C

Directory of
Special Libraries and
Information Centers

Directory of Special Libraries and Information Centers

7th Edition

A Guide to Special Libraries, Research Libraries, Information Centers, Archives, and Data Centers Maintained by Government Agencies, Business, Industry, Newspapers, Educational Institutions, Nonprofit Organizations, and Societies in the Fields of Science, Technology, Medicine, Law, Art, Religion, History, Social Sciences, and Humanistic Studies.

LOIS LENROOT-ERNT
Editor

BRIGITTE T. DARNAY
Associate Editor

VOLUME 2

Geographic and Personnel Indexes

GALE RESEARCH COMPANY • BOOK TOWER • DETROIT, MICHIGAN 48226

Sharon L. Stanton, *Senior Assistant Editor*

Holly M. Gudmundson, Carol C. Southward, Mary L. Wolf,
Assistant Editors

Carol Blanchard, *Production Supervisor*

Arthur Chartow, *Cover Design*

Directory of Special Libraries and Information Centers
Seventh Edition, in Three Volumes

Volume 1—Directory of Special Libraries and Information Centers
in the United States and Canada

Volume 2—Geographic and Personnel Indexes

Volume 3—New Special Libraries (a periodic supplement to Volume 1)

Copyright © 1963, 1968, 1974, 1977, 1979, 1981, 1982 by
Gale Research Company

Computerized photocomposition by
Computer Composition Corporation,
Madison Heights, Michigan

Library of Congress Catalog Card Number 82-6068 (set)
ISSN 0731-633X

Library of Congress Cataloging in Publication Data

Main entry under title:

Directory of special libraries and information centers.

    Vol. 2 has also subtitle: A guide to special
libraries, research libraries, information centers,
archives, and data centers maintained by government
agencies, business, industry, newspapers, educational
institutions, nonprofit organizations, and societies in
the fields of science, technology, medicine, law, art,
religion, history, social sciences, and humanistic
studies.
    Includes indexes.
    Contents: v. 1. Directory of special libraries and
information centers in the United States and Canada--
v. 2. Geographic and personnel indexes.
    1. Libraries, Special--Directories. 3. Information
services--Directories. I. Lenroot-Ernt, Lois.
Z731.D56   1982   026'.00025'7   82-81275
ISBN 0-8103-0261-6 (v. 1)   AACR2

Contents

Introduction

The "Geographic and Personnel Indexes" volume consists of selected parts of the entries which are arranged by library name in Volume 1, *Directory of Special Libraries and Information Centers in the United States and Canada.*

As the title of the volume indicates, the selected data have been rearranged in geographic sequence, with respect to libraries, and in alphabetical sequence, with respect to the personal names of professional staff. This volume makes it possible:

    1) to find libraries according to their geographical locations;

    2) to determine which and/or how many libraries are located in a specific city;

    3) to learn where a librarian is employed when only her/his name is known.

The entries in Volume 2 are brief and include only a library's name, address, head librarian and phone number. However, Volume 1 may be consulted to find additional details concerning founding date, staff size, subject specialty, number of holdings, publications and other features.

This volume is arranged in two sections, as follows:

GEOGRAPHIC INDEX—All libraries included in Volume 1 are reported in this section in geographic order by state or province and city in the following manner: first, the United States; next U.S. territories and possessions; last, Canada. Entries within each city are arranged alphabetically according to the name of the parent institution housing the special library.

PERSONNEL INDEX—This section, beginning on page 461, lists alphabetically by surname the professional staff of the special libraries and information centers listed in the Geographic Index and in Volume 1.

The editors will appreciate receiving suggestions from users regarding the arrangement of listings, the type of data provided, additional text or statistical data, or any other comments which will enable them to make the *Directory of Special Libraries and Information Centers* more helpful.

Abbreviations and Symbols

(State, Province and Territory)

UNITED STATES

AL	Alabama		MT	Montana
AK	Alaska		NE	Nebraska
AZ	Arizona		NV	Nevada
AR	Arkansas		NH	New Hampshire
CA	California		NJ	New Jersey
CO	Colorado		NM	New Mexico
CT	Connecticut		NY	New York
DE	Delaware		NC	North Carolina
DC	District of Columbia		ND	North Dakota
FL	Florida		OH	Ohio
GA	Georgia		OK	Oklahoma
HI	Hawaii		OR	Oregon
ID	Idaho		PA	Pennsylvania
IL	Illinois		RI	Rhode Island
IN	Indiana		SC	South Carolina
IA	Iowa		SD	South Dakota
KS	Kansas		TN	Tennessee
KY	Kentucky		TX	Texas
LA	Louisiana		UT	Utah
ME	Maine		VT	Vermont
MD	Maryland		VA	Virginia
MA	Massachusetts		WA	Washington
MI	Michigan		WV	West Virginia
MN	Minnesota		WI	Wisconsin
MS	Mississippi		WY	Wyoming
MO	Missouri			

U.S. TERRITORIES

AS	American Samoa		PR	Puerto Rico
GU	Guam		VI	Virgin Islands

CANADA

AB	Alberta		NS	Nova Scotia
BC	British Columbia		ON	Ontario
MB	Manitoba		PE	Prince Edward Island
NB	New Brunswick		PQ	Quebec
NF	Newfoundland		SK	Saskatchewan
NT	Northwest Territories		YT	Yukon Territory

An asterisk (*) after the library's name denotes a library that did not answer the three requests for updated information, but that is one the editors are reasonably certain exists.

A dagger (†) after the library's name denotes a library which did not reply but whose existence was verified in current secondary sources.

Section 1
GEOGRAPHIC INDEX

United States

ALABAMA

NORTHEAST ALABAMA REGIONAL MEDICAL CENTER - MEDICAL LIBRARY
400 East Tenth St.
Box 2208　　　　　　　　　　　　Phone: (205) 235-5877
Anniston, AL 36202　　　　　　　　Priscilla Lloyd, Med.Libn.

PARKER MEMORIAL BAPTIST CHURCH - LIBRARY *
Box 2104　　　　　　　　　　　　Phone: (205) 236-5628
Anniston, AL 36201　　　　　　　　Mrs. Gale Main, Libn.

AUBURN UNIVERSITY - ARCHITECTURE AND FINE ARTS LIBRARY
Dudley Hall　　　　　　　　　　　Phone: (205) 826-4510
Auburn, AL 36830　　　　　　　　Mary K. Dudman, Libn.

AUBURN UNIVERSITY - ARCHIVES
Ralph B. Draughon Library　　　　　　Phone: (205) 826-4465
Auburn, AL 36849　　　　　　　Dr. Allen W. Jones, Archv.

AUBURN UNIVERSITY - DEPARTMENT OF SPECIAL COLLECTIONS
University Libraries　　　　　　　　Phone: (205) 826-4500
Auburn, AL 36830　　　　　　Gene Geiger, Spec.Coll.Libn.

AUBURN UNIVERSITY - LEARNING RESOURCES CENTER
Haley Center　　　　　　　　　　Phone: (205) 826-4420
Auburn, AL 36830　　　　　　　Dr. C.D. Wright, Coord.

AUBURN UNIVERSITY - WATER RESOURCES RESEARCH INSTITUTE -
　INFORMATION CENTER *
205 Samford Hall　　　　　　　　　Phone: (205) 826-5075
Auburn, AL 36830　　　　　　　James C. Warman, Dir.

U.S.D.A. - AGRICULTURAL RESEARCH SERVICE - NATL. TILLAGE
　MACHINERY LABORATORY LIBRARY
Box 792　　　　　　　　　　　　Phone: (205) 887-8596
Auburn, AL 36830　　　　　　　William R. Gill, Dir.

AUBURN UNIVERSITY - INTERNATIONAL CENTER FOR AQUACULTURE -
　LIBRARY
Swingle Hall　　　　　　　　　　Phone: (205) 826-4786
Auburn University, AL 36849　　　　E.W. Shell, Dept.Hd.

AUBURN UNIVERSITY - VETERINARY MEDICAL LIBRARY
Veterinary Medical Complex　　　　　Phone: (205) 826-4780
Auburn University, AL 36849　　　Atha Louise Henley, Libn.

ALABAMA POWER COMPANY - LIBRARY
600 N. 18th St.
Box 2641　　　　　　　　　　　　Phone: (205) 323-5341
Birmingham, AL 35291　　　　　　Alison I. English, Libn.

AMERICAN CAST IRON PIPE COMPANY - TECHNICAL LIBRARY
2930 N. 16th St.
Box 2727
Birmingham, AL 35202

AMERICAN TRUCK HISTORICAL SOCIETY - LIBRARY
201 Office Park Dr.　　　　　　　　Phone: (205) 879-2131
Birmingham, AL 35223　　　　　Zoe S. James, Exec.Dir.

BALCH, BINGHAM, BAKER, HAWTHORNE, WILLIAMS & WARD - LIBRARY †
600 N. 18th St.
Box 306　　　　　　　　　　　　Phone: (205) 251-8100
Birmingham, AL 35201　　　　　　Joanna Chen, Libn.

BAPTIST MEDICAL CENTER - MEDICAL LIBRARY
701 Princeton Ave., S.W.　　　　　　Phone: (205) 783-3078
Birmingham, AL 35211　　　　　　Romilda F. Cook, Libn.

BAPTIST MEDICAL CENTERS-SAMFORD UNIVERSITY - IDA V. MOFFETT
　SCHOOL OF NURSING - L.R. JORDAN LIBRARY
820 Montclair Rd.　　　　　　　　Phone: (205) 591-2371
Birmingham, AL 35213　　　Jewell Alexender Carter, Lib.Dir.

BIRMINGHAM BOTANICAL GARDENS - HORACE HAMMOND MEMORIAL
　LIBRARY
2612 Lane Park Rd.　　　　　　　　Phone: (205) 879-1227
Birmingham, AL 35223　　　　　Gary G. Gerlach, Dir.

BIRMINGHAM MUSEUM OF ART - REFERENCE LIBRARY
2000 Eighth Ave., N.　　　　　　　Phone: (205) 254-2565
Birmingham, AL 35203　　　　　Richard N. Murray, Dir.

BIRMINGHAM NEWS - REFERENCE LIBRARY
2200 Fourth Ave., N.　　　　　　　Phone: (205) 325-2409
Birmingham, AL 35203　　　　　　Laurie Orr, Hd.Libn.

BIRMINGHAM PUBLIC AND JEFFERSON COUNTY FREE LIBRARY - ART AND
　MUSIC DEPARTMENT
2020 Park Place　　　　　　　　　Phone: (205) 254-2538
Birmingham, AL 35203　　　　　Jane F. Greene, Dept.Hd.

BIRMINGHAM PUBLIC AND JEFFERSON COUNTY FREE LIBRARY - COLLINS
　COLLECTION OF THE DANCE
2020 Park Place　　　　　　　　　Phone: (205) 254-2538
Birmingham, AL 35203　　　　　　Lois A. Eady, Cur.

BIRMINGHAM PUBLIC AND JEFFERSON COUNTY FREE LIBRARY -
　GOVERNMENT DOCUMENTS DEPARTMENT
2020 Park Place　　　　　　　　　Phone: (205) 254-2555
Birmingham, AL 35203　　Rebecca Scarborough, Hd., Govt.Doc.Dept.

BIRMINGHAM PUBLIC AND JEFFERSON COUNTY FREE LIBRARY - J. HUBERT
　SCRUGGS, JR. COLLECTION OF PHILATELY
2020 Park Place　　　　　　　　　Phone: (205) 254-2698
Birmingham, AL 35203　　　　　Marrin Y. Whiting, Cur.

BIRMINGHAM PUBLIC AND JEFFERSON COUNTY FREE LIBRARY - RUCKER
　AGEE CARTOGRAPHICAL COLLECTION
2020 Park Place　　　　　　　　　Phone: (205) 254-2534
Birmingham, AL 35203　　　　　Ruth S. Spence, Map Cur.

BIRMINGHAM PUBLIC AND JEFFERSON COUNTY FREE LIBRARY -
　TUTWILER COLLECTION OF SOUTHERN HISTORY AND LITERATURE
2020 Park Place　　　　　　　　　Phone: (205) 254-2534
Birmingham, AL 35203　　　　　Virginia Scott, Hd.Libn.

BIRMINGHAM PUBLIC AND JEFFERSON COUNTY FREE LIBRARY - YOUTH
　DEPARTMENT
2020 Park Place　　　　　　　　　Phone: (205) 254-2530
Birmingham, AL 35203　　　　　　Eva Yates, Hd.

BIRMINGHAM-SOUTHERN COLLEGE - CHARLES ANDREW RUSH LEARNING
　CENTER/LIBRARY
800 8th Ave., W.　　　　　　　　Phone: (205) 328-5250
Birmingham, AL 35204　　　　　Barbara G. Scott, Dir.

CARRAWAY METHODIST MEDICAL CENTER - MEDICAL LIBRARY
1615 N. 25th St.　　　　　　　　Phone: (205) 254-6265
Birmingham, AL 35234　　　Mrs. Bobby H. Powell, Med.Libn.

EYE FOUNDATION HOSPITAL - JOHN E. MEYER EYE FOUNDATION LIBRARY
1720 8th Ave., S.　　　　　　　　Phone: (205) 325-8505
Birmingham, AL 35233　　　　　Hugh Thomas, Med.Libn.

JEFFERSON COUNTY LAW LIBRARY
900 Jefferson County Court House　　　Phone: (205) 325-5628
Birmingham, AL 35263　　　　　　Linda Hand, Libn.

RUST ENGINEERING COMPANY - LIBRARY
Box 101　　　　　　　　　　　　Phone: (205) 254-4000
Birmingham, AL 35201　　　　Calberta O. Atkinson, Libn.

SAMFORD UNIVERSITY - BAPTIST HISTORICAL COLLECTION
Harwell G. Davis Library　　　　　　Phone: (205) 870-2749
Birmingham, AL 35209　　　　F. Wilbur Helmbold, Cur.

SAMFORD UNIVERSITY - CUMBERLAND SCHOOL OF LAW - CORDELL HULL
　LAW LIBRARY †
800 Lakeshore Dr.　　　　　　　　Phone: (205) 870-2714
Birmingham, AL 35209　　　　　Laurel R. Clapp, Libn.

GEOGRAPHIC *(vertical side tab)*

SAMFORD UNIVERSITY - HARWELL GOODWIN DAVIS LIBRARY
800 Lakeshore Dr.   Phone: (205) 870-2846
Birmingham, AL 35209   F. Wilbur Helmbold, Univ.Libn.

SOUTH HIGHLANDS HOSPITAL - MEDICAL LIBRARY
1127 S. 12th St.   Phone: (205) 250-7703
Birmingham, AL 35205   Dena Metts, Libn.

SOUTHEASTERN BIBLE COLLEGE - ROWE MEMORIAL LIBRARY
2901 Pawnee Ave. South   Phone: (205) 251-2311
Birmingham, AL 35205   Edith Taff, Libn.

SOUTHERN NATURAL GAS COMPANY, INC. - CORPORATE LIBRARY
Box 2563   Phone: (205) 325-7409
Birmingham, AL 35202   Regina Hinkle, Libn.

SOUTHERN RESEARCH INSTITUTE - THOMAS W. MARTIN MEMORIAL
    LIBRARY
2000 Ninth Ave., S.   Phone: (205) 323-6592
Birmingham, AL 35255   Mary L. Pullen, Lib.Mgr.

TEMPLE EMANU-EL - WILLIAM P. ENGEL LIBRARY
2100 Highland Ave.   Phone: (205) 933-8037
Birmingham, AL 35205   Adele Cohn, Libn.

U.S. DEPT. OF COMMERCE - INTERNATIONAL TRADE ADMINISTRATION -
    BIRMINGHAM DISTRICT OFFICE LIBRARY *
908 S. 20th St.   Phone: (205) 254-1331
Birmingham, AL 35205   Gayle C. Shelton, Jr., Dir.

U.S. VETERANS ADMINISTRATION (AL-Birmingham) - HOSPITAL MEDICAL
    LIBRARY
700 S. l9th St.   Phone: (205) 933-8101
Birmingham, AL 35233   Mary Ann Knotts, Chf., Lib.Serv.

UNIVERSITY OF ALABAMA IN BIRMINGHAM - LISTER HILL LIBRARY OF THE
    HEALTH SCIENCES
University Sta.   Phone: (205) 934-5460
Birmingham, AL 35294   Richard B. Fredericksen, Dir.

U.S. NATL. PARK SERVICE - RUSSELL CAVE NATL. MONUMENT - LIBRARY
                                            Phone: (205) 495-2672
Bridgeport, AL 35740   John Mapel, Unit Mgr.

ALABAMA STATE DEPARTMENT OF CONSERVATION & NATURAL
    RESOURCES - ALABAMA MARINE RESOURCES LAB. - LIBRARY
Box 189   Phone: (205) 861-2882
Dauphin Island, AL 36528   Donald G. Bland, Biologist Aide

MARINE ENVIRONMENTAL SCIENCES CONSORTIUM - LIBRARY †
Dauphin Island Sea Lab
Box 386   Phone: (205) 861-2141
Dauphin Island, AL 36528   Judy Stout, Libn.

U.S. FOOD & DRUG ADMINISTRATION - GULF COAST TECHNICAL SERVICES
    UNIT - LIBRARY
Box 158   Phone: (205) 861-2962
Dauphin Island, AL 36528

MONSANTO TEXTILES COMPANY - TECHNICAL CENTER LIBRARY *
                                            Phone: (205) 552-2223
Decatur, AL 35601

NORTH CENTRAL ALABAMA REGIONAL COUNCIL OF GOVERNMENTS -
    LIBRARY *
City Hall Tower, 5th Fl.
Box C   Phone: (205) 355-4515
Decatur, AL 35602

SOUTHEAST ALABAMA MEDICAL CENTER - LIBRARY
Box 6987   Phone: (205) 793-8111
Dothan, AL 36302   Kathy H. Dexter, Med.Lib.Dir.

NOLAND (Lloyd) HOSPITAL - DAVID KNOX MC KAMY MEDICAL LIBRARY
701 Ridgeway Rd.   Phone: (205) 783-5121
Fairfield, AL 35064   Elisabeth Burton, Libn.

FLORENCE CITY SCHOOLS - CENTRAL RESOURCE CENTER *
541 Riverview Dr.   Phone: (205) 766-3234
Florence, AL 35630   Lois E. Henderson, Lib.Supv.

U.S. ARMY HOSPITALS - NOBLE ARMY HOSPITAL - MEDICAL LIBRARY
                                            Phone: (205) 238-2411
Ft. McClellan, AL 36205   Pauline Mayhall, Med.Libn.

U.S. ARMY MILITARY POLICE SCHOOL - LIBRARY
Bldg. 3181, Rm. 10   Phone: (205) 238-3737
Ft. McClellan, AL 36201   Sybil P. Parker, Supv.Libn.

U.S. ARMY - AEROMEDICAL RESEARCH LABORATORY - SCIENTIFIC
    INFORMATION CENTER
Box 577   Phone: (205) 255-6919
Ft. Rucker, AL 36362   Sybil H. Bullock, Libn.

U.S. ARMY AVIATION TRAINING LIBRARY
Bldgs. 5906 & 5907
Drawer O   Phone: (205) 255-5014
Ft. Rucker, AL 36362   M.L. Durkin, Chf.Libn.

U.S. ARMY HOSPITALS - LYSTER ARMY HOSPITAL - MEDICAL LIBRARY
Bldg. 301
U.S. Army Aeromedical Center   Phone: (205) 255-4504
Ft. Rucker, AL 36362   Jeanette A. Chambers, Lib.Techn.

BAPTIST MEMORIAL HOSPITAL - MEDICAL LIBRARY
1007 Goodyear Ave.   Phone: (205) 492-1240
Gadsden, AL 35903   Willene L. Payne, Libn.

FIRST PRESBYTERIAN CHURCH OF GADSDEN - LIBRARY
530 Chestnut St.
Box 676   Phone: (201) 547-5747
Gadsden, AL 35902   Mrs. Tom Smith, Libn.

HOLY NAME OF JESUS HOSPITAL - MEDICAL LIBRARY †
600 S. 3rd St.   Phone: (205) 547-4911
Gadsden, AL 35901

U.S. AIR FORCE BASE - GUNTER BASE LIBRARY
                                            Phone: (205) 279-3179
Gunter AFS, AL 36114   Alta N. Hunt, Libn.

INTERNATIONAL ASSOCIATION OF EDUCATORS FOR WORLD PEACE -
    IAEWP CENTER OF INTERCULTURAL INFORMATION
Blue Springs Sta.
Box 3282   Phone: (205) 539-7205
Huntsville, AL 35810   Charles Mercieca, Exec. V.P.

MADISON COUNTY - ELBERT H. PARSONS PUBLIC LAW LIBRARY
205 East Side Sq.   Phone: (205) 536-5911
Huntsville, AL 35801   Cleo S. Cason, Libn.

NATIONAL SPELEOLOGICAL SOCIETY - NSS LIBRARY
1 Cave Ave.   Phone: (205) 852-1300
Huntsville, AL 35810   William W. Torode, Libn.

TELEDYNE BROWN ENGINEERING - TECHNICAL LIBRARY
Cummings Research Pk.   Phone: (205) 532-1433
Huntsville, AL 35807   Peggy Shelton, Chf.Libn.

U.S. NASA - MSFC LIBRARY
Code AS24L   Phone: (205) 453-1880
Marshall Space Flight Ctr., AL 35812   Charlotte H. Dabbs, Libn.

CIVIL AIR PATROL - NATIONAL HEADQUARTERS AEROSPACE EDUCATION
    REFERENCE LIBRARY
National Headquarters
Maxwell AFB, AL 36112

U.S. AIR FORCE - AIR UNIVERSITY - LIBRARY
                                            Phone: (205) 293-2606
Maxwell AFB, AL 36112   Robert B. Lane, Dir.

U.S. AIR FORCE - ALBERT F. SIMPSON HISTORICAL RESEARCH CENTER
                                            Phone: (205) 293-5958
Maxwell AFB, AL 36112   Lloyd H. Cornett, Jr., Dir.

HISTORIC MOBILE PRESERVATION SOCIETY - MITCHELL ARCHIVES
350 Oakleigh Pl.   Phone: (205) 432-1281
Mobile, AL 36604   Mrs. Carter Smith, Archv.

INTERNATIONAL PAPER COMPANY - ERLING RIIS RESEARCH LABORATORY
   - INFORMATION SERVICES
Box 2787   Phone: (205) 457-8911
Mobile, AL 36652   Barbara M. Broadhead, Supv.

INTERNATIONAL PAPER COMPANY - FOREST PRODUCTIVITY & RESEARCH
   - FOREST RESEARCH LIBRARY
Box 2328   Phone: (205) 457-8911
Mobile, AL 36652   Joy Walker Gallegos, Supv., Tech.Info.Serv.

MERCHANTS NATIONAL BANK OF MOBILE - EMPLOYEES LIBRARY †
58 St. Francis St.
Box 2527   Phone: (205) 690-1139
Mobile, AL 36652   Pat Looney, Libn.

MOBILE COUNTY PUBLIC LAW LIBRARY
County Court House   Phone: (205) 690-8436
Mobile, AL 36602   May Lowe, Libn.

MOBILE PUBLIC LIBRARY - SPECIAL COLLECTIONS DIVISION
704 Government St.   Phone: (205) 438-7094
Mobile, AL 36602   Robert J. Zietz, Hd.

MUSEUMS OF THE CITY OF MOBILE - MUSEUM REFERENCE LIBRARY
355 Government St.   Phone: (205) 438-7569
Mobile, AL 36602   Caldwell Delaney, Musm.Dir.

PROVIDENCE HOSPITAL & SCHOOL OF NURSING - PROVIDENCE HEALTH
   SCIENCE LIBRARY
Box 208   Phone: (205) 438-7869
Mobile, AL 36601   Mary Ann Donnell, Libn.

UNIVERSITY OF SOUTH ALABAMA - COLLEGE OF MEDICINE - BIOMEDICAL
   LIBRARY
Library 312   Phone: (205) 460-7043
Mobile, AL 36688   Robert Donnell, Dir.

UNIVERSITY OF SOUTH ALABAMA - LIBRARY - SPECIAL COLLECTIONS
                                                    Phone: (205) 460-7028
Mobile, AL 36688   Anita Bayles, Circ.Libn.

ALABAMA LEAGUE OF MUNICIPALITIES - LIBRARY
Box 1270   Phone: (205) 262-2566
Montgomery, AL 36102   John F. Watkins, Exec.Dir.

ALABAMA STATE DEPARTMENT OF ARCHIVES AND HISTORY
624 Washington Ave.   Phone: (205) 832-6510
Montgomery, AL 36130   Milo B. Howard, Jr., Dir.

ALABAMA STATE DEPARTMENT OF PUBLIC HEALTH - REFERENCE LIBRARY
206 State Office Bldg.   Phone: (205) 832-3194
Montgomery, AL 36130   Vonciel Davis, Info.Spec.

ALABAMA STATE DEVELOPMENT OFFICE - PLANNING DIVISION -
   PLANNING REFERENCE SERVICE
State Capitol   Phone: (205) 832-6400
Montgomery, AL 36130   John P. Worsham, Jr., Adm.

ALABAMA STATE SUPREME COURT - SUPREME COURT AND STATE LAW
   LIBRARY
Judicial Bldg., 445 Dexter Ave.   Phone: (205) 832-6410
Montgomery, AL 36130   William C. Younger, Dir.

ALABAMA STATE WATER IMPROVEMENT COMMISSION - LIBRARY
State Office Bldg.
Montgomery, AL 36130

BAPTIST MEDICAL CENTER - MEDICAL LIBRARY
2105 East South Blvd.   Phone: (205) 288-2100
Montgomery, AL 36198   Ruth Steffen, Libn.

ENVIRONMENTAL PROTECTION AGENCY - EASTERN ENVIRONMENTAL
   RADIATION LAB - LIBRARY
Box 3009   Phone: (205) 272-3402
Montgomery, AL 36193   Charles M. Petko

JACKSON HOSPITAL AND CLINIC - MEDICAL LIBRARY
1235 Forest Ave.   Phone: (205) 832-4000
Montgomery, AL 36106   Annelle Johnson, Med.Libn.

MONTGOMERY ADVERTISER AND ALABAMA JOURNAL - LIBRARY
200 Washington Ave.   Phone: (205) 262-1611
Montgomery, AL 36104   Peggy Ross, Libn.

MONTGOMERY COUNTY LAW LIBRARY
Box 1667   Phone: (205) 832-4950
Montgomery, AL 36192   Jean M. Bowar, Law Libn.

MONTGOMERY MUSEUM OF FINE ARTS - ART RESEARCH LIBRARY
440 S. McDonough St.   Phone: (205) 834-3490
Montgomery, AL 36104   Elizabeth B. Brown, Libn.

NORMANDALE BAPTIST CHURCH - MEDIA CENTER
Box 2615   Phone: (205) 288-6190
Montgomery, AL 36105   Thelma Reaves, Media Ctr.Dir.

SOUTHERN POVERTY LAW CENTER - KLANWATCH - LIBRARY
1001 S. Hull St.   Phone: (205) 264-0286
Montgomery, AL 36104   Randall Williams, Dir.

U.S. AIR FORCE HOSPITAL - MEDICAL LIBRARY (AL-Montgomery)
Maxwell AFB   Phone: (205) 293-5852
Montgomery, AL 36112   Patricia A. Kuther, Med.Lib.Techn.

U.S. VETERANS ADMINISTRATION (AL-Montgomery) - MEDICAL CENTER
   LIBRARY (142D)
215 Perry Hill Rd.   Phone: (205) 272-4670
Montgomery, AL 36193   Mara R. Wilhelm, Chf., Lib.Serv.

UNIVERSITY OF ALABAMA - JONES LAW INSTITUTE - LIBRARY
1500 East Fairview Ave.   Phone: (205) 832-5588
Montgomery, AL 36106   John R. Huthnance, Dir.

NORTHWEST ALABAMA COUNCIL OF LOCAL GOVERNMENTS - LIBRARY
Box 2603   Phone: (205) 383-3861
Muscle Shoals, AL 35660   Leon Graham, Exec.Dir.

TENNESSEE VALLEY AUTHORITY - TECHNICAL LIBRARY
National Fertilizer Development Ctr.   Phone: (205) 386-2871
Muscle Shoals, AL 35660   Shirley G. Nichols, Supv.Libn.

ALABAMA A & M UNIVERSITY - JOSEPH F. DRAKE MEMORIAL LEARNING
   RESOURCES CENTER
                                                    Phone: (205) 859-7309
Normal, AL 35762   Dr. Birdie O. Weir, Dir.

PRICHARD (Cleveland) MEMORIAL LIBRARY *
4559 Old Citronelle Hwy.   Phone: (205) 456-1979
Prichard, AL 36613   Johnnie Andrews, Jr., Dir.

U.S. ARMY - MISSILE COMMAND & MARSHALL SPACE FLIGHT CENTER -
   REDSTONE SCIENTIFIC INFORMATION CENTER
                                                    Phone: (205) 876-3251
Redstone Arsenal, AL 35898   James P. Clark, Dir.

U.S. ARMY MISSILE & MUNITIONS CENTER & SCHOOL - MMCS TECHNICAL
   LIBRARY
Bldg. 3323   Phone: (205) 876-7425
Redstone Arsenal, AL 35809   Eva M. Cathey, Adm.Libn.

DALLAS COUNTY CIRCUIT COURT - LIBRARY
Dallas County Courthouse
Box 1158   Phone: (205) 872-3461
Selma, AL 36701

WESTPOINT PEPPERELL RESEARCH CENTER - INFORMATION SERVICES
   LIBRARY
Box 398   Phone: (205) 756-7111
Shawmut, AL 36876   Philip D. Lawrence, Jr., Supv., Info.Serv.

REYNOLDS METALS COMPANY - REDUCTION RESEARCH LIBRARY
Box 1200   Phone: (205) 383-7141
Sheffield, AL 35660   Pamela Hendon, Libn.

FIRST BAPTIST CHURCH - LIBRARY
Box 162
Slocomb, AL 36375
Phone: (205) 886-2533
Norma Foster, Libn.

ALABAMA INSTITUTE FOR THE DEAF AND BLIND - LIBRARY FOR THE BLIND
AND PHYSICALLY HANDICAPPED
525 North Court St.
Talladega, AL 35160
Phone: (205) 362-1050
Gloria S. Lemaster, Libn.

TALLADEGA COUNTY LAW LIBRARY
Judicial Bldg.
Talladega, AL 35160
Phone: (205) 362-2050
Jeffrey A. Willis, Hd.Libn.

TROY STATE UNIVERSITY - LIBRARY
University Ave.
Troy, AL 36081
Phone: (205) 566-3000
Kenneth Croslin, Dir.

U.S. VETERANS ADMINISTRATION (AL-Tuscaloosa) - HOSPITAL MEDICAL
LIBRARY
Tuscaloosa, AL 35404
Phone: (205) 553-3760
Olivia S. Maniece, Chf.Libn.

U.S. VETERANS ADMINISTRATION (AL-Tuskegee) - MEDICAL CENTER
LIBRARY
Tuskegee, AL 36083
Phone: (205) 727-0550
Artemisia J. Junier, Chf.Libn.

TUSKEGEE INSTITUTE - DEPARTMENT OF ARCHITECTURE LIBRARY †
Phone: (205) 727-8351
Tuskegee Institute, AL 36088
Luester Williams, Lib.Asst.

TUSKEGEE INSTITUTE - DIVISION OF BEHAVIORAL SCIENCE RESEARCH -
SCIENCE INFORMATION CENTER
Carnegie Hall, 4th Fl.
Tuskegee Institute, AL 36088
Phone: (205) 727-8575
Dr. Paul L. Wall, Dir.

TUSKEGEE INSTITUTE - HOLLIS BURKE FRISSELL LIBRARY-ARCHIVES †
Phone: (205) 727-8888
Tuskegee Institute, AL 36088
Daniel T. Williams, Archv.

TUSKEGEE INSTITUTE - SCHOOL OF ENGINEERING LIBRARY †
Phone: (205) 727-8901
Tuskegee Institute, AL 36088
Frances F. Davis, Libn.

TUSKEGEE INSTITUTE - VETERINARY MEDICINE LIBRARY †
Phone: (205) 727-8307
Tuskegee Institute, AL 36088
Carolyn Ford, Libn.

AMERICAN COLLEGE OF HERALDRY - LIBRARY
Drawer CG
University, AL 35486
Dr. David P. Johnson

GEOLOGICAL SURVEY OF ALABAMA - LIBRARY †
Drawer O
University, AL 35486
Phone: (205) 349-2852
Dorothy L. Brady, Libn.

U.S. BUREAU OF MINES - TUSCALOOSA RESEARCH CENTER - REFERENCE
LIBRARY
Box L
University, AL 35486
Phone: (205) 758-0491
Susan Markham, Lib.Techn.

UNIVERSITY OF ALABAMA - BUSINESS LIBRARY
Box S
University, AL 35486
Phone: (205) 348-6096
Dorothy Eady Brown, Sr.Libn.

UNIVERSITY OF ALABAMA - COLLEGE OF COMMUNITY HEALTH SCIENCES -
HEALTH SCIENCES LIBRARY
Box 6331
University, AL 35486
Phone: (205) 348-4950
Lynn M. Fortney, Chf.Med.Libn.

UNIVERSITY OF ALABAMA - EDUCATION LIBRARY
Box S
University, AL 35486
Phone: (205) 348-6055
Gail T. Graves, Sr.Libn.

UNIVERSITY OF ALABAMA - ENGINEERING LIBRARY
Box S
University, AL 35486
Phone: (205) 348-6551
Phil Kitchens, Sr.Libn.

UNIVERSITY OF ALABAMA - OFFICE OF PLANNING AND OPERATIONS -
ADMINISTRATIVE RESEARCH LIBRARY
222 Rose Administration Bldg.
Box 6156
University, AL 35486
Phone: (205) 348-5184
John C. Pritchett, Adm.Res.Libn.

UNIVERSITY OF ALABAMA - SCHOOL OF LAW - ALABAMA LAW REVIEW -
LIBRARY
Box 1976
University, AL 35486
Phone: (205) 348-7191
Fred McCallum, Res.Ed.

UNIVERSITY OF ALABAMA - SCHOOL OF LAW LIBRARY
Box 6205
University, AL 35486
Phone: (205) 348-5925
Orrin M. Walker, Law Libn.

UNIVERSITY OF ALABAMA - SCIENCE LIBRARY
Box S
University, AL 35486
Phone: (205) 348-5959
John S. Langen, Sr.Libn.

UNIVERSITY OF ALABAMA - WILLIAM STANLEY HOOLE SPECIAL
COLLECTIONS LIBRARY
Box S
University, AL 35486
Phone: (205) 348-5512
Joyce H. Lamont, Cur.

ALASKA

ALASKA HEALTH SCIENCES LIBRARY
3211 Providence Dr.
Anchorage, AK 99504
Phone: (907) 263-1870
Stanley Truelson, Dir.

ALASKA STATE COURT SYSTEM - ALASKA COURT LIBRARIES
303 K St.
Anchorage, AK 99501
Phone: (907) 264-0585
Aimee Ruzicka, Law Libn.

ALASKA STATE DEPARTMENT OF COMMERCE AND ECONOMIC
DEVELOPMENT - ALASKA PIPELINE COMMISSION - LIBRARY *
338 Denali
McKay Bldg., 12th Fl.
Anchorage, AK 99502
Phone: (907) 279-0583
Eric Hansen, Res.Anl.

ANCHORAGE HISTORICAL AND FINE ARTS MUSEUM - ARCHIVES
121 W. Seventh Ave.
Anchorage, AK 99501
Phone: (907) 264-4326
M. Diane Brenner, Musm.Archv.

NATIONAL BANK OF ALASKA - HERITAGE LIBRARY AND MUSEUM
Northern Lights & C St.
Box 600
Anchorage, AK 99510
Phone: (907) 272-5544
Mrs. Vanny Davenport, Libn. & Cur.

SOHIO ALASKA PETROLEUM COMPANY - TECHNICAL LIBRARY †
3111 C St., Pouch 6-612
Anchorage, AK 99502
Phone: (907) 265-0594
Lorraine M. Culbert, Libn.

U.S. BUREAU OF LAND MANAGEMENT - ALASKA OUTER-CONTINENTAL
SHELF OFFICE - LIBRARY
620 E. 10th Ave.
Box 1159
Anchorage, AK 99510
Phone: (907) 276-2955
Linda Massengale, Clerical Asst.

U.S. DEPT. OF COMMERCE - INTERNATIONAL TRADE ADMINISTRATION -
ANCHORAGE DISTRICT OFFICE LIBRARY
701 C St.
Box 32
Anchorage, AK 99513
Phone: (907) 271-5041
Blaine D. Porter, Dir.

U.S. DEPT. OF THE INTERIOR - ALASKA RESOURCES LIBRARY
701 C St.
Box 36
Anchorage, AK 99513
Phone: (907) 271-5025
Martha L. Shepard, Libn.

U.S. DISTRICT COURT - LAW LIBRARY
701 C St.
Box 4
Anchorage, AK 99513
Phone: (907) 271-5655
Jane L. Lehman, Libn.

U.S. FISH & WILDLIFE SERVICE - LIBRARY †
813 D St.   Phone: (907) 276-3800
Anchorage, AK 99501   Janet Ballard, Lib.Techn.

U.S. NATL. PARK SERVICE - ALASKA AREA OFFICE - LIBRARY
540 W. 5th Ave.   Phone: (907) 271-4211
Anchorage, AK 99501   Frank Deckert, Interp.Spec.

UNIVERSITY OF ALASKA, ANCHORAGE - ARCTIC ENVIRONMENTAL
  INFORMATION AND DATA CENTER
707 A St.   Phone: (907) 279-4523
Anchorage, AK 99501   Barbara J. Sokolov, Ldr., Lib.Sci. Group

UNIVERSITY OF ALASKA, ANCHORAGE - LIBRARY
3211 Providence Dr.   Phone: (907) 263-1825
Anchorage, AK 99504   Jack O'Bar, Dir.

UNIVERSITY OF ALASKA - INSTITUTE OF SOCIAL & ECONOMIC RESEARCH
  - LIBRARY *
707 A St., Suite 206
Anchorage, AK 99501

U.S. NATL. MARINE FISHERIES SERVICE - AUKE BAY FISHERIES
  LABORATORY - FISHERIES RESEARCH LIBRARY
Box 155   Phone: (907) 789-7231
Auke Bay, AK 99821   Paula Johnson, Lib.Techn.

U.S. AIR FORCE BASE - EIELSON BASE LIBRARY
FL 5004, 5010 CSG/SSL   Phone: (907) 372-4184
Eielson AFB, AK 99702   Stella E. Ludwikowski, Adm.Libn.

U.S. AIR FORCE HOSPITAL - MEDICAL LIBRARY (AK-Elmendorf AFB)
                                                   Phone: (907) 752-3383
Elmendorf AFB, AK 99506   Mary M. Ezzel, Libn.

FAIRBANKS ENVIRONMENTAL CENTER - LIBRARY
218 Driveway   Phone: (907) 452-5021
Fairbanks, AK 99701   Ingrid Lustig, Office Mgr.

PHILOSOPHICAL HERITAGE INSTITUTE - LIBRARY OF ESOTERIC STUDIES
Box 80849   Phone: (907) 456-2245
Fairbanks, AK 99707   LaVedi Lafferty, Libn.

U.S. ARMY POST - FORT WAINWRIGHT - LIBRARY
Bldg. 3717   Phone: (907) 353-6114
Fairbanks, AK 99703   Isabelle Mudd, Adm.Libn.

U.S. FOREST SERVICE - INSTITUTE OF NORTHERN FORESTRY - LIBRARY *
                                                   Phone: (907) 479-7443
Fairbanks, AK 99701

UNIVERSITY OF ALASKA - ALASKA NATIVE LANGUAGE CENTER -
  RESEARCH LIBRARY
302 Chapman Bldg.   Phone: (907) 479-7874
Fairbanks, AK 99701

UNIVERSITY OF ALASKA - ALASKA AND THE POLAR REGIONS COLLECTION
  †
Elmer E. Rasmuson Library   Phone: (907) 479-7227
Fairbanks, AK 99701   Dr. Marvin Falk, Arctic Biblog.

UNIVERSITY OF ALASKA - BIO-MEDICAL LIBRARY
                                                   Phone: (907) 479-7442
Fairbanks, AK 99701   Dwight Ittner, Libn.

UNIVERSITY OF ALASKA - CENTER FOR CROSS-CULTURAL STUDIES -
  RESOURCE CENTER
                                                   Phone: (907) 479-7184
Fairbanks, AK 99701   Jim Stricks, Coord.

UNIVERSITY OF ALASKA - GEOPHYSICAL INSTITUTE LIBRARY
                                                   Phone: (907) 479-7503
Fairbanks, AK 99701

UNIVERSITY OF ALASKA - INSTITUTE OF MARINE SCIENCE - LIBRARY
                                                   Phone: (907) 479-7740
Fairbanks, AK 99701   Robert C. Williams, Libn.

UNIVERSITY OF ALASKA - RARE BOOKS, ARCHIVES & MANUSCRIPTS
  COLLECTIONS
Elmer E. Rasmuson Library   Phone: (907) 479-7261
Fairbanks, AK 99701   Paul H. McCarthy, Archv./Cur. of Mss.

UNIVERSITY OF ALASKA - WILDLIFE LIBRARY
Division of Life Sciences   Phone: (907) 479-7672
Fairbanks, AK 99701   Dr. Frederick C. Dean, Supv.

U.S. ARMY HOSPITALS - BASSETT ARMY HOSPITAL - MEDICAL LIBRARY
                                                   Phone: (907) 353-8194
Fort Wainwright, AK 99703   Pam Picray, Med.Libn.

U.S. FOOD & DRUG ADMINISTRATION - NATIONAL CENTER FOR
  TOXICOLOGICAL RESEARCH - LIBRARY
Jefferson, AK 72079   James Pat Craig, Hd.Libn.

ALASKA STATE DEPARTMENT OF ADMINISTRATION - STATE ARCHIVES
Pouch C   Phone: (907) 465-2275
Juneau, AK 99811   John M. Kinney, State Archv.

ALASKA STATE DEPARTMENT OF FISH AND GAME - LIBRARY
Subport Bldg.   Phone: (907) 465-4119
Juneau, AK 99801   Sondra Stanway, Libn.

ALASKA STATE DEPARTMENT OF LAW - ATTORNEY GENERAL'S LIBRARY
Pouch K, State Capitol Bldg.   Phone: (907) 465-3600
Juneau, AK 99811

ALASKA STATE DEPARTMENT OF TRANSPORTATION & PUBLIC FACILITIES
  - TECHNICAL LIBRARY
Box 1467   Phone: (907) 465-2461
Juneau, AK 99802   Carol Ottesen, Libn.

ALASKA STATE DIVISION OF STATE LIBRARIES & MUSEUMS - HISTORICAL
  LIBRARY
Pouch G   Phone: (907) 465-2925
Juneau, AK 99811   Phyllis J. DeMuth, Libn.

ALASKA STATE DIVISION OF STATE LIBRARIES & MUSEUMS - STATE
  LIBRARY
Pouch G, State Office Bldg.   Phone: (907) 465-2910
Juneau, AK 99811   Richard B. Engen, Dir.Lib. & Musm.Div.

ALASKA STATE LEGISLATURE/LEGISLATIVE AFFAIRS AGENCY -
  REFERENCE LIBRARY
Pouch Y, State Capitol   Phone: (907) 465-3808
Juneau, AK 99811   Jeanie Henry, Libn.

U.S. BUREAU OF MINES - ALASKA FIELD OPERATIONS CENTER LIBRARY
Box 550   Phone: (907) 364-2111
Juneau, AK 99802   Margaret J. Mattson, Libn.

U.S. DEPT. OF ENERGY - ALASKA POWER ADMINISTRATION - LIBRARY
Box 50   Phone: (907) 586-7405
Juneau, AK 99802   Wilma L. Stoddard, Plan.Div.Asst.

U.S. DISTRICT COURT - LIBRARY
709 W. 9th St.
Box 349   Phone: (907) 586-7458
Juneau, AK 99802   Vera N. Gordon, Dp.Ck.

U.S. FOREST SERVICE - PACIFIC NORTHWEST FOREST & RANGE
  EXPERIMENT STATION - FORESTRY SCIENCES LAB. LIBRARY
653 Federal Bldg.
Box 909   Phone: (907) 586-7301
Juneau, AK 99802   Carol A. Ayer, Libn.

ALASKA STATE COURT SYSTEM - KETCHIKAN LAW LIBRARY
State Office Bldg.,
415 Main St., Rm. 403   Phone: (907) 225-3196
Ketchikan, AK 99901   Berniece Cleveland, Act.Libn.

ALASKA STATE DEPARTMENT OF NATURAL RESOURCES - DIVISION OF
  GEOLOGICAL SURVEY - INFORMATION CENTER *
415 Main St.
Box 7438   Phone: (907) 225-4181
Ketchikan, AK 99901   Geraldine Zartman, Mining Info.Spec.

GEOGRAPHIC

GEOGRAPHIC *(vertical sidebar)*

TONGASS HISTORICAL SOCIETY, INC. - ROBBIE BARTHOLOMEW
  MEMORIAL LIBRARY
629 Dock St.   Phone: (907) 225-5600
Ketchikan, AK 99901   Virginia McGillvray, Dir.

ST. HERMAN'S ORTHODOX THEOLOGICAL SEMINARY - LIBRARY
414 Mission Rd.
Box 728   Phone: (907) 486-3524
Kodiak, AK 99615   Rev. Fr. Joseph P. Kreta, Dean

U.S. NATL. MARINE FISHERIES SERVICE - W.F. THOMPSON MEMORIAL
  LIBRARY †
Box 1638   Phone: (907) 486-3298
Kodiak, AK 99615   Dr. Alan J. Beardsley, Lab.Dir.

U.S. NATL. PARK SERVICE - DENALI NATL. PARK - LIBRARY
Box 9   Phone: (907) 683-2295
McKinley Park, AK 99755   Bill Truesdell, Chf. Naturalist

U.S. PUBLIC HEALTH SERVICE - ALASKA NATIVE HEALTH SERVICE -
  HEALTH SCIENCES LIBRARY
Mt. Edgecumbe Hospital
Box 4577   Phone: (907) 966-2411
Mt. Edgecumbe, AK 99835

NOME LIBRARY/KEGOAYAH KOZGA LIBRARY
Box 1168   Phone: (907) 443-5242
Nome, AK 99762   Dee McKenna, Libn.

UNIVERSITY OF ALASKA - ALASKA AGRICULTURAL EXPERIMENT STATION
  - LIBRARY
Box AE   Phone: (907) 745-3257
Palmer, AK 99645   Winston M. Laughlin, Soil Sci.

UNIVERSITY OF ALASKA - INSTITUTE OF MARINE SCIENCE - SEWARD
  MARINE STATION LIBRARY *
Box 617   Phone: (907) 224-5261
Seward, AK 99664   Robert C. Williams, Inst.Libn.

U.S. NATL. PARK SERVICE - SITKA NATL. HISTORICAL PARK - LIBRARY
Box 738   Phone: (907) 747-6281
Sitka, AK 99835   Ernest J. Suazo, Supt.

ALASKA STATE COURT SYSTEM - VALDEZ LAW LIBRARY *
Box 127   Phone: (907) 835-2266
Valdez, AK 99686   Aimee Ruzicka

VALDEZ HISTORICAL SOCIETY - VALDEZ HERITAGE ARCHIVES ALIVE
Box 6   Phone: (907) 835-4367
Valdez, AK 99686   Dorothy I. Clifton, Dir.

ARIZONA

U.S. NATL. PARK SERVICE - ORGAN PIPE CACTUS NATL. MONUMENT -
  LIBRARY
Rte. 1, Box 100
Ajo, AZ 85321   Robert Burgoon, Park Techn.

COCHISE COUNTY LAW LIBRARY
Drawer P   Phone: (602) 432-5703
Bisbee, AZ 85603   Herlinda Tafoya, Libn.

CASA GRANDE VALLEY HISTORICAL SOCIETY - MUSEUM LIBRARY
110 W. Florence Blvd.   Phone: (602) 836-2223
Casa Grande, AZ 85222   Kay Benedict, Cur.

AMERIND FOUNDATION, INC. - FULTON-HAYDEN MEMORIAL LIBRARY
                                      Phone: (602) 586-3003
Dragoon, AZ 85609   Mario N. Klimiades, Libn.

COCONINO COUNTY LAW LIBRARY
County Court House   Phone: (602) 774-5011
Flagstaff, AZ 86001   Jo Ann Rawlinson, Law Libn.

LOWELL OBSERVATORY - LIBRARY
                                      Phone: (602) 774-3358
Flagstaff, AZ 86002

MUSEUM OF NORTHERN ARIZONA - HAROLD S. COLTON MEMORIAL
  LIBRARY
Route 4, Box 720   Phone: (602) 774-5211
Flagstaff, AZ 86001   Dorothy A. House, Libn.

NORTHERN ARIZONA UNIVERSITY - LIBRARIES
Box 6022   Phone: (602) 523-2951
Flagstaff, AZ 86011   Robert E. Kemper, Dir.

NORTHERN ARIZONA UNIVERSITY - LIBRARIES - SPECIAL COLLECTIONS
  DIVISION
CU Box 6022   Phone: (602) 523-4730
Flagstaff, AZ 86011   Bill Mullane, Spec.Coll.Libn.

U.S. GEOLOGICAL SURVEY - FLAGSTAFF FIELD CENTER - BRANCH LIBRARY
2255 N. Gemini Dr.   Phone: (602) 779-3311
Flagstaff, AZ 86001   James R. Nation, Libn.

U.S. NATL. PARK SERVICE - WALNUT CANYON NATL. MONUMENT -
  LIBRARY
Rte. 1, Box 25   Phone: (602) 526-3367
Flagstaff, AZ 86001   Thomas E. White

U.S. NATL. PARK SERVICE - WUPATKI-SUNSET CRATER LIBRARY
Tuba Star Rte.   Phone: (602) 774-7000
Flagstaff, AZ 86001

PINAL COUNTY HISTORICAL SOCIETY, INC. - LIBRARY
2201 S. Main St.
Box 851   Phone: (602) 868-4382
Florence, AZ 85232   Mary A. Faul, Libn.

U.S. ARMY HOSPITALS - BLISS ARMY HOSPITAL - MEDICAL LIBRARY
                                      Phone: (602) 538-5668
Fort Huachuca, AZ 85613   CPT Carl Hendricks, Lib.Off.

U.S. ARMY INTELLIGENCE CENTER & SCHOOL - ACADEMIC LIBRARY
Alvarado Hall   Phone: (602) 538-5930
Ft. Huachuca, AZ 85613   Sylvia J. Webber, Chf.

AMERICAN GRADUATE SCHOOL OF INTERNATIONAL MANAGEMENT -
  LIBRARY
Thunderbird Campus   Phone: (602) 938-7620
Glendale, AZ 85306   Lora Jeanne Wheeler, Libn.

GILA COUNTY LAW LIBRARY
1400 E. Ash   Phone: (602) 425-3231
Globe, AZ 85501

U.S. NATL. PARK SERVICE - GRAND CANYON RESEARCH LIBRARY
Grand Canyon Natl. Park   Phone: (602) 638-2411
Grand Canyon, AZ 86023   Louise M. Hinchliffe, Lib.Techn.

MOHAVE MUSEUM OF HISTORY AND ARTS - LIBRARY
400 W. Beale St.   Phone: (602) 753-3195
Kingman, AZ 86401   Norma Hughes, Dir.

U.S. AIR FORCE BASE - LUKE BASE LIBRARY
                                      Phone: (602) 935-6301
Luke AFB, AZ 85309   Betty L. Horn, Base Libn.

AMERICAN COLLEGE OF NATURAL THERAPEUTICS & ARIZONA COLLEGE OF
  NATUROPATHIC MEDICINE - LIBRARY
Box 1406   Phone: (602) 969-5293
Mesa, AZ 85201   Zona P. Dial, Libn.

CHURCH OF JESUS CHRIST OF LATTER-DAY SAINTS - MESA BRANCH
  GENEALOGICAL LIBRARY
464 E. First Ave.   Phone: (602) 964-1200
Mesa, AZ 85204   Joseph H. Lindblom, Libn.

U.S. NATL. PARK SERVICE - PETRIFIED FOREST NATL. PARK - LIBRARY
                                      Phone: (602) 524-6228
Petrified Forest Natl. Park, AZ 86028   Susan J. Hepler

AMERICAN EXPRESS COMPANY - CARD DIVISION - WESTERN REGION
  OPERATIONS CENTER - SYSTEMS LIBRARY *
2423 E. Lincoln Dr.   Phone: (602) 248-3914
Phoenix, AZ 85016   Judith Kettner, Sys.Libn.

AMERICAN INDIAN BIBLE INSTITUTE - DOROTHY CUMMINGS MEMORIAL
    LIBRARY
10020 N. 15th Ave.   Phone: (602) 944-3335
Phoenix, AZ 85021   Ruth Gardiner, Libn.

ARIZONA PHOTOGRAPHIC ASSOCIATES, INC. - LIBRARY
2350 W. Holly   Phone: (602) 258-6551
Phoenix, AZ 85009   Dorothy McLaughlin, Dir.

ARIZONA STATE DEPARTMENT OF HEALTH SERVICES - PUBLIC HEALTH
    LIBRARY
1740 W. Adams   Phone: (602) 255-1013
Phoenix, AZ 85007   Charles L. Nelson, Sr.Libn.

ARIZONA STATE DEPARTMENT OF LIBRARY, ARCHIVES & PUBLIC
    RECORDS
State Capitol, 3rd Fl.   Phone: (602) 255-5240
Phoenix, AZ 85007   Sharon G. Womack, Dir.

ARIZONA STATE DEPARTMENT OF MINERAL RESOURCES - LIBRARY
State Fairgrounds   Phone: (602) 255-3791
Phoenix, AZ 85007   John H. Jett, Dir.

ARIZONA STATE ENERGY INFORMATION CENTER
1700 W. Washington, 5th Fl.   Phone: (602) 255-3303
Phoenix, AZ 85007   Jeannine Soucie, Info.Spec.

ARIZONA STATE HIGHWAY DEPARTMENT - LIBRARY
206 S. 17th Ave.   Phone: (602) 261-7350
Phoenix, AZ 85007   Fran Lewis, Libn.

ARIZONA STATE HOSPITAL - MEDICAL LIBRARY
2500 E. Van Buren   Phone: (602) 244-1331
Phoenix, AZ 85008   Marguerite Cooper, Med.Libn.

ARIZONA STATE OFFICE OF ECONOMIC PLANNING AND DEVELOPMENT -
    RESEARCH LIBRARY
1700 W. Washington, Rm. 400   Phone: (602) 255-5725
Phoenix, AZ 85007   Mary Silva, Libn.

ARIZONA STATE REGIONAL LIBRARY FOR THE BLIND AND PHYSICALLY
    HANDICAPPED
3120 E. Roosevelt   Phone: (602) 255-5578
Phoenix, AZ 85008   Richard C. Peel, Adm.Libn.

CENTRAL ARIZONA MUSEUM - LIBRARY & ARCHIVES
1242 N. Central Ave.   Phone: (602) 255-4470
Phoenix, AZ 85004   Janet Michaelieu, Libn.

DESERT BOTANICAL GARDEN - RICHTER LIBRARY
Papago Pk., 1200 N. Galvin Pkwy.
Box 5415   Phone: (602) 941-1217
Phoenix, AZ 85010   Jan Loechell, Libn.

GARRETT CORPORATION - GARRETT TURBINE ENGINE COMPANY -
    ENGINEERING LIBRARY
111 S. 34th St.
Box 5217   Phone: (602) 267-2062
Phoenix, AZ 85010   Dr. Nelson W. Hope, Hd.Libn.

GOOD SAMARITAN HOSPITAL - HEALTH SCIENCE LIBRARY
Box 2989   Phone: (602) 257-4353
Phoenix, AZ 85062   Betty J. Kjellberg, Libn.

GREYHOUND CORPORATION - LAW DEPARTMENT LIBRARY
Greyhound Tower
111 W. Clarendon Ave.
Phoenix, AZ 85077

HALL OF FLAME - RICHARD S. FOWLER MEMORIAL LIBRARY
6101 E. Van Buren   Phone: (602) 275-3473
Phoenix, AZ 85008   George F. Getz, Jr., Pres.

HEARD MUSEUM - LIBRARY
22 E. Monte Vista Rd.   Phone: (602) 252-8848
Phoenix, AZ 85004   Mary E. Graham, Libn.

HONEYWELL, INC. - HONEYWELL INFORMATION SYSTEMS - TECHNICAL
    LIBRARY
Box 6000   Phone: (602) 866-2639
Phoenix, AZ 85005   Vera Minkel, Mgr., Lib.Serv.

LEAGUE OF ARIZONA CITIES AND TOWNS - LIBRARY
1820 W. Washington St.   Phone: (602) 258-5786
Phoenix, AZ 85007   John J. DeBolske, Exec.Dir.

MARICOPA COUNTY GENERAL HOSPITAL - MEDICAL LIBRARY
2601 E. Roosevelt   Phone: (602) 267-5197
Phoenix, AZ 85008   Fernande Hebert, Med.Libn.

MARICOPA COUNTY LAW LIBRARY
East Court Bldg., 2nd Fl.
101 W. Jefferson St.   Phone: (602) 262-3461
Phoenix, AZ 85003   Elizabeth Kelley, Dir.

MARICOPA MEDICAL SOCIETY - LIBRARY †
2025 N. Central Ave.   Phone: (602) 252-8054
Phoenix, AZ 85004

MARICOPA TECHNICAL COMMUNITY COLLEGE - INDUSTRY EDUCATION
    CENTER LIBRARY
108 N. 40th St.   Phone: (602) 275-8500
Phoenix, AZ 85034   Fran R. Johnson, Libn.

MARICOPA TECHNICAL COMMUNITY COLLEGE - LIBRARY RESOURCE
    CENTER
106 E. Washington St.   Phone: (602) 258-7251
Phoenix, AZ 85004   Peg Smith, Dir.

MOTOROLA, INC. - INTEGRATED CIRCUITS DIVISION - TECHNICAL
    LIBRARY
Box 20906   Phone: (602) 962-2157
Phoenix, AZ 85036   C. Denise Ashford, Sr.Libn. & Mgr.

MOTOROLA, INC. - SEMICONDUCTOR PRODUCTS DIVISION - TECHNICAL
    LIBRARY
Box 2953   Phone: (602) 244-6065
Phoenix, AZ 85062   C. Denise Ashford, Sr.Libn. & Mgr.

O'CONNOR, CAVANAGH, ANDERSON, WESTOVER, KILLINGSWORTH,
    BESHEARS - LAW LIBRARY
3003 N. Central Ave., Suite 1800   Phone: (602) 263-3811
Phoenix, AZ 85012   Joan Ferrerio, Libn.

PHOENIX ART MUSEUM - LIBRARY
1625 N. Central Ave.   Phone: (602) 257-1222
Phoenix, AZ 85004   Clayton Kirking, Libn.

PHOENIX DAY SCHOOL FOR THE DEAF - LIBRARY/MEDIA CENTER
1935 W. Hayward Ave.   Phone: (602) 255-3448
Phoenix, AZ 85021   Donna L. Farman, Libn.

PHOENIX ELEMENTARY SCHOOLS - DISTRICT NO. 1 - CURRICULUM MEDIA
    CENTER
125 E. Lincoln St.   Phone: (602) 257-3774
Phoenix, AZ 85004   Barbara Randall, Coord.Instr.Sup.Serv.

PHOENIX GENERAL HOSPITAL - MEDICAL LIBRARY
Box 21331   Phone: (602) 279-4411
Phoenix, AZ 85036   Myrtle Idland, Libn.

PHOENIX NEWSPAPERS, INC. - LIBRARY
Box 1950   Phone: (602) 271-8555
Phoenix, AZ 85001   Marcy Bagley, Hd.Libn.

PHOENIX PLANNING DEPARTMENT - LONG RANGE PLANNING DIVISION -
    LIBRARY
Municipal Bldg., 6th Fl.
251 W. Washington St.   Phone: (602) 262-6881
Phoenix, AZ 85003   Catherine N. Donovan, Sec.

PUEBLO GRANDE MUSEUM - RESEARCH LIBRARY
4619 E. Washington St.   Phone: (602) 275-3452
Phoenix, AZ 85034   Chad T. Phinney, Musm.Asst.

GEOGRAPHIC

GEOGRAPHIC

ST. JOSEPH'S HOSPITAL - MEDICAL LIBRARY
350 W. Thomas Rd.
Box 2071   Phone: (602) 241-3299
Phoenix, AZ 85001   Evelyn S. Gorman, Dir., Lib.Serv.

ST. LUKE'S HOSPITAL MEDICAL CENTER - HEALTH-SCIENCES REFERENCE
LIBRARY
525 N. 18th St.   Phone: (602) 258-7373
Phoenix, AZ 85006   Beverly Hagen, Libn.

SALT RIVER PROJECT - LIBRARY
Box 1980   Phone: (602) 273-5304
Phoenix, AZ 85001   Mary J. Schalow, Libn.

SEMANTODONTICS, INC. - LIBRARY
Box 15668   Phone: (602) 955-5662
Phoenix, AZ 85060   Jim Rhode, Pres.

SPERRY CORPORATION - SPERRY FLIGHT SYSTEMS - ENGINEERING
LIBRARY
Box 21, 111   Phone: (602) 869-2278
Phoenix, AZ 85036   Pat DeVillier, Libn.

TEMPLE BETH ISRAEL - LIBRARY
3310 N. 10th Ave.   Phone: (601) 264-4428
Phoenix, AZ 85013   Mrs. Elliot Tempkin, Libn.

U-HAUL - RESEARCH AND LIBRARY SERVICES
2727 N. Central Ave.   Phone: (602) 263-6606
Phoenix, AZ 85004   Dona L. West, Hd.

UFO INFORMATION RETRIEVAL CENTER, INC.
9652 N. 31st Ave., G7   Phone: (602) 997-1523
Phoenix, AZ 85021   Thomas M. Olsen, Pres.

UNIDYNAMICS/PHOENIX, INC. - LIBRARY †
Box 2990   Phone: (602) 935-8011
Phoenix, AZ 85062

U.S.D.A. - AGRICULTURAL RESEARCH SERVICE - WATER CONSERVATION
LABORATORY LIBRARY
4331 E. Broadway Rd.   Phone: (602) 261-4356
Phoenix, AZ 85040   Yvonne Clayton, Lib.Tech.

U.S. DEPT. OF COMMERCE - INTERNATIONAL TRADE ADMINISTRATION -
PHOENIX DISTRICT OFFICE LIBRARY
Valley Bank Center
201 N. Central Ave., Suite 2950   Phone: (602) 261-3285
Phoenix, AZ 85037   Donald W. Fry, Dir.

U.S. PUBLIC HEALTH SERVICE HOSPITAL - PHOENIX INDIAN MEDICAL
CENTER - LIBRARY
4212 N. 16th St.   Phone: (602) 263-1200
Phoenix, AZ 85016   Rebekah G. Hinton, Libn.

U.S. VETERANS ADMINISTRATION (AZ-Phoenix) - HOSPITAL LIBRARY
Seventh St. & Indian School Rd.   Phone: (602) 277-5551
Phoenix, AZ 85012   Diane Wiesenthal, Chf., Lib.Serv.

VALLEY NATIONAL BANK - FINANCIAL RESEARCH LIBRARY
Box 71   Phone: (602) 261-2456
Phoenix, AZ 85001   J.T. Gorman, Info.Spec.

WESTERN ELECTRIC COMPANY, INC. - LIBRARY
505 N. 51st Ave.
Box 13369   Phone: (602) 233-5216
Phoenix, AZ 85002   Helen M. Corrales, Employee Serv.

SHARLOT HALL/PRESCOTT HISTORICAL SOCIETIES - LIBRARY/ARCHIVES
†
415 W. Gurley St.   Phone: (602) 445-3122
Prescott, AZ 86301   Sue Chamberlain, Archv.

U.S. VETERANS ADMINISTRATION (AZ-Prescott) - HEALTH SCIENCES
LIBRARY
                                     Phone: (602) 445-4860
Prescott, AZ 86313   William P. Price, Chf., Lib.Serv.

YAVAPAI COUNTY LAW LIBRARY
Rm. 404, County Courthouse   Phone: (602) 445-7450
Prescott, AZ 86301   Betty Loving, Hd.Libn.

CHURCH OF JESUS CHRIST OF LATTER-DAY SAINTS - SAFFORD-THATCHER
STAKES - GENEALOGICAL LIBRARY
Box 1218   Phone: (602) 428-3194
Safford, AZ 85546   Ervin Cluff, Libn.

ARMOUR RESEARCH CENTER - LIBRARY
15101 N. Scottsdale Rd.   Phone: (602) 991-3000
Scottsdale, AZ 85260   Lorraine Nesvig, Libn.

FOUNDATION FOR BLIND CHILDREN - LIBRARY
1201 North 85th Pl.   Phone: (602) 947-3744
Scottsdale, AZ 85257   Bess D. Kaplan, Materials Coord.

GREYHOUND CORPORATION - PATENT LAW DEPARTMENT LIBRARY
Armour Research Center
15101 N. Scottsdale Rd.   Phone: (602) 991-3000
Scottsdale, AZ 85260   Frank T. Barber, Chf., Patent Counsel

MOTOROLA, INC. - GOVERNMENT ELECTRONICS DIVISION - TECHNICAL
LIBRARY
8201 E. McDowell Rd.   Phone: (602) 949-3471
Scottsdale, AZ 85252   A.J. Kordalewski, Tech.Info.Mgr.

SCOTTSDALE MEMORIAL HOSPITAL - HEALTH SCIENCES LIBRARY
7400 E. Osborn Rd.   Phone: (602) 994-9616
Scottsdale, AZ 85251   Marihelen O'Connor, Med.Libn.

SINGLE DAD'S LIFESTYLE MAGAZINE - LIBRARY
Box 4842   Phone: (602) 998-0980
Scottsdale, AZ 85258   Robert A. Hirschfeld, Ed./Publ.

AMERICAN FEDERATION OF ASTROLOGERS, INC. - LIBRARY
6535 S. Rural Rd.
Box 22040   Phone: (602) 838-1751
Tempe, AZ 85282   Robert W. Cooper, Exec.Sec.

ARIZONA HISTORICAL FOUNDATION - HAYDEN LIBRARY
Arizona State University   Phone: (602) 966-8331
Tempe, AZ 85287   Dr. Geoffrey P. Mawn, Hist./Archv.

ARIZONA STATE UNIVERSITY - ARIZONA COLLECTIONS
Hayden Library   Phone: (602) 965-3145
Tempe, AZ 85287   Dr. Geoffrey P. Mawn, Cur.

ARIZONA STATE UNIVERSITY - CENTER FOR METEORITE STUDIES -
LIBRARY
                                     Phone: (602) 965-6511
Tempe, AZ 85281   Carleton B. Moore, Dir.

ARIZONA STATE UNIVERSITY - CHICANO STUDIES COLLECTION
Hayden Library   Phone: (602) 965-2594
Tempe, AZ 85287   Christine N. Marin, Chicano Biblog.

ARIZONA STATE UNIVERSITY - COLLEGE OF LAW - LIBRARY
Armstrong Hall   Phone: (602) 966-6141
Tempe, AZ 85282   Richard C. Dahl, Dir.

ARIZONA STATE UNIVERSITY - HOWE ARCHITECTURE LIBRARY
College of Architecture   Phone: (602) 965-6400
Tempe, AZ 85287   Katherine M. Weir, Hd.

ARIZONA STATE UNIVERSITY - LLOYD BIMSON MEMORIAL LIBRARY
College of Business Administration   Phone: (602) 965-6138
Tempe, AZ 85287   Robert F. Rose, Hd.Bus.Lib.

ARIZONA STATE UNIVERSITY - MUSIC LIBRARY
                                     Phone: (602) 965-3513
Tempe, AZ 85287   Arlys L. McDonald, Music Libn.

ARIZONA STATE UNIVERSITY - SPECIAL COLLECTIONS
University Library   Phone: (602) 965-6519
Tempe, AZ 85287   Marilyn Wurzburger, Hd., Spec.Coll.

ARIZONA STATE UNIVERSITY - UNIVERSITY ARCHIVES
University Archives Bldg.   Phone: (602) 965-7645
Tempe, AZ 85287   Alfred Thomas, Jr., Univ.Archv.

AERIAL PHENOMENA RESEARCH ORGANIZATION, INC. - APRO LIBRARY
2840 N. Country Club, No. 103   Phone: (602) 323-1825
Tucson, AZ 85716   Allen Benz, Libn.

**ARABIAN HORSE OWNERS FOUNDATION - W.R. BROWN MEMORIAL
    LIBRARY**
4633 E. Broadway, Suite 131   Phone: (602) 885-9159
Tucson, AZ 85711   Berta Cellers, Exec.Sec.

ARIZONA DAILY STAR - LIBRARY
4850 S. Park Ave.
Box 26807   Phone: (602) 294-4433
Tucson, AZ 85726   Elizabeth D. Miner, Chf.Libn.

ARIZONA HISTORICAL SOCIETY - LIBRARY
949 E. Second St.   Phone: (602) 882-5774
Tucson, AZ 85719   Margaret S. Bret-Harte, Hd.Libn.

ARIZONA-SONORA DESERT MUSEUM - LIBRARY
Rte. 9, Box 900   Phone: (602) 883-1380
Tucson, AZ 85704   Arthur A. Holton, Lib.Supv.

DIOCESE OF TUCSON - REGINA CLERI RESOURCE LIBRARY
8800 E. 22nd St.   Phone: (602) 886-5201
Tucson, AZ 85710   Sr. Bibiane Roy, O.P., Coord.

FIRST SOUTHERN BAPTIST CHURCH - LIBRARY
445 E. Speedway   Phone: (602) 623-5858
Tucson, AZ 85705   Ina Gable, Lib.Comm.Chm.

KINO COMMUNITY HOSPITAL - LIBRARY †
2800 E. Ajo Way   Phone: (602) 624-2721
Tucson, AZ 85713   Connie Skinner, Libn.

KITT PEAK NATIONAL OBSERVATORY - LIBRARY
Box 26732   Phone: (602) 327-5511
Tucson, AZ 85726   Cathaleen Van Atta, Libn.

L-5 SOCIETY - LIBRARY
1620 N. Park Ave.   Phone: (602) 622-6351
Tucson, AZ 85719   Gerald Driggers, Pres.

MOLLOY, JONES, DONAHUE, TRACHTA, CHILDERS & MALLAMO - LIBRARY †
Arizona Bank Plaza
Box 2268   Phone: (602) 622-3531
Tucson, AZ 85702   Paula H. Nordin, Libn.

NORTH AMERICAN RADIO ARCHIVES (NARA) - LIBRARY
3051 S. Jessica   Phone: (602) 790-2123
Tucson, AZ 85730   Steven K. Ham, Pres.

PALO VERDE HOSPITAL - MEDICAL LIBRARY
801 S. Prudence
Tucson, AZ 85710

PIMA COUNTY JUVENILE COURT CENTER - LIBRARY
2225 E. Ajo Way   Phone: (602) 882-2074
Tucson, AZ 85713   Sharon Hekman, Info.Dir.

PIMA COUNTY LAW LIBRARY
111 W. Congress   Phone: (602) 792-8456
Tucson, AZ 85701   Cecilia C. Torres, Law Libn.

PIMA COUNTY PLANNING DEPARTMENT - LIBRARY
131 W. Congress St.   Phone: (602) 792-8361
Tucson, AZ 85701   Paul Matty, Libn.

ST. MARK'S PRESBYTERIAN CHURCH - LIBRARY
3809 E. 3rd St.   Phone: (602) 325-1519
Tucson, AZ 85716

**ST. MARY'S HOSPITAL & HEALTH CENTER - RALPH FULLER MEDICAL
    LIBRARY**
1601 W. St. Mary's Rd.
Box 5386   Phone: (602) 622-5833
Tucson, AZ 85705   Jeffrey W. St. Clair, Med.Libn.

ST. THOMAS MORE CENTER - TIMOTHY PARKMAN MEMORIAL LIBRARY
1615 E. Second St.   Phone: (602) 327-6662
Tucson, AZ 85719   Thomas McGreevy, Dir.

TUCSON CITIZEN - LIBRARY
Box 26767   Phone: (602) 294-4433
Tucson, AZ 85726   Charlotte Kenan, Libn.

TUCSON CITY PLANNING DEPARTMENT - LIBRARY
Box 27210   Phone: (602) 791-4234
Tucson, AZ 85726   Olya T. Tymciurak, Libn.

TUCSON MEDICAL CENTER - MEDICAL LIBRARY
Box 42195   Phone: (602) 327-5461
Tucson, AZ 85733   Christee King, Med.Libn.

TUCSON MUSEUM OF ART - LIBRARY
140 N. Main   Phone: (602) 623-4881
Tucson, AZ 85705   Dorcas Worsley, Libn.

TUCSON PUBLIC LIBRARY - TUCSON GOVERNMENTAL REFERENCE LIBRARY
City Hall, Local Government Info.Ctr.
Box 27210   Phone: (602) 791-4041
Tucson, AZ 85726   Ann Berg, Libn.

U.S. NATL. PARK SERVICE - WESTERN ARCHEOLOGICAL CENTER - LIBRARY
1415 N. 6th Ave.
Box 41058   Phone: (602) 792-6896
Tucson, AZ 85717   Lori Grumet, Act.Hd.Libn.

**U.S. VETERANS ADMINISTRATION (AZ-Tucson) - MEDICAL CENTER
    LIBRARY**
S. 6th Ave.   Phone: (602) 792-1450
Tucson, AZ 85723   Nancy E. Myer, Chf.Libn.

UNIVERSITY OF ARIZONA - ARID LANDS INFORMATION CENTER
845 N. Park Ave.   Phone: (602) 626-4925
Tucson, AZ 85719   M. Justin Wilkinson, Prog.Dir.

**UNIVERSITY OF ARIZONA - ARIZONA BUREAU OF GEOLOGY & MINERAL
    TECHNOLOGY LIBRARY**
845 N. Park Ave.   Phone: (602) 626-2733
Tucson, AZ 85719   Thomas G. McGarvin, Dir.

**UNIVERSITY OF ARIZONA - ARIZONA COOPERATIVE WILDLIFE RESEARCH
    UNIT - RESEARCH COLLECTION**
218 Biological Sciences Bldg.   Phone: (602) 626-2500
Tucson, AZ 85721   Valery Catt, Unit Sec.

UNIVERSITY OF ARIZONA - ARIZONA HEALTH SCIENCES CENTER LIBRARY
1501 N. Campbell Ave.   Phone: (602) 626-6121
Tucson, AZ 85724   Thomas D. Higdon, Libn.

UNIVERSITY OF ARIZONA - ARIZONA STATE MUSEUM LIBRARY
                                        Phone: (602) 626-4695
Tucson, AZ 85721   Hans Bart, Musm.Libn.

UNIVERSITY OF ARIZONA - CENTER FOR CREATIVE PHOTOGRAPHY
843 E. University Blvd.   Phone: (602) 626-4636
Tucson, AZ 85719   Terence Pitts, Cur. of Photo Archv.

UNIVERSITY OF ARIZONA - COLLEGE OF ARCHITECTURE LIBRARY
                                        Phone: (602) 626-2498
Tucson, AZ 85721   S.W. Gresham, Libn.

UNIVERSITY OF ARIZONA - COLLEGE OF LAW LIBRARY
                                        Phone: (602) 626-1413
Tucson, AZ 85721   Ronald L. Cherry, Dir.

**UNIVERSITY OF ARIZONA - DIVISION OF ECONOMIC AND BUSINESS
    RESEARCH - LIBRARY**
College of Business
& Public Administration   Phone: (602) 626-2109
Tucson, AZ 85721   Holly A. Penix, Lib.Asst.

**UNIVERSITY OF ARIZONA - DIVISION OF MEDIA & INSTRUCTIONAL
    SERVICES - FILM LIBRARY**
Audiovisual Bldg.
1365 E. Speedway   Phone: (602) 626-3282
Tucson, AZ 85719   Katherine Holsinger, Film Lib.Mgr.

GEOGRAPHIC

UNIVERSITY OF ARIZONA ENVIRONMENTAL PSYCHOLOGY PROGRAM - LIBRARY
Dept. of Psychology
Tucson, AZ 85721
Phone: (602) 626-2921
William Ittelson, Dir.

UNIVERSITY OF ARIZONA - GOVERNMENT DOCUMENTS DEPARTMENT
University Library
Tucson, AZ 85721
Phone: (602) 626-4871
Cynthia E. Bower, Hd.Doc.Libn.

UNIVERSITY OF ARIZONA - INSTITUTE OF ATMOSPHERIC PHYSICS LIBRARY
PAS Bldg., Rm. 542
Tucson, AZ 85721
Phone: (602) 626-1211
Deirdre A. Campbell, Libn.

UNIVERSITY OF ARIZONA - LIBRARY SCIENCE COLLECTION
Graduate Library School
1515 E. First
Tucson, AZ 85721
Phone: (602) 626-3383
Cecil W. Wellborn, Hd.Libn.

UNIVERSITY OF ARIZONA - MAP COLLECTION
University Library
Tucson, AZ 85721
Phone: (602) 626-2596
Mary Lloyd Blakeley, Hd. Map Libn.

UNIVERSITY OF ARIZONA - MEDIA CENTER
Library
Tucson, AZ 85721
Phone: (602) 626-3441
Bonnie L. Woollet, Hd.

UNIVERSITY OF ARIZONA - MUSIC COLLECTION
Tucson, AZ 85721
Phone: (602) 626-2140
Dorman H. Smith, Hd. Music Libn.

UNIVERSITY OF ARIZONA - OPTICAL SCIENCES CENTER - READING ROOM
Tucson, AZ 85721
Phone: (602) 626-3143
Dr. Hyatt Gibbs, Supv.

UNIVERSITY OF ARIZONA - ORIENTAL STUDIES COLLECTION
University Library
Tucson, AZ 85721
Phone: (602) 626-3695
Riaz Ahmad, Hd.Libn.

UNIVERSITY OF ARIZONA - POETRY CENTER
1086 N. Highland Ave.
Tucson, AZ 85719
Phone: (602) 626-2462
Lois Shelton, Dir.

UNIVERSITY OF ARIZONA - SCIENCE-ENGINEERING LIBRARY
Tucson, AZ 85721
Phone: (602) 626-3706

UNIVERSITY OF ARIZONA - SPACE IMAGERY CENTER
Lunar & Planetary Laboratory
Tucson, AZ 85721
Phone: (602) 626-4861
Gail S. Georgenson, Res.Libn.

UNIVERSITY OF ARIZONA - SPECIAL COLLECTIONS DEPARTMENT
University Library
Tucson, AZ 85721
Phone: (602) 626-3435
Louis A. Hieb, Hd., Spec.Coll.

WESTERNERS INTERNATIONAL, A FOUNDATION - LIBRARY
College Sta., Box 3485
Tucson, AZ 85722
Carolyn Nelson, Libn.

NAVAJO NATION LIBRARY
Box K
Window Rock, AZ 86515
Phone: (602) 871-4941

U.S. ARMY - YUMA PROVING GROUND - FOREIGN INTELLIGENCE, SCIENTIFIC & TECHNICAL INFO.DIV. - TECHNICAL LIB.
Attn: STEYP-FIO-TL
Yuma, AZ 85364
Phone: (602) 328-2527
Theresa R. Butts, Chf.

YUMA COUNTY LAW LIBRARY
219 W. 2nd St., Court House
Yuma, AZ 85364
Phone: (602) 782-4534
Anna Margaret Sibley, Libn.

ARKANSAS

HENDERSON STATE UNIVERSITY - HUIE LIBRARY
Arkadelphia, AR 71923
Phone: (501) 246-5511
Dr. G. Garry Warren, Dir.Lrng.Rsrcs.

OUACHITA BAPTIST UNIVERSITY - RILEY LIBRARY
Arkadelphia, AR 71923
Phone: (501) 246-4531
Juanita Barnett, Libn.

BENTON SERVICES CENTER - MEDICAL LIBRARY
Benton, AR 72015
Phone: (501) 778-1111
Wilma Umberson, Med.Lib.Asst.

U.S. AIR FORCE BASE - BLYTHEVILLE BASE LIBRARY
Blytheville AFB, AR 72315
Lyn Manet, Libn.

MURPHY OIL CORPORATION - LAW DEPARTMENT LIBRARY
200 Jefferson St.
El Dorado, AR 71730
Phone: (501) 862-6411
Ann Ripley, Asst.

MURPHY OIL CORPORATION - LIBRARY
200 Jefferson St.
El Dorado, AR 71730
Phone: (501) 862-6411
Peggy H. Makepeace, Libn.

MURPHY OIL CORPORATION - TAX LIBRARY
200 Jefferson St.
El Dorado, AR 71730
Phone: (501) 862-6411
Harry Bain, Tax Mgr.

OZARK INSTITUTE - RURAL MEDIA CENTER LIBRARY
99 Spring St.
Box 549
Eureka Springs, AR 72632
Phone: (501) 253-7384
Marietta Edens, Libn.

ANTAEUS RESEARCH INSTITUTE - LIBRARY
2470 Gregg Ave.
Fayetteville, AR 72701
Phone: (501) 443-3050
Larry Horn, Libn.

U.S. FISH & WILDLIFE SERVICE - NATL. RESERVOIR RESEARCH LIBRARY
100 W. Rock St.
Fayetteville, AR 72701
Phone: (501) 521-3063
Kate H. Moore, Libn.

U.S. VETERANS ADMINISTRATION (AR-Fayetteville) - MEDICAL CENTER LIBRARY
Fayetteville, AR 72701
Phone: (501) 443-4301
Mary Fran Prottsman, Chf., Lib.Serv.

UNIVERSITY OF ARKANSAS, FAYETTEVILLE - CHEMISTRY LIBRARY
Chemistry Bldg.
Fayetteville, AR 72701
Phone: (501) 575-4601
Carolyn DeLille, Libn.

UNIVERSITY OF ARKANSAS, FAYETTEVILLE - FINE ARTS LIBRARY
Fayetteville, AR 72701
Phone: (501) 575-4708
Eloise E. McDonald, Hd.

UNIVERSITY OF ARKANSAS, FAYETTEVILLE - LAW LIBRARY
Fayetteville, AR 72701
Phone: (501) 575-5604
George E. Skinner, Dir.

UNIVERSITY OF ARKANSAS, FAYETTEVILLE - MEDICAL CENTER - NORTHWEST ARKANSAS HEALTH EDUCATION CENTER
1125 N. College
Fayetteville, AR 72701
Phone: (501) 521-7615
Connie Wilson, Libn.

UNIVERSITY OF ARKANSAS, FAYETTEVILLE - SPECIAL COLLECTIONS DIVISION
Fayetteville, AR 72701
Phone: (501) 575-4101
Samuel A. Sizer, Cur., Spec.Coll.

SEBASTIAN COUNTY LAW LIBRARY
503 Stephens Bldg.
Fort Smith, AR 72901
Phone: (501) 783-4730
Frances F. Newhouse, Libn.

SPARKS REGIONAL MEDICAL CENTER - REGIONAL HEALTH SCIENCES LIBRARY
1311 S. Eye St.
Fort Smith, AR 72901
Phone: (501) 441-4221
Grace Anderson, Libn.

GARLAND COUNTY HISTORICAL SOCIETY - ARCHIVES
914 Summer St.
Hot Springs, AR 71901
Phone: (501) 623-5875
Inez E. Cline, City/County Hist.

NATIONAL ASSOCIATION FOR GIFTED CHILDREN - LIBRARY
217 Gregory Dr.
Hot Springs, AR 71901
Phone: (501) 767-6933

WEYERHAEUSER COMPANY - SOUTHERN FORESTRY RESEARCH LIBRARY
Box 1060   Phone: (501) 624-8286
Hot Springs, AR 71901   Shirley Mink, Libn.

U.S. AIR FORCE BASE - LITTLE ROCK BASE LIBRARY †
Little Rock AFB   Phone: (501) 988-6979
Jacksonville, AR 72076   J.L. Clark, Base Libn.

ARKANSAS STATE UNIVERSITY MUSEUM - HISTORICAL LIBRARY
Drawer HH   Phone: (501) 972-2074
Jonesboro, AR 72467   Mary Coles, Musm. Registrar

ARKANSAS ARTS CENTER - ELIZABETH PREWITT TAYLOR MEMORIAL
    LIBRARY
Box 2137, MacArthur Pk.   Phone: (501) 372-4000
Little Rock, AR 72203   Evelyn McCoy, Libn.

ARKANSAS GAZETTE - NEWS LIBRARY
Box 1821   Phone: (501) 371-3740
Little Rock, AR 72203   Betty A. Turner, Hd.Libn.

ARKANSAS STATE DEPARTMENT OF POLLUTION CONTROL AND ECOLOGY -
    LIBRARY
8001 National Dr.
Box 9583   Phone: (501) 371-1701
Little Rock, AR 72209   Connie J. Yenner, Libn.

ARKANSAS STATE ENERGY OFFICE LIBRARY
One Capitol Mall   Phone: (501) 371-1370
Little Rock, AR 72201   Nancy C. Lewis, Libn.

ARKANSAS STATE HISTORY COMMISSION - ARCHIVES
One Capitol Mall   Phone: (501) 371-2141
Little Rock, AR 72201   Dr. John L. Ferguson, State Hist.

ARKANSAS STATE HOSPITAL - MEDICAL LIBRARY
4313 W. Markham St.   Phone: (501) 664-4500
Little Rock, AR 72201   Bernadine Bailey, Asst.Med.Libn.

ARKANSAS STATE LIBRARY †
One Capitol Mall   Phone: (501) 371-1524
Little Rock, AR 72201   Frances Nix, Assoc.Dir.

ARKANSAS STATE SUPREME COURT LIBRARY
Justice Bldg.   Phone: (501) 374-2512
Little Rock, AR 72201

ARKANSAS TERRITORIAL RESTORATION - LIBRARY
Third & Scott   Phone: (501) 371-2348
Little Rock, AR 72201   Dr. Priscilla McArthur, Educ.Coord.

BAPTIST MEDICAL CENTER SYSTEM - CENTRAL BAPTIST HOSPITAL
    LIBRARY
12th & Marshall   Phone: (501) 227-3235
Little Rock, AR 72201   Mrs. Theo H. Storey, Libn.

BAPTIST MEDICAL CENTER SYSTEM - MARGARET CLARK GILBREATH
    MEMORIAL LIBRARY
9600 W. 12th St.   Phone: (501) 227-2671
Little Rock, AR 72201   Auburn Steward, Libn.

METROPLAN, A COUNCIL OF GOVERNMENTS - PLANNING LIBRARY
Continental Bldg., Rm. 509
100 Main St.   Phone: (501) 372-3300
Little Rock, AR 72201   Joyce Messer, Dir., Finance/Adm.

REYNOLDS METALS COMPANY - ALUMINA DIVISION - TECHNICAL
    INFORMATION CENTER
One Union National Plaza, Suite 975   Phone: (501) 376-4037
Little Rock, AR 72201   Sherry Townsend, Tech.Libn.

ST. VINCENT INFIRMARY - MEDICAL LIBRARY
Markham & University   Phone: (501) 661-3991
Little Rock, AR 72201   Sr. Jean B. Roberts, S.C.N., Med.Libn.

U.S. VETERANS ADMINISTRATION (AR-Little Rock) - HOSPITAL LIBRARIES
300 E. Roosevelt Rd.   Phone: (501) 372-8361
Little Rock, AR 72206   George M. Zumwalt, Chf., Lib.Serv.

UNIVERSITY OF ARKANSAS, FAYETTEVILLE - TECHNOLOGY CAMPUS
    LIBRARY
1201 McAlmont St.
Box 3017   Phone: (501) 370-5178
Little Rock, AR 72203   Brent A. Nelson, Libn.

UNIVERSITY OF ARKANSAS AT LITTLE ROCK - PULASKI COUNTY LAW
    LIBRARY
400 W. Markham   Phone: (501) 371-1071
Little Rock, AR 72201   Ruth Brunson, Dir.

UNIVERSITY OF ARKANSAS MEDICAL SCIENCES CAMPUS - MEDICAL
    SCIENCES LIBRARY
4301 W. Markham   Phone: (501) 661-5980
Little Rock, AR 72201   Rose Hogan, Dir.

DREW COUNTY HISTORICAL SOCIETY - MUSEUM AND ARCHIVES
404 S. Main St.   Phone: (501) 367-7446
Monticello, AR 71655   Mrs. Clyde Rogers, Hostess

UNIVERSITY OF ARKANSAS, MONTICELLO - LIBRARY †
Box 3599   Phone: (501) 367-6811
Monticello, AR 71655   William F. Droessler, Libn.

WINROCK INTERNATIONAL LIVESTOCK RESEARCH AND TRAINING
    CENTER - INTERNATIONAL CENTER LIBRARY
Petit Jean Mountain, Rte. 3   Phone: (501) 727-5435
Morrilton, AR 72110   Joan Newton, Libn.

FIRST ASSEMBLY OF GOD - LIBRARY
22nd & Franklin Sts.   Phone: (501) 758-8553
North Little Rock, AR 72114   Joye Murry, Dir.

U.S. NATL. PARK SERVICE - PEA RIDGE NATL. MILITARY PARK - LIBRARY
                                                       Phone: (501) 451-8122
Pea Ridge, AR 72751   Billy D. Stout, Hist.

UNIVERSITY OF ARKANSAS, PINE BLUFF - JOHN BROWN WATSON
    MEMORIAL LIBRARY †
                                                       Phone: (501) 535-6700
Pine Bluff, AR 71601   Ada Jenkins, Lib.Asst.

ARKANSAS TECH UNIVERSITY - TOMLINSON LIBRARY
                                                       Phone: (501) 968-0304
Russellville, AR 72801   W.A. Vaughn, Libn.

BENTON COUNTY HISTORICAL SOCIETY - LIBRARY
Box 355   Phone: (501) 524-3217
Siloam Springs, AR 72761   J. Roger Huff, Sec./Ed.

ARKANSAS STATE UNIVERSITY - DEAN B. ELLIS LIBRARY
Box 2040   Phone: (501) 972-3078
State University, AR 72467   William Hansard, Lib.Dir.

U.S. FISH & WILDLIFE SERVICE - FISH FARMING EXPERIMENTAL STATION
    - LIBRARY
Box 860   Phone: (501) 673-8761
Stuttgart, AR 72160   Harry K. Dupree, Dir.

SOUTHWEST ARKANSAS REGIONAL ARCHIVES (SARA)
Box 134   Phone: (501) 983-2633
Washington, AR 71862   Mary Medearis, Dir.

CALIFORNIA

U.S. NAVY - NAVAL AIR STATION (Alameda) - LIBRARY
Bldg. 2, Wing 3   Phone: (415) 869-2519
Alameda, CA 94501   Barbara A. Arnott, Adm.Libn.

BRAUN (C.F.) COMPANY - REFERENCE LIBRARY
1000 S. Fremont Ave.   Phone: (213) 570-2233
Alhambra, CA 91802   Beverly Muller, Libn.

FIRST UNITED METHODIST CHURCH OF ALHAMBRA - LIBRARY
9 N. Almansor   Phone: (213) 289-4258
Alhambra, CA 91801   Dorothy Hooper, Chm., Lib.Comm.

GEOGRAPHIC

VINNELL CORPORATION - TECHNICAL SERVICES DIVISION LIBRARY
1145 Westminster Ave.   Phone: (213) 289-6281
Alhambra, CA 91802   Judith P. Jonsberg, Libn.

LA VINA HOSPITAL FOR RESPIRATORY DISEASES - MEDICAL LIBRARY †
3900 N. Lincoln Ave.   Phone: (213) 791-1241
Altadena, CA 91001   Grace M. Waser, Lib.Dir.

THEOSOPHICAL UNIVERSITY - LIBRARY
2416 N. Lake Ave.   Phone: (213) 798-8020
Altadena, CA 91001   John P. Van Mater, Libn.

ANAHEIM MEMORIAL HOSPITAL - MEDICAL LIBRARY
1111 W. LaPalma Ave.   Phone: (714) 999-6020
Anaheim, CA 92801   Carole J. Myrick, Med.Libn.

AUTOMATIC SPRINKLER COMPANY - INTERSTATE ELECTRONICS
    DIVISION - LIBRARY
1001 E. Ball Rd., Dept 2540
Box 3117   Phone: (714) 635-7210
Anaheim, CA 92803   Frances P. Zuehlsdorf, Libn.

GOOD SAMARITAN HOSPITAL OF ORANGE COUNTY, INC. - MEDICAL
    LIBRARY
1025 S. Anaheim Blvd.   Phone: (714) 533-6220
Anaheim, CA 92805   Jerome A. Holst, Med.Libn.

NORTHROP CORPORATION - ELECTRO-MECHANICAL DIVISION -
    TECHNICAL INFORMATION CENTER
500 E. Orangethorpe Ave.   Phone: (714) 871-5000
Anaheim, CA 92801   B.J. Duba, Mgr.

PSYNETICS FOUNDATION - LIBRARY
1212 E. Lincoln Ave.   Phone: (714) 533-2311
Anaheim, CA 92805   Marilyn Livingston, Off.Mgr.

ROCKWELL INTERNATIONAL - ANAHEIM INFORMATION CENTER
3370 Miraloma Ave.   Phone: (714) 632-3621
Anaheim, CA 92803   Victor J. Michel, Mgr.

UNITED STATES BORAX RESEARCH CORPORATION - RESEARCH LIBRARY
412 Crescent Way   Phone: (714) 774-2670
Anaheim, CA 92801   Betty J. Robson, Res.Libn.

PACIFIC UNION COLLEGE - PITCAIRN ISLANDS STUDY CENTER - LIBRARY
                    Phone: (707) 965-6241
Angwin, CA 94508   Taylor D. Ruhl, Libn.

CALIFORNIA THOROUGHBRED BREEDERS ASSOCIATION - CARLETON F.
    BURKE MEMORIAL LIBRARY
201 Colorado Pl.
Box 750   Phone: (213) 445-7800
Arcadia, CA 91006   E. Brownie Working, Libn.

ENGINEERING-SCIENCE, INC. - TECHNICAL LIBRARY
125 W. Huntington Dr.   Phone: (213) 445-7560
Arcadia, CA 91010   Carole S. Brady, Tech.Libn.

LOS ANGELES COUNTY DEPARTMENT OF ARBORETA AND BOTANIC
    GARDENS - PLANT SCIENCE LIBRARY
301 N. Baldwin Ave.   Phone: (213) 446-8251
Arcadia, CA 91006   Joan DeFato, Plant Sci.Libn.

NET ENERGY - ALTERNATIVE ENERGY LIBRARY
854 9th St.   Phone: (707) 822-5926
Arcata, CA 95521   Patricia Ferris, Info.Spec.

ATASCADERO STATE HOSPITAL - PROFESSIONAL LIBRARY
Drawer A   Phone: (805) 466-2200
Atascadero, CA 93422   Marie V. Logan, Sr.Libn.

UNIVERSITY OF SOUTHERN CALIFORNIA - CATALINA MARINE SCIENCE
    CENTER - LIBRARY
Big Fisherman Cove
Box 398   Phone: (213) 743-6792
Avalon, CA 90704

KERN COUNTY HEALTH DEPARTMENT - DR. MYRNIE A. GIFFORD PUBLIC
    HEALTH LIBRARY *
1700 Flower St.   Phone: (805) 861-3631
Bakersfield, CA 93305   Tsun Hai Lee, Dir. of Health Educ.

KERN COUNTY LAW LIBRARY
Courts & Administration Bldg., Rm. 301   Phone: (805) 861-2379
Bakersfield, CA 93301   Marian N. Smrekar, Law Libn.

KERN COUNTY MUSEUM - LIBRARY
3801 Chester Ave.   Phone: (805) 861-2132
Bakersfield, CA 93301   Christopher D. Brewer, Musm.Techn.

KERN COUNTY SUPERINTENDENT OF SCHOOLS OFFICE - INSTRUCTIONAL
    RESOURCES CENTER
5801 Sundale   Phone: (805) 861-2446
Bakersfield, CA 93309   Karl R. Hardin, Libn.

OCCIDENTAL EXPLORATION & PRODUCTION COMPANY - LIBRARY
5000 Stockdale Hwy.   Phone: (805) 395-8565
Bakersfield, CA 93309   Barbara Rogers, Lib.Supv.

WITCO CHEMICAL CORPORATION - GOLDEN BEAR DIVISION - R & D
    LIBRARY
Norris & Manor Dr.
Box 5446   Phone: (805) 393-7110
Bakersfield, CA 93388   Irma E. Johnson, Lib.Coord.

SAN GORGONIO PASS MEMORIAL HOSPITAL - MEDICAL LIBRARY
600 N. Highland Springs Ave.
Banning, CA 92220

U.S. AIR FORCE BASE - BEALE BASE LIBRARY
FL 4686   Phone: (916) 634-2706
Beale AFB, CA 95903   Jolaine B. Lamb, Base Libn.

CALIFORNIA MISSIONARY BAPTIST INSTITUTE - LIBRARY †
9246 Rosser
Box 848   Phone: (213) 925-4082
Bellflower, CA 90706   Edith Green, Libn.

SOUTHERN CALIFORNIA PERMANENTE MEDICAL CENTER - HEALTH
    SCIENCES LIBRARY/MEDIA CENTER
9400 E. Rosecrans Ave.   Phone: (213) 920-4247
Bellflower, CA 90706   Geraldine N. Graves, Dir., Lib.Serv.

TEXTRON, INC. - BELL AEROSPACE TEXTRON - DALMO VICTOR
    OPERATIONS - TECHNICAL LIBRARY
1515 Industrial Way   Phone: (415) 595-1414
Belmont, CA 94002

ALTA BATES HOSPITAL - STUART MEMORIAL LIBRARY
3001 Colby At Ashby   Phone: (415) 845-7110
Berkeley, CA 94705   Kay Kammerer, Health Sci.Libn.

ARMSTRONG COLLEGE - LIBRARY
2222 Harold Way   Phone: (415) 848-2500
Berkeley, CA 94704   Dr. Gary E. Tombleson, Coll.Libn.

BERKELEY PUBLIC LIBRARY - ART AND MUSIC DIVISION
2090 Kittredge St.   Phone: (415) 644-6785
Berkeley, CA 94704   Anne C. Nutting, Supv.Prog.Libn.

BERKELEY UNIFIED SCHOOL DISTRICT - CURRICULUM LIBRARY
1720 Oregon St.   Phone: (415) 644-6260
Berkeley, CA 94703   Scott McFarland, Prog.Supv.

CALIFORNIA SCHOOL OF PROFESSIONAL PSYCHOLOGY - BERKELEY
    LIBRARY
1900 Addison   Phone: (415) 548-5415
Berkeley, CA 94704   Karen Hildebrand, Libn.

CALIFORNIA STATE DEPARTMENT OF HEALTH SERVICES - VECTOR
    BIOLOGY AND CONTROL SECTION - LIBRARY
2151 Berkeley Way   Phone: (415) 843-7900
Berkeley, CA 94704   Edna Hernandez, Libn.

CETUS CORPORATION - RESEARCH LIBRARY
600 Bancroft Way   Phone: (415) 549-3300
Berkeley, CA 94710   George McGregor, Libn.

CLINICAL PHARMACOLOGY RESEARCH INSTITUTE - LIBRARY
2123 Addison St.
Berkeley, CA 94704

CUTTER LABORATORIES - LIBRARY
4th & Parker Sts.   Phone: (415) 420-5188
Berkeley, CA 94710   Hwei Wen Ng, Libn.

ECOLOGY CENTER - LIBRARY
2701 College Ave.   Phone: (415) 548-2221
Berkeley, CA 94705   Edward Spencer, Info.Coord.

FAR EAST MERCHANTS ASSOCIATION - FEMAS TRADE LIBRARY
1597 Curtis St.   Phone: (415) 527-3455
Berkeley, CA 94702   Ruth R. Goodman, Libn.

GRADUATE THEOLOGICAL UNION - LIBRARY
2400 Ridge Rd.   Phone: (415) 841-8222
Berkeley, CA 94709   John. D. Baker-Batsel, Dir.

HERRICK HOSPITAL AND HEALTH CENTER - PSYCHIATRIC LIBRARY
2001 Dwight Way   Phone: (415) 845-0130
Berkeley, CA 94704   Lois King Danton, Libn.

INFORMATION ON DEMAND
2511 Channing Way
Box 4536   Phone: (415) 841-1145
Berkeley, CA 94704   Sue Rugge, Pres.

INSTITUTE OF BUDDHIST STUDIES - LIBRARY
2717 Haste St.   Phone: (415) 849-2383
Berkeley, CA 94704   Haruyoshi Kusada, Dir.

INTERNATIONAL BIRD RESCUE RESEARCH CENTER - LIBRARY †
Aquatic Pk.   Phone: (415) 841-9086
Berkeley, CA 94710   Alice Berkner, Dir.

MAGNES (Judah L.) MEMORIAL MUSEUM - MORRIS GOLDSTEIN LIBRARY
2911 Russell St.   Phone: (415) 849-2710
Berkeley, CA 94705   Jane Levy, Libn./Archv.

MAGNES (Judah L.) MEMORIAL MUSEUM - WESTERN JEWISH HISTORY
    CENTER
2911 Russell St.   Phone: (415) 849-2710
Berkeley, CA 94705   Elaine Dorfman, Oral Hist.Div.Hd.

MEIKLEJOHN CIVIL LIBERTIES INSTITUTE - LIBRARY
1715 Francisco St.   Phone: (415) 848-0599
Berkeley, CA 94703   Ann Fagan Ginger, Dir.

METROPOLITAN TRANSPORTATION COMMISSION - ASSOCIATION OF BAY
    AREA GOVERNMENTS (ABAG) - LIBRARY
Hotel Claremont   Phone: (415) 849-3223
Berkeley, CA 94705   Dian Gillmar, Info.Coord.

NATIONAL HOUSING LAW PROJECT/NATIONAL ECONOMIC DEVELOPMENT
    AND LAW CENTER - LIBRARY
2150 Shattuck Ave., No.300   Phone: (415) 548-2600
Berkeley, CA 94704   Katherine Parkes, Libn.

SOCIETY FOR NUTRITION EDUCATION - SNE RESOURCE CENTER
2140 Shattuck Ave., Suite 1110   Phone: (415) 548-1363
Berkeley, CA 94704   Carolyn Franklin, Libn.

SOUTHEAST ASIA RESOURCE CENTER
Box 4000-D   Phone: (415) 548-2546
Berkeley, CA 94704   John Spragens, Jr., Co-Dir.

SYNERGY POWER INSTITUTE - LIBRARY
Box 9096   Phone: (415) 549-0839
Berkeley, CA 94709   James H. Craig, Dir.

U.S.D.A. - AGRICULTURAL RESEARCH SERVICE - WESTERN REGIONAL
    RESEARCH CENTER LIBRARY
    Phone: (415) 486-3351
Berkeley, CA 94710   Rena Schonbrun, Libn.

U.S. DEPT. OF ENERGY - LAWRENCE BERKELEY LABORATORY - LIBRARY
University of California
Bldg. 50B, Rm. 420   Phone: (415) 486-4626
Berkeley, CA 94720   Gloria Haire, Hd.Libn.

U.S. FOREST SERVICE - PACIFIC SOUTHWEST FOREST & RANGE
    EXPERIMENT STATION - WESTFORNET-BERKELEY
1960 Addison St.
Box 245   Phone: (415) 486-3173
Berkeley, CA 94701   Theodor B. Yerke, WESTFORNET Prog.Mgr.

UNIVERSITY OF CALIFORNIA, BERKELEY - ANTHROPOLOGY LIBRARY
230 Kroeber Hall   Phone: (415) 642-2400
Berkeley, CA 94720   Dorothy A. Koenig, Libn.

UNIVERSITY OF CALIFORNIA, BERKELEY - ASIAN AMERICAN STUDIES
    LIBRARY
3407 Dwinelle Hall   Phone: (415) 642-2218
Berkeley, CA 94720   Mrs. Wei Chi Poon, Hd.Libn.

UNIVERSITY OF CALIFORNIA, BERKELEY - ASTRONOMY-MATHEMATICS-
    STATISTICS-COMPUTER SCIENCES LIBRARY
100 Evans Hall   Phone: (415) 642-3381
Berkeley, CA 94720   Kimiyo T. Hom, Libn.

UNIVERSITY OF CALIFORNIA, BERKELEY - BANCROFT LIBRARY
    Phone: (415) 642-3781
Berkeley, CA 94720   James D. Hart, Dir.

UNIVERSITY OF CALIFORNIA, BERKELEY - BIOCHEMISTRY LIBRARY
430 Biochemistry Bldg.   Phone: (415) 642-5112
Berkeley, CA 94720   Rebecca Martin, Hd.Libn.

UNIVERSITY OF CALIFORNIA, BERKELEY - BIOLOGY LIBRARY
3503 Life Sciences Bldg.   Phone: (415) 642-2531
Berkeley, CA 94720   Rebecca Martin, Hd.Libn.

UNIVERSITY OF CALIFORNIA, BERKELEY - CENTER FOR CHINESE STUDIES
    - LIBRARY
12 Barrows Hall, Rm. 64   Phone: (415) 642-6510
Berkeley, CA 94720   Chi-Ping Chen, Libn.

UNIVERSITY OF CALIFORNIA, BERKELEY - CHEMISTRY LIBRARY
100 Hildebrand Hall   Phone: (415) 642-3753
Berkeley, CA 94720   George Vdovin, Libn.

UNIVERSITY OF CALIFORNIA, BERKELEY - CHICANO STUDIES LIBRARY
3408 Dwinelle Hall   Phone: (415) 642-3859
Berkeley, CA 94720   Francisco Garcia-Ayvens, Coord.

UNIVERSITY OF CALIFORNIA, BERKELEY - EARTH SCIENCES LIBRARY
230 Earth Sciences Bldg.   Phone: (415) 642-2997
Berkeley, CA 94720   Beatrice L. Lukens, Libn.

UNIVERSITY OF CALIFORNIA, BERKELEY - EAST ASIATIC LIBRARY
208 Durant Hall   Phone: (415) 642-2556
Berkeley, CA 94720   Richard S. Cooper, Act.Hd.

UNIVERSITY OF CALIFORNIA, BERKELEY - EDUCATION/PSYCHOLOGY
    LIBRARY
2600 Tolman Hall   Phone: (415) 642-4208
Berkeley, CA 94720   Catherine Gordon, Libn.

UNIVERSITY OF CALIFORNIA, BERKELEY - ENERGY AND RESOURCES
    PROGRAM - ENERGY INFORMATION CENTER
Rm. 100, Bldg. T-4   Phone: (415) 642-1004
Berkeley, CA 94720   Mari Wilson, Assoc.Libn.

UNIVERSITY OF CALIFORNIA, BERKELEY - ENTOMOLOGY LIBRARY
Wellman Hall, Rm. 210   Phone: (415) 642-2030
Berkeley, CA 94720   Esther Laine, Lib.Asst.

UNIVERSITY OF CALIFORNIA, BERKELEY - ENVIRONMENTAL DESIGN
    LIBRARY
210 Wurster Hall   Phone: (415) 642-4818
Berkeley, CA 94720   Arthur B. Waugh, Hd.

GEOGRAPHIC

UNIVERSITY OF CALIFORNIA, BERKELEY - FORESTRY LIBRARY
260 Mulford Hall   Phone: (415) 642-2936
Berkeley, CA 94720   Esther Johnson, Libn.

UNIVERSITY OF CALIFORNIA, BERKELEY - GIANNINI FOUNDATION OF
   AGRICULTURAL ECONOMICS - RESEARCH LIBRARY
248 Giannini Hall   Phone: (415) 642-7121
Berkeley, CA 94720   Grace Dote, Act.Hd.

UNIVERSITY OF CALIFORNIA, BERKELEY - GOVERNMENT DOCUMENTS
   DEPARTMENT
General Library   Phone: (415) 642-3287
Berkeley, CA 94720   Elizabeth Myers, Hd.

UNIVERSITY OF CALIFORNIA, BERKELEY - GRADUATE SCHOOL OF
   JOURNALISM - LIBRARY
607 Evans Hall   Phone: (415) 642-3384
Berkeley, CA 94720   David Brown, Libn.

UNIVERSITY OF CALIFORNIA, BERKELEY - INSTITUTE OF GOVERNMENTAL
   STUDIES - LIBRARY
Moses Hall, Rm. 109   Phone: (415) 642-5659
Berkeley, CA 94720   Jack Leister, Libn.

UNIVERSITY OF CALIFORNIA, BERKELEY - INST. OF INDUSTRIAL
   RELATIONS - LABOR OCCUPATIONAL HEALTH PROG.LIB.
2521 Channing Way   Phone: (415) 642-5507
Berkeley, CA 94720   Morris Davis, Exec. Program Dir.

UNIVERSITY OF CALIFORNIA, BERKELEY - INSTITUTE OF INDUSTRIAL
   RELATIONS LIBRARY
2521 Channing Way   Phone: (415) 642-4441
Berkeley, CA 94720   Nanette O. Sand, Libn.

UNIVERSITY OF CALIFORNIA, BERKELEY - INSTITUTE OF INTERNATIONAL
   STUDIES LIBRARY
340 Stephens Hall   Phone: (415) 642-3633
Berkeley, CA 94720   Colette Myles, Hd.

UNIVERSITY OF CALIFORNIA, BERKELEY - INSTITUTE OF
   TRANSPORTATION STUDIES LIBRARY
412 McLaughlin Hall   Phone: (415) 642-3604
Berkeley, CA 94720   Michael C. Kleiber, Hd.Libn.

UNIVERSITY OF CALIFORNIA, BERKELEY - LAW LIBRARY
230 Law Bldg.   Phone: (415) 642-4044
Berkeley, CA 94720   Preble Stolz, Law Libn.

UNIVERSITY OF CALIFORNIA, BERKELEY - LIBRARY SCHOOL LIBRARY
2 South Hall   Phone: (415) 642-2253
Berkeley, CA 94720   Virginia Pratt, Libn.

UNIVERSITY OF CALIFORNIA, BERKELEY - MAP ROOM
137 General Library   Phone: (415) 642-4940
Berkeley, CA 94720   Philip Hoehn, Map Libn.

UNIVERSITY OF CALIFORNIA, BERKELEY - MUSIC LIBRARY
240 Morrison Hall   Phone: (415) 642-2623
Berkeley, CA 94720   Vincent H. Duckles, Hd.

UNIVERSITY OF CALIFORNIA, BERKELEY - NATIVE AMERICAN STUDIES
   LIBRARY
3415 Dwinelle Hall   Phone: (415) 642-2793
Berkeley, CA 94720   Rosalie McKay, Libn.

UNIVERSITY OF CALIFORNIA, BERKELEY - NATURAL RESOURCES LIBRARY
40 Giannini Hall   Phone: (415) 642-4493
Berkeley, CA 94720   Lois Farrell, Hd.

UNIVERSITY OF CALIFORNIA, BERKELEY - OPTOMETRY LIBRARY
490 Minor Hall   Phone: (415) 642-1020
Berkeley, CA 94720   Alison Howard, Hd.

UNIVERSITY OF CALIFORNIA, BERKELEY - PHYSICS LIBRARY
                                   Phone: (415) 642-3122
Berkeley, CA 94720   Camille Wanat, Hd.

UNIVERSITY OF CALIFORNIA, BERKELEY - PUBLIC HEALTH LIBRARY
42 Earl Warren Hall   Phone: (415) 642-2511
Berkeley, CA 94720   Thomas J. Alexander, Hd.

UNIVERSITY OF CALIFORNIA, BERKELEY - SCIENCE & MATHEMATICS
   EDUCATION LIBRARY
Lawrence Hall of Science
Centennial Dr.   Phone: (415) 642-1334
Berkeley, CA 94720   Priscilla Mace Watson, Libn.

UNIVERSITY OF CALIFORNIA, BERKELEY - SEBASTIAN S. KRESGE
   ENGINEERING LIBRARY
Stephen D. Bechtel Engineering Center   Phone: (415) 642-3339
Berkeley, CA 94720   Judith Morton, Libn.

UNIVERSITY OF CALIFORNIA, BERKELEY - SOCIAL SCIENCE LIBRARY
30 Stephens Hall   Phone: (415) 642-0370
Berkeley, CA 94720   Geraldine Scalzo, Hd.

UNIVERSITY OF CALIFORNIA, BERKELEY - SOCIAL WELFARE LIBRARY
216 Haviland Hall   Phone: (415) 642-4432
Berkeley, CA 94720   Geraldine Scalzo, Hd.

UNIVERSITY OF CALIFORNIA, BERKELEY - SOUTH/SOUTHEAST ASIA
   LIBRARY SERVICE
438 Main Library   Phone: (415) 642-3095
Berkeley, CA 94720   Peter Ananda, Hd.

UNIVERSITY OF CALIFORNIA, BERKELEY - STATE DATA PROGRAM LIBRARY
Survey Research Center
2538 Channing Way   Phone: (415) 642-6571
Berkeley, CA 94720   Ilona Einowski, Libn.

UNIVERSITY OF CALIFORNIA, BERKELEY - UNIVERSITY EXTENSION -
   CONTINUING EDUCATION OF THE BAR - LIBRARY
2300 Shattuck Ave.   Phone: (415) 642-5343
Berkeley, CA 94704   Virginia Polak, Libn.

UNIVERSITY OF CALIFORNIA, BERKELEY - WATER RESOURCES CENTER
   ARCHIVES
North Gate Hall, Rm. 40   Phone: (415) 642-2666
Berkeley, CA 94720   Gerald J. Giefer, Libn.

UNIVERSITY OF CALIFORNIA - EXTENSION MEDIA CENTER
2223 Fulton St.   Phone: (415) 642-0460
Berkeley, CA 94720   Olga Knight, Mgr.

WOMEN'S HISTORY RESEARCH CENTER, INC. - WOMEN'S HISTORY
   LIBRARY
2325 Oak St.   Phone: (415) 548-1770
Berkeley, CA 94708   Laura X, Dir. & Pres.

WRIGHT INSTITUTE - GRADUATE DIVISION LIBRARY
2728 Durant Ave.   Phone: (415) 841-9230
Berkeley, CA 94704   Dorrie Matthews, Libn.

ACADEMY OF MOTION PICTURE ARTS AND SCIENCES - MARGARET
   HERRICK LIBRARY
8949 Wilshire Blvd.   Phone: (213) 278-4313
Beverly Hills, CA 90211   Terry T. Roach, Lib.Adm.

AMERICAN FILM INSTITUTE - CENTER FOR ADVANCED FILM STUDIES -
   CHARLES K. FELDMAN LIBRARY
501 Doheny Rd.   Phone: (213) 278-8777
Beverly Hills, CA 90210   Anne G. Schlosser, Lib.Dir.

BEVERLY HILLS PUBLIC LIBRARY - FINE ARTS DIVISION
444 N. Rexford Dr.   Phone: (213) 550-4720
Beverly Hills, CA 90210   Nick Cellini, Libn.

LESSER (Robert Charles) AND COMPANY - RESOURCE DEPARTMENT
8383 Wilshire Blvd., Suite 240   Phone: (213) 658-7600
Beverly Hills, CA 90211   Katherine Hanson, Mgr.

LITTON INDUSTRIES - LAW LIBRARY
360 N. Crescent Dr.   Phone: (213) 273-7860
Beverly Hills, CA 90210   W. Thomas Johnson, Law Libn.

LOMA LINDA UNIVERSITY - INSTITUTE FOR CANCER AND BLOOD
    RESEARCH - LIBRARY *
140 N. Robertson Blvd.   Phone: (213) 655-4706
Beverly Hills, CA 90211   Belle Gould, Libn.

ROBERT GORE RIFKIND FOUNDATION - ART LIBRARY AND GRAPHICS
    COLLECTION
9454 Wilshire Blvd.   Phone: (213) 278-0970
Beverly Hills, CA 90212   Karin Breuer, Cur.

SOUTHERN CALIFORNIA PSYCHOANALYTIC INSTITUTE - FRANZ
    ALEXANDER LIBRARY
9024 Olympic Blvd.   Phone: (213) 276-2455
Beverly Hills, CA 90211   Lena Pincus, Libn.

TWENTIETH CENTURY FOX FILM CORPORATION - RESEARCH LIBRARY
10201 W. Pico Blvd.
Box 900   Phone: (213) 277-2211
Beverly Hills, CA 90213   Kenneth Kenyon, Hd. of Res.Dept.

U.S. FOREST SERVICE - INYO NATL. FOREST - INFORMATION SERVICE
873 N. Main St.   Phone: (714) 873-5841
Bishop, CA 93514   Ray Schaaf, Info.Off.

BRANDEIS-BARDIN INSTITUTE - HOUSE OF THE BOOK
                                               Phone: (213) 348-7201
Brandeis, CA 93064   Hannah R. Kuhn, Spec.Libn.

NUTRILITE PRODUCTS, INC. - RESEARCH LIBRARY
5600 Beach Blvd.   Phone: (714) 521-3900
Buena Park, CA 90620   Jacqueline M. McCoy, Libn.

BURBANK COMMUNITY HOSPITAL - MEDICAL LIBRARY
466 E. Olive Ave.   Phone: (213) 846-3135
Burbank, CA 91501   Narciso M. Garganta, Med.Libn.

CRANE COMPANY - HYDRO-AIRE DIVISION - TECHNICAL LIBRARY
3000 Winona Ave.   Phone: (213) 842-6121
Burbank, CA 91510   Douglas Longyear, Engr.Dir.

DISNEY (Walt) PRODUCTIONS - ARCHIVES
500 S. Buena Vista   Phone: (213) 840-5424
Burbank, CA 91521   David R. Smith, Archv.

DISNEY (Walt) PRODUCTIONS - LIBRARY
500 S. Buena Vista   Phone: (213) 840-5326
Burbank, CA 91521   Mary Jo Terry, Libn.

LOCKHEED-CALIFORNIA COMPANY - TECHNICAL INFORMATION CENTER
Dept. 84-40, Bldg. U-51, Plant B-1   Phone: (213) 847-5646
Burbank, CA 91520   Stanley A. Elman, Mgr.

LOCKHEED CORPORATION - INTERNATIONAL MARKETING LIBRARY
Box 551, Bldg. 61   Phone: (213) 847-6527
Burbank, CA 91520   Betty Scanlon, Libn.

ST. JOSEPH MEDICAL CENTER - HEALTH SCIENCE LIBRARY
Buena Vista & Alameda Sts.   Phone: (213) 843-5111
Burbank, CA 91505   Sr. Naomi Hurd, S.P., Libn.

COEN COMPANY, INC. - TECHNICAL LIBRARY
1510 Rollins Rd.   Phone: (415) 697-0440
Burlingame, CA 94010   Clark Hutchason, Supv.

PENINSULA HOSPITAL AND MEDICAL CENTER - MEDICAL STAFF LIBRARY
1783 El Camino Real   Phone: (415) 697-4061
Burlingame, CA 94010   Prudence Harvey Hamilton, Chf.Libn.

WOODVIEW-CALABASAS PSYCHIATRIC HOSPITAL - LIBRARY
25100 Calabasas Rd.   Phone: (213) 888-7500
Calabasas, CA 91302   Ching-Fen Wu Tsiang, Libn.

CAMARILLO STATE HOSPITAL - PROFESSIONAL LIBRARY
                                               Phone: (805) 484-3661
Camarillo, CA 93010   Melvin C. Oathout, Libn.

ENVIRONMENTAL EDUCATION GROUP - LIBRARY
5762 Firebird Ct.   Phone: (213) 340-7309
Camarillo, CA 93010   Alan Arthur Tratner, Exec.Dir.

GEOTHERMAL WORLD CORPORATION - INFORMATION CENTER
5762 Firebird Ct.   Phone: (213) 342-4984
Camarillo, CA 91335   Alan A. Tratner, Dir.

ST. JOHN'S SEMINARY - EDWARD LAURENCE DOHENY MEMORIAL LIBRARY
5012 E. Seminary Rd.   Phone: (805) 482-2755
Camarillo, CA 93010   Rev. N.C. Eberhardt, C.M., Dir.Lib.Serv.

U.S. MARINE CORPS - CAMP PENDLETON LIBRARY SYSTEM †
Marine Corps Base
1122 E St.   Phone: (714) 725-5104
Camp Pendleton, CA 92055   Patrick J. Carney, Lib.Dir.

U.S. NAVY - NAVAL REGIONAL MEDICAL CENTER (Camp Pendleton) -
    MEDICAL LIBRARY
                                               Phone: (714) 725-1322
Camp Pendleton, CA 92055   Deborah G. Batey, Med.Libn.

QUADREX CORPORATION - INFORMATION & RESOURCE CENTER LIBRARY
1700 Dell Ave.   Phone: (408) 866-4510
Campbell, CA 95008   Margaret C. Ma, Libn.

HUGHES AIRCRAFT COMPANY - CANOGA PARK LIBRARY
Bldg. CP-2, Mail Sta. T-10
8433 Fallbrook Ave.   Phone: (213) 833-2400
Canoga Park, CA 91304   Donald C. Paul, Libn.

ROCKWELL INTERNATIONAL - ENERGY SYSTEMS GROUP - LIBRARY
8900 De Soto Ave.   Phone: (213) 341-1000
Canoga Park, CA 91304   Y.O. Fackler, Supv.

ROCKWELL INTERNATIONAL - ROCKETDYNE DIVISION - TECHNICAL
    INFORMATION CENTER
6633 Canoga Ave.   Phone: (213) 884-2575
Canoga Park, CA 91304   Laura J. Rainey, Mgr.

CARLSBAD CITY LIBRARY - SPECIAL COLLECTIONS DEPARTMENT
1250 Elm Ave.   Phone: (714) 438-5614
Carlsbad, CA 92008   Georgina D. Cole, Lib.Dir.

COMMUNITY HOSPITAL OF THE MONTEREY PENINSULA - MEDICAL STAFF
    LIBRARY †
Box HH   Phone: (408) 624-5311
Carmel, CA 93921   Marjorie V. Thorpe, Staff Libn.

HUMAN RESOURCES RESEARCH ORGANIZATION - CALIFORNIA LIBRARY
27857 Berwick Dr.
Carmel, CA 93923

AMERICAN RIVER HOSPITAL - ERLE M. BLUNDEN MEMORIAL LIBRARY
4747 Engle Rd.   Phone: (916) 486-2128
Carmichael, CA 95608   Carolyn Kopper, Health Sci.Libn.

NISSAN MOTOR CORPORATION - CORPORATE LIBRARY †
18501 S. Figueroa St.
Box 191   Phone: (213) 532-3111
Carson, CA 90247   Moon H. Kim, Libn.

PUREX CORPORATION - TECHNICAL LIBRARY
24600 S. Main St.
Box 6200   Phone: (213) 775-2111
Carson, CA 90749   Louise Y. Sakamoto, Libn.

U.S. AIR FORCE BASE - CASTLE BASE - BAKER LIBRARY
FL 4672, Bldg. 422   Phone: (209) 726-2630
Castle AFB, CA 95342   Enid L. Wilford, Base Libn.

LAUREL GROVE HOSPITAL - MEDICAL & DENTAL STAFF LIBRARY
19933 Lake Chabot Rd.   Phone: (415) 538-6464
Castro Valley, CA 94546   Marie Culwell, Staff Sec.

NILS PUBLISHING CO. - NATIONAL INSURANCE LAW SERVICE - LIBRARY
20675 Bahama St.   Phone: (213) 998-8830
Chatsworth, CA 91311   Annie Goodman, Coll.Coord.

WHITTAKER CORPORATION - TASKER SYSTEMS DIVISION - TECHNICAL
    LIBRARY
20131 Sunburst St.   Phone: (213) 341-3010
Chatsworth, CA 91311   Orlean Hinds, Libn.

GEOGRAPHIC

EDWARD-DEAN MUSEUM ART REFERENCE LIBRARY
9401 Oak Glen Rd.   Phone: (714) 845-2626
Cherry Valley, CA 92223   Mary Jo O'Neill, Musm.Dir.

CALIFORNIA STATE UNIVERSITY, CHICO - MERIAM LIBRARY
First & Hazel Sts.   Phone: (916) 895-6212
Chico, CA 95929   Dwight W. Shannon, Assoc.Dir.

U.S. NAVY - NAVAL WEAPONS CENTER - LIBRARY DIVISION
                                           Phone: (714) 939-2507
China Lake, CA 93555   S. Earl LaFon, Hd., Lib.Div.

ROHR INDUSTRIES - CORPORATE LIBRARY
Box 1516   Phone: (714) 575-3010
Chula Vista, CA 92012   James C. Fuscoe, Chf.Libn.

ROHR MARINE, INC. - TECHNICAL LIBRARY †
Box 2300   Phone: (714) 575-4122
Chula Vista, CA 92012   Hazel Jennings, Libn.

CITY OF INDUSTRY - RALPH W. MILLER GOLF LIBRARY
One Industry Hills Pkwy.
Box 3287   Phone: (213) 965-0861
City of Industry, CA 91744   Dr. Marjorie M. Ford, Libn.

BLAISDELL INSTITUTE FOR ADVANCED STUDY IN WORLD CULTURES AND
    RELIGIONS - LIBRARY
143 E. 10th St.   Phone: (714) 626-0521
Claremont, CA 91711

CALIFORNIA INSTITUTE OF PUBLIC AFFAIRS - LIBRARY
226 W. Foothill Blvd.
Box 10   Phone: (714) 624-5212
Claremont, CA 91711   T.C. Trzyna, Pres.

CLAREMONT COLLEGES - ELLA STRONG DENISON LIBRARY
Scripps College   Phone: (714) 621-8000
Claremont, CA 91711   Judy Harvey Sahak, Libn.

CLAREMONT COLLEGES - LIBRARY
800 Dartmouth   Phone: (714) 621-8000
Claremont, CA 91711   Patrick Barkey, Dir.

CLAREMONT COLLEGES - NORMAN F. SPRAGUE MEMORIAL LIBRARY
Harvey Mudd College   Phone: (714) 621-8000
Claremont, CA 91711   David Kuhner, Libn.

CLAREMONT COLLEGES - POMONA SCIENCE LIBRARIES
Pomona College   Phone: (714) 621-8000
Claremont, CA 91711   W. Brian Ebersole, Libn.

CLAREMONT GRADUATE SCHOOL - EDUCATIONAL RESOURCE &
    INFORMATION CENTER
Rm. 110, Harper Hall
Ninth & College   Phone: (714) 621-8000
Claremont, CA 91711   Kathleen Bernath, Interim Libn.

CLAREMONT GRADUATE SCHOOL - GEORGE G. STONE CENTER FOR
    CHILDREN'S BOOKS
Rm. 110, Harper Hall
Ninth & College   Phone: (714) 621-8000
Claremont, CA 91711   Kathleen Bernath, Interim Libn.

FRANCIS BACON FOUNDATION - LIBRARY
655 N. Dartmouth Ave.   Phone: (714) 624-6305
Claremont, CA 91711   Elizabeth S. Wrigley, Dir.-Libn.

RANCHO SANTA ANA BOTANIC GARDEN - LIBRARY
1500 N. College Ave.   Phone: (714) 626-3922
Claremont, CA 91711   Beatrice M. Beck, Libn.

SCHOOL OF THEOLOGY AT CLAREMONT - THEOLOGY LIBRARY
1325 N. College Ave.   Phone: (714) 626-3521
Claremont, CA 91711   Dr. Caroline Becker Whipple, Dir.

ARCHDIOCESE OF SAN FRANCISCO - CHANCERY ARCHIVES
Box 1799   Phone: (415) 994-5211
Colma, CA 94014   James Abajian, Archv.

WORLD LIFE RESEARCH INSTITUTE - LIBRARY †
23000 Grand Terrace Rd.   Phone: (714) 825-4773
Colton, CA 92324   Bruce W. Halstead, Lib.Dir.

CITY OF COMMERCE PUBLIC LIBRARY
5655 Jillson St.   Phone: (213) 722-6660
Commerce, CA 90040   Lois E. McClish, Dir.

CONTRA COSTA COUNTY SUPERINTENDENT OF SCHOOLS - ACCESS
    INFORMATION CENTER & PROFESSIONAL LIBRARY
2371 Stanwell Dr.   Phone: (415) 689-4353
Concord, CA 94520   Juliana Rousseau, Coord., Lib./Res.Serv

MOUNT DIABLO UNIFIED SCHOOL DISTRICT - TEACHERS' PROFESSIONAL
    LIBRARY
Willow Creek Center
1026 Mohr Lane   Phone: (415) 682-8000
Concord, CA 94518   Oral Lee, Prog.Adm.

U.S. NAVY - FLEET ANALYSIS CENTER (FLTAC) - LIBRARY
                                           Phone: (714) 736-4467
Corona, CA 91720   LaVaughn S. Knutson, Libn.

SHERMAN RESEARCH LIBRARY
614 Dahlia Ave.   Phone: (714) 673-1880
Corona Del Mar, CA 92625   Dr. William O. Hendricks, Dir.

BRUNSWICK CORPORATION - DEFENSE DIVISION - TECHNICAL LIBRARY
3333 Harbor Blvd.   Phone: (714) 546-8030
Costa Mesa, CA 92626   Clay Zlomke, Dir. of Engr.

FAIRVIEW STATE HOSPITAL - STAFF LIBRARY
2501 Harbor Blvd.   Phone: (714) 957-5394
Costa Mesa, CA 92626   Barbara Naylor, Sr.Libn.

SOUTHERN CALIFORNIA COLLEGE - O. COPE BUDGE LIBRARY †
55 Fair Dr.   Phone: (714) 556-3610
Costa Mesa, CA 92626   Kenneth L. Tracy, Hd.Libn.

PROCUREMENT ASSOCIATES - LIBRARY
733 N. Dodsworth Ave.   Phone: (213) 966-4576
Covina, CA 91724   Marie McDonald, Libn.

DEL NORTE COUNTY HISTORICAL SOCIETY - LIBRARY
577 H St.   Phone: (707) 464-3922
Crescent City, CA 95531   Judy Knitter, Pres.

DEL NORTE COUNTY LAW LIBRARY
Courthouse   Phone: (707) 464-4139
Crescent City, CA 95531   Patricia Lamb, Law Libn.

HUGHES AIRCRAFT COMPANY - COMPANY TECHNICAL DOCUMENT CENTER
Bldg. 6, Mail Sta. E 110
Centinela & Teale Sts.   Phone: (213) 391-0711
Culver City, CA 90230   Billy W. Campbell, Supv.

HUGHES AIRCRAFT COMPANY - INFORMATION RESOURCES SECTION
Bldg. 17, Mail Sta. J-145
Centinela & Teale Sts.   Phone: (213) 391-0711
Culver City, CA 90230   Clinton E. Merritt, Hd.,Info.Rsrcs.

HUGHES AIRCRAFT COMPANY - TECHNICAL LIBRARY
Bldg. 6, Mail Sta. D-117
Centinela & Teale Sts.   Phone: (213) 391-0711
Culver City, CA 90230   Mr. Masse Bloomfield, Supv.

METRO-GOLDWYN-MAYER, INC. - PICTURE RESEARCH LIBRARY
10202 W. Washington Blvd.   Phone: (213) 836-3000
Culver City, CA 90230   Bonnie Rothbart, Mgr.

SUMMA CORPORATION - HUGHES HELICOPTERS - LIBRARY †
Centinela & Teale Sts.   Phone: (213) 391-4451
Culver City, CA 90230   Dorothy K. Goss, Libn.

UNIVERSITY OF WEST LOS ANGELES - LAW LIBRARY
10811 W. Washington Blvd.   Phone: (213) 204-0000
Culver City, CA 90230   Dinah Granafei, Hd.Libn.

FOUR-PHASE SYSTEMS - CORPORATE LIBRARY
10700 N. De Anza Blvd.   Phone: (408) 255-0900
Cupertino, CA 95014   Linda McKell, Hd.Libn.

HEWLETT-PACKARD COMPANY - CUPERTINO LIBRARY *
11000 Wolfe Rd.   Phone: (408) 257-7000
Cupertino, CA 95014   Catherine Biggs, Libn.

TANDEM COMPUTERS, INC. - CORPORATE LIBRARY
19333 Vallco Pkwy.   Phone: (408) 725-6000
Cupertino, CA 95014   Selma Zinker, Lib.Supv.

MARY'S HELP HOSPITAL - LIBRARY †
1900 Sullivan Ave.   Phone: (415) 991-6700
Daly City, CA 94015   Marie Grace Abbruzzese, Libn.

GEOTHERMAL RESOURCES COUNCIL - LIBRARY
Box 98   Phone: (916) 758-2360
Davis, CA 95616   David N. Anderson, Exec.Dir.

UNIVERSITY OF CALIFORNIA, DAVIS - AGRICULTURAL ECONOMICS
BRANCH LIBRARY
University Library   Phone: (916) 752-1540
Davis, CA 95616   Mary Farrens, Libn.

UNIVERSITY OF CALIFORNIA, DAVIS - CALIFORNIA PRIMATE RESEARCH
CENTER - REFERENCE SERVICES
                                               Phone: (916) 752-0424
Davis, CA 95616   Pauline R. Frederick, Lib.Asst.

UNIVERSITY OF CALIFORNIA, DAVIS - ENVIRONMENTAL TOXICOLOGY
LIBRARY
                                               Phone: (916) 752-2562
Davis, CA 95616   Dr. Ming-Yu Li, Doc.Spec.

UNIVERSITY OF CALIFORNIA, DAVIS - F. HAL HIGGINS LIBRARY OF
AGRICULTURAL TECHNOLOGY
University Library   Phone: (916) 752-1621
Davis, CA 95616   C. Danial Elliott, Cur.

UNIVERSITY OF CALIFORNIA, DAVIS - GENERAL LIBRARY
                                               Phone: (916) 752-2110
Davis, CA 95616   Bernard Kreissman, Univ.Libn.

UNIVERSITY OF CALIFORNIA, DAVIS - HEALTH SCIENCES LIBRARY
                                               Phone: (916) 752-1214
Davis, CA 95616   Marjan Merala, Libn.

UNIVERSITY OF CALIFORNIA, DAVIS - INSTITUTE OF GOVERNMENTAL
AFFAIRS - LIBRARY
                                               Phone: (916) 752-2045
Davis, CA 95616   Nedjelko Dinko Suljak, Hd.Libn.

UNIVERSITY OF CALIFORNIA, DAVIS - PHYSICAL SCIENCES LIBRARY
University Library   Phone: (916) 752-1627
Davis, CA 95616   Scott Kennedy, Hd.Libn.

UNIVERSITY OF CALIFORNIA, DAVIS - SCHOOL OF LAW - LAW LIBRARY
                                               Phone: (916) 752-3322
Davis, CA 95616   Mortimer D. Schwartz, Law Libn.

U.S. NATL. PARK SERVICE - DEATH VALLEY NATL. MONUMENT - LIBRARY
                                               Phone: (714) 786-2331
Death Valley, CA 92328   Virgil J. Olson, Chf. Naturalist

LANDMARK CONSERVATORS - CABOTS OLD INDIAN PUEBLO MUSEUM
LIBRARY
67-616 E. Desert View Ave.   Phone: (714) 329-7610
Desert Hot Springs, CA 92240   Colbert H. Eyraud, Pres./Cur.

AEROJET ORDNANCE COMPANY - TECHNICAL LIBRARY
9236 E. Hall Rd.   Phone: (213) 923-7511
Downey, CA 90241   Fran Nimmo, Libn.

DOWNEY HISTORICAL SOCIETY MUSEUM - LIBRARY
12458 Rives Ave.
Box 554   Phone: (213) 869-7367
Downey, CA 90241   Barbara Callarman, Dir.

LOS ANGELES COUNTY - DEPARTMENT OF DATA PROCESSING - TECHNICAL
LIBRARY
9150 E. Imperial Hwy., Rm. R-118   Phone: (213) 771-5421
Downey, CA 90242   Millie Jones, Tech.Libn.

LOS ANGELES COUNTY SUPERINTENDENT OF SCHOOLS - PROFESSIONAL
REFERENCE CENTER
9300 E. Imperial Highway   Phone: (213) 922-6359
Downey, CA 90242   Margaret Marquette, Coord.

RANCHO LOS AMIGOS HOSPITAL - MEDICAL LIBRARY
7601 E. Imperial Hwy.   Phone: (213) 922-7696
Downey, CA 90242   Janet Judson, Med.Libn.

ROCKWELL INTERNATIONAL - SPACE BUSINESSES - TECHNICAL
INFORMATION CENTER
12214 Lakewood Blvd.   Phone: (213) 922-3807
Downey, CA 90241   Barbara E. White, Supv.

SIERRA COUNTY LAW LIBRARY
Courthouse   Phone: (916) 289-3271
Downieville, CA 95936

CITY OF HOPE NATIONAL MEDICAL CENTER - PINESS MEDICAL AND
SCIENTIFIC LIBRARY
                                               Phone: (213) 359-8111
Duarte, CA 91010   John L. Carrigan, Dir.

STEREO PHOTOGRAPHERS, COLLECTORS & ENTHUSIASTS CLUB - REEL
THREE-D ENTERPRISES - LIBRARY
Box 35   Phone: (213) 357-8345
Duarte, CA 91010   Susan Pinsky, Pub.

FOREMOST-MC KESSON - R & D CENTER LIBRARY
Box 2277   Phone: (415) 828-1440
Dublin, CA 94566   Joan La Manna, Libn.

U.S. NASA - DRYDEN FLIGHT RESEARCH CENTER - LIBRARY
                                               Phone: (805) 258-3311
Edwards, CA 93523   Karen J. Puffer, Libn.

U.S. AIR FORCE BASE - EDWARDS BASE LIBRARY †
FL 2805, 6510th ABG/SSL STOP 115   Phone: (805) 277-2375
Edwards AFB, CA 93523   O.M. Moyer, Libn.

U.S. AIR FORCE - FLIGHT TEST CENTER - TECHNICAL LIBRARY
6510 ABG/SSD, Stop 238   Phone: (805) 277-3606
Edwards AFB, CA 93523   Jean E. Dickinson, Chf., Tech.Lib.

IMPERIAL COUNTY LAW LIBRARY
Court House
El Centro, CA 92243   Patricia Seay, Law Libn.

ESPERANTO LEAGUE FOR NORTH AMERICA - ESPERANTO INFORMATION
SERVICE
Box 1129   Phone: (415) 653-0998
El Cerrito, CA 94530   Donald J. Harlow, Dir

JAPANESE-AMERICAN SOCIETY FOR PHILATELY - LIBRARY
Box 1049
El Cerrito, CA 94530   John R. Shively, Pres.

EL MONTE HISTORICAL SOCIETY - MUSEUM LIBRARY *
3100 Tyler Ave.   Phone: (213) 444-3813
El Monte, CA 91733   Lillian Wiggins, Dir.-Cur.

GOULD, INC. - NAVCOM SYSTEMS DIVISION - TECHNICAL LIBRARY †
Hoffman Electronic Pk.
4323 N. Arden Dr.   Phone: (213) 442-0123
El Monte, CA 91731   Barb Taylor, Act.Libn.

AGBABIAN ASSOCIATES - LIBRARY
250 N. Nash St.   Phone: (213) 640-0576
El Segundo, CA 90245   Elizabeth Tucker, Info.Dir.

COMPUTER SCIENCES CORPORATION - TECHNICAL LIBRARY
650 N. Sepulveda Blvd.   Phone: (213) 615-0311
El Segundo, CA 90245   Linda L. French, Mgr.

XEROX CORPORATION - LIBRARY
701 S. Aviation Blvd.
El Segundo, CA 90245
Phone: (213) 536-5222
Rose W. Kattlove, Hd.Libn.

SONOMA STATE HOSPITAL - PROFESSIONAL LIBRARY †
15060 Arnold Dr.
Box 1400
Eldridge, CA 95431
Phone: (707) 938-6000
Thella Pleasant, Libn.

JHK & ASSOCIATES - TECHNICAL LIBRARY - WEST
5801 Christie Ave., No. 220
Emeryville, CA 94608
Phone: (415) 428-2550
Richard Presby, Libn.

ENCINO HISTORICAL SOCIETY, INC. - LIBRARY
16756 Moorpark St.
Encino, CA 91436
Phone: (213) 784-4849
Helen B. Beiner, Coord.

CHURCH OF JESUS CHRIST OF LATTER-DAY SAINTS - EUREKA,
CALIFORNIA STAKE BRANCH GENEALOGICAL LIBRARY †
2734 Dolbeer St.
Eureka, CA 95501
Phone: (707) 443-7411
Grace M. Jones, Libn.

HUMBOLDT COUNTY LAW LIBRARY
Court House, 825 Fifth St.
Eureka, CA 95501
Phone: (707) 445-7201
Nancy A. Guy, Law Libn.

SOLANO COUNTY LAW LIBRARY
Hall of Justice, 600 Union Ave.
Fairfield, CA 94533
Phone: (707) 429-6501
Dwight C. Ely, Pres., Lib. Trustees

U.S. ARMY COMBAT DEVELOPMENTS EXPERIMENTATION COMMAND -
TECHNICAL INFORMATION CENTER
HQ USACDEC
Box 22
Ft. Ord, CA 93941
Phone: (408) 242-3757
Carolyn I. Alexander, Chf.Libn.

CALIFORNIA SCHOOL FOR THE BLIND - LIBRARY MEDIA CENTER
500 Walnut St.
Fremont, CA 94536
Phone: (415) 794-3800
Anne Lord, Libn., Media Spec.

CALIFORNIA STATE DEPARTMENT OF EDUCATION - SCHOOL FOR THE
DEAF LIBRARY
39350 Gallaudet Dr.
Fremont, CA 94538
Phone: (415) 794-3666
Elsa C. Kleinman, Libn.

CALIFORNIA SCHOOL OF PROFESSIONAL PSYCHOLOGY - FRESNO LIBRARY
1350 M St.
Fresno, CA 93721
Phone: (209) 486-8420
Inge Kauffman, Libn.

CALIFORNIA STATE - COURT OF APPEAL, 5TH APPELLATE DISTRICT - LAW
LIBRARY
5002 State Bldg.
Fresno, CA 93721
Phone: (209) 445-5491

CALIFORNIA STATE UNIVERSITY, FRESNO - DEPARTMENT OF SPECIAL
COLLECTIONS
Fresno, CA 93740
Phone: (209) 487-2595
Ronald J. Mahoney, Hd.

FRESNO CITY AND COUNTY HISTORICAL SOCIETY - ARCHIVES *
7160 W. Kearney Blvd.
Fresno, CA 93706
Phone: (209) 441-0862
Sharon Hiigel, Archv.

FRESNO COMMUNITY HOSPITAL - MEDICAL LIBRARY
Box 1232
Fresno, CA 93715
Phone: (209) 442-6000
Ann Keeney, Med.Libn.

FRESNO COUNTY DEPARTMENT OF EDUCATION - IMC-LIBRARY
2314 Mariposa St.
Fresno, CA 93721
Phone: (209) 488-3272
Stephen E. Goodson, Dir.

FRESNO COUNTY ECONOMIC OPPORTUNITIES COMMISSION - LIBRARY
2100 Tulare St., Rm. 503
Fresno, CA 93721

FRESNO COUNTY LAW LIBRARY
Fresno County Courthouse, Rm. 600
1100 Van Ness Ave.
Fresno, CA 93721
Phone: (209) 237-2227
Dorothy G. Morris, Libn.

FRESNO DIOCESAN LIBRARY
Box 1668
Fresno, CA 93717
Phone: (209) 237-5125
Denis J. Doherty, Hd.Libn. & Archv.

FRESNO GENEALOGICAL SOCIETY - LIBRARY
Box 1429
Fresno, CA 93718
Ruby Newell Jeter, Libn.

MENNONITE BRETHREN BIBLICAL SEMINARY - HIEBERT LIBRARY
1717 S. Chestnut Ave.
Fresno, CA 93702
Phone: (209) 251-7194
Adonijah Pauls, Libn.

O.K. SUPERMARKET - REAL ESTATE & SHOPPING CENTER DEVELOPMENT
INFORMATION CENTER
660 "O" St.
Fresno, CA 93721
Phone: (209) 485-3393
Richard Erganian, Info.Dir.

THOMAS, SNELL, JAMISON, RUSSELL, WILLIAMSON AND ASPERGER -
LIBRARY
Fresno's Towne House, 10th Fl.
Fresno, CA 93721
Phone: (209) 442-0600
Susan Herzog, Libn.

U.S.D.A. - AGRICULTURAL RESEARCH SERVICE - STORED-PRODUCT
INSECTS RESEARCH LABORATORY
5578 E. Air Terminal Dr.
Fresno, CA 93727
Phone: (209) 487-5310
Mr. A.P. Yerington, Res. Entomologist

U.S. VETERANS ADMINISTRATION (CA-Fresno) - HOSPITAL MEDICAL
LIBRARY
2615 E. Clinton Ave.
Fresno, CA 93703
Phone: (209) 227-2941
Cynthia K. Meyer, Chf., Lib.Serv.

VALLEY MEDICAL CENTER OF FRESNO - MEDICAL LIBRARY
445 S. Cedar Ave.
Fresno, CA 93702
Phone: (209) 453-5030
Vicky Christianson, Med.Libn.

WEST COAST BIBLE COLLEGE - MC BRAYER LIBRARY
6901 N. Maple Ave.
Fresno, CA 93710
Phone: (209) 299-7205

BECKMAN INSTRUMENTS, INC. - RESEARCH LIBRARY
2500 Harbor Blvd.
Fullerton, CA 92634
Phone: (714) 871-4848
Jean R. Miller, Chf.Libn.

CALIFORNIA STATE UNIVERSITY, FULLERTON - COLLECTION FOR THE
HISTORY OF CARTOGRAPHY
The Library, Rm. L444-B
800 N. State College Blvd., Box 4150
Fullerton, CA 92634
Phone: (714) 773-3444
Linda E. Herman, Spec.Coll.Libn.

CALIFORNIA STATE UNIVERSITY, FULLERTON - LIBRARY - FREEDOM
CENTER
Box 4150
Fullerton, CA 92634
Phone: (714) 773-3186
Lynn M. Coppel, Coord.

HUGHES AIRCRAFT COMPANY - GROUND SYSTEMS GROUP - TECHNICAL
LIBRARY
Bldg. 600/MSC 222
Box 3310
Fullerton, CA 92634
Phone: (714) 871-3232
Stanley B. Demes, Chf.Libn.

HUNT-WESSON FOODS - INFORMATION CENTER
1645 W. Valencia Dr.
Fullerton, CA 92634
Phone: (714) 871-2100
Joy Hastings, Mgr.Info.Ctr.

PACIFIC CHRISTIAN COLLEGE - HURST MEMORIAL LIBRARY
2500 E. Nutwood Ave.
Fullerton, CA 92631
Phone: (714) 879-3901
Jeffrey L. Wilson, Dir.

REILLY TRANSLATIONS - LIBRARY
Box 2917
Fullerton, CA 92633
Phone: (213) 697-7227
Michael M. Reilly, Dir.

ST. JUDE HOSPITAL & REHABILITATION CENTER - MEDICAL LIBRARY
101 E. Valencia Mesa Dr.
Fullerton, CA 92635
Phone: (714) 871-3280
Barbara Garside, Med.Libn.

SOUTHERN CALIFORNIA COLLEGE OF OPTOMETRY - M.B. KETCHUM
MEMORIAL LIBRARY
2001 Associated Rd.   Phone: (714) 870-7226
Fullerton, CA 92631   Mrs. Pat Carlson, Hd.Libn.

WESTERN STATE UNIVERSITY - COLLEGE OF LAW - LIBRARY
1111 N. State College Blvd.   Phone: (714) 738-1000
Fullerton, CA 92631   Frank Phillips, Univ.Libn.

AMERICAN AVIATION HISTORICAL SOCIETY - AAHS REFERENCE LIBRARY
Box 99   Phone: (714) 549-4818
Garden Grove, CA 92642   Douglas I. Pirus, Off.Mgr.

GARDEN GROVE HISTORICAL SOCIETY - E.G.WARE LIBRARY
12174 Euclid Ave.   Phone: (714) 530-8871
Garden Grove, CA 92640

LIBRARY OF VEHICLES
12172 Sheridan Ln.   Phone: (714) 636-9517
Garden Grove, CA 92640   W. Everett Miller, Libn. & Owner

ORANGE COUNTY TRANSIT DISTRICT - RESOURCE CENTER
11222 Acacia Pkwy.
Box 3005   Phone: (714) 971-6200
Garden Grove, CA 92642   Judy Schulz, Rsrcs.Spec.

HITCO - TECHNICAL LIBRARY
1600 W. 135th St.   Phone: (213) 329-4908
Gardena, CA 90249   Anita Hicks, Tech.Libn.

U.S. AIR FORCE BASE - GEORGE BASE LIBRARY
                                             Phone: (714) 269-3228
George AFB, CA 92392   Mrs. Frances Haysley, Base Libn.

JACK LONDON MUSEUM AND RESEARCH CENTER
14300 Arnold Dr.
Box 337   Phone: (707) 996-2888
Glen Ellen, CA 95442   Winifred Kingman, Libn.

GLENDALE ADVENTIST MEDICAL CENTER - LIBRARY
1509 Wilson Terrace   Phone: (213) 244-8000
Glendale, CA 91206   Eugenie Prime, Lib.Dir.

GLENDALE CITY - PLANNING DIVISION - TECHNICAL LIBRARY
633 E. Broadway   Phone: (213) 956-2140
Glendale, CA 91205   Ronald Larson, Principal Planner

GLENDALE PUBLIC LIBRARY - BRAND LIBRARY
1601 W. Mountain St.   Phone: (213) 956-2051
Glendale, CA 91201   Jane Hagan, Lib.Serv.Supv.

GLENDALE UNIVERSITY - COLLEGE OF LAW LIBRARY
220 N. Glendale Ave.   Phone: (213) 247-0770
Glendale, CA 91206   Karen G. Wood, Hd.Libn.

LOS ANGELES COLLEGE OF CHIROPRACTIC - HENRY G. HIGHLY LIBRARY
920 E. Broadway   Phone: (213) 240-7686
Glendale, CA 91205   Robin L. Lober, Dir.

REPUBLICAN ASSOCIATES OF LOS ANGELES COUNTY - RESEARCH LIBRARY
1153 N. Brand Blvd.   Phone: (213) 240-9100
Glendale, CA 91202   Mark S. Harmsen, Res.Dir.

SINGER COMPANY - LIBRASCOPE DIVISION - TECHNICAL INFORMATION
CENTER
833 Sonora Ave.   Phone: (213) 244-6541
Glendale, CA 91201   Nathan J. Sands, Mgr.

SONS OF THE REVOLUTION IN THE STATE OF CALIFORNIA SOCIETY -
LIBRARY
600 S. Central Ave.   Phone: (213) 240-1775
Glendale, CA 91204   Richard E. Coe, Lib.Dir.

TRAVENOL LABORATORIES, INC. - HYLAND DIVISION - RESEARCH LIBRARY
444 W. Glenoaks Blvd.
Box 1976   Phone: (714) 641-3500
Glendale, CA 91209   Monica Hermesch, Chf.Libn.

UNIVERSAL POSTAL UNION COLLECTORS - LIBRARY
53 Glenflow Court
Glendale, CA 91206   Raymond Reaber, Pres.

WED ENTERPRISES - RESEARCH LIBRARY
1401 Flower St.   Phone: (213) 956-7263
Glendale, CA 91201   Maryruth Orr, Libn.

WOLFE (Harvey G.) LIBRARY
Box 3514   Phone: (213) 241-7284
Glendale, CA 91201   Douglas L. Evans, Libn.

BURROUGHS CORPORATION - SANTA BARBARA PLANT - LIBRARY
6300 Hollister Ave.   Phone: (805) 964-6881
Goleta, CA 93017   Nailah Malik, Tech.Libn.

EG&G, INC. - SANTA BARBARA DIVISION - LIBRARY
130 Robin Hill Rd.
Box 98   Phone: (805) 967-0456
Goleta, CA 93017   Richard H. Clow, Libn.

GENERAL MOTORS CORPORATION - DELCO ELECTRONICS DIVISION -
TECHNICAL LIBRARY †
6767 Hollister Ave.   Phone: (805) 961-5080
Goleta, CA 93017   Kenneth C. Crombie, Tech.Libn.

HUGHES AIRCRAFT COMPANY - SANTA BARBARA RESEARCH CENTER -
TECHNICAL LIBRARY
75 Coromar Dr.   Phone: (805) 968-3511
Goleta, CA 93117   Susan K. Gentry, Tech.Libn.

HUMAN FACTORS RESEARCH, INC. - TECHNICAL LIBRARY *
5775 Dawson Ave.   Phone: (805) 964-0591
Goleta, CA 93017

OCEANOGRAPHIC SERVICES, INC. - TECHNICAL LIBRARY
25 Castilian Dr.   Phone: (805) 685-4521
Goleta, CA 93117   Susan L. Dillon, Libn.

RAYTHEON COMPANY - ELECTROMAGNETIC SYSTEMS DIVISION -
ENGINEERING LIBRARY
6380 Hollister Ave.   Phone: (805) 967-5511
Goleta, CA 93117   J.K. Thornburgh, Libn.

SANTA BARBARA COUNTY GENEALOGICAL SOCIETY - LIBRARY
Box 1174
Goleta, CA 93116   Ruth Scollin, Libn.

SUNRAE LEARNING RESOURCES CENTER
5679 Hollister Ave.   Phone: (805) 964-4483
Goleta, CA 93017   Kate Christensen, Libn.

BLOCH (Ernest) SOCIETY - ARCHIVES
Star Route 2   Phone: (707) 884-3473
Gualala, CA 95445   Lucienne Bloch Dimitroff, Sec.

KINGS COUNTY LAW LIBRARY
County Government Ctr.
Hanford, CA 93230   Jean H. Smith, Law Libn.

BAY HARBOR HOSPITAL - MEDICAL LIBRARY
1437 W. Lomita Blvd.   Phone: (213) 325-1221
Harbor City, CA 90710   Bella Kwong, Med.Libn.

NORTHROP CORPORATION - AIRCRAFT DIVISION - LIBRARY SERVICES
3901 W. Broadway   Phone: (213) 970-4136
Hawthorne, CA 90250   Hugo W. Jones, Libn.

ALAMEDA COUNTY LAW LIBRARY
South County Branch
224 W. Winton Ave.   Phone: (415) 881-6380
Hayward, CA 94544   Cossette T. Sun, Law Lib.Dir.

ALAMEDA COUNTY OFFICE OF EDUCATION - TEACHERS' PROFESSIONAL
LIBRARY
685 A St.   Phone: (415) 881-6372
Hayward, CA 94541   Loretta M. Chin, Libn.

GEOGRAPHIC

GEOGRAPHIC

ALAMEDA COUNTY PLANNING DEPARTMENT - STAFF LIBRARY *
399 Elmhurst St.   Phone: (415) 881-6401
Hayward, CA 94544

AQUATIC RESEARCH INSTITUTE - LIBRARY
2242 Davis Court   Phone: (415) 785-2216
Hayward, CA 94545   V. Parker, Libn.

KAISER-PERMANENTE MEDICAL CENTER - HAYWARD MEDICAL LIBRARY
27400 Hesperian Blvd.   Phone: (415) 784-5298
Hayward, CA 94545   Alice Pipes, Med.Libn.

KAISER-PERMANENTE MEDICAL CENTER - HEALTH INFORMATION CENTER
27400 Hesprian Blvd.
Hayward, CA 94545   Alice Pipes, Libn.

DE FOREST RESEARCH SERVICE - LIBRARY
780 North Gower St.   Phone: (213) 469-2271
Hollywood, CA 90038   Kellam de Forest, Dir.

HOMOSEXUAL INFORMATION CENTER - TANGENT GROUP
6758 Hollywood Blvd., No. 208   Phone: (213) 464-8431
Hollywood, CA 90028   Leslie Colfax, Libn.

MAX FACTOR & COMPANY - R & D LIBRARY
1655 N. McCadden Pl.   Phone: (213) 856-6648
Hollywood, CA 90028   Dawn A. Wingate, Tech.Libn.

MERCURY ARCHIVES
1574 Crossroads of the World   Phone: (213) 463-8000
Hollywood, CA 90028   Herbert L. Kornfeld, Dir.

TEMPLE ISRAEL OF HOLLYWOOD - JOSEPH H. CORWIN MEMORIAL LIBRARY
†
7300 Hollywood Blvd.   Phone: (213) 876-8330
Hollywood, CA 90046

CIBBARELLI & ASSOCIATES - INFORMATION SERVICES
Box 5337   Phone: (714) 842-6121
Huntington Beach, CA 92646   Pamela Cibbarelli, Pres.

MC DONNELL DOUGLAS CORPORATION - MC DONNELL DOUGLAS
    ASTRONAUTICS COMPANY - TECHNICAL LIBRARY SERVICES
5301 Bolsa Ave.   Phone: (714) 896-2317
Huntington Beach, CA 92647   E.G. Reed, Sect.Mgr.

UNITED STATES LIFESAVING ASSOCIATION - LIBRARY & INFORMATION
    CENTER
Box 366   Phone: (714) 226-6868
Huntington Beach, CA 92648   Byron Wear, Exec.Dir.

KOBE, INC. - ENGINEERING LIBRARY
3040 E. Slauson Ave.   Phone: (213) 588-1271
Huntington Park, CA 90255   Zenny Mamdani, Engr.Adm.Asst.

NAPA STATE HOSPITAL - WRENSHALL A. OLIVER PROFESSIONAL LIBRARY
Box A   Phone: (707) 255-6600
Imola, CA 94558   Corlan Dokken Johnson, Sr.Libn.

INYO COUNTY LAW LIBRARY
Drawer K   Phone: (714) 878-2411
Independence, CA 93526

SPECTROL ELECTRONICS CORPORATION - LIBRARY
17070 E. Gale Ave.
Box 1220   Phone: (213) 964-6565
Industry, CA 91749   James Roehrich, Eng. Standards Supv.

DANIEL FREEMAN HOSPITAL - VICTOR J. WACHA MEDICAL LIBRARY
333 N. Prairie Ave.   Phone: (213) 674-7050
Inglewood, CA 90301   Susan W. Wilson, Dir.

NORTHROP UNIVERSITY - ALUMNI LIBRARY †
1155 W. Arbor Vitae St.   Phone: (213) 776-5466
Inglewood, CA 90306   Chere Negaard, Dir., Lib.Serv.

PANEL DISPLAYS, INC. - TECHNICAL LIBRARY †
211 S. Hindry Ave.   Phone: (213) 641-6661
Inglewood, CA 90301   K.O. Fugate, Pres. & Libn.

WESTERN STATES COLLEGE OF ENGINEERING - LIBRARY †
970 W. Manchester Ave.
Inglewood, CA 90301

CHURCH OF JESUS CHRIST OF LATTER-DAY SAINTS - MT. WHITNEY
    BRANCH GENEALOGICAL LIBRARY †
Box 1090
Inyokern, CA 93527   Brigg Lewis, Libn.

ALLERGAN PHARMACEUTICALS, INC. - PROFESSIONAL INFORMATION
    SERVICES
2525 Dupont Dr.   Phone: (714) 752-4500
Irvine, CA 92713   Retha Z. Ott, Mgr.

FLUOR ENGINEERS AND CONSTRUCTORS, INC. - ENGINEERING LIBRARY
3333 Michelson Dr.   Phone: (714) 975-2000
Irvine, CA 92730   Pam Sammons, Tech.Libn.

HURTY-PECK LIBRARY OF BEVERAGE LITERATURE †
16950 Armstrong Ave.
Box 16039   Phone: (714) 557-1660
Irvine, CA 92714   A.W. Noling, Libn.

OCCIDENTAL RESEARCH CORPORATION - TECHNICAL INFORMATION
    CENTER
2100 S.E. Main
Box 19601   Phone: (714) 957-7450
Irvine, CA 92713   Dicksie C. Blackstock, Tech.Info.Mgr.

UNIVERSITY OF CALIFORNIA, IRVINE - BIOLOGICAL SCIENCES LIBRARY
Box 19556   Phone: (714) 833-6730
Irvine, CA 92713

UNIVERSITY OF CALIFORNIA, IRVINE - BIOMEDICAL LIBRARY
Box 19556   Phone: (714) 833-6652
Irvine, CA 92713   F. Raymond Long, Asst.Univ.Libn.

UNIVERSITY OF CALIFORNIA, IRVINE - INSTITUTE OF TRANSPORTATION
    STUDIES - RESOURCE CENTER †
Rm. 150 SST   Phone: (714) 833-5985
Irvine, CA 92717   Nancy M. Jacobus, Info.Spec.

UNIVERSITY OF CALIFORNIA, IRVINE - MUSEUM OF SYSTEMATIC BIOLOGY
    - LIBRARY
Box 19556   Phone: (714) 833-6447
Irvine, CA 92713

UNITED FARM WORKERS OF AMERICA, AFL-CIO - I.C. LIBRARY †
La Paz   Phone: (805) 822-5571
Keene, CA 93531   Peter Gines Velasco, Dir.

CHEVRON OIL FIELD RESEARCH COMPANY - TECHNICAL INFORMATION
    SERVICES
Box 446   Phone: (213) 694-7500
La Habra, CA 90631   Ann S. Coppin, Supv.

CALBIOCHEM-BEHRING CORPORATION - LIBRARY
10933 N. Torrey Pines Rd.   Phone: (714) 453-7331
La Jolla, CA 92037   Aznive Sabonjian, Libn.

COPLEY PRESS, INC. - JAMES S. COPLEY LIBRARY
7713 Herschel Ave.
Box 1530   Phone: (714) 454-0411
La Jolla, CA 92037   Richard Reilly, Cur.

LA JOLLA MUSEUM OF CONTEMPORARY ART - HELEN PALMER GEISEL
    LIBRARY
700 Prospect St.   Phone: (714) 454-3541
La Jolla, CA 92037   Gail Richardson, Libn.

LIBRARY ASSOCIATION OF LA JOLLA - ATHENAEUM MUSIC AND ARTS
    LIBRARY
1008 Wall St.   Phone: (714) 454-5872
La Jolla, CA 92037   Evelyn Neumann, Lib.Adm.

OCEAN ENGINEERING INFORMATION SERVICE
Box 989   Phone: (714) 454-1922
La Jolla, CA 92038   Dr. E. Sinha, Hd.

SCRIPPS CLINIC & RESEARCH FOUNDATION - KRESGE MEDICAL LIBRARY
10666 N. Tarrey Pines Rd.   Phone: (714) 455-8705
La Jolla, CA 92037   Jesse G. Neely, Libn.

SYSTEMS, SCIENCE AND SOFTWARE - TECHNICAL LIBRARY
Box 1620   Phone: (714) 453-0060
La Jolla, CA 92038   LaDonna L. Rowe, Libn.

TRAUB PLANT SCIENCE LIBRARY
2678 Prestwick Ct.
La Jolla, CA 92037   Dr. Hamilton P. Traub, Hd.

U.S. NATL. MARINE FISHERIES SERVICE - SOUTHWEST FISHERIES CENTER
   - LIBRARY
Box 271   Phone: (714) 453-2820
La Jolla, CA 92038   Dan Gittings, Libn.

UNIVERSITY OF CALIFORNIA, SAN DIEGO - BIOMEDICAL LIBRARY
                                             Phone: (714) 452-3253
La Jolla, CA 92093   Robert F. Lewis, Libn.

UNIVERSITY OF CALIFORNIA, SAN DIEGO - SCIENCE & ENGINEERING
   LIBRARY
C-075E   Phone: (714) 452-3257
La Jolla, CA 92093   Beverlee French, Libn.

UNIVERSITY OF CALIFORNIA, SAN DIEGO - SCRIPPS INSTITUTION OF
   OCEANOGRAPHY LIBRARY
                                             Phone: (714) 452-3274
La Jolla, CA 92093   William J. Goff, Libn.

UNIVERSITY OF CALIFORNIA, SAN DIEGO - UNIVERSITY LIBRARIES
                                             Phone: (714) 452-3336
La Jolla, CA 92093   Millicent D. Abell, Univ.Libn.

WESTERN BEHAVIORAL SCIENCES INSTITUTE - LIBRARY *
1150 Silverado St.   Phone: (714) 459-3811
La Jolla, CA 92037   P. Falck, Adm.Coord.

BIOLA COLLEGE, INC. - LIBRARY
13800 Biola Ave.   Phone: (213) 944-0351
La Mirada, CA 90639   Gerald L. Gooden, Dir.

DENNY'S INC. - COMPUTER SERVICES LIBRARY
14256 E. Firestone Blvd.   Phone: (714) 521-4152
La Mirada, CA 90637   Penny Shubnell, Tech.Libn.

UNIVERSITY OF LA VERNE - COLLEGE OF LAW - LIBRARY
1950 3rd St.   Phone: (714) 593-7184
La Verne, CA 91750   Suzanne Miller, Law Libn.

U.S. NATL. ARCHIVES & RECORDS SERVICE - FEDERAL ARCHIVES AND
   RECORDS CENTER, REGION 9
24000 Avila Rd.   Phone: (714) 831-4220
Laguna Niguel, CA 92677   Kenneth F. Rossman, Chf., Archv.Br.

U.S. ARMY - SPECIAL SERVICES DIVISION - SHARPE ARMY DEPOT -
   LIBRARY *
                                             Phone: (209) 982-2404
Lathrop, CA 95331   Elizabeth Reeve, Libn.

U.S. NAVY - NAVAL AIR STATION (Lemoore) - LIBRARY †
Bldg. 821   Phone: (209) 998-3144
Lemoore, CA 93245   Harriet Jean Chism, Sta.Libn.

U.S. DEPT. OF ENERGY - LAWRENCE LIVERMORE LAB. - TECHNICAL INFO.
   DEPT. LIBRARY
Box 808   Phone: (415) 422-5277
Livermore, CA 94550   John B. Verity, Lib.Mgr.

U.S. DEPT. OF ENERGY - SANDIA NATL. LABORATORIES, LIVERMORE -
   TECHNICAL LIBRARY
Box 969   Phone: (415) 422-2847
Livermore, CA 94550   M.A. Pound, Supv.

U.S. VETERANS ADMINISTRATION (CA-Livermore) - MEDICAL LIBRARY
                                             Phone: (415) 447-2560
Livermore, CA 94550   Jane H. Levie, Chf.Libn.

SAN JOAQUIN COUNTY HISTORICAL MUSEUM
Micke Grove Pk.
Box 21   Phone: (209) 368-9154
Lodi, CA 95240   Michael W. Bennett, Musm.Dir.

LOMA LINDA UNIVERSITY - DEL E. WEBB MEMORIAL LIBRARY
                                             Phone: (714) 796-7311
Loma Linda, CA 92350   George L. McAlister, Assoc.Dir.

LOMA LINDA UNIVERSITY - NIELS BJORN JORGENSEN MEMORIAL LIBRARY
School of Dentistry   Phone: (714) 796-0141
Loma Linda, CA 92350   Carol Richardson Boyko, Dir.

LA PURISIMA MISSION - ARCHIVES
La Purisima Mission State Historic Pk.
R.F.D. Box 102   Phone: (805) 733-3713
Lompoc, CA 93436   Ronald J. Dupuy, Interpretive Ranger

LOMPOC MUSEUM - LIBRARY *
200 South H St.   Phone: (805) 736-3888
Lompoc, CA 93436   Lucille Christie, Dir.

U.S. AIR FORCE BASE - VANDENBERG BASE LIBRARY
Vandenberg AFB, Bldg. 10317   Phone: (805) 866-6414
Lompoc, CA 93437   June G. Moyers, Base Libn.

ERTEC, WESTERN, INC. - LIBRARY
3777 Long Beach Blvd.   Phone: (213) 595-6611
Long Beach, CA 90807   Misty Sis Dincel, Info.Dir.

FIRST BAPTIST CHURCH OF LAKEWOOD - CHURCH LIBRARY
5336 Arbor Rd.   Phone: (213) 420-1471
Long Beach, CA 90808   Judy L. Hughes, Libn.

HISTORICAL SOCIETY OF LONG BEACH - ARCHIVES
Rancho Los Cerritos
4600 Virginia Rd.
Long Beach, CA 90807   Zona Gale Forbes, Archv.

LONG BEACH CITY COLLEGE - PACIFIC COAST CAMPUS LIBRARY
1305 E. Pacific Coast Hwy.   Phone: (213) 420-4548
Long Beach, CA 90806   John L. Ayala, Libn./Asst.Prof.

LONG BEACH COMMUNITY HOSPITAL - MEDICAL LIBRARY
1720 Termino Ave.   Phone: (213) 597-6655
Long Beach, CA 90801   Lois O. Clark, Med.Libn.

LONG BEACH INDEPENDENT, PRESS-TELEGRAM - LIBRARY
604 Pine Ave.   Phone: (213) 435-1161
Long Beach, CA 90844   Violet R. Phillips, Hd.Libn.

LONG BEACH MUSEUM OF ART - LIBRARY
2300 E. Ocean Blvd.   Phone: (213) 439-2119
Long Beach, CA 90803   Russell J. Moore, Dir.

LONG BEACH PUBLIC LIBRARY - CALIFORNIA PETROLEUM INDUSTRY
   COLLECTION
101 Pacific Ave.   Phone: (213) 437-2949
Long Beach, CA 90802   James Jackson, Hd., Sci.Tech.Dept.

LONG BEACH PUBLIC LIBRARY - FINE ARTS DEPARTMENT
101 Pacific Ave.   Phone: (213) 437-2949
Long Beach, CA 90802   Natalee Collier, Dept.Hd.

LONG BEACH PUBLIC LIBRARY - LITERATURE AND HISTORY DEPARTMENT
   †
101 Pacific Ave.   Phone: (213) 437-2949
Long Beach, CA 90802   Helene A. Silver, Dept.Hd.

LONG BEACH PUBLIC LIBRARY - RANCHO LOS CERRITOS MUSEUM -
   LIBRARY
4600 Virginia Rd.   Phone: (213) 424-9423
Long Beach, CA 90807   Keith Foster, Cur.

LONG BEACH UNIFIED SCHOOL DISTRICT - PROFESSIONAL LIBRARY
1260 E. 33rd St.
Long Beach, CA 90807

GEOGRAPHIC

LOS ANGELES COUNTY/LONG BEACH GENERAL HOSPITAL - MEDICAL
  LIBRARY
2597 Redondo Ave.   Phone: (213) 636-0784
Long Beach, CA 90806   Thomas P. Dengler, Med.Libn.

MC DONNELL DOUGLAS CORPORATION - DOUGLAS AIRCRAFT COMPANY -
  TECHNICAL LIBRARY
3855 Lakewood Blvd.   Phone: (213) 593-9541
Long Beach, CA 90846   P.M. Ackerman, Sect.Mgr.

MEMORIAL HOSPITAL MEDICAL CENTER OF LONG BEACH - MEDICAL
  LIBRARY
2801 Atlantic Ave.
Box 1428   Phone: (213) 595-3841
Long Beach, CA 90801   Frances Lyon, Dir. of Lib.Serv.

PACIFIC HOSPITAL OF LONG BEACH - MEDICAL STAFF LIBRARY
2776 Pacific Ave.
Box 1268   Phone: (213) 595-1911
Long Beach, CA 90801   Lois E. Harris, Dir., Lib. & AV Serv.

PORT ADVENTURE, WRATHER PORT PROPERTIES, LTD. - ARCHIVES &
  RESOURCE CENTER
RMS Queen Mary
Box 8   Phone: (213) 435-4747
Long Beach, CA 90801   Milton Schwartz, Hist.

ST. MARY MEDICAL CENTER - - BELLIS MEDICAL LIBRARY
1050 Linden Ave.
Box 887   Phone: (213) 435-4441
Long Beach, CA 90801   Emily L. Giustino, Dir.

U.S. NAVY - NAVAL SHIPYARD (Long Beach) - TECHNICAL LIBRARY
Code 202.4, Bldg. 300, Rm. 358   Phone: (213) 547-6515
Long Beach, CA 90822   Marianna Droescher Clark, Hd.Libn.

U.S. VETERANS ADMINISTRATION (CA-Long Beach) - MEDICAL CENTER
  LIBRARY
5901 E. Seventh St.   Phone: (213) 498-1313
Long Beach, CA 90822   Betty F. Connolly, Chf., Lib.Serv.

SOUTHWEST REGIONAL LABORATORY FOR EDUCATIONAL RESEARCH AND
  DEVELOPMENT - LIBRARY
4665 Lampson Ave.   Phone: (213) 598-7661
Los Alamitos, CA 90720   Louise D. Riedel, Libn.

CONGREGATION BETH AM - LIBRARY
26790 Arastradero Rd.   Phone: (415) 322-4661
Los Altos Hills, CA 94022   Ken Fehl, Chm., Lib.Comm.

FOOTHILL COLLEGE - ELECTRONICS MUSEUM - DE FOREST MEMORIAL
  ARCHIVES
12345 El Monte Rd.   Phone: (415) 948-8590
Los Altos Hills, CA 94022   Robert Seal, Cur.

AEROSPACE CORPORATION - CHARLES C. LAURITSEN LIBRARY
Box 92957   Phone: (213) 648-6738
Los Angeles, CA 90009   Edythe Moore, Mgr.Lib.Serv.

AMERICAN INSTITUTE OF AERONAUTICS AND ASTRONAUTICS - LIBRARY
9841 Airport Blvd., Suite 800   Phone: (213) 670-6642
Los Angeles, CA 90045

AMERICAN INSTITUTE OF FAMILY RELATIONS - ROSWELL H. JOHNSON
  RESEARCH LIBRARY
5287 Sunset Blvd.   Phone: (213) 465-5131
Los Angeles, CA 90027   Dr. Edward Peacock, Res.Dir.

AMERICAN SOCIETY OF MILITARY HISTORY - LIBRARY
1816 S. Figueroa St.   Phone: (213) 746-1776
Los Angeles, CA 90015   Donald Michelson, Exec.Dir.

ARNOLD SCHOENBERG INSTITUTE - ARCHIVES
University of Southern California   Phone: (213) 743-5393
Los Angeles, CA 90007   Clara Steuermann, Archv.

ASOCIACION NACIONAL PRO PERSONAS MAYORES - LIBRARY
1730 W. Olympic Blvd., Suite 401   Phone: (213) 487-1922
Los Angeles, CA 90015   Carmela G. Lacayo, Natl.Exec.Dir.

ATLANTIC-RICHFIELD COMPANY - GOVERNMENT RELATIONS
  INFORMATION RESOURCES CENTER
515 S. Flower St., Rm. 4010   Phone: (213) 486-0777
Los Angeles, CA 90071   Esther Eastman, Coord.

ATLANTIC-RICHFIELD COMPANY - HEADQUARTERS LIBRARY
Terminal Annex, Box 2679   Phone: (213) 486-2400
Los Angeles, CA 90051   Meryl H. Swanigan, Corp.Libn.

AUTOMOBILE CLUB OF SOUTHERN CALIFORNIA - HIGHWAY ENGINEERING
  DEPARTMENT LIBRARY
2601 S. Figueroa St.   Phone: (213) 741-4490
Los Angeles, CA 90007   Donnalee L. Simmons, Libn.

BANK OF AMERICA - SOUTHERN CALIFORNIA HEADQUARTERS - LAW
  LIBRARY
555 S. Flower St.   Phone: (213) 683-3101
Los Angeles, CA 90071   Rachael Gordon, Asst. Law Libn.

BARLOW HOSPITAL - ELKS LIBRARY
2000 Stadium Way   Phone: (213) 628-4165
Los Angeles, CA 90026   Rose Thompson, Libn.

BECHTEL POWER CORPORATION - LIBRARY
12400 E. Imperial Hwy.
Box 60860, Terminal Annex   Phone: (213) 864-6011
Los Angeles, CA 90060   Jean Gregory, Libn.

BRAILLE INSTITUTE OF AMERICA - LIBRARY
741 N. Vermont Ave.   Phone: (213) 660-3880
Los Angeles, CA 90029   Phyllis Cairns, Lib.Dir.

CALIFORNIA FEDERAL SAVINGS AND LOAN ASSOCIATION - MANAGEMENT
  LIBRARY
5670 Wilshire Blvd.   Phone: (213) 932-4655
Los Angeles, CA 90036   Kathleen T. Kahn, Libn.

CALIFORNIA HISTORICAL SOCIETY - HISTORY CENTER LIBRARY
6300 Wilshire Blvd.   Phone: (213) 651-5655
Los Angeles, CA 90048   Julia Brown, Mgr.

CALIFORNIA HOSPITAL MEDICAL CENTER - HEALTH SCIENCES LIBRARY
1414 South Hope St.   Phone: (213) 748-2411
Los Angeles, CA 90015   Anne G. Dillibe, Med.Libn.

CALIFORNIA SCHOOL OF PROFESSIONAL PSYCHOLOGY - LOS ANGELES
  LIBRARY
3755 Beverly Blvd.   Phone: (213) 665-4201
Los Angeles, CA 90004   Tobeylynn Birch, Hd.Libn.

CALIFORNIA STATE - COLORADO RIVER BOARD OF CALIFORNIA - LIBRARY
107 S. Broadway, Rm. 8103   Phone: (213) 620-4480
Los Angeles, CA 90012   Loretta E. Austen, Tech.Lib.Asst.

CALIFORNIA STATE - COURT OF APPEAL, 2ND APPELLATE DISTRICT - LAW
  LIBRARY
3580 Wilshire Blvd., Rm. 448   Phone: (213) 736-2661
Los Angeles, CA 90010   Cheryl Stanwood, Law Libn.

CALIFORNIA STATE DEPARTMENT OF JUSTICE - ATTORNEY GENERAL'S
  OFFICE - LAW LIBRARY
3580 Wilshire Blvd., Rm. 701   Phone: (213) 736-2196
Los Angeles, CA 90010   Janet T. Whitney, Supv.Libn.

CALIFORNIA STATE DEPARTMENT OF TRANSPORTATION - DISTRICT 7
  LIBRARY
120 S. Spring St.   Phone: (213) 620-5500
Los Angeles, CA 90012   Alyce L. Davis, Sr.Libn.

CALIFORNIA STATE UNIVERSITY, LOS ANGELES - SCIENCE/TECHNOLOGY
  REFERENCE ROOM
John F. Kennedy Memorial Library
5151 State University Dr.   Phone: (213) 224-2232
Los Angeles, CA 90032   Cornelia O. Balogh, Act.Hd.

CAPITAL RESEARCH COMPANY - RESEARCH LIBRARY
333 S. Hope St., 51st Fl.   Phone: (213) 486-9261
Los Angeles, CA 90071   S. Kathleen Reilly, Libn.

CARNATION COMPANY - LIBRARY
5045 Wilshire Blvd.   Phone: (213) 932-6558
Los Angeles, CA 90036   Vicki C. Giella, Info.Ctr.Coord.

CEDARS-SINAI MEDICAL CENTER - HEALTH SCIENCES INFORMATION
   CENTER
8700 Beverly Blvd.
Box 48956   Phone: (213) 855-3751
Los Angeles, CA 90048

CENTER FOR COMPUTER/LAW - LIBRARY
Box 54308 T.A.   Phone: (312) 623-3321
Los Angeles, CA 90054   Michael D. Scott, Exec.Dir.

CENTER FOR EARLY EDUCATION - LAURA M. ELLIS MEMORIAL LIBRARY
563 N. Alfred St.   Phone: (213) 655-4878
Los Angeles, CA 90048   Amy D. Cooper, Libn.

CHILDREN'S HOSPITAL OF LOS ANGELES - MEDICAL LIBRARY †
4650 Sunset Blvd.   Phone: (213) 663-3341
Los Angeles, CA 90027

CHURCH OF JESUS CHRIST OF LATTER-DAY SAINTS - SOUTHERN
   CALIFORNIA AREA GENEALOGICAL LIBRARY
10741 Santa Monica Blvd.   Phone: (213) 474-9990
Los Angeles, CA 90025   Fred E. Klingman, Pres.

CITIZENS' RESEARCH FOUNDATION - LIBRARY †
University of Southern California
Research Annex, 3716 S. Hope St.   Phone: (213) 743-5440
Los Angeles, CA 90007   Herbert E. Alexander, Dir.

CITIZENS SAVINGS ATHLETIC FOUNDATION - LIBRARY †
9800 S. Sepulveda Blvd.   Phone: (213) 670-7550
Los Angeles, CA 90045   W.R. Bill Schroeder, Mng.Dir.

COLEMAN AND COMPANY - LIBRARY *
5800 W. Century Blvd.
Box 90546
Los Angeles, CA 90009   D.R. Jenkins, Libn.

COLLEGE OF INSURANCE - WESTERN DIVISION - LIBRARY
3142 Wilshire Blvd.   Phone: (213) 738-9973
Los Angeles, CA 90010   Kathryn Lee, Libn.

COOPERS AND LYBRAND - LIBRARY
1000 W. 6th St.   Phone: (213) 481-1000
Los Angeles, CA 90017   June B. Williams, Libn.

CRAFT AND FOLK ART MUSEUM - LIBRARY/MEDIA RESOURCE CENTER
5814 Wilshire Blvd.   Phone: (213) 937-5544
Los Angeles, CA 90036   Joan M. Benedetti, Media Libn.

DAMES & MOORE - LIBRARY
1100 Glendon Ave., Suite 1000   Phone: (213) 879-9700
Los Angeles, CA 90024   Alice Ohst, Libn.

DANIEL, MANN, JOHNSON AND MENDENHALL - LIBRARY
3250 Wilshire Blvd.   Phone: (213) 381-3663
Los Angeles, CA 90010   Marlene Barkley, Corp.Libn.

DOCUMENTATION ASSOCIATES †
Box 84005   Phone: (213) 477-5081
Los Angeles, CA 90073   Susanna Shuster, Mgr., Search & Ret.

ECOLOGY CENTER OF SOUTHERN CALIFORNIA
P.O. Box 35473   Phone: (213) 559-9160
Los Angeles, CA 90035   Nancy Pearlman, Exec.Dir.

ECONOMICS RESEARCH ASSOCIATES - LIBRARY †
10960 Wilshire Blvd.   Phone: (213) 477-9585
Los Angeles, CA 90024   Barbara J. Thompson, Libn.

ERIC CLEARINGHOUSE FOR JUNIOR COLLEGES
University of California, Los Angeles
96 Powell Library   Phone: (213) 825-3931
Los Angeles, CA 90024   Arthur M. Cohen, Dir.

ERNST & WHINNEY - LIBRARY
515 S. Flower St.   Phone: (213) 977-4401
Los Angeles, CA 90071   Sherry du Roy, Libn.

FARMERS INSURANCE GROUP - LIBRARY
4680 Wilshire Blvd.   Phone: (213) 932-3200
Los Angeles, CA 90010   Tish Wallace, Libn.

FASHION INSTITUTE OF DESIGN & MERCHANDISING - RESOURCE AND
   RESEARCH CENTER
818 W. 7th St.   Phone: (231) 624-1200
Los Angeles, CA 90017   Kaycee Hale, Dir.

FIRST INTERSTATE BANK OF CALIFORNIA - LIBRARY
Terminal Annex
Box 3666   Phone: (213) 614-4097
Los Angeles, CA 90051   Peggy Wilson, Chf.Libn.

GATEWAYS HOSPITAL AND COMMUNITY MENTAL HEALTH CENTER -
   PROFESSIONAL LIBRARY
1891 Effie St.   Phone: (213) 666-0171
Los Angeles, CA 90026   Celia Palant, Libn.

GETTY OIL COMPANY, INC. - LIBRARY
3810 Wilshire Blvd.   Phone: (213) 381-7151
Los Angeles, CA 90005   Mary Krupp, Corp.Libn.

GIBSON, DUNN & CRUTCHER - LAW LIBRARY
515 S. Flower St.   Phone: (213) 488-7216
Los Angeles, CA 90071   Irwin G. Manley, Adm., Info.Serv.

GREATER LOS ANGELES ZOO ASSOCIATION - ANDREW NORMAN
   EDUCATION CENTER
5333 Zoo Dr.   Phone: (213) 661-2184
Los Angeles, CA 90027   E. Sue Blake, Libn.

GREENBERG AND GLUSKER - LIBRARY
1900 Avenue of the Stars
Los Angeles, CA 90067   Lisa Winslow, Law Libn.

GRIFFITH OBSERVATORY - LIBRARY
2800 E. Observatory Rd.   Phone: (213) 664-1181
Los Angeles, CA 90027   Dr. E.C. Krupp, Dir.

HANCOCK (Allan) FOUNDATION - HANCOCK LIBRARY OF BIOLOGY &
   OCEANOGRAPHY
University of Southern California
University Pk.   Phone: (213) 743-6005
Los Angeles, CA 90007   Florence E. Lewis, Act.Hd.Libn.

HEBREW UNION COLLEGE - JEWISH INSTITUTE OF RELIGION - FRANCES-
   HENRY LIBRARY
3077 University Ave.   Phone: (213) 749-3424
Los Angeles, CA 90007   Harvey P. Horowitz, Libn.

HILL, FARRER & BURRILL - LAW LIBRARY †
445 S. Figueroa St.
Union Bank Bldg., 34th Fl.   Phone: (213) 620-0460
Los Angeles, CA 90071   Fleur C. Osmanson, Libn.

HOLLYWOOD PRESBYTERIAN MEDICAL CENTER - HEALTH SCIENCES
   LIBRARY
1300 N. Vermont Ave.   Phone: (213) 660-3530
Los Angeles, CA 90027   Erika M. Hansen, Med.Libn.

HOSPITAL OF THE GOOD SAMARITAN - MEDICAL LIBRARY
616 S. Witmer St.   Phone: (213) 977-2326
Los Angeles, CA 90017   Elizabeth Sherson, Med.Libn.

HOUZE, SHOURDS & MONTGOMERY, INC. - RESEARCH LIBRARY
2029 Century Park East   Phone: (213) 522-6027
Los Angeles, CA 90067   Elaine Kuo, Res.Dir.

HUGHES AIRCRAFT COMPANY - EL SEGUNDO LIBRARY
Bldg. 512, Mail Sta. V-311
Box 92919   Phone: (213) 648-4192
Los Angeles, CA 90009   Vicky S. Huang, Libn.

IMMACULATE HEART COLLEGE - MUSIC LIBRARY †
2021 N. Western Ave.
Los Angeles, CA 90027   Phone: (213) 462-1301

INNER CITY CULTURAL CENTER - LANGSTON HUGHES MEMORIAL LIBRARY
1308 S. New Hampshire Ave.   Phone: (213) 387-1161
Los Angeles, CA 90006   Fred Beauford, Lib.Cons.

INSTITUTE OF THE AMERICAN MUSICAL, INC. - LIBRARY
121 N. Detroit St.   Phone: (213) 934-1221
Los Angeles, CA 90036   Miles M. Kreuger, Cur.

INSTITUTE FOR STUDIES OF DESTRUCTIVE BEHAVIORS AND THE SUICIDE
   PREVENTION CENTER - HAROLD M. HILDRETH MEMORIAL LIB.
1041 S. Menlo Ave.
Los Angeles, CA 90006

INTERNATIONAL POSTCARD COLLECTORS ASSOCIATION, INC. - LIBRARY
†
Loyola/Marymount University
7101 W. 80th St.   Phone: (213) 642-2788
Los Angeles, CA 90045

IRELL & MANELLA - LIBRARY
1800 Ave. of the Stars, Suite 900   Phone: (213) 277-1010
Los Angeles, CA 90067   Louise Laughlin Lieb, Hd.Libn.

JEWISH FEDERATION COUNCIL OF GREATER LOS ANGELES - PETER M.
   KAHN JEWISH COMMUNITY LIBRARY
6505 Wilshire Blvd.   Phone: (213) 663-8484
Los Angeles, CA 90048   Mrs. Hava Ben-Zvi, Libn.

JUNG (C.G.) INSTITUTE OF LOS ANGELES, INC. - LIBRARY
10349 West Pico Blvd.   Phone: (213) 556-1193
Los Angeles, CA 90064   Claire Oksner, Hd.Libn.

KADISON, PFAELZER, WOODARD, QUINN & ROSSI - LAW LIBRARY
707 Wilshire Blvd., 40th Fl.   Phone: (213) 688-9000
Los Angeles, CA 90017   Diane G. Sapienza, Law Libn.

KAISER FOUNDATION HOSPITAL - MANAGEMENT EFFECTIVENESS
   LIBRARY
4747 Sunset Blvd.   Phone: (213) 667-5460
Los Angeles, CA 90027   Linda Y. Yamamoto, Libn.

KAISER FOUNDATION HOSPITALS - MEDICAL LIBRARY
4867 Sunset Blvd.   Phone: (213) 667-8568
Los Angeles, CA 90027   Judith A. Dowd, Dept.Hd.

KINDEL & ANDERSON - LIBRARY
555 S. Flower St., 26th Fl.   Phone: (213) 680-2222
Los Angeles, CA 90071   Marie Wallace, Law Libn.

KING (Martin Luther, Jr.) GENERAL HOSPITAL - MEDICAL LIBRARY
12021 Wilmington Ave.   Phone: (213) 603-4068
Los Angeles, CA 90059   Ms. M. Moss Humphrey, Sr.Med.Libn.

LATHAM & WATKINS - LAW LIBRARY
555 S. Flower St.   Phone: (213) 485-1234
Los Angeles, CA 90071   Laura M. Strain, Law Libn.

LAWLER, FELIX & HALL - LAW LIBRARY
700 S. Flower St.   Phone: (213) 629-9513
Los Angeles, CA 90017   Frank Houdek, Libn.

LEVENTHAL (Kenneth) & COMPANY - LIBRARY
2049 Century Park E., 17th Fl.   Phone: (213) 277-0880
Los Angeles, CA 90067   Joan K. Krasner, Natl.Libn.

LILLICK MC HOSE & CHARLES, ATTORNEYS AT LAW - LAW LIBRARY †
707 Wilshire Blvd., 45th Fl.   Phone: (213) 620-9000
Los Angeles, CA 90017   Luramay Ellsworth, Law Libn.

LOCARE MOTION PICTURE RESEARCH GROUP - LIBRARY
910 N. Fairfax Ave.   Phone: (213) 656-4420
Los Angeles, CA 90046   Bebe Bergsten, Libn.

LOEB AND LOEB - LAW LIBRARY
One Wilshire Bldg., Suite 1600   Phone: (213) 629-0418
Los Angeles, CA 90017   Nella L. Jarett, Libn.

LOO MERIDETH & MC MILLAN - LAW LIBRARY
1800 Century Park East, Suite 200   Phone: (213) 277-0300
Los Angeles, CA 90067   Susan A. Miller, Libn.

LOS ANGELES CENTER FOR PHOTOGRAPHIC STUDIES - LIBRARY
814 S. Spring St.   Phone: (213) 623-9410
Los Angeles, CA 90014   Darryl Curran, Pres.

LOS ANGELES CHAMBER OF COMMERCE - RESEARCH DEPARTMENT
   LIBRARY
404 S. Bixel   Phone: (213) 629-0673
Los Angeles, CA 90017   Harry H. Hamparzumian, Mgr.

LOS ANGELES CITY ATTORNEY - LAW LIBRARY
200 N. Main, Rm. 1700   Phone: (213) 485-5400
Los Angeles, CA 90012   Sandee Mirell, Libn.

LOS ANGELES COUNTY DEPARTMENT OF HEALTH SERVICES-PREVENTIVE
   PUBLIC HEALTH - JOHN L. POMEROY MEMORIAL LIBRARY
313 N. Figueroa St., Rm. 906   Phone: (213) 974-7780
Los Angeles, CA 90012   Agnes Imbrie, Libn.

LOS ANGELES COUNTY - DEPARTMENT OF MENTAL HEALTH - LIBRARY
2415 W. Sixth St.   Phone: (213) 738-4730
Los Angeles, CA 90057   Edward E. Asawa, Libn.

LOS ANGELES COUNTY LAW LIBRARY
301 W. First St.   Phone: (213) 629-3531
Los Angeles, CA 90012   Richard T. Iamele, Libn.

LOS ANGELES COUNTY MEDICAL ASSOCIATION - LIBRARY
634 S. Westlake Ave.   Phone: (213) 483-4555
Los Angeles, CA 90057   Elizabeth S. Crahan, Dir.Lib.Serv.

LOS ANGELES COUNTY MUSEUM OF ART - RESEARCH LIBRARY
5905 Wilshire Blvd.   Phone: (213) 937-4250
Los Angeles, CA 90036   Eleanor C. Hartman, Musm.Libn.

LOS ANGELES COUNTY MUSEUM OF NATURAL HISTORY - RESEARCH
   LIBRARY
900 Exposition Blvd.   Phone: (213) 744-3387
Los Angeles, CA 90007   Katharine E. Donahue, Musm.Libn.

LOS ANGELES COUNTY/UNIVERSITY OF SOUTHERN CALIFORNIA MEDICAL
   CENTER - MEDICAL LIBRARIES
1200 N. State St.   Phone: (213) 226-7006
Los Angeles, CA 90033   Alice Reinhardt, Chf., Lib.Serv.

LOS ANGELES COUNTY/UNIVERSITY OF SOUTHERN CALIFORNIA MEDICAL
   CENTER - PEDIATRICS LIBRARY
1129 N. State St.
Los Angeles, CA 90033

LOS ANGELES - DEPARTMENT OF WATER AND POWER - LEGAL DIVISION -
   LAW LIBRARY ★
1520 General Office Bldg.
111 N. Hope St.   Phone: (213) 481-6309
Los Angeles, CA 90012   Ethel Hardy

LOS ANGELES HERALD-EXAMINER - NEWSPAPER LIBRARY
1111 S. Broadway   Phone: (213) 744-8420
Los Angeles, CA 90015   Ann E. Sausedo, Lib.Dir.

LOS ANGELES PSYCHOANALYTIC SOCIETY AND INSTITUTE - SIMMEL-
   FENICHEL LIBRARY
2014 Sawtelle Blvd.   Phone: (213) 478-6851
Los Angeles, CA 90025   Kathleen Matson, Libn.

LOS ANGELES PUBLIC LIBRARY - ART, MUSIC & RECREATION DEPARTMENT
630 W. Fifth St.   Phone: (213) 626-7461
Los Angeles, CA 90071   Katherine E. Grant, Dept.Mgr.

LOS ANGELES PUBLIC LIBRARY - AUDIO-VISUAL DEPARTMENT
630 W. Fifth St.   Phone: (213) 626-7461
Los Angeles, CA 90071   Richard V. Partlow, Dept.Mgr.

LOS ANGELES PUBLIC LIBRARY - BUSINESS & ECONOMICS DEPARTMENT
630 W. Fifth St.
Los Angeles, CA 90071
Phone: (213) 626-7461
Joan Bartel, Dept.Mgr.

LOS ANGELES PUBLIC LIBRARY - CHILDREN'S LITERATURE DEPARTMENT
630 W. Fifth St.
Los Angeles, CA 90071
Phone: (213) 626-7461
Serenna Day, Sr.Libn.

LOS ANGELES PUBLIC LIBRARY - FICTION DEPARTMENT
630 W. Fifth St.
Los Angeles, CA 90071
Phone: (213) 626-7461
Helene G. Mochedlover, Dept.Mgr.

LOS ANGELES PUBLIC LIBRARY - FOREIGN LANGUAGES DEPARTMENT
630 W. Fifth St.
Los Angeles, CA 90071
Phone: (213) 626-7461
Sylva N. Manoogian, Principal Libn.

LOS ANGELES PUBLIC LIBRARY - HISTORY DEPARTMENT
630 W. Fifth St.
Los Angeles, CA 90071
Phone: (213) 626-7461
Mary S. Pratt, Dept.Mgr.

LOS ANGELES PUBLIC LIBRARY - LITERATURE & PHILOLOGY DEPARTMENT
630 W. Fifth St.
Los Angeles, CA 90071
Phone: (213) 626-7461
Helene Mochedlover, Dept.Mgr.

LOS ANGELES PUBLIC LIBRARY - MUNICIPAL REFERENCE DEPARTMENT
530 City Hall E.
200 N. Main St.
Los Angeles, CA 90012
Phone: (213) 485-3791
Wilma J. Dewey, Libn.

LOS ANGELES PUBLIC LIBRARY - MUNICIPAL REFERENCE DEPARTMENT -
PLANNING DIVISION
City Hall, Rm. 618
200 N. Spring St.
Los Angeles, CA 90012
Phone: (213) 485-5077
Sarah D. Wolf, Libn.

LOS ANGELES PUBLIC LIBRARY - MUNICIPAL REFERENCE DEPARTMENT -
POLICE LIBRARY
150 N. Los Angeles St., Rm. 503
Los Angeles, CA 90012
Phone: (213) 485-3288
Bea Yasui, Sr.Libn.

LOS ANGELES PUBLIC LIBRARY - MUNICIPAL REFERENCE DEPARTMENT -
WATER & POWER LIBRARY
Rm. 518 GOB
Box 111
Los Angeles, CA 90051
Phone: (213) 481-4610
Donald F. Hinrichs, Sr.Libn.

LOS ANGELES PUBLIC LIBRARY - NEWSPAPER ROOM
630 W. Fifth St.
Los Angeles, CA 90071
Phone: (213) 646-7461
Dan Strehl, Libn.

LOS ANGELES PUBLIC LIBRARY - PHILOSOPHY & RELIGION DEPARTMENT
630 W. Fifth St.
Los Angeles, CA 90071
Phone: (213) 626-7461
Marilyn C. Wherley, Dept.Hd.

LOS ANGELES PUBLIC LIBRARY - SCIENCE & TECHNOLOGY DEPARTMENT
630 W. Fifth St.
Los Angeles, CA 90071
Phone: (213) 626-7461
Billie M. Connor, Principal Libn.

LOS ANGELES PUBLIC LIBRARY - SOCIAL SCIENCES DEPARTMENT
630 W. Fifth St.
Los Angeles, CA 90071
Phone: (213) 626-7461
Marilyn C. Wherley, Dept.Hd.

LOS ANGELES TIMES - EDITORIAL LIBRARY
Times-Mirror Square
Los Angeles, CA 90053
Phone: (213) 972-7181
Cecily J. Surace, Lib.Dir.

LOS ANGELES TRADE-TECHNICAL COLLEGE - LIBRARY
400 W. Washington Blvd.
Los Angeles, CA 90015
Phone: (213) 746-0800
Harold Eckes, Coord., Lrng.Rsrcs,Ctr.

LOYOLA LAW SCHOOL - LIBRARY
1440 W. 9th St.
Los Angeles, CA 90015
Phone: (213) 642-2934
Frederica M. Sedgwick, Dir.

MC CUTCHEN, BLACK, VERLEGER AND SHEA - LAW LIBRARY
600 Wilshire Blvd.
Los Angeles, CA 90007
Phone: (213) 381-3411
Stewart Annand, Libn.

MC KINSEY & COMPANY, INC. - INFORMATION CENTER
611 W. Sixth St.
Los Angeles, CA 90017
Phone: (213) 624-1414
Doris M. Lamar, Mgr., Info.Serv.

MARTIN (Albert C.) & ASSOCIATES - INFORMATION RESEARCH CENTER
445 S. Figueroa St.
Los Angeles, CA 90071
Phone: (213) 683-1900
Millie Nicholson, Libn.

MERCER (William M.), INC. - LIBRARY INFORMATION CENTER
3303 Wilshire Blvd.
Los Angeles, CA 90010
Phone: (213) 386-7840
Robert C. Costello

MOLYCORP, INC. - LIBRARY
Box 54945
Los Angeles, CA 90054
Phone: (213) 977-6932
Jean K. Martin, Lib.Mgr.

MORRISON & FOERSTER - LIBRARY
601 W. 5th St., 5th Fl.
Los Angeles, CA 90017
Phone: (213) 626-3800
Karen A. Mayers, Libn.

MOUNT ST. MARY'S COLLEGE - NEWMAN SEMINAR
Coe Memorial Library
12001 Chalon Rd.
Los Angeles, CA 90049
Phone: (213) 476-2237
Erika Condon, Lib.Dir.

MUSIC CENTER OPERATING COMPANY - ARCHIVES
135 N. Grand Ave.
Los Angeles, CA 90012
Phone: (213) 972-7499
Joel M. Pritkin, Cur.

NATIONAL CENTER FOR COMPUTER CRIME DATA
2700 N. Cahuenga Blvd., Suite 2113
Los Angeles, CA 90068
Phone: (213) 850-0509
Jay J. BloomBecker, Dir.

NATIONAL ECONOMIC RESEARCH ASSOCIATES, INC.
555 S. Flower St.
Los Angeles, CA 90071
Phone: (213) 628-0131
Joan B. Schlimgen, Res.Libn.

NATIONAL JEWISH INFORMATION SERVICE FOR THE PROPAGATION OF
JUDAISM - RESEARCH LIBRARY AND ARCHIVES
5174 W. 8th St.
Los Angeles, CA 90036
Phone: (213) 936-6033
Rachel D. Maggal, P.R. Dir.

NEUROPSYCHIATRIC INSTITUTE - MENTAL HEALTH INFORMATION
SERVICE
University of California, Los Angeles
Center for the Health Sciences
760 Westwood Plaza
Los Angeles, CA 90024
Phone: (213) 825-0597
Sherry Terzian, Dir.

OCCIDENTAL COLLEGE - MARY NORTON CLAPP LIBRARY
1600 Campus Rd.
Los Angeles, CA 90041
Phone: (213) 259-2852
Michael C. Sutherland, Spec.Coll.Libn.

OCCIDENTAL LIFE INSURANCE COMPANY OF CALIFORNIA - LAW LIBRARY
1150 S. Olive St.
Los Angeles, CA 90015
Phone: (213) 748-8111

O'MELVENY AND MYERS - INFORMATION SERVICES
611 W. 6th St.
Los Angeles, CA 90017
Phone: (213) 620-1120
Stanley Pearce, Dir., Info.Serv.

ONE, INC. - BLANCHE M. BAKER MEMORIAL LIBRARY
2256 Venice Blvd.
Los Angeles, CA 90006
Phone: (213) 735-5252
David G. Moore, Libn.

ORTHOPAEDIC HOSPITAL - RUBEL MEMORIAL LIBRARY
2400 S. Flower St.
Terminal Annex, Box 60132
Los Angeles, CA 90060
Phone: (213) 742-1530
Veena N. Vyas, Dir., Med.Lib.

PACIFIC LIGHTING CORPORATION - LAW LIBRARY
810 S. Flower St.
Los Angeles, CA 90017
Phone: (213) 689-3352
Terence Pragnell, Law Libn.

PACIFICA TAPE LIBRARY
5316 Venice Blvd.
Los Angeles, CA 90019
Phone: (213) 931-1625
Helen Kennedy, Dir.

GEOGRAPHIC

PARSONS SCHOOL OF DESIGN - OTIS ART INSTITUTE - LIBRARY
627 S. Carondelet St.   Phone: (213) 387-5288
Los Angeles, CA 90057   Neal Menzies, Hd.Libn.

PAUL, HASTINGS, JANOFSKY AND WALKER - LAW LIBRARY
555 S. Flower, 22nd Floor   Phone: (213) 489-4000
Los Angeles, CA 90071   Bobbie Johnson, Hd.Libn.

PEAT, MARWICK, MITCHELL & COMPANY - CENTRAL LIBRARY
555 S. Flower St.   Phone: (213) 972-4000
Los Angeles, CA 90071   Vickie Taylor, Hd.Libn.

PHILOSOPHICAL RESEARCH SOCIETY - RESEARCH LIBRARY
3910 Los Feliz Blvd.   Phone: (213) 663-2167
Los Angeles, CA 90027   Pearl M. Thomas, Libn.

POLISH AMERICAN CONGRESS - SOUTHERN CALIFORNIA-ARIZONA
    DIVISION - POLAND'S MILLENIUM LIBRARY *
3424 W. Adams Blvd.
Los Angeles, CA 90018   Danuta M. Zawadzki, V.P.

PRICE WATERHOUSE - LIBRARY
606 S. Olive St.   Phone: (213) 625-4583
Los Angeles, CA 90014   Mignon Veasley, Hd.Libn.

QUEEN OF ANGELS HOSPITAL - MEDICAL LIBRARY
2301 Bellevue Ave.   Phone: (213) 413-3000
Los Angeles, CA 90026

REISS-DAVIS CHILD STUDY CENTER - RESEARCH LIBRARY
3200 Motor Ave.   Phone: (213) 204-1666
Los Angeles, CA 90034   Leonore Freehling, Libn.

RIGHT TO LIFE LEAGUE OF SOUTHERN CALIFORNIA - LIBRARY †
301 S. Kingsley Dr.   Phone: (213) 380-8750
Los Angeles, CA 90020   Virginia Hoff, Libn.

ROCKWELL INTERNATIONAL - NORTH AMERICAN AIRCRAFT DIVISION -
    TECHNICAL INFORMATION CENTER
Box 92098   Phone: (213) 647-2961
Los Angeles, CA 90009   G.H. Capp, Supv.

ROUNCE AND COFFIN CLUB, LOS ANGELES - LIBRARY
Occidental College Library
1600 Campus Rd.   Phone: (213) 259-2852
Los Angeles, CA 90041   Mike Sutherland, Spec.Coll.Libn.

ST. VINCENT MEDICAL CENTER - HEALTH SCIENCES LIBRARY
2131 W. Third St.   Phone: (213) 484-5530
Los Angeles, CA 90057   Doreen B. Keough, Libn.

SECURITY PACIFIC NATIONAL BANK - BANK LIBRARY
333 S. Hope St.   Phone: (213) 613-8623
Los Angeles, CA 90071   Ann E. Wiedel, Hd.Libn.

SHAKESPEARE SOCIETY OF AMERICA - NEW PLACE RARE BOOK LIBRARY †
1107 N. Kings Rd.   Phone: (213) 650-0208
Los Angeles, CA 90069   Charla Hall, Libn.

SHEPPARD, MULLIN, RICHTER & HAMPTON - LAW LIBRARY †
333 S. Hope St., 48th Fl.   Phone: (213) 620-1780
Los Angeles, CA 90071   Debra K. Hogan, Libn.

SISTERS OF SOCIAL SERVICE - ARCHIVES
1120 Westchester Pl.   Phone: (213) 732-4807
Los Angeles, CA 90019   Sr. Jean Marie Renfro, Archv.

SOUTHERN CALIFORNIA ASSOCIATION OF GOVERNMENTS - INFORMATION
    RESOURCE CENTER
600 S. Commonwealth Ave.   Phone: (213) 385-1000
Los Angeles, CA 90005   Shelli Snyder, Libn.

SOUTHERN CALIFORNIA LIBRARY FOR SOCIAL STUDIES AND RESEARCH
6120 S. Vermont Ave.   Phone: (213) 759-6063
Los Angeles, CA 90044   Emil Freed, Dir.

SOUTHERN CALIFORNIA RAPID TRANSIT DISTRICT - LIBRARY †
425 S. Main St.   Phone: (213) 972-6467
Los Angeles, CA 90013   Nola Wolf, Libn.

SOUTHERN CALIFORNIA SOCIETY FOR PSYCHICAL RESEARCH, INC. -
    LIBRARY
                                          Phone: (213) 936-0904
Los Angeles, CA 90004   Andrew T. Shields, Lib.Coord.

SOUTHWEST MUSEUM - RESEARCH LIBRARY
Highland Park Sta., Box 128
Los Angeles, CA 90042   Phone: (213) 221-2163
                                          Ruth M. Christensen, Libn.

SOUTHWESTERN UNIVERSITY - SCHOOL OF LAW LIBRARY
675 S. Westmoreland Ave.   Phone: (213) 738-6725
Los Angeles, CA 90005   Linda Schulte, Act.Dir.

THEATRE AND FILM ARTS - INFORMATION CENTER
Ambassador Sta., Box 98   Phone: (213) 383-1083
Los Angeles, CA 90070   Carl Post, Owner

THOMPSON (J. Walter) COMPANY - RESEARCH LIBRARY
10100 Santa Monica Blvd.   Phone: (213) 553-8383
Los Angeles, CA 90067   D.W. Thomas, V.P.

TOSCO CORPORATION - INFORMATION CENTER
10100 Santa Monica Blvd.   Phone: (213) 552-7093
Los Angeles, CA 90067   Dennis D. Beckman, Libn.

TOUCHE ROSS AND COMPANY - LIBRARY
3700 Wilshire Blvd.   Phone: (213) 381-3251
Los Angeles, CA 90010   Kathy Tice, Libn.

UNCAP INTERNATIONAL, INC. - PROJECT COLLECTORS RESEARCH
    LIBRARY
2613 Huron St.   Phone: (213) 222-2012
Los Angeles, CA 90065   James J. O'Connell, III, Cur.

UNION BANK - LIBRARY
445 S. Figueroa St.   Phone: (213) 687-5259
Los Angeles, CA 90071   John D. Shea, Libn.

UNION OIL COMPANY OF CALIFORNIA - INTERNATIONAL EXPLORATION
    LIBRARY
461 S. Boylston St.   Phone: (213) 977-6381
Los Angeles, CA 90017   Elizabeth Higgason, Libn.

UNITED CHURCH OF RELIGIOUS SCIENCE - LIBRARY
3251 W. Sixth St.   Phone: (213) 388-2181
Los Angeles, CA 90075   Lorraine Norberg, Libn.

U.S. BUREAU OF THE CENSUS - REGIONAL DATA USER SERVICE - LOS
    ANGELES REGIONAL OFFICE - LIBRARY *
11777 San Vincente Blvd., 8th Fl.   Phone: (213) 824-7291
Los Angeles, CA 90049   E.J. (Bud) Steinfeld, Data User Serv.Off.

U.S. DEPT. OF ENERGY - LABORATORY OF BIOMEDICAL AND
    ENVIRONMENTAL SCIENCES - LIBRARY
University Of California, Los Angeles
900 Veteran Ave.   Phone: (213) 825-8741
Los Angeles, CA 90024   Joann L. Taylor, Dir.

U.S. DEPT. OF JUSTICE - UNITED STATES ATTORNEY, CENTRAL DISTRICT
    OF CALIFORNIA - LIBRARY
1214 U.S. Court House
312 N. Spring St.   Phone: (213) 688-2419
Los Angeles, CA 90012

U.S. VETERANS ADMINISTRATION (CA-Los Angeles) - MEDICAL RESEARCH
    LIBRARY
Wilshire & Sawtelle Blvds.
Los Angeles, CA 90073   Christine Anderson, Med.Res.Libn.

U.S. VETERANS ADMINISTRATION (CA-Los Angeles) - WADSWORTH
    MEDICAL LIBRARY
Wilshire & Sawtelle Blvds.   Phone: (213) 478-3711
Los Angeles, CA 90073   Christa Buswell, Chf., Lib.Serv.

UNITED WAY, INC., LOS ANGELES - LIBRARY
621 S. Virgil Ave.   Phone: (213) 736-1300
Los Angeles, CA 90005   Philip E. Ervin, Corp.Libn.

UNIVERSITY OF CALIFORNIA, LOS ANGELES - ACADEMY OF TELEVISION
  ARTS & SCIENCES - TELEVISION ARCHIVES
Theater Arts Dept.
1438 Melnitz Hall   Phone: (213) 825-4480
Los Angeles, CA 90024   Robert Rosen, Dir.

UNIVERSITY OF CALIFORNIA, LOS ANGELES - AFRICAN STUDIES CENTER -
  RESEARCH WORKSHOP & READING ROOM *
10367 Bunche Hall   Phone: (213) 825-2944
Los Angeles, CA 90024   Dr. Michael Lofchie, Dir.

UNIVERSITY OF CALIFORNIA, LOS ANGELES - AMERICAN INDIAN STUDIES
  CENTER - LIBRARY
3220 Campbell Hall   Phone: (213) 825-4591
Los Angeles, CA 90024   Velma S. Salabiye, Libn.

UNIVERSITY OF CALIFORNIA, LOS ANGELES - ARCHITECTURE & URBAN
  PLANNING LIBRARY
1302 Architecture Bldg.   Phone: (213) 825-2747
Los Angeles, CA 90024   Jon S. Greene, Libn.

UNIVERSITY OF CALIFORNIA, LOS ANGELES - ART DEPARTMENT - VISUAL
  RESOURCE COLLECTION & SERVICES
3239 Dickson Art Center
405 Hilgard Ave.   Phone: (213) 825-3725
Los Angeles, CA 90024   Sandra Ducoff Garber, Slide Cur.

UNIVERSITY OF CALIFORNIA, LOS ANGELES - ART LIBRARY
2250 Dickson Art Center   Phone: (213) 825-3817
Los Angeles, CA 90024   Joyce P. Ludmer, Art Libn.

UNIVERSITY OF CALIFORNIA, LOS ANGELES - ART LIBRARY - ELMER BELT
  LIBRARY OF VINCIANA
Dickson Art Center   Phone: (213) 825-3817
Los Angeles, CA 90024   Joyce Ludmer, Art Libn./Dir.

UNIVERSITY OF CALIFORNIA, LOS ANGELES - BIOMEDICAL LIBRARY
Center for Health Sciences   Phone: (213) 825-5781
Los Angeles, CA 90024   Gloria Werner, Libn.

UNIVERSITY OF CALIFORNIA, LOS ANGELES - BRAIN INFORMATION
  SERVICE *
Center for Health Sciences   Phone: (213) 825-6011
Los Angeles, CA 90024   Michael H. Chase, Dir.

UNIVERSITY OF CALIFORNIA, LOS ANGELES - CHEMISTRY LIBRARY
4238 Young Hall   Phone: (213) 825-3342
Los Angeles, CA 90024   Marion C. Peters, Libn.

UNIVERSITY OF CALIFORNIA, LOS ANGELES - DEPARTMENT OF SPECIAL
  COLLECTIONS
University Research Library, Fl. A   Phone: (213) 825-4988
Los Angeles, CA 90024   James V. Mink, Hd./Univ.Archv.

UNIVERSITY OF CALIFORNIA, LOS ANGELES - EDUCATION & PSYCHOLOGY
  LIBRARY
390 Powell Library Bldg.   Phone: (213) 825-4081
Los Angeles, CA 90024   Dr. Lorraine Mathies, Hd.

UNIVERSITY OF CALIFORNIA, LOS ANGELES - ENGINEERING &
  MATHEMATICAL SCIENCES LIBRARY
8270 Boelter Hall   Phone: (213) 825-3982
Los Angeles, CA 90024   Karen L. Andrews, Hd.Libn.

UNIVERSITY OF CALIFORNIA, LOS ANGELES - ENGLISH READING ROOM †
1120 Rolfe Hall   Phone: (213) 825-4511
Los Angeles, CA 90024   C. Dandridge-Perry, Hd.

UNIVERSITY OF CALIFORNIA, LOS ANGELES - ENVIRONMENTAL SCIENCE
  AND ENGINEERING - LIBRARY
2066 Enginneering I Bldg.   Phone: (213) 825-7332
Los Angeles, CA 90024

UNIVERSITY OF CALIFORNIA, LOS ANGELES - GEOLOGY-GEOPHYSICS
  LIBRARY
Geology Bldg., Rm. 4697   Phone: (213) 825-1055
Los Angeles, CA 90024   Jim O'Donnell, Act.Libn.

UNIVERSITY OF CALIFORNIA, LOS ANGELES - HOUSING, REAL ESTATE &
  URBAN LAND STUDIES PROGRAM COLLECTION
Graduate School of Management   Phone: (213) 825-3977
Los Angeles, CA 90024   Frank G. Mittelbach, Dir.

UNIVERSITY OF CALIFORNIA, LOS ANGELES - LAW LIBRARY †
School Of Law
405 Hilgard Ave.   Phone: (213) 825-7826
Los Angeles, CA 90024   Frederick E. Smith, Law Libn.

UNIVERSITY OF CALIFORNIA, LOS ANGELES - MANAGEMENT LIBRARY
Graduate School of Management   Phone: (213) 825-3138
Los Angeles, CA 90024   Eloisa G. Yeargain, Act.Hd.

UNIVERSITY OF CALIFORNIA, LOS ANGELES - MAP LIBRARY
Bunche Hall, Rm. A-253   Phone: (213) 825-3526
Los Angeles, CA 90024   Carlos B. Hagen, Hd.

UNIVERSITY OF CALIFORNIA, LOS ANGELES - MATHEMATICS READING
  ROOM
Mathematics Science Bldg., Rm. 5379   Phone: (213) 825-4930
Los Angeles, CA 90024   Sharon Marcus, Libn.

UNIVERSITY OF CALIFORNIA, LOS ANGELES - MUSIC LIBRARY
1102 Schoenberg Hall
405 Hilgard Ave.   Phone: (213) 825-4881
Los Angeles, CA 90024   Stephen Fry, Music Libn.

UNIVERSITY OF CALIFORNIA, LOS ANGELES - ORIENTAL LIBRARY
21617 University Research Library   Phone: (213) 825-4836
Los Angeles, CA 90024   Mr. Ik-Sam Kim, Hd.

UNIVERSITY OF CALIFORNIA, LOS ANGELES - PHYSICAL SCIENCES &
  TECHNOLOGY LIBRARIES
8251 Boelter Hall   Phone: (213) 825-6515
Los Angeles, CA 90024   Alan R. Benenfeld, Coord.

UNIVERSITY OF CALIFORNIA, LOS ANGELES - PHYSICS LIBRARY
213 Kinsey Hall   Phone: (213) 825-4792
Los Angeles, CA 90024   J. Wally Pegram, Libn.

UNIVERSITY OF CALIFORNIA, LOS ANGELES - PUBLIC AFFAIRS SERVICE
405 Hilgard   Phone: (213) 825-3135
Los Angeles, CA 90024   Eugenia Eaton, Hd.

UNIVERSITY OF CALIFORNIA, LOS ANGELES - THEATER ARTS LIBRARY
22478 University Research Library   Phone: (213) 825-4880
Los Angeles, CA 90024   Mrs. Audree Malkin, Libn.

UNIVERSITY OF CALIFORNIA, LOS ANGELES - UCLA FILM ARCHIVES
Department Of Theater Arts   Phone: (213) 825-4142
Los Angeles, CA 90024   Robert Rosen, Dir.

UNIVERSITY OF CALIFORNIA, LOS ANGELES - UCLA RADIO ARCHIVES
Department Of Theater Arts   Phone: (213) 825-7357
Los Angeles, CA 90024   Robert Rosen, Dir.

UNIVERSITY OF CALIFORNIA, LOS ANGELES - UNIVERSITY ELEMENTARY
  SCHOOL LIBRARY
405 Hilgard Ave.   Phone: (213) 825-4928
Los Angeles, CA 90024   Judith Kantor, Hd.Libn.

UNIVERSITY OF CALIFORNIA, LOS ANGELES - WATER RESOURCES CENTER
  ARCHIVES
2081 Engineering I   Phone: (213) 825-7734
Los Angeles, CA 90024   Beth R. Willard, Libn.

UNIVERSITY OF CALIFORNIA, LOS ANGELES - WILLIAM ANDREWS CLARK
  MEMORIAL LIBRARY
2520 Cimarron St.   Phone: (213) 731-8529
Los Angeles, CA 90018   Robert Vosper, Dir.

UNIVERSITY OF ORIENTAL STUDIES - INTERNATIONAL BUDDHIST
  MEDITATION CENTER LIBRARY
939 S. New Hampshire Ave.   Phone: (213) 487-1235
Los Angeles, CA 90006   Edward Krafchow, Libn.

UNIVERSITY OF SOUTHERN CALIFORNIA - ARCHITECTURE & FINE ARTS LIBRARY
824 W. 37th St.
Los Angeles, CA 90007
Phone: (213) 743-2798
Alson Clark, Libn.

UNIVERSITY OF SOUTHERN CALIFORNIA - CROCKER BUSINESS LIBRARY
University Pk.
Los Angeles, CA 90007
Phone: (213) 743-7348
Judith A. Truelson, Dir.

UNIVERSITY OF SOUTHERN CALIFORNIA - DENTISTRY LIBRARY
Box 77951
Los Angeles, CA 90007
Phone: (213) 743-2884
Frank O. Mason, Libn.

UNIVERSITY OF SOUTHERN CALIFORNIA - EDUCATION LIBRARY
3424 S. Hoover, University Pk.
Los Angeles, CA 90007
Phone: (213) 743-6249
Janet Harvey, Educ.Libn.

UNIVERSITY OF SOUTHERN CALIFORNIA - ETHEL PERCY ANDRUS GERONTOLOGY CENTER - GERONTOLOGICAL INFO. CENTER
3715 McClintock Ave.
Los Angeles, CA 90007
Phone: (213) 743-5990
Jean E. Mueller, Libn.

UNIVERSITY OF SOUTHERN CALIFORNIA - HEALTH SCIENCES CAMPUS - NORRIS MEDICAL LIBRARY
2025 Zonal Ave.
Los Angeles, CA 90033
Phone: (213) 224-7231
Nelson J. Gilman, Libn./Dir.

UNIVERSITY OF SOUTHERN CALIFORNIA - INSTITUTE OF SAFETY & SYSTEMS MANAGEMENT - LIBRARY
SSM 105, U.S.C.
Los Angeles, CA 90007
Phone: (213) 743-6253
Monir Ziaian, Hd.Libn.

UNIVERSITY OF SOUTHERN CALIFORNIA - LAW CENTER LIBRARY †
University Pk.
Los Angeles, CA 90007
Phone: (213) 743-6487
Albert Brecht, Dir.

UNIVERSITY OF SOUTHERN CALIFORNIA - LIBRARY - CINEMA LIBRARY
University Pk.
Los Angeles, CA 90007
Phone: (213) 743-6058
Robert Knutson, Hd., Dept.Spec.Coll.

UNIVERSITY OF SOUTHERN CALIFORNIA - LIBRARY - DEPARTMENT OF SPECIAL COLLECTIONS
University Pk.
Los Angeles, CA 90007
Phone: (213) 743-6058
Robert Knutson, Hd.

UNIVERSITY OF SOUTHERN CALIFORNIA - LIBRARY - DEPARTMENT OF SPECIAL COLLECTIONS - AMERICAN LITERATURE COLLECTION
University Library, University Pk.
Los Angeles, CA 90007
Phone: (213) 743-6058
William Jankos, Cur.

UNIVERSITY OF SOUTHERN CALIFORNIA - MUSIC LIBRARY
Doheney Library, University Pk.
Los Angeles, CA 90007
Phone: (213) 743-2525
Rodney D. Rolfs, Music Libn.

UNIVERSITY OF SOUTHERN CALIFORNIA - NASA INDUSTRIAL APPLICATION CENTER (NIAC)
Denney Research Bldg., 3rd Fl.
University Park
Los Angeles, CA 90007
Phone: (213) 743-6132
Radford G. King, Dir.

UNIVERSITY OF SOUTHERN CALIFORNIA - PHILOSOPHY LIBRARY *
University Library, University Pk.
Los Angeles, CA 90007
Phone: (213) 743-2634
Bridget Molloy, Libn.

UNIVERSITY OF SOUTHERN CALIFORNIA - POPULATION RESEARCH LABORATORY - LIBRARY
University Pk., Research Annex 385
Los Angeles, CA 90007
Phone: (213) 743-2950
Professor David M. Heer, Assoc.Dir.

UNIVERSITY OF SOUTHERN CALIFORNIA - SCHOOL OF LIBRARY & INFORMATION MANAGEMENT - LIBRARY
M.R. Fisher Bldg., University Pk.
Los Angeles, CA 90007
Phone: (213) 743-2869
Mae L. Furbeyre, Libn.

UNIVERSITY OF SOUTHERN CALIFORNIA - SCIENCE & ENGINEERING LIBRARY
University Pk.
Los Angeles, CA 90007
Phone: (213) 743-2118
A. Albert Baker, Hd.

UNIVERSITY OF SOUTHERN CALIFORNIA - SOCIAL WORK LIBRARY
University Park
Los Angeles, CA 90302
Phone: (213) 743-7932
Ruth Britton, Libn.

UNIVERSITY OF SOUTHERN CALIFORNIA - VON KLEINSMID LIBRARY
University Pk.
Los Angeles, CA 90007
Phone: (213) 743-7347
Mr. Lynn Sipe, Libn.

UNIVERSITY OF SOUTHERN CALIFORNIA - VON KLEINSMID LIBRARY - ORIENTALIA COLLECTION
University Pk.
Los Angeles, CA 90007
Phone: (213) 743-7347
Mr. Lynn Sipe, Libn.

UPDATA PUBLICATIONS, INC. - LIBRARY
1756 Westwood Blvd.
Los Angeles, CA 90024
Phone: (213) 474-5900
Sara Ferguson, Libn.

WEINSTEIN (Robert) MARITIME HISTORICAL COLLECTION
1253 S. Stanley Ave.
Los Angeles, CA 90019
Phone: (213) 936-0558

WEST COAST UNIVERSITY - UNIVERSITY CENTER LIBRARY
440 Shatto Pl.
Los Angeles, CA 90020
Phone: (213) 487-4433
Beth Howell, Dir. of Lib.

WESTERN CENTER ON LAW AND POVERTY, INC. - LIBRARY
3535 W. 6th St.
Los Angeles, CA 90020
Phone: (213) 487-7211
David McFadden, Coord. of Lib.Serv.

WESTERN COSTUME COMPANY - RESEARCH LIBRARY
5335 Melrose Ave.
Los Angeles, CA 90038
Phone: (213) 469-1451
Nancy S. Kinney, Dir.

WHITE MEMORIAL MEDICAL CENTER - COURVILLE-ABBOTT MEMORIAL LIBRARY
1720 Brooklyn Ave.
Los Angeles, CA 90033
Phone: (213) 268-5000
Joyce Marson, Dir.

WHITE MEMORIAL MEDICAL CENTER - NEUROLOGY LIBRARY
1720 Brooklyn Ave.
Los Angeles, CA 90033
Phone: (213) 268-5000
Joyce Marson, Dir.

WHITTIER COLLEGE - SCHOOL OF LAW - LIBRARY
5353 W. 3d St.
Los Angeles, CA 90020
Phone: (213) 938-3621
J. Denny Haythorn, Dir., Law Lib.

WILSHIRE BOULEVARD TEMPLE - SIGMUND HECHT LIBRARY
3663 Wilshire Blvd.
Los Angeles, CA 90010
Phone: (213) 388-2401
Mitzi Weinstein, Libn.

WOODBURY UNIVERSITY - LIBRARY
1027 Wilshire Blvd.
Los Angeles, CA 90017
Phone: (213) 482-8491
Dr. Everett L. Moore, Dir., Lib.Serv.

ZEITLIN PERIODICALS COMPANY, INC. - LIBRARY
817 S. La Brea Ave.
Los Angeles, CA 90036
Phone: (213) 933-7175
Stanley Zeitlin, Pres.

ZEITLIN & VER BRUGGE, BOOKSELLERS - LIBRARY
815 N. La Cienega Blvd.
Los Angeles, CA 90069
Phone: (213) 655-7581
Jacob Israel Zeitlin, Pres.

CALIFORNIA PROVINCE OF THE SOCIETY OF JESUS - JESUIT CENTER LIBRARY *
300 College Ave.
Box 489
Los Gatos, CA 95030
Phone: (408) 354-9240
Bro. Thomas A. Marshall, S.J., Libn.

ST. FRANCIS MEDICAL CENTER - MOTHER MACARIA HEALTH SCIENCE LIBRARY
3630 E. Imperial Hwy.
Lynwood, CA 90262
Phone: (213) 603-6045
Eva Kratz, Dir. of Lib.Serv.

U.S. AIR FORCE BASE - MC CLELLAN BASE LIBRARY
2852 ABG/SSL
McClellan AFB, CA 95652
Phone: (916) 643-4640
Julia A. Patterson, Libn.

MADERA COUNTY HISTORICAL SOCIETY - MUSEUM/LIBRARY
210 W. Yosemite Ave.
Box 478   Phone: (209) 673-0291
Madera, CA 93639   Rintha Robbins, Libn.

GETTY (J. Paul) MUSEUM - RESEARCH LIBRARY
17985 Pacific Coast Hwy.   Phone: (213) 459-2306
Malibu, CA 90265   Anne-Mieke Halbrook, Hd.Libn.

HUGHES AIRCRAFT COMPANY - HUGHES RESEARCH LABORATORIES
    LIBRARY
3011 Malibu Canyon Rd.   Phone: (213) 456-6411
Malibu, CA 90265   Tobyann Mandel, Libn.

MEDICAL PLANNING ASSOCIATES - LIBRARY
1601 Rambla Pacifico   Phone: (213) 456-2084
Malibu, CA 90265   Carolyn Mitchell, Libn.

PEPPERDINE UNIVERSITY - LAW LIBRARY
24255 Pacific Coast Hwy.   Phone: (213) 456-4647
Malibu, CA 90265   Nancy J. Kitchen, Law Libn.

PEPPERDINE UNIVERSITY - LIBRARY - SPECIAL COLLECTIONS
24255 Pacific Coast Hwy.   Phone: (213) 456-4243
Malibu, CA 90265   Dorothy W. Moore, Dir.

U.S. AIR FORCE BASE - MARCH BASE LIBRARY
                                           Phone: (714) 655-2203
March AFB, CA 92518   Robert D. Jones, Lib.Techn.

R & D ASSOCIATES - TECHNICAL INFORMATION SERVICES
4640 Admiralty Way
Box 9695   Phone: (213) 822-1715
Marina Del Rey, CA 90291   Margaret R. Anderson, Mgr.

UNIVERSITY OF SOUTHERN CALIFORNIA - INFORMATION SCIENCES
    INSTITUTE - LIBRARY
4676 Admiralty Way   Phone: (213) 822-1511
Marina Del Rey, CA 90291   Sally Hambridge, Libn.

EARTHMIND - LIBRARY
4844 Hirsch Rd.
Mariposa, CA 95338   Michael A. Hackleman, Res.Dir.

ALPINE COUNTY LAW LIBRARY
Box 158   Phone: (916) 694-2281
Markleeville, CA 96120   Joan G. Chacon, Alpine County Ck.

CONTRA COSTA COUNTY LAW LIBRARY
Court House   Phone: (415) 372-2783
Martinez, CA 94553   Jean Steffensen, Law Libn.

U.S. VETERANS ADMINISTRATION (CA-Martinez) - HOSPITAL LIBRARY
150 Muir Rd.   Phone: (415) 228-6800
Martinez, CA 94553   Dorothea E. Bennett, Chf., Lib.Serv.

U.S. AIR FORCE BASE - MATHER BASE LIBRARY *
                                           Phone: (916) 364-2942
Mather AFB, CA 95655

U.S. AIR FORCE HOSPITAL - MEDICAL LIBRARY (CA-Mather AFB)
                                           Phone: (916) 364-2115
Mather AFB, CA 95655   Melinda Barrett, Libn.

MENDOCINO ART CENTER - ART LIBRARY
Box 765   Phone: (707) 937-5818
Mendocino, CA 95460   Joan Burleigh, Libn.

ADDISON-WESLEY PUBLISHING COMPANY - SCHOOL DIVISION LIBRARY
2725 Sand Hill Rd.   Phone: (415) 854-0300
Menlo Park, CA 94025   Elede Toppy Hall, Libn.

ENVIROTECH CORPORATION - LIBRARY
3000 Sand Hill Rd.
Menlo Park, CA 94025

GNOSTIC CONCEPTS, INC. - TECHNICAL LIBRARY
2710 Sand Hill Rd.   Phone: (415) 854-4672
Menlo Park, CA 94025   Nancy J. Mandeville, Tech.Libn.

INFORMATION ACCESS CORPORATION - LIBRARY
404 Sixth Ave.   Phone: (415) 367-7171
Menlo Park, CA 94025   Gene Windels, Corp.Libn.

RAYCHEM CORPORATION - TECHNICAL LIBRARY
300 Constitution Dr.   Phone: (415) 329-3282
Menlo Park, CA 94025   Phyllis Oda, Libn.

ST. PATRICK'S SEMINARY - MC KEON MEMORIAL LIBRARY
320 Middlefield Rd.   Phone: (415) 322-2224
Menlo Park, CA 94025   John F. Mattingly, Dir.

SRI INTERNATIONAL - BUSINESS INTELLIGENCE PROGRAM -
    INFORMATION CENTER
333 Ravenswood Ave.   Phone: (415) 859-2400
Menlo Park, CA 94025   Edward F. Christie, Supv.

SRI INTERNATIONAL - LIBRARY AND RESEARCH INFORMATION SERVICES
    DEPARTMENT
333 Ravenswood Ave.   Phone: (415) 326-6200
Menlo Park, CA 94025   V. Lorraine Pratt, Dir.

STANFORD LINEAR ACCELERATOR CENTER - LIBRARY
2575 Sand Hill Rd.   Phone: (415) 854-3300
Menlo Park, CA 94305   Robert C. Gex, Libn.

U.S. GEOLOGICAL SURVEY - LIBRARY
345 Middlefield Rd., MS55   Phone: (415) 323-8111
Menlo Park, CA 94025   Eleanore E. Wilkins, Libn.

U.S. GEOLOGICAL SURVEY - NATL. CARTOGRAPHIC INFORMATION CENTER
    (NCIC) - WESTERN BRANCH
345 Middlefield Rd.   Phone: (415) 323-8111
Menlo Park, CA 94025   Lee Aggers, Chf., NCIC - W.

MERCED COMMUNITY MEDICAL CENTER - MEDICAL LIBRARY
290 E. 15th St.
Box 231   Phone: (209) 723-2861
Merced, CA 95340   Betty Maddalena, Med.Libn.

GOLDEN GATE BAPTIST THEOLOGICAL SEMINARY - LIBRARY
Strawberry Point   Phone: (415) 388-8080
Mill Valley, CA 94941   Cecil R. White, Libn.

U.S. NATL. PARK SERVICE - MUIR WOODS NATL. MONUMENT - LIBRARY
Mill Valley, CA 94941

HOLY FAMILY COLLEGE - MOTHER DOLORES MEMORIAL LIBRARY
159 Washington Blvd.
Box 3426   Phone: (415) 651-1639
Mission San Jose, CA 94538   Sr. Patricia Wittman, Lib.Dir.

BURROUGHS CORPORATION - LIBRARY
25725 Jeronimo Rd.   Phone: (714) 768-2685
Mission Viejo, CA 92691   M. Patricia Feeney, Libn.

DOCTORS' MEDICAL CENTER - PROFESSIONAL LIBRARY
1441 Florida Ave.
Box 4138   Phone: (209) 578-1211
Modesto, CA 95352   Margaret F. Luebke, Med.Libn.

GALLO (E. & J.) WINERY - LIBRARY
Box 1130   Phone: (209) 521-3230
Modesto, CA 95353   Rosemary Harris, Libn.

MC HENRY MUSEUM - LIBRARY
1402 I St.   Phone: (209) 577-5366
Modesto, CA 95354   Heidi L. Warner, Cur.

MODESTO BEE - EDITORIAL LIBRARY
Box 3928   Phone: (209) 524-4041
Modesto, CA 95352   Lillian Wendt, Libn.

SHELL DEVELOPMENT COMPANY - BIOLOGICAL SCIENCES RESEARCH
    CENTER - LIBRARY
Box 4248   Phone: (209) 545-0761
Modesto, CA 95352   Patt Snyder, Libn.

STANISLAUS COUNTY LAW LIBRARY
Rm. 224, Courthouse
Phone: (209) 526-6302
Modesto, CA 95354   Stephen Edward Munson, Law Libn.

STANISLAUS COUNTY MEDICAL SOCIETY - MEDICAL LIBRARY
Box 3271
Phone: (209) 526-6132
Modesto, CA 95353   Margie Felt, Med.Libn.

STANISLAUS COUNTY SCHOOLS - TEACHERS' PROFESSIONAL LIBRARY
801 County Center No. 3 Ct.
Phone: (209) 526-6593
Modesto, CA 95355   V. Ruth Smith, Hd.

SYSTEM DEVELOPMENT CORPORATION - ARPA RESEARCH LIBRARY
Unit 1
Phone: (415) 968-9061
Moffett Field, CA 94035   Roy McCabe, Mgr.

MC DONNELL DOUGLAS CORPORATION - ACTRON TECHNICAL LIBRARY †
700 Royal Oaks Dr.
Phone: (213) 359-8216
Monrovia, CA 91016   Stella A. Medigovich, Libn.

WORLD VISION INTERNATIONAL - INFORMATION RESOURCE CENTER
919 W. Huntington Dr.
Phone: (213) 574-9017
Monrovia, CA 91016   Mary Janss-Clary, Res.Assoc.

COLTON HALL MUSEUM - LIBRARY
Phone: (408) 372-8121
Monterey, CA 93940   Dorothy Chesbro Ronald, Cur.

CTB/MC GRAW-HILL - LIBRARY
Del Monte Research Park
Phone: (408) 649-7919
Monterey, CA 93940   Phyllis H. O'Donovan, Libn.

MARITIME MUSEUM (Allen Knight) - LIBRARY
550 Calle Principal
Box 805
Phone: (408) 375-2553
Monterey, CA 93940   G. Robert Giet, Libn.

MONTEREY HISTORY & ART ASSOCIATION - MAYO HAYES O'DONNELL LIBRARY
155 Van Buren St.
Box 805
Monterey, CA 93940   Mrs. Charles M. Bentley, Lib.Chm.

MONTEREY INSTITUTE OF INTERNATIONAL STUDIES - WILLIAM TELL COLEMAN LIBRARY †
425 Van Buren St.
Box 1978
Phone: (408) 649-3113
Monterey, CA 93940   Dr. Eva I.A. Schroeder, Dir.

U.S. ARMY - DEFENSE LANGUAGE INSTITUTE - ACADEMIC LIBRARY
Presidio, Bldg. 618
Phone: (408) 242-8206
Monterey, CA 93940   Gary D. Walter, Libn.

U.S. NAVY - NAVAL ENVIRONMENTAL PREDICTION RESEARCH FACILITY - TECHNICAL LIBRARY
Naval Postgraduate School
Annex Bldg. 22
Phone: (408) 646-2813
Monterey, CA 93940   Joanne M. May, Libn.

U.S. NAVY - NAVAL POSTGRADUATE SCHOOL - DUDLEY KNOX LIBRARY
Phone: (408) 646-2341
Monterey, CA 93940   Paul Spinks, Dir. of Libs.

MEXICAN-AMERICAN OPPORTUNITY FOUNDATION - INFORMATION AND REFERRAL SERVICE - RESOURCE CENTER
664 Monterey Pass Rd.
Phone: (213) 289-0286
Monterey Park, CA 91754   Lorraine M. Mirabel, Project Dir.

MORAGA HISTORICAL SOCIETY - ARCHIVES
St. Mary's College Library
Phone: (415) 376-4411
Moraga, CA 94575   Bro. L. Dennis Goodman, F.S.C.

CALIFORNIA STATE UNIVERSITY AND COLLEGES - MOSS LANDING MARINE LABORATORIES - LIBRARY
Box 223
Phone: (408) 633-3304
Moss Landing, CA 95039   Sheila Baldridge, Libn.

ACUREX CORPORATION - TECHNICAL LIBRARY
485 Clyde Ave.
Phone: (415) 964-3200
Mountain View, CA 94042   Cindy Hutchinson, Chf.Libn.

BNR INC. - INFORMATION RESOURCE CENTER
685A E. Middlefield Rd.
Phone: (415) 969-9170
Mountain View, CA 94043   Ms. L.S. Menashian, Mgr.

GTE PRODUCTS CORPORATION - SYLVANIA SYSTEMS GROUP - WESTERN DIVISION - LIBRARY
Box 188
Phone: (415) 966-3082
Mountain View, CA 94042   Julie del Fierro, Lib.Serv.Supv.

NIELSEN ENGINEERING & RESEARCH, INC. - LIBRARY
510 Clyde Ave.
Phone: (415) 968-9457
Mountain View, CA 94043   Jane Differding, Libn.

PACIFIC STUDIES CENTER - LIBRARY
867 W. Dana St., No. 204
Phone: (415) 969-1545
Mountain View, CA 94041   Leonard M. Siegel, Dir.

STAUFFER CHEMICAL COMPANY - MOUNTAIN VIEW RESEARCH CENTER LIBRARY
Box 760
Phone: (408) 739-0511
Mountain View, CA 94042   Martha L. Manion, Assoc.Libn.

U.S. NASA - AMES RESEARCH CENTER - LIBRARY
Moffett Field, Mail Stop 202-3
Phone: (415) 965-5157
Mountain View, CA 94035   Ralph W. Lewis, Chf., Lib.Br.

NAPA COUNTY HISTORICAL SOCIETY - GOODMAN LIBRARY
1219 First St.
Phone: (707) 224-1739
Napa, CA 94558   Jess Doud, Exec.Dir./Archv.

PARADISE VALLEY HOSPITAL - MEDICAL LIBRARY *
2400 E. Fourth St.
Phone: (714) 470-6311
National City, CA 92050   Janet R. Fuss, Libn.

NEVADA COUNTY HISTORICAL SOCIETY - SEARLS HISTORICAL LIBRARY
214 Church St.
Nevada City, CA 95959   Edwin L. Tyson, Libn.

NEVADA COUNTY LAW LIBRARY
Courthouse Annex
Phone: (916) 265-2461
Nevada City, CA 95959   Letha Baker, Law Libn.

NEW ALMADEN MERCURY MINING MUSEUM - LIBRARY
21570 Almaden Rd.
Box 1
Phone: (408) 268-7869
New Almaden, CA 95042   Constance B. Perham, Owner-Cur.

NORTHROP CORPORATION - VENTURA DIVISION - TECHNICAL INFORMATION CENTER
1515 Rancho Conejo Blvd.
Phone: (805) 498-3131
Newbury Park, CA 91320   Marjorie Raine, Lib.Asst.Sr.

LOS ANGELES BAPTIST COLLEGE - ROBERT L. POWELL MEMORIAL LIBRARY
21726 W. Placerita Canyon Rd.
Box 878
Phone: (805) 259-3540
Newhall, CA 91322   Agnes M. Holt, Libn.

FORD AEROSPACE & COMMUNICATIONS CORP. - AERONUTRONIC DIVISION - TECHNICAL INFORMATION SERVICES
Ford Rd.
Phone: (714) 759-5367
Newport Beach, CA 92663   L.H. Linder, Mgr.Tech.Info.Serv.

HOAG MEMORIAL HOSPITAL-PRESBYTERIAN - MEDICAL LIBRARY
301 Newport Blvd.
Box Y
Phone: (714) 645-8600
Newport Beach, CA 92663   Mrs. Ute Simons, Med.Libn.

HUGHES AIRCRAFT COMPANY - ENGINEERING LIBRARY
500 Superior Ave.
Phone: (714) 759-2492
Newport Beach, CA 92663   Barbara Squyres, Engr.Libn.

NEWPORT HARBOR ART MUSEUM - LIBRARY
850 San Clemente Dr.
Phone: (714) 759-1122
Newport Beach, CA 92660   Ruth Roe, Libn.

ROCKWELL INTERNATIONAL - NEWPORT BEACH INFORMATION CENTER
4311 Jamboree Blvd., (501-105)   Phone: (714) 833-4389
Newport Beach, CA 92660   K.H. Preston, Mgr.

CALIFORNIA STATE REHABILITATION CENTER - RESIDENT LIBRARY
Box 841   Phone: (714) 737-2683
Norco, CA 91760   Gerald O. Nelson, Libn.

WILDERNESS LEADERSHIP INTERNATIONAL - OUTDOOR LIVING LIBRARY
Wilderness Leadership Center
Box 770
North Fork, CA 96643   Phylis Austin, Libn.

CALIFORNIA STATE UNIVERSITY, NORTHRIDGE - LIBRARY - HEALTH
    SCIENCE COLLECTION
18111 Nordhoff St.   Phone: (213) 885-3012
Northridge, CA 91330   Snowdy Dodson, Sci.Ref.Libn.

SPACE VECTOR CORPORATION - LIBRARY
19631 Prairie St.
Northridge, CA 91324

3M - RIKER LABORATORIES, INC. - NORTHRIDGE LIBRARY
19901 Nordhoff St.   Phone: (213) 709-3100
Northridge, CA 91324   Edwin A. Staggs, Sr.Lit.Sci./Hd.Libn.

U.S. AIR FORCE BASE - NORTON BASE LIBRARY
          Phone: (714) 382-7119
Norton AFB, CA 92409   Robert R. DeBaun, Base Libn.

U.S. DEFENSE AUDIOVISUAL AGENCY - DEPOSITORY BRANCH (DAVA-N-
    LGD)
Norton Activity   Phone: (714) 382-2513
Norton AFB, CA 92409   Donald R. Loucks, Chf. Depository Branch

METROPOLITAN STATE HOSPITAL - STAFF LIBRARY
11400 Norwalk Blvd.   Phone: (213) 863-7011
Norwalk, CA 90650   G. Calvin Tooker, Libn.

NOVATO UNIFIED SCHOOL DISTRICT - INSTRUCTIONAL MATERIALS
    CENTER
1015 7th St.   Phone: (415) 897-4247
Novato, CA 94947   Annette Conklin, Rsrcs.Libn.

ALAMEDA-CONTRA COSTA MEDICAL ASSOCIATION - LIBRARY
1411 E. 31st St.   Phone: (415) 534-8055
Oakland, CA 94602   Julia T. Duboczy, Med.Libn.

ALAMEDA COUNTY LAW LIBRARY
1225 Fallon St.   Phone: (415) 874-5823
Oakland, CA 94612   Cossette T. Sun, Law Lib.Dir.

ALAMEDA COUNTY LIBRARY - BUSINESS & GOVERNMENT LIBRARY
2201 Broadway   Phone: (415) 874-5178
Oakland, CA 94612   David Lewallen, Br.Hd.

ARCHIVES OF CALIFORNIA ART
Oakland Museum, 1000 Oak St.   Phone: (415) 273-3005
Oakland, CA 94607   Christina Orr-Cahall, Chf.Cur. of Art

CALIFORNIA COLLEGE OF ARTS AND CRAFTS - MEYER LIBRARY
Broadway At College   Phone: (415) 653-8118
Oakland, CA 94618   Robert L. Harper, Hd.Libn.

CALIFORNIA STATE REGIONAL WATER QUALITY CONTROL BOARD, SAN
    FRANCISCO BAY REGION - LIBRARY
1111 Jackson St., Rm. 6040   Phone: (415) 464-1255
Oakland, CA 94618   Lawrence Kolb, Hd.

CENTER FOR INVESTIGATIVE REPORTING - LIBRARY
1419 Broadway, Rm. 600   Phone: (415) 835-8525
Oakland, CA 94612   Dan Noyes, Staff Writer/Libn.

CHILDREN'S HOSPITAL MEDICAL CENTER OF NORTHERN CALIFORNIA -
    MEDICAL LIBRARY
51st & Grove Sts.   Phone: (415) 654-5600
Oakland, CA 94609   Barbara Davenport, Med.Libn.

CHURCH OF JESUS CHRIST OF LATTER-DAY SAINTS - OAKLAND
    GENEALOGICAL BRANCH LIBRARY *
4780 Lincoln Ave.   Phone: (415) 531-3905
Oakland, CA 94602   Ernest W. Henderson, Chf.Libn.

CROSBY, HEAFEY, ROACH & MAY - LAW LIBRARY
1939 Harrison St.   Phone: (415) 834-4820
Oakland, CA 94612   Patrick O'Leary, Libn.

DATA CENTER - INVESTIGATIVE RESOURCE CENTER
464 19th St.   Phone: (415) 835-4692
Oakland, CA 94612   Harry Strharsky, Exec.Dir.

FITZGERALD, ABBOTT AND BEARDSLEY - LAW LIBRARY
1330 Broadway
Oakland, CA 94612   Lawrence R. Shepp

GLADMAN (Everett A.) MEMORIAL HOSPITAL - MEDICAL LIBRARY
2633 East 27th St.   Phone: (415) 536-8111
Oakland, CA 94601   Elizabeth Edelstein, Libn.

ISI CORPORATION - RESEARCH LIBRARY
Box 23330   Phone: (415) 832-1400
Oakland, CA 94623   Lynn Krekemeyer, Libn.

KAISER ENGINEERS, INC. - ENGINEERING LIBRARY
300 Lakeside Dr.
Box 23210   Phone: (415) 271-4375
Oakland, CA 94623   Elaine Zacher, Libn.

KAISER-PERMANENTE MEDICAL CENTER - HEALTH LIBRARY
280 W. MacArthur Blvd.   Phone: (415) 645-6569
Oakland, CA 94611   Eileen McAdam, Libn.

KAISER-PERMANENTE MEDICAL CENTER - MEDICAL LIBRARY
280 W. MacArthur Blvd.   Phone: (415) 428-5033
Oakland, CA 94611   Helen C. Sheward, Libn.

KAISER-PERMANENTE MEDICAL CENTERS, NORTHERN CALIFORNIA
    REGION - REGIONAL HEALTH LIBRARY SERVICES
3451 Piedmont Ave.   Phone: (415) 428-6569
Oakland, CA 94611   Caren K. Quay, Regional Cons.

MERRITT (Samuel) HOSPITAL - MEDICAL LIBRARY
Hawthorne & Webster Sts.   Phone: (415) 655-4000
Oakland, CA 94609   Linda Charlmyra Thomas, Med.Libn.

MILLS COLLEGE - MARGARET PRALL MUSIC LIBRARY
          Phone: (415) 632-2700
Oakland, CA 94613   Eva Kreshka, Tech.Serv.Libn.

OAKLAND CITY PLANNING DEPARTMENT - LIBRARY
City Hall, 6th Fl.   Phone: (415) 273-3941
Oakland, CA 94612   Marceia L. Borden, Asst. Planner

OAKLAND PUBLIC LIBRARY - ART, MUSIC, RECREATION
125 14th St.   Phone: (415) 273-3178
Oakland, CA 94612   Richard Colvig, Sr.Libn.

OAKLAND PUBLIC LIBRARY - ASIAN LIBRARY
449 9th St.   Phone: (415) 273-3400
Oakland, CA 94612   Judy Yung, Libn.

OAKLAND PUBLIC LIBRARY - CITYLINE INFORMATION SERVICE
Oakland City Hall
1421 Washington St.   Phone: (415) 444-2489
Oakland, CA 94612   MaryLou T. Martin, Libn.

OAKLAND PUBLIC LIBRARY - HANDICAPPED SERVICES
125 14th St.   Phone: (415) 273-3133
Oakland, CA 94612   Lydia Shireman, Libn.

OAKLAND PUBLIC LIBRARY - HISTORY/LITERATURE DIVISION
125 14th St.   Phone: (415) 273-3136
Oakland, CA 94612   Harrison Malan, Sr.Libn.

OAKLAND PUBLIC LIBRARY - INTERTRIBAL LIBRARY PROJECT
125 14th St.   Phone: (415) 273-3511
Oakland, CA 94612   Adelia Lines, Supv.

GEOGRAPHIC

OAKLAND PUBLIC LIBRARY - LATIN AMERICAN LIBRARY †
1900 Fruitvale Ave., Suite 1-A   Phone: (415) 532-7882
Oakland, CA 94601   Deborah Ruiz, Libn.

OAKLAND PUBLIC LIBRARY - SCIENCE/SOCIOLOGY DIVISION
125 14th St.   Phone: (415) 273-3138
Oakland, CA 94612   Richard Ragsdale, Sr.Libn.

OAKLAND PUBLIC SCHOOLS - PROFESSIONAL LIBRARY
1025 Second Ave.   Phone: (415) 836-2622
Oakland, CA 94606   Michael Winters, Lrng.Rsrcs.Spec.

OAKLAND TRIBUNE - LIBRARY
Box 24304   Phone: (415) 645-2745
Oakland, CA 94623   Seth Simpson, Libn.

SAFEWAY STORES, INC. - LIBRARY
201 Fourth St.   Phone: (415) 891-3175
Oakland, CA 94660   Elizabeth D. Williams, Lib.Mgr.

U.S. NAVY - NAVAL REGIONAL MEDICAL CENTER (Oakland) - MEDICAL
    LIBRARY
8750 Mountain Blvd.   Phone: (415) 639-2070
Oakland, CA 94627   Jane C. O'Sullivan, Adm.Libn.

UNIVERSITY OF CALIFORNIA, BERKELEY - NAVAL BIOSCIENCES
    LABORATORY - LIBRARY
Bldg. 844, Naval Supply Ctr.   Phone: (415) 832-5217
Oakland, CA 94625   Theresa Dundon, Libn.

WHALE CENTER - EXTINCT SPECIES MEMORIAL FUND - LIBRARY
3929 Piedmont Ave.   Phone: (415) 654-6621
Oakland, CA 94611   Maxine McCloskey, Exec.Dir.

ROSICRUCIAN FELLOWSHIP - LIBRARY
2220 Mission Ave.   Phone: (714) 757-6601
Oceanside, CA 92054   Gene Franzman, Libn.

KROTONA INSTITUTE OF THEOSOPHY - KROTONA LIBRARY
Krotona 2   Phone: (805) 646-2653
Ojai, CA 93023   Erna Achenbach, Hd.Libn.

THEOSOPHICAL BOOK ASSOCIATION FOR THE BLIND, INC.
Krotona 54   Phone: (805) 646-2121
Ojai, CA 93023   Dennis Gottschalk, Pres.

SUNKIST GROWERS, INC. - RESEARCH LIBRARY
760 E. Sunkist St.   Phone: (714) 983-9811
Ontario, CA 91761   Martha C. Nemeth, Tech.Libn.

HOLMES & NARVER, INC. - TECHNICAL LIBRARY *
999 Town & Country Rd.   Phone: (714) 973-1100
Orange, CA 92668   Connie Rickerson, Libn.

LOYOLA MARYMOUNT COLLEGE - ORANGE CAMPUS - LIBRARY
480 S. Batavia St.   Phone: (714) 633-8495
Orange, CA 92668   Sr. Therese Zickgraf, C.S.J., Libn.

ORANGE COUNTY MEDICAL CENTER - MEDICAL LIBRARY
101 City Dr., S.
Orange, CA 92668

ST. JOSEPH HOSPITAL - BURLEW MEDICAL LIBRARY
1100 Stewart Dr.   Phone: (714) 633-9111
Orange, CA 92668   Julie Smith, Med.Libn.

UNIVERSITY OF CALIFORNIA, IRVINE - MEDICAL CENTER LIBRARY
101 City Dr., S.   Phone: (714) 634-5798
Orange, CA 92668   Diana Lane, Act.Hd.

BUTTE COUNTY LAW LIBRARY
Courthouse, One Court St.   Phone: (916) 534-4611
Oroville, CA 95965   Evlyn L. Turner, Law Libn.

ST. JOHN'S HOSPITAL - HEALTH SCIENCE LIBRARY
333 N. F St.   Phone: (805) 487-7861
Oxnard, CA 93030   Joanne Kennedy, Libn.

PACIFIC GROVE MUSEUM OF NATURAL HISTORY - LIBRARY
165 Forest Ave.
Pacific Grove, CA 93950   Vernal L. Yadon, Musm.Dir.

STANFORD UNIVERSITY - HOPKINS MARINE STATION - LIBRARY
Cabrillo Point   Phone: (408) 373-0460
Pacific Grove, CA 93950   Alan Baldridge, Libn.

LIVING DESERT RESERVE - HAYNES MEMORIAL LIBRARY
Box 1775   Phone: (714) 346-5694
Palm Desert, CA 92261

YOUTH RESOURCES, INC. - AGRI-SILVICULTURE INSTITUTE LIBRARY
Box 4166   Phone: (714) 327-2639
Palm Springs, CA 92263

PATERSON AND CO. - LIBRARY
Box 1196   Phone: (805) 273-4252
Palmdale, CA 93550

ACQUIRE INFORMATION - INFORMATION CENTER *
605 Cowper St.   Phone: (415) 326-3996
Palo Alto, CA 94301   Myra Hodgson, Owner

ALZA CORPORATION - RESEARCH LIBRARY
950 Page Mill Rd.   Phone: (415) 494-5215
Palo Alto, CA 94304   Mary Susan Laird, Mgr., Lib.Serv.

AMERICAN INSTITUTES FOR RESEARCH - LIBRARY
1791 Arastradero Rd.
Box 1113   Phone: (415) 493-3550
Palo Alto, CA 94302   John French, Libn.

AMERICAN INSTITUTES FOR RESEARCH - PROJECT TALENT DATA BANK
Box 1113   Phone: (415) 493-3550
Palo Alto, CA 94302   Lauri Steel, Dir., Data Bank

BECKMAN INSTRUMENTS, INC. - SPINCO DIVISION - TECHNICAL LIBRARY
1117 California Ave.   Phone: (415) 326-1970
Palo Alto, CA 94304   Phyllis M. Browning, Sci.Info.Mgr.

DYNAPOL - LIBRARY
1454 Page Mill Rd.   Phone: (415) 494-5608
Palo Alto, CA 94304   Sharon R. Hamrick, Libn.

ELECTRIC POWER RESEARCH INSTITUTE - TECHNICAL LIBRARY
3412 Hillview Ave.   Phone: (415) 855-2355
Palo Alto, CA 94304   Stephen B. Parker, Libn.

FAIRCHILD - R & D LIBRARY
4001 Miranda Ave.   Phone: (415) 493-7250
Palo Alto, CA 94303

FIRST CONGREGATIONAL CHURCH - LIBRARY †
1985 Louis Rd.   Phone: (415) 856-6662
Palo Alto, CA 94303

FORD AEROSPACE & COMMUNICATIONS CORP. - WESTERN DEVELOPMENT
    LABORATORIES (WDL) - TECHNICAL LIBRARY
3939 Fabian Way   Phone: (415) 494-7400
Palo Alto, CA 94303   Cynthia Turgeon, Libn.

HEWLETT-PACKARD COMPANY - CORPORATE LIBRARY
1501 Page Mill Rd.   Phone: (415) 857-3091
Palo Alto, CA 94304   Mark H. Baer, Dir. Of Libs.

HEWLETT-PACKARD COMPANY - HP LABORATORIES - DEER CREEK
    LIBRARY
3500 Deer Creek Rd.   Phone: (415) 857-5205
Palo Alto, CA 94304   Nancy E. Lem, Libn.

LOCKHEED MISSILES & SPACE COMPANY, INC. - LOCKHEED INFORMATION
    SYSTEMS
Code 5280, 3460 Hillview Ave.   Phone: (415) 858-3810
Palo Alto, CA 94304   Dr. Roger K. Summit, Mgr.

LOCKHEED MISSILES & SPACE COMPANY, INC. - TECHNICAL
    INFORMATION CENTER
3251 Hanover St.   Phone: (415) 493-4411
Palo Alto, CA 94304   Arthur N. Fried, Supv.

PALO ALTO MEDICAL FOUNDATION - BARNETT-HALL MEDICAL LIBRARY
860 Bryant St.   Phone: (415) 321-4121
Palo Alto, CA 94301   Eileen Cassidy, Hd.Libn.

PALO ALTO UNIFIED SCHOOL DISTRICT - TEACHERS' PROFESSIONAL
  LIBRARY
480 E. Meadow Dr.   Phone: (415) 855-8360
Palo Alto, CA 94306   Theresa Regan, AV Matl.Instr.

PENINSULA CONSERVATION FOUNDATION - LIBRARY OF THE
  ENVIRONMENT
2253 Park Blvd.   Phone: (415) 328-5313
Palo Alto, CA 94306   Nancy S. Olson, Libn.

PENINSULA TIMES TRIBUNE - LIBRARY
245 Lytton Ave.
Box 300   Phone: (415) 326-1200
Palo Alto, CA 94302   Elizabeth R. Miller, Hd.Libn.

R & E RESEARCH ASSOCIATES - LIBRARY
936 Industrial   Phone: (415) 328-4531
Palo Alto, CA 94303   R. Reed, Pub.

SYNTEX, U.S.A. - CORPORATE LIBRARY/INFORMATION SERVICES
3401 Hillview Ave.   Phone: (415) 855-5431
Palo Alto, CA 94304   Nancy Baltis, Mgr.

SYSTEMS CONTROL, INC. - TECHNICAL LIBRARY
1801 Page Mill Rd.   Phone: (408) 494-1165
Palo Alto, CA 94304   Martha Liles, Libn.

SYVA COMPANY - RESEARCH LIBRARY
900 Arastradero Rd.   Phone: (415) 493-2200
Palo Alto, CA 94303   Louise Lohr, Libn.

U.S. VETERANS ADMINISTRATION (CA-Palo Alto) - HOSPITAL MEDICAL
  LIBRARIES
3801 Miranda Ave.   Phone: (415) 493-5000
Palo Alto, CA 94304   C.R. Gallimore, Chf., Lib.Serv.

VARIAN ASSOCIATES - TECHNICAL LIBRARY
611 Hansen Way   Phone: (415) 493-4000
Palo Alto, CA 94303   Kathrine E. Johnson, Mgr., Lib.Serv.

XEROX CORPORATION - PALO ALTO RESEARCH CENTER - TECHNICAL
  INFORMATION CENTER
3333 Coyote Hill Rd.   Phone: (415) 494-4042
Palo Alto, CA 94304   Giuliana A. Lavendel, Mgr.

ZOECON CORPORATION - LIBRARY
975 California Ave.   Phone: (415) 329-1130
Palo Alto, CA 94304   Carolyn A. Erickson, Libn.

NORTHROP CORPORATION - RESEARCH AND TECHNOLOGY CENTER -
  LIBRARY SERVICES
One Research Park   Phone: (213) 377-4811
Palos Verdes Peninsula, CA 90274   Kay E. Salm, Hd.Libn.

KAISER-PERMANENTE MEDICAL CENTER - PANORAMA CITY HEALTH
  SCIENCE LIBRARY
13652 Cantara St.   Phone: (213) 781-2361
Panorama City, CA 91402   Elaine Graham, Hd.Libn.

DOUGLAS OIL COMPANY OF CALIFORNIA - RESEARCH AND TECHNOLOGY
  DEPARTMENT - LIBRARY *
14700 Downey Ave.   Phone: (213) 531-2060
Paramount, CA 90723   Rita Foster, Libn.

UNIVERSITY OF CALIFORNIA - SAN JOAQUIN VALLEY AGRICULTURAL
  RESEARCH & EXTENSION CENTER
9240 S. Riverbend Ave.   Phone: (209) 646-2794
Parlier, CA 93648   Andrew S. Deal, Dir.

ART CENTER COLLEGE OF DESIGN - JAMES LEMONT FOGG MEMORIAL
  LIBRARY
1700 Lida St.   Phone: (213) 577-1700
Pasadena, CA 91103   Elizabeth Stockly, Lib.Dir.

AVERY INTERNATIONAL CORPORATION - RESEARCH CENTER LIBRARY
325 N. Altadena Dr.   Phone: (213) 799-0881
Pasadena, CA 91107   Joanne McKinney, Info.Spec.

BELL & HOWELL COMPANY - LIBRARY/TECHNICAL INFORMATION
  SERVICES
360 Sierra Madre Villa   Phone: (213) 796-9381
Pasadena, CA 91109   Beverly V. Busenbark, Mgr.Lib.Serv.

BURROUGHS CORPORATION - COMPUTER SYSTEMS GROUP - TECHNICAL
  INFORMATION RESOURCES CENTER †
460 Sierra Madre Villa   Phone: (213) 351-6551
Pasadena, CA 91109   Judy Atkinson, Mgr.

CALIFORNIA INSTITUTE OF TECHNOLOGY - AERONAUTICS LIBRARY
1201 E. California Blvd.   Phone: (213) 356-4521
Pasadena, CA 91125   Virginia N. Anderson, Libn.

CALIFORNIA INSTITUTE OF TECHNOLOGY - ASTROPHYSICS LIBRARY
1201 E. California Blvd.   Phone: (213) 356-4008
Pasadena, CA 91125   Helen Z. Knudsen, Libn.

CALIFORNIA INSTITUTE OF TECHNOLOGY - EARTHQUAKE ENGINEERING
  RESEARCH LIBRARY
201 Thomas Lab.   Phone: (213) 356-4227
Pasadena, CA 91125   Kenneth D. Graham, Libn.

CALIFORNIA INSTITUTE OF TECHNOLOGY - ENERGY RESEARCH LIBRARY
1201 California Blvd.   Phone: (213) 356-4521
Pasadena, CA 91125   Virginia N. Anderson, Libn.

CALIFORNIA INSTITUTE OF TECHNOLOGY - ENVIRONMENTAL
  ENGINEERING LIBRARY
136 W.M. Keck Laboratory (138-78)   Phone: (213) 356-4381
Pasadena, CA 91125   Rayma Harrison, Assoc.Libn.

CALIFORNIA INSTITUTE OF TECHNOLOGY - GEOLOGY LIBRARY
201 North Mudd Bldg.   Phone: (213) 356-6699
Pasadena, CA 91125   Daphne Plane, Libn.

CALIFORNIA INSTITUTE OF TECHNOLOGY - JET PROPULSION LABORATORY
  - LIBRARY
4800 Oak Grove Dr.   Phone: (213) 354-4200
Pasadena, CA 91103   D. Adel Wilder, Mgr., Lib.

CALIFORNIA INSTITUTE OF TECHNOLOGY - MUNGER AFRICANA LIBRARY
115 Baxter Hall   Phone: (213) 795-6811
Pasadena, CA 91125   Dr. Edwin S. Munger, Dir.

CALIFORNIA INSTITUTE OF TECHNOLOGY - ROBERT A. MILLIKAN
  MEMORIAL LIBRARY
1201 E. California Blvd.   Phone: (213) 356-6405
Pasadena, CA 91125   Johanna E. Tallman, Dir. of Libs.

CARNEGIE INSTITUTION OF WASHINGTON - MOUNT WILSON & LAS
  CAMPANAS OBSERVATORIES - LIBRARY
813 Santa Barbara St.   Phone: (213) 577-1122
Pasadena, CA 91101   Joan Gantz, Libn.

CONVERSE WARD DAVIS DIXON - CORPORATE LIBRARY
221 E. Walnut St., Suite 250   Phone: (213) 796-8200
Pasadena, CA 91101   Andrea B. Berman, Corp.Libn.

FULLER THEOLOGICAL SEMINARY - MC ALISTER LIBRARY
135 N. Oakland Ave.   Phone: (213) 449-1745
Pasadena, CA 91101   Christine C. Jewett, Libn.

GREENE AND GREENE LIBRARY
David B. Gamble House
4 Westmoreland Pl.   Phone: (213) 793-3334
Pasadena, CA 91103   LuVerne LaMotte, Chm., Lib.Comm.

HUNTINGTON MEMORIAL HOSPITAL - HEALTH SCIENCES LIBRARY
100 Congress St.   Phone: (213) 258-7869
Pasadena, CA 91105   Samir Zeind, Dir.

INTERNATIONAL INSTITUTE OF MUNICIPAL CLERKS - MANAGEMENT
  INFORMATION CENTER
160 N. Altadena Dr.   Phone: (213) 795-6153
Pasadena, CA 91107   John J. Hunnewell, Exec.Dir.

JEFFERSON (Thomas) RESEARCH CENTER - LIBRARY
1143 N. Lake Ave.　　　　　　　　Phone: (213) 798-0791
Pasadena, CA 91104　　　　　　　Frank G. Goble, Pres.

NORTON SIMON MUSEUM OF ART AT PASADENA - GALKA E. SCHEYER
　　ARCHIVES
411 W. Colorado Blvd.　　　　　　Phone: (213) 449-6840
Pasadena, CA 91105　　　　　　　Sara Campbell, Cur.

NORTON SIMON MUSEUM OF ART AT PASADENA - LIBRARY
411 W. Colorado Blvd.　　　　　　Phone: (213) 449-6840
Pasadena, CA 91105

PARSONS (Ralph M.) COMPANY - CENTRAL LIBRARY
100 W. Walnut St.　　　　　　　　Phone: (213) 440-3999
Pasadena, CA 91124　　　　　　　Alice M. Hamilton, Libn.

PASADENA FOUNDATION FOR MEDICAL RESEARCH - FILM LIBRARY *
99 N. El Molino Ave.　　　　　　　Phone: (213) 795-4343
Pasadena, CA 91101　　　　　　　William Opel, Exec.Dir.

PASADENA HISTORICAL SOCIETY - LIBRARY
470 W. Walnut St.　　　　　　　　Phone: (213) 577-1660
Pasadena, CA 91103　　　　　　　Sue Schechter

PASADENA PUBLIC LIBRARY - ALICE COLEMAN BATCHELDER MUSIC
　　LIBRARY
285 E. Walnut St.　　　　　　　　Phone: (213) 577-4049
Pasadena, CA 91101　　　Josephine M. Pletscher, Libn., Fine Art Div.

PASADENA PUBLIC LIBRARY - BUSINESS-TECHNOLOGY DIVISION
285 E. Walnut St.　　　　　　　　Phone: (213) 577-4052
Pasadena, CA 91101　　　　Anne Cain, Principal Libn.Ref.Serv.

PASADENA PUBLIC LIBRARY - FINE ARTS DIVISION
285 E. Walnut St.　　　　　　　　Phone: (213) 577-4049
Pasadena, CA 91101　　　Josephine M. Pletscher, Libn., Fine Arts Div.

PASADENA PUBLIC LIBRARY - REFERENCE DIVISION
285 E. Walnut St.　　　　　　　　Phone: (213) 577-4054
Pasadena, CA 91101　　　　Elaine Zorbas, Libn., Ref.Div.

ST. LUKE HOSPITAL - MEDICAL LIBRARY
2632 E. Washington Blvd., Bin 7021　　Phone: (213) 797-1141
Pasadena, CA 91109　　　　　　　Jacquelin Erwin, Libn.

TETRA TECH, INC. - LIBRARY
630 N. Rosemead Blvd.　　　　　　Phone: (213) 449-6400
Pasadena, CA 91107　　　　　　Charlene M. Baldwin, Libn.

XEROX ELECTRO-OPTICAL SYSTEMS - TECHNICAL LIBRARY
300 N. Halstead St.　　　　　　　Phone: (213) 351-2351
Pasadena, CA 91107　　　　　　Elizabeth P. Neeri, Libn.

PATTON STATE HOSPITAL - STAFF LIBRARY
3102 E. Highland Ave.　　　　　　Phone: (714) 862-8121
Patton, CA 92369　　　　　　　Mary Sue Stumberg, Libn.

DOW CHEMICAL U.S.A. - WESTERN DIVISION - LIBRARY
Box 1398　　　　　　　　　　　　Phone: (415) 432-5199
Pittsburg, CA 94565　　　　Mary Ellen Christensen, Libn.

UNION OIL COMPANY OF CALIFORNIA - TECHNICAL INFORMATION
　　CENTER
376 S. Valencia Ave.
Box 76
Placentia, CA 92621　　　　　　Phone: (714) 528-7201
　　　　　　　　　　　　　　　Barbara J. Orosz, Hd.Libn.

EL DORADO COUNTY LAW LIBRARY
495 Main St.　　　　　　　　　　Phone: (916) 626-2416
Placerville, CA 95667　　　　James Blackford, Lib.Adm.

CONTRA COSTA COUNTY - CENTRAL LIBRARY - LOCAL HISTORY
　　COLLECTION
1750 Oak Park Blvd.　　　　　　　Phone: (415) 944-3434
Pleasant Hill, CA 94523　　　　Ruth Russell, Hd., Ctrl.Lib.

CLOROX COMPANY - TECHNICAL LIBRARY
7200 Johnson Industrial Rd.
Box 493　　　　　　　　　　　　Phone: (415) 462-2100
Pleasanton, CA 94566　　　　Mary Anne Hoopes, Libn.

KAISER ALUMINUM & CHEMICAL CORPORATION - TECHNICAL
　　INFORMATION CENTER
Center for Technology
6177 Sunol Blvd.
Box 877　　　　　　　　　　　　Phone: (415) 462-1122
Pleasanton, CA 94566　　　　Gary Gerard, Mgr.

U.S. NAVY - NAVAL AIR STATION - TECHNICAL LIBRARY
Code 6860　　　　　　　　　　Phone: (805) 982-8156
Point Mugu, CA 93042　　　　I.K. Burtnett, Hd.Libn.

U.S. NATL. PARK SERVICE - POINT REYES NATL. SEASHORE - LIBRARY
　　　　　　　　　　　　　　　Phone: (415) 663-1093
Point Reyes, CA 94956　　　　Genevieve Hahn, Libn.

ATMANIKETAN ASHRAM - LIBRARY
1291 Weber St.　　　　　　　　Phone: (714) 629-8255
Pomona, CA 91768　　　　　Santosh Krinsky, Libn.

CALIFORNIA STATE POLYTECHNIC UNIVERSITY, POMONA - LIBRARY
3801 W. Temple Ave.　　　　　　Phone: (714) 598-4671
Pomona, CA 91768　　　　　Harold F. Wells, Dir.

GENERAL DYNAMICS CORPORATION - POMONA DIVISION - DIVISION
　　LIBRARY MZ 4-20
Box 2507　　　　　　　　　　　Phone: (714) 629-5111
Pomona, CA 91769　　　　　N.S. Fredrick, Chf.Libn.

LANTERMAN (Frank J.) STATE HOSPITAL - STAFF LIBRARY
3530 W. Pomona Blvd.
Box 100　　　　　　　　　　　　Phone: (714) 595-1221
Pomona, CA 91766　　　　　Eleanor E. Wash, Sr.Libn.

POMONA PUBLIC LIBRARY - SPECIAL COLLECTIONS DEPARTMENT
625 S. Garey Ave.
Box 2271　　　　　　　　　　　Phone: (714) 620-2033
Pomona, CA 91766　　　　　Halbert Watson, Libn.

POMONA VALLEY COMMUNITY HOSPITAL - MEDICAL LIBRARY
1798 N. Garey Ave.　　　　　　　Phone: (714) 623-8715
Pomona, CA 91767　　　　　Shirley Chervin, Libn.

U.S. NAVY - NAVAL CONSTRUCTION BATTALION CENTER - LIBRARY
Code 351　　　　　　　　　　　Phone: (805) 982-4411
Port Hueneme, CA 93043　　　Eleanor V. Manos, Libn.

U.S. NAVY - NAVAL SCHOOL - CIVIL ENGINEER CORPS OFFICERS -
　　MOREELL LIBRARY
　　　　　　　　　　　　　　　Phone: (805) 982-3241
Port Hueneme, CA 93043　　　Barbara J. Horn, Lib.Dir.

PORTERVILLE STATE HOSPITAL - MEDICAL LIBRARY
Box 2000　　　　　　　　　　　Phone: (209) 784-2000
Porterville, CA 93257　　　　Mary Jane Berry, Libn.

SIERRA VIEW DISTRICT HOSPITAL - MEDICAL LIBRARY
465 W. Putnam Ave.　　　　　　Phone: (209) 784-1110
Porterville, CA 93257　　　Marilyn R. Pankey, Dir., Med.Rec.

U.S. ARMY POST - PRESIDIO OF SAN FRANCISCO - POST LIBRARY SYSTEM
Bldg. 386　　　　　　　　　　　Phone: (415) 561-3448
Presidio of San Francisco, CA 94129　　Juanita Taylor, Chf.Libn.

EISENHOWER MEDICAL CENTER - WALTER M. LEUTHOLD MEDICAL
　　LIBRARY
39000 Bob Hope Dr.　　　　　　Phone: (714) 340-3911
Rancho Mirage, CA 92270　　Jean Atkinson, Chf.Med.Libn.

SALVATION ARMY SCHOOL FOR OFFICERS TRAINING - ELFTMAN
　　MEMORIAL LIBRARY
30840 Hawthorne Blvd.　　　　　Phone: (213) 377-0481
Rancho Palos Verdes, CA 90274　Lavonne D. Robertson, Hd.Libn.

TEHAMA COUNTY LAW LIBRARY
Court House, Rm. 20
Red Bluff, CA 96080   M. Hendricks, Lib.Ck.

CH2M HILL, INC. - INFORMATION CENTER
1525 Court St.
Box 2088   Phone: (916) 243-5831
Redding, CA 96001   Virginia Merryman, Libn.

SHASTA COUNTY LAW LIBRARY
Court House
Redding, CA 96001   Joan Odell, Law Libn.

LINCOLN MEMORIAL SHRINE - LIBRARY
120 4th St.
Box 751   Phone: (714) 793-6622
Redlands, CA 92373   Dr. Larry E. Burgess, Cur.

SAN BERNARDINO COUNTY MUSEUM - WILSON C. HANNA LIBRARY/
    RESEARCH LIBRARY
2024 Orange Tree Lane   Phone: (714) 792-1334
Redlands, CA 92373   Dr. Gerald A. Smith, Dir.

TRW, INC. - DEFENSE & SPACE SYSTEMS GROUP - TECHNICAL
    INFORMATION CENTER
One Space Park, Bldg. S., Rm. 1930   Phone: (213) 536-2631
Redondo Beach, CA 90278   C.D. Campbell, Act.Mgr.

AMERICAN ASSOCIATION OF BIOANALYSTS - SLIDE LIBRARY
Broadway Medical Laboratory, Inc.
2946 Broadway   Phone: (415) 366-5813
Redwood City, CA 94062   Mary E. Wood, Cur.

AMPEX CORPORATION - TECHNICAL LIBRARY MS 3-10
401 Broadway   Phone: (415) 367-3368
Redwood City, CA 94063   Gwyneth Heynes Mallinson, Mgr.Tech.Info.Serv.

SAN MATEO COUNTY EDUCATIONAL RESOURCES CENTER
333 Main St.   Phone: (415) 364-5600
Redwood City, CA 94063   Dr. Curtis May, Dir., Lib.Serv.

SAN MATEO COUNTY LAW LIBRARY
Hall Of Justice & Records   Phone: (415) 364-5600
Redwood City, CA 94063   Robert D. Harrington, Dir.

WILLIAMS-KUEBELBECK & ASSOCIATES, INC. - LIBRARY
611 Veterans Blvd., Suite 206   Phone: (415) 365-7202
Redwood City, CA 94063   Nancy Jane Myers, Libn.

CHEVRON RESEARCH COMPANY - TECHNICAL INFORMATION CENTER
576 Standard Ave.   Phone: (415) 237-4411
Richmond, CA 94802   P.E. Fischer, Mgr., Tech.Info.Ctr.

STAUFFER CHEMICAL COMPANY - DE GUIGNE TECHNICAL CENTER -
    RESEARCH LIBRARY
1200 S. 47th St.   Phone: (415) 231-1018
Richmond, CA 94804   Linda Saylor, Lib.Supv.

UNIVERSITY OF CALIFORNIA, BERKELEY - EARTHQUAKE ENGINEERING
    RESEARCH CENTER LIBRARY
1301 S. 46th St.   Phone: (415) 231-9403
Richmond, CA 94804   Aileen M. Donovan, Hd.

UNIVERSITY OF CALIFORNIA, BERKELEY - FOREST PRODUCTS LIBRARY
1301 S. 46th St.   Phone: (415) 231-9549
Richmond, CA 94804   Peter Evans, Libn.

GOLD PARACHUTE LIBRARY, ARCHIVES & TECHNICAL INFORMATION
    CENTER
741 W. Haloid Ave.
Ridgecrest, CA 93555   Dave Gold, Dir. & Archv.

MOORE (Julie) & ASSOCIATES - LIBRARY
3319 Avalon St., No. 14   Phone: (714) 684-0441
Riverside, CA 92059   Julie L. Moore, Bibliographer

RIVERSIDE COUNTY LAW LIBRARY
3535 Tenth St., Suite 100   Phone: (714) 787-2460
Riverside, CA 92501   Maxyne M. Wannemacher, Law Libn.

RIVERSIDE GENERAL HOSPITAL - MEDICAL LIBRARY
9851 Magnolia Ave.   Phone: (714) 351-7066
Riverside, CA 92503   Richard M. Butler, Dir., Medical Rec.

RIVERSIDE MUNICIPAL MUSEUM - LIBRARY *
3720 Orange St.   Phone: (714) 787-7273
Riverside, CA 92501

RIVERSIDE PRESS-ENTERPRISE COMPANY - EDITORIAL LIBRARY
3512 14th St.   Phone: (714) 684-1200
Riverside, CA 92502   Joan Minesinger, Chf.Libn.

UNIVERSITY OF CALIFORNIA, RIVERSIDE - BIO-AGRICULTURAL LIBRARY
                                       Phone: (714) 787-3238
Riverside, CA 92521   Isabel Dickinson, Hd.Libn.

UNIVERSITY OF CALIFORNIA, RIVERSIDE - DEPARTMENT OF
    ENTOMOLOGY - LIBRARY
                                       Phone: (714) 787-4315
Riverside, CA 92502   Saul I. Frommer, Sr.Musm.Sci.

UNIVERSITY OF CALIFORNIA, RIVERSIDE - EDUCATION SERVICES
    LIBRARY
Box 5900   Phone: (714) 787-3715
Riverside, CA 92517   Marie Genung, Hd., Educ.Serv.

UNIVERSITY OF CALIFORNIA, RIVERSIDE - ENGLISH DEPARTMENT
    LIBRARY
Humanities Bldg.   Phone: (714) 787-5301
Riverside, CA 92521   Elizabeth Lang, Hd.

UNIVERSITY OF CALIFORNIA, RIVERSIDE - GOVERNMENT PUBLICATIONS
    DEPARTMENT - LIBRARY
Box 5900   Phone: (714) 787-3226
Riverside, CA 92507   James Rothenberger, Dept.Hd.

UNIVERSITY OF CALIFORNIA, RIVERSIDE - MAP SECTION - LIBRARY
Box 5900   Phone: (714) 787-3226
Riverside, CA 92507   James Rothenberger, Gov.Pubn.Libn.

UNIVERSITY OF CALIFORNIA, RIVERSIDE - MUSIC LIBRARY
                                       Phone: (714) 787-3137
Riverside, CA 92521   John W. Tanno, Music Libn.

UNIVERSITY OF CALIFORNIA, RIVERSIDE - OFFICE OF TECHNICAL INFO. -
    STATEWIDE AIR POLLUTION RESEARCH CTR.
                                       Phone: (714) 787-5132
Riverside, CA 92521   Dr.James N. Pitts, Jr., Dir. SAPRC

UNIVERSITY OF CALIFORNIA, RIVERSIDE - PHYSICAL SCIENCES LIBRARY
                                       Phone: (714) 787-3511
Riverside, CA 92517   Richard W. Vierich, Hd.Libn.

UNIVERSITY OF CALIFORNIA, RIVERSIDE - SPECIAL COLLECTIONS
Box 5900   Phone: (714) 787-3233
Riverside, CA 92517   Clifford R. Wurfel, Assoc.Libn.

SAVAGE INFORMATION SERVICES
608 Silver Spur Rd., Suite 310   Phone: (213) 377-5032
Rolling Hills Estates, CA 90274   Gretchen Sue Savage, Pres.

ASSOCIATION OF BALLOON & AIRSHIP CONSTRUCTORS - TECHNICAL
    LIBRARY
Box 7
Rosemead, CA 91770   Donald E. Woodward, Pres.

DON BOSCO TECHNICAL INSTITUTE - LEE LIBRARY
1151 N. San Gabriel Blvd.   Phone: (213) 280-0451
Rosemead, CA 91770   Sr. M. Jean Ellen Shields, BVM, Hd.Libn.

SOUTHERN CALIFORNIA EDISON COMPANY - LIBRARY
2244 Walnut Grove Ave.
Box 800   Phone: (213) 572-2096
Rosemead, CA 91770   Mary L. Parker, Libn.

FIREARMS RESEARCH AND IDENTIFICATION ASSOCIATION - LIBRARY
18638 Alderbury Dr.   Phone: (213) 964-7885
Rowland Heights, CA 91748   John Armann Caudron, Pres.

GEOGRAPHIC

RIVERSIDE COUNTY HISTORICAL COMMISSION - LIBRARY
4600 Crestmore Rd.
Box 3507   Phone: (714) 787-2551
Rubidoux, CA 92509   Stephen Becker, Hist.

AEROJET-CHEMICAL CORPORATION - AEROJET TACTICAL PROPULSION
   COMPANY - TECHNICAL INFORMATION CENTER
Box 13400   Phone: (916) 355-4076
Sacramento, CA 95813   Rimma Mironeullo, Tech.Libn.

AMERICAN JUSTICE INSTITUTE - LIBRARY
1007 7th St., Suite 414   Phone: (916) 444-3096
Sacramento, CA 95814   Mary Jo Brazil, Libn.

CALIFORNIA AIR RESOURCES BOARD - LIBRARY
1102 Q St.
Box 2815   Phone: (916) 323-8377
Sacramento, CA 95812   Mark T. Edwards, Libn.

CALIFORNIA - STATE ARCHIVES
Archives Bldg., Rm. 130
1020 O St.   Phone: (916) 445-4293
Sacramento, CA 95814   John F. Burns, Chf. of Archv.

CALIFORNIA STATE BOARD OF EQUALIZATION - LAW LIBRARY
1020 North St., Rm. 289   Phone: (916) 445-7356
Sacramento, CA 95808   Barrie Griffith, Sr.Libn.

CALIFORNIA STATE DEPARTMENT OF ALCOHOL AND DRUG PROGRAMS -
   INFORMATION CLEARINGHOUSE
111 Capitol Mall   Phone: (916) 323-1873
Sacramento, CA 95814   Thomas D. Peck, Educ.Cons.

CALIFORNIA STATE DEPARTMENT OF TRANSPORTATION - LABORATORY
   LIBRARY
5900 Folsom Blvd.   Phone: (916) 739-2152
Sacramento, CA 95819   Eva K. Caro, Sr.Libn.

CALIFORNIA STATE DEPARTMENT OF TRANSPORTATION - LAW LIBRARY
1120 N St., Rm. 1315   Phone: (916) 445-2291
Sacramento, CA 95807   Lorna J. Flesher, Supv.Libn.

CALIFORNIA STATE DEPARTMENT OF TRANSPORTATION -
   TRANSPORTATION LIBRARY
1120 N St.   Phone: (916) 445-3230
Sacramento, CA 95807   Phyllis Newton, Supv.Libn.

CALIFORNIA STATE DEPARTMENT OF WATER RESOURCES - LAW LIBRARY
1416 Ninth St., Rm. 1118-13   Phone: (916) 445-2839
Sacramento, CA 95814   Frances Pearson, Libn.

CALIFORNIA STATE HEALTH & WELFARE AGENCY DATA CENTER -
   TECHNICAL LIBRARY UNIT
112 J St.   Phone: (916) 323-7739
Sacramento, CA 95814   Geraldine I. Fontes, Staff Serv.Anl.

CALIFORNIA STATE HEALTH AND WELFARE AGENCY -
   INTERDEPARTMENTAL LIBRARY
714 P St., Rm. 1800   Phone: (916) 445-8975
Sacramento, CA 95814   Thomas A. Dickson, Sr.Libn.

CALIFORNIA STATE LIBRARY
Library & Courts Bldg.
Box 2037   Phone: (916) 445-2585
Sacramento, CA 95809   Gary E. Strong, State Libn.

CALIFORNIA STATE OFFICE OF LEGISLATIVE COUNSEL - LIBRARY
3021 State Capitol   Phone: (916) 445-2609
Sacramento, CA 95814   Virginia Castro, Lib.Tech.Asst.

CALIFORNIA STATE OFFICE OF THE STATE ARCHITECT - ARCHITECTURE/
   ENGINEERING LIBRARY
1500 5th St.   Phone: (916) 445-8661
Sacramento, CA 95814   Rose A. Granados, Tech.Libn.

CALIFORNIA STATE POSTSECONDARY EDUCATION COMMISSION -
   LIBRARY
1020 Twelfth St.   Phone: (916) 322-8031
Sacramento, CA 95814   Elizabeth Testa, Sr.Libn.

CALIFORNIA STATE RESOURCES AGENCY - LIBRARY
117 Resources Bldg.
1416 Ninth St.   Phone: (916) 445-7752
Sacramento, CA 95814   Madeleine A. Darcy, Sr.Libn.

CALIFORNIA STATE UNIVERSITY, SACRAMENTO - LIBRARY - MEDIA
   SERVICES CENTER
2000 Jed Smith Dr.   Phone: (916) 454-6538
Sacramento, CA 95819   Sheila J. Marsh, Media Libn.

CALIFORNIA STATE UNIVERSITY, SACRAMENTO - LIBRARY - SCIENCE &
   TECHNOLOGY REFERENCE DEPARTMENT †
2000 Jed Smith Dr.   Phone: (916) 454-6373
Sacramento, CA 95819   Barbara A. Charlton, Assoc.Libn.

CH2M HILL CORP. - LIBRARY
555 Capitol Mall, Suite 1290   Phone: (916) 441-3955
Sacramento, CA 95814   Joy Steveson, Libn.

CROCKER ART MUSEUM - RESEARCH LIBRARY
216 O St.   Phone: (916) 446-4677
Sacramento, CA 95814   Richard Vincent West, Dir.

MC GEORGE SCHOOL OF LAW - LAW LIBRARY
University of the Pacific
3282 Fifth Ave.
Sacramento, CA 95817   Alice J. Murray, Law Libn.

SACRAMENTO AREA COUNCIL OF GOVERNMENTS - LIBRARY
800 H St.   Phone: (916) 441-5930
Sacramento, CA 95814   Rhonda R. Egan, Libn.

SACRAMENTO BEE - REFERENCE LIBRARY
21st & Q Sts.
Sacramento, CA 95814   Anna Michael, Libn.

SACRAMENTO CITY AND COUNTY MUSEUM - LIBRARY
1931 K St.   Phone: (916) 447-2958
Sacramento, CA 95814   James E. Henley, Dir. of Musm.

SACRAMENTO COUNTY LAW LIBRARY †
Court House
720 9th St.   Phone: (916) 444-5910
Sacramento, CA 95814   Alice P. McDonald, Libn.

SACRAMENTO-EL DORADO MEDICAL SOCIETY - PAUL H. GUTTMAN
   LIBRARY
5380 Elvas Ave.   Phone: (916) 452-2671
Sacramento, CA 95819   Georgann Johnston, Libn.

SACRAMENTO PUBLIC LIBRARY - BUSINESS & MUNICIPAL DEPARTMENT
828 I St.   Phone: (916) 449-5203
Sacramento, CA 95814   Dorothy Harvey, Dept.Hd.

SACRAMENTO UNION - EDITORIAL LIBRARY
301 Capitol Mall   Phone: (916) 442-7811
Sacramento, CA 95812   Robin E. Reidy, Libn.

SEARCH GROUP, INC. - LIBRARY
925 Secret River Dr.   Phone: (916) 392-2550
Sacramento, CA 95831   Thomas F. Wilson, Info.Mgr.

U.S. ARMY - CORPS OF ENGINEERS - SACRAMENTO DISTRICT -
   TECHNICAL INFORMATION CENTER
650 Capitol Mall   Phone: (916) 440-3404
Sacramento, CA 95814   Deborah A. Newton, District Libn.

U.S. BUREAU OF LAND MANAGEMENT - CALIFORNIA STATE OFFICE -
   LIBRARY
2800 Cottage Way   Phone: (916) 484-4253
Sacramento, CA 95825   Annisteen Pack, Mgt.Asst.

U.S. BUREAU OF RECLAMATION - LIBRARY
2800 Cottage Way   Phone: (916) 484-4404
Sacramento, CA 95825   Margaret Elder

UNIVERSITY OF CALIFORNIA, DAVIS - MEDICAL CENTER LIBRARY
4301 X St.   Phone: (916) 453-3529
Sacramento, CA 95817   Terri L. Malmgren, Libn.

NAPA VALLEY WINE LIBRARY ASSOCIATION - LIBRARY
Box 328
St. Helena, CA 94574
Phone: (707) 963-5244
Mrs. Clayla Davis, Lib.Dir.

SANATANA DHARMA FOUNDATION - GERTRUDE C. BERNER MEMORIAL
LIBRARY OF SPIRITUAL SCIENCES
3100 White Sulphur Springs Rd.
St. Helena, CA 94574
Phone: (707) 963-9487
Bette Rasmussen, Lib.Supv.

SILVERADO MUSEUM
1490 Library Lane
Box 409
St. Helena, CA 94574
Phone: (707) 963-3757
Ellen Shaffer, Cur.

MONTEREY COUNTY LAW LIBRARY
Courthouse
Salinas, CA 93901
Eleanor DeLashmitt, Libn.

SALINAS PUBLIC LIBRARY - JOHN STEINBECK LIBRARY
110 W. San Luis St.
Salinas, CA 93901
Phone: (408) 758-7311
John Gross, Dir.

CALAVERAS COUNTY LAW LIBRARY
Government Center
San Andreas, CA 95249
Phone: (209) 754-4252
Kenneth M. Foley, Chm.

CALAVERAS COUNTY MUSEUM AND ARCHIVES
30 N. Main St.
Box 1281
San Andreas, CA 95249
Phone: (209) 754-4203
Judith Cunningham, Dir./Cur.

CALIFORNIA STATE - COURT OF APPEAL, 4TH APPELLATE DISTRICT,
DIVISION TWO - LAW LIBRARY
303 W. Third St.
San Bernardino, CA 92401
Phone: (914) 383-4441
Helen Bradberry, Libn.

INTERNATIONAL CHRISTIAN SCHOOL OF THEOLOGY - GRADUATE
UNIVERSITY LIBRARY
Arrowhead Springs
San Bernardino, CA 92414
Phone: (714) 886-5224
Cyril Barber, Hd.Libn.

ST. BERNARDINE HOSPITAL - NORMAN F. FELDHEYM LIBRARY
2101 North Waterman Ave.
San Bernardino, CA 92404
Phone: (714) 883-8711
Gloria Arredondo, Libn.

SAN BERNARDINO COUNTY - ENVIRONMENTAL PUBLIC WORKS AGENCY -
LIBRARY
1111 E. Mill St.
San Bernardino, CA 92415
Phone: (714) 383-3438
Jane Young Bellamy, Libn.

SAN BERNARDINO COUNTY HISTORICAL ARCHIVES
104 W. Fourth St.
San Bernardino, CA 92415
Phone: (714) 383-3374
Jeanette Bernthaler, Act.Archv.

SAN BERNARDINO COUNTY LAW LIBRARY †
Court House Annex
San Bernardino, CA 92401
Phone: (714) 383-2701
Beulah M. Brown, Libn.

SAN BERNARDINO COUNTY MEDICAL CENTER - MEDICAL LIBRARY
780 E. Gilbert St.
San Bernardino, CA 92404
Phone: (714) 383-3367

SAN BERNARDINO SUN-TELEGRAM - LIBRARY
399 North D St.
San Bernardino, CA 92401
Phone: (714) 889-9666
Blanche A. Lewis, Libn.

U.S. NATL. ARCHIVES & RECORDS SERVICE - FEDERAL ARCHIVES AND
RECORDS CENTER, REGION 9
1000 Commodore Dr.
San Bruno, CA 94066
Phone: (415) 876-9009
Glenn Burchett, Chf., Archv.Br.

WESTERN HIGHWAY INSTITUTE - RESEARCH LIBRARY
1200 Bayhill Dr., Suite 112
San Bruno, CA 94066
Mae Frances Moore, Libn.

CROATIAN GENEALOGICAL SOCIETY - LIBRARY
1372 Rosewood Ave.
San Carlos, CA 94070
Phone: (415) 494-1112
Adam S. Eterovich, Dir.

GTE LENKURT, INC. - TECHNICAL LIBRARY, M679
1105 County Rd.
San Carlos, CA 94070
Phone: (415) 595-3000
Patrick R. Marshment, Tech.Libn.

LITTON INDUSTRIES - ELECTRON TUBE DIVISION - LIBRARY
960 Industrial Rd.
San Carlos, CA 94070
Phone: (415) 591-8411
Anne Vaughan, Libn.

VARIAN ASSOCIATES - EIMAC DIVISION - TECHNICAL LIBRARY
301 Industrial Way
San Carlos, CA 94070
Phone: (415) 592-1221

SAN CLEMENTE PRESBYTERIAN CHURCH - SUTHERLAND MEMORIAL
LIBRARY
119 Estrella Ave.
San Clemente, CA 92672
Phone: (714) 492-6158
Ethel Wolleson, Libn.

BURROUGHS CORPORATION - RANCHO BERNARDO TECHNICAL
INFORMATION CENTER
16701 W. Bernardo Dr.
San Diego, CA 92127
Phone: (714) 451-4438
Marianna Seeley, Libn.

CALIFORNIA SCHOOL OF PROFESSIONAL PSYCHOLOGY - SAN DIEGO
LIBRARY
3974 Sorrento Valley Blvd.
San Diego, CA 92121
Phone: (714) 453-6880
Richard Sanborn, Libn.

CALIFORNIA STATE DEPARTMENT OF JUSTICE - ATTORNEY GENERAL'S
OFFICE - LAW LIBRARY
110 West A St., Suite 600
San Diego, CA 92101
Phone: (714) 237-7642
Robert Shaw, Sr.Libn.

CALIFORNIA STATE DEPARTMENT OF TRANSPORTATION - DISTRICT 11
LIBRARY
2829 Juan St.
San Diego, CA 92110
Phone: (714) 237-6644
Peggy A. Ziesler, Libn.

CALIFORNIA WESTERN LAW SCHOOL - LIBRARY
350 Cedar St.
San Diego, CA 92101
Phone: (714) 239-0391
Chin Kim, Lib.Dir.

CENTER FOR WOMEN'S STUDIES AND SERVICES - CWSS LIBRARY
908 E St.
San Diego, CA 92101
Phone: (714) 233-8984
Lisa Cobbs, Libn.

CREATION-SCIENCE RESEARCH CENTER - INFORMATION CENTER
5466 Complex St.
San Diego, CA 92123
Phone: (714) 569-8673

CUBIC CORPORATION - LIBRARY
Box 80787
San Diego, CA 92138
Phone: (714) 277-6780
Pat Purser, Mgr., Tech.Lib.

FINE ARTS GALLERY OF SAN DIEGO - LIBRARY
Box 2107
San Diego, CA 92112
Phone: (714) 232-7931
Nancy J. Andrews, Libn.

FIRST PRESBYTERIAN CHURCH - CHRISTIAN EDUCATION DEPARTMENT -
LIBRARY
320 Date St.
San Diego, CA 92101
Phone: (714) 232-7513
L.A. Schworer, Sec./Christian Educ.

GENERAL ATOMIC COMPANY - LIBRARY
Box 81608
San Diego, CA 92138
Phone: (714) 455-3322
Richard J. Tommey, Libn.

GENERAL DYNAMICS CORPORATION - CONVAIR DIVISION - RESEARCH
LIBRARY
Box 80986
San Diego, CA 92138
Phone: (714) 277-8900
Urban J. Sweeney, Chf.Libn.

GENERAL DYNAMICS CORPORATION - DATAGRAPHIX, INC. - ENGINEERING
LIBRARY
Box 82449
San Diego, CA 92138
Phone: (714) 291-9960
Tom Packard, Engr.Libn.

GRAY, CARY, AMES & FRYE - LAW LIBRARY
525 B St., Suite 2100
San Diego, CA 92101
Phone: (714) 236-1661
June F. Mac Leod, Law Libn.

GEOGRAPHIC

HEWLETT-PACKARD COMPANY - SAN DIEGO DIVISION - TECHNICAL LIBRARY
16399 W. Bernardo Drive
San Diego, CA 92127
Phone: (714) 487-4100
Cherlyn A. Williams, Lib.Spec.

HIGGS, FLETCHER & MACK - LAW LIBRARY †
707 Broadway, Suite 1800
Box 568
San Diego, CA 92112
Phone: (714) 236-1551
Lauren Reznack, Law Libn.

INTERNATIONAL SKATEBOARD ASSOCIATION - LIBRARY
5466 Complex St., Unit 207
San Diego, CA 92123

JEWISH COMMUNITY CENTER - SAMUEL & REBECCA ASTOR JUDAICA LIBRARY
4079 54th St.
San Diego, CA 92105
Phone: (714) 583-3300
Mollie S. Harris, Hd.Libn.

KAISER-PERMANENTE MEDICAL CENTER - HEALTH SCIENCES LIBRARY
4647 Zion Ave.
San Diego, CA 92120
Phone: (714) 563-2190
Sheila Latus, Med.Libn.

LOGICON, INC. - TACTICAL & TRAINING SYSTEMS DIVISION LIBRARY
Box 80158
San Diego, CA 92138
Phone: (714) 455-1330
Paula Oquita, Libn.

LUCE, FORWARD, HAMILTON & SCRIPPS - LIBRARY
110 West A St.
San Diego, CA 92101
Phone: (714) 236-1414
June B. Williams, Libn.

MERCK & COMPANY, INC. - KELCO DIVISION - LITERATURE AND INFORMATION SERVICES
8355 Aero Dr.
San Diego, CA 92123
Phone: (714) 292-4900
Ann A. Jenkins, Adm.

MERCY HOSPITAL AND MEDICAL CENTER - JEAN FARB MEDICAL LIBRARY
4077 Fifth Ave.
San Diego, CA 92103
Phone: (714) 294-8024
Virginia Reed, Med.Libn.

MORRIS CERULLO WORLD EVANGELISM, INC. - SCHOOL OF MINISTRY LIBRARY
Box 700
San Diego, CA 92101
Phone: (714) 232-0161
Craig La Caille, Libn.

NATIONAL COUNCIL FOR YEAR-ROUND EDUCATION - LIBRARY
6401 Linda Vista Rd.
San Diego, CA 92111
Dr. Wayne White, Pres.

NESTE, BRUDIN & STONE, INC. - CORPORATE LIBRARY
Box 28100
San Diego, CA 92128
Phone: (714) 485-1500
Joan J. Sierecki, Corp.Libn.

PHOTOPHILE - LIBRARY
2311 Kettner Blvd.
San Diego, CA 92101
Phone: (714) 234-4431
Frankie Wright, Dir.

PRICE-POTTENGER NUTRITION FOUNDATION - LIBRARY
6035 University Ave.
San Diego, CA 92115
Phone: (714) 583-7450
Patricia Connolly, Cur.

REES-STEALY MEDICAL GROUP - LIBRARY
2001 Fourth Ave.
San Diego, CA 92101
Phone: (714) 234-6261
Margaret M. O'Rourke, Libn.

SALK INSTITUTE FOR BIOLOGICAL STUDIES - LIBRARY
Box 85800
San Diego, CA 92138
Phone: (714) 453-4100
Pauline K. Whalen, Libn.

SAN DIEGO AERO-SPACE MUSEUM - N. PAUL WHITTIER HISTORICAL AVIATION LIBRARY
2001 Pan America Plaza, Balboa Park
San Diego, CA 92101
Phone: (714) 234-8291
Brewster C. Reynolds, Archv.

SAN DIEGO COUNTY - DEPARTMENT OF EDUCATION - PROFESSIONAL RESOURCE AND DEVELOPMENT CENTER
6401 Linda Vista Rd.
San Diego, CA 92111
Phone: (714) 292-3608
Dr. Marvin Barbula, Director

SAN DIEGO COUNTY LAW LIBRARY
1105 Front St.
San Diego, CA 92101
Phone: (714) 236-2231
O. James Werner, Libn.

SAN DIEGO COUNTY LIBRARY - GOVERNMENTAL REFERENCE LIBRARY
602 County Administration Center
San Diego, CA 92101
Phone: (714) 236-2760
Magali Garcia-Kirwan, Libn.

SAN DIEGO ECOLOGY CENTER - LIBRARY
340 Kalmia St.
San Diego, CA 92101
Phone: (714) 235-0066
Gaye M. Dingeman, Libn.

SAN DIEGO GAS AND ELECTRIC COMPANY - LIBRARY
Box 1831
San Diego, CA 92112
Phone: (714) 232-4252
Marie A. Peelman, Hd.Libn.

SAN DIEGO HALL OF SCIENCE - BERNICE HARDING LIBRARY
Box 33303
San Diego, CA 92103
Phone: (714) 238-1233
J. Elaine Colter, Libn.

SAN DIEGO HISTORICAL SOCIETY - LIBRARY AND MANUSCRIPTS COLLECTION
Presidio Pk.
Box 81825
San Diego, CA 92138
Phone: (714) 297-3258
Sylvia Arden, Hd.Libn.

SAN DIEGO HISTORICAL SOCIETY - PHOTOGRAPH ARCHIVES
Box 1150
San Diego, CA 92112
Phone: (714) 232-9544
Larry Booth, Photo Archv.

SAN DIEGO MUSEUM OF MAN - SCIENTIFIC LIBRARY
1350 El Prado, Balboa Pk.
San Diego, CA 92101
Phone: (714) 239-2001
Jane Bentley, Libn.

SAN DIEGO PUBLIC LIBRARY - ART, MUSIC & RECREATION SECTION
820 E St.
San Diego, CA 92101
Phone: (714) 236-5810
Barbara Tuthill, Supv.Libn.

SAN DIEGO PUBLIC LIBRARY - CALIFORNIA ROOM
820 E St.
San Diego, CA 92101
Phone: (714) 236-5834
Rhoda E. Kruse, Sr.Libn.

SAN DIEGO PUBLIC LIBRARY - GENEALOGY ROOM
820 E St.
San Diego, CA 92101
Rhoda Kruse, Sr.Libn.

SAN DIEGO PUBLIC LIBRARY - HISTORY & WORLD AFFAIRS SECTION
820 E St.
San Diego, CA 92101
Phone: (714) 236-5820
Margaret Queen, Supv.Libn.

SAN DIEGO PUBLIC LIBRARY - LITERATURE & LANGUAGE SECTION
820 E St.
San Diego, CA 92101
Phone: (714) 236-5816
Anna Martinez, Sr.Libn.

SAN DIEGO PUBLIC LIBRARY - SCIENCE & INDUSTRY SECTION
820 E St.
San Diego, CA 92101
Phone: (714) 236-5813
Dorothy Van Nice, Sr.Libn.

SAN DIEGO PUBLIC LIBRARY - SOCIAL SCIENCES SECTION
820 E St.
San Diego, CA 92101
Phone: (714) 236-5564
Dorothy Grimm, Sr.Libn.

SAN DIEGO PUBLIC LIBRARY - WANGENHEIM ROOM
820 E St.
San Diego, CA 92101
Phone: (714) 236-5807
Eileen Boyle, Libn.

SAN DIEGO SOCIETY OF NATURAL HISTORY - NATURAL HISTORY MUSEUM LIBRARY
Box 1390
San Diego, CA 92112
Phone: (714) 232-3821
Judith C. Dyer, Libn.

SAN DIEGO STATE UNIVERSITY - BUREAU OF BUSINESS & ECONOMIC RESEARCH LIBRARY *
College of Business Administration
San Diego, CA 92182
Phone: (714) 265-6838
Robert P. Hungate, Act.Dir.

SAN DIEGO STATE UNIVERSITY - CENTER FOR PUBLIC ECONOMICS LIBRARY
San Diego, CA 92182
Phone: (714) 286-6707
Dr. George Babilot, Dir.

SAN DIEGO STATE UNIVERSITY - EUROPEAN STUDIES CENTER - LIBRARY
Phone: (714) 265-5928
San Diego, CA 92182   Dr. Leon Rosenstein, Dir.

SAN DIEGO STATE UNIVERSITY - GOVERNMENT PUBLICATIONS
DEPARTMENT
Phone: (714) 265-5832
San Diego, CA 92182   Charles Dintrone, Doc.Libn.

SAN DIEGO STATE UNIVERSITY - MALCOLM A. LOVE LIBRARY
Phone: (714) 265-6014
San Diego, CA 92182   Ned V. Joy, Act.Univ.Libn.

SAN DIEGO STATE UNIVERSITY - MEDIA & CURRICULUM CENTER
Phone: (714) 265-6757
San Diego, CA 92182   Dr. Stephen D. Fitt, Chm.

SAN DIEGO STATE UNIVERSITY - PUBLIC ADMINISTRATION RESEARCH
CENTER LIBRARY
Phone: (714) 286-6084
San Diego, CA 92182   Dr. Glenn W. Sparrow, Dir.

SAN DIEGO STATE UNIVERSITY - SAN DIEGO HISTORY RESEARCH CENTER
University Library   Phone: (714) 265-5751
San Diego, CA 92182   Stephen A. Colston, Dir.

SAN DIEGO STATE UNIVERSITY - SCIENCE DEPARTMENT
University Library   Phone: (714) 265-6715
San Diego, CA 92182   Lillian Chan, Sci.Libn.

SAN DIEGO STATE UNIVERSITY - SOCIAL SCIENCE RESEARCH
LABORATORY - LIBRARY
Phone: (714) 265-5845
San Diego, CA 92182   Paul J. Strand, Dir.

SAN DIEGO UNION-TRIBUNE PUBLISHING COMPANY - LIBRARY
350 Camino De La Reina   Phone: (714) 299-3131
San Diego, CA 92108   Sharon Stewart Reeves, Dir., Lib.Serv.

SCOTTISH RITE BODIES, SAN DIEGO - SCOTTISH RITE MASONIC LIBRARY
1895 Camino Del Rio   Phone: (714) 297-0395
San Diego, CA 92108   Granville K. Frisbie, Chm., Lib.Comm.

SEA WORLD, INC. - LIBRARY
1720 S. Shores Rd.   Phone: (714) 222-6353
San Diego, CA 92109   Carlo A. Mosca, Corp.Dir., Educ.

SHARP (Donald N.) MEMORIAL COMMUNITY HOSPITAL - HEALTH SCIENCE
LIBRARY
7901 Frost St.   Phone: (714) 292-2538
San Diego, CA 92123   Estelle Davis, Dir. of Lib.Serv.

SOLAR TURBINES INTERNATIONAL - LIBRARY
Box 80966   Phone: (714) 238-5992
San Diego, CA 92138   George Hall, Libn.

TELEDYNE RYAN AERONAUTICAL - TECHNICAL INFORMATION SERVICES
2701 N. Harbor Dr.   Phone: (714) 291-7311
San Diego, CA 92101   William E. Ebner, Chf.

U.S. NATL. PARK SERVICE - CABRILLO NATL. MONUMENT - LIBRARY &
INFORMATION CENTER
Box 6670   Phone: (714) 293-5450
San Diego, CA 92106

U.S. NAVY - FLEET COMBAT DIRECTION SYSTEMS SUPPORT ACTIVITY,
SAN DIEGO - DATA RESOURCE CENTER †
200 Catalina Blvd.   Phone: (714) 225-2697
San Diego, CA 92147   Marilyn Soldwisch, Lib.Techn.

U.S. NAVY - NAVAL AIR STATION (North Island) - LIBRARY
Bldg. 91   Phone: (714) 437-7041
San Diego, CA 92135   Anne Farley Kleehammer, Adm.Libn.

U.S. NAVY - NAVAL AMPHIBIOUS BASE (Coronado) - LIBRARY
Phone: (714) 437-2473
San Diego, CA 92155   Nadine Bangsberg, Base Libn.

U.S. NAVY - NAVAL ELECTRONICS ENGINEERING CENTER (San Diego) -
LIBRARY
4297 Pacific Hwy.
Box 80337   Phone: (714) 225-4474
San Diego, CA 92138   Ann R. Brasche, Tech.Libn

U.S. NAVY - NAVAL HEALTH RESEARCH CENTER - WALTER L. WILKINS BIO-
MEDICAL LIBRARY
Box 85122   Phone: (714) 225-6640
San Diego, CA 92138   Mary Aldous, Libn.

U.S. NAVY - NAVAL OCEAN SYSTEMS CENTER - TECHNICAL LIBRARY
Phone: (714) 225-6171
San Diego, CA 92152   Joan Ingersoll, Hd.

U.S. NAVY - NAVAL REGIONAL MEDICAL CENTER (San Diego) - THOMPSON
MEDICAL LIBRARY
Phone: (714) 233-2367
San Diego, CA 92134   Marilyn W. Schwartz, Chf.Libn.

U.S. NAVY - NAVAL STATION LIBRARY (San Diego)
Naval Station, Box 15   Phone: (714) 235-1403
San Diego, CA 92136   B.D. Howard, Supv.Libn.

U.S. NAVY - NAVAL SUPERVISOR OF SHIPBUILDING, CONVERSION AND
REPAIR - TECHNICAL LIBRARY
U.S. Naval Station, Code 2011
Box 119   Phone: (714) 235-2455
San Diego, CA 92136   Pat Merritt, Libn.

U.S. NAVY - NAVAL SUPPLY CENTER - TECHNICAL DIVISION - TECHNICAL
LIBRARY
937 North Harbor Dr.   Phone: (714) 235-3237
San Diego, CA 92132   Ivy Seaberry, Lib.Techn.

U.S. NAVY - NAVY PERSONNEL RESEARCH & DEVELOPMENT CENTER -
TECHNICAL LIBRARY
Code P106L   Phone: (714) 225-7971
San Diego, CA 92152   Marie D. McDowell, Libn.

U.S. VETERANS ADMINISTRATION (CA-San Diego) - MEDICAL CENTER
LIBRARY
3350 La Jolla Village Dr.   Phone: (714) 453-7500
San Diego, CA 92161   Connie Baker, Chf.Libn.

UNIVERSITY OF CALIFORNIA, SAN DIEGO - MEDICAL CENTER LIBRARY
225 Dickenson St.   Phone: (714) 294-6520
San Diego, CA 92103   Sue Ann Blaise, Hd.Libn.

UNIVERSITY OF SAN DIEGO - MARVIN & LILLIAN KRATTER LAW LIBRARY
Alcala Pk.   Phone: (714) 293-4541
San Diego, CA 92110   Joseph S. Ciesielski, Dir.

WESTERN STATE UNIVERSITY - COLLEGE OF LAW - LIBRARY
1333 Front St.   Phone: (714) 231-0300
San Diego, CA 92101   Judith Runyon Leyva, Law Libn.

ZOOLOGICAL SOCIETY OF SAN DIEGO - ERNST SCHWARZ LIBRARY
San Diego Zoo
Box 551   Phone: (714) 231-1515
San Diego, CA 92112   Michaele M. Robinson, Libn.

SEEK INFORMATION SERVICE
570 W. Terrace Dr.
Box 216   Phone: (714) 599-2132
San Dimas, CA 91773   M.T. Grenier, Pres.

HOLY CROSS HOSPITAL - HEALTH SCIENCE LIBRARY
15031 Rinaldi St.   Phone: (213) 365-8051
San Fernando, CA 91345   Nina M. Hull, Health Sci.Libn.

AIRCRAFT TECHNICAL PUBLISHERS - LIBRARY
655 Fourth St.   Phone: (415) 777-1515
San Francisco, CA 94107   Carol Bonner, V.P.

AMERICAN ACADEMY OF ASIAN STUDIES - LIBRARY
134-140 Church St.
San Francisco, CA 94114

AMERICAN HYPNOTISTS' ASSOCIATION - HYPNOSIS TECHNICAL CENTER
Glanworth Bldg., Suite 6
1159 Green St.   Phone: (415) 775-6130
San Francisco, CA 94109   Dr. Angela Bertuccelli, Libn.

AMERICAN INDIAN HISTORICAL SOCIETY - LIBRARY †
1451 Masonic Ave.   Phone: (415) 626-5235
San Francisco, CA 94117   Dr. Jeanette Henry

ASIAN ART MUSEUM OF SAN FRANCISCO - AVERY BRUNDAGE COLLECTION
Golden Gate Pk.   Phone: (415) 558-2993
San Francisco, CA 94118   Fred A. Cline, Jr., Libn.

ATHEARN, CHANDLER AND HOFFMAN - LIBRARY
111 Sutter St.
San Francisco, CA 94104

BA INVESTMENT MANAGEMENT CORPORATION - LIBRARY
555 California St.   Phone: (415) 622-6883
San Francisco, CA 94104   Lee Stocks, Lib.Serv.Mgr.

BANCROFT, AVERY AND MC ALISTER - LAW LIBRARY
601 Montgomery St., Suite 900   Phone: (415) 788-8855
San Francisco, CA 94111   Diane Huijgen, Dir., Lib.Serv.

BANCROFT-WHITNEY COMPANY - EDITORIAL LIBRARY †
301 Brannan St.   Phone: (415) 986-4410
San Francisco, CA 94107   Keltah T. Narbut, Libn.

BANK OF AMERICA, NT & SA - LAW LIBRARY
Dept. 3220
Box 37000   Phone: (415) 622-6040
San Francisco, CA 94137   Sharon K. French, Libn.

BANK OF AMERICA, NT & SA - REFERENCE LIBRARY
555 California St.
Box 37000   Phone: (415) 622-2068
San Francisco, CA 94137   Marydee Ojala, Lib.Mgr.

BANK OF AMERICA - SYSTEMS LIBRARY
1455 Market St., 18th Fl.   Phone: (415) 953-2375
San Francisco, CA 94137   Fay Hulett-Nelson, Supv.

BANK OF CALIFORNIA - BUSINESS RESEARCH LIBRARY
400 California St.   Phone: (415) 765-2116
San Francisco, CA 94145   Barbara Barton, Libn.

BAY AREA COUNCIL ON SOVIET JEWRY - ARCHIVES *
106 Baden St.   Phone: (415) 585-1400
San Francisco, CA 94131   Natasha Kats, Exec.Sec.

BECHTEL - AUDIO-VISUAL LIBRARY
Box 3965   Phone: (415) 768-5799
San Francisco, CA 94119   Doris Burbick, Libn.

BECHTEL - CENTRAL LIBRARY
50 Beale St.   Phone: (415) 768-5306
San Francisco, CA 94119   Betty Jo Hardison, Chf.Libn.

BECHTEL CIVIL & MINERALS, INC. - MINING & MINERALS BUSINESS
    DEVELOPMENT LIBRARY
Box 3965   Phone: (415) 768-7294
San Francisco, CA 94119   Teri Gomez, Adm.Asst.

BECHTEL - DATA PROCESSING LIBRARY
Box 3965   Phone: (415) 768-9015
San Francisco, CA 94119   Mercedes Dumlao, Libn.

BECHTEL - FINANCE LIBRARY
Box 3965   Phone: (415) 768-5166
San Francisco, CA 94119   Phyllis S. Morales, Finance Libn.

BECHTEL - GEOLOGY LIBRARY
Box 3965   Phone: (415) 786-5353
San Francisco, CA 94119   Gail Sorrough, Libn.

BECHTEL - LEGAL DEPARTMENT LIBRARY
Box 3965   Phone: (415) 768-5545
San Francisco, CA 94119   Patricia Boyd, Libn.

BECHTEL POWER CORPORATION - LIBRARY
Box 3965   Phone: (415) 768-1152
San Francisco, CA 94119   Stacia Kato, Hd.Libn.

BECHTEL POWER CORPORATION - TRUST & THRIFT INVESTMENTS
    CENTER *
Box 3965   Phone: (415) 768-6301
San Francisco, CA 94119   Marsha Edwards, Libn.

BOOK CLUB OF CALIFORNIA - LIBRARY
312 Sutter St.   Phone: (415) 781-7532
San Francisco, CA 94108

BRITISH CONSULATE-GENERAL - LIBRARY
120 Montgomery St.   Phone: (415) 981-3030
San Francisco, CA 94104   Vera Sklaar, Libn.

BROBECK, PHLEGER & HARRISON - LIBRARY
1 Market Plaza
Spear St. Tower   Phone: (415) 442-1054
San Francisco, CA 94105   Alice McKenzie, Libn.

BUREAU OF JEWISH EDUCATION - JEWISH COMMUNITY LIBRARY
601 14th Ave.   Phone: (415) 751-6983
San Francisco, CA 94118   Larry S. Moses, Exec.Dir.

CALIFORNIA ACADEMY OF SCIENCES - J.W. MAILLIARD, JR. LIBRARY
Golden Gate Park   Phone: (415) 221-5100
San Francisco, CA 94118   Ray Brian, Libn.

CALIFORNIA COLLEGE OF PODIATRIC MEDICINE - SCHMIDT MEDICAL
    LIBRARY
Box 7855, Rincon Annex   Phone: (415) 563-3444
San Francisco, CA 94120   Leonard P. Shapiro, Dir.

CALIFORNIA HISTORICAL SOCIETY - SCHUBERT HALL LIBRARY
2099 Pacific Ave.   Phone: (415) 567-1848
San Francisco, CA 94109   Bruce L. Johnson, Lib.Dir.

CALIFORNIA INSTITUTE OF INTEGRAL STUDIES - LIBRARY
3494 21st St.   Phone: (415) 648-1489
San Francisco, CA 94110   Vern Haddick, Lib.Dir.

CALIFORNIA MEDICAL ASSOCIATION - LIBRARY
731 Market St.   Phone: (415) 777-2000
San Francisco, CA 94103   Regina E. Chadwick, Hd.Libn.

CALIFORNIA REDWOOD ASSOCIATION - LIBRARY
One Lombard St.   Phone: (415) 392-7880
San Francisco, CA 94111

CALIFORNIA STATE AUTOMOBILE ASSOCIATION - LIBRARY
150 Van Ness Ave., B2-3F   Phone: (415) 565-2300
San Francisco, CA 94101   Pauline Jones Tighe, Libn.

CALIFORNIA STATE BANKING DEPARTMENT - LIBRARY
235 Montgomery St., Suite 750   Phone: (415) 557-4040
San Francisco, CA 94104   Paula Heiman, Libn.

CALIFORNIA STATE DEPARTMENT OF INDUSTRIAL RELATIONS - DIVISION
    OF LABOR STATISTICS AND RESEARCH LIBRARY
Box 603   Phone: (415) 557-2184
San Francisco, CA 94101   Ruth Mark, Res.Anl.

CALIFORNIA STATE DEPARTMENT OF JUSTICE - ATTORNEY GENERAL'S
    OFFICE LIBRARY
6248 State Bldg.   Phone: (415) 557-2177
San Francisco, CA 94102   Malcolm Reynolds, Sr.Libn.

CALIFORNIA STATE DEPARTMENT OF TRANSPORTATION - DISTRICT 4
    LIBRARY
Box 3366, Rincon Annex   Phone: (415) 557-3894
San Francisco, CA 94119   Alice Whitten, Lib.Tech.Asst.

CALIFORNIA STATE DIVISION OF MINES AND GEOLOGY - LIBRARY
Ferry Bldg.   Phone: (415) 557-0308
San Francisco, CA 94111   Angela Brunton, Libn.

CALIFORNIA STATE LIBRARY - SUTRO LIBRARY
2495 Golden Gate Ave.   Phone: (415) 557-0374
San Francisco, CA 94118   Gary F. Kurutz, Sutro Libn.

CALIFORNIA STATE SUPREME COURT LIBRARY †
4241 State Bldg. Annex
455 Golden Gate Ave.   Phone: (415) 557-1922
San Francisco, CA 94102   John A. Sigel

CASTLE & COOKE, INC. - LAW & GOVERNMENT DEPARTMENT
   INFORMATION CENTER
50 California St., 18th Fl.   Phone: (415) 986-3000
San Francisco, CA 94111   Betty Hardin, Supv.Libn.

CHILDREN'S HOSPITAL OF SAN FRANCISCO - EMGE MEDICAL LIBRARY
Box 3805   Phone: (415) 387-8700
San Francisco, CA 94119   Angie Durso, Libn.

CITY COLLEGE OF SAN FRANCISCO - HOTEL AND RESTAURANT
   DEPARTMENT - ALICE STATLER LIBRARY
50 Phelan Ave.   Phone: (415) 239-3460
San Francisco, CA 94112   Mary B. Smyth, Lib.Mgr.

COGSWELL COLLEGE - LIBRARY
600 Stockton St.   Phone: (415) 433-5550
San Francisco, CA 94108   Herbert E. Childs, Jr., Libn.

COLLEGE OF THE SAN FRANCISCO ART INSTITUTE - ANNE BREMER
   MEMORIAL LIBRARY
800 Chestnut St.   Phone: (415) 771-7020
San Francisco, CA 94133   Sharon Chickanzeff, Libn.

COOLEY, GODWARD, CASTRO, HUDDLESON & TATUM - LIBRARY
1 Maritime Plaza, 20th Fl.   Phone: (415) 981-5252
San Francisco, CA 94111   Mary J. Hays, Libn.

COOPERS AND LYBRAND - LIBRARY
333 Market St.   Phone: (415) 957-3000
San Francisco, CA 94105   Karen E. Ivy, Libn.

CROCKER NATIONAL BANK - LIBRARY
Box 38000   Phone: (415) 477-3581
San Francisco, CA 94138   Inga Govaars, Libn.

CROWN ZELLERBACH CORPORATION - CORPORATE INFORMATION
   CENTER
One Bush St.   Phone: (415) 823-5403
San Francisco, CA 94104   Gloria Capel, Adm.

DAVIES (Ralph K.) MEDICAL CENTER - FRANKLIN HOSPITAL MEDICAL
   LIBRARY
Castro & Duboce St.   Phone: (415) 565-6352
San Francisco, CA 94114   Anne Shew, Med.Libn.

DELOITTE, HASKINS & SELLS - AUDIT/MAS & TAX LIBRARY †
44 Montgomery St.   Phone: (415) 393-4328
San Francisco, CA 94104   Eunice J. Azzani, Libn.

DESIGN PROFESSIONALS FINANCIAL CORPORATION - LIBRARY
50 California St., 5th Fl.   Phone: (415) 433-1676
San Francisco, CA 94111   Annette C. Gaskin, Libn.

EARTHWORK - CENTER FOR RURAL STUDIES
3410 19th St.
San Francisco, CA 94110   Mark Ritchie

ENVIRONMENTAL IMPACT PLANNING CORPORATION - LIBRARY
319 Eleventh St.   Phone: (415) 626-9034
San Francisco, CA 94103   Cathleen Galloway Brown, Libn.

ENVIRONMENTAL PROTECTION AGENCY - REGION IX LIBRARY/
   INFORMATION CENTER
215 Fremont St.   Phone: (415) 556-1840
San Francisco, CA 94105   Jean Circiello, Libn.

ESHERICK, HOMSEY, DODGE & DAVIS - LIBRARY
2789 25th St.   Phone: (415) 285-9193
San Francisco, CA 94110   Fran Brunet, Libn.

FAR WEST LABORATORY FOR EDUCATIONAL RESEARCH AND
   DEVELOPMENT - LIBRARY AND ARCHIVES
1855 Folsom St.   Phone: (415) 565-3211
San Francisco, CA 94103   Lillian Chinn, Lib.Asst.

FASHION INSTITUTE OF DESIGN & MERCHANDISING - LIBRARY
790 Market St.   Phone: (415) 433-6691
San Francisco, CA 94102   Bronwein Rasmussen, Libn.

FEDERAL HOME LOAN BANK OF SAN FRANCISCO - LIBRARY
Box 7948   Phone: (415) 393-1215
San Francisco, CA 94120   Molly M. Skeen, Libn.

FEDERAL RESERVE BANK OF SAN FRANCISCO - RESEARCH LIBRARY
400 Sansome St.
Box 7702   Phone: (415) 397-2358
San Francisco, CA 94120   Phyllis A. Waggoner, Lib.Mgr.

FINE ARTS MUSEUMS OF SAN FRANCISCO - LIBRARY
M.H. De Young Memorial Museum
Golden Gate Pk.   Phone: (415) 558-2887
San Francisco, CA 94118   Jane Gray Nelson, Hd.Libn.

FIREMAN'S FUND INSURANCE COMPANIES - LIBRARY †
3333 California St.
Box 3395   Phone: (415) 929-2871
San Francisco, CA 94119   Oda Bali Hansen, Libn.

FOUNDATION CENTER - SAN FRANCISCO LIBRARY
312 Sutter St., 3rd Fl.   Phone: (415) 397-0902
San Francisco, CA 94108   Caroline McGilvray, Dir.

GARBELL RESEARCH FOUNDATION - LIBRARY
1714 Lake St.   Phone: (415) 752-0871
San Francisco, CA 94121

GENSTAR CORP. - LIBRARY
3 Embarcadero Center, Suite 2500
San Francisco, CA 94111   Jana Selph, Libn.

GEORGE (Henry) SCHOOL OF SOCIAL SCIENCE - RESEARCH LIBRARY
833 Market St., Rm. 1009   Phone: (415) 362-7944
San Francisco, CA 94103   Robert Scrofani, Exec. V.P.

GOETHE INSTITUTE - LIBRARY
530 Bush St.   Phone: (415) 391-0370
San Francisco, CA 94108   Helmi Schluter, Libn.

GOLDEN GATE UNIVERSITY - LIBRARIES
536 Mission St.   Phone: (415) 442-7242
San Francisco, CA 94105   Harold E. Korf, Dir.

GOLDEN GATE UNIVERSITY - SCHOOL OF LAW LIBRARY
536 Mission St.   Phone: (415) 442-7260
San Francisco, CA 94105   Nancy Carol Carter, Dir.

GRAND LODGE OF FREE AND ACCEPTED MASONS OF CALIFORNIA -
   LIBRARY AND MUSEUM
1111 California St.   Phone: (415) 776-7000
San Francisco, CA 94108   Robert A. Klinger, Grand Libn.

GUEDEL MEMORIAL ANESTHESIA CENTER - LIBRARY
2395 Sacramento St.
Box 7999
San Francisco, CA 94120   Harold R. Gibson, Libn.

HALL OF JUSTICE LIBRARY
850 Bryant St., Rm. 305   Phone: (415) 553-1763
San Francisco, CA 94103   Robert R. Schmidt, Libn.

HASSARD, BONNINGTON, ROGERS & HUBER - LIBRARY
44 Montgomery St., Suite 3500   Phone: (415) 781-8787
San Francisco, CA 94104   John E. Few, Libn.

HEALD COLLEGE OF ENGINEERING AND ARCHITECTURE - LIBRARY †
1215 Van Ness Ave.   Phone: (415) 441-5562
San Francisco, CA 94109

HELLER, EHRMAN, WHITE & MC AULIFFE - LIBRARY
44 Montgomery St., 30th Fl.   Phone: (415) 772-6105
San Francisco, CA 94104   Loretta Mak, Libn.

HOLOCAUST LIBRARY AND RESEARCH CENTER OF SAN FRANCISCO
601 14th Ave.   Phone: (415) 751-6983
San Francisco, CA 94118   Martin A. Kuhn, Lib.Cons.

INDUSTRIAL INDEMNITY COMPANY - LIBRARY
255 California St.   Phone: (415) 986-3535
San Francisco, CA 94120   L.R. Murata, Libn.

INSTITUTE FOR ADVANCED STUDY OF HUMAN SEXUALITY - RESEARCH LIBRARY
1523 Franklin St.   Phone: (415) 928-1133
San Francisco, CA 94109   Dr. Erwin J. Haeberle, Dir.

INSTITUTE FOR CHILDHOOD RESOURCES - LIBRARY
1169 Howard St.   Phone: (415) 864-1169
San Francisco, CA 94103   Stevanne Auerbach, Dir.

INTERNATIONAL ENGINEERING COMPANY, INC. - LIBRARY
180 Howard St.   Phone: (415) 442-7300
San Francisco, CA 94105   Louis I. Pigott, Jr., Libn.

INTERNATIONAL LONGSHOREMEN'S AND WAREHOUSEMEN'S UNION - ANNE RAND RESEARCH LIBRARY
1188 Franklin St.   Phone: (415) 775-0533
San Francisco, CA 94109   Carol Schwartz, Libn.

JANUS FOUNDATION - LIBRARY
2420 Sutter St.   Phone: (415) 563-0344
San Francisco, CA 94115   Janet L. Bergman, Libn.

JANUS INFORMATION FACILITY
1952 Union St.   Phone: (415) 567-0162
San Francisco, CA 94123   Paul A. Walker, Dir.

KAISER-PERMANENTE MEDICAL CENTER - SAN FRANCISCO MEDICAL LIBRARY
Box 7612   Phone: (415) 929-4100
San Francisco, CA 94120   Vincent Lagano, Med.Libn.

KENNEDY/JENKS ENGINEERS, INC. - LIBRARY
657 Howard St.   Phone: (415) 362-6065
San Francisco, CA 94105   Verda M. Hawkins, Libn.

LANDELS, RIPLEY & DIAMOND - LIBRARY
450 Pacific Ave.   Phone: (415) 788-5000
San Francisco, CA 94133   Jeanette S. Lizotte, Libn.

LANGLEY PORTER PSYCHIATRIC INSTITUTE - LIBRARY
University of California
401 Parnassus Ave.   Phone: (415) 681-8080
San Francisco, CA 94143   Lisa M. Dunkel, Libn.

LAUTZE & LAUTZE ACCOUNTANCY CORPORATION - RESOURCES DEVELOPMENT CENTER
100 Pine St.   Phone: (415) 362-1970
San Francisco, CA 94111   Linda Marion Feingold, Sr.Cons., Info.

LEEDS, HILL & JEWETT, INC. - LIBRARY
1275 Market St.   Phone: (415) 626-2070
San Francisco, CA 94103   Gregory B. Sedgwick, Libn.

LEVI STRAUSS & COMPANY - CORPORATE MARKETING INFORMATION CENTER
2 Embarcadero Center, Rm. 1530
San Francisco, CA 94106   Catherine Rock, Adm.

LINCOLN UNIVERSITY - LAW LIBRARY
281 Masonic Ave.   Phone: (415) 221-1212
San Francisco, CA 94118   Andrea Segall, Law Libn.

LUDLOW (Fitz Hugh) MEMORIAL LIBRARY
Box 99346
San Francisco, CA 94109   Michael R. Aldrich, Exec.Cur.

LUTHERAN CHURCH - MISSOURI SYNOD - CALIFORNIA, NEVADA AND HAWAII DISTRICT ARCHIVES
465 Woolsey St.   Phone: (415) 468-2336
San Francisco, CA 94134   Rev. Karl H. Wyneken

MC CUTCHEN, DOYLE, BROWN & ENERSEN - LAW LIBRARY
3 Embarcadero Ctr.   Phone: (415) 393-2198
San Francisco, CA 94111   Elizabeth S. Nicholson, Libn.

MC KINSEY & COMPANY, INC. - LIBRARY
555 California St., Suite 4800   Phone: (415) 981-0250
San Francisco, CA 94104   Linda L. Kraemer, Mgr., Info.Serv.

MAIN HURDMAN - LIBRARY †
Two Embarcadero, 25th Fl.   Phone: (415) 981-7720
San Francisco, CA 94111   Eileen Malley, Libn.

MANALYTICS, INC. - LIBRARY
625 Third St.   Phone: (415) 788-4143
San Francisco, CA 94107   Seyem Deus, Libn.

MECHANICS' INSTITUTE LIBRARY
57 Post St.   Phone: (415) 421-1750
San Francisco, CA 94104   Kathleen T. Pabst, Lib.Dir.

MEXICAN AMERICAN LEGAL DEFENSE AND EDUCATIONAL FUND - LIBRARY
28 Geary St., 6th Fl.   Phone: (415) 981-5800
San Francisco, CA 94108   Tyler Kelly, Libn.

MOBIL LAND DEVELOPMENT CORPORATION - LIBRARY
One Market Plaza, Spear Tower 1515   Phone: (415) 764-1500
San Francisco, CA 94105   Lolly Pineda, Libn.

MORRISON & FOERSTER - LAW LIBRARY
One Market Plaza
Spear St. Tower   Phone: (415) 777-6272
San Francisco, CA 94105   Carl Whitaker, Law Libn.

MOUNT ZION HOSPITAL AND MEDICAL CENTER - HARRIS M. FISHBON MEMORIAL LIBRARY
Box 7921   Phone: (415) 567-6600
San Francisco, CA 94120   Angela Green Wesling, Med.Libn.

MUSIC AND ARTS INSTITUTE OF SAN FRANCISCO - COLLEGE LIBRARY
2622 Jackson St.   Phone: (415) 567-1445
San Francisco, CA 94115   R. McKee, Dir.

NATIONAL MARITIME MUSEUM - J. PORTER SHAW LIBRARY
Foot of Polk St.   Phone: (415) 556-8177
San Francisco, CA 94109   David Hull, Principal Libn.

OLD ST. MARY'S CHURCH - PAULIST LIBRARY
614 Grant Ave.   Phone: (415) 362-0959
San Francisco, CA 94108   Walter Anthony, C.S.P., Dir.

ORRICK, HERRINGTON, ROWLEY & SUTCLIFFE - LIBRARY
600 Montgomery St.   Phone: (415) 392-1122
San Francisco, CA 94111   Cynthia Papermaster, Libn.

PACIFIC GAS AND ELECTRIC COMPANY - LAW LIBRARY
Box 7442   Phone: (415) 781-4211
San Francisco, CA 94106   Gary L. Stromme, Law Libn.

PACIFIC GAS AND ELECTRIC COMPANY - LIBRARY
77 Beale St.   Phone: (415) 781-4211
San Francisco, CA 94106   Louisa M. Shoupe, Libn.

PACIFIC MEDICAL CENTER & UNIVERSITY OF THE PACIFIC SCHOOL OF DENTISTRY - HEALTH SCIENCES LIBRARY
2395 Sacramento St.
Box 7999   Phone: (415) 563-4321
San Francisco, CA 94120   Harold R. Gibson, Libn.

PACIFIC TELEPHONE COMPANY - LIBRARY
140 New Montgomery St., Rm. 2620   Phone: (415) 542-2896
San Francisco, CA 94105   Lois Lambert, Libn.

PACIFIC-UNION CLUB - LIBRARY †
1000 California St.
San Francisco, CA 94108
Phone: (415) 775-1234
Natasha Wilkinson, Hd.Libn.

PEAT, MARWICK, MITCHELL & COMPANY - LIBRARY
San Francisco Internatl. Airport
Box 8007
San Francisco, CA 94128
Helen T. Rolen, Libn.

PETTIT & MARTIN - LIBRARY
600 Montgomery, 21st Floor
San Francisco, CA 94111
Phone: (415) 434-4000
Mary Staats, Libn.

PILLSBURY, MADISON AND SUTRO - LIBRARY
225 Bush St.
San Francisco, CA 94104
Phone: (415) 983-1130
George R. Davis, Chf.Libn.

PRESS CLUB OF SAN FRANCISCO - WILL AUBREY MEMORIAL LIBRARY
555 Post St., Rm. 428
San Francisco, CA 94102
Phone: (415) 775-7800
Harry R. Illman, Libn.

QUESTOR ASSOCIATES - LIBRARY
115 Sansome St., Suite 600
San Francisco, CA 94104
Phone: (415) 433-0300
Robert J. Townsend, Publishing Mgr.

RAND INFORMATION SYSTEMS, INC. - LIBRARY
98 Battery St., 4th Fl.
San Francisco, CA 94111
Phone: (415) 392-2500
Dr. Marc Hofstadter, Libn.

REDWOOD EMPIRE ASSOCIATION - LIBRARY
360 Post St., Suite 401
San Francisco, CA 94108
Phone: (415) 421-6554
Stuart Nixon, Gen.Mgr.

ROSENBERG CAPITAL MANAGEMENT - LIBRARY
One Market Plaza
Spear St. Tower, Suite 3910
San Francisco, CA 94105
Phone: (415) 777-5474
Cathy Goodwin, Libn.

ST. FRANCIS MEMORIAL HOSPITAL - WALTER F. SCHALLER MEMORIAL
LIBRARY
Box 7726
San Francisco, CA 94120
Phone: (415) 775-4321
Linda Grix, Med.Libn.

ST. LUKE'S HOSPITAL - MEDICAL LIBRARY
3555 Army St.
San Francisco, CA 94110
Phone: (415) 647-8600
Corazon O'S. Ismarin, Libn.

ST. MARY'S HOSPITAL AND MEDICAL CENTER - MEDICAL LIBRARY
450 Stanyan St.
San Francisco, CA 94117
Phone: (415) 668-1000
Eleanor Benelisha, Dir., Lib.Serv.

SAN FRANCISCO ACADEMY OF COMIC ART - LIBRARY
2850 Ulloa
San Francisco, CA 94116
Phone: (415) 681-1737
Bill Blackbeard, Dir.

SAN FRANCISCO CHRONICLE - LIBRARY
5th & Mission Sts.
San Francisco, CA 94103
Phone: (415) 777-1111
Suzanne Caster, Hd.Libn.

SAN FRANCISCO - CITY ATTORNEY'S OFFICE - LIBRARY
206 City Hall
San Francisco, CA 94102
Phone: (415) 558-4993
Ruth Stevenson, Law Libn.

SAN FRANCISCO COLLEGE OF MORTUARY SCIENCE - LIBRARY
1450 Post St.
San Francisco, CA 94109
Phone: (415) 567-0674
Dale W. Sly, Pres.

SAN FRANCISCO CONSERVATORY OF MUSIC - LIBRARY
1201 Ortega St.
San Francisco, CA 94122
Phone: (415) 564-8086
Lucretia Wolfe, Libn.

SAN FRANCISCO EXAMINER - LIBRARY
110 Fifth St.
San Francisco, CA 94103
Phone: (415) 777-7845
Judy Gerritts, Hd.Libn.

SAN FRANCISCO GENERAL HOSPITAL MEDICAL CENTER - BARNETT-
BRIGGS LIBRARY
1001 Potrero Ave.
San Francisco, CA 94110
Phone: (415) 821-8553
Miriam Hirsch, Med.Libn.

SAN FRANCISCO LAW LIBRARY
436 City Hall
San Francisco, CA 94102
Phone: (415) 558-4627
Harold E. Rowe, Libn.

SAN FRANCISCO LIGHTHOUSE CENTER FOR THE BLIND - LIBRARY
745 Buchanan St.
San Francisco, CA 94102
Phone: (415) 431-1481
Daniel Forer, Coord.

SAN FRANCISCO MUNICIPAL RAILWAY - PLANNING DIVISION LIBRARY
949 Presidio Ave.
San Francisco, CA 94115
Phone: (415) 558-5284
Buford Johnson, Transit Planner

SAN FRANCISCO MUSEUM OF MODERN ART - LOUISE S. ACKERMAN FINE
ARTS LIBRARY
McAllister at Van Ness
San Francisco, CA 94102
Phone: (415) 863-8800
Eugenie Candau, Libn.

SAN FRANCISCO PSYCHOANALYTIC INSTITUTE - LIBRARY
2420 Sutter St.
San Francisco, CA 94115
Phone: (415) 563-5815
Anne Morddel Drayton, Libn.

SAN FRANCISCO PUBLIC LIBRARY - BUSINESS LIBRARY
530 Kearny St.
San Francisco, CA 94108
Phone: (415) 558-3946
Gil McNamee, Principal Libn.

SAN FRANCISCO PUBLIC LIBRARY - SAN FRANCISCO HISTORY ROOM
Civic Ctr.
San Francisco, CA 94102
Phone: (415) 558-3940
Gladys Hansen, Archv.

SAN FRANCISCO PUBLIC LIBRARY - SPECIAL COLLECTIONS DEPARTMENT
Civic Ctr.
San Francisco, CA 94102
Phone: (415) 558-3940
Johanna Goldschmid, Spec.Coll.Libn.

SAN FRANCISCO STATE UNIVERSITY - FRANK V. DE BELLIS COLLECTION
1630 Holloway Ave.
San Francisco, CA 94132
Phone: (415) 469-1649
Serena De Bellis, Cur.

SAN FRANCISCO UNIFIED SCHOOL DISTRICT - TEACHERS PROFESSIONAL
LIBRARY
135 Van Ness Ave.
San Francisco, CA 94102
Phone: (415) 565-9272
Helen M. Jacobsen, Res.Libn.

SIERRA CLUB - WILLIAM E. COLBY MEMORIAL LIBRARY
530 Bush St.
San Francisco, CA 94108
Phone: (415) 981-8634
Barbara Lekisch, Rsrcs.Libn.

SIMPSON COLLEGE - START-KILGOUR MEMORIAL LIBRARY
801 Silver Ave.
San Francisco, CA 94134
Phone: (415) 334-7400
Miles S. Compton, Hd.Libn.

SOCIETY OF CALIFORNIA PIONEERS - JOSEPH A. MOORE LIBRARY
456 McAllister St.
San Francisco, CA 94102
Phone: (415) 861-5278
Grace E. Baker, Libn.

SOCIETY OF MAYFLOWER DESCENDANTS IN THE STATE OF CALIFORNIA -
LIBRARY
681 Market St., Rm. 670
San Francisco, CA 94105
Phone: (415) 781-8324
Ruth Wilbur, Libn.

SOHIO PETROLEUM COMPANY - CENTRAL LIBRARY AND INFORMATION
SERVICES
100 Pine St.
San Francisco, CA 94111
Phone: (415) 445-9511
Marion Dorosh, Libn.

STANDARD OIL COMPANY OF CALIFORNIA - LIBRARY
225 Bush St.
San Francisco, CA 94104
Phone: (415) 894-2945
Margaret J. Linden, Chf.Libn.

STONE, MARRACCINI & PATTERSON - RESEARCH & DEVELOPMENT
LIBRARY
455 Beach St.
San Francisco, CA 94133
Phone: (415) 775-7300
Ronnie Cadam, Libn.

STRYBING ARBORETUM SOCIETY - HELEN CROCKER RUSSELL LIBRARY
Golden Gate Pk.
9th Ave. & Lincoln Way
San Francisco, CA 94122
Phone: (415) 661-1316
Jane Gates, Hd.Libn.

GEOGRAPHIC

THELEN, MARRIN, JOHNSON & BRIDGES - LAW LIBRARY
Two Embarcadero Center   Phone: (415) 392-6320
San Francisco, CA 94111   Sue Dyer, Law Libn.

THEOSOPHICAL SOCIETY - SAN FRANCISCO LODGE LIBRARY *
414 Mason St., No. 703   Phone: (415) 781-1677
San Francisco, CA 94102   Sherman Smukler, Pres.

UNITED AIR LINES, INC. - ENGINEERING DEPARTMENT - LIBRARY
San Francisco International Airport   Phone: (415) 876-3730
San Francisco, CA 94128   Josephine J. Whitney, Tech.Libn.

UNITED STATES ANIMAL BANK, INC. - LIBRARY
Box 15426   Phone: (415) 856-6525
San Francisco, CA 94115

U.S. ARMY - CORPS OF ENGINEERS - SOUTH PACIFIC DIVISION - LIBRARY
630 Sansome St., Rm. 1216   Phone: (415) 556-5320
San Francisco, CA 94111   Eloise A. Sauer, Lib.Techn.

U.S. ARMY HOSPITALS - LETTERMAN ARMY MEDICAL CENTER - MEDICAL
     LIBRARY
Presidio, Bldg. 1100, Rm. 338   Phone: (415) 561-2465
San Francisco, CA 94129   Mary Elsie Caruso, Adm.Libn.

U.S. COURT OF APPEALS, 9TH CIRCUIT - LIBRARY
Box 5731   Phone: (415) 556-6129
San Francisco, CA 94101   Edward Chichura, Chf.Libn.

U.S. DEPT. OF HOUSING AND URBAN DEVELOPMENT - REGION IX - LIBRARY
450 Golden Gate Ave.
Box 36003
San Francisco, CA 94102

U.S. DISTRICT COURT - NORTHERN CALIFORNIA DISTRICT - LOUIS E.
     GOODMAN MEMORIAL LIBRARY
450 Golden Gate Ave.
Box 36060   Phone: (415) 556-7979
San Francisco, CA 94102   Nancy Warnke, Libn.

U.S. GENERAL ACCOUNTING OFFICE - SAN FRANCISCO REGIONAL OFFICE -
     LIBRARY
1275 Market St.   Phone: (415) 556-6200
San Francisco, CA 94103   Mary O. Vargo, Tech.Info.Spec.

U.S. HERITAGE CONSERVATION AND RECREATION SERVICE - PACIFIC
     SOUTHWEST REGIONAL OFFICE - LIBRARY
450 Golden Gate Ave.   Phone: (415) 556-8530
San Francisco, CA 94102   Irene A. Stachura, Libn.

U.S. NATL. PARK SERVICE - WESTERN REGIONAL OFFICE - REGIONAL
     RESOURCES LIBRARY
450 Golden Gate Ave., Rm. 14009
Box 36063   Phone: (415) 556-4165
San Francisco, CA 94102   Gordon Chappell, Regional Hist.

U.S. NAVY - NAVAL REGIONAL MEDICAL CENTER (Guam) - MEDICAL
     LIBRARY *
                                           Phone: (671) 344-9250
FPO San Francisco, CA 96630

U.S. NAVY - NAVAL STATION LIBRARY (Guam)
Box 174
FPO San Francisco, CA 96630   Beverly J. Endsley, Lib.Techn.

U.S. PUBLIC HEALTH SERVICE HOSPITAL - MEDICAL LIBRARY †
15th Ave. & Lake St.   Phone: (415) 752-1400
San Francisco, CA 94118   Marie A. Wegman, Libn.

U.S. VETERANS ADMINISTRATION (CA-San Francisco) - MEDICAL CENTER
     LIBRARY
42nd Ave. & Clement St.   Phone: (415) 221-4810
San Francisco, CA 94121   Cynthia A. Heathfield, Act.Chf.Libn.

UNIVERSITY OF CALIFORNIA, SAN FRANCISCO - HASTINGS COLLEGE OF
     THE LAW - LEGAL INFORMATION CENTER
198 McAllister St.   Phone: (415) 557-1354
San Francisco, CA 94102   Dan F. Henke, Libn.

UNIVERSITY OF CALIFORNIA, SAN FRANCISCO - LIBRARY
Parnassus Ave., 257-S   Phone: (415) 666-2334
San Francisco, CA 94143   David Bishop, Univ.Libn.

UNIVERSITY OF SAN FRANCISCO - SCHOOL OF LAW LIBRARY
Kendrick Hall   Phone: (415) 666-6679
San Francisco, CA 94117   Elizabeth-Anne Quigley, Law Libn.

UNIVERSITY OF SAN FRANCISCO - SPECIAL COLLECTIONS DEPT./
     DONOHUE RARE BOOK ROOM
Richard A. Gleeson Library
2130 Fulton St.   Phone: (415) 666-6718
San Francisco, CA 94117   D. Steven Corey, Spec.Coll.Libn.

UTAH INTERNATIONAL, INC. - LIBRARY
550 California St.   Phone: (415) 981-1515
San Francisco, CA 94104   Jerry McWilliams, Libn.

VIDEO FREE AMERICA - LIBRARY *
442 Shotwell St.   Phone: (415) 648-9040
San Francisco, CA 94110   Joanne Kelly, Lib.Dir.

WELLS FARGO BANK - HISTORY DEPARTMENT 921
475 Sansome St.   Phone: (415) 396-4157
San Francisco, CA 94111   Mary L. Morganti, P.R.Off./Asst.Corp.Archv.

WELLS FARGO BANK - LIBRARY
Box 44000   Phone: (415) 396-3744
San Francisco, CA 94144   Alice E. Hunsucker, Asst.V.P./Mgr.

WINE INSTITUTE - LIBRARY
165 Post St.   Phone: (415) 986-0878
San Francisco, CA 94108   Joan V. Ingalls, Libn.

WINE MUSEUM OF SAN FRANCISCO - CHRISTIAN BROTHERS RARE WINE
     BOOKS LIBRARY
633 Beach St.   Phone: (415) 673-6990
San Francisco, CA 94109   Mary M. Rodgers, Libn.

WOODWARD-CLYDE CONSULTANTS - ENVIRONMENTAL SYSTEMS
     DIVISION - LIBRARY
3 Embarcadero Center, Suite 700   Phone: (415) 956-7070
San Francisco, CA 94111   Harriet Annino, Libn.

WOODWARD-CLYDE CONSULTANTS, WESTERN REGION - TECHNICAL
     LIBRARY
3 Embarcadero Center, Suite 700   Phone: (415) 956-7070
San Francisco, CA 94111   Anne T. Harrigan, Libn.

WORLD AFFAIRS COUNCIL OF NORTHERN CALIFORNIA - LIBRARY
312 Sutter St., Suite 200   Phone: (415) 982-2541
San Francisco, CA 94108   Lone C. Beeson, Hd.Libn.

BIBLIOGRAPHIC RESEARCH LIBRARY
964 Chapel Hill Way   Phone: (408) 247-2810
San Jose, CA 95122   Robert B. Harmon, Res.Biblog.

CALIFORNIA STATE DEPARTMENT OF DEVELOPMENTAL SERVICES -
     PROFESSIONAL LIBRARY
Agnews Residential Facility   Phone: (408) 262-2100
San Jose, CA 95134   Lucy Flagg, Sr.Libn.

FMC CORPORATION - ORDNANCE ENGINEERING DIVISION - TECHNICAL
     LIBRARY
Box 1201   Phone: (408) 289-2852
San Jose, CA 95108   Sheila Smokey, Supv.Tech.Lib.

GENERAL ELECTRIC COMPANY - NUCLEAR ENERGY GROUP - LIBRARY
175 Curtner Ave.   Phone: (408) 925-3522
San Jose, CA 95125   Alleen Thompson, Mgr., Lib.

IBM CORPORATION - GENERAL PRODUCTS DIVISION - INFORMATION/
     LIBRARY/LEARNING CENTER
Dept. J17/Bldg. K15
555 Baily Ave.   Phone: (408) 463-4259
San Jose, CA 95150   Karen Takle Quinn, Dir.

IBM CORPORATION - GENERAL PRODUCTS DIVISION - TECHNICAL
    INFORMATION CENTER
G35/141
5600 Cottle Rd.   Phone: (408) 256-2908
San Jose, CA 95193   Ruth Winik, Mgr., Tech.Info.Ctr.

IBM CORPORATION - RESEARCH LIBRARY
Dept. K 25, Bldg. 280
5600 Cottle Rd.   Phone: (408) 256-2562
San Jose, CA 95193   W.T. Gallagher, Mgr.

INDIAN CENTER OF SAN JOSE, INC. - LIBRARY
3485 East Hills Dr.   Phone: (408) 259-9722
San Jose, CA 95127   Marilyn Woods, Libn.

NATIONAL LIBRARY OF SPORTS
San Jose Public Library
180 W. San Carlos St.   Phone: (408) 287-0993
San Jose, CA 95113   Wes Mathis, Lib.Dir.

ROSICRUCIAN ORDER, AMORC - ROSICRUCIAN RESEARCH LIBRARY
Rosicrucian Park   Phone: (408) 287-9171
San Jose, CA 95191   Clara Campbell, Libn.

SAN JOSE HEALTH CENTER - HEALTH SCIENCE LIBRARY
675 E. Santa Clara St.   Phone: (408) 998-3212
San Jose, CA 95114   Susan L. Russell, Mgr.

SAN JOSE HISTORICAL MUSEUM - LIBRARY
635 Phelan Ave.   Phone: (408) 287-2290
San Jose, CA 95112   Claudia Jurmain, Asst.Cur.

SAN JOSE MEDICAL CLINIC - STAFF LIBRARY
45 S. 17th St.   Phone: (408) 998-5551
San Jose, CA 95112   Kathleen V. Stone, Lib.Ck.

SAN JOSE STATE UNIVERSITY - LIBRARY - SCIENCE/ENGINEERING
    DEPARTMENT †
250 S. 4th St.   Phone: (408) 277-3388
San Jose, CA 95192   Loren Molieri, Sr.Asst.Libn.

SANTA CLARA COUNTY HEALTH DEPARTMENT - LIBRARY *
2220 Moorpark Ave.   Phone: (408) 279-6021
San Jose, CA 95128   Elizabeth C. Walters, Libn.

SANTA CLARA COUNTY HEALTH SYSTEMS AGENCY - LIBRARY
852 N. First St., 3rd Fl.   Phone: (408) 292-9572
San Jose, CA 95112   Carolyn V. Garbarino, Program Libn.

SANTA CLARA COUNTY LAW LIBRARY
191 N. First St.   Phone: (408) 299-3567
San Jose, CA 95113   J.W. Heckel, Law Libn.

SANTA CLARA COUNTY PLANNING DEPARTMENT - LIBRARY
County Government Center, East Wing
70 W. Hedding St.   Phone: (408) 299-2521
San Jose, CA 95110   Heidi Lutz, Adm.Asst./Libn.

SANTA CLARA VALLEY MEDICAL CENTER - MEDICAL LIBRARY
751 S. Bascom Ave.   Phone: (408) 279-5650
San Jose, CA 95128   Barbara A. Wilson, Med.Libn.

U.P.E.C. CULTURAL CENTER - J.A. FREITAS LIBRARY
1120-24 E. 14th St.   Phone: (408) 483-7676
San Leandro, CA 94577   Carlos Almeida, Dir.

CALIFORNIA POLYTECHNIC STATE UNIVERSITY - ROBERT E. KENNEDY
    LIBRARY
                                                   Phone: (805) 546-2344
San Luis Obispo, CA 93407   Dr. David B. Walch, Dir.

SAN LUIS OBISPO COUNTY LAW LIBRARY †
Courthouse, Rm. 309   Phone: (805) 549-5855
San Luis Obispo, CA 93401   Mary E. Gaydosh, Libn.

SAN LUIS OBISPO COUNTY PLANNING DEPARTMENT - TECHNICAL
    INFORMATION LIBRARY
102 Courthouse Annex   Phone: (805) 543-1550
San Luis Obispo, CA 93401   Paul C. Crawford, Plan.Dir.

INVISIBLE MINISTRY - COMMITTEE FOR AN EXTENDED LIFESPAN -
    LIBRARY
Box 37   Phone: (714) 746-9430
San Marcos, CA 92069   A. Stuart Otto, Dir.

PALOMAR COLLEGE - PHIL H. PUTNAM MEMORIAL LIBRARY
1140 Mission Rd.   Phone: (714) 744-1150
San Marcos, CA 92069   Bonnie L. Rogers, Dean, Instr.Rsrcs.

HUNTINGTON (Henry E.) LIBRARY, ART GALLERY AND BOTANICAL GARDENS
1151 Oxford Rd.   Phone: (213) 792-6141
San Marino, CA 91108   James Thorpe, Dir.

CALIFORNIA JOCKEY CLUB AT BAY MEADOWS - WILLIAM P. KYNE
    MEMORIAL LIBRARY
Box 5050   Phone: (415) 574-7223
San Mateo, CA 94402   Gretchen G. Kramer, Libn.

COYOTE POINT MUSEUM - RESOURCE CENTER
Coyote Point Dr.   Phone: (415) 342-7755
San Mateo, CA 94401   Celia Reidler, Educ.Dir.

PENINSULA TEMPLE BETH EL - LIBRARY *
1700 Alameda De Las Pulgas   Phone: (415) 341-7701
San Mateo, CA 94403   Ann Levin, Libn.

SAN MATEO COUNTY DEPARTMENT OF PUBLIC HEALTH AND WELFARE -
    LIBRARY
225 37th Ave.   Phone: (415) 573-2520
San Mateo, CA 94403   Judith Levy, Lib.Dir.

SAN MATEO COUNTY HISTORICAL ASSOCIATION - LIBRARY
1700 W. Hillsdale Blvd.
College of San Mateo Campus   Phone: (415) 574-6441
San Mateo, CA 94402   Marion C. Holmes, Archv.

BROOKSIDE HOSPITAL - MEDICAL STAFF LIBRARY
2000 Vale Rd.   Phone: (415) 235-7000
San Pablo, CA 94806   Barbara Dorham, Libn.

AMERICAN CETACEAN SOCIETY - NATIONAL LIBRARY
Box 4416   Phone: (213) 548-6279
San Pedro, CA 90731   Virginia C. Callahan, Libn.

LOGICON, INC. - TECHNICAL LIBRARY
255 W. 5th St.   Phone: (213) 831-0611
San Pedro, CA 90731   Nammy M. Cho, Lib.Hd.

LOS ANGELES - DEPARTMENT OF RECREATION AND PARKS - CABRILLO
    MARINE MUSEUM - LIBRARY
3720 Stephen White Dr.   Phone: (213) 548-7562
San Pedro, CA 90731   Dr. Susanne Lawrenz-Miller, Assoc.Dir.

SAN PEDRO PENINSULA HOSPITAL - MEDICAL LIBRARY
1300 W. 7th St.   Phone: (213) 832-3311
San Pedro, CA 90732   James H. Harlan, Libn.

AMERICAN MUSIC RESEARCH CENTER - LIBRARY
Dominican College   Phone: (415) 457-4440
San Rafael, CA 94901   Sr. Mary Dominic Ray, Dir.

COMMERCE CLEARING HOUSE, INC. - BUSINESS LIBRARY
Quail Hill   Phone: (415) 472-3100
San Rafael, CA 94903   Grace Houston, Libn.

DOMINICAN SISTERS - CONGREGATION OF THE HOLY NAME - ARCHIVES
1520 Grand Ave.   Phone: (415) 454-9221
San Rafael, CA 94901   Sr. Justin Barry, O.P., Archv.

MARIN COUNTY HISTORICAL SOCIETY - LIBRARY *
1125 B St. at Mission   Phone: (415) 454-8538
San Rafael, CA 94901   Elsie Mazzini, Dir.

MARIN COUNTY LAW LIBRARY
Hall of Justice, C-33   Phone: (415) 499-6355
San Rafael, CA 94903   Meyer W. Halpern, Hd. Law Libn.

GEOGRAPHIC

MARIN GENERAL HOSPITAL - LIBRARY
Box 2129
San Rafael, CA 94901
Phone: (415) 461-0100
Julie Kahl, Libn.

MARIN WILDLIFE CENTER - LIBRARY
76 Albert Park Lane
Box 957
San Rafael, CA 94915
Phone: (415) 454-6961
Alice C. Katzung, Dir.

SAN RAFAEL INDEPENDENT JOURNAL - NEWSPAPER LIBRARY
1040 B St.
San Rafael, CA 94901
Phone: (415) 454-3020
Larry Storbo, Libn.

SPIRITUAL COMMUNITY PUBLICATIONS - INFORMATION CENTER
Box 1080
San Rafael, CA 94902
Phone: (415) 457-2990
Parmatma Singh Khalsa, Pub.

AMERICAN MC GAW - TECHNICAL INFORMATION CENTER
Box 11887
Santa Ana, CA 92711
Phone: (714) 754-2066
Judy Labovitz, Supv.

BOWERS MEMORIAL MUSEUM - LIBRARY AND ARCHIVES
2002 N. Main St.
Santa Ana, CA 92706

GLOBAL ENGINEERING DOCUMENTS - LIBRARY
2625 Hickory St.
Santa Ana, CA 92707
Phone: (714) 540-9870
Jerome H. Lieblich, Pres.

MARQUANDIA SOCIETY FOR STUDIES IN HISTORY AND LITERATURE -
LIBRARY
408 E. Civic Center Dr., No. 203
Santa Ana, CA 92701
Phone: (714) 836-4777
A.S.T. Blackburn, Libn.

ORANGE COUNTY DEPARTMENT OF EDUCATION - LIBRARY
1300 S. Grand Ave., Bldg. B
Box 15029
Santa Ana, CA 92705
Phone: (714) 834-3980
Faith M. Herbert, Lib.Techn.

ORANGE COUNTY ENVIRONMENTAL MANAGEMENT AGENCY -
ADMINISTRATION/PLANNING LIBRARY
811 N. Broadway
Box 4048
Santa Ana, CA 92701
Mary D. Demecour, Libn.

ORANGE COUNTY LAW LIBRARY
515 N. Flower St.
Santa Ana, CA 92703
Phone: (714) 834-3397
Bethany J. Ochal, Dir.

ORANGE COUNTY SHERIFF/CORONER - FORENSIC SCIENCE SERVICES
LIBRARY
550 N. Flower St.
Box 449
Santa Ana, CA 92702
Phone: (714) 834-3073
Mr. J.L. Ragle, Lab.Dir.

RUTAN AND TUCKER - LIBRARY
401 Civic Center Dr., W.
Santa Ana, CA 92702
Phone: (714) 835-2200
Hazel Bader, Libn.

TRINITY UNITED PRESBYTERIAN CHURCH - LIBRARY
13922 Prospect Ave.
Santa Ana, CA 92705
Phone: (714) 544-7850
Gail Williams, Libn.

U.S. MARINE CORPS - EL TORO AIR STATION LIBRARY
Bldg. 280
Santa Ana, CA 92709
Phone: (714) 559-2569
Jeannette A. Kerr, Libn.

WESTERN MEDICAL CENTER - MEDICAL LIBRARY
1001 N. Tustin Ave.
Santa Ana, CA 92705
Phone: (714) 835-3555
Evelyn Simpson, Med.Libn.

AMERICAN BIBLIOGRAPHICAL CENTER - CLIO PRESS - THE INGE BOEHM
LIBRARY
2040 Alameda Padre Serra
Santa Barbara, CA 93103
Phone: (805) 963-4221
Dr. Joyce Duncan Falk, Dir.

BROOKS INSTITUTE OF PHOTOGRAPHY - LIBRARY
2020 Alameda Padre Serra
Santa Barbara, CA 93103
Phone: (805) 969-2291
James B. Maher, Libn.

COMMUNITY ENVIRONMENTAL COUNCIL, INC. - ECOLOGY CENTER
LENDING LIBRARY
924 Anacapa St., Suite B-4
Santa Barbara, CA 93101
Phone: (805) 962-2210
Kathy O'Neil, Ecology Ctr.Coord.

COTTAGE HOSPITAL - DAVID L. REEVES MEDICAL LIBRARY
320 W. Pueblo St.
Santa Barbara, CA 93105
Phone: (805) 966-7393
Mrs. Kevin J. Fay, Libn.

FIRST UNITED METHODIST CHURCH - MEMORIAL LIBRARY
Garden & Anapamu Sts.
Santa Barbara, CA 93101
Homer W. Freeman, Church Libn.

GENERAL RESEARCH CORPORATION - LIBRARY
Box 6770
Santa Barbara, CA 93111
Phone: (805) 964-7724
Kathryn Tammen, Supv., Acq.

INTERNATIONAL ACADEMY AT SANTA BARBARA - LIBRARY
2074 Alameda Padre Serra
Santa Barbara, CA 93103
Phone: (805) 965-5010
Helen K. Rocky, Dir.Lib.Serv.

KAMAN-TEMPO - TECHNICAL INFORMATION CENTER
P.O. Drawer QQ
Santa Barbara, CA 93102
Phone: (805) 965-0551
E.J. Martin, Mgr.

MISSION RESEARCH CORPORATION - TECHNICAL LIBRARY
735 State St.
P.O. Drawer 719
Santa Barbara, CA 93102
Phone: (805) 963-8761
Elaine Messier, Libn.

OUR LADY OF LIGHT LIBRARY
1500 Chapala
Santa Barbara, CA 93101
Phone: (805) 962-9708
Lucille Chinnici, Pres.

ST. FRANCIS HOSPITAL - MEDICAL LIBRARY
601 E. Micheltorena
Santa Barbara, CA 93103
Phone: (805) 962-7661
Marilyn Shearer, Libn.

SANTA BARBARA BOTANIC GARDEN - LIBRARY
1212 Mission Canyon Rd.
Santa Barbara, CA 93105
Phone: (805) 682-4726
Margaret Connors, Libn.

SANTA BARBARA COUNTY LAW LIBRARY
Court House
Santa Barbara, CA 93101
Phone: (805) 966-1611
Susan B. Crowley, Law Libn.

SANTA BARBARA HISTORICAL SOCIETY - GLEDHILL LIBRARY
136 E. De La Guerra St.
Box 578
Santa Barbara, CA 93102
Phone: (805) 966-1601
Dr. Robert Miller, Hd.

SANTA BARBARA MARICULTURE FOUNDATION - PACIFIC LIBRARY AND
INFORMATION CENTER
2416 Selrose Ln.
Santa Barbara, CA 93109

SANTA BARBARA MISSION ARCHIVE-LIBRARY
Old Mission, Upper Laguna St.
Santa Barbara, CA 93105
Phone: (805) 682-4713
Rev. Francis F. Guest, O.F.M., Archv.-Hist.

SANTA BARBARA MUSEUM OF ART - MUSEUM LIBRARY AND ARCHIVES
1130 State St.
Santa Barbara, CA 93101
Phone: (805) 963-4364
Ron Crozier, Libn.

SANTA BARBARA MUSEUM OF NATURAL HISTORY - LIBRARY
2559 Puesta del Sol Rd.
Santa Barbara, CA 93105
Phone: (805) 682-4711
Clifton F. Smith, Libn.

SANTA BARBARA NEWS PRESS - LIBRARY
De la Guerra Plaza
Drawer N-N
Santa Barbara, CA 93102
Phone: (805) 966-3911
Carol Wilson, Libn.

STONEHENGE STUDY GROUP - LIBRARY
2821 De La Vina St.
Santa Barbara, CA 93105
Phone: (805) 687-9350
Donald L. Cyr, Ed.

TRINITY EPISCOPAL CHURCH - LIBRARY
1500 State St.   Phone: (805) 965-7419
Santa Barbara, CA 93101   Edith P. Stickney, Libn.

UNIVERSITY OF CALIFORNIA, SANTA BARBARA - ARTS LIBRARY
                                                Phone: (805) 961-2850
Santa Barbara, CA 93106   William R. Treese, Hd.

UNIVERSITY OF CALIFORNIA, SANTA BARBARA - BLACK STUDIES LIBRARY
   UNIT
                                                Phone: (805) 961-2922
Santa Barbara, CA 93106   Anne Powers, Libn.

UNIVERSITY OF CALIFORNIA, SANTA BARBARA - DEPARTMENT OF
   SPECIAL COLLECTIONS
University Library   Phone: (805) 961-3420
Santa Barbara, CA 93106   Christian Brun, Dept.Hd.

UNIVERSITY OF CALIFORNIA, SANTA BARBARA - LIBRARY - CHICANO
   STUDIES COLLECTION
University Library   Phone: (805) 961-2756
Santa Barbara, CA 93106   Roberto G. Trujillo, Assoc.Libn./Unit Hd.

UNIVERSITY OF CALIFORNIA, SANTA BARBARA - MAP AND IMAGERY
   LABORATORY - LIBRARY
                                                Phone: (805) 961-2779
Santa Barbara, CA 93106   Larry Carver, Dept.Hd.

UNIVERSITY OF CALIFORNIA, SANTA BARBARA - SCIENCES-ENGINEERING
   LIBRARY
                                                Phone: (805) 961-2765
Santa Barbara, CA 93106   Alfred Hodina, Hd.

AMERICAN MICROSYSTEMS, INC. - INFORMATION CENTER
3800 Homestead Rd.   Phone: (408) 246-0330
Santa Clara, CA 95051   Nancy Kay Walton, Info./Rec.Ctr.Mgr.

AVANTEK, INC. - CORPORATE SERVICES LIBRARY
3175 Bowers Ave.   Phone: (408) 727-0700
Santa Clara, CA 95051   Maureen J. McManus, Libn.

FMC CORPORATION - CENTRAL ENGINEERING LABORATORIES - LIBRARY
1185 Coleman Ave.
Box 580   Phone: (408) 289-2529
Santa Clara, CA 95052   Keye L. Luke, Libn.

HEWLETT-PACKARD COMPANY - SANTA CLARA DIVISION LIBRARY
5301 Stevens Creek Blvd.   Phone: (408) 246-4300
Santa Clara, CA 95050   Diana Robba, Lib.Spec.

HYDRO RESEARCH SCIENCE - LIBRARY
3334 Victor Ct.   Phone: (408) 988-1027
Santa Clara, CA 95050   Sharon Tyler, Libn.

INTEL-TECHNICAL INFORMATION CENTER
2625 Walsh Ave. 4-106   Phone: (408) 987-6014
Santa Clara, CA 95051   Marge Boyd, Mgr.

MEMOREX CORPORATION - TECHNICAL INFORMATION CENTER
San Tomas At Central Expy.   Phone: (408) 987-3599
Santa Clara, CA 95052   Monica Ertel, Mgr.

TRITON MUSEUM OF ART - LIBRARY
1505 Warburton Ave.   Phone: (408) 248-4585
Santa Clara, CA 95050   Jo Farb Hernandez, Dir.

UNIVERSITY OF SANTA CLARA - ARCHIVES
Santa Clara, CA 95053   Gerald McKevitt, S.J., Dir.

UNIVERSITY OF SANTA CLARA - EDWIN A. HEAFEY LAW LIBRARY
University of Santa Clara Law School   Phone: (408) 984-4451
Santa Clara, CA 95053   Mary B. Emery, Libn.

DOMINICAN SANTA CRUZ HOSPITAL - MEDICAL LIBRARY
1555 Soquel Dr.   Phone: (408) 476-0220
Santa Cruz, CA 95065   Mrs. Merle Ochs, Med.Libn.

FOREST HISTORY SOCIETY, INC. - LIBRARY AND ARCHIVES
109 Coral St.   Phone: (408) 426-3770
Santa Cruz, CA 95060   Mary E. Johnson, Libn.

SANTA CRUZ COUNTY COMMUNITY RESOURCES AGENCY - PARCEL
   RECORDS AND RESEARCH LIBRARY
701 Ocean St., Rm. 420
Santa Cruz, CA 95060

SANTA CRUZ COUNTY LAW LIBRARY
701 Ocean St., Courts Bldg.   Phone: (408) 425-2211
Santa Cruz, CA 95060   Patricia J. Pfremmer, Law Libn.

UNIVERSITY OF CALIFORNIA, SANTA CRUZ - DEAN E. MC HENRY LIBRARY
                                                Phone: (408) 429-2801
Santa Cruz, CA 95064   Allan J. Dyson, Univ. Libn.

UNIVERSITY OF CALIFORNIA, SANTA CRUZ - MAP COLLECTION
McHenry Library Bldg.   Phone: (408) 429-2364
Santa Cruz, CA 95064   Stanley D. Stevens, Map Libn.

UNIVERSITY OF CALIFORNIA, SANTA CRUZ - REGIONAL HISTORY PROJECT
Dean E. McHenry Library   Phone: (408) 429-2847
Santa Cruz, CA 95064   Randall Jarrell, Dir.

UNIVERSITY OF CALIFORNIA, SANTA CRUZ - SCIENCE LIBRARY
                                                Phone: (408) 429-2050
Santa Cruz, CA 95064   Carolyn Miller, Sci.Libn.

BUSHMAN (Ted) LAW OFFICES - LIBRARY
Bushman Bldg., Box 1261   Phone: (805) 773-4200
Santa Maria, CA 93456   Ted Bushman, Libn.

GEMOLOGICAL INSTITUTE OF AMERICA - RESEARCH LIBRARY
1660 Stewart St.   Phone: (213) 829-2991
Santa Monica, CA 90404   Dona Mary Dirlam, Info./Res.

GENERAL TELEPHONE OF CALIFORNIA - FILM LIBRARY
2020 Santa Monica Blvd.   Phone: (213) 451-6147
Santa Monica, CA 90404   Pegi Matsuda, Film Libn.

MEALS FOR MILLIONS/FREEDOM FROM HUNGER FOUNDATION - LIBRARY
1800 Olympic Blvd.   Phone: (213) 829-5337
Santa Monica, CA 90406   Butzer Larson, Info.Spec.

PACIFIC-SIERRA RESEARCH CORPORATION - LIBRARY
1456 Cloverfield Blvd.   Phone: (213) 828-7461
Santa Monica, CA 90404   Christine L. Lincoln, Res.Libn.

PROSPEROS - LIBRARY
1441 Fourth St.   Phone: (213) 393-0287
Santa Monica, CA 90401

RAND CORPORATION - LIBRARY
1700 Main St.   Phone: (213) 393-0411
Santa Monica, CA 90406   Vivian J. Arterbery, Lib.Dir.

ST. JOHN'S HOSPITAL AND HEALTH CENTER - HOSPITAL LIBRARY †
1328 22nd St.   Phone: (213) 829-8494
Santa Monica, CA 90404   Cathey L. Pinckney, Libn.

SANTA MONICA HOSPITAL MEDICAL CENTER - MEDICAL LIBRARY
1225 15th St.   Phone: (213) 451-1511
Santa Monica, CA 90404   Lenore F. Orfirer, Librarian

SANTA MONICA PUBLIC LIBRARY - CALIFORNIA SPECIAL COLLECTION
1343 Sixth St.   Phone: (213) 451-5751
Santa Monica, CA 90401   Nancy Presley, Hd., Rd.Serv.

SOUTHERN CALIFORNIA INSTITUTE OF ARCHITECTURE - ARCHITECTURE
   AND URBAN PLANNING LIBRARY
1800 Berkeley St.   Phone: (213) 829-3482
Santa Monica, CA 90404   Rose Marie Rabin, Info.Dir.

SYSTEM DEVELOPMENT CORPORATION - LIBRARY
2500 Colorado Ave.   Phone: (213) 829-7511
Santa Monica, CA 90406   Ellen Sol, Supv.Lib.Oper.

GEOGRAPHIC

VIVITAR CORPORATION - TECHNICAL LIBRARY †
1630 Stewart St.
Santa Monica, CA 90406

ANATEC BIOLOGICAL LABORATORIES, INC. - LIBRARY
435 Tesconi Circle, No. 14   Phone: (707) 526-7200
Santa Rosa, CA 95401

COMMUNITY HOSPITAL - MEDICAL LIBRARY
3325 Chanate Rd.   Phone: (707) 544-3340
Santa Rosa, CA 95404   Joan Chilton, Med.Libn.

SONOMA COUNTY LAW LIBRARY
Hall of Justice, Rm. 213-J
600 Administration Dr.   Phone: (707) 527-2668
Santa Rosa, CA 95401   June B. Lewek, Law Libn.

SONOMA COUNTY PLANNING DEPARTMENT - LIBRARY
575 Administration Dr.   Phone: (707) 527-2931
Santa Rosa, CA 95401

BETHANY BIBLE COLLEGE - LIBRARY
800 Bethany Dr.   Phone: (408) 438-3800
Scotts Valley, CA 95066   Arnold McLellan, Hd.Libn.

SAN FERNANDO VALLEY COLLEGE OF LAW - LAW LIBRARY
8353 Sepulveda Blvd.   Phone: (213) 894-5711
Sepulveda, CA 91343   James G. Sherman, Lib.Dir.

U.S. VETERANS ADMINISTRATION (CA-Sepulveda) - BIOMEDICAL
    ENGINEERING & COMPUTING CENTER - LIBRARY *
V.A. Hospital   Phone: (213) 892-4358
Sepulveda, CA 91343   Fred J. Weibell, Chf./BECC

SUNKIST GROWERS, INC. - CORPORATE LIBRARY
14130 Riverside Dr.   Phone: (213) 986-4800
Sherman Oaks, CA 91423   Jill Thomas Platt, Corp.Libn.

GEOSCIENCE, LTD. - LIBRARY
410 S. Cedros Ave.   Phone: (714) 755-9396
Solana Beach, CA 92075   D. Gossett, Libn.

TUOLUMNE COUNTY LAW LIBRARY
Court House
2 S. Green St.   Phone: (209) 533-5675
Sonora, CA 95370   Janet Anderson, Law.Libn.

LEE PHARMACEUTICALS - LIBRARY
1444 Santa Anita Ave.   Phone: (213) 442-3141
South El Monte, CA 91733   Dr. A. Wells, Chf. of Doc.

KAISER-PERMANENTE MEDICAL CENTER - SOUTH SAN FRANCISCO
    HEALTH SCIENCES LIBRARY
1200 El Camino Real   Phone: (415) 876-0408
South San Francisco, CA 94080 Ysabel R. Bertolucci, Health Sci.Libn.

CARNEGIE INSTITUTION OF WASHINGTON - DEPARTMENT OF PLANT
    BIOLOGY - LIBRARY
290 Panama   Phone: (415) 325-1521
Stanford, CA 94305   Dr. Jeanette S. Brown, Dir.

CENTER FOR ADVANCED STUDY IN THE BEHAVIORAL SCIENCES - LIBRARY
202 Junipero Serra Blvd.   Phone: (415) 321-2052
Stanford, CA 94305   Margaret Amara, Libn.

STANFORD ENVIRONMENTAL LAW SOCIETY - LIBRARY
Stanford University Law School   Phone: (415) 497-4421
Stanford, CA 94305   William R. Nee, Vice Pres.

STANFORD UNIVERSITY - ART AND ARCHITECTURE LIBRARY
Nathan Cummings Art Bldg.   Phone: (415) 497-3408
Stanford, CA 94305   Alexander D. Ross, Hd.Libn.

STANFORD UNIVERSITY - BRANNER EARTH SCIENCES LIBRARY
School of Earth Sciences   Phone: (415) 497-2746
Stanford, CA 94305   Charlotte R.M. Derksen, Libn.

STANFORD UNIVERSITY - CENTRAL MAP COLLECTION
Cecil H. Green Library   Phone: (415) 497-1811
Stanford, CA 94305   Karyl Tonge, Map Libn.

STANFORD UNIVERSITY - COMMUNICATION LIBRARY
Redwood Hall
Stanford, CA 94305

STANFORD UNIVERSITY - CUBBERLEY EDUCATION LIBRARY
                                   Phone: (415) 497-2121
Stanford, CA 94305   Kenneth Parker, Libn.

STANFORD UNIVERSITY - DEPARTMENT OF SPECIAL COLLECTIONS
Cecil H. Green Library   Phone: (415) 497-4054
Stanford, CA 94305   Florian J. Shasky, Chf.

STANFORD UNIVERSITY - ENGINEERING LIBRARY
                                   Phone: (415) 497-1513
Stanford, CA 94305   Celine F. Walker, Chf., Sci.Dept.

STANFORD UNIVERSITY - FALCONER BIOLOGY LIBRARY
                                   Phone: (415) 497-1528
Stanford, CA 94305   Michael V. Sullivan, Hd.Libn.

STANFORD UNIVERSITY - FOOD RESEARCH INSTITUTE - LIBRARY
                                   Phone: (415) 497-3943
Stanford, CA 94305   Charles C. Milford, Libn.

STANFORD UNIVERSITY - HOOVER INSTITUTION ON WAR, REVOLUTION
    AND PEACE - LIBRARY
                                   Phone: (415) 497-2058
Stanford, CA 94305   Richard F. Staar, Assoc.Dir.Lib.Oper.

STANFORD UNIVERSITY - INSTITUTE FOR ENERGY STUDIES - ENERGY
    INFORMATION CENTER
Bldg. 500, Rm. 500A   Phone: (415) 497-3237
Stanford, CA 94305   Marian Rees, Assoc.Libn.

STANFORD UNIVERSITY - J. HUGH JACKSON LIBRARY
Graduate School Of Business   Phone: (415) 497-2161
Stanford, CA 94305   Bela Gallo, Dir.

STANFORD UNIVERSITY - LANE MEDICAL LIBRARY
Medical Center   Phone: (415) 497-6831
Stanford, CA 94305   Peter Stangl, Dir.

STANFORD UNIVERSITY - LAW LIBRARY
                                   Phone: (415) 497-2721
Stanford, CA 94305   Professor J. Myron Jacobstein, Law Libn.

STANFORD UNIVERSITY - MATHEMATICAL AND COMPUTER SCIENCES
    LIBRARY
Bldg. 380, Sloan Mathematics Center Phone: (415) 497-4672
Stanford, CA 94305   Harry P. Llull, Hd.Libn./Biblog.

STANFORD UNIVERSITY - MUSIC LIBRARY
The Knoll   Phone: (415) 497-2463
Stanford, CA 94305   Jerry Persons, Hd.Libn.

STANFORD UNIVERSITY - PHYSICS LIBRARY
                                   Phone: (415) 497-4342
Stanford, CA 94305   Virginia M. Kosanovic, Hd.Libn.

STANFORD UNIVERSITY - SWAIN LIBRARY OF CHEMISTRY AND CHEMICAL
    ENGINEERING
                                   Phone: (415) 497-9237
Stanford, CA 94305   Margaret Green Ryken, Hd.Libn.

STANFORD UNIVERSITY - TANNER MEMORIAL PHILOSOPHY LIBRARY
                                   Phone: (415) 497-1539
Stanford, CA 94305   Richard Lee, Libn.

STANFORD UNIVERSITY - UNIVERSITY ARCHIVES
Cecil H. Green Library   Phone: (415) 497-4055
Stanford, CA 94305   Roxanne-Louise Nilan, Univ.Archv.

PIONEER MUSEUM AND HAGGIN GALLERIES - ALMEDA MAY CASTLE
    PETZINGER LIBRARY
1201 N. Pershing   Phone: (209) 462-4116
Stockton, CA 95203   Raymond W. Hillman, Hist.Cur.

SAN JOAQUIN COUNTY LAW LIBRARY
County Court House, Rm. 300   Phone: (209) 944-2207
Stockton, CA 95202   Gertrudes J. Ladion, Law Libn.

SAN JOAQUIN LOCAL HEALTH DISTRICT - LIBRARY
1601 E. Hazelton Ave.
Box 2009   Phone: (209) 466-6781
Stockton, CA 95201   Patricia Woods, Health Educator

STOCKTON NEWSPAPERS INC. - STOCKTON RECORD LIBRARY
530 Market St.   Phone: (209) 943-6397
Stockton, CA 95201   Dorothy M. Frankhouse, Libn.

STOCKTON STATE HOSPITAL - PROFESSIONAL LIBRARY
510 El Magnolia   Phone: (209) 948-7181
Stockton, CA 95202   Walter Greening, Sr.Libn.

UNITED METHODIST CHURCH - NORTHERN CALIFORNIA-NEVADA
    CONFERENCE - J.A.B. FRY RESEARCH LIBRARY
University of the Pacific   Phone: (209) 946-2269
Stockton, CA 95211   Arthur Swann, Dir. of Archv.

UNIVERSITY OF THE PACIFIC - SCIENCE LIBRARY
Pharmacy Bldg.   Phone: (209) 946-2568
Stockton, CA 95211   Arthur W. Swann, Sci.Libn.

UNIVERSITY OF THE PACIFIC - STUART LIBRARY OF WESTERN
    AMERICANA
                                              Phone: (209) 946-2405
Stockton, CA 95211   Kathryn Kemp, Dir.

CALIFORNIA RAILWAY MUSEUM - LIBRARY
Star Rte. 283, Box 150   Phone: (415) 534-0071
Suisun City, CA 94585   Vernon J. Sappers, Cur.

ADVANCED MICRO DEVICES, INC. - TECHNICAL LIBRARY
901 Thompson Pl., m/s 1   Phone: (408) 749-2260
Sunnyvale, CA 94086   Pamela McCoy

AMDAHL CORPORATION - CORPORATE LIBRARY
1250 E. Arques Ave.   Phone: (408) 746-6376
Sunnyvale, CA 94086   Lourdes (Ludy) Dorilag, Mgr.

CONTROL DATA CORPORATION - LIBRARY
215 Moffett Park Dr.   Phone: (408) 744-5798
Sunnyvale, CA 94086   Jaxon K. Matthews, Libn.

ESL, INC./SUBSIDIARY OF TRW - RESEARCH LIBRARY
495 Java Dr.
Box 510   Phone: (408) 738-2888
Sunnyvale, CA 94086   Verna Van Velzer, Chf.Libn.

FRIENDS OF THE WESTERN PHILATELIC LIBRARY
Box 2219   Phone: (408) 245-9171
Sunnyvale, CA 94087   J.F. Hutton, Pres.

GENERAL ELECTRIC COMPANY - ADVANCED REACTOR SYSTEMS DEPT. -
    LIBRARY
310 DeGuigne Drive
Box 5020   Phone: (408) 738-7177
Sunnyvale, CA 94086   Dorothy Hutson, Mgr., Tech.Serv.

ITEK CORPORATION - APPLIED TECHNOLOGY DIVISION - TECHNICAL
    LIBRARY
645 Almanor Ave.   Phone: (408) 732-2710
Sunnyvale, CA 94086   Doron A. Dula, Tech.Libn.

LITTON MELLONICS - PROGRAM LIBRARY
1001 W. Maude Ave.   Phone: (408) 245-0795
Sunnyvale, CA 95070   Cynthia Rimbach, Software Libn.

SIGNETICS CORPORATION - LIBRARY
811 E. Arques Ave.   Phone: (408) 739-7700
Sunnyvale, CA 94086   Stephanie Jang, Libn.

SINGER COMPANY - LINK DIVISION - TECHNICAL LIBRARY
1077 E. Arques Ave.   Phone: (408) 732-3800
Sunnyvale, CA 94086   Carol V. Schwarz, Tech.Libn.

SUNNYVALE PATENT INFORMATION CLEARINGHOUSE
1500 Partridge Ave., Bldg. 7   Phone: (408) 738-5580
Sunnyvale, CA 94087   Mary-Jo DiMuccio, Prog.Mgr.

UNITED TECHNOLOGIES CORPORATION - CHEMICAL SYSTEMS DIVISION -
    LIBRARY
1050 E. Arques Ave.   Phone: (408) 739-4880
Sunnyvale, CA 94086   Harold E. Wilcox, Supv.

CALIFORNIA LUTHERAN COLLEGE - LIBRARY
                                              Phone: (805) 492-2411
Thousand Oaks, CA 91360   Aina Abrahamson, Lib.Dir.

ROCKWELL INTERNATIONAL - SCIENCE CENTER LIBRARY
1049 Camino Dos Rios
Box 1085   Phone: (805) 498-4545
Thousand Oaks, CA 91360   Helen M. Coogan, Supv., Lib.

H.M.S. BOUNTY SOCIETY, INTERNATIONAL - RESEARCH LIBRARY AND
    DEPOSITORY
174 Trinidad Dr.   Phone: (415) 435-9749
Tiburon, CA 94920   A. Munro Christian, Dir.

U.S. NATL. MARINE FISHERIES SERVICE - TIBURON LABORATORY LIBRARY
3150 Paradise Dr.   Phone: (415) 435-3149
Tiburon, CA 94920   Maureen Woods, Libn.

GARRETT CORPORATION - AIRESEARCH MANUFACTURING COMPANY -
    TECHNICAL LIBRARY
2525 W. 190th St.   Phone: (213) 323-9500
Torrance, CA 90509   Jana Jones, Sr.Libn.

LOS ANGELES COUNTY HARBOR UCLA MEDICAL CENTER - MEDICAL
    LIBRARY
1000 W. Carson St.   Phone: (213) 533-2372
Torrance, CA 90509   Eleanor Goodchild, Dir.Lib.Serv.

MAGNAVOX GOVERNMENT & INDUSTRIAL ELECTRONICS COMPANY -
    ADVANCED PRODUCTS DIVISION - LIBRARY †
2829 Maricopa Ave.   Phone: (213) 328-0770
Torrance, CA 90503   Janet L. Gutheim

TORRANCE MEMORIAL HOSPITAL MEDICAL CENTER - HEALTH SCIENCES
    LIBRARY
3330 W. Lomita Blvd.   Phone: (213) 325-9110
Torrance, CA 90509   Anita N. Klecker, Dir. of Lib.Serv.

U.S. AIR FORCE BASE - TRAVIS BASE LIBRARY
Mitchell Memorial Library
60 ABGp/SSL   Phone: (707) 438-5254
Travis AFB, CA 94535   Nina Jacobs, Libn.

U.S. AIR FORCE HOSPITAL - DAVID GRANT MEDICAL CENTER - LIBRARY
                                              Phone: (707) 438-3257
Travis AFB, CA 94535   V. Kay Hafner, Med.Libn.

GEORGE (Henry) SCHOOL OF LOS ANGELES - RESEARCH LIBRARY
10242 Mahogany Trail
Box 655   Phone: (213) 352-4141
Tujunga, CA 91042   Mrs. G.E. Pollard, Libn.

SEQUOIA GENEALOGICAL SOCIETY - INEZ L. HYDE MEMORIAL COLLECTION
Tulare Public Library
113 North F. St.
Tulare, CA 93274   Louise Longan, Libn.

U.S. NATL. PARK SERVICE - LAVA BEDS NATL. MONUMENT - LIBRARY
                                              Phone: (916) 667-2601
Tulelake, CA 96134   Robert A. Patton, Interp.Spec.

EMANUEL MEDICAL CENTER - MEDICAL LIBRARY
825 Delbon Ave.   Phone: (209) 634-9151
Turlock, CA 95380   Donna Cardoza, Lib.Ck.

MEDIC ALERT FOUNDATION INTERNATIONAL - CENTRAL REFERENCE FILE
    OF MEMBERSHIP †
1000 N. Palm
Box 1009   Phone: (209) 632-2371
Turlock, CA 95380   Alfred A. Hodder, Pres.

HELD-POAGE MEMORIAL HOME & RESEARCH LIBRARY
603 W. Perkins St.   Phone: (707) 462-6969
Ukiah, CA 95482   Mrs. Lila J. Lee, Libn.

MENDOCINO COUNTY LAW LIBRARY
Courthouse, Rm. 207   Phone: (707) 468-4481
Ukiah, CA 95482   Ginny Holmen, Law Libn.

UNIVERSAL CITY STUDIOS - RESEARCH DEPARTMENT LIBRARY
100 Universal City Plaza   Phone: (213) 985-4321
Universal City, CA 91608   Robert A. Lee, Hd., Res.Dept.

FIRST PRESBYTERIAN CHURCH - LIBRARY
869 N. Euclid Ave.   Phone: (714) 982-8811
Upland, CA 91786   Karin E. Martin, Libn.

SAN ANTONIO COMMUNITY HOSPITAL - WEBER MEMORIAL LIBRARY
999 San Bernardino Rd.   Phone: (714) 985-2811
Upland, CA 91786   Francena Johnston, Med.Libn.

CALIFORNIA STATE MEDICAL FACILITY - STAFF LIBRARY
1600 California Dr.   Phone: (707) 448-6841
Vacaville, CA 95696   Roberta Carson, Med.Rec.Libn.

CALIFORNIA INSTITUTE OF THE ARTS - LIBRARY
24700 McBean Pkwy.   Phone: (805) 255-1050
Valencia, CA 91355   Elizabeth Armstrong, Lib.Dir.

CALIFORNIA MARITIME ACADEMY LIBRARY †
Box 1392   Phone: (707) 644-5601
Vallejo, CA 94590   Paul W. O'Bannon, Sr.Libn.

U.S. NAVY - NAVAL SHIPYARD (Mare Island) - TECHNICAL LIBRARY
Code 202.3, Stop T-4   Phone: (707) 646-4306
Vallejo, CA 94592   Barbara Drellich, Hd., Tech.Info.Br.

VALLEJO NAVAL AND HISTORIC MUSEUM - LIBRARY
734 Marin St.   Phone: (707) 643-0022
Vallejo, CA 94590   Dorothy E. Marsden, Libn.

BIO-SCIENCE LABORATORIES - LIBRARY
7600 Tyrone Ave.   Phone: (213) 989-2520
Van Nuys, CA 91405   Dr. R. Beardslee, Asst.Dir.Res.

CARNATION RESEARCH LABORATORIES - LIBRARY
8015 Van Nuys Blvd.   Phone: (213) 787-7820
Van Nuys, CA 91412   Kathryn A. Stewart, Libn.

ITT CORPORATION - GILFILLAN ENGINEERING LIBRARY †
7821 Orion Ave.
Box 7713   Phone: (213) 988-2600
Van Nuys, CA 91409   Dawn N. Villere, Sr.Tech.Libn.

LITTON INDUSTRIES - DATA SYSTEMS DIVISION - ENGINEERING LIBRARY
8000 Woodley Ave.   Phone: (213) 781-8211
Van Nuys, CA 91409   Joe Ann Clifton, Mgr., Tech.Libs.

**LOS ANGELES COUNTY/OLIVE VIEW MEDICAL CENTER - HEALTH
    SCIENCES LIBRARY**
7533 Van Nuys Blvd.
Rm. 303, South Tower   Phone: (213) 997-1800
Van Nuys, CA 91405   Miriam Kafka, Act.Libn.

NATIONAL INVESTIGATIONS COMMITTEE ON UFOS - NEW AGE CENTER
7970 Woodman Ave., No 207   Phone: (213) 781-7704
Van Nuys, CA 91402   Denise Fay, Mgr.

**PRUDENTIAL INSURANCE COMPANY OF AMERICA - WESTERN HOME
    OFFICE - BUSINESS LIBRARY**
Box 9220   Phone: (213) 857-4682
Van Nuys, CA 91409   Hilda Holmes, Libn.

**VALLEY PRESBYTERIAN HOSPITAL - LIBRARY FOR MEDICAL AND HEALTH
    SCIENCES**
15107 Vanowen St.   Phone: (216) 782-6600
Van Nuys, CA 91405   Ann Miller Ryan, Med.Libn.

**U.S. AIR FORCE - WESTERN SPACE AND MISSILE CENTER - WSMC
    TECHNICAL LIBRARY**
Space and Missile Test Center   Phone: (805) 866-9745
Vandenberg AFB, CA 93437   Jessica Rich, Chf.Libn.

BEYOND BAROQUE FOUNDATION - LIBRARY
Old Venice City Hall
681 Venice Blvd.   Phone: (213) 822-3006
Venice, CA 90291   Jocelyn Fisher, Lib.Dir.

PACIFIC BIO-MARINE LABORATORIES, INC. - LIBRARY
Box 536   Phone: (213) 822-5757
Venice, CA 90291   Michael J. Fishman, Libn.

**CHURCH OF JESUS CHRIST OF LATTER-DAY SAINTS - VENTURA BRANCH
    GENEALOGICAL LIBRARY**
3501 Loma Vista Rd.
Box 3517   Phone: (805) 643-5607
Ventura, CA 93003   C. Perry Smith, Libn.

VENTURA COUNTY HISTORICAL SOCIETY - LIBRARY & ARCHIVES
100 E. Main St.   Phone: (805) 653-0323
Ventura, CA 93001   George M. Anderjack, Exec.Dir.

VENTURA COUNTY LAW LIBRARY
800 S. Victoria Ave.   Phone: (805) 654-2695
Ventura, CA 93009   Naydean L. Baker, Law Libn.

**VENTURA COUNTY RESOURCE MANAGEMENT AGENCY - TECHNICAL
    LIBRARY**
800 S. Victoria Ave.   Phone: (805) 654-2480
Ventura, CA 93009   Evelyn Adams, Tech.Libn.

VENTURA COUNTY STAR-FREE PRESS - LIBRARY
Box 6711   Phone: (805) 659-4111
Ventura, CA 93006   Sara J. Riley, Libn.

**TULARE COUNTY FREE LIBRARY - CALIFORNIA HISTORICAL RESEARCH
    COLLECTION**
200 W. Oak St.   Phone: (209) 733-8440
Visalia, CA 93277   Mary Anne Terstegge, Hist.Libn.

TULARE COUNTY LAW LIBRARY
County Civic Center, Rm. 1   Phone: (209) 733-6395
Visalia, CA 93291   Mary Anthony, Lib.Asst.II

SAN DIEGO COUNTY LAW LIBRARY - VISTA BRANCH
325 S. Melrose   Phone: (714) 758-6247
Vista, CA 92083   O. James Werner, Libn.

BROWN & CALDWELL - LIBRARY
1501 N. Broadway   Phone: (415) 937-9010
Walnut Creek, CA 94596   Bruce Hubbard, Libn.

**DOW CHEMICAL U.S.A. - WESTERN DIVISION RESEARCH LABORATORIES -
    LIBRARY**
2800 Mitchell Dr.   Phone: (415) 944-2064
Walnut Creek, CA 94598   Mary Lao, Libn.

JOHN MUIR MEMORIAL HOSPITAL - HEALTH SCIENCES LIBRARY
1601 Ygnacio Valley Rd.   Phone: (415) 939-3000
Walnut Creek, CA 94598   Helen M. Reyes, Libn.

WALNUT CREEK - CONTRA COSTA TIMES - LIBRARY
2640 Shadelands Dr.
Box 5088   Phone: (415) 935-2525
Walnut Creek, CA 94596   Ellen D. Wood, Libn.

**WALNUT CREEK HISTORICAL SOCIETY - SHADELANDS RANCH HISTORICAL
    MUSEUM - HISTORY ROOM**
2660 Ygnacio Valley Rd.   Phone: (415) 935-7871
Walnut Creek, CA 94598   Beverly C. Clemson, Musm.Dir.

TRINITY COUNTY LAW LIBRARY
Box R   Phone: (916) 623-2451
Weaverville, CA 96093   Carol Rose, Sec.

HONEYWELL, INC. - DEFENSE ELECTRONICS DIVISION, TRAINING AND CONTROL SYSTEMS OPERATION - TECHNICAL LIBRARY
1200 E. San Bernardino Rd.   Phone: (213) 331-0011
West Covina, CA 91790   Kathleen Seekatz, Libn,

NATIONAL ASSOCIATION OF PHYSICAL THERAPISTS - LIBRARY
Box 367
West Covina, CA 91793

BUNKER-RAMO CORPORATION - MAIN LIBRARY
31717 La Tienda Dr.   Phone: (213) 889-2211
Westlake, CA 91359   Mrs. Jan Krcmar, Chf.Libn.

ENVIRONMENTAL RESEARCH & TECHNOLOGY, INC. - WESTERN REGIONAL OFFICE - LIBRARY
2625 Townsgate Rd., Suite 360   Phone: (213) 889-5313
Westlake Village, CA 91361   Marcia Henry, Libn.

WHITTIER COLLEGE - DEPARTMENT OF GEOLOGY - FAIRCHILD AERIAL PHOTOGRAPH COLLECTION
                                            Phone: (213) 693-0771
Whittier, CA 90608   Dallas D. Rhodes, Cur.

BLUE CROSS OF SOUTHERN CALIFORNIA - LEGAL AND BUSINESS LIBRARY
21555 Oxnard St.   Phone: (213) 703-3160
Woodland Hills, CA 91367   Frances Baur Linke, Hd.Libn.

LITTON INDUSTRIES - GUIDANCE AND CONTROL SYSTEMS - LIBRARY
5500 Canago Ave.   Phone: (213) 887-3867
Woodland Hills, CA 91364   Joe Ann Clifton, Mgr., Info.Serv.

LOS ANGELES UNIFIED SCHOOL DISTRICTS - WEST VALLEY OCCUPATIONAL CENTER - LIBRARY
6200 Winnetka Ave.   Phone: (213) 346-3540
Woodland Hills, CA 91364

U.S. NATL. PARK SERVICE - YOSEMITE NATL. PARK - RESEARCH LIBRARY
Box 577   Phone: (209) 372-4461
Yosemite National Park, CA 95389   Mary Vocelka, Lib.Techn.

VETERANS HOME OF CALIFORNIA - LINCOLN MEMORIAL LIBRARY
                                            Phone: (707) 944-4279
Yountville, CA 94599   June A. Clunie, Libn.

SISKIYOU COUNTY LAW LIBRARY †
311 Fourth St., Courthouse   Phone: (916) 842-3531
Yreka, CA 96097   Patricia Howard, Libn.

SISKIYOU COUNTY MUSEUM - LIBRARY
910 S. Main St.   Phone: (916) 842-3836
Yreka, CA 96097   Eleanor Brown, Musm.Cur.

SUTTER COUNTY LAW LIBRARY
Court House   Phone: (916) 673-6544
Yuba City, CA 95991   Lillian R. Boss, Law Libn.

COLORADO

U.S.D.A. - AGRICULTURAL RESEARCH SERVICE - CENTRAL GREAT PLAINS RESEARCH STATION - LIBRARY
Box K   Phone: (303) 345-2259
Akron, CO 80720   Dr. D.E. Smika, Location Leader

ADAMS STATE COLLEGE - LIBRARY
                                            Phone: (303) 589-7781
Alamosa, CO 81102   Nellie N. Hasfjord, Dir.

ASPEN HISTORICAL SOCIETY - LIBRARY
620 W. Bleeker   Phone: (303) 925-3721
Aspen, CO 81611

ASPEN INSTITUTE FOR HUMANISTIC STUDIES - DAVID MAYER LIBRARY
1000 N. 3rd St.   Phone: (303) 925-7010
Aspen, CO 81611   Florence M. Kirwin, Libn.

ROARING FORK ENERGY CENTER - LIBRARY
Wheeler Opera House
Box 9950   Phone: (303) 925-8885
Aspen, CO 81612   Pip Klein, Coord.

AURORA PUBLIC SCHOOLS - PROFESSIONAL LIBRARY
Peoria Center, 875 Peoria St.   Phone: (303) 344-8060
Aurora, CO 80011   Bill Murray, Dir.

LUTHERAN CHURCH - MISSOURI SYNOD - COLORADO DISTRICT ARCHIVES
1591 Fulton St.
Box 488   Phone: (303) 364-9148
Aurora, CO 80040   Lyle Schaefer, District Archv.

NATIONAL WRITERS CLUB - LIBRARY
1450 S. Havana, Suite 620   Phone: (303) 751-7844
Aurora, CO 80012   Donald E. Bower, Dir.

U.S. ARMY HOSPITALS - FITZSIMONS ARMY MEDICAL CENTER - MEDICAL-TECHNICAL LIBRARY
Peoria & Colfax Sts.   Phone: (303) 341-8918
Aurora, CO 80045   Yvonne M. Rhodes, Adm.Libn.

GEM VILLAGE MUSEUM - GREEN MEMORIAL LIBRARY
39671 Highway 160   Phone: (303) 884-2811
Bayfield, CO 81122   Elizabeth X. Gilbert, Sec.-Tres.

BALL AEROSPACE SYSTEMS DIVISION - TECHNICAL LIBRARY
Boulder Industrial Park
Box 1062   Phone: (303) 441-4436
Boulder, CO 80306   Judy Dayhoff, Tech.Libn.

BOULDER HISTORICAL SOCIETY - PIONEER MUSEUM - LIBRARY
1655 Broadway   Phone: (303) 449-3464
Boulder, CO 80302   Leanne Sander, Dir.

BOULDER PUBLIC LIBRARY - MUNICIPAL GOVERNMENT REFERENCE CENTER
P.O. Drawer H, 1000 Canyon Blvd.   Phone: (303) 441-3100
Boulder, CO 80306   Virginia Braddock, Head, MGRC

BOULDER VALLEY MEDICAL LIBRARY
Boulder Community Hospital
1100 Balsam Ave.   Phone: (303) 442-8190
Boulder, CO 80302   Carol M. Boyer, Med.Libn.

BOULDER VALLEY PUBLIC SCHOOLS, REGION 2 - PROFESSIONAL LIBRARY
6500 E. Arapahoe Ave.   Phone: (303) 447-1010
Boulder, CO 80302   Carol Newman, Libn.

CAUSE - LIBRARY
737 29th St.   Phone: (303) 449-4430
Boulder, CO 80303   Charles R. Thomas, Exec.Dir.

ERIC CLEARINGHOUSE FOR SOCIAL STUDIES/SOCIAL SCIENCE EDUCATION - RESOURCE & DEMONSTRATION CENTER
Social Science Education Consortium
855 Broadway   Phone: (303) 492-8434
Boulder, CO 80302   Regina McCormick, Staff Assoc.

IBM CORPORATION - BOULDER LIBRARY
Dept. 419, Box 1900   Phone: (303) 447-5064
Boulder, CO 80302   Janet Hughes, Lib.Mgr.

NATIONAL CENTER FOR ATMOSPHERIC RESEARCH - HIGH ALTITUDE OBSERVATORY LIBRARY
Box 3000   Phone: (303) 494-5151
Boulder, CO 80307   Kathryn Strand, Libn.

NATIONAL CENTER FOR ATMOSPHERIC RESEARCH - MESA LIBRARY
Box 3000   Phone: (303) 494-5151
Boulder, CO 80307   Charles B. Wenger, Chf.Libn.

U.S. NATL. OCEANIC & ATMOSPHERIC ADMINISTRATION - ENVIRONMENTAL RESEARCH LABORATORIES - LIBRARY
325 Broadway   Phone: (303) 497-3271
Boulder, CO 80303   Joan Maier McKean, Chf., Lib.Serv.

GEOGRAPHIC

UNIVERSITY OF COLORADO, BOULDER - ART AND ARCHITECTURE LIBRARY
Phone: (303) 492-7955
Boulder, CO 80309   Joan McConkey, Res. & Plan.Libn.

UNIVERSITY OF COLORADO, BOULDER - AUDIOVISUAL/MICROFORMS
DEPARTMENT
Norlin Library, Rm. 136   Phone: (303) 492-6930
Boulder, CO 80302   Sharon Gause, Libn.

UNIVERSITY OF COLORADO, BOULDER - BUREAU OF ECONOMIC RESEARCH
LIBRARY
Economics Bldg. 208
Box 257   Phone: (303) 492-7413
Boulder, CO 80309   Dr. Bernard Udis

UNIVERSITY OF COLORADO, BOULDER - BUREAU OF GOVERNMENTAL
RESEARCH & SERVICE LIBRARY
125 Ketchum Bldg.
Box 330   Phone: (303) 492-8586
Boulder, CO 80309   R.D. Sloan, Jr., Dir./Govt.Serv.

UNIVERSITY OF COLORADO, BOULDER - BUSINESS RESEARCH DIVISION -
BUSINESS & ECONOMIC COLLECTION
Phone: (303) 492-8227
Boulder, CO 80309   C.R. Goeldner, Dir.

UNIVERSITY OF COLORADO, BOULDER - BUSINESS RESEARCH DIVISION -
TRAVEL REFERENCE CENTER
Phone: (303) 492-8227
Boulder, CO 80309   C.R. Goeldner, Dir.

UNIVERSITY OF COLORADO, BOULDER - EARTH SCIENCES LIBRARY
Phone: (303) 492-6133
Boulder, CO 80309   Anita Cochran, Lib.Techn.

UNIVERSITY OF COLORADO, BOULDER - EDUCATIONAL MEDIA CENTER
Stadium Bldg., Rm. 361   Phone: (303) 492-7341
Boulder, CO 80309   Dr. Elwood E. Miller, Dir.

UNIVERSITY OF COLORADO, BOULDER - EDUCATIONAL MEDIA CENTER -
NATIONAL CENTER FOR AUDIO TAPES
Stadium Bldg.   Phone: (303) 492-7341
Boulder, CO 80302

UNIVERSITY OF COLORADO, BOULDER - ENGINEERING LIBRARY
Phone: (303) 492-7120
Boulder, CO 80309   Jean D. Messimer, Libn.

UNIVERSITY OF COLORADO, BOULDER - GOVERNMENT PUBLICATIONS
DIVISION
Norlin Library   Phone: (303) 492-8834
Boulder, CO 80309   Catharine J. Reynolds, Hd., Govt.Pubn.

UNIVERSITY OF COLORADO, BOULDER - INSTITUTE OF ARCTIC & ALPINE
RESEARCH - LIBRARY
PSRB No. 1   Phone: (303) 492-5365
Boulder, CO 80309

UNIVERSITY OF COLORADO, BOULDER - INSTITUTE OF BEHAVIORAL
SCIENCE - IBS RESEARCH LIBRARY
IBS Bldg. 1   Phone: (303) 492-8340
Boulder, CO 80309   Diana Oldsen, Lib.Techn.

UNIVERSITY OF COLORADO, BOULDER - JOINT INSTITUTE FOR
LABORATORY ASTROPHYSICS - INFO. ANALYSIS CENTER
JILA   Phone: (303) 492-7801
Boulder, CO 80309   J.W. Gallagher, Act.Dir.

UNIVERSITY OF COLORADO, BOULDER - LAW LIBRARY
Fleming Law Bldg.   Phone: (303) 492-7534
Boulder, CO 80309   Oscar Miller, Law Libn.

UNIVERSITY OF COLORADO, BOULDER - MAP ROOM
Norlin Library   Phone: (303) 492-7578
Boulder, CO 80309

UNIVERSITY OF COLORADO, BOULDER - MATHEMATICS & PHYSICS
LIBRARY
Duane Physical Laboratories G140   Phone: (303) 492-8231
Boulder, CO 80309   Allen Wynne, Dept.Hd.

UNIVERSITY OF COLORADO, BOULDER - MUSIC LIBRARY
N-290 Warner Imig Music Bldg.   Phone: (303) 492-8093
Boulder, CO 80309   Arne Arneson, Music Libn.

UNIVERSITY OF COLORADO, BOULDER - SCHOOL OF LAW - ROCKY
MOUNTAIN MINERAL LAW FOUNDATION - RESEARCH LIBRARY
Fleming Law Bldg.
Box 405   Phone: (303) 449-0943
Boulder, CO 80309   Joan A. Reid, Legal Ed.

UNIVERSITY OF COLORADO, BOULDER - SCIENCE LIBRARY
Norlin Library   Phone: (303) 492-5136
Boulder, CO 80302   David Fagerstrom, Libn.

UNIVERSITY OF COLORADO, BOULDER - SPECIAL COLLECTIONS
DEPARTMENT
Norlin Library   Phone: (303) 492-6144
Boulder, CO 80309   Ellsworth Mason, Hd.

UNIVERSITY OF COLORADO, BOULDER - THERAPEUTIC RECREATION
INFORMATION CENTER (TRIC) *
Dept. of Physical Educ. & Recreation
Box 354
Boulder, CO 80309   Fred W. Martin, Dir.

UNIVERSITY OF COLORADO, BOULDER - WESTERN HISTORICAL
COLLECTION & UNIVERSITY ARCHIVES
Norlin Library   Phone: (303) 492-7242
Boulder, CO 80309   Dr. John A. Brennan, Cur.

UNIVERSITY OF COLORADO, BOULDER - WILLIAM M. WHITE BUSINESS
LIBRARY
Business Bldg.   Phone: (303) 492-8367
Boulder, CO 80309   Tracey Miller, Bus.Libn.

VOLUNTEER/THE NATIONAL CENTER FOR CITIZEN INVOLVEMENT -
LIBRARY
Box 4179   Phone: (303) 447-0492
Boulder, CO 80306   Debbie Boswell, Lib.Coord.

WESTERN INTERSTATE COMMISSION FOR HIGHER EDUCATION - LIBRARY
Drawer P   Phone: (303) 497-0284
Boulder, CO 80302   Karon M. Kelly, Libn.

WORLD DATA CENTER A - GLACIOLOGY
CIRES, Campus Box 449
University Of Colorado   Phone: (303) 492-5171
Boulder CO 80309   Roger G. Barry, Dir.

WORLD DATA CENTER A - SOLAR-TERRESTRIAL PHYSICS
Natl. Oceanic and Atmospheric Adm.
D63   Phone: (303) 497-6323
Boulder, CO 80303   J.H. Allen, Act.Dir.

DENVER THEOLOGICAL SEMINARY/BIBLE INSTITUTE - SAMUEL JAMES
BRADFORD MEMORIAL LIBRARY
1200 Miramonte St.
Broomfield, CO 80020   June Delnay, Libn.

ST. THOMAS MORE HOSPITAL - MEDICAL LIBRARY
1019 Sheridan St.   Phone: (303) 275-3381
Canon City, CO 81212   Mrs. James G. Bruner, Libn.

AMAX, INC. - CLIMAX MOLYBDENUM COMPANY - TECHNICAL LIBRARY
Phone: (303) 486-2150
Climax, CO 80429   Carol Dice, Libn.

AMERICAN NUMISMATIC ASSOCIATION - LIBRARY
818 N. Cascade   Phone: (303) 473-9142
Colorado Springs, CO 80903   Nancy Green, Libn.

CHEYENNE MOUNTAIN ZOOLOGICAL PARK - LIBRARY
Cheyenne Mountain Hwy.   Phone: (303) 633-0917
Colorado Springs, CO 80906   Bill Aragon, Educ.Coord.

COLORADO COLLEGE - CHARLES LEAMING TUTT LIBRARY
Phone: (303) 473-2233
Colorado Springs, CO 80903   George V. Fagan, Hd.Libn.

COLORADO SCHOOL FOR THE DEAF AND THE BLIND - MEDIA CENTER
Kiowa at Institute   Phone: (303) 636-5186
Colorado Springs, CO 80903   Janet L. Fleharty, Media Spec.

COLORADO SPRINGS FINE ARTS CENTER - REFERENCE LIBRARY AND
TAYLOR MUSEUM LIBRARY
30 W. Dale St.   Phone: (303) 634-5581
Colorado Springs, CO 80903   Roderick Dew, Libn.

COLORADO SPRINGS PUBLIC SCHOOLS - DISTRICT NO. 11 - TEACHERS'
PROFESSIONAL LIBRARY
1036 N. Franklin St.   Phone: (303) 635-6275
Colorado Springs, CO 80903   Sandy Patton, Libn.

EL PASO COUNTY LAW LIBRARY
104 Judicial Bldg.
20 E. Vermijo   Phone: (303) 471-5419
Colorado Springs, CO 80903   Margaret B. Walker, Libn.

FIRST PRESBYTERIAN CHURCH - LIBRARY
219 E. Bijou   Phone: (303) 634-4301
Colorado Springs, CO 80903   Mrs. John C. Gardner, Libn.

HEWLETT-PACKARD COMPANY - COLORADO SPRINGS DIVISION -
ENGINEERING RESOURCE CENTER
1900 Garden Of The Gods Rd.
Box 2197   Phone: (303) 598-1900
Colorado Springs, CO 80907   Jacquelyn Nichols, Libn.

KAMAN SCIENCES CORPORATION - LIBRARY
1500 Garden of the Gods Rd.
Box 7463   Phone: (303) 599-1777
Colorado Springs, CO 80933   Barbara A. Kinslow, Libn.

MEMORIAL HOSPITAL AND BETH-EL SCHOOL OF NURSING - MEDICAL-
NURSING LIBRARY
1400 E. Boulder   Phone: (303) 475-5182
Colorado Springs, CO 80901   Frances Meese, Libn.

NAZARENE BIBLE COLLEGE - LIBRARY
Box 15749   Phone: (303) 596-5110
Colorado Springs, CO 80935   Roger M. Williams, Hd.Libn./Archv.

PENROSE HOSPITAL - WEBB MEMORIAL LIBRARY
2215 N. Cascade Ave.   Phone: (303) 630-5000
Colorado Springs, CO 80907   Sister Dolores, S.C., Asst.Libn.

PIKES PEAK LIBRARY DISTRICT - LOCAL HISTORY COLLECTION
20 N. Cascade
Box 1579   Phone: (303) 473-2080
Colorado Springs, CO 80901   Nancy E. Loe, Hd.Libn.

PIONEERS' MUSEUM - LIBRARY AND ARCHIVES
215 S. Tejon St.   Phone: (303) 471-6650
Colorado Springs, CO 80903   Rosemary Hetzler, Hist.-Libn.

ST. FRANCIS HOSPITAL - DOCTORS' LIBRARY
East Pikes Peak Ave. & Prospect   Phone: (303) 636-8800
Colorado Springs, CO 80903   Sr. Mary Louis Wenzl, Lib.Ck.

SHEPARD'S/MC GRAW-HILL - LIBRARY
420 N. Cascade Ave.
Box 1235   Phone: (303) 475-7230
Colorado Springs, CO 80901   Gregory P. Harris, Libn.

WESTERN MUSEUM OF MINING & INDUSTRY - LIBRARY
1025 Northgate Rd.   Phone: (303) 495-2182
Colorado Springs, CO 80908   Claudia A. Spicer, Cur.

AMERICAN INSTITUTE OF ISLAMIC STUDIES - MUSLIM BIBLIOGRAPHIC
CENTER
Box 10398   Phone: (303) 936-0108
Denver, CO 80210   C.L. Geddes, Dir.

AMERICAN NATIONAL BUILDING - JOINT VENTURE LAW LIBRARY
818 17th St., Suite 730
Denver, CO 80202   Marie Harvey, Libn.

AMERICAN WATER WORKS ASSOCIATION - TECHNICAL LIBRARY AND
INFORMATION CENTER
6666 W. Quincy   Phone: (303) 794-7711
Denver, CO 80235   Kurt M. Keeley, Tech.Libn.

ARABIAN HORSE REGISTRY TRUST OF AMERICA - LIBRARY
3435 S. Yosemite St.   Phone: (303) 750-5689
Denver, CO 80231   William M. Riley, Jr., Exec.Dir.

ASSOCIATION FOR EXPERIENTIAL EDUCATION - LIBRARY
Box 4625
Denver, CO 80204   Stephanie Takis, Exec.Sec.

ASSOCIATION OF OPERATING ROOM NURSES - LIBRARY
10170 E. Mississippi Ave.   Phone: (303) 755-6300
Denver, CO 80231   Sara Katsh, Libn.

ATLANTIC-RICHFIELD COMPANY - TECHNICAL INFORMATION CENTER
555 17th St.
Anaconda Tower   Phone: (303) 575-4425
Denver, CO 80202   Marlene Bundy, Supv.

AUGUSTANA LUTHERAN CHURCH - LIBRARY
5000 E. Alameda Ave.   Phone: (303) 388-4678
Denver, CO 80222   Ellen Swanson, Chm.Lib.Comm.

BELL TELEPHONE LABORATORIES, INC. & WESTERN ELECTRIC, INC. -
TECHNICAL LIBRARY
11900 Pecos St.   Phone: (303) 451-4275
Denver, CO 80234   James H. Varner, Lib. Group Supv.

BETH ISRAEL HOSPITAL & GERIATRIC CENTER - HEALTH SCIENCE
LIBRARY
1601 Lowell Blvd.   Phone: (303) 825-2190
Denver, CO 80204   Bunny Braunger, Med.Libn.

BETHESDA HOSPITAL - PROFESSIONAL LIBRARY
4400 E. Iliff Ave.   Phone: (303) 758-1514
Denver, CO 80222   Dolores Leone, Educ.Dir.

BIBLIOGRAPHICAL CENTER FOR RESEARCH - ROCKY MOUNTAIN REGION,
INC.
245 Columbine, Suite 212   Phone: (303) 388-9261
Denver, CO 80206   JoAn S. Segal, Interim Exec.Dir.

CARLSON PROPERTIES, INC. - SECURITY LIFE LAW LIBRARY *
1820 Security Life Bldg.   Phone: (303) 629-6043
Denver, CO 80202   Gayle A. Jackson, Libn.

CHEVRON USA INC. - CENTRAL REGION - TECHNICAL LIBRARY
700 S. Colorado Blvd., Rm. 845   Phone: (303) 759-7347
Denver, CO 80222   Pat Mountain, Libn.

CHILDREN'S HOSPITAL - FORBES MEDICAL LIBRARY
1056 E. 19th Ave.   Phone: (303) 861-6400
Denver, CO 80218   Melanie R. Birnbach, Med.Libn.

CHRIST CENTERED MINISTRIES - COLLEGE OF THE ROCKIES - LIBRARY
740-750 Clarkson   Phone: (303) 832-1547
Denver, CO 80218

COLORADO HISTORICAL SOCIETY - STEPHEN H. HART LIBRARY
Colorado Heritage Ctr.
1300 Broadway   Phone: (303) 866-2305
Denver, CO 80203   Dr. Maxine Benson, Cur.

COLORADO MINING ASSOCIATION - LIBRARY
1515 Cleveland Place, Suite 410   Phone: (303) 534-1181
Denver, CO 80202

COLORADO STATE DEPARTMENT OF EDUCATION - INSTRUCTIONAL
MATERIALS CENTER FOR THE VISUALLY HANDICAPPED
1362 Lincoln St.   Phone: (303) 839-2181
Denver, CO 80203   W. Buck Schrotberger, Sr.Cons.

COLORADO STATE DEPARTMENT OF GAME, FISH AND PARKS - LIBRARY
6060 Broadway
Denver, CO 80216   Rita Green, Libn.

GEOGRAPHIC

COLORADO STATE DEPARTMENT OF NATURAL RESOURCES - COLORADO
 GEOLOGICAL SURVEY LIBRARY
1313 Sherman, Rm. 715   Phone: (303) 866-2611
Denver, CO 80203   Louise M. Slade, Staff Asst.

COLORADO STATE DEPARTMENT OF SOCIAL SERVICE - LIBRARY
1575 Sherman St.   Phone: (303) 866-2253
Denver, CO 80203   Susan Englese, Libn.

COLORADO STATE DIVISION OF EMPLOYMENT & TRAINING - LABOR
 MARKET INFORMATION LIBRARY
251 E. 12th Ave.   Phone: (303) 839-5833
Denver, CO 80203   Marvin H. Wojahn, Economist

COLORADO STATE DIVISION OF HIGHWAYS - TECHNICAL LIBRARY
4340 E. Louisiana Ave., Rm. 104   Phone: (303) 757-9220
Denver, CO 80222   Joylyn A. Privette, Adm. Clerk

COLORADO STATE DIVISION OF STATE ARCHIVES AND PUBLIC RECORDS
Dept. of Administration
1313 Sherman St., Rm. 1B20   Phone: (303) 839-2055
Denver, CO 80203   George E. Warren, State Archv.

COLORADO STATE LIBRARY
1362 Lincoln
Denver, CO 80203

COLORADO STATE PLANNING LIBRARY
1313 Sherman St., Rm. 520   Phone: (393) 839-2351
Denver, CO 80203   Philip Schmuck, Plan.Dir.

COLORADO STATE SUPREME COURT LIBRARY
B 112 State Judicial Bldg.
2 E. 14th Ave.   Phone: (303) 861-1111
Denver, CO 80203   Frances D. Campbell, Libn.

COLORADO STATE WATER CONSERVATION BOARD - LIBRARY
1313 Sherman St.   Phone: (303) 839-3441
Denver, CO 80203   J. William McDonald, Dir.

CONOCO, INC. - MINERALS LIBRARY
555 17th St.   Phone: (303) 575-6025
Denver, CO 80202   Sharon Brown, Libn.

CONSERVATIVE BAPTIST THEOLOGICAL SEMINARY - CAREY S. THOMAS
 LIBRARY
Univ.Pk.Sta.
Box 10,000   Phone: (303) 781-8691
Denver, CO 80210   Sarah Lyons, Libn.

DAVIS, GRAHAM & STUBBS/COLORADO NATIONAL BUILDING - CNB LAW
 LIBRARY
2500 Colorado National Bldg.
950 17th St.   Phone: (303) 892-9400
Denver, CO 80202   Gay Ellen Roesch, Law Libn.

DENVER ART MUSEUM - FREDERIC H. DOUGLAS LIBRARY OF
 ANTHROPOLOGY AND ART
100 W. 14th Ave. Pkwy.   Phone: (303) 575-2256
Denver, CO 80204   Margaret Goodrich, Libn.

DENVER BOTANIC GARDENS - HELEN K. FOWLER LIBRARY
909 York St.   Phone: (303) 575-2547
Denver, CO 80206   Solange G. Gignac, Libn.

DENVER MEDICAL SOCIETY - LIBRARY
1601 E. 19th Ave.   Phone: (303) 861-1221
Denver, CO 80218   Mary De Mund, Lib.Dir.

DENVER MUSEUM OF NATURAL HISTORY - LIBRARY
City Park   Phone: (303) 575-3610
Denver, CO 80205   Stephanie H. Stowe, Libn.

DENVER POST - LIBRARY
650 15th St.   Phone: (303) 297-1565
Denver, CO 80202   Kathryn Sweeney, Libn.

DENVER PUBLIC LIBRARY - ARCHERY COLLECTION
1357 Broadway   Phone: (303) 573-5152
Denver, CO 80203   Georgiana Tiff, Dept.Hd.

DENVER PUBLIC LIBRARY - CONSERVATION LIBRARY & REGIONAL
 ENERGY/ENVIRONMENT INFORMATION CENTER
1357 Broadway   Phone: (303) 573-5152
Denver, CO 80203   Linda L. Cumming, Subject Dept.Mgr.

DENVER PUBLIC LIBRARY - DENVER GENERAL HOSPITAL LIBRARY
W. 8th & Cherokee Sts.   Phone: (303) 893-7422
Denver, CO 80204   Anita F. Westwood, Med. Subject Spec.

DENVER PUBLIC LIBRARY - DOUGLAS COLLECTION OF FINE PRINTING
1357 Broadway
Denver, CO 80203

DENVER PUBLIC LIBRARY - EUGENE FIELD COLLECTION
1357 Broadway
Denver, CO 80203

DENVER PUBLIC LIBRARY - FISH AND WILDLIFE REFERENCE SERVICE
3840 York St., Unit I   Phone: (303) 571-4656
Denver, CO 80205   Eric G. Halverson, Proj.Mgr.

DENVER PUBLIC LIBRARY - FRIENDS OF MUSIC FOLK-MUSIC COLLECTION
1357 Broadway   Phone: (303) 573-5152
Denver, CO 80203   Georgiana Tiff, Dept.Hd.

DENVER PUBLIC LIBRARY - GENEALOGY DIVISION
1357 Broadway   Phone: (303) 573-5152
Denver, CO 80203   Joanne Classen, Subject Spec.

DENVER PUBLIC LIBRARY - ROSS-BARRETT HISTORICAL AERONAUTICS
 COLLECTION
1357 Broadway   Phone: (303) 573-5152
Denver, CO 80203

DENVER PUBLIC LIBRARY - WESTERN HISTORY DEPARTMENT
1357 Broadway   Phone: (303) 573-5152
Denver, CO 80203   Eleanor M. Gehres, Hd.

DENVER PUBLIC SCHOOL DISTRICT 1 - PROFESSIONAL LIBRARY
3800 York St., Bldg.1, Unit B   Phone: (303) 837-1000
Denver, CO 80205   Phyllis Dodd, Supv.

DENVER REGIONAL TRANSPORTATION DISTRICT - LIBRARY
1325 S. Colorado Blvd.   Phone: (303) 759-1000
Denver, CO 80465   Sheila Wirth, Libn.

DENVER ZOOLOGICAL GARDEN - LIBRARY
23rd & Steele   Phone: (303) 575-2432
Denver, CO 80205   Paul Linger, Asst.Dir.

EMMAUS LUTHERAN CHURCH - LIBRARY
3120 Irving St.   Phone: (303) 477-5358
Denver, CO 80211   Herbert Harms, Libn.

ENVIRONMENTAL PROTECTION AGENCY - NATIONAL ENFORCEMENT
 INVESTIGATIONS - LIBRARY
Denver Federal Ctr., Bldg. 53
Box 25227   Phone: (303) 234-5765
Denver, CO 80225   Mary Quinlivan, Libn.

ENVIRONMENTAL PROTECTION AGENCY - REGION VIII LIBRARY
1860 Lincoln St.   Phone: (303) 837-2560
Denver, CO 80295   Dolores D. Eddy, Regional Libn.

FORT LOGAN MENTAL HEALTH CENTER - MEDICAL LIBRARY †
3520 Oxford Ave., W.   Phone: (303) 761-0220
Denver, CO 80236   Bernice N. Stone, Supv.Libn.

GATES RUBBER COMPANY - TECHNICAL INFORMATION CENTER
999 S. Broadway
Box 5887   Phone: (303) 744-4150
Denver, CO 80217   Kathryn L. Mikol, Res.Libn.

GULF OIL CORPORATION - GULF MINERAL RESOURCES COMPANY -
  EXPLORATION LIBRARY
1720 S. Bellaire St.   Phone: (303) 758-1700
Denver, CO 80222   Marriott W. Smart, Libn.

HEBREW EDUCATIONAL ALLIANCE - LIBRARY †
1555 Stuart St.   Phone: (303) 629-0410
Denver, CO 80204

HOLLAND & HART - LIBRARY
Box 8749   Phone: (303) 575-8091
Denver, CO 80201   Thomas C. McNinch, Staff Attorney

HOUSTON INTERNATIONAL MINERALS CORPORATION - LIBRARY
1325 S. Colorado Blvd., Bldg. B   Phone: (303) 692-6200
Denver, CO 80122   Ann-Marie Vermillion, Hd.Libn.

ILIFF SCHOOL OF THEOLOGY - IRA J. TAYLOR LIBRARY
2233 S. University Blvd.   Phone: (303) 744-1287
Denver, CO 80210   Andrew D. Scrimgeour, Libn.

INTERNATIONAL CLARINET SOCIETY - BURNET C. TUTHILL RESEARCH
  LIBRARY †
University of Denver   Phone: (303) 753-3691
Denver, CO 80210   Jerry Pierce, Pres.

INTERNATIONAL FEDERATION OF PETROLEUM AND CHEMICAL WORKERS -
  LIBRARY
Box 6603   Phone: (303) 388-9237
Denver, CO 80206   Curtis J. Hogan, Gen.Sec.

JOHNS-MANVILLE CORPORATION - HEALTH, SAFETY & ENVIRONMENT
  LIBRARY & INFORMATION CENTER
Ken-Caryl Ranch   Phone: (303) 978-2580
Denver, CO 80217   Janet Doerfler McGrath, Coord.Info.Serv.

JOHNS-MANVILLE SALES CORPORATION - CORPORATE INFORMATION
  CENTER
Ken-Caryl Ranch
Box 5108   Phone: (303) 978-3440
Denver, CO 80217   Ann B. Michael, Chf.Libn.

JOHNS-MANVILLE SALES CORPORATION - RESEARCH INFORMATION
  CENTER
Box 5108   Phone: (303) 979-1000
Denver, CO 80217   Judy Gerber, Chf.Libn., R & D

LORETTO HEIGHTS COLLEGE - MAY BONFILS STANTON LIBRARY
3001 S. Federal Blvd.   Phone: (303) 936-8441
Denver, CO 80236   Agnes M. Myers, Dir.

MARTIN MARIETTA CORPORATION - DENVER DIVISION - RESEARCH
  LIBRARY
Box 179   Phone: (303) 973-5512
Denver, CO 80201   Jay R. McKee, Chf.Libn.

MEDICAL GROUP MANAGEMENT ASSOCIATION - INFORMATION SERVICE
4101 E. Louisiana Ave.   Phone: (303) 753-1111
Denver, CO 80222   Barbara U. Hamilton, Dir.

MERCY MEDICAL CENTER - LIBRARY AND MEDIA RESOURCES
  DEPARTMENT
1619 Milwaukee St.   Phone: (303) 388-6288
Denver, CO 80206   Rosalind Dudden, Dir. of Lib.Serv.

MOBIL OIL CORPORATION - E & P DIVISION LIBRARY
Box 5444, Terminal Annex   Phone: (303) 572-2287
Denver, CO 80217   M.G. Harris, Division Libn.

MOUNTAIN BELL TELEPHONE COMPANY - LIBRARY
1005 17th St., Rm. 180   Phone: (303) 624-4607
Denver, CO 80202   Ida M. Hooker, Libn.

MOUNTAIN STATES EMPLOYERS COUNCIL - INFORMATION CENTER
1790 Logan St.   Phone: (303) 839-5177
Denver, CO 80203   Joy Sandberg, Info.Ctr.Mgr.

NATIONAL CABLE TELEVISION INSTITUTE - LIBRARY †
Box 27277   Phone: (303) 697-4967
Denver, CO 80227   Roland D. Hieb, Exec.Dir.

NATIONAL JEWISH HOSPITAL & RESEARCH CENTER/NATIONAL ASTHMA
  CENTER - MEDICAL LIBRARY
3800 E. Colfax Ave.   Phone: (303) 388-4461
Denver, CO 80206   Helen-Ann Brown, Med.Libn.

PORTER MEMORIAL HOSPITAL - HARLEY E. RICE MEMORIAL LIBRARY
2525 S. Downing St.   Phone: (303) 778-1955
Denver, CO 80210   Teresa Martin, Med.Libn.

PRESBYTERIAN DENVER HOSPITAL - BRADFORD MEMORIAL LIBRARY
1719 E. 19th Ave.   Phone: (303) 839-6100
Denver, CO 80218   Sue Coldren, Libn.

PUBLIC SERVICE COMPANY OF COLORADO - LIBRARY
550 15th St.
Box 840   Phone: (303) 571-7084
Denver, CO 80201   Mary Ann Hamm, Libn.

REGIONAL TRANSPORTATION DISTRICT - LIBRARY
1325 S. Colorado Blvd.   Phone: (303) 759-1000
Denver, CO 80222   Sheila Wirth, Libn.

ROATH & BREGA, P.C. - LAW LIBRARY
1720 S. Bellaire   Phone: (303) 759-5400
Denver, CO 80222   Dorothy Norbie, Law Libn.

ROCKY MOUNTAIN ENERGY CO. - LIBRARY
10 Longs Peak Dr.
Box 2000   Phone: (303) 469-8844
Denver, CO 80020   Sunny McPhail, Libn.

ROCKY MOUNTAIN HOSPITAL - C. LLOYD PETERSON MEMORIAL LIBRARY
4701 E. Ninth Ave.   Phone: (303) 388-5588
Denver, CO 80220   Joann Roith, Libn.

ROCKY MOUNTAIN NEWS - LIBRARY
400 W. Colfax Ave.   Phone: (303) 892-5000
Denver, CO 80204   Paula Shonkwiler, Libn.

ROSE MEDICAL CENTER - LIBRARY
4567 E. 9th Ave.   Phone: (303) 320-2160
Denver, CO 80220   Nancy Simon, Med.Libn.

ST. ANTHONY HOSPITAL - MEMORIAL MEDICAL LIBRARY
4231 W. 16th Ave.   Phone: (303) 629-3790
Denver, CO 80204   Christine Y. Crespin, Supv.

ST. JOSEPH HOSPITAL - HEALTH SCIENCES LIBRARY
1835 Franklin St.   Phone: (303) 837-7188
Denver, CO 80218   Margaret Bandy, Libn.

ST. LUKE'S HOSPITAL - HEALTH SCIENCES LIBRARY
601 E. 19th Ave.   Phone: (303) 839-1000
Denver, CO 80203   Kate Smith, Libn.

ST. THOMAS SEMINARY - LIBRARY
1300 S. Steele   Phone: (303) 722-4687
Denver, CO 80210   Marguerite W. Travis, Libn.

SKIDMORE, OWINGS & MERRILL - LIBRARY
1675 Broadway   Phone: (303) 825-3100
Denver, CO 80202   Elizabeth Manne, Libn.

SOCIETY OF PHOTO-TECHNOLOGISTS - LIBRARY †
Box 9634   Phone: (303) 733-4047
Denver, CO 80011   Elsa Kaiser, Act.Dir.

SOUTHEAST METROPOLITAN BOARD OF COOPERATIVE SERVICES -
  PROFESSIONAL INFORMATION CENTER
3301 S. Monaco   Phone: (303) 757-6201
Denver, CO 80222   Carole Martinez, Mgr.

STANDARD & POOR'S COMPUSTAT SERVICES, INC. - DATA RESOURCE
  CENTER
Box 239   Phone: (303) 771-6510
Denver, CO 80112   Freddie S. Howard, Libn.

GEOGRAPHIC

STEARNS-ROGER ENGINEERING CORPORATION - TECHNICAL LIBRARY
4500 Cherry Creek
Box 5888   Phone: (303) 758-1122
Denver, CO 80217   R.M. Fletcher, Supv.

STONE AND WEBSTER ENGINEERING CORPORATION - TECHNICAL
    INFORMATION CENTER
Box 5406   Phone: (303) 770-7700
Denver, CO 80217   Susan Newhams, Libn.

SYMES BUILDING LAW LIBRARY
820-16th St., Suite 800   Phone: (303) 572-8778
Denver, CO 80202

UNION COLLEGE - DEPARTMENT OF NURSING LIBRARY †
2525 S. Downing   Phone: (303) 778-1955
Denver, CO 80205   Miriam Kerr, Libn.

UNITED BANK OF DENVER, N.A. - INFORMATION CENTER LIBRARY
1740 Broadway
Box 5247   Phone: (303) 861-8811
Denver, CO 80217   Carol Minor, Info.Ctr./Lib.Mgr.

UNITED BANK OF DENVER, N.A. - UNITED BANK CENTER - LAW LIBRARY
1700 Broadway
Tower Bldg., Suite 1215   Phone: (303) 861-4304
Denver, CO 80290   Breta M. Krodshen, Law Libn.

U.S. AIR FORCE - ACCOUNTING AND FINANCE CENTER - TECHNICAL
    LIBRARY
AFAFC/FL7040   Phone: (303) 320-7566
Denver, CO 80279   Alreeta Viehdorfer, Command Libn.

U.S. BUREAU OF THE CENSUS - REGIONAL DATA USER SERVICE - DENVER
    REGIONAL OFFICE - LIBRARY *
575 Union Blvd.
Box 25207   Phone: (303) 234-5825
Denver, CO 80225   Gerald O'Donnell, Data User Serv.Off.

U.S. BUREAU OF MINES - CHARLES W. HENDERSON MEMORIAL LIBRARY
Denver Federal Center, Bldg. 20   Phone: (303) 234-2817
Denver, CO 80225   Samuel P. Shepard, Libn.

U.S. BUREAU OF RECLAMATION - LIBRARY
Engineering & Research Center
Denver Federal Center, Box 25007   Phone: (303) 234-3019
Denver, CO 80225   Paul F. Mulloney, Chf., Lib.Br.

U.S. COURT OF APPEALS, 10TH CIRCUIT - LIBRARY
U.S. Court House, Rm. C 411   Phone: (303) 837-3591
Denver, CO 80294   John N. McNamara, Libn.

U.S. DEPT. OF HOUSING AND URBAN DEVELOPMENT - REGION VIII -
    LIBRARY
1405 Curtis St.   Phone: (303) 837-3431
Denver, CO 80202   Patsy Torres, Regional Libn.

U.S. DEPT. OF THE INTERIOR - OFFICE OF REGIONAL SOLICITOR - LAW
    LIBRARY
Bldg. 67, Rm. 1400
Denver Federal Center   Phone: (303) 234-3175
Denver, CO 80225   Sally Raines, Libn.

U.S. DEPT. OF LABOR - EMPLOYMENT & TRAINING ADMINISTRATION -
    REGION 8 TECHNICAL RESOURCE LIBRARY
1617 Federal Office Bldg.
1961 Stout St.   Phone: (303) 837-4573
Denver, CO 80294   Larry Wieland, Libn.

U.S. DEPT. OF LABOR - MINE SAFETY & HEALTH ADMINISTRATION -
    INFORMATIONAL SERVICES LIBRARY
Box 25367   Phone: (303) 234-4961
Denver, CO 80225   James A. Greenhalgh, Libn.

U.S. FISH & WILDLIFE SERVICE - WILDLIFE RESEARCH CENTER LIBRARY
Federal Center, Bldg. 16   Phone: (303) 234-4919
Denver, CO 80225   Mary F. Layman, Libn.

U.S. GEOLOGICAL SURVEY - DENVER LIBRARY
Denver Federal Ctr.
Stop 914, Box 25046   Phone: (303) 234-4133
Denver, CO 80225   Robert A. Bier, Jr., Chf.Libn.

U.S. GEOLOGICAL SURVEY - NATL. CARTOGRAPHIC INFORMATION CENTER
    (NCIC)
Federal Ctr., Stop 511
Box 25046   Phone: (303) 234-5722
Denver, CO 80225   James Keogh, Cartographer

U.S. GEOLOGICAL SURVEY - WATER RESOURCES DIVISION - COLORADO
    DISTRICT LIBRARY
Federal Center
Box 25046, Stop 415   Phone: (303) 234-3487
Denver, CO 80225   Barbara J. Condron, Libn.

U.S. HERITAGE CONSERVATION AND RECREATION SERVICE -
    INTERAGENCY ARCHEOLOGICAL SERVICE LIBRARY
Denver Federal Center
Box 25387   Phone: (303) 234-2560
Denver, CO 80225   Jack R. Rudy, Chf.

U.S. NATL. ARCHIVES & RECORDS SERVICE - FEDERAL ARCHIVES AND
    RECORDS CENTER, REGION 8
Denver Federal Center, Bldg. 48   Phone: (303) 234-3187
Denver, CO 80225

U.S. NATL. PARK SERVICE - ROCKY MOUNTAIN REGIONAL OFFICE -
    LIBRARY
655 Parfet St.
Box 25287   Phone: (303) 234-4443
Denver, CO 80225   Ruth A. Larison, Libn.

U.S. VETERANS ADMINISTRATION (CO-Denver) - HOSPITAL LIBRARY
1055 Clermont St.
Denver, CO 80220   Ruth E. Gilbert, Med.Libn.

UNIVERSITY OF COLORADO MEDICAL CENTER - DENISON MEMORIAL
    LIBRARY
4200 E. Ninth Ave.   Phone: (303) 394-7469
Denver, CO 80220   Charles Bandy, Dir.

UNIVERSITY OF COLORADO MEDICAL CENTER - RENE A. SPITZ
    PSYCHIATRIC LIBRARY
4200 E. Ninth Ave., C-268   Phone: (303) 394-7039
Denver, CO 80262   Frances G. McCreary, Libn.

UNIVERSITY OF DENVER - COLLEGE OF LAW - WESTMINSTER LAW
    LIBRARY
200 W. 14th Ave.   Phone: (303) 753-3405
Denver, CO 80204   Alfred J. Coco, Libn.

UNIVERSITY OF DENVER AND DENVER RESEARCH INSTITUTE - SOCIAL
    SYSTEMS RESEARCH AND EVALUATION LIBRARY
University of Denver   Phone: (303) 753-3382
Denver, CO 80208   Kim Jondro, Info.Spec.

UNIVERSITY OF DENVER - PENROSE LIBRARY
2150 E. Evans Ave.   Phone: (303) 753-2007
Denver, CO 80208   Morris Schertz, Dir.

COLORADO STATE DISTRICT COURT, 6TH JUDICIAL DISTRICT - LAW
    LIBRARY
                                            Phone: (303) 247-1301
Durango, CO 81301   Al Haas, Libn.

FORT LEWIS COLLEGE - CENTER OF SOUTHWEST STUDIES
Fort Lewis College Library   Phone: (303) 247-7456
Durango, CO 81301   Dr. Robert W. Delaney, Dir.

AMERICAN INSTITUTE OF TIMBER CONSTRUCTION - LIBRARY
333 W. Hampden Ave.   Phone: (303) 761-3212
Englewood, CO 80110   Paul T. Nicholas, Dir. of Engr.Serv.

ENGINEERING DYNAMICS, INC. - LIBRARY †
3925 S. Kalamath   Phone: (303) 761-4367
Englewood CO 80110   Howard McGregor, Libn.

FRYE-SILLS, INC. - LIBRARY
5500 S. Syracuse Circle   Phone: (303) 773-3900
Englewood, CO 80111   Libbie Gottschalk, Libn.

INFORMATION HANDLING SERVICES - LIBRARY *
15 Inverness Way E.   Phone: (303) 779-0600
Englewood, CO 80150   Ellin Barrett, Sr.Libn.

MICROMEDEX, INC. - PAUL DE HAEN DRUG INFORMATION SYSTEMS
2750 S. Shoshone St.   Phone: (303) 781-6683
Englewood, CO 80110

MORRIS ANIMAL FOUNDATION - LIBRARY †
45 Inverness Dr., E.
Englewood, CO 80112

SWEDISH MEDICAL CENTER - LIBRARY
501 E. Hampden Ave.   Phone: (303) 786-6616
Englewood, CO 80110   Marla M. Graber, Dir., Lib.Serv.

U.S. ARMY HOSPITALS - FORT CARSON ARMY HOSPITAL - MEDICAL
   LIBRARY
Bldg. 6235   Phone: (303) 579-3209
Ft. Carson, CO 80913   Mildred B. Owen, Med.Libn.

U.S. ARMY POST - FORT CARSON - LIBRARY
                                                Phone: (303) 579-2350
Ft. Carson, CO 80913   Roger M. Miller, Lib.Dir.

AMERICAN SOCIETY OF SUGAR BEET TECHNOLOGISTS - LIBRARY
Box 1546   Phone: (303) 482-8250
Fort Collins, CO 80522   James H. Fischer, Sec.-Tres.

COLORADO STATE DIVISION OF WILDLIFE - RESEARCH CENTER LIBRARY
317 W. Prospect   Phone: (303) 484-2836
Fort Collins, CO 80526   Mrs. Marian Hershcopf, Libn.

COLORADO STATE UNIVERSITY - ENGINEERING SCIENCES BRANCH
   LIBRARY
                                                Phone: (303) 491-8694
Fort Collins, CO 80523   Barbara L. Burke, Asst.Engr.Sci.Libn.

COLORADO STATE UNIVERSITY - GERMANS FROM RUSSIA PROJECT
   LIBRARY
History Department   Phone: (303) 491-6854
Fort Collins, CO 80523   John Newman, Proj.Archv.

COLORADO STATE UNIVERSITY - WILLIAM E. MORGAN LIBRARY
                                                Phone: (303) 491-5911
Fort Collins, CO 80523   LeMoyne W. Anderson, Dir. of Lib.

ENVIRONMENTAL RESEARCH & TECHNOLOGY, INC. - LIFE SCIENCES
   INFORMATION CENTER
Box 2105   Phone: (303) 493-8878
Fort Collins, CO 80522   Lynn Unsworth, Libn.

HEWLETT-PACKARD COMPANY - DESKTOP COMPUTER DIVISION - FORT
   COLLINS FACILITY LIBRARY
3404 E. Harmony Rd.   Phone: (303) 226-3800
Fort Collins, CO 80525   Jane Fiasconaro, Libn.

IDEAL BASIC INDUSTRIES - CEMENT DIVISION - RESEARCH DEPARTMENT
   - LIBRARY
Box 1667   Phone: (303) 482-5600
Fort Collins, CO 80522

POUDRE VALLEY MEMORIAL HOSPITAL - MEDIA RESOURCES LIBRARY
1024 Lemay Ave.   Phone: (303) 482-4111
Fort Collins, CO 80524   Carole Trask, Libn.

TELEDYNE WATER PIK - INFORMATION CENTER
1635 Blue Spruce Dr.   Phone: (303) 493-8600
Fort Collins, CO 80524   Priscilla Weddell, Libn.

U.S. FOREST SERVICE - ROCKY MOUNTAIN FOREST & RANGE EXPERIMENT
   STATION - LIBRARY
240 W. Prospect St.   Phone: (303) 482-7332
Fort Collins, CO 80521   Frances J. Barney, Libn.

AMAX EXPLORATION, INC. - SCIENCE LIBRARY
1707 Cole Blvd.   Phone: (303) 433-6151
Golden, CO 80401   Laura A. Christensen, Tech.Libn.

AMAX EXTRACTIVE RESEARCH & DEVELOPMENT, INC. - TECHNICAL
   INFORMATION CENTER
5950 McIntyre St.   Phone: (303) 279-7636
Golden, CO 80401   James W. Carter, Supv.

BUFFALO BILL MEMORIAL MUSEUM - INFORMATION CENTER
Rte. 5, Box 950   Phone: (303) 526-0747
Golden, CO 80401   Stanley W. Zamonski, Cur.

CHEVRON RESOURCES COMPANY - LIBRARY
1746 Colorado Blvd.   Phone: (303) 279-8692
Golden, CO 80401   Penelope F. Avcin, Hd.Libn.

COLORADO RAILROAD HISTORICAL FOUNDATION - LIBRARY
17155 W. 44th Ave.
Box 10   Phone: (303) 279-4591
Golden, CO 80401   Robert W. Richardson, Exec.Dir.

COLORADO SCHOOL OF MINES - ARTHUR LAKES LIBRARY
                                                Phone: (303) 279-0300
Golden, CO 80401   Hartley K. Phinney, Jr., Dir.

COORS (Adolph) COMPANY - TECHNICAL LIBRARY
Mail 105   Phone: (303) 279-6565
Golden, CO 80401   Mary Bond, Libn.

DAMES & MOORE - LIBRARY
1626 Cole Blvd.   Phone: (303) 232-6262
Golden, CO 80401   Marilyn Stark, Librarian

ROCKWELL INTERNATIONAL - ATOMICS INTERNATIONAL DIVISION -
   ROCKY FLATS PLANT - TECHNICAL LIBRARY †
Box 938   Phone: (303) 497-2863
Golden, CO 80401   Mary Ann Paliani, Lib.Mgr.

SOLAR ENERGY RESEARCH INSTITUTE - SOLAR ENERGY INFORMATION
   CENTER
1617 Cole Blvd.   Phone: (303) 231-1415
Golden, CO 80401   Jerome T. Maddock, Br.Chf.

TOSCO CORPORATION - TECHNICAL INFORMATION CENTER
18200 W. Hwy. 72   Phone: (303) 425-6021
Golden, CO 80401   Stephen O. Boyle, Tech.Info.Spec.

MESA COUNTY MEDICAL SOCIETY - DR. E.H. MUNRO MEDICAL LIBRARY
St. Mary's Hospital & Medical Ctr.   Phone: (303) 242-1550
Grand Junction, CO 81501   Cynthia M. Tharaud, Med.Libn.

MESA COUNTY VALLEY SCHOOL DISTRICT 51 - DEPARTMENT OF
   RESOURCES, RESEARCH AND DEVELOPMENT
410 Hill Ave.   Phone: (303) 245-1788
Grand Junction, CO 81501   Ted S. Brumbaugh, Dir.

MUSEUM OF WESTERN COLORADO - ARCHIVES
4th & Ute Sts.   Phone: (303) 242-0971
Grand Junction, CO 81501   John Brumgardt, Musm.Dir.

U.S. DEPT. OF ENERGY - GRAND JUNCTION OFFICE - TECHNICAL LIBRARY
Bendix Field Engineering Corp.
Box 1569   Phone: (303) 242-8621
Grand Junction, CO 81502-1569   Sara L. Murphy, Sr.Libn.

U.S. GEOLOGICAL SURVEY - WATER RESOURCES LIBRARY
Aspinall Federal Bldg., Rm. 223
Box 2027   Phone: (303) 245-5257
Grand Junction, CO 81502   D.L. Collins, Subdistrict Chf.

U.S. VETERANS ADMINISTRATION (CO-Grand Junction) - HOSPITAL
   MEDICAL LIBRARY
2121 North Ave.   Phone: (303) 242-0731
Grand Junction, CO 81501   Lynn L. Bragdon, Chf., Lib.Serv.

AMERICAN HISTORICAL SOCIETY OF GERMANS FROM RUSSIA - GREELEY
   PUBLIC LIBRARY
City Complex Bldg.   Phone: (303) 353-6123
Greeley, CO 80631   Esther Fromm, Archv./Dir.GPL

GEOGRAPHIC

GEOGRAPHIC

COLORADO STATE DISTRICT COURT - LAW LIBRARY †
Weld County Court House
Box 789   Phone: (303) 356-4000
Greeley, CO 80632   Joy W. Ahlborn, Hd.

GREELEY MUNICIPAL MUSEUM - LIBRARY
Civic Ctr. Complex, 919 7th St.   Phone: (303) 353-6123
Greeley, CO 80631   Peggy A. Ford, Musm.Coord.

WELD COUNTY GENERAL HOSPITAL - STAFF LIBRARY
16th St. at 17th Ave.
Greeley, CO 80631   Meta Shore, Libn.

AMC CANCER RESEARCH CENTER AND HOSPITAL - GRACE & PHILIP
    LICHTENSTEIN SCIENTIFIC LIBRARY
6401 W. Colfax Ave.   Phone: (303) 233-6501
Lakewood, CO 80214   Eleanor Krakauer, Libn.

FRENCH AMERICAN METALS CORPORATION - LIBRARY
9580 W. 14th Ave.   Phone: (303) 232-4966
Lakewood, CO 80215   Judith H. Bailey, Libn.

JEFFERSON COUNTY PUBLIC SCHOOLS R1 - PROFESSIONAL LIBRARY
    MEDIA CENTER
1209 Quail St.   Phone: (303) 231-2309
Lakewood, CO 80215   Christa K. Coon, Exec.Dir.Lib.Serv.

PROWERS COUNTY HISTORICAL SOCIETY - BIG TIMBERS MUSEUM -
    LIBRARY
North Santa Fe Trail
Box 362   Phone: (303) 336-2472
Lamar, CO 81052   Ernest L. Goshen, Cur.

LAKE COUNTY PUBLIC LIBRARY - SPECIAL COLLECTIONS
1115 Harrison Ave.   Phone: (303) 486-0569
Leadville, CO 80461   David R. Parry, Dir.

TABOR OPERA HOUSE - LIBRARY
308 Harrison Ave.   Phone: (303) 486-1147
Leadville, CO 80461   Evelyn E. Furman, Owner

LITTLETON AREA HISTORICAL MUSEUM - LIBRARY †
6028 S. Gallup   Phone: (303) 795-3850
Littleton, CO 80120   Robert J. McQuarle, Dir.

MARATHON OIL COMPANY - RESEARCH CENTER LIBRARY
7400 S. Broadway   Phone: (303) 794-2601
Littleton, CO 80160   Jan Thomas, Libn.

GREAT WESTERN SUGAR COMPANY - AGRICULTURAL RESEARCH CENTER -
    RESEARCH LIBRARY
Sugarmill Rd.   Phone: (303) 893-9680
Longmont, CO 80501   James F. Gonyou, Dir.

HEWLETT-PACKARD COMPANY - LOVELAND FACILITY LIBRARY
Box 301   Phone: (303) 667-5000
Loveland, CO 80537   Marsha Haugen, Libn.

U.S. AIR FORCE BASE - LOWRY BASE LIBRARY
Lowry Technical Training Ctr.   Phone: (303) 394-3093
Lowry AFB, CO 80230   Helen C. McClaughry, Base Libn.

U.S. NATL. PARK SERVICE - MESA VERDE NATL. PARK - MUSEUM LIBRARY
Box 38   Phone: (303) 529-4475
Mesa Verde Natl. Park, CO 81330   Joyce A. Attebery, Lib.Techn.

COLORADO STATE HOSPITAL - PROFESSIONAL LIBRARY
1600 W. 24th St.   Phone: (303) 543-1170
Pueblo, CO 81003   Helen Wack, Libn.

PARKVIEW EPISCOPAL HOSPITAL - MEDICAL LIBRARY
400 W. 16th St.   Phone: (303) 542-8680
Pueblo, CO 81003   Ms. Lyn Smith Hammond, Med.Libn.

PUEBLO REGIONAL PLANNING COMMISSION - LIBRARY
One City Hall Pl.
Box 1427   Phone: (303) 543-6006
Pueblo, CO 81002   Donald R. Vest, Libn.

ST. MARY-CORWIN HOSPITAL - FINNEY MEMORIAL LIBRARY
1008 Minnequa Ave.   Phone: (303) 561-5119
Pueblo, CO 81004   Shirley Harper, Med.Libn.

SOUTHERN COLORADO ECONOMIC DEVELOPMENT DISTRICT - REGIONAL
    PLANNING & DEVELOPMENT CENTER - DATA FILE †
415 Harrison   Phone: (303) 545-8680
Pueblo, CO 81004

U.S. DEPT. OF TRANSPORTATION - TRANSPORTATION TEST CENTER -
    TECHNICAL LIBRARY
Box 11449, Code RTC-32   Phone: (303) 545-5660
Pueblo, CO 81001   Ruth Mecklenburg, Tech.Lib.Spec.

UNIVERSITY OF SOUTHERN COLORADO - LIBRARY - SPECIAL COLLECTIONS
2200 Bonforte Blvd.   Phone: (303) 549-2361
Pueblo, CO 81001   Beverly A. Moore, Dir.

U.S. AIR FORCE ACADEMY - LAW LIBRARY
                                                Phone: (303) 472-3680
U.S. Air Force Academy, CO 80840   Col. M.E. Kinevan, Prof. of Law

U.S. AIR FORCE ACADEMY - LIBRARY
                                                Phone: (303) 472-2590
U.S. Air Force Academy, CO 80840   Lt.Col. Benjaman C. Glidden

U.S. AIR FORCE ACADEMY - MEDICAL LIBRARY
                                                Phone: (303) 472-5107
U.S. Air Force Academy, CO 80840   Paula Brockway, Libn.

CAMP DRESSER & MC KEE, INC. - CDM ENVIRONMENTAL LIBRARY
11455 W. 48th Ave.   Phone: (303) 422-0469
Wheat Ridge, CO 80033   Linda S. Elinoff, Libn.

COLORADO STATE HOME AND TRAINING SCHOOL - STAFF LIBRARY *
10285 Ridge Rd.   Phone: (303) 424-7791
Wheat Ridge, CO 80033   Clara A. Glover, Dir.

LUTHERAN MEDICAL CENTER - MEDICAL LIBRARY
8300 W. 38th Ave.   Phone: (303) 425-8565
Wheat Ridge, CO 80033   Susan B. Higginbotham, Med.Libn.

EASTMAN KODAK COMPANY - COLORADO DIVISION - ENGINEERING
    LIBRARY
Bldg. CS02A   Phone: (303) 686-7611
Windsor, CO 80551   Audrey Hoover, Libn.

CONNECTICUT

ABBEY OF REGINA LAUDIS, ORDER OF ST. BENEDICT - LIBRARY
                                                Phone: (203) 266-7727
Bethlehem, CT 06751   Mother Agnes, O.S.B., Libn.

ANDERSEN LABORATORIES, INC. - LIBRARY
1280 Blue Hills Ave.   Phone: (203) 242-0761
Bloomfield, CT 06002   Clement Valerio, Jr., Hd.

MONSANTO CORPORATION - PACKAGING DIVISION - TECHNICAL
    INFORMATION CENTER
101 Granby St.   Phone: (203) 242-6221
Bloomfield, CT 06002

ST. THOMAS SEMINARY LIBRARY - ALUMNI COLLECTION
467 Bloomfield Ave.   Phone: (201) 242-5573
Bloomfield, CT 06002   Rev. Charles B. Johnson, Dir.

BRIDGEPORT HOSPITAL - REEVES MEMORIAL LIBRARY
267 Grant St.   Phone: (203) 384-3254
Bridgeport, CT 06602   Violet Rigia, Libn.

BRIDGEPORT PUBLIC LIBRARY - HISTORICAL COLLECTIONS
925 Broad St.   Phone: (203) 576-7417
Bridgeport, CT 06604   David W. Palmquist, Hd., Hist.Coll.

BRIDGEPORT PUBLIC LIBRARY - TECHNOLOGY AND BUSINESS
    DEPARTMENT
925 Broad St.   Phone: (203) 576-7406
Bridgeport, CT 06604   E. Paul Jones, Hd.

CONNECTICUT STATE LIBRARY - LAW LIBRARY AT BRIDGEPORT
1061 Main St., 7th Fl.
New Court House
Phone: (203) 579-6237
Bridgeport, CT 06604
Robert Nathan Plotnick, Libn.

GENERAL ELECTRIC COMPANY - COMPUTER MANAGEMENT OPERATION
LIBRARY
Bldg. 30ES
1285 Boston Ave.
Phone: (203) 382-3921
Bridgeport, CT 06602
Wendy Bergel, Info.Spec.

PARK CITY HOSPITAL - CARLSON MEMORIAL HEALTH SCIENCES LIBRARY
695 Park Ave.
Phone: (203) 579-5097
Bridgeport, CT 06604
Suzanne Porter-Zadera, Dir.

REMINGTON ARMS COMPANY, INC. - RESEARCH LIBRARY
939 Barnum Ave.
Bridgeport, CT 06602

SACRED HEART UNIVERSITY - LIBRARY
5229 Park Ave.
Phone: (203) 374-9441
Bridgeport, CT 06606
Edward J. O'Hara, Univ.Libn.

ST. VINCENT'S MEDICAL CENTER - DANIEL T. BANKS HEALTH SCIENCE
LIBRARY *
2800 Main St.
Phone: (203) 576-5336
Bridgeport, CT 06606
Janet Goerig, Dir. of Lib.Serv.

WARNACO, INC. - MARKET RESEARCH LIBRARY †
325 Lafayette St.
Phone: (203) 579-8272
Bridgeport, CT 06602
Irene Miller, Libn.

AMERICAN CLOCK AND WATCH MUSEUM - EDWARD INGRAHAM LIBRARY
100 Maple St.
Phone: (203) 583-6070
Bristol, CT 06010
Mr. Chris H. Bailey, Cur. & Libn.

ASSOCIATED SPRING BARNES GROUP, INC. - TECHNICAL CENTER LIBRARY
Box 570
Phone: (203) 583-1331
Bristol, CT 06010
Laura S. Drasgow, Libn.

CRANDALL (Prudence) MEMORIAL MUSEUM - LIBRARY
Box 12
Phone: (203) 566-3005
Canterbury, CT 06331
Margaret W. Nareff, Cur.Asst.

FIRST CONGREGATIONAL CHURCH OF CHESHIRE - LIBRARY
Church Dr.
Phone: (203) 272-5323
Cheshire, CT 06410

CLINTON HISTORICAL SOCIETY - LIBRARY
Andrews Memorial Town Hall
Box 174
Phone: (203) 669-2164
Clinton, CT 06413
Dr. Jesse H. Buell, Libn.

COLEBROOK HISTORICAL SOCIETY - LIBRARY AND ARCHIVES
Phone: (314) 635-1850
Colebrook, CT 06021
Elaine Delarm, Cur.

CANTON HISTORICAL SOCIETY - LIBRARY
11 Front St.
Phone: (203) 693-2793
Collinsville, CT 06022
Jane L. Goedecke, Libn.

HOLY APOSTLES COLLEGE - LIBRARY
33 Prospect Hill Rd.
Cromwell, CT 06416

DANBURY HOSPITAL - HEALTH SCIENCES LEARNING CENTER
24 Hospital Ave.
Phone: (203) 744-2300
Danbury, CT 06810
Maryanne Witters, Dir.

DANBURY SCOTT-FANTON MUSEUM AND HISTORICAL SOCIETY - LIBRARY
45 Main St.
Phone: (203) 743-5200
Danbury, CT 06810
Dorothy T. Schling, Dir.

GROLIER INCORPORATED - LIBRARY
Sherman Tpk.
Phone: (203) 792-1200
Danbury, CT 06816
Chun Chuan Chang, Chf.Libn.

WESTERN CONNECTICUT STATE COLLEGE - RUTH A. HAAS LIBRARY
181 White St.
Phone: (203) 797-4052
Danbury, CT 06810
Katherine J. Sholtz, Dir. of Lib.Serv.

DUNLAP AND ASSOCIATES, INC. - LIBRARY
One Parkland Dr.
Phone: (203) 655-3971
Darien, CT 06820
Bernice Astheimer, Libn.

UNITED TECHNOLOGIES CORPORATION - LIBRARY
United Technologies Research Center
Phone: (203) 727-7120
East Hartford, CT 06108
Irving H. Neufeld, Chf., Lib.Sys.

VANDERBILT (R.T.) COMPANY, INC. - LIBRARY
33 Winfield St.
Phone: (203) 853-1400
East Norwalk, CT 06855
Jane Wilson, Libn.

ST. BERNARD'S PARISH - HAZARDVILLE CATHOLIC LIBRARY *
426 Hazard Ave.
Phone: (203) 749-6371
Enfield, CT 06082
Mrs. Stephen Klesczewski, Libn.

CONNECTICUT AUDUBON CENTER - LIBRARY
2325 Burr St.
Phone: (203) 259-6305
Fairfield, CT 06430
Leslie N. Corey, Jr., Exec.Dir.

FAIRFIELD HISTORICAL SOCIETY - REFERENCE AND RESEARCH LIBRARY
636 Old Post Rd.
Phone: (203) 259-1598
Fairfield, CT 06430
Irene K. Miller, Libn.

CENTER FOR FARM AND FOOD RESEARCH, INC. - LIBRARY
Box 88
Phone: (203) 824-5945
Falls Village, CT 06031
Lucille Sadwith, Dir.

AMERICAN NUCLEAR INSURERS - INFORMATION RECORDS CENTER
The Exchange, Bldg. 3
245 Farmington Ave.
Phone: (203) 677-7305
Farmington, CT 06032
Dottie Sherman, Info./Rec.Dir.

STAUFFER CHEMICAL COMPANY - TECHNICAL INFORMATION CENTER
400 Farmington Ave.
Phone: (203) 674-6312
Farmington, CT 06032
Joanna W. Eickenhorst, Tech.Info.Spec.

UNIVERSITY OF CONNECTICUT - HEALTH CENTER - LYMAN MAYNARD
STOWE LIBRARY
Phone: (203) 674-2547
Farmington, CT 06032
Ralph Arcari, Dir. Of Libs.

FUTURES GROUP, INC. - LIBRARY
76 Eastern Blvd.
Phone: (203) 633-3501
Glastonbury, CT 06033
Katherine H. Willson, Mgr., Info.Serv.

SALMON BROOK HISTORICAL SOCIETY - REFERENCE AND EDUCATIONAL
CENTER
208 Salmon Brook St.
Phone: (203) 653-2700
Granby, CT 06035
Mrs. B.M. Dewey, Cur.

SOUTH CONGREGATIONAL CHURCH - LIBRARY
Salmon Brook St.
Phone: (203) 653-7289
Granby, CT 06035

AMAX, INC. - CLIMAX MOLYBDENUM COMPANY - TECHNICAL
INFORMATION DEPARTMENT †
1 Greenwich Plaza
Phone: (203) 622-3587
Greenwich, CT 06830
Ellen Jones, Supv., Info.Serv.

AMAX, INC. - LAW LIBRARY
AMAX Center
Phone: (203) 622-3021
Greenwich, CT 06830
Virginia S. Grayson, Libn.

AMAX, INC. - LIBRARY
AMAX Center
Phone: (203) 622-3021
Greenwich, CT 06830
Virginia S. Grayson, Libn.

AMERICAN CAN COMPANY - BUSINESS INFORMATION CENTER
American Ln. - 1B8
Phone: (203) 552-2160
Greenwich, CT 06830
Estelle C. Adler, Adm.

AMERICAN CAN COMPANY - MARKETING INFORMATION LIBRARY
American Ln.
Phone: (203) 552-2639
Greenwich, CT 06830
Ruth Gruettner, Lib.Adm.

GEOGRAPHIC

AMERICAN CAN COMPANY - TECHNICAL INFORMATION CENTER
American Lane, Mail Code 2B2   Phone: (203) 552-3140
Greenwich, CT 06830   MaryAnn J. Mislavitz, Mgr., Tech.Info.

DMS, INC. - TECHNICAL LIBRARY
100 Northfield St.   Phone: (203) 661-7800
Greenwich, CT 06830   Frank Dahm, Dir.

GREENWICH HOSPITAL ASSOCIATION - GRAY CARTER LIBRARY
                    Phone: (203) 869-7000
Greenwich, CT 06830   Carmel Fedors, Med.Libn.

GREENWICH LIBRARY - ORAL HISTORY PROJECT
101 W. Putnam Ave.   Phone: (203) 622-7900
Greenwich, CT 06830   Frances Lee, Ref.Libn.

REDDY COMMUNICATIONS, INC. - INFORMATION/RESEARCH SERVICES
537 Steamboat Rd.   Phone: (203) 661-4800
Greenwich, CT 06830   Elizabeth A. Muskus, Mgr.Info./Res.Serv.

GENERAL DYNAMICS CORPORATION - ELECTRIC BOAT DIVISION -
DIVISION LIBRARY
Eastern Point Rd.   Phone: (203) 446-3481
Groton, CT 06340   Charles E. Giles, Chf.Libn.

PFIZER, INC. - CENTRAL RESEARCH TECHNICAL INFORMATION SERVICES
Eastern Point Rd.   Phone: (203) 445-5611
Groton, CT 06340   Dr. Jay S. Buckley, Jr., Dir.Tech.Info.

U.S. NAVY - NAVAL SUBMARINE MEDICAL RESEARCH LABORATORY -
MEDICAL LIBRARY
Naval Submarine Base New London
Box 900   Phone: (203) 449-3629
Groton, CT 06340   Elaine M. Gaucher, Libn.

U.S. NAVY - SUBMARINE BASE - SUBMARINE FORCE LIBRARY AND MUSEUM
Code 340, Box 16   Phone: (203) 449-3174
Groton, CT 06349   Gary R. Morrison, Dir.

GUILFORD KEEPING SOCIETY, INC. - LIBRARY
171 Boston St.
Box 363   Phone: (203) 453-3176
Guilford, CT 06437   Joel Helander, Lib.Comm.Chm.

WIRE ASSOCIATION INTERNATIONAL - LIBRARY
1570 Boston Post Rd.   Phone: (203) 453-2777
Guilford, CT 06437   Rochelle P. Kramer, Coord., Tech.Info.

CONGREGATION MISHKAN ISRAEL - ADULT LIBRARY
785 Ridge Rd.   Phone: (203) 288-3877
Hamden, CT 06517   Jay M. Brown, Chm., House Comm.

AETNA LIFE AND CASUALTY COMPANY - LIBRARY
151 Farmington Ave.   Phone: (203) 273-2946
Hartford, CT 06156   Kathryn W. Porter, Libn.

ARCHDIOCESE OF HARTFORD - CATHOLIC INFORMATION CENTER †
125 Market St.   Phone: (203) 522-0602
Hartford, CT 06103   Rev. Edward J. McLean, Exec.Dir.

ARTHUR ANDERSEN & CO. - LIBRARY
One Financial Plaza   Phone: (203) 522-2600
Hartford, CT 06103   Jenifer Berman, Libn.

CONNECTICUT GENERAL LIFE INSURANCE COMPANY - LIBRARY
                    Phone: (203) 726-4327
Hartford, CT 06152   Marian G. Lechner, Libn.

CONNECTICUT HISTORICAL SOCIETY - LIBRARY
1 Elizabeth St.   Phone: (203) 236-5621
Hartford, CT 06105   Elizabeth Abbe, Libn.

CONNECTICUT MUTUAL LIFE INSURANCE COMPANY - LIBRARY
140 Garden St.   Phone: (203) 727-6500
Hartford, CT 06115   Ellen Cartledge, Libn.

CONNECTICUT STATE DEPARTMENT OF EDUCATION - CHARLES D. HINE
LIBRARY
Box 2219   Phone: (203) 566-3867
Hartford, CT 06115   Dorothy W. Headspeth, Educ.Asst.Libn.

CONNECTICUT STATE DEPARTMENT OF HEALTH SERVICES - STANLEY H.
OSBORN MEDICAL LIBRARY
79 Elm St., Rm. 315   Phone: (203) 566-2198
Hartford, CT 06115   Margery A. Cohen, Libn.

CONNECTICUT STATE LIBRARY
231 Capitol Ave.   Phone: (203) 566-4777
Hartford, CT 06115   Clarence R. Walters, State Libn.

CONNECTICUT STATE LIBRARY - HARTFORD LAW BRANCH
95 Washington St.   Phone: (203) 566-3900
Hartford, CT 06106   Evangeline Luddy, Libn.

CONNECTICUT STATE LIBRARY - LIBRARY FOR THE BLIND AND
PHYSICALLY HANDICAPPED
90 Washington St.   Phone: (203) 566-3028
Hartford, CT 06106   Dale Jeske, Dir.

CONNECTICUT STATE OFFICE OF POLICY AND MANAGEMENT - LIBRARY
80 Washington St.   Phone: (203) 566-5803
Hartford, CT 06115   Lalitha Kali, Libn.

HARTFORD - CITY PLAN LIBRARY
550 Main St.   Phone: (203) 722-6500
Hartford, CT 06103   Pat Williams, Dir. of Planning

HARTFORD COURANT - NEWS LIBRARY
285 Broad St.   Phone: (203) 249-6411
Hartford, CT 06115   Kathleen McKula, News Libn.

HARTFORD HOSPITAL - HEALTH SCIENCE LIBRARIES
80 Seymour St.   Phone: (203) 524-2971
Hartford, CT 06115   Gertrude Lamb, Ph.D., Dir.

HARTFORD INSURANCE GROUP - CORPORATE LIBRARY
Hartford Plaza   Phone: (203) 547-5516
Hartford, CT 06115   Bonnie Jean Woodworth, Libn.

HARTFORD MEDICAL SOCIETY - LIBRARY
230 Scarborough St.   Phone: (203) 236-5613
Hartford, CT 06105   William E. Hart, M.D., Libn.

HARTFORD PUBLIC LIBRARY - ART, MUSIC AND RECREATION
DEPARTMENT
500 Main St.   Phone: (203) 525-9121
Hartford, CT 06103   Vernon Martin, Hd.

HARTFORD PUBLIC LIBRARY - BUSINESS, SCIENCE & TECHNOLOGY
DEPARTMENT
500 Main St.   Phone: (203) 525-9121
Hartford, CT 06103   Charles S. Griffen, Hd.

HARTFORD PUBLIC LIBRARY - REFERENCE AND GENERAL READING
DEPARTMENT
500 Main St.   Phone: (203) 525-9121
Hartford, CT 06103   Martha D. Nolan, Hd.

HARTFORD SEMINARY FOUNDATION - CASE MEMORIAL LIBRARY
77 Sherman St.   Phone: (203) 232-4451
Hartford, CT 06105   Nancy Lee Harney, Libn.

HARTFORD STATE TECHNICAL COLLEGE - GROM HAYES LIBRARY
401 Flatbush Ave.   Phone: (203) 527-4111
Hartford, CT 06106   Larry W. Yother, Libn.

INDUSTRIAL RISK INSURERS - IRI LIBRARY
85 Woodland St.   Phone: (203) 525-2601
Hartford, CT 06102   Anne S. Grise, Libn.

INSTITUTE OF LIVING - MEDICAL LIBRARY
400 Washington St.   Phone: (203) 278-7950
Hartford, CT 06106   Helen R. Lansberg, Dir.

INSTITUTE OF SOCIAL ETHICS - LIBRARY AND ARCHIVES †
Central Station, Box 3417   Phone: (203) 547-1281
Hartford, CT 06103   Foster Gunnison, Jr., Adm.

LIFE INSURANCE MARKETING AND RESEARCH ASSOCIATION - LIBRARY
Box 208   Phone: (203) 677-0033
Hartford, CT 06141   William J. Mortimer, Mgr., Lib./Ref.Serv.

MARK TWAIN MEMORIAL - LIBRARY
351 Farmington Ave.   Phone: (203) 247-0998
Hartford, CT 06105   Mr. Wynn Lee, Dir.

MORSE SCHOOL OF BUSINESS - LIBRARY
275 Asylum St.   Phone: (203) 522-2261
Hartford, CT 06103   Mary M. Shea, Libn.

MOUNT SINAI HOSPITAL - HEALTH SCIENCES LIBRARY
500 Blue Hills Ave.   Phone: (203) 242-4431
Hartford, CT 06112   Nancy B. Cohen, Dir.

NORTHEAST UTILITIES SERVICE COMPANY - LIBRARY
Box 270   Phone: (203) 666-6911
Hartford, CT 06101   Joan N. Terry, Libn.

PHOENIX MUTUAL LIFE INSURANCE COMPANY - LIBRARY
One American Row   Phone: (203) 278-1212
Hartford, CT 06115   Margaret Colton, Libn.

PROTESTANT EPISCOPAL CHURCH - EPISCOPAL DIOCESE OF
    CONNECTICUT - DIOCESAN LIBRARY AND ARCHIVES
Box A, Sta. A   Phone: (203) 233-4481
Hartford, CT 06106   Rev. Kenneth W. Cameron, Archv./Historapher

ST. FRANCIS HOSPITAL AND MEDICAL CENTER - SCHOOL OF NURSING
    LIBRARY
338 Asylum St.   Phone: (203) 249-9101
Hartford, CT 06103   Ruth P. Carroll, Dir.

STOWE-DAY FOUNDATION - LIBRARY
77 Forest St.   Phone: (203) 522-9258
Hartford, CT 06105   Joseph S. Van Why, Dir.

TRAVELERS INSURANCE COMPANIES - CORPORATE LIBRARY
One Tower Square   Phone: (203) 277-5048
Hartford, CT 06115   Marcia S. Russo, Corp.Libn. & Hist.

TRINITY COLLEGE - WATKINSON LIBRARY
300 Summit St.   Phone: (203) 527-3151
Hartford, CT 06106   Dr. Jeffrey H. Kaimowitz, Cur.

UNITED CHURCH OF CHRIST - CONNECTICUT CONFERENCE - ARCHIVES *
125 Sherman St.
Hartford, CT 06105   Rev. Wesley C. Ewert, Archv.

U.S. DEPT. OF COMMERCE - INTERNATIONAL TRADE ADMINISTRATION -
    HARTFORD DISTRICT OFFICE LIBRARY
Federal Office Bldg., Rm. 610B
450 Main St.   Phone: (203) 244-3530
Hartford, CT 06103

UNIVERSITY OF CONNECTICUT - INSTITUTE OF PUBLIC SERVICE -
    INTERNATIONAL LIBRARY *
1380 Asylum Ave.   Phone: (203) 233-9681
Hartford, CT 06105   John Tabor, Prog.Dir.

UNIVERSITY OF CONNECTICUT - SCHOOL OF BUSINESS ADMINISTRATION
    LIBRARY
39 Woodland St.   Phone: (203) 527-2149
Hartford, CT 06105   MaryKay W. Schnare, Libn.

WADSWORTH ATHENEUM - AUERBACH ART LIBRARY *
600 Main St.   Phone: (203) 278-2670
Hartford, CT 06103   Elizabeth G. Hoke, Libn.

YOUNG MEN'S CHRISTIAN ASSOCIATION OF METROPOLITAN HARTFORD,
    INC. - CAREER COUNSELING CENTER LIBRARY
160 Jewell St.   Phone: (203) 522-4183
Hartford, CT 06103   Dr. William N. Goodwin, Dir.

CONNECTICUT STATE LIBRARY - LAW LIBRARY AT LITCHFIELD
Court House, West St.   Phone: (203) 567-0598
Litchfield, CT 06759   Evelina E. Lemelin, Libn.

LITCHFIELD HISTORICAL SOCIETY - INGRAHAM LIBRARY
Box 385   Phone: (203) 567-5862
Litchfield, CT 06759

MADISON HISTORICAL SOCIETY, INC. - LIBRARY
853 Boston Post Rd.
Box 17   Phone: (203) 245-4567
Madison, CT 06443   William T. Mills, Pres.

MANCHESTER MEMORIAL HOSPITAL - LIBRARY *
71 Haynes St.   Phone: (203) 646-1222
Manchester, CT 06040   Anna B. Salo

MANSFIELD TRAINING SCHOOL - MEDICAL LIBRARY
Box 51
Mansfield Depot, CT 06251

ALTOBELLO (Henry D.) CHILDREN AND YOUTH CENTER - PROFESSIONAL
    COLLECTION
Undercliff Rd.   Phone: (203) 238-6085
Meriden, CT 06450   Joetta Poppalardo, Dir. of Prof.Ed.

CONNECTICUT POLICE ACADEMY - RESOURCE CENTER
285 Preston Ave.   Phone: (203) 238-6531
Meriden, CT 06450   Theresa A. Wyser, Libn.

INTERNATIONAL SILVER COMPANY - HISTORICAL LIBRARY
550 Research Pkwy.   Phone: (203) 238-8058
Meriden, CT 06450   Ed P. Hogan, Hist.

MERIDEN-WALLINGFORD HOSPITAL - HEALTH SCIENCES LIBRARY
181 Cook Ave.   Phone: (203) 238-0771
Meriden, CT 06450   Patricia C. Westbrook, Libn.

UNIROYAL, INC. - CORPORATE LIBRARY
Oxford Management & Research Ctr.   Phone: (203) 573-2000
Middlebury, CT 06749   M. Carr, Libn.

UNIROYAL, INC. - TECHNICAL LIBRARY
Research Bldg.
Oxford Management & Research Ctr.   Phone: (203) 573-4509
Middlebury, CT 06749   D.H. Winslow, Mgr.

CONNECTICUT VALLEY HOSPITAL - HALLOCK MEDICAL LIBRARY
Box 351   Phone: (203) 344-2304
Middletown, CT 06457   Mildred Asbell, Med.Libn.

GODFREY MEMORIAL LIBRARY
134 Newfield St.   Phone: (203) 346-4375
Middletown, CT 06457   Doris Post, Dir.

MIDDLESEX COUNTY HISTORICAL SOCIETY - LIBRARY *
151 Main St.   Phone: (203) 346-0746
Middletown, CT 06457

MIDDLESEX MEMORIAL HOSPITAL - HEALTH SCIENCES LIBRARY
28 Crescent St.   Phone: (203) 347-9471
Middletown, CT 06457   Nancy R. Thorne, Dir.

UNITED TECHNOLOGIES CORPORATION - PRATT & WHITNEY AIRCRAFT
    GROUP - MATERIALS ENGINEERING RESEARCH LIB.
Box 611   Phone: (203) 344-5138
Middletown, CT 06457   Beverly J. Esson, Libn.

WESLEYAN UNIVERSITY - ART LIBRARY
Davison Art Center   Phone: (203) 347-9411
Middletown, CT 06457   Richard H. Wood, Libn.

WESLEYAN UNIVERSITY - MUSIC DEPARTMENT - WORLD MUSIC
    ARCHIVES
                                        Phone: (203) 347-9411
Middletown, CT 06457

WESLEYAN UNIVERSITY - PSYCHOLOGY DEPARTMENT LIBRARY
Judd Hall   Phone: (203) 347-9411
Middletown, CT 06457

WESLEYAN UNIVERSITY - SCIENCE LIBRARY
Phone: (203) 347-9411
Middletown, CT 06457
William Calhoon, Sci.Libn.

XEROX CORPORATION - XEROX EDUCATION PUBLICATIONS - LIBRARY
245 Long Hill Rd.　　　　Phone: (203) 347-7251
Middletown, CT 06457
Harriet S. Osburn, Hd.Libn.

U.S. NATL. MARINE FISHERIES SERVICE - MILFORD LABORATORY LIBRARY
212 Rogers Ave.　　　　Phone: (203) 878-2459
Milford, CT 06460
Ronald G. Fontaine, Libn.

MYSTIC SEAPORT, INC. - G.W. BLUNT WHITE LIBRARY
Phone: (203) 536-2631
Mystic, CT 06355
Gerald E. Morris, Libn.

UNIROYAL, INC. - UNIROYAL CHEMICAL DIVISION - MANAGEMENT & TECHNICAL INFORMATION SERVICES/LIBRARY
Elm St.　　　　Phone: (203) 723-3252
Naugatuck, CT 06770
Eugene S. Hertel, Info.Sci.

CENTRAL CONNECTICUT STATE COLLEGE - ELIHU BURRITT LIBRARY
Wells St.　　　　Phone: (203) 827-7530
New Britain, CT 06050
Robert E. Massmann, Dir.

NEW BRITAIN GENERAL HOSPITAL - HEALTH SCIENCE LIBRARY
100 Grand St.　　　　Phone: (203) 224-5122
New Britain, CT 06050
Debora K. Stenberg, Lib.Dir.

NEW BRITAIN MUSEUM OF AMERICAN ART - LIBRARY
56 Lexington St.　　　　Phone: (203) 229-0257
New Britain, CT 06052
Lois L. Blomstrann, Asst. to Dir.

NEW BRITAIN YOUTH MUSEUM - RESOURCE CENTER
30 High St.　　　　Phone: (203) 225-3020
New Britain, CT 06051
Alan J. Krauss, Musm.Dir.

NEW CANAAN HISTORICAL SOCIETY - LIBRARY
13 Oenoke Ridge　　　　Phone: (203) 966-1776
New Canaan, CT 06840
Mary C. Durbrow, Libn.

NEW CANAAN NATURE CENTER ASSOCIATION, INC. - LIBRARY †
144 Oenoke Ridge　　　　Phone: (203) 966-9577
New Canaan, CT 06840
Mrs. John Sawhill, Dir.

SILVERMINE SCHOOL OF THE ARTS - LIBRARY
1037 Silvermine Rd.
New Canaan, CT 06840

AREA COOPERATIVE EDUCATIONAL SERVICES - TEACHER RESOURCE LIBRARY
800 Dixwell Ave.　　　　Phone: (203) 562-9967
New Haven, CT 06511
Virginia Evitts, Libn.

CONNECTICUT AGRICULTURAL EXPERIMENT STATION - OSBORNE LIBRARY
123 Huntington St.
Box 1106　　　　Phone: (203) 789-7265
New Haven, CT 06504
Paul Gough, Libn.

CONNECTICUT STATE LIBRARY - LAW LIBRARY AT NEW HAVEN
County Courthouse
235 Church St.　　　　Phone: (203) 789-7889
New Haven, CT 06510
Martha J. Sullivan, Lib.Adm.

HASKINS LABORATORIES - LIBRARY
270 Crown St.　　　　Phone: (203) 436-1774
New Haven, CT 06510
Nancy O'Brien, Libn.

HOSPITAL OF ST. RAPHAEL - HEALTH SCIENCES LIBRARY
1450 Chapel St.　　　　Phone: (203) 789-3330
New Haven, CT 06511
Patricia L. Wales, Dir., Lib.Serv.

HUMAN RELATIONS AREA FILES, INC.
755 Prospect St.　　　　Phone: (203) 777-2334
New Haven, CT 06520
Timothy J. O'Leary, Dir., File Res.

NEW HAVEN COLONY HISTORICAL SOCIETY - LIBRARY
114 Whitney Ave.　　　　Phone: (203) 562-4183
New Haven, CT 06510
Ottilia Koel, Libn. & Cur. of Mss.

OLIN CORPORATION - METALS RESEARCH LABORATORIES - METALS INFORMATION CENTER
91 Shelton Ave.　　　　Phone: (203) 789-5278
New Haven, CT 06511
Marcella C. Tammard, Libn.

OLIN CORPORATION - RESEARCH CENTER/INFORMATION CENTER
Box 30-275　　　　Phone: (203) 789-6038
New Haven, CT 06511
Dr. R.E. Maizell, Mgr.

SOUTHERN CONNECTICUT STATE COLLEGE - H.C. BULEY LIBRARY
501 Crescent St.　　　　Phone: (203) 397-4505
New Haven, CT 06515
Richard Hegel, Dir. of Lib.Serv.

UNITED ILLUMINATING COMPANY - LIBRARY
80 Temple St.　　　　Phone: (203) 787-7690
New Haven, CT 06506
Marie S. Richardson, Libn.

YALE UNIVERSITY - AMERICAN ORIENTAL SOCIETY LIBRARY
Sterling Memorial Library, Rm. 329
New Haven, CT 06520
Rutherford D. Rogers, Libn.

YALE UNIVERSITY - ANTHROPOLOGY LIBRARY
Kline Science Library
Box 6666　　　　Phone: (203) 436-0874
New Haven, CT 06511
Richard J. Dionne, Libn.

YALE UNIVERSITY - ART AND ARCHITECTURE LIBRARY
Art & Architecture Bldg.
Yale Sta., Box 1605A　　　　Phone: (203) 436-2055
New Haven, CT 06520
Nancy S. Lambert, Libn.

YALE UNIVERSITY - ARTS OF THE BOOK COLLECTION
Sterling Memorial Library　　　　Phone: (203) 436-2200
New Haven, CT 06520
Gay Walker, Cur.

YALE UNIVERSITY - BABYLONIAN COLLECTION
Sterling Memorial Library
120 High St.　　　　Phone: (203) 432-4725
New Haven, CT 06520
William W. Hallo, Cur.

YALE UNIVERSITY - BEINECKE RARE BOOK AND MANUSCRIPT LIBRARY
Wall & High Sts.　　　　Phone: (203) 436-0234
New Haven, CT 06520
Lawrence Dowler, Act.Libn.

YALE UNIVERSITY - BENJAMIN FRANKLIN COLLECTION
Sterling Memorial Library, Rm. 230　　　　Phone: (203) 436-8646
New Haven, CT 06520
Dorothy W. Bridgwater, Asst.Libn.

YALE UNIVERSITY - CLASSICS LIBRARY
Phelps Hall, 344 College St.　　　　Phone: (203) 436-1130
New Haven, CT 06520
Carla M. Lukas, Libn.

YALE UNIVERSITY - COLLECTION OF THE LITERATURE OF THE AMERICAN MUSICAL THEATRE
Sterling Memorial Library, Rm. 226　　　　Phone: (203) 436-1822
New Haven, CT 06520
Richard Warren, Jr., Cur.

YALE UNIVERSITY - COLLECTION OF MUSICAL INSTRUMENTS - LIBRARY
15 Hillhouse Ave.
Box 2117　　　　Phone: (203) 436-4935
New Haven, CT 06520
Richard Rephann, Dir.

YALE UNIVERSITY - COWLES FOUNDATION FOR RESEARCH IN ECONOMICS - LIBRARY
30 Hillhouse Ave.　　　　Phone: (203) 436-0249
New Haven, CT 06520
Karlee Gifford, Libn.

YALE UNIVERSITY - CRAWFORD COLLECTION ON THE MODERN DRAMA
Sterling Memorial Library, Rm. 409　　　　Phone: (203) 436-8335
New Haven, CT 06520
Robert Balay, Hd., Ref.Dept.

YALE UNIVERSITY - DIVINITY SCHOOL LIBRARY
409 Prospect St.　　　　Phone: (203) 436-8440
New Haven, CT 06510
Stephen L. Peterson, Libn.

YALE UNIVERSITY - EAST ASIAN COLLECTION
Sterling Memorial Library   Phone: (203) 436-4810
New Haven, CT 06520   Hideo Kaneko, Cur.

YALE UNIVERSITY - ECONOMIC GROWTH CENTER COLLECTION
140 Prospect St.   Phone: (203) 436-3412
New Haven, CT 06520   Billie I. Salter, Libn. for Social Sci.

YALE UNIVERSITY - ELIZABETHAN CLUB COLLECTION
459 College St.   Phone: (203) 436-8535
New Haven, CT 06511   Stephen R. Parks, Libn.

YALE UNIVERSITY - ENGINEERING AND APPLIED SCIENCE LIBRARY
Becton Ctr., 15 Prospect St.   Phone: (203) 432-4539
New Haven, CT 06520   Elizabeth Hayes, Hd.

YALE UNIVERSITY - FORESTRY LIBRARY
205 Prospect St.   Phone: (203) 436-0577
New Haven, CT 06511   Joseph A. Miller, Libn.

YALE UNIVERSITY - GEOLOGY LIBRARY
Box 6666   Phone: (203) 436-2480
New Haven, CT 06511   Harry D. Scammell, Libn.

YALE UNIVERSITY - INDOLOGICAL AND LINGUISTIC SEMINAR - LIBRARY
302 Hall of Graduate Studies
320 York St.   Phone: (203) 436-1862
New Haven, CT 06520   Professor Stanley Insler, Chm.

YALE UNIVERSITY - JOHN HERRICK JACKSON MUSIC LIBRARY
98 Wall St.   Phone: (203) 436-8240
New Haven, CT 06520   Harold E. Samuel, Libn.

YALE UNIVERSITY - KLINE SCIENCE LIBRARY
Kline Biology Tower, Rm. C-8   Phone: (203) 436-3710
New Haven, CT 06520   Richard J. Dionne, Sci.Libn.

YALE UNIVERSITY - LAW LIBRARY
127 Wall St.   Phone: (203) 436-2215
New Haven, CT 06520   Morris L. Cohen, Libn.

YALE UNIVERSITY - MANUSCRIPTS AND ARCHIVES
Sterling Memorial Library   Phone: (203) 432-4695
New Haven, CT 06520   Lawrence Dowler, Assoc.Libn.

YALE UNIVERSITY - MAP COLLECTION
Sterling Memorial Library, Map Rm.   Phone: (203) 436-8638
New Haven, CT 06520   Barbara B. McCorkle, Cur. of Maps

YALE UNIVERSITY - MATHEMATICS LIBRARY
12 Hillhouse Ave.
Yale Sta., Box 2155   Phone: (203) 436-0725
New Haven, CT 06520   Paul J. Lukasiewicz, Mathematics Libn.

YALE UNIVERSITY - MEDICAL LIBRARY
333 Cedar St.   Phone: (203) 436-4784
New Haven, CT 06510   Mary E. Feeney, Libn.

YALE UNIVERSITY - OBSERVATORY LIBRARY
260 Whitney Ave., J.W. Gibbs Laboratory
Box 6666   Phone: (203) 436-3460
New Haven, CT 06511   Linda Brown, Assoc.Libn.

YALE UNIVERSITY - ORNITHOLOGY LIBRARY
Peabody Museum, Bingham Lab.
170 Whitney Ave., Box 6666   Phone: (203) 436-8547
New Haven, CT 06511   Eleanor H. Stickney, Sr.Musm.Asst.

YALE UNIVERSITY - SCHOOL OF DRAMA LIBRARY
222 York St.
Yale Sta., Box 1903A   Phone: (203) 436-2213
New Haven, CT 06520   Pamela C. Jordan, Libn.

YALE UNIVERSITY - SEMITIC REFERENCE LIBRARY
314 Sterling Memorial Library
Yale University Library
New Haven, CT 06520   Edward A. Jajko, Near East Biblog.

YALE UNIVERSITY - SLAVIC & EAST EUROPEAN COLLECTIONS
Sterling Memorial Library   Phone: (203) 436-0230
New Haven, CT 06520   Tatiana Rannit, Cur.

YALE UNIVERSITY - SOCIAL SCIENCE LIBRARY
140 Prospect St.   Phone: (203) 436-3412
New Haven, CT 06520   Billie I. Salter, Libn. for Social Sci.

YALE UNIVERSITY - SOUTHEAST ASIA COLLECTION
Sterling Memorial Library   Phone: (203) 436-1092
New Haven, CT 06520   Charles R. Bryant, Cur.

YALE UNIVERSITY - STERLING CHEMISTRY LIBRARY
225 Prospect St.   Phone: (203) 436-3397
New Haven, CT 06520   A. Brandon Gulledge, Hd.

YALE UNIVERSITY - YALE CENTER FOR BRITISH ART - PHOTO ARCHIVE
2120 Yale Sta.   Phone: (203) 432-4594
New Haven, CT 06520   Dr. Anne-Marie Logan, Libn./Photo Archv.

**YALE UNIVERSITY - YALE CENTER FOR BRITISH ART - RARE BOOK
COLLECTION**
2120 Yale Sta.   Phone: (203) 432-4099
New Haven, CT 06520   Joan M. Friedman, Cur. Of Rare Books

**YALE UNIVERSITY - YALE CENTER FOR BRITISH ART - REFERENCE
LIBRARY**
2120 Yale Sta.   Phone: (203) 432-4594
New Haven, CT 06520   Dr. Anne-Marie Logan, Libn./Photo Archv.

**YALE UNIVERSITY - YALE COLLECTION OF HISTORICAL SOUND
RECORDINGS**
Sterling Memorial Library   Phone: (203) 436-1822
New Haven, CT 06520   Richard Warren, Jr., Cur.

ALLYN (Lyman) MUSEUM - LIBRARY
625 Williams St.   Phone: (203) 443-2345
New London, CT 06320   Mrs. Daniel Dinsmore, Libn.

CONNECTICUT COLLEGE - GREER MUSIC LIBRARY
                                               Phone: (203) 447-1911
New London, CT 06320   Philip Youngholm, Music Libn.

CONNECTICUT COLLEGE - LIBRARY - SPECIAL COLLECTIONS
Mohegan Ave.   Phone: (203) 442-1630
New London, CT 06320   Brian D. Rogers, Coll.Libn.

NEW LONDON COUNTY HISTORICAL SOCIETY - LIBRARY
Shaw Mansion, 11 Blinman St.   Phone: (203) 443-1209
New London, CT 06320   Elizabeth B. Knox, Sec./Libn./Cur.

U.S. COAST GUARD ACADEMY - LIBRARY
                                               Phone: (203) 443-8463
New London, CT 06320   D. Johnson, Libn.

**U.S. NAVY - NAVAL UNDERWATER SYSTEMS CENTER - NEW LONDON
TECHNICAL LIBRARY**
Bldg. 80   Phone: (203) 447-4276
New London, CT 06320   David L. Hanna, Hd.Libn.

WESTRECO, INC. - TECHNICAL LIBRARY
Boardman Rd.
Box 634   Phone: (203) 355-0911
New Milford, CT 06776   Jean Trapani, Mgr., Info.Serv.

**CEDARCREST REGIONAL HOSPITAL AND DEPARTMENT OF MENTAL HEALTH
- LIBRARY**
Russell Rd.   Phone: (203) 666-4613
Newington, CT 06111   Ceil Liberno, Act.Libn.

NEWINGTON CHILDREN'S HOSPITAL - PROFESSIONAL LIBRARY
181 E. Cedar St.   Phone: (203) 666-2461
Newington, CT 06111   Jean Long, Med.Libn.

**U.S. VETERANS ADMINISTRATION (CT-Newington) - HOSPITAL HEALTH
SCIENCES LIBRARY**
555 Willard Ave.   Phone: (203) 666-6951
Newington, CT 06111   Julie A. Lueders, Chf., Lib.Serv.

GEOGRAPHIC

GEOGRAPHIC

FAIRFIELD HILLS HOSPITAL - MEDICAL LIBRARY
Box W
Newtown, CT 06470
Phone: (203) 426-2531
Pauline A. Kruk, Libn.

WHITNEY (Eli) MUSEUM - LIBRARY
Route 139
North Branford, CT 00471
Phone: (203) 488-2157
Merrill K. Lindsay, Pres.

UPJOHN COMPANY - D.S. GILMORE RESEARCH LABORATORIES - RESEARCH
LIBRARY
410 Sackett Point Rd.
North Haven, CT 06473
Phone: (203) 281-2782
A. Munim Nashu, EPA Coord./Libn.

BURNDY LIBRARY
Electra Sq.
Norwalk, CT 06856
Phone: (203) 838-4444
Dr. Bern Dibner, Dir.

NORDEN SYSTEMS, INC. - TECHNICAL LIBRARY
Norden Pl.
Norwalk, CT 06856
Phone: (203) 852-4724
Estelle Thurman, Libn.

NORWALK HOSPITAL - R. GLEN WIGGANS MEMORIAL LIBRARY
24 Stevens St.
Norwalk, CT 06856
Phone: (203) 852-2793
Joan Sjostrom, Libn.

NORWALK STATE TECHNICAL COLLEGE - LIBRARY
181 Richards Ave.
Norwalk, CT 06854
Phone: (203) 838-0601
Rita Schara, Libn.

PERKIN-ELMER CORPORATION - CORPORATE LIBRARY
Main Ave.
Norwalk, CT 06856
Phone: (203) 762-4946
Margaret D. Wood, Mgr.

PURDUE FREDERICK COMPANY - RESEARCH LIBRARY
50 Washington St.
Norwalk, CT 06856
Phone: (203) 853-0123
Ellen Oberman Ingber, Info.Mgr.

BACKUS (William W.) HOSPITAL - MEDICAL/NURSING LIBRARY
326 Washington St.
Norwich, CT 06360
Phone: (203) 889-8331
Florence Lamoureux, Med.Libn.

BETH JACOB SYNAGOGUE - LIBRARY
400 New London Tpke.
Norwich, CT 06360
Phone: (203) 886-2459

NORWICH HOSPITAL - HEALTH SCIENCES LIBRARY
Box 508
Norwich, CT 06360
Phone: (203) 889-7361
Emily Court, Libn.

SOCIETY OF THE FOUNDERS OF NORWICH, CONNECTICUT - LEFFINGWELL
INN LIBRARY
348 Washington St.
Norwich, CT 06360
L.K. Edgerton, Libn.

CONDIESEL MOBILE EQUIPMENT - ENGINEERING LIBRARY
1700 E. Putnam Ave.
Old Greenwich, CT 06870
Phone: (203) 637-6140
Frances Darwick, Libn.

LYME HISTORICAL SOCIETY, INC. - ARCHIVES
Lyme St.
Old Lyme, CT 06371
Phone: (203) 434-5542
Jeffrey W. Andersen, Dir.

INDIAN AND COLONIAL RESEARCH CENTER, INC. - EVA BUTLER LIBRARY
Route 27
Old Mystic, CT 06372
Phone: (203) 536-9771
Kathleen Greenhalgh, Libn.

HUBBELL , INC. - LIBRARY
584 Derby-Milford Rd.
Orange, CT 06477
Phone: (203) 789-1100
Roger M. Search, V.P.Indus.Rel.

YARDNEY ELECTRIC CORPORATION - TECHNICAL INFORMATION CENTER
82 Mechanic St.
Pawcatuck, CT 06379
Phone: (203) 559-1100
Mrs. P. Lochner, Libn.

BELDING HEMINWAY COMPANY - BELDING CORTICELLI RESEARCH
CENTER - LIBRARY
Putnam, CT 06260
Phone: (203) 928-2784
E.J. Page, Chf. Chemist

NEW ENGLAND INSTITUTE - LIBRARY *
90 Grove St.
Box 308
Ridgefield, CT 06877
Phone: (203) 438-6591
M. Vaccaro, Asst.Libn.

SCHLUMBERGER-DOLL RESEARCH CENTER - LIBRARY
Box 307, Old Quarry Rd.
Ridgefield, CT 06810
Phone: (203) 438-2631
Henry Edmundson, Mgr.

CONNECTICUT STATE LIBRARY - LAW LIBRARY AT ROCKVILLE
Box 510
Rockville, CT 06066
Phone: (203) 875-6294
Virginia Scanlon, Libn.

ROCKVILLE GENERAL HOSPITAL - MEDICAL LIBRARY/RESOURCE ROOM
31 Union St.
Rockville, CT 06066
Phone: (203) 875-7537
Dorothea M. Zabilansky, Med.Libn.

ROCKY HILL HISTORICAL SOCIETY - ACADEMY HALL MUSEUM - LIBRARY
785 Old Main St.
Box 185
Rocky Hill, CT 06067
Phone: (203) 563-8710
Mrs. Dudley S. Cooke, Libn.

ROGERS CORPORATION - LURIE LIBRARY
Rogers, CT 06263
Phone: (203) 774-9605
Myrna D. Riquier, Libn.

SHARON HOSPITAL - HEALTH SCIENCES LIBRARY
W. Main St.
Sharon, CT 06069
Phone: (203) 364-5511
Jean Moore, Dir.

SIMSBURY HISTORICAL SOCIETY - SIMSBURY RESEARCH LIBRARY
800 Hopmeadow St.
Simsbury, CT 06070
Phone: (203) 658-2500
Robert A. Hawley, Dir.

SOMERS HISTORICAL SOCIETY - ARCHIVES
574 Main St.
Somers, CT 06071
Phone: (203) 749-7273
Jeanne K. DeBell, Cur.

HOFFREL INSTRUMENTS, INC. - LIBRARY
345 Wilson Ave.
South Norwalk, CT 06854
Phone: (203) 866-9205
Donald P. Relyes, Hd.

AMERICAN CYANAMID COMPANY - STAMFORD RESEARCH CENTER
LIBRARY *
1937 W. Main St.
Stamford, CT 06904
Phone: (203) 348-7331
Joan Gallagher, Libn.

AMF, INC. - TECHNICAL INFORMATION CENTER
689 Hope St.
Stamford, CT 06907
Phone: (203) 325-2211
Bobbi Bernard, Tech.Libn.

BARNES ENGINEERING COMPANY - LIBRARY
30 Commerce Rd.
Stamford, CT 06904
Phone: (203) 348-5381
Belle B. Shipe, Libn.

BUSINESS COMMUNICATIONS CO., INC. - LIBRARY
Box 2070C
Stamford, CT 06906
Phone: (203) 325-2208
Roger Memmott, Dir. of Oper.

CBS INC. - CBS TECHNOLOGY CENTER
227 High Ridge Rd.
Stamford, CT 06905
Phone: (203) 327-2000
Laura Kapnick, Chf.Libn.

CHAMPION INTERNATIONAL - CORPORATE INFORMATION CENTER
1 Champion Plaza
Stamford, CT 06921
Phone: (203) 358-7390
Phyllis Prince, Mgr.

CLAIROL, INC. - RESEARCH LIBRARY
2 Blachley Rd.
Stamford, CT 06902
Phone: (203) 357-5001
Theodora J. Reardon, Libn.

CONNECTICUT STATE BOARD OF EDUCATION - J.M. WRIGHT TECHNICAL
SCHOOL - LIBRARY *
Scalzi Pk.
Stamford, CT 06904
Phone: (203) 324-7363
Robert Dolan, Libn.

CRAWFORD AND RUSSELL, INC. - TECHNICAL LIBRARY
17 Amelia Pl.
Stamford, CT 06904
Phone: (203) 327-1450
Beth Steinhardt, Libn.

DORR-OLIVER INC. - CENTRAL TECHNOLOGY LIBRARY †
77 Havemeyer Lane
Phone: (203) 348-5871
Stamford, CT 06904

EASTER SEAL REHABILITATION CENTER OF SOUTHWESTERN
   CONNECTICUT - FRANCIS M. HARRISON MEMORIAL LIBRARY
26 Palmer's Hill Rd.
Phone: (203) 325-1544
Stamford, CT 06902
Ruth C. Adams, Libn.

FERGUSON LIBRARY - BUSINESS-TECHNOLOGY DEPARTMENT
96 Broad St.
Phone: (203) 964-1000
Stamford, CT 06901
Doris Goodlett, Hd., Adult Serv.

FINANCIAL ACCOUNTING STANDARDS BOARD (FASB) - LIBRARY
High Ridge Pk.
Phone: (203) 329-8401
Stamford, CT 06905
Marianne Losch, Libn.

KENNECOTT CORPORATION - CORPORATE PLANNING LIBRARY
10 Stamford Forum
Phone: (203) 964-3481
Stamford, CT 06940
Dina Lokets, Libn.

OLIN CORPORATION - BUSINESS INFORMATION CENTER
120 Long Ridge Rd.
Phone: (203) 356-2498
Stamford, CT 06904
L.A. Magistrate, Hd.

PITNEY BOWES - TECHNICAL INFORMATION CENTER
Walter Wheeler Dr.
Phone: (203) 853-0727
Stamford, CT 06904
Mary Lynn Ainsworth, Mgr.Tech.Info.Ctr.

STAMFORD CATHOLIC LIBRARY, INC.
195 Glenbrook Rd.
Phone: (203) 348-4422
Stamford, CT 06902
Mary D. Cash, Libn.

STAMFORD HISTORICAL SOCIETY - LIBRARY
713 Bedford St.
Phone: (203) 323-1975
Stamford, CT 06901

STAMFORD HOSPITAL - HEALTH SCIENCES LIBRARY
Shelburne Rd. & W. Broad St.
Phone: (203) 327-1234
Stamford, CT 06902
Jo Ann Morris, Dir.

TEXASGULF, INC. - RESEARCH LIBRARY
High Ridge Park
Phone: (203) 358-5135
Stamford, CT 06904
Patricia R. O'Shea, Corp.Libn.

XEROX CORPORATION - LAW LIBRARY
Phone: (203) 329-8700
Stamford, CT 06904
Geraldine McColgan Brown, Hd.Libn.

YORK RESEARCH CORPORATION - LIBRARY
One Research Dr.
Phone: (203) 325-1371
Stamford, CT 06906
Barbara A. Goodhouse, Libn.

STONINGTON HISTORICAL SOCIETY - WHITEHALL LIBRARY
Box 31
Stonington, CT 06378
Roger Williams, Jr., Libn.

MANSFIELD HISTORICAL SOCIETY - EDITH MASON LIBRARY
954 Storrs Rd.
Box 145
Phone: (203) 429-9789
Storrs, CT 06268
Roberta Smith, Pres.

MOLESWORTH INSTITUTE - LIBRARY AND ARCHIVES
143 Hanks Hill Rd.
Phone: (203) 486-2220
Storrs, CT 06268
Cecily Cardew, Lib.Dir. & Archv.

UNIVERSITY OF CONNECTICUT - CENTER FOR REAL ESTATE & URBAN
   ECONOMIC STUDIES - REFERENCE & DOCUMENTS ROOM
U-41-RE
Phone: (203) 486-3227
Storrs, CT 06268
Judith B. Paesani

UNIVERSITY OF CONNECTICUT - INSTITUTE FOR SOCIAL INQUIRY
Box U-164
Phone: (203) 486-4440
Storrs, CT 06268
Everett C. Ladd, Jr., Exec.Dir.

UNIVERSITY OF CONNECTICUT - INSTITUTE OF URBAN RESEARCH -
   LIBRARY
Phone: (203) 486-4518
Storrs, CT 06268
Jean W. Gosselin, Res.Asst.

UNIVERSITY OF CONNECTICUT - LABOR EDUCATION CENTER -
   INFORMATION CENTER
Bishop Bldg., Rm. 213
Phone: (203) 486-3417
Storrs, CT 06268
George E. O'Connell, Dir.

UNIVERSITY OF CONNECTICUT - LEARNING RESOURCES DIVISION -
   CENTER FOR INSTRUCTIONAL MEDIA & TECHNOLOGY
Phone: (203) 486-3080
Storrs, CT 06268
Cora Hahn, Dir.

UNIVERSITY OF CONNECTICUT - LIBRARY
Phone: (203) 486-2219
Storrs, CT 06268
John P. McDonald, Dir. of Libs.

UNIVERSITY OF CONNECTICUT - MAP LIBRARY
Phone: (203) 486-4589
Storrs, CT 06268
Thornton P. McGlamery, Map Libn.

UNIVERSITY OF CONNECTICUT - MUSIC LIBRARY
U-12
Phone: (203) 486-2502
Storrs, CT 06268
Dorothy McAdoo Bognar, Libn.

UNIVERSITY OF CONNECTICUT - PHARMACY LIBRARY AND LEARNING
   CENTER
Box U-92
Phone: (203) 486-2218
Storrs, CT 06268
O. James Purnell, III, Dir.

UNIVERSITY OF CONNECTICUT - PUERTO RICAN CENTER - ROBERTO
   CLEMENTE LIBRARY
Phone: (203) 486-2204
Storrs, CT 06268

UNIVERSITY OF CONNECTICUT - ROPER CENTER
Box U-164R
Phone: (203) 486-4440
Storrs, CT 06268
Everett C. Ladd, Exec.Dir.

AVCO CORPORATION - LYCOMING DIVISION - LIBRARY & INFORMATION
   CENTER
550 S. Main St.
Phone: (203) 378-8211
Stratford, CT 06497
Joseph P. Murphy, Chf.Tech.Info.Serv.

STRATFORD HISTORICAL SOCIETY - LIBRARY
967 Academy Hill
Box 382
Phone: (203) 378-0630
Stratford, CT 06497
Mrs. Einar M. Larson, Libn.

UNITED TECHNOLOGIES CORPORATION - SIKORSKY AIRCRAFT DIVISION -
   DIVISION LIBRARY
N. Main St.
Phone: (203) 386-4713
Stratford, CT 06602
Robert M. Knapik, Libn.

KENT MEMORIAL LIBRARY - HISTORICAL ROOM
50 N. Main St.
Phone: (203) 668-2325
Suffield, CT 06078
Anne W. Borg, Asst.Dir.

TORRINGTON HISTORICAL SOCIETY - LIBRARY
192 Main St.
Phone: (203) 482-8260
Torrington, CT 06790
Catherine Calhoun, Exec.Dir.

CHESEBROUGH-POND'S, INC. - RESEARCH LIBRARY
Trumbull Industrial Pk.
Phone: (203) 377-7100
Trumbull, CT 06611
Carol Gannon, Libn.

GAYLORD HOSPITAL - MEDICAL LIBRARY
Box 400
Phone: (203) 269-3344
Wallingford, CT 06492
Ruth Ford, Med.Libn.

WALLINGFORD HISTORICAL SOCIETY, INC. - LIBRARY
Box 73
Phone: (203) 269-6257
Wallingford, CT 06492
Charles R. Clulee, Pres. Emeritus

CONNECTICUT ELECTRIC RAILWAY ASSOCIATION, INC. - LIBRARY
   DEPARTMENT
Box 436
Phone: (203) 623-7417
Warehouse Point, CT 06088
W.E. Wood, Libn.

ATLANTIC-RICHFIELD COMPANY - ANACONDA INDUSTRIES - RESEARCH
   AND TECHNICAL CENTER LIBRARY
245 Freight St.
Box 747
Phone: (203) 574-8936
Waterbury, CT 06720
Catherine N. Judd, Libn.

GEOGRAPHIC

GEOGRAPHIC

BRONSON (Silas) LIBRARY - BUSINESS, INDUSTRY, AND TECHNOLOGY
DEPARTMENT †
267 Grand St.
Waterbury, CT 06702
Phone: (203) 574-8233
Blanche T. Clark, Dept.Hd.

CENTRAL NAUGATUCK VALLEY REGIONAL PLANNING AGENCY - LIBRARY
20 E. Main St.
Waterbury, CT 06702
Phone: (203) 757-0535
Duncan M. Graham, Exec.Dir.

CONNECTICUT STATE LIBRARY - LAW LIBRARY AT WATERBURY
Court House, 300 Grand St.
Waterbury, CT 06702
Phone: (203) 754-2644
Lucy L. Cyr, Libn.

ST. MARY'S HOSPITAL - FINKELSTEIN LIBRARY
56 Franklin St.
Waterbury, CT 06702
Phone: (203) 756-8351
Jean Fuller, Libn.

TIMEX CORPORATION - LEGAL & CORPORATE LIBRARY
Park Road Ext.
Waterbury, CT 06720
Phone: (203) 573-5268
Margaret Q. Orloske, Libn.

WATERBURY AMERICAN-REPUBLICAN - LIBRARY
389 Meadow St.
Waterbury, CT 06722
Phone: (203) 574-3636
Clarissa D. Laukaitis, Libn.

WATERBURY HOSPITAL HEALTH CENTER - HEALTH CENTER LIBRARY
64 Robbins St.
Waterbury, CT 06720
Phone: (203) 573-6136
Mrs. M.F. Carmichael, Lib.Dir.

WATERBURY STATE TECHNICAL COLLEGE - HELEN HAHLO LIBRARY
1460 W. Main St.
Waterbury, CT 06708
Phone: (203) 756-7035
John Kiernan, Jr., Hd.Libn.

EUGENE O'NEILL MEMORIAL THEATER CENTER, INC. - THEATER
COLLECTION AND LIBRARY *
305 Great Neck Rd.
Waterford, CT 06385
Phone: (203) 443-5378
Sally Thomas Pavetti, Cur.

OPTIKON LABORATORIES - LIBRARY
River Rd.
West Cornwall, CT 06796
Phone: (203) 672-6614
W. Covington

JAMAICA (B.W.I.) STUDY GROUP - LIBRARY
267 West Granby Rd.
West Granby, CT 06090
Phone: (203) 653-6736
Howard J. Gaston, Libn.

CHANDLER EVANS, INC. - COMPANY LIBRARY *
One Charter Oak Blvd.
West Hartford, CT 06101
Phone: (203) 236-0651
Christina Jablonowski, Libn.

FIRST CHURCH OF CHRIST CONGREGATIONAL - JOHN P. WEBSTER
LIBRARY
12 S. Main St.
West Hartford, CT 06107
Phone: (203) 233-9605
Rev. Lee K. Ellenwood, Dir.

UNIVERSITY OF CONNECTICUT - LAW SCHOOL LIBRARY
Greater Hartford Campus
West Hartford, CT 06117
Phone: (203) 523-4841
Shirley R. Bysiewicz, Law Libn.

UNIVERSITY OF CONNECTICUT - SCHOOL OF SOCIAL WORK - LIBRARY *
Greater Hartford Campus
West Hartford, CT 06117
Phone: (203) 523-4841
Lee Sellers, Libn.

UNIVERSITY OF HARTFORD - ANNE BUNCE CHENEY LIBRARY
200 Bloomfield Ave.
West Hartford, CT 06117
Phone: (203) 243-4397
Jean J. Miller, Libn.

UNIVERSITY OF HARTFORD - DANA SCIENCE & ENGINEERING LIBRARY
200 Bloomfield Ave., Dana Bldg.
West Hartford, CT 06117
Phone: (203) 243-4404
Frances T. Libbey, Sci./Engr.Libn.

UNIVERSITY OF HARTFORD - HARTT SCHOOL OF MUSIC - ALLEN
MEMORIAL LIBRARY
200 Bloomfield Ave.
West Hartford, CT 06117
Phone: (203) 243-4491
Ethel Bacon, Libn.

WEBSTER (Noah) FOUNDATION & HISTORICAL SOCIETY OF WEST
HARTFORD - LIBRARY
227 S. Main St.
West Hartford, CT 06107
Phone: (203) 521-5362
Elliott W. Hoffman, Dir.

MILES LABORATORIES, INC.- DELBAY PHARMACEUTICALS - RESEARCH
LIBRARY
400 Morgan Lane
West Haven, CT 06516
Phone: (203) 934-9221
J.P. Fatcheric, Mgr., Info./Doc.

U.S. VETERANS ADMINISTRATION (CT-West Haven) - MEDICAL CENTER
LIBRARY
West Spring St.
West Haven, CT 06516
Phone: (203) 932-5711
William Preston, Chf.Libn.

GREENWOOD PRESS - LIBRARY
88 Post Rd., W.
Box 5007
Westport, CT 06881
Phone: (203) 226-3571
Mary Kalb, Info.Dir.

HALL-BROOKE HOSPITAL - PROFESSIONAL LIBRARY
47 Long Lots Rd.
Westport, CT 06880
Phone: (203) 227-1251
Lynn Sabol, Libn.

HUMAN LACTATION CENTER, LTD. - LIBRARY
666 Sturges Hwy.
Westport, CT 06880
Phone: (203) 259-5995
Dana Raphael, Dir.

LIFWYNN FOUNDATION, INC. - LIBRARY
30 Turkey Hill Rd., S.
Westport, CT 06880
Phone: (203) 227-4139
Alfreda S. Galt, Sec.

NATURE CENTER FOR ENVIRONMENTAL ACTIVITIES - REFERENCE
LIBRARY
10 Woodside Ln.
Westport, CT 06880
Phone: (203) 227-7253
Mrs. Robert J. Amirault, Libn.

TECHNOMIC PUBLISHING CO., INC. - BUSINESS LIBRARY
265 Post Rd. West
Westport, CT 06880
Phone: (203) 226-7203
Richard Dunn, Lib.Dir.

WETHERSFIELD HISTORICAL SOCIETY - OLD ACADEMY MUSEUM LIBRARY
150 Main St.
Wethersfield, CT 06109
Phone: (203) 529-7656
C. Douglas Alves, Jr., Dir.

EASTERN CONNECTICUT STATE COLLEGE - CENTER FOR CONNECTICUT
STUDIES
J. Eugene Smith Library
Willimantic, CT 06226
Phone: (203) 456-2231
Dr. David M. Roth, Dir.

CRAFT CENTER MUSEUM - CRAFT CENTER LIBRARY
78 Danbury Rd.
Box 488
Wilton, CT 06897
Miss E. Gilbaine, Libn.

RICHARDSON-VICKS, INC. - MARKETING INFORMATION CENTER
10 Westport Rd.
Wilton, CT 06897
Phone: (203) 762-2222
Mary Lou Wells, Mgr.

STANDARD BRANDS INC. - LIBRARY
15 River Rd.
Wilton, CT 06897
Phone: (203) 762-2500
Melanie C. Sze, Libn.

WILTON HISTORICAL SOCIETY, INC. - LIBRARY *
249 Danbury Rd.
Wilton, CT 06897
Phone: (203) 762-7257
Mrs. William M. Morrison, Jr., Dir.

COMBUSTION ENGINEERING, INC. - POWER SYSTEMS GROUP LIBRARY
SERVICES
Dept. 6435-405
Windsor, CT 06095
Phone: (203) 688-1911
Zena C. Grot-Zakrzewski, Mgr.

EMHART INDUSTRIES, INC. - HARTFORD DIVISION LIBRARY
123 Day Hill Rd.
Box 700
Windsor, CT 06095
Phone: (203) 688-8551
Linda J. Gale, Libn.

WINDSOR HISTORICAL SOCIETY - LIBRARY
96 Palisado Ave.
Windsor, CT 06095
Phone: (203) 688-3813
Edwinna C. Hillemeier, Cur.

CONNECTICUT AERONAUTICAL HISTORICAL ASSOCIATION - LIBRARY
Bradley International Airport
Windsor Locks, CT 06096

DEXTER CORPORATION - C.H. DEXTER DIVISION - TECHNICAL LIBRARY
Two Elm St.   Phone: (203) 623-9801
Windsor Locks, CT 06096   Fred N. Masters, Jr., Mgr.Tech.Info.Rsrcs.

DELAWARE

GETTY REFINING AND MARKETING COMPANY - TECHNICAL LIBRARY
                                                    Phone: (302) 834-6247
Delaware City, DE 19706   A.J. Juhas, Libn.

GOVERNOR BACON HEALTH CENTER - MEDICAL LIBRARY
                                                    Phone: (302) 834-9201
Delaware City, DE 19706   Ivonne K. Go, Libn.

DELAWARE STATE ARCHIVES
Hall of Records   Phone: (302) 736-5318
Dover, DE 19901   Lawrence Henry, Dir.

DELAWARE STATE DEPARTMENT OF PUBLIC INSTRUCTION - LIBRARY
Townsend Bldg., Box 1402   Phone: (302) 736-4692
Dover, DE 19901   Carolyn W. Huff, Libn.

DELAWARE STATE DEPARTMENT OF TRANSPORTATION - LIBRARY
Rte. 113, Administrative Bldg.   Phone: (302) 678-4157
Dover, DE 19901   Juliana Cheng, Libn.

DELAWARE STATE - DIVISION OF LIBRARIES
630 State College Rd.   Phone: (302) 678-4748
Dover, DE 19901   Sylvia Short, State Libn.

DELAWARE STATE LAW LIBRARY IN KENT COUNTY
Kent County Courthouse   Phone: (302) 736-1525
Dover, DE 19901   Carol N. Russell, Law Libn.

DELAWARE STATE OFFICE OF MANAGEMENT, BUDGET & PLANNING -
   TECHNICAL LIBRARY
Townsend Bldg., 3rd Fl.   Phone: (302) 736-4271
Dover, DE 19901   Cora Bonniwell

DELAWARE STATE TRAVEL SERVICE - LIBRARY
630 State College Rd.
Box 1401   Phone: (302) 678-4254
Dover, DE 19901   Donald R. Mathewson, Tourism Coord.

U.S. AIR FORCE BASE - DOVER BASE LIBRARY
                                                    Phone: (302) 678-6246
Dover, DE 19901

DELAWARE MUSEUM OF NATURAL HISTORY - LIBRARY
Kennett Pike, Rte. 52
Box 3937   Phone: (302) 658-9111
Greenville, DE 19807   S. Homsey, Libn.

UNIVERSITY OF DELAWARE, NEWARK - COLLEGE OF MARINE STUDIES -
   MARINE STUDIES COMPLEX LIBRARY †
Harry L. Cannon Marine Studies Laboratory   Phone: (302) 645-4290
Lewes, DE 19958   Mildred B. Weer, Lib.Spec.

DELAWARE STATE HOSPITAL - MEDICAL LIBRARY
                                                    Phone: (302) 421-6368
New Castle, DE 19720   Ruth A. Irwin, Libn.

DELAWARE STATE GEOLOGICAL SURVEY - LIBRARY
101 Penny Hall
University of Delaware   Phone: (302) 738-2834
Newark, DE 19711   Robert R. Jordan, State Geologist

DU PONT DE NEMOURS (E.I.) & COMPANY, INC. - HASKELL LABORATORY
   FOR TOXICOLOGY & INDUSTRIAL MEDICINE - LIBRARY
Elkton Rd.   Phone: (302) 366-5225
Newark, DE 19711   Nancy S. Selzer, Libn.

DU PONT DE NEMOURS (E.I.) & COMPANY, INC. - STINE LABORATORY
   LIBRARY
Box 30   Phone: (302) 366-5354
Newark, DE 19711   V.B. Bredemeier, Libn.

INTERNATIONAL READING ASSOCIATION - LIBRARY
800 Barksdale Rd.
Box 8139   Phone: (302) 731-1600
Newark, DE 19711   Gloria M. Smith, Libn.

PIAGET (Jean) SOCIETY - LIBRARY
College of Education
University of Delaware   Phone: (609) 921-9000
Newark, DE 19711   Ellin Scholnick, Pres.

PRODUCE MARKETING ASSOCIATION - PMA INFORMATION CENTER
700 Barksdale Rd.   Phone: (302) 738-7100
Newark, DE 19711   J.S. Raybourn, Staff V.P., Commun.

UNIVERSITY OF DELAWARE, NEWARK - AGRICULTURAL LIBRARY †
002 Agricultural Hall   Phone: (302) 738-2530
Newark, DE 19711   Frederick B. Getze, Libn.

UNIVERSITY OF DELAWARE, NEWARK - ARCHIVES †
78 E. Delaware Ave.   Phone: (302) 738-2750
Newark, DE 19711   John M. Clayton, Jr., Archv.

UNIVERSITY OF DELAWARE, NEWARK - CHEMISTRY/CHEMICAL
   ENGINEERING LIBRARY †
202 Brown Laboratory   Phone: (302) 738-2993
Newark, DE 19711   Grace Love, Lib.Spec.

UNIVERSITY OF DELAWARE, NEWARK - COLLEGE OF URBAN AFFAIRS -
   LIBRARY †
Willard Hall Bldg.   Phone: (302) 738-2394
Newark, DE 19711   Mary Helen Callahan, Accounts Adm.

UNIVERSITY OF DELAWARE, NEWARK - EDUCATION RESOURCE CENTER †
015 Willard Hall   Phone: (302) 738-2335
Newark, DE 19711   Janet Dove, Dir.

UNIVERSITY OF DELAWARE, NEWARK - MATH-PHYSICS READING ROOM *
221 Sharp Laboratory   Phone: (302) 738-2661
Newark, DE 19711   Virginia Makeever, Lib.Techn.

BISSELL (Emily P.) HOSPITAL - MEDICAL LIBRARY
3000 Newport Gap Pike   Phone: (302) 998-2223
Wilmington, DE 19808   Lucille M. Reilly, Med.Sec.

COLUMBIA GAS SYSTEM SERVICE CORPORATION - LAW LIBRARY
20 Montchanin Rd.   Phone: (302) 429-5320
Wilmington, DE 19807   Kathryn C. Bossler, Law Libn.

DELAWARE ACADEMY OF MEDICINE - LIBRARY
1925 Lovering Ave.   Phone: (302) 656-1629
Wilmington, DE 19806   Gail P. Gill, Libn.

DELAWARE ART MUSEUM - LIBRARY
2301 Kentmere Pkwy.   Phone: (302) 571-9590
Wilmington, DE 19806   Mrs. Eugene Nixon, Libn.

DELAWARE LAW SCHOOL OF WIDENER UNIVERSITY - LAW LIBRARY
Concord Pike, Box 7475   Phone: (302) 478-5280
Wilmington, DE 19803   Richard Humphreys, Law Libn.

DU PONT (Alfred I.) INSTITUTE OF THE NEMOURS FOUNDATION LIBRARY
Box 269   Phone: (302) 573-3259
Wilmington, DE 19899   Mrs. Gene Schiefelbein, Libn.

DU PONT DE NEMOURS (E.I.) & COMPANY, INC. - CHEMICALS & PIGMENTS
   DEPT. - JACKSON LAB. LIBRARY
                                                    Phone: (609) 299-5000
Wilmington, DE 19898   W.B. McCormack, R&D Libn.

DU PONT DE NEMOURS (E.I.) & COMPANY, INC. - LAVOISIER LIBRARY
Central Research & Development Dept.
Experimental Sta.   Phone: (302) 772-2086
Wilmington, DE 19898   Frances E. Parsons, Lib.Supv.

DU PONT DE NEMOURS (E.I.) & COMPANY, INC. - LEGAL DEPARTMENT
   LIBRARY
6067 Du Pont Bldg.   Phone: (302) 774-3307
Wilmington, DE 19898   M. Jane Dicecco, Libn.

DU PONT DE NEMOURS (E.I.) & COMPANY, INC. - TECHNICAL LIBRARY
    SYSTEM - HEADQUARTERS
3155 Du Pont Bldg.
Tenth & Market Sts.   Phone: (302) 774-7232
Wilmington, DE 19898   Helen S. Strolle, Mgr.

DU PONT DE NEMOURS (E.I.) & COMPANY, INC. - TECHNICAL LIBRARY
    SYSTEM - LOUVIERS BRANCH
                                             Phone: (302) 366-3791
Wilmington, DE 19898   Marilyn L. Evans, Br.Supv.

DU PONT DE NEMOURS (E.I.) & COMPANY, INC. - TECHNICAL LIBRARY
    SYSTEM - PIONEERING RESEARCH LABORATORY BRANCH
Experimental Sta., Bldg. 302   Phone: (302) 772-3451
Wilmington, DE 19898   Mrs. Bohuslawa Z-P. Bass, Br.Supv.

DU PONT DE NEMOURS (E.I.) & COMPANY, INC. - TECHNICAL LIBRARY
    SYSTEM - TEXTILE RESEARCH LABORATORY BRANCH
Chestnut Run   Phone: (302) 999-3473
Wilmington, DE 19898   Mrs. Bohuslawa Z-P. Bass, Br.Supv.

ELEUTHERIAN MILLS HISTORICAL LIBRARY
Greenville
Box 3630   Phone: (302) 658-2400
Wilmington, DE 19807   Dr. Richmond D. Williams, Lib.Dir.

GOLDEY BEACOM COLLEGE - J. WILBUR HIRONS LIBRARY
4701 Limestone Rd.
Box 5500   Phone: (302) 998-8814
Wilmington, DE 19808   R.M. Beach, Dir.

HERCULES, INC. - LAW DEPARTMENT LIBRARY
910 Market St., 14th Fl.   Phone: (302) 575-7019
Wilmington, DE 19899   Mary M. McAteer, Law Libn.

HERCULES, INC. - LIBRARY
Hercules Tower, Rm. 1401-T
910 Market St.   Phone: (302) 575-5401
Wilmington, DE 19899   Barbara Beaman, Supv.

HERCULES, INC. - RESEARCH CENTER - TECHNICAL INFORMATION
    DIVISION
                                             Phone: (302) 995-3484
Wilmington, DE 19899   Robert N. Manning, Mgr.

HISTORICAL SOCIETY OF DELAWARE - LIBRARY †
505 Market Street Mall   Phone: (302) 655-7161
Wilmington, DE 19801   Gladys M. Coghlan, Dir. of Libs.

ICI AMERICAS INC. - ATLAS LIBRARY
                                             Phone: (302) 575-8231
Wilmington, DE 19897   Velga B. Rukuts, Libn.

LOMBARDY HALL FOUNDATION - LIBRARY
1611 Concord Pike
Box 7036   Phone: (302) 772-4286
Wilmington, DE 19803   Harold J. Littleton, Pres.

MOUNT CUBA ASTRONOMICAL OBSERVATORY - LAMBERT L. JACKSON
    MEMORIAL LIBRARY
Box 3915, Greenville   Phone: (302) 654-6407
Wilmington, DE 19807   Leo G. Glasser, Dir.

NEW CASTLE COUNTY LAW LIBRARY
Public Bldg./Courthouse   Phone: (302) 571-2437
Wilmington, DE 19801   Rene Yucht, Hd.Libn.

RIVERSIDE HOSPITAL - MEDICAL LIBRARY
Foolea Blvd.
Box 845   Phone: (302) 764-6120
Wilmington, DE 19802   Hilde Ingersoll, Lib.Asst.

ST. FRANCIS HOSPITAL, INC. - MEDICAL LIBRARY
7th & Clayton Sts.   Phone: (302) 421-4123
Wilmington, DE 19805   Sr. Paschal Marie Cantone, O.S.F., Libn.

U.S. VETERANS ADMINISTRATION (DE-Wilmington) - CENTER MEDICAL
    LIBRARY †
1601 Kirkwood Hwy.   Phone: (302) 994-2511
Wilmington, DE 19805   Don Passidomo, Chf.Libn.

WILMINGTON MEDICAL CENTER (Delaware Division) - MEDICAL STAFF
    LIBRARY
14th & Washington Ave.
Box 1668   Phone: (302) 428-2201
Wilmington, DE 19899   Helen St. Clair, Med.Libn.

WILMINGTON NEWS-JOURNAL COMPANY - LIBRARY
831 Orange St.   Phone: (302) 573-2038
Wilmington, DE 19899   Dorothy L. Brown, Libn.

DU PONT (Henry Francis) WINTERTHUR MUSEUM - LIBRARY
                                             Phone: (302) 656-8591
Winterthur, DE 19735   Dr. Frank H. Sommer, III, Hd. Of Lib.

DISTRICT OF COLUMBIA

U.S. AIR FORCE - OFFICE OF SCIENTIFIC RESEARCH - LIBRARY *
Bldg. 410   Phone: (202) 767-4910
Bolling AFB, DC 20332   Anthony G. Bialecki, Libn.

ACACIA MUTUAL LIFE INSURANCE COMPANY - LIBRARY
51 Louisiana Ave., N.W.   Phone: (202) 628-4506
Washington, DC 20001   Doris Waldecker, Libn.

ACADEMY OF AMERICAN FRANCISCAN HISTORY - LIBRARY
Box 34440   Phone: (301) 365-1763
Washington, DC 20034   Jesse Joseph Torres, Libn.

ACCREDITING COMMISSION ON EDUCATION FOR HEALTH SERVICES ADM.
    - RESOURCE CTR. FOR HEALTH SERVICES ADM. EDUCATION
One Dupont Circle, Suite 420   Phone: (202) 659-3939
Washington, DC 20036   Lydia S. Clary, Coord.

ACTION - LIBRARY
806 Connecticut Ave., N.W.   Phone: (202) 254-3308
Washington, DC 20525   Rita C. Warpeha, Chf.Libn.

AEROSPACE CORPORATION - WASHINGTON LIBRARY
955 L'Enfant Plaza, S.W., Suite 4000   Phone: (202) 488-6154
Washington, DC 20024   Patricia W. Green, Lib.Supv.

AEROSPACE INDUSTRIES ASSOCIATION OF AMERICA - LIBRARY
1725 DeSales St., N.W.   Phone: (202) 347-2315
Washington, DC 20036   Mrs. Billie Ann Perry, Libn.

AFRICAN-AMERICAN LABOR CENTER (AALC) - LIBRARY
1125 Fifteenth St., N.W.   Phone: (202) 293-3603
Washington, DC 20005   John T. Sarr, Pubn.Off.

AFRICAN BIBLIOGRAPHIC CENTER - STAFF RESOURCE LIBRARY
1346 Connecticut Ave., N.W., Rm. 901   Phone: (202) 223-1392
Washington, DC 20036   Linda Fink Matthews, Adm.Dir.

AHMADIYYA MOVEMENT IN ISLAM - MUSLIM LIBRARY
2141 Leroy Place, N.W.   Phone: (202) 232-3737
Washington, DC 20008   Ata Ullah Kaleem, Info.Dir.

AIR FORCE ASSOCIATION - RESEARCH LIBRARY
1750 Pennsylvania Ave., N.W.   Phone: (202) 637-3300
Washington, DC 20006

AIR TRANSPORT ASSOCIATION OF AMERICA - LIBRARY
1709 New York Ave., N.W.   Phone: (202) 872-4184
Washington, DC 20006   Mrs. Marion Mistrik, Libn.

AIRPORT OPERATORS COUNCIL INTERNATIONAL - LIBRARY
1700 K St., N.W.   Phone: (202) 296-3270
Washington, DC 20006   Theana Y. Kastens, V.P., Pub.Rel.

ALEXANDER GRAHAM BELL ASSOCIATION FOR THE DEAF - VOLTA BUREAU
    LIBRARY
3417 Volta Place, N.W.   Phone: (202) 337-5220
Washington, DC 20007   Suzanne Pickering Neel, Dir.Prof.Prog./Serv.

ALLIANCE TO SAVE ENERGY - LIBRARY
1925 K St., N.W., Suite 507   Phone: (202) 857-0668
Washington, DC 20006   Julia Stefanelli, Res.Assoc.

GEOGRAPHIC

ALUMINUM ASSOCIATION - INFORMATION CENTER
818 Connecticut Ave., N.W.   Phone: (202) 862-5100
Washington, DC 20006   Ellen J. Levin, Mgr., Info.Ctr.

AMERICAN ASSOCIATION FOR THE ADVANCEMENT OF SCIENCE - LIBRARY
1515 Massachusetts Ave., N.W.   Phone: (202) 467-4428
Washington, DC 20005   Janet Kegg, Libn.

AMERICAN ASSOCIATION OF MUSEUMS - MUSEUM RESOURCES AND
     INFORMATION SERVICE
1055 Thomas Jefferson St., N.W.
Washington, DC 20007   K.J. Sanborn, Ed.Asst.

AMERICAN ASSOCIATION OF UNIVERSITY WOMEN - EDUCATIONAL
     FOUNDATION LIBRARY AND ARCHIVES
2401 Virginia Ave., N.W.   Phone: (202) 785-7763
Washington, DC 20037   Mary K. Jordan, Libn./Archv.

AMERICAN BANKERS ASSOCIATION - LIBRARY
1120 Connecticut Ave., N.W.   Phone: (202) 467-4180
Washington, DC 20036   Joan Gervino, Dir.

AMERICAN CHEMICAL SOCIETY, INC. - LIBRARY
1155 16th St., N.W.   Phone: (202) 872-4509
Washington, DC 20036   Barbara Gallagher, Hd.Lib.Serv.

AMERICAN COLLEGE OF NURSING HOME ADMINISTRATORS - LIBRARY
4650 East-West Hwy.   Phone: (301) 652-8384
Washington, DC 20014   Helene Zubkoff, Ref./Info.Serv.Spec.

AMERICAN COLLEGE OF OBSTETRICIANS AND GYNECOLOGISTS -
     RESOURCE CENTER
600 Maryland Ave., S.W., Suite 300   Phone: (202) 638-5577
Washington, DC 20024   Pamela Van Hine, Libn.

AMERICAN COUNCIL ON EDUCATION - NATIONAL CENTER FOR HIGHER
     EDUCATION (NCHE) - LIBRARY
One Dupont Circle, Suite 640   Phone: (202) 833-4690
Washington, DC 20015   Judith De Serio, Dir.

AMERICAN COUNCIL OF LIFE INSURANCE - LIBRARY
1850 K St., N.W.   Phone: (202) 862-4050
Washington, DC 20006   Marjorie Gordon, Libn.

AMERICAN ENTERPRISE INSTITUTE FOR PUBLIC POLICY RESEARCH -
     LIBRARY
1150 17th St., N.W.   Phone: (202) 862-5831
Washington, DC 20036   Evelyn B. Caldwell, Libn.

AMERICAN FEDERATION OF LABOR AND CONGRESS OF INDUSTRIAL
     ORGANIZATIONS - LIBRARY
815 16th St., N.W.   Phone: (202) 637-5297
Washington, DC 20006   Dora Kelenson, Libn.

AMERICAN FEDERATION OF STATE, COUNTY AND MUNICIPAL EMPLOYEES,
     AFL-CIO (AFSCME) - INFORMATION CENTER
1625 L St., N.W.   Phone: (202) 452-4882
Washington, DC 20036   Jodie Fine, Supv.

AMERICAN FILM INSTITUTE - RESOURCE CENTER
JFK Center for the Performing Arts   Phone: (202) 828-4088
Washington, DC 20566   Deborah Davidson Boutchard, Libn.

AMERICAN FORESTRY ASSOCIATION - LIBRARY
1319 18th St., N.W.   Phone: (202) 467-5810
Washington, DC 20036

AMERICAN HELICOPTER SOCIETY - TECHNICAL INFORMATION
1325 18th St., N.W., Suite 103   Phone: (202) 659-9524
Washington, DC 20036   John F. Zugschwert, Exec.Dir.

AMERICAN HOME ECONOMICS ASSOCIATION - LIBRARY
2010 Massachusetts Ave., N.W.
Washington, DC 20036

AMERICAN INSTITUTE OF ARCHITECTS - LIBRARY
1735 New York Ave., N.W.   Phone: (202) 626-7493
Washington, DC 20006   Stephanie C. Byrnes, Libn.

AMERICAN INSTITUTES FOR RESEARCH - LIBRARY
1055 Thomas Jefferson St., N.W.   Phone: (202) 342-5000
Washington, DC 20007   Lily Griner, Libn.

AMERICAN LIBRARY ASSOCIATION - WASHINGTON OFFICE
110 Maryland Ave., N.E.
Box 54   Phone: (202) 547-4440
Washington, DC 20002   Eileen D. Cooke, Dir.

AMERICAN MEDICAL ASSOCIATION - WASHINGTON OFFICE LIBRARY
1776 K St., N.W.   Phone: (202) 857-1338
Washington, DC 20006   James H. Jackson, Dir.

AMERICAN NATIONAL METRIC COUNCIL - LIBRARY
1625 Massachusetts Ave., N.W.   Phone: (202) 232-4545
Washington, DC 20036   Katherine Tynberg, Dir. of Commun.

AMERICAN NEWSPAPER PUBLISHERS ASSOCIATION - LIBRARY
Box 17407
Dulles International Airport   Phone: (703) 620-9500
Washington, DC 20041   Yvonne L. Egertson, Libn.

AMERICAN PETROLEUM INSTITUTE - LIBRARY
2101 L St.   Phone: (202) 457-7269
Washington, DC 20037   Gladys E. Siegel, Libn.

AMERICAN PHARMACEUTICAL ASSOCIATION - FOUNDATION LIBRARY
2215 Constitution Ave., N.W.   Phone: (202) 628-4410
Washington, DC 20037   Lee Simmons, Libn.

AMERICAN PODIATRY ASSOCIATION - WILLIAM J. STICKEL MEMORIAL
     LIBRARY
20 Chevy Chase Circle, N.W.
Washington, DC 20015   Roberta McVeigh, Libn.

AMERICAN PSYCHIATRIC MUSEUM ASSOCIATION - LIBRARY AND
     ARCHIVES
1700 18th St., N.W.   Phone: (202) 232-7878
Washington, DC 20009   Zing Jung, Dir.

AMERICAN PUBLIC HEALTH ASSOCIATION - INTERNATIONAL HEALTH
     PROGRAMS - RESOURCE CENTER
1015 15th St., N.W.   Phone: (202) 789-5710
Washington, DC 20005   Maria Emma McMurtry, Mgr.

AMERICAN PUBLIC POWER ASSOCIATION - LIBRARY
2600 Virginia Ave., N.W.   Phone: (202) 342-7200
Washington, DC 20037   Katie King, Libn.

AMERICAN PUBLIC TRANSIT ASSOCIATION - LIBRARY
1225 Connecticut Ave., N.W., Suite 200   Phone: (202) 828-2843
Washington, DC 20036   Lynn J. Kennedy, Mgr.

AMERICAN RED CROSS - NATIONAL HEADQUARTERS LIBRARY
17th & D Sts., N.W.   Phone: (202) 857-3491
Washington, DC 20006   Roberta F. Biles, Lib.Dir.

AMERICAN SEED TRADE ASSOCIATION - LIBRARY
Suite 964 Executive Bldg.
1030 15th St., N.W.
Washington, DC 20005

AMERICAN SHORT LINE RAILROAD ASSOCIATION - LIBRARY
2000 Massachusetts Ave., N.W.   Phone: (202) 785-2250
Washington, DC 20036   P.H. Croft, Pres.

AMERICAN SOCIETY FOR AEROSPACE EDUCATION
1750 Pennsylvania Ave. N.W., Suite 1303   Phone: (202) 347-5187
Washington, DC 20006   Julie Bettenberg, Rsrcs.Ed.

AMERICAN SOCIETY OF APPRAISERS - INTERNATIONAL VALUATION
     SCIENCES CENTRE LIBRARY
Dulles Intl. Airport
Box 17265   Phone: (703) 620-3838
Washington, DC 20041   Suzann Allen, Hd.Libn.

AMERICAN SOCIETY OF ASSOCIATION EXECUTIVES - INFORMATION
     CENTRAL
1575 Eye St., N.W., 12th Fl.   Phone: (202) 626-2723
Washington, DC 20005   Elissa Matulis Myers, Dir., Res. & Info.

AMERICAN SOCIETY FOR INFORMATION SCIENCE - INFORMATION CENTER
1010 Sixteenth St., N.W.   Phone: (202) 659-3644
Washington, DC 20036

AMERICAN SOCIETY OF INTERNATIONAL LAW - LIBRARY
2223 Massachusetts Ave., N.W.   Phone: (202) 265-4313
Washington, DC 20008   Helen S. Philos, Libn.

AMERICAN SOCIETY OF NOTARIES - LIBRARY
810 18th St., N.W.   Phone: (202) 347-7303
Washington, DC 20006   Eugene E. Hines, Exec.Dir.

AMERICAN TELEPHONE & TELEGRAPH COMPANY - LONG LINES DEPARTMENT - GOVERNMENT COMMUNICATIONS LIBRARY
1120 20th St., N.W., 5th Fl.   Phone: (202) 457-3028
Washington, DC 20036   Mary B. Freeman, Staff Supv.-Lib.

AMERICAN TEXTILE MANUFACTURERS INSTITUTE (ATMI) - LIBRARY
1101 Connecticut Ave., N.W., No. 300   Phone: (202) 862-0573
Washington, DC 20036   Virginia A. McNitt, Libn.

AMERICAN TRUCKING ASSOCIATIONS, INC. - LIBRARY
1616 P St., N.W.   Phone: (202) 797-5291
Washington, DC 20036   Linda Rothbart, Libn.

AMERICAN UNIVERSITY - FOREIGN AREA STUDIES LIBRARY
5010 Wisconsin Ave., N.W.   Phone: (202) 686-2740
Washington, DC 20016   Gilda Nimer, Libn.

AMERICAN UNIVERSITY - WASHINGTON COLLEGE OF LAW - LIBRARY
Massachusetts & Nebraska Aves., N.W.   Phone: (202) 686-2625
Washington, DC 20016   Patrick E. Kehoe, Dir.

ANTIOCH SCHOOL OF LAW - LIBRARY
1624 Crescent Place, N.W.   Phone: (202) 265-9500
Washington, DC 20009   William P. Statsky, Libn.

APPALACHIAN REGIONAL COMMISSION - LIBRARY
1666 Connecticut Ave., N.W.   Phone: (202) 673-7845
Washington, DC 20235   Lisbeth L. Luke, Libn.

ARMENIAN ASSEMBLY CHARITABLE TRUST - LIBRARY AND INFORMATION CENTER
522 21st St., N.W.   Phone: (202) 332-3434
Washington, DC 20006   Ross Vartian, Adm.Dir.

ARMY AND NAVY CLUB - LIBRARY
Farragut Sq., N.W.   Phone: (202) 628-8400
Washington, DC 20006   John S. Mayfield, Libn.

ARNOLD AND PORTER - LIBRARY
1200 New Hampshire Ave., N.W.   Phone: (202) 872-3994
Washington, DC 20036   James W. Shelar, Libn.

ASSOCIATED GENERAL CONTRACTORS OF AMERICA - JAMES L. ALLHANDS MEMORIAL LIBRARY
1957 E St., N.W.   Phone: (202) 393-2040
Washington, DC 20006   John C. Ellis, Dir.

ASSOCIATION OF AMERICAN MEDICAL COLLEGES - ARCHIVES
One DuPont Circle, N.W.   Phone: (202) 828-0400
Washington, DC 20008   Mary H. Littlemeyer, Archv.

ASSOCIATION OF AMERICAN RAILROADS - ECONOMICS AND FINANCE DEPARTMENT - LIBRARY
American Railroads Bldg., Rm. 523   Phone: (202) 293-4068
Washington, DC 20036   John G. McLeod, Libn.

ASSOCIATION FOR CHILDHOOD EDUCATION INTERNATIONAL - LIBRARY
3615 Wisconsin Ave., N.W.   Phone: (202) 363-6963
Washington, DC 20016   Elvie Lou Luetge, Act.Exec.Dir.

ASSOCIATION FOR GERONTOLOGY IN HIGHER EDUCATION - RESOURCE LIBRARY
600 Maryland Ave., S.W., West Wing 201   Phone: (202) 484-7505
Washington, DC 20024   Elizabeth Douglass, Dir.

ASSOCIATION OF GOVERNING BOARDS OF UNIVERSITIES AND COLLEGES - TRUSTEE INFORMATION CENTER
One Dupont Circle, Suite 720   Phone: (202) 296-8400
Washington, DC 20036   Linda E. Henderson, Info.Ctr.Coord.

ASSOCIATION OF SCIENCE/TECHNOLOGY CENTERS - LIBRARY
1016 16th St., N.W.   Phone: (202) 452-0655
Washington, DC 20036   Sheila Grinell, Exec.Dir.

ASSOCIATION OF STUDENT INTERNATIONAL LAW SOCIETIES - INFORMATION CENTER
2223 Massachusetts Ave., N.W.   Phone: (202) 387-8467
Washington, DC 20008   Louis E. Emery, Exec.Sec.

ASSOCIATION FOR THE STUDY OF AFRO-AMERICAN LIFE AND HISTORY, INC. - CARTER G. WOODSON LIBRARY
1401 14th St., N.W.   Phone: (202) 667-2822
Washington, DC 20005   Sr. Anthony Scally, Chf.Libn.

ASSOCIATION OF TRIAL LAWYERS OF AMERICA - ATLA LIBRARY
1050 31st St., N.W.   Phone: (202) 965-3500
Washington, DC 20007   Keith Searls, Libn.

ATLANTIC COUNCIL OF THE UNITED STATES, INC. - LIBRARY
1616 H St., N.W.   Phone: (202) 347-9353
Washington, DC 20006   June Haley, Libn.

ATOMIC INDUSTRIAL FORUM - LIBRARY
7101 Wisconsin Ave.   Phone: (301) 654-9260
Washington, DC 20014   Audrey D. Duff, Libn.

AUSTRALIAN EMBASSY - LIBRARY
1601 Massachusetts Ave.   Phone: (202) 797-3166
Washington, DC 20036   C.M. Cooze, Libn.

BAR ASSOCIATION OF THE DISTRICT OF COLUMBIA - LIBRARY
3518 U.S. Court House Bldg.   Phone: (202) 426-7087
Washington, DC 22101   Elizabeth K. Van Horn, Libn.

BARBER (Richard J.) ASSOCIATES, INC. - LIBRARY *
1000 Connecticut Ave., N.W., Suite 707   Phone: (202) 785-0597
Washington, DC 20036   Elizabeth Schomer, Chf.Libn.

BIO-ENERGY COUNCIL - LIBRARY
1625 Eye St., N.W.   Phone: (202) 833-5656
Washington, DC 20006   Dr. Paul F. Bente, Exec.Dir.

BRAZILIAN-AMERICAN CULTURAL INSTITUTE, INC. - HAROLD E. WIBBERLEY, JR. LIBRARY
4201 Connecticut Ave., N.W., Suite 211   Phone: (202) 362-8334
Washington, DC 20008   Dr. Jose Neistein, Exec.Dir.

BROADCAST PIONEERS LIBRARY
1771 N St., N.W.   Phone: (202) 223-0088
Washington, DC 20036   Catharine Heinz, Dir.

BROOKINGS INSTITUTION - LIBRARY
1775 Massachusetts Ave., N.W.   Phone: (202) 797-6240
Washington, DC 20036   Laura Walker, Libn.

BUREAU OF NATIONAL AFFAIRS, INC. - LIBRARY AND INFORMATION CENTER
1231 25th St., N.W.   Phone: (202) 452-4466
Washington, DC 20037   Mildred Mason, Dir.

BUREAU OF SOCIAL SCIENCE RESEARCH - LIBRARY
1990 M St., N.W.   Phone: (202) 223-4300
Washington, DC 20036   Mary K. Hartz, Libn.

BUSINESS AND PROFESSIONAL WOMEN'S FOUNDATION - LIBRARY
2012 Massachusetts Ave., N.W.   Phone: (202) 293-1200
Washington, DC 20036   Katherine Dickson, Libn.

CANADIAN EMBASSY - LIBRARY
1771 N St., N.W.   Phone: (202) 785-1400
Washington, DC 20036   Ms. Merle G. Fabian, Libn.

CAPLIN & DRYSDALE - LIBRARY
1101 17th St., N.W., Suite 1100
Washington, DC 20036
Phone: (202) 862-5073
Karen M. Meyer, Law Libn.

CARMELITANA COLLECTION
1600 Webster St., N.E.
Washington, DC 20017
Phone: (202) 526-1221
Calvin Alderson, O.C., Dir.

CARNEGIE INSTITUTION OF WASHINGTON - GEOPHYSICAL LABORATORY
LIBRARY
2801 Upton St., N.W.
Washington, DC 20008
Phone: (202) 966-0334
Dolores M. Petry, Libn.

CARNEGIE INSTITUTION OF WASHINGTON - LIBRARY
1530 P St., N.W.
Washington, DC 20005
Phone: (202) 387-6411
Pat Parratt, Libn.

CARNEGIE INSTITUTION OF WASHINGTON - TERRESTRIAL MAGNETISM
DEPARTMENT LIBRARY
5241 Broad Branch Rd., N.W.
Washington, DC 20015
Phone: (202) 966-0863
Dorothy B. Dillin, Libn.

CATHOLIC UNIVERSITY OF AMERICA - CHEMISTRY LIBRARY
301 Maloney Bldg.
Washington, DC 20064
Phone: (202) 635-5389
N.L. Powell, Coord. Campus Libs.

CATHOLIC UNIVERSITY OF AMERICA - CLEMENTINE LIBRARY
Mullen Library, Rm. 400-401
Washington, DC 20064
Phone: (202) 635-5091
Carolyn T. Lee, Cur.

CATHOLIC UNIVERSITY OF AMERICA - DEPARTMENT OF ARCHIVES AND
MANUSCRIPTS
Mullen Library, Rm. 4
Washington, DC 20064
Phone: (202) 635-5065
Dr. Anthony Zito, Univ.Archv.

CATHOLIC UNIVERSITY OF AMERICA - ENGINEERING/ARCHITECTURE/
MATHEMATICS LIBRARY
200 Pangborn Bldg.
Washington, DC 20064
Phone: (202) 635-5167
B. Fortier, Libn.

CATHOLIC UNIVERSITY OF AMERICA - HUMANITIES LIBRARY
Mullen Library, Rm. 114
Washington, DC 20064
Phone: (202) 635-5075
Blue K. Gutekunst, Libn.

CATHOLIC UNIVERSITY OF AMERICA - LIBRARY SCIENCE LIBRARY
Marist Bldg.
620 Michigan Ave., N.E.
Washington, DC 20064
Phone: (202) 635-5092
Victor Okim, Libn.

CATHOLIC UNIVERSITY OF AMERICA - MUSIC LIBRARY
Ward Music Bldg.
Washington, DC 20064
Phone: (202) 635-5424
Elizabeth M. Libbey, Music Libn.

CATHOLIC UNIVERSITY OF AMERICA - NURSING/BIOLOGY LIBRARY
Washington, DC 20064
Phone: (202) 635-5411
N.L. Powell, Libn.

CATHOLIC UNIVERSITY OF AMERICA - OLIVEIRA LIMA LIBRARY
Washington, DC 20064
Phone: (202) 635-5059
Manoel Cardozo, Cur.

CATHOLIC UNIVERSITY OF AMERICA - PHYSICS LIBRARY
208 Keane Bldg.
Washington, DC 20064
Phone: (202) 635-5320
N.L. Powell, Coord., Campus Libs.

CATHOLIC UNIVERSITY OF AMERICA - ROBERT J. WHITE LAW LIBRARY
Leahy Hall
Washington, DC 20064
Phone: (202) 635-5155
John R. Valeri, Law Libn.

CATHOLIC UNIVERSITY OF AMERICA - SEMITICS - INSTITUTE OF
CHRISTIAN ORIENTAL RESEARCH (ICOR) LIBRARY
Mullen Library, Rm. 18
Washington, DC 20064
Phone: (202) 635-5091
Carolyn T. Lee, Cur.

CATHOLIC UNIVERSITY OF AMERICA - THEOLOGY/PHILOSOPHY/CANON
LAW/RELIGIOUS EDUCATION LIBRARY
Mullen Library, Rm. 300
Washington, DC 20064
Phone: (202) 635-5088
R.B. Miller, Libn.

CENTER FOR APPLIED RESEARCH IN THE APOSTOLATE - CARA RESEARCH
LIBRARY †
3700 Oakview Terrace, N.E.
Box 29150
Washington, DC 20017
Phone: (202) 832-2300
Sr. Frances A. Smith, R.S.C.J., Libn.

CENTER FOR COMMUNITY ECONOMIC DEVELOPMENT - LIBRARY
1320 19th St., N.W.
Washington, DC 20036
Phone: (202) 659-3986
Bene L. Durant, Libn.

CENTER OF CONCERN - INFORMATION CENTER
3700 13th St., N.E.
Washington, DC 20017
Phone: (202) 635-2757
Maria Riley, Ed.

CENTER FOR NATIONAL SECURITY STUDIES - CNSS LIBRARY
122 Maryland Ave., N.E.
Washington, DC 20002
Phone: (202) 544-5380
Monica Andres, Libn.

CENTER FOR WOMEN POLICY STUDIES - RESOURCE CENTER
2000 P St., N.W., Suite 508
Washington, DC 20036
Phone: (202) 872-1770
Lois A. West, Supv.

CHAMBER OF COMMERCE OF THE UNITED STATES OF AMERICA - LIBRARY
1615 H St., N.W.
Washington, DC 20062
Phone: (202) 659-6053
Rose Racine, Libn.

CHEMICAL MANUFACTURERS ASSOCIATION - LIBRARY
2501 M St., N.W.
Washington, DC 20037
Phone: (202) 328-4229
Jane Rasmussen, Libn.

CHEVY CHASE BAPTIST CHURCH - SEBRING MEMORIAL LIBRARY
5671 Western Ave., N.W.
Washington, DC 20015
May Kardell, Libn.

CHICAGO TRIBUNE PRESS SERVICE - WASHINGTON BUREAU - LIBRARY
1707 H St., N.W., 9th Fl.
Washington, DC 20006
Phone: (202) 785-9430
Carolyn J. Hardnett, Chf.Libn.

CHILDREN'S HOSPITAL/NATIONAL MEDICAL CENTER - HOSPITAL LIBRARY
111 Michigan Ave., N.W.
Washington, DC 20010
Phone: (202) 745-3195
Deborah D. Gilbert, Chf.Hosp.Libn.

CHRONICLE OF HIGHER EDUCATION - LIBRARY
1333 New Hampshire Ave., N.W.
Washington, DC 20036
Phone: (202) 828-3525
Edith Uunila, Asst.Ed.

CIGAR ASSOCIATION OF AMERICA - LIBRARY †
1120 19th St., N.W., Suite 410
Washington, DC 20036
Phone: (202) 466-3070

CITIZENS' ENERGY PROJECT, INC. - LIBRARY
1110 Sixth St., N.W., Suite 300
Washington, DC 20001
Phone: (202) 387-8998
Ken Bossong, Coord.

CITIZENS' ENERGY PROJECT, INC. - PASSIVE SOLAR FOUNDATION -
LIBRARY
1110 Sixth St., N.W., Suite 300
Washington, DC 20001
Phone: (202) 387-8998
Ken Bossong, Coord.

CLEARINGHOUSE ON CHILD ABUSE AND NEGLECT INFORMATION
Box 1182
Washington, DC 20013
Phone: (703) 558-8222
Joseph G. Wechsler, Dir.

CLEARINGHOUSE ON THE HANDICAPPED
U.S. Dept. of Education
Switzer Bldg., Rm. 3106
Washington, DC 20202
Phone: (202) 245-0080
Helga Roth, Chf., Clearinghouse

CLUB MANAGERS ASSOCIATION OF AMERICA - INFORMATION, RESEARCH
& STATISTICS DEPARTMENT
7615 Winterberry Place
Box 34482
Washington, DC 20817
Phone: (301) 229-3600

COHEN AND URETZ - LAW LIBRARY
1775 K St., N.W.
Washington, DC 20006
Phone: (202) 293-4740
Michael E. Boren, Libn.

GEOGRAPHIC

GEOGRAPHIC

COLLEGE OF PREACHERS - LIBRARY
3510 Woodley Rd., N.W.
Washington, DC 20016   Mildred Coleman, Libn.

COLUMBIA HISTORICAL SOCIETY - LIBRARY
1307 New Hampshire Ave., N.W.   Phone: (202) 785-2068
Washington, DC 20036   Perry G. Fisher, Exec.Dir./Libn.

COLUMBIA HOSPITAL FOR WOMEN - MEDICAL LIBRARY
2425 L St., N.W.   Phone: (202) 293-6560
Washington, DC 20037   Elizabeth M. Haggart, Libn.

COMMODITY FUTURES TRADING COMMISSION - LAW LIBRARY
2033 K St., N.W., Rm. 540   Phone: (202) 254-5901
Washington, DC 20581   Evangeline N. Jackson, Adm.Libn.

COMMUNICATIONS SATELLITE CORPORATION - CENTRAL LIBRARY
950 L'Enfant Plaza, S.W.   Phone: (202) 554-8833
Washington, DC 20024   Rita A. Carter, Libn.

COMMUNICATIONS WORKERS OF AMERICA - CWA INFORMATION LIBRARY
1925 K St., N.W.   Phone: (202) 785-6799
Washington, DC 20006   Jean Frankel, Libn.

CONAC - LIBRARY
Binational Ctr. for Education
2717 Ontario Rd., N.W., Suite 200   Phone: (202) 223-1174
Washington, DC 20009   Cecelia Bustamante-Barron, Libn.

CONFERENCE ON ECONOMIC PROGRESS - LIBRARY
2610 Upton St., N.W.   Phone: (202) 363-6222
Washington, DC 20008   Leon H. Keyserling, Pres./Dir.

CONGRESSIONAL BUDGET OFFICE - LIBRARY
House Office Bldg., Annex 2
2nd & D Sts., S.W.   Phone: (202) 225-4525
Washington, DC 20515   Jane T. Sessa, Libn.

CONGRESSIONAL INFORMATION SERVICE, INC.
4520 East-West Hwy.   Phone: (301) 654-1550
Washington, DC 20014   Paul P. Massa, Pres.

CONSERVATION FOUNDATION - LIBRARY
1717 Massachusetts Ave., N.W.   Phone: (202) 797-4300
Washington, DC 20036   Barbara K. Rodes, Libn.

CONSUMER PRODUCT SAFETY COMMISSION - LIBRARY INFORMATION
     SERVICES BRANCH
5401 Westbard Ave.   Phone: (301) 492-6546
Washington, DC 20207   Everlyne K. Murdock, Act.Dir.

CORCORAN SCHOOL OF ART - LIBRARY
17th & New York Ave., N.W.   Phone: (202) 638-3211
Washington, DC 20006   Ann Maginnis, Libn.

CORN REFINERS ASSOCIATION, INC. - CORN INDUSTRIES RESEARCH
     FOUNDATION - LIBRARY
1001 Connecticut Ave., N.W.   Phone: (202) 331-1634
Washington, DC 20036

COUNCIL FOR ADVANCEMENT AND SUPPORT OF EDUCATION - REFERENCE
     CENTER
Eleven Dupont Circle, N.W., Suite 400   Phone: (202) 328-5900
Washington, DC 20036   Cynthia Snyder, Dir.

COVINGTON AND BURLING - LIBRARY
1201 Pennsylvania Ave., N.W.   Phone: (202) 452-6150
Washington, DC 20004   Ellen P. Mahar, Libn.

DAIRY SOCIETY INTERNATIONAL - LIBRARY
3008 McKinley St., N.W.   Phone: (202) 363-3359
Washington, DC 20015   George W. Weigold, Mng.Dir.

DAMES & MOORE - LIBRARY
7101 Wisconsin Ave., Suite 700
Washington, DC 20014

DELOITTE HASKINS & SELLS - LIBRARY
1101 - 15th St., N.W., 9th Fl.   Phone: (202) 862-3548
Washington, DC 20005   Maria Wasowski, Libn.

DEMOCRATIC NATIONAL COMMITTEE - RESEARCH LIBRARY
1625 Massachusetts Ave., N.W.   Phone: (202) 797-5900
Washington, DC 20036   John Francis Bierlein, Dir.Res.Dev.

DISTILLED SPIRITS COUNCIL OF THE U.S., INC. - LIBRARY
1300 Pennsylvania Bldg.
425 13th St., N.W.   Phone: (202) 628-3544
Washington, DC 20004   Susan Ferber, Libn.

DISTRICT OF COLUMBIA - CORPORATION COUNSEL LAW LIBRARY
Rm. 302, District Bldg.
14th & E Sts., N.W.   Phone: (202) 727-6274
Washington, DC 20004   Deborah M. Murray, Law Libn.

DISTRICT OF COLUMBIA DEPARTMENT OF HOUSING AND COMMUNITY
     DEVELOPMENT LIBRARY
1133 North Capitol St., Rm. 203   Phone: (202) 535-1004
Washington, DC 20002   Anne L. Meglis, Libn.

DISTRICT OF COLUMBIA GENERAL HOSPITAL - LIBRARY
19th St. & Massachusetts Ave., S.E.   Phone: (202) 626-6349
Washington, DC 20003   Sara L. Moore, Libn.

DISTRICT OF COLUMBIA PUBLIC LIBRARY - ART DIVISION
Martin Luther King Memorial Library
901 G St., N.W.   Phone: (202) 727-1291
Washington, DC 20001   Lois Kent Stiles, Chf.

DISTRICT OF COLUMBIA PUBLIC LIBRARY - AUDIOVISUAL DIVISION
Martin Luther King Memorial Library
901 G St., N.W.   Phone: (202) 727-1265
Washington, DC 20001   Diane Henry, Chf.

DISTRICT OF COLUMBIA PUBLIC LIBRARY - BIOGRAPHY DIVISION
Martin Luther King Memorial Library
901 G St., N.W.   Phone: (202) 727-1234
Washington, DC 20001   Helen Bergan, Chf.

DISTRICT OF COLUMBIA PUBLIC LIBRARY - BLACK STUDIES DIVISION
Martin Luther King Memorial Library
901 G St., N.W.   Phone: (202) 727-1211
Washington, DC 20001   Alice B. Robinson, Chf.

DISTRICT OF COLUMBIA PUBLIC LIBRARY - BUSINESS, ECONOMICS &
     VOCATIONS DIVISION
Martin Luther King Memorial Library
901 G St., N.W.   Phone: (202) 727-1171
Washington, DC 20001   Wayne D. Kryszak, Chf.

DISTRICT OF COLUMBIA PUBLIC LIBRARY - CHILDREN'S DIVISION
Martin Luther King Memorial Library
901 G St., N.W.   Phone: (202) 727-1248
Washington, DC 20001   Barbara F. Geyger, Chf.

DISTRICT OF COLUMBIA PUBLIC LIBRARY - HISTORY AND GEOGRAPHY
     DIVISION
Martin Luther King Memorial Library
901 G St., N.W.   Phone: (202) 727-1161
Washington, DC 20001   Eleanor A. Bartlett, Chf.

DISTRICT OF COLUMBIA PUBLIC LIBRARY - LANGUAGE, LITERATURE
     &FOREIGN LANGUAGE DIVISION
Martin Luther King Memorial Library
901 G St., N.W.   Phone: (202) 727-1281
Washington, DC 20001   Octave S. Stevenson, Chf.

DISTRICT OF COLUMBIA PUBLIC LIBRARY - LIBRARY FOR THE BLIND AND
     PHYSICALLY HANDICAPPED
Martin Luther King Memorial Library
901 G St., N.W.   Phone: (202) 272-2142
Washington, DC 20001   Grace Lyons, Chf.

DISTRICT OF COLUMBIA PUBLIC LIBRARY - MUSIC & RECREATION
     DIVISION
Martin Luther King Memorial Library
901 G St., N.W.   Phone: (202) 727-1285
Washington, DC 20001   Mary Elliott, Chf.

DISTRICT OF COLUMBIA PUBLIC LIBRARY - PHILOSOPHY, PSYCHOLOGY
AND RELIGION DIVISION
Martin Luther King Memorial Library
901 G St., N.W.   Phone: (202) 727-1251
Washington, DC 20001   Vicky Rogers, Chf.

DISTRICT OF COLUMBIA PUBLIC LIBRARY - POPULAR LIBRARY
Martin Luther King Memorial Library
901 G St., N.W.   Phone: (202) 727-1295
Washington, DC 20001   Mildred R. Greene, Chf.

DISTRICT OF COLUMBIA PUBLIC LIBRARY - SOCIOLOGY, GOVERNMENT &
EDUCATION DIVISION
Martin Luther King Memorial Library
901 G St., N.W.   Phone: (202) 727-1261
Washington, DC 20001   Ann K. Ross, Chf.

DISTRICT OF COLUMBIA PUBLIC LIBRARY - TECHNOLOGY AND SCIENCE
DIVISION
Martin Luther King Memorial Library
901 G St., N.W.   Phone: (202) 727-1175
Washington, DC 20001   Barbara Lundquist, Chf.

DISTRICT OF COLUMBIA PUBLIC LIBRARY - WASHINGTONIANA DIVISION
Martin Luther King Memorial Library
901 G St., N.W.   Phone: (202) 727-1213
Washington, DC 20001   Roxanne Deane, Chf.

DISTRICT OF COLUMBIA PUBLIC SCHOOLS - DIVISION OF RESEARCH AND
EVALUATION - RESEARCH INFORMATION CENTER
415 12th St., N.W.   Phone: (202) 724-4249
Washington, DC 20004   Erika Robinson, Coord.

DISTRICT OF COLUMBIA TEACHERS COLLEGE - LIBRARY
1100 Harvard St., N.W.   Phone: (202) 673-7018
Washington, DC 20009   Lottie Wright, Supv.

DOMINICAN COLLEGE LIBRARY
487 Michigan Ave., N.E.   Phone: (202) 529-5300
Washington, DC 20017   Rev. J. Raymond Vandegrift, O.P., Libn.

DOW, LOHNES & ALBERTSON - LAW LIBRARY
1225 Connecticut Ave., Suite 500   Phone: (202) 862-8021
Washington, DC 20036   Susanne D. Thevenet, Libn.

EDISON ELECTRIC INSTITUTE - LIBRARY
1111 19th St., N.W.   Phone: (202) 828-7520
Washington, DC 20036   Ethel Tiberg, Mgr.Lib.Serv.

EMPLOYEE BENEFIT RESEARCH INSTITUTE - LIBRARY
1920 M St., N.W., Suite 520
Washington, DC 20036   Margaret B. Riordan, Libn.

ENGLISH-SPEAKING UNION OF THE U.S.A. - WASHINGTON D.C. BRANCH
LIBRARY
2131 S St., N.W.   Phone: (202) 234-4602
Washington, DC 20008   Eleanor Johnson, Libn.

ENVIRONMENTAL LAW INSTITUTE - LIBRARY
1346 Connecticut Ave., N.W.
Suite 620   Phone: (202) 452-9600
Washington, DC 20036   Futrell Iva, Libn.

ENVIRONMENTAL PROTECTION AGENCY - HEADQUARTERS LIBRARY
401 M St., S.W., Rm. 2404   Phone: (202) 755-0308
Washington, DC 20460   Sami Klein, Chf.

ERIC CLEARINGHOUSE ON HIGHER EDUCATION
George Washington University
One Dupont Circle, Suite 630   Phone: (202) 296-2597
Washington, DC 20036   Dr. Jonathan D. Fife, Dir.

ERIC CLEARINGHOUSE ON LANGUAGES AND LINGUISTICS
3520 Prospect St., N.W.   Phone: (703) 528-4312
Washington, DC 20007   John L.D. Clark, Dir.

ERIC CLEARINGHOUSE ON TEACHER EDUCATION
American Assn. of Colleges
For Teacher Education
One Dupont Circle, N.W., Suite 610   Phone: (202) 293-2450
Washington, DC 20036   Dean A. Schwanke, User Serv.Spec.

ESPERANTIC STUDIES FOUNDATION - LIBRARY
6451 Barnaby St., N.W.   Phone: (202) 362-3963
Washington, DC 20015   E. James Lieberman, Dir.

EUROPEAN COMMUNITY INFORMATION SERVICE - LIBRARY
2100 M St., N.W., Suite 707   Phone: (202) 862-9500
Washington, DC 20037   Ella Krucoff, Chf.Ref. & Doc.

EXPORT-IMPORT BANK OF THE UNITED STATES - LIBRARY
811 Vermont Ave., N.W.   Phone: (202) 566-8897
Washington, DC 20571   Theodora McGill, Libn.

FEDERAL ELECTION COMMISSION - NATIONAL CLEARINGHOUSE ON
ELECTION ADMINISTRATION - DOCUMENT CENTER
1325 K St., N.W.   Phone: (800) 424-9530
Washington, DC 20463   Gwenn Hofmann, Asst. to Dir.

FEDERAL RESERVE SYSTEM - BOARD OF GOVERNORS - LAW LIBRARY
20th & Constitution Ave., N.W.   Phone: (202) 452-3284
Washington, DC 20551   Judith M. Weiss, Law Libn.

FEDERAL RESERVE SYSTEM - BOARD OF GOVERNORS - RESEARCH LIBRARY
20th & Constitution Ave., N.W.   Phone: (202) 452-3332
Washington, DC 20551   Ann Roane Clary, Chf.Libn.

FERTILIZER INSTITUTE
1015 18th St., N.W.   Phone: (202) 466-2700
Washington, DC 20036   Donald N. Collins, V.P.Commun.

FOLGER SHAKESPEARE LIBRARY
201 E. Capitol St.   Phone: (202) 544-4600
Washington, DC 20003   Dr. O.B. Hardison, Jr., Dir.

FOOD MARKETING INSTITUTE - INFORMATION SERVICE
1750 K St., N.W.   Phone: (202) 452-8444
Washington, DC 20006   Barbara L. McBride, Mgr., Info.Serv.

FOREIGN CLAIMS SETTLEMENT COMMISSION OF THE UNITED STATES -
LIBRARY
1111 20th St., N.W., Rm. 401   Phone: (202) 653-6166
Washington, DC 20579   Karl D. Klauck, Dp.Gen.Couns.

FOREIGN SERVICES RESEARCH INSTITUTE - LIBRARY
Box 6317   Phone: (202) 362-1588
Washington, DC 20015   Ellspath Lawrence, Libn.

FOSTER ASSOCIATES, INC. - LIBRARY
1101 17th St., N.W.   Phone: (202) 296-2380
Washington, DC 20036   Nancy Valint, Libn.

FOUNDATION CENTER - WASHINGTON BRANCH LIBRARY
1001 Connecticut Ave., N.W., Suite 938   Phone: (202) 331-1400
Washington, DC 20036   Margot Brinkley, Dir.

FOUNDATION OF THE FEDERAL BAR ASSOCIATION - FEDERAL BAR
FOUNDATION LIBRARY
1815 H St., N.W.   Phone: (202) 638-1956
Washington, DC 20006   Richard M. Flynn, Libn.

FOUNDATION FOR PUBLIC AFFAIRS - RESOURCE CENTER
1220 16th St., N.W.   Phone: (202) 872-1750
Washington, DC 20036   Jane Sennett Long, Dir.

FOUNDATION FOR THE STUDY OF PRESIDENTIAL AND CONGRESSIONAL
TERMS - LIBRARY
1019 19th St., N.W., Suite 1010   Phone: (202) 466-2300
Washington, DC 20036   William M. Mecke, Asst.Dir.

FRANCISCAN FRIARS OF THE ATONEMENT - ATONEMENT SEMINARY
LIBRARY
145 Taylor St., N.E.   Phone: (202) 529-1114
Washington, DC 20017   Bro. Edward Rankey, S.A., Libn.

FRANCISCAN MONASTERY LIBRARY *
1400 Quincy St., N.E.   Phone: (202) 526-6800
Washington, DC 20017

GEOGRAPHIC

FRIENDS COMMITTEE ON NATIONAL LEGISLATION - LEGISLATIVE
LIBRARY
245 2nd St., N.E.   Phone: (202) 547-6000
Washington, DC 20002

FUND FOR PEACE - CENTER FOR DEFENSE INFORMATION
122 Maryland Ave., N.E.   Phone: (202) 543-0400
Washington, DC 20002   Richard Fieldhouse, Res.Libn.

FUND FOR PEACE - CENTER FOR INTERNATIONAL POLICY - INFORMATION
CENTER
120 Maryland Ave., N.E.   Phone: (202) 544-4666
Washington, DC 20002   Virginia Adams, Adm.Dir.

FUTURE HOMEMAKERS OF AMERICA - RESOURCE CENTER
2010 Massachusetts Ave., N.W.   Phone: (202) 833-1925
Washington, DC 20036   Polli Howard, Dir. of Commun.

GALLAUDET COLLEGE LIBRARY - SPECIAL COLLECTIONS
Seventh & Florida Aves., N.E.   Phone: (202) 651-5566
Washington, DC 20002   Fern Edwards, College Libn.

GENERAL COMMISSION ON CHAPLAINS AND ARMED FORCES PERSONNEL -
CHAPLAINS MEMORIAL LIBRARY
5100 Wisconsin Ave., N.W., Suite 310   Phone: (202) 686-1857
Washington, DC 20016   Edward I. Swanson, Dir.

GEORGE WASHINGTON UNIVERSITY - INSTITUTE FOR SINO-SOVIET
STUDIES LIBRARY
2130 H St., N.W.   Phone: (202) 676-7105
Washington, DC 20052   Alice E. Kopp, Libn.

GEORGE WASHINGTON UNIVERSITY - MEDICAL CENTER - PAUL
HIMMELFARB HEALTH SCIENCES LIBRARY
2300 Eye St., N.W.   Phone: (202) 676-2961
Washington, DC 20037   Shelley A. Bader, Dir.

GEORGE WASHINGTON UNIVERSITY - NATIONAL LAW CENTER - JACOB
BURNS LAW LIBRARY
716 20th St., N.W.   Phone: (202) 676-6646
Washington, DC 20052   Anita K. Head, Libn.

GEORGETOWN UNIVERSITY - BLOMMER SCIENCE LIBRARY
Reiss Science Bldg., 3rd Fl.
Box 37445   Phone: (202) 625-4733
Washington, DC 20013   Peg O'Rourke

GEORGETOWN UNIVERSITY - CENTER FOR POPULATION RESEARCH -
LIBRARY
3520 Prospect St., N.W.   Phone: (202) 625-4333
Washington, DC 20057   Thomas W. Merrick, Dir.

GEORGETOWN UNIVERSITY - EAST CAMPUS DATA LIBRARY
35th & N Sts., N.W.
249A Nevils Bldg.   Phone: (202) 625-4492
Washington, DC 20057   Bradley Reese, Dir.

GEORGETOWN UNIVERSITY - KENNEDY INSTITUTE OF ETHICS - CENTER
FOR BIOETHICS LIBRARY
3520 Prospect St., N.W.   Phone: (202) 625-2383
Washington, DC 20057   Doris Goldstein, Dir.Lib. & Info.Serv.

GEORGETOWN UNIVERSITY - LAW CENTER LIBRARY
600 New Jersey Ave., N.W.   Phone: (202) 624-8260
Washington, DC 20001   Elisabeth S. Jackson, Act. Law Libn.

GEORGETOWN UNIVERSITY - MEDICAL CENTER - DAHLGREN MEMORIAL
LIBRARY
3900 Reservoir Rd.   Phone: (202) 625-7673
Washington, DC 20007   Naomi C. Broering, Libn.

GEORGETOWN UNIVERSITY - SPECIAL COLLECTION DIVISION - LAUINGER
MEMORIAL LIBRARY
37th And O Sts., N.W.   Phone: (202) 635-3230
Washington, DC 20057   George M. Barringer, Spec.Coll.Libn.

GOVERNMENT RESEARCH CORPORATION - LIBRARY
1730 M St., N.W.   Phone: (202) 857-1400
Washington, DC 20036   Nancy R. Miller, Dir., Lib.Serv.

GRANGE-FARM FILM FOUNDATION - LIBRARY
1616 H St., N.W.   Phone: (202) 628-3507
Washington, DC 20006   Charles Dana Bennett, Spec.Cons.

GREATER SOUTHEAST COMMUNITY HOSPITAL - LURA HEALTH SCIENCES
LIBRARY
1310 Southern Ave., S.E.   Phone: (202) 574-6793
Washington, DC 20032   Brenda Lewis, Chf.Libn.

GREEN THUMB LIBRARY
1012 14th St., N.W.   Phone: (202) 789-5400
Washington, DC 20012   Fred Twombley, Sr.Adm.Asst.

GROUP HEALTH ASSOCIATION OF AMERICA, INC. - GERTRUDE STURGES
MEMORIAL LIBRARY
624 9th St., N.W.   Phone: (202) 737-4311
Washington, DC 20001   Nina M. Lane, Lib.Dir.

HAMMER, SILER, GEORGE ASSOCIATES - LIBRARY †
1140 Connecticut Ave., N.W.   Phone: (202) 223-1100
Washington, DC 20036   Bruce Kin Huie, Libn./Res.Asst.

HARVARD UNIVERSITY - CENTER FOR HELLENIC STUDIES - LIBRARY
3100 Whitehaven St., N.W.   Phone: (202) 234-3738
Washington, DC 20008   Jeno Platthy, Ph.D., Libn.

HARVARD UNIVERSITY - DUMBARTON OAKS CENTER FOR PRE-COLUMBIAN
STUDIES - LIBRARY
1703 32nd St., N.W.   Phone: (202) 342-3265
Washington, DC 20007   Carlos Arostegui, Asst.Cur.

HARVARD UNIVERSITY - DUMBARTON OAKS GARDEN LIBRARY OF THE
CENTER FOR STUDIES IN LANDSCAPE ARCHITECTURE
1703 32nd St., N.W.
Washington, DC 20007   Laura Byers, Libn.

HARVARD UNIVERSITY - DUMBARTON OAKS RESEARCH LIBRARY AND
COLLECTION
1703 32nd St., N.W.   Phone: (202) 342-3240
Washington, DC 20007   Irene Vaslef, Libn.

HIGHWAY USERS FEDERATION - LIBRARY
1776 Massachusetts Ave., N.W.   Phone: (202) 857-1225
Washington, DC 20036   Blanca Avila, Libn.

HJK&A ADVERTISING & PUBLIC RELATIONS - INFORMATION CENTER
2233 Wisconsin Ave., N.W.   Phone: (202) 333-0700
Washington, DC 20007   Ann Brinsmead, Info.Spec.

HOGAN & HARTSON - LIBRARY †
815 Connecticut Ave., N.W.   Phone: (202) 331-4604
Washington, DC 20006   R. Austin Doherty, Libn.

HOWARD UNIVERSITY - ARCHITECTURE & PLANNING LIBRARY
6th St. & Howard Pl., N.W.   Phone: (202) 636-7773
Washington, DC 20059   Mod Mekkawi, Libn.

HOWARD UNIVERSITY - BERNARD B. FALL COLLECTION
Founders Library, Room 300A   Phone: (202) 636-7261
Washington, DC 20059   Steven I. Yoon, Cur.

HOWARD UNIVERSITY - CHANNING POLLOCK THEATRE COLLECTION
University Library   Phone: (202) 636-7259
Washington, DC 20059   Marilyn E. Mahanand, Cur.

HOWARD UNIVERSITY - CHEMISTRY LIBRARY
525 College St., N.W.   Phone: (202) 636-6881
Washington, DC 20059   Doris Mitchell, Sci. & Tech.Libn.

HOWARD UNIVERSITY - ENGINEERING LIBRARY
2300 Sixth St., N.W.   Phone: (202) 636-6620
Washington, DC 20059   Doris Mitchell, Sci. & Tech.Libn.

HOWARD UNIVERSITY - FINE ARTS LIBRARY
                                    Phone: (202) 636-7071
Washington, DC 20059   Carrie M. Hackney, Libn.

HOWARD UNIVERSITY - HEALTH SCIENCES LIBRARY
600 W St., N.W.   Phone: (202) 636-6433
Washington, DC 20059   Joseph Forrest, Assoc.Dir.

HOWARD UNIVERSITY - HEALTH SCIENCES LIBRARY - PHARMACY ANNEX
2300 4th St.   Phone: (202) 636-6545
Washington, DC 20059   Mr. Jei Whan Kim, Libn.

HOWARD UNIVERSITY - MOORLAND-SPINGARN RESEARCH CENTER -
   LIBRARY DIVISION
500 Howard Pl., N.W.   Phone: (202) 636-7480
Washington, DC 20059   Michael R. Winston, Dir. of Ctr.

HOWARD UNIVERSITY - MOORLAND-SPINGARN RESEARCH CENTER -
   MANUSCRIPT DIVISION
500 Howard Pl., N.W.   Phone: (202) 636-7480
Washington, DC 20059   Dr. Michael R. Winston, Dir. of Ctr.

HOWARD UNIVERSITY - SCHOOL OF BUSINESS AND PUBLIC
   ADMINISTRATION - LIBRARY
2345 Sherman Ave., N.W.   Phone: (202) 636-7838
Washington, DC 20059   Lucille B. Smiley, Libn.

HOWARD UNIVERSITY - SCHOOL OF LAW - ALLEN MERCER DANIEL LAW
   LIBRARY
2900 Van Ness St., N.W.   Phone: (202) 686-6684
Washington, DC 20008   Obot A. Essien, Act. Law Libn.

HOWARD UNIVERSITY - SCHOOL OF RELIGION LIBRARY *
1240 Randolph St. N.E.   Phone: (202) 636-7282
Washington, DC 20017   Irene Owens, Libn.

HOWARD UNIVERSITY - SOCIAL WORK LIBRARY
6th St. & Howard Pl., N.W.   Phone: (202) 636-7316
Washington, DC 20059   Brenda J. Cox, Libn.

HUMAN RIGHTS INTERNET - LIBRARY
1502 Ogden St., N.W.   Phone: (202) 462-4320
Washington, DC 20010   Charles Lee Regan, Libn.

INDEPENDENT PETROLEUM ASSOCIATION OF AMERICA - INFORMATION
   SERVICE
1101 16th St., N.W.
Washington, DC 20036

INDIA - EMBASSY OF INDIA - LIBRARY OF THE INFORMATION SERVICE OF
   INDIA
2107 Massachusetts Ave., N.W.   Phone: (202) 265-5050
Washington, DC 20008   Baburaj Stephen, Libn.

INSTITUTE FOR LOCAL SELF-RELIANCE - LIBRARY †
1717 18th St., N.W.   Phone: (202) 232-4108
Washington, DC 20009   David Macgregor, Dir., Info. Access

INSTITUTE OF NAVIGATION - LIBRARY
815 15th St., N.W., Suite 832   Phone: (202) 783-4121
Washington, DC 20005   Frank B. Brady, Exec.Dir.

INSTITUTE OF TRANSPORTATION ENGINEERS - LIBRARY
525 School St., S.W., Suite 410   Phone: (703) 527-5277
Washington, DC 20024   Thomas W. Brahms, Exec.Dir.

INSURANCE INSTITUTE FOR HIGHWAY SAFETY - LIBRARY
600 New Hampshire Ave., Suite 300   Phone: (202) 333-0770
Washington, DC 20037   Christine A. Pruzin, Libn.

INTER-AMERICAN DEFENSE BOARD - LIBRARY †
2600 16th St., N.W. 6   Phone: (202) 387-7863
Washington, DC 20441   Olga M. Fernandez, Libn.

INTER-AMERICAN DEFENSE COLLEGE - LIBRARY
Fort McNair   Phone: (202) 693-8154
Washington, DC 20319   Mercedes M. Bailey, Chf.Libn.

INTER-AMERICAN DEVELOPMENT BANK - TECHNICAL INFORMATION
   CENTER
808 17th St., N.W.   Phone: (202) 634-8385
Washington, DC 20577   Ana I. Conde, Hd.

INTERFAITH FORUM ON RELIGION, ART AND ARCHITECTURE - LIBRARY
1777 Church St., N.W.   Phone: (202) 387-8333
Washington, DC 20036   Judith A. Miller, Exec.Dir.

INTERNATIONAL ASSOCIATION OF INDEPENDENT PRODUCERS - LIBRARY
   †
Box 1933   Phone: (202) 638-5595
Washington, DC 20013   Dr. Edward VonRothkirch, Dir.

INTERNATIONAL BROTHERHOOD OF TEAMSTERS, CHAUFFEURS,
   WAREHOUSEMEN AND HELPERS OF AMERICA - RES./EDUC. LIBRARY
25 Louisiana Ave., N.W.   Phone: (202) 624-6978
Washington, DC 20001   Betty Bourg, Hd.Libn.

INTERNATIONAL CITY MANAGEMENT ASSOCIATION - LIBRARY
1140 Connecticut Ave., N.W.   Phone: (202) 293-2200
Washington, DC 20036   Mary Od'Neal, Libn.

INTERNATIONAL COMMUNICATION AGENCY - LIBRARY
1750 Pennsylvania Ave., N.W.   Phone: (202) 724-9214
Washington, DC 20547   Jeanne R. Zeydel, Agency Libn.

INTERNATIONAL COMMUNICATION AGENCY - OFFICE OF THE ASSOCIATE
   DIRECTORATE FOR EDUCATIONAL & CULTURAL AFFAIRS
1717 H St., N.W., Rm. 700   Phone: (202) 632-6700
Washington, DC 20547   Richard D. Moore, Dir.

INTERNATIONAL FOOD POLICY RESEARCH INSTITUTE - LIBRARY
1776 Massachusetts Ave., N.W.   Phone: (202) 862-5614
Washington, DC 20036   Patricia W. Klosky, Libn.

INTERNATIONAL FRANCHISE ASSOCIATION - LIBRARY
1025 Connecticut Ave., N.W.   Phone: (202) 659-0790
Washington, DC 20036   Nancy B. Shaver, Libn.

INTERNATIONAL HUMAN RIGHTS LAW GROUP - LIBRARY
1700 K St., N.W.   Phone: (202) 659-5023
Washington, DC 20006   Amy R. Novick, Adm.Asst.

INTERNATIONAL LABOR OFFICE - WASHINGTON BRANCH LIBRARY
1750 New York Ave., N.W.   Phone: (202) 376-2315
Washington, DC 20006   Patricia S. Hord, Libn.

INTERNATIONAL MILITARY ARCHIVES
Government Box 30051
Washington, DC 20014   Helga K. Knoeppel, Libn.

INTERNATIONAL MONETARY FUND - LAW LIBRARY
700 19th St., N.W.   Phone: (202) 477-6148
Washington, DC 20431   Eliana D. Prebisch, Libn.

INTERNATIONAL MONETARY FUND/WORLD BANK - JOINT BANK-FUND
   LIBRARY
700 19th St., N.W.   Phone: (202) 477-3125
Washington, DC 20431   Maureen M. Moore, Libn.

INTERNATIONAL NUMISMATIC SOCIETY - LIBRARY
1100 17th St. N.W., Box 19386   Phone: (202) 223-4496
Washington, DC 20036   Charles R. Hoskins, Info.Dir.

INTERNATIONAL VISITORS INFORMATION SERVICE
1825 H St., N.W.   Phone: (202) 872-8747
Washington, DC 20006   Marianne H. Cruze, Exec.Dir.

INVESTMENT COMPANY INSTITUTE - LIBRARY
1775 K St., N.W.   Phone: (202) 293-7700
Washington, DC 20006   Cut Parker, Libn.

JAPAN ECONOMIC INSTITUTE OF AMERICA - LIBRARY
1000 Connecticut Ave., N.W.   Phone: (202) 296-5633
Washington, DC 20036

JOHNS HOPKINS UNIVERSITY - SCHOOL OF ADVANCED INTERNATIONAL
   STUDIES - SYDNEY R. & ELSA W. MASON LIBRARY
1740 Massachusetts Ave., N.W.   Phone: (202) 785-6296
Washington, DC 20036   Peter J. Promen, Libn.

GEOGRAPHIC

KIRKLAND & ELLIS - LIBRARY
1776 K St., N.W.   Phone: (202) 857-5109
Washington, DC 20006   Charles E. Kregel, Jr., Info.Mgr.

LEAGUE FOR INTERNATIONAL FOOD EDUCATION - LIBRARY
1126 16th St., N.W., Rm. 404   Phone: (202) 331-1658
Washington, DC 20036   Margaret Fowles, Libn.

LIBRARY OF CONGRESS - AFRICAN & MIDDLE EASTERN DIVISION
John Adams Bldg., Rm. 1040C   Phone: (202) 287-7937
Washington, DC 20540   Dr. Julian W. Witherell, Chf.

LIBRARY OF CONGRESS - AMERICAN FOLKLIFE CENTER
Thomas Jefferson Bldg. - G104D   Phone: (202) 287-6590
Washington, DC 20540   Alan Jabbour, Dir.

**LIBRARY OF CONGRESS - AMERICAN FOLKLIFE CENTER - ARCHIVE OF FOLK
  SONG**
Thomas Jefferson Bldg. - G136   Phone: (202) 287-5505
Washington, DC 20540   Joseph C. Hickerson, Hd.

LIBRARY OF CONGRESS - ASIAN DIVISION
John Adams Bldg., Rm. 1024   Phone: (202) 287-5420
Washington, DC 20540   Dr. Richard C. Howard, Act.Chf.

LIBRARY OF CONGRESS - CHILDREN'S LITERATURE CENTER
Thomas Jefferson Bldg., Rm. 140H   Phone: (202) 287-5535
Washington, DC 20540   Virginia Haviland, Chf.

LIBRARY OF CONGRESS - CONGRESSIONAL RESEARCH SERVICE
James Madison Memorial Bldg., LM213 Phone: (202) 287-5735
Washington, DC 20540   Gilbert Gude, Dir.

LIBRARY OF CONGRESS - COPYRIGHT PUBLIC INFORMATION OFFICE
James Madison Memorial Bldg., LM-401
101 Independence Ave., S.E.   Phone: (202) 287-8700
Washington, DC 20559   Victor Marton, Supv., Info. Unit

LIBRARY OF CONGRESS - EUROPEAN DIVISION
John Adams Bldg., Rm. 5244   Phone: (202) 287-5413
Washington, DC 20540   David H. Kraus, Act.Chf.

LIBRARY OF CONGRESS - GEN. READING ROOMS DIV.
Thomas Jefferson Bldg. - GRR B144 Phone: (202) 287-5530
Washington, DC 20540   Ellen Hahn, Chf.

**LIBRARY OF CONGRESS - GEN. READING ROOMS DIV. - MICROFORM
  READING ROOM SECTION**
Thomas Jefferson Bldg. - GRR 140B Phone: (202) 287-5471
Washington, DC 20540   Robert V. Gross, Hd.

**LIBRARY OF CONGRESS - GEN. READING ROOMS DIV. - THOMAS
  JEFFERSON READING ROOMS SECTION**
John Adams Bldg., Rm. 5010   Phone: (202) 287-5538
Washington, DC 20540   Gary D. Jensen, Hd.

LIBRARY OF CONGRESS - GEOGRAPHY & MAP DIVISION
James Madison Memorial Bldg., LMB01 Phone: (202) 287-6277
Washington, DC 20540   Dr. John A. Wolter, Chf.

LIBRARY OF CONGRESS - HISPANIC DIVISION
Thomas Jefferson Bldg., Rm. 239E   Phone: (202) 287-5256
Washington, DC 20540   William E. Carter, Chf.

**LIBRARY OF CONGRESS - JOHN F. KENNEDY CENTER FOR THE
  PERFORMING ARTS - THE PERFORMING ARTS LIBRARY**
John F. Kennedy Ctr.   Phone: (202) 287-6245
Washington, DC 20566   Peter J. Fay, Hd.Libn.

LIBRARY OF CONGRESS - LAW LIBRARY
James Madison Memorial Bldg., Rm. 240 Phone: (202) 287-5065
Washington, DC 20540   Carleton W. Kenyon, Law Libn.

**LIBRARY OF CONGRESS - LAW LIBRARY - AMERICAN-BRITISH LAW
  DIVISION**
James Madison Memorial Bldg., Rm. 235 Phone: (202) 287-5077
Washington, DC 20540   Marlene C. McGuirl, Chf.

LIBRARY OF CONGRESS - LAW LIBRARY - EUROPEAN LAW DIVISION
James Madison Memorial Bldg., Rm. 240 Phone: (202) 287-5088
Washington, DC 20540   Ivan Sipkov, Chf.

LIBRARY OF CONGRESS - LAW LIBRARY - FAR EASTERN LAW DIVISION
James Madison Memorial Bldg., Rm. 235 Phone: (202) 287-5085
Washington, DC 20540   Tao-Tai Hsia, Chf.

LIBRARY OF CONGRESS - LAW LIBRARY - HISPANIC LAW DIVISION
James Madison Memorial Bldg., Rm. 235 Phone: (202) 287-5070
Washington, DC 20540   Rubens Medina, Chf.

**LIBRARY OF CONGRESS - LAW LIBRARY - NEAR EASTERN AND AFRICAN
  LAW DIVISION**
James Madison Memorial Bldg., Rm. 240 Phone: (202) 287-5073
Washington, DC 20540   Zuhair E. Jwaideh, Chf.

LIBRARY OF CONGRESS - LOAN DIVISION
Thomas Jefferson Bldg. - G151   Phone: (202) 287-5441
Washington, DC 20540   Olive C. James, Chf.

LIBRARY OF CONGRESS - MANUSCRIPT DIVISION
John Adams Bldg., Rm. 3005   Phone: (202) 287-5388
Washington, DC 20540   Paul T. Heffron, Act.Chf.

**LIBRARY OF CONGRESS - MOTION PICTURE, BROADCASTING & RECORDED
  SOUND DIVISION**
John Adams Bldg., Rm. 1053   Phone: (202) 287-5840
Washington, DC 20540   Erik Barnouw, Chf.

LIBRARY OF CONGRESS - MUSIC DIVISION
Thomas Jefferson Bldg., Rm. G144   Phone: (202) 287-5507
Washington, DC 20540   Donald L. Leavitt, Chf.

**LIBRARY OF CONGRESS - NATIONAL LIBRARY SERVICE FOR THE BLIND
  AND PHYSICALLY HANDICAPPED**
Taylor St. Annex
1291 Taylor St., N.W.   Phone: (202) 287-5100
Washington, DC 20542   Frank Kurt Cylke, Dir.

LIBRARY OF CONGRESS - NATIONAL REFERRAL CENTER
John Adams Bldg., Rm. 5223   Phone: (202) 287-5670
Washington, DC 20540   Edward N. MacConomy, Chf.

LIBRARY OF CONGRESS - PRESERVATION OFFICE
John Adams Bldg., Rm. G1008   Phone: (202) 287-5212
Washington, DC 20540   Peter G. Sparks, Chf.

LIBRARY OF CONGRESS - PRINTS & PHOTOGRAPHS DIVISION
John Adams Bldg., Rm. 1051   Phone: (202) 287-5836
Washington, DC 20540   Oliver Jensen, Chf.

LIBRARY OF CONGRESS - RARE BOOK & SPECIAL COLLECTIONS DIVISION
Thomas Jefferson Bldg., Rm. 256   Phone: (202) 287-5434
Washington, DC 20540   William Matheson, Chf.

LIBRARY OF CONGRESS - SCIENCE & TECHNOLOGY DIVISION
John Adams Bldg., Rm. 5112   Phone: (202) 287-5639
Washington, DC 20540   John F. Price, Act.Chf.

**LIBRARY OF CONGRESS - SERIAL AND GOVERNMENT PUBLICATIONS
  DIVISION**
John Adams Bldg., Rm. 1040   Phone: (202) 287-5647
Washington, DC 20540   Donald F. Wisdom, Chf.

MC KINSEY & COMPANY, INC. - LIBRARY
1700 Pennsylvania Ave., N.W.   Phone: (202) 393-6820
Washington, DC 20006   Ann Robertson, Mgr., Info. & Anl.Serv.

MARIST COLLEGE - LIBRARY
220 Taylor St., N.E.   Phone: (202) 529-2821
Washington, DC 20017   Paul M. Cabrita, Hd.Libn.

METROPOLITAN WASHINGTON COUNCIL OF GOVERNMENTS - LIBRARY
1875 Eye St., N.W.   Phone: (202) 223-6800
Washington, DC 20006   Deborah J. Nuttall, Libn.

MIDDLE EAST INSTITUTE - GEORGE CAMP KEISER LIBRARY
1761 N St., N.W.   Phone: (202) 785-1141
Washington, DC 20036   Lois M. Khairallah, Libn.

MORGAN, LEWIS & BOCKIUS - LIBRARY
1800 M St., N.W.   Phone: (202) 872-7691
Washington, DC 20036   Victoria M. Ward, Law Libn.

MORRISON AND FOERSTER - BRANCH LAW LIBRARY
1920 N St., N.W., Suite 800   Phone: (202) 466-6060
Washington, DC 20036   Jane Amon, Libn.

MORTGAGE BANKERS ASSOCIATION OF AMERICA - LIBRARY
1125 15th St., N.W.   Phone: (202) 861-6580
Washington, DC 20005   Timothy S. Wolf, Libn.

MOTT RESEARCH GROUP - LIBRARY
3220 Rittenhouse St., N.W.   Phone: (202) 363-3809
Washington, DC 20015   Dorothy Williams Mott, Libn./Cur.

MOUNT VERNON PLACE UNITED METHODIST CHURCH - DESSIE M.
  HALLETT LIBRARY
900 Massachusetts Ave., N.W.   Phone: (202) 347-9620
Washington, DC 20001   Dessie M. Hallett, Libn.

MPR ASSOCIATES, INC. - LIBRARY
1140 Connecticut Ave., N.W.   Phone: (202) 659-2320
Washington, DC 20036   Alice McNamara, Libn.

NARCOTICS EDUCATION, INC. - SCHARFFENBERG MEMORIAL LIBRARY
6830 Laurel St., N.W.
Box 4390   Phone: (202) 723-4774
Washington, DC 20012   F.A. Soper, Dir.

NATHAN (Robert R.) ASSOCIATES, INC. - LIBRARY *
1200 18th St., N.W., Suite 200   Phone: (202) 393-2700
Washington, DC 20036   Jean Bow, Libn.

NATIONAL ACADEMY OF SCIENCES - NATIONAL ACADEMY OF
  ENGINEERING - LIBRARY
2101 Constitution Ave., N.W.   Phone: (202) 389-6272
Washington, DC 20418   James L. Olsen, Jr., Libn.

NATIONAL ACADEMY OF SCIENCES - NATIONAL RESEARCH COUNCIL -
  HIGHWAY RESEARCH INFORMATION SERVICE
Transportation Research Bd.
2101 Constitution Ave., N.W.   Phone: (202) 389-6358
Washington, DC 20418   Arthur B. Mobley, HRIS Mgr.

NATIONAL ACADEMY OF SCIENCES - NATIONAL RESEARCH COUNCIL -
  MARITIME RESEARCH INFORMATION SERVICE
Maritime Transportation Research Board
2101 Constitution Ave., N.W.   Phone: (202) 389-6687
Washington, DC 20418   Davis G. Mellor, MRIS Mgr.

NATIONAL ACADEMY OF SCIENCES - NATIONAL RESEARCH COUNCIL -
  RAILROAD RESEARCH INFORMATION SERVICE
Transportation Research Bd.
2101 Constitution Ave., N.W.   Phone: (202) 389-6611
Washington, DC 20418   Frederick N. Houser, Jr., RRIS Mgr.

NATIONAL ACADEMY OF SCIENCES - NATIONAL RESEARCH COUNCIL -
  TRANSPORTATION RESEARCH BOARD LIBRARY
2101 Constitution Ave., N.W.   Phone: (202) 389-6841
Washington, DC 20418   Janice W. Bain, Libn.

NATIONAL AERONAUTIC ASSOCIATION - LIBRARY
821 15th St., N.W.   Phone: (202) 347-2808
Washington, DC 20005   Milton M. Brown, Sec.

NATIONAL ASSOCIATION OF BROADCASTERS - LIBRARY
1771 N St., N.W.   Phone: (202) 293-3578
Washington, DC 20036   Susan M. Hill, Libn.

NATIONAL ASSOCIATION OF HOME BUILDERS - NATIONAL HOUSING
  CENTER LIBRARY
15th & M Sts., N.W.   Phone: (202) 452-0201
Washington, DC 20005   Margery M. Clark, Chf.Libn.

NATIONAL ASSOCIATION OF HOUSING AND REDEVELOPMENT OFFICIALS -
  RESOURCE CENTER
2600 Virginia Ave., N.W., Suite 404 Phone: (202) 333-2020
Washington, DC 20037   Mary L. Pike, Dp.Dir., Member Serv.

NATIONAL ASSOCIATION OF LIFE UNDERWRITERS - LIBRARY †
1922 F St., N.W.   Phone: (202) 331-6001
Washington, DC 20006   Jack E. Bobo, Exec.V.P.

NATIONAL ASSOCIATION OF RETAIL GROCERS OF THE U.S., INC. -
  LIBRARY
Box 17208   Phone: (703) 860-3300
Washington, DC 20041   Jane Arnwine, Info.Mgr.

NATIONAL ASSOCIATION OF SOCIAL WORKERS - RESOURCE CENTER †
1425 H St., N.W., Suite 600   Phone: (202) 628-6800
Washington, DC 20005   David N. Weber, Info./Res.Ctr.Coord.

NATIONAL BIOMEDICAL RESEARCH FOUNDATION - LIBRARY
Georgetown University Medical Ctr.
3900 Reservoir Rd., N.W.   Phone: (202) 625-2121
Washington, DC 20007   Doris K. Mela, Libn.

NATIONAL CENTER FOR HOUSING MANAGEMENT - TECHNICAL
  INFORMATION CENTER †
1228 M St., N.W.   Phone: (202) 872-1717
Washington, DC 20005   Beth A. Brown, Dir., Tech.Info.Ctr.

NATIONAL COAL ASSOCIATION - LIBRARY
Coal Bldg., 1130 17th St., N.W.   Phone: (202) 463-2641
Washington, DC 20036   Richard E. Niswander, Dir., Lib.Serv.

NATIONAL COMMISSION ON WORKING WOMEN - RESOURCE CENTER
1211 Connecticut Ave., N.W.   Phone: (202) 466-6770
Washington, DC 20036   Sally Steenland, Info.Spec.

NATIONAL COUNCIL ON THE AGING - LIBRARY
600 Maryland Ave., S.W.   Phone: (202) 223-6250
Washington, DC 20024   John B. Balkema, Libn.

NATIONAL COUNCIL OF SENIOR CITIZENS, INC. - LIBRARY
925 15th St., N.W.   Phone: (202) 347-8800
Washington, DC 20005   Ternan Treadway, Lib.Serv.Coord.

NATIONAL COUNCIL FOR U.S.-CHINA TRADE - LIBRARY
1050 17th St., N.W., Suite 350   Phone: (202) 828-8375
Washington, DC 20036   Marianna Graham, Libn.

NATIONAL ECONOMIC RESEARCH ASSOCIATES, INC. - LIBRARY
1800 M St., N.W.   Phone: (202) 466-3510
Washington, DC 20036   Jane Platt-Brown, Libn.

NATIONAL ECUMENICAL COALITION, INC. - LIBRARY
Georgetown Sta., Box 3554   Phone: (202) 833-2616
Washington, DC 20007   Bro. Scott Desmond, F.O.C., Libn.

NATIONAL EDUCATION ASSOCIATION - INFORMATION CENTER
1201 16th St., N.W.
Washington, DC 20036

NATIONAL ENDOWMENT FOR THE ARTS - ARTS LIBRARY/INFORMATION
  CENTER
2401 E St., N.W., Rm. 1256   Phone: (202) 634-7640
Washington, DC 20506   M. Christine Morrison, Arts Libn.

NATIONAL ENDOWMENT FOR THE ARTS - LAW LIBRARY
Office of the General Counsel
2401 E St., N.W.   Phone: (202) 634-6588
Washington, DC 20506   Susan Liberman, Asst. to Gen. Counsel

NATIONAL ENDOWMENT FOR THE HUMANITIES - LIBRARY
806 15th St., N.W.   Phone: (202) 724-0360
Washington, DC 20506   Jeannette D. Coletti, Libn.

NATIONAL FOREST PRODUCTS ASSOCIATION - INFORMATION CENTER
1619 Massachusetts Ave., N.W.   Phone: (202) 797-5836
Washington, DC 20036   Barbara A. Beall, Mgr.

GEOGRAPHIC

NATIONAL FOUNDATION FOR CONSUMER CREDIT - LIBRARY
1819 H St., N.W.   Phone: (202) 223-2040
Washington, DC 20006   Badra Wijegoonawardena

NATIONAL 4-H COUNCIL - COMMUNICATIONS DIVISION *
7100 Connecticut Ave.
Washington, DC 20015   Mary Bedford, Rsrcs./Reporting Coord.

NATIONAL GALLERY OF ART - DEPARTMENT OF EXTENSION PROGRAMS
Sixth and Constitution Ave., N.W.   Phone: (202) 737-4215
Washington, DC 20565   Ruth R. Perlin, Cur.-in-Charge

NATIONAL GALLERY OF ART - EDUCATION DIVISION SLIDE LIBRARY
Sixth and Constitution Ave., N.W.   Phone: (202) 737-4215
Washington, DC 20565   Anne von Rebhan, Chf. Slide Libn.

NATIONAL GALLERY OF ART - INDEX OF AMERICAN DESIGN
Sixth and Constitution Ave., N.W.   Phone: (202) 737-4215
Washington, DC 20565   Lina Steele, Cur.

NATIONAL GALLERY OF ART - LIBRARY
Sixth and Constitution, N.W.   Phone: (202) 737-4215
Washington, DC 20565   J.M. Edelstein, Chf.Libn.

NATIONAL GALLERY OF ART - PHOTOGRAPHIC ARCHIVES
Sixth and Constitution Ave., N.W.   Phone: (202) 737-4215
Washington, DC 20565   Ruth R. Philbrick, Cur.

NATIONAL GENEALOGICAL SOCIETY - LIBRARY
1921 Sunderland Pl., N.W.   Phone: (202) 785-2123
Washington, DC 20036   Jean D. Strahan, Libn.

NATIONAL GEOGRAPHIC SOCIETY - CARTOGRAPHIC DIVISION - MAP
   LIBRARY
17th & M Sts., N.W.   Phone: (202) 857-7000
Washington, DC 20036   Margery K. Barkdull, Map Libn.

NATIONAL GEOGRAPHIC SOCIETY - ILLUSTRATIONS LIBRARY
17th & M Sts., N.W.   Phone: (202) 857-7000
Washington, DC 20036   Fern Shrewsberry Dame, Illus.Libn.

NATIONAL GEOGRAPHIC SOCIETY - LIBRARY
16th & M Sts., N.W.   Phone: (202) 857-7787
Washington, DC 20036   Virginia Carter Hills, Libn.

NATIONAL GUARD ASSOCIATION OF THE UNITED STATES - LIBRARY
One Massachusetts Ave., N.W.
Washington, DC 20001   Col. Leslie H. Cross, Libn.

NATIONAL HOME STUDY COUNCIL - LIBRARY
1601 18th St., N.W.   Phone: (202) 234-5100
Washington, DC 20009   Jeanne Casey

NATIONAL INJURY INFORMATION CLEARINGHOUSE
5401 Westbard Ave.
Westwood Towers Bldg., Rm. 625   Phone: (301) 492-6424
Washington, DC 20207   Nancy S. Johnston, Dir.

NATIONAL INSTITUTE OF EDUCATION - EDUCATIONAL RESEARCH
   LIBRARY
1832 M St., N.W., Rm. 609   Phone: (202) 254-5060
Washington, DC 20208-1101   Charles D. Missar, Lib.Dir.

NATIONAL INSTITUTE OF MUNICIPAL LAW OFFICES - LIBRARY
1000 Connecticut Ave., N.W., Suite 800
Washington, DC 20036   Charles S. Rhyne, Gen.Couns.

NATIONAL LEAGUE OF CITIES - MUNICIPAL REFERENCE SERVICE
1301 Pennsylvania Ave., N.W.   Phone: (202) 626-3210
Washington, DC 20004   Olivia Kredel, Mgr.

NATIONAL LEGAL AID AND DEFENDER ASSOCIATION - LIBRARY
1625 K St., N.W.
Washington, DC 20006

NATIONAL ORGANIZATION FOR WOMEN (NOW) - ACTION CENTER
   LIBRARY
425 13th St., N.W., No. 1048   Phone: (202) 347-2279
Washington, DC 20004   Jenny Tipton, Libn.

NATIONAL PAINT AND COATINGS ASSOCIATION - TECHNICAL LIBRARY †
1500 Rhode Island Ave., N.W.   Phone: (202) 462-6272
Washington, DC 20005   Donna Kordoski, Libn.

NATIONAL PARKS AND CONSERVATION ASSOCIATION - LIBRARY
1701 18th St., N.W.
Washington, DC 20009

NATIONAL PASSENGER RAILROAD CORPORATION (AMTRAK) - COMPUTER
   SERVICES DEPARTMENT LIBRARY *
400 North Capitol St., N.W.   Phone: (202) 383-3652
Washington, DC 20001   Michelle Solomon, Tech.Ref.Libn.

NATIONAL PRESBYTERIAN CHURCH - WILLIAM S. CULBERTSON LIBRARY
4101 Nebraska Ave., N.W.   Phone: (202) 244-3300
Washington, DC 20016   Muriel M. Kirk, Libn.

NATIONAL PUBLIC RADIO - PROGRAM LIBRARY & AUDIO ARCHIVE
2025 M St., N.W.   Phone: (202) 822-2000
Washington, DC 20036   Susan T. Bau, Prog.Libn.

NATIONAL REHABILITATION INFORMATION CENTER
4407 8th St., N.E.
Catholic University of America   Phone: (202) 635-5826
Washington, DC 20017   Eleanor Biscoe, Dir.

NATIONAL RESOURCE CENTER FOR CONSUMERS OF LEGAL SERVICES -
   CLEARINGHOUSE
1302 18th St., N.W., Suite 303   Phone: (202) 659-8514
Washington, DC 20036   Linda Marcus, Clghse.Dept.

NATIONAL RESTAURANT ASSOCIATION - INFORMATION RESOURCE
   CENTER
311 First St., N.W.   Phone: (202) 638-6100
Washington, DC 20001   Joan E. Campbell, Info.Rsrcs.Ctr.Mgr.

NATIONAL RETIRED TEACHERS ASSN.-AMERICAN ASSN. OF RETIRED
   PERSONS - NATL. GERONTOLOGY RESOURCE CTR.
1909 K St., N.W.   Phone: (202) 872-4845
Washington, DC 20049   Paula M. Lovas, Hd.

NATIONAL RIFLE ASSOCIATION - TECHNICAL LIBRARY
1600 Rhode Island Ave., N.W.   Phone: (202) 828-6227
Washington, DC 20036   Joe Roberts, Ed.

NATIONAL RURAL ELECTRIC COOPERATIVE ASSOCIATION - NORRIS
   MEMORIAL LIBRARY
1800 Massachusetts Ave., N.W.   Phone: (202) 857-9788
Washington, DC 20036   Chuck Rice, Lib.Serv.Spec.

NATIONAL SCHOOL BOARDS ASSOCIATION - RESOURCE CENTER
1055 Thomas Jefferson St., N.W.   Phone: (202) 337-7666
Washington, DC 20007   Eve Shepard, Info.Coord.

NATIONAL SCIENCE FOUNDATION - LIBRARY
1800 G St., N.W.   Phone: (202) 632-4070
Washington, DC 20550   Herman Fleming, Rec./Rpt.Off.

NATIONAL SCIENCE TEACHERS ASSOCIATION - GLENN O. BLOUGH
   LIBRARY
1742 Connecticut Ave., N.W.   Phone: (202) 265-4150
Washington, DC 20009   Devon Griffith, Chf.Libn.

NATIONAL SHERIFFS' ASSOCIATION - EDUCATION AND RESOURCE
   CENTER
1250 Connecticut Ave., N.W., Suite 320
Washington, DC 20036

NATIONAL SOCIETY FOR AUTISTIC CHILDREN - INFORMATION &
   REFERRAL SERVICE
1234 Massachusetts Ave., N.W.   Phone: (202) 783-0125
Washington, DC 20005   Frank Warren, Dir.

NATIONAL SOCIETY, DAUGHTERS OF THE AMERICAN REVOLUTION -
   LIBRARY
1776 D St., N.W.   Phone: (202) 628-1776
Washington, DC 20006   Carolyn Leopold Michaels, Staff Libn.

NATIONAL SOCIETY FOR MEDICAL RESEARCH - NSMR DATA BANK
1029 Vermont Ave., N.W.   Phone: (202) 347-9565
Washington, DC 20005   William M. Samuels, Exec.Dir.

NATIONAL SOCIETY OF PROFESSIONAL ENGINEERS - INFORMATION
  CENTER
2029 K St., N.W.   Phone: (202) 337-0420
Washington, DC 20006   Donald G. Weinert, Exec.Dir.

NATIONAL TAX EQUALITY ASSOCIATION - LIBRARY
1000 Connecticut Ave. Bldg.   Phone: (202) 296-5424
Washington, DC 20036   Ray M. Stroupe, Pres.

NATIONAL TRUST FOR HISTORIC PRESERVATION - INFORMATION
  SERVICES
1785 Massachusetts Ave., N.W.   Phone: (202) 673-4000
Washington, DC 20036   Susan Shearer, Info.Serv.Coord.

NATIONAL WILDLIFE FEDERATION - FRAZIER MEMORIAL LIBRARY
1412 16th St., N.W.   Phone: (202) 797-6828
Washington, DC 20036   Jay D. Hair, Exec. V.P.

NATIONAL WOMAN'S PARTY - FLORENCE BAYARD HILLES LIBRARY
144 Constitution Ave., N.E.
Washington, DC 20002

NATIONAL YOUTH WORK ALLIANCE, INC. - CLEARINGHOUSE/LIBRARY
1346 Connecticut Ave., N.W.   Phone: (202) 785-0764
Washington, DC 20036   Thomas R. McCarthy, Dir.

NETHERLANDS EMBASSY - REFERENCE ROOM LIBRARY
4200 Linnean Ave., N.W.   Phone: (202) 244-5300
Washington, DC 20008

NEW TRANSCENTURY FOUNDATION - SECRETARIAT FOR WOMEN IN
  DEVELOPMENT - DOCUMENTATION CENTER
1789 Columbia Rd., N.W.
Washington, DC 20009   Patricia Harlan McClure, Dir.

NEW ZEALAND EMBASSY - LIBRARY
37 Observatory Circle, N.W.   Phone: (202) 328-4800
Washington, DC 20008   Mr. Trevor Hughes, Info.Off.

NEWSPAPER GUILD - HEYWOOD BROUN LIBRARY
1125 15th St., N.W.   Phone: (202) 296-2990
Washington, DC 20005   David J. Eisen, Dir. of Res. & Info.

NEWSWEEK, INC. - WASHINGTON BUREAU LIBRARY
1750 Pennsylvania Ave., N.W.
Suite 1220   Phone: (202) 626-2040
Washington, DC 20006   F. Joseph McHugh, Bureau Libn.

OBLATE COLLEGE - LIBRARY
391 Michigan Ave., N.E.   Phone: (202) 529-5244
Washington, DC 20017   Rev. George Croft, O.M.I., Hd.Libn.

ORGANIZATION OF AMERICAN STATES - COLUMBUS MEMORIAL LIBRARY
17th St. & Constitution Ave., N.W.   Phone: (202) 789-6040
Washington, DC 20006   Thomas L. Welch, Dir.

ORGANIZATION FOR ECONOMIC COOPERATION AND DEVELOPMENT -
  PUBLICATIONS AND INFORMATION CENTER
1750 Pennsylvania Ave., N.W.
Suite 1207   Phone: (202) 724-1857
Washington, DC 20006   Eric N. Ekers, Hd.

OVERSEAS DEVELOPMENT COUNCIL - LIBRARY
1717 Massachusetts Ave., N.W.   Phone: (202) 234-8701
Washington, DC 20036   James E. Boyle, Libn.

OVERSEAS PRIVATE INVESTMENT CORPORATION - LIBRARY
1129 20th St., N.W., Rm.711   Phone: (202) 632-0146
Washington, DC 20527   Myra Norton, Libn.

PAN AMERICAN HEALTH ORGANIZATION - DOCUMENTATION AND HEALTH
  INFORMATION OFFICE †
525 23rd St., N.W.   Phone: (202) 861-3200
Washington, DC 20037   Dr. Carlos A. Gamboa, Chf.

PATTON BOGGS AND BLOW - LAW LIBRARY
2550 M St., N.W.   Phone: (202) 223-4040
Washington, DC 20037   Kevin McCall, Libn.

PENSION BENEFIT GUARANTY CORPORATION - OFFICE OF THE GENERAL
  COUNSEL - LIBRARY
2020 K St., N.W., Suite 7200   Phone: (202) 254-4889
Washington, DC 20006   Luanne Kitchin, Libn.

PHARMACEUTICAL MANUFACTURERS ASSOCIATION - SCIENCE
  INFORMATION SERVICES
1155 15th St., N.W.   Phone: (202) 463-2000
Washington, DC 20005   Patricia Marsh O'Brien, Mgr., Sci.Info.Serv.

PIERSON, BALL & DOWD - LAW LIBRARY
1200 18th St., N.W.   Phone: (202) 331-8566
Washington, DC 20036   Sandra Parrish, Libn.

POPULATION CRISIS COMMITEE/DRAPER FUND - LIBRARY
1120 19th St., N.W., Suite 550   Phone: (202) 659-1833
Washington, DC 20036   Linda J. Carroll, Libn.

POPULATION REFERENCE BUREAU, INC. - LIBRARY/INFORMATION
  SERVICE
1337 Connecticut Ave., N.W.   Phone: (202) 785-4664
Washington, DC 20036   Barbara Bower, Tech.Info.Spec.

POTOMAC ELECTRIC POWER COMPANY - LIBRARY
1900 Pennsylvania Ave., N.W.   Phone: (202) 872-2361
Washington, DC 20068   Helen C. Jessup, Libn.

PROVIDENCE HOSPITAL - HEALTH SCIENCES LIBRARY
1150 Varnum St., N.E.   Phone: (202) 269-7141
Washington, DC 20017   Sister Frances Healy, Dir.

PUBLIC CITIZEN - CONGRESS WATCH - LIBRARY
215 Pennsylvania Ave., S.E.   Phone: (202) 546-4996
Washington, DC 20003   Susan Lillis, Libn.

PUBLIC LAW EDUCATION INSTITUTE - LIBRARY
1346 Connecticut Ave. N.W., Suite 610   Phone: (202) 296-7590
Washington, DC 20036   William J. Straub, Circ.Mgr.

RACHEL CARSON COUNCIL, INC. - LIBRARY
8940 Jones Mill Rd.   Phone: (301) 652-1877
Washington, DC 20015   Shirley A. Briggs, Exec.Dir.

RAND CORPORATION - LIBRARY
2100 M St., N.W.   Phone: (202) 296-5000
Washington, DC 20037   Casey Kane, Libn.

REDMOND (J.W.) COMPANY - LIBRARY
1750 Pennsylvania Ave., N.W.
Washington, DC 20006   June Johnson, Libn.

REFRIGERATION RESEARCH FOUNDATION - LIBRARY
Air Rights Bldg.
7315 Wisconsin Ave.   Phone: (301) 652-5674
Washington, DC 20014   Richard M. Powell, Exec.Dir.

REPUBLICAN NATIONAL COMMITTEE - RESEARCH LIBRARY
310 First St., S.E.   Phone: (202) 484-6626
Washington, DC 20003   Helen Ammen, Libn.

REVIEW & HERALD PUBLISHING ASSOCIATION - LIBRARY
6856 Eastern Ave., N.W.   Phone: (202) 723-3700
Washington, DC 20012   Patricia Ruth Hirsch, Libn.

ROYAL SWEDISH EMBASSY - LIBRARY-INFORMATION CENTER
Watergate 600, Suite 1200
600 New Hampshire Ave., N.W.   Phone: (202) 298-3500
Washington, DC 20037   Aasa Arvidson, Info.Off.

ST. ELIZABETHS HOSPITAL - HEALTH SCIENCES LIBRARY
Administration Bldg.   Phone: (202) 574-7274
Washington, DC 20032   Toby G. Port, Adm.Libn.

GEOGRAPHIC

ST. JOSEPH'S SEMINARY - LIBRARY *
1200 Varnum St., N.E.   Phone: (202) 526-4231
Washington, DC 20017

ST. PAUL'S COLLEGE - LIBRARY
3015 Fourth St., N.E.   Phone: (202) 832-6262
Washington, DC 20017   Lawrence E. Boadt, C.S.P., Libn.

SCANDINAVIAN COUNCIL FOR APPLIED RESEARCH - SCANDINAVIAN
    DOCUMENTATION CENTER
1120 19th St., N.W.   Phone: (202) 659-8659
Washington, DC 20036   Gundula Sundgren, Dir.

SCIENCE SERVICE, INC. - LIBRARY
1719 N St., N.W.   Phone: (202) 785-2255
Washington, DC 20036   Jane M. Livermore, Libn.

SCIENCE TRENDS - LIBRARY
National Press Bldg., Suite 233   Phone: (202) 393-0031
Washington, DC 20045   Arthur Kranish, Hd.

SCOTTISH RITE SUPREME COUNCIL - LIBRARY
1733 Sixteenth St. N.W.   Phone: (202) 232-3579
Washington, DC 20009   Inge Baum, Libn.

SEVENTH-DAY ADVENTISTS - GENERAL CONFERENCE - OFFICE OF
    ARCHIVES AND STATISTICS
6840 Eastern Ave. N.W.   Phone: (202) 723-0800
Washington, DC 20012   Dr. F. Donald Yost, Archv.

SHAW, PITTMAN, POTTS & TROWBRIDGE - LIBRARY
1800 M St., N.W.   Phone: (202) 822-1000
Washington, DC 20036   Carolyn P. Ahearn, Libn.

SHEA & GARDNER - LIBRARY
1800 Massachusetts Ave., N.W.   Phone: (202) 828-2069
Washington, DC 20036   Sue Perrine, Libn.

SIBLEY MEMORIAL HOSPITAL - MEDICAL LIBRARY
5255 Loughboro Rd., N.W.   Phone: (202) 363-9600
Washington, DC 20016   Annie B. Footman, Libn.

SILVER INSTITUTE - LIBRARY
1001 Connecticut Ave., N.W., Suite 1138 Phone: (202) 331-1485
Washington, DC 20036   Richard L. Davies, Exec.Dir.

SKIDMORE, OWINGS & MERRILL - LIBRARY
1201 Connecticut Ave., N.W.   Phone: (202) 828-0700
Washington, DC 20036   Kathleen L. Kalt, Libn.

SMITHSONIAN INSTITUTION - FREER GALLERY OF ART - LIBRARY
Twelfth & Jefferson Dr., S.W.   Phone: (202) 357-2091
Washington, DC 20560   Priscilla P. Smith, Libn.

SMITHSONIAN INSTITUTION - HIRSHHORN MUSEUM AND SCULPTURE
    GARDEN - LIBRARY
Independence Ave. & 8th St., S.W.   Phone: (202) 357-3223
Washington, DC 20560   Anna Brooke, Libn.

SMITHSONIAN INSTITUTION LIBRARIES
National Museum of Natural History
10th & Constitution Ave., N.W.   Phone: (202) 357-2240
Washington, DC 20560   Robert Maloy, Dir.

SMITHSONIAN INSTITUTION LIBRARIES - CENTRAL REFERENCE SERVICES
Central Library
10th & Constitution Ave., N.W.   Phone: (202) 357-2139
Washington, DC 20560   Jack Marquardt, Chf.

SMITHSONIAN INSTITUTION LIBRARIES - CONSERVATION ANALYTICAL
    LABORATORY - LIBRARY
Museum of American History, AB-070   Phone: (202) 357-2444
Washington, DC 20560   Karen Preslock, Libn.

SMITHSONIAN INSTITUTION LIBRARIES - MUSEUM OF AFRICAN ART -
    BRANCH LIBRARY
330 A St., N.E.   Phone: (202) 287-3490
Washington, DC 20560   Janet L. Stanley, Br.Libn.

SMITHSONIAN INSTITUTION LIBRARIES - MUSEUM REFERENCE CENTER
Arts & Industries Bldg., Rm. 2235   Phone: (202) 357-3101
Washington, DC 20560   Rhoda Ratner, Libn.

SMITHSONIAN INSTITUTION LIBRARIES - NATIONAL AIR AND SPACE
    MUSEUM - LIBRARY
National Air & Space Museum, Rm. 3000   Phone: (202) 357-3133
Washington, DC 20560   Catherine D. Scott, Libn.

SMITHSONIAN INSTITUTION LIBRARIES - NATIONAL MUSEUM OF
    AMERICAN HISTORY - LIBRARY
Museum of American History   Phone: (202) 357-2414
Washington, DC 20560   Frank A. Pietropaoli, Br.Libn.

SMITHSONIAN INSTITUTION LIBRARIES - NATIONAL MUSEUM OF
    NATURAL HISTORY - ANTHROPOLOGY BRANCH LIBRARY
Natural History Bldg., Rm. 330/331   Phone: (202) 357-1819
Washington, DC 20560   Janette K. Saquet, Libn.

SMITHSONIAN INSTITUTION LIBRARIES - NATIONAL MUSEUM OF
    NATURAL HISTORY - BOTANY BRANCH LIBRARY
Natural History Bldg.
10th & Constitution Ave.   Phone: (202) 357-2715
Washington, DC 20560   Ruth Schallert, Libn.

SMITHSONIAN INSTITUTION LIBRARIES - NATIONAL MUSEUM OF
    NATURAL HISTORY - ENTOMOLOGY BRANCH LIBRARY
Natural History Bldg.   Phone: (202) 357-2354
Washington, DC 20560

SMITHSONIAN INSTITUTION LIBRARIES - NATIONAL MUSEUM OF
    NATURAL HISTORY - LIBRARY
Natural History Bldg.
10th & Constitution Ave.   Phone: (202) 357-1496
Washington, DC 20560   Sylvia Churgin, Libn.

SMITHSONIAN INSTITUTION LIBRARIES - NATIONAL ZOOLOGICAL PARK -
    LIBRARY
                                         Phone: (202) 673-4771
Washington, DC 20008   Mary Clare Gray, Chf.Libn.

SMITHSONIAN INSTITUTION LIBRARIES - SPECIAL COLLECTIONS BRANCH
                                         Phone: (202) 357-1568
Washington, DC 20560   Ellen B. Wells, Chf.

SMITHSONIAN INSTITUTION - NATIONAL ANTHROPOLOGICAL ARCHIVES
Natl. Museum of
Natural History Bldg., Rm. 60-A
10th & Constitution Ave., N.W.   Phone: (202) 357-1986
Washington, DC 20560   Dr. Herman J. Viola, Dir.

SMITHSONIAN INSTITUTION - NATL. MUSEUM OF AMERICAN ART -
    INVENTORY OF AMERICAN PAINTINGS EXECUTED BEFORE 1914
8th And G Sts., N.W.   Phone: (202) 357-2941
Washington, DC 20560   Martha Shipman Andrews, Coord.

SMITHSONIAN INSTITUTION - NATL. MUSEUM OF AMERICAN ART/
    NATIONAL PORTRAIT GALLERY - LIBRARY
8th & F Sts., N.W.   Phone: (202) 357-1886
Washington, DC 20560   Katharine Martinez, Chf.Libn.

SMITHSONIAN INSTITUTION - NATL. MUSEUM OF AMERICAN ART -
    OFFICE OF VISUAL RSRCS. - SLIDE/PHOTOGRAPH ARCHIVE
8th & G Sts., N.W.   Phone: (202) 357-1626
Washington, DC 20560   Eleanor E. Fink, Chf.

SMITHSONIAN SCIENCE INFORMATION EXCHANGE, INC.
1730 M St., N.W., Rm. 300   Phone: (202) 634-3933
Washington, DC 20036   Dr. David F. Hersey, Pres.

SOCIETY OF THE CINCINNATI - ANDERSON HOUSE LIBRARY AND MUSEUM
2118 Massachusetts Ave., N.W.   Phone: (202) 785-2040
Washington, DC 20008   John D. Kilbourne, Dir.

SOCIETY OF FRIENDS - FRIENDS MEETING OF WASHINGTON - LIBRARY
2111 Florida Ave., N.W.   Phone: (202) 483-3310
Washington, DC 20008   Edith H. Leeds, Libn.

STEPTOE AND JOHNSON - LIBRARY
1250 Connecticut Ave., N.W.   Phone: (202) 223-4491
Washington, DC 20036   Stephen G. Margeton, Libn.

STRAYER COLLEGE - WILKES LIBRARY
601 13th St., N.W.   Phone: (202) 783-5180
Washington, DC 20005   H. Barbara Krell, Libn.

SUGAR ASSOCIATION, INC. - LIBRARY
1511 K St., N.W.   Phone: (202) 628-0189
Washington, DC 20005   Sarah Setton, Asst. to the Pres.

SULPHUR INSTITUTE - LIBRARY
1725 K St., N.W.   Phone: (202) 331-9660
Washington, DC 20006   J.S. Platou, Dir. of Info.

TAX FOUNDATION - LIBRARY
1875 Connecticut Ave., N.W.   Phone: (202) 328-4565
Washington, DC 20009   Marion Marshall, Libn.

TEMPLE SINAI - LIBRARY
3100 Military Rd., N.W.   Phone: (202) 363-6394
Washington, DC 20015   Phyllis Holman Weisbard, Libn.

TEXTILE MUSEUM - LIBRARY
2320 S St., N.W.   Phone: (202) 667-0442
Washington, DC 20008   Katherine T. Freshley, Libn.

TOBACCO INSTITUTE - LIBRARY
1875 Eye St., N.W., Suite 800   Phone: (202) 457-4800
Washington, DC 20006   R. David Albinson, Dir., Info.Serv.

TRADE RELATIONS COUNCIL OF THE UNITED STATES - LIBRARY
1001 Connecticut Ave., N.W.
Washington, DC 20036   Eugene L. Stewart, Exec.Sec.

TRANSPORTATION INSTITUTE - LIBRARY
923 15th St., N.W.   Phone: (202) 347-2590
Washington, DC 20005   Chung-Tai Shen, Chf.Libn.

TRINITY COLLEGE - ARCHIVES
          Phone: (202) 269-2220
Washington, DC 20017   Sr. Columba Mullaly, Archv.

TRUXTUN-DECATUR NAVAL MUSEUM - LIBRARY
1610 H St., N.W.   Phone: (202) 783-2573
Washington, DC 20006   Admiral J.L. Holloway, III, USN (Ret) Pres.

UNITED FOOD AND COMMERCIAL WORKERS INTERNATIONAL UNION -
LIBRARY
1775 K St., N.W.   Phone: (202) 223-3111
Washington, DC 20006   Ellen Newton, Libn.

UNITED METHODIST CHURCH - WESLEY THEOLOGICAL SEMINARY -
LIBRARY
4400 Massachusetts Ave., N.W.   Phone: (202) 363-0922
Washington, DC 20016   Roland E. Kircher, Dir.

U.S. ADVISORY COMMISSION ON INTERGOVERNMENTAL RELATIONS -
LIBRARY
1111 20th St., N.W.   Phone: (202) 653-5034
Washington, DC 20575   Patricia A. Koch, Libn.

U.S. AGENCY FOR INTERNATIONAL DEVELOPMENT - DEVELOPMENT
INFORMATION CENTER
320 21st St., N.W., Rm. 1656   Phone: (202) 632-8571
Washington, DC 20523   Joanne M. Paskar, Hd.

U.S. AIR FORCE - AIR FORCE SYSTEMS COMMAND - LIBRARY DIVISION
AFSC/MPSL, Andrews Air Force Base   Phone: (301) 981-2598
Washington, DC 20334   Eleanor A. Driscoll, Dir., Command Libs.

U.S. AIR FORCE - AIR FORCE SYSTEMS COMMAND - TECHNICAL
INFORMATION CENTER
Andrews AFB, MPSLT   Phone: (301) 981-3551
Washington, DC 20334

U.S. AIR FORCE BASE - ANDREWS BASE LIBRARY
FL 4425, Andrews AFB   Phone: (301) 981-6454
Washington, DC 20331   Virginia J. Snyder, Chf.Libn.

U.S. AIR FORCE BASE - BOLLING BASE LIBRARY
Bolling AFB   Phone: (202) 767-4251
Washington, DC 20332   Gloria Guffey, Libn.

U.S. AIR FORCE HOSPITAL - MALCOLM GROW MEDICAL CENTER - LIBRARY
Andrews AFB   Phone: (202) 981-2354
Washington, DC 20331   Eunice M. Lyon, Med.Libn.

U.S. AIR FORCE - OFFICE OF JUDGE ADVOCATE GENERAL - LEGAL
REFERENCE LIBRARY
1900 Half St., S.W., Rm. 5113   Phone: (202) 693-5638
Washington, DC 20324   William J. Zschunke, Libn.

U.S. ARMED FORCES INSTITUTE OF PATHOLOGY - ASH LIBRARY
Walter Reed Army Medical Ctr.   Phone: (202) 576-2983
Washington, DC 20012   Sally Allinson, Libn.

U.S. ARMS CONTROL AND DISARMAMENT AGENCY - LIBRARY
Dept. Of State Bldg., Rm. 5672
21st & Virginia Ave., N.W.   Phone: (703) 235-9550
Washington, DC 20451   Diane A. Ferguson, Libn.

U.S. ARMY - ARMED FORCES PEST MANAGEMENT BOARD - DEFENSE PEST
MANAGEMENT INFORMATION ANALYSIS CENTER
Walter Reed Army Medical Center
Forest Glen Section   Phone: (202) 427-5365
Washington, DC 20012   LTC Ralph R. Carestia, MSC, Hd.

U.S. ARMY - ARMY LIBRARY
The Pentagon, Rm. 1 A 518   Phone: (202) 695-5346
Washington, DC 20310   Mary L. Shaffer, Dir.

U.S. ARMY HOSPITALS - WALTER REED ARMY MEDICAL CENTER - MEDICAL
LIBRARY
Bldg. 2, Rm. 2G
Washington, DC 20012   Newton W. Rucker, Chf.Libn.

U.S. ARMY - OFFICE OF THE CHIEF OF ENGINEERS - LIBRARY
20 Massachusetts Ave., N.W.   Phone: (202) 272-0455
Washington, DC 20001   Sarah A. Mikel, Chf., Tech.Info.Div.

U.S. ARMY/U.S. AIR FORCE - OFFICES OF THE SURGEONS GENERAL -
JOINT MEDICAL LIBRARY
The Pentagon, Rm. 1B - 473   Phone: (202) 695-5752
Washington, DC 20310   Donna K. Griffitts, Adm.Libn.

U.S. ARMY - WALTER REED ARMY INSTITUTE OF RESEARCH - LIBRARY
Walter Reed Army Medical Center   Phone: (202) 576-3314
Washington, DC 20012   V. Lynn Gera, Lib.Adm.

UNITED STATES BEET SUGAR ASSOCIATION - LIBRARY
1156 Fifteenth St., N.W.
Washington, DC 20005   David C. Carter, Pres.

U.S. BUREAU OF MINES - ADMINISTRATIVE SERVICES - LIBRARY
2401 E St., N.W.   Phone: (202) 634-1116
Washington, DC 20241   Judy C. Jordan, Lib.Techn.

U.S. CIVIL AERONAUTICS BOARD - LIBRARY
Universal Bldg., Rm. 912
Connecticut & Florida Aves., N.W.   Phone: (202) 673-5101
Washington, DC 20428   Mary Louise Ransom, Libn.

U.S. COAST GUARD - OCEANOGRAPHIC UNIT - LIBRARY
Bldg. 159-E, Navy Yard Annex   Phone: (202) 426-4630
Washington, DC 20590   Neda Marie Taylor, Libn.

U.S. COMMISSION ON CIVIL RIGHTS - NATL. CLEARINGHOUSE LIBRARY
1121 Vermont Ave., N.W.   Phone: (202) 254-6636
Washington, DC 20425   Marija Matich Hughes, Chf.Libn.

U.S. COMPTROLLER OF THE CURRENCY - LIBRARY
490 L'Enfant Plaza, S.W., 5th Fl.   Phone: (202) 447-1843
Washington, DC 20219   Alice Bagwill, Libn.

U. S. CONFERENCE OF MAYORS - HANDGUN CONTROL CLEARINGHOUSE
1620 Eye St., N.W., Rm. 266   Phone: (202) 293-4911
Washington, DC 20006   Anne D. Garner, Dir.

U.S. COURT OF APPEALS, DISTRICT OF COLUMBIA CIRCUIT - LIBRARY
5518 U.S. Court House
3rd & Constitution Ave., N.W.   Phone: (202) 426-7187
Washington, DC 20001   Nancy Lazar, Libn.

U.S. COURT OF CLAIMS/U.S. COURT OF CUSTOMS & PATENT APPEALS -
    COURTS' LIBRARY
717 Madison Pl., N.W.   Phone: (202) 633-7291
Washington, DC 20005   LouElla Ingram, Libn.

U.S. COURT OF MILITARY APPEALS - LIBRARY †
450 E St., N.W.   Phone: (202) 693-7100
Washington, DC 20442   Mary S. Kuck, Libn.

U.S. CUSTOMS SERVICE - LIBRARY AND INFORMATION CENTER
1301 Constitution Ave., N.W., Rm. 3340   Phone: (202) 566-5642
Washington, DC 20229   Patricia M. Dobrosky, Dir.

U.S. DEFENSE AUDIOVISUAL AGENCY - STILL PHOTO DEPOSITORY - ARMY
    COLLECTION
                             Phone: (202) 697-5601
Washington, DC 20301   Jane C. Dickens, Act.Chf.

U.S. DEFENSE AUDIOVISUAL AGENCY - STILL PICTURE LIBRARY
Bldg. 168, NDW   Phone: (202) 433-2168
Washington, DC 20374   Roy K. Heitman, Hd.Ref.Br.

U.S. DEFENSE COMMUNICATIONS AGENCY - NATL. MILITARY COMMAND
    SYSTEM SUPPORT CENTER - TECHNICAL LIBRARY *
BF 679, The Pentagon   Phone: (202) 697-6469
Washington, DC 20301   Kathryn T. Zuzick, Libn.

U.S. DEFENSE COMMUNICATIONS AGENCY - TECHNICAL LIBRARY AND
    INFORMATION CENTER *
Headquarters, DCA, Code 222   Phone: (202) 692-2468
Washington, DC 20305   Janet Brooks, Chf.Libn.

U.S. DEFENSE INTELLIGENCE AGENCY - LIBRARY RTS-ZA
                             Phone: (202) 692-5311
Washington, DC 20301   H. Holzbauer, Chief Libn.

U.S. DEFENSE MAPPING AGENCY - HYDROGRAPHIC/TOPOGRAPHIC
    CENTER- SUPPORT DIVISION - SCIENTIFIC DATA DEPARTMENT
6500 Brookes Lane, N.W.   Phone: (301) 227-2080
Washington, DC 20315   Nicholas Argyropoulas, Act.Chf.Sup.Div.

U.S. DEFENSE NUCLEAR AGENCY - TECHNICAL LIBRARY DIVISION
                             Phone: (202) 325-7780
Washington, DC 20305   Betty L. Fox, Chf., Tech.Lib.Div.

U.S. DEPT. OF AGRICULTURE - ECONOMICS AND STATISTICS SERVICE -
    ESS REFERENCE CENTER
500 12th St., S.W., Rm. 147   Phone: (202) 447-4382
Washington, DC 20250   Cynthia Kenyon, Dir.

U.S.D.A. - NATIONAL AGRICULTURAL LIBRARY - LAW LIBRARY
Independence Ave. at 12th St., S.W.
Rm. 1406, S Bldg.   Phone: (202) 447-7751
Washington, DC 20250   Spurgeon D. Terry, Law Libn.

U.S. DEPT. OF AGRICULTURE - PHOTOGRAPHY DIVISION - PHOTOGRAPH
    LIBRARY
14th & Independence Ave., S.W.   Phone: (202) 447-6633
Washington, DC 20250

U.S. DEPT. OF COMMERCE - DEPARTMENTAL LIBRARY
14th & Constitution Ave., N.W.   Phone: (202) 377-3611
Washington, DC 20230   Stanley J. Bougas, Dir.

U.S. DEPT. OF COMMERCE - NATL. TECHNICAL INFORMATION SERVICE -
    PRODUCTIVITY INFORMATION CENTER
425 13th St., N.W., Suite 620   Phone: (202) 724-3369
Washington, DC 20004   Carol Ann Meares, Prog.Mgr.

U.S. DEPT. OF ENERGY - HEADQUARTERS LAW LIBRARY
1000 Independence Ave., S.W., Rm. 6A-166   Phone: (202) 252-4848
Washington, DC 20585   Oscar E. Strothers, Chf. Law Libn.

U.S. DEPT. OF ENERGY - LAW LIBRARY
Forrestal Bldg., Rm. 6A-156
1000 Independence Ave., S.W.   Phone: (202) 252-4848
Washington, DC 20585

U.S. DEPT. OF ENERGY - LIBRARY
Rm. G-042, Germantown   Phone: (301) 353-4301
Washington, DC 20545   C. Neil Sherman, Dir.

U.S. DEPT. OF HEALTH AND HUMAN SERVICES - DEPARTMENT LIBRARY
330 Independence Ave., S.W., Rm 1436 N.   Phone: (202) 245-6339
Washington, DC 20201   Charles F. Gately, Dir.

U.S. DEPT. OF HOUSING AND URBAN DEVELOPMENT - LIBRARY
451 Seventh St., S.W.   Phone: (202) 755-6376
Washington, DC 20410   Elsa S. Freeman, Dir.

U.S. DEPT. OF HOUSING & URBAN DEVELOPMENT - PHOTOGRAPHY LIBRARY
451 7th St., S.W., Rm. B-120   Phone: (202) 755-7305
Washington, DC 20410   David A. Murdock, Visual Info.Spec.

U.S. DEPT. OF THE INTERIOR - CENTER FOR INFORMATION AND LIBRARY
    SERVICES - LAW BRANCH
18th & C Sts., N.W.   Phone: (202) 343-4571
Washington, DC 20240   Carl Kessler, Chf.

U.S. DEPT. OF THE INTERIOR - INDIAN ARTS AND CRAFTS BOARD
Rm. 4004, 18th & C Sts., N.W.   Phone: (202) 343-2773
Washington, DC 20240   Robert G. Hart, Gen.Mgr.

U.S. DEPT. OF THE INTERIOR - NATURAL RESOURCES LIBRARY
18th & C Sts., N.W.   Phone: (202) 343-5821
Washington, DC 20240   Phillip M. Haymond, Chf., Info./Lib.Serv.Dir.

U.S. DEPT. OF JUSTICE - ANTITRUST DIVISION LIBRARY
10th & Pennsylvania Ave., N.W., Rm. 3310   Phone: (202) 633-2431
Washington, DC 20530   Susan N. Hunchar, Libn.

U.S. DEPT. OF JUSTICE - CIVIL DIVISION LIBRARY
10th & Pennsylvania Ave., N.W., Rm. 3344   Phone: (202) 633-3523
Washington, DC 20530   James S. Heller, Libn.

U.S. DEPT. OF JUSTICE - CIVIL RIGHTS DIVISION - LIBRARY
10th & Pennsylvania Ave., N.W., Rm. 7618   Phone: (202) 633-4098
Washington, DC 20530

U.S. DEPT. OF JUSTICE - CRIMINAL DIVISION - LIBRARY
10th & Pennsylvania Ave., N.W.   Phone: (202) 633-2383
Washington, DC 20530   Winifred M. Hart, Libn.

U.S. DEPT. OF JUSTICE - FEDERAL PRISON SYSTEM - LIBRARY
320 First St., N.W.   Phone: (202) 724-3029
Washington, DC 20534   Lloyd W. Hooker, Libn.

U.S. DEPT. OF JUSTICE - LAND AND NATURAL RESOURCES DIVISION
    LIBRARY
10th & Pennsylvania Ave., N.W., Rm. 2333   Phone: (202) 633-2768
Washington, DC 20530   Adelaide Loretta Brown, Libn.

U.S. DEPT. OF JUSTICE - MAIN LIBRARY
10th & Pennsylvania Ave., N.W., Rm. 5400   Phone: (202) 633-3775
Washington, DC 20530   Terry Appenzellar, Lib.Dir.

U.S. DEPT. OF JUSTICE - NATIONAL INSTITUTE OF JUSTICE - LIBRARY
633 Indiana Ave., N.W.   Phone: (301) 492-9149
Washington, DC 20531   Kathleen Reyering, Tech.Info.Spec.

U.S. DEPT. OF JUSTICE - TAX DIVISION LIBRARY
10th & Pennsylvania Ave., N.W., Rm. 4335   Phone: (202) 633-2819
Washington, DC 20530   Rachel R. Hecht, Libn.

U.S. DEPT. OF LABOR - LIBRARY
200 Constitution Ave., N.W.   Phone: (202) 523-6988
Washington, DC 20210   Andre C. Whisenton, Libn.

U.S. DEPT. OF LABOR - LIBRARY - LAW LIBRARY DIVISION
200 Constitution Ave., N.W., Rm. N-2439
Washington, DC 20210   Donald L. Martin, Law Libn.

U.S. DEPT. OF LABOR - OSHA - TECHNICAL DATA CENTER
200 Constitution Ave., N.W.
Rm. N-2439 Rear   Phone: (202) 523-9700
Washington, DC 20210   Thomas A. Towers, Dir.

U.S. DEPT. OF STATE - LIBRARY
                    Phone: (202) 632-0372
Washington, DC 20520   Conrad P. Eaton, Libn.

U.S. DEPT. OF STATE - OFFICE OF THE LEGAL ADVISER - LAW LIBRARY
Rm. 6422, Dept. of State   Phone: (202) 632-2628
Washington, DC 20520   M.L. Nash, Attorney, Libn.

U.S. DEPT. OF TRANSPORTATION - LIBRARY SERVICES DIVISION
400 7th St., S.W.   Phone: (202) 426-1792
Washington, DC 20590   Lucile E. Beaver, Lib.Dir.

U.S. DEPT. OF TRANSPORTATION - URBAN MASS TRANSPORTATION ADM. - TRANSPORTATION RESEARCH INFO. CENTER (TRIC)
400 7th St., S.W.   Phone: (202) 426-9157
Washington, DC 20590   Donald M. Chapman, Chf., Info.Serv.Div.

U.S. DEPT. OF THE TREASURY - INFORMATION SERVICES DIVISION - TREASURY DEPT. LIBRARY
Main Treasury Bldg., Rm. 5030   Phone: (202) 566-2777
Washington, DC 20220   Elisabeth S. Knauff, Mgr., Info.Serv.Div.

U.S. DRUG ENFORCEMENT ADMINISTRATION - LIBRARY
1405 Eye St., N.W.   Phone: (202) 633-1369
Washington, DC 20537   Morton S. Goren, Libn.

U.S. EQUAL EMPLOYMENT OPPORTUNITY COMMISSION - LIBRARY
2401 E St., N.W.   Phone: (202) 634-6990
Washington, DC 20506   Susan D. Taylor, Act.Commn.

U.S. EXECUTIVE OFFICE OF THE PRESIDENT - INFORMATION MANAGEMENT AND SERVICES DIVISION
G007 New Executive Office Bldg.
726 Jackson Place, N.W.   Phone: (202) 395-3654
Washington, DC 20503   Carolyn Brown, Dir.

U.S. FEDERAL COMMUNICATIONS COMMISSION - LIBRARY
1919 M St., N.W.   Phone: (202) 632-7100
Washington, DC 20554   Sheryl A. Segal, Lib.Dir.

U.S. FEDERAL DEPOSIT INSURANCE CORPORATION - LIBRARY
550 Seventeenth St., N.W.   Phone: (202) 389-4314
Washington, DC 20429   Carole Cleland, Chf.Libn.

U.S. FEDERAL HOME LOAN BANK BOARD - LAW LIBRARY
1700 G St., N.W.   Phone: (202) 377-6470
Washington, DC 20552   Joyce A. Potter, Libn.

U.S. FEDERAL HOME LOAN BANK BOARD - RESEARCH LIBRARY
1700 G St., N.W.   Phone: (202) 377-6296
Washington, DC 20552   Janet B. Smith, Libn.

U.S. FEDERAL JUDICIAL CENTER - INFORMATION SERVICE
1520 H St., N.W.   Phone: (202) 633-6365
Washington, DC 20005   Marsha Carey, Act.Info.Spec.

U.S. FEDERAL MARITIME COMMISSION - LIBRARY †
1100 L St., N.W.   Phone: (202) 523-5762
Washington, DC 20573   Mary Ellen Daffron, Libn.

U.S. FEDERAL TRADE COMMISSION - LIBRARY
6th St. & Pennsylvania Ave., N.W.   Phone: (202) 523-3871
Washington, DC 20580   Susanne B. Hendsey, Lib.Dir.

U.S. FEED GRAINS COUNCIL - COMMUNICATIONS DEPARTMENT - LIBRARY
1575 Eye St., N.W., Suite 1000   Phone: (202) 789-0789
Washington, DC 20005   Sara K. Schildt, Commun.Mgr.

U.S. FISH & WILDLIFE SERVICE - OFFICE OF AUDIO-VISUAL - LIBRARY
Dept. of the Interior   Phone: (202) 343-8770
Washington, DC 20240   Beatrice Boone, Visual Info.Spec.

U.S. FOOD & DRUG ADMINISTRATION - BUREAU OF FOODS LIBRARY
200 C St., S.W.   Phone: (202) 245-1235
Washington, DC 20204   Grayson Tabler, Libn.

U.S. FOREST SERVICE - PERMANENT PHOTOGRAPHIC COLLECTION
Box 2417, Rm. 51-RPE   Phone: (703) 235-8060
Washington, DC 20013   William G. Hauser, Visual Info.Off.

U.S. GENERAL ACCOUNTING OFFICE - TECHNICAL INFORMATION SOURCES AND SERVICES BRANCH
441 G St., N.W.   Phone: (202) 275-5180
Washington, DC 20548   Marju Parming, Mgr.

U.S. GENERAL SERVICES ADMINISTRATION - CONSUMER INFORMATION CENTER
18th & F St., N.W.   Phone: (202) 566-1794
Washington, DC 20405   David F. Peterson, Exec.Dir.

U.S. GENERAL SERVICES ADMINISTRATION - GSA LIBRARY
General Services Bldg., Rm. 1033
18th & F Sts., N.W.   Phone: (202) 566-0212
Washington, DC 20405   Gail L. Kohlhorst, Chf.

U.S. HOUSE OF REPRESENTATIVES - LIBRARY
B-18 Cannon Bldg.   Phone: (202) 225-0462
Washington, DC 20515   E. Raymond Lewis, Libn.

U.S. INTERNAL REVENUE SERVICE - LAW LIBRARY
Internal Revenue Service Bldg., Rm. 4324
1111 Constitution Ave., N.W.   Phone: (202) 566-6342
Washington, DC 20224   Anne B. Scheer, Libn.

U.S. INTERNATIONAL TRADE COMMISSION - LIBRARY
701 E St., N.W.   Phone: (202) 523-0013
Washington, DC 20436   Dorothy J. Berkowitz, Chf., Lib.Div.

U.S. INTERSTATE COMMERCE COMMISSION - LIBRARY
Twelfth & Constitution Ave., N.W.   Phone: (202) 275-7328
Washington, DC 20423   Mrs. Doris E. Watts, Libn.

U.S. LEAGUE OF SAVINGS ASSOCIATIONS - LIBRARY
1709 New York Ave., N.W.   Phone: (202) 637-8920
Washington, DC 20006   Katherine Harahan, Libn.

U.S. MARINE CORPS - HISTORICAL CENTER LIBRARY
Washington Navy Yard, Bldg. 58   Phone: (202) 433-4253
Washington, DC 20374   Lt.Col. Frank Martino, Hd.Sup.Br.

U.S. MARINE CORPS - MARINE BAND LIBRARY
Marine Barracks
Eighth & Eye Sts., S.E.   Phone: (202) 433-4298
Washington, DC 20390   Frank P. Byrne, Jr., Chf.Libn.

U.S. NASA - HEADQUARTERS LIBRARY
600 Independence Ave., S.W.   Phone: (202) 755-2210
Washington, DC 20546   Mary Elizabeth Anderson, Libn.

U.S. NATL. ARBORETUM - LIBRARY
24th & R Sts., N.E.   Phone: (202) 472-9264
Washington, DC 20002

U.S. NATL. ARCHIVES & RECORDS SERVICE - NATL. ARCHIVES
Eighth & Constitution Ave., N.W.   Phone: (202) 523-3218
Washington, DC 20408   Dr. Robert M. Warner, U.S.Archv.

U.S. NATL. ARCHIVES & RECORDS SERVICE - NATL. ARCHIVES - CENTER FOR CARTOGRAPHIC & ARCHITECTURAL ARCHIVES
8th & Pennsylvania Ave., N.W.   Phone: (202) 523-3062
Washington, DC 20408   William H. Cunliffe, Chf.

U.S. NATL. ARCHIVES & RECORDS SERVICE - NATL. ARCHIVES LIBRARY
Eighth & Pennsylvania Ave., N.W.   Phone: (202) 523-3049
Washington, DC 20408   Patricia A. Andrews, Act.Libn.

GEOGRAPHIC

U.S. NATL. ARCHIVES & RECORDS SERVICE - NATL. AUDIOVISUAL CENTER - INFORMATION SERVICES SECTION
Phone: (301) 763-1896
Washington, DC 20409   John McLean, Dir.

U.S. NATL. ARCHIVES & RECORDS SERVICE - WASHINGTON NATL. RECORDS CENTER
Phone: (301) 763-7000
Washington, DC 20409   Jack Saunders

U.S. NATL. BUREAU OF STANDARDS - ALLOY DATA CENTER
Bldg. 223, Rm. B-150   Phone: (301) 921-2917
Washington, DC 20234   Dr. R.M. Mehrabian, Dir.

U.S. NATL. BUREAU OF STANDARDS - ATOMIC ENERGY LEVELS DATA CENTER
Physics Bldg., Rm. A155   Phone: (301) 921-2011
Washington, DC 20234   Dr. William C. Martin, Physicist

U.S. NATL. BUREAU OF STANDARDS - CHEMICAL THERMODYNAMICS DATA CENTER
Chemistry Bldg., Rm. A158
Washington, DC 20234   David Garvin, Mgr.

U.S. NATL. BUREAU OF STANDARDS - DATA CENTER ON ATOMIC LINE SHAPES AND SHIFTS
Bldg. 221, Rm. A267   Phone: (301) 921-2071
Washington, DC 20234   Dr. W.L. Wiese, Dir.

U.S. NATL. BUREAU OF STANDARDS - DATA CENTER ON ATOMIC TRANSITION PROBABILITIES
A267 Physics Bldg.   Phone: (301) 921-2071
Washington, DC 20234   Dr. W.L. Wiese, Hd.

U. S. NATL. BUREAU OF STANDARDS - FIRE RESEARCH INFORMATION SERVICES
Bldg. 224, Rm. A252
Natl. Bureau Of Standards   Phone: (301) 921-3246
Washington, DC 20234   Nora H. Jason, Project Ldr.

U.S. NATL. BUREAU OF STANDARDS - FUNDAMENTAL CONSTANTS DATA CENTER
Bldg. 220, Rm. B258   Phone: (301) 921-2701
Washington, DC 20234   Dr. Barry N. Taylor, Chf.

U.S. NATL. BUREAU OF STANDARDS - ION KINETICS AND ENERGETICS DATA CENTER
A139 - Chemistry   Phone: (301) 921-2783
Washington, DC 20234   Dr. Sharon G. Lias, Res.Chem.

U.S. NATL. BUREAU OF STANDARDS - LIBRARY
EOI Administration Bldg.   Phone: (301) 921-3451
Washington, DC 20234   Patricia W. Berger, Chf., Lib.Div.

U.S. NATL. BUREAU OF STANDARDS - OFFICE OF STANDARD REFERENCE DATA - REFERENCE CENTER
A-320 Physics Bldg.   Phone: (301) 921-2228
Washington, DC 20234   Cynthia A. Goldman, Libn.

U.S. NATL. BUREAU OF STANDARDS - PHASE DIAGRAMS FOR CERAMISTS
Phone: (301) 921-2842
Washington, DC 20234   Lawrence P. Cook, Dir.

U.S. NATL. BUREAU OF STANDARDS - PHOTON AND CHARGED PARTICLE DATA CENTER
Radiation Physics Bldg.
Rm. C-313, NBS   Phone: (301) 921-2685
Washington, DC 20234   Martin Berger, Act.Dir.

U.S. NATL. CAPITAL PLANNING COMMISSION - LIBRARY
1325 G St., N.W., Rm. 1018   Phone: (202) 724-0203
Washington, DC 20576   Mrs. Laure H. Brown, Libn.

U.S. NATL. DEFENSE UNIVERSITY - LIBRARY
Fort Lesley J. McNair
4th & P Sts., S.W.   Phone: (202) 693-8437
Washington, DC 20319   J. Thomas Russell, Lib.Dir.

U.S. NATL. HIGHWAY TRAFFIC SAFETY ADMINISTRATION - TECHNICAL REFERENCE BRANCH
400 7th St., S.W., Rm. 5108   Phone: (202) 426-2768
Washington, DC 20590   A.R. Lawrence, Chf., Adm.Oper.Div.

U.S. NATL. LABOR RELATIONS BOARD - LAW LIBRARY
1717 Pennsylvania Ave., N.W., Rm. 900   Phone: (202) 254-9055
Washington, DC 20570   Barbara W. Hazelett, Adm.Libn.

U.S. NATL. OCEANIC & ATMOSPHERIC ADMINISTRATION - ENVIRONMENTAL DATA & INFO. SERV. - NATL. OCEANOGRAPHIC DATA CTR.
2001 Wisconsin Ave., Page Bldg. One   Phone: (202) 634-7500
Washington, DC 20235   Edward Ridley, Dir.

U.S. NATL. PARK SERVICE - FREDERICK DOUGLASS MEMORIAL HOME - LIBRARY
1411 W St., S.E.   Phone: (202) 678-1825
Washington, DC 20020   Essie Lawrence, Site Mgr.

U.S. NATL. PARK SERVICE - NATL. CAPITAL REGION - ROCK CREEK NATURE CENTER LIBRARY
5200 Glover Rd., N.W.   Phone: (202) 426-6829
Washington, DC 20015

U.S. NAVY - DEPARTMENT LIBRARY
Bldg. 220, Rm. 220
Washington Navy Yard   Phone: (202) 433-2386
Washington, DC 20374   Stanley Kalkus, Dir.

U.S. NAVY - NAVAL AIR SYSTEMS COMMAND - TECHNICAL LIBRARY
Phone: (202) 692-9006
Washington, DC 20361   Pat Stone, Hd.Libn.

U.S. NAVY - NAVAL HISTORICAL CENTER - NAVAL HISTORY DIVISION - OPERATIONAL ARCHIVES
Bldg. 210, Washington Navy Yard   Phone: (202) 433-3170
Washington, DC 20374   Dr. Dean C. Allard, Dir.

U.S. NAVY - NAVAL HISTORICAL CENTER - PHOTOGRAPHIC SECTION
CuP
Washington Navy Yard   Phone: (202) 433-2765
Washington, DC 20374

U.S. NAVY - NAVAL INTELLIGENCE SUPPORT CENTER - INFORMATION SERVICES DIVISION
4301 Suitland Rd.
Code 63   Phone: (202) 763-1606
Washington, DC 20390   Alice T. Cranor, Hd., Info.Serv.Div.

U.S. NAVY - NAVAL MILITARY PERSONNEL COMMAND - TECHNICAL LIBRARY
Arlington Annex, Rm. 1403   Phone: (202) 694-2073
Washington, DC 20370   Joyce A. Lane, Libn.

U.S. NAVY - NAVAL OBSERVATORY - MATTHEW FONTAINE MAURY MEMORIAL LIBRARY
34th and Massachusetts Ave., N.W.   Phone: (202) 254-4525
Washington, DC 20390   Brenda G. Corbin, Libn.

U.S. NAVY - NAVAL RESEARCH LABORATORY - RUTH H. HOOKER TECHNICAL LIBRARY *
Phone: (202) 767-2357
Washington, DC 20375   Peter H. Imhof, Libn.

U.S. NAVY - NAVAL RESEARCH LABORATORY - SHOCK AND VIBRATION INFORMATION CENTER
Code 5804   Phone: (202) 767-2220
Washington, DC 20375   Henry C. Pusey, Hd.

U.S. NAVY - NAVAL SEA SYSTEMS COMMAND - LIBRARY DOCUMENTATION BRANCH (SEA 9961)
Rm. 1S28, National Center, Bldg. 3   Phone: (202) 692-3349
Washington, DC 20362   Alan M. Lewis, Hd., Lib.Doc.Br.

U.S. NAVY - NAVAL SUPPLY SYSTEMS COMMAND - LIBRARY
Rm. 607, Bldg. 3, Crystal Mall   Phone: (202) 695-4704
Washington, DC 20376   James Crouch, Libn.

U.S. NAVY - OFFICE OF THE GENERAL COUNSEL - LAW LIBRARY
Crystal Plaza 5, Rm. 450   Phone: (202) 692-7378
Washington, DC 20360   Mary E. Williams, Libn.

U.S. NAVY - REGIONAL DATA AUTOMATION CENTER - TECHNICAL LIBRARY
Bldg. 143, Washington Navy Yard   Phone: (202) 433-5700
Washington, DC 20374   William H. Hagen, Libn.

U.S. NAVY - STRATEGIC SYSTEMS PROJECT OFFICE - TECHNICAL LIBRARY
                                            Phone: (202) 697-2852
Washington, DC 20376   June R. Gable, Tech.Lib.Br.Hd.

UNITED STATES NEWS PUBLISHING, INC. - LIBRARY
2300 N St., N.W.   Phone: (202) 861-2350
Washington, DC 20037   Luther A. Dawson, Lib.Dir.

U.S. OFFICE OF PERSONNEL MANAGEMENT - LIBRARY
1900 E St., N.W.   Phone: (202) 632-4432
Washington, DC 20415   Violet D. Swisher, Libn.

U. S. OFFICE OF TECHNOLOGY ASSESSMENT - INFORMATION CENTER
Congress of the United States   Phone: (202) 224-6994
Washington, DC 20510   Martha M. Dexter, Mgr., Info.Serv.

U.S. POSTAL SERVICE - LIBRARY
475 L'Enfant Plaza, S.W.   Phone: (202) 245-4021
Washington, DC 20260   Jane F. Kennedy, Gen.Mgr.

UNITED STATES RAILWAY ASSOCIATION - USRA DOCUMENT CENTER *
955 L'enfant Plaza, S.W.   Phone: (202) 426-9067
Washington, DC 20595   Elaine Kuo, Chf., Lib.Serv.

U.S. SECURITIES AND EXCHANGE COMMISSION - LIBRARY
500 N. Capitol St., N.W.   Phone: (202) 272-2618
Washington, DC 20549   Charlene C. Derge, Libn.

U.S. SENATE - LIBRARY
Capitol Bldg., Suite S-332   Phone: (202) 224-7106
Washington, DC 20510   Roger K. Haley, Libn.

U.S. SMALL BUSINESS ADMINISTRATION - REFERENCE LIBRARY
1441 L St., N.W.   Phone: (202) 653-6914
Washington, DC 20416   Margaret Hickey, Libn.

U.S. SOCIAL SECURITY ADMINISTRATION - BRANCH LIBRARY
Universal N. Bldg., Rm. 320-0
1875 Connecticut Ave. N.W.   Phone: (202) 673-5624
Washington, DC 20009   Octavio Alvarez, Libn.

U.S. SOIL CONSERVATION SERVICE - NATIONAL PHOTOGRAPHIC LIBRARY
Box 2890   Phone: (202) 447-7547
Washington, DC 20013   E. Joseph Larson, Pub.Info.Off.

UNITED STATES STUDENT ASSOCIATION - INFORMATION SERVICES
1220 G St., S.E.   Phone: (202) 667-6000
Washington, DC 20003   F.X. Viggiano, Exec.Dir.

U.S. SUPREME COURT - LIBRARY
One First St., N.E.   Phone: (202) 252-3000
Washington, DC 20543   Roger F. Jacobs, Libn.

U.S. TAX COURT - LIBRARY
400 Second St., N.W.   Phone: (202) 376-2707
Washington, DC 20217   Jeanne R. Bonynge, Libn.

U.S. TRAVEL DATA CENTER - LIBRARY
1899 L St., N.W.   Phone: (202) 293-1040
Washington, DC 20036   Dr. Douglas Frechtling, Dir.

U.S. VETERANS ADMINISTRATION (DC-Washington) - GENERAL COUNSEL'S
   LAW LIBRARY
810 Vermont Ave., N.W., Rm. 1039   Phone: (202) 389-2159
Washington, DC 20420   Nina Kahn, Law Libn.

U.S. VETERANS ADMINISTRATION (DC-Washington) - HEADQUARTERS
   CENTRAL OFFICE LIBRARY
Veterans Administration
810 Vermont Ave., N.W.   Phone: (202) 389-2430
Washington, DC 20420   Karen Renninger, Chf., Lib.Div.

U.S. VETERANS ADMINISTRATION (DC-Washington) - HEADQUARTERS
   LIBRARY DIVISION
Veterans Administration Bldg.
810 Vermont Ave., N.W.   Phone: (202) 389-2781
Washington, DC 20420   Karen Renninger, Chf., Lib.Div.

U.S. VETERANS ADMINISTRATION (DC-Washington) - MEDICAL CENTER
   LIBRARY †
50 Irving St., N.W.   Phone: (202) 745-8262
Washington, DC 20422   Mary Netzow, Chf.Libn.

UNIVERSAL SERIALS & BOOK EXCHANGE, INC. - DUPLICATE EXCHANGE
   CLEARINGHOUSE & INFORMATION CENTER
3335 V St., N.E.   Phone: (202) 529-2555
Washington, DC 20018   Alice D. Ball, Exec.Dir.

URBAN INSTITUTE - LIBRARY
2100 M St., N.W.   Phone: (202) 223-1950
Washington, DC 20037   Carol J. Pyke, Dir. of Lib.

URBAN LAND INSTITUTE - LIBRARY
1090 Vermont Ave., N.W., Suite 300   Phone: (202) 289-8500
Washington, DC 20005   Lois Steinberg, Libn.

VEGETARIAN INFORMATION SERVICE, INC. - INFORMATION CENTER
Box 5888   Phone: (301) 530-1737
Washington, DC 20014   Dr. Alex Hershaft, Libn.

WAPORA, INC. - LIBRARY
6900 Wisconsin Ave., N.W.   Phone: (202) 652-9520
Washington, DC 20015   Rhoda Granat, Libn.

WASHINGTON CATHEDRAL FOUNDATION - CATHEDRAL RARE BOOK
   LIBRARY
Mount St. Alban, N.W.
Washington, DC 20016

WASHINGTON HOSPITAL CENTER - MEDICAL LIBRARY
110 Irving St., N.W., Rm. 2A-21   Phone: (202) 541-6221
Washington, DC 20010   Marilyn Cook, Dir.

WASHINGTON METROPOLITAN AREA TRANSIT AUTHORITY - OFFICE OF
   PUBLIC AFFAIRS - LIBRARY
600 Fifth St., N.W.   Phone: (202) 637-1052
Washington, DC 20001   Cody Pfanstiehl, Dir.Pub.Aff.

WASHINGTON POST - LIBRARY †
1150 15th St., N.W.   Phone: (202) 223-7343
Washington, DC 20071   William Hifner, Libn.

WASHINGTON PSYCHOANALYTIC SOCIETY - ERNEST E. HADLEY
   MEMORIAL LIBRARY
4925 MacArthur Blvd., N.W.   Phone: (202) 338-5453
Washington, DC 20007   Mary W. Allen, Libn.

WATER POLLUTION CONTROL FEDERATION - LIBRARY
2626 Pennsylvania Ave.   Phone: (202) 337-2500
Washington, DC 20037   Rhoda Miller, Tech.Info. Aide

WATER RESOURCES CONGRESS - LIBRARY
955 L'Enfant Plaza North, S.W.
Suite 1101
Washington, DC 20024

WHALE PROTECTION FUND - ENVIRONMENTAL EDUCATION RESOURCE
   LIBRARY
1925 K St., N.W.   Phone: (202) 466-4996
Washington, DC 20006   Twig C. George, Educ.Coord.

WILDLIFE MANAGEMENT INSTITUTE - LIBRARY
709 Wire Bldg.
1000 Vermont Ave., N.W.   Phone: (202) 347-1774
Washington, DC 20005   Richard E. McCabe, Pub.Dir.

WILKINSON, CRAGUN AND BARKER - LIBRARY
1735 New York Ave., N.W.   Phone: (202) 783-4800
Washington, DC 20006   Kamla J. King, Libn.

GEOGRAPHIC

GEOGRAPHIC

WILMER, CUTLER & PICKERING - LAW LIBRARY
1666 K St., N.W.   Phone: (202) 872-6182
Washington, DC 20006   Elaine Mitchell, Dir. of Info.

WILSON (Woodrow) INTERNATIONAL CENTER FOR SCHOLARS - LIBRARY
Smithsonian Institution Bldg.   Phone: (202) 381-5850
Washington, DC 20560   Zdenek David, Libn.

WOODSTOCK THEOLOGICAL CENTER - LIBRARY
Georgetown University   Phone: (202) 625-3120
Washington, DC 20057   Henry J. Bertels, S.J., Libn.

WORLD BANK LAW LIBRARY
1818 H St., N.W. (N-718)   Phone: (202) 676-1288
Washington, DC 20433   Linda L. Thompson, Law Libn.

WORLD DATA CENTER A - OCEANOGRAPHY
Natl. Oceanic and Atmospheric Adm.   Phone: (202) 634-7249
Washington, DC 20235   James Churgin, Dir.

WORLD HUNGER EDUCATION SERVICE - LIBRARY
2000 P St., N.W., Suite 205   Phone: (202) 223-2995
Washington, DC 20036   Dr. Patricia L. Kutzner, Exec.Dir.

WORLD PEACE THROUGH LAW CENTER - INFORMATION CENTER
1000 Connecticut Ave., N.W.
Suite 800   Phone: (202) 466-5428
Washington, DC 20036   Margaret Henneberry, Exec.Dir.

FLORIDA

INSTITUTE OF INTERNAL AUDITORS, INC. - LIBRARY †
International Headquarters
249 Maitland Ave.   Phone: (305) 830-7600
Altamonte Springs, FL 32701

WALKER MEMORIAL HOSPITAL - LIBRARY
Box A
Avon Park, FL 33825

POLK COUNTY HISTORICAL AND GENEALOGICAL LIBRARY
495 N. Hendry Ave.
Box 1719   Phone: (813) 533-5146
Bartow, FL 33830   LaCona Raines Padgett, Hist.Libn.

POLK COUNTY LAW LIBRARY
Courthouse, Rm. 307   Phone: (813) 533-0411
Bartow, FL 33830   Kathy E. Griffis, Libn.

U.S. VETERANS ADMINISTRATION (FL-Bay Pines) - CENTER LIBRARY
                                       Phone: (813) 391-9644
Bay Pines, FL 33504   Ann A. Conlan, Libn.

UNIVERSITY OF FLORIDA - AGRICULTURAL RESEARCH & EDUCATION
   CENTER - BELLE GLADE LIBRARY
Inst. of Food & Agricultural Sciences
Drawer A   Phone: (305) 996-3062
Belle Glade, FL 33430

BOCA RATON COMMUNITY HOSPITAL - HEALTH SCIENCES LIBRARY
800 Meadows Rd.   Phone: (305) 395-7100
Boca Raton, FL 33432   Judy Andrews, Adm.Libn.

CRC PRESS, INC. - LIBRARY
2000 N.W. 24th St.   Phone: (305) 994-0555
Boca Raton, FL 33431   Janelle Sparks, Ed.

BETHESDA MEMORIAL HOSPITAL - MEDICAL LIBRARY
2815 S. Seacrest Blvd.   Phone: (305) 737-7733
Boynton Beach, FL 33435   Helen J. Warner, Libn.

SEMINARY OF ST. VINCENT DE PAUL - LIBRARY
Military Trail
Box 460   Phone: (305) 732-4424
Boynton Beach, FL 33435   Rev. John A. Crowley, Libn.

MANATEE COUNTY BAR ASSOCIATION - LAW LIBRARY
County Court House   Phone: (813) 748-4501
Bradenton, FL 33505   L. Marie Ingram, Law Libn.

MANATEE COUNTY PLANNING AND DEVELOPMENT DEPARTMENT -
   TECHNICAL REFERENCE LIBRARY
212 6th Ave., E.   Phone: (813) 748-4501
Bradenton, FL 33506

MANATEE MEMORIAL HOSPITAL - WENTZEL MEDICAL LIBRARY
206 2nd St., E.   Phone: (813) 746-5111
Bradenton, FL 33508   Jeanette Mosher, Med.Libn.

U.S. NATL. PARK SERVICE - DE SOTO NATL. MEMORIAL - LIBRARY
75th St., N.W.   Phone: (813) 792-0458
Bradenton, FL 33529   Guy L. LaChine, Supv. Park Techn.

UNIVERSITY OF FLORIDA - AGRICULTURAL RESEARCH & EDUCATION
   CENTER - BRADENTON LIBRARY
Inst. of Food & Agricultural Sciences
5007 60th St., E.   Phone: (813) 755-1568
Bradenton, FL 33508

COMMUNITY HOSPITAL OF BUNNELL - MEDICAL LIBRARY
Box 98   Phone: (904) 437-3034
Bunnell, FL 32010   Laine Bridges, Libn.

FLORIDA SOLAR ENERGY CENTER - LIBRARY
300 State Rd. 401   Phone: (305) 783-0300
Cape Canaveral, FL 32920   Iraida B. Rickling, Libn.

FLORIDA STATE HOSPITAL - HEALTH SCIENCE LIBRARY
                                       Phone: (904) 663-7205
Chattahoochee, FL 32324   Geneva N. Herring, Med.Libn.

FLORIDA STATE HOSPITAL - PATIENT/STAFF LIBRARY
                                       Phone: (904) 663-7453
Chattahoochee, FL 32324   Ann M. Bruce, Libn.

PINELLAS COUNTY LAW LIBRARY - CLEARWATER BRANCH
315 Court St.   Phone: (813) 448-2411
Clearwater, FL 33516   Margaret A. Nightingale, Libn.

SPERRY CORPORATION - SPERRY GYROSCOPE DIVISION - ENGINEERING
   LIBRARY
Box 4648   Phone: (813) 577-1900
Clearwater, FL 33518   Margaret M. Cort, Libn.

FELLOWSHIP OF RELIGIOUS HUMANISTS - BRANCH LIBRARY †
1044 Samar Rd.   Phone: (305) 783-8359
Cocoa Beach, FL 32931   Rev. Edwin H. Wilson, Hist.

TEMPLE JUDEA - MEL HARRISON MEMORIAL LIBRARY
5500 Granada Blvd.
Coral Gables, FL 33146   Zelda Harrison, Libn.

U.S. NATL. OCEANIC & ATMOSPHERIC ADMINISTRATION - LIBRARY &
   INFORMATION SERVICES DIV. - CORAL GABLES CENTER
Gables 1 Tower, Rm. 520   Phone: (305) 350-4498
Coral Gables, FL 33146   Robert Ting, Chf.Libn.

UNIVERSITY OF MIAMI - LOWE ART MUSEUM LIBRARY
1301 Miller Dr.   Phone: (305) 284-3535
Coral Gables, FL 33146   Ms. Zan Gay, Libn.

UNIVERSITY OF MIAMI - MORTON COLLECTANEA
Box 248204   Phone: (305) 284-3741
Coral Gables, FL 33124   Dr. Julia F. Morton, Dir.

UNIVERSITY OF MIAMI - SCHOOL OF LAW LIBRARY
Box 248087   Phone: (305) 284-2250
Coral Gables, FL 33124   Betty V. LeBus, Law Libn.

UNIVERSITY OF MIAMI - SCHOOL OF MUSIC - ALBERT PICK MUSIC
   LIBRARY
                                       Phone: (305) 284-2429
Coral Gables, FL 33124   Elsie Fardig, Music Libn.

UNIVERSITY OF MIAMI - SCIENCE/ENGINEERING COLLECTION
Box 248214   Phone: (305) 284-4126
Coral Gables, FL 33124   Thomas T. Rogero, Libn.

BROWARD COUNTY PUBLIC SCHOOLS - LEARNING RESOURCES -
   PROFESSIONAL LIBRARY
6650 Griffin Rd.   Phone: (305) 765-6153
Davie, FL 33314   Helen S. Mattison, Educ.Spec., Media

EMBRY RIDDLE AERONAUTICAL UNIVERSITY - LEARNING RESOURCES
   CENTER
Regional Airport   Phone: (904) 252-5561
Daytona Beach, FL 32014   M. Judy Luther, Dir./Learning Rsrcs.

FLORIDA REGIONAL LIBRARY FOR THE BLIND AND PHYSICALLY
   HANDICAPPED - MULTISTATE CENTER FOR THE SOUTH
Box 2299   Phone: (904) 252-4722
Daytona Beach, FL 32015   Billie Jean Ouellette, Dir.

FLORIDA STATE DIVISION OF BLIND SERVICES - FLORIDA REGIONAL LIB.
   FOR THE BLIND & PHYSICALLY HANDICAPPED
Box 2299   Phone: (904) 252-4722
Daytona Beach, FL 32015   Donald John Weber, Dir.

HALIFAX HISTORICAL SOCIETY, INC. - LIBRARY
Box 5051
Daytona Beach, FL 32018   Florence Donathan-Nordquist, Exec.Dir.

HALIFAX HOSPITAL MEDICAL CENTER - MEDICAL LIBRARY
Clyde Morris Blvd.   Phone: (904) 258-1611
Daytona Beach, FL 32014   Ken Mead, Dir.Med.Lib.

MUSEUM OF ARTS AND SCIENCES - BRUCE EVERETT BATES MEMORIAL
   LIBRARY
1040 Museum Blvd.   Phone: (904) 255-0285
Daytona Beach, FL 32014   Marjorie L. Sigerson, Libn.

PATRIOTIC EDUCATION, INC. - LIBRARY
Box 2121   Phone: (904) 252-3414
Daytona Beach, FL 32015   Sedgley Thornbury, Pres.

VOLUSIA COUNTY LAW LIBRARY
Courthouse Annex, Rm. 207
125 S. Orange Ave.   Phone: (904) 258-7000
Daytona Beach, FL 32014   Rae Mastropierro, Law Libn.

VOLUSIA COUNTY SCHOOL BOARD - TEACHERS' RESOURCE LIBRARY
729 Loomis Ave.
Box 1910   Phone: (904) 255-6475
Daytona Beach, FL 32015   Loretta O. Wright, Media Spec.

FIRST PRESBYTERIAN CHURCH - LIBRARY
724 N. Woodland Blvd.   Phone: (904) 734-6212
De Land, FL 32720   Dorthea Beiler, Libn.

FISH MEMORIAL HOSPITAL - MEDICAL LIBRARY
245 E. New York Ave.   Phone: (904) 734-2323
De Land, FL 32720   Paula Greenwood, Circuit Libn.

STETSON UNIVERSITY - CHEMISTRY LIBRARY
Box 1271   Phone: (904) 734-4121
De Land, FL 32720   James H. Delap, Chem. Professor

STETSON UNIVERSITY - FLORIDA BAPTIST HISTORICAL COLLECTION
Box 1353   Phone: (904) 734-2559
De Land, FL 32720   E. Earl Joiner, Cur.

STETSON UNIVERSITY - SCHOOL OF MUSIC LIBRARY
Woodland Blvd.   Phone: (904) 734-4121
De Land, FL 32720   Janice Jenkins, Music Libn.

WEST VOLUSIA MEMORIAL HOSPITAL - MEDICAL LIBRARY
Box 509   Phone: (904) 734-3320
De Land, FL 32720   Lawrence A. Welch, Adm.

U.S. AIR FORCE - ARMAMENT DIVISION, AIR FORCE ARMAMENT
   LABORATORY - TECHNICAL LIBRARY
                                                    Phone: (904) 882-3212
Eglin AFB, FL 32542   Frances M. Quinn, Chf.

U.S. AIR FORCE BASE - EGLIN BASE LIBRARY
                                                    Phone: (904) 882-5088
Eglin AFB, FL 32542   F.P. Morgan, Chf., Lib.Br.

AMERICAN EXPRESS COMPANY - SYSTEMS LIBRARY
777 American Expressway   Phone: (305) 473-7771
Fort Lauderdale, FL 33337   Sheila Abbie Goren, Sys.Libn.

BENDIX CORPORATION - BENDIX AVIONICS DIVISION - LIBRARY
2100 N.W. 62nd St.
Box 9414   Phone: (305) 776-4100
Fort Lauderdale, FL 33310   Patricia Ferguson, Libn.

BROWARD COUNTY HISTORICAL COMMISSION - LIBRARY & ARCHIVES
100-B S. New River Dr., E.   Phone: (305) 765-5872
Fort Lauderdale, FL 33301   Carolyn Kayne, Coord.

BROWARD COUNTY LAW LIBRARY
444 County Courthouse   Phone: (305) 765-4096
Fort Lauderdale, FL 33301   Estra R. Pillau, Libn.

DUNHILL COMPANY - BUSINESS RESEARCH LIBRARY
2430 W. Oakland Park Blvd.   Phone: (305) 484-8300
Fort Lauderdale, FL 33311   Estelle Rickles, Libn.

ENGLISH, MC CAUGHAN AND O'BRYAN - LAW LIBRARY
Box 14098   Phone: (305) 462-3301
Fort Lauderdale, FL 33302   Angela R. Stramiello, Libn.

FIRST FEDERAL SAVINGS & LOAN ASSOCIATION OF BROWARD COUNTY -
   CORPORATE LIBRARY
301 E. Las Olas Blvd.
Box 14370
Fort Lauderdale, FL 33302   Ava Goldman, Corp.Libn.

FORT LAUDERDALE HISTORICAL SOCIETY - LIBRARY & ARCHIVES
219 Southwest 2nd Ave.   Phone: (305) 463-4431
Fort Lauderdale, FL 33301   Daniel T. Hobby, Exec.Dir.

HOSPITAL EQUITIES, INC. - MEDICAL WORLD NEWS - LIBRARY
941 N.E. 19th Ave., Suite 307
Fort Lauderdale, FL 33064

INTERNATIONAL GAME FISH ASSOCIATION - INTERNATIONAL LIBRARY OF
   FISHES
3000 E. Las Olas Blvd.   Phone: (305) 467-0161
Fort Lauderdale, FL 33316   M.B. McCracken, Libn.

INTERNATIONAL SWIMMING HALL OF FAME - MUSEUM & LIBRARY
One Hall Of Fame Dr.   Phone: (305) 462-6536
Fort Lauderdale, FL 33316   Marion Washburn, Libn.

MARQUIS BIOGRAPHICAL LIBRARY SOCIETY, INC.
2810 E. Oakland Park Blvd., Suite 210
Fort Lauderdale, FL 33306

MOTOROLA, INC. - COMMUNICATION PRODUCTS DIVISION - TECHNICAL
   LIBRARY
8000 W. Sunrise Blvd.   Phone: (305) 475-5049
Fort Lauderdale, FL 33322   Mary Anne Foley, Tech.Libn.

SYSTEMS ENGINEERING LABORATORIES - TECHNICAL INFORMATION
   CENTER
6901 W. Sunrise Blvd.   Phone: (305) 587-2900
Fort Lauderdale, FL 33313   L. Susan Hayes, Info.Spec.

UNIVERSITY OF FLORIDA - AGRICULTURAL RESEARCH CENTER - FORT
   LAUDERDALE LIBRARY
Inst. of Food & Agricultural Sciences
3205 S.W. 70th Ave.   Phone: (305) 475-8990
Fort Lauderdale, FL 33314   Dr. William B. Ennis, Jr., Ctr.Dir.

ST. LUCIE COUNTY HISTORICAL MUSEUM - LIBRARY
414 Seaway Dr.   Phone: (305) 464-6635
Fort Pierce, FL 33450   Iva Jean Sherman, Dir.

ST. LUCIE COUNTY LAW LIBRARY
County Courthouse, 3rd Fl.
Fort Pierce, FL 33450   Annie M. Fain, Libn.

CH2M HILL SOUTHEAST, INC. - INFORMATION CENTER
7201 N.W. 11th Place   Phone: (904) 377-2442
Gainesville, FL 32602   Mary Gene Blanchard, Libn.

FIRST BAPTIST CHURCH - MEDIA CENTER †
425 W. University Ave.   Phone: (904) 376-2131
Gainesville, FL 32601   Mrs. Luther C. Hammond, Dir. of Lib.Serv.

**FLORIDA STATE DEPT. OF AGRICULTURE AND CONSUMER SERVICES -
    DIVISION OF PLANT INDUSTRY - LIBRARY**
Box 1269   Phone: (904) 372-3505
Gainesville, FL 32602   June B. Jacobson, Libn.

GAINESVILLE SUN - LIBRARY
Drawer A   Phone: (904) 378-1411
Gainesville, FL 32602   Robert Ivey, Libn.

SUNLAND CENTER AT GAINESVILLE - LIBRARY
Box 1150   Phone: (904) 376-5381
Gainesville, FL 32602   Susan L. Stephan, Libn.

TREE OF LIFE PRESS - LIBRARY AND ARCHIVES
420 N.E. Blvd.
Gainesville, FL 32601   Reva Pachefsky

U.S. VETERANS ADMINISTRATION (FL-Gainesville) - HOSPITAL LIBRARY
     Phone: (904) 376-1611
Gainesville, FL 32602   Marylyn E. Gresser, Chf., Lib.Serv.

UNIVERSITY OF FLORIDA - ARCHITECTURE & FINE ARTS LIBRARY
201 FAA   Phone: (904) 392-0222
Gainesville, FL 32611   Anna L. Weaver, AFA Libn.

UNIVERSITY OF FLORIDA - BALDWIN LIBRARY
308 Library East
Gainesville, FL 32611   Dr. Ruth Baldwin

**UNIVERSITY OF FLORIDA - BELKNAP COLLECTION FOR THE PERFORMING
    ARTS**
512 Library W.   Phone: (904) 392-0322
Gainesville, FL 32611   Sidney Ives, Libn.

UNIVERSITY OF FLORIDA - CENTER FOR WETLANDS REFERENCE LIBRARY
Phelps Laboratory   Phone: (904) 392-2424
Gainesville, FL 32611   G. Ronnie Best, Assoc.Dir.

UNIVERSITY OF FLORIDA - CHEMISTRY LIBRARY
216 Leigh Hall   Phone: (904) 392-0573
Gainesville, FL 32611   Carol Drum, Assoc.Libn.

**UNIVERSITY OF FLORIDA - COASTAL & OCEANOGRAPHIC ENGINEERING
    DEPARTMENT - COASTAL ENGINEERING ARCHIVES**
433 Weil Hall   Phone: (904) 392-2710
Gainesville, FL 32611   Lucile Lehmann, Archv.

UNIVERSITY OF FLORIDA - EDUCATION LIBRARY
1500 Norman Hall   Phone: (904) 392-0707
Gainesville, FL 32611   Tena L. Crenshaw, Libn.

UNIVERSITY OF FLORIDA - ENGINEERING & PHYSICS LIBRARY
410 Weil Hall   Phone: (904) 392-0987
Gainesville, FL 32611   Roger V. Krumm, Libn.

UNIVERSITY OF FLORIDA - FLORIDA STATE MUSEUM LIBRARY
Museum Rd.   Phone: (904) 392-1721
Gainesville, FL 32611   F. Wayne King, Dir.

UNIVERSITY OF FLORIDA - HUME LIBRARY
Inst. of Food & Agricultural Sciences
McCarty Hall
     Phone: (904) 392-1934
Gainesville, FL 32611   Albert C. Strickland, Libn.

UNIVERSITY OF FLORIDA - ISSER AND RAE PRICE LIBRARY OF JUDAICA
18 Library East   Phone: (904) 392-0308
Gainesville, FL 32611   Robert Singerman, Hd.

UNIVERSITY OF FLORIDA - J. HILLIS MILLER HEALTH CENTER LIBRARY
Box J-206   Phone: (904) 392-4016
Gainesville, FL 32611   Ted F. Srygley, Dir.

UNIVERSITY OF FLORIDA - LATIN AMERICAN COLLECTION
4th Fl., Library East   Phone: (904) 392-0360
Gainesville, FL 32611   Dr. Rosa Q. Mesa, Dir.

UNIVERSITY OF FLORIDA - LAW LIBRARY
     Phone: (904) 392-0418
Gainesville, FL 32611   Betty W. Taylor, Dir.

UNIVERSITY OF FLORIDA - MAP LIBRARY
Library East   Phone: (904) 392-0803
Gainesville, FL 32611   Dr. Helen Jane Armstrong, Map Libn.

UNIVERSITY OF FLORIDA - MUSIC LIBRARY
231 Music Bldg.   Phone: (904) 392-6678
Gainesville, FL 32611   Robena Eng Cornwell, Asst.Univ.Libn.

**UNIVERSITY OF FLORIDA - P.K. YONGE LABORATORY SCHOOL - MEAD
    LIBRARY**
1080 S.W. 11th Ave.   Phone: (904) 392-1506
Gainesville, FL 32611   Sarah Caroline Fergusan, Hd.Libn.

UNIVERSITY OF FLORIDA - P.K. YONGE LIBRARY OF FLORIDA HISTORY
4th Fl., Library West   Phone: (904) 392-0319
Gainesville, FL 32611   Elizabeth Alexander, Libn.

UNIVERSITY OF FLORIDA - RARE BOOKS & MANUSCRIPTS
531 Library West   Phone: (904) 392-0321
Gainesville, FL 32611   Sidney Ives, Libn.

UNIVERSITY OF FLORIDA - TRANSPORTATION RESEARCH CENTER
Civil Engineering Dept.
245 Weil Hall   Phone: (904) 392-6656
Gainesville, FL 32611

**UNIVERSITY OF FLORIDA - UNIVERSITY ARCHIVES AND UNIVERSITY
    COLLECTION**
303 Library East   Phone: (904) 392-6547
Gainesville, FL 32611

**UNIVERSITY OF FLORIDA - URBAN AND REGIONAL PLANNING DOCUMENTS
    COLLECTION**
Library West   Phone: (904) 392-0317
Gainesville, FL 32611   Margaret S. LeSourd, Assoc.Univ.Libn.

BAPTIST BIBLE INSTITUTE - IDA J. MC MILLAN LIBRARY *
1306 College Dr.   Phone: (904) 263-3261
Graceville, FL 32440   Professor Gail A. Moul, Libn.

**ENVIRONMENTAL PROTECTION AGENCY - ENVIRONMENTAL RESEARCH
    LABORATORY, GULF BREEZE - LIBRARY**
Sabine Island, 6   Phone: (904) 932-5311
Gulf Breeze, FL 32561   Andree Lowry, Libn.

UNIVERSITY OF FLORIDA - AGRICULTURAL RESEARCH CENTER - LIBRARY
Box 728   Phone: (904) 692-1792
Hastings, FL 32045   R.B. Workman, Assoc.Prof.

HIALEAH HOSPITAL - HEALTH SCIENCE LIBRARY
651 East 25th St.   Phone: (305) 835-4635
Hialeah, FL 33013   Yvonne Barkman, Health Sci.Libn.

HOBE SOUND BIBLE COLLEGE - LIBRARY
Box 1065   Phone: (305) 546-5534
Hobe Sound, FL 33455   Joy A. Day, Dir.

**SOUTH FLORIDA STATE HOSPITAL - MEDICAL AND PROFESSIONAL
    LIBRARY**
1000 S.W. 84th Ave.   Phone: (305) 983-4321
Hollywood, FL 33025   Mabel E. Harvey, Med.Libn.

**U.S. NATL. PARK SERVICE - EVERGLADES NATL. PARK - REFERENCE
    LIBRARY**
Box 279   Phone: (305) 245-5266
Homestead, FL 33030   Mrs. Alcyone B. Bradley, Libn.

**UNIVERSITY OF FLORIDA - AGRICULTURAL RESEARCH & EDUCATION
    CENTER - HOMESTEAD LIBRARY**
Inst. of Food & Agricultural Sciences
18905 S.W. 280th St.   Phone: (305) 247-4624
Homestead, FL 33031   A.A. Duncan, Ctr.Dir.

U.S. AIR FORCE BASE - HOMESTEAD BASE LIBRARY
FL4829, 31 CSG/SSL
Homestead AFB, FL 33039
Phone: (305) 257-8184
Lauren J. Aragon, Libn.

CHURCH OF JESUS CHRIST OF LATTER-DAY SAINTS - JACKSONVILLE,
FLORIDA BRANCH GENEALOGICAL LIBRARY
4087 Hendricks Ave.
Jacksonville, FL 32207
Phone: (904) 398-3487
Mary C. Kelley, Br. Genealogy Libn.

CUMMER GALLERY OF ART - LIBRARY
829 Riverside Ave.
Jacksonville, FL 32204
Phone: (904) 356-6857
Laura R. Joost, Chm., Lib.Comm.

DUVAL COUNTY LAW LIBRARY
220 Court House
Jacksonville, FL 32202
Phone: (904) 633-4756
Jack T. Sheng, Law Libn.

FLORIDA PUBLISHING CO. - EDITORIAL LIBRARY
1 Riverside Ave.
Jacksonville, FL 32202
Phone: (904) 359-4237
Martin L. Crotts, Dir.

FLORIDA STATE DEPT. OF HEALTH & REHABILITATIVE SERVICES - HRS
RESOURCE CENTER
1217 Pearl St.
Box 210
Jacksonville, FL 32231
Phone: (904) 354-3961
Carolyn Hall, Libn.

JACKSONVILLE ART MUSEUM - LIBRARY
4160 Boulevard Center Dr.
Jacksonville, FL 32207

JACKSONVILLE HEALTH EDUCATION PROGRAMS, INC. - BORLAND HEALTH
SCIENCES LIBRARY
580 W. 8th St.
Jacksonville, FL 32209
Phone: (904) 359-6516
Robert P. Hinz, Dir.

JACKSONVILLE PUBLIC LIBRARY - FLORIDA COLLECTION
122 N. Ocean St.
Jacksonville, FL 32202
Phone: (904) 633-3305
Mr. Carol Harris, Cur.

LUTHER RICE SEMINARY - BERTHA SMITH LIBRARY
1050 Hendricks Ave.
Jacksonville, FL 32207
Phone: (904) 396-2316
Gerald L. Marshall, Libn.

PRUDENTIAL INSURANCE COMPANY OF AMERICA - EMPLOYEES' BUSINESS
& RECREATIONAL LIBRARY
Prudential Dr.
Jacksonville, FL 32207
Phone: (904) 399-2002
Barbara K. Williams, Libn.

REYNOLDS, SMITH & HILLS - LIBRARY
4019 Blvd. Center Dr.
Jacksonville, FL 32201
Phone: (904) 396-2011
Laura S. Vollenweider, Libn.

RIVERSIDE PRESBYTERIAN CHURCH - JEAN MILLER LIBRARY
849 Park St.
Jacksonville, FL 32204
Elizabeth Myers

ST. LUKE'S HOSPITAL - MEDICAL LIBRARY †
1900 Boulevard
Jacksonville, FL 32206
Phone: (904) 356-1992
Margarette Wally, Libn.

SCM CORPORATION - ORGANIC CHEMICALS DIVISION - TECHNICAL
LIBRARY
Box 389
Jacksonville, FL 32201
Phone: (904) 764-1711
Marian M. Derfer, Supv.Lib./Info.Serv.

SEABOARD COAST LINE RAILROAD COMPANY - LAW LIBRARY
500 Water St.
Jacksonville, FL 32202
Phone: (904) 353-2011

U.S. NAVY - NAVAL REGIONAL MEDICAL CENTER (Jacksonville) - MEDICAL
LIBRARY †
Jacksonville, FL 32214
Phone: (904) 772-3439
Bettye W. Stilley, Med.Libn.

WESTINGHOUSE ELECTRIC CORPORATION - OFFSHORE POWER SYSTEMS
LIBRARY
8000 Arlington Expy.
Jacksonville, FL 32211
Phone: (904) 724-7700
Minnie G. Thurston, Supv., Lib.Serv.

FLORIDA INSTITUTE OF TECHNOLOGY - SCHOOL OF APPLIED TECHNOLOGY
- LIBRARY
1707 N.E. Indian River Dr.
Jensen Beach, FL 33457
Phone: (305) 334-4200
Eleanor S. Harris, Br.Libn.

U.S. NASA - JOHN F. KENNEDY SPACE CENTER - LIBRARY
SAN 302 - 9905
Kennedy Space Center, FL 32899
Phone: (305) 867-3600
M. Konjevich, Lib.Mgr.

U.S. NAVY - NAVAL AIR STATION (Key West) - LIBRARY
Bldg. 623A
Key West, FL 33040
Phone: (305) 296-3561
LCDR M. Gore, Lib.Off.

UNIVERSITY OF FLORIDA - AGRICULTURAL RESEARCH & EDUCATION
CENTER - LAKE ALFRED LIBRARY
Inst. of Food & Agricultural Sciences
700 Experiment Station Rd.
Lake Alfred, FL 33850
Phone: (813) 956-1151
Pamela K. Hearon, Asst.Libn.

U.S. VETERANS ADMINISTRATION (FL-Lake City) - MEDICAL CENTER
LIBRARY
Lake City, FL 32055
Phone: (904) 752-1400
Shirley Mabry, Chf., Lib.Serv.

COLLECTOR CIRCLE - LIBRARY
1313 S. Killian Dr.
Lake Park, FL 33403
Phone: (305) 845-6075
Roz Belford

ARCHBOLD BIOLOGICAL STATION OF THE AMERICAN MUSEUM OF
NATURAL HISTORY - LIBRARY
Rte. 2, Box 180
Lake Placid, FL 33852
Phone: (813) 465-2571
Fred E. Lohrer, Libn.

LAKELAND GENERAL HOSPITAL - MEDICAL LIBRARY
Drawer 448
Lakeland, FL 33802
Phone: (813) 683-0411
Cheryl R. Dee, Med.Libn.

POLK PUBLIC MUSEUM - MEMORIAL LIBRARY
800 E. Palmetto
Lakeland, FL 33801
Phone: (813) 688-7744
Bonnie Rohrbaugh, Chm.

WATSON CLINIC - MEDICAL LIBRARY
Box 1429
Lakeland, FL 33802
Phone: (813) 687-4000
Cheryl Dee, Med.Libn.

HOLLEY (A.G.) STATE HOSPITAL - BENJAMIN L. BROCK MEDICAL LIBRARY
Box 3084
Lantana, FL 33462
Phone: (305) 582-5666
Andree Sweek, Med.Rec.Libn.

NATIONAL ENQUIRER - RESEARCH DEPARTMENT LIBRARY
600 Southeast Coast Ave.
Lantana, FL 33464
Phone: (305) 586-1111
Martha Moppett, Res.Libn.

UNIVERSITY OF FLORIDA - AGRICULTURAL RESEARCH CENTER - LIBRARY
Inst. of Food & Agricultural Sciences
Box 388
Leesburg, FL 32748
Phone: (904) 787-3423
Dr. Gary W. Elmstrom, Ctr.Dir.

U.S. AIR FORCE BASE - MAC DILL BASE LIBRARY
MacDill AFB, FL 33608
Phone: (813) 830-3607
Jean L. Jacob, Base Libn.

FLORIDA AUDUBON SOCIETY - INFORMATION CENTER
921 S. Lake Sybelia Dr.
P.O. Drawer 7
Maitland, FL 32751

FLORIDA INSTITUTE OF TECHNOLOGY - LIBRARY
Box 1150
Melbourne, FL 32901
Phone: (305) 723-3701
Llewellyn L. Henson, Dir.

AMERICAN COUNCIL OF THE INTERNATIONAL INSTITUTE OF WELDING -
LIBRARY
2501 N.W. 7th St.
Miami, FL 33125
Phone: (305) 642-7090
H.W. Raths, Libn.

AMERICAN HOSPITAL SUPPLY CORPORATION - DADE DIVISION LIBRARY
1851 Delaware Pkwy.
Box 520672
Miami, FL 33152
Phone: (305) 633-6461
Patsy A. Bentley, Sr.Med.Libn.

GEOGRAPHIC

AMERICAN INDIAN REFUGEES - NATIVE LIBRARY
6701 S.W. 62nd Ave.
Miami, FL 33143

AMERIFIRST FEDERAL SAVINGS & LOAN - LIBRARY
One S.E. Third Ave.   Phone: (305) 577-6397
Miami, FL 33131   Emerita M. Cuesta, Res.Libn.

BAPTIST HOSPITAL OF MIAMI - HEALTH SCIENCES LIBRARY
8900 S.W. 88th St.   Phone: (305) 596-1960
Miami, FL 33176   Diane F. Ream, Med.Libn.

BETH DAVID CONGREGATION - HARRY SIMONS LIBRARY
2625 S.W. Third Ave.   Phone: (305) 854-3911
Miami, FL 33129

BLACKWELL, WALKER, GRAY, POWERS, FLICK & HOEHL - LAW LIBRARY
2400 Amerifirst Bldg.
One S.E. Third Ave.   Phone: (305) 358-8880
Miami, FL 33131   Dr. Cesar J. Armstrong, Res.Libn.

CENTRAL AGENCY FOR JEWISH EDUCATION - EDUCATIONAL RESOURCE
   CENTER/LIBRARY
4200 Biscayne Blvd.   Phone: (305) 576-3030
Miami, FL 33137   Shirley Wolfe, Dir.

DADE COUNTY LAW LIBRARY
321A County Court House   Phone: (305) 579-5422
Miami, FL 33130   Robert B. Wallace, Libn.

FAIRCHILD TROPICAL GARDEN - MONTGOMERY LIBRARY
10901 Old Cutler Rd.   Phone: (305) 667-1651
Miami, FL 33156   John Popenoe, Dir.

FLORIDA POWER & LIGHT COMPANY - CORPORATE LIBRARY
9250 W. Flagler St.
Box 529100   Phone: (305) 552-3210
Miami, FL 33152   Caryl Congleton, Libn.

FLORIDA STATE COURT OF APPEAL - 3RD DISTRICT - LAW LIBRARY
2001 S.W. 117th Ave.
Box 650307   Phone: (305) 552-2900
Miami, FL 33165   Rosemary E. Helsabeck, Libn.

GORGAS ARMY HOSPITAL - SAMUEL TAYLOR DARLING MEMORIAL LIBRARY
USA MEDDAC Panama
APO Miami, FL 34004   Barbara Poole, Chf. MEDDAC Libn.

GORGAS MEMORIAL LABORATORY OF TROPICAL AND PREVENTIVE
   MEDICINE, INC. - BIO-MEDICAL RESEARCH LIBRARY
Box 935
APO Miami, FL 34002   Prof. Manuel Victor De Las Casas, Dir. & Med.Libn.

HISTORICAL ASSOCIATION OF SOUTHERN FLORIDA - CHARLTON W.
   TEBEAU LIBRARY OF FLORIDA HISTORY
3280 S. Miami Ave., Bldg. B   Phone: (305) 854-3289
Miami, FL 33129   Rebecca A. Smith, Libn.

JACKSON MEMORIAL HOSPITAL - SCHOOL OF NURSING LIBRARY
1611 N.W. 12th Ave.   Phone: (305) 325-6833
Miami, FL 33136   Joseph B. Sowell, Med.Libn.

MERCY HOSPITAL - MEDICAL LIBRARY
3663 S. Miami Ave.   Phone: (305) 854-4400
Miami, FL 33133   Cornelia C. Pope, Libn.

METROPOLITAN DADE COUNTY PLANNING DEPARTMENT - LIBRARY/
   INFORMATION CENTER
909 S.E. 1st Ave., Suite 900   Phone: (305) 579-2826
Miami, FL 33131   Maria Luisa Perez, Libn.

MIAMI-DADE PUBLIC LIBRARY - ART AND MUSIC DIVISION
1 Biscayne Blvd.   Phone: (305) 579-5001
Miami, FL 33132   Barbara Edwards, Hd.

MIAMI-DADE PUBLIC LIBRARY - AUDIO/VISUAL DEPARTMENT
1 Biscayne Blvd.   Phone: (305) 579-5001
Miami, FL 33132   Michel Anguilano, AV Dir.

MIAMI-DADE PUBLIC LIBRARY - BUSINESS, SCIENCE AND TECHNOLOGY
   DEPARTMENT
1 Biscayne Blvd.   Phone: (305) 579-5001
Miami, FL 33132   Louise Maurer, Sci.Libn.

MIAMI-DADE PUBLIC LIBRARY - FEDERAL DOCUMENTS DIVISION
1 Biscayne Blvd.   Phone: (305) 579-3555
Miami, FL 33132   Arthur Cutlip, Fed.Doc.Libn.

MIAMI-DADE PUBLIC LIBRARY - FLORIDA COLLECTION
1 Biscayne Blvd.   Phone: (305) 579-5189
Miami, FL 33132   S.J. Boldrick, Libn.

MIAMI-DADE PUBLIC LIBRARY - FOREIGN LANGUAGES DIVISION
1 Biscayne Blvd.   Phone: (305) 579-5001
Miami, FL 33132   Alicia Godoy, Lang.Libn.

MIAMI-DADE PUBLIC LIBRARY - GENEALOGY ROOM
1 Biscayne Blvd.   Phone: (305) 579-5015
Miami, FL 33132   Edward F. Sintz, Dir.

MIAMI-DADE PUBLIC LIBRARY - URBAN AFFAIRS LIBRARY
1 Biscayne Blvd.   Phone: (305) 579-5487
Miami, FL 33132   Richard G. Frow, Libn.

MIAMI HERALD - LIBRARY
No. 1 Herald Plaza   Phone: (305) 350-2419
Miami, FL 33101   Luis Bueno, Lib.Dir.

MIAMI NEWS - LIBRARY
One Herald Plaza   Phone: (305) 350-2189
Miami, FL 33101   Joseph F. Wright, Hd.Libn.

NORTH SHORE HOSPITAL - MEDICAL LIBRARY *
9200 N.W. 11th Ave.   Phone: (305) 693-1100
Miami, FL 33150   Gladys Mese, Med.Libn.

PANAMA CANAL COMMISSION - LIBRARY-MUSEUM *
APO Miami, FL 34011   Beverly C. Williams, Libn.-Cur.

PAPANICOLAOU CANCER RESEARCH INSTITUTE AT MIAMI - RESEARCH
   LIBRARY
1155 N.W. 14th St.
Box 016188   Phone: (305) 324-5572
Miami, FL 33101

RACAL-MILGO, INC. - INFORMATION RESOURCES
8600 N.W. 41st St.   Phone: (305) 591-5186
Miami, FL 33166   Jan Stern

RYDER SYSTEM, INC. - INFORMATION CENTRAL
Box 520816   Phone: (305) 593-3535
Miami, FL 33152   Robert L. Pendell, Mgr.Info.Ctrl.

SMATHERS & THOMPSON - LAW LIBRARY
1301 Du Pont Bldg.   Phone: (305) 379-6523
Miami, FL 33131   Mary F. Cross, Libn.

SOUTH FLORIDA REGIONAL PLANNING COUNCIL - LIBRARY *
1515 N.W. 167th St., Suite 429   Phone: (305) 621-5871
Miami, FL 33169   Laila Kalaf, Info.Spec.

TEMPLE ISRAEL OF GREATER MIAMI - LIBRARY
137 N.E. 19th St.   Phone: (305) 573-5900
Miami, FL 33132   Beatrice T. Muskat, Libn.

U.S. AIR FORCE BASE - HOWARD BASE LIBRARY
FL 4810
Howard AFB
APO Miami, FL 34001   S.K. Murdoch, Base Libn.

U.S. ARMY SCHOOL OF THE AMERICAS - LIBRARY/LEARNING CENTER
Bldg. 400, MOLASC-SS
APO Miami, FL 34008   Rafael E. Coulson, Dir.

U.S. ARMY - TROPIC TEST CENTER - TECHNICAL INFORMATION CENTER
Fort Clayton
APO Miami, FL 34004   Hoyt Wilson Galloway, Tech.Info.Spec.

U.S. DEPT. OF COMMERCE - INTERNATIONAL TRADE ADMINISTRATION - MIAMI DISTRICT OFFICE LIBRARY
City National Bank Bldg., Rm. 821
25 W. Flagler St.   Phone: (305) 350-5267
Miami, FL 33130   Ivan A. Cosimi, Dir.

U.S. NATL. MARINE FISHERIES SERVICE - SOUTHEAST FISHERIES CENTER - MIAMI LAB. LIBRARY
75 Virginia Beach Dr.   Phone: (305) 361-4229
Miami, FL 33149   Julianne Josiek, Hd.Libn.

U.S. NATL. OCEANIC & ATMOSPHERIC ADMINISTRATION - LIBRARY & INFORMATION SERVICES DIVISION - MIAMI CENTER
15 Rickenbacker Causeway   Phone: (305) 361-4372
Miami, FL 33149   Robert N. Ting, Chf.Libn.

U.S. VETERANS ADMINISTRATION (FL-Miami) - HOSPITAL MEDICAL LIBRARY
1201 N.W. 16th St.   Phone: (305) 324-4455
Miami, FL 33125   Raissa Maurin, Chf.Libn.

UNIVERSITY OF MIAMI - DOROTHY & LEWIS ROSENSTIEL SCHOOL OF MARINE & ATMOSPHERIC SCIENCES - LIBRARY
4600 Rickenbacker Causeway   Phone: (305) 350-7207
Miami, FL 33149   Kay K. Hale, Libn.

UNIVERSITY OF MIAMI - SCHOOL OF MEDICINE - BASCOM PALMER EYE INSTITUTE - LIBRARY
Ann Bates Leach Eye Hospital
900 N.W. 17th St., Box 016880   Phone: (305) 547-6023
Miami, FL 33101   Reva Hurtes, Libn.

UNIVERSITY OF MIAMI - SCHOOL OF MEDICINE - LOUIS CALDER MEMORIAL LIBRARY
Box 016950   Phone: (305) 547-6441
Miami, FL 33101   Henry L. Lemkau, Jr., Dir.

VIZCAYA GUIDES LIBRARY
3251 S. Miami Ave.   Phone: (305) 579-2808
Miami, FL 33129   Alice Miller, Lib.Chm.

WALTON LANTAFF SCHROEDER & CARSON - LAW LIBRARY
900 Alfred I. DuPont Bldg.   Phone: (305) 379-6411
Miami, FL 33131   Joanne Camarasana, Libn.

FLORIDA STATE SUPREME COURT - 11TH JUDICIAL CIRCUIT - DADE COUNTY AUXILIARY LAW LIBRARY
420 Lincoln Rd., Suite 245   Phone: (305) 538-0314
Miami Beach, FL 33139   Conrad L. Painter, Br.Libn.

MIAMI HEART INSTITUTE - MEDICAL LIBRARY
4701 N. Meridian Ave.   Phone: (305) 672-1111
Miami Beach, FL 33140   Bronia Barbash, Libn.

MOUNT SINAI MEDICAL CENTER OF GREATER MIAMI - MEDICAL LIBRARY
4300 Alton Rd.   Phone: (305) 674-2840
Miami Beach, FL 33139   Isabel Ezquerra, Chf.Med.Libn.

NATIONAL NETWORK OF YOUTH ADVISORY BOARDS, INC. - TECHNICAL ASSISTANCE LIBRARY
Ocean View Branch
Box 402036   Phone: (305) 532-2607
Miami Beach, FL 33140   Stuart Alan Rado, Exec.Dir.

ST. FRANCIS HOSPITAL - MEDICAL LIBRARY
250 W. 63rd St.   Phone: (305) 868-5000
Miami Beach, FL 33141   Sr. Marguerite O'Connell, Ph.D., Libn.

TEMPLE BETH SHOLOM - LIBRARY
4144 Chase Ave.   Phone: (305) 538-7231
Miami Beach, FL 33140   Gloria Schwartz, Libn.

TEMPLE EMANU-EL - LIBRARY
1701 Washington Ave.   Phone: (305) 538-2503
Miami Beach, FL 33139   Ruth M. Abelow, Libn.

AMERICAN CYANAMID COMPANY - SANTA ROSA PLANT - LIBRARY
                                     Phone: (904) 994-5311
Milton, FL 32570   Dee Rogers, Libn.

ISOTTA FRASCHINI OWNERS ASSOCIATION - RESEARCH LIBRARY
3000 N. Tamiami Trail
Box 612
North Fort Meyers, FL 33903   H.B. Willis, Dir.

AMERICAN FEDERATION OF POLICE RESEARCH CENTER AND LIBRARY
1100 NE 125th St.   Phone: (305) 891-1700
North Miami, FL 33161   Sgt. James Gordon, Res. & Trng.Asst.

VOLTAIRE SOCIETY - LIBRARY
1837 N. Azalea St., Basswood   Phone: (813) 763-6853
Okeechobee, FL 33472   R.L. Marchfield, Pres.

AMERICAN LAWN BOWLS ASSOCIATION - LIBRARY
1524 Lake Shore Dr.   Phone: (305) 896-2178
Orlando, FL 32853   Harold L. Esch, Hist.

FLORIDA HOSPITAL - DOCTORS' MEDICAL LIBRARY
601 E. Rollins Ave.   Phone: (305) 896-6611
Orlando, FL 32803   Patricia N. Cole, Assoc.Libn.

MAGUIRE, VOORHIS AND WELLS - LIBRARY
135 Wall St.
Box 633
Orlando, FL 32801   John D. Vanston, Law Libn.

MARTIN MARIETTA CORPORATION - ORLANDO AEROSPACE DIVISION - INFORMATION CENTER
Box 5837 MP-30   Phone: (305) 352-2051
Orlando, FL 32855   Morton Meltzer, Mgr.

ORANGE COUNTY HISTORICAL COMMISSION - MUSEUM LIBRARY
812 E. Rollins St.
Loch Haven Park
Orlando, FL 32803   Frank Mendola, Libn.

ORANGE COUNTY LAW LIBRARY
County Court House   Phone: (305) 420-3240
Orlando, FL 32801   Sarilou A. Barrow, Libn.

ORLANDO MUNICIPAL REFERENCE LIBRARY
City Hall, 400 S. Orange Ave.   Phone: (305) 849-2249
Orlando, FL 32801   Phyllis D. Freedman, Libn.

ORLANDO SENTINEL STAR NEWSPAPER - LIBRARY
633 N. Orange Ave.
Box 2833   Phone: (305) 420-5510
Orlando, FL 32802   Judy L. Grimsley, Info.Rsrcs.Supv.

SUNLAND CENTER AT ORLANDO - MEDICAL LIBRARY
Box 3513   Phone: (305) 293-1421
Orlando, FL 32802   Elizabeth G. Lincoln, Dir., Med.Rec.

U.S.D.A. - AGRICULTURAL RESEARCH SERVICE - HORTICULTURAL RESEARCH LABORATORY LIBRARY
2120 Camden Rd.   Phone: (305) 898-6791
Orlando, FL 32803   Helen Louise Dudak, Libn.

U.S. NAVY - NAVAL RESEARCH LABORATORY - UNDERWATER SOUND REFERENCE DETACHMENT - TECHNICAL LIBRARY
755 Gatlin Ave.
Box 8337   Phone: (305) 859-5120
Orlando, FL 32856   Mel Ray, Libn.

U.S. NAVY - NAVAL TRAINING EQUIPMENT CENTER - TECHNICAL INFORMATION CENTER
                                     Phone: (305) 646-4797
Orlando, FL 32813

HISTORICAL SOCIETY OF PALM BEACH COUNTY - LIBRARY AND ARCHIVES
Henry Morrison Flagler Museum
One Whitehall Way, Box 1147   Phone: (305) 655-1492
Palm Beach, FL 33480   Maxine Wisner Banash, Dir.

SOCIETY OF THE FOUR ARTS - LIBRARY
Four Arts Plaza   Phone: (305) 655-7226
Palm Beach, FL 33480   Helen McKinney, Libn.

GEOGRAPHIC

GEOGRAPHIC

PROFESSIONAL GOLFERS' ASSOCIATION OF AMERICA - LIBRARY
100 Ave. of the Champions
Box 12458
Phone: (305) 626-3600
Palm Beach Gardens, FL 33410
Bernice H. Price, Libn.

U.S. NATL. MARINE FISHERIES SERVICE - SOUTHEAST FISHERIES CENTER
- PANAMA CITY LABORATORY - LIBRARY
3500 Delwood Beach Rd.
Phone: (904) 234-6541
Panama City, FL 32407
Rosalie Vaught, Libn.

U.S. NAVY - NAVAL COASTAL SYSTEMS CENTER - TECHNICAL LIBRARY *
Phone: (904) 234-4381
Panama City, FL 32407
Myrtle J. Rhodes, Supv.Libn.

U.S. AIR FORCE BASE - PATRICK BASE LIBRARY †
FL 2829
Phone: (305) 494-6881
Patrick AFB, FL 32925
Marie D. Jennings, Adm.Libn.

U.S. AIR FORCE HOSPITAL - MEDICAL LIBRARY (FL-Patrick **AFB**)
Phone: (305) 494-5501
Patrick AFB, FL 32925
Ted L. Williams, Med.Lib.Off.

BAPTIST HOSPITAL - MEDICAL LIBRARY
1000 W. Moreno
Phone: (904) 434-4877
Pensacola, FL 32505
Anabel Simon, Sr.Libn.

ESCAMBIA COUNTY HEALTH DEPARTMENT - LIBRARY
Box 12604
Phone: (904) 438-8571
Pensacola, FL 32574-2604
Barbara McCullough, Health Educ.

HISTORIC PENSACOLA PRESERVATION BOARD - LIBRARY
205 E. Zaragoza St.
Phone: (904) 434-1042
Pensacola, FL 32501
Linda V. Ellsworth, Hist.

MONSANTO TEXTILES COMPANY - TECHNICAL LIBRARY
Box 12830
Phone: (904) 968-8248
Pensacola, FL 32575
Farrell J. Allen, Sr.Tech.Libn.

PENSACOLA HISTORICAL SOCIETY - LELIA ABERCROMBIE HISTORICAL
LIBRARY
405 S. Adams St.
Phone: (904) 433-1559
Pensacola, FL 32501
Gordon N. Simons, Cur.

PENSACOLA MUSEUM OF ART - HARRY THORNTON MEMORIAL LIBRARY
407 S. Jefferson St.
Phone: (904) 432-6247
Pensacola, FL 32501
Ona C. Butler, Lib.Chm.

REICHOLD CHEMICALS, INC. - NEWPORT DIVISION LIBRARY
Box 1433
Phone: (904) 433-7621
Pensacola, FL 32596
Dr. J.H. Stump, Mgr. R & D

SACRED HEART HOSPITAL - MEDICAL LIBRARY
5151 N. 9th Ave.
Phone: (904) 476-7851
Pensacola, FL 32504
Florence V. Ruby, Med.Libn.

STILL WATERS FOUNDATION - LIBRARY
313 Petherton Place
Pensacola, FL 32506
Nora Nelson, Cur.

U.S. NAVY - NAVAL AEROSPACE MEDICAL INSTITUTE - LIBRARY
Bldg. 1953, Code 012
Phone: (904) 452-2256
Pensacola, FL 32508
Ruth T. Rogers, Adm.Libn.

U.S. NAVY - NAVAL AIR STATION (Pensacola) - LIBRARY
Bldg. 633
Phone: (904) 452-4362
Pensacola, FL 32508
Mabel B. McCullough, Hd.Libn.

UNIVERSITY HOSPITAL AND CLINIC - HERBERT L. BRYANS MEMORIAL
LIBRARY
1200 West Leonard St.
Phone: (904) 436-9199
Pensacola, FL 32501
Rosemary Milner Kiefer, Libn.

UNIVERSITY OF WEST FLORIDA - JOHN C. PACE LIBRARY - SPECIAL
COLLECTIONS
Phone: (904) 476-9500
Pensacola, FL 32504
Marie Scroggs, Spec.Coll.Asst.

WENTWORTH (T.T., Jr.) MUSEUM - LIBRARY
8382 Palafox Hwy.
Box 806
Phone: (904) 438-3638
Pensacola, FL 32594
T.T. Wentworth, Jr., Pres.

COCA-COLA COMPANY - FOODS DIVISION - CITRUS RESEARCH &
DEVELOPMENT TECHNICAL LIBRARY
Orange St.
Box 550
Phone: (305) 886-1568
Plymouth, FL 32768
Kay W. Wolfe, Libn.

UNIVERSITY OF FLORIDA - AGRICULTURAL RESEARCH & EDUCATION
CENTER - QUINCY LIBRARY
Rte. 3, Box 638
Quincy, FL 32351

WUESTHOFF MEMORIAL HOSPITAL - MEDICAL LIBRARY
110 Longwood Ave.
Box 6
Phone: (305) 636-2211
Rockledge, FL 32955
Nancy A. Hanson, Med.Libn.

FLAGLER HOSPITAL - MEDICAL LIBRARY
Marine St.
St. Augustine, FL 32084

FLORIDA SCHOOL FOR THE DEAF AND BLIND - LIBRARY FOR THE DEAF
Box 1209
Phone: (904) 824-1654
St. Augustine, FL 32084
Joan Embry, Hd.Libn.

HISTORIC ST. AUGUSTINE PRESERVATION BOARD - HISPANIC RESEARCH
LIBRARY
King & St. George Sts.
Box 1987
Phone: (904) 824-3355
St. Augustine, FL 32084
Jean Hinson, Act.Libn.

MARINELAND, INC. - RESEARCH LABORATORY
Route 1, Box 122
Phone: (904) 829-5607
St. Augustine, FL 32084
Robert L. Jenkins, Cur.

ST. AUGUSTINE HISTORICAL SOCIETY - LIBRARY
271 Charlotte St.
Phone: (904) 829-5514
St. Augustine, FL 32084
Jacqueline K. Bearden, Lib.Dir.

SOCIETY OF PHILATICIANS - LIBRARY
154 Laguna Ct.
St. Augustine, FL 32084
Ruth A. Northup, Libn.

BAYFRONT MEDICAL CENTER, INC. - HEALTH SCIENCES LIBRARY
701 6th St. S.
Phone: (813) 823-1234
St. Petersburg, FL 33701
Polly Jean Duffey, Health Sci.Libn.

E-SYSTEMS, INC. - ECI DIVISION - TECHNICAL INFORMATION CENTER
1501 72nd St., N.
Box 12248
St. Petersburg, FL 33733
Susan Weiss, Supv.

FLORIDA POWER CORPORATION - CORPORATE LIBRARY
Box 14042
Phone: (813) 866-5458
St. Petersburg, FL 33733
Carol Prevaux, Supv.

FLORIDA STATE DEPT. OF NATURAL RESOURCES - MARINE RESEARCH
LABORATORY - LIBRARY
100 Eighth Ave., S.E.
Phone: (813) 896-8626
St. Petersburg, FL 33701
Mary G. Krost, Libn.

GREENE, MANN, ROWE, STANTON, MASTRY & BURTON - LIBRARY
1030 First Federal Bldg.
Phone: (813) 896-7171
St. Petersburg, FL 33701
Cindy Schartner, Libn.

JIM WALTER RESEARCH CORPORATION - LIBRARY
10301 9th St., N.
Phone: (813) 576-4171
St. Petersburg, FL 33702
Jane Mueller, Chf.Libn.

MUSEUM OF FINE ARTS - ART REFERENCE LIBRARY
255 Beach Dr., N.
Phone: (813) 896-2667
St. Petersburg, FL 33701
Muriel S. Kirk, Coord. for Lib.

PASADENA PRESBYTERIAN CHURCH - LIBRARY
100 Pasadena Ave., N.   Phone: (813) 345-0148
St. Petersburg, FL 33710   Esther G. Bierbaum, Libn.

PINELLAS COUNTY JUVENILE WELFARE BOARD - MAILANDE W. HOLLAND
    LIBRARY
4140 49th St., N.   Phone: (813) 521-1853
St. Petersburg, FL 33709   Molly Gill, Libn.

PINELLAS COUNTY LAW LIBRARY - ST. PETERSBURG BRANCH
Judicial Bldg., Rm. 500
545 1st Ave., N.   Phone: (813) 893-5875
St. Petersburg, FL 33701   Martha F. Otting, Libn.

PINELLAS COUNTY SCHOOL BOARD - MIRROR LAKE/TOMLINSON
    EDUCATION CENTER - LIBRARY/MEDIA CENTER
709 Mirror Lake Dr.   Phone: (813) 821-4593
St. Petersburg, FL 33701   Helen G. Campbell, Media Spec.

ST. ANTHONY'S HOSPITAL, INC. - MEDICAL LIBRARY
601 12th St., N.   Phone: (813) 823-5111
St. Petersburg, FL 33705   Linda Jo Rowe, Libn.

ST. PETERSBURG HISTORICAL SOCIETY - LIBRARY AND ARCHIVES
335 Second Ave., N.E.   Phone: (813) 894-1052
St. Petersburg, FL 33701   Everett L. Lehnert, Pres.

ST. PETERSBURG - MUNICIPAL REFERENCE LIBRARY *
City Hall, Box 2842   Phone: (813) 893-7547
St. Petersburg, FL 33731   Toni Farrell, Law Libn.

ST. PETERSBURG TIMES AND EVENING INDEPENDENT - LIBRARY
490 First Ave., S.
Box 1121   Phone: (813) 893-8111
St. Petersburg, FL 33731   James S. Scofield, Chf.Libn.

SCIENCE CENTER OF PINELLAS - LIBRARY
7701 22nd Ave., N.   Phone: (813) 384-0027
St. Petersburg, FL 33710   Patricia Foran, Libn.

STETSON UNIVERSITY - COLLEGE OF LAW - CHARLES A. DANA LAW
    LIBRARY
1401 - 61st St., S.   Phone: (813) 345-1335
St. Petersburg, FL 33707   J. Lamar Woodard, Libn./Professor of Law

TAMPA BAY REGIONAL PLANNING COUNCIL - RESEARCH & INFORMATION
    LIBRARY
9455 Koger Blvd.   Phone: (813) 577-5151
St. Petersburg, FL 33702   Ann Harter, Libn.

EMR TELEMETRY-SANGAMO WESTON - TECHNICAL INFORMATION
    CENTER *
Box 3041   Phone: (813) 371-0811
Sarasota, FL 33578   Alice Armstrong, Libn.

MEMORIAL HOSPITAL - MEDICAL LIBRARY
1901 Arlington St.
Sarasota, FL 33579   Doris Marose, Dir., Med.Lib.

MOTE MARINE LABORATORY - DAVIS LIBRARY
1600 City Island Pk.   Phone: (813) 388-4441
Sarasota, FL 33577   Sarah L. Hartwell, Libn.

RINGLING (John and Mable) MUSEUM OF ART - ART RESEARCH LIBRARY
Box 1838   Phone: (813) 355-5101
Sarasota, FL 33578   Valentine L. Schmidt, Libn.

RINGLING SCHOOL OF ART AND DESIGN - LIBRARY
1191 27th St.   Phone: (813) 355-5259
Sarasota, FL 33580   Elsie H. Straight, Libn.

FLORIDA A&M UNIVERSITY - ARCH/TECH LIBRARY
B.B. Tech Center A-301, Box 164   Phone: (904) 599-3050
Tallahassee, FL 32307   Margaret F. Wilson, Asst.Univ.Libn.

FLORIDA A&M UNIVERSITY - SCHOOL OF PHARMACY LIBRARY
Box 78-A   Phone: (904) 599-3301
Tallahassee, FL 32307   Ida G. Adams, Interim Dir., LRC

FLORIDA STATE BOARD OF REGENTS - LIBRARY
107 W. Gaines St.   Phone: (904) 488-6826
Tallahassee, FL 32304   Carol Wade, Libn.

FLORIDA STATE DEPT. OF COMMERCE - RESEARCH LIBRARY
Collins Bldg., Rm. 401   Phone: (904) 487-2971
Tallahassee, FL 32301   Laurie Wischmeyer, Libn.

FLORIDA STATE DEPT. OF ENVIRONMENTAL REGULATION - LIBRARY
2600 Blair Stone Rd.   Phone: (904) 488-0870
Tallahassee, FL 32301   Kathleen Everall, Dir.

FLORIDA STATE DEPT. OF HEALTH & REHABILITATIVE SERVICES -
    RESOURCE CENTER
1317 Winewood Blvd., Bldg. 2, Rm. 118   Phone: (904) 487-2312
Tallahassee, FL 32301   Karen Ungurait, Rsrcs.Ctr.Coord.

FLORIDA STATE DEPT. OF LEGAL AFFAIRS - ATTORNEY GENERAL'S
    LIBRARY
Capitol Bldg.   Phone: (904) 488-6040
Tallahassee, FL 32301   Ann C. Kaklamanos, Libn.

FLORIDA STATE DEPT. OF NATURAL RESOURCES - BUREAU OF GEOLOGY
    LIBRARY
903 W. Tennessee St.   Phone: (904) 488-5139
Tallahassee, FL 32304   Mary Ann Cleveland, Libn. I

FLORIDA STATE DEPT. OF NATURAL RESOURCES - DIV. OF STATE LANDS -
    BUREAU OF STATE LAND MANAGEMENT - TITLE SECTION
3900 Commonwealth Blvd.   Phone: (904) 488-2290
Tallahassee, FL 32303   F.R. Williams, Adm. Land Records

FLORIDA STATE DEPT. OF STATE TREASURER - DIVISION OF INSURANCE -
    LEGAL BUREAU LIBRARY *
Rm. 428-A Larson Bldg.
200 E. Gaines St.   Phone: (904) 488-3243
Tallahassee, FL 32304   Alphia F. Stephens

FLORIDA STATE DEPT. OF TRANSPORTATION - CENTRAL REFERENCE
    LIBRARY
Burns Bldg.   Phone: (904) 488-8572
Tallahassee, FL 32301   Robert Morse, Libn.

FLORIDA STATE DIVISION OF ARCHIVES, HISTORY & RECORDS
    MANAGEMENT - FLORIDA STATE ARCHIVES
R.A. Gray Bldg.
500 S. Bronough   Phone: (904) 487-2073
Tallahassee, FL 32301   Ed Tribble, Archv.Supv.

FLORIDA STATE LEGISLATURE - DIVISION OF LEGISLATIVE LIBRARY
    SERVICES
701, The Capitol   Phone: (904) 488-2812
Tallahassee, FL 32304   B. Gene Baker, Dir.

FLORIDA STATE SUPREME COURT LIBRARY
Supreme Court Bldg.   Phone: (904) 488-8919
Tallahassee, FL 32304   Brian S. Polley, Libn.

FLORIDA STATE UNIVERSITY - CTR. FOR STUDIES IN VOCATIONAL EDUC.
    - FLORIDA EDUCATORS INFO. SERV.
Box 2617   Phone: (904) 644-6454
Tallahassee, FL 32304   Margaret Winkler, Coord.

FLORIDA STATE UNIVERSITY - FLORIDA PHOTOGRAPHIC ARCHIVES
Robert Manning Strozier Library, Rm. 66   Phone: (904) 644-1222
Tallahassee, FL 32306   Joan L. Morris, Hd., Photo Archives

FLORIDA STATE UNIVERSITY - INSTRUCTIONAL SUPPORT CENTER - FILM
    LIBRARY
                    Phone: (904) 644-2820
Tallahassee, FL 32306   Dr. John W. McLanahan, Dir.

FLORIDA STATE UNIVERSITY - LAW LIBRARY
                    Phone: (904) 644-1004
Tallahassee, FL 32306   Edwin M. Schroeder, Law Libn.

FLORIDA STATE UNIVERSITY - LIBRARY SCIENCE LIBRARY
Robert Manning Strozier Library   Phone: (904) 644-1803
Tallahassee, FL 32306   Adeline W. Wilkes, Libn.

GEOGRAPHIC

FLORIDA STATE UNIVERSITY - SPECIAL COLLECTIONS
Robert Manning Strozier Library   Phone: (904) 644-3271
Tallahassee, FL 32306   Opal M. Free, Hd.

FLORIDA STATE UNIVERSITY - WARREN D. ALLEN MUSIC LIBRARY
                                                   Phone: (904) 644-5028
Tallahassee, FL 32306   Dale L. Hudson, Music Libn.

METAL TREATING INSTITUTE - LIBRARY
1300 Executive Ctr. Dr., Suite 115
Tallahassee, FL 32301

STATE LIBRARY OF FLORIDA
R.A. Gray Bldg.   Phone: (904) 487-2651
Tallahassee, FL 32304   Barratt Wilkins, State Libn.

TALL TIMBERS RESEARCH STATION - LIBRARY
Rte. 1, Box 160   Phone: (904) 893-4153
Tallahassee, FL 32312   Andrea V. Gabriel, Libn.

CARLTON, FIELDS, WARD, EMMANUEL, SMITH & CUTLER, P.A. - LIBRARY
610 N. Florida Ave., 20th Fl.
Exchange Bldg.   Phone: (813) 223-5366
Tampa, FL 33602   Donald G. Ziegenfuss, Libn.

CHURCH OF JESUS CHRIST OF LATTER-DAY SAINTS - TAMPA BRANCH GENEALOGICAL LIBRARY
4106 E. Fletcher Ave.   Phone: (813) 971-2869
Tampa, FL 33617   Barbara M. Dalby, Libn.

FLORIDA HISTORICAL SOCIETY - LIBRARY
Univ. of South Florida Library   Phone: (813) 974-2732
Tampa, FL 33620   Paul Eugen Camp, Exec.Sec.

HILLSBOROUGH COUNTY HISTORICAL COMMISSION - LIBRARY
County Court House   Phone: (813) 272-5919
Tampa, FL 33602   Anthony P. Pizzo, Chm.

HILLSBOROUGH COUNTY LAW LIBRARY
County Court House
Tampa, FL 33602   William M. Bailey, Libn.

LUTHERAN CHURCH IN AMERICA - FLORIDA SYNOD - MULTI-MEDIA LIBRARY
3838 W. Cypress St.   Phone: (813) 876-7660
Tampa, FL 33607   Grace Little, Libn.

TAMPA GENERAL HOSPITAL - MEDICAL LIBRARY
Davis Islands   Phone: (813) 251-7328
Tampa, FL 33606   Marianne Hough, Dir., Med.Lib.

TAMPA TRIBUNE & TAMPA TIMES - LIBRARY
202 S. Parker St.   Phone: (813) 272-7665
Tampa, FL 33601   Louise N. LeGette, Chf.Libn.

UNIVERSITY OF SOUTH FLORIDA - MEDICAL CENTER LIBRARY
12901 N. 30th St.
Box 31   Phone: (813) 974-2399
Tampa, FL 33612   Fred D. Bryant, Dir.

WESTINGHOUSE ELECTRIC CORPORATION - TAMPA DIVISION - ENGINEERING LIBRARY
6001 S. Westshore Blvd.
Box 19218   Phone: (813) 837-7221
Tampa, FL 33686   Patricia A. Hinkle, Libn.

ANCLOTE PSYCHIATRIC CENTER - MEDICAL LIBRARY †
Box 1224   Phone: (813) 937-4211
Tarpon Springs, FL 33589   Carol Lynn, Med.Libn.

LAKE COUNTY LAW LIBRARY
315 W. Main St.
Lake County Courthouse   Phone: (904) 343-9730
Tavares, FL 32278   Pamela L. Woodworth, Libn.

GRAPHIC COMMUNICATIONS WORLD/TECHNICAL INFORMATION, INC. - LIBRARY
Box 3489   Phone: (305) 746-0998
Tequesta, FL 33458   A.E. Gardner, Libn.

HISTORICAL SOCIETY OF OKALOOSA & WALTON COUNTIES, INC. - MUSEUM LIBRARY
115 Westview Ave.   Phone: (904) 678-2615
Valparaiso, FL 32580   Christian LaRoche, Musm.Dir.

FLORIDA STATE MEDICAL ENTOMOLOGY LABORATORY LIBRARY
IFAS, University of Florida
Box 520   Phone: (305) 562-5435
Vero Beach, FL 32960   Carolee Zimmerman, Sec. II-Libn.

INDIAN RIVER MEMORIAL HOSPITAL - PROFESSIONAL LIBRARY
1000 36th St.   Phone: (305) 567-4311
Vero Beach, FL 32960   Elizabeth W. Knowles, Chm., Lib.Comm.

AMERICAN PSYCHOTHERAPY ASSOCIATION - LIBRARY
Box 2436
West Palm Beach, FL 33402   Sandra Simonds, Director

FLORIDA STATE - SOUTH FLORIDA WATER MANAGEMENT DISTRICT - REFERENCE CENTER
Box V   Phone: (305) 686-8800
West Palm Beach, FL 33402   Cynthia H. Plockelman, Ref.Libn.

GEE & JENSON ENGINEERS, ARCHITECTS, PLANNERS, INC. - LIBRARY
2019 Okeechobee Blvd.   Phone: (305) 683-3301
West Palm Beach, FL 33409   Helen M. Foster, Hd.Libn.

GOOD SAMARITAN HOSPITAL - RICHARD S. BEINECKE MEDICAL LIBRARY
Box 3166   Phone: (305) 655-5511
West Palm Beach, FL 33402   Elizabeth H. Day, Med.Ref.Libn.

NORTON GALLERY AND SCHOOL OF ART - LIBRARY
1451 S. Olive Ave.   Phone: (305) 832-5194
West Palm Beach, FL 33401   Lourdes Macy, Libn.

PALM BEACH COUNTY - LAW LIBRARY
339 Courthouse   Phone: (305) 837-2928
West Palm Beach, FL 33401   Marguerite H. Johnson, Law Libn.

ST. MARY'S HOSPITAL - HEALTH SCIENCES LIBRARY
901 45th St.   Phone: (305) 844-6300
West Palm Beach, FL 33407   Jennie Glock, Libn.

TEMPLE ISRAEL - LIBRARY
1901 N. Flagler Dr.   Phone: (305) 833-8421
West Palm Beach, FL 33407   Elsie Leviton, Chm., Lib.Comm.

TREVES (Ralph) WORKSHOP FEATURES - WORKSHOP PHOTOS
311 Lake Evelyn Dr.   Phone: (305) 683-5167
West Palm Beach, FL 33411   Ralph Treves, Owner

GESSLER CLINIC - MEDICAL LIBRARY
635 First St., North
Winter Haven, FL 33880

WINTER HAVEN HOSPITAL - J.G. CONVERSE MEMORIAL LIBRARY
200 Ave F., N.E.   Phone: (813) 293-1121
Winter Haven, FL 33880   Juanelle V. Hurt, Act.Libn.

ROLLINS COLLEGE - BEAL-MALTBIE SHELL MUSEUM - LIBRARY
Box 1037
Winter Park, FL 32789   Nancy Lea Burton, Cur.

WINTER PARK MEMORIAL HOSPITAL - MEDICAL STAFF LIBRARY
200 N. Lakemont Ave.   Phone: (305) 646-7049
Winter Park, FL 32792   Alice E. Hansen, Med.Libn.

GEORGIA

U.S. MARINE CORPS - LOGISTICS BASE, ALBANY, GA - TECHNICAL LIBRARY
                                                   Phone: (912) 439-6470
Albany, GA 31704   William J. Tynes, Libn.

ENVIRONMENTAL PROTECTION AGENCY - ENVIRONMENTAL RESEARCH LABORATORY, ATHENS - LIBRARY
College Station Rd.   Phone: (404) 546-3324
Athens, GA 30613   Charlotte C. Folk, Libn.

U.S.D.A. - AGRICULTURAL RESEARCH SERVICE - SOUTHERN REGION -
   RICHARD B. RUSSELL AGRICULTURAL RESEARCH CTR. LIB.
College Station Rd., Box 5677   Phone: (404) 546-3314
Athens, GA 30604   Benna Brodsky Thompson, Libn.

UNIVERSITY OF GEORGIA - DEPARTMENT OF RECORDS MANAGEMENT &
   UNIVERSITY ARCHIVES
4th Fl., Old Section,
Ilah Dunlap Little Memorial Library   Phone: (404) 542-8151
Athens, GA 30602   Dr. John Carver Edwards, Rec.Off./Archv.

UNIVERSITY OF GEORGIA - GOVERNMENT REFERENCE/DOCUMENTS
   SECTION
          Phone: (404) 542-8949
Athens, GA 30602   Sandra McAninch, Docs.Libn.

UNIVERSITY OF GEORGIA - LAW LIBRARY
          Phone: (404) 542-1923
Athens, GA 30602   Erwin C. Surrency, Law Libn.

UNIVERSITY OF GEORGIA - MANUSCRIPTS COLLECTION
University of Georgia Libraries   Phone: (404) 542-2972
Athens, GA 30602   Larry Gulley, Mss. Libn.

UNIVERSITY OF GEORGIA - RARE BOOKS DEPARTMENT
          Phone: (404) 542-2972
Athens, GA 30602   Robert M. Willingham, Act.Asst.Dir.

UNIVERSITY OF GEORGIA - RICHARD B. RUSSELL MEMORIAL LIBRARY
University of Georgia Libraries   Phone: (404) 542-5788
Athens, GA 30602   Sheryl Vogt, Hd.

UNIVERSITY OF GEORGIA - SCIENCE LIBRARY
Athens, GA 30602   Virginia Benjamin, Pub.Serv.Libn.

UNIVERSITY OF GEORGIA - SCIENCE LIBRARY - MAP COLLECTION
University of Georgia Libraries   Phone: (404) 542-4535
Athens, GA 30602   John Sutherland, Map Cur.

ALSTON, MILLER AND GAINES - LAW LIBRARY
1200 C & S National Bank Bldg.
35 Broad St.   Phone: (404) 586-1500
Atlanta, GA 30335   Anne H. Butler, Libn.

ATLANTA BUREAU OF PLANNING - LIBRARY
10 Pryor St., S.W., Suite 200   Phone: (404) 658-6400
Atlanta, GA 30303   John Wright Heath, Dir./Lib. & Info.Serv.

ATLANTA COLLEGE OF ART - LIBRARY
1280 Peachtree St.   Phone: (404) 892-3600
Atlanta, GA 30309   Jo Anne Paschall, Hd.Libn.

ATLANTA HISTORICAL SOCIETY - ARCHIVES
Box 12423   Phone: (404) 261-1837
Atlanta, GA 30355   John Kerwood, Dir.

ATLANTA LAW SCHOOL - LIBRARY
56 Tenth St., N.E.   Phone: (404) 872-0990
Atlanta, GA 30309   Michael E. Seigler, Law Libn.

ATLANTA NEWSPAPERS - REFERENCE LIBRARY
72 Marietta St., N.W.   Phone: (404) 526-5420
Atlanta, GA 30303   Diane C. Hunter, Dir.Lib.Serv.

ATLANTA PUBLIC LIBRARY - FOUNDATION COLLECTION
1 Margaret Mitchell Sq.   Phone: (404) 688-4636
Atlanta, GA 30303   Ann Bush, Cur.

ATLANTA PUBLIC LIBRARY - IVAN ALLEN, JR. DEPARTMENT OF SCIENCE,
   INDUSTRY AND GOVERNMENT
1 Margaret Mitchell Sq.   Phone: (404) 688-4636
Atlanta, GA 30303   Claudia Schmitt, Hd.

ATLANTA PUBLIC LIBRARY - SPECIAL COLLECTIONS DEPARTMENT
1 Margaret Mitchell Sq.   Phone: (404) 688-4636
Atlanta, GA 30303   Janice White Sikes, Cur.

ATLANTA UNIVERSITY - SCHOOL OF LIBRARY & INFORMATION STUDIES -
   LIBRARY
223 Chestnut St., S.W.   Phone: (404) 681-0251
Atlanta, GA 30314   Chih Wang, Libn.

ATLANTA UNIVERSITY - TREVOR ARNETT LIBRARY - SPECIAL
   COLLECTIONS †
273 Chestnut St., S.W.   Phone: (404) 681-0251
Atlanta, GA 30314   Gloria Mims, Hd., Spec.Coll.

CARVER BIBLE COLLEGE - LIBRARY
437 Nelson St., S.W.
Atlanta, GA 30302

CLARK COLLEGE - SOUTHERN CENTER FOR STUDIES IN PUBLIC POLICY -
   LIBRARY
240 Chestnut St., S.W.   Phone: (404) 522-8770
Atlanta, GA 30314   Mrs. Ollye G. Davis, Res.Libn.

COCA-COLA COMPANY - ARCHIVES & BUSINESS INFORMATION SERVICES
NAT-19, Drawer 1734   Phone: (404) 898-2124
Atlanta, GA 30301   Philip F. Mooney, Mgr.

COCA-COLA COMPANY - MARKETING INFORMATION CENTER
310 North Ave.   Phone: (404) 898-3314
Atlanta, GA 30301   Judy A. Cassell, Libn.

COCA-COLA COMPANY - TECHNICAL INFORMATION SERVICES
Box 1734   Phone: (404) 897-2008
Atlanta, GA 30301   Bernard Prudhomme, Mgr.

CRAWFORD W. LONG MEMORIAL HOSPITAL - LIBRARY †
35 Linden Ave., N.E.   Phone: (404) 892-4411
Atlanta, GA 30308   Mrs. Girija Vijay, Dir., Med.Lib.

DAMES & MOORE - LIBRARY
445 East Paces Ferry Rd., N.E., Suite 200   Phone: (404) 262-2915
Atlanta, GA 30305   Becky Kear, Librarian

DEKALB COUNTY BOARD OF EDUCATION - FERNBANK SCIENCE CENTER -
   LIBRARY
156 Heaton Park Dr., N.E.   Phone: (404) 378-4311
Atlanta, GA 30307   Mary Larsen, Libn.

EMORY UNIVERSITY - CHEMISTRY LIBRARY
440 Chemistry Bldg.   Phone: (404) 329-6618
Atlanta, GA 30322   Pamela E. Pickens, Chem.Libn.

EMORY UNIVERSITY - DIVISION OF LIBRARY AND INFORMATION
   MANAGEMENT LIBRARY
420 Candler Library Bldg.   Phone: (404) 329-6846
Atlanta, GA 30322   June L. Engle, Libn.

EMORY UNIVERSITY - DOCUMENTS DEPARTMENT
Woodruff Library   Phone: (404) 329-6880
Atlanta, GA 30322   Elizabeth A. McBride, Doc.Libn.

EMORY UNIVERSITY - PITTS THEOLOGY LIBRARY
Theology Bldg.   Phone: (404) 329-4166
Atlanta, GA 30322   Channing R. Jeschke, Libn.

EMORY UNIVERSITY - SCHOOL OF DENTISTRY - SHEPPARD W. FOSTER
   LIBRARY
1462 Clifton Rd., N.E.   Phone: (404) 329-6695
Atlanta, GA 30322   Lucy L. Duke, Libn.

EMORY UNIVERSITY - SCHOOL OF LAW LIBRARY †
Gambrell Hall   Phone: (404) 329-6823
Atlanta, GA 30322   A.C. Hinze, Law Libn.

EMORY UNIVERSITY - SCHOOL OF MEDICINE - A.W. CALHOUN MEDICAL
   LIBRARY
          Phone: (404) 329-5820
Atlanta, GA 30322   Miriam H. Libbey, Libn.

EMORY UNIVERSITY - SCIENCE LIBRARY
Woodruff Library   Phone: (404) 329-6885
Atlanta, GA 30322   Irene K. Mallison, Hd.Sci.Libn.

EMORY UNIVERSITY - SPECIAL COLLECTIONS DEPARTMENT
Woodruff Library Phone: (404) 329-6887
Atlanta, GA 30322 David E. Estes, Hd.

EMORY UNIVERSITY - YERKES REGIONAL PRIMATE CENTER - LIBRARY
Phone: (404) 329-7764
Atlanta, GA 30322 Nellie Johns, Lib.Coord.

ENVIRONMENTAL PROTECTION AGENCY - REGION IV LIBRARY
345 Courtland St. Phone: (404) 881-4216
Atlanta, GA 30308 Carolyn W. Mitchell, Hd.Libn.

EQUIFAX, INC. - CORPORATE LIBRARY
Box 4081 Phone: (404) 885-8320
Atlanta, GA 30302 Michael McDavid, Corp.Libn.

FEDERAL RESERVE BANK OF ATLANTA - RESEARCH LIBRARY
Box 1731 Phone: (404) 586-8829
Atlanta, GA 30301 Sara June McDavid, Libn.

FULTON COUNTY LAW LIBRARY
709 Courthouse
136 Pryor St., S.W. Phone: (404) 572-2330
Atlanta, GA 30303 Margaret D. Martin, Law Libn.

GENEALOGICAL LIBRARY FOR THE BLIND & PHYSICALLY HANDICAPPED,
INC. - GENEALOGICAL CENTER LIBRARY
15 Dunwoody Park, Suite 130 Phone: (404) 393-9777
Atlanta, GA 30338 Diane Dieterle, Dir.

GEORGIA BAPTIST MEDICAL CENTER - MEDICAL LIBRARY
300 Boulevard, N.E. Phone: (404) 659-4211
Atlanta, GA 30312 Fay E. Boyer, Med.Libn.

GEORGIA CONSERVANCY, INC. - LIBRARY
3110 Maple Dr., Suite 407 Phone: (404) 262-1967
Atlanta, GA 30305 Barbara M. Smith, Prog.Dir.

GEORGIA INSTITUTE OF TECHNOLOGY - PRICE GILBERT MEMORIAL
LIBRARY
Campus Dr. Phone: (404) 894-4510
Atlanta, GA 30332 Dr. Edward Graham Roberts, Dir.

GEORGIA INSTITUTE OF TECHNOLOGY - PRICE GILBERT MEMORIAL
LIBRARY - ARCHITECTURE LIBRARY
Campus Dr. Phone: (404) 894-4877
Atlanta, GA 30332 Frances Drew, Arch.Libn.

GEORGIA MUNICIPAL ASSOCIATION - LIBRARY *
Ten Pryor St., Suite 220 Phone: (404) 688-0472
Atlanta, GA 30303 W.E. George, Res.Dir.

GEORGIA-PACIFIC CORPORATION - TECHNICAL INFORMATION CENTER
Box 105041 Phone: (404) 491-6559
Atlanta, GA 30348 Deanna Morrow Hall, Mgr.Tech.Info.Rsrcs.

GEORGIA POWER COMPANY - LIBRARY
333 Piedmont Ave.
Box 4545 Phone: (404) 526-6857
Atlanta, GA 30302 Beth Ansley, Lib.Serv.Supv.

GEORGIA STATE DEPARTMENT OF ARCHIVES AND HISTORY - CENTRAL
RESEARCH LIBRARY
330 Capitol Ave., S.E. Phone: (404) 656-2350
Atlanta, GA 30334 Carroll Hart, State Archv. & Dir.

GEORGIA STATE DEPARTMENT OF EDUCATION - DIVISION OF PUBLIC
LIBRARY SERVICES
156 Trinity Ave., S.W. Phone: (404) 656-2461
Atlanta, GA 30303 Joe. B. Forsee, Dir.

GEORGIA STATE DEPARTMENT OF EDUCATION - LIBRARY FOR THE BLIND
& PHYSICALLY HANDICAPPED
1050 Murphy Ave., S.W. Phone: (404) 656-2465
Atlanta, GA 30310 Jim DeJarnatt, Dir.

GEORGIA STATE DEPARTMENT OF HUMAN RESOURCES - GEORGIA MENTAL
HEALTH INSTITUTE - ADDISON M. DUVAL LIBRARY
1256 Briarcliff Rd., N.E. Phone: (404) 894-5663
Atlanta, GA 30306 Brenda Scott, Dir. of Libs.

GEORGIA STATE DEPARTMENT OF HUMAN RESOURCES - LIBRARY
534-H, 47 Trinity Ave., S.W. Phone: (404) 656-4969
Atlanta, GA 30334 Miriam Boland, Lib.Dir.

GEORGIA STATE DEPARTMENT OF OFFENDER REHABILITATION -
REFERENCE/RESOURCE CENTER
800 Peachtree St., N.E. Phone: (404) 894-5383
Atlanta, GA 30365 Karen Rawls, Libn.

GEORGIA STATE DEPARTMENT OF TRANSPORTATION - RESEARCH
LIBRARY
15 Kennedy Dr. Phone: (404) 363-7567
Atlanta, GA 30050 Alfredia A. Scott, Libn.

GEORGIA STATE LIBRARY
301 Judicial Bldg.
40 Capitol Sq., S.W. Phone: (404) 656-3468
Atlanta, GA 30334 Carroll T. Parker, State Libn.

GEORGIA STATE OFFICE OF PLANNING AND BUDGET - STATE DATA
CENTER
270 Washington St., S.W., Rm. 608 Phone: (404) 656-2191
Atlanta, GA 30334 Thomas M. Wagner, Principal Planner

GEORGIA STATE SUPREME COURT LIBRARY †
Judicial Bldg., 5th Fl.
40 Capitol Sq., S.W. Phone: (404) 656-3439
Atlanta, GA 30334 Thomas R. Moran, Libn.

GEORGIA STATE SURVEYOR GENERAL DEPARTMENT - ARCHIVES
330 Capitol Ave.
Archives & Records Bldg. Phone: (404) 656-2367
Atlanta, GA 30334 Mr. Marion R. Hemperley, Dp. Surveyor Gen.

GEORGIA STATE UNIVERSITY - SMALL BUSINESS DEVELOPMENT CENTER
Box 869, University Plaza Phone: (404) 658-3550
Atlanta, GA 30303 Lee Quarterman, Assoc.Dir.

GEORGIA STATE UNIVERSITY - SOUTHERN LABOR ARCHIVES
Phone: (404) 658-2476
Atlanta, GA 30303 Leslie S. Hough, Archv.

GOETHE INSTITUTE ATLANTA - GERMAN CULTURAL CENTER - LIBRARY
400 Colony Sq. Phone: (404) 892-2226
Atlanta, GA 30361 Margit Rostock, Libn.

INTERDENOMINATIONAL THEOLOGICAL CENTER - LIBRARY *
671 Beckwith St., S.W. Phone: (404) 522-1744
Atlanta, GA 30314 Wilson N. Flemister, Libn.

JONES, BIRD & HOWELL, ATTORNEYS AT LAW - LIBRARY
75 Poplar St., N.W.
Haas-Howell Bldg. Phone: (404) 522-2508
Atlanta, GA 30335 Jane M. Gudelsky, Libn.

KILPATRICK & CODY - LIBRARY
3100 Equitable Bldg.
100 Peachtree St. Phone: (404) 572-6397
Atlanta, GA 30303 Kay Moller Todd, Libn.

KING (Martin Luther, Jr.) CENTER FOR SOCIAL CHANGE - KING LIBRARY AND
ARCHIVES
503 Auburn Ave. Phone: (404) 524-1956
Atlanta, GA 30312 D. Louise Cook, Archv.

KING & SPALDING - LAW LIBRARY †
2500 Trust Company Tower Phone: (404) 572-4808
Atlanta, GA 30303 Janice B. Welshhans, Libn.

LIFE OFFICE MANAGEMENT ASSOCIATION - INFORMATION CENTER
100 Colony Sq. Phone: (404) 892-7272
Atlanta, GA 30361 Patricia A. Toups, Libn.

MAC FARLANE & COMPANY, INC. - FRY CONSULTANTS INCORPORATED -
MANAGEMENT CENTRE
One Park Place, Suite 450 Phone: (404) 352-2293
Atlanta, GA 30318 Jane W. Nicely, Mgr.

MERCER UNIVERSITY - SOUTHERN COLLEGE OF PHARMACY - H. CUSTER
   NAYLOR LIBRARY
345 Boulevard, N.E.   Phone: (404) 688-6291
Atlanta, GA 30312   Elizabeth Christian Jackson, Libn.

METROPOLITAN ATLANTA RAPID TRANSIT AUTHORITY - LIBRARY
2200 Peachtree Summit
401 W. Peachtree St., N.E.
Atlanta, GA 30308   Phone: (404) 586-5000

NORTHSIDE HOSPITAL - WOODRUFF HEALTH SCIENCE LIBRARY
1000 Johnson Ferry Rd., N.E.   Phone: (404) 256-8744
Atlanta, GA 30342   Sharon Cann, Libn.

NUCLEAR ASSURANCE CORPORATION - INFORMATION CENTER
24 Executive Pk., W.   Phone: (404) 325-4200
Atlanta, GA 30329   Nancy G. Reinhold, Mgr.Info.Ctr.

PIEDMONT HOSPITAL - SAULS MEMORIAL LIBRARY
1968 Peachtree Rd., N.W.   Phone: (404) 355-7611
Atlanta, GA 30309   Connee Chandler Wethey, Med.Libn.

PORTMAN (John) & ASSOCIATES - LIBRARY
225 Peachtree St.   Phone: (404) 522-8811
Atlanta, GA 30303   Gayla Wingate, Libn./P.R.

POWELL, GOLDSTEIN, FRAZER & MURPHY - LIBRARY †
1100 C & S National Bank Bldg.   Phone: (404) 572-6600
Atlanta, GA 30303   Margarette M. Dye, Libn.

ST. JOSEPH'S HOSPITAL - RUSSELL BELLMAN LIBRARY *
5665 Peachtree Dunwoody Rd., N.E.   Phone: (404) 256-7040
Atlanta, GA 30342   Gail Waverchak, Med.Libn.

SCIENTIFIC-ATLANTA, INC. - LIBRARY
3845 Pleasantdale Rd.   Phone: (404) 449-2000
Atlanta, GA 30340   Corrie T. Lineback, Libn.

SMITH, CURRIE & HANCOCK - LAW LIBRARY †
233 Peachtree St., N.E.
2600 Peachtree Ctr., Harris Tower   Phone: (404) 521-3800
Atlanta, GA 30303   Elisa F. Kadish, Libn.

SOUTHERN BELL TELEPHONE AND TELEGRAPH COMPANY - LAW LIBRARY
1245 Hurt Bldg.   Phone: (404) 529-7937
Atlanta, GA 30303   Deborah D. Lawhon, Libn.

SOUTHERN REGIONAL COUNCIL, INC. - REFERENCE LIBRARY †
75 Marietta St., N.W.   Phone: (404) 522-8764
Atlanta, GA 30303   Stephen T. Suitts, Exec.Dir.

SOUTHERN REGIONAL EDUCATION BOARD - LIBRARY
130 Sixth St., N.W.   Phone: (404) 875-9211
Atlanta, GA 30313   Ann Hadley Carter, Res.Asst./Libn.

SUTHERLAND, ASBILL & BRENNAN - LIBRARY
3100 First National Bank Tower   Phone: (404) 658-8907
Atlanta, GA 30383   Linda Baker, Adm.Libn.

TECHNICAL ASSOCIATION OF THE PULP AND PAPER INDUSTRY - LIBRARY
One Dunwoody Pk.   Phone: (404) 394-6130
Atlanta, GA 30338   D.V. Lent, Tech.Info.Adm.

THORNDIKE, DORAN, PAINE AND LEWIS INC. - RESEARCH LIBRARY
233 Peachtree St., N.E., Suite 700   Phone: (404) 688-2782
Atlanta, GA 30303   Linda Swann Austin, Libn.

U.S. BUREAU OF THE CENSUS - REGIONAL DATA USER SERVICE - ATLANTA
   REGIONAL OFFICE - LIBRARY
1365 Peachtree St., N.E., Rm. 523   Phone: (404) 881-2274
Atlanta, GA 30309   Joseph T. Reilly, Data User Serv.Off.

U.S. CENTER FOR DISEASE CONTROL - BUREAU OF LABORATORIES -
   TECHNICAL INFORMATION SERVICES LIBRARY
1600 Clifton Rd. 30/35   Phone: (404) 452-4167
Atlanta, GA 30333   Christine Fralish, Lib.Techn.

U.S. CENTER FOR DISEASE CONTROL - CDC LIBRARY
1600 Clifton Rd., N.E.   Phone: (404) 329-3396
Atlanta, GA 30333   Mary Alice Mills, Dir.

U.S. DEPT. OF COMMERCE - INTERNATIONAL TRADE ADMINISTRATION -
   ATLANTA DISTRICT OFFICE LIBRARY
1365 Peachtree St., N.W., Suite 600   Phone: (404) 881-4873
Atlanta, GA 30309   Christine B. Brown, Trade Ref.Asst.

U.S. DEPT. OF HOUSING AND URBAN DEVELOPMENT - REGION IV - LIBRARY
Richard B. Russell Fed. Bldg., Rm. 722
75 Spring St., S.W.   Phone: (404) 221-3367
Atlanta, GA 30303   Mrs. Davide B. Williams, Regional Libn.

U.S. HERITAGE CONSERVATION AND RECREATION SERVICE -
   INFORMATION CLEARINGHOUSE †
75 Spring St., S.W., Suite 1176   Phone: (404) 221-3449
Atlanta, GA 30303   Linda Hall, Lib.Techn.

CHRONICLE-HERALD NEWS - LIBRARY
Box 936   Phone: (404) 724-0851
Augusta, GA 30903   Edward S. Mitchell, Jr., Libn.

GEORGIA REGIONAL HOSPITAL AT AUGUSTA - HOSPITAL LIBRARY
3405 Old Savannah Rd.
Box 5826   Phone: (404) 790-2399
Augusta, GA 30906   Barbara Avrett, Libn.

MEDICAL COLLEGE OF GEORGIA - LIBRARY
1120 15th St.   Phone: (404) 828-3441
Augusta, GA 30912   Thomas G. Basler, Dir. of Libs.

U.S. VETERANS ADMINISTRATION (GA-Augusta) - HOSPITAL LIBRARY *
                                             Phone: (404) 724-5116
Augusta, GA 30904   Dorothy K. Jones, Chf., Lib.Serv.

UNIVERSITY HOSPITAL - HEALTH SCIENCES LIBRARY
1350 Walton Way   Phone: (404) 722-9011
Augusta, GA 30910   Jane B. Wells, Libn.

SOUTHWIRE COMPANY - TECHNICAL LIBRARY
Fertilla St.   Phone: (404) 832-5080
Carrollton, GA 30119   Debbie Ballard, Tech.Libn.

WEST GEORGIA COLLEGE - SPECIAL COLLECTIONS DEPARTMENT †
                                             Phone: (404) 834-1370
Carrollton, GA 30117   Susan Smith, Asst.Libn.

COLUMBUS LEDGER-ENQUIRER - LIBRARY
17 W. 12th St.   Phone: (404) 324-5526
Columbus, GA 31902   Patricia F. Hardy, Libn.

COLUMBUS MUSEUM OF ARTS AND SCIENCES - CMAS RESEARCH LIBRARY
1251 Wynnton Rd.   Phone: (404) 323-3617
Columbus, GA 31906   William E. Scheele, Dir.

MEDICAL CENTER - SIMON SCHWOB MEDICAL LIBRARY
710 Center St.   Phone: (404) 324-4711
Columbus, GA 31902   Opal Bartlett, Libn.

WEST CENTRAL GEORGIA REGIONAL HOSPITAL - STAFF/PATIENT
   LIBRARY
3000 Schatulga Rd.
Box 6563   Phone: (404) 568-5236
Columbus, GA 31907   Linda A. Sears, Libn., Sr.

COLUMBIA THEOLOGICAL SEMINARY - JOHN BULOW CAMPBELL LIBRARY
701 Columbia Dr.   Phone: (404) 378-8821
Decatur, GA 30031   Dr. James A. Overbeck, Lib.Dir.

DEKALB GENERAL HOSPITAL - MEDICAL LIBRARY
2701 N. Decatur Rd.   Phone: (404) 292-4444
Decatur, GA 30033   Marilyn Osborne Gibbs, Med.Libn.

U.S. VETERANS ADMINISTRATION (GA-Atlanta) - HOSPITAL MEDICAL
   LIBRARY
1670 Clairmont Rd.   Phone: (404) 321-6111
Decatur, GA 30033   Eugenia H. Abbey, Chf.Libn.

GEOGRAPHIC

GEOGRAPHIC

U.S. VETERANS ADMINISTRATION (GA-Dublin) - CENTER LIBRARY
Phone: (912) 272-1210
Dublin, GA 31021   Mrs. Kodell M. Thomas, Chf., Lib.Serv.

U.S. FEDERAL AVIATION ADMINISTRATION - SOUTHERN REGION LIBRARY
3400 Norman Berry Dr.   Phone: (404) 763-7276
East Point, GA 30344   Doris P. Little, Libn.

U.S. NATL. ARCHIVES & RECORDS SERVICE - FEDERAL ARCHIVES AND
RECORDS CENTER, REGION 4
1557 St. Joseph Ave.   Phone: (404) 763-7474
East Point, GA 30344   Thomas G. Hudson, Dir.

UNIVERSITY OF GEORGIA - GEORGIA AGRICULTURAL EXPERIMENT
STATION LIBRARY
Phone: (404) 228-7238
Experiment, GA 30212   Carole L. Ledford, Libn.

U.S. ARMY HOSPITALS - MARTIN ARMY COMMUNITY HOSPITAL - MEDICAL
LIBRARY
Phone: (404) 544-1341
Ft. Benning, GA 31905   Elaine A. Tate, Med.Libn.

U.S. ARMY INFANTRY SCHOOL - LIBRARY
Infantry Hall, Bldg. 4   Phone: (404) 544-4053
Ft. Benning, GA 31905   Vivian S. Howard, Chf., Lrng.Rsrcs.

U.S. ARMY POST - FORT BENNING - RECREATION SERVICES LIBRARY
BRANCH
Bldg. 93   Phone: (404) 544-4911
Ft. Benning, GA 31905   Gwendolyn L. Redd, Supv.Libn.

U.S. ARMY HOSPITALS - D.D. EISENHOWER ARMY MEDICAL CENTER -
MEDICAL LIBRARY
Phone: (404) 791-6765
Ft. Gordon, GA 30905   Judy M. Krivanek, Med.Libn.

U.S. ARMY SIGNAL CENTER & FORT GORDON - CONRAD TECHNICAL
LIBRARY
Bldg. 29807   Phone: (404) 791-3922
Ft. Gordon, GA 30905   Margaret H. Novinger, Adm.Libn.

U.S. ARMY POST - FORT MC PHERSON - LIBRARY SYSTEM
Bldg. T-44   Phone: (404) 752-3218
Ft. McPherson, GA 30330   Lee W. Porter, Chf.Libn.

U.S. ARMY POST - FORT STEWART/HUNTER AAF LIBRARY SYSTEM
Box 3179   Phone: (912) 767-2260
Ft. Stewart, GA 31314   M. Malinda Johnson, Chf.Libn.

AMERICAN CAMELLIA SOCIETY - LIBRARY
Box 1217   Phone: (912) 967-2358
Fort Valley, GA 31030   Milton H. Brown, Exec.Sec.

FORT VALLEY STATE COLLEGE - HENRY ALEXANDER HUNT MEMORIAL
LEARNING RESOURCES CENTER
State College Dr.   Phone: (912) 825-6342
Fort Valley, GA 31030   Dorothy Haith, Libn.

NORTHEAST GEORGIA MEDICAL CENTER AND HALL SCHOOL OF NURSING/
BRENAU COLLEGE - LIBRARY
741 Spring St.   Phone: (404) 536-1114
Gainesville, GA 30505   Caroline Alday, Libn.

GRACEWOOD STATE SCHOOL AND HOSPITAL - LIBRARY
Phone: (404) 790-2183
Gracewood, GA 30812   Alice K. Garren, Libn.

CHEROKEE REGIONAL LIBRARY - GEORGIA HISTORY & GENEALOGICAL
ROOM *
305 S. Duke St.
Box 707   Phone: (404) 638-2992
LaFayette, GA 30728   William N. Kirchner, Dir.

CALLAWAY EDUCATIONAL ASSOCIATION - COLEMAN LIBRARY
Lincoln St.   Phone: (404) 882-0948
LaGrange, GA 30240   Mary Lou Dabbs, Hd.Libn.

BIBB COUNTY LAW LIBRARY
Bibb County Court House
New Annex, Rm. A500   Phone: (912) 745-6871
Macon, GA 31207

GEORGIA BAPTIST HISTORICAL SOCIETY - LIBRARY
Stetson Memorial Library   Phone: (912) 745-6811
Macon, GA 31207   Mary E. Overby, Spec.Coll.Asst.

GEORGIA STATE FORESTRY COMMISSION - LIBRARY †
Box 819   Phone: (912) 744-3231
Macon, GA 31202   Al Smith, Hd.

MACON TELEGRAPH AND NEWS - LIBRARY †
Broadway & Riverside Dr.   Phone: (912) 743-2621
Macon, GA 31208   Mamie Denson

MERCER UNIVERSITY - LAW SCHOOL - HALLIBURTON LAW LIBRARY
Phone: (912) 745-6811
Macon, GA 31201   Leah F. Chanin, Dir., Law Lib.

MERCER UNIVERSITY - MEDICAL SCHOOL LIBRARY
Phone: (912) 745-6811
Macon, GA 31207   Jocelyn Rankin, Dir., Med.Lib.

MIDDLE GEORGIA REGIONAL LIBRARY - WASHINGTON MEMORIAL
LIBRARY - GENEALOGICAL & HISTORICAL ROOM
1180 Washington Ave.   Phone: (912) 745-5813
Macon, GA 31201   Nancy C. Watson, Chf. of Genealogy

LOCKHEED-GEORGIA COMPANY - TECHNICAL INFORMATION
DEPARTMENT
86 S. Cobb Dr.   Phone: (404) 424-2928
Marietta, GA 30063   Charles K. Bauer, Mgr.

SOUTHERN TECHNICAL INSTITUTE - LIBRARY
Clay St.   Phone: (404) 424-7275
Marietta, GA 30060   John W. Pattillo, Dir.

U.S. NATL. PARK SERVICE - KENNESAW MOUNTAIN NATL. BATTLEFIELD
PARK - LIBRARY
Box 1167   Phone: (404) 427-4686
Marietta, GA 30061   Emmet A. Nichols, Chf. Interpreter

CENTRAL STATE HOSPITAL - MEDICAL LIBRARY
Phone: (912) 453-4153
Milledgeville, GA 31062   Aurelia S. Spence, Lib.Dir.

CENTRAL STATE HOSPITAL - MENTAL HEALTH LIBRARY
Phone: (912) 453-4371
Milledgeville, GA 31062   Kathy Ridley, Libn.

GEORGIA COLLEGE - INA DILLARD RUSSELL LIBRARY
231 W. Hancock   Phone: (912) 453-4047
Milledgeville, GA 31061   Janice C. Fennell, Lib.Dir.

GEORGIA COLLEGE - LEARNING RESOURCES CENTER
Phone: (912) 453-4714
Milledgeville, GA 31061

U.S. AIR FORCE BASE - MOODY BASE LIBRARY †
Phone: (912) 333-3539
Moody AFB, GA 31699   Madeleine A. Peyton, Libn.

AMERICAN INSTITUTE OF INDUSTRIAL ENGINEERS, INC. - LIBRARY
25 Technology Park/Atlanta   Phone: (404) 449-0460
Norcross, GA 30092   James H. Reeves, Mgr.Tech.Serv.

BELL TELEPHONE LABORATORIES, INC. & WESTERN ELECTRIC, INC. -
TECHNICAL LIBRARY
2000 Northeast Expy.   Phone: (404) 447-2803
Norcross, GA 30071   John T. Shaw, Lib. Group Supv.

CONTINENTAL TELEPHONE LABORATORIES - WALTER L. ROBERTS
TECHNICAL LIBRARY
270 Scientific Dr., Suite 10
Technology Park/Atlanta   Phone: (404) 448-2206
Norcross, GA 30092   Carol Goode, Libn.

SOUTHERN BAPTIST CONVENTION - FOREIGN MISSION BOARD - MISSIONARY ORIENTATION LIBRARY
Box 535
Pine Mountain, GA 31822
Phone: (404) 663-2235
Cary Ann Geron, Libn.

U.S. AIR FORCE BASE - ROBINS BASE LIBRARY
2853 ABG/SSL
Robins AFB, GA 31098
Phone: (912) 926-5411
Evelyn R. Jarman, Hd.

CARNEGIE LIBRARY - HENDERSON ROOM
607 Broad St.
Rome, GA 30161
Phone: (404) 291-7568
Beatrice Millican, Spec.Coll.Libn.

FLOYD MEDICAL CENTER - LIBRARY
Turner McCall Blvd.
Rome, GA 30161
Phone: (404) 295-5500
Mark W. Lashley, Med.Libn.

GEORGIA KRAFT COMPANY - TECHNICAL DEVELOPMENT CENTER LIBRARY
*
Box 1551
Rome, GA 30161
Phone: (404) 291-6920

HIGHTOWER (Sara) REGIONAL LIBRARY - BUSINESS LIBRARY
Box 277
Rome, GA 30161
Phone: (404) 291-9360
Jim L. Doyle, Bus.Libn.

NORTHWEST GEORGIA REGIONAL HOSPITAL AT ROME - MEDICAL LIBRARY
Phone: (404) 295-6060
Rome, GA 30161
James R. Fletcher, Lib.Ck.

SHORTER COLLEGE - MEMORABILIA ROOM
Phone: (404) 291-2121
Rome, GA 30161
Robert Gardner, Historian

THIELE KAOLIN COMPANY - RESEARCH & DEVELOPMENT LIBRARY
Box 1056
Sandersville, GA 31082
Phone: (912) 552-3951
Barbara W. Goodman, Tech.Sec.-Libn.

CANDLER GENERAL HOSPITAL - PROFESSIONAL LIBRARY
5353 Reynolds St.
Box 9787
Savannah, GA 31412
Phone: (912) 356-6011
Genevieve Mallis, Libn.

GEORGIA HISTORICAL SOCIETY - LIBRARY
W.B. Hodgson Hall
501 Whitaker St.
Savannah, GA 31499
Phone: (912) 944-2128
Anthony R. Dees, Dir.

GIRL SCOUTS OF THE USA - JULIETTE GORDON LOW GIRL SCOUT NATIONAL CENTER
142 Bull St.
Savannah, GA 31401
Phone: (912) 233-4501
Charlotte E. Parker, Dir.

HERTY FOUNDATION - LIBRARY
Brampton Rd.
Box 1963
Savannah, GA 31402
Phone: (912) 964-5541
J. Robert Hart, Dir.

ST. JOSEPH'S HOSPITAL - MEDICAL LIBRARY †
11705 Mercy Blvd.
Savannah, GA 31406
Phone: (912) 925-4100
Judy G. Henry, Libn.

SAVANNAH (City) - MUNICIPAL RESEARCH LIBRARY †
City Hall, Rm. 402
Box 1027
Savannah, GA 31402
Phone: (912) 233-9321
Glenda E. Anderson, Res.Libn.

SAVANNAH (City) - POLICE DEPARTMENT - LIBRARY
323 Oglethorpe Ave.
Box 1027
Savannah, GA 31402
Phone: (912) 233-9321
Glenda E. Anderson, Res.Libn.

SAVANNAH SCIENCE MUSEUM - ENERGY LIBRARY
4405 Paulsen St.
Savannah, GA 31405
Phone: (912) 355-6705
Jeff Klein, Energy Projects Dir.

U.S. ARMY - CORPS OF ENGINEERS - SAVANNAH DISTRICT - TECHNICAL LIBRARY
Box 889
Savannah, GA 31402
Phone: (912) 944-5461
James C. Dorsey, Chf., Tech.Lib.

U.S.D.A. - AGRICULTURAL RESEARCH SERVICE - STORED-PRODUCT INSECTS RESEARCH & DEVELOPMENT LAB. - LIBRARY
3401 Edwin St.
Box 22909
Savannah, GA 31403
Phone: (912) 233-7981
Charlene Freyermuth, Lib.Techn.

U.S. DEPT. OF COMMERCE - INTERNATIONAL TRADE ADMINISTRATION - SAVANNAH DISTRICT OFFICE LIBRARY
222 U.S. Courthouse & P.O. Bldg.
125-29 Bull St.
Box 9746
Savannah, GA 31412
Phone: (912) 232-4321
James W. McIntire, Dir.

UNIVERSITY OF GEORGIA - SKIDAWAY INSTITUTE OF OCEANOGRAPHY - LIBRARY
Box 13687
Savannah, GA 31406
Phone: (912) 356-2474
Alison S. Ricker Chesney, Libn.

COWETA GENEALOGICAL & HISTORICAL SOCIETY - LIBRARY
Rt. 1, Hwy. 54
Sharpsburg, GA 30277
Phone: (404) 251-2877
Norma Gunby, Owner

GEORGIA SOUTHERN COLLEGE - ARCHIVES/SPECIAL COLLECTIONS
College Library
Landrum Box 8074
Statesboro, GA 30460
Phone: (912) 681-5645
Andrew Penson, Asst.Ref.Libn.

AMERICAN HEMEROCALLIS SOCIETY - LIBRARY
c/o Mrs. Barbara Mitchell
501 Tallwood Dr.
Stone Mountain, GA 30083
Phone: (404) 292-5856
Ned Irish, Chm., Pubn.Comm.

ARCHBOLD (John D.) MEMORIAL HOSPITAL - RALPH PERKINS MEMORIAL LIBRARY
Gordon & Mimosa Sts.
Box 1018
Thomasville, GA 31792
Phone: (912) 226-4121
Susan Danner, Med.Libn.

ABRAHAM BALDWIN AGRICULTURAL COLLEGE - LIBRARY
ABAC Station
Tifton, GA 31794
Phone: (912) 386-3223
Mary Emma Henderson, Libn.

UNIVERSITY OF GEORGIA - GEORGIA COASTAL PLAIN EXPERIMENT STATION LIBRARY
Tifton, GA 31794
Phone: (404) 386-3447
Emory Cheek, Lib.Assoc.

TOCCOA FALLS COLLEGE - SEBY JONES LIBRARY
Box 38
Toccoa Falls, GA 30598
Phone: (404) 886-6831
Ruth Good, Hd.Libn.

U.S. NATL. PARK SERVICE - FORT PULASKI NATL. MONUMENT - LIBRARY
Box 98
Tybee Island, GA 31328
Phone: (912) 786-5787
Talley Kirkland, Hist.

SOUTH GEORGIA MEDICAL CENTER - MEDICAL LIBRARY
Box 1727
Valdosta, GA 31601
Phone: (912) 242-3450
Susan T. Danner, Med.Libn.

ROOSEVELT'S (Franklin D.) LITTLE WHITE HOUSE AND MUSEUM - ARCHIVES
Phone: (404) 655-3511
Warm Springs, GA 31830
Eloise Ousley, Supt.

HAWAII

HAWAIIAN SUGAR PLANTERS' ASSOCIATION EXPERIMENT STATION - LIBRARY
99-193 Aiea Heights Dr.
Box 1057
Aiea, HI 96701
Phone: (808) 487-5561
Mary O. Matsuoka, Libn.

CARLSMITH, CARLSMITH, WICHMAN & CASE - LIBRARY *
121 Waianuenue Ave.
Box 686
Hilo, HI 96720
Phone: (808) 935-6644
Raymond K. Hasegawa, Att.

GEOGRAPHIC

HAWAII STATE CIRCUIT COURT - 3RD CIRCUIT - LAW LIBRARY †
Federal Bldg., 75 Aupini St.
Box 1007   Phone: (808) 961-7226
Hilo, HI 96720

HILO HOSPITAL - FRED IRWIN MEDICAL LIBRARY †
1190 Waianuenue Ave.   Phone: (808) 961-4331
Hilo, HI 96720   Hazel M. Takemoto, Libn.

LYMAN HOUSE MEMORIAL MUSEUM - KATHRYN E. LYLE MEMORIAL
    LIBRARY
276 Haili St.   Phone: (808) 935-5021
Hilo, HI 96720   Christina R.N. Lothian, Archv./Libn.

U.S. NATL. PARK SERVICE - PU'UHONUA O HONAUNAU NATL. HISTORICAL
    PARK - LIBRARY
Box 129   Phone: (808) 328-2326
Honaunau, HI 96726   Blossom Sapp, Libn.

AMERICAN CANCER SOCIETY - HAWAII DIVISION - LIBRARY
200 N. Vineyard Blvd.   Phone: (808) 531-1662
Honolulu, HI 96817   Dotty Morgan, Pub.Educ.Dir.

AMERICAN LUNG ASSOCIATION OF HAWAII - LEARNING CENTER FOR
    LUNG HEALTH
245 N. Kukui St.   Phone: (808) 537-5966
Honolulu, HI 96817   Catherine C. Tamura, Learning Ctr.Coord.

BANK OF HAWAII - INFORMATION CENTER
Financial Plaza Tower Bldg., 20th Fl.
Box 2900   Phone: (808) 537-8375
Honolulu, HI 96846   Sally Campbell, Info.Mgr.

BISHOP (Bernice P.) MUSEUM - LIBRARY
1355 Kalihi St.
Box 19000-A   Phone: (808) 847-3511
Honolulu, HI 96819   Cynthia Timberlake, Libn.

CHAMBER OF COMMERCE OF HAWAII - INFORMATION OFFICE
Dillingham Bldg., 735 Bishop St.   Phone: (808) 531-4111
Honolulu, HI 96813   Miss Tatsuko Honjo, Dir., Info.Off.Serv.

EAST-WEST CULTURE LEARNING INSTITUTE - RESOURCE MATERIALS
    COLLECTION
East-West Ctr., 1777 East-West Rd.   Phone: (808) 948-7081
Honolulu, HI 96848   William Feltz, Res.Mtl.Spec.

EAST-WEST POPULATION INSTITUTE RESOURCE MATERIALS COLLECTION
East-West Ctr., 1777 East-West Rd.   Phone: (808) 944-7451
Honolulu, HI 96848   Alice D. Harris, Rsrcs.Mtls.Spec.

FIRST HAWAIIAN BANK - RESEARCH DIVISION LIBRARY
Box 3200   Phone: (808) 525-6229
Honolulu, HI 96847   Mary I. Kuramoto, Res.Libn.

HAWAII CHINESE HISTORY CENTER
111 N. King St., No. 410   Phone: (808) 521-5948
Honolulu, HI 96817   Violet L. Lai, Hd.Libn.

HAWAII EMPLOYERS COUNCIL - LIBRARY *
2682 Waiwai Loop   Phone: (808) 836-1511
Honolulu, HI 96819

HAWAII INSTITUTE OF GEOPHYSICS - LIBRARY
University Of Hawaii
2525 Correa Rd.   Phone: (808) 948-7040
Honolulu, HI 96822   Patricia E. Price, Libn.

HAWAII MEDICAL LIBRARY, INC.
1221 Punchbowl St.   Phone: (808) 536-9302
Honolulu, HI 96813   John A. Breinich, Dir.

HAWAII NEWSPAPER AGENCY - LIBRARY
News Bldg., 605 Kapiolani Blvd.   Phone: (808) 525-7669
Honolulu, HI 96813   Beatrice S. Kaya, Chf.Libn.

HAWAII PLANNED PARENTHOOD - FAMILY PLANNING INFORMATION
    CENTER (FPIC) - LIBRARY
1164 Bishop St., Suite 1220   Phone: (808) 531-1327
Honolulu, HI 96813   Marsha N. Tamura, FPIC Supv.

HAWAII STATE DEPARTMENT OF ACCOUNTING AND GENERAL SERVICES -
    PUBLIC ARCHIVES
Iolani Palace Grounds   Phone: (808) 548-2357
Honolulu, HI 96813   Agnes C. Conrad, State Archv.

HAWAII STATE DEPARTMENT OF EDUCATION - AUDIOVISUAL SERVICES
641 18th Ave.   Phone: (808) 732-2824
Honolulu, HI 96816   Franklin S. Tamaribuchi, TAC Spec.

HAWAII STATE DEPARTMENT OF HEALTH - HASTINGS H. WALKER
    MEDICAL LIBRARY
Leahi Hospital
3675 Kilauea Ave.   Phone: (808) 734-0221
Honolulu, HI 96816   Jean K. Yeg, Lib.Asst.

HAWAII STATE DEPARTMENT OF PLANNING & ECONOMIC DEVELOPMENT -
    LIBRARY
Box 2359   Phone: (808) 548-3059
Honolulu, HI 96804   Anthony M. Oliver, Libn.

HAWAII STATE - LEGISLATIVE REFERENCE BUREAU LIBRARY
State Capitol   Phone: (808) 548-7853
Honolulu, HI 96813   Hanako Kobayashi, Res.Libn.

HAWAII STATE LIBRARY - BUSINESS, SCIENCE, TECHNOLOGY UNIT
478 S. King St.
Honolulu, HI 96813   Hanako Nakamura, Hd.

HAWAII STATE LIBRARY - EDNA ALLYN ROOM
478 S. King St.   Phone: (808) 548-2341
Honolulu, HI 96813   Shirley S. Naito, Oahu Ch.Coord.

HAWAII STATE LIBRARY - FINE ARTS AND AUDIOVISUAL SECTION
478 S. King St.   Phone: (808) 548-2340
Honolulu, HI 96813   Eloise Van Niel, Act.Hd.

HAWAII STATE LIBRARY - HAWAII AND PACIFIC SECTION I
478 S. King St.   Phone: (808) 548-2346
Honolulu, HI 96813   Hatsue Matsushige, Section Hd.

HAWAII STATE LIBRARY - LANGUAGE, LITERATURE AND HISTORY
    SECTION
478 S. King St.   Phone: (808) 548-4166
Honolulu, HI 96813   Sandra Kolloge, Act.Libn.

HAWAII STATE LIBRARY - SERIALS SECTION
478 S. King St.   Phone: (808) 548-2389
Honolulu, HI 96813   Vincent Van Brocklin, Ser.Libn.

HAWAII STATE LIBRARY - SOCIAL SCIENCE AND PHILOSOPHY SECTION
478 S. King St.   Phone: (808) 548-2340
Honolulu, HI 96813

HAWAII STATE LIBRARY - STATE LIBRARY FOR THE BLIND AND
    PHYSICALLY HANDICAPPED
402 Kapahulu Ave.   Phone: (808) 732-7767
Honolulu, HI 96815   Lydia S. Ranger, Hd.Libn.

HAWAII STATE LIBRARY - YOUNG ADULT SECTION
478 S. King St.   Phone: (808) 548-2337
Honolulu, HI 96813   Colette F. H. Young, Oahu YA Coord.

HAWAII STATE SUPREME COURT - LAW LIBRARY
Judiciary Bldg.   Phone: (808) 548-7432
Honolulu, HI 96813   Momoe Tanaka, State Law Libn.

HAWAIIAN ELECTRIC CO., INC. - CORPORATE LIBRARY
Box 2750   Phone: (808) 548-7915
Honolulu, HI 96840   Deborah Knowlton, Corp.Libn.

HAWAIIAN ELECTRIC CO., INC. - ENGINEERING LIBRARY
820 Ward Ave.
Box 2750   Phone: (808) 548-7915
Honolulu, HI 96840   Deborah Knowlton, Corp.Libn.

HAWAIIAN HISTORICAL SOCIETY - MISSION-HISTORICAL LIBRARY
560 Kawaiahao St.   Phone: (808) 537-6271
Honolulu, HI 96813   Barbara E. Dunn, Libn.

HAWAIIAN MISSION CHILDREN'S SOCIETY - MISSION-HISTORICAL
 LIBRARY
553 S. King St.   Phone: (808) 531-0481
Honolulu, HI 96813   Mary Jane Knight, Libn.

HAWAIIAN TELEPHONE COMPANY - LIBRARY
1177 Bishop St.
Box 2200   Phone: (808) 546-2600
Honolulu, HI 96841   Michelle A. Pommer, Libn.

HONOLULU ACADEMY OF ARTS - AUDIOVISUAL CENTER
900 S. Beretania St.   Phone: (808) 538-3693
Honolulu, HI 96814   Brone Jameikis, Kpr.

HONOLULU ACADEMY OF ARTS - ROBERT ALLERTON LIBRARY
900 S. Beretania St.   Phone: (808) 538-3693
Honolulu, HI 96814   Anne T. Seaman, Libn.

HONOLULU (City And County) - MUNICIPAL REFERENCE AND RECORDS
 CENTER
558 S. King St.   Phone: (808) 523-4577
Honolulu, HI 96813   Marsha C. Petersen, Dir.

INTERNATIONAL TSUNAMI INFORMATION CENTER
Box 50027   Phone: (808) 546-2847
Honolulu, HI 96850   Dr. George Pararas-Carayannis, Dir.

KAISER FOUNDATION HOSPITALS - MEDICAL LIBRARY
1697 Ala Moana Blvd.   Phone: (808) 944-6149
Honolulu, HI 96815   Lois J. Clark, Libn.

KAPIOLANI-CHILDREN'S MEDICAL CENTER - KCMC MEDICAL LIBRARY
1319 Punahou St.   Phone: (808) 947-8573
Honolulu, HI 96826   Ikuko Uesato, Libn.

LEEWARD COMMUNITY COLLEGE - LIBRARY
96-045 Ala Ike   Phone: (808) 455-0210
Honolulu, HI 96782

LYON ASSOCIATES, INC. - BELT, COLLINS AND ASSOCIATES DIVISION -
 INFORMATION SERVICES
745 Fort St., 5th Fl.   Phone: (808) 521-5361
Honolulu, HI 96813   Anne H. Saiki, Libn.

NATIONAL SOCIETY, DAUGHTERS OF THE AMERICAN REVOLUTION -
 ALOHA CHAPTER - MEMORIAL LIBRARY
1914 Makiki Heights Dr.
Honolulu, HI 96822   Florine H. Greenwood, Libn.

PACIFIC AND ASIAN AFFAIRS COUNCIL - PACIFIC HOUSE LIBRARY †
2004 University Ave.   Phone: (808) 941-5355
Honolulu, HI 96816

PACIFIC SCIENTIFIC INFORMATION CENTER
Bernice P. Bishop Museum
1355 Kalihi St., Box 19000-A   Phone: (808) 847-3511
Honolulu, HI 96819   Edwin H. Bryan, Jr., Mgr.

ST. FRANCIS HOSPITAL - MEDICAL LIBRARY
2230 Liliha St.   Phone: (808) 547-6481
Honolulu, HI 96817   Elaine Hickey, Libn.

STRAUB CLINIC & HOSPITAL, INC. - ARNOLD LIBRARY
888 S. King St.   Phone: (808) 544-0317
Honolulu, HI 96813   Frances P. Smith, Libn.

U.S. ARMY MUSEUM, HAWAII - REFERENCE LIBRARY
Box 8064   Phone: (808) 543-2639
Honolulu, HI 96815   Thomas M. Fairfull, Musm.Dir.

U.S. DEPT. OF COMMERCE - INTERNATIONAL TRADE ADMINISTRATION -
 HONOLULU DISTRICT OFFICE LIBRARY
PJK Federal Bldg., Rm. 4106
Box 50026   Phone: (808) 546-8694
Honolulu, HI 96850   H. Tucker Gratz, Dir.

U.S. DISTRICT COURT LIBRARY
U.S. Court House
Box 50128   Phone: (808) 546-3163
Honolulu, HI 96850   Isabel T. Anduha, Court Libn.

U.S. FEDERAL AVIATION ADMINISTRATION - PACIFIC-ASIA REGION
 LIBRARY †
300 Ala Moana Blvd.
Box 4009   Phone: (808) 546-8313
Honolulu, HI 96813   William R. Ranger, Libn.

U.S. MARINE CORPS - CAMP H.M. SMITH LIBRARY †
                                                   Phone: (808) 477-6348
Honolulu, HI 96701   Capt. J.P. Cavasoz, Hd.

U.S. NATL. MARINE FISHERIES SERVICE - WESTERN PACIFIC PROGRAMS
 OFFICE - LIBRARY †
2750 Dole St.
Box 3830   Phone: (808) 946-2181
Honolulu, HI 98612   Hazel S. Nishimura, Libn.

U.S. NATL. PARK SERVICE - HAWAII VOLCANOES NATIONAL PARK -
 LIBRARY
                                                   Phone: (808) 967-7311
Honolulu, HI 96718   Kathleen English, Libn.

UNIVERSITY OF HAWAII - ASIA COLLECTION
Hamilton Library, 2550 The Mall   Phone: (808) 948-8116
Honolulu, HI 96822   Joyce Wright, Hd.

UNIVERSITY OF HAWAII - DEPARTMENT OF HISTORY - PACIFIC REGIONAL
 ORAL HISTORY PROGRAM - LIBRARY
2530 Dole St.   Phone: (808) 948-8486
Honolulu, HI 96822   Edward Beechert, Dir.

UNIVERSITY OF HAWAII - PACIFIC BIO-MEDICAL RESEARCH CENTER -
 LIBRARY
41 Ahui St.   Phone: (808) 531-3538
Honolulu, HI 96813   Dr. Barbara H. Gibbons, Assoc.Res.

UNIVERSITY OF HAWAII - PUBLIC SERVICES - GOVERNMENT DOCUMENTS,
 MAPS & MICROFORMS
Hamilton Library, 2550 The Mall   Phone: (808) 948-8230
Honolulu, HI 96822   Patricia Shelden, Hd.

UNIVERSITY OF HAWAII - SCHOOL OF PUBLIC HEALTH - REFERENCE ROOM
1960 East-West Rd.
Court D., Rm. 207   Phone: (808) 948-8666
Honolulu, HI 96822   Carol W. Arnold, Libn.

UNIVERSITY OF HAWAII - SOCIAL SCIENCE RESEARCH INSTITUTE
Porteus Hall 704, Maile Way   Phone: (808) 948-8930
Honolulu, HI 96822   Donald M. Topping, Dir.

UNIVERSITY OF HAWAII - SPECIAL COLLECTIONS - ARCHIVES
Sinclair Library, 2425 Campus Rd.   Phone: (808) 948-6673
Honolulu, HI 96822   Frances Jackson, Archv.

UNIVERSITY OF HAWAII - SPECIAL COLLECTIONS - HAWAIIAN
 COLLECTION
Hamilton Library, 2550 The Mall   Phone: (808) 948-8264
Honolulu, HI 96822   David Kittelson, Cur.

UNIVERSITY OF HAWAII - SPECIAL COLLECTIONS - PACIFIC COLLECTION
Hamilton Library, 2550 The Mall   Phone: (808) 948-8264
Honolulu, HI 96822   Renee Heyum, Cur.

UNIVERSITY OF HAWAII - SPECIAL COLLECTIONS - RARE BOOKS
Hamilton Library, 2550 The Mall   Phone: (808) 948-8230
Honolulu, HI 96822   Eleanor C. Au, Hd.Spec.Coll.

UNIVERSITY OF HAWAII - WAIKIKI AQUARIUM - LIBRARY
2777 Kalakaua Ave.   Phone: (808) 923-9741
Honolulu, HI 96815   Linda K. Dizon, Libn.

YEE (Alfred A.) & ASSOCIATES INC. - LIBRARY
1441 Kapiolani Blvd., Suite 810   Phone: (808) 946-3161
Honolulu, HI 96814   Ann L. Marsteller, Libn.

ST. CHRISTOPHER'S CHURCH - LIBRARY
Box 456   Phone: (808) 262-8176
Kailua, HI 96734

GEOGRAPHIC

HAWAII STATE HOSPITAL - MEDICAL LIBRARY
45-710 Keaahala Rd.   Phone: (808) 247-2191
Kaneohe, HI 96744   Diana C. Stephens, Med.Libn.

U.S. MARINE CORPS - KANEOHE AIR STATION LIBRARY
                                                Phone: (808) 257-3583
Kaneohe Bay, HI 96863   Murray R. Visser, Supv.Libn.

BRIGHAM YOUNG UNIVERSITY, HAWAII CAMPUS - JOSEPH F. SMITH
    LIBRARY AND MEDIA CENTER
55-220 Kulanui St.   Phone: (808) 293-9211
Laie, HI 96762   E. Curtis Fawson, Dir.

CHURCH OF JESUS CHRIST OF LATTER-DAY SAINTS - LAIE, HAWAII STAKE
    BRANCH GENEALOGICAL LIBRARY
                                                Phone: (808) 293-1154
Laie, HI 96762   Wesley A. Gleason, Libn.

WILCOX (G.N.) MEMORIAL HOSPITAL & HEALTH CENTER - MEDICAL
    LIBRARY
3420 Kuhio Hwy.   Phone: (808) 245-4811
Lihue, HI 96766   Edna Stoffel, Med.Lib.Techn.

U.S. NATL. PARK SERVICE - HALEAKALA NATL. PARK - LIBRARY
Box 369   Phone: (808) 572-9306
Makawao, HI 96768   Carol Beadle, Pk.Techn.

ALDRICH (Mariska) MEMORIAL FOUNDATION, INC. - LIBRARY OF RARE
    MUSIC *
2512 Komo Mai Dr.   Phone: (808) 456-2201
Pearl City, HI 96782   Anna Mary Anderson, Pres.

U.S. NAVY - NAVAL SHIPYARD (Pearl Harbor) - TECHNICAL LIBRARY
Code 250.4, Box 400   Phone: (808) 471-3408
Pearl Harbor, HI 96860   Lincoln H.S. Yu, Libn.

U.S. ARMY HOSPITALS - TRIPLER ARMY MEDICAL CENTER - MEDICAL
    LIBRARY
Tripler AMC, HI 96859   Linda Requena, Chf., Med.Lib.

HAWAII STATE CIRCUIT COURT - 2ND CIRCUIT - LAW LIBRARY
Box P   Phone: (808) 244-5227
Wailuku, HI 96793

MAUI HISTORICAL SOCIETY - RESEARCH LIBRARY
2375 A Main St.
Box 1018   Phone: (808) 244-3326
Wailuku, HI 96793   Virginia Wirtz, Musm.Dir.

OCEANIC INSTITUTE LIBRARY
Makapuu Point   Phone: (808) 259-7951
Waimanalo, HI 96795   Karen Conley, Libn.

U.S. AIR FORCE BASE - WHEELER BASE LIBRARY
FL 5296, 15 Air Base Squadron (SSL)   Phone: (808) 655-1867
Wheeler AFB, HI 96854   William B. Hassler, Base Libn.

IDAHO

ASSOCIATION OF IDAHO CITIES - LIBRARY
3314 Grace
Boise, ID 83706

BOISE BIBLE COLLEGE - LIBRARY
8695 Marigold   Phone: (208) 376-7731
Boise, ID 83704   Zella Chamberlain, Libn.

BOISE GALLERY OF ART - LIBRARY
670 South Julia Davis Dr.   Phone: (208) 345-8330
Boise, ID 83701

IDAHO STATE HISTORICAL SOCIETY - GENEALOGICAL LIBRARY
610 N. Julia Davis Dr.   Phone: (208) 334-2305
Boise, ID 83706   Frieda O. March, Chf.Libn.

IDAHO STATE HISTORICAL SOCIETY - LIBRARY AND ARCHIVES
610 N. Julia Davis Dr.   Phone: (208) 334-3356
Boise, ID 83702   James Davis, Libn.

IDAHO STATE LAW LIBRARY
Supreme Court Bldg.
451 W. State St.   Phone: (208) 334-3316
Boise, ID 83720   Laura M. Pershing, Law Libn.

IDAHO STATE LIBRARY
325 W. State St.   Phone: (208) 334-2150
Boise, ID 83702   Charles Bolles, State Libn.

IDAHO STATE LIBRARY - REGIONAL LIBRARY FOR THE BLIND AND
    PHYSICALLY HANDICAPPED
325 W. State St.   Phone: (208) 334-2150
Boise, ID 83702   Evva L. Larson, Asst.State Libn.

IDAHO STATESMAN - LIBRARY
1200 N. Curtis Rd.
Box 40   Phone: (208) 377-6435
Boise, ID 83707   Nancy Van Dinter, Chf.Libn.

MORRISON-KNUDSEN CO., INC. - RECORDS AND MICROGRAPHICS CENTER
Box 7808   Phone: (206) 345-5000
Boise, ID 83729   Julie Kreiensieck, Mgr.

ST. ALPHONSUS HOSPITAL - HEALTH SCIENCES LIBRARY
1055 N. Curtis Rd.   Phone: (208) 376-1211
Boise, ID 83706   Martha R. Stolz, Libn.

ST. LUKE'S HOSPITAL - MEDICAL LIBRARY
190 E. Bannock   Phone: (208) 386-2222
Boise, ID 83702   Karen M. Little, Dir.

U.S. DEPT. OF LABOR - OSHA - IDAHO AREA OFFICE - LIBRARY *
1315 W. Idaho St.   Phone: (208) 334-1867
Boise, ID 83702   David M. Bernard, Area Dir.

U.S. VETERANS ADMINISTRATION (ID-Boise) - HOSPITAL LIBRARY (142D)
Fifth & Fort   Phone: (208) 336-5100
Boise, ID 83702   Gordon Carlson, Chf.Libn.

COLLEGE OF IDAHO - REGIONAL STUDIES CENTER - LIBRARY
Boone Science Hall, Rm. 257   Phone: (208) 459-5214
Caldwell, ID 83605   Donna Parsons, Dir.

ARGONNE NATIONAL LABORATORY - ARGONNE-WEST TECHNICAL
    LIBRARY
Box 2528   Phone: (208) 526-7237
Idaho Falls, ID 83401   Cathleen M. Scalice, Tech.Libn.

CONSOLIDATED HOSPITALS OF IDAHO FALLS - MEDICAL LIBRARY
2525 South Blvd.
Box 2077   Phone: (208) 529-7128
Idaho Falls, ID 83401   Jean Hopkins, Libn.

ENERGY, INC. - TECHNICAL LIBRARY
Box 736   Phone: (208) 524-1000
Idaho Falls, ID 83401   Jacqueline Loop, Libn.

U.S. DEPT. OF ENERGY - IDAHO NATL. ENGINEERING LABORATORY -
    TECHNICAL LIBRARY
Box 1625   Phone: (208) 526-1195
Idaho Falls, ID 83401

WESTINGHOUSE ELECTRIC CORPORATION - NAVAL REACTOR FACILITY
    LIBRARY
Box 2068
Idaho Falls, ID 83401   Coy E. Stewart, Libn.

U.S.D.A. - AGRICULTURAL RESEARCH SERVICE - SNAKE RIVER
    CONSERVATION RESEARCH CENTER - LIBRARY
Route 1, Box 186   Phone: (208) 423-5582
Kimberly, ID 83341   A. Smith, Libn.

LEWISTON TRIBUNE LIBRARY
505 C St.   Phone: (208) 743-9411
Lewiston, ID 83501   Betty Dresser, Libn.

NEZ PERCE COUNTY LAW LIBRARY
Court House
Lewiston, ID 83501

POTLATCH CORPORATION - WESTERN WOOD PRODUCTS DIV.
ENGINEERING & TECHNICAL SERV. DEPT. - INFORMATION CTR. *
Box 1016   Phone: (208) 799-0123
Lewiston, ID 83501

LATAH COUNTY HISTORICAL SOCIETY - LIBRARY
110 S. Adams   Phone: (208) 882-1004
Moscow, ID 83843   Keith Petersen, Dir.

UNIVERSITY OF IDAHO - ARCHIVE OF PACIFIC NORTHWEST
ARCHAEOLOGY
Dept. of Sociology/Anthropology   Phone: (208) 885-6751
Moscow, ID 83843   Roderick Sprague, Dir.

UNIVERSITY OF IDAHO - BUREAU OF PUBLIC AFFAIRS RESEARCH -
LIBRARY
                                            Phone: (208) 885-6563
Moscow, ID 83843   Sid Duncombe, Dir.

UNIVERSITY OF IDAHO - HUMANITIES LIBRARY
                                            Phone: (208) 885-6584
Moscow, ID 83843   Margaret Newsome, Libn.

UNIVERSITY OF IDAHO - IDAHO WATER RESOURCES RESEARCH
INSTITUTE - TECHNICAL INFO. CENTER & READING ROOM
                                            Phone: (208) 885-6429
Moscow, ID 83843   A.R. Gittins, Act.Dir.

UNIVERSITY OF IDAHO - LAW LIBRARY
College Of Law   Phone: (208) 885-6521
Moscow, ID 83843   Walter H. McLeod, Libn.

UNIVERSITY OF IDAHO - SCIENCE AND TECHNOLOGY LIBRARY
                                            Phone: (208) 885-6235
Moscow, ID 83843   Rod Hardies, Libn.

UNIVERSITY OF IDAHO - SOCIAL SCIENCE LIBRARY
                                            Phone: (208) 885-6344
Moscow, ID 83843   Dennis Baird, Libn.

UNIVERSITY OF IDAHO - SPECIAL COLLECTIONS LIBRARY
                                            Phone: (208) 885-7951
Moscow, ID 83843   Charles A. Webbert, Libn.

OWYHEE COUNTY HISTORICAL COMPLEX MUSEUM - LIBRARY
                                            Phone: (208) 495-2319
Murphy, ID 83650   Beverly Ingraham, Dir.

IDAHO STATE UNIVERSITY - COLLEGE OF EDUCATION - INSTRUCTIONAL
MATERIALS CENTER
                                            Phone: (208) 236-2652
Pocatello, ID 83209   Arthur R. Cullen, Dir.

IDAHO STATE UNIVERSITY - IDAHO MUSEUM OF NATURAL HISTORY -
LIBRARY
Campus Box 8096   Phone: (208) 232-3168
Pocatello, ID 83209   Lucille Harten, Pubn.Ed.

IDAHO STATE UNIVERSITY LIBRARY - AUDIO-VISUAL SERVICES
Box 8064   Phone: (208) 236-3212
Pocatello, ID 83209   Khan M. Hassan, Asst.Libn./AV Serv.

IDAHO STATE UNIVERSITY LIBRARY - DOCUMENTS DIVISION
Box 8089   Phone: (208) 236-3202
Pocatello, ID 83209   Joseph Lu, Doc.Libn.

IDAHO STATE UNIVERSITY LIBRARY - HUMANITIES DIVISION
Box 8089   Phone: (208) 236-3202
Pocatello, ID 83209   Douglas Birdsall, Hum.Libn.

IDAHO STATE UNIVERSITY LIBRARY - SCIENCE DIVISION
Box 8089   Phone: (208) 236-3202
Pocatello, ID 83209   Bill Hatton, Sci.Libn.

IDAHO STATE UNIVERSITY LIBRARY - SOCIAL SCIENCE DIVISION
Box 8089   Phone: (208) 236-3202
Pocatello, ID 83209   Gary Domitz, Soc.Sci.Libn.

CHURCH OF JESUS CHRIST OF LATTER-DAY SAINTS - UPPER SNAKE RIVER
BRANCH GENEALOGICAL LIBRARY
Ricks College Library   Phone: (208) 356-2351
Rexburg, ID 83440   Neal S. Southwick, Libn.

UPPER SNAKE RIVER VALLEY HISTORICAL SOCIETY - LIBRARY
49 North Center
Box 244
Rexburg, ID 83440   Jerry Glenn, Libn.

BONNER COUNTY HISTORICAL SOCIETY, INC. - RESEARCH LIBRARY
Lakeside Pk.
Box 1063   Phone: (208) 263-2344
Sandpoint, ID 83864   Betty Dunlap

U.S. NATL. PARK SERVICE - NEZ PERCE NATL. HISTORICAL PARK -
LIBRARY
Box 93   Phone: (208) 843-2685
Spalding, ID 83551   Kenneth Adkisson, Chf.Interp.

MORITZ COMMUNITY HOSPITAL - DEAN PIEROSE MEMORIAL HEALTH
SCIENCES LIBRARY *
Box 86   Phone: (208) 622-3323
Sun Valley, ID 83353   Marina H. Zuetell, Health Sci.Libn.

ASGROW SEED COMPANY - RESEARCH CENTER
Box 1235   Phone: (208) 326-4321
Twin Falls, ID 83301   Leland R. Schweitzer, Mgr. Of Res.Lab.

ILLINOIS

ALTON MENTAL HEALTH CENTER - PROFESSIONAL LIBRARY
4500 College Ave.   Phone: (618) 465-5593
Alton, IL 62002   Thomas M. McConahey, Dir.Dev. & Training

ALTON TELEGRAPH PRINTING COMPANY - LIBRARY
111 E. Broadway   Phone: (618) 463-2573
Alton, IL 62002   Charlene Heard, Libn.

ST. JOSEPH HOSPITAL - INFORMATION SERVICES
915 E. 5th St.   Phone: (618) 463-5284
Alton, IL 62002   Judith Messerle, Dir.

CPC INTERNATIONAL - MOFFETT TECHNICAL LIBRARY
Box 345   Phone: (312) 458-2000
Argo, IL 60501   Janet K. Zupko, Mgr., Info.Serv.

ARGONNE NATIONAL LABORATORY - NATIONAL ENERGY SOFTWARE
CENTER
9700 S. Cass Ave.   Phone: (312) 972-7250
Argonne, IL 60439   Margaret K. Butler, Dir.

ARGONNE NATIONAL LABORATORY - TECHNICAL INFORMATION SERVICES
DEPARTMENT
9700 S. Cass Ave., Bldg. 203-C110   Phone: (312) 972-4221
Argonne, IL 60439   Hillis L. Griffin, Dir.

HONEYWELL, INC. - COMMERCIAL DIVISION - LIBRARY
1500 W. Dundee   Phone: (312) 870-5380
Arlington Heights, IL 60004   Paul M. Klekner, Libn.

NORTHWEST COMMUNITY HOSPITAL - MEDICAL LIBRARY
800 West Central Rd.   Phone: (312) 259-1000
Arlington Heights, IL 60005   Edith Salzman, Libn.

AURORA COLLEGE - JENKS MEMORIAL COLLECTION OF ADVENTUAL
MATERIALS
347 S. Gladstone   Phone: (312) 892-6431
Aurora, IL 60507   Moses C. Crouse, Cur.

AURORA HISTORICAL SOCIETY - MUSEUM LIBRARY
305 Cedar St.   Phone: (312) 897-9029
Aurora, IL 60507   Fred B. Graham, Jr., Cur.

GEOGRAPHIC

MERCY CENTER FOR HEALTH CARE SERVICES - MEDICAL LIBRARY
1325 N. Highland Ave.   Phone: (312) 859-2222
Aurora, IL 60506   Mary P. Murray, Libn.

AMERICAN CAN COMPANY - BARRINGTON TECHNICAL CENTER -
    TECHNICAL INFORMATION CENTER
433 N. Northwest Hwy.   Phone: (312) 381-1900
Barrington, IL 60010   Mary T. Gormley, Supv.

CAI - TECHNICAL LIBRARY
550 W. Northwest Hwy.   Phone: (312) 381-2400
Barrington, IL 60010   Steven Kormanak, Tech.Libn.

QUAKER OATS COMPANY - JOHN STUART RESEARCH LABORATORIES -
    RESEARCH LIBRARY
617 W. Main St.   Phone: (312) 381-1980
Barrington, IL 60010   Mary C. Piper, Staff-Lib.

WIGHT CONSULTING ENGINEERS, INC. - TECHNICAL LIBRARY
127 S. Northwest Hwy.   Phone: (312) 381-1800
Barrington, IL 60010   Sally M. Trainer, Sec.

FERMI NATIONAL ACCELERATOR LABORATORY - LIBRARY
Box 500   Phone: (312) 840-3401
Batavia, IL 60510   Roger S. Thompson, Libn.

LUTHERAN CHURCH - MISSOURI SYNOD - SOUTHERN ILLINOIS DISTRICT
    ARCHIVES
2408 Lebanon Ave.   Phone: (618) 234-4767
Belleville, IL 62221

ST. ELIZABETH'S HOSPITAL - HEALTH SCIENCE LIBRARY
211 S. Third St.   Phone: (618) 234-2120
Belleville, IL 62221   Michael A. Campese, Lib.Dir.

AMERICAN SOKOL EDUCATION AND PHYSICAL CULTURE ORGANIZATION -
    LIBRARY
6426 W. Cermak Rd.   Phone: (312) 795-6671
Berwyn, IL 60402   Lorraine Zdenek, Libn.

MAC NEAL MEMORIAL HOSPITAL - FRANK C. BECHT MEMORIAL LIBRARY
3249 S. Oak Park Ave.   Phone: (312) 797-3089
Berwyn, IL 60402   Mildred Lydigsen, Libn.

OLYMPIC SAVINGS AND LOAN ASSOCIATION - LIBRARY †
6201 W. Cermak Rd.   Phone: (312) 788-6201
Berwyn, IL 60402

ORDER OF SERVANTS OF MARY - EASTERN PROVINCE LIBRARY - MORINI
    MEMORIAL COLLECTION
3401 S. Home Ave.   Phone: (312) 484-0063
Berwyn, IL 60402   Rev. Conrad M. Borntrager, O.S.M., Archv.

BLOOMINGTON-NORMAL DAILY PANTAGRAPH - NEWSPAPER LIBRARY
301 W. Washington St.   Phone: (309) 829-9411
Bloomington, IL 61701   Diane Miller, Lib.Dir.

ILLINOIS AGRICULTURAL ASSOCIATION - IAA AND AFFILIATED
    COMPANIES LIBRARY
1701 Towanda Ave.
Box 2901
Bloomington, IL 61701   Phone: (309) 557-2550
                                         Rue E. Olson, Libn.

ILLINOIS WESLEYAN UNIVERSITY - THORPE MUSIC LIBRARY
                                         Phone: (309) 556-3003
Bloomington, IL 61701   Robert C. Delvin, Fine Arts Libn.

INSTITUTE FOR THEOLOGICAL & PHILOSOPHICAL STUDIES - LIBRARY
Box 3563
Bloomington, IL 61701   Dr. James Kurtz, Dir.

MC LEAN COUNTY BAR ASSOCIATION - ILLINOIS SUPREME COURT -
    LIBRARY
300 Peoples Bank Bldg.   Phone: (309) 827-8009
Bloomington, IL 61701   Loretta I. Talley

MC LEAN COUNTY HISTORICAL SOCIETY - MUSEUM AND LIBRARY
201 E. Grove St.   Phone: (309) 827-0428
Bloomington, IL 61701   Barbara Dunbar, Dir.

MENNONITE HOSPITAL AND SCHOOL OF NURSING - HEALTH SCIENCES
    LIBRARY
807 N. Main St.   Phone: (309) 827-4321
Bloomington, IL 61701   Carolyn McCown Anderson, Dir.

SECOND PRESBYTERIAN CHURCH - CAPEN MEMORIAL LIBRARY *
313 N. East St.   Phone: (309) 828-6297
Bloomington, IL 61701

STATE FARM MUTUAL AUTOMOBILE INSURANCE COMPANY - LAW LIBRARY
One State Farm Plaza   Phone: (309) 662-2780
Bloomington, IL 61701   Laura Garrett, Libn.

UNITED METHODIST CHURCH - CENTRAL ILLINOIS CONFERENCE -
    CONFERENCE HISTORICAL SOCIETY LIBRARY
1211 N. Park
Box 2050
Bloomington, IL 61701

AEROPHILATELIC FEDERATION OF THE AMERICAS - LIBRARY
Box 269   Phone: (312) 485-1109
Brookfield, IL 60513   Earl H. Wellman, Libn.

CHICAGO ZOOLOGICAL PARK - BROOKFIELD ZOO - LIBRARY
8400 W. 31st St.   Phone: (312) 485-0263
Brookfield, IL 60513   Mary Rabb, Libn.

ST. LOUIS UNIVERSITY - PARKS COLLEGE OF AERONAUTICAL
    TECHNOLOGY - LIBRARY
                                         Phone: (618) 337-7500
Cahokia, IL 62206   Nancy Nobbe, Libn.

FULTON COUNTY HISTORICAL AND GENEALOGICAL SOCIETY - RESEARCH
    ROOM
Parlin-Ingersoll Library
205 W. Chestnut   Phone: (309) 647-0328
Canton, IL 61520   Beverly Stewart, Hd.Libn.

GRAHAM HOSPITAL ASSOCIATION - MEDICAL STAFF LIBRARY
210 W. Walnut St.   Phone: (309) 647-5240
Canton, IL 61520   Mrs. Moneta Bedwell, Libn.

GRAHAM HOSPITAL ASSOCIATION - SCHOOL OF NURSING LIBRARY
210 W. Walnut St.   Phone: (309) 647-5240
Canton, IL 61520   Mrs. Moneta Bedwell, Libn.

GREATER EGYPT REGIONAL PLANNING AND DEVELOPMENT COMMISSION -
    LIBRARY-RESEARCH CENTER
Box 3160   Phone: (618) 549-3306
Carbondale, IL 62901   Kay Clary, Res.Anl.

SOUTHERN ILLINOIS UNIVERSITY, CARBONDALE - DEPARTMENT OF
    SOCIOLOGY - LIBRARY
                                         Phone: (618) 453-5718
Carbondale, IL 62901   Dr. Thomas G. Eynon, Dir.

SOUTHERN ILLINOIS UNIVERSITY, CARBONDALE - EDUCATION DIVISION
    LIBRARY
Morris Library   Phone: (618) 453-2274
Carbondale, IL 62901   Dr. Ruth Bauner, Educ.Div.Libn.

SOUTHERN ILLINOIS UNIVERSITY, CARBONDALE - HUMANITIES DIVISION
    LIBRARY
Morris Library   Phone: (618) 536-3391
Carbondale, IL 62901   Alan M. Cohn, Hum.Libn.

SOUTHERN ILLINOIS UNIVERSITY, CARBONDALE - SCHOOL OF LAW
    LIBRARY
                                         Phone: (618) 536-7711
Carbondale, IL 62901   Elizabeth Slusser Kelly, Law Lib.Dir.

SOUTHERN ILLINOIS UNIVERSITY, CARBONDALE - SCIENCE DIVISION
    LIBRARY
Morris Library   Phone: (618) 453-2700
Carbondale, IL 62901   George W. Black, Jr., Sci.Libn.

SOUTHERN ILLINOIS UNIVERSITY, CARBONDALE - SOCIAL STUDIES
    DIVISION LIBRARY
Morris Library   Phone: (618) 453-2708
Carbondale, IL 62901   James Fox, Soc.Stud.Libn.

SOUTHERN ILLINOIS UNIVERSITY, CARBONDALE - SPECIAL COLLECTIONS
Morris Library   Phone: (618) 453-2516
Carbondale, IL 62901   David V. Koch, Cur./Archv.

SOUTHERN ILLINOIS UNIVERSITY, CARBONDALE - UNDERGRADUATE
    LIBRARY
Morris Library   Phone: (618) 453-2818
Carbondale, IL 62901   Judith Ann Harwood, Libn.

MURRAY (Warren G.) DEVELOPMENTAL CENTER - LIBRARY
1717 W. Broadway   Phone: (618) 532-1811
Centralia, IL 62801   Edith Jacke, Libn.

ADLER CENTER - LIBRARY
2204 Griffith Dr.   Phone: (217) 333-4993
Champaign, IL 61820   Mu-Chin Cheng, Libn.

CHAMPAIGN COUNTY HISTORICAL MUSEUM - LIBRARY
709 W. University Ave.   Phone: (217) 356-1010
Champaign, IL 61820   Michael Cahall, Dir.

ERIC CLEARINGHOUSE ON ELEMENTARY AND EARLY CHILDHOOD
    EDUCATION
University of Illinois
1310 S. 6th St.   Phone: (217) 333-1386
Champaign, IL 61820   Lilian G. Katz, Dir.

ILLINOIS STATE GEOLOGICAL SURVEY - LIBRARY
615 E. Peabody   Phone: (217) 344-1481
Champaign, IL 61820   Mary Krick, Libn.

ILLINOIS STATE WATER SURVEY - LIBRARY
605 E. Springfield
Sta. A, Box 5050   Phone: (217) 333-4956
Champaign, IL 61820   Adele S. Douglass, Hd.Libn.

PARKLAND COLLEGE - LEARNING RESOURCE CENTER
2400 W. Bradley Ave.   Phone: (217) 351-2241
Champaign, IL 61820   David L. Johnson, Dir.

U.S. ARMY - CONSTRUCTION ENGINEERING RESEARCH LABORATORY - H.B.
    ZACKRISON MEMORIAL LIBRARY
Interstate Research Pk.
Box 4005   Phone: (217) 352-6511
Champaign, IL 61820   Martha A. Blake, Libn.

UNIVERSITY OF ILLINOIS - ILLINOIS STATE NATURAL HISTORY SURVEY -
    LIBRARY
196 Natural Resources Bldg.
607 E. Peabody   Phone: (217) 333-6892
Champaign, IL 61820   Doris Sublette, Libn.

UNIVERSITY OF ILLINOIS - INSTITUTE OF LABOR AND INDUSTRIAL
    RELATIONS LIBRARY
504 E. Armory   Phone: (217) 333-2380
Champaign, IL 61820   Margaret A. Chaplan, Libn.

UNIVERSITY OF ILLINOIS - LAW LIBRARY
104 Law Bldg.   Phone: (217) 333-2914
Champaign, IL 61820   Carol Boast, Act.Dir.

U.S. AIR FORCE BASE - CHANUTE BASE LIBRARY †
                                            Phone: (217) 495-3191
Chanute AFB, IL 61868

U.S. AIR FORCE BASE - CHANUTE BASE TECHNICAL BRANCH LIBRARY †
                                            Phone: (217) 495-3191
Chanute AFB, IL 61868   Bertha A. Steinbeck, Libn.

COLES COUNTY HISTORICAL SOCIETY - GREENWOOD SCHOOL MUSEUM -
    LIBRARY
800 Hayes Ave.   Phone: (217) 581-3310
Charleston, IL 61920   Dr. E. Duane Elbert, Musm.Cur.

EASTERN ILLINOIS UNIVERSITY - BOOTH LIBRARY
                                            Phone: (217) 581-2210
Charleston, IL 61920   Wilson Luquire, Dean., Lib.Serv.

ACADEMY OF THE STREET OF PUERTO RICAN CONGRESS - LIBRARY
Chicago Public Library
1909 W. Erie St.   Phone: (312) 772-4223
Chicago, IL 60622   Carlos C. Ruiz, Exec.Dir.

ADAMS ADVERTISING AGENCY, INC. - LIBRARY
111 N. Canal St.   Phone: (312) 922-0856
Chicago, IL 60606   Lee Arnold, Libn.

ADLER (Alfred) INSTITUTE - LIBRARY
159 N. Dearborn St.   Phone: (312) 346-3458
Chicago, IL 60601   Eugene McClory, Pres.

ADLER PLANETARIUM - LIBRARY
1300 S. Lake Shore Dr.   Phone: (312) 322-0304
Chicago, IL 60605   James Seevers, Adm.

AMERICAN BAR FOUNDATION - WILLIAM NELSON CROMWELL LIBRARY
1155 E. 60th St.   Phone: (312) 667-4700
Chicago, IL 60637   Olavi Maru, Libn.

AMERICAN COLLEGE OF HOSPITAL ADMINISTRATORS - RAY E. BROWN
    MANAGEMENT COLLECTION
840 N. Lakeshore Dr.   Phone: (312) 943-0544
Chicago, IL 60611   Diana Brown, Coord.

AMERICAN COLLEGE OF SURGEONS - LIBRARY
55 E. Erie St.   Phone: (312) 664-4050
Chicago, IL 60611   Mrs. Jeri A. Ryan, Libn.

AMERICAN CONSERVATORY OF MUSIC - LIBRARY
116 S. Michigan Ave.   Phone: (312) 263-4161
Chicago, IL 60603   Lauren Dennhardt, Libn.

AMERICAN DENTAL ASSOCIATION - BUREAU OF LIBRARY SERVICES
211 E. Chicago Ave.   Phone: (312) 440-2653
Chicago, IL 60611   Aletha A. Kowitz, Dir.

AMERICAN DIETETIC ASSOCIATION - LULU G. GRAVES MEMORIAL
    LIBRARY
430 N. Michigan Ave.
Chicago, IL 60611

AMERICAN DRY MILK INSTITUTE - LIBRARY
130 N. Franklin St.   Phone: (312) 782-4888
Chicago, IL 60606

AMERICAN FEDERATION OF SMALL BUSINESS - INFORMATION CENTER
407 S. Dearborn St., Rm. 980   Phone: (312) 427-0206
Chicago, IL 60605   Ira H. Latimer, Exec. V.P.

AMERICAN HOSPITAL ASSOCIATION - ASA S. BACON MEMORIAL LIBRARY
840 N. Lake Shore Dr.   Phone: (312) 280-6263
Chicago, IL 60611   Eloise C. Foster, Dir.

AMERICAN JUDICATURE SOCIETY - RESEARCH LIBRARY
200 W. Monroe St., Suite 1606   Phone: (312) 558-6900
Chicago, IL 60606   Timothy Pyne, Libn.

AMERICAN LIBRARY ASSOCIATION - HEADQUARTERS LIBRARY
50 E. Huron St.   Phone: (312) 944-6780
Chicago, IL 60611   Joel M. Lee, Libn.

AMERICAN MARKETING ASSOCIATION - INFORMATION CENTER
250 S. Wacker Dr.   Phone: (312) 648-0536
Chicago, IL 60606   Lorraine Caliendo, Dir.

AMERICAN MEDICAL ASSOCIATION - DIVISION OF LIBRARY AND
    ARCHIVAL SERVICES
535 N. Dearborn St.   Phone: (312) 751-6000
Chicago, IL 60610   Dr. Susan Crawford, Dir.

AMERICAN MEDICAL RECORD ASSOCIATION - FORE LIBRARY †
875 N. Michigan Ave., Suite 1850   Phone: (312) 787-2672
Chicago, IL 60611   Mary Kay Siebert, Libn.

AMERICAN OCCUPATIONAL MEDICAL ASSOCIATION - LIBRARY
150 N. Wacker Dr.   Phone: (312) 782-2166
Chicago, IL 60606   Dr. Donald L. Hoops, Exec.Dir.

GEOGRAPHIC

AMERICAN OSTEOPATHIC ASSOCIATION - ANDREW TAYLOR STILL
   MEMORIAL LIBRARY
212 E. Ohio St.   Phone: (312) 944-2713
Chicago, IL 60611   Barbara E. Peterson, Libn.

AMERICAN PUBLIC WORKS ASSOCIATION - INFORMATION SERVICE
1313 E. 60th St.   Phone: (312) 947-2583
Chicago, IL 60637   Mary K. Simon, Libn.

AMERICAN RAILWAY CAR INSTITUTE - LIBRARY
303 E. Wacker Dr.
Chicago, IL 60601   Elwyn T. Ahnquist, Pres.

AMERICAN SOCIETY OF ARTISTS, INC. - RESOURCE CENTER
1297 Merchandise Mart Plaza   Phone: (312) 751-2500
Chicago, IL 60654   Donald Metcoff, Libn.

AMERICAN SOCIETY OF BAKERY ENGINEERS - INFORMATION SERVICE
   AND LIBRARY †
2 N. Riverside Plaza, Rm. 1921   Phone: (312) 332-2246
Chicago, IL 60606   R.A. Fischer, Sec.-Treas.

AMERICANS UNITED FOR LIFE - AUL LEGAL DEFENSE FUND -
   INFORMATION CENTER
230 N. Michigan Ave., Suite 915   Phone: (312) 263-5029
Chicago, IL 60601   Margaret Black

ART INSTITUTE OF CHICAGO - RYERSON AND BURNHAM LIBRARIES
Michigan Ave. at Adams St.   Phone: (312) 443-3666
Chicago, IL 60603   Daphne C. Roloff, Dir.

ARTHUR ANDERSEN & CO. - LIBRARY
33 W. Monroe St.   Phone: (312) 580-0033
Chicago, IL 60603   Marilyn R. Murray, Libn.

ARTHUR YOUNG & COMPANY - LIBRARY
One IBM Plaza
Chicago, IL 60611   Helen Facto, Libn.

AUGUSTANA HOSPITAL AND HEALTH CARE CENTER - CARL A. HEDBERG
   HEALTH SCIENCE LIBRARY
411 W. Dickens Ave.   Phone: (312) 975-5109
Chicago, IL 60614   Elizabeth Clausen, Chf.Libn.

BAKER & MC KENZIE - LIBRARY
2800 Prudential Plaza   Phone: (312) 861-2915
Chicago, IL 60601   Frank Lukes, Law Libn.

BALZEKAS MUSEUM OF LITHUANIAN CULTURE - RESEARCH LIBRARY
4012 S. Archer Ave.   Phone: (312) 847-2441
Chicago, IL 60632   Jurgis Kasakaitis, Hd.Libn.

BANK MARKETING ASSOCIATION - INFORMATION CENTER
309 W. Washington St.   Phone: (312) 782-1442
Chicago, IL 60606   Bonnie Wang, Dir., Info.Serv.

BBDO CHICAGO - INFORMATION CENTER
410 N. Michigan Ave.   Phone: (312) 337-7860
Chicago, IL 60611   Ann Hullihan, Res.Libn.

BEATRICE FOODS CO. - RESEARCH CENTER LIBRARY
1526 South State St.   Phone: (312) 791-8292
Chicago, IL 60605   Carol Berger, Mgr., Lib./Info.Serv.

BELL & HOWELL EDUCATION GROUP - DE VRY INSTITUTE OF TECHNOLOGY
   - LEARNING RESOURCE CENTER
3300 N. Campbell Ave.   Phone: (312) 929-8500
Chicago, IL 60618   Gary A. Meszaros, Libn.

BERTRAND RUSSELL SOCIETY, INC. - LIBRARY
3802 N. Kenneth Ave.
Chicago, IL 60641   Donald W. Jackanicz, Co-Libn.

BILLINGTON, FOX & ELLIS - RESEARCH DEPARTMENT - LIBRARY
20 N. Wacker Drive   Phone: (312) 236-5000
Chicago, IL 60606

BITUMINOUS PIPE INSTITUTE - LIBRARY
221 N. La Salle St.
Chicago, IL 60601

BLUE CROSS AND BLUE SHIELD ASSOCIATIONS - LIBRARY
676 N. St. Clair   Phone: (312) 440-6147
Chicago, IL 60611   Mary T. Drazba, Sr.Dir.

BODINE ELECTRIC COMPANY - LIBRARY *
2500 W. Bradley Pl.   Phone: (312) 478-3515
Chicago, IL 60618

BOOZ, ALLEN & HAMILTON, INC. - LIBRARY
Three First National Plaza   Phone: (312) 346-1900
Chicago, IL 60602   Mark Hopman, Mgr.

BOZELL & JACOBS, INC. - CORPORATE INFORMATION CENTER
444 N. Michigan Ave.   Phone: (312) 644-9800
Chicago, IL 60611   Laura M. Johnson, Mgr.

BURNETT (Leo) COMPANY, INC. - INFORMATION CENTER †
Prudential Plaza, 4th Fl.   Phone: (312) 565-5959
Chicago, IL 60601   Elizabeth Redmond, Libn.

CAMPBELL-MITHUN, INC. - RESEARCH INFORMATION CENTER
111 E. Wacker Dr.   Phone: (312) 565-3800
Chicago, IL 60601   Steve Heffernan, Libn.

CANADIAN CONSULATE GENERAL - INFORMATION CENTER
310 S. Michigan Ave.   Phone: (312) 427-1031
Chicago, IL 60604   Carol A. Summers, Info.Mgr.

CATHOLIC THEOLOGICAL UNION - LIBRARY
5401 S. Cornell Ave.   Phone: (312) 324-8000
Chicago, IL 60615   Rev. Kenneth O'Malley, C.P., Lib.Dir.

CENTER FOR NEW SCHOOLS - RESOURCE CENTER †
59 E. Van Buren   Phone: (312) 939-7025
Chicago, IL 60605   Robert O. Slater, Res.Ctr.Coord.

CENTER FOR RESEARCH LIBRARIES
5721 S. Cottage Grove Ave.   Phone: (312) 955-4545
Chicago, IL 60637   Donald B. Simpson, Dir.

CENTER FOR THE STUDY OF ETHICS IN THE PROFESSIONS - LIBRARY
Illinois Institute of Technology
IIT Center   Phone: (312) 567-3017
Chicago, IL 60616   Martin Pimsler, Libn.

CENTRAL STATES INSTITUTE OF ADDICTIONS - LIBRARY
120 W. Huron St.   Phone: (312) 266-6100
Chicago, IL 60610   Mrs. Vi Springenberg

CHADWELL, KAYSER, RUGGLES, MC GEE & HASTINGS - LAW LIBRARY
233 S. Wacker Dr.
8500 Sears Tower   Phone: (312) 876-2209
Chicago, IL 60606   Betty Roizman, Libn.

CHAPMAN AND CUTLER - LAW LIBRARY
111 W. Monroe St.   Phone: (312) 726-6130
Chicago, IL 60603   Denis S. Kowalewski, Libn.

CHICAGO ACADEMY OF SCIENCES - MATTHEW LAUGHLIN MEMORIAL
   LIBRARY
2001 N. Clark St.   Phone: (312) 549-0606
Chicago, IL 60614   Louise Lunak, Libn.

CHICAGO BAR ASSOCIATION - LIBRARY
29 S. LaSalle St.   Phone: (312) 782-7348
Chicago, IL 60603   Stephen F. Czike, Exec.Libn.

CHICAGO BOARD OF EDUCATION - LIBRARY
228 N. LaSalle St., Rm. 846   Phone: (312) 641-4105
Chicago, IL 60601   Mary Ann Ross, Libn.

CHICAGO BOARD OF TRADE - LIBRARY
141 W. Jackson Blvd.   Phone: (312) 435-3552
Chicago, IL 60604   Laura J. Miracle, Libn.

CHICAGO COLLEGE OF OSTEOPATHIC MEDICINE - ALUMNI MEMORIAL
    LIBRARY
5200 S. Ellis Ave.   Phone: (312) 947-4380
Chicago, IL 60615   Dr. Arthur Hafner, Dir. of Libs.

CHICAGO COMPREHENSIVE HEALTH COUNCIL - ALCOHOLISM CENTER -
    LIBRARY
55 E. Jackson Blvd., Suite 1080   Phone: (312) 663-0610
Chicago, IL 60604

CHICAGO DEPARTMENT OF HUMAN SERVICES - LIBRARY
640 N. LaSalle St.   Phone: (312) 744-6653
Chicago, IL 60610   Janice Bradshaw, Supv.

CHICAGO HISTORICAL SOCIETY - SPECIAL COLLECTIONS
Clark St. at North Ave.   Phone: (312) 642-4600
Chicago, IL 60614

CHICAGO INSTITUTE FOR PSYCHOANALYSIS - MC LEAN LIBRARY
180 N. Michigan Ave.   Phone: (312) 726-6300
Chicago, IL 60601   Glenn E. Miller, Libn.

CHICAGO MUNICIPAL REFERENCE LIBRARY
City Hall, Rm. 1004   Phone: (312) 744-4992
Chicago, IL 60602   Joyce Malden, Libn.

CHICAGO PUBLIC LIBRARY CENTRAL LIBRARY - BUSINESS/SCIENCE/
    TECHNOLOGY DIVISION
425 N. Michigan Ave.   Phone: (312) 269-2814
Chicago, IL 60611   Emelie Shroder, Division Chief

CHICAGO PUBLIC LIBRARY CENTRAL LIBRARY - GENERAL INFORMATION
    SERVICES DIVISION-BIBLIOGRAPHIC & ILL CENTER
425 N. Michigan Ave.   Phone: (312) 269-2823
Chicago, IL 60611   Kathleen C. O'Meara, Hd.

CHICAGO PUBLIC LIBRARY CENTRAL LIBRARY - GENERAL INFORMATION
    SERVICES DIVISION - INFORMATION CENTER
425 N. Michigan Ave.   Phone: (312) 269-2800
Chicago, IL 60611   Bronwyn Parhad, Hd.

CHICAGO PUBLIC LIBRARY CENTRAL LIBRARY - GENERAL INFORMATION
    SERVICES DIV. - NEWSPAPERS & GEN. PERIODICALS CTR.
425 N. Michigan Ave.   Phone: (312) 269-2913
Chicago, IL 60611   Joy Gleason, Hd.

CHICAGO PUBLIC LIBRARY CENTRAL LIBRARY - GOVERNMENT
    PUBLICATIONS DEPARTMENT
425 N. Michigan Ave.   Phone: (312) 269-3002
Chicago, IL 60611   Kay Ihlenfeldt, Dept.Hd.

CHICAGO PUBLIC LIBRARY CENTRAL LIBRARY - PROFESSIONAL LIBRARY
425 N. Michigan Ave.   Phone: (312) 269-2965
Chicago, IL 60611   Mildred Vannorsdall, Prof.Lib.Libn.

CHICAGO PUBLIC LIBRARY CENTRAL LIBRARY - SOCIAL SCIENCES &
    HISTORY DIVISION
425 N. Michigan Ave.   Phone: (312) 269-2830
Chicago, IL 60611   Robert Baumruk, Div.Chf.

CHICAGO PUBLIC LIBRARY CULTURAL CENTER - AUDIOVISUAL CENTER
78 E. Washington St.   Phone: (312) 269-2910
Chicago, IL 60602   Barbara L. Flynn, Hd.

CHICAGO PUBLIC LIBRARY CULTURAL CENTER - FINE ARTS DIVISION -
    ART SECTION
78 E. Washington St.   Phone: (312) 269-2858
Chicago, IL 60602   Clarissa Erwin, Div.Chf.

CHICAGO PUBLIC LIBRARY CULTURAL CENTER - FINE ARTS DIVISION -
    MUSIC SECTION
78 E. Washington St.   Phone: (312) 269-2886
Chicago, IL 60602   Clarissa Erwin, Div.Chf.

CHICAGO PUBLIC LIBRARY CULTURAL CENTER - LITERATURE AND
    LANGUAGE DIVISION
78 E. Washington St.   Phone: (312) 269-2880
Chicago, IL 60602   David T. Bosca, Div.Chf.

CHICAGO PUBLIC LIBRARY CULTURAL CENTER - SPECIAL COLLECTIONS
    DIVISION
78 E. Washington St.   Phone: (312) 269-2926
Chicago, IL 60602   Susan Prendergast Schoelwer, Cur.

CHICAGO PUBLIC LIBRARY CULTURAL CENTER - THOMAS HUGHES
    CHILDREN'S LIBRARY
78 E. Washington St.   Phone: (312) 269-2835
Chicago, IL 60602   Lillian R. New, Hd.

CHICAGO PUBLIC LIBRARY CULTURAL CENTER - VIVIAN G. HARSH
    COLLECTION OF AFRO-AMERICAN HISTORY & LIT. †
9525 S. Halsted St.   Phone: (312) 881-6910
Chicago, IL 60628

CHICAGO-READ MENTAL HEALTH CENTER - PROFESSIONAL LIBRARY
4200 N. Oak Park Ave.   Phone: (312) 794-3746
Chicago, IL 60634   Ruth Greenberg, Libn.

CHICAGO REGIONAL TRANSPORTATION AUTHORITY - INFORMATION
    SERVICES - LIBRARY *
300 N. State St.   Phone: (312) 836-4000
Chicago, IL 60610   Connie Tinner, Supv., Info.Serv.

CHICAGO SINAI CONGREGATION - EMIL G. HIRSCH LIBRARY
5350 S. Shore Dr.   Phone: (312) 288-1600
Chicago, IL 60615   Matthew I. Derby, Rabbi

CHICAGO STATE UNIVERSITY - DOUGLAS LIBRARY
E. 95th St. & King Dr.   Phone: (312) 995-2254
Chicago, IL 60628   Dr. W. Patrick Leonard, Dean

CHICAGO SUN-TIMES - EDITORIAL LIBRARY
401 N. Wabash Ave.   Phone: (312) 321-2594
Chicago, IL 60611   Ernest Perez, Chf.Libn.

CHICAGO THEOLOGICAL SEMINARY - HAMMOND LIBRARY
5757 S. University Ave.   Phone: (312) 752-5757
Chicago, IL 60637   Rev. Neil W. Gerdes, Libn.

CHICAGO TRANSIT AUTHORITY - HAROLD S. ANTHON MEMORIAL LIBRARY
Merchandise Mart Plaza
Box 3555   Phone: (312) 664-7200
Chicago, IL 60654   Joseph Benson, Dir.

CHICAGO TRIBUNE - INFORMATION CENTER
435 N. Michigan Ave.   Phone: (312) 222-3871
Chicago, IL 60611   Barbara T. Newcombe, Mgr.

CHICAGO TRIBUNE - MARKETING LIBRARY
435 N. Michigan, 11th Fl.   Phone: (312) 222-3188
Chicago, IL 60610   Annette Cadwell, Hd. Marketing Libn.

CHILDREN'S MEMORIAL HOSPITAL - JOSEPH BRENNEMANN LIBRARY
2300 Children's Plaza   Phone: (312) 649-4505
Chicago, IL 60614   Leslie Goodale, Dir.

CNA INSURANCE - LIBRARY
CNA Plaza, Van Buren and Wabash   Phone: (312) 822-7630
Chicago, IL 60685   Sandra Masson, Libn.

COLLECTORS CLUB OF CHICAGO - LIBRARY
1029 N. Dearborn St.   Phone: (312) 642-7981
Chicago, IL 60610   Lester E. Winick, Lib.Comm.

COMMONWEALTH EDISON COMPANY - LIBRARY
Box 767   Phone: (312) 294-3064
Chicago, IL 60690   Barbara R. Kelly, Libn.

CONGREGATION KINS OF WEST ROGERS PARK - JORDAN E. FEUER
    LIBRARY
2800 W. North Shore   Phone: (312) 761-4000
Chicago, IL 60645   Mrs. Milton Greenstein, Libn.

GEOGRAPHIC

GEOGRAPHIC

CONGREGATION RODFEI ZEDEK - J.S. HOFFMAN MEMORIAL LIBRARY *
5200 Hyde Park Blvd.   Phone: (312) 752-4489
Chicago, IL 60615   Henrietta Schultz, Libn.

CONTINENTAL CHEMISTE CORPORATION - LIBRARY
2256 W. Ogden Ave.   Phone: (312) 226-2134
Chicago, IL 60612   Kenneth J. Kass, Chm.Bd. Of Dir.

CONTINENTAL ILLINOIS NATIONAL BANK AND TRUST COMPANY OF
    CHICAGO - INFORMATION SERVICES DIVISION
231 S. La Salle St.   Phone: (312) 828-8580
Chicago, IL 60693   Susan J. Montgomery, Mgr.

COOK COUNTY HOSPITAL - HEALTH SCIENCE LIBRARY
1900 W. Polk St.   Phone: (312) 633-7787
Chicago, IL 60612   Grace Auer, Coord. of Libs. & Archv.

COOK COUNTY HOSPITAL - TICE MEMORIAL LIBRARY †
720 S. Wolcott St.   Phone: (312) 633-6724
Chicago, IL 60612   Grace Auer, Hd.Med.Libn.

COOK COUNTY LAW LIBRARY
2900 Richard J. Daley Ctr.   Phone: (312) 443-5423
Chicago, IL 60602   William J. Powers, Jr., Exec. Law Libn.

COOK COUNTY LAW LIBRARY - CRIMINAL COURT BRANCH
2650 S. California Ave., Rm. 4D00   Phone: (312) 890-7396
Chicago, IL 60608   Bennie E. Martin, Chf.Libn.

COOK COUNTY STATE'S ATTORNEY'S OFFICE LIBRARY
500 Richard J. Daley Center   Phone: (312) 443-8723
Chicago, IL 60602

CRAIN COMMUNICATIONS, INC. - INFORMATION CENTER
740 N. Rush St.   Phone: (312) 649-5200
Chicago, IL 60611   Carol A. David, Libn.

CRERAR (John) LIBRARY
35 W. 33rd St.   Phone: (312) 225-2526
Chicago, IL 60616   William S. Budington, Exec.Dir./Libn.

DARTNELL CORPORATION - PUBLISHING-RESEARCH LIBRARY
4660 N. Ravenswood Ave.   Phone: (312) 561-4000
Chicago, IL 60640   Juanita Roberts, Libn.

DAWE'S LABORATORIES, LTD. - TECHNICAL AND AGRICULTURAL
    LIBRARIES
7100 N. Tripp Ave.   Phone: (312) 982-9540
Chicago, IL 60646   Marge Schrader, Libn.

DE LEUW, CATHER AND COMPANY - LIBRARY
165 W. Wacker Dr.   Phone: (312) 346-0424
Chicago, IL 60601   Leslie Ewing, Libn.

DE PAUL UNIVERSITY - LAW SCHOOL LIBRARY
25 E. Jackson Blvd.   Phone: (312) 321-7710
Chicago, IL 60604   Susan Beverly Kuklin, Dir.

DE PAUL UNIVERSITY, LINCOLN PARK CAMPUS LIBRARY - SPECIAL
    COLLECTIONS DEPARTMENT
2323 N. Seminary   Phone: (312) 321-7940
Chicago, IL 60614   Kathryn DeGraff, Spec.Coll.Libn.

DENOYER-GEPPERT COMPANY - EDITORIAL LIBRARY
5235 Ravenswood Ave.
Chicago, IL 60640   Dr. Daniel H. Franck, Libn.

DICK (A.B.) COMPANY - LIBRARY
5700 W. Touhy Ave.   Phone: (312) 763-1900
Chicago, IL 60648   Nelly Somerman, Libn.

DONORS FORUM OF CHICAGO - LIBRARY
208 S. LaSalle St., Rm. 600   Phone: (312) 726-4882
Chicago, IL 60604   Susan M. Levy, Libn.

DU SABLE MUSEUM OF AFRICAN AMERICAN HISTORY - LIBRARY
740 E. 56th Pl.   Phone: (312) 947-0600
Chicago, IL 60637   Dr. Margaret Burroughs, Libn.

DUFF AND PHELPS, INC. - RESEARCH LIBRARY
55 E. Monroe St., Suite 4000   Phone: (312) 263-2610
Chicago, IL 60603   Sheila A. Collins, Libn.

EDGEWATER HOSPITAL - MEDICAL LIBRARY
5700 N. Ashland Ave.   Phone: (312) 878-6000
Chicago, IL 60660   Marie Korczak, Dir., Lib.Serv.

ELRICK AND LAVIDGE, INC. - LIBRARY
10 S. Riverside Plaza   Phone: (312) 726-0666
Chicago, IL 60606   G. Birch Ripley, Libn.

ENCYCLOPAEDIA BRITANNICA, INC. - EDITORIAL LIBRARY
425 N. Michigan Ave.   Phone: (312) 321-7221
Chicago, IL 60611   Terry Miller, Ed.Libn.

ENVIRONMENTAL PROTECTION AGENCY - REGION V LIBRARY
230 S. Dearborn St., Rm. 1420   Phone: (312) 353-2022
Chicago, IL 60604   Ms. Lou W. Tilley, Regional Libn.

EVANGELICAL COVENANT CHURCH OF AMERICA - ARCHIVES AND
    HISTORICAL LIBRARY
North Park College
5125 N. Spaulding Ave.   Phone: (312) 583-2700
Chicago, IL 60625   Sigurd F. Westberg, Archv.

FEDERAL RESERVE BANK OF CHICAGO - LIBRARY
164 W. Jackson
Box 834   Phone: (312) 322-5824
Chicago, IL 60690   Dorothy Phillips, Adm.

FIELD MUSEUM OF NATURAL HISTORY - LIBRARY
Roosevelt Rd. & Lake Shore Dr.   Phone: (312) 922-9410
Chicago, IL 60605   W. Peyton Fawcett, Hd.Libn.

FIRST NATIONAL BANK OF CHICAGO - LIBRARY
One First National Plaza, Suite 0477   Phone: (312) 732-3590
Chicago, IL 60670   Martha Whaley, Libn.

FLEXIBLE CAREERS - LIBRARY
37 S. Wabash
Chicago, IL 60603   Gertrude D. Schwerin, Libn.

FOOTE CONE & BELDING - INFORMATION CENTER
401 N. Michigan Ave.   Phone: (312) 467-9200
Chicago, IL 60611   John Kok, Dir.

FRIEDMAN & KOVEN - LAW LIBRARY
208 S. LaSalle St.   Phone: (312) 346-8500
Chicago, IL 60604   Cynthia A. Lowe, Libn.

GRANT (Alexander) & COMPANY - CHICAGO OFFICE LIBRARY
600 Prudential Plaza   Phone: (312) 856-0200
Chicago, IL 60601   Susan T. Robertson, Libn.

GRANT HOSPITAL OF CHICAGO - LIBRARY
550 W. Webster Ave.   Phone: (312) 883-2230
Chicago, IL 60614   Dalia S. Kleinmuntz, Lib.Dir.

GREELEY AND HANSEN - LIBRARY
222 S. Riverside Plaza   Phone: (312) 648-1155
Chicago, IL 60606   Elizabeth L. Tanner, Libn.

HARRIS TRUST AND SAVINGS BANK - LIBRARY
111 W. Monroe St.   Phone: (312) 461-7625
Chicago, IL 60690   Elizabeth Dreazen, Info.Spec.

HAYES/HILL INCORPORATED - LIBRARY
20 N. Wacker Dr., Suite 3330   Phone: (312) 984-5250
Chicago, IL 60606   Sandra K. Rollheiser, Libn.

HEIDRICK & STRUGGLES, INC. - LIBRARY RESEARCH CENTER
125 S. Wacker Dr., Suite 2800   Phone: (312) 372-8811
Chicago, IL 60606   Gail Bush, Lib.Res.Mgr.

HELENE CURTIS INDUSTRIES, INC. - CORPORATE LIBRARY
4401 W. North Ave.   Phone: (312) 292-2280
Chicago, IL 60639   Jacquelyn B. Becker, Corp.Libn.

HENROTIN HOSPITAL - MEDICAL LIBRARY
111 West Oak St. Phone: (312) 440-7759
Chicago, IL 60610 Penny Thomas-Jackson, Med.Libn.

HISTORICAL PICTURES SERVICE, INC.
601 W. Randolph St. Phone: (312) 346-0599
Chicago, IL 60606 Jeane M. Williams, Archv.

HOLY CROSS HOSPITAL - HEALTH SCIENCE LIBRARY
2701 W. 68th St. Phone: (312) 434-6700
Chicago, IL 60629 Olivija Fistrovic, Med.Libn.

IIT RESEARCH INSTITUTE - COMPUTER SEARCH CENTER
10 W. 35th St. Phone: (312) 567-4341
Chicago, IL 60616 Gerald J. Yucuis, Mgr.

IIT RESEARCH INSTITUTE - GUIDANCE AND CONTROL INFORMATION
   ANALYSIS CENTER (GACIAC)
10 W. 35th St. Phone: (312) 567-4345
Chicago, IL 60616 Charles Smoots, Mgr.

ILLINOIS BELL TELEPHONE COMPANY - LIBRARY
HDQ 20 D
225 W. Randolph St. Phone: (312) 727-2668
Chicago, IL 60606 Marguerite J. Krynicki, Hd.Libn.

ILLINOIS BELL TELEPHONE COMPANY - PIONEER HISTORICAL LIBRARY †
225 W. Randolph St. Phone: (312) 727-7850
Chicago, IL 60606 Ellen Guske, Res.Libn.

ILLINOIS COLLEGE OF OPTOMETRY - CARL F. SHEPARD MEMORIAL
   LIBRARY
3241 S. Michigan Ave. Phone: (312) 225-1700
Chicago, IL 60616 Peter E. Weil, Libn.

ILLINOIS COLLEGE OF PODIATRIC MEDICINE - LIBRARY
1001 N. Dearborn St. Phone: (312) 280-2891
Chicago, IL 60610 Richard S. Klein, Dir., Lib.Serv.

ILLINOIS INSTITUTE OF TECHNOLOGY - HAROLD LEONARD STUART
   SCHOOL OF MANAGEMENT & FINANCE - LIBRARY
10 W. 31st St. Phone: (312) 567-5136
Chicago, IL 60616 Jerome A. Lom, Stuart Libn.

ILLINOIS INSTITUTE OF TECHNOLOGY - JAMES S. KEMPER LIBRARY
3300 S. Federal St. Phone: (312) 225-2526
Chicago, IL 60616 Herbert Biblo, Libn.

ILLINOIS MASONIC MEDICAL CENTER - NOAH VAN CLEEF MEDICAL
   MEMORIAL LIBRARY
836 W. Wellington Ave. Phone: (312) 525-2300
Chicago, IL 60657 Harriette M. Cluxton, Dir., Med.Lib.Serv.

ILLINOIS MASONIC MEDICAL CENTER - SCHOOL OF NURSING - DR. JOSEPH
   DEUTSCH MEMORIAL LIBRARY
826 W. Nelson Phone: (312) 525-2300
Chicago, IL 60657 Ann Markham, Coord.

ILLINOIS STATE BUREAU OF EMPLOYMENT SECURITY - LABOR MARKET
   INFORMATION CENTER
910 S. Mighigan Ave., Rm. 1255 Phone: (312) 793-5277
Chicago, IL 60605 Eunhee Choi, Libn.

ILLINOIS STATE INSTITUTE OF NATURAL RESOURCES - ENVIRONMENTAL
   INFORMATION CENTER
309 W. Washington Phone: (312) 793-7695
Chicago, IL 60606 Sheila E. Cassels, Res.Libn.

ILLINOIS STATE PSYCHIATRIC INSTITUTE - PROFESSIONAL LIBRARY
1601 W. Taylor St. Phone: (312) 996-1320
Chicago, IL 60612 Mrs. Kineret Lichtenstein, Libn.

INDUSTRIAL WORKERS OF THE WORLD - LIBRARY
3435 N. Sheffield, Suite 202 Phone: (312) 549-5045
Chicago, IL 60657

INLAND STEEL COMPANY - INDUSTRIAL RELATIONS LIBRARY
30 W. Monroe Phone: (312) 346-0300
Chicago, IL 60603 Barbara Morton, Libn.

INSTITUTE ON THE CHURCH IN URBAN-INDUSTRIAL SOCIETY - LIBRARY
5700 S. Woodlawn Phone: (312) 643-7111
Chicago, IL 60637 Richard P. Poethig, Dir.

INSTITUTE OF GAS TECHNOLOGY - TECHNICAL INFORMATION CENTER
3424 S. State St. Phone: (312) 567-3870
Chicago, IL 60616 H.L. Mensch, Assoc.Dir.

INSTITUTE FOR JUVENILE RESEARCH - PROFESSIONAL LIBRARY
1735 W. Taylor St. Phone: (312) 996-1675
Chicago, IL 60612 Areta V. Halibey, Hd.Libn.

INSURANCE SCHOOL OF CHICAGO - LIBRARY †
330 S. Wells Phone: (312) 427-2520
Chicago, IL 60606

INTERNATIONAL ASSOCIATION OF ASSESSING OFFICERS - RESEARCH
   AND TECHNICAL SERVICES DEPT. - LIBRARY
1313 E. 60th St. Phone: (312) 947-2050
Chicago, IL 60637 Stuart W. Miller, Info.Spec.

INTERNATIONAL COLLEGE OF SURGEONS HALL OF FAME - DR. JOSEPH
   MONTAGUE PROCTOLOGIC LIBRARY
1524 N. Lake Shore Dr. Phone: (312) 642-3555
Chicago, IL 60610 George F. Smith, M.D., Cur. & Dir.

INTERNATIONAL FOOD SERVICE EXECUTIVES ASSOCIATION - LIBRARY
111 E. Wacker Dr., Suite 600
Chicago IL 60601

INTERNATIONAL FOODSERVICE MANUFACTURERS ASSOCIATION -
   INFORMATION SERVICE †
875 N. Michigan, Suite 3460 Phone: (312) 944-3838
Chicago, IL 60611 Michael Hoffman, Dir. of Marketing

IRISH-AMERICAN CULTURAL ASSOCIATION - LIBRARY
10415 S. Western Phone: (312) 239-6760
Chicago, IL 60643 Cynthia L. Buescher, Libn.

ISHAM, LINCOLN & BEALE - LIBRARY
1 First National Plaza Phone: (312) 558-7488
Chicago, IL 60603 Margaret Lundahl, Libn.

JACKSON PARK HOSPITAL - MEDICAL LIBRARY
7531 South Stony Island Ave. Phone: (312) 947-7653
Chicago, IL 60649 Syed A. Maghrabi, Med.Ref.Libn.

JESUIT SCHOOL OF THEOLOGY IN CHICAGO - LIBRARY *
1100 E. 55th St. Phone: (312) 667-3500
Chicago, IL 60615 Dr. W. Earle Hilgert, Act.Libn.

JEWISH VOCATIONAL SERVICE - LIBRARY
1 S. Franklin Phone: (312) 346-6700
Chicago, IL 60606 Beverly B. Martin, Libn.

JOHNSON PUBLISHING COMPANY, INC. - LIBRARY
820 S. Michigan Ave. Phone: (312) 322-9320
Chicago, IL 60605 Pamela J. Cash, Libn.

KEARNEY (A.T.), INC. - INFORMATION CENTER
222 S. Riverside Plaza Phone: (312) 648-0111
Chicago, IL 60606 Kathryn Sheehan, Corp.Libn.

KENNEDY-KING COLLEGE - LIBRARY
6800 S. Wentworth Phone: (312) 962-3262
Chicago, IL 60621 Mrs. Noel R. Grego, Hd.

KIRKLAND & ELLIS - LIBRARY
200 E. Randolph Dr., 60th Fl. Phone: (312) 861-3200
Chicago, IL 60601 William D. Murphy, Libn.

KNIGHT (Lester B.) & ASSOCIATES, INC. - MANAGEMENT CONSULTING
   LIBRARY
549 W. Randolph St. Phone: (312) 346-2100
Chicago, IL 60606 Clarita M. Generao, Libn.

KORN/FERRY INTERNATIONAL - RESEARCH LIBRARY
120 S. Riverside Plaza, Suite 918 Phone: (312) 726-1841
Chicago, IL 60606 Margaret A. French, Dir. of Res./Midwest

GEOGRAPHIC

LA RABIDA CHILDREN'S HOSPITAL AND RESEARCH CENTER - LAWRENCE
MERCER PICK MEMORIAL LIBRARY
E. 65th St. at Lake Michigan   Phone: (312) 363-6700
Chicago, IL 60649   Dr. Burton J. Grossman, Chf. of Med. Staff

LAKE MICHIGAN FEDERATION - ENVIRONMENTAL LIBRARY
53 W. Jackson, No. 1710   Phone: (312) 427-5121
Chicago, IL 60604   Judy Kiriazis, Adm.Dir.

LIBRARY OF INTERNATIONAL RELATIONS
666 Lake Shore Dr.   Phone: (312) 787-7928
Chicago, IL 60611   Eloise ReQua, Dir.

LINCOLN PARK ZOOLOGICAL GARDENS - LIBRARY
2200 N. Cannon Dr.   Phone: (312) 294-4640
Chicago, IL 60614   Gail Miller, Libn.

LIQUID CARBONIC CORPORATION - RESEARCH AND DEVELOPMENT
LIBRARY †
135 S. LaSalle St.   Phone: (312) 855-2500
Chicago, IL 60603   Patricia Beckwith, Tech.Libn.

LITHUANIAN AMERICAN COMMUNITY OF THE U.S.A. - LITHUANIAN WORLD
ARCHIVES
5620 S. Claremont
Chicago, IL 60636   Ceslovas V. Grincevicius

LORD, BISSELL AND BROOK - LAW LIBRARY
115 S. LaSalle St.   Phone: (312) 443-0647
Chicago, IL 60603   Jane L. Gaddis, Libn.

LORETTO HOSPITAL - HEALTH SCIENCES LIBRARY
645 S. Central Ave.   Phone: (312) 626-4300
Chicago, IL 60644   Dimiter Etimov, Dir.

LOYOLA UNIVERSITY OF CHICAGO - CUDAHY MEMORIAL LIBRARY -
SPECIAL COLLECTIONS
6525 Sheridan Rd.   Phone: (312) 274-3000
Chicago, IL 60626

LOYOLA UNIVERSITY OF CHICAGO - LAW LIBRARY
1 E. Pearson St.   Phone: (312) 670-2952
Chicago, IL 60611   Francis R. Doyle, Law Libn.

LUTHERAN CHURCH IN AMERICA - ARCHIVES
Lutheran School of Theology at Chicago
1100 E. 55th St.   Phone: (312) 667-3500
Chicago, IL 60615   Joel W. Lundeen, Assoc.Archv.

LUTHERAN SCHOOL OF THEOLOGY AT CHICAGO - KRAUSS LIBRARY *
1100 E. 55th St.   Phone: (312) 667-3500
Chicago, IL 60615   Rev. Lowell Albee, Jr., Libn.

MC CORMICK THEOLOGICAL SEMINARY - LIBRARY †
5555 S. Woodlawn Ave.   Phone: (312) 241-7800
Chicago, IL 60637   Elvire R. Hilgert, Libn.

MC CRONE (Walter C.) ASSOCIATES - LIBRARY
2820 S. Michigan   Phone: (312) 842-7100
Chicago, IL 60616   Juliet Robinson, Libn.

MC DERMOTT, WILL & EMERY - LIBRARY
111 W. Monroe St.   Phone: (312) 372-2000
Chicago, IL 60603   Louis J. Covotsos, Hd.Libn.

MC KINSEY & COMPANY, INC. - LIBRARY
Two First National Plaza   Phone: (312) 368-0600
Chicago, IL 60603   L. Smith, Mgr., Info.Serv.

MARQUIS WHO'S WHO, INC. - RESEARCH DEPARTMENT LIBRARY
200 E. Ohio St.   Phone: (312) 787-2008
Chicago, IL 60611   Adele Hast, Editor-in-Chief

MARSHALL (John) LAW SCHOOL - LIBRARY
315 S. Plymouth Ct.   Phone: (312) 427-2737
Chicago, IL 60604   Randall T. Peterson, Dir.

MARSTELLER, INC. - LIBRARY
One E. Wacker Dr.   Phone: (312) 329-1100
Chicago, IL 60601   Ellen Steininger, Hd.Libn.

MAYER, BROWN & PLATT - LIBRARY
231 S. LaSalle St.   Phone: (312) 782-0600
Chicago, IL 60604   Janice B. Bentley, Libn.

MEADVILLE/LOMBARD THEOLOGICAL SCHOOL - LIBRARY
5701 S. Woodlawn Ave.   Phone: (312) 753-3196
Chicago, IL 60637   Rev. Neil W. Gerdes, Libn.

MERCY HOSPITAL & MEDICAL CENTER - MEDICAL LIBRARY
2510 S. King Dr.   Phone: (312) 567-2364
Chicago, IL 60616   Timothy T. Oh, Dir. of Lib.

MERRIAM CENTER LIBRARY
Charles E. Merriam Center
For Public Administration
1313 E. 60th St.   Phone: (312) 947-2162
Chicago, IL 60637   Patricia Coatsworth, Hd.Libn.

METAL LATH/STEEL FRAMING ASSOCIATION - LIBRARY
221 N. La Salle St.   Phone: (312) 346-1600
Chicago, IL 60601   Durward Humes, Mng.Dir.

METROPOLITAN PERIODICAL SERVICE
60 W. Walton St.   Phone: (312) 664-9366
Chicago, IL 60610   Irma M. Lucht, Dir.

METROPOLITAN SANITARY DISTRICT OF GREATER CHICAGO - TECHNICAL
LIBRARY
100 E. Erie St.   Phone: (312) 751-5782
Chicago, IL 60611   Rudolph C. Ellsworth, Libn.

MICHAEL REESE HOSPITAL & MEDICAL CTR. - DEPT. OF LIBRARY & MEDIA
RSRCS.
2908 S. Ellis Ave.   Phone: (312) 791-2474
Chicago, IL 60616   Dr. George Mozes, Dir.

MIDWEST STOCK EXCHANGE, INC. - LISTINGS DEPARTMENT
120 S. LaSalle St., Rm. 1200   Phone: (312) 368-2222
Chicago, IL 60603

MONTGOMERY WARD AND CO. - CORPORATE LIBRARY
One Montgomery Ward Plaza   Phone: (312) 467-2334
Chicago, IL 60671   Barbara J. Burnett, Libn.

MOODY BIBLE INSTITUTE - LIBRARY
820 N. LaSalle St.   Phone: (312) 329-4139
Chicago, IL 60610   Richard G. Schock, Dir.

MOODY BIBLE INSTITUTE - MOODYANA COLLECTION
820 N. LaSalle St.   Phone: (312) 329-4140
Chicago, IL 60610   Richard G. Schock, Dir.

MORTON-NORWICH PRODUCTS, INC. - LIBRARY
110 N. Wacker Dr.   Phone: (312) 621-5244
Chicago, IL 60606   Evelyn S. Kanarek, Libn.

MOUNT SINAI HOSPITAL MEDICAL CENTER - LEWISOHN MEMORIAL
LIBRARY
California Ave. at 15th St.   Phone: (312) 542-2056
Chicago, IL 60608   Emily Sobkowiak, Med.Libn.

MUSEUM OF CONTEMPORARY ART - LIBRARY
237 E. Ontario St.   Phone: (312) 943-7755
Chicago, IL 60611   Naomi Vine, Dir. of Educ.

MUSEUM OF SCIENCE & INDUSTRY - LIBRARY
57th St. & Lake Shore Dr.   Phone: (312) 684-1414
Chicago, IL 60637   Bernice Richter, Libn.

NATIONAL ANTI-VIVISECTION SOCIETY - LIBRARY
100 E. Ohio St.
Chicago, IL 60611

NATIONAL ASSOCIATION OF BOARDS OF PHARMACY - LIBRARY †
One E. Wacker Dr., Suite 2210
Chicago, IL 60601

NATIONAL ASSOCIATION OF REALTORS - HERBERT U. NELSON MEMORIAL
    LIBRARY
430 N. Michigan Ave.   Phone: (312) 440-8070
Chicago, IL 60611   Beverly F. Dordick, Libn.

NATIONAL ASSOCIATION OF SUGGESTION SYSTEMS - LIBRARY
435 N. Michigan Ave.   Phone: (312) 644-0075
Chicago, IL 60611

NATIONAL CLEARINGHOUSE FOR LEGAL SERVICES - LIBRARY
500 N. Michigan Ave., Suite 1940   Phone: (312) 353-2566
Chicago, IL 60611   Katherine Stevenson, Libn.

NATIONAL COLLEGE OF EDUCATION - CHICAGO CAMPUS LIBRARY
18 S. Michigan Ave.   Phone: (312) 621-9676
Chicago, IL 60603   Estela Radovancev, Lib./Media Spec.

NATIONAL CONFECTIONERS ASSOCIATION OF THE U.S. - LIBRARY †
36 S. Wabash Ave., Suite 1300   Phone: (312) 372-1492
Chicago, IL 60603   James E. Mack, Pres. & Gen.Coun.

NATIONAL INDUSTRIAL RECREATION ASSOCIATION - INFORMATION
    CENTER
20 N. Wacker Dr.   Phone: (312) 346-7575
Chicago, IL 60606   Patrick B. Stinson, Exec.Dir.

NATIONAL LIVESTOCK AND MEAT BOARD - MEAT INDUSTRY
    INFORMATION CENTER
444 N. Michigan Ave.   Phone: (312) 467-5520
Chicago, IL 60611   William D. Siarny, Jr., Dir.

NATIONAL SAFETY COUNCIL - LIBRARY
444 N. Michigan Ave.   Phone: (312) 527-4800
Chicago, IL 60611   Ruth K. Hammersmith, Dir.

NATIONAL SISTERS VOCATION CONFERENCE - LIBRARY
1307 S. Wabash Ave.   Phone: (312) 939-6180
Chicago, IL 60605   Sr. Gertrude Wemhoff, O.S.B., Exec.Dir.

NATIONAL TRANSLATIONS CENTER †
John Crerar Library
35 W. 33rd St.   Phone: (312) 225-2526
Chicago, IL 60616   Mrs. Ildiko D. Nowak, Chf.

NATIVE AMERICAN EDUCATIONAL SERVICES - NAES LIBRARY AND
    RESOURCE CENTER
4550 N. Hermitage   Phone: (312) 728-1662
Chicago, IL 60640   Armin Beck, Dean

NEEDHAM, HARPER & STEERS ADVERTISING, INC. - INFORMATION
    SERVICES
303 E. Wacker Dr.   Phone: (312) 861-0200
Chicago, IL 60601   Belle Mest, Mgr.Info.Serv.

NEWBERRY LIBRARY
60 W. Walton St.   Phone: (312) 943-9090
Chicago, IL 60610   Lawrence W. Towner, Pres./Libn.

NORTH PARK THEOLOGICAL SEMINARY - MELLANDER LIBRARY
5125 N. Spaulding Ave.   Phone: (312) 583-2700
Chicago, IL 60625   Norma S. Goertzen, Dir.

NORTHEASTERN ILLINOIS PLANNING COMMISSION - LIBRARY
400 W. Madison St.   Phone: (312) 454-0400
Chicago, IL 60606   Mildred L. Cutberth, Sr.Libn.

NORTHEASTERN ILLINOIS UNIVERSITY - LIBRARY
5500 N. St. Louis Ave.   Phone: (312) 583-4050
Chicago, IL 60625   Melvin R. George, Dir.

NORTHERN TRUST COMPANY - LIBRARY
50 S. LaSalle St.   Phone: (312) 630-6000
Chicago, IL 60675   Lois H. Cole, Hd.Libn.

NORTHWEST HOSPITAL - MEDICAL LIBRARY
5645 W. Addison St.   Phone: (312) 282-7000
Chicago, IL 60634   Beverly Yurschak, Libn.

NORTHWESTERN UNIVERSITY - DENTAL SCHOOL LIBRARY
311 E. Chicago Ave.   Phone: (312) 649-8332
Chicago, IL 60611   Minnie Orfanos, Libn.

NORTHWESTERN UNIVERSITY - HEALTH SCIENCES LIBRARY
303 E. Chicago Ave.   Phone: (312) 649-8133
Chicago, IL 60611   Cecile E. Kramer, Dir.

NORTHWESTERN UNIVERSITY - LAW SCHOOL LIBRARY
357 E. Chicago Ave.   Phone: (312) 649-8450
Chicago, IL 60611   George S. Grossman, Libn.

NORWEGIAN-AMERICAN HOSPITAL, INC. - SEUFERT MEMORIAL LIBRARY
1044 N. Francisco Ave.   Phone: (312) 278-8800
Chicago, IL 60622   Estrella De La Cruz, Libn.

OPEN LANDS PROJECT - LIBRARY
53 W. Jackson Blvd., Rm. 1015   Phone: (312) 427-4256
Chicago, IL 60604   Judith M. Stockdale, Exec.Dir.

OUR LADY OF SORROWS BASILICA - ARCHIVES
3121 W. Jackson Blvd.   Phone: (312) 638-5800
Chicago, IL 60612   Rev. Conrad M. Borntrager, O.S.M., Archv.

PANNELL KERR FORSTER - MANAGEMENT ADVISORY SERVICES - LIBRARY
122 S. Michigan Ave.   Phone: (312) 427-7955
Chicago, IL 60603   Ann L. Plous, Libn.

PEAT, MARWICK, MITCHELL & COMPANY - AUDIT/MCD LIBRARY
Peat Marwick Plaza
303 E. Wacker Dr.   Phone: (312) 938-1000
Chicago, IL 60601   Mary LaRue Geiser, Libn.

PEOPLES GAS LIGHT AND COKE COMPANY - LIBRARY
122 S. Michigan Ave., Rm. 727   Phone: (312) 431-4677
Chicago, IL 60603   Barbara Benchik, Chf.Libn.

PERKINS AND WILL ARCHITECTS, INC. - RESOURCE CENTER
309 W. Jackson Blvd.   Phone: (312) 427-9300
Chicago, IL 60606   John O'Neil, Specifier

PLAYBOY ENTERPRISES, INC. - PHOTO LIBRARY
919 N. Michigan Ave.   Phone: (312) 751-8000
Chicago, IL 60611   Clydia Jones, Pict.Libn.

POLISH MUSEUM OF AMERICA - LIBRARY AND ARCHIVES
984 Milwaukee Ave.   Phone: (312) 384-3352
Chicago, IL 60622   Rev. Donald Bilinski, O.F.M., Dir.

POPE, BALLARD, SHEPARD AND FOWLE - LIBRARY
69 W. Washington St.   Phone: (312) 630-4283
Chicago, IL 60602   Ronald E. Feret

PRC CONSOER, TOWNSEND, INC. - LIBRARY AND INFORMATION CENTER
3 Illinois Center
303 E. Wacker Dr., Suite 600   Phone: (312) 938-0300
Chicago, IL 60601   Mary T. Schramm, Libn.-Dir.

PRICE WATERHOUSE - LIBRARY †
200 E. Randolph Dr., Rm. 6200   Phone: (312) 565-1500
Chicago, IL 60601   E. Ann Raup, Libn.

RAVENSWOOD HOSPITAL MEDICAL CENTER - MEDICAL-NURSING LIBRARY
    †
4550 N. Winchester at Wilson   Phone: (312) 878-4300
Chicago, IL 60640   Mr. Zia Solomon Gilliana, Med.Libn.

REAL ESTATE RESEARCH CORPORATION - LIBRARY
72 W. Adams St.   Phone: (312) 346-5885
Chicago, IL 60603   Robert G. Luberda, Hd.Libn.

GEOGRAPHIC

**G
E
O
G
R
A
P
H
I
C**

RED CROSS OF CONSTANTINE - UNITED GRAND IMPERIAL COUNCIL - LIBRARY
14 E. Jackson Blvd., Suite 1700   Phone: (312) 427-5670
Chicago, IL 60604   Paul C. Rodenhauser, Grand Recorder

RESURRECTION HOSPITAL - MEDICAL LIBRARY & ALLIED HEALTH SCIENCES
7435 W. Talcott Rd.   Phone: (312) 774-8000
Chicago, IL 60631   Klara B. Goodrich, Med.Libn.

REYNOLDS (Russell) ASSOCIATES, INC. - LIBRARY
230 W. Monroe St.   Phone: (312) 782-9862
Chicago, IL 60606   Gerri Hilt, Dir. of Res.

ROCKWELL INTERNATIONAL - GRAPHIC SYSTEMS DIVISION - TECHNICAL INFORMATION CENTER *
3100 S. Central   Phone: (312) 656-8600
Chicago, IL 60650   Cathe Benda, Libn.

ROOKS, PITTS, FULLAGAR & POUST - LIBRARY
55 W. Monroe, No. 1500   Phone: (312) 372-5600
Chicago, IL 60603   Victoria A. Praemer, Hd.Libn.

ROOSEVELT UNIVERSITY - ARCHIVES
430 S. Michigan   Phone: (312) 341-3643
Chicago, IL 60614   Marcia Dellenbach, Archv.

ROOSEVELT UNIVERSITY - MUSIC LIBRARY
430 S. Michigan Ave.   Phone: (312) 341-3651
Chicago, IL 60605   Donald Draganski, Libn.

ROOSEVELT UNIVERSITY - ORAL HISTORY PROJECT IN LABOR HISTORY
430 S. Michigan   Phone: (312) 341-3763
Chicago, IL 60605   Elizabeth Balanoff, Dir.

ROSELAND COMMUNITY HOSPITAL - HEALTH SCIENCE LIBRARY
45 W. 111th St.   Phone: (312) 995-3191
Chicago, IL 60628   Mary T. Hanlon, Libn.

ROSS, HARDIES, O'KEEFE, BABCOCK & PARSONS - LAW LIBRARY
One IBM Plaza, 3100   Phone: (312) 467-9300
Chicago, IL 60611   Dot Paas, Libn.

RUSH UNIVERSITY AND MEDICAL CENTER - LIBRARY
600 S. Paulina St.   Phone: (312) 942-5950
Chicago, IL 60612   Doris Bolef, Dir.

ST. ANNE'S HOSPITAL - MEDICAL STAFF LIBRARY *
4950 W. Thomas St.   Phone: (312) 378-7100
Chicago, IL 60651   Claire Strelzoff, Libn.

ST. ANTHONY HOSPITAL - SPRAFKA MEMORIAL HEALTH SCIENCE LIBRARY
2875 W. 19th St.   Phone: (312) 521-1710
Chicago, IL 60623   Karen Ambrose, Lib.Cons.

ST. ELIZABETH'S HOSPITAL - LUKEN HEALTH SCIENCES LIBRARY *
1431 N. Claremont Ave.   Phone: (312) 278-2000
Chicago, IL 60622   Claire Strelzoff, Libn.

ST. JOSEPH HOSPITAL - LIBRARY
2900 N. Lake Shore   Phone: (312) 975-3038
Chicago, IL 60657   Katherine Wimmer, Dir., Lib.Serv.

ST. MARY OF NAZARETH HOSPITAL - SCHOOL OF NURSING LIBRARY
1127 N. Oakley Blvd.   Phone: (312) 384-5360
Chicago, IL 60622   Laurie Broadus, Libn.

ST. MARY OF NAZARETH HOSPITAL - SISTER STELLA LOUISE HEALTH SCIENCE LIBRARY
2233 W. Division St.   Phone: (312) 770-2219
Chicago, IL 60622   Janet S. Klieman, Med.Libn.

SARGENT & LUNDY ENGINEERS - TECHNICAL LIBRARY
55 E. Monroe St., Rm. 16P41   Phone: (312) 269-3524
Chicago, IL 60603   Helen P. Heisler, Libn.

SCIENCE RESEARCH ASSOCIATES, INC. - LIBRARY *
155 N. Wacker Dr.   Phone: (312) 984-2425
Chicago, IL 60606   Joan M. Piraino, Libn.

SEARS, ROEBUCK AND CO. - ARCHIVES, BUSINESS HISTORY AND INFORMATION CENTER
Sears Tower, Dept. 703   Phone: (312) 875-8321
Chicago, IL 60684   Lenore Swoiskin, Dir. of Archv.

SEARS, ROEBUCK AND CO. - MERCHANDISE DEVELOPMENT AND TESTING LABORATORY - LIBRARY, DEPARTMENT 817 †
Sears Tower, 23rd Fl.   Phone: (312) 875-5991
Chicago, IL 60684   Mary M. McCarron, Libn.

SEYFARTH, SHAW, FAIRWEATHER & GERALDSON - LIBRARY
55 E. Monroe St.   Phone: (312) 346-8000
Chicago, IL 60603   Kenneth C. Halicki, Libn.

SHEDD (John G.) AQUARIUM - LIBRARY
1200 S. Lake Shore Dr.   Phone: (312) 939-2426
Chicago, IL 60605   Dottie Dilts, Libn.

SIDLEY & AUSTIN - LIBRARY
One First National Plaza   Phone: (312) 329-5475
Chicago, IL 60603   Julie Farmar DeBoer, Libn.

SKIDMORE, OWINGS & MERRILL - LIBRARY/RESOURCE CENTER
33 W. Monroe St.   Phone: (312) 346-6161
Chicago, IL 60603   Ann Dutt, Libn.

SOCIETY OF REAL ESTATE APPRAISERS - LIBRARY
645 N. Michigan Ave.
Chicago, IL 60611

SONNENSCHEIN CARLIN NATH & ROSENTHAL - LIBRARY
8000 Sears Tower
233 S. Wacker Dr.   Phone: (312) 876-7906
Chicago, IL 60606   Lael Laning Bush, Hd.Libn.

SOUTH SHORE HOSPITAL - MEDICAL STAFF LIBRARY
8015 S. Luella Ave.   Phone: (312) 768-0810
Chicago, IL 60617   Maline Mars, Sec./Libn.

SPERTUS COLLEGE OF JUDAICA - NORMAN AND HELEN ASHER LIBRARY
618 S. Michigan Ave.   Phone: (312) 922-9012
Chicago, IL 60605   Richard W. Marcus, Hd.Libn.

STANDARD EDUCATIONAL CORPORATION - EDITORIAL LIBRARY
200 W. Monroe St.   Phone: (312) 346-7440
Chicago, IL 60606   David E. King, Libn.

STANDARD OIL COMPANY OF INDIANA - LIBRARY/INFORMATION CENTER
200 E. Randolph St.   Phone: (312) 856-5961
Chicago, IL 60601   Miss Vlasta L. Jurco, Mgr.

STEIN ROE AND FARNHAM - LIBRARY
150 S. Wacker Dr.   Phone: (312) 368-7840
Chicago, IL 60606   Nancy Hanfelder, Libn.

SWEDISH COVENANT HOSPITAL - JOSEPH G. STROMBERG LIBRARY OF THE HEALTH SCIENCES
5145 North California Ave.   Phone: (312) 878-8200
Chicago, IL 60625   Jan Zibrat, Med.Libn.

SWEDISH PIONEER HISTORICAL SOCIETY - SWEDISH PIONEER ARCHIVES
5125 N. Spaulding Ave.   Phone: (312) 583-5722
Chicago, IL 60625   Selma Jacobson, Cur.

SWIFT AND COMPANY - GENERAL OFFICE LIBRARY
115 W. Jackson Blvd.
Chicago, IL 60604

TECHNOMIC CONSULTANTS - INFORMATION CENTER
One N. Wacker Dr.   Phone: (312) 346-5900
Chicago, IL 60606   Karen J. Switt, Mgr., Info.Serv.

THOMPSON (J. Walter) COMPANY - INFORMATION CENTER
875 N. Michigan Ave.   Phone: (312) 664-6700
Chicago, IL 60611   Edward G. Strable, V.P., Dir.Info.Serv.

UKRAINIAN MEDICAL ASSOCIATION OF NORTH AMERICA - MEDICAL ARCHIVES AND LIBRARY †
2453 W. Chicago Ave.   Phone: (312) 234-7200
Chicago, IL 60622   Paul Pundy, Dir.

UNION CARBIDE CORPORATION - FILMS-PACKAGING DIVISION -
  TECHNICAL LIBRARY
6733 W. 65th St.   Phone: (312) 496-4286
Chicago, IL 60638   Mrs. Nijole K. Pupius, Tech.Libn.

UNITED CHARITIES OF CHICAGO - LIBRARY
64 E. Jackson Blvd.   Phone: (312) 939-5930
Chicago, IL 60604   Marie T. Burns, Libn./Rec.Mgr.

U.S. BUREAU OF THE CENSUS - REGIONAL DATA USER SERVICE - CHICAGO
  REGIONAL OFFICE - LIBRARY
55 E. Jackson Blvd., Rm. 1304   Phone: (312) 353-0980
Chicago, IL 60604   Stephen Laue, Data User Serv.Off.

U.S.D.A. - AGRICULTURAL RESEARCH SERVICE - NORTH CENTRAL REGION
  - MARKET PATHOLOGY RESEARCH LIBRARY
536 S. Clark St., Rm. 183   Phone: (312) 353-6678
Chicago, IL 60605   Dr. Louis Beraha, Res. Leader

U.S. DEPT. OF COMMERCE - INTERNATIONAL TRADE ADMINISTRATION -
  CHICAGO DISTRICT OFFICE LIBRARY
Mid-Continental Plaza Bldg., Rm. 1406
55 E. Monroe   Phone: (312) 353-4450
Chicago, IL 60603   Bernadine C. Roberson, Libn.

U.S. DEPT. OF JUSTICE - UNITED STATES ATTORNEY, NORTHERN
  DISTRICT OF ILLINOIS - LIBRARY
1500 Dirksen Federal Bldg.
219 S. Dearborn St.   Phone: (312) 353-5338
Chicago, IL 60604   Paula Giroux, Lib.Techn.

U.S. NATL. ARCHIVES & RECORDS SERVICE - FEDERAL ARCHIVES &
  RECORDS CENTER, REGION 5
7358 S. Pulaski Rd.   Phone: (312) 353-0161
Chicago, IL 60629   Peter W. Bunce, Chf., Archv.Br.

U.S. RAILROAD RETIREMENT BOARD - LIBRARY
844 Rush St.   Phone: (312) 751-4928
Chicago, IL 60611   Kay Collins, Libn.

U.S. SECURITIES AND EXCHANGE COMMISSION - PUBLIC REFERENCE
  LIBRARY
219 S. Dearborn, Rm. 1228   Phone: (312) 353-7433
Chicago, IL 60604   Donald J. Evers, Chf.Ref.Libn.

U.S. VETERANS ADMINISTRATION (IL-Chicago) - LAKESIDE HOSPITAL
  MEDICAL LIBRARY
333 E. Huron St.   Phone: (312) 943-6600
Chicago, IL 60611   Lydia Tkaczuk, Chf., Lib.Serv.

U.S. VETERANS ADMINISTRATION (IL-Chicago) - WESTSIDE HOSPITAL
  LIBRARY
820 S. Damen Ave.   Phone: (312) 666-6500
Chicago, IL 60612   Lynne D. Morris, Chf., Lib.Serv.

UNITED WAY OF METROPOLITAN CHICAGO - LIBRARY
72 W. Adams St.   Phone: (312) 263-1756
Chicago, IL 60603   Sally J. Barnum, Dir.

UNIVERSITY OF CHICAGO - ART LIBRARY
Regenstein Library
1100 E. 57th St.   Phone: (312) 753-3439
Chicago, IL 60637   Suzanne Lorimer, Art Libn.

UNIVERSITY OF CHICAGO - BUSINESS/ECONOMICS LIBRARY
Joseph Regenstein Library
1100 E. 57th St.   Phone: (312) 753-3428
Chicago, IL 60637   Jennette S. Rader, Bus.Econ.Libn.

UNIVERSITY OF CHICAGO - CHEMISTRY LIBRARY
5747 S. Ellis Ave.   Phone: (312) 753-3417
Chicago, IL 60637   Brenda Rice, Libn.

UNIVERSITY OF CHICAGO - DEPARTMENT OF ART - EPSTEIN ARCHIVE
Regenstein Library
1100 E. 57th St.   Phone: (312) 753-2887
Chicago, IL 60637

UNIVERSITY OF CHICAGO - ECKHART LIBRARY
Eckhart Hall, Second Fl.   Phone: (312) 753-3454
Chicago, IL 60637   Harriet E. Schnoor, Libn.

UNIVERSITY OF CHICAGO - FAR EASTERN LIBRARY
Regenstein Library
1100 E. 57th St.   Phone: (312) 753-4116
Chicago, IL 60637   James K.M. Cheng, Cur.

UNIVERSITY OF CHICAGO - DR. FRANK BILLINGS LIBRARY
Billings Hospital, 950 E. 59th St.
Box 406   Phone: (312) 947-5220
Chicago, IL 60637   Alison Baker, Med.Ref.Libn.

UNIVERSITY OF CHICAGO HOSPITALS & CLINICS - PHARMACEUTICAL
  SERVICES - DRUG INFORMATION CENTER
950 E. 59th St.   Phone: (312) 947-6046
Chicago, IL 60637   Steven L. Ifshin, Drug Info.Libn.

UNIVERSITY OF CHICAGO - HUMAN RESOURCES CENTER - A.G. BUSH
  LIBRARY
1225 E. 60th St.   Phone: (312) 753-2024
Chicago, IL 60637   Jennette Rader, Libn.

UNIVERSITY OF CHICAGO - LAW SCHOOL LIBRARY
1121 E. 60th St.   Phone: (312) 753-3425
Chicago, IL 60637   Judith M. Wright, Law Libn.

UNIVERSITY OF CHICAGO - MAP COLLECTION
Regenstein Library
1100 E. 57th St.
Chicago, IL 60637   Kathleen A. Zar, Map Libn.

UNIVERSITY OF CHICAGO - MUSIC COLLECTION
Regenstein Library
1100 E. 57th St.   Phone: (312) 753-3445
Chicago, IL 60637   Hans Lenneberg, Music Libn.

UNIVERSITY OF CHICAGO - NATIONAL OPINION RESEARCH CENTER -
  LIBRARY AND DATA ARCHIVES
6030 S. Ellis Ave.   Phone: (312) 753-1487
Chicago, IL 60637   Patrick Bova, Libn.

UNIVERSITY OF CHICAGO - SOCIAL SERVICES ADMINISTRATION LIBRARY
969 East 60th St.   Phone: (312) 753-3426
Chicago, IL 60637   Eileen Libby, Libn.

UNIVERSITY OF CHICAGO - SOUTH ASIA COLLECTION
1100 E. 57th St.   Phone: (312) 753-3765
Chicago, IL 60637   Maureen L. P. Patterson, Biblog./Hd.

UNIVERSITY OF CHICAGO - SPECIAL COLLECTIONS
Regenstein Library, 1100 E. 57th St.   Phone: (312) 753-4308
Chicago, IL 60637   Robert Rosenthal, Cur.

UNIVERSITY OF ILLINOIS, CHICAGO CIRCLE - LIBRARY - MAP SECTION
Box 8198   Phone: (312) 996-5277
Chicago, IL 60626   Marsha L. Selmer, Map Libn.

UNIVERSITY OF ILLINOIS, CHICAGO CIRCLE - SCIENCE LIBRARY
Science & Engineering South Bldg.
Box 7565   Phone: (312) 996-5396
Chicago, IL 60680   Cynthia A. Steinke, Libn.

UNIVERSITY OF ILLINOIS - CONSULTATION CLINIC FOR EPILEPSY -
  LIBRARY
Neuropsychiatric Institute, Rm.855-N
912 S. Wood St.
Chicago, IL 60612

UNIVERSITY OF ILLINOIS MEDICAL CENTER - LIBRARY OF THE HEALTH
  SCIENCES
1750 W. Polk St.   Phone: (312) 996-8974
Chicago, IL 60612   Irwin H. Pizer, Univ.Libn.

URBAN INVESTMENT AND DEVELOPMENT COMPANY - INFORMATION
  CENTER †
845 N. Michigan Ave.   Phone: (312) 440-3296
Chicago, IL 60611   Charles LaGrutta, Info.Ctr.Coord.

GEOGRAPHIC

GEOGRAPHIC

VANDERCOOK COLLEGE OF MUSIC - HARRY RUPPEL MEMORIAL LIBRARY
3209 S. Michigan Ave.   Phone: (312) 225-6288
Chicago, IL 60616   Sue A. Weyhmiller, Libn.

VELSICOL CHEMICAL CORPORATION - RESEARCH AND DEVELOPMENT DEPARTMENT - LIBRARY †
341 E. Ohio St., 3rd Fl.   Phone: (312) 670-4771
Chicago, IL 60611   June M. Snyder, Asst.Libn.

WARBURG PARIBAS BECKER, INC. - LIBRARY
Two First National Plaza   Phone: (312) 630-5592
Chicago, IL 60603   Joan T. Goodman, Supv.

WEIR (Paul) COMPANY - LIBRARY
20 N. Wacker Dr., Suite 2828   Phone: (312) 346-0275
Chicago, IL 60606   Mary A. Vacula, Libn.

WEISS (Louis A.) MEMORIAL HOSPITAL - L. LEWIS COHEN MEMORIAL MEDICAL LIBRARY
4646 N. Marine Dr.   Phone: (312) 878-8700
Chicago, IL 60640   Iris Sachs, Med.Libn.

WESTERN ELECTRIC COMPANY, INC. - TECHNICAL LIBRARY *
Hawthorne Sta.
Chicago, IL 60623

WILLIAM J. CAMPBELL LIBRARY OF THE UNITED STATES COURTS
219 S. Dearborn St., Rm. 1448   Phone: (312) 435-5661
Chicago, IL 60604   Janet Wishinsky, Libn.

WINSTON & STRAWN - LIBRARY
One 1st National Plaza   Phone: (312) 558-5740
Chicago, IL 60603   Linda Lockwood, Law Libn.

WORLD ASSOCIATION OF DOCUMENT EXAMINERS - WADE LIBRARY
111 N. Canal St.   Phone: (312) 930-9446
Chicago, IL 60606   Lee Arnold, Libn.

WORLD BOOK-CHILDCRAFT INTERNATIONAL, INC.- RESEARCH LIBRARY
Merchandise Mart Plaza   Phone: (312) 341-8777
Chicago, IL 60654   Indrani Embar, Hd.Libn.

WORLD WITHOUT WAR COUNCIL - MIDWEST LIBRARY
67 E. Madison, Suite 1417   Phone: (312) 236-7459
Chicago, IL 60603   Robert Woito, Pubn.Dir.

WRIGLEY (Wm., Jr.) COMPANY - CORPORATE LIBRARY
410 N. Michigan Ave.   Phone: (312) 644-2121
Chicago, IL 60611   Linda Hanrath, Corp.Libn.

WRIGLEY (Wm., Jr.) COMPANY - QUALITY ASSURANCE BRANCH LIBRARY
3535 S. Ashland Ave.   Phone: (312) 523-4040
Chicago, IL 60609   Elizabeth R. Cibulskis, Tech.Libn.

WRIGLEY (Wm., Jr.) COMPANY - RESEARCH & DEVELOPMENT LIBRARY
3535 S. Ashland Ave.   Phone: (312) 523-4040
Chicago, IL 60609   Elizabeth R. Cibulskis, Tech.Libn.

YOUTH NETWORK COUNCIL OF CHICAGO, INC. - CLEARINGHOUSE
1123 W. Washington Blvd.   Phone: (312) 226-1200
Chicago, IL 60607   Steve Sperling, Dir.

ST. JAMES HOSPITAL - MEDICAL LIBRARY
1423 Chicago Rd.   Phone: (312) 756-1000
Chicago Heights, IL 60411   Margaret A. Lindstrand, Libn.

ST. JOHN UNITED CHURCH OF CHRIST - LIBRARY
307 W. Clay St.   Phone: (618) 344-2526
Collinsville, IL 62234   Norma L. Fischer, Libn.

SOUTHWESTERN ILLINOIS METROPOLITAN AND REGIONAL PLANNING COMMISSION - TECHNICAL LIBRARY
203 W. Main St.   Phone: (618) 344-4250
Collinsville, IL 62234   Noal F. Gruenert, Info.Mgr.

LAKEVIEW MEDICAL CENTER - MEDICAL/NURSING LIBRARY
812 N. Logan Ave.   Phone: (217) 443-5000
Danville, IL 61832   Donna Judd, Libn.

U.S. VETERANS ADMINISTRATION (IL-Danville) - MEDICAL CENTER LIBRARY
    Phone: (217) 442-8000
Danville, IL 61832   Betsy Taylor, Chf., Lib.Serv.

ARCHER DANIELS MIDLAND COMPANY - RESEARCH LIBRARY
4666 Faries Pkwy.   Phone: (217) 424-5397
Decatur, IL 62526   Richard E. Wallace, Mgr.Info.Serv.

DECATUR DEPARTMENT OF COMMUNITY DEVELOPMENT - PLANNING LIBRARY
One Civic Center Plaza   Phone: (217) 424-2778
Decatur, IL 62523

DECATUR HERALD AND REVIEW - LIBRARY
601 E. William St.   Phone: (217) 422-7395
Decatur, IL 62523   Faye Spencer, Libn.

DECATUR MEMORIAL HOSPITAL - HEALTH SCIENCE LIBRARY
2300 N. Edward St.   Phone: (217) 877-8121
Decatur, IL 62526   John W. Law, Libn.

MACON COUNTY LAW LIBRARY
County Bldg.   Phone: (217) 422-7441
Decatur, IL 62523   Norman C. Higgs, Libn.

STALEY (A.E.) MANUFACTURING COMPANY - TECHNICAL INFORMATION CENTER
2200 E. Eldorado St.   Phone: (217) 423-4411
Decatur, IL 62525   Ann M. Seidman, Mgr.

BAXTER TRAVENOL LABORATORIES, INC. - BUSINESS AND LAW LIBRARY/ INFORMATION CENTER
2-2W, One Baxter Pkwy.   Phone: (312) 948-3881
Deerfield, IL 60015   Frank J. Locker, Supv.

JENSEN (Rolf) & ASSOCIATES - LIBRARY
100 Wilmot Rd.   Phone: (312) 948-0700
Deerfield, IL 60015   Lois Gorr Rosenberg, Libn.

CLEARINGHOUSE FOR SOCIOLOGICAL LITERATURE
Dept. of Sociology
Northern Illinois Univ.   Phone: (815) 753-0303
Dekalb, IL 60115   Hugo O. Engelmann, Ed.

DEKALB AGRESEARCH INC. - CORN RESEARCH CENTER - LIBRARY
Sycamore Rd.   Phone: (815) 758-3461
DeKalb, IL 60115   Dr. Charles F. Krull, V.P., Corn Res.

NORTHERN ILLINOIS UNIVERSITY - FARADAY LIBRARY †
Faraday Hall, Rm. 212   Phone: (815) 753-1257
DeKalb, IL 60115   Paul L. Knapp, Sci.Libn.

NORTHERN ILLINOIS UNIVERSITY - MUSIC LIBRARY †
175 Music Bldg.   Phone: (815) 753-1426
DeKalb, IL 60115   Gordon S. Rowley, Music Libn.

NORTHERN ILLINOIS UNIVERSITY - REGIONAL HISTORY CENTER
268 Swen Parson Hall   Phone: (815) 753-1094
DeKalb, IL 60115   Glen A. Gildemeister, Dir.

NORTHERN ILLINOIS UNIVERSITY - SOUTHEAST ASIA COLLECTION
Founders Memorial Library   Phone: (815) 753-1819
DeKalb, IL 60115   Lee Dutton, Libn.

NORTHERN ILLINOIS UNIVERSITY - UNIVERSITY ARCHIVES
    Phone: (815) 753-1779
DeKalb, IL 60115   Glen A. Gildemeister, Archv.

AMERICAN FOUNDRYMEN'S SOCIETY - TECHNICAL INFORMATION CENTER †
Golf & Wolf Rds.   Phone: (312) 824-0181
Des Plaines, IL 60016   Ann V. Duggan, Mgr., Lib.Serv.

BORG-WARNER CORPORATION - ROY C. INGERSOLL RESEARCH CENTER - LIBRARY
Wolf & Algonquin Sts.   Phone: (312) 827-3131
Des Plaines, IL 60018   Kathleen P. Oestreich, Mgr., Info.Serv.

DE SOTO, INC. - INFORMATION CENTER
1700 S. Mt. Prospect Rd.   Phone: (312) 391-9556
Des Plaines, IL 60018   Cathy Collins Kozelka, Mgr.

DES PLAINES HISTORICAL SOCIETY - JOHN BYRNE MEMORIAL LIBRARY
789 Pearson St.
Box 225   Phone: (312) 297-4912
Des Plaines, IL 60017   Terri Fraser, Musm.Dir.

DOALL COMPANY - LIBRARY
245 N. Laurel Ave.   Phone: (312) 824-1122
Des Plaines, IL 60016

FOREST INSTITUTE OF PROFESSIONAL PSYCHOLOGY - LIBRARY
555 Wilson Ln.   Phone: (312) 635-4333
Des Plaines, IL 60090   Donna E. Bush, Dir.Lib.Serv.

INDUSTRIAL MANAGEMENT SOCIETY - FILM LIBRARY
570 Northwest Hwy.   Phone: (312) 296-7189
Des Plaines, IL 60016   Lila Blondell, Film Lib.Mgr.

REFRIGERATION SERVICE ENGINEERS SOCIETY - LIBRARY
1666 Rand Rd.   Phone: (312) 297-6464
Des Plaines, IL 60016   Mr. Nari Sethna, Exec.Mgr.

SIEMENS GAMMASONICS, INC. - NUCLEAR MEDICAL DIVISION -
    RESEARCH LIBRARY
2000 Nuclear Dr.   Phone: (312) 635-3643
Des Plaines, IL 60018   Arlene M. Lowden, Libn.

UNITED STATES GYPSUM COMPANY - RESEARCH CENTER LIBRARY
1000 E. Northwest Hwy.   Phone: (312) 299-3381
Des Plaines, IL 60016   Marie Ehrmann, Libn.-in-Charge

UOP INC. - PATENT LIBRARY
Ten UOP Plaza   Phone: (312) 391-2008
Des Plaines, IL 60016   Mildred S. Bruhn, Supv.

UOP INC. - RESEARCH TECHNICAL INFORMATION CENTER
Ten UOP Plaza
Algonquin & Mt. Prospect Rds.   Phone: (312) 392-3361
Des Plaines, IL 60016   Leonore Rogalski, Supv.

DIXON DEVELOPMENTAL CENTER - LIBRARY †
2600 N. Brinton Ave.   Phone: (815) 288-5561
Dixon, IL 61021

BIBLIOGRAPHIC SERVICE
4912 Wallbank Ave.   Phone: (312) 969-2706
Downers Grove, IL 60515   Maude R. Hinson, Lib.Cons. & Res.

OLIN CORPORATION - BRASS DIVISION LIBRARY
                                             Phone: (618) 258-3198
East Alton, IL 62024   Barbara A. Allen, Libn.

CATERPILLAR TRACTOR COMPANY - TRAINING LIBRARY
Bldg. W   Phone: (309) 675-2724
East Peoria, IL 61630   Donald J. Noble, Supv.

TRI-COUNTY REGIONAL PLANNING COMMISSION - LIBRARY
Box 2200   Phone: (309) 694-4391
East Peoria, IL 61611   Robert L. Pinkerton, Exec.Dir.

MADISON COUNTY HISTORICAL SOCIETY - MUSEUM LIBRARY
715 N. Main St.   Phone: (618) 656-7562
Edwardsville, IL 62025   Anna Symanski, Supt.

SOUTHERN ILLINOIS UNIVERSITY, EDWARDSVILLE - DOCUMENTS
    COLLECTION
Lovejoy Library   Phone: (618) 692-2606
Edwardsville, IL 62026   Robert Fortado, Doc.Libn.

SOUTHERN ILLINOIS UNIVERSITY, EDWARDSVILLE - EDUCATION LIBRARY
Lovejoy Library   Phone: (618) 692-2906
Edwardsville, IL 62026   Don Smith, Educ.Libn.

SOUTHERN ILLINOIS UNIVERSITY, EDWARDSVILLE - HUMAN SERVICES
    LIBRARY
                                             Phone: (618) 692-2884
Edwardsville, IL 62026   Frances Schipkowski, Sec.-Libn.

SOUTHERN ILLINOIS UNIVERSITY, EDWARDSVILLE - HUMANITIES & FINE
    ARTS LIBRARY
Lovejoy Library   Phone: (618) 692-2670
Edwardsville, IL 62026   John Dustin, Hum.Libn.

SOUTHERN ILLINOIS UNIVERSITY, EDWARDSVILLE - RESEARCH &
    PROJECTS OFFICE LIBRARY
Graduate School   Phone: (618) 692-3162
Edwardsville, IL 62026   Kate Chappell, Rsrcs.Anl.

SOUTHERN ILLINOIS UNIVERSITY, EDWARDSVILLE - SCIENCE LIBRARY
Lovejoy Library   Phone: (618) 692-3828
Edwardsville, IL 62026   Robert Gerhardt, Sci.Libn.

SOUTHERN ILLINOIS UNIVERSITY, EDWARDSVILLE - SOCIAL SCIENCE/
    BUSINESS/MAP LIBRARY
Lovejoy Library   Phone: (618) 692-2422
Edwardsville, IL 62026   Marvin Soloman, Soc.Sci./Map Libn.

CHURCH OF THE BRETHREN GENERAL BOARD - BRETHREN HISTORICAL
    LIBRARY AND ARCHIVES
1451 Dundee Ave.   Phone: (312) 742-5100
Elgin, IL 60120   James R. Lynch, Archv.

ELGIN MENTAL HEALTH CENTER - ANTON BOISEN PROFESSIONAL LIBRARY
750 S. State St.   Phone: (312) 742-1040
Elgin, IL 60120   Jennifer Ford, Libn.

ALEXIAN BROTHERS MEDICAL CENTER - MEDICAL LIBRARY
800 W. Biesterfield Rd.   Phone: (312) 437-5500
Elk Grove Village, IL 60007   Jocelyn A. Bernholdt, Med.Libn.

CONGREGATION OF THE ALEXIAN BROTHERS - PROVINCIAL ARCHIVES
600 Alexian Way
Elk Grove Village, IL 60007   Bro. Roy Godwin, C.F.A., Prov.Archv.

ELMHURST HISTORICAL COMMISSION - LIBRARY
120 E. Park Ave.
Box 84   Phone: (312) 833-1457
Elmhurst, IL 60126   Lillian Harlan, Cur.

LIZZADRO MUSEUM OF LAPIDARY ART - LIBRARY
220 Cottage Hill Ave.   Phone: (312) 833-1616
Elmhurst, IL 60126   Judith Greene, Exec.Sec.

MEMORIAL HOSPITAL OF DU PAGE COUNTY - MEDICAL & HEALTH
    SCIENCES LIBRARY
200 Berteau Ave.   Phone: (312) 833-1400
Elmhurst, IL 60126   Pauline Ng, Dir.

AMERICAN ACADEMY OF PEDIATRICS - LIBRARY
1801 Hinman Ave.
Box 1034   Phone: (312) 869-4255
Evanston, IL 60204   Frances Curry, Libn.

AMERICAN HOSPITAL SUPPLY CORPORATION - CORPORATE INFORMATION
    CENTER
One American Plaza   Phone: (312) 866-4586
Evanston, IL 60201   Sharon I. Meyer, Corp.Libn.

BARTON-ASCHMAN ASSOCIATES, INC. - PLANNING LIBRARY †
820 Davis St.   Phone: (312) 491-1000
Evanston, IL 60201   Doris Bell, Mgr.

BETH EMET, THE FREE SYNAGOGUE - BRUCE GORDON MEMORIAL LIBRARY
    *
1224 Dempster   Phone: (312) 869-4230
Evanston, IL 60202

EVANSTON HISTORICAL SOCIETY - CHARLES GATES DAWES HOME -
    LIBRARY
225 Greenwood St.   Phone: (312) 475-3410
Evanston, IL 60201   Margaret Nicholsen, Libn.

EVANSTON HOSPITAL - WEBSTER MEDICAL LIBRARY
2650 Ridge Ave.   Phone: (312) 492-4585
Evanston, IL 60201   Rose Slowinski, Dir.

GEOGRAPHIC

GEOGRAPHIC

FIRST PRESBYTERIAN CHURCH - THOMAS E. BOSWELL MEMORIAL
  LIBRARY
1427 Chicago Ave.   Phone: (312) 864-1472
Evanston, IL 60201   Joan Borg, Libn.

GARRETT-EVANGELICAL/SEABURY-WESTERN THEOLOGICAL SEMINARIES
  LIBRARY †
2021 Sheridan Rd.   Phone: (312) 866-3900
Evanston, IL 60201

LEVERE MEMORIAL FOUNDATION - LIBRARY
1856 Sheridan Rd.   Phone: (312) 475-1856
Evanston, IL 60201   Kenneth D. Tracey, Exec.Dir.

NATIONAL COLLEGE OF EDUCATION - LEARNING RESOURCE CENTERS
2840 Sheridan Rd.   Phone: (312) 256-5150
Evanston, IL 60201   Marilyn A. Lester, Dir. of Lrng.Rsrcs.

NATIONAL FOUNDATION OF FUNERAL SERVICE - BERYL L. BOYER LIBRARY
1600-1612 Central St.   Phone: (312) 328-6545
Evanston, IL 60201   Dr. Joe A. Adams, Dir.

NATIONAL WOMAN'S CHRISTIAN TEMPERANCE UNION - FRANCES E.
  WILLARD MEMORIAL LIBRARY
1730 Chicago Ave.   Phone: (312) 864-1396
Evanston, IL 60201   Rosalita J. Leonard, Libn.

NORTHWESTERN UNIVERSITY - ARCHIVES
University Library   Phone: (312) 492-3354
Evanston, IL 60201   Patrick M. Quinn, Univ.Archv.

NORTHWESTERN UNIVERSITY - GEOLOGY LIBRARY
Locy Hall, Rm. 101   Phone: (312) 492-5525
Evanston, IL 60201   Marsha Gross, Geology Libn.

NORTHWESTERN UNIVERSITY - MAP COLLECTION
University Library   Phone: (312) 492-7603
Evanston, IL 60201   Mary Fortney, Map Libn.

NORTHWESTERN UNIVERSITY - MATHEMATICS LIBRARY
Lunt Bldg., Rm. 111   Phone: (312) 492-7627
Evanston, IL 60201   Zita Hayward, Lib.Asst.

NORTHWESTERN UNIVERSITY - MELVILLE J. HERSKOVITS LIBRARY OF
  AFRICAN STUDIES
University Library   Phone: (312) 492-7684
Evanston, IL 60201   Hans E. Panofsky, Cur. of Africana

NORTHWESTERN UNIVERSITY - MUSIC LIBRARY
                                     Phone: (312) 492-3434
Evanston, IL 60201   Don L. Roberts, Hd.

NORTHWESTERN UNIVERSITY - SEELEY G. MUDD LIBRARY FOR SCIENCE
  AND ENGINEERING
2233 Sheridan Rd.   Phone: (312) 492-3362
Evanston, IL 60201   Robert Michaelson, Hd.Libn.

NORTHWESTERN UNIVERSITY - TRANSPORTATION LIBRARY
                                     Phone: (312) 492-5273
Evanston, IL 60201   Mary Roy, Libn.

RUST-OLEUM CORPORATION - R & D LIBRARY
2301 Oakton St.   Phone: (312) 864-8200
Evanston, IL 60204   Yvonne Sor, Mgr.Info.Sci.

ST. FRANCIS HOSPITAL - SCHOOL OF NURSING LIBRARY
319 Ridge Ave.   Phone: (312) 492-6268
Evanston, IL 60202   Patricia Gibson, Libn.

WASHINGTON NATIONAL INSURANCE COMPANY - INFORMATION
  RESOURCES CENTER
1630 Chicago Ave.   Phone: (312) 866-3651
Evanston, IL 60201   Joy M. Blackburn, Libn.

LITTLE COMPANY OF MARY HOSPITAL - EDUCATION BUILDING LIBRARY
2800 W. 95th St.   Phone: (312) 422-6200
Evergreen Park, IL 60642   Rita Karner, Libn.

MATSUSHITA INDUSTRIAL COMPANY - TECHNICAL INFORMATION
  SERVICES LIBRARY
9401 W. Grand Ave.   Phone: (312) 451-1200
Franklin Park, IL 60131   Ted Rzeszewski, Mgr., Advan. R & D

MOTOROLA, INC. - SYSTEMS DIVISION - TECHNICAL LIBRARY
2553 N. Edgington   Phone: (312) 451-1000
Franklin Park, IL 60131   Sandra Hoogland, Libn.

HONEYWELL, INC. - MICRO SWITCH ENGINEERING LIBRARY
11 Spring St.   Phone: (815) 235-5609
Freeport, IL 61032   Vernelia Tedman, Libn.

GALESBURG COTTAGE HOSPITAL - HEALTH SERVICES LIBRARY
695 N. Kellogg St.   Phone: (309) 343-8131
Galesburg, IL 61401   Barbara Olson Bullis, Libn.

GALESBURG MENTAL HEALTH CENTER - HIMWICH LIBRARY OF THE
  NEUROSCIENCES
                                     Phone: (309) 244-2141
Galesburg, IL 61401   Yvonne Boynton, Med.Libn.

DU PAGE LIBRARY SYSTEM - SYSTEM CENTER
127 S. First St.
Box 268   Phone: (312) 232-8457
Geneva, IL 60134   Alice E. McKinley, Dir.

CHICAGO MOUNTAINEERING CLUB - JOHN SPECK MEMORIAL LIBRARY
739 Forest Ave.   Phone: (312) 469-3443
Glen Ellyn, IL 60137   George Pokorny, Libn.

FIRST UNITED METHODIST CHURCH - LIBRARY
424 Forest Ave.   Phone: (312) 469-3510
Glen Ellyn, IL 60137   Kathryn Collord, Libn.

NORTH SHORE CONGREGATION ISRAEL - OSCAR HILLEL PLOTKIN LIBRARY
1185 Sheridan Rd.   Phone: (312) 835-2632
Glencoe, IL 60022   Matalie Cohen, Libn.

GLENVIEW AREA HISTORICAL SOCIETY - LIBRARY
1121 Waukegan Rd.   Phone: (312) 724-2235
Glenview, IL 60025   Esther Roseman, Libn.

KRAFT, INC. - BUSINESS RESEARCH CENTER
Kraft Ct.   Phone: (312) 998-2465
Glenview, IL 60025   Melissa B. Mickey, Libn.

KRAFT, INC. - RESEARCH & DEVELOPMENT LIBRARY
801 Waukegan Rd.   Phone: (312) 998-3707
Glenview, IL 60025   Helen Pettway, Libn.

SCOTT, FORESMAN & COMPANY, INC. - EDITORIAL LIBRARY
1900 E. Lake Ave.   Phone: (312) 729-3000
Glenview, IL 60025   S. Donald Robertson, Hd.Libn.

ZENITH RADIO CORPORATION - ENGINEERING LIBRARY
1000 N. Milwaukee Ave.   Phone: (312) 391-8452
Glenview, IL 60025   Ruby Chu, Hd.Libn.

U.S. NAVY - NAVAL DENTAL RESEARCH INSTITUTE - LIBRARY
Naval Base, Bldg. 1-H   Phone: (312) 688-5647
Great Lakes, IL 60088   Myra J. Rouse, Libn.

U.S. NAVY - NAVAL REGIONAL MEDICAL CENTER (Great Lakes) - MEDICAL
  LIBRARY
Bldg. 200-H   Phone: (312) 688-4601
Great Lakes, IL 60088   Phyllis A. Gibbs, Med.Libn.

INGALLS MEMORIAL HOSPITAL - MEDICAL LIBRARY
One Ingalls Dr.   Phone: (312) 333-2300
Harvey, IL 60426   Carol Ross, Libn.

CONGREGATION SOLEL - LIBRARY †
1301 Clavey Rd.   Phone: (312) 433-3555
Highland Park, IL 60035   Mrs. Irving Hanig, Lib.Chm.

HIGHLAND PARK HISTORICAL SOCIETY - LIBRARY
326 Central Ave.
Box 56   Phone: (312) 432-7090
Highland Park, IL 60035   Henry X. Arenberg

NORTH SUBURBAN SYNAGOGUE BETH EL - MAXWELL ABBELL LIBRARY
1175 Sheridan Rd.   Phone: (312) 432-8900
Highland Park, IL 60035   Patricia Cohler, Libn.

MADDEN (John J.) ZONE CENTER - PROFESSIONAL LIBRARY
1200 S. 1st Ave.   Phone: (312) 345-9870
Hines, IL 60141   Flora L. Hawthorne, Libn.

U.S. VETERANS ADMINISTRATION (IL-Hines) - MEDICAL LIBRARY
Edward Hines, Jr. Medical Center   Phone: (312) 343-7200
Hines, IL 60141   Rose W. Fingeret, Chf.Libn.

HINSDALE SANITARIUM AND HOSPITAL - A.C. LARSON LIBRARY †
120 N. Oak St.   Phone: (312) 887-2868
Hinsdale, IL 60521   Richard L. Cook, Hosp.Libn.

JACKSONVILLE MENTAL HEALTH AND DEVELOPMENTAL CENTER - LIBRARY
  *
1201 S. Main St.   Phone: (217) 245-2111
Jacksonville, IL 62650   Lois E. Wells, Libn.

PASSAVANT MEMORIAL AREA HOSPITAL ASSOCIATION - SIBERT LIBRARY
1600 W. Walnut St.   Phone: (217) 245-9541
Jacksonville, IL 62650   Dorothy H. Knight, LR Coord.

ST. JOSEPH HOSPITAL - HEALTH SCIENCE LIBRARY
333 N. Madison St.   Phone: (815) 725-7133
Joliet, IL 60435   Catherine Siron, Coord., Lib.Serv.

SILVER CROSS HOSPITAL - MEDICAL LIBRARY
1200 Maple Rd.   Phone: (815) 729-7811
Joliet, IL 60432   Mary Ingmire, Libn.

ARMOUR PHARMACEUTICAL COMPANY - LIBRARY †
Rte. 50 N., Box 511   Phone: (815) 932-6771
Kankakee, IL 60901   Shirley Wells, Libn.

KANKAKEE COUNTY HISTORICAL SOCIETY - LIBRARY
Eighth & Water St.   Phone: (815) 932-5279
Kankakee, IL 60901   Don Des Lauriers, Cur.

RIVERSIDE MEDICAL CENTER - MEDICAL LIBRARY
350 N. Wall St.   Phone: (815) 933-1671
Kankakee, IL 60901   Sylvia N. O'Connor, Coord.Med.Lib.Serv.

SHAPIRO (Samuel H.) DEVELOPMENTAL CENTER - PROFESSIONAL LIBRARY
100 E. Jeffery St.   Phone: (815) 939-8419
Kankakee, IL 60901   Juanita Licht, Lib.Supv.

KENILWORTH HISTORICAL SOCIETY - KILNER LIBRARY
415 Kenilworth Ave.   Phone: (312) 251-2565
Kenilworth, IL 60043   George A. Veeder, Pres.

COMMUNITY MEMORIAL GENERAL HOSPITAL - LIBRARY
5101 Willow Springs Rd.   Phone: (312) 352-1200
La Grange, IL 60525   Patricia J. Grundke, Libn.

GENERAL MOTORS CORPORATION - ELECTRO-MOTIVE DIVISION -
  ENGINEERING LIBRARY
9301 55th St.   Phone: (312) 387-6706
La Grange, IL 60525   Eleanor Spolarich, Libn.

AMERICAN NUCLEAR SOCIETY - LIBRARY
555 N. Kensington Ave.   Phone: (312) 352-6611
La Grange Park, IL 60525   Lois S. Webster, Libn.

NORTH SUBURBAN LIBRARY SYSTEM & SUBURBAN LIBRARY SYSTEM -
  SUBURBAN AV SERVICE
920 Barnsdale Rd.   Phone: (312) 352-7671
La Grange Park, IL 60525   Leon L. Drolet, Jr., Dir.

LAKE FOREST COLLEGE - THOMAS OSCAR FREEMAN MEMORIAL LIBRARY
                                           Phone: (312) 234-3100
Lake Forest, IL 60045   Arthur H. Miller, Jr., Coll.Libn.

CHEMED CORPORATION - DEARBORN CHEMICAL (U.S.) LIBRARY
300 Genesee St.   Phone: (312) 483-8241
Lake Zurich, IL 60047   Martha M. Mitchell, Libn.

CONDELL MEMORIAL HOSPITAL - FOHRMAN LIBRARY
900 Garfield Ave.   Phone: (312) 362-2900
Libertyville, IL 60048   Emily Bergmann, Libn.

FIRST PRESBYTERIAN CHURCH - LIBRARY
225 W. Maple Ave.   Phone: (312) 362-2174
Libertyville, IL 60048

LAKE COUNTY FOREST PRESERVE DISTRICT - RYERSON NATURE LIBRARY
2000 N. Milwaukee Ave.   Phone: (312) 948-7750
Libertyville, IL 60048   Barbara J. Lahr, Supv. of Educ.

LINCOLN CHRISTIAN COLLEGE & SEMINARY - JESSIE C. EURY LIBRARY
Rte. 10 & Limit St.
Box 178   Phone: (217) 732-3168
Lincoln, IL 62656   Thomas M. Tanner, Libn.

HEWITT ASSOCIATES - LIBRARY
100 Half Day   Phone: (312) 295-5000
Lincolnshire, IL 60015   Loralie Van Sluys, Mgr.

ILLINOIS BENEDICTINE COLLEGE - THEODORE LOWNIK LIBRARY
5700 College Rd.   Phone: (312) 968-7270
Lisle, IL 60532   Bert A. Thompson, Dir., Lib.Serv.

MORTON ARBORETUM - STERLING MORTON LIBRARY
                                           Phone: (312) 968-0074
Lisle, IL 60532   Ian MacPhail, Libn.

ILLINOIS CANAL SOCIETY - LIBRARY
1109 Garfield St.   Phone: (815) 838-7316
Lockport, IL 60441   John M. Lamb, Info.Dir.

MIDWEST COLLEGE OF ENGINEERING - JOSEPH M. HARRER LIBRARY
440 S. Finley Rd.
Box 127   Phone: (312) 627-6850
Lombard, IL 60148   Margot Fruehe, Libn.

NATIONAL COLLEGE OF CHIROPRACTIC - LEARNING RESOURCE CENTER
200 E. Roosevelt Rd.   Phone: (312) 629-2000
Lombard, IL 60148   Patricia Brown, Dir.

WATER QUALITY ASSOCIATION - RESEARCH COUNCIL LIBRARY †
477 E. Butterfield Rd.   Phone: (312) 969-6400
Lombard, IL 60148   Douglas R. Oberhamer, Exec.Dir.

KEMPER GROUP - LIBRARY
Library, F-5   Phone: (312) 540-2229
Long Grove, IL 60049   Evelyn Giannini, Libn.

CLASSIC AMX CLUB, INTERNATIONAL - AMX LIBRARY
5731 Walker Ave.   Phone: (815) 877-5500
Loves Park, IL 61117   Larry G. Mitchell, Cur.

ARMAK COMPANY - RESEARCH LIBRARY
8401 W. 47th St.   Phone: (312) 442-7100
McCook, IL 60525   Lenore Africk, Chem.Libn.

AMERICAN CRITICAL CARE - INFORMATION CENTER
1600 Waukegan Rd.   Phone: (312) 473-3000
McGaw Park, IL 60085   Joan Fortune, Mgr.

WESTERN ILLINOIS UNIVERSITY - GEOGRAPHY & MAP LIBRARY
                                           Phone: (309) 298-1171
Macomb, IL 61455   John V. Bergen, Map Libn.

WESTERN ILLINOIS UNIVERSITY - LIBRARIES
                                           Phone: (309) 298-2411
Macomb, IL 61455   Pearce S. Grove, Dir.

MANTENO MENTAL HEALTH CENTER - STAFF LIBRARY
100 Barnard Rd.   Phone: (815) 468-3451
Manteno, IL 60950   Charlotte M. Morgan, Libn.

OLIN CORPORATION - SOLID PROPELLANT ORGANIZATION - RESEARCH
  LIBRARY
Drawer G
Marion, IL 62959

GEOGRAPHIC

U.S. VETERANS ADMINISTRATION (IL- Marion) - HOSPITAL LIBRARY *
Phone: (618) 997-5311
Marion, IL 62959   Virginia H. Moake, Chf., Lib.Serv.

MARISSA HISTORICAL & GENEALOGICAL SOCIETY - LIBRARY
Box 27
Marissa, IL 62257   Dorothy Greenwood, Libn.

LOYOLA UNIVERSITY OF CHICAGO - MEDICAL CENTER LIBRARY
2160 S. First Ave.   Phone: (312) 531-3192
Maywood, IL 60153   James C. Cox, Chf.Libn.

ALBERTO-CULVER COMPANY - RESEARCH LIBRARY
2525 Armitage Ave.   Phone: (312) 450-3313
Melrose Park, IL 60160   Ellen P. Gunther, Libn.

RICHARDSON COMPANY - LIBRARY/INFORMATION CENTER
2701 W. Lake St.   Phone: (312) 344-4300
Melrose Park, IL 60160   Candi Strecker, Libn.

WESTLAKE COMMUNITY HOSPITAL - LIBRARY
1225 Superior St.   Phone: (312) 681-3000
Melrose Park, IL 60160   Carol D. Strauss, Lib.Serv.Coord.

FORT MASSAC HISTORIC SITE - LIBRARY
Box 708   Phone: (618) 524-9321
Metropolis, IL 62960   Paul E. Fellows, Site Supt.

BLACK HAWK COLLEGE - LEARNING RESOURCES CENTER
6600 34th Ave.   Phone: (309) 796-1311
Moline, IL 61265   Donald C. Rowland, Dir.

DEERE & COMPANY - LAW LIBRARY
John Deere Rd.   Phone: (309) 752-4165
Moline, IL 61265   Fran Moffitt, Libn.

DEERE & COMPANY - LIBRARY
John Deere Rd.   Phone: (309) 752-4442
Moline, IL 61265   Betty Hagberg, Mgr.

LUTHERAN HOSPITAL - MEDICAL STAFF LIBRARY AND SCHOOL FOR
NURSES LIBRARY
501 10th Ave.   Phone: (309) 757-2912
Moline, IL 61265   Jeanne A. Gittings, Libn.

MOLINE DAILY DISPATCH - LIBRARY
1720 Fifth Ave.   Phone: (309) 764-4344
Moline, IL 61265   Marlene Gantt, Libn.

NORTHERN PETROCHEMICAL COMPANY - TECHNICAL CENTER LIBRARY
Phone: (815) 942-7558
Morris, IL 60450   Ingrid M. Voss, Libn.

CRANE PACKING COMPANY - TECHNICAL LIBRARY
6400 Oakton St.   Phone: (312) 967-3790
Morton Grove, IL 60053   Margaret W. Ashworth, Libn.

TRAVENOL LABORATORIES, INC. - LIBRARY
6301 Lincoln Ave.   Phone: (312) 965-4700
Morton Grove, IL 60053   Lois A. Bey, Mgr., Info.Ctr.

INSTITUTE OF ENVIRONMENTAL SCIENCES - LIBRARY
940 E. Northwest Hwy.   Phone: (312) 255-1561
Mt. Prospect, IL 60056   Betty L. Peterson, Exec.Dir.

NORTHWEST MUNICIPAL CONFERENCE - GOVERNMENT INFORMATION
CENTER
Mt. Prospect Public Library
10 S. Emerson St.   Phone: (312) 398-6460
Mt. Prospect, IL 60056   Kenneth L. Gross, Lib.Serv.Dir.

GOOD SAMARITAN HOSPITAL - HEALTH-SCIENCE LIBRARY
605 N. 12th St.   Phone: (618) 242-4600
Mt. Vernon, IL 62864   Debbie Greene, Libn.

ILLINOIS STATE - APPELLATE COURT, 5TH DISTRICT - LIBRARY †
14th & Main St.   Phone: (618) 242-3120
Mt. Vernon, IL 62864   Walter T. Simmons, Ck. of Court

INTERNATIONAL MINERALS & CHEMICAL CORPORATION - LIBRARY
421 E. Hawley St.   Phone: (312) 566-2600
Mundelein, IL 60060   Ruth Smedlund, Res.Libn.

ST. MARY OF THE LAKE SEMINARY - FEEHAN MEMORIAL LIBRARY
Phone: (312) 566-6401
Mundelein, IL 60060   Gloria Sieben, Libn.

BELL TELEPHONE LABORATORIES, INC. - TECHNICAL LIBRARY
Phone: (312) 690-2550
Naperville, IL 60540   Robert E. Furlong, Lib. Group Supv.

NALCO CHEMICAL COMPANY - TECHNICAL CENTER - INFORMATION
SERVICES
1801 Diehl Rd.   Phone: (312) 961-9500
Naperville, IL 60540   Marie Tashima, Supv., Info.Serv.

NORTH CENTRAL COLLEGE - LIBRARY
320 E. School Ave.   Phone: (312) 355-0597
Naperville, IL 60566   Harriet Arklie, Dir.

STANDARD OIL COMPANY OF INDIANA - CENTRAL RESEARCH LIBRARY
Amoco Research Center, Box 400   Phone: (312) 420-5545
Naperville, IL 60566   B. Camille Stryck, Staff Libn.

GARD, INC. - LIBRARY
7449 N. Natchez Ave.   Phone: (312) 647-9000
Niles, IL 60648   Ida Carter, Tech.Libn.

MEDICAL RESEARCH LABORATORIES - LIBRARY
7450 Natchez Ave.   Phone: (312) 792-2666
Niles, IL 60648   D. Mehta, V.P.

ILLINOIS STATE UNIVERSITY - MILNER LIBRARY †
Phone: (309) 438-3675
Normal, IL 61761   Joe W. Kraus, Dir.

ABBOTT LABORATORIES - ABBOTT INFORMATION SERVICES
1400 Sheridan Rd.   Phone: (312) 688-2513
North Chicago, IL 60064

U.S. VETERANS ADMINISTRATION (IL-North Chicago) - HOSPITAL LIBRARY
Phone: (312) 689-1900
North Chicago, IL 60064   Carl Worstell, Chf.Libn.

UNIVERSITY OF HEALTH SCIENCES/CHICAGO MEDICAL SCHOOL -
LIBRARY
3333 Green Bay Rd.   Phone: (312) 689-8010
North Chicago, IL 60064   Nancy W. Garn, Dir.

ALLSTATE INSURANCE COMPANY - LAW LIBRARY
Allstate Plaza, Building E5   Phone: (312) 291-5407
Northbrook, IL 60062   Alice Bruemner, Libn.

UNDERWRITERS LABORATORIES INC. - STANDARDS REFERENCE CENTER
333 Pfingsten Rd.   Phone: (312) 272-8800
Northbrook, IL 60062   A.N. Angonese, Sr.Assoc.Mng.Engr.

NATIONAL ASSOCIATION OF ANOREXIA NERVOSA AND ASSOCIATED
DISORDERS, INC. (ANAD) - LIBRARY
550 Frontage Rd., Suite 2020   Phone: (312) 831-3438
Northfield, IL 60093   June Garland, Adm.Asst.

GTE AUTOMATIC ELECTRIC LABORATORIES - LIBRARY †
400 N. Wolf Rd., A-6
Box 2317   Phone: (312) 681-7118
Northlake, IL 60164   Jane Yu Lee, Libn.

BETHANY AND NORTHERN BAPTIST THEOLOGICAL SEMINARIES - LIBRARY
Butterfield & Meyers Rds.   Phone: (312) 620-2214
Oak Brook, IL 60521   Murray L. Wagner, Hd.Libn.

CHICAGO BRIDGE & IRON COMPANY - TECHNICAL LIBRARY
800 Jorie Blvd.   Phone: (312) 654-7279
Oak Brook, IL 60521   Suzanne D. Beatty, Tech.Libn.

RADIOLOGICAL SOCIETY OF NORTH AMERICA, INC. - LIBRARY
1415 W. 22nd St.
Oak Brook Regency Towers, Suite 1150   Phone: (312) 920-2670
Oak Brook, IL 60521

SWIFT AND COMPANY - RESEARCH AND DEVELOPMENT INFORMATION
   CENTER
1919 Swift Dr.   Phone: (312) 325-9320
Oak Brook, IL 60521   Marcus Bornfleth, Hd.Info.Ctr.

OAK FOREST HOSPITAL - PROFESSIONAL LIBRARY
15900 S. Cicero Ave.   Phone: (312) 928-4200
Oak Forest, IL 60452   Delores I. Quinn, Libn.

PROFESSIONAL CONVENTION MANAGEMENT ASSOCIATION - LIBRARY
Box 99   Phone: (312) 272-4810
Oak Forest, IL 60452   Frank A. Gary, Exec.Dir.

CHRIST HOSPITAL - HOSPITAL LIBRARY
4440 West 95th St.   Phone: (312) 425-8000
Oak Lawn, IL 60453   Gerald Dujsik, Lib.Mgr.

EVANGELICAL SCHOOL OF NURSING - WOJNIAK MEMORIAL LIBRARY
9345 S. Kilbourn   Phone: (312) 425-8000
Oak Lawn, IL 60453   Gerald Dujsik, Lib.Mgr.

EMMAUS BIBLE SCHOOL - LIBRARY
156 N. Oak Park Ave.   Phone: (312) 383-7000
Oak Park, IL 60301   Ruth Marshall, Libn.

INSTITUTE FOR ADVANCED PERCEPTION - LIBRARY
719 S. Clarence Ave.   Phone: (312) 386-1742
Oak Park, IL 60304   Donna Marie Schroeppel, Exec.Sec.

OAK PARK PUBLIC LIBRARY - LOCAL AUTHOR AND HISTORY COLLECTIONS
834 Lake St.   Phone: (312) 383-8200
Oak Park, IL 60301   Barbara Ballinger, Hd.Libn.

WEST SUBURBAN HOSPITAL - WALTER LAWRENCE MEMORIAL LIBRARY
518 N. Austin Blvd.   Phone: (312) 383-6200
Oak Park, IL 60302   Julia B. Faust, Libn.

OGLESBY HISTORICAL SOCIETY - LIBRARY
Oglesby Public Library
128 W. Walnut   Phone: (815) 883-3619
Oglesby, IL 61348   Albert Moyle

RICHLAND MEMORIAL HOSPITAL - STAFF LIBRARY
800 East Locust   Phone: (618) 395-2131
Olney, IL 62450   Pat Humphrey, Dir.Med.Rec.Dept.

CHICAGO COLLEGE OF OSTEOPATHIC MEDICINE - OLYMPIA FIELDS
   HOSPITAL LIBRARY
203rd and Crawford   Phone: (312) 747-4000
Olympia Fields, IL 60461   Lois F. Hayes, Libn.

ILLINOIS STATE - APPELLATE COURT, 3RD DISTRICT - LIBRARY
1004 Columbus St.   Phone: (815) 434-5050
Ottawa, IL 61350   Sharon Smith, Libn.

PALOS COMMUNITY HOSPITAL - MEDICAL LIBRARY
80th Ave. at McCarthy Rd.   Phone: (312) 361-4500
Palos Heights, IL 60463   Jack G. Vainauskas, Med.Rec.Adm.

OUTLOOK - OUTLOOK ACCESS CENTER
105 Wolpers Rd.   Phone: (312) 481-6168
Park Forest, IL 60466   Jim Laukes, Ed.

AMERICAN SOCIETY OF ANESTHESIOLOGISTS - WOOD LIBRARY-MUSEUM
   OF ANESTHESIOLOGY
515 Busse Hwy.   Phone: (312) 825-5586
Park Ridge, IL 60068   Patrick Sim, Libn.

AMERICAN SOCIETY OF SAFETY ENGINEERS - TECHNICAL INFORMATION
   CENTER
850 Busse Hwy.   Phone: (312) 692-4121
Park Ridge, IL 60068   L. Hoogerhyde, Dir., Educ.

ASSOCIATION OF SCHOOL BUSINESS OFFICIALS OF THE U.S. & CANADA -
   RESEARCH CORPORATION LIBRARY
720 Garden St.
Park Ridge, IL 60068

BANK ADMINISTRATION INSTITUTE - INFORMATION CENTER
303 S. Northwest Hwy.   Phone: (312) 693-7300
Park Ridge, IL 60068   Claudette S. Warner, Libn.

DAMES & MOORE - CHICAGO LIBRARY
1550 Northwest Highway   Phone: (312) 297-6120
Park Ridge, IL 60068   Patricia Krzysiak, Libn.

LUTHERAN GENERAL HOSPITAL - LIBRARY
1775 Dempster St.   Phone: (312) 696-5494
Park Ridge, IL 60068   Joanne Crispen, Dir. of Lib.Serv.

DIRKSEN (Everett McKinley) CONGRESSIONAL LEADERSHIP RESEARCH
   CENTER - LIBRARY
Broadway & Fourth St.   Phone: (309) 347-7113
Pekin, IL 61554   Frank H. Mackaman, II, Exec.Dir.

BAHAI REFERENCE LIBRARY OF PEORIA
5209 N. University   Phone: (309) 691-9311
Peoria, IL 61614   Carolyn Henderer, Libn.

BRADLEY UNIVERSITY - VIRGINIUS H. CHASE SPECIAL COLLECTIONS
   CENTER - CHARLES A. BENNETT COLLECTION
Cullom-Davis Library   Phone: (309) 676-7611
Peoria, IL 61625   Charles J. Frey, Spec.Coll.Libn.

BRADLEY UNIVERSITY - VIRGINIUS H. CHASE SPECIAL COLLECTIONS
   CENTER - CHASE COLLECTION
Cullom-Davis Library   Phone: (309) 676-7611
Peoria, IL 61625   Charles J. Frey, Spec.Coll.Libn.

BRADLEY UNIVERSITY - VIRGINIUS H. CHASE SPECIAL COLLECTIONS
   CENTER - LINCOLN COLLECTIONS
Cullom-Davis Library   Phone: (309) 676-7611
Peoria, IL 61625   Charles J. Frey, Spec.Coll.Libn.

BRADLEY UNIVERSITY - VIRGINIUS H. CHASE SPECIAL COLLECTIONS
   CENTER - PEORIA HISTORICAL SOCIETY COLLECTIONS
Cullom-Davis Library   Phone: (309) 676-7611
Peoria, IL 61625   Charles J. Frey, Spec.Coll.Libn.

CATERPILLAR TRACTOR COMPANY - BUSINESS LIBRARY
100 N.E. Adams St.   Phone: (309) 675-4622
Peoria, IL 61629   Amy Wolf, Lib.Supv.

CATERPILLAR TRACTOR COMPANY - TECHNICAL INFORMATION CENTER
Technical Center   Phone: (309) 578-6118
Peoria, IL 61629   Carol E. Mulvaney, Tech.Libn.

METHODIST MEDICAL CENTER OF ILLINOIS - LEARNING RESOURCE
   CENTER
221 N.E. Glen Oak   Phone: (309) 672-5570
Peoria, IL 61636   Dorothy Mortimer, Libn.

METHODIST MEDICAL CENTER OF ILLINOIS - MEDICAL LIBRARY
221 N.E. Glen Oak   Phone: (309) 672-4937
Peoria, IL 61636   Trudy Landwirth, Dir.

PEORIA COUNTY LAW LIBRARY
Peoria County Court House, Rm. 209   Phone: (309) 672-6084
Peoria, IL 61602   Mary Louise Jacquin, Libn.

PEORIA HISTORICAL SOCIETY - HARRY L. SPOONER MEMORIAL LIBRARY
Bradley Univ., Cullom-Davis Library
Glenwood & Bradley Aves.   Phone: (309) 676-7611
Peoria, IL 61603   Charles Frey, Dir.

PROCTOR COMMUNITY HOSPITAL - MEDICAL LIBRARY
5409 N. Knoxville Ave.   Phone: (309) 691-4702
Peoria, IL 61614   Nancy Camacho, Libn.

ST. FRANCIS HOSPITAL - MEDICAL CENTER - MEDICAL LIBRARY *
530-616 N.E. Glen Oak Ave.   Phone: (309) 672-2210
Peoria, IL 61637   Mary Anne Parr, Med.Libn.

U.S.D.A. - AGRICULTURAL RESEARCH SERVICE - NORTHERN
   REGIONALRESEARCH CENTER LIBRARY
1815 N. University St.   Phone: (309) 685-4011
Peoria, IL 61604   Donald L. Blevins, Libn.

GEOGRAPHIC

GEOGRAPHIC

UNIVERSITY OF ILLINOIS MEDICAL CENTER - PEORIA SCHOOL OF
MEDICINE - LIBRARY OF THE HEALTH SCIENCES
123 S.W. Glendale Ave.   Phone: (309) 671-3095
Peoria, IL 61605   Michele Johns, Br.Libn.

WABCO - CONSTRUCTION AND MINING EQUIPMENT GROUP -
ENGINEERING TECHNICAL LIBRARY
2301 N.E. Adams St.   Phone: (309) 672-7143
Peoria, IL 61639   Grace L. Birkey, Libn.

ZELLER (George A.) MENTAL HEALTH CENTER - PROFESSIONAL LIBRARY
5407 N. University   Phone: (309) 691-2200
Peoria, IL 61614   Barbara Haun, Libn.

BUREAU COUNTY HISTORICAL SOCIETY - MUSEUM & LIBRARY
109 Park Ave. W.
Princeton, IL 61356   Mrs. Howard Hilliard, Cur.

HOUSEHOLD FINANCE CORPORATION - CORPORATE LIBRARY
2700 Sanders Rd.   Phone: (312) 564-5000
Prospect Heights, IL 60070   Win Sadecki, Corp.Libn.

HISTORICAL SOCIETY OF QUINCY AND ADAMS COUNTY - LIBRARY
425 S. 12th St.   Phone: (217) 222-3432
Quincy, IL 62301   Ned Broemmel, Pres.

SOCIETY FOR ACADEMIC ACHIEVEMENT - LIBRARY
220 WCU Bldg.
510 Maine St.   Phone: (217) 224-0570
Quincy, IL 62301   Leo W. Manning, Exec.Dir.

U.S. AIR FORCE HOSPITAL - MEDICAL LIBRARY (IL-Rantoul)
Chanute Air Force Base   Phone: (217) 495-3068
Rantoul, IL 61868   R.M. Lucas, Med.Libn.

CONCORDIA TEACHERS COLLEGE - KLINCK MEMORIAL LIBRARY
7400 Augusta St.   Phone: (312) 771-8300
River Forest, IL 60305   Henry R. Latzke, Dir., Lib.Serv.

AUGUSTANA COLLEGE - DENKMANN MEMORIAL LIBRARY
3520 7th Ave.   Phone: (309) 794-7266
Rock Island, IL 61201   John Caldwell, Dir. of Lib.

BLACKHAWK GENEALOGICAL SOCIETY - LIBRARY
Box 912
Rock Island, IL 61201   Mrs. F.T. Winthurst, Lib.Chm.

TRI-CITY JEWISH CENTER - JOSEPH AND BENJAMIN NEFF MEMORIAL
LIBRARY
1804 Seventh Ave.   Phone: (309) 788-3426
Rock Island, IL 61201

U.S. ARMY - ARMAMENT MATERIAL READINESS COMMAND - TECHNICAL
LIBRARY
DRSAR-LEP-L   Phone: (309) 794-4208
Rock Island, IL 61299   Phil Casey, Chf.

BURPEE ART MUSEUM/ROCKFORD ART ASSOCIATION - KATHERINE
PEARMAN MEMORIAL LIBRARY
737 N. Main St.   Phone: (815) 965-3131
Rockford, IL 61103   Martin Dewitt, Dir./Cur.

ROCKFORD MEMORIAL HOSPITAL - HEALTH SCIENCE LIBRARY
2400 N. Rockton Ave.   Phone: (815) 968-6861
Rockford, IL 61101   Prudence Dalrymple, Hosp.Libn.

ROCKFORD PUBLIC LIBRARY - BUSINESS, SCIENCE AND TECHNOLOGY
DIVISION
215 N. Wyman   Phone: (815) 965-6731
Rockford, IL 61101   Marie Phillips, Hd.

SINGER (H. Douglas) MENTAL HEALTH CENTER - LIBRARY
4402 North Main St.   Phone: (815) 987-7092
Rockford, IL 61105   Pat Ellison, Lib.Assoc.

SUNDSTRAND AVIATION - ENGINEERING LIBRARY
4747 Harrison Ave.   Phone: (815) 226-6753
Rockford, IL 61101   Mrs. Fran Genrich, Libn.

UNIVERSITY OF ILLINOIS MEDICAL CENTER - ROCKFORD SCHOOL OF
MEDICINE - LIBRARY OF THE HEALTH SCIENCES
1601 Parkview Ave.   Phone: (815) 987-7377
Rockford, IL 61101   Stuart J. Kolner, Br.Libn.

WINNEBAGO COUNTY LAW LIBRARY
Courthouse Bldg., 3rd Fl.
400 W. State St.   Phone: (815) 987-2514
Rockford, IL 61101   Roberta S. McGaw, Dir.

WOODWARD GOVERNOR CO. - WOODWARD LIBRARY
5001 N. Second St.   Phone: (815) 877-7441
Rockford, IL 61101   Ben Schleicher, Adm.Serv.Supv.

CHEMPLEX COMPANY - LIBRARY
3100 Golf Rd.   Phone: (312) 437-7800
Rolling Meadows, IL 60008   Frieda R. Oetting, Libn.

GOULD INC. - GOULD INFORMATION CENTER
40 Gould Center   Phone: (312) 640-4423
Rolling Meadows, IL 60008   Mala Laurin, Dir., Info.Serv.

LEWIS UNIVERSITY - LIBRARY
Rte. 53   Phone: (815) 838-0500
Romeoville, IL 60441   Richard L. Tubesing, Lib.Dir.

DAIRY RESEARCH, INC. - TECHNICAL INFORMATION SERVICE
6300 N. River Rd.   Phone: (312) 696-1870
Rosemont, IL 60018   William W. Menz, Vice-Pres., Res.

NATIONAL DAIRY COUNCIL - LIBRARY
6300 N. River Rd.   Phone: (312) 696-1020
Rosemont, IL 60018   Diana Culbertson, Libn.

AMERICAN VETERINARY MEDICAL ASSOCIATION - LIBRARY †
930 N. Meacham Rd.   Phone: (312) 885-8070
Schaumburg, IL 60196

MOTOROLA, INC. - COMMUNICATIONS GROUP LIBRARY
1301 E. Algonquin Rd.   Phone: (312) 576-3974
Schaumburg, IL 60196   Bonnie Hohhof, Mgr.

U.S. AIR FORCE ENVIRONMENTAL TECHNICAL APPLICATIONS CENTER -
AIR WEATHER SERVICE TECHNICAL LIBRARY
FL 4414   Phone: (618) 256-2625
Scott AFB, IL 62225   Col. Quenten L. Wilkes, Commander

U.S. AIR FORCE HOSPITAL MEDICAL CENTER - MEDICAL LIBRARY (IL-Scott
AFB)
                                          Phone: (618) 256-7437
Scott AFB, IL 62225   Blanche A. Savage, Med.Libn.

BRUNSWICK CORPORATION - MANAGEMENT LIBRARY
One Brunswick Plaza   Phone: (312) 470-4880
Skokie, IL 60077   Ruth Roberts, Mgt.Libn.

HEBREW THEOLOGICAL COLLEGE - SAUL SILBER MEMORIAL LIBRARY
7135 N. Carpenter Rd.   Phone: (312) 267-9800
Skokie, IL 60077   Leah Mishkin, Libn. & Cur.

PORTLAND CEMENT ASSOCIATION/CONSTRUCTION TECHNOLOGY
LABORATORIES - INFORMATION SERVICES SECTION
5420 Old Orchard Rd.   Phone: (312) 966-6200
Skokie, IL 60077   Marilynn Halasz, Mgr., Info.Serv.Sect.

RAND MC NALLY AND COMPANY - LIBRARY
8255 Central Park Ave.   Phone: (312) 673-9100
Skokie, IL 60076   Philip L. Forstall, Libn.

ST. PAUL LUTHERAN CHURCH AND SCHOOL - PARISH LIBRARY *
5201 Galitz   Phone: (312) 673-5030
Skokie, IL 60077

SEARLE (G.D.) & CO. - RESEARCH LIBRARY
4901 Searle Pkwy.   Phone: (312) 982-7990
Skokie, IL 60077   Susan Robb, Mgr., Res.Lib.

TEMPLE JUDEA MIZPAH - LIBRARY
8610 Niles Center Rd.   Phone: (312) 676-1566
Skokie, IL 60077   Claire Alport, Lib.Chm.

TRIODYNE INC. CONSULTING ENGINEERS - INFORMATION CENTER
7855 Gross Point Rd.   Phone: (312) 251-8536
Skokie, IL 60077   Beth A. Hamilton, Sr.Info.Sci.

SOUTH SUBURBAN GENEALOGICAL & HISTORICAL SOCIETY - LIBRARY
Box 96
South Holland, IL 60473   Marilyn Poe Laird, Hd.Libn.

DAUGHTERS OF UNION VETERANS OF THE CIVIL WAR - NATIONAL
   HEADQUARTERS LIBRARY
503 S. Walnut St.   Phone: (217) 544-0616
Springfield, IL 62704   Anna Kinnison, Natl.Tres.

DIOCESAN SEMINARY OF THE IMMACULATE CONCEPTION - LIBRARY
1903 E. Lake Dr.   Phone: (217) 529-2213
Springfield, IL 62707

ILLINOIS STATE BOARD OF EDUCATION - MEDIA AND RESOURCES CENTER
100 N. First St.   Phone: (217) 782-4433
Springfield, IL 62777   William E. Lohman, Mgr.

ILLINOIS STATE DEPARTMENT OF COMMERCE & COMMUNITY AFFAIRS -
   OFFICE OF POLICY & PROGRAMS - LIBRARY
222 S. College St.   Phone: (217) 782-1438
Springfield, IL 62706   W.W. Biermann, Chf., Res.

ILLINOIS STATE DEPARTMENT OF TRANSPORTATION - TECHNICAL
   REFERENCE LIBRARY
338 Administration Bldg.
2300 S. Dirksen Pkwy.   Phone: (217) 782-6680
Springfield, IL 62764   Gisela Motzkus, Libn.

ILLINOIS STATE HISTORICAL LIBRARY
Old State Capitol   Phone: (217) 782-4836
Springfield, IL 62706   Olive S. Foster, Act. State Hist.

ILLINOIS STATE INSTITUTE OF NATURAL RESOURCES - ENERGY
   INFORMATION LIBRARY
325 W. Adams St., Rm. 300   Phone: (217) 785-2388
Springfield, IL 62706   Sheila E. Cassels, Res.Libn.

ILLINOIS STATE LEGISLATIVE REFERENCE BUREAU
State House, Rm. 112   Phone: (217) 525-6625
Springfield, IL 62706   Mary Louise McCreary, Libn.

ILLINOIS STATE LIBRARY
Centennial Bldg.   Phone: (217) 782-2994
Springfield, IL 62756   Kathryn J. Gesterfield, Dir.

ILLINOIS STATE MUSEUM OF NATURAL HISTORY AND ART - TECHNICAL
   LIBRARY
                                               Phone: (217) 782-6623
Springfield, IL 62706   Orvetta Robinson, Libn. & Registrar

ILLINOIS STATE - OFFICE OF THE SECRETARY OF STATE - STATE
   ARCHIVES
Illinois State Archives Bldg.   Phone: (217) 525-4682
Springfield, IL 62756   John Daly, Dir.

ILLINOIS STATE - SUPREME COURT LIBRARY
Supreme Court Bldg.   Phone: (217) 525-2424
Springfield, IL 62706   Catherine Bradley, Law Libn.

LINCOLN LIBRARY - SANGAMON VALLEY COLLECTION
326 S. 7th St.   Phone: (217) 753-4910
Springfield, IL 62701   Edward J. Russo, Hd.

MC FARLAND MENTAL HEALTH CENTER - STAFF LIBRARY *
901 Southwind Rd.   Phone: (217) 782-2753
Springfield, IL 62703   Marie Rine, Libn.

PROTESTANT EPISCOPAL CHURCH - EPISCOPAL DIOCESE OF
   SPRINGFIELD, ILLINOIS - DIOCESAN CENTER LIBRARY
821 S. 2nd St.   Phone: (217) 525-2827
Springfield, IL 62704   Philip L. Shutt, Registrar/Historiographer

ST. JOHN'S HOSPITAL - HEALTH SCIENCE LIBRARY
800 E. Carpenter   Phone: (217) 544-6464
Springfield, IL 62702   Dorthada Groesch, Dir.

SANGAMON STATE UNIVERSITY - ORAL HISTORY OFFICE - LIBRARY
Brookens Library   Phone: (217) 786-6521
Springfield, IL 62708   Cullom Davis, Dir.

SCHNEPP (Kenneth H.) MEDICAL LIBRARY
800 N. Rutledge St.   Phone: (217) 788-3336
Springfield, IL 62781   Myrtle Smarjesse, Med.Libn.

SOUTHERN ILLINOIS UNIVERSITY - SCHOOL OF MEDICINE - MEDICAL
   LIBRARY
801 N. Rutledge
Box 3926   Phone: (217) 782-2658
Springfield, IL 62708   Dana M. McDonald, Dir.

SPRINGFIELD ART ASSOCIATION - MICHAEL VICTOR II ART LIBRARY
700 N. Fourth St.   Phone: (217) 523-2631
Springfield, IL 62702   William Bealmer, Dir.

SPRINGFIELD, ILLINOIS STATE JOURNAL & REGISTER - EDITORIAL
   LIBRARY
313 S. 6th St.   Phone: (217) 544-5711
Springfield, IL 62705   Sandra Vance, Libn.

MOULTRIE COUNTY HISTORICAL & GENEALOGICAL SOCIETY - MOULTRIE
   COUNTY HERITAGE CENTER
117 E. Harrison St.
Box MM   Phone: (217) 728-4085
Sullivan, IL 61951   Mary L. Storm, Libn.

TINLEY PARK MENTAL HEALTH CENTER - INSTRUCTIONAL MEDIA LIBRARY
7400 W. 183rd St.   Phone: (312) 532-7000
Tinley Park, IL 60477   Sally M. Cole, Libn.

U.S. INDUSTRIAL CHEMICALS COMPANY - TUSCOLA PLANT TECHNICAL
   LIBRARY AND INFORMATION CENTER
Box 218   Phone: (217) 253-3311
Tuscola, IL 61953   Lois C. Bodoh, Tech.Libn.

ILLINOIS RAILWAY MUSEUM - TECHNICAL LIBRARY
Box 431   Phone: (815) 923-4391
Union, IL 60180   James E. Kehrein, Libn.

CARLE FOUNDATION HOSPITAL - LIBRARY
611 W. Park St.   Phone: (217) 337-3011
Urbana, IL 61801   Kim K. Uden, Mgr., Lib.Serv.

CHAMPAIGN COUNTY HISTORICAL ARCHIVES
c/o Urbana Free Library
201 S. Race St.   Phone: (217) 367-4025
Urbana, IL 61801   Barbara Roberts, Dir.

CLARK DIETZ ENGINEERS - LIBRARY
211 N. Race St.   Phone: (217) 384-1400
Urbana, IL 61801   Felicia Bagby, Libn.

ERIC CLEARINGHOUSE ON READING AND COMMUNICATIONS SKILLS *
National Council of Teachers of English
1111 Kenyon Rd.   Phone: (217) 328-3870
Urbana, IL 61801   Dr. Bernard O'Donnell, Dir.

MERCY HOSPITAL - LIBRARY
1400 W. Park St.   Phone: (217) 337-2283
Urbana, IL 61801   Harriet Williamson, Dir.

NATIONAL COUNCIL OF TEACHERS OF ENGLISH - CURRICULUM LIBRARY
1111 Kenyon Rd.   Phone: (217) 328-3870
Urbana, IL 61801   Carolyn H. McMahon, Libn.

UNIVERSITY OF ILLINOIS - AGRICULTURE LIBRARY
226 Mumford Hall
1301 W. Gregory   Phone: (217) 333-2416
Urbana, IL 61801   John W. Beecher, Libn.

GEOGRAPHIC

GEOGRAPHIC

UNIVERSITY OF ILLINOIS - APPLIED LIFE STUDIES LIBRARY
Main Library, Rm. 146
1408 W. Gregory Dr.   Phone: (217) 333-3615
Urbana, IL 61801   Jane Armstrong, Libn.

UNIVERSITY OF ILLINOIS - ASIAN LIBRARY
325 Main Library
1408 W. Gregory Dr.   Phone: (217) 333-1501
Urbana, IL 61801   William S. Wong, Asst.Dir.

UNIVERSITY OF ILLINOIS - ASIAN LIBRARY - SOUTH AND WEST ASIAN
    DIVISION
329 Main Library
1408 W. Gregory Dr.   Phone: (217) 333-2492
Urbana, IL 61801   Narindar K. Aggarwal, Asst. Asian Libn.

UNIVERSITY OF ILLINOIS - BIOLOGY LIBRARY
101 Burrill Hall
407 S. Goodwin   Phone: (217) 333-3654
Urbana, IL 61801   Elisabeth B. Davis, Libn.

UNIVERSITY OF ILLINOIS - CHEMISTRY LIBRARY
257 Noyes Laboratory
505 S. Matthews   Phone: (217) 333-3737
Urbana, IL 61801   Dr. Lucille Wert, Chem.Libn.

UNIVERSITY OF ILLINOIS - CITY PLANNING AND LANDSCAPE
    ARCHITECTURE LIBRARY
203 Mumford Hall
1301 W. Gregory Dr.   Phone: (217) 333-0424
Urbana, IL 61801   Mary D. Ravenhall, Libn.

UNIVERSITY OF ILLINOIS - CLASSICS LIBRARY
419A Main Library
1408 W. Gregory Dr.   Phone: (217) 333-1124
Urbana, IL 61801   Suzanne Griffiths, Libn.

UNIVERSITY OF ILLINOIS - COMMERCE LIBRARY
Rm. 101, Main Library
1408 W. Gregory Dr.   Phone: (217) 333-3619
Urbana, IL 61801   Esther M. Clausen, Libn.

UNIVERSITY OF ILLINOIS - COMMUNICATIONS LIBRARY
122 Gregory Hall   Phone: (217) 333-2216
Urbana, IL 61801   Nancy Allen, Libn.

UNIVERSITY OF ILLINOIS - COORDINATED SCIENCE LABORATORY
    LIBRARY
1101 W. Springfield, Rm. 269 A   Phone: (217) 333-4368
Urbana, IL 61801   Kerry A. Keck, Libn.

UNIVERSITY OF ILLINOIS - DEPARTMENT OF COMPUTER SCIENCE
    LIBRARY
260 Digital Computer Laboratory   Phone: (217) 333-6777
Urbana, IL 61801   Professor S. Muroga, Chm.Lib.Comm.

UNIVERSITY OF ILLINOIS - DOCUMENTS LIBRARY
200d Main Library   Phone: (217) 333-1056
Urbana, IL 61801   Paula Watson, Hd.

UNIVERSITY OF ILLINOIS - EDUCATION AND SOCIAL SCIENCE LIBRARY
100 Main Library
1408 W. Gregory Dr.   Phone: (217) 333-2305
Urbana, IL 61801   Barton M. Clark, Libn.

UNIVERSITY OF ILLINOIS - ENGINEERING LIBRARY
221 Engineering Hall
1308 W. Green St.   Phone: (217) 333-3576
Urbana, IL 61801   Mrs. Sarojini Balachandran, Asst.Engr.Libn.

UNIVERSITY OF ILLINOIS - ENGLISH LIBRARY
321 Library
1408 W. Gregory Dr.   Phone: (217) 333-2220
Urbana, IL 61801   Melissa Cain, Libn.

UNIVERSITY OF ILLINOIS - GEOLOGY LIBRARY
223 Natural History Bldg.
1301 W. Green St.   Phone: (217) 333-1266
Urbana, IL 61801   Dederick C. Ward, Libn.

UNIVERSITY OF ILLINOIS - HIGHWAY TRAFFIC SAFETY CENTER - LIBRARY
404 Engineering Hall   Phone: (217) 333-1270
Urbana, IL 61801   Dr. John Baerwald, Dir., Coll. of Engr.

UNIVERSITY OF ILLINOIS - HISTORY AND PHILOSOPHY LIBRARY
424 Main Library
1408 W. Gregory Dr.   Phone: (217) 333-1091
Urbana, IL 61801   Martha Friedman, Libn.

UNIVERSITY OF ILLINOIS - HOME ECONOMICS LIBRARY
905 S. Goodwin Ave.   Phone: (217) 333-0748
Urbana, IL 61801   Barbara C. Swain, Libn.

UNIVERSITY OF ILLINOIS - ILLINOIS HISTORICAL SURVEY LIBRARY
1A Main Library
1408 W. Gregory Dr.   Phone: (217) 333-1777
Urbana, IL 61801   Professor Robert M. Sutton, Dir.

UNIVERSITY OF ILLINOIS - LIBRARY AND INFORMATION SCIENCE
    LIBRARY
306 Main Library
1408 W. Gregory Dr.   Phone: (217) 333-3804
Urbana, IL 61801   Patricia Stenstrom, Libn.

UNIVERSITY OF ILLINOIS - MAP AND GEOGRAPHY LIBRARY
418 Main Library
1408 W. Gregory Dr.   Phone: (217) 333-0827
Urbana, IL 61801   David A. Cobb, Libn.

UNIVERSITY OF ILLINOIS - MATHEMATICS LIBRARY
216 Altgeld Hall
1409 W. Green St.   Phone: (217) 333-0258
Urbana, IL 61801   Nancy D. Anderson, Libn.

UNIVERSITY OF ILLINOIS MEDICAL CENTER - LIBRARY OF THE HEALTH
    SCIENCES
102 Medical Sciences Bldg.   Phone: (217) 333-4893
Urbana, IL 61801   Phyllis Self, Libn.

UNIVERSITY OF ILLINOIS - MODERN LANGUAGES AND LINGUISTICS
    LIBRARY
425 Main Library
1408 W. Gregory Dr.   Phone: (217) 333-0076
Urbana, IL 61801   Sara de Mundo Lo, Libn.

UNIVERSITY OF ILLINOIS - MUSIC LIBRARY
Music Bldg.   Phone: (217) 333-1173
Urbana, IL 61801   William M. McClellan, Music Libn.

UNIVERSITY OF ILLINOIS - NEWSPAPER LIBRARY
Main Library, Rm. 1
1408 W. Gregory Dr.   Phone: (217) 333-1509
Urbana, IL 61801   William J. Maher, Libn.

UNIVERSITY OF ILLINOIS - PHYSICS/ASTRONOMY LIBRARY
204 Loomis Laboratory
1110 W. Green St.   Phone: (217) 333-2101
Urbana, IL 61801   Bernice Lord Hulsizer, Libn.

UNIVERSITY OF ILLINOIS - RARE BOOK ROOM
346 Main Library
1408 W. Gregory Dr.   Phone: (217) 333-3777
Urbana, IL 61801   N. Frederick Nash, Libn.

UNIVERSITY OF ILLINOIS - RICKER LIBRARY OF ARCHITECTURE AND ART
208 Architecture Bldg.   Phone: (217) 333-0224
Urbana, IL 61801   Dee Wallace, Libn.

UNIVERSITY OF ILLINOIS - SURVEY RESEARCH LABORATORY - SRL DATA
    ARCHIVE
1005 W. Nevada St.   Phone: (217) 333-2243
Urbana, IL 61801   Patricia Meece, Res.Info.Spec.

UNIVERSITY OF ILLINOIS - SURVEY RESEARCH LABORATORY - SURVEY
    AND CENSUS DATA LIBRARY
1005 W. Nevada St.   Phone: (217) 333-7109
Urbana, IL 61801   Mary A. Spaeth, Res.Info.Coord.

UNIVERSITY OF ILLINOIS - UNIVERSITY ARCHIVES
University Library, Rm. 19
1408 W. Gregory Dr.   Phone: (217) 333-0798
Urbana, IL 61801   Maynard Brichford, Univ.Archv.

UNIVERSITY OF ILLINOIS - VETERINARY MEDICINE LIBRARY
250 Veterinary Medicine Bldg.
1101 W. Peabody Dr.   Phone: (217) 333-2193
Urbana, IL 61801   David Self, Libn.

VANDALIA HISTORICAL SOCIETY - JAMES HALL LIBRARY
Little Brick House
621 St. Clair St.   Phone: (618) 283-0024
Vandalia, IL 62471   Mary Burtschi, Dir.

IROQUOIS COUNTY GENEALOGICAL SOCIETY - LIBRARY
103 W. Cherry St.
Watseka, IL 60970   Roxanne Frey, Libn.

LAKE COUNTY MUSEUM - LIBRARY AND INFORMATION CENTER
Lakewood Forest Preserve
Rte. 176 & Fairfield Rd.   Phone: (312) 526-7878
Wauconda, IL 60084   Gary Keller, Dir.

LAKE COUNTY LAW LIBRARY
18 N. County St.   Phone: (312) 689-6654
Waukegan, IL 60085   Joanne T. Baker, Law Libn.

LAKE COUNTY REGIONAL PLANNING COMMISSION - LIBRARY
803 County Bldg.   Phone: (312) 689-6350
Waukegan, IL 60085   Nancy Ross, Libn.-Ed.

VICTORY MEMORIAL HOSPITAL - MEDICAL LIBRARY
1324 N. Sheridan Rd.   Phone: (312) 688-3054
Waukegan, IL 60085   Helen Hewitt, Libn.

WAUKEGAN HISTORICAL SOCIETY - JOHN RAYMOND MEMORIAL LIBRARY
1917 Sheridan Rd.   Phone: (312) 623-7339
Waukegan, IL 60085   Phebe B. Booth, Libn.

WAUKEGAN NEWS-SUN - LIBRARY
100 Madison St.   Phone: (312) 689-6969
Waukegan, IL 60085   Barbara Apple, Libn.

CANTIGNY WAR MEMORIAL MUSEUM OF THE FIRST DIVISION - ARCHIVES
     ROOM
15151 Winfield Rd.   Phone: (312) 668-5161
Wheaton, IL 60187   Arthur Veysey, Gen.Mgr.

DU PAGE COUNTY LAW LIBRARY
Courthouse
201 Reber St.   Phone: (312) 682-7337
Wheaton, IL 60187   Charlean Eggert, Law Libn.

THEOSOPHICAL SOCIETY IN AMERICA - OLCOTT LIBRARY & RESEARCH
     CENTER
1926 N. Main St.
Box 270   Phone: (312) 668-1571
Wheaton, IL 60187   Swarna Wickremeratne, Lib.Hd.

WHEATON COLLEGE - BILLY GRAHAM CENTER LIBRARY
                                                 Phone: (312) 682-5194
Wheaton, IL 60187   Ferne L. Weimer, Act.Dir.

WHEATON COLLEGE - LIBRARY
501 E. Seminary   Phone: (312) 682-5101
Wheaton, IL 60187   P. Paul Snezek, Dir.

NORTH SUBURBAN LIBRARY SYSTEM - PROFESSIONAL INFORMATION
     CENTER
200 W. Dundee   Phone: (312) 459-1300
Wheeling, IL 60090   Patricia M. Hogan, Info.Libn.

WILMETTE HISTORICAL MUSEUM - LIBRARY
565 Hunter Rd.   Phone: (312) 256-5838
Wilmette, IL 60091

MORTON-NORWICH PRODUCTS, INC. - WOODSTOCK RESEARCH
     INFORMATION CENTER †
1275 Lake Ave.   Phone: (815) 338-1800
Woodstock, IL 60098   Valentina M. Woodruff, Info.Sci.

WESTINGHOUSE ELECTRIC CORPORATION - WESTINGHOUSE NUCLEAR
     TRAINING CENTER - INSTRUCTIONAL MEDIA CENTER
505 Shiloh Blvd.   Phone: (312) 872-4585
Zion, IL 60099   Gail Huffman, Libn.

INDIANA

ALFORD HOUSE/ANDERSON FINE ARTS CENTER - ART REFERENCE
     LIBRARY
226 W. 8th St.   Phone: (317) 649-1248
Anderson, IN 46016   Judith Dillingham, Asst. to Dir.

ANDERSON COLLEGE - SCHOOL OF THEOLOGY - BYRD MEMORIAL LIBRARY
                                                 Phone: (317) 649-9071
Anderson, IN 46011   Delena Goodman, Hd.Libn.

PARK PLACE CHURCH OF GOD - CARL KARDATZKE MEMORIAL LIBRARY
501 College Dr.
Anderson, IN 46012   Hazel Smith, Chm., Lib.Comm.

ST. JOHN'S MEMORIAL HOSPITAL - HEALTH SCIENCES LIBRARY
2015 Jackson St.   Phone: (317) 646-8264
Anderson, IN 46012   Adelia P. Seglin, Dir.

AUBURN-CORD-DUESENBERG MUSEUM - TRI-KAPPA COLLECTION OF
     AUBURN AUTOMOTIVE LITERATURE
1600 S. Wayne St.
Box 271   Phone: (219) 925-1444
Auburn, IN 46706   Gregg Buttermore, Archv.

INDIANA LIMESTONE INSTITUTE OF AMERICA, INC. - LIBRARY AND
     INFORMATION CENTER
Stone City Bank Bldg., Suite 400   Phone: (812) 275-4426
Bedford, IN 47421   William H. McDonald, Arch.Serv.Dir.

AGENCY FOR INSTRUCTIONAL TELEVISION (AIT) - RESEARCH LIBRARY
1111 W. 17th St.
Box A   Phone: (812) 339-2203
Bloomington, IN 47402   Anne Beversdorf, Libn.

INDIANA UNIVERSITY - ARCHIVES OF TRADITIONAL MUSIC
Maxwell Hall 057   Phone: (812) 337-8632
Bloomington, IN 47405   Frank J. Gillis, Dir.

INDIANA UNIVERSITY - BIOLOGY LIBRARY
Jordan Hall   Phone: (812) 337-9791
Bloomington, IN 47405   Kevin C. Quinn, Act.Hd.

INDIANA UNIVERSITY - BUSINESS LIBRARY
Business Bldg.   Phone: (812) 337-1957
Bloomington, IN 47405   Nevin W. Raber, Hd.

INDIANA UNIVERSITY - CHEMISTRY LIBRARY
                                                 Phone: (812) 337-9452
Bloomington, IN 47405   Gary Wiggins, Hd.

INDIANA UNIVERSITY - EAST ASIAN COLLECTION
                                                 Phone: (812) 337-9695
Bloomington, IN 47405   Shizue Matsuda, Libn.

INDIANA UNIVERSITY - EDUCATION LIBRARY
                                                 Phone: (812) 337-1798
Bloomington, IN 47405   Wilmer H. Baatz, Hd.

INDIANA UNIVERSITY - FINE ARTS LIBRARY
Fine Arts Ctr.   Phone: (812) 337-5743
Bloomington, IN 47405   Betty Jo Irvine, Hd.

INDIANA UNIVERSITY - FINE ARTS SLIDE LIBRARY
Fine Arts 415   Phone: (812) 337-6717
Bloomington, IN 47405   Eileen Fry, Slide Libn.

GEOGRAPHIC

INDIANA UNIVERSITY - FOLKLORE ARCHIVES
510 N. Fess Phone: (812) 337-3652
Bloomington, IN 47405 Timothy J. Kloberdanz, Hd.Archv.

INDIANA UNIVERSITY - FOLKLORE COLLECTION
10th And Jordan Sts. Phone: (812) 337-1550
Bloomington, IN 47405 Polly S. Grimshaw, Libn./Cur.

INDIANA UNIVERSITY - GEOGRAPHY AND MAP LIBRARY
301 Kirkwood Hall Phone: (812) 337-1108
Bloomington, IN 47405 Daniel Seldin, Hd.

INDIANA UNIVERSITY - GEOLOGY LIBRARY
Geology Bldg., 1005 E. Tenth St. Phone: (812) 337-7170
Bloomington, IN 47405 Lois Heiser, Act.Libn.

INDIANA UNIVERSITY - HEALTH, PHYSICAL EDUCATION & RECREATION LIBRARY
HPER Bldg. 031 Phone: (812) 337-4420
Bloomington, IN 47401 Patricia Steele, Br.Mgr.

INDIANA UNIVERSITY - INSTITUTE FOR URBAN TRANSPORTATION - RESOURCE CENTER
809 E. 9th St. Phone: (812) 337-8143
Bloomington, IN 47401 Mary Bassett, Sr. Staff Res.

INDIANA UNIVERSITY - JOURNALISM LIBRARY
Ernie Pyle Hall, 7th St.
Bloomington, IN 47405 Frances Wilhoit

INDIANA UNIVERSITY - LAW LIBRARY
School of Law Phone: (812) 337-9666
Bloomington, IN 47405 Colleen K. Pauwels, Dir.

INDIANA UNIVERSITY - LEARNING RESOURCE CENTER *
109 N. Jordan Ave. Phone: (812) 337-3675
Bloomington, IN 47405 Leslie D. Simpson, Supv.

INDIANA UNIVERSITY - LILLY LIBRARY
Phone: (812) 337-2452
Bloomington, IN 47405 William R. Cagle, Libn.

INDIANA UNIVERSITY - MEDICAL SCIENCES LIBRARY
251 Myers Hall Phone: (812) 337-3347
Bloomington, IN 47405 Julia S. Carter, Libn.

INDIANA UNIVERSITY - MUSEUM - MUSEUM LIBRARY
Student Bldg., Rm. 209 Phone: (812) 337-7224
Bloomington, IN 47405

INDIANA UNIVERSITY - MUSIC LIBRARY
School Of Music Library Phone: (812) 337-8541
Bloomington, IN 47405 Dr. David Fenske, Hd.Libn.

INDIANA UNIVERSITY - NEAR EASTERN COLLECTION
Phone: (812) 337-3403
Bloomington, IN 47405

INDIANA UNIVERSITY - OPTOMETRY BRANCH LIBRARY
Optometry Bldg. Phone: (812) 337-8629
Bloomington, IN 47405 Sabina Sinclair, Hd.

INDIANA UNIVERSITY - ORAL HISTORY RESEARCH PROJECT - LIBRARY
512 N. Fess Phone: (812) 337-2856
Bloomington, IN 47401 John Bodnar, Dir.

INDIANA UNIVERSITY - RESEARCH INSTITUTE FOR INNER ASIAN STUDIES - LIBRARY
Goodbody Hall 157 Phone: (812) 337-1605
Bloomington, IN 47405 Prof. Stephen Halkovic, Dir.

INDIANA UNIVERSITY - SCHOOL OF LIBRARY AND INFORMATION SCIENCE LIBRARY
Phone: (812) 337-5968
Bloomington, IN 47405

INDIANA UNIVERSITY - SCHOOL OF PUBLIC AND ENVIRONMENTAL AFFAIRS - LIBRARY
Poplars Research Ctr.
400 E. 7th St. Phone: (812) 337-4584
Bloomington, IN 47405 Michael Parrish, Hd.

INDIANA UNIVERSITY - SOCIAL STUDIES DEVELOPMENT CENTER - CURRICULUM RESOURCE CENTER
513 N. Park Phone: (812) 337-3584
Bloomington, IN 47405 Linda Kelty, Libn.

INDIANA UNIVERSITY - SWAIN HALL LIBRARY
Phone: (812) 337-2758
Bloomington, IN 47405 Douglas J. Leadenham, Hd.

INSTITUTE FOR SEX RESEARCH, INC. - LIBRARY AND INFORMATION SERVICE
416 Morrison Hall
Indiana University Phone: (812) 337-7686
Bloomington, IN 47405 Susan Matusak, Hd.Libn.

VISION INFORMATION PROGRAM, INC.
Box 1208 Phone: (812) 825-5777
Bloomington, IN 47401 Dr. Gordon G. Heath, Pres.

CAYLOR-NICKEL CLINIC AND HOSPITAL - MEDICAL LIBRARY
311 S. Scott St. Phone: (219) 824-3500
Bluffton, IN 46714 Patricia Niblick, Med.Libn.

MUSCATATUCK STATE HOSPITAL & TRAINING CENTER - RESIDENT AND STAFF DEVELOPMENT LIBRARY
Box 77 Phone: (812) 346-4401
Butlerville, IN 47223 William Bohall, Info.Spec.

BARTHOLOMEW COUNTY HISTORICAL SOCIETY - MUSEUM LIBRARY
524 Third St. Phone: (812) 372-3541
Columbus, IN 47201 Sue Wilgus, Musm.Dir.

CUMMINS ENGINE CO., INC. - LIBRARIES
M/C 50120, Box 3005 Phone: (812) 379-6959
Columbus, IN 47201

IRWIN MANAGEMENT COMPANY, INC. - LIBRARY
301 Washington St.
Columbus, IN 47201

BLOMMEL HISTORIC AUTOMOTIVE DATA COLLECTION - LIBRARY AND INFORMATION CENTER
Rte. 5 Phone: (317) 825-9259
Connersville, IN 47331 Henry H. Blommel, Collector-Dir.

U.S. NAVY - NAVAL WEAPONS SUPPORT CENTER - LIBRARY
Code 016 Phone: (812) 854-1615
Crane, IN 47522 Peggy Curran, Supv.Libn.

LAKE CIRCUIT COURT - LIBRARY
2293 N. Main Phone: (219) 738-2020
Crown Point, IN 46307 Beth Henderson, Libn.

EAST CHICAGO HISTORICAL SOCIETY - LIBRARY
East Chicago Public Library
1008 W. Chicago Ave. Phone: (219) 397-2453
East Chicago, IN 46312 Rose LeVan, Pres.

INLAND STEEL COMPANY - RESEARCH LABORATORIES - LIBRARY
3001 E. Columbus Dr. Phone: (219) 392-5824
East Chicago, IN 46312 Barbara Minne Banek, Libn.

ST. CATHERINE HOSPITAL - MC GUIRE MEMORIAL LIBRARY
4321 Fir St. Phone: (219) 392-7494
East Chicago, IN 46312 Madeline E. Downen, Supv.

ASSOCIATED MENNONITE BIBLICAL SEMINARIES - MENNONITE BIBLICAL SEMINARY - LIBRARY
3003 Benham Ave. Phone: (219) 295-3726
Elkhart, IN 46514 Paul Roten, Libn.

MILES LABORATORIES, INC. - LIBRARY RESOURCES AND SERVICES
1127 Myrtle St. Phone: (219) 264-8341
Elkhart, IN 46515 Margaret L. Lee, Dir.

DEACONESS HOSPITAL - HEALTH SCIENCE LIBRARY
600 Mary St. Phone: (812) 426-3385
Evansville, IN 47747 Millie H. Grunow, Med.Libn.

EVANSVILLE MUSEUM OF ARTS AND SCIENCE - LIBRARY
411 S.E. Riverside Dr.   Phone: (812) 425-2406
Evansville, IN 47713   Mary S. McNamee, Cur., Coll.

EVANSVILLE PSYCHIATRIC CHILDREN'S CENTER - STAFF LIBRARY
3330 E. Morgan Ave.   Phone: (812) 477-6436
Evansville, IN 47715   Juanita J. Massie, Med.Rec.Adm./Libn.

INDIANA STATE UNIVERSITY, EVANSVILLE - SPECIAL COLLECTIONS AND
    UNIVERSITY ARCHIVES
8600 University Blvd.   Phone: (812) 464-1896
Evansville, IN 47712   Gina R. Walker, Act.Archv.

LEGAL SERVICES ORGANIZATION OF INDIANA, INC. - LIBRARY
222 N.W. 3rd St.   Phone: (812) 426-1295
Evansville, IN 47708   Patricia Farris, Office Mgr.

MEAD JOHNSON AND COMPANY - MEAD JOHNSON INSTITUTE - LIBRARY
2404 Pennsylvania   Phone: (812) 426-7042
Evansville, IN 47721   Larry H. Higgins, Mgr., Educ.

MEAD JOHNSON AND COMPANY - MEAD JOHNSON RESEARCH CENTER -
    LIBRARY
    Phone: (812) 426-6546
Evansville, IN 47721   Alice Weisling, Res.Ctr.Libn.

SOUTHWESTERN INDIANA MENTAL HEALTH CENTER - LIBRARY
415 Mulberry   Phone: (812) 423-7791
Evansville, IN 47713   Donna Yuschak, Libn.

VANDERBURGH COUNTY LAW LIBRARY
City-County Courts Bldg., Rm. 214   Phone: (812) 426-5175
Evansville, IN 47708   Shirley Roll, Libn.

U.S. ARMY ADMINISTRATION CENTER - MAIN LIBRARY
Bldg. 400, Rm. 205   Phone: (317) 542-3891
Ft. Benjamin Harrison, IN 46216   Mrs. Marina Griner, Supv.Libn.

ALLEN COUNTY-FORT WAYNE HISTORICAL SOCIETY - LIBRARY AND
    MANUSCRIPT COLLECTIONS
302 E. Berry St.   Phone: (219) 426-2882
Fort Wayne, IN 46802   Doris Perry, Registrar

ALLEN COUNTY LAW LIBRARY
Courthouse, Rm. 105   Phone: (219) 423-7638
Fort Wayne, IN 46802   Charlotte A. Roberts, Law Libn.

ALLEN COUNTY PUBLIC LIBRARY - INDIANA COLLECTION
900 Webster St.   Phone: (219) 424-7241
Fort Wayne, IN 46802   Helen Colchin, Ref.Dept.Hd.

CENTRAL SOYA COMPANY, INC. - FOOD RESEARCH LIBRARY
1300 Fort Wayne National Bank Bldg.   Phone: (219) 489-1511
Fort Wayne, IN 46802   Margaret Campbell, Libn.

CONCORDIA THEOLOGICAL SEMINARY - LIBRARY
6600 N. Clinton   Phone: (219) 482-9611
Fort Wayne, IN 46825   Kenneth Pflueger, Dir., Lib.Serv.

CROSIER HOUSE OF STUDIES - LIBRARY
2620 E. Wallen Rd.   Phone: (219) 489-3521
Fort Wayne, IN 46825   Rev. Ervin J. Rausch, O.S.C., Hd.Libn.

FIRST FEDERAL SAVINGS AND LOAN ASSOCIATION OF FORT WAYNE -
    LIBRARY
719 Court St.   Phone: (219) 423-2377
Fort Wayne, IN 46801   Robert P. Norton, V.P.

FORT WAYNE BIBLE COLLEGE - S.A. LEHMAN MEMORIAL LIBRARY
919 W. Rudisill Blvd.   Phone: (219) 456-2111
Fort Wayne, IN 46807   Wava Bueschlen, Dir. of the Lib.

INDIANA INSTITUTE OF TECHNOLOGY - MC MILLEN LIBRARY
1600 E. Washington Blvd.   Phone: (219) 422-5561
Fort Wayne, IN 46803   Jeanne Hickling, Libn.

INDIANA UNIVERSITY/PURDUE UNIVERSITY AT FORT WAYNE - FINE ARTS
    LIBRARY †
1026 W. Berry St.   Phone: (219) 482-5201
Fort Wayne, IN 46804   Marilyn L. Murphy, Libn.

ITT CORPORATION - AEROSPACE/OPTICAL DIVISION - INFORMATION
    SERVICES CENTER
3700 E. Pontiac St.   Phone: (219) 423-9636
Fort Wayne, IN 46803   Cheryl A. Womack, Info. Data Spec.

LINCOLN NATIONAL LIFE FOUNDATION - LOUIS A. WARREN LINCOLN
    LIBRARY AND MUSEUM
1300 S. Clinton St.   Phone: (219) 424-5421
Fort Wayne, IN 46801   Mark E. Neely, Jr., Dir.

LINCOLN NATIONAL LIFE INSURANCE COMPANY - LAW LIBRARY
1300 S. Clinton St., 7th Fl.
Box 1110   Phone: (219) 424-5421
Fort Wayne, IN 46801   Jo Ann Aufdenkamp, Adm., Info.Serv.

LUTHERAN HOSPITAL OF FORT WAYNE, INC. - HEALTH SCIENCES LIBRARY
3024 Fairfield Ave.   Phone: (219) 458-2277
Fort Wayne, IN 46807   Raisa Cherniv, Dir.

MAGNAVOX COMPANY - ENGINEERING LIBRARY †
2131 S. Coliseum Blvd.   Phone: (219) 482-4411
Fort Wayne, IN 46803   Lydia Peralta, Libn.

PARKVIEW MEMORIAL HOSPITAL - PARKVIEW-METHODIST SCHOOL OF
    NURSING - LIBRARY
2200 Randallia Dr.   Phone: (219) 484-6636
Fort Wayne, IN 46805   Susan L. Farid, Libn.

PUBLIC LIBRARY OF FORT WAYNE AND ALLEN COUNTY, INDIANA -
    BUSINESS AND TECHNOLOGY DEPARTMENT
900 Webster St.   Phone: (219) 424-7241
Fort Wayne, IN 46802   Wesley Avins, Mgr.

ST. JOSEPH'S HOSPITAL - MEDICAL LIBRARY
700 Broadway   Phone: (219) 423-2614
Fort Wayne, IN 46802   Michael Sheets, Dir., Med.Lib.

ST. JOSEPH'S HOSPITAL - SCHOOL OF NURSING LIBRARY
735 W. Berry St.   Phone: (219) 423-2614
Fort Wayne, IN 46804   Gloria Uptgraft, Libn.

U.S. VETERANS ADMINISTRATION (IN-Fort Wayne) - HOSPITAL LIBRARY
1600 Randalia Dr.   Phone: (219) 743-5431
Fort Wayne, IN 46805   Enolia L. Stalnaker, Chf., Lib.Serv.

FRANKLIN COLLEGE - SPECIAL COLLECTIONS
Franklin College Library   Phone: (317) 736-8441
Franklin, IN 46131   Mary Alice Medlicott, Cur.

GARY POST-TRIBUNE - LIBRARY
1065 Broadway   Phone: (219) 886-5078
Gary, IN 46402   Louise K. Tucker, Libn.

INDIANA UNIVERSITY NORTHWEST - CALUMET REGIONAL ARCHIVES
Library, 3400 Broadway   Phone: (219) 980-6661
Gary, IN 46408   Robert Moran

INDIANA VOCATIONAL-TECHNICAL COLLEGE - RESOURCE CENTER
1440 E. 35th Ave.   Phone: (219) 981-1111
Gary, IN 46409   John M. Niemann, Dir.

LAKE COUNTY SUPERIOR COURT LIBRARY
400 Broadway, Rms. 3 & 4   Phone: (219) 886-3621
Gary, IN 46402   Frances Zukowski, Libn.

INDIANA NORTHERN GRADUATE SCHOOL OF PROFESSIONAL
    MANAGEMENT - LIBRARY
410 S. 10th St.
Box 1000   Phone: (317) 674-2900
Gas City, IN 46933   Viola M. Moore

HISTORICAL COMMITTEE OF THE MENNONITE CHURCH - ARCHIVES OF
    THE MENNONITE CHURCH
Goshen College   Phone: (219) 533-3161
Goshen, IN 46526   Leonard Gross, Archv.

MENNONITE HISTORICAL LIBRARY
Goshen College   Phone: (219) 533-3161
Goshen, IN 46526   John S. Oyer, Dir.

GEOGRAPHIC

**DE PAUW UNIVERSITY - ARCHIVES OF DE PAUW UNIVERSITY AND
INDIANA UNITED METHODISM**
Roy O. West Library
Phone: (317) 658-4501
Greencastle, IN 46135
David E. Horn, Archv.

PUTNAM COUNTY HISTORICAL SOCIETY - ARCHIVES
Roy O. West Library
DePauw University
Phone: (317) 658-4501
Greencastle, IN 46135

**ELI LILLY AND COMPANY - GREENFIELD LABORATORIES - LIBRARY
AGRICULTURAL SERVICE**
Box 708
Phone: (317) 462-8225
Greenfield, IN 46140
Bernas Downing, Supv., Lit.Serv.

HAMMOND HISTORICAL SOCIETY - CALUMET ROOM
564 State St.
Phone: (219) 931-5100
Hammond, IN 46320
Harold Ogg, Libn.

LA SALLE STEEL COMPANY - RESEARCH AND DEVELOPMENT LIBRARY †
1412 150th St.
Phone: (219) 853-6095
Hammond, IN 46327
Ruth Polito, Libn.

PURDUE UNIVERSITY - CALUMET LIBRARY
2233 171st St.
Phone: (219) 844-0520
Hammond, IN 46323
Bernard H. Holicky, Dir.

ST. MARGARET HOSPITAL - SALLIE M. TYRRELL, M.D. MEMORIAL LIBRARY
5454 Hohman Ave.
Phone: (219) 932-2300
Hammond, IN 46320
Marguerite Gima, Libn.

**BLACKFORD COUNTY HISTORICAL SOCIETY - MUSEUM AND BEESON
LIBRARY**
321 N. High St.
Box 264
Phone: (317) 348-1905
Hartford City, IN 47348
Dwight Mikkelson, Pres.

**NATIONAL RAILROAD CONSTRUCTION AND MAINTENANCE ASSOCIATION,
INC. - TECHNICAL REFERENCE LIBRARY**
9331 Waymond Ave.
Phone: (219) 924-1709
Highland, IN 46322
larry shields, Exec.Dir.

**HOBART HISTORICAL SOCIETY, INC. - MARIAM J. PLEAK MEMORIAL
LIBRARY AND ARCHIVE**
706 E. Fourth St.
Hobart, IN 46342
Elin B. Christianson, Cur.

ALL SOULS UNITARIAN CHURCH - E. BURDETTE BACKUS LIBRARY
5805 E. 56th St.
Phone: (317) 545-6005
Indianapolis, IN 46226
Marcia Blumenthal, Chm., Lib.Comm.

AMERICAN LEGION - FILM LIBRARY
Box 1055
Indianapolis, IN 46206
Thomas V. Hull, Libn.

AMERICAN LEGION - NATIONAL HEADQUARTERS - LIBRARY
700 N. Pennsylvania St.
Box 1055
Phone: (317) 635-8411
Indianapolis, IN 46206
Thomas V. Hull, Libn.

AMERICAN STATES INSURANCE COMPANY - LIBRARY
500 N. Meridian St.
Phone: (317) 262-6560
Indianapolis, IN 46207
Peggy L. Goss, Librarian

BAKER & DANIELS - LAW LIBRARY
810 Fletcher Trust Bldg.
Phone: (317) 636-4535
Indianapolis, IN 46204
Paula Schmidt, Libn.

**BELL TELEPHONE LABORATORIES, INC. & WESTERN ELECTRIC, INC. -
TECHNICAL LIBRARY**
2525 Shadeland Ave.
Phone: (317) 352-3347
Indianapolis, IN 46206
Bernard L. English, Lib. Group Supv.

BOEHRINGER MANNHEIM CORPORATION - BMC INFORMATION CENTER
8021 Knue Rd.
Box 50528
Phone: (317) 849-6635
Indianapolis, IN 46250
George L. Curran, III, Supv./Libn.

BUTLER UNIVERSITY - IRWIN LIBRARY
Hugh Thomas Miller Rare Book Rm.
46th & Sunset
Phone: (317) 283-9227
Indianapolis, IN 46208
Gisela Hersch, Rare Books Libn.

BUTLER UNIVERSITY - JORDAN COLLEGE OF FINE ARTS MUSIC LIBRARY
46th & Sunset
Phone: (317) 283-9243
Indianapolis, IN 46208
Phyllis Schoonover, Music Libn.

BUTLER UNIVERSITY - SCIENCE LIBRARY
46th & Sunset
Phone: (317) 283-9401
Indianapolis, IN 46208
Charla Banner, Sci.Libn.

CARTER (Larue D.) MEMORIAL HOSPITAL - MEDICAL LIBRARY
1315 W. 10th St.
Phone: (317) 634-8401
Indianapolis, IN 46202
Philip I. Enz, Adm.Libn.

CATHOLIC SEMINARY FOUNDATION OF INDIANAPOLIS - LIBRARY
4545 Northwestern Ave.
Phone: (317) 925-9095
Indianapolis, IN 46208
Ivan W. Hughes, O.S.B., Act.Libn.

CENTRAL STATE HOSPITAL - PROFESSIONAL LIBRARY
3000 W. Washington
Phone: (317) 639-3927
Indianapolis, IN 46222
Aurelia S. Baker, Libn.

CHILDREN'S MUSEUM OF INDIANAPOLIS - RAUH MEMORIAL LIBRARY
3000 N. Meridian St.
Phone: (317) 924-5431
Indianapolis, IN 46208
Scott Steven Loman, Libn.

CHRISTIAN CHURCH (Disciples of Christ), INC. - LIBRARY
222 S. Downey Ave.
Box 1986
Phone: (317) 353-1491
Indianapolis, IN 46206
Doris Autrey Kennedy, Libn.

CHRISTIAN THEOLOGICAL SEMINARY - LIBRARY
1000 W. 42nd St.
Phone: (317) 924-1331
Indianapolis, IN 46208
Mr. Leslie R. Galbraith, Libn.

COMMUNITY HOSPITAL OF INDIANAPOLIS, INC. - LIBRARY
1500 N. Ritter Ave.
Phone: (317) 353-5591
Indianapolis, IN 46219
Jean Bonner, Hospital Libn.

CURTIS PUBLISHING COMPANY - ARCHIVES
1100 Waterway Blvd.
Phone: (317) 634-1100
Indianapolis, IN 46202
Carol Brown McShane, Libn./Archv.

DOW CHEMICAL COMPANY - RESEARCH CENTER LIBRARY *
Box 68511
Phone: (317) 873-5311
Indianapolis, IN 46268
Maxine Tomlin, Libn.

ELI LILLY AND COMPANY - BUSINESS LIBRARY
307 E. McCarty St.
Phone: (317) 261-3241
Indianapolis, IN 46285
Helen E. Loftus, Dept.Hd.

ELI LILLY AND COMPANY - LILLY ARCHIVES
Lilly Center
307 E. McCarty St.
Phone: (317) 261-2173
Indianapolis, IN 46285
Anita Martin, Archv.

ELI LILLY AND COMPANY - SCIENTIFIC LIBRARY
307 E. McCarty St.
Phone: (317) 261-4452
Indianapolis, IN 46285
Adele Hoskin, Chf.Libn.

ESTERLINE ANGUS INSTRUMENT CORPORATION - COMPANY LIBRARY
1201 Main St.
Phone: (317) 244-7611
Indianapolis, IN 46224
Pamela S. Hilt, Co.Libn.

FIRST MERIDIAN HEIGHTS PRESBYTERIAN CHURCH - HUDELSON LIBRARY
4701 N. Central Ave.
Phone: (317) 283-1301
Indianapolis, IN 46205
Linda K. Harris, Chm., Lib.Comm.

**FMC CORPORATION - CHAIN DIVISION - ENGINEERING RESEARCH
CENTER LIBRARY**
220 S. Belmont Ave.
Box 346B
Indianapolis, IN 46206

GENERAL MOTORS CORPORATION - DETROIT DIESEL ALLISON DIVISION - LIBRARY
Plant No. 8
Box 894
Indianapolis, IN 46206
Phone: (317) 243-5651
W.H. Richardson, Libn.

HARRISON (Benjamin) MEMORIAL HOME - LIBRARY
1230 N. Delaware St.
Indianapolis, IN 46202
Phone: (317) 631-1898
Katherine Svarczkopf

HISTORIC LANDMARKS FOUNDATION OF INDIANA, INC. - INFORMATION CENTER
3402 Boulevard Pl.
Indianapolis, IN 46208
Phone: (317) 926-2301
J. Reid Williamson, Jr., Pres.

INDIANA ACADEMY OF SCIENCE - JOHN SHEPARD WRIGHT MEMORIAL LIBRARY
State Library, 140 N. Senate Ave.
Indianapolis, IN 46204
Phone: (317) 232-3675
Lois Burton, Libn.

INDIANA HISTORICAL SOCIETY - WILLIAM HENRY SMITH MEMORIAL LIBRARY
315 W. Ohio St.
Indianapolis, IN 46202
Phone: (317) 232-1879
Gayle Thornbrough, Dir.

INDIANA STATE BOARD OF HEALTH - JACOB T. OLIPHANT LIBRARY *
1330 W. Michigan St.
Indianapolis, IN 46206
Phone: (317) 633-8585
Billy Smith, Dir.

INDIANA STATE CHAMBER OF COMMERCE - RESEARCH LIBRARY
One Capitol Ave.
Indianapolis, IN 46204
Phone: (317) 634-6407
Max L. Moser, Dir.

INDIANA STATE COMMISSION ON PUBLIC RECORDS - ARCHIVES DIVISION
140 N. Senate Ave.
Indianapolis, IN 46204
Phone: (317) 232-3737
John J. Newman, Dp.Dir./Archv.

INDIANA STATE DEPARTMENT OF COMMERCE - ENERGY GROUP - LIBRARY
440 N. Meridian
Indianapolis, IN 46204
Phone: (317) 232-8940
Rebecca E. Mahoney, Libn.

INDIANA STATE DEPT. OF PUBLIC INSTRUCTION - PROFESSIONAL LIBRARY
229 State House
Indianapolis, IN 46204
Phone: (317) 927-0295
Phyllis M. Land, Dir., Div.Instr. Media

INDIANA STATE HIGHWAY COMMISSION - OFFICE OF HIGHWAY DEVELOPMENT - TECHNICAL LIBRARY
State Office Bldg.
100 N. Senate Ave.
Indianapolis, IN 46204
Phone: (317) 232-5485
Thomas E. Brethauer, Libn.

INDIANA STATE LEGISLATIVE SERVICES AGENCY - OFFICE OF CODE REVISION - LIBRARY *
Rm. 302 State House
Indianapolis, IN 46204
Phone: (317) 269-3550

INDIANA STATE LIBRARY
140 N. Senate Ave.
Indianapolis, IN 46204
Phone: (317) 232-3675
C. Ray Ewick, Dir.

INDIANA STATE LIBRARY - INDIANA DIVISION
140 N. Senate Ave.
Indianapolis, IN 46204
Phone: (317) 232-3668
Jean E. Singleton, Hd.Libn.

INDIANA STATE PLANNING SERVICES AGENCY - LIBRARY †
Harrison Bldg., 143 W. Market St.
Indianapolis, IN 46204
Phone: (317) 232-1497
Sandra R. Thompson, Libn.

INDIANA STATE SCHOOL FOR THE DEAF - LIBRARY
1200 E. 42nd St.
Indianapolis, IN 46205
Phone: (317) 924-4374
Irene Hodock, Libn.

INDIANA STATE SUPREME COURT - LAW LIBRARY
316 State House
Indianapolis, IN 46204
Phone: (317) 633-4640
Juanita A. Miller, Libn.

INDIANA UNIVERSITY - HERRON SCHOOL OF ART - LIBRARY
1701 N. Pennsylvania
Indianapolis, IN 46202
Phone: (317) 923-3651
Maudine B. Williams, Hd.Libn.

INDIANA UNIVERSITY - SCHOOL OF DENTISTRY LIBRARY
1121 W. Michigan St.
Indianapolis, IN 46202
Phone: (317) 264-7204
Marie Sparks, Lib.Dir.

INDIANA UNIVERSITY - SCHOOL OF LAW LIBRARY
735 W. New York St.
Indianapolis, IN 46202
Phone: (317) 264-4028
Prof. James F. Bailey, III, Dir. Law Lib.

INDIANA UNIVERSITY - SCHOOL OF MEDICINE LIBRARY
1100 W. Michigan St.
Indianapolis, IN 46223
Phone: (317) 264-7182
Mary Jane Laatz, Dir.

INDIANA UNIVERSITY/PURDUE UNIVERSITY AT INDIANAPOLIS - 38TH STREET CAMPUS LIBRARY
1201 E. 38th St.
Indianapolis, IN 46205
Phone: (317) 923-1325
Barbara B. Fischler, Hd., Pub.Serv.

INDIANA UNIVERSITY/PURDUE UNIVERSITY AT INDIANAPOLIS - UNIVERSITY LIBRARY
815 W. Michigan St.
Indianapolis, IN 46202
Phone: (317) 264-4101
Robert J. Bonner, Dir. of Libs.

INDIANAPOLIS BAR ASSOCIATION - LIBRARY †
One Indiana Sq.
Indianapolis, IN 46204
Phone: (317) 632-8240
Sandra L. Foster, Libn.

INDIANAPOLIS CENTER FOR ADVANCED RESEARCH - ARAC - NASA TECHNICAL INFORMATION CENTER
1201 E. 38th St.
Indianapolis, IN 46205
Phone: (317) 264-4644
John M. Ulrich, Dir.

INDIANAPOLIS - DEPARTMENT OF METROPOLITAN DEVELOPMENT - DIVISION OF PLANNING AND ZONING - LIBRARY
2041 City-County Bldg.
Indianapolis, IN 46204
Phone: (317) 633-3331
Brenda Mangine, Libn.

INDIANAPOLIS-MARION COUNTY PUBLIC LIBRARY - ARTS DIVISION
40 E. St. Clair St.
Indianapolis, IN 46204
Phone: (317) 269-1764
Claire Conner, Act.Div.Hd.

INDIANAPOLIS-MARION COUNTY PUBLIC LIBRARY - BUSINESS, SCIENCE AND TECHNOLOGY DIVISION
40 E. St. Clair St.
Indianapolis, IN 46204
Phone: (317) 269-1741
Barbara Frantz, Div.Hd.

INDIANAPOLIS-MARION COUNTY PUBLIC LIBRARY - FILM DIVISION
1435 N. Illinois St.
Indianapolis, IN 46202
Phone: (317) 269-1821
Jacqueline Ek, Div.Hd.

INDIANAPOLIS-MARION COUNTY PUBLIC LIBRARY - SOCIAL SCIENCE DIVISION
40 E. St. Clair St.
Indianapolis, IN 46204
Phone: (317) 269-1733
Lois Laube, Act.Div.Hd.

INDIANAPOLIS MOTOR SPEEDWAY HALL OF FAME MUSEUM - LIBRARY
4790 W. 16th St.
Indianapolis, IN 46222
Phone: (317) 241-2501
Jack L. Martin, Dir.

INDIANAPOLIS MUSEUM OF ART - REFERENCE LIBRARY
1200 W. 38th St.
Indianapolis, IN 46208
Phone: (317) 923-1331
Martha G. Blocker, Hd.Libn.

INDIANAPOLIS MUSEUM OF ART - SLIDE COLLECTION
1200 W. 38th St.
Indianapolis, IN 46208
Phone: (317) 923-1331
Carolyn J. Metz, Dir.

INDIANAPOLIS NEWSPAPERS, INC. - INDIANAPOLIS STAR AND INDIANAPOLIS NEWS - REFERENCE LIBRARY
307 N. Pennsylvania St.
Indianapolis, IN 46206
Phone: (317) 633-9293
Sandra Fitzgerald, Hd.Libn.

INDIANAPOLIS POWER & LIGHT COMPANY - CORPORATE COMMUNICATIONS SERVICES REFERENCE LIBRARY
Box 1595B
Indianapolis, IN 46206
Phone: (317) 261-8390
Anna Lyon Baker, Commun.Res.Coord.

GEOGRAPHIC

GEOGRAPHIC

INDIANAPOLIS PUBLIC SCHOOLS - TEACHERS LIBRARY
120 E. Walnut St.   Phone: (317) 266-4499
Indianapolis, IN 46204   Marjorie Percival, Hd.Libn.

KOSSUTH FOUNDATION - HUNGARIAN RESEARCH LIBRARY
Butler University
Indianapolis, IN 46208   Dr. Janos Horvath, Pres.

LEGAL SERVICES ORGANIZATION OF INDIANA, INC. - LIBRARY
107 N. Pennsylvania, Suite 800   Phone: (317) 639-4151
Indianapolis, IN 46204   La Donna Dunlap, Libn.

MARION COUNTY LAW LIBRARY
602 City County Bldg.   Phone: (317) 633-3643
Indianapolis, IN 46204   Lynn S. Connor, Libn.

METHODIST HOSPITAL OF INDIANA, INC. - LIBRARY
1604 N. Capitol Ave.   Phone: (317) 924-8021
Indianapolis, IN 46202   Joyce S. Allen, Lib.Mgr.

MUSEUM OF INDIAN HERITAGE - LIBRARY
Eagle Creek Park
6040 DeLong Rd.   Phone: (317) 293-4488
Indianapolis, IN 46254   P.A. Lawton, Registrar

NATIONAL INTERFRATERNITY CONFERENCE - LIBRARY
3901 W. 86th St.   Phone: (317) 297-1112
Indianapolis, IN 46268   Jack L. Anson, Exec.Dir.

NORTH AMERICAN ISLAMIC TRUST, INC. - LIBRARY
10900 W. Washington St.   Phone: (317) 839-9248
Indianapolis, IN 46231   Muhammad Badr, Gen.Mgr.

PROTESTANT EPISCOPAL CHURCH - DIOCESE OF INDIANAPOLIS, INDIANA
    - ARCHIVES
Indiana State Library
140 N. Senate Ave.   Phone: (317) 926-5454
Indianapolis, IN 46208   Roland G. Usher, Jr., Hist.

RCA CORPORATION - RCA CONSUMER ELECTRONICS LIBRARY
Bldg. 6-223, 600 N. Sherman Dr.   Phone: (317) 267-5925
Indianapolis, IN 46201   S.M. Tamer, Libn.

RESEARCH AND REVIEW SERVICE OF AMERICA - LIBRARY *
6213 La Pas Trail
Box 1727   Phone: (317) 297-4360
Indianapolis, IN 46206   Polly Stewart, Libn.

ST. VINCENT'S HOSPITAL - GARCEAU LIBRARY
2001 W. 86th St.   Phone: (317) 871-2095
Indianapolis, IN 46260   Virginia Durkin, Med.Libn.

UNION CARBIDE CORPORATION - LINDE DIVISION - TECHNICAL LIBRARY
1500 Polco St.   Phone: (317) 240-2520
Indianapolis, IN 46224   Mary Ann Brady, Libn.

U. S. GEOLOGICAL SURVEY - WATER RESOURCES DIVISION - LIBRARY
1819 N. Meridian St.   Phone: (317) 269-6594
Indianapolis, IN 46202   Rudolph R. Contreras, Act.Libn.

U.S. NAVY - NAVAL AVIONICS CENTER - TECHNICAL LIBRARY
21st & Arlington Ave.   Phone: (317) 353-3231
Indianapolis, IN 46218   Louise Boyd, Supv.

U.S. VETERANS ADMINISTRATION (IN-Indianapolis) - MEDICAL CENTER
    LIBRARY
1481 W. Tenth St.   Phone: (317) 635-7401
Indianapolis, IN 46202   Larry D. Weitkemper, Chf., Lib.Serv.

WINONA MEMORIAL HOSPITAL - HEALTH SCIENCES LIBRARY
3232 N. Meridian   Phone: (317) 927-2248
Indianapolis, IN 46208   Karen A. Davis, Med.Libn.

WISHARD (William N.) MEMORIAL HOSPITAL - PROFESSIONAL LIBRARY/
    MEDIA SERVICES
1001 W. 10th St.   Phone: (317) 630-7028
Indianapolis, IN 46202   Jana Bradley, Dir.

CLARK COUNTY MEMORIAL HOSPITAL - MEDICAL LIBRARY
1220 Missouri Ave.   Phone: (812) 283-2358
Jeffersonville, IN 47130   Charlotte Teresa Reynolds, Med.Libn.

CABOT CORPORATION - TECHNICAL INFORMATION CENTER
1020 W. Park Ave.   Phone: (317) 456-6140
Kokomo, IN 46901   Betty S. Hollis, Tech.Libn.

GENERAL MOTORS CORPORATION - DELCO ELECTRONICS DIVISION -
    TECHNICAL LIBRARY
Box 1104   Phone: (317) 459-7262
Kokomo, IN 46901   R.E. Sparks, Tech.Libn.

KOKOMO TRIBUNE - LIBRARY
300 N. Union   Phone: (317) 459-3121
Kokomo, IN 46901   Dawn L. North, Libn.

ST. JOSEPH MEMORIAL HOSPITAL - HEALTH SCIENCE LIBRARY
1907 W. Sycamore St.   Phone: (317) 452-5611
Kokomo, IN 46901   Bernice B. Ludewig, Libn.

LAFAYETTE JOURNAL AND COURIER - LIBRARY
217 N. 6th St.   Phone: (317) 423-5511
Lafayette, IN 47901   Marlene Bailey, Libn.

NATIONAL ASSOCIATION OF QUICK PRINTERS - INTERNATIONAL QUICK
    PRINTING FOUNDATION LIBRARY
Box 1250
Lafayette, IN 47902   Jill Schmidhammer, Exec.Dir.

ST. ELIZABETH HOSPITAL MEDICAL CENTER - MEMORIAL MEDICAL
    LIBRARY †
1501 Hartford St.   Phone: (317) 423-6143
Lafayette, IN 47904   Ruth P. Pape, Libn.

ST. ELIZABETH MEDICAL CENTER - SCHOOL OF NURSING LIBRARY
1508 Tippecanoe St.   Phone: (317) 423-6125
Lafayette, IN 47904   Evelyn S. Wigent, Libn.

TIPPECANOE COUNTY HISTORICAL ASSOCIATION - ALAMEDA
    MC COLLOUGH RESEARCH & GENEALOGY LIBRARY
909 South St.   Phone: (317) 742-8411
Lafayette, IN 47901   John M. Harris, Dir.

U.S. NATL. PARK SERVICE - LINCOLN BOYHOOD NATL. MEMORIAL VISITOR
    CENTER
                                    Phone: (812) 937-4757
Lincoln City, IN 47552   Warren D. Beach, Supt.

LOGANSPORT STATE HOSPITAL - MEDICAL LIBRARY †
R.R. 2   Phone: (219) 722-4141
Logansport, IN 46947   Terra Newton, Libn.

MADISON STATE HOSPITAL - CRAGMONT MEDICAL LIBRARY
                                    Phone: (812) 265-2611
Madison, IN 47250   Laura D. Fury, Libn.

MARION GENERAL HOSPITAL - MEDICAL LIBRARY
Wabash & Euclid Avenues   Phone: (317) 662-4607
Marion, IN 46952   Kay Lake, Dir., Educ.Servs.

RCA CORPORATION - PICTURE TUBE DIVISION - LIBRARY *
3301 S. Adams St.   Phone: (317) 662-1411
Marion, IN 46952   M. Morgan

U.S. VETERANS ADMINISTRATION (IN-Marion) - HOSPITAL MEDICAL
    LIBRARY
E. 38th St. at Home Ave.   Phone: (317) 674-3321
Marion, IN 46952   Joy E. Zuger, Chf., Lib.Serv.

WESLEYAN CHURCH - ARCHIVES & HISTORICAL LIBRARY
Box 2000   Phone: (317) 674-3301
Marion, IN 46952   Paul W. Thomas, Dir.

AMERICAN CAMPING ASSOCIATION - LIBRARY †
Bradford Woods   Phone: (317) 342-8456
Martinsville, IN 46151

BALL CORPORATION - BALL INFORMATION CENTER AND LAW LIBRARY
345 S. High St.   Phone: (317) 747-6420
Muncie, IN 47302   Peg Nelson, Libn.

BALL CORPORATION - RESEARCH LIBRARY
1509 S. Macedonia   Phone: (317) 747-6707
Muncie, IN 47302

BALL STATE UNIVERSITY - ALTHEA L. STOECKEL DELAWARE COUNTY
   ARCHIVES & LOCAL HISTORY COLLECTION
Bracken Library   Phone: (317) 285-7800
Muncie, IN 47306   David C. Tambo, Cur.

BALL STATE UNIVERSITY - BRACKEN LIBRARY - SPECIAL COLLECTIONS
Bracken Library, Rm. 210   Phone: (317) 285-5078
Muncie, IN 47306   Juanita J. Smith, Spec.Coll.Libn.

BALL STATE UNIVERSITY - COLLEGE OF ARCHITECTURE & PLANNING -
   LIBRARY
                                             Phone: (317) 285-4760
Muncie, IN 47306   Marjorie Joyner, Libn.

BALL STATE UNIVERSITY - MUSIC LIBRARY
                                             Phone: (317) 285-7356
Muncie, IN 47306   Dr. Nyal Williams, Music Libn.

LEGAL SERVICES ORGANIZATION OF INDIANA, INC. - DELAWARE COUNTY
   OFFICE - LIBRARY *
316 W. Washington St.   Phone: (317) 286-0943
Muncie, IN 47305   Beth Holland, Libn.

MUNCIE STAR-PRESS LIBRARY
High & Jackson Sts.   Phone: (317) 747-5767
Muncie, IN 47302   Breena L. Wysong, Libn.

HENRY COUNTY HISTORICAL SOCIETY - LIBRARY
Henry County Historical Bldg.
606 S. 14th St.   Phone: (317) 529-4028
New Castle, IN 47362   Janet Bush, Pres.

NEW CASTLE STATE HOSPITAL - MEDICAL LIBRARY
100 Van Nuys Rd.
Box 34   Phone: (317) 529-0900
New Castle, IN 47362   Jann Swinford, Media Dir.

NEW HARMONY WORKINGMEN'S INSTITUTE - LIBRARY AND MUSEUM
407 W. Tavern St.
Box 368   Phone: (812) 682-4806
New Harmony, IN 47631   Mary Aline Cook, Libn.

CONNER PRAIRIE PIONEER SETTLEMENT - RESEARCH DEPARTMENT
   LIBRARY
30 Conner Lane   Phone: (317) 773-3633
Noblesville, IN 46060   John Lauritz Larson, Hist.

CONGREGATION OF HOLY CROSS - MOREAU SEMINARY - LIBRARY
                                             Phone: (219) 283-7735
Notre Dame, IN 46556   Rev. Peter F. Mueller, C.S.C., Dir.

ENVIRONIC FOUNDATION INTERNATIONAL, INC. - LIBRARY AND FILES
Box 88   Phone: (219) 233-3357
Notre Dame, IN 46556   Patrick Horsbrugh, Chm.

ST. MARY'S COLLEGE - MUSIC SEMINAR ROOM †
Moreau Hall   Phone: (219) 284-4186
Notre Dame, IN 46556

THEATRE HISTORICAL SOCIETY COLLECTION
Box 101   Phone: (219) 283-3615
Notre Dame, IN 46556   B. Andrew Corsini, Dir. of Pubn.

UNIVERSITY OF NOTRE DAME - ARCHITECTURE LIBRARY
Architectural Bldg.   Phone: (219) 283-6654
Notre Dame, IN 46556   Geri Decker, Libn.

UNIVERSITY OF NOTRE DAME - ARCHIVES
607 Memorial Library   Phone: (219) 283-6447
Notre Dame, IN 46556   Wendy C. Schlereth, Archv.

UNIVERSITY OF NOTRE DAME - CENTER FOR THE STUDY OF HUMAN
   RIGHTS - READING ROOM
Law School, Rm. 301   Phone: (219) 283-6483
Notre Dame, IN 46556   Rita M. Kopczynski, Libn.

UNIVERSITY OF NOTRE DAME - CHEMISTRY/PHYSICS LIBRARY
Nieuwland Science Hall   Phone: (219) 283-7203
Notre Dame, IN 46556   Karla P. Goold, Libn.

UNIVERSITY OF NOTRE DAME - ENGINEERING LIBRARY
Engineering Bldg.   Phone: (219) 283-6665
Notre Dame, IN 46556   Robert J. Havlik, Engr.Libn.

UNIVERSITY OF NOTRE DAME - INTERNATIONAL STUDIES LIBRARY
1201 Memorial Library   Phone: (219) 283-6587
Notre Dame, IN 46556   Theodore B. Ivanus, Hd.

UNIVERSITY OF NOTRE DAME - LAW SCHOOL LIBRARY
Box 535   Phone: (219) 283-7024
Notre Dame, IN 46556   Kathleen Farmann, Law Libn.

UNIVERSITY OF NOTRE DAME - LIFE SCIENCES RESEARCH LIBRARY
Galvin Life Sciences Bldg.   Phone: (219) 283-7209
Notre Dame, IN 46556   Dorothy Coil, Libn.

UNIVERSITY OF NOTRE DAME - MATHEMATICS LIBRARY
Computing Center   Phone: (219) 283-7278
Notre Dame, IN 46556   Donna G. Gehring, Lib.Assoc.

UNIVERSITY OF NOTRE DAME - MEDIEVAL INSTITUTE LIBRARY
715 Memorial Library   Phone: (219) 283-6604
Notre Dame, IN 46556   Louis Jordan, Hd.

UNIVERSITY OF NOTRE DAME - RADIATION LABORATORY - RADIATION
   CHEMISTRY DATA CENTER
                                             Phone: (219) 283-6528
Notre Dame, IN 46556   Dr. Alberta B. Ross, Supv.

UNIVERSITY OF NOTRE DAME - RARE BOOKS AND SPECIAL COLLECTIONS
   DEPARTMENT
Memorial Library   Phone: (219) 283-6489
Notre Dame, IN 46556   Anton C. Masin, Hd.

OAKLAND CITY COLLEGE - FOUNDERS MEMORIAL LIBRARY
                                             Phone: (812) 749-4781
Oakland City, IN 47660   Ulah Wilder, Hd.Libn.

U.S. AIR FORCE BASE - GRISSOM BASE LIBRARY
Grissom AFB
Bldg. 575
                                             Phone: (317) 689-2056
Peru, IN 46971   Christopher Cupp, Libn.

INDIANA LAW ENFORCEMENT ACADEMY - DAVID F. ALLEN MEMORIAL
   LEARNING RESOURCES CENTER
Box 313   Phone: (317) 839-5191
Plainfield, IN 46168   Donna K. Zimmerman, Libn.

PLAINFIELD PUBLIC LIBRARY - GUILFORD TOWNSHIP HISTORICAL
   COLLECTION
1120 Stafford Rd.   Phone: (317) 839-6602
Plainfield, IN 46168   Susan Miller Carter, Hist.Libn.

MARSHALL COUNTY HISTORICAL SOCIETY MUSEUM - LIBRARY
317 W. Monroe St.   Phone: (219) 936-2306
Plymouth, IN 46563   Mary L. Durnan, Dir.

EARLHAM COLLEGE - JOSEPH MOORE MUSEUM - HADLEY LIBRARY
Box 68   Phone: (317) 962-6561
Richmond, IN 47374   Jon Branstrator, Musm.Dir.

EARLHAM COLLEGE - QUAKER COLLECTION
Lilly Library   Phone: (317) 962-6561
Richmond, IN 47374   Philip Shore, Assoc.Libn.

HAYES (Stanley W.) RESEARCH FOUNDATION - LIBRARY
Box 1404
Richmond, IN 47374   D.R. Hendricks, Pres.

GEOGRAPHIC

WAYNE COUNTY HISTORICAL MUSEUM - LIBRARY
1150 North A St.   Phone: (317) 962-5756
Richmond, IN 47374   William E. Reifsteck, Dir.

FULTON COUNTY HISTORICAL SOCIETY - LIBRARY
7th & Pontiac   Phone: (219) 223-4436
Rochester, IN 46975   Shirley Willard, Dir.

WASHINGTON COUNTY HISTORICAL SOCIETY - LIBRARY
Stevens Memorial Musm.
307 E. Market St.
Salem, IN 47167   Lulie Davis, Sec.-Libn.

THERMARK CORPORATION - TECHNICAL INFORMATION SERVICES
650 W. 67th Pl.   Phone: (219) 322-5030
Schererville, IN 46375   Irene Ganas, Tech.Info.Serv.Mgr.

INLOW CLINIC - LIBRARY
103 W. Washington St.
Box 370
Shelbyville, IN 46176

ART CENTER, INC. - LIBRARY
120 S. St. Joseph St.   Phone: (219) 284-9102
South Bend, IN 46601   Judy Oberhausen, Act.Dir./Cur.

BENDIX CORPORATION - BENDIX ENERGY CONTROLS DIVISION -
    ENGINEERING LIBRARY
717 Bendix Dr.   Phone: (219) 237-5976
South Bend, IN 46620   Mary Jane Brayfield, Libn.

DISCOVERY HALL MUSEUM - RESEARCH LIBRARY
120 S. St. Joseph St.   Phone: (219) 284-9714
South Bend, IN 46601   Marsha Mullin, Cur.

NORTHERN INDIANA HISTORICAL SOCIETY - FREDERICK ELBEL LIBRARY *
112 S. Lafayette Blvd.   Phone: (219) 284-9664
South Bend, IN 46601   James Sullivan, Musm.Dir.

ST. JOSEPH COUNTY LAW LIBRARY
Court House   Phone: (219) 284-9657
South Bend, IN 46601   Conie J. Frank, Libn.

DEBS (Eugene V.) FOUNDATION - LIBRARY
451 N. 8th St.   Phone: (812) 232-2163
Terre Haute, IN 47807   Curtis Culver, Exec.V.P.

INDIANA STATE UNIVERSITY - CONTINUING EDUCATION AND EXTENDED
    SERVICES - LIBRARY
Alumni Ctr.   Phone: (812) 232-6311
Terre Haute, IN 47809   Dr. Louis R. Jensen, Asst. Dean

INDIANA STATE UNIVERSITY - DEPARTMENT OF RARE BOOKS AND
    SPECIAL COLLECTIONS
Cunningham Memorial Library   Phone: (812) 232-6311
Terre Haute, IN 47809   Dr. Robert K. O'Neill, Dept.Hd.

INDIANA STATE UNIVERSITY - SCIENCE LIBRARY
Science Bldg.   Phone: (812) 232-6311
Terre Haute, IN 47809

INDIANA STATE UNIVERSITY - SPECIAL SERVICES AREA
Cunningham Memorial Library   Phone: (812) 232-6311
Terre Haute, IN 47809   Allen Keathley, Spec.Serv.Libn.

INDIANA STATE UNIVERSITY - TEACHING MATERIALS DIVISION
Cunningham Memorial Library   Phone: (812) 232-6311
Terre Haute, IN 47809   Louise W. Richards, Dept.Hd.

INTERNATIONAL MINERALS & CHEMICALS CORPORATION - IMC
    RESEARCH & DEVELOPMENT LIBRARY
1331 S. First St.
Box 207   Phone: (812) 232-0121
Terre Haute, IN 47808   Mr. T.C. Shane, Jr., Tech.Libn.

ROSE-HULMAN INSTITUTE OF TECHNOLOGY - JOHN A. LOGAN LIBRARY
5500 E. Wabash Ave.   Phone: (812) 877-1511
Terre Haute, IN 47803   Herman Cole, Jr., Dir.

VIGO COUNTY HISTORICAL SOCIETY - HISTORICAL MUSEUM OF THE
    WABASH VALLEY - LIBRARY
1411 S. 6th St.   Phone: (812) 235-9717
Terre Haute, IN 47802   Judy Calvert, Libn.

VIGO COUNTY PUBLIC LIBRARY - SPECIAL COLLECTIONS
One Library Square   Phone: (812) 232-1113
Terre Haute, IN 47807   Clarence Brink, Coord., Ref.Serv.

VIGO COUNTY SCHOOL CORPORATION - INSTRUCTIONAL MATERIALS
    CENTER
3000 College Ave.   Phone: (812) 238-4354
Terre Haute, IN 47803   Georgia R. Cole, Coord.

HISTORICAL SOCIETY OF PORTER COUNTY - LIBRARY
Porter County Museum Old Jail   Phone: (219) 464-8661
Valparaiso, IN 46383   Bertha Stalbaum, Musm.Cur.

LUTHERAN DEACONESS ASSOCIATION - DEACONESS HALL LIBRARY
Deaconess Hall, E. Union St.   Phone: (219) 464-5033
Valparaiso, IN 46383   Deaconess Louise Williams, Dir. of Serv.

VALPARAISO UNIVERSITY - LAW LIBRARY
Wesemann Hall   Phone: (219) 464-5438
Valparaiso, IN 46383   Matthew P. Downs, Law Libn.

OLD CATHEDRAL PARISH CHURCH - BRUTE LIBRARY
207 Church St.   Phone: (812) 882-7016
Vincennes, IN 47591   Esther Cunningham

VINCENNES UNIVERSITY - BYRON R. LEWIS HISTORICAL LIBRARY
                                          Phone: (812) 885-4330
Vincennes, IN 47591   Robert R. Stevens, Dir.

WABASH COUNTY HISTORICAL MUSEUM - HISTORICAL LIBRARY
Memorial Hall   Phone: (219) 563-5058
Wabash, IN 46992   Kenneth E. Gray, Cur.

ALLEN (J.C.) AND SON, INC. - LIBRARY
Box 2061   Phone: (317) 463-9614
West Lafayette, IN 47906

PURDUE UNIVERSITY - AVIATION TECHNOLOGY LIBRARY
Purdue Univ. Airport   Phone: (317) 494-7640
West Lafayette, IN 47907   Dennis H. Parks, Libn.

PURDUE UNIVERSITY - BIOCHEMISTRY LIBRARY
Biochemistry Bldg.   Phone: (317) 494-1621
West Lafayette, IN 47907   Martha J. Bailey, Life Sci.Libn.

PURDUE UNIVERSITY - CHEMISTRY LIBRARY
Chemistry Bldg.   Phone: (317) 494-2862
West Lafayette, IN 47907   John Pinzelik, Chem.Libn.

PURDUE UNIVERSITY - CINDAS - ELECTRONIC PROPERTIES INFORMATION
    CENTER
2595 Yeager Rd.   Phone: (317) 494-6300
West Lafayette, IN 47906   Y.S. Touloukian, Dir.

PURDUE UNIVERSITY - CINDAS - THERMOPHYSICAL PROPERTIES
    RESEARCH CENTER - LIBRARY
2595 Yeager Rd.   Phone: (317) 494-6300
West Lafayette, IN 47906   Y.S. Touloukian, Dir.

PURDUE UNIVERSITY - CINDAS - UNDERGROUND EXCAVATION AND ROCK
    PROPERTIES INFORMATION CENTER
2595 Yeager Rd.
West Lafayette, IN 47906

PURDUE UNIVERSITY - CONSUMER AND FAMILY SCIENCES LIBRARY
Stone Hall   Phone: (317) 494-2914
West Lafayette, IN 47907   Emily Alward, Libn.

GEOGRAPHIC

PURDUE UNIVERSITY - ENGINEERING LIBRARY
Potter Bldg.   Phone: (317) 494-2867
West Lafayette, IN 47907   Edwin D. Posey, Engr.Libn.

PURDUE UNIVERSITY - FILM LIBRARY
Stewart Center   Phone: (317) 749-6188
West Lafayette, IN 47907   Carl E. Snow, Film Libn.

PURDUE UNIVERSITY - GEOSCIENCES LIBRARY
Geosciences Bldg.   Phone: (317) 494-3264
West Lafayette, IN 47907   Dennis H. Parks, Act.Libn.

PURDUE UNIVERSITY - LIFE SCIENCE LIBRARY
Lilly Hall of Life Sciences   Phone: (317) 494-2910
West Lafayette, IN 47907   Martha J. Bailey, Life Sci.Libn.

PURDUE UNIVERSITY - MANAGEMENT AND ECONOMICS LIBRARY
Krannert Bldg.   Phone: (317) 494-2922
West Lafayette, IN 47907   John M. Houkes, Libn.

PURDUE UNIVERSITY - MATHEMATICAL SCIENCES LIBRARY
Mathematical Sciences   Phone: (317) 494-2855
West Lafayette, IN 47907   Richard L. Funkhouser, Libn.

PURDUE UNIVERSITY - PHARMACY LIBRARY
Pharmacy Bldg.   Phone: (317) 494-1416
West Lafayette, IN 47907   Theodora Andrews, Libn.

PURDUE UNIVERSITY - PHYSICS LIBRARY
Physics Bldg.   Phone: (317) 494-2858
West Lafayette, IN 47907   Dennis H. Parks, Act.Libn.

PURDUE UNIVERSITY - PSYCHOLOGICAL SCIENCES LIBRARY
Stanley Coulter Annex   Phone: (317) 494-2969
West Lafayette, IN 47907   Marjorie A. Zumstein, Psych.Libn.

PURDUE UNIVERSITY - VETERINARY MEDICAL LIBRARY
C.V. Lynn Hall, Rm. 108   Phone: (317) 494-2852
West Lafayette, IN 47907   Gretchen Stephens, Libn.

UNION BIBLE SEMINARY - LIBRARY *
434 S. Union St.   Phone: (317) 896-2025
Westfield, IN 46074

WESTVILLE CORRECTIONAL CENTER - STAFF LIBRARY
Box 473   Phone: (219) 785-2511
Westville, IN 46391   Catherine M. Mohlke, Dir., Lib.Serv.

RANDOLPH CIRCUIT COURT - LAW LIBRARY †
Courthouse, Rm. 307   Phone: (317) 584-7231
Winchester, IN 47394

FREE METHODIST CHURCH OF NORTH AMERICA - HISTORICAL LIBRARY
901 College Ave.   Phone: (219) 267-7656
Winona Lake, IN 46590   Evelyn Mottweiler, Libn.

GRACE THEOLOGICAL SEMINARY - LIBRARY
Wooster Rd.   Phone: (219) 267-8191
Winona Lake, IN 46590   Robert Ibach, Dir.

IOWA

IOWA STATE DEPARTMENT OF TRANSPORTATION - LIBRARY
800 Lincoln Way   Phone: (515) 296-1200
Ames, IA 50010   Josephine Said, Libn.

IOWA STATE UNIVERSITY - ENERGY AND MINERAL RESOURCES RESEARCH
    INSTITUTE - RARE EARTH INFORMATION CENTER
                                                             Phone: (515) 294-2272
Ames, IA 50011   Karl A. Gschneidner, Jr., Dir.

IOWA STATE UNIVERSITY - LIBRARY
                                                             Phone: (515) 294-1442
Ames, IA 50011   Warren B. Kuhn, Dean of Lib.Serv.

IOWA STATE UNIVERSITY - VETERINARY MEDICAL LIBRARY
                                                             Phone: (515) 294-2225
Ames, IA 50011   Sara Peterson, Hd.Libn.

U.S.D.A. - AGRICULTURAL RESEARCH SERVICE - NATL. ANIMAL DISEASE
    CENTER LIBRARY
Box 70   Phone: (512) 232-0250
Ames, IA 50010   Janice K. Eifling, Libn.

U.S. DEPT. OF ENERGY - AMES LABORATORY - DOCUMENT LIBRARY
Iowa State University   Phone: (515) 294-1856
Ames, IA 50011   Burton J. Gleason, Hd., Office of Info.

SOIL CONSERVATION SOCIETY OF AMERICA - H. WAYNE PRITCHARD
    LIBRARY
7515 N.E. Ankeny Rd.   Phone: (515) 289-2331
Ankeny, IA 50021   James L. Sanders, Asst.Ed.

CEDAR FALLS HISTORICAL SOCIETY - ROWND HISTORICAL LIBRARY
Cedar Falls Historical Museum
303 Clay St.   Phone: (319) 266-5149
Cedar Falls, IA 50613   Rosemary Beach, Dir.

UNIVERSITY OF NORTHERN IOWA - LIBRARY - SPECIAL COLLECTIONS
                                                             Phone: (319) 273-6307
Cedar Falls, IA 50613   Gerald L. Peterson, Spec.Coll.Libn.

CEDAR RAPIDS ART CENTER - HERBERT S. STAMATS ART LIBRARY
324 3rd St., S.E.   Phone: (319) 366-7503
Cedar Rapids, IA 52401

CEDAR RAPIDS PUBLIC LIBRARY - BUSINESS CENTER
428 Third Ave., S.E.   Phone: (319) 398-5123
Cedar Rapids, IA 52401   Roy Kenagy, Hd. Adult Serv.

FIRST LUTHERAN CHURCH - MEMORIAL LIBRARY
1000 3rd Ave., S.E.
Cedar Rapids, IA 52403   Elaine V. Mykleby, Libn.

GRAND LODGE OF IOWA, A.F. AND A.M. - IOWA MASONIC LIBRARY
813 First Ave., S.E.
Box 279   Phone: (319) 365-1438
Cedar Rapids, IA 52406   Tom Eggleston, Grand Sec.

LINN COUNTY BAR ASSOCIATION - LAW LIBRARY †
Linn County Court House   Phone: (319) 398-3449
Cedar Rapids, IA 52401   Susan Corey, Libn.

MERCY HOSPITAL - HEALTH SERVICES LIBRARY
701 Tenth St., S.E.   Phone: (319) 398-6165
Cedar Rapids, IA 52403   Stephanie Schulte, Libn.

ROCKWELL INTERNATIONAL - COLLINS DIVISIONS - INFORMATION
    CENTER
400 Collins Rd., N.E.   Phone: (319) 395-2138
Cedar Rapids, IA 52498   Mildred A. Lahr, Supv., Info.Ctr.

ST. LUKE'S METHODIST HOSPITAL - HEALTH SCIENCE LIBRARY
1026 A Ave., N.E.   Phone: (319) 398-7358
Cedar Rapids, IA 52402   Sally Harms, Dir.

MENTAL HEALTH INSTITUTE - HEALTH SCIENCE LIBRARY
1200 W. Cedar St.   Phone: (712) 225-2594
Cherokee, IA 51012   Tom Folkes, Health Sci.Libn.

SANFORD MUSEUM & PLANETARIUM - LIBRARY
117 E. Willow St.   Phone: (712) 225-3922
Cherokee, IA 51012   Robert W. Hoge, Dir.

CLARINDA MENTAL HEALTH INSTITUTION - RESIDENTS AND STAFF
    LIBRARY
Box 338   Phone: (712) 585-2161
Clarinda, IA 51632   Dorothy Horton, Libn.

CHEROKEE COUNTY HISTORICAL SOCIETY - RESEARCH CENTER
Box 247   Phone: (712) 436-2624
Cleghorn, IA 51014   Darleen Cummins, Pres.

GEOGRAPHIC

EDMUNDSON (Jennie) MEMORIAL HOSPITAL - LIBRARY
933 E. Pierce St.   Phone: (712) 328-6130
Council Bluffs, IA 51501   Patricia A. Blanchard, Libn.

BENDIX CORPORATION - INSTRUMENTS & LIFE SUPPORT DIVISION -
    ENGINEERING LIBRARY
2734 Hickory Grove Rd.   Phone: (319) 383-6387
Davenport, IA 52808   Kathryn Nitz, Tech.Libn.

DAVENPORT ART GALLERY - ART REFERENCE LIBRARY
1737 W. 12th St.   Phone: (319) 326-7804
Davenport, IA 52804   Gladys Hitchings, Libn.

MC GLADREY HENDRICKSON & COMPANY, C.P.A. - CENTRAL LIBRARY *
1017 Davenport Bank Bldg.   Phone: (319) 326-5111
Davenport, IA 52801   Carol Boykin, Libn.

MARYCREST COLLEGE - CONE LIBRARY †
1607 West 12th St.   Phone: (319) 326-9254
Davenport, IA 52804   Sr. Joan Sheil, Dir., Lib.Serv.

PALMER COLLEGE OF CHIROPRACTIC - LIBRARY
1000 Brady St.   Phone: (319) 324-1611
Davenport, IA 52803   Brian J. Greer, Dir.

PUTNAM MUSEUM - LIBRARY
1717 W. 12th St.   Phone: (319) 324-1933
Davenport, IA 52804   Joseph Cartwright, Dir.

SCOTT COUNTY BAR ASSOCIATION - GRANT LAW LIBRARY
416 W. 4th St.   Phone: (319) 326-8677
Davenport, IA 52801   Ginger F. Wolfe, Libn.

LUTHER COLLEGE - PREUS LIBRARY
                                         Phone: (319) 387-1163
Decorah, IA 52101   Leigh D. Jordahl, Hd.Libn.

AMERICAN ACADEMY OF PSYCHOTHERAPISTS - AAP TAPE LIBRARY
8450 Hickman Rd., Suite 14   Phone: (515) 278-8741
Des Moines, IA 50322   Dr. Herbert S. Roth, Dir.

AMERICAN INSTITUTE OF PARLIAMENTARIANS - LIBRARY
229 Army Post Rd., Suite B   Phone: (515) 287-5154
Des Moines, IA 50315   Lester L. Dahms, Exec.Dir.

BROADLAWNS MEDICAL CENTER - MEDICAL LIBRARY
18th & Hickman Rd.   Phone: (515) 282-2200
Des Moines, IA 50314   Charles Z. Hughes, Libn.

DES MOINES ART CENTER - LIBRARY
Greenwood Park   Phone: (515) 277-4405
Des Moines, IA 50312   Margaret Buckley, Libn.

DRAKE UNIVERSITY - COLLEGE OF PHARMACY - LIBRARY
28th & Forest Ave.   Phone: (515) 271-2172
Des Moines, IA 50311   Margaret Daly Granberg, Libn.

DRAKE UNIVERSITY - LAW LIBRARY
Carnegie Hall, 27th & Carpenter   Phone: (515) 271-2141
Des Moines, IA 50311   Juan F. Aguilar, Dir.

GRAND VIEW COLLEGE - ARCHIVES
1351 Grandview   Phone: (515) 266-2651
Des Moines, IA 50316   Thorvald Hansen, Archv.

IOWA GENEALOGICAL SOCIETY - LIBRARY
6000 Douglas, Box 3815   Phone: (515) 276-0287
Des Moines, IA 50322   Carl W. Nissly, Pres.

IOWA HOSPITAL ASSOCIATION - LIBRARY
600 5th Ave. Plaza.   Phone: (515) 288-1955
Des Moines, IA 50309   Deborah Van Egdom, Dir.Lib.Serv.

IOWA LUTHERAN HOSPITAL - DEPARTMENT OF LIBRARY SERVICES
University At Penn   Phone: (515) 283-5181
Des Moines, IA 50316   Wayne A. Pederson, Dir. of Lib.Serv.

IOWA METHODIST MEDICAL CENTER - OLIVER J. FAY MEMORIAL LIBRARY
1200 Pleasant St.   Phone: (515) 283-6490
Des Moines, IA 50308   Mary Wegner, Dir., Med.Lib.

IOWA METHODIST SCHOOL OF NURSING - MARJORIE GERTRUDE MORROW
    LIBRARY
1117 Pleasant St.   Phone: (515) 283-6453
Des Moines, IA 50309   Patricia Downey, Libn.

IOWA STATE COMMISSION FOR THE BLIND - LIBRARY FOR THE BLIND &
    PHYSICALLY HANDICAPPED
4th & Keosauqua Way   Phone: (515) 283-2601
Des Moines, IA 50309   Sine Olesen, Libn.

IOWA STATE DEPARTMENT OF ENVIRONMENTAL QUALITY - TECHNICAL
    LIBRARY
Henry A. Wallace Bldg.   Phone: (515) 281-8899
Des Moines, IA 50319   Cecilia Nelson, Lib.Assoc.

IOWA STATE DEPARTMENT OF HEALTH - FILM LIBRARY
State Historical Bldg.   Phone: (515) 281-4316
Des Moines, IA 50319   Eileen C. Devine, Dir.

IOWA STATE DEPARTMENT OF HEALTH - VITAL RECORDS - INFORMATION
    CENTER
Lucas State Office Bldg.   Phone: (515) 281-5871
Des Moines, IA 50319   Don R. Coughenour, Dir.

IOWA STATE DEPARTMENT OF HISTORY AND ARCHIVES - IOWA
    HISTORICAL LIBRARY
E. 12th & Grand Ave.
Historical Bldg.   Phone: (515) 281-5472
Des Moines, IA 50319   Lowell R. Wilbur, Libn.

IOWA STATE DEPARTMENT OF PUBLIC INSTRUCTION - RESOURCE
    CENTER
Grimes State Office Bldg.   Phone: (515) 281-3770
Des Moines, IA 50319   Lydia B. Thomas, Libn.

IOWA STATE DEPARTMENT OF SOCIAL SERVICES - LIBRARY
Hoover Bldg.   Phone: (515) 281-5925
Des Moines, IA 50319   Kay M. Elliott, Chf.Libn.

IOWA STATE LAW LIBRARY
State House   Phone: (515) 281-5125
Des Moines, IA 50319   James H. Gritton, Law Libn.

IOWA STATE LEGISLATIVE SERVICE BUREAU - LIBRARY
State House   Phone: (515) 281-3312
Des Moines, IA 50319   Serge H. Garrison, Bur.Dir.

IOWA STATE MEDICAL LIBRARY
Historical Bldg.
E. 12th & Grand Ave.   Phone: (515) 281-5772
Des Moines, IA 50319   Pamela Clark Rees, Dir.

LEAGUE OF IOWA MUNICIPALITIES - LIBRARY
900 Des Moines St., Suite 100   Phone: (515) 265-9961
Des Moines, IA 50316   Robert W. Harpster, Exec.Dir.

MERCY HOSPITAL - LEVITT HEALTH SCIENCES LIBRARY
1165 5th Ave.   Phone: (515) 247-4189
Des Moines, IA 50314   Lenetta Atkins, Libn.

OPEN BIBLE COLLEGE - CARRIE HARDY MEMORIAL LIBRARY
2633 Fleur Dr.   Phone: (515) 283-0478
Des Moines, IA 50321   Linda Jones, Libn.

REED LIBRARY OF FOOT & ANKLE
6000 Waterbury Circle   Phone: (515) 277-5756
Des Moines, IA 50312   Stewart E. Reed, D.P.M.

U.S. DEPT. OF COMMERCE - INTERNATIONAL TRADE ADMINISTRATION -
    DES MOINES DISTRICT OFFICE LIBRARY
817 Federal Bldg., 210 Walnut St.   Phone: (515) 284-4222
Des Moines, IA 50309   Jesse N. Durden, Dir.

U.S. VETERANS ADMINISTRATION (IA-Des Moines) - HOSPITAL LIBRARY
30th & Euclid Ave.   Phone: (515) 255-2173
Des Moines, IA 50310   Clare M. Jergens, Chf., Lib.Serv.

UNIVERSITY OF OSTEOPATHIC MEDICINE AND HEALTH SCIENCES -
    LIBRARY †
3200 Grand Ave.   Phone: (515) 271-1537
Des Moines, IA 50312   Mrs. Krishna Sahu, Dir.

AMERICAN LUTHERAN CHURCH - ARCHIVES
Wartburg Theological Seminary   Phone: (319) 556-8151
Dubuque, IA 52001   Robert C. Wiederaenders, Archv.

MERCY HEALTH CENTER - ANTHONY C. PFOHL HEALTH SCIENCE LIBRARY
Mercy Dr.   Phone: (319) 588-8140
Dubuque, IA 52001   James H. Lander, Lib.Mgr.

SCHOOLS OF THEOLOGY IN DUBUQUE - LIBRARIES
2570 Asbury Rd.   Phone: (319) 589-3100
Dubuque, IA 52001   Duncan Brockway, Dir., Lib.Serv.

XAVIER HOSPITAL - DOCTOR'S LIBRARY
Davis Ave.   Phone: (319) 556-8080
Dubuque, IA 52001   Betty A. Baule, Libn.

MAHARISHI INTERNATIONAL UNIVERSITY - SCIENCE OF CREATIVE
    INTELLIGENCE COLLECTION
                                            Phone: (515) 472-5301
Fairfield, IA 52556   Frank Dowd, Lib.Dir.

GLENWOOD STATE HOSPITAL SCHOOL - STAFF LIBRARY
711 S. Vine   Phone: (712) 527-4811
Glenwood, IA 51534   Renee Pape, Libn.

INDEPENDENCE MENTAL HEALTH INSTITUTE - MEDICAL LIBRARY
Box 111   Phone: (319) 334-2583
Independence, IA 50644   Lois J. Samek, Med.Libn.

AMERICAN COLLEGE TESTING PROGRAM - LIBRARY
Box 168   Phone: (319) 337-1165
Iowa City, IA 52243   Lois Renter, Hd.Libn.

IOWA GEOLOGICAL SURVEY - I.G.S. LIBRARY SERVICES
123 N. Capitol St.
Iowa City, IA 52242

LE BEACON PRESSE - SMALL PRESS COLLECTION
621 Holt Ave.   Phone: (319) 354-5447
Iowa City, IA 52240   K.S. Gormezano, Coord.

STATE HISTORICAL SOCIETY OF IOWA - LIBRARY
402 Iowa Ave.   Phone: (319) 338-5471
Iowa City, IA 52240   Peter H. Curtis, Hd.Libn.

U.S. VETERANS ADMINISTRATION (IA-Iowa City) - HOSPITAL LIBRARY
                                            Phone: (319) 338-0581
Iowa City, IA 52241   Jean C. Williams, Chf.Libn.

UNIVERSITY OF IOWA - ART LIBRARY
Art Bldg.   Phone: (319) 353-4440
Iowa City, IA 52242   Harlan Sifford, Libn.

UNIVERSITY OF IOWA - BOTANY-CHEMISTRY LIBRARY
                                            Phone: (319) 353-3707
Iowa City, IA 52242   Louise Zipp, Libn.

UNIVERSITY OF IOWA - BUSINESS LIBRARY
College of Business Administration
Phillips Hall   Phone: (319) 353-5803
Iowa City, IA 52242   Patricia H. Folley, Bus.Libn.

UNIVERSITY OF IOWA - ENGINEERING LIBRARY
106 Engineering Bldg.   Phone: (319) 353-5224
Iowa City, IA 52242   John W. Forys, Libn.

UNIVERSITY OF IOWA - GEOLOGY LIBRARY
136 Trowbridge Hall   Phone: (319) 353-4225
Iowa City, IA 52242   Louise Zipp, Libn.

UNIVERSITY OF IOWA - HEALTH SCIENCES LIBRARY
Health Sciences Library Bldg.   Phone: (319) 353-5382
Iowa City, IA 52242   David S. Curry, Libn.

UNIVERSITY OF IOWA - INSTITUTE OF URBAN AND REGIONAL RESEARCH -
    LIBRARY
N246 Oakdale Campus   Phone: (319) 353-3862
Iowa City, IA 52242   John W. Fuller, Dir.

UNIVERSITY OF IOWA - IOWA URBAN COMMUNITY RESEARCH CENTER -
    REFERENCE LIBRARY
117 Macbride Hall   Phone: (319) 353-4119
Iowa City, IA 52242

UNIVERSITY OF IOWA - LABORATORY FOR POLITICAL RESEARCH *
321A Schaeffer Hall   Phone: (319) 353-3103
Iowa City, IA 52242   Professor G.R. Boynton, Dir.

UNIVERSITY OF IOWA - LAW LIBRARY
Law Center   Phone: (319) 353-5968
Iowa City, IA 52242   George A. Strait, Dir.

UNIVERSITY OF IOWA - LIBRARY SCIENCE LIBRARY
Main Library   Phone: (319) 353-3946
Iowa City, IA 52242   Sandra S. Ballasch, Libn.

UNIVERSITY OF IOWA - MATHEMATICS LIBRARY
MacLean Hall   Phone: (319) 353-5939
Iowa City, IA 52242   John W. Forys, Libn.

UNIVERSITY OF IOWA - MUSIC LIBRARY
Music Bldg.   Phone: (319) 353-3797
Iowa City, IA 52242   Kathleen Haefliger, Libn.

UNIVERSITY OF IOWA - PHYSICS LIBRARY
Physics Research Center   Phone: (319) 353-4762
Iowa City, IA 52242   Jack W. Dickey, Libn.

UNIVERSITY OF IOWA - PSYCHOLOGY LIBRARY
                                            Phone: (319) 353-5345
Iowa City, IA 52242   Dorothy M. Persson, Libn.

UNIVERSITY OF IOWA - SPECIAL COLLECTIONS DEPARTMENT
Main Library   Phone: (319) 353-4854
Iowa City, IA 52242   Frank Paluka, Hd.

UNIVERSITY OF IOWA - ZOOLOGY LIBRARY
301 Zoology Bldg.   Phone: (319) 353-5419
Iowa City, IA 52242   Jack W. Dickey, Libn.

WOMEN'S RESOURCE AND ACTION CENTER - SOJOURNER TRUTH
    WOMEN'S RESOURCE LIBRARY
130 N. Madison   Phone: (319) 353-6265
Iowa City, IA 52242   Betsy Schwarz, Libn.

IOWA LAW ENFORCEMENT ACADEMY - LIBRARY
Camp Dodge
Box 130   Phone: (515) 278-9357
Johnston, IA 50131   Eva Giercuszkiewicz, Libn.

U.S. VETERANS ADMINISTRATION (IA-Knoxville) - MEDICAL CENTER
    LIBRARY
                                            Phone: (515) 842-3101
Knoxville, IA 50138

GRACELAND COLLEGE - FREDERICK MADISON SMITH LIBRARY
                                            Phone: (515) 784-3311
Lamoni, IA 50140   Volante H. Russell, Dir.

U.S. NATL. PARK SERVICE - EFFIGY MOUNDS NATL. MONUMENT - LIBRARY
Box K
McGregor, IA 52157   Thomas A. Munson, Supt.

MIDWEST OLD SETTLERS AND THRESHERS ASSOCIATION - OLD
    THRESHERS OFFICE - LIBRARY
R.R. 1   Phone: (319) 385-8937
Mount Pleasant, IA 52641   Lennis Moore, Adm.

GEOGRAPHIC

GEOGRAPHIC

MOUNT PLEASANT MENTAL HEALTH INSTITUTE - PROFESSIONAL LIBRARY
1200 E. Washington St.   Phone: (319) 385-7231
Mt. Pleasant, IA 52641   James Sommerville, Libn.

CORNELL COLLEGE - CHEMISTRY LIBRARY
West Science Hall   Phone: (319) 895-8811
Mount Vernon, IA 52314   Stuart Stiffler, Lib.Dir.

GRAIN PROCESSING CORPORATION - TECHNICAL INFORMATION CENTER,
    R&D
1600 Oregon St.
Box 349   Phone: (319) 264-4389
Muscatine, IA 52761   Maurene Failor, Libn.

WILLIAM PENN COLLEGE - WILCOX LIBRARY - SPECIAL COLLECTIONS
                                          Phone: (515) 673-8311
Oskaloosa, IA 52577   Marion E. Rains, Libn.

AIRPOWER MUSEUM - LIBRARY
Antique Airfield
Rte. 2, Box 172
Ottumwa, IA 52501

ST. JOSEPH HOSPITAL - LIBRARY
312 E. Alta Vista   Phone: (515) 684-4651
Ottumwa, IA 52501   Sr. Mary Christine Conaway, Libn.

CALHOUN COUNTY HISTORICAL MUSEUM - LIBRARY
680 Eighth St.
Rockwell City, IA 50579   Judy Webb, Libn.

JEWISH COMMUNITY CENTER - LIBRARY
525 14th St.   Phone: (712) 258-0618
Sioux City, IA 51105   Joseph C. Bluestein, Exec.Dir.

ST. LUKE'S MEDICAL CENTER - LIBRARY
2720 Stone Park Blvd.   Phone: (712) 279-3156
Sioux City, IA 51104   Barbara Knight, Libn.

SIOUX CITY ART CENTER ASSOCIATION - LIBRARY
513 Nebraska St.   Phone: (712) 279-6272
Sioux City, IA 51101   Marilyn Laufer, Educ.Cur.

WOODBURY COUNTY BAR ASSOCIATION - LIBRARY
7th & Douglas Sts.
Woodbury County Courthouse, 6th Fl.   Phone: (712) 279-6609
Sioux City, IA 51101   Mary McQuillen, Libn.

BUENA VISTA COLLEGE - L.E. & E.L. BALLOU LIBRARY
                                          Phone: (712) 749-2141
Storm Lake, IA 50588   Dr. Barbara R. Palling, Hd.Libn.

GROUT MUSEUM OF HISTORY AND SCIENCE - REFERENCE LIBRARY
503 South St.   Phone: (319) 234-6357
Waterloo, IA 50701   Dorothy Ackerson, Lib. Aide

JOHN DEERE PRODUCT ENGINEERING CENTER - LIBRARY
Box 8000   Phone: (319) 235-4668
Waterloo, IA 50704   YangHoon Rhee, Libn.

U.S. PRESIDENTIAL LIBRARIES - HERBERT HOOVER LIBRARY
                                          Phone: (319) 643-5301
West Branch, IA 52358   Thomas Thalken, Dir.

DELAVAN CORPORATION - ENGINEERING LIBRARY
Box 100   Phone: (515) 274-1561
West Des Moines, IA 50265   Gwen Hartman, Libn.

WOODWARD STATE HOSPITAL SCHOOL - RESIDENT LIBRARY
Main School Bldg.   Phone: (515) 438-2600
Woodward, IA 50276   Marjorie Vaagen, Libn./AV Spec.

WOODWARD STATE HOSPITAL SCHOOL - STAFF LIBRARY
                                          Phone: (515) 438-2600
Woodward, IA 50276   Marjorie Vaagen, Libn.

KANSAS

MUSEUM OF INDEPENDENT TELEPHONY - ARCHIVES COLLECTION
412 S. Campbell   Phone: (913) 263-2681
Abilene, KS 67410   Peg Chronister, Cur.

U.S. PRESIDENTIAL LIBRARIES - DWIGHT D. EISENHOWER LIBRARY
S.E. Fourth St.   Phone: (913) 263-4751
Abilene, KS 67410   Dr. John E. Wickman, Dir.

U.S. NATL. PARK SERVICE - CHEROKEE STRIP LIVING MUSEUM -
    RESEARCH LIBRARY
Box 230   Phone: (316) 442-6750
Arkansas City, KS 67005   Herbert Marshall, Dir.

CLARK COUNTY HISTORICAL SOCIETY - PIONEER MUSEUM - LIBRARY
430 W. Fourth   Phone: (316) 635-2227
Ashland, KS 67831   Florence E. Hurd, Cur.

BAKER UNIVERSITY - ARCHIVES AND HISTORICAL LIBRARY
Collins Library   Phone: (913) 594-6451
Baldwin City, KS 66006   Harold Kolling, Univ.Cur.

BAKER UNIVERSITY - QUAYLE RARE BIBLE COLLECTION
Baker University Library, Eighth St.   Phone: (913) 594-3422
Baldwin City, KS 66006   Dr. John M. Forbes, Dir. of Libs.

WYANDOTTE COUNTY MUSEUM - HARRY M. TROWBRIDGE RESEARCH
    LIBRARY
631 N 126th St.   Phone: (913) 721-1078
Bonner Springs, KS 66012   Tom A. Pfannenstiel, Musm.Dir.

CEDAR VALE REGIONAL HOSPITAL - LIBRARY
Cedar St.
Box 398   Phone: (316) 758-2266
Cedar Vale, KS 67024   Mrs. Dera C. Brunstad, Libn.

MARTIN AND OSA JOHNSON SAFARI MUSEUM - STOTT EXPLORERS
    LIBRARY
16 S. Grant St.   Phone: (316) 431-2730
Chanute, KS 66720   Sondra Alden, Musm.Dir.

SOD TOWN PIONEER HOMESTEAD MUSEUM - LIBRARY †
U.S. Hwy. 24, East
Box 393   Phone: (913) 462-2021
Colby, KS 67701   Ronald E. Thiel, Dir.

THOMAS COUNTY HISTORICAL SOCIETY - LIBRARY
1525 W. Fourth   Phone: (913) 462-6972
Colby, KS 67701   Helen L. Smith, Dir.

CLOUD COUNTY HISTORICAL MUSEUM - LIBRARY
7th & Broadway   Phone: (913) 243-2866
Concordia, KS 66901   Vernon Martin, Dir.

KANSAS HERITAGE CENTER - LIBRARY
Box 1275   Phone: (316) 227-2823
Dodge City, KS 67801   Jeanie Covalt, Res.Libn.

DOUGLASS HISTORICAL SOCIETY MUSEUM - MUSEUM ARCHIVES *
314 S. Forest St.
Douglass, KS 67039   Jean Valentine, Dir.

BUTLER COUNTY HISTORICAL SOCIETY - OLIVE CLIFFORD STONE LIBRARY
381 E. Central
Box 696   Phone: (316) 321-9333
El Dorado, KS 67042   Anna Louise Borger, Libn.

BIKELIBRARY
Box 276
Emporia, KS 66801   Larry S. Bonura, Dir.

EMPORIA STATE UNIVERSITY - WILLIAM ALLEN WHITE LIBRARY -
    SPECIAL COLLECTIONS
1200 Commercial   Phone: (316) 343-1200
Emporia, KS 66801   Mary E. Bogan, Spec.Coll.Libn.

FLINT HILLS AREA VOCATIONAL-TECHNICAL SCHOOL - LIBRARY
3301 W. 18th Ave. Phone: (316) 342-6404
Emporia, KS 66801 Jane M. Birchard, Libn.

U.S. ARMY COMMAND AND GENERAL STAFF COLLEGE - COMBINED ARMS
RESEARCH LIBRARY
Bell Hall Phone: (913) 684-3282
Fort Leavenworth, KS 66027 Martha A. Davis, Libn.

U.S. ARMY HOSPITALS - IRWIN ARMY HOSPITAL - MEDICAL LIBRARY
Bldg. 485 Phone: (913) 239-7874
Fort Riley, KS 66442 Phyllis J. Whiteside, Med.Libn.

U.S. ARMY POST - FORT RILEY - LIBRARIES †
Bldg. 6 Phone: (913) 239-2322
Fort Riley, KS 66442 Mary O'Laughlin, Chf.Libn.

U.S. CAVALRY MUSEUM - LIBRARY
Bldg. 30 Phone: (913) 239-2737
Fort Riley, KS 66442 Terry Van Meter, Dir.

WILSON COUNTY MUSEUM - LIBRARY
420 N. 7th Phone: (316) 378-3965
Fredonia, KS 66736 Mrs. Giles Greager, Hist.

HERTZLER RESEARCH FOUNDATION LIBRARY †
3rd & Chestnut St. Phone: (316) 835-2241
Halstead, KS 67056

ELLIS COUNTY HISTORICAL SOCIETY - ARCHIVES
Box 9 Phone: (913) 625-6577
Hays, KS 67601 Rev. Blaine Burkey, Archv./Hist.

FORT HAYS STATE UNIVERSITY - STERNBERG MEMORIAL MUSEUM -
LIBRARY
Phone: (913) 628-4286
Hays, KS 67601 Dr. Richard J. Zakrzewski, Musm.Dir.

FARMLAND INDUSTRIES, INC. - FARMLAND RESEARCH CENTER &
FARMLAND AGRISERVICES
960 N. Halstead Phone: (316) 663-5711
Hutchinson, KS 67501 Diane Simmons, Exec.Sec.

CENTRAL BAPTIST THEOLOGICAL SEMINARY - LIBRARY
Seminary Heights Phone: (913) 371-1544
Kansas City, KS 66102 Dr. Henry R. Moeller, Libn.

PROVIDENCE-ST. MARGARET HEALTH CENTER - LIBRARY
8929 Parallel Pkwy. Phone: (913) 596-4795
Kansas City, KS 66112 Betty A. Wilkinson, Libn.

U.S. BUREAU OF THE CENSUS - REGIONAL DATA USER SERVICE - KANSAS
CITY REGIONAL OFFICE - LIBRARY
One Gateway Center, Suite 500 Phone: (816) 374-4601
Kansas City, KS 66101 James F. Holmes, Prog.Coord.

UNIVERSITY OF KANSAS MEDICAL CENTER - COLLEGE OF HEALTH
SCIENCES AND HOSPITAL - CLENDENING LIBRARY
Rainbow Blvd. at 39th Phone: (913) 588-7166
Kansas City, KS 66103 Earl Farley, Dir.

WYANDOTTE COUNTY BAR LIBRARY
710 N. 7th St. Phone: (913) 342-4224
Kansas City, KS 66101 Rita Hollecker Kancel, Libn.

FORT LARNED HISTORICAL SOCIETY, INC. - SANTA FE TRAIL CENTER
LIBRARY
Rte. 3 Phone: (316) 285-2054
Larned, KS 67550 Ruth Olson, Archv.

LARNED STATE HOSPITAL - STAFF LIBRARY
Box 89 Phone: (316) 285-2131
Larned, KS 67550 Debbie Rahe, Lib.Ck.

U.S. NATL. PARK SERVICE - FORT LARNED NATL. HISTORIC SITE - LIBRARY
Rte. 3 Phone: (316) 285-3571
Larned, KS 67550 B. William Henry, Jr., Park Hist.

GOLF COURSE SUPERINTENDENTS ASSOCIATION OF AMERICA - GCSAA
LIBRARY
1617 St. Andrews Dr. Phone: (913) 841-2240
Lawrence, KS 66044 Ann Neuschafer, Membership Serv.Ck.

KANSAS STATE GEOLOGICAL SURVEY - MOORE HALL LIBRARY
1930 Ave. A, Campus W Phone: (913) 864-3965
Lawrence, KS 66044 Janice H. Sorensen, Libn.

UNIVERSITY OF KANSAS - ACADEMIC COMPUTER CENTER LIBRARY
Drawer 2007
Lawrence, KS 66045

UNIVERSITY OF KANSAS - CENTER FOR PUBLIC AFFAIRS
607 Blake Hall Phone: (913) 864-3701
Lawrence, KS 66045 Thelma Helyar, Libn.

UNIVERSITY OF KANSAS - CENTER FOR RESEARCH, INC.
Phone: (913) 864-3441
Lawrence, KS 66045

UNIVERSITY OF KANSAS - DEPARTMENT OF SPECIAL COLLECTIONS
Spencer Research Library Phone: (913) 864-4334
Lawrence, KS 66045 Alexandra Mason, Spec.Coll.Libn.

UNIVERSITY OF KANSAS - DOCUMENTS COLLECTION
Spencer Research Library Phone: (913) 864-4662
Lawrence, KS 66045 Marion L. Howey, Doc.Libn.

UNIVERSITY OF KANSAS - EAST ASIAN LIBRARY
Libraries Phone: (913) 864-4669
Lawrence, KS 66045 Eugene Carvalho, Libn.

UNIVERSITY OF KANSAS - KANSAS COLLECTION
220 Spencer Research Library Phone: (913) 864-4274
Lawrence, KS 66045 Sheryl K. Williams, Cur.

UNIVERSITY OF KANSAS - MAP LIBRARY
110 Spencer Library Phone: (913) 864-4420
Lawrence, KS 66045 Lewis Armstrong, Map Lib.Assoc.

UNIVERSITY OF KANSAS - MURPHY LIBRARY OF ART HISTORY
Helen Foresman Spencer Museum of Art Phone: (913) 864-3020
Lawrence, KS 66045 Susan V. Craig, Art Libn.

UNIVERSITY OF KANSAS - SCHOOL OF LAW LIBRARY
New Green Hall Phone: (913) 864-3025
Lawrence, KS 66045

UNIVERSITY OF KANSAS - SCIENCE LIBRARY
605 Malott Hall Phone: (913) 864-3465
Lawrence, KS 66045 Jeanne Richardson, Sci.Libn.

UNIVERSITY OF KANSAS - SLAVIC COLLECTION
Watson Library Phone: (913) 864-3957
Lawrence, KS 66045 George Jerkovich, Dir./Cur.

UNIVERSITY OF KANSAS - THOMAS GORTON MUSIC LIBRARY
448 Murphy Hall Phone: (913) 864-3496
Lawrence, KS 66045 Earl Gates, Libn.

UNIVERSITY OF KANSAS - UNIVERSITY ARCHIVES
Spencer Library Phone: (913) 864-4188
Lawrence, KS 66045 John M. Nugent, Univ.Archv.

UNIVERSITY OF KANSAS - WEALTHY BABCOCK MATHEMATICS LIBRARY
209 Strong Hall Phone: (913) 864-3440
Lawrence, KS 66045 Ruth D. Fauhl, Lib.Asst.

UNIVERSITY OF KANSAS - WILCOX COLLECTION OF CONTEMPORARY
POLITICAL MOVEMENTS
Kansas Collection, Spencer Library Phone: (913) 864-4274
Lawrence, KS 66045 Sheryl K. Williams, Cur., Kansas Coll.

ST. MARY COLLEGE - LIBRARY - SPECIAL COLLECTIONS
Phone: (913) 682-5151
Leavenworth, KS 66048 Sr. Mary Mark Orr, Hd., Spec.Coll.Dept.

GEOGRAPHIC

U.S. VETERANS ADMINISTRATION (KS-Leavenworth) - CENTER MEDICAL LIBRARY
Phone: (913) 682-2000
Leavenworth, KS 66048 Bennett F. Lawson, Chf., Lib.Serv.

MC PHERSON COLLEGE - MILLER LIBRARY
1600 E. Euclid Phone: (316) 241-0731
McPherson, KS 67460 Rowena Olsen, Libn.

AMERICAN INSTITUTE OF BAKING - LIBRARY
1213 Bakers Way Phone: (913) 537-4750
Manhattan, KS 66502 Ruth Emerson, Libn.

FREE UNIVERSITY NETWORK - PUBLICATIONS AND RESOURCES
1221 Thurston Phone: (913) 532-5866
Manhattan, KS 66502 William A. Draves, Natl.Coord.

KANSAS STATE UNIVERSITY - ARCHITECTURE AND DESIGN LIBRARY
Phone: (913) 532-5968
Manhattan, KS 66506 Dorothy Barnett, Libn.

KANSAS STATE UNIVERSITY - FARRELL LIBRARY
Phone: (913) 532-6516
Manhattan, KS 66506 Mary R. Magruder, Dean of Libs.

KANSAS STATE UNIVERSITY - FOOD AND FEED GRAIN INSTITUTE - SWANSON MEMORIAL LIBRARY
Phone: (913) 532-6161
Manhattan, KS 66506 Dr. Charles Deyoe

KANSAS STATE UNIVERSITY - HERBARIUM LIBRARY
Bushnell Hall Phone: (913) 532-6619
Manhattan, KS 66506 T.M. Barkley, Cur. of Herbarium

KANSAS STATE UNIVERSITY - INSTITUTE FOR ENVIRONMENTAL RESEARCH - LIBRARY
Dept. of Mechanical Engineering Phone: (913) 532-5620
Manhattan, KS 66506 Dr. F.H. Rohles

KANSAS STATE UNIVERSITY - PHYSICS LIBRARY
Phone: (913) 532-6827
Manhattan, KS 66506 Bernice Bartel, Libn.

KANSAS STATE UNIVERSITY - POPULATION RESEARCH LABORATORY - LIBRARY
Phone: (913) 532-5984
Manhattan, KS 66506 Donald J. Adamchak, Act.Dir.

KANSAS STATE UNIVERSITY - RESOURCES ON DEVELOPING COUNTRIES
Farrell Library Phone: (913) 532-6516
Manhattan, KS 66506 Sylvia J. Blanding, Libn.

KANSAS STATE UNIVERSITY - SPECIAL COLLECTIONS DEPARTMENT & UNIVERSITY ARCHIVES
Farrell Library Phone: (913) 532-6516
Manhattan, KS 66506 Evan W. Williams, Libn.

KANSAS STATE UNIVERSITY - VETERINARY MEDICAL LIBRARY
Phone: (913) 532-5673
Manhattan, KS 66506 E. Guy Coffee, Hd.Libn.

KANSAS STATE UNIVERSITY - WILLARD LIBRARY
Phone: (913) 532-6530
Manhattan, KS 66506 Pat Parris, Libn.

RILEY COUNTY GENEALOGICAL SOCIETY - LIBRARY
2005 Claflin Rd. Phone: (913) 539-3731
Manhattan, KS 66502 Mildred Loeffler, Libn.

RILEY COUNTY HISTORICAL SOCIETY - SEATON MEMORIAL LIBRARY
2309 Claflin Rd. Phone: (913) 537-2210
Manhattan, KS 66502 Cheryl Collins, Libn.

JOHNSON COUNTY MENTAL HEALTH CENTER - JOHN R. KEACH MEMORIAL LIBRARY
6000 Lamar Ave. Phone: (913) 384-1100
Mission, KS 66202 Heidi Simpson, Libn.

BETHEL COLLEGE - MENNONITE LIBRARY AND ARCHIVES
Phone: (316) 283-2500
North Newton, KS 67117 Robert Kreider, Dir.

MENNONITE CHURCH - WESTERN DISTRICT CONFERENCE - WESTERN DISTRICT LOAN LIBRARY
Box 66
North Newton, KS 67117 Mrs. J. Lloyd Spaulding, Libn.

NORTON STATE HOSPITAL - PROFESSIONAL LIBRARY
Phone: (913) 877-3301
Norton, KS 67654

OSAWATOMIE STATE HOSPITAL - RAPAPORT PROFESSIONAL LIBRARY - MENTAL HEALTH LIBRARY †
Phone: (913) 755-3151
Osawatomie, KS 66064 Helen Porter, Libn.

PARSONS STATE HOSPITAL AND TRAINING CENTER - MEDICAL LIBRARY
Box 738 Phone: (316) 421-6550
Parsons, KS 67357 Michael J. Haynes, Libn.

PITTSBURG STATE UNIVERSITY - LEONARD H. AXE LIBRARY
S. Joplin Phone: (316) 231-7000
Pittsburg, KS 66762 Stevens W. Hilyard, Lib.Dir.

LINN COUNTY HISTORICAL SOCIETY - LIBRARY
Box 137 Phone: (913) 352-8739
Pleasanton, KS 66075 Ivan Irwin, Pres.

KANSAS TECHNICAL INSTITUTE - TULLIS RESOURCE CENTER
1831 Crompton Rd. Phone: (913) 825-0275
Salina, KS 67401 Eleen M. Owen, Libn.

BAYVET - LIBRARY
12707 W. 63rd St. Phone: (913) 631-4800
Shawnee, KS 66201 Donna Walters, Libn.

UNIVERSITY OF KANSAS REGENTS CENTER - LIBRARY
9900 Mission Rd. Phone: (913) 341-4554
Shawnee Mission, KS 66206 Nancy J. Burich, Libn.

AMERICAN LUNG ASSOCIATION OF KANSAS - INFORMATION CENTER
Box 4426 Phone: (913) 272-9290
Topeka, KS 66604 Darrel Walton, Exec.Dir.

KANSAS STATE DEPARTMENT OF HEALTH & ENVIRONMENT - BUREAU OF HEALTH & ENVIRONMENTAL EDUCATION LIBRARY
Forbes AFB, Bldg. 321 Phone: (913) 296-3571
Topeka, KS 66620 Virginia Lockhart, Dir.

KANSAS STATE DEPARTMENT OF SOCIAL & REHABILITATION SERVICES - STAFF DEVELOPMENT TRAINING CENTER LIBRARY
2700 W. 6th St. Phone: (913) 296-4327
Topeka, KS 66606 Frank Roth, Lib.Asst.

KANSAS STATE ENERGY OFFICE - INFORMATION CENTER
214 West 6th Phone: (913) 296-2496
Topeka, KS 66603 Kay McEnulty, Energy Info./Educ.Coord.

KANSAS STATE HISTORICAL SOCIETY - LIBRARY
120 W. 10th St. Phone: (913) 296-3251
Topeka, KS 66612 Portia Allbert, Hd.Libn.

KANSAS STATE LIBRARY
State Capitol, 3rd Fl. Phone: (913) 296-3296
Topeka, KS 66612 Martha Tucker, Act. State Libn.

KANSAS STATE SUPREME COURT - LAW LIBRARY
Judicial Center
301 West 10th Phone: (913) 296-3257
Topeka, KS 66612 Roger D. Brooks, Law Libn.

LONDON CLUB - ARCHIVES
Box 4527
Topeka, KS 66604 F.D. Baranski, Archv.

MENNINGER FOUNDATION - ARCHIVES
Box 829
Topeka, KS 66601
Phone: (913) 234-9566
Verne B. Horne, Archv.

MENNINGER FOUNDATION - PROFESSIONAL LIBRARY
Box 829
Topeka, KS 66601
Phone: (913) 234-9566
Alice Brand, Chf.Libn.

SECURITY BENEFIT LIFE INSURANCE COMPANY - LIBRARY *
700 Harrison St.
Topeka, KS 66636
Phone: (913) 295-3000
Dorothy N. Wright, Libn.

STORMONT-VAIL REGIONAL MEDICAL CENTER AND SHAWNEE COUNTY
    MEDICAL SOCIETY - HEALTH SCIENCES LIBRARY *
1500 S.W. 10th St.
Topeka, KS 66606
Phone: (913) 354-6090
Shirley Borglund, Hd.Libn.

TOPEKA STATE HOSPITAL - STAFF LIBRARY
2700 W. 6th St.
Topeka, KS 66606
Phone: (913) 296-4411
Ellen M. Flesher, Libn.

U.S. VETERANS ADMINISTRATION (KS-Topeka) - DR. KARL A. MENNINGER
    MEDICAL LIBRARY
2200 Gage Blvd.
Topeka, KS 66622
Phone: (913) 272-3111
Norma R. Torkelson, Chf., Lib.Serv.

WASHBURN UNIVERSITY OF TOPEKA - SCHOOL OF LAW LIBRARY
1700 College Ave.
Topeka, KS 66621
Phone: (913) 295-6688
John E. Christensen, Dir.

CHISHOLM TRAIL MUSEUM - ARCHIVES AND LIBRARY
502 N. Washington Ave.
Wellington, KS 67152
Phone: (316) 326-2174
Marie Dobbin, Libn.

BOEING MILITARY AIRPLANE COMPANY - LIBRARY
3801 S. Oliver
Wichita, KS 67210
Phone: (316) 526-3801
C.H. Jones, Lib.Supv.

CESSNA AIRCRAFT COMPANY - WALLACE DIVISION - ENGINEERING
    LIBRARY
Box 7704
Wichita, KS 67277
Phone: (316) 946-6575
Ms. B.C. Parks, Libn.

FRIENDS UNIVERSITY - EDMUND STANLEY LIBRARY
2100 University Ave.
Wichita, KS 67213
Phone: (316) 261-5800
Hans Bynagle, Dir., Lrng.Res.

INSTITUTE OF LOGOPEDICS - TECHNICAL LIBRARY
2400 Jardine Dr.
Wichita, KS 67219
Phone: (316) 262-8271
Clyde Cochran Berger, Tech.Libn.

INTERNATIONAL REFERENCE ORGANIZATION IN FORENSIC MEDICINE
    AND SCIENCES - LIBRARY AND REFERENCE CENTER
Milton Helpern Center
Wichita State University
Box 95
Wichita, KS 67208
Phone: (316) 262-6211
Dr. William G. Eckert, Dir.

KANSAS STATE GEOLOGICAL SURVEY - WICHITA WELL SAMPLE LIBRARY
4150 Monroe
Wichita, KS 67209
Phone: (316) 943-2343
Lawrence Skalton, Geologist & Mgr.

MIDWEST HISTORICAL & GENEALOGICAL SOCIETY, INC. - LIBRARY
Box 1121
Wichita, KS 67201
Dorothy Bethel, Libn.

ST. FRANCIS HOSPITAL - MEDICAL/NURSING LIBRARY
929 N. St. Francis
Wichita, KS 67214
Phone: (316) 268-5979
Betty B. Wood, Med.Libn.

ST. JOSEPH MEDICAL CENTER - MEDICAL LIBRARY
3600 E. Harry
Wichita, KS 67218
Phone: (316) 685-1111
Carol Matulka, Med.Libn.

SEDGWICK COUNTY LAW LIBRARY †
700 Century Plaza Bldg.
Wichita, KS 67202
Phone: (316) 263-2251
Jonalou M. Pinnell, Libn.

U.S. VETERANS ADMINISTRATION (KS-Wichita) - MEDICAL CENTER
    LIBRARY
5500 E. Kellogg St.
Wichita, KS 67208
Phone: (316) 685-2221
Peter B. Fleming, Chf., Lib.Serv.

WESLEY MEDICAL CENTER - MC KIBBIN PROFESSIONAL LIBRARY
550 N. Hillside
Wichita, KS 67214
Phone: (316) 685-2151
Dorothy Binkley, Chf.Libn.

WICHITA ART ASSOCIATION, INC. - REFERENCE LIBRARY
9112 E. Central
Wichita, KS 67206
Phone: (316) 686-6687
John R. Rouse, Dir.

WICHITA ART MUSEUM - LIBRARY
619 Stackman Dr.
Wichita, KS 67203
Phone: (316) 264-6251
Lois F. Crane, Libn.

WICHITA EAGLE AND BEACON - LIBRARY †
Box 820
Wichita, KS 67203
Phone: (316) 268-6473

WICHITA PUBLIC LIBRARY - BUSINESS AND TECHNOLOGY DIVISION
223 S. Main
Wichita, KS 67202
Phone: (316) 262-0611
Larry DePiesse, Hd.

WICHITA-SEDGWICK COUNTY HISTORICAL MUSEUM - LIBRARY &
    ARCHIVES
204 S. Main
Wichita, KS 67202
Phone: (316) 686-0915
Robert A. Puckett, Dir.

WICHITA STATE UNIVERSITY - DEPARTMENT OF CHEMISTRY - LLOYD
    MC KINLEY MEMORIAL CHEMISTRY LIBRARY
1845 Fairmount
Wichita, KS 67208
Phone: (316) 689-3120
B. Jack McCormick

WICHITA STATE UNIVERSITY - SPECIAL COLLECTIONS
1845 Fairmount
Wichita, KS 67208
Phone: (316) 689-3590
Dale R. Schrag, Cur.

WICHITA STATE UNIVERSITY - THURLOW LIEURANCE MEMORIAL MUSIC
    LIBRARY
Walter Duerksen Fine Arts Center
Wichita, KS 67208
Phone: (316) 689-3506
David L. Austin, Hd.

SNYDER (H.L.) MEMORIAL RESEARCH FOUNDATION - LIBRARY
1407 Wheat Rd.
Winfield, KS 67156
Phone: (316) 221-4080
Barbara Smith, Libn.

UNITED METHODIST CHURCH - KANSAS WEST CONFERENCE - ARCHIVES
    AND HISTORY DEPOSITORY
Southwestern College Library
Winfield, KS 67156
Phone: (316) 221-4150
Irene Watson, Archv.

WINFIELD STATE HOSPITAL AND TRAINING CENTER - PROFESSIONAL AND
    MEDICAL LIBRARY
Phone: (316) 221-1200
Winfield, KS 67156
Mrs. Lee Fast, Lib.Ck.

KENTUCKY

LOUISVILLE SCHOOL OF ART - LIBRARY & MEDIA RESOURCE CENTER
The Cloister
800 E. Chestnut
Anchorage, KY 40204
Phone: (502) 245-8836
Mary Jane Benedict, Libn.

ASHLAND OIL, INC. - RESEARCH & DEVELOPMENT LIBRARY
Box 391
Ashland, KY 41101
Phone: (606) 739-4166
L.H. Workman, Libn.

BARTON MUSEUM OF WHISKEY HISTORY - LIBRARY
Bardstown, KY 40004
Oscar Getz, Founder

BEREA COLLEGE - HUTCHINS LIBRARY - SPECIAL COLLECTIONS
Phone: (606) 986-9341
Berea, KY 40404
Gerald F. Roberts, Spec.Coll.Libn.

U.S. FISH & WILDLIFE SERVICE - EAST CENTRAL RESERVOIR
INVESTIGATIONS LIBRARY
Federal Bldg.   Phone: (502) 843-4376
Bowling Green, KY 42101   Charles H. Walburg, Chf.

WESTERN KENTUCKY UNIVERSITY - FOLKLORE, FOLKLIFE, & ORAL
HISTORY ARCHIVES
Helm-Cravens Library   Phone: (502) 745-3951
Bowling Green, KY 42101   Robert O. Turek, Soc.Sci.Libn.

WESTERN KENTUCKY UNIVERSITY - KENTUCKY LIBRARY AND MUSEUM/
UNIVERSITY ARCHIVES
                                       Phone: (502) 745-2592
Bowling Green, KY 42101   Riley Handy, Hd., Spec.Coll.Dept.

NORTHERN KENTUCKY UNIVERSITY - SALMON P. CHASE COLLEGE OF LAW
- LIBRARY
1401 Dixie Hwy.   Phone: (606) 292-5394
Covington, KY 41011   Thomas P. Vergamini, Act. Law Lib.Dir.

ST. ELIZABETH MEDICAL CENTER - NORTH - MEDICAL LIBRARY
401 E. 20th St.   Phone: (606) 292-4048
Covington, KY 41014   Donald R. Smith, Libn.

ST. WALBURG CONVENT OF BENEDICTINE SISTERS OF COVINGTON,
KENTUCKY - ARCHIVES
2500 Amsterdam Rd.   Phone: (606) 331-6771
Covington, KY 41016   Sr. Teresa Wolking, O.S.B., Archv.

ST. ELIZABETH MEDICAL CENTER - SOUTH - LIBRARY
One Medical Village Dr.   Phone: (606) 344-2248
Edgewood, KY 41017   Mary Ann Middendorf, Asst.Libn.

SEMINARY OF ST. PIUS X - LIBRARY
Donaldson Rd.   Phone: (606) 371-4449
Erlanger, KY 41018   Frank J. Mazsick, Lib.Dir.

FERGUSON BAPTIST CHURCH - LIBRARY
602 Gover Ln.   Phone: (606) 679-1018
Ferguson, KY 42533   Dorothy Holloway, Dir.

U.S. ARMY HOSPITALS - FORT CAMPBELL ARMY HOSPITAL - MEDICAL
LIBRARY
                                       Phone: (502) 798-6620
Ft. Campbell, KY 42223   Lillian G. Graham, Med.Libn.

U.S. ARMY ARMOR SCHOOL - LIBRARY
Gaffey Hall, 2369
Old Ironsides Ave.   Phone: (502) 624-6231
Ft. Knox, KY 40121   William H. Hansen, Libn.

U.S. ARMY - PATTON MUSEUM OF CAVALRY & ARMOR - EMERT L. DAVIS
MEMORIAL LIBRARY
Box 208   Phone: (502) 624-6350
Ft. Knox, KY 40121   Philip M. Cavanaugh, Musm.Dir.

KENTUCKY COVERED BRIDGE ASSOCIATION - LIBRARY
62 Miami Pkwy.   Phone: (606) 441-7000
Fort Thomas, KY 41075   L.K. Patton, Exec.Dir.

KENTUCKY HISTORICAL SOCIETY - LIBRARY
Broadway, Old Capitol Annex
Box H   Phone: (502) 564-3016
Frankfort, KY 40601   Anne McDonnell, Lib.Mgr.

KENTUCKY STATE DEPARTMENT OF COMMERCE - DIVISION OF RESEARCH
- MAP LIBRARY
133 Holmes St.   Phone: (502) 564-4715
Frankfort, KY 40601   Bill Howard, Chf.

KENTUCKY STATE DEPARTMENT OF COMMERCE - LIBRARY
Capitol Plaza Office Tower   Phone: (502) 564-4886
Frankfort, KY 40601   Doris Arnold, Res.Libn.

KENTUCKY STATE DEPARTMENT OF EDUCATION - RESOURCE CENTER
Capital Plaza Tower   Phone: (502) 564-5385
Frankfort, KY 40601   Anne Hamilton, Dir.

KENTUCKY STATE DEPARTMENT FOR HUMAN RESOURCES - LIBRARY
275 E. Main St.   Phone: (502) 564-4530
Frankfort, KY 40601   Douglas Raisor, Supv.

KENTUCKY STATE DEPARTMENT OF LIBRARY & ARCHIVES - KENTUCKIANA
COLLECTION
Berry Hill
Box 537   Phone: (502) 564-2480
Frankfort, KY 40602   Annie S. Harrison, Libn.

KENTUCKY STATE EXECUTIVE DEPARTMENT FOR FINANCE LIBRARY -
OFFICE FOR POLICY AND MANAGEMENT
Capitol Annex, Rm. 200   Phone: (502) 564-7300
Frankfort, KY 40601   Shirley Wood, Lib.Asst.

KENTUCKY STATE LAW LIBRARY
State Capitol, Rm. 200   Phone: (502) 564-4848
Frankfort, KY 40601   Wesley Gilmer, Jr., State Law Libn.

KENTUCKY STATE LEGISLATIVE RESEARCH COMMISSION - LIBRARY
State Capitol, 4th Fl.   Phone: (502) 564-8100
Frankfort, KY 40601   Peggy King, Leg.Libn.

KENTUCKY CHRISTIAN COLLEGE - MEDIA CENTER
College Ave.   Phone: (606) 474-6613
Grayson, KY 41143   Kenneth L. Beck, Libn.

U.S. NATL. PARK SERVICE - ABRAHAM LINCOLN BIRTHPLACE NATL.
HISTORIC SITE - LIBRARY
Rte. 1   Phone: (502) 358-3874
Hodgenville, KY 42748   Nicholas J. Eason, Supt.

WESTERN STATE HOSPITAL - PROFESSIONAL LIBRARY
Russellville Rd.   Phone: (502) 886-4431
Hopkinsville, KY 42240   Margaret Crim Riley, Libn.

CELANESE PLASTICS & SPECIALTIES COMPANY - TECHNICAL CENTER -
RESEARCH LIBRARY
9800 Bluegrass Pkwy.   Phone: (502) 585-8053
Jeffersontown, KY 40299   Carol Ann Murray, Libn.

CENTRAL CHRISTIAN CHURCH - LIBRARY
205 E. Short St.
Box 1354   Phone: (606) 233-1551
Lexington, KY 40590   Walter A. Hehl, Hd.

COUNCIL OF STATE GOVERNMENTS - STATES INFORMATION CENTER
Iron Works Pike
Box 11910   Phone: (606) 252-2291
Lexington, KY 40578   Nanette D. Eichel, Info.Rsrcs.Coord.

EASTERN STATE HOSPITAL - RESOURCE LIBRARY
627 W. Fourth St.   Phone: (606) 255-1431
Lexington, KY 40508   Juanita H. Morrill, Libn.

EPISCOPAL THEOLOGICAL SEMINARY IN KENTUCKY - BROWNING
MEMORIAL LIBRARY
544 Sayre Ave.   Phone: (606) 255-9591
Lexington, KY 40508   Rev. Dieter G. Sierp, Lib.Dir.

IBM CORPORATION - INFORMATION SYSTEMS DIVISION - TECHNICAL
LIBRARY
New Circle Rd.   Phone: (606) 232-6044
Lexington, KY 40511   Jewell C. Castle, Lib.Mgr.

KEENELAND ASSOCIATION - LIBRARY
Keeneland Race Course
Box 1690   Phone: (606) 254-3412
Lexington, KY 40592   Doris Jean Waren, Libn.

LEXINGTON-FAYETTE URBAN COUNTY PLANNING COMMISSION -
TECHNICAL INFORMATION LIBRARY
227 N. Upper St.   Phone: (606) 252-8808
Lexington, KY 40507   Phil Choma, Exec.Dir.

LEXINGTON HERALD-LEADER - LIBRARY
Main & Midland Ave.   Phone: (606) 231-3334
Lexington, KY 40507   Linda L. Smith, Libn.

LEXINGTON TECHNICAL INSTITUTE - LIBRARY
Cooper Dr., Oswald Bldg.
Lexington, KY 40506
Phone: (606) 258-4919
Martha J. Birchfield, Dir.

LEXINGTON THEOLOGICAL SEMINARY - BOSWORTH MEMORIAL LIBRARY
S. Limestone St.
Lexington, KY 40508
Phone: (606) 252-0361
Roscoe M. Pierson, Libn.

ST. JOSEPH HOSPITAL - MEDICAL LIBRARY
One St. Joseph Dr.
Lexington, KY 40504
Phone: (606) 278-3436
Jerri Trimble, Asst.Libn.

U.S. VETERANS ADMINISTRATION (KY-Lexington) - MEDICAL CENTER
LIBRARY
Lexington, KY 40511
Phone: (606) 233-4511
Ethel F. Mullins, Chf., Lib.Serv.

UNIVERSITY OF KENTUCKY - AGRICULTURE LIBRARY
Agricultural Science Ctr., N.
Lexington, KY 40506
Phone: (606) 258-2758
Antoinette P. Powell, Libn.

UNIVERSITY OF KENTUCKY - ART LIBRARY
4 Margaret I. King Library, N.
Lexington, KY 40506
Phone: (606) 257-3938
Mary B. Davis, Art Libn.

UNIVERSITY OF KENTUCKY - BIOLOGICAL SCIENCES LIBRARY
Thomas Morgan Biological Sci. Bldg.
Rm. 313
Lexington, KY 40506
Phone: (606) 258-5889
Elizabeth B. Howard, Libn.

UNIVERSITY OF KENTUCKY - BUSINESS AND ECONOMICS INFORMATION
CENTER
M.I. King Library
Lexington, KY 40506

UNIVERSITY OF KENTUCKY - CHEMISTRY-PHYSICS LIBRARY
150 Chemistry-Physics Bldg.
Lexington, KY 40506
Phone: (606) 258-5954
Ellen P. Baxter, Libn.

UNIVERSITY OF KENTUCKY - EDUCATION LIBRARY
205 Dickey Hall
Lexington, KY 40506
Phone: (606) 258-4939
Jane N. White, Libn.

UNIVERSITY OF KENTUCKY - ENGINEERING LIBRARY
355 Anderson Hall
Lexington, KY 40506
Phone: (606) 258-2965
Russell H. Powell, Libn.

UNIVERSITY OF KENTUCKY - GEOLOGY LIBRARY
100 Bowman Hall
Lexington, KY 40506
Phone: (606) 258-5730
Vivian S. Hall, Libn.

UNIVERSITY OF KENTUCKY - HUNTER M. ADAMS ARCHITECTURE LIBRARY
College Of Architecture
200 Pence Hall
Lexington, KY 40506
Phone: (606) 257-1533
Harry Gilbert, Libn.

UNIVERSITY OF KENTUCKY - INSTITUTE FOR MINING AND MINERALS
RESEARCH - IMMR LIBRARY
Kentucky Energy Res. Laboratory
Iron Works Pike, Box 13 015
Lexington, KY 40583
Phone: (606) 252-5535
Theresa K. Wiley, Lib.Mgr.

UNIVERSITY OF KENTUCKY - LAW LIBRARY
College of Law
Lexington, KY 40506
Phone: (606) 258-8686
William James, Law Libn.

UNIVERSITY OF KENTUCKY - MATHEMATICS LIBRARY
Lexington, KY 40506
Phone: (606) 258-8253
Mildred Moore, Libn.

UNIVERSITY OF KENTUCKY - MEDICAL CENTER LIBRARY
Lexington, KY 40536
Phone: (606) 233-5300
Omer Hamlin, Jr., Dir.

UNIVERSITY OF KENTUCKY - MUSIC LIBRARY/LISTENING CENTER
116 Fine Arts Bldg.
Lexington, KY 40506
Phone: (606) 258-2800
Adelle G. Dailey, Music Libn.

AMERICAN AIR FILTER COMPANY, INC. - TECHNICAL LIBRARY
215 Central Ave.
Louisville, KY 40232
Phone: (502) 637-0011
Richard D. Rivers, Mgr.

AUDUBON HOSPITAL - MEDICAL LIBRARY
One Audubon Plaza
Louisville, KY 40217
Phone: (502) 636-7296
Elizabeth Fischer, Libn.

BELLARMINE COLLEGE - THOMAS MERTON STUDIES CENTER
Newburg Rd.
Louisville, KY 40205
Phone: (502) 452-8187
Robert E. Daggy, Cur.

BROWN AND WILLIAMSON TOBACCO CORPORATION - RESEARCH LIBRARY
1600 W. Hill St.
Box 35090
Louisville, KY 40232
Phone: (502) 774-7683
Cheryl M. Doty, Libn.

CONGREGATION OF THE PASSION - HOLY CROSS PROVINCE - PROVINCIAL
LIBRARY †
1924 Newburg Rd.
Louisville, KY 40205
Phone: (502) 451-2330
Fr. Germain Legere, C.P., Libn.

COURIER-JOURNAL AND LOUISVILLE TIMES - LIBRARY
525 W. Broadway
Louisville, KY 40202
Phone: (502) 582-4184
Doris J. Batliner, Chf.Libn.

DATA COURIER, INC. - LIBRARY SERVICES & ACQUISITIONS
620 S. Fifth St.
Louisville, KY 40202
Phone: (502) 582-4111
Betty Gaskins, Mgr.Lib.Serv.

DOUGLASS BOULEVARD CHRISTIAN CHURCH - LIBRARY
2005 Douglass Blvd.
Louisville, KY 40205
Phone: (502) 452-2629
Mrs. Eugene R. Cruikshank

FILSON CLUB - LIBRARY
118 W. Breckinridge St.
Louisville, KY 40203
Phone: (502) 582-3727
Martin F. Schmidt, Libn.

JEFFERSON COUNTY OFFICE OF HISTORIC PRESERVATION AND ARCHIVES
Fiscal Court Bldg., Rm. 100
Louisville, KY 40202
Phone: (502) 581-5761
Olivia Frederick, Cons.Archv.

JEFFERSON COUNTY PUBLIC LAW LIBRARY
Old Louisville Trust Bldg.
200 S. Fifth St.
Louisville, KY 40202
Phone: (502) 581-5943
Kent E. Metcalf, Dir.

KOSAIR CRIPPLED CHILDREN HOSPITAL - LIBRARY
982 Eastern Pkwy.
Louisville, KY 40217
Phone: (502) 637-7616
Barbara J. Burgin, Adm.Sec.

LOUISVILLE ACADEMY OF MUSIC - LIBRARY
2740 Frankfort Ave.
Louisville, KY 40206
Phone: (502) 893-7885
Robert B. French, Pres.

LOUISVILLE BAPTIST HOSPITALS, INC. - HAGAN LIBRARY
810 Barret Ave.
Louisville, KY 40204
Phone: (502) 566-3108
Garry Johnson, Dir.

LOUISVILLE DEPARTMENT OF LAW - LIBRARY
6th & Jefferson, Rm. 200
Louisville, KY 40202
Phone: (502) 587-3511
Marynell Haas, Libn.

LOUISVILLE FREE PUBLIC LIBRARY - FILM SERVICES
301 W. York St.
Louisville, KY 40203
Phone: (502) 584-4154
Aubrey N. Hamilton, Dept.Hd.

LOUISVILLE FREE PUBLIC LIBRARY - KENTUCKY DIVISION
Fourth & York Sts.
Louisville, KY 40203
Phone: (502) 584-4154
Mark Harris, Hd.

LOUISVILLE FREE PUBLIC LIBRARY - LIBRARY BROADCASTING
301 W. York St.
Louisville, KY 40203
Thomas A. Donoho, Dept.Hd.

LOUISVILLE AND JEFFERSON COUNTY PLANNING COMMISSION -
LOUISVILLE METROPOLITAN PLANNING LIBRARY
900 Fiscal Court Bldg.
Louisville, KY 40202
Phone: (502) 581-6230
Biljon Slifer, Adm.Asst.

LOUISVILLE PRESBYTERIAN THEOLOGICAL SEMINARY - LIBRARY
1044 Alta Vista Rd.   Phone: (502) 895-3411
Louisville, KY 40205   Ernest M. White, Libn.

MEIDINGER, INC. - INFORMATION CENTER
1400 Embassy Sq.   Phone: (502) 499-1240
Louisville, KY 40299   Albertha Hoeck, Mgr.

NATIONAL CRIME PREVENTION INSTITUTE - INFORMATION CENTER
University of Louisville, Shelby Campus   Phone: (502) 588-6987
Louisville, KY 40292   Barbara R. Bomar, Info.Mgr.

NATIONAL SOCIETY OF THE SONS OF THE AMERICAN REVOLUTION -
     GENEALOGY LIBRARY
1000 S. 4th St.   Phone: (502) 589-1776
Louisville, KY 40203   Mary Linda Cotten, Libn.

NORTON-CHILDREN'S HOSPITALS - MEDICAL LIBRARY
Box 35070   Phone: (502) 589-8171
Louisville, KY 40232   Holly S. Buchanan, Dir.

OUR LADY OF PEACE HOSPITAL - MEDICAL LIBRARY
2020 Newburg Rd.   Phone: (502) 451-3330
Louisville, KY 40232   Sr. Mary Agnella Collins, S.C.N., Dir.

ST. ANTHONY HOSPITAL - MEDICAL LIBRARY
1313 St. Anthony Pl.   Phone: (502) 587-1161
Louisville, KY 40204   Alma Hall Fielden, Adm.Asst., Med. Staff

STS. MARY AND ELIZABETH HOSPITAL - MEDICAL LIBRARY
4400 Churchman Ave.   Phone: (502) 361-6319
Louisville, KY 40215   Ruth Gendron, Dir.

SOUTHERN BAPTIST THEOLOGICAL SEMINARY - AUDIOVISUAL CENTER
2825 Lexington Rd.   Phone: (502) 897-4508
Louisville, KY 40206   Andrew B. Rawls, AV Libn.

SOUTHERN BAPTIST THEOLOGICAL SEMINARY - BILLY GRAHAM ROOM
2825 Lexington Rd.   Phone: (502) 897-4807
Louisville, KY 40206   Dr. Ronald F. Deering, Libn.

SOUTHERN BAPTIST THEOLOGICAL SEMINARY - CHURCH MUSIC LIBRARY
2825 Lexington Rd.   Phone: (502) 897-4712
Louisville, KY 40206   Martha C. Powell, Church Music Libn.

SOUTHERN BAPTIST THEOLOGICAL SEMINARY - JAMES P. BOYCE
     CENTENNIAL LIBRARY
2825 Lexington Rd.   Phone: (502) 897-4807
Louisville, KY 40206   Dr. Ronald F. Deering, Libn.

SPEED (J.B.) ART MUSEUM - LIBRARY
2035 S. Third St.   Phone: (502) 636-2893
Louisville, KY 40208   Mary Jane Benedict, Libn.

UNITED CATALYSTS, INC. - TECHNICAL LIBRARY
Box 32370   Phone: (502) 637-9751
Louisville, KY 40232   Betty B. Simms, Tech.Libn.

U. S. NAVY - NAVAL ORDNANCE STATION - TECHNICAL LIBRARY
                                            Phone: (502) 367-5609
Louisville, KY 40214   Elizabeth T. Miles, Lib.Techn.

U.S. VETERANS ADMINISTRATION (KY-Louisville) - HOSPITAL LIBRARY
800 Zorn Ave.   Phone: (502) 895-3401
Louisville, KY 40202   James F. Kastner, Chf.Libn.

UNIVERSITY HOSPITAL (Louisville General) - MEDICAL LIBRARY
323 E. Chestnut St.   Phone: (502) 589-4321
Louisville, KY 40202   Frances Frank, Libn.

UNIVERSITY OF LOUISVILLE - ALLEN R. HITE ART INSTITUTE - MARGARET
     M. BRIDWELL ART LIBRARY
Belknap Campus   Phone: (502) 588-6741
Louisville, KY 40208   Gail R. Gilbert, Hd., Art Lib.

UNIVERSITY OF LOUISVILLE - DEPARTMENT OF RARE BOOKS AND SPECIAL
     COLLECTIONS
Belknap Campus   Phone: (502) 588-6762
Louisville, KY 40292   George T. McWhorter, Cur.

UNIVERSITY OF LOUISVILLE - DWIGHT ANDERSON MEMORIAL MUSIC
     LIBRARY
2301 S. 3rd St.   Phone: (502) 588-5659
Louisville, KY 40292   Marion Korda, Libn.

UNIVERSITY OF LOUISVILLE - J.B. SPEED SCIENTIFIC SCHOOL - LIBRARY
Belknap Campus   Phone: (502) 588-6297
Louisville, KY 40208   George Lindauer, Libn.

UNIVERSITY OF LOUISVILLE - KORNHAUSER HEALTH SCIENCES LIBRARY
                                            Phone: (502) 588-5771
Louisville, KY 40292   Leonard M. Eddy, Dir.

UNIVERSITY OF LOUISVILLE - LIFE SCIENCES LIBRARY
Belknap Campus   Phone: (502) 588-5945
Louisville, KY 40208   Janardan M. Kulkarni, Sci.Libn.

UNIVERSITY OF LOUISVILLE - PHOTOGRAPHIC ARCHIVES
Belknap Campus   Phone: (502) 588-6752
Louisville, KY 40208   James C. Anderson, Cur.

UNIVERSITY OF LOUISVILLE - SCHOOL OF LAW LIBRARY
Belknap Campus   Phone: (502) 636-4731
Louisville, KY 40292   Gene W. Teitelbaum, Libn.

UNIVERSITY OF LOUISVILLE - SEBASTIAN S. KRESGE NATURAL SCIENCE
     LIBRARY
Belknap Campus   Phone: (502) 588-5986
Louisville, KY 40208   Janardan M. Kulkarni, Sci.Libn.

UNIVERSITY OF LOUISVILLE - UNIVERSITY ARCHIVES AND RECORDS
     CENTER
Ekstrom Library   Phone: (502) 588-6674
Louisville, KY 40292   William J. Morison, Dir./Univ.Archv.

UNIVERSITY OF LOUISVILLE - UNIVERSITY ARCHIVES AND RECORDS
     CENTER - ORAL HISTORY CENTER
Belknap Campus   Phone: (502) 588-6674
Louisville, KY 40292   Carl G. Ryant, Co-Dir.

HOPKINS COUNTY - REGIONAL MEDICAL CENTER - LIBRARY
Hospital Dr.   Phone: (502) 821-6430
Madisonville, KY 42431   Mark A. Ingram, Med.Libn.

U.S. NATL. PARK SERVICE - CUMBERLAND GAP NATL. HISTORICAL PARK -
     LIBRARY
Box 840   Phone: (606) 248-2817
Middlesboro, KY 40965   Wes Leishman, Interpretation Chf.

MOREHEAD STATE UNIVERSITY - CAMDEN-CARROLL LIBRARY
                                            Phone: (606) 783-2142
Morehead, KY 40351   Dr. Jack D. Ellis, Dir.

ST. CLAIRE MEDICAL CENTER - MEDICAL LIBRARY
Medical Circle   Phone: (606) 784-6661
Morehead, KY 40351   Patsy Wright, Libn.

MURRAY STATE UNIVERSITY - LIBRARY
                                            Phone: (502) 762-2291
Murray, KY 42071   Edwin C. Strohecker, Dean

OWENSBORO AREA MUSEUM - LIBRARY
2829 S. Griffith Ave.   Phone: (502) 683-0296
Owensboro, KY 42301   Joseph M. Ford, Musm.Dir.

OWENSBORO-DAVIESS COUNTY PUBLIC LIBRARY - KENTUCKY ROOM
450 Griffith Ave.   Phone: (502) 684-0211
Owensboro, KY 42301   Shelia E. Brown, Hd.

OWENSBORO MESSENGER-INQUIRER - LIBRARY
1401 Frederica St.   Phone: (502) 926-0123
Owensboro, KY 42301   Katherine Fiedler, Libn.

TEXAS GAS TRANSMISSION CORPORATION - LIBRARY
Box 1160   Phone: (502) 926-8686
Owensboro, KY 42301   Frieda Rhodes, Libn.

UNION CARBIDE CORPORATION - NUCLEAR DIVISION - PADUCAH PLANT
  LIBRARY
Box 1410   Phone: (502) 444-6311
Paducah, KY 42001   Betty Barbre, Asst.Libn.

LLOYD (Alice) COLLEGE - APPALACHIAN ORAL HISTORY PROJECT
                                        Phone: (606) 368-2101
Pippa Passes, KY 41844   Katherine R. Martin, Dir.

EASTERN KENTUCKY UNIVERSITY - JOHN GRANT CRABBE LIBRARY
                                        Phone: (606) 622-3606
Richmond, KY 40475   Ernest E. Weyhrauch, Dean Of Libs.

EASTERN KENTUCKY UNIVERSITY - LAW ENFORCEMENT LIBRARY
Stratton Bldg.   Phone: (606) 622-5234
Richmond, KY 40475   Verna Casey, Libn.

EASTERN KENTUCKY UNIVERSITY - MUSIC LIBRARY
                                        Phone: (606) 622-4944
Richmond, KY 40475   Elizabeth K. Baker, Libn.

MADISON COUNTY HISTORICAL SOCIETY, INC. - LIBRARY
101 W. Irvine St.   Phone: (606) 623-1720
Richmond, KY 40475   Mrs. Neal Colyer

GETHSEMANI ABBEY - LIBRARY †
                                        Phone: (502) 549-3117
Trappist, KY 40073   Fr. Hilarion Schmock, O.C.S.O., Libn.

KENTUCKY MOUNTAIN BIBLE INSTITUTE - GIBSON LIBRARY
                                        Phone: (606) 666-5000
Vancleve, KY 41385   Ava Smith, Libn.

ASBURY THEOLOGICAL SEMINARY - B.L. FISHER LIBRARY
                                        Phone: (606) 858-3581
Wilmore, KY 40390   D. William Faupel, Dir., Lib. Serv.

LOUISIANA

RAPIDES GENERAL HOSPITAL - MEDICAL LIBRARY
Box 7146   Phone: (318) 487-8111
Alexandria, LA 71301   Mrs. B.T. Dawkins, Libn.

ST. FRANCES CABRINI HOSPITAL - MEDICAL LIBRARY
3330 Masonic Dr.   Phone: (318) 487-1122
Alexandria, LA 71301   Sr. Dorothy Dardeau, Libn.

TRUE VINE MISSIONARY BAPTIST CHURCH - LIBRARY
831 Broadway Ave.
Box 1051   Phone: (318) 445-6730
Alexandria, LA 71301   Louise Humphrey, Libn.

U.S. VETERANS ADMINISTRATION (LA-Alexandria) - HOSPITAL MEDICAL
  LIBRARY
                                        Phone: (318) 473-0010
Alexandria, LA 71301   Nancy M. Guillet, Chf.Libn.

U.S. AIR FORCE BASE - BARKSDALE BASE LIBRARY
FL 4608   Phone: (318) 869-4449
Barksdale AFB, LA 71110   Ronald J. Ferland, Libn.

BATON ROUGE STATE-TIMES & MORNING ADVOCATE NEWSPAPERS -
  LIBRARY
525 Lafayette St.   Phone: (504) 383-1111
Baton Rouge, LA 70821   Mrs. Lou Thomas, Libn.

ETHYL CORPORATION - CHEMICAL DEVELOPMENT LIBRARY
Box 2246   Phone: (504) 359-2182
Baton Rouge, LA 70821   Lois M. Skinner, Libn.

EXXON COMPANY, U.S.A. - EXXON RESEARCH & DEVELOPMENT
  LABORATORIES LIBRARY †
Box 2226   Phone: (504) 359-7681
Baton Rouge, LA 70821

LONG (Earl K.) MEMORIAL HOSPITAL - MEDICAL LIBRARY
5825 Airline Highway   Phone: (504) 342-5256
Baton Rouge, LA 70805   Elaine P. O'Connor, Dir.

LOUISIANA STATE DEPT. OF COMMERCE - OFFICE OF COMMERCE &
  INDUSTRY - INDUSTRIAL DEVELOPMENT REFERENCE LIBRARY
Box 44185   Phone: (504) 342-5383
Baton Rouge, LA 70804   Doyle Ray Bellotte, Libn.

LOUISIANA STATE DEPARTMENT OF JUSTICE - OFFICE OF THE ATTORNEY
  GENERAL - HUEY P. LONG MEMORIAL LAW LIBRARY *
State Capitol, 25th Fl. W.
Box 44005   Phone: (504) 342-7013
Baton Rouge, LA 70804   Freda Jackson, Intern in Charge

LOUISIANA STATE DEPARTMENT OF NATURAL RESOURCES - DIVISION OF
  RESEARCH & DEVELOPMENT - LIBRARY
Box 44156   Phone: (504) 342-1270
Baton Rouge, LA 70804   Diane C. Duchamp, Info.Dir.

LOUISIANA STATE DEPARTMENT OF TRANSPORTATION DEVELOPMENT -
  OFFICE OF PUBLIC WORKS - TECHNICAL LIBRARY
Capitol Sta., Box 44155   Phone: (504) 342-7566
Baton Rouge, LA 70804   Dorothy D. McConnell, Libn.

LOUISIANA STATE LEGISLATIVE COUNCIL - DIVISION OF INFORMATION
  SERVICES
Box 44012   Phone: (504) 342-2431
Baton Rouge, LA 70804   Suzanne Hughes, Coord., Info.Serv.

LOUISIANA STATE LIBRARY
Box 131   Phone: (504) 342-4922
Baton Rouge, LA 70821   Thomas F. Jaques, State Libn.

LOUISIANA STATE OFFICE OF THE SECRETARY OF STATE - STATE
  ARCHIVES AND RECORDS SERVICE
Capitol Sta., Box 44125   Phone: (504) 342-5440
Baton Rouge, LA 70804   Dr. Donald J. Lemieux, State Archv./Dir.

LOUISIANA STATE PLANNING OFFICE - LIBRARY
Box 44426   Phone: (504) 342-7428
Baton Rouge, LA 70804   Kay W. McGinnis, Adm.Libn./Info.Spec.

LOUISIANA STATE UNIVERSITY - CENTER FOR ENGINEERING & BUSINESS
  ADMINISTRATION READING ROOM *
                                        Phone: (504) 388-8221
Baton Rouge, LA 70803   J.H. Hoover, Hd., Bus.Adm./Govt.Doc

LOUISIANA STATE UNIVERSITY - CHEMISTRY LIBRARY
Virginia Williams Hall   Phone: (504) 388-2530
Baton Rouge, LA 70803

LOUISIANA STATE UNIVERSITY - COASTAL STUDIES INSTITUTE -
  REFERENCE ROOM
L.S.U.   Phone: (504) 388-2395
Baton Rouge, LA 70803   Rowena Hill, Res.Assoc.

LOUISIANA STATE UNIVERSITY - COLLEGE OF DESIGN - DESIGN
  RESOURCE CENTER
136 Atkinson Hall   Phone: (504) 388-2665
Baton Rouge, LA 70803   Doris A. Wheeler, Design Libn.

LOUISIANA STATE UNIVERSITY - DEPARTMENT OF ARCHIVES AND
  MANUSCRIPTS
Troy H. Middleton Library, Rm. 202   Phone: (504) 388-2240
Baton Rouge, LA 70803   M. Stone Miller, Jr., Hd.

LOUISIANA STATE UNIVERSITY - E.A. MC ILHENNY NATURAL HISTORY
  COLLECTION
Library   Phone: (504) 388-6934
Baton Rouge, LA 70803   Kathryn Morgan, Cur.

LOUISIANA STATE UNIVERSITY - LAW LIBRARY
                                        Phone: (504) 388-8802
Baton Rouge, LA 70803   Lance E. Dickson, Dir.

LOUISIANA STATE UNIVERSITY - LIBRARY SCHOOL LIBRARY
Library, Rm. 232 A   Phone: (504) 388-4576
Baton Rouge, LA 70803   Mary Jane Kahao, Hd.

LOUISIANA STATE UNIVERSITY - LISTENING ROOMS
Library   Phone: (504) 388-2900
Baton Rouge, LA 70803   Glenn Walden, Hd.

LOUISIANA STATE UNIVERSITY - LOUISIANA ROOM
Library   Phone: (504) 388-2575
Baton Rouge, LA 70803   Evangeline Mills Lynch, Libn.

LOUISIANA STATE UNIVERSITY - NEWSPAPER-MICROFORM ROOMS
                                               Phone: (504) 388-4662
Baton Rouge, LA 70803   Deborah Honeychurch, Hd.

LOUISIANA STATE UNIVERSITY - RARE BOOK COLLECTION
Library   Phone: (504) 388-2575
Baton Rouge, LA 70803   Evangeline M. Lynch, Libn.

LOUISIANA STATE UNIVERSITY - REFERENCE SERVICES
                                               Phone: (504) 388-8875
Baton Rouge, LA 70803   Joyce C. Werner, Hd.

**LOUISIANA STATE UNIVERSITY - SCHOOL OF VETERINARY MEDICINE -
    LIBRARY**
                                               Phone: (504) 346-3173
Baton Rouge, LA 70803   Sue Loubiere, Libn.

**OUR LADY OF THE LAKE REGIONAL MEDICAL CENTER - SCHOOL OF
    NURSING LIBRARY**
5000 Hennessy Blvd.   Phone: (504) 769-3100
Baton Rouge, LA 70805   Dorothy D. Romero, Libn.

PUBLIC AFFAIRS RESEARCH COUNCIL OF LOUISIANA - RESEARCH LIBRARY
Box 3118   Phone: (504) 343-9204
Baton Rouge, LA 70821   Jan Brashear, Res.Libn.

SOUTHERN UNIVERSITY - LAW SCHOOL LIBRARY
Southern Branch Post Office   Phone: (504) 771-2552
Baton Rouge, LA 70813   Yvonne Fonvielle, Law Libn.

U.S. PUBLIC HEALTH SERVICE HOSPITAL - MEDICAL LIBRARY †
                                               Phone: (504) 642-7771
Carville, LA 70721   Anna Belle Steinbach, Med.Libn.

**TULANE UNIVERSITY OF LOUISIANA - DELTA REGIONAL PRIMATE
    RESEARCH CENTER - SCIENCE INFORMATION SERVICE**
                                               Phone: (504) 892-2040
Covington, LA 70433   James L. Paysse, Ed.Asst.

U.S. AIR FORCE BASE - ENGLAND BASE LIBRARY
                                               Phone: (318) 448-5760
England AFB, LA 71301   Rupert C. Thom, Libn.

U.S. ARMY HOSPITALS - FORT POLK ARMY HOSPITAL - MEDICAL LIBRARY
                                               Phone: (318) 537-2073
Fort Polk, LA 71459   Ina L. Nesbitt, Med.Libn.

SOUTHEASTERN LOUISIANA UNIVERSITY - L.A. SIMS MEMORIAL LIBRARY
Drawer 896, Univ. Sta.   Phone: (504) 549-2234
Hammond, LA 70402   F. Landon Greaves, Jr., Hd.Libn.

DIOCESE OF LAFAYETTE, LOUISIANA - ARCHIVES
Drawer 3387   Phone: (318) 361-5639
Lafayette, LA 70501   Rev. James F. Geraghty, Archv.

**UNIVERSITY OF SOUTHWESTERN LOUISIANA - CENTER FOR LOUISIANA
    STUDIES**
Box 4-0831   Phone: (318) 264-6027
Lafayette, LA 70504   Glenn R. Conrad, Dir.

**UNIVERSITY OF SOUTHWESTERN LOUISIANA - JEFFERSON CAFFERY
    LOUISIANA ROOM**
Dupre Library
302 E. St. Mary   Phone: (318) 264-6031
Lafayette, LA 70504   Dr. Frederick J. Stielow, Archv.

**UNIVERSITY OF SOUTHWESTERN LOUISIANA - ORNAMENTAL
    HORTICULTURE LIBRARY**
2206 Johnston St.   Phone: (318) 264-6064
Lafayette, LA 70506   Brenda Kosiba, Libn.

CITIES SERVICE COMPANY - PLASTICS TECHNICAL CENTER - LIBRARY
3409 Prien Lake Rd.   Phone: (318) 491-7121
Lake Charles, LA 70605   Ursula M. Jones, Tech.Libn.

SOUTHEAST LOUISIANA HOSPITAL - PROFESSIONAL LIBRARY
Box 3850   Phone: (504) 626-8161
Mandeville, LA 70448   Carol C. Adams, Libn.

**LOUISIANA STATE DEPT. OF CULTURE, RECREATION & TOURISM -
    MANSFIELD STATE COMMEMORATIVE AREA - MUSEUM & LIB.**
Rte. 2, Box 252   Phone: (318) 872-1474
Mansfield, LA 71052   Ernestiene Roundtree, Cur.

CONWAY (E.A.) MEMORIAL HOSPITAL - MEDICAL LIBRARY
Box 1881   Phone: (318) 387-8460
Monroe, LA 71201   Linda Darnell, Libn.

ALTON OCHSNER MEDICAL FOUNDATION - MEDICAL LIBRARY
1516 Jefferson Hwy.   Phone: (504) 834-7070
New Orleans, LA 70121   Janet Minnerath, Med.Libn.

AMISTAD RESEARCH CENTER - LIBRARY
400 Esplanade Ave.   Phone: (504) 944-0239
New Orleans, LA 70116   Clifton H. Johnson, Exec.Dir.

**AMOCO PRODUCTION COMPANY - NEW ORLEANS REGION - LIBRARY
    INFORMATION CENTER**
Box 50879   Phone: (504) 586-6572
New Orleans, LA 70150   Louise M. Seidler, Supv.

BUREAU OF GOVERNMENTAL RESEARCH - LIBRARY †
1308 Richards Bldg.   Phone: (504) 525-4152
New Orleans, LA 70112   John Brewer, Lib. Contact

CHARITY HOSPITAL - SCHOOL OF NURSING - LIBRARY
450 S. Claiborne Ave.   Phone: (504) 568-6431
New Orleans, LA 70112   Bruce T. Abbott, Coord.Lib.Serv.

DEUTSCH, KERRIGAN AND STILES - LAW LIBRARY
4700 One Shell Sq.   Phone: (504) 581-5141
New Orleans, LA 70139   Jean Sandel, Libn.

GULF SOUTH RESEARCH INSTITUTE - LIBRARY
Box 26518   Phone: (504) 283-4223
New Orleans, LA 70186   Jim Hobbs, Tech.Libn.

HISTORIC NEW ORLEANS COLLECTION - LIBRARY
533 Royal St.   Phone: (504) 523-7146
New Orleans, LA 70130   Kenneth T. Urquhart, Hd.,Mss.Div. & Lib.

HOTEL DIEU HOSPITAL - LIBRARY
Box 61262   Phone: (504) 588-3000
New Orleans, LA 70161   Georgia Gwin Sewell, Libn.

INTERNATIONAL HOUSE LIBRARY
Box 52020   Phone: (504) 522-3591
New Orleans, LA 70152   Mina L. Crais, Libn.

LAW LIBRARY OF LOUISIANA
100 Supreme Court Bldg.
301 Loyola Ave.   Phone: (504) 568-5705
New Orleans, LA 70112   Carol D. Billings, Dir.

LOUISIANA STATE MUSEUM - LOUISIANA HISTORICAL CENTER
751 Chartres St.   Phone: (504) 568-6979
New Orleans, LA 70116   Rose Lambert, Libn.

LOUISIANA STATE UNIVERSITY MEDICAL CENTER - LIBRARY
1542 Tulane Ave.   Phone: (504) 568-6100
New Orleans, LA 70112   John P. Ische, Dir.

LOYOLA UNIVERSITY (New Orleans) - LAW LIBRARY
6363 St. Charles Ave.   Phone: (504) 865-3426
New Orleans, LA 70118   Win-Shin S. Chiang, Law Libn.

MC DERMOTT INC. - CORPORATE INFORMATION CENTER
1010 Common St.   Phone: (504) 587-5799
New Orleans, LA 70112   Karen Furlow, Corp.Libn.

MERCY HOSPITAL OF NEW ORLEANS - MEDICAL LIBRARY
301 N. Jefferson Davis Pkwy. Phone: (504) 486-7361
New Orleans, LA 70119 Jean Leonard, Med.Libn.

NEW ORLEANS BAPTIST THEOLOGICAL SEMINARY - JOHN T. CHRISTIAN LIBRARY
4110 Seminary Pl. Phone: (504) 282-4455
New Orleans, LA 70126 Dr. Paul Gericke, Dir. of Lib.

NEW ORLEANS MUSEUM OF ART - FELIX J. DREYOUS LIBRARY
City Park
Box 19123 Phone: (504) 488-2631
New Orleans, LA 70179 Jeannette D. Downing, Libn.

NEW ORLEANS PSYCHOANALYTIC INSTITUTE, INC. - LIBRARY
3624 Coliseum St. Phone: (504) 899-5815
New Orleans, LA 70115 Dr. Samuel Rubin, Chm.

NEW ORLEANS PUBLIC LIBRARY - ART, MUSIC & RECREATION DIVISION
219 Loyola Ave. Phone: (504) 586-4938
New Orleans, LA 70140 Marilyn Wilkins, Div.Hd.

NEW ORLEANS PUBLIC LIBRARY - BUSINESS AND SCIENCE DIVISION
219 Loyola Ave. Phone: (504) 586-4917
New Orleans, LA 70140 Elizabeth O. Bedikian, Div.Hd.

NEW ORLEANS PUBLIC LIBRARY - FOREIGN LANGUAGE DIVISION
219 Loyola Ave. Phone: (504) 586-4943
New Orleans, LA 70140 Norka Diaz, Div.Hd.

NEW ORLEANS PUBLIC LIBRARY - LOUISIANA DIVISION
219 Loyola Ave. Phone: (504) 586-4912
New Orleans, LA 70140 Collin B. Hamer, Jr., Div.Hd.

SOUTHERN BAPTIST HOSPITAL - LEARNING RESOURCE CENTER
2700 Napoleon Ave. Phone: (504) 899-9311
New Orleans, LA 70175 Pauline Louviere, Dir.

SOUTHERN FOREST PRODUCTS ASSOCIATION - LIBRARY
Box 52468 Phone: (504) 443-4464
New Orleans, LA 70152 Marlene B. Hickman, Libn.

STANDARD OIL OF CALIFORNIA - CHEVRON U.S.A., INC. - EASTERN REGION LIBRARY
1111 Tulane Ave. Phone: (504) 521-6369
New Orleans, LA 70112 Bob Hatten, Libn.

TOURO INFIRMARY - HOSPITAL LIBRARY
1401 Foucher St., 10th Fl., M Bldg. Phone: (504) 897-8102
New Orleans, LA 70115 Patricia J. Greenfield, Hd., Lib.Serv.

TULANE UNIVERSITY OF LOUISIANA - ARCHITECTURE LIBRARY
Richardson Memorial Bldg. Phone: (504) 865-4409
New Orleans, LA 70118 Frances Hecker, Libn.

TULANE UNIVERSITY OF LOUISIANA - LATIN AMERICAN LIBRARY
Howard-Tilton Memorial Library Phone: (504) 865-6616
New Orleans, LA 70118 Thomas Niehaus, Dir.

TULANE UNIVERSITY OF LOUISIANA - LAW LIBRARY
School of Law Phone: (504) 866-2751
New Orleans, LA 70118 David A. Combe, Libn.

TULANE UNIVERSITY OF LOUISIANA - MATHEMATICS RESEARCH LIBRARY
Gibson Hall Phone: (504) 865-5727
New Orleans, LA 70118 Martha Mark, Libn.

TULANE UNIVERSITY OF LOUISIANA - MAXWELL MUSIC LIBRARY
Dixon Hall Phone: (504) 865-4527
New Orleans, LA 70118 Liselotte Andersson, Libn.

TULANE UNIVERSITY OF LOUISIANA - SCHOOL OF BUSINESS ADMINISTRATION - NORMAN MAYER LIBRARY
Phone: (504) 865-6111
New Orleans, LA 70118 Dorothy Whittemore, Dir.

TULANE UNIVERSITY OF LOUISIANA - SCHOOL OF MEDICINE - RUDOLPH MATAS MEDICAL LIBRARY
1430 Tulane Ave. Phone: (504) 588-5155
New Orleans, LA 70112 William D. Postell, Jr., Med.Libn.

TULANE UNIVERSITY OF LOUISIANA - SPECIAL COLLECTIONS DIVISION
Howard-Tilton Memorial Library Phone: (504) 865-6695
New Orleans, LA 70118 Ann S. Gwyn, Hd., Spec.Coll.

TULANE UNIVERSITY OF LOUISIANA - WILLIAM RANSOM HOGAN JAZZ ARCHIVE
Howard-Tilton Memorial Library Phone: (504) 865-5688
New Orleans, LA 70118 Curtis D. Jerde, Cur.

U.S. COURT OF APPEALS, 5TH CIRCUIT - LIBRARY
600 Camp St., Rm. 106 Phone: (504) 589-6510
New Orleans, LA 70130 Max G. Dodson, Chf. Law Libn.

U.S.D.A. - AGRICULTURAL RESEARCH SERVICE - SOUTHERN REGIONALRESEARCH CENTER
1100 Robert E. Lee Blvd.
Box 19687 Phone: (504) 589-7072
New Orleans, LA 70179 Dorothy B. Skau, Libn.

U.S. DEPT. OF COMMERCE - INTERNATIONAL TRADE ADMINISTRATION - NEW ORLEANS DISTRICT OFFICE LIBRARY
International Trade Mart, Rm. 432
2 Canal St. Phone: (504) 589-6546
New Orleans, LA 70130 Raymond E. Eveland, Dir.

U.S. FOREST SERVICE - SOUTHERN FOREST EXPERIMENT STATION LIBRARY
Rm. T-10210 Postal Service Bldg.
701 Loyola Ave. Phone: (504) 589-6798
New Orleans, LA 70113 Linda A. Korb, Libn.

U.S. PUBLIC HEALTH SERVICE HOSPITAL - HEALTH SCIENCES LIBRARY
210 State St. Phone: (504) 899-3441
New Orleans, LA 70118 Billy M. James, Chf./Health Sci.Lib.

U.S. VETERANS ADMINISTRATION (LA-New Orleans) - MEDICAL CENTER LIBRARY
1601 Perdido St. Phone: (504) 568-0811
New Orleans, LA 70146 Wilma B. Neveu, Chf.Libn.

XAVIER UNIVERSITY OF LOUISIANA - COLLEGE OF PHARMACY - LIBRARY
7325 Palmetto St. Phone: (504) 486-7411
New Orleans, LA 70125 Yvonne C. Hull, Libn.

CENTRAL LOUISIANA STATE HOSPITAL - MEDICAL AND PROFESSIONAL LIBRARY
Box 31 Phone: (318) 445-2421
Pineville, LA 71360 Benton Carol McGee, Med.Libn.

GREEN CLINIC - LIBRARY
709 S. Vienna St.
Box 310 Phone: (318) 255-3690
Ruston, LA 71270 Louise M. Allen, Libn.

LOUISIANA TECH UNIVERSITY - COLLEGE OF EDUCATION - EDUCATIONAL RESEARCH LIBRARY *
Tech Sta., Box 5108 Phone: (318) 257-4683
Ruston, LA 71272 Jeannette Logan, Sec.

LOUISIANA TECH UNIVERSITY - RESEARCH DIVISION/COLLEGE OF ADMINISTRATION AND BUSINESS - LIBRARY
Box 10318, Tech Sta. Phone: (318) 257-3701
Ruston, LA 71272 Dr. James Robert Michael, Dir.

ST. JOSEPH ABBEY - LIBRARY
Phone: (504) 892-1800
St. Benedict, LA 70457 Bro. Damien Hauck, O.S.B., Act.Libn.

ST. JOSEPH SEMINARY COLLEGE - PERE ROUQUETTE LIBRARY
Phone: (504) 892-9895
St. Benedict, LA 70457 Joseph M. Babin, Dir. of Lib.

AMERICAN ROSE SOCIETY - LIBRARY
Box 30,000 Phone: (318) 938-5402
Shreveport, LA 71130 Harold S. Goldstein, Exec.Dir.

FIRST METHODIST CHURCH - BLISS MEMORIAL LIBRARY
Head of Texas St. Phone: (318) 424-7771
Shreveport, LA 71101 Mrs. Dick Towery, Libn.

GEOGRAPHIC

LOUISIANA STATE UNIVERSITY MEDICAL CENTER - SCHOOL OF MEDICINE
  IN SHREVEPORT - LIBRARY
Box 33932   Phone: (318) 226-3442
Shreveport, LA 71130   Mr. Mayo Drake, Libn.

NORTHWESTERN STATE UNIVERSITY OF LOUISIANA - EUGENE P. WATSON
  LIBRARY - SHREVEPORT DIVISION
1800 Warrington Pl.   Phone: (318) 424-1827
Shreveport, LA 71101   Dorcas M.C. McCormick, Div.Hd.

NORTON (R.W.) ART GALLERY - REFERENCE-RESEARCH LIBRARY
4747 Creswell Ave.   Phone: (318) 865-4201
Shreveport, LA 71106   Jerry M. Bloomer, Libn.

PENNZOIL PRODUCTS COMPANY - RESEARCH DEPARTMENT LIBRARY
8015 St. Vincent Ave.
Box 6199   Phone: (318) 861-4531
Shreveport, LA 71106   Connie Bihon, Libn.

SCHUMPERT MEDICAL CENTER - MEDICAL LIBRARY
915 Margaret Place
Box 21976   Phone: (318) 227-4500
Shreveport, LA 71120   M. Willis, Med.Libn.

SHREVEPORT TIMES - LIBRARY
Box 222   Phone: (318) 424-0373
Shreveport, LA 71130   Christy J. Wrenn, Adm.Libn.

U.S. VETERANS ADMINISTRATION (LA-Shreveport) - MEDICAL CENTER
  LIBRARY
510 E. Stoner   Phone: (318) 221-8411
Shreveport, LA 71130   Shirley B. Hegenwald, Chf., Lib.Serv.

WESTERN ELECTRIC COMPANY, INC. - TECHNICAL LIBRARY
Box 31111   Phone: (318) 683-2543
Shreveport, LA 71130   Dorothy Wilson, Libn.

MAINE

ANDROSCOGGIN COUNTY LAW LIBRARY
County Bldg.   Phone: (207) 782-3121
Auburn, ME 04210   Hon. Thomas E. Delahanty, Libn.

ANDROSCOGGIN HISTORICAL SOCIETY - CLARENCE E. MARCH LIBRARY
2 Turner St., County Bldg.   Phone: (207) 784-0586
Auburn, ME 04210   Leon M. Norris, Exec.Sec. & Cur.

CENTRAL MAINE POWER COMPANY - LIBRARY SERVICES
Edison Dr.   Phone: (207) 623-3521
Augusta, ME 04336   Catharine Webber, Supv.

KENNEBEC COUNTY LAW LIBRARY †
95 State St.   Phone: (207) 623-9293
Augusta, ME 04330   Charles Stillman, Libn.

KENNEBEC VALLEY MEDICAL CENTER - MEDICAL LIBRARY
6 E. Chestnut St.   Phone: (207) 623-4711
Augusta, ME 04330   Mrs. Gabriel W. Kirkpatrick, Med.Libn.

MAINE STATE DEPARTMENT OF ENVIRONMENTAL PROTECTION &
  DEPARTMENT OF CONSERVATION - DEP-DOC JOINT LIBRARY
State House, Station 17   Phone: (207) 289-2691
Augusta, ME 04333   Priscilla Bickford, Libn.

MAINE STATE DEPARTMENT OF HUMAN SERVICES - DEPARTMENTAL
  LIBRARY
State House   Phone: (207) 289-3055
Augusta, ME 04333   Mary J. Wandersee, Libn.

MAINE STATE DEPARTMENT OF TRANSPORTATION - LIBRARY
Child St.
Augusta, ME 04333

MAINE STATE LAW AND LEGISLATIVE REFERENCE LIBRARY
State House, Station 43   Phone: (207) 289-2648
Augusta, ME 04333   Edith L. Hary, State Law Libn.

MAINE STATE LIBRARY
Cultural Bldg.   Phone: (207) 289-3561
Augusta, ME 04333   J. Gary Nichols, State Libn.

MAINE STATE MUSEUM - RESOURCE CENTER
State House, Station 83   Phone: (207) 289-2301
Augusta, ME 04333   Jane E. Radcliffe, Musm. Registrar

MAINE STATE OFFICE OF ENERGY RESOURCES - LIBRARY *
295 Water St.   Phone: (207) 289-3811
Augusta, ME 04330   Robert Michaud, Libn.

MEDICAL CARE DEVELOPMENT, INC. - LIBRARY
295 Water St.   Phone: (207) 622-7566
Augusta, ME 04330   Mary Anne Spindler, Libn.

U.S. VETERANS ADMINISTRATION (ME-Augusta) - CENTER LIBRARY
Togus Br., (402/142D)   Phone: (207) 623-8411
Augusta, ME 04330   Melda W. Page, Chf.Libn.

BANGOR MENTAL HEALTH INSTITUTE - HEALTH SCIENCES MEDIA CENTER
Box 926   Phone: (207) 947-6981
Bangor, ME 04401   Wendy Troiano, Libn.

BANGOR THEOLOGICAL SEMINARY - MOULTON LIBRARY
300 Union St.   Phone: (207) 942-6781
Bangor, ME 04401   Clifton Davis, Libn.

BEAL COLLEGE - LIBRARY
629 Main St.   Phone: (207) 947-7905
Bangor, ME 04401   M.J. Van Arsdale, Libn.

EASTERN MAINE MEDICAL CENTER - HEALTH SCIENCES LIBRARY
489 State St.   Phone: (207) 947-3711
Bangor, ME 04401   Jean S. Doty, Libn.

HUSSON COLLEGE - LIBRARY
One College Circle   Phone: (207) 945-5641
Bangor, ME 04401   Berneice Thompson, Libn.

PENOBSCOT BAR LIBRARY ASSOCIATION - LIBRARY
Penobscot County Court House
Bangor, ME 04401   Norman Minsky, Sec./Tres.

JACKSON LABORATORY - RESEARCH LIBRARY
                                         Phone: (207) 288-3371
Bar Harbor, ME 04609   Joan Staats, Sr. Staff Sci.

BATH MEMORIAL HOSPITAL - HEALTH SCIENCES LIBRARY †
23 Winship St.   Phone: (207) 443-5524
Bath, ME 04530   Cynthia A. Williams, Health Sci.Libn.

MAINE MARITIME MUSEUM - LIBRARY/ARCHIVES
963 Washington St.   Phone: (207) 443-6311
Bath, ME 04530   Marion Small, Asst.Cur.Coll.

SAGADAHOC COUNTY LAW LIBRARY
County Court House   Phone: (207) 443-9734
Bath, ME 04530

WALDO COUNTY LAW LIBRARY †
Waldo County Courthouse
73 Church St.
Belfast, ME 04915

FIBER MATERIALS, INC. - TECHNICAL LIBRARY
Biddeford Industrial Park   Phone: (207) 282-5911
Biddeford, ME 04005   Susan Milo, Tech.Libn.

UNIVERSITY OF NEW ENGLAND - LIBRARY †
605 Pool Rd.   Phone: (207) 282-1515
Biddeford, ME 04005   Gertrude B. Weir, Libn.

UNIVERSITY OF NEW ENGLAND - NEW ENGLAND COLLEGE OF
  OSTEOPATHIC MEDICINE - NECOM LIBRARY
11 Hills Beach Rd.   Phone: (207) 283-0171
Biddeford, ME 04005   Rosemary G. Kelley, Med.Libn.

BOOTHBAY THEATRE MUSEUM
Corey Ln.   Phone: (207) 633-4536
Boothbay, ME 04537   Franklyn Lenthall, Cur.

ST. ANDREWS HOSPITAL - MEDICAL LIBRARY
3 St. Andrews Lane   Phone: (207) 633-2121
Boothbay Harbor, ME 04538   Karen Roberts, Libn.

BOWDOIN COLLEGE - LIBRARY - SPECIAL COLLECTIONS
                                             Phone: (201) 725-8731
Brunswick, ME 04011   Dianne M. Gutscher, Cur.

BOWDOIN COLLEGE - PUBLIC AFFAIRS RESEARCH CENTER
Brunswick, ME 04011

REGIONAL MEMORIAL HOSPITAL - HEALTH SCIENCES LIBRARY
Baribeau Dr.   Phone: (207) 729-0181
Brunswick, ME 04011   Cynthia Williams, Libn.

CALAIS FREE LIBRARY
                                             Phone: (207) 454-3223
Calais, ME 04619   Helen R. Oliver, Libn.

CARY MEDICAL CENTER - HEALTH SCIENCE LIBRARY
Van Buren Rd.   Phone: (207) 498-3131
Caribou, ME 04736   Donna E. Cote-Thibodeau, Libn.

NYLANDER MUSEUM - LIBRARY *
393 Main St.   Phone: (207) 493-4474
Caribou, ME 04730   Clara Piper, Libn.

MAINE MARITIME ACADEMY - NUTTING MEMORIAL LIBRARY
                                             Phone: (207) 326-4311
Castine, ME 04421   Kenneth H. Anthony, LCDR, Hd.Libn.

DEER ISLE-STONINGTON HISTORICAL SOCIETY - LIBRARY
                                             Phone: (207) 348-2886
Deer Isle, ME 04627   Genice Welcome, Exec.Sec.

HAYSTACK MOUNTAIN SCHOOL OF CRAFTS - LIBRARY
                                             Phone: (207) 348-6946
Deer Isle, ME 04627   Stanley Clifford, Coord.

PISCATAQUIS COUNTY LAW LIBRARY
Court House Annex   Phone: (207) 564-2181
Dover-Foxcroft, ME 04426   Elaine H. Roberts, Libn.

HANCOCK COUNTY LAW LIBRARY, INC.
60 State St.   Phone: (207) 667-8177
Ellsworth, ME 04605   Margaret A. Cunningham, Libn.

MAINE AUDUBON SOCIETY - ENVIRONMENTAL INFORMATION SERVICE
Gilsland Farm, 118 U.S. Rte. 1   Phone: (207) 781-2330
Falmouth, ME 04105   Miriam Schneider, Libn.

FRANKLIN MEMORIAL HOSPITAL - TURNER MEMORIAL LIBRARY
RFD No. 2
Wilton Rd.   Phone: (207) 778-6031
Farmington, ME 04938   Marilyn G. Courtney, Med.Libn.

UNIVERSITY OF MAINE, FARMINGTON - MANTOR LIBRARY
                                             Phone: (207) 778-3501
Farmington, ME 04938   John P. Burnham, Hd.Libn.

HOULTON REGIONAL HOSPITAL - LIBRARY
20 Hartford St.   Phone: (207) 532-9471
Houlton, ME 04730   Cathy Bates, Med.Libn.

BRICK STORE MUSEUM - EDITH CLEAVES BARRY LIBRARY
117 Main St.
Box 117
                                             Phone: (207) 985-4802
Kennebunk, ME 04043   Sandra S. Armentrout, Dir.

BATES COLLEGE - LIBRARY - SPECIAL COLLECTIONS
                                             Phone: (207) 784-2949
Lewiston, ME 04240   Joseph J. Derbyshire, Libn.

CENTRAL MAINE MEDICAL CENTER - GERRISH-TRUE HEALTH SCIENCE
   LIBRARY
300 Main St.   Phone: (207) 795-2376
Lewiston, ME 04240

LE CENTRE D'HERITAGE FRANCO-AMERICAIN - LIBRARY
133 Lisbon St.   Phone: (207) 783-8143
Lewiston, ME 04240   JoAnne D. Lapointe, Cur.

ST. MARY'S GENERAL HOSPITAL - HEALTH SCIENCES LIBRARY
45 Golder St.   Phone: (207) 786-2901
Lewiston, ME 04240   Evelyn A. Greenlaw, Libn.

INTERNATIONAL BACKPACKERS ASSOCIATION - LIBRARY *
Box 85   Phone: (207) 794-6062
Lincoln Center, ME 04458   Charlotte Grover-Feild

U.S. AIR FORCE BASE - LORING BASE LIBRARY
                                             Phone: (207) 999-2416
Loring AFB, ME 04751   Sylvia J. Sefcik, Libn.

NATIONAL SOCIETY, DAUGHTERS OF THE AMERICAN REVOLUTION -
   HANNAH WESTON CHAPTER - BURNHAM TAVERN MUSEUM
Main & Free Sts.   Phone: (207) 255-4432
Machias, ME 04654   Valdine C. Atwood, Chm.

LEARNING INCORPORATED - LIBRARY
Learning Place   Phone: (207) 244-5015
Manset-Seawall, ME 04656   A.L. Welles, Dir.

THOREAU FELLOWSHIP PAPERS †
Fogler Library,
University of Maine, Orono   Phone: (207) 581-7781
Orono, ME 04473   Eric S. Flower, Hd., Spec.Coll.

UNIVERSITY OF MAINE, ORONO - NORTHEAST ARCHIVES OF FOLKLORE
   AND ORAL HISTORY
Dept. of Anthropology
S. Stevens Hall   Phone: (207) 581-7466
Orono, ME 04469   Edward D. Ives, Dir.

UNIVERSITY OF MAINE, ORONO - RAYMOND H. FOGLER LIBRARY - SPECIAL
   COLLECTIONS DEPARTMENT †
                                             Phone: (207) 581-7781
Orono, ME 04473   Eric S. Flower, Dept.Hd.

PEMAQUID HISTORICAL ASSOCIATION - HARRINGTON MEETING HOUSE -
   LIBRARY
Old Harrington Road   Phone: (207) 677-2587
Pemaquid, ME 04558

UNITED SOCIETY OF BELIEVERS - THE SHAKER LIBRARY
Shaker Village, Sabbathday Lake   Phone: (207) 926-4865
Poland Spring, ME 04274   Theodore E. Johnson, Dir.

ANDOVER COLLEGE - LIBRARY
335 Forest Ave.   Phone: (207) 774-6126
Portland, ME 04101   Irene H. Tuttle, Libn.

CUMBERLAND BAR ASSOCIATION - NATHAN AND HENRY B. CLEAVES LAW
   LIBRARY
County Court House, 142 Federal St.   Phone: (207) 773-9712
Portland, ME 04111   Ann Pierce, Libn.

GANNETT (Guy) PUBLISHING COMPANY - PRESS HERALD-EVENING
   EXPRESS LIBRARY
390 Congress St.   Phone: (207) 775-5811
Portland, ME 04104   Mary N. Sparrow, Chf.Libn.

JORDAN (Edward C.) CO., INC. - LIBRARY
Box 7050   Phone: (207) 775-5401
Portland, ME 04112   Janice Tisdale, Libn.

MAINE CHARITABLE MECHANIC ASSOCIATION - LIBRARY *
519 Congress St.   Phone: (207) 773-8396
Portland, ME 04111   Edith M. Riley, Libn.

GEOGRAPHIC

MAINE HISTORICAL SOCIETY - LIBRARY
485 Congress St.   Phone: (207) 774-1822
Portland, ME 04101   Thomas L. Gaffney, Dir.

MAINE MEDICAL CENTER - LIBRARY
22 Bramhall St.   Phone: (207) 871-2201
Portland, ME 04102   Robin M. Rand, Dir., Lib.Serv.

MERCY HOSPITAL - HEALTH SCIENCES LIBRARY
144 State St.   Phone: (207) 774-1461
Portland, ME 04101   Mary Jane Geer, Health Info.Spec.

PORTLAND SCHOOL OF ART - LIBRARY
97 Spring St.   Phone: (207) 773-1233
Portland, ME 04101   Joanne Waxman, Libn.

UNION MUTUAL LIFE INSURANCE COMPANY - CORPORATE INFORMATION
  CENTER
2211 Congress St.   Phone: (207) 780-2347
Portland, ME 04122   Phillip C. Kalloch, Jr., Supv., Info.Serv.

UNIVERSITY OF MAINE SCHOOL OF LAW - DONALD L. GARBRECHT LAW
  LIBRARY
246 Deering Ave.   Phone: (207) 780-4350
Portland, ME 04102   Penny A. Hazelton, Law Libn.

UNIVERSITY OF SOUTHERN MAINE - CENTER FOR RESEARCH & ADVANCED
  STUDY - RESEARCH CENTER LIBRARY
246 Deering Ave.   Phone: (207) 780-4411
Portland, ME 04102   Janet F. Brysh, Libn.

PINELAND CENTER - MEDIA CENTER
Box C   Phone: (207) 688-4811
Pownal, ME 04069   D. Lamontagne, Libn.

AROOSTOOK MEDICAL CENTER - A.R. GOULD DIVISION - HEALTH
  SCIENCES LIBRARY
151 Academy St.   Phone: (207) 769-2511
Presque Isle, ME 04769   Marilyn W. Dean, Lib.Supv.

UNIVERSITY OF MAINE, PRESQUE ISLE - LIBRARY
181 Main St.   Phone: (207) 764-0311
Presque Isle, ME 04769   Dr. Vernon Lindquist, Dir.

TRANET - LIBRARY
Box 567   Phone: (207) 864-2252
Rangeley, ME 04970   William N. Ellis, Exec.Dir.

FARNSWORTH (William A.) - LIBRARY AND ART MUSEUM
                                          Phone: (207) 596-6457
Rockland, ME 04841   Marius B. Peladeau, Dir.

FMC CORPORATION - MARINE COLLOIDS DIVISION - LIBRARY
Box 308   Phone: (207) 594-4436
Rockland, ME 04841   Barbara Swift, Libn.

KNOX COUNTY LAW LIBRARY
62 Union St.
Rockland, ME 04841   Rendle Jones, Libn.

MOUNT DESERT ISLAND BIOLOGICAL LABORATORY - LIBRARY
                                          Phone: (207) 288-3605
Salsbury Cove, ME 04672   Mary Rush, Libn.

PENOBSCOT MARINE MUSEUM - LIBRARY
Church St., Box 403   Phone: (207) 548-6634
Searsport, ME 04974   C.G. Lane, Jr., Dir.

UNIVERSITY OF MAINE, ORONO - IRA C. DARLING CENTER LIBRARY †
                                          Phone: (207) 563-3146
Walpole, ME 04573   Louise M. Dean, Libn.

COLBY COLLEGE - MILLER LIBRARY - SPECIAL COLLECTIONS
                                          Phone: (207) 873-1131
Waterville, ME 04901   J. Fraser Cocks, III, Cur., Spec.Coll.

MAINE CRIMINAL JUSTICE ACADEMY - MEDIA RESOURCES
93 Silver St.   Phone: (207) 873-2651
Waterville, ME 04901   Linda J. Dwelley, Media Resource Dir.

MID-MAINE MEDICAL CENTER - CLARA HODGKINS MEMORIAL HEALTH
  SCIENCES LIBRARY
                                          Phone: (207) 873-0621
Waterville, ME 04901   Cora M. Damon, Libn.

THOMAS COLLEGE - MARRINER LIBRARY
W. River Rd.   Phone: (207) 873-0771
Waterville, ME 04901   Richard A. Boudreau, Libn.

WATERVILLE HISTORICAL SOCIETY - LIBRARY AND ARCHIVES
64 Silver St.   Phone: (207) 872-9439
Waterville, ME 04901   Agatha Fullom, Cur. in Residence

MAINE STATE DEPARTMENT OF MARINE RESOURCES - FISHERIES
  RESEARCH STATION - LIBRARY
                                          Phone: (207) 633-5572
West Boothbay Harbor, ME 04575   Kimberly Douglas, Libn.

SCOTT PAPER COMPANY - S.D. WARREN COMPANY - RESEARCH LIBRARY
Research Laboratory   Phone: (207) 856-6911
Westbrook, ME 04092   Deborah G. Chandler, Info.Spec.

LINCOLN COUNTY LAW LIBRARY †
                                          Phone: (207) 882-7517
Wiscasset, ME 04578   George A. Cowan, Libn.

TRIGOM - RESEARCH LIBRARY
16 Lafayette St.
Box 481   Phone: (207) 846-3294
Yarmouth, ME 04096   Gregory M. Scott, Pres.

OLD GAOL MUSEUM - LIBRARY
Lindsay Rd. & York St.   Phone: (207) 363-3872
York, ME 03909   Eldridge H. Pendleton, Dir.

YORK HOSPITAL - MEDICAL LIBRARY
15 Hospital Dr.   Phone: (207) 363-4321
York, ME 03909   Darryl Hamson, Med.Libn.

MARYLAND

U.S. ARMY - CHEMICAL SYSTEMS LABORATORY - TECHNICAL LIBRARY
                                          Phone: (301) 671-2934
Aberdeen Proving Ground, MD 21010   C.R. Anaclerio, Chf., Tech.Lib.

U.S. ARMY - ENVIRONMENTAL HYGIENE AGENCY - LIBRARY
Bldg. E2100   Phone: (301) 671-4236
Aberdeen Proving Ground, MD 21010   Krishan S. Goel, Libn.

U.S. ARMY MEDICAL RESEARCH INSTITUTE OF CHEMICAL DEFENSE -
  WOOD TECHNICAL LIBRARY
                                          Phone: (301) 671-4135
Aberdeen Proving Ground, MD 21010   Patricia Pepin, Chf., Lib.Br.

U.S. ARMY ORDNANCE CENTER & SCHOOL - LIBRARY
Attn: ATSL-DAC-L, Bldg. 3071   Phone: (301) 278-4991
Aberdeen Proving Ground, MD 21005   Janice C. Weston, Chf.Libn.

U.S. ARMY - ELECTRONICS R & D COMMAND - HARRY DIAMOND
  LABORATORIES-TECHNICAL & VISUAL INFORMATION OFFICE
2800 Powder Mill Rd. (DELHD-TIA)   Phone: (202) 394-2767
Adelphi, MD 20783   John P. Carrier, Chf.

U.S. PUBLIC HEALTH SERVICE - NATL. INSTITUTE OF MENTAL HEALTH -
  MENTAL HEALTH STUDY CENTER LIBRARY
2340 University Blvd., E.   Phone: (301) 436-6340
Adelphi, MD 20783   Robert F. Clarke, Prog.Chf./Libn.

ANNE ARUNDEL COUNTY OFFICE OF PLANNING AND ZONING - LIBRARY
Arundel Center   Phone: (301) 224-1880
Annapolis, MD 21404   Alexander D. Speer, Planner

ANNE ARUNDEL GENERAL HOSPITAL - MEMORIAL LIBRARY
Franklin & Cathedral Sts.   Phone: (301) 267-1562
Annapolis, MD 21401   Sara Barnett Fretwell, Libn.

ARINC RESEARCH CORPORATION - TECHNICAL LIBRARY
2551 Riva Rd.   Phone: (301) 224-4000
Annapolis, MD 21401   William O. Lively, Libn.

ENVIRONMENTAL PROTECTION AGENCY - CENTRAL REGIONAL
  LABORATORY - LIBRARY
839 Bestgate Rd.   Phone: (301) 224-2740
Annapolis, MD 21401   Margaret Munro, Libn.

HISTORIC ANNAPOLIS, INC. - LIBRARY
194 Prince George St.   Phone: (301) 267-7619
Annapolis, MD 21401   Mrs. John Symonds, Pres.

IIT RESEARCH INSTITUTE - ELECTROMAGNETIC COMPATIBILITY
  ANALYSIS CENTER - TECHNICAL INFORMATION SERVICES
185 Admiral Cochrane   Phone: (301) 267-2251
Annapolis, MD 21402   Alison A. Storch, Mgr., Info.Serv.

MARYLAND MUNICIPAL LEAGUE - LIBRARY
76 Maryland Ave.   Phone: (301) 268-5514
Annapolis, MD 21401   Jon C. Burrell, Exec.Dir.

MARYLAND STATE DEPARTMENT OF LEGISLATIVE REFERENCE - LIBRARY
Legislative Services Bldg.
90 State Circle   Phone: (301) 269-2871
Annapolis, MD 21401   Lynda C. Davis, Act.Libn.

MARYLAND STATE DEPARTMENT OF NATURAL RESOURCES - LIBRARY
Tawes State Office Bldg.   Phone: (301) 269-3015
Annapolis, MD 21401   Shashi P. Thaper, Hd.Libn.

MARYLAND STATE HALL OF RECORDS COMMISSION - LIBRARY
College Ave. & St. John's St.   Phone: (301) 269-3915
Annapolis, MD 21404   Dr. Edward C. Papenfuse, Archv.

MARYLAND STATE LAW LIBRARY
361 Rowe Blvd.   Phone: (301) 269-3395
Annapolis, MD 21401   Michael S. Miller, Dir.

U.S. NAVAL ACADEMY - NIMITZ LIBRARY
                                 Phone: (301) 267-2194
Annapolis, MD 21402   Professor Richard A. Evans, Lib.Dir.

U.S. NAVAL INSTITUTE - ORAL HISTORY OFFICE
                                 Phone: (301) 268-6110
Annapolis, MD 21402   John T. Mason, Jr., Dir.

U.S. NAVAL INSTITUTE - REFERENCE & PHOTOGRAPHIC LIBRARY
                                 Phone: (301) 268-6110
Annapolis, MD 21402   Patty M. Maddocks, Dir.

U.S. BUREAU OF MINES - AVONDALE RESEARCH CENTER LIBRARY
4900 La Salle Rd.   Phone: (301) 436-7552
Avondale, MD 20782   Paul F. Moran, Libn.

AAI CORPORATION - TECHNICAL LIBRARY
Box 6767   Phone: (301) 628-3193
Baltimore, MD 21204   Joyce F. Peacock, Libn.

ABELL (A.S.) COMPANY - BALTIMORE SUNPAPERS - LIBRARY
501 N. Calvert   Phone: (301) 332-6253
Baltimore, MD 21202   Clement G. Vitek, Chf.Libn.

ADAMS EXPRESS COMPANY - LIBRARY
201 N. Charles St.   Phone: (301) 752-5900
Baltimore, MD 21201   Dorothy Marvel, Libn.

ALCOLAC, INC. - RESEARCH LIBRARY *
3440 Fairfield Rd.   Phone: (301) 355-2600
Baltimore, MD 21226   Frances C. Hummel, Res.Libn.

ALTERNATIVE PRESS CENTER - LIBRARY
Box 7229   Phone: (301) 243-2471
Baltimore, MD 21218   Peggy D'Adamo, Pres.

BALTIMORE CITY DEPARTMENT OF HOUSING AND COMMUNITY
  DEVELOPMENT - RESEARCH LIBRARY
222 E. Saratoga St., Rm. 450   Phone: (301) 396-4248
Baltimore, MD 21202   Mrs. Shifra Cohen, Res.Anl.

BALTIMORE CITY DEPARTMENT OF PLANNING - LIBRARY *
222 E. Saratoga St., 8th Fl.   Phone: (301) 396-5920
Baltimore, MD 21202   Charles Newton, Libn.

BALTIMORE CITY HOSPITALS - HAROLD E. HARRISON LIBRARY †
4940 Eastern Ave.   Phone: (301) 396-9030
Baltimore, MD 21224   Edlea Jones, Libn.

BALTIMORE CITY PUBLIC SCHOOLS - PROFESSIONAL MEDIA CENTER
181 North Bend Rd.   Phone: (301) 396-5348
Baltimore, MD 21229   Jacqueline M. Merchant, Libn.

BALTIMORE - DEPARTMENT OF LEGISLATIVE REFERENCE - LIBRARY
626 S. Calvert St., 10th Fl.   Phone: (301) 396-4730
Baltimore, MD 21202   Bernard F. Murphy, Dir.

BALTIMORE ECONOMIC DEVELOPMENT CORPORATION - LIBRARY
36 S. Charles St., Suite 2400   Phone: (301) 837-9305
Baltimore, MD 21201   Margaret R. Taylor, Dir., Marketing Res.

BALTIMORE GAS AND ELECTRIC COMPANY - LIBRARY
2nd Fl., Monument St. Warehouse
Box 1475   Phone: (301) 234-6292
Baltimore, MD 21203   Agnes M. Lindemon, Libn.

BALTIMORE HEBREW COLLEGE - JOSEPH MEYERHOFF LIBRARY
5800 Park Heights Ave.   Phone: (301) 466-7900
Baltimore, MD 21215   Jesse Mashbaum, Dir.

BALTIMORE MUSEUM OF ART - REFERENCE LIBRARY
Art Museum Dr.   Phone: (301) 396-6317
Baltimore, MD 21218   Joan Settle, Libn.

BALTIMORE NEWS AMERICAN LIBRARY
Lombard & South Sts.   Phone: (301) 752-1212
Baltimore, MD 21203   Clark F. Ickes, Chf.Libn.

BALTIMORE ZOO - ARTHUR R. WATSON LIBRARY
Druid Hill Pk.   Phone: (201) 396-7102
Baltimore, MD 21217   Ethel R. Hardee, Libn.

BENDIX CORPORATION - COMMUNICATIONS DIVISION - ENGINEERING
  LIBRARY
E. Joppa Rd.   Phone: (301) 823-2200
Baltimore, MD 21204   Phyllis Davis, Libn.

B'NAI B'RITH CAREER & COUNSELING SERVICES - LIBRARY
7818 Liberty Rd.   Phone: (301) 655-5100
Baltimore, MD 21207   Leon L. Lerner, Exec.Dir.

BON SECOURS HOSPITAL - HEALTH SCIENCES LIBRARY
2025 W. Fayette St.   Phone: (301) 233-7100
Baltimore, MD 21223   Rosemary Pool, Med.Libn.

CARMELITE MONASTERY - LIBRARY AND ARCHIVES
1318 Dulaney Valley Rd.   Phone: (301) 823-7415
Baltimore, MD 21204   Sr. Constance Fitz Gerald, Archv.

CARNEGIE INSTITUTION OF WASHINGTON - DEPARTMENT OF
  EMBRYOLOGY - LIBRARY
115 W. University Pkwy.   Phone: (301) 467-1414
Baltimore, MD 21210

CHESAPEAKE AND OHIO RAILROAD COMPANY - TRAFFIC RESEARCH
  DEPARTMENT - LIBRARY *
One Charles Ctr., 16th Fl.   Phone: (301) 237-3742
Baltimore, MD 21201   R.M. Ruddle, Mgr., Traffic Res.

CHILDREN'S HOSPITAL, INC. - MEDICAL LIBRARY †
3825 Greenspring Ave.   Phone: (301) 462-6800
Baltimore, MD 21211   Janet E.N. Bush, Med.Rec.Adm.

COMMUNITY COLLEGE OF BALTIMORE - BARD LIBRARY - SPECIAL
  COLLECTIONS
2901 Liberty Heights Ave.   Phone: (301) 396-0432
Baltimore, MD 21215   Minnie B. Hoch, Dir.

GEOGRAPHIC

ENGINEERING SOCIETY OF BALTIMORE, INC. - LIBRARY †
11 W. Mt. Vernon Pl. Phone: (301) 539-6914
Baltimore, MD 21201

ENOCH PRATT FREE LIBRARY - AUDIO-VISUAL DEPARTMENT
400 Cathedral St. Phone: (301) 396-4616
Baltimore, MD 21201 Helen W. Cyr, Hd.

ENOCH PRATT FREE LIBRARY - BUSINESS, SCIENCE AND TECHNOLOGY
 DEPARTMENT
400 Cathedral St. Phone: (301) 396-5316
Baltimore, MD 21201 Margaret L. Jacobs, Dept.Hd.

ENOCH PRATT FREE LIBRARY - FINE ARTS AND RECREATION
 DEPARTMENT
400 Cathedral St. Phone: (301) 396-5491
Baltimore, MD 21201 Joan Stahl, Dept.Hd.

ENOCH PRATT FREE LIBRARY - GEORGE PEABODY DEPARTMENT
17 E. Mt. Vernon Pl. Phone: (301) 396-5540
Baltimore, MD 21202 Lyn Hart, Dept.Hd.

ENOCH PRATT FREE LIBRARY - MARYLAND DEPARTMENT
400 Cathedral St. Phone: (301) 396-5468
Baltimore, MD 21201 Morgan H. Pritchett, Hd.

ENOCH PRATT FREE LIBRARY - SOCIAL SCIENCE AND HISTORY
 DEPARTMENT
400 Cathedral St. Phone: (301) 396-5430
Baltimore, MD 21201 Marva Belt, Hd.

FIDELITY & DEPOSIT COMPANY OF MARYLAND - LAW LIBRARY
724-725 Fidelity Bldg.
Box 1227 Phone: (301) 539-0800
Baltimore, MD 21203 Mary Teresa McHugh, Law Libn.

FLICKINGER FOUNDATION FOR AMERICAN STUDIES, INC. - LIBRARY
300 St. Dunstan's Rd. Phone: (301) 323-6284
Baltimore, MD 21212 B. Floyd Flickinger, Pres.

FRANK, BERNSTEIN, CONAWAY & GOLDMAN - LIBRARY
2 Hopkins Plaza, Suite 1300 Phone: (301) 547-0500
Baltimore, MD 21201 Nina Ogden, Libn.

GENERAL REFRACTORIES COMPANY - U.S. REFRACTORIES DIVISION -
 RESEARCH CENTER LIBRARY
Box 1673 Phone: (301) 355-3400
Baltimore, MD 21203 J.M. Castro, Libn.

GRAND LODGE OF ANCIENT FREE AND ACCEPTED MASONS OF MARYLAND -
 LIBRARY
225 N. Charles St. Phone: (301) 752-1198
Baltimore, MD 21201

GREATER BALTIMORE MEDICAL CENTER - DR. JOHN E. SAVAGE MEDICAL
 STAFF LIBRARY
6701 N. Charles St. Phone: (301) 828-2530
Baltimore, MD 21204 Michael Houck, Libn.

HEALTH AND WELFARE COUNCIL OF CENTRAL MARYLAND, INC. - STAFF
 REFERENCE LIBRARY
22 Light St. Phone: (301) 752-4146
Baltimore, MD 21202 Beverly G. Rubenstein, Libn.

INSECT CONTROL AND RESEARCH, INC. - LIBRARY
1330 Dillon Heights Ave. Phone: (301) 747-4500
Baltimore, MD 21228 Dr. Eugene J. Gerberg, Pres.

JOHNS HOPKINS HOSPITAL - DEPARTMENT OF RADIOLOGY - LIBRARY
601 N. Broadway Phone: (301) 955-6029
Baltimore, MD 21205 Elaine Pinkney, Libn.

JOHNS HOPKINS UNIVERSITY - CENTER FOR METROPOLITAN PLANNING
 AND RESEARCH - LIBRARY
Shriver Hall Phone: (301) 338-7169
Baltimore, MD 21218 Deniz Bilgin

JOHNS HOPKINS UNIVERSITY - DEPARTMENT OF EARTH AND PLANETARY
 SCIENCES - SINGEWALD READING ROOM
  Phone: (301) 366-3300
Baltimore, MD 21218 Dr. George W. Fisher, Professor

JOHNS HOPKINS UNIVERSITY - FERDINAND HAMBURGER, JR. ARCHIVES
3400 North Charles St. Phone: (301) 338-8323
Baltimore, MD 21218 Julia B. Morgan, Archv.

JOHNS HOPKINS UNIVERSITY - JOHN WORK GARRETT LIBRARY
Evergreen House, 4545 N. Charles St. Phone: (301) 338-7641
Baltimore, MD 21218 Jane Katz, Asst.Libn.

JOHNS HOPKINS UNIVERSITY - MILTON S. EISENHOWER LIBRARY -
 GOVERNMENT PUBN./MAPS/LAW LIBRARY
Charles & 34th Sts. Phone: (301) 338-8360
Baltimore, MD 21218 Diane K. Harvey, Libn.

JOHNS HOPKINS UNIVERSITY - POPULATION INFORMATION PROGRAM
624 N. Broadway Phone: (301) 955-8200
Baltimore, MD 21205 Dr. Phyllis T. Piotrow, Dir.

JOHNS HOPKINS UNIVERSITY - RESEARCH & DEVELOPMENT CENTER -
 CENTER FOR SOCIAL ORGANIZATION OF SCHOOLS
3505 N. Charles St. Phone: (301) 338-7570
Baltimore, MD 21218 John H. Hollifield, Asst.Dir.

JOHNS HOPKINS UNIVERSITY - SCHOOL OF HYGIENE AND PUBLIC HEALTH
 - INTERDEPARTMENTAL LIBRARY
615 N. Wolfe St. Phone: (301) 955-3028
Baltimore, MD 21205 Edward S. Terry, Dir.

JOHNS HOPKINS UNIVERSITY-SCHOOL OF HYGIENE & PUBLIC HEALTH-
 MATERNAL & CHILD HEALTH/POPULATION DYNAMICS LIB.
615 N. Wolfe St. Phone: (301) 955-3573
Baltimore, MD 21205 Linda Knarr, Libn.

JOHNS HOPKINS UNIVERSITY - SCHOOL OF MEDICINE - DEPARTMENT OF
 PEDIATRICS - BAETJER MEMORIAL LIBRARY
CMSC 2-104 Johns Hopkins Hospital Phone: (301) 955-3124
Baltimore, MD 21205 Judith Rosenberg, Libn.

JOHNS HOPKINS UNIVERSITY - SCHOOL OF MEDICINE - JOSEPH L.
 LILIENTHAL LIBRARY
Blalock Bldg., 10th Fl.
601 N. Broadway Phone: (301) 955-6641
Baltimore, MD 21205 Robin A. Kroft, Libn.

JOHNS HOPKINS UNIVERSITY - WILLIAM H. WELCH MEDICAL LIBRARY
1900 E. Monument St. Phone: (301) 955-3411
Baltimore, MD 21205 Richard A. Polacsek, M.D., Dir./Libn.

JOHNS HOPKINS UNIVERSITY - WILMER OPHTHALMOLOGICAL INSTITUTE
 - JONAS S. FRIEDENWALD LIBRARY †
Johns Hopkins Hospital
601 N. Broadway Phone: (301) 955-3127
Baltimore, MD 21205 Maria Tama Maggio, Lib.Techn.

KENNEDY (John F.) INSTITUTE - INTERDISCIPLINARY MULTI-MEDIA
 LIBRARY †
707 North Broadway Phone: (301) 955-4240
Baltimore, MD 21205

LIBRARY COMPANY OF THE BALTIMORE BAR - LIBRARY
618 Court House West Phone: (301) 727-0280
Baltimore, MD 21202 Kai-Yun Chiu, Law Libn.

LUTHERAN HOSPITAL OF MARYLAND - CHARLES G. REIGNER MEDICAL
 LIBRARY
730 Ashburton St. Phone: (301) 945-1600
Baltimore, MD 21216 Sharon Morris, Hd.Libn.

MARTIN MARIETTA LABORATORIES - LIBRARY
1450 S. Rolling Rd. Phone: (301) 247-0700
Baltimore, MD 21227 Rosalind P. Cheslock, Mgr.Info./Lib.Serv.

MARYLAND GENERAL HOSPITAL - MEDICAL STAFF LIBRARY †
827 Linden Ave. Phone: (301) 728-7900
Baltimore, MD 21201 Frances Gerber, Supv.

MARYLAND HISTORICAL SOCIETY - LIBRARY
201 W. Monument St.   Phone: (301) 685-3750
Baltimore, MD 21201   William B. Keller, Hd.Libn.

MARYLAND INSTITUTE, COLLEGE OF ART - DECKER LIBRARY
1400 Cathedral St.   Phone: (301) 669-9200
Baltimore, MD 21201   John Stoneham, Libn.

MARYLAND PHARMACEUTICAL ASSOCIATION - LIBRARY
Kelly Memorial Bldg.
650 W. Lombard St.   Phone: (301) 727-0746
Baltimore, MD 21201   David A. Banta, Exec.Dir.

MARYLAND STATE DEPARTMENT OF EDUCATION - DIVISION OF LIBRARY
    DEVELOPMENT & SERVICES - MEDIA SERVICES CENTER
200 W. Baltimore St.   Phone: (301) 659-2109
Baltimore, MD 21201   Elsie A. Leonard, Sect.Chf.

MARYLAND STATE DEPARTMENT OF HEALTH & MENTAL HYGIENE -
    LIBRARY †
201 W. Preston St.   Phone: (301) 383-2634
Baltimore, MD 21201   Yvette Dixon, Assoc.Libn.

MARYLAND STATE DEPARTMENT OF STATE PLANNING - LIBRARY
State Office Bldg., Rm. 1101
301 W. Preston St.   Phone: (301) 383-2439
Baltimore, MD 21201   Edlea K. Jones, Libn.

MARYLAND STATE ENERGY OFFICE - LIBRARY
301 W. Preston St., Suite 903   Phone: (301) 383-6810
Baltimore, MD 21201   Belle Fry

MARYLAND STATE HIGHWAY ADMINISTRATION - LIBRARY
707 Calvert St.   Phone: (301) 659-1420
Baltimore, MD 21202   Ruby D. Weston, Libn.

MARYLAND STATE LAW DEPARTMENT - ATTORNEY GENERAL'S OFFICE -
    LIBRARY
1 S. Calvert St., 13th Fl.   Phone: (301) 659-4093
Baltimore, MD 21202   Natalie S. Paymer, Libn.

MEDICAL AND CHIRURGICAL FACULTY OF THE STATE OF MARYLAND -
    LIBRARY
1211 Cathedral St.   Phone: (301) 539-0872
Baltimore, MD 21201   Joseph E. Jensen, Libn.

MERCY HOSPITAL - MC GLANNAN MEMORIAL LIBRARY
301 St. Paul Pl.   Phone: (301) 727-5400
Baltimore, MD 21202   Eileen W. Gillis, Libn.

MERCY HOSPITAL, INC. - NURSING LIBRARY
301 St. Paul Pl.   Phone: (301) 332-9228
Baltimore, MD 21202   Dolores H. Kaisler, Libn.

NATIONAL INSTITUTE ON AGING - GERONTOLOGY RESEARCH CENTER
4940 Eastern Ave.   Phone: (301) 396-9403
Baltimore, MD 21224   Octavio Alvarez, Libn.

NATURAL HISTORY SOCIETY OF MARYLAND - LIBRARY
2643 N. Charles St.   Phone: (301) 235-6116
Baltimore, MD 21218   C. Haven Kolb, Sec.

NER ISRAEL RABBINICAL COLLEGE - LIBRARY
400 Mt. Wilson Lane   Phone: (301) 484-7200
Baltimore, MD 21208

NORTH CHARLES GENERAL HOSPITAL - MEDICAL STAFF LIBRARY *
2724 N. Charles St.   Phone: (301) 338-2306
Baltimore, MD 21218   Bertha J. Shub, Libn.

PEABODY CONSERVATORY OF MUSIC - LIBRARY
21 E. Mt. Vernon Pl.   Phone: (301) 837-0600
Baltimore, MD 21202   Edwin A. Quist, Libn.

PEALE MUSEUM - MUSEUM ARCHIVES
225 Holliday St.   Phone: (301) 396-3523
Baltimore, MD 21202   Dennis K. McDaniel, Dir.

PIPER & MARBURY - LAW LIBRARY
36 S. Charles St., Suite 1100   Phone: (301) 539-2530
Baltimore, MD 21201   Loretta O. Yaller, Libn.

PROVIDENT HOSPITAL - HEALTH SCIENCES LIBRARY
2600 Liberty Heights Ave.   Phone: (301) 225-2352
Baltimore, MD 21215   Lorene S. Pita, Libn.

REGIONAL PLANNING COUNCIL - LIBRARY
2225 N. Charles St.   Phone: (301) 383-5864
Baltimore, MD 21218   Irva B. Nachlas, Libn.

ST. AGNES HOSPITAL - L.P. GUNDRY HEALTH SCIENCES LIBRARY
Caton & Wilkens Aves.   Phone: (301) 368-7565
Baltimore, MD 21229   Joanne Sutt, Med.Libn.

SCM CORPORATION - GLIDDEN-PIGMENTS DIVISION - ADRIAN JOYCE
    WORKS RESEARCH CENTER LIBRARY
3901 Glidden Rd.   Phone: (301) 633-6400
Baltimore, MD 21226   Nancy Freeman, Libn.

SEMMES, BOWEN & SEMMES - LAW LIBRARY
10 Light St.   Phone: (301) 539-5040
Baltimore, MD 21202   Helen Y. Harris, Libn.

SINAI HOSPITAL OF BALTIMORE, INC. - EISENBERG MEDICAL STAFF
    LIBRARY
Belvedere & Greenspring   Phone: (301) 367-7800
Baltimore, MD 21215   Rita Matcher, Dir., Lib.Serv.

SOUTH BALTIMORE GENERAL HOSPITAL - MEDICAL LIBRARY
3001 S. Hanover St.   Phone: (301) 354-1000
Baltimore, MD 21230   Barbara J. Nunno, Med.Libn.

STEAMSHIP HISTORICAL SOCIETY OF AMERICA - LIBRARY
Univ. of Baltimore Library
1420 Maryland Ave.   Phone: (301) 659-3134
Baltimore, MD 21201   James Foster, Ref.Libn.

UNION MEMORIAL HOSPITAL - DR. JOHN M.T. FINNEY, JR. MEMORIAL
    MEDICAL LIBRARY *
201 E. University Pkwy.   Phone: (301) 235-7200
Baltimore, MD 21218   Rena Snyder, Chf.Med.Libn.

UNION MEMORIAL HOSPITAL - NURSING SCHOOL LIBRARY
3301 N. Calvert St.   Phone: (301) 235-7200
Baltimore, MD 21218   Carolyn M. Daugherty, Libn.

UNION TRUST COMPANY OF MARYLAND - LIBRARY
133301 Baltimore & St. Paul Sts.
Box 1077   Phone: (301) 332-5369
Baltimore, MD 21203   Edna Abramson, Libn.

UNITED METHODIST HISTORICAL SOCIETY - BALTIMORE ANNUAL
    CONFERENCE - LOVELY LANE MUSEUM LIBRARY
2200 St. Paul St.   Phone: (301) 889-4458
Baltimore, MD 21218   Rev. Edwin Schell, Exec.Sec./Libn.

U.S. DEPT. OF COMMERCE - INTERNATIONAL TRADE ADMINISTRATION -
    BALTIMORE DISTRICT OFFICE LIBRARY
415 U.S. Customhouse
Gay & Lombard Sts.   Phone: (301) 962-3560
Baltimore, MD 21202   Mary T. Conrad, Trade Spec.

U.S. NATL. PARK SERVICE - FORT MC HENRY NATL. MONUMENT - LIBRARY
End of Fort Ave.   Phone: (301) 962-4290
Baltimore, MD 21230   Paul E. Plamann, Hist.

U.S. PUBLIC HEALTH SERVICE HOSPITAL - MEDICAL LIBRARY
3100 Wyman Park Dr.   Phone: (301) 338-3571
Baltimore, MD 21211   Mary P. Cornwell, Chf.

U.S. SOCIAL SECURITY ADMINISTRATION - LIBRARY
6401 Security Blvd.
Altmeyer Bldg., Rm. 570   Phone: (301) 594-1650
Baltimore, MD 21235   Rowena S. Sadler, Chf., Lib.Serv. & Info.Br

GEOGRAPHIC

GEOGRAPHIC

U.S. VETERANS ADMINISTRATION (MD-Baltimore) - MEDICAL CENTER
LIBRARY SERVICE (142D)
3900 Loch Raven Blvd.   Phone: (301) 467-9932
Baltimore, MD 21218   Deborah A. Gustin, Chf., Lib.Serv.

UNIVERSITY OF BALTIMORE - BALTIMORE REGION INSTITUTIONAL
STUDIES CENTER (BRISC)
847 N. Howard St.   Phone: (301) 727-6350
Baltimore, MD 21201   Adele Newburger, Assoc.Dir.

UNIVERSITY OF BALTIMORE - LAW LIBRARY
1420 Maryland Ave.   Phone: (301) 727-6350
Baltimore, MD 21201   Emily Greenberg, Dir.

UNIVERSITY OF MARYLAND, BALTIMORE - HEALTH SCIENCES LIBRARY
111 S. Greene St.   Phone: (301) 528-7545
Baltimore, MD 21201   Cyril C.H. Feng, Libn.

UNIVERSITY OF MARYLAND, BALTIMORE - SCHOOL OF LAW - MARSHALL
LAW LIBRARY
20 N. Paca St.   Phone: (301) 528-7400
Baltimore, MD 21201   Barbara S. Gontrum, Dir.

WALTERS ART GALLERY - LIBRARY
600 N. Charles St.   Phone: (301) 547-9000
Baltimore, MD 21201   Muriel Toppan, Ref.Libn.

WEINBERG & GREEN, ATTORNEYS-AT-LAW - LIBRARY
100 S. Charles St.   Phone: (301) 332-8620
Baltimore, MD 21201   Sally J. Miles, Libn.

WESTERN ELECTRIC COMPANY, INC. - TECHNICAL LIBRARY
2500 Broening Hwy., Rm. 200   Phone: (301) 563-6373
Baltimore, MD 21224   Miss R.M. Sawaryn, Ref.Libn.

WESTINGHOUSE ELECTRIC CORPORATION - DEFENSE & ELECTRONIC
SYSTEMS CENTER - TECHNICAL INFORMATION CENTER
MS 1204, Box 1693   Phone: (301) 765-2858
Baltimore, MD 21203   Ruth R. McCullough, Supv.

U.S.D.A. - HUMAN NUTRITION INFORMATION SERVICES - FOOD AND
NUTRITION INFORMATION CENTER
10301 Baltimore Blvd.   Phone: (301) 344-3719
Beltsville, MD 20705   Robyn Frank, Chf.

U.S.D.A. - NATIONAL AGRICULTURAL LIBRARY
10301 Baltimore Blvd.   Phone: (301) 344-3755
Beltsville, MD 20705   Richard A. Farley, Adm.

U.S. NATL. PARK SERVICE - ASSATEAGUE ISLAND NATL. SEASHORE -
LIBRARY
Rte. 2, Box 294   Phone: (301) 641-1441
Berlin, MD 21811   Larry G. Points, Chf.Interp.

ARTHRITIS INFORMATION CLEARINGHOUSE
Capital Systems Group Inc.
Box 34427   Phone: (301) 881-9411
Bethesda, MD 20034   Renee Schick, Project Dir.

BOOZ, ALLEN APPLIED RESEARCH, INC. - LIBRARY
4330 East-West Hwy.   Phone: (301) 951-2786
Bethesda, MD 20014   Linda Dodson, Libn.

DITTBERNER ASSOCIATES, INC. - LIBRARY
4903 Auburn Ave.   Phone: (301) 652-8350
Bethesda, MD 20014   Ingrid C.D. Mayr, Libn.

ERIC PROCESSING AND REFERENCE FACILITY
4833 Rugby Ave., Suite 303   Phone: (301) 656-9723
Bethesda, MD 20014   Wesley T. Brandhorst, Dir.

INTERNATIONAL INSTITUTE FOR RESOURCE ECONOMICS - LIBRARY
6210 Massachusetts Ave.   Phone: (301) 229-6066
Bethesda, MD 20016

NATIONAL INSTITUTE OF ARTHRITIS, METABOLISM & DIGESTIVE
DISEASES - OFFICE OF HEALTH RESEARCH REPORTS
                                         Phone: (301) 496-3583
Bethesda, MD 20205   Betsy Singer, Chf.

NATIONAL LIBRARY OF MEDICINE
                                         Phone: (301) 496-6308
Bethesda, MD 20209   Martin M. Cummings, M.D., Dir.

SOCIETY OF AMERICAN FORESTERS - LIBRARY
5400 Grosvenor Ln.   Phone: (301) 897-8720
Bethesda, MD 20014   Philip V. Petersen, Dir. of Info.

U.S. ARMED FORCES RADIOBIOLOGY RESEARCH INSTITUTE (AFRRI) -
LIBRARY SERVICES
National Naval Medical Ctr., Bldg.42   Phone: (301) 295-0428
Bethesda, MD 20014   Nannette M. Pope, Hd., Lib.Serv.

U.S. ARMY CONCEPTS ANALYSIS AGENCY - LIBRARY
8120 Woodmont Ave.   Phone: (301) 295-1530
Bethesda, MD 20014   Louise A. LeTendre, Chf.Libn.

U.S. NATL. INSTITUTES OF HEALTH - DIVISION OF COMPUTER RESEARCH
& TECHNOLOGY - LIBRARY
9000 Bethesda Pike
Bldg. 12A, Rm. 3018   Phone: (301) 496-1658
Bethesda, MD 20205   Ellen M. Chu, Libn.

U.S. NATL. INSTITUTES OF HEALTH - LIBRARY
9000 Rockville Pike
Bldg. 10, Rm. 1L-25   Phone: (301) 496-2447
Bethesda, MD 20205   John Smart, Act.Chf., Lib.Br.

U.S. NAVY - DAVID W. TAYLOR NAVAL SHIP RESEARCH AND DEVELOPMENT
CENTER - LIBRARY DIVISION
Code 522   Phone: (202) 227-1309
Bethesda, MD 20084   Dr. Michael Dankewych, Libn.

U.S. NAVY - EDWARD RHODES STITT LIBRARY
National Naval Medical Ctr.   Phone: (202) 295-1184
Bethesda, MD 20014   Jerry Meyer, Adm.Libn.

U.S. NAVY - NAVAL MEDICAL RESEARCH INSTITUTE - INFORMATION
SERVICES BRANCH
National Naval Medical Ctr.   Phone: (202) 295-0060
Bethesda, MD 20014

U.S. NAVY - NAVAL SCHOOL OF HEALTH SCIENCES - LIBRARY
National Naval Medical Ctr.
Bethesda, MD 20014   Phyllis R. Blum, Libn.

EASTERN SHORE HOSPITAL CENTER - PROFESSIONAL LIBRARY
R.D. 1
Box 800   Phone: (301) 228-0800
Cambridge, MD 21613   Estella C. Clendaniel, Supv., Lib. & Files

SPRING GROVE HOSPITAL CENTER - SULZBACHER MEMORIAL LIBRARY †
Wade Ave., Isidore Tuerk Bldg.   Phone: (301) 455-7824
Catonsville, MD 21228   Charles H. Johnson, Supv. Of Lib.

UNIVERSITY OF MARYLAND - SCHOOL OF MEDICINE - DEPT. OF
PSYCHIATRY - HELEN C. TINGLEY MEMORIAL LIBRARY
Maryland Psychiatric Research Ctr.
Box 3235
Catonsville, MD 21228

PRINCE GEORGE'S GENERAL HOSPITAL & MEDICAL CENTER - SAUL
SCHWARTZBACH MEMORIAL LIBRARY
                                         Phone: (301) 341-2440
Cheverly, MD 20785   Eleanor Kleman, Med.Libn.

AUDUBON NATURALIST SOCIETY OF THE CENTRAL ATLANTIC STATES,
INC. - LIBRARY
8940 Jones Mill Rd.   Phone: (301) 652-9188
Chevy Chase, MD 20015

FAUCETT (Jack) ASSOCIATES - LIBRARY
5454 Wisconsin Ave., Suite 1100   Phone: (301) 657-8223
Chevy Chase, MD 20015   Robert J. Skarr, Libn.

OHR KODESH CONGREGATION - SISTERHOOD LIBRARY
8402 Freyman Dr.   Phone: (301) 589-3880
Chevy Chase, MD 20015   Tamar Joy Kahn, Libn.

COMMUNICATIONS SATELLITE CORPORATION - TECHNICAL LIBRARY
22300 Comsat Dr.   Phone: (301) 428-4512
Clarksburg, MD 20734   Wayne Smith, Libn.

MILBOURNE & TULL RESEARCH CENTER - LIBRARY
10605 Lakespring Way   Phone: (301) 628-2490
Cockeysville, MD 21030   Willis Clayton Tull, Jr., Libn.

UNITARIAN AND UNIVERSALIST GENEALOGICAL SOCIETY - LIBRARY
10605 Lakespring Way   Phone: (301) 628-2490
Cockeysville, MD 21030   Willis Clayton Tull, Jr., Libn.

AMERICAN CORRECTIONAL ASSOCIATION - LIBRARY
4321 Hartwick Rd., Suite L-208   Phone: (301) 699-7600
College Park, MD 20740   Diana Travisono, Res.

ASPHALT INSTITUTE - RESEARCH LIBRARY
Asphalt Institute Bldg.   Phone: (301) 927-0422
College Park, MD 20740   Charles A. Mayer, Lib.Cons.

INTERNATIONAL FORTEAN ORGANIZATION - INFO RESEARCH LIBRARY
7317 Baltimore Ave.   Phone: (301) 779-1873
College Park, MD 20740   Paul J. Willis, Archv.

UNIVERSITY OF MARYLAND, COLLEGE PARK - BUREAU OF GOVERNMENTAL
   RESEARCH - LIBRARY
Social Sciences Bldg., Rm. 1218   Phone: (301) 454-2506
College Park, MD 20742

UNIVERSITY OF MARYLAND, COLLEGE PARK - COLLEGE OF LIBRARY &
   INFORMATION SERVICES - LIBRARY
                                                    Phone: (301) 454-6003
College Park, MD 20742   William G. Wilson, Libn.

UNIVERSITY OF MARYLAND, COLLEGE PARK - COMPUTER SCIENCE
   CENTER - PROGRAM LIBRARY
                                                    Phone: (301) 454-4261
College Park, MD 20742   Barbara Rush, Program Libn.

UNIVERSITY OF MARYLAND, COLLEGE PARK - LIBRARIES - ARCHITECTURE
   LIBRARY
                                                    Phone: (301) 454-4316
College Park, MD 20742   Berna E. Neal, Libn.

UNIVERSITY OF MARYLAND, COLLEGE PARK - LIBRARIES - ARCHIVES AND
   MANUSCRIPTS DEPARTMENT
                                                    Phone: (301) 454-4020
College Park, MD 20740   Mary A. Boccaccio, Hd./Univ.Archv.

UNIVERSITY OF MARYLAND, COLLEGE PARK - LIBRARIES - ART LIBRARY
                                                    Phone: (301) 454-2065
College Park, MD 20742   Courtney A. Shaw, Libn.

UNIVERSITY OF MARYLAND, COLLEGE PARK - LIBRARIES - CHARLES E.
   WHITE MEMORIAL LIBRARY
                                                    Phone: (301) 454-2609
College Park, MD 20742   Elizabeth W. McElroy, Libn.

UNIVERSITY OF MARYLAND, COLLEGE PARK - LIBRARIES - EAST ASIA
   COLLECTION
                                                    Phone: (301) 454-5459
College Park, MD 20742   Frank Joseph Shulman, Libn.

UNIVERSITY OF MARYLAND, COLLEGE PARK - LIBRARIES - ENGINEERING &
   PHYSICAL SCIENCES LIBRARY
                                                    Phone: (301) 454-3037
College Park, MD 20742   Herbert N. Foerstel, Hd.Libn.

UNIVERSITY OF MARYLAND, COLLEGE PARK - LIBRARIES -
   KATHERINEANNE PORTER ROOM
                                                    Phone: (301) 454-4020
College Park, MD 20742

UNIVERSITY OF MARYLAND, COLLEGE PARK - LIBRARIES - MARYLAND AND
   RARE BOOK ROOM
McKeldin Library   Phone: (301) 454-3035
College Park, MD 20742   Suellen M. Towers, Hd. Marylandia Dept.

UNIVERSITY OF MARYLAND, COLLEGE PARK - LIBRARIES - MUSIC LIBRARY
                                                    Phone: (301) 454-3036
College Park, MD 20742   Neil Ratliff, Fine Arts Libn.

UNIVERSITY OF MARYLAND, COLLEGE PARK - LIBRARIES - MUSIC LIBRARY
   - INTERNATIONAL PIANO ARCHIVES AT MARYLAND
McKeldin Library
College Park, MD 20742

UNIVERSITY OF MARYLAND, COLLEGE PARK - LIBRARIES - WOMEN'S
   STUDIES PAMPHLET COLLECTION
Reference Department
McKeldin Library   Phone: (301) 454-4097
College Park, MD 20742   Susan Cardinale, Coord.

UNIVERSITY OF MARYLAND, COLLEGE PARK - M. LUCIA JAMES
   CURRICULUM LIBRARY
College of Education   Phone: (301) 454-5466
College Park, MD 20742   Dr. Charles Brand, Dir.

UNIVERSITY OF MARYLAND, COLLEGE PARK - U.S. INFORMATION CENTER
   FOR THE UNIVERSAL DECIMAL CLASSIFICATION
College of Library & Info.Serv.   Phone: (301) 454-3785
College Park, MD 20742   Hans H. Wellisch, Dir.

GRACE (W.R.) AND COMPANY - RESEARCH DIVISION LIBRARY
7379 Route 32   Phone: (301) 531-4269
Columbia, MD 21044   Jeanette S. Hamilton, Supv., Info.Ctr.

HITTMAN ASSOCIATES, INC. - TECHNICAL INFORMATION DEPARTMENT -
   LIBRARY
9190 Red Branch Rd.   Phone: (301) 730-7800
Columbia, MD 21045   Masako Doi, Libn.

URBAN WILDLIFE RESEARCH CENTER, INC. - LIBRARY
10921 Trotting Ridge Way   Phone: (301) 596-9111
Columbia, MD 21044   Louise E. Dove, Res.Asst.

ALLEGANY COUNTY CIRCUIT COURT - LIBRARY
Court House, Washington St.   Phone: (301) 722-5633
Cumberland, MD 21502   Wanda Keller, Libn.

MEMORIAL HOSPITAL - MEDICAL AND NURSING LIBRARY
Memorial Ave.   Phone: (301) 777-4027
Cumberland, MD 21502   Mary E. Courtney, Libn.

SACRED HEART HOSPITAL - HEALTH SCIENCE LIBRARY
900 Seton Dr.   Phone: (301) 759-5229
Cumberland, MD 21502   Sr. Martha, Libn.

MEMORIAL HOSPITAL - HEALTH SCIENCES LIBRARY
S. Washington St.   Phone: (301) 822-1000
Easton, MD 21601   Maureen Molter, Libn.

SMITHSONIAN INSTITUTION LIBRARIES - CHESAPEAKE BAY CENTER FOR
   ENVIRONMENTAL STUDIES - LIBRARY
R.R. 4, Box 622   Phone: (202) 261-4190
Edgewater, MD 21037   Mary Clare Gray, Chf.Libn.

NATIONAL FIRE ACADEMY - LIBRARY
16825 S. Seton Ave.   Phone: (301) 447-6771
Emmitsburg, MD 21727   Adele M. Chiesa, Chf., Lrng.Rsrcs.Ctr.

U.S. ARMY - FORT MEADE MUSEUM - LIBRARY
                                                    Phone: (301) 677-6966
Ft. George G. Meade, MD 20755   David C. Cole, Cur.

U.S. ARMY - LANGUAGE TRAINING FACILITY - LIBRARY *
Bldg. 393
USA Education Ctr.   Phone: (301) 677-7255
Fort George G. Meade, MD 20755   Jere R. Ossont, Chf.

U.S. VETERANS ADMINISTRATION (MD-Fort Howard) - HOSPITAL LIBRARY
                                                    Phone: (301) 477-1800
Fort Howard, MD 21052   JoAnn Cuadra, Med.Libn.

FREDERICK CANCER RESEARCH CENTER - SCIENTIFIC LIBRARY
Box B   Phone: (301) 663-7261
Frederick, MD 21701   Michele M. Sansbury, Mgr.

GEOGRAPHIC

GEOGRAPHIC

FREDERICK COUNTY LAW LIBRARY
Court House
Frederick, MD 21701
Phone: (301) 663-8300
Janet D. Rippeon, Law Libn.

FREDERICK COUNTY PLANNING AND ZONING COMMISSION - LIBRARY
Winchester Hall, E. Church St.
Frederick, MD 21701
Phone: (301) 694-1153
Theresa K. Alexander, Sec.

FREDERICK MEMORIAL HOSPITAL - WALTER F. PRIOR MEDICAL LIBRARY †
Park Place & W. 7th St.
Frederick, MD 21701
Phone: (301) 694-3459
Linda M. Caldwell, Med.Libn.

U.S. ARMY MEDICAL BIOENGINEERING RESEARCH & DEVELOPMENT LABORATORY - TECHNICAL REFERENCE LIBRARY
Fort Detrick, Bldg. 568
Frederick, MD 21701
Phone: (301) 663-2502
Edna M. Snyder, Libn.

U.S. ARMY MEDICAL RESEARCH INSTITUTE OF INFECTIOUS DISEASES - MEDICAL LIBRARY *
Fort Detrick
Frederick, MD 21701
Phone: (301) 663-2720
Ruth S. Janssen, Libn.

FROSTBURG STATE COLLEGE - LIBRARY
Frostburg, MD 21532
Phone: (301) 689-4396
John Zimmerman, Lib.Dir.

BECHTEL POWER CORPORATION - LIBRARY
15740 Shady Grove Rd.
Gaithersburg, MD 20760
Phone: (301) 258-3000
Carol A. Bell, Hd.Libn.

INTERNATIONAL ASSOCIATION OF CHIEFS OF POLICE - CENTER FOR LAW ENFORCEMENT RESEARCH
11 Firstfield Rd.
Gaithersburg, MD 20760

NATIONAL INVESTIGATIONS COMMITTEE ON AERIAL PHENOMENA - INFORMATION CENTER
One Bank St., Suite 307
Gaithersburg, MD 20760

REMAC INFORMATION CORPORATION - INFORMATION CENTER
1200 Quince Orchard Blvd.
Gaithersburg, MD 20760
Phone: (301) 948-4550

U.S. NATL. BUREAU OF STANDARDS - STANDARDS INFORMATION SERVICE
Rm. A168 Technology Bldg.
Gaithersburg, MD 20234
Phone: (301) 921-2587
Terrance N. Troy, Group Leader

AEROSPACE CORPORATION - GERMANTOWN LIBRARY
20030 Century Blvd.
Germantown, MD 20767
Phone: (301) 428-2740
Karen W. Newton, Libn.

FAIRCHILD INDUSTRIES - TECHNICAL INFORMATION SERVICE - LIBRARY
Sherman Fairchild Technology Ctr.
Germantown, MD 20767
Phone: (301) 428-6415
Hazel M. More, Tech.Libn.

U.S. NASA - GODDARD SPACE FLIGHT CENTER - LIBRARY †
Greenbelt, MD 20771
Phone: (301) 344-6244
Adelaide A. DelFrate, Hd., Lib.Br.

BROOK LANE PSYCHIATRIC CENTER - MEDICAL LIBRARY
Box 1945
Hagerstown, MD 21740
Phone: (301) 733-0330

MACK TRUCKS, INC. - TECHNICAL INFORMATION CENTER - ENGINEERING DIVISION LIBRARY
1999 Pennsylvania Ave.
Hagerstown, MD 21740
Phone: (301) 733-8308
E.E. Stout, Engr.Adm.Coord.

WASHINGTON COUNTY HOSPITAL - LIBRARY
King & Antietam Sts.
Hagerstown, MD 21740
Phone: (301) 797-2355
Denise Lupp, Lib.Serv.Coord.

WASHINGTON COUNTY LAW LIBRARY †
Court House
Hagerstown, MD 21740
Phone: (301) 791-3115
Arthur J. Campbell, Jr., Libn.

WASHINGTON COUNTY MUSEUM OF FINE ARTS - LIBRARY
City Park, Box 423
Hagerstown, MD 21740
Phone: (301) 739-5727
Dixie Lee Washington, Exec.Sec.

MC CORMICK & CO. - R & D INFORMATION CENTER
204 Wight Ave.
Hunt Valley, MD 21031
Phone: (301) 667-7485
Merle I. Eiss, Supv.

DE SALES HALL SCHOOL OF THEOLOGY - LIBRARY *
5001 Eastern Ave.
Hyattsville, MD 20782
Phone: (301) 559-4022
Ward E. Gongoll, Hd.Libn.

U.S. NAVY - NAVAL EXPLOSIVE ORDNANCE DISPOSAL TECHNOLOGY CENTER - TECHNICAL LIBRARY
Indian Head, MD 20640
Phone: (301) 743-4738
Bonnie D. Davis, Adm.Libn.

U.S. NAVY - NAVAL ORDNANCE STATION - TECHNICAL LIBRARY
Indian Head, MD 20640
Phone: (301) 743-4742
Susan Pratt, Lib.Techn.

CAPITAL SYSTEMS GROUP, INC. - LIBRARY
11301 Rockville Pike
Kensington, MD 20795
Phone: (301) 881-9400
William A. Creager, Pres.

CAPITOL INSTITUTION OF TECHNOLOGY - CAPITOL TECH LIBRARY
10335 Kensington Pkwy.
Kensington, MD 20795
Phone: (301) 933-2599
Patricia H. Wissinger, Libn.

LITTON BIONETICS, INC. - SCIENTIFIC LIBRARY
5516 Nicholson Lane
Kensington, MD 20795
Phone: (301) 881-5600
E.M. Henderson, Libn.

EPILEPSY FOUNDATION OF AMERICA - LIBRARY
4351 Garden City Pkwy.
Landover, MD 20785

PRINCE GEORGE'S COUNTY SCHOOLS - PROFESSIONAL LIBRARY
8437 Landover Rd.
Landover, MD 20785
Phone: (301) 773-9790
Joyce E. Meucci, Lib.Assoc.

WASHINGTON BIBLE COLLEGE/CAPITAL BIBLE SEMINARY - OYER MEMORIAL LIBRARY
6511 Princess Garden Pkwy.
Lanham, MD 20801
Phone: (301) 552-1400
Carol A. Watson, Dir. Of Lib.Serv.

JOHNS HOPKINS UNIVERSITY - APPLIED PHYSICS LABORATORY - CHEMICAL PROPULSION INFORMATION AGENCY
Johns Hopkins Rd.
Laurel, MD 20810
Phone: (301) 953-7100
Ronald D. Brown, Group Supv.

JOHNS HOPKINS UNIVERSITY - APPLIED PHYSICS LABORATORY - R.E. GIBSON LIBRARY
Johns Hopkins Rd.
Laurel, MD 20810
Phone: (301) 953-7100
Robert R. Kepple, Libn.

U.S. FISH & WILDLIFE SERVICE - PATUXENT WILDLIFE RESEARCH CENTER LIBRARY
Laurel, MD 20811
Phone: (301) 776-4880
Lynda Garrett, Libn.

WESTVACO CORPORATION - LAUREL RESEARCH LIBRARY
Johns Hopkins Rd.
Laurel, MD 20810
Phone: (301) 792-9100
Marie L. Uhlmann, Res.Libn.

GENEALOGICAL PERIODICALS LIBRARY
3 Lombardy Dr.
Middletown, MD 21769
Phone: (301) 371-6293
George Ely Russell, Genealogist

WILSON (Thomas) CENTER - MEDICAL AND PROFESSIONAL LIBRARY *
Mount Wilson Lane
Mount Wilson, MD 21112
Phone: (301) 486-7676
Helene W. Jeng, Libn.

ROSEWOOD CENTER - MEDICAL AND PROFESSIONAL LIBRARY
Owings Mills, MD 21117
Phone: (301) 363-0300
June M. Boardman, Supv., Lib./Files

U.S. NATL. MARINE FISHERIES SERVICE - NORTHEAST FISHERIES CENTER
- OXFORD LAB. LIBRARY
Phone: (301) 226-5193
Oxford, MD 21654   Susie K. Hines, Libn.

TWIRLY BIRDS ARCHIVE
2200 Rosecroft Blvd.   Phone: (301) 567-4407
Oxon Hill, MD 20022   John M. Slattery, Hist.

U.S. NAVY - NAVAL AIR TEST CENTER - NAVAL AIR STATION -
ENGINEERING & TECHNICAL LIBRARY
Bldg. 407   Phone: (301) 863-3686
Patuxent River, MD 20670   Suzanne M. Ryder, Supv.Libn.

U.S. NAVY - NAVAL TEST PILOT SCHOOL - RESEARCH LIBRARY
Naval Air Test Ctr.   Phone: (301) 863-4411
Patuxent River, MD 20670   Robert B. Richards, Hd. of Academics

U.S. VETERANS ADMINISTRATION (MD-Perry Point) - HOSPITAL MEDICAL
LIBRARY
Phone: (301) 642-2411
Perry Point, MD 21902   Mr. Lynn F. Delozier, Chf.Libn.

LUNDEBERG MARYLAND SEAMANSHIP SCHOOL - LIBRARY
Phone: (301) 994-0010
Piney Point, MD 20674   Janice McAteer Smolek, Act.Dir./Lib.Serv.

BALTIMORE COUNTY GENERAL HOSPITAL - HEALTH SCIENCES LIBRARY
5401 Old Court Rd.   Phone: (301) 922-5700
Randallstown, MD 21133   Bettie S. Holmes, Libn.

AMERICAN OCCUPATIONAL THERAPY ASSOCIATION - REFERENCE
LIBRARY
1383 Piccard Dr.   Phone: (301) 770-2200
Rockville, MD 20850   Amy R. Bridgman, Libn.

AMERICAN TYPE CULTURE COLLECTION - LIBRARY
12301 Parklawn Dr.   Phone: (301) 881-2600
Rockville, MD 20852   Mary Jane Gantt, Info.Sci.

ASPEN SYSTEMS CORPORATION - LAW LIBRARY & INFORMATION CENTER
1600 Research Blvd.   Phone: (301) 251-5000
Rockville, MD 20850   Judy Meadows, Info.Mgr.

EG&G, INC. - WASHINGTON ANALYTICAL SERVICES CENTER -
INFORMATION CENTER
2150 Fields Rd.   Phone: (301) 840-3243
Rockville, MD 20850   Vanessa R.L. Schroader, Mgr.

FOI SERVICES, INC. - LIBRARY
12315 Wilkins Ave.   Phone: (301) 881-0410
Rockville, MD 20852   John E. Carey, Gen.Mgr.

FRANKLIN RESEARCH CENTER - NATIONAL SOLAR HEATING & COOLING
INFO. CTR.
Box 1607   Phone: (800) 523-2929
Rockville, MD 20850   Ken Bordner, Dir.

GEOMET TECHNOLOGIES INC. - INFORMATION CENTER
1801 Research Blvd., 5th Fl.   Phone: (301) 770-1500
Rockville, MD 20850   Vickilyn Gigante, Dir., Info.Sci.

GILLETTE MEDICAL EVALUATION LABORATORIES - INFORMATION CENTER
1413 Research Blvd.   Phone: (301) 424-2000
Rockville, MD 20850   Patrick J. Dexter, Info.Serv.Supv.

GILLETTE RESEARCH INSTITUTE - TECHNICAL LIBRARY
1413 Research Blvd.   Phone: (301) 424-2000
Rockville, MD 20850   Art Gamson, Libn.

INFORMATICS INC. - ISG LIBRARY
6011 Executive Blvd.   Phone: (301) 770-3000
Rockville, MD 20852   Judy C. Huffman, Libn.

INTERNATIONAL HIBERNATION SOCIETY
300 Dean Dr.
Rockville, MD 20851   Dr. Richard C. Simmonds, Exec.Sec.

JEWISH COMMUNITY CENTER OF GREATER WASHINGTON - KASS JUDAIC
LIBRARY
6125 Montrose Rd.   Phone: (301) 881-0100
Rockville, MD 20852   T.K. Feldman, Dir., Literary Arts Dept.

KING RESEARCH, INC. - CENTER FOR QUANTITATIVE SCIENCES - LIBRARY
6000 Executive Blvd.   Phone: (301) 881-6766
Rockville, MD 20852   Mary K. Yates, Libn.

MONTGOMERY COUNTY CIRCUIT COURT - LAW LIBRARY
Courthouse, 27 Courthouse Sq., 4th Fl.   Phone: (301) 279-8293
Rockville, MD 20850   Karen S. Lockard, Law Libn.

MONTGOMERY COUNTY HISTORICAL SOCIETY - LIBRARY
103 W. Montgomery Ave.   Phone: (301) 762-1492
Rockville, MD 20850   Jane C. Sween, Libn.

MONTGOMERY COUNTY PUBLIC SCHOOLS - PROFESSIONAL LIBRARY
850 N. Hungerford Dr.   Phone: (301) 279-3227
Rockville, MD 20850   Karen Dowling, Curric.Libn.

NATIONAL CLEARINGHOUSE FOR ALCOHOL INFORMATION - LIBRARY
Box 2345   Phone: (301) 468-2600
Rockville, MD 20852   Wendy Jhabvala, Dir.

NATIONAL CLEARINGHOUSE FOR FAMILY PLANNING INFORMATION
Box 2225   Phone: (301) 881-9400
Rockville, MD 20852   Anita P. Cowan, Dir.

NATIONAL CLEARINGHOUSE FOR MENTAL HEALTH INFORMATION
5600 Fishers Lane, Rm. 11A-33   Phone: (301) 443-4517
Rockville, MD 20857   Sylvaine L. Kenyon, Chf.

NATIONAL INSTITUTE ON DRUG ABUSE - RESOURCE CENTER
5600 Fishers Lane, Rm. 10A   Phone: (301) 443-6614
Rockville, MD 20857   Ilse Vada, Libn.

NUS CORPORATION - LIBRARY
4 Research Pl.   Phone: (301) 948-7010
Rockville, MD 20850   Jo Ann Merchant, Hd.Libn.

OFFICE ON SMOKING AND HEALTH - TECHNICAL INFORMATION CENTER
Park Bldg., Rm. 1-16
5600 Fishers Lane   Phone: (301) 443-1690
Rockville, MD 20857   Donald R. Shopland, Tech.Info.Off.

SMITHSONIAN INSTITUTION LIBRARIES - RADIATION BIOLOGY BRANCH
LIBRARY
12441 Parklawn Dr.   Phone: (301) 443-2307
Rockville, MD 20852   Mary Clare Gray, Libn.

TRACOR JITCO, INC. - RESEARCH RESOURCES INFORMATION CENTER
1776 E. Jefferson St.   Phone: (301) 881-4150
Rockville, MD 20852   Edward Post, Dir.

U.S. BUREAU OF ALCOHOL, TOBACCO AND FIREARMS - NATIONAL
LABORATORY LIBRARY
1401 Research Blvd.   Phone: (301) 443-1195
Rockville, MD 20850   Janet R. Damon, Libn.

U.S. DEPT. OF JUSTICE - NATIONAL INSTITUTE OF JUSTICE - NATL.
CRIMINAL JUSTICE REF. SERVICE
Box 6000   Phone: (202) 251-5500
Rockville, MD 20850   Georgette Semick, Prog.Dir.

U.S. FOOD & DRUG ADMINISTRATION - BUREAU OF DRUGS - MEDICAL
LIBRARY HFD-630 †
5600 Fishers Lane, Room 11B-07   Phone: (301) 443-3180
Rockville, MD 20857   Elizabeth C. Kelly, Dir., Med.Lib.

U.S. FOOD & DRUG ADMINISTRATION - BUREAU OF RADIOLOGICAL HEALTH
- LIBRARY
12720 Twinbrook Pkwy.   Phone: (301) 443-1038
Rockville, MD 20857   Mary G. Berkey, Libn.

U.S. FOOD & DRUG ADMINISTRATION - NATL. CLEARINGHOUSE FOR
POISON CONTROL CENTERS
5600 Fishers Lane   Phone: (301) 443-6260
Rockville, MD 20857   Mark I. Fow, Act.Dir.

GEOGRAPHIC

U.S. NATL. INSTITUTE FOR OCCUPATIONAL SAFETY AND HEALTH - REFERENCE ROOM
5600 Fishers Ln., Mail Stop 8A-29
Rockville, MD 20852

U.S. NATL. OCEANIC & ATMOSPHERIC ADMINISTRATION - LIBRARY AND INFORMATION SERVICES DIVISION
6009 Executive Blvd.　　　Phone: (301) 443-8287
Rockville, MD 20852　　Elizabeth J. Yeates, Chf., LISD

U.S. NATL. OCEANIC & ATMOSPHERIC ADM. - NATL. OCEAN SURVEY - PHYSICAL SCIENCE SERVICES BRANCH - MAP LIB.
Washington Science Ctr.　　Phone: (301) 443-8031
Rockville, MD 20852　　William A. Stanley, Chf.

U.S. PUBLIC HEALTH SERVICE - NATIONAL INSTITUTE OF MENTAL HEALTH - COMMUNICATION CENTER - LIBRARY
Parklawn Bldg., Rm. 15C-05
5600 Fishers Lane
Rockville, MD 20857　　Phone: (301) 443-4507
Angela Sirrocco, Chief

U.S. PUBLIC HEALTH SERVICE - PARKLAWN HEALTH LIBRARY
5600 Fishers Ln.　　　Phone: (301) 443-2673
Rockville, MD 20857　　Arthur L. Carrol, Lib.Dir.

CHESAPEAKE BAY MARITIME MUSEUM - LIBRARY
Box 636　　　Phone: (301) 745-2916
St. Michaels, MD 21663　Mary Ruth Robertson, Libn.

SALISBURY STATE COLLEGE - BLACKWELL LIBRARY
　　　Phone: (301) 546-3261
Salisbury, MD 21801　　James R. Thrash, Dir.

U.S. NATL. PARK SERVICE - ANTIETAM NATL. BATTLEFIELD - VISITOR CENTER LIBRARY
Box 158　　　Phone: (301) 432-5124
Sharpsburg, MD 21782　Betty J. Otto, Libn./Cur.

AMERICANS UNITED FOR SEPARATION OF CHURCH AND STATE - ARCHIVES
8120 Fenton St.　　　Phone: (301) 589-3707
Silver Spring, MD 20910　Morgan Dukes, Dir.Gen.Serv.

AUTOMATION INDUSTRIES, INC. - VITRO LABORATORIES DIVISION - ADMINISTRATIVE SUPPORT DEPARTMENT
14000 Georgia Ave.　　　Phone: (301) 871-4258
Silver Spring, MD 20910　Anthony Ciaravino, Dept.Hd.

COMPUTER SCIENCES CORPORATION - SYSTEMS SCIENCES DIVISION - TECHNICAL INFORMATION CENTER
8728 Colesville Rd.　　　Phone: (301) 589-1545
Silver Spring, MD 20910　Tenna Smelkinson, Mgr.

HOLY CROSS HOSPITAL OF SILVER SPRING - MEDICAL LIBRARY
1500 Forest Glen Road　　Phone: (301) 565-1211
Silver Spring, MD 20910　Bernetta Payne, Libn.

INDUSTRIAL UNION OF MARINE AND SHIPBUILDING WORKERS OF AMERICA - RESEARCH LIBRARY †
8121 Georgia Ave.　　　Phone: (301) 589-8820
Silver Spring, MD 20910

INSTITUTE FOR BEHAVIORAL RESEARCH - LIBRARY
2429 Linden Ln.　　　Phone: (301) 585-3915
Silver Spring, MD 20910　Ken Williams, Libn.

INTERNATIONAL FABRICARE INSTITUTE - RESEARCH CENTER LIBRARY
12251 Tech Rd.　　　Phone: (301) 622-1900
Silver Spring, MD 20904　Joe Salama

MARYLAND NATIONAL CAPITAL PARK AND PLANNING COMMISSION - LIBRARY
8787 Georgia Ave.　　　Phone: (301) 565-7507
Silver Spring, MD 20907　Janice C. Holt, Hd.Libn.

MASONIC SERVICE ASSOCIATION OF THE UNITED STATES - LIBRARY
8120 Fenton St.　　　Phone: (301) 588-4010
Silver Spring, MD 20910　Stewart M.L. Pollard, Exec.Sec.

NATIONAL CAPITAL HISTORICAL MUSEUM OF TRANSPORTATION - LIBRARY
Colesville Branch, Box 4007　Phone: (301) 384-9797
Silver Spring, MD 20904　Edmond Henderer, Libn.

NATIONAL MICROGRAPHICS ASSOCIATION - RESOURCE CENTER
8719 Colesville Rd.　　　Phone: (301) 587-8444
Silver Spring, MD 20910　Nila Zynjuk, Info.Coord.

NORTH AMERICAN TIDDLYWINKS ASSOCIATION - ARCHIVES
2701 Woodedge Rd.　　　Phone: (301) 933-3840
Silver Spring, MD 20906　Richard W. Tucker, Archv.

UNITED PRESBYTERIAN CHURCH OF THE ATONEMENT - LIBRARY
10613 Georgia Ave.　　　Phone: (301) 649-4131
Silver Spring, MD 20902　Ada P. Jorgensen, Libn.

U.S. NATL. INSTITUTES OF HEALTH - NATIONAL CANCER INSTITUTE - DIVISION OF CANCER TREATMENT - LIBRARY *
8300 Colesville Rd.　　　Phone: (301) 427-7477
Silver Spring, MD 20910　Eleanor Sloane, Supv.

U.S. NATL. OCEANIC & ATMOSPHERIC ADMINISTRATION - LIBRARY AND INFO. SERV. DIVISION - SILVER SPRING CENTER
8060 13th St.　　　Phone: (301) 427-7800
Silver Spring, MD 20910

U.S. NAVY - NAVAL SURFACE WEAPONS CENTER - WHITE OAK LIBRARY
White Oak　　　Phone: (202) 394-1922
Silver Spring, MD 20910　Dr. J. Marshal Hughes, II, Act.Hd.

WASHINGTON THEOLOGICAL UNION - LIBRARY
9001 New Hampshire Ave.　Phone: (301) 439-0551
Silver Spring, MD 20910　Mary M. Klein, Libn.

CALVERT MARINE MUSEUM - LIBRARY
Box 97　　　Phone: (301) 326-3719
Solomons, MD 20688　Ralph Eshelman, Dir.

U.S. BUREAU OF THE CENSUS - LIBRARY & INFORMATION SERVICES BRANCH
Federal Bldg. No. 3　　　Phone: (301) 763-5040
Suitland, MD 20233　Betty Baxtresser, Chf.

SPRINGFIELD HOSPITAL CENTER - MEDICAL LIBRARY
　　　Phone: (301) 795-2100
Sykesville, MD 21784　Elizabeth D. Mercer, Libn.

COLUMBIA UNION COLLEGE - THEOFIELD G. WEIS LIBRARY
7600 Flower Ave.　　　Phone: (301) 270-9200
Takoma Park, MD 20012　Margaret J. Von Hake, Libn.

WASHINGTON ADVENTIST HOSPITAL - MEDICAL LIBRARY
7600 Carroll Ave.　　　Phone: (301) 891-5261
Takoma Park, MD 20012　Lorraine Sweetland, Libn./Supv.

TELEDYNE ENERGY SYSTEMS - LIBRARY
110 W. Timonium Rd.　　Phone: (301) 252-8220
Timonium, MD 21093　Cathy Layne, Libn.

BALTIMORE COUNTY CIRCUIT COURT - LAW LIBRARY
401 Bosley Ave.　　　Phone: (301) 494-3086
Towson, MD 21204　Douglas T. Skeen, Ct.Libn.

MARYLAND STATE GOVERNOR'S COMMISSION ON LAW ENFORCEMENT - LIBRARY
One Investment Pl., Suite 700
Towson, MD 21204

ST. JOSEPH HOSPITAL - OTTO C. BRANTIGAN MEDICAL LIBRARY
7620 York Rd.　　　Phone: (301) 337-1210
Towson, MD 21204　Sr. Francis Marie, Libn.

ST. JOSEPH HOSPITAL - SISTER MARY ALVINA NURSING LIBRARY
7620 York Rd.　　　Phone: (301) 337-1641
Towson, MD 21204　Mary Weihs, Libn.

TOWSON STATE UNIVERSITY - GERHARDT LIBRARY OF MUSICAL
  INFORMATION *
Towson State University   Phone: (301) 321-2839
Towson, MD 21204   Edwin L. Gerhardt, Cur.

TOWSON STATE UNIVERSITY - GERHARDT MARIMBA & XYLOPHONE
  COLLECTION
Towson State University   Phone: (301) 321-2839
Towson, MD 21204   Edwin L. Gerhardt, Cur.

PRINCE GEORGE'S COUNTY CIRCUIT COURT - LAW LIBRARY
Courthouse
Box 580   Phone: (301) 952-3438
Upper Marlboro, MD 20870   Pamela J. Gregory, Law Libn.

PRINCE GEORGE'S COUNTY MEMORIAL LIBRARY SYSTEM - PUBLIC
  DOCUMENTS REFERENCE LIBRARY
County Adm.Bldg., Rm. 2198   Phone: (301) 952-3904
Upper Marlboro, MD 20870   Marjorie M. Miller, Doc.Libn.

CARROLL COUNTY BAR LIBRARY
Court House
Westminster, MD 21157   Florence Steger, Libn.

CARROLL COUNTY FARM MUSEUM - LANDON BURNS MEMORIAL LIBRARY
500 S. Center St.   Phone: (301) 848-7775
Westminster, MD 21157   Cindy Hofferberth, Dir. of Musm.

MASSACHUSETTS

NEW ENGLAND DEPOSIT LIBRARY, INC.
135 Western Ave.   Phone: (617) 782-8441
Allston, MA 02134   Edward J. Sweny, Libn.

WHITTIER HOME ASSOCIATION - LIBRARY
86 Friend St.   Phone: (617) 388-1337
Amesbury, MA 01913   Frieda Marion, Cur.

AMHERST COLLEGE - SCIENCE LIBRARY
                                           Phone: (413) 542-2076
Amherst, MA 01002   Eleanor T. Brown, Hd.

AMHERST COLLEGE - SPECIAL COLLECTIONS DEPARTMENT AND ARCHIVES
                                           Phone: (413) 542-2299
Amherst, MA 01002   John Lancaster, Libn. & Archv.

JONES LIBRARY
43 Amity St.   Phone: (413) 256-0246
Amherst, MA 01002   Anne K. Williamson, Cur.

NATIONAL YIDDISH BOOK EXCHANGE, INC. - LIBRARY
Box 969   Phone: (413) 584-1142
Amherst, MA 01004   Aaron Lansky, Exec.Dir.

UNIVERSITY OF MASSACHUSETTS, AMHERST - LABOR RELATIONS &
  RESEARCH CENTER LIBRARY
Draper Hall   Phone: (413) 545-2884
Amherst, MA 01003   Janice Tausky, Libn.

UNIVERSITY OF MASSACHUSETTS, AMHERST - LIBRARY - DEPARTMENT
  OF ARCHIVES AND MANUSCRIPTS
                                           Phone: (413) 545-2780
Amherst, MA 01003   Katherine Emerson, Archv.

UNIVERSITY OF MASSACHUSETTS, AMHERST - MORRILL BIOLOGICAL &
  GEOLOGICAL SCIENCES LIBRARY
214 Morrill Science Ctr.   Phone: (413) 545-2674
Amherst, MA 01003   James L. Craig, Libn.

UNIVERSITY OF MASSACHUSETTS, AMHERST - PHYSICAL SCIENCES
  LIBRARY
Graduate Research Ctr.   Phone: (413) 545-1370
Amherst, MA 01003   Vlasta K. Greenbie, Libn.

ADDISON GALLERY OF AMERICAN ART - LIBRARY
Phillips Academy   Phone: (617) 475-7515
Andover, MA 01810

ANDOVER HISTORICAL SOCIETY - CAROLINE M. UNDERHILL RESEARCH
  LIBRARY
97 Main St.   Phone: (617) 475-2236
Andover, MA 01810   Marsha Rooney, Dir./Cur.

HEWLETT-PACKARD COMPANY - ANDOVER DIVISION LIBRARY
1776 Minuteman Rd.   Phone: (617) 687-1501
Andover, MA 01810   Carol Miller, Libn.

PEABODY (Robert S.) FOUNDATION FOR ARCHEOLOGY - LIBRARY
Phillips Academy   Phone: (617) 475-0248
Andover, MA 01810   Dr. Richard S. MacNeish, Dir.

PHILLIPS ACADEMY - OLIVER WENDELL HOLMES LIBRARY - SPECIAL
  COLLECTIONS
                                           Phone: (617) 475-3400
Andover, MA 01810   Lynne Robbins, Dir.

ASHLAND HISTORICAL SOCIETY - LIBRARY
Box 321   Phone: (617) 881-3075
Ashland, MA 01721   Cynthia C. Winterhalter, Cur.

STURDY MEMORIAL HOSPITAL - HEALTH SCIENCES LIBRARY
211 Park St.   Phone: (617) 222-5200
Attleboro, MA 02703   Juliet I. Mansfield, Libn.

FIRST CONGREGATIONAL CHURCH OF AUBURN - LIBRARY
128 Central St.   Phone: (617) 832-2845
Auburn, MA 01501   Mrs. Leroy H. LaPlante, Chm.

CENTER FOR ACTION ON ENDANGERED SPECIES, INC. - LIBRARY
175 W. Main St.   Phone: (617) 772-0445
Ayer, MA 01432   Phoebe Wray, Exec.Dir.

NASHOBA COMMUNITY HOSPITAL - MEDICAL LIBRARY
200 Groton Rd.   Phone: (617) 772-0200
Ayer, MA 01432   Edythe Salzman, Libn.

BABSON COLLEGE - HORN LIBRARY
                                           Phone: (617) 235-1200
Babson Park, MA 02157   James A. Boudreau, Dir.

STURGIS LIBRARY
Rte. 6A   Phone: (617) 362-6636
Barnstable, MA 02630   Susan R. Klein, Hd.Libn.

BAIRD CORPORATION - TECHNICAL LIBRARY
125 Middlesex Tpke.   Phone: (617) 276-6390
Bedford, MA 01730   Frances G. Greene, Libn.

GCA CORPORATION - TECHNOLOGY DIVISION - LIBRARY
213 Burlington Rd.   Phone: (617) 275-5444
Bedford, MA 01730   Josephine Silvestro, Libn.

MILLIPORE CORPORATION - INFORMATION CENTER
Ashby Rd.   Phone: (617) 275-9200
Bedford, MA 01730   Leslie R. Jacobs, Libn.

MITRE CORPORATION - CORPORATE LIBRARY †
Box 208   Phone: (617) 271-7834
Bedford, MA 01730   Mary F. Leahy, Supv./Libn.

MITRE CORPORATION - TECHNICAL REPORT CENTER †
Box 208   Phone: (617) 271-2351
Bedford, MA 01730   Patricia J. McNulty, Supv.

RAYTHEON COMPANY - MISSILE SYSTEMS DIVISION - BEDFORD
  LABORATORIES - TECHNICAL INFORMATION CENTER
Hartwell Rd.   Phone: (617) 274-7100
Bedford, MA 01730   Lorraine Bick-Gregoire, Mgr.

U.S. AIR FORCE - AIR FORCE SYSTEMS COMMAND - AIR FORCE
  GEOPHYSICS LABORATORY - RESEARCH LIBRARY †
Hanscom Air Force Base   Phone: (617) 861-4895
Bedford, MA 01731   Evano L. Cunha, Chf.

U.S. VETERANS ADMINISTRATION (MA-Bedford) - HOSPITAL MEDICAL
  LIBRARY *
200 Springs Rd.   Phone: (617) 275-7500
Bedford, MA 01730

GEOGRAPHIC

GEOGRAPHIC

ARMENIAN LIBRARY AND MUSEUM OF AMERICA
Box 147
Belmont, MA 02178   Dr. Lucy Der Manuelian

BETH EL TEMPLE CENTER - CARL KALES MEMORIAL LIBRARY †
2 Concord Ave.   Phone: (617) 484-6668
Belmont, MA 02178

EARTHWATCH - LIBRARY
10 Juniper Rd.
Box 127   Phone: (617) 489-3030
Belmont, MA 02178   Brian Rosborough, Pres.

HABITAT INSTITUTE - ENVIRONMENTAL STUDIES LIBRARY
10 Juniper Rd.
Box 136   Phone: (617) 489-3850
Belmont, MA 02178   Elizabeth Howe, Prog.Dir.

INTERNATIONAL SOCIETY FOR PHILOSOPHICAL ENQUIRY - ARCHIVES
307 Pleasant St.   Phone: (617) 489-3170
Belmont, MA 02178   Robert J. Davis, Hist.

MC LEAN HOSPITAL - MEDICAL LIBRARY
                                        Phone: (617) 855-2460
Belmont, MA 02178   Hector Bossange, Dir.

BEVERLY HISTORICAL SOCIETY - LIBRARY AND ARCHIVES
Cabot House, 117 Cabot St.   Phone: (617) 922-1186
Beverly, MA 01915   John C. MacLean, Dir.

BEVERLY HOSPITAL - LIBRARY
Herrick St.   Phone: (617) 922-3000
Beverly, MA 01915   Margaret A. Firth, Libn.

VARIAN ASSOCIATES - RESEARCH LIBRARY
Salem Rd.   Phone: (617) 922-6000
Beverly, MA 01915   Katherine R. MacGregor, Libn.

CABOT CORPORATION - TECHNICAL INFORMATION CENTER
Concord Rd.   Phone: (617) 663-3455
Billerica, MA 01821   Hanna Friedenstein, Mgr.

AMERICAN CONGREGATIONAL ASSOCIATION - CONGREGATIONAL
  LIBRARY
14 Beacon St.   Phone: (617) 523-0470
Boston, MA 02108   Rev.Dr. Harold F. Worthley, Libn.

AMERICAN INSTITUTE OF MANAGEMENT - LIBRARY
607 Boylston St.   Phone: (617) 536-2503
Boston, MA 02116

AMERICAN METEOROLOGICAL SOCIETY - ABSTRACTS PROJECT - LIBRARY
45 Beacon St.   Phone: (617) 227-2425
Boston, MA 02108   Kenneth C. Spengler, Exec.Dir.

AMERICAN METEOROLOGICAL SOCIETY - BROOKS LIBRARY
45 Beacon St.   Phone: (617) 227-2425
Boston, MA 02108   Kenneth C. Spengler, Exec.Dir.

AMERICAN SOCIETY OF LAW & MEDICINE - SAGALL LIBRARY OF LAW,
  MEDICINE & HEALTH CARE
765 Commonwealth Ave., 16th Fl.   Phone: (617) 262-4990
Boston, MA 02215   A. Edward Doudera, J.D., Exec.Dir.

ANCIENT AND HONORABLE ARTILLERY COMPANY OF MASSACHUSETTS -
  LIBRARY
Faneuil Hall   Phone: (617) 227-1638
Boston, MA 02109   Lt.Col. Charles F. Hohr, Exec.Sec.

ANTHROPOLOGY RESOURCE CENTER (ARC) - CITIZENS INFORMATION
  CENTER
59 Temple Place, Suite 444   Phone: (617) 426-9286
Boston, MA 02111   Michael De Petrillo, Libn.

APPALACHIAN MOUNTAIN CLUB - LIBRARY
5 Joy St.   Phone: (617) 523-0636
Boston, MA 02108   C. Francis Belcher, Archv./Cons.

ART INSTITUTE OF BOSTON - LIBRARY
700 Beacon St.   Phone: (617) 262-1223
Boston, MA 02215   Susan M. Eisen, Libn.

ARTHUR ANDERSEN & CO. - LIBRARY
100 Federal St.   Phone: (617) 423-1400
Boston, MA 02110   Jean Fisher, Libn.

ASSOCIATED GRANTMAKERS OF MASSACHUSETTS, INC. -
  MASSACHUSETTS REGIONAL FOUNDATION LIBRARY
294 Washington St., Suite 501   Phone: (617) 426-2608
Boston, MA 02108   Philip Conley, Libn.

ASSOCIATED SYNAGOGUES OF MASSACHUSETTS - LIBRARY *
177 Tremont St.   Phone: (617) 426-1832
Boston, MA 02111   Rabbi Arnold Fine, Dir.

BERKLEE COLLEGE OF MUSIC - LIBRARY
1140 Boylston St.   Phone: (617) 266-1400
Boston, MA 02215   John Voigt, Libn.

BETH ISRAEL HOSPITAL - LASSOR AGOOS LIBRARY
330 Brookline Ave.   Phone: (617) 735-4225
Boston, MA 02215   Martha F. Cole, Libn.

BETTERLEY CONSULTING GROUP - TECHNICAL INFORMATION CENTER
200 Clarendon St.   Phone: (617) 267-4300
Boston, MA 02116   Kathleen Berggren

BINGHAM, DANA AND GOULD - LAW LIBRARY
100 Federal St.   Phone: (617) 357-9300
Boston, MA 02110   Patricia H. Kuba, Libn.

BOSTON ARCHITECTURAL CENTER - ALFRED SHAW AND EDWARD DURELL
  STONE LIBRARY
320 Newbury St.   Phone: (617) 536-9018
Boston, MA 02115   Susan Lewis, Hd.Libn.

BOSTON ATHENAEUM LIBRARY
10 1/2 Beacon St.   Phone: (617) 227-0270
Boston, MA 02108   Rodney Armstrong, Dir. & Libn.

(Boston) CENTRAL TRANSPORTATION PLANNING STAFF - LIBRARY
  SERVICES
27 School St., 2nd Fl.   Phone: (617) 523-3410
Boston, MA 02108   Ms. Toby Pearlstein, Libn.

BOSTON CITY HOSPITAL - MEDICAL LIBRARY
818 Harrison Ave.   Phone: (617) 424-4198
Boston, MA 02118   Lawrence Brenner, Sr.Med.Libn.

BOSTON CITY HOSPITAL - NURSING - MORSE-SLANGER LIBRARY
35 Northampton St.   Phone: (617) 424-4771
Boston, MA 02118   Jane Keating Latus, Hd.Libn.

BOSTON CONSERVATORY OF MUSIC - ALBERT ALPHIN MUSIC LIBRARY
8 The Fenway   Phone: (617) 536-6340
Boston, MA 02215   Cathy S. Balshone, Hd.Libn.

BOSTON GLOBE NEWSPAPER COMPANY - LIBRARY
135 Morrissey Blvd.   Phone: (617) 929-2540
Boston, MA 02107   Jennifer J. Chao, Libn.

BOSTON HERALD AMERICAN - REFERENCE LIBRARY
300 Harrison Ave.   Phone: (617) 426-3000
Boston, MA 02106   John Cronin, Chf.Libn.

(Boston) METROPOLITAN DISTRICT COMMISSION - LIBRARY
20 Somerset St.   Phone: (617) 727-5218
Boston, MA 02108   Albert A. Swanson, Archv.

BOSTON MUNICIPAL RESEARCH BUREAU - LIBRARY
294 Washington St.   Phone: (617) 482-3626
Boston, MA 02108   Harry M. Durning, Exec.Dir.

BOSTON PUBLIC LIBRARY - FINE ARTS DEPARTMENT
Copley Sq.
Box 286   Phone: (617) 536-5400
Boston, MA 02117   Florence Connolly, Cur.

BOSTON PUBLIC LIBRARY - GOVERNMENT DOCUMENTS, MICROTEXT,
  NEWSPAPERS
Copley Sq.
Box 286   Phone: (617) 536-5400
Boston, MA 02117   V. Lloyd Jameson, Div.Coord.

BOSTON PUBLIC LIBRARY - HUMANITIES REFERENCE
Copley Sq.
Box 286   Phone: (617) 536-5400
Boston, MA 02117   Raymond B. Agler, Coord.

BOSTON PUBLIC LIBRARY - KIRSTEIN BUSINESS BRANCH
20 City Hall Ave.   Phone: (617) 523-0860
Boston, MA 02108   Joseph E. Walsh, Bus.Br.Libn.

BOSTON PUBLIC LIBRARY - MUSIC DEPARTMENT
Copley Sq.
Box 286   Phone: (617) 536-5400
Boston, MA 02117   Ruth M. Bleecker, Cur. of Music

BOSTON PUBLIC LIBRARY - PRINTS
Copley Sq.
Box 286   Phone: (617) 536-5400
Boston, MA 02117   Sinclair H. Hitchings, Kpr. of Prints

BOSTON PUBLIC LIBRARY - RARE BOOKS AND MANUSCRIPTS
Copley Sq.
Box 286   Phone: (617) 536-5400
Boston, MA 02117   Dr. Laura V. Monti, Keeper

BOSTON PUBLIC LIBRARY - SCIENCE REFERENCE
Copley Sq.
Box 286   Phone: (617) 536-5400
Boston, MA 02117   Suzanne K. Gray, Coord.

BOSTON PUBLIC LIBRARY - SOCIAL SCIENCES
Copley Sq.
Box 286   Phone: (617) 536-5400
Boston, MA 02117   William R. Lewis, Coord.

BOSTON REDEVELOPMENT AUTHORITY - STAFF LIBRARY †
City Hall - 9th Fl.
One City Hall Sq.   Phone: (617) 722-4300
Boston, MA 02201   Pearl Hunt-McCain, Libn.

BOSTON SCHOOL COMMITTEE OF THE CITY OF BOSTON -
  ADMINISTRATION LIBRARY
26 Court St.   Phone: (617) 726-6449
Boston, MA 02108   Elizabeth F. Scannell

BOSTON STATE HOSPITAL - MEDICAL LIBRARY
591 Morton St.   Phone: (617) 436-6000
Boston, MA 02124   John B. Picott, Med.Libn.

BOSTON UNIVERSITY - AFRICAN STUDIES LIBRARY
771 Commonwealth Ave.   Phone: (617) 353-3726
Boston, MA 02215   Gretchen Walsh, Hd.

BOSTON UNIVERSITY - CHEMISTRY LIBRARY
685 Commonwealth Ave.   Phone: (617) 353-2537
Boston, MA 02215   Carlotta Crisp, Lib.Techn.

BOSTON UNIVERSITY - DEPARTMENT OF SPECIAL COLLECTIONS -
  NURSING ARCHIVES
771 Commonwealth Ave.   Phone: (617) 353-3696
Boston, MA 02215   Nancy L. Noel, Cur.

BOSTON UNIVERSITY - J. GORDON STRIPE, JR. PHYSICS LIBRARY
111 Cummington St.   Phone: (617) 353-2622
Boston, MA 02215   Hazel Agyemang, Supv.Lib.Asst.

BOSTON UNIVERSITY - KRASKER MEMORIAL FILM LIBRARY
765 Commonwealth Ave.   Phone: (617) 353-3272
Boston, MA 02215   Earl E. Adreani, Dir.

BOSTON UNIVERSITY - LUTZ MEMORIAL BIOLOGY LIBRARY
38 Cummington St.   Phone: (617) 353-3733
Boston, MA 02215   Steve Drenga, Supv.Lib.Asst.

BOSTON UNIVERSITY MEDICAL CENTER - ALUMNI MEDICAL LIBRARY
80 E. Concord St.   Phone: (617) 247-6187
Boston, MA 02118   Irene Christopher, Chf.Libn.

BOSTON UNIVERSITY - PAPPAS LAW LIBRARY
765 Commonwealth Ave.   Phone: (617) 353-3151
Boston, MA 02215   Robert L. Oakley, Dir.

BOSTON UNIVERSITY - SCHOOL OF THEOLOGY LIBRARY
745 Commonwealth Ave.   Phone: (617) 353-3034
Boston, MA 02215   William E. Zimpfer, Libn.

BOSTONIAN SOCIETY - LIBRARY
Old State House, 206 Washington St.   Phone: (617) 242-5614
Boston, MA 02109   Thomas W. Parker, Dir.

BOSTON'S MUSEUM OF TRANSPORTATION - LIBRARY
Museum Wharf
300 Congress St.   Phone: (617) 426-6633
Boston, MA 02210   Michele Order, Public Relations

BRIGHAM AND WOMEN'S HOSPITAL - ABRAMSON CENTER FOR
  INSTRUCTIONAL MEDIA
75 Francis St.   Phone: (617) 732-4075
Boston, MA 02115   Barbara R. Pollack, Dir., ACIM

BRIGHAM AND WOMEN'S HOSPITAL - PETER BENT BRIGHAM SCHOOL OF
  NURSING - LIBRARY
300 Brookline Ave.   Phone: (617) 732-5922
Boston, MA 02115   Ann B. Snyder, Libn.

CAMP DRESSER & MC KEE, INC. - HERMAN G. DRESSER LIBRARY
One Center Plaza   Phone: (617) 742-5151
Boston, MA 02108   Virginia Carroll, Libn.

CENTER FOR THE ANALYSIS OF HEALTH PRACTICES - LIBRARY
Harvard School of Public Health
677 Huntington Ave.   Phone: (617) 732-1060
Boston, MA 02115   Eleanor Druckman, Libn.

CHARLES RIVER ASSOCIATES, INC. - LIBRARY
Box 708   Phone: (617) 266-0500
Boston, MA 02117   Nancy Jandl, Tech.Info.Mgr.

CHILDREN'S MUSEUM - RESOURCE CENTER
Museum Wharf
300 Congress St.   Phone: (617) 426-6500
Boston, MA 02210   Caryl-Ann Feldman, Mgr., Rsrcs.Serv.

CHOATE, HALL AND STEWART - LAW LIBRARY
60 State St.   Phone: (617) 227-5020
Boston, MA 02109   Joy Plunket, Libn.

CHRISTIAN SCIENCE MONITOR - RESEARCH LIBRARY
One Norway St.   Phone: (617) 262-2300
Boston, MA 02115   Geoffrey Fingland, Libn.

COMMERCIAL UNION INSURANCE COMPANIES - RISK CONTROL
  TECHNICAL RESOURCE CENTER
One Beacon St.   Phone: (617) 786-2155
Boston, MA 02108   Margaret Preston, Tech.Res.Assoc.

CONGREGATION ADATH ISRAEL - LIBRARY
Longwood Ave. & The Riverway   Phone: (617) 566-3960
Boston, MA 02215   Elaine B. Wilton, Libn.

COOPERS AND LYBRAND - LIBRARY AND INFORMATION CENTER
100 Federal St.   Phone: (617) 423-4200
Boston, MA 02110   Susan J. Ackermann, Libn.

CRIME & JUSTICE FOUNDATION - MASCARELLO LIBRARY OF CRIMINAL
  JUSTICE
19 Temple Pl.   Phone: (617) 426-9800
Boston, MA 02111   Cynthia Brophy, Project Dir.

EARTHWORM, INC. - RECYCLING INFORMATION SERVICES
186 Lincoln St.   Phone: (617) 426-7344
Boston, MA 02111   Holly Gettings, Lib.Hd.

GEOGRAPHIC

EMERSON COLLEGE - ABBOT MEMORIAL LIBRARY
303 Berkeley St.   Phone: (617) 262-2010
Boston, MA 02116   Donna Tripp, Dir.

ENVIRONMENTAL PROTECTION AGENCY - REGION I LIBRARY
JFK Bldg., Rm. 2100-B   Phone: (617) 223-5791
Boston, MA 02203   Ruth K. Seidman, Libn.

FEDERAL RESERVE BANK OF BOSTON - LAW LIBRARY
600 Atlantic Ave.
Boston, MA 02106

FEDERAL RESERVE BANK OF BOSTON - RESEARCH LIBRARY †
600 Atlantic Ave., T-28   Phone: (617) 973-3393
Boston, MA 02210   Mary C. Vlantikas, Libn.

FIDELITY MANAGEMENT & RESEARCH COMPANY - LIBRARY
82 Devonshire St.   Phone: (617) 726-0293
Boston, MA 02109   Catharine Schoellkopf, Libn.

FIRST CHURCH OF CHRIST SCIENTIST - ARCHIVES AND LIBRARY
Christian Science Ctr.   Phone: (617) 262-2300
Boston, MA 02115   Lee Z. Johnson, Archv.

FIRST NATIONAL BANK OF BOSTON - LIBRARY
100 Federal St.   Phone: (617) 434-8440
Boston, MA 02110   Jane E. Gutowski, Libn.

FORSYTH DENTAL CENTER - PERCY HOWE MEMORIAL LIBRARY
140 The Fenway   Phone: (617) 262-5200
Boston, MA 02115   Roberta Oppenheim, Libn.

FRANKLIN INSTITUTE OF BOSTON - LIBRARY
41 Berkeley St.   Phone: (617) 423-4632
Boston, MA 02116   Bonnie L. Wilson, Libn.

FRENCH LIBRARY IN BOSTON, INC.
53 Marlborough St.   Phone: (617) 266-4351
Boston, MA 02116   Mylo Housen, Exec.Dir.

GARDNER (Isabella Stewart) MUSEUM, INC. - STAFF LIBRARY
2 Palace Rd.   Phone: (617) 566-1401
Boston, MA 02115

GENERAL THEOLOGICAL LIBRARY
14 Beacon St.   Phone: (617) 227-4557
Boston, MA 02108   Ruth Pragnell, Libn.

GILLETTE COMPANY - PERSONAL CARE DIVISION - INFORMATION CENTER
Box 2131   Phone: (617) 463-2800
Boston, MA 02106   M. McDonough, Asst.Libn.

GOETHE INSTITUTE BOSTON - LIBRARY
170 Beacon St.   Phone: (617) 262-6050
Boston, MA 02116   Dorothee Burney, Hd.Libn.

GOODWIN, PROCTER & HOAR - LAW LIBRARY
28 State St., 22nd Fl.   Phone: (617) 523-5700
Boston, MA 02109   Mary Jo Poburko, Hd.Libn.

GRAND LODGE OF MASSACHUSETTS, A.F. AND A.M. - LIBRARY
Masonic Temple, 186 Tremont St.   Phone: (617) 426-6040
Boston, MA 02111   Roberta A. Hankamer, Libn.

HALE AND DORR - LIBRARY
60 State St.   Phone: (617) 742-9100
Boston, MA 02109

HARVARD MUSICAL ASSOCIATION - LIBRARY
57A Chestnut St.   Phone: (617) 523-2897
Boston, MA 02108   Natalie Palme, Libn.

HARVARD UNIVERSITY - CENTER FOR POPULATION STUDIES LIBRARY
665 Huntington Ave.   Phone: (617) 732-1234
Boston, MA 02115   Wilma E. Winters, Libn.

HARVARD UNIVERSITY - GRADUATE SCHOOL OF BUSINESS
    ADMINISTRATION - BAKER LIBRARY
Soldiers Field Rd.   Phone: (617) 495-6395
Boston, MA 02163   Mary V. Chatfield, Libn.

HARVARD UNIVERSITY - SCHERING FOUNDATION LIBRARY OF HEALTH
    CARE
643 Huntington Ave.   Phone: (617) 732-2101
Boston, MA 02115   Anne Alach, Libn.

HARVARD UNIVERSITY - SCHOOL OF MEDICINE - LUCIEN HOWE LIBRARY
    OF OPHTHALMOLOGY †
243 Charles St.   Phone: (617) 523-7900
Boston, MA 02114   Charles Snyder, Libn.

HARVARD UNIVERSITY - SCHOOL OF PUBLIC HEALTH - HEALTH SERVICES
    LIBRARY †
677 Huntington Ave.   Phone: (617) 732-1146
Boston, MA 02115   Margaret A. Hewitt, Libn.

HARVARD UNIVERSITY - SCHOOLS OF MEDICINE, DENTAL MEDICINE AND
    PUBLIC HEALTH - FRANCIS A. COUNTWAY LIBRARY
10 Shattuck St.   Phone: (617) 732-2136
Boston, MA 02115   C. Robin LeSueur, Libn.

HERRICK AND SMITH - LAW LIBRARY
100 Federal St.   Phone: (617) 357-9000
Boston, MA 02110   Faith M. Lane, Libn.

HILL AND BARLOW - LIBRARY
225 Franklin St.   Phone: (617) 423-6200
Boston, MA 02110   Carol S. Wellington, Libn.

HOUGHTON MIFFLIN COMPANY - LIBRARY
One Beacon St.   Phone: (617) 725-5270
Boston, MA 02107   Guest Perry, Libn.

INSURANCE LIBRARY ASSOCIATION OF BOSTON
156 State St.   Phone: (617) 227-2087
Boston, MA 02109   Jean E. Lucey, Dir.

JENSEN ASSOCIATES, INC. - LIBRARY
84 State St.   Phone: (617) 227-8115
Boston, MA 02109   Janet C. Dwyer, Libn.

JOHN HANCOCK MUTUAL LIFE INSURANCE COMPANY - COMPANY LIBRARY
John Hancock Pl., Box 111   Phone: (617) 421-4524
Boston, MA 02117   Amy L. Wang, Libn.

JOSLIN DIABETES FOUNDATION, INC. - MEDICAL LIBRARY
One Joslin Pl.   Phone: (617) 723-9065
Boston, MA 02215   Mary P. Greene, Libn.

KEYSTONE CUSTODIAN FUNDS, INC. - LIBRARY
99 High St.   Phone: (617) 338-3435
Boston, MA 02104   Kathleen Young, Libn.

LIBERTY MUTUAL INSURANCE COMPANY - BUSINESS REFERENCE LIBRARY
175 Berkeley St.   Phone: (617) 357-9500
Boston, MA 02117   Ann M. McDonald, Dir.

LIBERTY MUTUAL INSURANCE COMPANY - LAW LIBRARY
175 Berkeley St.   Phone: (617) 357-9500
Boston, MA 02117   C.E. Procopio, Dir. of Law Libs.

LINDEMANN (Erich) MENTAL HEALTH CENTER - LIBRARY
25 Staniford St.   Phone: (617) 727-7280
Boston, MA 02114   Elizabeth Jones, Libn.

MAIN (Chas. T.), INC. - LIBRARY
Southeast Tower, Prudential Ctr.   Phone: (617) 262-3200
Boston, MA 02199   Hayden Mason, Libn.

MARINE PRODUCTS COMPANY - LIBRARY
333 W. First St.   Phone: (617) 268-0758
Boston, MA 02127   Dr. E. James Iorio, Mgr.

MASSACHUSETTS COLLEGE OF ART - LIBRARY
364 Brookline Ave.   Phone: (617) 731-2340
Boston, MA 02215   Benjamin Hopkins, Hd.Libn.

MASSACHUSETTS COLLEGE OF PHARMACY & ALLIED HEALTH SCIENCES -
    SHEPPARD LIBRARY
179 Longwood Ave.   Phone: (617) 732-2810
Boston, MA 02115   Barbara M. Hill, Libn.

MASSACHUSETTS FINANCIAL SERVICES - BUSINESS LIBRARY
200 Berkeley St.   Phone: (617) 423-3500
Boston, MA 02116

MASSACHUSETTS GENERAL HOSPITAL - SCHOOL OF NURSING - PALMER-
    DAVIS LIBRARY
40 Parkman St.
Boston, MA 02114

MASSACHUSETTS GENERAL HOSPITAL - TREADWELL AND PALMER-DAVIS
    LIBRARY
Fruit St.   Phone: (617) 726-8600
Boston, MA 02114   Jacqueline Bastille, Dir.

MASSACHUSETTS HISTORICAL SOCIETY - RESEARCH LIBRARY
1154 Boylston St.   Phone: (617) 536-1608
Boston, MA 02215   John D. Cushing, Libn.

MASSACHUSETTS HORTICULTURAL SOCIETY - LIBRARY
300 Massachusetts Ave.   Phone: (617) 536-9280
Boston, MA 02115   Judith Weinberg, Libn.

MASSACHUSETTS INSTITUTE OF TECHNOLOGY - NEUROSCIENCES
    RESEARCH PROGRAM - LIBRARY
165 Allandale   Phone: (617) 522-6700
Boston, MA 02130   George Adelman, Libn.

MASSACHUSETTS MENTAL HEALTH CENTER - CHARLES MAC FIE CAMPBELL
    MEMORIAL LIBRARY
74 Fenwood Rd.   Phone: (617) 734-1300
Boston, MA 02115   Alice H. Wolpert, Act.Libn.

MASSACHUSETTS MUNICIPAL ASSOCIATION - RESEARCH LIBRARY
131 Tremont St.   Phone: (617) 426-7272
Boston, MA 02111   James Segel, Exec.Dir.

MASSACHUSETTS REHABILITATION COMMISSION - LIBRARY
20 Providence St.   Phone: (617) 727-1140
Boston, MA 02116   June C. Holt, Libn.

MASSACHUSETTS STATE ARCHIVES DIVISION
55 State House   Phone: (617) 727-2816
Boston, MA 02133   Albert H. Whitaker, State Archv.

MASSACHUSETTS STATE BOARD OF LIBRARY COMMISSIONERS -
    REFERENCE AND RESEARCH LIBRARY
648 Beacon St.   Phone: (617) 267-9400
Boston, MA 02215   Roland Piggford, Act.Dir.

MASSACHUSETTS STATE DEPARTMENT OF THE ATTORNEY GENERAL -
    LIBRARY
McCormack Bldg., 20th Fl.
One Ashburton Pl.   Phone: (617) 727-1036
Boston, MA 02108   Ruth G. Matz, Chf.Libn.

MASSACHUSETTS STATE DEPARTMENT OF COMMERCE AND
    DEVELOPMENT - RESEARCH LIBRARY
100 Cambridge St.   Phone: (617) 727-3215
Boston, MA 02202   Adell Greene, Libn.

MASSACHUSETTS STATE DEPARTMENT OF COMMUNITY AFFAIRS -
    LIBRARY
100 Cambridge St.
Boston, MA 02202

MASSACHUSETTS STATE DEPARTMENT OF CORRECTION - CENTRAL
    OFFICE STAFF LIBRARY
State Office Bldg., 22nd Fl.
100 Cambridge St.   Phone: (617) 727-3312
Boston, MA 02202   Daniel P. LeClair, Res.Spec.

MASSACHUSETTS STATE DEPARTMENT OF EDUCATION - EDUCATIONAL
    REFERENCE CENTER †
31 St. James Ave.   Phone: (617) 727-5792
Boston, MA 02116

MASSACHUSETTS STATE DEPARTMENT OF LABOR & INDUSTRIES -
    REFERENCE LIBRARY
Leverett Saltonstall Bldg., Rm. 1101
100 Cambridge St.   Phone: (617) 727-3593
Boston, MA 02202   Claudia Kelly, Libn.

MASSACHUSETTS STATE DEPARTMENT OF PUBLIC HEALTH - CENTRAL
    LIBRARY
600 Washington St., Rm. 608   Phone: (617) 727-7170
Boston, MA 02111   Catherine Moore, Libn.

MASSACHUSETTS STATE DIVISION OF OCCUPATIONAL HYGIENE -
    SPECIAL TECHNICAL LIBRARY
39 Boylston St.   Phone: (617) 727-3982
Boston, MA 02116   Mary Lim, Libn.

MASSACHUSETTS STATE LIBRARY
341 State House   Phone: (617) 727-2590
Boston, MA 02133   James H. Fish, State Libn.

MASSACHUSETTS TAXPAYERS FOUNDATION, INC. - LIBRARY
One Federal St.   Phone: (617) 357-8500
Boston, MA 02110   Donald E. Buckholtz, Libn.

METCALF & EDDY, INC. - LIBRARY
50 Staniford St.   Phone: (617) 367-4087
Boston, MA 02114   Mary E. Lydon, Corp.Libn.

MINTZ, LEVIN, COHN, GLOVSKY AND POPEO - LAW LIBRARY *
One Center Plaza   Phone: (617) 742-5800
Boston, MA 02108

MUSEUM OF FINE ARTS - DEPARTMENT OF PHOTOGRAPHIC SERVICES -
    SLIDE & PHOTOGRAPH LIBRARY
465 Huntington Ave.   Phone: (617) 267-9300
Boston, MA 02115   Janice Sorkow, Mgr. Photographic Serv.

MUSEUM OF FINE ARTS - SCHOOL LIBRARY *
230 The Fenway   Phone: (617) 267-9300
Boston, MA 02115   Carol Bjork, Libn.

MUSEUM OF FINE ARTS - WILLIAM MORRIS HUNT MEMORIAL LIBRARY
465 Huntington Ave.   Phone: (617) 267-9300
Boston, MA 02115   Nancy S. Allen, Libn.

MUSEUM OF SCIENCE - LIBRARY
Science Pk.   Phone: (617) 723-2500
Boston, MA 02114   Edward D. Pearce, Libn.

NEW ENGLAND AQUARIUM - LIBRARY
Central Wharf   Phone: (617) 742-8830
Boston, MA 02110   Marilyn Murphy, Libn.

NEW ENGLAND BAPTIST HOSPITAL - MEDICAL STAFF LIBRARY
91 Parker Hill Ave.   Phone: (617) 738-5800
Boston, MA 02120   Dr. Paul E. Woodard, Chf.Libn.

NEW ENGLAND BAPTIST HOSPITAL - SCHOOL OF NURSING LIBRARY
220 Fisher Ave.   Phone: (617) 738-5800
Boston, MA 02120   Elizabeth Guiu, Libn.

NEW ENGLAND COLLEGE OF OPTOMETRY - LIBRARY
420 Beacon St.   Phone: (617) 266-2030
Boston, MA 02115   F. Eleanor Warner, Hd.Libn.

NEW ENGLAND CONSERVATORY OF MUSIC - HARRIET M. SPAULDING
    LIBRARY
33 Gainsborough St.   Phone: (617) 262-1120
Boston, MA 02115   Geraldine Ostrove, Dir.

NEW ENGLAND DEACONESS HOSPITAL - HORRAX LIBRARY
185 Pilgrim Rd.   Phone: (617) 732-8311
Boston, MA 02215   Paul Vaiginas, Libn.

NEW ENGLAND HISTORIC GENEALOGICAL SOCIETY - LIBRARY
101 Newbury St.   Phone: (617) 536-5740
Boston, MA 02116   Dr. James B. Bell, Dir.

NEW ENGLAND MERCHANTS NATIONAL BANK - LIBRARY
28 State St.   Phone: (617) 742-4000
Boston, MA 02106   Helen Mazareas, Libn.

NEW ENGLAND MUTUAL LIFE INSURANCE COMPANY - BUSINESS LIBRARY
501 Boylston St.   Phone: (617) 266-3700
Boston, MA 02117   Agnes Brite, Libn.

GEOGRAPHIC

GEOGRAPHIC

NEW ENGLAND NUCLEAR CORPORATION - TECHNICAL LIBRARY
549 Albany St.   Phone: (617) 482-9595
Boston, MA 02118   Pauline R. Leeds, Libn.

NEW ENGLAND REGIONAL COMMISSION (NERCOM) - REFERENCE LIBRARY
141 Milk St.   Phone: (617) 223-6380
Boston, MA 02109   Shirley M. Raynard, Ref.Libn.

NEW ENGLAND SCHOOL OF LAW - LIBRARY
126 Newbury St.   Phone: (617) 267-9655
Boston, MA 02116   Frank S.H. Bae, Law Libn.

NORTHEASTERN UNIVERSITY - LAW SCHOOL LIBRARY
400 Huntington Ave.   Phone: (617) 437-3338
Boston, MA 02115   Rajinder S. Walia, Law Libn.

PAN AMERICAN SOCIETY OF NEW ENGLAND - SHATTUCK LIBRARY *
75A Newbury St.   Phone: (617) 266-2248
Boston, MA 02116   Reid Andrews, Libn.

PAYETTE ASSOCIATES - LIBRARY
40 Isabella St.   Phone: (617) 423-0070
Boston, MA 02116   Sonja M. Nielsen, Corp.Libn.

PORTUGUESE CONTINENTAL UNION OF THE U.S.A. - LIBRARY
899 Boylston St.   Phone: (617) 536-2916
Boston, MA 02115   Francisco J. Mendonca, Supreme Sec.-Libn.

PRICE WATERHOUSE - INFORMATION CENTER
One Federal St.   Phone: (617) 423-7330
Boston, MA 02110   Jean M. Scanlan, Dir.

PROTESTANT EPISCOPAL CHURCH - EPISCOPAL DIOCESE OF
  MASSACHUSETTS - DIOCESAN LIBRARY AND ARCHIVES
1 Joy St.   Phone: (617) 742-4720
Boston, MA 02108   Robert L. Howie, Jr., Historiographer

PUTNAM COMPANIES - INVESTMENT RESEARCH LIBRARY
265 Franklin St.   Phone: (617) 423-4960
Boston, MA 02110   Mary H. Thomsen, Libn.

RELIGIOUS ARTS GUILD - MUSIC LIBRARY
25 Beacon St.   Phone: (617) 742-2100
Boston, MA 02108   Barbara M. Hutchins, Exec.Sec.

RETINA FOUNDATION - JOINT RESEARCH LIBRARY
20 Staniford St.   Phone: (617) 742-3140
Boston, MA 02114   Rose M. Miller, Libn.

ROPES & GRAY - CENTRAL LIBRARY
225 Franklin St.   Phone: (617) 423-6100
Boston, MA 02110   Cornelia Trubey, Libn.

SCUDDER, STEVENS & CLARK - LIBRARY
175 Federal St.   Phone: (617) 482-3990
Boston, MA 02110   Helen Doikos, Libn.

SHAWMUT BANK OF BOSTON, N.A. - LIBRARY
1 Federal St.
Box 2176   Phone: (617) 292-2296
Boston, MA 02106   Emilie Pugliano, Libn.

SIMMONS COLLEGE - SCHOOL OF LIBRARY SCIENCE - LIBRARY
300 The Fenway   Phone: (617) 738-2226
Boston, MA 02115   Michael Ann Moskowitz, Libn.

SIMMONS COLLEGE - SCHOOL OF SOCIAL WORK LIBRARY
51 Commonwealth Ave.   Phone: (617) 266-0806
Boston, MA 02116   Marilyn Smith Bregoli, Libn.

SOCIAL LAW LIBRARY
1200 Court House   Phone: (617) 523-0018
Boston, MA 02108   Edgar J. Bellefontaine, Libn.

SOCIETY FOR THE PRESERVATION OF NEW ENGLAND ANTIQUITIES -
  LIBRARY
141 Cambridge St.   Phone: (617) 227-3956
Boston, MA 02114   Elinor Reichlin, Libn.

STONE AND WEBSTER ENGINEERING CORPORATION - TECHNICAL
  INFORMATION CENTER
245 Summer St.   Phone: (617) 973-8891
Boston, MA 02110   Nancy M. Pellini, Mgr.

SUFFOLK UNIVERSITY - LAW LIBRARY
41 Temple St.   Phone: (617) 723-4700
Boston, MA 02152   Edward Bander, Law Libn.

SWEDENBORG LIBRARY AND BOOKSTORE
79 Newbury St.   Phone: (617) 262-5918
Boston, MA 02116   Rafael Guiu, Mgr.

THORNDIKE LIBRARY
1300 Court House   Phone: (617) 725-8078
Boston, MA 02108   Jean Roberts, Ed./Libn.

TUFTS UNIVERSITY - SCHOOLS OF MEDICINE, DENTAL MEDICINE &
  VETERINARY MEDICINE - HEALTH SCIENCES LIBRARY †
136 Harrison Ave.   Phone: (617) 956-6706
Boston, MA 02111   Edward P. Leavitt, Libn.

UNITARIAN-UNIVERSALIST ASSOCIATION - ARCHIVES
25 Beacon St.   Phone: (617) 742-2100
Boston, MA 02108   Carl Seaburg, Info.Off./Archv.

UNITED ENGINEERS & CONSTRUCTORS, INC. - BOSTON OFFICE - LIBRARY
100 Summer St.   Phone: (617) 338-6000
Boston, MA 02110   Esther Usher, Libn.

UNITED METHODIST CHURCH - SOUTHERN NEW ENGLAND CONFERENCE -
  HISTORICAL SOCIETY LIBRARY
745 Commonwealth Ave.   Phone: (617) 353-3034
Boston, MA 02215   William E. Zimpfer, Libn.

U.S. BUREAU OF THE CENSUS - REGIONAL DATA USER SERVICE - BOSTON
  REGIONAL OFFICE - LIBRARY
441 Stuart St., 10th Fl.   Phone: (617) 223-0668
Boston, MA 02116   Arthur G. Dukakis, Regional Dir.

U.S. COURT OF APPEALS, 1ST CIRCUIT - LIBRARY
1208 McCormack P.O. & Court House   Phone: (617) 223-2891
Boston, MA 02109   Karen M. Moss, Chf.Libn.

U.S. DEPT. OF COMMERCE - INTERNATIONAL TRADE ADMINISTRATION -
  BOSTON DISTRICT OFFICE LIBRARY
441 Stuart St., 10th Fl.   Phone: (617) 223-2381
Boston, MA 02116   Mary E. Lipinski

U.S. DEPT. OF HEALTH AND HUMAN SERVICES - REGION I INFORMATION
  CENTER
John F. Kennedy Bldg., Rm. 2411   Phone: (617) 223-7291
Boston, MA 02203   Robert A. Castricone, Info.Spec.

U.S. DEPT. OF HOUSING AND URBAN DEVELOPMENT - REGION I - LIBRARY
J.F.K. Federal Bldg.   Phone: (617) 223-4674
Boston, MA 02203   Christine A. Fraser, Libn.

U.S. GENERAL ACCOUNTING OFFICE - BOSTON REGIONAL OFFICE -
  TECHNICAL LIBRARY
100 Summer St., Suite 1907   Phone: (617) 223-6536
Boston, MA 02110   Irene Briggs, Tech.Info.Spec.

U.S. PRESIDENTIAL LIBRARIES - JOHN F. KENNEDY LIBRARY
Columbia Point on Dorchester Bay   Phone: (617) 929-4500
Boston, MA 02125   Dan H. Fenn, Jr., Dir.

U.S. PUBLIC HEALTH SERVICE HOSPITAL - MEDICAL LIBRARY
77 Warren St.   Phone: (617) 782-3400
Boston, MA 02135   Lora Robbins, Med.Libn.

U.S. VETERANS ADMINISTRATION (MA-Boston) - HOSPITAL MEDICAL
  LIBRARY
150 S. Huntington Ave.   Phone: (617) 739-3434
Boston, MA 02130   Patricia J. McGrath, Chf., Lib.Serv.

U.S. VETERANS ADMINISTRATION (MA-Boston) - OUTPATIENT CLINIC
  MEDICAL LIBRARY
17 Court St.   Phone: (617) 223-2082
Boston, MA 02108   Mary Ellen West, Lib.Techn.

WARNER & STACKPOLE - LAW LIBRARY
28 State St.   Phone: (617) 523-6250
Boston, MA 02109

WENTWORTH INSTITUTE OF TECHNOLOGY - LIBRARY
550 Huntington Ave.   Phone: (617) 442-9010
Boston, MA 02115   Lynn H. Robinson, Libn.

WIDETT, SLATER & GOLDMAN P.C. - LIBRARY
60 State St.   Phone: (617) 227-7200
Boston, MA 02109   Anne DiLoreto, Hd. Law Libn.

BRAINTREE HISTORICAL SOCIETY, INC. - LIBRARY
786 Washington St.   Phone: (617) 848-1640
Braintree, MA 02184   Mrs. Donald G. Maxham, Libn.

CAPE COD MUSEUM OF NATURAL HISTORY - LIBRARY AND INFORMATION
    CENTER
Main St.   Phone: (617) 896-3867
Brewster, MA 02631   Eileen Bush, Libn.

NEW ENGLAND FIRE & HISTORY MUSEUM - LIBRARY AND ARCHIVE
1439 Main St., Rte. 6A   Phone: (617) 896-5711
Brewster, MA 02631   Helen Berrien, Libn.

BRIDGEWATER STATE COLLEGE - CLEMENT C. MAXWELL LIBRARY
Shaw Rd.   Phone: (617) 697-8321
Bridgewater, MA 02434   Owen T.P. McGowan, Ph.D., Lib.Dir.

KENNEDY (Joseph P., Jr.) MEMORIAL HOSPITAL FOR CHILDREN - MEDICAL
    LIBRARY
30 Warren St.   Phone: (617) 254-3800
Brighton, MA 02135   Barbara L. McMurrough, Lib.Asst.

ST. ELIZABETH'S HOSPITAL - MEDICAL LIBRARY
736 Cambridge St.   Phone: (617) 782-7000
Brighton, MA 02135   Deborah T. Almquist, Libn.

ST. ELIZABETH'S HOSPITAL - SCHOOL OF NURSING - LIBRARY
235 Washington St.   Phone: (617) 782-7000
Brighton, MA 02135   Robert L. Loud, Libn.

ST. JOHN'S SEMINARY - LIBRARY
99 Lake St.   Phone: (617) 254-2610
Brighton, MA 02135   Rev. L.W. McGrath, Hd.

BROCKTON ART MUSEUM - FULLER MEMORIAL LIBRARY
Oak St. on Upper Porters Pond   Phone: (617) 588-6000
Brockton, MA 02140   Deedee Andrea Des Jardins, Libn.

BROCKTON DAILY ENTERPRISE AND BROCKTON TIMES-ENTERPRISE -
    LIBRARY †
60 Main St.   Phone: (617) 586-6200
Brockton, MA 02401   Bernice W. Johnson, Hd.Libn.

BROCKTON HOSPITAL - LIBRARY
680 Centre St.   Phone: (617) 586-2600
Brockton, MA 02402   Lovisa Kamenoff, Mgr., Lib.Serv.

CARDINAL CUSHING GENERAL HOSPITAL - STAFF LIBRARY
235 N. Pearl St.   Phone: (617) 588-4000
Brockton, MA 02401   Johanna M. Alexander, Med.Libn.

PLYMOUTH COUNTY LAW LIBRARY ASSOCIATION - BROCKTON LAW
    LIBRARY
72 Belmont St.   Phone: (617) 583-8250
Brockton, MA 02401   Kenneth E. MacMullen, Libn.

U.S. VETERANS ADMINISTRATION (MA-Brockton) - MEDICAL CENTER
    LIBRARY
Belmont St.   Phone: (617) 583-4500
Brockton, MA 02401   Suzanne Noyes, Chf., Lib.Serv.

BROOKLINE HOSPITAL - MEDICAL LIBRARY
165 Chestnut St.   Phone: (617) 734-1330
Brookline, MA 02146   Carole Foxman, Med.Libn.

EX-MOON INC. - BUSINESS LIBRARY
Box 62   Phone: (617) 734-5108
Brookline, MA 02146   Steven Hassan, Pres.

HEBREW COLLEGE - JACOB AND ROSE GROSSMAN LIBRARY
43 Hawes St.   Phone: (617) 232-8710
Brookline, MA 02146   Maurice S. Tuchman, Libn.

HELLENIC COLLEGE AND HOLY CROSS GREEK ORTHODOX SCHOOL OF
    THEOLOGY - COTSIDAS-TONNA LIBRARY
50 Goddard Ave.   Phone: (617) 731-3500
Brookline, MA 02146   Diane Paterakis, Act.Dir. Of Lib.

TEMPLE OHABEI SHALOM - LIBRARY
1187 Beacon St.   Phone: (617) 277-6610
Brookline, MA 02146   Selma Levine, Libn.

TEMPLE SINAI - LIBRARY †
50 Sewall Ave.   Phone: (617) 277-5888
Brookline, MA 02146   Walter Lechten, Principal, Relg.Sch.

ANALYTICAL SYSTEMS ENGINEERING CORPORATION - LIBRARY
5 Old Concord Rd.   Phone: (617) 272-7910
Burlington, MA 01803   Rayna Lee Norster, Librarian

DURACELL INTERNATIONAL, INC. - TECHNICAL INFORMATION CENTER
Northwest Industrial Pk.   Phone: (617) 272-4100
Burlington, MA 01803   Mildred Keller, Mgr./Tech.Info.Serv.

HIGH VOLTAGE ENGINEERING CORPORATION - LIBRARY
S. Bedford St.
Burlington, MA 01803

LAHEY CLINIC MEDICAL CENTER - RICHARD B. CATTELL MEMORIAL
    LIBRARY
41 Mall Rd.   Phone: (617) 273-8253
Burlington, MA 01803   Carol Spencer, Med.Libn.

MICROWAVE ASSOCIATES, INC. - LIBRARY
South Ave.   Phone: (617) 272-3000
Burlington, MA 01803   Christine S. Coburn, Libn.

RAYTHEON SERVICE COMPANY - LIBRARY
2 Wayside Rd., Spencer Laboratory   Phone: (617) 272-9300
Burlington, MA 01803   Jean Cameron, Libn.

RCA CORPORATION - G & CS - AUTOMATED SYSTEMS - ENGINEERING
    LIBRARY
Box 588   Phone: (617) 272-4000
Burlington, MA 01803   Veronica Hsu, Tech.Libn.

MASSACHUSETTS MARITIME ACADEMY - CAPTAIN CHARLES H. HURLEY
    LIBRARY
Taylor's Point
Box D   Phone: (617) 759-5761
Buzzards Bay, MA 02532   Maurice H. Bosse, Dir. of Lib.Serv.

ABT ASSOCIATES INC. - LIBRARY
55 Wheeler St.   Phone: (617) 492-7100
Cambridge, MA 02138   Linda H. Webb, Libn.

AMERICAN ASSOCIATION OF VARIABLE STAR OBSERVERS - MC ATEER
    LIBRARY
187 Concord Ave.   Phone: (617) 354-0484
Cambridge, MA 02138   Janet A. Mattei, Dir.

ARCHITECTS COLLABORATIVE - LIBRARY
46 Brattle St.   Phone: (617) 868-4200
Cambridge, MA 02138   Anne Hartmere, Libn.

ARTHUR D. LITTLE, INC. - BURLINGTON LIBRARY
17 Acorn Park   Phone: (617) 864-5770
Cambridge, MA 02140   Marcia J. Kindzerske, Libn.

ARTHUR D. LITTLE, INC. - MANAGEMENT LIBRARY
35 Acorn Pk.   Phone: (617) 864-5770
Cambridge, MA 02140   Edith B. Mintz, Hd. Libn.

GEOGRAPHIC

ARTHUR D. LITTLE, INC. - RESEARCH LIBRARY
25 Acorn Pk.   Phone: (617) 864-5770
Cambridge, MA 02140   Ann J. Wolpert, Hd.

BOLT BERANEK AND NEWMAN, INC. - LIBRARY
50 Moulton St.   Phone: (617) 491-1850
Cambridge, MA 02138   Margaret H. Troy, Hd.Libn.

CAMBRIDGE HISTORICAL COMMISSION - LIBRARY
City Hall Annex, 57 Inman St.   Phone: (617) 498-9040
Cambridge, MA 02139   Charles M. Sullivan, Exec.Dir.

CAMBRIDGE HOSPITAL - MEDICAL LIBRARY
1493 Cambridge St.
Cambridge, MA 02139   Mrs. James H. Stanton, Med.Libn.

CAMBRIDGE SCHOOL DEPARTMENT - TEACHERS' RESOURCE CENTER
459 Broadway   Phone: (617) 492-8000
Cambridge, MA 02138   Sheila Morshead, Libn./Media Spec.

CENTER FOR LAW AND EDUCATION - VICTORIA GREGORIAN LIBRARY
6 Appian Way   Phone: (617) 495-4666
Cambridge, MA 02138   Ralph G. Oppenheim, Dir.

COM/ENERGY SERVICES CO. - LIBRARY
675 Massachusetts Ave.   Phone: (617) 864-3100
Cambridge, MA 02139   Esther A. Reppucci, Supv., Lib./Rec.Ctr.

DRAPER (Charles Stark) LABORATORY, INC. - TECHNICAL INFORMATION CENTER
555 Technology Sq., Mail Sta. 74   Phone: (617) 258-3555
Cambridge, MA 02139   M. Hope Coffman, Mgr.

DYNATECH CORPORATION LIBRARY
99 Erie St.   Phone: (617) 868-8050
Cambridge, MA 02139   Jane I. Petschaft, Libn.

ENERGY RESOURCES COMPANY - TECHNICAL INFORMATION CENTER
185 Alewife Brook Pkwy.   Phone: (617) 661-3111
Cambridge, MA 02138   Pamela Shephard-Lupo, Lib.Mgr.

EVALUATION, DISSEMINATION & ASSESSMENT CENTER - EDAC RESEARCH LIBRARY
Lesley College
49 Washington Ave.   Phone: (617) 492-0505
Cambridge, MA 02140   Eugene E. Liu, Bilingual Res.Libn.

GRACE (W.R.) AND COMPANY - INDUSTRIAL CHEMICALS GROUP - LIBRARY
62 Whittemore Ave.   Phone: (617) 876-1400
Cambridge, MA 02140   Marjorie Metcalf, Libn.

HARVARD UNIVERSITY - ARCHIVES
Pusey Library   Phone: (617) 495-2461
Cambridge, MA 02138   Harley P. Holden, Cur.

HARVARD UNIVERSITY - ARNOLD ARBORETUM & GRAY HERBARIUM - LIBRARY
22 Divinity Ave.   Phone: (617) 495-2366
Cambridge, MA 02138   Barbara A. Callahan, Libn.

HARVARD UNIVERSITY - BIOLOGICAL LABORATORIES LIBRARY
16 Divinity Ave.   Phone: (617) 495-3944
Cambridge, MA 02138   Dorothy J. Solbrig, Libn.

HARVARD UNIVERSITY - CENTER FOR EUROPEAN STUDIES - LIBRARY
5 Bryant St.   Phone: (617) 495-4150
Cambridge, MA 02138   Paul Mattick, Jr., Libn.

HARVARD UNIVERSITY - CENTER FOR MIDDLE EASTERN STUDIES - LIBRARY
Coolidge Hall
1737 Cambridge St.   Phone: (617) 495-2173
Cambridge, MA 02138   Julie M. Blattner, Libn.

HARVARD UNIVERSITY - CENTER FOR SCIENCE AND INTERNATIONAL AFFAIRS LIBRARY
79 Boylston St.   Phone: (617) 495-1408
Cambridge, MA 02138   Lisbeth Bernstein, Libn.

HARVARD UNIVERSITY - CHEMISTRY LIBRARY
Converse Memorial Library   Phone: (617) 495-4079
Cambridge, MA 02138   Ludmila Birladeanu, Supv.

HARVARD UNIVERSITY - DIVINITY SCHOOL - ANDOVER-HARVARD THEOLOGICAL LIBRARY
45 Francis Ave.   Phone: (617) 495-5770
Cambridge, MA 02138   Maria Grossmann, Libn.

HARVARD UNIVERSITY - ECONOMIC BOTANY LIBRARY
10 Oxford St.   Phone: (617) 495-2326
Cambridge, MA 02138   Wesley Wong

HARVARD UNIVERSITY - EDA KUHN LOEB MUSIC LIBRARY
   Phone: (617) 495-2794
Cambridge, MA 02138   Michael Ochs, Libn.

HARVARD UNIVERSITY - FARLOW REFERENCE LIBRARY
20 Divinity Ave.   Phone: (617) 495-2369
Cambridge, MA 02138   Geraldine C. Kaye, Libn.

HARVARD UNIVERSITY - FINE ARTS LIBRARY
Fogg Art Museum   Phone: (617) 495-3373
Cambridge, MA 02138   Wolfgang Freitag, Libn.

HARVARD UNIVERSITY - GEOLOGICAL SCIENCES LIBRARY
24 Oxford St.   Phone: (617) 495-2029
Cambridge, MA 02138   Julian Green, Libn.

HARVARD UNIVERSITY - GODFREY LOWELL CABOT SCIENCE LIBRARY
Science Ctr., One Oxford St.   Phone: (617) 495-5353
Cambridge, MA 02138   Alan E. Erickson, Sci.Spec.

HARVARD UNIVERSITY - GORDON MC KAY LIBRARY - DIVISION OF APPLIED SCIENCES
Pierce Hall, 29 Oxford St.   Phone: (617) 495-2836
Cambridge, MA 02138   Julie Sandall Barlas, Libn.

HARVARD UNIVERSITY - GRADUATE SCHOOL OF DESIGN - FRANCES LOEB LIBRARY
Gund Hall   Phone: (617) 495-2574
Cambridge, MA 02138   Angela Giral, Libn.

HARVARD UNIVERSITY - GRADUATE SCHOOL OF EDUCATION - GUTMAN LIBRARY
Appian Way   Phone: (617) 495-4225
Cambridge, MA 02138   Inabeth Miller, Libn.

HARVARD UNIVERSITY - HARVARD UKRAINIAN RESEARCH INSTITUTE - REFERENCE LIBRARY
1581/83 Massachusetts Ave.   Phone: (617) 495-5224
Cambridge, MA 02138   Larisa Trolle, Libn.

HARVARD UNIVERSITY - HARVARD YENCHING INSTITUTE - LIBRARY
2 Divinity Ave.   Phone: (617) 495-2756
Cambridge, MA 02138   Eugene Wu, Libn.

HARVARD UNIVERSITY - HISTORY OF SCIENCE LIBRARY
Widener Library, Rm. 91
Cambridge, MA 02138   Erwin N. Hiebert

HARVARD UNIVERSITY - HOUGHTON LIBRARY
   Phone: (617) 495-2440
Cambridge, MA 02138   William H. Bond, Libn.

HARVARD UNIVERSITY - INSTITUTE FOR INTERNATIONAL DEVELOPMENT - LIBRARY
Coolidge Hall
1737 Cambridge St.   Phone: (617) 495-2173
Cambridge, MA 02138   Julie M. Blattner, Libn.

HARVARD UNIVERSITY - JOHN FITZGERALD KENNEDY SCHOOL OF GOVERNMENT - LIBRARY
79 Boylston St.   Phone: (617) 495-1302
Cambridge, MA 02138   Malcolm C. Hamilton, Libn.

HARVARD UNIVERSITY - JOHN K. FAIRBANK CENTER FOR EAST ASIAN RESEARCH - LIBRARY
1737 Cambridge St.   Phone: (617) 495-5753
Cambridge, MA 02138   Nancy Hearst, Libn.

HARVARD UNIVERSITY - LAW SCHOOL LIBRARY
Langdell Hall
Phone: (617) 495-3170
Cambridge, MA 02138
Harry Martin, Libn.

HARVARD UNIVERSITY - LITTAUER LIBRARY
Phone: (617) 495-2105
Cambridge, MA 02138
James Damaskos, Libn.

HARVARD UNIVERSITY - MAP COLLECTION
Pusey Library
Phone: (617) 495-2417
Cambridge, MA 02138
Frank E. Trout, Cur.

HARVARD UNIVERSITY - MATHEMATICAL LIBRARY
Science Center
Phone: (617) 495-2147
Cambridge, MA 02138
Philip A. Griffiths

HARVARD UNIVERSITY - MUSEUM OF COMPARATIVE ZOOLOGY - LIBRARY
Oxford St.
Phone: (617) 495-2475
Cambridge, MA 02138
Eva Jonas, Libn.

HARVARD UNIVERSITY - OAKES AMES ORCHID LIBRARY
University Herbarium
Phone: (617) 495-2360
Cambridge, MA 02138
Herman R. Sweet, Libn.

HARVARD UNIVERSITY - OBSERVATORY LIBRARY
60 Garden St.
Phone: (617) 495-5488
Cambridge, MA 02138
Estelle Karlin, Libn.

HARVARD UNIVERSITY - PHYSICS RESEARCH LIBRARY
450 Jefferson Library
Phone: (617) 495-2878
Cambridge, MA 02138
Nina McMaster, Libn.

HARVARD UNIVERSITY - PSYCHOLOGY RESEARCH LIBRARY
33 Kirkland St.
Phone: (617) 495-3858
Cambridge, MA 02138
Annelise Katz, Libn.

HARVARD UNIVERSITY - RADCLIFFE COLLEGE - MORSE MUSIC LIBRARY
59 Shepard St.
Phone: (617) 495-8730
Cambridge, MA 02138
Stephan B. Fuller, Music Libn.

HARVARD UNIVERSITY - ROBBINS LIBRARY
Emerson Hall
Phone: (617) 495-2193
Cambridge, MA 02138
Susan Neiman, Asst.Libn.

HARVARD UNIVERSITY - RUSSIAN RESEARCH CENTER - LIBRARY
Coolidge Hall Library
1737 Cambridge St.
Phone: (617) 495-4030
Cambridge, MA 02138
Susan Jo Gardos, Libn.

HARVARD UNIVERSITY - SOCIAL RELATIONS/SOCIOLOGY LIBRARY
22 Kirkland St.
Phone: (617) 495-3838
Cambridge, MA 02138
Annelise Katz

HARVARD UNIVERSITY - STATISTICS LIBRARY
Science Center
Phone: (617) 495-5496
Cambridge, MA 02138
William Glynn, Lib.Asst.

HARVARD UNIVERSITY - THEATRE COLLECTION
Pusey Library
Phone: (617) 495-2445
Cambridge, MA 02138
Jeanne T. Newlin, Cur.

HARVARD UNIVERSITY - TICKNOR LIBRARY
Boylston Hall
Phone: (617) 495-2559
Cambridge, MA 02138
Arlene Marcin, Lib.Supv.

HARVARD UNIVERSITY - TOZZER LIBRARY - PEABODY MUSEUM OF
ARCHAEOLOGY AND ETHNOLOGY
21 Divinity Ave.
Phone: (617) 495-2253
Cambridge, MA 02138
Nancy J. Schmidt, Libn.

HARVARD UNIVERSITY - W.E.B. DU BOIS INSTITUTE FOR AFRO-AMERICAN
RESEARCH - LIBRARY
Canaday Hall B
Phone: (617) 495-4192
Cambridge, MA 02138
Ruth Washington, Libn.

HARVARD UNIVERSITY - WOODBERRY POETRY ROOM
Lamont Library
Phone: (617) 495-2454
Cambridge, MA 02138
Stratis Haviaras, Cur.

INTERMETRICS INC. - LIBRARY
733 Concord Ave.
Phone: (617) 661-1840
Cambridge, MA 02138
Ann M. Wilson, Libn.

KALBA BOWEN ASSOCIATES - LIBRARY
12 Arrow St.
Phone: (617) 661-2624
Cambridge, MA 02138
John Adams, Libn./Info.Spec.

LINCOLN INSTITUTE OF LAND POLICY - LIBRARY
26 Trowbridge St.
Phone: (617) 661-3016
Cambridge, MA 02138
Mary J. O'Brien, Libn.

MASSACHUSETTS INSTITUTE OF TECHNOLOGY - AERONAUTICS AND
ASTRONAUTICS LIBRARY
Rm. 33-316
Phone: (617) 253-5665
Cambridge, MA 02139
Kate S. Herzog, Libn.

MASSACHUSETTS INSTITUTE OF TECHNOLOGY - BARKER ENGINEERING
LIBRARY
Rm. 10-500
Phone: (617) 253-5663
Cambridge, MA 02139
James M. Kyed, Hd., Engr.Libs.

MASSACHUSETTS INSTITUTE OF TECHNOLOGY - CENTER FOR POLICY
ALTERNATIVES - DOCUMENTS COLLECTION
Rm. E40-250
Phone: (617) 253-1659
Cambridge, MA 02139
Marilyn A. Reisse, Doc.Coord.

MASSACHUSETTS INSTITUTE OF TECHNOLOGY - CENTER FOR SPACE
RESEARCH - READING ROOM
Rm. 37-582
Phone: (617) 253-3746
Cambridge, MA 02139

MASSACHUSETTS INSTITUTE OF TECHNOLOGY - CHEMISTRY READING
ROOM
Rm. 18-480
Phone: (617) 253-1891
Cambridge, MA 02139

MASSACHUSETTS INSTITUTE OF TECHNOLOGY - CIVIL ENGINEERING
DEPT. - RALPH M. PARSONS LABORATORY - REF. RM.
Bldg. 48-411
Phone: (617) 253-2994
Cambridge, MA 02139
Chiang C. Mei, Prof.Civ.Engr.

MASSACHUSETTS INSTITUTE OF TECHNOLOGY - DEPARTMENT OF
CHEMICAL ENGINEERING READING ROOM
Room 66-365
Phone: (617) 253-6521
Cambridge, MA 02139

MASSACHUSETTS INSTITUTE OF TECHNOLOGY - DEPARTMENT OF
MATHEMATICS - READING ROOM
Rm. 2-285
Cambridge, MA 02139
Dr. Jonathan Sacks

MASSACHUSETTS INSTITUTE OF TECHNOLOGY - DEPARTMENT OF
NUTRITION AND FOOD SCIENCE - READING ROOM
Rm. 20A-213
Phone: (617) 253-7994
Cambridge, MA 02139
Julia J. Peterson, Libn.

MASSACHUSETTS INSTITUTE OF TECHNOLOGY - DEWEY LIBRARY
Hermann Bldg., E53-138
Phone: (617) 253-5677
Cambridge, MA 02139
Edgar W. Davy, Dewey Libn.

MASSACHUSETTS INSTITUTE OF TECHNOLOGY - DIVISION FOR STUDY
AND RESEARCH IN EDUCATION - READING ROOM
Rm. 20C-117
Phone: (617) 253-6047
Cambridge, MA 02139
Debra Banerjee, Sec.

MASSACHUSETTS INSTITUTE OF TECHNOLOGY - DYNAMICS OF
ATMOSPHERES AND OCEANS LIBRARY
Rm. 54-1427
Phone: (617) 253-2450
Cambridge, MA 02139
Jule G. Charney, Professor

MASSACHUSETTS INSTITUTE OF TECHNOLOGY - ENVIRONMENTAL
MEDICAL SERVICE - LIBRARY
77 Massachusetts Ave., Rm. 20B-23B
Phone: (617) 253-7983
Cambridge, MA 02139
Angela A. Grammatico, Libn.

MASSACHUSETTS INSTITUTE OF TECHNOLOGY - FRANCIS HART NAUTICAL
MUSEUM - LIBRARY
Room 5-329
Phone: (617) 253-4444
Cambridge, MA 02139
William A. Baker, Dir./Cur. of Musm.

GEOGRAPHIC

MASSACHUSETTS INSTITUTE OF TECHNOLOGY - HUMANITIES LIBRARY
Rm. 14S-200
Cambridge, MA 02139
Phone: (617) 253-5683
David S. Ferriero, Libn.

MASSACHUSETTS INSTITUTE OF TECHNOLOGY - INFORMATION
PROCESSING SERVICES - READING ROOM
Rm. 39-233
Cambridge, MA 02139
Phone: (617) 253-4105
Georgia M. Nagle, Rd.Rm.Adm.

MASSACHUSETTS INSTITUTE OF TECHNOLOGY - INSTITUTE ARCHIVES
AND SPECIAL COLLECTIONS
Hayden Library, Rm. 14N-118
Cambridge, MA 02139
Phone: (617) 253-5688
Helen W. Slotkin, Archv./Spec.Coll.Hd.

MASSACHUSETTS INSTITUTE OF TECHNOLOGY - LABORATORY FOR
COMPUTER SCIENCE - READING ROOM
545 Technology Sq., Rm. 114
Cambridge, MA 02139
Phone: (617) 253-5896
Jindriska Badal, Info.Spec.

MASSACHUSETTS INSTITUTE OF TECHNOLOGY - LINDGREN LIBRARY
Rm. 54-200
Cambridge, MA 02139
Phone: (617) 253-5679
Jean Eaglesfield, Lindgren Libn.

MASSACHUSETTS INSTITUTE OF TECHNOLOGY - M.I.T. MUSEUM AND
HISTORICAL COLLECTIONS
Bldg. N52
Cambridge, MA 02139
Phone: (617) 253-4444
Warren A. Seamans, Dir.

MASSACHUSETTS INSTITUTE OF TECHNOLOGY - MUSIC LIBRARY
Rm. 14E-109
Cambridge, MA 02139
Phone: (617) 253-5689
Linda I. Solow, Music Libn.

MASSACHUSETTS INSTITUTE OF TECHNOLOGY - PHYSICS READING ROOM
Rm. 26-152
Cambridge, MA 02139
Phone: (617) 253-1791
Fay D. Martin

MASSACHUSETTS INSTITUTE OF TECHNOLOGY - PSYCHOLOGY LIBRARY
Rm. E10-030
Cambridge, MA 02139
Phone: (617) 253-5755
Catherine Gibbes, Libn.

MASSACHUSETTS INSTITUTE OF TECHNOLOGY - RESEARCH LABORATORY
OF ELECTRONICS - DOCUMENT ROOM
Rm. 36-412
Cambridge, MA 02139
Phone: (617) 253-2566
John H. Hewitt, Libn.

MASSACHUSETTS INSTITUTE OF TECHNOLOGY - ROTCH LIBRARY OF
ARCHITECTURE AND PLANNING
Rm. 7-238
Cambridge, MA 02139
Phone: (617) 253-7052
Margaret DePopolo, Rotch Libn.

MASSACHUSETTS INSTITUTE OF TECHNOLOGY - ROTCH LIBRARY VISUAL
COLLECTIONS - LOUIS SKIDMORE ROOM
Room 7-304
Cambridge, MA 02139
Phone: (617) 253-7098

MASSACHUSETTS INSTITUTE OF TECHNOLOGY - SCIENCE FICTION
SOCIETY - LIBRARY
Rm. W20-421
Cambridge, MA 02139
Phone: (617) 253-1000

MASSACHUSETTS INSTITUTE OF TECHNOLOGY - SCIENCE LIBRARY
Rm. 14S-100
Cambridge, MA 02139
Phone: (617) 253-5680
Irma Y. Johnson, Science Libn.

MASSACHUSETTS INSTITUTE OF TECHNOLOGY - TRI-SERVICE LIBRARY
U.S. AFROTC DET 365
Rm. 20E-122
Cambridge, MA 02139
Phone: (617) 253-4472

MASSACHUSETTS INSTITUTE OF TECHNOLOGY - VON HIPPEL MATERIALS
CENTER READING ROOM
Rm. 13-2137
Cambridge, MA 02139
Phone: (617) 253-6840
Polly Baslock, Sr.Lib.Asst.

MEN'S RIGHTS, INC. - READING CENTER
Rindge Towers - 402, Suite 8J
Cambridge, MA 02140
Phone: (617) 547-5054
Fredric Hayward, Dir.

MIDDLESEX LAW LIBRARY ASSOCIATION - LIBRARY †
Superior Courthouse
Cambridge, MA 02141
Phone: (617) 494-4148
William Highgas, Jr., Libn.

MOUNT AUBURN HOSPITAL - HEALTH SCIENCES LIBRARY
330 Mt. Auburn St.
Cambridge, MA 02138
Phone: (617) 492-3500
M. Cherie Haitz, Dir.

POLAROID CORPORATION - RESEARCH LIBRARY
730 Main St.
Cambridge, MA 02139
Phone: (617) 577-3368
Charles E. Zerwekh, Tech.Info.Sys.Mgr.

RADCLIFFE COLLEGE - ARTHUR AND ELIZABETH SCHLESINGER LIBRARY ON
THE HISTORY OF WOMEN IN AMERICA
10 Garden St.
Cambridge, MA 02138
Phone: (617) 495-8647
Dr. Patricia M. King, Dir.

RADCLIFFE COLLEGE - HENRY A. MURRAY RESEARCH CENTER
10 Garden St.
Cambridge, MA 02138
Phone: (617) 495-8140
Anne Colby, Dir.

RAYTHEON COMPANY - BADGER AMERICA, INC. - LIBRARY
One Broadway
Cambridge, MA 02142
Phone: (617) 494-7565
Eleanor M. Rice, Libn.

RETORT, INC. - LIBRARY
Box 477
Cambridge, MA 02139
Phone: (617) 661-0962
E.H. Rosenberg, Pres.

SMITHSONIAN INSTITUTION LIBRARIES - ASTROPHYSICAL OBSERVATORY
- LIBRARY †
60 Garden St.
Cambridge, MA 02138
Phone: (617) 495-7264
Joyce Rey, Libn.

TECHNOLOGY & ECONOMICS, INC. - LIBRARY
2225 Massachusetts Ave.
Cambridge, MA 02140
Phone: (617) 491-1500
Pamela Enion, Libn.

U.S. DEPT. OF TRANSPORTATION - TRANSPORTATION SYSTEMS CENTER -
TECHNICAL REFERENCE CENTER
Kendall Sq.
Cambridge, MA 02142
Phone: (617) 494-2783
Hadassah Linfield, Dir.

U.S. NATL. PARK SERVICE - LONGFELLOW NATL. HISTORIC SITE - LIBRARY
105 Brattle St.
Cambridge, MA 02138
Phone: (617) 876-4491
Elizabeth B. Egbert, Libn.

WARNER-EDDISON ASSOCIATES, INC. - INFORMATION SERVICE
186 Alewife Brook Pkwy.
Cambridge, MA 02138
Phone: (617) 661-8124
Mona Couts, Info.Serv.Mgr.

WESTON SCHOOL OF THEOLOGY - LIBRARY
99 Brattle St.
Cambridge, MA 02138
Phone: (617) 868-3450
Allan J. Stifflear, Dir.

ZATOR COMPANY - LIBRARY
56 Boylston St.
Cambridge, MA 02138

CANTON HISTORICAL SOCIETY - LIBRARY †
1400 Washington St.
Canton, MA 02021
Phone: (617) 828-4962
Edward H. Bolster, Pres.

MASSACHUSETTS STATE HOSPITAL SCHOOL - MEDICAL LIBRARY
Randolph St.
Canton, MA 02021
Phone: (617) 828-2440
Janet Doherty, Libn.

U.S. COAST GUARD/AIR STATION - BASE LIBRARY
Otis AFB
Cape Cod, MA 02542
Phone: (617) 968-5062
Evelyn L. Norton, Act.Libn.

CHELMSFORD HISTORICAL SOCIETY - BARRETT-BYAM HOMESTEAD
LIBRARY
40 Byam Rd.
Chelmsford, MA 01824
Mrs. Donald Fogg, Curator

BOSTON COLLEGE - GRADUATE SCHOOL OF SOCIAL WORK LIBRARY
McGuinn Hall
Chestnut Hill, MA 02167
Phone: (617) 969-0100
Harriet Nemiccolo, Chf.Libn.

BOSTON COLLEGE - LIBRARY - BREHAUT BOSTONIAN COLLECTION
Phone: (617) 969-0100
Chestnut Hill, MA 02167   Frank J. Seegraber, Spec.Coll.Libn.

BOSTON COLLEGE - LIBRARY - FRANCIS THOMPSON COLLECTION
Phone: (617) 969-0100
Chestnut Hill, MA 02167   Frank J. Seegraber, Spec.Coll.Libn.

BOSTON COLLEGE - LIBRARY - IRISH COLLECTION
Phone: (617) 969-0100
Chestnut Hill, MA 02167   Frank Seegraber, Spec.Coll.Libn.

BOSTON COLLEGE - LIBRARY - NICHOLAS M. WILLIAMS ETHNOLOGICAL
COLLECTION
Phone: (617) 969-0100
Chestnut Hill, MA 02167   Frank J. Seegraber, Spec.Coll.Libn.

BOSTON COLLEGE - SCHOOL OF MANAGEMENT LIBRARY
Fulton Hall   Phone: (617) 969-0100
Chestnut Hill, MA 02167   Rhoda K. Channing, Libn.

BOSTON COLLEGE - SCHOOL OF NURSING LIBRARY
Cushing Hall   Phone: (617) 969-0100
Chestnut Hill, MA 02167   Mary L. Pekarski, Libn.

BOSTON COLLEGE - SCIENCE LIBRARY
Devlin Hall   Phone: (617) 969-0100
Chestnut Hill, MA 02167   F. Clifford McElroy, Sci.Libn.

TEMPLE MISHKAN TEFILA - HARRY AND ANNA FEINBERG LIBRARY
300 Hammond Pond Pkwy.   Phone: (617) 332-7770
Chestnut Hill, MA 02167   Sarah Lamstein, Libn.

CONCORD ANTIQUARIAN SOCIETY - LIBRARY OF RALPH WALDO EMERSON
Lexington Rd. & Cambridge Tpke.
Concord, MA 01742

ENVIRONMENTAL RESEARCH & TECHNOLOGY, INC. - INFORMATION
CENTER
696 Virginia Rd.   Phone: (617) 369-8910
Concord, MA 01742   Brenda Y. Allen, Libn.

GENRAD, INC. - LIBRARY
300 Baker Ave.   Phone: (617) 369-4400
Concord, MA 01742   Donna L. Vallancourt, Libn.

THOREAU LYCEUM - LIBRARY
156 Belknap St.   Phone: (617) 369-5912
Concord, MA 01742   Anne McGrath, Cur.

GTE SYLVANIA - ENGINEERING LIBRARY
100 Endicott St.   Phone: (617) 777-1900
Danvers, MA 01923   Dorothy M. Rich Oak, Libn.

HUNT MEMORIAL HOSPITAL - GEORGE B. PALMER MEMORIAL LIBRARY
75 Lindall St.   Phone: (617) 774-4400
Danvers, MA 01923   Yvonne I. Cretecos, Med.Libn.

PEABODY INSTITUTE LIBRARY - DANVERS ARCHIVAL CENTER
13 Page St.   Phone: (617) 774-0554
Danvers, MA 01923   Richard B. Trask, Town Archv.

DEDHAM HISTORICAL SOCIETY - LIBRARY
612 High St.   Phone: (617) 326-1385
Dedham, MA 02026   Muriel N. Peters, Libn.

NORFOLK COUNTY LAW LIBRARY
Superior Court House
650 High St.   Phone: (617) 326-1600
Dedham, MA 02026   Lois B. Russell, Libn.

HISTORIC DEERFIELD, INC. - HENRY N. FLYNT LIBRARY - POCUMTUCK
VALLEY MEMORIAL ASSOCIATION
Memorial St.
Box 53   Phone: (413) 774-5581
Deerfield, MA 01342   David R. Proper, Libn.

ICI AMERICAS INC. - WORKS EXPERIMENTAL DEPARTMENT LIBRARY
Main St.   Phone: (617) 669-6731
Dighton, MA 02715   Marie A. Medeiros, Libn.

CARNEY HOSPITAL - MEDICAL LIBRARY
2100 Dorchester Ave.   Phone: (617) 296-4000
Dorchester, MA 02124   Frances E. O'Brien, Med.Libn.

DORCHESTER HISTORICAL SOCIETY - ROBINSON-LEHANE LIBRARY
195 Boston St.   Phone: (617) 436-8367
Dorchester, MA 02125   Anthony Mitchell Sammarco, Libn.

LEWIS (Elma) SCHOOL OF FINE ARTS - LIBRARY †
122 Elm Hill Ave.   Phone: (617) 442-8820
Dorchester, MA 02121   Beverlee A. Blair, Lib.Asst.

NICHOLS COLLEGE - CONANT LIBRARY
Phone: (617) 943-1560
Dudley, MA 01570   Dr. William L. Cohn, Libn.

BATTELLE NEW ENGLAND RESEARCH LABORATORY - WILLIAM F. CLAPP
LABORATORIES, INC. - LIBRARY
Washington St.   Phone: (617) 934-5682
Duxbury, MA 02332   Lawrence W. Martin, Libn.

CONNECTICUT RIVER WATERSHED COUNCIL - LIBRARY
125 Combs Rd.   Phone: (413) 584-0057
Easthampton, MA 01027   Terry Blunt, Exec.Dir.

DUKES COUNTY HISTORICAL SOCIETY - LIBRARY
Cooke & School Sts.
Box 827   Phone: (617) 627-4441
Edgartown, MA 02539   Thomas E. Norton, Dir.

AVCO CORPORATION - AVCO-EVERETT RESEARCH LABORATORY -
LIBRARY *
2385 Revere Beach Pkwy.   Phone: (617) 389-3000
Everett, MA 02149   Lorraine T. Nazzaro, Libn.

WHIDDEN MEMORIAL HOSPITAL - LIBRARY
103 Garland St.   Phone: (617) 389-6270
Everett, MA 02173   Selma W. Eigner, Libn.

BRISTOL COUNTY BAR ASSOCIATION - FALL RIVER LAW LIBRARY
Superior Court House
441 N. Main St.   Phone: (617) 676-8971
Fall River, MA 02720   Mary L. Sullivan, Libn.

FALL RIVER HISTORICAL SOCIETY - LIBRARY
451 Rock St.   Phone: (617) 679-1071
Fall River, MA 02720   Florence C. Brigham, Cur.

MARINE MUSEUM AT FALL RIVER, INC. - LIBRARY
70 Water St.   Phone: (617) 674-3533
Fall River, MA 02722   John F. Gosson, Cur.

P.T. BOATS, INC. - LIBRARY, ARCHIVES & TECHNICAL INFORMATION
CENTER
U.S.S. Massachusetts, Battleship Cove   Phone: (617) 678-1100
Fall River, MA 02721   Frank J. Szczepaniak, P.T. Boat Coord.

ST. ANNE'S HOSPITAL - SULLIVAN MEDICAL LIBRARY
795 Middle St.   Phone: (617) 674-5741
Fall River, MA 02722   Elaine Rondeau, Libn.

TEMPLE BETH-EL - ZISKIND MEMORIAL LIBRARY
385 High St.   Phone: (617) 674-3529
Fall River, MA 02720   Ida C. Pollock, Libn.

BURBANK HOSPITAL - SCHOOL OF NURSING - GRACE GUMMO LIBRARY
Phone: (617) 345-4311
Fitchburg, MA 01420   Martha Smith, Libn.

FITCHBURG HISTORICAL SOCIETY - LIBRARY
50 Grove St.
Box 953
Fitchburg, MA 01420   Eleanora F. West, Cur. of Musm.

GEOGRAPHIC

FITCHBURG LAW LIBRARY
Court House, Elm St.
Fitchburg, MA 01420
Phone: (617) 345-6726
Ann E. O'Connor, Law Libn.

FITCHBURG STATE COLLEGE - LIBRARY
Pearl St.
Fitchburg, MA 01420
Phone: (617) 345-2151
William T. Casey, Lib.Dir.

U.S. ARMY HOSPITALS - CUTLER ARMY HOSPITAL - MEDICAL LIBRARY
Phone: (617) 796-2031
Ft. Devens, MA 01433
Mrs. Leslie R. Seidel, Med.Libn.

U.S. ARMY INTELLIGENCE SCHOOL, DEVENS - LIBRARY/LEARNING CENTER
Phone: (617) 796-3413
Ft. Devens, MA 01433
Ornella L. Pensyl, Chf.

FOXBORO COMPANY - RD & E LIBRARY
38 Neponset Ave.
Foxboro, MA 02035
Phone: (617) 543-8750
Helen E. Stevens, Tech.Libn.

AMERICAN HUMANE EDUCATION SOCIETY - HUMANE EDUCATION
  LIBRARY
450 Salem End Rd.
Framingham, MA 01701
Phone: (617) 879-5345
Marshail McKee, Libn.

CUSHING HOSPITAL - MEDICAL LIBRARY †
Dudley Rd.
Box 190
Framingham, MA 01701
Phone: (617) 872-4301
Dina R. Krauss, Med.Libn.

DENNISON MANUFACTURING COMPANY - RESEARCH LIBRARY
300 Howard St.
Framingham, MA 01701
Phone: (617) 879-0511
Eva M. Bonis, Res.Libn.

FRAMINGHAM UNION HOSPITAL - CESARE GEORGE TEDESCHI LIBRARY
115 Lincoln St.
Framingham, MA 01701
Phone: (617) 879-7111
Sandra Clevesy, Dir.Lib.Serv.

INTERNATIONAL DATA CORPORATION - INFORMATION CENTER
5 Speen St.
Framingham, MA 01701
Phone: (617) 872-8200
Mary A. Rezetka, Mgr.Info.Ctr.

NEW ENGLAND WILD FLOWER SOCIETY, INC. - LIBRARY
Hemenway Rd.
Framingham, MA 01701
Phone: (617) 877-7630
Mary M. Walker, Libn.

PRIME COMPUTER, INC. - INFORMATION CENTER
500 Old Connecticut Path
Framingham, MA 01701
Phone: (617) 879-2960
Linda Loring Shea, Corp.Libn.

CAPE ANN HISTORICAL ASSOCIATION - LIBRARY
27 Pleasant St.
Gloucester, MA 01930
Phone: (617) 283-0455
Deborah L. Goodwin, Cur.

AMERICAN INSTITUTE FOR ECONOMIC RESEARCH - E.C. HARWOOD
  LIBRARY
Division St.
Great Barrington, MA 01230
Phone: (413) 528-1216
Laura Tucker, Libn.

FRANKLIN COUNTY TRIAL COURT - LAW LIBRARIES
Court House
Greenfield, MA 01301
Phone: (413) 772-6580
Marilyn M. Lee, Law Libn.

HANDWRITING ANALYSIS RESEARCH - LIBRARY
91 Washington St.
Greenfield, MA 01301
Phone: (413) 774-4667
Robert E. Backman, Cur.

MAC LEISH (Archibald) COLLECTION
Greenfield Community College
One College Dr.
Greenfield, MA 01301
Phone: (413) 774-3131
Margaret E.C. Howland, Cur.

U.S. AIR FORCE BASE - HANSCOM BASE LIBRARY
Phone: (617) 861-2177
Hanscom AFB, MA 01731
Gerald T. Griffin, Chf., Lib.Br.

FRUITLANDS MUSEUMS - LIBRARY
Prospect Hill Rd.
R.R. 2, Box 87
Harvard, MA 01451
Phone: (617) 456-3924
Richard S. Reed, Musm.Dir.

DANVERS STATE HOSPITAL - MAC DONALD MEDICAL LIBRARY
Box 50
Hathorne, MA 01937
Phone: (617) 774-5000
Bonnie Stecher, Lib.Dir.

HOGAN (Charles V.) REGIONAL CENTER - REGIONAL RESOURCE LIBRARY
Box A
Hathorne, MA 01937
Phone: (617) 774-5000
Bonnie Stecher, Libn.

HOGAN (Charles V.) REGIONAL CENTER - STAFF LIBRARY
Box A
Hathorne, MA 01937
Phone: (617) 774-5000
Bonnie Stecher, Libn.

HAVERHILL MUNICIPAL (Hale) HOSPITAL - MEDICAL LIBRARY
40 Buttonwoods Ave.
Haverhill, MA 01830
Phone: (617) 372-7141
Eleanor Howard, Med. Libn.

HAVERHILL PUBLIC LIBRARY - SPECIAL COLLECTIONS DIVISION
99 Main St.
Haverhill, MA 01830
Phone: (617) 372-4663
Howard W. Curtis, Cur.

MONSANTO PLASTICS & RESINS COMPANY - PLASTICS DIV. -
  SPRINGFIELD PLANT - TECHNOLOGY LIBRARY
730 Worcester St.
Indian Orchard, MA 01151
Phone: (413) 788-6911
Lorraine M. Daudelin, Libn.

MONSANTO PLASTICS & RESINS COMPANY - RESINS DIVISION -
  TECHNOLOGY LIBRARY *
190 Grochmal Ave.
Indian Orchard, MA 01151
Phone: (413) 788-6911
Mary H. Sheehan, Libn.

FAULKNER HOSPITAL - INGERSOLL BOWDITCH LIBRARY
1153 Centre St.
Jamaica Plain, MA 02130
Phone: (617) 522-5800
Barbara P. Pastan, Lib.Dir.

SHATTUCK (Lemuel) HOSPITAL - MEDICAL LIBRARY
170 Morton St.
Jamaica Plain, MA 02130
Phone: (617) 522-8110
Beth C. Poisson, Libn.

LAKEVILLE HOSPITAL - HEALTH SCIENCES LIBRARY
Main St.
Lakeville, MA 02346
Phone: (617) 947-1231
Bonnie Hsu, Libn.

LAWRENCE EAGLE TRIBUNE - LIBRARY
Box 100
Lawrence, MA 01842
Phone: (617) 685-1000
Cheryl Lynch, Libn.

LAWRENCE GENERAL HOSPITAL - HEALTH SCIENCE LIBRARY
One General Street
Lawrence, MA 01842
Phone: (617) 683-4000
Carmel M. Gram, Dir. of Lib. Serv.

LAWRENCE LAW LIBRARY
Superior Court House
41 Appleton St.
Lawrence, MA 01840
Phone: (617) 687-7754
Natalie C. Ballard, Libn.

BERKSHIRE CHRISTIAN COLLEGE - DR. LINDEN J. CARTER LIBRARY
200 Stockbridge Rd.
Lenox, MA 01240
Phone: (413) 637-0838
Lois W. Jones, Dir. of Lib.

MASSACHUSETTS AUDUBON SOCIETY - BERKSHIRE SANCTUARIES -
  LIBRARY
Pleasant Valley Wildlife Sanctuary
Lenox, MA 01240
Phone: (413) 637-0320
Lowell McAllister, Dir.

HONEYWELL, INC. - ELECTRO-OPTICS CENTER - TECHNICAL LIBRARY
2 Forbes Rd.
Lexington, MA 02173
Phone: (617) 863-3756
Kathleen A. Long, Mgr., Tech.Info.Serv

INSTRUMENTATION LABORATORY, INC. - LIBRARY
113 Hartwell Ave.
Lexington, MA 02173
Phone: (617) 861-0710
Jacqueline R. Kates, Corp.Libn.

ITEK CORPORATION - OPTICAL SYSTEMS DIVISION - LIBRARY
10 Maguire Rd.
Lexington, MA 02173
Phone: (617) 276-2643
Dorothy Cowe, Libn.

LEXINGTON HISTORICAL SOCIETY, INC. - LIBRARY
Box 514
Lexington, MA 02173
Phone: (617) 861-0928
S. Lawrence Whipple, Archv.

LEXINGTON PUBLIC SCHOOLS - CURRICULUM RESOURCE CENTER *
9 Philip Rd.   Phone: (617) 862-7500
Lexington, MA 02173   Martha Stanton Angevine, Coord.

MASSACHUSETTS INSTITUTE OF TECHNOLOGY - LINCOLN LABORATORY
   LIBRARY
244 Wood St.   Phone: (617) 862-5500
Lexington, MA 02173   Jane H. Katayama, Lib.Mgr.

RAYTHEON COMPANY - BUSINESS INFORMATION CENTER
141 Spring St.   Phone: (617) 862-6600
Lexington, MA 02173   Mary T. Tice, Mgr.

RAYTHEON COMPANY - LAW LIBRARY *
Office of the General Counsel
141 Spring St.   Phone: (617) 862-6600
Lexington, MA 02173

WOMEN'S INTERNATIONAL NETWORK - LIBRARY
187 Grant St.   Phone: (617) 862-9431
Lexington, MA 02173   F.P. Hosken, Coord.

XEROX CORPORATION - GINN AND COMPANY LIBRARY
191 Spring St.   Phone: (617) 861-1670
Lexington, MA 02173   Constance J. LeBeau, Libn.

DE CORDOVA MUSEUM - LIBRARY
Sandy Pond Rd.   Phone: (617) 259-8371
Lincoln, MA 01773   Bee Warren, Libn.

MASSACHUSETTS AUDUBON SOCIETY - HATHEWAY ENVIRONMENTAL
   EDUCATION INSTITUTE
                                                Phone: (617) 259-9500
Lincoln, MA 01773   Louise Maglione, Libn.

INFORONICS, INC. - TECHNICAL LIBRARY
550 Newton Rd.   Phone: (617) 486-8976
Littleton, MA 01460   Sandra Dennis, Mgr., Lib.Serv.

LOWELL GENERAL HOSPITAL - HEALTH SCIENCE LIBRARY
295 Varnum Ave.   Phone: (617) 454-0411
Lowell, MA 01854   Joan Kaiser, Med.Libn.

MIDDLESEX LAW LIBRARY ASSOCIATION - LIBRARY
Superior Court House
360 Gorham St.   Phone: (617) 452-9301
Lowell, MA 01852   Madeline Neilon, Libn.

ST. JOHN'S HOSPITAL - HEALTH SCIENCE LIBRARY
Hospital Dr.   Phone: (617) 458-1411
Lowell, MA 01852   Gale Cogan, Dir.

ST. JOSEPH'S HOSPITAL - HEALTH SCIENCE LIBRARY
220 Pawtucket St.   Phone: (617) 453-1761
Lowell, MA 01854   Anne C. Dick, Libn.

SOCIETY FOR THE PRESERVATION OF COLONIAL CULTURE - LIBRARY
c/o 10th Foot Royal
Lincolnshire Regimental Assn.
52 New Spalding St.
Lowell, MA 01851

UNIVERSITY OF LOWELL, NORTH CAMPUS - ALUMNI/LYDON LIBRARY
University Ave.   Phone: (617) 452-5000
Lowell, MA 01854   Joseph V. Kopycinski, Dir.

UNIVERSITY OF LOWELL, NORTH CAMPUS - UNIVERSITY LIBRARIES -
   SPECIAL COLLECTIONS
1 Univ. of Lowell   Phone: (617) 454-7811
Lowell, MA 01854   Martha Mayo, Hd., Spec.Coll.

UNIVERSITY OF LOWELL RESEARCH FOUNDATION - LIBRARY
450 Aiken St.
Lowell, MA 01854

UNIVERSITY OF LOWELL, SOUTH CAMPUS - DANIEL H. O'LEARY LIBRARY
Wilder St.   Phone: (617) 452-5000
Lowell, MA 01854   Charles R. Meehan, Dir.

GENERAL ELECTRIC COMPANY - AIRCRAFT ENGINE GROUP - DR. C.W.
   SMITH TECHNICAL INFORMATION CENTER
1000 Western Ave.   Phone: (617) 594-5363
Lynn, MA 01910   Jacqueline M. Wannemacher, Mgr.

HASTINGS & SONS PUBLISHERS - DAILY EVENING ITEM - NEWSPAPER
   MORGUE
38 Exchange St.   Phone: (617) 593-7700
Lynn, MA 01903   NancyAnn Rogers, Res.Libn.

LYNN HISTORICAL SOCIETY, INC. - LIBRARY
125 Green St.   Phone: (617) 592-2465
Lynn, MA 01902   Miss Ludovine Hamilton, Libn.

MALDEN HISTORICAL SOCIETY - LIBRARY
36 Salem St.   Phone: (617) 324-0218
Malden, MA 02148   Dorathy L. Rothe, Cur.

MALDEN HOSPITAL - MEDICAL LIBRARY
Hospital Rd.   Phone: (617) 322-7560
Malden, MA 02148   Denise Corless, Libn.

MALDEN HOSPITAL - SCHOOL OF NURSING LIBRARY
Hospital Rd.   Phone: (617) 322-7560
Malden, MA 02148   Phyllis M. McAuliffe, Libn.

MANCHESTER HISTORICAL SOCIETY - LIBRARY
10 Union St.   Phone: (617) 526-7230
Manchester, MA 01944   Esther W. Proctor, Libn.

MARBLEHEAD HISTORICAL SOCIETY - JEREMIAH LEE MANSION - LIBRARY
161 Washington St.   Phone: (617) 631-1069
Marblehead, MA 01945

MARLBOROUGH HOSPITAL - HEALTH SCIENCE LIBRARY
57 Union St.   Phone: (617) 485-1121
Marlborough, MA 01752   Eleanor Kunen, Libn.

NEW ENGLAND TELEPHONE LEARNING CENTER - RESOURCE CENTER
280 Locke Dr.   Phone: (617) 480-2331
Marlborough, MA 01572   Mark F. Mancevice, Dir., Resource Ctr.

DIGITAL EQUIPMENT CORPORATION - CORPORATE LIBRARY
ML 4-3/A20, 146 Main St.   Phone: (617) 493-6231
Maynard, MA 01754   Ralph Coffman, Lib.Mgr.

CORNING GLASS WORKS/CORNING MEDICAL & SCIENTIFIC - DAVID R.
   STEINBERG MEMORIAL LIBRARY & INFO. CENTER
63 North St.   Phone: (617) 359-7711
Medfield, MA 02052   Joyce Newton, Info.Spec.

MEDFIELD HISTORICAL SOCIETY - LIBRARY
6 Pleasant St.
Box 233
Medfield, MA 02052   Laura H. Smith, Libn.

MEDFIELD STATE HOSPITAL - MEDICAL LIBRARY
Hospital Rd.   Phone: (617) 359-7312
Medfield, MA 02052   Jeanne Migliacci, Sr.Libn.

LAWRENCE MEMORIAL HOSPITAL OF MEDFORD - HEALTH SCIENCES
   LIBRARY
170 Governors Ave.   Phone: (617) 396-9250
Medford, MA 02155   Elaine V. LeGendre, Health Sci.Libn.

MEDFORD HISTORICAL SOCIETY - LIBRARY
10 Governor's Ave.   Phone: (617) 395-7863
Medford, MA 02155   Joseph Valeriani

TUFTS UNIVERSITY - MATHEMATICS-PHYSICS LIBRARY
Robinson Hall, Rm. 251   Phone: (617) 628-5000
Medford, MA 02155   Pauline A. Boucher, Asst.Sci.Libn.

GEOGRAPHIC

GEOGRAPHIC

TUFTS UNIVERSITY - RICHARD H. LUFKIN LIBRARY
Anderson Hall   Phone: (617) 628-5000
Medford, MA 02155   Wayne B. Powell, Sci./Engr.Libn.

TUFTS UNIVERSITY - ROCKWELL CHEMISTRY LIBRARY
62 Talbot Ave.   Phone: (617) 628-5000
Medford, MA 02155   Pauline A. Boucher, Asst.Sci.Libn.

AMERICAN SOCIETY OF ABDOMINAL SURGEONS - DONALD COLLINS
     MEMORIAL LIBRARY
675 Main St.   Phone: (617) 665-6102
Melrose, MA 02176   Dr. Blaise F. Alfano, Hd.Libn.

FIRST BAPTIST CHURCH - LIBRARY
561 Main St.   Phone: (617) 665-4470
Melrose, MA 02176   Ruth Richardson, Libn.

BON SECOURS HOSPITAL - MEDICAL HEALTH SCIENCE LIBRARY
70 East St.   Phone: (617) 683-8781
Methuen, MA 01844   Chin-Soon Han, Hd.Libn.

WATERS ASSOCIATES INC. - INFORMATION RESOURCE CENTER
Maple St.   Phone: (617) 478-2000
Milford, MA 01757   Carla J. Clayton, Mgr., Info.Serv.

CURRY COLLEGE - LOUIS R. LEVIN MEMORIAL LIBRARY
1071 Blue Hill Ave.   Phone: (617) 333-0500
Milton, MA 02186   Dr. Marshall Keys, Dir.

MUSEUM OF THE AMERICAN CHINA TRADE - ARCHIVES
215 Adams St.   Phone: (617) 696-1815
Milton, MA 02186   Dana D. Ricciardi, Registrar/Archv.

NANTUCKET HISTORICAL ASSOCIATION - PETER FOULGER LIBRARY
Broad St.
Nantucket, MA 02554   Edourd A. Stackpole, Hist.

NANTUCKET MARIA MITCHELL ASSOCIATION - LIBRARY
Vestal St.   Phone: (617) 228-9198
Nantucket, MA 02554   Dr. M. Jane Stroup, Libn.

LEONARD MORSE HOSPITAL - MEDICAL LIBRARY
67 Union St.   Phone: (617) 653-3400
Natick, MA 01760   M. Margaret Cheney, Med.Libn.

U.S. ARMY - NATICK RESEARCH AND DEVELOPMENT LABORATORIES -
     TECHNICAL LIBRARY
                                            Phone: (617) 653-1000
Natick, MA 01760   Eugene G. Beary, Libn.

GTE - COMMUNICATION SYSTEMS DIVISION - MAIN LIBRARY
77 A St.   Phone: (617) 449-2000
Needham Heights, MA 02194   Dorothy C. Hill, Supv. of Lib.

NEW BEDFORD FREE PUBLIC LIBRARY - GENEALOGY ROOM
613 Pleasant St.   Phone: (617) 999-6291
New Bedford, MA 02740   Paul Cyr, Libn.

NEW BEDFORD FREE PUBLIC LIBRARY - MELVILLE WHALING ROOM
613 Pleasant St.   Phone: (617) 999-6291
New Bedford, MA 02740   Paul Cyr, Cur.

NEW BEDFORD LAW LIBRARY
441 County St.   Phone: (617) 992-8077
New Bedford, MA 02740   Margaretha E.H. Birknes, Law Libn.

NEW BEDFORD STANDARD-TIMES LIBRARY
555 Pleasant St.   Phone: (617) 997-7411
New Bedford, MA 02740   Maurice G. Lauzon, Libn.

OLD DARTMOUTH HISTORICAL SOCIETY AND WHALING MUSEUM -
     LIBRARY
18 Johnny Cake Hill   Phone: (617) 997-0046
New Bedford, MA 02740   Richard C. Kugler, Dir.

SWAIN SCHOOL OF DESIGN - LIBRARY †
140 Orchard St.   Phone: (617) 997-7831
New Bedford, MA 02740   Angela M. Sciotti, Lib.Dir.

HISTORICAL SOCIETY OF OLD NEWBURY - LIBRARY
Cushing House Museum
98 High St.   Phone: (603) 462-2681
Newburyport, MA 01950   Wilhelmina V. Lunt, Cur.

IRISH FAMILY HISTORY SOCIETY - LIBRARY
173 Tremont St.   Phone: (617) 965-0939
Newton, MA 02158   Joseph M. Glynn, Jr., Dir.

JACKSON HOMESTEAD - LIBRARY & ARCHIVES
527 Washington St.   Phone: (617) 552-7238
Newton, MA 02158   Duscha S. Scott, Dir.

NEWTON PUBLIC SCHOOLS - TEACHERS' PROFESSIONAL LIBRARY
100 Walnut St.   Phone: (617) 552-7630
Newton, MA 02160   David S. Whiting, Coord.Libn./Media

SWEDENBORG SCHOOL OF RELIGION - LIBRARY
48 Sargent St.   Phone: (617) 244-0504
Newton, MA 02158   Marian Kirven, Libn.

ANDOVER NEWTON THEOLOGICAL SCHOOL - TRASK LIBRARY
169 Herrick Rd.   Phone: (617) 964-1100
Newton Centre, MA 02159   Ellis E. O'Neal, Jr., Libn.

BOSTON COLLEGE - LAW SCHOOL LIBRARY
885 Centre St.   Phone: (617) 969-0100
Newton Centre, MA 02159   Sharon Hamby, Dir.

NEWTON-WELLESLEY HOSPITAL - PAUL TALBOT BABSON MEMORIAL
     LIBRARY
2014 Washington St.   Phone: (617) 964-2800
Newton Lower Falls, MA 02162   Christine L. Bell, Dir.Lib.Serv.

ACTION FOR CHILDREN'S TELEVISION - ACT RESOURCE LIBRARY
46 Austin St.   Phone: (617) 527-7870
Newtonville, MA 02160   Paula Rohrlick, Rsrcs.Dir.

PONDVILLE HOSPITAL - MEDICAL LIBRARY †
Box 111   Phone: (617) 668-0385
Norfolk, MA 02081

NORTH ADAMS STATE COLLEGE - EUGENE L. FREEL LIBRARY - SPECIAL
     COLLECTIONS
Church St.   Phone: (413) 664-4511
North Adams, MA 01247

SPRAGUE ELECTRIC COMPANY - RESEARCH LIBRARY *
87 Marshall St.   Phone: (413) 664-4411
North Adams, MA 01247   Mary B. Mace, Libn.

BELL TELEPHONE LABORATORIES, INC. & WESTERN ELECTRIC, INC. -
     TECHNICAL LIBRARY
1600 Osgood St.   Phone: (617) 681-6752
North Andover, MA 01845   Mary E. Sexton, Lib. Group Supv.

MERRIMACK VALLEY TEXTILE MUSEUM - LIBRARY
800 Massachusetts Ave.   Phone: (617) 686-0191
North Andover, MA 01845   Helena Wright, Libn.

NORTH ANDOVER HISTORICAL SOCIETY - LIBRARY
Merrimack Valley Textile Museum
800 Massachusetts Ave.   Phone: (617) 686-0191
North Andover, MA 01845   Mary Flinn, Soc.Adm.

STONEHILL COLLEGE - ARNOLD B. TOFIAS INDUSTRIAL ARCHIVES
320 Washington St.   Phone: (617) 238-1081
North Easton, MA 02356   Louise M. Kenneally, Archv.

FORBES LIBRARY
20 West St.   Phone: (413) 584-8550
Northampton, MA 01060   Blaise Bisaillon, Dir.

HAMPSHIRE COUNTY LAW LIBRARY
Court House   Phone: (413) 586-2297
Northampton, MA 01060   Barbara Fell-Johnson, Libn.

NORTHAMPTON HISTORICAL SOCIETY - HISTORICAL COLLECTION
46-66 Bridge St.   Phone: (413) 584-6011
Northampton, MA 01060   Ruth E. Wilbur, Dir.

SMITH COLLEGE - ARCHIVES
                                                    Phone: (413) 584-2700
Northampton, MA 01063   Mary-Elizabeth Murdock, Coll.Archv.

SMITH COLLEGE - CLARK SCIENCE LIBRARY
                                                    Phone: (413) 584-2700
Northampton, MA 01063   David Vikre, Sci.Libn.

SMITH COLLEGE - HILLYER ART LIBRARY
Fine Arts Ctr.   Phone: (413) 584-2700
Northampton, MA 01063   Karen J. Harvey, Libn.

SMITH COLLEGE - RARE BOOK ROOM
                                                    Phone: (413) 584-2700
Northampton, MA 01063   Ruth Mortimer, Cur.

SMITH COLLEGE - SOPHIA SMITH COLLECTION - WOMEN'S HISTORY
    ARCHIVE
                                                    Phone: (413) 584-2700
Northampton, MA 01063   Mary-Elizabeth Murdock, Dir.

SMITH COLLEGE - WERNER JOSTEN LIBRARY FOR THE PERFORMING ARTS
Mendenhall Ctr.   Phone: (413) 584-2700
Northampton, MA 01063   Mary M. Ankudowich, Libn.

U.S. VETERANS ADMINISTRATION (MA-Northampton) - MEDICAL CENTER
    LIBRARY
N. Main St.   Phone: (413) 584-4040
Northampton, MA 01060   Marjorie E. Sullivan, Chf., Lib.Serv.

WHEATON COLLEGE - LIBRARY - FINE ARTS COLLECTION
                                                    Phone: (617) 285-7722
Norton, MA 02766   Kersti Tannberg, Fine Arts Libn.

BRIGGS ENGINEERING & TESTING COMPANY, INC. - LIBRARY
164 Washington St.   Phone: (617) 773-2780
Norwell, MA 02061   R. Wayne Crandlemere, Dir.

FACTORY MUTUAL SYSTEM - FACTORY MUTUAL RESEARCH CORPORATION
    - LIBRARY
1151 Boston-Providence Tpke.   Phone: (617) 762-4300
Norwood, MA 02062   Bruce P. Mattoon, V.P.

RAYTHEON DATA SYSTEMS COMPANY - LIBRARY
1415 Boston-Providence Tpke.   Phone: (617) 762-6700
Norwood, MA 01748   Hazel M. Higgins, Libn.

OXFORD MUSEUM - LIBRARY
339 Main St.   Phone: (617) 987-2882
Oxford, MA 01540   Gloria L. Edinburg, Dir.

OXFORD UNITED METHODIST CHURCH - OSCAR G. COOK MEMORIAL
    LIBRARY *
465 Main St.   Phone: (617) 987-5378
Oxford, MA 01540

PEABODY HISTORICAL SOCIETY - LIBRARY AND ARCHIVES *
35 Washington St.   Phone: (617) 531-0805
Peabody, MA 01960

HARVARD UNIVERSITY - HARVARD FOREST LIBRARY
Shaler Hall   Phone: (617) 724-3285
Petersham, MA 01366   Catherine M. Danahar, Libn.

PETERSHAM HISTORICAL SOCIETY, INC. - LIBRARY
Main St.   Phone: (617) 724-3380
Petersham, MA 01366   Mrs. D. Gale Haines, Libn.

BERKSHIRE ATHENAEUM - MUSIC AND ARTS DEPARTMENT
One Wendell Ave.   Phone: (413) 442-1559
Pittsfield, MA 01201   Jean Bousquet, Supv.Mus./Art Serv.

BERKSHIRE EAGLE - LIBRARY
33 Eagle St.   Phone: (413) 447-7311
Pittsfield, MA 01201   Madeline F. Winter, Libn.

BERKSHIRE MEDICAL CENTER - MEDICAL LIBRARY
725 North St.   Phone: (413) 499-4161
Pittsfield, MA 01201   Jutta Luhde, Libn.

GENERAL ELECTRIC COMPANY - ORDNANCE SYSTEMS - ENGINEERING
    LIBRARY
100 Plastics Ave., Rm. 2168   Phone: (413) 494-4207
Pittsfield, MA 01201   Ann B. Rauch, Tech.Libn.

GENERAL ELECTRIC COMPANY - WILLIAM STANLEY LIBRARY †
100 Woodlawn Ave.   Phone: (413) 494-3763
Pittsfield, MA 01201   Kenneth Lauderdale, Libn.

SHAKER COMMUNITY, INC. - LIBRARY
Box 898   Phone: (413) 447-7284
Pittsfield, MA 01201   John H. Ott, Dir.

PILGRIM SOCIETY - PILGRIM HALL LIBRARY
75 Court St.   Phone: (617) 746-1620
Plymouth, MA 02360   Laurence R. Pizer, Dir.

PLIMOTH PLANTATION, INC. - LIBRARY
Warren Ave.
Box 1620   Phone: (617) 746-1622
Plymouth, MA 02360   James W. Baker, Res.Libn.

GENERAL DYNAMICS CORPORATION - QUINCY SHIPBUILDING DIVISION
    LIBRARY
97 E. Howard St.   Phone: (617) 471-4200
Quincy, MA 02169   G. Richard Myers, Libn.

NATIONAL FIRE PROTECTION ASSOCIATION - CHARLES S. MORGAN
    LIBRARY
Batterymarch Park   Phone: (617) 328-9290
Quincy, MA 02269   Nancy Corrin, Mgr.

QUINCY HISTORICAL SOCIETY - LIBRARY
Adams Academy Bldg., 8 Adams St.   Phone: (617) 773-1144
Quincy, MA 02169   Lawrence J. Yerdon, Musm.Dir./Cur.

ADDISON-WESLEY PUBLISHING COMPANY - LIBRARY
Jacob Way   Phone: (617) 944-3700
Reading, MA 01867

SANDY BAY HISTORICAL SOCIETY AND MUSEUM - LIBRARY
40 King St.
Rockport, MA 01966   Dr. William D. Hoyt, Cur.

METROPOLITAN COUNCIL FOR EDUCATIONAL OPPORTUNITY - LIBRARY
55 Dimock St.   Phone: (617) 427-1545
Roxbury, MA 02119   Marcus J. Mitchell, Pub.Rel.Dir.

ESSEX COUNTY LAW LIBRARY
34 Federal St.   Phone: (617) 744-1240
Salem, MA 01240   J. Joseph Gilligan, Libn.

ESSEX INSTITUTE - JAMES DUNCAN PHILLIPS LIBRARY
132-134 Essex St.   Phone: (617) 744-3390
Salem, MA 01970   Bryant F. Tolles, Jr., Libn.

PEABODY MUSEUM OF SALEM - PHILLIPS LIBRARY
161 Essex St.   Phone: (617) 745-1876
Salem, MA 01970   Barbara B. Edkins, Libn.

SALEM HOSPITAL - MACK MEMORIAL HEALTH SCIENCES LIBRARY
81 Highland Ave.   Phone: (617) 744-6000
Salem, MA 01970   Nancy Fazzone, Dir., Lib.Serv.

SALEM STATE COLLEGE - CURRICULUM RESOURCES CENTER †
Library, 352 Lafayette St.   Phone: (617) 745-0556
Salem, MA 01970   Gertrude L. Fox, Libn.

SALEM STATE COLLEGE - LIBRARY †
Lafayette St.   Phone: (617) 745-0556
Salem, MA 01970   Neil B. Olson, Dir. of Libs.

SALEM STATE COLLEGE - STUDENT GOVERNMENT ASSOCIATION &
    LIBRARY - LIBRARY OF SOCIAL ALTERNATIVES †
                                                    Phone: (617) 745-0556
Salem, MA 01970   Mary Karonis, Coord.

U.S. NATL. PARK SERVICE - SALEM MARITIME NATL. HISTORIC SITE - LIBRARY
Custom House, Derby St.   Phone: (617) 744-4323
Salem, MA 01970   John M. Frayler, Cur.

YESTERYEARS MUSEUM ASSOCIATION, INC. - LIBRARY
Main & River Sts.   Phone: (617) 888-1711
Sandwich, MA 02563   Ronald F. Thomas, Libn./Treas.

U.S. NATL. PARK SERVICE - SAUGUS IRON WORKS NATL. HISTORIC SITE - LIBRARY
244 Central St.   Phone: (617) 233-0050
Saugus, MA 01906   Cynthia Pollack, Park Ranger

SCITUATE HISTORICAL SOCIETY - LIBRARY
Cudworth House, First Parish Rd.
Scituate, MA 02066   Mrs. Philip H. Wood, Libn.

KENDALL WHALING MUSEUM - LIBRARY
27 Everett St.
Box 297   Phone: (617) 784-5642
Sharon, MA 02067   Stuart Frank, Dir.

TEMPLE ISRAEL - LEONARD M. SANDHAUS MEMORIAL LIBRARY *
125 Pond St.   Phone: (617) 784-3986
Sharon, MA 02067   Annette Tovsky, Libn.

WORCESTER FOUNDATION FOR EXPERIMENTAL BIOLOGY - GEORGE F. FULLER LIBRARY
222 Maple St.   Phone: (617) 842-8921
Shrewsbury, MA 01545   Melinda Saffer, Lib.Dir.

SOMERVILLE HOSPITAL - CARR HEALTH SCIENCES LIBRARY
230 Highland Ave.   Phone: (617) 666-4400
Somerville, MA 02143   Janet P. Smith, Libn.

GORDON-CONWELL THEOLOGICAL SEMINARY - GODDARD LIBRARY
130 Essex St.   Phone: (617) 468-7111
South Hamilton, MA 01982   Robert Dvorak, Dir.

NATICK HISTORICAL SOCIETY - LIBRARY *
Bacon Free Library Bldg.   Phone: (617) 653-6730
South Natick, MA 01760   Anne K. Schaller, Dir.

BIRD MACHINE COMPANY, INC. - LIBRARY
Neponset St.   Phone: (617) 668-0400
South Walpole, MA 02071   Barbara E. Mangion, Libn.

U.S. NATL. PARK SERVICE - CAPE COD NATL. SEASHORE - LIBRARY
Marconi Station Site   Phone: (617) 349-3785
South Wellfleet, MA 02663   Michael Whatley, Act.Chf., Interp.

HARVARD UNIVERSITY - NEW ENGLAND REGIONAL PRIMATE RESEARCH CENTER - LIBRARY
One Pine Hill Dr.   Phone: (617) 481-0400
Southborough, MA 01772   Sydney Fingold, Libn.

AMERICAN OPTICAL CORPORATION - RESEARCH CENTER LIBRARY
     Phone: (617) 765-9711
Southbridge, MA 01550   C. Hermas Swope, Lib.Adm.

EDWARDS (Jacob) LIBRARY
236 Main St.   Phone: (617) 764-2544
Southbridge, MA 01550   Ronald G. Latham, Dir.

ST. JOSEPH'S ABBEY - LIBRARY
Rte. 31   Phone: (617) 885-3901
Spencer, MA 01562   Br. Luke Truhan, Libn.

BAYSTATE MEDICAL CENTER - LIBRARY
759 Chestnut St.   Phone: (413) 787-4293
Springfield, MA 01107   Jean Scougall, Dir.

CONNECTICUT VALLEY HISTORICAL MUSEUM - RESEARCH LIBRARY
194 State St.   Phone: (413) 732-3080
Springfield, MA 01103   Gregory Farmer, Dir.

HAMPDEN COUNTY LAW LIBRARY
Hall of Justice
50 State St.   Phone: (413) 781-8100
Springfield, MA 01103   John J. Kelly, Libn.

INVENTORS CLUB OF AMERICA - INVENTORS REFERENCE CENTER
121 Chestnut St.   Phone: (413) 733-3286
Springfield, MA 01101   Alexander T. Marinaccio, Supv.Lib./Tech.Serv.

MASSACHUSETTS COLLEGE OF PHARMACY & ALLIED HEALTH SCIENCES - HAMPDEN CAMPUS LIBRARY
1215 Wilbraham Rd.   Phone: (413) 782-3111
Springfield, MA 01119   Mark J. Gazillo, Pharmacy Libn.

MASSACHUSETTS MUTUAL LIFE INSURANCE COMPANY - LAW LIBRARY
1295 State St.   Phone: (413) 788-8411
Springfield, MA 01111   Joan M. Jacques, Libn.

MASSACHUSETTS MUTUAL LIFE INSURANCE COMPANY - LIBRARY
1295 State St.   Phone: (413) 788-8411
Springfield, MA 01111   Yvette M. Jensen, Libn.

MERCY HOSPITAL - MEDICAL & HOSPITAL INSERVICE LIBRARIES
233 Carew St.   Phone: (413) 781-9100
Springfield, MA 01104   Mary G. Manning, Libn.

NAISMITH MEMORIAL BASKETBALL HALL OF FAME - EDWARD J. AND GENA G. HICKOX LIBRARY
460 Alden St.
Highland Sta., Box 175   Phone: (413) 781-6500
Springfield, MA 01109   June Harrison Steitz, Subject Spec.

SMITH (George Walter Vincent) ART MUSEUM - LIBRARY
222 State St.   Phone: (413) 733-4214
Springfield, MA 01103   Richard Muhlberger, Dir.

SPRINGFIELD ACADEMY OF MEDICINE - HEALTH SCIENCE LIBRARY
1400 State St.   Phone: (413) 734-5445
Springfield, MA 01109   Mildred E. Martin, Libn.

SPRINGFIELD CITY LIBRARY - FINE ARTS DEPARTMENT
220 State St.   Phone: (413) 739-3871
Springfield, MA 01103   Karen A. Dorval, Fine Arts Supv.

SPRINGFIELD CITY LIBRARY - WARTIME PROPAGANDA COLLECTION
220 State St., Rice Hall   Phone: (413) 739-3871
Springfield, MA 01103   Joseph Carvalho, III, Coll.Libn.

SPRINGFIELD COLLEGE - BABSON LIBRARY
263 Alden St.   Phone: (413) 787-2340
Springfield, MA 01109   Gerald F. Davis, Lib.Dir.

SPRINGFIELD LIBRARY AND MUSEUMS ASSOCIATION - CATHERINE E. HOWARD MEMORIAL LIBRARY
236 State St.   Phone: (413) 733-1194
Springfield, MA 01103   Glen P. Ives, Musm.Dir.

SPRINGFIELD NEWSPAPERS - LIBRARY †
1860 Main St.   Phone: (413) 787-2411
Springfield, MA 01101   Judith I. Epstein, Libn.

WESTERN NEW ENGLAND COLLEGE - JOHN D. CHURCHILL MEMORIAL LIBRARY
1215 Wilbraham Rd.   Phone: (413) 782-3111
Springfield, MA 01119   Glenn H. Johnson, Jr., Dir.

WESTERN NEW ENGLAND COLLEGE - SCHOOL OF LAW LIBRARY
1215 Wilbraham Rd.   Phone: (413) 782-3111
Springfield, MA 01119   Donald J. Dunn, Law Libn.

CHESTERWOOD - LIBRARY
Box 248   Phone: (413) 298-3579
Stockbridge, MA 01262   Susan Frisch Lehrer, Cur.

RIGGS (Austen) CENTER, INC. - AUSTEN FOX RIGGS LIBRARY
     Phone: (413) 298-5511
Stockbridge, MA 01262   Helen Linton, Libn.

STOCKBRIDGE LIBRARY ASSOCIATION - HISTORICAL ROOM
Main & Elm Sts.   Phone: (413) 298-5501
Stockbridge, MA 01262   Pauline D. Pierce, Cur.

OLD STURBRIDGE VILLAGE - RESEARCH LIBRARY
                                          Phone: (617) 347-3362
Sturbridge, MA 01566   Etta Falkner, Libn.

CHURCH OF JESUS CHRIST OF LATTER-DAY SAINTS - BOSTON BRANCH
    GENEALOGICAL LIBRARY
250 Maynard Rd.   Phone: (617) 235-9892
Sudbury, MA 01776   Algy Alexander, Libn.

RAYTHEON COMPANY - EQUIPMENT DIVISION - TECHNICAL
    INFORMATION CENTER
528 Boston Post Rd.   Phone: (617) 443-9521
Sudbury, MA 01776   Joan Dexter, Libn.

SPERRY CORPORATION - RESEARCH CENTER LIBRARY
North Rd.   Phone: (617) 369-4000
Sudbury, MA 01776   H.A. Steeves, Libn.

BRISTOL COUNTY LAW LIBRARY
Superior Court House   Phone: (617) 824-7632
Taunton, MA 02780   Carol A. Francis, Libn.

OLD COLONY HISTORICAL SOCIETY - MUSEUM & LIBRARY
66 Church Green   Phone: (617) 822-1622
Taunton, MA 02780

TAUNTON STATE HOSPITAL - MEDICAL LIBRARY
Hodges Ave.   Phone: (617) 824-7551
Taunton, MA 02780

MASSACHUSETTS COMPUTER ASSOCIATES, INC. - LIBRARY
26 Princess St.   Phone: (617) 245-9540
Wakefield, MA 01880   Jane C. Cotreau, Libn.

AMERICAN JEWISH HISTORICAL SOCIETY - LIBRARY
2 Thornton Rd.   Phone: (617) 891-8110
Waltham, MA 02154   Nathan M. Kaganoff, Libn.

BENTLEY COLLEGE - SOLOMON R. BAKER LIBRARY
Beaver & Forest Sts.   Phone: (617) 891-2231
Waltham, MA 02254   Joyce A. Bennett, Dir.

BRANDEIS UNIVERSITY - GERSTENZANG SCIENCE LIBRARY
415 South St.   Phone: (617) 647-2534
Waltham, MA 02254   Phyllis Cutler, Asst.Univ.Libn.

CHARLES RIVER BROADCASTING COMPANY - WCRB LIBRARY
750 South St.   Phone: (617) 893-7080
Waltham, MA 02154   George C. Brown, Music Dir.

CORPORATE-TECH PLANNING - RESEARCH LIBRARY
275 Wyman St.   Phone: (617) 890-2600
Waltham, MA 02154   Susan M. Castro, Res.Libn.

GORE PLACE SOCIETY, INC. - LIBRARY
52 Gore St.   Phone: (617) 894-2798
Waltham, MA 02154   Charles Hammond, Dir.

GTE LABORATORIES - LIBRARY
40 Sylvan Rd.   Phone: (617) 890-8460
Waltham, MA 02154   David Jelley, Hd.Libn.

HELIX TECHNOLOGY CORPORATION - LIBRARY
266 Second Ave.   Phone: (617) 890-9400
Waltham, MA 02254   Carole B. Shutzer, Libn.

HEWLETT-PACKARD COMPANY - MEDICAL ELECTRONICS DIVISION -
    LIBRARY
175 Wyman St.   Phone: (617) 890-6300
Waltham, MA 02154   Susan Saraidaridis, Libn.

HONEYWELL, INC. - HONEYWELL INFORMATION SYSTEMS - INFORMATION
    AND LIBRARY SERVICES
200 Smith St., MS 423   Phone: (617) 895-3622
Waltham, MA 02154   Melissa Brokalakis, Mgr., Info./Lib.Serv

MOBIL TYCO SOLAR ENERGY CORPORATION - LIBRARY
16 Hickory Dr.   Phone: (617) 890-0909
Waltham, MA 02254   Dorothy O. Bergin, Libn.

RAYTHEON COMPANY - RESEARCH DIVISION - LIBRARY
28 Seyon St.   Phone: (617) 899-8400
Waltham, MA 02154   Madaleine Bennett, Libn.

SHRIVER (Eunice Kennedy) CENTER FOR MENTAL RETARDATION, INC. -
    LIBRARY
200 Trapelo Rd.   Phone: (617) 893-3500
Waltham, MA 02154   Jacklyn Collette, Libn.

U.S. NATL. ARCHIVES & RECORDS SERVICE - FEDERAL ARCHIVES AND
    RECORDS CENTER, REGION 1
380 Trapelo Rd.   Phone: (617) 894-2400
Waltham, MA 02154   Clifford Amsler, Jr., Dir.

WALTHAM HOSPITAL - MEDICAL LIBRARY
Hope Ave.   Phone: (617) 899-3300
Waltham, MA 02154   Cheryl K. Kowalski, Libn.

TOBEY HOSPITAL - STILLMAN LIBRARY
High St.   Phone: (617) 295-0880
Wareham, MA 02571   Phyllis L. Collins, Libn.

IONICS, INC. - RESEARCH DEPARTMENT LIBRARY
65 Grove St.   Phone: (617) 926-2500
Watertown, MA 02172   Lorraine C. Baron, Libn.

PERKINS SCHOOL FOR THE BLIND - SAMUEL P. HAYES RESEARCH LIBRARY
175 N. Beacon St.   Phone: (617) 924-3434
Watertown, MA 02172   Kenneth A. Stuckey, Res.Libn.

SASAKI ASSOCIATES, INC. - LIBRARY
64 Pleasant St.   Phone: (617) 926-3300
Watertown, MA 02172   Jeanne M. Clancy, Libn.

U.S. ARMY - MATERIALS & MECHANICS RESEARCH CENTER - TECHNICAL
    LIBRARY
                                          Phone: (617) 923-3460
Watertown, MA 02172   Margaret M. Murphy, Chf., Tech.Lib.

RAYTHEON COMPANY - EQUIPMENT DIVISION - TECHNICAL
    INFORMATION CENTER
Boston Post Rd.   Phone: (617) 358-2721
Wayland, MA 01778   Joanne Portsch, Libn.

EDUCATIONAL RECORDS BUREAU - LIBRARY
Bardwell Hall
37 Cameron St.   Phone: (617) 235-8920
Wellesley, MA 02181   R. Bruce McGill, Pres.

EG&G, INC. - CORPORATE HEADQUARTERS - BUSINESS & FINANCIAL
    REFERENCE LIBRARY
45 William St.   Phone: (617) 237-5100
Wellesley, MA 02181   Raymond J. Champoux

HONEYWELL, INC. - HONEYWELL INFORMATION SYSTEMS - CIC
    INFORMATION CENTER *
65 Walnut St.   Phone: (617) 552-1132
Wellesley, MA 02181   Kathy Ott, Lib.Supv.

INSTITUTE OF CERTIFIED TRAVEL AGENTS - LIBRARY
148 Linden St.   Phone: (617) 237-0280
Wellesley, MA 02181   David S. Claflin, Dir./Adm.

WELLESLEY COLLEGE - ARCHIVES
Wellesley College   Phone: (617) 235-0320
Wellesley, MA 02181   Wilma R. Slaight, Archv.

WELLESLEY COLLEGE - ART LIBRARY
Jewett Arts Ctr.   Phone: (617) 235-0320
Wellesley, MA 02181   Katherine D. Finkelpearl, Art Libn.

WELLESLEY COLLEGE - MUSIC LIBRARY
Jewett Arts Center   Phone: (617) 235-0320
Wellesley, MA 02181   Mary Wallace Davidson, Music Libn.

WELLESLEY COLLEGE - SCIENCE LIBRARY
Science Ctr.   Phone: (617) 235-0320
Wellesley, MA 02181   Irene S. Laursen, Science Libn.

FIRST CONGREGATIONAL CHURCH IN WELLESLEY HILLS - LIBRARY †
207 Washington St.   Phone: (617) 235-4424
Wellesley Hills, MA 02181   Mrs. Charles W. Homeyer, Jr., Libn.

SUN LIFE ASSURANCE COMPANY OF CANADA - REFERENCE LIBRARY
One Sun Life Executive Park   Phone: (617) 237-6030
Wellesley Hills, MA 02181   Pamela A. Gardner, Libn.

GORDON COLLEGE - WINN LIBRARY
255 Grapevine Rd.   Phone: (617) 927-2300
Wenham, MA 01984   John Beauregard, Dir.

NEW ENGLAND BOARD OF HIGHER EDUCATION - LIBRARY
68 Walnut Rd.   Phone: (617) 468-7341
Wenham, MA 01984   Janet R. Slinn, Info.Serv.Cons.

WENHAM HISTORICAL ASSOCIATION AND MUSEUM - COLONEL TIMOTHY
     PICKERING LIBRARY
132 Main St.   Phone: (617) 468-2377
Wenham, MA 01984   Eleanor E. Thompson, Dir.

DATA GENERAL CORPORATION - CORPORATE RESEARCH & DEVELOPMENT
     LIBRARY
MS A-1 4400 Computer Dr.   Phone: (617) 366-8911
Westborough, MA 01581   Mary DeMartin, Coord.Info. Center

NEW ENGLAND POWER COMPANY - TECHNICAL INFORMATION CENTER
25 Research Dr.   Phone: (617) 366-9011
Westborough, MA 01581   William J. McCall, Sr.Tech.Libn.

WESTFIELD STATE COLLEGE - GOVERNOR JOSEPH B. ELY MEMORIAL
     LIBRARY
Western Ave.   Phone: (413) 568-3311
Westfield, MA 01086   Kenneth W. Cotton, Lib.Dir.

BOSTON COLLEGE - WESTON OBSERVATORY - CATHERINE B. O'CONNOR
     LIBRARY
                                                    Phone: (617) 899-0950
Weston, MA 02193   F. Clifford McElroy, Sci.Libn.

CARDINAL SPELLMAN PHILATELIC MUSEUM, INC. - LIBRARY
235 Wellesley St.   Phone: (617) 894-6735
Weston, MA 02193   Shakuntala Gokahle, Libn.

POPE JOHN XXIII NATIONAL SEMINARY - LIBRARY
558 South Ave.   Phone: (617) 899-5500
Weston, MA 02193   Rev. James L. Fahey, Libn.

UNDERWOOD (William) COMPANY - LIBRARY
One Red Devil Lane   Phone: (617) 329-5300
Westwood, MA 02090   Ms. Lee Miller-Hartnett, Libn./Archv.

CLARK (Sterling and Francine) ART INSTITUTE - LIBRARY
South St.
Box 8   Phone: (413) 458-8109
Williamstown, MA 01267   Michael Rinehart, Libn.

WILLIAMS COLLEGE - CENTER FOR ENVIRONMENTAL STUDIES - LIBRARY
                                                    Phone: (413) 597-2500
Williamstown, MA 01267   Nancy E. Hanssen, Doc.Libn.

WILLIAMS COLLEGE - CHAPIN LIBRARY
Stetson Hall, 2nd Fl.
Box 426   Phone: (413) 597-2462
Williamstown, MA 01267   Robert L. Volz, Custodian

ABCOR, INC. - LIBRARY
850 Main St.   Phone: (617) 657-4250
Wilmington, MA 01887   Kathleen Morton, Libn.

AVCO CORPORATION - SYSTEMS DIVISION - RESEARCH LIBRARY
201 Lowell St.   Phone: (617) 657-2632
Wilmington, MA 01887   Elizabeth M. Howard, Libn.

DYNAMICS RESEARCH CORPORATION - LIBRARY *
60 Concord St.   Phone: (617) 658-6100
Wilmington, MA 01887   Mary E. Brindamour, Libn.

INSTRUMENTATION LABORATORY, INC. - ANALYTICAL INSTRUMENTS
     DIVISION - LIBRARY
Jonspin Rd.   Phone: (617) 658-5125
Wilmington, MA 01887   Jacqueline R. Kates, Corp.Libn.

FLAG RESEARCH CENTER - LIBRARY
3 Edgehill Rd.   Phone: (617) 729-9410
Winchester, MA 01890   M. Smith, Dir.

U.S. PUBLIC HEALTH SERVICE - WINCHESTER ENGINEERING &
     ANALYTICAL CENTER - LIBRARY
109 Holton St.   Phone: (617) 729-5700
Winchester, MA 01890   Barbara Murphy, Adm.Asst.

MASSACHUSETTS STATE DISTRICT COURT - FOURTH EASTERN
     MIDDLESEX DIVISION - LIBRARY
30 Pleasant St.   Phone: (617) 935-4000
Woburn, MA 01801   Gertrude M. Allen, Libn.

NORTHERN RESEARCH & ENGINEERING CORPORATION - LIBRARY
39 Olympia Ave.   Phone: (617) 935-9050
Woburn, MA 01801   Mary Frances O'Brien, Libn.

MARINE BIOLOGICAL LABORATORY - LIBRARY
                                                    Phone: (617) 548-3705
Woods Hole, MA 02543   Jane Fessenden, Libn.

U.S. NATL. MARINE FISHERIES SERVICE - NORTHEAST FISHERIES CENTER
     - LIBRARY
                                                    Phone: (617) 548-5123
Woods Hole, MA 02543   Judith Brownlow, Libn.

WOODS HOLE OCEANOGRAPHIC INSTITUTION - RESEARCH LIBRARY
                                                    Phone: (617) 548-1400
Woods Hole, MA 02543   Carolyn P. Winn, Res.Libn.

AMERICAN ANTIQUARIAN SOCIETY - LIBRARY
185 Salisbury St.   Phone: (617) 755-5221
Worcester, MA 01609   Marcus A. McCorison, Dir.

CLARK UNIVERSITY - GRADUATE SCHOOL OF GEOGRAPHY - GUY H.
     BURNHAM MAP-AERIAL PHOTOGRAPH LIBRARY
950 Main St.   Phone: (617) 793-7322
Worcester, MA 01610   Michael Dulka, Map/Geog.Libn.

EG&G, INC. - MASON RESEARCH INSTITUTE - LIBRARY *
57 Union St.   Phone: (617) 791-0931
Worcester, MA 01608   Evelyn M. Brann, Libn.

HIGGINS (John Woodman) ARMORY, INC. - MEMORIAL LIBRARY
100 Barber Ave.   Phone: (617) 853-6015
Worcester, MA 01606   Mrs. Erveen C. Lundberg, Hd.

HOLY CROSS COLLEGE - SCIENCE LIBRARY
                                                    Phone: (617) 793-2643
Worcester, MA 01610   Tony Stankus, Sci.Libn.

MEMORIAL HOSPITAL - HOMER GAGE LIBRARY
119 Belmont St.   Phone: (617) 793-6421
Worcester, MA 01605

NORTON COMPANY - LIBRARY/TECHNICAL INFORMATION CENTER
One New Bond St.   Phone: (617) 853-1000
Worcester, MA 01606   Judith M. Gleason, Tech.Info.Spec.

STATE MUTUAL LIFE ASSURANCE COMPANY OF AMERICA - LIBRARY
440 Lincoln St.   Phone: (617) 852-1000
Worcester, MA 01605   Wendell G. Small, Jr., Libn.

UNIVERSITY OF MASSACHUSETTS MEDICAL SCHOOL & WORCESTER
     DISTRICT MEDICAL SOCIETY - LIBRARY
55 N. Lake Ave.   Phone: (617) 856-2511
Worcester, MA 01605   Donald J. Morton, Dir.

WORCESTER ART MUSEUM - LIBRARY
55 Salisbury St.
Worcester, MA 01608
Phone: (617) 799-4406
Hollee Haswell, Libn.

WORCESTER CITY HOSPITAL - MEDICAL LIBRARY
26 Queen St.
Worcester, MA 01610
Phone: (617) 799-8186
Mary Anne Toner, Libn.

WORCESTER COUNTY HORTICULTURAL SOCIETY - LIBRARY
30 Elm St.
Worcester, MA 01608
Phone: (617) 752-4274
Wanda H. Sandberg, Libn.

WORCESTER COUNTY LAW LIBRARY
Court House
Worcester, MA 01608
Phone: (617) 756-2441
Mary A. Terpo, Law Libn.

WORCESTER FREE PUBLIC LIBRARY - REFERENCE AND RESEARCH
Salem Sq.
Worcester, MA 01608
Phone: (617) 752-3751
Norman E. Lovely, Hd., Ref. & Res.

WORCESTER HAHNEMANN HOSPITAL - SCHOOL OF NURSING LIBRARY †
281 Lincoln St.
Worcester, MA 01605
Phone: (617) 757-7751
R.S. Hunter, Libn.

WORCESTER HISTORICAL MUSEUM - LIBRARY
39 Salisbury St.
Worcester, MA 01608
Phone: (617) 753-8278
Jessica S. Goss, Libn.

WORCESTER POLYTECHNIC INSTITUTE - GEORGE C. GORDON LIBRARY
West St.
Worcester, MA 01609
Phone: (617) 753-1411
Albert G. Anderson, Jr., Hd.Libn.

WORCESTER STATE COLLEGE - LEARNING RESOURCES CENTER
486 Chandler St.
Worcester, MA 01602
Phone: (617) 752-7700
Bruce Plummer, Act.Dir.

WORCESTER TELEGRAM AND GAZETTE, INC. - LIBRARY
20 Franklin St.
Worcester, MA 01613
Phone: (617) 755-4321
Sharon C. Carter, Libn.

WORCESTER VOCATIONAL SCHOOLS - GEORGE I. ALDEN LIBRARY
26 Salisbury St.
Worcester, MA 01605
Phone: (617) 799-1945

MICHIGAN

BIXBY (Emma L.) HOSPITAL - PATMOS MEMORIAL LIBRARY
818 Riverside Ave.
Adrian, MI 49221
Phone: (517) 263-0711
Cinda Walton, Dir. of Med.Rec.

LENAWEE COUNTY HISTORICAL MUSEUM - LIBRARY
110 E. Church
Box 511
Adrian, MI 49221
Phone: (517) 265-6071
Charles N. Lindquist, Cur.

STAUFFER CHEMICAL COMPANY - SWS SILICONES - TECHNICAL LIBRARY
Sutton Rd.
Adrian, MI 49221
Phone: (517) 263-5711

U.S. VETERANS ADMINISTRATION (MI-Allen Park) - MEDICAL CENTER
LIBRARY SERVICE (142D) *
Phone: (313) 562-6000
Allen Park, MI 48101
Bill Leavens, Chf.

ALPENA COUNTY LAW LIBRARY *
Courthouse
Alpena, MI 49707
Phone: (517) 356-0395
Mabel Ann Joseph, Law Libn.

BESSER (Jesse) MUSEUM - LIBRARY
491 Johnson St.
Alpena, MI 49707
Phone: (517) 356-2202
Dennis Bodem, Dir.

AMAX, INC. - CLIMAX MOLYBDENUM COMPANY OF MICHIGAN - LIBRARY
1600 Huron Parkway
Ann Arbor, MI 48105
Phone: (313) 761-2300
Eva Maria Di Giulio, Libn.

ANN ARBOR NEWS - LIBRARY
340 E. Huron St.
Ann Arbor, MI 48106
Phone: (313) 994-6953
Mary Meernik, Libn.

COMMUNITY SYSTEMS FOUNDATION - NUTRITION PLANNING
INFORMATION SERVICE
1130 Hill St.
Ann Arbor, MI 48103
Phone: (313) 761-1357
Martha C. Gregg, Libn.

ENVIRONMENTAL RESEARCH INSTITUTE OF MICHIGAN - ERIM
INFORMATION CENTER
Box 8618
Ann Arbor, MI 48107
Phone: (313) 994-1200
Karen E. Pearce, Res.Libn.

ENVIRONMENTAL RESEARCH INSTITUTE OF MICHIGAN - INFRARED
INFORMATION AND ANALYSIS CENTER (IRIA)
Box 8618
Ann Arbor, MI 48107
Phone: (313) 994-1200
George J. Zissis, Dir.

ERIC CLEARINGHOUSE ON COUNSELING AND PERSONNEL SERVICES -
LEARNING RESOURCES CENTER
School of Education Bldg.
University of Michigan
Ann Arbor, MI 48109
Phone: (313) 764-9492
Helen L. Mamarchev, Coord.LRC

FIRST PRESBYTERIAN CHURCH - LIBRARY *
1432 Washtenaw Ave.
Ann Arbor, MI 48104
Phone: (313) 662-4466

GREAT LAKES BASIN COMMISSION - GREAT LAKES BASIN LIBRARY
3475 Plymouth Rd.
Box 999
Ann Arbor, MI 48106
Phone: (313) 668-2322
Barbara Kohler, Libn.

GUILD OF CARILLONNEURS IN NORTH AMERICA - ARCHIVES
900 Burton Memorial Tower
University of Michigan
Ann Arbor, MI 48109
Phone: (313) 764-2539
William De Turk, Archv.

INSTITUTE OF GERONTOLOGY - LIBRARY
University of Michigan
520 E. Liberty St.
Ann Arbor, MI 48109
Phone: (313) 763-1325
Willie M. Edwards, Hd.Libn.

KMS FUSION, INC. - FUSION LIBRARY
3941 Research Park Dr.
Box 1567
Ann Arbor, MI 48106
Phone: (313) 769-8500
Christine Bennet, Tech.Libn.

LUTHERAN CHURCH - MISSOURI SYNOD - MICHIGAN DISTRICT ARCHIVES
4090 Geddes Rd.
Ann Arbor, MI 48105
Phone: (313) 665-3691
Rev. Edwin A. Mueckler, Archv.

MATHEMATICAL REVIEWS - LIBRARY
611 Church St.
Ann Arbor, MI 48104
Phone: (313) 764-7228
Janice Seidler, Hd.Libn.

MICHIGAN MUNICIPAL LEAGUE - LIBRARY
1675 Green Rd.
Box 1487
Ann Arbor, MI 48106
Phone: (313) 662-3246
Carol Genco, Coord.Lib./Inquiry Serv.

MICHIGAN STATE DEPARTMENT OF NATURAL RESOURCES - INSTITUTE
FOR FISHERIES RESEARCH - LIBRARY
Univ. Musms. Annex,
University Of Michigan
Ann Arbor, MI 48109
Phone: (313) 663-3554
Margaret McClure, Libn.

NORTH AMERICAN STUDENTS OF COOPERATION - LIBRARY
Box 7293
Ann Arbor, MI 48107
Phone: (313) 663-0889
Sheila Ritter, Exec.Dir.

ST. JOSEPH MERCY HOSPITAL - RIECKER MEMORIAL LIBRARY
Box 995
Ann Arbor, MI 48106
Phone: (313) 572-3045
Metta T. Lansdale, Jr., Mgr., Lib.Serv.

U.S. FISH & WILDLIFE SERVICE - JOHN VAN OOSTEN GREAT LAKES
FISHERY RESEARCH LIBRARY
Great Lakes Fishery Laboratory
1451 Green Rd.
Ann Arbor, MI 48105
Phone: (313) 994-3331
Cynthia McCauley, Libn.

U.S. NATL. OCEANIC & ATMOSPHERIC ADMINISTRATION -
    ENVIRONMENTAL DATA & INFO. SERV. - GREAT LAKES LIBRARY †
2300 Washtenaw Ave.   Phone: (313) 668-2235
Ann Arbor, MI 48104   Barbara J. Carrick, Libn.

U.S. VETERANS ADMINISTRATION (MI-Ann Arbor) - HOSPITAL LIBRARY *
2215 Fuller Rd.   Phone: (313) 769-7100
Ann Arbor, MI 48105   Mary Elizabeth Batey, Chf.Libn.

UNIVERSITY OF MICHIGAN - AEROSPACE ENGINEERING DEPARTMENTAL
    LIBRARY
221 Aerospace Engineering Bldg.   Phone: (313) 764-9159
Ann Arbor, MI 48109   Sharon Bauerle, Sec./Libn.

UNIVERSITY OF MICHIGAN - ALFRED TAUBMAN MEDICAL LIBRARY
1135 E. Catherine   Phone: (313) 764-1210
Ann Arbor, MI 48109   L. Yvonne Wulff, Hd.

UNIVERSITY OF MICHIGAN - ART & ARCHITECTURE LIBRARY
2106 Art & Architecture Bldg.   Phone: (313) 764-1303
Ann Arbor, MI 48109   Peggy Ann Kusnerz, Libn.

UNIVERSITY OF MICHIGAN - ASIA LIBRARY
Hatcher Graduate Library, 4th Fl.   Phone: (313) 764-0406
Ann Arbor, MI 48109   Weiying Wan, Hd.

UNIVERSITY OF MICHIGAN - BUREAU OF GOVERNMENT LIBRARY
100A Rackham Bldg.   Phone: (313) 763-3185
Ann Arbor, MI 48109   Gertrude Stolper, Libn.

UNIVERSITY OF MICHIGAN - BUSINESS ADMINISTRATION LIBRARY
Graduate School of Business Adm.
Tappan & Monroe   Phone: (313) 764-1375
Ann Arbor, MI 48109   Nancy Evich, Act.Dir.

UNIVERSITY OF MICHIGAN - BUSINESS ADMINISTRATION LIBRARY -
    INDUSTRIAL RELATIONS SECTION
330 Graduate School of Business Adm.   Phone: (313) 764-3108
Ann Arbor, MI 48109   JoAnn Sokkar, Libn.

UNIVERSITY OF MICHIGAN - CENTER FOR CONTINUING EDUCATION OF
    WOMEN - LIBRARY
350 S. Thayer   Phone: (313) 764-6555
Ann Arbor, MI 48109   Patricia Padala, Libn.

UNIVERSITY OF MICHIGAN - CENTER FOR RESEARCH ON ECONOMIC
    DEVELOPMENT
240 Lorch Hall   Phone: (313) 763-6609
Ann Arbor, MI 48109   Carol R. Wilson, Libn.

UNIVERSITY OF MICHIGAN - CHEMISTRY LIBRARY
2000 Chemistry Bldg.   Phone: (313) 764-7337
Ann Arbor, MI 48109   Stephen C. Lucchetti, Libn.

UNIVERSITY OF MICHIGAN - COOPERATIVE INFORMATION CENTER FOR
    HOSPITAL MANAGEMENT STUDIES
M3039 School of Public Health   Phone: (313) 764-1394
Ann Arbor, MI 48109   Gene Regenstreif, Libn.

UNIVERSITY OF MICHIGAN - DENTISTRY LIBRARY
1100 Dentistry   Phone: (313) 764-1526
Ann Arbor, MI 48109   Susan Seger, Libn.

UNIVERSITY OF MICHIGAN - DEPARTMENT OF GEOLOGICAL SCIENCES -
    SUBSURFACE LABORATORY LIBRARY
1009 C.C. Little Bldg.
Ann Arbor, MI 48109   John "Stu" McDonald, Supv.

UNIVERSITY OF MICHIGAN - DEPARTMENT OF RARE BOOKS AND SPECIAL
    COLLECTIONS - LIBRARY
711 Hatcher Graduate Library   Phone: (313) 764-9377
Ann Arbor, MI 48109   Jane G. Flener, Act.Hd.

UNIVERSITY OF MICHIGAN - ENGINEERING-TRANSPORTATION LIBRARY
Undergraduate Library Bldg.   Phone: (313) 764-7494
Ann Arbor, MI 48109   Maurita P. Holland, Libn.

UNIVERSITY OF MICHIGAN - ENGLISH LANGUAGE INSTITUTE - LIBRARY
1013 North University Bldg.   Phone: (313) 764-2417
Ann Arbor, MI 48109   Elizabeth S. Benford, Libn.

UNIVERSITY OF MICHIGAN - FINE ARTS LIBRARY
103 Tappan Hall   Phone: (313) 764-5405
Ann Arbor, MI 48109   Valerie Meyer, Libn.

UNIVERSITY OF MICHIGAN - HIGHWAY SAFETY RESEARCH INSTITUTE -
    LIBRARY
Huron Pkwy. & Baxter Rd.   Phone: (313) 764-2171
Ann Arbor, MI 48109   Ann C. Grimm, Libn.

UNIVERSITY OF MICHIGAN - HIGHWAY SAFETY RESEARCH INSTITUTE -
    PUBLIC INFORMATION MATERIALS CENTER
Huron Pkwy. & Baxter Rd.   Phone: (313) 764-2171
Ann Arbor, MI 48109   Ann C. Grimm, Libn.

UNIVERSITY OF MICHIGAN - HISTORY OF ART DEPARTMENT - ARCHIVES
    OF ASIAN ART
519 S. State
4 Tappan Hall   Phone: (313) 764-5555
Ann Arbor, MI 48109   Joy Alexander, Cur.

UNIVERSITY OF MICHIGAN - HISTORY OF ART DEPARTMENT -
    COLLECTION OF SLIDES AND PHOTOGRAPHS
107 Tappan Hall   Phone: (313) 764-5404
Ann Arbor, MI 48109   Joy Alexander, Cur.

UNIVERSITY OF MICHIGAN - HOPWOOD ROOM
1006 Angell Hall   Phone: (313) 764-6296
Ann Arbor, MI 48109   Andrea Beauchamp, Prog.Coord.

UNIVERSITY OF MICHIGAN - HUMAN PERFORMANCE CENTER - LIBRARY
330 Packard Rd.
Ann Arbor, MI 48109

UNIVERSITY OF MICHIGAN - INSTITUTE FOR SOCIAL RESEARCH - ISR
    SOCIAL SCIENCE ARCHIVE *
Box 1248   Phone: (313) 763-5010
Ann Arbor, MI 48106   Janet Vavra, Tech.Dir.

UNIVERSITY OF MICHIGAN - INSTITUTE FOR SOCIAL RESEARCH -
    LIBRARY †
426 Thompson St.
Box 1248   Phone: (313) 764-8513
Ann Arbor, MI 48109   Mrs. Adye Bel Evans, Libn.

UNIVERSITY OF MICHIGAN - LAW LIBRARY
Legal Research Bldg.   Phone: (313) 764-9322
Ann Arbor, MI 48109   Beverley J. Pooley, Dir.

UNIVERSITY OF MICHIGAN - LIBRARY EXTENSION SERVICE
2360 Bonisteel Blvd.   Phone: (313) 764-9363
Ann Arbor, MI 48109   Dr. Jane Flener, Assoc.Dir., Pub.Serv.

UNIVERSITY OF MICHIGAN - LIBRARY SCIENCE LIBRARY
300 Hatcher Graduate Library   Phone: (313) 764-9375
Ann Arbor, MI 48109   Jean Loup, Libn.

UNIVERSITY OF MICHIGAN - MAP ROOM
825 Hatcher Graduate Library   Phone: (313) 764-0407
Ann Arbor, MI 48109   James O. Minton, Map Libn.

UNIVERSITY OF MICHIGAN - MATHEMATICS LIBRARY
3027 Angell Hall   Phone: (313) 764-7266
Ann Arbor, MI 48109   Jack W. Weigel, Libn.

UNIVERSITY OF MICHIGAN - MATTHAEI BOTANICAL GARDENS - LIBRARY
1800 N. Dixboro Rd.   Phone: (313) 764-1168
Ann Arbor, MI 48105   O. Jane LaRue, Coll. Botanist

UNIVERSITY OF MICHIGAN - MENTAL HEALTH RESEARCH INSTITUTE -
    LIBRARY
205 Washtenaw Pl.   Phone: (313) 764-4202
Ann Arbor, MI 48109   Anne C. Davis, Hd.Libn.

UNIVERSITY OF MICHIGAN - MICHIGAN HISTORICAL COLLECTIONS -
 BENTLEY HISTORICAL LIBRARY
1150 Beal   Phone: (313) 764-3482
Ann Arbor, MI 48109   Dr. Richard Doolen, Act.Dir.

UNIVERSITY OF MICHIGAN - MICHIGAN INFORMATION TRANSFER
 SOURCE (MITS)
413 Harlan Hatcher Graduate Library   Phone: (313) 763-5060
Ann Arbor, MI 48109   Anne K. Beaubien, Mgr./Coord.

UNIVERSITY OF MICHIGAN - MUSEUMS LIBRARY
2500 Museums Bldg.   Phone: (313) 764-0467
Ann Arbor, MI 48109   Patricia B. Devlin, Musm.Libn.

UNIVERSITY OF MICHIGAN - MUSIC LIBRARY
3250 Earl V. Moore Bldg., N. Campus   Phone: (313) 764-2512
Ann Arbor, MI 48109   Wallace S. Bjorke, Music Libn.

UNIVERSITY OF MICHIGAN - NATURAL SCIENCE AND NATURAL
 RESOURCES LIBRARY
3140 Kraus Bldg.   Phone: (313) 764-1494
Ann Arbor, MI 48109   Patricia B. Devlin, Libn.

UNIVERSITY OF MICHIGAN - NORTH ENGINEERING LIBRARY
1002 I.S.T. Bldg.   Phone: (313) 764-5298
Ann Arbor, MI 48109   Maurita Petersen Holland, Hd.

UNIVERSITY OF MICHIGAN - PHYSICS-ASTRONOMY LIBRARY
290 Dennison Bldg.   Phone: (313) 764-3442
Ann Arbor, MI 48109   Jack W. Weigel, Libn.

UNIVERSITY OF MICHIGAN - SCHOOL OF ED. & SCHOOL OF LIB.SCI. -
 INSTR. RESOURCES UNIT OF INSTR. STRATEGY SERV.
610 E. University   Phone: (313) 764-5427
Ann Arbor, MI 48109   Margaret Schmidt, Mgr.

UNIVERSITY OF MICHIGAN - SCHOOL OF PUBLIC HEALTH - CENTER FOR
 POPULATION PLANNING - REFERENCE COLLECTION
                                             Phone: (313) 763-5732
Ann Arbor, MI 48109

UNIVERSITY OF MICHIGAN - SCHOOL OF PUBLIC HEALTH - PUBLIC HEALTH
 LIBRARY
M2030 School of Public Health   Phone: (313) 764-5473
Ann Arbor, MI 48109   Mary Townsend, Libn.

UNIVERSITY OF MICHIGAN - SOCIAL WORK LIBRARY
1548 Frieze Bldg.   Phone: (313) 764-5169
Ann Arbor, MI 48109   Christina W. Neal, Libn.

UNIVERSITY OF MICHIGAN - WILLIAM L. CLEMENTS LIBRARY
S. University Ave.   Phone: (313) 764-2347
Ann Arbor, MI 48109   John C. Dann, Dir.

VELSICOL CHEMICAL CORPORATION - TECHNICAL INFORMATION CENTER
1975 Green Rd.   Phone: (313) 994-8000
Ann Arbor, MI 48105   Barbara V. Chandik, Supv., Tech.Info.

WARNER-LAMBERT/PARKE-DAVIS - RESEARCH LIBRARY †
2800 Plymouth Rd.   Phone: (313) 994-3500
Ann Arbor, MI 48105   Katherine Owen, Mgr., INFoRM

WASHTENAW COMMUNITY COLLEGE - LEARNING RESOURCE CENTER
4800 Huron River Dr.   Phone: (313) 973-3300
Ann Arbor, MI 48106   Adella B. Scott, Dir. of LRC

WASHTENAW COUNTY METROPOLITAN PLANNING COMMISSION -
 LIBRARY
306 County Bldg.
Box 8645   Phone: (313) 994-2435
Ann Arbor, MI 48107   Don A. Farmer, Sr. Planner

WILSON ORNITHOLOGICAL SOCIETY - JOSSELYN VAN TYNE MEMORIAL
 LIBRARY
University of Michigan
Museum of Zoology   Phone: (313) 764-0457
Ann Arbor, MI 48109   William A. Lunk, Chm. of Lib.Comm.

XEROX CORPORATION - UNIVERSITY MICROFILMS INTERNATIONAL -
 LIBRARY †
300 N. Zeeb Rd.   Phone: (313) 761-4700
Ann Arbor, MI 48106   Joseph J. Fitzsimmons, Pres.

BATTLE CREEK ART CENTER LIBRARY - MICHIGAN ART ARCHIVES
265 E. Emmett   Phone: (616) 963-1219
Battle Creek, MI 49017   Linda Poirier, Cur. of Coll.

BATTLE CREEK SANITARIUM HOSPITAL - MEDICAL LIBRARY
197 N. Washington Ave.   Phone: (616) 964-7121
Battle Creek, MI 49016   Joni Wildman, Dir.

COMMUNITY HOSPITAL ASSOCIATION - MEDICAL LIBRARY
183 West St.   Phone: (616) 963-5521
Battle Creek, MI 49016   Marilyn Cantrell, Dir.Med.Rec.

ENQUIRER AND NEWS - EDITORIAL REFERENCE LIBRARY
155 W. Van Buren St.   Phone: (616) 964-7161
Battle Creek, MI 49016   Wanda G. Halsey, Libn.

KELLOGG COMPANY - TECHNICAL LIBRARY SERVICES
235 Porter St.   Phone: (616) 966-2291
Battle Creek, MI 49016   Emily Weingartz, Info.Spec.

KINGMAN MUSEUM OF NATURAL HISTORY - LIBRARY
West Michigan Ave. at 20th St.   Phone: (616) 965-5117
Battle Creek, MI 49017   Robert Learner, Musm.Dir.

LEILA HOSPITAL AND HEALTH CENTER - MEDICAL LIBRARY
300 North Ave.   Phone: (616) 962-8551
Battle Creek, MI 49016   Sister Mary Georgia Brown, Libn.

U.S. DEFENSE LOGISTICS AGENCY - DEFENSE LOGISTICS SERVICES
 CENTER - LIBRARY
Federal Ctr.
50 N. Washington St.   Phone: (616) 962-6511
Battle Creek, MI 49016   Anna K. Winger, Libn.

U.S. VETERANS ADMINISTRATION (MI-Battle Creek) - HOSPITAL LIBRARY *
                                             Phone: (616) 966-5600
Battle Creek, MI 49016   Barbara L. Hill, Chf.Libn.

BAY COUNTY HISTORICAL SOCIETY - MUSEUM OF THE GREAT LAKES -
 LIBRARY
1700 Center Ave.   Phone: (517) 893-5733
Bay City, MI 48706   Kathleen Krueger, Registrar

BAY MEDICAL CENTER - HEALTH SCIENCES LIBRARY
1900 Columbus Ave.   Phone: (517) 894-3782
Bay City, MI 48706   Barbara Kormelink, Med.Libn.

HENDERSHOT BIBLIOGRAPHY & CONSULTANTS - LIBRARY
4114 Ridgewood
Bay City, MI 48706   Dr. Carl H. Hendershot, Publ.

WHIRLPOOL CORPORATION - TECHNICAL INFORMATION CENTER
Monte Rd.   Phone: (616) 926-5323
Benton Harbor, MI 49022   Clifford L. Tierney, Mgr.

ANDREWS UNIVERSITY - JAMES WHITE LIBRARY
                                             Phone: (616) 471-3264
Berrien Springs, MI 49104   Marley H. Soper, Act.Dir.

FERRIS STATE COLLEGE - LIBRARY
901 S. State St.   Phone: (616) 796-0461
Big Rapids, MI 49307   Mary M. Bower, Dir.

FERRIS STATE COLLEGE - SCHOOL OF PHARMACY - PERIODICAL READING
 ROOM
901 S. State St.   Phone: (616) 796-2641
Big Rapids, MI 49307   Mary M. Bower, Dir.

OUR LADY QUEEN OF MARTYRS - ST. LUCIAN LIBRARY
32460 S. Pierce   Phone: (313) 644-8620
Birmingham, MI 48009   Ruth Brady, Hd.Libn.

GEOGRAPHIC

GEOGRAPHIC

TEMPLE BETH EL - PRENTIS MEMORIAL LIBRARY
7400 Telegraph Rd.   Phone: (313) 851-1100
Birmingham, MI 48010   Marilyn R. Brenner, Libn.

CHURCH OF JESUS CHRIST OF LATTER-DAY SAINTS - DETROIT BRANCH
    GENEALOGICAL LIBRARY
425 N. Woodward   Phone: (313) 647-5671
Bloomfield Hills, MI 48103

CRANBROOK ACADEMY OF ART - LIBRARY
500 Lone Pine Rd.
Box 801   Phone: (313) 645-3328
Bloomfield Hills, MI 48013   Diane Vogt-O'Connor, Hd.Libn.

CRANBROOK INSTITUTE OF SCIENCE - LIBRARY
500 Lone Pine Rd.
Box 801   Phone: (313) 645-3238
Bloomfield Hills, MI 48013   Christine Bartz, Libn.

D'ARCY-MAC MANUS AND MASIUS - LIBRARY INFORMATION SERVICES
Long Lake at Woodward   Phone: (313) 646-1000
Bloomfield Hills, MI 48013   Lois W. Collet, Dir.

IRON COUNTY MUSEUM - ARCHIVES
Box 272   Phone: (906) 265-3942
Caspian, MI 49915   Marcia Bernhardt, Exhibits Coord.

CHRYSLER DEFENSE, INC. - ENGINEERING DIVISION - TECHNICAL
    LIBRARY
25999 Lawrence Ave.   Phone: (313) 497-0495
Center Line, MI 48015   Margaret VonRosen, Libn.

COLOMBIERE COLLEGE - LIBRARY
Box 189   Phone: (313) 625-5611
Clarkston, MI 48106   Rev. Stephen A. Meder, S.J., Libn.

DEARBORN HISTORICAL MUSEUM - RESEARCH DIVISION - ARCHIVES AND
    LIBRARY *
915 S. Brady St.   Phone: (313) 565-3000
Dearborn, MI 48124

FORD MOTOR COMPANY - TECHNICAL INFORMATION SECTION &
    ENGINEERING & RESEARCH LIBRARY
20000 Rotunda Dr.   Phone: (313) 323-1059
Dearborn, MI 48121   Douna Seiler Estry, Supv., Tech.Info.Sect.

HENRY FORD MUSEUM AND GREENFIELD VILLAGE - FORD ARCHIVES
Village Rd.   Phone: (313) 271-1620
Dearborn, MI 48121   Douglas A. Bakken, Dir., Ford Archv.

HENRY FORD MUSEUM AND GREENFIELD VILLAGE - ROBERT H. TANNAHILL
    RESEARCH LIBRARY
Village Rd.   Phone: (313) 271-1620
Dearborn, MI 48124   Douglas A. Bakken, Dir.

OAKWOOD HOSPITAL - MC LOUTH MEMORIAL HEALTH SCIENCE LIBRARY
18101 Oakwood Blvd.   Phone: (313) 336-3000
Dearborn, MI 48124   Sharon A. Phillips, Dir.

SOCIETY OF MANUFACTURING ENGINEERS - SME LIBRARY
One SME Dr.
Box 930   Phone: (313) 271-1500
Dearborn, MI 48128   Paulette Groen, Libn.

UNIVERSITY OF MICHIGAN - DEARBORN LIBRARY
4901 Evergreen Rd.   Phone: (313) 593-5400
Dearborn, MI 48128   C. Edward Wall, Hd.Libn.

AMERICAN CONCRETE INSTITUTE - LIBRARY
Box 19150   Phone: (313) 532-2600
Detroit, MI 48219   Betty Borschell, Libn.

AMERICAN NATURAL RESOURCE COMPANY - SYSTEM ECONOMIC LIBRARY
One Woodward Ave., 26th Fl.   Phone: (313) 965-2430
Detroit, MI 48226   Freddie Larriett, Lib.Asst.

BURROUGHS CORPORATION - CORPORATE INFORMATION RESEARCH
    CENTER *
Burroughs Place, Rm. 4C51   Phone: (313) 972-7350
Detroit, MI 48232   David R. Curry, Mgr.

BURROUGHS CORPORATION - LEGAL ACTIVITY LIBRARY
Burroughs Pl.   Phone: (313) 972-7895
Detroit, MI 48232   Bernice C. Frank, Law Libn.

BUSHNELL CONGREGATIONAL CHURCH - LIBRARY *
15000 Southfield Rd.   Phone: (313) 272-3550
Detroit, MI 48223   Mrs. George Unterburger, Lib.Cons.

CENTER FOR CREATIVE STUDIES/COLLEGE OF ART & DESIGN - LIBRARY
245 E. Kirby   Phone: (313) 872-3118
Detroit, MI 48202   Jean Peyrat, Libn.

CHILDREN'S HOSPITAL OF MICHIGAN - MEDICAL LIBRARY
3901 Beaubien   Phone: (313) 494-5322
Detroit, MI 48201   Michele S. Klein, Dir., Lib.Serv.

CHRYSLER CORPORATION - ENGINEERING DIVISION - ENGINEERING
    LIBRARY
Box 1118   Phone: (313) 956-4881
Detroit, MI 48073   Phyllis J. Sears, Supv.

CLARK, KLEIN AND BEAUMONT - LAW LIBRARY
1600 First Federal Bldg.
1001 Woodward Ave.   Phone: (313) 962-6492
Detroit, MI 48226

CONSTRUCTION CONSULTANTS, INC. - LIBRARY
900 Pallister   Phone: (313) 874-2770
Detroit, MI 48202   Joan M. Boram, Libn.

DETREX CHEMICAL INDUSTRIES, INC. - RESEARCH LABORATORIES -
    LIBRARY
Box 501
Detroit, MI 48232   Sondra E. Schader, Libn.

DETROIT BAR ASSOCIATION FOUNDATION - LIBRARY
600 Woodward Ave.   Phone: (313) 961-3507
Detroit, MI 48226   Elizabeth T. Stajniak, Libn.

DETROIT COLLEGE OF LAW - LIBRARY
130 E. Elizabeth St.   Phone: (313) 965-0150
Detroit, MI 48201   Mario A. Ceresa, Hd.Libn.

DETROIT EDISON COMPANY - INFORMATION SERVICES LIBRARY †
2000 Second Ave.   Phone: (313) 237-9216
Detroit, MI 48226   Susan D. Clement, Libn.

DETROIT FREE PRESS - LIBRARY
321 W. Lafayette   Phone: (313) 222-6897
Detroit, MI 48231   Michele Ann Kapecky, Chief Libn.

DETROIT GARDEN CENTER - LIBRARY
1460 E. Jefferson Ave.   Phone: (313) 259-6363
Detroit, MI 48207   Mrs. Donald B. Smith, Chm. Of Lib.

DETROIT INSTITUTE OF ARTS - RESEARCH LIBRARY
5200 Woodward Ave.   Phone: (313) 833-7926
Detroit, MI 48202   Francis Warren Peters, Jr., Libn.

DETROIT INSTITUTE OF TECHNOLOGY - JAMES C. GORDON MEMORIAL
    LIBRARY
2727 Second Ave.   Phone: (313) 962-0830
Detroit, MI 48201   Janet Krawulski, Hd.Libn.

DETROIT JAZZ CENTER - JAZZ ARCHIVE
2110 Park Ave.   Phone: (313) 962-4124
Detroit, MI 48201   John Sinclair, Dir.

DETROIT MACOMB HOSPITALS ASSOCIATION - HOSPITAL LIBRARY
690 Mullett   Phone: (313) 225-5185
Detroit, MI 48226   Lynn A. Sorensen, Corp.Dir. of Libs.

DETROIT NEWS - GEORGE B. CATLIN MEMORIAL LIBRARY
615 W. Lafayette St.   Phone: (313) 222-2110
Detroit, MI 48231   Betty W. Havlena, Chf.Libn.

DETROIT OSTEOPATHIC HOSPITAL CORPORATION - MEDICAL LIBRARY
12523 Third Ave.   Phone: (313) 869-1200
Detroit, MI 48203   Gayle Williams, Dir. of Libs.

DETROIT PUBLIC LIBRARY - BURTON HISTORICAL COLLECTION
5201 Woodward Ave.   Phone: (313) 833-1480
Detroit, MI 48202   Alice C. Dalligan, Chf.

DETROIT PUBLIC LIBRARY - BUSINESS AND FINANCE DEPARTMENT
5201 Woodward Ave.   Phone: (313) 833-1420
Detroit, MI 48202   Richard Barton, Chf.

DETROIT PUBLIC LIBRARY - FILM DEPARTMENT
5201 Woodward Ave.   Phone: (313) 833-1495
Detroit, MI 48202   Robert J. Garen, Chf.

DETROIT PUBLIC LIBRARY - FINE ARTS DEPARTMENT
5201 Woodward Ave.   Phone: (313) 833-1467
Detroit, MI 48202   Shirley Solvick, Chf.

DETROIT PUBLIC LIBRARY - FOREIGN LANGUAGE COLLECTION
Downtown Library, 121 Gratiot   Phone: (313) 833-9800
Detroit, MI 48226   Carol Ferrero, Foreign Lang.Spec.

DETROIT PUBLIC LIBRARY - GENERAL INFORMATION DEPARTMENT
5201 Woodward Ave.   Phone: (313) 833-1400
Detroit, MI 48202   Joseph F. Oldenburg, Chf.

DETROIT PUBLIC LIBRARY - HISTORY AND TRAVEL DEPARTMENT
5201 Woodward Ave.   Phone: (313) 833-1445
Detroit, MI 48202   Anna DiPiazza, Chf.

DETROIT PUBLIC LIBRARY - LABOR COLLECTION
5201 Woodward Ave.   Phone: (313) 833-1440
Detroit, MI 48202   Doris Detwiler, Chf.

DETROIT PUBLIC LIBRARY - LANGUAGE AND LITERATURE DEPARTMENT
5201 Woodward Ave.   Phone: (313) 833-1470
Detroit, MI 48202   Ann Rabjohns, Chf.

DETROIT PUBLIC LIBRARY - MUNICIPAL REFERENCE LIBRARY
Rm. 1004, City County Bldg.
2 Woodward Ave.   Phone: (313) 224-3885
Detroit, MI 48226   Richard Maciejewski, Chf.

DETROIT PUBLIC LIBRARY - MUSIC AND PERFORMING ARTS DEPARTMENT
5201 Woodward Ave.   Phone: (313) 833-1460
Detroit, MI 48201   Agatha Pfeiffer Kalkanis, Chf.

DETROIT PUBLIC LIBRARY - NATIONAL AUTOMOTIVE HISTORY
    COLLECTION
5201 Woodward   Phone: (313) 833-1456
Detroit, MI 48202   Margaretta Sandula, Chf.

DETROIT PUBLIC LIBRARY - PHILOSOPHY, RELIGION AND EDUCATION
    DEPARTMENT
5201 Woodward Ave.   Phone: (313) 833-1430
Detroit, MI 48202   Geraldine Frenette, Chf.

DETROIT PUBLIC LIBRARY - RARE BOOK DIVISION
5201 Woodward Ave.   Phone: (313) 833-1476
Detroit, MI 48202   Gloria A. Francis, Chf.

DETROIT PUBLIC LIBRARY - SOCIOLOGY AND ECONOMICS DEPARTMENT
5201 Woodward Ave.   Phone: (313) 833-1440
Detroit, MI 48202   Doris Detwiler, Chf.

DETROIT PUBLIC LIBRARY - TECHNOLOGY AND SCIENCE DEPARTMENT
5201 Woodward Ave.   Phone: (313) 833-1450
Detroit, MI 48202   George Unterburger, Chf.

DETROIT PUBLIC SCHOOLS - PROFESSIONAL LIBRARY
5057 Woodward Ave.   Phone: (313) 494-1626
Detroit, MI 48202   Charles V. Partridge, Libn.

DETROIT RECEIVING HOSPITAL & UNIVERSITY HEALTH CENTER - LIBRARY
4201 St. Antoine   Phone: (313) 494-4475
Detroit, MI 48201   Cherrie M. Mudloff, Libn.

DETROIT SYMPHONY ORCHESTRA - LIBRARY
Ford Auditorium, 20 Auditorium Dr.   Phone: (313) 961-0700
Detroit, MI 48226   Albert P. Steger, Libn.

DETROIT UNIVERSITY CLUB - LIBRARY
1411 E. Jefferson   Phone: (313) 567-9280
Detroit, MI 48207

DETROITBANK CORPORATION - RESEARCH LIBRARY
211 W. Fort   Phone: (313) 222-9377
Detroit, MI 48231   Carol Pollack, Chf.Libn.

DICKINSON, WRIGHT, MC KEAN, CUDLIP & MOON - LIBRARY
800 First National Bldg.   Phone: (313) 223-3500
Detroit, MI 48226   Valerie Hanafee, Libn.

DWORMAN (Thomas J.) - LIBRARY
20210 Archer   Phone: (313) 255-2132
Detroit, MI 48219   Thomas J. Dworman

DYKEMA, GOSSETT, SPENCER, GOODNOW & TRIGG - LAW LIBRARY
400 Renaissance Center, 35th Fl.   Phone: (313) 568-6715
Detroit, MI 48243   Palma Campo, Libn.

ERNST & WHINNEY - LIBRARY *
100 Renaissance Center, Suite 2300   Phone: (313) 354-4600
Detroit, MI 48243   Lynne Taft, Libn.

FRUEHAUF CORPORATION - RESEARCH AND DEVELOPMENT DIVISION -
    LIBRARY
6500 French Rd.
Box 238   Phone: (313) 267-1504
Detroit, MI 48232   Rita Van Assche Bueter, Libn.

GALE RESEARCH COMPANY - LIBRARY
Book Tower   Phone: (313) 961-2242
Detroit, MI 48226   Annie M. Brewer, Sr.Ed.

GENERAL ELECTRIC COMPANY - CARBOLOY SYSTEMS DEPARTMENT - CSD
    LIBRARY
Box 237, G.P.O.   Phone: (313) 536-9100
Detroit, MI 48232   Frances M. Briggs, Libn.

GENERAL MOTORS CORPORATION - CADILLAC MOTOR CAR DIVISION -
    ENGINEERING DIVISION LIBRARY
2860 Clark   Phone: (313) 554-5376
Detroit, MI 48232

GENERAL MOTORS CORPORATION - LEGAL STAFF LIBRARY
14-224 General Motors Bldg.
3044 W. Grand Blvd.   Phone: (313) 556-4010
Detroit, MI 48202   Lorraine A. Kulpa, Legal Staff Libn.

GENERAL MOTORS CORPORATION - PUBLIC RELATIONS STAFF LIBRARY
General Motors Bldg., Rm. 11-235
3044 W. Grand Blvd.   Phone: (313) 556-2051
Detroit, MI 48202   Nettie H. Seabrooks, Mgr.

GENERAL MOTORS CORPORATION - TAX SECTION LIBRARY
12-135 General Motors Bldg.   Phone: (313) 556-1567
Detroit, MI 48202   Geraldyne J. Musser, Asst.Libn.

GREAT LAKES MARITIME INSTITUTE - DOSSIN GREAT LAKES MUSEUM
    INFORMATION CENTER
Belle Isle   Phone: (313) 824-3157
Detroit, MI 48207   John F. Polacsek, Cur.

HARPER-GRACE HOSPITALS - DRUG INFORMATION CENTER
3990 John R St.   Phone: (313) 494-8626
Detroit, MI 48201   Gerald W. Zieg, Dir.

HARPER-GRACE HOSPITALS - GRACE HOSPITAL DIVISION - OSCAR LE
    SEURE PROFESSIONAL LIBRARY
18700 Meyers Rd.   Phone: (313) 927-3277
Detroit, MI 48235   Frances M. Phillips, Chf.Libn.

HARPER-GRACE HOSPITALS - HARPER HOSPITAL DIVISION - DEPARTMENT
    OF LIBRARIES
3990 John R St.   Phone: (313) 494-8264
Detroit, MI 48201   Barbara Coe Johnson, Dir. Of Libs.

GEOGRAPHIC

HENRY FORD HOSPITAL - FRANK J. SLADEN LIBRARY
2799 W. Grand Blvd.   Phone: (313) 876-2550
Detroit, MI 48202   Nardina L. Namath, Dir., Lib./AV Serv.

HUTZEL HOSPITAL - MEDICAL LIBRARY
4707 St. Antoine   Phone: (313) 494-7179
Detroit, MI 48201   Caryl L. Scheuer, Dir., Lib.Serv.

INSTITUTE OF GERONTOLOGY - GERONTOLOGY LEARNING RESOURCES
   CENTER
Wayne State University
203 Library Ct.   Phone: (313) 577-2221
Detroit, MI 48202   H. Jean Owens, Lib.Dir.

LAFAYETTE CLINIC - LIBRARY
951 E. Lafayette   Phone: (313) 256-9596
Detroit, MI 48207   Nancy E. Ward, Libn.

MERCY SCHOOL OF NURSING OF DETROIT - LIBRARY
2242 E. Grand Blvd.   Phone: (313) 923-5700
Detroit, MI 48211   Rebecca Christman, Libn.

MERRILL-PALMER INSTITUTE - EDNA NOBLE WHITE LIBRARY *
71 E. Ferry Ave.   Phone: (313) 875-7450
Detroit, MI 48202   Jeanne F. Thomas, Libn.

MERRILL-PALMER INSTITUTE - KRESGE HISTORICAL LIBRARY *
71 E. Ferry Ave.   Phone: (313) 875-7450
Detroit, MI 48202   Jeanne F. Thomas, Libn.

METROPOLITAN HOSPITAL - MEDICAL LIBRARY
1800 Tuxedo Ave.   Phone: (313) 869-3600
Detroit, MI 48206   William F. McQueen, Med.Libn.

MICHIGAN BELL TELEPHONE COMPANY - CORPORATE REFERENCE CENTER
1141 Headquarters Bldg.
444 Michigan Ave.   Phone: (313) 223-8040
Detroit, MI 48226   M. Elizabeth Moore, Human Rsrcs.Supv.

MICHIGAN CANCER FOUNDATION - LEONARD F. SIMONS RESEARCH
   LIBRARY
110 E. Warren   Phone: (313) 833-0710
Detroit, MI 48201   C.J. Glodek, Chf.Libn.

MICHIGAN OSTEOPATHIC MEDICAL CENTER, INC. - HEALTH SCIENCE
   LIBRARY
5435 Woodward Ave.   Phone: (313) 494-0470
Detroit, MI 48202   Carolyn A. Hough, Mgr.Lib.Serv.

MICHIGAN STATE DEPARTMENT OF LABOR - MICHIGAN EMPLOYMENT
   SECURITY COMMISSION - LIBRARY
7310 Woodward Ave., Rm. 706   Phone: (313) 876-5597
Detroit, MI 48202   Richard L. Daoust, Hd.Libn.

MOTOR VEHICLE MANUFACTURERS ASSOCIATION (MVMA) -
   COMMUNICATIONS LIBRARY
300 New Center Bldg.   Phone: (313) 872-4311
Detroit, MI 48202   Christina C. Kanabrodzki, Commun.Libn.

MOTOR VEHICLE MANUFACTURERS ASSOCIATION (MVMA) - PATENT
   RESEARCH LIBRARY
320 New Center Bldg.   Phone: (313) 872-4311
Detroit, MI 48202   James A. Wren, Mgr.

MOTOR VEHICLE MANUFACTURERS ASSOCIATION (MVMA) - STATISTICS
   INFORMATION CENTER
300 New Center Bldg.   Phone: (313) 872-4311
Detroit, MI 48202   Jacques J. Evers, Mgr.

MOTOR VEHICLE MANUFACTURERS ASSOCIATION (MVMA) - TECHNICAL
   LIBRARY
300 New Center Bldg.   Phone: (313) 872-4311
Detroit, MI 48202   Louis X. Barbalas, Tech.Libn.

MOUNT CARMEL MERCY HOSPITAL AND MEDICAL CENTER - MEDICAL
   LIBRARY
6071 W. Outer Dr.   Phone: (313) 864-5400
Detroit, MI 48235   Joan Luksik, Dir.

NATIONAL BANK OF DETROIT - LIBRARY
Box 116   Phone: (313) 225-2840
Detroit, MI 48232   Steven Wecker, Mgr., Lib.Serv.

NATIONAL BANK OF DETROIT - MONEY MUSEUM LIBRARY
200 Renaissance Center, Street Level   Phone: (313) 446-0713
Detroit, MI 48243   Susan E. Cherry, Mgr.

REHABILITATION INSTITUTE, INC. - MC PHERSON BROWNING MEMORIAL
   LIBRARY
261 Mack Blvd.   Phone: (313) 494-9759
Detroit, MI 48201   Daria Shackelford, Med.Libn./Dir.

ROSS ROY, INC. - RESEARCH LIBRARY
2751 E. Jefferson Ave.   Phone: (313) 568-6117
Detroit, MI 48207   Eloise Lewis, Libn.

SACRED HEART SEMINARY - COLLEGE LIBRARY
2701 W. Chicago Blvd.   Phone: (313) 868-2700
Detroit, MI 48206   Arnold M. Rzepecki, Libn.

ST. JOHN HOSPITAL - MEDICAL LIBRARY
22101 Moross Rd.   Phone: (313) 343-3733
Detroit, MI 48236   Marie K. Bolanos, Dir.

SAMARITAN HEALTH CENTER - DEACONESS HOSPITAL UNIT - MEDICAL
   LIBRARY
3245 E. Jefferson Ave.   Phone: (313) 259-2200
Detroit, MI 48207   Louann Stewart, Libn.

SCHERER (R.P.) CORPORATION - LIBRARY
9425 Grinnell Ave.   Phone: (313) 571-6100
Detroit, MI 48213   Mary Ellen Gilden, Libn.

SINAI HOSPITAL OF DETROIT - SAMUEL FRANK MEDICAL LIBRARY
6767 W. Outer Dr.   Phone: (313) 493-5140
Detroit, MI 48235   Barbara L. Finn, Dir. of Med.Lib.

SMITH, MIRO, HIRSCH & BRODY - LIBRARY
1100 Fisher Bldg.   Phone: (313) 874-4600
Detroit, MI 48202   Candace E. Gadwa, Hd. Legal Asst./Libn.

SOUTHEAST MICHIGAN COUNCIL OF GOVERNMENTS - LIBRARY
800 Book Bldg.   Phone: (313) 961-4266
Detroit, MI 48226   Pamela L. Lazar, Libn.

UNITED AUTOMOBILE, AEROSPACE & AGRICULTURAL IMPLEMENT
   WORKERS OF AMERICA - RESEARCH LIBRARY
8000 E. Jefferson Ave.   Phone: (313) 926-5388
Detroit, MI 48214   Melba Kibildis, Libn.

U.S. BUREAU OF THE CENSUS - REGIONAL DATA USER SERVICE - DETROIT
   REGIONAL OFFICE - LIBRARY
231 W. Lafayette St., Rm. 565   Phone: (313) 226-4675
Detroit, MI 48226   Timothy Jones, Data User Serv.Off.

U.S. DEPT. OF COMMERCE - INTERNATIONAL TRADE ADMINISTRATION -
   DETROIT DISTRICT OFFICE LIBRARY
445 Federal Bldg.
230 W. Fort St.   Phone: (313) 226-3650
Detroit, MI 48226   Raymond R. Riesgo, Dir.

UNIVERSITY OF DETROIT - EVENING COLLEGE OF BUSINESS AND
   ADMINISTRATION - LIBRARY
651 E. Jefferson   Phone: (313) 927-1525
Detroit, MI 48226   Judy Dyki, Libn.

UNIVERSITY OF DETROIT - LIBRARY MEDIA CENTER
4001 W. McNichols Rd.   Phone: (313) 927-1075
Detroit, MI 48221   Lois C. Bailey, Adm.Asst.

UNIVERSITY OF DETROIT - SCHOOL OF ARCHITECTURE - LIBRARY
4001 W. McNichols Rd.   Phone: (313) 927-1065
Detroit, MI 48221   Elaine Arnold, Libn.

UNIVERSITY OF DETROIT - SCHOOL OF DENTISTRY LIBRARY
2931 E. Jefferson Ave.   Phone: (313) 259-6622
Detroit, MI 48207   Victor DeSchryver, Libn.

UNIVERSITY OF DETROIT - SCHOOL OF LAW LIBRARY
651 E. Jefferson   Phone: (313) 961-5444
Detroit, MI 48226   Peter C. Schanck, Assoc.Prof./Lib.Dir.

UNIVERSITY OF MICHIGAN - DETROIT BRANCH LIBRARY
60 Farnsworth Ave.   Phone: (313) 832-1668
Detroit, MI 48202   Galen Avery, Tech.Lib.Asst.

WAYNE COUNTY CIRCUIT COURT - LAW LIBRARY
1407 City-County Bldg.   Phone: (313) 224-5265
Detroit, MI 48226   Kathleen Friedman, Law Libn.

WAYNE STATE UNIVERSITY - ARCHIVES OF LABOR AND URBAN AFFAIRS/
    UNIVERSITY ARCHIVES
Walter P. Reuther Library   Phone: (313) 577-4024
Detroit, MI 48202   Philip P. Mason, Dir.

WAYNE STATE UNIVERSITY - ARTHUR NEEF LAW LIBRARY
468 W. Ferry Mall   Phone: (313) 577-3925
Detroit, MI 48202   Georgia A. Clark, Law Libn.

WAYNE STATE UNIVERSITY - EDUCATION LIBRARY
     Phone: (313) 577-4035
Detroit, MI 48202   Theodore Manheim, Hd.

WAYNE STATE UNIVERSITY - FOLKLORE ARCHIVE
448 Purdy Library   Phone: (313) 577-4053
Detroit, MI 48202   Janet L. Langlois, Dir.

WAYNE STATE UNIVERSITY - G. FLINT PURDY LIBRARY
     Phone: (313) 577-4040
Detroit, MI 48202   K.L. Kaul, Hd.

WAYNE STATE UNIVERSITY - SCHOOL OF MEDICINE - VERA PARSHALL
    SHIFFMAN MEDICAL LIBRARY
4325 Brush St.   Phone: (313) 577-1088
Detroit, MI 48201   James F. Williams, II, Med.Libn.

WAYNE STATE UNIVERSITY - SCIENCE LIBRARY
     Phone: (313) 577-4066
Detroit, MI 48202   James F. Williams, II, Act.Sci.Libn.

CHURCH OF JESUS CHRIST OF LATTER-DAY SAINTS - LANSING BRANCH
    GENEALOGICAL LIBRARY
431 E. Saginaw
Box 801   Phone: (517) 332-2932
East Lansing, MI 48823   Azalia Benjamin, Branch Libn.

MICHIGAN EDUCATION ASSOCIATION - LIBRARY *
Box 673   Phone: (517) 332-6551
East Lansing, MI 48823   Mary Jane White, Info.Spec.

MICHIGAN STATE DEPARTMENT OF AGRICULTURE - LIBRARY
1615 S. Harrison Rd.   Phone: (517) 373-6410
East Lansing, MI 48823   Kathleen E. Callahan, Lib.Asst.

MICHIGAN STATE UNIVERSITY - AGRICULTURAL ECONOMICS REFERENCE
    ROOM
29 Agriculture Hall   Phone: (517) 355-6650
East Lansing, MI 48824   Pauline Sondag, Libn.

MICHIGAN STATE UNIVERSITY - ANIMAL INDUSTRIES REFERENCE ROOM
208 Anthony Hall   Phone: (517) 355-8483
East Lansing, MI 48824   Carole S. Armstrong, Sci.Br.Coord.

MICHIGAN STATE UNIVERSITY - ART/MAPS DIVISION
     Phone: (517) 353-4593
East Lansing, MI 48824   Shirlee A. Studt, Art Libn.

MICHIGAN STATE UNIVERSITY - BUSINESS LIBRARY
21 Eppley Ctr.   Phone: (517) 355-3380
East Lansing, MI 48824   William S. Stoddard, Bus.Libn.

MICHIGAN STATE UNIVERSITY - C.W. BARR PLANNING AND DESIGN
    LIBRARY
     Phone: (517) 353-3941
East Lansing, MI 48824   Beth J. Shapiro, Libn.

MICHIGAN STATE UNIVERSITY - CHEMISTRY LIBRARY
426 Chemistry Bldg.   Phone: (517) 355-8512
East Lansing, MI 48824   Bernice Wallace, Libn.

MICHIGAN STATE UNIVERSITY - DOCUMENTS DEPARTMENT
     Phone: (517) 353-8707
East Lansing, MI 48824   Eleanor J. Boyles, Doc.Libn.

MICHIGAN STATE UNIVERSITY - ENGINEERING LIBRARY
308 Engineering Bldg.   Phone: (517) 355-8536
East Lansing, MI 48824   Jackson Yang, Engr./Sci.Libn.

MICHIGAN STATE UNIVERSITY - G. ROBERT VINCENT VOICE LIBRARY
Main Library Bldg., W433-W437   Phone: (517) 335-5122
East Lansing, MI 48824   Dr. Maurice A. Crane, Hd.

MICHIGAN STATE UNIVERSITY - GEOLOGY LIBRARY
5 Natural Sciences Bldg.   Phone: (517) 353-7988
East Lansing, MI 48824   Carole S. Armstrong, Sci.Br.Coord.

MICHIGAN STATE UNIVERSITY - HIGHWAY TRAFFIC SAFETY CENTER -
    LIBRARY †
University Library   Phone: (517) 353-9309
East Lansing, MI 48824   Frank C. MacDougall, Libn.

MICHIGAN STATE UNIVERSITY - INSTRUCTIONAL MEDIA CENTER - FILM
    LIBRARY
     Phone: (517) 353-7850
East Lansing, MI 48824   Sue Ann Wilt, Libn.

MICHIGAN STATE UNIVERSITY - INTERNATIONAL LIBRARY
W310-316 University Library   Phone: (517) 355-2366
East Lansing, MI 48824   Dr. Eugene de Benko, Hd., Intl.Lib.

MICHIGAN STATE UNIVERSITY - INTERNATIONAL LIBRARY - SAHEL
    DOCUMENTATION CENTER
W-312 University Library   Phone: (517) 355-2397
East Lansing, MI 48824   Dr. Joseph J. Lauer, Ed. & Libn.

MICHIGAN STATE UNIVERSITY - LABOR AND INDUSTRIAL RELATIONS
    LIBRARY
Library E109   Phone: (517) 355-4647
East Lansing, MI 48824   Martha Jane Soltow, Libn.

MICHIGAN STATE UNIVERSITY - MICROFORMS DIVISION
     Phone: (517) 353-3120
East Lansing, MI 48824   Sally A. Boersema, Lib.Ck.

MICHIGAN STATE UNIVERSITY - MUSIC LIBRARY
     Phone: (517) 355-7660
East Lansing, MI 48824   Roseann Hammill, Music Libn.

MICHIGAN STATE UNIVERSITY - NON-FORMAL EDUCATION INFORMATION
    CENTER
College of Education
513 Erickson Hall   Phone: (517) 355-5522
East Lansing, MI 48824   Joan M. Claffey, Dir.

MICHIGAN STATE UNIVERSITY - PHYSICS-ASTRONOMY LIBRARY
Rm. 229, Physics-Astronomy Bldg.   Phone: (517) 355-9704
East Lansing, MI 48824   Carole S. Armstrong, Sci.Br.Coord.

MICHIGAN STATE UNIVERSITY - SCIENCE LIBRARY
     Phone: (517) 355-2347
East Lansing, MI 48824   Carole S. Armstrong, Sci.Br.Coord.

MICHIGAN STATE UNIVERSITY - SPECIAL COLLECTIONS DIVISION
University Library   Phone: (517) 355-3770
East Lansing, MI 48824   Jannette Fiore, Libn.

MICHIGAN STATE UNIVERSITY - SPECIAL COLLECTIONS DIVISION -
    RUSSEL B. NYE POPULAR CULTURE COLLECTION
University Library   Phone: (517) 355-3770
East Lansing, MI 48824   Jannette Fiore, Libn.

MICHIGAN STATE UNIVERSITY - UNIVERSITY ARCHIVES AND HISTORICAL
  COLLECTIONS
                                        Phone: (517) 355-2330
East Lansing, MI 48824   Dr. Frederick L. Honhart, Dir.

MICHIGAN STATE UNIVERSITY - UNIVERSITY CENTER FOR
  INTERNATIONAL REHABILITATION (UCIR) - RESOURCE LIBRARY
D-223 West Fee Hall   Phone: (517) 355-1824
East Lansing, MI 48824   James J. Mullin, Coord.Info.Sys.

MICHIGAN STATE UNIVERSITY - UNIVERSITY EXTENSION LIBRARY †
Main Library, Rm. WG-5   Phone: (517) 355-2345
East Lansing, MI 48824   Frank C. MacDougall, Libn.

MICHIGAN STATE UNIVERSITY - URBAN POLICY AND PLANNING LIBRARY
University Library   Phone: (517) 353-9304
East Lansing, MI 48824   Beth J. Shapiro, Libn.

MICHIGAN STATE UNIVERSITY - V.G. GROVE RESEARCH LIBRARY OF
  MATHEMATICS-STATISTICS
101-D Wells Hall   Phone: (517) 353-8852
East Lansing, MI 48824   Berle Reiter, Libn.

DELTA COUNTY HISTORICAL SOCIETY MUSEUM LIBRARY
Ludington Park, Box 1776
Escanaba, MI 49829   Louraine Ham, Pres.

BIRMINGHAM TEMPLE - LIBRARY
28611 W. Twelve Mile Rd.
Farmington, MI 48024   Phone: (313) 477-0177

BOTSFORD GENERAL HOSPITAL, OSTEOPATHIC - MEDICAL LIBRARY
28050 Grand River Ave.   Phone: (313) 476-7600
Farmington, MI 48024   Deborah L. Adams, Libn.

ETHYL CORPORATION - RESEARCH LABORATORIES - RESEARCH LIBRARY
1600 W. Eight Mile Rd.   Phone: (313) 399-9600
Ferndale, MI 48220   Betty Lee, Libn.

FIRST PRESBYTERIAN CHURCH OF FLINT - PEIRCE MEMORIAL LIBRARY †
746 S. Saginaw St.   Phone: (313) 234-8673
Flint, MI 48502   Elaine K. Forrest

FLINT DEPARTMENT OF COMMUNITY DEVELOPMENT - LIBRARY
1101 S. Saginaw St., Rm. 6   Phone: (313) 766-7355
Flint, MI 48502   Dianne Montgomery, Adm. Aide

FLINT INSTITUTE OF ARTS - LIBRARY †
1120 E. Kearsley St.   Phone: (313) 234-1695
Flint, MI 48503   Diane Oliver, Act.Libn.

FLINT JOURNAL - EDITORIAL LIBRARY
200 E. First St.   Phone: (313) 767-0660
Flint, MI 48502   David W. Larzelere, Chf.Libn.

FLINT NEWMAN CENTER - LIBRARY AND CATHOLIC INFORMATION
  CENTER
609 E. 5th Ave.   Phone: (313) 239-9391
Flint, MI 48503   Rev. James B. Bettendorf, Dir.

FLINT OSTEOPATHIC HOSPITAL - DR. E. HERZOG MEMORIAL MEDICAL
  LIBRARY
3921 Beecher Rd.   Phone: (313) 762-4587
Flint, MI 48502   Doris M. Blauet, Libn.

FLINT PUBLIC LIBRARY - ART, MUSIC & DRAMA DEPARTMENT
1026 E. Kearsley St.   Phone: (313) 232-7111
Flint, MI 48502   Forrest Alter, Hd.

FLINT PUBLIC LIBRARY - AUTOMOTIVE HISTORY COLLECTION
1026 E. Kearsley St.   Phone: (313) 232-7111
Flint, MI 48502   Joyce E. Peck, Dept.Hd.

FLINT PUBLIC LIBRARY - BUSINESS AND INDUSTRY DEPARTMENT
1026 E. Kearsley St.   Phone: (313) 232-7111
Flint, MI 48502   Joyce E. Peck, Dept.Hd.

FLINT PUBLIC LIBRARY - MICHIGAN ROOM
1026 E. Kearsley St.   Phone: (313) 232-7111
Flint, MI 48502   Judith J. Field, Hd., Gen.Ref.

GENERAL MOTORS CORPORATION - AC SPARK PLUG DIVISION -
  ENGINEERING LIBRARY
1300 N. Dort Hwy.   Phone: (313) 766-2655
Flint, MI 48556   Eileen L. Lane, Libn.

GENERAL MOTORS INSTITUTE - LIBRARY †
Chevrolet & Third Aves.   Phone: (313) 762-9500
Flint, MI 48502   William R. Elgood, Dir.

GENESEE COUNTY CIRCUIT COURT - LAW LIBRARY
401 County Court House   Phone: (313) 766-8896
Flint, MI 48502   Janet E. Patsy, Law Libn.

GENESEE-LAPEER-SHIAWASSEE REGION V PLANNING & DEVELOPMENT
  COMMISSION - LIBRARY
1602 W. Third Ave.   Phone: (313) 766-8593
Flint, MI 48504   Verna L. McColley, Lib.Techn.

HURLEY MEDICAL CENTER - HAMADY HEALTH SCIENCES LIBRARY
One Hurley Plaza   Phone: (313) 766-0427
Flint, MI 48502   Anthos Hungerford, Dir.

MC LAREN GENERAL HOSPITAL - MEDICAL LIBRARY
401 Ballenger Hwy.   Phone: (313) 762-2141
Flint, MI 48502   Lea Ann McGaugh, Med.Libn.

MOTT (Charles Stewart) FOUNDATION - LIBRARY
Mott Foundation Bldg.   Phone: (313) 238-5651
Flint, MI 48502   Eve Brown, Records Mgt.Supv.

NATIONAL HAMILTONIAN PARTY - HAMILTONIAN LIBRARY
434 Chalmers St.   Phone: (313) 234-5552
Flint, MI 48503   Albert Victor, Libn.

ST. JOSEPH HOSPITAL - HEALTH SCIENCES LIBRARY
302 Kensington Ave.   Phone: (313) 762-8519
Flint, MI 48502   RoseMary Carter, Med.Libn.

SLOAN (Alfred P., Jr.) MUSEUM - LIBRARY
1221 E. Kearsley St.   Phone: (313) 762-1170
Flint, MI 48503   Phillip C. Kwiatkowski, Dir.

GERBER PRODUCTS COMPANY - CORPORATE LIBRARY
445 State St.   Phone: (616) 928-2631
Fremont, MI 49412   Sherrie Anderson, Libn.

BLODGETT MEMORIAL MEDICAL CENTER - RICHARD ROOT SMITH LIBRARY
1840 Wealthy St., S.E.   Phone: (616) 774-7624
Grand Rapids, MI 49506   Brian Simmons, Med.Libn.

BUTTERWORTH HOSPITAL - MEDICAL LIBRARY
100 Michigan, N.E.   Phone: (616) 774-1655
Grand Rapids, MI 49503   Eileen M. Dechow, Med.Libn.

BUTTERWORTH HOSPITAL - SCHOOL OF NURSING LIBRARY †
335 Bostwick Ave., N.E.   Phone: (616) 774-1779
Grand Rapids, MI 49503   Betty Sherwood, Libn.

CALVIN COLLEGE AND SEMINARY - LIBRARY
3207 Burton St., S.E.   Phone: (616) 949-4000
Grand Rapids, MI 49506   Marvin E. Monsma, Dir.

FOREMOST INSURANCE COMPANY - LIBRARY
5800 Foremost Dr., S.E.
Box 2450   Phone: (616) 942-3550
Grand Rapids, MI 49501   Laurie Gebben, Libn.

GENERAL MOTORS CORPORATION - DIESEL EQUIPMENT DIVISION -
  LIBRARY *
2100 Burlingame, S.W.   Phone: (616) 247-5148
Grand Rapids, MI 49509   Warren W. Comport, Libn.

GRACE BIBLE COLLEGE - BULTEMA MEMORIAL LIBRARY
1011 Aldon St., S.W.
Box 910   Phone: (616) 538-2332
Grand Rapids, MI 49509   Guni Olson, Hd.Libn.

GRAND RAPIDS ART MUSEUM - MC BRIDE LIBRARY
155 N. Division
Grand Rapids, MI 49503
Phone: (616) 459-4676
Luci King, Lib.Chm.

GRAND RAPIDS LAW LIBRARY
1010 Old Kent Bldg.
Grand Rapids, MI 49503
Phone: (616) 454-9493
Marjorie C. Wilcox, Exec.Dir.

GRAND RAPIDS PRESS - REFERENCE LIBRARY
Press Plaza, Vandenberg Ctr.
Grand Rapids, MI 49502
Phone: (616) 459-1474
Diane L. Wheeler, Libn.

GRAND RAPIDS PUBLIC LIBRARY - FOUNDATION CENTER REGIONAL
    COLLECTION
60 Library Plaza, N.E.
Grand Rapids, MI 49503
Phone: (616) 456-4411
Hazel Baar, Ref.Libn.

GRAND RAPIDS PUBLIC LIBRARY - FURNITURE DESIGN COLLECTION
60 Library Plaza, N.E.
Grand Rapids, MI 49503
Phone: (616) 456-4410
Lucija Skuja, Art Libn.

GRAND RAPIDS PUBLIC LIBRARY - MICHIGAN ROOM
60 Library Plaza, N.E.
Grand Rapids, MI 49503
Phone: (616) 456-4424
Celene Idema, Hd.

KENDALL SCHOOL OF DESIGN - LEARNING RESOURCE CENTER
1110 College N.E.
Grand Rapids, MI 49503
Phone: (616) 451-2787
Ruth Hornbach, Hd.Libn.

LEAR SIEGLER, INC. - INSTRUMENT DIVISION - ENGINEERING LIBRARY
4141 Eastern Ave., S.E.
Grand Rapids, MI 49508
Phone: (616) 241-7467
N. Scott Brackett, Tech.Libn.

PACKAGING CORPORATION OF AMERICA - RESEARCH AND DEVELOPMENT
    LIBRARY
470 Market Ave., S.W.
Grand Rapids, MI 49503
Phone: (616) 459-4581
James J. Higgins, Dir.

PINE REST CHRISTIAN HOSPITAL - VAN NOORD HEALTH SCIENCES
    LIBRARY
6850 S. Division Ave.
Grand Rapids, MI 49508
Phone: (616) 455-5000
Thomas Van Dam, Libn.

REFORMED BIBLE COLLEGE - LIBRARY
1869 Robinson Rd.
Grand Rapids, MI 49506
Phone: (616) 458-6065
Joanne Boehm, Libn.

ST. MARY'S HOSPITAL - LIBRARY
200 Jefferson, S.E.
Grand Rapids, MI 49503
Phone: (616) 774-6243
Mary A. Hanson, Med.Libn.

WARNER, NORCROSS & JUDD - LIBRARY
900 Old Kent Bldg.
Grand Rapids, MI 49503
Phone: (616) 459-6121
Shannon Mitchell, Libn.

WESTVIEW CHRISTIAN REFORMED CHURCH - LIBRARY
2861 Leonard St., N.W.
Grand Rapids, MI 49504
Phone: (616) 453-3105

BON SECOURS HOSPITAL - HEALTH SCIENCE LIBRARY
468 Cadieux Rd.
Grosse Pointe, MI 48230
Phone: (313) 343-1619
Sr. M. Bernita, S.S.J., Lib.Dir.

COTTAGE HOSPITAL OF GROSSE POINTE - MEDICAL LIBRARY
159 Kercheval Ave.
Grosse Pointe Farms, MI 48236
Phone: (313) 884-8600
Carol Attar, Lib.Dir.

MACEDONIAN ETHNIC LIBRARY
920 Shoreham Rd.
Grosse Pointe Woods, MI 48236
Phone: (313) 886-3361
Adrijana Panoska Randolph, Dir./Libn.

FINNISH-AMERICAN HISTORICAL ARCHIVES
Suomi College
Hancock, MI 49930
Phone: (906) 482-5300
Esther Pekkala, Archv.Sec.

CHARLTON PARK VILLAGE AND MUSEUM - LIBRARY
2545 S. Charlton Park Rd.
Hastings, MI 49058
Phone: (616) 945-3775
Frank E. Walsh, Dir.

MICHIGAN STATE UNIVERSITY - W.K. KELLOGG BIOLOGICAL STATION -
    WALTER F. MOROFSKY MEMORIAL LIBRARY
3700 E. Gull Lake Dr.
Hickory Corners, MI 49060
Phone: (616) 671-5117
Carolyn Hammarskjold, Libn.

BASF WYANDOTTE CORPORATION - PIGMENTS DIVISION LIBRARY
491 Columbia Ave.
Holland, MI 49423
Phone: (616) 392-2391
Janice A. Wierenga, Libn.

DONNELLY MIRRORS, INC. - LIBRARY
414 East 40th St.
Holland, MI 49423
Phone: (616) 394-2268
Nancy Yetman, Tech.Libn.

HOLLAND COMMUNITY HOSPITAL - HOSPITAL AND MEDICAL STAFF
    LIBRARY
602 Michigan Ave.
Holland, MI 49423
Phone: (616) 392-5141
Marge Kars, Dir.

NETHERLANDS MUSEUM - ARCHIVES AND LIBRARY
City Hall, 3rd Fl.
Holland, MI 49423
Phone: (616) 392-3129
Dr. Willard Wichers, Musm.Dir.

WESTERN THEOLOGICAL SEMINARY - BEARDSLEE LIBRARY
Phone: (616) 392-8555
Holland, MI 49423
Norman J. Kansfield, Libn.

MICHIGAN TECHNOLOGICAL UNIVERSITY - INSTITUTE OF MINERAL
    RESEARCH
Phone: (906) 487-2600
Houghton, MI 49931

MICHIGAN TECHNOLOGICAL UNIVERSITY - INSTITUTE OF WOOD
    RESEARCH INFORMATION CENTER
Phone: (906) 487-2464
Houghton, MI 49931
Jeffrey C. Huestis, Coord./Res.Info.Serv

MICHIGAN TECHNOLOGICAL UNIVERSITY - LIBRARY
Phone: (906) 487-2500
Houghton, MI 49931
Lee J. Lebbin, Dir.

HILLCREST REGIONAL CENTER FOR DEVELOPMENTAL DISABILITIES -
    MEDICAL LIBRARY
600 County Farm Rd.
Box M-155
Howell, MI 48843
Phone: (517) 546-3270
Mary E. Wilkinson, Sec.

INTERLOCHEN CENTER FOR THE ARTS - MUSIC LIBRARY
Phone: (616) 276-9221
Interlochen, MI 49643
E. Delmer Weliver, Dir.

U.S. VETERANS ADMINISTRATION (MI-Iron Mountain) - MEDICAL CENTER
    LIBRARY
East H St.
Iron Mountain, MI 49801
Phone: (906) 774-3300
Phyllis E. Hildebrandt, Chf., Lib.Serv.

NATIONAL SKI HALL OF FAME AND MUSEUM - ROLAND PALMEDO NATIONAL
    SKI LIBRARY
Box 191
Ishpeming, MI 49849
Phone: (906) 486-9281
Ken Luostari, Lib.Dir.

CONSUMERS POWER COMPANY - LAW LIBRARY
212 W. Michigan Ave.
Jackson, MI 49201
Phone: (517) 788-1088
Beulah I. Standish, Libn.

CONSUMERS POWER COMPANY - PARNALL TECHNICAL LIBRARY
1945 Parnall Rd.
Jackson, MI 49201
Phone: (517) 788-0541
Kay E. Stevens, Libn.

SHARP (Ella) MUSEUM - LIBRARY
3225 Fourth St.
Jackson, MI 49203
Phone: (517) 787-2320
Natalie Field, Volunteer Hist.

BORGESS MEDICAL CENTER - LIBRARY
1521 Gull Rd.
Kalamazoo, MI 49001
Phone: (616) 383-7360
Linda M. Havens, Libn.

BRONSON METHODIST HOSPITAL - HEALTH SCIENCES LIBRARY
252 Lovell St., E.
Kalamazoo, MI 49007
Phone: (616) 383-6318
Jeanne L. Hartenstein, Dir.Lib.Serv.

FIRST PRESBYTERIAN CHURCH - LIBRARY
321 W. South St.   Phone: (616) 344-0119
Kalamazoo, MI 49006   Lillian B. Auducon

FIRST UNITED METHODIST CHURCH - ALLEN LIBRARY
212 S. Park St.   Phone: (616) 381-6340
Kalamazoo, MI 49006   Mildred S. Hedrick, Libn.

KALAMAZOO COUNTY LAW LIBRARY - JUDGE RAYMOND FOX MEMORIAL
   LIBRARY
227 W. Michigan Ave.   Phone: (616) 383-8950
Kalamazoo, MI 49007   C. Duke Hynek, Ct.Adm.

KALAMAZOO INSTITUTE OF ARTS - ART CENTER LIBRARY
314 S. Park St.   Phone: (616) 349-7775
Kalamazoo, MI 49007   Helen Sheridan, Hd.Libn.

KALAMAZOO NATURE CENTER - REFERENCE LIBRARY
7000 N. Westnedge Ave.   Phone: (616) 381-1575
Kalamazoo, MI 49007   Diane D. Worden, Libn.

KALSEC, INC. - LIBRARY
3711 W. Main   Phone: (616) 349-9711
Kalamazoo, MI 49005   Mary Sagar, Libn.

MICHIGAN AUDUBON SOCIETY - EDITH MUNGER LIBRARY
7000 N. Westnedge Ave.   Phone: (616) 344-8648
Kalamazoo, MI 49007   Patricia L. Adams, Off.Mgr.

UPJOHN COMPANY - BUSINESS LIBRARY 88-0
                                              Phone: (616) 323-6352
Kalamazoo, MI 49001   Valerie Noble, Hd.

UPJOHN COMPANY - CORPORATE TECHNICAL LIBRARY
301 Henrietta St.   Phone: (616) 385-6414
Kalamazoo, MI 49001   Lorraine Schulte, Mgr.

UPJOHN COMPANY - PATENT LAW DEPARTMENT - LIBRARY
Bldg. 32-1   Phone: (616) 385-7569
Kalamazoo, MI 49001   Helen B. Longwell, Libn.

WESTERN MICHIGAN UNIVERSITY - ARCHIVES AND REGIONAL HISTORY
   COLLECTIONS
                                              Phone: (616) 383-1826
Kalamazoo, MI 49008   Wayne C. Mann, Dir.

WESTERN MICHIGAN UNIVERSITY - BUSINESS LIBRARY
                                              Phone: (616) 383-1926
Kalamazoo, MI 49008   David McKee, Hd.Libn.

WESTERN MICHIGAN UNIVERSITY - DOCUMENTS LIBRARY
Waldo Library   Phone: (616) 383-4952
Kalamazoo, MI 49008   Louis Kiraldi, Hd.

WESTERN MICHIGAN UNIVERSITY - EDUCATIONAL RESOURCES CENTER
Sangren Hall   Phone: (616) 383-1666
Kalamazoo, MI 49008   Frederick R. Brail, Dir.

WESTERN MICHIGAN UNIVERSITY - INSTITUTE OF CISTERCIAN STUDIES
   LIBRARY
                                              Phone: (616) 383-1969
Kalamazoo, MI 49008   Beatrice Beech, Hd.Libn.

WESTERN MICHIGAN UNIVERSITY - MAP LIBRARY
Waldo Library   Phone: (616) 383-4952
Kalamazoo, MI 49008   Dr. Louis Kiraldi, Hd.

WESTERN MICHIGAN UNIVERSITY - MUSIC LIBRARY
Maybee Music Bldg.   Phone: (616) 383-1817
Kalamazoo, MI 49008   Greg Fitzgerald, Hd.Libn.

WESTERN MICHIGAN UNIVERSITY - PHYSICAL SCIENCES LIBRARY
3376 Rood Hall   Phone: (616) 383-4943
Kalamazoo, MI 49008   Beatrice Sichel, Hd.Libn.

WESTERN MICHIGAN UNIVERSITY - SCHOOL OF LIBRARIANSHIP -
   LABORATORY LIBRARY
                                              Phone: (616) 383-1877
Kalamazoo, MI 49008   Norman Frankel, Libn.

HOUGHTON COUNTY HISTORICAL SOCIETY - LIBRARY *
Highway M-26, Lock Box D   Phone: (906) 296-4121
Lake Linden, MI 49945   Joseph H. Hawke, Cur.

NORTH OAKLAND GENEALOGICAL SOCIETY - LIBRARY
845 S. Lapeer Rd.   Phone: (313) 693-1888
Lake Orion, MI 48035   Barbara Stafford, Pres.

MICHIGAN TECHNOLOGICAL UNIVERSITY - FORD FORESTRY CENTER -
   LIBRARY
                                              Phone: (906) 524-6181
L'Anse, MI 49946   Stephen Shetron, Sr.Res.Sci.

COOLEY (Thomas M.) LAW SCHOOL - LIBRARY
217 S. Capitol Ave.
Box 13038   Phone: (517) 371-5140
Lansing, MI 48901   Peter M. Kempel, Dir., Res.Serv.

INGHAM MEDICAL CENTER - JOHN W. CHI MEMORIAL MEDICAL LIBRARY
401 West Greenlawn Ave.   Phone: (517) 374-2270
Lansing, MI 48909   David G. Keddle, Dir.Med.Lib.

LANSING COMMUNITY COLLEGE - PROFESSIONAL RESOURCE CENTER
419 N. Capitol Ave.
Box 40010   Phone: (517) 373-7274
Lansing, MI 48901   James P. Platte, Dean/Div.Lrng.Rsrcs.

LANSING GENERAL HOSPITAL - OSTEOPATHIC - K.M. BAKER MEMORIAL
   LIBRARY
2800 Devonshire Ave.   Phone: (517) 377-8389
Lansing, MI 48909   Bethany Robertson, Med.Libn.

MACKINAC ISLAND STATE PARK COMMISSION - HISTORICAL RESEARCH
   COLLECTION
Box 30028   Phone: (517) 322-1319
Lansing, MI 48909   Keith R. Widder, Cur.

MICHIGAN STATE DEPARTMENT OF MENTAL HEALTH - LIBRARY
Lewis Cass Bldg., 6th Fl.   Phone: (517) 373-0408
Lansing, MI 48926   Laurel Minott, Libn.

MICHIGAN STATE DEPARTMENT OF NATURAL RESOURCES - GEOLOGICAL
   SURVEY DIVISION - LIBRARY
Box 30028
Lansing, MI 48909

MICHIGAN STATE DEPARTMENT OF PUBLIC HEALTH - LIBRARY
3500 N. Logan St.   Phone: (517) 373-1359
Lansing, MI 48909   Bill Nelton, Libn.

MICHIGAN STATE DEPARTMENT OF TRANSPORTATION -
   TRANSPORTATION LIBRARY
Box 30050   Phone: (517) 373-1545
Lansing, MI 48909   Norman J. Bunker, Libn.

MICHIGAN STATE HISTORY DIVISION - ARCHIVES
3405 N. Logan   Phone: (517) 373-0512
Lansing, MI 48918   David J. Olson, State Archv.

MICHIGAN STATE LEGISLATIVE COUNCIL - LEGISLATIVE SERVICE BUREAU
   LIBRARY
125 W. Allegan
Box 30036   Phone: (517) 373-0472
Lansing, MI 48909   Elliott Smith, Dir.

MICHIGAN STATE LIBRARY SERVICES
Box 30007   Phone: (517) 373-1580
Lansing, MI 48909   Francis X. Scannell, State Libn.

MICHIGAN STATE LIBRARY SERVICES - LAW LIBRARY
Law Bldg.
Box 30012   Phone: (517) 373-0630
Lansing, MI 48909   Charles B. Wolfe, State Law Libn.

SPARROW (Edward W.) HOSPITAL - MEDICAL LIBRARY
1215 E. Michigan Ave.
Box 30480   Phone: (517) 487-2788
Lansing, MI 48909   Doris H. Asher, Med.Libn.

STATE BAR OF MICHIGAN - LIBRARY
306 Townsend St.   Phone: (517) 372-9030
Lansing, MI 48933   Douglas L. Sweet, Dir., R. & D.

TRI-COUNTY REGIONAL PLANNING COMMISSION - INFORMATION
    RESOURCE CENTER
913 W. Holmes Rd., Suite 201   Phone: (517) 393-0342
Lansing, MI 48901   Kiley Rankin, Info.Coord.

OAKDALE REGIONAL CENTER FOR DEVELOPMENTAL DISABILITIES - STAFF
    LIBRARY
                                          Phone: (313) 664-2951
Lapeer, MI 48446   Carole Harrison, Lib.Coord.

CONGREGATION BETH ACHIM - JOSEPH KATKOWSKY LIBRARY
21100 W. Twelve Mile Rd.   Phone: (313) 352-8670
Livonia, MI 48076   Dr. Israel Wiener, Lib.Chm./Libn.

LIVONIA PUBLIC SCHOOLS - CURRICULUM STUDY CENTER
18000 Newburgh Rd.
Livonia, MI 48152

MADONNA COLLEGE - CURRICULUM LIBRARY
36600 Schoolcraft Rd.   Phone: (313) 591-1200
Livonia, MI 48150   Sr. M. Martina, Dir.

ST. MARY HOSPITAL - MEDICAL LIBRARY
36475 Five Mile Road   Phone: (313) 464-4800
Livonia, MI 48154   Sister Mary Clementine, Libn.

MASON COUNTY HISTORICAL SOCIETY - ROSE HAWLEY MUSEUM AND
    HISTORICAL LIBRARY
305 E. Filer St.   Phone: (616) 843-2001
Ludington, MI 49431   Virginia Gaines, Cur.

MEMORIAL MEDICAL CENTER OF WEST MICHIGAN - LIBRARY *
One Atkinson Dr.   Phone: (616) 843-2591
Ludington, MI 49431   Ruth Gustafson, Adm.Sec.

MANISTEE COUNTY HISTORICAL MUSEUM - FORTIER MEMORIAL LIBRARY
425 River St.   Phone: (616) 723-5531
Manistee, MI 49660   Steve Harold, Musm.Dir.

BISHOP BARAGA ASSOCIATION - ARCHIVES
444 S. Fourth St.
Marquette, MI 49855   Fr. N. Daniel Rupp, Archv.

MARQUETTE COUNTY HISTORICAL SOCIETY - J.M. LONGYEAR RESEARCH
    LIBRARY
213 N. Front St.   Phone: (906) 226-3571
Marquette, MI 49855   Frank O. Paull, Jr., Dir.

MARQUETTE GENERAL HOSPITAL - KEVIN F. O'BRIEN HEALTH SCIENCES
    LIBRARY
420 W. Magnetic   Phone: (906) 228-9440
Marquette, MI 49855   Mildred E. Kingsbury, Lib.Dir.

AMERICAN MUSEUM OF MAGIC - LIBRARY
107 E. Michigan   Phone: (616) 781-7666
Marshall, MI 49068   Robert Lund, Owner

CALHOUN COUNTY METROPOLITAN PLANNING COMMISSION - PLANNING
    LIBRARY
County Bldg., 315 W. Green St.
Marshall, MI 49068

MARSHALL HISTORICAL SOCIETY - ARCHIVES
Box 68   Phone: (616) 781-8544
Marshall, MI 49068   Deborah Sullivan, Pres.

MAYVILLE HISTORICAL MUSEUM - LIBRARY
22 Turner   Phone: (517) 843-6429
Mayville, MI 48744   Mrs. Willard Phelps, Dir. & Cur.

AUTOMOTIVE ORGANIZATION TEAM, INC. - LIBRARY
AOT Automotive Hall of Fame Bldg.
3225 Cook Rd.
Box 1742   Phone: (517) 631-5760
Midland, MI 48640   Dorothy M. Ross, Pres.

DOW CHEMICAL COMPANY - LEGAL LIBRARY
2030 Dow Center   Phone: (517) 636-6648
Midland, MI 48640   Doris L. Steiner, Supv.

DOW CHEMICAL COMPANY - TECHNICAL INFORMATION SERVICES -
    CENTRAL REPORT INDEX
566 Bldg.   Phone: (517) 636-3754
Midland, MI 48640   Paula B. Moses, Mgr.

DOW CHEMICAL COMPANY - TECHNICAL INFORMATION SERVICES -
    CHEMICAL LIBRARY
566 Bldg.
Box 1704   Phone: (517) 636-2246
Midland, MI 48640   Paula B. Moses, Mgr.

DOW CHEMICAL U.S.A. - BUSINESS INFORMATION CENTER
2020 Dow Center   Phone: (517) 636-3779
Midland, MI 48640   Phae H. Dorman, Supv.

DOW CORNING CORPORATION - BUSINESS INFORMATION CENTER
                                          Phone: (517) 496-5733
Midland, MI 48640   Fred Lee, Libn.

DOW CORNING CORPORATION - TECHNICAL INFORMATION SERVICE
    LIBRARY
                                          Phone: (517) 496-4957
Midland, MI 48640   Jane W. Allshouse, Libn.

MEMORIAL PRESBYTERIAN CHURCH - LIBRARY
1310 Ashman St.   Phone: (517) 835-6759
Midland, MI 48640

MIDLAND COUNTY HISTORICAL SOCIETY - ARCHIVES
1801 W. St. Andrews Dr.   Phone: (517) 835-7401
Midland, MI 48640   Kathryn Cummins, Dir.

MIDLAND HOSPITAL CENTER - HEALTH SCIENCES LIBRARY
4005 Orchard Dr.   Phone: (517) 631-7700
Midland, MI 48640   Carole Colter, Health Sci.Libn.

NORTHWOOD INSTITUTE - STROSACKER LIBRARY
3225 Cook Rd.   Phone: (517) 631-1600
Midland, MI 48640   Catherine Chen, Hd.Libn.

MONROE COUNTY HISTORICAL MUSEUM - ARCHIVES
126 S. Monroe St.   Phone: (313) 243-7137
Monroe, MI 48161   Patricia H. Hudson, Archv.

MONROE COUNTY LAW LIBRARY
Court House
Monroe, MI 48161   Margaret Weipert, Sec.

MONROE COUNTY LIBRARY SYSTEM - GENERAL GEORGE ARMSTRONG
    CUSTER COLLECTION
3700 S. Custer   Phone: (313) 241-5277
Monroe, MI 48161   Karen Stoll, Cur.

SOUTHEAST MICHIGAN REGIONAL FILM LIBRARY
c/o Monroe County Library System
3700 S. Custer Rd.   Phone: (313) 241-5277
Monroe, MI 48161   Bernard A. Margolis, Dir.

MACOMB INTERMEDIATE SCHOOL DISTRICT - BEAL LIBRARY
44001 Garfield Rd.   Phone: (313) 286-8800
Mt. Clemens, MI 48044   Richard J. Palmer, Libn.

MOUNT CLEMENS GENERAL HOSPITAL - STUCK MEDICAL LIBRARY
1000 Harrington Blvd.   Phone: (313) 468-1451
Mt. Clemens, MI 48043   Lynne L. Coles, Med.Libn.

ST. JOSEPH HOSPITAL OF MT. CLEMENS - MEDICAL LIBRARY
East Site, 215 North Ave.   Phone: (313) 286-8100
Mt. Clemens, MI 48043   Sandra A. Cryderman, Dir.

CENTRAL MICHIGAN UNIVERSITY - CLARKE HISTORICAL LIBRARY
                                          Phone: (517) 774-3352
Mt. Pleasant, MI 48859   John Cumming, Dir.

GEOGRAPHIC

EVANGELICAL COVENANT CHURCH - LIBRARY †
First St. & Muskegon Ave.   Phone: (616) 728-5385
Muskegon, MI 49440   Carolyn M. Brooks, Libn.

HACKLEY HOSPITAL - MEDICAL LIBRARY
1700 Clinton St.   Phone: (616) 726-3511
Muskegon, MI 49443   Elizabeth Seeley, Med.Libn.

MERCY HOSPITAL - HEALTH SCIENCES LIBRARY
1500 E. Sherman Blvd.   Phone: (616) 739-9341
Muskegon, MI 49443   Jean Parker, Libn.

MUSKEGON BUSINESS COLLEGE - LIBRARY
145 Apple Ave.   Phone: (616) 726-4904
Muskegon, MI 49442   Margaret Moon, Libn.

MUSKEGON CHRONICLE - EDITORIAL LIBRARY
981 Third St.   Phone: (616) 722-3161
Muskegon, MI 49443   Linda S. Thompson, Libn.

NORTHVILLE HISTORICAL SOCIETY - LIBRARY
No. 1 Griswold
Box 71   Phone: (313) 348-1845
Northville, MI 48167   Carol L. Butske, Libn.

NORTHVILLE REGIONAL PSYCHIATRIC HOSPITAL - PROFESSIONAL
    LIBRARY *
41001 W. 7 Mile Rd.   Phone: (313) 349-1800
Northville, MI 48167   Dianna L. Wesley, Med.Libn.

PLYMOUTH CENTER FOR HUMAN DEVELOPMENT - MEDICAL LIBRARY *
15480 Sheldon Rd.   Phone: (313) 453-1500
Northville, MI 48167   Christine Bartz, Med.Libn.

CONGREGATION BETH SHALOM - RABBI MORDECAI S. HALPERN MEMORIAL
    LIBRARY
14601 W. Lincoln Rd.   Phone: (313) 547-7970
Oak Park, MI 48237   Eleanor Smith, Libn.

UNIVERSITY OF MICHIGAN - BIOLOGICAL STATION LIBRARY
                                              Phone: (616) 539-8048
Pellston, MI 49769   Patricia B. Devlin, Libn.

BURNS (Dean C.) HEALTH SCIENCES LIBRARY
                                              Phone: (616) 348-4500
Petoskey, MI 49770   Kay Kelly, Med.Libn.

ADISTRA CORPORATION - R & D LIBRARY
101 Union St.   Phone: (313) 425-2600
Plymouth, MI 48170   John H. Dillon, Mgr.

BURROUGHS CORPORATION - TECHNICAL INFORMATION CENTER
41100 Plymouth Rd.   Phone: (313) 453-1400
Plymouth, MI 48170   Elizabeth A. Roller, Tech.Libn.

ST. JOHN'S PROVINCIAL SEMINARY - LIBRARY
44011 Five Mile Rd.   Phone: (313) 453-6200
Plymouth, MI 48170   Sr. Joy Miller, I.B.V.M., Libn.

ADAMS-PRATT OAKLAND COUNTY LAW LIBRARY
1200 N. Telegraph Rd.   Phone: (313) 858-0011
Pontiac, MI 48054   Richard L. Beer, Law Libn.

OAKLAND COUNTY GOVERNMENTAL REFERENCE LIBRARY
1200 N. Telegraph Rd.   Phone: (313) 858-0738
Pontiac, MI 48053   Phyllis Jose, Dir.

OAKLAND COUNTY HEALTH DIVISION - LIBRARY
1200 N. Telegraph Rd.   Phone: (313) 585-1308
Pontiac, MI 48053   Ellen B. McCooey, Health Sci.Libn.

OAKLAND COUNTY PIONEER AND HISTORICAL SOCIETY - LIBRARY &
    ARCHIVES
405 Oakland Ave.   Phone: (313) 338-6732
Pontiac, MI 48058   Sandra McVicker, Adm.Coord.

OAKLAND SCHOOLS - EDUCATIONAL RESOURCE CENTER
2100 Pontiac Lake Rd.   Phone: (313) 858-1961
Pontiac, MI 48054   Dr. Robert N. Johnson, Dir.

PONTIAC GENERAL HOSPITAL - LIBRARY
Seminole & W. Huron   Phone: (313) 857-7412
Pontiac, MI 48053   Naim K. Sahyoun, Dir. Of Libs.

PONTIAC OSTEOPATHIC HOSPITAL - MEDICAL LIBRARY
50 N. Perry St.   Phone: (313) 338-7271
Pontiac, MI 48058   Janis M. Fox, Libn.

ST. JOSEPH MERCY HOSPITAL - EDUCATIONAL RESOURCES
900 Woodward   Phone: (313) 858-3000
Pontiac, MI 48053   Mollie S. Lynch, Dir., Educ.Rsrcs.

ACHESON INDUSTRIES, INC. - CORPORATE INFORMATION CENTER
315 Peoples Bank Bldg.
Box 8   Phone: (313) 984-5583
Port Huron, MI 48060   Myles T. Musgrave, Asst. to V.P.

OAKLAND UNIVERSITY - LIBRARY
                                              Phone: (313) 377-2492
Rochester, MI 48063   George L. Gardiner, Dean of Lib.

BEAUMONT (William) HOSPITAL - MEDICAL LIBRARY
3601 W. Thirteen Mile Rd.   Phone: (313) 288-8340
Royal Oak, MI 48072   Joan M.B. Smith, Med.Libn.

AMERICAN ASSOCIATION OF CORRECTIONAL OFFICERS - LIBRARY
2309 State St., North Office   Phone: (517) 799-8208
Saginaw, MI 48602   Herbert Van Dusen, Libn.

MICHIGAN LUTHERAN SEMINARY - LIBRARY
2128 Court   Phone: (517) 793-1041
Saginaw, MI 48602   Milton P. Spaude, Libn. & Professor

SAGINAW COUNTY LAW LIBRARY
Courthouse, Rm. 215
111 S. Michigan Ave.   Phone: (517) 790-5490
Saginaw, MI 48602   David Cable, Adm.

SAGINAW HEALTH SCIENCES LIBRARY
1000 Houghton St., Suite 2000   Phone: (517) 771-6846
Saginaw, MI 48602   Dr. Janette Caputo, Dir.

SAGINAW OSTEOPATHIC HOSPITAL - LIBRARY *
515 N. Michigan Ave.   Phone: (517) 771-5100
Saginaw, MI 48602   Patricia A. Wolfgram, Libn.

U.S. VETERANS ADMINISTRATION (MI-Saginaw) - MEDICAL CENTER
    LIBRARY
1500 Weiss St.   Phone: (517) 793-2340
Saginaw, MI 48602   Nancy R. Dingman, Chf.Libn.

FIRST CONGREGATIONAL CHURCH - LIBRARY
2001 Niles Ave.   Phone: (616) 983-5519
St. Joseph, MI 49085   Florence Ritchie, Libn.

GENEALOGICAL ASSOCIATION OF SOUTHWESTERN MICHIGAN - MAUD
    PRESTON PALENSKE MEMORIAL LIBRARY
Box 573
St. Joseph, MI 49085   Marjorie Pearson, Res.Chm.

LAKE SUPERIOR STATE COLLEGE - MICHIGAN COLLECTION
                                              Phone: (906) 632-6841
Sault Ste. Marie, MI 49783   Dr. Frederick A. Michels, Dir.

U.S. ARMY - TACOM SUPPORT ACTIVITY-SELFRIDGE - RECREATION
    SERVICES LIBRARY
Bldg. 169   Phone: (313) 466-5238
Selfridge Air Natl. Guard Base, MI 48045   D. Louise MacLean, Libn.

AUTOMOTIVE INFORMATION COUNCIL - LIBRARY
28333 Telegraph Rd.   Phone: (313) 358-0290
Southfield, MI 48034   Peggy Pentecost, Info.Coord.

BENDIX CORPORATION CENTER - LIBRARY
Box 5047   Phone: (313) 827-5620
Southfield, MI 48037

BURNETT (Leo) COMPANY, INC. - RESEARCH LIBRARY †
26555 Evergreen Rd.   Phone: (313) 355-1900
Southfield, MI 48076

CONGREGATION SHAAREY ZEDEK - LEARNING RESOURCE CENTER
27375 Bell Rd.   Phone: (313) 357-5544
Southfield, MI 48034   Albert E. Karbal, Dir.

DUNS SCOTUS COLLEGE - LIBRARY
20000 W. Nine Mile Rd.   Phone: (313) 357-3070
Southfield, MI 48075

EATON CORPORATION - ENGINEERING & RESEARCH CENTER LIBRARY
Box 766   Phone: (313) 354-6979
Southfield, MI 48037   Mary E. Montgomery, Res.Libn.

FINNISH AMERICAN HISTORICAL SOCIETY OF MICHIGAN - LIBRARY
19885 Melrose
Southfield, MI 48075   Felix V. Jackonen, Pres.

GIFFELS ASSOCIATES, INC. - LIBRARY *
Box 5025   Phone: (313) 355-4600
Southfield, MI 48037   William H. Dukes, Libn.

MICHIGAN PSYCHOANALYTIC INSTITUTE - LIBRARY
16310 W. 12 Mile Rd., No. 204   Phone: (313) 559-5855
Southfield, MI 48076   Marlene Handler, Libn.

MIDRASHA COLLEGE OF JEWISH STUDIES - LIBRARY
21550 W. Twelve Mile Rd.   Phone: (313) 354-3130
Southfield, MI 48076   Sarah Bell, Libn.

PROVIDENCE HOSPITAL - PANZNER MEMORIAL LIBRARY †
16001 W. 9 Mile Rd.
Box 2043   Phone: (313) 424-3294
Southfield, MI 48037   Sharon Cohen, Dir. of Lib.Serv.

SANDY CORPORATION - RESEARCH & RETRIEVAL CENTER
16025 Northland Dr.   Phone: (313) 569-4000
Southfield, MI 48075   Judith Wilson, Dir.

SPILL CONTROL ASSOCIATION OF AMERICA - LIBRARY
17117 W. Nine Mile Rd., Suite 1040   Phone: (313) 552-0500
Southfield, MI 48075   Marc K. Shaye, General Counsel

INSTITUTE FOR ADVANCED PASTORAL STUDIES - REFERENCE LIBRARY
29129 Southfield Rd.   Phone: (313) 645-3180
Southfield Hills, MI 48076

FIRST BAPTIST CHURCH - LIBRARY
Exchange & Meridian   Phone: (616) 842-1974
Spring Lake, MI 49456

PIONEER STUDY CENTER
Box 1032   Phone: (616) 946-3151
Traverse City, MI 49684   Nancy Baxter, Dir.

TRAVERSE CITY REGIONAL PSYCHIATRIC HOSPITAL - STAFF LIBRARY
Elmwood & 11th Sts.   Phone: (616) 947-5550
Traverse City, MI 49684   Jane Nelson, Staff Libn.

RIVERSIDE OSTEOPATHIC HOSPITAL - RALPH F. LINDBERG MEMORIAL
    LIBRARY
150 Truax St.   Phone: (313) 676-4200
Trenton, MI 48183   Susan E. Skoglund, Libn.

ROCKWELL INTERNATIONAL - AUTOMOTIVE OPERATIONS DIVISION -
    REFERENCE CENTER
2135 W. Maple Rd.   Phone: (313) 435-1668
Troy, MI 48084   Donna M. Rzepka, Libn.

WALSH COLLEGE OF ACCOUNTANCY AND BUSINESS ADMINISTRATION -
    LIBRARY
3838 Livernois   Phone: (313) 689-8282
Troy, MI 48084   Gloria B. Ellis, Lib.Dir.

CLINTON RIVER WATERSHED COUNCIL - LIBRARY
8215 Hall Rd.   Phone: (313) 739-1122
Utica, MI 48087   Peggy B. Johnson, Exec.Sec.

WILLIAMS RESEARCH CORPORATION - LIBRARY
2280 W. Maple Rd.   Phone: (313) 624-5200
Walled Lake, MI 48088   Lydia O. Johnstone, Hd.Libn.

CAMPBELL-EWALD COMPANY - REFERENCE CENTER
30400 Van Dyke   Phone: (313) 574-3400
Warren, MI 48093   Elizabeth L. Smith, V.P. & Mgr.

GENERAL MOTORS CORPORATION - DESIGN STAFF INFORMATION CENTER
General Motors Technical Ctr.
12 Mile & Mound Rds.   Phone: (313) 575-1957
Warren, MI 48090   Mrs. Biljana Delevich, Design Libn.

GENERAL MOTORS CORPORATION - RESEARCH LABORATORIES LIBRARY
General Motors Technical Center
12 Mile & Mound Rd.   Phone: (313) 575-2736
Warren, MI 48090   Robert W. Gibson, Jr., Dept.Hd.

GENERAL MOTORS CORPORATION - TECHNICAL INFORMATION CENTER
Engineering Staff
General Motors Technical Ctr.   Phone: (313) 534-7070
Warren, MI 48090   Rebecca Obsniuk, Libn.

OXY METAL INDUSTRIES CORPORATION - ELECTROCHEMICAL LIBRARY †
21441 Hoover Rd.   Phone: (313) 497-9270
Warren, MI 48089   Lynn Pefley

SOUTH MACOMB HOSPITAL - DETROIT-MACOMB HOSPITALS
    ASSOCIATION MEDICAL LIBRARY
11800 Twelve Mile Rd.   Phone: (313) 573-5117
Warren, MI 48093   Victoria Staniszewski, Asst.Libn.

U.S. ARMY - TANK AUTOMOTIVE RESEARCH & DEVELOPMENT COMMAND -
    TECHNICAL LIBRARY SERVICES BRANCH
28251 Van Dyke   Phone: (313) 573-2470
Warren, MI 48090   Leon Burg, Chf., Tech.Info.Off.

WAYNE HISTORICAL MUSEUM - HISTORICAL COMMISSION ARCHIVES
No. 1, Town Sq.   Phone: (313) 722-0113
Wayne, MI 48184   Mildred Hanchett, Dir./Supv.

JEWISH COMMUNITY CENTER OF METROPOLITAN DETROIT - HENRY
    MEYERS MEMORIAL LIBRARY †
6600 W. Maple Rd.   Phone: (313) 661-1000
West Bloomfield, MI 48033

TEMPLE ISRAEL - LIBRARY
5725 Walnut Lake Rd.   Phone: (313) 661-5700
West Bloomfield, MI 48033   Bertha Wember, Libn.

WAYNE COUNTY GENERAL HOSPITAL - MEDICAL LIBRARY
2345 Merriman   Phone: (313) 274-3000
Westland, MI 48185   Louise Dorman, Act.Med.Libn.

BASF WYANDOTTE CORPORATION - CORPORATE LIBRARY
Box 111   Phone: (313) 282-3300
Wyandotte, MI 48192   Mrs. Gene Kennedy, Res.Libn.

EASTERN MICHIGAN UNIVERSITY - CENTER OF EDUCATIONAL RESOURCES
    - ARCHIVES/SPECIAL COLLECTIONS
                                             Phone: (313) 487-3423
Ypsilanti, MI 48197   Margaret Eide, Act.Archv.

EASTERN MICHIGAN UNIVERSITY - CENTER OF EDUCATIONAL RESOURCES
    - GOVERNMENT DOCUMENTS COLLECTION
                                             Phone: (313) 487-2280
Ypsilanti, MI 48197   Clare Beck, Govt.Doc.Libn.

EASTERN MICHIGAN UNIVERSITY - CENTER OF EDUCATIONAL RESOURCES
    - INSTRUCTIONAL MATERIALS CENTER
                                             Phone: (313) 487-0490
Ypsilanti, MI 48197   Margaret Best, Libn.

EASTERN MICHIGAN UNIVERSITY - CENTER OF EDUCATIONAL RESOURCES
  - MAP LIBRARY
                                        Phone: (313) 487-3191
Ypsilanti, MI 48197   Joanne Hansen, Sci. & Tech.Libn.

HUDSON ESSEX TERRAPLANE CLUB, INC. - LIBRARY
5765 Munger Rd.   Phone: (313) 434-3289
Ypsilanti, MI 48197   Charles Liskow, Libn.

YPSILANTI REGIONAL PSYCHIATRIC HOSPITAL - LIBRARY
Box A   Phone: (313) 434-3400
Ypsilanti, MI 48197   Bonnie A. Gasperini, Med.Libn.

FIRST CHRISTIAN REFORMED CHURCH - LIBRARY
15 S. Church St.
Zeeland, MI 49464   Betty G. Shoemaker, Church Libn.

HERMAN MILLER, INC. - RESOURCE CENTER
                                        Phone: (616) 772-3629
Zeeland, MI 49464   Linda M. Wagenveld, Mgr.

MINNESOTA

NORMAN COUNTY HISTORICAL SOCIETY - MEMORIAL MUSEUM LIBRARY
404 W. 5th Ave.   Phone: (218) 784-4911
Ada, MN 56510   Myrtle Rector, Cur.

FREEBORN COUNTY HISTORICAL SOCIETY - RESEARCH LIBRARY
North Bridge St.
Box 105   Phone: (507) 373-8003
Albert Lea, MN 56007   Valborg Hansing Berg, Libn.

ANOKA AREA VOCATIONAL TECHNICAL INSTITUTE - MEDIA CENTER
Box 191   Phone: (612) 427-1880
Anoka, MN 55303   Deborah J. Brude, Hd.Libn.

ANOKA COUNTY HISTORICAL GENEALOGICAL SOCIETY - LIBRARY
1900 3rd Ave. S.   Phone: (612) 421-0600
Anoka, MN 55303   Pat Schwappach, Musm.Dir.

ANOKA STATE HOSPITAL - LIBRARY
3300 4th Ave., N.   Phone: (612) 421-3940
Anoka, MN 55303   Harriet Moore, Libn.

MINNESOTA ZOOLOGICAL GARDEN - LIBRARY
12101 Johnny Cake Ridge Rd.   Phone: (612) 432-9010
Apple Valley, MN 55124   Angie Norell, Libn.

PINE COUNTY HISTORICAL SOCIETY - LIBRARY
Askov, MN 55704   Ron Nelson, Pres.

UNIVERSITY OF MINNESOTA - HORMEL INSTITUTE - LIBRARY
801 16th Ave., N.E.   Phone: (507) 433-8804
Austin, MN 55912   Jacqueline Budde, Libn.

MINNESOTA HISTORICAL SOCIETY - NORTH CENTRAL MINNESOTA
  HISTORICAL CENTER
Bemidji State University   Phone: (218) 755-3349
Bemidji, MN 56601   Judith McDonald, Dir.

OAK HILLS BIBLE INSTITUTE - LIBRARY
Oak Hills   Phone: (218) 751-8670
Bemidji, MN 56601   John Sanders, Libn.

OUR REDEEMERS LUTHERAN CHURCH - LIBRARY
Tenth St., S. & Oakwood Ave.   Phone: (612) 843-3151
Benson, MN 56215   Mrs. Gale W. Skold, Libn.

HONEYWELL, INC. - CORPORATE TECHNOLOGY CENTER LIBRARY
10701 Lyndale Ave., S.   Phone: (612) 887-4321
Bloomington, MN 55420   Michael McClellan, Libn.

BRAINERD STATE HOSPITAL - LIBRARY †
Box 349   Phone: (218) 829-1741
Brainerd, MN 56401   David C. Bauer, Libn.

CROW WING COUNTY HISTORICAL SOCIETY - MUSEUM LIBRARY
Court House
Brainerd, MN 56401   Catherine M. Ebert, Cur.

ST. FRANCIS HOSPITAL - COMMUNITY HEALTH SCIENCE LIBRARY
415 Oak St.
Breckenridge, MN 56520   Karen Engstrom, Dir. of Lib.Serv.

CAMBRIDGE STATE HOSPITAL - LIBRARY
                                        Phone: (612) 689-2121
Cambridge, MN 55008   Jean Peterson, Libn.

HAZELDEN FOUNDATION - STAFF & RESEARCH LIBRARIES
Box 11   Phone: (612) 257-4010
Center City, MN 55012   Joan A. Frederickson, Libn.

UNIVERSITY OF MINNESOTA - LANDSCAPE ARBORETUM - ELMER L. &
  ELEANOR J. ANDERSEN HORTICULTURAL LIBRARY
3675 Arboretum Dr.   Phone: (612) 443-2460
Chaska, MN 55318   June Rogier, Libn.

MINNESOTA STATE IRON RANGE RESOURCES & REHABILITATION BOARD -
  IRON RANGE RESEARCH CENTER
Box 392   Phone: (218) 254-5733
Chisholm, MN 55719   Joseph D. Engles, Dir.

ST. JOHN'S ABBEY AND UNIVERSITY - HILL MONASTIC MANUSCRIPT
  LIBRARY - BUSH CENTER
                                        Phone: (612) 363-3514
Collegeville, MN 56321   Dr. Julian G. Plante, Dir.

BECKER COUNTY HISTORICAL SOCIETY - WALTER D. BIRD MEMORIAL
  HISTORICAL LIBRARY
915 Lake Ave.   Phone: (218) 847-2938
Detroit Lakes, MN 56501   Otto F. Zeck, Musm.Cur.

DULUTH BAR LIBRARY ASSOCIATION
515 St. Louis County Court House   Phone: (218) 723-3563
Duluth, MN 55802   Michele Milinovich, Libn.

DULUTH HERALD & NEWS-TRIBUNE - LIBRARY
424 W. 1st St.   Phone: (218) 723-5309
Duluth, MN 55801   Laurie Hertzel, Libn.

MILLER-DWAN HOSPITAL AND MEDICAL CENTER - TILDERQUIST
  MEMORIAL MEDICAL LIBRARY
502 E. Second St.   Phone: (218) 727-8762
Duluth, MN 55805   Annelie Sober, Dir., Med.Lib.

MINNESOTA HISTORICAL SOCIETY - NORTHEAST MINNESOTA
  HISTORICAL CENTER
Library 375
University of Minnesota, Duluth   Phone: (218) 726-8526
Duluth, MN 55812   Judith Ann Trolander, Dir.

ST. LUKE'S HOSPITAL - MEDICAL LIBRARY
915 E. First St.   Phone: (218) 727-6636
Duluth, MN 55805   Edean Berglund, Libn.

UNIVERSITY OF MINNESOTA, DULUTH - HEALTH SCIENCE LIBRARY
2400 Oakland Ave.   Phone: (218) 726-8586
Duluth, MN 55812   Diana Ebro, Asst.Lib.Dir./Health Sci.

MTS SYSTEMS CORPORATION - INFORMATION SERVICES
8055 Mitchell Rd.   Phone: (612) 937-4000
Eden Prairie, MN 55344   LaDonna M. Thompson, Mgr.

FAIRVIEW SOUTHDALE HOSPITAL - MARY ANN KING HEALTH SCIENCES
  LIBRARY
6401 France Ave. S.   Phone: (612) 920-4400
Edina, MN 55435   Lisa C. Bjerken, Libn.

GRANT COUNTY HISTORICAL SOCIETY - LIBRARY
                                        Phone: (218) 685-4864
Elbow Lake, MN 56531   George M. Shervey, Pres.

LE SUEUR COUNTY HISTORICAL SOCIETY MUSEUM - LIBRARY
Box 557   Phone: (507) 267-4620
Elysian, MN 56028   James E. Hruska, Dir.

U.S. HOCKEY HALL OF FAME - LIBRARY
Hat Trick Ave.   Phone: (218) 749-5167
Eveleth, MN 55734   Roger A. Godin, Exec.Dir.

HENNEPIN COUNTY PARK RESERVE DISTRICT - LOWRY NATURE CENTER -
     LIBRARY *
Carver Park Reserve
Rt. 1, Box 690   Phone: (612) 472-4911
Excelsior, MN 55331   Dale Rock, Naturalist

MARTIN COUNTY HISTORICAL SOCIETY - PIONEER MUSEUM - LIBRARY
304 E. Blue Earth Ave.   Phone: (507) 235-5178
Fairmont, MN 56031   Catherine Harber, Supt.

FARIBAULT STATE HOSPITAL - LIBRARY
                                                  Phone: (507) 332-3274
Faribault, MN 55021   Mary K. Heltsley, Libn.

MINNESOTA LIBRARY FOR THE BLIND AND PHYSICALLY HANDICAPPED
                                                  Phone: (507) 332-3279
Faribault, MN 55021   Myrna Wright, Libn.

RICE COUNTY HISTORICAL SOCIETY - ARCHIVES
1814 Second Ave.
Box 5   Phone: (507) 332-2121
Faribault, MN 55021   Dr. Elvin Heiberg, Pres.

FERGUS FALLS STATE HOSPITAL - LIBRARY
Corner Of Fir & Union
Box 157   Phone: (218) 739-7327
Fergus Falls, MN 56537   Elizabeth Swenson, Libn.

LUTHERAN BRETHREN SCHOOLS - BIBLE COLLEGE AND SEMINARY LIBRARY
815 W. Vernon Ave.   Phone: (218) 739-3373
Fergus Falls, MN 56537   Donald W. Brue, Libn.

OTTER TAIL POWER COMPANY - LIBRARY
215 S. Cascade   Phone: (218) 736-5411
Fergus Falls, MN 56537   Sheila Martinson, Supv.Lib.Serv.

UNITY HOSPITAL - MEDICAL LIBRARY
550 Osborne Rd.   Phone: (612) 786-2200
Fridley, MN 55432   Stan W. Carlson, Dir. of Libs.

POPE COUNTY HISTORICAL SOCIETY & MUSEUM - LIBRARY
Hwy. No. 104 S. Glenwood   Phone: (612) 634-3293
Glenwood, MN 56334   Laura Vix, Off.Supv.

COURAGE CENTER LIBRARY
3915 Golden Valley Rd.   Phone: (612) 588-0811
Golden Valley, MN 55422   Mary Lindgren, Libn.

GOLDEN VALLEY HEALTH CENTER - MEDICAL LIBRARY
4101 Golden Valley Rd.   Phone: (612) 588-2771
Golden Valley, MN 55422   Carol Nordby, Lib.Ck.

COOK COUNTY HISTORICAL SOCIETY - GRAND MARAIS LIBRARY
                                                  Phone: (218) 387-1678
Grand Marais, MN 55604   Mary Alice Harbey, Libn.

U.S. NATL. PARK SERVICE - GRAND PORTAGE NATL. MONUMENT - LIBRARY
Box 666   Phone: (218) 387-2788
Grand Marais, MN 55604

BLACKWELL - PRIVATE LIBRARY
Box 184
Hastings, MN 55033

HONEYWELL, INC. - DEFENSE SYSTEMS DIVISION - ENGINEERING
     LIBRARY
600 Second St., N.   Phone: (612) 931-6603
Hopkins, MN 55343   Lawrence W. Werner, Libn.

KOOCHICHING COUNTY HISTORICAL SOCIETY - MUSEUM
Smokey Bear Park
214 6th St.
Box 1147   Phone: (218) 283-4316
International Falls, MN 56649   Mary Hilke, Exec.Sec. & Cur.

GREEN GIANT / PILLSBURY COMPANY - LIBRARY
1100 N. 4th St.   Phone: (612) 665-3515
Le Sueur, MN 56058   Sally Olson, Libn.

ST. GABRIEL'S HOSPITAL - LIBRARY
St. Joseph's Hall   Phone: (612) 632-5441
Little Falls, MN 56345

WEYERHAEUSER (Charles A.) MEMORIAL MUSEUM - LIBRARY
Box 239   Phone: (612) 632-4007
Little Falls, MN 56345   Jan Warner, Dir.

LAC QUI PARLE COUNTY HISTORICAL SOCIETY - HISTORIC CENTER
408 Park Ave., No. 2.   Phone: (612) 598-7678
Madison, MN 56256   Melvin S. Wroolie, Cur.

BETHANY LUTHERAN THEOLOGICAL SEMINARY - LIBRARY
447 N. Division St.   Phone: (507) 625-2977
Mankato, MN 56001   Milton H. Otto, Libn.

BLUE EARTH COUNTY HISTORICAL SOCIETY - HUBBARD HOUSE MUSEUM
     ARCHIVES
606 S. Broad St.   Phone: (507) 345-4154
Mankato, MN 56001

MANKATO STATE UNIVERSITY - LIBRARY
Memorial Library   Phone: (507) 389-6201
Mankato, MN 56001   Dale K. Carrison, Dean of Lib.

MINNESOTA HISTORICAL SOCIETY - SOUTHERN MINNESOTA HISTORICAL
     CENTER
Mankato State University   Phone: (507) 389-1029
Mankato, MN 56001   Dr. William E. Lass, Dir.

MINNESOTA HISTORICAL SOCIETY - SOUTHWEST MINNESOTA
     HISTORICAL CENTER
Southwest State University   Phone: (507) 537-7373
Marshall, MN 56258   Dr. David L. Nass, Dir.

ALTERNATIVE SOURCES OF ENERGY MAGAZINE - ENERGY INFORMATION
     REFERRAL SERVICE (EIRS)
107 S. Central Ave.
Milaca, MN 56353   Donald Marier, Dir.

ABBOTT-NORTHWESTERN HOSPITAL CORPORATION - HEALTH SCIENCES
     RESOURCE CENTER
2727 Chicago Ave.   Phone: (612) 874-4312
Minneapolis, MN 55407   Donna Johnson, Resource Ctr.Dir.

ADATH JESHURUN CONGREGATION - JENNY GROSS MEMORIAL LIBRARY
3400 Dupont, S.   Phone: (612) 824-2685
Minneapolis, MN 55408   Naomi Goldberg Honor, Libn.

ALEXANDER & ALEXANDER, INC. - NATIONAL PRODUCTION INFORMATION
     CENTER
400 South County Rd. 18, Suite 500   Phone: (612) 546-1628
Minneapolis, MN 55426   Laura E. Dirks, Libn.

AMERICAN COLLECTORS ASSOCIATION, INC. - ACA MEMORIAL LIBRARY
4040 W. 70th St.   Phone: (612) 926-6547
Minneapolis, MN 55435   Debra J. Ciskey, Libn.

AMERICAN HARDWARE MUTUAL INSURANCE COMPANY - LIBRARY
3033 Excelsior Blvd.   Phone: (612) 920-1400
Minneapolis, MN 55416   Sylvia Kamrud, Libn.

AMERICAN SWEDISH INSTITUTE - LIBRARY
2600 Park Ave., S.   Phone: (612) 871-4907
Minneapolis, MN 55407

ASSOCIATED COLLEGIATE PRESS/NATIONAL SCHOLASTIC PRESS
     ASSOCIATION - INFORMATION CENTER
720 Washington Ave., S.E., Suite 205
University of Minnesota   Phone: (612) 373-3180
Minneapolis, MN 55414   Tom Rolnicki, Exec.Dir.

AUGSBURG COLLEGE - GEORGE SVERDRUP LIBRARY AND MEDIA CENTER
731-21st Ave., S.   Phone: (612) 330-1017
Minneapolis, MN 55454   Margaret J. Anderson, Hd.Libn.

BARR ENGINEERING COMPANY - LIBRARY
6800 France Ave. S.   Phone: (612) 920-0655
Minneapolis, MN 55435   Francine Creme, Tech.Libn.

BARTON-ASCHMAN ASSOCIATES, INC. - RESOURCE CENTER
10 Cedar Square West
1610 S. Sixth St.   Phone: (612) 332-0421
Minneapolis, MN 55454   Janet Fabio, Libn.

BIBLE SCIENCE ASSOCIATION - RESEARCH CENTER †
2911 E. 42nd St.   Phone: (612) 724-1883
Minneapolis, MN 55406   Rev. Walter Lang, Exec.Dir.

CAMPBELL-MITHUN, INC. - LIBRARY
Northstar Ctr.   Phone: (612) 347-1509
Minneapolis, MN 55402   Virginia Ferestad, Hd.Libn.

CARGILL, INC. - INFORMATION CENTER
Box 9300   Phone: (612) 475-6498
Minneapolis, MN 55440   Julia Peterson, Mgr.

CARLSON COMPANIES - LIBRARY
12755 State Hwy. 55   Phone: (612) 540-5236
Minneapolis, MN 55441   Stella M. Rosow, Libn.

CHILDREN'S THEATRE COMPANY AND SCHOOL - LIBRARY
2400 Third Ave. S.   Phone: (612) 874-0500
Minneapolis, MN 55404   Ingrid A. Liss, Theater Sch.Asst.

CONTROL DATA CORPORATION - LIBRARY/INFORMATION CENTER
2800 E. Old Shakopee Rd.
Box 1249, Bldg. HQM 250   Phone: (612) 853-4229
Minneapolis, MN 55440   Gloria T. Andrew, Mgr.

CORRECTIONAL SERVICE OF MINNESOTA - LIBRARY
1427 Washington Ave., S.   Phone: (612) 340-5432
Minneapolis, MN 55454   Richard C. Ericson, Exec.Dir.

DAYTON HUDSON CORPORATION LIBRARY
777 Nicollet Mall   Phone: (612) 370-6769
Minneapolis, MN 55402   Barbara Miller, Corp.Libn.

DELOITTE HASKINS & SELLS - LIBRARY
1950 IDS Tower   Phone: (612) 339-9744
Minneapolis, MN 55402   Richard G. Reynen, Libn.

DONALDSON COMPANY, INC. - INFORMATION CENTER
Box 1299   Phone: (612) 887-3019
Minneapolis, MN 55440   Arlene Louton, Libn.

DORSEY, WINDHORST, HANNAFORD, WHITNEY & HALLADAY - LAW
    LIBRARY
2300 First National Bank Bldg.   Phone: (612) 340-2613
Minneapolis, MN 55402   Ann M. Carter, Libn.

DUNWOODY INDUSTRIAL INSTITUTE - JOHN A. BUTLER LEARNING CENTER
818 Wayzata Blvd.   Phone: (612) 374-5800
Minneapolis, MN 55403   Lillian V. Carlson, Libn.

EDGEWATER BAPTIST CHURCH - LIBRARY
5501 Chicago Ave.   Phone: (612) 827-3803
Minneapolis, MN 55417   Berdella Gustafson, Libn.

FAEGRE & BENSON - LAW LIBRARY
1300 Northwestern Bank Bldg.   Phone: (612) 371-5300
Minneapolis, MN 55402   Carolyn Scott, Libn.

FAIRVIEW COMMUNITY HOSPITALS - HEALTH SCIENCES LIBRARY
2312 S. Sixth St.   Phone: (612) 371-6545
Minneapolis, MN 55454   Linda McIntosh, Dir.

FEDERAL RESERVE BANK OF MINNEAPOLIS - LAW LIBRARY
250 Marquette Ave.   Phone: (612) 340-2412
Minneapolis, MN 55480   James M. Lyon, Dir.

FEDERAL RESERVE BANK OF MINNEAPOLIS - LIBRARY
250 Marquette, S.   Phone: (612) 340-2292
Minneapolis, MN 55480   Joanne E. Farley, Mgr., Lib.Serv.

FLUIDYNE ENGINEERING CORPORATION - TECHNICAL LIBRARY
5900 Olson Memorial Hwy.   Phone: (612) 544-2721
Minneapolis, MN 55422   Marlys J. Johnson, Tech.Libn.

GENERAL MILLS, INC. - GENERAL OFFICE LIBRARY/INFORMATION CENTER
9200 Wayzata Blvd.   Phone: (612) 540-3536
Minneapolis, MN 55426   Duane R. Day, Mgr.Lib.Serv.

GENERAL MILLS, INC. - JAMES FORD BELL TECHNICAL CENTER -
    TECHNICAL INFORMATION SERVICES
9000 Plymouth Ave., N.   Phone: (612) 540-2801
Minneapolis, MN 55427   Dr. William J. Mayer, Mgr.Tech.Info.Serv.

GENERAL MILLS, INC. - LAW LIBRARY
Box 1113   Phone: (612) 540-2047
Minneapolis, MN 55440   Rhonda Edonis Greenwood, Law Libn.

GENERAL MILLS, INC. - MARKETING RESEARCH INFORMATION CENTER
Box 1113   Phone: (612) 540-2070
Minneapolis, MN 55440   Judith A. Sassaman, Info.Spec.

GOLDEN VALLEY LUTHERAN COLLEGE - LIBRARY
6125 Olson Hwy.   Phone: (612) 542-1210
Minneapolis, MN 55422   Richard Serena, Libn.

GRAHAM (Billy) EVANGELISTIC ASSOCIATION - LIBRARY
1300 Harmon Place   Phone: (612) 338-0500
Minneapolis, MN 55403   Rev. Roger C. Palms, Ed.

GRAY, PLANT, MOOTY, MOOTY, AND BENNETT - LAW LIBRARY †
300 Roanoke Bldg.   Phone: (612) 343-2800
Minneapolis, MN 55402   Annette Jenson, Libn.

HANSEN (Clark Bradley) PRIVATE LIBRARY
3901 E. 49th St.   Phone: (612) 722-3630
Minneapolis, MN 55417   Clark B. Hansen, Dir.

HENKEL CORPORATION - HENNEPIN TECHNICAL CENTER LIBRARY
2010 E. Hennepin Ave.   Phone: (612) 378-8758
Minneapolis, MN 55413   Dr. Ronald R. Dueltgen, Mgr.-Tech.Info.Serv.

HENNEPIN COUNTY HISTORICAL SOCIETY - ARCHIVES
2303 Third Ave. S.   Phone: (612) 870-1329
Minneapolis, MN 55404   Donna Lind, Exec.Dir.

HENNEPIN COUNTY LAW LIBRARY
C2451 Government Ctr.   Phone: (612) 348-3022
Minneapolis, MN 55487   Anne W. Grande, Hd.Libn.

HENNEPIN COUNTY LIBRARY SYSTEM - GOVERNMENT CENTER
    INFORMATION LIBRARY
C-2359 Government Center
300 S. Sixth St.   Phone: (612) 348-2024
Minneapolis, MN 55487   Julie Setnosky, Sr.Libn.

HENNEPIN COUNTY MEDICAL CENTER - HEALTH SCIENCES LIBRARY
701 Park Ave.   Phone: (612) 347-2710
Minneapolis, MN 55415   Patricia A. Williams, Sr.Libn.

HOLY TRINITY LUTHERAN CHURCH - LIBRARY †
2730 E. 31st St.   Phone: (612) 729-8358
Minneapolis, MN 55406   Mae Cruys, Hd.Libn.

HONEYWELL, INC. - SYSTEMS & RESEARCH CENTER - LIBRARY
2600 Ridgeway Pkwy.
Box 312   Phone: (612) 378-4238
Minneapolis, MN 55440   Maro Theologides, Supv.

IDS LIFE INSURANCE COMPANY - LIBRARY
IDS Tower   Phone: (612) 372-3747
Minneapolis, MN 55402   M.C. Laughlin, Libn.

INTERNATIONAL FESTIVALS ASSOCIATION - LIBRARY
Commodore Court, 702 Wayzata Blvd.   Phone: (612) 377-4621
Minneapolis, MN 55403   Ken Walstad, Mng.Dir.

INVESTORS DIVERSIFIED SERVICES, INC. - INVESTMENT LIBRARY
IDS Tower   Phone: (612) 372-3429
Minneapolis, MN 55402   Mel Kirkpatrick, Libn.

JEWISH COMMUNITY CENTER OF GREATER MINNEAPOLIS - LIBRARY †
4330 S. Cedar Lake Rd.   Phone: (612) 377-8330
Minneapolis, MN 55416   Ruth Isaacson

JEWISH COMMUNITY RELATIONS COUNCIL - ANTI-DEFAMATION LEAGUE
    OF MINNESOTA-DAKOTAS - LIBRARY
15 S. 9th St. Bldg., Suite 400   Phone: (612) 338-7816
Minneapolis, MN 55402   Morton W. Ryweck, Dir.

LUTHERAN BROTHERHOOD INSURANCE SOCIETY - LB LIBRARY
625 Fourth Ave., S.   Phone: (612) 340-7269
Minneapolis, MN 55415   Jean Diersen, Libn.

LUTHERAN DEACONESS HOSPITAL - MEDICAL LIBRARY
2315 14th Ave., South   Phone: (612) 721-2933
Minneapolis, MN 55404   Susan Clark, Libn.

MARTIN/WILLIAMS ADVERTISING AGENCY - LIBRARY/INFORMATION
    CENTER
10 S. 5th St.   Phone: (612) 340-0800
Minneapolis, MN 55402   Robert B. Van Horn, Dir., Info.Serv.

MEDTRONIC, INC. - LIBRARY
3055 Old Hwy. 8
Box 1453   Phone: (612) 574-3154
Minneapolis, MN 55440   Leonard Bigelow, Mgr. of Lib.Serv.

MINITEX
30 Wilson Library, Univ. of Minnesota
309 19th Ave. S.   Phone: (612) 376-3925
Minneapolis, MN 55455   Alice E. Wilcox, Dir.

MINNEAPOLIS COLLEGE OF ART AND DESIGN - LIBRARY AND MEDIA
    CENTER
200 E. 25th St.   Phone: (612) 870-3291
Minneapolis, MN 55404   Richard Kronstedt, Hd.Libn.

MINNEAPOLIS INSTITUTE OF ARTS - ARTS RESOURCE AND INFORMATION
    CENTER
2400 Third Ave., S.   Phone: (612) 870-3131
Minneapolis, MN 55404   Robert C. Booker, Supv.

MINNEAPOLIS INSTITUTE OF ARTS - LIBRARY - EDITORIAL DEPARTMENT
2400 Third Ave., S.   Phone: (612) 874-0200
Minneapolis, MN 55404   Harold Peterson, Libn./Ed.-in-Chf.

MINNEAPOLIS PUBLIC LIBRARY & INFORMATION CENTER - ART, MUSIC &
    FILMS DEPARTMENT
300 Nicollet Mall   Phone: (612) 372-6520
Minneapolis, MN 55401   Marlea R. Warren, Dept.Hd.

MINNEAPOLIS PUBLIC LIBRARY & INFORMATION CENTER - BUSINESS AND
    SCIENCE DEPARTMENT
300 Nicollet Mall   Phone: (612) 372-6552
Minneapolis, MN 55401   Leonard J. Pignatello, Dept.Hd.

MINNEAPOLIS PUBLIC LIBRARY & INFORMATION CENTER -
    ENVIRONMENTAL CONSERVATION LIBRARY OF MINNESOTA
300 Nicollet Mall   Phone: (612) 372-6609
Minneapolis, MN 55401   Julia Copeland, Env.Consrv.Libn.

MINNEAPOLIS PUBLIC LIBRARY & INFORMATION CENTER - GOVERNMENT
    DOCUMENTS
300 Nicollet Mall   Phone: (612) 372-6534
Minneapolis, MN 55401   Helen E. Garnaas, Doc.Libn.

MINNEAPOLIS PUBLIC LIBRARY & INFORMATION CENTER - HISTORY
    DEPARTMENT
300 Nicollet Mall   Phone: (612) 372-6537
Minneapolis, MN 55401   Robert K. Bruce, Dept.Hd.

MINNEAPOLIS PUBLIC LIBRARY & INFORMATION CENTER - HUTTNER
    ABOLITION AND ANTI-SLAVERY COLLECTION
300 Nicollet Mall   Phone: (612) 372-6522
Minneapolis, MN 55401   Richard Hofstad, Athenaeum Libn.

MINNEAPOLIS PUBLIC LIBRARY & INFORMATION CENTER - KITTLESON
    WORLD WAR II COLLECTION
300 Nicollet Mall   Phone: (612) 372-6522
Minneapolis, MN 55401   Richard Hofstad, Athenaeum Libn.

MINNEAPOLIS PUBLIC LIBRARY & INFORMATION CENTER - LITERATURE
    AND LANGUAGE DEPARTMENT
300 Nicollet Mall   Phone: (612) 372-6540
Minneapolis, MN 55401   Dorothy D. Thews, Dept.Hd.

MINNEAPOLIS PUBLIC LIBRARY & INFORMATION CENTER - MINNEAPOLIS
    ATHENAEUM LIBRARY
300 Nicollet Mall   Phone: (612) 372-6522
Minneapolis, MN 55401   Richard Hofstad, Athenaeum Libn.

MINNEAPOLIS PUBLIC LIBRARY & INFORMATION CENTER - MUNICIPAL
    INFORMATION LIBRARY
City Hall, Rm. 302   Phone: (612) 348-8139
Minneapolis, MN 55415   Sylvia Frisch, Libn.

MINNEAPOLIS PUBLIC LIBRARY & INFORMATION CENTER - 19TH CENTURY
    AMERICAN STUDIES COLLECTION
N. Regional Library, Emerson Rm.
1315 Lowry Ave., N.   Phone: (612) 522-3333
Minneapolis, MN 55411

MINNEAPOLIS PUBLIC LIBRARY & INFORMATION CENTER - SOCIOLOGY
    DEPARTMENT
300 Nicollet Mall   Phone: (612) 372-6555
Minneapolis, MN 55401   Eileen Schwartzbauer, Dept.Hd.

MINNEAPOLIS PUBLIC SCHOOLS - SPECIAL SCHOOL DISTRICT 1 - BOARD
    OF EDUCATION LIBRARY
807 N.E. Broadway   Phone: (612) 348-6048
Minneapolis, MN 55413   Phyllis Thornley, Asst.Dir.

MINNEAPOLIS STAR AND TRIBUNE - LIBRARY
Fifth & Portland
Minneapolis, MN 55488   Robert A. Lopez, Hd.Libn.

MINNEAPOLIS TECHNICAL INSTITUTE - LIBRARY
1415 Hennepin Ave. S.   Phone: (612) 370-9471
Minneapolis, MN 55403   David L. Jenson, Libn.

MINNESOTA GAS COMPANY - LIBRARY
733 Marquette Ave.   Phone: (612) 372-4824
Minneapolis, MN 55402   Virginia B. Shirk, Libn.

MINNESOTA ORCHESTRA - MUSIC LIBRARY
1111 Nicollet Mall   Phone: (612) 371-5622
Minneapolis, MN 55403   James N. Berdahl, Libn.

MINNESOTA SCIENCE FICTION SOCIETY - LIBRARY
Box 2128, Loop Station   Phone: (612) 722-5217
Minneapolis, MN 55402   Dennis Lien, Contact Person

MINNESOTA STATE DEPARTMENT OF HEALTH - ROBERT N. BARR PUBLIC
    HEALTH LIBRARY
717 Delaware St., S.E.   Phone: (612) 296-5240
Minneapolis, MN 55440   Lynne Siemers, Libn.

MINNESOTA WOMEN'S CENTER - RESOURCE COLLECTION
University of Minnesota
324 Walter Library
117 Pleasant St., S.E.   Phone: (612) 373-3850
Minneapolis, MN 55455   Anne Truax, Dir.

MOUNT OLIVET LUTHERAN CHURCH - LIBRARY
5025 Knox Ave., S.   Phone: (612) 926-7651
Minneapolis, MN 55419   Bonnie Morris, Lib.Adm.

MOUNT SINAI HOSPITAL - MEDICAL LIBRARY
2215 Park Ave.   Phone: (612) 871-3700
Minneapolis, MN 55404   Susan J. McIntyre, Med.Libn.

NATIONAL CAR RENTAL SYSTEM, INC. - BUSINESS INFORMATION CENTER
7700 France Ave. S.   Phone: (612) 893-6380
Minneapolis, MN 55435   Nancy Luse, Info.Spec.

NATIONAL COUNCIL ON FAMILY RELATIONS - FAMILY RESOURCE &
    REFERRAL CENTER
1219 University Ave., S.E.   Phone: (612) 331-2774
Minneapolis, MN 55414   Margaret J. Bodley, Dir.

GEOGRAPHIC

GEOGRAPHIC

NATIONAL INDIAN EDUCATION ASSOCIATION - LIBRARY
Ivy Tower Bldg., 2nd Fl.
1115 Second Ave., S.   Phone: (612) 333-5341
Minneapolis, MN 55403   Joyce Yellowhammer, Libn./Data Anl.

NATIONAL PUBLICATIONS LIBRARY
7611 Oakland Ave.   Phone: (612) 861-2162
Minneapolis, MN 55423   Elmer Josephs, Libn.

NORTH CENTRAL BIBLE COLLEGE - T.J. JONES MEMORIAL LIBRARY
910 Elliot Ave., S.   Phone: (612) 332-3491
Minneapolis, MN 55404   Marvin Smith, Lib.Dir.

NORTH MEMORIAL MEDICAL CENTER - MEDICAL LIBRARY
3220 Lowry Ave., N.   Phone: (612) 588-0616
Minneapolis, MN 55422   Sherry A. Oleson, Dir.Med.Lib.Serv.

NORTHERN STATES POWER COMPANY - "ASK NSP" TAPE LIBRARY
414 Nicollet Mall   Phone: (612) 330-6000
Minneapolis, MN 55401   Mr. Lynn M. Gustafson, Supv.

NORTHWEST BANCORPORATION - LIBRARY
1200 Northwestern Bank Bldg.   Phone: (612) 372-8263
Minneapolis, MN 55480   Marilyn J. Schlee, Lib.Serv.Off.

NORTHWESTERN NATIONAL LIFE INSURANCE COMPANY - LIBRARY
20 Washington Ave., S.   Phone: (612) 372-5606
Minneapolis, MN 55440   Beth O'Connor, Libn.

ONAN CORPORATION - LIBRARY
1400 73rd Ave., N.E.   Phone: (612) 574-5000
Minneapolis, MN 55432   Ingrid F. Forde, Corp.Libn.

PEAT, MARWICK, MITCHELL & COMPANY - LIBRARY
1700 IDS Center   Phone: (612) 341-2222
Minneapolis, MN 55402   Donna J. Harnden, Hd.Libn.

PEAVEY COMPANY - CORPORATE INFORMATION CENTER
730 2nd Ave. S.   Phone: (612) 370-7506
Minneapolis, MN 55402   Pearl Hunt-McCain, Corp.Libn.

PICKWICK INTERNATIONAL, INC. - RESOURCE CENTER *
7500 Excelsior Blvd.   Phone: (612) 932-7675
Minneapolis, MN 55426   Celia L. Moore, Res.Asst.

PILLSBURY COMPANY - MAIN OFFICE MARKETING LIBRARY
803 Pillsbury Bldg.   Phone: (612) 330-4047
Minneapolis, MN 55402   Rachel Berry, Mgr.

PILLSBURY COMPANY - TECHNICAL INFORMATION CENTER
311 Second St., S.E.   Phone: (612) 330-4750
Minneapolis, MN 55414   James B. Tchobanoff, Mgr.

PILOTS INTERNATIONAL ASSOCIATION - LIBRARY
400 S. County Rd. 18   Phone: (612) 546-4075
Minneapolis, MN 55426   Laura E. Dirks, Libn.

RIDER, BENNETT, EGAN & ARUNDEL - LIBRARY
900 First Bank Place W.   Phone: (612) 340-7960
Minneapolis, MN 55402   Janet A. Jacobson, Libn.

**ST. LOUIS PARK MEDICAL CENTER-RESEARCH FOUNDATION - ARNESON
    LIBRARY**
5000 W. 39th St.   Phone: (612) 927-3097
Minneapolis, MN 55416   Barbara Latta, Hd.Libn.

ST. MARY'S HOSPITAL - STAFF LIBRARY
2414 S. 7th St.   Phone: (612) 338-2229
Minneapolis, MN 55454   Jacquelynn Carlson, Chf.Libn.

ST. OLAF LUTHERAN CHURCH - CARLSEN MEMORIAL LIBRARY †
29th & Emerson Ave., N.   Phone: (612) 529-7726
Minneapolis, MN 55411   Lorraine P. Kelly, Libn.

SONS OF NORWAY - NORTH STAR LIBRARY
1455 W. Lake St.   Phone: (612) 827-3611
Minneapolis, MN 55408   Bent Vanberg, Cons.

TEL-MED HEALTH INFORMATION SERVICE
Lutheran Deaconess Hospital
2315 14th Ave., S.   Phone: (612) 721-2933
Minneapolis, MN 55404   Linda Thomson, Dir.

TEMPLE ISRAEL - LIBRARY
2324 Emerson Ave., S.   Phone: (612) 377-9157
Minneapolis, MN 55405   Georgia Kalman, Libn.

THERMO KING CORPORATION - LIBRARY
314 W. 90th St.   Phone: (612) 887-2336
Minneapolis, MN 55420   Mrs. Rougean Schoenborn, Libn.

**TWIN CITY FEDERAL SAVINGS & LOAN ASSOCIATION - CORPORATE
    LIBRARY †**
801 Marquette Ave.   Phone: (612) 370-7006
Minneapolis, MN 55402   Marguerite Crepeau, Libn.

**UNITED METHODIST COMMN. ON ARCHIVES & HIST. - MINNESOTA
    ANNUAL CONFERENCE - ARCHIVES & HISTORICAL LIB.**
122 W. Franklin Ave., Rm. 400   Phone: (612) 870-3637
Minneapolis, MN 55404   Thelma Boeder, Archv./Exec.Dir.

U.S. BUREAU OF MINES - TWIN CITIES RESEARCH CENTER - LIBRARY
5629 Minnehaha Ave. S.   Phone: (612) 725-4503
Minneapolis, MN 55417   Merle Bernstein, Libn.

**U.S. DEPT. OF COMMERCE - INTERNATIONAL TRADE ADMINISTRATION -
    MINNEAPOLIS DISTRICT OFFICE LIBRARY**
108 Federal Bldg.
110 S. Fourth St.   Phone: (612) 725-2134
Minneapolis, MN 55401   Mary Hobbs, Trade Spec.

U.S. VETERANS ADMINISTRATION (MN-Minneapolis) - HOSPITAL LIBRARY
54th St. & 48th Ave., S.   Phone: (612) 725-6767
Minneapolis, MN 55417   Lionelle Elsesser, Chf.Libn.

UNIVERSITY OF MINNESOTA - AMES LIBRARY OF SOUTH ASIA
S-10 Wilson Library
309 19th Ave. S.   Phone: (612) 373-2890
Minneapolis, MN 55455   Henry Scholberg, Libn.

UNIVERSITY OF MINNESOTA - ARCHITECTURE LIBRARY
160 Architecture Bldg.
89 Church St. S.E.   Phone: (612) 373-2203
Minneapolis, MN 55455   A. Kristine Johnson, Libn.

UNIVERSITY OF MINNESOTA - ART LIBRARY
Walter Library, Rm. 208
117 Pleasant St. S.E.   Phone: (612) 373-2875
Minneapolis, MN 55455   Herbert Scherer, Art Libn.

UNIVERSITY OF MINNESOTA - AUDIO VISUAL LIBRARY SERVICE
3300 University Ave., S.E.   Phone: (612) 373-5452
Minneapolis, MN 55414   Judith A. Gaston, Dir.

**UNIVERSITY OF MINNESOTA - BELL MUSEUM OF NATURAL HISTORY -
    LIBRARY**
10 Church St. S.E.   Phone: (612) 373-7771
Minneapolis, MN 55455   Tom English, Libn.

UNIVERSITY OF MINNESOTA - BIOMEDICAL LIBRARY
Diehl Hall
505 Essex St., S.E.   Phone: (612) 373-5584
Minneapolis, MN 55455   Glenn L. Brudvig, Dir.

UNIVERSITY OF MINNESOTA - BUSINESS REFERENCE SERVICE
Wilson Library, 2nd Fl.
309 19th Ave., S.   Phone: (612) 373-4109
Minneapolis, MN 55455   Judy Wells, Bus.Libn.

UNIVERSITY OF MINNESOTA - CHEMISTRY LIBRARY
4 Walter Library
117 Pleasant St., S.E.   Phone: (612) 373-2375
Minneapolis, MN 55455   Beverly A. Lee, Libn.

**UNIVERSITY OF MINNESOTA - CHILDREN'S LITERATURE RESEARCH
    COLLECTIONS**
109 Walter Library
117 Pleasant St. S.E.   Phone: (612) 373-9731
Minneapolis, MN 55455   Dr. Karen Nelson Hoyle, Cur.

UNIVERSITY OF MINNESOTA - CLASSICS DEPARTMENT - SEMINAR
LIBRARY
310 Folwell Hall
9 Pleasant St. S.E.   Phone: (612) 373-3912
Minneapolis, MN 55455

UNIVERSITY OF MINNESOTA - CONSULTING GROUP ON INSTRUCTIONAL
DESIGN LIBRARY
205 Elliott Hall
75 E. River Rd.   Phone: (612) 373-5352
Minneapolis, MN 55455   Dr. Russell W. Burris, Dir.

UNIVERSITY OF MINNESOTA - DELOITTE HASKINS & SELLS TAX RESEARCH
ROOM
Wilson Library, 2nd Fl.
309 19th Ave., S.   Phone: (612) 373-4109
Minneapolis, MN 55455   Judy Wells, Bus.Libn.

UNIVERSITY OF MINNESOTA - DEPARTMENT OF LINGUISTICS -
LINGUISTICS LIBRARY
146 Klaeber Court
320 16th Ave., S.E.   Phone: (612) 373-5769
Minneapolis, MN 55455   Karen Frederickson, Sr.Sec.

UNIVERSITY OF MINNESOTA - DRUG INFORMATION SERVICE CENTER
3-106 Health Science Unit F
308 Harvard St., S.E.   Phone: (612) 376-7190
Minneapolis, MN 55455   Jon Clouse, Dir.

UNIVERSITY OF MINNESOTA - EAST ASIAN LIBRARY
Wilson Library, S-30
309 19th Ave. S.   Phone: (612) 373-3737
Minneapolis, MN 55455   Richard Wang, Hd.

UNIVERSITY OF MINNESOTA - ECONOMICS RESEARCH LIBRARY
525 Science Classroom Bldg.
222 Pleasant St., S.E.   Phone: (612) 373-5958
Minneapolis, MN 55455   Wendy Williamson, Graduate Res.Asst.

UNIVERSITY OF MINNESOTA - EDUCATION-PSYCHOLOGY-LIBRARY
SCIENCE LIBRARY
Walter Library, Rm. 206
117 Pleasant St. S.E.   Phone: (612) 373-3841
Minneapolis, MN 55455

UNIVERSITY OF MINNESOTA - ENGINEERING LIBRARY
Lind Hall, Rm. 128
207 Church St., S.E.   Phone: (612) 373-2957
Minneapolis, MN 55455   Raymond Bohling, Engr.Libn.

UNIVERSITY OF MINNESOTA - ERIC SEVAREID JOURNALISM LIBRARY
121 Murphy Hall
206 Church St., S.E.   Phone: (612) 373-3174
Minneapolis, MN 55455   Kathy Busterna, Libn.

UNIVERSITY OF MINNESOTA - FIRE CENTER
3300 University Ave. S.E.   Phone: (612) 376-3535
Minneapolis, MN 55414   Antona Richardson, Dir.

UNIVERSITY OF MINNESOTA - GEOLOGY LIBRARY
Pillsbury Hall, Rm. 204
310 Pillsbury Dr., S.E,   Phone: (612) 373-4052
Minneapolis, MN 55455   Marie Dvorzak, Libn.

UNIVERSITY OF MINNESOTA - GOVERNMENT PUBLICATIONS DIVISION
409 Wilson Library
309 19th Ave. S.   Phone: (612) 373-7813
Minneapolis, MN 55455   William LaBissoniere, Libn.

UNIVERSITY OF MINNESOTA - HAROLD SCOTT QUIGLEY CENTER OF
INTERNATIONAL STUDIES LIBRARY
1246 Social Sciences Bldg.
267 19th Ave. S.   Phone: (612) 373-2691
Minneapolis, MN 55455   Karen Farwell, Libn.

UNIVERSITY OF MINNESOTA - INDUSTRIAL RELATIONS CENTER -
REFERENCE ROOM
309 B.A., West Campus
271 19th Ave. S.   Phone: (612) 373-3681
Minneapolis, MN 55455   Georgianna Herman, Libn. & Supv.

UNIVERSITY OF MINNESOTA - INFORM
Wilson Library, 2nd Fl.
309 19th Ave., S.   Phone: (612) 373-5938
Minneapolis, MN 55455

UNIVERSITY OF MINNESOTA - JAMES FORD BELL LIBRARY
Wilson Library 472
309 19th Ave. S.   Phone: (612) 373-2888
Minneapolis, MN 55455   John Parker, Cur.

UNIVERSITY OF MINNESOTA - LAW LIBRARY
229 19th Ave. S.   Phone: (612) 373-2737
Minneapolis, MN 55455   Kathleen Price, Dir.

UNIVERSITY OF MINNESOTA - LITZENBERG-LUND LIBRARY
Box 395, Mayo Memorial Bldg.
420 Delaware St., S.E.   Phone: (612) 373-8851
Minneapolis, MN 55455

UNIVERSITY OF MINNESOTA - MAP DIVISION
Wilson Library, S-76
309 19th Ave. S.   Phone: (612) 373-2825
Minneapolis, MN 55455   J. Mai Treude, Libn.

UNIVERSITY OF MINNESOTA - MATHEMATICS LIBRARY
Vincent Hall, Rm. 310
206 Church St. S.E.   Phone: (612) 376-7207
Minneapolis, MN 55455   Margie L. Voelker, Libn.

UNIVERSITY OF MINNESOTA - MIDDLE EAST LIBRARY
S50 Wilson Library
309 19th Ave., S.   Phone: (612) 373-7804
Minneapolis, MN 55455   Nassif Youssif, Hd.

UNIVERSITY OF MINNESOTA - MINES, METALLURGY, & CHEMICAL
ENGINEERING LIBRARY
132 Amundson Hall
421 Washington Ave., S.E.   Phone: (612) 373-2313
Minneapolis, MN 55455   Mary C. O'Reilly, Libn.

UNIVERSITY OF MINNESOTA - MINNESOTA CENTER FOR PHILOSOPHY OF
SCIENCE - DEPARTMENTAL LIBRARY
309 Ford Hall
224 Church St. S.E.   Phone: (612) 373-2845
Minneapolis, MN 55455   Grover Maxwell, Dir.

UNIVERSITY OF MINNESOTA - MUSIC LIBRARY
103 Walter Library
117 Pleasant St., S.E.   Phone: (612) 373-3438
Minneapolis, MN 55455   Katharine Holum, Music Libn.

UNIVERSITY OF MINNESOTA - NEWMAN CENTER LIBRARY
1701 University Ave., S.E.   Phone: (612) 331-3437
Minneapolis, MN 55414   Colleen Brady, Libn.

UNIVERSITY OF MINNESOTA - OCCUPATIONAL INFORMATION LIBRARY
9 Eddy Hall
192 Pillsbury Dr., S.E.   Phone: (612) 373-5493
Minneapolis, MN 55455   Dr. Ellen Betz, Supv. of Lib.
Minneapolis, MN 55455

UNIVERSITY OF MINNESOTA - PHYSICS LIBRARY
260 Tate Lab. of Physics
116 Church St. S.E.   Phone: (612) 373-3362
Minneapolis, MN 55455   Don Marion, Libn.

UNIVERSITY OF MINNESOTA - PUBLIC ADMINISTRATION LIBRARY
365 Blegen Hall
269 19th Ave. S.   Phone: (612) 373-2892
Minneapolis, MN 55455   Eunice Bisbee Johnson, Sr.Lib.Asst.

GEOGRAPHIC

GEOGRAPHIC

UNIVERSITY OF MINNESOTA - ST. ANTHONY FALLS HYDRAULIC
    LABORATORY - LORENZ G. STRAUB MEMORIAL LIBRARY
Mississippi River at Third Ave., S.E.   Phone: (612) 373-2782
Minneapolis, MN 55414   Patricia Swanson, Ed.

UNIVERSITY OF MINNESOTA - SCANDINAVIAN COLLECTION
Wilson Library
309 19th Ave. S.   Phone: (612) 376-2550
Minneapolis, MN 55455   Mariann Tiblin, Biblog.

UNIVERSITY OF MINNESOTA - SOCIAL AND ADMINISTRATIVE PHARMACY
    READING ROOM
7-159 Health Sciences Unit F
308 Harvard St., S.E.   Phone: (612) 376-5325
Minneapolis, MN 55455   Dr. Albert I. Wertheimer, Dir.

UNIVERSITY OF MINNESOTA - SOCIAL WELFARE HISTORY ARCHIVES
c/o Wilson Library
309 19th Ave. S.   Phone: (612) 373-4420
Minneapolis, MN 55455   David Klaasen, Cur.

UNIVERSITY OF MINNESOTA - SPECIAL COLLECTIONS AND RARE BOOKS
Wilson Library
309 19th Ave. S.   Phone: (612) 373-2897
Minneapolis, MN 55455   Austin J. McLean, Chf., Spec.Coll.

UNIVERSITY OF MINNESOTA - STATISTICS LIBRARY
270a Vincent Hall
206 Church St., S.E.   Phone: (612) 373-3035
Minneapolis, MN 55455   Seymour Geisser, Dir.

UNIVERSITY OF MINNESOTA - UNDERGROUND SPACE CENTER - LIBRARY
11 Mines & Metallurgy
221 Church St. S.E.   Phone: (612) 376-5341
Minneapolis, MN 55455   Dr. Ray Sterling, Dir.

UNIVERSITY OF MINNESOTA - UNIVERSITY ARCHIVES
10 Walter Library
117 Pleasant St. S.E.   Phone: (612) 373-2891
Minneapolis, MN 55455   Maxine B. Clapp, Archv.

UNIVERSITY OF MINNESOTA - URBAN TRANSPORTATION COLLECTION
150 Experimental Engineering Bldg.
208 Union St. S.E.   Phone: (612) 373-2509
Minneapolis, MN 55455   Peggy R. Wolfe, Libn.

WALKER ART CENTER - STAFF REFERENCE LIBRARY
Vineland Pl.   Phone: (612) 375-7680
Minneapolis, MN 55403   Geraldine H. Owens, Lib.Asst.

OAK TERRACE NURSING HOME - DEPT. OF PUBLIC WELFARE MEDICAL
    LIBRARY
County Rd. 67   Phone: (612) 938-7621
Minnetonka, MN 55343   Susan F. Ager, Hd.Libn.

FOUR COUNTY LAW LIBRARY
Chippewa County Courthouse   Phone: (612) 269-6053
Montevideo, MN 56265   C.A. Rolloff, Sec.

CLAY COUNTY HISTORICAL SOCIETY - ARCHIVES
22 N. 8th St.
Box 501   Phone: (218) 233-4604
Moorhead, MN 56560   Kate Andrews, Adm.

MINNESOTA HISTORICAL SOCIETY - NORTHWEST MINNESOTA
    HISTORICAL CENTER
Moorhead State University Library   Phone: (218) 236-2812
Moorhead, MN 56560   Evelyn J. Swenson, Dir.

TRINITY LUTHERAN CHURCH - LIBRARY
210 S. 7th St.   Phone: (218) 236-1333
Moorhead, MN 56560   Rodney Erickson, Comm.Chm.

MOOSE LAKE STATE HOSPITAL - STAFF LIBRARY
1000 Lake Shore Dr.   Phone: (218) 485-4411
Moose Lake, MN 55767   John C. Flynn, Libn.

MINNESOTA HISTORICAL SOCIETY - WEST CENTRAL MINNESOTA
    HISTORICAL CENTER
University of Minnesota, Morris   Phone: (612) 589-2211
Morris, MN 56267   Dr. Wilbert H. Ahern, Dir.

UNITED THEOLOGICAL SEMINARY OF THE TWIN CITIES - LIBRARY
3000 Fifth St., N.W.   Phone: (612) 633-4311
New Brighton, MN 55112   Holt H. Graham, Dir.

BROWN COUNTY HISTORICAL SOCIETY - MUSEUM LIBRARY
Broadway & First North St.   Phone: (507) 354-2016
New Ulm, MN 56073   Paul Klammer, Musm.Dir.

MANKATO AREA VOCATIONAL-TECHNICAL INSTITUTE - LIBRARY
1920 Lee Blvd.   Phone: (507) 625-3441
North Mankato, MN 56001

NORWEGIAN-AMERICAN HISTORICAL ASSOCIATION - ARCHIVES
St. Olaf College   Phone: (507) 663-3221
Northfield, MN 55057   Charlotte Jacobson, Cur. Of Archv.

CROSIER SEMINARY - LIBRARY
                                              Phone: (612) 532-3103
Onamia, MN 56359   Richard McGrath, Dir.

AMERICAN ACADEMY OF OPTOMETRY - LIBRARY
Box 565
Owatonna, MN 55060   Dr. John N. Schoen, Sec.-Tres.

U.S. NATL. PARK SERVICE - PIPESTONE NATL. MONUMENT - LIBRARY &
    ARCHIVES
Box 727   Phone: (507) 825-5463
Pipestone, MN 56164   David L. Lane, Supt.

FIRST LUTHERAN CHURCH OF THE LUTHERAN CHURCH IN AMERICA -
    SCHENDEL MEMORIAL LIBRARY
615 5th St.   Phone: (612) 388-9311
Red Wing, MN 55066   Mrs. Delma Rigelman, Libn.

GOODHUE COUNTY HISTORICAL SOCIETY - LIBRARY
1166 Oak St.   Phone: (612) 388-6024
Red Wing, MN 55066   Orville K. Olson, Cur. of Musm.

OAK GROVE LUTHERAN CHURCH - MEMORIAL LIBRARY †
71st & Lyndale Ave., S.   Phone: (612) 869-4917
Richfield, MN 55423   Mrs. Forrest Carpenter, Libn.

WOODLAKE LUTHERAN CHURCH - LIBRARY †
7525 Oliver Ave., S.   Phone: (612) 866-8449
Richfield, MN 55423   Mrs. Duane Lundquist, Hd.

IBM CORPORATION - INFORMATION CENTER/LIBRARY
Dept. 205, Hwy. 52 & 37th St., N.W.   Phone: (507) 286-4462
Rochester, MN 55901   Ursula Shimek, Sr.Libn.

MAYO FOUNDATION - MAYO CLINIC LIBRARY
200 First St., S.W.   Phone: (507) 284-2061
Rochester, MN 55905   Jack D. Key, Libn.

MINNESOTA BIBLE COLLEGE - LIBRARY
920 Mayowood Rd., S.W.   Phone: (507) 288-4563
Rochester, MN 55901   Ardis C. Sawyer, Libn.

OLMSTED COUNTY HISTORICAL SOCIETY - LIBRARY AND ARCHIVES
Box 6411   Phone: (507) 282-9447
Rochester, MN 55903   Doris Blinks, Lib.Supv.

ROCHESTER METHODIST HOSPITAL - METHODIST KAHLER LIBRARY
                                              Phone: (507) 286-7425
Rochester, MN 55901   Jean M. Brose, Hd.Libn.

ROCHESTER POST-BULLETIN - NEWS LIBRARY
18 First Ave., S.E.   Phone: (507) 285-7730
Rochester, MN 55901   Marcy Sawyer, News Libn.

ST. MARY'S HOSPITAL - LIBRARY *
1216 2nd St., S.W.   Phone: (507) 285-5647
Rochester, MN 55901   Carole Clark, Libn.

SPERRY CORPORATION - SPERRY UNIVAC DIVISION - INFORMATION
    SERVICE CENTER
2276 Highcrest Dr.   Phone: (612) 633-6170
Roseville, MN 55113   Mary C. Biersborn, Mgr.

MINNESOTA HISTORICAL SOCIETY - CENTRAL MINNESOTA HISTORICAL
    CENTER
St. Cloud State University   Phone: (612) 255-3254
St. Cloud, MN 56301   Dr. Calvin W. Gower, Dir.

ST. CLOUD HOSPITAL - HEALTH SCIENCES LIBRARY
1406 Sixth Ave., N.   Phone: (612) 251-2700
St. Cloud, MN 56301   Judy Heeter, Libn.

U.S. VETERANS ADMINISTRATION (MN-St. Cloud) - MEDICAL CENTER
    LIBRARY
                                      Phone: (612) 252-1670
St. Cloud, MN 56301   Sanford J. Banker, Chf., Lib.Serv.

BETH EL SYNAGOGUE - MAX SHAPIRO LIBRARY
5224 W. 26th St.   Phone: (612) 920-3512
St. Louis Park, MN 55416   Barbara Bach, Libn.

HONEYWELL, INC. - RESIDENTIAL ENGINEERING LIBRARY
Mail Sta. Mn 52-1258, Parkdale Plaza
1660 S. Hwy. 100   Phone: (612) 542-6830
St. Louis Park, MN 55416   Elizabeth Hicks Howard, Tech.Libn.

METHODIST HOSPITAL - MEDICAL LIBRARY
6500 Excelsior Blvd.   Phone: (612) 932-5451
St. Louis Park, MN 55426   Pearly Rudin, Med.Libn.

AMERICAN HOIST & DERRICK CO. - ENGINEERING STANDARDS LIBRARY
63 S. Robert St.
St. Paul, MN 55107

BAPTIST GENERAL CONFERENCE - ARCHIVES
3949 Bethel Dr.   Phone: (612) 638-6282
St. Paul, MN 55112   G. David Guston, Archv.

BETHEL THEOLOGICAL SEMINARY - RESOURCE CENTER
3949 Bethel Dr.   Phone: (612) 641-6184
St. Paul, MN 55112   Norris Magnuson, Dir.

BETHESDA LUTHERAN MEDICAL CENTER - MEDICAL-NURSING LIBRARY
570 Capitol Blvd.   Phone: (612) 221-2291
St. Paul, MN 55103   Eileen M. Erlandson, Hd.Libn.

CENTRAL BAPTIST CHURCH - MEDIA CENTER
420 N. Roy   Phone: (612) 646-2751
St. Paul, MN 55104   Karen Johnson, Libn.

CHAMPION INTERNATIONAL - HOERNER WALDORF PACKAGING DIVISION
    - TECHNICAL CENTER LIBRARY
2280 Myrtle Ave.   Phone: (612) 641-4125
St. Paul, MN 55114   Jeanette Kustelski, Libn.

CHILDREN'S HOSPITAL, INC. - MEDICAL-NURSING LIBRARY
345 N. Smith Ave.   Phone: (612) 227-6521
St. Paul, MN 55102   Nancy M. Wesley, Libn.

COLLEGE OF ST. CATHERINE - LIBRARY - RUTH SAWYER COLLECTION
2004 Randolph Ave.   Phone: (612) 690-6555
St. Paul, MN 55105   Sr. Mary William Brady, Archv.

COLLEGE OF ST. CATHERINE - LIBRARY - WOMAN'S COLLECTION
2004 Randolph Ave.   Phone: (612) 690-6648
St. Paul, MN 55105   Margaret Conant, Hd., Rd.Serv. & ILL

COLLEGE OF ST. CATHERINE - PERFORMING ARTS LIBRARY
2004 Randolph Ave.   Phone: (612) 690-6696
St. Paul, MN 55105   Donald Bemis Jones, Libn.

COLLEGE OF ST. THOMAS - CELTIC LIBRARY
O'Shaughnessy Library   Phone: (612) 647-5318
St. Paul, MN 55105   John B. Davenport, Spec.Coll.Libn.

COMO ZOO - LIBRARY
Midway Pkwy. & Kaufman Dr.   Phone: (612) 488-4041
St. Paul, MN 55103   Nan Connor, Info.Dir.

CONCORDIA COLLEGE - BUENGER MEMORIAL LIBRARY
275 N. Syndicate   Phone: (612) 641-8240
St. Paul, MN 55104   Glenn W. Offermann, Hd.Libn.

CONWED CORPORATION - CORPORATE LIBRARY
444 Cedar St.
Box 43237   Phone: (612) 221-1139
St. Paul, MN 55164

CRIME CONTROL PLANNING BOARD - LIBRARY
444 Lafayette Rd., Rm. 607   Phone: (612) 296-2771
St. Paul, MN 55101

ECONOMICS LABORATORY, INC. - CORPORATE INFORMATION CENTER
Osborn Bldg.   Phone: (612) 451-5651
St. Paul, MN 55102   Dona M. Sontag Bradt, Mgr.

FARMERS UNION CENTRAL EXCHANGE, INC. - INFORMATION CENTER
Box 43089   Phone: (612) 451-5151
St.Paul, MN 55164   Margaret Ludvigsen, Mgr., Info.Serv.

FIRST BAPTIST CHURCH - LIBRARY
Ninth & Wacouta Sts.   Phone: (612) 222-0718
St. Paul, MN 55101   Ann Fitch, Libn.

GILLETTE CHILDREN'S HOSPITAL - PROFESSIONAL LIBRARY
200 E. University   Phone: (612) 291-2848
St. Paul, MN 55101

HAMLINE UNIVERSITY SCHOOL OF LAW - LIBRARY
1536 Hewitt Ave.   Phone: (612) 641-2344
St. Paul, MN 55104   Elizabeth Kelley, Libn.

HILL (James Jerome) REFERENCE LIBRARY
Fourth St. at Market   Phone: (612) 227-9531
St. Paul, MN 55102   Virgil F. Massman, Exec.Dir.

LEAGUE OF MINNESOTA CITIES - LIBRARY
300 Hanover Bldg.
480 Cedar St.   Phone: (612) 222-2861
St. Paul, MN 55101   Peter Tritz, Res.Dir.

LUTHER-NORTHWESTERN SEMINARY - LIBRARY
2375 Como Ave.   Phone: (612) 641-3225
St. Paul, MN 55108   Norman G. Wente, Libn.

MACALESTER COLLEGE - OLIN SCIENCE LIBRARY
1600 Grand Ave.   Phone: (612) 647-6344
St. Paul, MN 55105   Rosemary Salscheider, Supv.

MACALESTER COLLEGE - WEYERHAEUSER LIBRARY
Grand & Macalester Sts.   Phone: (612) 647-6345
St. Paul, MN 55105   Jean K. Archibald, Dir.

METROPOLITAN COUNCIL OF THE TWIN CITIES AREA - LIBRARY
300 Metro Sq.   Phone: (612) 227-9421
St. Paul, MN 55101   Mary D. Adams, Libn.

MIDWAY HOSPITAL - HEALTH SCIENCES LIBRARY
1700 University Ave.   Phone: (612) 641-5234
St. Paul, MN 55104   Carol Windham, Hd.Libn.

MIDWEST CHINA CENTER - MIDWEST CHINA ORAL HISTORY AND
    ARCHIVES COLLECTION
2375 Como Ave.   Phone: (612) 641-3238
St. Paul, MN 55108   Jane Baker Koons, Coord.

MIDWEST CHINA STUDY RESOURCE CENTER
2375 Como Ave., W.
Gullixson Hall, Rm. 308   Phone: (612) 641-3238
St. Paul, MN 55108   Richard Bohr, Dir.

MINNESOTA GEOLOGICAL SURVEY - LIBRARY
University of Minnesota
1633 Eustis St.   Phone: (612) 376-2794
St. Paul, MN 55108   Lynn Swanson, Sr.Lib.Asst.

GEOGRAPHIC

GEOGRAPHIC

MINNESOTA HISTORICAL SOCIETY - DIVISION OF ARCHIVES AND
MANUSCRIPTS
1500 Mississippi St.   Phone: (612) 296-6980
St. Paul, MN 55101   Sue E. Holbert, State Archv.

MINNESOTA HISTORICAL SOCIETY - FORT SNELLING BRANCH LIBRARY
Bldg. 27, Fort Snelling   Phone: (612) 726-1630
St. Paul, MN 55111

MINNESOTA HISTORICAL SOCIETY - REFERENCE LIBRARY
690 Cedar St.   Phone: (612) 296-2143
St. Paul, MN 55101   Patricia C. Harpole, Chf. of Ref.Lib.

MINNESOTA HISTORICAL SOCIETY - SPECIAL LIBRARIES
690 Cedar St.   Phone: (612) 296-2489
St. Paul, MN 55101   Bonnie Wilson, Hd.

MINNESOTA MUSEUM OF ART - LIBRARY
St. Peter St. at Kellogg Blvd.   Phone: (612) 224-7431
St. Paul, MN 55102   Leanne A. Klein, Libn.

MINNESOTA STATE ATTORNEY GENERAL - LAW LIBRARY
102 State Capitol Bldg.   Phone: (612) 296-8152
St. Paul, MN 55155   Anita Anderson, Libn.

MINNESOTA STATE BOARD OF ANIMAL HEALTH - LIBRARY
LL-70, Metro Square Bldg.
7th & Robert Sts.   Phone: (612) 296-2942
St. Paul, MN 55101   J.G. Flint, Sec.

MINNESOTA STATE DEPARTMENT OF EDUCATION - INTERAGENCY
RESOURCE AND INFORMATION CENTER
401-A Capitol Square Bldg.   Phone: (612) 296-6684
St. Paul, MN 55101   Pat Tupper, Lib.Prog.Dir.

MINNESOTA STATE DEPARTMENT OF EDUCATION - OFFICE OF PUBLIC
LIBRARIES AND INTERLIBRARY COOPERATION
301 Hanover Bldg.
480 Cedar St.   Phone: (612) 296-2821
St. Paul, MN 55101   William G. Asp, Dir.

MINNESOTA STATE DEPARTMENT OF PUBLIC SAFETY - (MINNESOTA)
STATE PATROL FILM LIBRARY
3800 N. Dunlap   Phone: (612) 482-5925
St. Paul, MN 55112   Janet Weber, Libn.

MINNESOTA STATE DEPARTMENT OF PUBLIC WELFARE - LIBRARY
Centennial Bldg., 1st Floor   Phone: (612) 296-1548
St. Paul, MN 55155   William G. McCarthy, Lib.Prog.Dir.

MINNESOTA STATE DEPARTMENT OF REVENUE - TAX LIBRARY
Centennial Office Bldg.
658 Cedar St.   Phone: (612) 296-1022
St. Paul MN 55145   Barry W. Fick, Legal Techn., Libn.

MINNESOTA STATE DEPARTMENT OF TRANSPORTATION - LIBRARY AND
INFORMATION SERVICES SECTION
B-10 State Transportation Bldg.   Phone: (612) 296-2385
St. Paul, MN 55155   Jerome C. Baldwin, Dir., Lib./Info.Serv

MINNESOTA STATE ENERGY AGENCY - LIBRARY
150 E. Kellogg Blvd., Rm. 980   Phone: (612) 296-8902
St. Paul, MN 55101   Donna Slamkowski, Res.Libn.

MINNESOTA STATE INFORMATION SYSTEMS DIVISION - LIBRARY
Centennial Office Bldg., 5th Fl.   Phone: (612) 296-4621
St. Paul, MN 55155   Arlene Kromminga, Libn.

MINNESOTA STATE LAW LIBRARY
117 University Ave.   Phone: (612) 296-2775
St. Paul, MN 55155   Marvin Roger Anderson, State Law Libn.

MINNESOTA STATE LEGISLATIVE REFERENCE LIBRARY
State Capitol, Rm. 111   Phone: (612) 296-3398
St. Paul, MN 55155   Linda F. Montgomery, Dir.

MINNESOTA STATE OFFICE OF ECONOMIC OPPORTUNITY - LIBRARY
690 American Center Bldg.   Phone: (612) 296-8810
St. Paul, MN 55101   Linda Woodstrom, Libn.

MINNESOTA STATE SERVICES FOR THE BLIND AND VISUALLY
HANDICAPPED - COMMUNICATION CENTER
1745 University Ave.   Phone: (612) 296-6723
St. Paul, MN 55104   Joanne Jonson, Dir.

MINNESOTA STATE WATER RESOURCES BOARD - LIBRARY
555 Wabasha St.   Phone: (612) 296-2840
St. Paul, MN 55102   Erling Weiberg, Exec.Sec.

MITCHELL (William) COLLEGE OF LAW - JOHN B. SANBORN LIBRARY
871 Summit Ave.   Phone: (612) 227-9171
St. Paul, MN 55105   Carol C. Florin, Lib.Dir.

MOUNT ZION HEBREW CONGREGATION - TEMPLE LIBRARY
1300 Summit Ave.   Phone: (612) 698-3881
St. Paul, MN 55105   Janice Leichter, Libn.

MUSICAL INSTRUMENT MUSEUM - LIBRARY
1124 Dionne St.   Phone: (612) 488-4303
St. Paul, MN 55113   William J. Kugler, Pres.

NORTHWESTERN COLLEGE OF CHIROPRACTIC - LIBRARY
1834 S. Mississippi River Blvd.   Phone: (612) 690-1735
St. Paul, MN 55116   Cheryl A. Bjerke, Dir.

OPPENHEIMER, WOLFF, FOSTER, SHEPARD & DONNELLY - LIBRARY
W-1781 First National Bank Bldg.   Phone: (612) 227-7271
St. Paul, MN 55101   Gretchen Haase, Libn.

ORPHAN VOYAGE - KAMMANDALE LIBRARY
57 N. Dale   Phone: (612) 224-5160
St. Paul, MN 55102   Jeanette G. Kamman, Dir.

PLANNED PARENTHOOD OF MINNESOTA - POPULATION RESOURCE CENTER
1965 Ford Parkway   Phone: (612) 698-2401
St. Paul, MN 55116   John A. Cunico, Dir. of Comm.Educ.

RAMSEY COUNTY HISTORICAL SOCIETY - JOSEPH E. KARTH RESEARCH
CENTER - LIBRARY
75 W. Fifth St., Rm. 323   Phone: (612) 222-0701
St. Paul, MN 55102

RAMSEY COUNTY LAW LIBRARY
1815 Court House   Phone: (612) 298-5208
St. Paul, MN 55102   Patricia K. Cummings, Libn.

RAMSEY COUNTY MEDICAL SOCIETY - BOECKMANN LIBRARY
345 N. Smith Ave.   Phone: (612) 224-3346
St. Paul, MN 55102   Mary Sandra Tarman, Libn.

ST. JOHN'S HOSPITAL - FREDERICK J. PLONDKE MEDICAL LIBRARY
403 Maria Ave.   Phone: (612) 228-3255
St. Paul, MN 55106   Jan Walton, Libn.

ST. JOSEPH'S HOSPITAL - JEROME MEDICAL LIBRARY *
69 W. Exchange St.   Phone: (612) 291-3193
St. Paul, MN 55102   Jacquelin Gionfriddo, Dir.

ST. PAUL CITY COUNCIL - RESEARCH LIBRARY
702 B City Hall   Phone: (612) 298-4163
St. Paul, MN 55102   John W. Connelly, Leg. & Res.Asst.

ST. PAUL DISPATCH-PIONEER PRESS - LIBRARY
55 E. Fourth St.   Phone: (612) 222-5011
St. Paul, MN 55101   Judith Katzung, Hd.Libn.

ST. PAUL FIRE & MARINE INSURANCE COMPANY - LIBRARY
385 Washington St.   Phone: (612) 221-8226
St. Paul, MN 55102   Eleanor Hamilton, Lib.Supv.

ST. PAUL FIRE & MARINE INSURANCE COMPANY - LOSS PREVENTION
DEPT. - TECHNICAL INFORMATION SERVICES
385 Washington St.   Phone: (612) 221-7470
St. Paul, MN 55102   Sharon Carter, Tech.Info.Serv.Supv.

ST. PAUL PUBLIC LIBRARY - ARTS AND AUDIO-VISUAL SERVICES
90 W. Fourth St.   Phone: (612) 224-3383
St. Paul, MN 55102   Delores Sundbye, Supv.

ST. PAUL PUBLIC LIBRARY - CIRCULATION ROOM
90 W. Fourth St.   Phone: (612) 224-3383
St. Paul, MN 55102   Ortha D. Robbins, Supv.

ST. PAUL PUBLIC LIBRARY - GOVERNMENT PUBLICATIONS OFFICE
90 W. 4th St.   Phone: (612) 292-6178
St. Paul, MN 55102   Rosamond T. Jacob, Libn.

ST. PAUL PUBLIC LIBRARY - HIGHLAND PARK BRANCH - PERRIE JONES
    MEMORIAL ROOM
1974 Ford Pkwy.   Phone: (612) 698-0823
St. Paul, MN 55116   Elizabeth McMonigal, Br.Libn.

ST. PAUL PUBLIC LIBRARY - REFERENCE ROOM
90 W. Fourth St.   Phone: (612) 224-3383
St. Paul, MN 55102   Judith W. Devine, Supv.

ST. PAUL PUBLIC LIBRARY - SCIENCE AND INDUSTRY ROOM
90 W. Fourth St.   Phone: (612) 292-6249
St. Paul, MN 55102   Beatrice I. Bailey, Supv.

ST. PAUL PUBLIC LIBRARY - VIDEO COMMUNICATIONS CENTER
1080 University Ave.   Phone: (612) 292-6336
St. Paul, MN 55104   Annette Salo, Libn.

ST. PAUL PUBLIC SCHOOLS INDEPENDENT SCHOOL DISTRICT 625 -
    DISTRICT PROFESSIONAL LIBRARY
360 Colborne St.   Phone: (612) 298-5675
St. Paul, MN 55102   Walter M. Ostrem, Libn.

ST. PAUL RAMSEY MEDICAL CENTER - MEDICAL LIBRARY
640 Jackson St.   Phone: (612) 221-3607
St. Paul, MN 55101   Mary Dwyer, Hd.Libn.

ST. PAUL SEMINARY - JOHN IRELAND MEMORIAL LIBRARY
2260 Summit Ave.   Phone: (612) 690-4355
St. Paul, MN 55105   Rev. Leo J. Tibesar, Dir.

ST. PAUL TECHNICAL VOCATIONAL LIBRARY
235 Marshall Ave.   Phone: (612) 221-1410
St. Paul, MN 55102   Fred Berndt, Libn.

SCIENCE MUSEUM OF MINNESOTA - LOUIS S. HEADLEY MEMORIAL
    LIBRARY
30 E. 10th St.   Phone: (612) 221-9488
St. Paul, MN 55101   Mary S. Finlayson, Libn.

SISTERS OF ST. JOSEPH OF CARONDELET - ST. PAUL PROVINCE -
    ARCHIVES
1884 Randolph Ave.   Phone: (612) 690-2481
St. Paul, MN 55105   Mary E. Kraft, C.S.J., Archv.

SPERRY CORPORATION - SPERRY UNIVAC DEFENSE SYSTEMS DIVISION -
    INFORMATION SERVICE CENTER
M.S. UOR25, Box 3525   Phone: (612) 456-2580
St. Paul, MN 55165   Faye V. Peterson, Supv.

3M - BUSINESS INFORMATION SERVICE
3M Center, 220-1C   Phone: (612) 733-9057
St. Paul, MN 55144   Aletta Moore, Supv.

3M - ENGINEERING INFORMATION SERVICES
Bldg. 21-BW   Phone: (612) 778-4406
St. Paul, MN 55144   William T. Greene, Mgr.

3M - LAW LIBRARY
Box 33428   Phone: (612) 733-1460
St. Paul, MN 55133   Virginia Groth, Libn.

3M - MERTLE LIBRARY
3M Center, Bldg. 235-1D   Phone: (612) 733-2592
St. Paul, MN 55144   Mary E. Baker, Libn.

3M - PATENT INFORMATION CENTER
3M Center, 201 2C-12   Phone: (612) 733-7670
St. Paul, MN 55144   Nancy E. Lambert, Supv.

3M - TECHNICAL COMMUNICATIONS CENTER
3M Center, 201-2CN   Phone: (612) 733-7148
St. Paul, MN 55144   Mary Lou Kovacic, Supv.

3M - 201 TECHNICAL LIBRARY
3M Center, 201-2S   Phone: (612) 733-2447
St. Paul, MN 55144   Kristin K. Oberts, Supv.

3M - 209 LIBRARY
3M Center, 209-BC   Phone: (612) 733-9794
St. Paul, MN 55144   Alice Bresnahan, Libn.

3M - 230 LIBRARY
3M Center, 230-1S   Phone: (612) 733-5017
St. Paul, MN 55144   Susan Rau Tome, Tech.Libn.

3M - 235 LIBRARY
3M Center, 234-1A-25   Phone: (612) 733-2592
St. Paul, MN 55144   Mary E. Baker, Libn.

3M - 236 LIBRARY
3M Center, 236-B   Phone: (612) 733-5751
St. Paul, MN 55144   Elaine L. Wardrop, Libn.

3M - 251 LIBRARY
3M Center, 251-2A   Phone: (612) 733-5236
St. Paul, MN 55144   Ramona Huppert, Libn.

3M - 270 LIBRARY
3M Center, 270-4A   Phone: (612) 733-3402
St. Paul, MN 55144   Eloise M. Jasken, Libn.

TOYS 'N THINGS, TRAINING & RESOURCE CENTER, INC.
906 N. Dale   Phone: (612) 488-7284
St. Paul, MN 55103   Jean M. Nicol, Libn.

U.S. ARMY - CORPS OF ENGINEERS - ST. PAUL DISTRICT - TECHNICAL
    LIBRARY
1135 U.S. Post Office & Custom House   Phone: (612) 725-5921
St. Paul, MN 55101   Jean Marie Schmidt, Libn.

U.S. COURT OF APPEALS, 8TH CIRCUIT - RESEARCH LIBRARY
543 Federal Bldg.
316 N. Robert St.   Phone: (612) 725-7177
St. Paul, MN 55101   David J. Maland, Libn.

U.S. FOREST SERVICE - NORTH CENTRAL FOREST EXPERIMENT STATION
    LIBRARY
1992 Folwell Ave.   Phone: (612) 642-5257
St. Paul, MN 55108   Floyd L. Henderson, Libn.

UNIVERSITY OF MINNESOTA - AGRICULTURAL EXTENSION SERVICE -
    EXTENSION HOME EOCNOMICS - INFO. CTR.
1985 Buford Ave.   Phone: (612) 373-0912
St. Paul, MN 55108   Kathy Mangum, Ext.Spec.

UNIVERSITY OF MINNESOTA - AGRICULTURAL EXTENSION SERVICE -
    MINNESOTA ANALYSIS & PLANNING SYSTEM
415 Coffey Hall
1420 Eckles Ave.   Phone: (612) 376-7003
St. Paul, MN 55108   David M. Nelson, Dir.

UNIVERSITY OF MINNESOTA - CENTER FOR YOUTH DEVELOPMENT AND
    RESEARCH - RESOURCE ROOM
48 McNeal Hall
1985 Buford Ave.   Phone: (612) 376-7624
St. Paul, MN 55108   Paula Simon, Teaching Spec.

UNIVERSITY OF MINNESOTA - HORTICULTURE EXTENSION CLINIC
155 Alderman Hall
1970 Folwell Ave.   Phone: (612) 373-1100
St. Paul, MN 55108   Deborah L. Brown, Ext. Horticulturist

UNIVERSITY OF MINNESOTA - IMMIGRATION HISTORY RESEARCH
    CENTER
826 Berry St.   Phone: (612) 373-5581
St. Paul, MN 55114   Rudolph J. Vecoli, Dir.

GEOGRAPHIC

GEOGRAPHIC

UNIVERSITY OF MINNESOTA - MANUSCRIPTS DIVISION
826 Berry St.   Phone: (612) 376-7271
St. Paul, MN 55114   Alan K. Lathrop, Cur.

UNIVERSITY OF MINNESOTA, ST. PAUL - BIOCHEMISTRY LIBRARY
406 Biological Sciences Ctr.
1445 Gortner Ave.   Phone: (612) 373-1582
St. Paul, MN 55108   Theodore Peck, Libn.

UNIVERSITY OF MINNESOTA, ST. PAUL - CENTRAL LIBRARY
1984 Buford Ave.   Phone: (612) 373-0904
St. Paul, MN 55108   Richard L. Rohrer, Dir.

UNIVERSITY OF MINNESOTA, ST. PAUL - DEPARTMENT OF VOCATIONAL &
    TECHNICAL EDUCATION - LIBRARY
Vocational & Technical Educ. Bldg.
1954 Buford   Phone: (612) 373-3838
St. Paul, MN 55108   Dr. Jerome Moss, Dir.

UNIVERSITY OF MINNESOTA, ST. PAUL - ENTOMOLOGY LIBRARY
1980 Folwell Ave.
375 Hodson Hall   Phone: (612) 373-1741
St. Paul, MN 55108

UNIVERSITY OF MINNESOTA, ST. PAUL - FORESTRY LIBRARY
Green Hall
1530 N. Cleveland Ave.   Phone: (612) 373-1407
St. Paul, MN 55108   Jean Albrecht, Libn.

UNIVERSITY OF MINNESOTA, ST. PAUL - HERBARIUM COLLECTION
St. Paul Campus Library
1984 Buford Ave.
St. Paul, MN 55108

UNIVERSITY OF MINNESOTA, ST. PAUL - PLANT PATHOLOGY LIBRARY
202 Stakman Hall
1519 Gortner Ave.   Phone: (612) 373-1669
St. Paul, MN 55108   Nina Jorgensen, Lib.Asst.

UNIVERSITY OF MINNESOTA, ST. PAUL - VETERINARY MEDICAL LIBRARY
450 Veterinary Science Bldg.
1971 Commonwealth Ave.   Phone: (612) 373-1455
St. Paul, MN 55108   Livija Carlson, Libn.

VOLUNTARY ACTION CENTER OF THE ST. PAUL AREA - LIBRARY
623 Endicott
141 E. 4th St.   Phone: (612) 222-0561
St. Paul, MN 55101   Magge Davern, Exec.Dir.

WANDERER PRESS - LIBRARY
201 Ohio St.   Phone: (612) 224-5733
St. Paul, MN 55107   Kathleen E. Walsh, Libn.

WESTERN LIFE INSURANCE COMPANY - LIBRARY
Box 43271   Phone: (612) 738-4589
St. Paul, MN 55164   Carole Steele, Libn.

GUSTAVUS ADOLPHUS COLLEGE - LUND MUSIC LIBRARY
        Phone: (507) 931-7365
St. Peter, MN 56082   Margo Wheeler, Music Lib.Asst.

NICOLLET COUNTY HISTORICAL SOCIETY - MUSEUM
400 S. 3rd St.   Phone: (507) 931-2160
St. Peter, MN 56082   Marjorie A. Schmidt, Sec.

ST. PETER REGIONAL TREATMENT CENTER - STAFF LIBRARY
100 Freeman Dr.   Phone: (507) 931-3000
St. Peter, MN 56082   Richard Whitmore, Libn.

LEWIS (Sinclair) INFORMATION & INTERPRETIVE CENTRE
Box 222   Phone: (612) 352-6892
Sauk Centre, MN 56378   Janet Campbell, Mgr.

NYBERG CARTOGRAPHIC COLLECTION
4946 Devonshire Circle   Phone: (612) 474-9011
Shorewood, MN 55331   Nancy Nyberg, Libn.

DAKOTA COUNTY HISTORICAL SOCIETY - LIBRARY AND MUSEUM
130 3rd Ave. N.   Phone: (612) 451-6260
South St. Paul, MN 55075   Frances Miller, Dir.

STILLWATER PUBLIC LIBRARY - MINNESOTA ROOM
223 N. 4th St.   Phone: (612) 439-1675
Stillwater, MN 55082   Lynne Bertalmio, Dir.

WASHINGTON COUNTY MUSEUM LIBRARY
602 N. Main St.   Phone: (612) 439-5956
Stillwater, MN 55082   Louise Johnson, Cur.

U.S. FISH & WILDLIFE SERVICE - SCIENCE REFERENCE LIBRARY
Federal Bldg., Fort Snelling   Phone: (612) 725-3576
Twin Cities, MN 55111   Veronica Siedle, Libn.

RANGE MENTAL HEALTH CENTER - LIBRARY
624 South 13th St.   Phone: (218) 749-2881
Virginia, MN 55792   JoAnne Matson, Sec.

CARVER COUNTY HISTORICAL SOCIETY, INC. - LIBRARY
119 S. Cherry St.   Phone: (612) 442-4234
Waconia, MN 55387   Francis Klein, Pres.

UNIVERSITY OF MINNESOTA TECHNICAL COLLEGE, WASECA - LEARNING
    RESOURCES CENTER
        Phone: (507) 835-1000
Waseca, MN 56093   William M. Andrews, Dir.

GRACE LUTHERAN CHURCH - LIBRARY
18360 Minnetonka Blvd.   Phone: (612) 473-2362
Wayzata, MN 55391   Betty LeDell, Libn.

KANDIYOHI COUNTY HISTORICAL SOCIETY - VICTOR E. LAWSON
    RESEARCH LIBRARY
610 NE Hwy. 71   Phone: (612) 235-1881
Willmar, MN 56201   Mona R. Nelson, Program Coord.

WILLMAR STATE HOSPITAL - LIBRARY
Box 1128   Phone: (612) 235-3322
Willmar, MN 56201   Linda Bjornberg, Libn.

COTTONWOOD COUNTY HISTORICAL SOCIETY - LIBRARY †
1157 River Rd.   Phone: (507) 831-1134
Windom, MN 56101   Sylvia Sykora, Cur.

MINNESOTA HISTORICAL SOCIETY - SOUTHEAST MINNESOTA
    HISTORICAL CENTER
Winona State University
122 Maxwell Library   Phone: (507) 457-2086
Winona, MN 55987   Dr. George E. Bates, Jr., Dir.

WESCHCKE (Carl L.) LIBRARY
1661 Woodbury Dr.   Phone: (612) 739-2490
Woodbury, MN 55125   Carl L. Weschcke, Pres.

MISSISSIPPI

DIVINE WORD SEMINARY OF ST. AUGUSTINE - LIBRARY
Ulman Ave.
Bay St. Louis, MS 39520

U.S. NAVY - NAVAL OCEANOGRAPHIC OFFICE - NAVY LIBRARY
NSTL Station   Phone: (601) 688-4597
Bay St. Louis, MS 39522   Katharine Wallace, Libn.

BLUE MOUNTAIN COLLEGE - MUSIC LIBRARY
        Phone: (601) 685-5711
Blue Mountain, MS 38610   Carolyn Mounce, Libn.

FIRST BAPTIST CHURCH - LIBRARY
First at Church St.   Phone: (601) 728-6272
Booneville, MS 38829   Stanley Barnett, Libn.

MISSISSIPPI BAPTIST CONVENTION BOARD - MISSISSIPPI BAPTIST
    HISTORICAL COMMISSION
Box 51   Phone: (601) 924-6172
Clinton, MS 39056   Alice G. Cox, Libn.

LOWNDES COUNTY LAW LIBRARY †
County Courthouse, Rm. 210   Phone: (601) 327-7880
Columbus, MS 39701   Shirlee Harvey, Libn.

MISSISSIPPI UNIVERSITY FOR WOMEN - SCHOOL OF EDUCATION -
    LIBRARY SCIENCE DIVISION
                                                   Phone: (601) 328-9100
Columbus, MS 39701   Dr. Maude Yow, Hd.

HERCULES, INC. - HATTIESBURG PLANT LABORATORY - LIBRARY
Box 1937   Phone: (601) 545-3450
Hattiesburg, MS 39401   Georgia Kay Carter, Supv. Chemist

UNIVERSITY OF SOUTHERN MISSISSIPPI - GEOLOGY DEPARTMENT -
    LIBRARY
Southern Sta., Box 8196   Phone: (601) 266-7196
Hattiesburg, MS 39401   Dr. Daniel A. Sundeen, Assoc. Professor

UNIVERSITY OF SOUTHERN MISSISSIPPI - MC CAIN LIBRARY
Southern Sta., Box 5148   Phone: (601) 266-4171
Hattiesburg, MS 39401   Claude E. Fike, Dir.

MISSISSIPPI VALLEY STATE UNIVERSITY - JAMES HERBERT WHITE
    LIBRARY *
                                                   Phone: (601) 254-9041
Itta Bena, MS 38941   Dr. Robbye R. Henderson, Hd.Libn.

CENTRAL PRESBYTERIAN CHURCH - LIBRARY †
1100 W. Capitol   Phone: (601) 353-2757
Jackson, MS 39203

JACKSON METROPOLITAN LIBRARY - INFORMATION AND REFERENCE
    DIVISION
301 N. State St.   Phone: (601) 352-3677
Jackson, MS 39201   Jack Mulkey, Dir.

MISSISSIPPI MUSEUM OF NATURAL SCIENCE - LIBRARY
111 N. Jefferson St.   Phone: (601) 354-7303
Jackson, MS 39202   Mary P. Stevens, Musm.Libn.

MISSISSIPPI STATE BOARD OF HEALTH - FILM LIBRARY
Box 1700   Phone: (601) 354-6639
Jackson, MS 39205   Mary Ann Elkin, Supv., Health Educ.

MISSISSIPPI STATE BOARD OF HEALTH - LIBRARY
2423 N. State St.
Box 1700   Phone: (601) 354-6614
Jackson, MS 39205   Marilyn Dee Bates, Libn.

MISSISSIPPI STATE BUREAU OF GEOLOGY - LIBRARY
2525 N. West St.
Box 5348   Phone: (601) 354-6228
Jackson, MS 39216   Anne Bellomy, Libn.

MISSISSIPPI STATE DEPARTMENT OF ARCHIVES AND HISTORY -
    ARCHIVES AND LIBRARY DIVISION
100 S. State St.
Box 571   Phone: (601) 354-6218
Jackson, MS 39205   Mrs. Madel J. Morgan, Dir., Archv. & Lib.Div.

MISSISSIPPI STATE DEPARTMENT OF PUBLIC WELFARE - JEAN GUNTER
    SOCIAL WELFARE LIBRARY
515 E. Amite St.
Box 352   Phone: (601) 354-0341
Jackson, MS 39205   Mary Ellen Simpson, Welfare Libn.

MISSISSIPPI STATE LAW LIBRARY
Gartin Justice Bldg.
Box 1040   Phone: (601) 354-7113
Jackson, MS 39205   Merle Buckley Upton, Libn.

MISSISSIPPI STATE LIBRARY COMMISSION
Box 3260   Phone: (601) 354-6369
Jackson, MS 39207   David M. Woodburn, Dir.

MISSISSIPPI STATE MEDICAL ASSOCIATION - LIBRARY
735 Riverside Dr.   Phone: (601) 354-5433
Jackson, MS 39216

MISSISSIPPI STATE RESEARCH AND DEVELOPMENT CENTER -
    INFORMATION SERVICES DIVISION
3825 Ridgewood Rd.
Drawer 2470   Phone: (601) 982-6324
Jackson, MS 39205   Natelle Isley, Mgr.

REFORMED THEOLOGICAL SEMINARY - LIBRARY
5422 Clinton Blvd.   Phone: (601) 922-4988
Jackson, MS 39209   Sharon Taylor, Dir.

ST. DOMINIC-JACKSON MEMORIAL HOSPITAL - LUTHER MANSHIP
    MEDICAL LIBRARY
969 Lakeland Drive   Phone: (601) 982-0121
Jackson, MS 39216   Clara Joorfetz, Libn.

UNITED METHODIST HISTORICAL SOCIETY - MISSISSIPPI CONFERENCE -
    ARCHIVES
Millsaps College Library   Phone: (601) 362-5009
Jackson, MS 39210

U.S. VETERANS ADMINISTRATION (MS-Jackson) - CENTER LIBRARY
1500 E. Woodrow Wilson   Phone: (601) 362-4471
Jackson, MS 39216   Carol Sistrunk, Chf.Libn.

U.S. AIR FORCE BASE - KEESLER BASE - MC BRIDE LIBRARY
3380ABG/SSL, Bldg. 2222   Phone: (601) 377-2604
Keesler AFB, MS 39534   Elizabeth A. DeCoux, Adm.Libn.

U.S. AIR FORCE HOSPITAL MEDICAL CENTER - MEDICAL LIBRARY (MS-
    Keesler AFB)
SGEL   Phone: (601) 377-2042
Keesler AFB, MS 39534   Rita F. Smith, Adm.Libn.

U.S. AIR FORCE - KEESLER TECHNICAL TRAINING CENTER - ACADEMIC
    LIBRARY
McClelland Hall, Bldg. 2818   Phone: (601) 377-4295
Keesler AFB, MS 39534   Frank Gadbois, Libn.

ROGERS (Lauren) LIBRARY AND MUSEUM OF ART
5th Ave. at 7th St.   Phone: (601) 428-4875
Laurel, MS 39440   Betty Mulloy, Libn.

ALCORN STATE UNIVERSITY - JOHN DEWEY BOYD LIBRARY *
Box 539   Phone: (601) 877-3711
Lorman, MS 39096   Epsy Y. Hendricks, Lib.Dir.

MISSISSIPPI STATE UNIVERSITY - MITCHELL MEMORIAL LIBRARY -
    SPECIAL COLLECTIONS
Box 5408   Phone: (601) 325-4225
Mississippi State, MS 39762   Frances N. Coleman, Act.Hd., Spec.Coll.

U.S. GEOLOGICAL SURVEY - NATIONAL MAPPING DIVISION ASSISTANCE
    FACILITY - LIBRARY
National Space Technology Labs   Phone: (601) 688-3541
NSTL Station, MS 39529   Frank Beatty, Libn.

U.S. NASA - NATL. SPACE TECHNOLOGY LABORATORIES - RESEARCH
    LIBRARY
                                                   Phone: (601) 688-3244
NSTL Station, MS 39529   Mary H. Bush, Chf.Libn.

GULF COAST RESEARCH LABORATORY - GORDON GUNTER LIBRARY
                                                   Phone: (601) 875-2244
Ocean Springs, MS 39564   Malcolm S. Ware, Sr.Libn.

U.S. NATL. MARINE FISHERIES SERVICE - FISHERIES LABORATORY -
    LIBRARY
Drawer 1207
Pascagoula, MS 39567

FIRST BAPTIST CHURCH - MATTIE D. HALL LIBRARY †
Front St.
Box 125   Phone: (601) 759-6378
Rosedale, MS 38769

MISSISSIPPI STATE AGRICULTURAL & FORESTRY EXPERIMENT STATION -
    DELTA BR. EXPERIMENT STA. LIBRARY
                                                   Phone: (601) 686-9311
Stoneville, MS 38776   Charlotte G. Pierce, Libn.

GEOGRAPHIC

GEOGRAPHIC

U.S. NATL. PARK SERVICE - NATCHEZ TRACE PARKWAY - LIBRARY & VISITOR CENTER
R.R. 1, NT-143
Tupelo, MS 38801
Phone: (601) 842-1572
John S. Mohlhenrich, Chf.Pk. Interpreter

UNIVERSITY OF MISSISSIPPI - ARCHIVES & SPECIAL COLLECTIONS/ MISSISSIPPIANA
University, MS 38677
Phone: (601) 232-7408
Dr. Thomas M. Verich, Archv.

UNIVERSITY OF MISSISSIPPI - BUREAU OF BUSINESS & ECONOMIC RESEARCH LIBRARY
School of Business Administration
University, MS 38677
Phone: (601) 232-7481

UNIVERSITY OF MISSISSIPPI - BUREAU OF GOVERNMENTAL RESEARCH LIBRARY
University, MS 38677
Phone: (601) 232-7401
Dorothy I. Wilson, Ed.Asst.

UNIVERSITY OF MISSISSIPPI - SCHOOL OF EDUCATION LIBRARY
School of Education Bldg.
University, MS 38677
Phone: (601) 232-7040
Joyce Taylor, Educ.Libn.

UNIVERSITY OF MISSISSIPPI - SCHOOL OF LAW LIBRARY
University, MS 38677
Phone: (601) 232-7361
A. Michael Beaird, Law Libn.

UNIVERSITY OF MISSISSIPPI - SCHOOL OF PHARMACY - AUSTIN A. DODGE PHARMACY LIBRARY
University, MS 38677
Phone: (601) 232-7381
Nancy F. Fuller, Libn.

MERCY REGIONAL MEDICAL CENTER LIBRARY
100 McAuley Dr.
Box 271
Vicksburg, MS 39180
Phone: (601) 636-2131
Frances Betts, Libn.

U.S. ARMY - CORPS OF ENGINEERS - LOWER MISSISSIPPI VALLEY DIV. - MISSISSIPPI RIVER COMMN. TECHNICAL LIB.
Box 80
Vicksburg, MS 39180
Phone: (601) 634-5880
Betty R. Johnson, Libn.

U.S. ARMY - ENGINEER WATERWAYS EXPERIMENT STATION - CONCRETE TECHNOLOGY INFORMATION ANALYSIS CENTER
Box 631
Vicksburg, MS 39180
Phone: (601) 634-3264
Bryant Mather, Dir.

U.S. ARMY - ENGINEER WATERWAYS EXPERIMENT STATION - HYDRAULIC ENGINEERING INFORMATION ANALYSIS CENTER
Box 631
Vicksburg, MS 39180
Phone: (601) 634-3368
Ellis B. Pickett, Dir.

U.S. ARMY - ENGINEER WATERWAYS EXPERIMENT STATION - PAVEMENTS & SOIL TRAFFICABILITY INFO. ANALYSIS CTR.
Box 631
Vicksburg, MS 39180
Phone: (601) 634-2795
Marvin P. Meyer, Dir.

U.S. ARMY - ENGINEER WATERWAYS EXPERIMENT STATION - SOIL MECHANICS INFORMATION ANALYSIS CENTER
Box 631
Vicksburg, MS 39180
Phone: (601) 634-3475
Paul F. Hadala, Dir.

U.S. ARMY - ENGINEER WATERWAYS EXPERIMENT STATION - TECHNICAL INFORMATION CENTER
Box 631
Vicksburg, MS 39180
Phone: (601) 634-2533
Al Sherlock, Chf., Tech.Info.Ctr.

VICKSBURG HOSPITAL, INC. - MEDICAL LIBRARY
3311 I-20 Frontage Rd.
Vicksburg, MS 39180
Phone: (601) 636-2611
Dinnie K. Johnston, Med.Libn.

VICKSBURG & WARREN COUNTY HISTORICAL SOCIETY - MC CARDLE LIBRARY
Old Court House Museum
Vicksburg, MS 39180
Phone: (601) 636-0741
Blanche Terry, Res.Dir.

MARY HOLMES COLLEGE - BARR LIBRARY - ORAL HISTORY COLLECTION
West Point, MS 39773
Phone: (601) 494-6820

MISSOURI

REHABILITATION RESEARCH FOUNDATION - LIBRARY
Box 266
Canton, MO 63435
Phone: (314) 767-5470
Dr. E.C. Grandstaff, Cur.

ST. FRANCIS MEDICAL CENTER - CAPE COUNTY MEMORIAL MEDICAL LIBRARY
211 St. Francis Dr.
Cape Girardeau, MO 63701
Phone: (314) 335-1251
Mrs. Kilja Israel, Libn.

LOGAN COLLEGE OF CHIROPRACTIC - LIBRARY
1851 Schoettler Rd.
Box 100
Chesterfield, MO 63107
Phone: (314) 227-2100
Harriett Hirschfeld, Hd.Libn.

ST. LOUIS COUNTY LAW LIBRARY
St. Louis County Govt. Ctr.
7900 Carondelet Ave.
Clayton, MO 63105
Phone: (314) 889-2726
Mary C. Dahm, Libn.

CHRISTMAS SEAL AND CHARITY STAMP SOCIETY - LIBRARY
1105 Pheasant Run
Columbia, MO 65201
Phone: (314) 442-8407
Dr. H. Denny Donnell, Jr., Hist./Libn.

ELLIS FISCHEL STATE CANCER HOSPITAL AND CANCER RESEARCH CENTER - LIBRARY & INFORMATION CENTER
Business Loop 70 & Garth Ave.
Columbia, MO 65201
Phone: (314) 875-2100
Charles A. O'Dell, Libn.

FIRST CHRISTIAN CHURCH - LIBRARY †
Walnut & Tenth Sts.
Columbia, MO 65201
Phone: (314) 449-7265

INVESTIGATIVE REPORTERS AND EDITORS, INC. - PAUL WILLIAMS MEMORIAL RESOURCE CENTER
220 Walter Williams Hall
University Of Missouri
Columbia, MO 65211
Phone: (314) 882-2024
John Ullmann

MISSOURI SCHOOL OF RELIGION - LIBRARY
Lowry & Ninth Sts.
Columbia, MO 65201
Phone: (314) 449-0071

NATIONAL ASSOCIATION OF ANIMAL BREEDERS - LIBRARY †
401 Bernadette Dr.
Box 1033
Columbia, MO 65205
Phone: (314) 445-4406
William M. Durfey, Exec.V.P.

ORTHOPEDIC FOUNDATION FOR ANIMALS - OFA HIP DYSPLASIA REGISTRY
Middlebush Farms, Hwy. 63 S.
Columbia, MO 65201
Phone: (314) 442-0418
L.A. Corwin, Jr., Proj.Dir.

STATE HISTORICAL SOCIETY OF MISSOURI - LIBRARY
Univ. of Missouri
Elmer Ellis Library
Columbia, MO 65201
Phone: (314) 443-3165
Dr. Richard S. Brownlee, Dir.

U.S. FISH & WILDLIFE SERVICE - COLUMBIA NATIONAL FISHERIES RESEARCH LABORATORY LIBRARY
Route 1
Columbia, MO 65201
Phone: (314) 442-2271
Dr. Richard Shoettger, Dir.

U.S. VETERANS ADMINISTRATION (MO-Columbia) - HOSPITAL LIBRARY
800 Stadium Rd.
Columbia, MO 65201
Phone: (314) 443-2511
Dale C. Davis, Chf., Lib.Serv.

UNIVERSITY OF MISSOURI - ENGINEERING LIBRARY
2017 Engineering Bldg.
Columbia, MO 65211
Phone: (314) 882-2379
Alfred H. Jones, Libn.

UNIVERSITY OF MISSOURI - FREEDOM OF INFORMATION CENTER
223 Walter Williams Hall
Box 858   Phone: (314) 882-4856
Columbia, MO 65205   Dr. Paul L. Fisher, Dir.

UNIVERSITY OF MISSOURI - GEOLOGY LIBRARY
201 Geology Bldg.   Phone: (314) 882-4860
Columbia, MO 65211   Robert Heidlage, Lib.Asst.

UNIVERSITY OF MISSOURI - HEALTH CARE TECHNOLOGY CENTER - HCTC
    INFORMATION CENTER *
137 Clark Hall   Phone: (314) 882-4906
Columbia, MO 65211   Arjun Reddy, Hd.

UNIVERSITY OF MISSOURI - JOURNALISM LIBRARY
117 Walter Williams Hall   Phone: (314) 882-7502
Columbia, MO 65202   Robert C. Hahn, Libn.

UNIVERSITY OF MISSOURI - MATH SCIENCES LIBRARY
206 Math Sciences Bldg.   Phone: (314) 882-7286
Columbia, MO 65211   Dulcie T. Mundy, Lib.Asst.

UNIVERSITY OF MISSOURI - MEDICAL LIBRARY †
M210 Medical Ctr.   Phone: (314) 882-8086
Columbia, MO 65211   Dean Schmidt, Dir.

UNIVERSITY OF MISSOURI - MUSEUM LIBRARY
Pickard Hall   Phone: (314) 882-3591
Columbia, MO 65211   Osmund Overby, Dir. of Musm.

UNIVERSITY OF MISSOURI - RESEARCH PARK LIBRARY
132 Dalton Research Ctr.   Phone: (314) 882-3527
Columbia, MO 65211

UNIVERSITY OF MISSOURI - SCHOOL OF LAW LIBRARY
Tate Hall   Phone: (314) 882-4597
Columbia, MO 65211   Susan D. Csaky, Assoc.Prof./Law Libn.

UNIVERSITY OF MISSOURI - VETERINARY MEDICAL LIBRARY
W218 Veterinary Medicine   Phone: (314) 882-2461
Columbia, MO 65211   Trenton Boyd, Libn.

UNIVERSITY OF MISSOURI - WESTERN HISTORICAL MANUSCRIPT
    COLLECTION/STATE HISTORICAL SOCIETY OF MISSOURI
23 Ellis Library   Phone: (314) 882-3660
Columbia, MO 65201   Nancy C. Prewitt, Assoc.Dir.

CONCEPTION ABBEY AND SEMINARY - LIBRARY
                                                Phone: (816) 944-2211
Conception, MO 64433   Rev. Norbert Schappler, Hd.Libn.

TEMPLE ISRAEL - PAUL PELTASON LIBRARY
10675 Ladue Rd.   Phone: (314) 432-8050
Creve Coeur, MO 63141   Mrs. Barry Katz

U.S. NATL. PARK SERVICE - GEORGE WASHINGTON CARVER NATIONAL
    MONUMENT - LIBRARY
Box 38   Phone: (417) 325-4151
Diamond, MO 64840   Gentry Davis, Supt.

KNOX COUNTY HISTORICAL SOCIETY - LIBRARY *
Edina, MO 63537   Stiefel J. Wilkerson, Pres.

MARITZ, INC. - LIBRARY
1355 N. Highway Dr.   Phone: (314) 225-4000
Fenton, MO 63026   Patty S. Slocombe, Libn.

MARITZ TRAVEL COMPANY - TRAVEL LIBRARY
1385 N. Highway Dr.   Phone: (314) 225-4000
Fenton, MO 63026   Sue Hamilton, Libn.

U.S. ARMY HOSPITALS - GENERAL LEONARD WOOD ARMY COMMUNITY
    HOSPITAL - MEDICAL LIBRARY
                                                Phone: (314) 368-9110
Ft. Leonard Wood, MO 65473   Mrs. Marian B. Strang, Med.Libn.

U.S. ARMY POST - FORT LEONARD WOOD - LIBRARY SYSTEM
Bldg. 1607   Phone: (314) 368-5431
Ft. Leonard Wood, MO 65473   Marcia Whipple, Chf.Libn.

FULTON STATE HOSPITAL - MEDICAL LIBRARY †
E. Fifth St.   Phone: (314) 642-3311
Fulton, MO 65251   Wilfrid S. Akiyama, Libn.

WESTMINSTER COLLEGE - WINSTON CHURCHILL MEMORIAL AND LIBRARY
7th & Westminster Ave.   Phone: (314) 642-3361
Fulton, MO 65251   Karolyn Dickson, Mgr.

MARK TWAIN MUSEUM - LIBRARY
208 Hill St.   Phone: (314) 221-9010
Hannibal, MO 63401   Henry Sweets, Cur.

WORLD ARCHEOLOGICAL SOCIETY - INFORMATION CENTER
Star Rt. 140-D, Lake Rd. 65-48   Phone: (417) 334-2377
Hollister, MO 65672   Ron Miller, Dir.

ASSOCIATION OF INTERNATIONAL COLLEGES & UNIVERSITIES - AICU
    INTERNATIONAL EDUCATION LIBRARY
1301 S. Noland Rd.   Phone: (816) 931-6374
Independence, MO 64055   John W. Johnston, Dir.

BLUE SPRINGS HISTORICAL SOCIETY - LIBRARY
3929 Milton Dr.   Phone: (816) 373-5309
Independence, MO 64055   Larry Wiebusch, Musm.Chm.

(The) INTERNATIONAL UNIVERSITY - INTERNATIONAL RELATIONS
    LIBRARY AND RESEARCH CENTER
1301 S. Noland Rd.   Phone: (816) 931-6374
Independence, MO 64055   Kathleen Thompson, Dir.

JACKSON COUNTY HISTORICAL SOCIETY - RESEARCH LIBRARY &
    ARCHIVES
Independence Sq. Courthouse, Rm.103   Phone: (816) 252-7454
Independence, MO 64050   Nancy M. Ehrlich, Dir.

REORGANIZED CHURCH OF JESUS CHRIST OF LATTER DAY SAINTS -
    LIBRARY & ARCHIVES
RLDS Auditorium
Box 1059   Phone: (816) 833-1000
Independence, MO 64051   Sara Hallier, Libn.

REORGANIZED CHURCH OF JESUS CHRIST OF LATTER DAY SAINTS -
    SERVICES TO THE BLIND
1001 Walnut
Box 1069   Phone: (816) 833-1000
Independence, MO 64051   Stephanie Kelley, Supv.

SPIRITUAL FRONTIERS FELLOWSHIP - LIBRARY
10819 Winner Rd.   Phone: (816) 254-8585
Independence, MO 64052

U.S. PRESIDENTIAL LIBRARIES - HARRY S TRUMAN LIBRARY
                                                Phone: (816) 833-1400
Independence, MO 64050   Dr. Benedict K. Zobrist, Dir.

COLE COUNTY HISTORICAL SOCIETY - MUSEUM AND LIBRARY
109 Madison   Phone: (314) 635-1850
Jefferson City, MO 65101   Lynn Rebbeor Shay, Cur.

LINCOLN UNIVERSITY OF MISSOURI - INMAN E. PAGE LIBRARY
                                                Phone: (314) 751-2325
Jefferson City, MO 65101   Mrs. Freddye G. Ashford, Univ.Libn.

MISSOURI STATE DIVISION OF COMMUNITY AND ECONOMIC
    DEVELOPMENT - RESEARCH LIBRARY
1014 Madison St.
Box 118   Phone: (314) 751-3674
Jefferson City, MO 65102   Steven Dust, Dir.

MISSOURI STATE LEGISLATIVE LIBRARY
State Capitol Bldg.   Phone: (314) 751-4633
Jefferson City, MO 65101   Anne Rottman, Libn.

MISSOURI STATE LIBRARY
308 E. High St.
Box 387   Phone: (314) 751-4214
Jefferson City, MO 65102   Charles O'Halloran, State Libn.

GEOGRAPHIC

GEOGRAPHIC

MISSOURI STATE SUPREME COURT LIBRARY
Supreme Court Bldg., High St.
Jefferson City, MO 65101
Phone: (314) 751-2636
D.A. Divilbiss, Hd.Libn.

OZARK BIBLE COLLEGE - LIBRARY
1111 N. Main St.
Box 518
Joplin, MO 64801
Phone: (417) 624-2518
Loren L. Dickey, Libn.

AMERICAN ACADEMY OF FAMILY PHYSICIANS - INFORMATION RESOURCE
DEPARTMENT
1740 W. 92nd St.
Kansas City, MO 64114
Phone: (816) 333-9700
Karen R. Carter, Mgr., Info.Rsrcs.Dept.

AMERICAN ECONOMIC DEVELOPMENT COUNCIL - AEDC LIBRARY
1207 Grand Ave., Suite 845
Kansas City, MO 64106
Phone: (816) 474-4558
Karen Amelung, Libn.

BAPTIST MEMORIAL HOSPITAL - LEARNING RESOURCES CENTER
6601 Rockhill Road
Kansas City, MO 64131
Phone: (816) 361-3500
Barbara Seiglar, Dir.

BENDIX CORPORATION - KANSAS CITY DIVISION - TECHNICAL
INFORMATION CENTER
2000 E. 95th St.
Box 1159
Kansas City, MO 64141
Phone: (816) 997-2694
Lucile Stratton, Libn.

BETH SHALOM CONGREGATION - BLANCHE AND IRA ROSENBLUM
MEMORIAL LIBRARY
9400 Wornall Rd.
Kansas City, MO 64114
Phone: (816) 363-3331
Frances Wolf, Libn.

BLACK & VEATCH CONSULTING ENGINEERS - CENTRAL LIBRARY
1500 Meadow Lake Pkwy.
Box 8405
Kansas City, MO 64114
Phone: (913) 967-2223
Leo M. Hack, Libn.

BURNS AND MC DONNELL ENGINEERING COMPANY - TECHNICAL LIBRARY
4600 E. 63rd St.
Box 173
Kansas City, MO 64141
Phone: (816) 333-4375
Adalene Stagner, Libn.

CHILDREN'S MERCY HOSPITAL - MEDICAL LIBRARY
24th at Gillham Rd.
Kansas City, MO 64108
Phone: (816) 234-3001
Judy Vermillion, Med.Libn.

CHURCH OF THE NAZARENE - HEADQUARTERS LIBRARY
6401 The Paseo
Kansas City, MO 64131
Phone: (816) 333-7000
Lorraine Krofft, Libn.

ENVIRONMENTAL PROTECTION AGENCY - REGION VII LIBRARY
324 E. 11th St.
Kansas City, MO 64106
Phone: (816) 374-3497
Connie McKenzie, Libn.

ERC CORPORATION - JUNE AUSTIN PARRISH MEMORIAL LIBRARY
Box 2088
Kansas City, MO 64142
Phone: (816) 283-5176
Jeanne Wood, Libn.

FARMLAND INDUSTRIES, INC. - J.W. CUMMINS MEMORIAL LIBRARY
3315 N. Oak Trafficway
Box 7305
Kansas City, MO 64116
Phone: (816) 459-6606
Sarah Davidson, Info.Spec.

FEDERAL RESERVE BANK OF KANSAS CITY - LAW LIBRARY
925 Grand Ave.
Kansas City, MO 64198
Phone: (816) 881-2557
Jann Faltermeier, Law Libn.

FEDERAL RESERVE BANK OF KANSAS CITY - RESEARCH LIBRARY
Kansas City, MO 64198
Phone: (816) 881-2676
Ellen M. Johnson, Libn.

HALLMARK CARDS, INC. - CREATIVE RESEARCH LIBRARY
25th & McGee
Kansas City, MO 64108
Phone: (816) 274-5525
Jon M. Henderson, Mgr., Lib.Serv.

HEART OF AMERICA GENEALOGICAL SOCIETY & LIBRARY, INC.
311 E. 12th St.
Kansas City, MO 64106
Phone: (816) 221-2685

JACKSON COUNTY LAW LIBRARY
Scarritt Bldg., 2nd Fl.
818 Grand Ave.
Kansas City, MO 64106
Phone: (816) 421-6115
Vivian Shaw, Libn.

KANSAS CITY ART INSTITUTE - LIBRARY
4415 Warwick Blvd.
Box 10360
Kansas City, MO 64111
Phone: (816) 561-4852
Ellen Lignell, Lib.Dir.

KANSAS CITY - CITY DEVELOPMENT DEPARTMENT - LIBRARY
City Hall, 414 E. 12th St.
Kansas City, MO 64106
Phone: (816) 274-1864
Alma Lee, Libn.

KANSAS CITY LIFE INSURANCE COMPANY - GENERAL LIBRARY AND
ARCHIVES
3520 Broadway
Kansas City, MO 64111
Phone: (816) 753-7000
Wanda L. Burks, Libn.

KANSAS CITY MUSEUM OF HISTORY AND SCIENCE - ARCHIVES
3218 Gladstone Blvd.
Kansas City, MO 64123
Phone: (816) 483-8300
Barbara M. Gorman, Cur. of Hist.

KANSAS CITY PUBLIC LIBRARY - ART AND MUSIC COLLECTION †
311 E. 12th St.
Kansas City, MO 64106
Phone: (816) 221-2685

KANSAS CITY PUBLIC LIBRARY - BUSINESS AND TECHNICAL COLLECTION
311 E. 12th St.
Kansas City, MO 64106
Phone: (816) 221-2685

KANSAS CITY PUBLIC LIBRARY - MISSOURI VALLEY ROOM †
311 E. 12th St.
Kansas City, MO 64106
Phone: (816) 221-2685

KANSAS CITY PUBLIC LIBRARY - PERIODICAL-MICROFILM COLLECTION †
311 E. 12th St.
Kansas City, MO 64106

KANSAS CITY TIMES-STAR - LIBRARY
1729 Grand Ave.
Kansas City, MO 64108
John J. Springer, Libn.

LATHROP, KOONTZ, RIGHTER, CLAGETT & NORQUIST - LIBRARY
2600 Mutual Benefit Life Bldg.
2345 Grand Ave.
Kansas City, MO 64108
Phone: (816) 842-0820
Mary Ann Leahy, Libn.

LINDA HALL LIBRARY
5109 Cherry St.
Kansas City, MO 64110
Phone: (816) 363-4600
Thomas D. Gillies, Dir.

MARION LABORATORIES, INC. - LIBRARY
Box 9627
Kansas City, MO 64134
Phone: (816) 761-2500
Jane Stehlik-Kokker, Mgr., Sci.Info.Serv.

MENORAH MEDICAL CENTER - ROBERT UHLMAN MEDICAL LIBRARY
4949 Rockhill Rd.
Kansas City, MO 64110
Phone: (816) 276-8172
Marjorie L. Terrill, Med.Libn.

MIDWEST RESEARCH INSTITUTE - PATTERSON REFERENCE LIBRARY AND
ECONOMICS REFERENCE CENTER
425 Volker Blvd.
Kansas City, MO 64110
Phone: (816) 753-7600
Marsha Cole, Hd.Libn.

MIDWESTERN BAPTIST THEOLOGICAL SEMINARY - LIBRARY
5001 N. Oak St. Trafficway
Kansas City, MO 64118
Phone: (816) 453-4600
Dr. K. David Weekes, Dir.

MISSOURI STATE COURT OF APPEALS, WESTERN DISTRICT - LIBRARY
Jackson County Court House
415 E. 12th
Kansas City, MO 64106
Phone: (816) 881-3293
Vickie Selby, Libn.

MOBAY CHEMICAL CORPORATION - AGRICULTURAL CHEMICALS DIVISION
- LIBRARY
Box 4913   Phone: (816) 242-2236
Kansas City, MO 64120   Cheryl Postlewait, Libn.

MODERN HANDCRAFT, INC. - RESEARCH LIBRARY
4251 Pennsylvania Ave.   Phone: (816) 531-5730
Kansas City, MO 64111

NATIONAL ASSOCIATION OF PARLIAMENTARIANS - TECHNICAL
INFORMATION CENTER
3706 Broadway, Suite 300   Phone: (816) 356-5693
Kansas City, MO 64111   Elaine Fulton, Exec.Sec.

NAZARENE THEOLOGICAL SEMINARY - WILLIAM BROADHURST LIBRARY
1700 E. Meyer Blvd.   Phone: (816) 333-6255
Kansas City, MO 64131   William C. Miller, Libn.

NELSON GALLERY-ATKINS MUSEUM - SPENCER ART REFERENCE LIBRARY
4525 Oak St.   Phone: (816) 561-4000
Kansas City, MO 64111   Stanley W. Hess, Libn.

OLD AMERICAN INSURANCE COMPANY - LIBRARY
4900 Oak St.
Kansas City, MO 64112   Kathryn Kufahl, Libn.

PANHANDLE EASTERN PIPE LINE COMPANY - TECHNICAL INFORMATION
CENTER *
Box 1348   Phone: (816) 753-2849
Kansas City, MO 64141   GeorJane Simmons, Libn.

RESEARCH MEDICAL CENTER - LOCKWOOD MEMORIAL LIBRARY
Meyer Blvd. & Prospect Ave.   Phone: (816) 276-4159
Kansas City, MO 64132   Gerald R. Kruse, Dir.

ST. JOSEPH HOSPITAL - HEALTH SCIENCE LIBRARY *
1000 Carondelet Dr.   Phone: (816) 942-4400
Kansas City, MO 64114   Mary Evans, Libn.

ST. LUKE'S HOSPITAL OF KANSAS CITY - MEDICAL LIBRARY
44th & Wornall Rd.   Phone: (816) 932-2333
Kansas City, MO 64111   Karen Horst, Dir. of Lib.Serv.

ST. MARY'S HOSPITAL - LIBRARY
101 Memorial Dr.   Phone: (816) 753-5700
Kansas City, MO 64108   Pamela Kay Drayson, Libn.

ST. MARY'S HOSPITAL MEDICAL EDUCATION FOUNDATION - MEDICAL
LITERATURE INFORMATION CENTER
101 Memorial Dr.   Phone: (816) 753-5700
Kansas City, MO 64108   Dr. George X. Trimble, Dir.

ST. PAUL SCHOOL OF THEOLOGY - DANA DAWSON LIBRARY
5123 Truman Rd.   Phone: (816) 483-9600
Kansas City, MO 64127   Dr. William S. Sparks, Libn.

SHOOK, HARDY & BACON - LIBRARY
Mercantile Bank Tower, Suite 2000
1101 Walnut   Phone: (816) 474-6550
Kansas City, MO 64106   Lori A. Hunt, Libn.

TRINITY LUTHERAN HOSPITAL - FLORENCE L. NELSON MEMORIAL LIBRARY
31st & Wyandotte   Phone: (816) 753-4600
Kansas City, MO 64108   Cami L. Loucks, Dir.

U.S. COURT OF APPEALS, 8TH CIRCUIT - LIBRARY
U.S. Court House, 811 Grand Ave.
Kansas City, MO 64106

U.S. DEPT. OF THE INTERIOR - OFFICE OF SURFACE MINING - LIBRARY
Scarritt Bldg.
818 Grand Ave.   Phone: (816) 374-5056
Kansas City, MO 64106   Renee M. Stewart, Lib.Techn.

U.S. FEDERAL AVIATION ADMINISTRATION - CENTRAL REGION LIBRARY
Federal Bldg., Rm. 1556
601 E. 12th St.   Phone: (816) 374-5486
Kansas City, MO 64106   Judy Shifrin, Chf., Lib.Serv.

U.S. NATL. ARCHIVES & RECORDS SERVICE - FEDERAL ARCHIVES AND
RECORDS CENTER, REGION 6
2306 E. Bannister Rd.   Phone: (816) 926-7271
Kansas City, MO 64131   Patrick Borders, Ctr.Dir.

U.S. VETERANS ADMINISTRATION (MO-Kansas City) - MEDICAL CENTER
LIBRARY
4801 Linwood Blvd.   Phone: (816) 861-4700
Kansas City, MO 64128   Shirley C. Ting, Chf., Lib.Serv.

UNIVERSITY OF HEALTH SCIENCES - LIBRARY
2105 Independence Blvd.   Phone: (816) 283-2451
Kansas City, MO 64124   Marilyn J. DeGeus, Dir. of Libs.

UNIVERSITY OF MISSOURI, KANSAS CITY - CONSERVATORY LIBRARY
Conservatory of Music
4420 Warwick Blvd.   Phone: (816) 363-4300
Kansas City, MO 64111   Jack L. Ralston, Libn.

UNIVERSITY OF MISSOURI, KANSAS CITY - HEALTH SCIENCES LIBRARY
2411 Holmes   Phone: (816) 474-4100
Kansas City, MO 64108   Gary D. Byrd, Chf.Libn.

UNIVERSITY OF MISSOURI, KANSAS CITY - LAW LIBRARY
School of Law, 5100 Rockhill Rd.   Phone: (816) 276-1650
Kansas City, MO 64110   Charles R. Dyer, Law Libn.

UNIVERSITY OF MISSOURI, KANSAS CITY - SCHOOL OF DENTISTRY
LIBRARY
650 E. 25th St.   Phone: (816) 234-0494
Kansas City, MO 64108   Ann Marie Corry, Libn.

UNIVERSITY OF MISSOURI, KANSAS CITY - SNYDER COLLECTION OF
AMERICANA
General Library, 5100 Rockhill Rd.   Phone: (816) 276-1534
Kansas City, MO 64110

UNIVERSITY OF MISSOURI, KANSAS CITY - TEDROW TRANSPORTATION
COLLECTION
General Library, 5100 Rockhill Rd.   Phone: (816) 276-1534
Kansas City, MO 64110

WADDELL AND REED, INC. - RESEARCH LIBRARY
Box 1343   Phone: (816) 283-4072
Kansas City, MO 64141   Betty J. Howerton, Hd.Libn.

WESTERN MISSOURI MENTAL HEALTH CENTER - LIBRARY
600 E. 22nd St.   Phone: (816) 471-3000
Kansas City, MO 64108   Ellen Bull, Med.Libn.

FIRST BAPTIST CHURCH - LIBRARY
300 St. Francis St.   Phone: (314) 888-4689
Kennett, MO 63857   Pearl Young, Libn.

KIRKSVILLE COLLEGE OF OSTEOPATHIC MEDICINE - A.T. STILL MEMORIAL
LIBRARY
                                                  Phone: (816) 626-2345
Kirksville, MO 63501   Georgia Walter, Dir. of Lib.

NORTHEAST MISSOURI STATE UNIVERSITY - PICKLER MEMORIAL
LIBRARY - SPECIAL COLLECTIONS
                                                  Phone: (816) 785-4626
Kirksville, MO 63501   George N. Hartje, Dir. of Lib.

WATKINS WOOLEN MILL STATE HISTORIC SITE - RESEARCH LIBRARY
Rte. 2, Box 270M   Phone: (816) 296-3357
Lawson, MO 64062   Ann M. Matthews, Historic Site Adm.

CLAY COUNTY ARCHIVES
Box 99
Liberty, MO 64068   Ron Fuenfhausen, Cur.

MISSOURI BAPTIST HISTORICAL COMMISSION LIBRARY
William Jewell College Library   Phone: (816) 781-3806
Liberty, MO 64068

NORTHWEST MISSOURI STATE UNIVERSITY - HORACE MANN LEARNING
CENTER
                                                  Phone: (816) 582-7141
Maryville, MO 64468   Kerry England, Libn.

NORTHWEST MISSOURI STATE UNIVERSITY - WELLS LIBRARY
Phone: (816) 582-7141
Maryville, MO 64468   Charles W. Koch, Dir.Lrng.Rsrcs.

AUDRAIN COUNTY HISTORICAL SOCIETY - ROSS HOUSE LIBRARY/
AMERICAN SADDLE HORSE MUSEUM LIBRARY
501 South Muldrow   Phone: (314) 581-3910
Mexico, MO 65265   Clara Kaiser, Libn./Genealogist

MISSOURI STATE CHEST HOSPITAL - MEDICAL LIBRARY
Phone: (417) 466-3711
Mount Vernon, MO 65712   Shirley Boucher, Libn.

WATER AND WASTEWATER TECHNICAL SCHOOL - LIBRARY
Box 370   Phone: (417) 451-2786
Neosho, MO 64850   Polly Bell, Libn.

FIRST BAPTIST CHURCH - LIBRARY
2205 Iron St.   Phone: (816) 842-1175
North Kansas City, MO 64116   Esther St. John, Hd.Libn.

MARK TWAIN RESEARCH FOUNDATION - LIBRARY
Phone: (314) 565-3570
Perry, MO 63462   Chester L. Davis, Exec.Sec.

ST. MARY'S SEMINARY - ST. MARY'S OF THE BARRENS LIBRARY
Phone: (314) 547-6300
Perryville, MO 63775   Rev. John J. Bagen, C.M., Libn.

SCHOOL OF THE OZARKS - RALPH FOSTER MUSEUM - LOIS BROWNELL
RESEARCH LIBRARY
Phone: (417) 334-6411
Point Lookout, MO 65726   Robert S. Esworthy, Dir.

U.S. VETERANS ADMINISTRATION (MO-Poplar Bluff) - MEDICAL CENTER
LIBRARY (142D)
Highway 67 North   Phone: (314) 686-4151
Poplar Bluff, MO 63901   Kwang Hee Streiff, Chf., Lib.Serv.

MISSOURI STATE DIVISION OF GEOLOGY AND LAND SURVEY - LIBRARY
Box 250   Phone: (314) 364-1752
Rolla, MO 65401   Marcia Cussins, Libn.

U.S. BUREAU OF MINES - ROLLA RESEARCH CENTER - LIBRARY
1300 Bishop Ave.
Box 280   Phone: (314) 364-3169
Rolla, MO 65401   Nellie G. Jonas, Libn.

UNIVERSITY OF MISSOURI, ROLLA - CURTIS LAWS WILSON LIBRARY
Phone: (314) 341-4227
Rolla, MO 65401   Ronald Bohley, Libn.

ST. CHARLES COUNTY HISTORICAL SOCIETY - LIBRARY AND ARCHIVES
101 S. Main St.
Box 455   Phone: (314) 723-2939
St. Charles, MO 63301   Emma Porter, Genealogist & Dir.

ST. JOSEPH HOSPITAL - MEDICAL LIBRARY
Third St. & First Capitol Drive   Phone: (314) 724-2810
St. Charles, MO 63301   Julia Wise

HEARST (Phoebe Apperson) HISTORICAL SOCIETY, INC. - MUSEUM CENTER
850 Walton
Box 1842   Phone: (314) 629-3186
St. Clair, MO 63077   Mabel Reed, Sec. In Charge

BUCHANAN COUNTY LAW LIBRARY
816 Corby Bldg.   Phone: (816) 279-0274
St. Joseph, MO 64501   Renee Douglass, Libn.

FIRST CHRISTIAN CHURCH - LIBRARY †
Tenth & Faraon Sts.   Phone: (816) 233-2556
St. Joseph, MO 64501

FLETCHER, MAYO, ASSOCIATES, INC. - LIBRARY
Sta. E, Box B   Phone: (816) 233-8261
St. Joseph, MO 64505   Sara Bockelman, Libn.

HUFFMAN MEMORIAL UNITED METHODIST CHURCH - LIBRARY
2802 Renick   Phone: (816) 233-0239
St. Joseph, MO 64507   Dorothy Thomann, Libn.

PHILIPS ROXANE, INC. - TECHNICAL INFORMATION CENTER
2621 N. Belt Hwy.   Phone: (816) 233-1385
St. Joseph, MO 64502   Norma Barnes, Libn.

ST. JOSEPH HOSPITAL - MEDICAL STAFF LIBRARY
923 Powell St.   Phone: (816) 271-5000
St. Joseph, MO 64501   Merylin Sickels, Med.Rec.Libn.

ST. JOSEPH MUSEUM - LIBRARY
Eleventh at Charles   Phone: (816) 232-8471
St. Joseph, MO 64501   Richard A. Nolf, Dir.

ST. JOSEPH STATE HOSPITAL - PROFESSIONAL LIBRARY
3400 Frederick Ave.
Box 263   Phone: (816) 232-8431
St. Joseph, MO 64502   Laura Egan, Med.Libn.

AMERICAN SOYBEAN ASSOCIATION - LIBRARY
777 Craig Rd.
Box 27300   Phone: (314) 432-1600
St. Louis, MO 63141   Paula Keller, Info.Spec.

ANHEUSER-BUSCH COMPANIES, INC. - CORPORATE LIBRARY
721 Pestalozzi   Phone: (314) 577-2669
St. Louis, MO 63118   Ann Hunter, Corp.Libn.

AUTOMATED LOGISTIC MANAGEMENT SYSTEMS AGENCY - LIBRARY
210 N. 12th St., Rm. 1232a   Phone: (314) 263-5955
St. Louis, MO 63101   Oneta M. Welch, Lib.Techn.

AUTOMOBILE CLUB OF MISSOURI - INFORMATION RESOURCE CENTER
201 Progress Pkwy.   Phone: (314) 576-7350
St. Louis, MO 63043   Muriel Lindsay, Libn.

BARNES HOSPITAL - SCHOOL OF NURSING LIBRARY & INSTRUCTIONAL
RESOURCE LABORATORY
416 S. Kingshighway Blvd.   Phone: (314) 454-2554
St. Louis, MO 63110   Rosemary Buhr, Libn.

BLISS (Malcolm) MENTAL HEALTH CENTER - ROBERT J. BROCKMAN
MEMORIAL LIBRARY
1420 Grattan St.   Phone: (314) 241-7600
St. Louis, MO 63104   William G. Heigold, Med.Libn.

BLUE CROSS HOSPITAL SERVICE, INC. - LIBRARY
4444 Forest Park Blvd.   Phone: (314) 658-4774
St. Louis, MO 63108   Mary Hebert, Libn.

CATHOLIC CENTRAL UNION OF AMERICA - CENTRAL BUREAU LIBRARY
3835 Westminster Pl.   Phone: (314) 371-1653
St. Louis, MO 63108   Harvey J. Johnson, Dir.

CATHOLIC HEALTH ASSOCIATION OF THE UNITED STATES -
INFORMATION RESOURCE CENTER
4455 Woodson Rd.   Phone: (314) 427-2500
St. Louis, MO 63134   Jacqueline Windler, Dir., Info.Rsrcs.Ctr.

CENTER FOR REFORMATION RESEARCH - LIBRARY
6477 San Bonita Ave.   Phone: (314) 727-6655
St. Louis, MO 63105   Dr. William Maltby, Exec.Dir.

CENTRAL INSTITUTE FOR THE DEAF - EDUCATIONAL RESEARCH LIBRARY
818 S. Euclid   Phone: (314) 652-3200
St. Louis, MO 63110   Mary M. Sicking, Libn.

CHRIST SEMINARY - SEMINEX LIBRARY
607 N. Grand Blvd.   Phone: (314) 534-7535
St. Louis, MO 63103   Lucille Hager, Dir.

CHRISTIAN BOARD OF PUBLICATION - MARION STEVENSON LIBRARY
2640 Pine St.   Phone: (314) 371-6900
St. Louis, MO 63166

CHRISTIAN CHURCH (Disciples of Christ), INC. - DIVISION OF HIGHER
  EDUCATION - LIBRARY
119 N. Jefferson Ave.   Phone: (314) 371-2050
St. Louis, MO 63103   Catherine F. Chambliss, Libn.

CONCORDIA HISTORICAL INSTITUTE - DEPARTMENT OF ARCHIVES AND
  HISTORY
801 DeMun Ave.   Phone: (314) 721-5934
St. Louis, MO 63105   Dr. August R. Suelflow, Dir.

CONCORDIA SEMINARY - LIBRARY
801 DeMun Ave.   Phone: (314) 721-5934
St. Louis, MO 63105   W. Larry Bielenberg, Dir., Lib.Serv.

COVENANT THEOLOGICAL SEMINARY - J. OLIVER BUSWELL, JR. LIBRARY
12330 Conway Rd., Creve Coeur   Phone: (314) 434-4044
St. Louis, MO 63141   Dr. Joseph H. Hall, Libn.

D'ARCY-MAC MANUS AND MASIUS - LIBRARY †
One S. Memorial Dr.   Phone: (314) 342-8600
St. Louis, MO 63102   Jean Kammer, Libn.

DEACONESS HOSPITAL - DRUSCH PROFESSIONAL LIBRARY
6150 Oakland Ave.   Phone: (314) 645-8510
St. Louis, MO 63139   Jane Whalen, Libn.

DOANE AGRICULTURAL SERVICE, INC. - INFORMATION CENTER
8900 Manchester Rd.   Phone: (314) 968-1000
St. Louis, MO 63144   Mary E. Aversa, Mgr.

EAST-WEST GATEWAY COORDINATING COUNCIL - REFERENCE AREA
112 N. 4th St., Suite 1200   Phone: (314) 421-4220
St. Louis, MO 63102   Henrietta Whiteside, Info.Serv.Coord.

ENVIRODYNE ENGINEERS, INC. - LIBRARY
12161 Lackland Rd.   Phone: (314) 434-6960
St. Louis, MO 63141   Kathryn Flowers, Libn.

FEDERAL RESERVE BANK OF ST. LOUIS - RESEARCH LIBRARY
Box 442   Phone: (314) 444-8552
St. Louis, MO 63166   Carol J. Thaxton, Hd.Libn.

FIELD (Eugene) HOUSE AND TOY MUSEUM - LIBRARY
634 S. Broadway   Phone: (314) 421-4689
St. Louis, MO 63102

GARDNER ADVERTISING COMPANY - INFORMATION CENTER
10 Broadway   Phone: (314) 444-2357
St. Louis, MO 63102   Delores Borders, Info.Ctr.Mgr.

GENERAL DYNAMICS CORPORATION - PUBLIC AFFAIRS LIBRARY
Pierre Laclede Ctr.   Phone: (314) 862-2440
St. Louis, MO 63105   Barbara Elliott, Chf.Libn.

HARRIS-STOWE STATE COLLEGE LIBRARY
3026 Laclede Ave.   Phone: (314) 533-3366
St. Louis, MO 63103   Martin Knorr, Dir.

INCARNATE WORD HOSPITAL - MEDICAL LIBRARY
3545 Lafayette Ave.   Phone: (314) 664-6500
St. Louis, MO 63104   Sr. Raymond Borgmeyer, Libn.

INTERNATIONAL BROTHERHOOD OF OLD BASTARDS, INC. - SIR THOMAS
  CRAPPER MEMORIAL ARCHIVES
2330 S. Brentwood Blvd.   Phone: (314) 961-9825
St. Louis, MO 63144   Bro. Jose "Bat" Guano, O.B., Chf. of Archv. & Seals

INTERNATIONAL CONSUMER CREDIT ASSOCIATION - DEPARTMENT OF
  EDUCATION LIBRARY
243 N. Lindbergh Blvd.   Phone: (314) 991-3030
St. Louis, MO 63141   Mary Alice Minney, Dir., Dept. of Educ.

INTERNATIONAL LIBRARY, ARCHIVES & MUSEUM OF OPTOMETRY
243 N. Lindbergh Blvd.   Phone: (314) 991-0324
St. Louis, MO 63141   Maria Dablemont, Libn.

JEWISH COMMUNITY CENTERS ASSOCIATION (JCCA) - TANNIE LEWIN
  JUDAICA LIBRARY
11001 Schuetz Rd.   Phone: (314) 432-5700
St. Louis, MO 63141   Lorraine K. Miller, Hd.Libn.

JEWISH HOSPITAL OF ST. LOUIS - ROTHSCHILD MEDICAL LIBRARY
216 S. Kingshighway   Phone: (314) 454-7208
St. Louis, MO 63110   Ruth Kelly, Libn.

JEWISH HOSPITAL OF ST. LOUIS - SCHOOL OF NURSING - MOSES
  SHOENBERG MEMORIAL LIBRARY
306 S. Kingshighway   Phone: (314) 454-8474
St. Louis, MO 63110   Alice Bruenjes, Hd.Libn.

JOHNSON (George) ADVERTISING - LIBRARY
755 New Ballas Rd., S.   Phone: (314) 569-3440
St. Louis, MO 63141   Marianne C. Goedeker, Libn.

KENRICK SEMINARY LIBRARY
7800 Kenrick Rd.   Phone: (314) 961-4320
St. Louis, MO 63119   Rev. Myron Gohmann, C.P., Hd.Libn.

KRUPNICK & ASSOCIATES, INC. - LIBRARY *
135 N. Meramec   Phone: (314) 862-9393
St. Louis, MO 63105   Cynthia A. Maritz, Libn.

LAW LIBRARY ASSOCIATION OF ST. LOUIS
1300 Civil Courts Bldg.   Phone: (314) 622-4386
St. Louis, MO 63101   Rosa Gahn Wright, Libn.

LEGAL SERVICES OF EASTERN MISSOURI, INC. - LIBRARY
625 N. Euclid Ave.
Field Sta., Box 4999A   Phone: (314) 367-1700
St. Louis, MO 63108   Helen R. Gibson, Libn.

LEWIS, RICE, TUCKER, ALLEN AND CHUBB - LAW LIBRARY
1400 Railway Exchange Bldg.
611 Olive St.   Phone: (314) 231-5833
St. Louis, MO 63101   Nancy M. Wiegand, Libn.

LUTHERAN CHURCH - MISSOURI SYNOD - COMMISSION ON WORSHIP
  LIBRARY *
500 N. Broadway   Phone: (314) 231-6969
St. Louis, MO 63102   Rev. Dr. Fred L. Precht, Exec.Sec.

LUTHERAN CHURCH - MISSOURI SYNOD - LUTHERAN LIBRARY FOR THE
  BLIND
3558 S. Jefferson Ave.   Phone: (314) 664-7000
St. Louis, MO 63118   Francine Lieneke, Serv.Dir.

LUTHERAN MEDICAL CENTER - MEDICAL LIBRARY *
2639 Miami St.   Phone: (314) 772-1456
St. Louis, MO 63118   Jean Monsivais, Secretary

MC DONNELL DOUGLAS CORPORATION - MC DONNELL AIRCRAFT LIBRARY
Dept. 022, Box 516   Phone: (314) 232-6134
St. Louis, MO 63166   C.E. Zoller, Mgr.

MC DONNELL PLANETARIUM - LIBRARY
5100 Clayton Rd., Forest Pk.   Phone: (314) 535-5811
St. Louis, MO 63110   Richard W. Heuermann, Lib.Info.Dir.

MALLINCKRODT, INC. - LIBRARY
Box 5439   Phone: (314) 695-5514
St. Louis, MO 63147   Juanita McCarthy, Corp.Libn.

MAY DEPARTMENT STORES COMPANY - INFORMATION CENTER
611 Olive St., Suite 1350   Phone: (314) 436-3300
St. Louis, MO 63101   Julia O'Neil, Dir.

MERCANTILE TRUST COMPANY - INTERNATIONAL LIBRARY
Box 14881   Phone: (314) 425-2867
St. Louis, MO 67178   Carrie Kempen, Libn.

MISSOURI BAPTIST HOSPITAL - MEDICAL LIBRARY
3015 N. Ballas Rd.   Phone: (314) 432-1212
St. Louis, MO 63131   Mildred Schupmann, Med.Libn.

MISSOURI BAPTIST HOSPITAL - SCHOOL OF NURSING LIBRARY
3015 N. Ballas Rd.   Phone: (314) 432-1212
St. Louis, MO 63131   Helen J. Seaton, Libn.

MISSOURI BOTANICAL GARDEN - LIBRARY
Box 299
St. Louis, MO 63166
Phone: (314) 772-7600
James R. Reed, Dir. of Lib.

MISSOURI HISTORICAL SOCIETY - ARCHIVES AND MANUSCRIPTS
Jefferson Memorial Bldg.
Forest Park
St. Louis, MO 63112
Phone: (314) 361-1424

MISSOURI HISTORICAL SOCIETY - PICTORIAL HISTORY COLLECTION
Jefferson Memorial Bldg.
Forest Park
St. Louis, MO 63112
Phone: (314) 361-1424
Judy Ciampoli, Cur.

MISSOURI HISTORICAL SOCIETY - RESEARCH LIBRARY
Jefferson Memorial Bldg.
Forest Park
St. Louis, MO 63112
Phone: (314) 361-1424
Anthony R. Crawford, Asst.Dir./Lib. & Archv.

MISSOURI INSTITUTE OF PSYCHIATRY LIBRARY
5400 Arsenal St.
St. Louis, MO 63139
Phone: (314) 644-8838
Connie Wolf, Libn.

MISSOURI STATE LIBRARY - WOLFNER MEMORIAL LIBRARY FOR THE BLIND & PHYSICALLY HANDICAPPED
1808 Washington
St. Louis, MO 63103
Phone: (314) 241-4227
Pennie D. Peterson, Coord.

MONSANTO COMPANY - ENGINEERING INFORMATION CENTER - F1EE
800 N. Lindbergh Blvd.
St. Louis, MO 63166
Phone: (314) 694-7133
Frank L. Reynard, Libn.

MONSANTO COMPANY - INFORMATION CENTER
800 N. Lindbergh Blvd.
Box 7090
St. Louis, MO 63177
Phone: (314) 694-4778
William A. Wilkinson, Mgr.

MUSEUM OF SCIENCE AND NATURAL HISTORY - LIBRARY
2 Oak Knoll Pk.
St. Louis, MO 63105
Phone: (314) 726-2888
Donn P. Brazier, Dir.

NATIONAL MUSEUM OF TRANSPORT - TRANSPORTATION REFERENCE LIBRARY
3015 Barrett Station Rd.
St. Louis, MO 63122
Phone: (314) 965-6885
Dr. John P. Roberts, Sec.

NOOTER CORPORATION - TECHNICAL LIBRARY
Box 451
St. Louis, MO 63166
Phone: (314) 621-6000
Barry Heuer, Libn.

NORCLIFF THAYER MFG. FACILITY - DIVISION OF REVLON, INC. - LIBRARY
319 S. 4th St.
St. Louis, MO 63102
Phone: (314) 621-2304
Joann Aldridge, R.N., Libn.

PET, INC. - CORPORATE INFORMATION CENTER
Box 392
St. Louis, MO 63166
Phone: (314) 622-6134
Laurence R. Walton, Corp.Libn.

PETROLITE CORPORATION - RESEARCH LIBRARY
369 Marshall Ave.
St. Louis, MO 63119
Phone: (314) 961-3500
Pauline C. Beinbrech, Libn.

PLANNED PARENTHOOD ASSOCIATION OF ST. LOUIS - FAMILY PLANNING LIBRARY
2202 S. Hanley Rd.
St. Louis, MO 63144
Phone: (314) 781-3800
Debbie Fuhrmann, Prog.Coord.

PROTESTANT EPISCOPAL CHURCH - MISSOURI DIOCESE - DIOCESAN ARCHIVES
1210 Locust St.
St. Louis, MO 63103
Phone: (314) 231-1220
Charles F. Rehkopf, Archv./Registrar

RALSTON PURINA COMPANY - TECHNICAL INFORMATION CENTER
Checkerboard Sq.
St. Louis, MO 63188
Phone: (314) 982-2150
Linda S. Lincks, Mgr.

ST. JOHN'S MERCY MEDICAL CENTER - JOHN YOUNG BROWN MEMORIAL LIBRARY
621 S. New Ballas Rd.
St. Louis, MO 63141
Phone: (314) 569-6340
Karen Pirino, Dir.

ST. LOUIS ART MUSEUM - RICHARDSON MEMORIAL LIBRARY
Forest Pk.
St. Louis, MO 63110
Phone: (314) 721-0067
Ann B. Abid, Libn.

ST. LOUIS CHILDREN'S HOSPITAL - BORDEN S. VEEDER LIBRARY
500 S. Kingshighway Blvd.
Box 14871
St. Louis, MO 63178
Phone: (314) 367-6880
Pamela M. Menne, Pediatrics Libn.

ST. LOUIS COLLEGE OF PHARMACY - O.J. CLOUGHLY ALUMNI LIBRARY
4588 Parkview Pl.
St. Louis, MO 63110
Phone: (314) 367-8700
Helen F. Silverman, Libn.

ST. LOUIS - COMPTROLLERS OFFICE - MICROFILM DEPARTMENT
City Hall, Rm. 1
Tucker & Market Sts.
St. Louis, MO 63103
Phone: (314) 622-4274
Edward J. Machowski, Mgr.

ST. LOUIS CONSERVATORY OF MUSIC AND SCHOOLS FOR THE ARTS - MAE M. WHITAKER LIBRARY
560 Trinity Ave.
St. Louis, MO 63130
Phone: (314) 863-3033
Marion Sherman, Libn.

ST. LOUIS HEARING AND SPEECH CENTER - LIBRARY
9526 Manchester
St. Louis, MO 63119
Phone: (314) 968-4710
Mrs. Corley Thompson, Exec.Dir.

ST. LOUIS MERCANTILE LIBRARY ASSOCIATION - LIBRARY
510 Locust St.
Box 633
St. Louis, MO 63188
Phone: (314) 621-0670
Elizabeth Kirchner, Hd.Libn.

ST. LOUIS METROPOLITAN MEDICAL SOCIETY - ST. LOUIS SOCIETY FOR MEDICAL AND SCIENTIFIC EDUCATION - LIBRARY
3839 Lindell Blvd.
St. Louis, MO 63108
Phone: (314) 371-5225
Audrey L. Berkley, Libn.

ST. LOUIS MUNICIPAL MEDICAL LIBRARY - CITY HOSPITAL 1
1515 Lafayette Ave.
St. Louis, MO 63104
Phone: (314) 231-3700
Mrs. Bernie Ferrell, Libn.

ST. LOUIS - POLICE LIBRARY
315 S. Tucker
St. Louis, MO 63102
Phone: (314) 444-5581
Cathy H. Reilly, Libn.

ST. LOUIS POST-DISPATCH - REFERENCE DEPARTMENT
900 N. Tucker Blvd.
St. Louis, MO 63101
Phone: (314) 621-1111
Nancy Williams Stoddard, Libn.

ST. LOUIS PSYCHOANALYTIC INSTITUTE - BETTY GOLDE SMITH MEMORIAL LIBRARY
4524 Forest Park Blvd.
St. Louis, MO 63108
Phone: (314) 361-7075
Rheba Symeonglou, Libn.

ST. LOUIS PUBLIC LIBRARY - APPLIED SCIENCE DEPARTMENT
1301 Olive St.
St. Louis, MO 63103
Phone: (314) 241-2288
Therese F. Dawson, Chf.Libn.

ST. LOUIS PUBLIC LIBRARY - ART DEPARTMENT
1301 Olive St.
St. Louis, MO 63103
Phone: (314) 241-2288
Martha Hilligoss, Chf.Libn.

ST. LOUIS PUBLIC LIBRARY - CAROL MC DONALD GARDNER RARE BOOK ROOM
1301 Olive St.
St. Louis, MO 63103
Phone: (314) 241-2288
R. David Weaver, Libn.

ST. LOUIS PUBLIC LIBRARY - CHILDREN'S LITERATURE ROOM
1301 Olive St.
St. Louis, MO 63103
Phone: (314) 241-2288
Julanne M. Good, Libn.

ST. LOUIS PUBLIC LIBRARY - FILM LIBRARY SERVICE
1624 Locust St.
St. Louis, MO 63103
Phone: (314) 241-2288
Rita Broughton, Film Libn.

ST. LOUIS PUBLIC LIBRARY - HISTORY AND GENEALOGY DEPARTMENT
1301 Olive St.
St. Louis, MO 63103
Phone: (314) 241-2288
Noel C. Holobeck, Chf.Libn.

ST. LOUIS PUBLIC LIBRARY - HUMANITIES AND SOCIAL SCIENCES
   DEPARTMENT
1301 Olive St.   Phone: (314) 241-2288
St. Louis, MO 63103   Edna J. Reinhold, Chf.Libn.

ST. LOUIS PUBLIC LIBRARY - POPULAR LIBRARY - MUSIC SECTION
1301 Olive St.   Phone: (314) 241-2288
St. Louis, MO 63103   Helen Taylor, Libn.

ST. LOUIS PUBLIC LIBRARY - READERS SERVICES/DOCUMENTS
   DEPARTMENT
1301 Olive St.   Phone: (314) 241-2288
St. Louis, MO 63103   Anne Watts, Supv.

ST. LOUIS UNIVERSITY - COLLEGE OF PHILOSOPHY AND LETTERS - FUSZ
   MEMORIAL LIBRARY
3700 W. Pine Blvd.   Phone: (314) 652-3700
St. Louis, MO 63108   Rev. J. Eugene Coomes, S.J., Libn.

ST. LOUIS UNIVERSITY - DIVINITY LIBRARY
Pius XII Library
3655 W. Pine Blvd.   Phone: (314) 658-3082
St. Louis, MO 63108   Rev. W. Charles Heiser, S.J., Libn.

ST. LOUIS UNIVERSITY - KNIGHTS OF COLUMBUS VATICAN FILM LIBRARY
Pius XII Memorial Library
3655 West Pine Blvd.
St. Louis, MO 63108   Charles J. Ermatinger, Vatican Film Libn.

ST. LOUIS UNIVERSITY - MEDICAL CENTER LIBRARY
1402 S. Grand Blvd.   Phone: (314) 664-9800
St. Louis, MO 63104   Francis O'Leary, Libn.

ST. LOUIS UNIVERSITY - SCHOOL OF LAW - LIBRARY
3700 Lindell Blvd.   Phone: (314) 658-2755
St. Louis, MO 63108   Eileen H. Searls, Law Libn.

ST. LOUIS ZOOLOGICAL PARK - LIBRARY
Forest Park
St. Louis, MO 63108   Charles Hoessle, Dp.Dir.

ST. LUKE'S HOSPITAL - LIBRARY
5535 Delmar Blvd.   Phone: (314) 361-1212
St. Louis, MO 63112   Kathy Mullen, Libn.

ST. LUKE'S HOSPITAL - SCHOOL OF NURSING LIBRARY
5555 Delmar Blvd.   Phone: (314) 361-1212
St. Louis, MO 63112   Sarah Deaver, Sch.Libn.

SOUTHWESTERN BELL TELEPHONE COMPANY - BUSINESS INFORMATION
   RESOURCE SERVICE
112 N. Fourth St., Rm. 1323   Phone: (314) 247-8696
St. Louis, MO 63102   Leah Matthews, Supv./Libn.

SVERDRUP & PARCEL AND ASSOCIATES, INC. - TECHNICAL LIBRARY
801 N. 11th Blvd.   Phone: (314) 436-7600
St. Louis, MO 63101   R.A. Bodapati, Libn.

ST. MARY'S HEALTH CENTER - HEALTH SCIENCES LIBRARY
6420 Clayton Rd.   Phone: (314) 768-8112
St. Louis, MO 63117   Candace W. Thayer, Libn.

SOCIETY OF ST. VINCENT DE PAUL - LIBRARY
4140 Lindell Blvd.
St. Louis, MO 63108   Dudley L. Baker, Exec.Sec.

TEAM FOUR INC. - LIBRARY
14 N. Newstead Ave.   Phone: (314) 533-2200
St. Louis, MO 63108   Linda Scott, Libn.

THIRD BAPTIST CHURCH - LIBRARY
620 N. Grand   Phone: (314) 533-7340
St. Louis, MO 63103   Elsie Swarm, Libn.

TRINITY UNITED CHURCH OF CHRIST - EDITH L. STOCK MEMORIAL
   LIBRARY
4700 S. Grand Blvd.   Phone: (314) 352-6645
St. Louis, MO 63111   Jean A. Allison, Chm., Lib.Comm.

UNIDYNAMICS/ST. LOUIS, INC. - LIBRARY
472 Paul Ave.   Phone: (314) 522-6700
St. Louis, MO 63135   Mae E. Chaudet, Libn.

UNION ELECTRIC COMPANY - LIBRARY
1901 Gratiot St.
Box 149   Phone: (314) 621-3222
St. Louis, MO 63166   Constance Ford, Chf.Libn.

UNITED NATIONS ASSOCIATION OF THE UNITED STATES OF AMERICA -
   GREATER ST. LOUIS CHAPTER - LIBRARY
7359 Forsyth Blvd.   Phone: (314) 721-1961
St. Louis, MO 63105   Alice W. Dunlop

U.S. ARMY - CORPS OF ENGINEERS - ST. LOUIS DISTRICT - LIBRARY
210 Tucker Blvd., N.   Phone: (314) 263-5675
St. Louis, MO 63101   Katharine Hayes, District Libn.

U.S. ARMY - TROOP SUPPORT COMMAND - STINFO AND REFERENCE
   LIBRARY
4300 Goodfellow   Phone: (314) 263-2345
St. Louis, MO 63120   Grace Feng, Supv.Libn.

U.S. COURT OF APPEALS, 8TH CIRCUIT - LIBRARY
U.S. Court & Customs House, Rm. 503   Phone: (314) 425-4930
St. Louis, MO 63101   Patricia Rodi Monk, Chf.Libn.

U.S. DEFENSE MAPPING AGENCY - AEROSPACE CENTER - TECHNICAL
   LIBRARY
Second & Arsenal Sts.   Phone: (314) 263-4267
St. Louis, MO 63118   Graham Rosenberger, Command Libn.

U.S. DEPT. OF COMMERCE - INTERNATIONAL TRADE ADMINISTRATION -
   ST. LOUIS DISTRICT OFFICE LIBRARY
120 S. Central Ave., Suite 400   Phone: (314) 425-3302
St. Louis, MO 63105   Donald R. Loso, Dir.

U.S. NATL. ARCHIVES & RECORDS SERVICE - NATL. PERSONNEL RECORDS
   CENTER
9700 Page Blvd.   Phone: (314) 263-7201
St. Louis, MO 63132   J.D. Kilgore, Dir.

U.S. NATL. PARK SERVICE - JEFFERSON NATL. EXPANSION MEMORIAL -
   LIBRARY
11 N. Fourth St.   Phone: (314) 425-6023
St. Louis, MO 63102   Steven D. Harrison, Musm.Spec.

U.S. VETERANS ADMINISTRATION (MO-St. Louis) - HOSPITAL LIBRARY
                                            Phone: (314) 652-4100
St. Louis, MO 63125   Anne R. Thornton, Chf.Libn.

UNIVERSITY OF MISSOURI, ST. LOUIS - EDUCATION LIBRARY
8001 Natural Bridge Rd.   Phone: (314) 553-5571
St. Louis, MO 63121   Virginia R. Workman, Hd., Educ.Lib.

UNIVERSITY OF MISSOURI, ST. LOUIS - THOMAS JEFFERSON LIBRARY
8001 Natural Bridge Rd.   Phone: (314) 553-5053
St. Louis, MO 63121   Ron Krash, Dir.

UNIVERSITY OF MISSOURI, ST. LOUIS - WESTERN HISTORICAL
   MANUSCRIPT COLLECTION/STATE HISTORICAL SOC. OF MISSOURI
Thomas Jefferson Library
8001 Natural Bridge Rd.   Phone: (314) 453-5143
St. Louis, MO 63121   Anne R. Kenney, Assoc.Dir.

WASHINGTON UNIVERSITY - ART & ARCHITECTURE LIBRARY
Steinberg Hall   Phone: (314) 889-5268
St. Louis, MO 63130   Imre Meszaros, Libn.

WASHINGTON UNIVERSITY - BIOLOGY LIBRARY
Life Sciences Bldg.   Phone: (314) 889-5405
St. Louis, MO 63130   Betty S. Galyon, Libn.

GEOGRAPHIC

WASHINGTON UNIVERSITY - BUSINESS ADMINISTRATION LIBRARY
School of Business Adm., Prince Hall   Phone: (314) 889-6334
St. Louis, MO 63130   Magda Buday, Bus.Libn.

WASHINGTON UNIVERSITY - CHEMISTRY LIBRARY
Louderman Hall   Phone: (314) 889-6591
St. Louis, MO 63130   Mary Jane Gwinn, Libn.

WASHINGTON UNIVERSITY - COMPUTER LABORATORIES REFERENCE ROOM
700 S. Euclid Ave.   Phone: (314) 454-3364
St. Louis, MO 63110   Monica Shieh, Res.Libn.

WASHINGTON UNIVERSITY - DENTISTRY LIBRARY
School of Dental Medicine
4559 Scott Ave.   Phone: (314) 454-0385
St. Louis, MO 63110   Kathy Gallagher, Libn.

WASHINGTON UNIVERSITY - DEPARTMENT OF SPECIAL COLLECTIONS
Olin Library   Phone: (314) 889-5495
St. Louis, MO 63130   Holly Hall, Hd.

WASHINGTON UNIVERSITY - DEPARTMENT OF TECHNOLOGY AND HUMAN AFFAIRS - LIBRARY
Box 1106   Phone: (314) 889-5494
St. Louis, MO 63130   David B. Bancroft, Staff Assoc.

WASHINGTON UNIVERSITY - EARTH AND PLANETARY SCIENCES LIBRARY
    Phone: (314) 889-5406
St. Louis, MO 63130   Deborah Hartwig, Libn.

WASHINGTON UNIVERSITY - EAST ASIAN LIBRARY
    Phone: (314) 889-5155
St. Louis, MO 63130   Ernest J. Tsai, Libn.

WASHINGTON UNIVERSITY - EDWARD MALLINCKRODT INSTITUTE OF RADIOLOGY LIBRARY
510 S. Kingshighway Blvd.   Phone: (314) 454-2565
St. Louis, MO 63110   Bettye J. Thomas, Libn./Sec.

WASHINGTON UNIVERSITY - GAYLORD MUSIC LIBRARY
6500 Forsyth   Phone: (314) 889-5560
St. Louis, MO 63130   Elizabeth R. Krause, Music Libn.

WASHINGTON UNIVERSITY - GEORGE WARREN BROWN SCHOOL OF SOCIAL WORK - LIBRARY & LEARNING RESOURCES CENTER
Box 1196   Phone: (314) 889-6633
St. Louis, MO 63130   Michael E. Powell, Dir.

WASHINGTON UNIVERSITY - PFEIFFER PHYSICS LIBRARY
Lindell & Skinker Blvds.   Phone: (314) 889-6215
St. Louis, MO 63130   B.M. Eickhoff, Physics Libn.

WASHINGTON UNIVERSITY - SCHOOL OF LAW - FREUND LAW LIBRARY
Mudd Bldg.
Box 1120   Phone: (314) 889-6459
St. Louis, MO 63130   Bernard D. Reams, Jr., Law Libn.

WASHINGTON UNIVERSITY - SCHOOL OF MEDICINE - DEPARTMENT OF PSYCHIATRY LIBRARY *
4940 Audubon Ave.   Phone: (314) 454-2774
St. Louis, MO 63110   Dr. Samuel B. Guze, Hd. of Dept.

WASHINGTON UNIVERSITY - SCHOOL OF MEDICINE LIBRARY
4580 Scott Ave.   Phone: (314) 454-3711
St. Louis, MO 63110   Dr. Estelle Brodman, Libn. & Prof.

ASSEMBLIES OF GOD GRADUATE SCHOOL - CORDAS C. BURNETT LIBRARY
1445 Boonville Ave.   Phone: (417) 862-2781
Springfield, MO 65802   Larry L. Haight, Libn.

CENTRAL BIBLE COLLEGE - LIBRARY
3000 N. Grant   Phone: (417) 833-2551
Springfield, MO 65802   Gerard J. Flokstra, Jr., Libn.

COX (Lester E.) MEDICAL CENTER - DOCTORS' LIBRARY
1423 N. Jefferson St.   Phone: (417) 836-3238
Springfield, MO 65802   Theresa Wimsatt, Asst.Dir., Med.Rec.

M.F.A. MILLING COMPANY - LIBRARY *
Main Off., Box 757   Phone: (417) 862-0772
Springfield, MO 65801   Michael B. Officer, Nutritionist

MISSOURI STATE COURT OF APPEALS, SOUTHERN DISTRICT - LAW LIBRARY
1018 Woodruff Bldg.   Phone: (417) 862-6314
Springfield, MO 65806   Carole Wingert, Law Libn.

ST. JOHN'S HOSPITAL - MEDICAL LIBRARY
1235 E. Cherokee   Phone: (417) 881-8811
Springfield, MO 65804   Sr. Lillian Clare, Libn.

ST. JOHN'S HOSPITAL - SCHOOL OF NURSING LIBRARY
1930 S. National Ave.   Phone: (417) 885-2104
Springfield, MO 65804   Aurora Sun, Libn.

SOUTHWEST MISSOURI STATE UNIVERSITY - MAP COLLECTION
349 University Library   Phone: (417) 836-5105
Springfield, MO 65802   James A. Coombs, Libn.

SPRINGFIELD ART MUSEUM - ART REFERENCE LIBRARY
1111 E. Brookside Dr.   Phone: (417) 866-2716
Springfield, MO 65807   Alice Brooker, Libn.

SPRINGFIELD-GREENE COUNTY PUBLIC LIBRARIES - EDWARD M. SHEPARD MEMORIAL ROOM
397 E. Central   Phone: (417) 869-4621
Springfield, MO 65801   Robin Rader, Ref.Libn.

MARK TWAIN BIRTHPLACE - RESEARCH LIBRARY
Mark Twain State Park   Phone: (314) 565-3449
Stoutsville, MO 65283   Stanley Fast, Historic Site Adm.

MISSOURI COUNCIL FOR HANDGUN CONTROL - LIBRARY
7207 Pershing Ave.   Phone: (314) 727-7563
University City, MO 63130   Eugene P. Schwartz, Chm.

UNIVERSITY CITY PUBLIC LIBRARY - RECORD COLLECTION
6701 Delmar
University City, MO 63130   Robert L. Miller, Libn.

MORGAN COUNTY HISTORICAL SOCIETY - LIBRARY
120 N. Monroe St.
Versailles, MO 65084   Mrs. Preston Hutchison, Supv.

CENTRAL MISSOURI STATE UNIVERSITY - WARD EDWARDS LIBRARY
    Phone: (816) 429-4141
Warrensburg, MO 64093   Rosalie Schell, Dir., Rd.Serv.

JOHNSON COUNTY HISTORICAL SOCIETY - HERITAGE LIBRARY
135 E. Pine St.   Phone: (816) 747-3381
Warrensburg, MO 64093   Mary Miller Smiser, Libn.

EDEN THEOLOGICAL SEMINARY - LIBRARY
475 E. Lockwood   Phone: (314) 961-3627
Webster Groves, MO 63119   Rev. Warren R. Mehl, Libn.

EVANGELICAL AND REFORMED HISTORICAL SOCIETY - EDEN ARCHIVES
475 E. Lockwood Ave.   Phone: (314) 961-3627
Webster Groves, MO 63119   Prof. Lowell H. Zuck, Libn.

U.S. AIR FORCE BASE - WHITEMAN BASE LIBRARY
    Phone: (816) 687-3089
Whiteman AFB, MO 65305   Byron C. Taylor, Base Libn.

MONTANA

ALTERNATIVE ENERGY RESOURCES ORGANIZATION (AERO) - LIBRARY
424 Stapleton Bldg.   Phone: (406) 259-1958
Billings, MT 59101   Katie Johnson

BILLINGS GAZETTE - NEWS LIBRARY
401 N. Broadway
Box 2507   Phone: (406) 657-1271
Billings, MT 59103   Odelta A. Thomsen, Libn.

BILLINGS PUBLIC SCHOOLS - INSTRUCTIONAL MATERIALS CENTER
504 North 29th St.   Phone: (406) 259-0291
Billings, MT 59101   W. Marshall Jones, Dir.

EASTERN MONTANA COLLEGE - LIBRARY - SPECIAL COLLECTIONS †
1500 N. 30th St.   Phone: (406) 657-2320
Billings, MT 59101   Aaron Hause, Act.Dir.

U.S. BUREAU OF LAND MANAGEMENT - MONTANA STATE OFFICE LIBRARY
222 N. 32nd St.
Box 30157   Phone: (406) 657-6671
Billings, MT 59107   Carolyn M. Nelson, Libn.

MONTANA STATE UNIVERSITY - VETERINARY RESEARCH LABORATORY -
    HUIDEKOPER LIBRARY
                                            Phone: (406) 994-4705
Bozeman, MT 59717   Kathryn Kaya, Libn.

ATLANTIC-RICHFIELD COMPANY - DEPARTMENT OF LAW - LIBRARY
600 Anaconda Bldg.
Box 689   Phone: (406) 723-4311
Butte, MT 59703   Jessica Eyde, Libn.

MONTANA COLLEGE OF MINERAL SCIENCE AND TECHNOLOGY - LIBRARY
W. Park St.   Phone: (406) 496-4281
Butte, MT 59701   Elizabeth Morrissett, Hd.Libn.

NATIONAL CENTER FOR APPROPRIATE TECHNOLOGY - LIBRARY
3040 Continental Dr.
Box 3838   Phone: (406) 723-5474
Butte, MT 59701   Raelen Williard, Libn.

ATLANTIC-RICHFIELD COMPANY - ANACONDA ALUMINUM COMPANY -
    COLUMBIA FALLS REDUCTION DIVISION - LIBRARY
Box 10   Phone: (406) 892-3261
Columbia Falls, MT 59912   Hilda Parry, Libn.

U.S. NATL. PARK SERVICE - CUSTER BATTLEFIELD NATL. MONUMENT -
    LIBRARY
Box 39   Phone: (406) 638-2622
Crow Agency, MT 59022   Neil Mangum, Hist.

WESTERN MONTANA COLLEGE - LUCY CARSON MEMORIAL LIBRARY
710 S. Atlantic   Phone: (406) 683-7541
Dillon, MT 59725   Kenneth A. Cory, Libn.

CARTER COUNTY MUSEUM - LIBRARY
Ekalaka, MT 59324

U.S. VETERANS ADMINISTRATION (MT-Fort Harrison) - CENTER LIBRARY
                                            Phone: (406) 442-6410
Fort Harrison, MT 59636   Maurice C. Knutson, Chf., Lib.Serv.

U.S. NATL. PARK SERVICE - BIGHORN CANYON NATL. RECREATION AREA -
    LIBRARY
Box 458   Phone: (406) 666-2412
Fort Smith, MT 59035   Theo D. Hugs, Park Techn.

UNITED METHODIST CHURCH - YELLOWSTONE ANNUAL CONFERENCE -
    ARCHIVES *
Box 167   Phone: (406) 737-4475
Geraldine, MT 59446   Rev. Ron Lang, Chm.

FRONTIER GATEWAY MUSEUM - LIBRARY
Frontage Rd., Box 1181
Glendive, MT 59330   Louise Cross, Cur.

COLUMBUS HOSPITAL - HEALTH SCIENCES LIBRARY
Box 5013   Phone: (406) 727-3333
Great Falls, MT 59403   Sr. Margaret LaPorte, Dir.

GREAT FALLS CLINIC - MEDICAL LIBRARY †
1220 Central Ave.   Phone: (406) 454-2171
Great Falls, MT 59401   Bethel Bolstad, Libn.

GREAT FALLS GENEALOGY SOCIETY - LIBRARY
Paris Gibson Sq.
1400 First Ave., N.   Phone: (406) 727-8255
Great Falls, MT 59405   Thelma L. Marshall, Libn.

BITTER ROOT VALLEY HISTORICAL SOCIETY - RAVALLI COUNTY MUSEUM
205 Bedford Ave.   Phone: (406) 363-3338
Hamilton, MT 59840   Erma Owings, Dir.

U.S. NATL. INSTITUTES OF HEALTH - NATL. INSTITUTE OF ALLERGY &
    INFECTIOUS DISEASES - ROCKY MOUNTAIN LAB. LIB.
                                            Phone: (406) 363-3211
Hamilton, MT 59840   Liza Serha, Libn.

NORTHERN MONTANA COLLEGE - LIBRARY †
                                            Phone: (406) 265-7821
Havre, MT 59501   Terrence A. Thompson, Dir. of Lib.

CARROLL COLLEGE - LIBRARY
                                            Phone: (406) 442-1295
Helena, MT 59601   Lois A. Fitzpatrick, Dir.

CHURCH OF JESUS CHRIST OF LATTER-DAY SAINTS - HELENA BRANCH
    GENEALOGICAL LIBRARY
1610 E. Sixth Ave.   Phone: (406) 443-1558
Helena, MT 59601   Esther M. Stratton, Br.Libn.

MONTANA HISTORICAL SOCIETY - LIBRARY/ARCHIVES
225 N. Roberts   Phone: (406) 449-2681
Helena, MT 59601

MONTANA STATE DEPARTMENT OF ADMINISTRATION - RESEARCH &
    INFORMATION SYSTEMS DIVISION - RESOURCE CENTER
1301 Lockey
Capitol Sta.   Phone: (406) 449-2896
Helena, MT 59620   Patricia A.B. Roberts, Res.Spec.

MONTANA STATE DEPARTMENT OF COMMERCE - TRAVEL PROMOTION
    BUREAU
                                            Phone: (406) 449-2654
Helena, MT 59620   Norma Tirrell, Chf.

MONTANA STATE DEPARTMENT OF NATURAL RESOURCES &
    CONSERVATION - RESEARCH & INFORMATION CENTER
32 S. Ewing   Phone: (406) 449-3647
Helena, MT 59601   Mildred Sullivan, Res.Spec.

MONTANA STATE LAW LIBRARY †
State Capitol Bldg.   Phone: (406) 449-3660
Helena, MT 59620   Claire Engel, State Law Libn.

KALISPELL REGIONAL HOSPITAL - MEDICAL LIBRARY
310 Sunnyview Ln.   Phone: (406) 755-5111
Kalispell, MT 59901   Susan Long, Libn.

U.S. FOREST SERVICE - FLATHEAD NATL. FOREST LIBRARY *
Box 147   Phone: (406) 755-5401
Kalispell, MT 59901

U.S. AIR FORCE BASE - MALMSTROM BASE LIBRARY
FL 4626   Phone: (406) 731-2748
Malmstrom AFB, MT 59402   Arden G. Hill, Libn.

U.S. VETERANS ADMINISTRATION (MT-Miles City) - MEDICAL CENTER
    LIBRARY
                                            Phone: (406) 232-3060
Miles City, MT 59301   Linda Thomsen, Lib.Techn.

ST. PATRICK HOSPITAL - LIBRARY
500 W. Broadway
Box 4587   Phone: (406) 543-7271
Missoula, MT 59806   Jody Anderson, Libn.

UNIVERSITY OF MONTANA - CAREER PLANNING RESOURCE CENTER †
The Lodge, Rm. 148   Phone: (406) 243-4711
Missoula, MT 59812   Gretchen Castle, Career Counselor

UNIVERSITY OF MONTANA - LAW SCHOOL LIBRARY †
                                            Phone: (406) 243-5603
Missoula, MT 59812   Maurice M. Michel, Law Libn.

UNIVERSITY OF MONTANA - MAUREEN & MIKE MANSFIELD LIBRARY -
    ARCHIVES †
                                            Phone: (406) 243-6800
Missoula, MT 59812   Dale L. Johnson, Archv.

GEOGRAPHIC

UNIVERSITY OF MONTANA - SCHOOL OF FORESTRY - COOPERATIVE FOREST AND CONSERVATION COLLECTION
Science Division, Mansfield Library
Phone: (406) 243-6411
Missoula, MT 59812
Robert Schipf, Sci.Libn.

WESTERN MONTANA CLINIC - LIBRARY
501 W. Broadway
Phone: (406) 721-5600
Missoula, MT 59807
Patricia A. Manlove, Libn.

WESTERN MONTANA SCIENTISTS' COMMITTEE FOR PUBLIC INFORMATION - MONTANA ENVIRONMENTAL LIBRARY
Univ. of Montana
758 Eddy St.
Phone: (406) 243-2282
Missoula, MT 59812
William D. Tomlinson, Dir.

YELLOWSTONE-BIGHORN RESEARCH ASSN. - LIBRARY †
Red Lodge, MT 59068

U.S. NATL. PARK SERVICE - GLACIER NATL. PARK - GEORGE C. RUHLE LIBRARY
Phone: (406) 888-5441
West Glacier, MT 59936
Beth Lucas, Pk.Libn.

U.S. NATL. PARK SERVICE - BIG HOLE NATL. BATTLEFIELD - LIBRARY
Box 237
Phone: (406) 689-2530
Wisdom, MT 59761
Alfred W. Schulmeyer, Supt.

NEBRASKA

U.S. NATL. PARK SERVICE - HOMESTEAD NATL. MONUMENT - RESEARCH LIBRARY
R.R. 3
Phone: (402) 223-3514
Beatrice, NE 68310
Vincent J. Halvorson, Supt.

FONTENELLE FOREST NATURE CENTER - REFERENCE LIBRARY
1111 Bellevue Blvd., N.
Phone: (402) 731-3140
Bellevue, NE 68005
Elaine Dertien, Libn.

DANA COLLEGE - C.A. DANA-LIFE LIBRARY
College Dr.
Phone: (402) 426-4101
Blair, NE 68008
Ronald D. Johnson, Lib.Dir.

CENTER FOR THE STUDY OF YOUTH DEVELOPMENT, BOYS TOWN - LIBRARY SERVICES DIVISION
Father Flanagan's Boys' Home
Phone: (402) 498-1420
Boys Town, NE 68010
Rebecca Danforth Dixon, Dir.

CUSTER COUNTY HISTORICAL SOCIETY - LIBRARY
225 S. 10th Ave.
Phone: (308) 872-2203
Broken Bow, NE 68822
David K. Wilson, Cur.

MERRICK COUNTY HISTORICAL MUSEUM - LIBRARY
Central City, NE 68826
T.C. Reeves, Pres.

NEBRASKA STATE HISTORICAL SOCIETY - FORT ROBINSON MUSEUM - RESEARCH LIBRARY
Box 304
Phone: (308) 665-2852
Crawford, NE 69339
Vance E. Nelson, Cur.

J-B PUBLISHING COMPANY - RESEARCH LIBRARY
430 Ivy Ave.
Phone: (402) 826-3356
Crete, NE 68333
William F. Rapp, Libn.

IOWA BEEF PROCESSORS, INC. - CORPORATE LIBRARY
Box 515
Phone: (402) 494-2061
Dakota City, NE 68731
Mary Ellen Hulse, Rec.Adm.

WASHINGTON COUNTY HISTORICAL ASSOCIATION - MUSEUM LIBRARY
14th & Monroe Sts.
Phone: (402) 468-5740
Fort Calhoun, NE 68023
Genevieve Slader, Libn./Cur.

DODGE COUNTY HISTORICAL SOCIETY - LOUIS E. MAY MUSEUM
1643 N. Nye
Phone: (402) 721-4515
Fremont, NE 68025
Loell R. Jorgensen, Musm.Dir.

EASTERN NEBRASKA GENEALOGICAL SOCIETY - LIBRARY
Box 541
Phone: (402) 721-9553
Fremont, NE 68025
Claire Mares, Ed.

U.S. NATL. PARK SERVICE - SCOTTS BLUFF NATL. MONUMENT - OREGON TRAIL MUSEUM ASSOCIATION - LIBRARY
Box 427
Phone: (308) 436-4340
Gerling, NE 69341
Russell Osborn, Chf. Ranger

HALL COUNTY MUSEUM BOARD - STUHR MUSEUM - LIBRARY AND ARCHIVES
3133 W. Highway 34
Phone: (308) 384-1380
Grand Island, NE 68801
Valerie Christensen, Res.Hist.

U.S. VETERANS ADMINISTRATION (NE-Grand Island) - HOSPITAL LIBRARY
2201 N. Broadwell St.
Phone: (308) 382-3660
Grand Island, NE 68801
H. Ronald Fox, Chf., Lib.Serv.

ADAMS COUNTY HISTORICAL SOCIETY - ARCHIVES
1330 N. Burlington Ave.
Box 102
Phone: (402) 463-5838
Hastings, NE 68901

FIRST PRESBYTERIAN CHURCH - LIBRARY
7th at Lincoln Ave.
Phone: (402) 462-5147
Hastings, NE 68901
Mrs. Harrold Shiffler, Libn.

HASTINGS REGIONAL CENTER - MEDICAL LIBRARY
Phone: (402) 463-2461
Hastings, NE 68901
Ruth Swingle, Libn.

KEARNEY STATE COLLEGE - CALVIN T. RYAN LIBRARY
905 W. 25th
Phone: (308) 236-4218
Kearney, NE 68847
John Mayeski, Dir. of Lib.

AMERICAN OLD TIME FIDDLERS ASSOCIATION - ARCHIVES †
6141 Morrill Ave.
Phone: (402) 466-5519
Lincoln, NE 68507
DeLores DeRyke, Pres.

CHRISTIAN RECORD BRAILLE FOUNDATION - CHRISTIAN RECORD FREE LENDING LIBRARY
4444 S. 52nd St.
Phone: (402) 488-0981
Lincoln, NE 68506
Wendell Carpenter, Coord., Rd.Serv.

LINCOLN GENERAL HOSPITAL - MEDICAL LIBRARY
2300 S. 16th St.
Phone: (402) 473-5332
Lincoln, NE 68502
Lucille Rosenberg, Libn.

LINCOLN JOURNAL-STAR - LIBRARY
926 P St.
Box 81709
Phone: (402) 473-7293
Lincoln, NE 68501
Patricia R. Loos, Dir.

NATIONAL GASOHOL COMMISSION - LIBRARY
521 S. 14th St., Suite 5
Phone: (402) 475-8044
Lincoln, NE 68508
Mitzi Earl, Info.Dir.

NEBRASKA STATE DEPARTMENT OF PUBLIC WELFARE - LIBRARY
301 Centennial Mall S., 5th Fl.
Box 95026
Phone: (402) 471-3121
Lincoln, NE 68509
Karen Christensen, Sec./Libn.

NEBRASKA STATE GAME AND PARKS COMMISSION - LIBRARY
2200 N. 33rd St.
Box 30370
Phone: (402) 464-0641
Lincoln, NE 68503
Carol A. Krueger, Agency Libn.

NEBRASKA STATE HISTORICAL SOCIETY - ARCHIVES
1500 R St.
Phone: (402) 471-3270
Lincoln, NE 68508
James E. Potter, State Archv.

NEBRASKA STATE HISTORICAL SOCIETY - LIBRARY
1500 R St.
Phone: (402) 471-3270
Lincoln, NE 68508
Ann Reinert, Libn.

NEBRASKA STATE LIBRARY
3rd. Floor S., Statehouse
Phone: (402) 432-2922
Lincoln, NE 68509
Reta Johnson, Dp.Libn.

NEBRASKA STATE LIBRARY COMMISSION
1420 P St.   Phone: (402) 471-2045
Lincoln, NE 68508   John Kopischke, Dir.

ST. ELIZABETH COMMUNITY HEALTH CENTER - MEDICAL LIBRARY
555 South 70th St.   Phone: (402) 488-7181
Lincoln, NE 68510   Willa Hassell, Libn.

UNITED METHODIST CHURCH - NEBRASKA CONFERENCE - HISTORICAL
  CENTER
Nebraska Wesleyan University
Lucas Bldg., 50th & St. Paul Sts.   Phone: (402) 464-2371
Lincoln, NE 68504   C. Edwin Murphy, Cur.

U.S. NATL. PARK SERVICE - MIDWEST ARCHEOLOGICAL CENTER -
  RESEARCH LIBRARY
Federal Bldg., Rm. 474
100 Centennial Mall N.   Phone: (402) 471-5392
Lincoln, NE 68508   Lynn M. Mitchell, Lib.Techn.

U.S. VETERANS ADMINISTRATION (NE-Lincoln) - MEDICAL CENTER
  LIBRARY
600 S. 70th St.   Phone: (402) 489-3802
Lincoln, NE 68510   Jean Landfield, Chf.Libn.

UNIVERSITY OF NEBRASKA, LINCOLN - ARCHITECTURE LIBRARY
104 Architecture Hall   Phone: (402) 472-1208
Lincoln, NE 68588   Kathleen A. Johnson

UNIVERSITY OF NEBRASKA, LINCOLN - C.Y. THOMPSON LIBRARY
East Campus   Phone: (402) 472-2802
Lincoln, NE 68583   Wayne R. Collings, Professor

UNIVERSITY OF NEBRASKA, LINCOLN - CHEMISTRY LIBRARY
Hamilton Hall 427   Phone: (402) 472-2739
Lincoln, NE 68588   Richard E. Voeltz, Assoc. Professor

UNIVERSITY OF NEBRASKA, LINCOLN - DENTISTRY LIBRARY
College of Dentistry, East Campus, Rm. 8   Phone: (402) 472-1323
Lincoln, NE 68583   Richard E. Voeltz, Assoc. Professor

UNIVERSITY OF NEBRASKA, LINCOLN - ENGINEERING LIBRARY
Nebraska Hall, 2nd Fl. W.   Phone: (402) 472-3411
Lincoln, NE 68588   Alan V. Gould, Asst. Professor

UNIVERSITY OF NEBRASKA, LINCOLN - GEOLOGY LIBRARY
Morrill Hall, Rm. 303   Phone: (402) 472-2653
Lincoln, NE 68588   Agnes Adams, Asst. Professor

UNIVERSITY OF NEBRASKA, LINCOLN - INSTRUCTIONAL MEDIA CENTER
Division of Continuing Studies   Phone: (402) 472-1910
Lincoln, NE 68588   Randy Bretz, Dir.

UNIVERSITY OF NEBRASKA, LINCOLN - LAW LIBRARY
College of Law Bldg., East Campus   Phone: (402) 472-3547
Lincoln, NE 68583   John D. Nelson, Law Libn.

UNIVERSITY OF NEBRASKA, LINCOLN - LIFE SCIENCES LIBRARY
Manter Hall 402   Phone: (402) 472-2756
Lincoln, NE 68588   Richard E. Voeltz, Assoc. Professor

UNIVERSITY OF NEBRASKA, LINCOLN - MATHEMATICS LIBRARY
Oldfather Hall, Rm. 807   Phone: (402) 472-3731
Lincoln, NE 68588   Agnes Adams, Asst. Professor

UNIVERSITY OF NEBRASKA, LINCOLN - PHYSICS LIBRARY
Behlen Laboratory, Rm. 263   Phone: (402) 472-1209
Lincoln, NE 68588   Agnes Adams, Asst. Professor

UNIVERSITY OF NEBRASKA, LINCOLN - UNIVERSITY ARCHIVES AND
  SPECIAL COLLECTIONS
303 Love Library   Phone: (402) 472-2531
Lincoln, NE 68588   Joseph G. Svoboda, Archv.

WOODMEN ACCIDENT & LIFE COMPANY - LIBRARY
1526 K St.
Box 82288   Phone: (402) 476-6500
Lincoln, NE 68501   Virgene K. Sloan, Libn.

NEWMAN GROVE CREAMERY COMPANY - LIBRARY *
Box 340
Newman Grove, NE 68758   Albert Henderson, Libn.

NORFOLK REGIONAL CENTER AND NORTHEAST MENTAL HEALTH CLINIC -
  STAFF LIBRARY
Box 1209   Phone: (402) 371-4343
Norfolk, NE 68701   Muriel V. Hillson, Libn.

U.S. AIR FORCE BASE - OFFUTT BASE LIBRARY
FL 4600   Phone: (402) 294-2533
Offutt AFB, NE 68113   Margaret A. Byrne, Libn.

U.S. AIR FORCE HOSPITAL - EHRLING BERGQUIST REGIONAL HOSPITAL -
  MEDICAL LIBRARY
                                                Phone: (402) 294-7301
Offutt AFB, NE 68113   Bobby Chapman, Libn.

U.S. AIR FORCE - STRATEGIC AIR COMMAND - LIBRARY SERVICES SAC
  (DPSO)
Offutt AFB, NE 68113   Loutrell E. Cavin

ARCHBISHOP BERGAN MERCY HOSPITAL - MEDICAL STAFF LIBRARY
7500 Mercy Rd.   Phone: (402) 398-6092
Omaha, NE 68124   Ken Oyer, Libn.

CREIGHTON UNIVERSITY - ALUMNI MEMORIAL LIBRARY
2500 California St.   Phone: (402) 449-2705
Omaha, NE 68178   Ray B. Means, Dir.

CREIGHTON UNIVERSITY - HEALTH SCIENCES LIBRARY
2500 California St.   Phone: (402) 449-2908
Omaha, NE 68178   Marjorie Wannarka, Dir.

CREIGHTON UNIVERSITY - LAW SCHOOL - KLUTZNICK LIBRARY
2500 California St.   Phone: (402) 449-2875
Omaha, NE 68178   Robert Q. Kelly, Dir.

DOUGLAS COUNTY LAW LIBRARY
Hall of Justice
17th & Farnam   Phone: (402) 444-7174
Omaha, NE 68183   Carol Gendler, Libn.

EPPLEY INSTITUTE FOR RESEARCH IN CANCER & ALLIED DISEASES -
  LIBRARY
University Of Nebraska Medical Ctr.
42nd & Dewey   Phone: (402) 541-7669
Omaha, NE 68105

GRACE COLLEGE OF THE BIBLE - LIBRARY
1515 S. Tenth St.   Phone: (402) 342-3377
Omaha, NE 68108   Norma McWilliams, Hd.Libn.

IMMANUEL MEDICAL CENTER - PROFESSIONAL LIBRARY
6901 N. 72nd St.   Phone: (402) 572-2345
Omaha, NE 68122   Dorothy B. Willis, Libn.

INTERNORTH - LAW LIBRARY
2223 Dodge St.
Omaha, NE 68102

INTERNORTH - LIBRARY
2223 Dodge St.   Phone: (402) 633-4298
Omaha, NE 68102   Marvin E. Lauver, Hd.Libn.

JEWISH FEDERATION OF OMAHA - LIBRARY
333 S. 132nd St.   Phone: (402) 334-8200
Omaha, NE 68154   Edythe Wolf, Dir.

JOSLYN ART MUSEUM - ART REFERENCE LIBRARY
2200 Dodge   Phone: (402) 342-3300
Omaha, NE 68102   Ann E. Birney, Libn.

KUTAK, ROCK & HUIE - LAW LIBRARY
1650 Farnam St.   Phone: (402) 346-6000
Omaha, NE 68102   Avis B. Forsman, Libn.

GEOGRAPHIC

GEOGRAPHIC

MUTUAL OF OMAHA/UNITED OF OMAHA - LIBRARY *
Box 1298
Omaha, NE 68101
Phone: (402) 978-2002
Marcella Chase, Libn.

NEBRASKA METHODIST HOSPITAL - LIBRARY
8303 Dodge St.
Omaha, NE 68114
Phone: (402) 390-4611
Angela Arner, Libn.

NEBRASKA PSYCHIATRIC INSTITUTE - LIBRARY †
602 S. 45th St.
Omaha, NE 68106
Phone: (402) 559-5000
Pauline B. Allen, Libn.

NEBRASKA TESTING LABORATORIES - LIBRARY
Elmwood Park Sta., Box 6075
Omaha, NE 68117
Phone: (402) 331-4453
Dan McCarthy, Pres.

OMAHA-COUNCIL BLUFFS METROPOLITAN AREA PLANNING AGENCY
(MAPA) - LIBRARY
7000 W. Center Rd., Suite 200
Omaha, NE 68106
Phone: (402) 444-6866
Dagnia Prieditis, Libn.

OMAHA PUBLIC LIBRARY - BUSINESS, SCIENCE & TECHNOLOGY
DEPARTMENT
215 S. 15th St.
Omaha, NE 68102
Phone: (402) 444-4817
Bernice Johns, Hd.

OMAHA WORLD-HERALD - LIBRARY
World Herald Square
Omaha, NE 68102
Bette Shrader, Libn.

UNION PACIFIC RAILROAD COMPANY - LIBRARY
1416 Dodge St.
Omaha, NE 68179
Phone: (402) 271-4785
A.L. Dermyer, Hd.Libn.

U.S. ARMY - CORPS OF ENGINEERS - OMAHA DISTRICT - LIBRARY
215 N. 17th St.
6014 U.S. Post Office & Courthouse
Omaha, NE 68102
Phone: (402) 221-3230
Valetta Sharp, Libn.

U.S. NATL. PARK SERVICE - MIDWEST REGIONAL OFFICE LIBRARY *
1709 Jackson St.
Omaha, NE 68102
Phone: (402) 221-3471
Emily Bolton, Pub.Info.Asst.

U.S. VETERANS ADMINISTRATION (NE-Omaha) - HOSPITAL LIBRARY
4101 Woolworth Ave.
Omaha, NE 68105
Phone: (402) 346-8800
Lois J. Inskeep, Chf., Lib.Serv.

UNIVERSITY OF NEBRASKA MEDICAL CENTER - MC GOOGAN LIBRARY OF
MEDICINE
42nd & Dewey Ave.
Omaha, NE 68105
Phone: (402) 559-4006
Robert M. Braude, Dir.

NEBRASKA STATE HISTORICAL SOCIETY - WILLA CATHER HISTORICAL
CENTER - ARCHIVES
Red Cloud, NE 68970
Phone: (402) 746-3285
Ann E. Billesbach, Cur.

SHERIDAN COUNTY HISTORICAL SOCIETY, INC. - AGNES & CLARENCE
BENSCHOTER MEMORIAL LIBRARY
Box 274
Rushville, NE 69360
Phone: (308) 327-2961
Robert Buchan, Cur.

CONCORDIA TEACHERS COLLEGE - LINK LIBRARY
800 N. Columbia Ave.
Seward, NE 68434
Phone: (402) 643-3651
Vivian A. Peterson, Dir., Lib.Serv.

WAYNE STATE COLLEGE - U.S. CONN LIBRARY
200 E. 10
Wayne, NE 68787
Phone: (402) 375-2200
Dr. Jack Middendorf, Dir.

NEVADA

U.S. BUREAU OF MINES - BOULDER CITY RESEARCH LIBRARY
500 Date St.
Boulder City, NV 89005
Phone: (702) 293-1033

U.S. BUREAU OF RECLAMATION - TECHNICAL LIBRARY †
1404 Colorado St.
Box 427
Boulder City, NV 89005
Phone: (702) 293-8570
Frances Phyler, Lib.Techn.

U.S. NATL. PARK SERVICE - LAKE MEAD NATL. RECREATION AREA -
LIBRARY
601 Nevada Hwy.
Boulder City, NV 89005
Phone: (702) 293-4041
David H. Huntzinger, Chf. Interpreter

FORESTA INSTITUTE FOR OCEAN AND MOUNTAIN STUDIES -
ENVIRONMENTAL STUDIES CENTER †
6205 Franktown Rd.
Carson City, NV 89701
Phone: (702) 882-6361
Shannon Porter, Libn.

NEVADA STATE DEPARTMENT OF TRANSPORTATION - MAP INFORMATION
LIBRARY
1263 S. Stewart St.
Carson City, NV 89712
Phone: (702) 885-5400
Jack Slansky, Chf. Cartographer

NEVADA STATE LIBRARY
Capitol Complex
Carson City, NV 89710
Phone: (702) 885-5130
Joseph J. Anderson, State Libn.

NEVADA STATE LIBRARY - DIVISION OF STATE, COUNTY AND MUNICIPAL
ARCHIVES
101 S. Fall St.
Carson City, NV 89710
Phone: (702) 885-5210
Joseph J. Anderson, State Libn.

NEVADA STATE MUSEUM
Capitol Complex
600 N. Carson St.
Carson City, NV 89710
Phone: (702) 885-4810
Scott Miller, Musm.Dir.

NEVADA STATE SUPREME COURT - LIBRARY
Supreme Court Bldg., Capitol Complex
Carson City, NV 89710
Phone: (702) 885-5140
Catherine Finnegan, Law Libn.

ELKO MEDICAL CLINIC - LIBRARY
762 14th St.
Elko, NV 89801
Phone: (702) 738-3111

NORTHEASTERN NEVADA MUSEUM - LIBRARY
1515 Idaho St.
Box 503
Elko, NV 89801
Phone: (702) 738-3418
Howard Hickson, Musm.Dir.

TITANIUM METALS CORPORATION OF AMERICA - HENDERSON TECHNICAL
LIBRARY
Box 2128
Henderson, NV 89015
Phone: (702) 564-2544
Sally Canada, Libn.

CHURCH OF JESUS CHRIST OF LATTER-DAY SAINTS - LAS VEGAS BRANCH
GENEALOGICAL LIBRARY
509 S. Ninth St.
Las Vegas, NV 89101
Phone: (701) 382-9695
Pauleen C. Foutz, Hd.Libn.

CLARK COUNTY DISTRICT HEALTH DEPARTMENT - LIBRARY
625 Shadow Ln.
Las Vegas, NV 89106
Phone: (702) 385-1291
Janet Dolan, Health Info.Spec.

CLARK COUNTY LAW LIBRARY
County Courthouse
200 E. Carson Ave.
Las Vegas, NV 89101
Phone: (702) 386-4011
Katherine Slocum Henderson, Lib.Dir.

EG&G, INC. - TECHNICAL LIBRARY
680 E. Sunset Rd.
Box 1912
Las Vegas, NV 89101
Phone: (702) 739-0660
Anna Lee Kaighn, Libn.

ENVIRONMENTAL PROTECTION AGENCY - ENVIRONMENTAL MONITORING
SYSTEMS LABORATORY - LIBRARY
Box 15027
Las Vegas, NV 89114
Phone: (702) 798-2648

FUTURE AVIATION PROFESSIONALS OF AMERICA (FAPA) - INFORMATION
CENTER
3000B S. Highland Dr.
Las Vegas, NV 89109
Phone: (702) 737-0897
W. Louis Smith, Pres.

LAS VEGAS REVIEW-JOURNAL - LIBRARY
Box 70
Las Vegas, NV 89125
Phone: (702) 383-0269
Glenda Harris, Libn.

REYNOLDS ELECTRICAL AND ENGINEERING COMPANY, INC. - TECHNICAL
LIBRARY
Box 14400
Las Vegas, NV 89114
Phone: (702) 986-0796
Mona C. Lupo, Tech.Libn.

SOUTHERN NEVADA MEMORIAL HOSPITAL - MEDICAL LIBRARY
2040 W. Charleston Blvd.
Las Vegas, NV 89102
Phone: (702) 383-2368
Jean O'Neill, Dir., Lib.Serv.

SUNRISE HOSPITAL MEDICAL CENTER - LIBRARY
3186 Maryland Pkwy.
Las Vegas, NV 89109
Phone: (702) 731-8210
Florence I. Jakus, Ed.D., Med.Libn.

U.S. AIR FORCE BASE - NELLIS BASE LIBRARY
Nellis AFB
Las Vegas, NV 89191
Phone: (702) 643-2280
Dorothy Hart, Base Libn.

U.S. DEPT. OF ENERGY - NEVADA OPERATIONS OFFICE - TECHNICAL
LIBRARY
Box 14100
Las Vegas, NV 89114
Phone: (702) 734-3371
Cynthia Ortiz, Libn.

UNIVERSITY OF NEVADA, LAS VEGAS - GAMING RESEARCH CENTER
4505 Maryland Pkwy.
Las Vegas, NV 89154
Phone: (702) 739-3252
Susan Anderl, Spec.Coll.Libn.

CLARK COUNTY COMMUNITY COLLEGE - LEARNING RESOURCES CENTER
3200 East Cheyenne Ave.
North Las Vegas, NV 89030
Phone: (702) 643-6060
Frank Hall Gafford, Jr., Dir.

HARRAH'S AUTOMOTIVE LIBRARY
Box 10
Reno, NV 89504
Phone: (702) 786-3232
Mike Moore, Parts & Res.Supv.

NATIONAL JUDICIAL COLLEGE - LAW LIBRARY
University of Nevada
Reno, NV 89557
Phone: (702) 784-6747
Kathleen Dion, Libn.

NEVADA HISTORICAL SOCIETY - LIBRARY †
1650 N. Virginia St.
Reno, NV 89503
Phone: (702) 784-6397
Peter L. Bandurraga, Dir.

NEVADA MENTAL HEALTH INSTITUTE - MEDICAL LIBRARY
Box 2460
Reno, NV 89505
Phone: (702) 322-6961
Alice L. Lohse, Libn.

NORTH AMERICAN RADIO ARCHIVES (NARA) - LENDING LIBRARY
Box 11962
Reno, NV 89510
S. Bland, Tape Libn.

ST. MARY'S HOSPITAL - MAX C. FLEISCHMANN MEDICAL LIBRARY
235 W. Sixth St.
Reno, NV 89520
Phone: (702) 789-3108
Kathleen L. Pratt, Info.Dir.

U.S. BUREAU OF MINES - RENO METALLURGY RESEARCH CENTER -
LIBRARY *
1605 Evans Ave.
Reno, NV 89520
Phone: (702) 784-5348
Janice Behers, Libn.

U.S. DEPT. OF COMMERCE - INTERNATIONAL TRADE ADMINISTRATION -
RENO DISTRICT OFFICE LIBRARY *
777 W. 2nd St., Rm. 120
Reno, NV 89503
Phone: (702) 784-5203
Joseph J. Jeremy, Dir.

UNIVERSITY OF NEVADA, RENO - DESERT RESEARCH INSTITUTE -
LIBRARY
Sage Bldg., Stead Campus
Reno, NV 89506
Phone: (702) 972-1676
Roberta K. Orcutt, D.R.I. Libn.

UNIVERSITY OF NEVADA, RENO - ENGINEERING LIBRARY
Scrugham Engineering Bldg., Rm. 231
Reno, NV 89557
Phone: (702) 784-6945
Mary Ansari, Engr.Libn.

UNIVERSITY OF NEVADA, RENO - LIFE AND HEALTH SCIENCES LIBRARY
Fleischmann College of Agriculture Bldg.
Reno, NV 89557
Phone: (702) 784-6616
Anne Amaral, Libn.

UNIVERSITY OF NEVADA, RENO - MACKAY SCHOOL OF MINES LIBRARY
Reno, NV 89557
Phone: (702) 784-6596
Linda P. Newman, Act. Mines Libn.

UNIVERSITY OF NEVADA, RENO - PHYSICAL SCIENCES LIBRARY
New Chemistry Bldg., Rm. 316
Reno, NV 89557
Phone: (702) 784-6716
Roberta K. Orcutt, Physical Sci.Libn.

UNIVERSITY OF NEVADA, RENO - RESEARCH AND EDUCATIONAL
PLANNING CENTER *
New Education Bldg., Rm. 201
Reno, NV 89557
Phone: (702) 784-4921
Len L. Trout, Dir.

UNIVERSITY OF NEVADA, RENO - SAVITT MEDICAL LIBRARY
Anderson Medical Sciences Bldg.
Reno, NV 89557
Phone: (702) 784-4625
Joan S. Zenan, Libn.

UNIVERSITY OF NEVADA, RENO - SPECIAL COLLECTIONS DEPARTMENT/
UNIVERSITY ARCHIVES
University Library
Reno, NV 89557
Phone: (702) 784-6538

WASHOE COUNTY LAW LIBRARY
Court House
Box 11130
Reno, NV 89520
Phone: (702) 785-4188
Mary Anne Royle, Law Lib.Dir.

WASHOE MEDICAL CENTER - MEDICAL LIBRARY
77 Pringle Way
Reno, NV 89520
Phone: (702) 785-5693
Pearl A. Atcheson, Dir., Med.Lib.

UNIVERSITY OF NEVADA, RENO - DESERT RESEARCH INSTITUTE - WATER
RESOURCES COLLECTION
7010 El Rancho Dr.
Sparks, NV 89431
Phone: (702) 673-7354
Roberta K. Orcutt, D.R.I. Libn.

NYE COUNTY LAW LIBRARY
Court House, Box 1271
Tonopah, NV 89049
Phone: (702) 482-6666

NEW HAMPSHIRE

ANDROSCOGGIN VALLEY HOSPITAL - MEDICAL LIBRARY
Page Hill Rd.
Berlin, NH 03570
Phone: (603) 752-2200
Florence Guitard, Libn.

NEW HAMPSHIRE VOCATIONAL-TECHNICAL COLLEGE - LIBRARY
Hanover St. Extension
Claremont, NH 03743
Phone: (603) 542-7744
Phil Prever, Libn.

NUMISMATICS INTERNATIONAL - LIBRARY
30 Pleasant St.
Colebrook, NH 03576
Granvyl Hulse, Libn.

NEW HAMPSHIRE ANTIQUARIAN SOCIETY - LIBRARY *
Route 1 (Main St. Hopkinton)
Concord, NH 03301
Rachael Johnson, Cur.

NEW HAMPSHIRE GOVERNOR'S COUNCIL ON ENERGY - ENERGY
INFORMATION CENTER *
2 1/2 Beacon St.
Concord, NH 03301
Phone: (603) 271-2711
Carol Waters, Dir. of Educ.

NEW HAMPSHIRE HISTORICAL SOCIETY - LIBRARY
30 Park St.
Concord, NH 03301
Phone: (603) 225-3381
John F. Page, Dir.

NEW HAMPSHIRE HOSPITAL - PROFESSIONAL LIBRARY
105 Pleasant St.
Concord, NH 03301
Phone: (603) 224-6531
David B. Washburn, Prof. Staff Libn.

GEOGRAPHIC

NEW HAMPSHIRE HOSPITAL - SCHOOL OF NURSING REFERENCE LIBRARY
105 Pleasant St.
Concord, NH 03301
Phone: (603) 224-6531
Kathleen B. Bingham, Libn.

NEW HAMPSHIRE MUNICIPAL ASSOCIATION - LIBRARY
Box 617
Concord, NH 03301
Phone: (603) 224-7447
John B. Andrews, Exec.Dir.

NEW HAMPSHIRE PUBLIC UTILITIES COMMISSION - LIBRARY
8010 Suncook Rd.
Concord, NH 03301
Phone: (603) 271-2452
Pamila J. Bartlett, Lib.Asst.

NEW HAMPSHIRE STATE DEPARTMENT OF EDUCATION - EDUCATIONAL INFORMATION OFFICE AND LIBRARY
State House Annex, Rm. 410P
Concord, NH 03301
Phone: (603) 271-2778
Bruce G. Ryan, Asst.Chf.

NEW HAMPSHIRE STATE DEPARTMENT OF HEALTH & WELFARE - OFFICE OF ALCOHOL & DRUG ABUSE PREVENTION - LIBRARY
Health & Welfare Bldg.
Hazen Dr.
Concord, NH 03301
Phone: (603) 271-3531
Barry Rhodes, Dp.Dir.

NEW HAMPSHIRE STATE DEPARTMENT OF PUBLIC WORKS AND HIGHWAYS - LIBRARY
State Office Bldg.
85 Loudon Rd.
Concord, NH 03301
Phone: (603) 271-2515
William L. Rollins, Info.Rep.

NEW HAMPSHIRE STATE DEPARTMENT OF STATE - DIVISION OF RECORDS MANAGEMENT & ARCHIVES
71 S. Fruit St.
Concord, NH 03301
Phone: (603) 271-2236
Frank C. Mevers, Archv./Dir.

NEW HAMPSHIRE STATE FISH AND GAME DEPARTMENT - MANAGEMENT AND RESEARCH DIVISION - LIBRARY *
Concord, NH 03301
Phone: (603) 271-2462

NEW HAMPSHIRE STATE LIBRARY
20 Park St.
Concord, NH 03301
Phone: (603) 271-2394
Shirley G. Adamovich, Act. State Libn.

NEW HAMPSHIRE STATE LIBRARY - DIVISION OF LAW AND LEGISLATIVE REFERENCE SERVICE
Supreme Court Bldg.
Loudon Rd.
Concord, NH 03301
Phone: (603) 271-3777
Constance T. Rinden, Law Libn.

NEW HAMPSHIRE STATE WATER SUPPLY AND POLLUTION CONTROL COMMISSION - LIBRARY
Health and Welfare Bldg., Hazen Dr.
Box 95
Concord, NH 03301
Phone: (603) 271-3503
Terrence P. Frost

PATENT, TRADEMARK AND COPYRIGHT RESEARCH FOUNDATION - LIBRARY *
Franklin Pierce Law Ctr.
Concord, NH 03301
Phone: (603) 228-1541

UNIVERSITY OF NEW HAMPSHIRE - BIOLOGICAL SCIENCES LIBRARY
Kendall Hall
Durham, NH 03824
Phone: (603) 862-1018
Lloyd H. Heidgerd, Br.Libn.

UNIVERSITY OF NEW HAMPSHIRE - CHEMISTRY LIBRARY
Parsons Hall
Durham, NH 03824
Phone: (603) 862-1083
Edward Dauphinais, Libn.

UNIVERSITY OF NEW HAMPSHIRE - DAVID G. CLARK MEMORIAL PHYSICS LIBRARY
DeMeritt Hall
Durham, NH 03824
Phone: (603) 862-2348
Edward Dauphinais, Sci.Br.Libn.

UNIVERSITY OF NEW HAMPSHIRE - DEPARTMENT OF MEDIA SERVICES - FILM LIBRARY
Dimond Library
Durham, NH 03824
Phone: (603) 862-2240
John D. Bardwell, Dir.

UNIVERSITY OF NEW HAMPSHIRE - ENGINEERING-MATH LIBRARY
Kingsbury Hall
Durham, NH 03824
Phone: (603) 862-1196
Edward J. Dauphinais, Libn.

UNIVERSITY OF NEW HAMPSHIRE - NEW HAMPSHIRE WATER RESOURCE RESEARCH CENTER - RESOURCE CENTER
108 Pettee Hall
Durham, NH 03824
Phone: (603) 862-2144

UNIVERSITY OF NEW HAMPSHIRE - SPECIAL COLLECTIONS
Dimond Library
Durham, NH 03824
Phone: (603) 862-2714
Barbara A. White, Spec.Coll.Libn.

MOUNT WASHINGTON OBSERVATORY - LIBRARY
Gorham, NH 03581
Phone: (603) 466-3388
Guy Gosselin, Dir.

MEETING HOUSE GREEN MEMORIAL AND HISTORICAL ASSOCIATION, INC. - TUCK MEMORIAL MUSEUM - LIBRARY
Meeting House Green
40 Park Ave.
Hampton, NH 03842
John M. Holman, Cur.

CREARE, INC. - LIBRARY
Box 71
Hanover, NH 03755
Phone: (603) 643-3800
Margaret Ackerson, Hd., Tech.Info.Serv.

DARTMOUTH COLLEGE - DANA BIOMEDICAL LIBRARY
Medical School
Hanover, NH 03755
Phone: (603) 646-2858
Shirley J. Grainger, Libn.

DARTMOUTH COLLEGE - FELDBERG LIBRARY
Hanover, NH 03755
Phone: (603) 646-2191
Margaret M. Link, Engr. & Bus.Libn.

DARTMOUTH COLLEGE - KRESGE PHYSICAL SCIENCES LIBRARY
Hanover, NH 03755
Phone: (603) 646-3564
Monique C. Cleland, Libn.

DARTMOUTH COLLEGE - MAP SECTION
Baker Library
Hanover, NH 03755
Phone: (603) 646-2579
Cheryl T. Naslund, Spec. Subject Asst.

DARTMOUTH COLLEGE - PADDOCK MUSIC LIBRARY
Hanover, NH 03755
Phone: (603) 646-3234
Patricia B. Fisken, Spec.Subj.Asst.

DARTMOUTH COLLEGE - SANBORN ENGLISH HOUSE LIBRARY
Hanover, NH 03755
Phone: (603) 646-2312
Charlotte S. McCanna

DARTMOUTH COLLEGE - SHERMAN ART LIBRARY
Carpenter Hall
Hanover, NH 03755
Phone: (603) 646-2305
Jeffrey L. Horrell, Art Libn.

DARTMOUTH COLLEGE - SPECIAL COLLECTIONS
Dartmouth College Library
Hanover, NH 03755
Phone: (603) 646-2571
Stanley W. Brown, Chf.Spec.Coll.

U.S. ARMY - COLD REGIONS RESEARCH & ENGINEERING LABORATORY - LIBRARY
Box 282
Hanover, NH 03755
Phone: (603) 643-3200
Nancy H. Cummings, Libn.

NEW HAMPSHIRE STATE DIVISION OF FORESTS AND LANDS - FOX FOREST LIBRARY
Fox State Forest
Hillsboro, NH 03244
Phone: (603) 464-3453
Philip Verrier, Res. Forester

CHESHIRE HOSPITAL - MEDICAL LIBRARY
580 Court St.
Keene, NH 03431
Phone: (603) 352-4111
Margie Dempsey, Libn.

KEENE STATE COLLEGE - WALLACE E. MASON LIBRARY
Appian Way
Keene, NH 03431
Phone: (603) 352-1909
Clifford S. Mead, Libn.

MARKEM CORPORATION - LIBRARY
150 Congress St.   Phone: (603) 352-1130
Keene, NH 03431   Terry Johnson, Libn.

NEW HAMPSHIRE VOCATIONAL-TECHNICAL COLLEGE - LIBRARY
Prescott Hill   Phone: (603) 524-8084
Laconia, NH 03246   Patty Bobula, Libn.

AMERICAN-CANADIAN GENEALOGICAL SOCIETY - LIBRARY
Box 668   Phone: (603) 623-1781
Manchester, NH 03105   Richard Gagnon, Libn.

ASSOCIATION CANADO-AMERICAINE - INSTITUT CANADO-AMERICAIN
Box 989   Phone: (603) 625-8577
Manchester, NH 03105   Robert B. Perreault, Libn.

CATHOLIC MEDICAL CENTER - HEALTH SCIENCE LIBRARY
100 McGregor St.   Phone: (603) 668-3545
Manchester, NH 03102   Marcia K. Allen, Libn.

MANCHESTER CITY LIBRARY - FINE ARTS DEPARTMENT
405 Pine St.   Phone: (603) 625-6485
Manchester, NH 03104   Ann W. Frank, Fine Arts Libn.

MANCHESTER CITY LIBRARY - NEW HAMPSHIRE ROOM
405 Pine St.   Phone: (603) 625-6485
Manchester, NH 03104

MANCHESTER HISTORIC ASSOCIATION - LIBRARY
129 Amherst St.   Phone: (603) 622-7531
Manchester, NH 03104   Elizabeth Lessard, Libn.

NEW HAMPSHIRE COLLEGE - SHAPIRO LIBRARY
2500 N. River Rd.   Phone: (603) 668-2211
Manchester, NH 03104   Richard Pantano, Dir.

ST. ANSELM'S COLLEGE - GEISEL LIBRARY
                                         Phone: (603) 669-1030
Manchester, NH 03102   Norma Creaghe, Libn.

U.S. VETERANS ADMINISTRATION (NH-Manchester) - MEDICAL CENTER
   LIBRARY
Smyth Rd.   Phone: (603) 624-4366
Manchester, NH 03104   Myra S. Pritchett, Chf.Libn.

KOLLSMAN INSTRUMENT COMPANY - TECHNICAL ENGINEERING LIBRARY
Daniel Webster Hwy., S.   Phone: (603) 889-2500
Merrimack, NH 03054   Richard C. Meischeid, Dir.

DANIEL WEBSTER COLLEGE - LIBRARY
University Dr.   Phone: (603) 883-3556
Nashua, NH 03063   Patience K. Jackson, Lib.Dir.

INGERSOLL-RAND COMPANY - ENGINEERING LIBRARY
150 Burke St.   Phone: (603) 882-2711
Nashua, NH 03061   Susan Webb, Libn.

NASHUA CORPORATION - TECHNICAL LIBRARY
44 Franklin St.   Phone: (603) 880-2537
Nashua, NH 03061   Kay Marquis, Tech.Libn.

NEW HAMPSHIRE VOCATIONAL-TECHNICAL COLLEGE - LIBRARY
505 Amherst St.   Phone: (603) 882-6923
Nashua, NH 03063   William A. McIntyre, Libn.

SANDERS ASSOCIATES, INC. - TECHNICAL LIBRARY
95 Canal St., NCA 1-1342   Phone: (603) 885-4143
Nashua, NH 03061   Mary Stevens, Mgr.Lib.Serv.

U.S. AIR FORCE BASE - PEASE BASE LIBRARY †
                                         Phone: (603) 430-0100
Pease AFB, NH 03801   Julie M. O'Brien, Libn.

PETERBOROUGH HISTORICAL SOCIETY - LIBRARY
Grove St., Box 58   Phone: (603) 924-3235
Peterborough, NH 03458   Mrs. Arvilla C. Tolman, Lib.Chm.

PLYMOUTH STATE COLLEGE - GEOGRAPHERS ON FILM COLLECTION
Plymouth, NH 03264   Maynard Weston Dow, Dir.

PLYMOUTH STATE COLLEGE - HERBERT H. LAMSON LIBRARY
                                         Phone: (603) 536-1550
Plymouth, NH 03264   Janice Gallinger, Dir.Lib.Serv./Cur.

PLYMOUTH STATE COLLEGE - HERBERT H. LAMSON LIBRARY - ROBERT
   FROST COLLECTION
                                         Phone: (604) 536-1550
Plymouth, NH 03264   Janice Gallinger, Dir.Lib.Serv./Cur.

ELEVENTH BOMBARDMENT GROUP (H) ASSOCIATION - ARCHIVES
1106 Maplewood Ave.   Phone: (603) 436-5835
Portsmouth, NH 03801   W.M. Cleveland, Hist.

NEW HAMPSHIRE VOCATIONAL-TECHNICAL COLLEGE - LIBRARY
150 Greenleaf Ave.   Phone: (603) 436-3423
Portsmouth, NH 03801   Nancy L. Dodge, Libn.

PEARL HARBOR SURVIVORS ASSOCIATION - ARCHIVES
1106 Maplewood Ave.   Phone: (603) 436-5835
Portsmouth, NH 03801   W. M. Cleveland, Hist.

PORTSMOUTH ATHENAEUM
9 Market Sq.
Box 848
Portsmouth, NH 03801   Jon R. Russ, Chm., Lib.Comm.

U.S. NAVY - NAVAL SHIPYARD (Portsmouth) - TECHNICAL LIBRARY
Code 863   Phone: (603) 439-1000
Portsmouth, NH 03801   Josephine Rafferty, Tech.Libn.

SALISBURY HISTORICAL SOCIETY - ARCHIVES *
Box 10   Phone: (603) 648-2431
Salisbury, NH 03268   Sylvia P. Barber, Cur.

GENERAL ELECTRIC COMPANY - METER BUSINESS DEPARTMENT -
   LIBRARY & DATA BUREAU *
130 Main St.   Phone: (603) 692-2100
Somersworth, NH 03878   J.R. Kemen, Spec.

TAMWORTH HISTORICAL SOCIETY - LIBRARY †
Center of Village
Tamworth, NH 03886

DIETRICH COLLECTION
RFD 1, West Farms Rd.   Phone: (603) 632-7156
West Canaan, NH 03741   Dr. R. Krystyna Dietrich, Dir.

WOLFEBORO HISTORICAL SOCIETY - PLEASANT VALLEY SCHOOLHOUSE -
   LIBRARY
S. Main St.
Wolfeboro, NH 03894   Joan E. Kimball, Pres./Cur.

NEW JERSEY

ATLANTIC CITY MEDICAL CENTER - MEDICAL LIBRARY
1925 Pacific Ave.   Phone: (609) 344-4081
Atlantic City, NJ 08401   Valerie E. Alexander, Lib.Supv.

PRINCETON ANTIQUES BOOKFINDERS - ART MARKETING REFERENCE
   LIBRARY
2915-17-31 Atlantic Ave.   Phone: (609) 344-1943
Atlantic City, NJ 08401   Robert Eugene, Cur.

U.S. FEDERAL AVIATION ADMINISTRATION - TECHNICAL CENTER
   LIBRARY †
                                         Phone: (609) 641-8200
Atlantic City Airport, NJ 08405   Clarence H. Abbott, Jr., Chf.

AMERICAN TELEPHONE & TELEGRAPH COMPANY - CORPORATE LIBRARY
295 N. Maple Ave., Rm. 4430C1   Phone: (201) 221-4143
Basking Ridge, NJ 07920   Phyllis Chiavetta, Chf.Libn.

GEOGRAPHIC

U.S. NATL. ARCHIVES & RECORDS SERVICE - FEDERAL ARCHIVES AND
   RECORDS CENTER, REGION 2
Bldg. 22-MOT   Phone: (201) 858-7245
Bayonne, NJ 07002   O.R. Whitelock, Dir.

AMERICAN TELEPHONE & TELEGRAPH COMPANY - LONG LINES
   DEPARTMENT - INFORMATION RESEARCH CENTER
Rm. 3B100   Phone: (201) 234-3280
Bedminster, NJ 07921   Jack Borbely, Mgr.

OAKITE PRODUCTS INC. - CHEMICAL RESEARCH LIBRARY
50 Valley Rd.   Phone: (201) 464-6900
Berkeley Heights, NJ 07922   Mary Ann Derkach, Libn.

BLOOMFIELD COLLEGE - GEORGE TALBOT HALL LIBRARY
467 Franklin St.   Phone: (201) 748-9000
Bloomfield, NJ 07003   Dr. Imre Gal, Chf.Libn.

LUMMUS COMPANY - LUMMUS TECHNICAL CENTER - TECHNICAL
   INFORMATION DEPARTMENT
1515 Broad St.   Phone: (201) 893-2251
Bloomfield, NJ 07003   Mary A. Ciaramella, Chf.Libn.

SCHERING-PLOUGH CORPORATION - PHARMACEUTICAL RESEARCH
   DIVISION - LIBRARY INFORMATION CENTER
60 Orange St.   Phone: (201) 743-6000
Bloomfield, NJ 07003   Rita L. Goodemote, Assoc.Dir.

WESTINGHOUSE ELECTRIC CORPORATION - LAMP DIVISIONS -
   ENGINEERING LIBRARY
One Westinghouse Plaza   Phone: (201) 429-3316
Bloomfield, NJ 07003   Shuchen Huang, Engr.Libn.

DIVINE WORD SEMINARY - LIBRARY
101 Park St.   Phone: (609) 298-0549
Bordentown, NJ 08505   John McCullough, Libn.

JOHNSTONE (E.R.) TRAINING & RESEARCH CENTER - PROFESSIONAL
   LIBRARY
Burlington St.   Phone: (609) 298-2500
Bordentown, NJ 08505   Herman H. Spitz, Dir. of Res.

AMERICAN CYANAMID COMPANY - CHEMICAL RESEARCH DIVISION -
   LIBRARY
                                                 Phone: (201) 356-2000
Bound Brook, NJ 08805   Joan L. Gallagher, Mgr.Tech.Info.

UNION CARBIDE CORPORATION - RESEARCH AND DEVELOPMENT LIBRARY
1 River Rd.   Phone: (201) 356-8000
Bound Brook, NJ 08805   Anna Coleman, Libn.

BRIDGETON HOSPITAL - HEALTH SCIENCES LIBRARY
Irving & Manheim Aves.   Phone: (609) 451-6600
Bridgeton, NJ 08302   Jeanne Garrison, Health Sci.Libn.

CUMBERLAND COUNTY LAW LIBRARY *
County Court House
W. Broad & Fayette Sts.   Phone: (609) 451-8000
Bridgeton, NJ 08302   John R. Reinard, Law Libn.

CUMBERLAND COUNTY PLANNING BOARD - TECHNICAL REFERENCE
   LIBRARY
800 E. Commerce St.   Phone: (609) 451-8000
Bridgeton, NJ 08302   Carl B. Holm, Principal Planner

BRIDGEWATER COURIER-NEWS - LIBRARY
1201 Route 22
Box 6600   Phone: (201) 722-8800
Bridgewater, NJ 08807   Linda H. Crow, Libn.

NATIONAL STARCH AND CHEMICAL CORPORATION - LIBRARY
10 Finderne Ave.
Box 6500   Phone: (201) 685-5082
Bridgewater, NJ 08807   Marianne Vago, Libn.

DEBORAH HEART AND LUNG CENTER - MEDICAL LIBRARY
One Trenton Rd.   Phone: (609) 893-6611
Browns Mills, NJ 08015   Carol A. Harris, Libn.

BURLINGTON COUNTY HISTORICAL SOCIETY - DELIA BIDDLE PUGH
   LIBRARY
457 High St.   Phone: (609) 386-4773
Burlington, NJ 08016   Isabel Corless, Libn.

CONVERSE WARD DAVIS DIXON - LIBRARY *
91 Roseland Ave.
Box 91   Phone: (201) 226-9191
Caldwell, NJ 07006

CAMDEN COUNTY BAR ASSOCIATION - LAW LIBRARY †
City Hall, Rm. 500   Phone: (609) 757-6703
Camden, NJ 08101   Lydia M. Rivera, Libn.

CAMDEN COUNTY HISTORICAL SOCIETY - LIBRARY
Park Blvd. & Euclid Ave.   Phone: (609) 964-3333
Camden, NJ 08103   Miriam Favorite, Libn.

CAMPBELL INSTITUTE FOR RESEARCH AND TECHNOLOGY - RESEARCH
   DEVELOPMENT LIBRARY
Campbell Pl.   Phone: (609) 964-4000
Camden, NJ 08101   B. Jespersen, Libn.

COOPER MEDICAL CENTER - REUBEN L. SHARP HEALTH-SCIENCE LIBRARY
6th & Stevens Sts.   Phone: (609) 964-6600
Camden, NJ 08103   Katherine Richards, Dir.

INSTITUTE FOR MEDICAL RESEARCH - LIBRARY
Copewood St.   Phone: (609) 966-7377
Camden, NJ 08103   Dorothy H. Gruber, Libn.

OUR LADY OF LOURDES HOSPITAL - MEDICAL LIBRARY
1600 Haddon Ave.   Phone: (609) 757-3548
Camden, NJ 08103   Fred Kafes, Libn.

OUR LADY OF LOURDES HOSPITAL - SCHOOL OF NURSING - LIBRARY
1565 Vesper Blvd.   Phone: (609) 757-3722
Camden, NJ 08103   Eleanor M. Kelly, Libn.

RCA CORPORATION - GSD - GOVERNMENT COMMUNICATIONS SYSTEMS -
   LIBRARY
Delaware Ave. & Cooper St.   Phone: (609) 338-3488
Camden, NJ 08102   Olive F. Whitehead, Mgr., Lib.Rsrcs.

RUTGERS UNIVERSITY, THE STATE UNIVERSITY OF NEW JERSEY -
   SCHOOL OF LAW LIBRARY †
Fifth & Penn Sts.   Phone: (609) 757-6173
Camden, NJ 08102   Arno Liivak, Law Libn.

WHITMAN (Walt) HOUSE - LIBRARY
330 Mickle St.   Phone: (609) 964-5383
Camden, NJ 08103   Eleanor Ray, Caretaker

CAPE MAY COUNTY HISTORICAL/GENEALOGICAL SOCIETY AND MUSEUM -
   LIBRARY
Rte. 9   Phone: (609) 465-3535
Cape May Court House, NJ 08210   Ella W. Kay, Cur.

NEW YORK SOCIETY OF MODEL ENGINEERS - LIBRARY *
341 Hoboken Rd.   Phone: (201) 939-9212
Carlstadt, NJ 07072   Stephen Szewczuk, Libn.

SUN CHEMICAL CORPORATION - RESEARCH LIBRARY
631 Central Ave.   Phone: (201) 933-4500
Carlstadt, NJ 07072   Florence Clark, Libn.

ESSEX COUNTY HOSPITAL CENTER - HAMILTON MEMORIAL LIBRARY
Box 500   Phone: (201) 239-1900
Cedar Grove, NJ 07009   Elizabeth B. Guarducci, Med.Libn.

BERLEX LABORATORIES, INC. - RESEARCH AND DEVELOPMENT DIVISION
   LIBRARY
110 E. Hanover Ave.   Phone: (201) 540-8700
Cedar Knolls, NJ 07927   Lorene Lingelbach, Libn.

CELANESE CORPORATION - CELANESE PLASTICS & SPECIALTIES
   COMPANY - INFORMATION CENTER
26 Main St.   Phone: (201) 635-2600
Chatham, NJ 07928   Mary Ann Bury, Info.Spec.

PHARMACO-MEDICAL DOCUMENTATION, INC. - RESEARCH LIBRARY
205 Main St.
Box 401   Phone: (201) 635-9500
Chatham, NJ 07928   Miss G. Wold, Res.Libn.

COMPUTER HORIZONS, INC. - LIBRARY
1050 Kings Hwy., N.   Phone: (609) 779-0911
Cherry Hill, NJ 08034

KENNEDY (John F.) MEMORIAL HOSPITAL - CHERRY HILL DIVISION -
    MEDICAL LIBRARY
Chapel Ave. & Cooper Landing Rd.   Phone: (609) 665-2000
Cherry Hill, NJ 08002   Amy Kaplan, Libn.

TEMPLE EMANUEL - LIBRARY
Cooper River Pkwy. at Donahue
Cherry Hill, NJ 08034   Rene Batterman, Libn.

TRINITY UNITED PRESBYTERIAN CHURCH - NORMAN S. HJORTH
    MEMORIAL LIBRARY
Rte. 70 & W. Gate Dr.   Phone: (609) 428-2050
Cherry Hill, NJ 08034   Bernice Ahlquist, Chm., Lib.Comm.

AB BOOKMAN PUBLICATIONS, INC. - LIBRARY
Box AB   Phone: (201) 772-0020
Clifton, NJ 07015   Ellen Chernofsky, Libn.

GIVAUDAN CORPORATION - LIBRARY
125 Delawanna Ave.   Phone: (201) 546-8563
Clifton, NJ 07014   Roberta F. Nugent, Chf.Libn.

SHULTON, INC. - RESEARCH AND DEVELOPMENT LIBRARY
697 Rte. 46   Phone: (201) 546-7148
Clifton, NJ 07015   Marcia Weiss, Libn.

WHITE (James T.) AND COMPANY - LIBRARY
1700 State Hwy. 3   Phone: (201) 773-9300
Clifton, NJ 07013

COUNCIL OF SCOTTISH CLAN ASSOCIATIONS INC. - LIBRARY
7 Wyndmoor Dr.
Convent Station, NJ 07961

GENERAL DRAFTING COMPANY, INC. - MAP LIBRARY
Canfield Rd.   Phone: (201) 538-7600
Convent Station, NJ 07961   H. Jane Masar, Libn.

CARTER-WALLACE, INC. - LIBRARY
                                           Phone: (609) 655-6297
Cranbury, NJ 08512   Arthur Hilscher, Dir.

CRANFORD HISTORICAL SOCIETY - MUSEUM LIBRARY *
124 N. Union Ave.
Cranford, NJ 07016   Arthur K. Burditt, Trustee & Libn.

CRANFORD UNITED METHODIST CHURCH - LIBRARY
201 E. Lincoln Ave.   Phone: (201) 276-0936
Cranford, NJ 07016   Laura Engel, Libn.

DAMES & MOORE - LIBRARY
6 Commerce Dr.   Phone: (201) 272-8300
Cranford, NJ 07016   Maxine S. Karesh, Libn.

U.S. ARMY - ARMAMENT RESEARCH & DEVELOPMENT COMMAND -
    SCIENTIFIC AND TECHNICAL INFORMATION DIVISION
ARRADCOM   Phone: (201) 328-2914
Dover, NJ 07801   Normand L. Varieur, Libn.

U.S. ARMY - PLASTICS TECHNICAL EVALUATION CENTER
ARRADCOM, Bldg. 3401   Phone: (201) 328-2778
Dover, NJ 07801   Alfred M. Anzalone, Adm.Libn.

SANDOZ COLORS & CHEMICALS - INFORMATION CENTER
Route 10   Phone: (201) 386-8430
East Hanover, NJ 07936   Robyn Aber, Info.Sci.

SANDOZ PHARMACEUTICALS - INFORMATION SERVICES
Route 10   Phone: (201) 386-8105
East Hanover, NJ 07936   Joyce G. Koelle, Mgr.

EXXON BIOMEDICAL SCIENCES INC. - LIBRARY
Box 235   Phone: (201) 474-2506
East Millstone, NJ 08873   Patricia Hodge, Libn.

EAST ORANGE GENERAL HOSPITAL - MEDICAL LIBRARY
300 Central Ave.   Phone: (201) 672-8400
East Orange, NJ 07019   Joann Mehalick, Supv. Of Lib.Serv.

GLOBAL EDUCATION ASSOCIATES - CURRICULUM RESOURCE LIBRARY
552 Park Ave.   Phone: (201) 675-1409
East Orange, NJ 07017   Sandy Graff, Hd.

TEMPLE SHAREY TEFILO - EDWARD EHRENKRANTZ LIBRARY
57 Prospect St.   Phone: (201) 678-0005
East Orange, NJ 07017   Ann R. Zeve, Libn.

U.S. VETERANS ADMINISTRATION (NJ-East Orange) - MEDICAL CENTER
    LIBRARY †
                                           Phone: (201) 676-1000
East Orange, NJ 07019   Calvin A. Zamarelli, Chf.Libn.

LEVER BROTHERS COMPANY - RESEARCH AND DEVELOPMENT DIVISION -
    RESEARCH LIBRARY
45 River Rd.   Phone: (201) 943-7100
Edgewater, NJ 07020   Terry Hauerstein, Info.Off.

ENGELHARD CORPORATION - TECHNICAL INFORMATION CENTER
Menlo Park   Phone: (201) 321-5271
Edison, NJ 08837   Roger L. Meyer, Mgr.Tech.Info.Serv.

ENVIRONMENTAL PROTECTION AGENCY - REGION II FIELD OFFICE -
    TECHNICAL LIBRARY
                                           Phone: (201) 321-6000
Edison, NJ 08817   Dorothy Szefczyk, Libn.

KENNEDY (John F.) MEDICAL CENTER - LIBRARY
James St.   Phone: (201) 321-7181
Edison, NJ 08817   Roberta Tipton, Libn.

MIDLANTIC NATIONAL BANK - TRUST DEPARTMENT LIBRARY
Metro Park Plaza
Box 600   Phone: (201) 266-6355
Edison, NJ 08818   Eileen Y. Logan, Hd.

MOBIL CHEMICAL COMPANY - RESEARCH & DEVELOPMENT - TECHNICAL
    INFORMATION CENTER
Box 240   Phone: (201) 321-6229
Edison, NJ 08817   Claire A. Holden, Supv., Info.Serv.

ELIZABETH GENERAL HOSPITAL & DISPENSARY - HEALTH SCIENCE
    LIBRARY
925 E. Jersey St.   Phone: (201) 289-8600
Elizabeth, NJ 07201   Catherine M. Boss, Dir.

FREE PUBLIC LIBRARY OF ELIZABETH, NJ - ART AND MUSIC DEPARTMENT
11 S. Broad St.   Phone: (201) 354-6060
Elizabeth, NJ 07202   Roman A. Sawycky, Supv.Libn.

ST. ELIZABETH HOSPITAL - HEALTH SCIENCES LIBRARY
210 Williamson St.   Phone: (201) 527-5371
Elizabeth, NJ 07207   Sr. Anne Guinee, Libn.

SEA-LAND SERVICE, INC. - CORPORATE INFORMATION CENTER
Box 1050   Phone: (201) 289-6000
Elizabeth, NJ 07207

SINGER COMPANY - SPG ENGINEERING - SEWING PRODUCTS GROUP -
    ENGINEERING LIBRARY
321 First St.   Phone: (201) 527-6884
Elizabeth, NJ 07207   Jeanette R. Koziol, Tech.Libn.

THORNTHWAITE (C.W.) ASSOCIATES LABORATORY OF CLIMATOLOGY -
    LIBRARY
Rural Delivery 1
Elmer, NJ 08318   William J. Superior, Pres.

ENGLEWOOD HOSPITAL - MEDICAL LIBRARY
350 Engle St.   Phone: (201) 894-3070
Englewood, NJ 07631   Katherine L. Lindner, Dir.

GEOGRAPHIC

GEOGRAPHIC

ENGLEWOOD HOSPITAL - SCHOOL OF NURSING LIBRARY *
350 Engle St.   Phone: (201) 568-3400
Englewood, NJ 07631   Patricia Young, Libn.

LIPTON (Thomas J.) INC. - RESEARCH LIBRARY
800 Sylvan Ave.   Phone: (201) 567-8000
Englewood Cliffs, NJ 07632   Gloria S. Bernstein, Mgr., Lib.Info.Serv.

TCR SERVICE, INC. - COMMON LAW LIBRARY
190 Sylvan Ave.   Phone: (201) 461-7475
Englewood Cliffs, NJ 07632

NORTHEASTERN BIBLE COLLEGE - LINCOLN MEMORIAL LIBRARY
12 Oak Lane   Phone: (201) 226-1074
Essex Fells, NJ 07021   Charmaine L. MacMullen, Act.Dir.

NABISCO, INC. - RESEARCH CENTER LIBRARY †
2111 Rte. 208   Phone: (201) 797-6800
Fair Lawn, NJ 07410   Sonia D. Meurer, Libn.

UNITED STATES GOLF ASSOCIATION - GOLF HOUSE LIBRARY
Golf House   Phone: (201) 234-2300
Far Hills, NJ 07931   Janet Seagle, Libn./Musm.Cur.

HUNTERDON COUNTY HISTORICAL SOCIETY - HIRAM E. DEATS MEMORIAL
LIBRARY
114 Main St.   Phone: (201) 782-1091
Flemington, NJ 08822   Norman C. Wittwer, Chm., Lib.Comm.

HUNTERDON MEDICAL CENTER - MEDICAL LIBRARY
Rte. 31   Phone: (201) 782-2121
Flemington, NJ 08822   Joyce G. White, M.D., Libn.

REXHAM CORPORATION - PACKAGING TECHNICAL LIBRARY
Box 111   Phone: (201) 782-4000
Flemington, NJ 08822   Anne T. Hand, Exec.Sec.

AUTOMATIC SWITCH COMPANY - ASCO LIBRARY
50 Hanover Rd.   Phone: (201) 966-2479
Florham Park, NJ 07932   Nancy G. Garvey, Libn.

BOOZ ALLEN & HAMILTON, INC. - FOSTER D. SNELL DIVISION -
INFORMATION CENTER †
66 Hanover Rd.   Phone: (201) 377-6700
Florham Park, NJ 07932   Pat Guida, Mgr.

EXXON CORPORATION - COMMUNICATIONS AND COMPUTER SCIENCE -
TECHNICAL LIBRARY
Box 153   Phone: (201) 765-5639
Florham Park, NJ 07932   P. Neubig, Ref.Sys.Supv.

EXXON RESEARCH AND ENGINEERING COMPANY - FLORHAM PARK
INFORMATION CENTER †
Box 101   Phone: (201) 765-6704
Florham Park, NJ 07932   J.A. Price, Sect.Hd.

GPU NUCLEAR - OYSTER CREEK TECHNICAL LIBRARY
Oyster Creek Nuclear Generating Sta.
Box 338
Forked River, NJ 08731   Carlyn Ewald, Tech.Libn.

U.S. ARMY HOSPITALS - WALSON ARMY HOSPITAL - MEDICAL LIBRARY
           Phone: (609) 562-5741
Ft. Dix, NJ 08640   Anne Bonnaffon, Med.Libn.

FORT LEE PUBLIC LIBRARY - SILENT FILM PHOTO COLLECTION
320 Main St.   Phone: (201) 592-3614
Fort Lee, NJ 07024   Rita Altomara, Project Coord.

U.S. ARMY - COMMUNICATIONS-ELECTRONICS COMMAND - TECHNICAL
LIBRARY
           Phone: (201) 532-1298
Fort Monmouth, NJ 07703   Ellen K. Dobi, Libn.

U.S. ARMY - COMMUNICATIONS SYSTEMS CENTER - ELECTRONICS
MUSEUM
Myer Hall, Ave. of Memories   Phone: (201) 532-2445
Fort Monmouth, NJ 07703   Edmond J. Norris, Dir.

U.S. ARMY - ELECTRONICS R & D COMMAND - TECHNICAL LIBRARY
DIVISION
Bldg. 2700   Phone: (201) 544-2237
Fort Monmouth, NJ 07703   William R. Werk, Chf.

MONMOUTH COUNTY HISTORICAL ASSOCIATION - LIBRARY
70 Court St.   Phone: (201) 462-1466
Freehold, NJ 07728   Gregory J. Plunges, Libn.

MONMOUTH COUNTY LAW LIBRARY
Court House   Phone: (201) 431-7079
Freehold, NJ 07728   Carolyn S. Geiling, Law Libn.

MONMOUTH COUNTY SOCIAL SERVICES - LIBRARY
Box 3000   Phone: (201) 431-6011
Freehold, NJ 07728   Cynthia Noia, Libn.

STEVENS (J.P.) AND CO., INC. - TECHNICAL CENTER LIBRARY
141 Lanza Ave.   Phone: (201) 772-7100
Garfield, NJ 07026   Teresa M. Jaworski, Libn.

GLASSBORO STATE COLLEGE - SAVITZ LEARNING RESOURCES CENTER
           Phone: (609) 445-6303
Glassboro, NJ 08028   Clara Kirner, Spec.Coll.Libn.

GLASSBORO STATE COLLEGE - SAVITZ LIBRARY - LLOYD V. MANWILLER
CURRICULUM LABORATORY
Rte. 322   Phone: (609) 445-5335
Glassboro, NJ 08028   Kathleen Kennedy, Educ.Libn.

ASSOCIATED TECHNICAL SERVICES, INC. - RESEARCH LIBRARY
855 Bloomfield Ave.   Phone: (201) 748-5673
Glen Ridge, NJ 07028   Leon Jacolev, Lib.Dir.

CUMBERLAND COUNTY HISTORICAL SOCIETY - LIBRARY
Pirate House
Box 16   Phone: (609) 455-4055
Greenwich, NJ 08323   Carl West, Libn.

GREYSTONE PARK PSYCHIATRIC HOSPITAL - HEALTH SCIENCE LIBRARY †
Box A   Phone: (201) 538-1800
Greystone Park, NJ 07950   Brian C. Hamilton, Libn.

BERGEN COUNTY HISTORICAL SOCIETY - LIBRARY
Johnson Public Library
274 Main St.
Hackensack, NJ 07601   M. Singleton, Libn.

BERGEN COUNTY LAW LIBRARY
Court House, Rm. 225
Main St.   Phone: (201) 646-2056
Hackensack, NJ 07601   Edna M. Oakley, Libn.

FAIRLEIGH DICKINSON UNIVERSITY - SCHOOL OF DENTISTRY LIBRARY
110 Fuller Pl.   Phone: (201) 836-6300
Hackensack, NJ 07601   Kathy Marousek, Act. Dental Libn.

HACKENSACK HOSPITAL - MEDICAL LIBRARY †
22 Hospital Pl.   Phone: (201) 487-4000
Hackensack, NJ 07601   Duressa Pujat, Libn.

NATIONAL COUNCIL ON CRIME AND DELINQUENCY - LIBRARY
Continental Plaza
411 Hackensack Ave.   Phone: (201) 488-0400
Hackensack, NJ 07601   Eugene Doleschal, Libn.

HACKETTSTOWN HISTORICAL SOCIETY - MUSEUM
106 Church St.   Phone: (201) 852-8797
Hackettstown, NJ 07840   Milton K. Thorp, Cur.

HISTORICAL SOCIETY OF HADDONFIELD - LIBRARY
343 King's Hwy. East   Phone: (609) 429-7375
Haddonfield, NJ 08033   Gertrude D. Hess, Libn.

AMES RUBBER CORPORATION - TECHNICAL INFORMATION CENTER †
2347 Ames Blvd.   Phone: (201) 827-9101
Hamburg, NJ 07419   E.H. Oster, Mgr., Info.Serv.

ANCORA PSYCHIATRIC HOSPITAL - HEALTH SCIENCES LIBRARY
Phone: (609) 561-1700
Hammonton, NJ 08037 Houston Seals, Libn. II

STUDIO SUPPLIERS ASSOCIATION - BUSINESS LIBRARY
548 Goffle Rd. Phone: (201) 427-9384
Hawthorne, NJ 07506 Donald Franz, Exec.Sec.

U.S. NATL. MARINE FISHERIES SERVICE - SANDY HOOK LABORATORY -
LIONEL A. WALFORD LIBRARY
Phone: (201) 872-0200
Highlands, NJ 07732 Claire L. Steimle, Act.Libn.

BURR (Aaron) ASSOCIATION - LIBRARY
Hightstown-Freehold Rd.
R.D. 1, Rte. 33, Box 429
Hightstown, NJ 08520 Samuel Engle Burr, Jr., Act.Libn.

NL INDUSTRIES, INC. - MARKETING & TECHNICAL INFORMATION SERVICE
Box 700 Phone: (609) 448-3200
Hightstown, NJ 08520 Halina Kan, Libn.

BRISTOL-MYERS PRODUCTS - TECHNICAL INFORMATION CENTER
225 Long Ave. Phone: (201) 926-6691
Hillside, NJ 07207 Mary F. Bondarovich, Mgr., Tech.Info.Ctr.

GENERAL FOODS CORPORATION - MAXWELL HOUSE DIVISION - RESEARCH
DEPARTMENT LIBRARY
1125 Hudson St. Phone: (201) 420-3309
Hoboken, NJ 07030 Anne Marie Civinskas, Libn.

PLASTICS INSTITUTE OF AMERICA - LIBRARY
Stevens Institute Of Technology
Castle Point Sta. Phone: (201) 792-1839
Hoboken, NJ 07030 Albert Spaak, Exec.Dir.

STEVENS INSTITUTE OF TECHNOLOGY - SAMUEL C. WILLIAMS LIBRARY
Castle Point Sta. Phone: (201) 420-5198
Hoboken, NJ 07030 Richard P. Widdicombe, Dir.

UNITED STATES TESTING COMPANY, INC. - LIBRARY †
1415 Park Ave. Phone: (201) 792-2400
Hoboken, NJ 07030 Dorothy M. Campbell, Libn.

BELL TELEPHONE LABORATORIES, INC. - TECHNICAL LIBRARY
Phone: (201) 949-5236
Holmdel, NJ 07733 John E. Cooper, Lib. Group Supv.

HOPEWELL MUSEUM - LIBRARY
28 E. Broad St. Phone: (609) 466-0103
Hopewell, NJ 08525 Beverly Weidl, Cur.

WESTERN ELECTRIC COMPANY, INC. - CORPORATE EDUCATION CENTER -
LIBRARY
Box 1000 Phone: (609) 639-4451
Hopewell, NJ 08525 J. Lonney, Sect.Chf.Tech.Lib.

HUDSON COUNTY LAW LIBRARY †
Hudson County Administration Bldg.
595 Newark Ave. Phone: (201) 792-3737
Jersey City, NJ 07306 Eric Mayer, Law Libn.

JERSEY CITY STATE COLLEGE - FORREST A. IRWIN LIBRARY
2039 Kennedy Blvd. Phone: (201) 547-3026
Jersey City, NJ 07305 Robert S. Nugent, Dir.

NATIONAL RAILWAY HISTORICAL SOCIETY - LIBRARY OF AMERICAN
TRANSPORTATION
Box 7 Phone: (609) 829-5204
Jobstown, NJ 08041 Earle P. Finkbiner, Libn.

WESTERN ELECTRIC COMPANY, INC. - KEARNY INFORMATION RESOURCE
CENTER
100 Central Ave. Phone: (201) 465-4373
Kearny, NJ 07032 Anna-Elizabeth Vugrinecz, Ref.Libn.

SCHERING-PLOUGH CORPORATION - BUSINESS INFORMATION CENTER -
LIBRARY
Galloping Hill Rd. Phone: (201) 931-3120
Kenilworth, NJ 07033 Esther M. Jankovics, Mgr.

U.S. NAVY - NAVAL AIR ENGINEERING CENTER - TECHNICAL LIBRARY,
CODE 1115
Naval Air Engineering Center Phone: (201) 323-2893
Lakehurst, NJ 08733 Deloris J. Swan, Lib.Off.

RIDER COLLEGE - FRANKLIN F. MOORE LIBRARY
2083 Lawrenceville Rd. Phone: (609) 896-0800
Lawrenceville, NJ 08648 Ross Stephen, College Libn.

RIDER COLLEGE - FRANKLIN F. MOORE LIBRARY - ART ROOM
2083 Lawrenceville Rd. Phone: (609) 896-0800
Lawrenceville, NJ 08648 Violet K. Devlin, Art Libn.

EXXON RESEARCH AND ENGINEERING COMPANY - INFORMATION
SERVICES
Box 121 Phone: (201) 474-3108
Linden, NJ 07036 Margaret H. Graham, Mgr.

SOCIETY FOR THE INVESTIGATION OF THE UNEXPLAINED - LIBRARY
Box 265 Phone: (201) 842-5229
Little Silver, NJ 07739 N. Warth, Sec.

FOSTER WHEELER DEVELOPMENT CORPORATION - RESEARCH
INFORMATION CENTER AND LIBRARY
9 Peach Tree Hill Rd. Phone: (201) 533-3663
Livingston, NJ 07039 Karlo J. Mirth, Mgr.

MOTION PICTURE SERVICES
Box 252 Phone: (201) 992-8194
Livingston, NJ 07039 Murray Mankowitz, Dir.

ST. BARNABAS MEDICAL CENTER - MEDICAL STAFF LIBRARY
Old Short Hills Rd. Phone: (201) 533-5050
Livingston, NJ 07039 A. Christine Connor, Med.Libn.

MONMOUTH MEDICAL CENTER - DR. FRANK J. ALTSCHUL MEDICAL
LIBRARY
Third & Pavilion Aves. Phone: (201) 870-5170
Long Branch, NJ 07740 John Conway, Dir.

U.S. VETERANS ADMINISTRATION (NJ-Lyons) - HOSPITAL LIBRARY
Phone: (201) 647-0180
Lyons, NJ 07939 Louise A. Geroulo, Chf., Lrng.Res.Serv.

U.S. AIR FORCE BASE - MC GUIRE BASE LIBRARY
Phone: (609) 724-4319
McGuire AFB, NJ 08641 Barbara-Ann Bomgardner, Base Libn.

DREW UNIVERSITY - LIBRARY
Rose Memorial Library Phone: (201) 377-3000
Madison, NJ 07940 Dr. Arthur E. Jones, Jr., Dir.

IMMACULATE CONCEPTION SEMINARY - LIBRARY
671 Ramapo Valley Rd. Phone: (201) 327-0300
Mahwah, NJ 07430 Rev. James C. Turro, Dir., Lib.Serv.

HAMMOND, INC. - EDITORIAL DEPARTMENT LIBRARY
515 Valley St. Phone: (201) 763-6000
Maplewood, NJ 07040 W.Z. Myers, Libn.

MADISON TOWNSHIP HISTORICAL SOCIETY - THOMAS WARNE
HISTORICAL MUSEUM AND LIBRARY
RD 1, Box 150 Phone: (201) 566-0348
Matawan, NJ 07747 Alvia D. Martin, Cur.

CONGREGATION BETH JACOB - GOODWIN FAMILY LIBRARY †
109 E. Maple Ave. Phone: (609) 662-4509
Merchantville, NJ 08109 Myra Tishler, Libn.

ROOSEVELT HOSPITAL - HEALTH SCIENCE LIBRARY
Box 151 Phone: (201) 321-6833
Metuchen, NJ 08840 Karen Rubin, Libn.

JOHNSON AND JOHNSON - CHICOPEE, INC. - RESEARCH DIVISION -
LIBRARY
2 Ford Ave.
Box 8 Phone: (201) 524-7872
Milltown, NJ 08850 Judith A. Hassert, Res.Libn.

GEOGRAPHIC

PERSONAL PRODUCTS COMPANY - RESEARCH & DEVELOPMENT LIBRARY
Van Liew Ave.   Phone: (201) 524-7544
Milltown, NJ 08850   Kathryn Hummer, Res.Libn.

WHEATON HISTORICAL ASSOCIATION - LIBRARY & RESEARCH OFFICE
Wheaton Village   Phone: (609) 825-6800
Millville, NJ 08332   Gay Le Cleire Taylor, Libn.

MONTCLAIR ART MUSEUM - LE BRUN LIBRARY
3 S. Mountain Ave.
Box 1582   Phone: (201) 744-5555
Montclair, NJ 07042   Edith A. Rights, Libn.

MONTCLAIR PUBLIC LIBRARY - LOCAL HISTORY FILE
50 S. Fullerton Ave.   Phone: (201) 744-0500
Montclair, NJ 07042   Michael Connell, Dir.

MOUNTAINSIDE HOSPITAL - SCHOOL OF NURSING LIBRARY
School of Nursing
Bay & Highland Aves.   Phone: (201) 746-6000
Montclair, NJ 07042   Patricia Regenberg, Libn.

LEHN & FINK PRODUCTS GROUP - LIBRARY †
225 Summit Ave.   Phone: (201) 391-8500
Montvale, NJ 07645   Eileen M. Matthews, Libn.

HENRY (J.J.) CO., INC. - ENGINEERING LIBRARY
West Park Dr.
Mt. Laurel Ind. Pk.   Phone: (609) 234-3880
Moorestown, NJ 08057   Lorraine Van Leir, Libn.

RCA CORPORATION - ENGINEERING LIBRARY
Borton Landing Rd., Bldg. 101-222   Phone: (609) 778-3394
Moorestown, NJ 08057   Natalia J. Mamchur, Mgr., Lib.Res.

WARNER-LAMBERT COMPANY - CORPORATE LIBRARY †
170 Tabor Rd.   Phone: (201) 540-2875
Morris Plains, NJ 07950   Nedra Behringer, Mgr., Corp.Lib.

ALLIED CORPORATION - BUSINESS LIBRARY
Box 1021 R   Phone: (201) 455-6061
Morristown, NJ 07960   Loretta Massari, Libn.

ALLIED CORPORATION - CORPORATE MEDICAL AFFAIRS LIBRARY
Columbia Rd.
Box 1021R   Phone: (201) 455-2283
Morristown, NJ 07960   Emma Gergely, Med.Libn.

ALLIED CORPORATION - LAW LIBRARY
Box 1057R   Phone: (201) 455-4445
Morristown, NJ 07960   Jeanne C. Seigle, Law Libn.

ALLIED CORPORATION - TECHNICAL INFORMATION SERVICE
Box 1021R   Phone: (201) 455-3014
Morristown, NJ 07960   Linnea Ditchey, Supv.

AMERICAN TELEPHONE & TELEGRAPH COMPANY - MORRISTOWN
    CORPORATE MARKETING LIBRARY
1776 On The Green   Phone: (201) 540-6439
Morristown, NJ 07960   Linda O'Brien, Ref.Libn.

BENEFICIAL MANAGEMENT CORPORATION - LIBRARY
Beneficial Bldg.   Phone: (201) 455-7209
Morristown, NJ 07208   Patricia A. Moffat, Libn.

CHURCH OF JESUS CHRIST OF LATTER-DAY SAINTS - MORRISTOWN, NEW
    JERSEY BRANCH GENEALOGICAL LIBRARY
283 James St.   Phone: (201) 539-5362
Morristown, NJ 07960   Ronald L. Wadsack, Libn.

CRUM AND FORSTER CORPORATION - CORPORATE LIBRARY
U.S. Insurance Group
305 Madison Ave.
Box 2387   Phone: (201) 455-0707
Morristown, NJ 07960   Rosemary W. Leckie, Corp.Libn.

DIAMOND SHAMROCK CORPORATION - PROCESS CHEMICALS DIVISION -
    LIBRARY †
350 Mt. Kemble Ave.
Box 2386-R   Phone: (201) 267-1000
Morristown, NJ 07960   Marilyn Swetell, Libn.

KEUFFEL AND ESSER COMPANY - CHEMICAL RESEARCH AND
    DEVELOPMENT LIBRARY
20 Whippany Rd.   Phone: (201) 285-5530
Morristown, NJ 07960   Gloria Hickey, Libn.

MORRIS COUNTY HISTORICAL SOCIETY - VICTORIAN RESOURCE LIBRARY
68 Morris Ave.   Phone: (201) 267-3465
Morristown, NJ 07960   Doris Philips, Libn.

MORRIS COUNTY LAW LIBRARY
Morris County Court House
Washington St.   Phone: (201) 285-6497
Morristown, NJ 07960   Karen B. Brunner, Law Libn.

MORRISTOWN JEWISH COMMUNITY CENTER - LIBRARY
177 Speedwell Ave.   Phone: (201) 538-9292
Morristown, NJ 07960   Frances Tillinger, Libn.

MORRISTOWN MEMORIAL HOSPITAL - LATHROPE HEALTH SCIENCES
    LIBRARY
100 Madison Ave., Rm. JB-80   Phone: (201) 540-5657
Morristown, NJ 07960   JoAnne M. Searle, Dir.

PITNEY, HARDIN & KIPP - LAW LIBRARY
163 Madison Ave.
Box 2008-R   Phone: (201) 267-3333
Morristown, NJ 07960   Julie L. von Schrader, Libn.

SILVER BURDETT COMPANY - EDITORIAL LIBRARY
250 James St.   Phone: (201) 538-0400
Morristown, NJ 07960   Jane Marie Schrader, Hd.Libn.

U.S. NATL. PARK SERVICE - MORRISTOWN NATIONAL HISTORICAL PARK -
    LIBRARY
230 Morris St.   Phone: (201) 539-2017
Morristown, NJ 07960   Thomas O. Smith, Libn.

BURLINGTON COUNTY LYCEUM OF HISTORY AND NATURAL SCIENCE -
    MOUNT HOLLY LIBRARY
307 High St.   Phone: (609) 267-7111
Mt. Holly, NJ 08060   Susan Lyons, Dir.

BURLINGTON COUNTY MEMORIAL HOSPITAL - HEALTH SCIENCES LIBRARY
175 Madison Ave.   Phone: (609) 267-0700
Mt. Holly, NJ 08060   Betsy O'Connor, Libn.

CHILDREN'S SPECIALIZED HOSPITAL - MEDICAL LIBRARY
150 New Providence Rd.   Phone: (201) 233-3720
Mountainside, NJ 07090   Emily L. Snitow, Libn.

AIRCO, INC. - CENTRAL RESEARCH LABORATORIES - INFORMATION
    CENTER
                                                 Phone: (201) 464-2400
Murray Hill, NJ 07974   Loretta J. Kiersky, Supv.

BELL TELEPHONE LABORATORIES, INC. - LIBRARIES AND INFORMATION
    SYSTEMS CENTER
600 Mountain Ave.   Phone: (201) 582-2854
Murray Hill, NJ 07974   R.A. Kennedy, Dir.

BELL TELEPHONE LABORATORIES, INC. - TECHNICAL LIBRARY
                                                 Phone: (201) 582-4612
Murray Hill, NJ 07974   Ann W. Talcott, Lib. Group Supv.

BRAUN (C.F.) COMPANY - MURRAY HILL DIVISION - ENGINEERING LIBRARY
Diamond Hill Rd.   Phone: (201) 464-9000
Murray Hill, NJ 07974   Marion C. Bale, Libn.

WILPUTTE CORPORATION - LIBRARY
152 Floral Ave.   Phone: (201) 464-5900
Murray Hill, NJ 07974   Roberta Sager, Tech.Libn.

JERSEY SHORE MEDICAL CENTER - MEDICAL LIBRARY
1945 Corlies Ave.   Phone: (201) 775-5500
Neptune, NJ 07753   Mr. Gian C. Hasija, Med.Libn.

CENTER FOR THE AMERICAN WOMAN & POLITICS - LIBRARY
Eagleton Institute, Rutgers University
Wood Lawn, Neilson Campus   Phone: (201) 932-9384
New Brunswick, NJ 08901   Kathy Stanwick, Asst.Dir.

GENEALOGICAL SOCIETY OF NEW JERSEY - MANUSCRIPT COLLECTIONS
Rutgers University Library,
College Ave.   Phone: (201) 932-7510
New Brunswick, NJ 08903   Donald A. Sinclair, Cur. of Spec.Coll.

JOHNSON AND JOHNSON - RESEARCH CENTER LIBRARY
                                                   Phone: (201) 524-5563
New Brunswick, NJ 08903   Claire R. McDonnell, Mgr.Info.Serv.

MIDDLESEX COUNTY LAW LIBRARY †
County Court House, 2nd Fl., E. Wing
1 Kennedy Square   Phone: (201) 745-3357
New Brunswick, NJ 08901   Roland A. Winter, Libn.

MIDDLESEX COUNTY PLANNING BOARD - LIBRARY
40 Livingston Ave.   Phone: (201) 246-5890
New Brunswick, NJ 08901   Marla Kalaitzis, Libn.

NEW BRUNSWICK THEOLOGICAL SEMINARY - GARDNER A. SAGE LIBRARY
21 Seminary Pl.   Phone: (201) 247-5241
New Brunswick, NJ 08901   D. LeRoy Engelhardt, Libn.

RUTGERS UNIVERSITY, THE STATE UNIVERSITY OF NEW JERSEY -
   ALEXANDER LIBRARY - EAST ASIAN LIBRARY
College Ave.   Phone: (201) 932-7161
New Brunswick, NJ 08903   Dr. Nelson Chou, Libn.

RUTGERS UNIVERSITY, THE STATE UNIVERSITY OF NEW JERSEY - ART
   LIBRARY
Voorhees Hall   Phone: (201) 932-7739
New Brunswick, NJ 08903   Ferris Olin, Art Libn.

RUTGERS UNIVERSITY, THE STATE UNIVERSITY OF NEW JERSEY -
   INSTITUTE OF MANAGEMENT/LABOR RELATIONS LIBRARY
                                                   Phone: (201) 932-9513
New Brunswick, NJ 08903   Bernard F. Downey, Libn.

RUTGERS UNIVERSITY, THE STATE UNIVERSITY OF NEW JERSEY -
   SPECIAL COLLECTIONS DEPT. †
Alexander Library
College Ave. & Huntington St.   Phone: (201) 932-1766
New Brunswick, NJ 08903   Donald A. Sinclair, Cur.

ST. PETER'S MEDICAL CENTER - LIBRARY
254 Easton Ave.   Phone: (201) 745-8600
New Brunswick, NJ 08903   Elizabeth McMullen, Hosp.Libn.

SQUIBB (E.R.) & SONS, INC. - SQUIBB INST. FOR MEDICAL RES. - SCIENCE
   INFO. DEPT. - NEW BRUNSWICK LIBRARY
Georges Rd.   Phone: (201) 545-1300
New Brunswick, NJ 08903   Mary S. Klein, Libn.

NEW PROVIDENCE HISTORICAL SOCIETY - LIBRARY
Springfield Ave.
New Providence, NJ 07974   Dorothy Mason, Hd.Libn.

COLLEGE OF MEDICINE AND DENTISTRY OF NEW JERSEY AT NEWARK -
   GEORGE F. SMITH LIBRARY
100 Bergen St.   Phone: (201) 456-4580
Newark, NJ 07103   Philip Rosenstein, Dir. of Libs.

ESSEX COUNTY COLLEGE - ALLIED HEALTH LEARNING RESOURCES CENTER
375 Osborne Terrace
Newark, NJ 07112

ESSEX COUNTY LAW LIBRARY
512 County Courts Bldg.
50 W. Market St.   Phone: (201) 961-7293
Newark, NJ 07102   Jill Wright, Law Libn.

MC CARTER & ENGLISH - LAW LIBRARY
550 Broad St.   Phone: (201) 622-4444
Newark, NJ 07102   Carol Lee Discavage, Libn.

NEW JERSEY HISTORICAL SOCIETY - LIBRARY
230 Broadway   Phone: (201) 483-3939
Newark, NJ 07104   Barbara Smith Irwin, Lib.Dir.

NEW JERSEY INSTITUTE OF TECHNOLOGY - ROBERT W. VAN HOUTEN
   LIBRARY
323 High St.   Phone: (201) 645-5306
Newark, NJ 07102   Morton Snowhite, Libn.

NEWARK BETH ISRAEL MEDICAL CENTER - DR. VICTOR PARSONNET
   MEMORIAL LIBRARY
201 Lyons Ave.   Phone: (201) 926-7233
Newark, NJ 07112   Lillian Bernstein, Libn.

NEWARK BOARD OF EDUCATION - TEACHERS' PROFESSIONAL LIBRARY
2 Cedar St.   Phone: (201) 733-7136
Newark, NJ 07102   Elberta H. Stone, Libn.

NEWARK MUSEUM ASSOCIATION - MUSEUM LIBRARY
49 Washington St.
Box 540   Phone: (201) 733-6640
Newark, NJ 07101   Margaret Di Salvi, Libn.

NEWARK PUBLIC LIBRARY - ART AND MUSIC DEPARTMENT
5 Washington St.
Box 630   Phone: (201) 733-7840
Newark, NJ 07101-0630   William J. Dane, Supv.

NEWARK PUBLIC LIBRARY - BUSINESS LIBRARY
34 Commerce St.   Phone: (201) 733-7849
Newark, NJ 07102   Leslie P. Rupprecht, Supv.

NEWARK PUBLIC LIBRARY - EDUCATION DIVISION
5 Washington St.
Box 630   Phone: (201) 733-7792
Newark, NJ 07101-0630   Frances Beiman, Principal Libn.

NEWARK PUBLIC LIBRARY - HUMANITIES DIVISION
5 Washington St.
Box 630   Phone: (201) 733-7800
Newark, NJ 07101-0630   Sally Hannigan, Principal Libn.

NEWARK PUBLIC LIBRARY - NEW JERSEY REFERENCE DIVISION
5 Washington St.
Box 630   Phone: (201) 733-7776
Newark, NJ 07101-0630   Charles F. Cummings, Supv.Libn.

NEWARK PUBLIC LIBRARY - SCIENCE AND TECHNOLOGY DIVISION
5 Washington St.
Box 630   Phone: (201) 733-7815
Newark, NJ 07101-0630   Nicholas W. Patton, Principal Libn.

NEWARK PUBLIC LIBRARY - SOCIAL SCIENCE DIVISION
5 Washington St.
Box 630   Phone: (201) 733-7782
Newark, NJ 07101-0630   Donald Fostel, Principal Libn.

PRUDENTIAL INSURANCE COMPANY OF AMERICA - CRISP MARKETING
   RESEARCH LIBRARY
14 Prudential Plaza   Phone: (201) 877-7583
Newark, NJ 07101   Barbara Gurdon Ciccone, Marketing Res.Asst.

PRUDENTIAL INSURANCE COMPANY OF AMERICA - DEYDEN BUSINESS
   LIBRARY
Prudential Plaza - 2W   Phone: (201) 877-6749
Newark, NJ 07101   Robert P. Fallon, Libn.

PRUDENTIAL INSURANCE COMPANY OF AMERICA - FINANCIAL LIBRARY
4 Prudential Plaza   Phone: (201) 877-6529
Newark, NJ 07107   Debra R.A. Bowne, Res.Assoc.

PRUDENTIAL INSURANCE COMPANY OF AMERICA - LAW LIBRARY
Gibralter Bldg., 5th Fl.   Phone: (201) 877-6804
Newark, NJ 07101   Vickie Riccardo-Markot, Law Libn.

PUBLIC SERVICE ELECTRIC AND GAS COMPANY - LIBRARY
80 Park Plaza, P3C
Box 570   Phone: (201) 430-7333
Newark, NJ 07101   Florine E. Hunt, Corp.Libn.

RUTGERS UNIVERSITY, THE STATE UNIVERSITY OF NEW JERSEY -
   INSTITUTE OF JAZZ STUDIES
Bradley Hall
Warren & High Sts.   Phone: (201) 648-5595
Newark, NJ 07102   Dan Morgenstern, Dir.

RUTGERS UNIVERSITY, THE STATE UNIVERSITY OF NEW JERSEY -
     JUSTICE HENRY ACKERSON LIBRARY OF LAW & CRIMINAL JUSTICE
Samuel I. Newhouse Ctr.
for Law & Justice
15 Washington St.   Phone: (201) 648-5675
Newark, NJ 07102   Charlie Harvey, Law Libn.

ST. MICHAEL MEDICAL CENTER - AQUINAS MEDICAL LIBRARY †
268 High St.   Phone: (201) 877-5471
Newark, NJ 07102   M.A. Strong, Med.Libn.

SETON HALL UNIVERSITY - SCHOOL OF LAW - LAW LIBRARY
1111 Raymond Blvd.   Phone: (201) 642-3994
Newark, NJ 07102   Richard G. Hutchins, Dir.

SHANLEY & FISHER - LAW LIBRARY
550 Broad St.   Phone: (201) 643-1220
Newark, NJ 07102   Maureen McGuire, Libn.

UNITED HOSPITALS MEDICAL CENTER OF NEWARK - LIBRARY AND
     INFORMATION SERVICES
15 S. Ninth St.   Phone: (201) 268-8774
Newark, NJ 07107   Rosary S. Gilheany, Mgr./Lib. & Ref.Serv

U.S. COURT OF APPEALS, 3RD CIRCUIT - BRANCH LIBRARY †
U.S. Post Office & Court House
Box 1068   Phone: (201) 645-3034
Newark, NJ 07101   Maryanne Murphy, Libn.

U.S. DEPT. OF JUSTICE - UNITED STATES ATTORNEY, DISTRICT OF NEW
     JERSEY - LAW LIBRARY
970 Broad St.   Phone: (201) 645-2387
Newark, NJ 07102   Martha Bomgardner, Libn.

UNEXPECTED WILDLIFE REFUGE - LIBRARY *
Unexpected Rd.
Newfield, NJ 08344   Hope Sawyer Buyukmihci, Sec.

SUSSEX COUNTY HISTORICAL SOCIETY - LIBRARY
82 Main St.   Phone: (201) 383-6010
Newton, NJ 07860   Howard E. Case

SUSSEX COUNTY LAW LIBRARY
Court House, 3 High St.   Phone: (201) 383-4590
Newton, NJ 07860   Barbara J. Smith, Ck. To Jury Comm.

DURO-TEST CORPORATION - TECHNICAL LIBRARY *
2321 Kennedy Blvd.   Phone: (201) 867-7000
North Bergen, NJ 07047   Dorothy Jakubczak, Tech.Libn.

HOFFMANN-LA ROCHE, INC. - BUSINESS INFORMATION CENTER
340 Kingsland St.   Phone: (201) 235-3901
Nutley, NJ 07110   Goldie Rosenberg, Mgr.

HOFFMANN-LA ROCHE, INC. - MISD TECHNICAL LIBRARY
Kingsland Rd., Bldg. 85
Nutley, NJ 07110

HOFFMANN-LA ROCHE, INC. - SCIENTIFIC LIBRARY
                                     Phone: (201) 235-3091
Nutley, NJ 07110   Phyllis Deline, Mgr.

ITT CORPORATION - ITT AVIONICS/DEFENSE COMMUNICATIONS
     DIVISION - TECHNICAL LIBRARY †
492 River Rd., Dept. 39212   Phone: (201) 284-2096
Nutley, NJ 07110   Stephanie Pawelek, Tech.Ck.

NUTLEY HISTORICAL SOCIETY MUSEUM - ALICE J. BICKERS LIBRARY
65 Church St.   Phone: (201) 667-5239
Nutley, NJ 07110   Caroline Evangelista, Cur./Hist.

WITCO CHEMICAL CORPORATION - TECHNICAL CENTER LIBRARY †
100 Bauer Dr.   Phone: (201) 337-5812
Oakland, NJ 07436   Miss Jo Therese Smith, Hd.

OCEAN CITY HISTORICAL MUSEUM - LIBRARY
409 Wesley Ave.   Phone: (609) 399-1801
Ocean City, NJ 08226   Cecelia H. Nelson, Cur.

BURNS AND ROE, INC. - TECHNICAL LIBRARY
800 Kinderkamack Rd.   Phone: (201) 265-2000
Oradell, NJ 07649   Mrs. Ujwal Ranadive, Tech.Libn.

PENICK CORPORATION RESEARCH LIBRARY
215 Watchung Ave.   Phone: (201) 673-1335
Orange, NJ 07050   Beth E. Pitcher, Res.Libn.

BERGEN PINES COUNTY HOSPITAL - MEDICAL LIBRARY
E. Ridgewood Ave.   Phone: (201) 967-4000
Paramus, NJ 07652   Victoria Gonzalez, Med.Libn.

DU PONT DE NEMOURS (E.I.) & COMPANY, INC. - PHOTO PRODUCTS
     DEPARTMENT - INFORMATION CENTER
                                     Phone: (201) 257-4600
Parlin, NJ 08859   Peggy J. Joplin, Supv.

BEECHAM PRODUCTS - WESTERN HEMISPHERE RESEARCH - LIBRARY
1500 Littleton Rd.   Phone: (201) 267-1200
Parsippany, NJ 07504   Caroline Perkons, Info.Serv.Spec.

GPU NUCLEAR - CORPORATE LIBRARY
100 Interpace Pkwy.   Phone: (201) 263-4900
Parsippany, NJ 07054   Winifred F. Sayers, Libn.

GPU NUCLEAR - TECHNICAL LIBRARY
100 Interpace Pkwy.
Parsippany, NJ 07054   Toby E. Necht, Tech.Libn.

ST. MARY'S HOSPITAL - MEDICAL ALLIED HEALTH SCIENCE LIBRARY
211 Pennington Ave.   Phone: (201) 473-1000
Passaic, NJ 07055   Sister Gertrude, S.C., Libn.

PASSAIC COUNTY HISTORICAL SOCIETY - LIBRARY
Lambert Castle, Valley Rd.   Phone: (201) 345-6900
Paterson, NJ 07503   Catherine Keene, Dir.

PATERSON NEWS - LIBRARY/NEWSPAPER MORGUE
1 News Plaza   Phone: (201) 274-2000
Paterson, NJ 07509   Sheldon Matson, Libn.

ST. JOSEPH'S HOSPITAL AND MEDICAL CENTER - HEALTH SCIENCES
     LIBRARY
703 Main St.   Phone: (201) 977-2104
Paterson, NJ 07503   Ruth Rosensweig, Dir.

MOBIL RESEARCH & DEVELOPMENT CORPORATION - PAULSBORO
     LABORATORY - TECHNICAL INFORMATION SERVICES
Box 300   Phone: (609) 423-1040
Paulsboro, NJ 08066   Phillip Q. Stumpf, Jr., Mgr.

DATA SYSTEMS ANALYSTS - TECHNICAL LIBRARY
North Park Dr. & Airport Hwy.   Phone: (609) 665-6088
Pennsauken, NJ 08109   Elizabeth Colabrese, Libn.

PERTH AMBOY GENERAL HOSPITAL - MEDICAL LIBRARY
530 New Brunswick Ave.   Phone: (201) 442-3700
Perth Amboy, NJ 08861   Catherine A. Hilman, Health Sci.Libn.

BAKER (J.T.) CHEMICAL COMPANY - RESEARCH LIBRARY
                                     Phone: (201) 859-2151
Phillipsburg, NJ 08865   Frances E. Steele, Tech.Libn.

INGERSOLL-RAND COMPANY - TECHNICAL LIBRARY
Memorial Pkwy.   Phone: (201) 859-8288
Phillipsburg, NJ 08865   Sharon L. Shiner, Libn.

WARREN HOSPITAL - MEDICAL LIBRARY *
185 Roseberry St.   Phone: (201) 859-1500
Phillipsburg, NJ 08865   Mary K. Shipley, Staff Sec.

AMERICAN TELEPHONE & TELEGRAPH COMPANY - BUSINESS & TECHNICAL
     RESOURCE CENTER
444 Hoes Ln.   Phone: (201) 699-2169
Piscataway, NJ 08854   Betty J. Kauffman, Hd.Libn.

BELL TELEPHONE LABORATORIES, INC. - TECHNICAL LIBRARY
6 Corporate Pl.   Phone: (201) 981-6500
Piscataway, NJ 08854   Don T. Ho, Lib. Group Supv.

COLGATE PALMOLIVE COMPANY - TECHNICAL INFORMATION CENTER
909 River Rd.   Phone: (201) 463-1212
Piscataway, NJ 08854   Monica Grover, Sect.Hd.

COLLEGE OF MEDICINE AND DENTISTRY OF NEW JERSEY - RUTGERS
    MEDICAL SCHOOL - MEDIA LIBRARY
University Heights   Phone: (201) 463-4460
Piscataway, NJ 08854   Adrienne Berenbaum, Libn.

COLLEGE OF MEDICINE & DENTISTRY OF NEW JERSEY - RUTGERS
    MEDICAL SCHOOL - OFFICE OF CONSUMER HEALTH EDUCATION
University Heights   Phone: (201) 463-4500
Piscataway, NJ 08854   Vivian K. Miller, Res.Coord.

RUTGERS UNIVERSITY, THE STATE UNIVERSITY OF NEW JERSEY -
    CENTER FOR URBAN POLICY RESEARCH LIBRARY
Kilmer Area, Bldg. 4051   Phone: (201) 932-3136
Piscataway, NJ 08854   Edward E. Duensing, Jr., Info.Mgr.

RUTGERS UNIVERSITY, THE STATE UNIVERSITY OF NEW JERSEY -
    CHEMISTRY LIBRARY
Wright Laboratory
University Heights Campus   Phone: (201) 932-2625
Piscataway, NJ 08854   Dr. Louis P. Torre, Physical Sci.Libn.

RUTGERS UNIVERSITY, THE STATE UNIVERSITY OF NEW JERSEY -
    COMPUTER REFERENCE CENTER
Busch Campus
Box 879 Hill Center   Phone: (201) 932-2296
Piscataway, NJ 08854   Donald G. White, Dir.

RUTGERS UNIVERSITY, THE STATE UNIVERSITY OF NEW JERSEY -
    GOTTSCHO PACKAGING INFORMATION CENTER
College of Engineering
Box 909   Phone: (201) 932-3044
Piscataway, NJ 08854   Darrell R. Morrow, Dir.

RUTGERS UNIVERSITY, THE STATE UNIVERSITY OF NEW JERSEY -
    LIBRARY OF SCIENCE & MEDICINE
Box 1029   Phone: (201) 932-3850
Piscataway, NJ 08854   Shirley W. Bolles, Libn.

RUTGERS UNIVERSITY, THE STATE UNIVERSITY OF NEW JERSEY -
    MATHEMATICAL SCIENCES LIBRARY
                                       Phone: (201) 932-3735
Piscataway, NJ 08854   Sylvia Walsh, Libn.

RUTGERS UNIVERSITY, THE STATE UNIVERSITY OF NEW JERSEY -
    PHYSICS LIBRARY
Busch Campus
Serin Physics Laboratory   Phone: (201) 932-2500
Piscataway, NJ 08854   Dr. Louis P. Torre, Phys.Sci.Libn.

RUTGERS UNIVERSITY, THE STATE UNIVERSITY OF NEW JERSEY -
    RUTGERS CENTER OF ALCOHOL STUDIES - LIBRARY
Smithers Hall, Busch Campus   Phone: (201) 932-4442
Piscataway, NJ 08854   Penny B. Page, Act.Libn.

RUTGERS UNIVERSITY, THE STATE UNIVERSITY OF NEW JERSEY -
    WAKSMAN INSTITUTE OF MICROBIOLOGY LIBRARY
Box 759   Phone: (201) 932-2906
Piscataway, NJ 08854   Helen Hoffman, Libn.

TENNECO CHEMICALS, INC. - LIBRARY
Box 365   Phone: (201) 752-5000
Piscataway, NJ 08854   Joan A. Carnahan, Mgr., Lib. & Info.Ctr.

BURROUGHS CORPORATION - ELECTRONIC COMPONENTS DIVISION -
    ENGINEERING LIBRARY
Box 1226   Phone: (201) 757-5000
Plainfield, NJ 07061

CRESCENT AVENUE PRESBYTERIAN CHURCH - LIBRARY
716 Watchung Ave.
Plainfield, NJ 07060

LOCKHEED ELECTRONICS COMPANY, INC. - TECHNICAL DOCUMENT
    CENTER AND LIBRARY †
1501 U.S. Hwy. 22, C.S. No. 1   Phone: (201) 757-1600
Plainfield, NJ 07061   Marie Knight, Tech.Libn.

MUHLENBERG HOSPITAL - E. GORDON GLASS, M.D., MEMORIAL LIBRARY
Park Ave. & Randolph Rd.   Phone: (201) 668-2005
Plainfield, NJ 07061   Jane McCarthy, Libn.

SEVENTH DAY BAPTIST HISTORICAL SOCIETY - LIBRARY
510 Watchung Ave.
Box 868   Phone: (201) 561-8700
Plainfield, NJ 07061   C. Harmon Dickinson, Act.Hist.

TEMPLE BETH EL - LIBRARY
225 E. Seventh St.   Phone: (201) 756-2333
Plainfield, NJ 07060   Irving Olian, Libn.

PRINCETON POLYMER LABORATORIES, INC. - LIBRARY
501 Plainsboro Rd.   Phone: (609) 799-2060
Plainsboro, NJ 08536   Donald E. Hudgin, Info.Dir.

CHILTON MEMORIAL HOSPITAL - MEDICAL LIBRARY
97 West Parkway   Phone: (201) 835-3700
Pompton Plains, NJ 07444   Janice Sweeton, Med.Libn.

AMERICAN CAN COMPANY - PRINCETON RESEARCH INFORMATION
    CENTER
Box 50   Phone: (609) 921-2510
Princeton, NJ 08540   Kathleen A. Giovannini, Info.Sci.

AMERICAN CYANAMID COMPANY - AGRICULTURAL RESEARCH DIVISION -
    TECHNICAL INFORMATION SERVICES
Box 400   Phone: (609) 799-0400
Princeton, NJ 08540   Judith C. Leondar, Mgr.

EDUCATIONAL TESTING SERVICE - CARL CAMPBELL BRIGHAM LIBRARY
Rosedale Rd.   Phone: (609) 921-9000
Princeton, NJ 08541   Janet Williams, Libn.

EDUCOM, INTERUNIVERSITY COMMUNICATIONS COUNCIL, INC. -
    LIBRARY
Rosedale Rd.
Box 364   Phone: (609) 921-7575
Princeton, NJ 08540   Eleanor G. Sayles, Libn.

ERIC CLEARINGHOUSE ON TESTS, MEASUREMENT AND EVALUATION
Educational Testing Service
Rosedale Rd.   Phone: (609) 734-5181
Princeton, NJ 08541   Dr. S. Donald Melville, Dir.

EXCERPTA MEDICA - DATABASE DIVISION
Box 3085   Phone: (609) 896-9450
Princeton, NJ 08540   Alex Adler, Pres.

FMC CORPORATION - CHEMICAL RESEARCH & DEVELOPMENT CENTER -
    TECHNICAL INFORMATION SERVICES
Box 8   Phone: (609) 452-2300
Princeton, NJ 08540   Paul Garwig, Mgr.Tech.Info.Serv.

FOUNDATION FOR STUDENT COMMUNICATION - LIBRARY AND RESOURCE
    CENTER
305 Aaron Burr Hall
Princeton University   Phone: (609) 921-1111
Princeton, NJ 08540   Reid A. Buch, Libn.

HISTORICAL SOCIETY OF PRINCETON - LIBRARY
158 Nassau St.   Phone: (609) 921-6817
Princeton, NJ 08540   W.S. Gunning, Chm.Lib.Comm.

INGERSOLL-RAND RESEARCH, INC. - TECHNICAL LIBRARY
Box 301   Phone: (609) 921-9103
Princeton, NJ 08540   Susan E. Collier, Tech.Libn.

INSTITUTE FOR ADVANCED STUDY - LIBRARIES
                                       Phone: (609) 924-4400
Princeton, NJ 08540

INSTITUTE FOR DEFENSE ANALYSES - COMMUNICATIONS RESEARCH
    DIVISION - LIBRARY
Thanet Rd.   Phone: (609) 924-4600
Princeton, NJ 08540   Jane P. Ciosek, Libn.

GEOGRAPHIC

JOHNSON (Robert Wood) FOUNDATION - LIBRARY
                              Phone: (609) 452-8701
Princeton, NJ 08540   Philip J. Gallagher, Libn.

MEDICAL CENTER AT PRINCETON - MEDICAL CENTER LIBRARY
253 Witherspoon St.   Phone: (609) 921-7700
Princeton, NJ 08540   Louise M. Yorke, Libn.

METAL POWDER INDUSTRIES FEDERATION - TECHNICAL INFORMATION
    CENTER
105 College Rd., E.   Phone: (609) 452-7700
Princeton, NJ 08540   Kempton H. Roll, Exec.Dir.

MOBIL RESEARCH & DEVELOPMENT CORPORATION - CENTRAL RESEARCH
    DIVISION LIBRARY
Box 1025   Phone: (609) 737-3000
Princeton, NJ 08540   Jean B. Clarke, Libn.

MOBIL RESEARCH & DEVELOPMENT CORPORATION - ENGINEERING
    DEPARTMENT - INFORMATION CENTER
Box 1026   Phone: (609) 737-3000
Princeton, NJ 08540   Elizabeth N. Mailloux, Mgr.

NEW JERSEY NEURO-PSYCHIATRIC INSTITUTE - PROFESSIONAL LIBRARY
Box 1000   Phone: (609) 466-0400
Princeton, NJ 08540   Donald W. Biggs, Sr.Libn.

PRINCETON THEOLOGICAL SEMINARY - SPEER LIBRARY †
Mercer St. & Library Pl.
Box 111   Phone: (609) 921-8300
Princeton, NJ 08540   Dr. Charles Willard, Libn.

PRINCETON UNIVERSITY - ASTRONOMY LIBRARY
Peyton Hall   Phone: (609) 452-3820
Princeton, NJ 08544   Peter Cziffra, Libn.

PRINCETON UNIVERSITY - BIOLOGY LIBRARY
Guyot Hall   Phone: (609) 452-3235
Princeton, NJ 08544   Helen Y. Zimmerberg, Libn.

PRINCETON UNIVERSITY - CHEMISTRY & BIOCHEMISTRY LIBRARY
Frick Chemical Laboratory   Phone: (609) 452-3238
Princeton, NJ 08544   Dr. David Goodman, Libn.

PRINCETON UNIVERSITY - DEPARTMENT OF ART & ARCHAEOLOGY - INDEX
    OF CHRISTIAN ART
McCormick Hall   Phone: (609) 452-3773
Princeton, NJ 08544   Isa Ragusa, Act.Dir.

PRINCETON UNIVERSITY - ENGINEERING LIBRARY
School of Engineering   Phone: (609) 452-3200
Princeton, NJ 08544   Dolores M. Hoelle, Libn.

PRINCETON UNIVERSITY - GEOLOGY LIBRARY
Guyot Hall   Phone: (609) 452-3267
Princeton, NJ 08544   David C. Stager, Geology Libn.

PRINCETON UNIVERSITY - GEST ORIENTAL LIBRARY AND EAST ASIAN
    COLLECTIONS
317 Palmer Hall   Phone: (609) 452-3183
Princeton, NJ 08544   Kang-i Sun Chang, Cur.

PRINCETON UNIVERSITY - INDUSTRIAL RELATIONS LIBRARY
                              Phone: (609) 452-4043
Princeton, NJ 08544   Kevin Barry, Libn.

PRINCETON UNIVERSITY - MARQUAND LIBRARY
McCormick Hall   Phone: (609) 452-3783
Princeton, NJ 08544   Mary M. Schmidt, Libn.

PRINCETON UNIVERSITY - MATHEMATICS, PHYSICS AND STATISTICS
    LIBRARY
                              Phone: (609) 452-3188
Princeton, NJ 08544   Peter Cziffra, Libn.

PRINCETON UNIVERSITY - MUSIC COLLECTION †
Firestone Library   Phone: (609) 452-3230
Princeton, NJ 08544   Paula Morgan, Music Libn.

PRINCETON UNIVERSITY - NEAR EAST COLLECTIONS
Firestone Library   Phone: (609) 452-3279
Princeton, NJ 08544   Eric Ormsby, Cur.

PRINCETON UNIVERSITY - OFFICE OF POPULATION RESEARCH - LIBRARY
21 Prospect Ave.   Phone: (609) 452-4874
Princeton, NJ 08544   Thomas Holzmann, Libn.

PRINCETON UNIVERSITY - PHONOGRAPH RECORD LIBRARY
Woolworth Center of Musical Studies   Phone: (609) 452-4251
Princeton, NJ 08544   Marjorie Hassen, Record Libn.

PRINCETON UNIVERSITY - PLASMA PHYSICS LIBRARY
Box 451   Phone: (609) 452-3254
Princeton, NJ 08544   Elizabeth Graydon, Libn.

PRINCETON UNIVERSITY - PLINY FISK LIBRARY OF ECONOMICS AND
    FINANCE
Firestone Library   Phone: (609) 452-3211
Princeton, NJ 08544   Louise Tompkins, Libn.

PRINCETON UNIVERSITY - PSYCHOLOGY LIBRARY
Green Hall   Phone: (609) 452-3239
Princeton, NJ 08544   Janice D. Welburn, Psych.Libn.

PRINCETON UNIVERSITY - PUBLIC ADMINISTRATION COLLECTION
Firestone Library   Phone: (609) 452-3209
Princeton, NJ 08544   Rosemary Allen Little, Libn.

PRINCETON UNIVERSITY - RARE BOOKS AND SPECIAL COLLECTIONS
Firestone Library   Phone: (609) 452-3184
Princeton, NJ 08544   Richard M. Ludwig, Asst.Libn.

PRINCETON UNIVERSITY - RICHARD HALLIBURTON MAP COLLECTION
Firestone Library   Phone: (609) 452-3214
Princeton, NJ 08544   Lawrence E. Spellman, Cur. of Maps

PRINCETON UNIVERSITY - URBAN AND ENVIRONMENTAL STUDIES
    LIBRARY
School of Architecture & Urban Planning   Phone: (609) 452-3256
Princeton, NJ 08544   F. Chen, Libn.

PRINCETON UNIVERSITY - WILLIAM SEYMOUR THEATER COLLECTION
Firestone Library   Phone: (609) 452-3223
Princeton, NJ 08544   Mary Ann Jensen, Cur.

PRINCETON UNIVERSITY - WOODROW WILSON SCHOOL OF PUBLIC AND
    INTERNATIONAL AFFAIRS - LIBRARY †
                              Phone: (609) 452-4848
Princeton, NJ 08544   Linda Oppenheim, Libn.

RCA CORPORATION - ASTRO-ELECTRONICS-GOVERNMENT SYSTEMS
    DIVISION - LIBRARY
Box 800   Phone: (609) 448-3400
Princeton, NJ 08540   Mary L. Pfann, Libn.

RCA CORPORATION - DAVID SARNOFF LIBRARY
201 Washington Rd.
Box 432   Phone: (609) 452-2700
Princeton, NJ 08540

RCA CORPORATION - RCA LABORATORIES - DAVID SARNOFF RESEARCH
    CENTER - LIBRARY
                              Phone: (609) 734-2608
Princeton, NJ 08540   Wendy Chu, Mgr.

SQUIBB (E.R.) AND SONS, INC. - SQUIBB INSTITUTE FOR MEDICAL
    RESEARCH - SCIENCE INFORMATION DEPARTMENT
Box 4000   Phone: (609) 921-4844
Princeton, NJ 08540   Helen Kosowski, Supv., Lib.Oper.

TEXTILE RESEARCH INSTITUTE - LIBRARY
601 Prospect Ave.
Box 625   Phone: (609) 924-3150
Princeton, NJ 08540   Helen M. Tornell, Libn.

UNION CAMP CORP. - R & D DIVISION LIBRARY
Box 412   Phone: (609) 896-1200
Princeton, NJ 08540   Helen Lee, Libn.

U.S. NATL. OCEANIC & ATMOSPHERIC ADMINISTRATION - GEOPHYSICAL
  FLUID DYNAMICS LABORATORY - LIBRARY
Box 308   Phone: (609) 452-6550
Princeton, NJ 08540   Philip Fraulino, Libn.

WESTERN ELECTRIC COMPANY, INC. - ENGINEERING RESEARCH CENTER -
  TECHNICAL LIBRARY
Box 900   Phone: (609) 639-2512
Princeton, NJ 08540   William H. Fisher, Hd.Libn.

WESTMINSTER CHOIR COLLEGE - TALBOTT LIBRARY
Hamilton Ave. at Walnut Ln.   Phone: (609) 921-3658
Princeton, NJ 08540   John G. Peck, Jr., Dir., Lib.Serv.

EMR PHOTOELECTRIC-SCHLUMBERGER LTD. - BUSINESS LIBRARY &
  TECHNICAL INFORMATION *
20 Wallace Rd.
Box 44   Phone: (609) 799-1000
Princeton Junction, NJ 08540   Angela Harris, Ck.

M AND T CHEMICALS, INC. - TECHNICAL & BUSINESS INFORMATION
  CENTER
Box 1104   Phone: (201) 499-2437
Rahway, NJ 07065   Marguerite K. Moran, Dir.

MERCK & COMPANY, INC. - LAW LIBRARY
Box 2000   Phone: (201) 574-5805
Rahway, NJ 07065   Elizabeth H. Penman, Libn.

MERCK & COMPANY, INC. - MERCK SHARP & DOHME RESEARCH
  LABORATORIES - RESEARCH INFORMATION SYSTEMS
126 E. Lincoln Ave.   Phone: (201) 574-4726
Rahway, NJ 07065   Arlene C. Peterson, Mgr., Res.Info.Sys.

MERCK & COMPANY, INC. - MERCK SHARP & DOHME RESEARCH
  LABORATORIES - RESEARCH LIBRARIES
                                      Phone: (201) 574-6046
Rahway, NJ 07065   Ilona Giedrys, Res.Libn.

ORTHO PHARMACEUTICAL CORPORATION - HARTMAN LIBRARY
U.S. Hwy. 202   Phone: (201) 524-2240
Raritan, NJ 08869   June Bente, Mgr.

RIVERVIEW HOSPITAL - MEDICAL LIBRARY †
35 Union St.   Phone: (201) 741-2700
Red Bank, NJ 07701   Cheryl Newman, Med.Libn.

AMERICAN POWER JET COMPANY - LIBRARY *
705 Grand Ave.   Phone: (201) 945-8203
Ridgefield, NJ 07657

VALLEY HOSPITAL - LIBRARY
Linwood Ave.   Phone: (201) 445-4900
Ridgewood, NJ 07451   Wanda Borgen, Med.Libn.

FAIRLEIGH DICKINSON UNIVERSITY - MESSLER LIBRARY - NEW JERSEY
  ROOM
Montross Ave.   Phone: (201) 933-5000
Rutherford, NJ 07070   Catharine M. Fogarty, NJ Room Libn.

SALEM COUNTY HISTORICAL SOCIETY - LIBRARY
79-83 Market St.   Phone: (609) 935-5004
Salem, NJ 08079   Lucille G. Magill

SALEM COUNTY LAW LIBRARY
92 Market St.   Phone: (609) 935-7510
Salem, NJ 08079   Michael W. Chewkanes, Law Ck.

SALEM COUNTY MEMORIAL HOSPITAL - DAVID W. GREEN MEDICAL
  LIBRARY
                                      Phone: (609) 935-1000
Salem, NJ 08079   Marion E. Schultz, Med.Libn.

MOSS ARCHIVES
Box 234   Phone: (201) 842-0336
Sea Bright, NJ 07760   George H. Moss, Jr.

ATLANTIC COUNTY HISTORICAL SOCIETY - LIBRARY
907 Shore Rd.
Box 301   Phone: (609) 927-5218
Somers Point, NJ 08244   Elaine Abrahamson, Libn.

ETHICON, INC. - SCIENTIFIC INFORMATION SERVICES
Rte. 22   Phone: (201) 524-3402
Somerville, NJ 08076   Dr. Charles G. Fritz, Dir.

HOECHST-ROUSSEL PHARMACEUTICALS, INC. - LIBRARY
Route 202-206, North   Phone: (201) 685-2394
Somerville, NJ 08840   Loretta F. Stangs, Mgr., Lib.Serv.

RCA CORPORATION - SOLID STATE DIVISION - LIBRARY
Rte. 202   Phone: (201) 685-6017
Somerville, NJ 08876   Barbara S. McCoy, Libn.

SOMERSET COUNTY LAW LIBRARY
Court House   Phone: (201) 725-4700
Somerville, NJ 08876   Sylvia Reuben, Law Libn.

ARCHAEOLOGICAL SOCIETY OF NEW JERSEY - LIBRARY
Rm. 8, Humanities Bldg.
Seton Hall University   Phone: (201) 762-6680
South Orange, NJ 07079   Joan E. Kraft, Chm., Lib.Comm.

SETON HALL UNIVERSITY - MC LAUGHLIN LIBRARY
405 South Orange Ave.   Phone: (201) 762-9000
South Orange, NJ 07079   Rev. James C. Sharp, Act.Univ.Libn.

SETON HALL UNIVERSITY - MAC MANUS COLLECTION
McLaughlin Library
405 South Orange Ave.   Phone: (201) 762-9000
South Orange, NJ 07079   Rev. William Noe Field, Libn.

SETON HALL UNIVERSITY - UNIVERSITY ARCHIVES
McLaughlin Library
405 South Orange Ave.   Phone: (201) 762-7052
South Orange, NJ 07079   Peter J. Wosh, Univ.Archv.

SOUTH MOUNTAIN LABORATORIES, INC. - LIBRARY
380 Lackawanna Pl.   Phone: (201) 762-0045
South Orange, NJ 07079   C.N. Mangieri, Dir.

ASARCO INC. - LIBRARY †
Central Research Dept.
901 Oak Tree Rd.   Phone: (201) 756-4800
South Plainfield, NJ 07080   Betty E. Hurlbert, Libn.

SPRINGFIELD HISTORICAL SOCIETY - LIBRARY
126 Morris Ave.
Box 124   Phone: (201) 467-3580
Springfield, NJ 07081   Madeline E. Lancaster, Pres.

VESTIGIA - LIBRARY
RD 2, Brookwood Rd.   Phone: (201) 347-3638
Stanhope, NJ 07874   Robert E. Jones, Pres.

CELANESE CORPORATION - SUMMIT RESEARCH LABORATORIES -
  TECHNICAL INFORMATION CENTER
Box 1000   Phone: (201) 522-7500
Summit, NJ 07901   Dr. Norman Barson, Supv.

CIBA-GEIGY CORPORATION - PHARMACEUTICALS DIVISION - SCIENTIFIC
  INFORMATION CENTER †
556 Morris Ave.   Phone: (201) 277-5544
Summit, NJ 07901   Dr. Karl Doebel, Dir.

OVERLOOK HOSPITAL - HEALTH SCIENCES LIBRARY
193 Morris Ave.   Phone: (201) 522-2119
Summit, NJ 07901   Kathleen A. Moeller, Dir., Lib.Serv.

FAIRLEIGH DICKINSON UNIVERSITY - WEINER LIBRARY - REFERENCE/
  GOVERNMENT DOCUMENTS DEPARTMENT
1000 River Rd.   Phone: (201) 692-2290
Teaneck, NJ 07666   Michelle Fanelli, Hd.

GEOGRAPHIC

GEOGRAPHIC

HOLY NAME HOSPITAL - MEDICAL LIBRARY
Teaneck Rd.   Phone: (201) 833-3014
Teaneck, NJ 07666   Leila M. Hover, Libn.

TEANECK PUBLIC LIBRARY - ORAL AND LOCAL HISTORY PROJECT
840 Teaneck Rd.   Phone: (201) 837-4171
Teaneck, NJ 07666   Hilda Lipkin, Dir.

TENAFLY PRESBYTERIAN CHURCH LIBRARY *
55 Magnolia Ave.   Phone: (201) 567-0111
Tenafly, NJ 07670

BENDIX CORPORATION - ENGINEERING REFERENCE LIBRARY
                                               Phone: (201) 288-2000
Teterboro, NJ 07608   Ethel Toth, Libn.

PERKIN-ELMER TECHNICAL SYSTEMS DIVISION - LIBRARY
106 Apple St.   Phone: (201) 747-7300
Tinton Falls, NJ 07724   Nancy Lynott, Tech.Libn.

OCEAN COUNTY LAW LIBRARY
Court House   Phone: (201) 244-2121
Toms River, NJ 08753   James P. Rutigliana, Asst.Ct.Adm.

CONGOLEUM CORPORATION - RESILIENT FLOORING DIVISION -
   TECHNICAL RESEARCH LIBRARY
Box 3127   Phone: (609) 587-1000
Trenton, NJ 08619   M. Sneid, Libn.

DELAWARE RIVER BASIN COMMISSION - TECHNICAL LIBRARY
25 State Police Dr.
Box 7360   Phone: (609) 883-9500
Trenton, NJ 08628   Mary Frances Wightman, Tech.Libn.

HELENE FULD MEDICAL CENTER - HEALTH SCIENCES LIBRARY
750 Brunswick Ave.   Phone: (609) 396-6575
Trenton, NJ 08638   Kathy Curcio, Dir.

MERCER MEDICAL CENTER - DAVID B. ACKLEY MEDICAL LIBRARY
446 Bellevue Ave.   Phone: (609) 396-4070
Trenton, NJ 08607   Mae E. Williams, Libn.

MOTOR BUS SOCIETY, INC. - LIBRARY
Box 7058
Trenton, NJ 08628   John P. Hoschek, Pres.

NEW JERSEY EDUCATION ASSOCIATION - RESEARCH LIBRARY
180 W. State St.
Box 1211   Phone: (609) 599-4561
Trenton, NJ 08607   E. Lynne Van Buskirk, Assoc.Dir.

NEW JERSEY OPTOMETRIC ASSOCIATION - DR. E.C. NUROCK LIBRARY
684 Whitehead Rd.   Phone: (609) 695-3456
Trenton, NJ 08648   David L. Knowlton, Exec.Dir.

NEW JERSEY STATE DEPARTMENT OF ENVIRONMENTAL PROTECTION -
   DIVISION OF WATER RESOURCES - LIBRARY
1474 Prospect St.
Box CN029   Phone: (609) 292-5519
Trenton, NJ 08625   Angelo R. Papa, Lib.Asst.

NEW JERSEY STATE DEPARTMENT OF ENVIRONMENTAL PROTECTION -
   GEOLOGICAL SURVEY - INFORMATION CENTER
Box 1390   Phone: (609) 292-2576
Trenton, NJ 08625   Frank J. Markewicz, Act. State Geologist

NEW JERSEY STATE DEPARTMENT OF HEALTH - LIBRARY
Box 1540   Phone: (609) 292-5693
Trenton, NJ 08625   Cathy A. Stout, Libn.

NEW JERSEY STATE DEPARTMENT OF LABOR AND INDUSTRY - LIBRARY
C.N. 110   Phone: (609) 292-2035
Trenton, NJ 08625   Stuart H. Anderson, Libn.

NEW JERSEY STATE DEPARTMENT OF LAW AND PUBLIC SAFETY -
   ATTORNEY GENERAL'S LIBRARY
State House Annex   Phone: (609) 292-4958
Trenton, NJ 08625   Moira O. Strong, Chf.Libn.

NEW JERSEY STATE LEAGUE OF MUNICIPALITIES - LIBRARY
407 W. State St.   Phone: (609) 695-3481
Trenton, NJ 08618   Jeanne G. Helmstetter, Res.Assoc.

NEW JERSEY STATE LIBRARY
185 W. State St.
Box 1898   Phone: (609) 292-6220
Trenton, NJ 08625   Barbara F. Weaver, State Libn.

NEW JERSEY STATE LIBRARY - BUREAU OF ARCHIVES & HISTORY
185 W. State St.
Box 1898   Phone: (609) 292-6260
Trenton, NJ 08625   Dr. William Wright, Hd.

NEW JERSEY STATE LIBRARY - BUREAU OF LAW AND REFERENCE
185 W. State St.
Box 1898   Phone: (609) 292-6210
Trenton, NJ 08625   Susan Roumfort, Hd.

NEW JERSEY STATE MUSEUM - LIBRARY
State Cultural Ctr., W. State St.
Box 1868   Phone: (609) 292-6308
Trenton, NJ 08625   Leah P. Sloshberg, Dir. of Musm.

ST. FRANCIS MEDICAL CENTER - HEALTH SCIENCES LIBRARY
601 Hamilton Ave.   Phone: (609) 599-5068
Trenton, NJ 08629   Harold N. Boyer, Dir.

THIOKOL CORPORATION - SPECIALTY CHEMICALS DIVISION LIBRARY
Box 8296   Phone: (609) 396-4001
Trenton, NJ 08650   Dorothy McLaughlin, Libn.

TRANSAMERICA DE LAVAL INC. - TECHNICAL LIBRARY
Box 8788   Phone: (609) 890-5445
Trenton, NJ 08650   Ann C. Hunt, Libn.

TRENTON FREE PUBLIC LIBRARY - ART & MUSIC DEPARTMENT
120 Academy St.
Box 2448   Phone: (609) 392-7188
Trenton, NJ 08608   James N. Kisthardt, Dept.Hd.

TRENTON FREE PUBLIC LIBRARY - BUSINESS AND TECHNOLOGY
   DEPARTMENT
120 Academy St.   Phone: (609) 392-7188
Trenton, NJ 08608   Nancy Van Ornam, Dept.Hd.

TRENTON FREE PUBLIC LIBRARY - TRENTONIANA COLLECTION
120 Academy St.   Phone: (609) 392-7188
Trenton, NJ 08608   Nan Wright, Hd., Ref.Dept.

TRENTON PSYCHIATRIC HOSPITAL - MEDICAL LIBRARY
Sullivan Way   Phone: (609) 396-8261
Trenton, NJ 08625   Elaine Scheuerer, Lib.Coord.

TRENTON STATE COLLEGE - ROSCOE L. WEST LIBRARY
Pennington Rd., CN550   Phone: (609) 771-1855
Trenton, NJ 08625   Dr. Paul Z. DuBois, Dir. of Lib.Serv.

TRENTON TIMES - LIBRARY
500 Perry St.   Phone: (609) 396-3232
Trenton, NJ 08605   Susan E. Connery, Dir.

U.S. NAVY - NAVAL AIR PROPULSION CENTER - TECHNICAL LIBRARY †
Box 7176   Phone: (609) 896-5600
Trenton, NJ 08628

W2ZI HISTORICAL WIRELESS MUSEUM - HISTORICAL WIRELESS LIBRARY
19 Blackwood Drive   Phone: (609) 882-6645
Trenton, NJ 08628   Ed G. Raser, Cur./Hist.

CPC INTERNATIONAL - BEST FOODS RESEARCH CENTER - INFORMATION
   CENTER †
1120 Commerce Ave.
Box 1534   Phone: (201) 688-9000
Union, NJ 07083   Anne Troop, Mgr., Info.Serv.

KEAN COLLEGE OF NEW JERSEY - INSTRUCTIONAL RESOURCE CENTER *
Morris Ave.   Phone: (201) 527-2073
Union, NJ 07083   Vincent V. Merlo, Dir., Media & Tech.

KEAN COLLEGE OF NEW JERSEY - NANCY THOMPSON LIBRARY
Phone: (201) 527-2017
Union, NJ 07083
Dr. Louis N. Nagy, Dir.

INTERNATIONAL FLAVORS AND FRAGRANCES, INC. - TECHNICAL
INFORMATION CENTER
1515 Hwy. 36
Phone: (201) 264-4500
Union Beach, NJ 07735
Bernard J. Mayers, Supv.

EDUCATIONAL FOUNDATION FOR HUMAN SEXUALITY - LIBRARY
Montclair State College
Valley Rd. & Normal Ave.
Upper Montclair, NJ 07043

MONTCLAIR STATE COLLEGE - HARRY A. SPRAGUE LIBRARY - SPECIAL
COLLECTIONS
Phone: (201) 893-4301
Upper Montclair, NJ 07043
Blanche W. Haller, Dir. of Lib.Serv.

MONTCLAIR STATE COLLEGE - NATIONAL ADULT EDUCATION
CLEARINGHOUSE/MULTIMEDIA CENTER
Montclair State College
Phone: (201) 893-4353
Upper Montclair, NJ 07043
Frances M. Spinelli, Dir.

WESTERN UNION CORPORATION - LIBRARY †
One Lake St.
Phone: (201) 825-5850
Upper Saddle River, NJ 07458
Alice Critchley, Mgr., Info.Ctr.

BETH ISRAEL CONGREGATION - LIBRARY
1015 E. Park Ave.
Phone: (609) 691-0852
Vineland, NJ 08360
Phyllis Zislin, Act.Dir.

BIOVIVAN RESEARCH INSTITUTE - LIBRARY
9 S. Eighth St.
Phone: (609) 692-1499
Vineland, NJ 08360
Herbert Schwartz, Res.Coord.

VINELAND HISTORICAL AND ANTIQUARIAN SOCIETY - LIBRARY
108 S. 7th St.
Phone: (609) 691-1111
Vineland, NJ 08360
Joseph E. Sherry, Libn.

SOUTH JERSEY REGIONAL FILM LIBRARY
Echelon Urban Ctr., Laurel Rd.
Phone: (609) 772-1642
Voorhees, NJ 08043
Katherine Schalk-Greene, Act.Dir.

WEST JERSEY HOSPITAL, EASTERN DIVISION - STAFF MEDICAL LIBRARY
Evesham Rd.
Phone: (609) 795-3000
Voorhees, NJ 08043
Jean I. Belsterling, Med.Libn.

CONSUMERS' RESEARCH, INC. - LIBRARY
Bowerstown Rd.
Washington, NJ 07882

AMERICAN CYANAMID COMPANY - BUSINESS INFORMATION CENTER
Berdan Ave.
Phone: (201) 831-3592
Wayne, NJ 07470
Claudia A. Gentner, Libn.

AMERICAN CYANAMID COMPANY - ENVIRONMENTAL SERVICES DIVISION
LIBRARY †
Berdan Ave.
Phone: (201) 831-1234
Wayne, NJ 07470
Frances Scholten, Libn.

GAF CORPORATION - TECHNICAL INFORMATION SERVICES
1361 Alps Rd.
Phone: (201) 628-3321
Wayne, NJ 07470
Ira Naznitsky, Supv.

PANDULLO QUIRK ASSOCIATES - LIBRARY
40 Galesi Dr.
Phone: (201) 785-2410
Wayne, NJ 07470
Kathryn Sullivan, Libn.

SINGER COMPANY - KEARFOTT DIVISION - TECHNICAL INFORMATION
CENTER †
150 Totowa Rd.
Phone: (201) 256-4000
Wayne, NJ 07470
B.R. Meade, Supv.

WILLIAM PATERSON COLLEGE OF NEW JERSEY - SARAH BYRD ASKEW
LIBRARY - SPECIAL COLLECTIONS
300 Pompton Rd.
Phone: (201) 595-2113
Wayne, NJ 07470
Dr. Robert L. Goldberg, Dir.

ORGANON, INC. - MEDICAL LIBRARY
375 Mt. Pleasant Ave.
Phone: (201) 325-4614
West Orange, NJ 07052
Jane E. Farrands, Libn.

U.S. NATL. PARK SERVICE - EDISON NATL. HISTORIC SITE - ARCHIVES
Main St. and Lakeside Ave.
Phone: (201) 736-0550
West Orange, NJ 07052
Arthur R. Abel, Archv.

BAKER (H.M.) ASSOCIATES - RESEARCH COLLECTION
266 E. Dudley Ave.
Westfield, NJ 07090
Helen M.B. Cushman, Dir.

PASCACK VALLEY HOSPITAL - DAVID GOLDBERG MEMORIAL MEDICAL
LIBRARY
Old Hook Rd.
Phone: (201) 664-4000
Westwood, NJ 07675
Margaret F. DeMarrais, Libn.

TELEDYNE ISOTOPES - RESEARCH LIBRARY
50 Van Buren Ave.
Phone: (201) 664-7070
Westwood, NJ 07675
Marie Mandel, Res.Libn.

BELL TELEPHONE LABORATORIES, INC. - TECHNICAL LIBRARY
Phone: (201) 386-2604
Whippany, NJ 07981
Mary Jane Miller, Lib. Group Supv.

KNOLL PHARMACEUTICAL COMPANY - RESEARCH LIBRARY
30 N. Jefferson Rd.
Phone: (201) 887-8300
Whippany, NJ 07981
Kerry L. Kushinka, Supv., Med./Sci.Info.

MORRIS COUNTY FREE LIBRARY - NEW JERSEY ROOM
30 East Hanover Ave.
Phone: (201) 285-6130
Whippany, NJ 07981
Evelyn L. Klingler, Ref.Libn.

NATIONAL ASSOCIATION OF PRECANCEL COLLECTORS, INC. - CHESTER
DAVIS MEMORIAL LIBRARY
5121 Park Blvd.
Phone: (609) 522-2569
Wildwood, NJ 08260
Glenn W. Dye, Sec.-Tres.

WILDWOOD HISTORICAL COMMISSION - WILDWOOD LIBRARY OF NEW
JERSEY HISTORY
4408 New Jersey Ave.
Phone: (609) 522-2444
Wildwood, NJ 08260
Mrs. George F. Boyer, Chairman

BURLINGTON COUNTY TIMES - LIBRARY
Route 130
Phone: (609) 877-1600
Willingboro, NJ 08046
Helen Rosser, Libn.

CURTISS-WRIGHT CORPORATION - LIBRARY SERVICES †
1 Passaic St.
Phone: (201) 777-2900
Wood-Ridge, NJ 07075
Frances Litchauer, Libn.

GLOUCESTER COUNTY HISTORICAL SOCIETY - LIBRARY
17 Hunter St.
Phone: (609) 845-4771
Woodbury, NJ 08096
Edith Hoelle, Libn.

UNDERWOOD-MEMORIAL HOSPITAL - LIBRARY †
N. Broad St. & W. Red Bank Ave.
Phone: (609) 845-0100
Woodbury, NJ 08096
Helen M. Metcalfe, Libn.

NEW MEXICO

GHOST RANCH CONFERENCE CENTER - GHOST RANCH LIBRARY †
Phone: (505) 685-4333
Abiquiu, NM 87510
Lidie Miller, Libn.

NEW MEXICO SCHOOL FOR THE VISUALLY HANDICAPPED - LIBRARY
1900 White Sands Blvd.
Phone: (505) 347-3505
Alamogordo, NM 88310
Wanda West, Libn.

U.S. AIR FORCE BASE - HOLLOMAN BASE LIBRARY
Holloman AFB
Phone: (505) 479-3939
Alamogordo, NM 88310
Wanda M. Goecke, Base Libn.

ALBUQUERQUE MUNICIPAL REFERENCE LIBRARY *
Albuquerque Public Library
501 Copper N.W.
Phone: (505) 766-7720
Albuquerque, NM 87103
Verna L. Wood, Bus./Govt.Spec.

GEOGRAPHIC

AMERICAN CLASSICAL COLLEGE - LIBRARY
Box 4526   Phone: (505) 843-7749
Albuquerque, NM 87106   Dr. C.M. Flumiani, Dir.

AMERICAN CLASSICAL COLLEGE - STOCK MARKET LIBRARY
Box 4526   Phone: (505) 843-7749
Albuquerque, NM 87106   Dr. C.M. Flumiani, Dir.

BERNALILLO COUNTY - DISTRICT COURT LAW LIBRARY †
415 Tijeras, N.W.
Box 488   Phone: (505) 242-2961
Albuquerque, NM 87103   Ray Romero, Hd.Libn.

CHURCH OF JESUS CHRIST OF LATTER-DAY SAINTS - ALBUQUERQUE
  BRANCH GENEALOGICAL LIBRARY
Box 3568   Phone: (505) 255-1227
Albuquerque, NM 87110   Don D. Seaman, Libn.

FIRST UNITED PRESBYTERIAN CHURCH - LIBRARY
215 Locust St., N.E.   Phone: (505) 247-9594
Albuquerque, NM 87102   Anita Odermann, Dir./Christian Educ.

LOVELACE BIOMEDICAL & ENVIRONMENTAL RESEARCH INSTITUTE, INC. -
  INHALATION TOXICOLOGY RESEARCH INST. - LIB.
Box 5890   Phone: (505) 844-2600
Albuquerque, NM 87115

MUSEUM OF ALBUQUERQUE - LIBRARY *
Box 1293   Phone: (505) 766-7878
Albuquerque, NM 87103   James C. Moore, Dir.

PRESBYTERIAN HOSPITAL - MEDICAL LIBRARY
1100 Central Ave., S.E.   Phone: (505) 243-9411
Albuquerque, NM 87102   Helen Saylor, Med.Libn.

ST. JOSEPH HOSPITAL - MEDICAL LIBRARY
400 Walter, N.E.   Phone: (505) 243-8811
Albuquerque, NM 87102   Melba Clark, Libn.

ST. THOMAS AQUINAS NEWMAN CENTER - LIBRARY
1815 Las Lomas Rd., N.E.   Phone: (505) 247-1094
Albuquerque, NM 87106   Betty Innerst, Libn.

SOUTHWEST RESEARCH & INFORMATION CENTER
Box 4524   Phone: (505) 262-1862
Albuquerque, NM 87106   Paul Robinson, Exec.Dir.

TINGLEY CRIPPLED CHILDREN'S HOSPITAL - MEDICAL LIBRARY
1128 University Blvd., N.E.
Albuquerque, NM 87102

U.S. DEPT. OF COMMERCE - INTERNATIONAL TRADE ADMINISTRATION -
  ALBUQUERQUE DISTRICT OFFICE LIBRARY †
505 Marquette Ave. N.W.   Phone: (505) 766-2386
Albuquerque, NM 87102   William E. Dwyer, Dir.

U.S. DEPT. OF ENERGY - NATIONAL ATOMIC MUSEUM - LIBRARY
Box 5400   Phone: (505) 844-4378
Albuquerque, NM 87115   Gwen R. Schreiner, Libn.

U.S. DEPT OF ENERGY - SANDIA NATL. LABORATORIES - TECHNICAL
  LIBRARY
Kirtland AFB East   Phone: (505) 844-2869
Albuquerque, NM 87185   Calla Ann Pepmueller, Mgr.

U.S. GEOLOGICAL SURVEY - WATER RESOURCES DIVISION - READING
  ROOM
Western Bank, Rm. 712
505 Marquette N.W.
Box 26659   Phone: (505) 766-2810
Albuquerque, NM 87125   Janie Jones Nelson, Libn.

U.S. NATL. PARK SERVICE - CHACO CENTER - LIBRARY
Box 26176   Phone: (505) 766-3545
Albuquerque, NM 87125   Thomas C. Windes, Supv.Archeo.

U.S. VETERANS ADMINISTRATION (NM-Albuquerque) - MEDICAL CENTER
  LIBRARY
2100 Ridgecrest Dr., S.E.   Phone: (505) 265-1711
Albuquerque, NM 87108   Sharon Johnson, Chf., Lib.Serv.

UNIVERSITY OF NEW MEXICO - BUREAU OF BUSINESS & ECONOMIC
  RESEARCH DATA BANK
Anderson School of Management Bldg.   Phone: (505) 277-2216
Albuquerque, NM 87131   Betsie Kasner, Hd., Info.Serv.

UNIVERSITY OF NEW MEXICO - DEPARTMENT OF ANTHROPOLOGY - CLARK
  FIELD ARCHIVES
Roma & University, N.E.   Phone: (505) 277-4524
Albuquerque, NM 87131   Carrie Wackerbarth, Lib.Mgr.

UNIVERSITY OF NEW MEXICO - FINE ARTS LIBRARY
                                                 Phone: (505) 277-2357
Albuquerque, NM 87131   James B. Wright, Libn.

UNIVERSITY OF NEW MEXICO - MEDICAL CENTER LIBRARY
North Campus   Phone: (505) 277-2548
Albuquerque, NM 87131   Erika Love, Dir.

UNIVERSITY OF NEW MEXICO - SCHOOL OF LAW LIBRARY
1117 Stanford, N.E.   Phone: (505) 277-6236
Albuquerque, NM 87131   Myron Fink, Libn.

UNIVERSITY OF NEW MEXICO - SLIDE LIBRARY
                                                 Phone: (505) 277-6415
Albuquerque, NM 87131   Arlene Richardson, Dir.

UNIVERSITY OF NEW MEXICO - SPECIAL COLLECTIONS DEPARTMENT
General Library   Phone: (505) 277-6451
Albuquerque, NM 87131   Donald Farren, Hd.

UNIVERSITY OF NEW MEXICO - TECHNOLOGY APPLICATION CENTER
                                                 Phone: (505) 277-3622
Albuquerque, NM 87131   Stanley A. Morain, Dir.

UNIVERSITY OF NEW MEXICO - TIREMAN LEARNING MATERIALS LIBRARY
                                                 Phone: (505) 277-3854
Albuquerque, NM 87131   Deborah Eagan, Libn.

UNIVERSITY OF NEW MEXICO - WILLIAM J. PARISH MEMORIAL LIBRARY
                                                 Phone: (505) 277-5912
Albuquerque, NM 87131   Judith Bernstein, Bus.Adm.Libn.

ARTESIA HISTORICAL MUSEUM AND ART CENTER - LIBRARY †
505 W. Richardson   Phone: (505) 748-2390
Artesia, NM 88210   Frances W. Collins, Dir. of Musm.

U.S. NATL. PARK SERVICE - AZTEC RUINS NATL. MONUMENT - LIBRARY
Box U   Phone: (505) 334-6174
Aztec, NM 87410   William L. Schart, Pk. Ranger

U.S. NATL. PARK SERVICE - CHACO CANYON NATL. MONUMENT - VISITOR
  CENTER LIBRARY
Star Rte.   Phone: (505) 786-5384
Bloomfield, NM 87413   James Trott, Archeo.

U.S. AIR FORCE BASE - CANNON BASE LIBRARY *
FL 4855   Phone: (505) 784-3311
Cannon AFB, NM 88101   M. Edith Pierce, Libn.

GUADALUPE MEDICAL CENTER - MEDICAL STAFF LIBRARY
2430 W. Pierce St.   Phone: (505) 887-6633
Carlsbad, NM 88220   Dorothy Eswein, Med.Rec.Dir./Libn.

U.S. NATL. PARK SERVICE - CARLSBAD CAVERNS NATL. PARK - LIBRARY
3225 National Parks Hwy.   Phone: (505) 885-8884
Carlsbad, NM 88220   Robert W. Peters, Interp.

SETON MEMORIAL LIBRARY & MUSEUM *
Philmont Scout Ranch & Explorer Base   Phone: (505) 376-2281
Cimarron, NM 87714   Bonita Tooley, Libn.

SAN JUAN COUNTY ARCHAEOLOGICAL RESEARCH CENTER & LIBRARY
Rte. 3, Box 858   Phone: (505) 632-2013
Farmington, NM 87401   Ouida Steward, Libn.

U.S. PUBLIC HEALTH SERVICE HOSPITAL - GALLUP INDIAN MEDICAL
  CENTER - MEDICAL LIBRARY
East Nizhoni Blvd.
Box 1337   Phone: (505) 722-1119
Gallup, NM 84301   Patricia V. Bradley, Med.Libn.

U.S. AIR FORCE - AIR FORCE SYSTEMS COMMAND - TECHNICAL
    INFORMATION CENTER
6585th Test Group   Phone: (505) 473-6511
Holloman AFB, NM 88330   William F. Whalen, Chf.

U.S. AIR FORCE BASE - KIRTLAND BASE LIBRARY
FL 4469   Phone: (505) 844-0795
Kirtland AFB, NM 87117   Robert C. Mathews, Act.Libn.

U.S. AIR FORCE HOSPITAL - MEDICAL LIBRARY (NM-Kirtland AFB)
                                     Phone: (505) 264-1086
Kirtland AFB, NM 87117   Alice T. Lee, Libn.

U.S. AIR FORCE WEAPONS LABORATORY - TECHNICAL LIBRARY
                                     Phone: (505) 844-7449
Kirtland AFB, NM 87117   Georgiana Hillyer, Chf., Tech.Lib.

ERIC CLEARINGHOUSE ON RURAL EDUCATION AND SMALL SCHOOLS
New Mexico State University
Box 3AP   Phone: (505) 646-2623
Las Cruces, NM 88003   Dr. Everett D. Edington, Dir.

NEW MEXICO STATE UNIVERSITY - PHYSICAL SCIENCE LABORATORY -
    TECHNICAL LIBRARY *
Box 3 PSL   Phone: (505) 522-9100
Las Cruces, NM 88003   Verla Daugherty, Tech.Libn.

NEW MEXICO STATE DEPARTMENT OF HOSPITALS - STATE HOSPITAL -
    ELLA P. KIEF MEMORIAL LIBRARY
Hot Springs Blvd.
Box 1388   Phone: (505) 425-6711
Las Vegas, NM 87701   Hazel Hurley, Libn.

IMMACULATE HEART OF MARY - PARISH LIBRARY
3700 Canyon Rd.   Phone: (505) 662-6193
Los Alamos, NM 87544

LOS ALAMOS COUNTY HISTORICAL MUSEUM - ARCHIVES
Fuller Lodge Cultural Ctr.
Box 43   Phone: (505) 662-6272
Los Alamos, NM 87544   Hedy M. Dunn, Musm.Mgr.

UNITED CHURCH OF LOS ALAMOS - LIBRARY
2525 Canyon Rd.   Phone: (505) 662-2971
Los Alamos, NM 87544   Mrs. Donald P. MacMillan, Libn.

U.S. NATL. PARK SERVICE - BANDELIER NATL. MONUMENT - LIBRARY
                                     Phone: (505) 672-3861
Los Alamos, NM 87544   Edward J. Greene, Supv.Pk.Ranger

UNIVERSITY OF CALIFORNIA - LOS ALAMOS NATIONAL LABORATORY -
    LIBRARY
MS-N362, Box 1663   Phone: (505) 667-4448
Los Alamos, NM 87545   J. Arthur Freed, Hd.Libn.

LOS LUNAS HOSPITAL AND TRAINING SCHOOL - LIBRARY AND RESOURCE
    CENTER
Box 1269   Phone: (505) 865-9611
Los Lunas, NM 87031   Sarah Knox Morley, Libn.

EASTERN NEW MEXICO UNIVERSITY - GOLDEN LIBRARY
                                     Phone: (505) 562-2624
Portales, NM 88130   Peggy M. Tozer, Lib.Dir.

SOUTHERN METHODIST UNIVERSITY - FORT BURGWIN RESEARCH CENTER
    - LIBRARY & HERBARIUM
Box 314   Phone: (505) 758-8322
Ranchos De Taos, NM 87557

CHAVES COUNTY DISTRICT COURT - LIBRARY
Box 1776
Roswell, NM 88201

FIRST BAPTIST CHURCH - MEDIA CENTER †
Box 1996   Phone: (505) 623-2640
Roswell, NM 88201   Jeannine Miller, Dir. of Media Ctr.

ROSWELL MUSEUM AND ART CENTER - ART LIBRARY
100 W. 11th St.   Phone: (505) 622-4700
Roswell, NM 88201   Wendell Ott, Dir.

BROTHERS THREE OF MORIARTY - LIBRARY
1917 Fort Union Dr.   Phone: (505) 982-2947
Santa Fe, NM 87501   John Bennett Shaw, Owner

EPISCOPAL CHURCH OF THE HOLY FAITH - PARISH LIBRARY
311 E. Palace Ave.
Box 1848   Phone: (505) 982-4447
Santa Fe, NM 87501   Katherine Landers, Libn.

MUSEUM OF NEW MEXICO - HISTORY LIBRARY
Box 2087   Phone: (505) 827-2343
Santa Fe, NM 87503

MUSEUM OF NEW MEXICO - LABORATORY OF ANTHROPOLOGY - LIBRARY
Box 2087   Phone: (505) 827-3241
Santa Fe, NM 87503   Laura J. Holt, Libn.

MUSEUM OF NEW MEXICO - MUSEUM OF FINE ARTS - LIBRARY
Box 2087   Phone: (505) 827-3165
Santa Fe, NM 87501   Alberta F. Donlan, Hd.Libn.

MUSEUM OF NEW MEXICO - MUSEUM OF INTERNATIONAL FOLK ART -
    LIBRARY
Box 2087   Phone: (505) 827-2544
Santa Fe, NM 87503   Judith Sellars, Libn.

MUSEUM OF NEW MEXICO - PHOTOGRAPHIC ARCHIVES
Box 2087   Phone: (505) 827-2559
Santa Fe, NM 87503   Arthur L. Olivas, Archv.

NEW MEXICO STATE COMMERCE AND INDUSTRY DEPT. - ECONOMIC
    DEVELOPMENT DIVISION - LIBRARY
Bataan Memorial Bldg.   Phone: (505) 827-5571
Santa Fe, NM 87503   Rosalie Howland, Libn.

NEW MEXICO STATE ENERGY AND MINERALS DEPARTMENT - LIBRARY
113 Washington St.
Box 2770   Phone: (505) 827-2471
Santa Fe, NM 87501   Kathleen LaPlante, Libn.

NEW MEXICO STATE LEGISLATIVE COUNCIL SERVICE - LIBRARY
334 State Capitol   Phone: (505) 827-3141
Santa Fe, NM 87503   E. Jean Peters, Hd.Libn.

NEW MEXICO STATE LIBRARY
Box 1629   Phone: (505) 827-2033
Santa Fe, NM 87503   Clifford E. Lange, State Libn.

NEW MEXICO STATE RECORDS CENTER AND ARCHIVES - DOROTHY
    WOODWARD RESEARCH ROOM
404 Montezuma St.   Phone: (505) 827-2321
Santa Fe, NM 87503   Bryan M. Miller, Chf., Archv.Serv.Div.

NEW MEXICO STATE SUPREME COURT - LAW LIBRARY
Supreme Court Bldg.
Drawer L   Phone: (505) 827-2515
Santa Fe, NM 87501   John P. Blum, Dir.

SCHOOL OF AMERICAN RESEARCH - LIBRARY
Box 2188   Phone: (505) 982-3583
Santa Fe, NM 87501   Elizabeth Y. Kingman, Libn.

SIERRA CLUB - ENVIRONMENTAL LIBRARY & INFORMATION CENTER
1709 Paseo De Peralta   Phone: (505) 983-2703
Santa Fe, NM 87501

SOUTHWEST FOUNDATION FOR AUDIOVISUAL RESOURCES - AV
    COLLECTION
Box 522
Santa Fe, NM 87501

U.S. BUREAU OF LAND MANAGEMENT - NEW MEXICO STATE OFFICE
    LIBRARY
Box 1449   Phone: (505) 988-6248
Santa Fe, NM 87501   Caren T. Cline, Supv.Mgt.Asst.

GEOGRAPHIC

GEOGRAPHIC

WHEELRIGHT MUSEUM - LIBRARY
704 Camino Lejo
Box 5153   Phone: (505) 982-4636
Santa Fe, NM 87502   Laryne Parrish, Musm.Cur.

U.S. NATL. PARK SERVICE - GILA CLIFF DWELLINGS NATL. MONUMENT -
    VISITOR CENTER LIBRARY
Rte. 11, Box 100   Phone: (505) 534-9461
Silver City, NM 88061

NEW MEXICO INSTITUTE OF MINING AND TECHNOLOGY - MARTIN SPEARE
    MEMORIAL LIBRARY
Campus Station   Phone: (505) 835-5614
Socorro, NM 87801   Beverly Hawks, Act.Dir.

SACRAMENTO PEAK OBSERVATORY - LIBRARY
                                             Phone: (505) 434-1390
Sunspot, NM 88349   Cecilia Miranda, Libn.

CARSON (Kit) MEMORIAL FOUNDATION - HISTORICAL RESEARCH LIBRARY
    AND ARCHIVES
E. Kit Carson Ave.
Box B   Phone: (505) 758-4741
Taos, NM 87571   Jack K. Boyer, Dir.

HARWOOD FOUNDATION LIBRARY OF THE UNIVERSITY OF NEW MEXICO
25 Ledoux St.
Box 766   Phone: (505) 758-3063
Taos, NM 87571   James Levy, Dir.

U.S. NATL. PARK SERVICE - FORT UNION NATL. MONUMENT - LIBRARY
                                             Phone: (505) 425-8025
Watrous, NM 87753   Carol M. Kruse, Unit Mgr.

U.S. ARMY - TRADOC SYSTEMS ANALYSIS ACTIVITY - TRASANA
    TECHNICAL LIBRARY
Attn: ATAA-SL   Phone: (505) 678-3135
White Sands Missile Range, NM 88002   Judy A. Hawthorne, Adm.Libn.

U.S. ARMY - WHITE SANDS MISSILE RANGE - TECHNICAL LIBRARY
    DIVISION
                                             Phone: (505) 678-1317
White Sands Missile Range, NM 88002   Laurel B. Saunders, Chf.

NEW YORK

ALBANY BUSINESS COLLEGE - LIBRARY
130 Washington Ave.   Phone: (518) 465-3449
Albany, NY 12210   Janet Mathews, Libn.

ALBANY INSTITUTE OF HISTORY AND ART - MC KINNEY LIBRARY
125 Washington Ave.   Phone: (518) 463-4478
Albany, NY 12210   James R. Hobin, Libn.

CAPITAL DISTRICT PSYCHIATRIC CENTER - LIBRARY
75 New Scotland Ave.   Phone: (518) 445-6608
Albany, NY 12208   Bill McKewen, Libn.

FIRST CHURCH IN ALBANY (Reformed) - LIBRARY
N. Pearl & Clinton Sq.   Phone: (518) 463-4449
Albany, NY 12210   E. Helen Gardner, Libn.

HISTORICAL SOCIETY OF EARLY AMERICAN DECORATION, INC. - LIBRARY
19 Dove St.
Albany, NY 12210   Mrs. Charles Coffin, Libn.

HOSPITAL EDUCATIONAL AND RESEARCH FUND - LILLIAN R. HAYT
    MEMORIAL LIBRARY
Center for Health Initiatives
15 Computer Dr., W.   Phone: (518) 458-7940
Albany, NY 12205   Elaine C. Rotman, Libn.

KEY BANK N.A. - INFORMATION CENTER
60 State St.   Phone: (518) 447-3594
Albany, NY 12207   Joy Longo, Libn.

MEMORIAL HOSPITAL - MEDICAL LIBRARY
Northern Blvd.   Phone: (518) 471-3264
Albany, NY 12204   G.A. McNamara, Libn.

NATIONAL CATHOLIC STEWARDSHIP COUNCIL - INFORMATION CENTER
1 Columbia Place   Phone: (518) 465-0233
Albany, NY 12207   Rev. James M. Mackey, Exec.Dir.

NEW YORK STATE CONFERENCE OF MAYORS AND MUNICIPAL OFFICIALS -
    LIBRARY
119 Washington Ave.   Phone: (518) 463-1185
Albany, NY 12210   Gordon C. Perry, Exec.Dir.

NEW YORK STATE DEPARTMENT OF AUDIT CONTROL - LIBRARY
Alfred E. Smith Office Bldg.   Phone: (518) 474-3419
Albany, NY 12236   Rita Wiers, Sr. Typist

NEW YORK STATE DEPARTMENT OF CIVIL SERVICE - LIBRARY
State Office Bldg. Campus, Bldg. No. 1   Phone: (518) 457-6494
Albany, NY 12239   Virginia McCarthy, Dept.Libn.

NEW YORK STATE DEPARTMENT OF COMMERCE - LIBRARY
99 Washington Ave.   Phone: (518) 474-5664
Albany, NY 12245   John J. Kilrain, Libn.

NEW YORK STATE DEPARTMENT OF ENVIRONMENTAL CONSERVATION -
    OFFICE OF EDUC. SERV. - INFORMATION SERVICE
50 Wolf Rd.   Phone: (518) 457-3720
Albany, NY 12233   Graham L. Cox, Dir., Eniviromental Educ.

NEW YORK STATE DEPARTMENT OF HEALTH - DIVISION OF
    LABORATORIES AND RESEARCH LIBRARY
Empire State Plaza   Phone: (518) 474-6172
Albany, NY 12201   Thomas Flynn, Dir.

NEW YORK STATE DEPARTMENT OF LAW - LIBRARY
The Capitol   Phone: (518) 474-3840
Albany, NY 12224   Thomas R. Heitz, Chf., Lib.Serv.

NEW YORK STATE DEPARTMENT OF MOTOR VEHICLES - RESEARCH
    LIBRARY
Swan St. Bldg., Empire State Plaza   Phone: (518) 474-0684
Albany, NY 12228   Frances A. Miller, Sr.Libn.

NEW YORK STATE DEPARTMENT OF STATE - LIBRARY
162 Washington Ave.   Phone: (518) 474-7144
Albany, NY 12231   Kathryn E. Jackson, Sr.Libn.

NEW YORK STATE DEPARTMENT OF TAXATION & FINANCE - TAX LIBRARY
Bureau of Research & Statistics
Taxation & Finance Bldg.   Phone: (518) 457-3512
Albany, NY 12227   Jacqueline Goot, Act.Libn.

NEW YORK STATE DEPARTMENT OF TRANSPORTATION - MAP
    INFORMATION UNIT
State Office Campus
Bldg. 4, Rm. 105   Phone: (518) 457-3555
Albany, NY 12232   Paul McElligott, Assoc.Cartographer

NEW YORK STATE DEPARTMENT OF TRANSPORTATION PLANNING
    DIVISION - LIBRARY
1220 Washington Ave.
Bldg. 4, Rm. 209   Phone: (518) 457-6920
Albany, NY 12232   Carol R. Olson, Asst.Libn.

NEW YORK STATE LIBRARY
Cultural Education Center
Empire State Plaza   Phone: (518) 474-7646
Albany, NY 12230   Peter Paulson, Dir.

NEW YORK STATE LIBRARY FOR THE BLIND AND VISUALLY HANDICAPPED
Cultural Education Center
Empire State Plaza   Phone: (518) 474-5935
Albany, NY 12230   Audrey Smith, Assoc.Libn.

NEW YORK STATE LIBRARY - HUMANITIES REFERENCE SERVICE
Cultural Education Center
Empire State Plaza   Phone: (518) 474-5958
Albany, NY 12230   Mildred Ledden, Assoc.Libn.

NEW YORK STATE LIBRARY - LAW/SOCIAL SCIENCE REFERENCE
    SERVICES
Cultural Education Center
Empire State Plaza   Phone: (518) 474-5943
Albany, NY 12230   Stephanie Welden, State Law Libn.

NEW YORK STATE LIBRARY - LEGISLATIVE AND GOVERNMENTAL
    SERVICES
Cultural Education Center
Empire State Plaza   Phone: (518) 474-3940
Albany, NY 12230   Mary Redmond, Principal Libn.

NEW YORK STATE LIBRARY - MANUSCRIPTS AND SPECIAL COLLECTION
Cultural Education Center
Empire State Plaza   Phone: (518) 474-4461
Albany, NY 12230   Peter R. Christoph, Assoc.Libn.

NEW YORK STATE LIBRARY - SCIENCES/HEALTH SCIENCES/TECHNOLOGY
    REFERENCE SERVICES
Cultural Education Center
Empire State Plaza   Phone: (518) 474-7040
Albany, NY 12230   Christine A. Bain, Assoc.Libn.

NEW YORK STATE MUSEUM AND SCIENCE SERVICE - MUSEUM LIBRARY
State Education Dept., Rm.3128 CEC
Empire State Plaza   Phone: (518) 474-5878
Albany, NY 12230   Eleanor A. Gossen, Libn.

NEW YORK STATE OFFICE OF MENTAL HEALTH - RESEARCH RESOURCE
    CENTER
44 Holland Ave.   Phone: (518) 474-7167
Albany, NY 12229   Paul G. Hillengas, Libn.

NEW YORK STATE PARKS AND RECREATION - DIVISION FOR HISTORIC
    PRESERVATION - FIELD SERVICES BUREAU - LIBRARY
Agencies Tower No. 1
Empire State Plaza   Phone: (518) 474-0479
Albany, NY 12238   Kathleen LaFrank, Libn.

NEW YORK STATE SUPREME COURT - APPELLATE DIVISION, 3RD JUDICIAL
    DEPARTMENT - LAW LIBRARY
Justice Bldg., Empire State Plaza
Capitol Station, Box 7288
Albany, NY 12224   Ronald J. Milkins

ST. PETER'S HOSPITAL - MEDICAL STAFF LIBRARY
632 New Scotland Ave.   Phone: (518) 454-1490
Albany, NY 12208   Laura E. Campaigne, Libn.

SUNY AT ALBANY - LIBRARY SCIENCE BRANCH *
Hawley Library
1400 Washington Ave.   Phone: (518) 457-8581
Albany, NY 12222   Ella G. Bruins, Asst.Libn.

SUNY - CENTRAL ADMINISTRATION RESEARCH LIBRARY
State University Plaza, Rm. S540   Phone: (518) 473-1070
Albany, NY 12246   M. Joan Tauber, Libn.

UNION UNIVERSITY - ALBANY COLLEGE OF PHARMACY - LIBRARY
106 New Scotland Ave.   Phone: (518) 445-5217
Albany, NY 12208   Lucille W. Brown, Libn.

UNION UNIVERSITY - ALBANY LAW SCHOOL - LIBRARY
80 New Scotland Ave.   Phone: (518) 445-2340
Albany, NY 12208   Dr. Henry P. Tseng, Law Libn.

UNION UNIVERSITY - ALBANY MEDICAL COLLEGE - SCHAFFER LIBRARY OF
    THE HEALTH SCIENCES
47 New Scotland Ave.   Phone: (518) 445-5534
Albany, NY 12208   Ursula Poland, Libn.

U. S. GEOLOGICAL SURVEY - WATER RESOURCES DIVISION - NEW YORK
    DISTRICT - LIBRARY
343 Court House
Box 1350   Phone: (518) 472-3107
Albany, NY 12201   Denise A. Wiltshire, Libn.

U.S. VETERANS ADMINISTRATION (NY-Albany) - MEDICAL CENTER
    LIBRARY (500/142-D)
113 Holland Ave.   Phone: (518) 462-3311
Albany, NY 12208   John F. Connors, Adm.Libn.

HUMAN RESOURCES CENTER - RESEARCH LIBRARY
I.U. Willets & Searingtown Rds.   Phone: (516) 747-5400
Albertson, NY 11507   Lenore R. Greenberg, Res.Libn.

NEW YORK STATE COLLEGE OF CERAMICS, ALFRED UNIVERSITY - SAMUEL
    R. SCHOLES LIBRARY OF CERAMICS
Harder Hall   Phone: (607) 871-2492
Alfred, NY 14802   Mr. Robin R.B. Murray, Dir.

SUNY - AGRICULTURAL AND TECHNICAL COLLEGE AT ALFRED - WALTER C.
    HINKLE MEMORIAL LIBRARY
                                                Phone: (607) 871-6313
Alfred, NY 14802   Barry Lash, Hd.Libn.

SUNY AT BUFFALO - CENTER FOR CURRICULUM PLANNING
Faculty of Educational Studies
17 Baldy Hall   Phone: (716) 636-2486
Amherst, NY 14260   Dr. Robert Harnack, Dir.

TEMPLE SHAAREY ZEDEK - LIBRARY *
Hartford & Getzville Rds.
Amherst, NY 14226   Grace Stern, Libn.

ART REFERENCE BUREAU, INC.
Box 137   Phone: (518) 329-0535
Ancram, NY 12502   Janet S. Allen, Pres.

CIBA-GEIGY CORPORATION - CORPORATE LIBRARY
Saw Mill River Rd.   Phone: (914) 478-3131
Ardsley, NY 10502   Mary T. McLaughlin, Libn.

AUBURN MEMORIAL HOSPITAL - LIBRARY/RESOURCE CENTER
5-19 Lansing St.   Phone: (315) 255-7231
Auburn, NY 13021   Anne Costello Tomlin, Dir.

CAYUGA MUSEUM OF HISTORY AND ART - LIBRARY & ARCHIVES
203 Genesee St.   Phone: (315) 253-8051
Auburn, NY 13021   Walter K. Long, Dir.

FOUNDATION HISTORICAL ASSOCIATION - SEWARD HOUSE *
33 South St.   Phone: (315) 252-1283
Auburn, NY 13021   Betty Mae Lewis, Cur.

NEW YORK STATE SUPREME COURT - 7TH JUDICIAL DISTRICT - LAW
    LIBRARY
Cayuga County Court House   Phone: (315) 253-1279
Auburn, NY 13021

SARATOGA COUNTY HISTORICAL SOCIETY - LIBRARY
Brookside   Phone: (518) 885-4000
Ballston Spa, NY 12020

GENESEE COUNTY - DEPARTMENT OF HISTORY - RESEARCH LIBRARY
131 W. Main St.   Phone: (716) 343-2550
Batavia, NY 14020   Susan L. Conklin, Hist.

U.S. VETERANS ADMINISTRATION (NY-Batavia) - MEDICAL CENTER
    LIBRARY
Redfield Pkwy.   Phone: (716) 343-7500
Batavia, NY 14020   Madeline A. Coco, Chf.Libn.

NEW YORK STATE SUPREME COURT - 7TH JUDICIAL DISTRICT - LAW
    LIBRARY *
Surrogates Court
13 Pulteney Sq.   Phone: (607) 776-7126
Bath, NY 14810   Ethel M. Lewis, Law Libn.

U.S. VETERANS ADMINISTRATION (NY-Bath) - CENTER LIBRARY
                                                Phone: (607) 776-2111
Bath, NY 14810   Paula F. Benson, Chf., Lib.Serv.

SOUTHSIDE HOSPITAL - MEDICAL LIBRARY
Montauk Hwy.   Phone: (516) 859-3111
Bay Shore, NY 11706   May Chariton, Libn.

GEOGRAPHIC

BEAR MOUNTAIN TRAILSIDE MUSEUMS - LIBRARY
Bear Mountain State Park
Bear Mountain, NY 10911
Phone: (914) 786-2701
John H. Mead, Musm.Supv.

QUEENS CHILDREN'S PSYCHIATRIC CENTER - LAURETTA BENDER CHILD PSYCHIATRY LIBRARY
74-03 Commonwealth Blvd.
Bellerose, NY 11426
Phone: (212) 464-2900
Isabella Black, Libn.

DAMIEN DUTTON SOCIETY FOR LEPROSY AID, INC. - LIBRARY
616 Bedford Ave.
Bellmore, NY 11710
Phone: (516) 221-5829
Howard E. Crouch, Pres.

LONG ISLAND LIBRARY RESOURCES COUNCIL, INC. (LILRC)
Box 31
Bellport, NY 11713
Phone: (516) 286-0400
David Wilder, Dir.

SUFFOLK COOPERATIVE LIBRARY SYSTEM - AUDIOVISUAL DEPT.
Box 187
Bellport, NY 11713
Phone: (516) 286-1600
Philip Levering, AV Cons.

ALLEGANY COUNTY MUSEUM - LIBRARY
Court House
Belmont, NY 14813
Phone: (716) 268-7612
Bill Greene, Hist.

GRUMMAN AEROSPACE CORPORATION - TECHNICAL INFORMATION CENTER
Plant 35
Bethpage, NY 11714
Phone: (516) 575-3912
Royal Scheiman, Chf.Libn.

BINGHAMTON GENERAL HOSPITAL - STUART B. BLAKELY MEMORIAL LIBRARY
Mitchell Ave.
Binghamton, NY 13903
Phone: (607) 771-2200
Maryanne Mattimore, Med.Libn.

BINGHAMTON PRESS AND SUN BULLETIN - LIBRARY
Vestal Pkwy. E.
Binghamton, NY 13901
Phone: (607) 798-1159
Gloria Keenan, Hd.Libn.

BINGHAMTON PSYCHIATRIC CENTER - PROFESSIONAL LIBRARY
425 Robinson St.
Binghamton, NY 13901
Phone: (607) 724-1391
Martha A. Mason, Sr.Libn.

BROOME COMMUNITY COLLEGE - CECIL C. TYRRELL LEARNING RESOURCES CENTER
Box 1017
Binghamton, NY 13902
Phone: (607) 772-5020
James D. Baker, Dir.

BROOME COUNTY HISTORICAL SOCIETY - LIBRARY AND ARCHIVES
30 Front St.
Binghamton, NY 13905
Phone: (607) 772-0660
Ross McGuire, Cur.

GAF CORPORATION - PROCESS DEVELOPMENT DEPARTMENT - RESEARCH LIBRARY †
40 Charles St.
Binghamton, NY 13902
Phone: (607) 774-3138
Mrs. J.A. Kluger, Libn.

NEW YORK STATE ELECTRIC AND GAS CORPORATION - CORPORATE TECHNICAL LIBRARY
4500 Vestal Pkwy., E.
Binghamton, NY 13902
Phone: (607) 729-2551
Melba H. Lewis, Libn.

NEW YORK STATE SUPREME COURT - 6TH JUDICIAL DISTRICT - LAW LIBRARY
107 Court House
Binghamton, NY 13901
Phone: (607) 772-2119
Doris E. Chase, Law Libn. I

SINGER COMPANY - LINK DIVISION - TECHNICAL LIBRARY
Colesville Rd.
Binghamton, NY 13902
H.A. Scala, Lib.Supv.

SUNY AT BINGHAMTON - CENTER FOR MEDIEVAL AND EARLY RENAISSANCE STUDIES
Binghamton, NY 13901
Paul Szarmach, Dir.

SUNY AT BINGHAMTON - FINE ARTS LIBRARY
Vestal Pkwy. E.
Binghamton, NY 13901
Phone: (607) 798-4927
Marion Hanscom, Spec.Coll./Fine Arts Libn

SUNY AT BINGHAMTON - SCIENCE LIBRARY
Vestal Pkwy. E.
Binghamton, NY 13901
Phone: (607) 798-2528
Marlene Tebo, Asst.Dir.

SUNY AT BINGHAMTON - SPECIAL COLLECTIONS
Glenn G. Bartle Library
Vestal Pkwy. E.
Binghamton, NY 13901
Phone: (607) 798-4844
Marion Hanscom, Spec.Coll.Libn

ADIRONDACK HISTORICAL ASSOCIATION - ADIRONDACK MUSEUM - RESEARCH LIBRARY
Blue Mountain Lake, NY 12812
Phone: (518) 352-7311
Craig Gilborn, Dir.

NORTH AMERICAN PHILIPS CORPORATION - PHILIPS LABORATORIES RESEARCH LIBRARY
345 Scarborough Rd.
Briarcliff Manor, NY 10510
Phone: (914) 762-0300
Betsy McIlvaine, Hd.Libn.

SUNY - COLLEGE AT BROCKPORT - DRAKE MEMORIAL LIBRARY
Brockport, NY 14420
Phone: (716) 395-2141
Dr. George W. Cornell, Dir. of Lib.Serv.

AMERICAN TEILHARD ASSOCIATION FOR THE FUTURE OF MAN - LIBRARY
Manhattan College
4513 Manhattan College Pkwy.
Bronx, NY 10471
Phone: (212) 920-0114
Donald P. Gray

BETH ABRAHAM HOSPITAL - PATIENT'S LIBRARY
612 Allerton Ave.
Bronx, NY 10467
Phone: (212) 920-5856
Pamela S. George, Social Worker

BRONX COUNTY BAR ASSOCIATION - LAW LIBRARY
851 Grand Concourse
Bronx, NY 10051
Phone: (212) 293-5600

BRONX COUNTY HISTORICAL SOCIETY - LIBRARY †
3266 Bainbridge Ave.
Bronx, NY 10467
Phone: (212) 881-8900
Laura Tosi, Lib.Assoc.

BRONX-LEBANON HOSPITAL CENTER - CONCOURSE DIVISION MEDICAL LIBRARY
1650 Grand Concourse
Bronx, NY 10457
Phone: (212) 588-7000
Gerardo Gomez, Libn.

BRONX-LEBANON HOSPITAL CENTER - FULTON DIVISION MEDICAL LIBRARY
1276 Fulton Ave., 169th St.
Bronx, NY 10456
Phone: (212) 588-7000
Nancy McClennahan, Libn.

CALVARY HOSPITAL - MEDICAL LIBRARY
1740-1770 Eastchester Rd.
Bronx, NY 10461
Phone: (212) 430-4600
Mary M. Carroll, Med.Libn.

FORDHAM UNIVERSITY - MULCAHY LIBRARY
Mulcahy Hall, 4th Fl.
Bronx, NY 10458
Phone: (212) 933-2233
Edmund P. Maloney, Circ.Libn.

FORDHAM UNIVERSITY - SPECIAL COLLECTIONS
Duane Library
Bronx, NY 10458
Phone: (212) 933-2233
Mary Riley, Chf.Ref.Libn.

HUDSON RIVER ENVIRONMENTAL SOCIETY - LIBRARY
675 West 252nd St.
Bronx, NY 10471
Phone: (212) 884-4199
Florence Smeraldi, Sec.

HUNTINGTON FREE LIBRARY - MUSEUM OF THE AMERICAN INDIAN - LIBRARY
9 Westchester Sq.
Bronx, NY 10461
Phone: (212) 829-7770
Mary B. Davis, Libn.

JOHN XXIII ECUMENICAL CENTER, INC. - CENTER FOR EASTERN CHRISTIAN STUDIES
2502 Belmont Ave.
Bronx, NY 10458
Phone: (212) 298-8752
Rev. John F. Long, S.J., Dir.

LINCOLN HOSPITAL - MEDICAL LIBRARY
234 E. 149th St.
Bronx, NY 10451
Phone: (212) 579-5745
Miss Milagros M. Paredes, Med.Libn.

LOYOLA REFERENCE LIBRARY
Fordham University
Keating Hall   Phone: (212) 841-5134
Bronx, NY 10458   Rev. Theodore Cunnion, S.J., Libn.

MANHATTAN COLLEGE - GROVER M. HERMANN ENGINEERING LIBRARY
Corlear Ave. & 238th St.   Phone: (212) 548-1400
Bronx, NY 10471   Richard A. Barry, Libn.

MANHATTAN COLLEGE - SONNTAG LIBRARY
Corlear Ave. & 238th St.   Phone: (212) 548-1400
Bronx, NY 10471   Bro. Philip Dowd, Lib.Dir.

MISERICORDIA HOSPITAL - MEDICAL LIBRARY
600 E. 233rd St.   Phone: (212) 920-9869
Bronx, NY 10466   William J. Record, Libn.

MISERICORDIA HOSPITAL - SCHOOL OF NURSING LIBRARY
4401 Bronx Blvd.   Phone: (212) 920-9825
Bronx, NY 10470   Denise L. Kirk, Libn.

NEW YORK BOTANICAL GARDEN - LIBRARY
                                                   Phone: (212) 220-8749
Bronx, NY 10458   Charles R. Long, Dir.

NEW YORK INSTITUTE FOR THE EDUCATION OF THE BLIND - WALTER
    BROOKS LIBRARY
999 Pelham Pkwy.   Phone: (212) 547-1234
Bronx, NY 10469   Helen C. Isherwood, Libn.

NEW YORK PUBLIC LIBRARY - BELMONT REGIONAL LIBRARY - ENRICO
    FERMI CULTURAL CENTER
610 E. 186th St.   Phone: (212) 933-6410
Bronx, NY 10458   Theresa K. Casile, Principal Libn.

NEW YORK ZOOLOGICAL SOCIETY - LIBRARY
185th St. & Southern Blvd.   Phone: (212) 220-5125
Bronx, NY 10460   Allegra Hamer, Asst. in Zoology

NORTH CENTRAL BRONX HOSPITAL - J. LEWIS AMSTER HEALTH SCIENCES
    LIBRARY
3424 Kossuth Ave.   Phone: (212) 920-7865
Bronx, NY 10467   Ms. Padma Chittampalli, Med.Libn.

REVLON RESEARCH CENTER, INC. - LIBRARY
945 Zerega Ave.   Phone: (212) 824-9000
Bronx, NY 10473   Dr. Hilda Feinberg, Mgr., Lib./Info.Serv.

SUNY - MARITIME COLLEGE - STEPHEN B. LUCE LIBRARY
Fort Schuyler   Phone: (212) 892-3004
Bronx, NY 10465   Richard H. Corson, Libn.

U.S. VETERANS ADMINISTRATION (NY-Bronx) - MEDICAL CENTER LIBRARY
130 W. Kingsbridge Rd.
Bronx, NY 10468   Margaret M. Kinney, Chf.Libn.

YESHIVA UNIVERSITY - ALBERT EINSTEIN COLLEGE OF MEDICINE - D.
    SAMUEL GOTTESMAN LIBRARY
1300 Morris Park Ave.   Phone: (212) 430-3108
Bronx, NY 10461   Charlotte K. Lindner, Dir. of Lib.

YESHIVA UNIVERSITY - ALBERT EINSTEIN COLLEGE OF MEDICINE - DEPT.
    OF ANESTHESIOLOGY - LIBRARY
Eastchester Rd. & Morris Park Ave.
Bldg. J, Rm. 1226
Bronx, NY 10461

YESHIVA UNIVERSITY - ALBERT EINSTEIN COLLEGE OF MEDICINE - DEPT.
    OF PSYCHIATRY - J. THOMPSON PSYCHIATRY LIB.
Bronx Municipal Hospital Center
NR 2E7A   Phone: (212) 430-5571
Bronx, NY 10461   Silvia Davidson, Libn.

YESHIVA UNIVERSITY - ALBERT EINSTEIN COLLEGE OF MEDICINE -
    SURGERY LIBRARY
Jacobi Hospital, Rm. 613
Pelham Pkwy. & Eastchester Rd.   Phone: (212) 430-5800
Bronx, NY 10461   E. Clurman, Sr.Ck.

LAWRENCE HOSPITAL - ASHLEY BAKER MORRILL LIBRARY
                                                   Phone: (914) 337-7300
Bronxville, NY 10708   Judith M. Topper, Med.Libn.

AMERICAN ASSOCIATION OF CRIMEAN TURKS, INC. - ISMAIL GASPIRALI
    LIBRARY †
4509 New Utrecht Ave.   Phone: (212) 438-9567
Brooklyn, NY 11219   Halim Saylik, Mgr.

AMSTAR CORPORATION - RESEARCH AND DEVELOPMENT LIBRARY
266 Kent Ave.   Phone: (212) 387-6800
Brooklyn, NY 11211   Joseph X. Cavano, Info.Spec.

ANTIQUE PHONOGRAPH MONTHLY - APM LIBRARY OF RECORDED SOUND
650 Ocean Ave.   Phone: (212) 941-6835
Brooklyn, NY 11226   Allen Koenigsberg, Dir.

BROOKDALE HOSPITAL MEDICAL CENTER - MARIE SMITH SCHWARTZ
    MEDICAL LIBRARY
Linden Blvd. & Rockaway Pkwy.   Phone: (212) 240-5312
Brooklyn, NY 11212   Sophie Winston, Chf.Med.Libn.

BROOKLYN BAR ASSOCIATION FOUNDATION, INC. - LIBRARY
123 Remsen St.
Brooklyn, NY 11201

BROOKLYN BOTANIC GARDEN - LIBRARY
1000 Washington Ave.   Phone: (212) 622-4433
Brooklyn, NY 11225   Marie G. Giasi, Libn.

BROOKLYN CHILDREN'S MUSEUM - CHILDREN'S RESOURCE LIBRARY
145 Brooklyn Ave.   Phone: (212) 735-4400
Brooklyn, NY 11213   Susan J. Pober, Libn.

BROOKLYN CHILDREN'S MUSEUM - STAFF RESEARCH LIBRARY
145 Brooklyn Ave.   Phone: (212) 735-4400
Brooklyn, NY 11213   Terry Foy-McCarthy, Staff Libn.

BROOKLYN COLLEGE OF THE CITY UNIVERSITY OF NEW YORK - MUSIC
    LIBRARY
417 Gershwin Hall   Phone: (212) 780-5289
Brooklyn, NY 11210   Prof. Dee Baily, Music Libn.

BROOKLYN DAILY LIBRARY
338 3rd Ave.   Phone: (212) 858-3300
Brooklyn, NY 11215   Lionel Klass, Ed. & Libn.

BROOKLYN HOSPITAL - MEDICAL LIBRARY
121 DeKalb Ave.   Phone: (212) 270-4367
Brooklyn, NY 11201   Saul Kuchinsky, Libn.

BROOKLYN LAW SCHOOL - LAW LIBRARY
250 Joralemon St.   Phone: (212) 625-2200
Brooklyn, NY 11201   Charlotte L. Levy, Libn.

BROOKLYN MUSEUM - ART REFERENCE LIBRARY
188 Eastern Pkwy.   Phone: (212) 638-5000
Brooklyn, NY 11238   Margaret B. Zorach, Chf.Libn.

BROOKLYN MUSEUM - WILBOUR LIBRARY OF EGYPTOLOGY
188 Eastern Pkwy.   Phone: (212) 638-5000
Brooklyn, NY 11238   Diane Guzman, Libn.

BROOKLYN PUBLIC LIBRARY - ART AND MUSIC DIVISION
Grand Army Plaza   Phone: (212) 780-7784
Brooklyn, NY 11238   Sue Sharma, Div.Chf.

BROOKLYN PUBLIC LIBRARY - AUDIO VISUAL DIVISION
Grand Army Plaza   Phone: (212) 780-7793
Brooklyn, NY 11238   Kenneth W. Axthelm, Div.Chf.

BROOKLYN PUBLIC LIBRARY - BUSINESS LIBRARY
280 Cadman Plaza W.   Phone: (212) 780-7800
Brooklyn, NY 11201   Sylvia Mechanic, Bus.Libn.

BROOKLYN PUBLIC LIBRARY - HISTORY, TRAVEL, RELIGION AND
    BIOGRAPHY DIVISION
Grand Army Plaza   Phone: (212) 780-7794
Brooklyn, NY 11238   Henri Veit, Div.Chf.

GEOGRAPHIC

BROOKLYN PUBLIC LIBRARY - LANGUAGE AND LITERATURE DIVISION
Grand Army Plaza
Brooklyn, NY 11238
Phone: (212) 780-7733
Monte Olenick, Div.Chf.

BROOKLYN PUBLIC LIBRARY - SCIENCE AND INDUSTRY DIVISION
Grand Army Plaza
Brooklyn, NY 11238
Phone: (212) 780-7745
Walter Wolff, Div.Chf.

BROOKLYN PUBLIC LIBRARY - SOCIAL SCIENCE DIVISION
Grand Army Plaza
Brooklyn, NY 11238
Phone: (212) 780-7746
Lillian Tudiver, Div.Chf.

CATHOLIC MEDICAL CENTER OF BROOKLYN & QUEENS, INC. - ST. MARY'S
HOSPITAL - MEDICAL ADMINISTRATIVE LIBRARY
170 Buffalo Ave.
Brooklyn, NY 11213
Phone: (212) 774-3600
Madeline A. Brown, Med.Libn.

CONEY ISLAND HOSPITAL - HAROLD FINK MEMORIAL LIBRARY
Ocean & Shore Pkwys.
Brooklyn, NY 11235
Phone: (212) 743-4100
Ronnie Joan Mark, Dir.

CUNY - NEW YORK CITY TECHNICAL COLLEGE LIBRARY/LEARNING
RESOURCE CENTER
300 Jay St.
Brooklyn, NY 11201
Phone: (212) 643-5240
Catherine T. Brody, Chf.Libn.

DI CYAN AND BROWN - LIBRARY
1486 E. 33rd St.
Brooklyn, NY 11234
Phone: (212) 252-8844

JEWISH HOSPITAL AND MEDICAL CENTER OF BROOKLYN - GREENPOINT
HOSPITAL AFFILIATION - MEDICAL LIBRARY
300 Skillman Ave.
Brooklyn, NY 11211
Phone: (212) 387-3010
Leon Elveson, Med.Libn.

JEWISH HOSPITAL AND MEDICAL CENTER OF BROOKLYN - MEDICAL &
NURSING LIBRARY
555 Prospect Pl.
Brooklyn, NY 11238
Phone: (212) 240-1795
Sharon R. Peterson, Med.Libn.

KINGSBORO PSYCHIATRIC CENTER - MEDICAL LIBRARY
681 Clarkson Ave.
Brooklyn, NY 11203
Phone: (212) 735-1273
Lenore J. Roach, Sr.Libn.

KINGSBOROUGH COMMUNITY COLLEGE - KINGSBOROUGH HISTORICAL
SOCIETY
2001 Oriental Blvd.
Brooklyn, NY 11235
Phone: (212) 934-5122
John B. Manbeck, Archv.

KINGSBROOK JEWISH MEDICAL CENTER - MEDICAL LIBRARY
Rutland Rd. & E. 49th St.
Brooklyn, NY 11203
Phone: (212) 756-9700
Mary E. Buchheit, Dir. of Med.Lib.

LONG ISLAND COLLEGE HOSPITAL - HOAGLAND MEDICAL LIBRARY
340 Henry St.
Brooklyn, NY 11201
Phone: (212) 780-1077
Gabriel Bakcsy, Dir.

LONG ISLAND HISTORICAL SOCIETY - LIBRARY
128 Pierrepont St.
Brooklyn, NY 11201
Phone: (212) 624-0890
Patricia A. Flavin, Libn.

LONG ISLAND UNIV. - ARNOLD & MARIE SCHWARTZ COLLEGE OF
PHARMACY & HEALTH SCIENCES - INTERNATL. DRUG INFO.CTR.
81 DeKalb Ave. at University Plaza
Brooklyn, NY 11201
Phone: (212) 622-8989
Jack M. Rosenberg, Dir.

LONG ISLAND UNIV. - ARNOLD & MARIE SCHWARTZ COLLEGE OF
PHARMACY & HEALTH SCIENCES - PHARMACEUTICAL STUDY CENTER
75 DeKalb Ave.
Brooklyn, NY 11201
Phone: (212) 330-2753
Wendell A. Guy, Dir.

LUTHERAN MEDICAL CENTER - MEDICAL LIBRARY
150 55th St.
Brooklyn, NY 11220
Phone: (212) 630-7200
Gretchen N. Duchac, Libn.

MAIMONIDES MEDICAL CENTER - MEDICAL LIBRARY
4802 Tenth Ave.
Brooklyn, NY 11219
Phone: (212) 270-7679
Lydia Friedman, Chf.Med.Libn.

MENORAH INSTITUTE - LIBRARY
1533 60th St.
Box FF
Brooklyn, NY 11219
Phone: (212) 435-0500
Rabbi N. Halberstam, Libn.

METHODIST HOSPITAL - HEALTH SCIENCES LIBRARY
506 6th St.
Brooklyn, NY 11215
Phone: (212) 780-3368
Edith A. Taub, Dir. of Libs.

METROPOLITAN JEWISH GERIATRIC CENTER - MAX B. & LOUISA S. MARKS
MEMORIAL MEDICAL LIBRARY †
4915 Tenth Ave.
Brooklyn, NY 11219
Phone: (212) 853-2800
Mary Stankevich, Libn.

NEW YORK CITY BOARD OF EDUCATION - RESOURCE CENTER -
CURRICULUM LIBRARY
131 Livingston St.
Brooklyn, NY 11201
Phone: (212) 596-4903
Bernard D. Schwartz, Res.Asst.

NEW YORK CITY TRANSIT AUTHORITY - LAW LIBRARY
370 Jay St., Rm. 1333
Brooklyn, NY 11201
Phone: (212) 330-4330

NEW YORK STATE SUPREME COURT - APPELLATE DIVISION, 2ND
JUDICIAL DEPARTMENT - LAW LIBRARY
45 Monroe Pl.
Brooklyn, NY 11202
Albert Esselborn, Esq., Libn.

NEW YORK STATE SUPREME COURT - 2ND JUDICIAL DISTRICT - LAW
LIBRARY
360 Adams St.
Brooklyn, NY 11201
Phone: (212) 643-8080
Libby F. Jessup, Principal Law Libn.

NOVOCOL CHEMICAL MANUFACTURING COMPANY, INC. - LIBRARY *
2911 Atlantic Ave.
Brooklyn, NY 11207
Phone: (212) 277-5400
Elias Epstein, Dir. of Res.

OFFICE OF BILINGUAL EDUCATION - RESOURCE LIBRARY AND
INFORMATION UNIT
131 Livingston St., Rm. 204
Brooklyn, NY 11201
Phone: (212) 858-5505
Carmen Gloria Burgos, Libn.

OSBORN LABORATORIES OF MARINE SCIENCES - NEW YORK AQUARIUM
LIBRARY
Boardwalk & W. 8th St.
Brooklyn, NY 11224
Phone: (212) 266-8500
G.D. Ruggieri, Ph.D., Dir.

POLISH SINGERS ALLIANCE OF AMERICA - LIBRARY
1217 78th St.
Brooklyn, NY 11228
Phone: (212) 254-6642
Michal Bartkow, Libn.

POLYTECHNIC INSTITUTE OF NEW YORK - SPICER LIBRARY
333 Jay St.
Brooklyn, NY 11201
Phone: (212) 643-8690
Leonard Cohan, Dir. of Libs.

PRATT INSTITUTE - LIBRARY
215 Ryerson St.
Brooklyn, NY 11205
Phone: (212) 636-3545
George Lowy, Dir.

ST. FRANCIS COLLEGE - JAMES A. KELLY INSTITUTE FOR LOCAL
HISTORICAL STUDIES - LIBRARY
180 Remsen St.
Brooklyn, NY 11201
Phone: (212) 522-2300
Arthur J. Konop, Dir.-Archv.

ST. JOHN'S EPISCOPAL HOSPITAL - NURSING AND MEDICAL LIBRARY
480 Herkimer St.
Brooklyn, NY 11213
Phone: (212) 467-7000
Dallas C. Hopson, Libn.

SUNY - DOWNSTATE MEDICAL CENTER - DEPARTMENT OF PSYCHIATRY
LIBRARY
606 Winthrop St.
Brooklyn, NY 11203
Phone: (212) 735-3915
Patricia Tomasulo, Libn.

SUNY - DOWNSTATE MEDICAL CENTER - MEDICAL RESEARCH LIBRARY OF
BROOKLYN †
450 Clarkson Ave.
Box 14
Brooklyn, NY 11203
Phone: (212) 270-1041
Kenneth E. Moody, Dir.

TEMPLE AHAVATH SHOLOM - RABBI A. ALAN STEINBACH LIBRARY
1609 Ave. R
Brooklyn, NY 11229

U.S. ARMY POST - FORT HAMILTON - LIBRARY
Bldg. 404   Phone: (212) 836-4100
Brooklyn, NY 11252   Amelia K. Sefton, Libn. I

U.S. DISTRICT COURT - EASTERN DISTRICT OF NEW YORK - LIBRARY
225 Cadman Plaza E.   Phone: (212) 330-7483
Brooklyn, NY 11201   Lillian B. Garrell, Law Libn.

U.S. VETERANS ADMINISTRATION (NY-Brooklyn) - MEDICAL CENTER
    LIBRARY
800 Poly Place   Phone: (212) 836-6600
Brooklyn, NY 11209   Barbara B. Goldberg, Chf.Libn.

YESHIVA TORAH VODAATH AND MESIFTA - TORAH VODAATH LIBRARY *
425 E. Ninth St.   Phone: (212) 941-8000
Brooklyn, NY 11218   Rabbi Isaac M. Traube, Ph.D., Libn.

ALBRIGHT-KNOX ART GALLERY - ART REFERENCE LIBRARY
1285 Elmwood Ave.   Phone: (716) 882-8700
Buffalo, NY 14222   Annette Masling, Libn.

ALLIED CORPORATION - CHEMICALS COMPANY - LIBRARY
20 Peabody St.   Phone: (716) 827-6229
Buffalo, NY 14210   Dr. J. Northcott, Supv.

BELL AEROSPACE TEXTRON - LAWRENCE D. BELL MEMORIAL LIBRARY
Box 1   Phone: (716) 297-1000
Buffalo, NY 14240   Lester M. Breslauer, Chf.Libn.

BRYANT AND STRATTON BUSINESS INSTITUTE - LIBRARY
1028 Main St.   Phone: (716) 884-9120
Buffalo, NY 14202   Shirley R. Rowland, Media Supv.

BUFFALO COURIER-EXPRESS - LIBRARY
795 Main St.   Phone: (716) 855-6583
Buffalo, NY 14240   Cynthia Hayes, Libn.

BUFFALO & ERIE COUNTY HISTORICAL SOCIETY - LIBRARY
25 Nottingham Ct.   Phone: (716) 873-9644
Buffalo, NY 14216   Robert L. Damm, Dir.

BUFFALO & ERIE COUNTY PUBLIC LIBRARY - BUSINESS AND LABOR
    DEPARTMENT
Lafayette Sq.   Phone: (716) 856-7525
Buffalo, NY 14203   Stanley P. Zukowski, Hd.

BUFFALO & ERIE COUNTY PUBLIC LIBRARY - EDUCATION, SOCIOLOGY,
    PHILOSOPHY & RELIGION DEPARTMENT
Lafayette Sq.   Phone: (716) 856-7525
Buffalo, NY 14203   Ann P. Miller, Hd.

BUFFALO & ERIE COUNTY PUBLIC LIBRARY - FILM DEPARTMENT
Lafayette Sq.   Phone: (716) 856-7525
Buffalo, NY 14203   Robert M. Gurn, Hd.

BUFFALO & ERIE COUNTY PUBLIC LIBRARY - HISTORY, TRAVEL AND
    GOVERNMENT DEPARTMENT
Lafayette Sq.   Phone: (716) 856-7525
Buffalo, NY 14203   Ruth Willet, Dept.Hd.

BUFFALO & ERIE COUNTY PUBLIC LIBRARY - LANGUAGE, LITERATURE AND
    ARTS DEPARTMENT
Lafayette Sq.   Phone: (716) 856-7525
Buffalo, NY 14203   Ann P. Miller, Hd.

BUFFALO & ERIE COUNTY PUBLIC LIBRARY - MUSIC DEPARTMENT
Lafayette Sq.   Phone: (716) 856-7525
Buffalo, NY 14203   Norma Jean Lamb, Hd.

BUFFALO & ERIE COUNTY PUBLIC LIBRARY - RARE BOOK ROOM
Lafayette Sq.   Phone: (716) 856-7525
Buffalo, NY 14203   William H. Loos, Cur.

BUFFALO & ERIE COUNTY PUBLIC LIBRARY - SCIENCE AND TECHNOLOGY
    DEPARTMENT
Lafayette Sq.   Phone: (716) 856-7525
Buffalo, NY 14203   Stanley P. Zukowski, Hd.

BUFFALO EVENING NEWS - LIBRARY
One News Plaza   Phone: (716) 849-4444
Buffalo, NY 14240   Sally G. Schlaerth, Hd.Libn.

BUFFALO GENERAL HOSPITAL, INC. - A.H. AARON MEDICAL LIBRARY
100 High St.   Phone: (716) 845-2888
Buffalo, NY 14203   Wentsing Liu, Dir.

BUFFALO PSYCHIATRIC CENTER - BPC LIBRARY
400 Forest Ave.   Phone: (716) 885-2261
Buffalo, NY 14213   Margaret Litzenberger, Asst.Libn.

BUFFALO SOCIETY OF NATURAL SCIENCES - RESEARCH LIBRARY
Buffalo Musm. of Science
Humboldt Pkwy.   Phone: (716) 896-5200
Buffalo, NY 14211   Marcia Morrison, Libn.

CALSPAN CORPORATION - TECHNICAL LIBRARY
4455 Genesee St.   Phone: (716) 632-7500
Buffalo, NY 14225   Betty Miller, Lib.Supv.

CHILDREN'S HOSPITAL OF BUFFALO - MEDICAL LIBRARY
219 Bryant St.   Phone: (716) 878-7304
Buffalo, NY 14222   Lucy Wargo, Med.Libn.

DEACONESS HOSPITAL - MEDICAL LIBRARY
1001 Humboldt Parkway   Phone: (716) 886-4400
Buffalo, NY 14208   Donna Browning, Med.Libn.

ECOLOGY & ENVIRONMENT, INC. - LIBRARY
195 Sugg Rd.
Box D   Phone: (716) 632-4491
Buffalo, NY 14225   Patricia Lufkin, Info.Spec.

ERIE COMMUNITY COLLEGE NORTH - LIBRARY RESOURCES CENTER
Main & Youngs Rd.   Phone: (716) 684-0800
Buffalo, NY 14221   Sylvia J. Moran, Coord.

ERIE COUNTY MEDICAL CENTER - MEDICAL LIBRARY
462 Grider St.   Phone: (716) 898-3939
Buffalo, NY 14215   Anthony Ciko, Sr.Med.Libn.

FILLMORE (Millard) HOSPITAL - KIDENEY HEALTH SCIENCES LIBRARY
3 Gates Circle   Phone: (716) 887-4848
Buffalo, NY 14209   Aniela Lichtenstein, Libn.

MARINE MIDLAND BANK - TECHNICAL INFORMATION CENTER
One Marine Midland Ctr., 4th Fl., W. Wing   Phone: (716) 843-5011
Buffalo, NY 14240   Eva M. Saintcross, Tech.Libn.

MERCY HOSPITAL - MEDICAL LIBRARY
565 Abbott Rd.   Phone: (716) 826-7000
Buffalo, NY 14220   Linda S. Karch, Libn.

NEW YORK STATE SUPREME COURT - 8TH JUDICIAL DISTRICT - LAW
    LIBRARY
92 Franklin St.   Phone: (716) 852-0712
Buffalo, NY 14202   Lois L. Crissey, Principal Law Libn.

PENNWALT CORPORATION - LUCIDOL DIVISION - RESEARCH LIBRARY
1740 Military Rd.   Phone: (716) 877-1740
Buffalo, NY 14240   David C. Noller, Tech.Info.Spec.

PHILLIPS, LYTLE, HITCHOCK, BLAINE AND HUBER - LIBRARY
3400 Maine Midland Ctr.   Phone: (716) 847-8400
Buffalo, NY 14203   Laura M. Bartolo, Libn.

ROSWELL PARK MEMORIAL INSTITUTE - MEDICAL AND SCIENTIFIC
    LIBRARY
666 Elm St.   Phone: (716) 845-5966
Buffalo, NY 14263   Ann P. Hutchinson, Lib.Dir.

ST. MARY'S SCHOOL FOR THE DEAF - PROFESSIONAL LIBRARY
2253 Main St.
Phone: (716) 834-7200
Buffalo, NY 14214
Collette Sangster, Dir.

SISTERS OF CHARITY HOSPITAL - MEDICAL STAFF LIBRARY
2157 Main St.
Phone: (716) 862-2846
Buffalo, NY 14214
Anne Cohen, Med.Libn.

SUNY AT BUFFALO - ARCHITECTURE & ENVIRONMENTAL DESIGN LIBRARY
Hayes Hall
Main Street Campus
Phone: (716) 831-3505
Buffalo, NY 14214
Jeannine Lee, Act.Hd.

SUNY AT BUFFALO - CHARLES B. SEARS LAW LIBRARY
O'Brian Hall, Amherst Campus
Phone: (716) 636-2048
Buffalo, NY 14260
Kathleen Carrick, Dir.

SUNY AT BUFFALO - HEALTH SCIENCES LIBRARY
Main St. Campus
Phone: (716) 831-3337
Buffalo, NY 14214
Mr. C.K. Huang, Dir.

SUNY AT BUFFALO - MUSIC LIBRARY
Baird Hall
Phone: (716) 831-2571
Buffalo, NY 14260
James Coover, Dir.

SUNY AT BUFFALO - POETRY/RARE BOOKS COLLECTION
University Libraries, 420 Capen Hall
Phone: (716) 636-2918
Buffalo, NY 14260
Robert J. Bertholf, Cur.

SUNY AT BUFFALO - SCIENCE AND ENGINEERING LIBRARY
Phone: (716) 636-2946
Buffalo, NY 14260
James K. Webster, Dir.

SUNY - COLLEGE AT BUFFALO - BURCHFIELD CENTER-WESTERN NEW YORK FORUM FOR AMERICAN ART
1300 Elmwood Ave.
Phone: (716) 878-6011
Buffalo, NY 14222
Gary A. Dayton, Libn./Archv.

SUNY - COLLEGE AT BUFFALO - EDWARD H. BUTLER LIBRARY
1300 Elmwood Ave.
Phone: (716) 878-6302
Buffalo, NY 14222
Mary C. Hall, Act.Dir.

SUNY - COLLEGE AT BUFFALO - GREAT LAKES LABORATORY - LIMNOLOGY LIBRARY
1300 Elmwood Ave.
Phone: (716) 878-5422
Buffalo, NY 14222
Theresa Wolfe, Libn.

SUNY - SCHOOL OF PHARMACY - DRUG INFORMATION SERVICE - LIBRARY
Erie County Medical Center
462 Grider St.
Phone: (716) 898-3927
Buffalo, NY 14215
Dr. Sue Rozek, Hd.

TEMPLE BETH ZION - LIBRARY
805 Delaware Ave.
Phone: (716) 886-7151
Buffalo, NY 14209
Donna J. Davidoff, Hd.Libn.

TEXTRON, INC. - SPENCER KELLOGG DIVISION - RESEARCH CENTER LIBRARY
4201 Genesee St.
Phone: (716) 852-5850
Buffalo, NY 14225
H.M. Schroeder, Tech.Info.Mgr.

U.S. DEPT. OF COMMERCE - INTERNATIONAL TRADE ADMINISTRATION - BUFFALO DISTRICT OFFICE LIBRARY
1312 Federal Bldg.
111 W. Huron St.
Phone: (716) 846-4191
Buffalo, NY 14202
Marilyn G. Kinsman

U.S. VETERANS ADMINISTRATION (NY-Buffalo) - MEDICAL CENTER LIBRARY SERVICE
3495 Bailey Ave.
Phone: (716) 834-9200
Buffalo, NY 14215
Michelle D. O'Connell, Chf., Lib.Serv.

BEECH-NUT FOODS CORPORATION - TECHNICAL LIBRARY
Church St.
Phone: (518) 673-3251
Canajoharie, NY 13317
Stephanie Price, Libn.

ONTARIO COUNTY HISTORICAL SOCIETY, INC. - ARCHIVES
55 N. Main St.
Phone: (716) 394-4975
Canandaigua, NY 14424
Robert Donald Muller, Dir.

U.S. VETERANS ADMINISTRATION (NY-Canandaigua) - MEDICAL CENTER LIBRARY (142D)
Phone: (315) 394-2000
Canandaigua, NY 14424
Deborah M. Lewek, Chf., Lib.Serv.

ST. LAWRENCE COUNTY HISTORY AND RESEARCH CENTER - LIBRARY
3 1/2 E. Main St.
Phone: (315) 386-8118
Canton, NY 13617
Mary H. Smallman, Hist.

U.S. VETERANS ADMINISTRATION (NY-Castle Point) - MEDICAL CENTER LIBRARY
Phone: (914) 831-2000
Castle Point, NY 12511
William E. Kane, Chf.Libn.

NEW YORK STATE SUPREME COURT - 3RD JUDICIAL DISTRICT - EMORY A. CHASE MEMORIAL LIBRARY
Greene County Court House, Main St.
Phone: (518) 943-3130
Catskill, NY 12414
Mrs. Armida M. Marafioti, Libn.

FRANKLIN (H.H.) CLUB - LIBRARY †
Cazenovia College
Cazenovia, NY 13035
C.C. Nash, Mgr.

TEMPLE BETH EL - BUDDY BERMAN MEMORIAL LIBRARY *
Broadway & Locust Ave.
Phone: (516) 569-2700
Cedarhurst, NY 11516
Mirel Touger, Libn.

CENTRAL ISLIP PSYCHIATRIC CENTER - HEALTH SCIENCE LIBRARY
Carlton Ave., Station H
Phone: (516) 234-6262
Central Islip, NY 11722
Mary Avlon, Libn.

FALKIRK HOSPITAL - LIBRARY
Box 194
Phone: (914) 928-2256
Central Valley, NY 10917
Maria Gern

SMITH MEMORIAL LIBRARY
Pratt & Miller Ave.
Phone: (716) 357-5844
Chautauqua, NY 14722
Mrs. Torrey Isaac, Libn.

MINER (Alice T.) COLONIAL COLLECTION - LIBRARY
Box 330
Phone: (518) 846-7336
Chazy, NY 12921
Lucille L. Czarnetzky, Cur.

MINER INSTITUTE FOR MAN AND ENVIRONMENT - MINER CENTER LIBRARY
SUNY College at Plattsburgh
Phone: (518) 564-2178
Chazy, NY 12921
Linda J. Masters, Lib.Tech.Asst.

ST. JOSEPH INTERCOMMUNITY HOSPITAL - MEDICAL STAFF LIBRARY
2605 Harlem Rd.
Phone: (716) 896-6300
Cheektowaga, NY 14225
Sister M. Tiburtia, F.S.S.J., Cons.

CIRCLEVILLE PRESBYTERIAN CHURCH - BOOK NOOK
Rte. 302 & Goshen Tpke.
Phone: (914) 361-2381
Circleville, NY 10919
Mrs. Ralph Tavino

CLIFTON SPRINGS HOSPITAL AND CLINIC - MEDICAL LIBRARY
Coulter Rd.
Phone: (315) 462-9561
Clifton Springs, NY 14432
Mary L. Button, Med. Record Libn.

SUNY - AGRICULTURAL AND TECHNICAL COLLEGE AT COBLESKILL - JARED VAN WAGENEN, JR. LEARNING RESOURCE CENTER
Phone: (518) 234-5841
Cobleskill, NY 12043
Eleanor M. Carter, Dir.

PUTNAM COUNTY HISTORICAL SOCIETY - FOUNDRY SCHOOL MUSEUM - REFERENCE LIBRARY
63 Chestnut St.
Phone: (914) 265-2781
Cold Spring, NY 10516
Carol F. Morse, Libn.

COLD SPRING HARBOR LABORATORY - MAIN LIBRARY
Box 100
Phone: (516) 692-6660
Cold Spring Harbor, NY 11724
Susan Gensel, Dir., Libs. & Marketing

WHALING MUSEUM SOCIETY, INC. - LIBRARY
Main St.
Box 25
Phone: (516) 367-3418
Cold Spring Harbor, NY 11724
Robert D. Farwell, Exec.Dir.

EDO CORPORATION - ENGINEERING LIBRARY
14-04 111th St.   Phone: (212) 445-6000
College Point, NY 11356   Charlotte K. Boardman, Libn.

BASSETT (Mary Imogene) HOSPITAL - MEDICAL LIBRARY
                                            Phone: (607) 547-6481
Cooperstown, NY 13326   Deborah Dalton, Libn.

NATIONAL BASEBALL HALL OF FAME AND MUSEUM - NATIONAL BASEBALL
    LIBRARY
                                            Phone: (607) 547-9988
Cooperstown, NY 13326   Clifford Kachline, Hist.

NEW YORK STATE HISTORICAL ASSOCIATION - LIBRARY
                                            Phone: (607) 547-2509
Cooperstown, NY 13326   Wendell Tripp, Chf., Lib.Serv.

COLLEGE CENTER OF THE FINGER LAKES - LIBRARY
22 W. Third St.   Phone: (607) 962-3134
Corning, NY 14830   Julia Lonnberg, Libn.

CORNING GLASS WORKS - TECHNICAL INFORMATION CENTER
Sullivan Pk.   Phone: (607) 974-3258
Corning, NY 14830   Raymond R. Barber, Libn.

CORNING MUSEUM OF GLASS - LIBRARY
Corning Glass Ctr., Centerway   Phone: (607) 937-5371
Corning, NY 14830   Dr. John H. Martin, Dir.

HARVARD UNIVERSITY - HARVARD BLACK ROCK FOREST LIBRARY
                                            Phone: (914) 534-4517
Cornwall, NY 12518   Jack J. Karnig, Forest Mgr.

QUEENS BOROUGH PUBLIC LIBRARY - LANGSTON HUGHES COMMUNITY
    LIBRARY AND CULTURAL CENTER
102-09 Northern Blvd.   Phone: (212) 651-1100
Corona, NY 11368   Andrew P. Jackson, Supv.

CORTLAND COUNTY HISTORICAL SOCIETY - LIBRARY
25 Homer Ave.   Phone: (607) 756-6071
Cortland, NY 13045   Shirley G. Heppell, Libn.

SUNY - COLLEGE AT CORTLAND - MEMORIAL LIBRARY
Prospect Terrace   Phone: (607) 753-2221
Cortland, NY 13045   Selby U. Gration, Dir. Of Libs.

U.S. FISH & WILDLIFE SERVICE - TUNISON LABORATORY OF FISH
    NUTRITION - LIBRARY
28 Gracie Rd.   Phone: (607) 753-9391
Cortland, NY 13045   Gary L. Rumsey, Dir.

GREENE COUNTY HISTORICAL SOCIETY - VEDDER MEMORIAL LIBRARY
R.D. 1, Box 10A   Phone: (518) 731-6822
Coxsackie, NY 12051   Raymond Beecher, Libn.

HUDSON INSTITUTE - LIBRARY
Quaker Ridge Rd.   Phone: (914) 762-0700
Croton-On-Hudson, NY 10520   Mildred Schneck, Libn.

WORLD MODELING ASSOCIATION - WMA LIBRARY
Box 100   Phone: (914) 737-8512
Croton-On-Hudson, NY 10520   Ruth Tolman, Pres.

MUSICAL MUSEUM - RESEARCH LIBRARY
Main St.   Phone: (315) 841-8774
Deansboro, NY 13328   Arthur H. Sanders, Cur.

NEW YORK STATE SUPREME COURT - 6TH JUDICIAL DISTRICT - LAW
    LIBRARY
Court House   Phone: (607) 746-2603
Delhi, NY 13753   Barbara B. Lewis, Lib.Ck.

O'CONNOR (Lindsay A. & Olive B.) HOSPITAL - LIBRARY
Andes Road, Route 28   Phone: (607) 746-2371
Delhi, NY 13753   Steve Oles, Libn.

SUNY - AGRICULTURAL AND TECHNICAL COLLEGE AT DELHI - LIBRARY †
                                            Phone: (607) 746-4107
Delhi, NY 13753   Herbert J. Sorgen, Libn.

STAUFFER CHEMICAL COMPANY - EASTERN RESEARCH CENTER
    INFORMATION SERVICES
Livingstone Ave.   Phone: (914) 693-1200
Dobbs Ferry, NY 10522   Ramona C.T. Crosby, Supv.Info.Serv.

DUNKIRK OBSERVER - LIBRARY †
8 E. Second St.   Phone: (716) 366-3000
Dunkirk, NY 14048

AURORA HISTORICAL SOCIETY - ELBERT HUBBARD LIBRARY AND MUSEUM
Village Hall, 571 Main St.
East Aurora, NY 14052   Kenneth Whitney, Co-Cur.

CHRIST THE KING SEMINARY - LIBRARY
711 Knox Rd.   Phone: (716) 652-8959
East Aurora, NY 14052   Rev. Bonaventure F. Hayes, O.F.M., Lib.Dir.

EAST HAMPTON FREE LIBRARY - LONG ISLAND COLLECTION
159 Main St.   Phone: (516) 324-0222
East Hampton, NY 11937   Dorothy T. King, Libn.

NASSAU COUNTY MEDICAL CENTER - HEALTH SCIENCES LIBRARY
2201 Hempstead Turnpike   Phone: (516) 542-3542
East Meadow, NY 11554

NASSAU COUNTY MUSEUM REFERENCE LIBRARY
Dwight D. Eisenhower Memorial Pk.   Phone: (516) 292-4292
East Meadow, NY 11554   Edward J. Smits, Dir.

SUNY AT STONY BROOK - HEALTH SCIENCES LIBRARY
Box 66   Phone: (516) 246-2512
East Setauket, NY 11733   Ruth Marcolina, Dir.

EASTCHESTER HISTORICAL SOCIETY - LIBRARY
Box 37   Phone: (914) 793-1900
Eastchester NY 10709   Madeline Schaeffer, Libn.

EDEN HISTORICAL SOCIETY - TOWN HISTORIAN'S OFFICE AND
    HISTORICAL SOCIETY LIBRARY
8584 S. Main St.   Phone: (716) 992-9141
Eden, NY 14057   Nathalie B. Leonard, Town Hist./Cur.

ESSEX COUNTY HISTORICAL SOCIETY - LIBRARY
Court St.   Phone: (518) 873-6466
Elizabethtown, NY 12932   Dorothy A. Plum, Libn.

MOUNT SINAI HOSPITAL SERVICES - CITY HOSPITAL CENTER AT
    ELMHURST - MEDICAL LIBRARY
79-01 Broadway   Phone: (212) 830-1538
Elmhurst, NY 11373   Stacey Saley, Chf.Med.Libn.

ARNOT ART MUSEUM - LIBRARY *
235 Lake St.
Elmira, NY 14901

ARNOT-OGDEN MEMORIAL HOSPITAL - WEY MEMORIAL LIBRARY
Roe Ave. at Grove St.   Phone: (607) 737-4101
Elmira, NY 14901   Katherine F. Mekos, Libn.

CHEMUNG COUNTY HISTORICAL SOCIETY, INC. - MRS. ARTHUR W. BOOTH
    LIBRARY
304 William St.   Phone: (607) 737-2900
Elmira, NY 14901   Lyman D. Gridley, Pres.

ELMIRA PSYCHIATRIC CENTER - PROFESSIONAL LIBRARY
Caller 1527   Phone: (607) 737-4769
Elmira, NY 14902   Victoria G. Pifalo, Asst.Libn.

ELMIRA STAR GAZETTE - LIBRARY
201 Baldwin St.   Phone: (607) 734-5151
Elmira, NY 14902   Jean Strong, Libn.

NATIONAL SOARING MUSEUM - LIBRARY & ARCHIVES
Harris Hill, R.D. 3   Phone: (607) 734-3128
Elmira, NY 14903   Shirley Sliwa, Dir.

NEW YORK STATE SUPREME COURT - 6TH JUDICIAL DISTRICT - LAW
    LIBRARY
Hazlett Bldg.   Phone: (607) 737-2983
Elmira, NY 14901   Julie H. McDowell, Libn.

GEOGRAPHIC

ST. JOSEPH'S HOSPITAL - HELENE FULD LEARNING RESOURCE CENTER
555 E. Market St.   Phone: (607) 733-6541
Elmira, NY 14902   Arlene C. Pien, Libn.

THATCHER GLASS MANUFACTURING CO. - RESEARCH CENTER LIBRARY
Box 265   Phone: (607) 737-3162
Elmira, NY 14902   Dorothy A. McCluskey, Adm.Asst.

PERGAMON INSTITUTE - LIBRARY
Maxwell House
Elmsford, NY 10523   Phone: (914) 592-7700
                    Miriam Margoshes, Libn.

IBM CORPORATION - SYSTEM PRODUCTS DIVISION - LIBRARY
Rte. 17C & Glendale Dr.
Box 6   Phone: (607) 755-3226
Endicott, NY 13760   Shirley K. Manaley, Libn.

MOUNT ST. ALPHONSUS THEOLOGICAL SEMINARY - LIBRARY
                    Phone: (914) 384-6550
Esopus, NY 12429   Joan W. Durand, Libn.

PENINSULA HOSPITAL CENTER - MEDICAL LIBRARY
51-15 Beach Channel Dr.   Phone: (212) 945-7100
Far Rockaway, NY 11691   Edith Rubinstein, Library Director

ST. JOHN'S EPISCOPAL HOSPITAL (South Shore Division) - MEDICAL
    LIBRARY
327 Beach 19th St.   Phone: (212) 471-8100
Far Rockaway, NY 11691   Esther Skolnik, Med.Libn.

FAIRCHILD INDUSTRIES - FAIRCHILD REPUBLIC COMPANY - ENGINEERING
    LIBRARY
Conklin St.   Phone: (516) 531-3497
Farmingdale, NY 11735   George A. Mauter, Supv.

FARMINGDALE PUBLIC SCHOOLS - PROFESSIONAL LIBRARY
Main St. School   Phone: (516) 752-6553
Farmingdale, NY 11735   Geoffrey L. Mattocks, Dir.

SUNY - AGRICULTURAL AND TECHNICAL COLLEGE AT FARMINGDALE -
    THOMAS D. GREENLEY LIBRARY
Melville Rd.   Phone: (516) 420-2011
Farmingdale, NY 11735   Sylvia S. Ewen, Chf.Libn.

VAN WYCK HOMESTEAD MUSEUM - LIBRARY
Rte. 9, Box 133   Phone: (914) 896-9560
Fishkill, NY 12524   Ruth B. Polhill, Libn.

ACADEMY OF AERONAUTICS - LIBRARY
LaGuardia Airport Sta.   Phone: (212) 429-6600
Flushing, NY 11371   JoAnn Jayne, Libn.

ATLAS TRAFFIC CONSULTANTS CORPORATION - TARIFF DEPARTMENT
    LIBRARY
18-42 College Point Blvd.   Phone: (212) 461-0556
Flushing, NY 11356   Daniel Coppola, Libn.

BOOTH MEMORIAL MEDICAL CENTER - MEDICAL LIBRARY
Main St. at Booth Memorial Ave.   Phone: (212) 670-1118
Flushing, NY 11355   Rita S. Maier, Lib.Dir.

QUEENS COLLEGE OF THE CITY UNIVERSITY OF NEW YORK - ETHNIC
    MATERIALS INFORMATION CENTER
Graduate School of Lib. & Info. Studies
64-15 Kissena Blvd.   Phone: (212) 520-7194
Flushing, NY 11367   David Cohen, Prog.Dir.

QUEENS COLLEGE OF THE CITY UNIVERSITY OF NEW YORK - PAUL
    KLAPPER LIBRARY - ART LIBRARY
                    Phone: (212) 520-7243
Flushing, NY 11367   Suzanna Simor, Art Libn.

QUEENS COLLEGE OF THE CITY UNIVERSITY OF NEW YORK - SCIENCE
    LIBRARY
65-30 Kissena Blvd.   Phone: (212) 520-7254
Flushing, NY 11367   Jackson B. Cohen, Hd., Sci.Lib.

MOHAWK-CAUGHNAWAGA MUSEUM - LIBRARY
R.D.1
Box 6   Phone: (518) 853-3646
Fonda, NY 12068   Wayne Lenig, Musm.Adm.

MONTGOMERY COUNTY - DEPARTMENT OF HISTORY AND ARCHIVES
Old Court House   Phone: (518) 853-3431
Fonda, NY 12068   Anita A. Smith, Hist.

ACADEMY OF MEDICINE OF THE COUNTY OF QUEENS, INC. - CARL M.
    BOETTIGER MEMORIAL LIBRARY †
112-25 Queens Blvd., 4th Fl.   Phone: (212) 268-7300
Forest Hills, NY 11375   Ella M. Abney, Libn.

GOLDWATER MEMORIAL HOSPITAL - HEALTH SCIENCES LIBRARY †
New York Univ. Medical Center Affiliate   Phone: (212) 750-6749
Franklin D. Roosevelt Island, NY 10044   Martin M. Leibovici, Libn.

NOSTALGIA PRESS, INC. - ARCHIVES AND PICTURE LIBRARY *
Box 293   Phone: (212) 288-3875
Franklin Square, NY 11010   Martin F. Jackson, Info.Dir.

SUNY - COLLEGE AT FREDONIA - MUSIC LIBRARY
                    Phone: (716) 673-3183
Fredonia, NY 14063   Joseph Chouinard, Music Libn.

NESTLE ENTERPRISES, INC. - TECHNICAL SERVICE DIVISION - LIBRARY
555 S. Fourth St.   Phone: (315) 598-1234
Fulton, NY 13069   Janice Burns, Libn.

ADELPHI UNIVERSITY - SCIENCE LIBRARY
                    Phone: (516) 663-1043
Garden City, NY 11530   Liselotte Matzka, Hd., Sci.Lib.

ADELPHI UNIVERSITY - SOCIAL WORK LIBRARY
                    Phone: (516) 560-8040
Garden City, NY 11530   Ragai N. Makar, Hd.Libn.

ENDO LABORATORIES, INC. - LIBRARY
1000 Stewart Ave.   Phone: (516) 832-2113
Garden City, NY 11530   Virginia Steinberger, Mgr.

MERCER (George Jr.) MEMORIAL SCHOOL OF THEOLOGY - LIBRARY
65 Fourth St.   Phone: (516) 248-4800
Garden City, NY 11530   Elizabeth D. Dupont, Libn.

NASSAU COUNTY MEDICAL SOCIETY - NASSAU ACADEMY OF MEDICINE -
    JOHN N. SHELL LIBRARY
1200 Stewart Ave.   Phone: (516) 832-2320
Garden City, NY 11530   Mary L. Westermann, Med.Libn.

GRAYMOOR ECUMENICAL INSTITUTE - CARDINAL SPELLMAN LIBRARY
Graymoor   Phone: (914) 424-3671
Garrison, NY 10524   Fr. John W. Coppinger, S.A., Libn.

LIVINGSTON COUNTY LAW LIBRARY
2 Court St.   Phone: (716) 243-2500
Geneseo, NY 14454   Alice Esposito, Libn.

SUNY - COLLEGE AT GENESEO - MILNE LIBRARY
                    Phone: (716) 245-5591
Geneseo, NY 14454   Richard C. Quick, Dir. of Coll.Libs.

CORNELL UNIVERSITY - NEW YORK STATE AGRICULTURAL EXPERIMENT
    STATION - LIBRARY †
W. North St.   Phone: (315) 787-2214
Geneva, NY 14456   Gail L. Hyde, Libn.

GENEVA HISTORICAL SOCIETY AND MUSEUM - JAMES D. LUCKETT
    MEMORIAL ARCHIVES
543 S. Main St.   Phone: (315) 789-5151
Geneva, NY 14456   Eleanore R. Clise, Chf.Archv.

BUREAU OF JEWISH EDUCATION - COMMUNITY LIBRARY
2640 N. Forest Rd.   Phone: (716) 689-8844
Getzville, NY 14068   Abraham F. Yanover, Exec.Dir.

COMMUNITY HOSPITAL AT GLEN COVE - MEDICAL LIBRARY
St. Andrews Ln.   Phone: (516) 676-5000
Glen Cove, NY 11542   Kathryn M. Gegan, Libn.

WEBB INSTITUTE OF NAVAL ARCHITECTURE - LIVINGSTON LIBRARY
Crescent Beach Rd.   Phone: (516) 671-0439
Glen Cove, NY 11542   Fred H. Forrest, Libn.

NEW YORK CHIROPRACTIC COLLEGE - LIBRARY
255 Valentines Ln., Old Brookville   Phone: (516) 686-7657
Glen Head, NY 11545   Lorraine Palmer, Libn.

LONG ISLAND JEWISH-HILLSIDE MEDICAL CENTER - HILLSIDE DIVISION -
    HEALTH SCIENCES LIBRARY
Box 38   Phone: (212) 470-4406
Glen Oaks, NY 11004   Joan L. Kauff, Chf.Med.Libn.

GLENS FALLS-QUEENSBURY HISTORICAL ASSN., INC. - CHAPMAN
    HISTORICAL MUSM. - RUSSELL M.L. CARSON MEMORIAL LIB.
348 Glen St.   Phone: (518) 793-2826
Glens Falls, NY 12801   Joseph A. Cutshall King, Dir.

HYDE COLLECTION
161 Warren St.   Phone: (518) 792-1761
Glens Falls, NY 12801

FIRST UNITED METHODIST CHURCH - JENNIE E. WEAVER MEMORIAL
    LIBRARY
7 Elm St.   Phone: (518) 725-9313
Gloversville, NY 12078

TROTTING HORSE MUSEUM - LIBRARY
240 Main St.   Phone: (914) 294-6330
Goshen, NY 10924   Philip A. Pines, Dir.

MOORE BUSINESS FORMS, INC. - RESEARCH CENTER LIBRARY
300 Lang Blvd.   Phone: (716) 773-0557
Grand Island, NY 14072   Betsy M. Waters, Lib.Supv.

TEMPLE BETH-EL - ARNOLD & MARIE SCHWARTZ LIBRARY
5 Old Mill Rd.   Phone: (516) 829-9465
Great Neck, NY 11021   Ruth Jacobskind, Libn.

U.S.D.A. - AGRICULTURAL RESEARCH SERVICE - PLUM ISLAND ANIMAL
    DISEASE CENTER LIBRARY
Box 848   Phone: (516) 323-2500
Greenport, NY 11944   Stephen Perlman, Libn.

LONG ISLAND UNIVERSITY - C.W. POST CENTER - PALMER GRADUATE
    LIBRARY SCHOOL LIBRARY †
B. Davis Schwartz Memorial Library   Phone: (516) 299-2826
Greenvale, NY 11548   Ellen Weinstein, Hd.

U.S. AIR FORCE HOSPITAL - MEDICAL LIBRARY (NY-Rome)
Griffiss Air Force Base   Phone: (315) 330-7713
Griffiss Air Force Base, NY 13441   Patricia Hayes, Med.Libn.

U.S. AIR FORCE - ROME AIR DEVELOPMENT CENTER - TECHNICAL LIBRARY
RADC (TSL)   Phone: (315) 330-7607
Griffiss AFB, NY 13441   Nel Mathys, Chf., Tech.Lib.

NEW YORK STATE NURSES ASSOCIATION - LIBRARY
2113 Western Ave.   Phone: (518) 456-9354
Guilderland, NY 12084   Barbara Van Nortwick, Lib.Dir.

WESTERN NEW YORK GENEALOGICAL SOCIETY, INC. - LIBRARY
18 Boxwood Circle
Box 338   Phone: (716) 649-4440
Hamburg, NY 14075   Donald C. Shaw, Libn.

AMERICAN MANAGEMENT ASSOCIATIONS - D.W. MITCHELL MEMORIAL
    LIBRARY
Box 88   Phone: (315) 824-2000
Hamilton, NY 13346   Madge Snyder, Libn.

COLGATE UNIVERSITY - ARCHIVES
                                                   Phone: (315) 824-1000
Hamilton, NY 13346   Howard D. Williams, Univ.Archv.

CURTISS (Glenn H.) MUSEUM OF LOCAL HISTORY - MINOR SWARTHOUT
    MEMORIAL LIBRARY
Lake & Main St.   Phone: (607) 569-2160
Hammondsport, NY 14840   Merrill Stickler, Dir.

AFRAM ASSOCIATES, INC. - AFRAMAILIBRARY
Beatrice Lewis Bldg.
68-72 E. 131st St.   Phone: (212) 281-6000
Harlem, NY 10037   Mr. Westcott, Dir.

INSTITUTE OF SOCIETY, ETHICS & THE LIFE SCIENCES - HASTINGS
    CENTER
360 Broadway   Phone: (914) 478-0500
Hastings On Hudson, NY 10706   Marna Howarth, Libn.

NUMAX ELECTRONICS, INC. - LIBRARY
720 Old Willets Path
Hauppauge, NY 11787

SUFFOLK ACADEMY OF MEDICINE - LIBRARY
850 Veterans Memorial Hwy.   Phone: (516) 724-7970
Hauppauge, NY 11787   Isabel V. Hathorn, Libn.

IBM CORPORATION - DATA PROCESSING PROGRAM INFORMATION
    DEPARTMENT *
40 Saw Mill River Rd.   Phone: (914) 345-5000
Hawthorne, NY 10532

GOWANDA PSYCHIATRIC CENTER - HEALTH SCIENCES LIBRARY
Rte. 62   Phone: (716) 532-3311
Helmuth, NY 14079   Mark Wudyka, Libn.

HOFSTRA UNIVERSITY - LIBRARY - SPECIAL COLLECTIONS
1000 Fulton Ave.   Phone: (516) 560-3387
Hempstead, NY 11550   Marguerite Regan, Asst. to Dean

HOFSTRA UNIVERSITY - SCHOOL OF LAW LIBRARY
                                                   Phone: (516) 560-3603
Hempstead, NY 11550   Eugene M. Wypyski, Libn.

INDUSTRIAL HOME FOR THE BLIND - NASSAU-SUFFOLK BRAILLE LIBRARY
320 Fulton Ave.   Phone: (516) 485-1234
Hempstead, NY 11550   Helen Lomax, Libn.

LONG ISLAND CATHOLIC - RESEARCH LIBRARY
Box 700   Phone: (516) 538-8800
Hempstead, NY 11551   Doris S. Bader, Libn.

NASSAU COUNTY DEPARTMENT OF HEALTH - DIVISION OF LABORATORIES
    & RESEARCH - MEDICAL LIBRARY
209 Main St.   Phone: (516) 483-9158
Hempstead, NY 11550   Madeline H. Burston, Pub. Health Adm.

HERKIMER COUNTY LAW LIBRARY
Court House, Main St.   Phone: (315) 867-1172
Herkimer, NY 13350   Jane C. Gilbert, Law Lib.Ck.

TEMPLE BETH JOSEPH - ROSE BASLOE LIBRARY †
North Prospect St.   Phone: (315) 866-4270
Herkimer, NY 13350

GENERAL INSTRUMENT CORPORATION, GOVERNMENT SYSTEMS DIVISION
    - ENGINEERING LIBRARY
600 West John St.   Phone: (516) 733-3000
Hicksville, NY 11802   Hilda N. Shevack, Logistics/Data Mgr.

LONG ISLAND LIGHTING COMPANY - LIBRARY
175 E. Old Country Rd.   Phone: (516) 733-4264
Hicksville, NY 11801   Patricia Clancy, Libn.

SERVO CORPORATION OF AMERICA - TECHNICAL LIBRARY
111 New South Rd.   Phone: (516) 938-9700
Hicksville, NY 11802   W. Decker, Libn.

AKWESASNE LIBRARY CULTURAL CENTER
                                                   Phone: (518) 358-2240
Hogansburg, NY 13655   Margaret M. Jacobs, Dir.

GEOGRAPHIC

ANTIQUE WIRELESS ASSOCIATION, INC. - LIBRARY
Main St. (East Bloomfield)
Holcomb, NY 14469   Bruce Kelley, Dir./Cur.

LEIBIGER (O.W.) RESEARCH LABORATORIES, INC. - TECHNICAL
INFORMATION CENTER †
48 Classic St.
Box 10   Phone: (518) 686-5841
Hoosick Falls, NY 12090   I. Leibiger, Hd.

IBM CORPORATION - GENERAL TECHNOLOGY DIVISION - EAST FISHKILL
FACILITY - LIBRARY
Rte. 52   Phone: (914) 897-6219
Hopewell Junction, NY 12533   Robert B. Murphy, Mgr.

WESTINGHOUSE ELECTRIC CORPORATION - ENGINEERING LIBRARY
Westinghouse Circle   Phone: (607) 796-3207
Horseheads, NY 14845   Shelden S. King, Engr.Libn.

NEW YORK STATE SUPREME COURT - 3RD JUDICIAL DISTRICT - LAW
LIBRARY
Court House
Hudson, NY 12534   Emily M. Wildey, Libn.

OLANA STATE HISTORIC SITE - LIBRARY
R.D. 2   Phone: (518) 828-0135
Hudson, NY 12534   James Ryan, Site Mgr.

HUNTINGTON HISTORICAL SOCIETY - LIBRARY
2 High St.   Phone: (516) 427-7045
Huntington, NY 11743   Agnes K. Packard, Libn.

SEMINARY OF THE IMMACULATE CONCEPTION - LIBRARY
West Neck Rd.   Phone: (516) 423-0483
Huntington, NY 11743   Dr. Jiri Lipa, Libn.

KLD ASSOCIATES, INC. - LIBRARY
300 Broadway   Phone: (516) 549-9803
Huntington Station, NY 11746

WHITMAN (Walt) BIRTHPLACE ASSOCIATION - LIBRARY AND MUSEUM
246 Walt Whitman Rd.   Phone: (516) 427-5240
Huntington Station, NY 11746   Bets Vondrasek, Cur.

CULINARY INSTITUTE OF AMERICA - KATHARINE ANGELL LIBRARY
North Rd.   Phone: (914) 452-9600
Hyde Park, NY 12538   Eileen De Vries, Libn.

U.S. NATL. PARK SERVICE - ROOSEVELT-VANDERBILT NATL. HISTORIC
SITES - MUSEUMS
                                                    Phone: (914) 229-9115
Hyde Park, NY 12538   Franceska Macsali, Site Libn.

U.S. PRESIDENTIAL LIBRARIES - FRANKLIN D. ROOSEVELT LIBRARY
Albany Post Rd.   Phone: (914) 229-8114
Hyde Park, NY 12538   William R. Emerson, Dir.

FOUNDATION FOR ECONOMIC EDUCATION - LIBRARY
30 S. Broadway   Phone: (914) 591-7230
Irvington-On-Hudson, NY 10533   Brian Summers, Libn.

CORNELL UNIVERSITY - AFRICANA STUDIES AND RESEARCH CENTER
LIBRARY
310 Triphammer Rd.   Phone: (607) 256-3822
Ithaca, NY 14853

CORNELL UNIVERSITY - ALBERT R. MANN LIBRARY
                                                    Phone: (607) 256-2285
Ithaca, NY 14853   Jeanne White, Act.Libn.

CORNELL UNIVERSITY - AUDIO-VISUAL RESOURCE CENTER
8 Research Park   Phone: (607) 256-2091
Ithaca, NY 14850   Carol Doolittle, AV Coord.

CORNELL UNIVERSITY - BAILEY HORTORIUM LIBRARY
                                                    Phone: (607) 256-2132
Ithaca, NY 14853   D.M. Bates, Dir.

CORNELL UNIVERSITY - DEPARTMENT OF MANUSCRIPTS AND ARCHIVES
101 Olin Research Library   Phone: (607) 256-3530
Ithaca, NY 14853   H. Thomas Hickerson, Chm.

CORNELL UNIVERSITY - ENGINEERING LIBRARY
Carpenter Hall   Phone: (607) 256-4318
Ithaca, NY 14853

CORNELL UNIVERSITY - ENTOMOLOGY LIBRARY
Comstock Hall   Phone: (607) 256-3265
Ithaca, NY 14853   David L. Thomas, Entomology Libn.

CORNELL UNIVERSITY - FINE ARTS LIBRARY
Sibley Dome   Phone: (607) 256-3710
Ithaca, NY 14853   Judith E. Holliday, Libn.

CORNELL UNIVERSITY - FLOWER VETERINARY LIBRARY
                                                    Phone: (607) 256-2083
Ithaca, NY 14853   Susanne K. Whitaker, Libn.

CORNELL UNIVERSITY - GRADUATE SCHOOL OF BUSINESS AND PUBLIC
ADMINISTRATION - LIBRARY
Malott Hall   Phone: (607) 256-3389
Ithaca, NY 14853   Betsy Ann Olive, Libn.

CORNELL UNIVERSITY - HISTORY OF SCIENCE COLLECTIONS
215 Olin Research Library   Phone: (607) 256-4033
Ithaca, NY 14853   David W. Corson, Hist. of Sci.Libn.

CORNELL UNIVERSITY - ICELANDIC COLLECTION
Olin Research Library   Phone: (607) 256-6462
Ithaca, NY 14853   Vilhjalmur Bjarnar, Cur.

CORNELL UNIVERSITY - JOHN M. ECHOLS COLLECTION ON SOUTHEAST
ASIA
Olin Library   Phone: (607) 256-4189
Ithaca, NY 14853   Giok Po Oey, Cur.

CORNELL UNIVERSITY - LABORATORY OF ORNITHOLOGY - LIBRARY
159 Sapsucker Woods Rd.   Phone: (607) 256-5056
Ithaca, NY 14853   Helen Lapham, Supv.

CORNELL UNIVERSITY - LABORATORY OF ORNITHOLOGY - LIBRARY OF
NATURAL SOUNDS
159 Sapsucker Woods Rd.   Phone: (607) 256-5056
Ithaca, NY 14853   Dr. James L. Gulledge, Dir.

CORNELL UNIVERSITY - LAW LIBRARY
Myron Taylor Hall   Phone: (607) 256-7236
Ithaca, NY 14853   Jane L. Hammond, Law Libn.

CORNELL UNIVERSITY - MAPS, MICROTEXT, NEWSPAPERS DEPARTMENT
Olin Research Library   Phone: (607) 256-5258
Ithaca, NY 14853   Marie Gast, Libn.

CORNELL UNIVERSITY - MARTIN P. CATHERWOOD LIBRARY OF
INDUSTRIAL AND LABOR RELATIONS
                                                    Phone: (607) 256-2277
Ithaca, NY 14853   Shirley F. Harper, Libn.

CORNELL UNIVERSITY - MATHEMATICS LIBRARY
                                                    Phone: (607) 256-5076
Ithaca, NY 14853   Steven W. Rockey, Supv.

CORNELL UNIVERSITY - MUSIC LIBRARY
225 Lincoln Hall   Phone: (607) 256-4011
Ithaca, NY 14853   Michael A. Keller, Music Libn.

CORNELL UNIVERSITY - PHYSICAL SCIENCES LIBRARY
Clark Hall   Phone: (607) 256-5288
Ithaca, NY 14853   Ellen Thomas, Libn.

CORNELL UNIVERSITY - PROGRAM ON PARTICIPATION AND LABOR-
MANAGED SYSTEMS - DOCUMENTATION CENTER
490 Uris Hall   Phone: (607) 256-4070
Ithaca, NY 14853   Hazel D. Gunn, Coord.

CORNELL UNIVERSITY - RARE BOOKS DEPARTMENT
Olin Research Library   Phone: (607) 256-4211
Ithaca, NY 14853   Donald Eddy, Libn.

CORNELL UNIVERSITY - RESOURCE INFORMATION LABORATORY
Box 22, Roberts Hall   Phone: (607) 256-6520
Ithaca, NY 14853   Eugenia M. Barnaba, Mgr., Tech.Serv.

CORNELL UNIVERSITY - SCHOOL OF HOTEL ADMINISTRATION LIBRARY
Statler Hall   Phone: (607) 256-3673
Ithaca, NY 14853   Margaret J. Oaksford, Libn.

CORNELL UNIVERSITY - SHOALS MARINE LABORATORY - LIBRARY
G14 Stimson Hall   Phone: (607) 256-3717
Ithaca, NY 14853   Linda Mahon, Adm.Sec.

CORNELL UNIVERSITY - WASON COLLECTION
Olin Library   Phone: (607) 256-4357
Ithaca, NY 14853   Diane E. Perushek, Cur.

**DEWITT HISTORICAL SOCIETY OF TOMPKINS COUNTY - ARCHIVE/
   LIBRARY**
116 N. Cayuga St.   Phone: (607) 273-8284
Ithaca, NY 14850   Craig Williams, Dir.

HINCKLEY FOUNDATION MUSEUM - LIBRARY
410 E. Seneca St.   Phone: (607) 273-7053
Ithaca, NY 14850   Marilyn Reed Holscher, Dir.

PALEONTOLOGICAL RESEARCH INSTITUTION - LIBRARY *
1259 Trumansburg Rd.   Phone: (607) 273-6623
Ithaca, NY 14850   Gloria Kulhawy, Libn.

THOMPSON (Boyce) INSTITUTE - LIBRARY
Cornell University
Tower Rd.   Phone: (607) 257-2030
Ithaca, NY 14853   Greta Colavito, Lib.Hd.

TOMPKINS COMMUNITY HOSPITAL - ROBERT BROAD MEDICAL LIBRARY
1285 Trumansburg Rd.   Phone: (607) 274-4407
Ithaca, NY 14850   Sally Turo, Libn.

LEXINGTON SCHOOL FOR THE DEAF - LIBRARY MEDIA CENTER
26-26 75th St.   Phone: (212) 899-8800
Jackson Heights, NY 11370   Marie-Ann Marchese, Lib.Coord.

**CATHOLIC MEDICAL CENTER OF BROOKLYN & QUEENS, INC. - CENTRAL
   MEDICAL LIBRARY**
88-25 153rd St.   Phone: (212) 290-3300
Jamaica, NY 11432   Sr. Regina Clare Woods, O.P., Coord./Med.Libs.

JAMAICA HOSPITAL - MEDICAL LIBRARY
89th Ave. & Van Wyck Expy.   Phone: (212) 657-1800
Jamaica, NY 11418   Carolyn Mansbach, Med.Libn.

**LONG ISLAND JEWISH-HILLSIDE MEDICAL CENTER - QUEENS HOSPITAL
   CENTER - MEDICAL LIBRARY**
82-68 164th St.   Phone: (212) 990-2795
Jamaica, NY 11432   Helen M. Pilikian, Chf.Med.Libn.

**NEW YORK STATE SUPREME COURT - 11TH JUDICIAL DISTRICT - LAW
   LIBRARY**
General Court House
88-11 Sutphin Blvd.   Phone: (212) 520-3140
Jamaica, NY 11435   Anne Gail Gash, Libn.

PAN AMERICAN WORLD AIRWAYS - CLIPPER HALL MUSEUM ARCHIVES
John F. Kennedy Airport
Pan Am Passenger Terminal Bldg.
Jamaica, NY 11430

PASSIONIST MONASTERY - LIBRARY
86-45 178th St.   Phone: (212) 739-6502
Jamaica, NY 11432   Rev. Paul J. Fullam, Libn.

QUEENS BOROUGH PUBLIC LIBRARY - ART AND MUSIC DIVISION
89-11 Merrick Blvd.   Phone: (212) 990-0755
Jamaica, NY 11432   Dorothea Wu, Div.Hd.

**QUEENS BOROUGH PUBLIC LIBRARY - HISTORY, TRAVEL & BIOGRAPHY
   DIVISION**
89-11 Merrick Blvd.   Phone: (212) 990-0762
Jamaica, NY 11432   Deborah Hammer, Div.Hd.

QUEENS BOROUGH PUBLIC LIBRARY - LANGUAGE & LITERATURE DIVISION
89-11 Merrick Blvd.   Phone: (212) 990-0763
Jamaica, NY 11432   Thomas S. Black, Div.Hd.

QUEENS BOROUGH PUBLIC LIBRARY - LONG ISLAND DIVISION
89-11 Merrick Blvd.   Phone: (212) 990-0770
Jamaica, NY 11432   Davis Erhardt, Div.Hd.

QUEENS BOROUGH PUBLIC LIBRARY - SCIENCE & TECHNOLOGY DIVISION
89-11 Merrick Blvd.   Phone: (212) 990-0760
Jamaica, NY 11432   John D. Brady, Jr., Div.Hd.

QUEENS BOROUGH PUBLIC LIBRARY - SOCIAL SCIENCES DIVISION
89-11 Merrick Blvd.   Phone: (212) 990-0761
Jamaica, NY 11432   Phyllis R. Poses, Div.Hd.

ST. JOHN'S UNIVERSITY - ASIAN COLLECTION
Grand Central & Utopia Pkwys.   Phone: (212) 990-6161
Jamaica, NY 11439   Hou Ran Ferng, Libn.

ST. JOHN'S UNIVERSITY - LAW LIBRARY
Fromkes Hall
Grand Central & Utopia Pkwys.   Phone: (212) 990-6161
Jamaica, NY 11439   John T. Saiz, Law.Libn.

ST. JOHN'S UNIVERSITY - LIBRARY
Grand Central & Utopia Pkwys.   Phone: (212) 990-6161
Jamaica, NY 11439   Rev. Lawrence A. Lonergan, C.M., Dir. of Libs.

U.S. FEDERAL AVIATION ADMINISTRATION - EASTERN REGION LIBRARY
Federal Bldg.
J.F. Kennedy Intl. Airport   Phone: (212) 995-3325
Jamaica, NY 11430

FENTON HISTORICAL SOCIETY - LIBRARY
67 Washington St.   Phone: (716) 661-2296
Jamestown, NY 14701   B. Dolores Thompson, Exec.Dir.

**TRW, INC. - BEARINGS DIVISION - RESEARCH & DEVELOPMENT
   TECHNICAL LIBRARY**
402 Chandler St.   Phone: (716) 661-2894
Jamestown, NY 14701   Harold E. Munson, Supv. Project

**WILSON (Charles S.) MEMORIAL HOSPITAL - LEARNING RESOURCES
   DEPARTMENT**
33-57 Harrison St.   Phone: (607) 773-6030
Johnson City, NY 13790   Shirley Edsall, Dir.

AUTHENTICATED NEWS INTERNATIONAL - PHOTO LIBRARY
29 Katohah Ave.   Phone: (914) 232-7726
Katonah, NY 10536   Sidney Polinsky, Mng.Ed.

**GARIBALDI AND MEUCCI MEMORIAL MUSEUM - LIBRARY OF THE ITALIAN
   RISORGIMENTO**
John Jay Homestead, Box AH   Phone: (914) 232-3667
Katonah, NY 10536   Lino S. Lipinsky de Orlov, Dir.

JAY (John) HOMESTEAD - JAY LIBRARY
Box A.H.   Phone: (914) 232-5651
Katonah, NY 10536   Linda E. McLean, Dir./Site Mgr.

SISTERS OF ST. MARY OF NAMUR - MOUNT ST. MARY RESEARCH CENTER
3756 Delaware Ave.   Phone: (716) 875-4705
Kenmore, NY 14217   Sr. M. Xavier Hefner, Archv./Libn.

COLUMBIA COUNTY HISTORICAL SOCIETY - HOUSE OF HISTORY LIBRARY
                                               Phone: (518) 758-9265
Kinderhook, NY 12106   Ruth Piwonka, Exec.Dir.

KINGS PARK PSYCHIATRIC CENTER - LIBRARY
Box A   Phone: (516) 544-2671
Kings Park, NY 11754   Mark Abramson, Sr.Libn.

U.S. MARITIME ADMINISTRATION - NATL. MARITIME RESEARCH CENTER - STUDY CENTER
Phone: (516) 482-8200
Kings Point, NY 11024   Rayma Feldman, Sr.Info.Spec.

U.S. MERCHANT MARINE ACADEMY - SCHUYLER OTIS BLAND MEMORIAL LIBRARY
Phone: (516) 482-8200
Kings Point, NY 11024   Elizabeth A. Fuseler, Libn.

IBM CORPORATION - SYSTEM COMMUNICATIONS DIVISION - SITE LIBRARY
Dept. 65P/840
Neighborhood Rd.   Phone: (914) 383-3574
Kingston, NY 12401   Ralph W. Hasenbalg, Mgr.

KINGSTON HOSPITAL - LIBRARY
396 Broadway   Phone: (914) 331-3131
Kingston, NY 12401   Linda Stopard, Libn.

NEW YORK STATE SUPREME COURT - 3RD JUDICIAL DISTRICT - LAW LIBRARY
Court House
Kingston, NY 12401   Harriett Straus, Libn.

SENATE HOUSE STATE HISTORIC SITE - LIBRARY & ARCHIVES
296 Fair St.   Phone: (914) 338-2786
Kingston, NY 12401   Leigh R. Jones, Historic Site Mgr.

ULSTER COUNTY PLANNING BOARD - LIBRARY
244 Fair St.
Box 1800   Phone: (914) 331-9300
Kingston, NY 12401   Dennis Doyle, Planner

OUR LADY OF VICTORY HOSPITAL - HOSPITAL LIBRARY *
55 Melroy at Ridge Rd.   Phone: (716) 825-8000
Lackawanna, NY 14218   Ann Hassett, Lib.Ck.

NEW YORK STATE SUPREME COURT - 4TH JUDICIAL DISTRICT - LAW LIBRARY
Warren County Municipal Ctr.   Phone: (518) 761-6443
Lake George, NY 12845   Marjorie P. Potter, Law Lib.Ck.

LAKE PLACID ASSOCIATION FOR MUSIC, DRAMA & ART - NETTIE MARIE JONES FINE ARTS LIBRARY
Saranac Ave. At Fawn Ridge   Phone: (518) 523-2591
Lake Placid, NY 12946   Suellen Linn, Lib.Dir.

TISSUE CULTURE ASSOCIATION - W. ALTON JONES CELL SCIENCE CENTER - GEORGE AND MARGARET GEY LIBRARY
Old Barn Rd.   Phone: (518) 523-2427
Lake Placid, NY 12946   A. Kathleen Hanlon, Libn.

PRC SPEAS - TECHNICAL LIBRARY
3003 New Hyde Park Rd.   Phone: (516) 488-6930
Lake Success, NY 11040

CAPITAL DISTRICT LIBRARY COUNCIL FOR REFERENCE AND RESEARCH RESOURCES - BIBLIOGRAPHIC CENTER
91 Fiddlers Lane   Phone: (518) 785-0798
Latham, NY 12110   Charles D. Custer, Exec.Dir.

SISTERS OF ST. JOSEPH OF CARONDELET - ALBANY PROVINCE - ARCHIVES
St. Joseph Provincial House
Watervliet Shaker Rd.   Phone: (518) 785-4575
Latham, NY 12110   Sister Susan Marie O'Connor, C.S.J., Archv.

TEMPLE ISRAEL - LIBRARY †
140 Central Ave.   Phone: (516) 239-1140
Lawrence, NY 11559   Donna Z. Lifland, Libn.

LE ROY HISTORICAL SOCIETY - LIBRARY
23 E. Main St.
Box 176   Phone: (716) 768-7433
Le Roy, NY 14482   Wesley G. Balla, Dir./Cur.

CATTARAUGUS COUNTY MEMORIAL AND HISTORICAL MUSEUM - LIBRARY
Court St.   Phone: (716) 938-9111
Little Valley, NY 14755   Lorna Spencer, Cur.

SCHUMANN MEMORIAL FOUNDATION, INC. - LIBRARY
2904 E. Lake Rd.   Phone: (716) 346-2745
Livonia, NY 14487   June M. Dickinson, Pres.

NIAGARA COUNTY HISTORICAL SOCIETY - LIBRARY AND ARCHIVES
215 Niagara St.   Phone: (716) 434-7433
Lockport, NY 14094   Jan J. Losi, Cur.

TEMPLE EMANU-EL - LIBRARY
455 Neptune Blvd.   Phone: (516) 431-4060
Long Beach, NY 11561   Rheba Rotgin, Libn.

POLYTECHNIC INSTITUTE OF NEW YORK - LONG ISLAND CENTER LIBRARY
Phone: (516) 694-5500
Long Island, NY 11735   Lorraine Schein, Hd.Libn.

NEW YORK BARTOK ARCHIVE
Box 717   Phone: (516) 569-1468
Lynbrook, NY 11563   Dr. Benjamin Suchoff, Trustee

WAYNE COUNTY HISTORICAL SOCIETY MUSEUM - LIBRARY
21 Butternut St.   Phone: (315) 946-4943
Lyons, NY 14489   Marjory Allen Perez, County Hist.

MOBIL CHEMICAL COMPANY - PLASTICS DIVISION - INFORMATION CENTER
Technical Center   Phone: (315) 986-6375
Macedon, NY 14502   Violanda O. Burns, Info.Anl.

HISTORICAL SOCIETY OF THE TOWN OF NORTH HEMPSTEAD - LIBRARY
220 Plandome Rd.   Phone: (516) 627-0590
Manhasset, NY 11030   F.J. Pistone, Pres.

MANTELL (C.L.) AND ASSOCIATES - LIBRARY *
447 Ryder Rd.
Manhasset, NY 11030

NORTH SHORE UNIVERSITY HOSPITAL - DANIEL CARROLL PAYSON MEDICAL LIBRARY *
Community Dr.   Phone: (516) 562-4324
Manhasset, NY 11030   Elsie Wilensky, Med.Libn.

MARYKNOLL FATHERS - PHOTO LIBRARY
Pines Bridge Rd.   Phone: (914) 941-7590
Maryknoll, NY 10545   Penny Ann Sandoval, Photo Libn.

MARYKNOLL SEMINARY - LIBRARY
Maryknoll, P.O.   Phone: (914) 941-7590
Maryknoll, NY 10545   Rev. Arthur E. Brown, M.M., Libn.

CHAUTAUQUA COUNTY LAW LIBRARY
Phone: (716) 753-4247
Mayville, NY 14757   Peggy Cross, Hd.Libn.

EATON CORPORATION - AIL DIVISION - RESEARCH LIBRARY
Walt Whitman Rd.   Phone: (516) 595-4400
Melville, NY 11747   Laurel D. Meyerhoff, Libn.

NEWSDAY, INC. - LIBRARY
235 Pinelawn Rd.   Phone: (516) 454-2335
Melville, NY 11747   Andrew V. Ippolito, Dir. of Lib. & Res.

MORTON RESEARCH CORPORATION - BUSINESS INFORMATION CENTER †
1745 Merrick Ave.   Phone: (516) 378-1066
Merrick, NY 11566   Judy Levin, Info.Mgr.

FMC CORPORATION - AGRICULTURAL CHEMICAL GROUP - RESEARCH AND DEVELOPMENT DEPT. - TECHNICAL LIBRARY
100 Niagara St.   Phone: (716) 735-3761
Middleport, NY 14105   Dr. P.E. Drummong, Mgr., Tech.Info.

HORTON (Elizabeth A.) MEMORIAL HOSPITAL - MEDICAL LIBRARY
60 Prospect Ave.   Phone: (914) 342-5561
Middletown, NY 10940   Laura Leese, Med.Libn.

MIDDLETOWN PSYCHIATRIC CENTER - MEDICAL LIBRARY
141 Monhagen Ave.
Box 1453   Phone: (914) 342-5511
Middletown, NY 10940   Frank C. Appell, Jr., Asst.Libn.

NEW YORK BOTANICAL GARDEN - CARY ARBORETUM - LIBRARY
Box AB   Phone: (914) 677-5343
Millbrook, NY 12545   Charles R. Long, Adm.Libn.

NASSAU COUNTY DEPARTMENT OF HEALTH - CENTRAL RESEARCH
    LIBRARY
240 Old Country Rd., Rm. 613   Phone: (516) 535-3368
Mineola, NY 11501   Evelyn Vaughn, Libn.

NASSAU COUNTY PLANNING COMMISSION - LIBRARY
222 Willis Ave.   Phone: (516) 535-2244
Mineola, NY 11501   Adele A. Siedlecki, Libn.

NASSAU COUNTY SUPREME COURT - 10TH JUDICIAL DISTRICT - LAW
    LIBRARY
100 Supreme Court Dr.   Phone: (516) 535-3883
Mineola, NY 11501   James J. Lodato, Principal Law Libn.

NASSAU HOSPITAL - BENJAMIN WHITE SEAMAN MEDICAL LIBRARY
259 First St.   Phone: (516) 663-2280
Mineola, NY 11501   Virginia I. Cook, Med.Libn.

NEW YORK STATE SUPREME COURT - 3RD JUDICIAL DISTRICT -
    HAMILTON ODELL LIBRARY
Sullivan County Court House
Monticello, NY 12701   Edith Schop, Libn.

NEW YORK STATE DEPARTMENT OF STATE - FIRE ACADEMY LIBRARY
600 College Ave.
Box K   Phone: (607) 535-7136
Montour Falls, NY 14865   Diana Zell, Asst.Libn.

SCHUYLER COUNTY HISTORICAL SOCIETY - LEE SCHOOL MUSEUM
Rte. 14 South
Box 651   Phone: (607) 535-9741
Montour Falls, NY 14865   Louise V. Stillman, Pres.

SCHUYLER COUNTY HISTORICAL SOCIETY - OLD BRICK TAVERN MUSEUM -
    RESEARCH LIBRARY
108 N. Catharine St.
Box 651   Phone: (607) 535-9741
Montour Falls, NY 14865   Betty D. Landon, Dir.

BLOCKED IRON CORPORATION - LIBRARY *
Albany Post Rd.   Phone: (914) 737-3900
Montrose, NY 10548

U.S. VETERANS ADMINISTRATION (NY-Montrose) - HOSPITAL LIBRARY
                                      Phone: (914) 737-4400
Montrose, NY 10548   Linda S. Polardino, Chf., Lib.Serv.

SUNY - AGRICULTURAL AND TECHNICAL COLLEGE AT MORRISVILLE -
    LIBRARY
                                      Phone: (315) 684-7055
Morrisville, NY 13408   Michael Gieryic, Hd.Libn.

NORTHERN WESTCHESTER HOSPITAL CENTER - HEALTH SCIENCES
    LIBRARY
                                      Phone: (914) 666-1259
Mount Kisco, NY 10549   Nona C. Willoughby, Hd.Libn.

CONSUMERS UNION FOUNDATION - CENTER FOR THE STUDY OF THE
    CONSUMER MOVEMENT - LIBRARY
256 Washington St.
Mt. Vernon, NY 10550

CONSUMERS UNION OF UNITED STATES, INC. - LIBRARY
256 Washington St.   Phone: (914) 664-6400
Mount Vernon, NY 10550   Lynn P. Freedman, Mgr.

SCHWARZ SERVICES INTERNATIONAL - LIBRARY
230 Washington St.   Phone: (914) 664-1100
Mt. Vernon, NY 10551   Mary Altomari, Libn.

HISTORICAL SOCIETY OF ROCKLAND COUNTY - LIBRARY
20 Zukor Rd.   Phone: (914) 634-9629
New City, NY 10956

CENTRAL NEW YORK ACADEMY OF MEDICINE - LIBRARY
210 Clinton St.   Phone: (315) 735-2204
New Hartford, NY 13413   Mildred D. Timmerman, Libn.

SPECIAL METALS CORPORATION - INFORMATION FACILITY
Middle Settlement Rd.   Phone: (315) 798-2936
New Hartford, NY 13413   R.F. McNally, Supv.Tech.Info.

LONG ISLAND JEWISH-HILLSIDE MEDICAL CENTER - HEALTH SCIENCES
    LIBRARY
270-05 76th Ave.   Phone: (212) 470-2673
New Hyde Park, NY 11042   Sandra Spurlock, Dir.Lib.Serv.

GEBBIE PRESS, INC. - HOUSE MAGAZINE LIBRARY
                                      Phone: (914) 255-7560
New Paltz, NY 12561   A. Gebbie, Pres.

HUGUENOT HISTORICAL SOCIETY, NEW PALTZ - LIBRARY
6 Brodhead Ave.,
Box 339   Phone: (914) 255-1660
New Paltz, NY 12561   Kenneth E. Hasbrouck, Dir.

HUGUENOT-THOMAS PAINE HISTORICAL ASSOCIATION OF NEW ROCHELLE
    - HUFELAND MEMORIAL LIBRARY
893 North Ave.   Phone: (914) 632-5376
New Rochelle, NY 10804   Ruth M. Phillips, Chm.

MEDICAL LETTER - LIBRARY
56 Harrison St.   Phone: (914) 235-0500
New Rochelle, NY 10801   Esther Manes, Libn.

NEW ROCHELLE HOSPITAL MEDICAL CENTER - J. MARSHALL PERLEY
    HEALTH SCIENCE LIBRARY
16 Guion Pl.   Phone: (914) 632-5000
New Rochelle, NY 10802   Helene D. Lambert, Med.Libn.

RICHARDSON-VICKS, INC. - VICK DIVISIONS RESEARCH & DEVELOPMENT
    - RESEARCH LIBRARY
56 Harrison St.   Phone: (914) 576-1500
New Rochelle, NY 10801   Susanne Silverman, Libn.

ACADEMY FOR EDUCATIONAL DEVELOPMENT, INC. - EDUCATIONAL
    FACILITIES LABORATORIES DIVISION - LIBRARY
680 Fifth Ave.   Phone: (212) 751-6214
New York, NY 10019

ACKERMAN INSTITUTE FOR FAMILY THERAPY, INC. - LIBRARY
149 E. 78th St.   Phone: (212) 879-4900
New York, NY 10021   Ruth Perl, Dir. of Res.

ADVERTISING RESEARCH FOUNDATION - LIBRARY
3 E. 54th St.   Phone: (212) 751-5656
New York, NY 10022   Elisabeth R. Proudfit, Mgr., Info.Ctr.

ADVISORY GROUP ON ELECTRON DEVICES - LIBRARY
201 Varick St., 11th Fl.   Phone: (212) 620-3374
New York, NY 10014   David Slater, Sec.

AESTHETIC REALISM FOUNDATION, INC. - LIBRARY
141 Greene St.   Phone: (212) 777-4490
New York, NY 10012   Richard Palumbo

AFRICAN-AMERICAN INSTITUTE - LIBRARY
833 United Nations Plaza
New York, NY 10017

AIR FRANCE - PUBLIC RELATIONS DEPARTMENT - LIBRARY
1350 Ave. of the Americas, 16th Fl.   Phone: (212) 841-7300
New York, NY 10019   Annie Fellenberg, Stud. & Doc.Adm.

ALLY AND GARGANO, INC. - INFORMATION CENTER
360 W. 31st St.   Phone: (212) 688-5300
New York, NY 10001   Marsha Cohen, Mgr., Info.Serv.

AMALGAMATED CLOTHING & TEXTILE WORKERS UNION, AFL-CIO -
    RESEARCH DEPARTMENT LIBRARY
15 Union Sq.   Phone: (212) 255-7800
New York, NY 10003   Irene Kuchta, Res.Libn.

GEOGRAPHIC

AMATEUR ASTRONOMERS ASSOCIATION - JANE H. DOUGLAS MEMORIAL
    LIBRARY
1010 Park Ave.
New York, NY 10028

AMERICAN ACADEMY AND INSTITUTE OF ARTS AND LETTERS - LIBRARY
633 W. 155th St.   Phone: (212) 368-5900
New York, NY 10032   Casindania P. Eaton, Libn.

AMERICAN ALPINE CLUB - LIBRARY
113 E. 90th St.   Phone: (212) 722-1628
New York, NY 10028   Horst Von Henning, Chm.Lib.Comm.

AMERICAN ARBITRATION ASSOCIATION - EASTMAN ARBITRATION
    LIBRARY
140 W. 51st St.   Phone: (212) 484-4129
New York, NY 10020   Laura Ferris Brown, Chf.Libn.

AMERICAN ASSOCIATION OF ADVERTISING AGENCIES - MEMBER
    INFORMATION SERVICE
666 3rd Ave.   Phone: (212) 682-2500
New York, NY 10017   Marilyn M. Bockman, V.P.

AMERICAN ASSOCIATION FOR JEWISH EDUCATION - LIBRARY
114 Fifth Ave.   Phone: (212) 675-5656
New York, NY 10011   Dr. Shimon Frost, Dir.

AMERICAN ASSOCIATION FOR JEWISH EDUCATION - NATIONAL
    EDUCATIONAL RESOURCE CENTER
114 Fifth Ave.   Phone: (212) 675-5656
New York, NY 10011   Carolyn S. Hessel, Coord.

AMERICAN ASSOCIATION OF OCCUPATIONAL HEALTH NURSES - LIBRARY
575 Lexington Ave.   Phone: (212) 355-7733
New York, NY 10022   Sylvia Bedell, Libn.

AMERICAN BANKER, INC. - LIBRARY †
525 W. 42nd St., 4th Fl.   Phone: (212) 563-1900
New York, NY 10036   Patricia Bluestein, Hd.Libn.

AMERICAN BIBLE SOCIETY - LIBRARY
1865 Broadway   Phone: (212) 581-7400
New York, NY 10023   Dr. Ivan H. Nothdurft, Supv.Off.

AMERICAN BROADCASTING COMPANIES, INC. - ABC NEWS INFORMATION
    CENTER
7 W. 66th St.   Phone: (212) 887-3796
New York, NY 10023   Madeline Cohen, Mgr., Lib.Serv.

AMERICAN BUSINESS PRESS, INC. - LIBRARY
205 E. 42nd St.   Phone: (212) 661-6360
New York, NY 10017   Evelyn G. French, Dir. Of Info.Sys.

AMERICAN CAN COMPANY - BUTTERICK FASHION MARKETING COMPANY -
    BUTTERICK ARCHIVES/LIBRARY †
161 Ave. of the Americas   Phone: (212) 620-2555
New York, NY 10013   Maureen Fitzpatrick, Gen.Serv.Mgr.

AMERICAN CANCER SOCIETY - FILM LIBRARY
777 Third Ave.   Phone: (212) 371-2900
New York, NY 10017   Stefan Bodnariuk, Supv. Film Ed.

AMERICAN CANCER SOCIETY - MEDICAL LIBRARY
777 Third Ave.   Phone: (212) 371-2900
New York, NY 10017   Dr. Sourya Henderson, Med.Libn.

AMERICAN CIVIL LIBERTIES UNION - LIBRARY/ARCHIVES †
132 W. 43rd St.   Phone: (212) 944-9800
New York, NY 10036   Barbara J. Eichman, Libn.

AMERICAN COLLEGE OF ORGONOMY, INC. - LIBRARY
Ansonia Sta., Box 565   Phone: (212) 734-8433
New York, NY 10028   David Blasband, Archv.

AMERICAN COUNCIL FOR THE ARTS - LIBRARY
570 Seventh Ave.   Phone: (212) 354-6655
New York, NY 10018   Robert Porter, Mgr., Info.Serv.

AMERICAN COUNCIL FOR NATIONALITIES SERVICE - LIBRARY AND
    INFORMATION CENTER
20 W. 40th St.   Phone: (212) 398-9142
New York, NY 10018   Wells C. Klein, Exec.Dir.

AMERICAN COUNCIL OF VOLUNTARY AGENCIES FOR FOREIGN SERVICE,
    INC. - TECH. ASSISTANCE INFO. CLEARING HOUSE
200 Park Ave. S., 11th Fl.   Phone: (212) 777-8210
New York, NY 10003   Mary Ellen Burgess, Exec.Sec.

AMERICAN CRAFT COUNCIL - LIBRARY
44 W. 53rd St., 2nd Fl.   Phone: (212) 397-0638
New York, NY 10019   Joanne Polster, Libn.

AMERICAN DRUGGIST MAGAZINE LIBRARY *
224 W. 57th St.
New York, NY 10019

AMERICAN ELECTRIC POWER SERVICE CORP. - LIBRARY
2 Broadway   Phone: (212) 440-9000
New York, NY 10004   Janet Bulger, Act.Libn.

AMERICAN EXPRESS COMPANY - CARD DIVISION - LIBRARY
125 Broad St., 17th Fl.   Phone: (212) 323-4961
New York, NY 10004   Sarika Mahant, Supv., Info.Sys.Adm

AMERICAN EXPRESS COMPANY - CARD INFORMATION CENTER
American Express Plaza   Phone: (212) 323-4146
New York, NY 10021   Joan B. Lurye, Mgr.

AMERICAN EXPRESS COMPANY - CORPORATE SYSTEMS &
    COMMUNICATIONS INFORMATION CENTER
125 Broad St., 11th Fl.   Phone: (212) 323-4063
New York, NY 10004   Stephanie Morrell, Corp.Tech.Libn.

AMERICAN EXPRESS COMPANY - TRAVELERS CHECK SYSTEMS AND DATA
    PROCESSING LIBRARY
55 Water St., 33rd Fl., 25th Fl.   Phone: (212) 938-7018
New York, NY 10041   Martha Wolberg, Libn.

AMERICAN FEDERATION OF STATE, COUNTY AND MUNICIPAL EMPLOYEES,
    AFL-CIO (AFSCME) - DC37 RESEARCH LIBRARY
140 Park Place   Phone: (212) 766-1032
New York, NY 10007   Evelyn Seinfeld, Libn.

AMERICAN FOUNDATION FOR THE BLIND - M.C. MIGEL MEMORIAL
    LIBRARY
15 W. 16th St.   Phone: (212) 620-2161
New York, NY 10011   Judith M. Kaplan, Hd.Libn.

AMERICAN HERITAGE PUBLISHING COMPANY, INC. - LIBRARY
10 Rockefeller Plaza   Phone: (212) 399-8931
New York, NY 10020   Laura A. Lane, Dir., Res.

AMERICAN HUNGARIAN LIBRARY AND HISTORICAL SOCIETY
215 E. 82nd St.   Phone: (212) 744-5298
New York, NY 10028

AMERICAN INSTITUTE OF AERONAUTICS AND ASTRONAUTICS -
    TECHNICAL INFORMATION SERVICE
555 W. 57th St.   Phone: (212) 247-6500
New York, NY 10019   Thomas J. Meskel, Adm.

AMERICAN INSTITUTE OF CERTIFIED PUBLIC ACCOUNTANTS - LIBRARY
1211 Ave. of the Americas   Phone: (212) 575-6322
New York, NY 10036   Karen Hegge Simmons, Chf.Libn.

AMERICAN INSTITUTE FOR MARXIST STUDIES - LIBRARY
20 E. 30th St.   Phone: (212) 689-4530
New York, NY 10016   Henry Klein, Libn.

AMERICAN INSTITUTE OF PHYSICS - CENTER FOR HISTORY OF PHYSICS -
    NIELS BOHR LIBRARY
335 E. 45th St.   Phone: (212) 661-9404
New York, NY 10017   John C. Aubry, Archv./Libn.

AMERICAN INSURANCE ASSOCIATION - ENGINEERING & SAFETY
    DEPARTMENT LIBRARY
85 John St.   Phone: (212) 433-5667
New York, NY 10038   Lynne Wizowski, Libn.

AMERICAN INSURANCE ASSOCIATION - LAW LIBRARY †
85 John St.   Phone: (212) 433-4400
New York, NY 10038   Lorna L. Beasley, Libn.

AMERICAN IRISH HISTORICAL SOCIETY - LIBRARY
991 Fifth Ave.   Phone: (212) 288-2263
New York, NY 10028   T.M. Bayne, Dir.

AMERICAN JEWISH COMMITTEE - BLAUSTEIN LIBRARY
165 E. 56th St.   Phone: (212) 751-4000
New York, NY 10022   Cyma M. Horowitz, Dir.

AMERICAN JEWISH COMMITTEE - WILLIAM E. WIENER ORAL HISTORY
    LIBRARY
165 E. 56th St.   Phone: (212) 751-4000
New York, NY 10022   Irma Kopp Krents, Dir.

AMERICAN JEWISH CONGRESS - CHARLES AND BERTIE G. SCHWARTZ
    JUDAICA READING ROOM & LIBRARY
Martin Steinberg Ctr. for Jewish Artists
15 E. 84th St.
New York, NY 10028

AMERICAN JEWISH CONGRESS-COMMISSION ON LAW, SOCIAL ACTION &
    URBAN AFFAIRS - SHAD POLIER MEMORIAL LIBRARY
15 E. 84th St.   Phone: (212) 879-4500
New York, NY 10028

AMERICAN JEWISH JOINT DISTRIBUTION COMMITTEE - ARCHIVES
60 E. 42nd St., Suite 1914   Phone: (212) 687-6200
New York, NY 10165   Rose Klepfisz, Dir., Archv.

AMERICAN JEWISH JOINT DISTRIBUTION COMMITTEE - LIBRARY †
60 E. 42nd St., Suite 1914   Phone: (212) 687-6200
New York, NY 10017   Miryam H. Block

AMERICAN JOURNAL OF NURSING COMPANY - SOPHIA F. PALMER
    MEMORIAL LIBRARY
555 W. 57th St.   Phone: (212) 582-8820
New York, NY 10019   Jacqueline Picciano, Libn.

AMERICAN KENNEL CLUB - LIBRARY
51 Madison Ave.   Phone: (212) 481-9245
New York, NY 10010   Roberta A. Vesley, Libn.

AMERICAN MANAGEMENT ASSOCIATIONS - LIBRARY
135 W. 50th St.   Phone: (212) 586-8100
New York, NY 10020   Claire A. Lambkin, Chf.Libn.

AMERICAN MERCHANT MARINE LIBRARY ASSOCIATION - PUBLIC LIBRARY
    OF THE HIGH SEAS
One World Trade Center, Suite 2601   Phone: (212) 775-1038
New York, NY 10048   Mace G. Mavroleon, Exec.Dir.

AMERICAN MIME, INC. - LIBRARY
61 4th Ave.   Phone: (212) 677-9276
New York, NY 10003   Paul J. Curtis, Dir.

AMERICAN MUSEUM OF NATURAL HISTORY - DEPARTMENT OF
    ICHTHYOLOGY - DEAN MEMORIAL LIBRARY
Central Park W. at 79th St.   Phone: (212) 873-1300
New York, NY 10024   Dr. Gareth Nelson, Cur.

AMERICAN MUSEUM OF NATURAL HISTORY - HAYDEN PLANETARIUM -
    RICHARD S. PERKIN LIBRARY
Central Park W. at 81st St.   Phone: (212) 873-1300
New York, NY 10024   Sandra Kitt, Libn.

AMERICAN MUSEUM OF NATURAL HISTORY - LIBRARY
Central Park W. at 79th St.   Phone: (212) 873-1300
New York, NY 10024   Nina J. Root, Chairperson

AMERICAN MUSEUM OF NATURAL HISTORY - OSBORN LIBRARY OF
    VERTEBRATE PALEONTOLOGY †
Central Park W. at 79th St.   Phone: (212) 873-1300
New York, NY 10024   Charlotte Holton, Libn.

AMERICAN MUSIC CENTER - LIBRARY
250 W. 54th St., Rm. 300   Phone: (212) 265-8190
New York, NY 10019   Jane Gottlieb, Libn.

AMERICAN NUMISMATIC SOCIETY - LIBRARY
Broadway at 155th St.   Phone: (212) 234-3130
New York, NY 10032   Francis D. Campbell, Jr., Libn.

AMERICAN PETROLEUM INSTITUTE - CENTRAL ABSTRACTING & INDEXING
    SERVICE
156 William St.
New York, NY 10038

AMERICAN-SCANDINAVIAN FOUNDATION - WILLIAM HENRY SCHOFIELD
    MEMORIAL LIBRARY
127 E. 73rd St.
New York, NY 10021

AMERICAN-SCOTTISH FOUNDATION, INC. - SCOTTISH RESEARCH
    LIBRARY
Box 537, Lenox Hill Sta.
New York, NY 10021   Lady Malcolm Douglas-Hamilton, Pres.

AMERICAN SOCIETY OF CIVIL ENGINEERS - INFORMATION SERVICES
345 E. 47th St.   Phone: (212) 644-7520
New York, NY 10017   Elan Garonzik, Ed. of Info.Serv.

AMERICAN SOCIETY FOR PSYCHICAL RESEARCH - LIBRARY
5 W. 73rd St.   Phone: (212) 799-5050
New York, NY 10023

AMERICAN SOCIETY OF TRAVEL AGENTS - LIBRARY †
711 Fifth Ave.   Phone: (212) 486-0700
New York, NY 10022   Arthur Schiff, Staff V.P.

AMERICAN STANDARDS TESTING BUREAU, INC. - SAM TOUR LIBRARY
40 Water St.   Phone: (212) 943-3157
New York, NY 10004   Mr. C. Chavis, Libn.

AMERICAN STOCK EXCHANGE - MARTIN J. KEENA MEMORIAL LIBRARY
86 Trinity Pl.   Phone: (212) 938-2280
New York, NY 10006   Karen E. Buchanan, Hd.Libn.

AMERICAN TELEPHONE & TELEGRAPH COMPANY - CORPORATE RESEARCH
    LIBRARY
195 Broadway, Rm. 850   Phone: (212) 393-3714
New York, NY 10007   Marianne V. Gupta, Chf.Libn.

AMERICAN TELEPHONE & TELEGRAPH COMPANY - EDITORIAL &
    HISTORICAL RESEARCH CENTER
195 Broadway, Rm. 412   Phone: (212) 393-4955
New York, NY 10007   Gary Doran, Mgr.

AMERICAN TELEPHONE & TELEGRAPH COMPANY - LAW LIBRARY
195 Broadway, Rm. 2511   Phone: (212) 393-3652
New York, NY 10007   Cynthia R. Arkin, Libn.

ANALYTICAL PSYCHOLOGY CLUB OF NEW YORK - KRISTINE MANN LIBRARY
28 E. 39th St.   Phone: (212) 697-7877
New York, NY 10016   Peggy Brooks, Lib.Chm.

ANCHOR FOUNDATION - LIBRARY OF SOCIAL HISTORY †
410 West St.   Phone: (212) 255-1767
New York, NY 10014   Barbara West, Dir.

ANIMAL LIBERATION, INC. - LIBRARY
319 W. 74th St.   Phone: (212) 874-1792
New York, NY 10023   Dudley Giehl, Pres.

ANIMAL MEDICAL CENTER - LIBRARY
510 E. 62nd St.   Phone: (212) 838-8100
New York, NY 10021   A. Christine MacMurray, Ed./Libn.

ANTHOLOGY FILM ARCHIVES - LIBRARY
80 Wooster St.   Phone: (212) 226-0010
New York, NY 10012   Mark Padnos, Dir.

ANTI-DEFAMATION LEAGUE OF B'NAI B'RITH - JACOB ALSON MEMORIAL
 LIBRARY
823 United Nations Plaza   Phone: (212) 689-7400
New York, NY 10017   Florence Lummer, Libn.

ARCHIVES OF AMERICAN ART/SMITHSONIAN INSTITUTION - NATIONAL
 HEADQUARTERS
41 E. 65th St.   Phone: (212) 826-5722
New York, NY 10021   W.E. Woolfenden, Dir.

ARGENTINE INFORMATION SERVICE CENTER †
60 E. 42nd St.   Phone: (212) 243-0522
New York, NY 10017   Anya Thompson, Ed.

ARGUS ARCHIVES, INC.
228 E. 49th St.   Phone: (212) 355-6140
New York, NY 10017   Jean Stewart, Res.Assoc.

ARGUS RESEARCH CORPORATION - LIBRARY
140 Broadway   Phone: (212) 425-7500
New York, NY 10005   Sara Mobley, Libn.

ARICA INSTITUTE, INC. - LIBRARY AND ARCHIVES
235 Park Ave. S.
New York, NY 10003   David J. Johnson, Libn./Archv.

ARMSTRONG AND COMPANY, INC. - LIBRARY
Two Park Ave.
New York, NY 10016

ARNHOLD AND S. BLEICHROEDER, INC. - LIBRARY
30 Broad St.   Phone: (212) 943-9200
New York, NY 10004   Michael L. Curtis, Libn.

ART INFORMATION CENTER, INC.
189 Lexington Ave.   Phone: (212) 725-0335
New York, NY 10016   Betty Chamberlain, Dir.

ART STUDENTS LEAGUE OF NEW YORK - LIBRARY
215 W. 57th St.   Phone: (212) 247-4510
New York, NY 10019   Rosina A. Florio, Exec.Dir.

ARTHUR ANDERSEN & CO. - LIBRARY †
1345 Ave. of the Americas   Phone: (212) 956-2815
New York, NY 10019   Louise Wagner, Libn.

ARTHUR YOUNG & COMPANY - LIBRARY
277 Park Ave.   Phone: (212) 922-4880
New York, NY 10172   Jeanne F. Mellon, Libn.

ARTISTS SPACE - COMMITTEE FOR THE VISUAL ARTS - UNAFFILIATED
 ARTISTS FILE
105 Hudson St.   Phone: (212) 226-3970
New York, NY 10013   Linda Shearer, Dir.

ASIA SOCIETY - LIBRARY
725 Park Ave.   Phone: (212) 288-6400
New York, NY 10021   Mary Anne Cartelli, Lib.Asst.

ASSOCIATED PRESS - NEWSPHOTO LIBRARY
50 Rockefeller Plaza   Phone: (212) 621-1913
New York, NY 10020   Grant Lamos, III, Dir.

ASSOCIATION OF AMERICAN PUBLISHERS - PUBLISHING EDUCATION
 INFORMATION SERVICE
One Park Ave.   Phone: (212) 689-8920
New York, NY 10016   Sandra Math, Libn.

ASSOCIATION OF AVERAGE ADJUSTERS OF THE UNITED STATES -
 LIBRARY
College of Insurance
123 William St.   Phone: (212) 962-4111
New York, NY 10038   Donald E. Carson, Libn.

ASSOCIATION OF THE BAR OF THE CITY OF NEW YORK - LIBRARY †
42 W. 44th St.   Phone: (212) 840-3550
New York, NY 10036   Anthony P. Grech, Libn.

ASSOCIATION OF CONSULTING MANAGEMENT ENGINEERS - LIBRARY
230 Park Ave.   Phone: (212) 697-9693
New York, NY 10169   Joseph J. Brady, Pres.

ASSOCIATION OF JUNIOR LEAGUES - RESOURCE CENTER †
825 Third Ave.   Phone: (212) 355-4380
New York, NY 10022   Ruth Ann Barrett, Prog.Info.Coord.

ASSOCIATION OF NATIONAL ADVERTISERS - LIBRARY
155 E. 44th St.   Phone: (212) 697-5950
New York, NY 10017   Rosemary Collins, Mgr.

ASSOCIATION OF PHILIPPINE COCONUT DESICCATORS - LIBRARY †
Times Sq. Sta., Box 787   Phone: (212) 929-0104
New York, NY 10036   Conrado A. Escudero, U.S. Rep.

AUSTEN (Jane) SOCIETY OF NORTH AMERICA - ARCHIVES
400 West 43rd St., 44-M   Phone: (212) 594-1507
New York, NY 10036   J. David Grey, Pres.

AUSTRALIAN INFORMATION SERVICE - REFERENCE LIBRARY/
 INFORMATION SERVICE
636 5th Ave.   Phone: (212) 245-4000
New York, NY 10020   H. Hurst, Dir., Info.Serv.

AUSTRIAN PRESS AND INFORMATION SERVICE
31 E. 69th St.   Phone: (212) 737-6400
New York, NY 10021   Peter C. Marboe, Dir.

AVON PRODUCTS, INC. - CENTRAL LIBRARY †
9 W. 57th St.   Phone: (212) 593-5375
New York, NY 10019   Regina Gottesman, Lib.Coord.

AYER (NW) INCORPORATED - AYER INFORMATION CENTER
1345 Ave. of the Americas   Phone: (212) 974-6414
New York, NY 10105   John J. Cummings, Dir. of AIC

AYERST LABORATORIES - MEDICAL INFORMATION CENTER
685 Third Ave.   Phone: (212) 878-5970
New York, NY 10017   George A. Laszlo, Mgr.

BACHE HALSEY STUART SHIELDS - RESEARCH DEPARTMENT LIBRARY
100 Gold St., 3rd Fl.   Phone: (212) 791-4819
New York, NY 10038

BAECK (Leo) INSTITUTE - LIBRARY
129 E. 73rd St.   Phone: (212) 744-6400
New York, NY 10021   Stephanie Stern, Libn.

BAKER & MC KENZIE - LAW LIBRARY
375 Park Ave.   Phone: (212) 751-5700
New York, NY 10022   D.W. Crandall, Libn.

BANK STREET COLLEGE OF EDUCATION - LIBRARY
610 W. 112 St.   Phone: (212) 663-7200
New York, NY 10025   Eleanor Kulleseid, Lib.Dir.

BANTAM BOOKS, INC. - LIBRARY
666 Fifth Ave.   Phone: (212) 765-6500
New York, NY 10019   Jos. A. Fayette, Libn.

BARNARD COLLEGE WOMEN'S CENTER - BIRDIE GOLDSMITH AST
 RESOURCE COLLECTION
100 Barnard Hall
3001 Broadway   Phone: (212) 280-2067
New York, NY 10027   Jane S. Gould, Dir., Women's Ctr.

BARRETT, SMITH, SCHAPIRO, SIMON & ARMSTRONG - LIBRARY
26 Broadway   Phone: (212) 422-8180
New York, NY 10004   Alice Arant-Cousins, Libn.

BARUCH (Bernard M.) COLLEGE OF THE CITY UNIVERSITY OF NEW YORK -
 LIBRARY
156 E. 25th St.   Phone: (212) 725-3112
New York, NY 10010   Harold Eiberson, Chf.Libn.

BATES (Ted) AND COMPANY - LIBRARY
1515 Broadway   Phone: (212) 869-3131
New York, NY 10036   Ms. Bert Schachter, Libn.

BATTEN, BARTON, DURSTINE, OSBORN, INC. - INFORMATION RETRIEVAL
  CENTER
383 Madison Ave. Phone: (212) 355-5800
New York, NY 10017 Paula Brown, Mgr.

BELGIAN CONSULATE GENERAL - LIBRARY
50 Rockefeller Plaza Phone: (212) 586-5110
New York, NY 10020 Mr. Jean De Ruyt, Consul

BENDER (Matthew) AND COMPANY, INC. - LIBRARY
235 E. 45th St. Phone: (212) 661-5050
New York, NY 10017 Rudolph Caughman, Chf.Libn.

BENTON AND BOWLES, INC. - LIBRARY
909 3rd Ave. Phone: (212) 758-6200
New York, NY 10022 Lois Burke, Libn.

BERLACK, ISRAELS AND LIBERMAN - LAW LIBRARY
26 Broadway Phone: (212) 248-6900
New York, NY 10004 Ben Schneberg, Law Libn.

BERNHARD (Arnold) AND COMPANY, INC. - BUSINESS LIBRARY
711 Third Ave. Phone: (212) 687-3965
New York, NY 10017 Gloria Napoli, Chf.Libn.

BERNHARD (Richard J.) MEMORIAL LIBRARY OF FEDERATION EMPLOYMENT
  & GUIDANCE SERVICE
215 Park Ave., S. Phone: (212) 777-4900
New York, NY 10003 Otto Kanocz, Chf.Libn.

BERNSTEIN (Sanford C.) & COMPANY, INC. - RESEARCH LIBRARY
717 5th Ave. Phone: (212) 486-6761
New York, NY 10022 Marcia A. Hylton, Corp.Libn.

BESSEMER TRUST COMPANY, N.A. - INVESTMENT LIBRARY
630 Fifth Ave. Phone: (212) 949-7830
New York, NY 10111 Merrill H. Lishan, Libn.

BETH ISRAEL MEDICAL CENTER - SEYMOUR J. PHILLIPS HEALTH SCIENCES
  LIBRARY
10 Nathan D. Perlman Pl. Phone: (212) 420-2168
New York, NY 10003 Arlene L. Freedman, Dir. of Lib.Serv.

BETTMANN ARCHIVE, INC.
136 E. 57th St. Phone: (212) 758-0362
New York, NY 10022 Melvin Gray, Pres.

BIGHAM, ENGLAR, JONES AND HOUSTON - LIBRARY
14 Wall St. Phone: (212) 732-4646
New York, NY 10005 Sharon M. Kallop, Libn.

BIRD S. COLER HOSPITAL - MEDICAL LIBRARY
Roosevelt Island Phone: (212) 688-9400
New York, NY 10044 Gina Buika, Ph.D., Dir.Med.Lib.

BLACK ECONOMIC RESEARCH CENTER - REFERENCE LIBRARY
112 W. 120th St. Phone: (212) 666-0345
New York, NY 10027 Robert Browne, Pres.

BLACKSTONE-SHELBURNE, INC. - PHOTO SERVICE
42 W. 48th St. Phone: (212) 736-9100
New York, NY 10036

BLUE CROSS/BLUE SHIELD OF GREATER NEW YORK - REFERENCE LIBRARY
3 Park Ave. Phone: (212) 481-2384
New York, NY 10016 Iona Prilop, Libn.

BOARD OF JEWISH EDUCATION OF GREATER NEW YORK - EDUCATIONAL
  RESOURCE LIBRARY
426 W. 58th St. Phone: (212) 245-8200
New York, NY 10019 Benjamin Miller, Media Libn.

BOOZ, ALLEN & HAMILTON, INC. - RESEARCH SERVICE
245 Park Ave. Phone: (212) 697-1900
New York, NY 10017 Ellen L. Miller, Mgr.Res.Serv.

BOTEIN, HAYS, SKLAR & HERZBERG - LIBRARY
200 Park Ave., Suite 3014 Phone: (212) 867-5500
New York, NY 10166 Donald Wecht, Libn.

BOWKER (R.R.) COMPANY - FREDERIC G. MELCHER LIBRARY
1180 Ave. of the Americas Phone: (212) 764-5126
New York, NY 10036 Jean Peters, Libn.

BRADFORD NATIONAL CORPORATION - LIBRARY *
100 Church St., 12th Fl. Phone: (212) 581-5800
New York, NY 10007 Rushel Sumergrade, Chf.Libn.

BRAKELEY, JOHN PRICE JONES, INC. - LIBRARY †
6 E. 43rd St. Phone: (212) 697-7120
New York, NY 10017 Rose M. Price, Libn.

BREED, ABBOTT & MORGAN - LIBRARY
153 E. 53rd St. Phone: (212) 888-0800
New York, NY 10022 Carol H. Barra, Hd.Libn.

BRIGER & ASSOCIATES - LIBRARY
299 Park Ave. Phone: (212) 758-4000
New York, NY 10017 Jacqueline Granek, Libn.

BRITISH INFORMATION SERVICES - LIBRARY
845 Third Ave. Phone: (212) 752-8400
New York, NY 10022 Margaret J. Gale, Libn.

BROWN BROTHERS HARRIMAN & CO. - RESEARCH LIBRARY
59 Wall St. Phone: (212) 483-5517
New York, NY 10005 Joanne Ultang, Libn.

BROWN, WOOD, IVEY, MITCHELL & PETTY - LIBRARY
One Liberty Plaza Phone: (212) 349-7500
New York, NY 10006 Connie L. Kluever, Libn.

BRUNDAGE, STORY & ROSE, INVESTMENT COUNSEL - LIBRARY
90 Broad St. Phone: (212) 269-3050
New York, NY 10004 Jacqueline Badome, Hd.Libn.

BURKE & BURKE - LAW LIBRARY
529 Fifth Ave. Phone: (212) 661-6600
New York, NY 10017 Peter Bartucca, Libn.

BURSON-MARSTELLER - INFORMATION SERVICE
866 Third Ave. Phone: (212) 752-6500
New York, NY 10022 Gayle Haring, Mgr., Info.Serv.

BUSINESS INTERNATIONAL - RESEARCH LIBRARY
One Dag Hammarskjold Plaza
Second Ave. & 47th St. Phone: (212) 750-6383
New York, NY 10017 Audrey L. Bott, Dir. of Lib.Serv.

C.I.T. FINANCIAL CORPORATION - LAW LIBRARY
650 Madison Ave. Phone: (212) 572-6500
New York, NY 10022 Doris McFalls, Libn.

C.I.T. FINANCIAL CORPORATION - REFERENCE LIBRARY
650 Madison Ave. Phone: (212) 572-6412
New York, NY 10022 Marguerite Zambotti, Ref.Libn.

CABRINI MEDICAL CENTER - DR. MASSIMO BAZZINI MEMORIAL LIBRARY
227 E. 19th St. Phone: (212) 725-6631
New York, NY 10003 Jeanne Becker, Med.Libn.

CAHILL, GORDON, & REINDEL - LAW LIBRARY
80 Pine St. Phone: (212) 825-0100
New York, NY 10005 Margaret J. Davenport, Libn.

CALTEX PETROLEUM CORPORATION - PLANNING AND ECONOMICS
  DEPARTMENT - LIBRARY
380 Madison Ave. Phone: (212) 697-2000
New York, NY 10017 Ray R. Cotter, Libn.

CANADIAN CONSULATE GENERAL - LIBRARY
1251 Ave. of the Americas Phone: (212) 586-2400
New York, NY 10020 Sheila Purse, Hd.Libn.

CANCER CARE, INC. - NATIONAL CANCER FOUNDATION LIBRARY
1 Park Ave. Phone: (212) 679-5700
New York, NY 10016 Paula Dragutsky, Libn.

GEOGRAPHIC

CARNEGIE ENDOWMENT FOR INTERNATIONAL PEACE - LIBRARY - NEW
   YORK CENTER
30 Rockefeller Plaza, 54th Fl.   Phone: (212) 572-8208
New York, NY 10020   Vivian D. Hewitt, Libn.

CARTER, LEDYARD AND MILBURN - LIBRARY †
2 Wall St.   Phone: (212) 732-3200
New York, NY 10005   Julius Pomerantz, Libn.

CASEY, LANE & MITTENDORF - LAW LIBRARY
26 Broadway   Phone: (212) 943-3000
New York, NY 10004   Joel L. Solomon, Libn.

CATALYST - INFORMATION CENTER
14 E. 60th St.   Phone: (212) 759-9700
New York, NY 10022   Gurley Turner, Dir. of Info.Serv.

CATHEDRAL OF ST. JOHN THE DIVINE - CATHEDRAL LIBRARY
Cathedral Heights   Phone: (212) 678-6910
New York, NY 10025   Madeleine L'Engle Franklin, Writer in Residence

CATHOLIC CENTER AT NEW YORK UNIVERSITY - CATHOLIC CENTER
   LIBRARY
58 Washington Sq. S.   Phone: (212) 674-7236
New York, NY 10012

CBS INC. - CBS LAW LIBRARY
51 W. 52nd St.   Phone: (212) 975-4260
New York, NY 10019   Jean L. Merenda, Law Libn.

CBS INC. - CBS NEWS - REFERENCE LIBRARY
524 W. 57th St.   Phone: (212) 975-2877
New York, NY 10019   Marcia G. Ratcliff, Dir.

CBS RECORDS - ARCHIVES
1350 Ave. of the Americas   Phone: (212) 975-4949
New York, NY 10019   Martine Vinces, Archv.

CENTER FOR LIBERTARIAN STUDIES
200 Park Ave. S., Suite 911   Phone: (212) 533-6600
New York, NY 10003   C.A. Drake

CENTER FOR MEDICAL CONSUMERS AND HEALTH INFORMATION - LIBRARY
237 Thompson St.   Phone: (212) 674-7105
New York, NY 10012   Arthur Levin, Dir.

CENTER FOR MODERN PSYCHOANALYTIC STUDIES - LIBRARY
16 W. 10th St.   Phone: (212) 260-7050
New York, NY 10011   C.Z. Meadow, Dir.

CENTER FOR NONPROFIT ORGANIZATION - LIBRARY
155 W. 72nd St., Suite 604   Phone: (212) 873-7580
New York, NY 10023   Howard E. Fischer, Dir.

CENTER ON SOCIAL WELFARE POLICY AND LAW - LIBRARY
95 Madison Ave., Rm. 701   Phone: (212) 679-3709
New York, NY 10016   Barbara J. Rios, Project Libn.

CENTER FOR THE STUDY OF HUMAN RIGHTS - LIBRARY
Columbia University
704 International Affairs Bldg.   Phone: (212) 280-2479
New York, NY 10027   Deborah Martinsen, Exec.Sec.

CENTER FOR THE STUDY OF THE PRESIDENCY - LIBRARY
926 Fifth Ave.   Phone: (212) 249-1200
New York, NY 10021   Sondra Blewer, Libn.

CENTRAL OPERA SERVICE - INFORMATION CENTER AND LIBRARY
c/o Metropolitan Opera
Lincoln Center   Phone: (212) 957-9871
New York, NY 10023   Maria F. Rich, Adm.Dir.

CENTURY ASSOCIATION - LIBRARY
7 W. 43rd St.   Phone: (212) 944-0090
New York, NY 10036   Andrew Zaremba, Libn.

CHADBOURNE, PARKE, WHITESIDE, & WOLFF - LIBRARY
30 Rockefeller Plaza, 24th Fl.   Phone: (212) 344-8900
New York, NY 10020   Jeannine R. Esswein, Libn.

CHASE MANHATTAN BANK, N.A. - INFORMATION CENTER
One Chase Manhattan Plaza, 9th Fl.   Phone: (212) 552-0014
New York, NY 10081   Catherine Reilly, Mgr.

CHASE MANHATTAN BANK, N.A. - SYSTEMS LIBRARY
One New York Plaza   Phone: (212) 676-3629
New York, NY 10004   Veronica Briggs, Libn.

CHASE TRADE INFORMATION CORPORATION - LIBRARY
One World Trade Ctr.   Phone: (212) 552-6869
New York, NY 10048   Galina Gorochow, Asst.Libn.

CHEMICAL BANK - RESEARCH LIBRARY
20 Pine St., Rm. 1915   Phone: (212) 770-3127
New York, NY 10015   Helen Traina, Asst.Sec.

CHEMISTS' CLUB LIBRARY - CHEMICAL INTERNATIONAL INFORMATION
   CENTER
52 E. 41st St.   Phone: (212) 679-6383
New York, NY 10017   Norma B. Mar, Libn.

CHILD WELFARE LEAGUE OF AMERICA, INC. - DOROTHY L. BERNHARD
   LIBRARY
67 Irving Pl.   Phone: (212) 254-7410
New York, NY 10003   Gwendolyn T. Davis, Info.Spec.

CHILD WELFARE LEAGUE OF AMERICA, INC. - INFORMATIONAL RESOURCE
   SERVICES
67 Irving Pl.   Phone: (212) 254-7410
New York, NY 10003   Dr. Jeanne Hunzeker, Dir.

CHILDREN'S BOOK COUNCIL - LIBRARY
67 Irving Pl.   Phone: (212) 254-2666
New York, NY 10003

CHINESE CULTURAL CENTER - INFORMATION & COMMUNICATION
   DIVISION - LIBRARY
159 Lexington Ave.   Phone: (212) 725-4950
New York, NY 10016   David C. Liu, Libn.

CHURCH OF THE BELOVED DISCIPLE - HOMOPHILE RESEARCH LIBRARY
348 W. 14th St.   Phone: (212) 242-6616
New York, NY 10014   Thor Wood, Libn.

CITIBANK, N.A. - FINANCIAL LIBRARY
399 Park Ave.   Phone: (212) 559-4559
New York, NY 10043   Conchita J. Pineda, Mgr.

CITIBANK, N.A. - INVESTMENT LIBRARY
One Citicorp Ctr.
153 E. 53rd St.   Phone: (212) 559-9620
New York, NY 10043   Caroline Marks, Hd.Libn.

CITIZENS HOUSING AND PLANNING COUNCIL OF NEW YORK - LIBRARY
20 W. 40th St.   Phone: (212) 391-9030
New York, NY 10018   Marian Sameth, Assoc.Dir.

CITIZENS UNION OF THE CITY OF NEW YORK - LIBRARY
15 Park Row   Phone: (212) 227-0342
New York, NY 10038   Vance Benguiat, Exec.Dir.

CLARK (William H.) ASSOCIATES, INC. - RESEARCH LIBRARY
330 Madison Ave.   Phone: (212) 661-8760
New York, NY 10017   Judith Stein, Dir. of Res.

CLEARINGHOUSE FOR ARTS INFORMATION - CENTER FOR ARTS
   INFORMATION
625 Broadway   Phone: (212) 677-7548
New York, NY 10012   Jana Jevnikar, Info.Coord.

CLEARY, GOTTLIEB, STEEN & HAMILTON - LIBRARY
One State St. Plaza   Phone: (212) 344-0600
New York, NY 10004   Karol M. Sokol, Libn.

COLLECTORS CLUB - LIBRARY
22 E. 35th St.   Phone: (212) 683-0559
New York, NY 10016   Werner Elias, Libn.

COLLEGE FOR HUMAN SERVICES - LIBRARY
345 Hudson St.   Phone: (212) 989-2002
New York, NY 10014   Loretta Capers, Libn.

COLLEGE OF INSURANCE - INSURANCE SOCIETY OF NEW YORK - LIBRARY
123 William St.   Phone: (212) 962-4111
New York, NY 10038   Donald Carson, Chf.Libn.

COLLEGE RETIREMENT EQUITIES FUND - CREF RESEARCH LIBRARY
730 Third Ave.   Phone: (212) 490-9000
New York, NY 10017   Linda Krauss, Libn.

COLUMBIA UNIVERSITY - AMBROSE MONELL ENGINEERING LIBRARY
422 Mudd   Phone: (212) 280-2976
New York, NY 10027   Patricia Davitt Maughan, Engr.Libn.

COLUMBIA UNIVERSITY - AVERY ARCHITECTURAL AND FINE ARTS
  LIBRARY
Broadway & 116th St.   Phone: (212) 280-3501
New York, NY 10027   Charling Chang Fagan, Libn.

COLUMBIA UNIVERSITY - BIOLOGICAL SCIENCES LIBRARY
914 Schermerhorn Hall   Phone: (212) 280-4715
New York, NY 10027   Georgeanne M. O'Riordan, Libn.

COLUMBIA UNIVERSITY - BURGESS-CARPENTER LIBRARY
406 Butler Library   Phone: (212) 280-4710
New York, NY 10027   Frederick Byrne, Libn.

COLUMBIA UNIVERSITY - BUTLER LIBRARY CIRCULATION DEPARTMENT
303 Butler Library   Phone: (212) 280-2235
New York, NY 10027   Robert Pepin, Hd.

COLUMBIA UNIVERSITY CANCER CENTER - INSTITUTE OF CANCER
  RESEARCH
701 W. 168th St.   Phone: (212) 694-6948
New York, NY 10032   Betty Rose Moore, Lib.Serv.Coord.

COLUMBIA UNIVERSITY - CENTER FOR POPULATION & FAMILY HEALTH -
  LIBRARY/INFORMATION PROGRAM
60 Haven Ave.   Phone: (212) 694-6985
New York, NY 10032   Susan K. Pasquariella, Hd.Libn.

COLUMBIA UNIVERSITY - CHEMISTRY LIBRARY
454 Chandler Hall   Phone: (212) 280-4709
New York, NY 10027   Elida B. Stein, Libn.

COLUMBIA UNIVERSITY - COLUMBIA COLLEGE LIBRARY
225 Butler Library   Phone: (212) 280-3534
New York, NY 10027   Frederick Byrne, Libn.

COLUMBIA UNIVERSITY - COLUMBIANA
210 Low Memorial Library   Phone: (212) 280-3786
New York, NY 10027   Paul R. Palmer, Cur.

COLUMBIA UNIVERSITY - DEPARTMENT OF ART HISTORY & ARCHAEOLOGY
  - PHOTOGRAPH COLLECTION
420 Schermerhorn Hall   Phone: (212) 280-5203
New York, NY 10027   Prof. Douglas Fraser, Rep.

COLUMBIA UNIVERSITY - EAST ASIAN LIBRARY
300 Kent   Phone: (212) 280-4318
New York, NY 10027   Philip Yampolsky, Libn.

COLUMBIA UNIVERSITY - GEOLOGY LIBRARY
601 Schermerhorn   Phone: (212) 280-4522
New York, NY 10027   Susan Klimley, Libn.

COLUMBIA UNIVERSITY - HEALTH SCIENCES LIBRARY
701 W. 168th St.   Phone: (212) 694-3688
New York, NY 10032   Rachael K. Goldstein, Libn.

COLUMBIA UNIVERSITY - HERBERT LEHMAN LIBRARY
420 W. 118th St.   Phone: (212) 280-4170
New York, NY 10027

COLUMBIA UNIVERSITY - LAW LIBRARY
Law School
435 W. 116th St.   Phone: (212) 280-3737
New York, NY 10027   Prof. Francis Gates, Law Libn.

COLUMBIA UNIVERSITY - LIBRARY SERVICE LIBRARY
606 Butler Library   Phone: (212) 280-3543
New York, NY 10027   Jo-Ann Michalak, Libn.

COLUMBIA UNIVERSITY - MATHEMATICS/SCIENCE LIBRARY
303 Mathematics   Phone: (212) 280-4712
New York, NY 10027   Suzanne Fedunok, Libn.

COLUMBIA UNIVERSITY - MUSIC LIBRARY
701 Dodge   Phone: (212) 280-4711
New York, NY 10027   Thomas T. Watkins, Libn.

COLUMBIA UNIVERSITY - ORAL HISTORY COLLECTION
Butler Library
Box 20   Phone: (212) 280-2273
New York, NY 10027   Elizabeth B. Mason, Act.Dir.

COLUMBIA UNIVERSITY - PATERNO LIBRARY
Casa Italiana, 1161 Amsterdam Ave.   Phone: (212) 280-2307
New York, NY 10027   Robert Connolly, Lib.Asst.

COLUMBIA UNIVERSITY - PHILOSOPHY LIBRARY
228 Butler Library   Phone: (212) 280-2259
New York, NY 10027   Frederick Byrne, Libn.

COLUMBIA UNIVERSITY - PHYSICS LIBRARY
810 Pupin Laboratories   Phone: (212) 280-3943
New York, NY 10027   Suzanne Fedunok, Libn.

COLUMBIA UNIVERSITY - PSYCHOLOGY LIBRARY
409 Schermerhorn Hall   Phone: (212) 280-4714
New York, NY 10027   Georgeanne M. O'Riordan, Libn.

COLUMBIA UNIVERSITY - RARE BOOK AND MANUSCRIPT LIBRARY
801 Butler Library   Phone: (212) 280-2231
New York, NY 10027   Kenneth A. Lohf, Libn.

COLUMBIA UNIVERSITY - SULZBERGER JOURNALISM LIBRARY
304 Journalism Bldg.
Broadway & 116th St.   Phone: (212) 280-3860
New York, NY 10027   Wade A. Doares, Libn.

COLUMBIA UNIVERSITY - THOMAS J. WATSON LIBRARY OF BUSINESS AND
  ECONOMICS
130 Uris Hall   Phone: (212) 280-4000
New York, NY 10027   Paula T. Kaufman, Libn.

COLUMBIA UNIVERSITY - WHITNEY M. YOUNG, JR. MEMORIAL LIBRARY OF
  SOCIAL WORK
309 International Affairs Bldg.   Phone: (212) 280-5159
New York, NY 10027   Celestine C. Tutt, Libn.

COMICS MAGAZINE ASSOCIATION OF AMERICA, INC. - LIBRARY
60 E. 42nd St., Suite 1807   Phone: (212) 682-8144
New York, NY 10017   J. Dudley Waldner, Exec.Sec.

COMPOSERS AND CHOREOGRAPHERS THEATRE, INC. - MASTER TAPE
  LIBRARY
225 Lafayette St., No. 906   Phone: (212) 925-3721
New York, NY 10012   John Watts, Pres.

CONDE NAST PUBLICATIONS, INC. - LIBRARY
350 Madison Ave.   Phone: (212) 880-8245
New York, NY 10017   Theodore Tarter, Cur.

CONFERENCE BOARD, INC. - INFORMATION SERVICE
845 3rd Ave.   Phone: (212) 759-0900
New York, NY 10022   Tamsen M. Hernandez, Dir.

CONGREGATION EMANU-EL - IVAN M. STELTENHEIM LIBRARY †
1 E. 65th St.   Phone: (212) 744-1400
New York, NY 10021   Marianne Winkler, Libn.

CONGREGATION SHEARITH ISRAEL - SOPHIE AND IVAN SALOMON LIBRARY
  COLLECTION
8 W. 70th St.   Phone: (212) 873-0300
New York, NY 10023   Anita Notrica, Libn.

CONSOLIDATED EDISON COMPANY OF NEW YORK, INC. - LIBRARY
4 Irving Pl., Rm. 1650-S   Phone: (212) 460-4228
New York, NY 10003   Steven Jaffe, Libn.

CONSULATE GENERAL OF INDIA - INFORMATION SERVICE OF INDIA
    LIBRARY †
3 E. 64th St.   Phone: (212) 879-7800
New York, NY 10021   Mrs. Pushpa Gupta, Libn.

CONSULATE GENERAL OF ISRAEL - LT. DAVID TAMIR LIBRARY AND
    READING ROOM
800 Second Ave.   Phone: (212) 697-5500
New York, NY 10017   Ralene Levy, Info.Off.

CONSULATE GENERAL OF JAPAN - JAPAN INFORMATION SERVICE -
    LIBRARY †
One Citicorp Center
153 E. 53rd St., 44th Fl.   Phone: (212) 986-1600
New York, NY 10022

CONSULATE GENERAL OF THE NETHERLANDS - PRESS AND CULTURAL
    SECTION *
One Rockefeller Plaza   Phone: (212) 246-1429
New York, NY 10020

COOPER UNION FOR THE ADVANCEMENT OF SCIENCE AND ART - LIBRARY
Cooper Sq.   Phone: (212) 254-6300
New York, NY 10003   Elizabeth A. Vajda, Coord. for Lib.Serv.

COOPERS AND LYBRAND - NATIONAL LIBRARY †
1251 Ave. of the Americas   Phone: (212) 536-2000
New York, NY 10020   Dorothy Kasman, Chf.Libn.

COPPER DEVELOPMENT ASSOCIATION, INC. - COPPER DATA CENTER
405 Lexington Ave.   Phone: (212) 953-7300
New York, NY 10017   Mary W. Covington, Supv.Tech.Info.

CORNELL UNIVERSITY - MEDICAL COLLEGE - LIBRARY
1300 York Ave.   Phone: (212) 472-5300
New York, NY 10021   Erich Meyerhoff, Libn.

COUDERT BROTHERS - LIBRARY
200 Park Ave.   Phone: (212) 973-3300
New York, NY 10166   Jane C. Rubens, Libn.

COUNCIL FOR FINANCIAL AID TO EDUCATION - LIBRARY
680 Fifth Ave.   Phone: (212) 541-4050
New York, NY 10019

COUNCIL ON FOREIGN RELATIONS - LIBRARY
58 E. 68th St.   Phone: (212) 734-0400
New York, NY 10021   Janet Rigney, Libn.

COUNCIL OF JEWISH FEDERATIONS - LIBRARY
575 Lexington Ave.   Phone: (212) 751-1311
New York, NY 10022   Zalman Alpert, Libn.

CRAVATH, SWAINE, AND MOORE - LAW LIBRARY
1 Chase Manhattan Plaza   Phone: (212) 422-3000
New York, NY 10005   Jean Strohofer, Libn.

CRESAP, MC CORMICK, AND PAGET, INC. - LIBRARY †
245 Park Ave., 30th Fl.   Phone: (212) 953-7157
New York, NY 10017   Helen Garvey, Libn.

CULVER PICTURES, INC. - LIBRARY
660 First Ave.   Phone: (212) 684-5054
New York, NY 10016   Roberts Jackson, Dir.

CUNNINGHAM AND WALSH, INC. - LIBRARY
260 Madison Ave.   Phone: (212) 683-4900
New York, NY 10016   Lawrence A. Anderson, Libn.

CUNY - CENTRO DE ESTUDIOS PUERTORRIQUENOS
445 W. 59th St.   Phone: (212) 489-5262
New York, NY 10019   Nelida Perez, Libn.

CUNY - CITY COLLEGE LIBRARY - ARCHITECTURE LIBRARY
3300 Broadway, Rm. 206   Phone: (212) 690-5329
New York, NY 10031   Sylvia H. Wright, Chf.Arch.Libn.

CUNY - CITY COLLEGE LIBRARY - COLLEGE ARCHIVES
Convent Ave. & W. 135th St.   Phone: (212) 690-5367
New York, NY 10031   Barbara J. Dunlap, Archv.

CUNY - CITY COLLEGE LIBRARY - MUSIC LIBRARY
Shepard Hall, Rm. 318A
Convent Ave. & W. 138th St.   Phone: (212) 690-4174
New York, NY 10031   Melva Peterson, Chf. Music Libn.

CUNY - CITY COLLEGE LIBRARY - SCIENCE/ENGINEERING DIVISION
St. Nicholas Terrace   Phone: (212) 690-8244
New York, NY 10031   Marlin Demlinger, Lib.Chf.

CUNY - CITY COLLEGE LIBRARY - SPECIAL COLLECTIONS
Convent Ave. & W. 135th St.   Phone: (212) 690-5367
New York, NY 10031   Barbara J. Dunlap, Libn.

CUNY - GRADUATE SCHOOL AND UNIVERSITY CENTER - LIBRARY
33 W. 42nd St.   Phone: (212) 790-4541
New York, NY 10036   Jane R. Moore, Chf.Libn.

CURTIS, MALLET-PREVOST, COLT AND MOSLE - LIBRARY †
100 Wall St., 15th Fl.   Phone: (212) 248-8111
New York, NY 10005   Janet P. Tidwell, Libn.

CYRUS J. LAWRENCE, INC. - LIBRARY
115 Broadway   Phone: (212) 962-2200
New York, NY 10006   Linda Moore, Libn.

DANCE FILMS ASSOCIATION, INC.
125 E. 23rd St., Rm. 401-A   Phone: (212) 598-9138
New York, NY 10010   Susan Braun, Pres.

DANCER FITZGERALD SAMPLE, INC. - LIBRARY
405 Lexington Ave.   Phone: (212) 661-0800
New York, NY 10017   Carolyn Gutierrez, Libn.

DANISH CONSULATE GENERAL - INFORMATION OFFICE
280 Park Ave.   Phone: (212) 697-5107
New York, NY 10017   Anette Essemann

D'ARCY-MAC MANUS AND MASIUS - LIBRARY
360 Madison Ave.   Phone: (212) 754-2382
New York, NY 10017   Sandra Philips, Libn.

DAVIS POLK & WARDWELL - LIBRARY
One Chase Manhattan Plaza   Phone: (212) 530-4267
New York, NY 10005   Nuchine Nobari, Chf.Libn.

DEAN WITTER REYNOLDS, INC. - LIBRARY
130 Liberty St.   Phone: (212) 524-2745
New York, NY 10006   Barbara C. White, Chf.Libn.

DEAN WITTER REYNOLDS, INC. - RESEARCH DEPARTMENT LIBRARY
5 World Trade Center   Phone: (212) 524-3596
New York, NY 10048   Beth Morris, Res.Dept.Libn.

DEBEVOISE, PLIMPTON, LYONS AND GATES - LAW LIBRARY
299 Park Ave.   Phone: (212) 752-6400
New York, NY 10017   Jeannette Newman, Asst.Libn.

DELL PUBLISHING COMPANY, INC. - LIBRARY
One Dag Hammarskjold Plaza   Phone: (212) 832-7300
New York, NY 10017   Janie Fabian, Libn.

DELOITTE HASKINS & SELLS - EXECUTIVE OFFICE LIBRARY
1114 Ave. of the Americas   Phone: (212) 790-0639
New York, NY 10036   Rhea Tabakin, Exec.Off.Libn.

DEWEY, BALLANTINE, BUSHBY, PALMER & WOOD - LIBRARY
140 Broadway   Phone: (212) 344-8000
New York, NY 10005   Gitelle Seer, Libn.

DIEBOLD GROUP, INC. - LIBRARY
475 Park Ave., S. Phone: (212) 755-0400
New York, NY 10016 Beth Seelick, Libn.

DILLON, READ & COMPANY, INC. - LIBRARY
46 William St. Phone: (212) 285-5690
New York, NY 10005 Nancy J. Bowles, Libn.

DIRECT MAIL/MARKETING ASSOCIATION, INC. - INFORMATION CENTER
6 E. 43rd St., 12th Fl. Phone: (212) 689-4977
New York, NY 10017 Karen Burns, Dir., Info. & Res.

DONALDSON, LUFKIN AND JENRETTE, INC. - CORPORATE LIBRARY
140 Broadway, 34th Fl. Phone: (212) 943-0300
New York, NY 10005 Leslie Anne Wheaton, Hd.Libn.

DONOVAN, LEISURE, NEWTON & IRVINE - LIBRARY
30 Rockefeller Plaza Phone: (212) 489-4293
New York, NY 10020 Albert P. Borner, Libn.

DOVER PUBLICATIONS, INC. - PICTORIAL ARCHIVES LIBRARY †
180 Varick St. Phone: (212) 255-3755
New York, NY 10014

DOW JONES & CO. - LIBRARY
22 Cortlandt Phone: (212) 285-5075
New York, NY 10007 Lottie Lindberg, Libn.

DREXEL BURNHAM LAMBERT INC. - RESEARCH LIBRARY
60 Broad St. Phone: (212) 480-6475
New York, NY 10004 Laura G. Ripin, Libn.

DREYFUS CORPORATION - LIBRARY
767 Fifth Ave. Phone: (212) 935-8405
New York, NY 10153 Cytheria Theodos, Dir.Info.Serv.

DUN AND BRADSTREET, INC. - BUSINESS LIBRARY
99 Church St. Phone: (212) 285-7304
New York, NY 10007 Mary Engelmann Murphy, Libn.

EBASCO SERVICES, INC. - CORPORATE ADMINISTRATION LIBRARY
2 World Trade Ctr., 92nd Fl. Phone: (212) 839-2062
New York, NY 10048 Martha Peppel, Hd.Libn.

EBERSTADT (F.) AND COMPANY - BUSINESS LIBRARY
61 Broadway Phone: (212) 480-0807
New York, NY 10006 Mrs. Pat Salandy, Libn.

ECUMENICAL LIBRARY
475 Riverside Dr., Rm. 1372 Phone: (212) 678-6082
New York, NY 10115 Patricia F. Brown, Libn.

EDITOR & PUBLISHER - LIBRARY †
575 Lexington Ave. Phone: (212) 752-7050
New York, NY 10022

EDUCATIONAL BROADCASTING CORPORATION - CHANNEL 13 RESEARCH
LIBRARY
356 W. 58th St. Phone: (212) 560-3063
New York, NY 10019 Victoria A. Dawson, Hd.Libn.

EDUCATIONAL FILM LIBRARY ASSOCIATION - LIBRARY AND INFORMATION
CENTER
43 W. 61st St., 9th Fl. Phone: (212) 246-4533
New York, NY 10023 Maryann Chach, Film Ref.Libn.

ELECTRIC RAILROADERS' ASSOCIATION - SPRAGUE MEMORIAL LIBRARY †
Grand Central Terminal
89 E. 42nd St. Phone: (212) 354-9587
New York, NY 10017 Carl Ramulus, Libn.

EMBROIDERERS' GUILD OF AMERICA, INC. - LIBRARY
6 E. 45th St. Phone: (212) 986-0460
New York, NY 10017 Grace R. Gutberlet, Lib.Chm.

ENGINEERING SOCIETIES LIBRARY
United Engineering Ctr.
345 E. 47th St. Phone: (212) 644-7611
New York, NY 10017 S.K. Cabeen, Dir.

ENGLISH-SPEAKING UNION OF THE U.S.A. - BOOKS ACROSS THE SEA
LIBRARY
16 E. 69th St. Phone: (212) 879-6800
New York, NY 10021 Mary Ellen Moll, Libn.

ENVIRONMENT INFORMATION CENTER, INC. *
48 W. 38th St. Phone: (212) 944-8500
New York, NY 10018 James G. Kollegger, Pres. & Pub.

ENVIRONMENTAL ACTION COALITION - LIBRARY/RESOURCE CENTER
417 Lafayette St. Phone: (212) 677-1601
New York, NY 10003 Carolyn Steiner, Office Mgr.

ENVIRONMENTAL PROTECTION AGENCY - REGION II LIBRARY
26 Federal Plaza, Rm. 1002 Phone: (212) 264-2881
New York, NY 10278 Herbert Luger, Regional Libn.

EQUITABLE LIFE ASSURANCE SOCIETY OF THE U.S. - GENERAL LIBRARY †
1285 Ave. of the Americas Phone: (201) 554-2491
New York, NY 10019 Jean Carrigan, Chf.Libn.

EQUITABLE LIFE ASSURANCE SOCIETY OF THE U.S. - MEDICAL LIBRARY †
1285 Ave. of the Americas Phone: (212) 554-2935
New York, NY 10019 Susan Voge, Med.Libn.

EQUITABLE LIFE ASSURANCE SOCIETY OF THE U.S. - TECHNICAL
INFORMATION CENTER
1285 Ave. of the Americas, Rm. 9A Phone: (212) 554-4064
New York, NY 10019 Kathryn Marsala, Mgr., Tech.Info.Ctr.

ERIC CLEARINGHOUSE ON URBAN EDUCATION
Box 40, Teachers College
Columbia University Phone: (212) 678-3437
New York, NY 10027 Dr. Erwin Flaxman, Dir.

ERNST & WHINNEY - DATA SYSTEMS LIBRARY
153 E. 53rd St. Phone: (212) 888-9100
New York, NY 10022 Janet Sorem, Hd.Libn.

ERNST & WHINNEY - INTERNATIONAL LIBRARY
153 E. 53rd St. Phone: (212) 888-9100
New York, NY 10022 Janet Sorem, Hd.Libn.

ERNST & WHINNEY - LIBRARY
153 E. 53 St. Phone: (212) 752-8100
New York, NY 10022 Janet Sorem, Hd.Libn.

ERNST & WHINNEY - TAX LIBRARY
153 E. 53rd St. Phone: (212) 888-9100
New York, NY 10022 Robin Ahern, Tax Libn.

EUROPEAN ART COLOR - PETER ADELBERG ARCHIVE
120 W. 70th St. Phone: (212) 877-9654
New York, NY 10023 Greta Adelberg, Pict.Libn.

EUROPEAN COMMUNITY INFORMATION SERVICE - LIBRARY
245 E. 47 St. Phone: (212) 371-3804
New York, NY 10017 Kerrie Buitrago, Chf.Info.Spec.

EXPLORERS CLUB - JAMES B. FORD MEMORIAL LIBRARY
46 E. 70th St. Phone: (212) 628-8383
New York, NY 10021

EXXON CORPORATION - LAW-TAX LIBRARY
1251 Ave. of the Americas, 45th Fl. Phone: (212) 398-3247
New York, NY 10020 Mary K. Moynihan, Libn.

EXXON CORPORATION - MEDICAL LIBRARY
1251 Ave. of the Americas Phone: (212) 398-2504
New York, NY 10020 Constance M. Lima, Libn.

FAMILY SERVICE ASSOCIATION OF AMERICA - LIBRARY
44 E. 23rd St. Phone: (212) 674-6100
New York, NY 10010 Eero Richmond, Ref.Libn.

FASHION INSTITUTE OF TECHNOLOGY - LIBRARY/MEDIA SERVICES
227 W. 27th St. Phone: (212) 760-7695
New York, NY 10001 John F. Touhey, Dir.

GEOGRAPHIC

FEDERAL RESERVE BANK OF NEW YORK - LAW LIBRARY DIVISION
33 Liberty St.   Phone: (212) 791-5012
New York, NY 10045   Rodney H. Congdon, Chf. Law Libn.

FEDERAL RESERVE BANK OF NEW YORK - RESEARCH LIBRARY
33 Liberty St.
New York, NY 10045   Jean Deuss, Chf.Libn.

FEHL (Fred) PHOTOGRAPHER - INFORMATION CENTER
415 W. 115th St.   Phone: (212) 662-2253
New York, NY 10025

FIDUCIARY TRUST COMPANY OF NEW YORK - RESEARCH LIBRARY
2 World Trade Ctr., 94th Fl.   Phone: (212) 466-4100
New York, NY 10048   Marilyn Armeit, Libn.

FINANCIAL EXECUTIVES RESEARCH FOUNDATION - LIBRARY
633 Third Ave.   Phone: (212) 953-0500
New York, NY 10017   Moreen Hopkins

FIND/SVP - LIBRARY
500 Fifth Ave.   Phone: (212) 354-2424
New York, NY 10110   Kathleen S. Bingham, Exec.V.P.

FIRST BOSTON CORPORATION - LIBRARY
20 Exchange Pl.   Phone: (212) 825-7781
New York, NY 10005   Julia B. Shibla, Asst.V.P./ Hd.Libn.

FISH AND NEAVE - LIBRARY
277 Park Ave.   Phone: (212) 826-1050
New York, NY 10172   Janet M. Stark, Libn.

FLUSHING HOSPITAL AND MEDICAL CENTER - MEDICAL LIBRARY
Parsons Blvd. & 45th Ave.   Phone: (212) 670-5653
New York, NY 11355   Maria Czechowicz, Dir.

FOOTE CONE & BELDING - LIBRARY †
200 Park Ave.   Phone: (212) 880-9128
New York, NY 10017   Ruth Fromkes, Info.Dir.

FORBES, INC. - LIBRARY
60 Fifth Ave.   Phone: (212) 620-2237
New York, NY 10011   Dolores Lataniotis, Libn.

FORD, BACON & DAVIS, INC. - LIBRARY
2 Broadway   Phone: (212) 344-3200
New York, NY 10004   Joan Frick, Libn.

FORD FOUNDATION - INVESTMENT RESEARCH LIBRARY
320 E. 43rd St., 9th Fl.   Phone: (212) 573-5221
New York, NY 10017   Mary Camper-Titsingh, Investment Res.Libn.

FORD FOUNDATION - LIBRARY
320 E. 43rd St.   Phone: (212) 573-5155
New York, NY 10017   Susan T. Newman, Libn.

FORDHAM UNIVERSITY - LIBRARY AT LINCOLN CENTER
W. 60th St. and Columbus Ave.   Phone: (212) 841-5130
New York, NY 10023   Clement J. Anzul, Libn.

FORDHAM UNIVERSITY - SCHOOL OF LAW LIBRARY
Lincoln Sq., 140 W. 62nd St.   Phone: (212) 956-6601
New York, NY 10023   Dr. Ludwik A. Teclaff, Professor/Libn.

FOUNDATION CENTER - NEW YORK - LIBRARY
888 7th Ave., 26th Fl.   Phone: (212) 975-1120
New York, NY 10019   Carol M. Kurzig, Dir.Pub.Serv.

FOUNDATION FOR CITIZEN EDUCATION - ANNA LORD STRAUSS LIBRARY
817 Broadway   Phone: (212) 677-5050
New York, NY 10003   Alice Vielehr, Libn.

FRANKLIN FURNACE ARCHIVE, INC. - LIBRARY
112 Franklin St.   Phone: (212) 925-4671
New York, NY 10013   Martha Wilson, Exec.Dir.

FREEDOM HOUSE - INFORMATION CENTER
20 W. 40th St.   Phone: (212) 730-7744
New York, NY 10018   Leonard R. Sussman, Exec.Dir.

FREELANCE PHOTOGRAPHERS GUILD, INC.
251 Park Ave. S.   Phone: (212) 777-4210
New York, NY 10010   Arthur Brackman, Pres.

FRENCH AMERICAN CULTURAL SERVICES AND EDUCATIONAL AID
  (FACSEA)
972 Fifth Ave.   Phone: (212) 737-9700
New York, NY 10021   Anne Marie Morotte, Exec.Dir.

FRENCH INSTITUTE/ALLIANCE FRANCAISE - LIBRARY
22 E. 60th St.   Phone: (212) 355-6100
New York, NY 10022   Fred J. Gitner, Libn.

FRICK ART REFERENCE LIBRARY
10 E. 71st St.   Phone: (212) 288-8700
New York, NY 10021   Helen Sanger, Libn.

FRIED, FRANK, HARRIS, SHRIVER, JACOBSON - LIBRARY & INFORMATION
  CENTER
1 New York Plaza   Phone: (212) 820-8000
New York, NY 10004   Stewart F. Deutsch, Exec.Libn.

FRITZSCHE, DODGE AND OLCOTT, INC. - RESEARCH LIBRARY
76 Ninth Ave.   Phone: (212) 929-4100
New York, NY 10011   Dr. Roman T. Koenig, Info.Dir.

FUND FOR MODERN COURTS - LIBRARY
36 W. 44th St., Rm. 711   Phone: (212) 575-1577
New York, NY 10036   Fern Schair, Exec.Dir.

GAF CORPORATION - LIBRARY
140 W. 51st St.   Phone: (212) 621-5000
New York, NY 10020   James J. Lamphere, Dir.Corp. Marketing Res.

GALLOWAY (Ewing) PHOTO AGENCY
342 Madison Ave.   Phone: (212) 986-2910
New York, NY 10017   Tom McGeough, Mgr.

GEERS GROSS ADV. INC. - LIBRARY
845 Third Ave.   Phone: (212) 350-9234
New York, NY 10022   Janet Jacquette, Libn.

GENERAL AMERICAN INVESTORS CO., INC. - LIBRARY
330 Madison Ave.   Phone: (212) 949-1763
New York, NY 10017   Jennifer Jones, Libn.

GENERAL MOTORS CORPORATION - ECONOMICS STAFF LIBRARY
767 Fifth Ave., 26th Fl.   Phone: (212) 486-5092
New York, NY 10153   Lourdes P. Lim, Libn.

GENERAL SOCIETY OF MECHANICS AND TRADESMEN OF THE CITY OF NEW
  YORK - LIBRARY
20 W. 44th St.   Phone: (212) 921-1767
New York, NY 10036   Margery Peters, Libn.

GENERAL THEOLOGICAL SEMINARY OF THE PROTESTANT EPISCOPAL
  CHURCH IN THE U.S.A. - ST. MARK'S LIBRARY
175 Ninth Ave.   Phone: (212) 243-5150
New York, NY 10011   Anne-Marie Salgat, Libn.

GEORGESON & COMPANY - LIBRARY
Wall St. Plaza   Phone: (212) 440-9949
New York, NY 10005   Barbara B. Vizoyan, Libn.

GERMAN INFORMATION CENTER - FEDERAL REPUBLIC OF GERMANY
410 Park Ave.   Phone: (212) 888-9840
New York, NY 10022

GIBBS AND COX, INC. - TECHNICAL INFORMATION CONTROL
  DEPARTMENT
40 Rector St.   Phone: (212) 487-2835
New York, NY 10006   R.R. Bertolette, Mgr.

GIRL SCOUTS OF THE USA - LIBRARY/ARCHIVES †
830 Third Ave. & 51st St.   Phone: (212) 940-7500
New York, NY 10022   Rosemary Guerin-Place, Libn./Archv.

GLOBE PHOTOS, INC. - LIBRARY
404 Park Ave., S.   Phone: (212) 689-1340
New York, NY 10016

GOETHE HOUSE NEW YORK - LIBRARY †
1014 Fifth Ave.   Phone: (212) 744-8310
New York, NY 10028   Freya Jeschke, Libn.

GOLD INFORMATION CENTER
Olympic Tower, 645 Fifth Ave.   Phone: (212) 688-0474
New York, NY 10022   Ms. Leslie Mirin Domino, Mgr.

GOLDMAN, SACHS AND COMPANY - LIBRARY
55 Broad St.   Phone: (212) 676-7400
New York, NY 10004   Elizabeth O'Mahoney, Libn.

GRAND LODGE OF NEW YORK, F. AND A.M. - LIBRARY AND MUSEUM
71 W. 23rd St.   Phone: (212) 741-4500
New York, NY 10010   Allan Boudreau, Dir. & Cur.

GRANGER COLLECTION
1841 Broadway   Phone: (212) 586-0971
New York, NY 10023   William Glover, Dir.

GREATER NEW YORK SAFETY COUNCIL, INC. - LIBRARY †
386 Park Ave., S.
New York, NY 10016

GREY ADVERTISING, INC. - RESEARCH LIBRARY
777 3rd Ave.   Phone: (212) 751-3500
New York, NY 10017   Genette P. Lieb, Libn.

GROLIER CLUB OF NEW YORK - LIBRARY
47 E. 60th St.   Phone: (212) 838-6690
New York, NY 10022   Robert Nikirk, Libn.

GUGGENHEIM (Solomon R.) MUSEUM - LIBRARY
1071 5th Ave.   Phone: (212) 860-1338
New York, NY 10028   Mary Joan Hall, Libn.

HACKETT (G.D.) PHOTOGRAPHY - ARCHIVES
130 W. 57th St.
New York, NY 10019   Gabriel D. Hackett, Owner, Ed.

HAIGHT, GARDNER, POOR AND HAVENS - LIBRARY
One State St. Plaza   Phone: (212) 344-6800
New York, NY 10004   Hortense Zeller, Libn.

HALCON SD GROUP, INC. - TECHNICAL INFORMATION CENTER
2 Park Ave.   Phone: (212) 689-1222
New York, NY 10016   Ruth Falco, Sr.Info.Spec.

HANDY ASSOCIATES, INC. - RESEARCH LIBRARY
245 Park Ave.   Phone: (212) 867-8444
New York, NY 10167   Ann Barry, Dir. Of Res.

HARCOURT BRACE JOVANOVICH, INC. - EDITORIAL LIBRARY
757 Third Ave.   Phone: (212) 888-3497
New York, NY 10017   Ron Coplen, Libn.

HARCOURT BRACE JOVANOVICH, INC. - PICTURE RESEARCH LIBRARY
757 Third Ave., 7th Fl.   Phone: (212) 888-3645
New York, NY 10017   Mudite Austrins, Pict.Libn.

HARKNESS (Edward S.) EYE INSTITUTE - JOHN M. WHEELER LIBRARY
635 W. 165th St.   Phone: (212) 694-2916
New York, NY 10032   Albertina F. Mount, Lib.Supv.

HARLEM HOSPITAL CENTER - LIBRARY
506 Lenox Ave.   Phone: (212) 694-8261
New York, NY 10037   Mr. Man D. Chowdhury, Libn.

HARPER & ROW, PUBLISHERS, INC. - SCHOOL DIVISION LIBRARY
10 E. 53rd St., 16th Fl.   Phone: (212) 593-7379
New York, NY 10022   Beth Murphy, Mgr., Lib. & Curric.Res.

HARVARD LIBRARY IN NEW YORK
27 W. 44th St.   Phone: (212) 840-6600
New York, NY 10036   Adrienne G. Fischier, Libn.

HASHOMER HATZAIR-ZIONIST YOUTH MOVEMENT - LIBRARY
150 Fifth Ave.   Phone: (212) 929-4955
New York, NY 10011   David Lutzker, Pres.

HAWKINS, DELAFIELD & WOOD - LIBRARY
67 Wall St.   Phone: (212) 952-4772
New York, NY 10005   Peggy Martin, Libn.

HEBREW UNION COLLEGE - JEWISH INSTITUTE OF RELIGION - KLAU
    LIBRARY
1 W. Fourth St.   Phone: (212) 674-5300
New York, NY 10012   Philip E. Miller, Libn.

HISPANIC INSTITUTE - LIBRARY †
Casa Hispanica, Columbia University
612 W. 116th St.   Phone: (212) 280-4187
New York, NY 10027

HISPANIC SOCIETY OF AMERICA - DEPARTMENT OF ICONOGRAPHY -
    GENERAL REFERENCE FILE
Broadway & 155th St.   Phone: (212) 926-2234
New York, NY 10032

HISPANIC SOCIETY OF AMERICA - LIBRARY
Broadway & 155th St.   Phone: (212) 926-2234
New York, NY 10032   Jean R. Longland, Cur.

HOLLAND SOCIETY OF NEW YORK - LIBRARY
122 E. 58th St.   Phone: (212) 759-1675
New York, NY 10022   Kenneth L. Demarest, Jr., Pres.

HOLY LAND MUSEUM & LIBRARY
Marble Collegiate Church
1 W. 29th St.   Phone: (212) 686-2770
New York, NY 10001   Henry Marsh, Cur.

HOME LIFE INSURANCE COMPANY - LIBRARY
253 Broadway   Phone: (212) 233-6400
New York, NY 10007   Jeannette L. Secunda, Libn.

HORTICULTURAL SOCIETY OF NEW YORK - PUBLIC REFERENCE LIBRARY
128 W. 58th St.   Phone: (212) 757-0915
New York, NY 10019   Valerie Bennett, Libn.

HOSPITAL FOR SPECIAL SURGERY - KIM BARRETT MEMORIAL LIBRARY
535 E. 70th St.   Phone: (212) 535-5500
New York, NY 10021   Munir U. Din, Med.Libn.

HOTEL SALES MANAGEMENT ASSOCIATION - SALES RESEARCH LIBRARY
362 Fifth Ave., Rm. 1100   Phone: (212) 868-3466
New York, NY 10001   Frank W. Berkman, Exec.Dir.

HOUSE BEAUTIFUL - STAFF LIBRARY
717 Fifth Ave.   Phone: (212) 935-4098
New York, NY 10022   Carolyn E. Chesney, Libn.

HUGHES, HUBBARD, AND REED - LIBRARY
One Wall St.   Phone: (212) 943-6500
New York, NY 10005   James Corbett, Libn.

HUGUENOT SOCIETY OF AMERICA - LIBRARY
122 E. 58th St.   Phone: (212) 755-0592
New York, NY 10022   W. Stephen Kratzenberg, Exec.Sec.

HUNTER COLLEGE OF THE CITY UNIVERSITY OF NEW YORK - HEALTH
    PROFESSIONS LIBRARY
440 E. 26th St.   Phone: (212) 481-4326
New York, NY 10010   Samuel J. Waddell, Chf.Libn.

HUNTER COLLEGE OF THE CITY UNIVERSITY OF NEW YORK - HUNTER
    COLLEGE SCHOOL OF SOCIAL WORK - LIBRARY
129 E. 79th St.   Phone: (212) 360-2646
New York, NY 10021   Charles W. Elder, Hd.Libn.

HUTTON (E.F.) & COMPANY, INC. - LIBRARY
One State Street Plaza, 19th Fl.   Phone: (212) 742-2970
New York, NY 10004   Sheila Sterling, Hd.Libn.

GEOGRAPHIC

ICD REHABILITATION AND RESEARCH CENTER - LIBRARY
340 E. 24th St.   Phone: (212) 679-0100
New York, NY 10010   Helen Stonehill, Chf.Libn.

IF EVERY FOOL, INC. - PERFORMING ARTS LIBRARY
143 Chambers St.   Phone: (212) 964-7240
New York, NY 10007   Diane L. Goodman, Dir.

INFORMATION TECHNOLOGY CENTER - LIBRARY
One World Trade Center   Phone: (212) 466-9100
New York, NY 10048   Richard VanAuken, Dir.

INSIDE SPORTS MAGAZINE - LIBRARY
444 Madison Ave.
New York, NY 10022   Ellen Donato, Res.Libn.

INSTITUTE FOR GLAUCOMA RESEARCH, INC. - CARL C. SWISHER LIBRARY
667 Madison Ave.
New York, NY 10021

INSTITUTE OF INTERNATIONAL EDUCATION - LIBRARY/
  COMMUNICATIONS
809 UN Plaza   Phone: (212) 883-8470
New York, NY 10017   Ruthann Evanoff, Info.Spec.

INSTITUTE OF JUDICIAL ADMINISTRATION - LIBRARY
One Washington Sq. Village   Phone: (212) 598-7721
New York, NY 10012   Philip Klingle, Libn.

INSTITUTE OF PUBLIC ADMINISTRATION - LIBRARY
55 W. 44th St.   Phone: (212) 730-5632
New York, NY 10036   Xenia W. Duisin, Libn.

INSTITUTE FOR PUBLIC TRANSPORTATION - LIBRARY *
211 E. 43rd St.   Phone: (212) 661-4370
New York, NY 10017   Beverly Dolinsky, Act.Dir.

INSTITUTE FOR RATIONAL LIVING - RESEARCH LIBRARY
45 E. 65th St.   Phone: (212) 535-0822
New York, NY 10021   Dr. Myra Josephs, Libn.

INSTITUTE FOR RESEARCH IN HYPNOSIS - BERNARD B. RAGINSKY
  RESEARCH LIBRARY
10 W. 66th St.   Phone: (212) 874-5290
New York, NY 10023   Dr. Milton V. Kline, Dir. of Institute

INSTITUTES OF RELIGION AND HEALTH - LIBRARY
3 W. 29th St.   Phone: (212) 725-7842
New York, NY 10001   Roslyn Roth, Chf.Libn.

INTERNATIONAL ADVERTISING ASSOCIATION - LIBRARY
475 Fifth Ave.   Phone: (212) 684-1583
New York, NY 10017

INTERNATIONAL CENTER OF PHOTOGRAPHY - ARCHIVES
1130 Fifth Ave.
New York, NY 10028   Miles Barth, Cur.

INTERNATIONAL CENTER OF PHOTOGRAPHY - LIBRARY RESOURCE
  CENTER
1130 Fifth Ave.   Phone: (212) 860-1787
New York, NY 10028   Lee Sievan, Resource Libn.

INTERNATIONAL COPPER RESEARCH ASSOCIATION, INC. - LIBRARY
708 Third Ave.   Phone: (212) 697-9355
New York, NY 10017

INTERNATIONAL COUNCIL OF SHOPPING CENTERS - LIBRARY
665 Fifth Ave.   Phone: (212) 421-8181
New York, NY 10022   Nancy G. Morley, Libn.

INTERNATIONAL LADIES' GARMENT WORKERS UNION - LIBRARY
1710 Broadway   Phone: (212) 265-7000
New York, NY 10019

INTERNATIONAL MICROWAVE POWER INSTITUTE - REFERENCE LIBRARY
211 E. 43rd St., Suite 302   Phone: (212) 867-4659
New York, NY 10017   R.P. Halpern, Adm.

INTERNATIONAL NICKEL COMPANY, INC. - LIBRARY
One New York Plaza   Phone: (212) 742-4061
New York, NY 10004   Linda G. Doty, Lib.Adm.

INTERNATIONAL PAPER COMPANY - CORPORATE INFORMATION CENTER
77 W. 45th St., Rm. 4326   Phone: (212) 536-5549
New York, NY 10036   Elizabeth Skerritt, Corp.Libn.

INTERNATIONAL PLANNED PARENTHOOD FEDERATION - WESTERN
  HEMISPHERE REGION - LIBRARY
105 Madison Ave.   Phone: (212) 679-2230
New York, NY 10016   Helen Szterenfeld, Hd.

INTERNATIONAL SOCIETY FOR REHABILITATION OF THE DISABLED/
  REHABILITATION INTERNATIONAL - LIBRARY
432 Park Ave., S.   Phone: (212) 679-6520
New York, NY 10016

INTERNATIONAL THEATRE INSTITUTE OF THE UNITED STATES, INC. -
  INTERNATIONAL THEATRE COLLECTION
1860 Broadway, Suite 1510   Phone: (212) 245-3950
New York, NY 10023   Elizabeth B. Burdick, Dir.

INTERNATIONAL THOMSON EDUCATIONAL PUBLISHING, INC. - EDITORIAL
  LIBRARY
135 W. 50th St.   Phone: (212) 265-8700
New York, NY 10020   Dorothy R. Allen, Libn.

IRELAND CONSULATE GENERAL - LIBRARY
580 Fifth Ave.   Phone: (212) 245-1010
New York, NY 10036   Hon. Sean Oh'Uiginn, Consul Gen.

IRI RESEARCH INSTITUTE, INC. - LIBRARY
One Rockefeller Plaza, Rm. 1401   Phone: (212) 581-1942
New York, NY 10020

IRVING TRUST COMPANY - BUSINESS LIBRARY
One Wall St.   Phone: (212) 487-6431
New York, NY 10015   Susan Stewart, Hd.Libn.

ISLANDS RESEARCH FOUNDATION, INC. - INFORMATION CENTER †
108 Prospect Tower
45 Tudor City Pl.
New York, NY 10017

ITALIAN CULTURE INSTITUTE - LIBRARY †
686 Park Ave.   Phone: (212) 879-4242
New York, NY 10021   Dr. Maria A. Gargotta, Hd.Libn.

ITT CORPORATION - HEADQUARTERS LIBRARY
320 Park Ave.   Phone: (212) 752-6000
New York, NY 10022   Margaret M. DeLorme, Mgr.

ITT CORPORATION - LEGAL DEPARTMENT LIBRARY
320 Park Ave.
New York, NY 10022   Beryl White, Law Libn.

IULIU MANIU AMERICAN ROMANIAN RELIEF FOUNDATION - LIBRARY
17 E. 79th St.
Box 1151
New York, NY 10028

IVIMEY (Muriel) LIBRARY
329 E. 62nd St.   Phone: (212) 752-5267
New York, NY 10021   Eleanor Yachnes, M.D., Chm., Lib.Comm.

JAPAN SOCIETY, INC. - LIBRARY
333 E. 47th St.   Phone: (212) 832-1155
New York, NY 10017   Tomie Mochizuki, Libn.

JEWISH BOARD OF FAMILY & CHILDREN SERVICES - LIBRARY
120 W. 57th St.   Phone: (212) 582-9100
New York, NY 10019   Teresa Kremer, Libn.

JEWISH BRAILLE INSTITUTE OF AMERICA, INC. - LIBRARY
110 E. 30th St.   Phone: (212) 889-2525
New York, NY 10016   Richard Borgersen, Lib.Dir.

JEWISH GUILD FOR THE BLIND - YOUNG MEN'S PHILANTHROPIC LEAGUE - CASSETTE LIBRARY
15 W. 65th St.   Phone: (212) 595-2000
New York, NY 10023   Bruce E. Massis, Dir.

JEWISH HISTORICAL SOCIETY OF NEW YORK, INC. - LIBRARY
Eight W. 70th St.   Phone: (212) 873-0300
New York, NY 10023   Steven W. Siegel, Exec.Sec.

JEWISH MEMORIAL HOSPITAL - IRVING DORFMAN MEMORIAL MEDICAL LIBRARY
Broadway & 196th St.   Phone: (212) 569-4700
New York, NY 10040   Theodora L.D. Lindt, Dir.

JEWISH MUSEUM - LIBRARY
1109 Fifth Ave.   Phone: (212) 860-1888
New York, NY 10028   Beverly Franco, Libn.

JEWISH THEOLOGICAL SEMINARY OF AMERICA - LIBRARY
3080 Broadway   Phone: (212) 749-8000
New York, NY 10027   Dr. Menahem Schmelzer, Libn.

JOCKEY CLUB - LIBRARY
380 Madison Ave.   Phone: (212) 599-1919
New York, NY 10017   Robert L. Melican, Exec.Dir.

JOHN JAY COLLEGE OF CRIMINAL JUSTICE OF THE CITY UNIVERSITY OF NEW YORK - REISMAN MEMORIAL LIBRARY
445 W. 59th St.   Phone: (212) 489-5169
New York, NY 10019   Professor Eileen Rowland, Chf.Libn.

JUILLIARD SCHOOL - LILA ACHESON WALLACE LIBRARY
Lincoln Center Plaza   Phone: (212) 799-5000
New York, NY 10023   Brinton Jackson, Libn.

JULIEN AND SCHLESINGER, P.C., ATTORNEYS-AT-LAW - LIBRARY †
2 Lafayette St., Suite 1006   Phone: (212) 962-8020
New York, NY 10007   Denise J. Mortner, Libn. & Off.Mgr.

KAYE, SCHOLER, FIERMAN, HAYS & HANDLER - LAW LIBRARY
425 Park Ave.   Phone: (212) 759-8400
New York, NY 10022   Gerald Goodhartz, Libn.

KELLEY, DRYE & WARREN - LAW LIBRARY
350 Park Ave.   Phone: (212) 752-5800
New York, NY 10022   Martha Goldman, Libn.

KENNEDY GALLERIES - ART LIBRARY
40 W. 57th St.   Phone: (212) 541-9600
New York, NY 10019   Cynthia Seibels, Libn.

KENYON & ECKHARDT ADVERTISING - INFORMATION CENTER
200 Park Ave.   Phone: (212) 880-2361
New York, NY 10017   Aina Geske, Hd.Libn.

KEYSTONE PRESS AGENCY, INC. - PICTURE LIBRARY
156 Fifth Ave.   Phone: (212) 924-8123
New York, NY 10010   Brian F. Alpert, Mng.Ed.

KIDDER, PEABODY AND COMPANY, INC. - LIBRARY †
10 Hanover Sq., 21st Fl.
Box 94   Phone: (212) 747-2504
New York, NY 10005   Annette F. Herbert, Libn.-Supv.

KNOEDLER (M.) AND COMPANY, INC. - LIBRARY
19 E. 70th St.   Phone: (212) 794-0569
New York, NY 10021   Nancy C. Little, Libn.

KOSCIUSZKO FOUNDATION - REFERENCE LIBRARY
15 E. 65th St.
New York, NY 10021

LABOR RESEARCH ASSOCIATION - LIBRARY
80 E. 11th St.   Phone: (212) 473-1042
New York, NY 10003   Dr. Joseph Harris, Res.Dir.

LANDAUER ASSOCIATES, INC. - INFORMATION CENTER
200 Park Ave., Suite 3710   Phone: (212) 687-2323
New York, NY 10166   Therese E. Byrne, Dir., Info.Serv.

LAZARD FRERES AND COMPANY - FINANCIAL LIBRARY †
One Rockefeller Plaza   Phone: (212) 489-6600
New York, NY 10020   Anne Mintz, Libn.

LEAGUE OF ARAB STATES - ARAB INFORMATION CENTER
747 Third Ave.   Phone: (212) 838-8700
New York, NY 10017   Marwan Kanafani, Info.Off.

LEBER KATZ, INC. - MARKETING INFORMATION CENTER LIBRARY
767 Fifth Ave.   Phone: (212) 826-3957
New York, NY 10022   Bonnie Tauber, Mgr.Info.Serv.

LEBHAR-FRIEDMAN, INC. - CHAIN STORE AGE - READER SERVICE RESEARCH LIBRARY
425 Park Ave.   Phone: (212) 689-4800
New York, NY 10022   Ruth Weselteer, Libn.

LEBOEUF, LAMB, LEIBY & MAC RAE - LIBRARY
140 Broadway, 31st Fl.   Phone: (212) 269-1100
New York, NY 10005   Ruth V. Mortensen, Libn.

LEGAL AID SOCIETY - LIBRARIES
15 Park Row   Phone: (212) 577-3333
New York, NY 10038   David Donaldson, Hd.Libn.

LEHMAN BROTHERS, KUHN, LOEB, INC. - LIBRARY
55 Water St.   Phone: (212) 558-2134
New York, NY 10041   Louise Stoops, Chf.Libn.

LENOX HILL HOSPITAL - HEALTH SCIENCES LIBRARY
100 E. 77th St.   Phone: (212) 794-4266
New York, NY 10021   Shirley E. Dansker, Dir.

LEVY (W.J.) CONSULTANTS CORPORATION - RESEARCH LIBRARY
30 Rockefeller Plaza   Phone: (212) 586-5263
New York, NY 10020   Ilse E. Kagan, Libn.

LEWIS (Frederic) INC. - PHOTOGRAPHIC LIBRARY
15 W. 38th St.   Phone: (212) 921-2850
New York, NY 10018   David Perton, Pres.

LINCOLN EDUCATIONAL FOUNDATION - LIBRARY OF INDIVIDUAL BUSINESS HISTORIES
299 Madison Ave., Rm. 503   Phone: (212) 697-2236
New York, NY 10017   Frank Wetzel, Libn.

LIONEL D. EDIE AND COMPANY, INC. - LIBRARY †
530 Fifth Ave., 4th Fl.   Phone: (212) 575-4211
New York, NY 10036   Kay Stock, Sr.Lib.Asst.

LOWENSTEIN (M.) CORPORATION - DESIGN RESEARCH LIBRARY
1430 Broadway   Phone: (212) 930-5610
New York, NY 10018   Colleen A. Ryan, Libn.

LUTHERAN COUNCIL IN THE U.S.A. - RECORDS AND INFORMATION CENTER - REFERENCE LIBRARY
360 Park Ave. S.   Phone: (212) 532-6350
New York, NY 10010   Alice M. Kendrick, Dir.

MC ADAMS (William Douglas), INC. - MEDICAL LIBRARY
110 E. 59th St.   Phone: (212) 759-6300
New York, NY 10022   Cecilia Tinio, Chf.Libn.

MC CANN-ERICKSON, INC. - LIBRARY †
485 Lexington Ave.   Phone: (212) 697-6000
New York, NY 10017   Katherine Dodge, Supv.Lib.Serv.

MC GRAW-HILL, INC. - BUSINESS WEEK MAGAZINE LIBRARY †
1221 Ave. of the Americas   Phone: (212) 997-3297
New York, NY 10020   Tessie Mantzoros, Libn.

MC GRAW-HILL, INC. - LIBRARY
1221 Ave. of the Americas   Phone: (212) 997-6829
New York, NY 10020   George Barlow, Chf.Libn.

MC GRAW-HILL PUBLICATIONS COMPANY - MARKETING INFORMATION CENTER †
1221 Ave. of the Americas   Phone: (212) 997-3222
New York, NY 10020   Ranulph F. Norman, Dir.

GEOGRAPHIC

MC KINSEY & COMPANY, INC. - INFORMATION SERVICES
55 E. 52nd St.   Phone: (212) 909-8400
New York, NY 10022   Valerie Knupp, Supv., Tech.Serv.

MACKAY - SHIELDS FINANCIAL CORPORATION - RESEARCH LIBRARY
551 Fifth Ave.   Phone: (212) 986-1100
New York, NY 10017   Hertha Ketcham, Libn.

MAGAZINE PUBLISHERS ASSOCIATION - MAGAZINE INFORMATION
   CENTER
575 Lexington Ave.   Phone: (212) 752-0055
New York, NY 10022   Annmaria Di Cesare, Mgr., Info.Serv.

MAIN HURDMAN - LIBRARY
55 E. 52nd St.   Phone: (212) 269-5800
New York, NY 10055   Marjorie Moyal, Libn.

MANHATTAN SCHOOL OF MUSIC - LIBRARY
120 Claremont Ave.   Phone: (212) 749-2802
New York, NY 10027   Nina Davis-Millis, Libn.

MANNES COLLEGE OF MUSIC - HARRY SCHERMAN LIBRARY
157 E. 74th St.   Phone: (212) 737-0700
New York, NY 10021   Barbara Railo, Hd.Libn.

MANUFACTURERS HANOVER TRUST COMPANY - CORPORATE LIBRARY/
   FINANCIAL LIBRARY DIVISION
350 Park Ave.   Phone: (212) 350-4733
New York, NY 10022   Ann Little, Libn.

MANUFACTURERS HANOVER TRUST COMPANY - CORPORATE LIBRARY/
   INVESTMENT LIBRARY DIVISION
600 Fifth Ave.   Phone: (212) 957-1356
New York, NY 10020   Ann Little, Libn.

MANUFACTURERS HANOVER TRUST COMPANY - INTERNATIONAL
   ECONOMICS DEPARTMENT - LIBRARY
46 E. 52nd St.
Box 932   Phone: (212) 350-5829
New York, NY 10022   Halina Osysko, Libn.

MARINE MIDLAND BANK - LIBRARY
140 Broadway, 9th Fl.   Phone: (212) 797-6473
New York, NY 10015   Joan W. Glazier, Lib.Off.

MARLBOROUGH GALLERY - LIBRARY
40 W. 57th St.   Phone: (212) 541-4900
New York, NY 10019   Dorothy W. Herman, Libn.

MARSCHALK COMPANY, INC. - LIBRARY †
1345 Ave. of the Americas   Phone: (212) 974-7700
New York, NY 10019

MARSH AND MC LENNAN, INC. - INFORMATION CENTER
1221 Ave. of the Americas   Phone: (212) 997-7800
New York, NY 10020   Susan Kucsma, Mgr.

MARSHALL, BRATTER, GREENE, ALLISON & TUCKER - LIBRARY
430 Park Ave.   Phone: (212) 421-7200
New York, NY 10022   Ivy Kaufman, Libn.

MATERNITY CENTER ASSOCIATION - REFERENCE LIBRARY
48 E. 92nd St.   Phone: (212) 369-7300
New York, NY 10028   Esther Hanchett, Libn.

MEDICAL LIBRARY CENTER OF NEW YORK
17 E. 102nd St.   Phone: (212) 427-1630
New York, NY 10029   William D. Walker, Dir.

MEMORIAL SLOAN-KETTERING CANCER CENTER - LEE COOMBE MEMORIAL
   LIBRARY
1275 York Ave.   Phone: (212) 794-7439
New York, NY 10021   Angelina Harmon, Libn.

MEMORY SHOP, INC. - MOVIE MEMORABILIA STILLS *
109 E. 12th St.   Phone: (212) 473-2404
New York, NY 10003   Mark Ricci, Owner

MENTAL HEALTH MATERIALS CENTER - INFORMATION RESOURCES
   CENTER FOR MENTAL HEALTH & FAMILY LIFE EDUCATION
30 E. 29th St.   Phone: (212) 889-5760
New York, NY 10016

MERCANTILE LIBRARY ASSOCIATION - MERCANTILE LIBRARY
17 E. 47th St.   Phone: (212) 755-6710
New York, NY 10017   Claire J. Roth, Lib.Dir.

MERRILL LYNCH PIERCE FENNER & SMITH, INC. - LIBRARY
One Liberty Plaza
165 Broadway   Phone: (212) 637-7420
New York, NY 10080   Rita A. Hughes, Chf. Libn.

MERRILL LYNCH WHITE WELD - CAPITAL MARKETS GROUP - LIBRARY
One Liberty Plaza, 42nd Fl.   Phone: (212) 637-2085
New York, NY 10080   Eva Vanek, Mgr.Lib.Serv.

METROMEDIA INC. - CORPORATE RESEARCH LIBRARY
485 Lexington Ave.   Phone: (212) 682-9100
New York, NY 10017   Francine Holzer, Hd.Libn.

METROPOLITAN HOSPITAL CENTER - DRAPER HALL LIBRARY †
1918 First Ave.   Phone: (212) 360-6957
New York, NY 10029   Mitchell A. Bogen, Libn.

METROPOLITAN HOSPITAL CENTER - FREDERICK M. DEARBORN MEDICAL
   LIBRARY
1901 First Ave.   Phone: (212) 360-6270
New York, NY 10029   Vivienne Whitson, Chf.Libn.

METROPOLITAN LIFE INSURANCE COMPANY - LAW LIBRARY
One Madison Ave.   Phone: (212) 578-3111
New York, NY 10010   Rita Barone, Law Libn.

METROPOLITAN LIFE INSURANCE COMPANY - LIBRARY
One Madison Ave., 1 M-R   Phone: (212) 578-3700
New York, NY 10010   Elizabeth McCloat, Libn.

METROPOLITAN MUSEUM OF ART - CLOISTERS LIBRARY
Fort Tryon Pk.   Phone: (212) 923-3700
New York, NY 10040   Suse Childs, Libn.

METROPOLITAN MUSEUM OF ART - DEPARTMENT OF PRINTS AND
   PHOTOGRAPHS
Fifth Ave. & 82nd St.   Phone: (212) 879-5500
New York, NY 10028   Colta Feller Ives, Cur.

METROPOLITAN MUSEUM OF ART - IRENE LEWISOHN COSTUME
   REFERENCE LIBRARY
Fifth Ave. & 82nd St.   Phone: (212) 879-5500
New York, NY 10028   Gordon Stone, Assoc.Musm.Libn.

METROPOLITAN MUSEUM OF ART - JUNIOR MUSEUM LIBRARY
Fifth Ave. & 82nd St.   Phone: (212) 879-5500
New York, NY 10028   Roberta M. Paine, Musm. Educator

METROPOLITAN MUSEUM OF ART - PHOTOGRAPH AND SLIDE LIBRARY
Fifth Ave. & 82nd St.   Phone: (212) 879-5500
New York, NY 10028   Margaret P. Nolan, Chf.Libn.

METROPOLITAN MUSEUM OF ART - ROBERT GOLDWATER LIBRARY OF
   PRIMITIVE ART
Fifth Ave. & 82nd St.   Phone: (212) 879-5500
New York, NY 10028   Allan D. Chapman, Musm.Libn.

METROPOLITAN MUSEUM OF ART - ROBERT LEHMAN COLLECTION -
   LIBRARY
Fifth Ave. & 82nd St.   Phone: (212) 879-5500
New York, NY 10028   Victoria S. Galban, Asst.Cur., Res.

METROPOLITAN MUSEUM OF ART - THOMAS J. WATSON LIBRARY
Fifth Ave. & 82nd St.   Phone: (212) 879-5500
New York, NY 10028   William B. Walker, Chf.Libn.

METROPOLITAN OPERA ASSOCIATION - ARCHIVES
Lincoln Ctr. Plaza   Phone: (212) 799-3100
New York, NY 10023   Heloise L. Pressey, Asst.Archv.

MILBANK, TWEED, HADLEY & MC CLOY - LIBRARY
1 Chase Manhattan Plaza   Phone: (212) 530-5200
New York, NY 10005   Gina Resnick, Libn.

MINORITY BUSINESS INFORMATION INSTITUTE, INC. - LIBRARY
295 Madison Ave., 12th Fl.   Phone: (212) 889-8220
New York, NY 10017   Claudia J. Gollop, Adm., Info.Serv.

MOBIL OIL CORPORATION - PUBLIC AFFAIRS SECRETARIAT
150 E. 42nd St., Rm. 606   Phone: (212) 883-2155
New York, NY 10017   E. Holmes Bearden, Mgr.

MODERN LANGUAGE ASSOCIATION - CENTER FOR BIBLIOGRAPHICAL
    SERVICES
62 Fifth Ave.   Phone: (212) 741-5590
New York, NY 10011   Eileen M. Mackesy, Dir.

MONKMEYER PRESS PHOTO SERVICE
15 E. 48th St.
New York, NY 10017   Hilde R. Monkmeyer, Hd.

MONTEFIORE HOSPITAL & MEDICAL CENTER - KARL CHERKASKY SOCIAL
    MEDICINE LIBRARY
111 E. 210th St.   Phone: (212) 920-5508
New York, NY 10467   Dr. Victor W. Sidel, Chm.Dept.Soc.Med.

MONTEFIORE HOSPITAL & MEDICAL CENTER - MEDICAL LIBRARY
111 E. 210 St.   Phone: (212) 920-4666
New York, NY 10467   Marjorie De Forest, Chf.Med.Libn.

MOODY'S INVESTORS SERVICE - INFORMATION CENTER
99 Church St.   Phone: (212) 553-0525
New York, NY 10007   Angelica Carroll, Mgr.

MORGAN GUARANTY TRUST COMPANY OF NEW YORK - REFERENCE
    LIBRARY
23 Wall St.   Phone: (212) 483-2175
New York, NY 10015   J. Robert Reuter, Libn.

MORGAN, LEWIS & BOCKIUS - LIBRARY
9 W. 57th St.   Phone: (212) 980-4562
New York, NY 10019   Janice E. Henderson, Libn.

MORGAN STANLEY & COMPANY, INC. - LIBRARY
1251 Ave. of the Americas   Phone: (212) 974-4369
New York, NY 10020   Sarah C. Jones, Dir.Lib.Serv.

MOTION PICTURE ASSOCIATION OF AMERICA - LIBRARY †
522 Fifth Ave.   Phone: (212) 840-6161
New York, NY 10036   Michael Linden, Dir. of Res.

MOUNT SINAI SCHOOL OF MEDICINE OF THE CITY UNIVERSITY OF NEW
    YORK - GUSTAVE L. & JANET W. LEVY LIBRARY
One Gustave L. Levy Pl.   Phone: (212) 650-7793
New York, NY 10029   Jane S. Port, Dir.

MOVIE STAR NEWS - PHOTOGRAPH COLLECTION
212 E. 14th St.   Phone: (212) 777-5564
New York, NY 10003   Paula Klaw, Pres.

MUDGE, ROSE, GUTHRIE & ALEXANDER - LIBRARY †
20 Broad St.   Phone: (212) 422-6767
New York, NY 10005   Mrs. C. Alvy, Libn.

MUSCULAR DYSTROPHY ASSOCIATION - LIBRARY
810 Seventh Ave.   Phone: (212) 586-0808
New York, NY 10019

MUSEUM OF THE CITY OF NEW YORK - THEATRE COLLECTION
103rd St. & Fifth Ave.   Phone: (212) 534-1672
New York, NY 10029   Dr. Mary C. Henderson, Cur.

MUSEUM OF MODERN ART - DEPARTMENT OF RIGHTS AND
    REPRODUCTIONS - AUDIOVISUAL ARCHIVES
11 W. 53rd St.   Phone: (212) 956-7255
New York, NY 10019   Esther M. Carpenter, Archv.

MUSEUM OF MODERN ART - FILM STUDY CENTER
11 W. 53rd St.   Phone: (212) 956-4212
New York, NY 10019   Charles Silver, Supv.

MUSEUM OF MODERN ART - LIBRARY
11 W. 53rd St.   Phone: (212) 956-7236
New York, NY 10019   Clive Phillpot, Dir.

MUTUAL OF NEW YORK - LAW LIBRARY
1740 Broadway   Phone: (212) 708-2235
New York, NY 10019   Janet Stoller, Libn.

MUTUAL OF NEW YORK - LIBRARY/INFORMATION SERVICE
1740 Broadway   Phone: (212) 708-2139
New York, NY 10019   Janet Stoller, Libn.

MYSTERY WRITERS OF AMERICA, INC. - MYSTERY LIBRARY
150 Fifth Ave.   Phone: (212) 255-7005
New York, NY 10011   Hillary Waugh, Exec. V.P.

NATIONAL ACADEMY OF DESIGN - LIBRARY
1083 Fifth Ave.   Phone: (212) 369-4880
New York, NY 10028   John H. Dobkin, Dir.

NATIONAL ASSOCIATION OF ACCOUNTANTS - LIBRARY
919 Third Ave.   Phone: (212) 754-9736
New York, NY 10022   Miriam J. Redrick, Mgr., Lib.Serv.

NATIONAL ASSOCIATION OF MUTUAL SAVINGS BANKS - LIBRARY †
200 Park Ave.   Phone: (212) 973-4704
New York, NY 10017   Antoinette Stapper, Libn.

NATIONAL ASSOCIATION OF PURCHASING MANAGEMENT, INC. -
    PURCHASING INFORMATION CENTER
11 Park Pl.   Phone: (212) 267-3677
New York, NY 10007   Mary Crowell, Libn.

NATIONAL AUDUBON SOCIETY - LIBRARY
950 Third Ave.   Phone: (212) 832-3200
New York, NY 10022   Michelle I. Epstein, Libn.

NATIONAL BROADCASTING COMPANY, INC. - INFORMATION UNIT -
    RESEARCH DEPARTMENT
30 Rockefeller Plaza, Rm. 1640   Phone: (212) 664-4243
New York, NY 10020   Doris B. Katz, Mgr.

NATIONAL BROADCASTING COMPANY, INC. - NEWS ARCHIVAL SERVICES
    LIBRARY
30 Rockefeller Plaza   Phone: (212) 664-3271
New York, NY 10020   Michael Francaviglia, Mgr.

NATIONAL BROADCASTING COMPANY, INC. - REFERENCE LIBRARY
30 Rockefeller Plaza   Phone: (212) 664-5307
New York, NY 10020   Vera Mayer, V.P., Info. & Archv.

NATIONAL CENTER ON WOMEN AND FAMILY LAW, INC. - INFORMATION
    CENTER
799 Broadway, Rm. 402   Phone: (212) 674-8200
New York, NY 10003   Laurie Woods, Exec.Dir.

NATIONAL CHAMBER OF COMMERCE FOR WOMEN - ELIZABETH LEWIN
    BUSINESS LIBRARY & INFORMATION CENTER
Box 745   Phone: (212) 532-6408
New York, NY 10159   Ray Wright, Res.Dir.

NATIONAL CONFERENCE OF CHRISTIANS AND JEWS - PAULA K. LAZRUS
    LIBRARY OF INTERGROUP RELATIONS
43 W. 57th St.   Phone: (212) 688-7530
New York, NY 10019   Edith G. Selig, Adm.Asst.

NATIONAL CONFERENCE ON SOVIET JEWRY (NCSJ) - RESEARCH BUREAU
10 E. 40th St., Suite 907   Phone: (212) 679-6122
New York, NY 10016   Myrna Shinbaum, Assoc.Dir.

NATIONAL COUNCIL ON ALCOHOLISM, INC. - LIBRARY †
733 Third Ave.   Phone: (212) 986-4433
New York, NY 10017   Betty Gold, Libn.

GEOGRAPHIC

NATIONAL COUNCIL OF CHURCHES OF CHRIST IN THE U.S.A. - INTL.
   AFFAIRS OFFICE - JOHN FOSTER DULLES LIB. & RESEARCH CTR. †
475 Riverside Dr., Rm. 572
New York, NY 10115

NATIONAL COUNCIL OF CHURCHES - INTERFAITH CENTER ON CORPORATE
   RESPONSIBILITY
475 Riverside Dr., Rm. 566   Phone: (212) 870-2293
New York, NY 10115   Valerie Heinonen, Res.Mgr.

NATIONAL COUNCIL OF THE YOUNG MEN'S CHRISTIAN ASSOCIATIONS OF
   THE U.S. - YMCA HISTORICAL LIBRARY †
291 Broadway   Phone: (212) 374-2042
New York, NY 10007   Ellen Sowchek, Libn.

NATIONAL ECONOMIC RESEARCH ASSOCIATES, INC. - LIBRARY
5 World Trade Ctr., 8th Fl.   Phone: (212) 524-7800
New York, NY 10048   Dolores Colgan, Libn.

NATIONAL EMPLOYMENT LAW PROJECT, INC. - LIBRARY
475 Riverside Dr., Suite 240   Phone: (212) 870-2121
New York, NY 10027   Andrue Scott, Lib.Info.Mgr.

NATIONAL ENERGY FOUNDATION - ENERGY REFERENCE AND RESOURCE
   CENTER
366 Madison Ave., Rm. 705   Phone: (212) 697-2920
New York, NY 10017   Ann Borden, Exec.V.P.

NATIONAL FILM BOARD OF CANADA - FILM LIBRARY
1251 Ave. of the Americas, 16th Fl.   Phone: (212) 586-5131
New York, NY 10020   Ken Shere, U.S. Gen.Mgr.

NATIONAL INVESTMENT LIBRARY
80 Wall St.   Phone: (212) 254-1700
New York, NY 10005   Kathe. Engro, Asst.Dir.

NATIONAL LEAGUE FOR NURSING, INC. - LIBRARY/RECORDS CENTER
10 Columbus Circle   Phone: (212) 582-1022
New York, NY 10019   Marion Koshar, Libn./Rec.Mgr.

NATIONAL MARINE MANUFACTURERS ASSOCIATION - INFORMATION
   CENTER
666 3rd Ave.   Phone: (212) 697-1100
New York, NY 10017   John A. Lamont, Info.Mgr.

NATIONAL MULTIPLE SCLEROSIS SOCIETY - MEDICAL LIBRARY
205 E. 42nd St.   Phone: (212) 986-3240
New York, NY 10017

NATIONAL MUNICIPAL LEAGUE - LIBRARY
47 E. 68th St.   Phone: (212) 535-5700
New York, NY 10021   Joan A. Casey, Lib.Dir.

NATIONAL PSYCHOLOGICAL ASSOCIATION FOR PSYCHOANALYSIS -
   GEORGE LAWTON MEMORIAL LIBRARY
150 W. 13th St.   Phone: (212) 924-7440
New York, NY 10011   Annabella B. Nelken, Exec.Adm.

NATIONAL RECORDS MANAGEMENT COUNCIL - LIBRARY
60 E. 42nd St.   Phone: (212) 697-0290
New York, NY 10017   Robert A. Shiff, Pres.

NATIONAL SOCIETY TO PREVENT BLINDNESS - CONRAD BERENS LIBRARY
79 Madison Ave.   Phone: (212) 684-3505
New York, NY 10016   Raymond A. Jeri, Libn.Asst.

NATIONAL TRAINING CENTER OF POLYGRAPH SCIENCE - TECHNICAL
   INFORMATION CENTER
57 W. 57th St., Suite 1109
New York, NY 10019   Richard O. Arther, Dir.

NEEDHAM, HARPER & STEERS ADVERTISING, INC. - RESEARCH LIBRARY
909 Third Ave.   Phone: (212) 758-7600
New York, NY 10022   Alice Vallinos, Res.Libn.

NEIGHBORHOOD PLAYHOUSE SCHOOL OF THE THEATRE - IRENE LEWISOHN
   LIBRARY
340 E. 54th St.   Phone: (212) 688-3770
New York, NY 10022   Alice G. Owen, Libn.

NEW SCHOOL FOR SOCIAL RESEARCH - RAYMOND FOGELMAN LIBRARY
65 Fifth Ave.   Phone: (212) 741-7902
New York, NY 10003   Michael Lordi, Lib.Dir.

NEW YORK ACADEMY OF MEDICINE - LIBRARY
2 E. 103rd St.   Phone: (212) 876-8200
New York, NY 10029   Brett A. Kirkpatrick, Libn.

NEW YORK CITY BOARD OF EDUCATION - DIVISION OF SPECIAL
   EDUCATION - SPECIAL EDUC. TRAINING & RESOURCE CTR.
400 First Ave.   Phone: (212) 686-6120
New York, NY 10010   Jan Cable, Libn.

NEW YORK CITY COMMISSION ON HUMAN RIGHTS - LIBRARY †
52 Duane St.   Phone: (212) 233-4410
New York, NY 10007   Laura Fisher, Libn.

NEW YORK CITY HUMAN RESOURCES ADMINISTRATION - MC MILLAN
   LIBRARY
109 E. 16th St.   Phone: (212) 460-8555
New York, NY 10003   Harold W. Benson, Libn.

NEW YORK CITY HUMAN RESOURCES ADMINISTRATION - MEDICAL
   ASSISTANCE PROGRAM - MEDICAID LIBRARY
330 W. 34th St., Rm. 370   Phone: (212) 790-3988
New York, NY 10001   Barry L. Cohen, MAP Libn.

NEW YORK CITY - LAW DEPARTMENT - CORPORATION COUNSEL'S
   LIBRARY
100 Church St.   Phone: (212) 566-4418
New York, NY 10007   Jacob Wexler, Libn.

NEW YORK CITY - MUNICIPAL REFERENCE AND RESEARCH CENTER
31 Chambers St.   Phone: (212) 566-4285
New York, NY 10007   Solomon Jacobson, Dir.

NEW YORK CITY - MUNICIPAL REFERENCE AND RESEARCH CENTER -
   HAVEN EMERSON PUBLIC HEALTH LIBRARY
125 Worth St., Rm. 223   Phone: (212) 566-5169
New York, NY 10013   Solomon Becker, Chf.Libn.

NEW YORK CITY - OFFICE OF CHIEF MEDICAL EXAMINER - MILTON
   HELPERN LIBRARY OF LEGAL MEDICINE
520 First Ave.   Phone: (212) 340-0102
New York, NY 10016   Ellen R. Brenner, Libn.

NEW YORK CITY POLICE DEPARTMENT - POLICE ACADEMY LIBRARY
235 E. 20th St.   Phone: (212) 477-9723
New York, NY 10003   John Preston, Libn.

NEW YORK CITY - PUBLIC HEALTH LABORATORIES - WILLIAM HALLOCK
   PARK MEMORIAL LIBRARY
455 First Ave.   Phone: (212) 340-4700
New York, NY 10016   Shirley Chapin, Libn.

NEW YORK COLLEGE OF PODIATRIC MEDICINE - DR. SIDNEY DRUSKIN
   MEMORIAL LIBRARY †
53-55 E. 124th St., 3rd Fl.   Phone: (212) 427-8400
New York, NY 10035   Oksana Karaczewsky, Hd.Libn.

NEW YORK COUNTY - DISTRICT ATTORNEY'S OFFICE LIBRARY
One Hogan Pl.   Phone: (212) 553-9344
New York, NY 10013   Madeleine Fenster, Libn.

NEW YORK COUNTY LAWYERS' ASSOCIATION - LIBRARY
14 Vesey St.   Phone: (212) 267-6646
New York, NY 10007   Edward M. O'Connell, Law Libn.

NEW YORK COUNTY SURROGATE'S COURT - LAW LIBRARY †
31 Chambers St., Rm. 401   Phone: (212) 374-8275
New York, NY 10007   Nadine A. Dubson, Libn.

NEW YORK DAILY NEWS - LIBRARY
220 E. 42nd St.   Phone: (212) 949-3569
New York, NY 10017   John C. Hodgson, Chf.Libn.

NEW YORK EYE AND EAR INFIRMARY - BERNARD SAMUELS LIBRARY
310 E. 14th St.   Phone: (212) 598-1431
New York, NY 10003   Miriam Adorno, Libn.

NEW YORK GENEALOGICAL AND BIOGRAPHICAL SOCIETY - GENEALOGICAL
  RESEARCH LIBRARY
122-6 E. 58th St.   Phone: (212) 755-8532
New York, NY 10022   James P. Gregory, Libn.

NEW-YORK HISTORICAL SOCIETY - LIBRARY
170 Central Park W.   Phone: (212) 873-3400
New York, NY 10024   Dr. Larry E. Sullivan, Libn.

NEW YORK HOSPITAL-CORNELL MEDICAL CENTER - OSKAR DIETHELM
  HISTORICAL LIBRARY
525 E. 68th St.   Phone: (212) 472-6434
New York, NY 10021   Phyllis Rubinton, Libn.

NEW YORK INFIRMARY BEEKMAN DOWNTOWN HOSPITAL - ELISHA
  WALKER STAFF LIBRARY
170 William St.   Phone: (212) 233-5300
New York, NY 10273   Lois Sook, Med.Libn.

NEW YORK LAW INSTITUTE - LIBRARY
120 Broadway, Rm. 932   Phone: (212) 732-8720
New York, NY 10005   Sieglinde H. Rothschild, Libn.

NEW YORK LAW SCHOOL - LIBRARY
57 Worth St.   Phone: (212) 966-3500
New York, NY 10013   Andrew Simak, Hd.Libn.

NEW YORK LIFE INSURANCE COMPANY - LAW LIBRARY
51 Madison Ave., Rm. 1101   Phone: (212) 576-6458
New York, NY 10010   Margaret Butler, Law Libn.

NEW YORK LIFE INSURANCE COMPANY - MEDICAL DEPARTMENT LIBRARY
51 Madison Ave.   Phone: (212) 576-6246
New York, NY 10010   Thomas Jernigan, M.D., Med.Dir.

NEW YORK LIFE INSURANCE COMPANY - NEW YORK LIFE LIBRARY
51 Madison Ave.   Phone: (212) 576-6738
New York, NY 10010   Gail W. Johnson, Sr.Libn.

NEW YORK MEDICAL COLLEGE - DEPARTMENT OF PSYCHIATRY - LIBRARY
Metropolitan Hospital Ctr.
1901 First Ave., Rm. 10M13   Phone: (212) 360-7285
New York, NY 10029   Lorna Macdonald, Libn.

NEW YORK ORTHOPAEDIC HOSPITAL - RUSSELL A. HIBBS LIBRARY
622 W. 168th St.   Phone: (212) 694-3294
New York, NY 10032   Jack E. Termine, Med.Libn.

NEW YORK POST - LIBRARY
210 South St.   Phone: (212) 349-5000
New York, NY 10002   Merrill F. Sherr, Hd.Libn.

NEW YORK PSYCHOANALYTIC INSTITUTE - ABRAHAM A. BRILL LIBRARY
247 E. Eighty-Second St.   Phone: (212) 879-6900
New York, NY 10028   Katharine B. Wolpe, Libn.

NEW YORK PUBLIC LIBRARY - ANNEX SECTION - NEWSPAPERS AND OTHER
  RESEARCH MATERIALS COLLECTION
521 W. 43rd St.   Phone: (212) 930-0847
New York, NY 10036   Richard L. Hill, First Asst., Annex

NEW YORK PUBLIC LIBRARY - ANNEX SECTION - PATENTS COLLECTION
521 W. 43rd St.   Phone: (212) 930-0850
New York, NY 10036   Richard L. Hill, First Asst., Annex

NEW YORK PUBLIC LIBRARY - ARENTS COLLECTION OF BOOKS IN PARTS
  AND ASSOCIATED MATERIALS
Fifth Ave. & 42nd St., Rm. 324   Phone: (212) 930-0801
New York, NY 10018   Joseph T. Rankin, Cur.

NEW YORK PUBLIC LIBRARY - ARENTS TOBACCO COLLECTION
Fifth Ave. & 42nd St., Rm. 324   Phone: (212) 930-0801
New York, NY 10018   Joseph T. Rankin, Cur.

NEW YORK PUBLIC LIBRARY - ART, PRINTS & PHOTOGRAPHS DIVISION -
  ART AND ARCHITECTURE COLLECTION
Fifth Ave. & 42nd St., Rm. 313   Phone: (212) 930-0834
New York, NY 10018   Joseph T. Rankin, Act.Chf.

NEW YORK PUBLIC LIBRARY - ART, PRINTS & PHOTOGRAPHS DIVISION -
  PRINT ROOM
Fifth Ave. & 42nd St., Rm. 308   Phone: (212) 930-0817
New York, NY 10018   Joseph T. Rankin, Act.Kpr.

NEW YORK PUBLIC LIBRARY - BERG COLLECTION
Fifth Ave. & 42nd St., Rm. 318, 320   Phone: (212) 930-0802
New York, NY 10018   Dr. Lola L. Szladits, Cur.

NEW YORK PUBLIC LIBRARY - DONNELL LIBRARY CENTER
20 W. 53rd St.   Phone: (212) 621-0613
New York, NY 10019   Philip Gerrard, Supv.Coord.Libn.

NEW YORK PUBLIC LIBRARY - DONNELL LIBRARY CENTER - CENTRAL
  CHILDREN'S ROOM
20 W. 53rd St.   Phone: (212) 621-0636
New York, NY 10019   Angeline Moscatt, Supv.Libn.

NEW YORK PUBLIC LIBRARY - DONNELL LIBRARY CENTER - FILM LIBRARY
20 W. 53rd St.   Phone: (212) 621-0609
New York, NY 10019   Marie Nesthus, Principal Libn.

NEW YORK PUBLIC LIBRARY - DONNELL LIBRARY CENTER - FOREIGN
  LANGUAGE LIBRARY
20 W. 53rd St.   Phone: (212) 621-0641
New York, NY 10019   Bosiljka Stevanovic, Supv.Libn.

NEW YORK PUBLIC LIBRARY - DONNELL LIBRARY CENTER - NATHAN
  STRAUS YOUNG ADULT LIBRARY
20 W. 53rd St.   Phone: (212) 621-0633
New York, NY 10019   Beryl Eber, Supv.Libn.

NEW YORK PUBLIC LIBRARY - DONNELL LIBRARY CENTER - RECORD
  LIBRARY
20 W. 53rd St.   Phone: (212) 621-0624
New York, NY 10019   Margaret Pyle Greenhall, Supv.Libn.

NEW YORK PUBLIC LIBRARY - EARLY CHILDHOOD RESOURCE AND
  INFORMATION CENTER
66 Leroy St.   Phone: (212) 929-0815
New York, NY 10014   Hannah N. Scheffler, Dir.

NEW YORK PUBLIC LIBRARY - ECONOMIC AND PUBLIC AFFAIRS DIVISION
Fifth Ave. & 42nd St., Rm. 228   Phone: (212) 930-0750
New York, NY 10018   Edward Di Roma, Div.Chf.

NEW YORK PUBLIC LIBRARY - GENERAL LIBRARY OF THE PERFORMING
  ARTS
111 Amsterdam Ave.   Phone: (212) 870-1630
New York, NY 10023   George L. Mayer, Coord.

NEW YORK PUBLIC LIBRARY - GENERAL RESEARCH DIVISION
Fifth Ave. & 42nd St.   Phone: (212) 930-0831
New York, NY 10011   Rodney Phillips, Chf.

NEW YORK PUBLIC LIBRARY - JEWISH DIVISION
Fifth Ave. & 42nd St., Rm. 84   Phone: (212) 930-0601
New York, NY 10018   Leonard S. Gold, Div.Chf.

NEW YORK PUBLIC LIBRARY - LOCAL HISTORY AND GENEALOGY DIVISION
Fifth Ave. & 42nd St., Rm. 315G   Phone: (212) 930-0829
New York, NY 10018   Gunther E. Pohl, Div.Chf.

NEW YORK PUBLIC LIBRARY - MAP DIVISION
Fifth Ave. & 42nd St., Rm. 117   Phone: (212) 930-0587
New York, NY 10018   Gerard L. Alexander, Div.Chf.

NEW YORK PUBLIC LIBRARY - MICROFORM DIVISION
Fifth Ave. & 42nd St.   Phone: (212) 930-0838
New York, NY 10018   Thomas Bourke, Chf.

NEW YORK PUBLIC LIBRARY - MID-MANHATTAN LIBRARY
455 Fifth Ave.   Phone: (212) 340-0833
New York, NY 10016   Julia J. Brody, Chf.

NEW YORK PUBLIC LIBRARY - MID-MANHATTAN LIBRARY - ART LIBRARY
455 Fifth Ave.   Phone: (212) 790-6486
New York, NY 10016   Rebecca Siekevitz, Supv.Libn.

GEOGRAPHIC

NEW YORK PUBLIC LIBRARY - MID-MANHATTAN LIBRARY - GENERAL
REFERENCE SERVICE/EDUCATION
455 Fifth Ave.   Phone: (212) 340-0861
New York, NY 10016   Eleanor Radwan, Sr. Principal Libn.

NEW YORK PUBLIC LIBRARY - MID-MANHATTAN LIBRARY - HISTORY AND
SOCIAL SCIENCES DEPARTMENT
455 Fifth Ave.   Phone: (212) 340-0890
New York, NY 10016   Robert C. Sheehan, Sr. Principal Libn.

NEW YORK PUBLIC LIBRARY - MID-MANHATTAN LIBRARY - LEARNER'S
ADVISORY SERVICE
455 Fifth Ave.   Phone: (212) 340-0835
New York, NY 10016   Barbara Shapiro, Supv.Libn.

NEW YORK PUBLIC LIBRARY - MID-MANHATTAN LIBRARY - LITERATURE
AND LANGUAGE DEPARTMENT
455 Fifth Ave.   Phone: (212) 340-0875
New York, NY 10016   Eric Steele, Sr. Principal Libn.

NEW YORK PUBLIC LIBRARY - MID-MANHATTAN LIBRARY - PICTURE
COLLECTION
455 Fifth Ave.   Phone: (212) 790-6101
New York, NY 10016   Lenore Cowan, Cur.

NEW YORK PUBLIC LIBRARY - MID-MANHATTAN LIBRARY - PROJECT
ACCESS
455 Fifth Ave.   Phone: (212) 340-0843
New York, NY 10016   Belle Weinberg, Sr.Libn.

NEW YORK PUBLIC LIBRARY - MID-MANHATTAN LIBRARY - READERS'
ADVISER'S OFFICE
455 Fifth Ave.   Phone: (212) 340-0866
New York, NY 10016   Adele Greenberg, Rd.Adv.

NEW YORK PUBLIC LIBRARY - MID-MANHATTAN LIBRARY - SCIENCE/
BUSINESS DEPARTMENT
455 Fifth Ave.   Phone: (212) 340-0873
New York, NY 10016   Donald G. Alexis, Supv.Libn./Bus.Coll.

NEW YORK PUBLIC LIBRARY - ORIENTAL DIVISION
Fifth Ave. & 42nd St., Rm. 219   Phone: (212) 930-0716
New York, NY 10018   E. Christian Filstrup, Div.Chf.

NEW YORK PUBLIC LIBRARY - PERFORMING ARTS RESEARCH CENTER -
BILLY ROSE THEATRE COLLECTION
111 Amsterdam Ave.   Phone: (212) 870-1639
New York, NY 10023   Dorothy Swerdlove, Cur.

NEW YORK PUBLIC LIBRARY - PERFORMING ARTS RESEARCH CENTER -
DANCE COLLECTION
111 Amsterdam Ave.   Phone: (212) 799-2200
New York, NY 10023   Genevieve Oswald, Cur.

NEW YORK PUBLIC LIBRARY - PERFORMING ARTS RESEARCH CENTER -
MUSIC DIVISION
111 Amsterdam Ave.   Phone: (212) 870-1650
New York, NY 10023   Frank C. Campbell, Chf.

NEW YORK PUBLIC LIBRARY - PERFORMING ARTS RESEARCH CENTER -
RODGERS & HAMMERSTEIN ARCHIVES OF RECORDED SOUND
111 Amsterdam Ave.   Phone: (212) 799-2200
New York, NY 10023   David Hall, Chf.

NEW YORK PUBLIC LIBRARY - RARE BOOKS & MANUSCRIPTS DIVISION -
MANUSCRIPTS AND ARCHIVES COLLECTION
476 Fifth Ave., Rm. 319   Phone: (212) 930-0804
New York, NY 10018

NEW YORK PUBLIC LIBRARY - RARE BOOKS & MANUSCRIPTS DIVISION -
RARE BOOK COLLECTION
Fifth Ave. & 42nd St.   Phone: (212) 930-0820
New York, NY 10018

NEW YORK PUBLIC LIBRARY - REGIONAL LIBRARY FOR THE BLIND AND
PHYSICALLY HANDICAPPED
166 Ave. of the Americas   Phone: (212) 925-1014
New York, NY 10013   Barbara Nugent, Regional Br.Libn.

NEW YORK PUBLIC LIBRARY - SCHOMBURG CENTER FOR RESEARCH IN
BLACK CULTURE
515 Lenox Ave.   Phone: (212) 862-4000
New York, NY 10037   John Miller, Act.Chf.

NEW YORK PUBLIC LIBRARY - SCIENCE AND TECHNOLOGY RESEARCH
CENTER
Fifth Ave. & 42nd St., Rm. 121   Phone: (212) 930-0573
New York, NY 10018   Robert G. Krupp, Chf.

NEW YORK PUBLIC LIBRARY - SLAVONIC DIVISION
Fifth Ave. & 42nd St., Rm. 216, 223   Phone: (212) 930-0714
New York, NY 10018   Dr. Victor Koressaar, Div.Chf.

NEW YORK PUBLIC LIBRARY - SPENCER COLLECTION
Fifth Ave. & 42nd St., Rm. 324   Phone: (212) 930-0801
New York, NY 10018   Joseph T. Rankin, Cur.

NEW YORK SOCIETY LIBRARY
53 E. 79th St.   Phone: (212) 288-6900
New York, NY 10021   Mark Piel, Libn.

NEW YORK STATE DEPARTMENT OF LABOR - LABOR STAFF ACADEMY
LIBRARY
2 World Trade Ctr., Rm. 34-18   Phone: (212) 488-2689
New York, NY 10047   Ms. R. Ashley Hibbard, Asst.Libn.

NEW YORK STATE DEPARTMENT OF LABOR - RESEARCH LIBRARY
2 World Trade Ctr., Rm. 6826   Phone: (212) 488-6295
New York, NY 10047   Gloria Weinrich, Sr.Libn.

NEW YORK STATE DEPARTMENT OF LABOR - WORKERS' COMPENSATION
BOARD - LIBRARY
2 World Trade Ctr.
39th Fl., Rm. 3901   Phone: (212) 488-3103
New York, NY 10047   Donald H. Holley, Assoc. Attorney

NEW YORK STATE DEPARTMENT OF LAW - NEW YORK CITY LIBRARY
2 World Trade Center, Rm. 4749   Phone: (212) 488-7446
New York, NY 10047   Joan Kain, Sr.Libn.

NEW YORK STATE DIVISION OF HOUSING AND COMMUNITY RENEWAL -
REFERENCE ROOM
2 World Trade Center, 60th Fl.   Phone: (212) 488-4968
New York, NY 10047   William T. Mikell, Sr. Clerk

NEW YORK STATE DIVISION OF HUMAN RIGHTS - REFERENCE LIBRARY
2 World Trade Center, 53rd Fl.   Phone: (212) 488-5372
New York, NY 10047

NEW YORK STATE DIVISION OF SUBSTANCE ABUSE SERVICES - BUREAU
OF TRAINING & RESOURCE DEVELOPMENT - RESOURCE CENTER
350 Broadway, 4th Fl.   Phone: (212) 966-7600
New York, NY 10013   Binu Chaudhuri, Res.Ctr.Coord.

NEW YORK STATE METROPOLITAN TRANSPORTATION AUTHORITY -
LIBRARY
347 Madison Ave., 10th Fl.   Phone: (212) 878-7414
New York, NY 10017   Erwyn Khan, Libn.

NEW YORK STATE OFFICE OF MENTAL HEALTH - NEW YORK STATE
PSYCHIATRIC INSTITUTE - LIBRARY
722 W. 168 St.   Phone: (212) 568-4000
New York, NY 10032   James W. Montgomery, Dir.

NEW YORK STATE SUPREME COURT - APPELLATE DIVISION, 1ST JUDICIAL
DEPARTMENT - LAW LIBRARY
27 Madison Ave.   Phone: (212) 532-1000
New York, NY 10010   Stephen R. Grotsky, Libn.

NEW YORK STATE TRIAL LAWYERS ASSOCIATION - LIBRARY
132 Nassau St., Suite 200
New York, NY 10038   Anne J. Quashen, Exec.Dir.

NEW YORK STOCK EXCHANGE - RESEARCH LIBRARY †
11 Wall St., Rm. 1702   Phone: (212) 623-5049
New York, NY 10005   Jean E. Tobin, Libn.

NEW YORK TELEPHONE COMPANY - LAW LIBRARY
1095 Ave. of the Americas   Phone: (212) 395-6158
New York, NY 10036   Cornelia E. Mahon, Law Libn.

NEW YORK THEOLOGICAL SEMINARY - LIBRARY
5 W. 29th St.   Phone: (212) 532-4012
New York, NY 10001   Eleanor Soler, Libn.

NEW YORK TIMES - CORPORATE RECORDS LIBRARY
229 W. 43rd St.   Phone: (212) 556-1958
New York, NY 10036   Daniel J. McGlynn, Corp. Records Mgr.

NEW YORK TIMES - MUSEUM OF THE PRINTED WORD
229 W. 43rd St.
New York, NY 10036

NEW YORK TIMES - PHOTO LIBRARY
229 W. 43rd St.   Phone: (212) 556-7220
New York, NY 10036   Arthur Aaron, Supv.

NEW YORK TIMES - REFERENCE LIBRARY
229 W. 43rd St.   Phone: (212) 556-7428
New York, NY 10036

NEW YORK UNIVERSITY - COURANT INSTITUTE OF MATHEMATICAL
    SCIENCES - LIBRARY
251 Mercer St.   Phone: (212) 460-7301
New York, NY 10012   Nancy Gubman, Dir.

NEW YORK UNIVERSITY - DENTAL CENTER - JOHN & BERTHA E.
    WALDMANN MEMORIAL LIBRARY
345 E. 24th St.   Phone: (212) 481-5874
New York, NY 10010   Roy C. Johnson, Libn.

NEW YORK UNIVERSITY - ELMER HOLMES BOBST LIBRARY - FROST
    LIBRARY
70 Washington Square South   Phone: (212) 598-3756
New York, NY 10012   Dr. John Frost, Cur.

NEW YORK UNIVERSITY - FALES LIBRARY - DIVISION OF SPECIAL
    COLLECTIONS
Bobst Library
70 Washington Sq., S.   Phone: (212) 598-3756
New York, NY 10012   Dr. Theodore Grieder, Cur.

NEW YORK UNIVERSITY - FILM LIBRARY
26 Washington Pl.   Phone: (212) 598-2251
New York, NY 10003   Daniel Lesser, Dir.

NEW YORK UNIVERSITY - GRADUATE SCHOOL OF BUSINESS
    ADMINISTRATION - LIBRARY
100 Trinity Pl.   Phone: (212) 285-6230
New York, NY 10006   Ronald F. Dow, Dir.

NEW YORK UNIVERSITY - INSTITUTE OF FINE ARTS - PHOTOGRAPHIC
    ARCHIVE
1 East 78th St.   Phone: (212) 988-5550
New York, NY 10021   Suzanne Babineau-Simenauer, Cur.

NEW YORK UNIVERSITY MEDICAL CENTER - FREDERICK L. EHRMAN
    MEDICAL LIBRARY
550 First Ave.   Phone: (212) 340-5393
New York, NY 10016   Gilbert J. Clausman, Libn.

NEW YORK UNIVERSITY - SCHOOL OF LAW LIBRARY
40 Washington Sq., S.   Phone: (212) 598-3040
New York, NY 10012   Julius J. Marke, Law Libn.

NEW YORK UNIVERSITY - STEPHEN CHAN LIBRARY OF FINE ARTS
1 E. 78th St.   Phone: (212) 988-5550
New York, NY 10021   Evelyn Samuel, Hd.Libn.

NEW YORK UNIVERSITY - TAMIMENT LIBRARY
70 Washington Sq., S.   Phone: (212) 598-3708
New York, NY 10012   Dorothy Swanson, Libn.

NEW YORK UNIVERSITY - UNITED NATIONS COLLECTION
Bobst Library
70 Washington Sq., S.   Phone: (212) 598-3609
New York, NY 10012   Peter B. Allison, Docs.Libn.

NEW ZEALAND CONSULATE GENERAL - LIBRARY
630 Fifth Ave., Suite 530   Phone: (212) 586-0060
New York, NY 10111   Nicholas Lorimer, Info. Officer

NEWMONT MINING CORPORATION - TECHNICAL ENGINEERING LIBRARY
300 Park Ave.   Phone: (212) 980-1111
New York, NY 10022   Loretta Herrmann, Libn.

NEWSOM (Earl) & COMPANY, INC. - LIBRARY
10 East 53rd St.   Phone: (212) 755-4664
New York, NY 10022   Joan M. Reicherter, Libn.

NEWSPAPER ADVERTISING BUREAU, INC. - INFORMATION CENTER
485 Lexington Ave.   Phone: (212) 557-1822
New York, NY 10017   Ann Brady, Hd., Info.Ctr.

NEWSPAPER COMICS COUNCIL - LIBRARY AND INFORMATION CENTER
260 Madison Ave.   Phone: (212) 689-8210
New York, NY 10016   Mrs. T.G. Keller, Libn.

NEWSWEEK, INC. - LIBRARY
444 Madison Ave.   Phone: (212) 350-2494
New York, NY 10022   Ted Slate, Lib.Dir.

92ND STREET YOUNG MEN'S AND YOUNG WOMEN'S HEBREW
    ASSOCIATION - BUTTENWIESER LIBRARY
1395 Lexington Ave.   Phone: (212) 427-6000
New York, NY 10028   Susan Vogelstein, Lib.Dir.

NORTH AMERICAN JEWISH STUDENTS' NETWORK - NEW JEWISH MEDIA
    PROJECT - LIBRARY
1 Park Ave., Suite 418   Phone: (212) 679-0600
New York, NY 10016

NORTH AMERICAN PHILIPS CORPORATION - LIBRARY
100 E. 42nd St.
New York, NY 10017

NORTH GENERAL HOSPITAL - MEDICAL LIBRARY
1919 Madison Ave.   Phone: (212) 650-4000
New York, NY 10035   Jana Martin, Med.Libn.

OGILVY & MATHER, INC. - RESEARCH LIBRARY
2 E. 48th St.   Phone: (212) 688-6100
New York, NY 10017   Joanne Winiarski, Hd.Libn.

OLWINE, CONNELLY, CHASE, O'DONNELL & WEYHER - LAW LIBRARY
299 Park Ave.   Phone: (212) 688-0400
New York, NY 10171   Martin Cullen, Libn.

ONE TO ONE - RESOURCE CENTER
One Lincoln Plaza
63rd & Broadway   Phone: (212) 874-2410
New York, NY 10023   Mariette Bates, Resource Ctr.Coord.

OPPENHEIMER & CO., INC. - LIBRARY †
One New York Plaza, 32nd Fl.   Phone: (212) 825-4264
New York, NY 10004   Carter Crawford, Libn.

ORGANIZATION RESOURCES COUNSELORS, INC. - INFORMATION CENTER
1211 Ave. of the Americas   Phone: (212) 575-7511
New York, NY 10036   Mary J. DuVal, Libn.

OXFORD UNIVERSITY PRESS, INC. - LIBRARY
200 Madison Ave.   Phone: (212) 679-7300
New York, NY 10016   Clare Marie Hess, Libn.

PACE UNIVERSITY - LIBRARY
Pace Plaza   Phone: (212) 285-3331
New York, NY 10038   Henry Birnbaum, Univ.Libn.

PACKAGING INSTITUTE, USA - LIBRARY AND RESOURCE CENTER
20 E. 46th St., Suite 603   Phone: (212) 687-8874
New York, NY 10017   Harold M. Beckman, Exec.Dir.

PAINE WEBBER INC. - PAINE WEBBER BLYTH EASTMAN - LIBRARY
1221 Ave. of the Americas   Phone: (212) 730-8839
New York, NY 10020   Barbara A. Fody, Hd.Libn.

PAINE WEBBER INC. - PAINE WEBBER MITCHELL HUTCHINS - LIBRARY
140 Broadway   Phone: (212) 437-7465
New York, NY 10005   June Fackler, Libn.

PAN AMERICAN WORLD AIRWAYS - CORPORATE LIBRARY
200 Park Ave., Rm. 904   Phone: (212) 880-1917
New York, NY 10017   Liwa Chiu, Libn.

PANNELL KERR FORSTER - LIBRARY
420 Lexington Ave.   Phone: (212) 867-8000
New York, NY 10017   Eleanor Sabo, Libn.

PARADE PUBLICATIONS, INC. - LIBRARY
750 Third Ave., 7th Fl.   Phone: (212) 573-7188
New York, NY 10017   Paul Cook, Lib.Dir.

PARAPSYCHOLOGY FOUNDATION - EILEEN J. GARRETT LIBRARY
228 E. 71st St.   Phone: (212) 628-1550
New York, NY 10021   Wayne Norman, Libn.

PARK AVENUE SYNAGOGUE - ROTHSCHILD LIBRARY
50 E. 87th St.   Phone: (212) 369-2600
New York, NY 10028   Amy Louise Frey, Libn.

PARKER, CHAPIN, FLATTAU AND KLIMPL - LIBRARY †
530 Fifth Ave.   Phone: (212) 840-6200
New York, NY 10036   Helene W. Nelson, Libn.

PARSONS, BRINCKERHOFF, QUADE & DOUGLAS - LIBRARY
250 W. 34th St.   Phone: (212) 239-6458
New York, NY 10001   Sarah L. Warner, Libn.

PARSONS SCHOOL OF DESIGN - ADAM L. GIMBEL DESIGN LIBRARY
66 Fifth Ave.   Phone: (212) 741-8914
New York, NY 10011   Christiane C. Collins, Hd.Libn.

PAUL, WEISS, RIFKIND, WHARTON AND GARRISON - LIBRARY
345 Park Ave.   Phone: (212) 644-8235
New York, NY 10022   Paul B. Gloeckner, Chf.Libn.

PAYNE WHITNEY PSYCHIATRIC CLINIC LIBRARY
New York Hospital
525 E. 68th St.   Phone: (212) 472-6442
New York, NY 10021   Phyllis Rubinton, Libn.

PEAT, MARWICK, MITCHELL & COMPANY - ACCOUNTING AND AUDITING
     LIBRARY
345 Park Ave.   Phone: (212) 872-5982
New York, NY 10022   Michael J. Ready, Hd.Libn.

PEN AND BRUSH INC. - LIBRARY
16 E. Tenth St.   Phone: (212) 475-3669
New York, NY 10003   Mercy Dobell Wolfe, Pres.

PENNEY (J.C.) COMPANY, INC. - LAW LIBRARY
1301 Ave. of the Americas   Phone: (212) 957-8488
New York, NY 10019   Teresa E. Wrenn, Law Libn.

PENNIE & EDMONDS - LAW LIBRARY
330 Madison Ave.   Phone: (212) 986-8686
New York, NY 10017   Jurate Antioco, Libn.

PERSHING & CO. INC. - RESEARCH LIBRARY †
120 Broadway   Phone: (212) 902-3000
New York, NY 10005   Lourdes E. Baez, Libn.

P'EYLIM-AMERICAN YESHIVA STUDENT UNION - LIBRARY
3 W. 16th St.
New York, NY 10011

PFIZER, INC. - PFIZER PHARMACEUTICALS LIBRARY
235 E. 42nd St.   Phone: (212) 573-2966
New York, NY 10017   Charlotte Baran, Mgr., Prof.Info.

PFORZHEIMER (Carl & Lily) FOUNDATION, INC. - CARL H. PFORZHEIMER
     LIBRARY
41 E. 42nd St., Rm. 815   Phone: (212) 697-7217
New York, NY 10017   Mihai H. Handrea, Libn.

PHOTO RESEARCHERS, INC. - LIBRARY
60 E. 56th St.   Phone: (212) 758-3420
New York, NY 10022   Jane S. Kinne, Pres.

PHOTO TRENDS - LIBRARY
1328 Broadway   Phone: (212) 279-2130
New York, NY 10001   R. Eugene Keesee, Owner

PICTORIAL PARADE INC. - LIBRARY
130 W. 42nd St.   Phone: (212) 840-2026
New York, NY 10036   Baer M. Frimer, Pres.

PIERPONT MORGAN LIBRARY
29 E. 36th St.   Phone: (212) 685-0008
New York, NY 10016   Charles A. Ryskamp, Dir.

PILSUDSKI (Jozef) INSTITUTE OF AMERICA FOR RESEARCH IN THE
     MODERN HISTORY OF POLAND - LIBRARY
381 Park Ave., S.   Phone: (212) 683-4342
New York, NY 10016   Michael Budny, V.P.

PLANNED PARENTHOOD FEDERATION OF AMERICA, INC. - KATHARINE
     DEXTER MC CORMICK LIBRARY
810 Seventh Ave.   Phone: (212) 541-7800
New York, NY 10019   Gloria A. Roberts, Hd. Libn.

POETRY SOCIETY OF AMERICA - VAN VOORHIS LIBRARY
15 Gramercy Park   Phone: (212) 254-9628
New York, NY 10003   Deborah Gimelson, Adm.Dir.

POINT OF PURCHASE ADVERTISING INSTITUTE - INFORMATION CENTER
60 E. 42nd St.   Phone: (212) 682-7041
New York, NY 10165   Howard Stumpf, Pres.

POLISH INSTITUTE OF ARTS AND SCIENCES IN AMERICA, INC. -
     RESEARCH LIBRARY †
59 E. 66th St.   Phone: (212) 988-4338
New York, NY 10021

POPULATION COUNCIL - BIO-MEDICAL LIBRARY †
Rockefeller University
York Ave. & 66th St.   Phone: (212) 570-8000
New York, NY 10021

POPULATION COUNCIL - LIBRARY
1 Dag Hammarskjold Plaza   Phone: (212) 644-1620
New York, NY 10017   H. Neil Zimmerman, Libn.

PORT AUTHORITY OF NEW YORK AND NEW JERSEY - LIBRARY
55 N., One World Trade Ctr.   Phone: (212) 466-4062
New York, NY 10048   Jane M. Janiak, Chf.Libn.

POSTGRADUATE CENTER FOR MENTAL HEALTH - EMIL A. GUTHEIL
     MEMORIAL LIBRARY
124 E. 28th St.   Phone: (212) 689-7700
New York, NY 10016   Mrs. Lee Mackler, Dir. of Lib.

PRACTISING LAW INSTITUTE - LIBRARY
810 Seventh Ave.   Phone: (212) 765-5700
New York, NY 10019   Henry W. Enberg, II, Legal Ed.

PRATT INSTITUTE - PRATT/PHOENIX SCHOOL OF DESIGN LIBRARY
160 Lexington Ave.   Phone: (212) 685-2973
New York, NY 10016   Peter Kelley, Coord.

PRICE WATERHOUSE - NATIONAL INFORMATION CENTER
1251 Ave. of the Americas   Phone: (212) 489-8900
New York, NY 10020   Masha Zipper, Mgr.

PRICE WATERHOUSE - NEW YORK OFFICE INFORMATION CENTER
153 E. 53rd St.   Phone: (212) 371-2000
New York, NY 10022   Patricia R. Pauth, Adm.

PRICE WATERHOUSE - TAX LIBRARY
153 E. 53rd St.   Phone: (212) 371-2000
New York, NY 10022   Deborah A. Cappiello, Tax Libn.

PRINCETON LIBRARY IN NEW YORK
15 W. 43rd St.   Phone: (212) 840-6400
New York, NY 10036   Paula Matta, Libn.

PROGRAM PLANNERS, INC. - LIBRARY/INFORMATION CENTER
230 W. 41st St.   Phone: (212) 840-2600
New York, NY 10036   Stanley Grill, Libn.

PROGRESSIVE GROCER - RESEARCH LIBRARY
708 Third Ave.   Phone: (212) 490-1000
New York, NY 10017   Shirley Palmer, Res.Libn.

PROJECT FOR PUBLIC SPACES - LIBRARY
875 Ave. of the Americas   Phone: (212) 581-6553
New York, NY 10001   Kathleen Love, Res.Dir.

PROSKAUER, ROSE, GOETZ & MENDELSOHN - LIBRARY
300 Park Ave.   Phone: (212) 593-9400
New York, NY 10022   Marsha Pront, Hd.Libn.

PROTESTANT EPISCOPAL CHURCH - EPISCOPAL DIOCESE OF NEW YORK -
    ARCHIVES
1047 Amsterdam Ave.   Phone: (212) 678-6977
New York, NY 10025   Judith Johnson, Archv.

PROTESTANT EPISCOPAL CHURCH EXECUTIVE COUNCIL - HENRY KNOX
    SHERRILL RESOURCE CENTER
Episcopal Church Center
815 Second Ave.   Phone: (212) 867-8400
New York, NY 10017   Avis E. Harvey, Rsrcs./Info.Off.

PUBLIC AFFAIRS INFORMATION SERVICE
11 W. 40th St.   Phone: (212) 736-6629
New York, NY 10018   Wilhelm Bartenbach, Exec.Dir.

PUBLIC EDUCATION ASSOCIATION - LIBRARY
20 W. 40th St.   Phone: (212) 354-6100
New York, NY 10018   Judith Baum, Libn.

PUBLIC RELATIONS SOCIETY OF AMERICA - INFORMATION CENTER
845 Third Ave.   Phone: (212) 826-1776
New York, NY 10022   Mary W. Wilson, Dir.

PUTNEY, TWOMBLY, HALL & HIRSON - LAW LIBRARY
250 Park Ave.   Phone: (212) 661-8700
New York, NY 10017

RACQUET AND TENNIS CLUB - LIBRARY
370 Park Ave.   Phone: (212) 753-9700
New York, NY 10022   Gerard J. Belliveau, Jr., Libn.

RADIO ADVERTISING BUREAU - MARKETING INFORMATION CENTER
485 Lexington Ave.   Phone: (212) 599-6659
New York, NY 10017   Irene Kossowsky, Dir.

RADIO FREE EUROPE/RADIO LIBERTY - REFERENCE LIBRARY
1775 Broadway   Phone: (212) 397-5343
New York, NY 10019   Irene V. Dutikow, Dir.

RAILROAD ENTHUSIASTS NEW YORK DIVISION, INC. - WILLIAMSON
    LIBRARY
Box 1318
New York, NY 10017   Charles Grossman, Libn.

READER'S DIGEST - ADVERTISING AND MARKETING LIBRARY
200 Park Ave.   Phone: (212) 972-3730
New York, NY 10017   Helen Fledderus, Libn.

RECORDING FOR THE BLIND, INC. - MASTER TAPE LIBRARY
215 E. 58th St.   Phone: (212) 751-0860
New York, NY 10022   Sandra J. Bonner, Dir. of Lib.Serv.

RECORDING INDUSTRY ASSOCIATION OF AMERICA - REFERENCE LIBRARY
888 7th Ave., 9th Fl.   Phone: (212) 765-4330
New York, NY 10019   Stephen Traiman, Exec.Dir.

REFERENCE PICTURES, INC.
100 Fifth Ave.   Phone: (212) 242-9535
New York, NY 10011   Dolph Morse, Pres.

REGIONAL PLAN ASSOCIATION, INC. - LIBRARY
235 E. 45th St.   Phone: (212) 682-7750
New York, NY 10017   Thelma Vanderberg, Libn.

REID AND PRIEST - LAW LIBRARY
40 Wall St.   Phone: (212) 344-2233
New York, NY 10005   Morton Barad, Libn.

RELIGIOUS NEWS SERVICE - LIBRARY AND MORGUE
43 W. 57th St.   Phone: (212) 688-7094
New York, NY 10019

RELIGIOUS NEWS SERVICE - PHOTOGRAPH LIBRARY
43 W. 57th St.   Phone: (212) 688-7094
New York, NY 10019   Jim Hansen, Hd.

REPERTOIRE INTERNATIONAL D'ICONOGRAPHIE MUSICALE - RESEARCH
    CENTER FOR MUSICAL ICONOGRAPHY - LIBRARY
Grad. Ctr., CUNY, Dept. of Music
33 W. 42nd St.   Phone: (212) 790-4282
New York, NY 10036

RESEARCH CENTER FOR RELIGION & HUMAN RIGHTS IN CLOSED
    SOCIETIES - INFORMATION CENTER
475 Riverside Dr., Suite 448   Phone: (212) 870-2481
New York, NY 10115   Rev. B.S. Hruby, Exec.Dir.

RESEARCH & EDUCATION ASSOCIATION - LIBRARY
505 Eighth Ave.   Phone: (212) 695-9487
New York, NY 10018   C. Fuchs

RESEARCH FOUNDATION FOR JEWISH IMMIGRATION, INC. - ARCHIVES
570 7th Ave., 16th Fl.   Phone: (212) 869-8611
New York, NY 10018   Herbert A. Strauss, Coord. of Res.

RESEARCH INSTITUTE OF AMERICA - INFORMATION SERVICES CENTER
589 Fifth Ave.   Phone: (212) 755-8900
New York, NY 10017   C.B. Hayden, Adm. of Info.Serv.

RESEARCH INSTITUTE FOR THE STUDY OF MAN - LIBRARY
162 E. 78th St.   Phone: (212) 535-8448
New York, NY 10021   Judith Selakoff, Libn.

ROCKEFELLER FOUNDATION - LIBRARY
1133 Ave. of the Americas   Phone: (212) 869-8500
New York, NY 10036   Muriel Regan, Libn.

ROCKEFELLER UNIVERSITY - LIBRARY
1230 York Ave.   Phone: (212) 360-1274
New York, NY 10021   Sonya Wohl Mirsky, Libn./Cur., Spec.Coll.

ROGERS & WELLS - LAW LIBRARY
200 Park Ave.   Phone: (212) 972-5432
New York, NY 10166   Raphael Gonzalez, Libn.

ROMANIAN LIBRARY
200 E. 38th St.   Phone: (212) 687-0180
New York, NY 10016   Adrian Petrescu, Dir.

ROOSEVELT HOSPITAL - MEDICAL LIBRARY
428 W. 59th St.   Phone: (212) 554-6872
New York, NY 10019   Winifred Lieber, Libn.

ROSENMAN, COLIN, FREUND, LEWIS & COHEN - LAW LIBRARY
575 Madison Ave.   Phone: (212) 644-7004
New York, NY 10022   John A. Coar, Adm.Libn.

ST. CLARE'S HOSPITAL & HEALTH CENTER - MEDICAL LIBRARY
415 W. 51st St.   Phone: (212) 586-1500
New York, NY 10019   Dianne Kovitz Weiss, Libn.

ST. LUKE'S HOSPITAL CENTER - NURSING LIBRARY
Amsterdam Ave. at 114th St.   Phone: (212) 870-6195
New York, NY 10025   Geraldine Allerman, Dir., Staff Educ.

ST. LUKE'S HOSPITAL CENTER - RICHARD WALKER BOLLING MEMORIAL
    MEDICAL LIBRARY
Amsterdam Ave. at 114th St.   Phone: (212) 870-1861
New York, NY 10025   Nancy Mary Panella, Libn.

ST. VINCENT'S HOSPITAL AND MEDICAL CENTER - MEDICAL LIBRARY
153 W. Eleventh St.   Phone: (212) 790-7811
New York, NY 10011   Agnes T. Frank, Dir.

ST. VINCENT'S HOSPITAL - SCHOOL OF NURSING LIBRARY
27 Christopher St.   Phone: (212) 790-8486
New York, NY 10014   Marie C. Medici, Libn.

SALES & MARKETING EXECUTIVES INTERNATIONAL - MARKETING
    INFORMATION CENTER
380 Lexington Ave.   Phone: (212) 986-9300
New York, NY 10168   Adele N. Bendes, Mgr.

SALES AND MARKETING MANAGEMENT - LIBRARY
633 Third Ave.   Phone: (212) 986-4800
New York, NY 10017   Aileen Jenkins, Libn.

SALMAGUNDI CLUB - LIBRARY
47 Fifth Ave.   Phone: (212) 255-7740
New York, NY 10003

SALOMON BROTHERS - CORPORATE FINANCE LIBRARY
One New York Plaza, 46th Fl.   Phone: (212) 747-7933
New York, NY 10004   Beverly J. Glad, V.P. & Dir.

SALVATION ARMY - ARCHIVES AND RESEARCH CENTER
145 W. 15th St.   Phone: (212) 620-4392
New York, NY 10011   Thomas Wilsted, Archv./Adm.

SALVATION ARMY - EDUCATION DEPARTMENT LIBRARY
120-130 W. 14th St.   Phone: (212) 620-4994
New York, NY 10011   Mrs. Major Gordon Sharp

SANDERSON AND PORTER - LIBRARY
26 Broadway, 10th Fl.
New York, NY 10004

SANGER (Margaret) CENTER-PLANNED PARENTHOOD NEW YORK CITY -
    ABRAHAM STONE LIBRARY
380 Second Ave.   Phone: (212) 677-6474
New York, NY 10010   Jeanne Swinton, Libn.

SCHOLASTIC MAGAZINES - EDITORIAL DEPARTMENT - LIBRARY
50 W. 44th St.   Phone: (212) 944-7700
New York, NY 10036   Lucy Evankow, Chf.Libn.

SCHOLASTIC MAGAZINES - SCHOLASTIC MATERIALS CENTER -
    CURRICULUM LIBRARY †
50 W. 44th St.   Phone: (212) 867-7700
New York, NY 10036

SCHOOL OF VISUAL ARTS - LIBRARY
209 E. 23rd St.   Phone: (212) 679-7350
New York, NY 10010   Zuki Landau, Chf.Libn.

SCHRODER (J. Henry) BANK & TRUST COMPANY - LIBRARY
One State St.   Phone: (212) 269-6500
New York, NY 10015   Juliette Levinton, Libn.

SCIENCE ASSOCIATES/INTERNATIONAL, INC. - LIBRARY
1841 Broadway   Phone: (212) 265-4995
New York, NY 10023   Roxy Bauer, Libn.

SCUDDER, STEVENS & CLARK - LIBRARY
345 Park Ave.   Phone: (212) 350-8371
New York, NY 10022   Jackie Malone, Libn.

SEAGRAM (Joseph E.) & SONS, INC. - CORPORATE LIBRARY
800 Third Ave.   Phone: (212) 572-7871
New York, NY 10022   Alice Gross, Corp.Libn.

SEAMEN'S CHURCH INSTITUTE OF NEW YORK - JOSEPH CONRAD LIBRARY
15 State St.   Phone: (212) 269-2710
New York, NY 10004   Robert S. Wolk, Libn.

SELIGMAN (J.&W.) & CO. INCORPORATED - RESEARCH LIBRARY
One Bankers Trust Pl.   Phone: (212) 432-4002
New York, NY 10006   Elena Eckhouse, Libn.

SEWARD & KISSEL - LIBRARY
Wall Street Plaza   Phone: (212) 248-2800
New York, NY 10005   Robert J. Davis, Libn.

SHEARMAN & STERLING - LIBRARY
53 Wall St., Rm. 718   Phone: (212) 483-1000
New York, NY 10005   Jack S. Ellenberger, Libn.

SHEARSON LOEB RHOADES, INC. - RESEARCH LIBRARY
14 Wall St.   Phone: (212) 577-5253
New York, NY 10005   Elizabeth R. Boutinon, Chf.Libn.

SHEVCHENKO SCIENTIFIC SOCIETY, INC. - LIBRARY AND ARCHIVES
302-304 W. 13th St.   Phone: (212) 929-7622
New York, NY 10014   Dr. Wasyl Lew, Dir.

SHOSTAL ASSOCIATES, INC.
60 E. 42nd St.   Phone: (212) 687-0696
New York, NY 10165

SIMAT, HELLIESEN, AND EICHNER - LIBRARY
708 Third Ave.   Phone: (212) 682-8455
New York, NY 10017   William J. Ehlers, Libn.

SIMPSON, THACHER & BARTLETT - LIBRARY †
1 Battery Park Plaza   Phone: (212) 483-9000
New York, NY 10004   John S. Marsh, Libn.

SIMULATIONS PUBLICATIONS, INC. - SPI MILITARY LIBRARY
257 Park Ave. S.   Phone: (212) 673-4103
New York, NY 10010   David J. Ritchie, Libn.

SKADDEN, ARPS, SLATE, MEAGHER & FLOM - LIBRARY
919 3rd Ave.   Phone: (212) 371-6000
New York, NY 10022   Carrie Hirtz, Libn.

SKIDMORE, OWINGS & MERRILL - LIBRARY
400 Park Ave.   Phone: (212) 759-2121
New York, NY 10028   Frances C. Gretes, Libn.

SMITH BARNEY, HARRIS UPHAM & COMPANY, INC. - LIBRARY
1345 Ave. of the Americas   Phone: (212) 399-6294
New York, NY 10105   Morton R. Brown, Libn.

SMITHSONIAN INSTITUTION LIBRARIES - COOPER-HEWITT MUSEUM OF
    DESIGN - DORIS & HENRY DREYFUSS MEMORIAL STUDY CENTER
2 E. 91st St.   Phone: (212) 860-6887
New York, NY 10028   Robert C. Kaufmann, Libn.

SMYTHE (R.M.) AND COMPANY - OBSOLETE AND INACTIVE SECURITIES
    LIBRARY
24 Broadway   Phone: (212) 668-1880
New York, NY 10004   Diana E. Herzog, Sec./Treas.

SOAP AND DETERGENT ASSOCIATION - LIBRARY
475 Park Ave., S. at 32nd St.   Phone: (212) 725-1262
New York, NY 10016   Rose D. Api, Off.Mgr.

SOCIETAS CAMPANARIORUM - LIBRARY
Riverside Church
490 Riverside Dr.   Phone: (212) 749-7000
New York, NY 10027   James R. Lawson, Libn.

SOCIETE CULINAIRE PHILANTHROPIQUE DE NEW YORK, INC. - LIBRARY
250 W. 57th St., Rm. 1532   Phone: (212) 246-6754
New York, NY 10019   Henri Deltieure, Pres.

SOCIETY OF COSMETIC CHEMISTS - LIBRARY
1995 Broadway, 17th Fl.   Phone: (212) 532-7320
New York, NY 10023   Dr. Hilda Feinberg, Chm., Lib.Comm.

SOCIETY OF FRIENDS - NEW YORK YEARLY MEETING - RECORDS
    COMMITTEE - HAVILAND RECORDS ROOM
15 Rutherford Pl.   Phone: (212) 673-6866
New York, NY 10003   Elizabeth Haas Moger, Kpr.

SOCIETY OF WOMEN ENGINEERS - INFORMATION CENTER
345 E. 47th St., Rm. 305   Phone: (212) 644-7855
New York, NY 10017

SOHO CENTER FOR VISUAL ARTISTS - LIBRARY
110 Prince St.   Phone: (212) 226-1993
New York, NY 10012   Kristen Cooney Crawford, Libn.

SONS OF THE REVOLUTION IN THE STATE OF NEW YORK - LIBRARY
Fraunces Tavern Museum
Broad & 54 Pearl Sts.   Phone: (212) 425-1776
New York, NY 10004

SOUTH STREET SEAPORT MUSEUM - LIBRARY
203 Front St.   Phone: (212) 766-9089
New York, NY 10038   Norman J. Brouwer, Ship Hist.

SPECIAL LIBRARIES ASSOCIATION - INFORMATION SERVICES
235 Park Ave., S.   Phone: (212) 477-9250
New York, NY 10003   Wanda D. Kemp, Mgr., Info.Serv.

SPENCE-CHAPIN SERVICES TO FAMILIES AND CHILDREN - CHARLOTTE
    TOWLE MEMORIAL LIBRARY
6 E. 94th St.   Phone: (212) 369-0300
New York, NY 10028   Leilani Straw, Asst.Dir.

SPERRY CORPORATION - BUSINESS PLANNING LIBRARY
1290 Avenue of the Americas   Phone: (212) 956-3476
New York, NY 10019   William C. Patterson, Dir.

SPERRY CORPORATION - LAW LIBRARY
1290 Avenue of the Americas   Phone: (212) 484-4444
New York, NY 10104   Rosemarie Scirica, Lib.Adm.

SPERRY CORPORATION - SPERRY UNIVAC NEW YORK TECHNICAL LIBRARY
1290 Avenue of the Americas   Phone: (212) 956-2060
New York, NY 10019   Robert G. Bertley, Libn.

SPERRY AND HUTCHINSON COMPANY - MARKET RESEARCH LIBRARY
330 Madison Ave., 9th Fl.   Phone: (212) 983-2000
New York, NY 10017   Mary J. LaFlare, Mgr., Lib.Serv.

STACK'S RARE COIN COMPANY OF NEW YORK - TECHNICAL INFORMATION
    CENTER
123 W. 57th St.   Phone: (212) 582-2580
New York, NY 10019   James C. Risk, Mgr., Tech.Oper.

STANDARD & POOR'S CORPORATION - LIBRARY
25 Broadway   Phone: (212) 248-3918
New York, NY 10004   Dennis F. Jensen, Lib.Mgr.

STEP FAMILY FOUNDATION, INC. - LIBRARY
333 West End Ave.   Phone: (212) 877-3244
New York, NY 10023   Jeannette Lofas, Exec.Dir.

STERLING DRUG, INC. - WINTHROP LABORATORIES - MEDICAL LIBRARY
90 Park Ave.   Phone: (212) 972-6256
New York, NY 10016   Irene Frisch, Lib.Dir.

STOCKPHOTOS, INC. - LIBRARY
60 E. 42nd St.   Phone: (212) 421-8980
New York, NY 10017   Lori Stevens, Dir.

STONE AND WEBSTER MANAGEMENT CONSULTANTS, INC. - INFORMATION
    CENTER/LIBRARY †
90 Broad St., 17th Fl.   Phone: (212) 269-4224
New York, NY 10004   Mrs. D.O. Wright, Mgr.

SULLIVAN AND CROMWELL - LIBRARY †
125 Broad St.   Phone: (212) 558-4000
New York, NY 10004   Helene A. Weatherill, Libn.

SUNY - COLLEGE OF OPTOMETRY - HAROLD KOHN MEMORIAL VISUAL
    SCIENCE LIBRARY
100 E. 24th St.   Phone: (212) 477-7965
New York, NY 10010   Margaret Lewis, Libn.

SWEDENBORG FOUNDATION - LIBRARY
139 E. 23rd St.   Phone: (212) 673-7310
New York, NY 10010   Darrell Ruhl, Exec.Dir.

SWEDISH CONSULATE GENERAL - SWEDISH INFORMATION SERVICE
825 Third Ave.   Phone: (212) 751-5900
New York, NY 10022   Ragnhild Wallin, Libn.

SYMMERS, FISH AND WARNER - RESEARCH LIBRARY
111 E. 50th St.   Phone: (212) 751-6400
New York, NY 10022   Roberta J. Anas, Hd.Libn.

TAMS ENGINEERS, ARCHITECTS & PLANNERS - LIBRARY
655 Third Ave.   Phone: (212) 867-1777
New York, NY 10017   Emily Candelmo, Libn.

TAYLOR BUSINESS INSTITUTE - LIBRARY
One Penn Plaza   Phone: (212) 279-0510
New York, NY 10001   Roslyn Arnstein, Libn.

TEACHERS COLLEGE - LIBRARY
Columbia University
Box 307   Phone: (212) 678-3494
New York, NY 10027   Jane P. Franck, Dir.

TEACHERS INSURANCE AND ANNUITY ASSOCIATION OF AMERICA -
    BUSINESS LIBRARY
730 Third Ave.   Phone: (212) 490-9000
New York, NY 10017   Kathleen Kelleher, Libn.

TELEVISION INFORMATION OFFICE OF THE NATIONAL ASSOCIATION OF
    BROADCASTERS - RESEARCH SERVICES †
745 Fifth Ave., 17th Fl.   Phone: (212) 759-6800
New York, NY 10022   James Poteat, Mgr., Res.Serv.

THOMPSON (J. Walter) COMPANY - INFORMATION CENTER
466 Lexington Ave.   Phone: (212) 210-7000
New York, NY 10017   Nancy Terry Munger, Mgr., Info.Serv.

THREE LIONS, INC. - LIBRARY *
150 Fifth Ave.   Phone: (212) 691-8640
New York, NY 10011

TIME, INC. - LIBRARY
Time & Life Bldg.
Rockefeller Center   Phone: (212) 556-3746
New York, NY 10020   Benjamin Lightman, Chf.Libn.

TIME, INC. - SPORTS LIBRARY
Radio City Sta., Box 614   Phone: (212) 841-3397
New York, NY 10019   Lester Annenberg, Hd.Libn.

TOBACCO MERCHANTS ASSOCIATION OF THE U.S. - HOWARD S. CULLMAN
    LIBRARY
1220 Broadway   Phone: (212) 239-4435
New York, NY 10001   R. Robert Sengstacken, Libn.

TOUCHE ROSS AND COMPANY - BUSINESS LIBRARY
1633 Broadway   Phone: (212) 489-1600
New York, NY 10019   Harold W. Miller, Chf.Libn.

TOWERS, PERRIN, FORSTER & CROSBY, INC. - INFORMATION CENTER
600 Third Ave.   Phone: (212) 661-5080
New York, NY 10016   Joseph M. Simmons, Mgr.

TOWNSEND-GREENSPAN & COMPANY, INC. - LIBRARY
1 New York Plaza, 35th Fl.   Phone: (212) 943-9515
New York, NY 10004   Janet L. Waitz, Libn.

TRANS WORLD AIRLINES, INC. - CORPORATE LIBRARY
605 Third Ave.   Phone: (212) 557-6055
New York, NY 10158   Esther L. Giles, Corp.Libn.

TRAPHAGEN SCHOOL OF FASHION - LIBRARY
257 Park Ave., S.   Phone: (212) 673-0300
New York, NY 10010   Barbara German, Libn.

TRI-STATE REGIONAL PLANNING COMMISSION - LIBRARY
One World Trade Ctr., 82nd Fl.   Phone: (212) 938-3313
New York, NY 10048   Louise A. Heller, Libn.

GEOGRAPHIC

TURKISH TOURISM AND INFORMATION OFFICE
821 United Nations Plaza
New York, NY 10017
Phone: (212) 687-2194
Ibrahim Sipit, Dir.

TURTLE BAY MUSIC SCHOOL - LIBRARY
244 E. 52nd St.
New York, NY 10022
Phone: (212) 753-8811
Lilien Weintraub, Libn.

TWENTIETH CENTURY FUND - LIBRARY
41 E. 70th St.
New York, NY 10021
Phone: (212) 535-4441
Nettie Gerduk, Libn.

UKRAINIAN ENGINEERS SOCIETY OF AMERICA - LIBRARY
2 East 79th St.
New York, NY 10021
Phone: (212) 535-7676
Basil Mysak

UNION OF AMERICAN HEBREW CONGREGATIONS - SYNAGOGUE
ARCHITECTURAL AND ART LIBRARY
838 Fifth Ave.
New York, NY 10021
Phone: (212) 249-0100
Myron E. Schoen, Dir.

UNION CARBIDE CORPORATION - BUSINESS LIBRARY
270 Park Ave., Rm. 9-101
New York, NY 10017
Phone: (212) 551-4301
L. Arless Leve, Mgr.

UNION CARBIDE CORPORATION - LAW DEPARTMENT LIBRARY
270 Park Ave., 47th Fl.
New York, NY 10017
Phone: (212) 551-6472
Carolyn A. Lareau, Libn.

UNION CARBIDE CORPORATION - LINDE DIVISION - COMMUNICATIONS
LIBRARY
270 Park Ave.
New York, NY 10017
Phone: (212) 551-4604
Helen Walsh, Ldr., Res. Group

UNION CLUB - LIBRARY
101 E. 69th St.
New York, NY 10021
Phone: (212) 734-5400
Helen M. Allen, Libn.

UNION DIME SAVINGS BANK - INFORMATION CENTER
1065 Ave. of the Americas
New York, NY 10018
Phone: (212) 221-2057
Mary L. Callinan, Mgr.

UNION LEAGUE CLUB LIBRARY
38 E. 37th St.
New York, NY 10016
Phone: (212) 685-3800
Jane Reed, Libn.

UNION THEOLOGICAL SEMINARY - LIBRARY
Reinhold Niebuhr Place
3041 Broadway
New York, NY 10027
Phone: (212) 662-7100
Richard D. Spoor, Dir.

UNITED CEREBRAL PALSY OF NEW YORK CITY, INC. - LIBRARY
122 E. 23rd St.
New York, NY 10010
Phone: (212) 677-7400
Richard Gordon, Lib.Mgr.

UNITED CHURCH BOARD FOR WORLD MINISTRIES - LIBRARY
475 Riverside Dr.
New York, NY 10027
Virginia Stowe, Libn.

UNITED HOSPITAL FUND OF NEW YORK - REFERENCE LIBRARY
3 E. 54th St.
New York, NY 10022
Phone: (212) 754-1080
Christine Bahr, Libn.

UNITED LODGE OF THEOSOPHISTS - THEOSOPHY HALL - LIBRARY
347 E. 72nd St.
New York, NY 10021
Phone: (212) 535-2230
Anita Atkins, Hd.Libn.

UNITED NATIONS - CENTRE ON TRANSNATIONAL CORPORATIONS -
LIBRARY
United Nations
New York, NY 10017
Rana Singh, Dir., Info.Anl.Div.

UNITED NATIONS HEADQUARTERS - DAG HAMMARSKJOLD LIBRARY
United Nations
New York, NY 10017
Phone: (212) 754-7412
Vladimir Orlov, Dir.

UNITED NEIGHBORHOOD CENTERS OF AMERICA, INC. - LIBRARY
232 Madison Ave.
New York, NY 10016

U.S. ARMY IN EUROPE (USAREUR) - LIBRARY AND RESOURCE CENTER
H Q USAREUR and Seventh Army
APO New York, NY 09403
Duane G. Nahley, Supv.Libn.

U.S. BUREAU OF THE CENSUS - REGIONAL DATA USER SERVICE - NEW
YORK REGIONAL OFFICE - LIBRARY *
26 Federal Plaza, Rm. 37-100
New York, NY 10278
Phone: (212) 264-4730
Jeffrey L. Hall, Data User Serv.Off.

U.S. COAST GUARD - TAMPA MEMORIAL LIBRARY †
Governors Island, Bldg. S251
New York, NY 10004
Phone: (212) 264-8694
Bessie Seymour

U.S. COMMITTEE FOR UNICEF - INFORMATION CENTER ON CHILDREN'S
CULTURES
331 E. 38th St.
New York, NY 10016
Phone: (212) 686-5522
Melinda Greenblatt, Dir.-Libn.

U.S. COURT OF APPEALS, 2ND CIRCUIT - LIBRARY
U.S. Court House, Rm. 2501, Foley Sq.
New York, NY 10007
Phone: (212) 791-1052
Margaret J. Evans, Chf.Libn.

U.S. CUSTOMS COURT - LIBRARY †
One Federal Plaza
New York, NY 10007
Phone: (212) 264-2816
Margaret J. Evans, Libn.

U.S. CUSTOMS SERVICE - REGION II - LAW LIBRARY
6 World Trade Ctr., Rm. 732
New York, NY 10048
Phone: (212) 466-4579
Ann Marie D'Ambrosio, Lib.Techn.

U.S. DEPT. OF COMMERCE - INTERNATIONAL TRADE ADMINISTRATION -
NEW YORK DISTRICT OFFICE LIBRARY
26 Federal Plaza
New York, NY 10278
Phone: (212) 264-0630
Stuart Werner, Tech.Info.Spec.

U.S. DEPT. OF ENERGY - HEALTH & SAFETY LABORATORY LIBRARY
376 Hudson St.
New York, NY 10014
Phone: (212) 620-3606
Michael P. Durso, Libn.

U.S. DEPT. OF HOUSING AND URBAN DEVELOPMENT - REGION II - LIBRARY
26 Federal Plaza, Rm. 1304
New York, NY 10007
Phone: (212) 264-8175
Susan J. Heller, Regional Libn.

U.S. DEPT. OF JUSTICE - UNITED STATES ATTORNEY, SOUTHERN
DISTRICT OF NEW YORK - LIBRARY
One St. Andrew's Plaza, 6th Fl.
New York, NY 10007
Phone: (212) 791-0029
Barbara J. Zelenko, Hd.Libn.

U.S. DEPT. OF LABOR - BUREAU OF LABOR STATISTICS - INFORMATION
AND ADVISORY SECTION
1515 Broadway
New York, NY 10036
Phone: (212) 944-3121
Martin Karlin, Chf.

U.S. INDUSTRIAL CHEMICALS COMPANY - LIBRARY
99 Park Ave.
New York, NY 10016
Phone: (212) 949-5299
Peggy F. Presson, Libn.

U.S. NASA - GODDARD INSTITUTE FOR SPACE STUDIES - LIBRARY
2880 Broadway
New York, NY 10025
Phone: (212) 678-5613

U.S. NATL. PARK SERVICE - STATUE OF LIBERTY NATL. MONUMENT -
AMERICAN MUSEUM OF IMMIGRATION - LIBRARY
Liberty Island
New York, NY 10004
Phone: (212) 732-1236
Paul O. Weinbaum, Musm.Cur.

UNITED STATES TRADEMARK ASSOCIATION - LAW LIBRARY
6 E. 45th St.
New York, NY 10017
Phone: (212) 986-5880
Charlotte Jones, Staff Assoc./Libn.

UNITED STATES TRUST COMPANY - INVESTMENT LIBRARY
45 Wall St.
New York, NY 10005
Phone: (212) 425-4500
Trudy Daley, Chf.Libn.

U.S. VETERANS ADMINISTRATION (NY-New York) - MEDICAL CENTER
LIBRARY †
408 First Ave. at E. 24th St.
New York, NY 10010
Phone: (212) 686-7500
Malvin Vitriol, Chf.Libn.

U.S. VETERANS ADMINISTRATION (NY-New York) - OFFICE OF
TECHNOLOGY TRANSFER - REFERENCE COLLECTION
252 Seventh Ave., 3rd Fl. Phone: (212) 620-6670
New York, NY 10001 Lily W. Hom, Tech.Info.Spec.

UNIVERSIDAD BORICUA - PUERTO RICAN RESEARCH & RESOURCES
CENTER, INC. - REFERENCE LIBRARY
3755 Broadway Phone: (212) 865-9000
New York, NY 10032 Aurora Gomez, Libn.

UNIVERSITY CLUB LIBRARY
1 W. 54th St. Phone: (212) 572-3418
New York, NY 10019 Guy St. Clair, Dir.

VIDEO TAPE NETWORK, INC. - LIBRARY *
115 E. 62nd St. Phone: (212) 759-8735
New York, NY 10021 John A. Friede, Pres.

VOCATIONAL FOUNDATION, INC. - INFORMATION CENTER
44 E. 23rd St.
New York, NY 10010

WALL STREET JOURNAL - LIBRARY
22 Cortlandt St. Phone: (212) 285-5075
New York, NY 10007 Lottie Lindberg, Libn.

WALTER HAMPDEN - EDWIN BOOTH THEATER COLLECTION AND LIBRARY
The Players, 16 Gramercy Pk. Phone: (212) 228-7610
New York, NY 10003 Louis A. Rachow, Cur.Libn.

WEBSTER & SHEFFIELD - LIBRARY
One Rockefeller Plaza Phone: (212) 582-3370
New York, NY 10020 Clare Blaser, Libn.

WENDER, MURASE & WHITE - LIBRARY
400 Park Ave. Phone: (212) 832-3333
New York, NY 10022 Elizabeth Cohen Mayer, Libn.

WENNER-GREN FOUNDATION FOR ANTHROPOLOGICAL RESEARCH -
LIBRARY
1865 Broadway Phone: (212) 957-8750
New York, NY 10023 L. Osmundsen, Pres.

WERTHEIM AND COMPANY, INC. - RESEARCH LIBRARY
200 Park Ave. Phone: (212) 578-0426
New York, NY 10017 Joanne Johannessen, Libn.

WEST END COLLEGIATE CHURCH - LIBRARY
West End Ave. at 77th St.
New York, NY 10024

WESTERN ELECTRIC COMPANY, INC. - GENERAL BUSINESS LIBRARY †
222 Broadway Phone: (212) 571-4884
New York, NY 10038 Edna E. George, Libn.

WESTERN ELECTRIC COMPANY, INC. - PUBLIC RELATIONS LIBRARY †
195 Broadway, Rm. 1642 Phone: (212) 571-5115
New York, NY 10007 Mrs. Young Hi Quick, Ref.Libn.

WHITCOM INVESTMENT COMPANY - RESEARCH LIBRARY
Time & Life Bldg., Rm. 4600
110 W. 51st St. Phone: (212) 582-2300
New York, NY 10020 Sharon Leach, Res.Dir.

WHITE AND CASE - LIBRARY
14 Wall St. Phone: (212) 732-1040
New York, NY 10005 John J. Banta, Chf. Law Libn.

WHITMAN & RANSOM - LIBRARY
522 Fifth Ave. Phone: (212) 575-5800
New York, NY 10036 Annetta C. Guidotti, Law Libn.

WHITNEY MUSEUM OF AMERICAN ART - LIBRARY
945 Madison Ave. Phone: (212) 570-3649
New York, NY 10021 May FitzGerald, Libn.

WIDE WORLD PHOTOS, INC.
50 Rockefeller Plaza Phone: (212) 621-1930
New York, NY 10020 Paul M. Cliffard, Gen. Sales Mgr.

WILEY AND SONS, INC. - LIBRARY
605 Third Ave.
New York, NY 10158

WILLIAM-FREDERICK PRESS - PAMPHLET LIBRARY
308 E. 79th St. Phone: (212) 722-7272
New York, NY 10021 Alvin Levin, Libn.

WILLIAMS CO., INC. - MEDICAL LIBRARY
767 5th Ave.
New York, NY 10022

WILLKIE FARR & GALLAGHER - LIBRARY
153 E. 53rd St. Phone: (212) 935-8000
New York, NY 10022 Judith T. Opatrny, Libn.

WINDELS, MARX, DAVIES & IVES - LIBRARY
51 W. 51st St. Phone: (212) 977-9600
New York, NY 10019 Huguette Streuli, Libn.

WINTHROP, STIMSON, PUTNAM AND ROBERTS - LIBRARY
40 Wall St. Phone: (212) 943-0700
New York, NY 10005 Nancy J. Haab, Libn.

WOMEN ARTISTS NEWS - ARCHIVES
Grand Central Sta.
Box 3304 Phone: (212) 666-6990
New York, NY 10163 Cindy Lyle, Adm.

WOMEN'S ACTION ALLIANCE, INC. - LIBRARY
370 Lexington Ave. Phone: (212) 532-8330
New York, NY 10017 Jane Williamson, Libn.

WORLD ZIONIST ORGANIZATION - AMERICAN SECTION - ZIONIST
ARCHIVES AND LIBRARY
515 Park Ave. Phone: (212) 753-2167
New York, NY 10022 Sylvia Landress, Dir. & Libn.

XAVIER SOCIETY FOR THE BLIND - NATIONAL CATHOLIC PRESS AND
LIBRARY FOR THE VISUALLY HANDICAPPED *
154 E. 23rd St.
New York, NY 10010 Anthony F. LaBau, Dir.

YALE CLUB OF NEW YORK CITY - LIBRARY
50 Vanderbilt Ave. Phone: (212) 661-2070
New York, NY 10017 David T. Dale, Libn.

YESHIVA UNIVERSITY - HEDI STEINBERG LIBRARY
Stern College for Women
245 Lexington Ave. Phone: (212) 481-0570
New York, NY 10016 Edith Lubetski, Hd.Libn.

YESHIVA UNIVERSITY - LANDOWNE-BLOOM LIBRARY †
55 Fifth Ave., 12th Fl. Phone: (212) 790-0236
New York, NY 10003 Paul Devyatkin, Libn.

YESHIVA UNIVERSITY - MENDEL GOTTESMAN LIBRARY OF HEBRAICA AND
JUDAICA
500 W. 185th St. Phone: (212) 960-5382
New York, NY 10033 Sarah N. Levy, Supv.Libn.

YIDDISH LEAGUE - LIBRARY
200 W. 72nd St. Phone: (212) 787-6675
New York, NY 10023 Leybl Kahn, Libn.

YIVO INSTITUTE FOR JEWISH RESEARCH - LIBRARY AND ARCHIVES
1048 Fifth Ave. Phone: (212) 535-6700
New York, NY 10028 Marek Web, Chf.Archv.

YOUNG (Morris N. & Chesley V.) MNEMONICS LIBRARY
270 Riverside Dr. Phone: (212) 233-2344
New York, NY 10025 Morris N. Young, M.D., Dir.

YOUNG AND RUBICAM INTERNATIONAL - LIBRARY †
285 Madison Ave., 10th Fl. Phone: (212) 953-3075
New York, NY 10017 Celestine G. Frankenberg, Dir. of Lib.Serv.

GEOGRAPHIC

YOUNG WOMEN'S CHRISTIAN ASSOCIATION - NATIONAL BOARD - LIBRARY
600 Lexington Ave.　　　　　Phone: (212) 753-4700
New York, NY 10022　　　　　Elizabeth D. Norris, Libn./Hist.

NEW YORK STATE SUPREME COURT - 9TH JUDICIAL DISTRICT - LAW LIBRARY
104 Second St.
Newburgh, NY 12550　　　　　Ann McClean, Law Lib.Ck.

WASHINGTON'S HEADQUARTERS AND MUSEUM - LIBRARY
84 Liberty St.　　　　　Phone: (914) 562-1195
Newburgh, NY 12550　　　　　E.J. Townsend, Mgr.

AIRCO CARBON - RESEARCH LIBRARY
Packard Rd. & 47th St.　　　　　Phone: (716) 285-6971
Niagara Falls, NY 14302　　　　　Rita Smith, Res.Libn.

ELKEM METALS COMPANY - TECHNOLOGY CENTER - HAYNES-BECKET MEMORIAL LIBRARY
4625 Royal Ave.
Box 1344　　　　　Phone: (716) 286-7497
Niagara Falls, NY 14302　　　　　Thomas K. Lindsey, Libn.

HOOKER CHEMICAL CORPORATION - TECHNICAL INFORMATION CENTER
Box 8　　　　　Phone: (716) 773-8531
Niagara Falls, NY 14302　　　　　Dr. Irving Gordon, Supv.

KENNECOTT CORPORATION - CARBORUNDUM COMPANY - INFORMATION CENTER
Buffalo Ave.
Box 1054　　　　　Phone: (716) 278-2571
Niagara Falls, NY 14302　　　　　Marjorie L. Popovich, Hd., Info.Serv.

TAM CERAMICS, INC. - LIBRARY
Hyde Park Blvd.
Niagara Falls, NY 14305　　　　　Cheryl J. Ujeski, Sec., Tech.Dept.

MOORE-COTTRELL SUBSCRIPTION AGENCIES - SERIALS REFERENCE LIBRARY
　　　　　Phone: (716) 534-5221
North Cohocton, NY 14868　　　　　Ruth C. Kanner, Dir. of Info.Serv.

ROCKEFELLER UNIVERSITY - ROCKEFELLER ARCHIVE CENTER
Hillcrest, Pocantico Hills　　　　　Phone: (914) 631-4505
North Tarrytown, NY 10591　　　　　Dr. Joseph W. Ernst, Dir.

HOOKER CHEMICAL & PLASTICS CORPORATION - DUREZ DIVISION - LABORATORY LIBRARY
Walck Rd.
North Tonawanda, NY 14120

NORTHPORT PUBLIC SCHOOLS - TEACHERS' PROFESSIONAL LIBRARY *
110 Elwood Rd.
Northport, NY 11768　　　　　Edwin Sorensen, Hd.

U.S. VETERANS ADMINISTRATION (NY-Northport) - HOSPITAL LIBRARY
　　　　　Phone: (516) 261-4400
Northport, NY 11768　　　　　Larry D. Weitkemper, Chf.Libn.

CHENANGO MEMORIAL HOSPITAL - MEDICAL LIBRARY
179 N. Broad St.　　　　　Phone: (607) 335-4159
Norwich, NY 13815　　　　　Ann L. Slocum, Med.Libn.

MORTON-NORWICH PRODUCTS, INC. - NORWICH PHARMACAL COMPANY - R&D DEPT. - LIBRARY INFORMATION GROUP
Box 191　　　　　Phone: (607) 335-2539
Norwich, NY 13815　　　　　Donald A. Windsor, Leader, Lib. & Info Group

NEW YORK STATE SUPREME COURT - 6TH JUDICIAL DISTRICT - LAW LIBRARY
West Park Pl.
Norwich, NY 13815　　　　　Bethany L. Ginther, Libn.

FELLOWSHIP OF RECONCILIATION - LIBRARY
Box 171　　　　　Phone: (914) 358-4601
Nyack, NY 10960　　　　　Rebekah Ray-Crichton, Libn.

NYACK COLLEGE - LIBRARY
　　　　　Phone: (914) 358-1710
Nyack, NY 10960　　　　　May K. Leo, Libn.

STIEFEL LABORATORIES, INC. - RESEARCH INSTITUTE LIBRARY
　　　　　Phone: (518) 239-6901
Oak Hill, NY 12460　　　　　Loretta Lounsbury, Act.Libn.

SOUTH NASSAU COMMUNITIES HOSPITAL - JULES REDISH MEMORIAL MEDICAL LIBRARY
Oceanside Rd.　　　　　Phone: (516) 764-2600
Oceanside, NY 11572　　　　　Claire Joseph, Libn.

DIOCESE OF OGDENSBURG - ARCHIVES
622 Washington St.
Box 369　　　　　Phone: (315) 393-2920
Ogdensburg, NY 13669　　　　　Rev. Lawrence E. Cotter, Archv.

HEPBURN (A. Barton) HOSPITAL - MEDICAL LIBRARY
214 King St.　　　　　Phone: (315) 393-3600
Ogdensburg, NY 13669　　　　　M. Bridget Doyle, Med.Libn.

NEW YORK STATE OFFICE OF MENTAL HEALTH - ST. LAWRENCE PSYCHIATRIC CENTER - LIBRARY
Station A　　　　　Phone: (315) 393-3000
Ogdensburg, NY 13669　　　　　Eleanor Cunningham, Lib.Techn.

WADHAMS HALL SEMINARY - COLLEGE LIBRARY
Riverside Dr.　　　　　Phone: (315) 393-4231
Ogdensburg, NY 13669　　　　　Rev. Richard S. Sturtz, Hd.Libn.

SHAKER MUSEUM FOUNDATION - EMMA B. KING LIBRARY
　　　　　Phone: (518) 794-9100
Old Chatham, NY 12136　　　　　R. Peter Laskovski, Musm.Dir. & Libn.

NORTHEASTERN LOGGERS ASSOCIATION, INC. - LIBRARY
Box 69
Old Forge, NY 13420

NEW YORK INSTITUTE OF TECHNOLOGY - CENTER FOR ENERGY POLICY AND RESEARCH - ENERGY INFORMATION CENTER
　　　　　Phone: (516) 686-7765
Old Westbury, NY 11568　　　　　Mickie Watterson, Assoc.Dir.Info.Sys.

NEW YORK INSTITUTE OF TECHNOLOGY - LIBRARY †
Wheatley Rd.　　　　　Phone: (516) 686-7657
Old Westbury, NY 11568　　　　　Margaretta W. Smith, Dir. of Libs.

MADISON COUNTY HISTORICAL SOCIETY - LIBRARY
435 Main St.
Box 415　　　　　Phone: (315) 363-4136
Oneida, NY 13421　　　　　John H. Braunlein, Dir.

SUNY - COLLEGE AT ONEONTA - JAMES M. MILNE LIBRARY
　　　　　Phone: (607) 431-2723
Oneonta, NY 13820　　　　　Richard D. Johnson, Dir. of Libs.

BECTON, DICKINSON IMMUNODIAGNOSTICS - TECHNICAL RESEARCH AND DEVELOPMENT LIBRARY †
Mountain View Ave.　　　　　Phone: (914) 359-2700
Orangeburg, NY 10962　　　　　Olga Mancebo, Libn.

ROCKLAND RESEARCH INSTITUTE - ROCKLAND HEALTH SCIENCES LIBRARY
Bldg. 37　　　　　Phone: (914) 359-1050
Orangeburg, NY 10962　　　　　Lois Cohan, Libn.

OSSINING HISTORICAL SOCIETY MUSEUM - LIBRARY
196 Croton Ave.　　　　　Phone: (914) 762-4851
Ossining, NY 10562　　　　　John Drittler, Chf.Libn.

FORT ONTARIO - LIBRARY
Ft. Ontario　　　　　Phone: (315) 343-4711
Oswego, NY 13126　　　　　Wallace Workmaster, Historic Site Mgr.

NEW YORK STATE SUPREME COURT - 4TH JUDICIAL DISTRICT - LAW LIBRARY
Court House, E. Oneida St.　　　　　Phone: (315) 342-0550
Oswego, NY 13126　　　　　Janice Drumm Matthews, Law Lib.Ck.

SUNY - COLLEGE AT OSWEGO - PENFIELD LIBRARY
Phone: (315) 341-3122
Oswego, NY 13126
B. Anne Commerton, Dir.

IBM CORPORATION - FEDERAL SYSTEMS DIVISION - AVIONICS SYSTEMS -
LIBRARY
Phone: (607) 687-2121
Owego, NY 13827
Charles F. Balz, Project Mgr.

TIOGA COUNTY HISTORICAL SOCIETY MUSEUM - LIBRARY
110-112 Front St.
Phone: (607) 687-2460
Owego, NY 13827
William Lay, Jr., Musm.Cur.

PLANTING FIELDS ARBORETUM - HORTICULTURAL LIBRARY
Planting Fields Rd.
Phone: (516) 922-1130
Oyster Bay, NY 11771
Elizabeth K. Reilley, Libn.

COLUMBIA UNIVERSITY - LAMONT-DOHERTY GEOLOGICAL OBSERVATORY
- GEOSCIENCE LIBRARY
Phone: (914) 359-2900
Palisades, NY 10964
Susan Klimley, Libn.

BROOKHAVEN MEMORIAL HOSPITAL - MEDICAL LIBRARY
101 Hospital Rd.
Phone: (516) 654-7774
Patchogue, NY 11772
Mrs. Freddie Borock, Libn.

AKIN HALL ASSOCIATION - AKIN FREE LIBRARY
Quaker Hill
Phone: (914) 855-5099
Pawling, NY 12564
James Mandracchia, Libn.

AMERICAN CYANAMID COMPANY - LEDERLE LABORATORIES DIVISION -
SUBBAROW MEMORIAL LIBRARY
N. Middletown Rd.
Phone: (914) 735-5000
Pearl River, NY 10965
Dr. M.G. Howell, Hd., Tech.Info.Serv.

LAWLER MATUSKY & SKELLY ENGINEERS - LIBRARY
One Blue Hill Plaza
Phone: (914) 735-8300
Pearl River, NY 10965
Katharine S. Thomas, Info.Sci.

ORANGE AND ROCKLAND UTILITIES, INC. - LIBRARY
1 Blue Hill Plaza
Phone: (914) 627-2680
Pearl River, NY 10965
Esther B. Clifford, Libn.

ROSENBERG (Paul) ASSOCIATES - LIBRARY
330 Fifth Ave.
Phone: (914) 738-2266
Pelham, NY 10803
M. Hill, Libn.

CHAMPLAIN VALLEY - PHYSICIANS HOSPITAL MEDICAL CENTER -
MEDICAL LIBRARY
100 Beekman St.
Phone: (518) 561-2000
Plattsburgh, NY 12901
Judith El Reedy, Med.Libn.

SUNY - COLLEGE AT PLATTSBURGH - SPECIAL COLLECTIONS
Benjamin F. Feinberg Library
Phone: (518) 564-3180
Plattsburgh, NY 12901
Dr. Bruce Stark, Dir.

PACE UNIVERSITY, PLEASANTVILLE/BRIARCLIFF - LIBRARY
861 Bedford Rd.
Phone: (914) 769-3200
Pleasantville, NY 10570
William J. Murdock, Lib.Dir.

READER'S DIGEST - INDEX
Phone: (914) 769-7000
Pleasantville, NY 10570
Adrienne M. Bova, Ed.

LIFE SAVERS, INC. - RESEARCH AND DEVELOPMENT DIVISION -
TECHNICAL INFORMATION CENTER
N. Main St.
Phone: (914) 937-3200
Port Chester, NY 10573
Rita D. Reade, Libn.

MUSEUM OF CARTOON ART - LIBRARY
Comly Ave.
Phone: (914) 939-0234
Port Chester, NY 10573
Ellen J. Armstrong, Mgr.

GRAVURE RESEARCH INSTITUTE - LIBRARY
22 Manhasset Ave.
Phone: (516) 883-6670
Port Washington, NY 11050
Harvey F. George, Res.Dir.

GREENVALE EDITORIAL SERVICES, INC. - LIBRARY
2 Haven Ave.
Phone: (516) 944-8066
Port Washington, NY 11050
Joan Casson Sauer, Libn.

CLARKSON COLLEGE OF TECHNOLOGY - EDUCATIONAL RESOURCES
CENTER
Phone: (315) 268-2292
Potsdam, NY 13676
Ottilie H. Rollins, Assoc.Dir.

SUNY - COLLEGE AT POTSDAM - CRANE MUSIC LIBRARY
Phone: (315) 268-3019
Potsdam, NY 13676
Sally Skyrm, Music Libn.

SUNY - COLLEGE AT POTSDAM - FREDERICK W. CRUMB MEMORIAL
LIBRARY
Pierrepont Ave.
Phone: (315) 268-4991
Potsdam, NY 13676
Dr. Thomas M. Peischl, Dir. of Libs.

DUTCHESS COUNTY DEPARTMENT OF PLANNING - INFORMATION CENTER
47 Cannon St.
Phone: (914) 485-9890
Poughkeepsie, NY 12601
Charles J. Murphy, Pub.Info.Off.

DUTCHESS COUNTY GENEALOGICAL SOCIETY - LIBRARY
LDS Church
Spackenkill Rd., Box 708
Poughkeepsie, NY 12602

DUTCHESS COUNTY MENTAL HEALTH LIBRARY
230 North Rd.
Phone: (914) 485-9700
Poughkeepsie, NY 12601
Barbara B. Pantridge, Libn.

IBM CORPORATION - LIBRARY
Box 390
Phone: (914) 463-1630
Poughkeepsie, NY 12602
Gabrielle S. Nelson, Mgr.

NEW YORK SCHOOL OF PSYCHIATRY AND HUDSON RIVER PSYCHIATRIC
CENTER - MEDICAL LIBRARY *
Branch B
Phone: (914) 452-8000
Poughkeepsie, NY 12601
Dan Wood, Libn.

NEW YORK STATE SUPREME COURT - 9TH JUDICIAL DISTRICT - JOSEPH F.
BARNARD MEMORIAL LAW LIBRARY ASSOCIATION
Court House, 10 Market St.
Phone: (914) 485-9874
Poughkeepsie, NY 12601
Catherine A. Maher, Sr. Law Lib.Ck.

ST. FRANCIS HOSPITAL - MEDICAL LIBRARY
North Rd.
Phone: (914) 471-2000
Poughkeepsie, NY 12601
Mrs. Howard Wilson, Med.Libn.

VASSAR BROTHERS HOSPITAL - MEDICAL LIBRARY
Reade Pl.
Phone: (914) 454-8500
Poughkeepsie, NY 12601
Mrs. Howard A. Wilson, Med.Libn.

VASSAR COLLEGE - ART LIBRARY
Phone: (914) 452-7000
Poughkeepsie, NY 12601
Janis Ekdahl, Art Libn.

VASSAR COLLEGE - GEORGE SHERMAN DICKINSON MUSIC LIBRARY
Phone: (914) 452-7000
Poughkeepsie, NY 12601
Robert E. Parks, Music Libn.

CREEDMOOR PSYCHIATRIC CENTER - HEALTH SCIENCES LIBRARY
80-45 Winchester Blvd.
Phone: (212) 464-7500
Queens Village, NY 11427
Susan Taubman, Lrng.Rsrcs.Coord.

BASF WYANDOTTE CORPORATION - DEVELOPMENT LABORATORY -
LIBRARY *
36 Riverside Ave.
Phone: (518) 465-4511
Rensselaer, NY 12144

ST. ANTHONY-ON-HUDSON THEOLOGICAL LIBRARY
St. Anthony-On-Hudson
Phone: (518) 463-2261
Rensselaer, NY 12144
Rev. Peter D. Fehlner, Libn.

IN-FACT - RESEARCH AND INFORMATION SERVICE
Righter Rd.
Box 151
Phone: (518) 797-5154
Rensselaerville, NY 12147
Katherine H. Storms, Info.Spec.

ASTOR HOME FOR CHILDREN - PROFESSIONAL LIBRARY
36 Mill St. Phone: (914) 876-4081
Rhinebeck, NY 12572 William J. Nichols, Libn.

CENTRAL SUFFOLK HOSPITAL - MEDICAL LIBRARY
1300 Roanoke Ave. Phone: (516) 369-6088
Riverhead, NY 11901 Anne Kirsch, Libn.

NEW YORK STATE SUPREME COURT - 10TH JUDICIAL DISTRICT - LAW LIBRARY
Court House, Rm. 210
Griffing Ave. Phone: (516) 727-4700
Riverhead, NY 11901 Lynn C. Fullshire, Sr. Law Libn.

SUFFOLK COUNTY HISTORICAL SOCIETY - LIBRARY
300 W. Main St. Phone: (516) 727-2881
Riverhead, NY 11901 Betty M. Carpenter, Libn.

AMERICAN BAPTIST HISTORICAL SOCIETY - SAMUEL COLGATE BAPTIST HISTORICAL LIBRARY
1106 S. Goodman St. Phone: (716) 473-1740
Rochester, NY 14620 William H. Brackney, Exec.Dir.

BAUSCH & LOMB, INC. - CORPORATE LIBRARY
1400 N. Goodman St. Phone: (716) 338-6053
Rochester, NY 14602 Delsa I. Benz, Corp.Libn.

BAUSCH & LOMB, INC. - SOFLENS DIVISION - SOFLENS TECHNICAL INFORMATION CENTER *
1400 N. Goodman St. Phone: (716) 338-6427
Rochester, NY 14602 Susan Quinn, Tech.Info.Spec.

CENTER FOR GOVERNMENTAL RESEARCH, INC. - LIBRARY
37 S. Washington St. Phone: (716) 325-6360
Rochester, NY 14608 Christine Ryan, Libn.

COLGATE ROCHESTER/BEXLEY HALL/ CROZER THEOLOGICAL SEMINARIES - AMBROSE SWASEY LIBRARY
1100 S. Goodman St. Phone: (716) 271-1320
Rochester, NY 14620 Peter N. VandenBerge, Dir. of Lib.Serv.

CONVALESCENT HOSPITAL FOR CHILDREN - LIBRARY
2075 Scottsville Rd. Phone: (716) 436-4442
Rochester, NY 14623 Christine S. Bonati, Libn.

DANISH BAPTIST GENERAL CONFERENCE OF AMERICA - ARCHIVES
American Baptist Historical Society
1106 S. Goodman St. Phone: (716) 473-1740
Rochester, NY 14620 William H. Brackney, Exec.Dir.

EASTMAN DENTAL CENTER - BASIL G. BIBBY LIBRARY
625 Elmwood Ave. Phone: (716) 275-5010
Rochester, NY 14620 June Glaser, Libn.

EASTMAN KODAK COMPANY - BUSINESS LIBRARY
343 State St. Phone: (716) 724-3041
Rochester, NY 14650 M. Lois Gauch, Libn.

EASTMAN KODAK COMPANY - ENGINEERING LIBRARY
Kodak Park Division, Bldg. 23 Phone: (716) 722-2356
Rochester, NY 14650 Raymond W. Curtin, Libn.

EASTMAN KODAK COMPANY - HEALTH, SAFETY AND HUMAN FACTORS LABORATORY - LIBRARY
Kodak Park Division, Bldg. 320 Phone: (716) 458-1000
Rochester, NY 14650 Rita B. Stack, Libn.

EASTMAN KODAK COMPANY - KODAK APPARATUS DIVISION - LIBRARY
901 Elmgrove Rd. Phone: (716) 726-2127
Rochester, NY 14650 Marie Jean Bonn, Supv.Libn.

EASTMAN KODAK COMPANY - PHOTOGRAPHIC TECHNOLOGY DIVISION - LIBRARY
Kodak Park Division Phone: (716) 722-2341
Rochester, NY 14650 Ruth H. Donoghue, Supv., Info.Serv.

EASTMAN KODAK COMPANY - RESEARCH LABORATORIES - RESEARCH LIBRARY
Kodak Park Division, Bldg. 83 Phone: (716) 722-2723
Rochester, NY 14650 Elizabeth W. Kraus, Info.Assoc./Lib.Mgr.

FRENCH (R.T.) COMPANY - TECHNICAL LIBRARY
Box 23450 Phone: (716) 482-8000
Rochester, NY 14692 P.C. Verrioli, Libn.

GARDEN CENTER OF ROCHESTER - LIBRARY
5 Castle Park Phone: (716) 473-5130
Rochester, NY 14620 Mrs. Robert Baschnagel, Libn.

GENERAL RAILWAY SIGNAL CO. - TECHNICAL LIBRARY
801 West Ave.
Box 600 Phone: (716) 436-2020
Rochester, NY 14602 Kathy Ciarpelli, Libn.

GENESEE HOSPITAL - SAMUEL J. STABINS, M.D., HEALTH SCIENCES LIBRARY
224 Alexander St. Phone: (716) 263-6305
Rochester, NY 14607 Sally M. Gerling, Chf.Libn.

HIGHLAND HOSPITAL OF ROCHESTER - THE WILLIAMS HEALTH SCIENCES LIBRARY
South Ave. at Bellevue Dr. Phone: (716) 473-2200
Rochester, NY 14620 Helen King Murphy, Dir.

HIGHLAND PARK HERBARIUM - LIBRARY *
375 Westfall Rd. Phone: (716) 244-4640
Rochester, NY 14620 James W. Kelly, Cur.

INTERNATIONAL MUSEUM OF PHOTOGRAPHY AT GEORGE EASTMAN HOUSE - LIBRARY
900 East Ave. Phone: (716) 271-3361
Rochester, NY 14607 Andrew Eskind, Act.Dir.

LANDMARK SOCIETY OF WESTERN NEW YORK - WENRICH MEMORIAL LIBRARY
130 Spring St. Phone: (716) 546-7029
Rochester, NY 14608 Cynthia Howk, Libn.

LINCOLN FIRST BANK, NA, INC. - LINCOLN FIRST LIBRARY
One Lincoln First Square Phone: (716) 262-2306
Rochester, NY 14643 Alla F. Levi, Dir. of Lib. Serv.

MIXING EQUIPMENT COMPANY, INC. - MIXCO R&D LIBRARY
135 Mt. Read Blvd. Phone: (716) 436-5550
Rochester, NY 14611 Maryann Kerwin, Libn.

MONROE COMMUNITY HOSPITAL - HEALTH SCIENCES LIBRARY
435 E. Henrietta Rd. Phone: (716) 473-4080
Rochester, NY 14603 Elinor Reynolds, Med.Libn.

MONROE COUNTY HISTORIAN'S DEPARTMENT - LIBRARY
115 South Ave.
Rochester, NY 14604 Shirley C. Husted, County Hist.

MONROE DEVELOPMENTAL CENTER - STAFF/PARENT LIBRARY
620 Westfall Rd. Phone: (716) 461-2800
Rochester, NY 14620 Tamara Strubel, Asst.Libn.

NEW YORK STATE ARCHEOLOGICAL ASSOCIATION - LIBRARY
657 East Ave.
Box 1480 Phone: (716) 271-4320
Rochester, NY 14603 Charles F. Hayes, III, Res.Dir.

NEW YORK STATE SUPREME COURT - APPELLATE DIVISION, 4TH JUDICIAL DEPARTMENT - LAW LIBRARY
525 Hall of Justice Phone: (716) 428-5480
Rochester, NY 14614 Joseph T. Pascucci, Libn.

NIXON, HARGRAVE, DEVANS & DOYLE - LAW LIBRARY †
Lincoln First Tower
Box 1051 Phone: (716) 546-8000
Rochester, NY 14603 Sharon A. Hayden, Libn.

PARK RIDGE HOSPITAL - MEDICAL LIBRARY
1555 Long Pond Rd. Phone: (716) 225-7150
Rochester, NY 14626 Eileen P. Shirley, Libn.

PENNWALT CORPORATION - PENNWALT PHARMACEUTICAL DIVISION - RESEARCH LIBRARY
755 Jefferson Rd., Box 1710 Phone: (716) 475-9000
Rochester, NY 14603 Rita Conyne, Res.Libn.

ROCHESTER ACADEMY OF MEDICINE - LIBRARY
1441 East Ave. Phone: (716) 271-1313
Rochester, NY 14610

ROCHESTER BUSINESS INSTITUTE - BETTY CRONK MEMORIAL LIBRARY
339 East Ave. Phone: (716) 325-7290
Rochester, NY 14604 Shirley Nagg, Libn.

ROCHESTER GAS AND ELECTRIC CORPORATION - TECHNICAL
INFORMATION CENTER
89 East Ave. Phone: (716) 546-2700
Rochester, NY 14649 Linda L. Phillips, Tech.Info.Coord.

ROCHESTER GENERAL HOSPITAL - LILLIE B. WERNER HEALTH SCIENCES
LIBRARY
1425 Portland Ave. Phone: (716) 338-4743
Rochester, NY 14621 Bernie Todd Smith, Libn.

ROCHESTER HISTORICAL SOCIETY - LIBRARY
485 East Ave. Phone: (716) 271-2705
Rochester, NY 14607

ROCHESTER INSTITUTE OF TECHNOLOGY - CHEMISTRY GRADUATE
RESEARCH LIBRARY
One Lomb Memorial Dr. Phone: (716) 475-2520
Rochester, NY 14623 Christine DeGolyer, Chem.Libn.

ROCHESTER INSTITUTE OF TECHNOLOGY - MELBERT B. CARY, JR.
GRAPHIC ARTS COLLECTION
School of Printing Phone: (716) 475-2408
Rochester, NY 14623 David Pankow, Libn.

ROCHESTER INSTITUTE OF TECHNOLOGY - NATIONAL TECHNICAL
INSTITUTE FOR THE DEAF - STAFF RESOURCE CENTER
Lyndon Baines Johnson Bldg., Rm. 2490
1 Lomb Memorial Dr. Phone: (716) 475-6823
Rochester, NY 14623 Audrey Ritter, Rsrcs.Spec.

ROCHESTER INSTITUTE OF TECHNOLOGY - TECHNICAL & EDUCATION
CENTER FOR THE GRAPHIC ARTS - GRAPHIC ARTS INFO.SERV.
One Lomb Memorial Dr. Phone: (716) 475-2791
Rochester, NY 14623 Lily Shung, Tech.Libn.

ROCHESTER INSTITUTE OF TECHNOLOGY - WALLACE MEMORIAL LIBRARY
One Lomb Memorial Dr. Phone: (716) 475-2565
Rochester, NY 14623 Gary D. MacMillan, Dir.

ROCHESTER MUSEUM AND SCIENCE CENTER - LIBRARY
657 East Ave.
Box 1480 Phone: (716) 271-4320
Rochester, NY 14603 Janice Tauer Wass, Libn.

ROCHESTER MUSEUM AND SCIENCE CENTER - STRASENBURGH
PLANETARIUM - TODD LIBRARY
657 East Ave. Phone: (716) 244-6060
Rochester, NY 14607 Dr. William Gutsch, Staff Astronomer

ROCHESTER PSYCHIATRIC CENTER - PROFESSIONAL LIBRARY
1600 South Ave. Phone: (716) 473-3230
Rochester, NY 14620 Helen A. Vogel, Libn.

ROCHESTER PUBLIC LIBRARY - ART DIVISION
115 South Ave. Phone: (716) 428-7332
Rochester, NY 14604 Mary Lee Miller, Hd.

ROCHESTER PUBLIC LIBRARY - BUSINESS AND SOCIAL SCIENCE DIVISION
115 South Ave. Phone: (716) 428-7328
Rochester, NY 14604 June Rogoff, Hd.

ROCHESTER PUBLIC LIBRARY - EDUCATION AND RELIGION DIVISION
115 South Ave. Phone: (716) 428-7330
Rochester, NY 14604 Robert D. Murphy, Hd.

ROCHESTER PUBLIC LIBRARY - HISTORY AND TRAVEL DIVISION
115 South Ave. Phone: (716) 428-7323
Rochester, NY 14604 Winn McCray, Hd.

ROCHESTER PUBLIC LIBRARY - LITERATURE AND RECREATION DIVISION
115 South Ave. Phone: (716) 428-7315
Rochester, NY 14604 William J. Cuseo, Hd.

ROCHESTER PUBLIC LIBRARY - LOCAL HISTORY DIVISION
115 South Ave. Phone: (716) 428-7338
Rochester, NY 14604 Wayne Arnold, Hd.

ROCHESTER PUBLIC LIBRARY - REYNOLDS AUDIO-VISUAL DEPARTMENT
115 South Ave. Phone: (716) 428-7335
Rochester, NY 14604 Robert Barnes, Hd.

ROCHESTER PUBLIC LIBRARY - SCIENCE AND TECHNOLOGY DIVISION
115 South Ave. Phone: (716) 428-7327
Rochester, NY 14604 Judith Prevratil, Hd.

ROCHESTER TIMES-UNION AND ROCHESTER DEMOCRAT & CHRONICLE -
LIBRARY
55 Exchange St. Phone: (716) 232-7100
Rochester, NY 14614 Peter Ford, Lib.Dir.

ST. BERNARD'S INSTITUTE - LIBRARY
1100 S. Goodman Phone: (716) 271-1320
Rochester, NY 14620 Rev. Sebastian A. Falcone, Dean

SENECA ZOOLOGICAL SOCIETY - LIBRARY
2222 St. Paul St. Phone: (716) 342-2744
Rochester, NY 14621 Daniel R. Michalowski, Park Dir.

SINGER COMPANY - EDUCATION DIVISION - TECHNICAL LIBRARY
3750 Monroe Ave.
Rochester, NY 14603

STRONG (Margaret Woodbury) MUSEUM - LIBRARY
700 Allen Creek Rd. Phone: (716) 381-1818
Rochester, NY 14618 Elaine M. Challacombe, Libn.

SYBRON CORPORATION - PFAUDLER COMPANY - TECHNICAL LIBRARY
Box 1600 Phone: (716) 235-1000
Rochester, NY 14603 Candice M. Johnson, Libn.

SYBRON CORPORATION - TAYLOR INSTRUMENT PROCESS CONTROL
DIVISION - TECHNICAL INFORMATION CENTER
95 Ames St. Phone: (716) 235-5000
Rochester, NY 14601 Mary Jo Eiser, Libn.

TEMPLE BETH EL - LIBRARY
139 Winton Rd., S. Phone: (716) 473-1770
Rochester, NY 14610 Anna S. Kirshenbaum, Libn.

TEMPLE B'RITH KODESH - LIBRARY
2131 Elmwood Ave. Phone: (716) 244-7060
Rochester, NY 14618 Bertha Cravets, Libn.

UNIVERSITY OF ROCHESTER - ASIA LIBRARY
Rush Rhees Library, River Campus Phone: (716) 275-4489
Rochester, NY 14627 Datta S. Kharbas, Hd.

UNIVERSITY OF ROCHESTER - CARLSON LIBRARY
Hutchison Hall, River Campus Phone: (716) 275-4465
Rochester, NY 14627 Arleen Somerville, Hd.

UNIVERSITY OF ROCHESTER - CHARLOTTE WHITNEY ALLEN LIBRARY
490 University Ave. Phone: (716) 275-4765
Rochester, NY 14607 Beryl Nesbit, Libn.

UNIVERSITY OF ROCHESTER - DEPARTMENT OF ENERGY LIBRARY
400 Elmwood Ave.
Rochester, NY 14642

UNIVERSITY OF ROCHESTER - DEPARTMENT OF RARE BOOKS,
MANUSCRIPTS & ARCHIVES
River Campus Phone: (716) 275-4477
Rochester, NY 14627 Peter Dzwonkoski, Hd.

UNIVERSITY OF ROCHESTER - EASTMAN SCHOOL OF MUSIC - SIBLEY
MUSIC LIBRARY
44 Swan St. Phone: (716) 275-3018
Rochester, NY 14604 Dr. Ruth Watanabe, Libn.

UNIVERSITY OF ROCHESTER - EDUCATION LIBRARY
Rush Rhees Library   Phone: (716) 275-4481
Rochester, NY 14627   Kathleen McGowan, Educ.Libn.

UNIVERSITY OF ROCHESTER - ENGINEERING AND GEOLOGY LIBRARY
Gavett Hall   Phone: (716) 275-4486
Rochester, NY 14627   J.W. Holladay, Hd.

UNIVERSITY OF ROCHESTER - FINE ARTS LIBRARY
Rush Rhees Library, River Campus   Phone: (716) 275-4476
Rochester, NY 14627   Stephanie Frontz, Hd.

UNIVERSITY OF ROCHESTER - LABORATORY FOR LASER ENERGETICS -
       LIBRARY
250 E. River Rd.   Phone: (716) 275-5768
Rochester, NY 14623   Janice Holladay, Libn.

UNIVERSITY OF ROCHESTER - MANAGEMENT LIBRARY
Rush Rhees Library, River Campus   Phone: (716) 275-4482
Rochester, NY 14627   Edward P. Wass, Act.Hd.

UNIVERSITY OF ROCHESTER - PHYSICS-OPTICS-ASTRONOMY LIBRARY
374 Bausch & Lomb Bldg.   Phone: (716) 275-4469
Rochester, NY 14627   Loretta Caren, Hd.

UNIVERSITY OF ROCHESTER - SCHOOL OF MEDICINE & DENTISTRY -
       EDWARD G. MINER LIBRARY
601 Elmwood Ave.   Phone: (716) 275-3364
Rochester, NY 14642   Lucretia McClure, Med.Libn.

XEROX CORPORATION - XEROX SQUARE LIBRARY †
Xerox Sq. 105   Phone: (716) 423-5223
Rochester, NY 14644   Cecelia E. Rice, Mgr.

CENTRAL SYNAGOGUE OF NASSAU COUNTY - HELEN BLAU MEMORIAL
       LIBRARY
430 DeMott Ave.   Phone: (516) 766-4300
Rockville Centre, NY 11570   Barbara Gresack, Libn.

MERCY HOSPITAL - MEDICAL LIBRARY
1000 N. Village Ave.   Phone: (516) 255-2255
Rockville Centre, NY 11361   Carol L. Reid, Med.Libn.

IIT RESEARCH INSTITUTE - RELIABILITY ANALYSIS CENTER *
RADC (RBRAC)
Griffiss Air Force Base   Phone: (315) 330-4151
Rome, NY 13441   Charles E. Ehrenfried, Tech.Dir.

JERVIS PUBLIC LIBRARY
613 N. Washington St.   Phone: (315) 336-4570
Rome, NY 13440   William A. Dillon, Dir.

ROME HISTORICAL SOCIETY - ELAINE & WILLIAM E. SCRIPTURE
       MEMORIAL LIBRARY
200 Church St.   Phone: (315) 336-5870
Rome, NY 13440   Joseph G. Vincent, Exec.Dir.

BRYANT LIBRARY - LOCAL HISTORY COLLECTION
Paper Mill Rd.   Phone: (516) 621-2240
Roslyn, NY 11576   Anthony M. Cucchiara, Cur.

ST. FRANCIS HOSPITAL - MEDICAL LIBRARY
Port Washington Blvd.   Phone: (516) 627-6200
Roslyn, NY 11576   Byrnice Hurt, Med.Libn.

AYERST LABORATORIES, INC. - INFORMATION CENTER
Maple St.   Phone: (518) 297-6611
Rouses Point, NY 12979   Christina Ransom, Mgr.Info.Ctr.

ITT CONTINENTAL BAKING COMPANY - RESEARCH LABORATORIES
       LIBRARY
Halstead Ave.
Box 731   Phone: (914) 899-0380
Rye, NY 10580   Jocelyn Rosen, Supv.Tech.Info.Serv.

SLOAN-KETTERING INSTITUTE FOR CANCER RESEARCH - DONALD S.
       WALKER LABORATORY - C.P. RHOADS MEMORIAL LIBRARY
145 Boston Post Rd.   Phone: (914) 698-1100
Rye, NY 10580   Alison Morrow, Libn.

ST. BONAVENTURE UNIVERSITY - FRANCISCAN INSTITUTE LIBRARY
                                                Phone: (716) 375-2105
St. Bonaventure, NY 14778   Dr. Louis J. Reith, Rare Book Libn.

BOCES - ORLEANS-NIAGARA EDUCATIONAL COMMUNICATIONS CENTER
4124 Saunders Settlement Rd.
Niagara East - Box 310D   Phone: (716) 731-4146
Sanborn, NY 14132   Marie Sharp, Mgr.

NASSAU COUNTY MUSEUM LIBRARY AT SANDS POINT
Middle Neck Rd.   Phone: (516) 671-0300
Sands Point, NY 11050   Richard A. Winsche, Hist.

TRUDEAU INSTITUTE IMMUNOBIOLOGICAL RESEARCH LABORATORIES -
       LIBRARY *
Box 59   Phone: (518) 891-3080
Saranac Lake, NY 12983   Joyce Ward, Libn.

ESPEY MFG. & ELECTRONICS CORP. - COMPONENT SPECIFICATIONS
       LIBRARY
Ballston at Congress Aves.
Box 422   Phone: (518) 584-4100
Saratoga Springs, NY 12866   Cathi Jackson, Libn.

HISTORICAL SOCIETY OF SARATOGA SPRINGS - MUSEUM AND LIBRARY
Casino, Congress Park
Box 216   Phone: (518) 584-6920
Saratoga Springs, NY 12866   Heidi A. Fuge, Lib. & Musm.Dir.

NEW YORK STATE SUPREME COURT - 4TH JUDICIAL DISTRICT - LAW
       LIBRARY
2 City Hall   Phone: (518) 584-4862
Saratoga Springs, NY 12866   Renita V. Johnson, Court Libn.

SUNY - EMPIRE STATE COLLEGE - LEARNING RESOURCES CENTER
2 Union Ave.
Saratoga Springs, NY 12866

WEINBERG NATURE CENTER - LIBRARY
455 Mamaroneck Rd.   Phone: (914) 723-4784
Scarsdale, NY 10583   Peter J. Woodcock, Naturalist/Dir.

ELLIS HOSPITAL - MEDICAL-NURSING LIBRARY
1101 Nott St.   Phone: (518) 382-4381
Schenectady, NY 12308   Dorothy Dralle, Libn.

GENERAL ELECTRIC COMPANY - CORPORATE RESEARCH & DEVELOPMENT
       - WHITNEY LIBRARY
Box 8   Phone: (518) 385-8791
Schenectady, NY 12301   Maryde Fahey King, Mgr.

GENERAL ELECTRIC COMPANY - MAIN LIBRARY
One River Rd.   Phone: (518) 385-3652
Schenectady, NY 12345   Julia Hewitt, Mgr.

GENERAL ELECTRIC COMPANY - TECHNICAL INFORMATION EXCHANGE
Bldg. 81, Rm. A133
One River Rd.   Phone: (518) 385-3615
Schenectady, NY 12345   P.A. Oliver, Mgr.

SCHENECTADY CHEMICALS, INC. - W. HOWARD WRIGHT RESEARCH
       CENTER - LIBRARY
2750 Balltown Rd.   Phone: (518) 346-8711
Schenectady, NY 12309   Elizabeth H. Groot, Mgr., Tech.Info.Serv.

SCHENECTADY COUNTY HISTORICAL SOCIETY - LIBRARY AND ARCHIVES
32 Washington Ave.   Phone: (518) 374-0263
Schenectady, NY 12305   Mrs. C.A. Church, Archv.

SCHENECTADY GAZETTE - LIBRARY
332 State St.   Phone: (518) 374-4141
Schenectady, NY 12301   Colleen J. Daze, Libn.

SCHENECTADY MUSEUM - LIBRARY *
Nott Terrace Heights   Phone: (518) 382-7890
Schenectady, NY 12308

UNION COLLEGE CHARACTER RESEARCH PROJECT - LIBRARY
207 State St.
Phone: (518) 370-6012
Schenectady, NY 12305
Hanford D. Wright, Hd.

UNION UNIVERSITY - DUDLEY OBSERVATORY - LIBRARY
69 Union Ave.
Phone: (518) 382-7583
Schenectady, NY 12308
Rita Spenser, Act.Libn.

U.S. DEPT. OF ENERGY - KNOLLS ATOMIC POWER LABORATORY -
LIBRARIES
Box 1072
Phone: (518) 393-6611
Schenectady, NY 12301
J. Olivia Yunker, Supv.

SCHOHARIE COUNTY HISTORICAL SOCIETY - REFERENCE LIBRARY
Old Stone Fort Museum, N. Main St.
Phone: (518) 295-7192
Schoharie, NY 12157
Helene S. Farrell, Dir.

SENECA FALLS HISTORICAL SOCIETY - LIBRARY
55 Cayuga St.
Phone: (315) 568-8412
Seneca Falls, NY 13148
Ann M. Hermann, Dir.

SHELTER ISLAND HISTORICAL SOCIETY - ARCHIVES
Havens House
Phone: (516) 749-0025
Shelter Island, NY 11964
Margaret Joyce, Chairwoman

ROGERS ENVIRONMENTAL EDUCATION CENTER - GEORGE W. HOTCHKIN
MEMORIAL LIBRARY
Box Q
Phone: (607) 674-2861
Sherburne, NY 13460
Nell Miller, Libn.

BENDIX CORPORATION - ELECTRICAL COMPONENTS DIVISION -
ENGINEERING LIBRARY
Phone: (607) 563-5605
Sidney, NY 13838
Betty L. Burnham, Libn.

SMITHTOWN HISTORICAL SOCIETY - LIBRARY
Route 25A
Phone: (516) 265-6768
Smithtown, NY 11787
Louise P. Hall, Dir.

SMITHTOWN LIBRARY
1 North Country Rd.
Phone: (516) 265-2072
Smithtown, NY 11787
Peter McCann Gillard, Act.Dir.

ALLIED CORPORATION - CHEMICALS COMPANY - SYRACUSE RESEARCH
LABORATORY - LIBRARY
Box 6
Phone: (315) 487-4151
Solvay, NY 13209
Betty L. Emery, Libn.

SOMERS HISTORICAL SOCIETY - LIBRARY AND ARCHIVES
Box 336
Phone: (914) 277-4977
Somers, NY 10589
Florence S. Oliver, Archv.

CRAIG DEVELOPMENTAL CENTER - MARGARET A. KENNGOTT MEMORIAL
LIBRARY OF THE HEALTH SCIENCES
Phone: (716) 658-2221
Sonyea, NY 14556
Rose M. Cipriano, Act.Libn.

PARRISH ART MUSEUM - MOSES & IDA SOYER FINE ART LIBRARY
25 Job's Ln.
Phone: (516) 283-2118
Southampton, NY 11968

SOUTHOLD HISTORICAL SOCIETY MUSEUM - LIBRARY
Main Rd. & Maple Ln.
Phone: (516) 765-5500
Southold, NY 11971
George D. Wagoner, Dir.

CENTER FOR MIGRATION STUDIES - LIBRARY
209 Flagg Pl.
Phone: (212) 351-8800
Staten Island, NY 10304
Nancy F. Avrin, Libn./Archv.

MARCHAIS (Jacques) CENTER OF TIBETAN ARTS, INC. - LIBRARY
338 Lighthouse Ave.
Phone: (212) 987-3478
Staten Island, NY 10306
Sigrid Sidrow, Libn.

NEW YORK STATE INSTITUTE FOR BASIC RESEARCH IN MENTAL
RETARDATION - LIBRARY
1050 Forest Hill Rd.
Phone: (212) 698-1122
Staten Island, NY 10314
Lawrence Black, Sr.Libn.

NEW YORK STATE SUPREME COURT - 2ND JUDICIAL DISTRICT - LAW
LIBRARY
County Court House
Phone: (212) 447-4748
Staten Island, NY 10301
Edward C. Wagner, Libn.

ST. JOHN'S UNIVERSITY, NOTRE DAME CAMPUS - LIBRARY
300 Howard Ave.
Phone: (212) 447-4343
Staten Island, NY 10301
William V. Stone, Libn.

SEA VIEW HOSPITAL AND HOME - MEDICAL LIBRARY
460 Brielle Ave.
Phone: (212) 390-8689
Staten Island, NY 10314
Selma Amtzis, Med.Libn.

STATEN ISLAND COOPERATIVE CONTINUUM - EDUCATIONAL RESOURCE
CENTER
130 Stuyvesant Pl., Rm. 704
Phone: (212) 390-7985
Staten Island, NY 10301
John Gino, Prog.Dir.

STATEN ISLAND DEVELOPMENTAL CENTER - LEARNING RESOURCES
CENTER †
2760 Victory Blvd., Bldg. 4
Staten Island, NY 10314

STATEN ISLAND HISTORICAL SOCIETY - LIBRARY
Court & Center Sts.
Phone: (212) 351-1611
Staten Island, NY 10306
Stephen C. Barto, Res.Assoc.

STATEN ISLAND HOSPITAL - MEDICAL STAFF LIBRARY *
450 Seaview Ave.
Phone: (212) 390-9000
Staten Island, NY 10305
Song Ja Oh, Dir.

STATEN ISLAND INSTITUTE OF ARTS AND SCIENCES - HIGH ROCK PARK
CONSERVATION CENTER - LIBRARY
200 Nevada Ave.
Phone: (212) 987-6233
Staten Island, NY 10306
Evelyn Hare, Libn.

STATEN ISLAND INSTITUTE OF ARTS AND SCIENCES - LIBRARY
75 Stuyvesant Pl.
Phone: (212) 727-1135
Staten Island, NY 10301
Gail K. Schneider, Adm.Libn.

STATEN ISLAND ZOOLOGICAL SOCIETY - LIBRARY
614 Broadway
Phone: (212) 442-3101
Staten Island, NY 10310

U.S. PUBLIC HEALTH SERVICE HOSPITAL - CHARLES FERGUSON MEDICAL
LIBRARY
Phone: (212) 447-3010
Staten Island, NY 10304
Marie R. McManus, Chf.Libn.

WAGNER COLLEGE - HORRMANN LIBRARY
631 Howard Ave.
Phone: (212) 390-3006
Staten Island, NY 10301
Y. John Auh, Hd.Libn.

U.S. NATL. PARK SERVICE - SARATOGA NATL. HISTORICAL PARK -
LIBRARY
R.D. 2, Box 33
Phone: (518) 664-9821
Stillwater, NY 12170
Michael Phillips, Chf.Hist.

INSTITUTE FOR ADVANCED STUDIES OF WORLD RELIGIONS - LIBRARY
Melville Memorial Library, 5th Fl.
SUNY at Stony Brook
Phone: (516) 246-8366
Stony Brook, NY 11794
C.T. Shen, Pres./Libn.

MUSEUMS AT STONY BROOK - KATE STRONG HISTORICAL LIBRARY
Rte. 25A
Phone: (516) 751-0066
Stony Brook, NY 11790
Janice Gray Armstrong, Libn.

SUNY AT STONY BROOK - BIOLOGICAL SCIENCES LIBRARY
Phone: (516) 246-5662
Stony Brook, NY 11794
Doris Williams, Libn.

SUNY AT STONY BROOK - CHEMISTRY LIBRARY
Phone: (516) 246-5664
Stony Brook, NY 11794
Esther C. Linkletter, Hd.

SUNY AT STONY BROOK - DEPARTMENT OF SPECIAL COLLECTIONS
Phone: (516) 246-3615
Stony Brook, NY 11794
Evert Volkersz, Libn.

SUNY AT STONY BROOK - EARTH AND SPACE SCIENCES LIBRARY
Phone: (516) 246-3616
Stony Brook, NY 11794
Rosalind Walcott, ESS Libn.

SUNY AT STONY BROOK - ENGINEERING LIBRARY
Phone: (516) 246-7724
Stony Brook, NY 11794
Kenneth W. Furst, Libn.

SUNY AT STONY BROOK - ENVIRONMENTAL INFORMATION SERVICE
Phone: (516) 246-5975
Stony Brook, NY 11794
David Allen, Libn.

SUNY AT STONY BROOK - MAP LIBRARY
Phone: (516) 246-5975
Stony Brook, NY 11794
Barbara A. Shupe, Libn.

SUNY AT STONY BROOK - MATHEMATICS-PHYSICS LIBRARY
Physics Bldg., C Fl.
Phone: (516) 246-5666
Stony Brook, NY 11794
Sherry Chang, Libn.

SUNY AT STONY BROOK - MUSIC LIBRARY
Phone: (516) 246-5660
Stony Brook, NY 11794
Judith Kaufman, Libn.

AVON PRODUCTS, INC. - TECHNICAL INFORMATION CENTER LIBRARY
Division St.
Phone: (914) 357-2000
Suffern, NY 10901
Rosa K. Conlon, Sect.Mgr.

SALVATION ARMY SCHOOL FOR OFFICERS TRAINING - BRENGLE MEMORIAL LIBRARY
201 Lafayette Ave.
Phone: (914) 357-3500
Suffern, NY 10901
Maj. Lorraine Sacks, Libn.

HARRIS CORPORATION - PRD ELECTRONICS DIVISION - INFORMATION CENTER
6801 Jericho Tpke.
Phone: (516) 364-0400
Syosset, NY 11791
Eleanor Pienitz, Libn., Info.Spec.

NORTH SHORE SYNAGOGUE - CHARLES COHN MEMORIAL LIBRARY
83 Muttontown Rd.
Phone: (516) 921-2282
Syosset, NY 11791
Elaine Charnow, Libn.

U.S. GEOLOGICAL SURVEY - WATER RESOURCES DIVISION - NEW YORK SUBDISTRICT - LIBRARY
5 Aerial Way
Phone: (516) 938-8830
Syosset, NY 11791
Joan Bachmann, Lib. Aid

WATER INFORMATION CENTER, INC.
The North Shore Atrium
6800 Jericho Tpke.
Syosset, NY 11791
David W. Miller, Pres.

AGWAY, INC. - CORPORATE LIBRARY
Box 4933
Phone: (315) 477-6408
Syracuse, NY 13221
Ron Herrgesell, Libn.

BORDEN INC. - RESEARCH CENTRE - LIBRARY
600 N. Franklin St.
Phone: (315) 474-8526
Syracuse, NY 13204
Carol Lenz Taylor, Libn.

BRISTOL-MYERS COMPANY - BRISTOL LABORATORIES - LIBRARY AND INFORMATION SERVICES
Box 657
Phone: (315) 432-2232
Syracuse, NY 13201
John S. Silvin, Dir.

CANAL MUSEUM - RESEARCH LIBRARY AND DOCUMENTATION CENTER
Canal Museum Administration Bldg.
315 Water St.
Phone: (315) 471-0593
Syracuse, NY 13202
Todd S. Weseloh, Libn./Archv.

CARRIER CORPORATION - LOGAN LEWIS LIBRARY
Research Division, Carrier Pkwy.
Box 4808
Phone: (315) 432-6306
Syracuse, NY 13221
Jennifer Huitfeldt, Mgr., Info.Res.

CENTRAL NEW YORK REGIONAL PLANNING & DEVELOPMENT BOARD - LIBRARY & INFORMATION CENTER
700 E. Water St., Midtown Plaza
Phone: (315) 422-8276
Syracuse, NY 13210
Paul Jasek, Res.Asst.

COMMUNITY-GENERAL HOSPITAL OF GREATER SYRACUSE - STAFF LIBRARY
Broad Rd.
Phone: (315) 492-5500
Syracuse, NY 13215
Jessica Boysen, Staff Libn.

CROUSE-IRVING MEMORIAL HOSPITAL - LIBRARY
736 Irving Ave.
Phone: (315) 424-6380
Syracuse, NY 13210
Eden J. Gruenberg, Libn.

ERIC CLEARINGHOUSE ON INFORMATION RESOURCES
Syracuse Univ., School of Education
150 Marshall St.
Phone: (315) 423-3640
Syracuse, NY 13210
Dr. Donald Ely, Dir.

EVERSON MUSEUM OF ART - LIBRARY *
401 Harrison St.
Phone: (315) 474-6064
Syracuse, NY 13202
Barbara C. Polowy, Libn.

GENERAL ELECTRIC COMPANY - ELECTRONICS PARK LIBRARY *
Electronics Park, Bldg. 3, Rm. 154
Phone: (315) 456-2023
Syracuse, NY 13221
Connie Steward, Mgr.

HANCOCK, ESTABROOK, RYAN, SHOVE & HUST - LAW LIBRARY
One Mony Plaza
Phone: (315) 471-3151
Syracuse, NY 13202
Judy A. Lauer, Libn.

LAUBACH LITERACY INTERNATIONAL, INC. - LIBRARY
1320 Jamesville Ave.
Box 131
Phone: (315) 422-9121
Syracuse, NY 13210
Jeannette Smithee, Libn.

LITERACY VOLUNTEERS OF AMERICA, INC. - LIBRARY
623 Midtown Plaza
700 E. Water St.
Phone: (315) 474-7039
Syracuse, NY 13210
Barbara J. MacDonald, Supv.

MAC KENZIE, SMITH, LEWIS, MICHELL & HUGHES - LAW LIBRARY
600 Onondaga Savings Bank Bldg.
Phone: (315) 474-7571
Syracuse, NY 13202
Cynthia J. Kesler, Libn.

MANUFACTURERS ASSOCIATION OF CENTRAL NEW YORK - LIBRARY
770 James St.
Phone: (315) 474-4201
Syracuse, NY 13203
Mary F. Pennock, Lib.Assoc.

NEW YORK STATE SUPREME COURT - APPELLATE DIVISION, 4TH JUDICIAL DEPARTMENT - LAW LIBRARY
500 Court House
Phone: (315) 425-2063
Syracuse, NY 13202
Susan M. Wood, Libn.

ONONDAGA COUNTY PUBLIC LIBRARY - ART AND MUSIC DEPARTMENT
335 Montgomery St.
Phone: (415) 473-4492
Syracuse, NY 13202
Beatrice N. Marble, Dept.Hd.

ONONDAGA COUNTY PUBLIC LIBRARY - BUSINESS AND INDUSTRIAL DEPARTMENT
335 Montgomery St.
Phone: (315) 473-4493
Syracuse, NY 13202
Evelyn B. Phelps, Dept.Hd.

ONONDAGA COUNTY PUBLIC LIBRARY - LOCAL HISTORY AND GENEALOGY DEPARTMENT
335 Montgomery St.
Phone: (315) 473-6801
Syracuse, NY 13202
Gerald J. Parsons, Dept.Hd.

ONONDAGA HISTORICAL ASSOCIATION - LIBRARY
311 Montgomery St.
Phone: (315) 422-9948
Syracuse, NY 13202

ST. JOSEPH'S HOSPITAL HEALTH CENTER - MEDICAL AND SCHOOL OF NURSING LIBRARIES
301 Prospect Ave.
Phone: (315) 424-5053
Syracuse, NY 13203
Mr. V. Juchimek, Hd.Libn.

SUNY - COLLEGE OF ENVIRONMENTAL SCIENCE AND FORESTRY - F. FRANKLIN MOON LIBRARY
Phone: (315) 470-6715
Syracuse, NY 13210
Donald F. Webster, Dir.

SUNY - UPSTATE MEDICAL CENTER LIBRARY
766 Irving Ave.   Phone: (315) 473-4580
Syracuse, NY 13210   Evelyn L. Hoey, Dir.

SYRACUSE RESEARCH CORPORATION - LIBRARY
Merrill Lane   Phone: (315) 425-5200
Syracuse, NY 13210   Mary E. O'Neill, Res.Libn.

SYRACUSE UNIVERSITY - CHEMISTRY LIBRARY
308 Bowne Hall   Phone: (315) 423-2212
Syracuse, NY 13210

SYRACUSE UNIVERSITY - E.S. BIRD LIBRARY - AREA STUDIES
    DEPARTMENT
                                             Phone: (315) 423-4176
Syracuse, NY 13210   Gurnek Singh, Dept.Hd./Asian Bibl.

SYRACUSE UNIVERSITY - E.S. BIRD LIBRARY - FINE ARTS DEPARTMENT
                                             Phone: (315) 423-2440
Syracuse, NY 13210   Donald Seibert, Dept.Hd.

SYRACUSE UNIVERSITY - E.S. BIRD LIBRARY - HUMANITIES DEPARTMENT
                                             Phone: (315) 423-4243
Syracuse, NY 13210

SYRACUSE UNIVERSITY - E.S. BIRD LIBRARY - SOCIAL SCIENCES
    DEPARTMENT
                                             Phone: (315) 423-3715
Syracuse, NY 13210   Carl Braun, Dept.Hd.

SYRACUSE UNIVERSITY - ENGINEERING & LIFE SCIENCES LIBRARY
105 Carnegie   Phone: (315) 423-2160
Syracuse, NY 13210   Pauline M. Miller, Hd.Sci. & Tech.Dept.

SYRACUSE UNIVERSITY - GEOLOGY LIBRARY
300 Heroy Geology Lab   Phone: (315) 423-3337
Syracuse, NY 13210   Eileen Snyder, Libn.

SYRACUSE UNIVERSITY - GEORGE ARENTS RESEARCH LIBRARY FOR
    SPECIAL COLLECTIONS
E.S. Bird Library   Phone: (315) 423-2585
Syracuse, NY 13210   Sidney F. Huttner, Hd.

SYRACUSE UNIVERSITY - LAW LIBRARY
E.I. White Hall   Phone: (315) 423-2528
Syracuse, NY 13210   Thomas C. Kingsley, Libn.

SYRACUSE UNIVERSITY - MATHEMATICS LIBRARY
308 Carnegie Bldg.   Phone: (315) 423-2092
Syracuse, NY 13210   Nancy Rude, Asst.Biblog.

SYRACUSE UNIVERSITY - PHYSICS LIBRARY
208 Physics Bldg.   Phone: (315) 423-2692
Syracuse, NY 13210   Eileen Snyder, Libn.

SYRACUSE UNIVERSITY - SCHOOL OF EDUCATION - EDUCATIONAL
    RESOURCE CENTER
150 Marshall St.   Phone: (315) 423-3800
Syracuse, NY 13210   Dr. Tom Rusk Vickery, Dir.

U.S. VETERANS ADMINISTRATION (NY-Syracuse) - MEDICAL CENTER
    LIBRARY
Irving Ave. & University Pl.   Phone: (315) 476-7461
Syracuse, NY 13210   June M. Mitchell, Chf., Lib.Serv.

CHEM SYSTEMS INC. - INFORMATION CENTER
303 S. Broadway   Phone: (914) 631-2828
Tarrytown, NY 10591   Milton B. Wenger, Info.Spec.

HISTORICAL SOCIETY OF THE TARRYTOWNS - HEADQUARTERS LIBRARY
19 Grove St. & 1 Grove St.   Phone: (914) 631-8374
Tarrytown, NY 10591   Adelaide R. Smith, Cur.

RAYMOND, PARISH, PINE & WEINER, INC. - LIBRARY
555 White Plains Rd.   Phone: (914) 631-9003
Tarrytown, NY 10591   Vera E. Albert, Libn.

SLEEPY HOLLOW RESTORATIONS, INC. - SPECIAL LIBRARY & ARCHIVES
150 White Plains Rd.   Phone: (914) 631-8200
Tarrytown, NY 10591   Hollee Haswell, Libn.

TEACHER AUTHOR LEAGUE OF AMERICA - LIBRARY
177 White Plains Rd., Suite 60-F
Tarrytown, NY 10591

TECHNICON INSTRUMENTS CORPORATION - LIBRARY
511 Benedict Ave.   Phone: (914) 631-8000
Tarrytown, NY 10591   L.E. Billyou, Libn.

UNION CARBIDE CORPORATION - I.S. INFORMATION CENTER
Spine Bldg., Level 02
Saw Mill River Rd.
Tarrytown, NY 10591   Maureen D. Flanagan, Libn.

UNION CARBIDE CORPORATION - LIBRARY & TECHNICAL INFORMATION
    SERVICE †
Tarrytown Technical Center   Phone: (914) 789-3700
Tarrytown, NY 10591   Joan Schechtman, Mgr.

LETCHWORTH VILLAGE DEVELOPMENTAL CENTER - ISAAC N. WOLFSON
    LIBRARY
                                             Phone: (914) 947-1000
Thiells, NY 10984   Cherie Werbel, Sr.Libn.

FORT TICONDEROGA MUSEUM - LIBRARY
Box 390   Phone: (518) 585-2821
Ticonderoga, NY 12883   Jane M. Lape, Cur.-Libn.

TEMPLE BETH EL - LIBRARY
2368 Eggert Rd.   Phone: (716) 836-3762
Tonawanda, NY 14150   Sandra Freed Gralnick, Libn.

UNION CARBIDE CORPORATION - LINDE DIVISION - TECHNICAL LIBRARY
Box 44   Phone: (716) 879-2031
Tonawanda, NY 14150   Sandra C. Anderson, Tech.Libn.

HUDSON VALLEY COMMUNITY COLLEGE - DWIGHT MARVIN LEARNING
    RESOURCES CENTER *
80 Vandenburgh Ave.   Phone: (518) 283-1100
Troy, NY 12180   James F. McCoy, Dir.

NEW YORK STATE SUPREME COURT - 3RD JUDICIAL DISTRICT - LAW
    LIBRARY
Court House, 2nd St. Annex
Rensselaer County   Phone: (518) 270-5238
Troy, NY 12180   Mary S. Burch, Law Libn.

NORTON COMPANY - COATED ABRASIVE DIVISION - TECHNICAL LIBRARY
Box 808   Phone: (518) 273-0100
Troy, NY 12181   P.E. Smith, Tech.Serv.Adm.

RENSSELAER COUNTY HISTORICAL SOCIETY - LIBRARY
59 Second St.   Phone: (518) 272-7232
Troy, NY 12180   Mrs. Frederick R. Walsh, Dir.

RENSSELAER POLYTECHNIC INSTITUTE - ARCHITECTURE LIBRARY
                                             Phone: (518) 270-6465
Troy, NY 12181   Virginia S. Bailey

RENSSELAER POLYTECHNIC INSTITUTE - FOLSOM LIBRARY
                                             Phone: (518) 270-6673
Troy, NY 12181   James C. Andrews, Dir. of Lib.

ST. MARY'S HOSPITAL - MEDICAL STAFF LIBRARY
1300 Massachusetts Ave.   Phone: (518) 272-5000
Troy, NY 12180   Audna T. Clum, Libn.

SAMARITAN HOSPITAL - MEDICAL LIBRARY
2215 Burdett Ave.   Phone: (518) 271-3200
Troy, NY 12180   Annie J. Smith, Med.Libn.

TROY TIMES RECORD - LIBRARY
501 Broadway   Phone: (518) 272-2000
Troy, NY 12181   Ingrid Sharke, Libn.

GEOGRAPHIC

REVLON HEALTH CARE GROUP - INFORMATION SERVICES DEPARTMENT
One Scarsdale Rd.   Phone: (914) 779-6300
Tuckahoe, NY 10707   Amy M. Levine, Dir., Info.Serv.

ST. VLADIMIR'S ORTHODOX THEOLOGICAL SEMINARY - FR. GEORGES
  FLOROVSKY LIBRARY
575 Scarsdale Rd.   Phone: (914) 961-8313
Tuckahoe, NY 10707   Paul D. Garrett, Libn.

WESTCHESTER COUNTY HISTORICAL SOCIETY - LIBRARY
43 Read Ave.   Phone: (914) 337-1753
Tuckahoe, NY 10707   Elizabeth G. Fuller, Libn.

CINTICHEM, INC. - LIBRARY
Box 816   Phone: (914) 351-2131
Tuxedo, NY 10987   Mary Ruth Bateman, Tech.Libn.

INTERNATIONAL PAPER COMPANY - CORPORATE RESEARCH &
  DEVELOPMENT DIVISION - TECHNICAL INFORMATION CENTER
Box 797   Phone: (914) 351-2101
Tuxedo, NY 10987   Bernadette Marasco, Sr.Tech.Info.Spec.

NEW YORK UNIVERSITY MEDICAL CENTER - INSTITUTE OF
  ENVIRONMENTAL MEDICINE - LIBRARY
Long Meadow Rd., Sterling Forest   Phone: (914) 351-4232
Tuxedo, NY 10987   Christine M. Singleton, Res.Libn.

U.S. DEPT. OF ENERGY - BROOKHAVEN NATL. LABORATORY - TECHNICAL
  INFORMATION DIVISION
                                                Phone: (516) 282-3489
Upton, NY 11973   Mary Winkels, Mgr., Tech.Info.Div.

GENERAL ELECTRIC COMPANY - AIRCRAFT EQUIPMENT DIVISION -
  INFORMATION RESOURCES
901 Broad St.   Phone: (315) 797-1000
Utica, NY 13503   Catherine Walsh, Supv.

HERKIMER-ONEIDA COUNTIES COMPREHENSIVE PLANNING PROGRAM -
  LIBRARY
800 Park Ave.   Phone: (315) 798-5721
Utica, NY 13501   Michael Gapin, Prog.Dir.

INTERNATIONAL ASSOCIATION FOR IDENTIFICATION - LIBRARY
Box 139   Phone: (315) 732-2897
Utica, NY 13503   Walter G. Hoetzer, Sec./Treas.

MASONIC MEDICAL RESEARCH LABORATORY - LIBRARY
2150 Bleecker St.   Phone: (315) 735-2217
Utica, NY 13501   Irma S. Tuttle, Libn.

MOHAWK VALLEY COMMUNITY COLLEGE - LIBRARY
1101 Sherman Dr.   Phone: (315) 792-5408
Utica, NY 13501   Alice B. Griffith, Lib.Dir.

MUNSON-WILLIAMS-PROCTOR INSTITUTE - ART REFERENCE AND MUSIC
  LIBRARY
310 Genesee St.   Phone: (315) 797-0000
Utica, NY 13502   Barbara C. Polowy, Libn.

NEW YORK STATE SUPREME COURT - 5TH JUDICIAL DISTRICT - LAW
  LIBRARY †
Oneida County Court House   Phone: (315) 798-5703
Utica, NY 13501   Doris M. Ravina, Libn.

ONEIDA HISTORICAL SOCIETY - LIBRARY
318 Genesee St.   Phone: (315) 797-0000
Utica, NY 13502   Alice C. Dodge, Libn.

ST. ELIZABETH'S HOSPITAL - NURSING SCHOOL LIBRARY
2215 Genesee St.   Phone: (315) 798-5209
Utica, NY 13503   Ann M. Kelly, Libn.

UTICA/MARCY PSYCHIATRIC CENTER - MARCY CAMPUS PROFESSIONAL
  LIBRARY
1213 Court St.   Phone: (315) 736-3301
Utica, NY 13502   Janina Strife, Sr.Libn.

UTICA/MARCY PSYCHIATRIC CENTER - UTICA CAMPUS LIBRARY
  SERVICES
1213 Court St.   Phone: (315) 797-6800
Utica, NY 13502   Toms E. Smith, Sr.Libn.

UTICA MUTUAL INSURANCE COMPANY - REFERENCE AND LAW LIBRARY
Box 530   Phone: (315) 735-3321
Utica, NY 13503   Nora Morse, Ref.Libn.

UTICA OBSERVER DISPATCH & UTICA DAILY PRESS - LIBRARY †
221 Oriskany Plaza   Phone: (315) 792-5004
Utica, NY 13503   Virginia Malecki

NEW YORK MEDICAL COLLEGE AND THE WESTCHESTER ACADEMY OF
  MEDICINE - WESTCHESTER MEDICAL CENTER LIBRARY
New York Medical College
Basic Sciences Bldg.   Phone: (914) 347-5237
Valhalla, NY 10595   Donald E. Roy, Dir.

PEPSICO, INC. - INFORMATION CENTER
100 Stevens Ave.
Valhalla, NY 10595   Helen Regan, Libn.

WESTCHESTER COUNTY MEDICAL CENTER - HEALTH SCIENCES LIBRARY
                                                Phone: (914) 347-7033
Valhalla, NY 10595   Joan Giordano, Med.Libn.

TOLSTOY FOUNDATION CENTER - TOLSTOY LIBRARY *
Lake Rd.   Phone: (914) 268-6551
Valley Cottage, NY 10989   George T. Spudeiko, Hd.Libn.

FRANKLIN GENERAL HOSPITAL - MEDICAL LIBRARY
900 Franklin Ave.   Phone: (516) 825-8800
Valley Stream, NY 11580   Kathryn A. Boccieri, Libn.

MADISON COUNTY LAW LIBRARY
Court House
Wampsville, NY 13163

WARSAW HISTORICAL SOCIETY - LIBRARY *
15 Perry Ave.
Warsaw, NY 14569   Lewis H. Bishop

GENERAL ELECTRIC COMPANY - SILICONE PRODUCTS DIVISION - LIBRARY
                                                Phone: (518) 237-3330
Waterford, NY 12188   Marianne K. Pouliott, Libn.

WATERLOO LIBRARY AND HISTORICAL SOCIETY †
31 E. Williams St.   Phone: (315) 539-3313
Waterloo, NY 13165   Elizabeth A. Stetz, Libn.

JEFFERSON COUNTY HISTORICAL SOCIETY - LIBRARY
228 Washington St.   Phone: (315) 782-3491
Watertown, NY 13601   Margaret W.M. Shaeffer, Dir.

MERCY HOSPITAL OF WATERTOWN - HEALTH SCIENCE LIBRARY
218 Stone St.   Phone: (315) 782-7400
Watertown, NY 13601   Jeffrey M. Garvey, Libn.

NEW YORK STATE SUPREME COURT - 5TH JUDICIAL DISTRICT -
  WATERTOWN LAW LIBRARY
Court House   Phone: (315) 785-3064
Watertown, NY 13601   Patrica B. Donaldson, Libn.

U.S. ARMY - ARMAMENT RESEARCH & DEVELOPMENT COMMAND - BENET
  WEAPONS LABORATORY - TECHNICAL LIBRARY
Watervliet Arsenal
Attn: DRDAR-LCB-TL   Phone: (518) 266-5613
Watervliet, NY 12189   George K. Vrooman, Chf., Sci./Tech.Info.

AMERICAN LIFE FOUNDATION AND STUDY INSTITUTE - AMERICANA
  RESEARCH LIBRARY
Old Irelandville, Box 349   Phone: (607) 535-4737
Watkins Glen, NY 14891   John Crosby Freeman, Dir.

PRANG-MARK SOCIETY - LIBRARY
Old Irelandville   Phone: (607) 535-4004
Watkins Glen, NY 14891   L. M. Goodman, Coord.

XEROX CORPORATION - TECHNICAL INFORMATION CENTER
Box 305   Phone: (716) 422-3505
Webster, NY 14580   Michael D. Majcher, Mgr.

PILGRIM PSYCHIATRIC CENTER - HEALTH SCIENCES LIBRARY
                                                      Phone: (516) 231-8000
West Brentwood, NY 11717   Aime Atlas, Sr.Libn.

HELEN HAYES HOSPITAL - LIBRARY
Route 9W   Phone: (914) 947-3000
West Haverstraw, NY 10993   Kathleen Kuczynski, Lib.Dir.

CONSTITUTION ISLAND ASSOCIATION, INC. - WARNER HOUSE LIBRARY *
Box 41   Phone: (914) 446-8676
West Point, NY 10996

U.S. ARMY - MILITARY ACADEMY - ARCHIVES
                                                      Phone: (914) 938-2017
West Point, NY 10996   Ed Cass, Archv.

U.S. ARMY - MILITARY ACADEMY - LIBRARY
                                                      Phone: (914) 938-2209
West Point, NY 10966   Egon A. Weiss, Libn.

SUFFOLK MARINE MUSEUM - HERVEY G. SMITH RESEARCH LIBRARY
Montauk Hwy.   Phone: (516) 567-1733
West Sayville, NY 11796   Gertrude Welte, Registrar

HOUGHTON COLLEGE - BUFFALO SUBURBAN CAMPUS - ADA M. KIDDER
    MEMORIAL LIBRARY
910 Union Rd.   Phone: (716) 674-6363
West Seneca, NY 14224   Ruth G. Butler, Libn.

BOARD OF COOPERATIVE EDUCATIONAL SERVICES OF NASSAU COUNTY
    (BOCES) - NASSAU EDUC. RSRCS. CTR. (NERC)
111 Cantiague Rock Rd.   Phone: (516) 931-8121
Westbury, NY 11590

METCO INC. - ENGINEERING LIBRARY
1101 Prospect Ave.   Phone: (516) 334-1300
Westbury, NY 11590   Peter H. Leonard, Dir.

CHAUTAUQUA COUNTY HISTORICAL SOCIETY - LIBRARY
McClurg Mansion, Village Park   Phone: (716) 326-2977
Westfield, NY 14787   Maxine Smith, Hostess/Libn.

GENERAL FOODS CORPORATION - MARKETING INFORMATION CENTER
250 North St.   Phone: (914) 683-3911
White Plains, NY 10625   Lois Seulowitz, Mgr.

GENERAL FOODS CORPORATION - TECHNICAL CENTER - TARRYTOWN
    TECHNICAL INFORMATION CENTER
                                                      Phone: (914) 683-6827
White Plains, NY 10625   Elinor Cohen, Adm., Tech.Info.Serv.

IBM CORPORATION - DP COMMUNICATIONS LIBRARY †
1133 Westchester Ave.   Phone: (914) 696-2382
White Plains, NY 10604   Anne A. Austin, Manager

MALCOLM PIRNIE, INC. - TECHNICAL LIBRARY
2 Corporate Park Dr.   Phone: (914) 694-2100
White Plains, NY 10602   Myron E. Menewitch, Tech.Libn.

MARCH OF DIMES BIRTH DEFECTS FOUNDATION - REFERENCE ROOM
1275 Mamaroneck Ave.   Phone: (914) 428-7100
White Plains, NY 10605   Sandra Schepis, Libn.

MENTAL HEALTH ASSOCIATION OF WESTCHESTER COUNTY - LIBRARY
29 Sterling Ave.   Phone: (914) 949-6741
White Plains, NY 10606   Mary H. Johnson, Libn.

NEW YORK HOSPITAL - CORNELL MEDICAL CENTER, WESTCHESTER
    DIVISION - MEDICAL LIBRARY
21 Bloomingdale Rd.   Phone: (914) 682-9100
White Plains, NY 10605   Lillian A. Wahrow, Med.Libn.

NEW YORK STATE SUPREME COURT - 9TH JUDICIAL DISTRICT - LAW
    LIBRARY
Westchester County Court House
111 Grove St., 9th Fl.   Phone: (914) 682-2574
White Plains, NY 10601   Harriet E. Smith, Principal Law Libn.

PACE UNIVERSITY - SCHOOL OF LAW LIBRARY
78 N. Broadway   Phone: (914) 682-7272
White Plains, NY 10603   Bardie C. Wolfe, Jr., Law Libn./Professor

PHARMACEUTICAL SOCIETY OF THE STATE OF NEW YORK - ACADEMY OF
    PHARMACY LIBRARY *
925 Westchester Ave.   Phone: (914) 428-2626
White Plains, NY 10604

WHITE PLAINS HOSPITAL - BERTON LATTIN MEMORIAL MEDICAL LIBRARY
E. Post Rd. at Davis Ave.   Phone: (914) 682-4799
White Plains, NY 10601   Marion C. Renz, Dir.

COUNCIL ON NATIONAL LITERATURES - INFORMATION CENTER
Box 81   Phone: (212) 767-8380
Whitestone, NY 11357   Anne Paolucci, Exec.Dir.

WILLARD PSYCHIATRIC CENTER - PROFESSIONAL LIBRARY *
                                                      Phone: (607) 869-3111
Willard, NY 14588   Steven Scott Krompf, Chf., Lib.Serv.

HARLEM VALLEY PSYCHIATRIC CENTER - INTERDISCIPLINARY LIBRARY
                                                      Phone: (914) 832-6611
Wingdale, NY 12594   Virginia Lewandowski, Libn.

BURNS AND ROE, INC. - JAMES MACLEAN TECHNICAL LIBRARY
185 Crossways Park Dr.   Phone: (516) 677-2300
Woodbury, NY 11797   Emerenciana S. Santos, Tech.Libn.

BULOVA (Joseph) SCHOOL OF WATCHMAKING - LIBRARY
40-24 62nd St.   Phone: (212) 424-2929
Woodside, Queens, NY 11377   James M. Devaney, Dir.

MIDDLEBURY HISTORICAL SOCIETY - MIDDLEBURY ACADEMY MUSEUM
    LIBRARY *
22 S. Academy St.   Phone: (716) 495-6495
Wyoming, NY 14591   Mary D. Wilson, Sec.

LORAL ELECTRONIC SYSTEMS - TECHNICAL INFORMATION CENTER
999 Central Park Ave.   Phone: (914) 968-2800
Yonkers, NY 10704   Terry Mozorosky, Tech.Info.Spec.

POLYCHROME CORPORATION - RESEARCH & DEVELOPMENT LIBRARY †
137 Alexander St.   Phone: (914) 965-8800
Yonkers, NY 10702   Cynthia Zapf, Libn.

ST. JOHN'S RIVERSIDE HOSPITAL - MEDICAL LIBRARY
967 N. Broadway   Phone: (914) 963-3535
Yonkers, NY 10701   Helen A. Vocasek, Dir., Med.Rec.

ST. JOSEPH'S MEDICAL CENTER - MEDICAL LIBRARY
127 S. Broadway   Phone: (914) 965-6700
Yonkers, NY 10701   Ann Gorghan, Libn.

ST. JOSEPH'S SEMINARY - ARCHBISHOP CORRIGAN MEMORIAL LIBRARY †
Dunwoodie   Phone: (914) 968-6200
Yonkers, NY 10704   Richard P. Breaden, Lib.Dir.

YONKERS GENERAL HOSPITAL - MEDICAL LIBRARY
127 Ashburton Ave.   Phone: (914) 965-8200
Yonkers, NY 10701   Lucila R. Samson, Med.Libn.

YONKERS HISTORICAL SOCIETY - LIBRARY
Hudson River Museum
511 Warburton Ave.   Phone: (914) 969-5622
Yonkers, NY 10701   Olga C. Kourre, Libn.

YONKERS PUBLIC LIBRARY - FINE ARTS DEPARTMENT
1500 Central Park Ave.   Phone: (914) 337-1500
Yonkers, NY 10710   Martita Schwarz, Dept.Hd.

YONKERS PUBLIC LIBRARY - REFERENCE & INFORMATION SERVICES
7 Main St.   Phone: (914) 337-1500
Yonkers, NY 10701   Elinor L. Upton, Tech.Libn.

IBM CORPORATION - THOMAS J. WATSON RESEARCH CENTER LIBRARY
Box 218   Phone: (914) 945-1415
Yorktown Heights, NY 10598   J.W. Leonard, Mgr.

OLD FORT NIAGARA ASSOCIATION - LIBRARY
Box 169
Youngstown, NY 14174
Phone: (716) 745-7611
Brian Leigh Dunnigan, Exec.Dir.

NORTH CAROLINA

MOORE, GARDNER & ASSOCIATES, INC. - LIBRARY
Box 728
Asheboro, NC 27203
Phone: (919) 625-6111
Louise C. Johnston, Libn.

MOUNTAIN AREA HEALTH EDUCATION CENTER - HEALTH SCIENCES
LIBRARY
501 Biltmore Ave.
Asheville, NC 28801
Phone: (704) 258-0881
Linda C. Butson, Libn.

U.S. FOREST SERVICE - SOUTHEASTERN FOREST EXPERIMENT STATION
LIBRARY †
Box 2570
Asheville, NC 28802
Phone: (704) 258-2850
Margaret Jean Taylor, Libn.

U.S. NATL. OCEANIC & ATMOSPHERIC ADM. - ENVIRONMENTAL DATA &
INFO. SERV. - NATL. CLIMATIC CTR. LIBRARY
Federal Bldg., D542x2
Asheville, NC 28801
Phone: (704) 258-2850
Joseph M. Bauman, Chf., User Serv.

U.S. VETERANS ADMINISTRATION (NC-Asheville) - MEDICAL CENTER
LIBRARY
Asheville, NC 28805
Phone: (704) 298-7911
Richard Haver, Chf.Libn.

WORLD DATA CENTER A - METEOROLOGY AND NUCLEAR RADIATION
Natl. Oceanic and Atmospheric Adm.
Environmental Data & Info.Serv.
Federal Bldg.
Asheville, NC 28801
Phone: (704) 258-2850
H.L. Suits, Dir.

COUNTRY DOCTOR MUSEUM - LIBRARY
Vance St.
Box 34
Bailey, NC 27807
Phone: (919) 235-4165
Joyce R. Cooper, Exec.Sec.

DUKE UNIVERSITY - MARINE LABORATORY - A.S. PEARSE MEMORIAL
LIBRARY
Beaufort, NC 28516
Phone: (919) 728-2111
Jean S. Williams, Sr.Lib.Asst.

U.S. NATL. MARINE FISHERIES SERVICE - SOUTHEAST FISHERIES CENTER
- BEAUFORT LABORATORY LIBRARY †
Beaufort, NC 28516
Phone: (919) 728-4595
Ann Bowman Hall, Libn.

U.S. NATL. PARK SERVICE - CAPE LOOKOUT NATL. SEASHORE - LIBRARY
415 Front St.
Beaufort, NC 28516
Phone: (919) 728-2121
Philip R. Brueck, Chf., Park Oper.

BELMONT ABBEY COLLEGE - ABBOT VINCENT TAYLOR LIBRARY
Belmont, NC 28012
Phone: (704) 825-3711
Jane Freeman, Libn.

GULF RESOURCES AND CHEMICAL CORPORATION - LITHIUM
CORPORATION OF AMERICA, INC. - RESEARCH LIBRARY
Box 795
Bessemer City, NC 28016
Phone: (704) 692-2282
JoAnn Trull, Libn.

APPALACHIAN STATE UNIVERSITY - BELK LIBRARY
Boone, NC 28608
Phone: (704) 262-2186
Richard T. Barker, Libn.

APPALACHIAN STATE UNIVERSITY - MUSIC LIBRARY
I.G. Greer Music Bldg.
Boone, NC 28608
Phone: (704) 262-2292
Joan O. Falconer, Music Libn.

BREVARD COLLEGE - JAMES A. JONES LIBRARY - FINE ARTS DIVISION
Brevard, NC 28712
Phone: (704) 883-8292
Mary Margaret Houk, Dir.

FIRST BAPTIST CHURCH - LIBRARY
Gaston & Morgan Sts.
Brevard, NC 28712
Phone: (704) 883-8251
Edna Bryson, Libn.

CAMPBELL UNIVERSITY - SCHOOL OF LAW - LAW LIBRARY
Box 458
Buies Creek, NC 27506
Phone: (919) 893-4111
Karen C. Sorvari, Dir. of Res.

UMSTEAD (John) HOSPITAL - LEARNING RESOURCE CENTER
Butner, NC 27509
Phone: (919) 575-7259
Brenda M. Ellis, Libn.

U.S. NAVY - NAVAL REGIONAL MEDICAL CENTER (Camp Lejeune) - MEDICAL
LIBRARY
Camp Lejeune, NC 28542
Phone: (919) 451-4570
Betty Frazelle, Lib.Techn.

UNIVERSITY OF NORTH CAROLINA, CHAPEL HILL - CENTER FOR EARLY
ADOLESCENCE - INFORMATION SERVICES DIVISION
Carr Mill Mall, Suite 223
Carrboro, NC 27510
Phone: (919) 966-1148
David Sheaves, Info.Serv.Coord.

ASSOCIATION FOR POPULATION/FAMILY PLANNING LIBRARIES &
INFORMATION CENTERS INTERNATIONAL
c/o Carolina Population Center Library
University Square - East 300A
Chapel Hill, NC 27514
Alice D. Harris, Pres.

BLUE CROSS AND BLUE SHIELD OF NORTH CAROLINA - INFORMATION
CENTER
5901 Chapel Hill-Durham Blvd.
Box 2291
Chapel Hill, NC 27514
Phone: (919) 489-7431
Tera B. White, Mgr., Corp.Info.Serv.

CAROLINA LIBRARY SERVICES
137 E. Rosemary St.
Chapel Hill, NC 27514
Phone: (919) 929-4870
Eva C. Metzger, Dir.

CAROLINA POPULATION CENTER - LIBRARY
University Sq., 123 W. Franklin St.
Chapel Hill, NC 27514
Phone: (919) 933-3081
Patricia E. Shipman, Hd.Libn.

KXE6S VEREIN CHESS SOCIETY - SPECIAL/RESEARCH LIBRARY - EAST
DIVISION
Box 2066
Chapel Hill, NC 27514
Steven Leslie Buntin, Bibliothecar

PSYCHICAL RESEARCH FOUNDATION - DAVID WAYNE HOOKS MEMORIAL
LIBRARY
214 Pittsboro St.
Chapel Hill, NC 27514
Phone: (919) 968-4956

SOUTHEAST INSTITUTE - LIBRARY †
100 Eastowne
Box 2183
Chapel Hill, NC 27514
Phone: (919) 929-1171
Vann Joines, Pres.

UNIVERSITY OF NORTH CAROLINA, CHAPEL HILL - ART LIBRARY
Ackland Art Ctr.
Chapel Hill, NC 27514
Phone: (919) 933-2397
Philip A. Rees, Art Libn.

UNIVERSITY OF NORTH CAROLINA, CHAPEL HILL - CHEMISTRY LIBRARY
269 Venable Hall 045-A
Chapel Hill, NC 27514
Phone: (919) 933-1188
T. Jimmy Dickerson, Libn.

UNIVERSITY OF NORTH CAROLINA, CHAPEL HILL - GEOLOGY LIBRARY
Mitchell Hall 029-A
Chapel Hill, NC 27514
Phone: (919) 933-2386
Miriam Sheaves, Dept.Libn.

UNIVERSITY OF NORTH CAROLINA, CHAPEL HILL - HEALTH SCIENCES
LIBRARY
Chapel Hill, NC 27514
Phone: (919) 966-2111
Samuel Hitt, Dir.

UNIVERSITY OF NORTH CAROLINA, CHAPEL HILL - HIGHWAY SAFETY
RESEARCH CENTER - LIBRARY
Trailer 13, CTP, 197 A
Chapel Hill, NC 27514
Phone: (919) 933-2202
Beth A. Boone, Libn.

UNIVERSITY OF NORTH CAROLINA, CHAPEL HILL - INSTITUTE OF
 GOVERNMENT - LIBRARY
Box 990   Phone: (919) 966-5381
Chapel Hill, NC 27514   Rebecca Ballentine, Libn.

UNIVERSITY OF NORTH CAROLINA, CHAPEL HILL - INSTITUTE OF
 OUTDOOR DRAMA - ARCHIVES
202 Graham Memorial Hall   Phone: (919) 933-1328
Chapel Hill, NC 27514   Mark R. Sumner, Dir.

UNIVERSITY OF NORTH CAROLINA, CHAPEL HILL - INSTITUTE FOR
 RESEARCH IN SOCIAL SCIENCE - DATA LIBRARY
Manning Hall 026A, Rm. 10   Phone: (919) 933-3061
Chapel Hill, NC 27514   Diana McDuffee, Dir.

UNIVERSITY OF NORTH CAROLINA, CHAPEL HILL - JOHN N. COUCH
 LIBRARY
301 Coker Hall 010-A   Phone: (919) 933-3783
Chapel Hill, NC 27514   William R. Burk, Botany Libn.

UNIVERSITY OF NORTH CAROLINA, CHAPEL HILL - LAW LIBRARY
Van Hecke-Wettach Bldg.   Phone: (919) 933-1321
Chapel Hill, NC 27514   Mary W. Oliver, Law Libn.

UNIVERSITY OF NORTH CAROLINA, CHAPEL HILL - MATHEMATICS-
 PHYSICS-STATISTICS LIBRARY
Phillips Hall   Phone: (919) 933-2323
Chapel Hill, NC 27514   Dana Sally, Libn.

UNIVERSITY OF NORTH CAROLINA, CHAPEL HILL - MUSIC LIBRARY
Hill Hall   Phone: (919) 933-1030
Chapel Hill, NC 27514   Margaret F. Lospinuso, Music Libn.

UNIVERSITY OF NORTH CAROLINA, CHAPEL HILL - NORTH CAROLINA
 COLLECTION
University Library   Phone: (919) 933-1172
Chapel Hill, NC 27514   H.G. Jones, Cur.

UNIVERSITY OF NORTH CAROLINA, CHAPEL HILL - RARE BOOK
 COLLECTION
Wilson Library 024A   Phone: (919) 933-1143
Chapel Hill, NC 27514   Paul S. Koda, Cur.

UNIVERSITY OF NORTH CAROLINA, CHAPEL HILL - SCHOOL OF LIBRARY
 SCIENCE LIBRARY
114 Manning Hall   Phone: (919) 933-8361
Chapel Hill, NC 27514   Ellen Anderson, Libn.

UNIVERSITY OF NORTH CAROLINA, CHAPEL HILL - SOUTHERN HISTORICAL
 COLLECTION & MANUSCRIPTS DEPARTMENT
Wilson Library 024A   Phone: (919) 933-1345
Chapel Hill, NC 27514   Carolyn A. Wallace, Dir./Cur.

UNIVERSITY OF NORTH CAROLINA, CHAPEL HILL - ZOOLOGY LIBRARY
213 Wilson Hall 046A   Phone: (919) 933-2264
Chapel Hill, NC 27514   John Darling, Libn.

CHARLOTTE LAW BUILDING ASSN. - CHARLOTTE LAW LIBRARY
730 E. Trade St.   Phone: (704) 334-4912
Charlotte, NC 28202   Elizabeth F. Ledford, Libn.

CHARLOTTE AND MECKLENBURG COUNTY PUBLIC LIBRARY - CAROLINA
 ROOM
310 N. Tryon St.   Phone: (704) 374-2980
Charlotte, NC 28202   Mary Louise Phillips, Local Hist.Libn.

CHARLOTTE AND MECKLENBURG COUNTY PUBLIC LIBRARY - TEXTILE
 COLLECTION
310 N. Tryon St.   Phone: (704) 374-2725
Charlotte, NC 28202   Mae S. Tucker, Asst.Dir.Lib.Serv.

CHARLOTTE-MECKLENBURG SCHOOLS - CURRICULUM RESEARCH CENTER
428 W. Boulevard   Phone: (704) 376-0122
Charlotte, NC 28203   Bettye D. McCain, Hd., Media Spec.

CHARLOTTE MEMORIAL HOSPITAL AND MEDICAL CENTER - MEDICAL
 LIBRARY OF MECKLENBURG COUNTY/LRC OF CHARLOTTE AHEC
Box 32681   Phone: (704) 373-3129
Charlotte, NC 28232   Donna Keklock, Chf.Libn.

CHARLOTTE OBSERVER AND THE CHARLOTTE NEWS - LIBRARY
600 S. Tryon St.
Box 32188   Phone: (704) 369-6889
Charlotte, NC 28232   Sara Gesler, Hd.Libn.

CROMPTON & KNOWLES CORPORATION - DYES AND CHEMICALS DIVISION
 - CENTRAL INFORMATION SERVICE
3001 N. Graham   Phone: (704) 372-5890
Charlotte, NC 28206

DUKE POWER COMPANY - DAVID NABOW LIBRARY
                                               Phone: (704) 373-4095
Charlotte, NC 28242   Peggy B. Lambert, Libn.

GEO-TECH ARCHIVES LTD. - PALEONTOLOGICAL RESEARCH LABORATORY -
 LIBRARY
3616 Garden Club Ln.   Phone: (704) 552-0102
Charlotte, NC 28210   Mary Elizabeth Carson, Libn.

MARTIN MARIETTA CHEMICALS - SODYECO DIVISION - TECHNICAL
 LIBRARY
Box 33429   Phone: (704) 827-4351
Charlotte, NC 28233   Jacqueline N. Kirkman, Tech.Libn.

MERCY SCHOOL OF NURSING - LIBRARY
1921 Vail Ave.   Phone: (704) 379-5845
Charlotte, NC 28207   Barbara Duval, Libn.

MIDREX CORPORATION - LIBRARY
One NCNB Plaza   Phone: (704) 373-1600
Charlotte, NC 28280   Josef Schmid, Jr., Libn.

MINT MUSEUM OF ART - LIBRARY
501 Hempstead Pl.
Box 6011   Phone: (704) 334-9723
Charlotte, NC 28207   Sara H. Wolf, Libn.

MINT MUSEUM OF HISTORY - LASSITER LIBRARY
3500 Shamrock Dr.   Phone: (704) 568-1774
Charlotte, NC 28215   Linda Skinner, Libn.

NATIONAL ASSOCIATION OF HOSIERY MANUFACTURERS - LIBRARY
Box 4098   Phone: (704) 372-4200
Charlotte, NC 28204   S.M. Berry, Pres.

NCNB - LIBRARY
Box 120   Phone: (704) 374-5842
Charlotte, NC 28255   Andrea White, Stat.Asst./Libn.

PRESBYTERIAN HOSPITAL - SCHOOL OF NURSING - LIBRARY
Box 33549   Phone: (704) 371-4258
Charlotte, NC 28233   Darlene F. Byrd, Media Spec.

U.S. BUREAU OF THE CENSUS - REGIONAL DATA USER SERVICE -
 CHARLOTTE REGIONAL OFFICE - LIBRARY
230 S. Tryon St., Suite 800   Phone: (704) 371-6144
Charlotte, NC 28202   Lawrence E. McNutt, Data User Serv.Off.

DUKE POWER COMPANY - STEAM PRODUCTION DEPARTMENT -
 INFORMATION RESOURCE CENTER (IRC)
Box 666   Phone: (704) 875-1686
Cornelius, NC 28031   Ella B. Scarborough, Supv. IRC

U.S. NATL. PARK SERVICE - MOORES CREEK NATL. BATTLEFIELD - LIBRARY
Box 69   Phone: (919) 283-5591
Currie, NC 28435   Terry H. Mitchell, Park Techn.

DUKE UNIVERSITY - ARCHIVES
341 Perkins   Phone: (919) 684-5637
Durham, NC 27706   William E. King, Univ.Archv.

DUKE UNIVERSITY - BIOLOGY-FORESTRY LIBRARY
                                               Phone: (919) 684-2381
Durham, NC 27706   Bertha Livingstone, Libn.

DUKE UNIVERSITY - CENTER FOR DEMOGRAPHIC STUDIES - REFERENCE
 LIBRARY
2117 Campus Dr.   Phone: (919) 684-6126
Durham, NC 27706   Michael McFee, Libn.

GEOGRAPHIC

DUKE UNIVERSITY - CHEMISTRY LIBRARY
Phone: (919) 684-3004
Durham, NC 27706   Kitty Porter, Libn.

DUKE UNIVERSITY - DIVINITY SCHOOL LIBRARY
Phone: (919) 684-3691
Durham, NC 27706   Donn Michael Farris, Libn.

DUKE UNIVERSITY - MATH-PHYSICS LIBRARY
233 Physics Bldg.   Phone: (919) 684-8118
Durham, NC 27706   Mary Ann Wilkins, Libn.

DUKE UNIVERSITY - MEDICAL CENTER LIBRARY
Phone: (919) 684-2092
Durham, NC 27710   Warren Bird, Dir.

DUKE UNIVERSITY - MUSIC LIBRARY
Phone: (919) 684-6449
Durham, NC 27708   J. Samuel Hammond, Libn.

DUKE UNIVERSITY - SCHOOL OF ENGINEERING LIBRARY
Phone: (919) 684-2371
Durham, NC 27706   Eric J. Smith, Libn.

DUKE UNIVERSITY - SCHOOL OF LAW LIBRARY
Phone: (919) 684-2847
Durham, NC 27706   Richard Danner, Dir.

DURHAM COUNTY HOSPITAL CORPORATION - WATTS SCHOOL OF
   NURSING - LIBRARY
3643 N. Roxboro Rd.   Phone: (919) 471-3411
Durham, NC 27704   Priscilla W. Hoover, Libn.

DURHAM HERALD-SUN NEWSPAPER - LIBRARY
115 Market St.   Phone: (919) 682-8181
Durham, NC 27702   Barbara P. Semonche, Chf.Libn.

FOUNDATION FOR RESEARCH ON THE NATURE OF MAN - INSTITUTE FOR
   PARAPSYCHOLOGY - RESEARCH LIBRARY
6847 College Sta.   Phone: (919) 688-8241
Durham, NC 27708   G. Rani Rao, Libn.

LIGGETT & MYERS TOBACCO CO. - INFORMATION SERVICES
Research Department
Box 1572
Durham, NC 27702

NORTH CAROLINA CENTRAL UNIVERSITY - LAW LIBRARY
Phone: (919) 683-6244
Durham, NC 27707   Douglas W. Martin, Law Libn.

NORTH CAROLINA CENTRAL UNIVERSITY - SCHOOL OF LIBRARY SCIENCE -
   LIBRARY
J.E. Shepard Library   Phone: (919) 683-6400
Durham, NC 27707   Alice S. Richmond, Libn.

U.S. VETERANS ADMINISTRATION (NC-Durham) - MEDICAL CENTER
   LIBRARY
Fulton St. & Erwin Rd.   Phone: (919) 286-0411
Durham, NC 27705   Michael M. Blanton, Chf.Libn.

AMERICAN ENKA COMPANY - BUSINESS AND TECHNICAL LIBRARY
Phone: (704) 667-6936
Enka, NC 28728   Ruth H. Easter, Libn.

FIRST BAPTIST CHURCH - STINCEON IVEY MEMORIAL LIBRARY †
Box 663   Phone: (919) 628-6371
Fairmont, NC 28340   Mrs. Jack Waters, Lib.Asst.

CUMBERLAND COUNTY HOSPITAL SYSTEM, INC. - CAPE FEAR VALLEY
   HOSPITAL - MEDICAL LIBRARY
Box 2000   Phone: (919) 323-6708
Fayetteville, NC 28302   Ann Stephens, Dir.

CUMBERLAND COUNTY PUBLIC LIBRARY - NORTH CAROLINA FOREIGN
   LANGUAGE CENTER
328 Gillespie St.   Phone: (919) 483-5022
Fayetteville, NC 28301   Patrick M. Valentine, Foreign Lang.Libn.

FAYETTEVILLE AREA HEALTH EDUCATION CENTER - LIBRARY
Box 64699
1601 Owen Dr.   Phone: (919) 323-1152
Fayetteville, NC 28306   Patricia J. Powell, Libn.

FAYETTEVILLE PUBLISHING COMPANY - NEWSPAPER LIBRARY
Box 849   Phone: (919) 323-4848
Fayetteville, NC 28302   Daisy D. Maxwell, Libn.

U.S. VETERANS ADMINISTRATION (NC-Fayetteville) - HOSPITAL LIBRARY
Phone: (919) 488-2120
Fayetteville, NC 28301   Yvonne L. Morse, Chf., Lib.Serv.

U.S. NATL. PARK SERVICE - CARL SANDBURG HOME NATL. HISTORIC SITE
   - MUSEUM/LIBRARY
Box 395   Phone: (704) 693-4178
Flat Rock, NC 28731   Benjamin Davis, Supt.

U.S. ARMY HOSPITALS - WOMACK ARMY HOSPITAL - MEDICAL LIBRARY *
Phone: (919) 396-0205
Fort Bragg, NC 28307   Cecilia C. Edwards, Med.Libn.

U.S. ARMY INSTITUTE FOR MILITARY ASSISTANCE - MARQUAT MEMORIAL
   LIBRARY †
Rm. 140, Kennedy Hall   Phone: (919) 396-9383
Fort Bragg, NC 28307   Marian O. Nance, Libn.

U.S. ARMY POST - FORT BRAGG - LIBRARY
Phone: (919) 396-1691
Fort Bragg, NC 28307   Evelyn B. Stephan, Chf.Libn.

SCHIELE MUSEUM OF NATURAL HISTORY AND PLANETARIUM - LIBRARY
1500 E. Garrison Blvd.
Box 953   Phone: (704) 864-3962
Gastonia, NC 28052   Richard A. Stout, Dir.

CARTER (William) COLLEGE & EVANGELICAL THEOLOGICAL SEMINARY -
   WAGNER-KEVETTER LIBRARY
2306 E. Ash St.   Phone: (919) 735-0831
Goldsboro, NC 27530   Dr. Doris Byrd Thomas, Libn.

WAYNE COMMUNITY COLLEGE - LEARNING RESOURCE CENTER
Caller Box 8002   Phone: (919) 735-5151
Goldsboro, NC 27530

ALAMANCE COUNTY PLANNING DEPARTMENT - LIBRARY
124 W. Elm St.
Graham, NC 27253

BENNETT COLLEGE - THOMAS F. HOLGATE LIBRARY - SPECIAL
   COLLECTIONS
Phone: (919) 273-4431
Greensboro, NC 27420   Ednita W. Bullock, Hd.Libn.

BURLINGTON INDUSTRIES, INC. - LIBRARY INFORMATION SERVICES
Box 20288
Greensboro, NC 27420   Darlene L. Ball, Mgr.

CENTER FOR CREATIVE LEADERSHIP - LIBRARY
5000 Laurinda Dr.   Phone: (919) 288-7210
Greensboro, NC 27402   Frank H. Freeman, Dir.

CIBA-GEIGY CORPORATION - TECHNICAL INFORMATION SERVICE
410 Swing Rd.   Phone: (919) 292-7100
Greensboro, NC 27409   Leonard Parker, Mgr., Tech.Info.Serv.

CONE MILLS CORPORATION - LIBRARY
1106 Maple St.   Phone: (919) 379-6215
Greensboro, NC 27405   Arletta M. Kluttz, Libn.

CONE (Moses H.) MEMORIAL HOSPITAL - MEDICAL LIBRARY
1200 N. Elm St.   Phone: (919) 379-4484
Greensboro, NC 27420   Ann W. Ellington, Med.Libn.

FIRST BAPTIST CHURCH - LIBRARY
1000 W. Friendly
Box 5443   Phone: (919) 274-3286
Greensboro, NC 27403   Charlotte M. Bell, Dir., Media Serv.

GREENSBORO DAILY NEWS AND RECORD - LIBRARY
Box 20848   Phone: (919) 373-7044
Greensboro, NC 27420   B.D. Isaacs, Lib.Dir.

GREENSBORO HISTORICAL MUSEUM
130 Summit Ave.   Phone: (919) 373-2043
Greensboro, NC 27401   William J. Moore, Dir. of Mus.

GREENSBORO MASONIC MUSEUM LIBRARY *
426 W. Market St.
Box 1043   Phone: (919) 273-8502
Greensboro, NC 27401

GREENSBORO PLANNING & COMMUNITY DEVELOPMENT DEPARTMENT -
   LIBRARY
Drawer W-2   Phone: (919) 373-2144
Greensboro, NC 27402   Arthur Davis, III, Data & Anl.Spec.

GREENSBORO PUBLIC LIBRARY - BUSINESS LIBRARY
201 N. Greene St.   Phone: (919) 373-2471
Greensboro, NC 27402   Ms. Lebby B. Lamb, Bus.Libn.

GUILFORD COLLEGE - LIBRARY
5800 W. Friendly Ave.   Phone: (919) 292-5511
Greensboro, NC 27410   Dr. Herbert Poole, Dir.

LORILLARD RESEARCH CENTER LIBRARY
420 English St.
Box 21688   Phone: (919) 373-6895
Greensboro, NC 27420   Audree D. Anthony, Lib.Supv.

NORTH CAROLINA AGRICULTURAL & TECHNICAL STATE UNIVERSITY - F.D.
   BLUFORD LIBRARY
312 Market St.   Phone: (919) 379-7783
Greensboro, NC 27411   Dr. Myrtle C. Bennett, Dir., Lib.Serv.

U.S. DEPT. OF COMMERCE - INTERNATIONAL TRADE ADMINISTRATION -
   GREENSBORO DISTRICT OFFICE LIBRARY
203 Federal Bldg., West Market St.   Phone: (919) 378-5345
Greensboro, NC 27402   Joel B. New, Dir.

UNIVERSITY OF NORTH CAROLINA, GREENSBORO - DANCE COLLECTION
Jackson Library, Special Collections   Phone: (919) 379-5246
Greensboro, NC 27412   Emilie Mills, Spec.Coll.Libn.

UNIVERSITY OF NORTH CAROLINA, GREENSBORO - GEORGE HERBERT
   COLLECTION
Jackson Library, Special Collections   Phone: (919) 379-5246
Greensboro, NC 27412

UNIVERSITY OF NORTH CAROLINA, GREENSBORO - LOIS LENSKI
   COLLECTION
Jackson Library, Special Collections   Phone: (919) 379-5246
Greensboro, NC 27412

UNIVERSITY OF NORTH CAROLINA, GREENSBORO - LUIGI SILVA
   COLLECTION
Jackson Library, Special Collections   Phone: (919) 379-5246
Greensboro, NC 27412

UNIVERSITY OF NORTH CAROLINA, GREENSBORO - PHYSICAL EDUCATION
   HISTORY COLLECTION
Jackson Library, Special Collections   Phone: (919) 379-5246
Greensboro, NC 27412

UNIVERSITY OF NORTH CAROLINA, GREENSBORO - PRINTING COLLECTION
Jackson Library, Special Collections   Phone: (919) 379-5246
Greensboro, NC 27412

UNIVERSITY OF NORTH CAROLINA, GREENSBORO - RANDALL JARRELL
   COLLECTION
Jackson Library, Special Collections   Phone: (919) 379-5246
Greensboro, NC 27412

UNIVERSITY OF NORTH CAROLINA, GREENSBORO - SAUL BAIZERMAN
   ARCHIVE
Jackson Library, Special Collections   Phone: (919) 379-5246
Greensboro, NC 27412

UNIVERSITY OF NORTH CAROLINA, GREENSBORO - WAY & WILLIAMS
   COLLECTION
Jackson Library, Special Collections   Phone: (919) 379-5246
Greensboro, NC 27412

UNIVERSITY OF NORTH CAROLINA, GREENSBORO - WOMAN'S COLLECTION
Jackson Library, Special Collections   Phone: (919) 379-5246
Greensboro, NC 27412

WESTERN ELECTRIC COMPANY, INC. - GUILFORD CENTER LIBRARY
I-85 & Mt. Hope Church Rd.
Box 25000   Phone: (919) 697-5012
Greensboro, NC 27420   Edward H. Uhler, Libn.

BURROUGHS WELLCOME COMPANY - PLANT LIBRARY
US 13 and SR 1584   Phone: (919) 758-3436
Greenville, NC 27834   Robert Lee Hadden, Libn.

EAST CAROLINA UNIVERSITY - HEALTH SCIENCES LIBRARY
                                             Phone: (919) 757-6961
Greenville, NC 27834   JoAnn Bell, Dir.

TECHNICAL COLLEGE OF ALAMANCE - TECHNICAL LIBRARY
Box 623   Phone: (919) 578-2002
Haw River, NC 27265

FURNITURE LIBRARY ASSOCIATION
1009 N. Main St.   Phone: (919) 883-4011
High Point, NC 27262   N.I. Bienenstock, Cur.

CALDWELL COMMUNITY COLLEGE AND TECHNICAL INSTITUTE - LEARNING
   RESOURCE CENTER *
1000 Hickory Blvd.   Phone: (704) 728-4323
Hudson, NC 28638   Marischa B. Cooke, Dir.

GUILFORD TECHNICAL INSTITUTE - LEARNING RESOURCE CENTER
Box 309   Phone: (919) 292-1101
Jamestown, NC 27282   Mertys W. Bell, Dean, LRC

U.S. NATL. PARK SERVICE - KINGS MOUNTAIN NATL. MILITARY PARK -
   LIBRARY
Box 31   Phone: (803) 936-7508
Kings Mountain, NC 28086   James J. Anderson, Hist.

DU PONT DE NEMOURS (E.I.) & COMPANY, INC. - DACRON RESEARCH
   LABORATORY - TECHNICAL LIBRARY
Box 800   Phone: (919) 522-6463
Kinston, NC 28501   Louis G. Boccetti, Libn.

UNITED METHODIST CHURCH - GENERAL COMMISSION ON ARCHIVES AND
   HISTORY - LIBRARY AND ARCHIVES
Box 488   Phone: (704) 456-9433
Lake Junaluska, NC 28745   Evelyn Sutton, Libn.

ST. ANDREWS PRESBYTERIAN COLLEGE - MUSIC LIBRARY *
Laurinburg, NC 28352

U.S. NATL. PARK SERVICE - CAPE HATTERAS NATL. SEASHORE LIBRARY
Rte. 1, Box 675   Phone: (919) 473-2111
Manteo, NC 27954   Donetta Livesay, Lib.Techn.

HISTORICAL FOUNDATION OF THE PRESBYTERIAN AND REFORMED
   CHURCHES - LIBRARY AND ARCHIVES
Box 847   Phone: (704) 669-7061
Montreat, NC 28757   Jerrold Lee Brooks, Dir.

UNIVERSITY OF NORTH CAROLINA - INSTITUTE OF MARINE SCIENCES -
   LIBRARY
3407 Arendell St.
Box 809   Phone: (919) 726-6841
Morehead City, NC 28557   Dr. W.E. Fahy, Professor of Zoology

BROUGHTON HOSPITAL - MEDICAL LIBRARY
1000 S. Sterling St.   Phone: (704) 433-2303
Morganton, NC 28655   Mary E. Bush, Libn.

MOUNT OLIVE COLLEGE - FREE WILL BAPTIST HISTORICAL COLLECTION
Moye Library   Phone: (919) 658-2502
Mount Olive, NC 28365   Gary Fenton Barefoot, Libn.

GEOGRAPHIC

GEOGRAPHIC

COMMITTEE ON DIAGNOSTIC READING TESTS, INC. - LIBRARY
Phone: (704) 693-5223
Mountain Home, NC 28758   Dr. Frances Oralind Triggs, Chm.

NORTH CAROLINA STATE DEPARTMENT OF CULTURAL RESOURCES -
  TRYON PALACE RESTORATION - LIBRARY
613 Pollock St.
Box 1007   Phone: (919) 638-5109
New Bern, NC 28560   Donald R. Taylor, Adm.

CATAWBA COUNTY HISTORICAL MUSEUM - LIBRARY
U.S. Hwy. 321   Phone: (704) 465-0383
Newton, NC 28658   Sidney Halma, Dir.

OLIN CORPORATION - FINE PAPER AND FILM GROUP - TECHNICAL
  LIBRARY
Box 200   Phone: (704) 877-2339
Pisgah Forest, NC 28768   Martha M. Sellers, Tech.Libn.

U.S. AIR FORCE BASE - POPE BASE LIBRARY
Phone: (919) 394-2791
Pope AFB, NC 28308   Patrick D. Colucci, Base Libn.

CAROLINA POWER & LIGHT COMPANY - CORPORATE LIBRARY
411 Fayetteville St.
Box 1551   Phone: (919) 836-6790
Raleigh, NC 27602   Anne P. Carmichael, Corp.Libn.

DOROTHEA DIX HOSPITAL - F.T. FULLER STAFF LIBRARY
Phone: (919) 733-5111
Raleigh, NC 27611   Spanola Eubanks, Dir., Lib.Serv.

NEWS AND OBSERVER PUBLISHING COMPANY - LIBRARY
215 S. McDowell St.   Phone: (919) 821-1234
Raleigh, NC 27602   Lany W. McDonald, Libn.

NORTH CAROLINA GEOLOGICAL SURVEY - LIBRARY
Box 27687   Phone: (919) 733-2424
Raleigh, NC 27611   Alberta McKay, Libn.

NORTH CAROLINA MUSEUM OF ART - ART REFERENCE LIBRARY
Cultural Resources Dept.
107 E. Morgan St.   Phone: (919) 733-7568
Raleigh, NC 27611   Dr. Anna Dvorak, Libn.

NORTH CAROLINA STATE DEPT. OF CULTURAL RESOURCES - DIV. OF
  ARCHIVES AND HISTORY - ARCHIVES & RECORDS SECTION
109 E. Jones St.   Phone: (919) 733-3952
Raleigh, NC 27611   T.W. Mitchell, Chf.

NORTH CAROLINA STATE DEPARTMENT OF CULTURAL RESOURCES -
  DIVISION OF THE STATE LIBRARY
109 E. Jones St.   Phone: (919) 829-4129
Raleigh, NC 27611   David McKay, Dir./State Libn.

NORTH CAROLINA STATE DEPARTMENT OF CULTURAL RESOURCES -
  LIBRARY FOR THE BLIND AND PHYSICALLY HANDICAPPED
1811 North Blvd.   Phone: (919) 733-4376
Raleigh, NC 27635   Charles H. Fox, Chf.Spec.Serv.Sect.

NORTH CAROLINA STATE DEPARTMENT OF HUMAN RESOURCES -
  DIVISION OF HEALTH SERVICES - PUBLIC HEALTH LIBRARY
Box 2091   Phone: (919) 733-7389
Raleigh, NC 27602   Elnora H. Turner, Pub. Health Libn.

NORTH CAROLINA STATE DEPT. OF NATURAL RESOURCES & COMMUNITY
  DEVELOPMENT - DIV. OF COMMUNITY ASSISTANCE LIB. *
Box 27687   Phone: (919) 829-2850
Raleigh, NC 27611   Christine Coxe, Libn.

NORTH CAROLINA STATE DEPT. OF NATURAL RESOURCES & COMMUNITY
  DEVELOPMENT - ENVIRONMENTAL MGT. LIBRARY
512 N. Salisbury St., 7th Fl.
Box 27687   Phone: (919) 733-5064
Raleigh, NC 27611   Donna Lucier, Libn.

NORTH CAROLINA STATE DEPARTMENT OF PUBLIC INSTRUCTION -
  EDUCATION INFORMATION CENTER
Education Bldg.   Phone: (919) 733-7094
Raleigh, NC 27611   Ann Fowler, Coord.

NORTH CAROLINA STATE LEGISLATIVE LIBRARY
Legislative Bldg.   Phone: (919) 733-7778
Raleigh, NC 27611   Vivian Payne Halperen, Libn.

NORTH CAROLINA STATE MUSEUM - H.H. BRIMLEY MEMORIAL LIBRARY
102 N. Salisbury St.
Box 27647
Raleigh, NC 27611   Ray E. Ashton, Dir. of Educ.

NORTH CAROLINA STATE SUPREME COURT LIBRARY
Box 28006   Phone: (919) 733-3425
Raleigh, NC 27611   Frances H. Hall, Libn.

NORTH CAROLINA STATE UNIVERSITY - BURLINGTON TEXTILE LIBRARY
Box 5006   Phone: (919) 737-3231
Raleigh, NC 27650   Georgia H. Rodeffer, Textiles Libn.

NORTH CAROLINA STATE UNIVERSITY - D.H. HILL LIBRARY
Box 5007   Phone: (919) 737-2843
Raleigh, NC 27650   Isaac T. Littleton, Dir.

NORTH CAROLINA STATE UNIVERSITY - FOREST RESOURCES LIBRARY
4012 Biltmore Hall   Phone: (919) 737-2306
Raleigh, NC 27650   Pamela E. Puryear, Libn.

NORTH CAROLINA STATE UNIVERSITY - HARRYE LYONS DESIGN LIBRARY
209 Brooks Hall
Box 5398   Phone: (919) 737-2207
Raleigh, NC 27650   Maryellen LoPresti, Libn.

NORTH CAROLINA STATE UNIVERSITY - SOUTHERN WATER RESOURCES
  SCIENTIFIC INFORMATION CENTER
D.H. Hill Library
Box 5007   Phone: (919) 737-2683
Raleigh, NC 27650   Jean M. Porter, Supv.

NORTH CAROLINA STATE UNIVERSITY - TOBACCO LITERATURE SERVICE
2314 D.H. Hill Library
Box 5007   Phone: (919) 737-2837
Raleigh, NC 27650   Carmen M. Marin, Dir.

REX HOSPITAL - LIBRARY
4420 Lake Boone Trail   Phone: (919) 828-6211
Raleigh, NC 27607   Dorothy T. McCallum, Libn.

WAKE COUNTY MEDICAL CENTER - MEDICAL LIBRARY
3000 New Bern Ave.   Phone: (919) 755-8528
Raleigh, NC 27610   Virginia B. Whitney, Med.Libn.

AMERICAN ASSOCIATION OF TEXTILE CHEMISTS AND COLORISTS -
  LIBRARY
Box 12215   Phone: (919) 549-8141
Research Triangle Park, NC 27709   George J. Mandikos, Tech.Dir.

BECTON, DICKINSON & COMPANY - RESEARCH CENTER LIBRARY
Box 12016   Phone: (919) 549-8641
Research Triangle Park, NC 27709   Dora Zia, Res.Libn.

BURROUGHS WELLCOME COMPANY - LIBRARY
3030 Cornwallis Rd.   Phone: (919) 541-9090
Research Triangle Park, NC 27709   Ildiko Trombitas, Hd., Tech.Info.Dept.

ENVIRONMENTAL PROTECTION AGENCY - DIVISION OF METEOROLOGY -
  INFORMATION SERVICE CENTER
Phone: (919) 541-4536
Research Triangle Park, NC 27711   Evelyn M. Poole-Kober, Tech.Info.Ck.

ENVIRONMENTAL PROTECTION AGENCY - LIBRARY SERVICES
MD 35   Phone: (919) 541-2777
Research Triangle Park, NC 27711   Libby Smith, Libn.

IBM CORPORATION - SYSTEM COMMUNICATIONS DIVISION - LIBRARY
Dept. 609/Bldg. 060
Box 12195   Phone: (919) 543-5942
Research Triangle Park, NC 27709   Ann Williams, Mgr.

INSTRUMENT SOCIETY OF AMERICA - LIBRARY
67 Alexander Dr.
Box 12277
Research Triangle Park, NC 27709   Vickie Dempsey, Pubn.Coord.

INTERNATIONAL FERTILITY RESEARCH PROGRAM - LIBRARY
Triangle Dr.   Phone: (919) 549-0517
Research Triangle Park, NC 27709   William Barrows, Info.Coord.

MONSANTO COMPANY - TRIANGLE PARK DEVELOPMENT CENTER, INC. -
   LIBRARY
Box 12274   Phone: (919) 549-8111
Research Triangle Park, NC 27709   Barbara Best Nichols, Libn.

NATIONAL HUMANITIES CENTER - LIBRARY
Box 12256   Phone: (919) 549-0661
Research Triangle Park, NC 27709   Walter Alan Tuttle, Libn.

NATIONAL INSTITUTE OF ENVIRONMENTAL HEALTH SCIENCES -
   ENVIRONMENTAL TERATOLOGY INFORMATION CENTER
Box 122233   Phone: (919) 541-3214
Research Triangle Park, NC 27709   Florence E. Jordan, Tech.Info.Spec.

NATIONAL INSTITUTE OF ENVIRONMENTAL HEALTH SCIENCES - LIBRARY
Box 12233   Phone: (919) 541-3426
Research Triangle Park, NC 27709   W. Davenport Robertson, Hd.Libn.

NORTH CAROLINA STATE SCIENCE AND TECHNOLOGY RESEARCH CENTER
Box 12235   Phone: (919) 549-0671
Research Triangle Park, NC 27709   Dr. James E. Vann, Dir.

UNION CARBIDE AGRICULTURAL PRODUCTS COMPANY, INC. - LIBRARY
T.W. Alexander Dr.
Box 12014
Research Triangle Park, NC 27709   Constance J. Lavoy, Lib.Serv.Supv.

U.S. ARMY RESEARCH OFFICE - TECHNICAL LIBRARY
Box 12211   Phone: (919) 549-0641
Research Triangle Park, NC 27709   Brenda Mann, Libn.

NORTH CAROLINA STATE JUSTICE ACADEMY - LEARNING RESOURCE
   CENTER
Drawer 99   Phone: (919) 525-4151
Salemburg, NC 28385   Donald K. Stacy, Libn.

HOOD THEOLOGICAL SEMINARY - LIVINGSTONE COLLEGE - LIBRARY
W.J. Walls Ctr.
800 W. Thomas St.   Phone: (704) 633-7960
Salisbury, NC 28144   Rev.Mrs. Willie L. Aldrich, Hd. Libn.

LUTHERAN CHURCH IN AMERICA - NORTH CAROLINA SYNOD - ARCHIVES
Box 2049   Phone: (704) 633-4861
Salisbury, NC 28144   Rev. David L. Martin, Sec./Archv.

ROWAN MEMORIAL HOSPITAL - MC KENZIE MEMORIAL LIBRARY
612 Mocksville Ave.   Phone: (704) 636-3311
Salisbury, NC 28144   Mary J. Peck, AHEC Libn./Coord.

ROWAN PUBLIC LIBRARY - EDITH M. CLARK HISTORY ROOM
201 W. Fisher St.
Box 4039   Phone: (704) 633-5578
Salisbury, NC 28144   Patricia G. Rosenthal, Hist./Genealogy Libn.

U.S. VETERANS ADMINISTRATION (NC-Salisbury) - HOSPITAL LIBRARY
1601 Brenner Ave.   Phone: (704) 636-2351
Salisbury, NC 28144   Lucile C. Owsley, Chf., Lib.Serv.

CENTRAL CAROLINA TECHNICAL COLLEGE - LEARNING RESOURCE CENTER
1105 Kelly Dr.   Phone: (919) 775-5401
Sanford, NC 27330   Jim Foster, Dir.Lrng.Rsrc.Ctr.

SWANSBORO HISTORICAL ASSOCIATION, INC. - RESEARCH FILES
Box 21   Phone: (919) 326-5361
Swansboro, NC 28584   Tucker R. Littleton, Hist.

MONTGOMERY TECHNICAL INSTITUTE - LEARNING RESOURCES CENTER
Drawer 487   Phone: (919) 572-3691
Troy, NC 27371   Gay R. Russell, Libn.

NATIONAL SHARECROPPERS FUND/RURAL ADVANCEMENT FUND - F.P.
   GRAHAM RESOURCE CENTER
Rte. 3, Box 95   Phone: (704) 851-9346
Wadesboro, NC 28170   Cary Fowler, Prog.Dir.

ST. JOHN'S MUSEUM OF ART, INC. - LIBRARY
114 Orange St.   Phone: (919) 763-0281
Wilmington, NC 28401   Alan Aiches, Dir.

WILMINGTON STAR-NEWS NEWSPAPERS, INC. - LIBRARY
1103 S. 17th St.
Box 840   Phone: (919) 343-2309
Wilmington, NC 28402   Patricia Shoaf, Libn.

WILSON MEMORIAL HOSPITAL - LIBRARY/LEARNING CENTER
1705 S. Tarboro St.   Phone: (919) 339-8253
Wilson, NC 27893   Marian H. Spencer, Lib.Dir.

FORSYTH MEMORIAL HOSPITAL - JOHN C. WHITAKER LIBRARY
3333 Silas Creek Pkwy.   Phone: (919) 773-3995
Winston-Salem, NC 27103   Sandra L. Lawson, Med.Libn.

MORAVIAN CHURCH IN AMERICA - SOUTHERN PROVINCE - MORAVIAN
   ARCHIVES
Drawer M, Salem Sta.   Phone: (919) 722-1742
Winston-Salem, NC 27108   Mary Creech, Archv.

MORAVIAN MUSIC FOUNDATION, INC. - LIBRARY
20 Cascade Ave.   Phone: (919) 725-0651
Winston-Salem, NC 27108   James Boeringer, Dir.

OLD SALEM, INC. - LIBRARY
Drawer F, Salem Sta.   Phone: (919) 723-3688
Winston-Salem, NC 27108   Gene T. Capps, Dir., Dept. of Educ.

OLD SALEM, INC. - MUSEUM OF EARLY SOUTHERN DECORATIVE ARTS
   (MESDA) - LIBRARY
Drawer F, Salem Sta.   Phone: (919) 722-6148
Winston-Salem, NC 27108   Bradford L. Rauschenberg

PIEDMONT BIBLE COLLEGE - GEORGE M. MANUEL MEMORIAL LIBRARY
716 Franklin St.   Phone: (919) 725-8345
Winston-Salem, NC 27101   William P. Thompson, Libn.

REYNOLDA HOUSE, INC. - LIBRARY
Reynolda Rd.
Box 11765   Phone: (919) 725-5325
Winston-Salem, NC 27106   Ruth Mullen, Libn.

REYNOLDS (R.J.) INDUSTRIES, INC. - MANAGEMENT INFORMATION
   LIBRARY
401 N. Main St.   Phone: (919) 777-2652
Winston-Salem, NC 27102   Barry K. Miller, Corp.Libn.

REYNOLDS (R.J.) TOBACCO COMPANY - MARKETING INTELLIGENCE
   LIBRARY
203 Reynolds Bldg.   Phone: (919) 777-5636
Winston-Salem, NC 27102   Diane S. Burrows, Marketing Res.Coord.

REYNOLDS (R.J.) TOBACCO COMPANY - R&D INFORMATION SYSTEMS
   LIBRARY
Chestnut at Belews St.   Phone: (919) 777-6554
Winston-Salem, NC 27102   Tom W. Stamey, Mgr., R&D

WAKE FOREST UNIVERSITY - BABCOCK GRADUATE SCHOOL OF
   MANAGEMENT - LIBRARY
Box 7689, Reynolda Sta.   Phone: (919) 761-5414
Winston-Salem, NC 27109   Jean B. Hopson, Lib.Dir.

WAKE FOREST UNIVERSITY - BAPTIST COLLECTION
University Library   Phone: (919) 761-5472
Winston-Salem, NC 27109   John R. Woodard, Jr., Dir.

WAKE FOREST UNIVERSITY - BOWMAN GRAY SCHOOL OF MEDICINE -
   LIBRARY
300 S. Hawthorne Rd.   Phone: (919) 727-4691
Winston-Salem, NC 27103   Michael D. Sprinkle, Dir.

WAKE FOREST UNIVERSITY - LAW LIBRARY
Reynolda Sta., Box 7206   Phone: (919) 761-5438
Winston-Salem, NC 27109   Kenneth A. Zick, II, Dir.

GEOGRAPHIC

WINSTON-SALEM FOUNDATION - FOUNDATION CENTER REGIONAL
 LIBRARY
229 First Union Bldg.   Phone: (919) 725-2382
Winston-Salem, NC 27101   Sara N. Willard, Supv.

WINSTON-SALEM JOURNAL AND SENTINEL - LIBRARY
418 N. Marshall   Phone: (919) 727-7275
Winston-Salem, NC 27102   Marilyn H. Rollins, Ref.Dept.Mgr.

WINSTON-SALEM STATE UNIVERSITY - O'KELLY LIBRARY
                                           Phone: (919) 761-2128
Winston-Salem, NC 27102   Belinda Daniels, Act.Libn.

YADKIN COUNTY HISTORICAL SOCIETY - LIBRARY
Yadkin County Public Library
E. Main St.
Box 607
Yadkinville, NC 27055   Frances H. Casstevens, Pres.

NORTH DAKOTA

BISMARCK TRIBUNE - LIBRARY
707 E. Front Ave.
Box 1498   Phone: (701) 223-2500
Bismarck, ND 58501   Kelli J. Herman, Libn.

MARY COLLEGE - LIBRARY
Apple Creek Rd.   Phone: (701) 255-4681
Bismarck, ND 58501   Cheryl M. Bailey, Dir.

NORTH DAKOTA STATE DEPARTMENT OF HEALTH - HEALTH EDUCATION
 FILM & STAFF JOURNAL LIBRARY
Capitol Bldg.   Phone: (701) 224-2367
Bismarck, ND 58505   Kathleen Zimmerman, Libn.

NORTH DAKOTA STATE HIGHWAY DEPARTMENT - LIBRARY
North Dakota State Capitol Grounds   Phone: (701) 224-2560
Bismarck, ND 58505   Mr. LaMoyne Splichal, Libn.

NORTH DAKOTA STATE LIBRARY
Highway 83, N.   Phone: (701) 224-2490
Bismarck, ND 58505   Richard J. Wolfert, State Libn.

NORTH DAKOTA STATE SUPREME COURT LAW LIBRARY
State Capitol, 2nd Fl.   Phone: (701) 224-2227
Bismarck, ND 58505   Elmer J. Dewald, Law Libn.

QUAIN AND RAMSTAD CLINIC - MEDICAL LIBRARY
221 N. Fifth St.   Phone: (701) 222-5390
Bismarck, ND 58501   Harriet Kling, Med.Libn.

STATE HISTORICAL SOCIETY OF NORTH DAKOTA - RESEARCH AND
 REFERENCE DIVISION
Heritage Center   Phone: (701) 224-2668
Bismarck, ND 58505

NORTH DAKOTA STATE UNIVERSITY - BOTTINEAU BRANCH AND
 INSTITUTE OF FORESTRY - LIBRARY
First & Simrall Blvd.   Phone: (701) 228-2277
Bottineau, ND 58318   Mary Claire Thorleifson, Libn.

DICKINSON STATE COLLEGE - STOXEN LIBRARY
                                           Phone: (701) 227-2135
Dickinson, ND 58601   Bernnett Reinke, Lib.Dir.

ST. JOSEPH'S HOSPITAL - LIBRARY
7th St. W.   Phone: (701) 225-7267
Dickinson, ND 58601   Martha Sacchini, Med.Libn.

FORUM PUBLISHING CO. - LIBRARY
Box 2020   Phone: (701) 235-7311
Fargo, ND 58102   Andrea H. Halgrimson, Hd.Libn.

LUTHERAN HOSPITALS AND HOMES SOCIETY OF AMERICA - LIBRARY
Box 2087   Phone: (701) 293-9053
Fargo, ND 58107   Mary L. Littlefield, Sec.Lib.Comm.

NEUROPSYCHIATRIC INSTITUTE - LIBRARY
700 1st Ave. S.   Phone: (701) 235-5354
Fargo, ND 58103   Diane Nordeng, Libn.

NORTH DAKOTA STATE UNIVERSITY - DIVISION OF INDEPENDENT STUDY
 - FILM LIBRARY
State University Sta.
Box 5036   Phone: (701) 237-8907
Fargo, ND 58105   Lillian M. Wadnizak, Lib.Mgr.

NORTH DAKOTA STATE UNIVERSITY - INSTITUTE FOR REGIONAL STUDIES
University Dr. & 12th Ave., N.   Phone: (701) 237-8914
Fargo, ND 58105   John E. Bye, Cur.Mss.

NORTH DAKOTA STATE UNIVERSITY - LIBRARY
University Sta.   Phone: (701) 237-8876
Fargo, ND 58105   K.L. Janecek, Dir.

NORTH DAKOTA STATE UNIVERSITY - UPPER GREAT PLAINS
 TRANSPORTATION INSTITUTE - INFORMATION CENTER
                                           Phone: (701) 237-7767
Fargo, ND 58105   Gene C. Griffin, Dir.

ST. LUKE'S HOSPITAL - LIBRARY †
5th St. N. at Mills Ave.   Phone: (701) 280-5571
Fargo, ND 58122   Marcia Stephens, Dir. of Lib.Serv.

TEMPLE BETH EL - MAX & ANN GOLDBERG LIBRARY
809 11th Ave., S.   Phone: (701) 232-0441
Fargo, ND 58103

U.S. VETERANS ADMINISTRATION (ND-Fargo) - CENTER LIBRARY
                                           Phone: (701) 232-3241
Fargo, ND 58102   Glenn E. Hasse, Chf.Libn.

UNITED HOSPITAL - LIBRARY
1200 S. Columbia Rd.   Phone: (701) 780-5146
Grand Forks, ND 58201   Nancy L. Devereux, Libn.

U.S. DEPT. OF ENERGY - GRAND FORKS ENERGY TECHNOLOGY CENTER
 LIBRARY
University Sta., Box 8213   Phone: (701) 795-8131
Grand Forks, ND 58202

UNIVERSITY OF NORTH DAKOTA - CHEMISTRY LIBRARY
224 Abbott Hall   Phone: (701) 777-2741
Grand Forks, ND 58202   Evelyn Cole

UNIVERSITY OF NORTH DAKOTA - DEPARTMENT OF SPECIAL
 COLLECTIONS
Chester Fritz Library   Phone: (701) 777-4625
Grand Forks, ND 58202   Dan Rylance, Cur.

UNIVERSITY OF NORTH DAKOTA - EDUCATIONAL RESOURCES
 INFORMATION CENTER
Chester Fritz Library   Phone: (701) 777-2617
Grand Forks, ND 58202   Patricia Berntsen, ERIC/Per.Coord.

UNIVERSITY OF NORTH DAKOTA - ENGINEERING LIBRARY
Harrington Hall, University Sta.   Phone: (701) 777-3040
Grand Forks, ND 58202   Ruth Peterson

UNIVERSITY OF NORTH DAKOTA - GEOLOGY LIBRARY
Leonard Hall, University Sta.   Phone: (701) 777-3221
Grand Forks, ND 58202   Mindy Pinkneg

UNIVERSITY OF NORTH DAKOTA - INSTITUTE FOR ECOLOGICAL STUDIES -
 ENVIRONMENTAL RESOURCE CENTER
103 Chandler Hall   Phone: (701) 777-2851
Grand Forks, ND 58202   Richard E. Frank, Assoc.Dir.

UNIVERSITY OF NORTH DAKOTA - MATH-PHYSICS LIBRARY
211 Witmer Hall   Phone: (701) 777-2911
Grand Forks, ND 58202

UNIVERSITY OF NORTH DAKOTA - OLAF H. THORMODSGARD LAW LIBRARY
                                           Phone: (701) 777-2204
Grand Forks, ND 58201   Rita T. Reusch, Dir.

UNIVERSITY OF NORTH DAKOTA - SCHOOL OF MEDICINE - HARLEY E. FRENCH MEDICAL LIBRARY
Phone: (701) 777-3993
Grand Forks, ND 58202
Lila Pedersen, Asst.Dir.

U.S. AIR FORCE - STRATEGIC AIR COMMAND - 321 CSG/SS - LIBRARY
FL 4659
Phone: (701) 594-6725
Grand Forks AFB, ND 58205
Wynne A. Tysdal, Adm.Libn.

STEELE COUNTY HISTORICAL SOCIETY - ARCHIVES
Steele Ave.
Phone: (701) 945-2394
Hope, ND 58046
Helen Parkman, Cur.

NORTH DAKOTA FARMERS UNION - LULU EVANSON RESOURCE LIBRARY
Box 651
Phone: (701) 252-2340
Jamestown, ND 58401
Karl Limvere, Info.Asst.

NORTH DAKOTA STATE HOSPITAL - DEPARTMENT OF LIBRARY SERVICES - HEALTH SCIENCE LIBRARY
Box 476
Phone: (701) 253-2679
Jamestown, ND 58401
L. Fay Domek, Lib.Dir.

U.S. FISH & WILDLIFE SERVICE - NORTHERN PRAIRIE WILDLIFE RESEARCH CENTER LIBRARY
Box 1747
Phone: (701) 252-5363
Jamestown, ND 58401
Eileen Bartels, Libn.

U.S. NATL. PARK SERVICE - THEODORE ROOSEVELT NATL. PARK - LIBRARY
Phone: (701) 623-4466
Medora, ND 58645
Michele Hellickson, Interpretation Chf.

MINOT DAILY NEWS - LIBRARY *
301-303 Fourth St., S.E.
Phone: (701) 852-3341
Minot, ND 58701
Betty Rogstad, Libn.

MINOT STATE COLLEGE - MEMORIAL LIBRARY
Phone: (701) 857-3200
Minot, ND 58701
George C. Clark, Hd.Libn.

NORTHWEST BIBLE COLLEGE - LIBRARY
1900 8th Ave., S.E.
Phone: (701) 852-3781
Minot, ND 58701
Clyde R. Root, Hd.Libn.

TRINITY MEDICAL CENTER - ANGUS L. CAMERON MEDICAL LIBRARY †
Trinity Professional Bldg.
20 Fourth Ave., S.W.
Phone: (701) 857-5435
Minot, ND 58701
Frances E. Cockrum, AHEC Libn.

TRINITY MEDICAL CENTER - SCHOOL OF NURSING LIBRARY
S. Main And 4th Ave.
Phone: (701) 839-9229
Minot, ND 58701
Mildred A. Morgan, Libn.

U.S. AIR FORCE BASE - MINOT BASE LIBRARY
91 CSG/SSL
Phone: (701) 727-4761
Minot AFB, ND 58705
Geraldine Y. Brosman, Libn.

ASSUMPTION ABBEY - LIBRARY
Phone: (701) 974-3315
Richardson, ND 58652
Bro. Paul Nyquist, Hd.Libn.

NORTH DAKOTA STATE SCHOOL OF SCIENCE - MILDRED JOHNSON LIBRARY
Phone: (701) 671-2298
Wahpeton, ND 58075
Jerald Stewart, Lib.Dir.

OHIO

OHIO NORTHERN UNIVERSITY - COLLEGE OF LAW - JAY P. TAGGART MEMORIAL LAW LIBRARY
Phone: (419) 634-9921
Ada, OH 45810
Dr. Robert T. Begg, Hd.Libn.

OHIO NORTHERN UNIVERSITY - HETERICK MEMORIAL LIBRARY
Phone: (419) 634-9921
Ada, OH 45810
J. Wayne Baker, Lib.Dir.

AKRON ART MUSEUM - LIBRARY
70 E. Market St.
Phone: (216) 376-9185
Akron, OH 44308
Marcianne Herr, Cur. of Educ.

AKRON BEACON JOURNAL - REFERENCE LIBRARY
44 E. Exchange St.
Phone: (216) 375-8514
Akron, OH 44328
Catherine M. Tierney, Chf.Libn.

AKRON CITY HEALTH DEPARTMENT - PUBLIC HEALTH LIBRARY
177 S. Broadway
Phone: (216) 375-2960
Akron, OH 44308
Dr. C. William Keck, Dir. of Health

AKRON - DEPARTMENT OF PLANNING AND URBAN RENEWAL AND METROPOLITAN AREA TRANSPORTATION STUDY - LIBRARY
403 Municipal Bldg.
Phone: (216) 375-2091
Akron, OH 44308
Louise A. Morris, Libn.

AKRON GENERAL MEDICAL CENTER - J.D. SMITH MEMORIAL LIBRARY
400 Wabash Ave.
Phone: (216) 384-6242
Akron, OH 44307
Lois Arnold, Med.Libn.

AKRON LAW LIBRARY
Summit County Court House
Phone: (216) 379-5734
Akron, OH 44308
Rosemarie Chrisant, Lib.Dir.

AKRON-SUMMIT COUNTY PUBLIC LIBRARY - BUSINESS, LABOR AND GOVERNMENT DIVISION
55 S. Main St.
Phone: (216) 762-7621
Akron, OH 44326
William G. Johnson, Div.Hd.

AKRON-SUMMIT COUNTY PUBLIC LIBRARY - SCIENCE AND TECHNOLOGY DIVISION
55 S. Main St.
Phone: (216) 762-7621
Akron, OH 44326
Joyce McKnight, Div.Hd.

AMERICAN CHEMICAL SOCIETY, INC. - RUBBER DIVISION - JOHN H. GIFFORD MEMORIAL LIBRARY & INFORMATION CTR.
Bierce Library, University of Akron
Phone: (216) 375-7197
Akron, OH 44325
Ruth Murray, Lit.Chem.

FIRESTONE TIRE AND RUBBER COMPANY - BUSINESS LIBRARY
1200 Firestone Pkwy.
Phone: (216) 379-6650
Akron, OH 44317
Betty Watson, Libn.

FIRESTONE TIRE AND RUBBER COMPANY - CENTRAL RESEARCH LIBRARY
1200 Firestone Pkwy.
Phone: (216) 379-7430
Akron, OH 44317
S. Koo, Sr.Res.Libn.

FIRESTONE TIRE AND RUBBER COMPANY - DEFENSE RESEARCH AND PRODUCTS DIVISION - LIBRARY
1200 Firestone Pkwy.
Phone: (216) 379-7467
Akron, OH 44317
Thomas DeMan

GENERAL TIRE AND RUBBER COMPANY - RESEARCH DIVISION INFORMATION CENTER
2990 Gilchrist Rd.
Phone: (216) 798-3496
Akron, OH 44305
Lois Brock, Libn.

GOODRICH (B.F.) COMPANY - AKRON INFORMATION CENTER
500 S. Main St.
Phone: (216) 379-4368
Akron, OH 44318
Virginia Gallicchio, Supv.

GOODYEAR AEROSPACE CORPORATION - LIBRARY
1210 Massillon Rd.
Phone: (216) 796-2557
Akron, OH 44315
Louise Lariccia, Libn.

GOODYEAR TIRE AND RUBBER COMPANY - BUSINESS INFORMATION CENTER
1144 E. Market St.
Phone: (216) 794-2790
Akron, OH 44316
Dori Rogers, Bus.Info.Spec.

GOODYEAR TIRE AND RUBBER COMPANY - TECHNICAL INFORMATION CENTER
142 Goodyear Blvd.
Phone: (216) 796-6540
Akron, OH 44316
Judy E. Hale, Mgr., Info.Serv.

HIGH STREET CHRISTIAN CHURCH - H.A. VALENTINE MEMORIAL LIBRARY
131 S. High St.
Phone: (216) 434-1039
Akron, OH 44308
Mrs. Robert E. Ling, Libn.

INTERNATIONAL SOAP BOX DERBY - LIBRARY
789 Derby Downs Dr.   Phone: (216) 733-8723
Akron, OH 44306   Jeff Iula, Adm.Asst.

MONSANTO COMPANY - RUBBER CHEMICALS RESEARCH LIBRARY
260 Springside Dr.   Phone: (216) 666-4111
Akron, OH 44313   Paul Ferrin, Libn.

NORTHEAST OHIO FOUR COUNTY REGIONAL PLANNING & DEVELOPMENT
    ORGANIZATION - TECHNICAL INFORMATION CENTER
137 S. Main St.   Phone: (216) 253-4196
Akron, OH 44308   Linda Brown, Libn.

NORTON COMPANY - CHAMBERLAIN LABORATORIES - TECHNICAL
    LIBRARY
Box 350   Phone: (216) 673-5860
Akron, OH 44309   Jan York, Libn.

ST. THOMAS HOSPITAL - MEDICAL LIBRARY
444 N. Main St.   Phone: (216) 379-1111
Akron, OH 44310   Linda E. Bunyan, Med.Libn.

UNIVERSITY OF AKRON - ARCHIVES OF THE HISTORY OF AMERICAN
    PSYCHOLOGY
                    Phone: (216) 375-7285
Akron, OH 44325   John A. Popplestone, Dir.

UNIVERSITY OF AKRON - SCHOOL OF LAW - C. BLAKE MC DOWELL
    LIBRARY
Law Center   Phone: (216) 375-7447
Akron, OH 44325   Paul Richert, Law Libn.

BABCOCK AND WILCOX COMPANY - RESEARCH CENTER LIBRARY
Box 835   Phone: (216) 821-9110
Alliance, OH 44601   Elmer H. Fisher, Supv., Info.Serv.

MOUNT UNION COLLEGE - STURGEON MUSIC LIBRARY
Cope Music Hall   Phone: (216) 823-3206
Alliance, OH 44601   Becky C. Thomas, Music Libn.

STARK COUNTY LAW LIBRARY ASSOCIATION - ALLIANCE BRANCH LAW
    LIBRARY *
City Hall   Phone: (216) 823-6181
Alliance, OH 44601

MC GILL & SMITH ENGINEERS, ARCHITECTS & PLANNERS - LIBRARY
119 W. Main St.   Phone: (513) 753-4430
Amelia, OH 45102   Patricia A. Cutrell, Lib. Media Tech.Asst.

NORDSON CORPORATION - TECHNICAL INFORMATION DEPARTMENT
555 Jackson St.   Phone: (216) 988-9411
Amherst, OH 44001   Agnes K. Bacon, Dept.Hd.

ASHLAND THEOLOGICAL SEMINARY - ROGER DARLING MEMORIAL LIBRARY
910 Center St.   Phone: (419) 289-4126
Ashland, OH 44805   Rev. Bradley E. Weidenhamer, Libn.

AMERICAN HARP SOCIETY REPOSITORY
52 Charles   Phone: (202) 287-6321
Athens, OH 45701   Lucile H. Jennings, Proj.Dir.

ATHENS COUNTY LAW LIBRARY
Courthouse, 3rd Fl.   Phone: (614) 592-2077
Athens, OH 45701   Sheila Klinebriel, Libn.

ATHENS MENTAL HEALTH CENTER - STAFF LIBRARY
Richland Ave.   Phone: (614) 592-3031
Athens, OH 45701   Judy McGinn, Staff Libn.

OHIO UNIVERSITY - DEPARTMENT OF ARCHIVES AND SPECIAL
    COLLECTIONS
Alden Library   Phone: (614) 594-5755
Athens, OH 45701   Gary A. Hunt, Hd.

OHIO UNIVERSITY - FINE ARTS COLLECTION
Alden Library   Phone: (614) 594-5065
Athens, OH 45701   Anne Braxton, Fine Arts Libn.

OHIO UNIVERSITY - HEALTH SCIENCES LIBRARY
                    Phone: (614) 594-6581
Athens, OH 45701   Anne S. Goss, Hd.Libn.

OHIO UNIVERSITY - MAP COLLECTION
Alden Library   Phone: (614) 594-5240
Athens, OH 45701   Theodore Foster, Map Libn.

OHIO UNIVERSITY - MUSIC/DANCE LIBRARY
Music Bldg.   Phone: (614) 594-5733
Athens, OH 45701   Dan O. Clark, Libn.

OHIO UNIVERSITY - SOUTHEAST ASIA COLLECTION
Alden Library   Phone: (614) 594-6958
Athens, OH 45701   Lian The-Mulliner, Hd.Libn.

OHIO VALLEY HEALTH SERVICES FOUNDATION, INC. - LIBRARY
One Blue Line Ave.   Phone: (614) 592-4457
Athens, OH 45701   Sandra Porter, Adm.Asst.

GOODRICH (B.F.) COMPANY - GOODRICH CHEMICAL DIVISION TECHNICAL
    CENTER - INFORMATION CENTER
Box 122   Phone: (216) 933-6181
Avon Lake, OH 44012

BABCOCK AND WILCOX COMPANY - FOSSIL POWER GENERATION
    DIVISION - TECHNICAL LIBRARY
20 S. Van Buren Ave.   Phone: (216) 753-4511
Barberton, OH 44203   Gloria H. Broaddus, Libn.

BARBERTON CITIZENS HOSPITAL - MEDICAL LIBRARY †
Tuscora Pk.   Phone: (216) 745-1611
Barberton, OH 44203   Helen Young, Adm.Coord.

PPG INDUSTRIES, INC. - CHEMICAL DIVISION - RESEARCH LIBRARY
Box 31   Phone: (216) 848-4161
Barberton, OH 44203   Diana M. Danko, Supv.Info.Serv.

CLERMONT COUNTY LAW LIBRARY ASSOCIATION
Courthouse, Main St.   Phone: (513) 732-7109
Batavia, OH 45103   Eda C. Watson, Libn.

CLEVELAND COLLEGE OF JEWISH STUDIES - AARON GARBER LIBRARY
26500 Shaker Blvd.   Phone: (216) 464-4050
Beachwood, OH 44122   Zipora Leiby, Chf.Libn.

BEDFORD HISTORICAL SOCIETY - LIBRARY
30 S. Park St.
Box 282   Phone: (216) 232-3925
Bedford, OH 44146   Richard J. Squire, Dir.

FERRO CORPORATION - FERRO CHEMICAL DIVISION - FERRO CHEMICAL
    LIBRARY
7040 Krick Rd.   Phone: (216) 641-8580
Bedford, OH 44146   Mary Jane Campbell, Libn.

BALDWIN-WALLACE COLLEGE - CHEMISTRY LIBRARY
Berea, OH 44017

BALDWIN-WALLACE COLLEGE - RIEMENSCHNEIDER BACH INSTITUTE -
    BACH LIBRARY
Merner-Pfeiffer Hall
49 Seminary St.   Phone: (216) 826-2207
Berea, OH 44017   Dr. Elinore Barber, Dir., Bach Inst.

BLUFFTON COLLEGE - MENNONITE HISTORICAL LIBRARY
                    Phone: (419) 358-8015
Bluffton, OH 45817   Delbert Gratz, Libn.

BOWLING GREEN STATE UNIVERSITY - CENTER FOR ARCHIVAL
    COLLECTIONS
Library, 5th Fl.   Phone: (419) 372-2411
Bowling Green, OH 43403   Dr. Richard J. Wright, Dir.

BOWLING GREEN STATE UNIVERSITY - POPULAR CULTURE LIBRARY
                    Phone: (419) 372-2450
Bowling Green, OH 43403   Nancy Steen, Hd.Libn.

WOOD COUNTY HISTORICAL SOCIETY - HISTORICAL MUSEUM LIBRARY
13360 County Home Rd.   Phone: (419) 352-0967
Bowling Green, OH 43402   Lyle Fletcher, Archv.

WOOD COUNTY LAW LIBRARY
County Office Bldg., 1st Fl.   Phone: (419) 353-3921
Bowling Green, OH 43402   Brenda Woodruff, Law Libn.

GOODRICH (B.F.) COMPANY - RESEARCH AND DEVELOPMENT CENTER -
    BRECKSVILLE INFORMATION CENTER
9921 Brecksville Rd.   Phone: (216) 526-4311
Brecksville, OH 44141   Carol A. Lioce, Mgr., Info.Ctr.

U.S. VETERANS ADMINISTRATION (OH-Brecksville) - HOSPITAL LIBRARY
10000 Brecksville Rd.   Phone: (216) 526-3030
Brecksville, OH 44141   Nancy S. Tesmer, Chf., Lib.Serv.

BROADVIEW DEVELOPMENTAL CENTER - REGIONAL STAFF LIBRARY
9543 Broadview Rd.   Phone: (216) 526-5000
Broadview Heights, OH 44147   Noreen M. Kenney, Regional Libn.

GEAUGA COUNTY HISTORICAL SOCIETY - LIBRARY
14653 E. Park St.   Phone: (216) 834-1492
Burton, OH 44021   Marlene F. Collins, Off.Mgr.

CAMBRIDGE MENTAL HEALTH & DEVELOPMENTAL CENTER - STAFF &
    RESIDENT RESOURCE CENTER
Rte. 21 N.   Phone: (614) 439-1371
Cambridge, OH 43725   Nancy Bolin, Dir. Resource Serv.

GUERNSEY COUNTY LAW LIBRARY
Court House
Cambridge, OH 43725   Frank Leyshon, Libn.

AULTMAN HOSPITAL - MEDICAL LIBRARY
2600 6th St., S.W.   Phone: (216) 452-9911
Canton, OH 44710   Leah R. Lloyd, Libn.

AULTMAN HOSPITAL - SCHOOL OF NURSING LIBRARY
2614 6th St., S.W.   Phone: (216) 452-9911
Canton, OH 44710   Violet Russell, Coord.Lrng.Rsrcs.

MERCY SCHOOL OF NURSING - E.O. MORROW LIBRARY
1320 Timken Mercy Dr., N.W.   Phone: (216) 489-1140
Canton, OH 44708   Jane Clarke, Dir.

OHIO POWER COMPANY - LIBRARY
301 Cleveland Ave., S.W.   Phone: (216) 456-8173
Canton, OH 44701   J.M. Beck, Libn.

PRO FOOTBALL HALL OF FAME - LIBRARY/RESEARCH CENTER
2121 Harrison Ave., N.W.   Phone: (216) 456-8207
Canton, OH 44708   Anne Monnot, Libn.

STARK COUNTY HISTORICAL SOCIETY - RAMSAYER LIBRARY
McKinley Musm. of Hist., Sci. & Industry
749 Hazlett Ave., N.W.
Box 483   Phone: (216) 455-7043
Canton, OH 44701

STARK COUNTY LAW LIBRARY ASSOCIATION - LAW LIBRARY
Court House, Fourth Fl.   Phone: (216) 456-2330
Canton, OH 44702   Martha M. Cox, Dir.

TIMKEN COMPANY - RESEARCH LIBRARY
1835 Deuber Ave.   Phone: (216) 453-4511
Canton, OH 44706   A.T. Brown, Libn.

TIMKEN MERCY HOSPITAL - MEDICAL LIBRARY
1320 Timken Mercy Dr.   Phone: (216) 489-1462
Canton, OH 44708   Jane L. Clark, Dir., Med.Lib.Serv.

ST. CHARLES SEMINARY - LIBRARY
Carthagena, OH 45822

MERCER COUNTY LAW LIBRARY
Court House   Phone: (419) 586-2122
Celina, OH 45822   Carolyn Leffler, Asst.Sec.

GEAUGA COUNTY LAW LIBRARY
Court House   Phone: (216) 285-2222
Chardon, OH 44024   Violet R. Amnasan, Libn.

MEAD CORPORATION - LIBRARY
Central Research Laboratories   Phone: (614) 772-3588
Chillicothe, OH 45601   Jane M. White, Libn.

U.S. NATL. PARK SERVICE - MOUND CITY GROUP NATL. MONUMENT -
    LIBRARY
16062 State Route 104   Phone: (614) 774-1125
Chillicothe, OH 45601   Kenneth Apschnikat, Supt.

U.S. VETERANS ADMINISTRATION (OH-Chillicothe) - HOSPITAL LIBRARY
                                          Phone: (614) 773-1141
Chillicothe, OH 45601   Barbara A. Schultz, Chf., Lib.Serv.

AMERICAN WATCHMAKERS INSTITUTE - LIBRARY
3700 Harrison Ave.   Phone: (513) 661-3838
Cincinnati, OH 45211   Mrs. Michael Danner, Libn.

ARCHDIOCESE OF CINCINNATI - ARCHIVES
6616 Beechmont Ave.   Phone: (513) 731-9229
Cincinnati, OH 45230   Fr. M. Edmund Hussey, Archv.

BETHESDA HOSPITAL - INFORMATION RESOURCE CENTER
619 Oak St.   Phone: (513) 559-6337
Cincinnati, OH 45206   Margaret Gomien, Libn.

CARSTAB CORPORATION - RESEARCH LIBRARY
West St.   Phone: (513) 554-1554
Cincinnati, OH 45215   Christine J. Gadker, Res.Libn.

CHILDREN'S HOSPITAL RESEARCH FOUNDATION - RESEARCH LIBRARY
Elland & Bethesda Sts.   Phone: (513) 559-4300
Cincinnati, OH 45229   Margaret L. Moutseous, Lib.Dir.

CHRIST HOSPITAL INSTITUTE OF MEDICAL RESEARCH - LIBRARY
2141 Auburn Ave.   Phone: (513) 369-2540
Cincinnati, OH 45219   Lisa L. McCormick, Res.Libn.

CINCINNATI ART MUSEUM - LIBRARY
Eden Pk.   Phone: (513) 721-5204
Cincinnati, OH 45202   Patricia P. Rutledge, Libn.

CINCINNATI CITY PLANNING COMMISSION - PLANNING AND
    MANAGEMENT SUPPORT SYSTEM LIBRARY
City Hall, Rm. 141
801 Plum St.   Phone: (513) 352-3441
Cincinnati, OH 45202   Kevin Shepard, Dir.

CINCINNATI ELECTRONICS CORPORATION - TECHNICAL LIBRARY
2630 Glendale-Milford Rd.   Phone: (513) 563-6000
Cincinnati, OH 45241   Lois D. Hammond, Chf.Tech.Libn.

CINCINNATI HISTORICAL SOCIETY - LIBRARY
Eden Park   Phone: (513) 241-4622
Cincinnati, OH 45202   Laura L. Chace, Libn.

CINCINNATI LAW LIBRARY ASSOCIATION
601 Courthouse   Phone: (513) 632-8372
Cincinnati, OH 45202   Carol E. Meyer, Hd.Libn.

CINCINNATI MILACRON, INC. - CORPORATE INFORMATION CENTER
4701 Marburg Ave.   Phone: (513) 841-8879
Cincinnati, OH 45209   Rory L. Chase, Corp.Libn.

CINCINNATI MUNICIPAL REFERENCE LIBRARY
Rm. 224, City Hall   Phone: (513) 352-3309
Cincinnati, OH 45202   Hila O. Foley, Libn.

CINCINNATI MUSEUM OF NATURAL HISTORY - LIBRARY
1720 Gilbert Ave.   Phone: (513) 621-3889
Cincinnati, OH 45202   DeVere Burt, Musm.Dir.

CINCINNATI POST - LIBRARY
800 Broadway   Phone: (513) 352-2785
Cincinnati, OH 45202   Elmer L. Geers, Libn.

CINCINNATI PUBLIC SCHOOLS - PROFESSIONAL LIBRARY †
230 E. Ninth St.   Phone: (513) 369-4734
Cincinnati, OH 45202   Paul J. Lee, Libn.

CORVA LIBRARY
19 Garfield Place   Phone: (513) 621-2434
Cincinnati, OH 45252   Susanne Gilliam, Libn.

DEACONESS HOSPITAL - SCHOOL OF NURSING - RICHARD W. ANGERT
   MEMORIAL LIBRARY
415 Straight St.   Phone: (513) 559-2285
Cincinnati, OH 45219   Valerie J. Eliot, Libn.

DINSMORE, SHOHL, COATES & DEUPREE - LIBRARY
2100 Fountain Sq. Plaza
511 Walnut St.   Phone: (513) 621-6747
Cincinnati, OH 45202   Doris Kaplan, Libn.

DOW CHEMICAL COMPANY - MERRELL DOW PHARMACEUTICALS, INC. -
   RESEARCH CENTER LIBRARY
2110 E. Galbraith Rd.   Phone: (513) 948-9111
Cincinnati, OH 45215   Elaine Besterman, Mgr.Lib.Serv.

DRACKETT COMPANY - RESEARCH AND DEVELOPMENT LIBRARY
5020 Spring Grove Ave.   Phone: (513) 632-1449
Cincinnati, OH 45232   Mary Jane Ennis, Res.Libn.

EMERY INDUSTRIES, INC. - RESEARCH LIBRARY
4900 Este Ave.   Phone: (513) 482-2157
Cincinnati, OH 45232   B.A. Bernard, Res.Libn.

ENGINEERS AND SCIENTISTS OF CINCINNATI - LIBRARY
1349 E. McMillan St.
Cincinnati, OH 45206

ENVIRONMENTAL PROTECTION AGENCY - ANDREW W. BREIDENBACH
   ENVIRONMENTAL RESEARCH CTR., CINCINNATI - TECH.LIB.
26 W. St. Clair Ave.   Phone: (513) 684-7701
Cincinnati, OH 45268   JoAnn Johnson, Chf., Lib.Serv.

GENERAL ELECTRIC COMPANY - AIRCRAFT ENGINE GROUP - LAW LIBRARY
Mail Drop F44   Phone: (513) 243-2298
Cincinnati, OH 45215

GENERAL ELECTRIC COMPANY - AIRCRAFT ENGINE GROUP - TECHNICAL
   INFORMATION CENTER
Bldg. 700, N-32   Phone: (513) 243-4333
Cincinnati, OH 45215   James J. Brady, Mgr.

GOOD SAMARITAN HOSPITAL - MEDICAL LIBRARY
3217 Clifton Ave.   Phone: (513) 872-2433
Cincinnati, OH 45220   Kathleen D. Connick, Med.Libn.

HEBREW UNION COLLEGE - JEWISH INSTITUTE OF RELIGION - AMERICAN
   JEWISH ARCHIVES
3101 Clifton Ave.   Phone: (513) 221-1875
Cincinnati, OH 45220   Professor Jacob R. Marcus, Dir.

HEBREW UNION COLLEGE - JEWISH INSTITUTE OF RELIGION - AMERICAN
   JEWISH PERIODICAL CENTER
3101 Clifton Ave.   Phone: (513) 221-1875
Cincinnati, OH 45220   Jacob R. Marcus, Dir.

HEBREW UNION COLLEGE - JEWISH INSTITUTE OF RELIGION - KLAU
   LIBRARY
3101 Clifton Ave.   Phone: (513) 221-1875
Cincinnati, OH 45220   Herbert C. Zafren, Lib.Dir.

HOME MISSIONERS OF AMERICA - GLENMARY NOVITIATE LIBRARY *
Box 46404   Phone: (513) 874-8900
Cincinnati, OH 45246   Thomas J. Meehan, Libn.

INTERNATIONAL THESPIAN SOCIETY - LIBRARY
3368 Central Pkwy.   Phone: (513) 559-1996
Cincinnati, OH 45225   Ronald L. Longstreth, Exec.Sec.

JEWISH HOSPITAL OF CINCINNATI - MEDICAL LIBRARY
3200 Burnet Ave.   Phone: (513) 872-3136
Cincinnati, OH 45229   Melanie F. McGuire, Med.Libn.

JEWISH HOSPITAL OF CINCINNATI SCHOOL OF NURSING - NURSE'S
   REFERENCE LIBRARY
3161 Harvey Ave.   Phone: (513) 872-3534
Cincinnati, OH 45229   Alice W. Neumann, Instr./Media Coord.

K.K. BENE ISRAEL/ROCKDALE TEMPLE - SIDNEY G. ROSE MEMORIAL
   LIBRARY
8501 Ridge Rd.   Phone: (513) 891-9900
Cincinnati, OH 45236   Mrs. Seymour Miller, Libn.

KINNEY (A.M.) INC. - LIBRARY
2900 Vernon Place   Phone: (513) 281-2900
Cincinnati, OH 45219   Donna L. Middendorf, Libn.

KZF, INC. - KZF LIBRARY
2830 Victory Pkwy.   Phone: (513) 281-7723
Cincinnati, OH 45206   Dennis O. Hamilton, Lib.Dir.

LLOYD LIBRARY AND MUSEUM
917 Plum St.   Phone: (513) 721-3707
Cincinnati, OH 45202   John B. Griggs, Libn.

METCUT RESEARCH ASSOCIATES, INC. - MACHINABILITY DATA CENTER
3980 Rosslyn Dr.   Phone: (513) 271-9510
Cincinnati, OH 45209   John F. Kahles, Dir.

MIAMI PURCHASE ASSOCIATION FOR HISTORIC PRESERVATION -
   LIBRARY AND INFORMATION CENTER
812 Dayton St.   Phone: (513) 721-4506
Cincinnati, OH 45214   Cecelia S. Grineff, Registrar

MOUNT ST. MARY'S SEMINARY OF THE WEST - LIBRARY
6616 Beechmont Ave.   Phone: (513) 231-2223
Cincinnati, OH 45230   Sr. Deborah Harmeling, O.S.B., Hd.Libn.

NATIONAL ASSOCIATION FOR CREATIVE CHILDREN AND ADULTS (NACCA)
   - LIBRARY
8080 Springvalley Dr.   Phone: (513) 631-1777
Cincinnati, OH 45236   Ann Fabe Isaacs, Hd.

NLO, INC. - LIBRARY
Box 39158   Phone: (513) 738-1151
Cincinnati, OH 45239   Rosemary H. Gardewing, Lib.Asst.

OHIO COVERED BRIDGE COMMITTEE - LIBRARY
18 Elm Ave.   Phone: (513) 761-1789
Cincinnati, OH 45215   John A. Diehl, Libn.

PEDCO GROUP LIBRARY
Chester Towers
11499 Chester Rd.   Phone: (513) 782-4770
Cincinnati, OH 45246   Janet L. Zieleniewski, Libn.

PROCTER & GAMBLE COMPANY - IVORYDALE TECHNICAL CENTER -
   LIBRARY
                                             Phone: (901) 454-8310
Cincinnati, OH 45217   Alberta Weisgerber, Lib.Mgr.

PROCTER & GAMBLE COMPANY - LIBRARY
Box 599
Cincinnati, OH 45201   Marcia Cahall, Libn.

PROCTER & GAMBLE COMPANY - MIAMI VALLEY LABORATORIES -
   TECHNICAL LIBRARY
Box 39175
Cincinnati, OH 45247   E. Heaton

PROCTER & GAMBLE COMPANY - WINTON HILL TECHNICAL CENTER -
   TECHNICAL LIBRARY
6090 Center Hill Rd.   Phone: (513) 977-7257
Cincinnati, OH 45224   Irene L. Myers, Sect.Hd.

PUBLIC LIBRARY OF CINCINNATI AND HAMILTON COUNTY - ART AND
   MUSIC DEPARTMENT
800 Vine St.   Phone: (513) 369-6954
Cincinnati, OH 45202   R. Jayne Craven, Hd., Art & Music

PUBLIC LIBRARY OF CINCINNATI AND HAMILTON COUNTY - DEPARTMENT
OF RARE BOOKS & SPECIAL COLLECTIONS
800 Vine St.   Phone: (513) 369-6957
Cincinnati, OH 45202   Yeatman Anderson III, Cur.

PUBLIC LIBRARY OF CINCINNATI AND HAMILTON COUNTY - EDUCATION
AND RELIGION DEPARTMENT
800 Vine St.   Phone: (513) 369-6940
Cincinnati, OH 45202   Jane E. Wagner, Hd.

PUBLIC LIBRARY OF CINCINNATI AND HAMILTON COUNTY - EXCEPTIONAL
CHILDREN'S DIVISION
800 Vine St.   Phone: (513) 369-6065
Cincinnati, OH 45202   Miss Coy K. Hunsucker, Hd.

PUBLIC LIBRARY OF CINCINNATI AND HAMILTON COUNTY - FILMS AND
RECORDINGS CENTER
800 Vine St.   Phone: (513) 369-6924
Cincinnati, OH 45202   Patrice Callaghan, Hd.

PUBLIC LIBRARY OF CINCINNATI AND HAMILTON COUNTY - GOVERNMENT
AND BUSINESS DEPARTMENT
800 Vine St.   Phone: (513) 369-6932
Cincinnati, OH 45202   Paul Hudson, Hd.

PUBLIC LIBRARY OF CINCINNATI AND HAMILTON COUNTY - HISTORY AND
LITERATURE DEPARTMENT
800 Vine St.   Phone: (513) 369-6905
Cincinnati, OH 45202   J. Richard Abell, Hd.

PUBLIC LIBRARY OF CINCINNATI AND HAMILTON COUNTY - HISTORY AND
LITERATURE DEPARTMENT - MAP UNIT
800 Vine St.   Phone: (513) 369-6909
Cincinnati, OH 45202   Carl G. Marquette, Jr., Map Libn.

PUBLIC LIBRARY OF CINCINNATI AND HAMILTON COUNTY -
INSTITUTIONS/BOOKS BY MAIL
800 Vine St.   Phone: (513) 369-6070
Cincinnati, OH 45202   Keith Kuhn, Interim Supv.

PUBLIC LIBRARY OF CINCINNATI AND HAMILTON COUNTY - LIBRARY FOR
THE BLIND AND PHYSICALLY HANDICAPPED
444 W. 3rd St.   Phone: (513) 369-6075
Cincinnati, OH 45202   Mary Jo Holcomb, Regional Libn.

PUBLIC LIBRARY OF CINCINNATI AND HAMILTON COUNTY - SCIENCE AND
INDUSTRY DEPARTMENT
800 Vine St.   Phone: (513) 369-6936
Cincinnati, OH 45202   Rosemary Gaiser, Hd.

ST. FRANCIS-ST. GEORGE HOSPITAL - HEALTH SCIENCES LIBRARY
1860 Queen City Ave.   Phone: (513) 244-5122
Cincinnati, OH 45214   Carol Mayor, Libn.

ST. THOMAS INSTITUTE - LIBRARY
1842 Madison Rd.   Phone: (513) 861-3460
Cincinnati, OH 45206   Sr. M. Virgil Ghering, O.P., Libn.

STERLING DRUG, INC. - HILTON-DAVIS CHEMICAL COMPANY DIVISION -
LIBRARY
2235 Langdon Farm Rd.   Phone: (513) 841-4074
Cincinnati, OH 45237   Dorothy B. Breyley, Libn.

TAFT MUSEUM - LIBRARY
316 Pike St.   Phone: (513) 241-0343
Cincinnati, OH 45202   Katherine Hanna, Dir.

TAFT, STETTINIUS & HOLLISTER - LAW LIBRARY
First National Bank Ctr.   Phone: (513) 381-2838
Cincinnati, OH 45202   Maureen T. Willig, Libn.

U.S. COURT OF APPEALS, 6TH CIRCUIT - LIBRARY
617 U.S. Court House & Post Office Bldg.   Phone: (513) 684-2958
Cincinnati, OH 45202   Frank Payne, Libn.

U.S. DEPT. OF COMMERCE - INTERNATIONAL TRADE ADMINISTRATION -
CINCINNATI DISTRICT OFFICE LIBRARY
10504 Federal Office Bldg.
550 Main St.   Phone: (513) 684-2944
Cincinnati, OH 45202   Gordon B. Thomas, Dir.

U.S. NATL. INSTITUTE FOR OCCUPATIONAL SAFETY & HEALTH -
CLEARINGHOUSE FOR OCCUPATIONAL SAFETY & HEALTH INFO.
Robert A. Taft Laboratory
4676 Columbia Pkwy.   Phone: (513) 684-8321
Cincinnati, OH 45226   Vivian Morgan, Hd.

U.S. VETERANS ADMINISTRATION (OH-Cincinnati) - MEDICAL CENTER
LIBRARY
3200 Vine St.
Cincinnati, OH 45220   Cynthia R. Sterling, Libn.

UNIVERSITY AFFILIATED CINCINNATI CENTER FOR DEVELOPMENTAL
DISORDERS - RESEARCH LIBRARY
Pavilion Bldg.
Elland & Bethesda Aves.   Phone: (513) 559-4626
Cincinnati, OH 45229   Dorothy A. Gilroy, Libn.

UNIVERSITY OF CINCINNATI - COLLEGE CONSERVATORY OF MUSIC -
GORNO MEMORIAL MUSIC LIBRARY
101 Emery Hall   Phone: (513) 475-4471
Cincinnati, OH 45221   Robert O. Johnson, Libn.

UNIVERSITY OF CINCINNATI - DEPARTMENT OF ENVIRONMENTAL HEALTH
LIBRARY
Kettering Laboratory Library
3223 Eden Ave.   Phone: (513) 872-5771
Cincinnati, OH 45267   Evelyn M. Widner, Sr.Res.Assoc.

UNIVERSITY OF CINCINNATI - DESIGN, ARCHITECTURE & ART LIBRARY
800 Alms Bldg.   Phone: (513) 475-3238
Cincinnati, OH 45221   Elizabeth D. Byrne, Hd.Libn.

UNIVERSITY OF CINCINNATI - ENGINEERING LIBRARY
880 Baldwin Hall   Phone: (513) 475-3761
Cincinnati, OH 45221   Dorothy F. Byers, Hd.

UNIVERSITY OF CINCINNATI - GEOLOGY LIBRARY
103 Old Tech Bldg.   Phone: (513) 475-4332
Cincinnati, OH 45221   Richard A. Spohn, Hd.

UNIVERSITY OF CINCINNATI - JOHN MILLER BURNAM CLASSICAL LIBRARY
671 Blegen   Phone: (513) 475-6724
Cincinnati, OH 45221   Jean Susorney Wellington, Classics Libn.

UNIVERSITY OF CINCINNATI - MATHEMATICS LIBRARY
840 Old Chemistry Bldg.   Phone: (513) 475-4449
Cincinnati, OH 45221   Olga Dobur, Hd.

UNIVERSITY OF CINCINNATI - MEDICAL CENTER LIBRARIES - COLLEGE OF
NURSING & HEALTH - LEVI MEMORIAL LIBRARY
Vine St. & St. Clair Ave.   Phone: (513) 872-5543
Cincinnati, OH 45219   Mildred Turcotte, Libn.

UNIVERSITY OF CINCINNATI - MEDICAL CENTER LIBRARIES - HEALTH
SCIENCES LIBRARY
231 Bethesda Ave.   Phone: (513) 872-5627
Cincinnati, OH 45267   Billie Broaddus, Hd.

UNIVERSITY OF CINCINNATI - MEDICAL CENTER LIBRARIES - HISTORY OF
HEALTH SCIENCES LIBRARY AND MUSEUM
Eden & Bethesda Aves., Wherry Hall   Phone: (513) 872-5120
Cincinnati, OH 45267   Charles Isetts, Hd.

UNIVERSITY OF CINCINNATI - MEDICAL CENTER LIBRARIES - MEDIA
RESOURCES CENTER
231 Bethesda Ave.   Phone: (513) 872-4173
Cincinnati, OH 45267   Kumar Dontamsetti, Hd.

UNIVERSITY OF CINCINNATI - OBSERVATORY LIBRARY
Observatory Pl.   Phone: (513) 475-2331
Cincinnati, OH 45208   Marianne Wells, Libn.

UNIVERSITY OF CINCINNATI - OESPER CHEMISTRY-BIOLOGY LIBRARY
Brodie A-3, Rm. 503   Phone: (513) 475-4524
Cincinnati, OH 45221   Dorice Des Chene, Hd.

UNIVERSITY OF CINCINNATI - OMI COLLEGE OF APPLIED SCIENCE -
TIMOTHY C. DAY TECHNICAL LIBRARY
100 E. Central Pkwy.   Phone: (513) 475-6553
Cincinnati, OH 45210   John P. Hiestand, Libn.

GEOGRAPHIC

GEOGRAPHIC

UNIVERSITY OF CINCINNATI - PHYSICS LIBRARY
406 Braunstein Hall
Cincinnati, OH 45221
Phone: (513) 475-2331
Marianna Wells, Hd.

UNIVERSITY OF CINCINNATI - ROBERT S. MARX LAW LIBRARY
Law School
Cincinnati, OH 45221
Phone: (513) 475-3016
Jorge L. Carro, Hd.Libn.

UNIVERSITY OF CINCINNATI - SPECIAL COLLECTIONS DEPARTMENT
Central Library, Rm. 462
Cincinnati, OH 45221
Phone: (513) 475-6459
Alice M. Vestal, Hd.

WESTERN AND SOUTHERN LIFE INSURANCE CO. - LIBRARY
400 Broadway
Cincinnati, OH 45202
Phone: (513) 421-1800
Virginia Custer, Libn.

WESTMINSTER PRESBYTERIAN CHURCH - JOHN H. HOLMES LIBRARY
4991 Cleves Warsaw Pike
Cincinnati, OH 45238
Phone: (513) 921-1623
E. Allen, Libn.

WESTWOOD FIRST PRESBYTERIAN CHURCH - WALTER LORENZ MEMORIAL
LIBRARY
3011 Harrison Ave.
Cincinnati, OH 45211
Phone: (513) 661-6846
Marian B. McNair, Libn.

WISE (Isaac M.) TEMPLE - RALPH COHEN MEMORIAL LIBRARY
8329 Ridge Rd.
Cincinnati, OH 45236
Phone: (513) 793-2556
Judith S. Carsch, Libn.

YOUNG MEN'S MERCANTILE LIBRARY ASSOCIATION - LIBRARY
414 Walnut St.
Cincinnati, OH 45202
Phone: (513) 621-0717
Jean M. Springer, Exec.Dir.

ZOOLOGICAL SOCIETY OF CINCINNATI - MEDIA CENTER
3400 Vine St.
Cincinnati, OH 45220
Phone: (513) 281-3700
Zona Wilkinson, Media Ctr.Coord.

PICKAWAY COUNTY LAW LIBRARY
Courthouse
Box 87
Circleville, OH 43113
William Ammer, Treas.

AFRO-AMERICAN CULTURAL AND HISTORICAL SOCIETY MUSEUM -
LIBRARY †
1839 E. 81st St.
Cleveland, OH 44103
Phone: (216) 231-2131
Icabod Flewellen, Dir.

ALCAN ALUMINUM CORPORATION - CORPORATE LIBRARY
100 Erieview Plaza
Cleveland, OH 44114
Phone: (216) 523-6860
Winifred B. Bowes, Libn.

BAKER AND HOSTETLER - LIBRARY
3200 National City Ctr.
Cleveland, OH 44114
Phone: (216) 621-0200
Alvin M. Podboy, Libn.

BRUSH WELLMAN, INC. - TECHNICAL LIBRARY
17876 St. Clair Ave.
Cleveland, OH 44110
Phone: (216) 486-4200
Nancie J. Skonezny, Libn.

CARROLL (John) UNIVERSITY - SEISMOLOGICAL LIBRARY
Cleveland, OH 44118
Phone: (216) 491-4361
Ann Mell, Libn.

CASE WESTERN RESERVE UNIVERSITY - APPLIED SOCIAL SCIENCES
LIBRARY
School of Applied Social Sciences
2035 Abington Rd.
Cleveland, OH 44106
Phone: (216) 368-2302
Vlatka Ivanisevic, Libn.

CASE WESTERN RESERVE UNIVERSITY - LAW LIBRARY
11075 East Blvd.
Cleveland, OH 44106
Phone: (216) 368-2792
Simon L. Goren, Law Libn.

CASE WESTERN RESERVE UNIVERSITY - MATTHEW A. BAXTER SCHOOL OF
LIBRARY & INFORMATION SCIENCE
Newton D. Baker Bldg.
10950 Euclid Ave.
Cleveland, OH 44106
Phone: (216) 368-3524
Bettina R. MacAyeal, Libn.

CASE WESTERN RESERVE UNIVERSITY - SEARS LIBRARY
10900 Euclid Ave.
Cleveland, OH 44106
Phone: (216) 368-4244
David Goding, Hd.Libn.

CATHOLIC UNIVERSE BULLETIN - LIBRARY
Chancery Bldg., 1027 Superior Ave.
Cleveland, OH 44114
Phone: (216) 696-6525
Edgar Barmann, Mng.Ed.

CLEVELAND CLINIC EDUCATION FOUNDATION - MEDICAL LIBRARY/
AUDIOVISUAL CENTER †
9500 Euclid Ave.
Cleveland, OH 44106
Phone: (216) 444-5698
Elizabeth Joy, Hd.Med.Libn.

CLEVELAND COUNCIL ON WORLD AFFAIRS - LIBRARY AND PAMPHLET SHOP
601 Rockwell Ave.
Cleveland, OH 44114
Phone: (216) 781-3730

CLEVELAND - DEPARTMENT OF LAW LIBRARY †
211 City Hall
601 Lakeside Ave.
Cleveland, OH 44114
Phone: (216) 664-2656
Jan Ryan Novak, Dept.Hd.

CLEVELAND ELECTRIC ILLUMINATING COMPANY - LAW LIBRARY
Public Square
Box 5000
Cleveland, OH 44101
Phone: (216) 622-9800
Frank U. Sowell, Jr., Assoc. Legal Anl.

CLEVELAND ELECTRIC ILLUMINATING COMPANY - LIBRARY
Public Square, Rm. 504
Box 5000
Cleveland, OH 44101
Phone: (216) 622-9800
Gerrard Roberts, Libn.

CLEVELAND HEALTH SCIENCES LIBRARY
2119 Abington Rd.
Cleveland, OH 44106
Phone: (216) 368-3426
Robert G. Cheshier, Dir.

CLEVELAND HEALTH SCIENCES LIBRARY - ALLEN MEMORIAL LIBRARY
11000 Euclid Ave.
Cleveland, OH 44106
Phone: (216) 368-3640
Lydia Holian, Assoc.Dir.

CLEVELAND HEALTH SCIENCES LIBRARY - HEALTH CENTER LIBRARY
2119 Abington Rd.
Cleveland, OH 44106
Phone: (216) 368-3426
Marjorie Saunders, Assoc.Dir.

CLEVELAND HEALTH SCIENCES LIBRARY - HOWARD DITTRICK MUSEUM OF
HISTORICAL MEDICINE
11000 Euclid Ave.
Cleveland, OH 44106
Phone: (216) 368-3648
Dr. Patsy A. Gerstner, Chf.Cur.

CLEVELAND HEARING AND SPEECH CENTER - LUCILE DAUBY GRIES
MEMORIAL LIBRARY
11206 Euclid Ave.
Cleveland, OH 44106
Phone: (216) 231-8787
Ali Emdad, Libn.

CLEVELAND INSTITUTE OF ART - JESSICA R. GUND MEMORIAL LIBRARY
11141 East Blvd.
Cleveland, OH 44106
Phone: (216) 421-4322
Karen D. Tschudy, Lib.Dir.

CLEVELAND INSTITUTE OF MUSIC - LIBRARY
11021 East Blvd.
Cleveland, OH 44106
Phone: (216) 791-5165
Karen Miller, Libn.

CLEVELAND LAW LIBRARY
404 County Court House
Cleveland, OH 44113
Phone: (216) 861-5070
Arthur W. Fiske, Libn.

CLEVELAND METROPARKS ZOOLOGICAL PARK - LIBRARY *
Brookside Pk.
Cleveland, OH 44109
Phone: (216) 661-6500

CLEVELAND METROPOLITAN GENERAL HOSPITAL - HAROLD H.
BRITTINGHAM MEMORIAL LIBRARY
3395 Scranton Rd.
Cleveland, OH 44109
Phone: (216) 398-6000
Carol Morrison, Chf.Libn.

CLEVELAND MUSEUM OF ART - LIBRARY
11150 East Blvd.
Cleveland, OH 44106
Phone: (216) 421-7340
Jack Perry Brown, Libn.

CLEVELAND MUSEUM OF NATURAL HISTORY - HAROLD TERRY CLARK
  LIBRARY
Wade Oval, University Circle   Phone: (216) 231-4600
Cleveland, OH 44106   Mary Baum, Libn.

CLEVELAND MUSIC SCHOOL SETTLEMENT - KULAS LIBRARY *
11125 Magnolia St.   Phone: (216) 421-5809
Cleveland, OH 44106   Mary Louise Emery, Libn. & Instr.

CLEVELAND PRESS - LIBRARY
901 Lakeside Ave.   Phone: (216) 623-6740
Cleveland, OH 44114   Thomas Barensfeld, Libn.

CLEVELAND PSYCHIATRIC INSTITUTE - KARNOSH LIBRARY
1708 Aiken Ave.   Phone: (216) 661-6200
Cleveland, OH 44109   Anna L. Harris, Libn.

CLEVELAND PSYCHOANALYTIC SOCIETY - LIBRARY
11328 Euclid Ave., No. 205   Phone: (216) 229-2111
Cleveland, OH 44106   Norine E. Wild, Libn.

CLEVELAND PUBLIC LIBRARY - BUSINESS, ECONOMICS & LABOR
  DEPARTMENT
325 Superior Ave.   Phone: (216) 623-2927
Cleveland, OH 44114   Marcella Matejka, Dept.Hd.

CLEVELAND PUBLIC LIBRARY - CHILDREN'S LITERATURE DEPARTMENT
325 Superior Ave.   Phone: (216) 623-2834
Cleveland, OH 44114   Miss Roger Mae Johnson, Dept.Hd.

CLEVELAND PUBLIC LIBRARY - DOCUMENTS COLLECTION
325 Superior Ave.   Phone: (216) 623-2870
Cleveland, OH 44114   Elizabeth Fannon, Dept.Hd.

CLEVELAND PUBLIC LIBRARY - FINE ARTS DEPARTMENT
325 Superior Ave.   Phone: (216) 623-2848
Cleveland, OH 44114   Joan Hoagland, Dept.Hd.

CLEVELAND PUBLIC LIBRARY - FOREIGN LITERATURE DEPARTMENT
325 Superior Ave.   Phone: (216) 623-2895
Cleveland, OH 44114   Natalia B. Bezugloff, Dept.Hd.

CLEVELAND PUBLIC LIBRARY - GENERAL REFERENCE DEPARTMENT
325 Superior Ave.   Phone: (216) 623-2856
Cleveland, OH 44114   Joan L. Sorger, Dept.Hd.

CLEVELAND PUBLIC LIBRARY - HISTORY AND GEOGRAPHY DEPARTMENT
325 Superior Ave.   Phone: (216) 623-2864
Cleveland, OH 44114   Donald Tipka, Dept.Hd.

CLEVELAND PUBLIC LIBRARY - JOHN G. WHITE COLLECTION OF FOLKLORE,
  ORIENTALIA, & CHESS
325 Superior Ave.   Phone: (216) 623-2818
Cleveland, OH 44114   Alice N. Loranth, Hd.

CLEVELAND PUBLIC LIBRARY - LITERATURE DEPARTMENT
325 Superior Ave.   Phone: (216) 623-2881
Cleveland, OH 44114   Lucille R. Troph, Dept.Hd.

CLEVELAND PUBLIC LIBRARY - POPULAR LIBRARY DEPARTMENT
325 Superior Ave.   Phone: (216) 623-2842
Cleveland, OH 44114   John Philip Ferguson, Dept.Hd.

CLEVELAND PUBLIC LIBRARY - PUBLIC ADMINISTRATION LIBRARY
601 Lakeside Ave.   Phone: (216) 623-2919
Cleveland, OH 44114   Jan Ryan Novak, Dept.Hd.

CLEVELAND PUBLIC LIBRARY - ROBERT HAYS GRIES TOBACCO
  COLLECTION
325 Superior Ave.   Phone: (216) 623-2818
Cleveland, OH 44114

CLEVELAND PUBLIC LIBRARY - SCIENCE AND TECHNOLOGY DEPARTMENT
325 Superior Ave.   Phone: (216) 623-2932
Cleveland, OH 44114   Jean Z. Piety, Hd.

CLEVELAND PUBLIC LIBRARY - SOCIAL SCIENCES DEPT.
325 Superior Ave.   Phone: (216) 623-2860
Cleveland, OH 44114   Thelma J. Morris, Dept.Hd.

CLEVELAND STATE UNIVERSITY - JOSEPH W. BARTUNEK III LAW LIBRARY
Euclid Ave. At E. 18th St.   Phone: (216) 687-2250
Cleveland, OH 44115   Anita L. Morse, Prof., Dir. Law Lib.

CONSOLIDATED NATURAL GAS SERVICE CO., INC. - RESEARCH
  DEPARTMENT LIBRARY
11001 Cedar Ave.   Phone: (216) 421-6310
Cleveland, OH 44106   Carol A. Brown, Tech.Res.Libn.

COOPER SCHOOL OF ART - LIBRARY †
1951 W. 26th St.   Phone: (216) 241-1486
Cleveland, OH 44113   Barbara Hammerlund, Hd.Libn.

CUYAHOGA COUNTY REGIONAL PLANNING COMMISSION - LIBRARY *
415 The Arcade   Phone: (216) 861-6805
Cleveland, OH 44114   Robert Parry, Dp.Dir.

DANA CORPORATION - WEATHERHEAD DIVISION - LIBRARY AND
  TECHNICAL INFORMATION CENTER
300 E. 131st St.   Phone: (216) 451-5200
Cleveland, OH 44108   Inez Sifleet, Libn.

DUNHAM TAVERN MUSEUM - LIBRARY
6709 Euclid Ave.   Phone: (216) 431-1060
Cleveland, OH 44103   Elizabeth Martel, Libn.

EATON CORPORATION - CORPORATE LIBRARY
100 Erieview Plaza
Cleveland, OH 44114

ERNST & WHINNEY - NATIONAL OFFICE LIBRARY
2000 National City Ctr.   Phone: (216) 861-5000
Cleveland, OH 44114   Naomi Clifford, Natl.Off.Libn.

FAIRMOUNT TEMPLE - SAM AND EMMA MILLER LIBRARY
23737 Fairmount Blvd.   Phone: (216) 464-1330
Cleveland, OH 44122   Susan Scheps, Libn.

FAIRVIEW GENERAL HOSPITAL - HEALTH MEDIA CENTER
18101 Lorain Ave.   Phone: (216) 476-7118
Cleveland, OH 44111   Susan Favorite, Dir.

FEDERAL RESERVE BANK OF CLEVELAND - RESEARCH LIBRARY
Box 6387   Phone: (216) 241-2800
Cleveland, OH 44101   Elizabeth Maynard, Libn.

FIRST CATHOLIC SLOVAK UNION OF U.S.A. AND CANADA
3289 E. 55th St.   Phone: (216) 341-3355
Cleveland, OH 44127   Stephen F. Ungvarsky, Exec.Sec.

FOUNDATION CENTER - CLEVELAND - KENT H. SMITH LIBRARY
739 National City Bank Bldg.   Phone: (216) 861-1933
Cleveland, OH 44114   Jeanne Bohlen, Dir.

GARDEN CENTER OF GREATER CLEVELAND - ELEANOR SQUIRE LIBRARY
East Blvd.   Phone: (216) 721-1600
Cleveland, OH 44106   Richard T. Isaacson, Libn.

GENERAL ELECTRIC COMPANY - LIGHTING RESEARCH AND TECHNICAL
  SERVICES OPERATIONS - LIBRARY
Nela Park   Phone: (216) 266-3216
Cleveland, OH 44112   Sue Vincelli, Libn.

GENERAL ELECTRIC COMPANY - REFRACTORY METAL PRODUCTS
  DEPARTMENT - LIBRARY †
21800 Tungsten Rd.   Phone: (216) 266-3736
Cleveland, OH 44117   Patricia A. Loucka, Libn.

GOULD, INC. - GOULD INFORMATION CENTER
540 E. 105th St.   Phone: (216) 851-5500
Cleveland, OH 44108   Barbara Sanduleak, Supv., Lib.Serv.

GOULD, INC. - OCEAN SYSTEMS DIVISION - OCEAN SYSTEMS
  INFORMATION CENTER
18901 Euclid Ave.   Phone: (216) 486-8300
Cleveland, OH 44117   Robert J. Rittenhouse, Tech.Info.Spec.

GEOGRAPHIC

GEOGRAPHIC

HAYES (Max S.) VOCATIONAL SCHOOL - LIBRARY
4600 Detroit Ave.
Cleveland, OH 44102
Phone: (216) 631-1528
Robert Stephen, Libn.

HURON ROAD HOSPITAL - LIBRARY AND AUDIOVISUAL CENTER
13951 Terrace Rd.
Cleveland, OH 44112
Phone: (216) 261-8106
Sara W. Baker, Dir.Lib.Serv.

JONES, DAY, REAVIS & POGUE - LIBRARY
1700 Union Commerce Bldg.
Cleveland, OH 44115
Phone: (216) 696-3939
Sharon R. McIntyre, Libn.

LUTHERAN MEDICAL CENTER - C. W. NEVEL MEMORIAL LIBRARY
2609 Franklin Blvd.
Cleveland, OH 44113
Phone: (216) 696-4300
Rosary H. Martin, Med.Libn.

MC GEAN CHEMICAL COMPANY, INC. - RESEARCH LABORATORY LIBRARY
Box 09087
Cleveland, OH 44109
Phone: (216) 441-4900
Charlotte L. Conklin, Libn.

MC KEE (Davy) CORPORATION - INFORMATION RESOURCE CENTER
6200 Oak Tree Blvd.
Cleveland, OH 44131
Phone: (216) 524-9300
Ruth W. Parratt, Libn.

MC KINSEY & COMPANY, INC. - BUSINESS RESEARCH LIBRARY
100 Erieview Plaza
Cleveland, OH 44114
Phone: (216) 696-1313
Lauren C. Rowe, Mgr., Info.Serv.

MARSCHALK COMPANY, INC. - LIBRARY
601 Rockwell Ave.
Cleveland, OH 44114
Phone: (216) 687-8859
Marie Kane, Libn.

MELDRUM AND FEWSMITH, INC. - BUSINESS INFORMATION LIBRARY
1220 Huron Rd.
Cleveland, OH 44115
Phone: (216) 241-2141
Laura Gusky, Supv.

MIDLAND-ROSS CORPORATION - LIBRARY
20600 Chagrin Blvd.
Cleveland, OH 44122
Phone: (216) 491-8400
Diane Greenbaum, Libn.

MOUNT SINAI HOSPITAL OF CLEVELAND - GEORGE H. HAYS MEMORIAL LIBRARY
University Circle
Cleveland, OH 44106
Phone: (216) 795-6000
Pamela Alderman, Chf.Med.Libn.

NORTHEAST OHIO AREAWIDE COORDINATING AGENCY - RESEARCH LIBRARY
1501 Euclid Ave.
Cleveland, OH 44115
Phone: (216) 241-2414
Lee Wachtel, Res.Libn.

OHIO COLLEGE OF PODIATRIC MEDICINE - LIBRARY
10515 Carnegie Ave.
Cleveland, OH 44106
Phone: (216) 231-3300
Judy Mehl, Libn.

PENTON/IPC - MARKETING INFORMATION CENTER
614 Superior Ave., W.
Cleveland, OH 44113
Phone: (216) 696-0300
Kenneth Long, Mgr.

PLAIN DEALER PUBLISHING COMPANY - LIBRARY
1801 Superior Ave.
Cleveland, OH 44114
Phone: (216) 344-4195
Grace D. Parch, Lib.Dir.

PLANNED PARENTHOOD OF CLEVELAND, INC. - LIBRARY
2027 Cornell Rd.
Cleveland, OH 44106
Phone: (216) 721-4700
Shelley B. Matthews, Exec.Sec.

PREFORMED LINE PRODUCTS COMPANY - RESEARCH & ENGINEERING LIBRARY
Box 91129
Cleveland, OH 44101
Phone: (216) 461-5200
Edwina T. Barron, Libn.

REPUBLIC STEEL CORPORATION - RESEARCH CENTER LIBRARY
6801 Brecksville Rd.
Cleveland, OH 44131
Phone: (216) 524-5100
Kathryn A. Woolard, Libn.

ST. ALEXIS HOSPITAL - HEALTH SCIENCES LIBRARY
5163 Broadway Ave.
Cleveland, OH 44127
Phone: (216) 641-3300
Jean Stanley, Dir., Lib.Serv.

ST. LUKE'S HOSPITAL - MEDICAL LIBRARY
11311 Shaker Blvd.
Cleveland, OH 44104
Phone: (216) 368-7691
Pam Billick, Dir.

ST. MARY SEMINARY - LIBRARY
1227 Ansel Rd.
Cleveland, OH 44108
Phone: (216) 721-2100
Steven Kiczek, Libn.

ST. VINCENT CHARITY HOSPITAL - LIBRARY
2351 E. 22nd St.
Cleveland, OH 44115
Phone: (216) 861-6200
Joanne Billiar, Hd.Libn.

SHERWIN-WILLIAMS COMPANY - COMMERCIAL INTELLIGENCE LIBRARY
Box 6520
Cleveland, OH 44101
Phone: (216) 566-2000
Lillian Burkhardt, Adm.

SHERWIN-WILLIAMS COMPANY - TECHNICAL LIBRARY
601 Canal Rd.
Cleveland, OH 44113

SLOVAK WRITERS AND ARTISTS ASSOCIATION - SLOVAK INSTITUTE - LIBRARY †
St. Andrew's Abbey
2900 East Blvd.
Cleveland, OH 44104
Phone: (216) 521-7288
Fr. Nicholas Sprinc, Sec.

SQUIRE, SANDERS & DEMPSEY - LAW LIBRARY
1800 Union Commerce Bldg.
Cleveland, OH 44115
Phone: (216) 696-9200
Vivian S. Balester, Hd.Libn.

TEMPLE LIBRARY
University Circle & Silver Pk.
Cleveland, OH 44106
Phone: (216) 791-7755
Beth Dwoskin, Libn.

TRW, INC. - ENGINEERING LIBRARY
23555 Euclid Ave.
Cleveland, OH 44117
Phone: (216) 383-3417
Elizabeth Barrett, Libn.

UKRAINIAN MUSEUM - ARCHIVES
1202 Kenilworth Ave.
Cleveland, OH 44113
Phone: (216) 661-3038
Alexander Fedynsky, Dir.

UNION CARBIDE CORPORATION - BATTERY PRODUCTS DIVISION - TECHNICAL INFORMATION CENTER
1280 W. 73rd St.
Cleveland, OH 44102
Phone: (216) 631-3100
Claire Marie Langkau, Libn.

UNION CARBIDE CORPORATION - PARMA TECHNICAL CENTER - TECHNICAL INFORMATION SERVICE
Box 6116
Cleveland, OH 44101
Phone: (216) 433-8600
Meredith S. Wright, Mgr.

U.S. DEPT. OF COMMERCE - INTERNATIONAL TRADE ADMINISTRATION - CLEVELAND DISTRICT OFFICE LIBRARY
666 Euclid Ave., Rm. 600
Cleveland, OH 44114
Phone: (216) 522-4750
Zelda W. Milner, Dir.

U.S. NASA - LEWIS RESEARCH CENTER - LIBRARY
21000 Brookpark Rd.
Cleveland, OH 44135
Phone: (216) 433-4000
Dorothy Morris, Chf., Lib.

U.S. VETERANS ADMINISTRATION (OH-Cleveland) - HOSPITAL LIBRARY
10701 East Blvd.
Cleveland, OH 44106
Phone: (216) 791-3800
Nancy S. Tesmer, Chf.Libn.

UNIVERSITY HOSPITALS OF CLEVELAND & CASE WESTERN RESERVE UNIVERSITY - DEPT. OF PATHOLOGY - LIBRARY
2085 Adelbert Rd.
Cleveland, OH 44106
Phone: (216) 368-2482
Susan M. Lucas, Libn.

VISTRON CORPORATION - LIBRARY
1604 Midland Bldg.
Cleveland, OH 44115
Phone: (216) 575-5715
Esther Palevsky, Libn.

WESTERN RESERVE HISTORICAL SOCIETY - LIBRARY
10825 E. Blvd.
Cleveland, OH 44106
Phone: (216) 721-5722
Kermit J. Pike, Dir.

WOMAN'S GENERAL HOSPITAL - MEDICAL LIBRARY
1940 E. 101st St.   Phone: (216) 421-3100
Cleveland, OH 44106   Jeanine M. Harkonen, Circuit Libn.

CONGREGATION BETH AM - DOROTHY G. FELDMAN LIBRARY
3557 Washington Blvd.   Phone: (216) 321-1000
Cleveland Heights, OH 44118   Mrs. Louis L. Powers, Libn.

PARK SYNAGOGUE LIBRARY
3300 Mayfield Rd.   Phone: (216) 371-2244
Cleveland Heights, OH 44118   Ethel I. Saferin, Libn.

ACCURAY CORPORATION - ENGINEERING LIBRARY
650 Ackerman Rd.   Phone: (614) 261-2000
Columbus, OH 43202   Patricia Daley, Libn.

AGUDAS ACHIM CONGREGATION - STEIN MEMORIAL LIBRARY
2767 E. Broad St.   Phone: (614) 237-2747
Columbus, OH 43209   Mrs. William Goldsmith, Libn.

AMERICAN CERAMIC SOCIETY - LIBRARY
65 Ceramic Dr.   Phone: (614) 268-8645
Columbus, OH 43214   Joanna Dobson, Libn.

AMERICAN SOCIETY FOR NONDESTRUCTIVE TESTING - LIBRARY AND
    INFORMATION CENTER
Box 21142   Phone: (614) 488-7921
Columbus, OH 43221   Michael P. Walcoff, Mgr.

ASHLAND CHEMICAL COMPANY - TECHNICAL INFORMATION CENTER
Box 2219   Phone: (614) 889-3281
Columbus, OH 43221   Priscilla Ratliff, Supv.

BATTELLE-COLUMBUS LABORATORIES - COPPER DATA CENTER
505 King Ave.   Phone: (614) 424-7679
Columbus, OH 43201   R.A. Gubiotti, Oper.Mgr.

BATTELLE-COLUMBUS LABORATORIES - DIVER EQUIPMENT INFORMATION
    CENTER
505 King Ave.   Phone: (614) 424-7207
Columbus, OH 43201   Ruth Linebaugh, Mgr.

BATTELLE-COLUMBUS LABORATORIES - LIBRARY
505 King Ave.   Phone: (614) 424-6424
Columbus, OH 43201   Henry A. Rawles, Jr., Mgr.Lib.Serv.

BATTELLE-COLUMBUS LABORATORIES - MECHANICAL PROPERTIES DATA
    CENTER
505 King Ave.   Phone: (614) 424-5892
Columbus, OH 43201   Harold Mindlin, Dir.

BATTELLE-COLUMBUS LABORATORIES - METALS AND CERAMICS
    INFORMATION CENTER
505 King Ave.   Phone: (614) 424-5000
Columbus, OH 43201   Harold Mindlin, Dir.

BATTELLE-COLUMBUS LABORATORIES - RAPIDLY SOLIDIFIED MATERIALS
    (RaSoMat) - RESOURCE CENTER
505 King Ave.   Phone: (614) 424-4324
Columbus, OH 43201   Dr. R.S. Carbonara

BATTELLE-COLUMBUS LABORATORIES - STACK GAS EMISSION CONTROL
    COORDINATION CENTER - LIBRARY
505 King Ave.   Phone: (614) 424-7885
Columbus, OH 43201   Joseph H. Oxley, Mgr.

BATTELLE-COLUMBUS LABORATORIES - TACTICAL TECHNOLOGY CENTER
505 King Ave.   Phone: (614) 424-5047
Columbus, OH 43201   J.T. Brown, Mgr.

BELL TELEPHONE LABORATORIES, INC. & WESTERN ELECTRIC, INC. -
    TECHNICAL LIBRARY
6200 E. Broad St.   Phone: (614) 868-3696
Columbus, OH 43213   Beverly A. Kaushagen, Lib. Group Supv.

CAPITAL UNIVERSITY - CHEMISTRY LIBRARY
2199 E. Main St.   Phone: (614) 236-6500
Columbus, OH 43209   Albert F. Maag, Univ.Libn.

CAPITAL UNIVERSITY - LAW SCHOOL LIBRARY
665 S. High St.   Phone: (614) 445-8634
Columbus, OH 43215   Leverett L. Preble, III, Hd. Law Libn./Prof.

CENTER FOR HUMANE OPTIONS IN CHILDBIRTH EXPERIENCES (CHOICE) -
    LIBRARY
1300 Morse Rd., Suite 200   Phone: (614) 436-2191
Columbus, OH 43229   Barbi Cantrell, Cons.

CENTRAL OHIO TRANSIT AUTHORITY - LIBRARY
1600 McKinley Ave.   Phone: (614) 228-3831
Columbus, OH 43222   Oliva Piper

CHEMICAL ABSTRACTS SERVICE - LIBRARY
Box 3012   Phone: (614) 421-6940
Columbus, OH 43210   Robert S. Tannehill, Jr., Lib.Mgr.

CIRCUS HISTORICAL SOCIETY - LIBRARY
2515 Dorset Rd.
Columbus, OH 43221   Fred D. Pfening, Jr.

COLUMBIA GAS SYSTEM SERVICE CORPORATION - RESEARCH LIBRARY
1600 Dublin Rd.   Phone: (614) 486-3681
Columbus, OH 43215   Camille Duer Greenwald, Libn.

COLUMBUS COLLEGE OF ART AND DESIGN - PACKARD LIBRARY
47 N. Washington Ave.   Phone: (614) 224-9101
Columbus, OH 43215   Chilin Yu, Libn.

COLUMBUS DEVELOPMENTAL CENTER - GOVE SCHOOL LIBRARY
1601 W. Broad St.   Phone: (614) 272-0509
Columbus, OH 43223   Laura T. Barndt, Libn./Media Techn.

COLUMBUS DISPATCH - EDITORIAL LIBRARY
34 S. Third St.   Phone: (614) 461-5039
Columbus, OH 43216   James Hunter, Libn.

COLUMBUS DOMINICAN EDUCATION CENTER
Nelson & Johnston Rds.   Phone: (614) 252-2137
Columbus, OH 43219   Sr. Caritas Litzinger, Libn.

COLUMBUS LAW LIBRARY ASSOCIATION
Franklin County Hall of Justice, 10th Fl. Phone: (614) 221-4181
Columbus, OH 43215   Virginia B. Capute, Law Libn.

COLUMBUS PUBLIC SCHOOLS - TEACHERS' PROFESSIONAL LIBRARY
889 E. 17th Ave.   Phone: (614) 225-2815
Columbus, OH 43211   Hugh A. Durbin, Dir.

COLUMBUS TECHNICAL INSTITUTE - EDUCATIONAL RESOURCES CENTER †
550 E. Spring St.
Box 1609   Phone: (614) 227-2400
Columbus, OH 43216   Linda Landis Cofer, Supv., ERC

DOCTORS HOSPITAL - MEDICAL LIBRARY
1087 Dennison Ave.   Phone: (614) 421-4113
Columbus, OH 43201   Joseph Muzzo, Dir.

ERIC CLEARINGHOUSE ON ADULT, CAREER AND VOCATIONAL EDUCATION
    - NATL. CTR. FOR RESEARCH IN VOCATIONAL EDUC.
Ohio State University
1960 Kenny Rd.   Phone: (614) 486-3655
Columbus, OH 43210   Juliet V. Miller, Dir.

ERIC CLEARINGHOUSE FOR SCIENCE, MATHEMATICS AND
    ENVIRONMENTAL EDUCATION
Ohio State University
1200 Chambers Rd.   Phone: (614) 422-6717
Columbus, OH 43212   Robert W. Howe, Dir.

FEDERATION FOR UNIFIED SCIENCE EDUCATION - FUSE CENTER LIBRARY
231 Battell Hall of Science
Capital University   Phone: (614) 236-6816
Columbus, OH 43209   Dr. Victor M. Showalter, Dir.

FRANKLIN COUNTY HISTORICAL SOCIETY - CENTER OF SCIENCE &
    INDUSTRY - CLEMENTS HISTORY MEMORIAL LIBRARY
280 E. Broad St.   Phone: (614) 228-5613
Columbus, OH 43215   Daniel F. Prugh, Dir., Hist./Pub.Rel.

GEOGRAPHIC

FRANKLIN UNIVERSITY - LIBRARY
201 S. Grant Ave.
Columbus, OH 43215
Phone: (614) 224-6237
Mr. Allyn Ehrhardt, Libn.

GRANT HOSPITAL - MEDICAL LIBRARY
309 E. State St.
Columbus, OH 43215
Phone: (614) 461-3467
Nancy Cohen, Med.Libn.

ITT NORTH - LIBRARY
Box 20345
Columbus, OH 43220
Phone: (614) 548-4301
Gerald M. Hay, Libn.

MERRILL (Charles E.) PUBLISHING COMPANY - LIBRARY
1300 Alum Creek Dr.
Columbus, OH 43216
Phone: (614) 258-8441
Marcia Earnest, Libn.

MOUNT CARMEL MEDICAL CENTER - MOTHER M. CONSTANTINE MEMORIAL LIBRARY
793 W. State St.
Columbus, OH 43222
Phone: (614) 225-5214
Pamela M. Elwell, Libn.

NATIONWIDE MUTUAL INSURANCE COMPANY - LIBRARY
1 Nationwide Plaza
Columbus, OH 43216
Phone: (614) 227-6154
Jean French, Chf.Libn.

OHIO DOMINICAN COLLEGE - LIBRARY
1216 Sunbury Rd.
Columbus, OH 43219
Phone: (614) 253-2741
Sr. Suzanne Uhrhane, Lib.Adm.

OHIO HISTORICAL SOCIETY - ARCHIVES-LIBRARY
I-71 & 17th Ave.
Columbus, OH 43211
Phone: (614) 466-1500
Dr. Dennis East, Hd.

OHIO INSTITUTE OF TECHNOLOGY - LIBRARY
1350 Alum Creek Dr.
Columbus, OH 43209
Phone: (614) 253-7291
Dan L. Kniesner, Libn.

OHIO STATE ATTORNEY GENERAL'S OFFICE - LAW LIBRARY
30 E. Broad St., 17th Fl.
Columbus, OH 43215
Phone: (614) 466-2465
Marianne Gigante, Libn.

OHIO STATE DEPARTMENT OF ENERGY - ODOE LIBRARY
30 E. Broad St., 34th Fl.
Columbus, OH 43215
Phone: (614) 466-7915
Riek A. Oldenquist, Libn.

OHIO STATE DEPARTMENT OF TAXATION - RESEARCH AND STATISTICS LIBRARY
State Office Tower
Box 530
Columbus, OH 43216
Phone: (614) 469-3960
Stanley L. Shriver, Libn.

OHIO STATE DEPARTMENT OF TRANSPORTATION - LIBRARY
25 S. Front St.
Box 899
Columbus, OH 43216
Phone: (614) 466-7680
Ellen Haider, Libn.

OHIO STATE DIVISION OF GEOLOGICAL SURVEY - LIBRARY
Fountain Sq., Bldg. B
Columbus, OH 43224
Phone: (614) 466-5344
Madge Fitak, Geologist

OHIO STATE INDUSTRIAL COMMISSION - DIVISION OF SAFETY AND HYGIENE - RESOURCE CENTER
246 N. High St.
Box 16512
Columbus, OH 43215
Phone: (614) 466-7388
Rosemary Larkins, Libn.

OHIO STATE LEGISLATIVE REFERENCE BUREAU - LIBRARY †
State House, Rm. 10
Columbus, OH 43215
Phone: (614) 466-3031
Mary S. Duffey, Libn.

OHIO STATE LEGISLATIVE SERVICE COMMISSION - RESEARCH LIBRARY
State House
Columbus, OH 43215
Phone: (614) 466-5312
Edith S. Woodward, Lib.Adm.

OHIO STATE SCHOOL FOR THE BLIND - LIBRARY
5220 N. High St.
Columbus, OH 43214
Phone: (614) 888-8211
Beverly Kessler, Libn.

OHIO STATE SUPREME COURT LAW LIBRARY
30 E. Broad St., 4th Fl.
Columbus, OH 43215
Phone: (614) 466-2044
Paul S. Fu, Law Libn.

OHIO STATE UNIVERSITY - AGRICULTURE LIBRARY
2120 Fyffe Rd.
Columbus, OH 43210
Phone: (614) 422-6125
Susan Emerson, Hd.Libn.

OHIO STATE UNIVERSITY - BIOLOGICAL SCIENCES LIBRARY
1735 Neil Ave.
Columbus, OH 43210
Phone: (614) 422-1744
Sharon Schwerzel, Hd.Libn.

OHIO STATE UNIVERSITY - BLACK STUDIES LIBRARY
1858 Neil Ave.
Columbus, OH 43210
Phone: (614) 422-8403
Eleanor M. Daniel, Hd.Libn.

OHIO STATE UNIVERSITY - CALCULATOR INFORMATION CENTER
1200 Chambers Rd.
Columbus, OH 43212
Phone: (614) 422-8509
Marilyn N. Suydam, Dir./Prof.Math.Educ.

OHIO STATE UNIVERSITY - CENTER FOR LAKE ERIE AREA RESEARCH - LAKE ERIE LIBRARY
484 W. 12th Ave.
Columbus, OH 43210
Phone: (614) 422-8949
Charles E. Herdendorf, Dir.

OHIO STATE UNIVERSITY - CHEMISTRY LIBRARY
140 W. 18th Ave.
Columbus, OH 43210
Phone: (614) 422-1118
Virginia E. Yagello, Hd.Libn.

OHIO STATE UNIVERSITY - CHILDREN'S HOSPITAL LIBRARY
700 Children's Drive
Columbus, OH 43205
Phone: (614) 461-2375
Robert J. Stout, Hd.

OHIO STATE UNIVERSITY - COLE MEMORIAL LIBRARY OF THE PHYSICS AND ASTRONOMY DEPARTMENT
174 W. 18th Ave.
Columbus, OH 43210
Phone: (614) 422-7894
Virginia E. Yagello, Hd.Libn.

OHIO STATE UNIVERSITY - COMMERCE LIBRARY
1810 College Rd.
Columbus, OH 43210
Phone: (614) 422-2136

OHIO STATE UNIVERSITY - DISASTER RESEARCH CENTER - LIBRARY
128 Derby
154 N. Oval Mall
Columbus, OH 43210
Phone: (614) 422-5916
C. Indue, Libn.

OHIO STATE UNIVERSITY - EAST ASIAN COLLECTION
1858 Neil Ave. Mall
Columbus, OH 43210
Phone: (614) 422-3502
David Y. Hu, Biblog.

OHIO STATE UNIVERSITY - EAST EUROPEAN AND SLAVIC READING ROOM
Main Library, Rm. 300
1858 Neil Ave. Mall
Columbus, OH 43210
Phone: (614) 422-2073
G. Koolemans Beynen, Slavic Biblog.

OHIO STATE UNIVERSITY - EDUCATION LIBRARY
1945 N. High St.
Columbus, OH 43210
Phone: (614) 422-6275
Laura Blomquist, Hd.Libn.

OHIO STATE UNIVERSITY - ENGINEERING LIBRARY
112 Caldwell Lab.
2024 Neil Ave.
Columbus, OH 43210
Phone: (614) 422-2852
Mary Jo Arnold, Hd.Libn.

OHIO STATE UNIVERSITY - ENGLISH, COMMUNICATION AND THEATRE GRADUATE LIBRARY
Main Library
1858 Neil Ave. Mall
Columbus, OH 43210
Phone: (614) 422-2786
Richard Centing, Hd.

OHIO STATE UNIVERSITY - ENGLISH DEPARTMENT LIBRARY
Derby Hall
154 N. Oval Mall
Columbus, OH 43210
Phone: (614) 422-6357
Louise H. Smith, Libn.

OHIO STATE UNIVERSITY - FINE ARTS LIBRARY
Sullivant Hall
1813 N. High St.
Columbus, OH 43210
Phone: (614) 422-6184
Susan Wyngaard, Hd.Libn.

OHIO STATE UNIVERSITY - FOREIGN LANGUAGES GRADUATE LIBRARY
1858 Neil Ave.   Phone: (614) 422-2594
Columbus, OH 43210   Ms. Ana R. Llorens, Hd.Libn.

OHIO STATE UNIVERSITY - HEALTH SCIENCES LIBRARY
376 W. 10th Ave.   Phone: (614) 422-9810
Columbus, OH 43210   Elizabeth J. Sawyers, Dir.

OHIO STATE UNIVERSITY - HILANDAR ROOM
308 Main Library
1858 Neil Ave.   Phone: (614) 422-0634
Columbus, OH 43210   Gabriella Petrovics, Act.Libn.

OHIO STATE UNIVERSITY - HISTORY, POLITICAL SCIENCE, AND
    PHILOSOPHY GRADUATE LIBRARY
Main Library
1858 Neil Ave.   Phone: (614) 422-2393
Columbus, OH 43210   George P. Schoyer, Hd.Libn.

OHIO STATE UNIVERSITY - HOME ECONOMICS LIBRARY
Campbell Hall
1787 Neil Ave.   Phone: (614) 422-4220
Columbus, OH 43210   Neosha Mackey, Hd.Libn.

OHIO STATE UNIVERSITY - INSTITUTE OF POLAR STUDIES - GOLDTHWAIT
    POLAR LIBRARY
125 S. Oval Mall   Phone: (614) 422-6531
Columbus, OH 43210   Deborah Jones Vavra, Libn.

OHIO STATE UNIVERSITY - JOURNALISM LIBRARY
242 W. 18th Ave.   Phone: (614) 422-8747
Columbus, OH 43210   Eleanor Block, Hd.Libn.

OHIO STATE UNIVERSITY - JUDAICA LIBRARY
1858 Neil Ave. Mall   Phone: (614) 422-3362
Columbus, OH 43210   Amnon Zipin, Jewish Stud.Libn.

OHIO STATE UNIVERSITY - LATIN AMERICAN STUDIES READING ROOM
    AND LIBRARY
Main Library
1858 Neil Ave.   Phone: (614) 422-8959
Columbus, OH 43210   George C. Hart, Biblog.

OHIO STATE UNIVERSITY - LAW LIBRARY
College of Law
1659 N. High St.   Phone: (614) 422-6691
Columbus, OH 43210   Mathew F. Dee, Dir.

OHIO STATE UNIVERSITY - MAP GRADUATE LIBRARY
1858 Neil Ave.   Phone: (614) 422-2393
Columbus, OH 43210   George P. Schoyer, Hd.Libn.

OHIO STATE UNIVERSITY - MATERIALS ENGINEERING LIBRARY
2041 N. College Rd.   Phone: (614) 422-9614
Columbus, OH 43210   Mary Jo Arnold, Hd.Libn.

OHIO STATE UNIVERSITY - MATHEMATICS LIBRARY
231 W. 18th St.   Phone: (614) 422-2009
Columbus, OH 43210   Janina Talat-Kielpsz, Hd.Libn.

OHIO STATE UNIVERSITY - MECHANIZED INFORMATION CENTER (MIC)
1858 Neil Ave. Mall   Phone: (614) 422-3480
Columbus, OH 43210   Bernard Bayer, Hd.

OHIO STATE UNIVERSITY - MIDDLE EAST/ISLAMICA READING ROOM
Thompson Library, Rm. 320
1858 Neil Ave. Mall   Phone: (614) 422-3362
Columbus, OH 43210   Marsha McClintock, Middle East Libn.

OHIO STATE UNIVERSITY - MUSIC LIBRARY
186 Sullivant Hall
1813 N. High St.   Phone: (614) 422-2319
Columbus, OH 43210   Thomas Heck, Hd.Libn.

OHIO STATE UNIVERSITY - OHIO COOPERATIVE WILDLIFE RESEARCH
    UNIT - LIBRARY
1735 Neil Ave.   Phone: (614) 422-6112
Columbus, OH 43210   Dr. Theodore A. Bookhout, Unit Leader

OHIO STATE UNIVERSITY - ORTON MEMORIAL LIBRARY OF GEOLOGY
155 S. Oval Dr.   Phone: (614) 422-2428
Columbus, OH 43210   Regina Brown, Hd.Libn.

OHIO STATE UNIVERSITY - PHARMACY LIBRARY
Pharmacy Bldg.
500 W. 12th Ave.   Phone: (614) 422-6078
Columbus, OH 43210   Virginia Hall, Hd.Libn.

OHIO STATE UNIVERSITY - SOCIAL WORK LIBRARY
1947 College Rd.   Phone: (614) 422-6627
Columbus, OH 43210   Mrs. Toyo S. Kawakami, Hd.Libn.

OHIO STATE UNIVERSITY - THEATRE RESEARCH INSTITUTE
1089 Drake Union
1849 Cannon Dr.   Phone: (614) 422-6614
Columbus, OH 43210   Alan Woods, Dir.

OHIO STATE UNIVERSITY - TOPAZ MEMORIAL LIBRARY
College Of Optometry
338 W. Tenth Ave.   Phone: (614) 422-1888
Columbus, OH 43210

OHIO STATE UNIVERSITY - VETERINARY MEDICINE LIBRARY
1900 Coffey Rd.   Phone: (614) 422-6107
Columbus, OH 43210   Roberta A. Garrett, Hd.Libn.

OHIO STATE UNIVERSITY - WOMEN'S STUDIES LIBRARY
1858 Neil Ave. Mall   Phone: (614) 422-3035
Columbus, OH 43210   Adrienne Zahniser, Hd.Libn.

OHIOANA LIBRARY ASSOCIATION - OHIOANA LIBRARY AND ARCHIVES
1105 Ohio Departments Bldg.
65 S. Front St.   Phone: (614) 466-3831
Columbus, OH 43215   Kathy A. Babeaux, Libn.

OTTAWA INSTITUTE - IRENE HOLM MEMORIAL LIBRARY
1465 Osborn Dr.   Phone: (614) 486-5028
Columbus, OH 43221   Ms. Bobbi Wilson, Libn.

PUBLIC UTILITIES COMMISSION OF OHIO - LIBRARY
375 S. High St.   Phone: (614) 466-7153
Columbus, OH 43215   Elza O. Fodor, Libn.

RIVERSIDE METHODIST HOSPITAL - LIBRARY RESOURCE CENTER
3535 Olentangy River Rd.   Phone: (614) 261-5230
Columbus, OH 43214   Josephine W. Yeoh, Dir.

ROCKWELL INTERNATIONAL - TECHNICAL INFORMATION CENTER
4300 E. Fifth Ave.
Box 1259   Phone: (614) 239-3131
Columbus, OH 43216   J.A. Seidwitz, Mgr.

ROSS LABORATORIES - LIBRARY
625 Cleveland Ave.   Phone: (614) 227-3503
Columbus, OH 43216   Linda Mitro Hopkins, Mgr.

ST. ANTHONY HOSPITAL - MEDICAL LIBRARY *
1450 Hawthorne Ave.   Phone: (614) 253-8877
Columbus, OH 43203   M. Diane Mess, Lib.Supv.

SOCIETY OF FRIENDS - OHIO YEARLY MEETING - WESTGATE FRIENDS
    LIBRARY
3750 Sullivant Ave.   Phone: (614) 274-5131
Columbus, OH 43228   William T. Peters, Lit.Coord.

STATE LIBRARY OF OHIO
65 S. Front St.   Phone: (614) 466-2693
Columbus, OH 43215   Richard M. Cheski, State Libn.

TIN RESEARCH INSTITUTE, INC. - LIBRARY & INFORMATION CENTER
1353 Perry St.   Phone: (614) 424-6200
Columbus, OH 43201   Daniel J. Maykuth, Mgr.

TRINITY LUTHERAN SEMINARY - LIBRARY
2199 E. Main St.   Phone: (614) 236-7116
Columbus, OH 43209   Donald L. Huber, Libn.

GEOGRAPHIC

GEOGRAPHIC

U.S. DEFENSE LOGISTICS AGENCY - DEFENSE CONSTRUCTION SUPPLY CENTER - TECHNICAL DATA PROCESSING BRANCH
3990 E. Broad St.   Phone: (614) 236-3075
Columbus, OH 43215   Robert A. Brown, Chf.

FALLSVIEW PSYCHIATRIC HOSPITAL - STAFF LIBRARY
330 Broadway E.   Phone: (216) 929-8301
Cuyahoga Falls, OH 44221   David Allen, Libn.

AULLWOOD AUDUBON CENTER AND FARM - LIBRARY
1000 Aullwood Rd.   Phone: (513) 890-7360
Dayton, OH 45414   Evelyn Pereny, Libn.

CHEMINEER, INC. - LIBRARY
Box 1123   Phone: (513) 898-1111
Dayton, OH 45401   Dr. David S. Dickey, Technical Dir.

CHILDREN'S MEDICAL CENTER - LIBRARY
One Children's Plaza   Phone: (513) 226-8307
Dayton, OH 45404   Jane R. Bottoms, Libn.

DAYTON ART INSTITUTE - LIBRARY
Forest & Riverview Aves.   Phone: (513) 223-5277
Dayton, OH 45401   Helen L. Pinkney, Libn.

DAYTON CHILDREN'S PSYCHIATRIC HOSPITAL - LIBRARY
141 Firwood Dr.   Phone: (513) 258-0445
Dayton, OH 45419   Velma Y. Church, Med.Rec.Libn.

DAYTON LAW LIBRARY †
505 Montgomery County Courts Bldg.
41 N. Perry St.   Phone: (513) 225-4505
Dayton, OH 45422   Betty Busch, Libn.

DAYTON MENTAL HEALTH CENTER - STAFF LIBRARY
2611 Wayne Ave.   Phone: (513) 258-0440
Dayton, OH 45420   Leonard Skonecki, Libn.

DAYTON AND MONTGOMERY COUNTY PUBLIC LIBRARY - INDUSTRY AND SCIENCE DIVISION
215 E. Third St.   Phone: (513) 224-1651
Dayton, OH 45402   Martha A. Overwein, Hd.

DAYTON AND MONTGOMERY COUNTY PUBLIC LIBRARY - LITERATURE AND FINE ARTS DIVISION
215 E. Third St.   Phone: (513) 224-1651
Dayton, OH 45402   Donald T. Paul, Hd.

DAYTON AND MONTGOMERY COUNTY PUBLIC LIBRARY - NON-PRINT MEDIA CENTER
215 E. Third St.   Phone: (513) 224-1651
Dayton, OH 45402   Theodore J. Nunn, Jr., Hd.

DAYTON AND MONTGOMERY COUNTY PUBLIC LIBRARY - SOCIAL SCIENCES DIVISION
215 E. Third St.   Phone: (513) 224-1651
Dayton, OH 45402   Laura J. Smith, Hd.

DAYTON NEWSPAPERS INC. - REFERENCE LIBRARY
37 S. Ludlow St.   Phone: (513) 225-2430
Dayton, OH 45402   Mr. Harish Trivedi, Ref. & Res.Dir.

ENGINEERS' CLUB OF DAYTON - LIBRARY
110 E. Monument Ave.   Phone: (513) 228-2148
Dayton, OH 45402   Jane E. Vermillion, Libn.

FRANCISCAN FATHERS OF CINCINNATI, OHIO - ST. LEONARD COLLEGE - LIBRARY
8100 Clyo Rd.   Phone: (513) 433-0480
Dayton, OH 45459   Betty A. O'Brien, Lib.Dir.

GOOD SAMARITAN HOSPITAL - SHANK MEMORIAL LIBRARY
2222 Philadelphia Dr.   Phone: (513) 278-2612
Dayton, OH 45406   Elizabeth A. Robinson, Libn.

GRANDVIEW HOSPITAL - MEDICAL LIBRARY
405 Grand Ave.   Phone: (513) 226-3379
Dayton, OH 45405   Loma Pallman, Dir.

MEAD CORPORATION - CORPORATE LIBRARY
Corporate Plaza N.E.   Phone: (513) 222-6323
Dayton, OH 45463   Susan Kremer, Corp.Libn./Anl.

MEAD CORPORATION - MEAD PAPERS - MEAD LIBRARY OF IDEAS
Courthouse Plaza, N.E.   Phone: (513) 222-6323
Dayton, OH 45463   Sonya Mitchell, Dir.

MIAMI VALLEY HOSPITAL - MEMORIAL MEDICAL LIBRARY
One Wyoming St.   Phone: (513) 223-6192
Dayton, OH 45409   Margaret C. Hardy, Dir.

MIAMI VALLEY REGIONAL PLANNING COMMISSION - LIBRARY
117 S. Main St., Suite 200   Phone: (513) 223-6323
Dayton, OH 45402   John Vining, Exec.Dir.

MONSANTO RESEARCH CORPORATION - DAYTON LABORATORY LIBRARY †
1515 Nicholas Rd.
Sta. B, Box 8   Phone: (513) 268-3411
Dayton, OH 45407   Dorothy T. Crabtree, Libn.

NCR CORPORATION - TECHNICAL LIBRARY
Engineering & Manufacturing-Dayton
Building 28, 3rd Fl.   Phone: (513) 445-7032
Dayton, OH 45479   Vicki Stouder, Libn.

ST. ELIZABETH MEDICAL CENTER - HEALTH SCIENCES LIBRARY
601 Miami Blvd., W.   Phone: (513) 223-3141
Dayton, OH 45408   Lenore D. Pursch, Med.Libn.

SOCIETY OF MARY - CINCINNATI PROVINCE - ARCHIVES
University of Dayton
Box 472   Phone: (513) 229-2724
Dayton, OH 45469   Rev. Robert E. Brown, S.M., Archv.

STANDARD REGISTER COMPANY - CORPORATE LIBRARY
                                     Phone: (513) 223-6181
Dayton, OH 45401   Dorothea P. Adkinson, Libn.

TEMPLE ISRAEL - RABBI LOUIS WITT MEMORIAL LIBRARY
1821 Emerson Ave.   Phone: (513) 278-9621
Dayton, OH 45406   Jeanne B. Goldzwig, Libn.

U.S. AIR FORCE - AERONAUTICAL LABORATORIES - TECHNICAL LIBRARY
Wright-Patterson AFB, Bldg. 22   Phone: (513) 255-3630
Dayton, OH 45433   Dorothy Siegfried, Chf.

U.S. DEFENSE LOGISTICS AGENCY - DEFENSE ELECTRONICS CENTER - LIBRARY
1507 Wilmington Pike
Dayton, OH 45444

U.S. VETERANS ADMINISTRATION (OH-Dayton) - CENTER LIBRARY
4100 W. Third St.   Phone: (513) 268-6511
Dayton, OH 45428   Betty Bogen, Chf., Lib.Serv.

UNITED THEOLOGICAL SEMINARY - LIBRARY
1810 Harvard Blvd.   Phone: (513) 278-5817
Dayton, OH 45406   Elmer J. O'Brien, Libn.

UNIVERSITY OF DAYTON - LAW SCHOOL LIBRARY
300 College Park   Phone: (513) 229-2315
Dayton, OH 45469   Dr. Jose D. Coutin, Dir.

UNIVERSITY OF DAYTON - MARIAN LIBRARY
300 College Park   Phone: (513) 229-4214
Dayton, OH 45469   Rev. Theodore Koehler, S.M., Dir.

UNIVERSITY OF DAYTON - ROESCH LIBRARY - SPECIAL COLLECTIONS
College Park Ave.   Phone: (513) 229-4221
Dayton, OH 45469   Linda Keir Hinrichs, Spec.Coll.Libn.

UNIVERSITY OF DAYTON - SCHOOL OF EDUCATION - CURRICULUM MATERIALS CENTER
300 College Park, Chaminade Hall   Phone: (513) 229-3140
Dayton, OH 49469   Sr. Catherine Rudolph, OSF, Dir.

WRIGHT STATE UNIVERSITY - ARCHIVES & SPECIAL COLLECTIONS
Phone: (513) 873-2092
Dayton, OH 45435   Dr. Patrick B. Nolan, Hd.

WRIGHT STATE UNIVERSITY - HEALTH SCIENCES LIBRARY
3640 Colonel Glenn Hwy.   Phone: (513) 873-2266
Dayton, OH 45435   Raymond A. Palmer, Libn.

DELAWARE COUNTY LAW LIBRARY
Court House   Phone: (614) 363-4632
Delaware, OH 43015   Sherman Moist, Libn.

METHODIST THEOLOGICAL SCHOOL IN OHIO - LIBRARY
Box 1204   Phone: (614) 363-1146
Delaware, OH 43015   John B. McTaggart, Dir., Lib.Serv.

OCLC, INC. - LIBRARY
Box 7777   Phone: (614) 764-6000
Dublin, OH 43017   Ann T. Dodson, Mgr.

ELYRIA CHRONICLE-TELEGRAM - LIBRARY
225 East Ave.   Phone: (216) 329-7000
Elyria, OH 44036   Jeanne D. Meredith, Libn.

ELYRIA MEMORIAL HOSPITAL - LIBRARY
630 E. River St.   Phone: (216) 323-3221
Elyria, OH 44035   Linda Masek, Hd.Libn.

LORAIN COUNTY HISTORICAL SOCIETY - GERALD HICKS MEMORIAL
LIBRARY
509 Washington Ave.   Phone: (216) 322-3341
Elyria, OH 44035   Mary Jeffries, Cat.

LORAIN COUNTY LAW LIBRARY ASSOCIATION - LIBRARY
3rd Fl., Courthouse   Phone: (216) 322-5024
Elyria, OH 44035   Eleanor E. Pietch, Libn.

COURIER - LIBRARY
701 W. Sandusky St.   Phone: (419) 422-5151
Findlay, OH 45840   Betty B. Edie, Libn.

HANCOCK COUNTY LAW LIBRARY ASSOCIATION
Hancock County Courthouse   Phone: (419) 423-1756
Findlay, OH 45840   Sue Dillon, Libn.

MARATHON OIL COMPANY - LAW LIBRARY
539 S. Main St., Rm. 854-M   Phone: (419) 422-2121
Findlay, OH 45840   Durand S. Dudley, Sr. Law Libn.

WINEBRENNER THEOLOGICAL SEMINARY - LIBRARY
701 E. Melrose Ave.   Phone: (419) 422-4824
Findlay, OH 45840   Elizabeth Harpst, Adm.Libn.

HAYES (Rutherford B.) PRESIDENTIAL CENTER - LIBRARY
1337 Hayes Ave.   Phone: (419) 332-2081
Fremont, OH 43420   Leslie H. Fishel, Jr., Dir.

SANDUSKY COUNTY LAW LIBRARY
Courthouse, Park Ave.   Phone: (419) 332-6411
Fremont, OH 43420   Thomas B. Stahl, Law Libn.

HOLZER MEDICAL CENTER - SCHOOL OF NURSING - LIBRARY
First Ave.   Phone: (614) 446-5264
Gallipolis, OH 45631   Marge Adkins, Lib.Ck.

OWENS-CORNING FIBERGLAS CORPORATION - TECHNICAL DATA CENTER
Granville, OH 43023   Betty Nethers, Mgr.

GREENVILLE LAW LIBRARY
Court House   Phone: (513) 548-1430
Greenville, OH 45331   Helen V. Pierce, Libn.

BUTLER COUNTY LAW LIBRARY ASSOCIATION
Court House Annex   Phone: (513) 867-5714
Hamilton, OH 45011   Anita K. Shew, Law Libn.

CHAMPION INTERNATIONAL - CHAMPION PAPERS TECHNICAL LIBRARY
Knightsbridge Dr.   Phone: (513) 868-4578
Hamilton, OH 45020   Paul F. Bryant, Tech.Libn.

FORT HAMILTON-HUGHES MEMORIAL HOSPITAL CENTER - SOHN
MEMORIAL HEALTH SERVICES LIBRARY
630 Eaton Ave.   Phone: (513) 867-2310
Hamilton, OH 45013   Lois Protzman, Libn.

MERCY NORTH HOSPITAL - HEALTH SCIENCES LIBRARY
116 Dayton St.   Phone: (513) 896-3000
Hamilton, OH 45011   Frances McCullough, Libn.

BLESSED SACRAMENT SEMINARY - LIBRARY *
5384 Wilson Mills Rd.   Phone: (216) 442-3410
Highland Heights, OH 44143

HIGHLAND COUNTY LAW LIBRARY
High & Main Sts., Court House   Phone: (513) 393-2422
Hillsboro, OH 45133   Michelle Vanzant, Law Libn.

SOUTHERN OHIO GENEALOGICAL SOCIETY - REFERENCE LIBRARY
879 W. Main St.
Box 414
Hillsboro, OH 45133   Marie A. Knott, Libn.

HUDSON LIBRARY AND HISTORICAL SOCIETY
22 Aurora St.   Phone: (216) 653-6658
Hudson, OH 44236   Thomas L. Vince, Libn. & Cur.

FERRO CORPORATION - LIBRARY
7500 E. Pleasant Valley Rd.   Phone: (216) 641-8580
Independence, OH 44131   Kathleen Fuller, Hd.Libn.

JACKSON COUNTY LAW LIBRARY
Court House
Jackson, OH 45640   M. Murphy, Lib. Custodian

KENT STATE UNIVERSITY - AMERICAN HISTORY RESEARCH CENTER
Library   Phone: (216) 672-2411
Kent, OH 44242   Dr. James W. Geary, Dir.

KENT STATE UNIVERSITY - ARCHIVES
Library   Phone: (216) 672-2411
Kent, OH 44242   James W. Geary, Univ.Archv.

KENT STATE UNIVERSITY - AUDIOVISUAL SERVICES
330 University Library   Phone: (216) 672-3456
Kent, OH 44242   Charles Hunger, Dir., AV Serv.

KENT STATE UNIVERSITY - CHEMISTRY/PHYSICS LIBRARY
312 Williams Hall   Phone: (216) 672-2532
Kent, OH 44242   Julia Cannan, Coord.

KENT STATE UNIVERSITY - COMPUTER ASSISTED AND SELF INSTRUCTION
CENTER
265 Library   Phone: (216) 672-2889
Kent, OH 44242   Patrick C. Boyden, Dir.

KENT STATE UNIVERSITY - DEPARTMENT OF SPECIAL COLLECTIONS
University Library   Phone: (216) 672-2270
Kent, OH 44242   Dean H. Keller, Cur.

KENT STATE UNIVERSITY - DOCUMENTS DEPARTMENT
370 Library   Phone: (216) 672-2388
Kent, OH 44242   Virginia Crowl, Doc.Libn.

KENT STATE UNIVERSITY - MAP LIBRARY
406 McGilvery Hall   Phone: (216) 672-2243
Kent, OH 44240   Julia Cannan, Coord.

KENT STATE UNIVERSITY - MUSIC LIBRARY
D5 Music & Speech Bldg.   Phone: (216) 672-2004
Kent, OH 44242   Judith B. McCarron, Music Lib.Coord.

KETTERING COLLEGE OF MEDICAL ARTS - LEARNING RESOURCES CENTER
3737 Southern Blvd.   Phone: (513) 296-7201
Kettering, OH 45429   Edward Collins, Libn.

KETTERING MEMORIAL HOSPITAL - MEDICAL LIBRARY
3535 Southern Blvd.   Phone: (513) 298-4331
Kettering, OH 45429   Joseph P. Stoia, Med.Libn.

NATIONAL FEDERATION OF LOCAL CABLE PROGRAMMERS - LIBRARY †
3700 Far Hills Ave., Suite 109
Kettering, OH 45429   Sue Miller Buske, Exec.Dir.

LAKEWOOD HISTORICAL SOCIETY - LIBRARY
14710 Lake Ave.   Phone: (216) 221-7343
Lakewood, OH 44107   Mrs. James Sekerka, Cur.

LAKEWOOD HOSPITAL - MEDICAL LIBRARY
14519 Detroit Ave.   Phone: (216) 521-4200
Lakewood, OH 44107   Dorothy Jorgens, Dir.

ANCHOR HOCKING CORPORATION - CORPORATE LIBRARY
2980 W. Fair Ave.   Phone: (614) 687-2403
Lancaster, OH 43130   Peggy J. Myers, Corp.Libn.

ARCAIR COMPANY - LIBRARY
Box 406   Phone: (614) 653-5618
Lancaster, OH 43130   Dottie Young, Libn.

WARREN COUNTY HISTORICAL SOCIETY - MUSEUM AND LIBRARY
105 S. Broadway
Box 223   Phone: (513) 932-1817
Lebanon, OH 45036   Mrs. Elva R. Adams, Dir. & Libn.

WARREN COUNTY LAW LIBRARY
500 Justice Dr.   Phone: (614) 932-4040
Lebanon, OH 45036   Barbara Bronson, Libn.

ALLEN COUNTY HISTORICAL SOCIETY - ELIZABETH M. MAC DONELL
   MEMORIAL LIBRARY
620 W. Market St.   Phone: (419) 222-9426
Lima, OH 45801   Anna B. Selfridge, Asst.Cur./Mss., Archv.

ALLEN COUNTY LAW LIBRARY
Court House, 4th Fl.
Lima, OH 45801   Ruth Laudahn, Act.Libn.

LIMA MEMORIAL HOSPITAL - HEALTH SCIENCES LIBRARY
Linden & Mobel Sts.   Phone: (419) 228-3335
Lima, OH 45804   Margaret S. Cutter, Libn.

LIMA STATE HOSPITAL - RESIDENTS & PROFESSIONAL LIBRARY †
North West St.   Phone: (419) 227-4631
Lima, OH 45801   Charles W. Lee, Dir.

ST. RITA'S MEDICAL CENTER - MEDICAL LIBRARY
730 W. Market St.   Phone: (419) 227-3361
Lima, OH 45801   Sharon Eversole, Libn.

WESTINGHOUSE ELECTRIC CORPORATION - ELECTRICAL SYSTEMS
   DIVISION - TECHNICAL LIBRARY
Box 989   Phone: (419) 226-3210
Lima, OH 45802   R. James Heine

WAGNALLS MEMORIAL - LIBRARY
150 E. Columbus St.   Phone: (614) 837-4765
Lithopolis, OH 43136   Jerry Neff, Dir.

MADISON COUNTY LAW LIBRARY
Court House   Phone: (614) 852-9515
London, OH 43140   Kristina J. Bridgman, Law Libn.

ST. JOSEPH HOSPITAL - MEDICAL STAFF LIBRARY
205 W. 20th St.   Phone: (216) 245-6851
Lorain, OH 44052   Elizabeth Wakefield, Dir.

MORGAN COUNTY BAR ASSOCIATION - LIBRARY
Court House
McConnelsville, OH 43756   William Safranek, Libn.

KINGWOOD CENTER - LIBRARY
900 Park Ave. W.   Phone: (419) 522-0211
Mansfield, OH 44906   Marjorie Dickinson, Libn.

RICHLAND COUNTY LAW LIBRARY
Court House   Phone: (419) 524-9944
Mansfield, OH 44902   Arthur W. Negin, Libn./V.P.

OHIO HISTORICAL SOCIETY - CAMPUS MARTIUS MUSEUM - LIBRARY
601 Second St.   Phone: (614) 373-3750
Marietta, OH 45750   John B. Briley, Mgr.

WASHINGTON COUNTY LAW LIBRARY
Court House, Second & Putnam Sts.
Marietta, OH 45750

MARION COUNTY LAW LIBRARY
Court House   Phone: (614) 387-5871
Marion, OH 43302   Hazel Aldrich, Ck.

SMITH (Frederick C.) CLINIC - MEDICAL LIBRARY
1040 Delaware Ave.   Phone: (614) 387-0850
Marion, OH 43302   Doris P. Hurn, Libn.

SCOTT (O.M.) AND SONS - INFORMATION SERVICES
Dwight G. Scott Research Center   Phone: (513) 644-0011
Marysville, OH 43041   Carol B. Grise, Supv., Info.Serv.

DOCTORS HOSPITAL INC. OF STARK COUNTY - MEDICAL LIBRARY
400 Austin Ave., N.W.   Phone: (216) 837-7371
Massillon, OH 44646   Christine J. Williams, Dir.Lib.Serv.

STARK COUNTY LAW LIBRARY ASSOCIATION - MASSILLON BRANCH LAW
   LIBRARY *
City Hall   Phone: (216) 837-4271
Massillon, OH 44646

MEDINA COUNTY LAW LIBRARY ASSOCIATION
Court House, 93 Public Sq.   Phone: (216) 723-3641
Medina, OH 44256   Stan Scheetz, Libn.

HOLDEN ARBORETUM - WARREN H. CORNING LIBRARY
Sperry Rd.   Phone: (216) 946-4400
Mentor, OH 44060   Paul C. Spector

LAKE COUNTY HISTORICAL SOCIETY - PERCY KENDALL SMITH LIBRARY
   FOR HISTORICAL RESEARCH
8095 Mentor Ave.   Phone: (216) 255-8722
Mentor, OH 44060   Carl Thomas Engel, Libn.

LIBRARY OF HENRY J. GRUND
4897 Corduroy Rd.
Mentor Headlands
Mentor, OH 44060   Henry J. Grund, II, Dir.

AMERICAN SOCIETY FOR METALS - METALS INFORMATION
                                     Phone: (216) 338-5151
Metals Park, OH 44073   William A. Weida, Libn.

MONARCH MARKING SYSTEMS - TECHNICAL LIBRARY
1 Kohnle Dr.   Phone: (513) 865-2082
Miamisburg, OH 45342   Mrs. Artence Walton, Tech.Dir.

MONSANTO RESEARCH CORPORATION - MOUND FACILITY - TECHNICAL
   INFORMATION CENTER
Box 32   Phone: (513) 865-3942
Miamisburg, OH 45342   Hermina Brinkmeier, Supv., Lib. & Rec.

ARMCO, INC. - TECHNICAL INFORMATION CENTER
703 Curtis St.   Phone: (513) 425-2596
Middletown, OH 45043   David C. Heckard, Mgr.

MIDDLETOWN HOSPITAL ASSOCIATION - ADA I. LEONARD MEMORIAL
   LIBRARY
105 McKnight Dr.   Phone: (513) 422-2111
Middletown, OH 45042   Ursula S. Boettcher, Libn.

HOLMES COUNTY LAW LIBRARY
Court House   Phone: (216) 674-5086
Millersburg, OH 44654   Thomas D. Gindlesberger, Law Libn.

KNOX COMMUNITY HOSPITAL - MEDICAL LIBRARY
117 E. High St.   Phone: (614) 397-5555
Mount Vernon, OH 43050   Havilah Phelps, Libn.

HENRY COUNTY LAW LIBRARY
Court House
Napoleon, OH 43545   James Donovan, Sec.-Tres.

HOCKING TECHNICAL COLLEGE - LIBRARY
Rt. 1   Phone: (614) 753-3591
Nelsonville, OH 45764   Margy L. Kramer, Libn.

TUSCARAWAS COUNTY GENEALOGICAL SOCIETY - LIBRARY
Box 141
New Philadelphia, OH 44663   Ruth Gary, Libn.

TUSCARAWAS COUNTY LAW LIBRARY ASSOCIATION
Court House, Rm. 208   Phone: (216) 364-3703
New Philadelphia, OH 44663   Doris V. Couts, Libn.

DAWES ARBORETUM - LIBRARY
7770 Jacksontown Rd., S.E.   Phone: (614) 323-2355
Newark, OH 43055   Alan D. Cook, Horticulturist

HEISEY COLLECTORS OF AMERICA, INC. - HCA LIBRARY & ARCHIVES
Sixth & Church Sts.   Phone: (614) 345-2932
Newark, OH 43055   Louise Ream, Pres.

LICKING COUNTY LAW LIBRARY ASSOCIATION *
22 1/2 N. Second St.   Phone: (614) 345-6400
Newark, OH 43055   Hon. Virginia Weiss, Libn.

LICKING MEMORIAL HOSPITAL - MEDICAL LIBRARY
1320 W. Main St.   Phone: (614) 344-0331
Newark, OH 43055   Mrs. Lindsay Freytag, Dir.

HOOVER COMPANY - ENGINEERING DIVISION LIBRARY
101 E. Maple St.   Phone: (216) 499-9200
North Canton, OH 44720

SAGAMORE HILLS CHILDREN'S PSYCHIATRIC HOSPITAL - STAFF MEDICAL
    LIBRARY
11910 Dunham Rd.   Phone: (614) 467-7955
Northfield, OH 44067   Karen Parsons, Libn.

WESTERN RESERVE PSYCHIATRIC HABILITATION CENTER - STAFF
    LIBRARY
Box 305   Phone: (216) 467-7131
Northfield, OH 44067   Libby Bryan, Libn.

GILFORD INSTRUMENT LABORATORIES, INC. - TECHNICAL LIBRARY †
132 Artino St.   Phone: (216) 774-1041
Oberlin, OH 44074   Marjorie Mulder, Libn.

OBERLIN COLLEGE - CLARENCE WARD ART LIBRARY
Allen Art Bldg.   Phone: (216) 775-8635
Oberlin, OH 44074   David J. Patten, Art Libn.

OBERLIN COLLEGE - CLASS OF 1904 SCIENCE LIBRARY AND PHYSICS
    READING ROOM
Kettering Hall   Phone: (216) 775-8310
Oberlin, OH 44074   Eleanor S. Fairbanks, Sci.Libn.

OBERLIN COLLEGE - CONSERVATORY OF MUSIC - MARY M. VIAL MUSIC
    LIBRARY
                                  Phone: (216) 775-8280
Oberlin, OH 44074   John E. Druesedow, Jr., Dir.

MC GUFFEY (William Holmes) HOUSE AND MUSEUM - LIBRARY
Spring & Oak Sts.   Phone: (513) 529-4917
Oxford, OH 45056   Sterling Cook, Cur.

MIAMI UNIVERSITY - ART AND ARCHITECTURE LIBRARY
Alumni Hall   Phone: (513) 529-3219
Oxford, OH 45056   Joann Olson, Hum.Libn.

MIAMI UNIVERSITY - MUSIC LIBRARY
Ctr. for Performing Arts   Phone: (513) 529-2017
Oxford, OH 45056   Edith Miller, Hum.Libn.

MIAMI UNIVERSITY - SCIENCE LIBRARY
                                  Phone: (513) 529-7527
Oxford, OH 45056   Marian C. Winner, Hd.Sci.Libn.

MIAMI UNIVERSITY - SCRIPPS FOUNDATION FOR RESEARCH IN
    POPULATION PROBLEMS & GERONTOLOGY CENTER - LIBRARY
Hoyt Library   Phone: (513) 529-2914
Oxford, OH 45056

MIAMI UNIVERSITY - WALTER HAVIGHURST SPECIAL COLLECTIONS
    LIBRARY
King Library   Phone: (513) 529-2537
Oxford, OH 45056   Helen Ball, Cur. of Spec.Coll.

DIAMOND SHAMROCK CORPORATION - CORPORATE LIBRARY
Box 348   Phone: (216) 357-3475
Painesville, OH 44077   Marilyn Graubart, Mgr.Lib.Serv.

LAKE COUNTY MEMORIAL HOSPITAL EAST - MEDICAL LIBRARY
71 E. High St.   Phone: (216) 352-4481
Painesville, OH 44077   Carolyn Tyx, Health Info.Rsrcs.

KAISER FOUNDATION HOSPITALS - MEDICAL LIBRARY
12301 Snow Rd.   Phone: (216) 362-2086
Parma, OH 44130   Marlene Saul, Med.Libn.

PENINSULA LIBRARY AND HISTORICAL SOCIETY
6105 Riverview Rd.   Phone: (216) 657-2291
Peninsula, OH 44264   Fredericka A. Hagerty, Libn.

B'NAI JESHURUN TEMPLE ON THE HEIGHTS - JACK JACOBSON MEMORIAL
    LIBRARY
27501 Fairmount Blvd.   Phone: (216) 932-1820
Pepper Pike, OH 44124

GOODYEAR TIRE AND RUBBER COMPANY - GOODYEAR ATOMIC
    CORPORATION - TECHNICAL LIBRARY
Box 628   Phone: (614) 289-2331
Piketon, OH 45661   Robert P. Holland, Supv.

MEIGS COUNTY LAW LIBRARY
Court House   Phone: (614) 992-7430
Pomeroy, OH 45769   Karen Story, Libn.

PORTSMOUTH BAR AND LAW LIBRARY
Scioto County Court House, 3rd Fl. Phone: (614) 353-8319
Portsmouth, OH 45662   Dave Spears, Libn.

PORTSMOUTH RECEIVING HOSPITAL - MEDICAL LIBRARY
25th & Elmwood   Phone: (614) 354-2804
Portsmouth, OH 45662   Linda S. Collins, Libn.

OHIO STATE UNIVERSITY - FRANZ THEODORE STONE LABORATORY -
    LIBRARY
Box 138   Phone: (419) 285-2341
Put-In-Bay, OH 43456   Dr. Ronald L. Stuckey, Cur.

U.S. NATL. PARK SERVICE - PERRY'S VICTORY & INTERNATIONAL PEACE
    MEMORIAL - LIBRARY
Box 78   Phone: (419) 285-2184
Put-In-Bay, OH 43456   Alford J. Banta, Supt.

PORTAGE COUNTY HISTORICAL SOCIETY, INC. - LIBRARY AND MUSEUM
6549-51 N. Chestnut St.   Phone: (216) 297-3523
Ravenna, OH 44266   Betty J. Widger, Genealogist

GENERAL ELECTRIC COMPANY - LAMP GLASS & COMPONENTS LIBRARY
24400 Highland Rd.   Phone: (216) 266-3653
Richmond Heights, OH 44143   Jeanne Parker

STEEL FOUNDERS' SOCIETY OF AMERICA - LIBRARY
20611 Center Ridge Rd.   Phone: (216) 333-9600
Rocky River, OH 44116   Cheryl Hallstrom, Commun.Dir.

NORTHEASTERN OHIO UNIVERSITIES COLLEGE OF MEDICINE - BASIC
    MEDICAL SCIENCES LIBRARY
                                  Phone: (216) 325-2511
Rootstown, OH 44272   Karen Brewer, Dir.

BELMONT COUNTY LAW LIBRARY †
Court House   Phone: (614) 695-2121
St. Clairsville, OH 43950

GEOGRAPHIC

GEOGRAPHIC

JENNINGS LIBRARY
437 Jennings Ave.
Salem, OH 44460
Phone: (216) 337-3348
Dale E. Shaffer, Lib.Cons. & Dir.

ERIE COUNTY LAW LIBRARY †
Court House, 1st Fl.
Sandusky, OH 44870
Phone: (419) 626-4823
Robin A. Muratori, Libn.

PROVIDENCE HOSPITAL - SCHOOL OF NURSING LIBRARY
1912 Hayes Ave.
Sandusky, OH 44870
Phone: (419) 625-8450
Deborah Sutter, Media Coord.

INSTITUTE FOR CENTRAL EUROPEAN RESEARCH - LIBRARY
2950 Warrensville Ctr. Rd.
Shaker Heights, OH 44122
Phone: (216) 752-9927
W.K. Von Uhlenhorst-Ziechmann, Dir.

SHAKER HEIGHTS CITY SCHOOL DISTRICT - GARVIN LIBRARY
3468 Lee Rd.
Shaker Heights, OH 44120
Phone: (216) 921-1400
Ellen M. Stepanian, Dir. of Lib. Media

MSC CENTER LIBRARY
Route 4
Shelby, OH 44875
Phone: (419) 747-4772
Rev. Denis C. Brunelle, M.S.C., Libn.

SHELBY COUNTY LAW LIBRARY
Court House
Sidney, OH 45365
Phone: (513) 498-4541
Rita Miller, Libn.

WARNER & SWASEY COMPANY - RESEARCH DIVISION LIBRARY
28999 Aurora Rd.
Solon, OH 44139
Phone: (216) 368-6144
Susan M. Kroll, Libn.

CLARK COUNTY HISTORICAL SOCIETY - LIBRARY
Memorial Hall, 300 W. Main St.
Springfield, OH 45504
Phone: (513) 324-0657
George H. Berkhofer, Exec.Dir.

COMMUNITY HOSPITAL OF SPRINGFIELD & CLARK COUNTY - HEALTH SCIENCES LIBRARY
2615 E. High St.
Springfield, OH 45501
Phone: (513) 325-0531
Jane Violet, Libn.

HYMN SOCIETY OF AMERICA - LIBRARY
Wittenberg University
Springfield, OH 45501
Phone: (513) 327-6308
W. Thomas Smith, Exec.Dir.

MERCY MEDICAL CENTER - HEALTH SCIENCES LIBRARY
1343 Fountain
Springfield, OH 45501
Phone: (513) 390-5000
Marietta Wilson, Libn.

SPRINGFIELD ART CENTER - LIBRARY
107 Cliff Park Rd.
Springfield, OH 45501
Phone: (513) 325-4673
Mary McG. Miller, Chm. of Lib.Comm.

SPRINGFIELD BAR AND LAW LIBRARY ASSOCIATION - LIBRARY
Clark County Court House, 3rd Fl.
Springfield, OH 45502
Phone: (513) 324-5871
A.F. Hohlmayer, Libn.

WITTENBERG UNIVERSITY - THOMAS LIBRARY
Springfield, OH 45501
Phone: (513) 327-7016
Bob Lee Mowery, Dir.

BARIUM AND CHEMICALS, INC. - RESEARCH LIBRARY
County Rd. 44
Box 218
Steubenville, OH 43952
Phone: (614) 282-9776
Eleanor R. Naylor, Libn.

JEFFERSON COUNTY LAW LIBRARY
Courthouse
Steubenville, OH 43952
Phone: (614) 283-4111
Christine K. Firm, Libn.

OHIO VALLEY HOSPITAL - HEALTH SCIENCES LIBRARY
380 Summit Ave.
Steubenville, OH 43952
Phone: (614) 283-7400
Kathryn Pasquarella, Med.Libn.

SCM CORPORATION - GLIDDEN COATINGS & RESINS DIV./DURKEE FOODS DIV. - TECHNICAL INFORMATION SERVICES
Joyce Research Ctr.
16651 Sprague Rd.
Strongsville, OH 44136
Phone: (216) 771-5121
Maria Jones McSweeney, Mgr.

TALLMADGE HISTORICAL SOCIETY - LIBRARY & ARCHIVES *
One Tallmadge Circle
Tallmadge, OH 44278
Phone: (216) 633-1098
James B. Hillegas, Pres.

ANTIQUE AND HISTORIC GLASS FOUNDATION - LIBRARY
Box 7413
Toledo, OH 43615
Phone: (419) 531-5679
Carl U. Fauster, Dir.

FARM LABOR ORGANIZING COMMITTEE - LIBRARY
714 1/2 S. St. Clair St.
Toledo, OH 43609
Phone: (419) 243-3456

FULLER, HENRY, HODGE & SNYDER - LIBRARY †
12th Fl., Edison Plaza
300 Madison Ave.
Toledo, OH 43604
Phone: (419) 255-8220
James Hodge, Jr., Partner

LIBBEY-OWENS-FORD COMPANY - CORPORATE LIBRARY
811 Madison Ave.
Toledo, OH 43695
Phone: (419) 247-4862
Patricia B. Jones, Corp.Libn.

LIBBEY-OWENS-FORD COMPANY - TECHNICAL CENTER - LIBRARY
1701 E. Broadway
Toledo, OH 43605
Phone: (419) 247-4367
Jeanne M. Keogh, Libn.

MARSHALL, MELHORN, COLE, HUMMER & SPITZER - LIBRARY
1434 Natl. Bank Bldg.
Toledo, OH 43604
Phone: (419) 243-4200
Nancy Harris, Libn.

MEDICAL COLLEGE OF OHIO AT TOLEDO - RAYMON H. MULFORD LIBRARY
3000 Arlington Ave.
Toledo, OH 43614
Phone: (419) 381-4223
R.M. Watterson, Libn.

MERCY HOSPITAL - EDWARD L. BURNS HEALTH SCIENCES LIBRARY
2200 Jefferson Ave.
Toledo, OH 43624
Phone: (419) 259-1327
Thomas R. Sink, Dir. of Lib.Serv.

MIDLAND-ROSS CORPORATION - THERMAL SYSTEMS TECHNICAL CENTER - LIBRARY
900 N. Westwood Ave.
Box 985
Toledo, OH 43696
Phone: (419) 537-6133
Jean Raynock, Libn.

OWENS-CORNING FIBERGLAS CORPORATION - LAW DEPARTMENT LIBRARY
Fiberglas Tower 26
Toledo, OH 43659
Phone: (419) 248-7787
Sharon G.S. Sobel, Law Libn.

OWENS-ILLINOIS, INC. - BUSINESS INFORMATION SERVICES
Owens-Illinois Bldg., Box 1035
Toledo, OH 43666
Phone: (419) 247-1788
Laura Kauffmann, Libn.

OWENS-ILLINOIS, INC. - TECHNICAL INFORMATION SERVICES
1700 N. Westwood Ave.
Toledo, OH 43666
Phone: (419) 247-9320
Shirley Taylor, Supv.

PARKVIEW OSTEOPATHIC HOSPITAL - LIBRARY
1920 Parkwood Ave.
Toledo, OH 43624
Phone: (419) 242-8471
Donna McLain, Lib.Cons.

RIVERSIDE HOSPITAL - MEDICAL LIBRARY
1530 Superior St.
Toledo, OH 43604
Phone: (419) 729-5151
Kay Deffenbaugh, Libn.

ST. VINCENT HOSPITAL AND MEDICAL CENTER - HEALTH SCIENCE LIBRARY
2213 Cherry St.
Toledo, OH 43608
Phone: (419) 259-4324
Jack W. Shaffer, Dir.

SAMBORN, STEKETEE, OTIS & EVANS, INC. - RESOURCE & INFORMATION CENTER
1001 Madison Ave.
Toledo, OH 43624
Phone: (419) 255-3830
Lorraine R. DeVenney, Libn.

SHUMAKER, LOOP & KENDRICK - LIBRARY
811 Madison Ave., Suite 500
Toledo, OH 43624
Phone: (419) 241-4201
Martha Esbin, Law Libn.

TELEDYNE CAE CORPORATION - ENGINEERING LIBRARY
1330 Laskey Rd.   Phone: (419) 470-3027
Toledo, OH 43612   Marlene S. Dowdell, Libn.

TOLEDO BLADE - LIBRARY
541 Superior St.   Phone: (419) 259-7265
Toledo, OH 43660   Kathleen L. Trimble, Hd.Libn.

TOLEDO EDISON COMPANY - LIBRARY
Edison Plaza   Phone: (419) 259-5279
Toledo, OH 43652   Catherine Witker, Libn.Techn.

TOLEDO HOSPITAL - LIBRARY
2142 N. Cove Blvd.   Phone: (419) 473-4404
Toledo, OH 43606   Linda Fankhauser, Dir.

TOLEDO LAW ASSOCIATION LIBRARY
Lucas County Court House   Phone: (419) 259-8951
Toledo, OH 43624   Deborah J. Cannaday, Libn./Dir.

TOLEDO-LUCAS COUNTY PLAN COMMISSIONS - LIBRARY
Renaissance Municipal Bldg.
415 N. St. Clair St.
Toledo, OH 43604

TOLEDO-LUCAS COUNTY PUBLIC LIBRARY - BUSINESS DEPARTMENT
325 Michigan St.   Phone: (419) 255-7055
Toledo, OH 43624   Dorothy R. McHenry, Hd.

TOLEDO-LUCAS COUNTY PUBLIC LIBRARY - FINE ARTS AND AUDIO
  SERVICE DEPARTMENT
325 Michigan St.   Phone: (419) 255-7055
Toledo, OH 43624   Paula J. Baker, Hd.

TOLEDO-LUCAS COUNTY PUBLIC LIBRARY - HISTORY-TRAVEL-BIOGRAPHY
  DEPARTMENT
325 Michigan St.   Phone: (419) 255-7055
Toledo, OH 43624   Donald C. Barnette, Jr., Dept.Hd.

TOLEDO-LUCAS COUNTY PUBLIC LIBRARY - LITERATURE/FICTION
  DEPARTMENT
325 Michigan St.   Phone: (419) 255-7055
Toledo, OH 43624   William S. Granger, Hd.

TOLEDO-LUCAS COUNTY PUBLIC LIBRARY - LOCAL HISTORY & GENEALOGY
  DEPARTMENT
325 Michigan St.   Phone: (419) 255-7055
Toledo, OH 43624   Morgan J. Barclay, Hd., Local Hist.

TOLEDO-LUCAS COUNTY PUBLIC LIBRARY - SCIENCE AND TECHNOLOGY
  DEPARTMENT
325 Michigan St.   Phone: (419) 255-7055
Toledo, OH 43624   Mary B. Hubbard, Hd.

TOLEDO-LUCAS COUNTY PUBLIC LIBRARY - SOCIAL SCIENCE & GENERAL
  INFORMATION DEPARTMENT
325 Michigan St.   Phone: (419) 255-7055
Toledo, OH 43624   Marcia Learned Au, Hd.

TOLEDO MENTAL HEALTH CENTER - LIBRARY AND INFORMATION
  SERVICES †
Caller 10002   Phone: (419) 381-8349
Toledo, OH 43699   Peg Cordner, Supv., Lib.Serv.

TOLEDO MUSEUM OF ART - ART REFERENCE LIBRARY
Box 1013   Phone: (419) 255-8000
Toledo, OH 43697   Anne O. Reese, Hd.Libn.

UNIVERSITY OF TOLEDO - COLLEGE OF LAW LIBRARY †
2801 W. Bancroft St.   Phone: (419) 537-2733
Toledo, OH 43606   Janet L. Wallin, Law Libn.

UNIVERSITY OF TOLEDO - WARD M. CANADAY CENTER
William S. Carlson Library   Phone: (419) 537-2443
Toledo, OH 43606   David J. Martz, Jr., Dir.

HOBART BROTHERS COMPANY - TECHNICAL CENTER - JOHN H.
  BLANKENBUEHLER MEMORIAL LIBRARY
Trade Square E.   Phone: (513) 339-6011
Troy, OH 45373   Martha A. Baker, Libn.

MIAMI COUNTY LAW LIBRARY *
Court House
Box 130   Phone: (513) 335-8341
Troy, OH 45373   Helen Carstensen, Libn.

WYANDOT COUNTY HISTORICAL SOCIETY - WYANDOT MUSEUM - LIBRARY
130 S. 7th St.   Phone: (419) 294-3857
Upper Sandusky, OH 43351   Frances Smith, Cur.

CHAMPAIGN COUNTY LAW LIBRARY
County Court House   Phone: (513) 652-2222
Urbana, OH 43078   Judy K. Burnett, Libn.

VAN WERT COUNTY LAW LIBRARY
Court House, 3rd Fl.   Phone: (419) 238-6935
Van Wert, OH 45891

GREAT LAKES HISTORICAL SOCIETY - CLARENCE METCALF RESEARCH
  LIBRARY
480 Main St.   Phone: (216) 967-3467
Vermilion, OH 44089   Dr. Robert M. Hosler

UNITED CHURCH OF CHRIST EVANGELICAL AND REFORMED - CHURCH
  LIBRARY
Grand & Ohio Sts.   Phone: (216) 967-3559
Vermilion, OH 44089

AUGLAIZE COUNTY LAW LIBRARY
Court House   Phone: (419) 738-3124
Wapakoneta, OH 45895   Ron Miller, Attorney

TRUMBULL MEMORIAL HOSPITAL - SCHOOL OF NURSING LIBRARY
1350 East Market St.   Phone: (216) 841-9372
Warren, OH 44484   Dorothy Stambaugh, Libn.

TRUMBULL MEMORIAL HOSPITAL - WEAN MEDICAL LIBRARY
1350 E. Market St.   Phone: (216) 841-9379
Warren, OH 44482   Patricia J. Dull, Med.Libn.

WARREN GENERAL HOSPITAL - MEDICAL STAFF LIBRARY
667 Eastland Ave., S.E.   Phone: (216) 399-7541
Warren, OH 44484   Rene Taranta, Med.Libn.

FAYETTE COUNTY LAW LIBRARY †
Fayette County Court House   Phone: (614) 335-6371
Washington Court House, OH 43160

FULTON COUNTY LAW LIBRARY ASSOCIATION - LAW LIBRARY
Court House   Phone: (419) 335-8863
Wauseon, OH 43567   Marilyn Horner, Libn.

ADAMS COUNTY LAW LIBRARY
Courthouse
West Union, OH 45693   Roy E. Gabbert, Libn.

CHURCH OF JESUS CHRIST OF LATTER-DAY SAINTS - CLEVELAND, OHIO
  STAKE BRANCH GENEALOGICAL LIBRARY
25000 Westwood Rd.   Phone: (216) 777-1518
Westlake, OH 44145   Mary Phelps, Libn.

ST. JOHN AND WEST SHORE HOSPITAL - MEDIA CENTER
29000 Center Ridge Rd.   Phone: (216) 835-6020
Westlake, OH 44145   Jennifer Jung, Dir.

LUBRIZOL CORPORATION - CHEMICAL LIBRARY
29400 Lakeland Blvd.   Phone: (216) 943-4200
Wickliffe, OH 44092   Dr. Horton Dunn, Jr., Supv., Info.Serv.

OTZER HASFORIM OF TELSHE YESHIVA - RABBI A.N. SCHWARTZ LIBRARY
28400 Euclid Ave.   Phone: (216) 943-5300
Wickliffe, OH 44092   Rabbi Binyomin Grunwald, Hd.Libn.

PAYNE THEOLOGICAL SEMINARY - R.C. RANSOM MEMORIAL LIBRARY
Wilberforce-Clifton Rd.   Phone: (513) 376-2946
Wilberforce, OH 45384   Fabienne R. Johns, Hd.Libn.

LAKE COUNTY MEMORIAL HOSPITAL WEST - MEDICAL LIBRARY
36000 Euclid Ave.   Phone: (216) 951-9700
Willoughby, OH 44094   Carolyn Tyx, Circuit Libn.

SCHOOL OF FINE ARTS - LIBRARY
38660 Mentor Ave.   Phone: (216) 951-7500
Willoughby, OH 44094   Edith Reed, Act.Libn.

WILMINGTON COLLEGE - CURRICULUM MATERIALS CENTER *
                                          Phone: (513) 382-6661
Wilmington, OH 45177   George Winsor, Professor of Educ.

MONROE COUNTY LAW LIBRARY *
Court House
Woodsfield, OH 43793   Helen L. English, Libn.

BELL & HOWELL COMPANY - MICRO PHOTO DIVISION - MICROFORMS
    ARCHIVE
Old Mansfield Rd.   Phone: (216) 264-6666
Wooster, OH 44691   Pamela A. Myers, Mgr.Info.Serv.

LATHROP (Norman) ENTERPRISES - LIBRARY
2342 Star Dr.
Box 198   Phone: (216) 262-5587
Wooster, OH 44691   Mary Lou Lathrop, Mgr.

OHIO STATE AGRICULTURAL RESEARCH AND DEVELOPMENT CENTER -
    LIBRARY
                                          Phone: (216) 264-1021
Wooster, OH 44691   Constance Britton, Libn.

OHIO STATE UNIVERSITY - AGRICULTURAL TECHNICAL INSTITUTE -
    LIBRARY
                                          Phone: (216) 264-3911
Wooster, OH 44691   Phoebe F. Phillips, Hd.Libn.

WAYNE COUNTY LAW LIBRARY ASSOCIATION
Wayne County Courthouse   Phone: (216) 262-5561
Wooster, OH 44691   Betty K. Schuler, Libn.

AVIATION SAFETY INSTITUTE - ASI TECHNICAL LABS. - LIBRARY
893 High St., Suite J
Box 304   Phone: (614) 885-4242
Worthington, OH 43085   John B. Galipault, Pres.

NATIONAL WATER WELL ASSOCIATION - GROUND WATER LIBRARY/
    INFORMATION CENTER
500 W. Wilson Bridge Rd.   Phone: (614) 846-9355
Worthington, OH 43085   Jean Poland, Info.Serv.Mgr.

OHIO STATE UNIVERSITY - CENTER FOR HUMAN RESOURCE RESEARCH -
    LIBRARY
5701 N. High St.   Phone: (614) 422-7337
Worthington, OH 43085   Julian Larson, Libn.

PONTIFICAL COLLEGE JOSEPHINUM - A.T. WEHRLE MEMORIAL LIBRARY
N. High St.   Phone: (614) 885-2376
Worthington, OH 43085

WORTHINGTON HISTORICAL SOCIETY - LIBRARY
50 W. New England Ave.   Phone: (614) 885-1247
Worthington, OH 43085   Lillian Skeele, Libn.

U.S. AIR FORCE BASE - WRIGHT-PATTERSON GENERAL LIBRARY †
FL 2300, Kittyhawk Ctr.   Phone: (513) 257-4815
Wright-Patterson AFB, OH 45433   Theresa J. Knasiak, Adm.Libn.

U.S. AIR FORCE HOSPITAL MEDICAL CENTER - MEDICAL LIBRARY (OH-
    Wright-Patterson AFB)
SGEL   Phone: (513) 257-4506
Wright-Patterson AFB, OH 45433   Jo-Ann D. Suleiman, Biomed.Libn.

U.S. AIR FORCE INSTITUTE OF TECHNOLOGY - LIBRARY
Bldg. 640, Area B   Phone: (513) 255-5894
Wright-Patterson AFB, OH 45433   Virginia E. Eckel, Dir.

U.S. AIR FORCE MUSEUM - RESEARCH DIVISION LIBRARY
Bldg. 489, Area B   Phone: (513) 255-3284
Wright-Patterson AFB, OH 45433   Charles G. Worman, Chf., Res.Div.

U.S. AIR FORCE - WRIGHT AERONAUTICAL LABORATORIES - AEROSPACE
    STRUCTURES INFORMATIONAL ANALYSIS CENTER
AFWAL/FIBR (ASIAC)   Phone: (513) 255-6688
Wright-Patterson AFB, OH 45431   Gordon R. Negaard, Dir.

GREENE COUNTY DISTRICT LIBRARY - GREENE COUNTY ROOM
76 E. Market St.   Phone: (513) 376-2995
Xenia, OH 45385   Julie M. Overton, Coord., Local Hist.

GREENE COUNTY LAW LIBRARY
Court House   Phone: (513) 376-5115
Xenia, OH 45385   Jill LeSourd, Libn.

COMMUNITY SERVICE, INC. - LIBRARY
114 E. Whiteman St.   Phone: (513) 767-2161
Yellow Springs, OH 45387   Jane Folmer, Dir.

FELLOWSHIP OF RELIGIOUS HUMANISTS - LIBRARY
105 W. North College St.
Yellow Springs, OH 45387   Edwin H. Wilson, Hist.

GLEN HELEN ASSOCIATION - LIBRARY
Glen Helen Bldg.
405 Corry St.   Phone: (513) 767-7375
Yellow Springs, OH 45387   Mrs. George Asakawa, Libn.

KETTERING (Charles F.) RESEARCH LABORATORY - LIBRARY
150 E. South College St.   Phone: (513) 767-7271
Yellow Springs, OH 45387   Janice Williams, Libn.

AMERICAN AMBULANCE ASSOCIATION - INFORMATION CENTER †
1919 Market St.   Phone: (216) 744-4161
Youngstown, OH 44507   Daniel Becker

BUTLER INSTITUTE OF AMERICAN ART - LIBRARY *
524 Wick Ave.   Phone: (216) 743-1711
Youngstown, OH 44502   C. Singer, Assoc.Dir.

MAHONING LAW LIBRARY
Court House   Phone: (216) 747-2000
Youngstown, OH 44503   Lucille G. DeMoss, Law Libn.

PUBLIC LIBRARY OF YOUNGSTOWN AND MAHONING COUNTY - SCIENCE
    AND INDUSTRY DIVISION
305 Wick Ave.   Phone: (216) 744-8636
Youngstown, OH 44503   Orin D. Cole, Hd.

ST. ELIZABETH HOSPITAL MEDICAL CENTER - MEDICAL LIBRARY
1044 Belmont Ave.   Phone: (216) 746-7231
Youngstown, OH 44501   Barbara G. Rosenthal, Med.Libn.

ST. ELIZABETH HOSPITAL MEDICAL CENTER - SCHOOL OF NURSING
    LIBRARY
1044 Belmont Ave.   Phone: (216) 746-7211
Youngstown, OH 44501   Doris L. Crawford, Libn.

WOODSIDE RECEIVING HOSPITAL - STAFF RESOURCE LIBRARY/
    PATIENTS' LIBRARY
800 E. Indianola Ave.   Phone: (216) 788-8712
Youngstown, OH 44502   Carol L. Homrighausen, Libn.

YOUNGSTOWN HOSPITAL ASSOCIATION - HEALTH SCIENCES LIBRARY
345 Oak Hill Ave.   Phone: (216) 747-0751
Youngstown, OH 44501   Wendy Hawk Mady, Hd.Libn.

BETHESDA HOSPITAL - CHILDBIRTH EDUCATION LIBRARY †
2951 Maple Ave.   Phone: (614) 454-4000
Zanesville, OH 43701   Jean Shaw

BETHESDA HOSPITAL - LIBRARY AND EDUCATION SERVICES †
2951 Maple Ave.   Phone: (614) 454-4220
Zanesville, OH 43701   Patty Y. Hartley, Dir.

MUSKINGUM LAW LIBRARY
Court House   Phone: (614) 452-9143
Zanesville, OH 43701   Helen Porter, Libn.

ZANESVILLE ART CENTER - LIBRARY
620 Military Rd.   Phone: (614) 452-0741
Zanesville, OH 43701   Dr. Charles Dietz, Dir.

OKLAHOMA

EAST CENTRAL OKLAHOMA STATE UNIVERSITY - OKLAHOMA
ENVIRONMENTAL INFORMATION/MEDIA CENTER
Phone: (405) 332-8000
Ada, OK 74820   John Walker, Dir.

ENVIRONMENTAL PROTECTION AGENCY - ROBERT S. KERR
ENVIRONMENTAL RESEARCH LABORATORY - LIBRARY
Box 1198   Phone: (405) 332-8800
Ada, OK 74820   Ms. LoRene Fuller, Libn.

U.S. AIR FORCE BASE - ALTUS BASE LIBRARY
FL 4419   Phone: (405) 482-8670
Altus AFB, OK 73521   A. Lucille Lowrie, Libn.

NORTHWESTERN OKLAHOMA STATE UNIVERSITY - LIBRARY
Phone: (405) 327-1700
Alva, OK 73717   Ray D. Lau, Lib.Dir.

SAMUEL ROBERTS NOBLE FOUNDATION, INC. - BIOMEDICAL DIVISION
LIBRARY
Rte. 1   Phone: (405) 223-5810
Ardmore, OK 73401   Virginia Huebsch, Libn.

BARTLESVILLE PUBLIC LIBRARY - HISTORY ROOM
6th & Johnstone   Phone: (918) 336-2133
Bartlesville, OK 74003   Herbert E. Winn, Libn.

PHILLIPS (FRANK) FOUNDATION, INC. - WOOLAROC MUSEUM - LIBRARY
Phone: (515) 438-2600
Bartlesville, OK 74003   Linda Stone, Cur. of Art

PHILLIPS PETROLEUM COMPANY - ENGINEERING LIBRARY
11 A3 Phillips Bldg.   Phone: (918) 661-5911
Bartlesville, OK 74004   Norma Benefiel, Off.Serv.Supv.

PHILLIPS PETROLEUM COMPANY - EXPLORATION & PRODUCTION GROUP -
LIBRARY
439 Frank Phillips Bldg.   Phone: (918) 661-5514
Bartlesville, OK 74004   Annabeth Bearer, Tech.Res. Analyst

PHILLIPS PETROLEUM COMPANY - GAS & GAS LIQUIDS DIVISION -
LIBRARY †
5 D-2 Phillips Bldg.   Phone: (918) 661-5803
Bartlesville, OK 74004   Ollie Mae Burdett, Hd.Libn.

PHILLIPS PETROLEUM COMPANY - RESEARCH & DEVELOPMENT
DEPARTMENT - TECHNICAL INFORMATION BRANCH
Phillips Research Ctr.   Phone: (918) 661-3435
Bartlesville, OK 74004   David R. Weiser, Mgr.

U.S. DEPT. OF ENERGY - BARTLESVILLE ENERGY TECHNOLOGY CENTER
LIBRARY
Cudahy & Virginia Sts.
Box 1398   Phone: (918) 336-2400
Bartlesville, OK 74003   Elizabeth Mohr, Adm.Libn.

DAVIS (J.M.) GUN MUSEUM - RESEARCH LIBRARY
333 N. Lynn Riggs Blvd.
Box 966   Phone: (918) 341-5707
Claremore, OK 74017   Sue E.G. Cook, Exec.Sec.

WILL ROGERS LIBRARY
121 N. Weenonah   Phone: (918) 341-1564
Claremore, OK 74017   Geraldine Warmack, Libn.

EASTERN ORTHODOX CATHOLIC CHURCH IN AMERICA - THREE
HIERARCHS SEMINARY LIBRARY
Rt. 1, Paradise Valley   Phone: (405) 466-3960
Coyle, OK 73027   Kay Adair, Libn.

SOUTHEASTERN OKLAHOMA STATE UNIVERSITY - KERR INDUSTRIAL
APPLICATIONS CENTER - LIBRARY
Phone: (405) 924-6822
Durant, OK 74701   Dr. James S. Harmon, Dir.

CENTRAL STATE UNIVERSITY - LIBRARY
100 N. University Dr.   Phone: (405) 341-2980
Edmond, OK 73034   Dr. John L. Lolley, Dir. of Lib.Serv.

CANADIAN COUNTY HISTORICAL MUSEUM - LIBRARY
Wade & Grand Sts.   Phone: (405) 232-5121
El Reno, OK 73036   Mrs. Frank C. Ball, Cur.

PHILLIPS UNIVERSITY - GRADUATE SEMINARY LIBRARY
University Sta., Box 2218   Phone: (405) 237-4433
Enid, OK 73701   John Sayre, Dir.

ST. MARY'S HOSPITAL - LIBRARY
305 S. Fifth St.   Phone: (405) 233-6100
Enid, OK 73701   Jean McDaniel, Libn.

U.S. ARMY FIELD ARTILLERY SCHOOL - MORRIS SWETT LIBRARY
Snow Hall, Rm. 16   Phone: (405) 351-4525
Ft. Sill, OK 73503   Lester L. Miller, Jr., Supv.Libn.

WESTERN STATE HOSPITAL - MEDICAL LIBRARY
Phone: (405) 766-2311
Fort Supply, OK 73841   Vi Thomas, Libn.

PANHANDLE STATE UNIVERSITY - NO MAN'S LAND HISTORICAL MUSEUM -
LIBRARY
Sewel St.
Box 278   Phone: (405) 349-2670
Goodwell, OK 73939   Dr. Harold S. Kachel, Cur.

LANGSTON UNIVERSITY - MELVIN B. TOLSON BLACK HERITAGE CENTER †
2nd Fl., Page Hall Annex   Phone: (405) 466-2231
Langston, OK 73050   Rosalind Savage, Cur.

MUSEUM OF THE GREAT PLAINS - GREAT PLAINS RESEARCH LIBRARY AND
ARCHIVES
601 Ferris
Box 68   Phone: (405) 353-5675
Lawton, OK 73502   Jeane Bothe, Cur.Spec.Coll.

OKLAHOMA GEOLOGICAL SURVEY - OKLAHOMA GEOPHYSICAL
OBSERVATORY LIBRARY
Box 8   Phone: (918) 366-4152
Leonard, OK 74043   Charles J. Mankin, Dir.

BACONE COLLEGE - LIBRARY
East Shawnee   Phone: (918) 683-4581
Muskogee, OK 74401   Frances A. Donelson, Lib.Dir.

OKLAHOMA SCHOOL FOR THE BLIND - PARKVIEW LIBRARY
3300 Gibson St.
Box 309   Phone: (918) 682-6641
Muskogee, OK 74401   Marjorie Moske, Libn.

U.S. VETERANS ADMINISTRATION (OK-Muskogee) - MEDICAL CENTER
LIBRARY
Honor Heights Dr.   Phone: (918) 683-3261
Muskogee, OK 74401   Larry L. Shea, Chf., Lib.Serv.

APPLIED TECHNOLOGY CORPORATION - LIBRARY
Box FF   Phone: (405) 364-5431
Norman, OK 73070

CENTRAL STATE HOSPITAL - PROFESSIONAL LIBRARY
Box 151   Phone: (405) 321-4880
Norman, OK 73069   Jane Marie Hamilton, Med.Libn.

NORMAN MUNICIPAL HOSPITAL - HEALTH SCIENCE LIBRARY
901 N. Porter
Box 1308   Phone: (405) 321-1700
Norman, OK 73030   Jacalyn E. Mosnat, Libn.

U.S. POSTAL SERVICE - TRAINING & DEVELOPMENT INSTITUTE -
TECHNICAL CENTER LIBRARY
Box 1800   Phone: (405) 325-1001
Norman, OK 73070   Maureen D. Flynn, Libn.

GEOGRAPHIC

UNIVERSITY OF OKLAHOMA - ART LIBRARY
Jacobson Hall, Rm. 203
Norman, OK 73019
Phone: (405) 325-2841
Donald E. Koozer, Supv.

UNIVERSITY OF OKLAHOMA - CENTER FOR ECONOMIC AND MANAGEMENT RESEARCH
307 W. Brooks St., Rm. 4
Norman, OK 73019
Phone: (405) 325-2931
Patty Staggs, Libn.

UNIVERSITY OF OKLAHOMA - CHEMISTRY-MATHEMATICS LIBRARY
Physical Sciences Center, 207
Norman, OK 73019
Phone: (405) 325-5628
Jeanne G. Howard, Libn.

UNIVERSITY OF OKLAHOMA - ENGINEERING LIBRARY
Norman, OK 73019
Phone: (405) 325-2941
Jean Poland, Libn.

UNIVERSITY OF OKLAHOMA - GEOLOGY LIBRARY
830 Van Vleet Oval, Rm. 103
Norman, OK 73019
Phone: (405) 325-6451
Claren M. Kidd, Libn.

UNIVERSITY OF OKLAHOMA - HARRY W. BASS COLLECTION IN BUSINESS HISTORY
401 W. Brooks
Norman, OK 73019
Phone: (405) 325-3941
Dr. Daniel Wren, Cur.

UNIVERSITY OF OKLAHOMA - HISTORY OF SCIENCE COLLECTIONS
401 W. Brooks, Rm. 339
Norman, OK 73019
Phone: (405) 325-2741
Duane H.D. Roller, Cur.

UNIVERSITY OF OKLAHOMA - LAW LIBRARY
300 Timberdell Rd.
Norman, OK 73019
Phone: (405) 325-4311
Laura N. Gasaway, Dir.

UNIVERSITY OF OKLAHOMA - LIMITED ACCESS COLLECTION
401 W. Brooks, Rm. 440
Norman, OK 73019
Phone: (405) 325-2048
Duane H.D. Roller, Cur.

UNIVERSITY OF OKLAHOMA - MUSIC LIBRARY
Norman, OK 73019
Phone: (405) 325-4243
Jan Seifert, Fine Arts Libn.

UNIVERSITY OF OKLAHOMA - OKLAHOMA BIOLOGICAL STATION LIBRARY *
Norman, OK 73019
Phone: (405) 564-2463
Dr. Loren G. Hill, Dir.

UNIVERSITY OF OKLAHOMA - PHYSICS-ASTRONOMY LIBRARY
Norman, OK 73019
Phone: (405) 325-3962
Jeanne Howard, Libn.

UNIVERSITY OF OKLAHOMA - SCHOOL OF ARCHITECTURE LIBRARY
Norman, OK 73019
Phone: (405) 325-5521
Ilse Davis, Lib.Techn.

UNIVERSITY OF OKLAHOMA - SCHOOL OF DRAMA LIBRARY
Norman, OK 73019
Phone: (405) 325-4201
Jan Seifert, Fine Arts Libn.

UNIVERSITY OF OKLAHOMA - WESTERN HISTORY COLLECTIONS
630 Parrington Oval, Rm. 452
Norman, OK 73019
Phone: (405) 325-3641
John S. Ezell, Cur.

UNIVERSITY OF OKLAHOMA - WESTERN HISTORY COLLECTIONS - LIBRARY DIVISION
Monnet Hall, Rm. 300
Norman, OK 73019
Phone: (405) 325-3641
John S. Ezell, Cur.

AMATEUR SOFTBALL ASSOCIATION - ASA RESEARCH CENTER AND LIBRARY
2801 N.E. 50th St.
Oklahoma City, OK 73136
Phone: (405) 424-5266
Bill Plummer, III, Comm.Coord.

ANTA CORPORATION - LIBRARY
101 N. Robinson, Suite 1400
Oklahoma City, OK 73102
Phone: (405) 272-9321
Shirley Hilbert-Price, Anl.

BAPTIST MEDICAL CENTER - WANN LANGSTON MEMORIAL LIBRARY
3300 Northwest Expy.
Oklahoma City, OK 73112
Phone: (405) 949-3766
Phyllis Bennett, Dir., Med.Lib.

HTB, INC. - TECHNICAL INFORMATION CENTER
Box 1845
Oklahoma City, OK 73101
Phone: (405) 525-7451
Retha Robertson, Libn.

INTERSTATE OIL AND GAS COMPACT COMMISSION - LIBRARY
900 N.E. 23rd St.
Box 53127
Oklahoma City, OK 73152
Phone: (405) 525-3556
W. Timothy Dowd, Exec.Dir.

KERR-MC GEE CORPORATION - MC GEE LIBRARY
Box 25861
Oklahoma City, OK 73125
Phone: (405) 270-3358
Tom W. Harrison, Mgr.

MERCY HEALTH CENTER LIBRARY †
4300 W. Memorial Rd.
Oklahoma City, OK 73120
Phone: (405) 755-1515
Dorothy Williams, Libn.

NATIONAL COWBOY HALL OF FAME & WESTERN HERITAGE CENTER - RESEARCH LIBRARY OF WESTERN AMERICANA
1700 N.E. 63rd St.
Oklahoma City, OK 73111
Phone: (405) 478-2250
Mr. A.J. Tytgat, Educ.Dir.

NINETY-NINES, INC. - LIBRARY
Will Rogers World Airport
Box 59965
Oklahoma City, OK 73159
Phone: (405) 685-7969
Dorothy Niekamp, Libn.

OKLAHOMA ART CENTER - LIBRARY
Plaza Circle, Fair Park
3113 Pershing Blvd.
Oklahoma City, OK 73107
Lowell Adams, Dir.

OKLAHOMA CHRISTIAN COLLEGE - OKLAHOMA LIVING LEGENDS
North Eastern & Memorial Rd.
Oklahoma City, OK 73111
Phone: (405) 478-1661
Pendleton Woods, Dir.

OKLAHOMA CITY METROPOLITAN LIBRARY SYSTEM - BUSINESS-SCIENCE SECTION
131 Dean A. McGee Ave.
Oklahoma City, OK 73102
Phone: (405) 235-0571
Elsie Bell, Chf., Main Lib.

OKLAHOMA CITY UNIVERSITY - LAW LIBRARY
Oklahoma City, OK 73106
Phone: (405) 521-5271
William J. Beintema, Law Libn.

OKLAHOMA COUNTY LAW LIBRARY
County Courthouse, Rm. 247
Oklahoma City, OK 73102
Phone: (405) 236-2727
Betty A. Skaggs, Libn.

OKLAHOMA GAS AND ELECTRIC COMPANY - LIBRARY
Box 321
Oklahoma City, OK 73101
Phone: (405) 272-3191
Ms. Pat Tucker, Libn.

OKLAHOMA HISTORICAL SOCIETY - DIVISION OF LIBRARY RESOURCES
Historical Bldg.
Oklahoma City, OK 73105
Phone: (405) 521-2491
Vicki Sullivan, Dir., Lib.Rsrcs.

OKLAHOMA REGIONAL LIBRARY FOR THE BLIND AND PHYSICALLY HANDICAPPED
1108 N.E. 36th St.
Oklahoma City, OK 73111
Phone: (405) 521-3514
Bill McIlvain, Adm.Libn.

OKLAHOMA STATE DEPARTMENT OF ENERGY - ENERGY INFORMATION CENTER
4400 N. Lincoln Blvd., Suite 251
Oklahoma City, OK 73105
Phone: (405) 521-3941
S.K. Arnold, Energy Info.Spec.

OKLAHOMA STATE DEPARTMENT OF HEALTH - INFORMATION & REFERRAL HEALTHLINE
N.E. 10th & Stonewall
Box 53551
Oklahoma City, OK 73152
Phone: (405) 271-4725
Dorothy Hall, Dir.

OKLAHOMA STATE DEPARTMENT OF LIBRARIES
200 N.E. 18th St.
Oklahoma City, OK 73105
Phone: (405) 521-2502
Robert L. Clark, Jr., Dir.

OKLAHOMA STATE UNIVERSITY - OKLAHOMA CITY BRANCH - TECHNICAL
  INSTITUTE LIBRARY
900 N. Portland   Phone: (405) 947-4421
Oklahoma City, OK 73107   Annette Duffy, Hd.Libn.

OKLAHOMA WATER RESOURCES BOARD - LIBRARY
1000 N.E. 10th, 12th Fl.
Box 53585   Phone: (405) 271-2555
Oklahoma City, OK 73152   Susan E. Lutz, Lib.Techn.

PRESBYTERIAN HOSPITAL - MEDICAL LIBRARY
N.E. 13th and Lincoln Blvd.   Phone: (405) 271-4266
Oklahoma City, OK 73104   Dorothy Williams, Lib.Dir.

ST. ANTHONY HOSPITAL - O'DONOGHUE MEDICAL LIBRARY *
1000 N. Lee St.
Box 205   Phone: (405) 231-1811
Oklahoma City, OK 73102   Robert J. Lefkowitz, Libn.

ST. FRANCIS CENTER FOR CHRISTIAN RENEWAL - ECUMENICAL LIBRARY
Box 32180
Oklahoma City, OK 73123

U.S. COURT OF APPEALS, 10TH CIRCUIT - OKLAHOMA CITY GENERAL
  LIBRARY
200 N.W. 4th St.   Phone: (405) 232-7441
Oklahoma City, OK 73102   Sharon Ware

U.S. DEPT. OF TRANSPORTATION - TRANSPORTATION SAFETY INSTITUTE
  - TECHNICAL REFERENCE SERVICE †
6500 S. MacArthur Blvd.   Phone: (405) 686-4611
Oklahoma City, OK 73125   Virginia C. Hughes, Mgr.

U.S. FEDERAL AVIATION ADMINISTRATION - AERONAUTICAL CENTER
  LIBRARY, AAC-44D
6500 S. MacArthur
Box 25082   Phone: (405) 686-4709
Oklahoma City, OK 73125   Virginia C. Hughes, Libn.

U.S. VETERANS ADMINISTRATION (OK-Oklahoma City) - HOSPITAL LIBRARY
921 N.E. 13th St.   Phone: (405) 272-9876
Oklahoma City, OK 73104   Verlean Delaney, Chf.Libn.

UNIVERSITY OF OKLAHOMA - HEALTH SCIENCES CENTER - DEPARTMENT
  OF SURGERY LIBRARY
Oklahoma Memorial Hospital
Box 26307 - ET 2009   Phone: (405) 271-5506
Oklahoma City, OK 73125   Linda R. O'Rourke, Med.Libn.

UNIVERSITY OF OKLAHOMA - HEALTH SCIENCES CENTER LIBRARY
1000 Stanton L. Young Blvd.
Box 26901   Phone: (405) 271-2285
Oklahoma City, OK 73190   C.M. Thompson, Dir.

WESTMINSTER PRESBYTERIAN CHURCH - LIBRARY
4400 N. Shartel   Phone: (405) 524-2204
Oklahoma City, OK 73118   Richard Hershberger, Assoc.Min.

WILSON FOODS, INC. - RESEARCH LIBRARY
4545 Lincoln Blvd.   Phone: (405) 525-4781
Oklahoma City, OK 73105

CREEK INDIAN MEMORIAL ASSOCIATION - CREEK COUNCIL HOUSE
  MUSEUM - LIBRARY
Town Square
106 W. 6th St.   Phone: (918) 756-2324
Okmulgee, OK 74447   Bruce M. Shackelford, Cur./Dir.

OKLAHOMA STATE UNIVERSITY - SCHOOL OF TECHNICAL TRAINING -
  OKMULGEE BRANCH LIBRARY
                                         Phone: (918) 756-6211
Okmulgee, OK 74447   Becky Kirkbride, Libn.

CONOCO, INC. - RESEARCH AND DEVELOPMENT DEPARTMENT -
  TECHNICAL INFORMATION SERVICES
                                         Phone: (405) 767-4719
Ponca City, OK 74601   Dr. Harold H. Eby, Dir.

PONCA CITY CULTURAL CENTER MUSEUM - LIBRARY
1000 E. Grand Ave.   Phone: (405) 762-6123
Ponca City, OK 74601   Diane Dembicki, Musm.Cur.

NATIONAL CLEARINGHOUSE OF REHABILITATION TRAINING MATERIALS -
  REFERENCE COLLECTION
Oklahoma State University
115 Old USDA Bldg.   Phone: (405) 624-7650
Stillwater, OK 74074   Paul Gaines, Proj.Dir.

NATIONAL WRESTLING HALL OF FAME - LIBRARY
405 W. Hall of Fame Ave.   Phone: (405) 377-5242
Stillwater, OK 74074   Doris Dellinger, Libn.

OKLAHOMA STATE DEPARTMENT OF VOCATIONAL AND TECHNICAL
  EDUCATION - CURRICULUM DIVISION
1515 W. 6th Ave.   Phone: (405) 377-2000
Stillwater, OK 74074   Susan K. Hedrick, Libn.

OKLAHOMA STATE UNIVERSITY - AUDIO VISUAL CENTER
University Library   Phone: (405) 624-7212
Stillwater, OK 74074   Dr. Woodfin G. Harris, Dir.

OKLAHOMA STATE UNIVERSITY - BIOLOGICAL SCIENCES DIVISION
University Library   Phone: (405) 624-6309
Stillwater, OK 74074   Sheila G. Johnson, Biological Sci.Libn.

OKLAHOMA STATE UNIVERSITY - CURRICULUM MATERIALS LABORATORY
University Library   Phone: (405) 624-6310
Stillwater, OK 74074   Anne K. Hoyt, Hd.

OKLAHOMA STATE UNIVERSITY - DOCUMENTS DIVISION
University Library   Phone: (405) 624-6546
Stillwater, OK 74074   Vicki W. Phillips, Libn.

OKLAHOMA STATE UNIVERSITY - HUMANITIES DIVISION
University Library   Phone: (405) 624-6544
Stillwater, OK 74074   Kim Fisher, Hd., Hum.Div.

OKLAHOMA STATE UNIVERSITY - PHYSICAL SCIENCES AND ENGINEERING
  DIVISION
University Library   Phone: (405) 624-6305
Stillwater, OK 74074   Calvin Brewer, Libn.

OKLAHOMA STATE UNIVERSITY - SOCIAL SCIENCE DIVISION
University Library   Phone: (405) 624-6540
Stillwater, OK 74074   Edward G. Hollman, Hd., Soc.Sci.Div.

OKLAHOMA STATE UNIVERSITY - SPECIAL COLLECTIONS AND MAPS
University Library   Phone: (405) 624-6311
Stillwater, OK 74074   Heather M. Lloyd, Ref.Libn.

OKLAHOMA STATE UNIVERSITY - VETERINARY MEDICINE LIBRARY
University Library   Phone: (405) 624-6655
Stillwater, OK 74074   LaVerne K. Jones, Libn.

U.S. NATL. PARK SERVICE - CHICKASAW NATL. RECREATION AREA -
  TRAVERTINE NATURE CENTER LIBRARY
Box 201   Phone: (405) 622-3165
Sulphur, OK 73086   Bert L. Speed, Chf.Pk. Interpreter

CHEROKEE NATIONAL HISTORICAL SOCIETY, INC. - LIBRARY AND
  ARCHIVES
Box 515
TSA-LA-GI   Phone: (918) 456-6007
Tahlequah, OK 74464   M.A. Hagerstrand, Exec.V.P.

NORTHEASTERN OKLAHOMA STATE UNIVERSITY - JOHN VAUGHAN
  LIBRARY/LEARNING RESOURCES CENTER
                                         Phone: (918) 456-5511
Tahlequah, OK 74464   Dr. Brad Agnew, Interim Dir.

OKLAHOMA VETERANS CENTER - TALIHINA DIVISION - LIBRARY
Box 488   Phone: (918) 567-2251
Talihina, OK 74571   Betty L. Davis, Libn.

U.S. AIR FORCE BASE - TINKER BASE LIBRARY
2854 ABG/SSL, Bldg. 5702   Phone: (405) 734-3083
Tinker AFB, OK 73145   Doris Ellis Haglund, Base Libn.

GEOGRAPHIC

U.S. AIR FORCE HOSPITAL - MEDICAL LIBRARY (OK-Tinker AFB) *
Phone: (405) 734-8373
Tinker AFB, OK 73145   Barbara J. Ryan, Med.Libn.

OKLAHOMA HISTORICAL SOCIETY - CHICKASAW COUNCIL HOUSE LIBRARY
Court House Sq.
Box 717   Phone: (405) 371-3351
Tishomingo, OK 73460   Beverly J. Wyatt, Site Agent

AMERICAN AIRLINES, INC. - ENGINEERING LIBRARY
3800 N. Mingo Rd.   Phone: (918) 832-2821
Tulsa, OK 74151   Mike Rusk, Tech.Libn.

AMERICAN ASSOCIATION OF PETROLEUM GEOLOGISTS - LIBRARY
1444 S. Boulder
Box 979   Phone: (918) 584-2555
Tulsa, OK 74101   Kathy Shanks, Libn.

AMOCO PRODUCTION COMPANY - LAW DEPARTMENT LIBRARY
Box 591   Phone: (918) 581-3523
Tulsa, OK 74102   Sally Shipley

AMOCO PRODUCTION COMPANY - RESEARCH CENTER LIBRARY †
Box 591   Phone: (918) 664-3238
Tulsa, OK 74102   Carolyn Beson, Supv., Tech.Info.Serv.

CITIES SERVICE COMPANY - CHEMICALS AND MINERALS MARKET
    RESEARCH LIBRARY
201 Bldg.
Box 300   Phone: (918) 586-4892
Tulsa, OK 74102   C. Carol Guy, Libn.

CITIES SERVICE COMPANY - ERG - RESEARCH LIBRARY
1133 N. Lewis
Box 50408   Phone: (918) 586-2524
Tulsa, OK 74150   Linda L. Hill, Mgr.

CITIES SERVICE COMPANY - LEGAL DIVISION LIBRARY
110 W. Seventh St.
Box 300   Phone: (918) 586-2272
Tulsa, OK 74102   Alberta Baker, Libn.

FIRST UNITED METHODIST CHURCH - LIBRARY
1115 S. Boulder   Phone: (918) 587-9481
Tulsa, OK 74119   Marie Tongue, Dir. of Lib.Serv.

GETTY REFINING AND MARKETING COMPANY - LAW LIBRARY
Box 1650   Phone: (918) 560-6000
Tulsa, OK 74102

GILCREASE (Thomas) INSTITUTE OF AMERICAN HISTORY AND ART -
    LIBRARY
1400 N. 25th West Ave.   Phone: (918) 531-5311
Tulsa, OK 74127   G.P. Edwards, Sr.Cur.

INDIAN NATIONS COUNCIL OF GOVERNMENTS - LIBRARY
707 S. Houston   Phone: (918) 584-7526
Tulsa, OK 74127   Ginger Garbacz, Plan.Anl./Libn.

OKLAHOMA COLLEGE OF OSTEOPATHIC MEDICINE & SURGERY - LIBRARY
Box 2280   Phone: (918) 582-1972
Tulsa, OK 74101   Linda L. Roberts, Coll.Libn.

OKLAHOMA OSTEOPATHIC HOSPITAL - L.C. BAXTER MEDICAL LIBRARY
Ninth St. at Jackson Ave.   Phone: (918) 587-2561
Tulsa, OK 74127   S. Jane Cooper, Hd.Med.Libn.

OKLAHOMA SCHOOL OF BUSINESS - LIBRARY
4770 S. Harvard Ave.   Phone: (918) 742-3311
Tulsa, OK 74135   Carolyn S. McCauley, Libn.

OKLAHOMA WELL LOG LIBRARY, INC.
837 Mayo Bldg.   Phone: (918) 582-6188
Tulsa, OK 74103   Jan Jennings, Mgr./Libn.

ORAL ROBERTS UNIVERSITY - HEALTH SCIENCES LIBRARY
7777 S. Lewis
Box 2187   Phone: (918) 494-4949
Tulsa, OK 74171   Timothy C. Judkins, Asst.Dir.

ORAL ROBERTS UNIVERSITY - LAW LIBRARY
7777 S. Lewis
Box 2187   Phone: (918) 492-6161
Tulsa, OK 74171   David W. Dunn, Law Libn.

ORAL ROBERTS UNIVERSITY - LIBRARY - HOLY SPIRIT RESEARCH CENTER
Box 2187   Phone: (918) 495-6898
Tulsa, OK 74171   Karen Robinson, Libn.

OZARK-MAHONING COMPANY - RESEARCH LIBRARY †
1870 S. Boulder   Phone: (918) 585-2661
Tulsa, OK 74119

PUBLIC SERVICE COMPANY OF OKLAHOMA - REFERENCE CENTER
212 E. 6th St.
Box 201   Phone: (918) 599-2367
Tulsa, OK 74119   Jean Thompson, Supv.

ROCKWELL INTERNATIONAL - TECHNICAL INFORMATION CENTER *
2000 N. Memorial Dr.
Box 51308   Phone: (918) 835-3111
Tulsa, OK 74151   Wenona Hurd, Lib. Attendant

ST. FRANCIS HOSPITAL - HEALTH SCIENCES LIBRARY
6161 S. Yale Ave.   Phone: (918) 494-1210
Tulsa, OK 74177   Darryl Logan, Med.Libn.

ST. JOHN MEDICAL CENTER - HEALTH SCIENCES LIBRARY
1923 S. Utica   Phone: (918) 744-2970
Tulsa, OK 74104   Geneva N. Norvell, Libn.

SOUTHWESTERN ART ASSOCIATION - PHILBROOK ART CENTER - LIBRARY
Box 52510   Phone: (918) 741-7941
Tulsa, OK 74152   Thomas E. Young, Libn.

TULSA CITY-COUNTY LIBRARY SYSTEM - BUSINESS AND TECHNOLOGY
    DEPARTMENT
400 Civic Ctr.   Phone: (918) 581-5211
Tulsa, OK 74103   J. Craig Buthod, Dept.Hd.

TULSA COUNTY LAW LIBRARY
Tulsa County Court House, Rm. 242
500 S. Denver   Phone: (918) 584-0471
Tulsa, OK 74103   Rena C. Hanton, Libn.

TULSA WORLD-TULSA TRIBUNE - LIBRARY DEPARTMENT †
315 S. Boulder Ave.
Box 1770   Phone: (918) 583-2161
Tulsa, OK 74102   Lucy Towry, Libn.

TULSA ZOOLOGICAL PARK - LIBRARY
5701 E. 36th St., N.   Phone: (918) 835-8471
Tulsa, OK 74115   Carol Eames, Educ.Cur.

UNIVERSITY OF TULSA - COLLEGE OF ENGINEERING & PHYSICAL
    SCIENCES - DIVISION OF INFORMATION SERVICES
1133 N. Lewis Ave.   Phone: (918) 592-6000
Tulsa, OK 74110   J.A. Bailey, Dir.

UNIVERSITY OF TULSA - COLLEGE OF LAW LIBRARY
3120 E. Fourth Pl.   Phone: (918) 939-6351
Tulsa, OK 74104   Alan Ogden, Law Libn.

UNIVERSITY OF TULSA - SIDNEY BORN TECHNICAL LIBRARY
600 S. College   Phone: (918) 592-6000
Tulsa, OK 74104   James T. Murray, Tech.Libn.

WILLIAMS BROTHERS ENGINEERING COMPANY - TECHNICAL
    INFORMATION CENTER
6600 S. Yale Ave.   Phone: (918) 496-5655
Tulsa, OK 74177   Kay Kittrell, Dir.

U.S. AIR FORCE BASE - VANCE BASE LIBRARY
Phone: (405) 237-2121
Vance AFB, OK 73701   Tom L. Kirk, Chf.Libn.

SOUTHWESTERN OKLAHOMA STATE UNIVERSITY - AL HARRIS LIBRARY
Phone: (405) 772-6611
Weatherford, OK 73096   Sheila Wilder Hoke, Lib.Dir.

OREGON

SOUTHERN OREGON STATE COLLEGE - LIBRARY
1250 Siskiyou Blvd.　　　　　　　　　Phone: (503) 482-6445
Ashland, OR 97520　　　　　　　　Richard E. Moore, Lib.Dir.

COLUMBIA RIVER MARITIME MUSEUM - LIBRARY
1618 Exchange St.　　　　　　　　　Phone: (503) 325-2323
Astoria, OR 97103　　　　　　　　　Larry D. Gilmore, Cur.

U.S. JOB CORPS - TONGUE POINT CENTER - INSTRUCTIONAL MEDIA
　CENTER
Astoria, OR 97103

OREGON GRADUATE CENTER FOR STUDY AND RESEARCH - LIBRARY
19600 N.W. Walker Rd.　　　　　　　Phone: (503) 645-1121
Beaverton, OR 97006　　　　　　　Maureen G. Seaman, Libn.

OREGON REGIONAL PRIMATE RESEARCH CENTER - LIBRARY
505 N.W. 185th Ave.　　　　　　　　Phone: (503) 645-1141
Beaverton, OR 97006　　　　　　　　Isabel McDonald, Libn.

TEKTRONIX, INC. - CORPORATE LIBRARY
Box 500, MS 50-210　　　　　　　　Phone: (503) 644-0161
Beaverton, OR 97077　　　　　　　　Julianne Jedeka, Lib.Mgr.

KAISER SUNNYSIDE MEDICAL CENTER - LIBRARY
10180 S.E. Sunnyside Rd.
Clackamas, OR 97015　　　　　　　Ann H. Haines, Med.Libn.

OREGON STATE DEPARTMENT OF FISH AND WILDLIFE - LIBRARY
17330 S.E. Evelyn St.
Clackamas, OR 97015　　　　　　Shirley M. McKinney, Libn.

ENVIRONMENTAL PROTECTION AGENCY - ENVIRONMENTAL RESEARCH
　LABORATORY, CORVALLIS - LIBRARY
200 S.W. 35th St.　　　　　　　　　Phone: (503) 757-4731
Corvallis, OR 97330　　　　　　　Betty M. McCauley, Libn.

HEWLETT-PACKARD COMPANY - CORVALLIS DIVISION TECHNICAL
　INFORMATION CENTER
1000 N.E. Circle Blvd.　　　　　　　Phone: (503) 757-2000
Corvallis, OR 97330　　　　　　　　Shari Morwood, Dir.

OREGON STATE UNIVERSITY - SCHOOL OF FORESTRY - FRL LIBRARY
　　　　　　　　　　　　　　　　Phone: (503) 753-9166
Corvallis, OR 97331　　　　　　　Mary B. Scroggins, Libn.

OREGON STATE UNIVERSITY - WATER RESOURCES RESEARCH INSTITUTE
　- LIBRARY
Covell Hall 115　　　　　　　　　　Phone: (503) 754-4022
Corvallis, OR 97331　　　　　　　Peter C. Klingeman, Dir.

OREGON STATE UNIVERSITY - WILLIAM JASPER KERR LIBRARY
　　　　　　　　　　　　　　　　Phone: (503) 754-3411
Corvallis, OR 97331　　　　　Rodney K. Waldron, Dir. Of Libs.

PROTESTANT EPISCOPAL CHURCH - EPISCOPAL DIOCESE OF EASTERN
　OREGON - ARCHIVES
Box 98
Cove, OR 97824　　　　　　　　Rev. Louis L. Perkins, Hist.

U.S. NATL. PARK SERVICE - CRATER LAKE NATL. PARK - LIBRARY
Box 7
Crater Lake, OR 97604　　　　Henry M. Tanski, Jr., Asst.Interp.

CHURCH OF JESUS CHRIST OF LATTER-DAY SAINTS - EUGENE, OREGON
　BRANCH GENEALOGICAL LIBRARY
3550 W. 18th Ave.　　　　　　　　Phone: (503) 343-3741
Eugene, OR 97402　　　　　　　　Shirlee A. Bird, Libn.

ERIC CLEARINGHOUSE ON EDUCATIONAL MANAGEMENT
University of Oregon Library　　　　Phone: (503) 686-5043
Eugene, OR 97403　　　　　　　　Philip K. Piele, Dir.

EUGENE HEARING AND SPEECH CENTER - LIBRARY †
1202 Almaden
Box 2087　　　　　　　　　　　　Phone: (503) 485-8521
Eugene, OR 97402　　　　　　　Ned Risbrough, Exec.Dir.

EUGENE HOSPITAL AND CLINIC - DOCTORS' LIBRARY †
1162 Willamette St.　　　　　　　　Phone: (503) 687-6000
Eugene, OR 97401　　　Dr. Byron Musa, Chm., Lib. Committee

EUGENE REGISTER-GUARD - NEWS LIBRARY
975 High St.
Box 10188　　　　　　　　　　　Phone: (503) 485-1234
Eugene, OR 97440　　　　　　　Marijoy Rubaloff, Libn.

LANE COUNCIL OF GOVERNMENTS - LIBRARY
Public Service Bldg.
125 E. 8th　　　　　　　　　　　Phone: (503) 687-4283
Eugene, OR 97401　　　　　　JoAnn McCauley, Info.Coord.

LANE COUNTY LAW LIBRARY
Courthouse　　　　　　　　　　　Phone: (503) 687-4337
Eugene, OR 97401　　　　　　　Mary E. Clayton, Law Libn.

LANE COUNTY MUSEUM - SPECIAL COLLECTIONS & ARCHIVES
740 W. 13th Ave.　　　　　　　　Phone: (503) 687-4239
Eugene, OR 97402　　　　　　　　Edward Nolan, Archv.

NORTHWEST CHRISTIAN COLLEGE - LEARNING RESOURCE CENTER
828 E. 11th　　　　　　　　　　　Phone: (503) 343-1641
Eugene, OR 97401　　　　　　　Margaret W. Hewitt, Dir.

OREGON CENTER FOR GERONTOLOGY AT THE UNIVERSITY OF OREGON -
　RESOURCE CENTER
1627 Agate St.　　　　　　　　　Phone: (503) 686-4207
Eugene, OR 97403　　　　　　　　Jennifer Ware, Libn.

OREGON RESEARCH INSTITUTE - LIBRARY
195 W. 12th Ave.
Eugene, OR 97401　　　　　　　　Linda Rargus, Lib.Mgr.

SACRED HEART GENERAL HOSPITAL AND MEDICAL CENTER - LIBRARY
　SERVICES
1200 Alder St.
Box 10905　　　　　　　　　　　Phone: (503) 686-6837
Eugene, OR 97440　　　　　Debbie Graham, Dir., Lib.Serv.

UNIVERSITY OF OREGON - ARCHITECTURE AND ALLIED ARTS BRANCH
　LIBRARY
　　　　　　　　　　　　　　　　Phone: (503) 686-3637
Eugene, OR 97403　　　　　　　　R.R. McCready, Libn.

UNIVERSITY OF OREGON - BUREAU OF GOVERNMENTAL RESEARCH AND
　SERVICE LIBRARY
Box 3177　　　　　　　　　　　　Phone: (503) 686-3048
Eugene, OR 97403　　　　　　　Katherine G. Eaton, Libn.

UNIVERSITY OF OREGON - CAREER INFORMATION CENTER
Susan Campbell Hall　　　　　　　Phone: (503) 686-3235
Eugene, OR 97403　　　　June F. Wyant, Career Info.Spec.

UNIVERSITY OF OREGON - CAREER INFORMATION SYSTEM
247 Hendricks Hall　　　　　　　　Phone: (503) 686-3872
Eugene, OR 97403　　　　　　　Bruce McKinlay, Dir.

UNIVERSITY OF OREGON - COLLEGE OF BUSINESS ADMINISTRATION -
　DIVISION OF RESEARCH
140 Gilbert Hall
Eugene, OR 97403

UNIVERSITY OF OREGON - CURRICULUM AND JUVENILE COLLECTIONS
University Library　　　　　　　　Phone: (503) 686-3074
Eugene, OR 97403　　　Laurene E. Zaporozhetz, Ref.Libn., Educ.

UNIVERSITY OF OREGON - DEPARTMENT OF ENGLISH - RANDALL V. MILLS
　ARCHIVES OF NORTHWEST FOLKLORE
　　　　　　　　　　　　　　　　Phone: (503) 686-3925
Eugene, OR 97401　　　　　　　　J. Barre Toelken

GEOGRAPHIC

UNIVERSITY OF OREGON - EDUCATIONAL POLICY AND MANAGEMENT
   DIVISION - RESOURCE CENTER
College of Education   Phone: (503) 686-5072
Eugene, OR 97403   Constance Hixson, Libn.

UNIVERSITY OF OREGON - ENVIRONMENTAL STUDIES CENTER
                                            Phone: (503) 686-5006
Eugene, OR 97403   Al Urquhart, Dir.

UNIVERSITY OF OREGON - GOVERNMENT DOCUMENTS SECTION
University Library   Phone: (503) 686-3070
Eugene, OR 97403   Thomas A. Stave, Hd.

UNIVERSITY OF OREGON - INSTRUCTIONAL MEDIA CENTER
University Library   Phone: (503) 686-3091
Eugene, OR 97403   George Bynon, Dir.

UNIVERSITY OF OREGON - LAW LIBRARY
                                            Phone: (503) 686-3088
Eugene, OR 97403   Richard H. Surles, Jr., Libn.

UNIVERSITY OF OREGON - MAP LIBRARY
165 Condon Hall   Phone: (503) 686-3051
Eugene, OR 97403

UNIVERSITY OF OREGON - MATHEMATICS LIBRARY
University Library
Eugene, OR 97403

UNIVERSITY OF OREGON - MICROFORMS AND RECORDINGS DEPARTMENT
University Library   Phone: (503) 686-3080
Eugene, OR 97403   Rory Funke, Hd.

UNIVERSITY OF OREGON - ORIENTALIA COLLECTION
University Library   Phone: (503) 686-3114
Eugene, OR 97403   Wen Kai Kung, Cat.Libn. & Biblog.

UNIVERSITY OF OREGON - SCIENCE BRANCH LIBRARY
University Library   Phone: (503) 686-3075
Eugene, OR 97403   Luise E. Walker, Hd.Libn.

UNIVERSITY OF OREGON - SPECIAL COLLECTIONS DIVISION
University Library   Phone: (503) 686-3069
Eugene, OR 97403   Kenneth Duckett, Cur.

PACIFIC UNIVERSITY - SCHOOL OF MUSIC - LIBRARY
College Way   Phone: (503) 357-6151
Forest Grove, OR 97116   Norma M. Cooper, Music Libn.

OREGON ELECTRIC RAILWAY HISTORICAL SOCIETY, INC. - TROLLEY PARK
   - LIBRARY
Star Route, Box 1318   Phone: (503) 357-3574
Glenwood, OR 97120   William Hayes, Hist.

JOSEPHINE COUNTY LAW LIBRARY †
Courthouse   Phone: (503) 474-5181
Grants Pass, OR 97526   A.M. Foster, County Ck.

WASHINGTON COUNTY LAW LIBRARY †
Courthouse   Phone: (503) 648-8880
Hillsboro, OR 97123   Ann Karlen, Libn.

WASHINGTON COUNTY MUSEUM - LIBRARY
641 E. Main St.   Phone: (503) 648-8601
Hillsboro, OR 97123   Dr. Robert W. Keeler, Cur.

SOUTHERN OREGON HISTORICAL SOCIETY - RESEARCH LIBRARY
206 N. 5th St.
Box 480   Phone: (503) 899-1847
Jacksonville, OR 97530   Richard H. Engeman, Libn.

COLLIER STATE PARK LOGGING MUSEUM - LIBRARY
Box 428   Phone: (503) 884-5145
Klamath Falls, OR 97601   Alfred D. Collier, Cur.

KLAMATH COUNTY - LOYD DELAP LAW LIBRARY
Court House   Phone: (503) 882-2501
Klamath Falls, OR 97601   Ruth Rice, Law Libn.

OREGON INSTITUTE OF TECHNOLOGY - LEARNING RESOURCES CENTER
Oretech Branch P.O.   Phone: (503) 882-6321
Klamath Falls, OR 97601   Charles H. Kemp, Dir.

JACKSON COUNTY LAW LIBRARY
Jackson County Justice Bldg.   Phone: (503) 776-7214
Medford, OR 97501   Toni VanDeusen, Libn.

MEDFORD MAIL TRIBUNE - LIBRARY
Box 1108   Phone: (503) 776-4493
Medford, OR 97501   Kathryn Harper, Libn.

OREGON COLLEGE OF EDUCATION - LIBRARY
234 Monmouth Ave.   Phone: (503) 838-1220
Monmouth, OR 97361   Dr. Clarence Gorchels, Dir.

OREGON STATE UNIVERSITY - MARINE SCIENCE CENTER - LIBRARY
                                            Phone: (503) 867-3011
Newport, OR 97365   Marilyn Guin, Libn.

OREGON STATE UNIVERSITY - SCHOOL OF OCEANOGRAPHY - NORTHWEST
   COASTAL INFORMATION CENTER (NCIC)
Marine Science Center   Phone: (503) 867-3011
Newport, OR 97365   John Morgan, Hd.Res.Lit.Anl.

AMERICAN-NEPAL EDUCATION FOUNDATION - WOOD NEPAL LIBRARY
Box ANEF   Phone: (503) 842-4024
Oceanside, OR 97134   Hugh B. Wood, Libn.

EASTERN OREGON HOSPITAL AND TRAINING CENTER - PROFESSIONAL
   LIBRARY
Box A   Phone: (503) 276-1711
Pendleton, OR 97801

BASSIST COLLEGE - LIBRARY
923 S.W. Taylor St.   Phone: (503) 228-6528
Portland, OR 97201   Norma H. Bassist, Libn.

CH2M HILL, INC. - LIBRARY
200 S.W. Market St., 12th Fl.   Phone: (503) 224-9190
Portland, OR 97201   Nancy Beth Kenney, Libn.

COLUMBIA CHRISTIAN COLLEGE - LIBRARY
200 N.E. 91st Ave.   Phone: (503) 255-7060
Portland, OR 97220   Annette B. Cates, Libn.

CONTEMPORARY CRAFTS ASSOCIATION - LIBRARY
3934 S.W. Corbett Ave.
Portland, OR 97201   LaVerne Kuchler, Act.Libn.

EMANUEL HOSPITAL - LIBRARY SERVICES
2801 N. Gantenbein Ave.   Phone: (503) 280-3558
Portland, OR 97227   Katherine W. Rouzie, Dir., Lib.Serv.

ESCO CORP. - LIBRARY
Box 10123   Phone: (503) 228-2141
Portland, OR 97210   Leroy Finch, Sr. Metallurgist

FIRST NATIONAL BANK OF OREGON - LIBRARY *
1300 S.W. 5th
Box 3131   Phone: (503) 225-3725
Portland, OR 97208   Sue Pettis, Libn.

FLOATING POINT SYSTEMS, INC. - TECHNICAL LIBRARY
Box 23489   Phone: (503) 641-3151
Portland, OR 97223   Richard Grahner, Hd.Libn.

GEORGIA-PACIFIC CORPORATION - ARCHIVE
900 S.W. 5th Ave.   Phone: (503) 222-5561
Portland, OR 97204   Mary A. Grant, Archv.

GEORGIA-PACIFIC CORPORATION - HISTORICAL MUSEUM
900 S.W. 5th Ave.   Phone: (503) 222-5561
Portland, OR 97204   Richard M. Thompson, Info.Spec./Musm.Mgr.

GOOD SAMARITAN HOSPITAL AND MEDICAL CENTER - LIBRARY
1015 N.W. 22nd Ave.   Phone: (503) 229-7336
Portland, OR 97210   Melvina Stell, Hd.Libn.

HYSTER COMPANY - TECHNICAL INFORMATION SERVICES
2902 N.E. Clackamas   Phone: (503) 280-7405
Portland, OR 97208   Ruth Jahnke, Libn.

INDUSTRIAL FORESTRY ASSOCIATION - LIBRARY
225 S.W. Broadway, Rm. 400   Phone: (503) 222-9505
Portland, OR 97205   Mike Sullivan, Dir. of Pub. Affairs

KAISER FOUNDATION HOSPITALS - HEALTH SERVICES RESEARCH CENTER
    LIBRARY
4610 S.E. Belmont St.   Phone: (503) 233-5631
Portland, OR 97215   Leslie Webb Wykoff, Libn.

KAISER PERMANENTE MEDICAL CENTER - MEDICAL LIBRARY
5055 N. Greeley Ave.   Phone: (503) 285-9321
Portland, OR 97217   Patricia Hanley, Med.Libn.

LAMB-WESTON - BUSINESS RESEARCH CENTER
Box 23517   Phone: (503) 639-8612
Portland, OR 97223   Anne Vixie, Bus.Res.Spec.

LEWIS AND CLARK LAW SCHOOL - NORTHWESTERN SCHOOL OF LAW -
    PAUL L. BOLEY LAW LIBRARY
10015 S.W. Terwilliger Blvd.   Phone: (503) 244-1181
Portland, OR 97219   Prof. Peter S. Nycum, Law Libn.

LIBRARY ASSOCIATION OF PORTLAND - ART AND MUSIC DEPARTMENT
801 S.W. Tenth Ave.   Phone: (503) 223-7201
Portland, OR 97205   Barbara K. Padden, Hd.

LIBRARY ASSOCIATION OF PORTLAND - GENERAL INFORMATION
    DEPARTMENT - FOUNDATION CENTER
801 S.W. 10th Ave.   Phone: (503) 223-7201
Portland, OR 97205   Ann Austin, Dept.Hd.

LIBRARY ASSOCIATION OF PORTLAND - LITERATURE AND HISTORY
    DEPARTMENT
801 S.W. Tenth Ave.   Phone: (503) 223-7201
Portland, OR 97205   Elizabeth Anne Johnson, Dept.Hd.

LIBRARY ASSOCIATION OF PORTLAND - OREGON COLLECTION
801 S.W. Tenth Ave.   Phone: (503) 223-7201
Portland, OR 97205   Elizabeth Anne Johnson

LIBRARY ASSOCIATION OF PORTLAND - SOCIAL SCIENCE AND SCIENCE
    DEPARTMENT
801 S.W. Tenth Ave.   Phone: (503) 223-7201
Portland, OR 97205   Jim Takita, Dept.Hd.

MAZAMAS - LIBRARY *
909 N.W. Nineteenth Ave.   Phone: (503) 227-2345
Portland, OR 97209

MILLER, NASH, YERKE, WIENER & HAGER - LIBRARY
900 S.W. Fifth Ave.   Phone: (503) 224-5858
Portland, OR 97204   Leslie Meserve, Libn.

MULTNOMAH LAW LIBRARY
Court House   Phone: (503) 248-3394
Portland, OR 97204   Jacquelyn J. Jurkins, Law Libn.

MULTNOMAH SCHOOL OF THE BIBLE - JOHN AND MARY MITCHELL LIBRARY
8435 N.E. Glisan St.   Phone: (503) 255-0332
Portland, OR 97220   James F. Scott, Hd.Libn.

NATIONAL COLLEGE OF NATUROPATHIC MEDICINE - LIBRARY
510 S.W. 3rd Ave.   Phone: (503) 226-3745
Portland, OR 97204   Friedhelm Kirchfeld, Libn.

NORTHWEST REGIONAL EDUCATIONAL LABORATORY - CLEARINGHOUSE
    FOR APPLIED PERFORMANCE TESTING (CAPT)
300 S.W. Sixth Ave.   Phone: (503) 248-6800
Portland, OR 97204   Richard J. Stiggins, Coord.

NORTHWEST REGIONAL EDUCATIONAL LABORATORY - INFORMATION
    CENTER/LIBRARY
300 S.W. Sixth Ave.   Phone: (503) 248-6800
Portland, OR 97204   M. Margaret Rogers, Dir.Info.Serv.

OREGON HISTORICAL SOCIETY - LIBRARY
1230 S.W. Park Ave.   Phone: (503) 222-1741
Portland, OR 97205   Louis Flannery, Chf.Libn.

OREGON STATE DEPARTMENT OF GEOLOGY AND MINERAL INDUSTRIES -
    LIBRARY
1005 State Office Bldg.   Phone: (503) 229-5580
Portland, OR 97201   Klaus Neuendorf, Libn.

OREGONIAN LIBRARY
1320 S.W. Broadway   Phone: (503) 221-8131
Portland, OR 97201   Doris N. Smith, Chf.Libn.

PACIFIC POWER AND LIGHT COMPANY - LIBRARY
920 S.W. Sixth Ave.   Phone: (503) 243-4095
Portland, OR 97204   William L. Hutchinson, Mgr.Lib.& Files

PORTLAND ART MUSEUM - LIBRARY
1219 S.W. Park   Phone: (503) 226-2811
Portland, OR 97205   Emily Evans, Libn.

PORTLAND BUREAU OF PLANNING - LIBRARY
621 S.W. Alder   Phone: (503) 248-4140
Portland, OR 97205   Karol Koon, Libn.

PORTLAND GENERAL ELECTRIC - CORPORATE AND TECHNICAL LIBRARIES
121 S.W. Salmon St., TB-5   Phone: (503) 226-8695
Portland, OR 97204   Helene K. Etheredge, Supv.Libn.

PORTLAND PUBLIC SCHOOLS - PROFESSIONAL LIBRARY
501 N. Dixon St.
Box 3107
Portland, OR 97208   Phone: (503) 249-2000

PORTLAND STATE UNIVERSITY - AUDIO-VISUAL SERVICES
Box 1151   Phone: (503) 229-4514
Portland, OR 97207   Frank F. Kuo, Dir.

PORTLAND STATE UNIVERSITY - COMMUNITY SERVICES UNIT -
    CONTINUING EDUCATION FILM LIBRARY
1633 S.W. Park Ave.   Phone: (503) 229-4890
Portland, OR 97207   Glenn R. Boettcher, Dir.Libn.

PORTLAND STATE UNIVERSITY - MIDDLE EAST STUDIES CENTER
Box 751   Phone: (503) 229-3609
Portland, OR 97207   C. Thomas Pfingsten, Dir.

PORTLAND STATE UNIVERSITY - SCIENCE LIBRARY
Box 1151   Phone: (503) 229-4735
Portland, OR 97207   Dr. J.J. Kohut, Sci.Libn.

PROVIDENCE MEDICAL CENTER - MEDICAL LIBRARY
700 N.E. 47th Ave.   Phone: (503) 234-8211
Portland, OR 97213   Miriam Palmer, Med.Libn.

RADER COMPANIES, INC. - INFORMATION CENTER
6005 N.E. 82nd Ave.   Phone: (503) 255-5330
Portland, OR 97220   Colleen Joy Sobieski, Mgr., Info.Ctr.

REED COLLEGE - PHYSICS LIBRARY †
Dept. of Physics   Phone: (503) 771-1112
Portland, OR 97202   Nicholas A. Wheeler, Prof.

ST. VINCENT HOSPITAL AND MEDICAL CENTER - HEALTH SCIENCES
    LIBRARY †
9205 S.W. Barnes Rd.   Phone: (503) 297-4411
Portland, OR 97225   Edith H. Throckmorton, Dir.

SETON, JOHNSON & ODELL, INC. - TECHNICAL INFORMATION CENTER *
317 S.W. Adler St.   Phone: (503) 226-3921
Portland, OR 97204   James K. Farley, Tech.Info.Spec.

SPEARS, LUBERSKY, CAMPBELL, & BLEDSOE - LIBRARY
800 Pacific Bldg.   Phone: (503) 226-6151
Portland, OR 97204   Jacqueline Revel McInnis, Libn.

UNION PACIFIC RAILROAD COMPANY - LAW LIBRARY
628 Pittock Block   Phone: (503) 249-2711
Portland, OR 97208   L. James Bergmann, Gen. Solicitor

GEOGRAPHIC

GEOGRAPHIC

U.S. ARMY - CORPS OF ENGINEERS - PORTLAND DISTRICT - LIBRARY
Box 2946 Phone: (503) 221-6016
Portland, OR 97208 Christian P. Hurd, District Libn.

U.S. BANCORP - RESOURCE LIBRARY
555 S.W. Oak St. Phone: (503) 225-5816
Portland, OR 97204 Lois A. Stutheit, Libn.

U.S. COURT OF APPEALS, 9TH CIRCUIT - LIBRARY
Pioneer Courthouse Phone: (503) 221-6042
Portland, OR 97204 Jane E. Gay, Libn.

U.S. DEPT. OF COMMERCE - INTERNATIONAL TRADE ADMINISTRATION -
PORTLAND DISTRICT OFFICE LIBRARY
1220 S.W. 3rd Ave., Rm. 618 Phone: (503) 221-3001
Portland, OR 97204 Lloyd R. Porter, Dir.

U.S. DEPT. OF ENERGY - BONNEVILLE POWER ADMINISTRATION - LIBRARY
1002 N.E. Holladay St.
Box 3621 Phone: (503) 234-3361
Portland, OR 97208 Matthew F. Cullen, Hd., Lib.

U.S. DISTRICT COURT - DISTRICT OF OREGON - LIBRARY
529 U.S. Courthouse
620 S.W. Main Phone: (503) 221-6042
Portland, OR 97219 Jane E. Gay, Libn.

U.S. VETERANS ADMINISTRATION (OR-Portland) - MEDICAL LIBRARY
3710 S.W. U.S. Veterans Hospital Rd.
Box 1035 Phone: (503) 222-9221
Portland, OR 97201 Mrs. Nymah L. Trued, Chf., Lib.Serv.

UNIVERSITY OF OREGON HEALTH SCIENCES CENTER - DENTAL LIBRARY †
611 S.W. Campus Dr. Phone: (503) 225-8822
Portland, OR 97201 Carol C. Laxer, Dental Libn.

UNIVERSITY OF OREGON - HEALTH SCIENCES CENTER - LIBRARY
3181 S.W. Sam Jackson Park Rd.
Box 573 Phone: (503) 225-8026
Portland, OR 97207 James E. Morgan, Dir.

WALLA WALLA COLLEGE - SCHOOL OF NURSING PROFESSIONAL LIBRARY
10345 S.E. Market Phone: (503) 239-6115
Portland, OR 97216 Shirley A. Cody, Libn.

WARNER-PACIFIC COLLEGE - OTTO F. LINN LIBRARY
2219 S.E. 68th Ave. Phone: (503) 775-4368
Portland, OR 97215 Dr. William M. Orr, Gen.Lib.Adm.

WASHINGTON PARK ZOO - LIBRARY
4001 S.W. Canyon Rd. Phone: (503) 226-1561
Portland, OR 97221 Warren J. Iliff, Dir.

WESTERN CONSERVATIVE BAPTIST SEMINARY - CLINE-TUNNELL LIBRARY
5511 S.E. Hawthorne Blvd. Phone: (503) 233-8561
Portland, OR 97215 Michael B. Winter, Lib.Dir.

WESTERN EVANGELICAL SEMINARY - GEORGE HALLAUER MEMORIAL
LIBRARY
4200 S.E. Jennings Ave. Phone: (503) 654-5182
Portland, OR 97222 Ralph L. Ewbank, Libn.

WESTERN STATES CHIROPRACTIC COLLEGE - W.A. BUDDEN MEMORIAL
LIBRARY
2900 N.E. 132nd Ave. Phone: (503) 256-3180
Portland, OR 97230 Judy Bar-Tzur, Libn.

DOUGLAS COUNTY MUSEUM - LAVOLA BAKKEN MEMORIAL LIBRARY
Box 1550 Phone: (503) 440-4507
Roseburg, OR 97470 Ella Mae Young, Res.Hist.

FIRST PRESBYTERIAN CHURCH - LIBRARY
823 S.E. Lane Phone: (503) 673-5559
Roseburg, OR 97470 Nancy Nixon, Libn.

COLUMBIA COUNTY HISTORICAL SOCIETY - MUSEUM
Old Courthouse Phone: (503) 397-2805
St. Helens, OR 97051 Mildred Lain, Hist.

OREGON STATE DEPARTMENT OF AGRICULTURE - INFORMATION SERVICE
- LIBRARY
Agriculture Bldg.
635 Capitol St., N.E.
Salem, OR 97310

OREGON STATE DEPARTMENT OF EDUCATION - RESOURCE/
DISSEMINATION CENTER
700 Pringle Parkway, S.E. Phone: (503) 378-8471
Salem, OR 97310 George Katagiri, Coord., Instr.Tech.

OREGON STATE DEPARTMENT OF ENERGY - LIBRARY
102 Labor & Industries Bldg.
Salem, OR 97310

OREGON STATE DEPARTMENT OF LAND CONSERVATION AND
DEVELOPMENT - LIBRARY
1175 Court St., N.E. Phone: (503) 378-2980
Salem, OR 97310 Dixie Ziemer, Libn.

OREGON STATE DEPARTMENT OF REVENUE - LIBRARY
State Office Bldg., Rm. 508 Phone: (503) 378-3727
Salem, OR 97310 Kay Stroup, Libn.

OREGON STATE DEPARTMENT OF TRANSPORTATION - LIBRARY
127 Transportation Bldg. Phone: (503) 378-6268
Salem, OR 97310 Faith Steffen, Libn.

OREGON STATE HOSPITAL - MEDICAL LIBRARY
2600 Center St., N.E. Phone: (503) 378-2266
Salem, OR 97310 Dr. Narain B. Jetmalani, Dir., Ed. & Res.

OREGON STATE LIBRARY
State Library Bldg. Phone: (503) 378-4274
Salem, OR 97310 Marcia Lowell, State Libn.

OREGON STATE LIBRARY - SERVICES FOR THE BLIND AND PHYSICALLY
HANDICAPPED
555 13th St., N.E. Phone: (503) 378-3849
Salem, OR 97301 Patricia A. Kirk, Dir.

OREGON STATE SCHOOL FOR THE BLIND - MEDIA CENTER
700 Church St., S.E. Phone: (503) 378-8025
Salem, OR 97310 Delphie Schuberg, Libn.

OREGON STATE SCHOOL FOR THE DEAF - LIBRARY
999 Locust St., N.E. Phone: (503) 378-6252
Salem, OR 97310 Adoracion A. Alvarez, Curric.Dir.

OREGON STATE SUPREME COURT LIBRARY
Phone: (503) 378-6030
Salem, OR 97310 Roger Andrus, Libn.

OREGON STATE WATER RESOURCES DEPARTMENT - LIBRARY &
INFORMATION CENTER
555 13th St., N.E.
Salem, OR 97310

SALEM HOSPITAL - HEALTH SCIENCES LIBRARY AND INFORMATION
CENTER
665 Winter St., S.E.
Box 14001 Phone: (503) 370-5377
Salem, OR 97309 Dye Kuni, Dir., Lib.Serv.

WILLAMETTE UNIVERSITY - LAW LIBRARY
Winter & Ferry Sts. Phone: (503) 370-6386
Salem, OR 97301 Richard F. Breen, Jr., Law Libn.

AMUNDSON ASSOCIATES - PLANNING REFERENCE LIBRARY †
Box F Phone: (503) 746-8231
Springfield, OR 97477 Robert S. Furrer

NICHOLS MUSEUM - LIBRARY
400 E. Scenic Dr.
The Dalles, OR 97058

TILLAMOOK COUNTY PIONEER MUSEUM - LIBRARY
2106 Second St. Phone: (503) 842-4553
Tillamook, OR 97141 M. Wayne Jensen, Dir.

PENNSYLVANIA

ABINGTON MEMORIAL HOSPITAL - WILMER MEMORIAL MEDICAL LIBRARY
Phone: (215) 885-4000
Abington, PA 19001
Patricia M. Insetta, Libn.

ALUMINUM COMPANY OF AMERICA - ALCOA LABORATORIES -
INFORMATION DEPARTMENT
Phone: (412) 337-2283
Alcoa Center, PA 15069
V.J. Sapp, Lib.Supv.

AIR PRODUCTS AND CHEMICALS, INC. - INFORMATION SERVICES -
TREXLERTOWN LIBRARY
Box 538
Phone: (215) 481-7292
Allentown, PA 18105
Valerie K. Tucci, Mgr., Info.Serv.

ALLENTOWN ART MUSEUM - RESEARCH LIBRARY
5th & Court Sts.
Box 117
Phone: (215) 432-4333
Allentown, PA 18105
Peter F. Blume, Cur.

ALLENTOWN CALL-CHRONICLE - NEWSPAPER LIBRARY
6th & Linden Sts.
Box 1260
Phone: (215) 820-6523
Allentown, PA 18105
Lois A. Doncevic, Sr.Libn.

ALLENTOWN HOSPITAL ASSOCIATION - HEALTH SCIENCES LIBRARY
17th & Chew Sts.
Phone: (215) 821-2263
Allentown, PA 18102
Barbara J. Iobst, Med.Libn.

ALLENTOWN STATE HOSPITAL - HEIM MEMORIAL LIBRARY
1700 Hanover Ave.
Phone: (215) 821-6265
Allentown, PA 18103
Margaret M. Caffrey, Libn.

BELL TELEPHONE LABORATORIES, INC. & WESTERN ELECTRIC, INC. -
TECHNICAL LIBRARY
555 Union Blvd.
Phone: (215) 439-7648
Allentown, PA 18103
Mary L. Coakley, Lib. Group Supv.

CONGREGATION KENESETH ISRAEL - LIBRARY
2227 Chew St.
Phone: (215) 435-9074
Allentown, PA 18104
Dale Honig, Lib. Chairperson

LEHIGH COUNTY HISTORICAL SOCIETY - SCOTT ANDREW TREXLER II
MEMORIAL LIBRARY
Old Court House
Fifth & Hamilton Sts.
Phone: (215) 435-1072
Allentown, PA 18101
Mrs. C. Spencer Allen, Libn.

LEHIGH COUNTY LAW LIBRARY
County Court House
5th & Hamilton Sts., Box 1548
Phone: (215) 820-3308
Allentown, PA 18105
James L. Weirbach, Esq., Law Libn.

MUHLENBERG COLLEGE - JOHN A.W. HAAS LIBRARY
Phone: (215) 433-3191
Allentown, PA 18104
Patricia Ann Sacks, Dir. of Libs.

RAILWAYS TO YESTERDAY, INC. - LEHIGH VALLEY TRANSPORTATION
RESEARCH CENTER
12th and Cumberland Sts.
2nd Fl., General Office
Phone: (215) 797-6687
Allentown, PA 18103
Douglas E. Peters, Hist./Libn.

SACRED HEART HOSPITAL - WILLIAM A. HAUSMAN MEDICAL LIBRARY
4th & Chew Sts.
Phone: (215) 821-3280
Allentown, PA 18102
Joan Daptula, R.R.L., Libn.

TREXLER (Harry C.) MASONIC LIBRARY
Masonic Temple
Fulton & Linden Sts.
Phone: (215) 434-2831
Allentown, PA 18102
Paul R. Breitenstein, Libn.

PPG INDUSTRIES, INC. - COATINGS AND RESINS DIVISION - RESEARCH
CENTER LIBRARY †
Rosanna Dr.
Box 9
Phone: (412) 487-4500
Allison Park, PA 15101
Helen Lamrey, Supv., Info.Serv.

ALTOONA AREA PUBLIC LIBRARY & DISTRICT CENTER - PENNSYLVANIA
ROOM
1600 Fifth Ave.
Phone: (814) 946-0417
Altoona, PA 16602
Nancy Temple, Techn.

ALTOONA HOSPITAL - GLOVER MEMORIAL MEDICAL AND NURSING
LIBRARY
Howard Ave. & 7th St.
Phone: (814) 946-2318
Altoona, PA 16603
Mary Lou Grinch, Chf. of Lib.Serv.

ALTOONA MIRROR - LIBRARY
1000 Green Ave.
Box 2008
Phone: (814) 946-7457
Altoona, PA 16603
Esther Barnes, Libn.

MERCY HOSPITAL - SCHOOL OF NURSING LIBRARY
2613 8th Ave.
Phone: (814) 944-1681
Altoona, PA 16602
Sr. Mary Theodore, C.S.F.N., Libn.

U.S. VETERANS ADMINISTRATION (PA-Altoona) - MEDICAL CENTER
LIBRARY
Phone: (814) 943-8164
Altoona, PA 16603
Rose Altberg, Chf.Libn.

TEMPLE UNIVERSITY - CENTRAL LIBRARY SYSTEM - AMBLER CAMPUS
LIBRARY
Meetinghouse Rd.
Phone: (215) 643-1200
Ambler, PA 19002
Esther Bloomsburgh, Libn.

CENTER FOR THE HISTORY OF AMERICAN NEEDLEWORK - LIBRARY
Old Economy Village
14th & Church Sts.
Phone: (412) 266-6440
Ambridge, PA 15003
Rachel Maines, Dir.

PENNSYLVANIA STATE HISTORICAL & MUSEUM COMMISSION - OLD
ECONOMY LIBRARY
14th & Church Sts.
Phone: (412) 266-4500
Ambridge, PA 15003

EVANGELICAL UNITED BRETHREN CHURCH - HISTORICAL SOCIETY OF THE
EASTERN CONFERENCE - ARCHIVES ROOM
Gossard Memorial Library
Lebanon Valley College
Phone: (717) 867-4411
Annville, PA 17003
Rev. Herbert R. Blouch, Conf.Hist.

FAIRCHILD-WESTON SYSTEMS INC. - WESTON CONTROLS DIVISION -
TECHNICAL LIBRARY
Kennedy Dr.
Phone: (717) 876-1500
Archbald, PA 18403
Arlene F. Kohl, Tech.Libn.

HEWLETT-PACKARD COMPANY - AVONDALE DIVISION LIBRARY
Route 41 & Starr Rd.
Phone: (215) 268-2281
Avondale, PA 19311
Shirley Boyd, Clerk

PHILADELPHIA ASSOCIATION FOR PSYCHOANALYSIS - LOUIS S. KAPLAN
MEMORIAL LIBRARY
15 St. Asaph's Rd.
Bala Cynwyd, PA 19004
June M. Strickland, Libn.

BAKER (Michael, Jr.), INC. - LIBRARY
4301 Dutch Ridge Rd.
Box 280
Phone: (412) 495-7711
Beaver, PA 15009
Ruth J. Williams, Libn.

BEAVER COUNTY BAR ASSOCIATION - LAW LIBRARY
Court House
Phone: (412) 728-5700
Beaver, PA 15009
Jean Watson, Libn.

BEAVER COUNTY TIMES - LIBRARY
400 Fair Ave.
Box 400
Phone: (412) 775-3200
Beaver, PA 15009
Dorothy L. Basar, Hd.Libn.

MEDICAL CENTER OF BEAVER COUNTY - HEALTH SCIENCES LIBRARY
1000 Dutch Ridge Rd.
Phone: (412) 728-7000
Beaver, PA 15009
Patricia M. Coghlan, Dir.

GEOGRAPHIC

RESOURCE & RESEARCH CENTER FOR BEAVER COUNTY & LOCAL HISTORY
Carnegie Free Library
1301 7th Ave.   Phone: (412) 846-4340
Beaver Falls, PA 15010   Vivian C. McLaughlin, Dir.

CENTRE COUNTY LAW LIBRARY
Court House
Bellefonte, PA 16823

PENNSYLVANIA STATE FISH COMMISSION LIBRARY - BENNER SPRING
   FISH RESEARCH STATION
R.D. 1, Box 200 C   Phone: (814) 355-4837
Bellefonte, PA 16823   Thomas R. Bender, Jr., Biolog.

CHRIST UNITED METHODIST CHURCH - LIBRARY †
44 Highland Rd.   Phone: (412) 835-6621
Bethel Park, PA 15102

BETHLEHEM STEEL CORPORATION - BERNARD D. BROEKER LAW LIBRARY
Martin Tower Bldg., Rm. 2027   Phone: (215) 694-5002
Bethlehem, PA 18016   David D. Hendley, Libn.

BETHLEHEM STEEL CORPORATION - SCHWAB MEMORIAL LIBRARY
Martin Tower   Phone: (215) 694-3325
Bethlehem, PA 18016   Ann W. Streiff, Dir.

BETHLEHEM STEEL CORPORATION - TECHNICAL INFORMATION
Homer Research Laboratories   Phone: (215) 694-6938
Bethlehem, PA 18016   W.M. Perry, Supv.

COLLEGE PLACEMENT COUNCIL, INC. - RESOURCE INFORMATION CENTER
Box 2263   Phone: (215) 868-1421
Bethlehem, PA 18001   Susan McGouldrick, Res.Assoc.

DIOCESE OF ALLENTOWN - PRO-LIFE LIBRARY
1135 Stefko Blvd.   Phone: (215) 691-0380
Bethlehem, PA 18017   Sr. M. Irene, O.S.F., Libn.

G & W NATURAL RESOURCES GROUP - ZERBE RESEARCH CENTER -
   TECHNICAL LIBRARY
1 Highland Ave.   Phone: (215) 866-9249
Bethlehem, PA 18017   Faith I. Gensler, Libn.

HISTORIC BETHLEHEM INC. - LIBRARY/ARCHIVES
516 Main St.   Phone: (215) 868-6311
Bethlehem, PA 18018   Susan Finkel, Cur.

LEHIGH UNIVERSITY - MART SCIENCE AND ENGINEERING LIBRARY
15 East Packer Ave., Bldg. 8   Phone: (215) 861-3075
Bethlehem, PA 18015   Sharon Siegler, Hd., Pub.Serv.

MORAVIAN CHURCH IN AMERICA - NORTHERN PROVINCE - MORAVIAN
   ARCHIVES
41 W. Locust St.   Phone: (215) 866-3255
Bethlehem, PA 18018   Vernon H. Nelson, Archv.

MORAVIAN COLLEGE - REEVES LIBRARY
Main St. at Elizabeth Ave.   Phone: (215) 865-0741
Bethlehem, PA 18018   Henry L. Williams, Libn.

ST. LUKE'S HOSPITAL OF BETHLEHEM, PENNSYLVANIA - AUDIOVISUAL
   LIBRARY
Ostrum St.   Phone: (215) 691-4341
Bethlehem, PA 18014   Eileen M. Miller, Libn.

ST. LUKE'S HOSPITAL OF BETHLEHEM, PENNSYLVANIA - TREXLER NURSES'
   LIBRARY
Bishopthorpe & Ostrum St.   Phone: (215) 691-4355
Bethlehem, PA 18015   Linda Beach, Libn.

ST. LUKE'S HOSPITAL OF BETHLEHEM, PENNSYLVANIA - W.L. ESTES, JR.
   MEMORIAL LIBRARY
801 Ostrum St.   Phone: (215) 691-4227
Bethlehem, PA 18015   Maria D. Collette, Med.Libn.

U.S. NATL. PARK SERVICE - HOPEWELL VILLAGE NATL. HISTORIC SITE -
   LIBRARY
R.D. 2, Box 345   Phone: (215) 582-8773
Birdsboro PA 19508   Elizabeth E. Disrude, Supt.

BLOOMSBURG STATE COLLEGE - HARVEY A. ANDRUSS LIBRARY
                                               Phone: (717) 389-2900
Bloomsburg, PA 17815   William V. Ryan, Dir.Lib.Serv.

SPERRY CORPORATION - SPERRY UNIVAC COMPUTER SYSTEMS -
   INFORMATION CENTER
Township Line & Union Meeting Rds.
Box 500   Phone: (215) 542-2458
Blue Bell, PA 19424   Alma B. Campbell, Mgr.

ALLEGHENY LUDLUM STEEL CORPORATION - RESEARCH CENTER
   TECHNICAL LIBRARY
Alabama & Pacific Aves.
Brackenridge, PA 15014

BRADFORD HOSPITAL - DOCTORS' MEMORIAL LIBRARY
Interstate Pkwy.   Phone: (814) 368-4761
Bradford, PA 16701   Genevieve R. Chiodo, Dir., Med.Rec.

PENNSYLVANIA STATE DEPARTMENT OF PUBLIC WELFARE - MENTAL
   HEALTH AND MEDICAL LIBRARY
Mayview State Hospital   Phone: (412) 221-7500
Bridgeville, PA 15017   William A. Suvak, Jr., Libn. II

UNIVERSAL-CYCLOPS SPECIALTY STEEL DIVISION - TECHNICAL
   INFORMATION CENTER
Mayer St.   Phone: (412) 221-8000
Bridgeville, PA 15017   Helen Chappel, Sec.

ROHM & HAAS COMPANY - RESEARCH DIVISION - INFORMATION
   SERVICES DEPT. - LIBRARY
Box 718   Phone: (215) 785-8055
Bristol, PA 19007   Barbara G. Prewitt, Adm.Mgr.

BROCKWAY GLASS COMPANY, INC. - ENGINEERING AND RESEARCH
   CENTER LIBRARY
Engineering & Research Ctr.   Phone: (814) 261-5213
Brockway, PA 15824   Ed McKinley

U.S. FOREST SERVICE - NORTHEASTERN FOREST EXPERIMENT STATION
   LIBRARY
370 Reed Rd.   Phone: (215) 461-3105
Broomall, PA 19008   Gladys D. Daines, Info.Off.

ACADEMY OF THE NEW CHURCH - LIBRARY
2815 Huntingdon Pike
Box 278-68   Phone: (215) 947-0203
Bryn Athyn, PA 19009   Mary Alice Carswell, Dir.

AMERICAN COLLEGE - VANE B. LUCAS MEMORIAL LIBRARY
270 S. Bryn Mawr Ave.   Phone: (215) 896-4507
Bryn Mawr, PA 19010   Maureen E. Strazdon, Libn.

AMERICAN COLLEGE - VANE B. LUCAS MEMORIAL LIBRARY - ORAL
   HISTORY CENTER & ARCHIVES
270 Bryn Mawr Ave.   Phone: (215) 525-9500
Bryn Mawr, PA 19010   Marjorie Amos Fletcher, Dir.

BRYN MAWR COLLEGE - GEOLOGY LIBRARY
                                               Phone: (215) 525-1000
Bryn Mawr, PA 19010   Anne Pringle, Hd., Sci. & Psych.Libs.

BRYN MAWR HOSPITAL - MEDICAL LIBRARY
                                               Phone: (215) 896-3160
Bryn Mawr, PA 19010   L.D. Gundry, Chf.Med.Libn.

BRYN MAWR HOSPITAL - MEDICAL LIBRARY - NURSING DIVISION
Lindsay Ave.   Phone: (215) 896-3084
Bryn Mawr, PA 19010   L.D. Gundry, Chf.Med.Libn.

BUTLER COUNTY LAW LIBRARY
Court House   Phone: (412) 285-4731
Butler, PA 16001   Dolores Bradrick, Law Libn.

BUTLER COUNTY MEMORIAL HOSPITAL - RUTH ARMSTRONG MEMORIAL
   MEDICAL LIBRARY
East Brady St. Extension   Phone: (412) 283-6666
Butler, PA 16001   Rita V. Liebler, Hosp.Libn.

U.S. VETERANS ADMINISTRATION (PA-Butler) - MEDICAL CENTER LIBRARY
Phone: (412) 287-4781
Butler, PA 16001   Dianne Hohn, Chf., Lib.Serv.

PENNSYLVANIA BLUE SHIELD - RESEARCH LIBRARY
Erford Rd.   Phone: (717) 763-3807
Camp Hill, PA 17011   Jill Benko, Res.Sec.

WESTERN CENTER - LIBRARY
333 Curry Hill Rd.   Phone: (412) 745-0700
Canonsburg, PA 15317

CUMBERLAND COUNTY HISTORICAL SOCIETY & HAMILTON LIBRARY
21 N. Pitt St.
Box 626   Phone: (717) 249-7610
Carlisle, PA 17013   Warren J. Gates, Pres.

CUMBERLAND COUNTY LAW LIBRARY
Court House, S. Hanover St.   Phone: (717) 243-3221
Carlisle, PA 17013   Mary S. Rykoskey, Libn.

DICKINSON COLLEGE - LIBRARY - SPECIAL COLLECTIONS
College Library   Phone: (717) 245-1399
Carlisle, PA 17013   Martha Calvert Slotten, Cur.

DICKINSON SCHOOL OF LAW - SHEELY-LEE LAW LIBRARY
150 S. College St.   Phone: (717) 243-4611
Carlisle, PA 17013   James R. Fox, Law Libn.

U.S. ARMY MILITARY HISTORY INSTITUTE
Phone: (717) 245-4139
Carlisle Barracks, PA 17013   Col. Donald P. Shaw, Dir.

U.S. ARMY WAR COLLEGE - LIBRARY
Phone: (717) 245-3660
Carlisle Barracks, PA 17013   Barbara E. Stevens, Dir.

NATIONAL STANDARDS COUNCIL OF AMERICAN EMBROIDERERS - NSCAE
LIBRARY
Carnegie Office Park
600 Bell Ave.   Phone: (412) 279-0299
Carnegie, PA 15106   Yvonne R. Moossy, Libn.

WOODVILLE STATE HOSPITAL - PROFESSIONAL LIBRARY
Phone: (412) 279-2000
Carnegie, PA 15106   Mary Thompson, Libn.

BRANDYWINE CONSERVANCY, INC. - BRANDYWINE RIVER MUSEUM
LIBRARY & STUDY CENTER
Box 141   Phone: (215) 388-7601
Chadds Ford, PA 19317   Ruth Bassett, Libn.

FRANKLIN COUNTY LAW LIBRARY
Court House   Phone: (717) 263-4809
Chambersburg, PA 17201   Janet J. Schug, Libn.

CROZER CHESTER MEDICAL CENTER - MEDICAL LIBRARY
15th St. & Upland Ave.   Phone: (215) 447-2600
Chester, PA 19013   Elizabeth R. Warner, Med.Libn.

DELAWARE COUNTY HISTORICAL SOCIETY - LIBRARY
Box 1036, Widener University   Phone: (215) 874-6444
Chester, PA 19013   Edna S. Sweely, Cur.

LINDSAY LAW LIBRARY †
Widener Univ.
Wolfgram Memorial Library   Phone: (215) 872-3821
Chester, PA 19013

WIDENER UNIVERSITY - WOLFGRAM MEMORIAL LIBRARY
17th & Walnut Sts.   Phone: (215) 876-5551
Chester, PA 19013   Theresa Taborsky, Lib.Dir.

SPRING GARDEN COLLEGE - LIBRARY
102 E. Mermaid Ln.   Phone: (215) 242-3700
Chestnut Hill, PA 19118   Mildred Glushakow, Dir.

HERCULES, INC. - PICCO RESINS DIVISION - LIBRARY
120 State St.   Phone: (412) 233-8600
Clairton, PA 15025   Curtis W. DeWalt, Tech.Libn.

CLARION COUNTY HISTORICAL SOCIETY - LIBRARY/MUSEUM
18 Grant St.   Phone: (814) 226-4450
Clarion, PA 16214   Elisabeth S. Fulmer, Sec./Libn.

CLARION STATE COLLEGE - RENA M. CARLSON LIBRARY
Phone: (814) 226-2343
Clarion, PA 16214   Dan W. Graves, Dir. of Libs.

BAPTIST BIBLE COLLEGE OF PENNSYLVANIA - RICHARD J. MURPHY
MEMORIAL LIBRARY
538 Venard Rd.   Phone: (717) 587-1172
Clarks Summit, PA 18411   David C. McClain, Hd.Libn.

CLEARFIELD LAW LIBRARY
Phone: (816) 781-8062
Clearfield, PA 16830   Carl Soderlund, Libn.

LUKENS STEEL COMPANY - TECHNICAL LIBRARY
Phone: (215) 383-2674
Coatesville, PA 19320   Gloria R. Hartley, Tech.Libn.

U.S. VETERANS ADMINISTRATION (PA-Coatesville) - MEDICAL CENTER
LIBRARY
Phone: (215) 384-7711
Coatesville, PA 19320   Alice M. VonderLindt, Chf., Lib.Serv.

NATIONAL ASSOCIATION OF WATCH AND CLOCK COLLECTORS MUSEUM -
LIBRARY
514 Poplar St.
Box 33   Phone: (717) 684-8261
Columbia, PA 17512   W.H. Francillon, Pres.

QUAKER CHEMICAL CORPORATION - TECHNICAL INFORMATION CENTER
Phone: (215) 828-4250
Conshohocken, PA 19428   Ellen B. Morrow, Mgr.

KTA-TATOR ASSOCIATES, INC. - LIBRARY
2020 Montour St.   Phone: (412) 262-2663
Coraopolis, PA 15108   Dr. Thor Johndahl, Lab.Dir.

CORRY AREA HISTORICAL SOCIETY - LIBRARY
Box 107
Corry, PA 16407   Mrs. Keppel Tiffany

U.S. NATL. PARK SERVICE - ALLEGHENY PORTAGE RAILROAD NATL.
HISTORIC SITE - LIBRARY
Lemon House
Box 247   Phone: (814) 886-8176
Cresson, PA 16630   Dean R. Garrett, Chf.

DANVILLE STATE HOSPITAL - MEDICAL LIBRARY †
Phone: (717) 275-7011
Danville, PA 17821

GEISINGER MEDICAL CENTER - MEDICAL LIBRARY
N. Academy Ave.   Phone: (717) 275-6463
Danville, PA 17821   Britain G. Roth, Mgr., Lib.Serv.

GEISINGER MEDICAL CENTER - SCHOOL OF NURSING LIBRARY
Phone: (717) 275-6288
Danville, PA 17822   Claire A. Huntington, Libn.

MERCY CATHOLIC MEDICAL CENTER - HEALTH SCIENCES LIBRARY
Lansdowne & Baily Rd.   Phone: (215) 586-2050
Darby, PA 19023   Janet Clinton, Chf. of Lib.Serv.

BUCKS COUNTY HISTORICAL SOCIETY - SPRUANCE LIBRARY
Pine & Ashland Sts.   Phone: (215) 345-0210
Doylestown, PA 18901   Terry A. McNealy, Lib.Dir.

BUCKS COUNTY LAW LIBRARY
Court House   Phone: (215) 348-2911
Doylestown, PA 18901   Katharine P. Lehnig, Law Libn.

GEOGRAPHIC

BUCKS COUNTY PLANNING COMMISSION STAFF LIBRARY
22-28 S. Main St.   Phone: (215) 348-2911
Doylestown, PA 18901   Jeff A. Vey, Info.Spec.

DELAWARE VALLEY COLLEGE OF SCIENCE AND AGRICULTURE - JOSEPH
     KRAUSKOPF MEMORIAL LIBRARY
     Phone: (215) 345-1500
Doylestown, PA 18901   Constance R. Shook, Hd.Libn.

AMERICAN SOCIETY OF ANCIENT INSTRUMENTS - LIBRARY
1205 Blythe Ave.   Phone: (215) 849-3333
Drexel Hill, PA 19026   Frederick Stad, V.P.

EAGLEVILLE HOSPITAL AND REHABILITATION CENTER - HENRY S.
     LOUCHHEIM MEDICAL LIBRARY
Box 45   Phone: (215) 539-6000
Eagleville, PA 19408   Patricia C. Moretti, Dir.Lib.Serv.

WESTINGHOUSE ELECTRIC CORPORATION - LIBRARY 3-S-14
700 Braddock Ave.   Phone: (412) 256-2414
East Pittsburgh, PA 15112   Vincent J. Mirabello, Lib.Ck.

EAST STROUDSBURG STATE COLLEGE - LIBRARY
     Phone: (717) 424-3465
East Stroudsburg, PA 18301   Russell J. Emele, Dir. Of Lib.

ANPA RESEARCH INSTITUTE - LIBRARY
1350 Sullivan Trail
Box 598   Phone: (215) 253-6155
Easton, PA 18042   Erwin Jaffe, Dir. Of Res.

EASTON HOSPITAL - MEDICAL LIBRARY
21st & Lehigh Sts.   Phone: (215) 250-4130
Easton, PA 18042   Mary James, Libn.

LAFAYETTE COLLEGE - AMERICAN FRIENDS OF LAFAYETTE COLLECTION
David Bishop Skillman Library   Phone: (215) 253-6281
Easton, PA 18042   Robert G. Gennett, Spec.Coll.Libn.

LAFAYETTE COLLEGE - KIRBY LIBRARY OF GOVERNMENT AND LAW †
     Phone: (215) 250-5398
Easton, PA 18042   Mercedes Benitez Sharpless, Libn.

NORTHAMPTON COUNTY HISTORICAL AND GENEALOGICAL SOCIETY -
     HISTORICAL MUSEUM AND LIBRARY
101 S. Fourth St.   Phone: (215) 253-1222
Easton, PA 18042   Bruce Drinkhouse, Pres.

NORTHAMPTON COUNTY LAW LIBRARY
7th & Washington Sts.   Phone: (215) 253-4292
Easton, PA 18042   George A. Gollub, Law Libn.

PENNSYLVANIA CANAL SOCIETY - CANAL MUSEUM - RESEARCH LIBRARY
Hugo Moore Park
Box 877   Phone: (215) 258-7155
Easton, PA 18042   Marsha L. Kleedorfer, Cur.

CAMBRIA COUNTY FREE LAW LIBRARY
Courthouse   Phone: (814) 427-5440
Ebensburg, PA 15931   Judy Patterson, Libn.

CAMBRIA COUNTY HISTORICAL SOCIETY - MUSEUM & LIBRARY
521 W. High St.   Phone: (814) 472-6674
Ebensburg, PA 15931   Sara Leishman, Cur.

BISHOP'S MILL HISTORICAL INSTITUTE - SOL FEINSTONE LIBRARY
Ridley Creek State Park   Phone: (215) 353-1777
Edgemont, PA 19028   Marie A. Martin, Exec.Sec.

EDINBORO STATE COLLEGE - BARON-FORNESS LIBRARY
     Phone: (814) 732-2780
Edinboro, PA 16444   Saul Weinstein, Dir.

ENSANIAN PHYSICOCHEMICAL INSTITUTE - INFORMATION CENTER FOR
     GRAVITATION CHEMISTRY
Box 98   Phone: (814) 225-3296
Eldred, PA 16731   Elizabeth A. Ensanian, Chf.Libn.

ELIZABETHTOWN COLLEGE - ZUG MEMORIAL LIBRARY - ARCHIVES
     Phone: (717) 367-1151
Elizabethtown, PA 17022   Anna M. Carper, Dir.

UNITED STATES SPACE EDUCATION ASSOCIATION - USSEA MEDIA
     CENTER
746 Turnpike Rd.   Phone: (717) 367-3265
Elizabethtown, PA 17022   Stephen M. Cobaugh, Intl.Pres.

BETH SHOLOM CONGREGATION - JOSEPH & ELIZABETH SCHWARTZ
     LIBRARY
Foxcroft & Old York Rd.   Phone: (215) 887-1342
Elkins Park, PA 19117   David J. Salaman, Libn.

CONGREGATION ADATH JESHURUN - GOTTLIEB MEMORIAL LIBRARY
York & Ashbourne Rds.   Phone: (215) 635-1337
Elkins Park, PA 19117   Carole G. Ozeroff, Libn.

REFORM CONGREGATION KENESETH ISRAEL - MEYERS LIBRARY
York Rd. & Township Line   Phone: (215) 887-8700
Elkins Park, PA 19117

ELWYN INSTITUTE - PROFESSIONAL LIBRARY
     Phone: (215) 566-8800
Elwyn, PA 19063   Joyce Lentz, Staff Libn.

CAMERON COUNTY HISTORICAL SOCIETY - LITTLE MUSEUM
R.R. 2, Box 54   Phone: (814) 483-3636
Emporium, PA 15834   Mrs. Merle L. Bowser, Pres.

HISTORICAL SOCIETY OF THE COCALICO VALLEY - MUSEUM AND LIBRARY
249 W. Main St.   Phone: (717) 733-1616
Ephrata, PA 17522   Clarence E. Spohn, Cur.

PENNSYLVANIA STATE HISTORICAL & MUSEUM COMMISSION - EPHRATA
     CLOISTER - LIBRARY
632 W. Main St.   Phone: (717) 733-6600
Ephrata, PA 17522   John L. Kraft, Adm.

AMERICAN STERILIZER COMPANY - LIBRARY
2424 W. 23rd St.   Phone: (814) 452-3100
Erie, PA 16512   Janis M. Ruben, Info.Spec.

ANSHE HESED TEMPLE - LIBRARY
10th & Liberty Sts.   Phone: (814) 454-2426
Erie, PA 16502   Rose Tanner, Chm.

CONGREGATION BRITH SHALOM - MORRIS P. RADOV JEWISH CENTER
     LIBRARY *
3207 State St.   Phone: (814) 454-2431
Erie, PA 16508   Rabbi Geoffery Botnick

ERIE COUNTY HISTORICAL SOCIETY
Cashiers House, 417 State St.   Phone: (814) 454-1813
Erie, PA 16501   J.H. Bailey, Pres.

ERIE COUNTY LAW LIBRARY
Court House   Phone: (814) 456-8851
Erie, PA 16501   Sharon Craig, Libn.

FIRST UNITED PRESBYTERIAN CHURCH OF THE COVENANT - BRITTAIN
     LIBRARY
250 W. 7th St.   Phone: (814) 456-4243
Erie, PA 16501   Louise Loesel, Libn.

GENERAL ELECTRIC COMPANY - DIRECT CURRENT MOTOR AND
     GENERATOR DEPARTMENT - LIBRARY
3001 E. Lake Rd.   Phone: (814) 455-5466
Erie, PA 16531

GENERAL ELECTRIC COMPANY - TRANSPORTATION TECHNOLOGY CENTER
     - TECHNICAL INFORMATION CENTER
Bldg. 14, Rm. 123A
2901 E. Lake Rd.   Phone: (814) 455-5466
Erie, PA 16531   Robert H. Berry, Tech.Info.Spec.

HAMMERMILL PAPER COMPANY - CENTRAL RESEARCH - TECHNICAL
     LIBRARY
East Lake Rd.
Box 1440   Phone: (814) 456-8811
Erie, PA 16533

HAMOT MEDICAL CENTER - LIBRARY SERVICES
201 State St.   Phone: (814) 455-6711
Erie, PA 16512   Patricia A. Dalrymple, Dir., Lib.Serv.

ST. MARK'S SEMINARY - LIBRARY
429 E. Grandview Blvd.   Phone: (814) 864-3005
Erie, PA 16504   Rev. Thomas C. Kelley, Rector

ST. VINCENT HEALTH CENTER - HEALTH SCIENCE LIBRARY
232 W. 25th St.   Phone: (814) 459-4000
Erie, PA 16512   Joni M. Alex, Med.Libn.

MINE SAFETY APPLIANCES COMPANY - MSA RESEARCH CORPORATION -
    CALLERY CHEMICAL COMPANY - LIBRARY
                                                        Phone: (412) 538-3510
Evans City, PA 16033   Barbara Boutwell, Libn.

FOOTE MINERAL COMPANY - LIBRARY †
Rte. 100   Phone: (215) 363-6500
Exton, PA 19341

NEWCOMEN SOCIETY IN NORTH AMERICA - THOMAS NEWCOMEN LIB. IN
    STEAM TECHNOLOGY & INDUSTRIAL HISTORY
412 Newcomen Rd.   Phone: (215) 363-6600
Exton, PA 19335   Nancy Arnold, Libn./Cur.

U.S. NATL. PARK SERVICE - FORT NECESSITY NATL. BATTLEFIELD -
    LIBRARY
The National Pike   Phone: (412) 329-5512
Farmington, PA 15437   Robert Warren, Supt.

SHENANGO VALLEY OSTEOPATHIC HOSPITAL - MEDICAL LIBRARY †
2200 Memorial Dr. Extended   Phone: (412) 981-3500
Farrell, PA 16121   Ethelnel Baron, Hospital Libn.

BUDD COMPANY TECHNICAL LIBRARY
375 Commerce Dr.   Phone: (215) 643-2950
Fort Washington, PA 19034   Dale Ann Rodenhaver, Mgr.

HONEYWELL, INC. - PROCESS CONTROLS DIVISION - INFORMATION
    CENTER, M.S. 221
1100 Virginia Dr.   Phone: (215) 641-3982
Fort Washington, PA 19034   Jean L. Hurd, Sr.Info.Sys.Spec.

MC NEIL LABORATORIES - LIBRARY
Camp Hill Rd.
Fort Washington, PA 19034   M.E. Rountree, Hd.Libn.

WILLIAM H. RORER, INC. - RESEARCH LIBRARY
500 Virginia Dr.   Phone: (215) 628-6358
Fort Washington, PA 19034   Catherine Heslin, Libn.

VENANGO COUNTY LAW LIBRARY
Court House
Corner 12th & Liberty Sts.   Phone: (814) 437-6871
Franklin, PA 16323   Julia I. McNamara, Law Libn.

FRANKLIN MINT - INFORMATION RESEARCH SERVICES
                                                        Phone: (215) 459-6374
Franklin Center, PA 19091   Nancy Davis, Dir.

PENNSYLVANIA STATE HISTORICAL & MUSEUM COMMISSION -
    PENNSYLVANIA LUMBER MUSEUM - LIBRARY *
Box K   Phone: (814) 435-2652
Galeton, PA 16922   Dolores M. Buchsen

ADAMS COUNTY HISTORICAL SOCIETY - LIBRARY
Drawer A, Schmucker Hall
Seminary Campus   Phone: (717) 334-4723
Gettysburg, PA 17325   Dr. Charles Glatfelter, Dir.

ADAMS COUNTY LAW LIBRARY †
Court House   Phone: (717) 334-6781
Gettysburg, PA 17325   Mary C. Grim, Libn.

GETTYSBURG COLLEGE - DEPARTMENT OF CHEMISTRY - LIBRARY
Breidenbaugh Hall
Gettysburg, PA 17325   Lillian S. Jackson, Chem. Faculty

GETTYSBURG COLLEGE - MUSSELMAN LIBRARY - SPECIAL COLLECTIONS
                                                        Phone: (717) 334-3131
Gettysburg, PA 17325   James H. Richards, Jr., Libn.

LUTHERAN THEOLOGICAL SEMINARY - A.R. WENTZ LIBRARY
66 W. Confederate Ave.   Phone: (717) 334-6286
Gettysburg, PA 17325   Donald N. Matthews, Libn.

U.S. NATL. PARK SERVICE - GETTYSBURG NATL. MILITARY PARK -
    CYCLORAMA CENTER LIBRARY
                                                        Phone: (717) 334-1124
Gettysburg, PA 17325   Thomas J. Harrison, Chf., Prof.Serv.

DEACONESS COMMUNITY LUTHERAN CHURCH OF AMERICA - LUTHERAN
    DEACONESS COMMUNITY LIBRARY
801 Merion Sq. Rd.   Phone: (215) 642-8838
Gladwyne, PA 19035   Sr. Dorothy Goff, Libn.

CARMEL UNITED PRESBYTERIAN CHURCH - MEMORIAL LIBRARY
100 Edge Hill Rd.   Phone: (215) 887-1074
Glenside, PA 19038   Mrs. James T. Eaton, Libn.

BRETHREN IN CHRIST CHURCH AND MESSIAH COLLEGE - ARCHIVES
Messiah College   Phone: (717) 766-2511
Grantham, PA 17027   Dr. E. Morris Sider, Archv.

CITIZENS LAW LIBRARY
202 Courthouse Sq.   Phone: (412) 834-2191
Greensburg, PA 15601   Peter P. Cherellia, Libn.

WESTMORELAND COUNTY MUSEUM OF ART - ART REFERENCE LIBRARY
221 N. Main St.   Phone: (412) 837-1500
Greensburg, PA 15601   Jeffrey P. Rouse, Registrar

WESTMORELAND HOSPITAL - HEALTH EDUCATION CENTER
532 W. Pittsburgh St.   Phone: (412) 832-4087
Greensburg, PA 15601   Beverly M. McMahon, Libn.

HAMBURG CENTER FOR THE MENTALLY RETARDED - STAFF LIBRARY
                                                        Phone: (215) 562-7511
Hamburg, PA 19526   Marie D. Fortney, Libn.

AMP, INC. - TECHNICAL INFORMATION CENTER
Box 3608, Res. Div.   Phone: (717) 780-8131
Harrisburg, PA 17105   Kay Birula, Mgr.

DAUPHIN COUNTY LAW LIBRARY
Dauphin County Court House   Phone: (717) 234-7001
Harrisburg, PA 17101   Catherine Lanzino, Libn.

HARRISBURG HOSPITAL - HOSPITAL LIBRARY
S. Front St.   Phone: (717) 782-5511
Harrisburg, PA 17101   Cheryl A. Capitani, Dir., Lib./Media Serv.

HARRISBURG STATE HOSPITAL - STAFF LIBRARY †
Cameron & Maclay Sts.
Pouch A   Phone: (717) 787-9555
Harrisburg, PA 17105   Wayne Miller, Libn.

HISTORICAL SOCIETY OF DAUPHIN COUNTY - LIBRARY
219 S. Front St.   Phone: (717) 233-3462
Harrisburg, PA 17104   Ralph D. Huston, Pres.

MC NEES, WALLACE AND NURICK - LIBRARY
100 Pine St.
Box 1166   Phone: (717) 236-9341
Harrisburg, PA 17108   Mary E. Rinesmith, Libn.

PATRIOT NEWS COMPANY - NEWS LIBRARY
312 Market St.
Box 2265   Phone: (717) 255-8402
Harrisburg, PA 17105   Deanna Beeching, Hd.Libn.

PENNSYLVANIA PUBLIC UTILITY COMMISSION - LIBRARY
Box 3265   Phone: (717) 787-4466
Harrisburg, PA 17120   Thais Gardy, Libn.

GEOGRAPHIC

PENNSYLVANIA STATE DEPARTMENT OF COMMUNITY AFFAIRS - LIBRARY
202 S. Office Bldg.
Box 155   Phone: (717) 787-6904
Harrisburg, PA 17120   Nan C. Burg, Libn.

PENNSYLVANIA STATE DEPARTMENT OF ENVIRONMENTAL RESOURCES -
    BUREAU OF TOPOGRAPHIC & GEOLOGIC SURVEY LIB.
916 Executive House Apts.
Second & Chestnut Sts.   Phone: (717) 783-8077
Harrisburg, PA 17120   Sandra Blust, Libn.

PENNSYLVANIA STATE DEPT. OF ENVIRONMENTAL RESOURCES -
    ENVIRONMENTAL PROTECTION TECHNICAL REFERENCE LIBRARY
Fulton Bldg., 13th Fl.
Box 2063   Phone: (717) 787-9646
Harrisburg, PA 17120   Wanda R. Bell, Libn.

PENNSYLVANIA STATE DEPARTMENT OF JUSTICE - OFFICE OF ATTORNEY
    GENERAL LAW LIBRARY
1525 Strawberry Square   Phone: (717) 787-3176
Harrisburg, PA 17120   Catherine T. Stambaugh, Libn.

PENNSYLVANIA STATE DEPARTMENT OF TRANSPORTATION -
    TRANSPORTATION INFORMATION CENTER
903 Transportation & Safety Bldg.   Phone: (717) 787-6527
Harrisburg, PA 17120   Judy Gutshall, Libn.

PENNSYLVANIA STATE HISTORICAL & MUSEUM COMMISSION - DIVISION
    OF ARCHIVES AND MANUSCRIPTS
William Penn Memorial Museum
& Archives Bldg.
Box 1026   Phone: (717) 787-3051
Harrisburg, PA 17120   Harry E. Whipkey, State Archv.

PENNSYLVANIA STATE HISTORICAL & MUSEUM COMMISSION -
    REFERENCE LIBRARY
William Penn Memorial Museum & Archives Bldg.
Box 1026   Phone: (717) 787-2701
Harrisburg, PA 17120   Carol W. Tallman, Lib.Techn.

PENNSYLVANIA STATE - JOINT STATE GOVERNMENT COMMISSION -
    LIBRARY
108 Finance Bldg.   Phone: (717) 787-6803
Harrisburg, PA 17120   Donna Dort, Libn.

PENNSYLVANIA STATE - LEGISLATIVE REFERENCE BUREAU LIBRARY
Box 1127   Phone: (717) 787-4816
Harrisburg, PA 17120   Susan A. Kline, Libn.

PENNSYLVANIA STATE LIBRARY
Forum Bldg.
Walnut St. & Commonwealth Ave.   Phone: (717) 783-5968
Harrisburg, PA 17105   Elliot L. Shelkrot, State Libn.

POLYCLINIC MEDICAL CENTER - MEDICAL STAFF LIBRARY
Third St. & Polyclinic Ave.   Phone: (717) 782-4292
Harrisburg, PA 17105   Suzanne M. Shultz, Libn.

HATBORO BAPTIST CHURCH - LIBRARY
32 N. York Ave.   Phone: (215) 675-8400
Hatboro, PA 19040   Carolyn Zimmerman, Libn.

BIBLICAL THEOLOGICAL SEMINARY - LIBRARY
200 N. Main St.
Box 9   Phone: (215) 368-5000
Hatfield, PA 19440   James C. Pakala, Libn.

HAVERFORD COLLEGE - TREASURE ROOM AND QUAKER COLLECTION
Haverford College Library   Phone: (215) 649-9600
Haverford, PA 19041   Edwin B. Bronner, Cur.

HAVERFORD TOWNSHIP HISTORICAL SOCIETY - LIBRARY
Box 825
Havertown, PA 19083   Margaret E. Johnston, Cur.

GILMAN MUSEUM - LIBRARY
At the Cave   Phone: (215) 838-8767
Hellertown, PA 18055   Naomi P. Gilman, Info.Dir.

ANTIQUE AUTOMOBILE CLUB OF AMERICA - AACA AUTOMOBILE
    REFERENCE COLLECTION
501 W. Governor Rd.   Phone: (717) 534-1910
Hershey, PA 17033   Kim M. Miller, Libn.

HERSHEY FOODS CORPORATION - COMMUNICATIONS CENTER
1025 Reese Ave.   Phone: (717) 534-5106
Hershey, PA 17033   William M. Woodruff, Tech.Comm.Spec.

PENNSYLVANIA STATE UNIVERSITY - COLLEGE OF MEDICINE - GEORGE T.
    HARRELL LIBRARY
Milton S. Hershey Medical Center   Phone: (717) 534-8629
Hershey, PA 17033   Lois J. Lehman, Libn.

BLAIR COUNTY LAW LIBRARY
County Court House   Phone: (814) 695-5541
Hollidaysburg, PA 16648   June C. Ringdal, Law Libn.

SWIGART MUSEUM - LIBRARY
Museum Pk., Box 214   Phone: (814) 643-3000
Huntingdon, PA 16652   William E. Swigart, Jr., Exec.Dir.

HISTORICAL AND GENEALOGICAL SOCIETY OF INDIANA COUNTY -
    LIBRARY AND ARCHIVES
Silas M. Clark House
S. Sixth & Wayne Ave.   Phone: (412) 463-9600
Indiana, PA 15701   Clarence D. Stephenson, Co-Cur.

INDIANA COUNTY LAW LIBRARY
Court House   Phone: (412) 465-2661
Indiana, PA 15701   Bonnie Brady, Law Libn.

INDIANA UNIVERSITY OF PENNSYLVANIA - COGSWELL MUSIC LIBRARY
Cogswell Hall   Phone: (412) 357-2892
Indiana, PA 15705   Calvin Elliker, Music Libn.

INDIANA UNIVERSITY OF PENNSYLVANIA - UNIVERSITY LIBRARY
                                           Phone: (412) 357-2340
Indiana, PA 15705   William E. Lafranchi, Dir. of Libs./Media Rsrcs

CARRIER CORPORATION - ELLIOTT COMPANY - ENGINEERING LIBRARY
N. Fourth St.   Phone: (412) 527-2811
Jeannette, PA 15644   Geri K. Keitzer, Libn.

MONSOUR MEDICAL CENTER - HEALTH SERVICES LIBRARY
70 Lincoln Way, East   Phone: (412) 527-1511
Jeannette, PA 15644   Edith Gross, Med.Libn.

JENKINTOWN LIBRARY - PENNSYLVANIA COLLECTION
York & Vista Rds.   Phone: (215) 884-0593
Jenkintown, PA 19046   Joyce E. Baur, Libn.

OLD YORK ROAD HISTORICAL SOCIETY - ARCHIVES *
Abington Library Society
Jenkintown, PA 19046   James A. Lindemann, Libn.

CARBON COUNTY LAW LIBRARY
Court House   Phone: (717) 325-3111
Jim Thorpe, PA 18229   Benjamin A. Lesniak, Libn.

CONEMAUGH VALLEY MEMORIAL HOSPITAL - MEDICAL STAFF LIBRARY
1086 Franklin St.   Phone: (814) 536-6671
Johnstown, PA 15905   Fred L. Wilson, Jr., Med. Staff Libn.

FIRST LUTHERAN CHURCH - PARISH LIBRARY
415 Vine St.   Phone: (814) 536-7521
Johnstown, PA 15901   Elizabeth J. Will, Libn.

LONGWOOD GARDENS, INC. - LIBRARY
                                           Phone: (215) 388-6741
Kennett Square, PA 19348   Enola Jane N. Teeter, Libn.

TAYLOR (Bayard) MEMORIAL LIBRARY
216 E. State St.   Phone: (215) 444-2702
Kennett Square, PA 19348   Joseph A. Lordi, Dir.

UNIVERSITY OF PENNSYLVANIA - NEW BOLTON CENTER - JEAN AUSTIN
    DU PONT LIBRARY
382 W. Street Rd.   Phone: (215) 444-5800
Kennett Square, PA 19348   Alice K. Holton, Lib.Serv.Asst.

PENNSYLVANIA RESOURCES AND INFORMATION CENTER FOR SPECIAL
  EDUCATION
1013 W. 9th Ave.   Phone: (215) 265-7321
King of Prussia, PA 19406   Kathleen S. Ewell, Dir.

PENNWALT CORPORATION - TECHNICAL DIVISION LIBRARY
900 First Ave.   Phone: (215) 265-3200
King Of Prussia, PA 19406   Kathryn M. Donovan, Mgr.

RESEARCH & INFORMATION SERVICES FOR EDUCATION - MONTGOMERY
  COUNTY INTERMEDIATE UNIT LIBRARY
198 Allendale Rd.
King Of Prussia, PA 19406

NESBITT MEMORIAL HOSPITAL - LIBRARY
562 Wyoming Ave.   Phone: (717) 288-1411
Kingston, PA 18704   Katherine L. McCrea, Libn.

KUTZTOWN STATE COLLEGE - ROHRBACH LIBRARY
                                        Phone: (215) 683-3511
Kutztown, PA 19530   John K. Amrhein, College Libn.

PQ CORPORATION - RESEARCH LIBRARY
Box 258   Phone: (215) 825-5000
Lafayette Hill, PA 19444   Geraldine R. James, Libn.

ARMSTRONG WORLD INDUSTRIES, INC. - MANAGEMENT REFERENCE
  SERVICES
Liberty & Charlotte Sts.
Box 3001   Phone: (717) 397-0611
Lancaster, PA 17604   Margaret B. Boyer, Libn.

ARMSTRONG WORLD INDUSTRIES, INC. - TECHNICAL CENTER -
  TECHNICAL INFORMATION SERVICES
2500 Columbia Ave.   Phone: (717) 397-0611
Lancaster, PA 17604   Dr. Joseph M. Judge, Mgr.

EVANGELICAL AND REFORMED HISTORICAL SOCIETY - LANCASTER
  CENTRAL ARCHIVES AND LIBRARY
Lancaster Theological Seminary
555 W. James St.   Phone: (717) 393-0654
Lancaster, PA 17603   Florence M. Bricker, Dir. Of Archv.

FRANKLIN AND MARSHALL COLLEGE - BIOLOGY LIBRARY
                                        Phone: (717) 291-4118
Lancaster, PA 17604

FRANKLIN AND MARSHALL COLLEGE - CHEMISTRY DEPARTMENT -
  WILLIAM SHAND, JR. MEMORIAL LIBRARY
                                        Phone: (717) 291-4123
Lancaster, PA 17604   Dr. Claude Yoder, Chm.

FRANKLIN AND MARSHALL COLLEGE - DEPARTMENT OF PHYSICS - LIBRARY
                                        Phone: (717) 291-4136
Lancaster, PA 17604   Dr. Sutter, Chm.

FRANKLIN AND MARSHALL COLLEGE - FACKENTHAL LIBRARY - SPECIAL
  COLLECTIONS
                                        Phone: (717) 291-4216
Lancaster, PA 17604   Peter C. Haskell, Dir.

FRANKLIN AND MARSHALL COLLEGE - PSYCHOLOGY LIBRARY
                                        Phone: (717) 291-4202
Lancaster, PA 17604

JAMES BUCHANAN FOUNDATION FOR THE PRESERVATION OF WHEATLAND
  - LIBRARY
1120 Marietta Ave.   Phone: (717) 392-8721
Lancaster, PA 17603   Sally S. Cahalan, Dir.

LANCASTER BIBLE COLLEGE - STOLL MEMORIAL LIBRARY
901 Eden Rd.   Phone: (717) 569-7071
Lancaster, PA 17601   Mary L. Walters, Hd.Libn. & Asst.Prof.

LANCASTER COUNTY HISTORICAL SOCIETY - LIBRARY
Willson Bldg.
230 N. President Ave.   Phone: (717) 392-4633
Lancaster, PA 17603   Salinda M. Matt, Libn.

LANCASTER GENERAL HOSPITAL - MUELLER HEALTH SCIENCES LIBRARY
555 N. Duke St.   Phone: (717) 299-5511
Lancaster, PA 17604   Virginia H. Engle, Libn.

LANCASTER LAW LIBRARY
50 N. Duke St.
Box 3480   Phone: (717) 299-8090
Lancaster, PA 17604   Christine Harvan, Libn.

LANCASTER MENNONITE HISTORICAL SOCIETY - LIBRARY
2215 Millstream Rd.   Phone: (717) 393-9745
Lancaster, PA 17602   Carolyn C. Wenger, Dir.

LANCASTER NEWSPAPERS - LIBRARY
8 W. King St.   Phone: (717) 291-8773
Lancaster, PA 17603   Helen L. Everts, Libn.

LANCASTER THEOLOGICAL SEMINARY OF THE UNITED CHURCH OF CHRIST
  - PHILIP SCHAFF LIBRARY
555 W. James St.   Phone: (717) 393-0654
Lancaster, PA 17603   Ernest Duerrehuhl, Act.Libn.

PENNSYLVANIA FARM MUSEUM OF LANDIS VALLEY - LIBRARY
2451 Kissel Hill Rd.   Phone: (717) 569-0401
Lancaster, PA 17601   Robert L. Sieber, Dir.

RCA CORPORATION - LIBRARY
New Holland Pike   Phone: (717) 397-7661
Lancaster, PA 17604   Mary K. Noll, Libn.

ST. JOSEPH HOSPITAL - HOSPITAL LIBRARY
250 College Ave.
Box 3509   Phone: (717) 291-8119
Lancaster, PA 17604   Eileen B. Doudna, Libn.

PHILADELPHIA COLLEGE OF BIBLE - SCOFIELD-HILL MEMORIAL LIBRARY
Langhorne Manor   Phone: (215) 752-5800
Langhorne, PA 19047   Julius C. Bosco, Dir.

CALVARY BAPTIST THEOLOGICAL SEMINARY - LIBRARY
Valley Forge Rd. & Sumneytown Pike   Phone: (215) 368-7538
Lansdale, PA 19446   James F. Stitzinger, Libn.

MENNONITE HISTORICAL LIBRARY OF EASTERN PENNSYLVANIA
1000 Forty Foot Rd.   Phone: (215) 362-2675
Lansdale, PA 19446   Joseph S. Miller, Adm.

LATROBE AREA HOSPITAL - MEDICAL & NURSING LIBRARIES
W. Second Ave.   Phone: (412) 537-1275
Latrobe, PA 15650   Marsha E. Gelman, Med.Libn.

ST. VINCENT COLLEGE AND ARCHABBEY - LIBRARY
                                        Phone: (412) 539-9761
Latrobe, PA 15650   Rev. Fintan R. Shoniker, O.S.B., Dir.

ST. VINCENT COLLEGE AND ARCHABBEY - MUSIC LIBRARY
Latrobe, PA 15650

ST. VINCENT COLLEGE AND ARCHABBEY - PHYSICS DEPARTMENTAL
  LIBRARY
Latrobe, PA 15650

LAURELTON CENTER - LIBRARY
                                        Phone: (717) 922-3311
Laurelton, PA 17835   Jane G. Slack, Libn.

GOOD SAMARITAN HOSPITAL - KROHN MEMORIAL LIBRARY
4th & Walnut Sts.   Phone: (717) 272-7611
Lebanon, PA 17042   Susan Foltz, Libn.

LEBANON COUNTY HISTORICAL SOCIETY - LIBRARY
924 Cumberland St.   Phone: (717) 272-1473
Lebanon, PA 17042

U.S. VETERANS ADMINISTRATION (PA-Lebanon) - MEDICAL CENTER
  LIBRARY
State Drive   Phone: (717) 272-6621
Lebanon, PA 17042   Norma W. Haskins, Chf., Lib.Serv.

GEOGRAPHIC

GEOGRAPHIC

LEHIGH-NORTHAMPTON COUNTIES JOINT PLANNING COMMISSION - LIBRARY
Allentown-Bethlehem-Easton Airport
Government Bldg. Phone: (215) 264-4544
Lehigh Valley, PA 18103 Penn Clissold, Libn.

LITERATURE SERVICE ASSOCIATES
Rd. 3
Box 352 B
Lehighton, PA 18235

PENNSYLVANIA DUTCH FOLK CULTURE SOCIETY, INC. - BAVER MEMORIAL LIBRARY
Phone: (215) 562-4803
Lenhartsville, PA 19534 Florence Baver, Mgr.

BUCKNELL UNIVERSITY - ARCHIVES
Phone: (717) 524-1493
Lewisburg, PA 17837 Dr. Robert R. Gross, Archv.

BUCKNELL UNIVERSITY - ELLEN CLARKE BERTRAND LIBRARY
Phone: (717) 524-3056
Lewisburg, PA 17837 Mary Jane Stoneburg, Hd., Per.Dept.

MIFFLIN COUNTY HISTORICAL SOCIETY - LIBRARY AND MUSEUM *
The McCoy House
17 N. Main St.
Lewistown, PA 17044 Helen McNitt, Libn.

MIFFLIN COUNTY LAW LIBRARY
Box 746 Phone: (717) 248-7332
Lewistown, PA 17044

CONOCO COAL DEVELOPMENT COMPANY - TECHNICAL LIBRARY
Phone: (412) 831-6688
Library, PA 15129 Janice M. Metzger, Libn.

FORT LIGONIER MEMORIAL FOUNDATION - HENRY BOUQUET ROOM
S. Market St. Phone: (412) 238-9701
Ligonier, PA 15658 J. Martin West, Dir./Cur.

LINCOLN UNIVERSITY - LANGSTON HUGHES MEMORIAL LIBRARY - SPECIAL COLLECTIONS
Phone: (215) 932-8300
Lincoln University, PA 19352 Sophy H. Cornwell, Spec.Coll.Libn.

UNIVERSITY OF PITTSBURGH - PYMATUNING LABORATORY OF ECOLOGY - LIBRARY
Phone: (814) 683-5813
Linesville, PA 16424 Dr. Richard T. Hartman, Dir.

PENNSYLVANIA STATE DEPARTMENT OF HEALTH - BUREAU OF LABORATORIES LIBRARY
Pickering Way & Welsh Pool Rd. Phone: (215) 436-3464
Lionville, PA 19353 Leonard Sideman, Libn.

AMERICAN COLOR AND CHEMICAL CORPORATION, INC. - LIBRARY
Mt. Vernon St. Phone: (717) 748-6747
Lock Haven, PA 17745

LOCK HAVEN STATE COLLEGE - GEORGE B. STEVENSON LIBRARY
Phone: (717) 893-2309
Lock Haven, PA 17745 Robert S. Bravard, Dir.

FULTON COUNTY HISTORICAL SOCIETY - LIBRARY
Box 115
McConnellsburg, PA 17233

OHIO VALLEY GENERAL HOSPITAL - PROFESSIONAL LIBRARY
Heckel Rd. Phone: (412) 777-6159
McKee's Rock, PA 15136 Mary Evans, Libn.

MC KEESPORT HOSPITAL - HEALTH SERVICES LIBRARY
1500 Fifth Ave. Phone: (412) 664-2363
McKeesport, PA 15132 Daphne Lynn, Dir.

WESTINGHOUSE ELECTRIC CORPORATION - NUCLEAR ENERGY SYSTEMS - ADVANCED REACTORS DIVISION - LIBRARY
Waltz Mill Site
Box 158 Phone: (412) 722-5301
Madison, PA 15663 Ann Chernega, Lib.Mgr.

AMERICAN INSTITUTE FOR PROPERTY & LIABILITY UNDERWRITERS - INSURANCE INSTITUTE OF AMERICA - LIBRARY
Providence & Sugartown Rds. Phone: (215) 644-2100
Malvern, PA 19355 Kim Holston, Libn./Sec.

MANSFIELD STATE COLLEGE - AUDIOVISUAL CENTER
North Hall, Rm. 23 Phone: (717) 662-4138
Mansfield, PA 16933 Ronald E. Remy, AV Dir.

MANSFIELD STATE COLLEGE - BUTLER MUSIC LIBRARY
Phone: (717) 662-4365
Mansfield, PA 16933 Pauline Borodkin, Hd. Music Libn.

AIR PRODUCTS AND CHEMICALS, INC. - HOUDRY LABORATORIES - INFORMATION SERVICES
Box 427 Phone: (215) 485-1135
Marcus Hook, PA 19061 Mary E. Bongiorno, Sr.Info.Spec.

SUN COMPANY - LIBRARY & INFORMATION SERVICE
Box 1135 Phone: (215) 485-1121
Marcus Hook, PA 19061 Norman D. Morphet, Sect.Chf.

ALLEGHENY COLLEGE - WALTER M. SMALL GEOLOGY LIBRARY
Alden Hall Phone: (814) 724-2350
Meadville, PA 16335 Margaret L. Moser, Libn.

CRAWFORD COUNTY BAR ASSOCIATION - LAW LIBRARY
Court House, Rm. 212 Phone: (814) 336-1151
Meadville, PA 16335 William K. Reid, Libn.

CRAWFORD COUNTY HISTORICAL SOCIETY - LIBRARY AND ARCHIVES †
848 N. Main St. Phone: (814) 724-6080
Meadville, PA 16335 Robert Ilisevich, Libn.

MEADVILLE CITY HOSPITAL - HUMMER LIBRARY
751 Liberty St. Phone: (814) 336-3121
Meadville, PA 16335 Barbara Ewing, Libn.

DELAWARE COUNTY LAW LIBRARY
Courthouse Phone: (215) 891-2380
Media, PA 19063 Charlotte H. Hewlings, Libn.

DELAWARE COUNTY PLANNING COMMISSION - LIBRARY AND DATA SECTION
3rd & Orange Sts. Phone: (215) 891-2381
Media, PA 19063 Jane Taggart Quinn, Libn.

MERCER COUNTY HISTORICAL SOCIETY - LIBRARY AND ARCHIVES
119 S. Pitt St. Phone: (412) 662-3490
Mercer, PA 16137 David M. Miller, Pres.

MERCER COUNTY LAW LIBRARY
Court House
Mercer, PA 16137 Olive L. Griffin, Libn.

AKIBA HEBREW ACADEMY - JOSEPH N. FIRST LIBRARY
N. Highland Ave. & Old Lancaster Rd.
Merion, PA 19066

BUTEN MUSEUM OF WEDGWOOD - LIBRARY
246 N. Bowman Ave. Phone: (215) 664-6601
Merion, PA 19066 David Buten, Dir.

TEMPLE ADATH ISRAEL - RUBEN LIBRARY †
Old Lancaster Rd. & Highland Ave. Phone: (215) 664-3241
Merion, PA 19066 Phyllis Mirsky, Libn.

SNYDER COUNTY HISTORICAL SOCIETY, INC. - LIBRARY
30 E. Market St.
Box 276 Phone: (717) 837-6191
Middleburg, PA 17842 Gladys Corman, Ck.

GPU NUCLEAR - TMI TECHNICAL LIBRARY
Three Mile Island Nuclear Generating Sta.
Box 480 Phone: (717) 948-8105
Middletown, PA 17057 Joan L. Parrick, Tech.Libn.

MILLERSVILLE STATE COLLEGE - HELEN A. GANSER LIBRARY
                                    Phone: (717) 872-3607
Millersville, PA 17551   John S. Maine, Lib.Dir.

ST. JOE MINERALS CORPORATION - RESEARCH DEPARTMENT
     INFORMATION CENTER
Box A   Phone: (412) 774-1020
Monaca, PA 15061   Sallie Smith, Tech.Libn.

BITUMINOUS COAL RESEARCH, INC. - LIBRARY
350 Hochberg Rd.
Box 278   Phone: (412) 327-1600
Monroeville, PA 15146   Mary Ann Sakoian, Libn.

FORBES HEALTH SYSTEM - EAST SUBURBAN HEALTH CENTER LIBRARY
2570 Haymaker Rd.   Phone: (412) 273-2422
Monroeville, PA 15146   Margaret C. Lietman, Dir. of Libs.

KOPPERS COMPANY, INC. - TECHNICAL INFORMATION GROUP
440 College Park Dr.   Phone: (412) 327-3000
Monroeville, PA 15146   Eugene P. Meckly, Libn.

UNITED STATES STEEL CORPORATION - RESEARCH LABORATORY -
     TECHNICAL INFORMATION CENTER
MS 88   Phone: (412) 372-1212
Monroeville, PA 15146   Angela R. Pollis, Staff Supv.

SUSQUEHANNA COUNTY HISTORICAL SOCIETY AND FREE LIBRARY
     ASSOCIATION
Monument Square   Phone: (717) 278-1881
Montrose, PA 18801   Marion F. Baker, Libn.

MUNCY HISTORICAL SOCIETY AND MUSEUM OF HISTORY - HISTORICAL
     LIBRARY
40 N. Main St.   Phone: (717) 546-3431
Muncy, PA 17756   Thomas J. Clegg, Pres.

EVANGELICAL SCHOOL OF THEOLOGY - ROSTAD LIBRARY
121 S. College St.   Phone: (717) 866-5775
Myerstown, PA 17067   Terry M. Heisey, Libn.

MORAVIAN HISTORICAL SOCIETY - WHITEFIELD HOUSE
214 E. Center St.
Nazareth, PA 18064

FIRST CHRISTIAN CHURCH - LIBRARY
On The Diamond
New Castle, PA 16101   Mrs. H.E. McEwen, Libn.

HIGHLAND UNITED PRESBYTERIAN CHURCH - LIBRARY
708 Highland Ave.   Phone: (412) 654-7391
New Castle, PA 16101   Elizabeth Milholland, Libn.

JAMESON MEMORIAL HOSPITAL - SCHOOL OF NURSING LIBRARY
W. Garfield Ave.   Phone: (412) 658-9001
New Castle, PA 16105   Joan T. Whitman, Libn.

LYON'S BUSINESS COLLEGE - LIBRARY
316 Rhodes Pl.   Phone: (412) 658-9066
New Castle, PA 16103   Grace Lyon, Hd.Libn.

NEW CASTLE PUBLIC LIBRARY - PENNSYLVANIA HISTORY ROOM
106 E. North St.   Phone: (412) 658-6659
New Castle, PA 16101   Helen M. Roux, Dir.

NORTHMINSTER UNITED PRESBYTERIAN CHURCH - LIBRARY
2434 Wilmington Rd.   Phone: (412) 658-9051
New Castle, PA 16105   Helen Sloat, Church Libn.

SPERRY CORPORATION - SPERRY NEW HOLLAND - ENGINEERING LIBRARY
500 Diller Ave.   Phone: (717) 354-1358
New Holland, PA 17557   Tammy Mast, Libn.

ATLANTIC-RICHFIELD COMPANY - ARCO CHEMICAL COMPANY -
     RESEARCH & ENGINEERING TECHNICAL INFORMATION CENTER
3801 West Chester Pike   Phone: (215) 586-4700
Newton Square, PA 19073   Anthony J. Costanzo, Tech.Info.Supv.

NEWTOWN HISTORIC ASSOCIATION, INC. - LIBRARY
Centre Ave. & Court St.   Phone: (215) 968-4004
Newtown, PA 18940   Claire Hennessy, Dir.

DELTIOLOGISTS OF AMERICA - LIBRARY
3709 Gradyville Rd.   Phone: (215) 353-1689
Newtown Square, PA 19073   James L. Lowe, Dir.

MONTGOMERY COUNTY LAW LIBRARY
Court House   Phone: (215) 278-3806
Norristown, PA 19404   Arthur S. Zanan, Law Libn.

MONTGOMERY COUNTY PLANNING COMMISSION - RESEARCH LIBRARY
Court House   Phone: (215) 278-3726
Norristown, PA 19404   Florence Bailey

MONTGOMERY HOSPITAL - MEDICAL LIBRARY
Powell & Fornance St.   Phone: (215) 631-3232
Norristown, PA 19401   Alberta T. O'Brien, Med.Libn.

PENNSYLVANIA STATE DEPARTMENT OF PUBLIC WELFARE - NORRISTOWN
     STATE HOSPITAL - PROFESSIONAL/STAFF SERVICES LIBRARY
c/o Professional Library, Bldg. 11   Phone: (215) 631-2948
Norristown, PA 19401   Raymond Frank Roedell, Jr., Dir.

LEEDS AND NORTHRUP COMPANY - TECHNICAL CENTER LIBRARY
Dickerson Rd.   Phone: (215) 643-2000
North Wales, PA 19454   Adina Zupanick, Mgr., Lib.Serv.

COLUMBIA COUNTY HISTORICAL SOCIETY - LIBRARY
Box 197   Phone: (717) 683-6011
Orangeville, PA 17859   Edna Lynn, Exec.Sec.

PAOLI MEMORIAL HOSPITAL - ROBERT M. WHITE MEMORIAL LIBRARY
Lancaster Pike   Phone: (215) 648-1218
Paoli, PA 19301   Doris J. Rickards, Med.Libn.

MID-VALLEY HOSPITAL ASSOCIATION - PHYSICIAN'S MEDICAL LIBRARY
1400 Main St.   Phone: (717) 489-7546
Peckville, PA 18452   Arline Ham, Med.Rec.Adm.

SCHWENKFELDER LIBRARY
                                    Phone: (215) 679-7175
Pennsburg, PA 18073   Peter C. Erb, Assoc.Dir.

SOCIETY OF COSTA RICA COLLECTORS (SOCORICO) - EARL FOSSOM
     MEMORIAL LIBRARY
1120 N. 7th St.
Perkasie, PA 18944   M.F. Mosser, Libn.

ACADEMY OF NATURAL SCIENCES - LIBRARY
19th & The Parkway   Phone: (215) 299-1040
Philadelphia, PA 19103   Sylva Baker, Hd.Libn.

ADLER BARISH DANIELS LEVIN & CRESKOFF - LIBRARY
Rohm & Haas Bldg., 2nd Fl.   Phone: (215) 923-8900
Philadelphia, PA 19106   Susan J. Falken, Libn.

AMERICAN ASSOCIATION OF MEDICO-LEGAL CONSULTANTS - LIBRARY
Park Towne Pl., N-105
2200 Benjamin Franklin Pkwy.   Phone: (215) 561-2121
Philadelphia, PA 19130   Arlene Goldman, Libn.

AMERICAN HOME PRODUCTS CORPORATION - WYETH LABORATORIES
     DIVISION LIBRARY
Box 8299   Phone: (215) 688-4400
Philadelphia, PA 19101   John E. James, Supv., Lib.Serv.

AMERICAN LAW INSTITUTE - LIBRARY
4025 Chestnut St.   Phone: (215) 243-1658
Philadelphia, PA 19104   Loretta U. McConnell, Libn.

AMERICAN PHILOSOPHICAL SOCIETY - LIBRARY
105 S. Fifth St.   Phone: (215) 627-0706
Philadelphia, PA 19106   Dr. Edward C. Carter, II, Libn.

AMERICAN SOCIETY FOR TESTING AND MATERIALS - INFORMATION
     CENTER
1916 Race St.   Phone: (215) 299-5474
Philadelphia, PA 19103   Dolores G. Collyer, Adm.

GEOGRAPHIC

GEOGRAPHIC

AMERICAN SWEDISH HISTORICAL MUSEUM - NORD LIBRARY
1900 Pattison Ave. Phone: (215) 389-1776
Philadelphia, PA 19145 Karin Persson, Adm.Asst.

ANTIOCH UNIVERSITY - LEARNING RESOURCE CENTER
401 N. Broad Phone: (215) 629-1370
Philadelphia, PA 19108 William B. Saunders, Libn./External Coord.

ARCHDIOCESE OF PHILADELPHIA - CATHOLIC INFORMATION CENTER
936 Market St. Phone: (215) 587-3520
Philadelphia, PA 19107 Rev.Msgr. Raymond Teller, Dir.

AREA COUNCIL FOR ECONOMIC EDUCATION (ACEE) - LIBRARY †
254 Suburban Sta. Bldg.
1617 John F. Kennedy Blvd. Phone: (215) 564-3504
Philadelphia, PA 19103

ATHENAEUM OF PHILADELPHIA
219 S. Sixth St. Phone: (215) 925-2688
Philadelphia, PA 19106 Dr. Roger W. Moss, Jr., Exec.Dir.

BALCH INSTITUTE FOR ETHNIC STUDIES - LIBRARY
18 S. 7th St.
Philadelphia, PA 19106 Roy H. Tryon, Lib.Dir.

BALLARD, SPAHR, ANDREWS AND INGERSOLL - LAW LIBRARY †
30 S. 17th St., 20th Fl. Phone: (215) 564-1800
Philadelphia, PA 19103 Shari Y. Liu, Libn.

BELLET (Samuel) LIBRARY OF LAW, MEDICINE AND BEHAVIORAL SCIENCE
201E Piersol Bldg. H.U.P. Phone: (215) 662-2848
Philadelphia, PA 19104 Victoria K. Evalds, Libn.

BETH DAVID REFORM CONGREGATION - JEWEL K. MARKOWITZ LIBRARY
5220 Wynnefield Ave. Phone: (215) 473-8438
Philadelphia, PA 19131 Mrs. Jerome Apfel, Chm.

BIOSCIENCES INFORMATION SERVICE - BIOLOGICAL ABSTRACTS - LIBRARY
2100 Arch St. Phone: (215) 568-4016
Philadelphia, PA 19103 Janet M. Sherr, Group Ldr.

BLUE CROSS OF GREATER PHILADELPHIA - E.A. VAN STEENWYK MEMORIAL LIBRARY
1333 Chestnut St.
16th Fl., Widener Bldg. Phone: (215) 448-5400
Philadelphia, PA 19107 Judith Delbaum, Libn.

B'NAI B'RITH CAREER & COUNSELING SERVICES - LIBRARY
1405 Locust St. Phone: (215) 545-1455
Philadelphia, PA 19102 Julius S. Romanoff, Exec.Dir.

BOCKUS RESEARCH INSTITUTE - LIBRARY
19th & Lombard Sts. Phone: (215) 893-2372
Philadelphia, PA 19146 Marta Lee Bussard, Adm.

BOEING VERTOL COMPANY - LYDIA RANKIN TECHNICAL LIBRARY
Box 16858 Phone: (215) 522-2536
Philadelphia, PA 19142 Beth Evanson, Libn.

CATALYTIC, INC. - LIBRARY
Centre Square West
1500 Market St. Phone: (215) 864-8559
Philadelphia, PA 19102 Mary J. Kober, Dir.

CHESTNUT HILL HOSPITAL - SCHOOL OF NURSING LIBRARY
8835 Germantown Ave.
Philadelphia, PA 19118 Maude H. Meyerend, Libn.

CHILDREN'S HOSPITAL OF PHILADELPHIA - MEDICAL LIBRARY
34th & Civic Center Blvd. Phone: (215) 596-9673
Philadelphia, PA 19104 Mrs. Swaran Lata Chopra, Dir., Med.Lib.

CLIVEDEN - LIBRARY
6401 Germantown Ave. Phone: (215) 848-1777
Philadelphia, PA 19144 Raymond V. Shepherd, Jr., Adm.

COLLEGE OF PHYSICIANS OF PHILADELPHIA - LIBRARY AND MEDICAL DOCUMENTATION SERVICE
19 S. 22nd St. Phone: (215) 561-6050
Philadelphia, PA 19103 Anthony Aguirre, Lib.Dir.

COLONIAL PENN GROUP, INC. - INFORMATION RESEARCH CENTER
5 Penn Center Plaza Phone: (215) 988-7414
Philadelphia, PA 19181 Orest Borys, Sr.Info.Spec.

COMMUNITY COLLEGE OF PHILADELPHIA - EDUCATION RESOURCES CENTER
34 S. 11th St. Phone: (215) 569-3680
Philadelphia, PA 19107 Sidney August, Dir.

CONGREGATION RODEPH SHALOM - LIBRARY
1338 Mount Vernon St. Phone: (215) 627-6747
Philadelphia, PA 19123 Mildred Kurland, Libn.

CURTIS INSTITUTE OF MUSIC - LIBRARY
Rittenhouse Sq.
1726 Locust St. Phone: (215) 893-5265
Philadelphia, PA 19103 Elizabeth Walker, Libn.

CUSHMAN (Charlotte) CLUB - THEATRE RESEARCH LIBRARY
239 S. Camac St. Phone: (215) 735-4676
Philadelphia, PA 19107

DAY & ZIMMERMANN, INC. - LIBRARY
1818 Market St., 21st Fl. Phone: (215) 299-8222
Philadelphia, PA 19103 Jenny Kuan, Libn.

DECHERT, PRICE AND RHOADS - LIBRARY
3400 Centre Sq. W.
1500 Market St. Phone: (215) 972-3453
Philadelphia, PA 19102 Susan Jane Gibbons, Libn.

DELOITTE HASKINS & SELLS - LIBRARY
2500 Three Girard Plaza Phone: (215) 569-3500
Philadelphia, PA 19102 Lenka Berlin, Libn.

DREXEL UNIVERSITY LIBRARIES - GENERAL LIBRARY
32nd & Chestnut Sts. Phone: (215) 895-2755
Philadelphia, PA 19104 Michael Halperin, Hd., Gen.Lib.

DREXEL UNIVERSITY LIBRARIES - SCIENCE AND TECHNOLOGY LIBRARY
32nd & Chestnut Sts. Phone: (215) 895-2765
Philadelphia, PA 19104 William Page, Hd.Sci. & Tech.Lib.

DRINKER, BIDDLE & REATH - LAW LIBRARY
1100 Philadelphia National Bank Bldg.
Broad & Chestnut Sts. Phone: (215) 988-2951
Philadelphia, PA 19107 Nancy H. Rosenberg, Hd., Law Lib.

DROPSIE UNIVERSITY - LIBRARY
Broad & York Sts. Phone: (215) 229-1566
Philadelphia, PA 19132 Prof. Hayim Y. Sheynin, Lib.Dir.

DU PONT DE NEMOURS (E.I.) & COMPANY, INC. - MARSHALL LABORATORY LIBRARY
3500 Grays Ferry Ave.
Box 3886 Phone: (215) 339-6314
Philadelphia, PA 19146 Virginia L. Maier, Libn.

DUANE, MORRIS & HECKSCHER - LAW LIBRARY
1500 One Franklin Plaza Phone: (215) 854-6248
Philadelphia, PA 19102 Teresa N. Clarkson, Libn.

EASTERN BAPTIST THEOLOGICAL SEMINARY - LIBRARY
Lancaster Ave. & City Line Phone: (215) 896-5000
Philadelphia, PA 19151 Rev. R. David Koch, Libn.

EINSTEIN (Albert) MEDICAL CENTER - DAROFF DIVISION - MEDICAL LIBRARY
5th & Reed Sts. Phone: (215) 465-1100
Philadelphia, PA 19147 Rena E. Hawes, Lib.Dir.

EINSTEIN (Albert) MEDICAL CENTER - NORTHERN DIVISION - LURIA MEDICAL LIBRARY †
York & Tabor Roads Phone: (215) 329-0700
Philadelphia, PA 19141 Marion H. Silverman, Dir.

EINSTEIN (Albert) MEDICAL CENTER - SCHOOL OF NURSING LIBRARY
11th & Tabor Rds.   Phone: (215) 329-0700
Philadelphia, PA 19141   Mary M. McCrory, Libn.

ENVIRONMENTAL PROTECTION AGENCY - REGION III LIBRARY
Curtis Bldg., 6th & Walnut Sts.   Phone: (215) 597-0580
Philadelphia, PA 19106   Diane M. McCreary, Libn.

EPISCOPAL HOSPITAL - MEDICAL LIBRARY
Front St. & Lehigh Ave.   Phone: (215) 427-7487
Philadelphia, PA 19125   Margaret Flanagan, Libn.

FARM JOURNAL, INC. - MARKETING RESEARCH LIBRARY
230 W. Washington Sq.   Phone: (215) 574-1360
Philadelphia, PA 19105   Christina Rega, Libn.

FARNHAM (Frank C.) COMPANY, INC. - LIBRARY
1930 Chestnut St., 8th Fl.   Phone: (215) 567-1500
Philadelphia, PA 19103   Katherine C. Jordan, Sci.Ed.

FEDERAL RESERVE BANK OF PHILADELPHIA - LIBRARY
Box 66   Phone: (215) 574-6540
Philadelphia, PA 19105   Aileen C. Boer, Libn.

FELLOWSHIP COMMISSION - LIBRARY †
260 S. 17th St.
Philadelphia, PA 19102

FIDELITY MUTUAL LIFE INSURANCE COMPANY - LIBRARY ARCHIVES
Fidelity Mutual Life Bldg.   Phone: (215) 977-8093
Philadelphia, PA 19101   Renee Walker, Libn.

FIRST PENNSYLVANIA BANK, N.A. - MARKETING INFORMATION CENTER †
Center Sq. Tower, 40th Fl.
16th & Market Sts.   Phone: (215) 786-8354
Philadelphia, PA 19101   Vernice W. Berry, Mgr.

FOREIGN POLICY RESEARCH INSTITUTE - LIBRARY
3508 Market St., Suite 350   Phone: (215) 382-2054
Philadelphia, PA 19104   Alan H. Luxenberg, Res.Libn.

FRANKFORD HOSPITAL - HOSPITAL LIBRARIES
Frankford Ave. & Wakeling St.   Phone: (215) 831-2182
Philadelphia, PA 19124   Dianne E. Rose, Med.Libn.

FRANKFORD HOSPITAL - SCHOOL OF NURSING - STUDENT LIBRARY
4918 Penn St.   Phone: (215) 831-2372
Philadelphia, PA 19124   Dianne Rose, Med.Libn.

FRANKLIN INSTITUTE - LIBRARY
20th & Benjamin Franklin Pkwy.   Phone: (215) 448-1224
Philadelphia, PA 19103   Emerson W. Hilker, Dir.

FRANKLIN RESEARCH CENTER - SCIENCE INFORMATION SERVICES *
20th & Benjamin Franklin Pkwy.   Phone: (215) 448-1227
Philadelphia, PA 19103   Alec Peters, Dept.Dir.

FREE LIBRARY OF PHILADELPHIA - ART DEPARTMENT
Logan Sq.   Phone: (215) 686-5403
Philadelphia, PA 19103   Miriam L. Lesley, Hd.

FREE LIBRARY OF PHILADELPHIA - BUSINESS, SCIENCE AND INDUSTRY
  DEPARTMENT
Logan Sq.   Phone: (215) 686-5394
Philadelphia, PA 19103   Alex S. Weinbaum, Hd.

FREE LIBRARY OF PHILADELPHIA - EDUCATION, PHILOSOPHY, RELIGION
  DEPARTMENT
Logan Sq.   Phone: (215) 686-5392
Philadelphia, PA 19103   Esther J. Maurer, Hd.

FREE LIBRARY OF PHILADELPHIA - EDWIN A. FLEISHER COLLECTION OF
  ORCHESTRAL MUSIC
Logan Sq.   Phone: (215) 686-5313
Philadelphia, PA 19103   Sam Dennison, Cur.

FREE LIBRARY OF PHILADELPHIA - FILMS DEPARTMENT
Logan Sq.   Phone: (215) 686-5367
Philadelphia, PA 19103   Steven J. Mayover, Lib. Film Oper.Supv.

FREE LIBRARY OF PHILADELPHIA - GOVERNMENT PUBLICATIONS
  DEPARTMENT
Logan Sq.   Phone: (215) 686-5330
Philadelphia, PA 19103   Clifford P. Crowers, Hd.

FREE LIBRARY OF PHILADELPHIA - LIBRARY FOR THE BLIND AND
  PHYSICALLY HANDICAPPED
919 Walnut St.   Phone: (215) 925-3213
Philadelphia, PA 19107   Michael P. Coyle, Hd.

FREE LIBRARY OF PHILADELPHIA - LITERATURE DEPARTMENT
Logan Sq.   Phone: (215) 686-5402
Philadelphia, PA 19103   Maryann Baker, Hd.

FREE LIBRARY OF PHILADELPHIA - MERCANTILE LIBRARY
1021 Chestnut St.   Phone: (215) 627-1231
Philadelphia, PA 19107   James B. Woy, Hd.

FREE LIBRARY OF PHILADELPHIA - MICROFORMS AND NEWSPAPERS
  DEPARTMENT
Logan Sq.   Phone: (215) 686-5431
Philadelphia, PA 19103   Bohdan W. Mysko, Hd.

FREE LIBRARY OF PHILADELPHIA - MUSIC DEPARTMENT
Logan Sq.   Phone: (215) 686-5316
Philadelphia, PA 19103   Frederick J. Kent, Hd.

FREE LIBRARY OF PHILADELPHIA - MUSIC DEPARTMENT - DRINKER
  LIBRARY OF CHORAL MUSIC
Logan Sq.   Phone: (215) 686-5364
Philadelphia, PA 19103   Frederick J. Kent, Hd.

FREE LIBRARY OF PHILADELPHIA - PRINT AND PICTURE COLLECTION
Logan Sq.   Phone: (215) 686-5405
Philadelphia, PA 19103   Robert F. Looney, Cur.

FREE LIBRARY OF PHILADELPHIA - RARE BOOK DEPARTMENT
Logan Sq.   Phone: (215) 686-5416
Philadelphia, PA 19103   Howell J. Heaney, Rare Book Libn.

FREE LIBRARY OF PHILADELPHIA - SOCIAL SCIENCE & HISTORY
  DEPARTMENT
Logan Sq.
Philadelphia, PA 19103   William Handley, Hd.

FREE LIBRARY OF PHILADELPHIA - SOCIAL SCIENCE & HISTORY
  DEPARTMENT - MAP COLLECTION
Logan Sq.   Phone: (215) 686-5397
Philadelphia, PA 19103   J.B. Post, Map Libn.

FREE LIBRARY OF PHILADELPHIA - THEATRE COLLECTION
Logan Sq.   Phone: (215) 686-5427
Philadelphia, PA 19103   Geraldine Duclow, Libn.-In-Charge

FRIENDS HOSPITAL - NORMAN D. WEINER PROFESSIONAL LIBRARY
Roosevelt Blvd. & Adams Ave.   Phone: (215) 831-4763
Philadelphia, PA 19124   Donna M. Zoccola, Libn.

GAY TASK FORCE (ALA-SRRT) - INFORMATION CENTER
Box 2383   Phone: (215) 471-3322
Philadelphia, PA 19103   Barbara Gittings, Coord.

GENEALOGICAL SOCIETY OF PENNSYLVANIA - LIBRARY †
1300 Locust St.   Phone: (215) 545-0391
Philadelphia, PA 19107

GENERAL ELECTRIC COMPANY - RSD BRANCH LIBRARY
3198 Chestnut St.   Phone: (215) 823-3405
Philadelphia, PA 19104   Frances Berg, Br.Libn.

GENERAL ELECTRIC COMPANY - SPACE/RSD LIBRARIES
Box 8555   Phone: (215) 962-4700
Philadelphia, PA 19101   Larry Chasen, Mgr.

GEOGRAPHICAL SOCIETY OF PHILADELPHIA - LIBRARY †
21 S. 12th St., Rm. 909   Phone: (215) 563-0127
Philadelphia, PA 19107

GEOGRAPHIC

GERMAN SOCIETY OF PENNSYLVANIA - JOSEPH HORNER MEMORIAL
    LIBRARY
611 Spring Garden St.   Phone: (215) 627-4365
Philadelphia, PA 19123   Christine E. Richardson, Libn.

GERMANTOWN FRIENDS MEETING - FRIENDS FREE LIBRARY
5418 Germantown Ave.   Phone: (215) 438-6023
Philadelphia, PA 19144   Sara G. Woy, Hd.Libn.

GERMANTOWN HISTORICAL SOCIETY - LIBRARY
5214 Germantown Ave.   Phone: (215) 844-0514
Philadelphia, PA 19144   Leonard Rossiter Denis, Libn.

GERMANTOWN HOSPITAL AND MEDICAL CENTER - MEDICAL STAFF
    LIBRARY
One Penn Blvd.   Phone: (215) 438-9700
Philadelphia, PA 19144   Kathleen A. Leigh, Libn.

GERMANTOWN HOSPITAL AND MEDICAL CENTER - NURSING SCHOOL
    LIBRARY
One Penn Blvd.   Phone: (215) 438-9700
Philadelphia, PA 19144   Kathleen A. Leigh, Libn.

GIRARD BANK - INFORMATION CENTER
Girard Plaza   Phone: (215) 585-3313
Philadelphia, PA 19101   Laurel J. Tumbler, Mgr.

GRADUATE HOSPITAL - LIBRARY
One Graduate Plaza   Phone: (215) 893-2401
Philadelphia, PA 19146   Diane M. Farny, Libn.

GRAND LODGE OF FREE AND ACCEPTED MASONS OF PENNSYLVANIA -
    LIBRARY
Masonic Temple, 1 N. Broad St.   Phone: (215) 567-4190
Philadelphia, PA 19107   Frank W. Bobb, Libn. & Cur.

GRATZ COLLEGE - LIBRARY
10th St. & Tabor Rd.   Phone: (215) 329-3363
Philadelphia, PA 19141   Michael Grunberger, Libn.

GRAY PANTHERS - NATIONAL OFFICE LIBRARY
3635 Chestnut St.
Philadelphia, PA 19104   Jean G. Hopper, Libn.

GREAT LAKES COLLEGES ASSOCIATION - PHILADELPHIA URBAN SEMESTER
    - LIBRARY
1227-29 Walnut St.   Phone: (215) 574-9490
Philadelphia, PA 19107   Margit L. Linforth, Libn.

HAHNEMANN MEDICAL COLLEGE & HOSPITAL - WARREN H. FAKE LIBRARY
245 N. 15th St.   Phone: (215) 448-7186
Philadelphia, PA 19102   Eleanora M. Kenworthy, Dir.

HAR ZION TEMPLE - IVA AND MATTHEW RUZOSKER LIBRARY
Hazy's Ford & Hollow Rd.   Phone: (215) 667-5000
Philadelphia, PA 19072   Jessie Rubenstone, Libn.

HAY ASSOCIATES - RESEARCH LIBRARY
229 S. 18th St., Rittenhouse Sq.   Phone: (215) 875-2300
Philadelphia, PA 19103   Lynn Dunwody, Res.Libn.

HISTORICAL SOCIETY OF PENNSYLVANIA - LIBRARY
1300 Locust St.   Phone: (215) 732-6200
Philadelphia, PA 19107   John H. Platt, Libn.

HOLY FAMILY COLLEGE - LIBRARY
Grant & Frankford Aves.   Phone: (215) 637-7703
Philadelphia, PA 19114   Sr. M. Kathryn Dobbs, C.S.F.N., Dir.

HOUSING ASSOCIATION OF DELAWARE VALLEY - LIBRARY
1317 Filbert St., Suite 523   Phone: (215) 563-4050
Philadelphia, PA 19107   Anthony Lewis, Mng.Dir.

HUEBNER (S.S.) FOUNDATION FOR INSURANCE EDUCATION - LIBRARY
W-145 Dietrich Hall
University of Pennsylvania   Phone: (215) 243-7621
Philadelphia, PA 19104   Elizabeth W. Gillies, Libn.

INA CORPORATION - LIBRARY
1600 Arch St.   Phone: (215) 241-4677
Philadelphia, PA 19101   Jeannette E. Ballard, Libn.

INSTITUTE FOR CANCER RESEARCH - LIBRARY
7701 Burholme Ave., Fox Chase   Phone: (215) 728-2711
Philadelphia, PA 19111   Jane M. Bosley, Libn.

INSTITUTE OF THE PENNSYLVANIA HOSPITAL - MEDICAL LIBRARY †
111 N. 49th St.   Phone: (215) 829-2765
Philadelphia, PA 19139   June M. Strickland, Libn.

INSTITUTE FOR SCIENTIFIC INFORMATION
3501 Market St.
University City Science Ctr.   Phone: (215) 386-0100
Philadelphia, PA 19104   Susan S. Jones, Jrnl.Serv.Mgr.

JEFFERSON (Thomas) UNIVERSITY - CARDEZA FOUNDATION - TOCANTINS
    MEMORIAL LIBRARY
1015 Walnut St.   Phone: (215) 928-8474
Philadelphia, PA 19107   Allan J. Erslev, M.D., Dir.

JEFFERSON (Thomas) UNIVERSITY - SCOTT MEMORIAL LIBRARY
11th & Walnut Sts.   Phone: (215) 928-6994
Philadelphia, PA 19107   John A. Timour, Libn.

JENKINS (Theodore F.) MEMORIAL LAW LIBRARY COMPANY - LIBRARY
Widener Bldg., 10th Fl.
1339 Chestnut St.   Phone: (215) 686-5692
Philadelphia, PA 19107   Jill L. Kremer, Dir.

KEAN ARCHIVES
1320 Locust St.   Phone: (215) 735-1812
Philadelphia, PA 19107   Manuel Kean, Owner

KLAUDER (Louis T.) & ASSOCIATES - LIBRARY
2000 Philadelphia Natl. Bank Bldg.   Phone: (215) 563-2570
Philadelphia, PA 19107   Nancy C. Todd, Libn.

LAMBERT (Harold M.) STUDIOS - LIBRARY
2801 W. Cheltenham Ave.
Box 27310   Phone: (215) 224-1400
Philadelphia, PA 19150   Raymond Lambert, Owner

LANKENAU HOSPITAL - MEDICAL LIBRARY
Lancaster & City Line Aves.   Phone: (215) 645-2698
Philadelphia, PA 19151   Loann Scarpato, Med.Libn.

LANKENAU HOSPITAL - SCHOOL OF NURSING LIBRARY
City Ave. & 64th St.   Phone: (215) 642-3931
Philadelphia, PA 19151   Sr. Alma Koder, Libn.

LIBRARY COMPANY OF PHILADELPHIA
1314 Locust St.   Phone: (215) 546-3181
Philadelphia, PA 19107   Edwin Wolf, II, Libn.

LUTHERAN CHURCH IN AMERICA - BOARD OF PUBLICATION - LIBRARY
2900 Queen Ln.   Phone: (215) 848-6800
Philadelphia, PA 19129   Charlotte J. Odman, Libn.

LUTHERAN THEOLOGICAL SEMINARY - KRAUTH MEMORIAL LIBRARY
7301 Germantown Ave.   Phone: (215) 248-4616
Philadelphia, PA 19119   The Rev. David J. Wartluft, Lib.Dir.

MARQUETTE COPPERSMITHING COMPANY - LIBRARY
Box 4584   Phone: (215) 877-9362
Philadelphia, PA 19131   T.T. Hill, Libn.

MARRIAGE COUNCIL OF PHILADELPHIA - DIVISION OF FAMILY STUDY AND
    MARRIAGE COUNCIL LIBRARY
4025 Chestnut St.   Phone: (215) 382-6680
Philadelphia, PA 19104

MEDICAL COLLEGE OF PENNSYLVANIA - ARCHIVES AND SPECIAL
    COLLECTIONS ON WOMEN IN MEDICINE
3300 Henry Ave.   Phone: (215) 842-6910
Philadelphia, PA 19129   Sandra L. Chaff, Dir.

MEDICAL COLLEGE OF PENNSYLVANIA - EASTERN PENNSYLVANIA
   PSYCHIATRIC INSTITUTE - LIBRARY
Henry Ave. & Abbottsford Rd.   Phone: (215) 842-4510
Philadelphia, PA 19129   Terry Wiggins, Hd.Libn.

MERCY CATHOLIC MEDICAL CENTER - MISERICORDIA DIVISION - HEALTH
   SCIENCES LIBRARY
54th & Cedar Ave.   Phone: (215) 747-7600
Philadelphia, PA 19143   Janet Clinton, Chf. of Lib.Serv.

METHODIST HOSPITAL - LIBRARY
2301 S. Broad St.   Phone: (215) 339-5133
Philadelphia, PA 19148

METROPOLITAN HOSPITAL - LIBRARY
201 N. Eighth St., Rm. 208   Phone: (215) 238-2312
Philadelphia, PA 19106   Marjorie Greenfield, Libn.

MICRODOC - TECHNICAL DOCUMENTATION COLLECTION
815 Carpenter Ln.   Phone: (215) 848-4545
Philadelphia, PA 19119   Thomas F. Deahl, Micropublisher

MILITARY ORDER OF THE LOYAL LEGION OF THE UNITED STATES - WAR
   LIBRARY AND MUSEUM
1805 Pine St.   Phone: (215) 735-8196
Philadelphia, PA 19103   Russ A. Pritchard, Dir.

MONELL CHEMICAL SENSES CENTER - LIBRARY
3500 Market St.   Phone: (215) 243-6666
Philadelphia, PA 19104

MONTGOMERY, MC CRACKEN, WALKER & RHOADS - LIBRARY
3 Pkwy.   Phone: (215) 563-0650
Philadelphia, PA 19102   L.B. Beardwood, Libn.

MOORE COLLEGE OF ART - LIBRARY
20th & Race Sts.   Phone: (215) 568-4515
Philadelphia, PA 19103   Marjorie Bilk, Lib.Dir.

MORGAN, LEWIS & BOCKIUS - LIBRARY
123 S. Broad St.   Phone: (215) 491-9633
Philadelphia, PA 19109   Linda C. Roach, Libn.

MORRIS (Robert) ASSOCIATES - LIBRARY
1616 Philadelphia Natl. Bank Bldg.   Phone: (215) 665-2850
Philadelphia, PA 19107   Susan M. Kelsay, Asst.Dir.

NATIONAL ACTION/RESEARCH ON THE MILITARY-INDUSTRIAL COMPLEX -
   LIBRARY
1501 Cherry St.   Phone: (215) 241-7175
Philadelphia, PA 19102   David Goodman

NATIONAL FEDERATION OF ABSTRACTING AND INDEXING SERVICES
112 S. 16th St.   Phone: (215) 563-2406
Philadelphia, PA 19102   M. Lynne Neufeld, Exec.Dir.

NAZARETH HOSPITAL - MEDICAL LIBRARY
2601 Holme Ave.   Phone: (215) 335-6000
Philadelphia, PA 19152   Shirley M. Betz, Dir.

NEW SCHOOL OF MUSIC, INC. - ALICE TULLY LIBRARY
301 S. 21st St.   Phone: (215) 732-3966
Philadelphia, PA 19103   Virginia B. Emerson, Libn.

NORTHEASTERN HOSPITAL - SCHOOL OF NURSING LIBRARY
2301 E. Allegheny Ave.   Phone: (215) 291-3168
Philadelphia, PA 19134   James W. Osborne, Libn.

OVERBROOK SCHOOL FOR THE BLIND - LIBRARY
64th St. & Malvern Ave.   Phone: (215) 877-0313
Philadelphia, PA 19151   Frances M. Burke, Libn.

PARKVIEW HOSPITAL - LIBRARY
1331 E. Wyoming Ave.   Phone: (215) 533-8400
Philadelphia, PA 19124   Grace Toll, Libn.

PENN MUTUAL LIFE INSURANCE COMPANY - LAW LIBRARY
Independence Sq.   Phone: (215) 629-0600
Philadelphia, PA 19172   Doris Nardin, Major Lib.Ck.

PENN VIRGINIA CORPORATION - LIBRARY
2500 Fidelity Bldg.   Phone: (302) 545-6600
Philadelphia, PA 19109   Ben Payne, Libn.

PENNSYLVANIA ACADEMY OF THE FINE ARTS - LIBRARY
Broad & Cherry Sts.   Phone: (215) 972-7611
Philadelphia, PA 19102   Marietta P. Bushnell, Libn.

PENNSYLVANIA AREA LIBRARY NETWORK AND UNION LIBRARY
   CATALOGUE OF PENNSYLVANIA
3420 Walnut St.   Phone: (215) 382-7031
Philadelphia, PA 19104   James G. Schoenung, Exec.Dir.

PENNSYLVANIA COLLEGE OF OPTOMETRY - ALBERT FITCH MEMORIAL
   LIBRARY
1200 W. Godfrey Ave.   Phone: (215) 424-5900
Philadelphia, PA 19141   Marita J. Krivda, Libn.

PENNSYLVANIA COLLEGE OF PODIATRIC MEDICINE - AUDIOVISUAL
   LIBRARY
Race at Eighth St.
Philadelphia, PA 19107   John Harris, Libn.

PENNSYLVANIA COLLEGE OF PODIATRIC MEDICINE - CHARLES E. KRAUSZ
   LIBRARY
Eighth St. at Race   Phone: (215) 629-0300
Philadelphia, PA 19107   Frances E. Peters, Libn.

PENNSYLVANIA ECONOMY LEAGUE - EASTERN DIVISION - LIBRARY
215 S. Broad St.   Phone: (215) 985-0510
Philadelphia, PA 19107   Ellen Brennan, Libn.

PENNSYLVANIA HORTICULTURAL SOCIETY - LIBRARY
325 Walnut St.   Phone: (215) 625-8268
Philadelphia, PA 19106   Mary Lou Wolfe, Libn.

PENNSYLVANIA HOSPITAL - DEPARTMENT FOR SICK AND INJURED -
   HISTORICAL LIBRARY
Eighth & Spruce Sts.   Phone: (215) 829-3998
Philadelphia, PA 19107   Caroline Morris, Libn.-Archv.

PENNSYLVANIA HOSPITAL - DEPARTMENT FOR SICK AND INJURED -
   MEDICAL LIBRARY
Eighth & Spruce Sts.   Phone: (215) 829-3998
Philadelphia, PA 19107   Caroline Morris, Libn.-Archv.

PEPPER, HAMILTON AND SCHEETZ - LAW LIBRARY
123 S. Broad St.   Phone: (215) 893-3080
Philadelphia, PA 19109   Robyn Beyer, Libn.

PERELMAN ANTIQUE TOY MUSEUM - LIBRARY
270 S. 2nd St.   Phone: (215) 922-1070
Philadelphia, PA 19106   Cindy Haveson, Cur.

PHILADELPHIA BOARD OF EDUCATION - PEDAGOGICAL LIBRARY
21st St. & Parkway   Phone: (215) 299-7783
Philadelphia, PA 19103   Helen E. Howe, Hd.Libn.

PHILADELPHIA BULLETIN - NEWS LIBRARY
30th & Market Sts.   Phone: (215) 662-7630
Philadelphia, PA 19101   George D. McDowell, Lib.Dir.

PHILADELPHIA - CITY ARCHIVES
City Hall, Dept. of Records   Phone: (215) 686-2272
Philadelphia, PA 19107   Allen Weinberg, City Archv.

PHILADELPHIA CITY PLANNING COMMISSION - LIBRARY
City Hall Annex, 14th Fl.
Juniper & Filbert Sts.   Phone: (215) 686-4637
Philadelphia, PA 19103

PHILADELPHIA COLLEGE OF ART - LIBRARY
Broad & Spruce Sts.   Phone: (215) 893-3126
Philadelphia, PA 19102   Hazel Gustow, Dir.

PHILADELPHIA COLLEGE OF OSTEOPATHIC MEDICINE - O.J. SNYDER
   MEMORIAL MEDICAL LIBRARY
4150 City Ave.   Phone: (215) 581-6526
Philadelphia, PA 19131   Dr. Shanker H. Vyas, Dir. Of Libs.

PHILADELPHIA COLLEGE OF THE PERFORMING ARTS - LIBRARY †
250 S. Broad St.   Phone: (215) 545-6200
Philadelphia, PA 19102   Kent Christensen, Libn.

PHILADELPHIA COLLEGE OF PHARMACY AND SCIENCE - JOSEPH W.
  ENGLAND LIBRARY
42nd St. & Woodland Ave.   Phone: (215) 596-8960
Philadelphia, PA 19104   Carol Hansen Fenichel, Dir.Lib.Serv.

PHILADELPHIA COLLEGE OF TEXTILES AND SCIENCE - PASTORE LIBRARY
School House Lane & Henry Ave.   Phone: (215) 951-2840
Philadelphia, PA 19144   Wilfred A. Frisby, Dir. Of Lib.Serv.

PHILADELPHIA COMMUNITY LEGAL SERVICES, INC. - LAW LIBRARY
Sylvania House
1324 Locust St.   Phone: (215) 893-5368
Philadelphia, PA 19107   Diane F. Tierney, Libn.

PHILADELPHIA CORPORATION FOR AGING - LIBRARY
Penn Square Bldg.
1317 Filbert St., Rm. 415   Phone: (215) 241-8207
Philadelphia, PA 19107   Steven J. Bell, Ref.Libn.

PHILADELPHIA COURT OF COMMON PLEAS - LAW LIBRARY
City Hall, Rm. 600   Phone: (215) 686-3799
Philadelphia, PA 19107   James M. Clark, Libn.

PHILADELPHIA ELECTRIC COMPANY - LIBRARY
2301 Market St.   Phone: (215) 841-4357
Philadelphia, PA 19101   Dorothy N. Sherman, Libn.

PHILADELPHIA HISTORICAL COMMISSION - LIBRARY
1313 City Hall Annex   Phone: (215) 686-4543
Philadelphia, PA 19107   Dr. Richard Tyler, Hist.

PHILADELPHIA MARITIME MUSEUM - LIBRARY
321 Chestnut St.   Phone: (215) 925-5439
Philadelphia, PA 19106   Dorothy H. Mueller, Libn.

PHILADELPHIA MUSEUM OF ART - LIBRARY
Box 7646   Phone: (215) 763-8100
Philadelphia, PA 19101   Barbara Sevy, Libn.

PHILADELPHIA MUSEUM OF ART - SLIDE LIBRARY
Parkway At 26th St.   Phone: (215) 763-8100
Philadelphia, PA 19130   Ben Kessler, Slide Libn.

PHILADELPHIA NEWSPAPERS, INC. - INQUIRER AND DAILY NEWS LIBRARY
400 N. Broad St.   Phone: (215) 854-2825
Philadelphia, PA 19101   Joseph D. DiMarino, Mgr.Lib./Info.Ctr.

PHILADELPHIA ORCHESTRA ASSOCIATION - LIBRARY
Academy of Music
1420 Locust St.   Phone: (215) 893-1929
Philadelphia, PA 19102   Clinton F. Nieweg, Principal Libn.

PHILADELPHIA PSYCHIATRIC CENTER - PROFESSIONAL LIBRARY
Ford Rd. & Monument Ave.   Phone: (215) 877-2000
Philadelphia, PA 19131   Fern Zalin, Libn.

PHILADELPHIA PSYCHOANALYTIC INSTITUTE - LIBRARY *
111 N. 49th St.   Phone: (215) 474-5748
Philadelphia, PA 19139   Mrs. M.R. Cooper, Exec.Asst.

PHILADELPHIA STATE HOSPITAL - STAFF LIBRARY
Research & Education Bldg.
14000 Roosevelt Blvd.   Phone: (215) 671-4111
Philadelphia, PA 19114   Greta Clark, Libn.

PIERCE JUNIOR COLLEGE - LIBRARY †
1420 Pine St.   Phone: (215) 545-6400
Philadelphia, PA 19102   James R. McAuliffe, Hd.Libn.

PLANNED PARENTHOOD OF SOUTHEASTERN PENNSYLVANIA - RESOURCE
  CENTER
1220 Sansom St.   Phone: (215) 629-2828
Philadelphia, PA 19107   Michele A. Belluomini, Dir.

PROTESTANT EPISCOPAL CHURCH - DIOCESE OF PENNSYLVANIA -
  INFORMATION CENTER
IVB Bldg., Suite 2616
1700 Market St.   Phone: (215) 567-6650
Philadelphia, PA 19103   Rev. John F. Hardwick, Dir., Plan/Prog.

PROVIDENT MUTUAL LIFE INSURANCE COMPANY OF PHILADELPHIA -
  LIBRARY
46th & Market Sts.   Phone: (215) 474-7000
Philadelphia, PA 19101   Tikvah S. Shulman, Libn.

RAHENKAMP, SACHS, WELLS AND ASSOCIATES, INC. - PLANNING LIBRARY
1717 Spring Garden St.   Phone: (215) 568-7545
Philadelphia, PA 19130   Robert W. Ditmer, Dir. of Info.Res.

RAWLE AND HENDERSON - LAW LIBRARY
211 S. Broad St.   Phone: (215) 875-4000
Philadelphia, PA 19107   Hope S. Ridge, Libn.

RECONSTRUCTIONIST RABBINICAL COLLEGE - MORDECAI M. KAPLAN
  LIBRARY
2308 N. Broad St.   Phone: (215) 223-8121
Philadelphia, PA 19132   Jennifer Gabriel, Libn.

REFORMED EPISCOPAL CHURCH - THEOLOGICAL SEMINARY - KUEHNER
  MEMORIAL LIBRARY
4225 Chestnut St.   Phone: (215) 222-5158
Philadelphia, PA 19104   Walter G. Truesdell, Libn.

RESEARCH FOR BETTER SCHOOLS, INC. - RESOURCE CENTER
444 N. Third St.   Phone: (215) 574-9300
Philadelphia, PA 19123   Marian L. Chapman, Dir.

ROBERTS (H. Armstrong) COMPANY - STOCK PICTURE LIBRARY
4203 Locust St.   Phone: (215) 386-6300
Philadelphia, PA 19104   H. Armstrong Roberts, III, Pres.

ROHM & HAAS COMPANY - HOME OFFICE LIBRARY
Independence Mall W.   Phone: (215) 592-3631
Philadelphia, PA 19105   Ellen Castellan Dotterrer, Lib.Supv.

ROSENBACH MUSEUM & LIBRARY †
2010 De Lancey Pl.   Phone: (215) 732-1600
Philadelphia, PA 19103   Suzanne Bolan, Dir.

ROXBOROUGH MEMORIAL HOSPITAL - SCHOOL OF NURSING AND MEDICAL
  STAFF LIBRARY
5800 Ridge Ave.   Phone: (215) 483-9900
Philadelphia, PA 19128   Linda C. Stanley, Libn.

SADTLER RESEARCH LABORATORIES, INC. - LIBRARY
3316 Spring Garden St.   Phone: (215) 382-7800
Philadelphia, PA 19104   Bernadette Steiner, Libn.

ST. AGNES MEDICAL CENTER - HEALTH SCIENCES LIBRARY
1900 S. Broad St.   Phone: (215) 339-4448
Philadelphia, PA 19145   Angelina Caponigro, Hd.Libn.

ST. CHARLES BORROMEO SEMINARY - RYAN MEMORIAL LIBRARY
Overbrook   Phone: (215) 839-3760
Philadelphia, PA 19151   Rev. John B. DeMayo, Dir. of Libs.

ST. CHRISTOPHER'S HOSPITAL FOR CHILDREN - MEDICAL LIBRARY *
2600 N. Lawrence St.   Phone: (215) 427-5374
Philadelphia, PA 19133   Patricia A. Rose, Med.Libn.

ST. JOSEPH'S UNIVERSITY - ACADEMY OF FOOD MARKETING - CAMPBELL
  LIBRARY
54th & City Line Ave.   Phone: (215) 879-7489
Philadelphia, PA 19131   Anna Mae Penrose, Libn.

ST. JOSEPH'S UNIVERSITY - INSTITUTE OF INDUSTRIAL RELATIONS -
  LIBRARY
54th & City Line Ave.   Phone: (215) 879-7660
Philadelphia, PA 19131   Edward J. Mullaly, S.J., Assoc.Dir.

SCHEIE EYE INSTITUTE - LIBRARY
Myrin Circle, 51 N. 39th St.   Phone: (215) 662-8148
Philadelphia, PA 19104   Michael P. Toner, Lib.Dir.

SCHNADER, HARRISON, SEGAL & LEWIS - LIBRARY
1719 Packard Bldg.   Phone: (215) 988-2111
Philadelphia, PA 19102   Susanne E. Hahn, Libn.

SCHUYLKILL VALLEY NATURE CENTER - LIBRARY
8480 Hagy's Mill Rd.   Phone: (215) 482-7300
Philadelphia, PA 19128   Karin James, Libn.

SCOTT PAPER COMPANY - MARKETING LIBRARY
                                      Phone: (215) 521-5000
Philadelphia, PA 19113   Eva K. Butler, Libn.

SCOTT PAPER COMPANY - RESEARCH LIBRARY & TECHNICAL
  INFORMATION SERVICE
Scott Plaza 3   Phone: (215) 521-5000
Philadelphia, PA 19113   George Burna, Mgr.

SETTLEMENT MUSIC SCHOOL - BLANCHE WOLF KOHN LIBRARY
416 Queen St.   Phone: (215) 336-0400
Philadelphia, PA 19147   Ellen Formanek, Libn.

SISTERS OF THE HOLY FAMILY OF NAZARETH - IMMACULATE CONCEPTION
  PROVINCE - ARCHIVES
Grant & Frankford Aves.   Phone: (215) 637-6464
Philadelphia, PA 19114   Sr. M. Theodosette, Archv.

SMITH, KLINE & FRENCH LABORATORIES - MARKETING RESEARCH
  LIBRARY
1500 Spring Garden St.   Phone: (215) 854-5328
Philadelphia, PA 19101   Anna Smyth, Marketing Libn.

SMITH, KLINE & FRENCH LABORATORIES - RESEARCH AND DEVELOPMENT
  LIBRARY
1500 Spring Garden St.   Phone: (215) 854-5593
Philadelphia, PA 19101   Judith C. Bitting, Libn.

SOCIETY OF FRIENDS - PHILADELPHIA YEARLY MEETING - LIBRARY
1515 Cherry St.   Phone: (215) 241-7220
Philadelphia, PA 19102   Mary Davidson, Libn.

SOUTHEASTERN PENNSYLVANIA TRANSPORTATION AUTHORITY -
  LIBRARY
130 S. 9th St., 20th Fl.   Phone: (215) 574-7387
Philadelphia, PA 19107   Joanne P. Feinstein, Libn.

SPACE FUTURES SOCIETY - LIBRARY
1627 Spruce St.
Philadelphia, PA 19103   Ronald P. Smolin, Libn.

STRADLEY, RONON, STEVENS & YOUNG - LAW LIBRARY
1100 One Franklin Plaza   Phone: (215) 564-8000
Philadelphia, PA 19102   Linda-Jean Smith, Libn.

TEMPLE UNIVERSITY - CENTRAL LIBRARY SYSTEM - AUDIO UNIT
Broad & Montgomery   Phone: (215) 787-8205
Philadelphia, PA 19122   Leslie K. Greer, Audio Libn.

TEMPLE UNIVERSITY - CENTRAL LIBRARY SYSTEM - BIOLOGY LIBRARY
248 Life Science Bldg.   Phone: (215) 787-8878
Philadelphia, PA 19122   Robin Pachtman, Biblog.Asst.

TEMPLE UNIVERSITY - CENTRAL LIBRARY SYSTEM - CENTER CITY
  LIBRARY
1619 Walnut St.   Phone: (215) 787-6950
Philadelphia, PA 19103   Cornelia Tucker, Libn.

TEMPLE UNIVERSITY - CENTRAL LIBRARY SYSTEM - CHEMISTRY LIBRARY
Beury Hall, 1st Fl.   Phone: (215) 787-7120
Philadelphia, PA 19122   Dolores Michalak, Biblog.Asst.

TEMPLE UNIVERSITY - CENTRAL LIBRARY SYSTEM - COLLEGE OF
  ENGINEERING - TECHNOLOGY LIBRARY
12th & Norris Sts.   Phone: (215) 787-7828
Philadelphia, PA 19122   Arlene R. Keller, Libn.

TEMPLE UNIVERSITY - CENTRAL LIBRARY SYSTEM - CONTEMPORARY
  CULTURE COLLECTION
13th & Berks Sts.   Phone: (215) 787-8667
Philadelphia, PA 19122

TEMPLE UNIVERSITY - CENTRAL LIBRARY SYSTEM - CONWELLANA-
  TEMPLANA COLLECTION
13th & Berks Sts.   Phone: (215) 787-8240
Philadelphia, PA 19122   Miriam I. Crawford, Cur.

TEMPLE UNIVERSITY - CENTRAL LIBRARY SYSTEM - MATHEMATICAL
  SCIENCES LIBRARY
407 Computer Sciences Bldg.   Phone: (215) 787-8434
Philadelphia, PA 19122   Sandra Thompson, Biblog.Asst.

TEMPLE UNIVERSITY - CENTRAL LIBRARY SYSTEM - NATIONAL
  IMMIGRATION ARCHIVES
Balch Institute Bldg.
18 S. 7th St.   Phone: (215) 922-3454
Philadelphia, PA 19106   Stephanie A. Morris, Cur.

TEMPLE UNIVERSITY - CENTRAL LIBRARY SYSTEM - PHYSICS LIBRARY
209A Barton Hall   Phone: (215) 787-7649
Philadelphia, PA 19122   Rhea Mihalism, Biblog.Asst.

TEMPLE UNIVERSITY - CENTRAL LIBRARY SYSTEM - RARE BOOK &
  MANUSCRIPT COLLECTION
13th & Berks St.   Phone: (215) 787-8230
Philadelphia, PA 19122   Thomas M. Whitehead, Hd., Spec.Coll.Dept.

TEMPLE UNIVERSITY - CENTRAL LIBRARY SYSTEM - SCHOOL OF SOCIAL
  ADMINISTRATION - LIBRARY
565 Ritter Hall Annex   Phone: (215) 787-1209
Philadelphia, PA 19122   Harriet Segal, Biblog.Asst.

TEMPLE UNIVERSITY - CENTRAL LIBRARY SYSTEM - SCIENCE FICTION
  COLLECTION
13th & Berks St.   Phone: (215) 787-8230
Philadelphia, PA 19122   Cornelia King, Libn.

TEMPLE UNIVERSITY - CENTRAL LIBRARY SYSTEM - TYLER SCHOOL OF
  FINE ARTS - LIBRARY
Beech & Penrose Aves.   Phone: (215) 224-7575
Philadelphia, PA 19126   Mary Ivy Bayard, Libn.

TEMPLE UNIVERSITY - CENTRAL LIBRARY SYSTEM - TYLER SCHOOL OF
  FINE ARTS - SLIDE LIBRARY
Beech & Penrose Aves.   Phone: (215) 224-7575
Philadelphia, PA 19126   Edith Zuckerman, Slide Cur.

TEMPLE UNIVERSITY - CENTRAL LIBRARY SYSTEM - URBAN ARCHIVES
13th & Berks Sts.   Phone: (215) 787-8257
Philadelphia, PA 19122   Dr. Fredric Miller, Cur.

TEMPLE UNIVERSITY - CENTRAL LIBRARY SYSTEM - ZAHN
  INSTRUCTIONAL MATERIALS CENTER
13th & Columbia Ave.   Phone: (215) 787-8481
Philadelphia, PA 19122   Linda Sekula, Hd.Libn.

TEMPLE UNIVERSITY - HEALTH SCIENCES CENTER - LIBRARY
N. Broad & Tioga Sts.   Phone: (215) 221-4032
Philadelphia, PA 19140   Ruth Y. Diamond, Dir.

TEMPLE UNIVERSITY HOSPITAL - HEALTH SCIENCES CENTER -
  DEPARTMENT OF RADIOLOGY - LIBRARY
3401 N. Broad St.   Phone: (215) 221-4226
Philadelphia, PA 19140   Linda M. Quick, Libn.

TEMPLE UNIVERSITY - LAW LIBRARY
N. Broad St. & Montgomery Ave.   Phone: (215) 787-7892
Philadelphia, PA 19122   John Lindsey, Law Professor/Law Libn.

TRW, INC. - PHILADELPHIA LABORATORIES - RESEARCH & DEVELOPMENT
  LIBRARY
401 N. Broad St.   Phone: (215) 922-8900
Philadelphia, PA 19108   Ruth Capolino, Libn.

UNION LEAGUE OF PHILADELPHIA - LIBRARY
140 S. Broad St.   Phone: (215) 563-6500
Philadelphia, PA 19102   James G. Mundy, Jr., Libn.

UNITED ENGINEERS & CONSTRUCTORS, INC. - LIBRARY
30 S. 17th St.
Box 8223   Phone: (215) 422-3374
Philadelphia, PA 19101   Rose Antipin, Libn.

GEOGRAPHIC

UNITED METHODIST CHURCH - PHILADELPHIA ANNUAL CONFERENCE -
　HISTORICAL SOCIETY LIBRARY
326 New St.　　　　　　　　　　Phone: (215) 925-7788
Philadelphia, PA 19106　　　　　Brian McCloskey, Adm.

UNITED PRESBYTERIAN CHURCH IN THE U.S.A. - PRESBYTERIAN
　HISTORICAL SOCIETY - LIBRARY
425 Lombard St.　　　　　　　　Phone: (215) 627-1852
Philadelphia, PA 19147　　　　　William B. Miller, Sec.

U.S. ARMY - CORPS OF ENGINEERS - PHILADELPHIA DISTRICT -
　TECHNICAL LIBRARY
2nd & Chestnut Sts.　　　　　　Phone: (215) 597-3610
Philadelphia, PA 19106　　　　Pamela Wiwel, District Libn.

U.S. BUREAU OF THE CENSUS - REGIONAL DATA USER SERVICE -
　PHILADELPHIA REGIONAL OFFICE - LIBRARY *
Federal Bldg., Rm. 9244
600 Arch St.　　　　　　　　　　Phone: (215) 597-8314
Philadelphia, PA 19106　　　David Lewis, Data User Serv.Off.

U.S. COURT OF APPEALS, 3RD CIRCUIT - LIBRARY †
U.S. Court House
601 Market St.　　　　　　　　　Phone: (215) 597-2009
Philadelphia, PA 19106　　　Dorothy A. Cozzolino, Libn.

U.S. DEFENSE LOGISTICS AGENCY - DEFENSE INDUSTRIAL SUPPLY
　CENTER - TECHNICAL DATA MANAGEMENT OFFICE
700 Robbins Ave.　　　　　　　Phone: (215) 697-2757
Philadelphia, PA 19111　　　G. Dorney, Chf.Tech. Data Mgr.

U.S. DEFENSE LOGISTICS AGENCY - DEFENSE PERSONNEL SUPPORT CTR. -
　DIRECTORATE OF MED. MATERIEL TECH. LIBRARY
2800 S. 20th St., Bldg. 9-4-F　　　Phone: (215) 952-2110
Philadelphia, PA 19101　　　Gerald J. Ziccardi, Med.Libn.

U.S.D.A. - AGRICULTURAL RESEARCH SERVICE - EASTERN REGIONAL
　RESEARCH CENTER LIBRARY
600 E. Mermaid Lane　　　　　Phone: (215) 233-6602
Philadelphia, PA 19118　　　Wendy H. Kramer, Adm.Libn.

U.S. DEPT. OF COMMERCE - INTERNATIONAL TRADE ADMINISTRATION -
　PHILADELPHIA DISTRICT OFFICE LIBRARY
9448 Federal Bldg.
600 Arch St.　　　　　　　　　　Phone: (215) 597-2850
Philadelphia, PA 19106　　　Patrick P. McCabe, Dir.

U.S. DEPT. OF HOUSING AND URBAN DEVELOPMENT - REGION III -
　LIBRARY
6th and Walnut St.
Curtis Bldg., Rm. 989　　　　　Phone: (215) 597-2685
Philadelphia, PA 19106　　　Beverly R. Taplinger, Lib.Techn.

U.S. INTERAGENCY ADVANCED POWER GROUP - POWER INFORMATION
　CENTER †
Franklin Research Center
20th & Race Sts.　　　　　　　Phone: (215) 448-1145
Philadelphia, PA 19103　　　Joyce E. Falkenstein, Dp.Dir.

U.S. NATL. ARCHIVES & RECORDS SERVICE - FEDERAL ARCHIVES AND
　RECORDS CENTER, REGION 3
5000 Wissahickon Ave.　　　　Phone: (215) 951-5591
Philadelphia, PA 19144　　　Charles T. Glessner, Dir.

U.S. NATL. PARK SERVICE - INDEPENDENCE NATL. HISTORICAL PARK -
　LIBRARY
313 Walnut St.　　　　　　　　Phone: (215) 597-8047
Philadelphia, PA 19106　　　Martin I. Yoelson, Chf.Pk.Hist.

U.S. NAVY - NAVAL REGIONAL MEDICAL CENTER (Philadelphia) - MEDICAL
　LIBRARY
17th & Pattison Aves.　　　　　Phone: (215) 755-8314
Philadelphia, PA 19145　　　Giovina Cavacini, Libn.

U.S. NAVY - NAVAL SHIP SYSTEMS ENGINEERING STATION
　HEADQUARTERS - TECHNICAL LIBRARY
Bldg. 619, Naval Base　　　　　Phone: (215) 755-3922
Philadelphia, PA 19112　　　Pearl O. Robinson, Libn.

U.S. NAVY - NAVAL SHIPYARD (Philadelphia) - TECHNICAL LIBRARY
Philadelphia Naval Base　　　　Phone: (215) 755-3657
Philadelphia, PA 19112　　　Alice R. Murray, Libn.

U.S. VETERANS ADMINISTRATION (PA-Philadelphia) - MEDICAL CENTER
　LIBRARY
University & Woodland Aves.　　Phone: (215) 382-2400
Philadelphia, PA 19104　　　David E. Falger, Chf., Lib.Serv.

UNIVERSITY OF PENNSYLVANIA - ANNENBERG SCHOOL OF
　COMMUNICATIONS - LIBRARY
3620 Walnut St.　　　　　　　Phone: (215) 243-7027
Philadelphia, PA 19104　　　Sandra B. Grilikhes, Hd.Libn.

UNIVERSITY OF PENNSYLVANIA - ARCHIVES AND RECORDS CENTER
North Arcade, Franklin Field　　Phone: (215) 243-7024
Philadelphia, PA 19104　　　Francis James Dallett, Archv.

UNIVERSITY OF PENNSYLVANIA - BIDDLE LAW LIBRARY
100 S. 34th St./I4　　　　　　Phone: (215) 243-7478
Philadelphia, PA 19104　　　Richard Sloane, Libn.

UNIVERSITY OF PENNSYLVANIA - DEPARTMENT OF FOLKLORE & FOLKLIFE
　- ARCHIVE
417 Logan Hall　　　　　　　　Phone: (215) 243-7352
Philadelphia, PA 19104　　　Dr. Kenneth Goldstein, Hd.

UNIVERSITY OF PENNSYLVANIA - EDGAR FAHS SMITH MEMORIAL
　COLLECTION IN THE HISTORY OF CHEMISTRY
Van Pelt Library CH　　　　　Phone: (215) 243-7088
Philadelphia, PA 19104　　　Dr. Arnold W. Thackray, Cur.

UNIVERSITY OF PENNSYLVANIA - ENERGY CENTER - DRL BASEMENT
　ENERGY LIBRARY
3831 Walnut St.　　　　　　　Phone: (215) 243-5340
Philadelphia, PA 19104　　　Dr. Alan H. Struth, Lib.Dir.

UNIVERSITY OF PENNSYLVANIA - FINE ARTS LIBRARY
Furness Bldg./CK　　　　　　　Phone: (215) 243-8325
Philadelphia, PA 19104　　　Alan E. Morrison, Libn.

UNIVERSITY OF PENNSYLVANIA - GEOLOGY MAP LIBRARY
Hayden Hall
240 S. 33rd St.　　　　　　　Phone: (215) 243-5630
Philadelphia, PA 19104　　　Carol Faul, Map Libn.

UNIVERSITY OF PENNSYLVANIA - HENRY CHARLES LEA LIBRARY
Van Pelt Library
3420 Walnut St.　　　　　　　Phone: (215) 243-7088
Philadelphia, PA 19104

UNIVERSITY OF PENNSYLVANIA - HERMAN BEERMAN LIBRARY
University Hospital
3400 Spruce St.　　　　　　　Phone: (215) 662-2571
Philadelphia, PA 19104　　　Susan Cleveland, Dir.

UNIVERSITY OF PENNSYLVANIA - HORACE HOWARD FURNESS MEMORIAL
　LIBRARY
Van Pelt Library
3420 Walnut St.　　　　　　　Phone: (215) 243-7552
Philadelphia, PA 19104　　　Dr. Roland Mushat Frye, Cur.

UNIVERSITY OF PENNSYLVANIA - JOHN PENMAN WOOD MEMORIAL
　LIBRARY OF NATIONAL DEFENSE
Hollenback Ctr./M1
3000 South St.　　　　　　　Phone: (215) 243-7757
Philadelphia, PA 19104　　　Margaret Brinkley, Adm.Asst.

UNIVERSITY OF PENNSYLVANIA - JOHNSON RESEARCH FOUNDATION
　LIBRARY
Richards Bldg.
37th & Hamilton Walk　　　　　Phone: (215) 243-4387
Philadelphia, PA 19104

UNIVERSITY OF PENNSYLVANIA - LIPPINCOTT LIBRARY
3420 Walnut St./CH　　　　　Phone: (215) 243-5924
Philadelphia, PA 19104　　　Eleanor B. Allen, Hd.Libn.

UNIVERSITY OF PENNSYLVANIA - MATHEMATICS-PHYSICS-ASTRONOMY LIBRARY
Rittenhouse Laboratory/E1
Philadelphia, PA 19104
Phone: (215) 243-8173
Marion A. Kreiter, Libn.

UNIVERSITY OF PENNSYLVANIA - MEDICAL & BIOLOGICAL SCIENCES LIBRARY
Johnson Pavilion/G2
36th & Hamilton Walk
Philadelphia, PA 19104
Phone: (215) 243-8020
Eleanor Goodchild, Libn.

UNIVERSITY OF PENNSYLVANIA - MOORE SCHOOL OF ELECTRICAL ENGINEERING LIBRARY
200 South 33rd St./D2
Philadelphia, PA 19104
Phone: (215) 243-8135
Holly C.K.S. Lucas, Libn.

UNIVERSITY OF PENNSYLVANIA - MORRIS ARBORETUM LIBRARY
9414 Meadowbrook Ave.
Philadelphia, PA 19118
Phone: (215) 247-5777
Karen D. Stevens, Libn.

UNIVERSITY OF PENNSYLVANIA - MUSEUM LIBRARY
33rd & Spruce Sts./F1
Philadelphia, PA 19104
Phone: (215) 243-7840
Jean S. Adelman, Libn.

UNIVERSITY OF PENNSYLVANIA - POPULATION STUDIES CENTER - DEMOGRAPHY LIBRARY
3718 Locust Walk
Philadelphia, PA 19174
Phone: (215) 243-5375
Adele B. Burns, Res.Biblog.

UNIVERSITY OF PENNSYLVANIA - SCHOOL OF DENTAL MEDICINE - LEON LEVY LIBRARY
4001 Spruce St./A1
Philadelphia, PA 19104
Phone: (215) 243-8969
John M. Whittock, Jr., Libn.

UNIVERSITY OF PENNSYLVANIA - SCHOOL OF SOCIAL WORK - SMALLEY LIBRARY OF SOCIAL WORK
Caster Bldg./C3
3701 Locust Walk
Philadelphia, PA 19104
Phone: (215) 243-5508
Evelyn Butler, Libn.

UNIVERSITY OF PENNSYLVANIA - SCHOOL OF VETERINARY MEDICINE - C.J. MARSHALL MEMORIAL LIBRARY
3800 Spruce St./H1
Philadelphia, PA 19104
Phone: (215) 243-8874
Lillian Bryant, Libn.

UNIVERSITY OF PENNSYLVANIA - TOWNE SCIENTIFIC LIBRARY
220 S. 33rd St./D3
Philadelphia, PA 19104
Phone: (215) 243-7266
Holly C.K.S. Lucas, Act.Hd.

UNIVERSITY OF PENNSYLVANIA - WISTAR INSTITUTE OF ANATOMY & BIOLOGY - LIBRARY
36th & Spruce Sts.
Philadelphia, PA 19104
Phone: (215) 243-3508
J. A. Hunter, Libn.

WAGNER FREE INSTITUTE OF SCIENCE - LIBRARY
17th St. & Montgomery Ave.
Philadelphia, PA 19121
Robert Chambers, Dir.

WESTINGHOUSE ELECTRIC CORPORATION - STEAM TURBINE GENERATOR DIVISION - TECHNICAL LIBRARY
Lester Branch
Box 9175
Philadelphia, PA 19113
Phone: (215) 595-4203
Hilary C. Johnson, Tech.Libn.

WESTMINSTER THEOLOGICAL SEMINARY - MONTGOMERY LIBRARY
Chestnut Hill
Philadelphia, PA 19118
Phone: (215) 887-5511
Robert J. Kepple, Libn.

WHITE & WILLIAMS - LIBRARY
1234 Market St.
Philadelphia, PA 19107
Phone: (215) 854-7126
Margaret S. Fallon, Libn.

WILLET STAINED GLASS STUDIOS - LIBRARY
10 E. Moreland Ave.
Philadelphia, PA 19118
Phone: (215) 247-5721
Helene Weis, Libn.

WILLS EYE HOSPITAL AND RESEARCH INSTITUTE - ARTHUR J. BEDELL MEMORIAL LIBRARY
Ninth & Walnut Sts.
Philadelphia, PA 19107
Phone: (215) 928-3287
Fleur Weinberg, Dir.

WOLF, BLOCK, SCHORR & SOLIS-COHEN - LIBRARY †
Packard Bldg., 12th Fl.
Philadelphia, PA 19102
Phone: (215) 569-4000
Mary-Louise Fleisher, Libn.

ZOOLOGICAL SOCIETY OF PHILADELPHIA - LIBRARY
34th St. & Girard Ave.
Philadelphia, PA 19104
Phone: (215) 243-1100
Doris Ryall, Libn.

FIRST PRESBYTERIAN CHURCH - LIBRARY
Main St.
Phoenixville, PA 19460
Phone: (215) 933-8816
Elizabeth Holden, Libn.

VALLEY FORGE CHRISTIAN COLLEGE - LIBRARY
Phoenixville, PA 19460
Phone: (215) 935-0450
Dorsey Reynolds, Libn.

ACTION-HOUSING, INC. - LIBRARY & HOUSING INFORMATION CENTER
2 Gateway Ctr.
Pittsburgh, PA 15222
Phone: (412) 281-2102
Terri F. Gould, Dir. of Educ.

AIR POLLUTION CONTROL ASSOCIATION - LIBRARY †
Box 2861
Pittsburgh, PA 15230
Phone: (412) 621-1090

ALLEGHENY COUNTY - DEPARTMENT OF PLANNING - LIBRARY
429 Forbes Ave., 12th Fl.
Pittsburgh, PA 15219
Phone: (412) 355-4353
Patricia M. Carle, Lib.Cons.

ALLEGHENY COUNTY HEALTH DEPARTMENT - LIBRARY
40th St. & Penn Ave.
Pittsburgh, PA 15224
Phone: (412) 578-8028
Carol Schmitt, Libn.

ALLEGHENY COUNTY LAW LIBRARY
921 City-County Bldg.
Pittsburgh, PA 15219
Phone: (412) 355-5353
Joel Fishman, Law Libn.

ALLEGHENY GENERAL HOSPITAL - MEDICAL LIBRARY
320 E. North Ave.
Pittsburgh, PA 15212
Phone: (412) 237-3041
Lillian Fisher, Hd.Libn.

ALUMINUM COMPANY OF AMERICA - CORPORATE LIBRARY
325 Alcoa Bldg.
Pittsburgh, PA 15219
Phone: (412) 553-4482
Nancy J. Furlan, Info.Serv.Adm.

BLUE CROSS OF WESTERN PENNSYLVANIA - IN-HOUSE BUSINESS LIBRARY
1 Smithfield St.
Pittsburgh, PA 15222
Phone: (412) 255-8220
Connie Ferguson, Libn.

BYZANTINE CATHOLIC SEMINARY OF SAINTS CYRIL AND METHODIUS - BYZANTINE SEMINARY LIBRARY
3605 Perrysville Ave.
Pittsburgh, PA 15214
Phone: (412) 321-8383
Rev. Gary Powell, Dir. of Lib.

CARNEGIE LIBRARY OF PITTSBURGH - BUSINESS DIVISION
Frick Bldg. Mezzanine
437 Grant St.
Pittsburgh, PA 15219
Phone: (412) 281-5945
Miriam S. Lerch, Div.Hd.

CARNEGIE LIBRARY OF PITTSBURGH - CENTRAL CHILDREN'S ROOM HISTORICAL COLLECTION
4400 Forbes Ave.
Pittsburgh, PA 15213
Phone: (412) 622-3122
Amy Kellman, Hd. Of Ch.Dept.

CARNEGIE LIBRARY OF PITTSBURGH - MUSIC AND ART DEPARTMENT
4400 Forbes Ave.
Pittsburgh, PA 15213
Phone: (412) 622-3105
Ida Reed, Hd.

CARNEGIE LIBRARY OF PITTSBURGH - PENNSYLVANIA DIVISION
4400 Forbes Ave.
Pittsburgh, PA 15213
Phone: (412) 622-3154
Maria Zini, Hd.

CARNEGIE LIBRARY OF PITTSBURGH - SCIENCE AND TECHNOLOGY DEPARTMENT
4400 Forbes Ave.
Pittsburgh, PA 15213
Phone: (412) 622-3138
Catherine Brosky, Hd.

CARNEGIE-MELLON UNIVERSITY - AUDIO VISUAL SERVICES *
Hunt Library, Frew St.
Pittsburgh, PA 15213
Phone: (412) 578-2430
Stephanie Evancho, Dir.

GEOGRAPHIC

GEOGRAPHIC

CARNEGIE-MELLON UNIVERSITY - ENGINEERING & SCIENCE LIBRARY
Schenley Park　　　　　　　　　　　Phone: (412) 578-2428
Pittsburgh, PA 15213　　　　Mark H. Kibbey, Hd.Eng./Sci.Libn.

CARNEGIE-MELLON UNIVERSITY - HUNT INSTITUTE FOR BOTANICAL DOCUMENTATION - LIBRARY
Schenley Park　　　　　　　　　　　Phone: (412) 578-2434
Pittsburgh, PA 15213　　　　　　　Robert W. Kiger, Dir.

CARNEGIE-MELLON UNIVERSITY - HUNT LIBRARY
Schenley Park　　　　　　　　　　　Phone: (412) 578-2447
Pittsburgh, PA 15213　　　Thomas J. Michalak, Dir.Univ.Libs.

CARNEGIE-MELLON UNIVERSITY - MELLON INSTITUTE LIBRARY
4400 Fifth Ave.　　　　　　　　　　Phone: (412) 578-3172
Pittsburgh, PA 15213　　　　　　　Mary J. Volk, Libn.

CARNEGIE MUSEUM OF NATURAL HISTORY - LIBRARY
4400 Forbes Ave.　　　　　　　　　Phone: (412) 622-3264
Pittsburgh, PA 15213　　　　　　Anna R. Tauber, Libn.

CHILDREN'S HOSPITAL OF PITTSBURGH - BLAXTER MEMORIAL LIBRARY
125 De Soto St.　　　　　　　　　　Phone: (412) 647-5288
Pittsburgh, PA 15213　　　　　　　Nancy Dunn, Libn.

COLT INDUSTRIES - CRUCIBLE RESEARCH CENTER - LIBRARY
Box 88　　　　　　　　　　　　　　Phone: (412) 923-2955
Pittsburgh, PA 15230　　　　Patricia J. Aducci, Tech.Libn.

CONSOLIDATION COAL COMPANY - EXPLORATION LIBRARY *
Consol Plaza
1800 Washington Rd.　　　　　　　Phone: (412) 831-4513
Pittsburgh, PA 15241　　　　　　Peter Stamoolis, Libn.

DIOCESE OF PITTSBURGH - LEARNING MEDIA CENTER *
201 Market St.　　　　　　　　　　Phone: (412) 456-3120
Pittsburgh, PA 15222

DRAVO CORPORATION - LIBRARY
1 Oliver Plaza　　　　　　　　　　Phone: (412) 566-5075
Pittsburgh, PA 15222　　　　　Alice P. Estes, Lib.Mgr.

DUQUESNE UNIVERSITY - LAW LIBRARY
600 Forbes Ave.　　　　　　　　　Phone: (412) 434-6293
Pittsburgh, PA 15282　　　　Frank Yining Liu, Law Libn.

EAST LIBERTY PRESBYTERIAN CHURCH - LIBRARY
Penn Mall at Highland Ave.　　　　Phone: (412) 441-3800
Pittsburgh, PA 15206

ENERGY IMPACT ASSOCIATES, INC. - LIBRARY
Box 1899　　　　　　　　　　　　Phone: (412) 351-5800
Pittsburgh, PA 15230　　　　　Jacqueline Dasch, Libn.

EYE AND EAR HOSPITAL OF PITTSBURGH - BLAIR-LIPPINCOTT LIBRARY
230 Lothrop St.　　　　　　　　　Phone: (412) 647-2287
Pittsburgh, PA 15213　　　　Bruce Johnston, Med.Libn.

FEDERAL RESERVE BANK OF CLEVELAND - PITTSBURGH BRANCH LIBRARY
717 Grant St.　　　　　　　　　　Phone: (412) 261-7800
Pittsburgh, PA 15230　　　　　D. Craft, Act.Libn.

FORBES HEALTH SYSTEM - COLUMBIA HEALTH CENTER LIBRARY
Penn Ave. & West St.　　　　　　Phone: (412) 247-2541
Pittsburgh, PA 15221　　　　Margaret C. Lietman, Dir.

FORBES HEALTH SYSTEM - CORPORATE OFFICE LIBRARY
Finley Bldg., 500 Finley St.　　　Phone: (412) 665-3570
Pittsburgh, PA 15206　　Margaret C. Lietman, Dir., Lib.Sci.Dept.

FORBES HEALTH SYSTEM - PITTSBURGH SKILLED NURSING CENTER LIBRARY
Frankstown Ave. at Washington Blvd.　Phone: (412) 665-3050
Pittsburgh, PA 15206　　Margaret C. Lietman, Dir./Dept. for Sys.

FOUNDATION FOR THE STUDY OF CYCLES INC. - LIBRARY
124 S. Highland Ave.　　　　　　Phone: (412) 441-1666
Pittsburgh, PA 15206　　　　Gertrude F. Shirk, Ed.

GRAPHIC ARTS TECHNICAL FOUNDATION - E.H. WADEWITZ MEMORIAL LIBRARY
4615 Forbes Ave.　　　　　　　　Phone: (412) 621-6941
Pittsburgh, PA 15213　　　　　Janice L. Lloyd, Libn.

GULF OIL CORPORATION - BUSINESS RESEARCH LIBRARY
Box 1166　　　　　　　　　　　Phone: (412) 263-6040
Pittsburgh, PA 15230　　　　Judy Van Horn, Lib.Supv.

GULF RESEARCH AND DEVELOPMENT COMPANY - TECHNICAL INFORMATION SERVICES
Drawer 2038　　　　　　　　　　Phone: (412) 665-6000
Pittsburgh, PA 15230　　Tina B. Ross, Dir.Tech.Info.Serv.

HARBISON-WALKER REFRACTORIES COMPANY - GARBER RESEARCH CENTER LIBRARY
Box 98037　　　　　　　　　　　Phone: (412) 562-6200
Pittsburgh, PA 15227　　　　Harriet Gillespie, Res.Libn.

HEALTH EDUCATION CENTER LIBRARY
200 Ross St.　　　　　　　　　　Phone: (412) 392-3165
Pittsburgh, PA 15219　　　　Dorothy B. Melamed, Libn.

HEALTH AND WELFARE PLANNING ASSOCIATION OF ALLEGHENY COUNTY - LIBRARY
200 Ross St.　　　　　　　　　　Phone: (412) 261-6010
Pittsburgh, PA 15219　　　Mary Lou Charlton, Libn.

HEBREW INSTITUTE OF PITTSBURGH - SOL ROSENBLOOM LIBRARY
6401 Forbes Ave.　　　　　　　Phone: (412) 521-1100
Pittsburgh, PA 15217　　　　　Pauline Milch, Libn.

HEINZ (H.J.) COMPANY - LIBRARY
1062 Progress St.
Box 57　　　　　　　　　　　　Phone: (412) 237-5948
Pittsburgh, PA 15230　　　　Nancy M. Wright, Libn.

HISTORICAL SOCIETY OF WESTERN PENNSYLVANIA - LIBRARY
4338 Bigelow Blvd.　　　　　　Phone: (412) 681-5533
Pittsburgh, PA 15213

INDUSTRIAL HEALTH FOUNDATION, INC. - LIBRARY
5231 Centre Ave.　　　　　　　Phone: (412) 687-2100
Pittsburgh, PA 15232　　Jane F. Brislin, Dir.Info.Serv.

JONES AND LAUGHLIN STEEL CORPORATION - COMMERCIAL LIBRARY
1600 W. Carson St.　　　　　　Phone: (412) 227-4354
Pittsburgh, PA 15263　　　　Nancy Owens, Libn.

JONES AND LAUGHLIN STEEL CORPORATION - GRAHAM LIBRARY
900 Agnew Rd.　　　　　　　　Phone: (412) 884-1000
Pittsburgh, PA 15227　　　Joanne S. Klein, Tech.Libn.

KM&G INTERNATIONAL INC. - LIBRARY SERVICES
Four Gateway Ctr.　　　　　　Phone: (412) 456-3600
Pittsburgh, PA 15222　　Florence V. Merkel, Lib.Supv.

KNOW, INC.
Box 86031　　　　　　　　　　Phone: (412) 241-4844
Pittsburgh, PA 15221　　　　F. Scardina, Educ.Dir.

KOPPERS COMPANY, INC. - ENGINEERING AND CONSTRUCTION DIVISION - INFORMATION SERVICE
510 Chamber of Commerce Bldg.
Pittsburgh, PA 15219　　Catherine A. Emish, Coord., Info.Serv.

MAGEE-WOMENS HOSPITAL - HOWARD ANDERSON POWER MEMORIAL LIBRARY
Forbes Ave. & Halket St.　　　Phone: (412) 647-4288
Pittsburgh, PA 15213　　　Velma Axelrod, Med.Libn.

MELLON BANK, N.A. - LIBRARY
Mellon Sq.　　　　　　　　　　Phone: (412) 232-4312
Pittsburgh, PA 15230　　　Patricia H. Riordan, Libn.

MERCK & COMPANY, INC. - CALGON CORPORATION - INFORMATION CENTER
Box 1346　　　　　　　　　　Phone: (412) 777-8203
Pittsburgh, PA 15230　　Marie Louise Stonehouse, Mgr.

GEOGRAPHIC

MERCY HOSPITAL - MEDICAL STAFF LIBRARY
Pride & Locust Sts.
Phone: (412) 232-7520
Pittsburgh, PA 15219
Suzanne A. Gabarry, Libn.

MERCY HOSPITAL - SCHOOL OF NURSING LIBRARY
1401 Blvd. of the Allies
Phone: (412) 232-7963
Pittsburgh, PA 15219
Veronica C. Harrison, Libn.

METROPOLITAN PITTSBURGH PUBLIC BROADCASTING, INC. - WQED LIBRARY
4802 Fifth Ave.
Phone: (412) 622-1524
Pittsburgh, PA 15213
Jeanette Blackston, Lib.Serv.Adm.

MINE SAFETY APPLIANCES COMPANY - BUSINESS LIBRARY
600 Penn Ctr. Blvd.
Phone: (412) 273-5131
Pittsburgh, PA 15235
Hilda M. Reitzel, Libn.

MINE SAFETY APPLIANCES COMPANY - TECHNICAL LIBRARY
201 N. Braddock Ave.
Phone: (412) 273-5600
Pittsburgh, PA 15208
Hilda M. Reitzel, Libn.

MOBAY CHEMICAL CORPORATION - INFORMATION CENTER †
Penn Lincoln Pkwy., W.
Phone: (412) 923-2700
Pittsburgh, PA 15205
Edwin G. La Quay, Libn.

NATIONAL FLAG FOUNDATION - FLAG PLAZA LIBRARY
Flag Plaza
Phone: (412) 261-1776
Pittsburgh, PA 15219
George F. Cahill, Pres.

NORTH HILLS PASSAVANT HOSPITAL - MEDICAL LIBRARY
9100 Babcock Blvd.
Phone: (412) 366-1000
Pittsburgh, PA 15237
Margaret U. Trevanion, Med.Libn.

NUS CORPORATION - TECHNICAL LIBRARY
Box 330
Phone: (412) 788-1080
Pittsburgh, PA 15230
Kathryn E. Marlow, Libn.

PENNSYLVANIA ECONOMY LEAGUE - WESTERN DIVISION - LIBRARY
Two Gateway Ctr.
Phone: (412) 471-1477
Pittsburgh, PA 15222
Judith A. Eves, Libn.

PENNSYLVANIA STATE HISTORICAL & MUSEUM COMMISSION - FORT PITT MUSEUM - LIBRARY
Point State Park
Phone: (412) 281-9284
Pittsburgh, PA 15222
Robert J. Trombetta, Dir.

PEOPLES NATURAL GAS COMPANY - LAW LIBRARY
2 Gateway Ctr.
Phone: (412) 471-5100
Pittsburgh, PA 15222
Edison W. Keener, Att.

PITTSBURGH BOARD OF EDUCATION - PROFESSIONAL LIBRARY
635 Ridge Ave.
Phone: (412) 231-1939
Pittsburgh, PA 15212
Dorothy Hopkins, Libn.

PITTSBURGH CORNING CORPORATION - TECHNICAL LIBRARY
800 Presque Isle Dr.
Pittsburgh, PA 15239

PITTSBURGH HISTORY & LANDMARKS FOUNDATION - JAMES D. VAN TRUMP LIBRARY
One Landmarks Sq.
Phone: (412) 322-1204
Pittsburgh, PA 15212
Arthur P. Ziegler, Jr.

PITTSBURGH PRESS - LIBRARY
Boulevard of the Allies
Phone: (412) 263-1480
Pittsburgh, PA 15230
Eileen E. Finster, Libn.

PITTSBURGH THEOLOGICAL SEMINARY - CLIFFORD E. BARBOUR LIBRARY
616 N. Highland Ave.
Phone: (412) 362-5610
Pittsburgh, PA 15206
Dikran Y. Hadidian, Libn.

PORT AUTHORITY OF ALLEGHENY COUNTY - TRANSIT RESEARCH LIBRARY
Beaver & Island Ave.
Phone: (412) 237-7334
Pittsburgh, PA 15233
Lydia S. Pratt, Libn.

PPG INDUSTRIES, INC. - FIBER GLASS RESEARCH CENTER - LIBRARY
Box 2844
Phone: (412) 782-5130
Pittsburgh, PA 15230
Jacqueline A. Maxin, Supv.Info.Serv.

PPG INDUSTRIES, INC. - GENERAL OFFICE LIBRARY
One Gateway Center
Phone: (412) 434-3177
Pittsburgh, PA 15222
Esther Pacetti, Libn.

PPG INDUSTRIES, INC. - GLASS RESEARCH CENTER - INFORMATION SERVICES
Box 11472
Phone: (412) 274-8800
Pittsburgh, PA 15238
Jane Bookmyer, Supv.

PSYCHOLOGICAL SERVICE OF PITTSBURGH - LIBRARY
100 Fifth Ave.
Phone: (412) 261-1333
Pittsburgh, PA 15222
Beth A. Hough, Libn.

REED, SMITH, SHAW AND MC CLAY - LAW LIBRARY
747 Union Trust Bldg.
Phone: (412) 288-3340
Pittsburgh, PA 15219
Barbara Rose Stewart, Hd.Libn.

REFORMED PRESBYTERIAN THEOLOGICAL SEMINARY - LIBRARY
7418 Penn Ave.
Phone: (412) 731-8690
Pittsburgh, PA 15208
Rachel George, Libn.

ROCKWELL INTERNATIONAL - BUSINESS RESEARCH CENTER †
600 Grant St.
Phone: (412) 565-5880
Pittsburgh, PA 15219
Ruth T. Gunning, Mgr.

ROCKWELL INTERNATIONAL - GENERAL INDUSTRIES OPERATIONS - INFORMATION CENTER
400 N. Lexington Ave.
Phone: (412) 247-3095
Pittsburgh, PA 15208
Mohsen M. Farid, Mgr., Info.Rsrcs.

ST. CYRIL AND METHODIUS BYZANTINE CATHOLIC SEMINARY - LIBRARY
3605 Perrysville Ave.
Phone: (412) 321-8383
Pittsburgh, PA 15214
Rev. Gary Powell, O.F.M.Cap., Libn.

ST. MARGARET MEMORIAL HOSPITAL - PAUL TITUS MEMORIAL LIBRARY AND SCHOOL OF NURSING LIBRARY
4631 Davison St.
Phone: (412) 622-7090
Pittsburgh, PA 15201

SHADYSIDE HOSPITAL - JAMES FRAZER HILLMAN HEALTH SCIENCES LIBRARY
5230 Centre Ave.
Phone: (412) 622-2415
Pittsburgh, PA 15232
Malinda Fetkovich, Dir.

SOUTH HILLS HEALTH SYSTEM - BEHAN HEALTH SCIENCE LIBRARY
Coal Valley Rd.
Box 18119
Phone: (412) 664-5780
Pittsburgh, PA 15236
William Rose, Dir.Lib./Media Serv.

U.S. DEPT. OF COMMERCE - INTERNATIONAL TRADE ADMINISTRATION - PITTSBURGH DISTRICT OFFICE LIBRARY
2002 Federal Bldg.
1000 Liberty Ave.
Phone: (412) 644-2850
Pittsburgh, PA 15222
William M. Bradley, Dir.

UNITED STATES STEEL CORPORATION - COMMERCIAL INFORMATION CENTER
600 Grant St., Rm. 1818
Phone: (412) 433-3459
Pittsburgh, PA 15230
Nancy J. Suvak, Res.Supv.

U.S. VETERANS ADMINISTRATION (PA-Pittsburgh) - HOSPITAL LIBRARY
Highland Dr.
Phone: (412) 363-4900
Pittsburgh, PA 15206
Pauline M. Mason, Chf., Lib.Serv.

U.S. VETERANS ADMINISTRATION (PA-Pittsburgh) - MEDICAL LIBRARY
University Dr. C
Phone: (412) 683-3000
Pittsburgh, PA 15240
Tuula Beazell, Chf.Libn.

UNIVERSITY OF PITTSBURGH - AFRO-AMERICAN COLLECTION
Hillman Library
Phone: (412) 624-4447
Pittsburgh, PA 15260
Jeffrey S. Jackson, Libn.

UNIVERSITY OF PITTSBURGH - ALLEGHENY OBSERVATORY - LIBRARY
159 Riverview Airway
Phone: (412) 321-2400
Pittsburgh, PA 15260
Paul J. Kobulnicky, Libn.

UNIVERSITY OF PITTSBURGH - ARCHIVES
363 Hillman Library
Phone: (412) 624-4428
Pittsburgh, PA 15260
Dr. Marilyn P. Whitmore, Univ.Archv.

GEOGRAPHIC

UNIVERSITY OF PITTSBURGH - ARCHIVES OF INDUSTRIAL SOCIETY
363-H., Hillman Library
Univ. of Pittsburgh
Phone: (412) 624-4429
Pittsburgh, PA 15260
Frank A. Zabrosky, Cur.

UNIVERSITY OF PITTSBURGH - BEVIER ENGINEERING LIBRARY
126 Benedum Hall
Phone: (412) 624-4484
Pittsburgh, PA 15261
Homer I. Bernhardt, Hd.

UNIVERSITY OF PITTSBURGH - CENTER FOR INTERNATIONAL STUDIES
Forbes Quadrangle
Phone: (412) 624-1234
Pittsburgh, PA 15260
Jan P. Miller, Gen.Mgr.

UNIVERSITY OF PITTSBURGH - CHEMISTRY LIBRARY
200 Alumni Hall
Phone: (412) 624-5026
Pittsburgh, PA 15260
Paul J. Kobulnicky, Libn.

UNIVERSITY OF PITTSBURGH - COMPUTER SCIENCE LIBRARY
200 Alumni Hall
Phone: (412) 624-6462
Pittsburgh, PA 15260
Paul Kobulnicky, Libn.

UNIVERSITY OF PITTSBURGH - DARLINGTON MEMORIAL LIBRARY
Cathedral of Learning
Phone: (412) 624-4491
Pittsburgh, PA 15260
Charles E. Aston, Jr., Coord.

UNIVERSITY OF PITTSBURGH - EAST ASIAN LIBRARY
234 Hillman Library
Phone: (412) 624-4457
Pittsburgh, PA 15260
Dr. Thomas Kuo, Cur.

UNIVERSITY OF PITTSBURGH - ECONOMICS/COLLECTION IN REGIONAL
ECONOMICS
Mervis Hall, Rm. 430
139 University Pl.
Phone: (412) 624-4492
Pittsburgh, PA 15260
Susan Neuman, Libn.

UNIVERSITY OF PITTSBURGH - EDUCATIONAL RESOURCES INFORMATION
CENTER COLLECTION
233 Hillman Library
Phone: (412) 624-4528
Pittsburgh, PA 15260
Jean R. Aiken, Info.Libn.

UNIVERSITY OF PITTSBURGH - FALK LIBRARY OF THE HEALTH SCIENCES
Scaife Hall, 2nd Fl.
Phone: (412) 624-2521
Pittsburgh, PA 15261
Laurabelle Eakin, Dir.

UNIVERSITY OF PITTSBURGH - FOSTER HALL COLLECTION
Forbes Ave.
Phone: (412) 624-4100
Pittsburgh, PA 15260
Fletcher Hodges, Jr., Cur.

UNIVERSITY OF PITTSBURGH - GRADUATE SCHOOL OF BUSINESS LIBRARY
1501 Cathedral of Learning
Phone: (412) 624-6408
Pittsburgh, PA 15260
Mildred S. Myers, Dir.

UNIVERSITY OF PITTSBURGH - GRADUATE SCHOOL OF PUBLIC HEALTH
LIBRARY
130 De Soto St.
Phone: (412) 624-3016
Pittsburgh, PA 15261
Patti K. Corbett, Dir.

UNIVERSITY OF PITTSBURGH - GRADUATE SCHOOL OF PUBLIC &
INTERNATIONAL AFFAIRS LIBRARY
Forbes Quadrangle, 1st Fl. West
Phone: (412) 624-4738
Pittsburgh, PA 15260
Nicholas C. Caruso, Libn.

UNIVERSITY OF PITTSBURGH - HENRY CLAY FRICK FINE ARTS LIBRARY
Phone: (412) 624-4124
Pittsburgh, PA 15260
Anne W. Gordon, Libn.

UNIVERSITY OF PITTSBURGH - HUMAN RELATIONS AREA FILES
G16 Hillman Library
Phone: (412) 624-4449
Pittsburgh, PA 15260
Jean R. Aiken, Info.Libn.

UNIVERSITY OF PITTSBURGH - LANGLEY HALL LIBRARY
A-217 Langley Hall
Phone: (412) 624-4489
Pittsburgh, PA 15260
D.L. Johnston, Libn.

UNIVERSITY OF PITTSBURGH - LATIN AMERICAN COLLECTION
171 Hillman Library
Phone: (412) 624-4425
Pittsburgh, PA 15260
Eduardo Lozano, Biblog.

UNIVERSITY OF PITTSBURGH - LAW LIBRARY
3900 Forbes Ave.
Phone: (412) 624-6213
Pittsburgh, PA 15260
Jenni Parrish, Dir.

UNIVERSITY OF PITTSBURGH - MATHEMATICS LIBRARY
809 Schenley Hall
Phone: (412) 624-4488
Pittsburgh, PA 15260
Homer I. Bernhardt, Hd.

UNIVERSITY OF PITTSBURGH - NASA INDUSTRIAL APPLICATIONS CENTER
710 L.I.S. Bldg.
Phone: (412) 624-5212
Pittsburgh, PA 15260
Paul W. McWilliams, Dir.

UNIVERSITY OF PITTSBURGH - PHYSICS LIBRARY
208 Engineering Hall
Phone: (412) 624-4482
Pittsburgh, PA 15260
Paul J. Kobulnicky, Libn.

UNIVERSITY OF PITTSBURGH - PRESBYTERIAN UNIVERSITY HOSPITAL -
MEDICAL LIBRARY
DeSoto at O'Hara Sts.
Phone: (412) 647-3287
Pittsburgh, PA 15213
Mrs. Bianka M. Hesz, Med.Libn.

UNIVERSITY OF PITTSBURGH - READING/COMMUNICATIONS RESOURCE
CENTER
Forbes Quadrangle
Phone: (412) 624-1311
Pittsburgh, PA 15260
Dr. Allen Berger, Dir.

UNIVERSITY OF PITTSBURGH - SCHOOL OF EDUCATION - INTERNATIONAL
& DEVELOPMENT EDUCATION PROGRAM CLEARINGHOUSE
Learning Resource Center
IN10 Forbes Quadrangle
Phone: (412) 624-3271
Pittsburgh, PA 15260
Carmelita Lavayna Portugal, Dir.

UNIVERSITY OF PITTSBURGH - SCHOOL OF LIBRARY & INFORMATION
SCIENCE - INTL. LIB. INFO. CTR.
135 N. Bellefield Ave.
Phone: (412) 624-3398
Pittsburgh, PA 15260
Dr. Richard Krzys, Dir.

UNIVERSITY OF PITTSBURGH - SCHOOL OF LIBRARY & INFORMATION
SCIENCE - LIBRARY
135 N. Bellefield Ave.
LIS Bldg., 3rd Fl.
Phone: (412) 624-5238
Pittsburgh, PA 15260
Jean Kindlin, Dir., Lib. & Media Serv.

UNIVERSITY OF PITTSBURGH - SCHOOL OF SOCIAL WORK - BUHL LIBRARY
Hillman Library
Phone: (412) 624-4456
Pittsburgh, PA 15260
Dolores Williams, Libn.

UNIVERSITY OF PITTSBURGH - SPECIAL COLLECTIONS DEPARTMENT
363 Hillman Library
Phone: (412) 624-4430
Pittsburgh, PA 15260
Charles E. Aston, Jr., Coord.

UNIVERSITY OF PITTSBURGH - THEODORE M. FINNEY MUSIC LIBRARY
Music Bldg.
Phone: (412) 624-4130
Pittsburgh, PA 15260
Norris L. Stephens, Libn.

UNIVERSITY OF PITTSBURGH - UNIVERSITY CENTER FOR INSTRUCTIONAL
RESOURCES
G-20 Hillman Library
Phone: (412) 624-4468
Pittsburgh, PA 15260
Dr. J. Fred Gage, Dir.

UNIVERSITY OF PITTSBURGH - WESTERN PSYCHIATRIC INSTITUTE AND
CLINIC - LIBRARY
3811 O'Hara St.
Phone: (412) 624-2378
Pittsburgh, PA 15261
Lucile S. Stark, Dir.

WESTERN PENNSYLVANIA GENEALOGICAL SOCIETY - LIBRARY
4338 Bigelow Blvd.
Phone: (412) 681-5533
Pittsburgh, PA 15213
Helen M. Wilson, Libn.

WESTINGHOUSE ELECTRIC CORPORATION - NUCLEAR ENERGY SYSTEMS -
INFORMATION RESOURCES †
Box 355
Phone: (412) 373-4200
Pittsburgh, PA 15230
Mary Vasilakis, Mgr.

WESTINGHOUSE ELECTRIC CORPORATION - RESEARCH LABORATORIES -
LIBRARY †
1310 Beulah Rd.
Phone: (412) 256-3463
Pittsburgh, PA 15235
Anita Newell, Mgr.

WESTMINSTER PRESBYTERIAN CHURCH - LIBRARY †
2040 Washington Rd.   Phone: (412) 835-6630
Pittsburgh, PA 15241   Mrs. R.L. Hutchison, Libn.

EMERGENCY CARE RESEARCH INSTITUTE - LIBRARY
5200 Butler Pike   Phone: (215) 825-6000
Plymouth Meeting, PA 19462   Linda Wengel, Hd.Libn.

POTTSTOWN MEMORIAL MEDICAL CENTER - MEDICAL STAFF LIBRARY
High St. & Firestone Blvd.   Phone: (215) 327-7000
Pottstown, PA 19464   Marilyn D. Chapis, Med. Staff Libn.

SANDERS & THOMAS, INC. - LIBRARY
11 Robinson St.   Phone: (215) 326-4600
Pottstown, PA 19464   Carol S. Leh, Tech.Libn.

OHEB ZEDECK SYNAGOGUE CENTER - LIBRARY
2300 Mahantongo St.   Phone: (717) 622-4320
Pottsville, PA 17901   Dr. David Lazar, Rabbi

POTTSVILLE HOSPITAL AND WARNE CLINIC - MEDICAL LIBRARY
Jackson & Mauch Chunk Sts.   Phone: (717) 622-6120
Pottsville, PA 17901   Marguerite Schoenfelder, Libn.

SCHUYLKILL COUNTY LAW LIBRARY
Court House   Phone: (717) 622-5570
Pottsville, PA 17901   Constance H. Pugh, Libn.

ROSICRUCIAN FRATERNITY - LIBRARY †
Beverly Hall
Box 220   Phone: (215) 536-5168
Quakertown, PA 18951   Emerson M. Clymer, Pres.

RESSLER (Martin E.) - PRIVATE MUSIC LIBRARY
R.D. 2, Box 173   Phone: (717) 529-2463
Quarryville, PA 17566   Martin E. Ressler, Owner

CABRINI COLLEGE - HOLY SPIRIT LIBRARY
Eagle & King of Prussia Rds.   Phone: (215) 687-2100
Radnor, PA 19087   Claire Skerrett, Lib.Dir.

CHILTON COMPANY - MARKETING & ADVERTISING INFORMATION CENTER
One Chilton Way   Phone: (215) 687-8200
Radnor, PA 19089   Donald Altmaier, V.P., Mktg.Serv.

PENNSYLVANIA STATE UNIVERSITY, RADNOR CENTER FOR GRADUATE
    STUDIES AND CONTINUING EDUCATION - LIBRARY
259 Radnor-Chester Rd.   Phone: (215) 293-9860
Radnor, PA 19087   Vera Hospodka, Hd.Libn.

BELL TELEPHONE LABORATORIES, INC. & WESTERN ELECTRIC, INC. -
    TECHNICAL LIBRARY
2525 N. 11th St.   Phone: (215) 929-7990
Reading, PA 19603   Ann M. Buck, Lib. Group Supv.

BERKS COUNTY LAW LIBRARY
Court House   Phone: (215) 375-6121
Reading, PA 19601   Linda Fuerle Fisk, Libn.

CABOT CORPORATION - READING RESEARCH & DEVELOPMENT LIBRARY
Box 1462   Phone: (215) 921-5262
Reading, PA 19603   Brenda C. Hehr, Libn.

CARPENTER TECHNOLOGY CORPORATION - RESEARCH AND DEVELOPMENT
    CENTER LIBRARY
Box 662   Phone: (215) 371-2583
Reading, PA 19603   Wendy M. Holt, Assoc.Libn.

GILBERT ASSOCIATES, INC. - CORPORATE LIBRARY †
Box 1498   Phone: (215) 775-2600
Reading, PA 19603

GPU NUCLEAR - LIBRARY
Rte. 183 & Van Reed Rd.   Phone: (215) 371-1001
Reading, PA 19601   Winifred F. Sayers, Libn.

HISTORICAL SOCIETY OF BERKS COUNTY - LIBRARY
940 Centre Ave.   Phone: (215) 375-4375
Reading, PA 19601   Aimee Devine Sanders, Lib.Cons.

KESHER ZION SYNAGOGUE SISTERHOOD - LIBRARY
Perkiomen & Hill Aves.   Phone: (215) 372-3818
Reading, PA 19602   Rachel Yaffee, Libn.

METROPOLITAN EDISON COMPANY - SYSTEM LIBRARY
2800 Pottsville Pike   Phone: (215) 929-3601
Reading, PA 19605

PENNSYLVANIA STATE UNIVERSITY, BERKS CAMPUS - LIBRARY
R.D. 5, Tulpehocken Rd.
Box 2150   Phone: (215) 375-4211
Reading, PA 19608   Sally S. Small, Hd.Libn.

POLYMER CORPORATION - LIBRARY
501 Crescent Ave.   Phone: (215) 929-5858
Reading, PA 19603   Mrs. C.J. Arbogast, Libn.

READING HOSPITAL - MEDICAL LIBRARY
Sixth & Spruce Sts.   Phone: (215) 378-6399
Reading, PA 19603   Melinda R. Paquette, Med.Libn.

READING HOSPITAL - SCHOOL OF NURSING LIBRARY
                                             Phone: (215) 378-6359
Reading, PA 19603   Carolyn V. Unruh, Libn.

READING PUBLIC MUSEUM AND ART GALLERY - REFERENCE LIBRARY
500 Museum Rd.   Phone: (215) 371-5850
Reading, PA 19611   Bruce L. Dietrich, Dir.

READING SCHOOL DISTRICT PLANETARIUM - LIBRARY
1211 Parkside Dr., S.   Phone: (215) 371-5854
Reading, PA 19611   Bruce L. Dietrich, Dir. of Planetarium

ST. JOSEPH HOSPITAL - HEALTH SCIENCES LIBRARY
12th & Walnut Sts.   Phone: (215) 378-2390
Reading, PA 19603   Jean E. McLaughlin, Libn.

ROSEMONT COLLEGE - GERTRUDE KISTLER MEMORIAL LIBRARY - SPECIAL
    COLLECTIONS
                                             Phone: (215) 527-0200
Rosemont, PA 19010   Sr. M. Dennis Lynch, S.H.C.J., Lib.Dir.

AIRCO CARBON - RESEARCH AND DEVELOPMENT LIBRARY
800 Theresa St.   Phone: (814) 834-2801
St. Marys, PA 15857   Rebecca Mattivi, Libn.

PURE CARBON CO., INC. - ENGINEERING LIBRARY
441 Hall Ave.   Phone: (814) 781-1573
St. Marys, PA 15857   Betty J. Aaron, Libn.

PACKER (Robert) HOSPITAL - MEDICAL LIBRARY
Guthrie Sq.   Phone: (717) 888-6666
Sayre, PA 18840   E. Jean Antes, Med.Ref.Libn.

HISTORIC SCHAEFFERSTOWN, INC. - THOMAS R. BRENDLE MEMORIAL
    LIBRARY & MUSEUM
N. Market St.
Schaefferstown, PA 17088   Mrs. Paul Skewis

CK-PERMANENT PRESS - PARMAR ELDALIEVA LIBRARY
1846 Bundy St.
Scranton, PA 18508   Rumil of Cameloford, Libn.

LACKAWANNA BAR ASSOCIATION - LAW LIBRARY
Court House   Phone: (717) 342-8089
Scranton, PA 18503   Marita E. Paparelli, Law Libn.

LACKAWANNA HISTORICAL SOCIETY - LIBRARY AND ARCHIVES
232 Monroe Ave.   Phone: (717) 344-3841
Scranton, PA 18510   William P. Lewis, Exec.Dir.

MARYWOOD COLLEGE - LEARNING RESOURCES CENTER
2300 Adams Ave.   Phone: (717) 348-6260
Scranton, PA 18509   James P. Clarke, Lib.Dir.

MERCY HOSPITAL - MEDICAL LIBRARY
746 Jefferson Ave.   Phone: (717) 348-7800
Scranton, PA 18510   Sr. Elizabeth Anne Brandreth, Libn.

GEOGRAPHIC

MERCY HOSPITAL - SCHOOL OF NURSING - LIBRARY
520 Jefferson Ave.   Phone: (717) 344-8571
Scranton, PA 18501   Marie McAndrew, Libn.

ST. ANN'S PASSIONIST MONASTERY - LIBRARY
1230 St. Ann St.   Phone: (717) 347-5691
Scranton, PA 18504

SCRANTON TRIBUNE AND SCRANTONIAN - LIBRARY
336 N. Washington Ave.   Phone: (717) 344-7221
Scranton, PA 18503   Hal Lewis, Libn.

GRAND VIEW HOSPITAL - MEDICAL RESOURCE LIBRARY
Lawn Ave.   Phone: (215) 257-3611
Sellersville, PA 18960   Freda Clark Agnew, Med.Libn.

DIXMONT STATE HOSPITAL - PERSONNEL LIBRARY
                                           Phone: (412) 761-1780
Sewickley, PA 15143   Ta-Liang Daisy Yao, Libn.

SHARON GENERAL HOSPITAL - MEDICAL STAFF LIBRARY
740 E. State St.   Phone: (412) 983-3911
Sharon, PA 16146   Eugenia Christenson, Libn.

SHARON GENERAL HOSPITAL - SCHOOL OF NURSING - LIBRARY
740 E. State St.   Phone: (412) 983-3911
Sharon, PA 16146   Eugenia Christenson, Libn.

WESTINGHOUSE ELECTRIC CORPORATION - MEDIUM POWER
    TRANSFORMER DIV. - SHARON ENGINEERING LIBRARY
469 Sharpsville Ave.
Sharon, PA 16146   S.G. Vargo, Mgr.

MERCER COUNTY REGIONAL PLANNING COMMISSION - LIBRARY
Sharpsville Ctr. Plaza
94 E. Shenango St.   Phone: (412) 962-5787
Sharpsville, PA 16150   Leslie B. Spaulding, Libn.

SHIPPENSBURG HISTORICAL SOCIETY - ARCHIVES
Shippensburg Public Library
West King St.   Phone: (717) 532-4508
Shippensburg, PA 17257

SHIPPENSBURG STATE COLLEGE - EZRA LEHMAN MEMORIAL LIBRARY
                                           Phone: (717) 532-1463
Shippensburg, PA 17257

MC KEAN COUNTY LAW LIBRARY
Court House   Phone: (814) 887-5571
Smethport, PA 16749   Phyllis P. Anderson, Libn.

HISTORICAL AND GENEALOGICAL SOCIETY OF SOMERSET COUNTY -
    COUNTY HISTORICAL LIBRARY AND RESEARCH CENTER
Somerset Historical Ctr., R.F.D. 2   Phone: (814) 445-6077
Somerset, PA 15501

PENNSYLVANIA STATE DEPARTMENT OF PUBLIC WELFARE - SOMERSET
    STATE HOSPITAL - LIBRARY
Box 631   Phone: (814) 445-6501
Somerset, PA 15501   Eve Kline, Libn./Dir.

SOMERSET COUNTY LAW LIBRARY †
                                           Phone: (814) 445-5545
Somerset, PA 15501   Irene Coffroth, Libn.

UNION NATIONAL BANK AND TRUST COMPANY - LIBRARY
Univest Bldg.
14 Main St.   Phone: (215) 723-9841
Souderton, PA 18964   Gladys Detweiler, Libn.

PENNHURST CENTER - STAFF LIBRARY
324 Buchanan Bldg.   Phone: (215) 948-3500
Spring City, PA 19475   Thomas Hudson, Coord., Lib.Serv.

GLATFELTER (P.H.) COMPANY - RESEARCH LIBRARY
                                           Phone: (717) 225-4711
Spring Grove, PA 17362   Jean Bailey, Libn.

ROHM & HAAS COMPANY - RESEARCH DIVISION - INFORMATION
    SERVICES DEPARTMENT
727 Norristown Rd.   Phone: (215) 641-7816
Spring House, PA 19477   Dr. Frederick H. Owens, Mgr.

TRI-COUNTY HOSPITAL - MEDICAL LIBRARY
Sproul & Thomson Rds.
Springfield, PA 19064   Barbara Rivers, Libn.

AMERICAN PHILATELIC RESEARCH LIBRARY
Box 338   Phone: (814) 237-3803
State College, PA 16801   Steven A. Pla, Libn.

PENNSYLVANIA STATE UNIVERSITY - APPLIED RESEARCH LABORATORY -
    LIBRARY
Box 30   Phone: (814) 865-6621
State College, PA 16801   Charles G. Murphy, Sr.Asst.Libn.

ROY (Milton) CO. LABORATORY GROUP - APPLIED SCIENCE DIVISION -
    LIBRARY ★
Box 440   Phone: (814) 238-2406
State College, PA 16801

SINGER COMPANY - HRB-SINGER, INC. - TECHNICAL INFORMATION
    CENTER
Science Pk.   Phone: (814) 238-4311
State College, PA 16801   Karen L. Moore, Tech.Libn.

BROWN BROTHERS - PHOTOGRAPH COLLECTION
                                           Phone: (717) 689-9688
Sterling, PA 18463   Harry B. Collins, Jr., Pres.

DOWDEN, HUTCHINSON & ROSS, INC. - REFERENCE LIBRARY
523 Sarah St.
Stroudsburg, PA 18360

MONROE COUNTY HISTORICAL SOCIETY - LIBRARY AND MUSEUM
Ninth & Main Sts.
Stroud Community House   Phone: (717) 421-7703
Stroudsburg, PA 18360

MONROE COUNTY LAW LIBRARY
Court House   Phone: (717) 424-5100
Stroudsburg, PA 18360   Kennard Lewis, Esq., Chm.Lib.Comm.

NORTHUMBERLAND COUNTY LAW LIBRARY
Court House   Phone: (717) 286-0147
Sunbury, PA 17801   Pauline M. Sokalzuk, Law Libn.

FOX CONSULTING AND LIBRARY SERVICE
309 Yale Ave.   Phone: (215) 543-2801
Swarthmore, PA 19081   Jane G. Fox, Libn.

SWARTHMORE COLLEGE - DANIEL UNDERHILL MUSIC LIBRARY
                                           Phone: (215) 447-7232
Swarthmore, PA 19081   George K. Huber, Music Libn.

SWARTHMORE COLLEGE - DU PONT SCIENCE LIBRARY
                                           Phone: (215) 544-7900
Swarthmore, PA 19081   Emi K. Horikawa, Libn.

SWARTHMORE COLLEGE - FRIENDS HISTORICAL LIBRARY
                                           Phone: (215) 447-7496
Swarthmore, PA 19081   J. William Frost, Dir.

SWARTHMORE COLLEGE - FRIENDS HISTORICAL LIBRARY - PEACE
    COLLECTION
McCabe Library   Phone: (215) 447-7500
Swarthmore, PA 19081   J. Richard Kyle, Cur.

SWARTHMORE COLLEGE - SPROUL OBSERVATORY LIBRARY
                                           Phone: (215) 544-7900
Swarthmore, PA 19081   Emi K. Horikawa, Libn.

ATLAS POWDER COMPANY - RESEARCH & DEVELOPMENT LABORATORY -
    LIBRARY
Box 271   Phone: (717) 386-4121
Tamaqua, PA 18252   Charlotte D. Fisler, Libn.

PENNSYLVANIA STATE HISTORICAL & MUSEUM COMMISSION - DRAKE
WELL MUSEUM - LIBRARY
R.D. 3   Phone: (814) 827-2797
Titusville, PA 16354

BETZ LABORATORIES, INC. - RESEARCH LIBRARY
4636 Somerton Rd.   Phone: (215) 355-3300
Trevose, PA 19047   Joan E. Goldberg, Tech.Libn.

EASTERN STATE SCHOOL AND HOSPITAL - STAFF LIBRARY
3740 Lincoln Hwy.   Phone: (215) 671-3389
Trevose, PA 19047   Elizabeth Sorg, Libn.

FAYETTE COUNTY LAW LIBRARY
Court House
Uniontown, PA 15401   Elnora E. Mullooly, Libn.

UNIONTOWN HOSPITAL ASSOCIATION - MEDICAL LIBRARY
500 W. Berkeley St.   Phone: (412) 437-4531
Uniontown, PA 15401   Nina Stith, Med.Libn.

PENNSYLVANIA STATE UNIVERSITY - ARCHITECTURE READING ROOM
207 Engineering Unit C   Phone: (814) 863-0511
University Park, PA 16802   Jean Smith, Libn.

PENNSYLVANIA STATE UNIVERSITY - ARTS LIBRARY
University Library, Rm. E405   Phone: (814) 865-6481
University Park, PA 16802   Jean Smith, Hd.Libn.

PENNSYLVANIA STATE UNIVERSITY - AUDIOVISUAL SERVICES
Special Services Bldg.   Phone: (814) 865-6314
University Park, PA 16802   Robert L. Allen, Hd.

PENNSYLVANIA STATE UNIVERSITY - CENTER FOR AIR ENVIRONMENT
STUDIES - INFORMATION CENTER
225 Fenske Laboratory   Phone: (814) 865-1415
University Park, PA 16802   Elizabeth J. Carroll, Adm.Asst.

PENNSYLVANIA STATE UNIVERSITY - EARTH AND MINERAL SCIENCES
LIBRARY
105 Deike Bldg.   Phone: (814) 865-9517
University Park, PA 16802   Emilie T. McWilliams, Hd.

PENNSYLVANIA STATE UNIVERSITY - ENGINEERING LIBRARY
325 Hammond Bldg.   Phone: (814) 865-3451
University Park, PA 16802   Thomas W. Conkling, Hd.

PENNSYLVANIA STATE UNIVERSITY - FROST ENTOMOLOGICAL MUSEUM -
TAXONOMIC RESEARCH LIBRARY
106 Patterson Bldg.   Phone: (814) 865-1895
University Park, PA 16802   Ke Chung Kim, Cur.

PENNSYLVANIA STATE UNIVERSITY - INSTITUTE FOR POLICY RESEARCH
AND EVALUATION - LIBRARY
N253 Burrowes   Phone: (814) 865-9561
University Park, PA 16802   Mary Jane Johnson, Sec.

PENNSYLVANIA STATE UNIVERSITY - INSTITUTE OF PUBLIC
ADMINISTRATION - LIBRARY
211 Burrowes Bldg.   Phone: (814) 865-2536
University Park, PA 16802   Robert D. Lee

PENNSYLVANIA STATE UNIVERSITY - INSTITUTE FOR RESEARCH ON LAND
AND WATER RESOURCES - LIBRARY
Land & Water Research Bldg.   Phone: (814) 863-0140
University Park, PA 16802   Eunice Roe, Project Assoc.

PENNSYLVANIA STATE UNIVERSITY - LIFE SCIENCES LIBRARY
E205 E. Pattee Library   Phone: (814) 865-7056
University Park, PA 16802   Keith Roe, Hd.

PENNSYLVANIA STATE UNIVERSITY - MAPS SECTION
Pattee Library   Phone: (814) 863-0094
University Park, PA 16802   Karl H. Proehl, Map Libn.

PENNSYLVANIA STATE UNIVERSITY - MATHEMATICS LIBRARY
110 McAllister Bldg.   Phone: (814) 865-6822
University Park, PA 16802   C.J. McKown, Hd.

PENNSYLVANIA STATE UNIVERSITY - PHYSICAL SCIENCES LIBRARY
230 Davey Laboratory   Phone: (814) 865-7617
University Park, PA 16802   C.J. McKown, Hd.

PENNSYLVANIA STATE UNIVERSITY - TRANSPORTATION INSTITUTE
WORKING COLLECTION
Research Bldg. B   Phone: (814) 865-1891
University Park, PA 16802   Del Sweeney, Info.Spec.

SPORTS RESEARCH INSTITUTE - LIBRARY
Pennsylvania State University
109 Sports Research Bldg.   Phone: (814) 865-9543
University Park, PA 16802   Patricia McMullen, Sec.

HAVERFORD STATE HOSPITAL - MEDICAL LIBRARY
3500 Darby Rd.   Phone: (215) 525-9620
Upper Darby, PA 19041   Joyce Matheson, Dir., Lib.Serv.

AMERICAN BAPTIST CHURCHES IN THE U.S.A. - BOARD OF EDUCATIONAL
MINISTRIES - EDITORIAL LIBRARY
                                                   Phone: (215) 768-2378
Valley Forge, PA 19481   Dorothy A. Martin, Libn.

AMERICAN BAPTIST CHURCHES IN THE U.S.A. - BOARD OF
INTERNATIONAL MINISTRIES - LIBRARY AND CENTRAL FILES
                                                   Phone: (215) 768-2365
Valley Forge, PA 19481   Priscilla B. Shaw, Libn.

AMERICAN BAPTIST CHURCHES IN THE U.S.A. - BOARD OF NATIONAL
MINISTRIES - LIBRARY & RECORDS MANAGEMENT
                                                   Phone: (215) 768-2383
Valley Forge, PA 19481   Mrs. Henrene George, Supv.

COMBUSTION ENGINEERING, INC. - C-E REFRACTORIES - RESEARCH &
DEVELOPMENT LIBRARY
Box 828   Phone: (215) 337-1100
Valley Forge, PA 19482   Dolores A. Belanger, Res.Libn.

FREEDOMS FOUNDATION AT VALLEY FORGE - LIBRARY
                                                   Phone: (215) 933-8825
Valley Forge, PA 19481   Harold Badger, Libn.

HOUGHTON (E.F.) TECHNICAL CENTER - LIBRARY
Madison & Van Buren Aves.   Phone: (215) 666-4000
Valley Forge, PA 19482

PHILADELPHIA QUARTZ COMPANY - BUSINESS/ENGINEERING
INFORMATION CENTER
Box 840   Phone: (215) 293-7352
Valley Forge, PA 19482   Frieda S. Mecray, Info.Spec.

VALLEY FORGE HISTORICAL SOCIETY - LIBRARY *
                                                   Phone: (215) 783-0535
Valley Forge, PA 19481   John F. Reed, Cur., Doc.

AUGUSTINIAN HISTORICAL INSTITUTE - LIBRARY
Villanova University, Falvey Hall   Phone: (215) 527-2100
Villanova, PA 19085   Marcese W. Downey, Libn.

VILLANOVA UNIVERSITY - PULLING LAW LIBRARY
Garey Hall   Phone: (215) 527-2100
Villanova, PA 19085   Charlie R. Harvey, Libn./Asst.Prof.

OHEV SHALOM SYNAGOGUE - RAY DOBLITZ MEMORIAL LIBRARY
2 Chester Rd.   Phone: (215) 874-1465
Wallingford, PA 19086   Virginia Coleman, Libn.

PENDLE HILL - QUAKER COLLECTION
                                                   Phone: (215) 566-4507
Wallingford, PA 19086   Yuki T. Brinton, Libn.

FISCHER & PORTER CO. - CORPORATE ENGINEERING LIBRARY
125 E. County Line Rd.   Phone: (215) 674-6834
Warminster, PA 18974   Cheryl A. Cherry, Libn.

U.S. NAVY - NAVAL AIR DEVELOPMENT CENTER - TECHNICAL
INFORMATION BRANCH
Technical Services Dept.   Phone: (215) 441-2429
Warminster, PA 18974   Dora Huang, Br.Hd.Libn.

GEOGRAPHIC

WARREN COUNTY HISTORICAL SOCIETY - LIBRARY AND ARCHIVES
Box 427   Phone: (814) 723-1795
Warren, PA 16365   Mrs. Conrad Brunke, Libn.

WARREN LIBRARY ASSOCIATION - LIBRARY †
205 Market St.
Box 489   Phone: (814) 723-4650
Warren, PA 16365   Robert C. Johnston, Ref.Libn.

WARREN STATE HOSPITAL - MEDICAL LIBRARY
Box 249   Phone: (814) 723-5500
Warren, PA 16365   Daryl G. Ellsworth, Libn.

SOCIETY OF AUTOMOTIVE ENGINEERS - SAE LIBRARY
400 Commonwealth Dr.   Phone: (412) 776-4841
Warrendale, PA 15096   Janet Jedlicka, Libn./Res.Ck.

THE WHEELMEN - LIBRARY †
1479 Guinea Ln.
Warrington, PA 18976   Dorothy Koehler, Hon.Libn.

WASHINGTON COUNTY HISTORICAL AND MUSEUM SOCIETY - LE MOYNE HOUSE LIBRARY
LeMoyne House, 49 E. Maiden St.   Phone: (412) 225-6740
Washington, PA 15301   Nancy Berry Saxon, Dir.

WASHINGTON COUNTY LAW LIBRARY
Court House   Phone: (412) 228-6747
Washington, PA 15301   Jane M. Fulcher, Law Libn.

WASHINGTON HOSPITAL - MEDICAL-NURSES' LIBRARY
155 Wilson Ave.   Phone: (412) 225-7000
Washington, PA 15301   Mary D. Leif, Libn.

DAVID LIBRARY OF THE AMERICAN REVOLUTION
River Rd.
Rte. 32, Box 48   Phone: (215) 493-6776
Washington Crossing, PA 18977   Joseph J. Felcone, Libn.

EARLY AMERICAN INDUSTRIES ASSOCIATION - LIBRARY
Washington Crossing Historic Park   Phone: (213) 493-4076
Washington Crossing, PA 18977   Daniel B. Reibel, Dir.

PENNSYLVANIA STATE HISTORICAL & MUSEUM COMMISSION - FORT LE BOEUF MUSEUM - LIBRARY
123 S. High St.
Box 231   Phone: (814) 796-4113
Waterford, PA 16441   Patricia Leiphart, Historic Site Mgr.

RADNOR HISTORICAL SOCIETY - RESEARCH LIBRARY
Finley House
113 W. Beech Tree Ln.   Phone: (215) 688-2668
Wayne, PA 19087   Mrs. R.I. Cummin

WAYNE PRESBYTERIAN CHURCH - LIBRARY
125 E. Lancaster Ave.   Phone: (215) 688-8700
Wayne, PA 19087   Anne Pringle, Hd.Libn.

GREENE COUNTY HISTORICAL SOCIETY - LIBRARY AND MUSEUM
R.F.D. 2   Phone: (412) 627-9513
Waynesburg, PA 15370   Kathryn Gooden, Libn.

GREENE COUNTY LAW LIBRARY †
Court House   Phone: (412) 852-1171
Waynesburg, PA 15370   Wanda B. Smith, Libn.

AMERICAN HOME PRODUCTS CORPORATION - WYETH LABORATORIES DIVISION - ANTIBIOTICS LABORATORIES LIBRARY †
611 E. Nield St.   Phone: (215) 696-3100
West Chester, PA 19380   Beverly L. Cantor, Tech.Libn.

CHESTER COUNTY HISTORICAL SOCIETY - LIBRARY
225 N. High St.   Phone: (215) 692-4800
West Chester, PA 19380   Rosemary B. Philips, Libn.

CHESTER COUNTY LAW AND MISCELLANEOUS LIBRARY ASSOCIATION
Court House   Phone: (215) 431-6166
West Chester, PA 19380   Eileen M. Macbeth, Libn.

WEST CHESTER STATE COLLEGE - FRANCIS HARVEY GREEN LIBRARY - SPECIAL COLLECTIONS
                                              Phone: (215) 436-2643
West Chester, PA 19380   Frank Q. Helms, Dir. of Lib.Serv.

WEST CHESTER STATE COLLEGE - MUSIC LIBRARY
Swope Hall, College Ave.   Phone: (215) 436-2430
West Chester, PA 19380   Ruth Weidner, Music Libn.

WESTON (Roy F.), INC. - TECHNICAL INFORMATION CENTER AND LIBRARY
Weston Way   Phone: (215) 692-3030
West Chester, PA 19380   Margo Dinniman, Sr.Info.Spec.

U.S. DEPT. OF ENERGY - BETTIS ATOMIC POWER LABORATORY - LIBRARY
Box 79   Phone: (412) 462-5000
West Mifflin, PA 15122   Mary Louise Frazee, Libn.

MERCK & COMPANY, INC. - MERCK SHARP & DOHME RESEARCH LABORATORIES - LIBRARY SERVICES
                                              Phone: (215) 661-6026
West Point, PA 19486   Evelyn W. Armstrong, Mgr.

WHITE HAVEN CENTER - STAFF LIBRARY
Oley Valley Rd.   Phone: (717) 443-9564
White Haven, PA 18661   Frances M. McSpedon, Libn.

KING'S COLLEGE - D. LEONARD CORGAN LIBRARY
14 W. Jackson St.   Phone: (717) 824-9931
Wilkes-Barre, PA 18711   Judith Tierney, Spec.Coll.Libn.

MERCY HOSPITAL - MEDICAL LIBRARY
25 Church St.   Phone: (717) 826-3699
Wilkes-Barre, PA 18765   Barbara Nanstiel, Coord. of Lib.Serv.

ROSENN, JENKINS & GREENWALD, ATTORNEYS AT LAW - LIBRARY
15 S. Franklin St.   Phone: (717) 826-5663
Wilkes-Barre, PA 18711   Evelyn Tomasovic, Libn.

U.S. VETERANS ADMINISTRATION (PA-Wilkes-Barre) - MEDICAL CENTER LIBRARY
1111 E. End Blvd.   Phone: (717) 824-3521
Wilkes-Barre, PA 18711   Betsy S. Schreder, Chf.Libn.

WILKES-BARRE GENERAL HOSPITAL - HOSPITAL LIBRARY
Auburn & River Sts.   Phone: (717) 829-8111
Wilkes-Barre, PA 18764   Rosemarie Kazda Taylor, Dir., Lib.Serv.

WILKES-BARRE LAW AND LIBRARY ASSOCIATION †
Courthouse, Rm. 23   Phone: (717) 822-6712
Wilkes-Barre, PA 18711

WILKES COLLEGE - EARTH AND ENVIRONMENTAL SCIENCES READING ROOM
Box 111   Phone: (717) 824-4651
Wilkes-Barre, PA 18766   Dr. Bruce Berryman, Chm.

WILKES COLLEGE - INSTITUTE OF REGIONAL AFFAIRS - LIBRARY †
165 S. Franklin St.   Phone: (717) 824-4651
Wilkes-Barre, PA 18766   Andrew Shaw, Jr., Dir.

WYOMING HISTORICAL AND GEOLOGICAL SOCIETY - BISHOP MEMORIAL LIBRARY
49 S. Franklin St.   Phone: (717) 823-6244
Wilkes-Barre, PA 18701   William H. Siener, Exec.Dir.

BRODART, INC. - REFERENCE LIBRARY
1609 Memorial Ave.   Phone: (717) 326-2461
Williamsport, PA 17705   Richard A. Russell, Libn.

DIVINE PROVIDENCE HOSPITAL - MEDICAL LIBRARY
1100 Grampian Blvd.   Phone: (717) 326-8153
Williamsport, PA 17701   Janet Anderson, Med.Rec.Adm.

LYCOMING COUNTY LAW LIBRARY
Court House, 3rd Fl.   Phone: (717) 327-2475
Williamsport, PA 17701   Charles Hunt, Law Libn.

WILLIAMSPORT AREA COMMUNITY COLLEGE - SLOAN FINE ARTS LIBRARY
1005 W. 3rd St.
Williamsport, PA 17701   David P. Siemsen, Dir., Lib.Serv.

WILLIAMSPORT HOSPITAL - LEARNING RESOURCES CENTER
777 Rural Ave.   Phone: (717) 322-7861
Williamsport, PA 17701   Michael Heyd, Dir.

FORD AEROSPACE & COMMUNICATIONS CORP. - COMMUNICATIONS
    SYSTEMS LIBRARY
3900 Welsh Rd.
Willow Grove, PA 19090

MAIN LINE REFORM TEMPLE - LIBRARY
410 Montgomery Ave.   Phone: (215) 649-7800
Wynnewood, PA 19096   Betty Graboyes, Libn.

BORG-WARNER CORPORATION - YORK DIVISION - ENGINEERING LIBRARY
Box 1592   Phone: (717) 846-7890
York, PA 17405   Doris Dellinger, Libn.

HISTORICAL SOCIETY OF YORK COUNTY - LIBRARY AND ARCHIVES
250 E. Market St.   Phone: (717) 848-1587
York, PA 17403   Landon Chas. Reisinger, Libn.

SCHOOL OF LIVING - RALPH BORSODI MEMORIAL LIBRARY
Deep Run Center
Box 3233   Phone: (717) 755-1561
York, PA 17402   S.N. Owbird, Libn.

YORK COUNTY LAW LIBRARY
Court House   Phone: (717) 854-0754
York, PA 17401   Margaret A. Dize, Libn.

YORK COUNTY PLANNING COMMISSION - LIBRARY
118 Pleasant Acres Rd.   Phone: (717) 757-2647
York, PA 17402   Gayle Y. Heagy, Libn.

YORK HOSPITAL - LIBRARY
1001 S. George St.   Phone: (717) 771-2495
York, PA 17405   Barbara H. Bevan, Chf.Libn.

RHODE ISLAND

BARRINGTON COLLEGE - LIBRARY
Middle Hwy.   Phone: (401) 246-1200
Barrington, RI 02806   Eleanor C. Wilson, Libn.

BRISTOL HISTORICAL AND PRESERVATION SOCIETY - LIBRARY *
48 Court St.   Phone: (401) 253-5705
Bristol, RI 02809   Helene L. Tessler, Cur.-Libn.

RHODE ISLAND STATE DEPARTMENT OF SOCIAL AND REHABILITATIVE
    SERVICES - STAFF DEVELOPMENT LIBRARY
600 New London Ave.   Phone: (401) 464-3111
Cranston, RI 02920   Joyce McGee

NEW ENGLAND WIRELESS & STEAM MUSEUM, INC. - LIBRARY
697 Tillinghast Rd.   Phone: (401) 884-1710
East Greenwich, RI 02818   Robert W. Merriam

ALLENDALE MUTUAL INSURANCE COMPANY - LIBRARY
Allendale Park
Box 7500   Phone: (401) 275-4500
Johnston, RI 02919   Ann Hinnov, Libn.

METASCIENCE FOUNDATION - LIBRARY
Box 32   Phone: (401) 783-8683
Kingston, RI 02881   Marc Seifer, Dir.

PETTAQUAMSCUTT HISTORICAL SOCIETY - LIBRARY
1348 Kingstown Rd.   Phone: (401) 783-1328
Kingston, RI 02881

UNIVERSITY OF RHODE ISLAND - ART DEPARTMENT - SLIDE LIBRARY
Fine Arts Center   Phone: (401) 792-5821
Kingston, RI 02881   Cynthia A. Pankiewicz, Cur.

UNIVERSITY OF RHODE ISLAND - INTERNATIONAL CENTER FOR MARINE
    RESOURCE DEVELOPMENT - LIBRARY
Main Library   Phone: (401) 792-2938
Kingston, RI 02881   Mary Jane Beardsley, Libn.

UNIVERSITY OF RHODE ISLAND - RHODE ISLAND ORAL HISTORY PROJECT
Dept. of History   Phone: (401) 792-2528
Kingston, RI 02881   Dr. James Findlay, Professor of Hist.

UNIVERSITY OF RHODE ISLAND - SPECIAL COLLECTIONS
Library   Phone: (401) 792-2594
Kingston, RI 02881   David C. Maslyn, Hd.

ISOCHEM RESINS COMPANY - LIBRARY
99 Cook St.   Phone: (401) 723-2100
Lincoln, RI 02865   Alice L. Cabana, Libn.

ENVIRONMENTAL PROTECTION AGENCY - ENVIRONMENTAL RESEARCH
    LABORATORY, NARRAGANSETT - LIBRARY
South Ferry Rd.   Phone: (401) 789-1071
Narragansett, RI 02882   Rose Ann Gamache, Libn.

UNIVERSITY OF RHODE ISLAND, NARRAGANSETT BAY - PELL MARINE
    SCIENCE LIBRARY *
                                             Phone: (401) 792-6161
Narragansett, RI 02882   Kenneth T. Morse, Chf.Libn.

UNIVERSITY OF RHODE ISLAND - SEA GRANT MARINE ADVISORY SERVICE
Watkins Bldg., Bay Campus   Phone: (401) 792-6211
Narragansett, RI 02882   Walter J. Gray, Dir.

UNIVERSITY OF RHODE ISLAND, NARRAGANSETT BAY - DIVISION OF
    MARINE RESOURCES - MARINE AWARENESS CENTER
Graduate School of Oceanography   Phone: (401) 792-6183
Narragansett Bay, RI 02882   Prentice K. Stout, Marine Educ.Spec.

INTERNATIONAL TENNIS HALL OF FAME AND TENNIS MUSEUM - LIBRARY
Newport Casino, 194 Bellevue Ave.   Phone: (401) 846-4567
Newport, RI 02840   Robert S. Day, Exec.Dir.

NEWPORT HISTORICAL SOCIETY - LIBRARY
82 Touro St.   Phone: (401) 846-0813
Newport, RI 02840   Madeline H. Wordell, Libn.

NEWPORT HOSPITAL - INA MOSHER HEALTH SCIENCES LIBRARY
Friendship St.   Phone: (401) 846-6400
Newport, RI 02840   Tosca N. Carpenter, Hd.Libn.

U.S. NAVY - NAVAL EDUCATION AND TRAINING CENTER - LIBRARY
Bldg. 114   Phone: (401) 841-3044
Newport, RI 02840   James F. Aylward, Adm.Libn.

U.S. NAVY - NAVAL REGIONAL MEDICAL CENTER (Newport) - MEDICAL
    LIBRARY
Cypress & Third Sts.   Phone: (401) 841-1180
Newport, RI 02840   Winifred M. Jacome, Lib.Techn.

U.S. NAVY - NAVAL UNDERWATER SYSTEMS CENTER - NEWPORT
    TECHNICAL LIBRARY
                                             Phone: (401) 841-4338
Newport, RI 02840   Mary Barravecchia, Dir.

U.S. NAVY - NAVAL WAR COLLEGE - LIBRARY
                                             Phone: (401) 841-2641
Newport, RI 02840   Earl R. Schwass, Dir.

ST. JOSEPH HOSPITAL, OUR LADY OF FATIMA UNIT - HEALTH SCIENCE
    LIBRARY
200 High Service Ave.   Phone: (401) 456-3060
North Providence, RI 02904   Kathleen C. McAvoy, Libn.

PAWTUCKET MEMORIAL HOSPITAL - HEALTH SCIENCES LIBRARY
Prospect & Pond Sts.   Phone: (401) 722-6000
Pawtucket, RI 02860   Carol-Ann Rausch, Med.Libn.

GEOGRAPHIC

SLATER MILL HISTORIC SITE - RESEARCH LIBRARY
Roosevelt Ave.
Box 727   Phone: (401) 725-8638
Pawtucket, RI 02862   Stephen Victor, Dp.Dir.

RAYTHEON COMPANY - SUBMARINE SIGNAL DIVISION - TECHNICAL
   INFORMATION CENTER
1847 W. Main Rd.
Box 360   Phone: (401) 847-8000
Portsmouth, RI 02871   Mark F. Baldwin, Mgr., Tech.Info.Sys.

AUDUBON SOCIETY OF RHODE ISLAND - HARRY S. HATHAWAY LIBRARY OF
   NATURAL HISTORY AND CONSERVATION
40 Bowen St.   Phone: (401) 521-1670
Providence, RI 02903   Tim Rumage, Libn.

BROWN UNIVERSITY - ART DEPARTMENT SLIDE ROOM
Box 1861, List Art Bldg.
64 College St.   Phone: (401) 863-3218
Providence, RI 02912   Norine Duncan Cashman, Cur.

BROWN UNIVERSITY - JOHN CARTER BROWN LIBRARY
                                                Phone: (401) 863-2725
Providence, RI 02912   Thomas R. Adams, Libn.

BROWN UNIVERSITY - POPULATION STUDIES AND TRAINING CENTER -
   DEMOGRAPHY LIBRARY
Sociology Dept., Box 1916   Phone: (401) 863-2668
Providence, RI 02912   Sidney Goldstein, Dir.

BROWN UNIVERSITY - SCIENCES LIBRARY
Brown Univ. Library, Box I   Phone: (401) 863-2405
Providence, RI 02912   Ann K. Randall, Asst.Univ.Libn.

BROWN UNIVERSITY - SPECIAL COLLECTIONS †
John Hay Library
20 Prospect St.   Phone: (401) 863-2146
Providence, RI 02912   Samuel A. Streit, Spec.Coll.Libn.

BUTLER HOSPITAL - ISAAC RAY MEDICAL LIBRARY
345 Blackstone Blvd.   Phone: (401) 456-3869
Providence, RI 02906   Erika Schmidt, Libn.

INTERNATIONAL RAILROAD & TRANSPORTATION POSTCARD COLLECTORS
   CLUB - LIBRARY
Box 6782
Providence, RI 02940   Robert J. Andrews, Pres.

JOHNSON & WALES COLLEGE - PAUL FRITZSCHE CULINARY LIBRARY
1 Washington Ave.   Phone: (401) 456-1161
Providence, RI 02903   David B. Puffer, Lib.Dir.

KEYES ASSOCIATES - LIBRARY
321 S. Main St.   Phone: (401) 861-2900
Providence, RI 02903   Carole E. Twombly, Libn.

MIRIAM HOSPITAL - MEDICAL LIBRARY
164 Summit Ave   Phone: (401) 274-3700
Providence, RI 02906   Ann LeClaire, Dir., Lib.Serv.

PROVIDENCE ATHENAEUM - LIBRARY
251 Benefit St.   Phone: (401) 421-6970
Providence, RI 02903   Sylvia Moubayed, Hd.Libn.

PROVIDENCE COLLEGE - PHILLIPS MEMORIAL LIBRARY
River Ave. at Eaton St.   Phone: (401) 865-2242
Providence, RI 02918   Joseph H. Doherty, Dir.

PROVIDENCE JOURNAL COMPANY - NEWS LIBRARY
75 Fountain St.   Phone: (401) 277-7390
Providence, RI 02902   Joseph O. Mehr, Libn.

PROVIDENCE PUBLIC LIBRARY - ART AND MUSIC DEPARTMENT
150 Empire St.   Phone: (401) 521-7722
Providence, RI 02903   Susan R. Waddington, Dept.Hd.

PROVIDENCE PUBLIC LIBRARY - BUSINESS-INDUSTRY-SCIENCE
   DEPARTMENT
150 Empire St.   Phone: (401) 521-7722
Providence, RI 02903   Marcia DiGregorio, Dept.Hd.

RHODE ISLAND HISTORICAL SOCIETY - LIBRARY
121 Hope St.   Phone: (401) 331-0448
Providence, RI 02906

RHODE ISLAND HOSPITAL - PETERS HEALTH SCIENCES LIBRARY
                                                Phone: (401) 277-4671
Providence, RI 02902   Irene Lathrop, Dir. of Lib.Serv.

RHODE ISLAND JEWISH HISTORICAL ASSOCIATION - LIBRARY
130 Sessions St.
Providence, RI 02906   Eleanor F. Horvitz, Libn. & Archv.

RHODE ISLAND MEDICAL SOCIETY - LIBRARY
106 Francis St.   Phone: (401) 331-3208
Providence, RI 02903   Judith L. Zimmer, Libn.

RHODE ISLAND PUBLIC EXPENDITURE COUNCIL - LIBRARY
126 N. Main St.   Phone: (401) 521-6320
Providence, RI 02903   Gary S. Sasse, Exec.Dir.

RHODE ISLAND SCHOOL OF DESIGN - LIBRARY
2 College St.   Phone: (401) 331-3511
Providence, RI 02865   Jeanne Borden, Hd.Libn.

RHODE ISLAND STATE ARCHIVES
State House, Rm. 43, Smith St.   Phone: (401) 277-2353
Providence, RI 02903   Phyllis Peloquin Silva, Dir.

RHODE ISLAND STATE DEPARTMENT OF COMMUNITY AFFAIRS -
   REFERENCE LIBRARY
150 Washington St.   Phone: (401) 277-2857
Providence, RI 02903   Donald J. Boisvert, Libn.

RHODE ISLAND STATE DEPARTMENT OF ECONOMIC DEVELOPMENT -
   RESEARCH DIVISION LIBRARY
7 Jackson Walkway   Phone: (401) 277-2601
Providence, RI 02903   John A. Iemma, Asst.Dir., DED

RHODE ISLAND STATE DEPARTMENT OF EDUCATION - EDUCATION
   INFORMATION SERVICES
235 Promenade St.   Phone: (401) 277-2035
Providence, RI 02908   Irene P. Smith, Cons.

RHODE ISLAND STATE DEPARTMENT OF ELDERLY AFFAIRS - LIBRARY
79 Washington St.   Phone: (401) 277-2858
Providence, RI 02903   Eve M. Goldberg

RHODE ISLAND STATE DEPARTMENT OF HEALTH - GERTRUDE E. STURGES
   MEMORIAL LIBRARY
75 Davis St., Rm. 407   Phone: (401) 277-2506
Providence, RI 02908   J.G. Paster, Libn.

RHODE ISLAND STATE DEPARTMENT OF STATE LIBRARY SERVICES
95 Davis St.   Phone: (401) 277-2726
Providence, RI 02908   Fay Zipkowitz, Dir.

RHODE ISLAND STATE LAW LIBRARY
County Court House, 250 Benefit St.   Phone: (401) 277-3275
Providence, RI 02903   Edward V. Barlow, Law Libn.

RHODE ISLAND STATE LIBRARY
State House   Phone: (401) 277-2473
Providence, RI 02903   Elliott E. Andrews, State Libn.

ROGER WILLIAMS GENERAL HOSPITAL - HEALTH SCIENCES LIBRARY
825 Chalkstone Ave.   Phone: (401) 456-2036
Providence, RI 02908   Hadassah Stein, Libn.

ST. FRANCIS MONASTERY AND CHAPEL - ST. FRANCIS CHAPEL
   INFORMATION CENTER & FREE-LENDING LIBRARY
20 Page St.   Phone: (401) 331-6510
Providence, RI 02903   Rev. John Bosco Valente, O.F.M., Libn.

ST. JOSEPH HOSPITAL, OUR LADY OF PROVIDENCE UNIT - HEALTH
   SCIENCE LIBRARY
21 Peace St.   Phone: (401) 456-4035
Providence, RI 02907   Ruth E. Szabo, Med.Libn.

SOCIETY OF FRIENDS - NEW ENGLAND YEARLY MEETING OF FRIENDS -
  ARCHIVES
Rhode Island Historical Society
121 Hope St.   Phone: (401) 331-8575
Providence, RI 02906   Thyra Jane Foster, Cur.

TEMPLE BETH-EL - WILLIAM G. BRAUDE LIBRARY
70 Orchard Ave.   Phone: (401) 331-6070
Providence, RI 02906   Allan Metz, Libn.

TEMPLE EMANU-EL - CONGREGATIONAL LIBRARY
99 Taft Ave.   Phone: (401) 331-1616
Providence, RI 02906   Lillian Schwartz, Libn.

U.S. VETERANS ADMINISTRATION (RI-Providence) - HOSPITAL LIBRARY
Davis Park   Phone: (401) 521-1700
Providence, RI 02908   Lucy R. Butler, Chf., Lib.Serv.

WILLIAMS PARK - PARK MUSEUM OF NATURAL HISTORY & PLANETARIUM -
  MUSEUM LIBRARY/RESOURCE CENTER
Providence, RI 02905

WOMEN & INFANTS HOSPITAL OF RHODE ISLAND - HEALTH SCIENCES
  INFORMATION CENTER
50 Maude St.   Phone: (401) 274-1100
Providence, RI 02908   Patricia L. Thibodeau, Dir.

BRADLEY (Emma Pendleton) HOSPITAL - AUSTIN T. AND JUNE ROCKWELL
  LEVY LIBRARY
1011 Veterans Memorial Pkwy.   Phone: (401) 434-3400
Riverside, RI 02915   Carolyn A. Waller, Libn.

BRYANT COLLEGE OF BUSINESS ADMINISTRATION - EDITH M. HODGSON
  MEMORIAL LIBRARY
                                            Phone: (401) 231-1200
Smithfield, RI 02917   Dr. John P. Hannon, Dir.

LEESONA CORPORATION - LIBRARY
333 Strawberry Field Rd.   Phone: (401) 739-7100
Warwick, RI 02887   Rita F. Manocchio, Libn.

METROPOLITAN PROPERTY & LIABILITY INSURANCE COMPANY - LAW &
  BUSINESS LIBRARY
700 Quaker Ln.   Phone: (401) 827-2658
Warwick, RI 02886   Kevin J. Carty, Libn.

NATIONAL FOUNDATION FOR GIFTED AND CREATIVE CHILDREN - LIBRARY
395 Diamond Hill Rd.   Phone: (401) 942-2253
Warwick, RI 02886   Marie Friedel, Exec.Dir.

SEMINARY OF OUR LADY OF PROVIDENCE - LIBRARY
R.R. 1 Warwick Neck Ave.
Warwick, RI 02889

WESTERLY HOSPITAL - MEDICAL LIBRARY
Wells St.   Phone: (401) 596-4961
Westerly, RI 02891   Natalie V. Lawton, Libn.

UNION SAINT-JEAN-BAPTISTE - MALLET LIBRARY
One Social St.   Phone: (401) 769-0520
Woonsocket, RI 02895   Bro. Felician, S.C., Libn.

STAGECOACH HOUSE MUSEUM - LIBRARY *
Main St.   Phone: (401) 539-7768
Wyoming, RI 02898   Susan O. Lindquist, Libn.

SOUTH CAROLINA

U.S. DEPT. OF ENERGY - SAVANNAH RIVER LAB. - TECHNICAL INFO.
  SERVICE LIBRARY
Savannah River Laboratory
E.I. Du Pont De Nemours and Company
Aiken, SC 29808   M.S. Feldman, Libn.

CAMDEN DISTRICT HERITAGE FOUNDATION - RESEARCH ARCHIVES
Box 710   Phone: (803) 432-9841
Camden, SC 29020   Hope Cooper, Adm.

CAROLINA ART ASSOCIATION - LIBRARY & SOUTH CAROLINA ART
  ARCHIVES
Gibbes Art Gallery
135 Meeting St.   Phone: (803) 722-2706
Charleston, SC 29401

CHARLESTON EVENING POST/NEWS AND COURIER - LIBRARY
134 Columbus St.
Box 758   Phone: (803) 577-7111
Charleston, SC 29402   Louise N. Mazorol, Chf.Libn.

CHARLESTON LIBRARY SOCIETY
164 King St.   Phone: (803) 723-9912
Charleston, SC 29401   Catherine E. Sadler, Libn.

CHARLESTON MUSEUM - LIBRARY
121 Rutledge Ave.   Phone: (803) 722-2996
Charleston, SC 29401   K. Sharon Bennett, Libn.

CITADEL - THE MILITARY COLLEGE OF SOUTH CAROLINA - ARCHIVES/
  MUSEUM
The Citadel   Phone: (803) 792-6846
Charleston, SC 29409   LCDR Mal J. Collet, Dir.

CITADEL - THE MILITARY COLLEGE OF SOUTH CAROLINA - DANIEL
  LIBRARY
                                            Phone: (803) 723-0711
Charleston, SC 29409   Col. James M. Hillard, Dir. Of Libs.

DALCHO HISTORICAL SOCIETY OF THE PROTESTANT EPISCOPAL CHURCH
  IN SOUTH CAROLINA - LIBRARY AND ARCHIVES
Box 2127   Phone: (803) 722-4075
Charleston, SC 29403   George W. Williams, Pres.

HUGUENOT SOCIETY OF SOUTH CAROLINA - LIBRARY
25 Chalmers St.   Phone: (803) 723-3235
Charleston, SC 29401

MEDICAL UNIVERSITY OF SOUTH CAROLINA - LIBRARY
171 Ashley Ave.   Phone: (803) 792-2374
Charleston, SC 29425   Warren A. Sawyer, Dir.

SOUTH CAROLINA HISTORICAL SOCIETY - LIBRARY
Fireproof Bldg.
Meeting & Chalmers Sts.   Phone: (803) 723-3225
Charleston, SC 29401   Gene Waddell, Dir.

SOUTH CAROLINA STATE WILDLIFE AND MARINE RESOURCES DEPT. -
  LIBRARY
P.O. Box 12559   Phone: (803) 795-6350
Charleston, SC 29412   Marilyn Lewis, Marine Rsrcs.Libn.

U.S. NAVY - NAVAL SHIPYARD (Charleston) - TECHNICAL LIBRARY
Naval Base   Phone: (803) 743-3843
Charleston, SC 29408   D.C. Woody, Act.Techn.

U.S. AIR FORCE BASE - CHARLESTON BASE LIBRARY *
                                            Phone: (803) 554-3134
Charleston AFB, SC 29404   Mrs. Halcyon S. Robinson, Libn.

CLEMSON UNIVERSITY - EMERY A. GUNNIN ARCHITECTURAL LIBRARY
Lee Hall   Phone: (803) 656-3081
Clemson, SC 29631   Dillman B. Sorrells, Arch.Lib.Spec.

CLEMSON UNIVERSITY - ROBERT MULDROW COOPER LIBRARY
                                            Phone: (803) 656-3026
Clemson, SC 29631   Joseph Boykin, Dir.

SOUTH CAROLINA STATE DEPARTMENT OF MENTAL RETARDATION -
  WHITTEN CENTER LIBRARY & MEDIA RESOURCE SERVICES
Box 239   Phone: (803) 833-2736
Clinton, SC 29325   Mr. Hsiu-Yun Keng, Dir.

BAPTIST MEDICAL CENTER - AMELIA WHITE PITTS MEMORIAL LIBRARY
Taylor at Marion St.   Phone: (803) 771-5281
Columbia, SC 29220   Lois W. Smith, Libn.

GEOGRAPHIC

BARUCH (Belle W.) INSTITUTE FOR MARINE BIOLOGY AND COASTAL
 RESEARCH - LIBRARY
University of South Carolina
Columbia, SC 29208
Phone: (803) 777-5288
Ms. V. Smith, Adm.Asst.

BRYAN (G. Werber) PSYCHIATRIC HOSPITAL - PROFESSIONAL LIBRARY
220 Faison Dr.
Columbia, SC 29203
Phone: (803) 758-4839
Virginia S. McEachern, Libn.

COLUMBIA BIBLE COLLEGE - LEARNING RESOURCES CENTER
7435 Monticello Rd.
Box 3122
Columbia, SC 29230
Phone: (803) 754-4100
Laura Braswell, Act.Dir. of LRC

COLUMBIA MUSEUMS OF ART & SCIENCE - LIBRARY
1112 Bull St.
Columbia, SC 29201
Phone: (803) 799-2810
Cassandra S. Gissendanner, Hd.

HALL (William S.) PSYCHIATRIC INSTITUTE - PROFESSIONAL LIBRARY
Box 119
Columbia, SC 29202
Phone: (803) 758-5370
Mrs. Neeta N. Shah, Chf.Med.Libn.

LUTHERAN THEOLOGICAL SOUTHERN SEMINARY - LONEBERGER
 MEMORIAL LIBRARY
4201 Main St.
Columbia, SC 29203
Phone: (803) 786-5150
William Richard Fritz, Sr., Libn.

MUNICIPAL ASSOCIATION OF SOUTH CAROLINA - LIBRARY AND
 REFERENCE CENTER
1213 Lady St.
Box 11558
Columbia, SC 29201
Phone: (803) 799-9574
Edward J. Kinghorn, Jr., Staff Assoc.

NATIONAL ASSOCIATION FOR SPORT & PHYSICAL EDUCATION (NASPE) -
 MEDIA RESOURCE CENTER
University of South Carolina
Dept. of Physical Education
Columbia, SC 29208
Phone: (803) 777-3172
Dr. Richard C. Hohn, Dir.

RICHLAND MEMORIAL HOSPITAL - JOSEY MEMORIAL MEDICAL LIBRARY
3301 Harden St.
Columbia, SC 29203
Phone: (803) 765-6312
Kay F. Harwood, Libn.

SOUTH CAROLINA CONFEDERATE RELIC ROOM & MUSEUM - LIBRARY
World War Memorial Bldg.
Sumter St. At Pendleton
Columbia, SC 29201
Phone: (803) 758-2144

SOUTH CAROLINA STATE DEPARTMENT OF ARCHIVES & HISTORY -
 ARCHIVES SEARCH ROOM
Capitol Sta., Box 11669
Columbia, SC 29211
Phone: (803) 758-5816
Charles E. Lee, Dir.

SOUTH CAROLINA STATE DEPARTMENT OF HEALTH & ENVIRONMENTAL
 CONTROL - EDUCATIONAL RESOURCE CENTER
2600 Bull St.
Columbia, SC 29201
Phone: (803) 758-5448
Michael Kronenfeld, Dir.

SOUTH CAROLINA STATE DEPARTMENT OF MENTAL RETARDATION -
 MIDLANDS CENTER LIBRARY
8301 Farrow Rd.
Columbia, SC 29203
Phone: (803) 758-4434
Mrs. Clannie H. Washington, Libn.

SOUTH CAROLINA STATE ENERGY EXTENSION SERVICE - ENERGY
 INFORMATION CENTER
Box 11469
Columbia, SC 29211
Phone: (803) 758-3181
Debbie Bowdler, Energy Info.Spec.

SOUTH CAROLINA STATE GEOLOGICAL SURVEY - LIBRARY
Harbison Forest Rd.
Columbia, SC 29210
Phone: (803) 758-6431
Arthur Maybin

SOUTH CAROLINA STATE LIBRARY
1500 Senate St.
Box 11469
Columbia, SC 29211
Phone: (803) 758-3181
Betty E. Callaham, State Libn.

SOUTH CAROLINA STATE SUPREME COURT - LIBRARY
Box 11330
Columbia, SC 29211
Phone: (803) 758-3741
Elizabeth A. Sprott, Libn.

U.S. VETERANS ADMINISTRATION (SC-Columbia) - HOSPITAL LIBRARY
Garners Ferry Rd.
Columbia, SC 29201
Phone: (803) 776-4000
Charletta P. Felder, Chf., Lib.Serv.

UNIVERSITY OF SOUTH CAROLINA - BUREAU OF GOVERNMENTAL
 RESEARCH AND SERVICE - LIBRARY
Columbia, SC 29208
Phone: (803) 777-8156
Sandra T. Cowen, Res.Anl./Libn.

UNIVERSITY OF SOUTH CAROLINA - COLEMAN KARESH LAW LIBRARY
Law Center
Columbia, SC 29208
Phone: (803) 777-5942
Steve Huang, Asst. Law Libn.

UNIVERSITY OF SOUTH CAROLINA - MAP LIBRARY
Calcott Bldg.
Columbia, SC 29208
Phone: (803) 777-2802
David C. McQuillan, Map Libn.

UNIVERSITY OF SOUTH CAROLINA - SCHOOL OF MEDICINE LIBRARY
VA Hospital
Columbia, SC 29201
Phone: (803) 777-4858
R. Thomas Lange, Chf.Med.Libn.

UNIVERSITY OF SOUTH CAROLINA - SOUTH CAROLINIANA LIBRARY
Columbia, SC 29208
Phone: (803) 765-3131
E.L. Inabinett, Libn.

UNIVERSITY OF SOUTH CAROLINA - THOMAS COOPER LIBRARY - RARE
 BOOKS & SPECIAL COLLECTIONS DEPARTMENT
Columbia, SC 29201
Phone: (803) 777-8154
Roger Mortimer, Hd., Spec.Coll.

UNIVERSITY OF SOUTH CAROLINA - UNIVERSITY ARCHIVES
McKissick Museums
Columbia, SC 29208
Phone: (803) 777-7251
Barry H. Rosen, Dir./Archv.

WILBUR SMITH AND ASSOCIATES - LIBRARY
1301 Gervais St.
Box 92
Columbia, SC 29202
Phone: (803) 771-8844
Marilyn F. Stebbins, Libn.

DARLINGTON COUNTY HISTORICAL COMMISSION - DARLINGTON COUNTY
 ARCHIVES
Court House, Rm. 307
Darlington, SC 29532
Horace Fraser Rudisill, Hist.

GRACE (W.R.) AND COMPANY - CRYOVAC DIVISION - TECHNICAL LIBRARY
Box 464
Duncan, SC 29334
Phone: (803) 439-4121
Margaret M. Ezell, Tech.Libn.

TOMPKINS (D.A.) MEMORIAL LIBRARY
Courthouse Square
Box 468
Edgefield, SC 29824
Phone: (803) 637-6437
Mrs. M.H. Mims, Libn.

FLORENCE-DARLINGTON TECHNICAL COLLEGE - LIBRARY
Drawer 8000
Florence, SC 29501
Phone: (803) 662-8151
Jeronell White, Lib.Dir.

FLORENCE DEVELOPMENT DIVISION - RESEARCH AND PLANNING LIBRARY
City-County Complex, Drawer FF
Florence, SC 29501
Phone: (803) 665-3141
Elizabeth Shaw, Libn.

PEE DEE AREA HEALTH EDUCATION CENTER LIBRARY
McLeod Regional Medical Ctr.
555 E. Cheves St.
Florence, SC 29501
Phone: (803) 667-2275
Nancy J. Smith, Libn.

U.S. ARMY POST - FORT JACKSON - LIBRARY
Bldg. 4679
Ft. Jackson, SC 29207
Phone: (803) 751-4826

BOB JONES UNIVERSITY - CHURCH MINISTRIES RESOURCE LAB
Greenville, SC 29614
Phone: (803) 242-5100
Mrs. James Berg, Supv.

BOB JONES UNIVERSITY - MUSIC LIBRARY
Phone: (803) 242-5100
Greenville, SC 29614   Dr. Karen S. Wilson, Music Libn.

BOB JONES UNIVERSITY - SCHOOL OF EDUCATION - MEDIA CENTER
Phone: (803) 242-5100
Greenville, SC 29614   Bill Yost, Supv.

FURMAN UNIVERSITY LIBRARY - SPECIAL COLLECTIONS
Phone: (803) 294-2194
Greenville, SC 29613   Dr. J. Glen Clayton, Spec.Coll.Libn.

GREENVILLE COUNTY PLANNING COMMISSION - PLANNING TECHNICAL
LIBRARY
Courthouse Annex, Box 1947   Phone: (803) 298-8671
Greenville, SC 29602   Robin Hughes Gordon, Econ. Planner

GREENVILLE GENERAL HOSPITAL - MEDICAL LIBRARY
701 Grove Rd.   Phone: (803) 242-8628
Greenville, SC 29605   Susan Chappell, Med.Libn.

GREENVILLE MENTAL HEALTH CENTER - LIBRARY
715 Grove Rd.   Phone: (803) 242-8058
Greenville, SC 29605   Laura F. Pitzer, Libn.

GREENVILLE TECHNICAL COLLEGE - LEARNING RESOURCES CENTER
Box 5539   Phone: (803) 242-3170
Greenville, SC 29606   Martin R. Pautz, Dean, Lrng.Rsrcs.

HOLLINGSWORTH (John D.) ON WHEELS, INC. - INFORMATION SERVICES
Box 516   Phone: (803) 297-1000
Greenville, SC 29602   Rick Carter, Info.Spec.

PLATT SACO LOWELL CORPORATION - ENGINEERING LIBRARY
Drawer 2327   Phone: (803) 859-3211
Greenville, SC 29602   Donald H. Feldman, Mgr.

POLYMER INDUSTRIES - LIBRARY
Roberts Road
Box 2184   Phone: (803) 244-5351
Greenville, SC 29602   Piper L. Hemphill, Libn.

MONSANTO TEXTILES COMPANY - LIBRARY
Box 1057
Greenwood, SC 29646   Mildred Upton, Libn.

PIEDMONT TECHNICAL COLLEGE - LIBRARY
P.O. Drawer 1467, Emerald Rd.   Phone: (803) 223-8357
Greenwood, SC 29646   Daniel D. Koenig, Dir.Lrng.Rscrs.

AMERICAN HOECHST - FILMS DIVISION - TECHNICAL INFORMATION
CENTER
Box 1400   Phone: (803) 877-8471
Greer, SC 29651   Judith Duffie, Info.Spec.

UNITED MERCHANTS AND MANUFACTURING COMPANY - RESEARCH
CENTER LIBRARY *
Box 64   Phone: (803) 593-4461
Langley, SC 29834   Larry G. Smith, Mgr., Anl.Serv.

MARION COUNTY MEMORIAL HOSPITAL - LIBRARY
1108 N. Main St.   Phone: (803) 423-3210
Marion, SC 29571   Ann Finney, Educ.Dir.

BROOKGREEN GARDENS - LIBRARY
Phone: (803) 237-4218
Murrells Inlet, SC 29576   G.L. Tarbox, Jr., Dir.

U.S. AIR FORCE BASE - MYRTLE BEACH BASE LIBRARY
Phone: (803) 238-7086
Myrtle Beach AFB, SC 29577   Jean L. Cady, Base Libn.

TRIDENT TECHNICAL COLLEGE - NORTH CAMPUS LIBRARY
7000 Rivers Ave.   Phone: (803) 572-6095
North Charleston, SC 29405   Marion L. Vogel, Dean of Lrng.Rsrcs.

WESTVACO CORPORATION - INFORMATION SERVICES CENTER
Box 5207   Phone: (803) 744-8231
North Charleston, SC 29406   Elizabeth deLiesseline, Info.Spec.

ORANGEBURG-CALHOUN TECHNICAL COLLEGE - GRESSETTE LEARNING
RESOURCE CENTER
Highway 601 N.
Drawer 1767   Phone: (803) 536-0311
Orangeburg, SC 29115   Margaret F. Huff, Dean, LRC

PENDLETON DISTRICT HISTORICAL AND RECREATIONAL COMMISSION -
REFERENCE LIBRARY
125 E. Queen St.
Box 234   Phone: (803) 646-3782
Pendleton, SC 29670   Hurley Badders, Commn.Dir.

TRI-COUNTY TECHNICAL COLLEGE - LIBRARY
Box 587   Phone: (803) 646-8361
Pendleton, SC 29670   Dr. Stephen B. Walter, Dir., L.R.C.

CELANESE CORPORATION - CELANESE FIBERS COMPANY - TECHNICAL
LIBRARY
Cherry Rd. Sta.   Phone: (803) 366-4121
Rock Hill, SC 29730   Donna Adams, Libn.

MUSEUM OF YORK COUNTY - EDUCATIONAL LIBRARY
Mt. Gallant Rd.
Rte. 4, Box 211
Rock Hill, SC 29730

YORK TECHNICAL COLLEGE - LIBRARY *
U.S. 21 Bypass   Phone: (803) 324-3130
Rock Hill, SC 29730   Amanda Yu, Libn.

CALHOUN COUNTY MUSEUM - ARCHIVES AND LIBRARY
303 Butler St.   Phone: (803) 874-3964
St. Matthews, SC 29135   Virginia D. Carroll, Libn.

MILLIKEN RESEARCH CORPORATION - RESEARCH LIBRARY
Box 1927   Phone: (803) 573-2340
Spartanburg, SC 29304   Don Miles, Res.Libn.

SPARTANBURG GENERAL HOSPITAL - HEALTH SCIENCES LIBRARY
101 E. Wood St.   Phone: (803) 573-6220
Spartanburg, SC 29303   Fay J. Henderson, Dir.Lib.Serv.

UNITED METHODIST COMMN. ON ARCHIVES & HISTORY - SOUTH
CAROLINA CONFERENCE - HISTORICAL LIBRARY
Wofford College
Spartanburg, SC 29301   Herbert Hucks, Jr., Cur.

WOFFORD COLLEGE - SANDOR TESZLER LIBRARY - ARCHIVES
N. Church St.   Phone: (803) 585-4821
Spartanburg, SC 29301   Herbert Hucks, Jr., Archv.

WOFFORD COLLEGE - SANDOR TESZLER LIBRARY - LITTLEJOHN RARE
BOOK ROOM
N. Church St.   Phone: (803) 585-4821
Spartanburg, SC 29301   Frank J. Anderson, Libn.

STATE PARK HEALTH CENTER - PATIENTS' AND MEDICAL LIBRARY
Box 115   Phone: (803) 758-4694
State Park, SC 29147   Evelyn Russ, Libn.

OLD SLAVE MART MUSEUM - LIBRARY
Box 446   Phone: (803) 883-3797
Sullivan's Island, SC 29482   Judith Wragg Chase, Lib.Dir.

U.S. NATL. PARK SERVICE - FORT SUMTER NATL. MONUMENT - LIBRARY
1214 Middle St.   Phone: (803) 883-3123
Sullivan's Island, SC 29482   Brien Varnado, Supt.

SUMTER AREA TECHNICAL COLLEGE - LIBRARY †
506 N. Guignard Dr.   Phone: (803) 773-9371
Sumter, SC 29150   Fannie M. Davis, Dir.

SOUTH DAKOTA

LUTHERAN CHURCH LIBRARY ASSOCIATION - BETHLEHEM LUTHERAN
LIBRARY
215 Fourth Ave., S.E.   Phone: (605) 225-9740
Aberdeen, SD 57401

GEOGRAPHIC

PRESENTATION COLLEGE - LIBRARY
1500 North Main
Phone: (605) 225-0420
Aberdeen, SD 57401
Ellen F. Hall, Lib.Dir.

SOUTH DAKOTA STATE UNIVERSITY - DEPARTMENT OF WILDLIFE &
FISHERIES SCIENCES - RESEARCH LIBRARY
Brookings, SD 57007

SOUTH DAKOTA STATE UNIVERSITY - HILTON M. BRIGGS LIBRARY
Phone: (605) 688-5106
Brookings, SD 57007
Dr. Leon Raney, Dean of Lib.

U.S. VETERANS ADMINISTRATION (SD-Fort Meade) - MEDICAL CENTER
LIBRARY
Phone: (605) 347-2511
Fort Meade, SD 57741
Jack D. Seymour, Chf., Lib.Serv.

U.S. VETERANS ADMINISTRATION (SD-Hot Springs) - CENTER LIBRARY
Phone: (605) 745-4101
Hot Springs, SD 57747
John E. Akers, Med.Libn.

U.S. NATL. PARK SERVICE - BADLANDS NATL. MONUMENT - LIBRARY
Box 6
Phone: (605) 433-5361
Interior, SD 57750
Midge Johnston, Bus.Mgr.

DAKOTA STATE COLLEGE - KARL E. MUNDT LIBRARY
Phone: (605) 256-3551
Madison, SD 57042
Joseph T. Paulukonis, Dir.

MADISON COMMUNITY HOSPITAL - HEALTH-SCIENCE LIBRARY
917 N. Washington Ave.
Phone: (605) 256-6551
Madison, SD 57042
Donna Sullivan, Lib.Mgr.

UNITED METHODIST CHURCH - SOUTH DAKOTA CONFERENCE -
COMMITTEE ON ARCHIVES AND HISTORY - LIBRARY
1331 W. University Ave.
Phone: (605) 996-6552
Mitchell, SD 57301
Barbara Rich Sorenson, Archv.

SOUTH DAKOTA STATE DEPARTMENT OF EDUCATION & CULTURAL
AFFAIRS - ARCHIVES RESOURCE CENTER
East Highway Bypass
Phone: (605) 773-3173
Pierre, SD 57501
Lawrence Hibpshman, State Archv.

SOUTH DAKOTA STATE HISTORICAL RESOURCE CENTER
Memorial Bldg.
Phone: (605) 773-3615
Pierre, SD 57501
Rosemary Evetts, Libn.

SOUTH DAKOTA STATE LIBRARY
State Library Bldg.
Phone: (605) 773-3131
Pierre, SD 57501
Clarence L. Coffindaffer, State Libn.

SOUTH DAKOTA STATE OFFICE OF ENERGY POLICY - LIBRARY
Capitol Lake Plaza
Phone: (605) 773-3603
Pierre, SD 57501
David Sell, Policy Anl.

SOUTH DAKOTA STATE SUPREME COURT - LIBRARY
State Capitol
Pierre, SD 57501
V. Biddle, Asst.Libn.

NATIONAL COLLEGE - THOMAS JEFFERSON LIBRARY
Box 1780
Phone: (605) 394-4943
Rapid City, SD 57709
Linda L. Watson, Dir.

RAPID CITY REGIONAL HOSPITAL - HEALTH SCIENCES LIBRARY
1011 11th St.
Phone: (605) 394-3059
Rapid City, SD 57701
Bonnie R. Mack, Dept.Mgr./Lib.Serv.

SOUTH DAKOTA SCHOOL OF MINES & TECHNOLOGY - DEVEREAUX LIBRARY
500 St. Joseph St.
Phone: (605) 394-2418
Rapid City, SD 57701
Harry E. Welsh, Dir.

AUGUSTANA COLLEGE - CENTER FOR WESTERN STUDIES
29th & Summit Sts.
Phone: (605) 336-4007
Sioux Falls, SD 57102
Sven Froiland, Dir.

FIRST BAPTIST CHURCH - LIBRARY
1401 S. Covell
Phone: (605) 336-0966
Sioux Falls, SD 57105
Chris Carstensen, Libn.

GREAT PLAINS ZOO - REFERENCE LIBRARY
Sioux Falls Park & Recreation Dept.
600 E. 7th
Phone: (605) 339-7059
Sioux Falls, SD 57102
Keith Halverson, Zoo Dir.

MC KENNAN HOSPITAL - MEDICAL LIBRARY
800 E. 21st St.
Phone: (605) 339-8088
Sioux Falls, SD 57101
A. James Bothmer, Med.Libn.

NORTH AMERICAN BAPTIST SEMINARY - KAISER-RAMAKER LIBRARY
1321 W. 22nd St.
Phone: (605) 336-6805
Sioux Falls, SD 57105
George W. Lang, Lib.Adm.

PROTESTANT EPISCOPAL CHURCH - EPISCOPAL DIOCESE OF SOUTH
DAKOTA - ARCHIVES
200 17th St.
Phone: (605) 338-9751
Sioux Falls, SD 57101
Alan M. Schwartz, Archv.

SIOUX FALLS ARGUS-LEADER - LIBRARY
200 S. Minnesota
Phone: (605) 336-1130
Sioux Falls, SD 57102
Perry Swenson, Libn.

SIOUX VALLEY HOSPITAL - MEDICAL LIBRARY
1100 S. Euclid Ave.
Phone: (605) 336-3440
Sioux Falls, SD 57105
Kay Hasegawa, Libn.

SIOUXLAND HERITAGE MUSEUMS - PETTIGREW MUSEUM - LIBRARY
131 N. Duluth Ave.
Phone: (605) 339-7097
Sioux Falls, SD 57104
Ms. Lee N. McLaird, Cur. of Collections

U.S. GEOLOGICAL SURVEY - EROS DATA CENTER - DON L. KULOW
MEMORIAL LIBRARY
EROS Data Center
Phone: (605) 594-6511
Sioux Falls, SD 57198
Sharon Kadinger, Libn.

U.S. VETERANS ADMINISTRATION (SD-Sioux Falls) - HOSPITAL LIBRARY †
2501 W. 22nd St.
Phone: (605) 336-3230
Sioux Falls, SD 57101
Barbara McDowell, Chf., Lib.Serv.

BLACK HILLS STATE COLLEGE - CURRICULUM LIBRARY
Berry Library-Learning Ctr.
University St.
Phone: (605) 642-6833
Spearfish, SD 57783
Anne Richardson, Libn.

BLACK HILLS STATE COLLEGE - E.Y. BERRY LIBRARY-LEARNING CENTER
Phone: (605) 642-6833
Spearfish, SD 57783
Dr. W. Edwin Erickson, Dir.

UNIVERSITY OF SOUTH DAKOTA, SPRINGFIELD - CARL G. LAWRENCE
LIBRARY
Phone: (605) 369-2296
Springfield, SD 57062

AMERICAN INDIAN RESEARCH PROJECT - LIBRARY
University of South Dakota
16 Dakota Hall
Phone: (605) 677-5208
Vermillion, SD 57069
Dr. Richmond L. Clow, Dir.

OVER (W.H.) MUSEUM - LIBRARY
University of South Dakota
Phone: (605) 677-5228
Vermillion, SD 57069
Julia R. Vodicka, Musm.Dir.

SHRINE TO MUSIC MUSEUM
University of South Dakota
Box 194
Phone: (605) 677-5306
Vermillion, SD 57069
Andre P. Larson, Dir.

UNIVERSITY OF SOUTH DAKOTA - BUSINESS RESEARCH BUREAU
School of Business
Phone: (605) 677-5287
Vermillion, SD 57069
Dr. Jerry Johnson, Dir.

UNIVERSITY OF SOUTH DAKOTA - CHEMISTRY LIBRARY
Pardee Laboratory
Phone: (605) 677-5487
Vermillion, SD 57069

UNIVERSITY OF SOUTH DAKOTA - CHRISTIAN P. LOMMEN HEALTH
SCIENCES LIBRARY
School of Medicine
Phone: (605) 677-5347
Vermillion, SD 57069
Patrick W. Brennen, Dir.

UNIVERSITY OF SOUTH DAKOTA - GOVERNMENTAL RESEARCH LIBRARY
Phone: (605) 677-5242
Vermillion, SD 57069   Mitchel Beville, Assoc.Dir.

UNIVERSITY OF SOUTH DAKOTA - I.D. WEEKS LIBRARY - RICHARDSON
ARCHIVES
Phone: (605) 677-5371
Vermillion, SD 57069   John N. Olsgaard, Archv.

UNIVERSITY OF SOUTH DAKOTA - MC KUSICK LAW LIBRARY
Phone: (605) 677-5259
Vermillion, SD 57069   Eileen Bouniol, Law Libn.

SACRED HEART HOSPITAL - MEDICAL LIBRARY AND INFORMATION
CENTER
W. 4th St.   Phone: (605) 665-9371
Yankton, SD 57078   Mary Heinbokel, Med.Libn.

SOUTH DAKOTA HUMAN SERVICES CENTER - MEDICAL LIBRARY
Box 76   Phone: (605) 665-3671
Yankton, SD 57078   Mary Lou Kostel, Libn.

TENNESSEE

ARLINGTON DEVELOPMENTAL CENTER - PROFESSIONAL LIBRARY
11293 Memphis-Arlington Rd.   Phone: (901) 867-2921
Arlington, TN 38002   Christine B. Gavin, Instr. Media Spec.

ARNOLD ENGINEERING DEVELOPMENT CENTER - LIBRARY
Phone: (615) 455-2611
Arnold Air Force Sta., TN 37389   Gay D. Goethert, Lib.Supv.

BEECHAM, INC. - BEECHAM LABORATORIES - MEDICAL LIBRARY
501 5th St.   Phone: (615) 764-5141
Bristol, TN 37620   Peggy Rutsis, Med.Libn.

OLIN CORPORATION - CHEMICALS - CHARLESTON TECHNICAL
INFORMATION CENTER
Phone: (615) 336-2251
Charleston, TN 37310   Barbara C. Suttles, Coord.

CHATTANOOGA-HAMILTON COUNTY REGIONAL PLANNING COMMISSION -
LIBRARY
100 E. 11th St.
City Hall Annex, Rm. 200   Phone: (615) 757-5216
Chattanooga, TN 37402

CHATTANOOGA TIMES - LIBRARY †
117 E. 10th St.
Box 951   Phone: (615) 756-1234
Chattanooga, TN 37402   Trina McLeod, Libn.

CHATTEM DRUG AND CHEMICAL COMPANY - RESEARCH LIBRARY *
1715 W. 38th St.   Phone: (615) 821-4571
Chattanooga, TN 37409

COMBUSTION ENGINEERING, INC. - METALLURGICAL AND MATERIALS
LIBRARY
911 W. Main St.   Phone: (615) 265-4631
Chattanooga, TN 37402   Nell T. Holder, Libn.

ERLANGER MEDICAL CENTER - MEDICAL LIBRARY
975 E. Third St.   Phone: (615) 755-7498
Chattanooga, TN 37403   Margarette D. Koplan, Chf.Libn.

ERLANGER MEDICAL CENTER - SCHOOL OF NURSING - SARAH C. BARTON
LIBRARY
975 E. Third St.   Phone: (615) 755-7861
Chattanooga, TN 37403   Margarette D. Koplan, Chf.Libn.

HUNTER MUSEUM OF ART - REFERENCE LIBRARY
Bluff View   Phone: (615) 267-0968
Chattanooga, TN 37403   Diana W. Suarez, Cur. of Educ.

TENNESSEE VALLEY AUTHORITY - MAPS AND SURVEYS BRANCH - MAP
INFORMATION AND RECORDS UNIT
101 Haney Bldg.   Phone: (615) 755-2122
Chattanooga, TN 37401   J.L. Dodd, Supv.

TENNESSEE VALLEY AUTHORITY - TECHNICAL LIBRARY
100-401 Bldg.   Phone: (615) 755-2811
Chattanooga, TN 37401   Nancy F. Atkins, Supv., Lib.Serv.

CLARKSVILLE LEAF-CHRONICLE COMPANY - LIBRARY
200 Commerce St.   Phone: (615) 552-1808
Clarksville, TN 37040   Lesley S. Potts, Libn.

SOUTHERN MISSIONARY COLLEGE - MC KEE LIBRARY - SPECIAL
COLLECTIONS
Box 629   Phone: (615) 396-4290
Collegedale, TN 37315   Charles E. Davis, Dir. of Libs./Archv.

POLK (James K.) ANCESTRAL HOME - LIBRARY
301 S. Seventh St.
Box 741   Phone: (615) 388-2354
Columbia, TN 38401   Lucinda Pool, Exec.Dir.

CITIES SERVICE COMPANY - LIBRARY
Highway 68   Phone: (615) 496-7919
Copperhill, TN 37317   George DeWitt

GREAT LAKES RESEARCH CORPORATION - RESEARCH LIBRARY
Box 1031   Phone: (615) 543-3111
Elizabethton, TN 37643   Joan Warden, Libn.

U.S. NATL. PARK SERVICE - GREAT SMOKY MOUNTAINS NATL. PARK -
SUGARLANDS VISITOR CENTER
Phone: (615) 436-5615
Gatlinburg, TN 37738   Claryse D. Myers, Libn.

TUSCULUM COLLEGE - INSTRUCTIONAL MATERIALS CENTER
Box 88   Phone: (615) 639-3751
Greeneville, TN 37743   Dr. Shirley S. Beck, Chm., Div. of Prof.Educ.

U.S. NATL. PARK SERVICE - ANDREW JOHNSON NATL. HISTORIC SITE -
LIBRARY
College at Depot   Phone: (615) 638-3551
Greeneville, TN 37743   Hugh A. Lawing, Hist.

LINCOLN MEMORIAL UNIVERSITY - ABRAHAM LINCOLN LIBRARY AND
MUSEUM
Harrogate, TN 37752   Edgar G. Archer, Dir.

JACKSON-MADISON COUNTY GENERAL HOSPITAL - LEARNING CENTER
708 West Forest Ave.   Phone: (901) 424-0424
Jackson, TN 38301   Linda G. Farmer, Med.Libn.

EAST TENNESSEE STATE UNIVERSITY, QUILLEN-DISHNER COLLEGE OF
MEDICINE - DEPT. OF LEARNING RSRCS. - MEDICAL LIBRARY
Box 23290A   Phone: (615) 928-6426
Johnson City, TN 37614   Janet S. Fisher, Asst. Dean

NATIONAL STORYTELLING RESOURCE CENTER
Box 112   Phone: (615) 753-2171
Jonesboro, TN 37659   Martha Gillette, Adm.Asst.

JOHNSON BIBLE COLLEGE - GLASS MEMORIAL LIBRARY
Phone: (615) 573-4517
Kimberlin Heights Station, TN 37920   Helen E. Lemmon, Libn.

EASTMAN KODAK COMPANY - TENNESSEE EASTMAN COMPANY - BUSINESS
LIBRARY
Box 511   Phone: (615) 246-2111
Kingsport, TN 37662   Sandra H. Boyd, Lib.Asst.

EASTMAN KODAK COMPANY - TENNESSEE EASTMAN COMPANY -
RESEARCH LIBRARY
Box 511   Phone: (615) 246-2111
Kingsport, TN 37662   Michael W. Ubaldini, Res.Libn.

HOLSTON VALLEY HOSPITAL AND MEDICAL CENTER - HEALTH SCIENCE
LIBRARY
Ravine St.   Phone: (615) 246-3322
Kingsport, TN 37662   Angela C. England, Med.Libn.

EAST TENNESSEE BAPTIST HOSPITAL - HEALTH SCIENCES LIBRARY
Box 1788   Phone: (615) 632-5618
Knoxville, TN 37920   Mary Evelyn Lynn, Libn.

GEOGRAPHIC

FIRST CHRISTIAN CHURCH - WINONA ROEHL LIBRARY
211 W. 5th Ave.   Phone: (615) 522-0545
Knoxville, TN 37917   Mrs. E.R. Snyder, Libn.

FORT SANDERS REGIONAL MEDICAL CENTER - MEDICAL/NURSING
    LIBRARY
1915 White Ave.   Phone: (615) 971-1293
Knoxville, TN 37916   Nedra Cook, Libn.

KNOX COUNTY GOVERNMENTAL LIBRARY
Knox County Court House, Rm. 310   Phone: (615) 523-2257
Knoxville, TN 37902   Katherine Meredith Douglas, Libn.

KNOXVILLE-KNOX COUNTY METROPOLITAN PLANNING COMMISSION -
    LIBRARY
City-County Bldg., Suite 403   Phone: (615) 521-2500
Knoxville, TN 37902   Gretchen F. Beal, Libn.

KNOXVILLE-KNOX COUNTY PUBLIC LIBRARY SYSTEM - MC CLUNG
    HISTORICAL COLLECTION
Lawson McGhee Library
500 W. Church Ave.   Phone: (615) 523-0781
Knoxville, TN 37902   William J. MacArthur, Jr., Hd.

MUNICIPAL TECHNICAL ADVISORY SERVICE - LIBRARY
                                   Phone: (615) 974-5301
Knoxville, TN 37916   Carol C. Hewlett, Libn.

ST. MARY'S MEDICAL CENTER, INC. - MEDICAL LIBRARY
Oak Hill Ave.   Phone: (615) 971-7916
Knoxville, TN 37917   Martha H. Dickens, Libn.

ST. MARY'S MEDICAL CENTER, INC. - SCHOOL OF NURSING LIBRARY
Celeste Hall, Emerald Ave.   Phone: (615) 971-7839
Knoxville, TN 37917   Beth Barret, Libn.

STUDENTS' MUSEUM, INC. - LIBRARY
516 Beaman St.
Chilhowee Pk., Box 6108   Phone: (615) 637-1121
Knoxville, TN 37914   Edna W. Clark, Dir.

TENNESSEE STATE SUPREME COURT - LAW LIBRARY
Supreme Court Bldg., 719 Locust St. Phone: (615) 524-4537
Knoxville, TN 37902   Mamie H. Winstead, Libn.

TENNESSEE VALLEY AUTHORITY - LAW LIBRARY
400 Commerce Ave. (E10 C65)   Phone: (615) 632-4391
Knoxville, TN 37902   Bonnie M. Holmes, Supv. Law Lib.Serv.

TENNESSEE VALLEY AUTHORITY - MAP SALES OFFICE
400 Commerce Ave. (WP A3)   Phone: (615) 632-2717
Knoxville, TN 37902   Harold Donahue, Hd. Clerk

TENNESSEE VALLEY AUTHORITY - TECHNICAL LIBRARY
400 Commerce Ave.   Phone: (615) 632-3464
Knoxville, TN 37902   Jesse C. Mills, Chf.Libn.

UNIVERSITY OF TENNESSEE - AGRICULTURE-VETERINARY MEDICINE
    LIBRARY
Veterinary Medicine Teaching Hospital Phone: (615) 974-7338
Knoxville, TN 37916   Aubrey H. Mitchell, Libn.

UNIVERSITY OF TENNESSEE - CENTER FOR THE HEALTH SCIENCES -
    PRESTON MEDICAL LIBRARY
1924 Alcoa Hwy.   Phone: (615) 971-3237
Knoxville, TN 37920   Martha C. Childs, Libn.

UNIVERSITY OF TENNESSEE - COLLEGE OF LAW LIBRARY
1505 W. Cumberland Ave.   Phone: (615) 974-4381
Knoxville, TN 37916   David K. Brennan, Libn.

UNIVERSITY OF TENNESSEE - JOINT RESEARCH CENTERS LIBRARY
423 South Stadium Hall   Phone: (615) 974-4251
Knoxville, TN 37916   Joe R. Stines, Hd.Libn.

UNIVERSITY OF TENNESSEE - MUSIC LIBRARY
Music Bldg., Rm. 301   Phone: (615) 974-3474
Knoxville, TN 37916   Pauline S. Bayne, Libn.

UNIVERSITY OF TENNESSEE - SCIENCE-ENGINEERING LIBRARY
672 Buehler Hall   Phone: (615) 974-3270
Knoxville, TN 37916   Don Jett, Hd.Libn.

UNIVERSITY OF TENNESSEE - SPECIAL COLLECTIONS
                                   Phone: (615) 974-4480
Knoxville, TN 37916   John Dobson, Spec.Coll.Libn.

BLOUNT MEMORIAL HOSPITAL - LESLIE R. LINGEMAN MEMORIAL MEDICAL
    LIBRARY
New Walland Highway   Phone: (615) 983-7211
Maryville, TN 37801   Miriam B. Williamson, Libn.

AMERICAN BLAKE FOUNDATION - RESEARCH LIBRARY
Memphis State University
Dept. Of English   Phone: (901) 454-2653
Memphis, TN 38152   Dr. Roger R. Easson, Exec.Dir.

AMERICAN CONTRACT BRIDGE LEAGUE - ALBERT H. MOREHEAD
    MEMORIAL LIBRARY
2200 Democrat Rd.   Phone: (901) 332-5586
Memphis, TN 38116   Edith Simon, Libn.

BAPTIST MEMORIAL HOSPITAL - JOHN L. MC GEHEE LIBRARY
899 Madison Ave.   Phone: (901) 522-5140
Memphis, TN 38146   Donna L. Davis, Med.Libn.

BAPTIST MEMORIAL HOSPITAL - SCHOOL OF NURSING - LIBRARY
999 Monroe   Phone: (901) 522-4309
Memphis, TN 38104   Sherry Young, Libn.

BARTHOLOMEW (Harland) AND ASSOCIATES, INC. - LIBRARY
188 Jefferson Ave.   Phone: (901) 527-3521
Memphis, TN 38103   Jennifer B. Fox, Libn.

BROOKS MEMORIAL ART GALLERY - LIBRARY †
Overton Pk.   Phone: (901) 726-5266
Memphis, TN 38112   Letitia B. Proctor, Libn.

CENTER FOR SOUTHERN FOLKLORE - ARCHIVES
1216 Peabody Ave.
Box 40105   Phone: (901) 726-4205
Memphis, TN 38104   Frank Fourmy, Archv.

DIXON GALLERY AND GARDENS - LIBRARY
4339 Park Ave.   Phone: (901) 761-5250
Memphis, TN 38117   Michael Milkovich, Dir.

GRACE (W.R.) AND COMPANY - AGRICULTURAL CHEMICALS GROUP -
    PLANNING SERVICES LIBRARY
100 N. Main Bldg.
Box 277   Phone: (901) 522-2385
Memphis, TN 38101   Carolyn Wilhite, Libn.

HARDING GRADUATE SCHOOL OF RELIGION - L.M. GRAVES MEMORIAL
    LIBRARY
1000 Cherry Rd.   Phone: (901) 761-1354
Memphis, TN 38117   Annie May Alston Lewis, Libn.

HOLIDAY INNS, INC. - RESEARCH SERVICES INFORMATION CENTER
3742 Lamar Ave.   Phone: (901) 369-5993
Memphis, TN 38195   Vanessa Patterson, Supv., Res.Serv.

MEMPHIS ACADEMY OF ARTS - G. PILLOW LEWIS MEMORIAL LIBRARY †
Overton Pk.   Phone: (901) 726-4085
Memphis, TN 38112   Robert M. Scarlett, Libn.

MEMPHIS BOTANIC GARDEN FOUNDATION, INC. - GOLDSMITH CIVIC
    GARDEN CTR. - SYBILE MALLOY MEMORIAL LIBRARY
750 Cherry Rd.   Phone: (901) 685-1566
Memphis, TN 38117   Clara M. Wright, Adm.Ck.

MEMPHIS COMMERCIAL APPEAL - LIBRARY
495 Union Ave.   Phone: (901) 529-2781
Memphis, TN 38101   Eugene Brady, Libn.

MEMPHIS MENTAL HEALTH INSTITUTE - JAMES A. WALLACE LIBRARY
865 Poplar Ave.
Box 4966   Phone: (901) 529-7768
Memphis, TN 38104   Josephine Maddry, Lib.Techn.

MEMPHIS PINK PALACE MUSEUM - LIBRARY
3050 Central Ave.   Phone: (901) 454-5600
Memphis, TN 38111   Natalie B. Jalenak, Libn.

MEMPHIS-SHELBY COUNTY BAR ASSOCIATION LIBRARY
Court House   Phone: (901) 527-7041
Memphis, TN 38103   Mary Sue Boushe, Law Libn.

MEMPHIS-SHELBY COUNTY OFFICE OF PLANNING AND DEVELOPMENT -
     LIBRARY
City Hall, Rm. 419
125 N. Main St.   Phone: (901) 528-2601
Memphis, TN 38103   Marilyn A. Meeks, Libn.

MEMPHIS-SHELBY COUNTY PUBLIC LIBRARY AND INFORMATION CENTER -
     MEMPHIS ROOM COLLECTIONS
1850 Peabody Ave.   Phone: (901) 528-2961
Memphis, TN 38104   James R. Johnson, Hd., Hist. & Travel

MEMPHIS-SHELBY COUNTY PUBLIC LIBRARY AND INFO. CTR. - SCIENCE/
     BUSINESS/SOCIAL SCIENCES DEPT.
1850 Peabody Ave.   Phone: (901) 528-2984
Memphis, TN 38104   Sallie Johnson, Dept.Hd.

MEMPHIS STATE UNIVERSITY LIBRARIES - ART SLIDE LIBRARY
Department of Art
Jones Hall, Rm. 220   Phone: (901) 454-2071
Memphis, TN 38152   Mary Alice Martin, Slide Cur.

MEMPHIS STATE UNIVERSITY LIBRARIES - BUREAU OF EDUCATIONAL
     RESEARCH AND SERVICES - LIBRARY
College of Education
302 Ball Bldg.   Phone: (901) 454-2362
Memphis, TN 38152   Dr. John R. Petry, Libn.

MEMPHIS STATE UNIVERSITY LIBRARIES - C.H. NASH MUSEUM LIBRARY
1987 Indian Village Dr.   Phone: (901) 785-3160
Memphis, TN 38109   Gerald P. Smith, Cur.

MEMPHIS STATE UNIVERSITY LIBRARIES - CHEMISTRY LIBRARY
                                                       Phone: (901) 454-2625
Memphis, TN 38152   Sharon Banker, Lib.Asst.

MEMPHIS STATE UNIVERSITY LIBRARIES - ENGINEERING LIBRARY
Central Ave.   Phone: (901) 454-2179
Memphis, TN 38152   Pamela Palmer, Libn.

MEMPHIS STATE UNIVERSITY LIBRARIES - MISSISSIPPI VALLEY
     COLLECTION
                                                       Phone: (901) 454-2210
Memphis, TN 38152   Eleanor McKay, Cur.

MEMPHIS STATE UNIVERSITY LIBRARIES - MUSIC LIBRARY
Central Ave.   Phone: (901) 454-2556
Memphis, TN 38152   Ann Viles, Music Libn.

MEMPHIS STATE UNIVERSITY LIBRARIES - SCHOOL OF LAW LIBRARY
                                                       Phone: (901) 454-2426
Memphis, TN 38152   Sara Turley Cole, Law Libn.

MEMPHIS STATE UNIVERSITY LIBRARIES - SPEECH AND HEARING CENTER
     LIBRARY
807 Jefferson Ave.   Phone: (901) 525-2682
Memphis, TN 38104   Edwin Frank, Lib.Asst.

MEMPHIS STATE UNIVERSITY - PLANNING LIBRARY
226 Johnson Hall   Phone: (901) 454-2161
Memphis, TN 38152   Gail Findlay, Libn.

MEMPHIS THEOLOGICAL SEMINARY - LIBRARY
168 E. Pkwy. S.   Phone: (901) 458-8232
Memphis, TN 38104

NATIONAL COTTON COUNCIL OF AMERICA - LIBRARY
1918 N. Parkway   Phone: (901) 274-9030
Memphis, TN 38112   Carolyn Robertson, Libn.

P.T. BOATS, INC. - LIBRARY, ARCHIVES & TECHNICAL INFORMATION
     CENTER - NATIONAL HEADQUARTERS
Box 109   Phone: (901) 272-9980
Memphis, TN 38101   J.M. "Boats" Newberry, Founder & Dir.

PLOUGH, INC. - RESEARCH LIBRARY
Box 377   Phone: (901) 320-2702
Memphis, TN 38151   Martha Hurst, Libn.

PROCTER & GAMBLE COMPANY - BUCKEYE CELLULOSE CORPORATION-
     CELLULOSE & SPECIALTIES DIV. TECH. INFO. SERV.
2899 Jackson Ave.   Phone: (901) 454-8310
Memphis, TN 38108   Ruth McLallen, Tech.Info.Mgr.

ST. JOSEPH HOSPITAL - HEALTH SCIENCE LIBRARY
220 Overton   Phone: (901) 529-2874
Memphis, TN 38105   Gail Findley, Libn.

ST. JUDE CHILDREN'S RESEARCH HOSPITAL - RESEARCH LIBRARY
332 N. Lauderdale
Box 318   Phone: (901) 525-8381
Memphis, TN 38101   Mary Edith Walker, Med.Libn.

SHILOH MILITARY TRAIL, INC. - LIBRARY
Box 17386   Phone: (901) 454-5600
Memphis, TN 38117   Edward F. Williams, III, Res.Hist.

SOUTHERN COLLEGE OF OPTOMETRY - WILLIAM P. MAC CRACKEN, JR.
     MEMORIAL LIBRARY
1245 Madison Ave.   Phone: (901) 725-0180
Memphis, TN 38104   Nancy Gatlin, Libn.

STATE TECHNICAL INSTITUTE AT MEMPHIS - GEORGE E. FREEMAN
     LIBRARY
5983 Macon Cove   Phone: (901) 388-1200
Memphis, TN 38134   Rosa S. Burnett, Libn.

U.S. ARMY - CORPS OF ENGINEERS - MEMPHIS DISTRICT - LIBRARY
668 Clifford Davis Federal Bldg.   Phone: (901) 521-3584
Memphis, TN 38103   Jacque Patterson, Libn.

U.S. DEPT. OF COMMERCE - INTERNATIONAL TRADE ADMINISTRATION -
     MEMPHIS DISTRICT OFFICE LIBRARY
147 Jefferson Ave., Rm. 710   Phone: (901) 521-3213
Memphis, TN 38103   Bradford H. Rice, Dir.

U.S. DEPT. OF DEFENSE - DEFENSE INDUSTRIAL PLANT EQUIPMENT
     CENTER - TECHNICAL DATA REPOSITORY & LIBRARY
Airways Blvd.   Phone: (901) 744-5549
Memphis, TN 38114   Johnny F. Murray, Chf., Lib.

U.S. VETERANS ADMINISTRATION (TN-Memphis) - MEDICAL CENTER
     LIBRARY
1030 Jefferson Ave.   Phone: (901) 523-8990
Memphis, TN 38104   Mary Virginia Taylor, Chf., Lib.Serv.

UNIVERSITY OF TENNESSEE - CENTER FOR THE HEALTH SCIENCES
     LIBRARY
800 Madison Ave.   Phone: (901) 528-5638
Memphis, TN 38163   Jess A. Martin, Dir.

U.S. NAVY - NAVAL AIR STATION (Memphis) - LIBRARY
                                                       Phone: (901) 872-5683
Millington, TN 38054   Frances E. Smith, Libn.

U.S. NAVY - NAVAL REGIONAL MEDICAL CENTER (Memphis) - GENERAL AND
     MEDICAL LIBRARY †
                                                       Phone: (901) 872-5846
Millington, TN 38054   Allen Carter, Libn.

U.S. VETERANS ADMINISTRATION (TN-Johnson City) - HOSPITAL LIBRARY
                                                       Phone: (615) 926-1171
Mountain Home, TN 37684   Mary Jane Crutchfield, Chf.Libn.

U.S. NATL. PARK SERVICE - STONES RIVER NATL. BATTLEFIELD - LIBRARY
Old Nashville Hwy.
Rte. 10, Box 401   Phone: (615) 893-9501
Murfreesboro, TN 37130   Donald E. Magee, Pk.Supt.

GEOGRAPHIC

GEOGRAPHIC

U.S. VETERANS ADMINISTRATION (TN-Murfreesboro) - MEDICAL CENTER LIBRARY
Phone: (615) 893-1360
Murfreesboro, TN 37130
David N. Pennington, Chf., Lib.Serv.

ALADDIN INDUSTRIES - LIBRARY
703 Murfreesboro Rd.
Phone: (615) 748-3427
Nashville, TN 37210
Nancy S. Rumsey, Info.Spec.

AMERICAN BAPTIST THEOLOGICAL SEMINARY - T.L. HOLCOMB LIBRARY
1800 White's Creek Pike
Phone: (615) 262-1369
Nashville, TN 37207
Dorothy B. Lucas, Libn.

AVCO CORPORATION - AEROSTRUCTURES DIVISION - ENGINEERING LIBRARY *
Box 210
Phone: (615) 361-2472
Nashville, TN 38102
Martha G. Hardee, Libn.

BAPTIST HOSPITAL - LIBRARY
2000 Church St.
Phone: (615) 329-5373
Nashville, TN 37236
Vickie Overstreet, Libn.

BIOMEDICAL COMPUTING TECHNOLOGY INFORMATION CENTER
R-1302
Vanderbilt Medical Center
Phone: (615) 322-2385
Nashville, TN 37232

COUNTRY MUSIC FOUNDATION - LIBRARY AND MEDIA CENTER
4 Music Square E.
Phone: (615) 256-7008
Nashville, TN 37203
Danny R. Hatcher, Dir.

CRAWFORD (F. Marion) MEMORIAL SOCIETY - BIBLIOTHECA CRAWFORDIANA
Saracinesca House
3610 Meadowbrook Ave.
Phone: (615) 292-9695
Nashville, TN 37205
John C. Moran, Dir.

CUMBERLAND MUSEUM AND SCIENCE CENTER - LIBRARY
800 Ridley Ave.
Phone: (615) 242-1858
Nashville, TN 37203
Mary S. Thieme, Cur. of Coll.

DARGAN-CARVER LIBRARY
127 Ninth Ave., N.
Phone: (615) 251-2133
Nashville, TN 37234

DISCIPLES OF CHRIST HISTORICAL SOCIETY - LIBRARY
1101 19th Ave., S.
Phone: (615) 327-1444
Nashville, TN 37212
David I. McWhirter, Dir. of Lib./Archv.

FISK UNIVERSITY - MOLECULAR SPECTROSCOPY RESEARCH LABORATORY - LIBRARY
Box 8
Phone: (615) 329-8620
Nashville, TN 37203
E. Silberman, Professor/Dir.

FISK UNIVERSITY - SPECIAL COLLECTIONS DEPARTMENT
17th at Jackson St.
Phone: (615) 329-9111
Nashville, TN 37203
Ann Allen Shockley, Assoc.Libn./Archv.

HOSPITAL CORPORATION OF AMERICA - RESEARCH/INFORMATION SERVICES
One Park Plaza
Box 550
Phone: (615) 327-9551
Nashville, TN 37202
Lisa Ogletree, Mgr., Res./Info.Serv.

INTERNATIONAL ROCK AND ROLL MUSIC ASSOCIATION, INC. - LIBRARY
Box 50111
Phone: (615) 352-1443
Nashville, TN 37025
Bernard G. Walters, Pres.

JEWISH FEDERATION OF NASHVILLE AND MIDDLE TENNESSEE - ARCHIVES
3500 West End Ave.
Phone: (615) 297-3588
Nashville, TN 37205
Annette R. Levy, Dir.

MEHARRY MEDICAL COLLEGE - MEDICAL LIBRARY - LEARNING RESOURCES CENTER
1005 18th Ave., N.
Phone: (615) 327-6319
Nashville, TN 37208
Bernice Armstead, Act.Lib.Dir.

NASHVILLE BANNER - LIBRARY
1100 Broadway
Phone: (615) 255-5401
Nashville, TN 37202
Sally P. Moran, Libn.

NASHVILLE AND DAVIDSON COUNTY METROPOLITAN PLANNING COMMISSION - LIBRARY
Lindsley Hall
730 Second Ave. S.
Phone: (615) 259-6268
Nashville, TN 37201
Wanda Lucia Moore, Libn./Ed.

NASHVILLE GENERAL HOSPITAL - HEALTH SCIENCE LIBRARY
72 Hermitage Ave.
Phone: (615) 259-5657
Nashville, TN 37210
Stephanie Towle, Libn.

NASHVILLE - METROPOLITAN DEPARTMENT OF PUBLIC HEALTH - LENTZ HEALTH CENTER LIBRARY
311 23rd Ave., N.
Phone: (615) 327-9313
Nashville, TN 37203
Jenny Patterson, Libn.

NASHVILLE STATE TECHNICAL INSTITUTE - EDUCATIONAL RESOURCE CENTER
120 White Bridge Rd.
Phone: (615) 741-1229
Nashville, TN 37209
Carolyn Householder, Hd.

PEABODY COLLEGE FOR TEACHERS - KENNEDY CENTER - MATERIALS LIBRARY
Box 62
Phone: (615) 327-8154
Nashville, TN 37203
Mrs. Jamesie Rodney, Mgr.

PUBLIC LIBRARY OF NASHVILLE AND DAVIDSON COUNTY - BUSINESS INFORMATION SERVICE
222 Eighth Ave., N.
Phone: (615) 244-4700
Nashville, TN 37203
Alyne R. Gundlach, Chf.

SCARRITT COLLEGE FOR CHRISTIAN WORKERS - VIRGINIA DAVIS LASKEY LIBRARY
1104 19th Ave., S.
Phone: (615) 327-2700
Nashville, TN 37203
Leo Rippy, Jr., Dir., Lib.Serv.

TENNESSEAN - LIBRARY
1100 Broadway
Phone: (615) 255-1221
Nashville, TN 37202
Sandra Roberts, Libn.

TENNESSEE BOTANICAL GARDENS & FINE ARTS CENTER - MINNIE RITCHEY & JOEL OWSLEY CHEEK LIBRARY
Cheek Rd.
Phone: (615) 356-3306
Nashville, TN 37205
Jym Knight, Chf.Libn.

TENNESSEE STATE COMMISSION ON AGING - LIBRARY
700 Tennessee Bldg.
535 Church St.
Phone: (615) 741-2056
Nashville, TN 37219
Mason Rowe, Res.Anl.

TENNESSEE STATE COMMISSION FOR HUMAN DEVELOPMENT - RESOURCE LIBRARY *
C3-305 Cordell Hull Bldg.
Phone: (615) 741-2424
Nashville, TN 37219

TENNESSEE STATE DEPARTMENT OF AGRICULTURE - LOU WALLACE LIBRARY
Ellington Agricultural Center
Melrose Sta., Box 40627
Phone: (615) 741-1456
Nashville, TN 37204
Paulette C. Fewell, Dir. of Info./Ed.

TENNESSEE STATE DEPARTMENT OF CONSERVATION - DIVISION OF GEOLOGY - LIBRARY
G-5 State Office Bldg.
Phone: (615) 741-2726
Nashville, TN 37219
Robert A. Hershey, Dir./State Geologist

TENNESSEE STATE DEPARTMENT OF ECONOMIC & COMMUNITY DEVELOPMENT - LIBRARY
1014 Andrew Jackson Office Bldg.
Phone: (615) 741-1995
Nashville, TN 37219
Edith Snider, Libn.

TENNESSEE STATE DEPARTMENT OF EMPLOYMENT SECURITY - RESEARCH & STATISTICS SECTION
519 Cordell Hull Bldg.
Phone: (615) 741-2284
Nashville, TN 37219
Joe Cummings, Chf. of Res. & Stat.

TENNESSEE STATE DEPARTMENT OF HUMAN SERVICES - LIBRARY *
111 7th Ave. N.   Phone: (615) 741-3692
Nashville, TN 37203   Wilma W. Beard

TENNESSEE STATE DEPARTMENT OF PUBLIC HEALTH - FILM LIBRARY *
State Office Bldg., Ben Allen Rd.   Phone: (615) 741-2745
Nashville, TN 37216   Kathleen P. Kunzelman, Film Libn.

TENNESSEE STATE DEPARTMENT OF PUBLIC HEALTH - MCH/HWP
   RESOURCE CENTER
TDPH State Office Bldg.
Ben Allen Rd.   Phone: (615) 741-7276
Nashville, TN 37216   Gary Miles, Resource Ctr.Dir.

TENNESSEE STATE DEPARTMENT OF TRANSPORTATION - LIBRARY
James K. Polk Bldg., Suite 900   Phone: (615) 741-2330
Nashville, TN 37219   Ruth S. Letson, Libn.

TENNESSEE STATE ENERGY AUTHORITY - LIBRARY
707 Capitol Blvd. Bldg.   Phone: (615) 741-6677
Nashville, TN 37219   David Snider, Libn.

TENNESSEE STATE LAW LIBRARY
Supreme Court Bldg.
401 Seventh Ave., N.   Phone: (615) 741-2016
Nashville, TN 37219   G. Alvis Winstead, Dir. & Libn.

TENNESSEE STATE LEGISLATIVE LIBRARY
G-16 War Memorial Bldg.   Phone: (615) 741-3091
Nashville, TN 37219   Julie J. McCown, Leg.Libn.

TENNESSEE STATE LIBRARY AND ARCHIVES - ARCHIVES & MANUSCRIPTS
   SECTION
Seventh Ave., N.   Phone: (615) 741-2561
Nashville, TN 37219   Lexie Jean Brown Waggener, Dir.

TENNESSEE STATE LIBRARY - LIBRARY FOR THE BLIND AND PHYSICALLY
   HANDICAPPED †
729 Church St.   Phone: (615) 741-3915
Nashville, TN 37203   Miss Francis H. Ezell, Dir.

TENNESSEE STATE LIBRARY - STATE LIBRARY DIVISION
403 7th Ave., N.   Phone: (615) 741-2764
Nashville, TN 37219   Miss Kendall Cram, Dir.

TENNESSEE STATE PLANNING OFFICE - LIBRARY
1800 Polk Bldg.
505 Deadrick St.   Phone: (615) 741-2363
Nashville, TN 37219   Eleanor J. Burt, Libn.

TENNESSEE STATE PUBLIC SERVICE COMMISSION - LEGAL DEPARTMENT -
   LIBRARY
C1-103 Cordell Hull Bldg.   Phone: (615) 741-3191
Nashville, TN 37219   Henry Walker, Gen. Counsel

TENNESSEE VALLEY BANCORP - LIBRARY
One Commerce Pl.   Phone: (615) 749-3227
Nashville, TN 37239   John H. Thurman, Libn.

UNITED METHODIST PUBLISHING HOUSE - LIBRARY
201 Eighth Ave., S.   Phone: (615) 749-6335
Nashville, TN 37202   Rosalyn Lewis, Libn.

U.S. VETERANS ADMINISTRATION (TN-Nashville) - MEDICAL CENTER
   LIBRARY SERVICE *
1310 24th Ave., S.   Phone: (615) 327-4751
Nashville, TN 37203   Barbara A. Meadows, Chf.Libn.

UPPER ROOM DEVOTIONAL LIBRARY, MUSEUM AND ARCHIVES
1908 Grand Ave.   Phone: (615) 327-2700
Nashville, TN 37203   Dale E. Bilbrey, Libn./Musm.Coord.

VANDERBILT UNIVERSITY LAW LIBRARY
School of Law   Phone: (615) 322-2568
Nashville, TN 37203   Igor I. Kavass, Dir.

VANDERBILT UNIVERSITY LIBRARY - CENTRAL DIVISION - ARTS LIBRARY
21st Ave., S.   Phone: (615) 322-4887
Nashville, TN 37203   Jack Robertson, Arts Libn.

VANDERBILT UNIVERSITY LIBRARY - CENTRAL DIVISION - SARAH
   SHANNON STEVENSON SCIENCE LIBRARY
Vanderbilt University   Phone: (615) 322-2775
Nashville, TN 37203

VANDERBILT UNIVERSITY LIBRARY - DIVINITY LIBRARY
419 21st Ave., S.   Phone: (615) 322-2865
Nashville, TN 37203   Dorothy Ruth Parks, Dir.

VANDERBILT UNIVERSITY LIBRARY - DIVINITY LIBRARY - KESLER
   CIRCULATING LIBRARY
419 21st Ave., S.   Phone: (615) 322-2865
Nashville, TN 37203   Dorothy Ruth Parks, Dir.

VANDERBILT UNIVERSITY LIBRARY - DYER OBSERVATORY
Sta. B
Box 1803   Phone: (615) 373-4897
Nashville, TN 37235   Ellen Ellis, Libn.

VANDERBILT UNIVERSITY LIBRARY - EDUCATION LIBRARY
Peabody College for Teachers
Box 325   Phone: (615) 327-8184
Nashville, TN 37203   David Kearley, Dir.

VANDERBILT UNIVERSITY LIBRARY - EDUCATION LIBRARY - PEABODY
   COLLECTION OF BOOKS ON CHILDREN
Box 325   Phone: (615) 327-8184
Nashville, TN 37203   JoAnn Mulvihill, Libn.

VANDERBILT UNIVERSITY LIBRARY - MUSIC LIBRARY
Peabody College for Teachers   Phone: (615) 327-8081
Nashville, TN 37203   Shirley Marie Watts, Libn.

VANDERBILT UNIVERSITY LIBRARY - OWEN GRADUATE SCHOOL OF
   MANAGEMENT - MANAGEMENT LIBRARY
2505 W. End Ave.   Phone: (615) 322-2534
Nashville, TN 37203   Shirley Hallblade, Dir.

VANDERBILT UNIVERSITY LIBRARY - SPECIAL COLLECTIONS
   DEPARTMENT
21st Ave., S.   Phone: (615) 322-2807
Nashville, TN 37203   Marice Wolfe, Hd.

VANDERBILT UNIVERSITY LIBRARY - TELEVISION NEWS ARCHIVE
                                                   Phone: (615) 322-2927
Nashville, TN 37203   James P. Pilkington, Adm.

VANDERBILT UNIVERSITY - MEDICAL CENTER LIBRARY
                                                   Phone: (615) 322-2292
Nashville, TN 37232   T. Mark Hodges, Dir.

TENNESSEE VALLEY AUTHORITY - DIVISION OF FORESTRY, FISHERIES
   AND WILDLIFE DEVELOPMENT - LIBRARY
Forestry Bldg.   Phone: (615) 494-7173
Norris, TN 37828   Janice P. McDonnell, Libn.

COMPARATIVE ANIMAL RESEARCH LABORATORY - CARL REFERENCE
   LIBRARY
1299 Bethel Valley Rd.   Phone: (615) 576-4023
Oak Ridge, TN 37830   M. Ruth Kerr, Libn.

NATIONAL LIBRARY OF MEDICINE - TOXICOLOGY DATA BANK
Oak Ridge Natl. Laboratory   Phone: (615) 574-7805
Oak Ridge, TN 37830   Dr. Po-Yung Lu, Dir.

OAK RIDGE ASSOCIATED UNIVERSITIES - MEDICAL HEALTH SCIENCES
   DIVISION LIBRARY
Box 117   Phone: (615) 576-3070
Oak Ridge, TN 37830   Marion H. Garber, Libn.

UNION CARBIDE CORPORATION - NUCLEAR DIVISION - OAK RIDGE
   GASEOUS DIFFUSION PLANT LIBRARY
Box P   Phone: (615) 574-9694
Oak Ridge, TN 37830   John T. Phillips, Lib.Supv.

U.S. DEPT. OF ENERGY - TECHNICAL INFORMATION CENTER - FILM
   LIBRARY
Box 62   Phone: (615) 576-1285
Oak Ridge, TN 37830   Willie E. Clark, Film Libn.

GEOGRAPHIC

GEOGRAPHIC

U.S. DEPT. OF ENERGY - TECHNICAL INFORMATION CENTER - REFERENCE
  CENTER
Box 62   Phone: (615) 576-6837
Oak Ridge, TN 37830   Joseph G. Coyne, Mgr.

U.S. OAK RIDGE NATL. LABORATORY - CONTROLLED FUSION ATOMIC DATA
  CENTER
Bldg. 6003, Box X   Phone: (615) 574-4704
Oak Ridge, TN 37830   D.H. Crandall, Dir.

U.S. OAK RIDGE NATL. LABORATORY - INFORMATION CENTER FOR
  INTERNAL EXPOSURE
Box X   Phone: (615) 574-6261
Oak Ridge, TN 37830   S.R. Bernard, Dir.

U.S. OAK RIDGE NATL. LABORATORY - INFORMATION DIVISION -
  ENVIRONMENTAL MUTAGEN INFORMATION CENTER
Box Y   Phone: (615) 574-7871
Oak Ridge, TN 37830   John S. Wassom, Dir.

U.S. OAK RIDGE NATL. LABORATORY - LIBRARIES
Box X   Phone: (615) 574-6722
Oak Ridge, TN 37830   R.R. Dickison, Chf.Libn.

U.S. OAK RIDGE NATL. LABORATORY - NUCLEAR DATA PROJECT †
Box X   Phone: (615) 483-8611
Oak Ridge, TN 37830   M.J. Martin, Dir.

U.S. OAK RIDGE NATL. LABORATORY - NUCLEAR SAFETY INFORMATION
  CENTER
Bldg. 9711-1, Box Y   Phone: (615) 483-8611
Oak Ridge, TN 37830   W.B. Cottrell, Dir.

U.S. OAK RIDGE NATL. LABORATORY - RADIATION SHIELDING
  INFORMATION CENTER
Box X   Phone: (615) 574-6176
Oak Ridge, TN 37830   Betty F. Maskewitz, Dir.

U.S. OAK RIDGE NATL. LABORATORY - TOXICOLOGY INFORMATION
  RESPONSE CENTER
Bldg. 2024, Box X   Phone: (615) 576-1743
Oak Ridge, TN 37830   Susan G. Winslow, Dir.

ROCKY MOUNT HISTORICAL ASSOCIATION - LIBRARY
Route 2, Box 70   Phone: (615) 538-7396
Piney Flats, TN 37686   Cindy Penix, Libn.

HUGHES (Thomas) LIBRARY
Box 8   Phone: (615) 628-2441
Rugby, TN 37733   Barbara Stagg Paylor, Libn.

UNIVERSITY OF THE SOUTH - SCHOOL OF THEOLOGY LIBRARY
                                          Phone: (615) 598-5931
Sewanee, TN 37375   Thomas E. Camp, Libn.

U.S. NATL. PARK SERVICE - SHILOH NATL. MILITARY PARK - LIBRARY
                                          Phone: (901) 689-5275
Shiloh, TN 38376   Zeb V. McKinney, Supt.

UNIVERSITY OF TENNESSEE - SPACE INSTITUTE LIBRARY
                                          Phone: (615) 455-0631
Tullahoma, TN 37388   Helen B. Mason, Res. Facility Libn.

TEXAS

ABILENE REPORTER-NEWS - LIBRARY
Box 30   Phone: (915) 673-4271
Abilene, TX 79604   Anne Bell, Libn.

ABILENE STATE SCHOOL - SPECIAL LIBRARY
Box 451   Phone: (915) 692-4053
Abilene, TX 79604   Mary H. Harlow, Libn.

CRESCENT HEIGHTS BAPTIST CHURCH - LIBRARY
1902 N. Mockingbird Ln.   Phone: (915) 677-3749
Abilene, TX 79603   Mrs. Bill Jonas, Dir. of Lib.Serv.

FIRST BAPTIST CHURCH - MEDIA LIBRARY
Box 85   Phone: (915) 673-5031
Abilene, TX 79604   Ruth Dahlstrom, Libn.

HENDRICK MEDICAL CENTER - MARY MEEK SCHOOL OF NURSING -
  LIBRARY
N. 19th & Hickory Sts.   Phone: (915) 677-3551
Abilene, TX 79601   Mrs. Frances Brookreson, Libn.

UNITED METHODIST CHURCH - NORTHWEST TEXAS ANNUAL CONFERENCE
  - COMMISSION ON ARCHIVES AND HISTORY
McMurray College
Jay-Rollins Library
Box 296   Phone: (915) 692-4130
Abilene, TX 79697   Jewell Posey, Archv.

U.S. AIR FORCE BASE - DYESS BASE LIBRARY
Dyess AFB   Phone: (915) 696-2618
Abilene, TX 79607   Edith V. Roebuck, Libn.

AMARILLO COLLEGE - LEARNING RESOURCE CENTER
Box 447   Phone: (806) 376-5111
Amarillo, TX 79178   George E. Huffman, Dir.

AMARILLO GENEALOGICAL SOCIETY - LIBRARY
Amarillo Public Library
Box 2171   Phone: (806) 378-3054
Amarillo, TX 79189   Alice Green, Hd.Libn.

AMARILLO GLOBE-NEWS LIBRARY †
9th & Harrison Sts.   Phone: (806) 376-4488
Amarillo, TX 79166

M.P.K. OMEGA COMPANY - B.O.T.I. SPECIAL RESEARCH COLLECTION
3615 Carson   Phone: (806) 355-9369
Amarillo, TX 79109   Jacques Cantrell, Libn.

M.P.K. OMEGA COMPANY - BIOSCIENCE LIBRARY
3615 Carson   Phone: (806) 355-9369
Amarillo, TX 79109   Jacques Cantrell, Corp.Libn.

MASON & HANGER-SILAS MASON COMPANY, INC. - PANTEX PLANT -
  TECHNICAL LIBRARY
Box 30020   Phone: (806) 335-1581
Amarillo, TX 79177   Sue Sutphin, Tech.Libn.

SOUTHWESTERN PUBLIC SERVICE COMPANY - LIBRARY
Box 1261   Phone: (806) 378-2741
Amarillo, TX 79170   Gloria Branham, Libn.

TEXAS STATE - COURT OF APPEALS - 7TH SUPREME JUDICIAL DISTRICT
  AND POTTER COUNTY - LAW LIBRARY *
Potter County Courthouse   Phone: (806) 376-4266
Amarillo, TX 79101   Doyce Mallett, Law Libn.

TEXAS STATE TECHNICAL INSTITUTE, MID-CONTINENT CAMPUS -
  LIBRARY †
Box 11117   Phone: (806) 335-2316
Amarillo, TX 79111   Cynthia Sadler, Hd.Libn.

TEXAS TECH UNIVERSITY - HEALTH SCIENCES CENTER - REGIONAL
  ACADEMIC HEALTH CENTER LIBRARY
1400 Wallace Blvd.   Phone: (806) 355-8961
Amarillo, TX 79106   Carolyn Patrick, Assoc.Dir.

UNITED STATES MUSEUM LIBRARIAN SOCIETY - BUSINESS AND ARCHIVAL
  LIBRARY
3615 Carson
Amarillo, TX 79109

U.S. VETERANS ADMINISTRATION (TX-Amarillo) - HOSPITAL LIBRARY
                                          Phone: (806) 355-9703
Amarillo, TX 79106   Cheryl A. Hale, Chf., Lib.Serv.

ARLINGTON BAPTIST COLLEGE - EARL K. OLDHAM LIBRARY
3001 W. Division   Phone: (817) 265-6331
Arlington, TX 76012   Sandra H. Tanner, Libn.

BAUDER FASHION COLLEGE - LIBRARY
508 S. Center St.   Phone: (817) 277-6666
Arlington, TX 76010   Jane Kennedy, Libn.

COMPUTER AIDED MANUFACTURING-INTERNATIONAL, INC. (CAM-I) -
    LIBRARY
611 Ryan Plaza Dr., Suite 1107   Phone: (817) 265-5328
Arlington, TX 76011   Joanne E. Cruz, Lib.Coord.

JET RESEARCH CENTER, INC. - TECHNICAL INFORMATION AND SCIENCE
    LIBRARY
Box 246   Phone: (817) 572-2321
Arlington, TX 76010   Marion R. Baker, Info.Ret.

NORTH CENTRAL TEXAS COUNCIL OF GOVERNMENTS - REGIONAL
    INFORMATION SERVICE CENTER
Drawer COG
1201 N. Watson Rd., Suite 270   Phone: (817) 640-3300
Arlington, TX 76011   Gail A. Nichols, Adm.Asst.

SURGIKOS - RESEARCH LIBRARY
2500 Arbrook Blvd.
Box 130   Phone: (817) 277-8141
Arlington, TX 76010   W.B. Scroggs, Res.Libn.

UNIVERSITY OF TEXAS, ARLINGTON - LIBRARY - DIVISION OF SPECIAL
    COLLECTIONS AND ARCHIVES
Box 19497   Phone: (817) 273-3391
Arlington, TX 76019   Dr. Charles C. Colley, Dir.

ALLIED HEALTH SCIENCES LIBRARY
707 E. 14th St.   Phone: (512) 476-6461
Austin, TX 78701   Keith A. Drake, Act.Med.Libn.

AUSTIN AMERICAN STATESMAN - LIBRARY
308 Guadalupe   Phone: (512) 397-1212
Austin, TX 78701   Kay Guleke, Hd.Libn.

AUSTIN PRESBYTERIAN THEOLOGICAL SEMINARY - STITT LIBRARY
106 W. 27th St.   Phone: (512) 472-6736
Austin, TX 78705   Calvin Klemt, Libn.

AUSTIN PUBLIC LIBRARY - AUSTIN-TRAVIS COUNTY COLLECTION
810 Guadalupe   Phone: (512) 472-5433
Austin, TX 78701   Audray Bateman, Cur.

AUSTIN STATE HOSPITAL - STAFF LIBRARY
4110 Guadalupe St.   Phone: (512) 452-0381
Austin, TX 78751   Nancy H. Dobson, Libn.

CITE RESOURCE CENTER
211 E. 7th St.
Southwest Tower   Phone: (512) 476-6861
Austin, TX 78701   Jan B. Anderson, Mgr.

ELECTRO-MECHANICS COMPANY - LIBRARY †
Box 1546   Phone: (512) 451-8273
Austin, TX 78767   Laelle B. Marshall, Exec.Sec.

EPISCOPAL THEOLOGICAL SEMINARY OF THE SOUTHWEST - LIBRARY
Box 2247   Phone: (512) 472-4134
Austin, TX 78768   Harold H. Booher, Libn.

IBM CORPORATION - ENGINEERING LIBRARY
11400 Burnet Rd., Dept. 449-045-3
Austin, TX 78758   Cynthia A. Dyess, Libn.

INTERNATIONAL OIL SCOUTS ASSOCIATION - LIBRARY
Box 2121   Phone: (512) 472-3357
Austin, TX 78768   Barbara Lockstedt, Mgr.

MOTOROLA, INC. - MOS INTEGRATED CIRCUITS DIVISION -
    INFORMATION CENTER
3501 Ed Bluestein Blvd.   Phone: (512) 928-2600
Austin, TX 78721   Jacqueline Bass Davis, Dir., Info.Serv.

PROTESTANT EPISCOPAL CHURCH - ARCHIVES
Box 2247   Phone: (512) 472-6816
Austin, TX 78768   Dr. Virginia Nelle Bellamy, Archv.

PUBLIC UTILITY COMMISSION OF TEXAS - LIBRARY
7800 Shoal Creek Blvd.   Phone: (512) 458-0251
Austin, TX 78757   Martha M. Bartow, Hd.Libn.

RADIAN CORPORATION - LIBRARY
8500 Shoal Creek Blvd.
Box 9948   Phone: (512) 454-4797
Austin, TX 78766   Barbara J. Maxey, Sr.Libn.

SMALL, CRAIG & WERKENTHIN - LIBRARY
2600 Austin Natl. Bank Tower   Phone: (512) 472-8355
Austin, TX 78701   Kim J. Tomlin, Libn.

SOUTHWEST EDUCATIONAL DEVELOPMENT LABORATORY - LIBRARY
211 E. 7th   Phone: (512) 476-6861
Austin, TX 78701

STEVENS (Charles E.) AMERICAN ATHEIST LIBRARY AND ARCHIVES INC. †
2210 Hancock Dr.   Phone: (512) 458-1244
Austin, TX 78756   Madalyn Murray O'Hair, Archv.

TEXACO CHEMICAL COMPANY, INC. - TECHNICAL LITERATURE SECTION
Box 15730   Phone: (512) 459-6543
Austin, TX 78761   Ferne C. Allan, Supv., Tech.Lit.Sect.

TEXAS ADVISORY COMMISSION ON INTERGOVERNMENTAL RELATIONS -
    INFORMATION CENTER
Box 13206   Phone: (512) 475-3728
Austin, TX 78711

TEXAS CATHOLIC HISTORICAL SOCIETY - CATHOLIC ARCHIVES OF TEXAS
Capitol Sta., Box 13327   Phone: (512) 476-4888
Austin, TX 78711   Sr. M. Dolores Kasner, O.P., Dir.

TEXAS EDUCATION AGENCY - RESOURCE CENTER LIBRARY
150 E. Riverside Dr.   Phone: (512) 475-3567
Austin, TX 78704   Linda Kemp, Libn.

TEXAS INSTRUMENTS, INC. - AUSTIN SITE LIBRARY
Box 2909--MS/2207   Phone: (512) 250-7421
Austin, TX 78769   Sara Jane Lee, Site Libn.

TEXAS MEDICAL ASSOCIATION - MEMORIAL LIBRARY
1801 Lamar Blvd.   Phone: (512) 477-6704
Austin, TX 78701   Betty Afflerbach, Libn.

TEXAS MEMORIAL MUSEUM - LIBRARY
24th & Trinity   Phone: (512) 471-1604
Austin, TX 78705   W.G. Reeder, Dir.

TEXAS MUNICIPAL LEAGUE - LIBRARY
1020 Southwest Tower   Phone: (512) 478-6601
Austin, TX 78701   Gary N. Watkins, Asst. to Dir.

TEXAS NUCLEAR DIVISION - LIBRARY
9101 Research Blvd.
Box 9267
Austin, TX 78766

TEXAS RESEARCH LEAGUE - LIBRARY
Box 12456   Phone: (512) 472-3127
Austin, TX 78711   Judy Wright, Libn.

TEXAS STATE AERONAUTICS COMMISSION - LIBRARY & INFORMATION
    CENTER
Capitol Sta., Box 12607   Phone: (512) 475-3985
Austin, TX 78711   Nonie Mitchel, Libn.

TEXAS STATE AIR CONTROL BOARD - LIBRARY
6330 Hwy. 290 E.   Phone: (512) 451-5711
Austin, TX 78723   Clyde Biggs, Off.Serv.Supv.

TEXAS STATE BUREAU OF ECONOMIC GEOLOGY - WELL SAMPLE AND CORE
    LIBRARY
Balcones Research Center
10100 Burnet Rd.   Phone: (512) 835-3042
Austin, TX 78757   George Donaldson, Cur.

GEOGRAPHIC

TEXAS STATE - COURT OF APPEALS - 3RD SUPREME JUDICIAL DISTRICT -
  LAW LIBRARY
Capitol Sta., Box 12547   Phone: (512) 475-2441
Austin, TX 78711

TEXAS STATE DEPARTMENT OF AGRICULTURE - LIBRARY
Stephen F. Austin Bldg., Rm. 915
Box 12847   Phone: (512) 475-6467
Austin, TX 78711   Virginia Hall, Libn.

TEXAS STATE DEPARTMENT OF HEALTH - LIBRARY
1100 W. 49th St.   Phone: (512) 458-7559
Austin, TX 78756   Toni Connell, Lib.Ck.

TEXAS STATE DEPARTMENT OF HUMAN RESOURCES - LIBRARY
Box 2960   Phone: (512) 458-8568
Austin, TX 78769   Diana Boardman Houston, Libn.

TEXAS STATE DEPARTMENT OF MENTAL HEALTH & MENTAL RETARDATION
  - CENTRAL OFFICE LIBRARY
Capitol Sta., Box 12668   Phone: (512) 454-3761
Austin, TX 78711   Sandy Coyle, Libn.

TEXAS STATE DEPARTMENT OF WATER RESOURCES - WATER RESOURCES
  RESEARCH LIBRARY
Stephen F. Austin Bldg., Rm. 511
Capitol Sta., Box 13087   Phone: (512) 475-3781
Austin, TX 78711   Wicky Sleight, Hd.Libn.

TEXAS STATE EMPLOYMENT COMMISSION - TEC LIBRARY
15th & Congress   Phone: (512) 397-4491
Austin, TX 78778   Kaye Hanson, Adm.Techn.

TEXAS STATE INDUSTRIAL COMMISSION - RESEARCH LIBRARY
Capitol Sta., Box 12728   Phone: (512) 472-5059
Austin, TX 78711   Charles Newell, Statistician

TEXAS STATE LAW LIBRARY
Supreme Court Bldg., Box 12367   Phone: (512) 475-3807
Austin, TX 78711   Marian O. Boner, Dir.

TEXAS STATE LEGISLATIVE REFERENCE LIBRARY
Capitol Sta., Box 12488   Phone: (512) 475-4626
Austin, TX 78711   James R. Sanders, Dir.

TEXAS STATE LIBRARY
Capitol Sta., Box 12927   Phone: (512) 475-2166
Austin, TX 78711   Dr. Dorman H. Winfrey, Dir. & Libn.

TEXAS STATE LIBRARY - INFORMATION SERVICES DIVISION
Capitol Sta., Box 12927   Phone: (512) 475-2996
Austin, TX 78711   Al Quinn, Div.Dir.

TEXAS STATE LIBRARY - LIBRARY SCIENCE COLLECTION
Box 12927   Phone: (512) 475-3564
Austin, TX 78711   Anne Ramos, Libn.

TEXAS STATE LIBRARY - TEXAS ARCHIVES DIVISION
1201 Brazos St.
Box 12927   Phone: (512) 475-2445
Austin, TX 78711   Dr. David B. Gracy, II, Dir.

TEXAS STATE PARKS & WILDLIFE DEPARTMENT - LIBRARY
4200 Smith School Rd.   Phone: (512) 475-4950
Austin, TX 78744   Elaine Byrne, Libn.

TEXAS STATE - RAILROAD COMMISSION OF TEXAS - CENTRAL RECORDS
1124 South IH 35   Phone: (512) 445-1318
Austin, TX 78711   Mrs. Patsy S. Nance, Libn.

TRACOR, INC. - TECHNICAL LIBRARY
6500 Tracor Ln.   Phone: (512) 926-2800
Austin, TX 78721   Nancy P. McCandless, Tech.Libn.

UNITED DAUGHTERS OF THE CONFEDERACY - TEXAS CONFEDERATE
  MUSEUM LIBRARY
112 E. 11th   Phone: (512) 472-2596
Austin, TX 78701   Ethel J. McCutcheon, Musm.Cur.

U.S. AIR FORCE BASE - BERGSTROM BASE LIBRARY *
Bergstrom AFB   Phone: (512) 385-4100
Austin, TX 78743   Louise St. John, Base Libn.

U.S. PRESIDENTIAL LIBRARIES - LYNDON B. JOHNSON LIBRARY †
2313 Red River   Phone: (512) 397-5137
Austin, TX 78705   Harry J. Middleton, Dir.

UNIVERSITY OF TEXAS, AUSTIN - ARCHITECTURE & PLANNING LIBRARY
General Libraries, BTL 200   Phone: (512) 471-1844
Austin, TX 78712   Carole Cable, Arch./Fine Arts Libn

UNIVERSITY OF TEXAS, AUSTIN - ASIAN COLLECTION
General Libraries, MAI 316   Phone: (512) 471-3135
Austin, TX 78712   Kevin Lin, Libn.

UNIVERSITY OF TEXAS, AUSTIN - BENSON LATIN AMERICAN COLLECTION
General Libraries, SRH 1.109   Phone: (512) 471-3818
Austin, TX 78712   Laura Gutierrez-Witt, Libn.

UNIVERSITY OF TEXAS, AUSTIN - BUREAU OF BUSINESS RESEARCH -
  INFORMATION SERVICES
Box 7459, University Sta.   Phone: (512) 471-1616
Austin, TX 78712   Rita J. Wright, Soc.Sci./Res.Assoc.

UNIVERSITY OF TEXAS, AUSTIN - BUREAU OF ECONOMIC GEOLOGY
  READING ROOM *
Geology Bldg. 515   Phone: (512) 471-1534
Austin, TX 78712   Roselle Girard, Res.Sci.Assoc.

UNIVERSITY OF TEXAS, AUSTIN - CENTER FOR ENERGY STUDIES - ENERGY
  INFORMATION SERVICE
ENS 143
Austin, TX 78712   Carol J. Dunning, Res.Assoc.

UNIVERSITY OF TEXAS, AUSTIN - CENTER FOR INTERCULTURAL STUDIES
  IN FOLKLORE AND ETHNOMUSICOLOGY - LIBRARY *
Student Services Bldg., Rm. 203   Phone: (512) 471-1288
Austin, TX 78712   Dr. Richard Bauman, Dir.

UNIVERSITY OF TEXAS, AUSTIN - CHEMISTRY LIBRARY
General Libraries, WEL 2.132   Phone: (512) 471-1303
Austin, TX 78712   Aubrey E. Skinner, Libn.

UNIVERSITY OF TEXAS, AUSTIN - CLASSICS LIBRARY
General Libraries, WAG 1   Phone: (512) 471-5742
Austin, TX 78712   Bernice M. Dawson, Lib.Asst.

UNIVERSITY OF TEXAS, AUSTIN - ENGINEERING LIBRARY
General Libraries, ECJ 1.300   Phone: (512) 471-1610
Austin, TX 78712   Susan B. Ardis, Libn.

UNIVERSITY OF TEXAS, AUSTIN - EUGENE C. BARKER TEXAS HISTORY
  CENTER
General Libraries, SRH 2.109   Phone: (512) 471-5961
Austin, TX 78712   Dr. Don E. Carleton, Hd.Libn./Archv.

UNIVERSITY OF TEXAS, AUSTIN - FILM LIBRARY
EDA F-22   Phone: (512) 471-3573
Austin, TX 78712   Jane Hazelton, Media Coord.

UNIVERSITY OF TEXAS, AUSTIN - FINE ARTS LIBRARY
General Libraries, FAB 3.200   Phone: (512) 471-4777
Austin, TX 78712   Carole Cable, Arch./Fine Arts Libn

UNIVERSITY OF TEXAS, AUSTIN - GEOLOGY LIBRARY
General Libraries, GEO 302   Phone: (512) 471-1257
Austin, TX 78712   Martin Smith, Libn.

UNIVERSITY OF TEXAS, AUSTIN - HOGG FOUNDATION FOR MENTAL
  HEALTH - LIBRARY
W.C. Hogg Bldg., Rm. 301   Phone: (512) 471-5041
Austin, TX 78712   Anita Faubion, Libn.

UNIVERSITY OF TEXAS, AUSTIN - HUMANITIES RESEARCH CENTER
Box 7219   Phone: (512) 471-1833
Austin, TX 78712   Decherd Turner, Dir.

UNIVERSITY OF TEXAS, AUSTIN - LINGUISTICS RESEARCH CENTER -
    LIBRARY
HRC 3.342   Phone: (512) 471-4566
Austin, TX 78712   Dr. Helen-Jo J. Hewitt

UNIVERSITY OF TEXAS, AUSTIN - LYNDON B. JOHNSON SCHOOL OF PUBLIC
    AFFAIRS LIBRARY
General Libraries
Sid Richardson Hall, Unit 3.243   Phone: (512) 471-4486
Austin, TX 78712   Olive Forbes, Hd.Libn.

UNIVERSITY OF TEXAS, AUSTIN - MIDDLE EAST COLLECTION
General Libraries, MAI 316   Phone: (512) 471-4675
Austin, TX 78712   Abazar Sepehri, Libn.

UNIVERSITY OF TEXAS, AUSTIN - NATURAL FIBERS INFORMATION
    CENTER
University Sta., Box 8180   Phone: (512) 471-1063
Austin, TX 78712   Mary Green, Act.Dir.

UNIVERSITY OF TEXAS, AUSTIN - ORAL BUSINESS HISTORY PROJECT *
BEB 500
Austin, TX 78712

UNIVERSITY OF TEXAS, AUSTIN - PERRY-CASTANEDA LIBRARY -
    DOCUMENTS COLLECTION
General Libraries, PCL 2.400   Phone: (512) 471-3813
Austin, TX 78712   Barbara Turman, Libn.

UNIVERSITY OF TEXAS, AUSTIN - PERRY-CASTANEDA LIBRARY - MAP
    COLLECTION
PCL 1.102   Phone: (512) 471-5937
Austin, TX 78712   John Burlinson, Map Libn.

UNIVERSITY OF TEXAS, AUSTIN - PHYSICS-MATHEMATICS-ASTRONOMY
    LIBRARY
General Libraries, RLM 4.200   Phone: (512) 471-7539
Austin, TX 78712   John H. Sandy, Libn.

UNIVERSITY OF TEXAS, AUSTIN - POPULATION RESEARCH CENTER
    LIBRARY
1800 Main Bldg.   Phone: (512) 471-5514
Austin, TX 78712   Doreen S. Goyer, Hd.Libn.

UNIVERSITY OF TEXAS, AUSTIN - SCIENCE LIBRARY
General Libraries, MAI 220   Phone: (512) 471-1475
Austin, TX 8712   Betty J. White, Libn.

UNIVERSITY OF TEXAS SCHOOL OF LAW - TARLTON LAW LIBRARY
2500 Red River   Phone: (512) 471-7726
Austin, TX 78705   Roy M. Mersky, Dir. Of Res.

EXXON COMPANY, U.S.A. - TECHNICAL SERVICES - ENGINEERING LIBRARY
Box 3950   Phone: (713) 428-4487
Baytown, TX 77520   Bethany Picard, Libn.

EXXON RESEARCH AND ENGINEERING COMPANY - LIBRARY
Box 4178   Phone: (713) 428-5100
Baytown, TX 77520   Geraldine Gieger, Res.Libn.

BAPTIST HOSPITAL OF SOUTHEAST TEXAS - MEDICAL LIBRARY
Box 1591   Phone: (713) 832-5160
Beaumont, TX 77704   Deloris Blake, Med.Libn.

BEAUMONT ART MUSEUM - LIBRARY
1111 9th St.   Phone: (713) 832-3432
Beaumont, TX 77702   Kay Paris, Musm.Dir.

BEAUMONT ENTERPRISE & JOURNAL - LIBRARY
380 Walnut
Box 3071   Phone: (713) 833-3311
Beaumont, TX 77704   Jeanne E. Houston, Libn.

DU PONT DE NEMOURS (E.I.) & COMPANY, INC. - POLYMER PRODUCTS
    LIBRARY
Box 3269   Phone: (713) 727-9606
Beaumont, TX 77704   Roberta L. Howard, Tech.Libn.

GULF STATES UTILITIES COMPANY - CORPORATE LIBRARY
Box 2951   Phone: (713) 838-6631
Beaumont, TX 77704   Karen S. McConnell, Corp.Libn.

LAMAR UNIVERSITY - MARY AND JOHN GRAY LIBRARY
Lamar Univ. Sta., Box 10021   Phone: (713) 838-8313
Beaumont, TX 77710   Marjorie Wheeler, Ref.Dept.Hd.

ST. ELIZABETH HOSPITAL - HEALTH SCIENCES LIBRARY
2830 Calder Ave.
Box 5405   Phone: (713) 892-7171
Beaumont, TX 77702   Deborah Boone, Libn.

U.S. VETERANS ADMINISTRATION (TX-Big Spring) - HOSPITAL LIBRARY †
2400 S. Gregg St.   Phone: (915) 263-7361
Big Spring, TX 79720

RAYBURN (Sam) FOUNDATION - SAM RAYBURN LIBRARY
                                            Phone: (214) 583-2455
Bonham, TX 75418   H.G. Dulaney, Lib.Dir.

U.S. VETERANS ADMINISTRATION (TX-Bonham) - SAM RAYBURN
    MEMORIAL VETERANS CENTER MEDICAL LIBRARY
                                            Phone: (214) 583-2111
Bonham, TX 75418   D.C. Linn, Chf., Lib.Serv.

HUBER (J.M.) CORPORATION - RESEARCH LIBRARY
Box 2831   Phone: (806) 274-6331
Borger, TX 79006   Wanetca Reynolds, Libn.

BRAZOSPORT MUSEUM OF NATURAL SCIENCE - LIBRARY
400 College Dr.   Phone: (713) 265-7831
Brazosport, TX 77531

U.S. AIR FORCE - AEROSPACE MEDICAL DIVISION - SCHOOL OF
    AEROSPACE MEDICINE - STRUGHOLD AEROMEDICAL LIBRARY
                                            Phone: (516) 536-3322
Brooks AFB, TX 78235   Fred W. Todd, Chf.Libn.

U.S. AIR FORCE - HUMAN RESOURCES LABORATORY - LIBRARY
                                            Phone: (512) 536-2651
Brooks AFB, TX 78235   Orrine L. Woinowsk, Adm.Libn.

PAYNE (Howard) UNIVERSITY - CURRICULUM LIBRARY
Walker Memorial Library   Phone: (915) 646-2502
Brownwood, TX 76801   Rebecca Clausen, Lib.Supv.

PANHANDLE-PLAINS HISTORICAL MUSEUM - HISTORIC RESEARCH CENTER
Wt. Sta., Box 967   Phone: (806) 655-7191
Canyon, TX 79016   Claire R. Kuehn, Archv.-Libn.

WEST TEXAS STATE UNIVERSITY - CORNETTE LIBRARY
W.T. Sta., Box 748   Phone: (806) 656-2761
Canyon, TX 79016   Frank M. Blackburn, Univ.Libn.

U.S. AIR FORCE HOSPITAL - MEDICAL LIBRARY (TX-Carswell AFB) †
                                            Phone: (817) 735-7579
Carswell AFB, TX 76127   Loraine Ward, Med.Libn.

NORTHWOOD INSTITUTE OF TEXAS - FREEDOM EDUCATION CENTER
Box 58   Phone: (214) 291-7466
Cedar Hill, TX 75104   James R. Bromley, Dir.

NORTHWOOD INSTITUTE OF TEXAS - LIBRARY
Box 58   Phone: (214) 291-1541
Cedar Hill, TX 75104   Carla W. Bryan, Libn.

NORTHWOOD INSTITUTE OF TEXAS - ROSALIND KRESS HALEY LIBRARY
Box 58   Phone: (214) 291-7466
Cedar Hill, TX 75104   Sheryl J. Brown, Dir.

ATLANTIC-RICHFIELD COMPANY - ARCO CHEMICAL COMPANY - LYONDELL
    PLANT LIBRARY
Box 777   Phone: (713) 452-8147
Channelview, TX 77530   Virginia Wood, Lib.Supv.

FOOD PROTEIN RESEARCH AND DEVELOPMENT CENTER - LIBRARY
Texas A & M University, F.E. Box 183   Phone: (713) 845-2741
College Station, TX 77843   Dr. E.W. Lusas, Dir.

GEOGRAPHIC

GEOGRAPHIC

TEXAS A & M UNIVERSITY - ARCHIVES & MANUSCRIPTS COLLECTIONS
Sterling C. Evans Library   Phone: (713) 845-1815
College Station, TX 77843   Dr. Charles R. Schultz, Univ.Archv.

TEXAS A & M UNIVERSITY - MAP DEPARTMENT
Sterling C. Evans Library   Phone: (713) 845-1024
College Station, TX 77843   Susan S. Lytle, Map Libn.

TEXAS A & M UNIVERSITY - MEDICAL SCIENCES LIBRARY
Veterinary Adm. Bldg., Rm. 101   Phone: (713) 845-7427
College Station, TX 77843   Virginia L. Algermissen, Dir.

TEXAS A & M UNIVERSITY - REFERENCE DIVISION
Sterling C. Evans Library   Phone: (713) 845-5741
College Station, TX 77843   Katherine M. Jackson, Hd., Ref.Div.

TEXAS A & M UNIVERSITY - SPECIAL COLLECTIONS DIVISION
Sterling C. Evans Library   Phone: (713) 845-1951
College Station, TX 77843   Donald A. Dyal, Hd., Spec.Coll.Div.

TEXAS A & M UNIVERSITY - TECHNICAL REPORTS DEPARTMENT
Sterling C. Evans Library   Phone: (713) 845-2551
College Station, TX 77843   Loretto M. Long, Hd.

TEXAS A & M UNIVERSITY - THERMODYNAMICS RESEARCH CENTER
Texas Engineering Experiment Station   Phone: (713) 846-8765
College Station, TX 77843   Dr. Kenneth R. Hall, Dir.

TEXAS STATE FOREST SERVICE - LIBRARY
Texas A&M University   Phone: (713) 845-2641
College Station, TX 77843

AMERICAN NAME SOCIETY - PLACE NAME SURVEY OF THE UNITED STATES
   - LIBRARY
James Gilliam Gee Library
East Texas State University   Phone: (214) 886-5251
Commerce, TX 75428   Dr. Fred Tarpley, Natl.Dir.

EAST TEXAS STATE UNIVERSITY - JAMES GILLIAM GEE LIBRARY
East Texas Sta.   Phone: (214) 886-5717
Commerce, TX 75428   Mary E. Cook, Dir. Of Lib.Serv.

EAST TEXAS STATE UNIVERSITY - ORAL HISTORY PROGRAM
James Gilliam Gee Library
East Texas Sta.   Phone: (214) 886-5738
Commerce, TX 75428   James Conrad, Coord.

ART MUSEUM OF SOUTH TEXAS - LIBRARY
1902 N. Shoreline
Box 1010   Phone: (512) 884-3844
Corpus Christi, TX 78403   Susan Walker-Atchison, Cur.

CELANESE CORPORATION - CELANESE CHEMICAL COMPANY, INC. -
   TECHNICAL CENTER - LIBRARY
Box 9077   Phone: (512) 241-2343
Corpus Christi, TX 78408   Robert C. Wilkerson, Mgr.Adm.Sys.

CORPUS CHRISTI CALLER-TIMES - LIBRARY
Box 9136   Phone: (512) 884-2011
Corpus Christi, TX 78408   Linda James, Libn.

CORPUS CHRISTI MUSEUM - STAFF LIBRARY
1919 N. Water St.   Phone: (512) 883-2862
Corpus Christi, TX 78401   Aalbert Heine, Musm.Dir.

DRISCOLL FOUNDATION CHILDREN'S HOSPITAL - MEDICAL LIBRARY †
Box 6530   Phone: (512) 854-5341
Corpus Christi, TX 78411   Becky Melton, Lib.Mgr.

MEMORIAL MEDICAL CENTER - HEALTH SCIENCES LIBRARY
2606 Hospital Blvd.
Box 5280   Phone: (512) 881-4197
Corpus Christi, TX 78405   Charles A. Brown, Dir. of Lib.

PPG INDUSTRIES, INC. - CHEMICAL DIVISION - RESEARCH LIBRARY
Box 4026   Phone: (512) 883-4301
Corpus Christi, TX 78408   Ivan C. Trombley, Libn.

SPOHN HOSPITAL - MEDICAL LIBRARY
1436 Third St.   Phone: (512) 884-2041
Corpus Christi, TX 78404   Linda Neargardner, Dir.

U.S. NAVY - NAVAL AIR STATION (Corpus Christi) - LIBRARY †
Station Library, Bldg. 5   Phone: (512) 939-3574
Corpus Christi, TX 78419

U.S. NAVY - NAVAL REGIONAL MEDICAL CENTER (Corpus Christi) - MEDICAL
   LIBRARY †
                                             Phone: (512) 939-3863
Corpus Christi, TX 78419   Frances A. Hewlett, Med.Libn.

CROSBY COUNTY PIONEER MEMORIAL - CCPM HISTORICAL COLLECTION/
   MUSEUM LIBRARY
101 Main St.
Box 386   Phone: (806) 675-2331
Crosbyton, TX 79322   Verna Anne Wheeler, Exec.Dir.

AKIN, GUMP, STRAUSS, HAUER & FELD LAW LIBRARY
2800 Republic National Bank Bldg.   Phone: (214) 655-2800
Dallas, TX 75201   Joan Hass, Hd.Libn.

AMERICAN HEART ASSOCIATION - LIBRARY/RECORDS CENTER
7320 Greenville Ave.   Phone: (214) 750-5408
Dallas, TX 75231   Mary Halliburton, Mgr.

ATLANTIC-RICHFIELD COMPANY - ARCO OIL AND GAS COMPANY -
   RESEARCH & DEVELOPMENT TECHNICAL INFORMATION CENTER
Box 2819   Phone: (214) 422-6965
Dallas, TX 75221   Inge Loncaric, Supv.

BAYLOR UNIVERSITY, DALLAS - LIBRARY
3402 Gaston Ave.   Phone: (214) 820-2372
Dallas, TX 75246   Marcel C. Carol, Libn.

BISHOP COLLEGE - ZALE LIBRARY - BANKS AFRO-AMERICAN HERITAGE
   COLLECTION
3837 Simpson-Stuart Rd.   Phone: (214) 372-8134
Dallas, TX 75241   Dennis M. Hawkins, Pub.Serv.Libn.

BURGESS INDUSTRIES - ENGINEERING LIBRARY
8101 Carpenter Fwy.   Phone: (214) 631-1410
Dallas, TX 75247   Ernest L. Black, Mgr.

CAMPBELL TAGGART, INC. - RESEARCH DIVISION - LIBRARY
3401 Haggar Way   Phone: (214) 358-9424
Dallas, TX 75222   Sue Hammond, Libn.

CARRINGTON, COLEMAN, SLOMAN & BLUMENTHAL - LIBRARY
2500 South Tower
Plaza of the Americas   Phone: (214) 741-2121
Dallas, TX 75201   Dorothy H. Clary, Libn.

CHURCH OF THE INCARNATION - MARMION LIBRARY
3966 McKinney Ave.   Phone: (214) 521-5101
Dallas, TX 75204   Willa H. Johnson, Libn.

CITIZENS ASSOCIATION FOR SOUND ENERGY (CASE) - LIBRARY
Box 4123   Phone: (214) 946-9446
Dallas, TX 75208   Juanita Ellis, Pres.

CORE LABORATORIES, INC. - LIBRARY
7501 Stemmons
Box 47547   Phone: (214) 631-8270
Dallas, TX 75247   Christine B. Dobson, Libn.

CRISWELL CENTER FOR BIBLICAL STUDIES - LIBRARY
525 N. Ervay   Phone: (214) 742-3111
Dallas, TX 75201   Brenda G. Warren, Dir. of Lib.

DALLAS BIBLE COLLEGE - GOULD MEMORIAL LIBRARY †
8733 LaPrada Dr.   Phone: (214) 328-7171
Dallas, TX 75228   John R. Stanley, Libn.

DALLAS CHRISTIAN COLLEGE - LIBRARY
2700 Christian Pkwy.   Phone: (214) 241-3371
Dallas, TX 75234

DALLAS CIVIC GARDEN CENTER - LIBRARY
Corner First & Forest Aves., Fair Park
Box 26194   Phone: (214) 428-7476
Dallas, TX 75226   John J. Hill, Dir.

DALLAS COUNTY LAW LIBRARY
Government Ctr. Bldg.   Phone: (214) 749-8481
Dallas, TX 75202   Sheila C. Porter, Libn.

DALLAS HISTORICAL SOCIETY - RESEARCH CENTER
Hall of State, Fair Park
Box 26038   Phone: (214) 421-5136
Dallas, TX 75226   John W. Crain, Dir.

DALLAS MANAGEMENT SERVICES LIBRARY
City Hall   Phone: (214) 670-4248
Dallas, TX 75201   Kathryn W. Martin, Libn.

DALLAS MORNING NEWS - REFERENCE DEPARTMENT
Communications Center   Phone: (214) 745-8302
Dallas, TX 75265   Barbara C. May, Ref.Ed.

DALLAS MUSEUM OF FINE ARTS - REFERENCE LIBRARY †
Fair Park
Box 26250   Phone: (214) 421-4187
Dallas, TX 75226   Donna E. Rhein, Dir.

DALLAS POWER AND LIGHT COMPANY - RESEARCH LIBRARY
1506 Commerce St., Rm. 1801   Phone: (214) 698-7000
Dallas, TX 75201   Mrs. I. Naraine, Libn.

DALLAS PUBLIC LIBRARY - ARCHIVES AND RESEARCH CENTER FOR TEXAS
   AND DALLAS HISTORY
1954 Commerce   Phone: (214) 748-9071
Dallas, TX 75201   Katherine P. Jagoe, Hd., Res.Ctr.

DALLAS PUBLIC LIBRARY - BUSINESS AND TECHNOLOGY DIVISION
1954 Commerce St.   Phone: (214) 748-9071
Dallas, TX 75201   Sarabeth Sullivan, Div.Hd.

DALLAS PUBLIC LIBRARY - FILM SERVICE
1954 Commerce St.   Phone: (214) 748-9071
Dallas, TX 75201   Julie Travis, Supv.

DALLAS PUBLIC LIBRARY - FINE ARTS DIVISION
1954 Commerce St.   Phone: (214) 748-9071
Dallas, TX 75201

DALLAS PUBLIC LIBRARY - GENEALOGY COLLECTION
1954 Commerce St.   Phone: (214) 748-9071
Dallas, TX 75201   Lloyd DeWitt Bockstruck, Head

DALLAS PUBLIC LIBRARY - GOVERNMENT PUBLICATIONS DIVISION
1954 Commerce St.   Phone: (214) 748-9071
Dallas, TX 75201   Milton G. Ternberg, Hd.

DALLAS PUBLIC LIBRARY - HISTORY AND SOCIAL SCIENCES DIVISION
1954 Commerce St.   Phone: (214) 748-9071
Dallas, TX 75201   Thomas M. Bogie, Hd.

DALLAS PUBLIC LIBRARY - HUMANITIES DIVISION
1954 Commerce St.   Phone: (214) 748-9071
Dallas, TX 75201   Frances Bell, Hd.

DALLAS PUBLIC LIBRARY - RARE BOOK ROOM
1954 Commerce St.   Phone: (214) 748-9071
Dallas, TX 75201   Marvin H. Stone, Fine Coll.Libn.

DALLAS SKILLS CENTER - LEARNING LAB
1403 Corinth
Dallas, TX 75215   Cynthia A. Teter, Lrng.Ctr.Instr.

DALLAS THEOLOGICAL SEMINARY - MOSHER LIBRARY
3909 Swiss Ave.   Phone: (214) 824-3094
Dallas, TX 75204   Dr. John A. Witmer, Dir.

DALLAS TIMES-HERALD - LIBRARY
1101 Pacific St.
Box 5445   Phone: (214) 744-6240
Dallas, TX 75202   Elaine B. Walden, Libn.

DEGOLYER AND MAC NAUGHTON - LIBRARY
One Energy Sq.   Phone: (214) 368-6391
Dallas, TX 75206   Eleanor Maclay

E-SYSTEMS, INC. - GARLAND DIVISION - TECHNICAL LIBRARY
Box 226118   Phone: (214) 272-0515
Dallas, TX 75266   Charlene Morris, Tech.Libn.

EAST DALLAS CHRISTIAN CHURCH - HAGGARD MEMORIAL LIBRARY †
629 N. Peak St.   Phone: (214) 824-8185
Dallas, TX 75246   Mrs. Alfred C. Grosse, Lib.Chm.

ENVIRONMENTAL PROTECTION AGENCY - REGION VI LIBRARY
First International Bldg.
1201 Elm St.   Phone: (214) 767-7341
Dallas, TX 75270   Yvonne Lev, Libn.

FEDERAL RESERVE BANK OF DALLAS - RESEARCH LIBRARY
400 S. Akard St.   Phone: (214) 651-6392
Dallas, TX 75222   Victoria M. Roberts, Res.Libn.

FIRST BAPTIST CHURCH OF DALLAS - FIRST BAPTIST ACADEMY - GEORGE
   W. TRUETT MEMORIAL LIBRARY
1707 San Jacinto   Phone: (214) 742-3111
Dallas, TX 75201   Mildred L. Lively, Dir. of Lib.Serv.

FRITO-LAY, INC. - LIBRARY
Box 35034   Phone: (214) 351-7298
Dallas, TX 75235   Rosemary Barrett, Libn.

GEOLOGICAL INFORMATION LIBRARY OF DALLAS (GILD)
One Energy Sq., Suite 100
4925 Greenville Ave.   Phone: (214) 363-1078
Dallas, TX 75206   G. Frederick Shepherd, Dir.

GEOTRONICS LABORATORIES, INC. - LIBRARY
115 West Greenbriar Lane   Phone: (214) 946-7573
Dallas, TX 75208

GRACE (W.R.) AND COMPANY - NATURAL RESOURCES GROUP - LIBRARY
3400 First International Bldg.   Phone: (214) 658-1030
Dallas, TX 75270   Jane Freeman, Mgr.

GREATER DALLAS PLANNING COUNCIL - LIBRARY AND INFORMATION
   CENTER
Fidelity Union Tower, 16th Fl.   Phone: (214) 748-2274
Dallas, TX 75201   William L. Moore, Exec.Dir.

HIGHLAND PARK METHODIST CHURCH - LIBRARY
3300 Mockingbird Ln.   Phone: (214) 521-3111
Dallas, TX 75205   Mary Cochran, Libn.

HIGHLAND PARK PRESBYTERIAN CHURCH - MADELINE ROACH MEYERCORD
   LIBRARY
3821 University Blvd.   Phone: (214) 526-7457
Dallas, TX 75205   Mrs. David P. Smith, Chm.

INTERNATIONAL INSTITUTE FOR ROBOTICS - LIBRARY
Box 210708
Dallas, TX 75211   Dale Cowsert, Dir.

JOHNSON SWANSON & BARBEE - LIBRARY
4700 First International Bldg.   Phone: (214) 746-7059
Dallas, TX 75270   Carol Marks, Libn.

LIFE PLANNING/HEALTH SERVICES - LIBRARY/MEDIA SERVICES
2727 Oaklawn, Suite 228   Phone: (214) 522-0290
Dallas, TX 75219   Martha Brewer, Dp.Dir.

LIQUID PAPER CORPORATION - EMPLOYEE LIBRARY
9130 Markville
Box 225909   Phone: (214) 783-2600
Dallas, TX 75265   Emily C. Lin, Libn.

LONE STAR GAS COMPANY - RESEARCH LIBRARY
301 S. Harwood St.   Phone: (214) 670-2662
Dallas, TX 75201   Charlotte W. Vinson, Chf.Libn.

GEOGRAPHIC

MARY KAY COSMETICS, INC. - TECHNICAL INFORMATION CENTER
1330 Regal Row   Phone: (214) 638-6750
Dallas, TX 75247   Patricia Thompson, Tech.Info.Coord.

METHODIST HOSPITALS OF DALLAS - MEDICAL LIBRARY
301 W. Colorado   Phone: (214) 946-8181
Dallas, TX 75222   Mary J. Jarvis, Med.Libn.

MOBIL EXPLORATION AND PRODUCING SERVICES INC. - MEPSI LIBRARY
Box 900   Phone: (214) 658-4779
Dallas, TX 75221   Mary Lee Freeman, Libn.

MOBIL PIPE LINE COMPANY - ENGINEERING LIBRARY *
Box 900   Phone: (214) 658-2039
Dallas, TX 75221   K.E. Anderson, Mgr. of Engr.

MOBIL RESEARCH & DEVELOPMENT CORPORATION - FIELD RESEARCH LABORATORY LIBRARY
Box 900   Phone: (214) 333-6111
Dallas, TX 75221   Ammarette Roberts, Mgr., Tech.Info.Serv.

PARK CITIES BAPTIST CHURCH - LIBRARY
3933 Northwest Pkwy.   Phone: (214) 369-8211
Dallas, TX 75225   Peggy Gooch, Dir.

ROCKWELL INTERNATIONAL - ELECTRONICS OPERATIONS - DALLAS INFORMATION CENTER
Dallas Information Center 407-120   Phone: (214) 996-6022
Dallas, TX 75207   Wanda Fox, Mgr.

ST. MATTHEW'S EPISCOPAL CATHEDRAL - LIBRARY †
5100 Ross Ave.   Phone: (214) 823-8134
Dallas, TX 75206   Mrs. Sam E. Johnson, Act.Libn.

ST. PAUL HOSPITAL - C.B. SACHER LIBRARY
5909 Harry Hines Blvd.   Phone: (214) 689-2390
Dallas, TX 75235   Barbara D. Pace, Med.Libn.

SOUTHERN METHODIST UNIVERSITY - FIKES HALL OF SPECIAL COLLECTIONS AND DEGOLYER LIBRARY
Central University Libraries, SMU Sta.   Phone: (214) 692-2253
Dallas, TX 75275   Clifton H. Jones, Dir.

SOUTHERN METHODIST UNIVERSITY - METHODIST HISTORICAL COLLECTIONS
Bridwell Library   Phone: (214) 692-2363
Dallas, TX 75275   Rev. Roger L. Loyd, Cur.

SOUTHERN METHODIST UNIVERSITY - PERKINS SCHOOL OF THEOLOGY - LIBRARY
Bridwell Library   Phone: (214) 692-3483
Dallas, TX 75275   Jerry D. Campbell, Libn.

SOUTHERN METHODIST UNIVERSITY - SCIENCE/ENGINEERING LIBRARY
     Phone: (214) 692-2276
Dallas, TX 75275   Devertt D. Bickston, Libn.

SOUTHERN METHODIST UNIVERSITY - UNDERWOOD LAW LIBRARY
     Phone: (214) 692-3258
Dallas, TX 75275   Earl C. Borgeson, Libn.

SOUTHERN UNION COMPANY - CENTRAL RECORDS & LIBRARY
First International Bldg., Suite 1800   Phone: (214) 748-8511
Dallas, TX 75270   Gerald McWhorter, Records Coord.

SOUTHERN UNION COMPANY - LEGAL LIBRARY
First International Bldg., Suite 1800   Phone: (214) 748-8511
Dallas, TX 75270

SOUTHWEST MUSEUM OF SCIENCE & TECHNOLOGY/THE SCIENCE PLACE - LIBRARY
Fair Park, Box 11158   Phone: (214) 428-8351
Dallas, TX 75223   Linda C. Lewis, Musm.Dir.

TEMPLE EMANU-EL - ALEX F. WEISBERG LIBRARY
8500 Hillcrest   Phone: (214) 368-3613
Dallas, TX 75225   Donna Berliner, Libn.

TEXAS EMPLOYERS INSURANCE ASSOCIATION - ENGINEERING INFORMATION CENTER
Box 2759   Phone: (214) 653-8100
Dallas, TX 75221   Gay Bethel, Info.Res.Spec.

TEXAS INSTRUMENTS, INC. - INFORMATION SYSTEMS & SERVICES LIBRARY
Box 225621, M/S 988   Phone: (214) 995-5182
Dallas, TX 75265   Cecilia Tung, Libn.

TEXAS INSTRUMENTS, INC. - NORTH BUILDING LIBRARY
Box 226015, MS 211   Phone: (214) 995-2803
Dallas, TX 75265   Frances Dort, Libn.

TEXAS INSTRUMENTS, INC. - RESEARCH BUILDING LIBRARY
Box 225936, MS 135   Phone: (214) 995-2407
Dallas, TX 75265   Nancy Newins, Libn.

TEXAS INSTRUMENTS, INC. - SEMICONDUCTOR BUILDING LIBRARY
Box 225012, MS 20   Phone: (214) 995-2511
Dallas, TX 75265   Kathy Nordhaus, Libn.

TEXAS MID-CONTINENT OIL & GAS ASSOCIATION - LIBRARY
1341 W. Mockingbird Lane, Suite 1111-E   Phone: (214) 634-8610
Dallas, TX 75247   Joyce Nettles, Res.Libn.

TEXAS STATE - COURT OF APPEALS - 5TH SUPREME JUDICIAL DISTRICT - LAW LIBRARY
Dallas County Courthouse
Dallas, TX 75202

TEXAS WOMAN'S UNIVERSITY, DALLAS CENTER - F.W. AND BESSIE DYE MEMORIAL LIBRARY
1810 Inwood Rd.   Phone: (214) 631-3836
Dallas, TX 75235   Tommy M. Yardley, Coord., Health Sci.Lib.

THOMPSON & KNIGHT - LIBRARY
2300 Republic National Bank Bldg.   Phone: (214) 655-7568
Dallas, TX 75201   Jane Ward, Libn.

TRACY-LOCKE ADVERTISING AND PUBLIC RELATIONS, INC. - LIBRARY
Texas Commerce Bank Tower
Plaza of the Americas
Box 50129   Phone: (214) 742-3131
Dallas, TX 75250   Nancy M. Clausen, Mgr. of Info.Serv.

TRINITY UNIVERSITY - DALLAS THEATER CENTER LIBRARY
3636 Turtle Creek Blvd.   Phone: (214) 526-0109
Dallas, TX 75219   Marian Mitchell, Libn.

U.S. ARMY AND AIR FORCE EXCHANGE SERVICE - CENTRAL LIBRARY AD-M
     Phone: (214) 330-3337
Dallas, TX 75222   Anne Murray, Libn.

U.S. ARMY - CORPS OF ENGINEERS - SOUTHWESTERN DIVISION - LIBRARY
1114 Commerce St.   Phone: (214) 767-2325
Dallas, TX 75242   Maxine C. Smith, Libn.

U.S. BUREAU OF THE CENSUS - REGIONAL DATA USER SERVICE - DALLAS REGIONAL OFFICE - LIBRARY
Earle Caball Federal Bldg.
1100 Commerce St.   Phone: (214) 767-0625
Dallas, TX 75242   Valerie McFarland, Data User Serv.Off.

U.S. DEPT. OF COMMERCE - INTERNATIONAL TRADE ADMINISTRATION - DALLAS DISTRICT OFFICE LIBRARY
1110 Commerce St., Rm. 7A5   Phone: (214) 767-0544
Dallas, TX 75242   C. Carmon Stiles, Dir.

U.S. VETERANS ADMINISTRATION (TX-Dallas) - MEDICAL CENTER LIBRARY SERVICE
4500 S. Lancaster Rd.   Phone: (214) 376-5451
Dallas, TX 75216   Barbara W. Huckins, Chf., Lib.Serv.

UNIVERSITY OF TEXAS, DALLAS - CALLIER CENTER FOR COMMUNICATIONS DISORDERS - LIBRARY
1966 Inwood Rd.   Phone: (214) 638-1100
Dallas, TX 75235   Norma Jean Foster, Hd. of Lib.Serv.

UNIVERSITY OF TEXAS HEALTH SCIENCE CENTER, DALLAS - LIBRARY
5323 Harry Hines Blvd.   Phone: (214) 688-3368
Dallas, TX 75235   Jean K. Miller, Dir.

VOUGHT CORPORATION - TECHNICAL INFORMATION CENTER
9314 W. Jefferson St.
Box 225907   Phone: (214) 266-4660
Dallas, TX 75265   T.P. McGinty, Chf.Libn.

WADLEY INSTITUTES OF MOLECULAR MEDICINE - RESEARCH INSTITUTE
   LIBRARY
9000 Harry Hines Blvd.   Phone: (214) 351-8111
Dallas, TX 75235   Kathryn Manning, Libn.

XEROX CORPORATION - OFFICE SYSTEMS DIVISION - INFORMATION
   SERVICES/LIBRARY
1341 W. Mockingbird Ln.   Phone: (214) 689-6027
Dallas, TX 75247   Marjorie A. Henderson, Mgr., Info.Serv./Lib.

BOY SCOUTS OF AMERICA - LIBRARY
Box 61030   Phone: (214) 659-2280
Dallas/Fort Worth Airport, TX 75261   Ann L. McVicar, Libn.

AMERICAN AIRLINES, INC. - CORPORATE LIBRARY
Box 61616   Phone: (214) 355-1464
Dallas/Ft. Worth Airport, TX 75261   Carla Martindell Felsted, Libn.

WISE COUNTY HISTORICAL COMMISSION ARCHIVE
1602 S. College
Box 427   Phone: (817) 627-5586
Decatur, TX 76234   Rosalie Gregg, Exec.Dir.

SHELL OIL COMPANY - DEER PARK MANUFACTURING COMPLEX - LIBRARY
Box 999   Phone: (713) 476-6565
Deer Park, TX 77536

SOUTHWEST TEXAS GENEALOGICAL ASSOCIATION - LIBRARY
308 Ave. K
Del Rio, TX 78840

U.S. AIR FORCE BASE - LAUGHLIN BASE LIBRARY *
Laughlin AFB   Phone: (512) 298-5119
Del Rio, TX 78840   William Darcy, Base Libn.

AMERICAN DONKEY AND MULE SOCIETY - INFORMATION OFFICE
Rte. 5, Box 65   Phone: (817) 382-6845
Denton, TX 76201   Betsy Hutchins, Info.Off.

INSTITUTO INTERAMERICANO - LIBRARY †
1133 N. Texas Sta.   Phone: (817) 382-6686
Denton, TX 76203   Carl B. Compton, Dir.

NORTH TEXAS STATE UNIVERSITY - ORAL HISTORY COLLECTION
University Sta., Box 13734   Phone: (817) 788-2558
Denton, TX 76203   Dr. Ronald E. Marcello, Coord.

TEXAS WOMAN'S UNIVERSITY - LIBRARY SCIENCE LIBRARY
School of Library Science   Phone: (817) 387-2418
Denton, TX 76204   Samuel J. Marino, Act.Libn.

TEXAS WOMAN'S UNIVERSITY - LIBRARY SCIENCE LIBRARY - PROYECTO
   LEER *
School of Library Science
Denton, TX 76204   Dr. Ana Cleveland, Dir.

TEXAS WOMAN'S UNIVERSITY - SPECIAL COLLECTIONS
Bralley Memorial Library
TWU Sta., Box 23715   Phone: (817) 566-6415
Denton, TX 76204   Jean L. Glasgow, Spec.Coll.Libn.

TEXAS STATE - COURT OF APPEALS - 11TH SUPREME JUDICIAL DISTRICT
   - LAW LIBRARY
                                          Phone: (817) 629-2638
Eastland, TX 76448

HIDALGO COUNTY LAW LIBRARY
Courthouse, Box 215   Phone: (512) 383-1853
Edinburg, TX 78539   Aurora Rutledge, Libn.

CHURCH OF JESUS CHRIST OF LATTER-DAY SAINTS - EL PASO BRANCH
   GENEALOGICAL LIBRARY
3651 Douglas Ave.   Phone: (915) 565-9711
El Paso, TX 79903   H. Leroy Taylor, Libn.

EL PASO COUNTY LAW LIBRARY
508 City-County Bldg.
500 San Antonio St.   Phone: (915) 543-2917
El Paso, TX 79901   June D. Haggin, Libn.

EL PASO HERALD-POST - LIBRARY
401 Mills St.   Phone: (915) 747-6950
El Paso, TX 79999   Trinidad B. Acosta, Libn.

EL PASO NATURAL GAS COMPANY - TECHNICAL INFORMATION CENTER
Box 1492   Phone: (915) 543-3085
El Paso, TX 79978   Anne S. Wise, Coord.

EL PASO PUBLIC LIBRARY - GENEALOGY SECTION
501 N. Oregon St.   Phone: (915) 541-4873
El Paso, TX 79901   Jeanne C. Reynolds, Genealogy Libn.

EL PASO PUBLIC LIBRARY - SOUTHWEST RESEARCH COLLECTION
501 N. Oregon St.   Phone: (916) 543-3815
El Paso, TX 79901

FIRST PRESBYTERIAN CHURCH - LIBRARY †
1340 Murchison Dr.   Phone: (915) 533-7551
El Paso, TX 79902   J. Rodgers Spencer, Assoc. Pastor

TEXAS TECH UNIVERSITY - HEALTH SCIENCES CENTER - REGIONAL
   ACADEMIC HEALTH CENTER LIBRARY
4800 Alberta Ave.   Phone: (915) 533-3020
El Paso, TX 79905   Dona Roush, Assoc.Dir.

U.S. ARMY HOSPITALS - WILLIAM BEAUMONT ARMY MEDICAL CENTER -
   MEDICAL LIBRARY †
Bldg. 7777   Phone: (915) 569-3121
El Paso, TX 79920   Merle Alexander, Med.Libn.

U.S. NATL. PARK SERVICE - CHAMIZAL NATL. MEMORIAL - LIBRARY
109 N. Oregon, Suite 1316
Box 722   Phone: (915) 543-7780
El Paso, TX 79944   Richard Razo, Interp.Spec.

UNIVERSITY OF TEXAS, EL PASO - EDUCATION LIBRARY
College of Education   Phone: (915) 747-5417
El Paso, TX 79968   Jean Stevens, Hd.

UNIVERSITY OF TEXAS, EL PASO - INSTITUTE OF ORAL HISTORY
Liberal Arts 339   Phone: (915) 747-5488
El Paso, TX 79968   Dr. Oscar J. Martinez, Dir.

UNIVERSITY OF TEXAS, EL PASO - LIBRARY
                                          Phone: (915) 747-5684
El Paso, TX 79968   Fred W. Hanes, Dir. Of Libs.

UNIVERSITY OF TEXAS, EL PASO - LIBRARY - DOCUMENTS/MAPS LIBRARY
Library Annex   Phone: (915) 747-5685
El Paso, TX 79968   Brenda McDonald, Act.Hd.

UNIVERSITY OF TEXAS, EL PASO - LIBRARY - S.L.A. MARSHALL MILITARY
   HISTORY COLLECTION
Rm. 139   Phone: (915) 747-5697
El Paso, TX 79968   Thomas Burdett, Cur.

UNIVERSITY OF TEXAS, EL PASO - - NURSING/MEDICAL LIBRARY
                                          Phone: (915) 533-6094
El Paso, TX 79968   Esperanza A. Moreno, Hd.Libn.

UNIVERSITY OF TEXAS, EL PASO - SCIENCE/ENGINEERING/
   MATHEMATICS LIBRARY
Library Annex   Phone: (915) 747-5138
El Paso, TX 79968   Fletcher C. Newman, Hd.

U.S. ARMY AIR DEFENSE SCHOOL - LIBRARY †
Bldg. 2, Wing E
Box 5040   Phone: (915) 568-5781
Ft. Bliss, TX 79916   Delfina C. Galloway, Chf.Libn.

GEOGRAPHIC

GEOGRAPHIC

U.S. ARMY SERGEANTS MAJOR ACADEMY - OTHON O. VALENT LEARNING
    RESOURCES CENTER
Bldg. 11203   Phone: (915) 568-8176
Ft. Bliss, TX 79918   Marijean Murray, Supv.Libn.

HARVARD UNIVERSITY - RADIO ASTRONOMY STATION - LIBRARY
                                         Phone: (915) 426-3201
Fort Davis, TX 79734   A. Maxwell, Project Dir.

U.S. NATL. PARK SERVICE - FORT DAVIS NATL. HISTORIC SITE - LIBRARY
Box 1456   Phone: (915) 426-3225
Fort Davis, TX 79734   Douglas C. McChristian, Supt.

U.S. ARMY HOSPITALS - DARNALL ARMY HOSPITAL - MEDICAL LIBRARY
                                         Phone: (817) 685-4717
Ft. Hood, TX 76544   Frank M. Norton, Med.Libn.

U.S. ARMY - LANGUAGE TRAINING FACILITY - LIBRARY
Bldg. 4404   Phone: (817) 685-6392
Ft. Hood, TX 76544   Claire B. Curtice, Libn.

U.S. ARMY POST - FORT HOOD - MSA DIVISION - CASEY MEMORIAL
    LIBRARY
Bldg. 18000   Phone: (817) 685-5202
Ft. Hood, TX 76544   M.F. Hardin

U.S. ARMY - ACADEMY OF HEALTH SCIENCES - STIMSON LIBRARY †
                                         Phone: (512) 221-2116
Ft. Sam Houston, TX 78234   Lowell M. Robinson, Chf.Libn.

U.S. ARMY HOSPITALS - BROOKE ARMY MEDICAL CENTER - MEDICAL
    LIBRARY
                                         Phone: (512) 221-4119
Ft. Sam Houston, TX 78234

ALCON LABORATORIES, INC. - RESEARCH & DEVELOPMENT LIBRARY
6201 S. Fwy.
Box 1959   Phone: (817) 293-0450
Fort Worth, TX 76101   Darlene Fleming, Sci.Libn.

ALL SAINTS EPISCOPAL HOSPITAL - F.M. CORSELIUS LIBRARY
1400 Enderly Pl.
Box 31   Phone: (817) 926-2544
Fort Worth, TX 76101   Alma Enis, Libn.

CARTER (Amon) MUSEUM OF WESTERN ART - LIBRARY
3501 Camp Bowie Blvd.
Box 2365   Phone: (817) 738-1933
Fort Worth, TX 76107   Nancy G. Wynne, Libn.

CARTER & BURGESS, INC. ENGINEERS & PLANNERS - LIBRARY
1100 Macon   Phone: (817) 335-2611
Fort Worth, TX 76102   Julia W. Sweet, Libn.

COASTAL ECOSYSTEMS MANAGEMENTS, INC. - LIBRARY *
3600 Hulen St.   Phone: (817) 731-3727
Fort Worth, TX 76107   Elizabeth L. Parker, Libn.

FIRST NATIONAL BANK OF FORT WORTH - LIBRARY
Box 2260   Phone: (817) 390-6161
Fort Worth, TX 76101   Bonner Garmon, Libn.

FORT WORTH ART MUSEUM - LIBRARY
1309 Montgomery St.   Phone: (817) 738-9215
Fort Worth, TX 76107   David Ryan, Dir.

FORT WORTH PUBLIC LIBRARY - BUSINESS AND TECHNOLOGY
    DEPARTMENT
300 Taylor St.   Phone: (817) 870-7727
Fort Worth, TX 76102

FORT WORTH PUBLIC LIBRARY - BUSINESS AND TECHNOLOGY
    DEPARTMENT - EARTH SCIENCE LIBRARY
300 Taylor St.   Phone: (817) 870-7727
Fort Worth, TX 76102

FORT WORTH PUBLIC LIBRARY - HUMANITIES DEPARTMENT
300 Taylor St.   Phone: (817) 870-7717
Fort Worth, TX 76102   Heather L. Goebel, Hd.

FORT WORTH PUBLIC LIBRARY - SOUTHWEST AND GENEALOGY
    DEPARTMENT
300 Taylor St.   Phone: (817) 870-7740
Fort Worth, TX 76102   Patricia Chadwell, Hd.

FORT WORTH STAR-TELEGRAM - LIBRARY
400 W. 7th St.   Phone: (817) 390-7740
Fort Worth, TX 76102   Hettie Arleth, Chf.Libn.

GENERAL DYNAMICS CORPORATION - FORT WORTH DIVISION -
    RESEARCH LIBRARY *
Grant's Lane, MZ2246
Box 748   Phone: (817) 732-4811
Fort Worth, TX 76101   P. Roger De Tonnancour, Chf.Libn.

HARRIS HOSPITAL - MEDICAL LIBRARY *
1300 W. Cannon St.   Phone: (817) 334-6474
Fort Worth, TX 76104   Vaida Durham, Libn.

JOHN PETER SMITH HOSPITAL - MARIETTA MEMORIAL MEDICAL LIBRARY
1500 S. Main   Phone: (817) 921-3431
Fort Worth, TX 76104   Sharon Louise Isler, Med.Libn.

KIMBELL ART MUSEUM - LIBRARY
Will Rogers Rd. W.
Box 9440   Phone: (817) 332-8451
Fort Worth, TX 76107

RESEARCH SERVICES CORPORATION - INSTITUTE FOR MICROCRYSTAL
    POLYMER RESEARCH - LIBRARY
5280 Trail Lake Dr.   Phone: (817) 292-4271
Fort Worth, TX 76133   Naomi L. Matous, Libn.

ST. JOSEPH HOSPITAL - MEDICAL AND NURSING LIBRARY
1401 S. Main St.   Phone: (817) 336-9371
Fort Worth, TX 76104   Jesse Pierrard, Libn.

SOUTHWESTERN BAPTIST THEOLOGICAL SEMINARY - FLEMING LIBRARY
Box 22000-2E   Phone: (817) 923-1921
Fort Worth, TX 76122   Keith C. Wills, Dir. of Libs.

TARRANT COUNTY LAW LIBRARY
2nd Fl., Civil Courts Bldg.   Phone: (817) 334-1481
Fort Worth, TX 76102   Frances Perry, Law Libn.

TEXAS CHRISTIAN UNIVERSITY - INSTITUTE OF BEHAVIORAL RESEARCH -
    DRUG ABUSE COUNCIL LIBRARY
                                         Phone: (817) 921-7674
Fort Worth, TX 76129   Nancy J. Bruce, Lib.Supv.

TEXAS CHRISTIAN UNIVERSITY - INSTITUTE OF BEHAVIORAL RESEARCH -
    DRUG ABUSE EPIDEMIOLOGY DATA CENTER
                                         Phone: (817) 921-7674
Fort Worth, TX 76129   Dr. LaVerne D. Knezek, Assoc.Dir.

TEXAS CHRISTIAN UNIVERSITY - INSTITUTE OF BEHAVIORAL RESEARCH -
    TECHNICAL LIBRARY
                                         Phone: (817) 921-7672
Fort Worth, TX 76129   Nancy Bruce, Lib.Supv.

TEXAS CHRISTIAN UNIVERSITY - MARY COUTS BURNETT LIBRARY - BRITE
    DIVINITY SCHOOL COLLECTION
                                         Phone: (817) 921-7106
Fort Worth, TX 76129   Robert A. Olsen, Jr., Libn.

TEXAS CHRISTIAN UNIVERSITY - MUSIC LIBRARY
                                         Phone: (817) 921-7000
Fort Worth, TX 76129   Sheila Madden, Music Libn.

TEXAS COLLEGE OF OSTEOPATHIC MEDICINE - MEDICAL LIBRARY
Camp Bowie at Montgomery   Phone: (817) 735-2464
Fort Worth, TX 76107   Bobby R. Carter, Dir. of Lib.Serv.

TEXAS ELECTRIC SERVICE COMPANY - LIBRARY
115 W. 7th St.
Box 970   Phone: (817) 336-9411
Fort Worth, TX 76101   Melba Connelley, Libn.

TEXTRON, INC. - BELL HELICOPTER COMPANY - TECHNICAL LIBRARY
Box 482   Phone: (817) 280-3608
Fort Worth, TX 76101   Carol A. Barrett, Engr.Libn.

TRAVIS AVENUE BAPTIST CHURCH - MAURINE HENDERSON LIBRARY
3041 Travis Ave.   Phone: (817) 924-4266
Fort Worth, TX 76110   Mrs. S.H. Henderson, Libn.

U.S. AIR FORCE BASE - CARSWELL BASE LIBRARY
Carswell AFB   Phone: (817) 735-5230
Fort Worth, TX 76127   Christine R. Lain, Libn.

U.S. ARMY - CORPS OF ENGINEERS - FORT WORTH DISTRICT - TECHNICAL
   LIBRARY
819 Taylor St.
Box 17300   Phone: (817) 334-2138
Fort Worth, TX 76102   Craig L. Pelz, Libn.

U.S. DEPT. OF HOUSING AND URBAN DEVELOPMENT - REGION VI - LIBRARY
221 W. Lancaster, 8th Fl.
Box 2905   Phone: (817) 870-5420
Fort Worth, TX 76113   Susan M. Hayes, Regional Libn.

U.S. FEDERAL AVIATION ADMINISTRATION - SOUTHWEST REGION
   LIBRARY *
Box 1689   Phone: (817) 624-4911
Fort Worth, TX 76101

U.S. NATL. ARCHIVES & RECORDS SERVICE - FEDERAL ARCHIVES AND
   RECORDS CENTER, REGION 7 *
4900 Hemphill, Bldg. 1
Box 6216   Phone: (817) 334-5515
Fort Worth, TX 76115   Kent Carter, Chf., Archv.Br.

DOW CHEMICAL U.S.A. - TEXAS DIVISION - LIBRARY
                                             Phone: (713) 238-3513
Freeport, TX 77541   J.P. Eben, Supv.

ROSENBERG LIBRARY - ARCHIVES DEPARTMENT
2310 Sealy Ave.   Phone: (713) 765-5845
Galveston, TX 77550   Jane A. Kenamore, Archv.

TEMPLE B'NAI ISRAEL - LASKER MEMORIAL LIBRARY
3006 Ave. O   Phone: (713) 765-5796
Galveston, TX 77550   Mrs. Sidney R. Kay

TEXAS A & M UNIVERSITY AT GALVESTON - LIBRARY
Mitchell Campus
Pelican Island, Box 1675   Phone: (713) 744-7161
Galveston, TX 77553   Elizabeth A. Fuseler, Libn.

U.S. ARMY - CORPS OF ENGINEERS - GALVESTON DISTRICT - LIBRARY
Box 1229   Phone: (713) 763-1211
Galveston, TX 77553   Frank Gately, Libn.

U.S. NATL. MARINE FISHERIES SERVICE - SOUTHEAST FISHERIES CENTER
   - GALVESTON LABORATORY LIBRARY
4700 Avenue U   Phone: (713) 763-1211
Galveston, TX 77550   Eileen M. McVey, Libn.

UNIVERSITY OF TEXAS, AUSTIN - MARINE SCIENCE INSTITUTE -
   GEOPHYSICS LABORATORY - LIBRARY
700 The Strand   Phone: (713) 765-2914
Galveston, TX 77550   Josefa A. York, Libn.

UNIVERSITY OF TEXAS MEDICAL BRANCH - MOODY MEDICAL LIBRARY
                                             Phone: (713) 765-1971
Galveston, TX 77550   Emil F. Frey, Dir.

GENERAL ELECTRODYNAMICS CORPORATION - LIBRARY †
4430 Forest Ln.   Phone: (214) 276-1161
Garland, TX 75040

U.S. AIR FORCE BASE - GOODFELLOW BASE LIBRARY
Bldg. 712   Phone: (915) 653-3231
Goodfellow AFB, TX 76908   Martha K. Sumpter, Libn.

GRAND PRAIRIE COMMUNITY HOSPITAL - DR. PHIL R. RUSSELL LIBRARY
2709 Hospital Blvd.   Phone: (214) 641-5086
Grand Prairie, TX 76010

E-SYSTEMS, INC. - DIVISION LIBRARY
Box 1056   Phone: (214) 454-4580
Greenville, TX 75401   Joleta Moore, Supv.

MORGAN (J. Harris) LAW OFFICE - LAW LIBRARY *
Box 556   Phone: (214) 455-3183
Greenville, TX 75401   Mrs. Almarine Morgan, Libn.

TEXAS STATE TECHNICAL INSTITUTE, RIO GRANDE CAMPUS - LIBRARY
                                             Phone: (512) 425-4922
Harlingen, TX 78550   Michael D. Buck, Dir. of Lib.

TEXAS BAPTIST INSTITUTE/SEMINARY - LIBRARY
1300 Longview Dr.
Box 570   Phone: (214) 657-6543
Henderson, TX 75652   James A. Kirkland, Libn.

DEAF SMITH GENERAL HOSPITAL - LIBRARY
801 E. 3rd St.   Phone: (806) 364-2141
Hereford, TX 79045   Vicky L. Higgins, Dir.Med.Rec.

HILL JUNIOR COLLEGE - CONFEDERATE RESEARCH CENTER AND GUN
   MUSEUM
                                             Phone: (817) 582-2555
Hillsboro, TX 76645   AnnieLee Wright, Libn.

AMERICAN BRAHMAN BREEDERS ASSOCIATION - LIBRARY
1313 La Concha Ln.   Phone: (713) 795-4444
Houston, TX 77054   Cecilia Cowart, Dir., Commun.

AMERICAN GENERAL CAPITAL MANAGEMENT, INC. - RESEARCH LIBRARY
Box 3121   Phone: (713) 522-1111
Houston, TX 77001   Betty J. Mohrman, Libn.

AMERICAN SOCIETY FOR MEDICAL TECHNOLOGY - LIBRARY †
330 Meadowfern Dr.   Phone: (713) 893-7072
Houston, TX 77067

AMOCO INTERNATIONAL OIL COMPANY - LIBRARY INFORMATION CENTER
16825 Northchase Dr.   Phone: (713) 931-2584
Houston, TX 77060   Eloise F. Martinez, Supv.

ARNOLD, WHITE & DURKEE - LIBRARY
2100 Transco Tower   Phone: (713) 621-9100
Houston, TX 77056   Sharan Zwick, Libn.

ARTHUR ANDERSEN & CO. - BUSINESS LIBRARY
711 Louisiana, Suite 700   Phone: (713) 237-2718
Houston, TX 77338   Ann Ghist, Libn.

BAKER & BOTTS - LAW LIBRARY
3000 One Shell Plaza   Phone: (713) 229-1412
Houston, TX 77002   Melissa Colbert, Libn.

BECHTEL POWER CORPORATION - LIBRARY
Box 2166   Phone: (713) 850-2365
Houston, TX 77001   Jean Adams, Libn.

BONNER & MOORE ASSOCIATES, INC. - LIBRARY
2727 Allen Pkwy.   Phone: (713) 522-6800
Houston, TX 77019   Ann T. Kelley, Info.Spec.

BRACEWELL & PATTERSON - LAW LIBRARY
2900 South Tower, Pennzoil Place   Phone: (713) 223-2900
Houston, TX 77002   Susan Mims, Libn.

BROWN & ROOT, INC. - TECHNICAL LIBRARY
Box 3   Phone: (713) 676-8693
Houston, TX 77001   Kathy Hubbard, Hd.Libn.

BUTLER, BINION, RICE, COOK, & KNAPP - LAW LIBRARY
1100 Esperson Bldg.   Phone: (713) 237-3140
Houston, TX 77002   Nell Booker, Libn.

CAMERON IRON WORKS, INC. - LIBRARY
Box 1212   Phone: (713) 939-3789
Houston, TX 77001   Norma A. Gries, Libn.

CAUDILL ROWLETT SCOTT - LIBRARY
1111 W. Loop S.
Box 22427   Phone: (713) 621-9600
Houston, TX 77027   Nancy S. Acker, Libn.

CENTRAL PRESBYTERIAN CHURCH - LIBRARY
3788 Richmond Ave.   Phone: (713) 621-2424
Houston, TX 77027   J.J. Britton, Libn.

CHEVRON GEOSCIENCES COMPANY - LIBRARY
Box 36487   Phone: (713) 781-3030
Houston, TX 77036   Francine Rorabaugh, Libn.

COLUMBIA GULF TRANSMISSION COMPANY - ENGINEERING LIBRARY
Box 683   Phone: (713) 621-1200
Houston, TX 77001   Jayne F. Young, Engr.Libn.

CONOCO, INC. - INTERNATIONAL EXPLORATION AND PRODUCTION
    LIBRARY †
Box 2197   Phone: (713) 965-2499
Houston, TX 77001   Olga Camero, Supv., Lib.Serv.

CONTINENTAL CARBON COMPANY - TECHNICAL LIBRARY †
10500 Richmond Ave.
Box 42817   Phone: (713) 975-5802
Houston, TX 77042   Linda M. Malisheski, Libn.

DAMES & MOORE - LIBRARY AND INFORMATION CENTER
4321 Directors Row, Suite 200   Phone: (713) 688-4541
Houston, TX 77092   Pat Howes, Librarian

DOW CHEMICAL U.S.A. - ENGINEERING AND CONSTRUCTION SERVICES
    LIBRARY †
Box 3387   Phone: (713) 978-2971
Houston, TX 77001   Alice Harris, Libn.

DRESSER INDUSTRIES, INC. - MAGCOBAR RESEARCH LIBRARY
10201 Westheimer, Bldg. 1A, Rm. 100   Phone: (713) 784-6611
Houston, TX 77042   Dr. Aliyah Von Nussbaumer, Res.Libn.

ESOTERIC PHILOSOPHY CENTER, INC. - LIBRARY
517 Lovett Blvd.   Phone: (713) 526-5998
Houston, TX 77006   Jannah Gibson, Libn.

ESSO EASTERN, INC. - LIBRARY
Box 1415   Phone: (713) 656-7346
Houston, TX 77001   Carrie W. Eagon, Libn.

EXXON COMPANY, U.S.A. - EXPLORATION LIBRARY
Box 4279, Rm. 3350   Phone: (713) 999-9257
Houston, TX 77001   Roza Ekimov, Libn.

EXXON COMPANY, U.S.A. - GENERAL SERVICES - LIBRARY
Box 2180   Phone: (713) 656-5915
Houston, TX 77001   Mary L. Moore, Libn.

EXXON COMPANY, U.S.A. - LAW LIBRARY
Box 2180   Phone: (713) 656-2019
Houston, TX 77001   Mrs. Del Wherry, Libn.

FIRST PRESBYTERIAN CHURCH - EWING MEMORIAL LIBRARY
5300 S. Main   Phone: (713) 526-2525
Houston, TX 77004   Elizabeth Orr, Libn.

FLUOR ENGINEERS AND CONSTRUCTORS, INC. - FLUOR HOUSTON LIBRARY
Box 35000   Phone: (713) 662-3960
Houston, TX 77035   Camille M. Powell, Libn.

FLUOR OCEAN SERVICES, INC. - ENGINEERING LIBRARY
6200 Hillcroft
Box 36878   Phone: (713) 776-4369
Houston, TX 77036   Juanna I. Gee, Libn.

FUGRO GULF, INC. - LIBRARY
5884 Point West Dr.   Phone: (713) 777-2641
Houston, TX 77036   Gloria Bellis, Libn.

FULBRIGHT & JAWORSKI - LIBRARY
Bank of the Southwest Bldg.   Phone: (713) 651-5151
Houston, TX 77002   Jane D. Holland, Libn.

GENERAL ELECTRIC COMPANY - APOLLO SYSTEMS - TECHNICAL AND
    SERVICES SUPPORT LIBRARY
Box 58408   Phone: (713) 332-4511
Houston, TX 77058   C.E. Colburn, Libn.

GETTY OIL COMPANY, INC. - RESEARCH CENTER LIBRARY
10201 Westpark Dr.
Box 42214   Phone: (713) 972-1749
Houston, TX 77042   Elaine P. Adams, Supv., Lib.Serv.

GULF COAST BIBLE COLLEGE - CHARLES EWING BROWN LIBRARY
911 W. 11th St.   Phone: (713) 862-3800
Houston, TX 77008   Ronald W. Kriesel, Hd.Libn.

GULF COAST WASTE DISPOSAL AUTHORITY - RESEARCH AND
    DEVELOPMENT LIBRARY *
910 Bay Area Blvd.   Phone: (713) 488-4115
Houston, TX 77058   Lisa Wills, Libn.

GULF COMPANIES - LAW LIBRARY
Box 3725   Phone: (713) 754-3172
Houston, TX 77001   Martha C. Nash, Law Libn.

GULF OIL CHEMICALS COMPANY - BUSINESS INFORMATION CENTER
Box 3766
Houston, TX 77001   Joel A. Beale, Libn.

GULF OIL CHEMICALS COMPANY - HOUSTON RESEARCH LIBRARY
Box 79070   Phone: (713) 754-7421
Houston, TX 77079   R.C. Sartorius, Info.Anl.

GULF OIL CORPORATION - GS & T CORPORATE ENGINEERING LIBRARY
Box 1357   Phone: (713) 754-3624
Houston, TX 77001   Margaret A. Sirman, Libn.

GULF REFINING & MARKETING COMPANY - LIBRARY AND INFORMATION
    CENTER
Box 2100   Phone: (713) 226-1632
Houston, TX 77001   Stanley E. Brewer, Chf.Libn.

HARRIS COUNTY HERITAGE SOCIETY - LIBRARY
1100 Bagby St.   Phone: (713) 223-8367
Houston, TX 77002   Mrs. T.J. Burnett, Jr., Chm.

HARRIS COUNTY LAW LIBRARY
101 Civil Courts Bldg.   Phone: (713) 221-5183
Houston, TX 77002   Eugene Chambers, Dir., Law Lib.

HERMANN HOSPITAL - SCHOOL OF VOCATIONAL NURSING LIBRARY
1203 Ross Sterling   Phone: (713) 797-4080
Houston, TX 77030   Helen C. Harrell, Dir.

HOUSTON ACADEMY OF MEDICINE - TEXAS MEDICAL CENTER LIBRARY
Jesse H. Jones Lib. Bldg.   Phone: (713) 797-1230
Houston, TX 77030   Richard Lyders, Exec.Dir.

HOUSTON CHRONICLE - EDITORIAL LIBRARY
Box 4260   Phone: (713) 220-7313
Houston, TX 77210   Sherry Ray, Libn.

HOUSTON CITY AVIATION DEPARTMENT - LIBRARY
Box 60106   Phone: (713) 443-1714
Houston, TX 77205   Trudy Schindewolf, Adm. Aide

HOUSTON - CITY LEGAL DEPARTMENT - LAW LIBRARY
4th Fl. City Hall
Box 1562   Phone: (713) 222-5151
Houston, TX 77001   Edward A. Cazares, City Attorney

HOUSTON LIGHTING & POWER COMPANY - LIBRARY *
Box 1700   Phone: (713) 228-9211
Houston, TX 77001   Catherine Robichaux, Libn.

HOUSTON MUSEUM OF NATURAL SCIENCE - REFERENCE LIBRARY
1 Hermann Circle Dr.   Phone: (713) 526-4273
Houston, TX 77030   Carl H. Ailsen, Act.Dir.

HOUSTON OIL & MINERALS CORPORATION - LIBRARY
1100 Louisiana   Phone: (713) 658-3420
Houston, TX 77002   Olive Tyson, Libn.

HOUSTON POST - LIBRARY/INFORMATION CENTER
                                   Phone: (713) 840-5830
Houston, TX 77001   Kathy Foley, Chf.Libn.

HOUSTON PUBLIC LIBRARY - ARCHIVES AND MANUSCRIPT DEPARTMENT
500 McKinney St.   Phone: (713) 224-5441
Houston, TX 77002   Dr. Louis J. Marchiafava, Archv.

HOUSTON PUBLIC LIBRARY - BUSINESS, SCIENCE & TECHNOLOGY
    DEPARTMENT
500 McKinney Ave.   Phone: (713) 224-5441
Houston, TX 77002   Brenda Peabody Tirrell, Dept.Hd.

HOUSTON PUBLIC LIBRARY - CLAYTON LIBRARY CENTER FOR
    GENEALOGICAL RESEARCH
5300 Caroline St.   Phone: (713) 524-0101
Houston, TX 77004   Maxine Alcorn, Libn.

HOUSTON PUBLIC LIBRARY - FILM COLLECTION DEPARTMENT
500 McKinney Ave.   Phone: (713) 224-5441
Houston, TX 77002   Syma Zerkow, Dept.Hd.

HOUSTON PUBLIC LIBRARY - FINE ARTS & RECREATION DEPARTMENT
500 McKinney Ave.   Phone: (713) 224-5441
Houston, TX 77002   John Harvath, Dept.Hd.

HOUSTON PUBLIC LIBRARY - SPECIAL COLLECTIONS DEPARTMENT
500 McKinney Ave.   Phone: (713) 224-5441
Houston, TX 77002   Donna Grove, Dept.Hd.

HOUSTON PUBLIC LIBRARY - TEXAS AND LOCAL HISTORY DEPARTMENT
500 McKinney Ave.   Phone: (713) 224-5441
Houston, TX 77002   Dorothy Glasser, Dept.Hd.

HUGHES TOOL COMPANY - BUSINESS AND TECHNICAL LIBRARY
Box 2539   Phone: (713) 924-2583
Houston, TX 77001   Madge L. Wilkins, Libn.

IBM CORPORATION - DP LIBRARY
Two Riverway   Phone: (713) 940-2554
Houston, TX 77056   Agnete V. Katherman, Libn.

(The) INSTITUTE FOR REHABILITATION AND RESEARCH (TIRR) -
    INFORMATION SERVICES CENTER
1333 Moursund Ave.   Phone: (713) 797-1440
Houston, TX 77025   Kay Lindloff, Libn.

INSTITUTE FOR STORM RESEARCH - LIBRARY
4104 Mt. Vernon   Phone: (713) 529-4891
Houston, TX 77006   Dr. John C. Freeman, Hd.

JACOBS ENGINEERING GROUP - TECHNICAL INFORMATION SERVICES
    DEPARTMENT
Box 53495   Phone: (713) 626-2020
Houston, TX 77052   Elizabeth L. Soles, Hd.Libn.

JOHNSON (Bernard) INC. - TECHNICAL LIBRARY
5050 Westheimer   Phone: (713) 622-1400
Houston, TX 77056   Mitzi Binder, Libn.

KELLOGG (M.W.) - RESEARCH INFORMATION DIVISION
16200 Park Row
Industrial Park Ten   Phone: (713) 492-2500
Houston, TX 77084   Bonnie A. Phillips, Supv.

KORN/FERRY INTERNATIONAL - LIBRARY
1100 Milam, Suite 3400   Phone: (713) 651-1834
Houston, TX 77002   Laura L. Sorrell, Dir. of Res.

LOCKWOOD, ANDREWS & NEWNAM, INC. - INFORMATION CENTER
1500 City West Blvd.   Phone: (713) 226-6900
Houston, TX 77042   Diane E. Walker, Info.Ctr.Coord.

LUMMUS COMPANY - TECHNICAL LIBRARY
3000 S. Post Oak Rd.
Box 22105   Phone: (713) 871-3120
Houston, TX 77027   June Parchman, Libn.

LUNAR AND PLANETARY INSTITUTE - LIBRARY/INFORMATION CENTER
3303 NASA Rd., No. 1   Phone: (713) 486-2135
Houston, TX 77058   Frances B. Waranius, Lib./Info.Ctr.Mgr.

LUNAR AND PLANETARY INSTITUTE - PLANETARY IMAGE CENTER
3303 NASA Rd., No. 1   Phone: (713) 486-2172
Houston, TX 77058   Ron Weber, Photo/Cart.Mgr.

MC CLELLAND ENGINEERS, INC. - CORPORATE LIBRARY
Box 37321   Phone: (713) 772-3701
Houston, TX 77036   Pat M. Johnson, Corp.Libn.

MENTAL HEALTH AND MENTAL RETARDATION AUTHORITY OF HARRIS
    COUNTY - INFORMATION RESOURCE CENTER
2501 Dunstan
Box 25381   Phone: (713) 526-2871
Houston, TX 77005   Jacqueline Woods, Adm.Techn. III

MICHIGAN WISCONSIN PIPELINE COMPANY - LIBRARY *
5075 Westheimer, Suite 1100 W.   Phone: (713) 623-0300
Houston, TX 77056   Sue Haley, Tech.Asst.

MOBIL PRODUCING TEXAS & NEW MEXICO INC. - INFORMATION
    RESOURCE CENTER
Nine Greenway Plaza, Suite 2700   Phone: (713) 871-5621
Houston, TX 77046   Susan Kutscher Hughes, Info.Rsrcs.Coord.

MUSEUM OF FINE ARTS, HOUSTON - LIBRARY
1001 Bissonnet   Phone: (713) 526-1361
Houston, TX 77005   Linda Nelson, Libn.

NATIONAL COLLEGE OF DISTRICT ATTORNEYS - RESOURCE CENTER *
College of Law
University of Houston   Phone: (713) 749-1571
Houston, TX 77004   Ann Fikes, Commun.Mgr.

NL BAROID PETROLEUM SERVICES - TECHNICAL LIBRARY
2404 Southwest Freeway
Box 1675   Phone: (713) 527-1282
Houston, TX 77001   Mary H. Boris, Libn.

PEAT, MARWICK, MITCHELL & COMPANY - LIBRARY
4300 One Shell Plaza   Phone: (713) 224-4262
Houston, TX 77002   Charlotte Curtis-Kohrs, Supv., Lib.Serv.

PRUDENTIAL INSURANCE COMPANY OF AMERICA - BUSINESS LIBRARY
Box 2075   Phone: (713) 663-5909
Houston, TX 77001   Claire Moffett, Bus.Libn.

RICE UNIVERSITY - ART LIBRARY
Box 1892   Phone: (713) 527-4832
Houston, TX 77001   Jet Marie Prendeville, Art Libn.

RICE UNIVERSITY - GOVERNMENT DOCUMENTS AND MICROFORMS
    DEPARTMENT
Fondren Library
Box 1892   Phone: (713) 527-8101
Houston, TX 77001   Barbara Kile, Hd.

RICE UNIVERSITY - WOODSON RESEARCH CENTER
Fondren Library, Box 1892   Phone: (713) 527-8101
Houston, TX 77001   Nancy Boothe Parker, Dir.

ST. JOSEPH HOSPITAL - HOSPITAL HEALTH SCIENCE LIBRARY
1919 LaBranch   Phone: (713) 757-1000
Houston, TX 77002   Sr. M. Catherine Finlay, CCVI, Dir.

GEOGRAPHIC

ST. LUKE'S EPISCOPAL & TEXAS CHILDREN'S HOSPITALS - MEDICAL
LIBRARY
6621 Fannin St.   Phone: (715) 791-3054
Houston, TX 77030   Robert C. Park, Dir. of Lib. Serv.

ST. MARY'S SEMINARY - CARDINAL BERAN LIBRARY
9845 Memorial Dr.   Phone: (713) 681-5544
Houston, TX 77024   Constance Walker, Libn.

SCHLUMBERGER WELL SERVICES - ENGINEERING LIBRARY
5000 Gulf Fwy.
Box 2175   Phone: (713) 928-4411
Houston, TX 77001   Margaret Kuo, Libn.

SHELL DEVELOPMENT COMPANY - BELLAIRE RESEARCH CENTER LIBRARY
Box 481   Phone: (713) 663-2293
Houston, TX 77001   Aphrodite Mamoulides, Lib.Supv.

SHELL DEVELOPMENT COMPANY - WESTHOLLOW RESEARCH CENTER
LIBRARY †
3333 Hwy. 6 S.
Box 1378   Phone: (713) 493-7530
Houston, TX 77001   Shirley Thompson, Supv. of Lib.

SHELL OIL COMPANY - INFORMATION & LIBRARY SERVICES
Box 587   Phone: (713) 241-1017
Houston, TX 77001   Marilyn K. Johnson, Mgr.

SHRINERS HOSPITAL FOR CRIPPLED CHILDREN - ORTHOPEDIC LIBRARY
1402 Outerbelt Dr.   Phone: (713) 797-1616
Houston, TX 77025   Lillian Nicholson, Libn.

SOUTH TEXAS COLLEGE OF LAW - LIBRARY
1220 Polk St.   Phone: (713) 659-8040
Houston, TX 77002   F.H. Thompson, Law Libn.

SOUTHERN BIBLE COLLEGE - WORDEN MC DONALD LIBRARY *
10950 Beaumont Hwy.   Phone: (713) 675-2351
Houston, TX 77028   Judy Mitchell, Hd.Libn.

TAUB (Ben) GENERAL HOSPITAL - DOCTOR'S MEDICAL LIBRARY
1502 Taub Loop   Phone: (713) 791-7441
Houston, TX 77025   Angie Ortiz, Lib.Ck.

TENNECO, INC. - CORPORATE LIBRARY
2143 Tenneco Bldg.
Box 2511   Phone: (713) 757-2788
Houston, TX 77001   Charles Suessmuth, Chf.Libn.

TENNECO, INC. - TENNECO OIL COMPANY - GEOLOGICAL RESEARCH
LIBRARY
Tenneco Bldg., 24th Fl., 1010 Milam
Box 2511   Phone: (713) 757-2310
Houston, TX 77001   Wilda Wiley, Libn.

TEXAS EASTERN TRANSMISSION CORPORATION - LIBRARY †
1221 McKinney
Box 2521   Phone: (713) 759-3533
Houston, TX 77001   Ms. Kay Bailey, Libn.

TEXAS INSTRUMENTS - HOUSTON SITE LIBRARY
Box 1443 MS/6947   Phone: (713) 490-2981
Houston, TX 77001   Helen Manning, Libn.

TEXAS RESEARCH INSTITUTE OF MENTAL SCIENCES - LIBRARY
1300 Moursund   Phone: (713) 797-1976
Houston, TX 77030   Felicia S. Chuang, Libn.

TEXAS SOUTHERN UNIVERSITY - LIBRARY - HEARTMAN COLLECTION
3201 Wheeler   Phone: (713) 527-7149
Houston, TX 77004   Dorothy H. Chapman, Cur.

TEXAS SOUTHERN UNIVERSITY - PHARMACY LIBRARY
3201 Wheeler Ave.   Phone: (713) 527-7160
Houston, TX 77004   Barbara Ritcherson, Pharmacy Libn.

TEXAS SOUTHERN UNIVERSITY - THURGOOD MARSHALL SCHOOL OF LAW -
LIBRARY †
3201 Wheeler Ave.   Phone: (713) 527-7125
Houston, TX 77004   Anna T. James, Libn.

TEXAS STATE - COURT OF APPEALS - 1ST SUPREME JUDICIAL DISTRICT -
LAW LIBRARY
604 Harris County Civil Courts Bldg.   Phone: (713) 228-8311
Houston, TX 77002

3D/INTERNATIONAL - CORPORATE LIBRARY
1900 West Loop South, Suite 200   Phone: (713) 781-7141
Houston, TX 77027   Goldie C. Domingue, Dir., Info.Rsrcs.

TRANSCONTINENTAL GAS PIPE LINE CORPORATION - LIBRARY
Box 1396   Phone: (713) 871-2321
Houston, TX 77001   Cheryl L. Watson, Libn.

TRUNKLINE GAS COMPANY - GENERAL LIBRARY
Box 1642   Phone: (713) 664-3401
Houston, TX 77001   Hershall Stair, Libn.

TURNER, COLLIE & BRADEN, INC. - LIBRARY AND INFORMATION SERVICES
Box 13089   Phone: (713) 780-4100
Houston, TX 77019   Mary Kathryn Hubbard, Mgr.

UNDERWOOD, NEUHAUS & COMPANY INC. - CORPORATE FINANCE
DEPARTMENT - LIBRARY
724 Travis St.   Phone: (713) 221-2086
Houston, TX 77002   Velma Shields, Libn.

UNION TEXAS PETROLEUM CORPORATION - LIBRARY
Box 2120   Phone: (713) 960-7044
Houston, TX 77001   Betty J. Backus

U.S. DEPT. OF COMMERCE - INTERNATIONAL TRADE ADMINISTRATION -
HOUSTON DISTRICT OFFICE LIBRARY
515 Rusk Ave., Rm. 2625   Phone: (713) 226-4231
Houston, TX 77002   Bernice Hardeman

U. S. NASA - LYNDON B. JOHNSON SPACE CENTER - SPACE LIFE SCIENCES
ARCHIVAL LIBRARY
JM65, Johnson Space Center   Phone: (713) 483-2889
Houston, TX 77058   Harold Davis, Tech. Monitor

U.S. NASA - LYNDON B. JOHNSON SPACE CENTER - TECHNICAL LIBRARY
                                             Phone: (713) 483-6268
Houston, TX 77058   Albert F. Kelly, Chf., Tech.Lib.Br.

U.S. VETERANS ADMINISTRATION (TX-Houston) - MEDICAL CENTER
LIBRARY *
2002 Holcombe Blvd.   Phone: (713) 795-4411
Houston, TX 77211

UNIVERSITY OF HOUSTON - AUDIOVISUAL SERVICES
4800 Calhoun   Phone: (713) 749-2361
Houston, TX 77004   Joseph R. Schroeder, Dir.

UNIVERSITY OF HOUSTON - COLLEGE OF OPTOMETRY LIBRARY
4800 Calhoun, Rm. 2225   Phone: (713) 749-2411
Houston, TX 77004   Suzanne Ferimer, Dir., Lrng.Rsrcs.

UNIVERSITY OF HOUSTON - COLLEGE OF PHARMACY LIBRARY
133 Science & Research II Bldg.   Phone: (713) 749-1566
Houston, TX 77004   Derral Parkin, Libn.

UNIVERSITY OF HOUSTON - FRANZHEIM ARCHITECTURE LIBRARY
Cullen Blvd.   Phone: (713) 749-1193
Houston, TX 77004   Margaret Culbertson, Libn.

UNIVERSITY OF HOUSTON - LAW LIBRARY
3801 Calhoun   Phone: (713) 749-3191
Houston, TX 77004   Jon S. Schultz, Dir.

UNIVERSITY OF HOUSTON - MUSIC LIBRARY
106 Fine Arts   Phone: (713) 749-2534
Houston, TX 77004   Helen Garrett, Supv.

UNIVERSITY OF HOUSTON - SCHOOL OF MUSIC - WOODY HERMAN
ARCHIVES
                                             Phone: (713) 749-1116
Houston, TX 77004   Robert L. Briggs, Libn.

UNIVERSITY OF TEXAS HEALTH SCIENCE CENTER, HOUSTON - DENTAL
    BRANCH LIBRARY
Box 20068   Phone: (713) 792-4094
Houston, TX 77025   Lorrayne B. Webb, Libn.

UNIVERSITY OF TEXAS - M.D. ANDERSON HOSPITAL AND TUMOR
    INSTITUTE - RESEARCH MEDICAL LIBRARY
Texas Medical Center   Phone: (713) 792-2282
Houston, TX 77030   Marie Harvin, Res.Med.Libn.

VINSON & ELKINS - LAW LIBRARY
First City National Bank Bldg.   Phone: (713) 651-2678
Houston, TX 77002   Karl T. Gruben, Libn.

WEINER'S STORES, INC. - LIBRARY
Box 2612   Phone: (713) 688-1331
Houston, TX 77001   Gloria Bellis, Libn.

WESTERN GEOPHYSICAL COMPANY OF AMERICA - R & D LIBRARY
Box 2469   Phone: (713) 789-9600
Houston, TX 77001   Ching-Cheng Ting, R & D Libn.

WITCO CHEMICAL CORPORATION - LIBRARY
3200 Brookfield   Phone: (713) 433-7281
Houston, TX 77045   Paul Berger, Group Mgr.

HUNTSVILLE MEMORIAL HOSPITAL - SCHOOL OF VOCATIONAL NURSING -
    EARNESTINE CANNON MEMORIAL LIBRARY *
3000 I-45
Box 479   Phone: (713) 291-3411
Huntsville, TX 77340   Joan N. Davis, Dir.

SAM HOUSTON STATE UNIVERSITY - LIBRARY †
                                           Phone: (713) 295-6211
Huntsville, TX 77340

FLINTKOTE BUILDING PRODUCTS COMPANY - CORPORATE R&D LIBRARY
Flintkote Plaza
580 Decker Dr.   Phone: (214) 659-9800
Irving, TX 75062

GRUY (H.J.) & ASSOCIATES, INC. - LIBRARY
150 W. Carpenter Fwy.   Phone: (214) 659-3200
Irving, TX 75062   Nancy Cooper, Dir., Lib./Info.Serv.

BAPTIST MISSIONARY ASSOCIATION THEOLOGICAL SEMINARY - KELLAR
    LIBRARY
1410 E. Pine St.
Box 1797   Phone: (214) 586-2501
Jacksonville, TX 75766   James C. Blaylock, Libn.

JEFFERSON HISTORICAL SOCIETY AND MUSEUM - ARCHIVES
223 Austin St.
Drawer G   Phone: (214) 665-2775
Jefferson, TX 75657   Mrs. Jack Bullard, Cur.

U.S. NATL. PARK SERVICE - LYNDON B. JOHNSON NATL. HISTORICAL PARK
    - LIBRARY
Box 329   Phone: (512) 868-7128
Johnson City, TX 78636   John T. Tiff, Hist.

U.S. VETERANS ADMINISTRATION (TX-Kerrville) - HEALTH SCIENCES
    LIBRARY
                                           Phone: (512) 896-2020
Kerrville, TX 78028   Elsie B. Branton, Chf., Lib.Serv.

SAN JACINTO MUSEUM OF HISTORY ASSOCIATION - LIBRARY
3800 Park Rd.   Phone: (713) 479-2421
La Porte, TX 77571   J.C. Martin, Dir.

CONSERVATION DISTRICTS FOUNDATION - DAVIS CONSERVATION
    LIBRARY
408 E. Main St.
Box 776   Phone: (713) 332-3402
League City, TX 77573   Laurie Sundborg, Libn.

TEXAS STATE LIBRARY - TEXAS ARCHIVES DIVISION - SAM HOUSTON
    REGIONAL LIBRARY AND RESEARCH CENTER
Farm Road 1011
Box 989   Phone: (713) 336-7097
Liberty, TX 77575   H. Joyce Calhoon, Dir.-Archv.

CHURCH OF JESUS CHRIST OF LATTER-DAY SAINTS - LONGVIEW BRANCH
    GENEALOGICAL LIBRARY
West Pine St.
Box 296   Phone: (214) 759-2194
Longview, TX 75604

EASTMAN KODAK COMPANY - TEXAS EASTMAN COMPANY - BUSINESS
    LIBRARY
Box 7444   Phone: (214) 757-6611
Longview, TX 75602   Carol Underwood, Bus.Libn.

EASTMAN KODAK COMPANY - TEXAS EASTMAN COMPANY - RESEARCH
    LIBRARY
Box 7444   Phone: (214) 757-6611
Longview, TX 75602   Jack T. Buchanan, Res.Libn.

FIRST BAPTIST CHURCH - JOHN L. WHORTON MEDIA CENTER
Box 2188   Phone: (214) 758-0681
Longview, TX 75601   Sandra Trippett, Dir.

LE TOURNEAU COLLEGE - MARGARET ESTES LIBRARY
Box 7001   Phone: (214) 753-0231
Longview, TX 75607   Rachel Miley, Dir., Lib.Serv.

HIGHLAND HOSPITAL, INC. - MEDICAL LIBRARY
2412 - 50th St.   Phone: (806) 795-8251
Lubbock, TX 79412   Margaret Bussey, Med.Libn.

LUBBOCK CHRISTIAN COLLEGE - MOODY LIBRARY
5601 W. 19th St.   Phone: (806) 792-3221
Lubbock, TX 79407

METHODIST HOSPITAL AND SCHOOL OF NURSING - LIBRARY
3615 19th St.   Phone: (806) 793-4180
Lubbock, TX 79410   June Rayburn, Libn.

TEXAS TECH UNIVERSITY - DEPARTMENT OF MATHEMATICS - LIBRARY
Box 4319
Lubbock, TX 79409

TEXAS TECH UNIVERSITY - HEALTH SCIENCES CENTER - LIBRARY OF THE
    HEALTH SCIENCES
                                           Phone: (806) 743-2200
Lubbock, TX 79430   Charles W. Sargent, Ph.D., Dir.

TEXAS TECH UNIVERSITY - LIBRARY
                                           Phone: (806) 742-2261
Lubbock, TX 79409   R.C. Janeway, Dir. of Lib.Serv.

TEXAS TECH UNIVERSITY - LIBRARY - DOCUMENTS DEPARTMENT
                                           Phone: (806) 742-2268
Lubbock, TX 79409   Mary Ann Higdon, Doc.Libn.

TEXAS TECH UNIVERSITY - SCHOOL OF LAW LIBRARY
                                           Phone: (806) 742-3794
Lubbock, TX 79409   Jane G. Olm, Law Libn.

TEXAS TECH UNIVERSITY - SOUTHWEST COLLECTION
Box 4090   Phone: (806) 742-3749
Lubbock, TX 79409   David Murrah, Univ.Archv.

U.S. AIR FORCE BASE - REESE BASE LIBRARY
Reese AFB   Phone: (806) 885-4511
Lubbock, TX 79489   Mary E. Rinas, Libn.

MEMORIAL HOSPITAL - MEDICAL LIBRARY
Box 1447   Phone: (713) 634-8111
Lufkin, TX 75902   Nancy Anderson, Dir., Med.Rec.

TEXAS STATE FOREST SERVICE - TEXAS FOREST PRODUCTS LABORATORY
    - LIBRARY
Box 310   Phone: (713) 632-6666
Lufkin, TX 75901   Kim Mericle, Libn.

FIRST BAPTIST CHURCH - E.F. WALKER MEMORIAL LIBRARY
218 N. Magnolia
Box 90   Phone: (512) 875-2227
Luling, TX 78648   Mrs. Raymond Matthews, Libn.

GEOGRAPHIC

GEOGRAPHIC

FIRST BAPTIST CHURCH - LIBRARY
1200 Beech St.   Phone: (512) 686-7418
McAllen, TX 78501   Mrs. Hans Wells, Dir.

HERCULES, INC. - AEROSPACE DIVISION - MC GREGOR TECHNICAL
   INFORMATION CENTER
Box 548   Phone: (817) 840-2811
McGregor, TX 76657   D.A. Browne, Pubn.Coord.

COLLIN MEMORIAL HOSPITAL - MEDICAL LIBRARY
1800 N. Graves St.   Phone: (214) 542-2641
McKinney, TX 75069   Joan L. Thomas, Libn.

MC KINNEY JOB CORPS - LIBRARY
1501 N. Church St.
Box 750   Phone: (214) 542-2623
McKinney, TX 75069   Lois Stewart, Libn.

U.S. VETERANS ADMINISTRATION (TX-Marlin) - MEDICAL CENTER LIBRARY
   SERVICE (142D)
1016 Ward St.   Phone: (817) 833-3511
Marlin, TX 76661   Elsie B. Branton, Adm.Libn.

EAST TEXAS BAPTIST COLLEGE - MAMYE JARRETT LEARNING CENTER
1209 North Grove   Phone: (214) 938-2636
Marshall, TX 75670   E.M. Adams, Jr., Libn.

HARRISON COUNTY HISTORICAL MUSEUM - LIBRARY
Peter Whetstone Sq.   Phone: (214) 938-2680
Marshall, TX 75670   Mrs. Solon G. Hughes, Dir.

ICI AMERICAS INC. - DARCO EXPERIMENTAL LABORATORY LIBRARY
Box 790   Phone: (214) 938-9211
Marshall, TX 75670

MIDLAND COUNTY PUBLIC LIBRARY - SCI-TECH SECTION LIBRARY
Box 1191   Phone: (915) 683-2708
Midland, TX 79702   Mrs. R. Harris, Tech.Libn.

PALOMINO HORSE BREEDERS OF AMERICA - LIBRARY
Box 249   Phone: (817) 325-2513
Mineral Wells, TX 76067   Robert J. Shiflet, Exec. V.P.

STEPHEN F. AUSTIN STATE UNIVERSITY - STEEN LIBRARY - SPECIAL
   COLLECTIONS DEPARTMENT
SFA Sta., Box 13055   Phone: (713) 569-4101
Nacogdoches, TX 75962   Linda Cheves Nicklas, Spec.Coll.Libn.

FORT BELKNAP ARCHIVES, INC. - LIBRARY
Box 68   Phone: (817) 549-1856
Newcastle, TX 76372   K.F. Neighbours, Archv.

EL PASO PRODUCTS COMPANY - RESEARCH AND DEVELOPMENT LIBRARY
Box 3986   Phone: (915) 333-8497
Odessa, TX 79760   R.A. Landis, Info. Chemist

ODESSA AMERICAN - EDITORIAL LIBRARY
4th & Jackson Sts.   Phone: (915) 337-4661
Odessa, TX 79760   Gail Covey, Libn.

DU PONT DE NEMOURS (E.I.) & COMPANY, INC. - POLYMER PRODUCTS
   DEPARTMENT - TECHNICAL LIBRARY
Sabine River Works
Box 1089   Phone: (713) 886-6418
Orange, TX 77630   Patsy Holland, Tech.Libn.

CABOT CORPORATION - LIBRARY
Box 1101   Phone: (806) 669-2596
Pampa, TX 79065   Delores Martin, Libn.

CARSON COUNTY SQUARE HOUSE MUSEUM - INFORMATION CENTER
Box 276   Phone: (806) 537-3118
Panhandle, TX 79068   Jo Stewart Randel, Dir.

TEXAS CHIROPRACTIC COLLEGE - MAE HILTY MEMORIAL LIBRARY
5912 Spencer Hwy.   Phone: (713) 487-1170
Pasadena, TX 77505   Mara U. Umpierre, Hd.Libn.

UNIVERSITY OF TEXAS - MARINE SCIENCE LABORATORY - LIBRARY
                                        Phone: (512) 749-6723
Port Aransas, TX 78373   Ruth Grundy, Libn.

ST. MARY HOSPITAL - HEALTH SCIENCE LIBRARY
3600 Gates Blvd.   Phone: (713) 985-7431
Port Arthur, TX 77640   Sister Mary Patricius, Dir.

AMERICAN SCIENCE FICTION ASSOCIATION - ASFA LIBRARY
Box 10   Phone: (702) 361-4703
Port Neches, TX 77651   P.G. Silvers, Hd., Lib.Serv.

PRAIRIE VIEW A & M COLLEGE OF TEXAS - W.R. BANKS LIBRARY *
Third St.
Box T   Phone: (713) 857-3311
Prairie View, TX 77445   Frank Francis, Jr., Hd.Libn.

U.S. AIR FORCE - AIR FORCE MANPOWER AND PERSONNEL CENTER -
   MORALE, WELFARE & RECREATION DIVISION - LIBRARIES SECTION
AFMPC/MPCSOA   Phone: (512) 652-3037
Randolph AFB, TX 78148   Tony Dakan, Dir., USAF Libs.

U.S. AIR FORCE - AIR TRAINING COMMAND - LIBRARY PROGRAM ATC/
   DPSOL
                                        Phone: (512) 652-2438
Randolph AFB, TX 78150   Duane A. Johnson, Command Libn.

U.S. AIR FORCE BASE - RANDOLPH BASE LIBRARY
                                        Phone: (512) 652-2617
Randolph AFB, TX 78250   Nova C. Maddox, Chf.Libn.

U.S. AIR FORCE HOSPITAL - MEDICAL LIBRARY (TX-Reese AFB) *
                                        Phone: (806) 885-4511
Reese AFB, TX 79489   Gary C. Sutton, Master Sgt.

DAWGWOOD RESEARCH LIBRARY
Oak & Ymbacion Sts.   Phone: (512) 526-2451
Refugio, TX 78377   Hobart Huson, Owner

ANDERSON CLAYTON FOODS - W.L. CLAYTON RESEARCH CENTER
3333 N. Central Expy.   Phone: (214) 231-6121
Richardson, TX 75080   Irmgarde Martin, Libn.

SUN PRODUCTION COMPANY - INFORMATION RESOURCES CENTER
503 N. Central Expy.
Box 936   Phone: (214) 699-3148
Richardson, TX 75080   Margaret Anderson, Libn.

TEXAS STATE PARKS & WILDLIFE DEPARTMENT - MARINE LABORATORY
   LIBRARY *
Box 1707   Phone: (512) 729-2328
Rockport, TX 78382   T.L. Heffernan, Lab.Supv.

FORT CONCHO REFERENCE LIBRARY
213 E. Ave. D   Phone: (915) 655-9121
San Angelo, TX 76903   Wayne Daniel, Libn./Archv.

GENERAL TELEPHONE COMPANY OF THE SOUTHWEST - E.H. DANNER
   LIBRARY OF TELEPHONY
2701 S. Johnson St.
Box 1001   Phone: (915) 944-5149
San Angelo, TX 76901   Aline H. Taylor, Libn.

ASSUMPTION SEMINARY - LIBRARY
2600 W. Woodlawn   Phone: (512) 734-5137
San Antonio, TX 78284   John R. McGrath, Libn.

BAPTIST MEMORIAL HOSPITAL SYSTEM - BRUCE A. GARRETT MEMORIAL
   LIBRARY & MEDIA CENTER
111 Dallas St.   Phone: (512) 222-8431
San Antonio, TX 78286   Martha E. Knott, Chf.Libn.

BEXAR COUNTY LAW LIBRARY
Court House, 5th Fl.   Phone: (512) 227-8822
San Antonio, TX 78205   Jimmy Alleson, Libn.

BEXAR COUNTY MEDICAL LIBRARY
202 W. French Place
Box 12678   Phone: (512) 734-6691
San Antonio, TX 78212   Lynne Ricketts, Libn.

CONGREGATION AGUDAS ACHIM - BERNARD RUBENSTEIN LIBRARY
1201 Donaldson Ave.   Phone: (512) 736-4216
San Antonio, TX 78228   Marie Bartman, Libn.

DAUGHTERS OF THE REPUBLIC OF TEXAS - LIBRARY
Box 2599   Phone: (512) 225-1071
San Antonio, TX 78299   Sharon R. Crutchfield, Dir.

FIRST BAPTIST CHURCH - LIBRARY
515 McCullough Ave.   Phone: (512) 226-0363
San Antonio, TX 78215   Virginia Patterson, Libn.

MC NAY (Marion Koogler) ART INSTITUTE - LIBRARY
Box 6069   Phone: (512) 824-5368
San Antonio, TX 77509   Mrs. John P. Leeper, Libn.

MATTHEWS & NOWLIN - LIBRARY
1500 Alamo National Bldg.   Phone: (512) 226-4211
San Antonio, TX 78205   Judy K. Lytle, Libn.

OBLATE COLLEGE OF THE SOUTHWEST - LIBRARY
285 Oblate Dr.   Phone: (512) 341-1366
San Antonio, TX 78216   James Maney, Lib.Dir.

ORDER OF DAEDALIANS - NATIONAL HEADQUARTERS - LIBRARY AND
    INFORMATION CENTER
Bldg. 1635
Kelly Air Force Base   Phone: (512) 924-9485
San Antonio, TX 78241   Col. (Ret.) Robert Morris, Ed.

OUR LADY OF THE LAKE UNIVERSITY - OLD SPANISH MISSIONS
    HISTORICAL RESEARCH LIBRARY
411 S.W. 24th St.   Phone: (512) 434-6711
San Antonio, TX 78285   Fr. Benedict Leutenegger, Archv.

OUR LADY OF THE LAKE UNIVERSITY - WORDEN SCHOOL OF SOCIAL
    SERVICE - LIBRARY
411 S.W. 24th St.   Phone: (512) 434-6711
San Antonio, TX 78285   Margaret Pittman Munke, Libn.

PIPER (Minnie Stevens) FOUNDATION - FUNDING INFORMATION LIBRARY
201 N. St. Mary's St., Suite 101A   Phone: (512) 227-4333
San Antonio, TX 78205   Candes Chumney, Supv.

PLANNED PARENTHOOD CENTER OF SAN ANTONIO - SOUTH CENTRAL
    REGIONAL LIBRARY
106 Warren St.   Phone: (512) 227-2227
San Antonio, TX 78212   Ginger Cave, Dir., Community Rel.

ST. MARY'S UNIVERSITY - LAW LIBRARY
One Camino Santa Maria   Phone: (512) 436-3435
San Antonio, TX 78284   Paul F. Ferguson, Dir.

SAN ANTONIO COLLEGE - SPECIAL COLLECTIONS
1001 Howard St.   Phone: (512) 734-7311
San Antonio, TX 78284   James O. Wallace, Dir.

SAN ANTONIO CONSERVATION SOCIETY - LIBRARY
107 King William St.   Phone: (512) 224-6163
San Antonio, TX 78204   Mrs. Eyrle G. Johnson, Libn.

SAN ANTONIO EXPRESS AND NEWS - LIBRARY
Box 2171   Phone: (512) 225-7411
San Antonio, TX 78297   Judy Robinson, Hd.Libn.

SAN ANTONIO MUSEUM ASSOCIATION - WITTE MEMORIAL MUSEUM
    RESEARCH LIBRARY
3801 Broadway   Phone: (512) 826-0647
San Antonio, TX 78209   Linda M. Hardberger, Libn.

SAN ANTONIO PUBLIC LIBRARY - ART, MUSIC AND FILMS DEPARTMENT
203 S. St. Mary's St.   Phone: (512) 299-7795
San Antonio, TX 78205   Mary A. Wright, Hd.

SAN ANTONIO PUBLIC LIBRARY - BUSINESS, SCIENCE AND TECHNOLOGY
    DEPARTMENT
203 S. St. Mary's St.   Phone: (512) 299-7800
San Antonio, TX 78205   James Sosa, Hd.

SAN ANTONIO PUBLIC LIBRARY - HARRY HERTZBERG CIRCUS COLLECTION
210 W. Market St.   Phone: (512) 299-7810
San Antonio, TX 78205   Betty Claire King, Hd.

SAN ANTONIO PUBLIC LIBRARY - HISTORY, SOCIAL SCIENCE AND
    GENERAL REFERENCE DEPARTMENT
203 S. St. Mary's St.   Phone: (512) 299-7813
San Antonio, TX 78205   Marie Berry, Hd.

SAN ANTONIO PUBLIC LIBRARY - LITERATURE, PHILOSOPHY AND
    RELIGION DEPARTMENT
203 S. St. Mary's St.   Phone: (512) 299-7817
San Antonio, TX 78205   Helen K. Halloran, Hd.

SAN ANTONIO STATE CHEST HOSPITAL - HEALTH SCIENCE LIBRARY
Highland Hills Sta.
Box 23340   Phone: (512) 534-8857
San Antonio, TX 78223   Patricia Beaman, Libn.

SAN ANTONIO STATE HOSPITAL - STAFF LIBRARY
Highland Hills Sta.
Box 23310   Phone: (512) 532-8811
San Antonio, TX 78223   Beth M. Stenberg, Med.Libn.

SANTA ROSA MEDICAL CENTER - HEALTH SCIENCE LIBRARY
519 W. Houston St.
Sta. A, Box 7330   Phone: (512) 228-2284
San Antonio, TX 78285   Marjorie McFarland, Libn.

SOUTHWEST FOUNDATION FOR RESEARCH AND EDUCATION - PRESTON G.
    NORTHROP MEMORIAL LIBRARY
Box 28147   Phone: (512) 674-1410
San Antonio, TX 78284   Maureen D. Funnell, Libn.

SOUTHWEST RESEARCH INSTITUTE - NONDESTRUCTIVE TESTING
    INFORMATION ANALYSIS CENTER
Drawer 28510   Phone: (512) 684-5111
San Antonio, TX 78284   Richard T. Smith, Dir.

SOUTHWEST RESEARCH INSTITUTE - THOMAS BAKER SLICK MEMORIAL
    LIBRARY
Drawer 28510   Phone: (512) 684-5111
San Antonio, TX 78284   Edwin F. Vaught, Libn.

SOUTHWEST TEXAS METHODIST HOSPITAL - MEDICAL-NURSING &
    PATIENT LIBRARY
7700 Floyd Curl Dr.   Phone: (512) 696-1200
San Antonio, TX 78229   Eileen T. Lively, Libn.

SYMPHONY SOCIETY OF SAN ANTONIO - SYMPHONY LIBRARY
109 Lexington Ave., Suite 207   Phone: (512) 225-6161
San Antonio, TX 78205   James R. Dotson, Libn.

TEXAS STATE - COURT OF APPEALS - 4TH SUPREME JUDICIAL DISTRICT -
    LAW LIBRARY
500 Bexar County Courthouse
San Antonio, TX 78205

TRINITY UNIVERSITY - LIBRARY
715 Stadium Dr.
Box 56   Phone: (512) 736-8121
San Antonio, TX 78284   Robert A. Houze, Lib.Dir.

UNITED SERVICES AUTOMOBILE ASSOCIATION - CORPORATE LIBRARY
    AND INFORMATION CENTER
USAA Bldg.   Phone: (512) 690-2900
San Antonio, TX 78288   Patricia A. Pratchett, Mgr., Lib.Serv.

U.S. AIR FORCE BASE - KELLY BASE - SPECIAL SERVICES LIBRARY
Kelly AFB   Phone: (512) 925-3214
San Antonio, TX 78241   Melvin P. McElfresh, Libn.

U.S. AIR FORCE - ELECTRONIC SECURITY COMMAND - GENERAL LIBRARY
6923 SPTS/SSL   Phone: (512) 925-2617
San Antonio, TX 78243   Dale T. Ogden, Libn.

U.S. AIR FORCE MEDICAL CENTER - WILFORD HALL U.S.A.F. MEDICAL
    CENTER - MEDICAL LIBRARY (SGEL)
Lackland AFB   Phone: (512) 671-7204
San Antonio, TX 78236   Judith A. Arnn, Med.Libn.

GEOGRAPHIC

GEOGRAPHIC

UNIVERSITY OF TEXAS HEALTH SCIENCE CENTER, SAN ANTONIO -
LIBRARY
7703 Floyd Curl Dr.   Phone: (512) 691-6271
San Antonio, TX 78284   Dr. David A. Kronick, Libn.

UNIVERSITY OF TEXAS HEALTH SCIENCE CENTER, SAN ANTONIO -
BRADY/GREEN EDUCATIONAL RESOURCES CENTER
527 N. Leona St.   Phone: (512) 223-6361
San Antonio, TX 78284   Rajia C. Tobia, Libn.

UNIVERSITY OF TEXAS - INSTITUTE OF TEXAN CULTURES AT SAN
ANTONIO - LIBRARY
801 S. Bowie St.
Box 1226   Phone: (512) 226-7651
San Antonio, TX 78294   Deborah S. Large, Dir.Lib.Serv.

ZACHRY (H.B.) COMPANY - CENTRAL RECORDS AND LIBRARY
Box 21130   Phone: (512) 922-1213
San Antonio, TX 78285   Cindy Hall, Libn.

FIRST UNITED METHODIST CHURCH - GERTRUDE CALLIHAN MEMORIAL
LIBRARY *
129 W. Hutchinson
Box 2490   Phone: (512) 392-3848
San Marcos, TX 78666   Hilda Carlisle, Lib.Chm.

SOUTHWEST TEXAS STATE UNIVERSITY - LEARNING RESOURCES CENTER
J.C. Kellam Bldg.   Phone: (512) 245-2132
San Marcos, TX 78666   Louis C. Moloney, Dir., LRC

U.S. AIR FORCE HOSPITAL - SHEPPARD REGIONAL HOSPITAL - MEDICAL
LIBRARY
    Phone: (817) 851-6647
Sheppard AFB, TX 76311   Maxine Gustafson, Libn.

U.S. AIR FORCE SCHOOL OF HEALTH CARE SCIENCES - ACADEMIC LIBRARY
MSTL/114, Bldg. 1900   Phone: (817) 851-2256
Sheppard AFB, TX 76311   Theodore C. Kennedy, Supv.Libn.

NORTH PARK BAPTIST CHURCH - LIBRARY
2605 Rex Cruse Dr.   Phone: (214) 892-8429
Sherman, TX 75090   Mrs. Jack Raidt, Dir. of Lib.Serv.

WELDER (Rob & Bessie) WILDLIFE FOUNDATION - LIBRARY
Box 1400   Phone: (512) 364-2643
Sinton, TX 78387   Kay Drawe, Libn.

WESTERN TEXAS COLLEGE - LEARNING RESOURCE CENTER
    Phone: (915) 573-8511
Snyder, TX 79549   L.V. Anderson, Dir. of Lib.Serv.

SUNSET TRADING POST-OLD WEST MUSEUM - LIBRARY
Rte. 1   Phone: (817) 872-2027
Sunset, TX 76270   Jack Glover, Owner

RAILROAD AND PIONEER MUSEUM, INC. - LIBRARY
710 Jack Baskin St.
Box 5126   Phone: (817) 778-6873
Temple, TX 76501   Melinda Herzog, Dir.

SCOTT & WHITE MEMORIAL HOSPITAL - MEDICAL LIBRARY
2401 S. 31st St.   Phone: (817) 774-2228
Temple, TX 76501   Mary H. Spoede, Med.Libn.

SLAVONIC BENEVOLENT ORDER OF THE STATE OF TEXAS - LIBRARY,
ARCHIVES, MUSEUM
520 N. Main St.   Phone: (817) 773-1575
Temple, TX 76501   Otto Hanus, Libn./Cur.

TEXAS CENTRAL COUNTIES CENTER FOR MENTAL HEALTH & MENTAL
RETARDATION SERVICES - INFO. RESOURCE CENTER *
Box 1025   Phone: (817) 778-4841
Temple, TX 76501   Kathy Amburn, Coord.

U.S. VETERANS ADMINISTRATION (TX-Temple) - CENTER MEDICAL
LIBRARY
1901 S. First St.   Phone: (817) 778-4811
Temple, TX 76501   Mary E. Curtis, Chf., Lib.Serv.

TERRELL STATE HOSPITAL - MEDICAL LIBRARY
Box 70   Phone: (214) 563-6452
Terrell, TX 75160   Lillian Squires, Libn.

TEXARKANA HISTORICAL SOCIETY & MUSEUM - LIBRARY
219 State Line Ave.
Box 2343   Phone: (214) 793-4831
Texarkana, TX 75501   Katy Caver, Cur.

TEXAS STATE - COURT OF APPEALS - 6TH SUPREME JUDICIAL DISTRICT -
LAW LIBRARY *
401 Texas City Hall
Third & Texas   Phone: (214) 794-2576
Texarkana, TX 75501

U.S. ARMY - MATERIEL DEVELOPMENT & READINESS COMMAND (DARCOM)
- INTERN TRAINING CENTER LIBRARY
Red River Army Depot   Phone: (214) 838-3430
Texarkana, TX 75507   Frank M. London, Libn.

MONSANTO CHEMICAL INTERMEDIATES COMPANY - PROCESS
TECHNOLOGY DEPARTMENT - LIBRARY
Box 1311   Phone: (713) 945-4431
Texas City, TX 77590   Effie N. Birdwell, Sr.Libn.

UNION CARBIDE CORPORATION - SOLVENTS & INTERMEDIATES DIVISION
- PLANT LIBRARY †
3300 Fifth Ave. S.
Box 471   Phone: (713) 945-7411
Texas City, TX 77590   Jean Croix, Hd.

CHAPARRAL GENEALOGICAL SOCIETY - LIBRARY
410 W. Market St.
Box 606   Phone: (713) 356-8866
Tomball, TX 77375   Audra Gray, Libn.

MEDICAL CENTER HOSPITAL - BELL-MARSH MEMORIAL LIBRARY *
1000 S. Beckham St.
Drawer 6400   Phone: (214) 597-0351
Tyler, TX 75711   Mrs. Rae Dowdy, Med. Staff Sec.

TYLER COURIER-TIMES-TELEGRAPH - LIBRARY *
Box 2030   Phone: (214) 597-8111
Tyler, TX 75701   Leoma Pratt, Libn.

DU PONT DE NEMOURS (E.I.) & COMPANY, INC. - VICTORIA PLANT LIBRARY
Box 2626   Phone: (512) 573-3211
Victoria, TX 77901   Debbie A. Ganem, Libn.

VICTORIA COLLEGE - LIBRARY - TEXAS AND LOCAL HISTORY COLLECTION
2200 E. Red River   Phone: (512) 573-3295
Victoria, TX 77901   Dr. R.W. Shook, Dir.

BAYLOR UNIVERSITY - ARMSTRONG BROWNING LIBRARY
Box 6336   Phone: (817) 755-3566
Waco, TX 76706   Dr. Jack W. Herring, Dir.

BAYLOR UNIVERSITY - CONGRESSIONAL COLLECTION
Box 245   Phone: (817) 755-3530
Waco, TX 76798   James Rogers, Dir.

BAYLOR UNIVERSITY - CROUCH MUSIC LIBRARY
Moody Memorial Library
Box 6307   Phone: (817) 755-1366
Waco, TX 76706   Bessie Hess Smith, Libn.

BAYLOR UNIVERSITY - DEPARTMENT OF GEOLOGY - FERDINAND ROEMER
GEOLOGICAL LIBRARY
Moody Library   Phone: (817) 755-2361
Waco, TX 76703   H.H. Beaver, Chm.

BAYLOR UNIVERSITY - J.M. DAWSON CHURCH-STATE RESEARCH CENTER -
LIBRARY
Box 380   Phone: (817) 755-1519
Waco, TX 76706   Julie Sams, Adm.Asst.

BAYLOR UNIVERSITY - LAW LIBRARY †
Box 6342   Phone: (817) 755-2168
Waco, TX 76706   Della M. Geyer, Law Libn.

BAYLOR UNIVERSITY - STRECKER MUSEUM LIBRARY
Richardson Bldg.   Phone: (817) 755-1110
Waco, TX 76703   Dr. Bryce C. Brown, Musm.Dir.

BAYLOR UNIVERSITY - TEXAS COLLECTION
Carroll Library Bldg.
Box 6396   Phone: (817) 755-1268
Waco, TX 76706   Kent Keeth, Dir.

FIRST BAPTIST CHURCH - I.C. ANDERSON LIBRARY
Fifth & Webster Sts.   Phone: (817) 754-0328
Waco, TX 76706   Ginger Sutcliffe, Dir. of Lib.Serv.

MC LENNAN COUNTY LAW LIBRARY
Box 1606   Phone: (817) 753-7341
Waco, TX 76703   Mary Padgett

MASONIC GRAND LODGE OF TEXAS - LIBRARY AND MUSEUM
Box 446   Phone: (817) 753-7395
Waco, TX 76703   Janet Melton, Asst.Libn.

TEXAS STATE TECHNICAL INSTITUTE, WACO CAMPUS - LEARNING
    RESOURCE CENTER
                                           Phone: (817) 799-3611
Waco, TX 76705   Linda K. Myers, Dir., LRC

U.S. VETERANS ADMINISTRATION (TX-Waco) - MEDICAL CENTER LIBRARY
Memorial Dr.   Phone: (817) 752-6581
Waco, TX 76703   Barbara H. Hobbs, Chf., Lib.Serv.

WACO-MC LENNAN COUNTY LIBRARY - SPECIAL COLLECTIONS
    DEPARTMENT †
1717 Austin Ave.   Phone: (817) 754-0189
Waco, TX 76701   Sue Kethley, Libn.

STAR OF THE REPUBLIC MUSEUM - LIBRARY
Box 317   Phone: (713) 878-2461
Washington, TX 77880   D. Ryan Smith, Dir.

SOUTHWESTERN ASSEMBLIES OF GOD COLLEGE - P.C. NELSON MEMORIAL
    LIBRARY
1200 Sycamore   Phone: (214) 937-2341
Waxahachie, TX 75165   Mr. Murl M. Winters, Dir.Info.Serv.

AMERICAN SUFFOLK HORSE ASSOCIATION (ASHA) - LIBRARY
15 B Roden
Wichita Falls, TX 76311   Mary Margaret M. Read, Sec.

U.S. AIR FORCE BASE - SHEPPARD BASE LIBRARY
Sheppard AFB   Phone: (817) 851-2687
Wichita Falls, TX 76311   Billie A. Owens, Libn.

WICHITA FALLS STATE HOSPITAL - MEDICAL LIBRARY
Box 300   Phone: (817) 692-1220
Wichita Falls, TX 76301   Grace E. Smith, Libn.

WICHITA GENERAL HOSPITAL - MEDICAL LIBRARY
1600 - 8th St.   Phone: (817) 723-1461
Wichita Falls, TX 76301   Marge Bohack, Hd.Libn.

WICHITA SCOUTING CO-OP, INC. - OIL INFORMATION LIBRARY
813 Hamilton Bldg.   Phone: (817) 322-4241
Wichita Falls, TX 76301   Dorothy Shilts, Libn.

UTAH

U.S. NATL. PARK SERVICE - TIMPANOGOS CAVE NATL. MONUMENT -
    LIBRARY
Rte. 2, Box 200   Phone: (801) 756-4497
American Fork, UT 84003   Jerry Yarbrough, Chf.Pk. Ranger

U.S. BUREAU OF INDIAN AFFAIRS - OFFICE OF TECHNICAL ASSISTANCE &
    TRAINING (OTAT) - PROFESSIONAL LIBRARY †
Box 66   Phone: (801) 734-2071
Brigham City, UT 84302   Ray D. Reese, Libn.

SOUTHERN UTAH STATE COLLEGE - LIBRARY - SPECIAL COLLECTIONS
    DEPARTMENT
300 W. Center St.   Phone: (801) 586-4411
Cedar City, UT 84720   Inez S. Cooper, Spec.Coll.Libn.

U.S. ARMY - DUGWAY PROVING GROUND - TECHNICAL LIBRARY
                                           Phone: (801) 522-3565
Dugway, UT 84022   Joseph L. Buelna, Chf., Tech.Lib.

U.S. NATL. PARK SERVICE - DINOSAUR NATL. MONUMENT - QUARRY
    VISITOR CENTER - LIBRARY
Box 128   Phone: (801) 789-2115
Jensen, UT 84035   Dennis B. Davies, Chf. Naturalist-Dir.

UTAH WATER RESEARCH LABORATORY - LIBRARY
Utah State Univ.   Phone: (801) 752-4100
Logan, UT 84322   Blanche B. Taylor, Libn.

HERCULES, INC. - BACCHUS WORKS INFORMATION SERVICES
Box 98   Phone: (801) 297-5911
Magna, UT 84044   Dorothy H. Alley, Ref.Libn.

BROWNING ARMS COMPANY - LIBRARY *
Route 1
Morgan, UT 84050

MC KAY DEE HOSPITAL CENTER - EDUCATIONAL MEDIA CENTER
3939 Harrison Blvd.   Phone: (801) 399-4141
Ogden, UT 84409   Marjorie J. Seeger, Libn.

ST. BENEDICT'S HOSPITAL - HEALTH SCIENCES LIBRARY
5475 S. 500 East   Phone: (801) 479-2055
Ogden, UT 84403   Bette M. Light, Med.Libn.

U.S. FOREST SERVICE - INTERMOUNTAIN FOREST & RANGE EXPERIMENT
    STATION - LIBRARY
Forest Service Bldg., 507 25th St.   Phone: (801) 626-3697
Ogden, UT 84401   Elizabeth G. Close, Tech.Info.Spec.

WEBER COUNTY LAW LIBRARY
Municipal Bldg.   Phone: (801) 399-8466
Ogden, UT 84401   Grace A. Rost, Libn.

CHURCH OF JESUS CHRIST OF LATTER-DAY SAINTS - PRICE BRANCH
    GENEALOGICAL LIBRARY
85 E. 4th N.   Phone: (801) 637-2071
Price, UT 84501   Grant Lee Hanson, Libn.

BRIGHAM YOUNG UNIVERSITY - HUMANITIES AND ARTS DIVISION
    LIBRARY
University Library   Phone: (801) 378-4005
Provo, UT 84602   Blaine H. Hall, Div.Coord.

BRIGHAM YOUNG UNIVERSITY - J. REUBEN CLARK LAW SCHOOL LIBRARY
B.Y.U.   Phone: (801) 378-3593
Provo, UT 84602   David A. Thomas, Law Libn.

BRIGHAM YOUNG UNIVERSITY - RELIGION AND HISTORY DIVISION
    LIBRARY
University Library   Phone: (801) 378-3933
Provo, UT 84602   Donald H. Howard, Div.Coord.

BRIGHAM YOUNG UNIVERSITY - SCIENCE DIVISION LIBRARY
University Library   Phone: (801) 378-2986
Provo, UT 84602   Carol T. Smith, Div.Coord.

BRIGHAM YOUNG UNIVERSITY - SOCIAL SCIENCE DIVISION LIBRARY
University Library   Phone: (801) 378-3809
Provo, UT 84602   Susan Fales, Div.Coord.

BRIGHAM YOUNG UNIVERSITY - SPECIAL COLLECTIONS
University Library   Phone: (801) 378-2932
Provo, UT 84602   Chad Flake, Cur.

BRIGHAM YOUNG UNIVERSITY - UTAH VALLEY BRANCH GENEALOGICAL
    LIBRARY
Harold B. Lee Library, Rm. 4226   Phone: (801) 378-3934
Provo, UT 84602   Roger C. Flick, Libn.

GEOGRAPHIC

UTAH STATE HOSPITAL - LIBRARY
East Center St.   Phone: (801) 373-4400
Provo, UT 84601   Janinn Chilte, Libn.

UTAH VALLEY HOSPITAL - MEDICAL LIBRARY
1034 N. 500 W.   Phone: (801) 373-7850
Provo, UT 84601   Gregory R. Patterson, Med.Libn.

CHURCH OF JESUS CHRIST OF LATTER-DAY SAINTS - ST. GEORGE BRANCH
    GENEALOGICAL LIBRARY *
Box 417
St. George, UT 84770   Abram Owen Young, Libn.

CHURCH OF JESUS CHRIST OF LATTER-DAY SAINTS - GENEALOGICAL
    LIBRARY
50 E. North Temple St.   Phone: (801) 531-2331
Salt Lake City, UT 84150   David M. Mayfield, Dir.

CHURCH OF JESUS CHRIST OF LATTER-DAY SAINTS - HISTORICAL
    DEPARTMENT - CHURCH LIBRARY-ARCHIVES
50 E. North Temple St.   Phone: (801) 531-2745
Salt Lake City, UT 84150   Donald T. Schmidt, Dir., Lib.Archv.

DESERET NEWS - LIBRARY
30 E. First S.   Phone: (801) 237-2155
Salt Lake City, UT 84111   Connie Christensen, Libn.

EIMCO PMD TECHNOLOGY & DEVELOPMENT - TECHNICAL LIBRARY †
414 West 300 South
Box 300   Phone: (801) 526-2492
Salt Lake City, UT 84110   Linda Kothe, Libn.

HOLY CROSS HOSPITAL - MEDICAL LIBRARY
1045 E. First South St.   Phone: (801) 350-4060
Salt Lake City, UT 84102   Sr. M. Fidelia, Med.Libn.

INTERGALACTIC CORP. - LIBRARY
3585 Via Terra
Salt Lake City, UT 84115   Douglas MacGregor, Dir.

L.D.S. HOSPITAL - MEDICAL LIBRARY
325 Eighth Ave.   Phone: (801) 350-1054
Salt Lake City, UT 84143   Mr. Terry L. Heyer, Lib.Dir.

NORTH AMERICAN WEATHER CONSULTANTS - TECHNICAL LIBRARY
1141 E. 3900 S. A130
Salt Lake City, UT 84117   Carol Robinson Simpson, Libn.

ST. MARK'S HOSPITAL - LIBRARY
1200 East 3900 South St.   Phone: (801) 268-7004
Salt Lake City, UT 84117   Kerry F. Skidmore, Libn.

SALT LAKE CITY SCHOOLS - INSTRUCTIONAL MEDIA CENTER
1575 S. State   Phone: (801) 322-1471
Salt Lake City, UT 84115   Marion Karpisek, Hd.

SALT LAKE TRIBUNE - LIBRARY
143 South Main St.   Phone: (801) 237-2001
Salt Lake City, UT 84111   Laurene A. Sowby, Libn.

SPERRY CORPORATION - SPERRY UNIVAC - LIBRARY/TECHNICAL
    INFORMATION CENTER
322 North 2200 West   Phone: (801) 539-5222
Salt Lake City, UT 84116   Phyllis J. Tadlock, Libn.

STOVE KING - LIBRARY
1116 Capistrano Dr.   Phone: (801) 261-2495
Salt Lake City, UT 84116   Clarence Froman, Owner

TERRA TEK - TECHNICAL LIBRARY
420 Wakara Way
University Research Park   Phone: (801) 582-2220
Salt Lake City, UT 84108   Kim M. Green, Libn.

U.S. BUREAU OF MINES - SALT LAKE CITY RESEARCH CENTER - LIBRARY
729 Arapeen Dr.   Phone: (801) 524-6111
Salt Lake City, UT 84108   A.B. Whitehead, Supv., Tech.Sup.

U.S. DEPT. OF COMMERCE - INTERNATIONAL TRADE ADMINISTRATION -
    SALT LAKE CITY DISTRICT OFFICE LIBRARY
304 U.S. Post Office Bldg.
350 S. Main St.   Phone: (801) 524-5116
Salt Lake City, UT 84101   Stephen P. Smoot, Dir.

U.S. VETERANS ADMINISTRATION (UT-Salt Lake City) - HOSPITAL MEDICAL
    LIBRARY
500 Foothill Dr.   Phone: (801) 582-1565
Salt Lake City, UT 84148   Cherryi M. Povey, Chf., Lib.Serv.

UNIVERSITY OF UTAH - CENTER FOR PUBLIC AFFAIRS AND
    ADMINISTRATION - RESEARCH LIBRARY
214 Orson Spencer Hall   Phone: (801) 581-6781
Salt Lake City, UT 84112   Susan K. Gibbons, Libn.

UNIVERSITY OF UTAH - HUMAN RELATIONS AREA FILES
Marriott Library   Phone: (801) 581-7024
Salt Lake City, UT 84112   Mark W. Emery, Ref.Libn.

UNIVERSITY OF UTAH - INSTRUCTIONAL MEDIA SERVICES
207 Milton Bennion Hall   Phone: (801) 581-6112
Salt Lake City, UT 84112   Stephen H. Hess, Dir.

UNIVERSITY OF UTAH - LAW LIBRARY
College of Law   Phone: (801) 581-6438
Salt Lake City, UT 84112   Ms. Lane Wilkins, Dir.

UNIVERSITY OF UTAH - MAP LIBRARY
158 Marriott Library   Phone: (801) 581-7533
Salt Lake City, UT 84112   Barbara Cox, Map Libn.

UNIVERSITY OF UTAH - MATHEMATICS LIBRARY
121 JWB   Phone: (801) 581-6208
Salt Lake City, UT 84112   Christine Zeidner, Sci. & Engr.Libn.

UNIVERSITY OF UTAH - MIDDLE EAST LIBRARY
Marriott Library   Phone: (801) 581-6208
Salt Lake City, UT 84112

UNIVERSITY OF UTAH - NON-PRINT SERVICES
Marriott Library, 4th Fl.   Phone: (801) 581-6283
Salt Lake City, UT 84112   Ronald Read, Hd.

UNIVERSITY OF UTAH - SPECIAL COLLECTIONS DEPARTMENT
Marriott Library   Phone: (801) 581-8863
Salt Lake City, UT 84112   Dr. Everett L. Cooley, Asst.Dir./Univ.Archv.

UNIVERSITY OF UTAH - SPENCER S. ECCLES HEALTH SCIENCES LIBRARY
                                         Phone: (801) 581-8771
Salt Lake City, UT 84112   Priscilla M. Mayden, Dir.

UPPER COLORADO RIVER COMMISSION - LIBRARY *
355 S. Fourth East St.
Salt Lake City, UT 84111   Paul L. Billhymer, Libn.

UTAH STATE ARCHIVES
State Capitol, Rm. 28   Phone: (801) 533-5250
Salt Lake City, UT 84114   T. Harold Jacobsen, State Archv.

UTAH STATE BOARD OF EDUCATION - U-CRIS PROGRAM
Division of Program Adm.
250 E. Fifth, S.   Phone: (801) 533-5061
Salt Lake City, UT 84111   Robert Olson, Info.Ret.Spec.

UTAH STATE HISTORICAL SOCIETY - RESEARCH LIBRARY
300 Rio Grande   Phone: (801) 533-5808
Salt Lake City, UT 84105   Jay M. Haymond, Libn.

UTAH STATE LAW LIBRARY
332 State Capitol Bldg.   Phone: (801) 533-5280
Salt Lake City, UT 84114   Geoffrey J. Butler, Law Libn.

UTAH STATE LIBRARY
2150 South 300 West, Suite 16   Phone: (801) 533-5875
Salt Lake City, UT 84115   Russell L. Davis, Dir.

UTAH STATE LIBRARY - BLIND AND PHYSICALLY HANDICAPPED PROGRAM
    - REGIONAL LIBRARY
2150 South 300 West, Suite 16   Phone: (801) 533-5855
Salt Lake City, UT 84115   Gerald Buttars, Dir.

UTAH STATE LIBRARY - FILM PROGRAM
2150 South 300 West, Suite 9   Phone: (801) 533-5875
Salt Lake City, UT 84115   Kirk Matheson, Hd.

UTAH STATE - 3RD JUDICIAL DISTRICT - SALT LAKE COUNTY LAW
    LIBRARY
A-222 Hall of Justice   Phone: (801) 535-7518
Salt Lake City, UT 84111   Jim Burris, Law Libn.

WHO AM I - LIBRARY
57 W. South Temple, No. 554
Salt lake City, UT 84101   P.W. McMullin, Exec.Dir.

U.S. NATL. PARK SERVICE - ZION NATL. PARK - LIBRARY
                                          Phone: (801) 772-3256
Springdale, UT 84767   Victor L. Jackson, Chf. Naturalist

DINOSAUR NATURAL HISTORY MUSEUM - REFERENCE LIBRARY
235 E. Main St.
Box 396   Phone: (801) 789-3799
Vernal, UT 84078   Alden Hamblin, Dir.

VERMONT

CANFIELD MEMORIAL LIBRARY - RUSSELL VERMONTIANA COLLECTION
                                          Phone: (802) 375-6153
Arlington, VT 05250   Mary Henning, Libn.

CARMELITE MONASTERY - LIBRARY OF THE IMMACULATE HEART OF MARY
Beckley Hill   Phone: (802) 476-8362
Barre, VT 05641   Sr. Jeanne M. Gonyon, Libn.

CENTRAL VERMONT HOSPITAL - MEDICAL LIBRARY
Box 547   Phone: (802) 229-9121
Barre, VT 05641   Betty-Jean Eastman, Med.Libn.

ASSOCIATION OF NORTH AMERICAN DIRECTORY PUBLISHERS - PRICE &
    LEE COMPANY DIRECTORY LIBRARY
Box 317
Bellows Falls, VT 05101   Pat Lentocha

BENNINGTON MUSEUM - GENEALOGICAL LIBRARY
W. Main St.   Phone: (802) 442-2180
Bennington, VT 05201   Charles G. Bennett, Genealogical Libn.

BLACKMER (Samuel H.) MEMORIAL LIBRARY
County Court House   Phone: (802) 442-8528
Bennington, VT 05201

PUTNAM (Henry W.) MEMORIAL HOSPITAL - MEDICAL LIBRARY
100 Hospital Dr.   Phone: (802) 442-6361
Bennington, VT 05201   Jack Hall, Med.Libn.

BRANDON TRAINING SCHOOL - LIBRARY
                                          Phone: (802) 247-5711
Brandon, VT 05733   Lorna Z. Whitehorne, Libn.

AUSTINE SCHOOL - LIBRARY
120 Maple St.   Phone: (802) 254-4571
Brattleboro, VT 05301   John I. Enola, Libn.

BRATTLEBORO MEMORIAL HOSPITAL - MEDICAL LIBRARY
9 Belmont Ave.   Phone: (802) 257-0341
Brattleboro, VT 05301   Martha J. Fenn, Libn.

BRATTLEBORO RETREAT - MEDICAL LIBRARY
75 Linden St.   Phone: (802) 257-7785
Brattleboro, VT 05301   Jane Rand, Dir. of Lib.Serv.

EXPERIMENT IN INTERNATIONAL LIVING - SCHOOL FOR INTERNATIONAL
    TRAINING - DONALD B. WATT LIBRARY
Kipling Rd.   Phone: (802) 257-7751
Brattleboro, VT 05301   Shirley Capron, Pub.Serv.Libn.

NEW ENGLAND SOLAR ENERGY ASSOCIATION - LIBRARY
14 Green St.
Box 541   Phone: (802) 254-2386
Brattleboro, VT 05301   Larry Sherwood, Exec.Dir.

MUSEUM OF THE AMERICAS - LIBRARY
                                          Phone: (802) 276-3386
Brookfield, VT 05036   Earle W. Newton, Dir.

GENERAL ELECTRIC COMPANY - AIRCRAFT EQUIPMENT DIVISION -
    ARMAMENT SYSTEMS DEPT. ENGINEERING LIBRARY *
Lakeside Ave.   Phone: (802) 658-1500
Burlington, VT 05401   Raymond M. Palmer, Tech.Libn.

UNIVERSITY OF VERMONT - CHEMISTRY/PHYSICS LIBRARY
                                          Phone: (802) 656-2268
Burlington, VT 05405   Elizabeth Dole, Ref.Libn.

UNIVERSITY OF VERMONT - DIVISION OF HEALTH SCIENCES - CHARLES A.
    DANA MEDICAL LIBRARY
Given Bldg.   Phone: (802) 656-2200
Burlington, VT 05405   Ellen Gillies, Med.Libn.

UNIVERSITY OF VERMONT - PRINGLE HERBARIUM - LIBRARY
Botany Dept.   Phone: (802) 656-3221
Burlington, VT 05405   David S. Barrington, Cur.

UNIVERSITY OF VERMONT - WILBUR COLLECTION OF VERMONTIANA
Bailey/Howe Library   Phone: (802) 656-2020
Burlington, VT 05405   John Buechler, Hd., Spec.Coll.

CASTLETON HISTORICAL SOCIETY - MUSEUM LIBRARY *
Main St.   Phone: (802) 468-2226
Castleton, VT 05735   Mrs. Finley Shepard, Cur.

CASTLETON STATE COLLEGE - CALVIN COOLIDGE LIBRARY - LEARNING
    RESOURCES CENTER
                                          Phone: (802) 468-5611
Castleton, VT 05735   Dr. Edward A. Scott, Dir.

AMERICAN SOCIETY OF DOWSERS, INC. - LIBRARY
                                          Phone: (802) 684-3417
Danville, VT 05828   Paul S. Sevigny, Pres.

IBM CORPORATION - GENERAL TECHNOLOGY DIVISION - INFORMATION
    CENTER/LEARNING CENTER
                                          Phone: (802) 769-2331
Essex Junction, VT 05452   C. Allen Merritt, Mgr.

WALKER MUSEUM - LIBRARY
Fairlee, VT 05045

CHAPMAN (Bruce) COMPANY - LIBRARY
                                          Phone: (802) 843-2321
Grafton, VT 05146   William Chapman, Libn.

GRAFTON HISTORICAL MUSEUM
Main St.   Phone: (802) 843-2388
Grafton, VT 05146   Helen M. Pettengill, Musm.Dir.

MUSEUM OF AMERICAN FLY FISHING, INC. - LIBRARY
                                          Phone: (802) 362-3300
Manchester, VT 05254

PORTER MEDICAL CENTER - MEDICAL LIBRARY AND INFORMATION
    SERVICE
South St.   Phone: (802) 388-7901
Middlebury, VT 05753   Barbara P. Lande, Libn.

SHELDON ART MUSEUM - GOVERNOR JOHN W. STEWART & MR. & MRS.
    CHARLES M. SWIFT RESEARCH CENTER LIBRARY
2 Park St.   Phone: (802) 388-2117
Middlebury, VT 05753   Polly C. Darnell, Libn.

NATIONAL LIFE INSURANCE COMPANY - LIBRARY
National Life Dr.   Phone: (802) 229-3278
Montpelier, VT 05602   Saba L. Foster, Chf.Libn.

GEOGRAPHIC

GEOGRAPHIC

VERMONT HISTORICAL SOCIETY - LIBRARY *
Pavilion Bldg., 109 State St. Phone: (802) 828-2291
Montpelier, VT 05602 Laura P. Abbott, Libn.

VERMONT STATE AGENCY OF ADMINISTRATION - PUBLIC RECORDS DIVISION
133 State St. Phone: (802) 828-3288
Montpelier, VT 05602 John Yacavoni, Asst.Dir.

VERMONT STATE DEPARTMENT OF LIBRARIES
State Office Bldg. Post Office Phone: (802) 828-3261
Montpelier, VT 05602 Patricia E. Klinck, State Libn.

VERMONT STATE OFFICE OF THE SECRETARY OF STATE - ARCHIVES AND STATE PAPERS DIVISION
Pavilion Bldg. Phone: (802) 828-2363
Montpelier, VT 05602 Marlene B. Wallace, Archv. & Ed.

NORTH COUNTRY HOSPITAL AND HEALTH CENTER, INC. - INFORMATION CENTER
Prouty Dr. Phone: (802) 334-7331
Newport, VT 05855 Estelle Raymond, Info.Ctr.Techn.

GIFFORD MEMORIAL HOSPITAL - HEALTH INFORMATION CENTER
44 S. Main St. Phone: (802) 728-3366
Randolph, VT 05060 Patience L. Crowley, Dir.

VERMONT TECHNICAL COLLEGE - HARTNESS LIBRARY
Phone: (802) 728-3391
Randolph Center, VT 05061 Dewey F. Patterson, Lib.Dir.

CENTRAL VERMONT PUBLIC SERVICE CORPORATION - TECHNICAL INFORMATION CENTER
77 Grove St. Phone: (802) 773-2711
Rutland, VT 05701 Olga M. Compton, Mgr., TIC

RUTLAND HOSPITAL - HEALTH SCIENCE LIBRARY
Allen St. Phone: (802) 775-7111
Rutland, VT 05701 Cherie L. Goderwis, R.N., Dir.

NORTHWESTERN MEDICAL CENTER - INFORMATION CENTER
Fairfield St. Phone: (802) 524-2161
St. Albans, VT 05478 June C. Wakefield, Info.Ctr.Dir.

FAIRBANKS MUSEUM AND PLANETARIUM - LIBRARY
Main and Prospect Sts. Phone: (802) 748-2378
St. Johnsbury, VT 05819 Howard B. Reed, Assoc.Dir., Musm.Coll.

NORTHEASTERN VERMONT REGIONAL HOSPITAL - INFORMATION CENTER/LIBRARY
Hospital Dr. Phone: (802) 748-8141
St. Johnsbury, VT 05819 Eleanor Simons, Libn.

SHELBURNE MUSEUM, INC. - RESEARCH LIBRARY
Phone: (802) 985-3346
Shelburne, VT 05482 Leslie A. Hasker, Lib.Asst.

VERMONT LAW SCHOOL - LIBRARY
Chelsea St. Phone: (802) 763-8303
South Royalton, VT 05068 W. Leslie Peat, Law Libn.

SPRINGFIELD HOSPITAL - INFORMATION CENTER LIBRARY
25 Ridgewood Rd. Phone: (802) 885-2151
Springfield, VT 05156 Holly H. Eddy, Med.Libn.

MILLHOUSE BUNDY PERFORMING & FINE ARTS CENTER - LIBRARY
Phone: (802) 496-2206
Waitsfield, VT 05673

VERMONT STATE HOSPITAL - AGENCY OF HUMAN SERVICES LIBRARY
103 S. Main St.
Waterbury, VT 05676 Susan Longenecker, Chf.Libn.

U.S. VETERANS ADMINISTRATION (VT-White River Jct.) - ALLIED HEALTH SCIENCES LIBRARY
Phone: (802) 295-9369
White River Junction, VT 05001 John A. Package, Chf., Lib.Serv.

FANNY ALLEN HOSPITAL - INFORMATION CENTER
101 College Pkwy. Phone: (802) 655-1234
Winooski, VT 05404 Ann M. Bousquet, Med.Libn.

VERMONT INSTITUTE OF NATURAL SCIENCES - LIBRARY
Church Hill Rd. Phone: (802) 457-2779
Woodstock, VT 05091 Sarah B. Laughlin, Dir.

WOODSTOCK HISTORICAL SOCIETY, INC. - JOHN COTTON DANA LIBRARY
26 Elm St. Phone: (802) 457-1822
Woodstock, VT 05091 John Martin, Pres.

VIRGINIA

ALEXANDRIA CITY PUBLIC SCHOOLS - EDUCATIONAL MEDIA CENTER - NICHOLS PROFESSIONAL LIBRARY
3801 W. Braddock Rd. Phone: (703) 998-9045
Alexandria, VA 22302 Dale W. Brown, Dir.

ALEXANDRIA GAZETTE - LIBRARY
Box 119
Alexandria, VA 22313

ALEXANDRIA HOSPITAL - HEALTH SCIENCES LIBRARY †
4320 Seminary Rd. Phone: (703) 370-9000
Alexandria, VA 22314 Libby Hamilton, Libn.

ALEXANDRIA LIBRARY - LLOYD HOUSE
220 N. Washington St. Phone: (703) 838-4577
Alexandria, VA 22314 Jeanne G. Plitt, Dir.

AMERICAN ORTHOTIC AND PROSTHETIC ASSOCIATION - LIBRARY
717 Pendleton St. Phone: (703) 836-7114
Alexandria, VA 22314 William L. McCulloch, Exec.Dir.

ASSOCIATION OF AVIATION & SPACE MUSEOLOGISTS - INFORMATION CENTER
6203 Yellowstone Dr. Phone: (703) 941-4724
Alexandria, VA 22312 Douglas Campbell, Dir.

ATLANTIC RESEARCH CORPORATION - LIBRARY
5390 Cherokee Ave. Phone: (703) 642-4178
Alexandria, VA 22314 Ellen Lebovitz, Libn.

CONTROL DATA CORPORATION - GOVERNMENT SYSTEMS LIBRARY
1800 N. Beauregard St. Phone: (703) 998-4606
Alexandria, VA 22311 Barbara B. Harris, Libn.

FIRST CHRISTIAN CHURCH - LIBRARY
2723 King St. Phone: (703) 549-3911
Alexandria, VA 22302 Sue Solomon, Libn.

FORT WARD MUSEUM - DOROTHY C.S. STARR CIVIL WAR RESEARCH LIBRARY
4301 W. Braddock Rd. Phone: (703) 838-4848
Alexandria, VA 22304 Wanda S. Dowell, Cur.

HARRIS & GIFFORD - LIBRARY
520 N. Washington St. Phone: (202) 628-8700
Alexandria, VA 22314 R.A. Gifford, Owner

HUMAN RESOURCES RESEARCH ORGANIZATION - VAN EVERA LIBRARY †
300 N. Washington St. Phone: (703) 549-3611
Alexandria, VA 22314 Mrs. Lonnie J. Elliott, Libn.

IFI/PLENUM DATA COMPANY - LIBRARY
302 Swann Ave. Phone: (703) 683-1085
Alexandria, VA 22301 Harry M. Allcock, V.P.

JHK & ASSOCIATES - TECHNICAL LIBRARY - EAST
4660 Kenmore Ave. Phone: (703) 370-2411
Alexandria, VA 22304 Richard Presby, Dir.

OCTAMERON ASSOCIATES, INC. - RESEARCH LIBRARY
820 Fontaine St. Phone: (703) 836-1019
Alexandria, VA 22302 Karen Stokstad, Libn.

TIME-LIFE BOOKS INC. - REFERENCE LIBRARY
777 Duke St.   Phone: (703) 960-5353
Alexandria, VA 22314   Louise D. Forstall, Hd.Libn.

UNITED FRESH FRUIT AND VEGETABLE ASSOCIATION - LIBRARY
N. Washington at Madison   Phone: (703) 836-3410
Alexandria, VA 22314   Charles Magoon, Dir. of Res.

U.S. ARMY - ADJUTANT GENERAL - LIBRARY DIVISION
Hoffman Bldg. I, Rm. 1450   Phone: (703) 325-9700
Alexandria, VA 22331   Nellie B. Strickland, Div.Chf.

U.S. ARMY INSTITUTE OF HERALDRY - LIBRARY
5010 Duke St.
Bldg. 15, Cameron Sta.   Phone: (202) 274-6544
Alexandria, VA 22314   Herbert M. Pastan, Libn.

U.S. ARMY - MATERIEL DEVELOPMENT & READINESS COMMAND -
   HEADQUARTERS - TECHNICAL LIBRARY
5001 Eisenhower Ave.   Phone: (202) 274-8152
Alexandria, VA 22333   John Fragale, Jr., Chf.

U.S. BUREAU OF LAND MANAGEMENT - EASTERN STATES OFFICE LIBRARY
350 S. Pickett St.
Alexandria, VA 22304   Belynda B. Bradshaw, Mgt.Asst.

U.S. DEFENSE LOGISTICS AGENCY - HEADQUARTERS LIBRARY
Cameron Sta.   Phone: (202) 274-6055
Alexandria, VA 22314   Barbara Ralston, Chf.

U.S. DEFENSE TECHNICAL INFORMATION CENTER
Cameron Sta.   Phone: (202) 274-7633
Alexandria, VA 22314   Hubert E. Sauter, Adm.

U.S. DEFENSE TECHNICAL INFORMATION CENTER - TECHNICAL LIBRARY
Cameron Sta., Bldg. 5   Phone: (202) 274-6833
Alexandria, VA 22314   Elaine Burress, Libn.

U.S. NAVY - CENTER FOR NAVAL ANALYSES - LIBRARY
2000 N. Beauregard St.   Phone: (703) 998-3580
Alexandria, VA 22311   Karen N. Domabyl, Libn.

U.S. NAVY - NAVAL FACILITIES ENGINEERING COMMAND - TECHNICAL
   LIBRARY
Hoffman Bldg. 2, 200 Stovall St.   Phone: (703) 325-8507
Alexandria, VA 22332   Cynthia K. Neyland, Libn.

U.S. NAVY - OFFICE OF THE JUDGE ADVOCATE GENERAL - LAW LIBRARY
Hoffman Bldg. No. 2
200 Stovall St.   Phone: (202) 325-9565
Alexandria, VA 22332   Richard S. Barrows, Libn.

UNITED WAY OF AMERICA - INFORMATION CENTER †
801 N. Fairfax St.   Phone: (703) 836-7100
Alexandria, VA 22314   Henry M. Smith, Dir.

VIRGINIA THEOLOGICAL SEMINARY - BISHOP PAYNE LIBRARY
Seminary Rd. & Quaker Ln.   Phone: (703) 370-6602
Alexandria, VA 22304   J.H. Goodwin, Libn.

VSE CORPORATION - TECHNICAL LIBRARY
2550 Huntington Ave.   Phone: (703) 960-4600
Alexandria, VA 22303   Merriel T. Whitehead, Libn.

WESTMINSTER PRESBYTERIAN CHURCH - LIBRARY †
2701 Cameron Mills Rd.   Phone: (703) 549-4766
Alexandria, VA 22302   Esther M. Cook, Libn.

AMELIA HISTORICAL LIBRARY - JACKSON MEMORIAL LIBRARY
Box 21
Amelia, VA 23002   Mrs. D.H. Flippin, Chm.

U.S. NATL. PARK SERVICE - APPOMATTOX COURT HOUSE NATL.
   HISTORICAL PARK - LIBRARY
Box 218   Phone: (703) 352-8987
Appomattox, VA 24522   Ronald Wilson, Pk.Hist.

AMERICAN GAS ASSOCIATION - LIBRARY
1515 Wilson Blvd.   Phone: (703) 841-8415
Arlington, VA 22209   Steven J. Dorner, Mgr., Lib.Serv.

AMERICAN GEAR MANUFACTURERS ASSOCIATION - LIBRARY
1901 N. Fort Myer Dr., Suite 1000   Phone: (703) 525-6000
Arlington, VA 22209

AMERICAN PATENT LAW ASSOCIATION - PATENT LAW LIBRARY
2001 Jefferson Davis Hwy., Suite 203   Phone: (703) 521-1680
Arlington, VA 22202

AMERICAN PSYCHOLOGICAL ASSOCIATION - ARTHUR W. MELTON
   LIBRARY
1400 N. Uhle St.   Phone: (202) 833-7590
Arlington, VA 22201   Elizabeth B. Lawton, Libn.

AMERICAN WATERWAYS OPERATORS, INC. - LIBRARY
1600 Wilson Blvd., Suite 1101   Phone: (703) 841-9300
Arlington, VA 22209   Neil D. Schuster, V.P., Res.

ANALYTIC SERVICES, INC. - TECHNICAL LIBRARY
400 Army-Navy Dr.   Phone: (703) 979-0700
Arlington, VA 22202   Francie G. Binion

ARCHITECTURAL WOODWORK INSTITUTE - LIBRARY †
2310 S. Walter Reed Dr.   Phone: (703) 671-9100
Arlington, VA 22206

ARLINGTON COUNTY CENTRAL LIBRARY - VIRGINIANA COLLECTION
1015 N. Quincy St.   Phone: (703) 527-4777
Arlington, VA 22201   Sara Collins, Virginiana Libn.

ARLINGTON COUNTY CENTRAL LIBRARY - ZONTA ORAL HISTORY
   COLLECTION
1015 N. Quincy St.   Phone: (703) 527-4777
Arlington, VA 22201   Sara Collins, Virginiana Libn.

ARLINGTON HISTORICAL SOCIETY - ARCHIVES
Box 402
Arlington, VA 22210   Ruth M. Ward, Archv.

ARLINGTON HOSPITAL - DOCTORS' LIBRARY †
1701 N. George Mason Dr.   Phone: (703) 558-6524
Arlington, VA 22205   Olga Taylor, Libn.

ARLINGTON PUBLIC SCHOOLS - PROFESSIONAL LIBRARY
1426 N. Quincy St.   Phone: (703) 558-2836
Arlington, VA 22207   Gina Parish, Mgr.

ASBESTOS INFORMATION ASSOCIATION/NORTH AMERICA - TECHNICAL
   AND MEDICAL FILES
1745 Jefferson Davis Hwy., Suite 509   Phone: (703) 979-1150
Arlington, VA 22202   N. Hluchyj, Asst. for Govt.Aff.

CABLE TELEVISION INFORMATION CENTER
1800 N. Kent St., Suite 1007   Phone: (703) 528-6846
Arlington, VA 22209   Harold E. Horn, Pres.

COMPUTER & COMMUNICATIONS INDUSTRY ASSOCIATION - RESEARCH
   LIBRARY
1500 Wilson Blvd., Suite 512   Phone: (703) 524-1360
Arlington, VA 22209

DATA USE AND ACCESS LABORATORIES (DUALABS) - LIBRARY
1601 N. Kent St., Suite 900   Phone: (703) 525-1480
Arlington, VA 22209   Deborah S. Pomerance, Libn.

EDUCATIONAL RESEARCH SERVICE - LIBRARY
1800 N. Kent St.   Phone: (703) 243-2100
Arlington, VA 22209   Josephine Franklin, Coord., Info.Serv.

GEORGE MASON UNIVERSITY - SCHOOL OF LAW - LIBRARY †
3401 N. Fairfax Dr.   Phone: (703) 841-2652
Arlington, VA 22201   Stephen J. Burnett, Dir.

HERNER AND COMPANY - LIBRARY
1700 N. Moore St.   Phone: (703) 558-8238
Arlington, VA 22209   Nancy D. Wright, V.P. for Lib.Serv.

INSTITUTE FOR DEFENSE ANALYSES - TECHNICAL INFORMATION SERVICES
400 Army-Navy Dr.   Phone: (703) 558-1456
Arlington, VA 22202   Ruth S. Smith, Mgr.

INTERNATIONAL BUSINESS FORMS INDUSTRIES/PRINTING INDUSTRIES OF AMERICA - LIBRARY †
1730 N. Lynn St.   Phone: (703) 841-9191
Arlington, VA 22209

MC CARTHY (Walter T.) LAW LIBRARY †
1400 N. Courthouse Rd.
Court House, Rm. 501   Phone: (703) 558-2243
Arlington, VA 22201   Betty J. Waldow, Exec.Dir.

NATIONAL MENTAL HEALTH ASSOCIATION - CLIFFORD BEERS MEMORIAL LIBRARY
1800 N. Kent St.   Phone: (703) 528-6405
Arlington, VA 22209   Lynn Schultz-Writsel, Act.Dir.

NATIONAL RECREATION AND PARK ASSOCIATION - JOSEPH LEE MEMORIAL LIBRARY AND INFORMATION CENTER
1601 N. Kent St.
Arlington, VA 22209   Dr. Madeleine J. Wilkins, Mgr.

SYSTEM PLANNING CORPORATION - RESEARCH LIBRARY
1500 Wilson Blvd.   Phone: (703) 841-2878
Arlington, VA 22209   Linda S. Glickman, Hd.Libn.

TAX EXECUTIVES INSTITUTE, INC. - TEI INFORMATION SYSTEM
1616 N. Ft. Myer Dr., 14th Fl.   Phone: (703) 522-3535
Arlington, VA 22209   William L. Lynch, Mng.Dir.

TRW, INC. - INFORMATION CENTER
1000 Wilson Blvd., Suite 2700   Phone: (703) 276-5016
Arlington, VA 22209   Kathleen Galiher Ott, Mgr.

U.S. DEFENSE AUDIOVISUAL AGENCY - ARLINGTON STILL PHOTO DEPOSITORY
1221 S. Fern St.   Phone: (202) 695-1147
Arlington, VA 22202   Virginia Fincik, Chf.

U.S. DEPT. OF STATE - FOREIGN SERVICE INSTITUTE LIBRARY
1400 Key Blvd.   Phone: (703) 235-8717
Arlington, VA 22209   Mary C. Schloeder, Libn.

U.S. NAVY - OFFICE OF NAVAL RESEARCH - LIBRARY
633 Ballston Tower, No. 1
800 N. Quincy St.   Phone: (202) 696-4415
Arlington, VA 22217   Frances M. Chang, Libn.

U.S. PATENT & TRADEMARK OFFICE - SCIENTIFIC LIBRARY
2021 Jefferson Davis Hwy.   Phone: (703) 557-2955
Arlington, VA 22202   Henry Rosicky, Prog.Mgr.

VIRGINIA POLYTECHNIC INSTITUTE AND STATE UNIVERSITY - ARCHITECTURE LIBRARY
Cowgill Hall   Phone: (703) 961-6182
Blacksburg, VA 24061   Robert E. Stephenson, Arch.Libn.

VIRGINIA POLYTECHNIC INSTITUTE AND STATE UNIVERSITY - CAROL M. NEWMAN LIBRARY
     Phone: (703) 961-5593
Blacksburg, VA 24061   H. Gordon Bechanan, Dir. of Libs.

AMERICAN SECURITY COUNCIL EDUCATION FOUNDATION - SOL FEINSTONE LIBRARY
     Phone: (703) 825-1776
Boston, VA 22713   John M. Fisher, Pres.

UNIVERSITY OF VIRGINIA - BLANDY EXPERIMENTAL FARM LIBRARY
Box 175   Phone: (703) 837-1758
Boyce, VA 22620   Thomas E. Ewert, Dir.

BRIDGEWATER COLLEGE - ALEXANDER MACK MEMORIAL LIBRARY - SPECIAL COLLECTIONS
     Phone: (703) 828-2501
Bridgewater, VA 22812   Orland (Jack) Wages, Libn.

INSTITUTE OF CHARTERED FINANCIAL ANALYSTS - LIBRARY
University of Virginia
Ednam Forest   Phone: (804) 977-6600
Charlottesville, VA 22903

INSTITUTE OF TEXTILE TECHNOLOGY - TEXTILE INFORMATION SERVICES - ROGER MILLIKEN TEXTILE LIBRARY
Rte. 250 W.   Phone: (804) 296-5511
Charlottesville, VA 22902   Linda Justus, Libn.

NATIONAL RADIO ASTRONOMY OBSERVATORY - LIBRARY
Edgemont Rd.   Phone: (804) 296-0211
Charlottesville, VA 22901   Sarah S. Martin, Libn.

SPERRY CORPORATION - SPERRY MARINE SYSTEMS - ENGINEERING LIBRARY
Rte. 29 North   Phone: (804) 973-0100
Charlottesville, VA 22906   Mrs. O. Bray, Libn.

U.S. ARMY - JUDGE ADVOCATE GENERAL'S SCHOOL - LIBRARY
     Phone: (804) 293-9824
Charlottesville, VA 22901   R. Vivian Hebert, Law Libn.

UNIVERSITY OF VIRGINIA - ARTHUR J. MORRIS LAW LIBRARY
School of Law   Phone: (804) 924-3384
Charlottesville, VA 22901   Larry B. Wenger

UNIVERSITY OF VIRGINIA - BIOLOGY/PSYCHOLOGY LIBRARY
Gilmer Hall   Phone: (804) 924-3529
Charlottesville, VA 22901   Sandra Bennett, Libn.

UNIVERSITY OF VIRGINIA - CHEMISTRY LIBRARY
Chemistry Bldg.   Phone: (804) 924-3159
Charlottesville, VA 22901   Robert La Rue, Libn.

UNIVERSITY OF VIRGINIA - CLIFTON WALLER BARRETT LIBRARY
Alderman Library   Phone: (804) 924-3366
Charlottesville, VA 22901   Joan S. Crane, Cur.Amer.Lit.

UNIVERSITY OF VIRGINIA - COLGATE DARDEN GRADUATE SCHOOL OF BUSINESS ADMINISTRATION - LIBRARY
Box 6550   Phone: (804) 924-7321
Charlottesville, VA 22906   Henry Wingate, Libn.

UNIVERSITY OF VIRGINIA - EDUCATION LIBRARY
Ruffner Hall, Emmet St.
Charlottesville, VA 22903   Helen B. Anthony, Libn.

UNIVERSITY OF VIRGINIA - ENGINEERING LIBRARY
Thornton Hall   Phone: (804) 924-3046
Charlottesville, VA 22901   James W. Zerwick, Engr.Libn.

UNIVERSITY OF VIRGINIA - FISKE KIMBALL FINE ARTS LIBRARY
Bayly Dr.   Phone: (804) 924-7024
Charlottesville, VA 22903   Mary C. Dunnigan, Libn.

UNIVERSITY OF VIRGINIA - MATHEMATICS-ASTRONOMY LIBRARY
Mathematics-Astronomy Bldg.   Phone: (804) 924-7806
Charlottesville, VA 22901   Roma Reed, Libn.

UNIVERSITY OF VIRGINIA MEDICAL CENTER - CLAUDE MOORE HEALTH SCIENCES LIBRARY
Box 234   Phone: (804) 924-5464
Charlottesville, VA 22908   Terry A. Thorkilson, Dir. & Assoc.Prof.

UNIVERSITY OF VIRGINIA MEDICAL CENTER - DEPARTMENT OF NEUROLOGY - ELIZABETH J. OHRSTROM LIBRARY
Box 394   Phone: (804) 924-2676
Charlottesville, VA 22908   Dr. T.R. Johns, Dept.Chm.

UNIVERSITY OF VIRGINIA - MUSIC LIBRARY
Old Cabell Hall   Phone: (804) 924-7041
Charlottesville, VA 22901   Evan Bonds, Music Libn.

UNIVERSITY OF VIRGINIA - PHYSICS LIBRARY
Physics Bldg.   Phone: (804) 924-3781
Charlottesville, VA 22901   Judith Kirwan, Libn.

UNIVERSITY OF VIRGINIA - SCIENCE/TECHNOLOGY INFORMATION
    CENTER
Clark Hall   Phone: (804) 924-7209
Charlottesville, VA 22901   Edwina H. Pancake, Dir.

UNIVERSITY OF VIRGINIA - TRACY W. MC GREGOR LIBRARY
Alderman Library   Phone: (804) 924-3366
Charlottesville, VA 22901   William H. Runge, Cur.

VIRGINIA STATE DEPARTMENT OF CONSERVATION & ECONOMIC
    DEVELOPMENT - DIVISION OF MINERAL RESOURCES LIBRARY
McCormick Rd.
Box 3667   Phone: (804) 293-5121
Charlottesville, VA 22903

U.S. NAVY - NAVAL SURFACE WEAPONS CENTER - CENTER LIBRARY
Mail Code X-20   Phone: (703) 663-8994
Dahlgren, VA 22448   Dr. J. Marshal Hughes, II, Ctr.Libn.

DAN RIVER, INC. - RESEARCH LIBRARY
                                              Phone: (804) 799-7103
Danville, VA 24541   W.K. Adams, Asst. to Res.Dir.

MEMORIAL HOSPITAL - MEDICAL LIBRARY
142 S. Main St.   Phone: (804) 799-4418
Danville, VA 24541   Edith K. Ledford, Med.Libn.

MEMORIAL HOSPITAL - SCHOOL OF PROFESSIONAL NURSING - LIBRARY
Simpson Hall
Danville, VA 24541   Edith K. Ledford, Libn.

NATIONAL TOBACCO-TEXTILE MUSEUM - LIBRARY AND INFORMATION
    CENTER *
614 Lynn St.   Phone: (804) 797-9437
Danville, VA 24541   Samuel W. Price, Dir.

FAIRFAX COUNTY - COMPREHENSIVE PLANNING LIBRARY
4100 Chain Bridge Rd.
Fairfax, VA 22030   James L. Linard, Res.Libn.

FAIRFAX COUNTY LAW LIBRARY
Court House, Rm. 66   Phone: (703) 691-2170
Fairfax, VA 22030   Judith G. Caratenuto, Law Libn.

FAIRFAX COUNTY PUBLIC LIBRARY - BUSINESS & TECHNICAL SECTION
3915 Chain Bridge Rd.   Phone: (703) 691-2121
Fairfax, VA 22030   B.G. Sleight, Libn.

FAIRFAX COUNTY PUBLIC LIBRARY - VIRGINIA ROOM
3915 Chain Bridge Rd.   Phone: (703) 691-2123
Fairfax, VA 22030   Suzanne S. Levy, Libn.

FAIRFAX COUNTY PUBLIC SCHOOLS - PROFESSIONAL REFERENCE LIBRARY
    IN EDUCATION
3500 Old Lee Hwy.   Phone: (703) 591-4514
Fairfax, VA 22030   Betty Chilton, Lib.Spec.

AMERICAN AUTOMOBILE ASSOCIATION - LIBRARY
8111 Gatehouse Rd.   Phone: (703) 222-6466
Falls Church, VA 22047   Sue Williams, Libn.

AMERICAN GEOLOGICAL INSTITUTE - GEO-REF RETROSPECTIVE SEARCH
    SERVICE
5205 Leesburg Pike   Phone: (703) 379-2480
Falls Church, VA 22041   John Mulvihill, Dir.

AMERICAN PERSONNEL AND GUIDANCE ASSOCIATION - HEADQUARTERS
    OFFICE LIBRARY
5203 Leesburg Pike   Phone: (703) 820-4700
Falls Church, VA 22041   Sylvia Nisenoff, Prof.Info.Spec.

AMERICAN SOCIETY OF PHOTOGRAMMETRY - HEINZ GRUNER LIBRARY
105 N. Virginia Ave.   Phone: (703) 534-6617
Falls Church, VA 22046   William D. French, Exec.Dir.

ARCANE ORDER - LIBRARY
Studio of Contemplation
2904 Rosemary Lane
Falls Church, VA 22042   Sandra Elizabeth H. Merriman, Cur.

ARMED FORCES COMMUNICATIONS AND ELECTRONICS ASSOCIATION -
    LIBRARY
5205 Leesburg Pike, Suite 300   Phone: (703) 820-5028
Falls Church, VA 22041   Pat Veneziani, Adm.

COMPUTER SCIENCES CORPORATION - TECHNICAL LIBRARY
6565 Arlington Blvd.   Phone: (703) 533-8877
Falls Church, VA 22046   Ramona Briggs, Mgr.Tech.Lib.

E-SYSTEMS, INC. - MELPAR DIVISION - TECHNICAL LIBRARY
7700 Arlington Blvd.   Phone: (703) 560-5000
Falls Church, VA 22046   Mary A. Albertson, Libn.

FAIRFAX HOSPITAL - JACOB D. ZYLMAN MEMORIAL LIBRARY
3300 Gallows Rd.   Phone: (703) 698-3234
Falls Church, VA 22046   Alice J. Sheridan, Dir.

NATIONAL ALLIANCE OF SENIOR CITIZENS - LIBRARY †
101 Park Washington Ct.   Phone: (703) 241-9181
Falls Church, VA 22046   C.C. Clinkscales, III, Natl.Dir.

SYSTEMATICS GENERAL CORPORATION - LIBRARY *
2922 Telestar Ct.   Phone: (703) 698-8500
Falls Church, VA 22042   Andrew L. Johnson, Libn.

U.S. ARMY OPERATIONAL TEST & EVALUATION AGENCY (OTEA) -
    TECHNICAL LIBRARY
5600 Columbia Pike   Phone: (703) 756-2234
Falls Church, VA 22041   Ava Dell Headley, Libn.

FRANKLIN COUNTY HISTORICAL SOCIETY - STANLEY LIBRARY
Ferrum College   Phone: (703) 365-2121
Ferrum, VA 24088   J.B. Mitchell, Hd.Libn.

U.S. ARMY - ARMY MOBILITY EQUIPMENT RESEARCH & DEVELOPMENT
    COMMAND - TECHNICAL LIBRARY
                                              Phone: (703) 664-5840
Ft. Belvoir, VA 22060   Gloria J. Holland, Chf., Tech.Lib.Div.

U.S. ARMY COMPUTER SYSTEMS COMMAND - TECHNICAL LIBRARY
ACSC-DST (Annex), Stop H-9   Phone: (703) 756-5491
Ft. Belvoir, VA 22060   Grace Corbin, Tech.Info.Spec.

U.S. ARMY - CORPS OF ENGINEERS - COASTAL ENGINEERING RESEARCH
    CENTER - LIBRARY
Kingman Bldg.   Phone: (202) 325-7375
Ft. Belvoir, VA 22060   Bennie F. Maddox, Chf., Libn.

U.S. ARMY ENGINEER SCHOOL - LIBRARY
Bldg. 270   Phone: (703) 664-2524
Ft. Belvoir, VA 22060   Elizabeth F. Slawson, Engr.Libn.

U.S. ARMY - ENGINEER TOPOGRAPHIC LABORATORIES - SCIENTIFIC &
    TECHNICAL INFORMATION CENTER †
                                              Phone: (703) 664-3834
Ft. Belvoir, VA 22060   Natalie E. Kothe, Chf.

U.S. ARMY POST - FORT BELVOIR - VAN NOY LIBRARY
Bldg. 1024   Phone: (703) 664-1045
Ft. Belvoir, VA 22060   Madge J. Busey, Dir.

U.S. ARMY HOSPITALS - MC DONALD USA COMMUNITY HOSPITAL -
    MEDICAL LIBRARY
                                              Phone: (804) 878-2897
Ft. Eustis, VA 23604   Helen O. Hearn, Libn.

U.S. ARMY - RESEARCH AND TECHNOLOGY LABS (AVRADCOM) - APPLIED
    TECH. LABORATORY - TECHNICAL LIB.
                                              Phone: (804) 878-2963
Ft. Eustis, VA 23604   Virginia Kurbjun, Libn.

U.S. ARMY HOSPITALS - KENNER ARMY HOSPITAL - MEDICAL LIBRARY
                                              Phone: (804) 734-1339
Ft. Lee, VA 23801   Betty K. Lewis, Libn.

U.S. ARMY - LOGISTICS LIBRARY
Bunker Hall   Phone: (703) 734-1797
Ft. Lee, VA 23801   Raymon Trisdale, Chf.

GEOGRAPHIC

CASEMATE MUSEUM - LIBRARY
Box 341
Phone: (804) 727-3935
Ft. Monroe, VA 23651
R. Cody Phillips, Musm.Cur.

U.S. ARMY - TRAINING AND DOCTRINE COMMAND - TECHNICAL LIBRARY
Bldg. 133
Phone: (804) 727-2821
Ft. Monroe, VA 23651
Frances M. Doyle, Supv.Libn.

MONROE (James) MUSEUM AND MEMORIAL LIBRARY
908 Charles St.
Phone: (703) 373-8426
Fredericksburg, VA 22401
Donald W. Baldwin, Chm., Bd. of Regt.

U.S. NATL. PARK SERVICE - FREDERICKSBURG & SPOTSYLVANIA NATL. MILITARY PARK - LIBRARY
Box 679
Phone: (703) 373-4461
Fredericksburg, VA 22401
Robert K. Krick, Chf.Hist.

WASHINGTON (Mary) HOSPITAL - LIBRARY
2300 Fall Hill Ave.
Phone: (703) 373-4110
Fredericksburg, VA 22401
Joan S. Bulley, Dir. of Lib.Serv.

VIRGINIA INSTITUTE OF MARINE SCIENCE LIBRARY
Phone: (804) 642-2111
Gloucester Point, VA 23062
Susan O. Barrick, Libn.

HAMPTON GENERAL HOSPITAL - MEDICAL LIBRARY
3120 Victoria Blvd.
Phone: (703) 722-7921
Hampton, VA 23669
Minette Brooks, Med.Libn.

HAMPTON INSTITUTE - COLLIS P. HUNTINGTON MEMORIAL LIBRARY
Phone: (804) 727-5371
Hampton, VA 23668
Jason C. Grant, III, Dir.

U.S. NASA - LANGLEY RESEARCH CENTER - TECHNICAL LIBRARY MS 185 *
Phone: (804) 827-2786
Hampton, VA 23665
Jane S. Hess, Hd., Tech.Lib.Br.

U.S. VETERANS ADMINISTRATION (VA-Hampton) - MEDICAL CENTER LIBRARY
Phone: (804) 722-9961
Hampton, VA 23667
M. Eileen Hickey, Chf., Lib.Serv.

U.S. NATL. PARK SERVICE - BOOKER T. WASHINGTON NATL. MONUMENT - LIBRARY
Rte. 1, Box 195
Phone: (703) 721-2094
Hardy, VA 24101
Bill Wilcox, Chf., Interp.

EASTERN MENNONITE COLLEGE - MENNO SIMONS HISTORICAL LIBRARY AND ARCHIVES
Phone: (703) 433-2771
Harrisonburg, VA 22801
Grace Showalter, Libn.

HARRISONBURG-ROCKINGHAM HISTORICAL SOCIETY AND MUSEUM - JOHN W. WAYLAND LIBRARY
301 S. Main St.
Box 1141
Phone: (703) 434-4762
Harrisonburg, VA 22801
Julia A. Drinkard, Info.Dir.

ROCKINGHAM MEMORIAL HOSPITAL - HEALTH SCIENCES LIBRARY
738 South Mason St.
Phone: (703) 433-8311
Harrisonburg, VA 22801
Ilene N. Smith, Med.Libn.

HOLLINS COLLEGE - MUSIC DEPARTMENT - ERICH RATH LIBRARY - LISTENING CENTER
Phone: (703) 362-6511
Hollins College, VA 24020
John Diercks, Chm.

AMERICAN BRANDS, INC. - AMERICAN TOBACCO COMPANY - DEPARTMENT OF RESEARCH & DEVELOPMENT LIBRARY
Box 899
Phone: (804) 748-4561
Hopewell, VA 23860
Dorothy D. Robben, Supv., Lib. & Rec.

MARY BALL WASHINGTON MUSEUM AND LIBRARY, INC.
Box 97
Phone: (804) 462-7280
Lancaster, VA 22503
Ann Lewis Burrows, Exec.Dir.

U.S. AIR FORCE BASE - LANGLEY BASE LIBRARY
FL 4800
Phone: (804) 764-3078
Langley AFB, VA 23665
David A.L. Smith, Libn.

U.S. AIR FORCE - TACTICAL AIR COMMAND - LANGLEY BASE LIBRARY
Phone: (804) 764-3319
Langley AFB, VA 23665
David A.L. Smith, Chf.Libn.

HISTORIC LEXINGTON FOUNDATION - GARLAND GRAY CENTER FOR JACKSON STUDIES
Stonewall Jackson House
8 E. Washington St.
Lexington, VA 24450
Barbara L. Crawford, Act.Dir.

MARSHALL (George C.) RESEARCH FOUNDATION - GEORGE C. MARSHALL RESEARCH LIBRARY
Box 920
Phone: (703) 463-7103
Lexington, VA 24450
Dr. Fred L. Hadsel, Dir.

ROCKBRIDGE HISTORICAL SOCIETY - LIBRARY/ARCHIVES
101 E. Washington
Phone: (703) 911-1352
Lexington, VA 24450
Charles W. Turner, Libn.

VIRGINIA MILITARY INSTITUTE - PRESTON LIBRARY
Phone: (703) 463-6228
Lexington, VA 24450
James E. Gaines, Hd.Libn.

WASHINGTON & LEE UNIVERSITY - LAW LIBRARY
Lewis Hall
Phone: (703) 463-3157
Lexington, VA 24450
Sarah K. Wiant, Dir.

GUNSTON HALL PLANTATION - HOUSE MUSEUM - LIBRARY
Phone: (703) 550-9220
Lorton, VA 22079
Bennie Brown, Jr., Libn.

PETTIT'S MUSEUM OF MOTORING MEMORIES - LIBRARY
Box 445
Louisa, VA 23093

BABCOCK AND WILCOX COMPANY - NUCLEAR POWER GENERATION DIVISION - LIBRARY
3315 Old Forest Rd.
Phone: (804) 384-5111
Lynchburg, VA 24501
Ruth H. Johnson, Tech.Libn.

LYNCHBURG TRAINING SCHOOL AND HOSPITAL - PROFESSIONAL LIBRARY *
Box 1098
Phone: (804) 528-6171
Lynchburg, VA 24505
Virginia White, Libn.

VIRGINIA BAPTIST HOSPITAL - BARKSDALE MEDICAL LIBRARY AND SCHOOL OF NURSING LIBRARY
3300 Rivermont Ave.
Phone: (804) 384-4608
Lynchburg, VA 24503
Anne M. Nurmi, Libn.

BDM CORPORATION - CORPORATE LIBRARY
7915 Jones Branch Dr.
Phone: (703) 821-5181
McLean, VA 22102
Dana D. Mallett, Corp.Libn.

DECISIONS AND DESIGNS, INC. - LIBRARY
8400 Westpark Dr., Suite 600
Box 907
Phone: (703) 821-2828
McLean, VA 22101
Vicki Holcomb, Libn.

GENERAL RESEARCH CORPORATION - LIBRARY
Westgate Research Pk.
Phone: (703) 893-5900
McLean, VA 22102
Patricia M. Wolf, Dir.

JRB ASSOCIATES, INC. - OCCUPATIONAL HEALTH & SAFETY LIBRARY
8400 Westpark Dr.
Phone: (703) 827-8108
McLean, VA 22102
Madeleine Babb, Libn.

MITRE CORPORATION - LIBRARY
1820 Dolley Madison Blvd.
Phone: (703) 827-6481
McLean, VA 22102
Paula M. Strain, Mgr., Info.Serv.

PLANNING RESEARCH CORPORATION - LIBRARY SERVICES DEPARTMENT
7600 Old Springhouse Rd.
Phone: (703) 893-1800
McLean, VA 22101
Lura Ann Dillard, Mgr.Lib.Serv.Dept.

PRC VOORHEES - LIBRARY
7798 Old Springhouse Rd.
Phone: (703) 893-4310
McLean, VA 22102
Sally Mason, Lib.Res.Asst.

QUEST RESEARCH CORPORATION - LIBRARY
6858 Old Dominion Dr.   Phone: (703) 821-3200
McLean, VA 22101   Gay Takakoshi, Libn.

SAN MARTIN SOCIETY OF WASHINGTON, DC - INFORMATION CENTER
1128 Balls Hill Rd.   Phone: (703) 356-3055
McLean, VA 22101   Dr. Christian Garcia-Godoy, Pres.

SCIENCE APPLICATIONS, INC. - INFORMATION CENTER
1710 Goodridge Dr.
Box 1303   Phone: (703) 821-4300
McLean, VA 22102   John W. Crabbe, Dir. of Info.Serv.

TRW, INC. - DEFENSE & SPACE SYSTEMS GROUP - TECHNICAL LIBRARY †
7600 Colshire Dr.   Phone: (703) 734-6243
McLean, VA 22102   Mary Ronan-Clark, Lib.Mgr.

TRW INC. - ENERGY SYSTEMS PLANNING DIVISION - LIBRARY
8301 Greensboro Dr.   Phone: (703) 734-6558
McLean, VA 22102   Ellen L. Berman, Mgr.

U.S. NATL. PARK SERVICE - ARLINGTON HOUSE, THE ROBERT E. LEE
   MEMORIAL - LIBRARY
Turkey Run Park   Phone: (703) 557-0613
McLean, VA 22101   Ann Fuqua, Site Mgr.

PRINCE WILLIAM COUNTY SCHOOLS - STAFF LIBRARY
Box 389   Phone: (703) 791-3111
Manassas, VA 22110   Marianna L. Durst, Staff Libn.

U.S. NATL. PARK SERVICE - MANASSAS NATL. BATTLEFIELD PARK -
   LIBRARY *
Box 1830   Phone: (703) 754-7107
Manassas, VA 22110   R. Brien Varnardo, Pk.Supt.

SOUTHWESTERN STATE HOSPITAL - PROFESSIONAL LIBRARY
Box 670   Phone: (703) 783-3171
Marion, VA 24354   Kathleen G. Overbay, Dir., Lib.Serv.

MEMORIAL HOSPITAL OF MARTINSVILLE - MEDICAL LIBRARY
Commonwealth Blvd.   Phone: (703) 632-2911
Martinsville, VA 24112   Mary Alice Sherrard, Libn.

NATIONAL SPORTING LIBRARY, INC.
Box 1335   Phone: (703) 687-6542
Middleburg, VA 22117   Judith Ozment, Libn.

AMERICAN HORTICULTURAL SOCIETY - HAROLD B. TUKEY MEMORIAL
   LIBRARY
Natl. Center for American Horticulture   Phone: (703) 768-5700
Mount Vernon, VA 22121   Jane Steffey, Dir., Adv.Serv.

MOUNT VERNON LADIES' ASSOCIATION OF THE UNION - RESEARCH AND
   REFERENCE LIBRARY
                                         Phone: (703) 780-2000
Mount Vernon, VA 22121   Ellen McCallister, Libn.

COLLEGE OF WILLIAM AND MARY - VIRGINIA ASSOCIATED RESEARCH
   CAMPUS LIBRARY
12070 Jefferson Ave.   Phone: (804) 877-9231
Newport News, VA 23606   Nancy S. Harris, Libn.

MARINERS MUSEUM - LIBRARY
                                         Phone: (804) 595-0368
Newport News, VA 23606   Ardie L. Kelly, Libn.

NEWPORT NEWS DAILY PRESS, INC. - LIBRARY
7505 Warwick Blvd.
Box 746   Phone: (804) 244-8421
Newport News, VA 23607   Theresa M. Hammond, Dir.Lib.Serv.

NEWPORT NEWS SHIPBUILDING AND DRY DOCK COMPANY - LIBRARY
   SERVICES DEPARTMENT
                                         Phone: (804) 380-2610
Newport News, VA 23607   D.E. Rawls, Lib.Supv.

RIVERSIDE HOSPITAL - HEALTH SCIENCES LIBRARY
J. Clyde Morris Blvd.   Phone: (804) 599-2175
Newport News, VA 23601   Peggy Rogers, Med.Libn.

SCHUYLER TECHNICAL LIBRARY
615 Brandywine Dr.   Phone: (804) 877-5860
Newport News, VA 23602   Gilbert S. Bahn, Hd.

U.S. ARMY TRANSPORTATION - TECHNICAL INFORMATION AND RESEARCH
   CENTER
Ft. Eustis   Phone: (804) 878-5563
Newport News, VA 23604   Janelle S. Williams, Libn.

WAR MEMORIAL MUSEUM OF VIRGINIA - RESEARCH LIBRARY
9285 Warwick Blvd.   Phone: (804) 247-8523
Newport News, VA 23607   Eliza E. Embrey, Libn.

CHRYSLER MUSEUM - ART REFERENCE LIBRARY
Olney Rd. & Mowbray Arch   Phone: (804) 622-1211
Norfolk, VA 23510   Amy Navratil Ciccone, Libn.

DE PAUL HOSPITAL - DR. HENRY BOONE MEMORIAL LIBRARY
Kingsley Ln. & Granby St.   Phone: (804) 489-5270
Norfolk, VA 23505   Ramona C. Parrish, Libn.

DE PAUL HOSPITAL - SCHOOL OF NURSING LIBRARY
150 Kingsley Ln.   Phone: (804) 489-5386
Norfolk, VA 23505   Elinor B. Arsic, Libn.

EASTERN VIRGINIA MEDICAL SCHOOL - MOORMAN MEMORIAL LIBRARY
700 Olney Rd., Box 1980   Phone: (804) 446-5845
Norfolk, VA 23501   Anne Cramer, Dir.

MAC ARTHUR (General Douglas) MEMORIAL - LIBRARY AND ARCHIVES
One MacArthur Sq.   Phone: (804) 441-2256
Norfolk, VA 23510   Lyman H. Hammond, Jr., Dir.

NORFOLK BOTANICAL GARDENS - LIBRARY
Airport Rd.   Phone: (804) 855-0194
Norfolk, VA 23518   Ada M. Washington, Libn./Ck.

NORFOLK AND PORTSMOUTH BAR ASSOCIATION - LAW LIBRARY
1105 Virginia National Bank Bldg.   Phone: (804) 622-3152
Norfolk, VA 23510   William J. Davis, Exec.Dir.

NORFOLK PUBLIC LIBRARY - SARGEANT MEMORIAL ROOM
301 City Hall Ave.
Norfolk, VA 23510   Lucile B. Portlock, Hd.

NORFOLK STATE COLLEGE - W.K. KELLOGG SOCIAL SCIENCE RESEARCH
   CENTER - LIBRARY
2401 Corprew Ave.   Phone: (804) 623-8435
Norfolk, VA 23504   Angela Perkins

U.S. ARMED FORCES STAFF COLLEGE - LIBRARY
7800 Hampton Blvd.   Phone: (804) 444-5155
Norfolk, VA 23511   Lois V. Leach, Libn.

U.S. NAVY - COMMAND OPERATIONAL TEST AND EVALUATION FORCE -
   TECHNICAL AND PROFESSIONAL LIBRARY
U.S. Naval Station   Phone: (804) 444-5619
Norfolk, VA 23511   Mildred W. Smith, Hd.

U.S. NAVY - FLEET ANTI-SUBMARINE WARFARE TRAINING CENTER,
   ATLANTIC - TACTICAL LIBRARY
                                         Phone: (703) 444-4026
Norfolk, VA 23511   Elizabeth Evans, Libn.

U.S. NAVY - NAVAL AMPHIBIOUS SCHOOL - JOHN SIDNEY MC CAIN
   AMPHIBIOUS WARFARE LIBRARY
Bldg. 3504   Phone: (804) 464-7467
Norfolk, VA 23521   Carolyn G. Jones, Dir., Lib.Serv.

U.S. NAVY - SCHOOL OF MUSIC - REFERENCE LIBRARY
NAVPHI Base, Little Creek   Phone: (703) 464-7511
Norfolk, VA 23521

VIRGINIA NATIONAL BANK - LIBRARY
One Commercial Pl.
Box 600   Phone: (804) 441-4419
Norfolk, VA 23501   June E. Smink, Libn.

GEOGRAPHIC

VIRGINIAN-PILOT & LEDGER-STAR - LIBRARY
150 W. Brambleton Ave.   Phone: (804) 446-2242
Norfolk, VA 23510   Ann Kinken Johnson, Hd.Libn.

AMERICAN WORK HORSE MUSEUM - LIBRARY
                                          Phone: (703) 338-6290
Paeonian Springs, VA 22129   Frank Joy Hopkins, Chf.Libn.

ALLIED CORPORATION - FIBERS & PLASTICS COMPANY - TECHNICAL
    CENTER LIBRARY
Box 31   Phone: (804) 520-3617
Petersburg, VA 23803   Mrs. R.P. Murphy, Libn.

CENTRAL STATE HOSPITAL - HEALTH SCIENCES LIBRARY
Box 4030   Phone: (804) 861-7517
Petersburg, VA 23803   Mr. P.D. Upadhyaya, Med.Libn.

PETERSBURG GENERAL HOSPITAL - MEDICAL LIBRARY MEDIA SERVICES
801 S. Adams St.   Phone: (804) 732-7220
Petersburg, VA 23803   Mary Grace H. Brown, Med.Libn./Media Serv.Dir.

U.S. NATL. PARK SERVICE - PETERSBURG NATL. BATTLEFIELD - LIBRARY
Box 549   Phone: (804) 732-3531
Petersburg, VA 23803

VIRGINIA STATE UNIVERSITY - JOHNSTON MEMORIAL LIBRARY
Box JJ   Phone: (804) 520-6171
Petersburg, VA 23803   Catherine V. Bland, Dir., Lib.Serv.

MARYVIEW HOSPITAL - DOCTORS' LIBRARY
3636 High St.   Phone: (804) 398-2331
Portsmouth, VA 23707   Peggy A. Zultanky, Libn.

PORTSMOUTH GENERAL HOSPITAL - MEDICAL LIBRARY
900 Leckie St.   Phone: (804) 398-4000
Portsmouth, VA 23704   Robie Hammond, Sec.

PORTSMOUTH PUBLIC LIBRARY - LOCAL HISTORY ROOM
601 Court St.   Phone: (804) 393-8501
Portsmouth, VA 23704   Octavia Parrish, Lib.Asst.

U.S. NAVY - NAVAL REGIONAL MEDICAL CENTER (Portsmouth) - MEDICAL
    LIBRARY
                                          Phone: (804) 398-5386
Portsmouth, VA 23708   Suad Jones, Med.Libn.

U.S. NAVY - NAVAL SHIPYARD (Norfolk) - TECHNICAL LIBRARY
Code 202.3, Bldg. 29, 2nd Fl.   Phone: (703) 393-5580
Portsmouth, VA 23709   Ilene M. Wagner, Tech.Libn.

VIRGINIA CHEMICALS, INC. - LIBRARY
3340 W. Norfolk Rd.   Phone: (703) 483-7213
Portsmouth, VA 23703   Barbara Smith, Libn.

U.S. DEPT. OF JUSTICE - FEDERAL BUREAU OF INVESTIGATION - F.B.I.
    ACADEMY - LEARNING RESOURCE CENTER
                                          Phone: (703) 640-6131
Quantico, VA 22135   Edward D. Kenney, Libn.

U.S. MARINE CORPS - EDUCATION CENTER - JAMES CARSON
    BRECKINRIDGE LIBRARY & AMPHIBIOUS WARFARE RESEARCH FACILITY
Marine Corps Development &
Education Command   Phone: (703) 640-2248
Quantico, VA 22134   David C. Brown, Adm.Libn.

U.S. NAVY - NAVAL REGIONAL MEDICAL CENTER (Quantico) - MEDICAL
    LIBRARY
                                          Phone: (703) 640-2595
Quantico, VA 22035   Marjorie L. Starr, Libn.

AMERICAN ALLIANCE FOR HEALTH, PHYSICAL EDUCATION, RECREATION &
    DANCE - INFORMATION CENTER FOR THE HANDICAPPED
1900 Association Dr.   Phone: (202) 833-5547
Reston, VA 22091   Julian U. Stein, Dir.

ERIC CLEARINGHOUSE ON HANDICAPPED & GIFTED CHILDREN - CEC
    INFORMATION SERVICES
Council for Exceptional Children
1920 Association Dr.   Phone: (703) 620-3660
Reston, VA 22091   Lynn Smarte, Asst.Dir./User Serv.

HARDWOOD PLYWOOD MANUFACTURERS ASSOCIATION - LIBRARY
1825 Michael Faraday Dr.
Box 2789   Phone: (703) 435-2900
Reston, VA 22090   Clark E. McDonald, Mng.Dir.

NATIONAL COUNCIL OF TEACHERS OF MATHEMATICS - TEACHER/
    LEARNING CENTER
1906 Association Dr.   Phone: (703) 620-9840
Reston, VA 22091   Joseph R. Caravella, Dir., Prof.Serv.

U.S. GEOLOGICAL SURVEY - LIBRARY
National Ctr., Mail Stop 950   Phone: (703) 860-6671
Reston, VA 22092   George H. Goodwin, Jr., Chf.Libn.

U.S. GEOLOGICAL SURVEY - NATL. CARTOGRAPHIC INFORMATION CENTER
    (NCIC)
507 National Center   Phone: (703) 860-6045
Reston, VA 22092   Alan R. Stevens, Act.Chf.

U.S. GEOLOGICAL SURVEY - WATER RESOURCES DIVISION - NATL. WATER
    DATA STORAGE & RETRIEVAL SYSTEM
National Ctr., Mail Stop 437   Phone: (703) 860-6879
Reston, VA 22092   Philip Cohen, Chf. Hydrologist

BLUE CROSS AND BLUE SHIELD OF VIRGINIA - PLANS LIBRARY
2015 Staples Mill Rd.
Box 27401   Phone: (804) 359-7177
Richmond, VA 23279   Frank Johns, Libn.

BRAILLE CIRCULATING LIBRARY, INC.
2700 Stuart Ave.   Phone: (804) 359-3743
Richmond, VA 23220   Robert N. Gordon, Exec.Dir.

CONFEDERATE MEMORIAL LITERARY SOCIETY - MUSEUM OF THE
    CONFEDERACY - ELEANOR S. BROCKENBROUGH LIBRARY
1201 E. Clay St.   Phone: (804) 649-1861
Richmond, VA 23219   Edward D.C. Campbell, Jr., Dir.

DU PONT DE NEMOURS (E.I.) & COMPANY, INC. - TECHNICAL LIBRARY
    SYSTEM - SPRUANCE RESEARCH LABORATORY BRANCH
Box 27001
Spunbonded Products, Nomex Division   Phone: (804) 743-2616
Richmond, VA 23261   Carolyn K. Markwood, Libn.

FEDERAL RESERVE BANK OF RICHMOND - RESEARCH LIBRARY
Box 27622   Phone: (804) 643-1250
Richmond, VA 23261   Ruth M.E. Cannon, Libn.

FIRST BAPTIST CHURCH OF RICHMOND - LIBRARY †
Monument & Boulevard   Phone: (804) 355-8637
Richmond, VA 23220

HUNTON & WILLIAMS - LAW LIBRARY
707 E. Main St.
Box 1535   Phone: (804) 788-8245
Richmond, VA 23212   Mr. Beverley Butler, Hd.Libn.

MC GUIRE, WOODS AND BATTLE - LAW LIBRARY
1400 Ross Bldg.   Phone: (804) 644-4131
Richmond, VA 23219   Ann B. Roberts, Libn.

PHILIP MORRIS, U.S.A. - RESEARCH CENTER LIBRARY
Box 26583   Phone: (804) 271-2877
Richmond, VA 23261   Marian Z. DeBardeleben, Res.Libn.

REVEILLE UNITED METHODIST CHURCH - REVEILLE MEMORIAL LIBRARY
4200 Cary Street Rd.   Phone: (804) 359-6041
Richmond, VA 23221   Mrs. W. Gordon Binns, Libn.

REYNOLDS METALS COMPANY - CORPORATE INFORMATION CENTER
6601 W. Broad St.   Phone: (804) 281-2804
Richmond, VA 23261   Kathie P. Anderson, Corp.Libn.

REYNOLDS METALS COMPANY - PACKAGING DIVISION - TECHNOLOGY
    LIBRARY
2101 Reymet Rd.   Phone: (804) 743-6649
Richmond, VA 23234   Lorna K. Joyner, Libn.

REYNOLDS METALS COMPANY - TECHNICAL INFORMATION SERVICES
LIBRARY
Fourth & Canal Sts.
Box 27003
Phone: (804) 788-7409
Richmond, VA 23261
Mary R. Harris, Libn.

RICHMOND MEMORIAL HOSPITAL - MEDICAL AND NURSING SCHOOL
LIBRARY
1300 Westwood Ave.
Phone: (804) 359-6961
Richmond, VA 23227
Lynne Turman, Libn.

RICHMOND NEWSPAPERS, INC. - LIBRARY
333 E. Grace St.
Phone: (703) 649-6283
Richmond, VA 23213
Mary Morris Watt, Libn.

RICHMOND PUBLIC LIBRARY - ART AND MUSIC DEPARTMENT †
101 E. Franklin St.
Phone: (804) 780-4740
Richmond, VA 23219
Myra L. Kight, Hd.

RICHMOND PUBLIC LIBRARY - BUSINESS, SCIENCE & TECHNOLOGY
DEPARTMENT †
101 E. Franklin St.
Phone: (804) 780-8223
Richmond, VA 23219
Elizabeth Engle Askew, Sr.Libn.

RICHMOND PUBLIC SCHOOLS - CURRICULUM MATERIALS CENTER *
301 N. Ninth St.
Phone: (804) 780-5370
Richmond, VA 23219
Delores Z. Pretlow, Libn.

ST. MARY'S HOSPITAL - HEALTH SCIENCES LIBRARY
5801 Bremo Rd.
Phone: (804) 281-8247
Richmond, VA 23229
Sandra Heath Parham, Libn.

ST. PAUL'S EPISCOPAL CHURCH - LIBRARY
815 E. Grace St.
Phone: (703) 643-3589
Richmond, VA 23219
Jean LeRoy, Lib.Cons.

SOUTHERN BAPTIST CONVENTION - FOREIGN MISSION BOARD - JENKINS
MEMORIAL RESEARCH CENTER
3806 Monument Ave.
Phone: (804) 353-0151
Richmond, VA 23230

UNION THEOLOGICAL SEMINARY IN VIRGINIA - LIBRARY
3401 Brook Rd.
Phone: (804) 355-0671
Richmond, VA 23227
Dr. John B. Trotti, Libn.

UNITED DAUGHTERS OF THE CONFEDERACY - CAROLINE MERIWETHER
GOODLETT LIBRARY
U.D.C. Headquarters Bldg.
328 North Blvd.
Phone: (804) 355-1636
Richmond, VA 23220
Dorothy L. Barrett, Chm., Lib.Comm.

U.S. COURT OF APPEALS, 4TH CIRCUIT - LIBRARY
U.S. Courthouse, Rm. 424
Tenth & Main Sts.
Phone: (703) 782-2291
Richmond, VA 23219
Iris C. Stevenson, Chf.Libn.

U.S. DEFENSE LOGISTICS AGENCY - DEFENSE GENERAL SUPPLY CENTER -
CENTER LIBRARY
Phone: (804) 275-3215
Richmond, VA 23297
Yvonne H. Oakley, Ctr.Libn.

U.S. DEPT. OF COMMERCE - INTERNATIONAL TRADE ADMINISTRATION -
RICHMOND DISTRICT OFFICE LIBRARY
8010 Federal Bldg.
400 N. 8th St.
Phone: (804) 782-2246
Richmond, VA 23240
Philip A. Ouzts, Dir.

U.S. NATL. PARK SERVICE - RICHMOND NATL. BATTLEFIELD PARK -
LIBRARY
3215 E. Broad St.
Phone: (804) 226-1981
Richmond, VA 23223
Patrice Ferrell, Pk. Ranger

U.S. VETERANS ADMINISTRATION (VA-Richmond) - HOSPITAL LIBRARY
1201 Broad Rock Rd.
Phone: (804) 231-9011
Richmond, VA 23249
Bernice B. Walker, Med.Libn.

UNITED VIRGINIA BANK - INFORMATION CENTER
Box 26665
Phone: (804) 782-7452
Richmond, VA 23261
Marion L. Hart, AVP-Info.Serv.

UNIVERSITY OF RICHMOND - MUSIC LIBRARY
Phone: (804) 285-6398
Richmond, VA 23173
Bonlyn G. Hall, Libn.

VALENTINE MUSEUM - LIBRARY
1015 E. Clay St.
Phone: (804) 649-0711
Richmond, VA 23219
Sarah Shields, Cur.

VIRGINIA BAPTIST HISTORICAL SOCIETY - LIBRARY
University of Richmond
Box 34
Phone: (804) 285-6324
Richmond, VA 23173
Fred Anderson, Exec.Dir.

VIRGINIA COMMONWEALTH UNIVERSITY - JAMES BRANCH CABELL
LIBRARY - SPECIAL COLLECTIONS
901 Park Ave.
Phone: (804) 257-1108
Richmond, VA 23284
Daniel A. Yanchisin, Spec.Coll.Libn.

VIRGINIA COMMONWEALTH UNIVERSITY - MEDICAL COLLEGE OF
VIRGINIA - TOMPKINS-MC CAW LIBRARY
MCV Sta., Box 667
Phone: (804) 786-0823
Richmond, VA 23298
J. Craig McLean, Libn.

VIRGINIA ELECTRIC & POWER COMPANY - LIBRARY
One James River Plaza
Box 26666
Phone: (804) 771-3659
Richmond, VA 23261
Ann B. Flanagan, Libn.

VIRGINIA HISTORICAL SOCIETY - LIBRARY
428 North Blvd.
Phone: (804) 358-4901
Richmond, VA 23220
Paul C. Nagel, Dir.

VIRGINIA MUSEUM OF FINE ARTS - LIBRARY
Boulevard & Grove Ave.
Box 7260
Phone: (804) 257-0827
Richmond, VA 23221
Betty A. Stacy, Libn.

VIRGINIA STATE DEPARTMENT OF EDUCATION - DIVISION OF
MANAGEMENT INFORMATION SERVICES - LIBRARY
Box 6Q
Phone: (804) 786-2068
Richmond, VA 23216
Dr. Jan L. Harris, Supv.

VIRGINIA STATE DEPARTMENT OF GENERAL SERVICES - DIVISION OF
CONSOLIDATED LABORATORY SERVICES LIBRARY
1 N. 14th St., Rm. 274
Richmond, VA 23219

VIRGINIA STATE DEPARTMENT OF TRANSPORTATION SAFETY - FILM
LIBRARY
300 Turner Rd.
Phone: (804) 276-9600
Richmond, VA 23225
Nancy Arrowood, Film Libn.

VIRGINIA STATE DIVISION OF JUSTICE AND CRIME PREVENTION -
LIBRARY
8501 Mayland Dr.
Phone: (804) 281-9276
Richmond, VA 23229
Stephen E. Squire, Libn.

VIRGINIA STATE DIVISION OF LEGISLATIVE SERVICES - REFERENCE
LIBRARY
State Capitol, Box 3-AG
Phone: (804) 786-1861
Richmond, VA 23208

VIRGINIA STATE LAW LIBRARY
1101 E. Broad St.
Phone: (804) 786-2075
Richmond, VA 23219
Marjorie D. Kirtley, Law Libn.

VIRGINIA STATE LIBRARY
Capitol St.
Phone: (804) 786-8929
Richmond, VA 23219
Donald Haynes, State Libn.

VIRGINIA STATE LIBRARY FOR THE VISUALLY AND PHYSICALLY
HANDICAPPED
1901 Roane St.
Phone: (804) 786-8016
Richmond, VA 23222
Marylu Gates, Act.Libn.

VIRGINIA STATE OFFICE OF EMERGENCY & ENERGY SERVICES - ENERGY
INFORMATION AND SERVICES CENTER
310 Turner Rd.
Phone: (804) 745-3245
Richmond, VA 23225
Kathy Erickson, Supv.

GEOGRAPHIC

VIRGINIA STATE WATER CONTROL BOARD - LIBRARY
2111 N. Hamilton St.
Box 11143   Phone: (804) 257-6340
Richmond, VA 23230   Pat Vanderland

VIRGINIA UNION UNIVERSITY - WILLIAM J. CLARK LIBRARY
1500 N. Lombardy St.   Phone: (804) 359-9331
Richmond, VA 23220   Verdelle V. Bradley, Libn.

HAYES, SEAY, MATTERN & MATTERN - TECHNICAL LIBRARY
1315 Franklin Rd., S.W.
Box 13446   Phone: (703) 343-6971
Roanoke, VA 24034   Nancy H. Seamans, Libn.

ROANOKE LAW LIBRARY
210 Campbell Ave., S.W.   Phone: (703) 981-2268
Roanoke, VA 24011   Clayne Calhoun, Libn.

ROANOKE MEMORIAL HOSPITALS - MEDICAL LIBRARY
Belleview at Jefferson St.
Box 13367   Phone: (703) 981-7371
Roanoke, VA 24033   Lucy D. Glenn, Chf.Med.Libn.

ROANOKE VALLEY HISTORICAL SOCIETY - LIBRARY
Box 1904   Phone: (703) 344-3418
Roanoke, VA 24018   Nomeka B. Sours, Exec.Sec.

TIMES-WORLD CORPORATION - NEWSPAPER LIBRARY
Box 2491   Phone: (703) 981-3279
Roanoke, VA 24010   Richard Hancock, Libn.

CONSUMER EDUCATION RESOURCE NETWORK (CERN)
1555 Wilson Blvd., Suite 600   Phone: (703) 522-4616
Rosslyn, VA 22209   Anita Simendinger, Info.Sys.Mgr.

LEWIS-GALE HOSPITAL CORPORATION - LEWIS-GALE MEDICAL LIBRARY
1900 Electric Rd.   Phone: (703) 989-4261
Salem, VA 24153   Audrey D. Lachowicz, Med.Libn.

U.S. VETERANS ADMINISTRATION (VA-Salem) - MEDICAL CENTER LIBRARY
                                       Phone: (703) 982-2463
Salem, VA 24153   Jean A. Kennedy, Chf.Libn.

SPOTSYLVANIA HISTORICAL ASSOCIATION, INC. - RESEARCH MUSEUM
  AND LIBRARY
Court House, Box 64   Phone: (703) 582-5672
Spotsylvania, VA 22553   Frances L.N. Waller, Libn.

ENSCO, INC. - TECHNICAL LIBRARY
5408 A Port Royal Rd.   Phone: (703) 321-9000
Springfield, VA 22151   Sue E. Littlepage, Res.Libn.

LOGETRONICS, INC. - INFORMATION CENTER *
7001 Loisdale Rd.   Phone: (703) 971-1400
Springfield, VA 22150   Janet Duckworth, Libn.

U.S. DEPT. OF COMMERCE - NATL. TECHNICAL INFORMATION SERVICE
5285 Port Royal Rd.   Phone: (703) 487-4600
Springfield, VA 22161

WASHINGTON GAS LIGHT COMPANY - LIBRARY
6801 Industrial Rd.   Phone: (703) 750-4440
Springfield, VA 22151   Marc L. Davis, Libn.

WESTERN STATE HOSPITAL - MEDICAL LIBRARY
Box 2500   Phone: (703) 885-9387
Staunton, VA 24401   Richard D. Wills, Libn.

WILSON (Woodrow) BIRTHPLACE FOUNDATION, INC. - RESEARCH LIBRARY
  & ARCHIVES
20 N. Coalter St.
Box 24   Phone: (703) 885-0897
Staunton, VA 24401   Dr. Katharine L. Brown, Exec.Dir.

LEE (Robert E.) MEMORIAL ASSOCIATION, INC. - JESSIE BALL DU PONT
  MEMORIAL LIBRARY
Stratford Hall Plantation   Phone: (804) 493-8572
Stratford, VA 22558   Dr. Ralph Draughon, Jr., Libn./Hist.

OBICI (Louise) MEMORIAL HOSPITAL - LIBRARY
Box 1100   Phone: (804) 539-1511
Suffolk, VA 23434   Claudia J. Byers, RRA, Dir.Med.Rec.

AMERICAN SYMPHONY ORCHESTRA LEAGUE - LIBRARY
Box 669   Phone: (703) 281-1230
Vienna, VA 22180   Catherine French, Chf.Exec.Off.

BOEING COMPUTER SERVICES COMPANY - TECHNICAL LIBRARY
7980 Gallows Ct.   Phone: (703) 821-6062
Vienna, VA 22180   Cheryl Gore, Lib.Mgr.

PAGE COMMUNICATIONS ENGINEERS, INC. - INFORMATION CENTER
801 Follin Ln.   Phone: (703) 938-4000
Vienna, VA 22180   Eileen C. Durham, Libn.

ASSOCIATION FOR RESEARCH AND ENLIGHTENMENT - ARE BRAILLE
  LIBRARY
Box 595   Phone: (804) 428-3588
Virginia Beach, VA 23451   Alma Crovatt, Libn.

ASSOCIATION FOR RESEARCH AND ENLIGHTENMENT - EDGAR CAYCE
  FOUNDATION - LIBRARY
Box 595   Phone: (804) 428-3588
Virginia Beach, VA 23451   Stephen Jordan, Lib.Mgr.

VIRGINIA BEACH PUBLIC LIBRARY SYSTEM - MUNICIPAL REFERENCE
  LIBRARY
Municipal Ctr.   Phone: (804) 427-4644
Virginia Beach, VA 23456   Kathleen G. Hevey, Municipal Ref.Coord.

VIRGINIA BEACH PUBLIC LIBRARY SYSTEM - ROBERT S. WAHAB, JR.
  PUBLIC LAW LIBRARY
Municipal Ctr.   Phone: (804) 427-4419
Virginia Beach, VA 23456   Robert P. Miller, Jr., Law Lib.Coord.

VIRGINIA STATE TRUCK AND ORNAMENTALS RESEARCH STATION -
  LIBRARY
1444 Diamond Springs Rd.   Phone: (804) 464-3528
Virginia Beach, VA 23455   Amy DesRoches, Libn.

U.S. NASA - WALLOPS FLIGHT CENTER - TECHNICAL LIBRARY
                                       Phone: (804) 824-3411
Wallops Island, VA 23337   Jane N. Foster, Adm.Spec.

INTERTECHNOLOGY/SOLAR CORPORATION - LIBRARY *
100 Main St.   Phone: (703) 347-7900
Warrenton, VA 22186   Pamela R. Goetze, Libn.

DU PONT DE NEMOURS (E.I.) & COMPANY, INC. - BENGER LABORATORY -
  LIBRARY
                                       Phone: (703) 949-8141
Waynesboro, VA 22980   Myrtle F. Hanger, Libn.

VIRGINIA STATE DEPARTMENT OF CORRECTIONS - ACADEMY FOR STAFF
  DEVELOPMENT - LIBRARY
500 N. Winchester Ave.
Box 2215   Phone: (703) 943-3141
Waynesboro, VA 22980   Kathryn C. Denney, Libn.

ABBY ALDRICH ROCKEFELLER FOLK ART CENTER - LIBRARY
307 S. England St.
Drawer C   Phone: (804) 229-1000
Williamsburg, VA 23185   Anne Watkins, Registrar/Libn.

BADISCHE CORPORATION - LIBRARY
Drawer D   Phone: (804) 887-6335
Williamsburg, VA 23185   Friederika Groves, Libn.

COLLEGE OF WILLIAM AND MARY - EARL GREGG SWEM LIBRARY
                                       Phone: (804) 253-4405
Williamsburg, VA 23185   Clifford Currie, Libn.

COLLEGE OF WILLIAM AND MARY - MARSHALL-WYTHE LAW LIBRARY
                                       Phone: (804) 253-4680
Williamsburg, VA 23185   Caroline C. Heriot, Law Libn.

COLONIAL WILLIAMSBURG - AUDIO-VISUAL LIBRARY
Phone: (804) 229-1000
Williamsburg, VA 23185   Patricia G. Maccubbin, Chf.Libn.

COLONIAL WILLIAMSBURG - RESEARCH LIBRARY & ARCHIVES
Box C   Phone: (804) 229-1000
Williamsburg, VA 23185   Louise A. Merriam, Libn.

EASTERN STATE HOSPITAL - PROFESSIONAL LIBRARY
Drawer A   Phone: (804) 253-5457
Williamsburg, VA 23185   Barbara Dike, Libn.

INSTITUTE OF EARLY AMERICAN HISTORY AND CULTURE - KELLOCK
    LIBRARY
Box 220   Phone: (804) 229-2771
Williamsburg, VA 23185   Patricia Higgs, Supv.

NATIONAL CENTER FOR STATE COURTS - LIBRARY
300 Newport Ave.   Phone: (804) 253-2000
Williamsburg, VA 23185   Margaret Maes Axtmann, Libn.

SHENANDOAH COLLEGE & CONSERVATORY OF MUSIC - HOWE LIBRARY
Phone: (703) 667-8714
Winchester, VA 22601   Nancy H. Moore, Adm.Libn.

WINCHESTER MEMORIAL HOSPITAL - HEALTH SCIENCES LIBRARY
South Stewart St.   Phone: (703) 662-4121
Winchester, VA 22601   Beth A. Layton, Libn.

U.S. NAVY - NAVAL WEAPONS STATION - LIBRARY
Bldg. 705   Phone: (804) 887-4726
Yorktown, VA 23691   Jacqueline W. Slivka, Libn.

WASHINGTON

WHITE RIVER VALLEY HISTORICAL SOCIETY MUSEUM - LIBRARY
918 H St., S.E.   Phone: (206) 939-2783
Auburn, WA 98002   LaVerna J. Conrad, Libn.

ENI COMPANIES - INFORMATION CENTER
1417 116th Ave. N.E., C-C21611   Phone: (206) 453-7000
Bellevue, WA 98009   Katharine H. Ricklefs, Lib.Techn.

NORTHWEST PULP AND PAPER ASSOCIATION - TECHNICAL INFORMATION
    CENTER
555 116th Ave., N.E., Suite 266
Bellevue, WA 98004

PUGET SOUND POWER AND LIGHT COMPANY LIBRARY
Puget Power Bldg.   Phone: (206) 454-6363
Bellevue, WA 98009   Susan Campbell Ball, Libn.

HUXLEY COLLEGE OF ENVIRONMENTAL STUDIES - ENVIRONMENTAL
    CENTER
ESC 535, Huxley College   Phone: (206) 676-3974
Bellingham, WA 98225

SPIE - THE INTERNATIONAL SOCIETY FOR OPTICAL ENGINEERING -
    LIBRARY
405 Fieldston Rd.
Box 10   Phone: (206) 676-3290
Bellingham, WA 98225   Joseph Yaver, Exec.Dir.

WESTERN WASHINGTON UNIVERSITY - CENTER FOR PACIFIC
    NORTHWEST STUDIES
Bellingham, WA 98225   Dr. James W. Scott, Dir.

WESTERN WASHINGTON UNIVERSITY - DEPARTMENT OF GEOGRAPHY
    AND REGIONAL PLANNING - MAP LIBRARY
Arntzen Hall 101   Phone: (206) 676-3272
Bellingham, WA 98225   Janet Collins, Map Cur.

WHATCOM/ISLAND HEALTH SERVICES - LIBRARY
3201 Ellis St.   Phone: (206) 734-5400
Bellingham, WA 98225   Betty Jo Jensen, Med.Libn.

HAKLUYT MINOR - LIBRARY
9206 N.E. 180th St.   Phone: (206) 485-2124
Bothell, WA 98011   Richard G. McCloskey, Dir.

U.S. NAVY - NAVAL REGIONAL MEDICAL CENTER (Bremerton) - MEDICAL
    LIBRARY
Phone: (206) 478-4269
Bremerton, WA 98314   Jane Easley, Lib.Adm.

WASHINGTON STATE LIBRARY - RAINIER SCHOOL STAFF LIBRARY
Rainier School   Phone: (206) 829-1111
Buckley, WA 98321   Lynn Red, Libn.

CROWN ZELLERBACH CORPORATION - CENTRAL RESEARCH LIBRARY
Phone: (206) 834-4444
Camas, WA 98607   Darlene Olson, Supv.Adm.Serv.

WEYERHAEUSER COMPANY - WESTERN FORESTRY RESEARCH CENTER -
    LIBRARY
Box 420   Phone: (206) 736-8241
Centralia, WA 98531   Donna Loucks, Libn.

LEWIS COUNTY HISTORICAL MUSEUM - LIBRARY
599 N.W. Front St.   Phone: (206) 748-0831
Chehalis, WA 98532   Jill Kangas, Musm.Dir.

LEWIS COUNTY LAW LIBRARY
Box 357   Phone: (206) 748-9121
Chehalis, WA 98532   Jan Draper, Act.Libn.

EASTERN WASHINGTON UNIVERSITY - INSTRUCTIONAL MEDIA CENTER
Phone: (509) 359-2265
Cheney, WA 99004   Jerome S. Donen, Dir.

EASTERN WASHINGTON UNIVERSITY - LIBRARY
Phone: (509) 359-2261
Cheney, WA 99004   Charles H. Baumann, Univ.Libn.

EASTERN WASHINGTON UNIVERSITY - MUSIC LIBRARY
Phone: (509) 359-7843
Cheney, WA 99004   Karen Olson, Hd.

WALLA WALLA COLLEGE - CURRICULUM LIBRARY
Smith Hall   Phone: (509) 527-2221
College Place, WA 99324   Camille Wood, Dir.

U.S. NATL. PARK SERVICE - COULEE DAM NATL. RECREATION AREA - FORT
    SPOKANE VISITOR CENTER *
Star Rte., Box 30   Phone: (509) 725-2715
Davenport, WA 99122   Steve Shrader, District Ranger

CENTRAL WASHINGTON UNIVERSITY - LIBRARY - CURRICULUM
    LABORATORY
Phone: (509) 963-1641
Ellensburg, WA 98926   Ann Donovan, Curriculum Libn.

CENTRAL WASHINGTON UNIVERSITY - LIBRARY DOCUMENTS
    DEPARTMENT
Phone: (509) 963-1541
Ellensburg, WA 98926   Ruth Dahlgren Hartman, Hd.

CENTRAL WASHINGTON UNIVERSITY - MAP LIBRARY
Phone: (509) 963-1541
Ellensburg, WA 98926   Peter Stark, Map Libn.

CENTRAL WASHINGTON UNIVERSITY - MEDIA LIBRARY SERVICES
Bouillon Complex No. 105-107   Phone: (509) 963-2861
Ellensburg, WA 98926   Ann Elizabeth McLean, Coord. Media Serv.

CENTRAL WASHINGTON UNIVERSITY - MUSIC LIBRARY
Phone: (509) 963-1841
Ellensburg, WA 98926   Paul Emmons, Music Libn.

FLUKE (John) MANUFACTURING CO., INC. - LIBRARY
6920 Seaway Blvd.
Everett, WA 98206   Gladys Cloakey, Libn.

GEOGRAPHIC

PROVIDENCE HOSPITAL, EVERETT - HEALTH INFORMATION NETWORK
SERVICES (HINS)
Pacific & Nassau
Box 1067   Phone: (206) 258-7550
Everett, WA 98206   Shirley C. Lewis, Dir.Lib.Serv.

SNOHOMISH COUNTY LAW LIBRARY
County Court House   Phone: (206) 259-5326
Everett, WA 98201   Christine Taylor, Libn.

U.S. AIR FORCE BASE - FAIRCHILD BASE LIBRARY
FL 4620   Phone: (509) 247-5556
Fairchild AFB, WA 99011   Virginia A. Mather, Libn.

U.S. AIR FORCE HOSPITAL - TECHNICAL LIBRARY
USAFH/SGQA   Phone: (509) 247-2763
Fairchild AFB, WA 99011   Connie Forwood, Libn.

WEYERHAEUSER COMPANY - ARCHIVES
33606 30th Ave., S.   Phone: (206) 924-5052
Federal Way, WA 98477   Linda Edgerly, Archv.

FORT LEWIS MILITARY MUSEUM - MUSEUM RESEARCH LIBRARY
Main St., Bldg. 4320   Phone: (206) 967-5524
Fort Lewis, WA 98433   Barbara A. Bower, Dir.

U.S. ARMY POST - FORT LEWIS - LIBRARY SYSTEM
Bldg. 2109   Phone: (206) 967-7736
Fort Lewis, WA 98433   Patricia A. Louderback, Chf.Libn.

WASHINGTON STATE LIBRARY - WESTERN STATE HOSPITAL - STAFF
LIBRARY
                                          Phone: (206) 756-9635
Fort Steilacoom, WA 98494   Sary Taurytzky, Libn.

UNIVERSITY OF WASHINGTON - FRIDAY HARBOR LABORATORIES -
LIBRARY
NJ-22   Phone: (206) 378-2501
Friday Harbor, WA 98250   Thomas D. Moritz, Libn.

LUTHERAN BIBLE INSTITUTE - LIBRARY
Providence Heights   Phone: (206) 392-0400
Issaquah, WA 98027   Rev. Loring Younce, Hd.Libn.

FOURNIER NEWSPAPERS - LIBRARY
600 S. Washington St.
Box 130   Phone: (206) 872-6674
Kent, WA 98031   Frances Wright, Libn.

KENWORTH TRUCK CO. - DIVISION LIBRARY
Box 1000   Phone: (206) 828-5255
Kirkland, WA 98033   Maureen McCrea, Libn.

NORTHWEST COLLEGE OF THE ASSEMBLIES OF GOD - HURST LIBRARY
11102 N.E. 53rd Ave.
Box 579   Phone: (206) 822-8266
Kirkland, WA 98033   Ruth Petty, Libn.

SKAGIT COUNTY HISTORICAL MUSEUM - HISTORICAL REFERENCE
LIBRARY
Box 32   Phone: (206) 466-3365
La Conner, WA 98257   Barbara Cantwell, Libn.

WASHINGTON STATE DEPARTMENT OF NATURAL RESOURCES - DIVISION
OF GEOLOGY AND EARTH RESOURCES - LIBRARY
Bldg One, Row 6
4224 6th Ave., S.E.   Phone: (206) 753-3647
Lacey WA 98503   Connie J. Manson, Libn.

MONTICELLO MEDICAL CENTER - MEDICAL STAFF LIBRARY
Box 638   Phone: (206) 423-5850
Longview, WA 98632   Margaret B. Geering, Coord., Med. Staff Serv.

U.S. FISH & WILDLIFE SERVICE - ABERNATHY SALMON CULTURAL
DEVELOPMENT CENTER - RESEARCH & INFO. CENTER
1440 Abernathy Rd.   Phone: (206) 425-6072
Longview, WA 98632   David A. Leith, Dir.

WASHINGTON STATE LIBRARY - EASTERN STATE HOSPITAL LIBRARY
Box A   Phone: (509) 299-4276
Medical Lake, WA 99022   Neal Van Der Voorn, Libn.

WASHINGTON STATE LIBRARY - LAKELAND VILLAGE BRANCH LIBRARY
Box 200   Phone: (509) 299-5089
Medical Lake, WA 99022   Neal Van Der Voorn, Inst.Serv.Libn.

GRAYS HARBOR COUNTY LAW LIBRARY
Courthouse, 2nd Fl.   Phone: (206) 249-5311
Montesano, WA 98563   E. Urquhart, Libn.

SKAGIT COUNTY LAW LIBRARY †
County Court House, 2nd Fl.   Phone: (206) 336-9313
Mount Vernon, WA 98273   Don Vaught, Libn.

ALIVE FELLOWSHIP OF HARMONIOUS LIVING - LIBRARY
Star Route Box 86   Phone: (206) 376-4755
Olga, WA 98279   Steven Jungerberg, Sec.

STATE CAPITOL HISTORICAL ASSOCIATION - LIBRARY AND PHOTO
ARCHIVES
211 W. 21st Ave.   Phone: (206) 753-2580
Olympia, WA 98501

WASHINGTON STATE ATTORNEY GENERAL'S LIBRARY
Temple Of Justice   Phone: (206) 753-2681
Olympia, WA 98504   Phil Bunker, Law Libn.

WASHINGTON STATE DEPARTMENT OF ECOLOGY - TECHNICAL LIBRARY
                                          Phone: (206) 753-2959
Olympia, WA 98504   Jeanne M. Rensel, Hd.

WASHINGTON STATE DEPARTMENT OF REVENUE - RESEARCH AND
INFORMATION DIVISION - LIBRARY
414 Gen.Adm.Bldg.   Phone: (206) 753-5516
Olympia, WA 98504   Gary O'Neil, Dir. Of Res.

WASHINGTON STATE DEPARTMENT OF TRANSPORTATION - LIBRARY
Highway Administration Bldg.   Phone: (206) 753-2107
Olympia, WA 98504   Barbara Russo, Libn.

WASHINGTON STATE ENERGY OFFICE - LIBRARY
400 E. Union St.   Phone: (206) 754-1369
Olympia, WA 98504   Ginger Alexander, Libn.

WASHINGTON STATE LAW LIBRARY
Temple of Justice   Phone: (206) 753-6525
Olympia, WA 98504   C.E. Bolden, State Law Libn.

WASHINGTON STATE LIBRARY
State Library Bldg.   Phone: (206) 753-5592
Olympia, WA 98504   Roderick G. Swartz, State Libn.

WASHINGTON STATE OFFICE OF SECRETARY OF STATE - DIVISION OF
ARCHIVES AND RECORD MANAGEMENT
Archives & Records Ctr.
12th & Washington   Phone: (206) 753-5467
Olympia, WA 98504   Sidney McAlpin, State Archv.

NORTH OLYMPIC LIBRARY SYSTEM - PORT ANGELES BRANCH - PACIFIC
NORTHWEST ROOM
207 S. Lincoln St.   Phone: (206) 452-9253
Port Angeles, WA 98362   Peggy M. Brady, Hd.Ref.Dept.

U.S. NATL. PARK SERVICE - OLYMPIC NATL. PARK - PIONEER MEMORIAL
MUSEUM - LIBRARY
2800 Hurricane Ridge Rd.   Phone: (206) 452-4501
Port Angeles, WA 98362   Henry C. Warren, Chf.Pk. Naturalist

KITSAP COUNTY LAW LIBRARY
614 Division St.   Phone: (206) 876-7140
Port Orchard, WA 98366

ABUNDANT LIFE SEED FOUNDATION - LIBRARY
1029 Lawrence   Phone: (206) 385-5660
Port Townsend, WA 98368   Forest Roth-Shomer, Dir.

JEFFERSON COUNTY HISTORICAL SOCIETY - RESEARCH CENTER
City Hall, Madison St.   Phone: (205) 385-1003
Port Townsend, WA 98368   Deborah McBride, Res. Staff

INFORMATION FUTURES - INFORMATION CENTER
2217 College Station   Phone: (509) 332-5726
Pullman, WA 99163   Gerald R. Brong, Dir.

WASHINGTON ARCHAEOLOGICAL RESEARCH CENTER - LIBRARY
Washington State Univ.
Commons Hall 322   Phone: (509) 335-8566
Pullman, WA 99164   Lloyd E. Whelchel, Rec.Libn.

WASHINGTON STATE UNIVERSITY - EDUCATION LIBRARY
130 Cleveland Hall   Phone: (509) 335-1591
Pullman, WA 99164   Carolyn A. Hook, Hd.

WASHINGTON STATE UNIVERSITY - HOLLAND LIBRARY
                                                Phone: (509) 335-2691
Pullman, WA 99164   Ronald Force, Asst.Dir.Pub.Serv.

WASHINGTON STATE UNIVERSITY - MANUSCRIPTS, ARCHIVES, & SPECIAL
    COLLECTIONS
                                                Phone: (509) 335-6691
Pullman, WA 99164   John F. Guido, Hd.

WASHINGTON STATE UNIVERSITY - OWEN SCIENCE AND ENGINEERING
    LIBRARY
                                                Phone: (509) 335-2671
Pullman, WA 99164   Elizabeth P. Roberts, Hd.

WASHINGTON STATE UNIVERSITY - PRIMATE RESEARCH CENTER
    LIBRARY
                                                Phone: (509) 335-1507
Pullman, WA 99164   Francis A. Young, Dir.

WASHINGTON STATE UNIVERSITY - VETERINARY MEDICAL/PHARMACY
    LIBRARY
170 Wegner Hall   Phone: (509) 335-9556
Pullman, WA 99164   Vicki F. Croft, Hd.

GOOD SAMARITAN HOSPITAL - LIBRARY
407 14th Ave., S.E.   Phone: (206) 848-6661
Puyallup, WA 98371   Linda Ziemke, Dir.

SUNDSTRAND DATA CONTROL, INC. - LIBRARY
Overlake Industrial Pk.   Phone: (206) 885-8420
Redmond, WA 98052   Madeline Sienda, Libn.

VALLEY GENERAL HOSPITAL - LIBRARY
400 S. 43rd St.   Phone: (206) 228-3450
Renton, WA 98055   Dr. Hugh MacMahon, Chm., Lib.Comm.

WASHINGTON STATE DEPARTMENT OF VETERANS AFFAIRS - STAFF
    LIBRARY
Washington Veterans' Home   Phone: (206) 876-7605
Retsil, WA 98378   John Jackson, Staff Libn.

CHURCH OF JESUS CHRIST OF LATTER-DAY SAINTS - TRI-CITIES BRANCH
    GENEALOGICAL LIBRARY
1720 Thayer   Phone: (509) 946-0111
Richland, WA 99352   Pat Ballowe, Hd.Libn.

EXXON NUCLEAR CO., INC. - RESEARCH & TECHNOLOGY CENTER LIBRARY
2955 George Washington Way   Phone: (509) 943-7386
Richland, WA 99352   Lydia H. Lee, Libn.

U.S. DEPT. OF ENERGY - PACIFIC NORTHWEST LABORATORY - TECHNICAL
    INFO. SECT.
Battelle Memorial Institute
Box 999   Phone: (509) 376-5451
Richland, WA 99352   W.A. Snyder, Mgr., Tech.Info.

UNIVERSITY OF WASHINGTON - GRADUATE SCHOOL - JOINT CENTER FOR
    GRADUATE STUDY - LIBRARY
100 Sprout Rd.   Phone: (509) 943-3176
Richland, WA 99352   Beverly Jane Cooper, Libn.

WASHINGTON PUBLIC POWER SUPPLY SYSTEM - LIBRARY
3000 George Washington Way
Box 968   Phone: (509) 372-6337
Richland, WA 99352   Verna Hawkins, Lib.Spec.

BECK (R.W.) & ASSOCIATES - LIBRARY
Tower Bldg., 7th Ave. at Olive Way   Phone: (206) 622-5000
Seattle, WA 98101   Enid Miller Slivka, Libn.

BOEING COMPANY - SEATTLE SERVICES DIVISION - HISTORICAL
    SERVICES AND ARCHIVES
Box 3707   Phone: (206) 655-4586
Seattle, WA 98124   Paul Spitzer, Adm.

BOEING COMPANY - SEATTLE SERVICES DIVISION - KENT TECHNICAL
    LIBRARY
Box 3707, M/S 8K-38   Phone: (206) 773-0590
Seattle, WA 98124   Solange V. McIntyre, Lib.Mgr.

BOEING COMPANY - SEATTLE SERVICES DIVISION - RENTON LIBRARY
Box 3707, Mail Stop 74-60   Phone: (206) 237-2445
Seattle, WA 98124   Nancy L. Wilson, Lib.Mgr.

CHILDREN'S ORTHOPEDIC HOSPITAL & MEDICAL CENTER - HOSPITAL
    LIBRARY
4800 Sand Point Way N.E.   Phone: (206) 634-5081
Seattle, WA 98105   Tamara A. Turner, Dir.

CORNISH INSTITUTE - LIBRARY
710 E. Roy St.   Phone: (206) 329-0901
Seattle, WA 98102   Ronald G. McComb, Hd.Libn.

DAMES & MOORE - SEATTLE OFFICE LIBRARY
155 N.E. 100th St., Suite 500   Phone: (206) 523-0560
Seattle, WA 98125   Ruth Van Dyke, Libn.

ENVIRONMENTAL PROTECTION AGENCY - REGION X LIBRARY
1200 Sixth Ave.   Phone: (206) 442-1289
Seattle, WA 98101   Ms. Arvella Weir, Regional Libn.

FRYE (Charles and Emma) ART MUSEUM - LIBRARY
704 Terry Ave.
Box 3005   Phone: (206) 622-9250
Seattle, WA 98114   Mrs. W.S. Greathouse, Pres.

GROUP HEALTH COOPERATIVE OF PUGET SOUND - MEDICAL LIBRARY
200 15th Ave., E.   Phone: (206) 326-6093
Seattle, WA 98112   Tagalie Atcher, Dir.

HONEYWELL, INC. - HONEYWELL MARINE SYSTEMS OPERATIONS -
    TECHNICAL INFORMATION CENTER
5303 Shilshole Ave., N.W.   Phone: (206) 789-2000
Seattle, WA 98107   Christy Mackey, Libn.

KING COUNTY LAW LIBRARY
601 County Courthouse
Seattle, WA 98104   James J. McArdle, Libn.

KING COUNTY MASONIC LIBRARY ASSOCIATION - LIBRARY *
Harvard & E. Pine St.   Phone: (206) 324-0110
Seattle, WA 98122   Erwin L. Hippe, Libn.

KING COUNTY YOUTH SERVICE CENTER - LIBRARY
1211 E. Alder   Phone: (206) 323-9500
Seattle, WA 98122   Julie Ann Oiye, Libn.

KRAMER CHIN AND MAYO INC. - LIBRARY
1917 First Ave.   Phone: (206) 447-5301
Seattle, WA 98101   Gretchen K. Leslie, Libn.

MUNICIPAL RESEARCH AND SERVICES CENTER OF WASHINGTON -
    LIBRARY
4719 Brooklyn Ave., N.E.   Phone: (206) 543-9050
Seattle, WA 98105   Lynne DeMerritt, Libn.

NORTHWEST HOSPITAL - EFFIE M. STOREY LEARNING CENTER
1551 North 120th   Phone: (206) 364-0500
Seattle, WA 98133   Marilyn R. Carlson, Libn.

GEOGRAPHIC

PACIFIC COAST BANKING SCHOOL - LIBRARY
1218 Third Ave., Suite 500   Phone: (206) 624-7618
Seattle, WA 98101   Mrs. Marciel Tomich, Registrar

PACIFIC SCIENCE CENTER FOUNDATION - LIBRARY
200 Second Ave., N.   Phone: (206) 625-9333
Seattle, WA 98109   Michael Olivere, Adm.Asst.

PERKINS, COIE, STONE, OLSEN & WILLIAMS - LAW LIBRARY
1900 Washington Bldg.   Phone: (206) 682-8770
Seattle, WA 98101   Jane Stewart, Librarian

PLYMOUTH CONGREGATIONAL CHURCH - VIDA B. VAREY LIBRARY
1217 6th Ave.
Seattle, WA 98101   Jeannette W. Squire, Libn.

POPULATION DYNAMICS, INC. - INFORMATION CENTER
3829 Aurora Ave., N.   Phone: (206) 632-5030
Seattle, WA 98103

PORT OF SEATTLE - LIBRARY
Box 1209   Phone: (206) 587-4979
Seattle, WA 98111   Edgar G. Ribback, Libn.

PRESTON, THORGRIMSON, ELLIS & HOLMAN - LIBRARY
2000 IBM Bldg.   Phone: (206) 623-7580
Seattle, WA 98101   Viola A. Bird, Libn.

PROVIDENCE MEDICAL CENTER - MEDICAL LIBRARY
500 17th Ave., C-34008   Phone: (206) 326-5621
Seattle, WA 98124   Kathleen Murray, Med.Libn.

PSYCHOANALYTIC ASSOCIATION OF SEATTLE - LIBRARY
4029 E. Madison St.   Phone: (206) 324-6611
Seattle, WA 98112   Adolph M. Gruhn, Chm., Lib.Comm.

PUGET SOUND COUNCIL OF GOVERNMENTS - LIBRARY
Grand Central on the Park
216 First Ave., S.   Phone: (206) 464-7090
Seattle, WA 98104   Cam McIntosh, Libn.

RAINIER NATIONAL BANK - INFORMATION CENTER
Box 3966
Seattle, WA 98124   Vivienne C. Burke, Asst.V.P./Mgr.

SAFECO INSURANCE COMPANY - LIBRARY
Safeco Plaza   Phone: (206) 545-5505
Seattle, WA 98185   Esther Delaney, Libn.

SCHICK SHADEL HOSPITAL - MEDICAL LIBRARY
Box 48149   Phone: (206) 244-8100
Seattle, WA 98166   Mary Jane McInturff, Med.Libn.

SEATTLE ART MUSEUM - LIBRARY
Volunteer Park   Phone: (206) 447-4686
Seattle, WA 98112   Elizabeth De Fato, Libn.

SEATTLE-FIRST NATIONAL BANK - LIBRARY
Box 3586   Phone: (206) 583-4056
Seattle, WA 98124   Jeannette M. Privat, A.V.P. & Mgr.

SEATTLE & KING COUNTY HISTORICAL SOCIETY - SOPHIE FRYE BASS
    LIBRARY OF NORTHWEST AMERICANA
Museum of History & Industry
2161 E. Hamlin St.   Phone: (206) 324-1125
Seattle, WA 98112   Mary-Thadia d'Hondt, Archv./Libn.

SEATTLE POST-INTELLIGENCER - NEWSPAPER LIBRARY
6th & Wall Sts.   Phone: (206) 628-8357
Seattle, WA 98111   Florence Frye, Chf.Libn.

SEATTLE PUBLIC LIBRARY - ART AND MUSIC DEPARTMENT †
1000 Fourth Ave.   Phone: (206) 625-4969
Seattle, WA 98104   Carolyn J. Holmquist, Hd.

SEATTLE PUBLIC LIBRARY - BUSINESS AND SCIENCE DEPARTMENT
1000 Fourth Ave.   Phone: (206) 625-4977
Seattle, WA 98104   James B. Taylor, Dept.Hd.

SEATTLE PUBLIC LIBRARY - DOUGLASS-TRUTH BRANCH LIBRARY
23rd Ave. & E. Yesler Way   Phone: (206) 625-4900
Seattle, WA 98122   Kay Johnson, South Reg.Libn.

SEATTLE PUBLIC LIBRARY - EDUCATION, PSYCHOLOGY, SOCIOLOGY,
    SPORTS DEPARTMENT
1000 Fourth Ave.   Phone: (206) 625-4822
Seattle, WA 98104   Lonita M. Walton, Dept.Hd.

SEATTLE PUBLIC LIBRARY - GOVERNMENTAL RESEARCH ASSISTANCE
    LIBRARY
Municipal Bldg.
600 Fourth Ave.   Phone: (206) 625-4868
Seattle, WA 98104   Barbara Guptill, Mng.Libn.

SEATTLE PUBLIC LIBRARY - HISTORY, GOVERNMENT AND BIOGRAPHY
    DEPARTMENT
1000 Fourth Ave.   Phone: (206) 625-4893
Seattle, WA 98104   Jean Coberly, Hd., History Dept.

SEATTLE PUBLIC LIBRARY - LITERATURE, LANGUAGES, PHILOSOPHY &
    RELIGION DEPARTMENT
1000 Fourth Ave.   Phone: (206) 625-4898
Seattle, WA 98104   Nancy Wildin, Hd.

SEATTLE PUBLIC LIBRARY - MEDIA & PROGRAM SERVICES
1000 Fourth Ave.   Phone: (206) 625-4986
Seattle, WA 98104   Kandy B. Brandt, Hd.

SEATTLE PUBLIC LIBRARY - WASHINGTON REGIONAL LIBRARY FOR THE
    BLIND AND PHYSICALLY HANDICAPPED
811 Harrison St.   Phone: (206) 464-6699
Seattle, WA 98129   Jan Ames, Regional Libn.

SEATTLE TIMES - LIBRARY †
Fairview N. & John
Box 70   Phone: (206) 464-2311
Seattle, WA 98111   Beverly Russell, Libn.

SEATTLE TRUST & SAVINGS BANK - LIBRARY
804 Second Ave.   Phone: (206) 223-2052
Seattle, WA 98040   Dorothy S. Hughes, Libn.

SEATTLE WEAVERS' GUILD - LIBRARY *
Museum of History & Industry
2161 E. Hamlin St.   Phone: (206) 324-1125
Seattle, WA 98112   Mildred K. Sherwood, Libn.

SHANNON & WILSON, INC. - TECHNICAL LIBRARY *
1105 N. 38th St.   Phone: (206) 632-8020
Seattle, WA 98103   Jean Boucher, Libn.

SISTERS OF PROVIDENCE - SACRED HEART PROVINCE - ARCHIVES
4800 37th Ave., S.W.   Phone: (206) 937-4600
Seattle, WA 98126   Sr. Rita Bergamini, S.P., Archv.

SWEDISH HOSPITAL MEDICAL CENTER - REFERENCE LIBRARY
747 Summit Ave.   Phone: (206) 292-2484
Seattle, WA 98104   Jean C. Anderson, Chf.Libn.

TEMPLE DE HIRSCH SINAI - LIBRARY
1511 E. Pike
Seattle, WA 98122   Susan L. Mautner, Libn.

TRA ARCHITECTURE ENGINEERING PLANNING INTERIORS - LIBRARY
215 Columbia   Phone: (206) 682-1133
Seattle, WA 98104   Ann R. McQuaid, Libn.

U.S. ARMY - CORPS OF ENGINEERS - SEATTLE DISTRICT - LIBRARY
Box C-3755   Phone: (206) 764-3728
Seattle, WA 98124   Mary Pritchard, District Libn.

U.S. BUREAU OF THE CENSUS - REGIONAL DATA USER SERVICE - SEATTLE
    REGIONAL OFFICE - LIBRARY
1700 Westlake Ave., N.   Phone: (206) 442-7080
Seattle, WA 98174   Betty J. Owens, Libn.

U.S. DEPT. OF LABOR - OSHA - REGIONAL LIBRARY
909 First Ave., Rm. 6003   Phone: (206) 442-5930
Seattle, WA 98174   Judith Robertson, Libn.

U.S. GENERAL SERVICES ADMINISTRATION - NORTHWEST FEDERAL
    REGIONAL COUNCIL - LIBRARY
M.S. 132 Arcade Plaza Bldg.
1321 Second Ave.   Phone: (206) 442-5554
Seattle, WA 98101   Mariley Ferens, Libn.

U.S. NATL. ARCHIVES & RECORDS SERVICE - FEDERAL ARCHIVES AND
    RECORDS CENTER, REGION 10
6125 Sand Point Way   Phone: (206) 442-4502
Seattle, WA 98115   Phillip E. Lothyan, Chf., Archv.Br.

U.S. NATL. MARINE FISHERIES SERVICE - NATIONAL MARINE MAMMAL
    LABORATORY - LIBRARY
7600 Sand Point Way N.E., Bldg. 32   Phone: (206) 442-4580
Seattle, WA 98115   Sherry Pearson, Tech.Info.Spec.

U.S. NATL. MARINE FISHERIES SERVICE - NORTHWEST & ALASKA
    FISHERIES CENTER - LIBRARY
2725 Montlake Blvd., E.   Phone: (206) 442-7795
Seattle, WA 98112   Patricia Cook, Libn.

U.S. NAVY - NAVAL SUPPORT ACTIVITY - LIBRARY
Bldg. 47   Phone: (206) 527-3577
Seattle, WA 98115   Bob Kinstdahl, Libn.

U.S. PUBLIC HEALTH SERVICE HOSPITAL - MEDICAL SERVICE LIBRARY †
1131 14th Ave. S.   Phone: (206) 324-7650
Seattle, WA 98114   Ms. Seungja Song, Med.Libn.

U.S. VETERANS ADMINISTRATION (WA-Seattle) - HOSPITAL MEDICAL
    LIBRARY
4435 Beacon Ave., S.   Phone: (206) 762-1010
Seattle, WA 98108   Martha Leredu, Chf., Lib.Serv.

UNIVERSITY CONGREGATIONAL CHURCH - LIBRARY
4515 16th Ave., N.E.   Phone: (206) 524-2322
Seattle, WA 98105   Gertrude Wulfekoetter, Libn.

UNIVERSITY OF WASHINGTON - ARCHITECTURE - URBAN PLANNING
    LIBRARY
334 Gould Hall, JO-30   Phone: (206) 543-4067
Seattle, WA 98195   Betty L. Wagner, Libn.

UNIVERSITY OF WASHINGTON - ART LIBRARY
101 Art Bldg., DM-10   Phone: (206) 543-0648
Seattle, WA 98195   Marietta M. Ward, Libn.

UNIVERSITY OF WASHINGTON - ART SLIDE COLLECTION
120 Art Bldg., DM-10   Phone: (206) 543-0649
Seattle, WA 98195   Mildred Ellquist Thorson, Preparator

UNIVERSITY OF WASHINGTON - BUSINESS ADMINISTRATION BRANCH
    LIBRARY
100 Balmer Hall, DJ-10   Phone: (206) 543-4360
Seattle, WA 98195   Anne B. Passarelli, Hd.Libn.

UNIVERSITY OF WASHINGTON - CENTER FOR STUDIES IN DEMOGRAPHY
    AND ECOLOGY - LIBRARY
102 Savery Hall, DK-40   Phone: (206) 543-5035
Seattle, WA 98195   Thomas W. Pullum, Dir.

UNIVERSITY OF WASHINGTON - CHEMISTRY-PHARMACY LIBRARY
192 Bagley Hall, BG-20   Phone: (206) 543-1603
Seattle, WA 98195   Irmgard Rutherford, Libn.

UNIVERSITY OF WASHINGTON - COMPUTING INFORMATION CENTER
3737 Brooklyn N.E., HG-45   Phone: (206) 543-8519
Seattle, WA 98105   Darlene Myers, Mgr.

UNIVERSITY OF WASHINGTON - CURRICULUM MATERIALS SECTION
Suzzallo Library, FM-25   Phone: (206) 543-2725
Seattle, WA 98195   Jean Belch, Libn.

UNIVERSITY OF WASHINGTON - DRAMA LIBRARY
25 Drama-TV Bldg., BH-20   Phone: (206) 543-5148
Seattle, WA 98195   Liz Fugate, Libn.

UNIVERSITY OF WASHINGTON - EAST ASIA LIBRARY
322 Gowen Hall, DO-27   Phone: (206) 543-4490
Seattle, WA 98195   Karl Lo, Hd.

UNIVERSITY OF WASHINGTON - ENGINEERING LIBRARY
202 Engineering Library Bldg., FH-15   Phone: (206) 543-0740
Seattle, WA 98195   Harold N. Wiren, Hd.Libn.

UNIVERSITY OF WASHINGTON - FISHERIES-OCEANOGRAPHY LIBRARY
151 Oceanography Teaching Bldg., WB-30   Phone: (206) 543-4279
Seattle, WA 98195   Yasuko T. Fukano, Hd.Libn.

UNIVERSITY OF WASHINGTON - FOREST RESOURCES LIBRARY
60 Bloedel Hall, AQ-15   Phone: (206) 543-2758
Seattle, WA 98195   Barbara B. Gordon, Libn.

UNIVERSITY OF WASHINGTON - GEOGRAPHY LIBRARY
415 Smith Hall, DP-10   Phone: (206) 543-5244
Seattle, WA 98195   Anna Chiong, Libn.

UNIVERSITY OF WASHINGTON - GOVERNMENT PUBLICATIONS DIVISION
Suzzalo Library, FM-25   Phone: (206) 543-1937
Seattle, WA 98195   Eleanor L. Chase, Hd.Libn.

UNIVERSITY OF WASHINGTON - HEALTH SCIENCES LIBRARY
T-231 Health Sciences, SB-55   Phone: (206) 543-5530
Seattle, WA 98195   Gerald J. Oppenheimer, Dir.

UNIVERSITY OF WASHINGTON - HEALTH SCIENCES LIBRARY - K.K.
    SHERWOOD LIBRARY
Harborview Medical Ctr.
325 9th Ave., ZA-43   Phone: (206) 223-3360
Seattle, WA 98104   Sharon Babcock, Lib.Supv.

UNIVERSITY OF WASHINGTON - LAW SCHOOL LIBRARY
School of Law
1100 N.E. Campus Pkwy., JB-20   Phone: (206) 543-4089
Seattle, WA 98105   Robert C. Berring, Jr., Law Libn.

UNIVERSITY OF WASHINGTON - MAP SECTION
Suzzallo Library, FM-25   Phone: (206) 543-9392
Seattle, WA 98195   Steven Z. Hiller, Libn.

UNIVERSITY OF WASHINGTON - MATHEMATICS RESEARCH LIBRARY
C306 Padelford, GN-50   Phone: (206) 543-7296
Seattle, WA 98195   Heidi Mercado, Libn.

UNIVERSITY OF WASHINGTON - MUSIC LIBRARY
113 Music Bldg., DN-10   Phone: (206) 543-1168
Seattle, WA 98195   David A. Wood, Hd.Libn.

UNIVERSITY OF WASHINGTON - NATURAL SCIENCES LIBRARY
Suzzallo Library, FM-25   Phone: (206) 543-1243
Seattle, WA 98195   Sarah C. Michalak, Hd.Libn.

UNIVERSITY OF WASHINGTON - PHILOSOPHY LIBRARY
331 Savery, DK-50   Phone: (206) 543-5856
Seattle, WA 98195   Carol Weibel, Libn.

UNIVERSITY OF WASHINGTON - PHYSICS-ASTRONOMY LIBRARY
219 Physics Bldg., FM-15   Phone: (206) 543-2988
Seattle, WA 98195   Martha Austin, Libn.

UNIVERSITY OF WASHINGTON - POLITICAL SCIENCE LIBRARY
220 Smith Hall, DP 25   Phone: (206) 543-2389
Seattle, WA 98195   Al Fritz, Libn.

UNIVERSITY OF WASHINGTON - REGIONAL PRIMATE RESEARCH CENTER -
    PRIMATE INFORMATION CENTER
SJ-50   Phone: (206) 543-4376
Seattle, WA 98195   Maryeva W. Terry, Mgr.

UNIVERSITY OF WASHINGTON - SCHOOL OF NUTRITION SCIENCES AND
    TEXTILES - COSTUME AND TEXTILE STUDY CENTER
45 Drama-TV Bldg., DL-10   Phone: (206) 543-1739
Seattle, WA 98195   Krista Turnbull, Cur.

GEOGRAPHIC

UNIVERSITY OF WASHINGTON - SOCIAL WORK LIBRARY
Social Work/Speech-Hearing Bldg., JH-30   Phone: (206) 545-2180
Seattle, WA 98195   Guela G. Johnson, Libn.

UNIVERSITY OF WASHINGTON - SPECIAL COLLECTIONS DIVISION -
    HISTORICAL PHOTOGRAPHY COLLECTION
Suzzallo Library, FM-25   Phone: (206) 543-0742
Seattle, WA 98195

UNIVERSITY OF WASHINGTON - SPECIAL COLLECTIONS DIVISION -
    PACIFIC NORTHWEST COLLECTION
Suzzallo Library, FM-25   Phone: (206) 543-1929
Seattle, WA 98195   Andrew F. Johnson, Libn.

UNIVERSITY OF WASHINGTON - UNIVERSITY ARCHIVES & MANUSCRIPT
    DIVISION - MANUSCRIPT COLLECTION
Suzzallo Library, FM-25   Phone: (206) 543-1879
Seattle, WA 98195   Richard Berner, Hd.Libn.

UNIVERSITY OF WASHINGTON - UNIVERSITY ARCHIVES & MANUSCRIPT
    DIVISION - UNIVERSITY ARCHIVES
3902 Cowlitz Rd., HO-10   Phone: (206) 543-6509
Seattle, WA 98195   Richard C. Berner, Univ.Archv.

WALDO GENERAL HOSPITAL - MEDICAL LIBRARY
10560 5th, N.E.
Box 25167   Phone: (206) 364-2050
Seattle, WA 98125   Janet Schnall, Consulting Libn.

WASHINGTON MUTUAL SAVINGS BANK - INFORMATION CENTER &
    DIETRICH SCHMITZ MEMORIAL LIBRARY
1101 2nd Ave.
Box 834   Phone: (206) 464-4501
Seattle, WA 98111   Marcella C. Gaar, Libn.

WASHINGTON STATE DEPARTMENT OF COMMERCE AND ECONOMIC
    DEVELOPMENT - TOURISM DEVELOPMENT DIVISION
312 First Ave., N.   Phone: (206) 753-5610
Seattle, WA 98109   W.D. Taylor, Dir.

WOODLAND PARK ZOOLOGICAL GARDENS - LIBRARY
5500 Phinney Ave., N.   Phone: (206) 782-1265
Seattle, WA 98103   Mary C. Hopkins, Libn.

ITT RAYONIER, INC. - OLYMPIC RESEARCH DIVISION - LIBRARY
409 E. Harvard St.   Phone: (206) 426-4461
Shelton, WA 98584   Patricia A. Tostevin, Libn.

KITSAP COUNTY HISTORICAL MUSEUM - LIBRARY †
Washington & Byron   Phone: (206) 692-1949
Silverdale, WA 98383   Mrs. Sigurd Olsen, Musm.Dir.

DIOCESE OF SPOKANE - DIOCESAN CHANCERY ARCHIVES
1023 W. Riverside Ave.
Box 1453   Phone: (509) 456-7100
Spokane, WA 99210   Rev. Edward J. Kowrach, Archv.

EASTERN WASHINGTON STATE HISTORICAL SOCIETY - LIBRARY
Cheney Cowles Memorial Museum
W. 2316 First Ave.   Phone: (509) 456-3931
Spokane, WA 99204   Elinor C. Kelly, Libn.

FINCH ARBORETUM - LIBRARY
W. 3404 Woodland Blvd.
Spokane, WA 99204

GONZAGA UNIVERSITY - CROSBY LIBRARY
502 E. Boone Ave.   Phone: (509) 328-4220
Spokane, WA 99258   Robert L. Burr, Dir.

GONZAGA UNIVERSITY SCHOOL OF LAW - LIBRARY
600 E. Sharp Ave.
Box 3528   Phone: (509) 328-4220
Spokane, WA 99220   Dennis J. Stone, Law Libn.

HOLLISTER-STIER LABORATORIES - LIBRARY
Box 3145 Terminal Annex
Spokane, WA 99220   E.L. Foubert, Jr.

INTERCOLLEGIATE CENTER FOR NURSING EDUCATION - LIBRARY
W. 2917 Ft. George Wright Dr.   Phone: (509) 326-7270
Spokane, WA 99204   Robert M. Pringle, Jr., Hd.Libn.

MOLDENHAUER ARCHIVES
1011 Comstock Ct.   Phone: (509) 747-4555
Spokane, WA 99203   Hans Moldenhauer, Dir.

SACRED HEART MEDICAL CENTER - HEALTH SCIENCES LIBRARY
W. 101 8th St.   Phone: (509) 455-3094
Spokane, WA 99204   Elizabeth J. Guilfoil, Dir.

ST. LUKE'S MEMORIAL HOSPITAL - A.M. JOHNSON MEMORIAL LIBRARY
South 711 Cowley   Phone: (509) 838-4771
Spokane, WA 99210   Loren A. Gothberg, Chm., Lib.Comm.

SOCIETY OF JESUS - OREGON PROVINCE ARCHIVES
Crosby Library, Gonzaga University
E. 502 Boone Ave.   Phone: (509) 328-4220
Spokane, WA 99258   Rev. Clifford Carroll, S.J., Archv.

SPOKANE COUNTY LAW LIBRARY
1020 Paulsen Bldg.   Phone: (509) 456-3680
Spokane, WA 99201   Emily E. Wadden, Law Libn.

SPOKANE MEDICAL LIBRARY
W. 35 8th Ave.   Phone: (509) 747-5777
Spokane, WA 99204   Cora R. Wilson, Libn.

SPOKANE SPOKESMAN-REVIEW AND DAILY CHRONICLE - NEWSPAPER
    REFERENCE LIBRARY
508 Chronicle Bldg.   Phone: (509) 455-6891
Spokane, WA 99210   Robert A. Neswick, Mgr.

SPOKANE VALLEY PIONEER MUSEUM, INC. - LIBRARY †
E. 10303 Sprague Ave.   Phone: (509) 924-4994
Spokane, WA 99206   Virginia Straughan, Archv.

U.S. GEOLOGICAL SURVEY - WESTERN MINERAL RESOURCES LIBRARY
656 U.S. Court House
920 W. Riverside Ave.   Phone: (509) 456-4677
Spokane, WA 99201   Anita W. Tarbert, Lib.Techn.

U.S. VETERANS ADMINISTRATION (WA-Spokane) - MEDICAL CENTER
    LIBRARY
N. 4815 Assembly St.   Phone: (509) 328-4521
Spokane, WA 99208   Ruth A. Jones, Chf., Lib.Serv.

WHITWORTH COLLEGE - SCIENCE LIBRARY
          Phone: (509) 489-3550
Spokane, WA 99218

ABAM ENGINEERS, INC. - TECHNICAL LIBRARY
500 S. 336th, Suite 200
Federal Way   Phone: (206) 952-6100
Tacoma, WA 98003   Patricia Williams, Tech.Libn.

AMERICAN PLYWOOD ASSOCIATION - INFORMATION CENTER
Box 11700   Phone: (206) 272-2283
Tacoma, WA 98411   June Packer, Rec.Mgr.

ASBURY UNITED METHODIST CHURCH - LIBRARY *
5601 S. Puget Sound
Box 9448   Phone: (206) 472-4239
Tacoma, WA 98409   Mrs. Roy Teter, Jr., Libn.

CHURCH OF JESUS CHRIST OF LATTER-DAY SAINTS - TACOMA BRANCH
    GENEALOGY LIBRARY *
1518 S. Woodlawn   Phone: (206) 564-1103
Tacoma, WA 98465   Clifton M. Foreman, Libn.

FAITH EVANGELICAL LUTHERAN SEMINARY - LIBRARY
3504 N. Pearl
Box 7186   Phone: (206) 752-2020
Tacoma, WA 98407   Rev. Osborne Y. Bruland, Libn.

PIERCE COUNTY LAW LIBRARY
123 County-City Bldg.   Phone: (206) 593-4346
Tacoma, WA 98402   Faye L. Reese, Libn.

PIERCE COUNTY MEDICAL LIBRARY
315 South K St.
Box 5277   Phone: (206) 572-5340
Tacoma, WA 98405   Ms. Marion VonBruck, Medical Librarian

ST. JOSEPH HOSPITAL AND HEALTH CARE CENTER - MEDICAL LIBRARY
1718 South I St.
Box 2197   Phone: (206) 627-4101
Tacoma, WA 98401   Hermione Anderson, Libn.

TACOMA NEWS TRIBUNE - LIBRARY
1950 South State St.   Phone: (206) 597-8629
Tacoma, WA 98411   Mr. N.L. Kirkland, Libn.

TACOMA PUBLIC LIBRARY - SPECIAL COLLECTIONS
1102 Tacoma Ave. S.   Phone: (206) 572-2000
Tacoma, WA 98402   Kevin Hegarty, Dir.

U.S. AIR FORCE BASE - MC CHORD BASE LIBRARY
McChord AFB   Phone: (206) 984-2126
Tacoma, WA 98438   Dorothy Hulbush, Libn.

U.S. ARMY HOSPITALS - MADIGAN ARMY MEDICAL CENTER - MEDICAL
   LIBRARY
Box 375   Phone: (206) 967-6782
Tacoma, WA 98431   Elizabeth C. Bolden, Libn.

U.S. ARMY HOSPITALS - MADIGAN ARMY MEDICAL CENTER - MORALE
   SUPPORT LIBRARY
                                             Phone: (206) 967-6198
Tacoma, WA 98431   Bonita J. Tucker, Adm.Libn.

U.S. VETERANS ADMINISTRATION (WA-Tacoma) - MEDICAL CENTER
   LIBRARY
American Lake   Phone: (206) 582-8440
Tacoma, WA 98493   Dennis L. Levi, Chf., Lib.Serv.

UNIVERSITY OF PUGET SOUND - SCHOOL OF LAW LIBRARY
8811 South Tacoma Way   Phone: (206) 756-3320
Tacoma, WA 98499   Anita M. Steele, Dir.

WASHINGTON STATE HISTORICAL SOCIETY - LIBRARY
315 N. Stadium Way   Phone: (206) 593-2830
Tacoma, WA 98403   Frank L. Green, Libn.

WEYERHAEUSER COMPANY - CORPORATE LIBRARY
CH 4-W   Phone: (206) 924-3030
Tacoma, WA 98477   Karin H. Williams, Corp.Libn.

WEYERHAEUSER COMPANY - TECHNICAL INFORMATION CENTER *
                                             Phone: (206) 924-6268
Tacoma, WA 98477   H.W. Haigh, Mgr.

WASHINGTON STATE SUPERINTENDENT OF PUBLIC INSTRUCTION -
   RESOURCE INFORMATION CENTER
7510 Armstrong St., S.W.
Mailstop Fg -11   Phone: (206) 753-6731
Tumwater WA 98504   Mrs. Bobbie J. Patterson, Coord.

BOISE CASCADE CORPORATION - PULP & PAPER RESEARCH LIBRARY
909 W. Seventh St.   Phone: (206) 695-4477
Vancouver, WA 98660   Vernon N. Gagnon, Libn.

CLARK COUNTY LAW LIBRARY
Court House, Rm. 302
Box 5000   Phone: (206) 699-2268
Vancouver, WA 98668   Barbara Rowland, Libn.

CLARK COUNTY REGIONAL PLANNING COUNCIL - LIBRARY *
1408 Franklin
Box 5000   Phone: (206) 699-2361
Vancouver, WA 98668

PACIFIC NORTHWEST RIVER BASINS COMMISSION - INFORMATION
   DEPARTMENT
1 Columbia River   Phone: (206) 696-7551
Vancouver, WA 98660   David Ricks, Planner

ST. JOSEPH COMMUNITY HOSPITAL - LIBRARY
600 N.E. 92nd Ave.
Box 1687   Phone: (206) 256-2045
Vancouver, WA 98668   Sylvia E. MacWilliams, Lib.Coord.

U.S. NATL. PARK SERVICE - FORT VANCOUVER NATL. HISTORIC SITE -
   LIBRARY
1501 E. Evergreen Blvd.   Phone: (206) 696-7655
Vancouver, WA 98661   Kent J. Taylor, Supv./Pk. Ranger

U.S. VETERANS ADMINISTRATION (WA-Vancouver) - HOSPITAL LIBRARY
Fourth Plain & O Sts.   Phone: (206) 696-4061
Vancouver, WA 98661   Mrs. Nymah L. Trued, Chf., Lib.Serv.

VANCOUVER MEMORIAL HOSPITAL - R.D. WISWALL MEMORIAL LIBRARY
3400 Main St.
Box 1657   Phone: (206) 696-5143
Vancouver, WA 98663   Sylvia E. MacWilliams, Lib.Coord.

WASHINGTON STATE SCHOOL FOR THE DEAF - LEARNING RESOURCE
   CENTER
611 Grand Blvd.
Box 5187   Phone: (206) 696-6223
Vancouver, WA 98668   James Randall, Dir.

U.S. VETERANS ADMINISTRATION (WA-Walla Walla) - HOSPITAL LIBRARY
77 Wainwright Dr.   Phone: (509) 525-5200
Walla Walla, WA 99362   Max J. Merrell, Chf.Libn.

WALLA WALLA COUNTY LAW LIBRARY †
Court House   Phone: (509) 529-2280
Walla Walla, WA 99362   Ben R. Forcier, Jr., Libn.

CENTRAL WASHINGTON HOSPITAL - HEALTH SCIENCES LIBRARY
1211 Rosewood
Box 1887   Phone: (509) 662-1511
Wenatchee, WA 98801   Jane Belt, Libn.

ENVIRONMENTAL PROTECTION AGENCY - WENATCHEE PESTICIDES
   RESEARCH BRANCH - LIBRARY
Box 219   Phone: (509) 662-4243
Wenatchee, WA 98801   Janice Scheunemann, Adm.Ck.

ST. ELIZABETH HOSPITAL - HEALTH SCIENCES LIBRARY
110 S. Ninth Ave.   Phone: (509) 575-5073
Yakima, WA 98902   Sr. Irene Charron, S.P., Med.Libn.

WASHINGTON STATE HERITAGE COUNCIL - INFORMATION CENTER
924 S. 16th Ave.   Phone: (509) 575-9878
Yakima, WA 98902   Jack Lines, Pres.

YAKIMA COUNTY LAW LIBRARY
Yakima County Court House   Phone: (509) 457-5452
Yakima, WA 98901   C.A. Erickson, Libn.

YAKIMA VALLEY GENEALOGICAL SOCIETY - LIBRARY
Box 445   Phone: (509) 248-1328
Yakima, WA 98907   Ellen Brzoska, Libn.

YAKIMA VALLEY MUSEUM AND HISTORICAL ASSOCIATION - LIBRARY
2105 Tieton Dr.   Phone: (509) 248-0747
Yakima, WA 98902   Frances A. Hare, Archv.

WEST VIRGINIA

CHESAPEAKE & OHIO HISTORICAL SOCIETY, INC. - C & O ARCHIVAL
   COLLECTION
Box 417
Alderson, WV 24910   Thomas W. Dixon, Jr., Pres.

U.S. NATIONAL MINE HEALTH AND SAFETY ACADEMY - LEARNING
   RESOURCE CENTER
Airport Rd.
Box 1166   Phone: (304) 255-0451
Beckley, WV 25801   Dr. Leslie E. Woelflin, Chf., Lrng.Res.Ctr.

GEOGRAPHIC

GEOGRAPHIC

U.S. VETERANS ADMINISTRATION (WV-Beckley) - MEDICAL CENTER
LIBRARY
200 Veterans Ave.   Phone: (304) 255-2121
Beckley, WV 25801   Shelley C. Doman, Chf., Lib.Serv.

BETHANY COLLEGE - CHEMISTRY LIBRARY
Richardson Hall of Science   Phone: (304) 829-7711
Bethany, WV 26032   Rosalie Draper, Ck.

APPALACHIAN BIBLE COLLEGE - LIBRARY
                                           Phone: (304) 877-6428
Bradley, WV 25818   John VanPuffelen, Libn.

WEST VIRGINIA WESLEYAN COLLEGE - ANNIE MERNER PFEIFFER LIBRARY
College Ave.   Phone: (304) 473-8059
Buckhannon, WV 26201   Keith P. Burns, Dir., Lib.Serv.

OLD CHARLES TOWN LIBRARY, INC.
200 E. Washington St.   Phone: (304) 725-2208
Charles Town, WV 25414   Anna M. Shewbridge, Libn.

CHARLESTON AREA MEDICAL CENTER - GENERAL DIVISION - MEDICAL
LIBRARY
Box 1393   Phone: (304) 348-6219
Charleston, WV 25325   Mary A. Davis, Libn.

CHARLESTON GAZETTE-MAIL - LIBRARY
1001 Virginia St., E.   Phone: (304) 348-4888
Charleston, WV 25330   Ron Miller, Hd.Libn.

COLUMBIA GAS TRANSMISSION CORPORATION - LAW LIBRARY
Box 1273   Phone: (304) 346-0951
Charleston, WV 25325   Nina K. Angle, Law Libn.

FIRST PRESBYTERIAN CHURCH OF CHARLESTON - LIBRARY
16 Broad St.   Phone: (304) 343-8961
Charleston, WV 25301

NATIONAL TRACK AND FIELD HALL OF FAME OF THE U.S.A. - LIBRARY
1524 Kanawha Blvd., E.   Phone: (304) 345-0087
Charleston, WV 25311   Dr. Jack W. Rose, Exec.Dir.

SUNRISE FOUNDATION, INC. - LIBRARY
746 Myrtle Rd.   Phone: (304) 344-8035
Charleston, WV 25314

SURFACE MINING RESEARCH LIBRARY
Box 5024   Phone: (304) 342-0717
Charleston, WV 25311   Norman Kilpatrick, Dir.

U.S. DEPT. OF COMMERCE - INTERNATIONAL TRADE ADMINISTRATION -
CHARLESTON DISTRICT OFFICE LIBRARY
3000 New Federal Office Bldg.
500 Quarrier St.   Phone: (304) 343-6181
Charleston, WV 25301   Roger L. Fortner, Dir.

WEST VIRGINIA STATE ATTORNEY GENERAL - LAW LIBRARY
Rm. 26E, State Capitol   Phone: (304) 348-2021
Charleston, WV 25305

WEST VIRGINIA STATE DEPT. OF AGRICULTURE - PLANT PEST CONTROL &
LABORATORY SERVICES DIVISION LIBRARY
Capitol Bldg.   Phone: (304) 348-2212
Charleston, WV 25305

WEST VIRGINIA STATE DEPARTMENT OF CULTURE AND HISTORY -
ARCHIVES AND HISTORY LIBRARY
Cultural Center, Capitol Complex   Phone: (304) 348-0230
Charleston, WV 26505   Rodney A. Pyles, Dir.

WEST VIRGINIA STATE DEPARTMENT OF EDUCATION - EDUCATIONAL
MEDIA CENTER
1900 Washington St., Rm. B346   Phone: (304) 348-3925
Charleston, WV 25305   Carolyn R. Skidmore, Lib.Dir.

WEST VIRGINIA STATE DEPARTMENT OF HIGHWAYS - RIGHT OF WAY
DIVISION LIBRARY
1900 Washington St., E.   Phone: (304) 348-3195
Charleston, WV 25305

WEST VIRGINIA STATE DEPARTMENT OF NATURAL RESOURCES -
DIVISION OF WATER RESOURCES - LIBRARY
1201 Greenbrier St.
Charleston, WV 25311

WEST VIRGINIA STATE DEPARTMENT OF WELFARE - LIBRARY
307 Jefferson St.   Phone: (304) 348-8834
Charleston, WV 25305   Joy B. Jones, Libn.

WEST VIRGINIA STATE GOVERNOR'S OFFICE OF ECON. & COMMUNITY
DEV. - GOECD COMMUNITY DEVELOPMENT DIV. - LIBRARY
State Capitol Complex, B-548 Bldg. 6   Phone: (304) 348-2246
Charleston, WV 25305   Thomas H. Pendleton, Mgr.

WEST VIRGINIA STATE GOVERNOR'S OFFICE OF ECONOMIC &
COMMUNITY DEVELOPMENT - TRAVEL DEVELOPMENT DIVISION
Bldg. 6, Room B-564
1900 Washington St., E.   Phone: (304) 348-2286
Charleston, WV 25305   Joseph R. Fowler, Jr., Dir.

WEST VIRGINIA STATE LEGISLATIVE REFERENCE LIBRARY
Rm. 415, Main Unit, Capitol Bldg.   Phone: (304) 348-2153
Charleston, WV 25305   Mary Del Cont, Libn.

WEST VIRGINIA STATE LIBRARY COMMISSION - FILM SERVICES
DEPARTMENT
Science and Cultural Ctr.   Phone: (304) 348-3976
Charleston, WV 25305   Steve Fesenmaier, Film Libn.

WEST VIRGINIA STATE LIBRARY COMMISSION - REFERENCE LIBRARY
Science and Cultural Center   Phone: (304) 348-2045
Charleston, WV 25305   Karen E. Goff, Ref.Libn.

WEST VIRGINIA STATE SUPREME COURT OF APPEALS - STATE LAW
LIBRARY
Rm. E-320, Capitol Bldg.   Phone: (304) 348-2607
Charleston, WV 25305   John E. Montgomery, Dir.

WEST VIRGINIA UNIVERSITY MEDICAL CENTER - CHARLESTON DIVISION
- LEARNING RESOURCES CENTER
3110 Mac Corkle Ave., S.E.   Phone: (304) 347-1285
Charleston, WV 25304   Patricia Powell, Libn.

SPACE AND UNEXPLAINED CELESTIAL EVENTS RESEARCH SOCIETY -
LIBRARY
Box 2228   Phone: (304) 269-2719
Clarksburg, WV 26301

U.S. VETERANS ADMINISTRATION (WV-Clarksburg) - MEDICAL CENTER
LIBRARY SERVICE *
                                           Phone: (304) 623-3461
Clarksburg, WV 26301   Mary E. Conway, Chf., Lib.Serv.

U.S. NATL. PARK SERVICE - HARPERS FERRY CENTER LIBRARY
                                           Phone: (304) 535-6371
Harpers Ferry, WV 25425   David Nathanson, Chf.Libn.

U.S. NATL. PARK SERVICE - HARPERS FERRY NATL. HISTORICAL PARK -
LIBRARY
Box 65   Phone: (304) 535-6371
Harpers Ferry, WV 25425   Hilda E. Staubs, Musm.Techn.

BOONE COUNTY GENEALOGICAL SOCIETY - LIBRARY
Box 10   Phone: (304) 369-4675
Hewett, WV 25108

BUCK (Pearl S.) BIRTHPLACE FOUNDATION - LIBRARY
Box 126   Phone: (304) 653-4430
Hillsboro, WV 24946

CABELL HUNTINGTON HOSPITAL - HEALTH SCIENCE LIBRARY
1340 Hal Greer Blvd.   Phone: (304) 696-2605
Huntington, WV 25701   Deborah L. Woodburn, Health Sci.Libn.

HUNTINGTON ALLOYS, INC. - TECHNOLOGY LIBRARY
Guyan River Rd.
Box 1958   Phone: (304) 696-6260
Huntington, WV 25720   Lola W. McClure, Tech.Libn.

HUNTINGTON GALLERIES - REFERENCE LIBRARY
Park Hills   Phone: (304) 529-2701
Huntington, WV 25701   Elizabeth A. Bostwick, Libn.

MARSHALL UNIVERSITY - JAMES E. MORROW LIBRARY - SPECIAL
    COLLECTIONS
                                                   Phone: (304) 696-2320
Huntington, WV 25701   Lisle G. Brown, Cur.

MARSHALL UNIVERSITY - RESEARCH COORDINATING UNIT FOR
    VOCATIONAL EDUCATION
                                                   Phone: (304) 696-3180
Huntington, WV 25701   Kristine Standifur, Res.Asst.

MARSHALL UNIVERSITY - SCHOOL OF MEDICINE - HEALTH SCIENCE
    LIBRARIES
Marshall University Campus   Phone: (304) 696-6426
Huntington, WV 25701   Ann Howard, Dir.

ST. MARY'S HOSPITAL - MEDICAL LIBRARY
                                                   Phone: (304) 696-6807
Huntington, WV 25701   Kay Gibson, Med.Libn.

U.S. VETERANS ADMINISTRATION (WV-Huntington) - MEDICAL CENTER
    LIBRARY
1540 Spring Valley Dr.   Phone: (304) 429-6741
Huntington, WV 25704   Evelyn J. Schaffer, Chf., Lib.Serv.

U.S. FISH & WILDLIFE SERVICE - NATIONAL FISHERIES CENTER -
    TECHNICAL INFORMATION SERVICE
Route 3, Box 40-A   Phone: (304) 725-8461
Kearneysville, WV 25430   Joyce A. Mann, Tech.Info.Off.

GREENBRIER HISTORICAL SOCIETY - ARCHIVES *
North House, Church St.   Phone: (304) 645-3503
Lewisburg, WV 24901   Frances A. Swope, Archv.

U.S. VETERANS ADMINISTRATION (WV-Martinsburg) - CENTER MEDICAL
    LIBRARY
                                                   Phone: (304) 263-0811
Martinsburg, WV 25401   Barbara S. Adams, Chf.Libn.

WEST VIRGINIA INSTITUTE OF TECHNOLOGY - VINING LIBRARY
Fayette Pike   Phone: (304) 442-3141
Montgomery, WV 25136   Victor C. Young, Dir.

AMERICAN ASSOCIATION OF COST ENGINEERS - LIBRARY
308 Monongahela Bldg.   Phone: (304) 296-8444
Morgantown, WV 26505   Kenneth K. Humphreys, Exec.Dir.

U.S. DEPT. OF ENERGY - MORGANTOWN ENERGY TECHNOLOGY CENTER
    LIBRARY
Box 880   Phone: (304) 599-7183
Morgantown, WV 26505   S. Elaine Pasini, Libn.

WEST VIRGINIA STATE GEOLOGICAL AND ECONOMIC SURVEY - LIBRARY
Box 879   Phone: (304) 292-6331
Morgantown, WV 26505   Ruth I. Hayhurst, Libn.

WEST VIRGINIA UNIVERSITY - BUREAU FOR GOVERNMENT RESEARCH
    LIBRARY
                                                   Phone: (304) 293-4030
Morgantown, WV 26506

WEST VIRGINIA UNIVERSITY - CREATIVE ARTS CENTER - MUSIC LIBRARY
                                                   Phone: (304) 293-4505
Morgantown, WV 26506   Ruby Canning, Libn.

WEST VIRGINIA UNIVERSITY - LAW LIBRARY
Law School   Phone: (304) 293-5309
Morgantown, WV 26506   William E. Johnson, Law Libn./Professor

WEST VIRGINIA UNIVERSITY - MEDICAL CENTER LIBRARY
Basic Sciences Bldg.   Phone: (304) 293-2113
Morgantown, WV 26506   Robert Murphy, Libn.

WEST VIRGINIA UNIVERSITY - WEST VIRGINIA COLLECTION
University Library   Phone: (304) 293-3240
Morgantown, WV 26506   George Parkinson, Cur.

MOBAY CHEMICAL CORPORATION - RESEARCH LIBRARY
                                                   Phone: (304) 455-4400
New Martinsville, WV 26155   Douglas A. Portmann, Tech.Libn.

PPG INDUSTRIES, INC. - CHEMICAL DIVISION - NATRIUM RESEARCH AND
    DEVELOPMENT LIBRARY
Box 191   Phone: (304) 455-2200
New Martinsville, WV 26155   Alice K. Johnson, Libn.

WEST VIRGINIA SCHOOLS FOR THE DEAF AND BLIND - WV SCHOOL FOR
    THE BLIND LIBRARY
                                                   Phone: (304) 822-3521
Romney, WV 26757   Leslie Durst, Libn.

UNION CARBIDE CORPORATION - ENGINEERING DEPARTMENT LIBRARY
Box 8361   Phone: (304) 747-4608
South Charleston, WV 25303   Julia Adkins, Libn.

UNION CARBIDE CORPORATION - RESEARCH AND DEVELOPMENT LIBRARY
Bldg. 770
Box 8361   Phone: (304) 747-5119
South Charleston, WV 25303   Alice S. Behr, Tech.Libn.

WEST VIRGINIA STATE DEPARTMENT OF HEALTH - STATE HYGIENIC
    LABORATORY - LIBRARY
167 11th Ave.   Phone: (304) 348-3530
South Charleston, WV 25303

BORG-WARNER CORPORATION - CHEMICALS LIBRARY
Box 68   Phone: (304) 863-7335
Washington, WV 26181   Sharon D. Watson, Libn.

NATIONAL STEEL CORPORATION - RESEARCH CENTER LIBRARY
                                                   Phone: (304) 797-2837
Weirton, WV 26062   Elizabeth W. Fulton, Sr.Res.Libn.

STEVENS CLINIC HOSPITAL - LIBRARY
U.S. 52, East   Phone: (304) 436-3161
Welch, WV 24801   Karen Peery, Libn.

WEST LIBERTY STATE COLLEGE - ELBIN LIBRARY
                                                   Phone: (304) 336-8035
West Liberty, WV 26074   Donald R. Strong, Libn.

OGLEBAY INSTITUTE - MANSION MUSEUM LIBRARY
Oglebay Park   Phone: (304) 242-7272
Wheeling, WV 26003   T. Patrick Brennan, Cur.

OHIO COUNTY LAW LIBRARY
City-County Bldg.   Phone: (304) 234-3634
Wheeling, WV 26003   Nancy C. Obecny, Law Libn.

OHIO VALLEY MEDICAL CENTER - HUPP MEDICAL LIBRARY †
2000 Eoff St.   Phone: (304) 234-8771
Wheeling, WV 26003   Eleanor Shonn, Med.Libn.

WHEELING HOSPITAL, INC. - HENRY G. JEPSON MEMORIAL LIBRARY
Medical Pk.   Phone: (304) 243-3308
Wheeling, WV 26003   Anne S. Loner, Med.Libn.

WISCONSIN

AID ASSOCIATION FOR LUTHERANS - CORPORATE LIBRARY
4321 N. Ballard Rd.   Phone: (414) 734-5721
Appleton, WI 54919   Ordelle Aaker, Libn.

INSTITUTE OF PAPER CHEMISTRY - LIBRARY
1043 E. South River St.
Box 1039   Phone: (414) 734-9251
Appleton, WI 54912   Mary L. Scribner, Hd.Libn.

JUSTICE SYSTEM TRAINING ASSOCIATION - PSYCHO-MOTOR SKILL
    DESIGN ARCHIVE
Box 356   Phone: (414) 731-8893
Appleton, WI 54912   Kevin Parsons, Dir.

GEOGRAPHIC

OUTAGAMIE COUNTY LAW LIBRARY
410 S. Walnut St.
Appleton, WI 54911   Phone: (414) 735-5347

ST. ELIZABETH HOSPITAL - HEALTH SCIENCE LIBRARY
1506 S. Oneida St.   Phone: (414) 731-5261
Appleton, WI 54911   Mary M. Bayorgeon, Dir., Lib.Serv.

CIRCUS WORLD MUSEUM - LIBRARY
415 Lynn St.   Phone: (608) 356-8341
Baraboo, WI 53913   Robert L. Parkinson, Chf.Libn. & Hist.

INTERNATIONAL CRANE FOUNDATION - LIBRARY
City View Rd.   Phone: (608) 356-9462
Baraboo, WI 53913   Joan Fordham, Adm.

SAUK COUNTY HISTORICAL SOCIETY, INC. - HISTORICAL MUSEUM LIBRARY
531 Fourth Ave.   Phone: (608) 356-6016
Baraboo, WI 53913   Ora Brice, Cur.

BELOIT COLLEGE - HERBERT V. KOHLER SCIENCE LIBRARY
     Phone: (608) 365-3391
Beloit, WI 53511   Glenn Remelts, Hd.Pub.Serv./Br.Lib.

BELOIT HISTORICAL SOCIETY - BARTLETT MEMORIAL MUSEUM - LIBRARY
2149 St. Lawrence Ave.   Phone: (608) 365-3811
Beloit, WI 53511   Joseph W. Rhodes, Dir.

COLT INDUSTRIES - FM ENGINE DIVISION LIBRARY
701 Lawton St.   Phone: (608) 364-4411
Beloit, WI 53511   Wesley A. Brill, Act.Adm.

HOLY FAMILY CONVENT - LIBRARY
     Phone: (414) 862-2010
Benet Lake, WI 53102   Sr. Maris Stella Doran, O.S.B., Libn.

ST. BENEDICT'S ABBEY - BENET LIBRARY
     Phone: (414) 396-4311
Benet Lake, WI 53102   Bro. Vincent Wedig, O.S.B., Libn.

MONROE, JUNEAU, JACKSON COUNTY, WISCONSIN GENEALOGY WORKSHOP - LIBRARY
Rte. 3, Box 253   Phone: (608) 378-4388
Black River Falls, WI 54615   Carolyn Habelman, Pres.

ELMBROOK MEMORIAL HOSPITAL - MARY BETH CURTIS HEALTH SCIENCE LIBRARY
19333 W. North Ave.   Phone: (414) 782-2222
Brookfield, WI 53005   Harvada Oitzinger, Dir.

INTERNATIONAL FOUNDATION OF EMPLOYEE BENEFIT PLANS - INFORMATION CENTER
18700 W. Bluemound Rd.   Phone: (414) 786-6700
Brookfield, WI 53005   Jack Baltes, Dir., Info.Serv.

NATIONAL ASSOCIATION OF INSURANCE COMMISSIONERS - NAIC INFORMATION CENTER
350 Bishops Way   Phone: (414) 784-9540
Brookfield, WI 53005   Cheryl A. Adamski, Libn.

NORTHERN WISCONSIN CENTER FOR THE DEVELOPMENTALLY DISABLED - LIBRARY/INSTRUCTIONAL MATERIALS CENTER
E. Park Ave.
Box 340   Phone: (715) 723-5542
Chippewa Falls, WI 54729   Robert Carlsen, Teacher-Libn.

ST. JOSEPH'S HOSPITAL - HEALTH SCIENCE LIBRARY
2661 County Trunk I   Phone: (715) 723-1811
Chippewa Falls, WI 54729   Carolyn Kowalkowski, Dir.

LADISH CO. - METALLURGICAL DEPARTMENT LIBRARY
5481 S. Packard Ave.
Cudahy, WI 53110   Patrick Berry, Libn.

TRINITY MEMORIAL HOSPITAL - LIBRARY
5900 S. Lake Dr.   Phone: (414) 769-9000
Cudahy, WI 53110   Mrs. Pat Cameron, Libn.

ST. NORBERT ABBEY - AUGUSTINE LIBRARY
1016 N. Broadway   Phone: (414) 336-1321
De Pere, WI 54115   Rev. G.G. Claridge, Libn. & Archv.

WISCONSIN SCHOOL FOR THE DEAF - JOHN R. GANT LIBRARY
309 W. Walworth Ave.   Phone: (414) 728-6477
Delavan, WI 53115   Betty E. Watkins, Libn.

CHIPPEWA VALLEY MUSEUM, INC. - LIBRARY
9 Carson Park Dr.
Box 1204   Phone: (715) 834-7871
Eau Claire, WI 54701   Alberta Rommelmeyer, Archv.

DISTRICT ONE TECHNICAL INSTITUTE - LIBRARY - EDUCATIONAL RESOURCE CENTER
620 W. Clairemont Ave.   Phone: (715) 836-4756
Eau Claire, WI 54701   Lorraine Kearney, Coord., Lib.Serv.

LUTHER HOSPITAL - MEDICAL LIBRARY
1221 Whipple St.   Phone: (715) 839-3248
Eau Claire, WI 54701   Eileen Emberson, Dir.Lib.Serv.

SACRED HEART HOSPITAL - MEDICAL LIBRARY
900 W. Clairemont Ave.   Phone: (715) 839-4330
Eau Claire, WI 54701   Bruno Warner, Libn.

LAKELAND COUNSELING CENTER - LIBRARY
Box 1005, Hwy. NN   Phone: (414) 723-5400
Elkhorn, WI 53121   Ruby Bill, Libn.

LAKELAND HOSPITAL - MEDICAL LIBRARY
Hwy. NN
Box 1002   Phone: (414) 723-2960
Elkhorn, WI 53121   Mary Bray, Libn.

SOUTHWEST WISCONSIN VOCATIONAL-TECHNICAL INSTITUTE - LEARNING RESOURCES CENTER *
Bronson Blvd.   Phone: (608) 822-3262
Fennimore, WI 53809   Harold Krubsack, Dir.

MORAINE PARK TECHNICAL INSTITUTE - LEARNING RESOURCE CENTER
235 N. National Ave.   Phone: (414) 922-8611
Fond Du Lac, WI 54935   Judy Denor, Lib.Spec.

ST. AGNES HOSPITAL - LIBRARY
430 E. Division St.   Phone: (414) 921-2300
Fond Du Lac, WI 54935   Sr. Mary David Boyle, C.S.A., Libn.

WISCONSIN STATE - FOND DU LAC COUNTY LAW LIBRARY
Court House   Phone: (414) 921-5600
Fond Du Lac, WI 54935   Mary E. Scharf, Law Libn.

HOARD HISTORICAL MUSEUM - LIBRARY
407 Merchant Ave.   Phone: (414) 563-4521
Fort Atkinson, WI 53538   Hannah Swart, Cur.

NORLAND CORPORATION - TECHNICAL LIBRARY *
R4 Norland Dr.   Phone: (414) 563-8456
Fort Atkinson, WI 53538   Jean Badura, Tech.Libn.

BELLIN MEMORIAL HOSPITAL - HEALTH SCIENCES LIBRARY
744 S. Webster Ave.
Box 1700   Phone: (414) 468-3693
Green Bay, WI 54305   Shelley Jordan, Libn.

BROWN COUNTY MENTAL HEALTH CENTER - H.H. HUMPHREY MEMORIAL STAFF LIBRARY
2900 St. Anthony Dr.   Phone: (414) 468-1136
Green Bay, WI 54301   Nancy Hillen, Lib.Mgr.

DURANT FAMILY REGISTRY - LIBRARY
2700 Timber Ln.   Phone: (414) 499-8797
Green Bay, WI 54303   Jeff Gillis, Hd.

GREEN BAY PRESS-GAZETTE - LIBRARY
435 E. Walnut St.   Phone: (414) 435-4411
Green Bay, WI 54305   Diane L. Laes, Libn.

NEVILLE PUBLIC MUSEUM - LIBRARY
129 S. Jefferson St.
Green Bay, WI 54301   Phone: (414) 497-3767

NORTHEAST WISCONSIN TECHNICAL INSTITUTE - LEARNING RESOURCE
    CENTER
2740 W. Mason   Phone: (414) 497-3190
Green Bay, WI 54303   Mary Hein, Libn.

ST. VINCENT HOSPITAL - MEDICAL LIBRARY
835 S. VanBuren St.
Box 1221   Phone: (414) 433-8172
Green Bay, WI 54305   Joan M. Bower, R.R.A.

SCHREIBER FOODS, INC. - LIBRARY
425 Pine St.
Box 610   Phone: (414) 437-7601
Green Bay, WI 54305   Karen K. Braatz, Info.Spec.

UNIVERSITY OF WISCONSIN, GREEN BAY - AREA RESEARCH CENTER
2420 Nicolet Dr.   Phone: (414) 465-2383
Green Bay, WI 54302   Dorothy L. Heinrich, Spec.Coll.Libn.

BOERNER BOTANICAL GARDENS - HORTICULTURE REFERENCE LIBRARY *
Whitnall Park
5879 S. 92nd St.
Hales Corners, WI 53130   Phone: (414) 421-1130

EXPERIMENTAL AIRCRAFT ASSOCIATION - AIR MUSEUM FOUNDATION,
    INC. - RESEARCH LIBRARY
11311 W. Forest Home Ave.
Box 469
Hales Corners, WI 53130

SACRED HEART MONASTERY - LEO DEHON LIBRARY
7331 S. Lovers Lane Rd.   Phone: (414) 425-8300
Hales Corners, WI 53130   Sr. Agnese Jasko, P.H.J.C., Libn.

BLACKHAWK TECHNICAL INSTITUTE, JANESVILLE - LEARNING MATERIALS
    CENTER *
Prairie Ave., Rte. 3   Phone: (608) 756-4121
Janesville, WI 53545   Grace Sweeney, Libn.

MERCY HOSPITAL - MEDICAL LIBRARY
1000 Mineral Point   Phone: (608) 756-6749
Janesville, WI 53545   Lois J. Zuehlke, Lib.Dir.

ROCK COUNTY HEALTH CARE CENTER - STAFF LIBRARY
Box 351   Phone: (608) 755-2542
Janesville, WI 53545   Claudia M. Cramer, Libn.

ROCK COUNTY HISTORICAL SOCIETY - ARCHIVES OF ROCK COUNTY
    HISTORY
10 S. High
Box 896   Phone: (608) 752-4519
Janesville, WI 53545   Ruth Widdicombe, Archv./Libn.

WISCONSIN STATE DEPARTMENT OF PUBLIC INSTRUCTION - SCHOOL FOR
    THE VISUALLY HANDICAPPED - LIBRARY
1700 W. State St.   Phone: (608) 755-2950
Janesville, WI 53545   Jean Wolski, Libn.

COUNTRYSIDE HOME - STAFF LIBRARY
Hwy. W.   Phone: (414) 674-3170
Jefferson, WI 53549   Catherine M. Rueth, Sec./Libn.

GATEWAY VOCATIONAL TECHNICAL & ADULT EDUCATION DISTRICT -
    LEARNING RESOURCES CENTER
3520 30th Ave.   Phone: (414) 656-6924
Kenosha, WI 53141   Frank Burbank, Coord.Instr.Rsrcs.

KENOSHA ACHIEVEMENT CENTER - LIBRARY *
1218 79th St.   Phone: (414) 658-1687
Kenosha, WI 53140   Betty Anderson

KENOSHA COUNTY HISTORICAL SOCIETY - HISTORICAL MUSEUM LIBRARY
6300 3rd Ave.   Phone: (414) 654-5770
Kenosha, WI 53140   Phil Sander, Musm.Dir.

KENOSHA MEMORIAL HOSPITAL - HEALTH SCIENCES LIBRARY
6308 Eighth Ave.   Phone: (414) 656-2120
Kenosha, WI 53140   Esther L. Puhek, Libn.

KENOSHA NEWS - NEWSPAPER LIBRARY †
715 58th St.   Phone: (414) 657-1000
Kenosha, WI 53141   Bernice L. Nagy, Libn.

KENOSHA PUBLIC MUSEUM - LIBRARY
Civic Center, 5608 10th Ave.   Phone: (414) 656-6026
Kenosha, WI 53140   Stephen H. Schwartz, Dir.

ST. CATHERINE'S HOSPITAL - MEDICAL LIBRARY
3556 Seventh Ave.   Phone: (414) 656-3230
Kenosha, WI 53140   Mary Sipsma, Med.Libn.

SOCIETY FOR THE PRESERVATION AND ENCOURAGEMENT OF BARBER
    SHOP QUARTET SINGING IN AMERICA - OLD SONGS LIBRARY
6315 Third Ave.
Box 575   Phone: (414) 654-9111
Kenosha, WI 53141   Ruth Marks, Harmony Found.Adm.

UNIVERSITY OF WISCONSIN, PARKSIDE - UNIVERSITY ARCHIVES AND
    AREA RESEARCH CENTER
Box 2000   Phone: (414) 553-2411
Kenosha, WI 53141   Nicholas C. Burckel, Dir.

DAIRYLAND POWER COOPERATIVE - LIBRARY
2615 E. Ave. South   Phone: (608) 788-4000
La Crosse, WI 54601   Dolly Matthes, Rec.Coord.

LA CROSSE LUTHERAN HOSPITAL - HEALTH SCIENCES LIBRARY
1910 South Ave.   Phone: (608) 785-0530
La Crosse, WI 54601   LaVerne Samb, Libn.

ST. FRANCIS MEDICAL CENTER - HEALTH SCIENCES LIBRARY
615 S. 10th St.   Phone: (608) 785-0940
La Crosse, WI 54601   Sr. Regine Lang, Libn.

U.S. FISH & WILDLIFE SERVICE - NATIONAL FISHERY RESEARCH
    LABORATORY LIBRARY
National Fishery Research Laboratory
Box 818   Phone: (608) 783-6451
La Crosse, WI 54601   Rosalie A. Schnick, Tech.Info.Spec.

UNIVERSITY OF WISCONSIN, LA CROSSE - AUDIOVISUAL CENTER - FILM
    LIBRARY
1705 State St.   Phone: (608) 785-8040
La Crosse, WI 54601   Gary Goorough, Film Libn.

UNIVERSITY OF WISCONSIN, LA CROSSE - CENTER FOR CONTEMPORARY
    POETRY
Murphy Library
1631 Pine St.   Phone: (608) 785-8511
La Crosse, WI 54601   Edwin L. Hill, Spec.Coll.Libn.

UNIVERSITY OF WISCONSIN, LA CROSSE - CURRICULUM AND
    INSTRUCTION CENTER
Morris Hall   Phone: (608) 785-8651
La Crosse, WI 54601   Alice Hagar, Media Libn.

UNIVERSITY OF WISCONSIN, LA CROSSE - MURPHY LIBRARY
1631 Pine St.   Phone: (608) 785-8507
La Crosse, WI 54601   Dale Gresseth, Chm.

VITERBO COLLEGE - ZOELLER FINE ARTS LIBRARY
815 S. Ninth   Phone: (608) 784-0040
La Crosse, WI 54601   Sr. Rosella Namer, Fine Arts Libn.

WESLEY UNITED METHODIST CHURCH - LIBRARY
8th & King Sts.   Phone: (608) 782-3018
La Crosse, WI 54601   Johnina Wardwell, Libn.

WESTERN WISCONSIN TECHNICAL INSTITUTE - LIBRARY
6th & Vine Sts.   Phone: (608) 785-9142
La Crosse, WI 54601   Mrs. Thuan T. Tran, Hd.Libn.

GEOGRAPHIC

AMERICAN SOCIETY OF AGRONOMY - INFORMATION CENTER
677 S. Segoe Rd.   Phone: (608) 274-1212
Madison, WI 53711

CAPITAL TIMES NEWSPAPER - LIBRARY
1901 Fish Hatchery Rd.   Phone: (608) 252-6412
Madison, WI 53715   Ann Lund, Libn.

CREDIT UNION NATIONAL ASSOCIATION - INFORMATION RESOURCE
   CENTER
5710 W. Mineral Point Rd.
Box 431   Phone: (608) 231-4170
Madison, WI 53701   Judith Sayrs, Ref.Libn.

DANE COUNTY LAW LIBRARY
230 City-County Bldg.
210 Monona Ave.   Phone: (608) 266-4230
Madison, WI 53709   Lorraine Breszee, Libn.

DANE COUNTY REGIONAL PLANNING COMMISSION - LIBRARY
City-County Bldg., Rm. 114   Phone: (608) 266-4137
Madison, WI 53709   Ellen Chin, Libn.

FOREST PRODUCTS RESEARCH SOCIETY - ABSTRACT INFO. DIGEST
   SERVICE - INFORMATION CTR.
2801 Marshall Ct.   Phone: (608) 231-1361
Madison, WI 53705   Joni M. Hermanson, Info.Sys.Dir.

GREATER MADISON CHAMBER OF COMMERCE - MATERIALS REFERENCE
   LIBRARY
Box 71   Phone: (608) 256-8348
Madison, WI 53701   Robert Brennan, Pres.

MADISON AREA TECHNICAL COLLEGE - TECHNICAL CENTER LIBRARY
2125 Commercial Ave.   Phone: (608) 266-5025
Madison, WI 53704   Janet B. Jeffcott, Tech.Libn.

MADISON BUSINESS COLLEGE - LIBRARY
1110 Spring Harbor Dr.   Phone: (608) 238-4266
Madison, WI 53705   Mary T. Boyd, Libn.

MADISON GENERAL HOSPITAL - MEMORIAL LIBRARY
202 South Park St.   Phone: (608) 267-6202
Madison, WI 53715   Dona Bowman, Med.Libn.

MADISON GENERAL HOSPITAL - NURSING EDUCATION - MAUDE WEBSTER
   MIDDLETON LIBRARY
1010 Mound St.   Phone: (608) 267-6250
Madison, WI 53715   Vicki Schluge, Instr.Rsrcs.Mgr.

MADISON METROPOLITAN SCHOOL DISTRICT - EDUCATION REFERENCE
   LIBRARY
545 W. Dayton St.   Phone: (608) 266-6188
Madison, WI 53703   Maryfaith Fox, Ref.Libn.

MADISON PUBLIC LIBRARY - ART AND MUSIC DIVISION
201 W. Mifflin   Phone: (608) 266-6311
Madison, WI 53703   Beverly Brager, Supv.

MADISON PUBLIC LIBRARY - BUSINESS AND SCIENCE DIVISION
201 W. Mifflin St.   Phone: (608) 266-6333
Madison, WI 53703   Philip Sullivan, Supv.

MADISON PUBLIC LIBRARY - LITERATURE AND SOCIAL SCIENCES
201 W. Mifflin St.   Phone: (608) 266-6350
Madison, WI 53703   Natalie Tinkham, Supv.Libn.

MADISON PUBLIC LIBRARY - MUNICIPAL REFERENCE SERVICE
City-County Bldg., Rm. 103B
210 Monona Ave.   Phone: (608) 266-6316
Madison, WI 53709   Ann Waidelich, Libn.

MAYER (Oscar) & COMPANY - RESEARCH DEPARTMENT LIBRARY
Box 7188   Phone: (608) 241-3311
Madison, WI 53707   Thomas R. Whitemarsh, Res.Libn.

MENDOTA MENTAL HEALTH INSTITUTE - LIBRARY MEDIA CENTER
301 Troy Dr.   Phone: (608) 244-2411
Madison, WI 53704   Margaret Tielke Grinnell, Act.Dir.

METHODIST HOSPITAL - LIBRARY
309 W. Washington Ave.
Madison, WI 53703   Mary Alice Kuehling, Libn.

RALTECH SCIENTIFIC SERVICES - LIBRARY
3301 Kinsman Blvd.
Box 7545   Phone: (608) 241-4471
Madison, WI 53707   Patricia Riese, Libn.

RAY-O-VAC CORP. - TECHNOLOGY CENTER LIBRARY
630 Forward Dr.   Phone: (608) 252-7400
Madison, WI 53711   Barbara A. Lazewski, Tech.Libn.

ST. MARIA GORETTI PARISH LIBRARY *
5405 Flad Ave.   Phone: (608) 271-8081
Madison, WI 53711

STATE HISTORICAL SOCIETY OF WISCONSIN - ARCHIVES DIVISION
816 State St.   Phone: (608) 262-3338
Madison, WI 53706   F. Gerald Ham, State Archv. & Dir.

STATE HISTORICAL SOCIETY OF WISCONSIN - LIBRARY
816 State St.   Phone: (608) 262-3421
Madison, WI 53706   Peter Draz, Hd.Libn.

TRINITY LUTHERAN CHURCH - LIBRARY
1904 Winnebago St.   Phone: (608) 249-8527
Madison, WI 53704   Sharon Kenyon, Libn.

U.S. FOREST SERVICE - FOREST PRODUCTS LABORATORY LIBRARY
Box 5130   Phone: (608) 264-5712
Madison, WI 53705   Roger Scharmer, Libn.

U.S. GEOLOGICAL SURVEY - WATER RESOURCES DIVISION - LIBRARY
1815 University Ave.   Phone: (608) 262-2488
Madison, WI 53706   Marla Wallace, Lib.Techn.

U.S. VETERANS ADMINISTRATION (WI-Madison) - WILLIAM S. MIDDLETON
   MEMORIAL VETERANS HOSPITAL - LIBRARY
2500 Overlook Terrace   Phone: (608) 256-1901
Madison, WI 53705   Anne Taylor, Chf., Lib.Serv.

UNIVERSITY OF WISCONSIN, MADISON - AFRICAN STUDIES
   INSTRUCTIONAL MATERIALS CENTER
Teachers Education Bldg.
225 N. Mills St.   Phone: (608) 263-4178
Madison, WI 53706   Joseph Adjaye, Outreach Spec.

UNIVERSITY OF WISCONSIN, MADISON - ARCHIVES
B134 Memorial Library   Phone: (608) 262-3290
Madison, WI 53706   J. Frank Cook, Dir.

UNIVERSITY OF WISCONSIN, MADISON - BIOLOGY LIBRARY
Birge Hall   Phone: (608) 262-2740
Madison, WI 53706   Gordon R. Luce, Jr., Libn.

UNIVERSITY OF WISCONSIN, MADISON - BOTANY DEPARTMENT -
   HERBARIUM LIBRARY
158 Birge Hall   Phone: (608) 262-2792
Madison, WI 53706   H.H. Iltis, Dir. of Herbarium

UNIVERSITY OF WISCONSIN, MADISON - BUREAU OF AUDIOVISUAL
   INSTRUCTION - LIBRARY
1327 University Ave.
Box 2093   Phone: (608) 262-1644
Madison, WI 53701   Dr. Hal F. Riehle, Dir.

UNIVERSITY OF WISCONSIN, MADISON - CARTOGRAPHIC LABORATORY -
   MAP AND AIR PHOTO LIBRARY
384 Science Hall
550 N. Park St.   Phone: (608) 262-1471
Madison, WI 53706   Mary Galneder, Map Libn.

UNIVERSITY OF WISCONSIN, MADISON - CENTER FOR DEMOGRAPHY -
   LIBRARY
3216 Social Science Bldg.   Phone: (608) 262-2182
Madison, WI 53706   Ruth Sandor, Libn.

UNIVERSITY OF WISCONSIN, MADISON - CENTER FOR HEALTH SCIENCES
  LIBRARIES
1305 Linden Dr.   Phone: (608) 262-6594
Madison, WI 53706   Virginia Holtz, Dir.

UNIVERSITY OF WISCONSIN, MADISON - CHEMISTRY LIBRARY
Chemistry Bldg.   Phone: (608) 262-2942
Madison, WI 53706   Kendall Rouse, Libn.

UNIVERSITY OF WISCONSIN, MADISON - COLLEGE OF ENGINEERING -
  TECHNICAL REPORTS CENTER
Kurt F. Wendt Library
215 N. Randall Ave.   Phone: (608) 262-6845
Madison, WI 53706   Jean Gilbertson, Libn.

UNIVERSITY OF WISCONSIN, MADISON - COMPUTER SCIENCES-
  COMPUTING CENTER-STATISTICS STAFF COLLECTION
1210 W. Dayton St., Rm. 3134   Phone: (608) 262-2055
Madison, WI 53706   Frieda S. Cohn, Spec.

UNIVERSITY OF WISCONSIN, MADISON - COOPERATIVE CHILDREN'S
  BOOK CENTER (CCBC)
Helen C. White Hall, Rm. 4289-4290
600 N. Park St.   Phone: (608) 263-3721
Madison, WI 53706   Ginny Moore Kruse, Dir.

UNIVERSITY OF WISCONSIN, MADISON - DATA AND PROGRAM LIBRARY
  SERVICE *
4452 Social Science Bldg.   Phone: (608) 262-7962
Madison, WI 53706   Martin David, Dir.

UNIVERSITY OF WISCONSIN, MADISON - DEPARTMENT OF PSYCHIATRY -
  LITHIUM INFORMATION CENTER
600 Highland Ave.   Phone: (608) 263-6171
Madison, WI 53792   Dr. James W. Jefferson, Co-Dir.

UNIVERSITY OF WISCONSIN, MADISON - DEPARTMENT OF RURAL
  SOCIOLOGY - APPLIED POPULATION LAB. - LIBRARY
Agriculture Hall, Rm. 420   Phone: (608) 262-3029
Madison, WI 53706   Stephen J. Tordella, Spec.

UNIVERSITY OF WISCONSIN, MADISON - DEPARTMENT OF URBAN AND
  REGIONAL PLANNING - GRADUATE RESEARCH CENTER
Music Hall
925 Lathrop Dr.   Phone: (608) 262-1004
Madison, WI 53706   Janet F. Kline, Libn.

UNIVERSITY OF WISCONSIN, MADISON - F.B. POWER PHARMACEUTICAL
  LIBRARY
School of Pharmacy
425 N. Charter St.   Phone: (608) 262-2894
Madison, WI 53706   Dolores Nemec, Libn.

UNIVERSITY OF WISCONSIN, MADISON - GEOGRAPHY LIBRARY
250 Science Hall   Phone: (608) 262-1706
Madison, WI 53706   Miriam E. Kerndt, Libn.

UNIVERSITY OF WISCONSIN, MADISON - GEOLOGY-GEOPHYSICS LIBRARY
440 Weeks Hall   Phone: (608) 262-8956
Madison, WI 53706   Nancy L. Crossfield, Libn.

UNIVERSITY OF WISCONSIN, MADISON - GERALD G. SOMERS GRADUATE
  REFERENCE ROOM
8432 Social Science Bldg.
1180 Observatory Dr.   Phone: (608) 262-6195
Madison, WI 53706   Virginia Wolters, Libn.

UNIVERSITY OF WISCONSIN, MADISON - INSTITUTE FOR RESEARCH IN
  THE HUMANITIES - LIBRARY
Old Observatory   Phone: (608) 262-3855
Madison, WI 53706

UNIVERSITY OF WISCONSIN, MADISON - KOHLER ART LIBRARY
Elvehjem Museum of Art
800 University Ave.   Phone: (608) 263-2256
Madison, WI 53706   William C. Bunce, Dir. & Hd.Libn.

UNIVERSITY OF WISCONSIN, MADISON - KURT F. WENDT ENGINEERING
  LIBRARY
215 N. Randall Ave.   Phone: (608) 262-7980
Madison, WI 53706   Prof. LeRoy G. Zweifel, Dir.

UNIVERSITY OF WISCONSIN, MADISON - LABORATORY OF LIMNOLOGY -
  LIBRARY
                                             Phone: (608) 262-2840
Madison, WI 53706   Dr. J.J. Magnuson, Dir. Of Lib.

UNIVERSITY OF WISCONSIN, MADISON - LAND TENURE CENTER - LIBRARY
434 Steenbock Memorial Library
550 Babcock Dr.   Phone: (608) 262-1240
Madison, WI 53706   Beverly R. Phillips, Libn.

UNIVERSITY OF WISCONSIN, MADISON - LAW LIBRARY
                                             Phone: (608) 262-1128
Madison, WI 53706   Maurice Leon, Dir.

UNIVERSITY OF WISCONSIN, MADISON - LAW SCHOOL- CRIMINAL
  JUSTICE REFERENCE & INFORMATION CENTER
L140 Law Bldg.   Phone: (608) 262-1499
Madison, WI 53706   Sue L. Center, Dir.

UNIVERSITY OF WISCONSIN, MADISON - LIBRARY SCHOOL LIBRARY
600 N. Park St.   Phone: (608) 263-2960
Madison, WI 53706   Sally Davis, Libn.

UNIVERSITY OF WISCONSIN, MADISON - MARINE ENVIRONMENT
  READING ROOM
1225 W. Dayton St., Room 1229   Phone: (608) 262-1585
Madison, WI 53706

UNIVERSITY OF WISCONSIN, MADISON - MATHEMATICS LIBRARY
B224 Van Vleck Hall   Phone: (608) 262-3596
Madison, WI 53706   Shirley Tan Shen, Libn.

UNIVERSITY OF WISCONSIN, MADISON - MILLS MUSIC LIBRARY
B162 Memorial Library
728 State St.   Phone: (608) 263-1884
Madison, WI 53706   Lenore Coral, Libn.

UNIVERSITY OF WISCONSIN, MADISON - NIEMAN-GRANT JOURNALISM
  READING ROOM
2130 Vilas Communication Hall
821 University Ave.   Phone: (608) 263-3387
Madison, WI 53706   Ellen H. Hammond, Libn.

UNIVERSITY OF WISCONSIN, MADISON - PHYSICS LIBRARY
1150 University Ave.   Phone: (608) 262-9500
Madison, WI 53706   Sandra Moline, Hd.

UNIVERSITY OF WISCONSIN, MADISON - PLANT PATHOLOGY
  DEPARTMENT - MEMORIAL LIBRARY
1630 Linden Dr.   Phone: (608) 262-1410
Madison, WI 53706   Helen H. Kuntz, Lib.Supv.

UNIVERSITY OF WISCONSIN, MADISON - POULTRY SCIENCE DEPARTMENT
  - HALPIN MEMORIAL LIBRARY
Animal Science Bldg., Rm. 214
1675 Observatory Dr.   Phone: (608) 262-1243
Madison, WI 53706   Louis C. Arrington, Prof.

UNIVERSITY OF WISCONSIN, MADISON - SCHOOL OF EDUCATION -
  HISTORICAL MATERIALS COLLECTION
Education Bldg., Box 66
1000 Bascom Mall   Phone: (608) 263-6575
Madison, WI 53706   Prof. Lola R. Pierstorff, Dir.

UNIVERSITY OF WISCONSIN, MADISON - SCHOOL OF EDUCATION -
  INSTRUCTIONAL MATERIALS CENTER
Teacher Education Bldg.
225 N. Mills St.   Phone: (608) 263-4750
Madison, WI 53706   Deane W. Hill, Dir.

UNIVERSITY OF WISCONSIN, MADISON - SCHOOL OF SOCIAL WORK -
  RESEARCH & INSTRUCTIONAL MEDIA CENTER
425 Henry Mall, Rm. 163   Phone: (608) 263-3663
Madison, WI 53706   Dennis Rinzel, Media Dir.

UNIVERSITY OF WISCONSIN, MADISON - SCHOOL OF SOCIAL WORK -
   VIRGINIA L. FRANKS MEMORIAL LIBRARY
425 Henry Mall, Rm. 230   Phone: (608) 263-3840
Madison, WI 53706   Thurston Davini, Libn.

UNIVERSITY OF WISCONSIN, MADISON - SEMINARY OF MEDIEVAL
   SPANISH STUDIES - LIBRARY
1120 Van Hise Hall   Phone: (608) 262-2529
Madison, WI 53706   Lloyd Kasten, Prof.

UNIVERSITY OF WISCONSIN, MADISON - STEENBOCK MEMORIAL LIBRARY
          Phone: (608) 262-9990
Madison, WI 53706   Daisy T. Wu, Dir.

UNIVERSITY OF WISCONSIN, MADISON - THEORETICAL CHEMISTRY
   INSTITUTE - LIBRARY
1101 University Ave., Rm. 8326   Phone: (608) 262-1511
Madison, WI 53706   Prof. Phillip R. Certain

UNIVERSITY OF WISCONSIN, MADISON - UNIVERSITY CENTER FOR
   COOPERATIVES LIBRARY
Lowell Hall, Rm. 524
610 Langdon St.   Phone: (608) 262-3251
Madison, WI 53706   MaryJean McGrath, Act.Libn.

UNIVERSITY OF WISCONSIN, MADISON - VOCATIONAL EDUCATION
   RESOURCE MATERIALS CENTER
1263 B Educational Sciences   Phone: (608) 263-2929
Madison, WI 53706   Geraldine Strey, Libn.

UNIVERSITY OF WISCONSIN, MADISON - WASHBURN OBSERVATORY -
   WOODMAN ASTRONOMICAL LIBRARY
6521 Sterling Hall
475 N. Charter St.   Phone: (608) 262-1320
Madison, WI 53706   Marcia Lynn Cooke, Libn.

UNIVERSITY OF WISCONSIN, MADISON - WATER RESOURCES CENTER -
   LIBRARY
1975 Willow Dr.   Phone: (608) 262-3069
Madison, WI 53706   Sarah L. Calcese, Libn.

UNIVERSITY OF WISCONSIN, MADISON - WILLIAM A. SCOTT BUSINESS
   LIBRARY
School of Business, Bascom Hall
500 Lincoln Dr.   Phone: (608) 262-5935
Madison, WI 53706   Marilyn Hicks, Bus.Libn.

UNIVERSITY OF WISCONSIN, MADISON - WILLIAM A. SCOTT BUSINESS
   LIBRARY - JOHNSON FOUNDATION COLLECTION *
School Of Business
1155 Observatory Dr.   Phone: (608) 263-2120
Madison, WI 53706   Randall B. Dunham, Prof.

UNIVERSITY OF WISCONSIN, MADISON - WISCONSIN CENTER FOR FILM
   AND THEATER RESEARCH
Vilas Communication Hall   Phone: (608) 262-9706
Madison, WI 53706   Tino Balio, Dir.

UNIVERSITY OF WISCONSIN, MADISON - WISCONSIN REGIONAL PRIMATE
   RESEARCH CENTER - PRIMATE LIBRARY
1223 Capitol Court   Phone: (608) 263-3512
Madison, WI 53706   Lawrence Jacobsen, Libn.

UNIVERSITY OF WISCONSIN, MADISON - ZOOLOGICAL MUSEUM LIBRARY
L.E. Noland Bldg.
250 N. Mills St.   Phone: (608) 262-3766
Madison, WI 53706   E. Elizabeth Pillaert, Cur.

VESTERHEIM GENEALOGICAL CENTER/NORWEGIAN-AMERICAN MUSEUM
   - LIBRARY
4909 Sherwood Rd.   Phone: (608) 271-8826
Madison, WI 53711   Gerhard B. Naeseth, Libn.

VISITING NURSE SERVICE, INC. - LIBRARY *
328 E. Lakeside St.   Phone: (608) 257-6710
Madison, WI 53715

WISCONSIN ALUMNI RESEARCH FOUNDATION - LIBRARY
614 N. Walnut St.
Box 7365   Phone: (608) 263-2848
Madison, WI 53707   Lila N. Hillyer, Libn.

WISCONSIN HOSPITAL ASSOCIATION - MEMORIAL LIBRARY
5721 Odana Rd.   Phone: (608) 274-1820
Madison, WI 53719   Pat Craven, Libn.

WISCONSIN STATE BOARD OF VOCATIONAL, TECHNICAL & ADULT
   EDUCATION - RESEARCH COORDINATING UNIT RESOURCE CTR.
4802 Sheboygan Ave., HFSOB, 7th Fl.   Phone: (608) 266-3705
Madison, WI 53702   Roland Krogstad, Dir.

WISCONSIN STATE DEPARTMENT OF ADMINISTRATION - LIBRARY
Gen. Executive Facility II
101 S. Webster St.   Phone: (608) 266-0035
Madison, WI 53702   JoAnn Howlett, Libn.

WISCONSIN STATE DEPARTMENT OF JUSTICE - LAW LIBRARY
123 W. Washington, Rm. 349   Phone: (608) 266-0325
Madison, WI 53702   Michael F. Bemis, Law Libn.

WISCONSIN STATE DEPARTMENT OF PUBLIC INSTRUCTION - LIBRARY
125 S. Webster St., 4th Fl.   Phone: (608) 266-2529
Madison, WI 53702   Marjorie D. Westergard, Libn.

WISCONSIN STATE DEPARTMENT OF PUBLIC INSTRUCTION - WISCONSIN
   DISSEMINATION PROJECT (WDP)
125 S. Webster St.
Box 7841   Phone: (608) 266-2127
Madison, WI 53707   Loretta Harmatuck, Coord.

WISCONSIN STATE DEPARTMENT OF TRANSPORTATION - LIBRARY
4802 Sheboygan Ave., Rm. 901
Box 7913   Phone: (608) 266-0724
Madison, WI 53707   Cordell Klyve, Libn.

WISCONSIN STATE DIVISION FOR LIBRARY SERVICES - REFERENCE AND
   LOAN LIBRARY
2109 S. Stoughton Rd.   Phone: (608) 266-1053
Madison, WI 53716   Peter Hamon, Dir.

WISCONSIN STATE JOURNAL - LIBRARY
Box 8058   Phone: (608) 252-6112
Madison, WI 53708   Ronald J. Larson, Hd.Libn.

WISCONSIN STATE LAW LIBRARY
310 E., State Capitol   Phone: (608) 266-1424
Madison, WI 53702   Marcia J. Koslov, State Law Libn.

WISCONSIN STATE LEGISLATIVE REFERENCE BUREAU
State Capitol   Phone: (608) 266-0341
Madison, WI 53702   H. Rupert Theobald, Chf.

WISCONSIN STATE MEDICAL SOCIETY - LIBRARY
330 E. Lakeside St.
Box 1109   Phone: (608) 257-6781
Madison, WI 53701   Mary Angell, Mng.Ed./Libn.

WISCONSIN STATE OFFICE OF THE COMMISSIONER OF INSURANCE -
   LIBRARY
123 W. Washington Ave., 7th Fl.   Phone: (608) 266-0376
Madison, WI 53702   Sharon Dowd

HOLY FAMILY HOSPITAL - HEALTH SCIENCE LIBRARY
21st & Western Ave.   Phone: (414) 684-2260
Manitowoc, WI 54220   Dan Eckert, Libn.

RAHR - WEST MUSEUM AND CIVIC CENTER - LIBRARY
Park St. at N. 8th
Manitowoc, WI 54220

MARINETTE COUNTY LAW LIBRARY
Court House, 1926 Hall Ave.   Phone: (715) 735-3371
Marinette, WI 54143   Don E. Phillips, Ck. of Court

MARSHFIELD CLINIC - MEDICAL CENTER LIBRARY
1000 N. Oak   Phone: (715) 387-5183
Marshfield, WI 54449   Albert Zimmermann, Med.Ed., Libn.

ST. JOSEPH'S HOSPITAL - SCHOOL OF NURSING - LEARNING RESOURCE
  CENTER
509 St. Joseph Ave.   Phone: (715) 387-7374
Marshfield, WI 54449   Margaret A. Allen, Libn.

MEDICAL ASSOCIATES - HEALTH CENTER - LIBRARY
W180 N7950 Town Hall Rd.   Phone: (414) 255-2500
Menomonee Falls, WI 53051   Kirsten R. Shelstad, Lib.Dir.

UNIVERSITY OF WISCONSIN, STOUT - LIBRARY LEARNING CENTER -
  MEDIA RETRIEVAL SERVICES
                                                 Phone: (715) 232-1184
Menomonie, WI 54751   John J. Jax, Dir.

WISCONSIN LUTHERAN SEMINARY - LIBRARY
6633 W. Wartburg Circle   Phone: (414) 242-2331
Mequon, WI 53092   Rev. Martin O. Westerhaus, Libn.

ALLEN-BRADLEY COMPANY - CORPORATE LIBRARY
1201 S. 2nd St.
Box 2086   Phone: (414) 671-2000
Milwaukee, WI 53201   Agnes G. Rice, Libn.

ALLIS-CHALMERS CORPORATION - ADVANCED TECHNOLOGY CENTER -
  LIBRARY *
Box 512   Phone: (414) 475-2102
Milwaukee, WI 53201   R.A. Schlueter, Libn.

ALVERNO COLLEGE - RESEARCH CENTER ON WOMEN
3401 S. 39th St.   Phone: (414) 671-5400
Milwaukee, WI 53215   Lola Stuller, Libn.

AMERICAN APPRAISAL COMPANY - LIBRARY
525 E. Michigan St.   Phone: (414) 271-7240
Milwaukee, WI 53201   Stella Lorenz, Libn.

AMERICAN GEOGRAPHICAL SOCIETY COLLECTION OF THE UNIVERSITY OF
  WISCONSIN, MILWAUKEE - GOLDA MEIR LIBRARY
Box 399   Phone: (414) 963-6282
Milwaukee, WI 53201   Roman Drazniowsky, Cur.

AMERICAN SOCIETY FOR QUALITY CONTROL - LIBRARY
161 W. Wisconsin Ave.   Phone: (414) 272-8575
Milwaukee, WI 53203   Robert Abbott, Tech.Dir.

AMF/HARLEY-DAVIDSON MOTOR CO. - ENGINEERING LIBRARY
3700 W. Juneau Ave.
Box 653
Milwaukee, WI 53201

ASCENSION LUTHERAN CHURCH - LIBRARY
1236 S. Layton Blvd.   Phone: (414) 671-5066
Milwaukee, WI 53215   Lorraine Pike, Libn.

AUTOTROL CORPORATION - BIO-SYSTEMS DIVISION - INFORMATION
  CENTER *
5855 N. Glen Park Rd.   Phone: (414) 228-9100
Milwaukee, WI 53209   Dannette H. Lank, Info.Res.Spec.

BEIHOFF MUSIC CORPORATION - SHEET MUSIC DEPARTMENT
5040 W. North Ave.   Phone: (414) 442-3920
Milwaukee, WI 53208   Robert F. Loomer, Mgr.

CATHOLIC SOCIAL SERVICES - LIBRARY
206 E. Michigan St.   Phone: (414) 271-2881
Milwaukee, WI 53202   Anne Kozlowski, Coord.

CITIZENS' GOVERNMENTAL RESEARCH BUREAU, INC.
125 E. Wells St., Rm. 616   Phone: (414) 276-8240
Milwaukee, WI 53202   Norman N. Gill, Exec.Dir.

COLUMBIA HOSPITAL - MEDICAL LIBRARY
2025 E. Newport Ave.   Phone: (414) 961-3858
Milwaukee, WI 53211   Ruth Holst, Med.Libn.

COLUMBIA HOSPITAL - SCHOOL OF NURSING LIBRARY
2121 E. Newport Ave.   Phone: (414) 961-3533
Milwaukee, WI 53211   Shirley S. Chan, Libn.

COMMUNITY RELATIONS-SOCIAL DEVELOPMENT COMMISSION -
  RESEARCH LIBRARY
161 W. Wisconsin Ave., Rm. 7146   Phone: (414) 272-5600
Milwaukee, WI 53203   Gary McMillan, Res.Spec.

CONGREGATION EMANU-EL B'NE JESHURUN - RABBI DUDLEY WEINBERG
  LIBRARY
2419 E. Kenwood Blvd.   Phone: (414) 964-4100
Milwaukee, WI 53211   Shirley Rumack, Libn.

CONGREGATION SHALOM - SHERMAN PASTOR MEMORIAL LIBRARY
7630 N. Santa Monica Blvd.   Phone: (414) 352-9288
Milwaukee, WI 53217   Ellen Mandelman, Libn.

DE SALES PREPARATORY SEMINARY - LIBRARY *
3501 S. Lake Dr.   Phone: (414) 744-5026
Milwaukee, WI 53207

DEFENSE RESEARCH INSTITUTE, INC. - BRIEF BANK
1100 W. Wells St.   Phone: (414) 272-5995
Milwaukee, WI 53233   Fred L. Bardenwerper, Asst.Res.Dir.

EATON CORPORATION - CUTLER-HAMMER LIBRARY
Box 463-464, 4201 N. 27th St.   Phone: (414) 442-7800
Milwaukee, WI 53201   Herbert J. Seuss, Corp.Libn.

FOLEY & LARDNER - LIBRARY
777 E. Wisconsin Ave.   Phone: (414) 271-2400
Milwaukee, WI 53202   Noreen Link, Libn.

GOOD SAMARITAN MEDICAL CENTER - DEACONESS HOSPITAL CAMPUS -
  HEALTH SCIENCE LIBRARY
620 N. 19th St.   Phone: (414) 933-9600
Milwaukee, WI 53233   Julia Woodward Schleif, Libn.

GOOD SAMARITAN MEDICAL CENTER - LUTHERAN CAMPUS - EVANS
  MEMORIAL LIBRARY
2200 W. Kilbourn Ave.
Milwaukee, WI 53233   Ann Towell, Med.Libn.

GUITAR FOUNDATION OF AMERICA - ARCHIVE
C/O Wisconsin Conservatory Of Music
1584 N. Prospect Ave.
Milwaukee, WI 53202   George Lindquist, Assoc.Archv.

HISTORIC WALKER'S POINT, INC. - LIBRARY
734 S. 5th St.   Phone: (414) 645-9222
Milwaukee, WI 53204   Diane Kealty, Pres.

HOPE LUTHERAN CHURCH - LIBRARY
1115 N. 35th St.
Milwaukee, WI 53208   Mrs. Arthur Damkoehler, Libn.

JOHNSON CONTROLS - BATTERY DIVISION - TECHNICAL LIBRARY
5757 N. Green Bay Ave.   Phone: (414) 228-2382
Milwaukee, WI 53201   Marian Rauch, Tech.Libn.

JOHNSON CONTROLS, INC. - CORPORATE INFO. CTR./LIBRARY M47
507 E. Michigan St.
Box 423   Phone: (414) 277-4687
Milwaukee, WI 53201   Mary F. Kaczmarek, Libn.

KALMBACH PUBLISHING COMPANY - INFORMATION CENTER
1027 N. Seventh St.   Phone: (414) 272-2060
Milwaukee, WI 53233   George H. Drury, Info.Chf.

KRAUSE MILLING COMPANY - TECHNICAL LIBRARY
4222 W. Burnham St.   Phone: (414) 272-6200
Milwaukee, WI 53215   Pamela C. Atwood, Lib.Asst.

MARQUETTE UNIVERSITY - DEPARTMENT OF SPECIAL COLLECTIONS AND
  UNIVERSITY ARCHIVES
Memorial Library
1415 W. Wisconsin Ave.   Phone: (414) 224-7256
Milwaukee, WI 53233   Charles B. Elston, Dept.Hd.

GEOGRAPHIC

MARQUETTE UNIVERSITY - FOUNDATION CENTER REGIONAL REFERENCE
  COLLECTION
Memorial Library
1415 W. Wisconsin Ave.   Phone: (414) 224-1515
Milwaukee, WI 53233   Susan Hopwood, Found.Coll.Libn.

MARQUETTE UNIVERSITY - LEGAL RESEARCH CENTER
1103 W. Wisconsin Ave.   Phone: (414) 224-7031
Milwaukee, WI 53233   Robert L. Starz, Law Libn.

MARQUETTE UNIVERSITY - MEMORIAL LIBRARY
1415 W. Wisconsin Ave.   Phone: (414) 224-7214
Milwaukee, WI 53233   William M. Gardner, Dir. of Libs.

MARQUETTE UNIVERSITY - SCIENCE LIBRARY
560 N. Sixteenth St.   Phone: (414) 224-3396
Milwaukee, WI 53233   Jay H. Kirk, Sci.Libn.

MEDICAL COLLEGE OF WISCONSIN - TODD WEHR LIBRARY
8701 Watertown Plank Rd.
Box 26509   Phone: (414) 257-8323
Milwaukee, WI 53226   Bessie A. Stein, Lib.Dir.

MGIC INVESTMENT CORPORATION - CORPORATE LIBRARY
MGIC Plaza   Phone: (414) 347-6409
Milwaukee, WI 53202   Peg Peterson, Corp.Libn.

MILLER BREWING COMPANY - RESEARCH AND TECHNICAL LIBRARY
3939 W. Highland Blvd.   Phone: (414) 931-3640
Milwaukee, WI 53201   Joanne L. Schwarz, Hd.Libn., Sci. & Tech.

MILWAUKEE ACADEMY OF MEDICINE - LIBRARY
8701 Watertown Plank Rd.
Box 26509
Milwaukee, WI 53226   John P. Mullooly, M.D., Libn.

MILWAUKEE AREA TECHNICAL COLLEGE - RASCHE MEMORIAL LIBRARY
1015 N. Sixth St.   Phone: (414) 278-6205
Milwaukee, WI 53203   Richard E. Meerdink, District Libn.

MILWAUKEE ART CENTER - LIBRARY
750 N. Lincoln Memorial Dr.   Phone: (414) 271-9508
Milwaukee, WI 53202   Betty Karow, Libn.

MILWAUKEE CHILDREN'S HOSPITAL - HEALTH SCIENCES LIBRARY
Box 1997   Phone: (414) 931-4121
Milwaukee, WI 53201   Margaret Wold, Health Sci.Libn.

MILWAUKEE COUNTY BOARD OF SUPERVISORS - RESEARCH LIBRARY *
901 N. 9th St., Room 201   Phone: (414) 278-4952
Milwaukee, WI 53233   Terrence Cooley, Res.Anl.

MILWAUKEE COUNTY HISTORICAL SOCIETY - LIBRARY AND ARCHIVES
910 N. Third St.   Phone: (414) 273-8288
Milwaukee, WI 53203   Robert G. Carroon, Cur.

MILWAUKEE COUNTY LAW LIBRARY
Rm. 307, Courthouse
901 N. 9th St.   Phone: (414) 278-4321
Milwaukee, WI 53233   Divinia J. Astraquillo, Law Libn.

MILWAUKEE COUNTY MENTAL HEALTH COMPLEX - MICHAEL KASAK
  LIBRARY
9455 Watertown Plank Rd.   Phone: (414) 257-7381
Milwaukee, WI 53226   Anna M. Green, Libn.

MILWAUKEE INSTITUTE OF ART & DESIGN - LIBRARY
207 N. Milwaukee St.   Phone: (414) 276-7889
Milwaukee, WI 53202   Terry Marcus, Libn.

MILWAUKEE - LEGISLATIVE REFERENCE BUREAU - LEGISLATIVE LIBRARY
City Hall, Rm. 404
200 E. Wells St.   Phone: (414) 278-2295
Milwaukee, WI 53202   Jean B. Tyler, Dir.

MILWAUKEE PUBLIC LIBRARY - ART, MUSIC AND RECREATION SECTION
814 W. Wisconsin Ave.   Phone: (414) 278-3043
Milwaukee, WI 53233   June M. Edlhauser, Coord. of Fine Arts

MILWAUKEE PUBLIC LIBRARY - HUMANITIES DIVISION - LOCAL HISTORY
  AND MARINE ROOM
814 W. Wisconsin Ave.   Phone: (414) 278-3074
Milwaukee, WI 53233   Paul Woehrmann, Local Hist.Libn.

MILWAUKEE PUBLIC LIBRARY - SCIENCE & BUSINESS DIVISION
814 W. Wisconsin Ave.   Phone: (414) 278-3043
Milwaukee, WI 53233   Theodore Cebula, Coord.Sci./Bus.Div.

MILWAUKEE PUBLIC LIBRARY - WISCONSIN ARCHITECTURAL ARCHIVE
814 W. Wisconsin Ave.   Phone: (414) 278-3897
Milwaukee, WI 53233

MILWAUKEE PUBLIC MUSEUM - REFERENCE LIBRARY
800 W. Wells St.   Phone: (414) 278-2736
Milwaukee, WI 53233   Judith Campbell Turner, Sect.Hd., Libn.

MILWAUKEE SCHOOL OF ENGINEERING - WALTER SCHROEDER LIBRARY
500 E. Kilbourn Ave.
Box 644   Phone: (412) 277-7180
Milwaukee, WI 53201   Mary Ann Schmidt, Libn.

MILWAUKEE URBAN OBSERVATORY - URBAN INFORMATION CENTER
University Of Wisconsin, Milwaukee
Box 413   Phone: (414) 963-4271
Milwaukee, WI 53201   Miriam Poluy, Assoc.Dir.

MOUNT CARMEL LUTHERAN CHURCH - LIBRARY
8424 W. Center St.   Phone: (414) 771-1270
Milwaukee, WI 53222   Verna A. Weller, Libn.

MOUNT SINAI MEDICAL CENTER - MEDICAL LIBRARY
Box 342   Phone: (414) 289-8318
Milwaukee, WI 53201   Deborah A. Hall, Dir.

NATIONAL INVESTMENT SERVICES OF AMERICA, INC. - LIBRARY
815 E. Mason St.
Box 2143   Phone: (414) 271-6540
Milwaukee, WI 53201   Debbie Chapin, Libn.

NORTH UNITED PRESBYTERIAN CHURCH - LIBRARY
3410 W. Silver Spring Dr.   Phone: (414) 466-1870
Milwaukee, WI 53209

NORTHWEST GENERAL HOSPITAL - MEDICAL LIBRARY
5310 W. Capitol Dr.   Phone: (414) 447-8599
Milwaukee, WI 53216   Coralyn Marks, Lib.Dir.

NORTHWESTERN MUTUAL LIFE INSURANCE COMPANY - LAW LIBRARY
720 E. Wisconsin Ave.   Phone: (414) 271-1444
Milwaukee, WI 53202   Jane Marshall, Law Libn.

NORTHWESTERN MUTUAL LIFE INSURANCE COMPANY - MEDICAL LIBRARY
720 E. Wisconsin Ave.   Phone: (414) 271-1444
Milwaukee, WI 53202   Virginia Murphy, Med.Libn.

NORTHWESTERN MUTUAL LIFE INSURANCE COMPANY - REFERENCE
  LIBRARY
720 E. Wisconsin Ave.   Phone: (414) 271-1444
Milwaukee, WI 53202   Patricia H. Ehr, Hd.Libn.

OUR SAVIOR'S LUTHERAN CHURCH - LIBRARY *
3022 W. Wisconsin Ave.   Phone: (414) 342-5252
Milwaukee, WI 53208   Kenneth E. Nordby, Lay Asst.

OUTBOARD MARINE CORPORATION - RESEARCH CENTER LIBRARY *
4109 N. 27th
Box 663   Phone: (414) 447-5400
Milwaukee, WI 53201   Cynthia Meinhardt, Libn.

PABST BREWING COMPANY - P-L BIOCHEMICALS, INC. - RESEARCH
  LIBRARY
1037 W. McKinley Ave.   Phone: (414) 347-7448
Milwaukee, WI 53205   Marie Fendry, Res.Libn.

PALLOTTINE PROVINCIALATE LIBRARY
5424 W. Blue Mound Rd.   Phone: (414) 258-0653
Milwaukee, WI 53208   Rev. Jerome Kuskowski, S.A.C., Libn.

PLANNED PARENTHOOD ASSOCIATION OF WISCONSIN - RESOURCE
    CENTER
1135 W. State St.   Phone: (414) 271-8116
Milwaukee, WI 53233   Helen Gordon, Libn.

PRINCE OF PEACE LUTHERAN CHURCH - LIBRARY
4419 S. Howell Ave.   Phone: (414) 483-3828
Milwaukee, WI 53207   Mrs. Robert Heinritz, Hd.Libn.

QUARLES & BRADY - LIBRARY
780 N. Water St.   Phone: (414) 277-5000
Milwaukee, WI 53202   Susan Howdle, Libn.

REINHART, BOERNER, VAN DEUREN, NORRIS & RIESELBACH - LIBRARY
1800 Marine Plaza   Phone: (414) 271-1190
Milwaukee, WI 53202   Carol Bannen, Libn.

REXNORD, INC. - TECHNICAL LIBRARY
5101 W. Beloit Rd.
Box 2022   Phone: (414) 643-2725
Milwaukee, WI 53214   Linda L. Le Veille, Info.Spec.

ROA FILMS - LIBRARY
1696 N. Astor St.   Phone: (414) 271-0861
Milwaukee, WI 53202   Jean Larson, Exec. V.P.

ST. FRANCIS HOSPITAL - HEALTH SCIENCE LEARNING CENTER
3237 S. 16th St.   Phone: (414) 647-5156
Milwaukee, WI 53215   Joy Shong, Libn.

ST. FRANCIS SEMINARY - SALZMANN LIBRARY
3257 South Lake Dr.   Phone: (414) 483-1979
Milwaukee, WI 53207   Rev. Lawrence Miech, Lib.Dir.

ST. JOSEPH'S HOSPITAL - SAMUEL ROSENTHAL MEMORIAL LIBRARY
5000 W. Chambers St.   Phone: (414) 447-2194
Milwaukee, WI 53210   M. Frances McManimon, Med.Libn.

ST. LUKE'S HOSPITAL - MEDICAL LIBRARY
2900 W. Oklahoma Ave.   Phone: (414) 647-7357
Milwaukee, WI 53215   Midge Wos, Hd.Libn.

ST. MARY'S HOSPITAL - MEMORIAL LIBRARY
2323 N. Lake Dr.
Box 503   Phone: (414) 289-7000
Milwaukee, WI 53201   Jean M. Truscott, Libn.

ST. MICHAEL'S HOSPITAL - REGNER HEALTH SCIENCES LIBRARY
2400 W. Villard Ave.   Phone: (414) 263-8477
Milwaukee, WI 53209   Joan Yanicke, Dir., Lib.Serv.

SCHLITZ (Joseph) BREWING COMPANY - MARKETING RESEARCH LIBRARY
Box 614   Phone: (414) 224-5617
Milwaukee, WI 53201   A. Pamela Reichmann, Libn.

SMITH (A.O.) CORPORATION - TECHNICAL LIBRARY
Box 584   Phone: (414) 447-4683
Milwaukee, WI 53201   Larry Medley, Libn.

SOUTHEASTERN WISCONSIN HEALTH SYSTEMS AGENCY - LIBRARY
735 N. 5th St.   Phone: (414) 271-9788
Milwaukee, WI 53203   Karen Budahn, Libn.

SQUARE D COMPANY - LIBRARY
4041 N. Richards St.   Phone: (414) 332-2000
Milwaukee, WI 53212   Julie Schwartz, Libn.

U.S. DEFENSE CONTRACT ADMINISTRATION - SERVICES MANAGEMENT
    AREA LIBRARY
744 N. 4th St.   Phone: (414) 272-8180
Milwaukee, WI 53203   Joan Schumacher, QA Data Ck.

U.S. DEPT. OF COMMERCE - INTERNATIONAL TRADE ADMINISTRATION -
    MILWAUKEE DISTRICT OFFICE LIBRARY
Federal Bldg.
517 E. Wisconsin Ave.   Phone: (414) 291-3473
Milwaukee, WI 53203   Russell H. Leitch, Dir.

UNIVERSAL FOODS CORPORATION - TECHNICAL INFORMATION SERVICES
6143 N. 60th St.   Phone: (414) 271-6755
Milwaukee, WI 53218   Aileen Mundstock, Tech.Info.Spec.

UNIVERSITY OF WISCONSIN, MILWAUKEE - AREA RESEARCH CENTER
2311 E. Hartford Ave.   Phone: (414) 963-5402
Milwaukee, WI 53201   Wilbur Stolt, Archv.

UNIVERSITY OF WISCONSIN, MILWAUKEE - GOLDA MEIR LIBRARY -
    CURRICULUM COLLECTION
Box 604   Phone: (414) 963-4074
Milwaukee, WI 53201   Julie Czisny, Educ.Libn.

UNIVERSITY OF WISCONSIN, MILWAUKEE - GRADUATE SCHOOL - OFFICE
    OF RESEARCH - INFORMATION LIBRARY
Box 413   Phone: (414) 963-4063
Milwaukee, WI 53201   Victor J. Larson, Info.Spec.

UNIVERSITY OF WISCONSIN, MILWAUKEE - GREENE MEMORIAL MUSEUM -
    LIBRARY
3367 N. Downer Ave.
Milwaukee, WI 53201

UNIVERSITY OF WISCONSIN, MILWAUKEE - INSTITUTE OF WORLD
    AFFAIRS - RESEARCH LIBRARY
Bolton 659
Box 413   Phone: (414) 963-4251
Milwaukee, WI 53201   David Garnham, Dir.

UNIVERSITY OF WISCONSIN, MILWAUKEE - MORRIS FROMKIN MEMORIAL
    COLLECTION
2311 E. Hartford Ave.   Phone: (414) 963-5402
Milwaukee, WI 53201   Stanley Mallach, Biblog.

UNIVERSITY OF WISCONSIN, MILWAUKEE - MUSIC COLLECTION
2311 E. Hartford Ave.
Box 604   Phone: (414) 963-5529
Milwaukee, WI 53201   Richard E. Jones, Music Libn.

UOP INC. - BOSTROM DIVISION - ENGINEERING LIBRARY *
133 W. Oregon St.   Phone: (414) 271-4122
Milwaukee, WI 53201   E.T. Seifullin, Supv.Engr.Adm.

VALUATION RESEARCH CORPORATION - CORPORATE RESEARCH AND
    REFERENCE LIBRARY
250 E. Wisconsin Ave.   Phone: (414) 271-8662
Milwaukee, WI 53202   Don F. Schwamb, Dir.

WISCONSIN CONSERVATORY OF MUSIC - LIBRARY
1584 N. Prospect Ave.   Phone: (414) 276-4350
Milwaukee, WI 53202   Brian Jonathan Gerl, Dir.

WISCONSIN GAS COMPANY - CORPORATE AND LAW LIBRARY
626 E. Wisconsin Ave.   Phone: (414) 291-6666
Milwaukee, WI 53202   Carolyn A. Rennebohm, Libn.

WISCONSIN INFORMATION SERVICE
161 W. Wisconsin Ave., Rm. 7071   Phone: (414) 276-0760
Milwaukee, WI 53203   Marianne Oberbrunner, Proj.Coord.

ST. LAWRENCE SEMINARY - LIBRARY *
                                                 Phone: (414) 753-3911
Mount Calvary, WI 53057   Rev. Francis J. Heidenreich, Libn.

NASHOTAH HOUSE - LIBRARY
                                                 Phone: (414) 646-3371
Nashotah, WI 53058   James Dunkly, Libn.

AMERICAN CAN COMPANY - NEENAH TECHNICAL CENTER - TECHNICAL
    INFORMATION CENTER
1915 Marathon Ave.   Phone: (414) 729-8169
Neenah, WI 54956   Cheryl Lamb, Info.Sci.

BERGSTROM ART CENTER AND MUSEUM - ART REFERENCE LIBRARY
165 N. Park Ave.
Neenah, WI 54956

GEOGRAPHIC

GEOGRAPHIC

KELLER (J.J.) & ASSOCIATES, INC. - RESEARCH CENTER/LIBRARY
  SERVICES
145 W. Wisconsin Ave.   Phone: (414) 722-2848
Neenah, WI 54956   John K. Breese, Mgr.-RC/LS

KIMBERLY-CLARK CORPORATION - LIBRARY
2100 Winchester Rd.
Box 999   Phone: (414) 729-5261
Neenah, WI 54956   Mary E. Sutliff, Tech.Libn.

THEDA CLARK REGIONAL MEDICAL CENTER - HEALTH SCIENCES LIBRARY
130 2nd St.   Phone: (414) 722-6904
Neenah, WI 54956   Muriel Witt, Dir. of Lib.Serv.

NEW BERLIN MEMORIAL HOSPITAL - LIBRARY
13750 W. National Ave.   Phone: (414) 782-2700
New Berlin, WI 53151   June Regis, Staff Libn.

WISCONSIN INDIANHEAD TECHNICAL INSTITUTE, NEW RICHMOND
  CAMPUS - LEARNING RESOURCE CENTER
1019 S. Knowles Ave.   Phone: (715) 246-6561
New Richmond, WI 54017   David D. Hartung, Libn.

MILWAUKEE AREA TECHNICAL COLLEGE - SOUTH CAMPUS LIBRARY
6665 S. Howell Ave.   Phone: (414) 762-2500
Oak Creek, WI 53154   Louise Weber, Lib.Techn.

MEMORIAL HOSPITAL AT OCONOMOWOC - HEALTH SCIENCES LIBRARY
791 East Summit Ave.   Phone: (414) 567-0371
Oconomowoc, WI 53066   Mary Kaye Lintner, Health Sci.Libn.

OSHKOSH PUBLIC MUSEUM - LIBRARY & ARCHIVES
1331 Algoma Blvd.   Phone: (414) 424-0452
Oshkosh, WI 54901   Kitty A. Hobson, Archv.

PAINE ART CENTER AND ARBORETUM - LIBRARY
1410 Algoma Blvd.   Phone: (414) 235-4530
Oshkosh, WI 54901   Corinne H. Spoo, Hd.

UNITED METHODIST CHURCH - WISCONSIN CONFERENCE - ARCHIVES
1174 Algoma Blvd.   Phone: (414) 231-2800
Oshkosh, WI 54901   Kitty A. Hobson, Archv./Hist.Libn.

UNIVERSITY OF WISCONSIN, OSHKOSH - UNIVERSITY LIBRARIES AND
  LEARNING RESOURCES
800 Algoma Blvd.   Phone: (414) 424-3333
Oshkosh, WI 54901   J. Daniel Vann, Exec.Dir.

UNIVERSITY OF WISCONSIN, PLATTEVILLE - KARRMANN LIBRARY
                                         Phone: (608) 342-1688
Platteville, WI 53818   Jerome P. Daniels, Dir.

WISCONSIN STATE DEPARTMENT OF NATURAL RESOURCES - MAC KENZIE
  ENVIRONMENTAL EDUCATION CENTER
Rte. 1   Phone: (608) 635-4498
Poynette, WI 53955   Robert Wallen, Naturalist

FRANCISCAN FRIARS - ASSUMPTION FRIARY LIBRARY
Franciscan Center
143 E. Pulaski St.   Phone: (414) 822-3291
Pulaski, WI 54162   Joseph Krymkowski, O.F.M., Libn.

GIRL SCOUTS OF RACINE COUNTY, INC. - LIBRARY *
816 6th St.
Racine, WI 53403   Betsy Marron, Prog.Serv.Dir.

INTERNATIONAL BANK NOTE SOCIETY - LIBRARY †
Box 1222
Racine, WI 53405   Milan Alusic, Sec.

JOHNSON (S.C.) AND SON, INC. - TECHNICAL & BUSINESS INFORMATION
  CENTER
1525 Howe St.   Phone: (414) 554-2372
Racine, WI 53403   E.L. Schaut, Tech.Mgr.

RACINE COUNTY HISTORICAL MUSEUM, INC. - REFERENCE LIBRARY OF
  GENEALOGY AND LOCAL HISTORY
701 Main St.   Phone: (414) 637-8585
Racine, WI 53403   Gilbert D. Stieg, Dir.

RACINE JOURNAL TIMES - LIBRARY
212 4th St.   Phone: (414) 634-3322
Racine, WI 53403   Karolyn Cotton, Libn.

WALKER MANUFACTURING CO. - LIBRARY
1201 Michigan Blvd.
Racine, WI 53402   Glenn Heisa, Libn.

WESTERN PUBLISHING COMPANY, INC. - CORPORATE TRAINING CENTER
  LIBRARY
1220 Mound Ave.   Phone: (414) 633-2431
Racine, WI 53404   Richard H. Popp, Mgr., Corp. Training

WISCONSIN STATE - RACINE COUNTY LAW LIBRARY
730 Wisconsin Ave.   Phone: (414) 636-3517
Racine, WI 53403   Lawrence E. Flynn, Ck. of Courts

YOUNG RADIATOR COMPANY - LIBRARY
2825 Four Mile Rd.   Phone: (414) 639-1010
Racine, WI 53404   Sandra Kraft, Libn.

RIPON HISTORICAL SOCIETY - LIBRARY
508 Watson St.
Box 274   Phone: (414) 748-5354
Ripon, WI 54971   George H. Miller, Cur.

UNIVERSITY OF WISCONSIN, RIVER FALLS - CHALMER DAVEE LIBRARY
120 E. Cascade Ave.   Phone: (715) 425-3321
River Falls, WI 54022   Richard A. Cooklock, Dir.

UNIVERSITY OF WISCONSIN, RIVER FALLS - CHALMER DAVEE LIBRARY -
  AREA RESEARCH CENTER
                                         Phone: (715) 425-3567
River Falls, WI 54022   Timothy L. Ericson, Archv.

AMERICAN CAN COMPANY - RESEARCH AND DEVELOPMENT LIBRARY
                                         Phone: (715) 359-6544
Rothschild, WI 54474   Marion Haase, Libn.

STERLING DRUG, INC. - ZIMPRO INC. - REFERENCE AND RESOURCE
  CENTER
Military Rd.   Phone: (715) 359-7211
Rothschild, WI 54474   Christine L. Kensmoe, Libn.

LAND, INC. - LIBRARY
Route 1
525 River Rd.   Phone: (715) 423-7996
Rudolph, WI 54475   Naomi Jacobson, Co-Chm.

ST. NICHOLAS HOSPITAL - HEALTH SCIENCES LIBRARY
1601 N. Taylor Dr.   Phone: (414) 459-4713
Sheboygan, WI 53081   Kathleen Blaser, Libn.

SHEBOYGAN PRESS LIBRARY
632 Center Ave.   Phone: (414) 457-7711
Sheboygan, WI 53081   Janice Hildebrand, Libn.

DOMINICAN EDUCATION CENTER - LIBRARY *
                                         Phone: (608) 748-4411
Sinsinawa, WI 53824

MONROE COUNTY LOCAL HISTORY ROOM & LIBRARY
Courthouse Annex North, Rte. 2   Phone: (608) 269-3175
Sparta, WI 54656   Audrey Johnson, Act. County Hist.

AMERICAN PLAYERS THEATRE, INC. (APT) - LIBRARY
Route 3   Phone: (608) 588-7401
Spring Green, WI 53588   Margaret L. Hayes, Libn.

ST. MICHAEL'S HOSPITAL - HEALTH SCIENCES LIBRARY
900 Illinois Ave.   Phone: (715) 344-4400
Stevens Point, WI 54481   Barbara DeWeerd, Libn.

SENTRY LIBRARY
1800 N. Point Dr.
Box 200   Phone: (715) 346-6788
Stevens Point, WI 54481   Irene A. Dobbert, Corp.Libn.

UNIVERSITY OF WISCONSIN, STEVENS POINT - JAMES H. ALBERTSON
    CENTER FOR LEARNING RESOURCES
                                                Phone: (715) 346-2540
Stevens Point, WI 54481   Allen F. Barrows, Dir. of Pub.Serv.

DOUGLAS COUNTY HISTORICAL MUSEUM - LIBRARY
906 E. 2nd St.   Phone: (715) 394-5712
Superior, WI 54880   James E. Lundsted, Dir. Of Musm.

DOUGLAS COUNTY LAW LIBRARY
Court House   Phone: (715) 394-0237
Superior, WI 54880   Carol Wittke, Libn.

UNIVERSITY OF WISCONSIN, SUPERIOR - JIM DAN HILL LIBRARY *
800 Grand   Phone: (715) 392-1116
Superior, WI 54880   Eugene T. Lundholm, Hd.Libn.

WISCONSIN INDIANHEAD TECHNICAL INSTITUTE, SUPERIOR CAMPUS -
    LIBRARY
600 N. 21st St.   Phone: (715) 394-6677
Superior, WI 54880   Donald Rantala, LRC Spec.

U.S. VETERANS ADMINISTRATION (WI-Tomah) - HOSPITAL LIBRARY
Tomah, WI 54660   William E. Nielsen, Chf.Libn.

SOUTHERN WISCONSIN CENTER FOR THE DEVELOPMENTALLY DISABLED -
    LIBRARY †
Box 100   Phone: (414) 878-2411
Union Grove, WI 53182

WATERTOWN HISTORICAL SOCIETY - ARCHIVES
919 Charles St.   Phone: (414) 261-2796
Watertown, WI 53094   Dr. E.C. Kiessling, Pres.

MALEDICTA: INTERNATIONAL RESEARCH CENTER FOR VERBAL
    AGGRESSION, INC. - ARCHIVES
331 S. Greenfield Ave.   Phone: (414) 542-5853
Waukesha, WI 53186   Dr. Reinhold A. Aman, Pres.

SOUTHEASTERN WISCONSIN REGIONAL PLANNING COMMISSION -
    REFERENCE LIBRARY
916 N. East Ave.   Phone: (414) 547-6721
Waukesha, WI 53186   Thomas D. Patterson, Libn.

WAUKESHA COUNTY HISTORICAL MUSEUM - RESEARCH CENTER
101 W. Main St.   Phone: (414) 544-8430
Waukesha, WI 53186   Jean Penn Loerke, Musm.Dir./Hist.

WAUKESHA FREEMAN - NEWSPAPER LIBRARY
200 Park Pl.   Phone: (414) 542-2501
Waukesha, WI 53186   Lorrayne Mathews, Libn.

WAUKESHA MEMORIAL HOSPITAL - MEDICAL LIBRARY
725 American Ave.   Phone: (414) 544-2150
Waukesha, WI 53186   Jean V. Hawkins, Med.Libn.

RIVERSIDE COMMUNITY MEMORIAL HOSPITAL - HEALTH SCIENCE
    LIBRARY
500 Riverside Dr.   Phone: (715) 258-1000
Waupaca, WI 54981   Mary Hanegraaf, Libn.

LUTHERAN CHURCH - MISSOURI SYNOD - NORTH WISCONSIN DISTRICT
    ARCHIVES
3103 Seymour Ln.   Phone: (715) 845-8241
Wausau, WI 54401   Rev. Ronald W. Goetsch, Archv.

MARATHON COUNTY HISTORICAL MUSEUM - LIBRARY
403 McIndoe St.   Phone: (715) 848-6143
Wausau, WI 54401   Maryanne C. Norton, Libn.

WAUSAU INSURANCE COMPANIES - LIBRARY
2000 Westwood Dr.   Phone: (715) 847-8504
Wausau, WI 54401   Douglas H. Lay, Dir., Lib.Serv.

BETHANY UNITED METHODIST CHURCH - LIBRARY
7265 W. Center St.   Phone: (414) 258-2868
Wauwatosa, WI 53210   Barbara A. Jones, Libn.

MILWAUKEE PSYCHIATRIC HOSPITAL - LIBRARY
1220 Dewey Ave.   Phone: (414) 258-2600
Wauwatosa, WI 53213   Darlyne Ritter, Libn.

WEST ALLIS MEMORIAL HOSPITAL - MEDICAL LIBRARY
8901 W. Lincoln Ave.   Phone: (414) 321-2200
West Allis, WI 53227   Joan A. Clausz, Med.Libn.

UNIVERSITY OF WISCONSIN, WHITEWATER - LIBRARY & LEARNING
    RESOURCES
800 W. Main St.   Phone: (414) 472-1000
Whitewater, WI 53190   Ronald Fingerson, Dean

UNIVERSITY OF CHICAGO - YERKES OBSERVATORY LIBRARY
                                           Phone: (414) 245-5555
Williams Bay, WI 53191   J.A. Lola, Asst. in Chg.

WINNEBAGO MENTAL HEALTH INSTITUTE - MEDICAL LIBRARY
Box H   Phone: (414) 235-4910
Winnebago, WI 54985   Mary Campfield, Dir. of Lib.Serv.

CONSOLIDATED PAPERS, INC. - RESEARCH AND DEVELOPMENT LIBRARY
Box 50   Phone: (715) 422-3768
Wisconsin Rapids, WI 54494   Helen W. Sanborn, Supv.Info.Serv.

U.S. VETERANS ADMINISTRATION (WI-Wood) - MEDICAL CENTER
    LIBRARY
                                           Phone: (414) 384-2000
Wood, WI 53193   Jeanne A. Holcomb, Med.Libn.

HOWARD YOUNG MEDICAL CENTER - HEALTH SCIENCE LIBRARY
Box 470   Phone: (715) 356-5222
Woodruff, WI 54568   Debra L. Gilles, Libn.

WYOMING

U.S. BUREAU OF LAND MANAGEMENT - CASPER DISTRICT OFFICE -
    LIBRARY †
951 Union Blvd.
Box 2834   Phone: (307) 265-5550
Casper, WY 82602   Trudy Closson, Rec.Mgr.

U.S. DEPT. OF COMMERCE - INTERNATIONAL TRADE ADMINISTRATION -
    CHEYENNE DISTRICT OFFICE LIBRARY
Federal O'Mahoney Ctr., Rm. 6022
2120 Capitol Ave.   Phone: (307) 778-2220
Cheyenne, WY 82001   Lowell O. Burns, Dir.

U.S. VETERANS ADMINISTRATION (WY-Cheyenne) - CENTER LIBRARY
2360 E. Pershing Blvd.   Phone: (307) 778-7550
Cheyenne, WY 82001   Edwina M. Hubbard, Libn.

WYOMING STATE ARCHIVES, MUSEUMS AND HISTORICAL DEPARTMENT
Barrett Bldg.   Phone: (307) 777-7518
Cheyenne, WY 82002   Michael J. Boyle, Dir.

WYOMING STATE DEPARTMENT OF ECONOMIC PLANNING AND
    DEVELOPMENT - LIBRARY
Barrett Bldg.   Phone: (307) 777-7284
Cheyenne, WY 82002   Anne W. McGowan, Lib.Mgr.

WYOMING STATE DEPARTMENT OF HEALTH & SOCIAL SERVICE - HEALTH
    INFORMATION LIBRARY *
State Office Building West   Phone: (307) 777-7363
Cheyenne, WY 82002   Jeani P. Thomas, Libn.

WYOMING STATE LAW LIBRARY
Supreme Court Bldg.   Phone: (307) 777-7509
Cheyenne, WY 82002   Albert W. St. Clair, Law Libn.

WYOMING STATE LIBRARY
Supreme Court & State Library Bldg.   Phone: (307) 777-7281
Cheyenne, WY 82002   Wayne Johnson, State Libn.

BUFFALO BILL HISTORICAL CENTER - HAROLD MC CRACKEN RESEARCH
    LIBRARY
Box 1000   Phone: (307) 587-4771
Cody, WY 82414   Michael Kelly, Libn./Archv.

PARK COUNTY BAR ASSOCIATION - LAW LIBRARY
Court House, 1002 Sheridan Ave.   Phone: (307) 587-2204
Cody, WY 82414   William P. Rohrbach, Chm.

GRAND ENCAMPMENT MUSEUM, INC. - LIBRARY
                                          Phone: (307) 327-5310
Encampment, WY 82325   Vera Oldman, Pres., Musm.Corp.

WYOMING STATE HOSPITAL - MEDICAL LIBRARY
Box 177   Phone: (307) 789-3464
Evanston, WY 82930   Charles D. Bright, Supv.

U.S. NATL. PARK SERVICE - FORT LARAMIE NATL. HISTORIC SITE -
     LIBRARY
Box 178   Phone: (307) 837-2221
Fort Laramie, WY 82212   Lewis A. Eaton, Park Techn.

SWEETWATER COUNTY MUSEUM - INFORMATION CENTER
50 W. Flaming Gorge Ave.   Phone: (307) 875-2611
Green River, WY 82935   Henry F. Chadey, Dir.

NATIONAL OUTDOOR LEADERSHIP SCHOOL - OUTDOOR EDUCATION
     RESOURCE LIBRARY
Box AA   Phone: (307) 332-4381
Lander, WY 82520   Kevin Hildebrant, Chf.Instr.

GEOLOGICAL SURVEY OF WYOMING - PUBLIC RECORDS SECTION
Box 3008, University Sta.   Phone: (307) 742-2054
Laramie, WY 82071   Gary B. Glass, Deputy Dir.

LARAMIE PLAINS MUSEUM ASSOCIATION - LIBRARY
603 Ivinson   Phone: (307) 742-4448
Laramie, WY 82070   Joyce S. Wright, Musm.Dir.

U.S.D.A. - AGRICULTURAL RESEARCH SERVICE - HONEY BEE PESTICIDES/
     DISEASES RESEARCH LABORATORY - LIBRARY
University of Wyoming
University Sta., Box 3168
Laramie, WY 82071   Phone: (307) 766-2281
                               W.T. Wilson, Res. Entomologist

U.S. DEPT. OF ENERGY - LARAMIE ENERGY TECHNOLOGY CENTER LIBRARY
University Sta., Box 3395   Phone: (307) 721-2201
Laramie, WY 82071   B.J. Davidson, Libn.

UNIVERSITY OF WYOMING - ANIMAL SCIENCE DIVISION - WOOL LIBRARY
University Sta.
Box 3354   Phone: (307) 766-5212
Laramie, WY 82071   Svend-Aage Larsen, Assoc.Prof.

UNIVERSITY OF WYOMING - GEOLOGY LIBRARY
S.H. Knight Geology Bldg.   Phone: (307) 766-3374
Laramie, WY 82071   Josephine Battisti, Geology Lib.Mgr.

UNIVERSITY OF WYOMING - LAW LIBRARY
College of Law   Phone: (307) 766-5175
Laramie, WY 82071   Catherine Mealey, Law Libn./Prof.

UNIVERSITY OF WYOMING - PETROLEUM HISTORY AND RESEARCH
     CENTER LIBRARY
William Robertson Coe Library
Box 3334   Phone: (307) 766-4114
Laramie, WY 82071   Gene M. Gressley, Archv.

UNIVERSITY OF WYOMING - SCIENCE AND TECHNOLOGY LIBRARY
University Sta., Box 3262   Phone: (307) 766-5065
Laramie, WY 82071   Linda S. Keiter, Coord., Sci.Lib.Serv.

UNIVERSITY OF WYOMING - WATER RESOURCES RESEARCH INSTITUTE -
     LIBRARY
                                          Phone: (307) 766-2143
Laramie, WY 82071   Paul A. Rechard, Dir.

UNIVERSITY OF WYOMING - WESTERN HISTORY RESEARCH CENTER
     LIBRARY
William Robertson Coe Library
Box 3334   Phone: (307) 766-4114
Laramie, WY 82071   Gene M. Gressley, Dir.

CHURCH OF JESUS CHRIST OF LATTER-DAY SAINTS - LOVELL, WYOMING
     BRANCH GENEALOGICAL LIBRARY
50 W. Main St.
Box 547   Phone: (307) 548-2963
Lovell, WY 82431   Barbara C. Bassett, Libn.

U.S. NATL. PARK SERVICE - GRAND TETON NATL. PARK - LIBRARY
Drawer 170   Phone: (307) 733-2880
Moose, WY 83012   John Daugherty, Pk.Hist.

WESTON COUNTY HISTORICAL SOCIETY - ANNA MILLER MUSEUM -
     LIBRARY
Box 698   Phone: (307) 746-4188
Newcastle, WY 82701   Mabel E. Brown, Dir.

U.S. VETERANS ADMINISTRATION (WY-Sheridan) - MEDICAL CENTER
     LIBRARY
                                          Phone: (307) 672-3473
Sheridan, WY 82801   Carol N. Conner, Chf., Lib.Serv.

U.S. NATL. PARK SERVICE - YELLOWSTONE LIBRARY AND MUSEUM
     ASSOCIATION
Box 117   Phone: (307) 344-7381
Yellowstone National Park, WY 82190 Valerie Black, Lib.Techn.

U.S. Territories & Possessions

AMERICAN SAMOA

FELETI PACIFIC LIBRARY †
Fagatogo Village
Pago Pago, AS 96799   Olive Atisanoe, Lib.Mgr.

GUAM

FLORES (Nieves M.) MEMORIAL LIBRARY
Box 652
Agana, GU 96910   Magdalena S. Taitano, Territorial Libn.

GUAM MEMORIAL HOSPITAL AUTHORITY - MEDICAL LIBRARY
Box AX   Phone: (717) 646-5801
Agana, GU 96910   Juliana C. Salumbides, Med.Libn.

UNIVERSITY OF GUAM - MICRONESIAN AREA RESEARCH CENTER -
   PACIFIC COLLECTION
U.O.G. Sta.   Phone: (717) 734-2921
Mangilao, GU 96913   Dirk A. Ballendorf, Dir.

PUERTO RICO

CORNELL UNIVERSITY - ARECIBO OBSERVATORY - LIBRARY
Box 995   Phone: (809) 878-2612
Arecibo, PR 00612   Arisleida Hernandez, Libn.

PUERTO RICAN CULTURE INSTITUTE - LUIS MUNOZ RIVERA LIBRARY AND
   MUSEUM †
Luis Munoz Rivera St. No.10
Barranquitas, PR 00618   Maria L. Valencia, Libn.

EVANGELICAL SEMINARY OF PUERTO RICO - JUAN DE VALDES LIBRARY
Ave. Ponce De Leon 776   Phone: (809) 751-6483
Hato Rey, PR 00918   Hector Ruben Sanchez, Lib.Dir.

FESTIVAL CASALS, INC. - PUERTO RICO INDUSTRIAL DEVELOPMENT
   COMPANY - CONSERVATORIO DE MUSICA - LIBRARY
Ave. Roosevelt Y Lamar   Phone: (809) 751-0160
Hato Rey, PR 00918   Ines Mora Gordon, Libn.

PUERTO RICO - GENERAL COURT OF JUSTICE - OFFICE OF COURT
   ADMINISTRATION - LIBRARY DIVISION
Call Box 22-A   Phone: (809) 764-2739
Hato Rey, PR 00919   Nidia Miranda Graterole, Dir.

UNIVERSITY OF PUERTO RICO - HUMACAO UNIVERSITY COLLEGE -
   LIBRARY
Bo. Tejas, CUH-Sta.   Phone: (809) 852-2525
Humacao, PR 00661   Oneida R. de Ortiz, Dir.

CENTER FOR ENERGY AND ENVIRONMENT RESEARCH - READING ROOM
College Sta.   Phone: (809) 832-1408
Mayaguez, PR 00708   Jeanette Valentin Marty, Asst.Libn.

PUERTO RICO DEPARTMENT OF HEALTH - RAMON EMETERIO BETANCES
   MEDICAL LIBRARY
Bo. Sabalos, Carr. no. 2
Box 1868   Phone: (809) 832-8686
Mayaguez, PR 00708   Myrna Y. Ramirez, Libn.

UNIVERSITY OF PUERTO RICO - MAYAGUEZ CAMPUS - LIBRARY *
                    Phone: (809) 832-4040
Mayaguez, PR 00708   Miguel Angel Ortiz, Dir.

UNIVERSITY OF PUERTO RICO - MAYAGUEZ CAMPUS - MARINE SCIENCES
   LIBRARY †
                    Phone: (809) 832-4040
Mayaguez, PR 00708   Vicente Lopez, Libn.

UNIVERSITY OF PUERTO RICO - MAYAGUEZ CAMPUS - TECHNICAL
   INFORMATION CENTER
College Station   Phone: (809) 832-4040
Mayaguez, PR 00708   Lueny Morell de Ramirez, Dir.

CATHOLIC UNIVERSITY OF PUERTO RICO - MONSIGNOR JUAN FREMIOT
   TORRES OLIVER LAW LIBRARY
Ave. Las Americas   Phone: (809) 844-4150
Ponce, PR 00732   Noelia Padua, Dir.

U.S. VETERANS ADMINISTRATION (PR-San Juan) - HOSPITAL LIBRARY *
Carretera 21   Phone: (809) 764-4545
Rio Piedras, PR 00921   Raquel A. Walters, Chf., Lib.Serv.

UNIVERSITY OF PUERTO RICO - AGRICULTURAL EXPERIMENT STATION -
   LIBRARY *
Box H   Phone: (809) 764-0000
Rio Piedras, PR 00928   Joan P. Hayes, Libn.

UNIVERSITY OF PUERTO RICO - COLLEGE OF EDUCATION - SELLES SOLA
   MEMORIAL COLLECTION
                    Phone: (809) 764-0000
Rio Piedras, PR 00931   Lina B. Morales, Hd.Libn.

UNIVERSITY OF PUERTO RICO - GRADUATE SCHOOL OF PLANNING -
   LIBRARY
UPR Sta., Box BE   Phone: (809) 764-0000
Rio Piedras, PR 00931   Martha Torres-Irizarry, Libn.

UNIVERSITY OF PUERTO RICO - HISTORICAL RESEARCH CENTER
University Sta., Box 22802   Phone: (809) 764-0000
Rio Piedras, PR 00931   Dr. Aida R. Caro Costas, Dir.

UNIVERSITY OF PUERTO RICO - LAW SCHOOL LIBRARY
Box L   Phone: (809) 764-0000
Rio Piedras, PR 00931   Carmelo Delgado Cintron, Law Libn.

UNIVERSITY OF PUERTO RICO - MEDICAL SCIENCES CAMPUS - LIBRARY
Box 5067   Phone: (809) 767-9626
Rio Piedras, PR 00936   Aura J. Panepinto, Dir.

UNIVERSITY OF PUERTO RICO - NATURAL SCIENCE LIBRARY
Box 22446   Phone: (809) 764-0000
Rio Piedras, PR 00931   Giovanna Del Pilar Barber, Hd.

UNIVERSITY OF PUERTO RICO - PUERTO RICAN COLLECTION
UPR Sta., Box C   Phone: (809) 764-0000
Rio Piedras, PR 00931   Dr. Mercedes Saenz, Hd.

UNIVERSITY OF PUERTO RICO - SCHOOL OF PUBLIC ADMINISTRATION -
   LIBRARY
                    Phone: (809) 764-0000
Rio Piedras, PR 00931   Magda Rivera Colon, Libn.

ASHFORD MEMORIAL COMMUNITY HOSPITAL - MEDICAL LIBRARY
1451 Ashford Ave.
Box 32   Phone: (809) 724-2160
San Juan, PR 00902

CARIBBEAN REGIONAL LIBRARY
UPR Sta., Box 21927   Phone: (809) 764-0000
San Juan, PR 00931   Ramon Arroyo-Carrion, Dir.

PUERTO RICO - ATENEO PUERTORRIQUENO - BIBLIOTECA *
Ave. Ponce De Leon
Parada 2, Apartado 1180   Phone: (809) 722-1258
San Juan, PR 00902   Clara S. De Lergier, Chf.Libn.

PUERTO RICO - DEPARTMENT OF HEALTH - MEDICAL LIBRARY
Ant. Hospital de Psiquiatria -
Bo. Monacillos
Call Box 70184   Phone: (809) 767-6060
San Juan, PR 00936   Josefina Santiago Ortiz, Libn.

PUERTO RICO - DEPARTMENT OF HEALTH - MENTAL HEALTH LIBRARY *
Asst. Secretariat for Mental Health
Box G.P.O. 61   Phone: (809) 781-5660
San Juan, PR 00936   Consuelo Serrano Romero, Libn.

PUERTO RICO - DEPARTMENT OF JUSTICE - LIBRARY
50 Fortaleza St.   Phone: (809) 724-6869
San Juan, PR 00902   Antonio Nadal, Hd. Law Libn.

**PUERTO RICO - INSTITUTE OF PUERTO RICAN CULTURE - ARCHIVO
    GENERAL DE PUERTO RICO ***
Ponce De Leon 500, Apartado 4184   Phone: (809) 722-2113
San Juan, PR 00905   Miguel Angel Nieves, Dir.

**PUERTO RICO - INSTITUTE OF PUERTO RICAN CULTURE - LA CASA DEL
    LIBRO**
Calle Del Cristo 225
Box 2265   Phone: (809) 723-0354
San Juan, PR 00903   David Jackson McWilliams, Dir.

PUERTO RICO - OFFICE OF BUDGET & MANAGEMENT - LIBRARY
254 Cruz St.
Box 3228   Phone: (809) 725-9420
San Juan, PR 00904   Gladys Santiago, Hd.Libn.

PUERTO RICO - OFFICE OF CRIMINAL JUSTICE
Forta Leza No. 50
San Juan, PR 00902

PUERTO RICO - SUPREME COURT - LAW LIBRARY
Box 2392   Phone: (809) 723-3863
San Juan, PR 00903   Doris Asencio-Toro, Hd.Libn.

**U.S. DEPT. OF COMMERCE - INTERNATIONAL TRADE ADMINISTRATION -
    SAN JUAN DISTRICT OFFICE LIBRARY ***
Federal Post Office Bldg., Rm. 659   Phone: (809) 753-4555
San Juan, PR 00918   Enrique Vilella, Dir.

U.S. DISTRICT COURT - LEGAL LIBRARY †
Box 3671   Phone: (809) 722-0844
San Juan, PR 00904

UNIVERSITY OF PUERTO RICO - GENERAL LIBRARY
Jose M. Lazaro Memorial Library
Box C   Phone: (809) 764-0000
San Juan, PR 00931   Rafael R. Delgado, Dir.

**UNIVERSITY OF PUERTO RICO - GRADUATE SCHOOL OF LIBRARIANSHIPS -
    LIBRARY**
Box 21906   Phone: (809) 764-0000
San Juan, PR 00931   Vilma Rivera Bayron, Libn.

CARIBBEAN CENTER FOR ADVANCED STUDIES - LIBRARY
Minillas Sta., Box 41246   Phone: (809) 725-2458
Santurce, PR 00940   Betsaida Velez, Libn.

**INTERAMERICAN UNIVERSITY - SCHOOL OF LAW - DOMINGO TOLEDO
    ALAMO LAW LIBRARY**
1610 Fernandez Juncos Ave.
Box 8897   Phone: (809) 727-1930
Santurce, PR 00910   Prof. Carlos R. Davis, Dir.

PUERTO RICO - OFFICE OF PERSONNEL - LIBRARY *
Fernandez Juncos Sta.
Box 8476   Phone: (809) 723-4300
Santurce, PR 00910   Ana Mercedes Lupianez De Gonzalez, Libn.

PUERTO RICO - STATE DEPARTMENT OF CONSUMER AFFAIRS - LIBRAY *
Minillas Govt. Center
North Tower, 5th Fl.   Phone: (809) 726-7555
Santurce, PR 00940   Israel Rivera, Libn.

VIRGIN ISLANDS

**COLLEGE OF THE VIRGIN ISLANDS - CARIBBEAN RESEARCH INSTITUTE -
    LIBRARY**
CRI Library   Phone: (809) 774-1252
St. Thomas, VI 00801   Anna Mae Brown-Comment, Supv., Info.Serv.

**COLLEGE OF THE VIRGIN ISLANDS - FOUNDATION CENTER REGIONAL
    COLLECTION**
Paiewonsky Library   Phone: (809) 774-1252
St. Thomas, VI 00801   Jeff Clark, Supv.

**VIRGIN ISLANDS - DEPARTMENT OF CONSERVATION & CULTURAL AFFAIRS
    - BUREAU OF LIBRARIES AND MUSEUMS**
Charlotte Amalie
Box 390   Phone: (809) 774-3407
St. Thomas, VI 00801   Dr. Henry C. Chang, Dir.

Canada

ALBERTA

ALPINE CLUB OF CANADA - LIBRARY
Box 160
Banff, AB T0L 0C0
Phone: (403) 762-2291
A.M. Daffern, Club Libn.

ARCHIVES OF THE CANADIAN ROCKIES
Box 160
Banff, AB T0L 0C0
Phone: (403) 762-2291
E.J. Hart, Adm.

MINERAL SPRINGS HOSPITAL - MEDICAL LIBRARY
Box 1050
Banff, AB T0L 0C0
Phone: (403) 762-2222
Mrs. E. Heikkila, Dir., Med.Rec.

CANADA - AGRICULTURE CANADA - RESEARCH STATION, BEAVERLODGE - LIBRARY
Box 29
Beaverlodge, AB T0H 0C0
Phone: (403) 354-2212
Dr. L.P.S. Spangelo, Dir.

ALBERTA ALCOHOLISM AND DRUG ABUSE COMMISSION - LIBRARY
3rd Fl., 1177 11th Ave., S.W.
Calgary, AB T2R 0G5
Phone: (403) 244-2727
Molly Taylor, Lib.Techn.

ALBERTA - DEPARTMENT OF THE ATTORNEY GENERAL - JUDGES' LAW LIBRARY
611 4th St., S.W.
Calgary, AB T2P 1T5
Phone: (403) 261-7475
Melody M. Hainsworth, Libn.

ALBERTA - ENERGY RESOURCES CONSERVATION BOARD - LIBRARY
640 5th Ave., S.W.
Calgary, AB T2P 3G4
Phone: (403) 261-8242
Liz Johnson, Libn.

ALBERTA HEART FOUNDATION - LIBRARY
2011 10th Ave., S.W.
Calgary, AB T3C 0K4
Phone: (403) 244-0786
Emily Alstad, Educ.Coord.

ALBERTA MENTAL HEALTH SERVICES - LIBRARY *
3rd Fl., Ford Tower
633 6th Ave., S.W.
Calgary, AB T2P 2Y5
Phone: (403) 261-7483
K.L. Walsh, Chm., Lib.Comm.

AMOCO CANADA PETROLEUM COMPANY, LTD. - LIBRARY INFORMATION CENTER
Amoco Canada Bldg.
444 7th Ave., S.W., Rm. 1012
Calgary, AB T2P 0Y2
Phone: (403) 233-1963
Frances M. Drummond, Supv.

ANGLICAN CHURCH OF CANADA - DIOCESE OF CALGARY - ANGLICAN ARCHIVES
Special Collections Library
University of Calgary
Calgary, AB T2N 1N4
Phone: (403) 269-1905
Rev. D.J. Carter, Archv.

ARCTIC INSTITUTE OF NORTH AMERICA - LIBRARY
University Of Calgary Library
2500 University Dr., N.W.
Calgary, AB T2N 1N4
Phone: (403) 284-5966
W.R. Maes, Northern Stud.Libn.

ATKINS (Gordon) AND ASSOCIATES ARCHITECTS LTD. - LIBRARY
1909 17th Ave., S.W.
Calgary, AB T2T 0E9
Phone: (403) 245-4545
Rosalind Innes, Libn.

BAKER CENTRE - SERVICES FOR THE HANDICAPPED - LIBRARY
P.O. Box 72
Calgary, AB T2P 2H2
Phone: (403) 261-7506
Marilyn Forester, Spec. Projects Coord.

BENNETT JONES - LIBRARY
3200 Shell Centre
400 4th Ave., S.W.
Calgary, AB T2P 0X9
Phone: (403) 267-3226
Jennifer Martison, Libn.

BEREAN BIBLE COLLEGE - LIBRARY
460 31st Ave., N.W.
Box 3900, Postal Station B
Calgary, AB T2M 4N2
Phone: (403) 230-3424
Mary M. Macomber, Libn.

CALGARY BOARD OF EDUCATION - PROFESSIONAL LIBRARY
3610 9th St. S.E.
Calgary, AB T2G 3C5
Phone: (403) 268-8581
Jane Webb, Libn.

CALGARY CENTENNIAL PLANETARIUM & AERO-SPACE MUSEUM - LIBRARY & ARCHIVES
Box 2100
Calgary, AB T2P 2M5
Phone: (403) 264-2030

CALGARY ECO-CENTRE SOCIETY - ENVIRONMENTAL INFORMATION CENTRE
204-223 12th Ave., S.W.
Calgary, AB T2R 0G9
Phone: (403) 263-6106
Valerie Jobson, Mgr.

CALGARY GENERAL HOSPITAL - LIBRARY SERVICES
841 Centre Ave., E.
Calgary, AB T2E 0A1
Phone: (403) 268-9234
Elizabeth Kirchner, Chf.Med.Libn.

CALGARY HERALD - LIBRARY
215 16th St., S.E.
Calgary, AB T2G 3P2
Phone: (403) 269-6361
Karen Liddiard, Chf.Libn.

CALGARY PLANNING DEPARTMENT - INFORMATION SERVICES
Box 2100
Calgary, AB T2P 2M5
Phone: (403) 268-5449
Patricia J. Drake, Hd., Info.Serv.

CALGARY SOCIAL SERVICE DEPARTMENT - LIBRARY
Box 2100
Calgary, AB T2P 2M5
Phone: (403) 268-5111
Tahani Sarophim

CALGARY SUN - LIBRARY
830 10th Ave., S.W.
Calgary, AB T2R 0B1
Phone: (403) 263-7730
Marilyn Wood, Libn.

CALGARY ZOOLOGICAL SOCIETY - LIBRARY
St. George's Island
Calgary, AB T2G 3H4
Phone: (403) 265-9310
Patricia Schroeder, Libn./Rec.Ck.

CANADA - GEOLOGICAL SURVEY OF CANADA - INSTITUTE OF SEDIMENTARY & PETROLEUM GEOLOGY - LIBRARY
3303 33rd St., N.W.
Calgary, AB T2L 2A7
Phone: (403) 284-0324
Marian Jones, Libn.

CANADA - PARKS CANADA, WESTERN REGION - LIBRARY
Sta. M, P.O. Box 2989
Calgary, AB T2P 3H8
Phone: (403) 231-4455
R.P. Morgan, Libn.

CANADIAN ETHNIC STUDIES ASSOCIATION - RESEARCH CENTRE
University of Calgary
2500 University Dr., N.W.
Calgary, AB T2N 1N4
Phone: (403) 284-7257
Dr. James S. Frideres, Dir.

CANADIAN MUSIC CENTRE - PRAIRIE REGION LIBRARY
9th Fl., Library Tower
University of Calgary
Calgary, AB T2N 1N4
Phone: (403) 284-7403
Christine Purvis, Regional Dir.

CANADIAN WESTERN NATURAL GAS COMPANY LIMITED - LIBRARY
140 6th Ave., S.W.
Calgary, AB T2P 0P6
Phone: (403) 245-7403
Shelley J. Weatherhead, Libn.

CHEVRON STANDARD, LTD. - LIBRARY
400 5th Ave., S.W.
Calgary, AB T2P 0L7
Phone: (403) 267-5910
Terri Pieschel, Libn.

CHURCH OF JESUS CHRIST OF LATTER-DAY SAINTS - CALGARY INSTITUTE OF RELIGION - LIBRARY
3120 32nd Ave. N.W.
Calgary, AB T2N 1N7
Phone: (403) 282-5426
Merlin Olsen, Dir.

ESSO RESOURCES CANADA LIMITED - LIBRARY INFORMATION CENTRE
237 4th Ave., S.W.
Calgary, AB T2P 0H6
Phone: (403) 237-4500
Larson Brodner, Supv.

GEOGRAPHIC

ESSO RESOURCES CANADA LIMITED - RESEARCH DEPARTMENT LIBRARY
339 50th Ave., S.E.   Phone: (403) 259-0303
Calgary, AB T2G 2B3   Vicki Kohse, Res.Dept.Libn.

FOOTHILLS HOSPITAL SCHOOL OF NURSING - LIBRARY
1403 29th St. N.W.   Phone: (403) 270-1460
Calgary, AB T2N 2T9   Ruth MacRae, Lib.Asst.

FOOTHILLS PIPE LINES (Yukon) LTD. - LIBRARY
205 5th Ave., S.W., No. 1600   Phone: (403) 237-1480
Calgary, AB T2P 2V7   Laverna Marchese, Libn.

GEOPHOTO SERVICES, LTD. - LIBRARY
906 12th Ave., S.W.
Calgary, AB T2R 1K7

GLENBOW-ALBERTA INSTITUTE - LIBRARY & ARCHIVES
130 9th Ave., S.E.   Phone: (403) 245-4741
Calgary, AB T2G 0P3   Leonard J. Gottselig, Chf.Libn.

GULF CANADA LIMITED - LIBRARY
P.O. Box 130   Phone: (403) 233-3804
Calgary, AB T2P 3C5   Ms. D. Budrevics, Sr.Libn.

HOLY CROSS HOSPITAL OF CALGARY - MEDICAL LIBRARY
2210 2nd St., S.W.   Phone: (403) 266-7231
Calgary, AB T2S 1S6   Mumtaz Jivraj, Med.Libn.

HOME OIL COMPANY, LTD. - LIBRARY
2300 Home Oil Tower
324 8th Ave., S.W.   Phone: (403) 232-7207
Calgary, AB T2P 2Z5   Rodney Anne Muir, Libn.

HUDSON'S BAY OIL & GAS COMPANY, LTD. - CORPORATE LIBRARY
700 Second St., S.W.   Phone: (403) 231-6051
Calgary, AB T2P 0X5   C.G. Harvey, Libn.

INSURANCE INSTITUTE OF SOUTHERN ALBERTA - LIBRARY
630 8th Ave., S.W., No. 601   Phone: (403) 266-3427
Calgary, AB T2P 1G6   Kathleen Schwabl, Sec.

LAW SOCIETY OF ALBERTA - CALGARY LIBRARY
611 4th St., S.W.   Phone: (403) 261-6148
Calgary, AB T2P 1T5   Melody M. Hainsworth, Libn.

MC KINNON, ALLEN & ASSOCIATES (Western), LTD. - RESEARCH LIBRARY
631 42nd Ave., S.E.   Phone: (403) 243-4345
Calgary, AB T2G 1Y7   Vi Sommerfeld, Corp.Sec.

MASON AND COMPANY - LIBRARY
1110 Bow Valley Sq. 2
205 5th Ave., S.W.   Phone: (403) 263-2190
Calgary, AB T2P 2V7   Lou Selgensen, Libn.

MOBIL OIL CANADA, LTD. - LIBRARY
P.O. Box 800   Phone: (403) 268-7785
Calgary, AB T2P 2J7   Kathleen V. McNeely, Libn.

MONTREAL ENGINEERING COMPANY, LTD. - CALGARY LIBRARY
900 One Palliser Sq.
125 9th Ave. S.E.   Phone: (403) 263-1680
Calgary, AB T2G 0P6   Beverley Bendell, Libn.

NORCEN ENERGY RESOURCES LIMITED - LIBRARY
715 5th Ave., S.W.   Phone: (403) 231-0887
Calgary, AB T2P 2X7   Gwendolyn Cameron, Libn.

PANARCTIC OILS LTD. - LIBRARY
703 6th Ave., S.W.
Box 190   Phone: (403) 269-0329
Calgary, AB T2P 2H6   Susan Tyrrell, Libn.

PETRO-CANADA - LIBRARY SERVICES
727 7th Ave. S.W.
P.O. Box 2844   Phone: (403) 232-8000
Calgary, AB T2P 2M7   Maryan Meadows, Hd.Libn.

ST. DAVID'S UNITED CHURCH - LIBRARY †
2606 32nd Ave., N.W.   Phone: (403) 284-2276
Calgary, AB T2M 2R2   Molly Webb

ST. VLADIMIR'S UKRAINIAN GREEK ORTHODOX CHURCH - LIBRARY OF ST.
  VLADIMIR
400 Meredith Rd., N.E.   Phone: (403) 277-6269
Calgary, AB T2E 5A6   Mykola Woron, Hd.Libn.

SALVATION ARMY GRACE HOSPITAL - MEDICAL STAFF LIBRARY
1402 8th Ave., N.W.   Phone: (403) 284-1141
Calgary, AB T2N 1B9   Dr. A. Rothwell, Chm., Lib.Comm.

SHELL CANADA RESOURCES LIMITED - TECHNICAL LIBRARY
P.O. Box 100   Phone: (403) 232-3512
Calgary, AB T2P 2H5   Sheila J. Jepps, Hd.Libn.

SOUTHERN ALBERTA INSTITUTE OF TECHNOLOGY - ALBERTA COLLEGE OF
  ART - LIBRARY
1301 16th Ave., N.W.   Phone: (403) 284-8665
Calgary, AB T2M 0L4   Mike Parkinson, Lib.Supv.

SOUTHERN ALBERTA INSTITUTE OF TECHNOLOGY - LEARNING RESOURCES
  CENTRE
1301 16th Ave., N.W.   Phone: (403) 284-8647
Calgary, AB T2M 0L4   R.F. Peters, Hd., LRC

SPROULE ASSOCIATES, LTD. - LIBRARY
Postal Sta. D, Box 6525
Calgary, AB T2P 2E1

SUNCOR INC. - LIBRARY
500 4th Ave., S.W.
P.O. Box 38   Phone: (403) 269-8128
Calgary, AB T2P 2V5   Pat Strong, Libn.

SWEDISH CONSULATE - LIBRARY
420 47th Ave., S.W.   Phone: (403) 243-1093
Calgary, AB T2S 1C4   R. Zoumer, Consul

TOTAL PETROLEUM (North America), LTD. - LIBRARY
639 5th Ave., S.W., 12th Fl.   Phone: (403) 265-9080
Calgary, AB T2P 0M9   KumKum Kabir, Libn.

UNION OIL COMPANY OF CANADA, LTD. - LIBRARY
335 8th Ave., S.W.
P.O. Box 999   Phone: (403) 268-0303
Calgary, AB T2P 2K6   Julie Graham, Libn.

UNIVERSITY OF CALGARY - EDUCATION MATERIALS CENTER
2500 University Dr. N.W.   Phone: (403) 284-5637
Calgary, AB T2N 1N4   Philomena Hauck, Dir.

UNIVERSITY OF CALGARY - ENVIRONMENT-SCIENCE-TECHNOLOGY
  LIBRARY
2500 University Dr., N.W.   Phone: (403) 284-5966
Calgary, AB T2N 1N4   Hazel Fry, Area Hd.

UNIVERSITY OF CALGARY - FILM LIBRARY
2500 University Dr., N.W.   Phone: (403) 284-6146
Calgary, AB T2N 1N4   Jennie Paine, Film Libn.

UNIVERSITY OF CALGARY - KANANASKIS CENTRE FOR ENVIRONMENTAL
  RESEARCH - LIBRARY
                                                 Phone: (403) 284-5355
Calgary, AB T0L 0H0   Grace LeBel, Libn.

UNIVERSITY OF CALGARY - LAW LIBRARY
2500 University Dr., N.W.   Phone: (403) 284-5090
Calgary, AB T2N 1N4   Gail Starr, Law Libn.

UNIVERSITY OF CALGARY - MEDICAL LIBRARY
Health Sciences Centre   Phone: (403) 284-6858
Calgary, AB T2N 1N4   Andras Kirchner, Med.Libn.

UNIVERSITY OF CALGARY - SPECIAL COLLECTIONS DIVISION
2500 University Dr., N.W.   Phone: (403) 284-5972
Calgary, AB T2N 1N4   Apollonia Steele, Spec.Coll.Libn.

WALSH YOUNG - LIBRARY
1500 Guinness House   Phone: (403) 263-8490
Calgary, AB T2P 0Z8   Susan L. Ross, Libn.

CAMROSE LUTHERAN COLLEGE - LIBRARY
4503 50th St.   Phone: (403) 672-3381
Camrose, AB T4V 2R3   Asgeir Ingibergsson, Hd.Libn.

CANADIAN UNION COLLEGE - LIBRARY
Box 430   Phone: (403) 782-6461
College Heights, AB T0C 0Z0   Keith H. Clouten, Libn.

MOUNTAIN VIEW BIBLE COLLEGE - LIBRARY
Box 190   Phone: (403) 335-3337
Didsbury, AB T0M 0W0   Sharon E. Quantz, Libn.

AFRICAN LITERATURE ASSOCIATION - SECRETARIAT LIBRARY
University Of Alberta
Dept. Of Comparative Literature   Phone: (403) 432-5535
Edmonton, AB T6G 2E6   Stephen H. Arnold, Sec.-Treas., Ed.

ALBERTA ALCOHOLISM AND DRUG ABUSE COMMISSION - LIBRARY
10909 Jasper Ave., 7th Fl.   Phone: (403) 427-7303
Edmonton, AB T5J 3M9   Susan Dingle-Cliff, Libn.

ALBERTA ASSOCIATION OF REGISTERED NURSES - LIBRARY
10256 112th St.   Phone: (403) 426-0160
Edmonton, AB T5K 1M6   Lloanne Walker, Libn.

ALBERTA - DEPARTMENT OF ADVANCED EDUCATION AND MANPOWER -
    LIBRARY
9th Fl., East Tower
11160 Jasper Ave.   Phone: (403) 427-5590
Edmonton, AB T5K 0L1   Pauline T. Howatt, Hd.Libn.

ALBERTA - DEPARTMENT OF THE ATTORNEY GENERAL - ATTORNEY
    GENERAL LAW LIBRARY
4th Fl., N. Wing
9833 109th St.   Phone: (403) 427-5021
Edmonton, AB T5K 2E8   Andrew Balazs, Dept.Libn.

ALBERTA - DEPARTMENT OF CONSUMER AND CORPORATE AFFAIRS -
    RESOURCE CENTRE
7th Fl., 10065 Jasper Ave.   Phone: (403) 427-5215
Edmonton, AB T5J 3B1   Rean Modien, Lib.Techn.

ALBERTA - DEPARTMENT OF CULTURE - DEPARTMENTAL LIBRARY
CN Tower, 11th Fl.
10004 104th Ave.   Phone: (403) 427-2571
Edmonton, AB T5J 0K5   Lucy M. Pana, Dept.Libn.

ALBERTA - DEPARTMENT OF CULTURE - HISTORICAL RESOURCES LIBRARY
12845 102nd Ave.   Phone: (403) 452-2150
Edmonton, AB T5N 0M6   Mrs. J. Toon, Libn.

ALBERTA - DEPARTMENT OF ECONOMIC DEVELOPMENT - LIBRARY
11th Fl., Pacific Plaza
10909 Jasper Ave.   Phone: (403) 427-4957
Edmonton, AB T5J 3M8   Linda Giffen, Libn.

ALBERTA - DEPARTMENT OF EDUCATION - LIBRARY
4th Fl., Devonian Bldg.
11160 Jasper Ave.   Phone: (403) 427-2985
Edmonton, AB T5K 0L2   Helen Skirrow, Coord., Lib.Serv.

ALBERTA - DEPARTMENT OF ENERGY AND NATURAL RESOURCES - LIBRARY
    †
9th Fl., South Tower, Petroleum Plaza
9915 108th St.   Phone: (403) 427-7425
Edmonton, AB T5K 2C9   Carole Dawson, Chf.Libn.

ALBERTA - DEPARTMENT OF ENERGY AND NATURAL RESOURCES - MAP &
    AIR PHOTO REFERENCE LIBRARY
2nd Fl. W., North Tower, Petroleum Plaza
9945 108th St.   Phone: (403) 427-7417
Edmonton, AB T5K 2G6   Alice S. Chen, Supv.

ALBERTA - DEPARTMENT OF THE ENVIRONMENT - LIBRARY
14th Fl., Oxbridge Place
9820 106th St.   Phone: (403) 427-6132
Edmonton, AB T5K 2J6   Ione Hooper, Libn.

ALBERTA - DEPARTMENT OF FEDERAL AND INTERGOVERNMENTAL
    AFFAIRS - LIBRARY
14th Fl., South Tower
10030 107th St.   Phone: (403) 427-2611
Edmonton, AB T5J 3E4   Anita E. Duncan, Lib.Techn.

ALBERTA - DEPARTMENT OF HOSPITALS AND MEDICAL CARE - HOSPITAL
    SERVICES LIBRARY
11010 101st St., 5th Fl.
Box 2222   Phone: (403) 427-8720
Edmonton, AB T5J 2P4   Margaret Bradfield, Lib.Techn.

ALBERTA - DEPARTMENT OF HOUSING AND PUBLIC WORKS - HOUSING
    LIBRARY
10050 112th St., 4th Fl.   Phone: (403) 427-8144
Edmonton, AB T5K 1L9   Dolores Ogilvie, Libn.

ALBERTA - DEPARTMENT OF LABOUR - BUILDING STANDARDS BRANCH
    RESOURCE CENTRE
10339 124th St., 201   Phone: (403) 427-6461
Edmonton, AB T5N 3W1

ALBERTA - DEPARTMENT OF LABOUR - LABOUR LIBRARY
10808 99th Ave., Rm. 501   Phone: (403) 427-8531
Edmonton, AB T5K 0G2   Wendy Kinsella, Hd.Libn.

ALBERTA - DEPARTMENT OF MUNICIPAL AFFAIRS - LIBRARY
9925 107th St., 9th Fl.   Phone: (403) 427-4829
Edmonton, AB T5K 2H9   Bettie Bayrak, Libn.

ALBERTA - DEPARTMENT OF SOCIAL SERVICES & COMMUNITY HEALTH -
    LIBRARY
6th Fl., Seventh St. Plaza
10030 107th St.   Phone: (403) 427-7272
Edmonton, AB T5J 3E4   Judy Sponholz, Dept.Libn.

ALBERTA - DEPARTMENT OF TOURISM AND SMALL BUSINESS - LIBRARY
1900 Capitol Sq.
10065 Jasper Ave.   Phone: (403) 427-3685
Edmonton, AB T5J 0H4   Glenna Winter, Dept.Libn.

ALBERTA - DEPARTMENT OF TRANSPORTATION - LIBRARY
9630 106th St.   Phone: (403) 427-8802
Edmonton, AB T5K 2B8   D. Smith, Libn.

ALBERTA - ENVIRONMENT COUNCIL - INFORMATION CENTRE
2100 College Plaza, Tower 3
8215 112th St.   Phone: (403) 427-5792
Edmonton, AB T6G 2M4   Colleen MacLachlan, Libn.

ALBERTA - GOVERNMENT SERVICES - INFORMATION SERVICES DIVISION
    LIBRARY
9515 107th St., Rm 259   Phone: (403) 427-2353
Edmonton, AB T5K 2C4   Danielle Bugeaud, Libn.

ALBERTA HOSPITAL ASSOCIATION - RESOURCE CENTRE
10025 108th St., 6th Floor   Phone: (403) 423-1776
Edmonton, AB T5J 1K9   Patricia Baxter, Libn.

ALBERTA HOSPITAL - LIBRARY †
Box 307   Phone: (403) 973-2268
Edmonton, AB T5J 2J7   Margaret Pierre, Lib.Techn. (Supv.)

ALBERTA HUMAN RIGHTS COMMISSION - LIBRARY
10053 111th St., Rm. 501
Edmonton, AB T5K 2H8

ALBERTA - LEGISLATIVE ASSEMBLY OF ALBERTA - LEGISLATURE LIBRARY
216 Legislature Bldg.   Phone: (403) 427-2473
Edmonton, AB T5K 2B6   D.B. McDougall, Legislative Libn.

ALBERTA MENTAL HEALTH SERVICES - CLINIC LIBRARY
5th Fl., 9942 108th St.
Edmonton, AB T5K 2J5

GEOGRAPHIC

ALBERTA - OFFICE OF THE OMBUDSMAN - OMBUDSMAN'S LIBRARY
1630 Phipps-McKinnon Bldg.
10020 101A Ave.　　　　Phone: (403) 427-2756
Edmonton, AB T5J 3G2　　　　Ms. D. Harry, Supv.

ALBERTA - PUBLIC UTILITIES BOARD - LIBRARY
Manulife Bldg., 11th Floor
10055 106th St.　　　　Phone: (403) 427-4901
Edmonton, AB T5J 2Y2　　　　James E. McKee, Lib.Techn.

ALBERTA RESEARCH COUNCIL - ALBERTA OIL SANDS INFORMATION CENTRE
6th Fl., Highfield Pl.
10010 106th St.　　　　Phone: (403) 427-8382
Edmonton, AB T5J 3L8　　　　Helga Radvanyi, Mgr.

ALBERTA RESEARCH COUNCIL - LIBRARY SERVICES
4445 Calgary Trail S.　　　　Phone: (403) 438-1810
Edmonton, AB T6H 5R7　　　　Sharon M. Gee, Chf.Libn.

ALBERTA RESEARCH COUNCIL - SOLAR & WIND ENERGY RESEARCH PROGRAM (SWERP) INFORMATION CENTRE
5th Fl., Terrace Plaza
4445 Calgary Trail S.　　　　Phone: (403) 453-1808
Edmonton, AB T6H 5R7　　　　Karen D. Beliveau, Coord.

ALBERTA SCHOOL FOR THE DEAF - L.A. BROUGHTON LIBRARY
6240 113th St.　　　　Phone: (403) 434-1481
Edmonton, AB T6H 3L2　　　　Charmaine Muise, Teacher/Libn.

ALBERTA SOCIETY FOR AUTISTIC CHILDREN - LIBRARY
Edmonton School for Autistic Children
7330 113th St.　　　　Phone: (403) 435-0161
Edmonton, AB T6G 1L6

ALBERTA TEACHERS' ASSOCIATION - LIBRARY
11010 142nd St., Barnett House　　　　Phone: (403) 453-2411
Edmonton, AB T5N 2R1　　　　Donna Dryden, Libn.

ALBERTA - TREASURY DEPARTMENT - BUREAU OF STATISTICS LIBRARY
7th Fl., Sir Frederick W. Haultain Bldg.
10820 98th Ave.　　　　Phone: (403) 427-3058
Edmonton, AB T5K 0C8　　　　Christine Minailo, Lib.Techn.

ALBERTA - TREASURY DEPARTMENT - LIBRARY SERVICES
404 Terrace Bldg.
9515 107th St.　　　　Phone: (403) 427-7595
Edmonton, AB T5K 2C3　　　　J. Robin Brown, Dept.Libn.

ALBERTA - WORKERS' HEALTH SAFETY & COMPENSATION - OCCUPATIONAL HEALTH & SAFETY DIVISION - LIBRARY
Oxbridge Pl., 3rd Fl.
9820 106th St.　　　　Phone: (403) 427-4671
Edmonton, AB T5K 2J6　　　　W. Keith McLaughlin, Libn.

ASSOCIATED ENGINEERING SERVICES, LTD. - INFORMATION CENTRE
13140 St. Albert Trail　　　　Phone: (403) 453-8111
Edmonton, AB T5L 4R8　　　　M. Davidson, Libn.

CAMSELL (Charles) GENERAL HOSPITAL - PETER WILCOCK LIBRARY
12815 115th Ave.　　　　Phone: (403) 452-8770
Edmonton, AB T5M 3A4　　　　Janet Jacobson, Med.Libn.

CANADA - ATMOSPHERIC ENVIRONMENT SERVICE - WESTERN REGION HEADQUARTERS LIBRARY
Argyll Centre
6325 103rd St.　　　　Phone: (403) 437-1250
Edmonton, AB T6H 5H6　　　　Larry Winstone, Meteorologist

CANADA - CANADIAN FORESTRY SERVICE - NORTHERN FOREST RESEARCH CENTRE - LIBRARY
5320 122nd St.　　　　Phone: (403) 435-7323
Edmonton, AB T6H 3S5　　　　D. Robinson, Libn.

CANADA - CANADIAN WILDLIFE SERVICE - WESTERN AND NORTHERN REGION LIBRARY
10th Fl., 9942 108th St.　　　　Phone: (403) 425-5891
Edmonton, AB T5K 2J5　　　　Peter A. Jordan, Regional Libn.

CANADA - NATIONAL FILM BOARD OF CANADA - EDMONTON DISTRICT OFFICE - FILM LIBRARY
Centennial Bldg.
10031 103rd Ave.　　　　Phone: (403) 420-3010
Edmonton, AB T5J 0G9

CANADA - STATISTICS CANADA - ADVISORY SERVICES - EDMONTON REFERENCE CENTRE †
1000, 10025 106th St.　　　　Phone: (403) 420-3027
Edmonton, AB T5J 1G9

CANADA - TRANSPORT CANADA - CANADIAN AIR TRANSPORTATION ADMINISTRATION - WESTERN REGIONAL LIBRARY
Federal Bldg.
9820 107th St., Rm. 10-76　　　　Phone: (403) 420-3801
Edmonton, AB T5K 1G3　　　　P.J. Nelson, Regional Libn.

CANADIAN UTILITIES LIMITED - LIBRARY
10040 104th St.　　　　Phone: (403) 420-7039
Edmonton, AB T5J 2V6　　　　Donna I. Humphries, Libn.

CONSULATE-GENERAL OF JAPAN - JAPANESE CONSULATE LIBRARY
10020 - 100th St., Suite 2600　　　　Phone: (403) 422-3752
Edmonton, AB T5J 0N4

CROSS CANCER INSTITUTE - LIBRARY
11560 University Ave.　　　　Phone: (403) 432-8593
Edmonton, AB T6G 1Z2　　　　Katherine Sharma, Libn.

EDMONTON ART GALLERY - REFERENCE LIBRARY
2 Sir Winston Churchill Sq.　　　　Phone: (403) 429-6781
Edmonton, AB T5J 2C1　　　　Brenda Banks, Libn.

EDMONTON CITY ARCHIVES
10105 112th Ave.　　　　Phone: (403) 479-2069
Edmonton, AB T5G 0H1　　　　Helen LaRose, Supv., Archv.

EDMONTON CITY PLANNING DEPARTMENT - LIBRARY/RESOURCE CENTRE
11th Fl., Phipps-McKinnon Bldg.
10020 101A Ave.　　　　Phone: (403) 428-2665
Edmonton, AB T5J 3G2　　　　Coreen Douglas, Libn.

EDMONTON GENERAL HOSPITAL - HEALTH SCIENCES LIBRARY
11111 Jasper Ave.　　　　Phone: (403) 482-4421
Edmonton, AB T5K 0L4　　　　Jake VandeBrink, Hd.Libn.

EDMONTON JOURNAL - LIBRARY
101 St. & 100 Ave.
Box 2421　　　　Phone: (403) 420-1920
Edmonton, AB T5J 2S6　　　　Patricia Garneau, Libn.

EDMONTON POWER - LIBRARY
600 Centennial Library　　　　Phone: (403) 428-4302
Edmonton, AB T5J 2V4　　　　Janet C. Marren, Libn.

EDMONTON PUBLIC SCHOOL BOARD - LEARNING RESOURCES PROFESSIONAL LIBRARY
10010 107A Ave.　　　　Phone: (403) 429-5621
Edmonton, AB T5H 0Z8　　　　Alma A. Webster, Supv. Of Lrng.Rsrcs.

EDMONTON SEPARATE SCHOOL BOARD - PROFESSIONAL LIBRARY
9807 106th St.　　　　Phone: (403) 429-7631
Edmonton, AB T5K 1C2　　　　C. Hornby, Res.Libn.

EDMONTON SOCIAL SERVICES DEPARTMENT - LIBRARY
CN Tower, 6th Fl.
10004 - 104 Ave.　　　　Phone: (403) 428-5927
Edmonton, AB T5J 0K1

EDMONTON SUN - NEWSPAPER LIBRARY
9405 50th St.　　　　Phone: (403) 468-5111
Edmonton, AB T6B 2T4　　　　John M. Sinclair, Libn.

GCG ENGINEERING PARTNERSHIP - LIBRARY
17420 Stony Plain Rd.　　　　Phone: (403) 483-8094
Edmonton, AB T5S 1K6　　　　Heather Grimble, Lib.Techn.

GENSTAR CEMENT, LTD. - TECHNICAL LIBRARY
Sta. D, P.O. Box 3961   Phone: (403) 452-8290
Edmonton, AB T5L 4P8   Mrs. D.A. Bales, Sec.

GOOD SAMARITAN SOCIETY - LIBRARY
Good Samaritan Auxiliary Hospital
9649 71st Ave.   Phone: (403) 439-6381
Edmonton, AB T6E 5J2   Geraldine Ridge, Libn.

HANSON MATERIALS ENGINEERING (Western) LTD. - BUSINESS LIBRARY
18th St. and 75th Ave.
R.R.2   Phone: (403) 464-7916
Edmonton, AB T6C 4E6   Norma Armstrong, Libn.

HARDY ASSOCIATES (1978) LTD. - LIBRARY
4810 93rd St.
Box 746   Phone: (403) 436-2152
Edmonton, AB T5J 2L4   Jean Crozier, Dir. Of Lib.Serv.

HEALTH COMPUTER INFORMATION BUREAU
10504A-169th St.   Phone: (403) 489-4553
Edmonton, AB T5P 3X6   Steven A. Huesing, HCIB Secretariat

INSTITUTE OF LAW RESEARCH AND REFORM - LIBRARY
402 Law Centre
University of Alberta   Phone: (403) 432-5291
Edmonton, AB T6G 2H5   Marlene Welton, Lib.Asst.

LAW SOCIETY OF ALBERTA - EDMONTON LIBRARY
Law Courts Bldg., 1A Churchill Sq.   Phone: (403) 423-7601
Edmonton, AB T5J 0R2   Shih-Sheng Hu, Chf.Prov. Law Libn.

MISERICORDIA HOSPITAL - WEINLOS MEDICAL LIBRARY
16940 87th Ave.   Phone: (403) 484-8811
Edmonton, AB T5R 4H5   Linda Herman, Med.Libn.

NEWMAN THEOLOGICAL COLLEGE - LIBRARY †
R.R. 8   Phone: (403) 459-6656
Edmonton, AB T5L 4H8   Shirley Anne Threndyle, Libn.

NORTHERN ALBERTA INSTITUTE OF TECHNOLOGY - LEARNING RESOURCE
   CENTRE
11762 106th St.   Phone: (403) 477-4375
Edmonton, AB T5G 2R1   Miss Jean Paul, Chf.Libn.

NORTHWEST BIBLE COLLEGE - J.C. COOKE LIBRARY
11617 106th Ave.   Phone: (403) 452-0808
Edmonton, AB T5H 0S1   Braden S. Fawcett, Libn.

QUEEN'S BENCH - COURT OF APPEAL JUDGES' LIBRARY
Law Courts Bldg.
1A Churchill Sq.
Edmonton, AB T5J 0R2   Shih-Sheng Hu, Chf.Prov. Law Libn.

ROYAL ALEXANDRA HOSPITAL - MEDICAL LIBRARY
10240 Kingsway Ave.   Phone: (403) 474-3431
Edmonton, AB T5H 3V9   Deana Dryden, Libn.

ROYAL ALEXANDRA HOSPITAL - SCHOOL OF NURSING LIBRARY
10240 Kingsway Ave.   Phone: (403) 474-3431
Edmonton, AB T5H 3V9   E. Pass, Libn.

ST. STEPHEN'S COLLEGE - LIBRARY
University of Alberta   Phone: (403) 439-7311
Edmonton, AB T6G 2J6   Ruth Schrag, Libn. & Church Archv.

STANLEY ASSOCIATES ENGINEERING, LTD. - LIBRARY
11748 Kingsway Ave.   Phone: (403) 453-3441
Edmonton, AB T5G 0X5   Catherine Wang, Libn.

SYNCRUDE CANADA, LTD. - RESEARCH DEPARTMENT LIBRARY
P.O. Box 5790   Phone: (403) 464-8400
Edmonton, AB T6C 4G3   Peter J. Bates, Info.Spec.

UKRAINIAN WOMEN'S ASSOCIATION OF CANADA - UKRAINIAN MUSEUM
   OF CANADA - LIBRARY
10611 110th Ave.   Phone: (403) 424-1530
Edmonton, AB T5H 1H7   Mrs. J. Verchomin, Dir.

UNIVERSITY OF ALBERTA - BOREAL INSTITUTE FOR NORTHERN STUDIES -
   LIBRARY
CW 401 Biological Sciences Bldg.   Phone: (403) 432-4409
Edmonton, AB T6G 2E9   Mrs. G.A. Cooke, Libn.

UNIVERSITY OF ALBERTA - CENTRE FOR THE STUDY OF MENTAL
   RETARDATION - LIBRARY
6-123A Education II   Phone: (403) 432-4439
Edmonton, AB T6G 2E1   Barbara McGowan, Sec.

UNIVERSITY OF ALBERTA - COMPUTING SCIENCE READING ROOM
604 General Services Bldg.   Phone: (403) 432-3977
Edmonton, AB T6G 2H1   Jennifer Penny, Libn.

UNIVERSITY OF ALBERTA - FACULTE ST-JEAN - BIBLIOTHEQUE
8406 91st St.   Phone: (403) 466-2196
Edmonton, AB T6C 4G9   Georges Durocher, Libn.

UNIVERSITY OF ALBERTA - GOVERNMENT PUBLICATIONS
                                                  Phone: (403) 432-3776
Edmonton, AB T6G 2J8   Sally Manwaring, Hd., Govt.Pubn.Lib.

UNIVERSITY OF ALBERTA - H.T. COUTTS EDUCATION LIBRARY
Faculty of Education Bldg.   Phone: (403) 432-5555
Edmonton, AB T6G 2G5   B.J. Busch, Hd.

UNIVERSITY OF ALBERTA - HEALTH SCIENCES LIBRARY
                                                  Phone: (403) 432-3791
Edmonton, AB T6G 2J8   Phyllis J. Russell, Health Sci.Libn.

UNIVERSITY OF ALBERTA - HUMANITIES AND SOCIAL SCIENCES LIBRARY
Rutherford North   Phone: (403) 432-4674
Edmonton, AB T6G 2E1   Mohan Sharma, Hd.

UNIVERSITY OF ALBERTA - LAW LIBRARY
Law Centre   Phone: (403) 432-5560
Edmonton, AB T6G 2H5   Lillian MacPherson, Law Libn.

UNIVERSITY OF ALBERTA - NUCLEAR PHYSICS LIBRARY
Nuclear Research Centre   Phone: (403) 432-3637
Edmonton, AB T6G 2N5   G.M.T. Tratt, Sec.

UNIVERSITY OF ALBERTA - POPULATION RESEARCH LIBRARY
Dept. of Sociology   Phone: (403) 432-3916
Edmonton, AB T6H 2H2   Susan Major, Libn.

UNIVERSITY OF ALBERTA - SCIENCE LIBRARY
                                                  Phone: (403) 432-3785
Edmonton, AB T6G 2J8   David Jones, Act.Hd.

UNIVERSITY OF ALBERTA - SPECIAL COLLECTIONS
Cameron Library   Phone: (403) 432-5998
Edmonton, AB T6G 2J8   John W. Charles, Spec.Coll.Libn.

UNIVERSITY OF ALBERTA - UNIVERSITY MAP COLLECTION
B-7 H.M. Tory Bldg.   Phone: (403) 432-4760
Edmonton, AB T6G 2H4   R. Whistance-Smith, Univ. Map Curator

FAIRVIEW COLLEGE - LEARNING RESOURCES CENTRE
Box 3000   Phone: (403) 835-2213
Fairview, AB T0H 1L0   Olive V. Lancaster, Libn.

SYNCRUDE CANADA, LTD. - OPERATIONS LIBRARY
Postal Bag 4009, Zone 3060   Phone: (403) 791-8431
Fort McMurray, AB T9H 3L1   Anita Thomas, Lib.Techn.

SHERRITT GORDON MINES, LTD. - RESEARCH CENTRE LIBRARY
                                                  Phone: (403) 998-6419
Fort Saskatchewan, AB T8L 2P2   J. Derek Sim, Libn.

GRANDE PRAIRIE GENERAL HOSPITAL - LIBRARY
10409 98th St.
Grande Prairie, AB T8V 2E8   S. Black, Libn.

CANADA - AGRICULTURE CANADA - RESEARCH STATION, LACOMBE -
   LIBRARY
                                                  Phone: (403) 782-3316
Lacombe, AB T0C 1S0   D.E. Waldern, Dir.

GEOGRAPHIC

GEOGRAPHIC

ALBERTA - DEPARTMENT OF THE ATTORNEY GENERAL - LAW SOCIETY
   LIBRARY
Court House   Phone: (403) 329-3266
Lethbridge, AB T1J 0P5   Mrs. J. Kiprick, Libn.

CANADA - AGRICULTURE CANADA - RESEARCH STATION, LETHBRIDGE -
   LIBRARY
                          Phone: (403) 327-4561
Lethbridge, AB T1J 4B1   John P. Miska, Area Coord.

OLDS COLLEGE - LEARNING RESOURCES CENTRE
Box 760   Phone: (403) 556-8243
Olds, AB T0M 1P0   Garry Grisak, Lib.Coord.

ALBERTA HOSPITAL PONOKA - STAFF LIBRARY
P.O. Box 1000   Phone: (403) 783-3351
Ponoka, AB T0C 2H0   Peter Managhan, Staff Libn.

CANADA - DEFENCE RESEARCH ESTABLISHMENT SUFFIELD - LIBRARY
                          Phone: (403) 544-3701
Ralston, AB T0J 2N0   Linda A. Berg, Lib.Techn.

MICHENER CENTRE - STAFF LIBRARY
Box 5002   Phone: (403) 343-5936
Red Deer, AB T4N 5Y5   Judith Benson, Libn.

RED DEER ADVOCATE - NEWSPAPER LIBRARY
4703 50th St.   Phone: (403) 343-2400
Red Deer, AB T4N 5W9   Patricia J. Goulet, Libn.

NORTH AMERICAN BAPTIST COLLEGE - LIBRARY
11523 23rd Ave.   Phone: (403) 988-5571
South Edmonton, AB T6H 4N7   Arnold Rapske, Libn.

PRAIRIE BIBLE INSTITUTE - LIBRARY
                          Phone: (403) 443-5511
Three Hills, AB T0M 2A0   Ron Jordahl, Libn.

WAINWRIGHT GENERAL HOSPITAL - MEDICAL LIBRARY
Box 820   Phone: (403) 842-3324
Wainwright, AB T0B 4P0   Lorraine Murray, Health Rec.Adm.

REYNOLDS MUSEUM - LIBRARY
4118 57th St.   Phone: (403) 352-5201
Wetaskiwin, AB T9A 2B6   Stanley G. Reynolds, Cur.

BRITISH COLUMBIA

BRITISH COLUMBIA INSTITUTE OF TECHNOLOGY - LIBRARY SERVICES
   DIVISION
3700 Willingdon Ave.   Phone: (604) 434-5734
Burnaby, BC V5G 3H2   Joseph E. Carver, Dean of Lib.Serv.

BRITISH COLUMBIA - MINISTRY OF HEALTH - MENTAL HEALTH SERVICES
   LIBRARY *
3405 Willingdon Ave.   Phone: (604) 434-4247
Burnaby, BC V5G 3H4   Joy Fourchalk, Libn.

BRITISH COLUMBIA TELEPHONE COMPANY - BUSINESS LIBRARY
5th Fl., 3777 Kingsway   Phone: (604) 432-2671
Burnaby, BC V5H 3Z7   Miss E.B. Murray, Libn.

BURNABY GENERAL HOSPITAL - DR. H.H.W. BROOKE MEMORIAL LIBRARY
3935 Kincaid St.   Phone: (604) 434-4211
Burnaby, BC V5G 2X6   Mr. Hoong Lim, Libn.

BURNABY AND NEW WESTMINSTER SCHOOL BOARDS - REGIONAL FILM
   LIBRARY SERVICES *
Schou Educational Centre
4041 Canada Way   Phone: (604) 437-4511
Burnaby, BC V5G 1G6   R. Donald Lyon, Coord.

BURNABY SCHOOL BOARD - DISTRICT RESOURCE CENTRE *
Schou Educational Centre
4041 Canada Way   Phone: (604) 437-4511
Burnaby, BC V5G 1G6   R. Donald Lyon, Coord.

BURNABY SCHOOL BOARD - TEACHERS' PROFESSIONAL LIBRARY †
Schou Educational Centre
4041 Canada Way   Phone: (604) 437-4511
Burnaby, BC V5G 1G6

MICROTEL PACIFIC RESEARCH LTD. - TECHNICAL LIBRARY
105-4664 Lougheed Hwy.   Phone: (604) 294-0414
Burnaby, BC V5C 5T5   V. Renzetti, Tech.Libn.

SIMON FRASER UNIVERSITY - LIBRARY - SPECIAL COLLECTIONS
                          Phone: (604) 291-3261
Burnaby, BC V5A 1S6   T.C. "Ted" Dobb, Univ.Libn.

CANADIAN MILITARY ENGINEERS MUSEUM - LIBRARY
M.P.O. 612   Phone: (604) 858-3311
C.F.B. Chilliwack, BC V0X 2E0

WESTERN PENTECOSTAL BIBLE COLLEGE - LIBRARY
Box 1000   Phone: (604) 853-7491
Clayburn, BC V0X 1E0   Rev. Laurence M. Van Kleek, Libn.

BRITISH COLUMBIA LAW LIBRARY FOUNDATION - KAMLOOPS
   COURTHOUSE LIBRARY
Court Annex, 1165 Battle St.   Phone: (604) 374-7415
Kamloops, BC V2C 2N4   Denise Caldwell, Area Libn.

CANADA - AGRICULTURE CANADA - RESEARCH STATION, KAMLOOPS -
   LIBRARY
3015 Ord Rd.   Phone: (604) 376-5565
Kamloops, BC V2B 7V8

KOOTENAY LAKE HISTORICAL SOCIETY - LIBRARY
Box 537   Phone: (604) 353-2525
Kaslo, BC V0G 1M0   Roy E. Green, Cur.

COMINCO LTD. - SULLIVAN MINE LIBRARY
P.O. Box 2000
Kimberley, BC V1A 2G3   Mrs. E.E. Gold, Libn.

YASODHARA ASHRAM SOCIETY - LIBRARY
Box 9   Phone: (604) 227-9220
Kootenay Bay, BC V0B 1X0   Swami Sivananda Radha

LANGLEY SCHOOL DISTRICT - RESOURCE CENTRE
19740 32nd Ave.   Phone: (604) 530-5151
Langley, BC V3A 4S1   Shirley D. Fisher-Fleming, Educ. Media Coord.

WESTMINSTER ABBEY - LIBRARY
Mission, BC V2V 4J2   Boniface Aicher, O.S.B., Libn.

CANADA - FISHERIES & OCEANS - PACIFIC BIOLOGICAL STATION -
   LIBRARY
                          Phone: (604) 758-5202
Nanaimo, BC V9R 5K6   G. Miller, Libn.

NANAIMO AND DISTRICT MUSEUM SOCIETY - ARCHIVES
100 Cameron Rd.   Phone: (604) 753-1821
Nanaimo, BC V9R 2X1   Barrie Hardcastle, Cur.

BRITISH COLUMBIA - MINISTRY OF FORESTS - NELSON FOREST REGION
   LIBRARY
518 Lake St.   Phone: (604) 354-4181
Nelson, BC V1L 4C6   Chris F. Thompson, Regional Res.Off.

CHAMBER OF MINES OF EASTERN BRITISH COLUMBIA - BUREAU OF
   INFORMATION
215 Hall St.   Phone: (604) 352-5242
Nelson, BC V1L 5X4   George Murray, Mgr.

DAVID THOMPSON UNIVERSITY CENTRE - SPECIAL COLLECTIONS
820 Tenth St.   Phone: (604) 352-2241
Nelson, BC V1L 3C7   Ronald J. Welwood, Chm.

INTERNATIONAL PACIFIC SALMON FISHERIES COMMISSION - LIBRARY
Box 30   Phone: (604) 521-3771
New Westminster, BC V3L 4X9   Mrs. Fumi Sato, Libn.

LOCKHEED PETROLEUM SERVICES LTD. - ENGINEERING LIBRARY †
610 Derwent Way
New Westminster, BC V3M 5P8 Ronald V. Simmer, Libn.

ROYAL COLUMBIAN HOSPITAL - LIBRARY
330 E. Columbia St. Phone: (604) 520-4255
New Westminster, BC V3L 3W7 Ms. S. Abzinger, Libn.

LIONS GATE HOSPITAL - DR. H. CARSON GRAHAM MEMORIAL LIBRARY
230 E. 13th St. Phone: (604) 988-3131
North Vancouver, BC V7L 2L7 Myrra N. Marshall, Libn.

CANADA - NATIONAL RESEARCH COUNCIL - CISTI - DOMINION RADIO
ASTROPHYSICAL OBSERVATORY - LIBRARY
Box 248 Phone: (604) 497-5321
Penticton, BC V2A 6K3 W. Gully, Libn.

BRITISH COLUMBIA - MINISTRY OF HEALTH - MENTAL HEALTH PROGRAMS
- STAFF REFERENCE LIBRARY
Riverview Hospital
500 Lougheed Hwy. Phone: (604) 521-1911
Port Coquitlam, BC V3C 1J0 Min-Ja Laubental, Dir., Lib.Serv.

PRINCE GEORGE CITIZEN - NEWSPAPER LIBRARY
150 Brunswick St. Phone: (604) 562-2441
Prince George, BC V2L 4T1 Lynda Jane Williams, Libn.

BRITISH COLUMBIA GENEALOGICAL SOCIETY - REFERENCE LIBRARY
Box 94371 Phone: (604) 274-3659
Richmond, BC V7C 1J3 Alice Marwood, Libn.

BRITISH COLUMBIA - MINISTRY OF EDUCATION - PROVINCIAL
EDUCATIONAL MEDIA CENTRE
7351 Elmbridge Way Phone: (604) 278-4961
Richmond, BC V6X 1B8 B.A. Black, Dir.

ROSSLAND MUSEUM - ARCHIVES
Box 26 Phone: (604) 362-7722
Rossland, BC V0G 1Y0 E. Pierpoint, Cur.

CANADA - AGRICULTURE CANADA - SAANICHTON RESEARCH & PLANT
QUARANTINE STATION - LIBRARY
8801 E. Saanich Rd. Phone: (604) 656-1173
Sidney, BC V8L 1H3 Peggy Watson, Libn.

CANADA - FISHERIES & OCEANS - INSTITUTE OF OCEAN SCIENCES -
LIBRARY
9860 W. Saanich Rd.
Box 6000 Phone: (604) 656-8392
Sidney, BC V8L 4B2 Sharon Thomson, Libn.

CANADA - AGRICULTURE CANADA - RESEARCH STATION, SUMMERLAND -
LIBRARY
Phone: (604) 494-7711
Summerland, BC V0H 1Z0 Vivienne B. Smith, Libn.

BRITISH COLUMBIA - MINISTRY OF FORESTS - TRAINING SCHOOL
LIBRARY *
9800 140th St. Phone: (604) 585-1101
Surrey, BC V3T 4M5 J.B. Cawston, Principal

SURREY MUSEUM - ARCHIVES
Cloverdale
Box 1006 Phone: (604) 574-5744
Surrey, BC V3S 4P5 D.R. Hooser, Cur.

COMINCO LTD. - CENTRAL TECHNICAL LIBRARY
Phone: (604) 364-4409
Trail, BC V1R 4L8 Robert G. Lewis, Lib.Supv.

WILLIAMS (C.S.) CLINIC - LIBRARY
901 Helena St. Phone: (604) 368-5211
Trail, BC V1R 3X4 Dr. L. Simonetta, Lib.Chm.

ANGLICAN CHURCH OF CANADA - PROVINCIAL SYNOD OF BRITISH
COLUMBIA AND THE YUKON - ARCHIVES
6050 Chancellor Blvd. Phone: (604) 228-9031
Vancouver, BC V6T 1X3 R.G. Walker, Archv.

BRITISH COLUMBIA ALCOHOL AND DRUG PROGRAMS - LIBRARY
1755 W. Broadway, 2nd Fl. Phone: (604) 873-0263
Vancouver, BC V6J 4S5 W. Holmes, Lib.Techn.

BRITISH COLUMBIA CENTRAL CREDIT UNION - RESOURCE CENTRE
P.O. Box 2038 Phone: (604) 734-2511
Vancouver, BC V6B 3R9 Valerie Redston, Libn.

BRITISH COLUMBIA - COUNCIL OF FOREST INDUSTRIES OF BRITISH
COLUMBIA - LIBRARY
1500/1055 W. Hastings St. Phone: (604) 684-0211
Vancouver, BC V6E 2H1 Sheila Foley, Libn.

BRITISH COLUMBIA HEALTH ASSOCIATION (BCHA) - LIBRARY
440 Cambie St. Phone: (604) 683-7421
Vancouver, BC V7H 1M9 Carolyn Hall, Lib.Techn.

BRITISH COLUMBIA HYDRO & POWER AUTHORITY - ENGINEERING
LIBRARY
555 W. Hastings St.
Box 12121 Phone: (604) 663-2894
Vancouver, BC V6B 4T6 Elizabeth Preston, Asst.Libn.

BRITISH COLUMBIA HYDRO & POWER AUTHORITY - LIBRARY
970 Burrard St. Phone: (604) 663-2416
Vancouver, BC V6Z 1Y3 Eleanor Haydock, Libn.

BRITISH COLUMBIA - JUDGES' LIBRARY - SUPERIOR & COUNTY COURTS
Law Courts, 800 Smithe St. Phone: (604) 668-2799
Vancouver, BC V6Z 2E1 A. Rector, Libn.

BRITISH COLUMBIA LAW LIBRARY FOUNDATION - VANCOUVER
COURTHOUSE LIBRARY
800 Smithe St. Phone: (604) 689-7295
Vancouver, BC V6Z 2E1 Maureen B. McCormick, Exec.Dir.

BRITISH COLUMBIA LIONS SOCIETY FOR CRIPPLED CHILDREN - LIBRARY
177 W. 7th
Vancouver, BC V5Y 1K5

BRITISH COLUMBIA - MINISTRY OF HUMAN RESOURCES - LIBRARY †
800 Cassiar St. Phone: (604) 387-6415
Vancouver, BC V8W 2Z2 M.J. Love, Libn.

BRITISH COLUMBIA RESEARCH COUNCIL - LIBRARY
3650 Wesbrook Mall Phone: (604) 224-4331
Vancouver, BC V6S 2L2 Viona Coates, Libn.

BRITISH COLUMBIA RESEARCH COUNCIL - URANIUM INFORMATION
CENTRE
3650 Wesbrook Mall Phone: (604) 224-4331
Vancouver, BC V6S 2L2 Viona Coates, Res.Libn.

BRITISH COLUMBIA TEACHERS' FEDERATION - RESOURCES CENTRE
105 2235 Burrard St. Phone: (604) 731-8121
Vancouver, BC V6J 3H9

BRITISH COLUMBIA UTILITIES COMMISSION - LIBRARY
2100-1177 W. Hastings St. Phone: (604) 689-1831
Vancouver, BC V6E 2L3 C. Brian Tu, Libn.

BRITISH COLUMBIA - WORKER'S COMPENSATION BOARD - LIBRARY
5255 Heather St. Phone: (604) 266-0211
Vancouver, BC V5Z 3L8 Barbara L. Sanderson, Libn.

BRITISH COLUMBIA AND YUKON CHAMBER OF MINES - LIBRARY
840 W. Hastings St. Phone: (604) 681-5328
Vancouver, BC V6C 1C8 Jack M. Patterson, Mgr.

BULL, HOUSSER AND TUPPER - LIBRARY
3000 Royal Centre
1055 W. Georgia
P.O. Box 11130 Phone: (604) 687-6575
Vancouver, BC V6E 3R3 Susan Daly, Libn.

CANADA - AGRICULTURE CANADA - RESEARCH STATION, VANCOUVER -
LIBRARY
6660 N.W. Marine Dr. Phone: (604) 224-4355
Vancouver, BC V6T 1X2 C.M. Cutler, Area Coord.

GEOGRAPHIC

CANADA - ATMOSPHERIC ENVIRONMENT SERVICE - PACIFIC REGION - LIBRARY
700-1200 W. 73rd Ave.   Phone: (604) 732-4830
Vancouver, BC V6P 6H9   D.A. Faulkner, Meteorologist

CANADA - FISHERIES & OCEANS - FISHERIES MANAGEMENT REGIONAL LIBRARY
1090 W. Pender St.   Phone: (604) 666-3851
Vancouver, BC V6E 2P1   Paulette Westlake, Lib.Techn.

CANADA - GEOLOGICAL SURVEY OF CANADA - LIBRARY
100 W. Pender St., 5th Fl.   Phone: (604) 666-3812
Vancouver, BC V6B 1R8   Mary Akehurst, Libn.

CANADA - HEALTH AND WELFARE CANADA - HEALTH PROTECTION BRANCH - REGIONAL LIBRARY
1001 W. Pender St., 6th Fl.   Phone: (604) 666-3147
Vancouver, BC V6E 2M7   Elizabeth Hardacre, Lib.Techn.

CANADA - STATISTICS CANADA - ADVISORY SERVICES - VANCOUVER REFERENCE CENTRE
1145 Robson St.   Phone: (604) 666-3695
Vancouver, BC V6E 3W8   C.G. Lenoski, Asst. Regional Dir.

CANADIAN MUSIC CENTRE - LIBRARY
3-2007 W. 4th Ave.   Phone: (604) 734-4622
Vancouver, BC V6J 1N3   Colin Miles, Regional Dir.

CANCER CONTROL AGENCY OF BRITISH COLUMBIA - LIBRARY
2656 Heather St.   Phone: (604) 873-6212
Vancouver, BC V5Z 3J3   David Noble, Libn.

CARR (Emily) COLLEGE OF ART - LIBRARY
1399 Johnston St.
Granville Island
Vancouver, BC V6H 3R9   Phone: (604) 687-2345
                                  Ken Chamberlain, Hd.Libn.

CHINESE NATIONALIST LEAGUE OF CANADA - LIBRARY †
529 Gore Ave.   Phone: (604) 681-6022
Vancouver, BC V6A 2Z6   James K. Cheng, Chf.Libn.

COLLEGE OF PHYSICIANS AND SURGEONS OF BRITISH COLUMBIA - MEDICAL LIBRARY SERVICE
1807 W. 10th Ave.   Phone: (604) 736-5551
Vancouver, BC V6J 2A9   C. William Fraser, Dir.

COMINCO LTD. - INFORMATION SERVICES
200 Granville Sq., 24th Fl.   Phone: (604) 682-0611
Vancouver, BC V6C 2R2   David A. Pepper, Chf.Libn.

CP AIR - ENGINEERING LIBRARY
One Grant McConachie Way
Vancouver International Airport
Vancouver, BC V7B 1V1   Phone: (604) 273-5211

FARRIS, VAUGHAN, WILLS & MURPHY - LIBRARY
700 W. Georgia St.
Box 10026
Vancouver, BC V7Y 1B3   Phone: (604) 684-9151
                                      Fiona Anderson, Libn.

FORINTEK CANADA CORP. - WESTERN LABORATORY - LIBRARY
6620 N.W. Marine Dr.   Phone: (604) 224-3221
Vancouver, BC V6T 1X2   Mrs. Marion E. Johnson, Libn.

GREATER VANCOUVER REGIONAL DISTRICT - LIBRARY
2034 W. 12th Ave.   Phone: (604) 731-1155
Vancouver, BC V6J 2G2   Frances Christopherson, Libn.

MAC MILLAN BLOEDEL RESEARCH LIMITED - LIBRARY
3350 E. Broadway   Phone: (604) 254-5151
Vancouver, BC V5M 4E6   Diana Wilimovsky, Libn.

MACRAE, MONTGOMERY & CUNNINGHAM - LIBRARY
555 Burrard St., No. 1585   Phone: (604) 689-5755
Vancouver, BC V7N 2A5   Jane Wostradowski, Libn.

NORTHWEST BAPTIST THEOLOGICAL COLLEGE AND SEMINARY - LIBRARY
3358 S.E. Marine Dr.   Phone: (604) 433-2475
Vancouver, BC V5S 3W3   Diane Scott, Libn.

PACIFIC PRESS, LTD. - PRESS LIBRARY
2250 Granville St.   Phone: (604) 732-2519
Vancouver, BC V6H 3G2   Shirley E. Mooney, Libn.

PLACER DEVELOPMENT, LTD. - LIBRARY
800-1030 W. Georgia St.   Phone: (604) 682-7082
Vancouver, BC V6E 3A8   Linda Martin, Libn.

PRICE WATERHOUSE - AUDIT LIBRARY
1075 W. Georgia St., No. 1500   Phone: (604) 682-4711
Vancouver, BC V6E 3G1   Janet A. Parkinson, Libn.

REGISTERED NURSES' ASSOCIATION OF BRITISH COLUMBIA - LIBRARY
2855 Arbutus St.   Phone: (604) 736-7331
Vancouver, BC V6K 2N3   Jean Molson, Libn.

ROYAL BANK OF CANADA - LIBRARY
1055 W. Georgia St.
P.O. Box 11141
Vancouver, BC V6E 3S5   Phone: (604) 665-4069
                                      Judy Kornfeld, Libn.

RUSSELL AND DUMOULIN - LIBRARY
MacMillan Bloedel Bldg., 17th Fl.
1075 W. Georgia St.   Phone: (604) 688-3411
Vancouver, BC V6E 3G2   Diana E. Hunt, Libn.

ST. PAUL'S HOSPITAL - HEALTH SCIENCES LIBRARY
1081 Burrard St.   Phone: (604) 682-2344
Vancouver, BC V6Z 1Y6   Roberta S. Wong, Health Sci.Libn.

SHAUGHNESSY HOSPITAL - HEALTH SCIENCES LIBRARY
4500 Oak St.   Phone: (604) 875-2222
Vancouver, BC V6H 3N1   Deborah Newstead, Lib.Techn.

TALMUD TORAH SCHOOL - LIBRARY
998 W. 26th Ave.   Phone: (604) 736-5213
Vancouver, BC V5Z 2G1   Nancy McLean, Libn.

TOUCHE, ROSS AND COMPANY - LIBRARY AND INFORMATION CENTER
Suite 700 Board of Trade
1177 W. Hastings   Phone: (604) 683-8641
Vancouver, BC V6E 2L2   Linda G. King, Libn.

UNITED WAY OF THE LOWER MAINLAND - LIBRARY
1625 W. 8th Ave.   Phone: (604) 731-7781
Vancouver, BC V5S 4A1   Timmy Timms, Libn.

UNIVERSITY OF BRITISH COLUMBIA - ASIAN STUDIES LIBRARY
Asian Centre   Phone: (604) 228-2427
Vancouver, BC V6T 1W5   Miss Tung-King Ng, Hd.

UNIVERSITY OF BRITISH COLUMBIA - BIOMEDICAL BRANCH LIBRARY
Vancouver General Hospital
700 W. 10th Ave.   Phone: (604) 873-5441
Vancouver, BC V5Z 1L5   George C. Freeman, Hd.Biomed.Br.

UNIVERSITY OF BRITISH COLUMBIA - CHARLES CRANE MEMORIAL LIBRARY
1874 East Mall   Phone: (604) 228-6111
Vancouver, BC V6T 1W5   Paul E. Thiele, Libn. & Hd.

UNIVERSITY OF BRITISH COLUMBIA - CURRICULUM LABORATORY
Scarfe Bldg., 2125 Main Mall   Phone: (604) 228-5378
Vancouver, BC V6T 1Z5   Howard Hurt, Hd.

UNIVERSITY OF BRITISH COLUMBIA - DATA LIBRARY
6356 Agricultural Rd., Rm. 206   Phone: (604) 228-5587
Vancouver, BC V6T 1W5   Ms. Laine Ruus, Hd., Data Lib.

UNIVERSITY OF BRITISH COLUMBIA - DEPARTMENT OF GEOGRAPHY - MAP AND AIR PHOTO LIBRARY
2075 Wesbrook Pl.   Phone: (604) 228-3048
Vancouver, BC V6T 1W5   Rosemary J. Hadley, Map Libn.

UNIVERSITY OF BRITISH COLUMBIA - FINE ARTS DIVISION
University Library, 1956 Main Mall   Phone: (604) 228-2720
Vancouver, BC V6T 1Y3   Melva J. Dwyer, Hd.

UNIVERSITY OF BRITISH COLUMBIA - GOVERNMENT PUBLICATIONS &
   MICROFORMS DIVISIONS
University Library   Phone: (604) 228-2584
Vancouver, BC V6T 1Y3   Suzanne Dodson, Hd.

UNIVERSITY OF BRITISH COLUMBIA - HUMANITIES DIVISION
University Library   Phone: (604) 228-2411
Vancouver, BC V6T 1Y3   Charles F. Forbes, Hd.

UNIVERSITY OF BRITISH COLUMBIA - INSTITUTE OF ANIMAL RESOURCE
   ECOLOGY - LIBRARY
2204 Main Mall   Phone: (604) 228-3324
Vancouver, BC V6T 1W5   Ann Nelson, Hd.

UNIVERSITY OF BRITISH COLUMBIA - LAW LIBRARY
1822 East Mall   Phone: (604) 228-2275
Vancouver, BC V6T 1W5   Thomas J. Shorthouse, Law Libn.

UNIVERSITY OF BRITISH COLUMBIA - MAC MILLAN FORESTRY/
   AGRICULTURE LIBRARY
MacMillan Bldg., 2357 Main Mall   Phone: (604) 228-3445
Vancouver, BC V6T 2A2   Mary W. Macaree, Hd.

UNIVERSITY OF BRITISH COLUMBIA - MAP DIVISION
University Library   Phone: (604) 228-2231
Vancouver, BC V6T 1Y3   Maureen F. Wilson, Hd.

UNIVERSITY OF BRITISH COLUMBIA - MARJORIE SMITH LIBRARY
School of Social Work
6201 Cecil Green Pk. Rd.   Phone: (604) 228-2242
Vancouver, BC V6T 1W5   Elsie deBruijn, Hd.

UNIVERSITY OF BRITISH COLUMBIA - MATHEMATICS LIBRARY
1984 Main Mall   Phone: (604) 228-2667
Vancouver, BC V6T 1W5   Rein J. Brongers, Hd.

UNIVERSITY OF BRITISH COLUMBIA - MUSIC LIBRARY
6361 Memorial Rd.   Phone: (604) 228-3589
Vancouver, BC V6T 1W5   Hans Burndorfer, Hd.

UNIVERSITY OF BRITISH COLUMBIA - SCHOOL OF LIBRARIANSHIP
   READING ROOM
                                         Phone: (604) 228-2446
Vancouver, BC V6T 1W5   Margaret Burke, Libn.

UNIVERSITY OF BRITISH COLUMBIA - SCIENCE DIVISION
University Library   Phone: (604) 228-3295
Vancouver, BC V6T 1Y3   Rein J. Brongers, Hd.

UNIVERSITY OF BRITISH COLUMBIA - SOCIAL SCIENCES DIVISION
University Library   Phone: (604) 228-2725
Vancouver, BC V6T 1Y3   Lois J. Carrier, Hd.

UNIVERSITY OF BRITISH COLUMBIA - SPECIAL COLLECTIONS DIVISION
University Library
1956 Main Mall   Phone: (604) 228-2521
Vancouver, BC V6T 1Y3   Anne Yandle, Hd.

UNIVERSITY OF BRITISH COLUMBIA - SPENCER ENTOMOLOGICAL MUSEUM
   - LIBRARY
Dept. of Zoology   Phone: (604) 228-3379
Vancouver, BC V6T 2A9

UNIVERSITY OF BRITISH COLUMBIA - WILSON RECORDINGS COLLECTION
1958 Main Mall   Phone: (604) 228-2534
Vancouver, BC V6T 1W5   Doug Kaye, Hd.

UNIVERSITY OF BRITISH COLUMBIA - WOODWARD BIOMEDICAL LIBRARY
2198 Health Sciences Mall   Phone: (604) 228-2762
Vancouver, BC V6T 1W5   Anna R. Leith, Hd.

VANCOUVER ART GALLERY - LIBRARY
1145 W. Georgia St.   Phone: (604) 682-5621
Vancouver, BC V6E 3H2   Jean Martin, Libn.

VANCOUVER MUSEUMS & PLANETARIUM ASSOCIATION - LIBRARY AND
   RESOURCE CENTRE
1100 Chestnut St.   Phone: (604) 736-4431
Vancouver, BC V6J 3J9   Norah McLaren, Libn.

VANCOUVER PUBLIC LIBRARY - BUSINESS & ECONOMICS DIVISION
750 Burrard St.   Phone: (604) 682-5911
Vancouver, BC V6Z 1X5   Barbara Bell, Act.Hd.

VANCOUVER SCHOOL OF THEOLOGY - LIBRARY
6050 Chancellor Blvd.   Phone: (604) 228-9031
Vancouver, BC V6T 1X3   Paul Nathanson, Libn.

VANCOUVER TEACHERS' PROFESSIONAL LIBRARY
Teacher Centre, 123 E. 6th Ave.   Phone: (604) 874-2617
Vancouver, BC V5T 1J6   Linda Dunbar, Lib.Techn.

VANCOUVER VOCATIONAL INSTITUTE - LIBRARY
250 West Pender St.   Phone: (604) 681-8111
Vancouver, BC V6B 159   Ross M. Henderson, Libn.

ART GALLERY OF GREATER VICTORIA - LIBRARY
1040 Moss St.   Phone: (604) 384-4101
Victoria, BC V8V 4P1   Susan Vial, Libn.

BRITISH COLUMBIA - JUDGES' LIBRARY - SUPERIOR & COUNTY COURTS
Law Courts, 850 Burdett Ave.
Victoria, BC V8W 1B4

BRITISH COLUMBIA - LEGISLATIVE LIBRARY
Legislative Bldgs.   Phone: (604) 387-6510
Victoria, BC V8V 1X4   J.G. Mitchell, Legislative Libn.

BRITISH COLUMBIA - MINISTRY OF EDUCATION - LIBRARY
Douglas Bldg., Government St.   Phone: (604) 387-6279
Victoria, BC V8V 1X4   Norma Lofthouse, Libn.

BRITISH COLUMBIA - MINISTRY OF ENERGY, MINES AND PETROLEUM
   RESOURCES - LIBRARY
Douglas Bldg., Rm. 430   Phone: (604) 387-6407
Victoria, BC V8V 1X4   S.E. Ferris

BRITISH COLUMBIA - MINISTRY OF ENVIRONMENT - LIBRARY
780 Blanshard   Phone: (604) 387-5194
Victoria, BC V8W 2H1   Marg Palmer, Ministerial Libn.

BRITISH COLUMBIA - MINISTRY OF ENVIRONMENT - MAPS LIBRARY
Parliament Bldgs.   Phone: (604) 387-3174
Victoria, BC V8V 1X5   G.H. Harris, Supv.

BRITISH COLUMBIA - MINISTRY OF ENVIRONMENT - WASTE
   MANAGEMENT BRANCH LIBRARY
Parliament Bldgs.
Victoria, BC V8V 4S5

BRITISH COLUMBIA - MINISTRY OF FORESTS - LIBRARY
Parliament Bldgs.
1450 Government St.   Phone: (604) 387-3628
Victoria, BC V8W 3E7   S.E. Barker, Mgr.

BRITISH COLUMBIA - MINISTRY OF HEALTH - LIBRARY
1515 Blanshard St., 5th Fl.   Phone: (604) 387-6627
Victoria, BC V8W 3C8   Elizabeth M. Woodworth, Libn.

BRITISH COLUMBIA - MINISTRY OF INDUSTRY & SMALL BUSINESS
   DEVELOPMENT - LIBRARY
Legislative Bldgs.   Phone: (604) 387-3765
Victoria, BC V8V 1X4   Helen G. Bruce, Libn.

BRITISH COLUMBIA - MINISTRY OF LANDS, PARKS AND HOUSING - PARKS
   LIBRARY
Parliament Bldgs.   Phone: (604) 387-1978
Victoria, BC V8V 1X4   Shirley Desrosiers, Libn.

BRITISH COLUMBIA - MINISTRY OF TOURISM - PHOTOGRAPHIC LIBRARY
1117 Wharf St., 3rd Fl.   Phone: (604) 387-6490
Victoria, BC V8W 2Z3   K.L. Gibbs, Act.Dir.

BRITISH COLUMBIA - PROVINCIAL ARCHIVES
Legislative Bldgs.   Phone: (604) 387-5885
Victoria, BC V8V 1X4   John A. Bovey, Prov.Archv.

GEOGRAPHIC

GEOGRAPHIC

BRITISH COLUMBIA - PROVINCIAL ARCHIVES - MAP DIVISION
655 Belleville St.   Phone: (604) 387-6516
Victoria, BC V8V 1X4   Geoff Castle, Archv.

CAMOSUN COLLEGE - LIBRARY/MEDIA SERVICES
1950 Lansdowne Rd.   Phone: (605) 592-1281
Victoria, BC V8P 5J2   Catherine Winter, Coord.

CANADA - CANADIAN FORESTRY SERVICE - PACIFIC FOREST RESEARCH
    CENTRE - LIBRARY
506 W. Burnside Rd.   Phone: (604) 388-3811
Victoria, BC V8Z 1M5   Alice Solyma, Libn.

CANADA - DEFENCE RESEARCH ESTABLISHMENT PACIFIC - LIBRARY †
Forces Mail Office   Phone: (604) 388-1665
Victoria, BC V0S 1B0   J.A. Wilson, Libn.

CANADA - NATIONAL RESEARCH COUNCIL - CISTI - DOMINION
    ASTROPHYSICAL OBSERVATORY - LIBRARY
5071 W. Saanich Rd.
R.R. 5   Phone: (604) 388-0298
Victoria, BC V8X 3X3   Eric S. LeBlanc, Libn.

LAW SOCIETY OF BRITISH COLUMBIA - VICTORIA LIBRARY †
No. 300, 1148 Hornby St.   Phone: (604) 688-9461
Victoria, BC V6Z 2C4   Hugh Lockhart, Libn.

MARITIME MUSEUM OF BRITISH COLUMBIA - LIBRARY
28-30 Bastion Square   Phone: (604) 385-4222
Victoria, BC V8W 1H9   A.K. Cameron, Dir.

PEARSON (Lester B.) COLLEGE OF THE PACIFIC - LIBRARY
RR 1   Phone: (604) 478-5591
Victoria, BC V8X 3W9   Margaret McAvity, Libn.

ROYAL ROADS MILITARY COLLEGE - LIBRARY
                                                  Phone: (604) 388-1483
Victoria, BC V0S 1B0   C.C. Whitlock, Chf.Libn.

UNIVERSITY OF VICTORIA - KATHARINE MALTWOOD COLLECTION
P.O. Box 1700   Phone: (604) 477-6911
Victoria, BC V8W 2Y2   Martin Segger, Cur.

UNIVERSITY OF VICTORIA - LAW LIBRARY †
P.O. Box 2300   Phone: (604) 477-6911
Victoria, BC V8W 3B1   Diana M. Priestly, Law Libn.

UNIVERSITY OF VICTORIA - MC PHERSON LIBRARY - CURRICULUM
    LABORATORY
P.O. Box 1800   Phone: (604) 477-6911
Victoria, BC V8W 2Y3   Donald E. Hamilton, Educ.Libn.

UNIVERSITY OF VICTORIA - MC PHERSON LIBRARY - MUSIC & AUDIO
    COLLECTION
P.O. Box 1800   Phone: (604) 477-6911
Victoria, BC V8W 2Y3   Sandra Benet, Music Libn.

UNIVERSITY OF VICTORIA - MC PHERSON LIBRARY - SPECIAL
    COLLECTIONS
Box 1700   Phone: (604) 477-6911
Victoria, BC V8W 2Y2   Howard B. Gerwing, Rare Bks.Libn.

UNIVERSITY OF VICTORIA - MC PHERSON LIBRARY - UNIVERSITY MAP
    COLLECTION
P.O. Box 1800   Phone: (604) 477-6911
Victoria, BC V8W 2Y3   M.A. Brian Turnbull, Map Cur.

VICTORIA GENERAL HOSPITAL - HEALTH SCIENCES LIBRARY †
841 Fairfield Rd.   Phone: (604) 388-9121
Victoria, BC V8V 3B6   George E.A. Zizka, Libn.

VICTORIA MEDICAL SOCIETY/ROYAL JUBILEE HOSPITAL - LIBRARY
1900 Fort St.   Phone: (604) 595-9723
Victoria, BC V8R 1J8   Johann van Reenen, Libn.

VICTORIA TIMES-COLONIST - LIBRARY
P.O. Box 300   Phone: (604) 382-7211
Victoria, BC V8W 2N4   Corinne Wong, Libn.

CANADA - ENVIRONMENTAL PROTECTION SERVICE - LIBRARY
3rd Fl., Kapilano 100
Park Royal South   Phone: (604) 666-6711
West Vancouver, BC V7T 1A2   Lorelei Pettit, Lib.Ck.

MANITOBA

BRANDON GENERAL HOSPITAL - LIBRARY SERVICES
150 McTavish Ave., E.   Phone: (204) 728-3321
Brandon, MB R7A 2B3   Kathy Eagleton, Dir.

BRANDON MENTAL HEALTH CENTRE - REFERENCE AND LENDING LIBRARY
Box 420   Phone: (204) 728-7110
Brandon, MB R7A 5Z5   Marjorie G. McKinnon, Lib.Techn.

BRANDON UNIVERSITY - CHRISTIE EDUCATION LIBRARY
Eighteenth St.   Phone: (204) 728-9520
Brandon, MB R7A 6A9   Mrs. T.S. Gonzales, Libn.

BRANDON UNIVERSITY - MUSIC LIBRARY †
Music Bldg.   Phone: (204) 728-9520
Brandon, MB R7A 6A9   June D. Jones, Music Libn.

CANADA - AGRICULTURE CANADA - RESEARCH STATION, MORDEN -
    LIBRARY
P.O. Box 3001   Phone: (204) 822-4471
Morden, MB R0G 1J0   Mrs. B. Cowan

WINNIPEG BIBLE COLLEGE/WINNIPEG THEOLOGICAL SEMINARY -
    LIBRARY
                                                  Phone: (204) 284-2923
Otterburne, MB R0A 1G0   R. Curt Rice, Lib.Dir.

ATOMIC ENERGY OF CANADA, LTD. - WNRE LIBRARY
Whiteshell Nuclear Research Establishment   Phone: (204) 753-2311
Pinawa, MB R0E 1L0   Gladys Gibson, Chf.Libn.

DELTA WATERFOWL RESEARCH STATION - LIBRARY
R.R. 1   Phone: (204) 857-9125
Portage La Prairie, MB R1N 3A1   Shirley Rutledge, Libn.

MANITOBA - DEPARTMENT OF HEALTH - MANITOBA SCHOOL - MEMORIAL
    LIBRARY
Box 1190   Phone: (204) 857-3403
Portage La Prairie, MB R1N 3C6   Mr. W.D. Bates, Lib.Supv.

COLLEGE UNIVERSITAIRE DE ST. BONIFACE - BIBLIOTHEQUE
    UNIVERSITAIRE
200 Ave. De La Cathedrale   Phone: (204) 233-0210
Saint-Boniface, MB R2H 0H7   Marcel Boulet, Hd.Libn.

MANITOBA - CENTRE DE RESSOURCES EDUCATIVES FRANCAISES DU
    MANITOBA
200, Ave. de la Cathedrale   Phone: (204) 237-6671
Saint Boniface, MB R2H 0H7   Arsene Huberdeau, Dir.

SELKIRK MENTAL HEALTH CENTRE - CENTRAL LIBRARY
Box 9600   Phone: (204) 482-3810
Selkirk, MB R1A 2B5   John English, Dir., Nursing Educ.

ROYAL CANADIAN ARTILLERY MUSEUM - LIBRARY
Canadian Forces Base   Phone: (204) 765-2282
Shilo, MB R0K 2A0

MENNONITE VILLAGE MUSEUM (Canada) INC. - LIBRARY
Box 1136   Phone: (204) 326-9661
Steinbach, MB R0A 2A0   Peter Goertzen, Mgr.

ALCOHOLISM FOUNDATION OF MANITOBA - WILLIAM POTOROKA
    MEMORIAL LIBRARY
1580 Dublin Ave.   Phone: (204) 775-8601
Winnipeg, MB R3B 0L4   Diana Ringstrom, Libn.

CANADA - AGRICULTURE CANADA - CANADIAN GRAIN COMMISSION -
    LIBRARY
303 Main St., Rm. 1001   Phone: (204) 949-3360
Winnipeg, MB R3C 3G7   Lee Teal, Libn.

**CANADA - AGRICULTURE CANADA - RESEARCH STATION, WINNIPEG -
LIBRARY**
195 Dafoe Rd.   Phone: (204) 269-2100
Winnipeg, MB R3T 2M9   M. Malyk, Libn.

**CANADA - ATMOSPHERIC ENVIRONMENT SERVICE - CENTRAL REGION
LIBRARY**
266 Graham Ave.
9th Fl., Post Office Bldg.   Phone: (204) 949-4389
Winnipeg, MB R3C 3V4   R.R. Tortorelli, Sci.Serv.Techn.

**CANADA - EMPLOYMENT & IMMIGRATION CANADA - PUBLIC AFFAIRS
LIBRARY**
167 Lombard Ave., Rm. 190   Phone: (204) 949-3781
Winnipeg, MB R3B 0T6   Win Kennedy, Regional Mgr.

CANADA - FISHERIES & OCEANS - FRESHWATER INSTITUTE LIBRARY
501 University Crescent   Phone: (204) 269-7379
Winnipeg, MB R3T 2N6   K. Eric Marshall, Libn.

**CANADA - STATISTICS CANADA - ADVISORY SERVICES - WINNIPEG
REFERENCE CENTRE**
602 General Post Office
266 Graham Ave.
Winnipeg, MB R3C 0K4   Phone: (204) 949-4020
                                    Mr. W.S. Pawluk, Asst. Regional Dir.

CANADIAN BROADCASTING CORPORATION - MUSIC & RECORD LIBRARY
541 Portage Ave.
P.O. Box 160   Phone: (204) 775-8351
Winnipeg, MB R2Y 1H3   Don R. McLaren, Sr.Libn.

**CANADIAN MENTAL HEALTH ASSOCIATION - MANITOBA DIVISION
LIBRARY**
330 Edmonton St.
Winnipeg, MB R3B 2L2

CRAFTS GUILD OF MANITOBA - LIBRARY
183 Kennedy St.   Phone: (204) 943-1190
Winnipeg, MB R3C 1S6   Betty Andrich, Chm.

DEER LODGE HOSPITAL - MEDICAL REFERENCE LIBRARY
2109 Portage Ave.   Phone: (204) 837-1301
Winnipeg, MB R3J 0L3   J.L. Saunders, Libn.

DUCKS UNLIMITED (Canada) - LIBRARY
1190 Waverley St.   Phone: (204) 477-1760
Winnipeg, MB R3T 2E2

GERMAN SOCIETY OF WINNIPEG - LIBRARY
121 Charles St.   Phone: (204) 589-7724
Winnipeg, MB R2W 4A6

GRAND LODGE OF MANITOBA, A.F. AND A.M. - MASONIC LIBRARY
Masonic Memorial Temple
420 Corydon Ave.   Phone: (204) 284-2423
Winnipeg, MB R3L 0N8   W.F.L. Hyde, Grand Libn.

GREAT-WEST LIFE ASSURANCE COMPANY - LIBRARY
60 Osborne St., N.   Phone: (204) 946-9225
Winnipeg, MB R3C 3A5   Mary F. Keelan, Libn.

HUDSON'S BAY COMPANY ARCHIVES
Manitoba Archives Bldg.
200 Vaughan St.   Phone: (204) 944-3971
Winnipeg, MB R3C 0P8   Shirlee Anne Smith, Kpr.

HUDSON'S BAY COMPANY - LIBRARY
Hudson's Bay House
77 Main St.   Phone: (204) 943-0881
Winnipeg, MB R3C 2R1   Carol Preston, Libn.

LAW SOCIETY OF MANITOBA - LIBRARY
Law Courts Bldg., Broadway Ave.   Phone: (204) 943-5277
Winnipeg, MB R3C 0V7   Garth Niven, Chf.Libn.

MANITOBA ASSOCIATION OF REGISTERED NURSES - LIBRARY
647 Broadway   Phone: (204) 774-3477
Winnipeg, MB R3C 0X2   Eleanor Gowerluk, Lib.Techn.

MANITOBA CANCER TREATMENT AND RESEARCH FOUNDATION - LIBRARY
700 Bannatyne Ave.   Phone: (204) 787-2136
Winnipeg, MB R3C 1N7   Isobel M. Steedman, Libn.

**MANITOBA - DEPT. OF CONSUMER & CORPORATE AFFAIRS &
ENVIRONMENT - DEPT. REFERENCE SERV. - CONSUMER AFF. LIB.**
1023-405 Broadway Ave.   Phone: (204) 944-3319
Winnipeg, MB R3C 3L6   S. Norma Godavari, Libn.

**MANITOBA - DEPT. OF CONSUMER & CORPORATE AFFAIRS &
ENVIRONMENT - DEPT. REF. SERV. - ENVIRONMENTAL MGT. LIB.**
139 Tuxedo Ave.
Box 7
Winnipeg, MB R3N 0H6   S. Norma Gadavari, Libn.

**MANITOBA - DEPARTMENT OF ECONOMIC DEVELOPMENT AND TOURISM -
LIBRARY**
648-155 Carlton St.   Phone: (204) 944-2036
Winnipeg, MB R3C 3H8   F. Helen Paine, Libn.

MANITOBA - DEPARTMENT OF EDUCATION - LIBRARY
1181 Portage Ave., Main Fl.
Box 3   Phone: (204) 786-0218
Winnipeg, MB R3G 0T3   John Tooth, Hd.Libn.

**MANITOBA - DEPARTMENT OF HEALTH - ANNA E. WELLS MEMORIAL
LIBRARY**
202-880 Portage Ave.   Phone: (204) 786-5867
Winnipeg, MB R3G 0P1   Marilyn J. Hernandez, Health Libn.

MANITOBA - DEPARTMENT OF NATURAL RESOURCES - LIBRARY
1495 St. James St.
Box 26   Phone: (204) 786-9299
Winnipeg, MB R3H 0W9   Irene Hamerton, Libn.

MANITOBA - HEALTH SERVICES COMMISSION - LIBRARY †
599 Empress St.   Phone: (204) 786-7398
Winnipeg, MB R3C 2T6   Daphne A.T. Kowal, Libn.

MANITOBA HYDRO - LIBRARY
Box 815   Phone: (204) 474-3614
Winnipeg, MB R3C 2P4   M. Gardiner, Libn.

MANITOBA INDIAN CULTURAL EDUCATION CENTRE - PEOPLES LIBRARY *
119 Sutherland Ave.   Phone: (204) 942-0228
Winnipeg, MB R2W 3C9   V. Chalmers, Lib.Dir.

MANITOBA - LEGISLATIVE LIBRARY
200 Vaughan St., Main Floor   Phone: (204) 946-7214
Winnipeg, MB R3C 0P8   Joyce Irvine, Act.Leg.Libn.

MANITOBA MUSEUM OF MAN AND NATURE - LIBRARY
190 Rupert Ave.   Phone: (204) 956-2830
Winnipeg, MB R3B 0N2   Valerie Hatten, Libn.

MANITOBA - PROVINCIAL ARCHIVES OF MANITOBA
Manitoba Archives Bldg.
200 Vaughan St.   Phone: (204) 944-3971
Winnipeg, MB R3C 1T5   Peter Bower, Prov.Archv.

MENNONITE BRETHREN BIBLE COLLEGE - LIBRARY
77 Henderson Hwy.   Phone: (204) 667-9560
Winnipeg, MB R2L 1L1   Herbert Giesbrecht, College Libn.

MISERICORDIA GENERAL HOSPITAL - HOSPITAL LIBRARY
99 Cornish Ave.   Phone: (204) 774-6581
Winnipeg, MB R3C 1A2   Sharon Allentuck, Hosp.Libn.

RED RIVER COMMUNITY COLLEGE - LEARNING RESOURCES CENTRE
2055 Notre Dame Ave.   Phone: (204) 632-2232
Winnipeg, MB R3H 0J9   Patricia Bozyk Porter, Chf.Libn.

RICHARDSON SECURITIES OF CANADA, LTD. - RESEARCH LIBRARY
One Lombard Place, 29th Fl.   Phone: (204) 988-5940
Winnipeg, MB R3B 0Y2   Agnes Unger, Libn.

**SOCIETY FOR CRIPPLED CHILDREN AND ADULTS OF MANITOBA - STEPHEN
SPARLING LIBRARY**
825 Sherbrook St.   Phone: (204) 786-5601
Winnipeg, MB R3A 1M5   Barbara Wolfe, Libn.

GEOGRAPHIC

UKRAINIAN CULTURAL AND EDUCATIONAL CENTRE - LIBRARY
184 Alexander Ave., E.   Phone: (204) 942-0218
Winnipeg, MB R3B 0L6   Orysia Tracz, Libn.

UNITED GRAIN GROWERS LTD. - LIBRARY
433 Main St.
Box 6600   Phone: (204) 944-5572
Winnipeg, MB R3C 3A7   Carole Rogers, Libn.

UNIVERSITY OF MANITOBA - ADMINISTRATIVE STUDIES LIBRARY
                    Phone: (204) 474-8440
Winnipeg, MB R3T 2N2   Judith Head, Hd.Libn.

UNIVERSITY OF MANITOBA - AGRICULTURE LIBRARY
                    Phone: (204) 474-9457
Winnipeg, MB R3T 2N2   Judith Harper, Hd.

UNIVERSITY OF MANITOBA - ARCHITECTURE & FINE ARTS LIBRARY
                    Phone: (204) 474-9216
Winnipeg, MB R3T 2N2   Peter Anthony, Hd.Libn.

UNIVERSITY OF MANITOBA - ARCHIVES AND SPECIAL COLLECTIONS
331 Elizabeth Dafoe Library   Phone: (204) 474-9986
Winnipeg, MB R3T 2N2   Richard E. Bennett, Hd.

UNIVERSITY OF MANITOBA - DENTAL LIBRARY
780 Bannatyne Ave.   Phone: (204) 786-3635
Winnipeg, MB R3E 0W3   Doris Pritchard, Hd.Libn.

UNIVERSITY OF MANITOBA - EDUCATION LIBRARY
                    Phone: (204) 474-9976
Winnipeg, MB R3T 2N2   Doreen Shanks, Hd.Libn.

UNIVERSITY OF MANITOBA - ENGINEERING LIBRARY
                    Phone: (204) 474-9445
Winnipeg, MB R3T 2N2   Yong-Ja Cho, Hd.Libn.

UNIVERSITY OF MANITOBA - LAW LIBRARY
Robson Hall   Phone: (204) 474-9995
Winnipeg, MB R3T 2N2   Denis Marshall, Hd.Libn.

UNIVERSITY OF MANITOBA - MEDICAL LIBRARY
Medical College Bldg.
770 Bannatyne Ave.   Phone: (204) 786-4342
Winnipeg, MB R3T 0W3   Audrey M. Kerr, Hd.Med.Libn.

UNIVERSITY OF MANITOBA - MUSIC READING ROOM
223 Music Bldg.   Phone: (204) 474-9567
Winnipeg, MB R3T 2N2   Peter Anthony, Adm.Hd.

UNIVERSITY OF MANITOBA - REFERENCE SERVICES DEPARTMENT - MAP AND ATLAS COLLECTION
Elizabeth Dafoe Library   Phone: (204) 474-9844
Winnipeg, MB R3T 2N2   Hugh Larimer, Map Libn.

UNIVERSITY OF MANITOBA - ST. JOHN'S COLLEGE - LIBRARY
400 Dysart Rd.   Phone: (204) 474-8542
Winnipeg, MB R3T 2M5   Dr. A.E. Millward, Libn.

UNIVERSITY OF MANITOBA - ST. PAUL'S COLLEGE - LIBRARY
                    Phone: (204) 474-8585
Winnipeg, MB R3T 2M6   Fr. Harold Drake, Hd.

UNIVERSITY OF MANITOBA - SCIENCE LIBRARY
                    Phone: (204) 474-8171
Winnipeg, MB R3T 2N2   Vladimir Simosko, Hd.Sci.Libn.

UNIVERSITY OF MANITOBA - SLAVIC COLLECTION
Elizabeth Dafoe Library   Phone: (204) 474-9681
Winnipeg, MB R3T 2N2   John Muchin, Hd., Slavic Coll.

WINNIPEG ART GALLERY - CLARA LANDER LIBRARY
300 Memorial Blvd.   Phone: (204) 786-6641
Winnipeg, MB R3C 1V1   David W. Rozniatowski, Libn.

WINNIPEG CLINIC - LIBRARY
425 St. Mary Ave.   Phone: (204) 957-1900
Winnipeg, MB R3C 0N2   S. Loeppky, Libn.

WINNIPEG DEPARTMENT OF ENVIRONMENTAL PLANNING - LIBRARY
100 Main St.   Phone: (204) 985-5174
Winnipeg, MB R3C 1A5   Gordon Courage, Hd.

WINNIPEG FREE PRESS - LIBRARY †
300 Carlton St.   Phone: (204) 943-9331
Winnipeg, MB R3C 3C1   Mrs. E. Langer, Libn.

WINNIPEG HEALTH SCIENCES CENTRE - LIBRARY SERVICES
700 McDermot Ave.   Phone: (204) 787-2743
Winnipeg, MB R3E 0T2   Barbara Greeniaus, Dir., Lib.Serv.

WINNIPEG SCHOOL DIVISION NO. 1 - TEACHERS LIBRARY AND RESOURCE CENTRE
1180 Notre Dame Ave.   Phone: (204) 943-3541
Winnipeg, MB R3E 0P2   Gerald R. Brown, Chf.Libn.

WINNIPEG SOCIAL PLANNING COUNCIL - LIBRARY
412 McDermot Ave.   Phone: (204) 943-2561
Winnipeg, MB R3A 0A9   E.T. Sale, Exec.Dir.

NEW BRUNSWICK

FRASER INC. - CENTRAL TECHNICAL DEPARTMENT LIBRARY
                    Phone: (506) 735-5551
Edmundston, NB E3V 1S9   Floyd G. Hinton, Mgr., Process Dev.

BARRISTERS' SOCIETY OF NEW BRUNSWICK - LAW LIBRARY
Justice Bldg., Queen St.   Phone: (506) 453-2500
Fredericton, NB E3B 5C2   Diane Hanson, Prov. Law Libn.

CANADA - AGRICULTURE CANADA - RESEARCH STATION, FREDERICTON - LIBRARY
Box 20280   Phone: (506) 452-3260
Fredericton, NB E3B 4Z7   Donald B. Gammon, Area Coord. Atlantic

CANADA - CANADIAN FORESTRY SERVICE - MARITIMES FOREST RESEARCH CENTRE - LIBRARY
P.O. Box 4000   Phone: (506) 452-3541
Fredericton, NB E3B 5P7   Barry Barner, Libn.

CHALMERS (Dr. Everett) HOSPITAL - DR. GARFIELD MOFFATT HEALTH SCIENCES LIBRARY
Box 9000   Phone: (506) 452-5431
Fredericton, NB E3B 5N5   Cietta M. Babineau, Lib.Asst.

NEW BRUNSWICK ASSOCIATION OF REGISTERED NURSES - LIBRARY
231 Saunders St.   Phone: (506) 454-5591
Fredericton, NB E3B 1N6   Judith Heron, Libn.

NEW BRUNSWICK - DEPARTMENT OF AGRICULTURE - LIBRARY
P.O. Box 6000
Fredericton, NB E3B 5H1

NEW BRUNSWICK - DEPARTMENT OF THE ENVIRONMENT - LIBRARY
P.O. Box 6000   Phone: (506) 453-3700
Fredericton, NB E3B 5H1   Geraldine L. King, Libn.

NEW BRUNSWICK - DEPARTMENT OF NATURAL RESOURCES - FORESTS BRANCH LIBRARY
P.O. Box 6000   Phone: (506) 453-2485
Fredericton, NB E3B 5H1   Irma R. Long, Lib.Asst.

NEW BRUNSWICK - DEPARTMENT OF YOUTH, RECREATION & CULTURAL RESOURCES - NEW BRUNSWICK LIBRARY SERVICE
P.O. Box 6000   Phone: (506) 453-2354
Fredericton, NB E3B 5H1   Agnez Hall, Dir.Lib.Serv.

NEW BRUNSWICK ELECTRIC POWER COMMISSION - LIBRARY
527 King St.
P.O. Box 2000   Phone: (506) 453-4353
Fredericton, NB E3B 4X1   Aileen W. Humes, Libn.

NEW BRUNSWICK - LEGISLATIVE LIBRARY
Legislative Bldg.
P.O. Box 6000   Phone: (506) 453-2338
Fredericton, NB E3B 5H1   Jocelyn LeBel, Dir.

NEW BRUNSWICK - PROVINCIAL ARCHIVES OF NEW BRUNSWICK
Box 6000   Phone: (506) 453-2637
Fredericton, NB E3B 5H1   Marion Beyea, Prov.Archv.

NEW BRUNSWICK RESEARCH AND PRODUCTIVITY COUNCIL - LIBRARY
P.O. Box 6000   Phone: (506) 455-8994
Fredericton, NB E3B 5H1   Bonnie J. Ellis, Lib.Supv.

UNIVERSITY OF NEW BRUNSWICK - EDUCATION RESOURCE CENTRE
D'Avray Hall
P.O. Box 7500   Phone: (506) 453-3516
Fredericton, NB E3B 5H5   Andrew Pope, Educ.Libn.

UNIVERSITY OF NEW BRUNSWICK - ENGINEERING LIBRARY
Sir Edmund Head Hall
P.O. Box 7500   Phone: (506) 453-4747
Fredericton, NB E3B 5H5   Everett R. Dunfield, Engr.Libn.

UNIVERSITY OF NEW BRUNSWICK - LAW LIBRARY
Ludlow Hall
Bag Service No. 44999   Phone: (506) 453-4669
Fredericton, NB E3B 6C9   Anne Crocker, Law Libn.

UNIVERSITY OF NEW BRUNSWICK - SCIENCE LIBRARY
P.O. Box 7500   Phone: (506) 453-3566
Fredericton, NB E3B 5H5   Ezster L.K. Schwenke, Libn.

YORK REGIONAL LIBRARY - BIBLIOTHEQUE DR. MARGUERITE MICHAUD
715 Priestman St.   Phone: (506) 455-1740
Fredericton, NB E3B 5W7   Mona Guerrette, Libn.

MONCTON HOSPITAL - HEALTH SCIENCES LIBRARY
135 MacBeath Ave.   Phone: (506) 855-1600
Moncton, NB E1C 6Z8   Mrs. I.W. Wallace, Libn.

UNIVERSITE DE MONCTON - BIBLIOTHEQUE DE DROIT
                                                  Phone: (506) 858-4569
Moncton, NB E1A 3E9   Simonne Clermont, Law Libn.

UNIVERSITE DE MONCTON - CENTRE D'ETUDES ACADIENNES
                                                  Phone: (506) 858-4076
Moncton, NB E1A 3E9   Ronald Leblanc, Libn.

UNIVERSITE DE MONCTON - FACULTE DES SCIENCES DE L'EDUCATION -
    CENTRE DE RESSOURCES PEDAGOGIQUES
                                                  Phone: (506) 858-4356
Moncton, NB E1A 3E9   Berthe Boudreau, Dir.

MIRAMICHI HOSPITAL - HEALTH SCIENCES LIBRARY
P.O. Box 420   Phone: (506) 622-1340
Newcastle, NB E1V 3M5   Audrey D. Somers, Educ.Coord.

OLD MANSE LIBRARY
225 Mary St.   Phone: (506) 622-0453
Newcastle, NB E1V 1Z3   Edith MacAllister, Libn.

CANADA - CANADIAN WILDLIFE SERVICE - ATLANTIC REGION LIBRARY
Box 1590   Phone: (506) 536-3025
Sackville, NB E0A 3C0   F. Helen Anderson, Libn.

MOUNT ALLISON UNIVERSITY - ALFRED WHITEHEAD MEMORIAL MUSIC
    LIBRARY
                                                  Phone: (506) 536-2040
Sackville, NB E0A 3C0   Gwendolyn Creelman

MOUNT ALLISON UNIVERSITY - WINTHROP P. BELL COLLECTION OF
    ACADIANA
Ralph Pickard Bell Library   Phone: (506) 536-2040
Sackville, NB E0A 3C0   Margaret Fancy, Spec.Coll.Libn.

CANADA - FISHERIES & OCEANS - BIOLOGICAL STATION LIBRARY
                                                  Phone: (506) 529-8854
St. Andrews, NB E0G 2X0   Ms. C.R. Garnett, Libn.

INTERNATIONAL ATLANTIC SALMON FOUNDATION - LIBRARY
P.O. Box 429   Phone: (506) 529-3818
St. Andrews, NB E0G 2X0   Mrs. Lee Sochasky, Prog.Coord.

CHURCH OF ENGLAND INSTITUTE - LIBRARY
116 Princess St.   Phone: (506) 693-2295
Saint John, NB E2L 1K4   Mrs. F.H. Burton, Mgr.

NEW BRUNSWICK MUSEUM - REFERENCE & RESEARCH LIBRARIES
277 Douglas Ave.   Phone: (506) 693-1196
Saint John, NB E2K 1E5   Carol Rosevear, Libn.

NEW BRUNSWICK TELEPHONE COMPANY, LTD. - EDUCATIONAL LIBRARY
One Brunswick Sq.
Box 1430   Phone: (506) 693-6845
Saint John, NB E2L 4K2   Patricia J. Blenkhorn, Libn.

CARLETON MEMORIAL HOSPITAL - HEALTH SCIENCES LIBRARY
Box 400   Phone: (506) 328-3391
Woodstock, NB E0J 2B0   Mary M. Sprague, Dir.

NEWFOUNDLAND

WESTERN MEMORIAL REGIONAL HOSPITAL - HEALTH SCIENCE LIBRARY
West Valley Rd.   Phone: (709) 634-5101
Corner Brook, NF A2H 6J7   Walter S. MacPherson, Libn.

LABRADOR CITY COLLEGIATE - LIBRARY
213 Matthew Ave.   Phone: (709) 944-2232
Labrador City, NF A2V 2J9   Leo Cote, Libn.

CANADA - AGRICULTURE CANADA - RESEARCH STATION, ST. JOHN'S
    WEST - LIBRARY
Brookfield Rd.
P.O. Box 7098   Phone: (709) 737-4619
St. John's, NF A1E 3Y3

CANADA - CANADIAN FORESTRY SERVICE - NEWFOUNDLAND FOREST
    RESEARCH CENTRE - LIBRARY
P.O. Box 6028   Phone: (709) 726-7330
St. John's, NF A1C 5X8   Catherine E. Philpott, Libn.

CANADA - FISHERIES & OCEANS - NEWFOUNDLAND REGIONAL LIBRARY
P.O. Box 5667   Phone: (709) 737-2022
St. John's, NF A1C 5X1   Audrey Conroy, Libn.

CANADA - STATISTICS CANADA - ADVISORY SERVICES - ST. JOHN'S
    REFERENCE CENTRE
Viking Bldg. 3rd Fl., Crosbie Rd.
Box 8556   Phone: (709) 737-4073
St. John's, NF A1B 3P2

COLLEGE OF FISHERIES, NAVIGATION, MARINE ENGINEERING AND
    ELECTRONICS - LIBRARY
P.O. Box 4920, Parade St.   Phone: (709) 726-5272
St. John's, NF A1C 5R3   Mabel Farmer, Libn.

COLLEGE OF TRADES AND TECHNOLOGY - LIBRARY
P.O. Box 1693   Phone: (709) 753-9360
St. John's, NF A1C 5P7   Patricia Rahal, Libn.

COLLEGE OF TRADES AND TECHNOLOGY - MEDICAL LIBRARY
Topsail Campus
P.O. Box 1693   Phone: (709) 368-2001
St. John's, NF A1C 5P7   Patricia Rahal, Libn.

GRACE GENERAL HOSPITAL - CHESLEY A. PIPPY, JR. MEDICAL LIBRARY
LeMarchant Rd.   Phone: (709) 778-6796
St. John's, NF A1E 1P9   Elizabeth Duggan, Med.Libn.

GRACE GENERAL HOSPITAL - SCHOOL OF NURSING LIBRARY
LeMarchant Rd.   Phone: (709) 778-6645
St. John's, NF A1E 1P9   Catherine Ryan, Libn.

JANEWAY (Dr. Charles A.) CHILD HEALTH CENTRE - JANEWAY MEDICAL
    LIBRARY
Pleasantville   Phone: (709) 778-4344
St. John's, NF A1A 1R8   Joan E. Wheeler, Lib.Techn.

GEOGRAPHIC

LAW SOCIETY OF NEWFOUNDLAND - LIBRARY
Court House, Duckworth St.
P.O. Box 1028 Phone: (709) 753-7770
St. John's, NF A1C 5M3 Suzanna Duke, Libn.

MEMORIAL UNIVERSITY OF NEWFOUNDLAND - CENTRE FOR NEWFOUNDLAND STUDIES
Elizabeth Ave. Phone: (709) 753-1200
St. John's, NF A1B 3Y1 Anne Hart, Hd.

MEMORIAL UNIVERSITY OF NEWFOUNDLAND - DEPARTMENT OF GEOGRAPHY - MAP LIBRARY
Phone: (709) 753-1200
St. John's, NF A1B 3X9 Gladys Deutsch, Lib.Asst. IV/Supv.

MEMORIAL UNIVERSITY OF NEWFOUNDLAND - EDUCATION LIBRARY
Elizabeth Ave. Phone: (709) 753-1200
St. John's, NF A1C 5S7 Barbara J. Eddy, Educ.Libn.

MEMORIAL UNIVERSITY OF NEWFOUNDLAND - FOLKLORE AND LANGUAGE ARCHIVE
Phone: (709) 737-8401
St. John's, NF A1C 5S7 Neil V. Rosenberg, Dir.

MEMORIAL UNIVERSITY OF NEWFOUNDLAND - HEALTH SCIENCES LIBRARY
Health Science Centre
300 Prince Philip Dr. Phone: (709) 737-6672
St. John's, NF A1B 3V6 Isabel Hunter, Hd.Libn.

MEMORIAL UNIVERSITY OF NEWFOUNDLAND - OCEAN ENGINEERING INFORMATION CENTRE
Phone: (709) 737-8377
St. John's, NF A1B 3X5 Judith A. Whittick, Info.Res.

NEWFOUNDLAND - DEPARTMENT OF EDUCATION - INSTRUCTIONAL MATERIALS LIBRARY
Bldg. 951, Pleasantville Phone: (709) 737-2619
St. John's, NF A1A 1R2 D. Nanayakkara, Libn.

NEWFOUNDLAND - DEPARTMENT OF JUSTICE - LAW LIBRARY
Confederation Bldg. Phone: (709) 737-2861
St. John's, NF A1C 5T7 Mona B. Pearce, Libn.

NEWFOUNDLAND - DEPARTMENT OF MINES AND ENERGY - MINERAL DEVELOPMENT DIVISION - LIBRARY
95 Bonaventure Ave. Phone: (709) 737-3159
St. John's, NF A1C 5T7 Genie Power, Lib.Techn.

NEWFOUNDLAND - DEPARTMENT OF RURAL DEVELOPMENT - RESOURCE CENTRE
Confederation Bldg. Phone: (709) 737-3172
St. John's, NF A1C 5T7 Philip I. Mullett, Info.Spec.

NEWFOUNDLAND AND LABRADOR DEVELOPMENT CORPORATION LTD. - LIBRARY
44 Torbay Rd.
P.O. Box 9548 Phone: (709) 753-3560
St. John's, NF A1A 2Y4 Heddy M. Peddle, Libn.

NEWFOUNDLAND - LEGISLATIVE LIBRARY †
House of Assembly, Confederation Bldg.
P.O. Box 4750 Phone: (709) 737-3604
St. John's, NF A1C 5T7 N.J. Richards, Legislative Libn.

NEWFOUNDLAND LIGHT & POWER COMPANY, LTD. - CENTRAL RECORDS LIBRARY
P.O. Box 8910, Kenmount Road Phone: (709) 737-5645
St. John's, NF A1B 3P6 Cyril C. Morgan, Supv.

NEWFOUNDLAND - PROVINCIAL ARCHIVES OF NEWFOUNDLAND AND LABRADOR
Colonial Bldg., Military Rd. Phone: (709) 753-9390
St. John's, NF A1C 2C9 David J. Davis, Prov.Archv.

NEWFOUNDLAND - PUBLIC LIBRARY SERVICES
Arts & Culture Centre
Allandale Rd. Phone: (709) 737-3964
St. John's, NF A1B 3A3 Pearce J. Penney, Chf.Prov.Libn.

ST. CLARE'S MERCY HOSPITAL - MEDICAL LIBRARY
St. Clare Ave. Phone: (709) 778-3414
St. John's, NF A1C 5B8 Eileen E. Woll, Lib.Techn.

WATERFORD HOSPITAL - HEALTH SERVICES LIBRARY
Waterford Bridge Rd. Phone: (709) 368-6061
St. John's, NF A1E 4J8 Daniel Peyton, Libn.

NORTHWEST TERRITORIES

CANADA - INDIAN & NORTHERN AFFAIRS CANADA - INUVIK SCIENTIFIC RESOURCE CENTRE - LIBRARY
P.O. Box 1430 Phone: (403) 979-3838
Inuvik, NT X0E 0T0 C.P. Lewis, Scientist-In-Charge

CANADA - NATIONAL DEFENCE - NORTHERN REGION REFERENCE LIBRARY
Northern Region Headquarters
Evans Block, P.O. Box 6666 Phone: (403) 873-4011
Yellowknife, NT X0E 1H0 Capt. J.A. MacDonald, Lib.Off.

NORTHWEST TERRITORIES - GOVERNMENT IN-SERVICE LIBRARY
Phone: (403) 873-7628
Yellowknife, NT X1A 2L9 G. Anderson, Act.Libn.

NOVA SCOTIA

MARITIME RESOURCE MANAGEMENT SERVICE - INFORMATION CENTRE
P.O. Box 310 Phone: (902) 667-7231
Amherst, NS B4H 3Z5 C. Bradley Fay, Mgr.

ST. FRANCIS XAVIER UNIVERSITY - COADY INTERNATIONAL INSTITUTE - MARIE MICHAEL LIBRARY
Phone: (902) 867-3964
Antigonish, NS B2G 1C0 Sr. Berthold Mackey, Chf.Libn.

ST. MARTHA'S HOSPITAL - SCHOOL OF NURSING LIBRARY
25 Bay St. Phone: (902) 863-2830
Antigonish, NS B2G 2G5 Sr. Marilyn Curry, Libn.

CANADA - ATMOSPHERIC ENVIRONMENT SERVICE - ATLANTIC REGIONAL LIBRARY
5th Fl., 1496 Bedford Hwy. Phone: (902) 835-9529
Bedford, NS B4A 1E5 Dr. A.D.J. O'Neill, Chf., Sci.Serv.

BEDFORD INSTITUTE OF OCEANOGRAPHY - LIBRARY
Box 1006 Phone: (902) 426-3675
Dartmouth, NS B2Y 4A2 J. Elizabeth Sutherland, Hd.

CANADA - DEFENCE RESEARCH ESTABLISHMENT ATLANTIC - LIBRARY
P.O. Box 1012 Phone: (902) 426-3100
Dartmouth, NS B2Y 3Z7 Donna I. Collins, Hd.Info.Serv. Group

CANADA - TRANSPORT CANADA - CANADIAN COAST GUARD, MARITIMES REGION - MARINE LIBRARY
602-46 Portland St.
P.O. Box 1013 Phone: (902) 426-5182
Dartmouth, NS B2Y 3Z7 Mrs. Gaylan Ritchie, Regional Marine Libn.

HERMES ELECTRONICS LTD. - LIBRARY
Box 1005 Phone: (902) 466-7491
Dartmouth, NS B2Y 4A1 Vaila S. Mowat, Hd., Engr.Doc.

NOVA SCOTIA HOSPITAL - HEALTH SCIENCE LIBRARY
P.O. Box 1004 Phone: (902) 469-7500
Dartmouth, NS B2Y 3Z9 Marjorie A. Cox

NOVA SCOTIA RESEARCH FOUNDATION CORPORATION - LIBRARY †
100 Fenwick St.
P.O. Box 790 Phone: (902) 424-8670
Dartmouth, NS B2Y 3Z7 Helen I. Hendry, Libn.

CAPE BRETON MINERS' MUSEUM - LIBRARY *
Quarry Point Phone: (902) 849-4522
Glace Bay, NS B1A 5T8 Thomas Miller, Cat.

ATLANTIC PROVINCES ECONOMIC COUNCIL - LIBRARY
One Sackville Place   Phone: (902) 422-6516
Halifax, NS B3J 1K1   L. Duffy

ATLANTIC SCHOOL OF THEOLOGY - LIBRARY
640 Francklyn St.   Phone: (902) 423-7986
Halifax, NS B3H 3B5   Alice W. Harrison, Libn.

CAMP HILL HOSPITAL - HEALTH SCIENCES LIBRARY
1763 Robie St.   Phone: (902) 423-1371
Halifax, NS B3H 3G2   Verona Hall, Lib.Asst.

CANADA - FISHERIES & OCEANS - SCOTIA-FUNDY REGIONAL LIBRARY
P.O. Box 550   Phone: (902) 426-3972
Halifax, NS B3J 2S7   Anna Oxley, Regional Libn.

CANADA - NATIONAL DEFENCE - CAMBRIDGE MILITARY LIBRARY
Royal Artillery Pk., Queen St.   Phone: (902) 426-5142
Halifax, NS B3J 2H9   W.R. MacNeil, Sec.

CANADA - NATIONAL RESEARCH COUNCIL - ATLANTIC RESEARCH
    LABORATORY - LIBRARY
1411 Oxford St.   Phone: (902) 426-8250
Halifax, NS B3H 3Z1   Annabelle Taylor, Libn.

CANADA - STATISTICS CANADA - ADVISORY SERVICES - HALIFAX
    REFERENCE CENTRE
1256 Barrington St., 3rd Fl.   Phone: (902) 426-5331
Halifax, NS B3J 1Y6

CANADIAN BROADCASTING CORPORATION - MUSIC & RECORD LIBRARY
5600 Sackville St.
Box 3000   Phone: (902) 422-8311
Halifax, NS B3J 3E9   David S. Leadbeater, Sr.Rec.Libn.

DALHOUSIE UNIVERSITY - INSTITUTE OF PUBLIC AFFAIRS - LIBRARY
6086 University Ave.   Phone: (902) 424-2526
Halifax, NS B3H 1W7   Faustina Chen, Libn.

DALHOUSIE UNIVERSITY - KIPLING COLLECTION
University Library   Phone: (902) 424-3615
Halifax, NS B3H 4H8

DALHOUSIE UNIVERSITY - LAW LIBRARY
Weldon Law Bldg.   Phone: (902) 424-2124
Halifax, NS B3H 3J5   Christian L. Wiktor, Law Libn.

DALHOUSIE UNIVERSITY - MACDONALD SCIENCE LIBRARY
University Library   Phone: (902) 424-2059
Halifax, NS B3H 4J3   Sylvia J. Fullerton, Asst.Univ.Libn.Sci.

DALHOUSIE UNIVERSITY - MARITIME SCHOOL OF SOCIAL WORK -
    LIBRARY
6420 Coburg Rd.   Phone: (902) 424-3760
Halifax, NS B3H 3J5   Mrs. Jean O. Hattie, Libn.

DALHOUSIE UNIVERSITY - W.K. KELLOGG HEALTH SCIENCES LIBRARY
Sir Charles Tupper Medical Bldg.   Phone: (902) 424-2458
Halifax, NS B3H 4H7   Ann Nevill, Health Sci.Libn.

GRACE MATERNITY HOSPITAL - MEDICAL LIBRARY
5821 University Ave.   Phone: (902) 422-6501
Halifax, NS B3H 1W3   Donna M. Gallivan, Dir., Med.Rec.Dept.

HALIFAX BOARD OF TRADE - LIBRARY
Suite 400, 5251 Duke St.   Phone: (902) 422-6447
Halifax, NS B3J 1P3   G.H. Lummis, Mgr.

HALIFAX INFIRMARY - HEALTH SERVICES LIBRARY †
1335 Queen St.   Phone: (902) 428-3058
Halifax, NS B3J 2H6   Dr. Anitra Laycock, Libn.

HALIFAX REGIONAL VOCATIONAL SCHOOL - LIBRARY
1825 Bell Rd.   Phone: (902) 422-8301
Halifax, NS B3H 2Z4   Joann Morris, Libn.

IZAAK WALTON KILLAM HOSPITAL FOR CHILDREN - MEDICAL STAFF
    LIBRARY
5850 University Ave.   Phone: (902) 424-3055
Halifax, NS B3H 3G9   Hilda Van Rooyen, Med.Libn.

MARITIME TELEGRAPH & TELEPHONE CO. LTD. - INFORMATION RESOURCE
    CENTRE
P.O. Box 880   Phone: (902) 421-4570
Halifax, NS B3J 2W3   Joan E. Fage, Libn.

MOUNT SAINT VINCENT UNIVERSITY - LIBRARY
166 Bedford Hwy.   Phone: (902) 443-4450
Halifax, NS B3M 2J6   Mr. L. Bianchini, Hd.Libn.

NOVA SCOTIA - ATTORNEY GENERAL'S LIBRARY
Provincial Bldg.
P.O. Box 7   Phone: (902) 424-7699
Halifax, NS B3J 2L6   Margaret Murphy, Libn.

NOVA SCOTIA BARRISTERS' SOCIETY - LIBRARY
Law Courts, 1815 Upper Water St.   Phone: (902) 422-1491
Halifax, NS B3J 1S7   Linda M. Keddy, Libn.

NOVA SCOTIA COLLEGE OF ART AND DESIGN - LIBRARY
5163 Duke St.   Phone: (902) 422-7381
Halifax, NS B3J 3J6   John Murchie, Lib.Dir.

NOVA SCOTIA COMMISSION ON DRUG DEPENDENCY - LIBRARY AND
    INFORMATION CENTRE
4th Fl., 5668 South St.   Phone: (902) 424-4270
Halifax, NS B3J 1A6   Eleanor Cardoza, Libn.

NOVA SCOTIA - DEPARTMENT OF CULTURE, RECREATION AND FITNESS -
    LIBRARY
P.O. Box 864   Phone: (902) 424-7734
Halifax, NS B3J 2V2   Genni Archibald, Lib.Off.

NOVA SCOTIA - DEPARTMENT OF DEVELOPMENT - LIBRARY
5151 George St., 8th Fl.
P.O. Box 519   Phone: (902) 424-5807
Halifax, NS B3J 2R7   Donald Purcell, Libn.

NOVA SCOTIA - DEPARTMENT OF EDUCATION - EDUCATION MEDIA
    SERVICES
5250 Spring Garden Rd.   Phone: (902) 424-5445
Halifax, NS B3J 1E8   B.F. Hart, Educ. Media Serv.

NOVA SCOTIA - DEPARTMENT OF LABOUR AND MANPOWER - LIBRARY
P.O. Box 697   Phone: (902) 424-4313
Halifax, NS B3J 2T8   Marie DeYoung, Libn.

NOVA SCOTIA - DEPARTMENT OF MINES & ENERGY - LIBRARY
P.O. Box 1087   Phone: (902) 424-8633
Halifax, NS B3J 2X1   Valerie Brisco, Res.Asst.

NOVA SCOTIA - DEPARTMENT OF SOCIAL SERVICES - LIBRARY
P.O. Box 696   Phone: (902) 424-4383
Halifax, NS B3J 2T7   Jane Phillips, Libn.

NOVA SCOTIA - LEGISLATIVE LIBRARY
Province House   Phone: (902) 424-5932
Halifax, NS B3J 2P8   Shirley B. Elliott, Legislative Libn.

NOVA SCOTIA MUSEUM - LIBRARY
1747 Summer St.   Phone: (902) 429-4610
Halifax, NS B3H 3A6   S. Whiteside, Libn.

NOVA SCOTIA POWER CORPORATION - LIBRARY
Box 910   Phone: (902) 424-2928
Halifax, NS B3J 2W5   Barbara N. MacKenzie, Libn.

NOVA SCOTIA - PROVINCIAL LIBRARY
5250 Spring Garden Rd.   Phone: (902) 424-5439
Halifax, NS B3J 1E8   Mrs. Carin Somers, Dir.

NOVA SCOTIA - PUBLIC ARCHIVES OF NOVA SCOTIA
6016 University Ave.   Phone: (902) 423-9115
Halifax, NS B3H 1W4   Hugh A. Taylor, Prov.Archv.

ST. MARY'S UNIVERSITY - PATRICK POWER LIBRARY
                                            Phone: (902) 422-7361
Halifax, NS B3H 3C3   Ronald A. Lewis, Univ.Libn.

TECHNICAL UNIVERSITY OF NOVA SCOTIA - LIBRARY
Barrington & Bishop St.
P.O. Box 1000   Phone: (902) 429-8300
Halifax, NS B3J 2X4   Mohammad Riaz Hussain, Libn.

UNITED CHURCH OF CANADA - MARITIME CONFERENCE ARCHIVES
Pine Hill Divinity Hall   Phone: (902) 429-4819
Halifax, NS B3H 3B5   Rev. Neil A. MacLeod, Archv.

UNIVERSITY OF KING'S COLLEGE - KING'S COLLEGE LIBRARY
                                           Phone: (902) 423-8428
Halifax, NS B3H 2A1   Mrs. J.E. Lane, Chf.Libn.

VICTORIA GENERAL HOSPITAL - HEALTH SCIENCES LIBRARY
                                           Phone: (902) 429-3497
Halifax, NS B3H 2Y9   Joyce A. Kublin, Coord.Lib./AV Serv.

CANADA - AGRICULTURE CANADA - RESEARCH STATION, KENTVILLE -
    LIBRARY
                                           Phone: (902) 678-2171
Kentville, NS B4N 1J5   Jerry Miner, Libn.

FORTRESS OF LOUISBOURG NATIONAL HISTORIC PARK - LIBRARY
P.O. Box 160   Phone: (902) 733-2280
Louisbourg, NS B0A 1M0   Margaret MacMullin, Libn.

CANADA - TRANSPORT CANADA - CANADIAN COAST GUARD COLLEGE -
    LIBRARY
P.O. Box 4500   Phone: (902) 539-2115
Sydney, NS B1P 6L1   David N. MacSween, Libn.

COLLEGE OF CAPE BRETON - BEATON INSTITUTE ARCHIVES
Box 5300   Phone: (506) 564-6393
Sydney, NS B1P 6J1   Dr. R.J. Morgan, Dir.

NOVA SCOTIA AGRICULTURAL COLLEGE - LIBRARY
Box 550   Phone: (902) 895-1571
Truro, NS B2N 5E3   B. Sodhi, Libn.

ACADIA UNIVERSITY - SCIENCE LIBRARY
Box 70   Phone: (902) 542-2201
Wolfville, NS B0P 1X0   Dr. Nirmal K. Jain, Hd., Sci.Div.

FIREFIGHTERS' MUSEUM OF NOVA SCOTIA - LIBRARY & INFORMATION
    CENTER
451 Main St.   Phone: (902) 742-5525
Yarmouth, NS B5A 1G9   Helen Goodwin, Cur.

YARMOUTH COUNTY HISTORICAL SOCIETY - LIBRARY
22 Collins St.   Phone: (902) 742-5539
Yarmouth, NS B5A 3C8   Helen Hall, Libn.

ONTARIO

MISSISSIPPI VALLEY CONSERVATION AUTHORITY - R. TAIT MC KENZIE
    RESEARCH LIBRARY
R.R. 1, The Mill of Kintail   Phone: (613) 256-3610
Almonte, ON K0A 1A0

FORT MALDEN NATIONAL HISTORIC PARK - LIBRARY & ARCHIVES
P.O. Box 38   Phone: (519) 736-5416
Amherstburg, ON N9V 2Z2   Sally Snyder, Libn.

SIMCOE COUNTY LAW ASSOCIATION - LIBRARY
30 Poyntz St.   Phone: (715) 728-1221
Barrie, ON L4M 1M1   Eleanor Garner, Act.Libn.

LOYALIST COLLEGE OF APPLIED ARTS & TECHNOLOGY - ANDERSON
    RESOURCE CENTRE
Box 4200   Phone: (613) 962-9501
Belleville, ON K8N 5B9   Ronald H. Boyce, Hd., Lib.Serv.

CANADA - NATIONAL DEFENCE - CANADIAN FORCES MEDICAL SERVICES
    SCHOOL - LIBRARY *
Canadian Forces Base   Phone: (705) 424-1200
Borden, ON L0M 1C0   Mrs. Marion Thomson, Libn.

ONTARIO PROVINCIAL POLICE - TRAINING BRANCH LIBRARY
Queen & McLaughlin Rd.
Box 266
Brampton, ON L6V 2L1   S/Sgt. F.C. Harvey

BRANT COUNTY MUSEUM - LIBRARY
57 Charlotte St.   Phone: (519) 752-2483
Brantford, ON N3T 2W6   William R. Robbins

AEL MICROTEL LIMITED - LIBRARY
100 Strowger Blvd.
Brockville, ON K6V 5W8

BRANT (Joseph) MEMORIAL HOSPITAL - HOSPITAL LIBRARY
1230 Northshore Blvd.   Phone: (416) 632-3730
Burlington, ON L7R 4C4   Janice McMillan, Hosp.Libn.

CANADA CENTRE FOR INLAND WATERS - LIBRARY
867 Lakeshore Rd.
Box 5050   Phone: (416) 637-4282
Burlington, ON L7R 4A6   Eve Dowie, Hd., Lib.Serv.

CANADIAN CANNERS, LTD. - RESEARCH CENTRE - LIBRARY
1101 Walker's Line   Phone: (416) 335-9700
Burlington, ON L7N 2G4   Gisela Smithson, Tech.Libn.

WESTINGHOUSE CANADA LTD. - ELECTRONICS DIVISION LIBRARY
777 Walker's Lane
P.O. Box 5009   Phone: (416) 528-8811
Burlington, ON L7R 4B3   E. Jackson, Libn.

LEIGH INSTRUMENTS, LTD. - ENGINEERING & AEROSPACE DIVISION -
    TECHNICAL LIBRARY
P.O. Box 82   Phone: (613) 257-3883
Carleton Place, ON K7C 3P3   Betty G. Robertson, Info.Sec.

ATOMIC ENERGY OF CANADA, LTD. - TECHNICAL INFORMATION BRANCH -
    MAIN LIBRARY
Chalk River Nuclear Labs.   Phone: (613) 687-5581
Chalk River, ON K0J 1J0   H. Greenshields, Chf.Libn.

UNION GAS, LTD. - LIBRARY SERVICE †
50 Keil Dr., N.   Phone: (519) 352-3100
Chatham, ON N7M 5M1   Mrs. A. Steen

CANADIAN NUMISMATIC ASSOCIATION - LIBRARY *
P.O. Box 503   Phone: (705) 737-0845
Collingwood, ON L9Y 4B2   Maria A. Ford, Libn.

CANADA - PARKS CANADA, ONTARIO REGION LIBRARY
40 Fifth St., E.   Phone: (613) 933-9712
Cornwall, ON K6H 5V4   Michel R. Jesmer, Lib.Techn.

CANADA - TRANSPORT CANADA - TRAINING INSTITUTE - TECHNICAL
    INFORMATION CENTRE
1950 Montreal Rd.
Bag Service 5400   Phone: (613) 938-4344
Cornwall, ON K6H 6L2   Dianne Harding, Libn.

ST. LAWRENCE COLLEGE OF APPLIED ARTS AND TECHNOLOGY - LEARNING
    RESOURCE CENTRE
2 Belmont St.   Phone: (613) 933-6080
Cornwall, ON K6H 4Z1   Norah Fourney, Hd.Libn.

ALCOHOL AND DRUG CONCERNS, INC. - AUDIOVISUAL LIBRARY
15 Gervais Dr., Rm. 603   Phone: (416) 449-4933
Don Mills, ON M3C 1Y8   Miss O. Hussey, Commun.Sec.

BANK OF NOVA SCOTIA - OPERATIONS LIBRARY
10 Gateway Blvd.   Phone: (416) 424-3551
Don Mills, ON M3C 3A1   Penni Lee, Sys.Libn.

CANADIAN GAS RESEARCH INSTITUTE - LIBRARY
55 Scarsdale Rd.   Phone: (416) 447-6465
Don Mills, ON M3B 2R3

CANADIAN REAL ESTATE ASSOCIATION - LIBRARY
99 Duncan Mill Rd.   Phone: (416) 445-9910
Don Mills, ON M3B 1Z2   Mary Lynn Weatherwax, Libn.

CANADIAN RESEARCH INSTITUTE - LIBRARY
85 Curlew Dr.
Don Mills, ON M3A 2R2

CIVIC GARDEN CENTRE - LIBRARY
777 Lawrence Ave., E.   Phone: (416) 445-1552
Don Mills, ON M3C 1P2   Pamela MacKenzie, Libn.

IBM CANADA, LTD. - DP CENTRAL LIBRARY
1150 Eglinton Ave. E.   Phone: (416) 443-2043
Don Mills, ON M3C 1H7   Susan H. Johnston, Hd.Libn.

IBM CANADA, LTD. - GENERAL BUSINESS GROUP LIBRARY
101 Valleybrook Dr.   Phone: (416) 443-4465
Don Mills, ON M3B 3H1   Anne F. Martin, GBG Libn.

IBM CANADA, LTD. - LABORATORY LIBRARY
1150 Eglinton Ave., E.   Phone: (416) 443-3136
Don Mills, ON M3C 1H7   Ms. R.H. Yan, Lab.Libn.

INDUSMIN, LTD. - TECHNICAL CENTRE LIBRARY
1933 Leslie St.   Phone: (416) 445-6720
Don Mills, ON M3B 2M3

MARSHALL MACKLIN MONAGHAN LIMITED - LIBRARY
275 Duncan Mill Rd.   Phone: (416) 449-2500
Don Mills, ON M3B 2Y1

ONTARIO FEDERATION OF LABOUR - RESOURCE CENTRE
15 Gervais Dr., Suite 202   Phone: (416) 441-2731
Don Mills, ON M3C 1Y8   Duncan J. MacDonald, Res.Coord.

ONTARIO FILM INSTITUTE - LIBRARY & INFORMATION CENTRE
770 Don Mills Rd.   Phone: (416) 429-4100
Don Mills, ON M3C 1T3   Sherie Brethour, Libn.

ONTARIO SCIENCE CENTRE - AUDIO VISUAL LIBRARY
770 Don Mills Rd.   Phone: (416) 429-4100
Don Mills, ON M3C 1T3

ONTARIO SCIENCE CENTRE - LIBRARY
770 Don Mills Rd.   Phone: (416) 429-4100
Don Mills, ON M3C 1T3   Dale Munro, Libn.

ORTHO PHARMACEUTICAL (Canada), LTD. - LIBRARY
19 Green Belt Dr.   Phone: (416) 444-4461
Don Mills, ON M3C 1L9   Mrs. Marta Bodnar, Libn.

SOUTHAM COMMUNICATIONS LTD. - LIBRARY
1450 Don Mills Rd.   Phone: (416) 445-6641
Don Mills, ON M3B 2X7   Eileen M. Wise, Libn.

CANADA - ATMOSPHERIC ENVIRONMENT SERVICE - LIBRARY
4905 Dufferin St.   Phone: (416) 667-4500
Downsview, ON M3H 5T4   Mary M. Skinner, Chf.Lib.Serv.Div.

CANADA - DEFENCE AND CIVIL INSTITUTE OF ENVIRONMENTAL
    MEDICINE - SCIENTIFIC INFORMATION CENTRE
1133 Sheppard Ave., W.
P.O. Box 2000   Phone: (416) 633-4240
Downsview, ON M3M 3B9   Anthony Cheung, Chf.Libn.

DE HAVILLAND AIRCRAFT OF CANADA, LTD. - ENGINEERING LIBRARY
Garratt Blvd.   Phone: (416) 633-7310
Downsview, ON M3K 1Y5   Mrs. C. Parsons, Libn.

DELLCREST CHILDREN'S CENTRE - LIBRARY
1645 Sheppard Ave. W.   Phone: (416) 633-0515
Downsview, ON M3M 2X4   Lois Elliott, Libn.

NATIONAL INSTITUTE ON MENTAL RETARDATION - JOHN ORR FOSTER
    NATIONAL REFERENCE LIBRARY
Kinsmen Bldg., York University
4700 Keele St.   Phone: (416) 661-9611
Downsview, ON M3J 1P3   Mrs. Edward Armour, Coord.Natl.Ref.Serv.

NORTH YORK PUBLIC LIBRARY - MULTILINGUAL MATERIALS DEPARTMENT
120 Martin Ross Ave.   Phone: (416) 667-1060
Downsview, ON M3J 2L4   Diane Dragasevich, Libn./Supv.

ONTARIO - MINISTRY OF TRANSPORTATION AND COMMUNICATIONS -
    LIBRARY AND INFORMATION CENTRE
Central Bldg., Rm. 149
1201 Wilson Ave.   Phone: (416) 248-3591
Downsview, ON M3M 1J8   Stefanie A. Pavlin, Hd., Lib.Serv.

UNIVERSITY OF TORONTO - INSTITUTE FOR AEROSPACE STUDIES -
    LIBRARY
4925 Dufferin St.   Phone: (416) 667-7712
Downsview, ON M3H 5T6   Asta Luik, Libn.

WORKMEN'S COMPENSATION BOARD OF ONTARIO - HOSPITAL &
    REHABILITATION CENTRE - MEDICAL LIBRARY
115 Torbarrie Rd.   Phone: (416) 244-1761
Downsview, ON M3L 1G8   Catherine W. Wilson, Libn.

YORK-FINCH GENERAL HOSPITAL - DR. THOMAS J. MALCHO MEMORIAL
    LIBRARY
2111 Finch Ave., W.   Phone: (416) 744-2500
Downsview, ON M3N 1N1   Joyce Jones, Dir.

YORK UNIVERSITY - FACULTY OF EDUCATION - EDUCATION CENTRE *
S166 Ross Bldg.
4700 Keele St.   Phone: (416) 667-2395
Downsview, ON M3J 1P3   Nancy Kasper, Educ.Libn.

YORK UNIVERSITY - FILM LIBRARY
Scott Library
4700 Keele St.   Phone: (416) 667-2546
Downsview, ON M3J 2R2

YORK UNIVERSITY - GOVERNMENT DOCUMENTS/ADMINISTRATIVE
    STUDIES LIBRARY
113 Administrative Studies Bldg.
4700 Keele St.   Phone: (416) 667-2545
Downsview, ON M3J 2R6   F. Anne Cannon, Hd.

YORK UNIVERSITY - INSTITUTE FOR BEHAVIOURAL RESEARCH - DATA
    BANK
4700 Keele St.   Phone: (416) 667-3026
Downsview, ON M3J 2R6   Professor A.H. Richmond

YORK UNIVERSITY - LAW LIBRARY
4700 Keele St.   Phone: (416) 667-3939
Downsview, ON M3J 2R5   Professor B.J. Halevy, Libn.

YORK UNIVERSITY - LISTENING ROOM
Scott Library, Rm. 409
4700 Keele St.   Phone: (416) 667-3694
Downsview, ON M3J 2R2   Julie Stockton, Hd.

YORK UNIVERSITY - MAP LIBRARY
Scott Library, Rm. 115
4700 Keele St.   Phone: (416) 667-3353
Downsview, ON M3J 2R2   Janet Allin, Supv.

YORK UNIVERSITY - RARE BOOKS AND SPECIAL COLLECTIONS
Scott Library, Rm. 305
4700 Keele St.   Phone: (416) 667-2457
Downsview, ON M3J 2R2   Nancy O'Reilly, Attendant

YORK UNIVERSITY - STEACIE SCIENCE LIBRARY
4700 Keele St.   Phone: (416) 667-3927
Downsview, ON M3J 2R3   Brian B. Wilks, Sci.Libn.

YORK UNIVERSITY - UNIVERSITY ARCHIVES
105 Scott Library
4700 Keele St.   Phone: (416) 667-3306
Downsview, ON M3J 2R2   Hartwell Bowsfield, Univ.Archv.

CONSUMERS GLASS COMPANY LIMITED - PLASTICS PACKAGING DIVISION
    LIBRARY
701 Evans Ave., Suite 401   Phone: (416) 232-3275
Etobicoke, ON M9C 1A3   Barbara Presho, Libn.

ETOBICOKE BOARD OF EDUCATION - RESOURCE LIBRARY
1 Civic Centre Court   Phone: (416) 626-4360
Etobicoke, ON M9C 2B3   Alice Guignard, Coord.

GEOGRAPHIC

VARIAN CANADA INC. - TECHNICAL LIBRARY *
45 River Dr.　　　　　　　　　　　　Phone: (416) 457-4130
Georgetown, ON L7G 2J4　　　　　　　Rhonda Barber, Libn.

CONESTOGA COLLEGE OF APPLIED ARTS & TECHNOLOGY, GUELPH CENTRE
　- HEALTH SCIENCES DIV. LEARNING RESOURCE CENTRE
70 Westmount Rd.　　　　　　　　Phone: (519) 824-2950
Guelph, ON N1H 5H7　　　　　　　　　Joy Weiss, Libn.

UNIROYAL, LTD. - RESEARCH LABORATORIES LIBRARY
120 Huron St.　　　　　　　　　　Phone: (519) 822-3790
Guelph, ON N1H 6N3　　　　　　　　　Lorna P. Cole, Libn.

UNIVERSITY OF GUELPH - HUMANITIES AND SOCIAL SCIENCES DIVISION -
　MAP COLLECTION
McLaughlin Library　　　　　　　　Phone: (519) 824-4120
Guelph, ON N1G 2W1　　　　　　Mrs. F. Francis, Ref.Libn.

UNIVERSITY OF GUELPH - LIBRARY
McLaughlin Library　　　　　　　　Phone: (519) 824-4120
Guelph, ON N1G 2W1　　　　　Margaret L. Beckman, Chf.Libn.

WELLINGTON COUNTY BOARD OF EDUCATION - EDUCATION LIBRARY
500 Victoria Rd., N.　　　　　　　Phone: (519) 822-4420
Guelph, ON N1E 6K2　　　　R.E. Monkhouse, Educ. Media Cons.

NORTHERN COLLEGE - HAILEYBURY SCHOOL OF MINES - LIBRARY
Latchford St.
P.O. Box 849　　　　　　　　　　Phone: (705) 672-3376
Haileybury, ON P0J 1K0　　　　　　　Maureen Taeger, Libn.

ART GALLERY OF HAMILTON - MURIEL ISABEL BOSTWICK LIBRARY
123 King St. W.　　　　　　　　　Phone: (416) 527-6610
Hamilton, ON L8P 4S8　　　　Andrew J. Oko, Cur., Hist.Coll.

BAPTIST CONVENTION OF ONTARIO AND QUEBEC - CANADIAN BAPTIST
　ARCHIVES
McMaster Divinity College　　　　　Phone: (416) 525-9140
Hamilton, ON L8S 4K1　　　　　　　Judith Colwell, Libn.

DOFASCO INC. - MAIN OFFICE LIBRARY
1330 Burlington St. E.
P.O. Box 460　　　　　　　　　　Phone: (416) 544-3761
Hamilton, ON L8N 3J5　　　　　　　Mrs. Mina Gucma, Libn.

DOFASCO INC. - RESEARCH INFORMATION CENTRE
1390 Burlington St., E.
Box 460　　　　　　　　　　　　Phone: (416) 544-3761
Hamilton, ON L8N 3J5　　　　　　　Ann M. Duff, Res.Libn.

HAMILTON ACADEMY OF MEDICINE - LIBRARY
286 Victoria Ave., N.　　　　　　　Phone: (416) 528-1611
Hamilton, ON L8L 5G4　　　　　　Bessie J. McKinlay, Libn.

HAMILTON BOARD OF EDUCATION - EDUCATION CENTRE LIBRARY
100 Main St., W.　　　　　　　　Phone: (416) 527-5092
Hamilton, ON L8P 1H6　　　　　E. Birgit Langhammer, Libn.

HAMILTON CITY HALL - LIBRARY
71 Main St., W.　　　　　　　　　Phone: (416) 527-0241
Hamilton, ON L8N 3T4　　　S.G. Hollowell, Supv., Rec.Div.

HAMILTON LAW ASSOCIATION - LAW LIBRARY
50 Main St., E.　　　　　　　　　Phone: (416) 522-1563
Hamilton, ON L8N 1E9　　　　　　W. Hearder-Moan, Libn.

HAMILTON PUBLIC LIBRARY - SPECIAL COLLECTIONS
55 York Blvd.　　　　　　　　　Phone: (416) 529-8111
Hamilton, ON L8R 3K1　　　　　Judith McAnanama, Chf.Libn.

HAMILTON SPECTATOR - REFERENCE LIBRARY
44 Frid St.　　　　　　　　　　Phone: (416) 526-3315
Hamilton, ON L8N 3G3　　　　　Jean M. Tebbutt, Chf.Libn.

MC MASTER UNIVERSITY - ARCHIVES AND RESEARCH COLLECTIONS
　DIVISION
Mills Memorial Library　　　　　　Phone: (416) 525-9140
Hamilton, ON L8S 4L6　　　　　　Mr. G.R. Hill, Chf.Libn.

MC MASTER UNIVERSITY - BUSINESS LIBRARY
Innis Room, Mills Memorial Library　　Phone: (416) 525-9140
Hamilton, ON L8S 4L6　　　　　Sheila Pepper, Bus.Libn.

MC MASTER UNIVERSITY - HEALTH SCIENCES LIBRARY
1400 Main St., W.　　　　　　　Phone: (416) 525-9140
Hamilton, ON L8S 4J9　　　Beatrix H. Robinow, Health Sci.Libn.

MC MASTER UNIVERSITY - MAP LIBRARY
Burke Science Bldg.　　　　　　　Phone: (416) 525-9140
Hamilton, ON L8S 4K1　　　　　　Kate Donkin, Map Cur.

MC MASTER UNIVERSITY - THODE LIBRARY OF SCIENCE & ENGINEERING
　　　　　　　　　　　　　　Phone: (416) 525-9140
Hamilton, ON L8S 4P5　　Harold Siroonian, Sci. & Engr.Libn.

MC MASTER UNIVERSITY - URBAN DOCUMENTATION CENTRE
1200 Main St. West　　　　　　　Phone: (416) 525-9140
Hamilton, ON L8S 4K1　　　Cathy Moulder, Documentalist

MOHAWK COLLEGE OF APPLIED ARTS AND TECHNOLOGY - HEALTH
　SCIENCES LIBRARY RESOURCE CENTRE
P.O. Box 2034　　　　　　　　　Phone: (416) 389-4461
Hamilton, ON L8N 3T2　　　　　　　June Shore, Libn.

MOHAWK COLLEGE OF APPLIED ARTS AND TECHNOLOGY - MOHAWK
　LIBRARY RESOURCE CENTRE
P.O. Box 2034　　　　　　　　　Phone: (416) 389-4461
Hamilton, ON L8N 3T2　　　Sandra M. Black, Act.Chf.Libn.

ONTARIO - MINISTRY OF HEALTH - PSYCHIATRIC BRANCH - LIBRARY
　RESOURCE CENTRE ***
P.O. Box 585　　　　　　　　　Phone: (416) 388-2511
Hamilton, ON L9C 3N6　　　　　　Mary McManus, Libn.

PROCTER & GAMBLE INC. - PRODUCT DEVELOPMENT LIBRARY
P.O. Box 589, Burlington St., E.
Hamilton, ON L8N 3L5

ROYAL BOTANICAL GARDENS - LIBRARY
Box 399　　　　　　　　　　　Phone: (416) 527-1158
Hamilton, ON L8N 3H8　　　Ina Vrugtman, Botanical Libn.

ST. JOSEPH'S HOSPITAL - DRUG INFORMATION CENTRE
50 Charlton Ave., E.　　　　　　Phone: (416) 522-4941
Hamilton, ON L8N 1Y4　Mrs. D.A. Thompson, Dir. of Pharm.Serv.

ST. JOSEPH'S HOSPITAL - HOSPITAL LIBRARY
50 Charlton Ave., E.　　　　　　Phone: (416) 522-4941
Hamilton, ON L8N 1Y4　　　　　　Mrs. S. Rogers

ST. PETER'S HOSPITAL - PROFESSIONAL LIBRARY
88 Maplewood Ave.
Hamilton, ON L8M 1W9　　　　　　Joan Osburn, Libn.

SOCIETY OF MANAGEMENT ACCOUNTANTS OF CANADA - RESOURCE
　CENTRE †
154 Main St., E.
Box 176　　　　　　　　　　　Phone: (416) 525-4100
Hamilton, ON L8N 3C3　　　　　　　Helen Hill, Libn.

STELCO INC. - CENTRAL LIBRARY
Stelco Tower
100 King St., W.　　　　　　　　Phone: (416) 528-2511
Hamilton, ON L8N 3T1　　Larraine P. Murphy, Off.Serv.Supv.-Lib.Serv.

STELCO INC. - ENGINEERING SERVICES LIBRARY
100 King St., W.　　　　　　　　Phone: (416) 528-2511
Hamilton, ON L8N 3T1　　　　　　J.A. De Young, Libn.

STELCO INC. - RESEARCH LIBRARY
Stelco Tower
100 King St., W.　　　　　　　　Phone: (416) 528-2511
Hamilton, ON L8N 3T1　　　　　David Rosenplot, Libn.

CHRISTIAN FARMERS FEDERATION OF ONTARIO - FOUND. FOR CHRISTIAN
　ALTERNATIVES IN AGRICULTURE-LIBRARY
Box 694　　　　　　　　　　　Phone: (519) 338-2921
Harriston, ON N0G 1Z0　Elbert van Donkersgoed, Res. & Policy Dir.

CANADA - AGRICULTURE CANADA - RESEARCH STATION, HARROW -
LIBRARY
    Phone: (519) 738-2251
Harrow, ON N0R 1G0   Eric A. Champagne, Libn.

CIP RESEARCH, LTD. - LIBRARY
    Phone: (613) 632-4121
Hawkesbury, ON K6A 2H4   Mrs. M.E. Cranford, Libn.

NOTRE DAME HOSPITAL - LIBRARY
1405 Edward St.   Phone: (705) 362-4291
Hearst, ON P0L 1N0   Mary Kellie, Inservice Coord.

ERCO INDUSTRIES, LTD. - LIBRARY
2 Gibbs Rd.   Phone: (416) 239-7111
Islington, ON M9B 1R1   Douglas G. Suarez, Corp.Libn.

NORTHERN TELECOM CANADA, LTD. - BUSINESS SYSTEMS LIBRARY
304 The East Mall   Phone: (416) 232-2000
Islington, ON L5N 1B3   Karen J. Ryan, Data Adm.Libn.

NORTHERN TELECOM CANADA, LTD. - NT LIBRARY
304 The East Mall   Phone: (416) 232-2000
Islington, ON M9B 6E4   Eileen Daniel, Libn.

KEMPTVILLE COLLEGE OF AGRICULTURAL TECHNOLOGY - LIBRARY
    Phone: (613) 258-3414
Kemptville, ON K0G 1J0   Alison Meikle, Libn.

ONTARIO - MINISTRY OF AGRICULTURE AND FOOD - VETERINARY
SERVICES LABORATORY LIBRARY
    Phone: (613) 258-3804
Kemptville, ON K0G 1J0   George C. Fisher, Hd.

ALCAN INTERNATIONAL LTD. - KINGSTON LABORATORIES - LIBRARY
P.O. Box 8400   Phone: (613) 549-4500
Kingston, ON K7L 4Z4   Miss E.M. Vanags, Hd.

CANADA - NATIONAL DEFENCE - FORT FRONTENAC LIBRARY
Fort Frontenac   Phone: (613) 545-5829
Kingston, ON K7K 2X8   Mr. S.K. Kamra, Chf.Libn.

DU PONT CANADA, INC. - CUSTOMER TECHNICAL CENTRE LIBRARY
P.O. Box 3500   Phone: (613) 544-6000
Kingston, ON K7L 5A1

DU PONT CANADA, INC. - RESEARCH CENTRE LIBRARY
P.O. Box 5000   Phone: (613) 544-6400
Kingston, ON K7L 5A5   B.F. Swerbrick, Libn.

KINGSTON GENERAL HOSPITAL - MEDICAL LIBRARY
Stuart St.   Phone: (613) 547-5023
Kingston, ON K7L 2V7   Enid Scott, Libn.

KINGSTON PSYCHIATRIC HOSPITAL - STAFF LIBRARY
Bag 603   Phone: (613) 546-1101
Kingston, ON K7L 4X3   Mae Morley, Libn.

ONGWANADA HOSPITAL - PENROSE & HOPKINS DIVISIONS - PENROSE
DIVISION LIBRARY
117 Park St.   Phone: (613) 544-9611
Kingston, ON K7L 1J9   Margaret Garrigan

QUEEN'S UNIVERSITY AT KINGSTON - ART LIBRARY
Ontario Hall   Phone: (613) 547-2633
Kingston, ON K7L 5C4   Eve Albrich, Art/Music Libn.

QUEEN'S UNIVERSITY AT KINGSTON - BIOLOGY LIBRARY
Earl Hall, Barrie St.   Phone: (613) 547-2896
Kingston, ON K7L 5C4   Mrs. J. Stevenson, Lib.Asst.

QUEEN'S UNIVERSITY AT KINGSTON - BRACKEN LIBRARY
    Phone: (613) 547-5753
Kingston, ON K7L 3N6   Virginia Parker, Libn.

QUEEN'S UNIVERSITY AT KINGSTON - CHEMISTRY LIBRARY
Frost Wing, Gordon Hall   Phone: (613) 547-2636
Kingston, ON K7L 5C4   Janet Innis, Lib.Asst.

QUEEN'S UNIVERSITY AT KINGSTON - CIVIL ENGINEERING LIBRARY
Ellis Hall   Phone: (613) 547-5546
Kingston, ON K7L 5C4   Mrs. P. Egan, Lib.Asst.

QUEEN'S UNIVERSITY AT KINGSTON - DOCUMENTS LIBRARY
Mackintosh-Corry Hall   Phone: (613) 547-6138
Kingston, ON K7L 5C4   S. Casey, Doc.Libn.

QUEEN'S UNIVERSITY AT KINGSTON - DUPUIS HALL LIBRARY
Division & Clergy Sts.
Kingston, ON K7L 5C4   Mrs. B. Walls, Lib.Asst.

QUEEN'S UNIVERSITY AT KINGSTON - EDUCATION LIBRARY
Duncan McArthur Hall   Phone: (613) 547-6286
Kingston, ON K7L 3N6   Mrs. F. Gwendolyn Wright, Chf.Educ.Libn.

QUEEN'S UNIVERSITY AT KINGSTON - ELECTRICAL ENGINEERING
LIBRARY
Fleming Hall
Kingston, ON K7L 5C4   Judy Young, Lib.Asst.

QUEEN'S UNIVERSITY AT KINGSTON - GEOLOGICAL SCIENCES LIBRARY
Miller Hall, Bruce Wing   Phone: (613) 547-2653
Kingston, ON K7L 5C4   Donald A. Redmond, Geology Libn.

QUEEN'S UNIVERSITY AT KINGSTON - INDUSTRIAL RELATIONS CENTRE -
LIBRARY
    Phone: (613) 547-6917
Kingston, ON K7L 3N6   Carol Williams, Libn.

QUEEN'S UNIVERSITY AT KINGSTON - LAW LIBRARY
Sir John A. Macdonald Hall   Phone: (613) 547-5934
Kingston, ON K7L 3N6   Irene Bessette; Libn.

QUEEN'S UNIVERSITY AT KINGSTON - MAP AND AIR PHOTO LIBRARY
Mackintosh-Corry Hall   Phone: (613) 547-6193
Kingston, ON K7L 5C4   Kathy Harding, Lib.Asst.

QUEEN'S UNIVERSITY AT KINGSTON - MATHEMATICS LIBRARY
Jeffery Hall   Phone: (613) 547-5720
Kingston, ON K7L 5C4   Mrs. D. Nuttall, Lib.Asst.

QUEEN'S UNIVERSITY AT KINGSTON - MECHANICAL ENGINEERING
LIBRARY
McLaughlin Hall, Stuart St.   Phone: (613) 547-2714
Kingston, ON K7L 5C4   Mrs. K. Paget, Lib.Asst.

QUEEN'S UNIVERSITY AT KINGSTON - MUSIC LIBRARY
Harrison-LeCaine Hall   Phone: (613) 547-2873
Kingston, ON K7L 5C4   Eve Albrich, Art/Music Libn.

QUEEN'S UNIVERSITY AT KINGSTON - PHYSICS LIBRARY
Stirling Hall, Queen's Crescent   Phone: (613) 547-2739
Kingston, ON K7L 5C4   Catherine Johnson, Lib.Asst.

QUEEN'S UNIVERSITY AT KINGSTON - PSYCHOLOGY LIBRARY
Humphrey Hall   Phone: (613) 547-3172
Kingston, ON K7L 5C4   Helen Cobb, Lib.Asst.

QUEEN'S UNIVERSITY AT KINGSTON - SPECIAL COLLECTIONS
Douglas Library   Phone: (613) 547-3030
Kingston, ON K7L 5C4   William F.E. Morley, Cur., Spec.Coll.

ROYAL MILITARY COLLEGE OF CANADA - MASSEY LIBRARY & SCIENCE/
ENGINEERING LIBRARY
    Phone: (613) 545-7330
Kingston, ON K7L 2W3   Keith Crouch, Chf.Libn.

ST. LAWRENCE COLLEGE OF APPLIED ARTS AND TECHNOLOGY - LEARNING
RESOURCE CENTRE
King & Portsmouth Sts.
Box 6000   Phone: (613) 544-5400
Kingston, ON K7L 5A6   Sherwin Raichman, Hd.

ST. MARY'S OF THE LAKE HOSPITAL - GIBSON MEDICAL LIBRARY
340 Union St. W.   Phone: (613) 544-5220
Kingston, ON K7L 5A2   Penny G. Levi, Libn.

GEOGRAPHIC

KITCHENER-WATERLOO ART GALLERY - ELEANOR CALVERT MEMORIAL
LIBRARY
101 Queen St. N.   Phone: (519) 579-5860
Kitchener, ON N2H 6P7   Nancy Francis, Libn.

KITCHENER-WATERLOO HOSPITAL - HEALTH SCIENCES LIBRARY
835 King St., W.   Phone: (519) 742-3611
Kitchener, ON N2G 1G3   Thelma Bisch, Libn.

KITCHENER-WATERLOO OVERSEAS AID INC. - GLOBAL COMMUNITY
CENTRE - LIBRARY *
94 Queen St. S.   Phone: (519) 743-7111
Kitchener, ON N2G 1V9   Stephen Allen

KITCHENER-WATERLOO RECORD - LIBRARY
225 Fairway Rd., S.   Phone: (519) 579-2231
Kitchener, ON N2G 4E5   Penny Coates, Libn.

ST. MARY'S HOSPITAL - MEDICAL LIBRARY
911B Queen's Blvd.   Phone: (519) 744-3311
Kitchener, ON N2M 1B2   Marilyn Mathews, Libn.

WATERLOO HISTORICAL SOCIETY - LIBRARY
Kitchener Public Library
85 Queen St.N.   Phone: (519) 743-0271
Kitchener, ON N2H 2H1   Albert I. Hunsberger, Pres.

GLENGARRY GENEALOGICAL SOCIETY - HIGHLAND HERITAGE LIBRARY
11 Oak St.
P.O. Box 460   Phone: (613) 347-3771
Lancaster, ON K0C 1N0   Alex W. Fraser, Pres.

POINT PELEE NATIONAL PARK - LIBRARY
R.R. 1   Phone: (519) 326-1161
Leamington, ON N8H 3V4   Rob Watt, Chief Pk. Naturalist

CANADA - AGRICULTURE CANADA - LONDON RESEARCH CENTRE LIBRARY
University Sub Post Office   Phone: (519) 679-4452
London, ON N6A 5B7   J. Giesbrecht, Area Coord.

COLLEGE OF FAMILY PHYSICIANS OF CANADA - CANADIAN LIBRARY OF
FAMILY MEDICINE
University Of Western Ontario
Medical Sciences Bldg.   Phone: (519) 679-2537
London, ON N6A 5C1   Dorothy Fitzgerald, Libn.

DIVINE WORD INTERNATIONAL RELIGIOUS EDUCATION CENTRE -
LIBRARY
Box 2400   Phone: (519) 439-7211
London, ON N6A 4G3   Maria Lopez De Heredia, Libn.

FANSHAWE COLLEGE OF APPLIED ARTS AND TECHNOLOGY - LEARNING
RESOURCE CENTRE - VICTORIA CAMPUS LIBRARY
P.O. Box 4005, Sta. C   Phone: (519) 433-6157
London, ON N5W 5H1   Jennifer Morrissey, Libn.

FANSHAWE COLLEGE OF APPLIED ARTS AND TECHNOLOGY - MAIN
LIBRARY
P.O. Box 4005   Phone: (519) 452-4350
London, ON N5W 5H1   Annette K. Frost, Hd., Lib.Serv.

HURON COLLEGE - SILCOX MEMORIAL LIBRARY
1349 Western Rd.   Phone: (519) 438-7224
London, ON N6G 1H3   Victoria Ripley, Chf.Libn.

LABATT BREWING COMPANY LIMITED - CENTRAL RESEARCH LI BRARY
150 Simcoe St.
Box 5050   Phone: (519) 673-5324
London, ON N6A 4M3   Marliese Lehwaldt, Hd.Libn.

LONDON FREE PRESS PUBLISHING COMPANY, LTD. - EDITORIAL LIBRARY
369 York St.   Phone: (519) 679-1111
London, ON N6A 4G1   Edythe Cusack, Libn.

LONDON PUBLIC LIBRARIES AND MUSEUMS - CFPL NEWSCLIPS
305 Queens Ave.   Phone: (519) 432-7166
London, ON N6B 3L7

LONDON PUBLIC LIBRARIES AND MUSEUMS - LONDON ROOM
305 Queens Ave.   Phone: (519) 432-7166
London, ON N6B 3L7   Glen Curnoe, Libn.

MIDDLESEX LAW ASSOCIATION - LIBRARY
Box 5600, 80 Dundas St.   Phone: (519) 679-7046
London, ON N6A 2P3   J.V. Gulliver, Libn./Adm.

ST. JOSEPH'S HOSPITAL - MEDICAL LIBRARY
268 Grosvenor St.   Phone: (519) 439-3271
London, ON N6A 4V2   Louise Lin, Coord., Lib.Serv.

ST. PETER'S SEMINARY - LIBRARY
1040 Waterloo St., N.   Phone: (519) 432-1824
London, ON N6A 3Y1   Lois Cote, Libn.

SILVERWOOD INDUSTRIES, LTD. - RESEARCH & DEVELOPMENT LIBRARY
Box 2185   Phone: (519) 672-9111
London, ON N6A 4E5   Nancy J. Kearns, Info.Dir.

SOLCAN, LTD. - LIBRARY
RR 3   Phone: (519) 473-0501
London, ON N6A 4B7   R.K. Swartman, Pres.

3M CANADA - TECHNICAL INFORMATION CENTRE
Box 5757   Phone: (519) 451-2500
London, ON N6A 4T1   Lorraine Polk, Tech.Libn.

UNIVERSITY OF WESTERN ONTARIO - CPRI LIBRARY *
Box 2460   Phone: (519) 471-2540
London, ON N6A 4G6   Asta Hansen, Libn.

UNIVERSITY OF WESTERN ONTARIO - D.B. WELDON LIBRARY -
DEPARTMENT OF SPECIAL COLLECTIONS
                                             Phone: (519) 679-6289
London, ON N6A 3K7   Beth Miller, Libn.

UNIVERSITY OF WESTERN ONTARIO - D.B. WELDON LIBRARY - REGIONAL
COLLECTION
                                             Phone: (519) 679-6213
London, ON N6A 3K7   Edward Phelps, Libn.

UNIVERSITY OF WESTERN ONTARIO - DEPARTMENT OF GEOGRAPHY - MAP
LIBRARY *
                                             Phone: (519) 679-3424
London, ON N6A 5C2   Serge A. Sauer, Map Cur.

UNIVERSITY OF WESTERN ONTARIO - ENGINEERING LIBRARY
                                             Phone: (519) 679-6119
London, ON N6A 3K7   Bogdana Brajsa, Libn.

UNIVERSITY OF WESTERN ONTARIO - FACULTY OF EDUCATION LIBRARY
Althouse College
1137 Western Rd.   Phone: (519) 679-3488
London, ON N6G 1G7   Anna Holman, Libn.

UNIVERSITY OF WESTERN ONTARIO - HEALTH SCIENCES LIBRARY
Medical Bldg.   Phone: (519) 679-3911
London, ON N6A 5C1   Larry C. Lewis, Libn.

UNIVERSITY OF WESTERN ONTARIO - LAW LIBRARY
                                             Phone: (519) 679-2857
London, ON N6A 3K7   Dr. Margaret A. Banks, Libn.

UNIVERSITY OF WESTERN ONTARIO - MUSIC LIBRARY
                                             Phone: (519) 679-2466
London, ON N6A 3K7   Merwin Lewis, Libn.

UNIVERSITY OF WESTERN ONTARIO - NATURAL SCIENCES LIBRARY
Natural Sciences Centre
1151 Richmond St.   Phone: (519) 679-6601
London, ON N6A 3K7   John Macpherson, Libn.

UNIVERSITY OF WESTERN ONTARIO - SCHOOL OF BUSINESS
ADMINISTRATION - BUSINESS LIBRARY & INFORMATION CENTRE
                                             Phone: (519) 679-3255
London, ON N6A 3K7   Alan Burk, Libn.

UNIVERSITY OF WESTERN ONTARIO - SCHOOL OF LIBRARY & INFORMATION SCIENCE - LIBRARY
Phone: (519) 679-3542
London, ON N6A 5B9
Pat Nicholls, Chf.Libn.

WESTMINSTER INSTITUTE FOR ETHICS AND HUMAN VALUES - LIBRARY
Westminster College
Phone: (519) 673-0046
London, ON N6G 2M2
Nancy H. Margolis, Libn.

DU PONT CANADA, INC. - MAITLAND WORKS LIBRARY
P.O. Box 611
Phone: (613) 348-3611
Maitland, ON K0E 1P0
H.M. Perrott, Libn.

ONTARIO - MINISTRY OF NATURAL RESOURCES - NATURAL RESOURCES LIBRARY - MAPLE
Southern Research Sta.
Phone: (416) 832-2761
Maple, ON L0J 1E0
Sandra Louet, Mgr.

HURONIA HISTORICAL PARKS - RESOURCE CENTRE
P.O. Box 160
Phone: (705) 526-7838
Midland, ON L4R 4K8
Mrs. M. Quealey, Supv., Lib.Serv.

SIMCOE COUNTY ARCHIVES
R.R. 2
Phone: (705) 726-9300
Minesing, ON L0L 1Y0
Peter P. Moran, Archv.

ABITIBI-PRICE INC. - RESEARCH CENTRE LIBRARY
Sheridan Park
Phone: (416) 822-4770
Mississauga, ON L5K 1A9
Joy A. Armstrong, Libn.

ATOMIC ENERGY OF CANADA, LTD. - ENGINEERING COMPANY LIBRARY
Sheridan Park Research Community
Phone: (416) 823-9040
Mississauga, ON L5K 1B2
Christine C. Byrne, Hd.

BEAK CONSULTANTS LTD. - LIBRARY
6870 Goreway Dr.
Phone: (416) 671-2600
Mississauga, ON L4V 1L9
Kim Rowan, Libn.

C-I-L INC. - CHEMICALS RESEARCH LABORATORY LIBRARY
2101 Hadwen Rd.
Sheridan Park
Phone: (416) 823-7160
Mississauga, ON L5K 2L3
Joan L. Leishman, Libn.

CANADA SYSTEMS GROUP - REFERENCE LIBRARY
2599 Speakman Dr.
Phone: (416) 822-5200
Mississauga, ON L5K 1B1
Janet Bycio, Libn.

CIBA-GEIGY (Canada) LTD. - PHARMACEUTICAL LIBRARY
6860 Century Ave.
Mississauga, ON L5N 2W5
Heather Dansereau, Med.Libn.

COMINCO LTD. - PRODUCT RESEARCH CENTRE LIBRARY
Sheridan Park
Phone: (416) 822-2022
Mississauga, ON L5K 1B4
Kalinka Szachlewicz, Libn.

DIVERSEY WYANDOTTE INC. - RESEARCH CENTRE LIBRARY
2645 Royal Windsor Dr.
Phone: (416) 822-3511
Mississauga, ON L5J 1L1
Mrs. M. Bennett, Sec.

DOMGLAS INC. - CORPORATE LIBRARY
2070 Hadwen Rd.
Phone: (416) 823-3860
Mississauga, ON L5K 2C9
Mary MacKinnon

DU PONT CANADA, INC. - CENTRAL LIBRARY
Streetsville Postal Sta., Box 2300
Phone: (416) 821-5781
Mississauga, ON L5M 2J4
Martha Pettit, Libn.

DU PONT CANADA, INC. - PATENT DIVISION LIBRARY
Streetsville Postal Sta., Box 2200
Phone: (416) 821-5504
Mississauga, ON L5M 2H3
Joan Leedale, Libn.

DUNLOP RESEARCH CENTRE - LIBRARY
Sheridan Park
Phone: (416) 822-4711
Mississauga, ON L5K 1Z8
Shirley A. Morrison, Libn.

DURACELL INC. - RESEARCH LIBRARY
2333 N. Sheridan Way
Sheridan Park
Mississauga, ON L5K 1A7
Irene Sillius, Lib.Techn.

GOLDER (H.Q.) & ASSOCIATES - LIBRARY †
3151 Wharton Way
Phone: (416) 625-0094
Mississauga, ON L4X 2B6
Mary Anne Smyth, Lib.Techn.

GULF CANADA LIMITED - RESEARCH & DEVELOPMENT DEPARTMENT - LIBRARY
2489 N. Sheridan Way
Sheridan Park
Phone: (416) 822-6770
Mississauga, ON L5K 1A8
Ann Neilson, Libn.

INCO METALS COMPANY - J. ROY GORDON RESEARCH LABORATORY
Sheridan Park
Phone: (416) 822-3322
Mississauga, ON L5K 1Z9
L. Green, Libn.

NCR CANADA LTD. - MIRS LIBRARY
6865 Century Ave.
Phone: (416) 826-9000
Mississauga, ON L5N 2E2
Ms. Virve M. Tremblay, MIRS Libn.

ONTARIO RESEARCH FOUNDATION - LIBRARY
Sheridan Park
Phone: (416) 822-4111
Mississauga, ON L5K 1B3
Carl K. Wei, Libn.

PEEL COUNTY BOARD OF EDUCATION - J.A. TURNER PROFESSIONAL LIBRARY
73 King St., W.
Phone: (416) 279-6010
Mississauga, ON L5B 1H5
Mr. B. Levin, Chf.Res.Off.

SHERIDAN COLLEGE OF APPLIED ARTS AND TECHNOLOGY - SCHOOL OF DESIGN - LIBRARY
1460 S. Sheridan Way
Phone: (416) 274-3685
Mississauga, ON L5H 1Z7
Cathy Zuraw, Hd.Libn.

SMITH, KLINE & FRENCH CANADA, LTD. - MEDICAL/MARKETING LIBRARY
1940 Argentia Rd.
Phone: (416) 821-2200
Mississauga, ON L5N 2V7
Janet B. Hillis, Lib.Techn.

SPERRY UNIVAC COMPUTER SYSTEMS - LIBRARY
55 City Centre Dr.
Phone: (416) 270-3030
Mississauga, ON L5B 1M4
B. Figol, Lib.Mgr.

UNITED COOPERATIVES OF ONTARIO - HARMAN LIBRARY
Sta. A, P.O. Box 527
Phone: (416) 270-3560
Mississauga, ON L5A 3A4
Helen Carnell, Libn.

XEROX RESEARCH CENTRE OF CANADA - TECHNICAL INFORMATION CENTRE
2480 Dunwin Dr.
Phone: (416) 828-6200
Mississauga, ON L5L 1J9
Betty A. Bassett, Mgr., Tech.Info.Ctr.

LENNOX AND ADDINGTON COUNTY MUSEUM - LIBRARY & ARCHIVES
97 Thomas St., E.
Box 160
Phone: (613) 354-3027
Napanee, ON K7R 3M3
Jane Foster, Dir.

ONTARIO - MINISTRY OF AGRICULTURE AND FOOD - VETERINARY SERVICES LABORATORY LIBRARY
Box 790
Phone: (705) 647-6701
New Liskeard, ON P0J 1P0

ACRES CONSULTING SERVICES, LTD. - LIBRARY
5259 Dorchester Rd.
Box 1001
Phone: (416) 354-3831
Niagara Falls, ON L2E 6W1
Mrs. A. McKay, Libn.

MOUNT CARMEL SPIRITUAL CENTER - TOELLE MEMORIAL LIBRARY
7035 Portage Rd.
Phone: (416) 356-4113
Niagara Falls, ON L2G 7B7

NIAGARA PARKS COMMISSION - SCHOOL OF HORTICULTURE - HORTICULTURAL LIBRARY
P.O. Box 150
Phone: (416) 356-8554
Niagara Falls, ON L2E 6T2
Ruth Stoner, Lib.Techn.

NORTON RESEARCH CORPORATION (Canada) LTD. - LIBRARY
8001 Daly St.
Phone: (416) 295-4311
Niagara Falls, ON L2G 6S2
Wende Cournoyea, Exec.Sec.

NIAGARA HISTORICAL SOCIETY - LIBRARY *
43 Castle Reigh St.   Phone: (416) 468-3912
Niagara on the Lake, ON L0S 1J0   Deborah Rose, Cur.

FOREST PRODUCTS ACCIDENT PREVENTION ASSOCIATION - LIBRARY
Box 270   Phone: (705) 472-4120
North Bay, ON P1B 8H2   James Nugent

NORTH BAY COLLEGE EDUCATION CENTRE - LIBRARY
Box 5001, Gormanville Rd.   Phone: (705) 474-7600
North Bay, ON P1B 8K9   J.G. Poff, Hd.Libn.

SEARLE (G.D.) & CO. OF CANADA, LIMITED - LIBRARY
400 Iroquois Shore Rd.   Phone: (416) 844-1040
Oakville, ON L6H 1M5   Marilyn Lee

SHELL CANADA LIMITED - OAKVILLE RESEARCH CENTRE - SHELL
   RESEARCH CENTRE LIBRARY
P.O. Box 2100   Phone: (416) 827-1141
Oakville, ON L6J 5C7   Mr. Lan C. Sun, Libn.

WELDING INSTITUTE OF CANADA - LIBRARY
391 Burnhamthorpe Rd. E.   Phone: (416) 487-5415
Oakville, ON L6J 6C9   Bruce Bryan, Libn.

HURONIA REGIONAL CENTRE - LIBRARY
Box 1000   Phone: (705) 326-7361
Orillia, ON L3V 6L2   Christie MacMillan, Libn.

LEACOCK (Stephen) MEMORIAL HOME - LIBRARY *
Old Brewery Bay   Phone: (705) 324-9357
Orillia, ON L3V 6K8   Jay Cody, Dir./Cur.

DURHAM COLLEGE OF APPLIED ARTS AND TECHNOLOGY - LIBRARY
Simcoe St., N.
Box 385   Phone: (416) 576-0210
Oshawa, ON L1H 7L7   Susan Barclay, Chf.Libn.

AGUDATH ISRAEL CONGREGATION - MALCA PASS MEMORIAL LIBRARY
1400 Coldrey Ave.
Ottawa, ON K1Z 7P9   Frieda Lauterman, Libn.

ALGONQUIN COLLEGE OF APPLIED ARTS & TECHNOLOGY - RESOURCE
   CENTRES †
1385 Woodroffe Ave.   Phone: (613) 725-7301
Ottawa, ON K2G 1V8   James Feeley, Dir.

ASSOCIATION OF UNIVERSITIES AND COLLEGES OF CANADA - LIBRARY
151 Slater St.   Phone: (613) 563-3670
Ottawa, ON K1P 5N1   Hazel J. Roberts, Hd.Libn.

ATOMIC ENERGY OF CANADA, LTD. - COMMERCIAL PRODUCTS LIBRARY
Sta. J, P.O. Box 6300   Phone: (613) 592-2790
Ottawa, ON K2A 3W3   Herb Fletcher, Libn.

ATOMIC ENERGY CONTROL BOARD - LIBRARY
P.O. Box 1046   Phone: (613) 995-1359
Ottawa, ON K1P 5S9   Helen Booth, Libn.

BANK OF CANADA - LIBRARY
245 Sparks St.   Phone: (613) 563-8201
Ottawa, ON K1A 0G9   Sheila Balatti, Chf.Libn.

BELL-NORTHERN RESEARCH LTD. - TECHNICAL INFORMATION CENTRE
P.O. Box 3511, Station C   Phone: (613) 596-2467
Ottawa, ON K1Y 4H7   Maureen Towaij, Mgr.

BOY SCOUTS OF CANADA - MUSEUM & ARCHIVES OF CANADIAN SCOUTING
1345 Base Line Rd.
Sta. F, Box 5151   Phone: (613) 224-5131
Ottawa, ON K2C 3G7   Patrick M.O. Evans, Cur.

BOY SCOUTS OF CANADA - NATIONAL LIBRARY
1345 Base Line Rd.
Sta. F, Box 5151   Phone: (613) 224-5131
Ottawa, ON K2C 3G7   Mrs. M. Crampton, Libn.

BREWERS ASSOCIATION OF CANADA - LIBRARY
151 Sparks St., Suite 805   Phone: (613) 232-9601
Ottawa, ON K1P 5E3

CANADA - AGRICULTURE CANADA - ANIMAL DISEASES RESEARCH
   INSTITUTE LIBRARY
Sta. H., P.O. Box 11300   Phone: (613) 998-9320
Ottawa, ON K2H 8P9

CANADA - AGRICULTURE CANADA - ANIMAL RESEARCH INSTITUTE
   LIBRARY
Genetics Bldg.   Phone: (613) 994-9719
Ottawa, ON K1A 0C6

CANADA - AGRICULTURE CANADA - ENTOMOLOGY RESEARCH LIBRARY
K.W. Neatby Bldg., Rm. 4061
Central Experimental Farm   Phone: (613) 994-9733
Ottawa, ON K1A 0C6   Ruth Sharrett, Entomology Res.Libn.

CANADA - AGRICULTURE CANADA - LIBRARIES DIVISION
Sir John Carling Bldg., Rm. 245   Phone: (613) 995-7851
Ottawa, ON K1A 0C5   M.L. Morton, Dir., Lib.Div.

CANADA - AGRICULTURE CANADA - NEATBY LIBRARY
K.W. Neatby Bldg., Rm. 3032
Central Experimental Farm   Phone: (613) 994-9657
Ottawa, ON K1A 0C6   Marcel Charette, Ck. In Charge

CANADA - AGRICULTURE CANADA - PLANT RESEARCH LIBRARY
Biosystematics Research Inst., Bldg. 49   Phone: (613) 996-1665
Ottawa, ON K1A 0C6   Eva Gavora, Libn.

CANADA - AGRICULTURE CANADA - RESEARCH STATION, OTTAWA -
   LIBRARY
                                             Phone: (613) 995-9428
Ottawa, ON K1A 0C6

CANADA - AIR POLLUTION TECHNICAL INFORMATION SECTION
APCD-EPS   Phone: (819) 997-3204
Ottawa, ON K1A 1C8   Mary Frances Laughton, Hd.

CANADA - CANADA CENTRE FOR REMOTE SENSING - TECHNICAL
   INFORMATION SERVICE
717 Belfast Rd.   Phone: (613) 995-1210
Ottawa, ON K1A 0Y7   Brian McGurrin, Hd.

CANADA - CANADIAN ADVISORY COUNCIL ON THE STATUS OF WOMEN -
   DOCUMENTATION CENTRE
Sta. B, Box 1541   Phone: (613) 995-8284
Ottawa, ON K1P 5R5   Barbara Hicks, Libn.

CANADA - CANADIAN RADIO-TELEVISION AND TELECOMMUNICATIONS
   COMMISSION - LIBRARY
                                             Phone: (819) 997-4484
Ottawa, ON K1A 0N2   Ms. M.A. Anschutz, Libn.

CANADA - CANADIAN TRANSPORT COMMISSION - LIBRARY
                                             Phone: (819) 997-7160
Ottawa, ON K1A 0N9   Marty H. Lovelock, Libn.

CANADA - CANADIAN WILDLIFE SERVICE - ONTARIO REGION LIBRARY
1725 Woodward Dr., 5th Fl.   Phone: (613) 998-4693
Ottawa, ON K1A 0E7   Katherine L. Mahoney, Libn.

CANADA - CONSUMER AND CORPORATE AFFAIRS CANADA -
   DEPARTMENTAL LIBRARY
                                             Phone: (819) 997-1632
Ottawa, ON K1A 0C9   Corinne MacLaurin, Chf.Libn.

CANADA - CONSUMER AND CORPORATE AFFAIRS CANADA - PATENT AND
   COPYRIGHT OFFICE
                                             Phone: (613) 997-2525
Ottawa, ON K1A 0C9   Wm. Berdnikoff, Hd.

CANADA - DEFENCE RESEARCH ESTABLISHMENT OTTAWA - LIBRARY
                                             Phone: (613) 596-9386
Ottawa, ON K1A 0Z4   Tina Matiisen, Hd.Info.Serv.

CANADA - DEPARTMENT OF COMMUNICATIONS - COMMUNICATIONS
  RESEARCH CENTRE LIBRARY
Sta. H., P.O. Box 11490   Phone: (613) 596-9250
Ottawa, ON K2H 8S2   Callista Kelly, Libn.

CANADA - DEPARTMENT OF COMMUNICATIONS - LIBRARY &
  INFORMATION RETRIEVAL SERVICES
300 Slater St., Rm. 1420   Phone: (613) 593-4037
Ottawa, ON K1A 0C8   Michel Granger, Chf.Libn.

CANADA - DEPARTMENT OF FINANCE - FINANCE/TREASURY BOARD
  LIBRARY
Place Bell Canada, 17 Fl.
160 Elgin St.   Phone: (613) 996-5491
Ottawa, ON K1A 0G5   Mr. T. Reid, Chf.Libn.

CANADA - DEPARTMENT OF INSURANCE - LIBRARY
140 O'Connor St., 16th Fl.
East Tower   Phone: (613) 996-5162
Ottawa, ON K1A 0H2   Luanne Larose, Lib.Techn.

CANADA - DEPARTMENT OF JUSTICE - LIBRARY
Justice Bldg.
Kent & Wellington Sts.   Phone: (613) 995-0144
Ottawa, ON K1A 0H8   Susan Geggie, Dir.Lib.Serv.

CANADA - ECONOMIC COUNCIL OF CANADA - LIBRARY
Sta. B., P.O. Box 527   Phone: (613) 993-1914
Ottawa, ON K1P 5V6   Irene Lackner, Libn.

CANADA - EMPLOYMENT & IMMIGRATION CANADA - LIBRARY
                                             Phone: (819) 994-2603
Ottawa, ON K1A 0J9   P.E. Sunder-Raj, Chf.Libn.

CANADA - ENERGY, MINES & RESOURCES CANADA - CANMET - LIBRARY
555 Booth St.   Phone: (613) 995-4132
Ottawa, ON K1A 0G1   Gloria M. Peckham, Chf.Libn.

CANADA - ENERGY, MINES & RESOURCES CANADA - EARTH PHYSICS
  BRANCH LIBRARY
1 Observatory Crescent   Phone: (613) 995-5558
Ottawa, ON K1A 0Y3   W.M. Tsang, Chf.Libn.

CANADA - ENERGY, MINES & RESOURCES CANADA - GEOGRAPHICAL
  SERVICES DIRECTORATE - MAP RESOURCE CENTRE
615 Booth St.
Ottawa, ON K1A 0E9

CANADA - ENERGY, MINES & RESOURCES CANADA - RESOURCE
  ECONOMICS LIBRARY
580 Booth St.   Phone: (613) 995-9466
Ottawa, ON K1A 0E4   F.B. Scollie, Chf.Libn.

CANADA - ENERGY, MINES & RESOURCES CANADA - SURVEYS & MAPPING
  BRANCH - LIBRARY
615 Booth St.   Phone: (613) 995-4071
Ottawa, ON K1A 0E9   Valerie E. Hoare, Chf.Libn.

CANADA - ENERGY, MINES & RESOURCES CANADA - SURVEYS & MAPPING
  BRANCH - NATIONAL AIR PHOTO LIBRARY
615 Booth St.   Phone: (613) 995-4650
Ottawa, ON K1A 0E9   Dianne Rombough, Hd.

CANADA - ENVIRONMENT CANADA - LIBRARY SERVICES BRANCH
                                             Phone: (613) 997-1767
Ottawa, ON K1A 1C7   Mrs. A.M. Bystram, Dir., Lib.Serv.Br.

CANADA - EXTERNAL AFFAIRS CANADA - LIBRARY
Sussex Dr.   Phone: (613) 992-8733
Ottawa, ON K1A 0G2   Ruth Margaret Thompson, Dir.

CANADA - FARM CREDIT CORPORATION CANADA - LIBRARY
Sta. D, Box 2314   Phone: (613) 995-8295
Ottawa, ON K1P 6J9   Ginette Michel, Info.Off.

CANADA - FISHERIES & OCEANS - LIBRARY
240 Sparks St., 8th Fl. W.   Phone: (613) 995-9991
Ottawa, ON K1A 0E6   C.S. Boyle, Dir., Lib.Serv.

CANADA - GEOLOGICAL SURVEY OF CANADA - LIBRARY
601 Booth St., Rm. 350   Phone: (613) 995-4151
Ottawa, ON K1A 0E8   Miss A.E. Bourgeois, Hd.Lib.Serv.

CANADA - HEALTH AND WELFARE CANADA - DEPARTMENTAL LIBRARY
  SERVICES
Brooke Claxton Bldg., Rm. 374
Tunney's Pasture   Phone: (613) 992-5743
Ottawa, ON K1A 0K9   Daphne Dolan, Chf.

CANADA - HEALTH AND WELFARE CANADA - LIBRARY SERVICES
Sir F.G. Banting Research Centre, 3rd Fl., E.
Ross Ave., Tunney's Pasture   Phone: (613) 593-7603
Ottawa, ON K1A 0L2

CANADA - IMMIGRATION APPEAL BOARD - LIBRARY
116 Lisgar St.   Phone: (613) 995-6486
Ottawa, ON K1A 0K1   Philippa Wall, Hd.

CANADA - INDIAN & NORTHERN AFFAIRS CANADA - DEPARTMENTAL
  LIBRARY
Terrasses de la Chaudiere   Phone: (819) 997-0799
Ottawa, ON K1A 0H4   Kamra Ramma, Hd.Libn.

CANADA - INDUSTRY, TRADE & COMMERCE - CANADIAN GOVERNMENT
  OFFICE OF TOURISM
Tourism Reference & Data Centre
235 Queen St.   Phone: (613) 995-2754
Ottawa, ON K1A 0H6   Rae Bradford, Mgr.

CANADA - INDUSTRY, TRADE & COMMERCE - LIBRARY
235 Queen St.   Phone: (613) 992-4947
Ottawa, ON K1A 0H6   Stephan Rush, Chf.Libn.

CANADA - LABOUR CANADA - LIBRARY
                                             Phone: (819) 997-3540
Ottawa, ON K1A 0J2   V.S. MacKelvie, Chf.Libn.

CANADA - LABOUR CANADA - OCCUPATIONAL SAFETY AND HEALTH
  BRANCH - TECHNICAL RESOURCE CENTRE
                                             Phone: (819) 997-3100
Ottawa, ON K1A 0J3   John S.N. Chan, Libn.

CANADA - LABOUR RELATIONS BOARD - LIBRARY
Pearson Bldg., Tower D
Fourth Floor   Phone: (613) 995-0895
Ottawa, ON K1A 0X8   Judith Rubin, Libn.

CANADA - LAW REFORM COMMISSION OF CANADA - LIBRARY
130 Albert St., Rm. 809   Phone: (613) 995-8648
Ottawa, ON K1A 0L6   E. Irene Roy, Libn.

CANADA - LIBRARY OF PARLIAMENT
Parliament Bldgs.   Phone: (613) 995-7113
Ottawa, ON K1A 0A9   Erik J. Spicer, Parliamentary Libn.

CANADA - METRIC COMMISSION - SIM RESEARCH UNIT
240 Sparks St.   Phone: (613) 996-8584
Ottawa, ON K1A 0H5   J. Cameron, Res.Mgr.

CANADA - MINISTRY OF STATE FOR SCIENCE AND TECHNOLOGY -
  LIBRARY
270 Albert St.   Phone: (613) 992-7851
Ottawa, ON K1A 1A1   Carol P. Barton, Libn.

CANADA - MORTGAGE AND HOUSING CORPORATION - CANADIAN
  HOUSING INFORMATION CENTRE
Ground Fl., Annex, Montreal Rd.   Phone: (613) 746-4611
Ottawa, ON K1A 0P7   Monica Welch, Mgr.

CANADA - NATIONAL DEFENCE - DIRECTORATE OF HISTORY LIBRARY
National Defence Headquarters   Phone: (613) 992-7849
Ottawa, ON K1A 0K2   Dr. W.A.B. Douglas, Dir.

CANADA - NATIONAL DEFENCE - MAPPING AND CHARTING
  ESTABLISHMENT TECHNICAL LIBRARY
615 Booth St.   Phone: (613) 995-4411
Ottawa, ON K1A 0K2   Master Corporal Therien, Libn.

CANADA - NATIONAL DEFENCE - NATIONAL DEFENCE MEDICAL CENTRE - MEDICAL LIBRARY
Alta Vista Dr.
Ottawa, ON K1A 0K6
Phone: (613) 733-6600
Philip B. Allan, Med.Libn.

CANADA - NATIONAL DEFENCE - NDHQ LIBRARY
101 Colonel By Drive, 2NT
Ottawa, ON K1A 0K2
Phone: (613) 996-0831
Mr. R. Van Den Berg, Dept.Libn.

CANADA - NATIONAL DEFENCE - NDHQ TECHNICAL LIBRARY
Bldg. 155W, CFB Ottawa (N)
Ottawa, ON K1A 0K2
Phone: (613) 993-2105
L. Workman, Libn.

CANADA - NATIONAL DEFENCE - OFFICE OF THE JUDGE ADVOCATE GENERAL - LIBRARY
National Defence Headquarters
Ottawa, ON K1A 0K2
Phone: (613) 992-4813
W.J. Kenney, Law Ck.

CANADA - NATIONAL ENERGY BOARD - LIBRARY
473 Albert St., Rm. 962
Ottawa, ON K1A 0E5
Phone: (613) 996-0375
Mrs. M.J. Hurley, Mgr.

CANADA - NATIONAL FILM BOARD OF CANADA - PHOTOTHEQUE
Tunney's Pasture
Ottawa, ON K1A 0M9
Phone: (613) 593-5826
Lise Krueger, Photo Libn.

CANADA - NATIONAL GALLERY OF CANADA - LIBRARY
75 Albert St., 4th Fl.
Ottawa, ON K1A 0M8
Phone: (613) 995-6245
J.E.B. Hunter, Chf.Libn.

CANADA - NATIONAL MUSEUMS OF CANADA - CANADIAN CONSERVATION INSTITUTE LIBRARY
Ottawa, ON K1A 0M8
Phone: (613) 998-3721

CANADA - NATIONAL MUSEUMS OF CANADA - CANADIAN WAR MUSEUM - LIBRARY
330 Sussex Dr.
Ottawa, ON K1A 0M8
Phone: (613) 996-4708
Mr. L. Kosche, Libn.

CANADA - NATIONAL MUSEUMS OF CANADA - LIBRARY
Ottawa, ON K1A 0M8
Phone: (613) 998-3923
Valerie Monkhouse, Chf.Lib.Div.

CANADA - NATIONAL MUSEUMS OF CANADA - PHOTOGRAPHIC DIVISION LIBRARY
Ottawa, ON K1A 0M8
Phone: (613) 998-9433
Mr. C. Kirby

CANADA - NATIONAL RESEARCH COUNCIL - CANADA INSTITUTE FOR SCIENTIFIC AND TECHNICAL INFORMATION (CISTI)
Montreal Rd.
Ottawa, ON K1A 0S2
Phone: (613) 993-1600
Elmer V. Smith, Dir.

CANADA - NATIONAL RESEARCH COUNCIL - CISTI - AERONAUTICAL & MECHANICAL ENGINEERING BRANCH
Montreal Rd., Bldg M-2
Ottawa, ON K1A 0R6
Phone: (613) 993-2431
Louise Fletcher, Libn.

CANADA - NATIONAL RESEARCH COUNCIL - CISTI - BUILDING RESEARCH BRANCH
Montreal Rd.
Ottawa, ON K1A 0R6
Phone: (613) 993-2466
Joyce Waudby-Smith, Libn.

CANADA - NATIONAL RESEARCH COUNCIL - CISTI - CHEMISTRY BRANCH
Montreal Rd. Laboratories
Ottawa, ON K1A 0R9
Phone: (613) 993-2266
Nancy Ross, Libn.

CANADA - NATIONAL RESEARCH COUNCIL - CISTI - ELECTRICAL ENGINEERING BRANCH
Montreal Rd.
Ottawa, ON K1A 0R6
Phone: (613) 993-2006

CANADA - NATIONAL RESEARCH COUNCIL - CISTI - ENERGY BRANCH
Bldg. M-55, Montreal Rd.
Ottawa, ON K1A 0S2
Phone: (613) 993-3861

CANADA - NATIONAL RESEARCH COUNCIL - CISTI - PHYSICS BRANCH
Division of Physics, Bldg. M-36
Ottawa, ON K1A 0S1
Phone: (613) 993-2483
Mary Buskirk, Libn.

CANADA - NATIONAL RESEARCH COUNCIL - CISTI - SUSSEX BRANCH LIBRARY
100 Sussex Dr.
Ottawa, ON K1A 0R6
Phone: (613) 992-9151
Margaret Schade, Libn.

CANADA - NATIONAL RESEARCH COUNCIL - CISTI - UPLANDS BRANCH
Montreal Rd.
Ottawa, ON K1A 0R6
Phone: (613) 998-3327
Alma Gorman, Hd.

CANADA - OFFICE OF THE COMMISSIONER OF OFFICIAL LANGUAGES - LIBRARY
66 Slater St., 20th Fl.
Ottawa, ON K1A 0T8
Phone: (613) 995-7717
Beryl Hunter

CANADA - POST OFFICE DEPARTMENT - LIBRARY
Sir Alexander Campbell Bldg.
Riverside Dr.
Ottawa, ON K1A 0B1
Phone: (613) 998-4463

CANADA - PRIVY COUNCIL OFFICE - LIBRARY
Blackburn Bldg.
Ottawa, ON K1A 0A3
Phone: (613) 992-7608

CANADA - PUBLIC ARCHIVES OF CANADA - FEDERAL ARCHIVES DIVISION
395 Wellington St.
Ottawa, ON K1A 0N3
Phone: (613) 996-8507
D.L. McDonald, Dir.

CANADA - PUBLIC ARCHIVES OF CANADA - LIBRARY
395 Wellington St.
Ottawa, ON K1A 0N3
Phone: (613) 992-2669
Normand St. Pierre, Chf.Libn.

CANADA - PUBLIC ARCHIVES OF CANADA - MANUSCRIPT DIVISION
395 Wellington St.
Ottawa, ON K1A 0N3
Phone: (613) 995-8094
R.S. Gordon, Dir.

CANADA - PUBLIC ARCHIVES OF CANADA - NATIONAL ETHNIC ARCHIVES
395 Wellington St.
Ottawa, ON K1A 0N3
Phone: (613) 996-7453
Walter Neutel, Chf.

CANADA - PUBLIC ARCHIVES OF CANADA - NATL. FILM, TELEVISION & SOUND ARCHIVES - DOCUMENTATION & PUB. SERV.
395 Wellington St.
Ottawa, ON K1A 0N3
Phone: (613) 995-1311
Jana Vosikovska, Chf.

CANADA - PUBLIC ARCHIVES OF CANADA - NATIONAL MAP COLLECTION
395 Wellington St.
Ottawa, ON K1A 0N3
Phone: (613) 992-0468
Betty Kidd, Dir.

CANADA - PUBLIC SERVICE COMMISSION - LIBRARY SERVICES DIVISION
Esplanade-Laurier Bldg., Rm. 938, Tower 2
300 Laurier Ave.
Ottawa, ON K1A 0M7
Phone: (613) 996-6365
A. Campbell, Libn.

CANADA - PUBLIC SERVICE STAFF RELATIONS BOARD - LIBRARY
Sta. B, P.O. Box 1525
Ottawa, ON K1P 5V2
Phone: (613) 992-3584
Charlene Elgee, Hd. & Ref.Libn.

CANADA - PUBLIC WORKS CANADA - INFORMATION, RESEARCH & LIBRARY SERVICES
Sir Charles Tupper Bldg.
Ottawa, ON K1A 0M2
Phone: (613) 998-8350
Mr. R. Gagnon, Chf.Libn.

CANADA - PUBLIC WORKS CANADA - OFFICE OF THE DOMINION FIRE COMMISSIONER - RESOURCE CENTRE
Riverside Drive
Ottawa, ON K1A 0M2
Phone: (613) 998-4773
Mr. J.L. Novak, Fire Res.Off.

CANADA - REGIONAL ECONOMIC EXPANSION - LIBRARY
Ottawa, ON K1A 0M4
Phone: (613) 997-6074
Diane Bays, Chf.Libn.

CANADA - REVENUE CANADA - CUSTOMS & EXCISE LIBRARY
Connaught Bldg., 2nd Fl.
Ottawa, ON K1A 0L5
Phone: (613) 995-0007
Dianne L. Parsonage, Dept.Libn.

CANADA - REVENUE CANADA - CUSTOMS & EXCISE - SCIENTIFIC AND
TECHNICAL INFORMATION CENTRE
79 Bentley Ave. Phone: (613) 998-9155
Ottawa, ON K1A 0L5 Marion Boyd, Info.Serv.Techn.

CANADA - REVENUE CANADA - TAXATION LIBRARY
Head Office, 875 Heron Rd. Phone: (613) 996-9896
Ottawa, ON K1A 0L8 Lorraine Wilkinson, Chf., Lib.Serv.

CANADA SAFETY COUNCIL (CSC) - LIBRARY
1765 St. Laurent Blvd. Phone: (613) 521-6881
Ottawa, ON K1G 3V4 Joseph M. Grabetz, Libn.

CANADA - SCIENCE COUNCIL OF CANADA - LIBRARY
100 Metcalfe St. Phone: (613) 996-3818
Ottawa, ON K1P 5M1 Ms. Frances Bonney, Libn.

CANADA - SECRETARY OF STATE - TRANSLATION BUREAU -
DOCUMENTATION DIRECTORATE
Phone: (819) 997-3857
Ottawa, ON K1A 0M5 Suzanne Richer, Dir.

CANADA - SOLICITOR GENERAL CANADA - CRIMINOLOGY
DOCUMENTATION CENTRE
340 Laurier Ave. W. Phone: (613) 992-0857
Ottawa, ON K1A 0P8 Heather Moore, Chf.

CANADA - STATISTICS CANADA - LIBRARY
R.H. Coats Bldg., Tunney's Pasture Phone: (613) 992-2365
Ottawa, ON K1A 0T6 Georgia Ellis, Chf.Libn.

CANADA - SUPPLY & SERVICE CANADA - CANADIAN GOVERNMENT
EXPOSITIONS CENTRE - TECHNICAL LIBRARY
440 Coventry Rd. Phone: (613) 993-9732
Ottawa, ON K1A 0T1 Margaret T. Leahy, Libn.

CANADA - SUPREME COURT OF CANADA - LIBRARY
Supreme Court Bldg., Wellington St. Phone: (613) 995-6354
Ottawa, ON K1A 0J1 Peter Freeman, Chf.Libn.

CANADA - TAX REVIEW BOARD - TAX LIBRARY
381 Kent St. Phone: (613) 996-4762
Ottawa, ON K2P 0M1 S.R. Perrin, Spec. Projects Off.

CANADA - TELESAT CANADA - COMPANY LIBRARY
333 River Rd. Phone: (613) 746-5920
Ottawa, ON K1L 8B9 Eileen Foster, Lib.Mgr.

CANADA - TRANSPORT CANADA - LIBRARY & INFORMATION CENTRE
Place de Ville, Tower C Phone: (613) 992-4529
Ottawa, ON K1A 0N5 Serge G. Campion, Chf.Libn.

CANADA - TRANSPORT CANADA - ST. LAWRENCE SEAWAY AUTHORITY -
INFORMATION OFFICE
Place De Ville, 320 Queen St. Phone: (613) 992-3949
Ottawa, ON K1R 5A3

CANADA - VETERANS AFFAIRS CANADA - LIBRARY
284 Wellington St. Phone: (613) 593-4155
Ottawa, ON K1A 0P4 J. Cousineau, Lib.Mgr.

CANADIAN BROADCASTING CORPORATION - HEAD OFFICE LIBRARY
1500 Bronson Ave.
P.O. Box 8478 Phone: (613) 731-3111
Ottawa, ON K1G 3J5 N. Deschamps, Ref.Libn.

CANADIAN COUNCIL ON SOCIAL DEVELOPMENT - LIBRARY
Sta. C, Box 3505 Phone: (613) 728-1865
Ottawa, ON K1Y 4G1 Ms. Pat Redhead, Libn.

CANADIAN DENTAL ASSOCIATION - SYDNEY WOOD BRADLEY MEMORIAL
LIBRARY
1815 Alta Vista Dr. Phone: (613) 523-1770
Ottawa, ON K1G 3Y6 J.G. D'Aoust, D.D.S., Libn.

CANADIAN EXPORT ASSOCIATION - LIBRARY
99 Bank St., Suite 250 Phone: (613) 238-8888
Ottawa, ON K1P 6B9 J.D. Moore, Sec.

CANADIAN FILM INSTITUTE - NATIONAL SCIENCE FILM LIBRARY
75 Albert St., Suite B20 Phone: (613) 232-2495
Ottawa, ON K1P 5E7 Peter Dyson-Bonter, Dir., N.S.F.L.

CANADIAN HOSPITAL ASSOCIATION - BLACKADER LIBRARY
410 Laurier W., Suite 800 Phone: (613) 238-8005
Ottawa, ON K1R 7T6 Diane Thomson, Lib.Dir.

CANADIAN HUNGER FOUNDATION - LIBRARY SERVICE
323 Chapel St. Phone: (613) 237-0180
Ottawa, ON K1N 7Z2 Valerie Melnikoff, Info.Off.

CANADIAN LABOUR CONGRESS - LIBRARY
2841 Riverside Dr. Phone: (613) 521-3400
Ottawa, ON K1V 8X7 Dawn Dobson, Libn.

CANADIAN LAW INFORMATION COUNCIL - RESOURCE CENTRE FOR
COMPUTERS AND LAW
Place de Ville, Suite 2010
112 Kent St. Phone: (613) 236-9766
Ottawa, ON K1P 5P2 Shirley A. Lounder, Dir. of Res.

CANADIAN MEDICAL ASSOCIATION - LIBRARY
1867 Alta Vista Dr.
P.O. Box 8650 Phone: (613) 731-9331
Ottawa, ON K1G 0G8 Kathleen Beaudoin, Libn.

CANADIAN NURSES ASSOCIATION - HELEN K. MUSSALLEM LIBRARY
50 The Driveway Phone: (613) 237-2133
Ottawa, ON K2P 1E2 Linda Solomon Shiff, Libn.

CANADIAN TEACHERS' FEDERATION - GEORGE G. CROSKERY MEMORIAL
LIBRARY
110 Argyle Ave. Phone: (613) 232-1505
Ottawa, ON K2P 1B4 Geraldine Channon, Dir.Res. & Info.Serv

CANADIAN WILDLIFE FEDERATION - REFERENCE LIBRARY &
INFORMATION CENTRE
1673 Carling Ave. Phone: (613) 725-2191
Ottawa, ON K2A 1C4 Luba Mycio, Pub. Affairs

CANADIAN WOOD COUNCIL - LIBRARY
85 Albert St., Suite 800 Phone: (613) 235-7221
Ottawa, ON K1P 6A4 D.H. Wilson, Dir. of Educ.

CARLETON COUNTY LAW LIBRARY
Court House, 2 Daly Ave. Phone: (613) 233-7386
Ottawa, ON K1N 6E2 Wanda T. Walsh, Libn.

CARLETON UNIVERSITY - MACODRUM LIBRARY - MAP LIBRARY
D299 Loeb Bldg., Colonel By Drive Phone: (613) 231-4392
Ottawa, ON K1S 5B6 Barbara E. Farrell, Map Libn.

CARLETON UNIVERSITY - NORMAN PATERSON SCHOOL OF
INTERNATIONAL AFFAIRS - RESOURCE CENTRE
Colonel By Drive Phone: (613) 231-7182
Ottawa, ON K1B 5B6 Jane Beaumont, Coord.

CHILDREN'S HOSPITAL OF EASTERN ONTARIO - MEDICAL LIBRARY
401 Smyth Rd. Phone: (613) 737-2206
Ottawa, ON K1H 8L1 Margaret P.J. Taylor, Dir., Lib.Serv.

COLLEGE DOMINICAIN DE PHILOSOPHIE ET DE THEOLOGIE -
BIBLIOTHEQUE
96 Empress Ave. Phone: (613) 233-5696
Ottawa, ON K1R 7G2 Jean-Jacques Robillard, Chf.Libn./Info.Dir.

CONFERENCE BOARD OF CANADA - LIBRARY & INFORMATION CENTER
25 McArthur Rd., Suite 100 Phone: (613) 746-1261
Ottawa, ON K1L 6R3 Diane Lutz, Dir., Info.Serv.

ELDORADO NUCLEAR, LTD. - RESEARCH & DEVELOPMENT LIBRARY
400-255 Albert St. Phone: (613) 238-5222
Ottawa, ON K1P 6A9 Mary Cochrane, Libn.

EXPORT DEVELOPMENT CORPORATION - LIBRARY
110 O'Connor St.
Box 655 Phone: (613) 237-2570
Ottawa, ON K1P 5T9 Ann James, Libn.

FORINTEK CANADA CORPORATION - EASTERN FOREST PRODUCTS
    LABORATORY - LIBRARY
800 Montreal Rd.   Phone: (613) 744-0963
Ottawa, ON K1G 3Z5   Marjorie Wickens, Libn.

GOETHE INSTITUTE OTTAWA - GERMAN CULTURAL CENTRE - LIBRARY
300 Slater St.   Phone: (613) 235-5124
Ottawa, ON K1P 6A6   Dr. Wolfgang Kort, Dir.

INSTITUT CANADIEN-FRANCAIS D'OTTAWA - LIBRARY
316 Dalhousie St.   Phone: (613) 234-1288
Ottawa, ON K1N 7E7   Yves Franche, Libn.

INTERNATIONAL COMMUNICATION AGENCY, UNITED STATES OF
    AMERICA - LIBRARY SERVICE
150 Wellington St., 3rd Fl.   Phone: (613) 238-5045
Ottawa, ON K1P 5A4   Margaret Dohan, Libn.

INTERNATIONAL DEVELOPMENT RESEARCH CENTRE - LIBRARY
Box 8500   Phone: (613) 996-2321
Ottawa, ON K1G 3H9   Martha Stone, Act. Centre Libn.

INTERNATIONAL JOINT COMMISSION - LIBRARY
100 Metcalfe St., 18th Fl.   Phone: (613) 995-2984
Ottawa, ON K1P 5M1   C.T. Ferguson, Asst.Sec.

JEWISH COMMUNITY CENTRE - LIBRARY
151 Chapel St.   Phone: (613) 232-7306
Ottawa, ON K1N 7Y2   Miriam Paghis, Libn.

LE DROIT - CENTRE DE DOCUMENTATION
375, Rue Rideau   Phone: (613) 237-3050
Ottawa, ON K1N 5Y7   Alice Mimeault, Documentaliste

METROPOLITAN LIFE INSURANCE COMPANY - LIBRARY
99 Bank St.   Phone: (613) 231-3531
Ottawa, ON K1P 5A3   Marjorie A. Purvis, Commun.Res.Supv.

NATIONAL LIBRARY OF CANADA
395 Wellington St.   Phone: (613) 995-9481
Ottawa, ON K1A 0N4   Dr. J.G. Sylvestre, Natl.Libn.

NATIONAL LIBRARY OF CANADA - CANADIAN INDIAN RIGHTS COLLECTION
395 Wellington St.   Phone: (613) 995-9481
Ottawa, ON K1A 0N4   Denise Dufour, Ref.Asst.

NATIONAL LIBRARY OF CANADA - COMPUTER-BASED REFERENCE
    SERVICES
395 Wellington   Phone: (613) 992-5190
Ottawa, ON K1A 0N4   Helen Rogers, Chf.

NATIONAL LIBRARY OF CANADA - LIBRARY DOCUMENTATION CENTRE
395 Wellington   Phone: (613) 995-8717
Ottawa, ON K1A 0N4   Beryl L. Anderson, Chf.

NATIONAL LIBRARY OF CANADA - MULTILINGUAL BIBLIOSERVICE
        Phone: (819) 997-9930
Ottawa, ON K1A 0N4   Marie F. Zielinska, Chf.

NATIONAL LIBRARY OF CANADA - MUSIC DIVISION
395 Wellington   Phone: (613) 996-3377
Ottawa, ON K1A 0N4   Dr. Helmut Kallmann, Chf.

NATIONAL LIBRARY OF CANADA - NEWSPAPER DIVISION
395 Wellington   Phone: (613) 996-3515
Ottawa, ON K1A 0N4   Lois Burrell, Chf.

NATIONAL LIBRARY OF CANADA - OFFICIAL PUBLICATIONS DIVISION
395 Wellington   Phone: (613) 996-3842
Ottawa, ON K1A 0N4   Mr. J. Lariviere, Chf.

NATIONAL LIBRARY OF CANADA - RARE BOOKS AND MANUSCRIPTS
    DIVISION
395 Wellington   Phone: (613) 996-1318
Ottawa, ON K1A 0N4   Liana Van der Bellen, Chf.

NATIONAL LIBRARY OF CANADA - REFERENCE AND BIBLIOGRAPHY
    SECTION
395 Wellington   Phone: (613) 995-9481
Ottawa, ON K1A 0N4   Ursula Schultz, Act.Hd.

NAVY LEAGUE OF CANADA - NATIONAL OFFICE - LIBRARY
4 Queen Elizabeth Dr.   Phone: (613) 232-2784
Ottawa, ON K2P 2H9   F.B. Caldwell, Dir. of Programmes

OBLATE FATHERS - BIBLIOTHEQUE DESCHATELETS
175 Main   Phone: (613) 237-0580
Ottawa, ON K1S 1C3   Leo Laberge, Dir.

OTTAWA CITIZEN - LIBRARY
1101 Baxter Rd.
Box 5020   Phone: (613) 829-9100
Ottawa, ON K2C 3M4   Steven Proulx, Chf.Libn.

OTTAWA CIVIC HOSPITAL - DR. GEORGE S. WILLIAMSON HEALTH
    SCIENCES LIBRARY
1053 Carling Ave.   Phone: (613) 725-4450
Ottawa, ON K1Y 4E9   Mabel C. Brown, Dir., Lib.Serv.

OTTAWA GENERAL HOSPITAL - MEDICAL LIBRARY †
501 Smyth Rd.   Phone: (613) 737-8530
Ottawa, ON K1H 8L6   Cecile Fournier, Libn.

OTTAWA PUBLIC LIBRARY - OTTAWA ROOM
120 Metcalfe St.
Ottawa, ON K1P 5M2

RIVERSIDE HOSPITAL - SCOBIE MEMORIAL LIBRARY
1967 Riverside Dr.   Phone: (613) 731-6710
Ottawa, ON K1H 7W9   Mrs. W.N. White, Libn.

ROADS AND TRANSPORTATION ASSOCIATION OF CANADA - TECHNICAL
    INFORMATION SERVICE
1765 St. Laurent Blvd.   Phone: (613) 521-4052
Ottawa, ON K1G 3V4   Mrs. Francoise Carriere, Tech.Info.Off.

ROYAL CANADIAN MOUNTED POLICE - LAW ENFORCEMENT REFERENCE
    CENTRE
1200 Alta Vista Dr.   Phone: (613) 993-3225
Ottawa, ON K1A 0R2   N. Grattan Garrett, Libn.

ROYAL SOCIETY OF CANADA - LIBRARY
344 Wellington St.   Phone: (613) 992-3468
Ottawa, ON K1A 0N4   E.H.P. Garneau, Exec.Sec.

ST. VINCENT HOSPITAL - LIBRARY †
60 Cambridge St.   Phone: (613) 233-4041
Ottawa, ON K1R 7A5   Line Crete, Lib.Techn.

SPORT INFORMATION RESOURCE CENTRE
333 River Rd.   Phone: (613) 746-5357
Ottawa, ON K1L 8B9   Gilles Chiasson, Mgr.

STANDARDS COUNCIL OF CANADA - STANDARDS INFORMATION DIVISION
350 Sparks St.   Phone: (613) 238-3222
Ottawa, ON K1R 7S8   M. Crainey, Mgr.

TRAFFIC INJURY RESEARCH FOUNDATION OF CANADA - LIBRARY
171 Nepean St., 6th Fl.   Phone: (613) 238-5235
Ottawa, ON K2P 0B4

TRANSCANADA TELEPHONE SYSTEM - INFORMATION CENTRE
410 Laurier St. W.   Phone: (613) 560-3953
Ottawa, ON K1P 6H5   Brenda Schroh, Info.Spec.

UNIVERSITE ST-PAUL D'OTTAWA - BIBLIOTHEQUE
223 Main   Phone: (613) 236-1393
Ottawa, ON K1S 1C4   Gaston Rioux, O.M.I., Chf.Libn.

UNIVERSITY OF OTTAWA - INSTITUTE FOR INTERNATIONAL
    COOPERATION - DOCUMENTATION CENTRE
14 Henderson   Phone: (613) 231-4240
Ottawa, ON K1N 6N5   William D. Ward, Coord.

UNIVERSITY OF OTTAWA - LAW LIBRARY
Fauteux Hall, 57 Copernicus St.   Phone: (613) 231-4943
Ottawa, ON K1N 6N5   Jules Lariviere, Libn.

GEOGRAPHIC

UNIVERSITY OF OTTAWA - MAP LIBRARY
Morisset Library
65 Hastey St., Rm. 353   Phone: (613) 231-6830
Ottawa, ON K1N 9A5   Aileen Desbarats, Hd.

UNIVERSITY OF OTTAWA - MORISSET LIBRARY
65 Hastey St.   Phone: (613) 231-6880
Ottawa, ON K1N 9A5   Yvon Richer, Univ.Chf.Libn.

UNIVERSITY OF OTTAWA - MUSIC LIBRARY
One Stewart St.   Phone: (613) 231-5717
Ottawa, ON K1N 6H7   Debra Begg, Libn.

UNIVERSITY OF OTTAWA - SCHOOL OF NURSING LIBRARY
Colonel By Bldg., 770 King Edward   Phone: (613) 231-3218
Ottawa, ON K1J 7X8   Myra Owen, Libn.

UNIVERSITY OF OTTAWA - TEACHER EDUCATION LIBRARY
651 Cumberland St.   Phone: (613) 231-5986
Ottawa, ON K2P 1L3   Jan Kolaczek, Libn.

UNIVERSITY OF OTTAWA - VANIER MEDICAL, SCIENCE & ENGINEERING
    LIBRARY
11 Somerset St., E.   Phone: (613) 231-2324
Ottawa, ON K1N 9A4   Dr. David Holmes, Dir.

VANIER INSTITUTE OF THE FAMILY - RESOURCE & INFORMATION CENTRE
151 Slater St., Suite 207   Phone: (613) 232-7115
Ottawa, ON K1P 5H3   Susan L. Campbell, Libn./Res.

NORWICH-EATON - FILM LIBRARY
Box 2005   Phone: (519) 442-6361
Paris, ON N3L 3T8   Sharon Godden, Adm.Supv.

CANADIAN GENERAL ELECTRIC COMPANY, LTD. - ENGINEERING LIBRARY
107 Park St., N.   Phone: (705) 742-7711
Peterborough, ON K9J 7B5   Leida Madisso, Act.Libn.

SIR SANFORD FLEMING COLLEGE OF APPLIED ARTS & TECHNOLOGY -
    LIBRARIES
Brealey Dr.   Phone: (705) 743-5610
Peterborough, ON K9J 7B1   Janice Coughlin, Lib.Supv.

PRINCE EDWARD HEIGHTS - RESIDENT RECORDS LIBRARY
Box 440   Phone: (613) 476-2104
Picton, ON K0K 2T0   Deborah Norton, Health Rec.Adm.

CANADIAN THOROUGHBRED HORSE SOCIETY - LIBRARY
Box 172   Phone: (416) 675-3602
Rexdale, ON M9W 5L1   D.M. Amos, Mgr.

ETOBICOKE GENERAL HOSPITAL - MEDICAL LIBRARY
101 Humber College Blvd.   Phone: (416) 744-3334
Rexdale, ON M9V 1R8   Joyce Gitt, Lib.Techn.

GARRETT MANUFACTURING, LTD. - ENGINEERING LIBRARY
255 Attwell Dr.   Phone: (416) 675-1411
Rexdale, ON M9W 5B8   Louis J. Hale, Standards Engr.

HUMBER COLLEGE OF APPLIED ARTS & TECHNOLOGY - LIBRARY
205 Humber College Blvd.   Phone: (416) 675-3111
Rexdale, ON M9W 5L7   Audrey MacLellan, Chf.Libn.

THISTLETOWN REGIONAL CENTRE - LIBRARY
51 Panorama Court   Phone: (416) 741-1210
Rexdale, ON M9V 4L8   Priscilla Wagner, Libn.

UNIVERSITY OF TORONTO - DAVID DUNLAP OBSERVATORY - LIBRARY
P.O. Box 360   Phone: (416) 884-2112
Richmond Hill, ON L4C 4Y6   Lynda Colbeck, Libn.

RIDGETOWN COLLEGE OF AGRICULTURAL TECHNOLOGY - LIBRARY
                                                Phone: (519) 674-5456
Ridgetown, ON N0P 2C0   Mrs. I. R. Roadhouse, Libn.

BROCK UNIVERSITY - DEPARTMENT OF GEOGRAPHY - MAP LIBRARY
Decew Campus   Phone: (416) 684-7201
St. Catharines, ON L2S 3A1   Olga Slachta, Map Libn.

RODMAN HALL ARTS CENTRE - ART LIBRARY
109 St. Paul Crescent   Phone: (416) 684-2925
St. Catharines, ON L2S 1M3   Barbara Todd, Educ.Off.

ST. CATHARINES HISTORICAL MUSEUM - LIBRARY
343 Merritt St.   Phone: (416) 227-2962
St. Catharines, ON L2T 1K7   Mr. Arden Phair, Adm./Cur.

SHAVER HOSPITAL FOR CHEST DISEASES - HEALTH SCIENCES LIBRARY
541 Glenridge Ave.   Phone: (416) 685-1381
St. Catharines, ON L2R 6S5   Ruth Prince, Dir.

ST. THOMAS PSYCHIATRIC HOSPITAL - LIBRARY SERVICES
Box 2004   Phone: (519) 631-8510
St. Thomas, ON N5P 3V9   Iris Becker-Zawadowski, Libn.

DOW CHEMICAL OF CANADA, LTD. - LIBRARY
P.O. Box 1012   Phone: (519) 339-3663
Sarnia, ON N7T 7K7   Barbara R. Buchanan, Libn.

IMPERIAL OIL, LTD. - RESEARCH TECHNICAL INFORMATION CENTRE
Box 3022   Phone: (519) 339-2471
Sarnia, ON N7T 7M1   N.J. Gaspar, Hd., Info.Serv.

POLYSAR, LTD. - INFORMATION CENTRE
Vidal St., S.   Phone: (519) 337-8251
Sarnia, ON N7T 7M2   Dorothy J. Clarkson, Supv.

CANADA - CANADIAN FORESTRY SERVICE - GREAT LAKES FOREST
    RESEARCH CENTRE - LIBRARY
P.O. Box 490   Phone: (705) 949-9461
Sault Ste. Marie, ON P6A 5M7   Sandra Burt, Libn.

CANADA - FISHERIES & OCEANS - SEA LAMPREY CONTROL CENTRE -
    LIBRARY
Huron St., Ship Canal P.O.   Phone: (705) 949-1102
Sault Ste. Marie, ON P6A 1P0   B.G.H. Johnson, Biologist

GENERAL HOSPITAL - HEALTH SCIENCES LIBRARY
941 Queen St. E.   Phone: (705) 254-5181
Sault Ste. Marie, ON P6A 2B8   Kathy You, Libn.

CANADA - HEALTH AND WELFARE CANADA - HEALTH PROTECTION
    BRANCH - TORONTO REGIONAL LIBRARY
2301 Midland Ave.   Phone: (416) 291-4231
Scarborough, ON M1P 4R7   S. Brockhurst, Lib.Techn.

CENTENNIAL COLLEGE OF APPLIED ARTS & TECHNOLOGY - ASHTONBEE
    CAMPUS RESOURCE CENTRE
P.O. Box 631, Sta. A   Phone: (416) 694-3241
Scarborough, ON M1K 5E9   Wendy Scott, Campus Libn.

CENTENNIAL COLLEGE OF APPLIED ARTS & TECHNOLOGY - EAST YORK
    CAMPUS RESOURCE CENTRE
P.O. Box 631, Sta. A   Phone: (416) 469-5981
Scarborough, ON M1K 5E9   Ron Wood, Campus Libn.

CENTENNIAL COLLEGE OF APPLIED ARTS & TECHNOLOGY - PROGRESS
    CAMPUS RESOURCE CENTRE
Sta. A, P.O. Box 631   Phone: (416) 439-7180
Scarborough, ON M1K 5E9   Judy Downs, Campus Libn.

CENTENNIAL COLLEGE OF APPLIED ARTS & TECHNOLOGY - WARDEN
    WOODS CAMPUS RESOURCE CENTRE
Sta. A, P.O. Box 631   Phone: (416) 694-3241
Scarborough, ON M1K 5E9   Annetta Turner, Campus Libn.

CONSUMERS' GAS COMPANY - LIBRARY SERVICES
P.O. Box 650   Phone: (416) 492-5490
Scarborough, ON M1K 5E3   Donna M. Ivey, Supv., Lib.Serv.

MASARYK MEMORIAL INSTITUTE INC. - LIBRARY
450 Scarborough Golf Club Rd.
Scarborough, ON M1G 1H1

ST. AUGUSTINE'S SEMINARY - LIBRARY
2661 Kingston Rd.   Phone: (416) 261-7207
Scarborough, ON M1M 1M3   Sr. Madeline Connolly, Libn.

SCARBOROUGH BOARD OF EDUCATION - A.B. PATTERSON PROFESSIONAL LIBRARY
140 Borough Dr., Level 2 Phone: (416) 296-7515
Scarborough, ON M1P 4N6 MaryLu Brennan, Supv.

SCARBOROUGH GENERAL HOSPITAL - HEALTH SCIENCES LIBRARY
3050 Lawrence Ave., E. Phone: (416) 438-2911
Scarborough, ON M1P 2V5 Anne Kubjas, Health Sci.Libn.

SCARBOROUGH PUBLIC LIBRARY - FILM SERVICES
Campbell District Library
496 Birchmount Rd. Phone: (416) 698-1191
Scarborough, ON M1K 1N8 K. Elder, Film Coord.

SCARBOROUGH RESOURCE CENTRE
Scarborough Civic Centre
150 Borough Dr. Phone: (416) 438-7215
Scarborough, ON M1P 4N7 Dave Hawkins, Mgr.

WARNER-LAMBERT CANADA, LTD. - REFERENCE LIBRARY
2200 Eglinton Ave., E. Phone: (416) 750-2360
Scarborough, ON M1K 5C9 Edna Allen, Ref.Libn.

WARNER-LAMBERT CANADA, LTD. - TECHNICAL LIBRARY
2200 Eglinton Ave., E. Phone: (416) 750-2402
Scarborough, ON M1K 5C9 Susan Underdown, Tech.Libn.

GALLERY/STRATFORD - JOHN MARTIN LIBRARY
54 Romeo St. Phone: (519) 271-5271
Stratford, ON N5A 4S9 Bruce White, Coord., Educ. & Ext.

CAMBRIAN COLLEGE OF APPLIED ARTS AND TECHNOLOGY - LIBRARY *
1400 Barrydowne Rd., Station A Phone: (705) 566-8101
Sudbury, ON P3A 3V8 Bernard Bregaint, Mgr., Lib.Serv.

LAURENTIAN HOSPITAL - MEDICAL LIBRARY
41 Ramsey Lake Rd. Phone: (705) 522-2200
Sudbury, ON P3E 5J1 Simone Hamilton, Supv.

LAURENTIAN UNIVERSITY - MAIN LIBRARY
Ramsey Lake Rd. Phone: (705) 675-1151
Sudbury, ON P3E 2C6 Andrzej H. Mrozewski, Chf.Libn.

LAURENTIAN UNIVERSITY - SCHOOL OF EDUCATION - LIBRARY
Ramsey Lake Rd. Phone: (705) 675-1151
Sudbury, ON P3E 2C6 Lionel Bonin, Libn.

LAURENTIAN UNIVERSITY - SCIENCE AND ENGINEERING LIBRARY
Ramsey Lake Rd. Phone: (705) 675-1151
Sudbury, ON P3E 2C6 Robert M. Wilson, Sci. & Engr.Libn.

ONTARIO - MINISTRY OF EDUCATION - EDUCATION CENTER LIBRARY
199 Larch St., 7th Fl. Phone: (705) 566-3480
Sudbury, ON P3E 5P9 George Whalen, Libn.

SUDBURY GENERAL HOSPITAL - HOSPITAL LIBRARY
700 Paris St., Station B Phone: (705) 674-3181
Sudbury, ON P3E 3B5 D.M. Hawryliuk, Libn.

UNIVERSITY OF SUDBURY - ARCHIVES *
Phone: (705) 673-5661
Sudbury, ON P3E 2C6 Robert Toupin, Dir.

UNIVERSITY OF SUDBURY - LIBRARY
Phone: (705) 673-5661
Sudbury, ON P3E 2C6 Stanislaw Chojnacki, Dir. of Lib.

FALCONBRIDGE NICKEL MINES, LTD. - METALLURGICAL LABORATORIES INFORMATION SERVICES
Box 900 Phone: (416) 889-6221
Thornhill, ON L3T 4A8 Doris George, Libn.

ONTARIO PAPER COMPANY, LTD. - LIBRARY
Allanburg Rd. Phone: (416) 227-1121
Thorold, ON L2V 3Z5 Isabelle Ridgway, Libn.

CONFEDERATION COLLEGE OF APPLIED ARTS & TECHNOLOGY - RESOURCE CENTRE
Box 398 Phone: (807) 475-6241
Thunder Bay, ON P7C 4W1 C.C. Frewin, Dir.

LAKEHEAD UNIVERSITY - CHANCELLOR PATERSON LIBRARY
Oliver Rd. Phone: (807) 345-2121
Thunder Bay, ON P7B 5E1 Donald J. Sharp, Act.Chf.Libn.

LAKEHEAD UNIVERSITY - EDUCATION LIBRARY
Oliver Road Phone: (807) 345-2121
Thunder Bay, ON P7B 5E1 Mr. J. Arnot, Educ.Libn.

ROYAL COMMISSION ON THE NORTHERN ENVIRONMENT - LIBRARY
215 Red River Rd., Suite 201 Phone: (807) 345-3658
Thunder Bay, ON P7B 1A5 Jan Nelson, Act.Libn.

ST. JOSEPH'S GENERAL HOSPITAL - MEDICAL LIBRARY
P.O. Box 3251
Thunder Bay, ON P7B 5G7 Laurie Hill, Libn.

ACADEMY OF MEDICINE, TORONTO - WILLIAM BOYD LIBRARY
288 Bloor St., W. Phone: (416) 964-7088
Toronto, ON M5S 1V8 Sheila Swanson, Libn.

ACRES CONSULTING SERVICES, LTD. - TORONTO LIBRARY
480 University Ave. Phone: (416) 595-2063
Toronto, ON M5G 1V2 Elske Bosma, Libn.

ALCOHOLISM AND DRUG ADDICTION RESEARCH FOUNDATION - LIBRARY
33 Russell St. Phone: (416) 595-6144
Toronto, ON M5S 2S1 R.J. Hall, Libn.

AMES (A.E.) AND COMPANY, LTD. - LIBRARY
320 Bay St. Phone: (416) 867-4058
Toronto, ON M5H 2P7 Wilberta M. Malcom, Libn.

ANGLICAN CHURCH OF CANADA - CHURCH HOUSE LIBRARY
600 Jarvis St. Phone: (416) 924-9192
Toronto, ON M4Y 2J6 Alice Marie Hedderick, Libn.

ANGLICAN CHURCH OF CANADA - DIOCESE OF TORONTO - DIOCESAN LIBRARY & RESOURCE CENTRE †
135 Adelaide St., E. Phone: (416) 924-9121
Toronto, ON M5C 1L8 Anne Tanner, Diocesan Libn.

ANGLICAN CHURCH OF CANADA - GENERAL SYNOD ARCHIVES
600 Jarvis St. Phone: (416) 924-9192
Toronto, ON M4Y 2J6 Mrs. Terry Thompson, Archv.

ANTHROPOSOPHICAL SOCIETY IN CANADA - RUDOLPH STEINER LIBRARY
81 Lawton Blvd. Phone: (416) 488-2886
Toronto, ON M4V 1Z6 Barbara Gunther, Libn.

ANTIQUE AND CLASSIC CAR CLUB OF CANADA - LIBRARY
19 Richmond St. W., Suite 302 Phone: (416) 621-9743
Toronto, ON M5H 1Y9 Peter Weatherhead, Pubn.Chm.

ART GALLERY OF ONTARIO - AUDIO-VISUAL CENTRE
317 Dundas St. W. Phone: (416) 361-0414
Toronto, ON M5T 1G4 Catherine Goldsmith, Hd., AV Ctr.

ART GALLERY OF ONTARIO - EDWARD P. TAYLOR REFERENCE LIBRARY
317 Dundas St. W. Phone: (416) 361-0414
Toronto, ON M5T 1G4 Karen McKenzie, Hd.Libn.

ARTHRITIS SOCIETY - NATIONAL OFFICE LIBRARY
920 Yonge St., Suite 420 Phone: (416) 967-1414
Toronto, ON M4W 3J7 Joan-Mary Attwood, Libn.

ARTHUR ANDERSEN & CO. - LIBRARY
Toronto Dominion Ctr.
Box 29 Phone: (416) 366-6243
Toronto, ON M5K 1B9 Mary O'Neill, Libn.

BAKER, LOVICK, LTD. - INFORMATION RETRIEVAL CENTRE
60 Bloor St., W.
Toronto, ON M4W 3B8

BANK OF NOVA SCOTIA - LIBRARY
44 King St., W. Phone: (416) 866-6257
Toronto, ON M5H 1H1 Beverley Kent, Chf.Libn.

BECHTEL CANADA LIMITED - ENGINEERING CONSULTANTS - LIBRARY
250 Bloor St., E., 15th Fl.　　　　　　　　Phone: (416) 928-1671
Toronto, ON M4W 3K5　　　　　　　　　Elke M. Warwas, Libn.

BELL CANADA - O.R. INFORMATION RESOURCE CENTRE
393 University Ave., 6th Fl.　　　　　　　Phone: (416) 599-7096
Toronto, ON M5G 1W9　　　　　　　　　Vivian Lung, Libn.

BELL-NORTHERN RESEARCH LTD. - TECHNICAL INFORMATION CENTRE
522 University Ave.　　　　　　　　　　　Phone: (416) 598-0196
Toronto, ON M5G 1W7

BETH TZEDEC SYNAGOGUE - CONGREGATIONAL LIBRARY
1700 Bathurst St.　　　　　　　　　　　　Phone: (416) 781-3511
Toronto, ON M5P 3K3　　　　　　　　　Samuel Simchovitch, Libn.

BLAKE, CASSELS & GRAYDON - LIBRARY
Commerce Court West
P.O. Box 25　　　　　　　　　　　　　　Phone: (416) 863-2650
Toronto, ON M5L 1A9　　　　　　　　　Judith A. Smith, Libn.

BLANEY, PASTERNAK, SMELA & WATSON - LAW LIBRARY
365 Bay St., Suite 1100　　　　　　　　Phone: (416) 364-9421
Toronto, ON M5H 2V4　　　　　　　　　Arlene Levy, Libn.

BOARD OF TRADE OF METROPOLITAN TORONTO - RESOURCE CENTRE
3 First Canadian Pl.
Box 60　　　　　　　　　　　　　　　　Phone: (416) 366-6811
Toronto, ON M5X 1C1　　　　　　　　　Janis Campbell, Res.Libn.

BRINCO LIMITED - LIBRARY
20 King St. W., 10th Fl.　　　　　　　　Phone: (416) 868-6970
Toronto, ON M5H 1C4　　　　　　Deborah M. Kelly, Corp.Libn.

BUILT ENVIRONMENT COORDINATORS LIMITED - BEC INFORMATION
　　SYSTEM (BIS)
1947 Avenue Rd.　　　　　　　　　　　Phone: (416) 783-4277
Toronto, ON M5M 4A2　　　　　　　Constance Wheeler, Dir.

BUREAU OF MUNICIPAL RESEARCH - LIBRARY
73 Richmond St. W., Suite 404　　　　　Phone: (416) 363-9265
Toronto, ON M5H 2A1　　　　　　　　　Alice E. Bull, Libn.

BURNS FRY LIMITED - RESEARCH LIBRARY
1 First Canadian Place
P.O. Box 150　　　　　　　　　　　　　Phone: (416) 365-4444
Toronto, ON M5X 1H3　　　　　　　　　Ann Rait, Libn.

C-I-L PAINTS INC. - PAINT RESEARCH LABORATORY LIBRARY
1300 Castlefield Ave.　　　　　　　　　Phone: (416) 787-2411
Toronto, ON M6B 1G5　　　　　　M. Elaine Fitzpatrick, Libn.

CAMPBELL, GODFREY & LEWTAS - LIBRARY
Toronto Dominion Centre
Box 36　　　　　　　　　　　　　　　Phone: (416) 362-2401
Toronto, ON M5K 1C5　　　　　　　　Clare-Marie Lyons, Libn.

CANADA - ENVIRONMENTAL PROTECTION SERVICE - ONTARIO REGION
　　LIBRARY †
25 St. Clair Ave. E., 7th Fl.　　　　　　Phone: (416) 966-5840
Toronto, ON M6P 4B9　　　　　　Nancy L. Urbankiewicz, Libn.

CANADA LIFE ASSURANCE COMPANY - LIBRARY
330 University Ave.　　　　　　　　　　Phone: (416) 597-1456
Toronto, ON M5G 1R8　　　　　　　　Gloria F.L. Johns, Libn.

CANADA - NATIONAL DEFENCE - CANADIAN FORCES COLLEGE - KEITH
　　HODSON MEMORIAL LIBRARY †
215 Yonge Blvd.　　　　　　　　　　　Phone: (416) 484-5742
Toronto, ON M5M 3H9　　　　　　　　Mary Ash, Chf.Libn.

CANADA - NATIONAL DEFENCE - CANADIAN FORCES COLLEGE - STAFF
　　SCHOOL LIBRARY
1107 Avenue Rd.　　　　　　　　　　　Phone: (416) 484-5645
Toronto, ON M5N 2E4　　　　　Coby Oates, Techn.-In-Charge

CANADA - STATISTICS CANADA - ADVISORY SERVICES - TORONTO
　　REFERENCE CENTRE
25 St. Clair Ave., E., 10th Fl.　　　　　Phone: (416) 966-6586
Toronto, ON M4T 1M4　　　　　　Sandra McIntyre, Data Off.

CANADA WIRE AND CABLE, LTD. - TECHNICAL LIBRARY
147 Laird Dr.　　　　　　　　　　　　Phone: (416) 421-0440
Toronto, ON M4G 3W1　　　　　Dianne Crompton, Lib.Techn.

CANADIAN ASSOCIATION - LATIN AMERICA AND CARIBBEAN -
　　INFORMATION CENTRE
42 Charles St., E.　　　　　　　　　　Phone: (416) 964-6068
Toronto, ON M4Y 1T4　　　　　　　Maria A. Escriu, Libn.

CANADIAN BOOK PUBLISHERS' COUNCIL - LIBRARY
45 Charles St., E.　　　　　　　　　　Phone: (416) 964-7231
Toronto, ON M4Y 1S2

CANADIAN BROADCASTING CORPORATION - MUSIC LIBRARY
Sta. A., Box 500　　　　　　　　　　Phone: (416) 925-3311
Toronto, ON M5W 1E6　　　John P. Lawrence, Coord. Music Lib.

CANADIAN BROADCASTING CORPORATION - PROGRAM ARCHIVES (Sound)
Sta. A, Box 500　　　　　　　　　　Phone: (416) 925-3311
Toronto, ON M5W 1E6　　　　　　　Pat Kellogg, Supv.

CANADIAN BROADCASTING CORPORATION - RECORD LIBRARY †
Sta. A, Box 500　　　　　　　　　　Phone: (416) 925-3311
Toronto, ON M5W 1E6　　　　　John P. Lawrence, Coord.

CANADIAN BROADCASTING CORPORATION - REFERENCE LIBRARY
415 Yonge St.
Sta. A, Box 500　　　　　　　　　　Phone: (416) 925-3311
Toronto, ON M5W 1E6　　　　　Elizabeth Jenner, Hd.Libn.

CANADIAN BROADCASTING CORPORATION - TV CURRENT AFFAIRS
　　LIBRARY
Sta. A, Box 500　　　　　　　　　　Phone: (416) 925-3311
Toronto, ON M5W 1E6　　　　　　Cynthia Fisher, Libn.

CANADIAN COUNCIL OF CHRISTIANS AND JEWS - JOHN D. HAYES LIBRARY
　　OF HUMAN RELATIONS
49 Front St., E.　　　　　　　　　　Phone: (416) 368-8026
Toronto, ON M5E 1B3　　　　　　　Jeane Kotick, Libn.

CANADIAN CREDIT INSTITUTE - CREDIT RESEARCH AND LENDING
　　LIBRARY
931 Yonge St.
Sta. F, Box 500　　　　　　　　　　Phone: (416) 962-9911
Toronto, ON M4Y 2L8　　　　　W.J. Hambly, Registrar

CANADIAN EDUCATION ASSOCIATION - LIBRARY
252 Bloor St., W.　　　　　　　　　Phone: (416) 924-7721
Toronto, ON M5S 1V5　　　　　　　Diane Sibbett, Libn.

CANADIAN FOUNDATION FOR ECONOMIC EDUCATION - RESOURCE
　　CENTRE
252 Bloor St. W., Suite 560　　　　　Phone: (416) 968-2236
Toronto, ON M5S 1V5　　　Judith Jackson, Resource Ctr.Dir.

CANADIAN GAY ARCHIVES - LIBRARY
Sta. A, Box 639　　　　　　　　　　Phone: (416) 863-6320
Toronto, ON M5W 1G2　　　James A. Fraser, Collective Member

CANADIAN GENERAL ELECTRIC COMPANY, LTD. - CORPORATE
　　INFORMATION CENTRE
Commerce Court Postal Station
P.O. Box 417　　　　　　　　　　　Phone: (416) 862-5598
Toronto, ON M5L 1J2　　　　　　Norman Cheesman, Mgr.

CANADIAN HEARING SOCIETY - LIBRARY
60 Bedford Rd.　　　　　　　　　　Phone: (416) 964-9595
Toronto, ON M5R 2K2　　　　　　　Dorothy Scott, Libn.

CANADIAN IMPERIAL BANK OF COMMERCE - INFORMATION CENTRE
Head Office - Commerce Court　　　　Phone: (416) 862-3053
Toronto, ON M5L 1A2　　　　　　　Jane Cooney, Mgr.

CANADIAN INSTITUTE OF INTERNATIONAL AFFAIRS - LIBRARY
15 King's College Circle　　　　　　Phone: (416) 979-1851
Toronto, ON M5S 2V9　　　　　　Jane R. Barrett, Libn.

GEOGRAPHIC

GEOGRAPHIC

CANADIAN JEWELLERS INSTITUTE - LIBRARY
100 Front St. W.
Phone: (416) 368-8372
Toronto, ON M5J 1E3
Betty Smith, Ck.

CANADIAN MEMORIAL CHIROPRACTIC COLLEGE - C.C. CLEMMER LIBRARY
1900 Bayview Ave.
Phone: (416) 482-2340
Toronto, ON M4G 3E6
J. Claire Callaghan, Dir.

CANADIAN MENTAL HEALTH ASSOCIATION - LIBRARY
2160 Yonge St., 3rd Fl.
Phone: (416) 484-7750
Toronto, ON M4S 2Z3

CANADIAN MUSIC CENTRE - LIBRARY
1263 Bay St.
Phone: (416) 961-6601
Toronto, ON M5R 2C1
H.A. Mutsaers, Libn.

CANADIAN NATIONAL INSTITUTE FOR THE BLIND - NATIONAL LIBRARY
   SERVICES
1929 Bayview Ave.
Phone: (416) 486-2579
Toronto, ON M4G 3E8
Francoise Hebert, Exec.Dir.

CANADIAN NATIONAL RAILWAYS - CANADIAN NATIONAL
   TELECOMMUNICATIONS - GREAT LAKES REGION LIBRARY †
151 Front St., W., Rm. 342
Phone: (416) 860-2418
Toronto, ON M5J 1G1
Shirley K. Smith, Libn.

CANADIAN NUCLEAR ASSOCIATION - CNA LIBRARY
111 Elizabeth St., 11th Fl.
Phone: (416) 977-6152
Toronto, ON M5G 1P7
David McArthur, Libn.

CANADIAN PARAPLEGIC ASSOCIATION - LIBRARY
520 Sutherland Dr.
Phone: (416) 422-5640
Toronto, ON M4G 3V9
Peter Bernauer, Libn./Info.Off.

CANADIAN PRESS - LIBRARY
36 King St., E.
Phone: (416) 364-0321
Toronto, ON M5C 2L9
Elizabeth Shewan, Libn.

CANADIAN RED CROSS SOCIETY - LIBRARY
95 Wellesley St., E.
Phone: (416) 923-6692
Toronto, ON M4Y 1H6
Mrs. C. Pepper, Libn.

CANADIAN REHABILITATION COUNCIL FOR THE DISABLED - CRCD
   RESOURCE CENTRE
One Yonge St., Suite 2110
Phone: (416) 862-0340
Toronto, ON M5E 1E8
Maureen Vasey, Dir., Info.Serv.

CANADIAN RESTAURANT & FOODSERVICES ASSOCIATION - RESOURCE
   CENTRE
80 Bloor St. W., Suite 904
Phone: (416) 923-8416
Toronto, ON M5S 2V1
Joyce Reynolds, Info.Spec.

CANADIAN STANDARDS ASSOCIATION - INFORMATION CENTRE
178 Rexdale Blvd.
Phone: (416) 744-4058
Toronto, ON M9W 1R3
Brenda M. Esson, Mgr.Info.Rsrcs. Group

CANADIAN TAX FOUNDATION - LIBRARY
130 Adelaide St., W.
Phone: (416) 593-4657
Toronto, ON M5H 3P5
Marjorie Robinson, Libn.

CANADIAN TROTTING ASSOCIATION - STANDARDBRED CANADA LIBRARY
233 Evans Ave.
Phone: (416) 252-3565
Toronto, ON M8Z 1J6
Margaret Neal, Coord. & Info.Spec.

CENTRAL BAPTIST SEMINARY - DR. W. GORDON BROWN MEMORIAL
   LIBRARY
95 Jonesville Crescent
Phone: (416) 752-1976
Toronto, ON M4A 1H3
Ruth L. Kraulis, Libn.

CENTRE FOR CHRISTIAN STUDIES - LIBRARY †
77 Charles St., W.
Phone: (416) 923-1168
Toronto, ON M5S 1K5
Mrs. Elfa M. Davidson, Libn.

CITADEL GENERAL ASSURANCE COMPANY - INFORMATION CENTRE
1075 Bay St.
Phone: (416) 928-8539
Toronto, ON M5S 2W5
Christine Macdonald, Libn.

CLARKE INSTITUTE OF PSYCHIATRY - FARRAR LIBRARY *
250 College St.
Phone: (416) 979-2221
Toronto, ON M5T 1R8
Ms. D. Stewardson, Libn./Archv.

CLARKSON, GORDON /WOODS, GORDON - LIBRARY
Box 251, Toronto Dominion Centre
Phone: (416) 864-1234
Toronto, ON M5K 1J7
Mrs. Jean Parriss, Libn.

COLLINS CANADA - TIC LIBRARY
150 Bartley Dr.
Phone: (416) 757-1101
Toronto, ON M4A 1C7
Joan Ann Hall, Libn.

CONFEDERATION LIFE INSURANCE COMPANY - LIBRARY
321 Bloor St., E.
Phone: (416) 967-8326
Toronto, ON M4W 1H1
Lynne M. Cousins, Libn.

CONSERVATION COUNCIL OF ONTARIO - LIBRARY
45 Charles St. E., 6th Fl.
Phone: (416) 961-6830
Toronto, ON M4Y 1S2
Arthur M. Timms, Exec.Dir.

CRANE (J.W.) MEMORIAL LIBRARY
351 Christie St.
Phone: (416) 537-6000
Toronto, ON M6G 3C3
Elaine DuWors, Libn.

CRAVEN FOUNDATION - AUTOMOTIVE REFERENCE LIBRARY *
760 Lawrence Ave., W.
Phone: (416) 789-3432
Toronto, ON M6A 1B8
Frank Francis, Gen.Mgr.

CROWN LIFE INSURANCE COMPANY - LAW LIBRARY
120 Bloor St., E.
Phone: (416) 928-4563
Toronto, ON M4W 1B8
Mari White, Law Libn.

CROWN LIFE INSURANCE COMPANY - LIBRARY
120 Bloor St., E.
Phone: (416) 928-4650
Toronto, ON M4W 1B8
H. Elizabeth Angus, Libn.

CURRIE, COOPERS & LYBRAND, LTD. - LIBRARY/INFORMATION CENTRE
145 King St., W.
Phone: (416) 366-1921
Toronto, ON M5H 1J8
Stephen K. Abram, Libn.

DOCTORS HOSPITAL - MEDICAL LIBRARY
45 Brunswick Ave.
Phone: (416) 923-5411
Toronto, ON M5S 2M1
Mrs. Tsai-O Wong, Libn.

EAST YORK BOARD OF EDUCATION - PROFESSIONAL LIBRARY
840 Coxwell Ave.
Phone: (416) 465-4631
Toronto, ON M4C 2V3
Martha Pluscauskas, Coord.

ECUMENICAL FORUM OF CANADA - LIBRARY
11 Madison Ave.
Phone: (416) 924-9351
Toronto, ON M5R 2S2
Ms. M. MacKinnon, Libn.

FALCONBRIDGE NICKEL MINES, LTD. - FALCONBRIDGE INFORMATION
   CENTRE
Commerce Court West
P.O. Box 40
Phone: (416) 863-7227
Toronto, ON M5L 1B4
Stewart Collett, Mgr.

FASKEN & CALVIN, BARRISTERS AND SOLICITORS - LIBRARY
Toronto Dominion Centre, Box 30
Phone: (416) 366-8381
Toronto, ON M5K 1C1
Bettina Hakala, Libn.

FINANCIAL TIMES OF CANADA - LIBRARY
920 Yonge St., Suite 500
Phone: (416) 922-1133
Toronto, ON M4W 3L5
Jane Wachna, Libn.

FOSTER ADVERTISING COMPANY, LTD. - INFORMATION CENTRE †
40 St. Clair Ave., W.
Phone: (416) 924-8090
Toronto, ON M4V 1M6
M.E. Bowen, Libn.

FRASER AND BEATTY - LIBRARY
First Canadian Place, P.O. Box 100
Phone: (416) 863-4527
Toronto, ON M5X 1B2
Joan Hudson, Libn.

GENERAL FOODS, LTD. - INFORMATION CENTRE
Terminal A, P.O. Box 4019
Phone: (416) 481-4211
Toronto, ON M5W 1J6
Carol Symon, Supv., Info.Ctr.

GEORGE BROWN COLLEGE OF APPLIED ARTS & TECHNOLOGY - ARCHIVES
Sta. B, Box 1015   Phone: (416) 967-1212
Toronto, ON M5T 2T9   John L. Hardy, Archv.

GEORGE BROWN COLLEGE OF APPLIED ARTS & TECHNOLOGY - LIBRARY
Sta. B, Box 1015   Phone: (416) 967-1212
Toronto, ON M5T 2T9   Rita L. Edwards, Dir./Lib. & AV Serv.

GLAXO CANADA, LTD. - REFERENCE LIBRARY †
1025 The Queensway   Phone: (416) 252-2281
Toronto, ON M8Z 5S6   Dr. V. Chivers Wilson, Libn.

GOETHE INSTITUTE TORONTO - LIBRARY
1067 Yonge St.   Phone: (416) 924-3327
Toronto, ON M4W 2L2   Ulla Habekost, Libn.

GOODMAN AND GOODMAN - LIBRARY
101 Richmond St., W., Suite 1500   Phone: (416) 862-1500
Toronto, ON M5H 1V5   Michele L. Miles, Libn.

GULF CANADA LIMITED - CENTRAL LIBRARY
800 Bay St.
P.O. Box 460, Station A   Phone: (416) 924-4141
Toronto, ON M5W 1E5   Wendy A. Davis, Sr.Libn.

HAWKER SIDDELEY CANADA INC. - ORENDA DIVISION - ENGINEERING
    LIBRARY
Box 6001, A.M.F.
Toronto, ON L5P 1B3

HAYHURST (F.H.) COMPANY, LTD. - MEDIA RESEARCH LIBRARY
55 Eglinton Ave., East   Phone: (416) 487-4371
Toronto, ON M4P 1G9   Ann Sargent, Libn./Media Res.Asst.

HOCKEY HALL OF FAME - LIBRARY
Exhibition Place   Phone: (416) 595-1345
Toronto, ON M6K 3C3   M.H. (Lefty) Reid, Dir. & Cur.

HOSPITAL FOR SICK CHILDREN - HOSPITAL LIBRARY
555 University Ave.   Phone: (416) 597-1500
Toronto, ON M5G 1X8   Irene Jeryn, Libn.

IMPERIAL LIFE ASSURANCE COMPANY - LIBRARY
95 St. Clair Ave., W.   Phone: (416) 923-6661
Toronto, ON M4V 1N7   P. Stewart, Libn.

IMPERIAL OIL, LTD. - BUSINESS INFORMATION CENTRE
111 St. Clair Ave., W.   Phone: (416) 924-9111
Toronto, ON M5W 1K3   Mary M. Greenwood, Mgr.

INCO METALS COMPANY - BUSINESS LIBRARY
1 First Canadian Pl.
Box 44   Phone: (416) 361-7640
Toronto, ON M5X 1C4   Cynthia M. Smith, Chf.Libn.

INCO METALS COMPANY - EXPLORATION LIBRARY
1 First Canadian Place
Box 44   Phone: (416) 361-7511
Toronto, ON M5X 1C4   Mrs. Neftalie Abrenica, Libn.

INDUSTRIAL ACCIDENT PREVENTION ASSOCIATION - LIBRARY
2 Bloor St., E.   Phone: (416) 965-8888
Toronto, ON M4W 3C2   Marion Frank, Res.Libn.

INSTITUTE OF CHARTERED ACCOUNTANTS OF ONTARIO - THE MERRILEES
    LIBRARY
69 Bloor St., E.   Phone: (416) 962-1841
Toronto, ON M4W 1B3   Theresa Wolak, Libn.

INTERGOVERNMENTAL COMMITTEE ON URBAN & REGIONAL RESEARCH
    (ICURR)
123 Edward St., Suite 625   Phone: (416) 966-5629
Toronto, ON M5G 1E2   Tanya Wanio, Info.Coord.

JEWISH PUBLIC LIBRARY OF TORONTO
22 Glen Park Ave.   Phone: (416) 781-6282
Toronto, ON M6B 2B9   Rabbi Z. Wolkenstein, Exec.Dir.

LAW SOCIETY OF UPPER CANADA - GREAT LIBRARY
Osgoode Hall, 130 Queen St., W.   Phone: (416) 362-4741
Toronto, ON M5H 2N6   Glen W. Howell, Act.Chf.Libn.

MC CARTHY AND MC CARTHY - LIBRARY
Toronto Dominion Ctr.
P.O. Box 48   Phone: (416) 362-1812
Toronto, ON M5K 1E6   Mary Percival, Libn.

MC KIM ADVERTISING, LTD. - RESEARCH SERVICES LIBRARY
Commerce Court East, P.O. Box 99   Phone: (416) 863-5471
Toronto, ON M5L 1E1

MC LEOD YOUNG WEIR LIMITED - INFORMATION CENTRE
Commercial Union Tower
Toronto-Dominion Centre, Box 433   Phone: (416) 863-7737
Toronto, ON M5K 1M2   Marie Gadula, Libn.

MC MILLAN, BINCH - LIBRARY
Royal Bank Plaza
P.O. Box 38   Phone: (416) 865-7031
Toronto, ON M5J 2J7   Judith A. Ryll, Libn.

MACLEAN-HUNTER, LTD. - LIBRARY
481 University Ave.   Phone: (416) 596-5244
Toronto, ON M5W 1A7   Marian Duncan, Lib.Mgr.

MANUFACTURERS LIFE INSURANCE COMPANY - BUSINESS LIBRARY
200 Bloor St., E.   Phone: (416) 928-4104
Toronto, ON M4W 1E5   Oriole Anderson, Libn.

MARSH & MC LENNAN - INFORMATION CENTRE
1 First Canadian Pl.
P.O. Box 58   Phone: (416) 868-2623
Toronto, ON M5X 1G2   Angela Agostino, Libn.

MASSEY COLLEGE - LIBRARY
4 Devonshire Place   Phone: (416) 978-2893
Toronto, ON M5S 2E1   Desmond G. Neill, Libn.

MERCER (William M.) LTD. - LIBRARY/INFORMATION CENTRE
1 First Canadian Pl., 56th Fl.
P.O. Box 59   Phone: (416) 868-2989
Toronto, ON M5X 1G3   Laurence Pellan, Libn.

METROPOLITAN TORONTO ASSOCIATION FOR THE MENTALLY RETARDED -
    HOWARD E. BACON MEMORIAL LIBRARY
8 Spadina Rd.   Phone: (416) 968-0650
Toronto, ON M5R 2S7   Adrienne Wykes, Lib.Asst.

METROPOLITAN TORONTO LIBRARY - AUDIO VISUAL SERVICES
789 Yonge St.   Phone: (416) 928-5185
Toronto, ON M4W 2G8   Laura Murray, AV Coord.

METROPOLITAN TORONTO LIBRARY - BIBLIOGRAPHIC CENTRE &
    INTERLOAN
789 Yonge St.   Phone: (416) 928-5182
Toronto, ON M4W 2G8   Robert H.S. Yu, Hd.

METROPOLITAN TORONTO LIBRARY - BUSINESS DEPARTMENT
789 Yonge St.   Phone: (416) 928-5256
Toronto, ON M4W 2G8   Patricia Dye, Hd.

METROPOLITAN TORONTO LIBRARY - CANADIAN HISTORY DEPARTMENT
Baldwin Room, 789 Yonge St.   Phone: (416) 928-5275
Toronto, ON M4W 2G8   Edith G. Firth, Hd.

METROPOLITAN TORONTO LIBRARY - FINE ART DEPARTMENT
789 Yonge St.   Phone: (416) 928-5214
Toronto, ON M4W 2G8   Alan Suddon, Hd.

METROPOLITAN TORONTO LIBRARY - GENERAL REFERENCE DEPARTMENT
789 Yonge St.   Phone: (416) 928-5211
Toronto, ON M4W 2G8   Anne Mack, Hd.

METROPOLITAN TORONTO LIBRARY - HISTORY DEPARTMENT
789 Yonge St.   Phone: (416) 928-5267
Toronto, ON M4W 2G8   Michael Pearson, Hd.

GEOGRAPHIC

METROPOLITAN TORONTO LIBRARY - LANGUAGES CENTRE
789 Yonge St.   Phone: (416) 928-5280
Toronto, ON M4W 2G8   Barbara Gunther, Hd.

METROPOLITAN TORONTO LIBRARY - LITERATURE DEPARTMENT
789 Yonge St.   Phone: (416) 928-5284
Toronto, ON M4W 2G8   Katherine McCook, Hd.

METROPOLITAN TORONTO LIBRARY - MUNICIPAL REFERENCE LIBRARY
City Hall, Nathan Phillips Square   Phone: (416) 928-5357
Toronto, ON M5H 2N1   Margot Hewings, Hd.

METROPOLITAN TORONTO LIBRARY - MUSIC DEPARTMENT
789 Yonge St.   Phone: (416) 928-5224
Toronto, ON M4W 2G8   Isabel Rose, Hd.

METROPOLITAN TORONTO LIBRARY - NEWSPAPER UNIT
789 Yonge St.   Phone: (416) 928-5254
Toronto, ON M4W 2G8   Alan Suddon, Hd. of Unit

METROPOLITAN TORONTO LIBRARY - SCIENCE & TECHNOLOGY
   DEPARTMENT
789 Yonge St.   Phone: (416) 928-5234
Toronto, ON M4W 2G8   Margaret Walshe, Hd.

METROPOLITAN TORONTO LIBRARY - SOCIAL SCIENCES DEPARTMENT
789 Yonge St.   Phone: (416) 928-5246
Toronto, ON M4W 2G8   Abdus Salam, Hd.

METROPOLITAN TORONTO LIBRARY - THEATRE DEPARTMENT
789 Yonge St.   Phone: (416) 928-5230
Toronto, ON M4W 2G8   Heather McCallum, Hd.

METROPOLITAN TORONTO PLANNING DEPARTMENT - LIBRARY
City Hall, 11th Fl., East Tower   Phone: (416) 367-8101
Toronto, ON M5H 2N1   Pamela J. Smith, Libn.

METROPOLITAN TORONTO SCHOOL BOARD - LIBRARY
155 College St., 3rd Fl.   Phone: (416) 598-4620
Toronto, ON M5T 1P6   Barbara Beardsley, Educ.Res.Off.

METROPOLITAN (Toronto) SEPARATE SCHOOL BOARD - PROFESSIONAL
   LIBRARY †
146 Laird Dr.   Phone: (416) 421-8950
Toronto, ON M4G 3V8   Patricia A. Berry, Chf.Libn.

MIDLAND DOHERTY, LTD. - LIBRARY
Box 25, Commercial Union Tower
Toronto Dominion Centre   Phone: (416) 361-6063
Toronto, ON M5K 1B5   Ilme Regina, Hd.

MIGRAINE FOUNDATION - LIBRARY
390 Brunswick Ave.   Phone: (416) 920-4916
Toronto, ON M5R 2Z4   David Jones, Chm., Lib.Comm.

MOUNT SINAI HOSPITAL - SIDNEY LISWOOD LIBRARY
600 University Ave.   Phone: (416) 596-4614
Toronto, ON M6S 4C6   Eleanor Hayes, Libn.

NEEDHAM, HARPER & STEERS OF CANADA, LTD. - INFORMATION SERVICES
   CENTRE
130 Adelaide St., W.   Phone: (416) 364-1492
Toronto, ON M5H 3P5   Linda Dominitz, Res.Asst.

NORANDA SALES CORPORATION, LTD. - SALES LIBRARY
Commerce Court W.
Box 45   Phone: (416) 867-7036
Toronto, ON M5L 1B6   Karen Hammond, Libn.

NORTH AMERICAN LIFE ASSURANCE COMPANY - LIBRARY *
105 Adelaide St., W.
Toronto, ON M5H 1R1

NORTHERN MINER - LIBRARY
7 Labatt Ave.   Phone: (416) 368-3481
Toronto, ON M5A 1Z1   Mrs. M. Murray, Libn.

NORTHERN PIGMENT LIMITED - TECHNICAL LIBRARY †
P.O. Box One, Station N   Phone: (416) 251-1161
Toronto, ON M8V 3S5   Duncan Wills

ONTARIO - ARCHIVES OF ONTARIO - LIBRARY
Ministry of Culture & Recreation
77 Grenville St.   Phone: (416) 965-4030
Toronto, ON M7A 2R9   Ethelyn Harlow, Libn.

ONTARIO CANCER INSTITUTE - LIBRARY
500 Sherbourne St.   Phone: (416) 924-0671
Toronto, ON M4X 1K9   Carol A. Morrison, Libn.

ONTARIO - CIVIL SERVICE COMMISSION - LIBRARY
Frost Bldg. South
Parliament Bldgs., Queen's Park   Phone: (416) 965-7096
Toronto, ON M7A 1Z5   Mary Williams, Libn.

ONTARIO COLLEGE OF ART - LIBRARY/AUDIOVISUAL CENTRE
100 McCaul St.   Phone: (416) 362-5311
Toronto, ON M5T 1W1   Ian Carr-Harris, Dir.

ONTARIO CRAFTS COUNCIL - CRAFT RESOURCE CENTRE
346 Dundas St., W.   Phone: (416) 977-3551
Toronto, ON M5T 1G5   Ted Rickard, Libn.

ONTARIO ECONOMIC COUNCIL - LIBRARY
81 Wellesley St. E.   Phone: (416) 965-4315
Toronto, ON M4Y 1H6   Ann M. Chin, Libn.

ONTARIO EDUCATIONAL COMMUNICATIONS AUTHORITY - MEDIA
   RESOURCE CENTRE
P.O. Box 200, Station Q   Phone: (416) 484-2652
Toronto, ON M4T 2T1   Cheryl Zimmerman, Chf.Libn.

ONTARIO HYDRO - LIBRARY
700 University Ave.   Phone: (416) 592-2719
Toronto, ON M5G 1X6   Doreen Taylor, Chf.Libn.

ONTARIO - LAND COMPENSATION BOARD - LIBRARY †
10 King St. East   Phone: (416) 965-6027
Toronto, ON M5C 1C3   Y. Fernandes, Sec.

ONTARIO - LEGISLATIVE ASSEMBLY - LEGISLATIVE LIBRARY RESEARCH
   AND INFORMATION SERVICES
Legislative Bldg., Queen's Park   Phone: (416) 965-4545
Toronto, ON M7A 1A2   R. Brian Land, Dir.

ONTARIO LOTTERY CORPORATION - LIBRARY
2 Bloor St. W., 24th Fl.   Phone: (416) 961-6262
Toronto, ON M4W 3H8   Suzanne Kemper, Libn.

ONTARIO MEDICAL ASSOCIATION - LIBRARY
240 St. George St.   Phone: (416) 925-3264
Toronto, ON M5R 2P4   Jan Greenwood, Libn.

ONTARIO - MINISTRY OF AGRICULTURE AND FOOD - LIBRARY
Legislative Bldgs.   Phone: (416) 965-1816
Toronto, ON M7A 2B2   Ken Sundquist, Libn.

ONTARIO - MINISTRY OF THE ATTORNEY GENERAL - JUDGES' LIBRARY *
Osgoode Hall, Queen St., W.   Phone: (416) 363-4101
Toronto, ON M5H 2N5   Anne Brown, Judges' Libn.

ONTARIO - MINISTRY OF THE ATTORNEY GENERAL - LIBRARY
18 King St. E., 3rd Fl.   Phone: (416) 965-4714
Toronto, ON M5C 1C5   Elaine Norman, Libn.

ONTARIO - MINISTRY OF COMMUNITY AND SOCIAL SERVICES - MINISTRY
   LIBRARY †
880 Bay St., 6th Fl.   Phone: (416) 965-2300
Toronto, ON M7A 1E9   Irene Shlapak, Hd.Libn.

ONTARIO - MINISTRY OF CONSUMER AND COMMERCIAL RELATIONS -
   LIBRARY
555 Yonge St., 1st Fl.   Phone: (416) 963-0200
Toronto, ON M7A 2H6   Elizabeth Morgan, Libn.

ONTARIO - MINISTRY OF CORRECTIONAL SERVICES - LIBRARY SERVICES
2001 Eglinton Ave., E.   Phone: (416) 750-3481
Toronto, ON M1L 4P1   T.J.B. Anderson, Chf.Libn.

ONTARIO - MINISTRY OF CULTURE AND RECREATION - LIBRARIES AND
   COMMUNITY INFORMATION
7th Fl., 77 Bloor St. W.   Phone: (416) 965-2696
Toronto, ON M7A 2R9   Grace Buller, Act.Dir.

ONTARIO - MINISTRY OF CULTURE AND RECREATION - LIBRARY/
   RESOURCE CENTRE
77 Bloor St. W., 9th Fl.   Phone: (416) 965-6763
Toronto, ON M7A 2R9   Mrs. M.B. Howard, Coord.

ONTARIO - MINISTRY OF CULTURE AND RECREATION - MAP LIBRARY
77 Grenville St.   Phone: (416) 965-4030
Toronto, ON M7A 2R9   John W. Fortier, Archv.

ONTARIO - MINISTRY OF CULTURE AND RECREATION - PLANNING AND
   TECHNICAL SERVICES
77 Bloor St. W., 4th Fl.   Phone: (416) 965-0322
Toronto, ON M7A 2R9   John Shipman, Tech.Res.

ONTARIO - MINISTRY OF EDUCATION - INFORMATION CENTRE
Mowat Block, 13th Fl., Queen's Park   Phone: (416) 965-1451
Toronto, ON M7A 1L2   Carol Fordyce, Mgr.

ONTARIO - MINISTRY OF ENERGY - LIBRARY †
56 Wellesley St., W., 12th Fl.   Phone: (416) 965-9175
Toronto, ON M7A 2B7   Nancy Musgrove, Libn.

ONTARIO - MINISTRY OF THE ENVIRONMENT - LIBRARY
135 St. Clair Ave., W.   Phone: (416) 965-7978
Toronto, ON M4V 1P5   N.J. McIlroy, Libn.

ONTARIO - MINISTRY OF GOVERNMENT SERVICES - TECHNICAL
   REFERENCE LIBRARY
1200 Bay St., 4th Fl.   Phone: (416) 965-2965
Toronto, ON M5R 2A5   Lori Page, Educ.Serv.Coord.

ONTARIO - MINISTRY OF HEALTH - LIBRARY
15 Overlea Blvd.   Phone: (416) 965-7881
Toronto, ON M4H 1A9   Veronica Brunka, Lib.Supv.

ONTARIO - MINISTRY OF HEALTH - PUBLIC HEALTH LABORATORIES -
   LIBRARY
Postal Terminal A, Box 9000   Phone: (416) 248-3165
Toronto, ON M5W 1R5   Doris A. Standing, Libn.

ONTARIO - MINISTRY OF HOUSING - LIBRARY
56 Wellesley St., W., 2nd Fl.   Phone: (416) 965-9720
Toronto, ON M7A 2K4   Frank Szucs, Libn.

ONTARIO - MINISTRY OF INDUSTRY AND TOURISM - INFORMATION
   CENTRE
Hearst Block, Queen's Park   Phone: (416) 965-3365
Toronto, ON M7A 2E2   Maureen Enge, Mgr.

ONTARIO - MINISTRY OF INDUSTRY AND TOURISM - PHOTOGRAPH
   LIBRARY
900 Bay St., Hearst Block, 10th Fl.
Queen's Park   Phone: (416) 965-5411
Toronto, ON M7A 2E3

ONTARIO - MINISTRY OF LABOUR - LIBRARY
400 University Ave.   Phone: (416) 965-1641
Toronto, ON M7A 1T7   Douglas Armstrong, Hd.Libn.

ONTARIO - MINISTRY OF LABOUR - ONTARIO LABOUR RELATIONS BOARD -
   LIBRARY
400 University Ave., 4th Fl.   Phone: (416) 965-0206
Toronto, ON M7A 1V4   Barbara Mathias, Libn.

ONTARIO - MINISTRY OF NATURAL RESOURCES - MINES LIBRARY
77 Grenville St.   Phone: (416) 965-1352
Toronto, ON M5S 1B3   Nancy Thurston, Libn.

ONTARIO - MINISTRY OF NATURAL RESOURCES - NATURAL RESOURCES
   LIBRARY
Whitney Block, Rm. 4540
Queen's Park   Phone: (416) 965-6319
Toronto, ON M7A 1W3   Sandra Louet, Mgr.

ONTARIO - MINISTRY OF NORTHERN AFFAIRS - LIBRARY
10 Wellesley St. E., 9th Fl.   Phone: (416) 965-7577
Toronto, ON M4Y 1G2   Glenda J. Schultz, Libn.

ONTARIO - MINISTRY OF REVENUE - LIBRARY
77 Bloor St. W., 3rd Fl.
Queen's Park   Phone: (416) 965-3892
Toronto, ON M7A 1X8   Lorna Brown, Libn.

ONTARIO - MINISTRY OF THE SOLICITOR GENERAL - CENTRE OF
   FORENSIC SCIENCES - H. WARD SMITH LIBRARY
25 Grosvenor St.   Phone: (416) 965-2561
Toronto, ON M7A 2G8   Grace B. Kopec, Libn.

ONTARIO - MINISTRY OF THE SOLICITOR GENERAL - OFFICE OF THE FIRE
   MARSHAL LIBRARY
590 Keele St., Rm. 341   Phone: (416) 965-4855
Toronto, ON M6N 4X2   Nancy Carlucci, Libn.

ONTARIO - MINISTRY OF TREASURY AND ECONOMICS - LIBRARY
   SERVICES BRANCH
Frost Bldg. North, 1st Fl.
Queen's Park   Phone: (416) 965-2314
Toronto, ON M7A 1Y7   Barbara Weatherhead, Dir.

ONTARIO NURSES ASSOCIATION - ONA LIBRARY
415 Yonge St., 14th Fl.   Phone: (416) 977-1975
Toronto, ON M5B 2E7   Kathy O'Hara, Lib.Techn.

ORTHOPAEDIC AND ARTHRITIC HOSPITAL - LIBRARY
43 Wellesley St., E.   Phone: (416) 967-8545
Toronto, ON M4Y 1H1   Sheila M. Lethbridge, Libn.

PEAT, MARWICK & PARTNERS - LIBRARY
Commerce Court West   Phone: (416) 863-3440
Toronto, ON M5L 1B2   Mrs. S.A. Layton, Libn.

POLAR GAS PROJECT - LIBRARY
Commerce Court W.
Box 90   Phone: (416) 869-2675
Toronto, ON M5L 1H3   Jennifer M. Wentworth, Libn.

PRICE WATERHOUSE - NATIONAL RESEARCH LIBRARY
Toronto Dominion Centre
P.O. Box 51   Phone: (416) 863-1133
Toronto, ON M5K 1G1   Dorothy L. Sedgwick, Libn.

PROCTOR & REDFERN, CONSULTING ENGINEERS - LIBRARY
75 Eglinton Ave., E.   Phone: (416) 486-5225
Toronto, ON M4P 1H3   Mrs. Tran Dam, Hd.Libn.

PRUDENTIAL LIFE INSURANCE COMPANY OF AMERICA - BUSINESS
   LIBRARY
King & Yonge Sts.   Phone: (416) 366-6971
Toronto, ON M5H 1B7   J. Ireland, Libn.

QUEEN STREET MENTAL HEALTH CENTRE - HEALTH SCIENCES LIBRARY †
1001 Queen St., W.   Phone: (416) 535-8501
Toronto, ON M6J 1H3   Mary Ann Georges, Staff Libn.

REED STENHOUSE, LTD. - RESEARCH DEPARTMENT LIBRARY
Toronto Dominion Centre
P.O. Box 250   Phone: (416) 868-5520
Toronto, ON M5K 1J6   G.R.E. Bromwich, V.P., Res. & Info.Dept.

REGIS COLLEGE - LIBRARY
15 St. Mary St.   Phone: (416) 922-0536
Toronto, ON M4Y 2R5   Rev. Vincent MacKenzie, S.J., Chf.Libn.

REGISTERED NURSES' ASSOCIATION OF ONTARIO - LIBRARY
33 Price St.   Phone: (416) 923-3523
Toronto, ON M4W 1Z2   Mary Boite, Libn.

GEOGRAPHIC

RIO ALGOM, LTD. - LIBRARY
120 Adelaide St., W.   Phone: (416) 367-4299
Toronto, ON M5H 1W5   Penny Lipman, Libn.

ROYAL ASTRONOMICAL SOCIETY OF CANADA - NATIONAL LIBRARY
124 Merton St., 4th Fl.   Phone: (416) 484-4960
Toronto, ON M4S 2Z2   Frederic L. Troyer, Libn.

ROYAL BANK OF CANADA - INFORMATION RESOURCES
Royal Bank Plaza   Phone: (416) 865-2780
Toronto, ON M5H 2J5   Jane Dysart, Chf.Libn.

ROYAL CANADIAN MILITARY INSTITUTE - LIBRARY
426 University Ave.   Phone: (416) 597-0286
Toronto, ON M5G 1S9   Lt.Col. W.G. Heard, Cur.

ROYAL ONTARIO MUSEUM - CANADIANA GALLERY LIBRARY
14 Queen's Park Crescent, W.   Phone: (416) 978-6738
Toronto, ON M5S 2C6   Janet Holmes, Cur.Asst.

ROYAL ONTARIO MUSEUM - FAR EASTERN LIBRARY
100 Queen's Park   Phone: (416) 978-3653
Toronto, ON M5S 2C6   Betty Kingston, Libn.

ROYAL ONTARIO MUSEUM - LIBRARY
100 Queen's Park   Phone: (416) 928-3671
Toronto, ON M5S 2C6   Gene Wilburn, Hd.Libn.

ROYAL TRUST CORPORATION OF CANADA - INVESTMENT RESEARCH
 LIBRARY
Sta. A, P.O. Box 7500   Phone: (416) 867-2928
Toronto, ON M5W 1P9   Anita Frank, Libn.

RYERSON POLYTECHNICAL INSTITUTE - LEARNING RESOURCES CENTRE
50 Gould St.   Phone: (416) 595-5322
Toronto, ON M5B 1E8   John North, Dir.

RYERSON POLYTECHNICAL INSTITUTE - LIBRARY ARTS DEPT. - LIBRARY
50 Gould St.   Phone: (416) 595-5285
Toronto, ON M5B 1E8   Dean Tudor, Chm.

ST. JOSEPH'S HEALTH CENTRE - GEORGE PENNAL LIBRARY
30 The Queensway   Phone: (416) 534-9531
Toronto, ON M6R 1B5

ST. MICHAEL'S HOSPITAL - HEALTH SCIENCE LIBRARY
30 Bond St.   Phone: (416) 360-4941
Toronto, ON M5B 1W8   Anita Wong, Dir.

ST. VLADIMIR INSTITUTE - UKRAINIAN LIBRARY
620 Spadina Ave.   Phone: (416) 923-8266
Toronto, ON M5S 2H4   Vera Skop, Libn.

SHELL CANADA LIMITED - TECHNICAL LIBRARY
505 University Ave.
Toronto, ON M5G 1X4   Miss S. Tattershall, Hd., Lib.Sect.

SOCIETY OF FRIENDS - FRIENDS HOUSE LIBRARY
60 Lowther Ave.   Phone: (416) 921-0368
Toronto, ON M5R 1C7   Christine Manville

STRATHY, ARCHIBALD AND SEAGRAM - LAW LIBRARY
3801 Commerce Court W.
Box 438   Phone: (416) 863-7525
Toronto, ON M5L 1J3   Catherine J. McLoughlin, Libn.

SUN LIFE ASSURANCE COMPANY OF CANADA - REFERENCE LIBRARY
Sta. A., P.O. Box 4150   Phone: (416) 869-6908
Toronto, ON M5W 2C9   Mary Walsh, Chf.Libn.

SUNNYBROOK MEDICAL CENTRE - HEALTH SCIENCES LIBRARY
2075 Bayview Ave.   Phone: (416) 486-3880
Toronto, ON M4N 3M5   Linda McFarlane, Health Sci.Libn.

THOMSON, ROGERS, BARRISTERS & SOLICITORS - LIBRARY †
390 Bay St., Suite 3100   Phone: (416) 868-3100
Toronto, ON M5H 1W2   Dianne D. Sydij, Libn.

TORONTO BOARD OF EDUCATION - EDUCATION CENTRE LIBRARY
155 College St.   Phone: (416) 598-4931
Toronto, ON M5T 1P6   F. Eugene Gattinger, Coord., Lib.Serv.

TORONTO CITY PLANNING AND DEVELOPMENT DEPARTMENT - LIBRARY
City Hall   Phone: (416) 367-7182
Toronto, ON M5H 2N2   Georgina Moravec, Libn.

TORONTO CITY RECORDS AND ARCHIVES DIVISION
City Hall   Phone: (416) 367-7042
Toronto, ON M5H 2N2   R. Scott James, Dir. of Rec./City Archv.

TORONTO DOMINION BANK - DEPARTMENT OF ECONOMIC RESEARCH -
 LIBRARY
55 King St., W.   Phone: (416) 866-8068
Toronto, ON M5K 1A2   Ruth P. Smith, Libn.

TORONTO EAST GENERAL HOSPITAL - DOCTORS' LIBRARY
825 Coxwell Ave.   Phone: (416) 461-8272
Toronto, ON M4C 3E7   Katherine Hauw, Libn.

TORONTO GENERAL HOSPITAL - FUDGER MEDICAL LIBRARY
101 College St.   Phone: (416) 595-3549
Toronto, ON M5G 1L7   Mrs. D. Cowper, Libn.

TORONTO GLOBE AND MAIL, LTD. - LIBRARY
444 Front St., W.   Phone: (416) 598-5075
Toronto, ON M5V 2S9   Amanda Valpy, Chf.Libn.

TORONTO INSTITUTE OF MEDICAL TECHNOLOGY - LIBRARY
222 St. Patrick St.   Phone: (416) 596-3123
Toronto, ON M5T 1V4   Margaret Mitchell, Libn.

TORONTO PUBLIC LIBRARY - CANADIANA COLLECTION OF CHILDREN'S
 BOOKS
40 St. George St.
Boys and Girls House   Phone: (416) 593-5350
Toronto, ON M5S 2E4   Margaret Crawford Maloney, Hd.

TORONTO PUBLIC LIBRARY - LILLIAN H. SMITH COLLECTION OF
 CHILDREN'S BOOKS
40 St. George St.
Boys And Girls House   Phone: (416) 593-5350
Toronto, ON M5S 2E4   Margaret Crawford Maloney, Hd.

TORONTO PUBLIC LIBRARY - MARGUERITE G. BAGSHAW COLLECTION
40 St. George St.
Boys and Girls House   Phone: (416) 593-5162
Toronto, ON M5S 2E4   Stephen Lee, Bagshaw Comm.Chm.

TORONTO PUBLIC LIBRARY - OSBORNE COLLECTION OF EARLY CHILDREN'S
 BOOKS
40 St. George St.
Boys and Girls House   Phone: (416) 593-5350
Toronto, ON M5S 2E4   Margaret Crawford Maloney, Hd.

TORONTO PUBLIC LIBRARY - SPACED-OUT LIBRARY
40 St. George St.   Phone: (416) 593-5351
Toronto, ON M5S 2E4   Doris Mehegan, Hd.

TORONTO STAR, LTD. - LIBRARY
One Yonge St.   Phone: (416) 367-2420
Toronto, ON M5E 1E6   Carol Lindsay, Chf.Libn.

TORONTO STOCK EXCHANGE - LIBRARY
55 Yonge St., 8th Fl.   Phone: (416) 868-5326
Toronto, ON M5E 1J8   Shirley Foster, Libn.

TORONTO SUN - LIBRARY
333 King St., E.   Phone: (416) 868-2257
Toronto, ON M5A 3X5   Julie Kirsh, Chf.Libn.

TORONTO TRANSIT COMMISSION - ENGINEERING & CONSTRUCTION
 LIBRARY
1900 Yonge St.   Phone: (416) 534-9511
Toronto, ON M4S 1Z2   Frances Villanti, Lib.Techn.

TORONTO TRANSIT COMMISSION - HEAD OFFICE LIBRARY
1900 Yonge St.   Phone: (416) 481-4252
Toronto, ON M4S 1Z2   Adrian Gehring, Lib.Techn.

TORONTO WESTERN HOSPITAL - HEALTH SCIENCES LIBRARY
399 Bathurst St.   Phone: (416) 369-5750
Toronto, ON M5T 2S8   Elizabeth A. Reid, Dir.

TORY, TORY, DESLAURIERS & BINNINGTON - LIBRARY
Royal Bank Plaza, Suite 3400
P.O. Box 20   Phone: (416) 865-0040
Toronto, ON M5J 2K1   Laurel Murdoch, Libn.

TOUCHE, ROSS & COMPANY/TOUCHE ROSS & PARTNERS - LIBRARY
100 King St. W.
Box 12, First Canadian Pl.   Phone: (416) 364-4242
Toronto, ON M5X 1B3   Barbara Dance, Libn.

UNION CARBIDE CANADA, LTD. - REFERENCE LIBRARY
123 Eglinton Ave., E.   Phone: (416) 487-1311
Toronto, ON M4P 1J3   K. Martha Nagata, Libn.

UNITED CHURCH OF CANADA - CENTRAL ARCHIVES
Birge-Carnegie Bldg., Victoria Univ.
Queen's Park   Phone: (416) 978-3832
Toronto, ON M5S 2C4   Rev. Glenn Lucas, Archv./Hist.

UNIVERSITY OF TORONTO - A.E. MAC DONALD OPHTHALMIC LIBRARY
1 Spadina Crescent   Phone: (416) 978-2635
Toronto, ON M5S 2J5   Madeline Ahad, Res.Sec./Libn.

UNIVERSITY OF TORONTO - ANTHROPOLOGY READING ROOM
Sidney Smith Hall, Rm. 560A
100 St. George St.   Phone: (416) 978-3296
Toronto, ON M5S 1A1   Tessa J. Ireland, Sec.

UNIVERSITY OF TORONTO - AUDIO-VISUAL LIBRARY
                                                Phone: (416) 978-6084
Toronto, ON M5S 2E8   Liz Avison, Hd.Libn.

UNIVERSITY OF TORONTO - CENTRE OF CRIMINOLOGY - LIBRARY
130 St. George St., Suite 8055   Phone: (416) 978-7068
Toronto, ON M5S 1A5   Catherine J. Matthews, Libn.

UNIVERSITY OF TORONTO - CENTRE FOR INDUSTRIAL RELATIONS -
    INFORMATION SERVICE
                                                Phone: (416) 978-2928
Toronto, ON M5S 2E8   Elizabeth Perry, Act.Libn.

UNIVERSITY OF TORONTO - DEPARTMENT OF BOTANY LIBRARY
Botany Bldg., Rm. 202
6 Queen's Pk.   Phone: (416) 978-3538
Toronto, ON M5S 1A1   Ellen Chamberlain, Sec.

UNIVERSITY OF TORONTO - DEPARTMENT OF CHEMISTRY LIBRARY
Lash-Miller Bldg., Rms. 429-433
Willcocks & St. George Sts.   Phone: (416) 978-3587
Toronto, ON M5S 2T4   Donna Allen, Sec.

UNIVERSITY OF TORONTO - DEPARTMENT OF COMPUTER SCIENCE
    LIBRARY
McLennan Physical Labs.
60 St. George St.   Phone: (416) 978-2987
Toronto, ON M5S 2E7   Stephanie Johnston, Libn.

UNIVERSITY OF TORONTO - DEPARTMENT OF GEOLOGY - COLEMAN
    LIBRARY
Mining Bldg., Rm. 316
170 College St.   Phone: (416) 978-3024
Toronto, ON M5S 1A1   L.A. Eschenauer, Sec.

UNIVERSITY OF TORONTO - DEPARTMENT OF MEDICAL RESEARCH
    LIBRARY
Banting & Best Institute, Rm. 304
112 College St.   Phone: (416) 978-2588
Toronto, ON M5G 1L6   C. Baier, Sec.

UNIVERSITY OF TORONTO - DEPARTMENT OF PHYSICS LIBRARY
McLennan Physical Labs., Rm. 211
Russell & Huron Sts.   Phone: (416) 978-5788
Toronto, ON M5S 1A7   B. Chu, Libn.

UNIVERSITY OF TORONTO - DEPARTMENT OF ZOOLOGY LIBRARY
Ramsey-Wright Bldg., Rm. 225
St. George & Harbord Sts.   Phone: (416) 978-3515
Toronto, ON M5S 1A1   R. O'Grady, Sec.

UNIVERSITY OF TORONTO - EAST ASIAN LIBRARY
280 Huron St.   Phone: (416) 928-3300
Toronto, ON M5S 1A1   Anna U, Libn.

UNIVERSITY OF TORONTO - FACULTY OF DENTISTRY LIBRARY
124 Edward St., Rm. 202   Phone: (416) 978-2796
Toronto, ON M5G 1G6   Susan Goddard, Faculty Libn.

UNIVERSITY OF TORONTO - FACULTY OF EDUCATION LIBRARY
371 Bloor St., W.   Phone: (416) 978-3224
Toronto, ON M5S 2R7   Mary Shortt, Chf.Libn.

UNIVERSITY OF TORONTO - FACULTY OF ENGINEERING LIBRARY
20 St. George St.   Phone: (416) 978-6109
Toronto, ON M5S 1A4   E.S. Brown

UNIVERSITY OF TORONTO - FACULTY OF FORESTRY LIBRARY
Forestry Bldg., Rm. 102
45 St. George St.   Phone: (416) 978-6016
Toronto, ON M5S 1A1   Jean Bohne, Libn.

UNIVERSITY OF TORONTO - FACULTY OF LAW LIBRARY
78 Queen's Park   Phone: (416) 978-3719
Toronto, ON M5S 1A1   Christine Attalai, Act.Chf.Libn.

UNIVERSITY OF TORONTO - FACULTY OF LIBRARY SCIENCE LIBRARY
140 St. George St.   Phone: (416) 978-7060
Toronto, ON M5S 1A1   Diane Henderson, Chf.Libn.

UNIVERSITY OF TORONTO - FACULTY OF MANAGEMENT STUDIES LIBRARY
246 Bloor St., W.   Phone: (416) 978-3421
Toronto, ON M5S 1V4   Barbara Dance, Libn.

UNIVERSITY OF TORONTO - FACULTY OF MUSIC LIBRARY
Edward Johnson Bldg.   Phone: (416) 978-3734
Toronto, ON M5S 1A1   Kathleen McMorrow, Libn.

UNIVERSITY OF TORONTO - FACULTY OF PHARMACY - R.O. HURST
    LIBRARY
25 Russell St.   Phone: (416) 978-2870
Toronto, ON M5S 1A1   Barbara A. Gallivan, Libn.

UNIVERSITY OF TORONTO - FINE ARTS LIBRARY
100 St. George St.   Phone: (416) 978-3290
Toronto, ON M5S 1A1   Andrea Retfalvi, Libn.

UNIVERSITY OF TORONTO - GENERAL LIBRARY - SCIENCE AND MEDICINE
    DEPARTMENT
                                                Phone: (416) 978-2284
Toronto, ON M5S 1A5   Mrs. G. Heaton, Hd.

UNIVERSITY OF TORONTO - INSTITUTE OF CHILD STUDY - LIBRARY
45 Walmer Rd.   Phone: (416) 978-5086
Toronto, ON M5R 2X2   Miriam Herman, Lib.Techn.

UNIVERSITY OF TORONTO - INSTITUTE FOR POLICY ANALYSIS - LIBRARY
150 St. George St.   Phone: (416) 928-8623
Toronto, ON M5S 2E9   U. Gutenburg, Lib.Techn.

UNIVERSITY OF TORONTO - KNOX COLLEGE - CAVEN LIBRARY
59 St. George St.   Phone: (416) 979-2532
Toronto, ON M5S 2E6   A. Burgess, Libn.

UNIVERSITY OF TORONTO - MAP LIBRARY
130 St. George St., Rm. 1001   Phone: (416) 978-3372
Toronto, ON M5S 1A5   Joan Winearls, Map Libn.

UNIVERSITY OF TORONTO - MATHEMATICS LIBRARY
Sidney Smith Hall, Rm. 2124
100 St. George St.   Phone: (416) 978-8624
Toronto, ON M5S 1A1   Chibeck Graham, Libn.

UNIVERSITY OF TORONTO - PATHOLOGY LIBRARY
Banting Institute, Rms. 108-109
100 College St.   Phone: (416) 978-2558
Toronto, ON M5G 1L5   Sophia Duda, Libn.

UNIVERSITY OF TORONTO - PONTIFICAL INSTITUTE OF MEDIAEVAL
    STUDIES - LIBRARY
113 St. Joseph   Phone: (416) 921-3151
Toronto, ON M5S 1J4   Rev. D.F. Finlay, Libn.

UNIVERSITY OF TORONTO - ST. MICHAEL'S COLLEGE - JOHN M. KELLY
    LIBRARY
113 St. Joseph St.   Phone: (416) 921-3151
Toronto, ON M5S 1J4   Rev. J. Bernard Black, Libn.

UNIVERSITY OF TORONTO - SCHOOL OF ARCHITECTURE AND PLANNING
    LIBRARY
230 College St.   Phone: (416) 978-2649
Toronto, ON M5S 1A1   Pamela Manson-Smith, Libn.

UNIVERSITY OF TORONTO - THOMAS FISHER RARE BOOK LIBRARY
120 St. George St.   Phone: (416) 978-5285
Toronto, ON M5S 1A5   Richard G. Landon, Dept.Hd.

UNIVERSITY OF TORONTO - UNIVERSITY ARCHIVES
Fisher Library
120 St. George St.   Phone: (416) 978-2277
Toronto, ON M5S 1A5   David W. Rudkin, Univ.Archv.

UNIVERSITY OF TORONTO - UNIVERSITY OF TRINITY COLLEGE - LIBRARY
2 Hoskin Ave.   Phone: (416) 978-2653
Toronto, ON M5S 1H8   L. Corman, Libn.

UNIVERSITY OF TORONTO - VICTORIA UNIVERSITY - LIBRARY
71 Queen's Park Crescent, E.   Phone: (416) 928-3821
Toronto, ON M5S 1K7   Dr. Robert C. Brandeis, Libn.

UNIVERSITY OF TORONTO - WYCLIFFE COLLEGE - LEONARD LIBRARY
Hoskin Ave.   Phone: (416) 979-2870
Toronto, ON M5S 1H7   Lorna Hassell, Libn.

UNIVERSITY OF TORONTO/YORK UNIVERSITY JOINT PROGRAM IN
    TRANSPORTATION - INFORMATION SERVICE
Centre for Urban & Community Studies
150 St. George St.   Phone: (416) 978-6424
Toronto, ON M5S 1A1   Ann Poole, Libn.

UPPER CANADA RAILWAY SOCIETY, INC. - LIBRARY †
Box 122, Terminal A
Toronto, ON M5W 1A2

URBAN TRANSPORTATION DEVELOPMENT CORPORATION - LIBRARY
2 St. Clair Ave., W.   Phone: (416) 961-9569
Toronto, ON M4V 1L7   Robert Aarhus, Hd.Libn.

VICKERS & BENSON LTD. - RESOURCE CENTRE
22 St. Clair Ave., E.   Phone: (416) 925-9393
Toronto, ON M4T 2T3   Winston F. Fletcher, Res.Dir.

WELLESLEY HOSPITAL - LIBRARY
160 Wellesley St., E.   Phone: (416) 966-6617
Toronto, ON M4Y 1J3   Verla E. Empey, Libn.

WESTON RESEARCH CENTRE - LIBRARY
1047 Yonge St.   Phone: (416) 922-5100
Toronto, ON M4W 2L3   Mrs. Lusi Wong, Info.Mgr.

WOMEN'S COLLEGE HOSPITAL - MEDICAL LIBRARY
76 Grenville St.   Phone: (416) 966-7468
Toronto, ON M5S 1B2   Margaret Robins, Med.Libn.

WOMEN'S COLLEGE HOSPITAL - PSORIASIS EDUCATION AND RESEARCH
    CENTRE
60 Grosvenor St.   Phone: (416) 964-0247
Toronto, ON M5S 1B6   Dr. R. Schachter, Dir.

WOOD GUNDY LTD. - LIBRARY
Royal Trust Tower
P.O. Box 274   Phone: (416) 362-4433
Toronto, ON M5K 1M7   Anne Baumann, Libn.

WORLD TRADE CENTRE TORONTO - LIBRARY
60 Harbour St.   Phone: (416) 863-2156
Toronto, ON M5J 1B7   Sally Graham, Libn.

YORK BOROUGH BOARD OF EDUCATION - PROFESSIONAL LIBRARY
2 Trethewey Dr.   Phone: (416) 653-2270
Toronto, ON M6M 4A8   Sheila Moll, Libn.

YORK COUNTY LAW ASSOCIATION - COURT HOUSE LIBRARY
361 University Ave.   Phone: (416) 965-7488
Toronto, ON M5G 1T3   Anna M. MacIver

CANADA - AGRICULTURE CANADA - RESEARCH STATION, VINELAND
    STATION - LIBRARY
                                          Phone: (416) 562-4113
Vineland Station, ON L0R 2E0   N. Gibson-McDonald, Libn.

ONTARIO - MINISTRY OF AGRICULTURE AND FOOD - HORTICULTURAL
    RESEARCH INSTITUTE OF ONTARIO - LIBRARY
                                          Phone: (416) 562-4141
Vineland Station, ON L0R 2E0   Judith Wanner, Libn.

CONRAD GREBEL COLLEGE - LIBRARY/ARCHIVES
                                          Phone: (519) 885-0220
Waterloo, ON N2L 3G6   Samuel Steiner, Libn. & Archv.

MUTUAL LIFE ASSURANCE COMPANY OF CANADA - LIBRARY
227 King St.   Phone: (519) 888-2262
Waterloo, ON N2J 1R2   Leslie Day, Libn.

UNIVERSITY OF WATERLOO - DANA PORTER ARTS LIBRARY
                                          Phone: (519) 885-1211
Waterloo, ON N2L 3G1   Murray C. Shepherd, Univ.Libn.

UNIVERSITY OF WATERLOO - ENGINEERING, MATHEMATICS & SCIENCE
    DIVISIONAL LIBRARY
                                          Phone: (519) 885-1211
Waterloo, ON N2L 3G1   Carolynne Presser, Asst.Libn.

UNIVERSITY OF WATERLOO - ONLINE INFORMATION RETRIEVAL SYSTEM
    FOR THE SOCIOLOGY OF LEISURE & SPORT (SIRLS)
                                          Phone: (519) 885-1211
Waterloo, ON N2L 3G1   Betty Smith, Documentalist

UNIVERSITY OF WATERLOO - UNIVERSITY MAP LIBRARY
Environmental Studies Bldg., Rm. 246   Phone: (519) 885-1211
Waterloo, ON N2L 3G1   Richard Hugh Pinnell, Map Libn.

WILFRID LAURIER UNIVERSITY - LIBRARY
75 University Ave., W.   Phone: (519) 884-1970
Waterloo, ON N2L 3C5   Erich R.W. Schultz, Univ.Libn.

NIAGARA COLLEGE OF APPLIED ARTS AND TECHNOLOGY - LEARNING
    RESOURCE CENTRE
Woodlawn Rd.
Box 1005   Phone: (416) 735-2211
Welland, ON L3B 5S2   Stephen J. Kees, Chf.Libn.

ALGONQUIN PARK MUSEUM - LIBRARY & ARCHIVES
Box 219   Phone: (705) 633-5592
Whitney, ON K0J 2M0   Ronald G. Tozer, Interp.Serv.Supv.

BANK OF MONTREAL - TECHNICAL INFORMATION CENTRE
245 Consumers Rd.   Phone: (416) 493-2440
Willowdale, ON M2J 1S2   Janice Reynolds, Tech.Libn.

C-I-L INC. - CENTRAL LIBRARY
P.O. Box 200   Phone: (416) 226-6110
Willowdale, ON M2N 5S8   Linda Cobbett, Libn.

C-I-L INC. - PATENT AND LAW LIBRARY
P.O. Box 200   Phone: (416) 226-6110
Willowdale, ON M2N 5S8   Y. DeSouza, Libn.

CANADA - PUBLIC WORKS CANADA - ONTARIO REGIONAL LIBRARY
4900 Yonge St.   Phone: (416) 224-4235
Willowdale, ON M2N 6A6   Rocco Cornacchia, Reg.Libn.

COMMONWEALTH MICROFILM LIBRARY
760 Gordon Baker Rd.   Phone: (416) 497-8140
Willowdale, ON M2H 3B4   Lorne Mann, Dir.

CONNAUGHT LABORATORIES, LTD. - BALMER NEILLY LIBRARY
1755 Steeles Ave., W.   Phone: (416) 667-2921
Willowdale, ON M2R 3T4   Elaine Selke, Libn.

DATACROWN, INC. - LIBRARY
650 McNicoll Ave.   Phone: (416) 497-1012
Willowdale, ON M2H 2E1   Lucille Slack, Mgr., Lib.Serv.

MACLAREN ENGINEERS PLANNERS & SCIENTISTS INC. - LIBRARY
1220 Sheppard Ave. E., Suite 100   Phone: (416) 499-0880
Willowdale, ON M2K 2T8   Agnes M. Croxford, Libn.

NORTH YORK BOARD OF EDUCATION - F.W. MINKLER LIBRARY
Education Administration Ctr.
5050 Yonge St.   Phone: (416) 225-4661
Willowdale, ON M2N 5N8   H.P. Greaves, Chf.Libn.

NORTH YORK GENERAL HOSPITAL - W. KEITH WELSH LIBRARY
4001 Leslie St.   Phone: (416) 492-4748
Willowdale, ON M2K 1E1   Marianne E. Brett, Hosp.Libn.

NORTH YORK PUBLIC LIBRARY - CANADIANA COLLECTION
35 Fairview Mall Dr.   Phone: (416) 494-6838
Willowdale, ON M2J 4S4   David B. Kotin, Hd.

NORTH YORK PUBLIC LIBRARY - URBAN AFFAIRS SECTION
5126 Yonge St.   Phone: (416) 225-8891
Willowdale, ON M2N 5N9   Mary N. Budd, Libn.

ONTARIO BIBLE COLLEGE/ONTARIO THEOLOGICAL SEMINARY - J.
   WILLIAM HORSEY LIBRARY
25 Ballyconnor Ct.   Phone: (416) 226-6380
Willowdale, ON M2M 4B3   James Johnson, Libn.

ONTARIO GENEALOGICAL SOCIETY - LIBRARY
c/o Canadiana Collection
North York Public Library
35 Fairview Mall Dr.   Phone: (416) 494-6838
Willowdale, ON M2J 4S4   Grant Brown, Libn.

ONTARIO PUPPETRY ASSOCIATION - LIBRARY
171 Avondale Ave.   Phone: (416) 222-9029
Willowdale, ON M2N 2V4   Dorothy McKay, Adm.Asst.

SENECA COLLEGE OF APPLIED ARTS AND TECHNOLOGY - RESOURCE
   CENTRE
1255 Sheppard Ave. E.   Phone: (416) 494-8900
Willowdale, ON M2K 1E2   Faye Ozden, Supv.

ESSEX LAW ASSOCIATION - LIBRARY
County Court House
245 Windsor Ave.   Phone: (519) 252-8418
Windsor, ON N9A 1J2   Anne Matthewman, Libn.

HOTEL-DIEU OF ST. JOSEPH HOSPITAL - MEDICAL LIBRARY
1030 Ouellette Ave.   Phone: (519) 252-3631
Windsor, ON N9A 1E1   Toni Janik, Hosp.Libn.

INTERNATIONAL JOINT COMMISSION - GREAT LAKES REGIONAL OFFICE
   LIBRARY
100 Ouellette Ave., 8th Fl.   Phone: (519) 256-7821
Windsor, ON N9A 6T3   Patricia Murray, Libn./Tech.Ed.

SALVATION ARMY GRACE HOSPITAL - LIBRARY
339 Crawford Ave.   Phone: (519) 255-2245
Windsor, ON N9A 5C6   Mrs. A. Henshaw, Libn.

UNIVERSITY OF WINDSOR - FACULTY OF EDUCATION LIBRARY
600 Third Concession Rd.   Phone: (519) 969-0520
Windsor, ON N9E 1A5   Thomas J. Robinson, Educ.Libn.

UNIVERSITY OF WINDSOR - PAUL MARTIN LAW LIBRARY
                                                  Phone: (519) 253-4232
Windsor, ON N9B 3P4   Paul T. Murphy, Law Libn.

WALKER (Hiram) HISTORICAL MUSEUM - REFERENCE LIBRARY
254 Pitt St., W.   Phone: (519) 253-1812
Windsor, ON N9A 5L5   R. Alan Douglas, Cur.

WINDSOR STAR - LIBRARY
167 Ferry St.   Phone: (519) 256-5511
Windsor, ON N9A 4M5   Frances Curry, Libn.

ONTARIO - MINISTRY OF COMMUNITY AND SOCIAL SERVICES - RESOURCE
   LIBRARY
Highway 59N
P.O. Box 310   Phone: (519) 539-1251
Woodstock, ON N4S 7X9   Frances Thompson, Libn.

WESTERN ONTARIO BREEDERS, INC. - LIBRARY
Hwy. 59 N.
P.O. Box 457   Phone: (519) 539-9831
Woodstock, ON N4S 7Y7   Howard D. Start, Dir.

PRINCE EDWARD ISLAND

CANADA - AGRICULTURE CANADA - RESEARCH STATION,
   CHARLOTTETOWN - LIBRARY
P.O. Box 1210   Phone: (902) 892-5461
Charlottetown, PE C1A 7M8   Barrie Stanfield, Libn.

CONFEDERATION CENTRE ART GALLERY AND MUSEUM - ART REFERENCE
   LIBRARY
P.O. Box 848   Phone: (902) 892-2464
Charlottetown, PE C1A 7L9   Mark Holton, Cur.

PRINCE EDWARD ISLAND - DEPARTMENT OF EDUCATION - MEDIA CENTRE
202 Richmond St.   Phone: (902) 894-3786
Charlottetown, PE C1A 1J2   Bill Ledwell, Chf. of Educ. Media

PRINCE EDWARD ISLAND - DEPARTMENT OF HEALTH AND SOCIAL
   SERVICES - HEALTH BRANCH CENTRAL LIBRARY
Box 3000   Phone: (902) 892-5471
Charlottetown, PE C1A 7P1   Marilyn Bell, Lib.Supv.

PRINCE EDWARD ISLAND HERITAGE FOUNDATION - GENEALOGICAL
   COLLECTION
P.O. Box 922   Phone: (902) 892-0789
Charlottetown, PE C1A 7L9   Miss Orlo Jones, Genealogical Coord.

PRINCE EDWARD ISLAND - LEGISLATIVE LIBRARY
Confederation Centre Library
P.O. Box 7000   Phone: (902) 892-7932
Charlottetown, PE C1A 8G8   Brenda Brady, Libn.

PRINCE EDWARD ISLAND - PLANNING LIBRARY
Box 2000   Phone: (902) 892-3504
Charlottetown, PE C1A 7N8   Marion Kielly, Libn.

PRINCE EDWARD ISLAND - PUBLIC ARCHIVES
P.O. Box 1000   Phone: (902) 892-7949
Charlottetown, PE C1A 7M4   N.J. de Jong, Prov.Archv.

UNIVERSITY OF PRINCE EDWARD ISLAND - ROBERTSON LIBRARY
                                                  Phone: (902) 892-1243
Charlottetown, PE C1A 4P3   M.C. Crockett, Chf.Libn.

PRINCE COUNTY HOSPITAL - MEDICAL LIBRARY
                                                  Phone: (902) 436-9131
Summerside, PE C1N 2A9   Dr. J.P. Schaefer, Dir.

QUEBEC

HOTEL-DIEU D'ARTHABASKA - MEDICAL LIBRARY-DOCUMENTATION
   SERVICE
5 Quesnel St.   Phone: (819) 357-2031
Arthabaska, PQ G6P 6N2   Micheline LeClair, Lib.Techn.

GEOGRAPHIC

ALCAN INTERNATIONAL, LTD. - TECHNICAL INFORMATION CENTRE
P.O. Box 250   Phone: (418) 548-1121
Arvida, PQ G7S 4K8   Ms. P. Leclerc, Chf.Libn.

CENTRE HOSPITALIER ROBERT-GIFFARD - BIBLIOTHEQUE
  PROFESSIONNELLE
2601, De La Canardiere   Phone: (418) 663-5300
Beauport, PQ G1J 2G3   Yolande Plamondon, Techn.

CIP INC. NATURE CENTRE - LIBRARY
R.R. 2   Phone: (819) 242-6066
Calumet, PQ J0V 1B0   John Morrison, Ck.

JARDIN ZOOLOGIQUE DE QUEBEC - BIBLIOTHEQUE
8191 Ave. Du Zoo   Phone: (418) 643-2310
Charlesbourg, PQ G1G 4G4   Jeannine Gagne, Responsable

SEMINAIRE DE CHICOUTIMI - BIBLIOTHEQUE
679 Rue Chabanel   Phone: (418) 549-1786
Chicoutimi, PQ G7H 1Z7   Clement-Jacques Simard, Dir.

SOCIETE HISTORIQUE DU SAGUENAY - BIBLIOTHEQUE
C.P. 456
Chicoutimi, PQ G7H 5C8   Roland Belanger, Archv.

JEWISH CONVALESCENT HOSPITAL CENTRE - HEALTH SCIENCES
  INFORMATION CENTRE
3205 Alton Goldbloom   Phone: (514) 688-9550
Chomedey, Laval, PQ H7V 1R2   Irene Deborah Shanefield, Med.Libn.

SIDBEC-DOSCO LTEE. - CENTRE DE DOCUMENTATION
C.P. 1000   Phone: (514) 587-2091
Contrecoeur, PQ J0L 1C0   Lise Brosseau, Libn.

CANADA - DEFENCE RESEARCH ESTABLISHMENT VALCARTIER - LIBRARY
P.O. Box 8800   Phone: (418) 844-4271
Courcelette, PQ G0A 1R0   Real Menard, Chf.Libn.

CONSOLIDATED-BATHURST INC. - RESEARCH CENTRE LIBRARY
                                                             Phone: (819) 538-3341
Grand Mere, PQ G9T 5L2   Gilberte Angel, Libn.

CENTRE HOSPITALIER DE L'HOTEL-DIEU DE GASPE - MEDICAL LIBRARY
                                                             Phone: (418) 368-3301
Havre De Gaspe, PQ G0C 1S0   Mathilda Adams, Responsable

CANADA - CANADIAN INTERNATIONAL DEVELOPMENT AGENCY -
  DEVELOPMENT INFORMATION CENTRE
200 Promenade Du Portage   Phone: (819) 997-6212
Hull, PQ K1A 0G4   Monique Legere, Dir.

CANADA - SECRETARY OF STATE - LIBRARY
15 Eddy St., 2nd Fl.   Phone: (819) 997-5467
Hull, PQ K1A 0M5   Claire Renaud-Frigon, Chf.Libn.

EDDY (E.B.) FOREST PRODUCTS, LTD. - LIBRARY
P.O. Box 600
Hull, PQ J8X 3Y7   J.D. Hall, Mgr., R & D

UNIVERSITE DU QUEBEC A HULL - BIBLIOTHEQUE
C.P. 1250, Succursale B   Phone: (819) 776-8381
Hull, PQ J8X 3X7   Andre Chenier, Directeur

CENTRE HOSPITALIER REGIONAL DE LANAUDIERE - BIBLIOTHEQUE
  MEDICALE
1000 Ste-Anne Blvd.   Phone: (514) 759-8222
Joliette, PQ J6E 6J2   Francine Garneau, Bibliothecaire

MUSEE D'ART DE JOLIETTE - BIBLIOTHEQUE
145 rue Wilfrid-Corbeil   Phone: (514) 756-0311
Joliette, PQ J6E 3Z3   Carmen Delorme Toupin, Animator

COLLEGE DE JONQUIERE - CENTRE DE RESSOURCES EDUCATIVES
65 St. Hubert   Phone: (418) 547-2191
Jonquiere, PQ G7X 7W2   Jean-Pierre Dufour, Coord.

BROME COUNTY HISTORICAL SOCIETY - ARCHIVES *
P.O. Box 690   Phone: (514) 243-6782
Knowlton, PQ J0E 1V0   Marion L. Phelps, Cur. & Archv.

CANADA - AGRICULTURE CANADA - EXPERIMENTAL FARM LIBRARY
C.P. 400   Phone: (418) 856-3141
La Pocatiere, PQ G0R 1Z0   Eric Comeau, Dir.

COLLEGE DE STE-ANNE-DE-LA-POCATIERE - BIBLIOTHEQUE
100 Ave. Painchaud   Phone: (418) 856-3082
La Pocatiere, PQ G0R 1Z0   Marcel Mignault, Hd.

COLLEGE DE STE-ANNE-DE-LA-POCATIERE - SOCIETE HISTORIQUE-DE-LA-
  COTE-DU-SUD - BIBLIOTHEQUE
                                                             Phone: (418) 856-1525
La Pocatiere, PQ G0R 1Z0   Guy Theberge, Sec.

INSTITUT DE TECHNOLOGIE AGRICOLE - RESEARCH LIBRARY
                                                             Phone: (418) 856-1110
La Pocatiere, PQ G0R 1Z0   Rene-Daniel Langlois, Libn.

BUILDING PRODUCTS OF CANADA LTD. - LIBRARY †
10500 Cote De Liesse Rd., Suite 200   Phone: (514) 636-6810
Lachine, PQ H8T 3E3   Mrs. C. Rose, Libn.

DOMINION ENGINEERING WORKS, LTD. - LIBRARY
795 1st Ave.   Phone: (514) 634-3411
Lachine, PQ H8S 2S8   Celine Bourdages, Libn.

SEAGRAM COMPANY, LTD. - INFORMATION CENTRE, LIBRARY & ARCHIVES
225 LaFleur Ave.   Phone: (514) 366-2410
LaSalle, PQ H8R 3T9   Don J. Deans, Mgr.

WARNOCK HERSEY PROFESSIONAL SERVICES LTD. - LIBRARY †
128 Elmslie St.   Phone: (514) 366-3100
LaSalle, PQ H8R 1V8   Gwendolyn Hazlett, Libn.

FOREIGN MISSIONS SOCIETY OF QUEBEC - LIBRARY *
60 Desnoyers St.   Phone: (514) 667-4190
Laval, PQ H7G 1A4   Florian Vachon, Lib.Dir.

CONFEDERATION DES CAISSES POPULAIRES ET D'ECONOMIE DESJARDINS
  DU QUEBEC - CENTRE DE DOCUMENTATION
100 Ave. Des Commandeurs   Phone: (418) 835-2468
Levis, PQ G6V 7N5   Louise Tremblay

HOTEL-DIEU DE LEVIS - BIBLIOTHEQUE MEDICALE
143 Rue Wolfe   Phone: (418) 833-7121
Levis, PQ G6V 3Z1   Colette Pasquis-Audant, Libn.

CANADA - HEALTH AND WELFARE CANADA - HEALTH PROTECTION
  BRANCH - REGIONAL LIBRARY
1001 Ouest Boul. St. Laurent, Ch. 321   Phone: (514) 283-5472
Longueuil, PQ J4K 1C7   Eleanora Ferenczy, Regional Libn.

INSTITUT NAZARETH ET LOUIS-BRAILLE - BIBLIOTHEQUE PUBLIQUE
1255 Beauregard   Phone: (514) 463-1710
Longueil, PQ J4K 2M3   Suzanne Olivier, Directrice

PRATT AND WHITNEY AIRCRAFT OF CANADA, LTD. - LIBRARY
P.O. Box 10   Phone: (514) 677-9411
Longueuil, PQ J4K 4X9   Joyce Charlebois, Libn.

HOPITAL DE MONT-JOLI, INC. - BIBLIOTHEQUE
800 Sanatorium   Phone: (418) 775-7261
Mont-Joli, PQ G5H 3L6   Sylvie Dupuis, Lib.Techn.

ABBOTT LABORATORIES, LTD. - COMPANY LIBRARY
Sta. A, P.O. Box 6150   Phone: (514) 341-6880
Montreal, PQ H3C 3K6   Genevieve Heroux, Lib.Techn.

AIR CANADA - LIBRARY
1 Place Ville Marie, 38th Fl.   Phone: (514) 874-4841
Montreal, PQ H3B 3P7   Iris L. Land, Mgr., Lib.Serv.

ALCAN ALUMINIUM, LTD. - GROUP INFORMATION CENTRE
One Place Ville Marie
Box 6090   Phone: (514) 877-2610
Montreal, PQ H3C 3H2   Ellen A. Johnston, Chf.Libn.

ANGLICAN CHURCH OF CANADA - DIOCESE OF MONTREAL - ARCHIVES †
Synod Office, 1444 Union Ave.   Phone: (514) 845-6211
Montreal, PQ H3A 2B8   Rev. Canon M.A. Hughes, Adm.Off.

ASSELIN, BENOIT, BOUCHER, DUCHARME, LAPOINTE, INC. - LIBRARY
   DEPARTMENT
85 W. Ste. Catherine   Phone: (514) 282-9650
Montreal, PQ H2X 3P4   Chantale Dion

ASSOCIATION DES MEDECINS DE LANGUE FRANCAISE DU CANADA -
   UNION MEDICALE DU CANADA - RESEARCH LIBRARY
1440 St. Catherine St. W., Suite 510   Phone: (514) 866-2053
Montreal, PQ H3G 2P9   G. Faucher, Asst. To The Ed.

ASSOCIATION DES UNIVERSITES PARTIELLEMENT OU ENTIEREMENT DE
   LANGUE FRANCAISE - BIBLIOTHEQUE
B.P. 6128, Universite de Montreal   Phone: (514) 343-6630
Montreal, PQ H3C 3J7   Francoise Sorieul

ATOMIC ENERGY OF CANADA, LTD. - ENGINEERING COMPANY LIBRARY
1600 Dorchester Blvd. W.   Phone: (514) 934-4311
Montreal, PQ H3H 1P9   Susan Nish, Techn.

AVIATION ELECTRIC, LTD. - TECHNICAL DATA SECTION LIBRARY †
St. Laurent
P.O. Box 2140   Phone: (514) 744-2811
Montreal, PQ H4L 4X8   R. Warrick, Mgr.Tech.Serv.

AYERST LABORATORIES - RESEARCH LIBRARY †
Box 6115   Phone: (514) 744-6771
Montreal, PQ H3C 3J1   Nicole Barrette-Pilon, Libn.

BANK OF MONTREAL - HEAD OFFICE LIBRARY
129 St. James Street W.   Phone: (514) 877-6890
Montreal, PQ H2Y 1L6   Nancy C. Leclerc, Chf.Libn./Mgr.

BANK OF MONTREAL - OPERATIONS & SYSTEMS LIBRARY
Box 6002   Phone: (514) 877-8235
Montreal, PQ H3C 3B1   Kae Vickery, Lib.Supv.

BARREAU DE MONTREAL - BIBLIOTHEQUE
Palais De Justice   Phone: (514) 873-3083
Montreal, PQ H2Y 1B6   Arthur Perrault, Libn.

BEAUCHEMIN-BEATON-LAPOINTE, INC. - BBL LIBRARY
1134 Ste-Catherine St., West   Phone: (514) 871-9555
Montreal, PQ H3B 1H4   Ginette Dumont, Lib.Techn.

BELL CANADA - INFORMATION RESOURCE CENTRE
1050 Beaver Hall Hill, 1st Fl.   Phone: (514) 870-8500
Montreal, PQ H3C 3G4   B. Eskelson, Mgr.

BELL CANADA - LAW LIBRARY
1050 Beaver Hall Hill, Rm. 1500   Phone: (514) 861-6550
Montreal, PQ H3C 3G4   Patricia Young, Law Libn.

BELL CANADA - TELEPHONE HISTORICAL COLLECTION
1050 Beaver Hall Hill, Rm. 820   Phone: (514) 870-2224
Montreal, PQ H3C 3G4   Miss E.M.L. Geraghty, Hist.

BIBLIOTHEQUE DE LA VILLE DE MONTREAL - CINEMATHEQUE
880 Roy St. E., Suite 200   Phone: (514) 872-3680
Montreal, PQ H2L 1E6   Lise D. Bourassa, Coord. AV Serv.

BIBLIOTHEQUE DE LA VILLE DE MONTREAL - COLLECTION GAGNON
1210 Sherbrooke St., E.   Phone: (514) 872-5923
Montreal, PQ H2L 1L9   Carmen Catelli, Hd.

B'NAI BRITH HILLEL FOUNDATION AT MC GILL UNIVERSITY - LIBRARY
3460 Stanley St.   Phone: (514) 845-9171
Montreal, PQ H3A 1R8   Leon Wasser, Libn.

C.I. POWER SERVICES - INFORMATION CENTRE
2020 University St., Suite 1800   Phone: (514) 285-1414
Montreal, PQ H3A 2A5   Judith Joba, Info.Spec.

C.L.S.C. METRO - FAMILY LIFE EDUCATION SERVICES - PEEL CENTRE
   LIBRARY †
3647 Peel St.   Phone: (514) 844-8435
Montreal, PQ H3A 1X1   Mrs. J.M. Elder, Libn.

CAE ELECTRONICS, LTD. - ENGINEERING REFERENCE LIBRARY
8585 Cote de Liesse Rd.   Phone: (514) 341-6780
Montreal, PQ H4T 1G6   Mrs. S. Holloway

CANADA - EMPLOYMENT & IMMIGRATION CANADA - QUEBEC REGIONAL
   LIBRARY
550 Sherbrooke St., W., Rm. 424   Phone: (514) 283-4695
Montreal, PQ H3A 1B9   Claudine Lussier, Dir.

CANADA - NATIONAL FILM BOARD OF CANADA - FILM PREVIEW LIBRARY
3155 Cote De Liesse Rd.   Phone: (514) 333-3180
Montreal, PQ H4N 2N4   Antoinette LaPointe, Film Libn.

CANADA - NATIONAL FILM BOARD OF CANADA - REFERENCE LIBRARY
Sta. A, P.O. Box 6100   Phone: (514) 333-3141
Montreal, PQ H3C 3H5   Rose-Aimee Todd, Chf.Libn.

CANADA - NATIONAL RESEARCH COUNCIL - CISTI - INDUSTRIAL
   MATERIALS RESEARCH INSTITUTE LIBRARY
750 Rue Bel-Air   Phone: (514) 935-8513
Montreal, PQ H4C 2K3   Louise Venne, Libn.

CANADA - REGIONAL ECONOMIC EXPANSION - GOVERNMENT
   DOCUMENTATION CENTRE
800 Square Victoria, C.P. 247   Phone: (514) 283-7266
Montreal, PQ H4Z 1E8   Rita Desilets, Ck.

CANADA - SECRETARY OF STATE - TRANSLATION BUREAU - LIBRARY
Tour De La Cite, C.P. 970   Phone: (514) 283-7519
Montreal, PQ H2W 2R1   Cecile Mondou, Hd.Libn.

CANADA - STATISTICS CANADA - ADVISORY SERVICES - MONTREAL
   REFERENCE CENTRE
Alexis Nihon Plaza, 7th Fl.
1500 Atwater St.   Phone: (514) 283-5725
Montreal, PQ H3Z 1Y2   Paul J. Legare, Asst. Regional Dir.

CANADA - TRANSPORT CANADA - TRANSPORTATION DEVELOPMENT
   CENTRE - LIBRARY
1000 Sherbrooke St., W.
P.O. Box 549   Phone: (514) 283-4084
Montreal, PQ H3A 2R3   Judith Nogrady, Hd.

CANADAIR, LTD. - COMPANY LIBRARY †
P.O. Box 6087   Phone: (514) 744-1511
Montreal, PQ H3C 3G9   Margaret Levesque

CANADIAN AMATEUR MUSICIANS-MUSICIENS AMATEURS DU CANADA
   (CAMMAC) - MUSIC LIBRARY
4450 Sherbrooke St., W.   Phone: (514) 935-2272
Montreal, PQ H3Z 1E6   Grace Prince, Libn.

CANADIAN BROADCASTING CORPORATION - ENGINEERING
   HEADQUARTERS LIBRARY
7925 Cote St. Luc Rd.   Phone: (514) 488-2551
Montreal, PQ H4W 1R5   Mrs. E. Mercer, Act.Libn.

CANADIAN BROADCASTING CORPORATION - LIBRARY
C.P. 6000   Phone: (514) 285-3854
Montreal, PQ H3C 3A8   Michelle Bachand, Hd.Libn.

CANADIAN BROADCASTING CORPORATION - MUSIC SERVICES LIBRARY
1400 Dorchester Blvd., E.
P.O. Box 6000   Phone: (514) 285-3900
Montreal, PQ H3C 3A8   Claude Gagnon, Hd. Music Serv.

CANADIAN CENTRE FOR ECUMENISM - LIBRARY
2065 W. Sherbrooke   Phone: (514) 937-9176
Montreal, PQ H3H 1G6   Reginald Goulet, S.J., Libn.

CANADIAN INSTITUTE OF HYPNOTISM - LIBRARY
Medical Towers Bldg., Suite 51
3465 Cote Des Neiges Rd.   Phone: (514) 937-4488
Montreal, PQ H3H 1T7   Jeanne Rigaud, Coord.

CANADIAN JEWISH CONGRESS - LIBRARY & ARCHIVES
1590 Ave. Docteur Penfield   Phone: (514) 931-7531
Montreal, PQ H3G 1C5   Judith Nefsky, Archv.

GEOGRAPHIC

CANADIAN LIQUID AIR, LTD. - E & C LIBRARY
1155 Sherbrooke St., W.
Phone: (514) 842-5431
Montreal, PQ H3A 1H8
Doris Hammond, Libn.

CANADIAN MARCONI COMPANY - LIBRARY
2442 Trenton Ave.
Phone: (514) 341-7630
Montreal, PQ H3P 1Y9
Mrs. M. Benjamin, Libn.

CANADIAN MUSIC CENTRE - LIBRARY †
1259 Rue Berri, Suite 300
Phone: (514) 849-9175
Montreal, PQ H2L 4C7
Louise Laplante, Regional Dir.

**CANADIAN NATIONAL INSTITUTE FOR THE BLIND - QUEBEC DIVISION
LIBRARY †**
1181 Guy St.
Phone: (514) 931-7221
Montreal, PQ H3H 2K6
Micheline Taillon, Lib.Supv.

CANADIAN NATIONAL RAILWAYS - DECHIEF LIBRARY
935 Lagauchetiere St., W.
B.P. 8100
Phone: (514) 877-4407
Montreal, PQ H3C 3N4
Kathleen Elliott, Sr.Libn.

CANADIAN NATIONAL RAILWAYS - PHOTOGRAPHIC LIBRARY
P.O. Box 8100
Phone: (514) 877-4834
Montreal, PQ H3C 3N4
R. Susan Gallagher, Sys.Photo.Libn.

**CANADIAN NATIONAL RAILWAYS - PUBLIC AFFAIRS DEPARTMENT
LIBRARY**
935 Lagauchetiere St., W.
Phone: (514) 877-5584
Montreal, PQ H3C 3N4
Dorothy Webb, Ed.Res.Supv.

CANADIAN OLYMPIC ASSOCIATION - LIBRARY/INFORMATION SERVICES
Olympic House, Cite Du Havre
Phone: (514) 861-3371
Montreal, PQ H3C 3R4
Sylvia Doucette, Info.Serv.

CANADIAN PACIFIC, LTD. - CORPORATE LIBRARY/INFORMATION CENTRE
Windsor Station
Sta. A, P.O. Box 6042
Phone: (514) 395-6617
Montreal, PQ H3C 3E4
Diane Wolfenden, Corp.Libn.

CANADIAN PSYCHOANALYTIC SOCIETY - LIBRARY
7000 Cote Des Neiges Rd.
Phone: (514) 738-6105
Montreal, PQ H3S 2C1
Nadia Gargour, Adm.Sec.

CANADIAN RAILROAD HISTORICAL ASSOCIATION - LIBRARY *
Canadian Railway Museum
Sta. B, P.O. Box 22
Phone: (514) 632-2410
Montreal, PQ H3B 3J5
Dr. R.V.V. Nicholls, Archv./Libn.

CANADIAN TELEPHONE EMPLOYEES' ASSOCIATION - LIBRARY
Place Du Canada, Rm. 1465
Phone: (514) 861-9963
Montreal, PQ H3B 2N2
Miss E.A. Fenton

**CANADIAN TOBACCO MANUFACTURERS COUNCIL - SMOKING & HEALTH
LIBRARY**
1808 Sherbrooke St., W.
Phone: (514) 937-7428
Montreal, PQ H3H 1E5
Myrna Cain, Council Libn.

CANATOM INC. - LIBRARY
C.P. 420, Tour De La Bourse
Phone: (514) 879-4810
Montreal, PQ H4Z 1K3
Marie-Anna Myers, Hd., Lib.Dept.

CEGEP DU VIEUX MONTREAL - LIBRARY
255 Ontario St. E.
Station N, P.O. Box 1444
Phone: (514) 279-1759
Montreal, PQ H2X 3M8

CELANESE CANADA, INC. - LIBRARY
800 Dorchester Blvd., W.
Phone: (514) 871-5789
Montreal, PQ H3B 1X9
Miss L. Trevaskis, Libn.

**CENTRE D'ANIMATION, DE DEVELOPPEMENT ET DE RECHERCHE EN
EDUCATION - BIBLIOTHEQUE**
1940 Est, Blvd. Henri-Bourassa
Phone: (514) 381-8891
Montreal, PQ H2B 1S2
Jean-Luc Roy, Libn.

CENTRE D'ETUDES DU TOURISME - TECHNICAL INFORMATION CENTRE
C.P. 8000, Succursale A
Phone: (514) 282-9613
Montreal, PQ H3C 3L4
Mureille Bourque, Documentaliste

CENTRE HOSPITALIER COTE-DES-NEIGES - CENTRE DE DOCUMENTATION
4565 Queen Mary Rd.
Phone: (514) 344-3905
Montreal, PQ H3W 1W5
Jocelyne Blain-Juneau, Chf.Libn.

CENTRE HOSPITALIER JACQUES-VIGER - BIBLIOTHEQUE MEDICALE
1051 St. Hubert St.
Phone: (514) 842-7181
Montreal, PQ H2L 3Y5
Jocelyne Blain-Juneau, Chf.Libn.

CENTRE HOSPITALIER STE. JEANNE D'ARC - BIBLIOTHEQUE MEDICALE
3570 Rue St. Urbain
Phone: (514) 842-6141
Montreal, PQ H2X 2N8
Louise Lemay, Chf.Libn.

CENTRE INTERCULTUREL MONCHANIN - BIBLIOTHEQUE
4917 St-Urbain
Phone: (514) 288-7229
Montreal, PQ H2T 2W1
Real Bathalon, Lib.Techn.

CENTRE DE READAPTATION LETHBRIDGE - MEDICAL LIBRARY
7005 Boul. De Maisonneuve W.
Phone: (514) 487-1770
Montreal, PQ H4B 1T3
Jane Petrov, Libn.

CENTRE DE RECHERCHES EN RELATIONS HUMAINES - BIBLIOTHEQUE
2715 Cote St. Catherine Rd.
Phone: (514) 738-8076
Montreal, PQ H3T 1B6
Prof. Noel Mailloux

**CENTRE DE SERVICES SOCIAUX DU MONTREAL METROPOLITAIN -
BIBLIOTHEQUE**
1001 Est Boul. De Maisonneuve
Phone: (514) 527-7261
Montreal, PQ H2L 4R5
Rosemarie Benoit, Hd.Libn.

**CHAIT, SALOMON, GELBER, REIS, BRONSTEIN, LITVACK, ECHENBERG &
LIPPER - LIBRARY**
1 Place Ville Marie, Suite 1901
Phone: (514) 879-1353
Montreal, PQ H3B 2C3
Shake Hagopian, Libn.

**CHARETTE, FORTIN, HAWEY & COMPANY/TOUCHE, ROSS & COMPANY -
LIBRARY**
One Place Ville Marie
Royal Bank Bldg.
Phone: (514) 861-8531
Montreal, PQ H3B 2A3
Nancy Bouchard, Libn.

CINEMATHEQUE NATIONALE DU QUEBEC
360 McGill
Phone: (514) 873-2234
Montreal, PQ H2Y 3E9
Mme. Gairiepy, Dir.

CINEMATHEQUE QUEBECOISE - ARCHIVES & FILM MUSEUM
335 Blvd. De Maisonneuve E.
Phone: (514) 845-8118
Montreal, PQ H2X 1K1
Robert Daudelin, Exec.Dir.

**CINEMATHEQUE QUEBECOISE - CENTRE DE DOCUMENTATION
CINEMATOGRAPHIQUE**
335 Blvd. de Maisonneuve E.
Phone: (514) 873-6753
Montreal, PQ H2X 1K1
Pierre Allard, Chf.Libn.

CLARKSON GORDON - BUSINESS LIBRARY
630 Dorchester Blvd., West
Phone: (514) 875-6060
Montreal, PQ H3B 1T9
Linda Cunnington, Hd.Libn.

CLINICAL RESEARCH INSTITUTE OF MONTREAL - MEDICAL LIBRARY
110 Pine Ave., W.
Phone: (514) 842-1481
Montreal, PQ H2W 1R7
Lorraine Bielmann, Hd.Libn.

**COMMISSION DES ECOLES CATHOLIQUES DE MONTREAL - BIBLIOTHEQUE
CENTRALE**
3737 Sherbrooke E.
Phone: (514) 525-6001
Montreal, PQ H1X 3B3

COMPAGNIE DE JESUS - BIBLIOTHEQUE DE THEOLOGIE
5605 Decelles Ave.
Phone: (514) 737-1465
Montreal, PQ H3T 1W4
Claude-Roger Nadeau, S.J., Dir.

**CONCORDIA UNIVERSITY - LOYOLA CAMPUS - DRUMMOND SCIENCE
LIBRARY**
7141 Sherbrooke St., W.
Phone: (514) 482-0320
Montreal, PQ H4B 1R6
Caroline M. Knowles, Libn.

**CONCORDIA UNIVERSITY - LOYOLA CAMPUS - GEORGES P. VANIER
LIBRARY**
7141 Sherbrooke St., W.
Phone: (514) 482-0320
Montreal, PQ H4B 1R6
Irene Sendek, Hd. Loyola Libs.

CONCORDIA UNIVERSITY - SIR GEORGE WILLIAMS CAMPUS - GUIDANCE
    INFORMATION CENTRE
1455 De Maisonneuve Blvd., W.   Phone: (514) 879-4443
Montreal, PQ H3G 1M8   Marlis Hubbard, Libn.

CONCORDIA UNIVERSITY - SIR GEORGE WILLIAMS CAMPUS - NORRIS
    LIBRARY
1455 De Maisonneuve Blvd., W.   Phone: (514) 879-5891
Montreal, PQ H3G 1M8   Dr. Paul-Emile Filion, Dir. of Libs.

CONCORDIA UNIVERSITY - SIR GEORGE WILLIAMS CAMPUS - SCIENCE &
    ENGINEERING LIBRARY
1455 De Maisonneuve Blvd., W.   Phone: (514) 879-4188
Montreal, PQ H3G 1M8   Z. Jirkovsky, Hd.

CONFERENCE DES RECTEURS ET DES PRINCIPAUX DES UNIVERSITES DU
    QUEBEC - CENTRE DE DOCUMENTATION
2 Complexe Desjardins, Suite 1817
C.P. 124   Phone: (514) 288-8524
Montreal, PQ H3B 1B3   Marie Brie-Berard, Documentaliste

CORPORATION PROFESSIONNELLE DES MEDECINS DU QUEBEC -
    INFORMATHEQUE
1440 Ste. Catherine St., W., Rm. 914   Phone: (514) 878-4441
Montreal, PQ H3G 1S5   Marthe Dumont Salvail, Hd.Libn.

CURRIE, COOPERS & LYBRAND, LTD. - INFORMATION CENTRE
630 Dorchester Blvd., W.   Phone: (514) 866-3721
Montreal, PQ H3B 1W5   Johan Mady, Libn.

DEUTZ DIESEL (Canada) LIMITED - BUSINESS LIBRARY
4660 Hickmore   Phone: (514) 735-4411
Montreal, PQ H4T 1K2   Sharon E. McKay, Info.Dir.

DISADA PRODUCTIONS LTD. - WALT DISNEY MEMORIAL LIBRARY
5788 Notre Dame de Grace Ave.   Phone: (514) 489-0527
Montreal, PQ H4A 1M4   Sherrill Barth, Libn.

DOMINICAINS DE ST-ALBERT-LE-GRAND, MONTREAL - INSTITUT
    D'ETUDES MEDIEVALES - BIBLIOTHEQUE
2715 Chemin de la Cote Ste-Catherine   Phone: (514) 739-9868
Montreal, PQ H3T 1B6   Yvon-D. Gelinas, O.P., Hd.Libn.

DOMTAR, INC. - CENTRAL LIBRARY
P.O. Box 7210   Phone: (514) 282-5039
Montreal, PQ H3C 3M1   Elyse Therrien, Libn.

DOUGLAS HOSPITAL CENTRE - STAFF LIBRARY
6875 La Salle Blvd.
Montreal, PQ H4H 1R3   E. Mancina, Chf.Libn.

ECOLE DES HAUTES ETUDES COMMERCIALES DE MONTREAL -
    BIBLIOTHEQUE
5255 Decelles Ave.   Phone: (514) 343-4481
Montreal, PQ H3T 1V6   Rodolphe Lavergne, Chf.Libn.

ECOLE POLYTECHNIQUE - BIBLIOTHEQUE
C.P. 6079, Succursale A   Phone: (514) 344-4847
Montreal, PQ H3C 3A7   Roger Bonin, Dir.

FEDERAL BUSINESS DEVELOPMENT BANK - LIBRARY
360, rue St-Jacques W., Suite 320   Phone: (514) 283-7632
Montreal, PQ H2Y 1P5   Julia E. McIntosh, Hd.Libn.

FEDERATION DES ADMINISTRATEURS DES SERVICES DE SANTE ET DES
    SERVICES SOCIAUX DU QUEBEC - BIBLIOTHEQUE †
4237 Rue Bordeaux   Phone: (514) 526-0875
Montreal, PQ H2H 1Z4   Claude Magnon, Dir.

FEDERATION DES MEDECINS OMNIPRACTICIENS DU QUEBEC - TECHNICAL
    INFORMATION CENTRE
1440 Ouest Ste-Catherine, Suite 1100   Phone: (514) 878-1911
Montreal, PQ H3G 1R8   Ghislaine Lincourt, Adm.

FRASER-HICKSON INSTITUTE, MONTREAL - FREE LIBRARY
4855 Kensington Ave.   Phone: (514) 489-5301
Montreal, PQ H3X 3S6   Margery W. Trenholme, Chf.Libn.

GESTAS INC. - DOCUMENTATION CENTER
410 St. Nicolas St.   Phone: (514) 288-5611
Montreal, PQ H2Y 2P5   Monique Dumont, Libn.

GOETHE INSTITUTE MONTREAL - GERMAN CULTURAL CENTRE - LIBRARY
Place Bonaventure
P.O. Box 428   Phone: (514) 866-1081
Montreal, PQ H5A 1B8   Elisabeth Morf, Libn.

GRAND SEMINAIRE DE MONTREAL - BIBLIOTHEQUE
2065 Sherbrooke, W.   Phone: (514) 932-9918
Montreal, PQ H3H 1G6   Rev. Jacques Viger, S.S., Hd.Libn.

THE GROUP CSL INC. - LIBRARY *
Sta. A, Box 100
Montreal, PQ H3C 2R7

HOPITAL JEAN-TALON - BIBLIOTHEQUE MEDICALE
1385 E. Jean-Talon   Phone: (514) 273-5151
Montreal, PQ H2E 1S6   Pierrette Galarneau, Libn.

HOPITAL LOUIS H. LAFONTAINE - BIBLIOTHEQUE
7401 Rue Hochelaga   Phone: (514) 253-8200
Montreal, PQ H1N 3M5   Camil Lemire, Med.Libn.

HOPITAL MAISONNEUVE-ROSEMONT - SERVICE DES BIBLIOTHEQUES
5415 De L'Assomption Blvd.   Phone: (514) 254-8341
Montreal, PQ H1T 2M4   Helene Lauzon, Hd.Libn.

HOPITAL NOTRE DAME - MEDICAL LIBRARY
C.P. 1560, Succ. C.   Phone: (514) 876-6862
Montreal, PQ H2L 4K8   Marcelle L'Esperance, Chf.Libn.

HOPITAL RIVIERE-DES-PRAIRIES - BIBLIOTHEQUE DU PERSONNEL
7070 boul. Perras   Phone: (514) 323-7260
Montreal, PQ H1E 1A4   Noella Martineau, Med.Libn.

HOPITAL DU SACRE COEUR - PAVILLON ALBERT-PREVOST - MEDICAL
    LIBRARY
6555 Gouin Blvd., W.   Phone: (514) 333-4284
Montreal, PQ H4K 1B3   Margareth Page, Techn.,Docs.

HOPITAL STE-JUSTINE - CENTRE D'INFORMATION SUR LA SANTE DE
    L'ENFANT †
3175, Chemin Cote Ste-Catherine   Phone: (514) 731-4931
Montreal, PQ H3T 1C5   Pierrette Bubuc, Hd.

HOPITAL ST-LUC - BIBLIOTHEQUE MEDICALE †
1058 St. Denis St.   Phone: (514) 285-1525
Montreal, PQ H2X 3J4   Rene Cote, Chf.Libn.

HORNER (Frank W.), LTD. - RESEARCH LIBRARY
5485 Ferrier St.   Phone: (514) 731-3931
Montreal, PQ H4P 1M6   Miss R. Robinson, Adm.Asst.

HOTEL-DIEU DE MONTREAL - CENTRE DE DOCUMENTATION
3840 Rue St-Urbain   Phone: (514) 844-0161
Montreal, PQ H2W 1T8   Ginette Boyer, Libn.

HYDRO-QUEBEC - BIBLIOTHEQUE
75 Dorchester Blvd., W.   Phone: (514) 289-2149
Montreal, PQ H2Z 1A4   Claude-Andre Bonin, Chf.Libn.

HYDRO-QUEBEC - DIRECTION RECHERCHE ECONOMIQUE - CENTRE DE
    DOCUMENTATION
870 Est. boul de Maisonneuve   Phone: (614) 289-6806
Montreal, PQ H2L 4S8   Sylvie Perron, Analyste

IBM CANADA, LTD. - EASTERN REGION REFERENCE LIBRARY †
5 Place Ville Marie   Phone: (514) 874-6271
Montreal, PQ H3B 2G2   Mrs. X. Corber, Sr.Info.Proc.

IMASCO FOODS, LTD. - LIBRARY
4945 Ontario St., E.   Phone: (514) 255-2811
Montreal, PQ H1V 1M2   Louise Pichet, Libn.

IMPERIAL TOBACCO LTD. - CORPORATE LIBRARY
P.O. Box 6500   Phone: (514) 932-6161
Montreal, PQ H3C 3L6   Yolande Mukherjee, Corp.Libn.

GEOGRAPHIC

IMPERIAL TOBACCO LTD. - RESEARCH LIBRARY
734 Bourget St.
Montreal, PQ H4C 2M7
Phone: (514) 932-6161
Miss R. Ayoung, Res.Libn.

INDUSTRIAL ACCIDENT PREVENTION ASSOCIATION - TECHNICAL
INFORMATION LIBRARY
50 Place Cremazie, Suite 812
Montreal, PQ H2P 2T5
Phone: (514) 389-8295
Lise Locas, Libn.

INDUSTRIAL GRAIN PRODUCTS, LTD. - RESEARCH & DEVELOPMENT
LIBRARY
995 Mill St.
P.O. Box 6089
Montreal, PQ H3C 3H1
Phone: (514) 866-7961
Muriel Henri, Libn.

INFORMATECH - CENTRE QUEBECOIS DE BANQUES D'INFORMATION
SCIENTIFIQUE ET TECHNIQUE
3467 Rue Durocher
Montreal, PQ H2X 2C6
Phone: (514) 845-2206
Antony Gervais, Dir.

INSTITUT CANADIEN D'EDUCATION DES ADULTES - CENTRE DE
DOCUMENTATION
506 E. Ste-Catherine, Suite 800
Montreal, PQ H2L 2C7
Phone: (514) 842-2766
Micheline Seguin, Documentaliste

INSTITUT D'HISTOIRE DE L'AMERIQUE FRANCAISE (1970) - RESEARCH
CENTRE LIBRARY
257-261 Ave. Bloomfield
Montreal, PQ H2V 3R6
Phone: (514) 271-8264
Rene Durocher, Pres.

INSTITUT PHILIPPE PINEL - LIBRARY
10905 Henri-Bourassa Blvd., E.
Montreal, PQ H1C 1H1
Phone: (514) 648-8461
Normand Beaudet, Bibliotechnicien

INSTITUTE OF OCCUPATIONAL AND ENVIRONMENTAL HEALTH - ARCHIVES
Crown Trust Bldg., Suite 410
1130 Sherbrooke St., W.
Montreal, PQ H3A 2M8
Phone: (514) 844-4955
Therese Brien, Exec.Sec.

INTERNATIONAL CIVIL AVIATION ORGANIZATION - LIBRARY
Place De L'Aviation Internationale
1000 Sherbrooke St., W.
Box 400
Montreal, PQ H3A 2R2
Phone: (514) 285-8208
Mrs. Fathia Ismail, Libn.

INTERNATIONAL INSTITUTE OF STRESS - LIBRARY AND DOCUMENTATION
CENTER
659 Milton St.
Montreal, PQ H2X 1W6
Phone: (514) 288-2707
Marianne Timm, Chf. Documentalist

ITALIAN CULTURAL SERVICE - LIBRARY
1200 Dr. Penfield Ave.
Montreal, PQ H3A 1A9
Phone: (514) 849-3473
Dr. Gioganni Battaglia, Dir.

JARDIN BOTANIQUE DE MONTREAL - BIBLIOTHEQUE
4101 Sherbrooke St., E.
Montreal, PQ H1X 2B2
Phone: (514) 872-4543
Jeno Arros, Botanist

JEWISH PUBLIC LIBRARY OF MONTREAL
5151 Cote St. Catherine Rd.
Montreal, PQ H3W 1M6
Phone: (514) 735-6535
Paul Trepman, Dir.

JOHNSON AND JOHNSON, LTD. - RESEARCH LIBRARY
7101 Notre Dame St., E.
Montreal, PQ H1N 2G4
Phone: (514) 252-5029
Lilian Smyth, Res.Libn.

KLOCKNER STADLER HURTER, LTD. - LIBRARY
1600 Dorchester Blvd., W.
Montreal, PQ H3H 1P9

LA PRESSE, LTEE. - CENTRE DE DOCUMENTATION
7 Ouest, Rue St-Jacques
Montreal, PQ H2Y 1K9
Phone: (514) 285-7007
Fernand Drouin, Dir.

LE DEVOIR - CENTRE DE DOCUMENTATION
211, Rue Du St-Sacrement
Montreal, PQ H2Y 1X1
Phone: (514) 844-3361
Gilles Pare, Libn.

LIVESTOCK FEED BOARD OF CANADA - LIBRARY
5180 Queen Mary Rd., Suite 400
Montreal, PQ H3W 3E7
Phone: (514) 283-7505
A. Douglas Mutch

LOVELL LITHO & PUBLICATIONS INC. - LIBRARY
423 St. Nicholas St.
Montreal, PQ H2Y 2P4

MC GILL UNIVERSITY - ALLAN MEMORIAL INSTITUTE OF PSYCHIATRY -
LIBRARY
1025 Pine Ave., W.
Montreal, PQ H3A 1A1
Phone: (514) 842-1251
Felicitas Kirchenberger, Act.Libn.

MC GILL UNIVERSITY - BLACKADER LIBRARY OF ARCHITECTURE/
LAUTERMAN LIBRARY OF ART
3459 McTavish St.
Montreal, PQ H3A 1Y1
Phone: (514) 392-4960

MC GILL UNIVERSITY - BLACKER/WOOD LIBRARY OF ZOOLOGY AND
ORNITHOLOGY
Redpath Library Bldg.
3459 McTavish St.
Montreal, PQ H3A 1Y1
Phone: (514) 392-4955
Eleanor MacLean, Libn.

MC GILL UNIVERSITY - BOTANY-GENETICS LIBRARY
Stewart Biological Sciences Bldg.
1205 Dr. Penfield Ave.
Montreal, PQ H3A 1B1
Phone: (514) 392-5829
Wendy Patrick, Libn.

MC GILL UNIVERSITY - CENTRE FOR DEVELOPING AREA STUDIES -
DOCUMENTATION CENTRE
815 Sherbrooke St. W.
Montreal, PQ H3A 2K6
Phone: (514) 392-5342
Marjorie Neilson, Documentalist

MC GILL UNIVERSITY - DENTISTRY LIBRARY
Strathcona Anatomy & Dentistry Bldg.
3640 University St.
Montreal, PQ H3A 2B2
Phone: (514) 392-4926
Jean Fensom, Libn.

MC GILL UNIVERSITY - DEPARTMENT OF RARE BOOKS & SPECIAL
COLLECTIONS
McLennan Library Bldg.
3459 McTavish St.
Montreal, PQ H3A 1Y1
Phone: (514) 392-4973
Elizabeth Lewis, Rare Book Libn.

MC GILL UNIVERSITY - EDUCATION LIBRARY
3700 McTavish St.
Montreal, PQ H3A 1Y2
Phone: (514) 392-8849
Joan Gagne, Educ.Libn.

MC GILL UNIVERSITY - EDUCATION LIBRARY - SAM RABINOVITCH
MEMORIAL COLLECTION
3700 McTavish St.
Montreal, PQ H3A 1Y2
Phone: (514) 392-8849
Joan Gagne, Educ.Libn.

MC GILL UNIVERSITY - ENGINEERING LIBRARY
Macdonald Engineering Bldg.
817 Sherbrooke St. W.
Montreal, PQ H3A 2K6
Phone: (514) 392-5913
Jadwiga Wygnanski, Libn.

MC GILL UNIVERSITY - EXPERIMENTAL SURGERY LIBRARY
Donner Bldg.
740 Dr. Penfield Ave.
Montreal, PQ H3A 1A4
Phone: (514) 392-4858
Brenda Bewick, Libn.

MC GILL UNIVERSITY - FRENCH CANADA STUDIES PROGRAMME -
REFERENCE LIBRARY
3475 Peel St.
Montreal, PQ H3A 1W7
Phone: (514) 392-5200
Professor Yvan Lamonde, Dir.

MC GILL UNIVERSITY - HOWARD ROSS LIBRARY OF MANAGEMENT
Bronfman Bldg.
1001 Sherbrooke St., W.
Montreal, PQ H3A 1G5
Phone: (514) 392-5795
Marjorie Judah, Libn.

MC GILL UNIVERSITY - ISLAMIC STUDIES LIBRARY
Stephen Leacock Bldg., 9th Fl.
855 Sherbrooke St. W.
Montreal, PQ H3A 2T7
Phone: (514) 392-5197
Raja Dirlik, Libn.

MC GILL UNIVERSITY - LABOUR AGREEMENTS DATA BANK
1001 Sherbrooke St., W.   Phone: (514) 392-6771
Montreal, PQ H3A 1G5   Dr. Charles Steinberg

MC GILL UNIVERSITY - LAW LIBRARY
New Chancellor Day Hall
3644 Peel St.   Phone: (514) 392-5060
Montreal, PQ H3A 1W9   Michael Renshawe, Law Libn.

MC GILL UNIVERSITY - LIBRARY SCIENCE LIBRARY
McLennan Library Bldg.
3459 McTavish St.   Phone: (514) 392-5931
Montreal, PQ H3A 1Y1   Stephanie Both, Libn.

MC GILL UNIVERSITY - MAP AND AIR PHOTO LIBRARY
524 Burnside Hall
805 Sherbrooke St. W.   Phone: (514) 392-5492
Montreal, PQ H3A 2K6   Lorraine Dubreuil

MC GILL UNIVERSITY - MARINE SCIENCES LIBRARY
3620 University St.   Phone: (514) 392-5723
Montreal, PQ H3A 2B2   Robert Freese, Area Libn.

MC GILL UNIVERSITY - MARVIN DUCHOW MUSIC LIBRARY
Strathcona Music Bldg.
555 Sherbrooke St., W.   Phone: (514) 392-4530
Montreal, PQ H3A 1E3   Kathleen M. Toomey, Libn.

MC GILL UNIVERSITY - MATHEMATICS LIBRARY
1105 Burnside Hall
805 Sherbrooke St., W.   Phone: (514) 392-8273
Montreal, PQ H3A 2K6   Robert T. Freese, Area Libn.

MC GILL UNIVERSITY - MEDICAL LIBRARY
McIntyre Medical Sciences Bldg.
3655 Drummond St.   Phone: (514) 392-3056
Montreal, PQ H3G 1Y6   Frances Groen, Life Sci. Area Libn.

MC GILL UNIVERSITY - METEOROLOGY LIBRARY
704 Burnside Hall
805 Sherbrooke St. W.   Phone: (514) 392-8237
Montreal, PQ H3A 2K6   Robert Freese, Area Libn.

MC GILL UNIVERSITY - NORTHERN STUDIES LIBRARY
1020 Pine Ave., W.   Phone: (514) 392-8233
Montreal, PQ H3A 1A2   Robert Freese, Area Libn.

MC GILL UNIVERSITY - NURSING LIBRARY
Wilson Hall
3506 University St.   Phone: (514) 392-5027
Montreal, PQ H3A 2A7   Mrs. M.A. Flower, Libn.

MC GILL UNIVERSITY - OSLER LIBRARY
McIntyre Medical Sciences Bldg.
3655 Drummond St.   Phone: (514) 392-4329
Montreal, PQ H3G 1Y6   Philip Teigen, Osler Libn.

MC GILL UNIVERSITY - PHYSICAL SCIENCES LIBRARY
Frank Dawson Adams Bldg.
3450 University St.   Phone: (514) 392-4929
Montreal, PQ H3A 2A7   Robert Freese, Libn.

MC GILL UNIVERSITY - RELIGIOUS STUDIES LIBRARY
William & Henry Birks Bldg.
3520 University St.   Phone: (514) 392-4832
Montreal, PQ H3A 2A7   Norma Johnston, Hd.Libn.

MC GILL UNIVERSITY - RUTHERFORD PHYSICS LIBRARY
3600 University St.   Phone: (514) 392-4785
Montreal, PQ H3A 2T8   Robert Freese, Area Libn.

MC GILL UNIVERSITY - SCHOOL OF HUMAN COMMUNICATION DISORDERS
  - LIBRARY
1266 Pine Ave., W.   Phone: (514) 392-5966
Montreal, PQ H3G 1A8   Dr. James C. McNutt, Assoc. Professor

MC GILL UNIVERSITY - SOCIAL WORK LIBRARY
Wilson Hall
3506 University   Phone: (514) 392-5046
Montreal, PQ H3A 2A7   Eva Raby, Libn.

MAIMONIDES HOSPITAL & HOME FOR THE AGED - POLLACK LIBRARY
5795 Caldwell Ave.   Phone: (514) 483-2121
Montreal, PQ H4W 1W3   Sheindel Bresinger, Libn.

MAISON BELLARMIN LIBRARY
25 W. Jarry   Phone: (514) 387-2541
Montreal, PQ H2P 1S6   Edmond E. Desrochers, Dir.

MARIANOPOLIS COLLEGE - LIBRARY
3880 Cote des Neiges Rd.   Phone: (514) 931-8792
Montreal, PQ H3H 1W1   Dr. Roman R. Grodzicky, Chf.Libn.

MECHANICS' INSTITUTE OF MONTREAL - ATWATER LIBRARY
1200 Atwater Ave.   Phone: (514) 935-7344
Montreal, PQ H3Z 1X4   Heather Connolly, Chf.Libn.

MOLSON BREWERIES OF CANADA, LTD. - INFORMATION CENTRE
1555 Notre Dame St., E.   Phone: (514) 527-5151
Montreal, PQ H2L 2R5   Sheila Globus, Tech.Libn.

MONTREAL ASSOCIATION FOR THE MENTALLY RETARDED -
   DOCUMENTATION CENTRE †
5915 Henri Bourassa St., W.   Phone: (514) 336-0684
Montreal, PQ H4R 1B7   Helene Lauzon, Documentalist

MONTREAL BOARD OF TRADE - INFORMATION CENTRE
1080 Beaver Hall Hill, 6th Fl.   Phone: (514) 878-4651
Montreal, PQ H2Z 1S9   Jeannette Lemay, Supv.

MONTREAL CANCER INSTITUTE - LIBRARY
1560 Sherbrooke St., E.   Phone: (514) 876-7078
Montreal, PQ H2L 4M1   Helene Harnois, Lib.Techn.

MONTREAL CHEST HOSPITAL CENTRE - MEDICAL LIBRARY
3650 St. Urbain St.   Phone: (514) 849-5201
Montreal, PQ H2X 2P4   Marianne Constantine, Med.Libn.

MONTREAL CHILDREN'S HOSPITAL - MEDICAL LIBRARY
2300 Tupper St.   Phone: (514) 937-8511
Montreal, PQ H3H 1P3   Dorothy Sirois, Med.Libn.

MONTREAL CITY PLANNING DEPARTMENT - LIBRARY †
85 Notre-Dame St., E.
Montreal, PQ H2Y 1B5

MONTREAL ENGINEERING COMPANY, LTD. - LIBRARY
Box 6088, Station A   Phone: (514) 286-3519
Montreal, PQ H3C 3Z8   Penelope H. Kamichaitis, Libn.

MONTREAL GAZETTE - LIBRARY
250 St. Antoine St. W.
P.O. Box 4300, Place d'Armes   Phone: (514) 282-2771
Montreal, PQ H2Y 3S1   Agnes McFarlane, Libn.

MONTREAL GENERAL HOSPITAL - MEDICAL LIBRARY
1650 Cedar Ave.   Phone: (514) 937-6011
Montreal, PQ H3G 1A4   Kathryn Vaughn, Chf.Med.Libn.

MONTREAL GENERAL HOSPITAL - NURSES LIBRARY
Room 3808, Montreal General Hospital   Phone: (514) 937-6011
Montreal, PQ H3G 1A4   Mrs. S.L. Turner, Lib.Techn.

MONTREAL MILITARY AND MARITIME MUSEUM - MACDONALD STEWART
   LIBRARY
P.O. Box 1024, Station A   Phone: (514) 861-6738
Montreal, PQ H3C 2W9   Elizabeth F. Hale, Cons.

MONTREAL MUSEUM OF FINE ARTS - LIBRARY †
3400 Ave. du Musee   Phone: (514) 285-1600
Montreal, PQ H3G 1K3   Juanita M. Toupin, Libn.

MONTREAL NEUROLOGICAL INSTITUTE - LIBRARY
3801 University St.   Phone: (514) 284-4651
Montreal, PQ H3A 2B4   Marina M. Boski, Libn.

MONTREAL URBAN COMMUNITY TRANSIT COMMISSION - LIBRARY
159 St. Antoine St., W., Rm. 912   Phone: (514) 877-6046
Montreal, PQ H2Z 1H3   Victor Itesco, Hd.Libn.

GEOGRAPHIC

GEOGRAPHIC

MONTREAL YOUNG WOMEN'S CHRISTIAN ASSOCIATION - LIBRARY
1355 Dorchester Blvd., W.　　　　Phone: (514) 866-9941
Montreal, PQ H3G 1T3

MUSEE D'ART CONTEMPORAIN - CENTRE DE DOCUMENTATION
Cite Du Havre　　　　　Phone: (514) 873-2878
Montreal, PQ H3C 3R4　　　　Isabelle Montplaisir, Libn.

NATIONAL THEATRE SCHOOL OF CANADA - THEATRICAL LIBRARY
5030 St. Denis St.　　　　Phone: (514) 842-7954
Montreal, PQ H2J 2L8　　　　Beatrice De-Vreeze, Hd.Libn.

NESBITT, THOMSON AND COMPANY, LTD. - RESEARCH LIBRARY
355 St. James St., W.　　　　Phone: (514) 844-0131
Montreal, PQ H2Y 1P1　　　　Ms. L. Cahill, Libn.

NORANDA MINES LTD. - CCR DIVISION - PROCESS DEVELOPMENT LIBRARY
P.O. Box 338, Place D'Armes　　　　Phone: (514) 645-8861
Montreal, PQ H2Y 3H2　　　　J.P. Thiriar, Supt.

NORTHERN TELECOM CANADA, LTD. - LIBRARY & TECHNICAL
INFORMATION CENTRE
P.O. Box 6122, Sta. A　　　　Phone: (514) 634-3511
Montreal, PQ H3C 3J4　　　　Miss M.Y. Pollock, Mgr.

OGILVY, RENAULT - LIBRARY
One Place Ville Marie, Suite 700　　　　Phone: (514) 875-5424
Montreal, PQ H3B 1Z7　　　　Mrs. M. Elvidge, Libn.

ORATOIRE ST-JOSEPH - CENTRE DE DOCUMENTATION
3800 Queen Mary Rd.　　　　Phone: (514) 733-8211
Montreal, PQ H3V 1H6　　　　Aime Trottier, Libn.

ORDRE DES INFIRMIERES ET DES INFIRMIERS DU QUEBEC - CENTRE DE
DOCUMENTATION
4200 Dorchester, W.　　　　Phone: (514) 935-2501
Montreal, PQ H3Z 1V4　　　　Denise Mailhot, Libn.

POLISH INSTITUTE OF ARTS AND SCIENCES IN CANADA - POLISH LIBRARY
McGill University
3479 Peel St.　　　　Phone: (514) 392-5958
Montreal, PQ H3A 1W7　　　Dr. Anna Poray-Wybranowski, Chf.Libn.

PRESBYTERIAN COLLEGE - LIBRARY
3495 University St.　　　　Phone: (514) 288-5257
Montreal, PQ H3A 2A8　　　　Rev. Daniel Shute, Libn.

PRICE WATERHOUSE - LIBRARY †
1200 McGill College Ave., Suite 2300　　　　Phone: (514) 879-9050
Montreal, PQ H3B 2G4　　　　Martha Nugent

PROTESTANT SCHOOL BOARD OF GREATER MONTREAL - PROFESSIONAL
LIBRARY
6000 Fielding Ave.　　　　Phone: (514) 482-6000
Montreal, PQ H3X 1T4　　　　M.E. Montague, Lib.Techn.

QUEBEC PROVINCE - BIBLIOTHEQUE NATIONALE DU QUEBEC
1700, Rue St-Denis　　　　Phone: (514) 873-2155
Montreal, PQ H2X 3K6　　M. Jean-Remi Brault, Conservateur En Chef

QUEBEC PROVINCE - CAISSE DE DEPOT ET PLACEMENT DU QUEBEC -
LIBRARY
C.P. 74, Tour de la Bourse　　　　Phone: (514) 873-2460
Montreal, PQ H4Z 1B4　　　　Pauline Lefebvre Gour, Libn.

QUEBEC PROVINCE - MINISTERE DES AFFAIRES SOCIALES -
BIBLIOTHEQUE †
6161 St-Denis, Ch. 416　　　　Phone: (514) 873-3695
Montreal, PQ H2S 2R5　　　　Gerard Darlington, Libn.

QUEBEC PROVINCE - MINISTERE DE L'EDUCATION - CENTRALE DES
BIBLIOTHEQUES - CENTRE DOCUMENTAIRE
1685 Est, Rue Fleury　　　　Phone: (514) 381-8891
Montreal, PQ H2C 1T1　　　　Gertrude S. DeCarufel, Hd.Libn.

QUEBEC PROVINCE - MINISTERE DU LOISIR, DE LA CHASSE ET DE LA
PECHE - BIBLIOTHEQUE DE LA FAUNE
5075, Rue Fullum　　　　Phone: (514) 873-4693
Montreal, PQ H2H 2K3　　　　Richard Mathieu, Chf.Libn.

QUEBEC PROVINCE - MINISTERE DU TRAVAIL ET DE LA MAIN-D'OEUVRE -
BIBLIOTHEQUE
255 Est, Boul. Cremazie　　　　Phone: (514) 873-3624
Montreal, PQ H2M 1L5　　　　Roch Mercier, Libn.

QUEBEC PROVINCE - OFFICE DES COMMUNICATIONS SOCIALES -
BIBLIOTHEQUE *
4005 De Bellechasse　　　　Phone: (514) 526-9165
Montreal, PQ H1X 1J6　　　　Alice Blain, Dir.

QUEBEC PROVINCE - REGIE DE L'ELECTRICITE ET DU GAZ -
BIBLIOTHEQUE
2100 rue Drummond　　　　Phone: (514) 873-2452
Montreal, PQ H3G 1X1　　　　Marielle Bernard, Lib.Techn.

QUEBEC PROVINCE - SERVICE GENERAL DES MOYENS D'ENSEIGNEMENT -
CENTRE DE DOCUMENTATION *
600 Rue Fullum, 5th Fl.　　　　Phone: (514) 873-3973
Montreal, PQ H2K 4L1　　　　Jean Sarrazin, Act.Dir.

QUEEN ELIZABETH HOSPITAL OF MONTREAL - HOSPITAL LIBRARY
2100 Marlowe Ave.　　　　Phone: (514) 488-2311
Montreal, PQ H4A 3L6　　　　Ms. S.L. Mullan, Lib.Techn.

RADIO QUEBEC - CENTRE DES RESSOURCES DOCUMENTAIRES
1000 Fullum　　　　Phone: (514) 873-5243
Montreal, PQ H2K 3L7　　　　Nicole Charest, Dir.

READER'S DIGEST MAGAZINES LIMITED - EDITORIAL LIBRARY
215 Redfern Ave.　　　　Phone: (514) 934-0751
Montreal, PQ H3Z 2V9　　　　Colette Nishizaki, Libn.

ROBINSON, CUTLER, SHEPPARD, BORENSTEIN, SHAPIRO, LANGLOIS &
FLAM - LAW LIBRARY
800 Place Victoria, Suite 612　　　　Phone: (514) 878-2631
Montreal, PQ H4Z 1H6　　　Lesley-Ann Lawrence, Law Libn.

ROYAL BANK OF CANADA - INFORMATION RESOURCES
P.O. Box 6001　　　　Phone: (514) 874-2452
Montreal, PQ H3C 3A9　　　　Anthea Downing, Chf.Libn.

ROYAL BANK OF CANADA - TAXATION LIBRARY
Royal Bank of Canada Bldg.　　　　Phone: (514) 874-7075
Montreal, PQ H3C 3A9　　　　Franki Elliott, Res.Asst.

ROYAL CANADIAN ORDNANCE CORPS MUSEUM - LIBRARY
6560 Hochelaga St.
P.O. Box 6109　　　　Phone: (514) 255-8811
Montreal, PQ H3C 3H7　　　　Leo Lavigne, Cur.

ROYAL VICTORIA HOSPITAL - MEDICAL LIBRARY †
687 Pine Ave., W.　　　　Phone: (514) 842-1231
Montreal, PQ H3A 1A1　　　Sandra R. Duchow, Chf.Med.Libn.

ROYAL VICTORIA HOSPITAL - OBSTETRICS & GYNAECOLOGY LIBRARY
687 Pine Ave., W.　　　　Phone: (514) 842-1251
Montreal, PQ H3A 1A1　　　　Elaine Waddington, Libn.

ST. MARY'S HOSPITAL - MEDICAL LIBRARY
3830 Lacombe　　　　Phone: (514) 344-3317
Montreal, PQ H3T 1M5　　　　Lucile Lavigueur, Libn.

SHAWINIGAN CONSULTANTS INC. - LIBRARY
620 Dorchester West　　　　Phone: (514) 878-9311
Montreal, PQ H3B 1N8　　　　Mrs. D.J. Leonard, Libn.

SHERWIN-WILLIAMS COMPANY OF CANADA, LTD. - TECHNICAL LIBRARY
2875 Centre St.　　　　Phone: (514) 933-8611
Montreal, PQ H3K 1K4　　　　Shirley Brown, Libn.

SIR MORTIMER B. DAVIS JEWISH GENERAL HOSPITAL - INSTITUTE OF
COMMUNITY & FAMILY PSYCHIATRY - LIBRARY
4333 Cote St. Catherine Rd.　　　　Phone: (514) 341-6211
Montreal, PQ H3T 1E2　　　　Ruth Stilman, Libn.

SIR MORTIMER B. DAVIS JEWISH GENERAL HOSPITAL - LADY DAVIS
INSTITUTE FOR MEDICAL RESEARCH - RESEARCH LIBRARY
3755 Cote St. Catherine Rd.　　　　Phone: (514) 342-3620
Montreal, PQ H3T 1E2　　　　Arlene Greenberg, Libn.

SIR MORTIMER B. DAVIS JEWISH GENERAL HOSPITAL - MEDICAL LIBRARY
3755 Cote St. Catherine Rd.   Phone: (514) 342-3111
Montreal, PQ H3T 1E2   Arlene Greenberg, Chf.Med.Libn.

SNC GROUP - LIBRARY
1 Complexe Desjardins, C.P. 10   Phone: (514) 282-9551
Montreal, PQ H5B 1C8   Madeleine C.-Lambert, Chf.Libn.

SOCIETE D'ARCHEOLOGIE ET DE NUMISMATIQUE DE MONTREAL -
    BIBLIOTHEQUE †
280 Est, Rue Notre-Dame   Phone: (514) 861-7182
Montreal, PQ H2Y 1C5   Margot Albert, Sec.

SOCIETE DE DEVELOPPEMENT DE LA BAIE JAMES - SERVICE
    DOCUMENTATION
800 Est, Boul. de Maisonneuve   Phone: (514) 284-0270
Montreal, PQ H2L 4M6   Nicole Cote, Dir.

SOCIETE D'ENERGIE DE LA BAIE JAMES - CENTRE DE DOCUMENTATION-
    ENVIRONNEMENT
800 Est, Boul. de Maisonneuve
Place Dupuis, 8th Floor   Phone: (514) 844-3741
Montreal, PQ H2L 4M8   Sylvie Charron, Director

SOCIETE HISTORIQUE DE MONTREAL - BIBLIOTHEQUE
4420, Rue Saint-Denis
Montreal, PQ H2J 2L1

SOCIETE NATIONALE DE DIFFUSION EDUCATIVE ET CULTURELLE -
    SERVICE D'INFORMATION SONDEC †
8770 Langelier, Rm. 230   Phone: (514) 324-4010
Montreal, PQ H1P 3E8   Yvon Lewis, Dir.

SQUIBB CANADA INC. - MEDICAL LIBRARY
2365 Cote De Liesse Rd.   Phone: (514) 331-7423
Montreal, PQ H4N 2M7   Vicky Esposito, Clinical Data Coord.

TA ASSOCIATES - INFORMATION CENTER
1801 McGill College Ave.   Phone: (514) 281-2753
Montreal, PQ H3A 2N4   Betty Kahane, Libn.

TOWERS, PERRIN, FORSTER & CROSBY - INFORMATION CENTRE
800 Dorchester W., Suite 3010   Phone: (514) 866-7652
Montreal, PQ H3B 1X9   Amy Scowen, Libn.

UNIVERSITE DE MONTREAL - AMENAGEMENT-BIBLIOTHEQUE
C.P. 6128, Succursale A   Phone: (514) 343-6009
Montreal, PQ H3C 3J7   Jacqueline Pelletier, Libn.

UNIVERSITE DE MONTREAL - BIBLIOTHECONOMIE-BIBLIOTHEQUE
C.P. 6128, Succursale A   Phone: (514) 343-6047
Montreal, PQ H3C 3J7

UNIVERSITE DE MONTREAL - BIBLIOTHEQUE PARA-MEDICALE
C.P. 6128, Succursale A   Phone: (514) 343-7490
Montreal, PQ H3C 3J7   Johanne Hopper, Libn.

UNIVERSITE DE MONTREAL - BIBLIOTHEQUE DE LA SANTE
C.P. 6128, Succursale A   Phone: (514) 343-7810
Montreal, PQ H3C 3J7   Therese Peternell, Libn.

UNIVERSITE DE MONTREAL - BIOLOGIE-BIBLIOTHEQUE
C.P. 6128, Succursale A   Phone: (514) 343-6801
Montreal, PQ H3C 3J7   Vesna Blazina, Libn.

UNIVERSITE DE MONTREAL - BOTANIQUE-BIBLIOTHEQUE
4101 Est, Rue Sherbrooke   Phone: (514) 872-2702
Montreal, PQ H1X 2B2   Nicole Taillefer-Witty, Libn.

UNIVERSITE DE MONTREAL - CENTRE D'ETUDES ET DE DOCUMENTATION
    EUROPEENNES
3150 Rue Jean-Brillant
C.P. 6128, Succursale A   Phone: (514) 343-7870
Montreal, PQ H3T 1V6   Lucie Bouchard, Documentaliste

UNIVERSITE DE MONTREAL - CENTRE INTERNATIONAL DE CRIMINOLOGIE
    COMPAREE - DOCUMENTATION CENTRE
C.P. 6128, Succursale A   Phone: (514) 343-6534
Montreal, PQ H3C 3J7   Jacqueline DePlaen, Hd., Doc.Serv.

UNIVERSITE DE MONTREAL - CENTRE NATIONAL D'INFORMATION ET DE
    RECHERCHE SUR L'AIDE JURIDIQUE *
C.P. 6128, Succursale A   Phone: (514) 343-7961
Montreal, PQ H3C 3J7   Jean-Paul Reid, Libn.

UNIVERSITE DE MONTREAL - CENTRE DE RECHERCHE SUR LES
    TRANSPORTS - DOCUMENTATION CENTRE
C.P. 6128, Succursale A   Phone: (514) 343-6949
Montreal, PQ H3C 3J7   Sylvie Hetu, Libn.

UNIVERSITE DE MONTREAL - CENTRE DE RECHERCHES CARAIBES -
    BIBLIOTHEQUE
C.P. 6128
Montreal, PQ H3C 3J7   Dr. Victor Pichi, Dir.

UNIVERSITE DE MONTREAL - CHIMIE-BIBLIOTHEQUE
C.P. 6128, Succursale A   Phone: (514) 343-6459
Montreal, PQ H3C 3J7   Corinne Haumont, Libn.

UNIVERSITE DE MONTREAL - DEPARTEMENT DE DEMOGRAPHIE - SERVICE
    DE LA RECHERCHE DOCUMENTATION
C.P. 6128, Succursale A   Phone: (514) 343-7567
Montreal, PQ H3C 3J7   Isabelle Laperle, Documentaliste

UNIVERSITE DE MONTREAL - DROIT-BIBLIOTHEQUE
C.P. 6206, Succursale A   Phone: (514) 343-6132
Montreal, PQ H3C 3T6   Paquerette Ranger, Libn.

UNIVERSITE DE MONTREAL - ECOLE DE TRADUCTION - CENTRE DE
    DOCUMENTATION TERMINOLOGIQUE BILINGUE
C.P. 6128, Succursale A   Phone: (514) 343-7296
Montreal, PQ H3C 3J7

UNIVERSITE DE MONTREAL - EDUCATION PHYSIQUE-BIBLIOTHEQUE
C.P. 6128, Succursale A   Phone: (514) 343-6714
Montreal, PQ H3C 3J7   Lise Mayrand, Libn.

UNIVERSITE DE MONTREAL - EDUCATION/PSYCHOLOGIE/
    COMMUNICATION-BIBLIOTHEQUE
C.P. 6128, Succursale A   Phone: (514) 343-6638
Montreal, PQ H3C 3J7   Marielle Durand, Libn.

UNIVERSITE DE MONTREAL - GEOLOGIE-BIBLIOTHEQUE
C.P. 6128, Succursale A   Phone: (514) 343-6831
Montreal, PQ H3C 3J7   Clement Arwas, Libn.

UNIVERSITE DE MONTREAL - INFORMATIQUE-BIBLIOTHEQUE
C.P. 6128, Succursale A   Phone: (514) 343-6819
Montreal, PQ H3C 3J7   Louis Sarrasin, Libn.

UNIVERSITE DE MONTREAL - MATHEMATIQUES-BIBLIOTHEQUE
C.P. 6128, Succursale A   Phone: (514) 343-6703
Montreal, PQ H3C 3J7   Rita Paquette, Libn.

UNIVERSITE DE MONTREAL - MUSIQUE-BIBLIOTHEQUE
C.P. 6128, Succursale A   Phone: (514) 343-6432
Montreal, PQ H3C 3J7   Claude Soulard, Libn.

UNIVERSITE DE MONTREAL - OPTOMETRIE-BIBLIOTHEQUE
C.P. 6128, Succursale A   Phone: (514) 343-7674
Montreal, PQ H3C 3J7   Denise Lacroix, Libn.

UNIVERSITE DE MONTREAL - PHYSIQUE-BIBLIOTHEQUE
C.P. 6128, Succursale A   Phone: (514) 343-6613
Montreal, PQ H3C 3J7   Janine Cadet, Libn.

UNIVERSITE DE MONTREAL - PSYCHO-EDUCATION-BIBLIOTHEQUE
750 Est, Boul. Gouin   Phone: (514) 382-2977
Montreal, PQ H2C 1A6   Yolande Beaudoin, Libn.

UNIVERSITE DE MONTREAL - SCIENCES HUMAINES ET SOCIALES-
    BIBLIOTHEQUE
C.P. 6202, Succursale A   Phone: (514) 343-7424
Montreal, PQ H3C 3T2   Richard Greene, Libn.

UNIVERSITE DE MONTREAL - THEOLOGIE-PHILOSOPHIE BIBLIOTHEQUE
C.P. 6128, Succursale A   Phone: (514) 343-6592
Montreal, PQ H3C 3J7   Francoise Beaudet

GEOGRAPHIC

UNIVERSITE DU QUEBEC A MONTREAL - BIBLIOTHEQUE DES ARTS
C.P. 8889, Succursale A Phone: (514) 282-4655
Montreal, PQ H3C 3P8 Daphne Dufresne, Chf.Libn.

UNIVERSITE DU QUEBEC A MONTREAL - BIBLIOTHEQUE DE MUSIQUE
C.P. 8889, Succursale A Phone: (514) 282-3934
Montreal, PQ H3C 3P8 Renald Beaumier, Dir.

UNIVERSITE DU QUEBEC A MONTREAL - BIBLIOTHEQUE DES SCIENCES
C.P. 8889, Succursale A Phone: (514) 282-7317
Montreal, PQ H3C 3P8 Conrad Corriveau, Dir.

UNIVERSITE DU QUEBEC A MONTREAL - BIBLIOTHEQUE DES SCIENCES DE L'EDUCATION
C.P. 8889, Succursale A Phone: (514) 282-3884
Montreal, PQ H3C 3P8 Marcel Dupuis, Dir.

UNIVERSITE DU QUEBEC A MONTREAL - BIBLIOTHEQUES DES SCIENCES JURIDIQUES
1255 rue St-Denis
C.P. 8889, Succursale A Phone: (514) 282-6184
Montreal, PQ H3C 3P8 Micheline Drapeau, Director

UNIVERSITE DU QUEBEC A MONTREAL - CARTOTHEQUE
C.P. 8889, Succursale A Phone: (514) 282-4371
Montreal, PQ H3C 3P8 Bernard Chouinard, Responsable

UNIVERSITE DU QUEBEC A MONTREAL - CENTRE DE DOCUMENTATION ECONOMIE-ADMINISTRATION
C.P. 8889, Succursale A Phone: (514) 282-6136
Montreal, PQ H3C 3P8 Monique Cote, Libn.

UNIVERSITE DU QUEBEC A MONTREAL - CENTRE DE DOCUMENTATION EN SCIENCES HUMAINES
C.P. 8889, Succursale A Phone: (514) 282-6138
Montreal, PQ H3C 3P8 Louis Le Borgne, Documentaliste

UNIVERSITE DU QUEBEC A MONTREAL - INSTITUT NATIONAL DE LA RECHERCHE SCIENTIFIQUE - CARTOTHEQUE
3465 Durocher, Local 225 Phone: (514) 842-4191
Montreal, PQ H2X 2C6 Christiane Desmarais, Cartothecaire

URBARC CANADA - LIBRARY
2500 Bates Rd.
Montreal, PQ H3S 1A6 Claude La Haye, Documentaliste

VILLE MARIE SOCIAL SERVICE CENTRE - LIBRARY
4018 St. Catherine W. Phone: (514) 989-1885
Montreal, PQ H3Z 1P2 Leatrice Maurice, Libn.

ZITTRER, SIBLIN, STEIN, LEVINE - LIBRARY
4115 Sherbrooke St., West Phone: (514) 933-1112
Montreal, PQ H3Z 1K9 Norman Daitchman

QUEBEC PROVINCE - MINISTERE DU LOISIR, DE LA CHASSE ET DE LA PECHE - BIBLIOTHEQUE DE LA FAUNE
9530 Rue de la Faune Phone: (418) 643-8554
Orsainville, PQ G1G 5E5 Francine Morneau, Bibliotechnicienne

UNION CARBIDE CANADA, LTD. - PLASTICS & CHEMICALS TECHNICAL CENTRE LIBRARY
10555 Metropolitan Blvd., E.
C.P. 700 Phone: (514) 645-5311
Pointe-Aux-Trembles, PQ H1B 5K8 A.M. de Jesus, Libn.

FOREST ENGINEERING RESEARCH INSTITUTE OF CANADA - LIBRARY
143 Place Frontenac Phone: (514) 694-1140
Pointe Claire, PQ H9R 4Z7 Christel Mukhopadhyay, Libn.

NORANDA RESEARCH CENTRE - LIBRARY
240 Hymus Blvd. Phone: (514) 697-6640
Pointe Claire, PQ H9R 1G5 Shirley Courtis, Libn.

PULP AND PAPER RESEARCH INSTITUTE OF CANADA - LIBRARY
570 St. John's Blvd. Phone: (514) 697-4110
Pointe Claire, PQ H9R 3J9 Alison Finnemore, Libn.

MERCK FROSST LABORATORIES - RESEARCH LIBRARY
P.O. Box 1005 Phone: (514) 695-7920
Pointe Claire-Dorval, PQ H9R 4P8 Claire B. Kelly, Res.Libn.

ASSOCIATION DE PARALYSIE CEREBRALE DU QUEBEC, INC. - CENTRE DE DOCUMENTATION
525 Boul. Hamel Est, Suite A-50 Phone: (418) 529-5371
Quebec, PQ G1M 2S8 Rock Gadreau, Dir.

CENTRALE DE L'ENSEIGNEMENT DU QUEBEC - CENTRE DE DOCUMENTATION
2336 Chemin Ste-Foy Phone: (418) 658-5711
Quebec, PQ G1V 4E5 Guy Duchesne

CENTRE HOSPITALIER CHRIST-ROI - BIBLIOTHEQUE MEDICALE
300, Boul. Wilfrid-Hamel Phone: (418) 687-1711
Quebec, PQ G1M 2R9 Gratien Gelinas, Bibliothecaire

CENTRE HOSPITALIER DE L'UNIVERSITE LAVAL - BIBLIOTHEQUE DES SCIENCES DE LA SANTE
2705 Boul. Laurier Phone: (418) 656-8188
Quebec, PQ G1X 3L9 Beatrice Sato, Chf.

CONSERVATOIRE D'ART DRAMATIQUE DE QUEBEC - BIBLIOTHEQUE
30 St-Denis Phone: (418) 643-2139
Quebec, PQ G1R 4B6 Georgette Laki, Bibliothecaire

HOPITAL DE L'ENFANT-JESUS - BIBLIOTHEQUE MEDICALE
1401 18e Rue Phone: (418) 694-5686
Quebec, PQ G1J 1Z4 Madeleine Dumais, Responsable

HOPITAL ST-FRANCOIS D'ASSISE - MEDICAL & ADMINISTRATIVE LIBRARY
10 De L'Espinay Phone: (418) 529-7311
Quebec, PQ G1L 3L5 Sr. Marie-Paule Genest, S.F.A., Chf.Libn.

HOPITAL ST-SACREMENT - BIBLIOTHEQUE MEDICALE
1050 Chemin Ste-Foy Phone: (418) 688-7560
Quebec, PQ G1S 4L8 Bernadette Drolet, Chf.Libn.

HOTEL-DIEU DU SACRE-COEUR DE JESUS - BIBLIOTHEQUE MEDICALE †
1, Ave. Du Sacre-Coeur Phone: (418) 529-6851
Quebec, PQ G1N 2W1 Christian Martel, Lib.Techn.

INDUSTRIAL GENERAL INSURANCE COMPANY - LIBRARY †
1080 St. Louis Rd.
Box 1907 Phone: (418) 688-8210
Quebec, PQ G1K 7M3 N. Demers, Sec.

LAURENTIENNE COMPAGNIE D'ASSURANCE - LIBRARY
500 Est Grande-Allee Phone: (418) 647-5359
Quebec, PQ G1R 2J7 Louise de Bellefeville, Tech.Libn.

LITERARY AND HISTORICAL SOCIETY OF QUEBEC - LIBRARY †
44 St. Stanislas St. Phone: (418) 694-9147
Quebec, PQ G1R 4H3 Cynthia Dooley, Libn.

MONASTERE DES URSULINES - ARCHIVES DES URSULINES DE QUEBEC †
C.P. 760 Phone: (418) 692-2523
Quebec, PQ G1R 4T1

MUSEE DU QUEBEC - BIBLIOTHEQUE
Parc des Champs de Bataille Phone: (418) 643-7134
Quebec, PQ G1S 1C8 Francois Lafortune, Chf.Libn.

QUEBEC PROVINCE - LEGISLATURE DU QUEBEC - BIBLIOTHEQUE †
Hotel du Gouvernement Phone: (418) 643-2896
Quebec, PQ G1A 1A5 Jacques Premont, Dir.

QUEBEC PROVINCE - MINISTERE DES AFFAIRES CULTURELLES - CENTRE DE DOCUMENTATION
225 Grande-Allee Est Phone: (418) 643-6330
Quebec, PQ G1R 1G5 Real Dumoulin, Chf.

QUEBEC PROVINCE - MINISTERE DES AFFAIRES MUNICIPALES - CENTRE DE DOCUMENTATION
1039 De La Chevrotiere, 26th Fl. Phone: (418) 643-6570
Quebec, PQ G1R 4Z3 Ernest Bertrand Roy, Responsable

QUEBEC PROVINCE - MINISTERE DES AFFAIRES SOCIALES -
INFORMATHEQUE *
1075 Chemin Ste-Foy   Phone: (418) 643-6392
Quebec, PQ G1S 4N4   Paul Dubois, Dir.

QUEBEC PROVINCE - MINISTERE DE L'AGRICULTURE, DES PECHERIES ET
DE L'ALIMENTATION - CENTRE DE DOCUMENTATION
200-A, Chemin Ste-Foy   Phone: (418) 643-2428
Quebec, PQ G1R 4X6   Michele Aodette, Responsable

QUEBEC PROVINCE - MINISTERE DES COMMUNICATIONS - BIBLIOTHEQUE
ADMINISTRATIVE
1037 De La Chevrotiere, Edifice G   Phone: (418) 643-1515
Quebec, PQ G1R 4Y7   Monique Charbonneau, Lib.Dir.

QUEBEC PROVINCE - MINISTERE DES CONSOMMATEURS, COOPERATIVES
ET INSTITUTIONS FINANCIERES - BIBLIOTHEQUE
800 Place D'Youville, 7th Fl.   Phone: (418) 643-5236
Quebec, PQ G1R 4Y5   Francine Breton, Bibliotechnicienne

QUEBEC PROVINCE - MINISTERE DE L'ENERGIE ET DES RESSOURCES -
BIBLIOTHEQUE *
200-B Ste-Foy Rd.   Phone: (418) 643-6004
Quebec, PQ G1R 4X7   Andre Lamarre, Hd.Libn.

QUEBEC PROV. - MIN. DE L'ENERGIE ET DES RESSOURCES - CENTRE DE
DOCUMENTATION ET DE RENSEIGNEMENTS
1530 blvd. de l'Entente   Phone: (418) 643-4624
Quebec, PQ G1S 4N6   Normand Guerette, Dir.

QUEBEC PROVINCE - MINISTERE DE L'INDUSTRIE, DU COMMERCE ET DU
TOURISME - BIBLIOTHEQUE MINISTERIELLE
710 Place d'Youville, local 203   Phone: (418) 643-5081
Quebec, PQ G1R 4Y4   Mario Day, Bibliothecaire

QUEBEC PROVINCE - OFFICE DE PLANIFICATION ET DE DEVELOPPEMENT
DU QUEBEC - BIBLIOTHEQUE
1060 Rue Conroy, Bloc 2, 1er Etage   Phone: (418) 643-1607
Quebec, PQ G1R 5E6   Suzanne Plante-Garneau

QUEBEC PROVINCE - REGIE DES RENTES - CENTRE DE DOCUMENTATION
C.P. 5200   Phone: (418) 643-8250
Quebec, PQ G1K 7S9   Nicole Paquin, Libn.

REED LTD. - TECHNICAL INFORMATION CENTRE
Enquiry & Reference Dept.
Box 1487   Phone: (418) 694-6580
Quebec, PQ G1K 7H9   Jim Drake, Libn.

SEMINAIRE DE QUEBEC - ARCHIVES
Box 460   Phone: (418) 694-3981
Quebec, PQ G1R 4R7   Rev. Georges Drouin, Archiviste

SOLEIL LIMITEE - CENTRE DE DOCUMENTATION
390 E. St. Vallier   Phone: (418) 647-3369
Quebec, PQ G1K 7J6   Pierre Mathieu, Dir.

UNIVERSITE DU QUEBEC A RIMOUSKI - CARTOTHEQUE
300, Avenue Des Ursulines   Phone: (418) 724-1669
Rimouski, PQ G5L 3A1   Yves Michaud, Map Libn.

COLLEGE DU NORD-OUEST - BIBLIOTHEQUE
425 College Blvd.
Box 8000   Phone: (819) 762-0931
Rouyn, PQ J9X 5M5   Serge Allard, Dir.

UNIVERSITE DU QUEBEC - CEUAT BIBLIOTHEQUE
446, rue Gagne
Box 8000   Phone: (819) 762-0971
Rouyn, PQ J9X 5M5   Serge Allard, Dir.

SEMINAIRE ST-ALPHONSE - BIBLIOTHEQUE
10026 Rue Royale   Phone: (418) 827-2751
Ste. Anne de Beaupre, PQ G0A 3C0   Robert Boucher, Dir.

CANADA - FISHERIES & OCEANS - R&D DIRECTORATE - ARCTIC
BIOLOGICAL STATION LIBRARY
555 St. Pierre Blvd.   Phone: (514) 457-3660
Ste. Anne-De-Bellevue, PQ H9X 3R4   June Currie, Libn.

DOMTAR, INC. - RESEARCH CENTRE LIBRARY
C.P. 300   Phone: (514) 457-6810
Ste. Anne de Bellevue PQ H9X 3L7   Barbara G. Bolton, Libn.

MC GILL UNIVERSITY - MACDONALD COLLEGE - BRACE RESEARCH
INSTITUTE LIBRARY
P.O. Box 900   Phone: (514) 457-2000
Ste. Anne De Bellevue, PQ H9X 1C0   Mrs. A. Ives, Adm. & Info.Serv.

MC GILL UNIVERSITY - MACDONALD COLLEGE - LIBRARY
Barton Bldg.
2111 Lakeshore Rd.   Phone: (514) 457-2000
Ste. Anne De Bellevue, PQ H9X 1C0   Janet Finlayson, Hd.Libn.

SPAR AEROSPACE LTD. - LIBRARY †
21025 Trans-Canada Hwy.
Box 850   Phone: (514) 457-2150
Ste. Anne De Bellevue, PQ H9X 3R2   Shirley L. Edwards, Lib.Adm.

CANADA - AGRICULTURE CANADA - RESEARCH STATION, STE-FOY -
LIBRARY
2560 Hochelaga Blvd.   Phone: (418) 694-4017
Ste. Foy, PQ G1V 2J3   Paul R. Venne, Area Coord., Quebec

CANADA - CANADIAN FORESTRY SERVICE - LAURENTIAN FOREST
RESEARCH CENTRE - LIBRARY
C.P. 3800, 1080 Route Du Vallon   Phone: (418) 694-3989
Ste. Foy, PQ G1V 4C7   Monique Kroon, Libn.

CENTRE DE RECHERCHE INDUSTRIELLE DU QUEBEC - DIRECTION DE
L'INFORMATION TECHNOLOGIQUE (DIT)
333 Rue Franquet   Phone: (418) 659-1550
Ste. Foy, PQ G1V 4C7   Francois Labrousse

COMPLEXE SCIENTIFIQUE DU QUEBEC - SERVICE DE DOCUMENTATION ET
DE BIBLIOTHEQUE
2700 Einstein C-I-I   Phone: (418) 643-9730
Ste. Foy, PQ G1P 3W8

QUEBEC PROVINCE - ARCHIVES NATIONALES DU QUEBEC - BIBLIOTHEQUE
C.P. 10450   Phone: (418) 643-2167
Ste. Foy, PQ G1V 4N1   Colette Barry, Libn.

QUEBEC PROVINCE - MINISTERE DE LA JUSTICE - BIBLIOTHEQUE
1200, Route De L'Eglise
Edifice Delta, 4th Fl.   Phone: (418) 643-8409
Ste. Foy, PQ G1V 4M1   Michel Ricard, Agent de Recherche

QUEBEC PROVINCE - MINISTERE DU REVENU - BIBLIOTHEQUE
3800, Rue Marly   Phone: (418) 643-6214
Ste. Foy, PQ G1X 4A5   Pierre-Paul Blais, Dir.

SOCIETE QUEBECOISE D'INITIATIVES PETROLIERES - DOCUMENTATION
CENTRE
3340 de la Perade   Phone: (418) 651-9543
Ste. Foy, PQ G1X 2L7   Gilles Dion, Chf.

UNIVERSITE LAVAL - BIBLIOTHEQUE †
Cite Universitaire   Phone: (418) 656-3343
Ste. Foy, PQ G1K 7P4   Celine R. Cartier, Dir.

UNIVERSITE LAVAL - BIBLIOTHEQUE SCIENTIFIQUE †
Pavillon Vachon
Cite Universitaire   Phone: (418) 656-3967
Ste. Foy, PQ G1K 7P4   Gilles Deschatelets, Chf.

UNIVERSITE LAVAL - CENTRE D'ETUDES NORDIQUES (CEN) - CENTRE DE
DOCUMENTATION *
Pavillon de la Tour des Arts   Phone: (418) 656-3340
Ste. Foy, PQ G1K 7P4   Serge Payette, Dir.

UNIVERSITE LAVAL - INTERNATIONAL CENTRE FOR RESEARCH ON
BILINGUALISM *
Pavillon Casault, 6th Fl.   Phone: (418) 656-3232
Ste. Foy, PQ G1K 7P4   Diane G. Garand, Libn.

UNIVERSITE DU QUEBEC - ECOLE NATIONALE D'ADMINISTRATION
PUBLIQUE - CENTRE DE DOCUMENTATION
Pavillon Katimavik
945, ave. Wolfe   Phone: (418) 657-2473
Ste. Foy, PQ G1V 3J9   Jean-Marc Alain, Coord.

GEOGRAPHIC

UNIVERSITE DU QUEBEC - MEDIATHEQUE
2875, Boul. Laurier　　　　Phone: (418) 657-2578
Ste. Foy, PQ G1V 2M3　　　　Yvon Isabel, Directeur

CEGEP ST-JEAN SUR RICHELIEU - BIBLIOTHEQUE †
30 Blvd. Du Seminaire
C.P. 310　　　　Phone: (514) 347-5301
St. Jean, PQ J3B 5J4　　　　Michel Robert, Chf.Libn.

COLLEGE MILITAIRE ROYAL DE ST-JEAN - LIBRARY
　　　　Phone: (514) 346-2131
St. Jean, PQ J0J 1R0　　　　Armand Lamirande, Chf.Libn.

CANADA - AGRICULTURE CANADA - RESEARCH STATION, ST-JEAN - LIBRARY
P.O. Box 457　　　　Phone: (514) 346-4494
St. Jean-Sur-Richelieu, PQ J3B 6Z8　　　　Ian Wallace, Libn.

COMPAGNIE DE JESUS - JESUITS LIBRARY
C.P. 130　　　　Phone: (514) 438-3593
St. Jerome, PQ J7Z 5T8　　　　Joseph Cossette, S.J., Lib.Dir.

CANADA - ATMOSPHERIC ENVIRONMENT SERVICE - QUEBEC REGION - BIBLIOTHEQUE REGIONALE
100 Blvd. Alexis-Nihon, 3rd Fl.　　　　Phone: (514) 333-3020
St. Laurent, PQ H4M 2N6　　　　Jacques Miron, Off.-In-Charge

COLLEGE DE MUSIQUE SAINTE-CROIX - BIBLIOTHEQUE *
637 Sainte-Croix Blvd.　　　　Phone: (514) 747-6521
St. Laurent, PQ H4L 3X7　　　　Lucienne Nadeau, Dir.

HOPITAL NOTRE DAME DE L'ESPERANCE - BIBLIOTHEQUE †
1275 Cote Vertu　　　　Phone: (514) 747-4771
St. Laurent, PQ H4L 4V2　　　　Sr. Gemma Emond, Med.Libn.

COLLEGE LIONEL-GROULX - BIBLIOTHEQUE
100 Rue Duquet　　　　Phone: (514) 430-3120
Ste. Therese, PQ J7E 3G6　　　　Gaetan Hebert, Media Coord.

MC GILL UNIVERSITY - SUB-ARCTIC RESEARCH STATION LIBRARY
Box 790　　　　Phone: (418) 585-2489
Schefferville, PQ G0G 2T0　　　　Douglas R. Barr, Mgr.

CENTRE HOSPITALIER HOTEL-DIEU DE SHERBROOKE - BIBLIOTHEQUE
580 S. Bowen St.　　　　Phone: (819) 569-2551
Sherbrooke, PQ J1G 2E8　　　　Louise Saucier, Chf.Libn.

GRAND SEMINAIRE DES SAINTS APOTRES - BIBLIOTHEQUE
130 Cathedrale, C.P. 430　　　　Phone: (819) 563-9934
Sherbrooke, PQ J1H 5K1　　　　Irene Desruisseaux, Sec.

MONASTERE DES PERES REDEMPTORISTES - BIBLIOTHEQUE †
871 Rue Ontario　　　　Phone: (819) 562-2677
Sherbrooke, PQ J1J 3S1　　　　Laurent Tousegnant, Libn.

SOCIETE D'HISTOIRE DES CANTONS DE L'EST - BIBLIOTHEQUE
P.O. Box 1141　　　　Phone: (819) 562-0616
Sherbrooke, PQ J1H 5L5　　　　Monique Choquette-Habel, Sec./Archv.

UNIVERSITE DE SHERBROOKE - FACULTE DE MEDECINE - BIBLIOTHEQUE
Centre Hospitalier Universitaire　　　　Phone: (819) 565-2095
Sherbrooke, PQ J1H 5N4　　　　Germain Chouinard, Dir.

Q.I.T. - FER ET TITANE INC. - BIBLIOTHEQUE
B.P. 560　　　　Phone: (514) 742-6671
Sorel, PQ J3P 5P6　　　　C. Stroemgren, Libn.

UNIVERSITE DE MONTREAL - MEDECINE VETERINAIRE-BIBLIOTHEQUE
C.P. 5000　　　　Phone: (514) 773-8521
St-Hyacinthe, PQ J2S 7C6　　　　Jean-Paul Jette, Dir.

HOPITAL DU HAUT-RICHELIEU - BIBLIOTHEQUE MEDICALE
920, boul. du Seminaire　　　　Phone: (514) 348-6101
St-Jean, PQ J3A 1B7　　　　Helene Heroux-Bouchard, Lib.Techn.

MISSISQUOI HISTORICAL SOCIETY - CORNELL MILL MUSEUM - REFERENCE LIBRARY & ARCHIVES
Box 186
Stanbridge East, PQ J0J 2H0　　　　Margaret Ellis, Archv.

ASBESTOS CORPORATION, LTD. - PRODUCT RESEARCH & DEVELOPMENT LIBRARY
835 Mooney St.
P.O. Box 9　　　　Phone: (418) 335-9171
Thetford Mines, PQ G6G 5S1　　　　Robert B. Steele, Res. Chemist

CEGEP DE TROIS-RIVIERES - BIBLIOTHEQUE
3500 De Courval　　　　Phone: (819) 376-1721
Trois-Rivieres, PQ G9A 5E6　　　　Denis Simard, Dir.

CENTRE HOSPITALIER COOKE - BIBLIOTHEQUE MEDICALE ET ADMINISTRATIVE *
3450 Rue Ste-Marguerite　　　　Phone: (819) 375-7713
Trois-Rivieres, PQ G8Z 1X3　　　　Helene H. Bouchard, Bibliotechnicienne

CENTRE HOSPITALIER ST-JOSEPH - BIBLIOTHEQUE MEDICALE ET ADMINISTRATIVE
731 Rue Ste-Julie　　　　Phone: (819) 379-8112
Trois-Rivieres, PQ G9A 1Y1　　　　Solange De-Rouyn, Chf.

SEMINAIRE ST-JOSEPH - BIBLIOTHEQUE
858 Laviolette
C.P. 548　　　　Phone: (819) 378-5167
Trois-Rivieres, PQ G9A 5J1　　　　Jerome Laperriere, Dir.

SEMINAIRE DES TROIS RIVIERES - ARCHIVES
858 Laviolette
C.P. 548
Trois-Rivieres, PQ G9A 5J1　　　　Jules Bettez, Dir.

UNIVERSITE DU QUEBEC A TROIS-RIVIERES - CARTOTHEQUE
Pavillon Michel Sarrazin
C.P. 500　　　　Phone: (819) 376-5351
Trois-Rivieres, PQ G9A 5H7　　　　Marie Lefebvre, Cartothecaire

HYDRO-QUEBEC - INSTITUT DE RECHERCHE - BIBLIOTHEQUE
1800, Montee Ste-Julie　　　　Phone: (514) 652-8324
Varennes, PQ J0L 2P0　　　　Michel Leclerc, Chf.

HOFFMANN-LA ROCHE, LTD. - CORPORATE LIBRARY
1000 Blvd. Roche　　　　Phone: (514) 487-8425
Vaudreuil, PQ J7V 6B3　　　　Mr. C.G.D. Hoare, Supv., Sci.Info.

BELL-NORTHERN RESEARCH LTD. - TECHNICAL INFORMATION CENTRE
3 Place Du Commerce, Suite 500　　　　Phone: (514) 761-5831
Verdun, PQ H3E 1H6　　　　Ghislaine Gauthier, Br.Libn.

CENTRE HOSPITALIER DE VERDUN - BIBLIOTHEQUE MEDICALE
4000 Blvd. Lasalle　　　　Phone: (514) 761-3551
Verdun, PQ H4G 2A3　　　　Mrs. Andree N. Mandeville, Libn.

SASKATCHEWAN

BATTLEFORD NATIONAL HISTORIC PARK - CAMPBELL INNES MEMORIAL LIBRARY
Box 70　　　　Phone: (306) 937-2621
Battleford, SK S0M 0E0　　　　Mrs. M.A. Simpson, Supt.

ST. CHARLES SCHOLASTICATE - LIBRARY
Box 99　　　　Phone: (306) 937-2355
Battleford, SK S0M 0E0　　　　Aloysius Kedl

BRIERCREST BIBLE INSTITUTE - ARCHIBALD LIBRARY †
　　　　Phone: (306) 756-2321
Caronport, SK S0H 0S0　　　　Allan R. Johnson, Libn.

SASKATCHEWAN - DEPARTMENT OF NORTHERN SASKATCHEWAN - LIBRARY
Box 5000　　　　Phone: (306) 425-2033
La Ronge, SK S0J 1L0　　　　Ida Studer, Libn.

ALDERSGATE COLLEGE - WILSON MEMORIAL LIBRARY
Box 460　　　　Phone: (306) 692-1816
Moose Jaw, SK S6H 4P1　　　　Ruth Huston, Dir.

MOOSE JAW LAW SOCIETY - LIBRARY †
Court House   Phone: (306) 693-6105
Moose Jaw, SK S6H 4P1   Paul Bozak, Libn.

ST. PETER'S ABBEY & COLLEGE - LIBRARY
Box 10   Phone: (306) 682-2581
Muenster, SK S0K 2Y0   Bede Hubbard, Libn.

SASKATCHEWAN HOSPITAL - DEPARTMENT OF PSYCHIATRIC SERVICES -
   STAFF LIBRARY
P.O. Box 39   Phone: (306) 445-9411
North Battleford, SK S9A 2X8   Doris Allan, Libn.

SASKATCHEWAN - DEPARTMENT OF TOURISM AND RENEWABLE
   RESOURCES - FISH MANAGEMENT DIVISION LIBRARY
Government Bldg.
Prince Albert, SK S6V 1B5   Brian Christensen, Resource Off.

SASKATCHEWAN - DEPARTMENT OF TOURISM AND RENEWABLE
   RESOURCES - FORESTRY BRANCH LIBRARY
Government Bldg., Rm. 300
49 12th St. E.   Phone: (306) 922-3133
Prince Albert, SK S6V 1B5   Janelle D. Johnston, Clerk

VICTORIA UNION HOSPITAL - MEDICAL LIBRARY
1200 24th St., W.   Phone: (306) 764-1551
Prince Albert, SK S6V 5T4   Joan I. Ryan, Med.Rec.Libn.

ALCOHOLISM COMMISSION OF SASKATCHEWAN - LIBRARY
3475 Albert St.   Phone: (306) 565-4656
Regina, SK S4S 6X6   Susan Whittick, Libn.

CAMPION COLLEGE - LIBRARY
University of Regina   Phone: (306) 586-4242
Regina, SK S4S 0A2   Myfanwy Truscott, Libn.

CANADA - AGRICULTURE CANADA - REGIONAL DEVELOPMENT &
   INTERNATIONAL AFFAIRS LIBRARY
101-2050 Cornwall St.   Phone: (306) 569-5545
Regina, SK S4P 2K6

CANADA - AGRICULTURE CANADA - RESEARCH STATION, REGINA -
   LIBRARY
5000 Wascana Pkwy.
Box 440   Phone: (306) 585-0255
Regina, SK S4P 3A2   H.C. Vanstone, Lib.Techn.

CANADA - REGIONAL ECONOMIC EXPANSION - PRAIRIE FARM
   REHABILITATION ADMINISTRATION - LIBRARY
Motherwell Bldg.   Phone: (306) 569-5100
Regina, SK S4P 0R5   Charlene Kosack, Libn.

CANADA - STATISTICS CANADA - ADVISORY SERVICES - REGINA
   REFERENCE CENTRE
530 Midtown Centre   Phone: (306) 359-5405
Regina, SK S4P 2B6   D. Lawrance, Regional Adv.

CANADIAN BIBLE COLLEGE/CANADIAN THEOLOGICAL COLLEGE -
   ARCHIBALD FOUNDATION LIBRARY
4400 Fourth Ave.   Phone: (306) 545-1515
Regina, SK S4T 0H8   Marguerite Porter, Dir., Lib. Serv.

LAW SOCIETY OF SASKATCHEWAN - LIBRARY
Court House
P.O. Box 5032   Phone: (306) 569-8020
Regina, SK S4P 3E4   Douglass T. MacEllven, Dir.

PASQUA HOSPITAL - HEALTH SCIENCES LIBRARY
4101 Dewdney Ave.   Phone: (306) 527-9641
Regina, SK S4T 1A5   Leona Lang, Dir.

PLAINS HEALTH CENTRE - DR. W.A. RIDDELL HEALTH SCIENCES LIBRARY
4500 Wascana Pkwy.   Phone: (306) 584-6210
Regina, SK S4S 5W9   Beth Silzer, Dir.

REGINA CITY - PLANNING DEPARTMENT - LIBRARY
P.O. Box 1790   Phone: (306) 569-7533
Regina, SK S4P 3C8   Helene Stewart, Libn.

REGINA GENERAL HOSPITAL - MEDICAL LIBRARY
1440 14th Ave.   Phone: (306) 359-4444
Regina, SK S4P 0W5   Mrs. A. Belva Park, Med.Libn.

ROYAL CANADIAN MOUNTED POLICE - CENTENNIAL MUSEUM LIBRARY
P.O. Box 6500   Phone: (306) 359-5837
Regina, SK S4P 3J7   Malcolm J.H. Wake, Dir.

SASKATCHEWAN ARCHIVES BOARD
Library Bldg., University of Regina   Phone: (306) 565-4068
Regina, SK S4S 0A2   Ian E. Wilson, Prov.Archv.

SASKATCHEWAN ARTS BOARD - LIBRARY
200 Lakeshore Dr.   Phone: (306) 565-4056
Regina, SK S4S 0B3

SASKATCHEWAN CANCER FOUNDATION - ALLAN BLAIR MEMORIAL CLINIC
   - LIBRARY
1555 Pasqua St.   Phone: (306) 527-9651
Regina, SK S4T 4L8

SASKATCHEWAN - DEPARTMENT OF AGRICULTURE - LIBRARY
Walter Scott Bldg.   Phone: (306) 565-5151
Regina, SK S4S 0B1   Rhona Wright, Libn.

SASKATCHEWAN - DEPARTMENT OF THE ATTORNEY GENERAL - COURT OF
   APPEAL LIBRARY
Court House, 2425 Victoria Ave.   Phone: (306) 565-5411
Regina, SK S4P 3V7   Rita M. Lidster, Libn.

SASKATCHEWAN - DEPARTMENT OF CONSUMER AND COMMERICAL
   AFFAIRS - RESOURCE CENTRE
1871 Smith St.   Phone: (306) 565-5549
Regina, SK S4P 3V7   Edith Berg, Coord.

SASKATCHEWAN - DEPARTMENT OF CO-OPERATION - LIBRARY
2055 Albert St.   Phone: (306) 565-5807
Regina, SK S4P 3V7   Rae French, Resource Ctr.Coord.

SASKATCHEWAN - DEPARTMENT OF EDUCATION - RESOURCE CENTRE
2220 College Ave.   Phone: (306) 565-5977
Regina, SK S4P 3V7   Jane Naisbitt, Libn.

SASKATCHEWAN - DEPARTMENT OF THE ENVIRONMENT - LIBRARY
5th Fl., 1855 Victoria Ave.   Phone: (306) 565-6125
Regina, SK S4P 3V5   Mrs. Shannon G. Bellamy, Supv.

SASKATCHEWAN - DEPARTMENT OF HEALTH - LIBRARY
3475 Albert St.   Phone: (306) 565-3090
Regina, SK S4S 6X6   M. Smigarowski, Lib.Supv.

SASKATCHEWAN - DEPARTMENT OF HIGHWAYS AND TRANSPORTATION -
   PLANNING BRANCH LIBRARY
1855 Victoria Ave.   Phone: (306) 565-4777
Regina, SK S4P 3V5   Dr. M.U. Hassan, Libn.

SASKATCHEWAN - DEPARTMENT OF INDUSTRY AND COMMERCE -
   LIBRARY
Saskatchewan Power Bldg., 7th Fl.   Phone: (306) 565-2232
Regina, SK S4P 3V7   Lionel Poitras, Res.Off.

SASKATCHEWAN - DEPARTMENT OF LABOUR - LIBRARY
1914 Hamilton St.   Phone: (306) 565-2429
Regina, SK S4P 4V4   Fraser Russell, Libn.

SASKATCHEWAN - DEPARTMENT OF LABOUR - OCCUPATIONAL HEALTH
   AND SAFETY DIVISION - LIBRARY
1150 Rose St.   Phone: (306) 565-4494
Regina, SK S4R 3V7   Susan Johnson, Libn.

SASKATCHEWAN - DEPARTMENT OF LABOUR - WOMEN'S DIVISION -
   RESOURCE CENTRE
1914 Hamilton St.   Phone: (306) 565-2465
Regina, SK S4P 4Y4   Jane Coombe, Educ.Ext.Coord.

SASKATCHEWAN - DEPARTMENT OF REVENUE, SUPPLY & SERVICES -
   SYSTEMS CENTRE LIBRARY
3rd Fl., T.C. Douglas Bldg.
3475 Albert St.   Phone: (306) 565-2090
Regina, SK S4S 6X6   Heather D. Haig, Lib.Techn.

GEOGRAPHIC

SASKATCHEWAN - DEPARTMENT OF SOCIAL SERVICES - LIBRARY
1920 Broad St.   Phone: (306) 565-3605
Regina, SK S4P 3V6   Janice Watson, Lib.Techn.

SASKATCHEWAN - DEPARTMENT OF URBAN AFFAIRS - LIBRARY
1791 Rose St.
Regina, SK S4P 3V7

SASKATCHEWAN GENEALOGICAL SOCIETY - LIBRARY
Box 1894
Regina, SK S4P 3E1   Laura M. Hanowski, Libn.

SASKATCHEWAN INDIAN FEDERATED COLLEGE - LIBRARY
University of Regina
C-4, Classroom Bldg.   Phone: (306) 584-8333
Regina, SK S4S 0A2   Heather West, Libn.

SASKATCHEWAN - LEGISLATIVE LIBRARY
234 Legislative Bldg.   Phone: (306) 565-2277
Regina, SK S4S 0B3   Christine MacDonald, Legislative Libn.

SASKATCHEWAN MUSEUM OF NATURAL HISTORY - LIBRARY
Dept. of Culture and Youth
Wascana Park   Phone: (306) 565-2808
Regina, SK S4P 3V7   Ruby Apperley, Supv., Museum Serv.

SASKATCHEWAN - PHOTOGRAPHIC AND ART DIVISION - LIBRARY
Legislative Bldg., Rm. 3   Phone: (306) 565-6298
Regina, SK S4S 0B3   Dorothy McMillan, Photo Libn.

SASKATCHEWAN PIPING INDUSTRY JOINT TRAINING BOARD - LIBRARY †
1366 Cornwall St.   Phone: (306) 522-4237
Regina, SK S4R 2H5   Jill Collins

SASKATCHEWAN POWER CORPORATION - LIBRARY
2025 Victoria Ave.   Phone: (306) 525-7650
Regina, SK S4P 0S1   H. Philley, Lib.Ck.

SASKATCHEWAN - PROVINCIAL LIBRARY
1352 Winnipeg St.   Phone: (306) 565-2972
Regina, SK S4P 3V7   Merry Harbottle, Act.Prov.Libn.

SASKATCHEWAN WHEAT POOL - REFERENCE LIBRARY
2625 Victoria Ave.   Phone: (306) 569-4480
Regina, SK S4P 2Y6   A.D. McLeod, Res.Dir.

UNIVERSITY OF REGINA - BILINGUAL CENTRE - LIBRARY
College West No. 218   Phone: (306) 584-4177
Regina, SK S4S 0A5

UNIVERSITY OF REGINA - CANADIAN PLAINS RESEARCH CENTER INFORMATION SYSTEM
                                            Phone: (306) 584-4758
Regina, SK S4S 0A2   Margaret Scratch, Coord., Info.Serv.

UNIVERSITY OF REGINA - EDUCATION BRANCH LIBRARY
                                            Phone: (306) 584-4642
Regina, SK S4S 0A2   Del Affleck, Hd.

UNIVERSITY OF REGINA - MAP LIBRARY
                                            Phone: (306) 584-4401
Regina, SK S4S 0A2   Mrs. Anwar S. Qureshi, Map Libn.

WASCANA HOSPITAL - HEALTH SCIENCES LIBRARY
Ave. G & 23rd Ave.   Phone: (306) 359-9230
Regina, SK S4S 0A5   Darlene Jones, Dir.

WASCANA INSTITUTE OF APPLIED ARTS AND SCIENCES - RESOURCE & INFORMATION CENTRE
4635 Wascana Pkwy.
Box 556   Phone: (306) 565-4321
Regina, SK S4P 3A3   Pran Vohra, Supv./Chf.Libn.

CANADA - AGRICULTURE CANADA - RESEARCH STATION, SASKATOON - LIBRARY
107 Science Cresc.   Phone: (306) 343-8214
Saskatoon, SK S7N 0X2   Marlene Glen, Libn.

CANADA - CANADIAN WILDLIFE SERVICE - PRAIRIE MIGRATORY BIRD RESEARCH CENTRE - LIBRARY
115 Perimeter Rd.   Phone: (306) 665-4087
Saskatoon, SK S7N 0X4   Dorothy Lapp, Lib.Techn.

CANADA - NATIONAL RESEARCH COUNCIL - PRAIRIE REGIONAL LABORATORY LIBRARY
                                            Phone: (306) 343-9541
Saskatoon, SK S7N 0W9   Flora Chen, Libn.

CO-OPERATIVE COLLEGE OF CANADA - LIBRARY SERVICES
141 105th St., W.   Phone: (306) 373-0474
Saskatoon, SK S7N 1N3   Leona Olson, Libn.

ELIASON (Frank) CENTRE - HEALTH SCIENCES LIBRARY
2003 Arlington Ave.   Phone: (306) 373-2151
Saskatoon, SK S7J 2H6   Patricia Jarvis

KELSEY INSTITUTE OF APPLIED ARTS AND SCIENCES - LEARNING RESOURCES CENTRE
P.O. Box 1520   Phone: (306) 664-6417
Saskatoon, SK S7K 3R5   D.F. Robertson, Dir.

LAW SOCIETY OF SASKATCHEWAN - BARRISTERS LIBRARY
Court House
520 Spadina Crescent E.   Phone: (306) 664-5141
Saskatoon, SK S7K 3G7   Peta Bates, Libn.

MOHYLA INSTITUTE - LIBRARY AND ARCHIVES
1240 Temperance St.   Phone: (306) 653-1944
Saskatoon, SK S7N 0P1   F.J. Kindrachuk, Rector

SASKATCHEWAN INDIAN CULTURAL COLLEGE - LIBRARY
Box 3085   Phone: (306) 244-1146
Saskatoon, SK S7K 3S9   David L. Sparvier, Coord.

SASKATCHEWAN RESEARCH COUNCIL - LIBRARY
30 Campus Dr.   Phone: (306) 242-6494
Saskatoon, SK S7N 0X1   Sharon E. Neary, Libn.

SASKATCHEWAN TEACHERS' FEDERATION - STEWART RESOURCES CENTRE
2317 Arlington Ave.
Box 1108   Phone: (306) 373-1660
Saskatoon, SK S7K 3N3   Ms. S.M. Dyer, Libn.

SASKATOON CANCER CLINIC - LIBRARY & SIGGA COOK MEMORIAL LIBRARY
University Hospital   Phone: (306) 343-9565
Saskatoon, SK S7N 0X0   Agnes Stanek, Ck.

SASKATOON GALLERY AND CONSERVATORY CORPORATION - MENDEL ART GALLERY - LIBRARY
950 Spadina Crescent E.
P.O. Box 569   Phone: (306) 664-9610
Saskatoon, SK S7K 3L6   Joan Steel, Libn.

SASKATOON STAR-PHOENIX - LIBRARY
204 5th Ave., N.   Phone: (306) 664-8223
Saskatoon, SK S7K 2P1   Don Perkins, Libn.

UKRAINIAN WOMEN'S ASSOCIATION OF CANADA - UKRAINIAN MUSEUM OF CANADA - LIBRARY
910 Spadina Crescent E.   Phone: (306) 244-3800
Saskatoon, SK S7K 3H5   Marie Kishchuk, Act.Dir.

UNIVERSITY OF SASKATCHEWAN - EDUCATION BRANCH LIBRARY
                                            Phone: (306) 343-3793
Saskatoon, SK S7N 0W0   Margaret Baldock, Libn.

UNIVERSITY OF SASKATCHEWAN - ENGINEERING BRANCH LIBRARY
                                            Phone: (306) 343-2062
Saskatoon, SK S7N 0W0   Edna Wilson, Lib.Asst.

UNIVERSITY OF SASKATCHEWAN - GEOLOGY BRANCH LIBRARY
                                            Phone: (306) 343-4358
Saskatoon, SK S7N 0W0   Lise St. Arnaud, Lib.Asst.

UNIVERSITY OF SASKATCHEWAN - HEALTH SCIENCES LIBRARY
Phone: (306) 343-3168
Saskatoon, SK S7N 0W0 Dr. Wilma Sweaney, Libn.

UNIVERSITY OF SASKATCHEWAN - INSTITUTE FOR NORTHERN STUDIES -
LIBRARY
John G. Diefenbaker Centre Phone: (306) 343-4318
Saskatoon, SK S7N 0W0 R. Gyorgy, Libn.

UNIVERSITY OF SASKATCHEWAN - LAW LIBRARY
Phone: (306) 343-4273
Saskatoon, SK S7N 0W0 E. Stanek, Law Libn.

UNIVERSITY OF SASKATCHEWAN - LUTHERAN THEOLOGICAL SEMINARY -
OTTO OLSON MEMORIAL LIBRARY †
114 Seminary Crescent Phone: (306) 343-8204
Saskatoon, SK S7N 0X3 Mrs. M. Kinzel, Libn.

UNIVERSITY OF SASKATCHEWAN - PHYSICS BRANCH LIBRARY
Phone: (306) 343-4934
Saskatoon, SK S7N 0W0 Lori Horky, Lib.Asst.

UNIVERSITY OF SASKATCHEWAN - ST. ANDREW'S COLLEGE - LIBRARY
Phone: (306) 343-6631
Saskatoon, SK S7N 0W3 Rosa Ho, Libn.

UNIVERSITY OF SASKATCHEWAN - ST. THOMAS MORE COLLEGE -
SHANNON LIBRARY
1437 College Dr. Phone: (306) 343-4561
Saskatoon, SK S7N 0W6 Dr. Margot King, Libn.

UNIVERSITY OF SASKATCHEWAN - SPECIAL COLLECTIONS - SHORTT
LIBRARY OF CANADIANA
University Library Phone: (306) 343-4514
Saskatoon, SK S7N 0W0 Shirley Perkins, Hd.

UNIVERSITY OF SASKATCHEWAN - THORVALDSON LIBRARY
Thorvaldson Bldg. Phone: (306) 343-2956
Saskatoon, SK S7N 0W0 Lily Chin, Lib.Asst.

UNIVERSITY OF SASKATCHEWAN - WESTERN COLLEGE OF VETERINARY
MEDICINE - LIBRARY
Phone: (306) 343-3249
Saskatoon, SK S7N 0W0 John V. James, Libn.

WESTERN DEVELOPMENT MUSEUM - GEORGE SHEPHERD LIBRARY
2610 Lorne Ave., S.
P.O. Box 1910 Phone: (306) 652-8900
Saskatoon, SK S7K 3S5

CANADA - AGRICULTURE CANADA - RESEARCH STATION, SWIFT CURRENT
- LIBRARY
Box 1030 Phone: (306) 773-4621
Swift Current, SK S9H 3X2 Karen E. Wilton, Libn.

PSYCHIATRIC CENTRE - STAFF LIBRARY
Box 1056 Phone: (306) 842-5461
Weyburn, SK S4H 2L4 Helen Sayyeau

SOURIS VALLEY EXTENDED CARE HOSPITAL - LIBRARY
Box 2001 Phone: (306) 842-7481
Weyburn, SK S4H 2L7 W.D. Wallin, Dir., Finance

UNITED STATES SPACE EDUCATION ASSOCIATION - G.L. BORROWMAN
ASTRONAUTICS LIBRARY
P.O. Box 1032
Weyburn, SK S4H 2L3 Gerald L. Borrowman, Chf.

NOTRE DAME COLLEGE - LANE HALL MEMORIAL LIBRARY - SPECIAL
COLLECTIONS
Box 280
Wilcox, SK S0G 5E0

YUKON TERRITORY

YUKON TERRITORY - DEPARTMENT OF LIBRARY AND INFORMATION
RESOURCES - YUKON ARCHIVES
2071 Second Ave. Phone: (403) 667-5321
Whitehorse, YT Y1A 2C6 Miriam McTiernan, Territorial Archv.

GEOGRAPHIC

Section 2
PERSONNEL INDEX

For phone numbers, street addresses, and zip codes of libraries cited in Personnel Index listings, consult Section 1—Geographic Index.

A

Aaker, Ordelle, Libn.
AID ASSOCIATION FOR LUTHERANS -
CORPORATE LIBRARY □ Appleton, WI

Aarhus, Robert, Hd.Libn.
URBAN TRANSPORTATION DEVELOPMENT
CORPORATION - LIBRARY □ Toronto, ON

Aaron, Arthur, Supv.
NEW YORK TIMES - PHOTO LIBRARY □ New
York, NY

Aaron, Betty J., Libn.
PURE CARBON CO., INC. - ENGINEERING
LIBRARY □ St. Marys, PA

Aaron, Robert D., Ref.Libn.
ATLANTA NEWSPAPERS - REFERENCE LIBRARY
□ Atlanta, GA

Abajian, James, Archv.
ARCHDIOCESE OF SAN FRANCISCO -
CHANCERY ARCHIVES □ Colma, CA

Abatelli, Carol, Asst.Libn., Slides
COOPER UNION FOR THE ADVANCEMENT OF
SCIENCE AND ART - LIBRARY □ New York, NY

Abbas, R.M., Tech.Libn.
GENERAL ELECTRIC COMPANY - AIRCRAFT
ENGINE GROUP - TECHNICAL INFORMATION
CENTER □ Cincinnati, OH

Abbe, Elizabeth, Libn.
CONNECTICUT HISTORICAL SOCIETY -
LIBRARY □ Hartford, CT

Abbey, Eugenia H., Chf.Libn.
U.S. VETERANS ADMINISTRATION (GA-Atlanta)
- HOSPITAL MEDICAL LIBRARY □ Decatur, GA

Abbey, Karen, Hd., Cat.
UNIVERSITY OF MICHIGAN - DEARBORN
LIBRARY □ Dearborn, MI

Abbott, Bruce T., Coord.Lib.Serv.
CHARITY HOSPITAL - SCHOOL OF NURSING -
LIBRARY □ New Orleans, LA

Abbott, Clarence H., Jr., Chf.
U.S. FEDERAL AVIATION ADMINISTRATION -
TECHNICAL CENTER LIBRARY† □ Atlantic City
Airport, NJ

Abbott, Laura P., Libn.
VERMONT HISTORICAL SOCIETY - LIBRARY □
Montpelier, VT

Abbott, Robert, Tech.Dir.
AMERICAN SOCIETY FOR QUALITY CONTROL -
LIBRARY □ Milwaukee, WI

Abbruzzese, Marie Grace, Libn.
MARY'S HELP HOSPITAL - LIBRARY† □ Daly
City, CA

Abdelghani, Hoda, Libn.
CALIFORNIA INSTITUTE OF TECHNOLOGY -
GEOLOGY LIBRARY □ Pasadena, CA

Abdullah, Bilquis, Dp.Libn.
ROCKLAND RESEARCH INSTITUTE - ROCKLAND
HEALTH SCIENCES LIBRARY □ Orangeburg, NY

Abel, Arthur R., Archv.
U.S. NATL. PARK SERVICE - EDISON NATL.
HISTORIC SITE - ARCHIVES □ West Orange, NJ

Abel, Wanda, Ref.Libn.
OHIO STATE SUPREME COURT LAW LIBRARY □
Columbus, OH

Abell, J. Richard, Hd.
PUBLIC LIBRARY OF CINCINNATI AND
HAMILTON COUNTY - HISTORY AND
LITERATURE DEPARTMENT □ Cincinnati, OH

Abell, Millicent D., Univ.Libn.
UNIVERSITY OF CALIFORNIA, SAN DIEGO -
UNIVERSITY LIBRARIES □ La Jolla, CA

Abelow, Ruth M., Libn.
TEMPLE EMANU-EL - LIBRARY □ Miami Beach,
FL

Abelson, Rabbi Kassel, Supv.
BETH EL SYNAGOGUE - MAX SHAPIRO LIBRARY
□ St. Louis Park, MN

Abend, Beth, Gen.Libn.
FRIED, FRANK, HARRIS, SHRIVER, JACOBSON -
LIBRARY & INFORMATION CENTER □ New York,
NY

Aber, Robyn, Info.Sci.
SANDOZ COLORS & CHEMICALS -
INFORMATION CENTER □ East Hanover, NJ

Abernathy, Sandra, Circ.Supv.
ASBURY THEOLOGICAL SEMINARY - B.L.
FISHER LIBRARY □ Wilmore, KY

Abid, Ann B., Libn.
ST. LOUIS ART MUSEUM - RICHARDSON
MEMORIAL LIBRARY □ St. Louis, MO

Ables, Linda, Libn.
OKLAHOMA REGIONAL LIBRARY FOR THE
BLIND AND PHYSICALLY HANDICAPPED □
Oklahoma City, OK

Ablove, Gayle, Cat.
ROSWELL PARK MEMORIAL INSTITUTE -
MEDICAL AND SCIENTIFIC LIBRARY □ Buffalo,
NY

Abney, Ella M., Libn.
ACADEMY OF MEDICINE OF THE COUNTY OF
QUEENS, INC. - CARL M. BOETTIGER
MEMORIAL LIBRARY† □ Forest Hills, NY

Abraham, Lynn, Assoc.Libn.
SIMPSON, THACHER & BARTLETT - LIBRARY† □
New York, NY

Abrahamian, Aina, Lib.Dir.
CALIFORNIA LUTHERAN COLLEGE - LIBRARY □
Thousand Oaks, CA

Abrahamson, Edythe, Libn.
MINNEAPOLIS PUBLIC LIBRARY &
INFORMATION CENTER - BUSINESS AND
SCIENCE DEPARTMENT □ Minneapolis, MN

Abrahamson, Elaine, Libn.
ATLANTIC COUNTY HISTORICAL SOCIETY -
LIBRARY □ Somers Point, NJ

Abram, Stephen K., Libn.
CURRIE, COOPERS & LYBRAND, LTD. -
LIBRARY/INFORMATION CENTRE □ Toronto,
ON

Abramowicz, Dina, Chf.Libn.
YIVO INSTITUTE FOR JEWISH RESEARCH -
LIBRARY AND ARCHIVES □ New York, NY

Abrams, Douglas, Tech.Serv.Dir.
UTAH STATE LIBRARY □ Salt Lake City, UT

Abrams, F., Hd., Ref./Coll.Dev.
UNIVERSITY OF WATERLOO - ENGINEERING,
MATHEMATICS & SCIENCE DIVISIONAL
LIBRARY □ Waterloo, ON

Abramson, Edna, Libn.
UNION TRUST COMPANY OF MARYLAND -
LIBRARY □ Baltimore, MD

Abramson, Jenifer, Asst.Cat.
LOYOLA LAW SCHOOL - LIBRARY □ Los Angeles,
CA

Abramson, Mark, Sr.Libn.
KINGS PARK PSYCHIATRIC CENTER - LIBRARY
□ Kings Park, NY

Abrenica, Mrs. Neftalie, Libn.
INCO METALS COMPANY - EXPLORATION
LIBRARY □ Toronto, ON

Abzinger, Ms. S., Libn.
ROYAL COLUMBIAN HOSPITAL - LIBRARY □
New Westminster, BC

Achenbach, Erna, Hd.Libn.
KROTONA INSTITUTE OF THEOSOPHY -
KROTONA LIBRARY □ Ojai, CA

Acker, Nancy S., Libn.
CAUDILL ROWLETT SCOTT - LIBRARY □
Houston, TX

Ackerman, Dorothy P., Per. & Tech.Serv.Libn.
U.S. ARMY POST - FORT JACKSON - LIBRARY □
Ft. Jackson, SC

Ackerman, Ellen, Supv., Ref.Serv.
CONFERENCE BOARD, INC. - INFORMATION
SERVICE □ New York, NY

Ackerman, Katherine, Libn.
CHICAGO TRIBUNE - INFORMATION CENTER □
Chicago, IL

Ackerman, P.M., Sect.Mgr.
MC DONNELL DOUGLAS CORPORATION -
DOUGLAS AIRCRAFT COMPANY - TECHNICAL
LIBRARY □ Long Beach, CA

Ackermann, Susan J., Libn.
COOPERS AND LYBRAND - LIBRARY AND
INFORMATION CENTER □ Boston, MA

Ackerson, Dorothy, Lib. Aide
GROUT MUSEUM OF HISTORY AND SCIENCE -
REFERENCE LIBRARY □ Waterloo, IA

Ackerson, Margaret, Hd., Tech.Info.Serv.
CREARE, INC. - LIBRARY □ Hanover, NH

Ackert, Elizabeth, Lib.Asst.
COLONIAL WILLIAMSBURG - RESEARCH
LIBRARY & ARCHIVES □ Williamsburg, VA

Ackroyd, Lynn, Ref.Libn.
BRITISH COLUMBIA LAW LIBRARY
FOUNDATION - VANCOUVER COURTHOUSE
LIBRARY □ Vancouver, BC

Acosta, Trinidad B., Libn.
EL PASO HERALD-POST - LIBRARY □ El Paso, TX

Acton, Anne, Asst.Libn.
NEW ENGLAND SCHOOL OF LAW - LIBRARY □
Boston, MA

Adach, Ms. S., Data Lib. Programmer
UNIVERSITY OF BRITISH COLUMBIA - DATA
LIBRARY □ Vancouver, BC

Adair, Kay, Libn.
EASTERN ORTHODOX CATHOLIC CHURCH IN
AMERICA - THREE HIERARCHS SEMINARY
LIBRARY □ Coyle, OK

Adam, Mrs. Rohini, Ref.Libn.
MC GILL UNIVERSITY - PHYSICAL SCIENCES
LIBRARY □ Montreal, PQ

Adamchak, Donald J., Act.Dir.
KANSAS STATE UNIVERSITY - POPULATION
RESEARCH LABORATORY - LIBRARY □
Manhattan, KS

Adamo, Clare, Asst.Libn.
FRITZSCHE, DODGE AND OLCOTT, INC. -
RESEARCH LIBRARY □ New York, NY

Adamovich, Shirley G., Act. State Libn.
NEW HAMPSHIRE STATE LIBRARY □ Concord,
NH

Adams, Agnes, Asst. Professor
UNIVERSITY OF NEBRASKA, LINCOLN -
GEOLOGY LIBRARY □ Lincoln, NE

Adams, Agnes, Asst. Professor
UNIVERSITY OF NEBRASKA, LINCOLN -
MATHEMATICS LIBRARY □ Lincoln, NE

Adams, Agnes, Asst. Professor
UNIVERSITY OF NEBRASKA, LINCOLN -
PHYSICS LIBRARY □ Lincoln, NE

Adams, Barbara S., Chf.Libn.
U.S. VETERANS ADMINISTRATION (WV-
Martinsburg) - CENTER MEDICAL LIBRARY □
Martinsburg, WV

Adams, Carol C., Libn.
SOUTHEAST LOUISIANA HOSPITAL -
PROFESSIONAL LIBRARY □ Mandeville, LA

Adams, Deborah L., Libn.
BOTSFORD GENERAL HOSPITAL, OSTEOPATHIC
- MEDICAL LIBRARY □ Farmington, MI

Adams, Donna, Libn.
CELANESE CORPORATION - CELANESE FIBERS
COMPANY - TECHNICAL LIBRARY □ Rock Hill,
SC

Adams, E.M., Jr., Libn.
EAST TEXAS BAPTIST COLLEGE - MAMYE
JARRETT LEARNING CENTER □ Marshall, TX

Adams, Elaine P., Supv., Lib.Serv.
GETTY OIL COMPANY, INC. - RESEARCH
CENTER LIBRARY □ Houston, TX

Adams, Mrs. Elva R., Dir. & Libn.
WARREN COUNTY HISTORICAL SOCIETY -
MUSEUM AND LIBRARY □ Lebanon, OH

Adams, Evelyn, Tech.Libn.
VENTURA COUNTY RESOURCE MANAGEMENT
AGENCY - TECHNICAL LIBRARY □ Ventura, CA

Adams, Geraldine, Gen.Ref.
OKLAHOMA STATE DEPARTMENT OF
LIBRARIES □ Oklahoma City, OK

Adams, Ida G., Interim Dir., LRC
FLORIDA A&M UNIVERSITY - SCHOOL OF
PHARMACY LIBRARY □ Tallahassee, FL

Adams, Jacqueline, Hd., Acq.Sect.
NORTHWESTERN UNIVERSITY - HEALTH
SCIENCES LIBRARY □ Chicago, IL

Adams, Jean, Libn.
BECHTEL POWER CORPORATION - LIBRARY □
Houston, TX

Adams, Jeanne, Program Serv.Adm.
WOODSIDE RECEIVING HOSPITAL - STAFF
RESOURCE LIBRARY/PATIENTS' LIBRARY □
Youngstown, OH

Adams, Dr. Joe A., Dir.
NATIONAL FOUNDATION OF FUNERAL SERVICE
- BERYL L. BOYER LIBRARY □ Evanston, IL

Adams, John, Libn./Info.Spec.
KALBA BOWEN ASSOCIATES - LIBRARY □
Cambridge, MA

Adams, John, Univ. Photographer
UNIVERSITY OF NEW HAMPSHIRE -
DEPARTMENT OF MEDIA SERVICES - FILM
LIBRARY □ Durham, NH

Adams, Karen, Info.Spec.
MIAMI VALLEY REGIONAL PLANNING
COMMISSION - LIBRARY □ Dayton, OH

Adams, Lowell, Dir.
OKLAHOMA ART CENTER - LIBRARY □ Oklahoma
City, OK

Adams, Mary D., Libn.
METROPOLITAN COUNCIL OF THE TWIN
CITIES AREA - LIBRARY □ St. Paul, MN

Adams, Mathilda, Responsable
CENTRE HOSPITALIER DE L'HOTEL-DIEU DE
GASPE - MEDICAL LIBRARY □ Havre De Gaspe,
PQ

Adams, Patricia L., Off.Mgr.
MICHIGAN AUDUBON SOCIETY - EDITH
MUNGER LIBRARY □ Kalamazoo, MI

Adams, Patricia L., Sr.Mss.Spec.
UNIVERSITY OF MISSOURI, ST. LOUIS -
WESTERN HISTORICAL MANUSCRIPT
COLLECTION/STATE HISTORICAL SOC. OF
MISSOURI □ St. Louis, MO

Adams, Mrs. R. Burns, Tech.Serv.Libn.
TECHNICAL UNIVERSITY OF NOVA SCOTIA -
LIBRARY □ Halifax, NS

Adams, Raquel, Cat.
UTAH STATE LIBRARY □ Salt Lake City, UT

Adams, Ruth C., Libn.
EASTER SEAL REHABILITATION CENTER OF
SOUTHWESTERN CONNECTICUT - FRANCIS M.
HARRISON MEMORIAL LIBRARY □ Stamford, CT

Adams, Sally L., Day Supv.
INDIANAPOLIS NEWSPAPERS, INC. -
INDIANAPOLIS STAR AND INDIANAPOLIS
NEWS - REFERENCE LIBRARY □ Indianapolis, IN

Adams, Thomas R., Libn.
BROWN UNIVERSITY - JOHN CARTER BROWN
LIBRARY □ Providence, RI

Adams, Tommy, Hd.Archv.Proc.
TENNESSEE STATE LIBRARY AND ARCHIVES -
ARCHIVES & MANUSCRIPTS SECTION □
Nashville, TN

Adams, Virginia, Info.Spec.
FIDELITY MANAGEMENT & RESEARCH
COMPANY - LIBRARY □ Boston, MA

Adams, Virginia, Adm.Dir.
FUND FOR PEACE - CENTER FOR
INTERNATIONAL POLICY - INFORMATION
CENTER □ Washington, DC

Adams, Virginia M., Libn.
OLD DARTMOUTH HISTORICAL SOCIETY AND
WHALING MUSEUM - LIBRARY □ New Bedford,
MA

Adams, W.K., Asst. to Res.Dir.
DAN RIVER, INC. - RESEARCH LIBRARY □
Danville, VA

Adamski, Cheryl A., Libn.
NATIONAL ASSOCIATION OF INSURANCE
COMMISSIONERS - NAIC INFORMATION
CENTER □ Brookfield, WI

Adamson, L. Kurt, Hd.Pub.Serv.
BOSTON UNIVERSITY - PAPPAS LAW LIBRARY
□ Boston, MA

Adamson, Martha, Ref.Libn.
U.S. AIR FORCE WEAPONS LABORATORY -
TECHNICAL LIBRARY □ Kirtland AFB, NM

Adan, A.
DOW CHEMICAL COMPANY - TECHNICAL
INFORMATION SERVICES - CHEMICAL
LIBRARY □ Midland, MI

Addis, Louise, Asst.Libn.
STANFORD LINEAR ACCELERATOR CENTER -
LIBRARY □ Menlo Park, CA

Addison, Barbara, Cat.
SWARTHMORE COLLEGE - FRIENDS
HISTORICAL LIBRARY - PEACE COLLECTION □
Swarthmore, PA

Addison, Marion, Libn.
METROPOLITAN TORONTO LIBRARY - HISTORY
DEPARTMENT □ Toronto, ON

Adelberg, Greta, Pict.Libn.
EUROPEAN ART COLOR - PETER ADELBERG
ARCHIVE □ New York, NY

Adele, Sr. M., Asst.Archv.
SISTERS OF THE HOLY FAMILY OF NAZARETH -
IMMACULATE CONCEPTION PROVINCE -
ARCHIVES □ Philadelphia, PA

Adelman, George, Libn.
MASSACHUSETTS INSTITUTE OF TECHNOLOGY
- NEUROSCIENCES RESEARCH PROGRAM -
LIBRARY □ Boston, MA

Adelman, Jean S., Libn.
UNIVERSITY OF PENNSYLVANIA - MUSEUM
LIBRARY □ Philadelphia, PA

Aderhold, Margaret, Supv., User Serv.
AUTOMATION INDUSTRIES, INC. - VITRO
LABORATORIES DIVISION - ADMINISTRATIVE
SUPPORT DEPARTMENT □ Silver Spring, MD

Adjaye, Joseph, Outreach Spec.
UNIVERSITY OF WISCONSIN, MADISON -
AFRICAN STUDIES INSTRUCTIONAL
MATERIALS CENTER □ Madison, WI

Adkins, Gail, Acq.Libn.
SOUTHERN ILLINOIS UNIVERSITY - SCHOOL OF
MEDICINE - MEDICAL LIBRARY □ Springfield, IL

Adkins, Julia, Libn.
UNION CARBIDE CORPORATION -
ENGINEERING DEPARTMENT LIBRARY □ South
Charleston, WV

Adkins, Marge, Lib.Ck.
HOLZER MEDICAL CENTER - SCHOOL OF
NURSING - LIBRARY □ Gallipolis, OH

Adkinson, Dorothea P., Libn.
STANDARD REGISTER COMPANY - CORPORATE
LIBRARY □ Dayton, OH

Adkisson, Kenneth, Chf.Interp.
U.S. NATL. PARK SERVICE - NEZ PERCE NATL.
HISTORICAL PARK - LIBRARY □ Spalding, ID

Adler, Alex, Pres.
EXCERPTA MEDICA - DATABASE DIVISION □
Princeton, NJ

Adler, Estelle C., Adm.
AMERICAN CAN COMPANY - BUSINESS
INFORMATION CENTER □ Greenwich, CT

Adorno, Miriam, Libn.
NEW YORK EYE AND EAR INFIRMARY -
BERNARD SAMUELS LIBRARY □ New York, NY

Adreani, Earl E., Dir.
BOSTON UNIVERSITY - KRASKER MEMORIAL
FILM LIBRARY □ Boston, MA

Adrian-Neufeld, Audrey, Asst.Libn.
WINNIPEG BIBLE COLLEGE/WINNIPEG
THEOLOGICAL SEMINARY - LIBRARY □
Otterburne, MB

Aducci, Patricia J., Tech.Libn.
COLT INDUSTRIES - CRUCIBLE RESEARCH
CENTER - LIBRARY □ Pittsburgh, PA

Affleck, Del, Hd.
UNIVERSITY OF REGINA - EDUCATION
BRANCH LIBRARY □ Regina, SK

Afflerbach, Betty, Libn.
TEXAS MEDICAL ASSOCIATION - MEMORIAL
LIBRARY □ Austin, TX

Africano, Theresa, Libn.
ST. AGNES MEDICAL CENTER - HEALTH
SCIENCES LIBRARY □ Philadelphia, PA

Africk, Lenore, Chem.Libn.
ARMAK COMPANY - RESEARCH LIBRARY □
McCook, IL

Agajanian, A.H., Biblog.
IBM CORPORATION - GENERAL TECHNOLOGY
DIVISION - EAST FISHKILL FACILITY -
LIBRARY □ Hopewell Junction, NY

Agar, Mrs. W.S., Hist.Stud.Libn.
INSTITUTE FOR ADVANCED STUDY -
LIBRARIES □ Princeton, NJ

Ager, Susan F., Hd.Libn.
OAK TERRACE NURSING HOME - DEPT. OF
PUBLIC WELFARE MEDICAL LIBRARY □
Minnetonka, MN

Aggarwal, Narindar, Asst. Asian Libn.
UNIVERSITY OF ILLINOIS - ASIAN LIBRARY □
Urbana, IL

Aggarwal, Narindar K., Asst. Asian Libn.
UNIVERSITY OF ILLINOIS - ASIAN LIBRARY -
SOUTH AND WEST ASIAN DIVISION □ Urbana,
IL

Aggers, Lee, Chf., NCIC - W.
U.S. GEOLOGICAL SURVEY - NATL.
CARTOGRAPHIC INFORMATION CENTER
(NCIC) - WESTERN BRANCH □ Menlo Park, CA

Agler, Raymond B., Coord.
BOSTON PUBLIC LIBRARY - HUMANITIES
REFERENCE □ Boston, MA

Agner, Pamela, Patients' Libn.
U.S. VETERANS ADMINISTRATION (FL-Miami) -
HOSPITAL MEDICAL LIBRARY □ Miami, FL

Agnes, Mother, O.S.B., Libn.
ABBEY OF REGINA LAUDIS, ORDER OF ST.
BENEDICT - LIBRARY □ Bethlehem, CT

Agnew, Dr. Brad, Interim Dir.
NORTHEASTERN OKLAHOMA STATE
UNIVERSITY - JOHN VAUGHAN LIBRARY/
LEARNING RESOURCES CENTER □ Tahlequah,
OK

Agnew, Christopher, Mss.Libn.
HISTORICAL SOCIETY OF DELAWARE -
LIBRARY† □ Wilmington, DE

Agnew, Freda Clark, Med.Libn.
GRAND VIEW HOSPITAL - MEDICAL RESOURCE
LIBRARY □ Sellersville, PA

Agostino, Angela, Libn.
MARSH & MC LENNAN - INFORMATION CENTRE
□ Toronto, ON

Agriesti, Paul A., Deputy State Libn.
NEW MEXICO STATE LIBRARY □ Santa Fe, NM

Aguece, Debra, Ref.Libn.
NEW YORK PUBLIC LIBRARY - BELMONT
REGIONAL LIBRARY - ENRICO FERMI
CULTURAL CENTER □ Bronx, NY

Aguilar, Juan F., Dir.
DRAKE UNIVERSITY - LAW LIBRARY □ Des
Moines, IA

Aguirre, Anthony, Lib.Dir.
COLLEGE OF PHYSICIANS OF PHILADELPHIA -
LIBRARY AND MEDICAL DOCUMENTATION
SERVICE □ Philadelphia, PA

Aguirre, Anthony, Assoc.Dir.
UNIVERSITY OF CONNECTICUT - HEALTH
CENTER - LYMAN MAYNARD STOWE LIBRARY □
Farmington, CT

Agyemang, Hazel, Supv.Lib.Asst.
BOSTON UNIVERSITY - J. GORDON STRIPE, JR.
PHYSICS LIBRARY □ Boston, MA

Ahad, Madeline, Res.Sec./Libn.
UNIVERSITY OF TORONTO - A.E. MAC DONALD
OPHTHALMIC LIBRARY □ Toronto, ON

Ahearn, Carolyn P., Libn.
SHAW, PITTMAN, POTTS & TROWBRIDGE -
LIBRARY □ Washington, DC

Ahearn, Marg, Chf.Ref.Serv.
CANADA - MORTGAGE AND HOUSING
CORPORATION - CANADIAN HOUSING
INFORMATION CENTRE □ Ottawa, ON

Alexander, Joy, Cur.
UNIVERSITY OF MICHIGAN - HISTORY OF ART
DEPARTMENT - COLLECTION OF SLIDES AND
PHOTOGRAPHS □ Ann Arbor, MI
Alexander, Mrs. Lee G., Archv.
ATLANTA UNIVERSITY - TREVOR ARNETT
LIBRARY - SPECIAL COLLECTIONS† □ Atlanta,
GA
Alexander, Merle, Med.Libn.
U.S. ARMY HOSPITALS - WILLIAM BEAUMONT
ARMY MEDICAL CENTER - MEDICAL LIBRARY†
□ El Paso, TX
Alexander, Rondal, Data Anl. Planner
GREENSBORO PLANNING & COMMUNITY
DEVELOPMENT DEPARTMENT - LIBRARY □
Greensboro, NC
Alexander, Samuel O., Ser.Libn.
LAKEHEAD UNIVERSITY - CHANCELLOR
PATERSON LIBRARY □ Thunder Bay, ON
Alexander, Susanna, Assoc. State Libn.
MISSOURI STATE LIBRARY □ Jefferson City,
MO
Alexander, Terri, AV
UNIVERSITY OF HEALTH SCIENCES - LIBRARY
□ Kansas City, MO
Alexander, Theresa K., Sec.
FREDERICK COUNTY PLANNING AND ZONING
COMMISSION - LIBRARY □ Frederick, MD
Alexander, Thomas J., Hd.
UNIVERSITY OF CALIFORNIA, BERKELEY -
PUBLIC HEALTH LIBRARY □ Berkeley, CA
Alexander, Valerie E., Lib.Supv.
ATLANTIC CITY MEDICAL CENTER - MEDICAL
LIBRARY □ Atlantic City, NJ
Alexanian, Ann, Asst.Libn.-Ref.
PRICE WATERHOUSE - NATIONAL
INFORMATION CENTER □ New York, NY
Alexis, Donald G., Supv.Libn./Bus.Coll.
NEW YORK PUBLIC LIBRARY - MID-
MANHATTAN LIBRARY - SCIENCE/BUSINESS
DEPARTMENT □ New York, NY
Alfano, Dr. Blaise F., Hd.Libn.
AMERICAN SOCIETY OF ABDOMINAL
SURGEONS - DONALD COLLINS MEMORIAL
LIBRARY □ Melrose, MA
Alford, Carolyn S., Lib.Techn.
U.S. ARMS CONTROL AND DISARMAMENT
AGENCY - LIBRARY □ Washington, DC
Alford, Marybel, Media Spec.
FLORIDA SCHOOL FOR THE DEAF AND BLIND -
LIBRARY FOR THE DEAF □ St. Augustine, FL
Alfred, Judy, Med.Libn.
U.S. VETERANS ADMINISTRATION (IN-
Indianapolis) - MEDICAL CENTER LIBRARY □
Indianapolis, IN
Algermissen, Virginia L., Dir.
TEXAS A & M UNIVERSITY - MEDICAL
SCIENCES LIBRARY □ College Station, TX
Algon, Jacqueline, Sr.Pubn.Coord.
MERCK & COMPANY, INC. - MERCK SHARP &
DOHME RESEARCH LABORATORIES -
RESEARCH INFORMATION SYSTEMS □ Rahway,
NJ
Alig, Katharine, Sr.Libn.
AIRCO, INC. - CENTRAL RESEARCH
LABORATORIES - INFORMATION CENTER □
Murray Hill, NJ
Alimena, Diane M., Ref.Libn.
BELL TELEPHONE LABORATORIES, INC. -
TECHNICAL LIBRARY □ Murray Hill, NJ
Alkes, Doris, Hd., Acq.Sect.
U.S. DEPT. OF ENERGY - BROOKHAVEN NATL.
LABORATORY - TECHNICAL INFORMATION
DIVISION □ Upton, NY
Alladice, Darryl, Info.Spec.
ERIC CLEARINGHOUSE ON URBAN EDUCATION
□ New York, NY
Allain, Carmel, Cat.
UNIVERSITE DE MONCTON - BIBLIOTHEQUE DE
DROIT □ Moncton, NB

Allan, Doris, Libn.
SASKATCHEWAN HOSPITAL - DEPARTMENT OF
PSYCHIATRIC SERVICES - STAFF LIBRARY □
North Battleford, SK
Allan, Ferne C., Supv., Tech.Lit.Sect.
TEXACO CHEMICAL COMPANY, INC. -
TECHNICAL LITERATURE SECTION □ Austin, TX
Allan, Gary, Doc.Libn.
CARROLL COLLEGE - LIBRARY □ Helena, MT
Allan, Michael F., Asst.Libn.
UNION CARBIDE CORPORATION - BATTERY
PRODUCTS DIVISION - TECHNICAL
INFORMATION CENTER □ Cleveland, OH
Allan, Philip B., Med.Libn.
CANADA - NATIONAL DEFENCE - NATIONAL
DEFENCE MEDICAL CENTRE - MEDICAL
LIBRARY □ Ottawa, ON
Allard, Dr. Dean C., Dir.
U.S. NAVY - NAVAL HISTORICAL CENTER -
NAVAL HISTORY DIVISION - OPERATIONAL
ARCHIVES □ Washington, DC
Allard, Francois, Ref.Libn.
QUEBEC PROVINCE - MINISTERE DES
AFFAIRES SOCIALES - INFORMATHEQUE □
Quebec, PQ
Allard, Laurette
GRAND SEMINAIRE DE MONTREAL -
BIBLIOTHEQUE □ Montreal, PQ
Allard, Pierre, Chf.Libn.
CINEMATHEQUE QUEBECOISE - CENTRE DE
DOCUMENTATION CINEMATOGRAPHIQUE □
Montreal, PQ
Allard, Serge, Dir.
COLLEGE DU NORD-OUEST - BIBLIOTHEQUE □
Rouyn, PQ
Allard, Serge, Dir.
UNIVERSITE DU QUEBEC - CEUAT
BIBLIOTHEQUE □ Rouyn, PQ
Allard, Ursula, Cat.
MITCHELL (William) COLLEGE OF LAW - JOHN B.
SANBORN LIBRARY □ St. Paul, MN
Allbert, Portia, Hd.Libn.
KANSAS STATE HISTORICAL SOCIETY -
LIBRARY □ Topeka, KS
Allcock, Harry M., V.P.
IFI/PLENUM DATA COMPANY - LIBRARY □
Alexandria, VA
Allen, Barbara, Cat.Libn.
UNIVERSITY OF DENVER - COLLEGE OF LAW -
WESTMINSTER LAW LIBRARY □ Denver, CO
Allen, Barbara A., Libn.
OLIN CORPORATION - BRASS DIVISION
LIBRARY □ East Alton, IL
Allen, Betty, Sr.Sec.
GEORGIA STATE UNIVERSITY - SMALL
BUSINESS DEVELOPMENT CENTER □ Atlanta,
GA
Allen, Bonnie, Coord.Acq.
NORTHERN ARIZONA UNIVERSITY - LIBRARIES
□ Flagstaff, AZ
Allen, Brenda Y., Libn.
ENVIRONMENTAL RESEARCH & TECHNOLOGY,
INC. - INFORMATION CENTER □ Concord, MA
Allen, Mrs. C. Spencer, Libn.
LEHIGH COUNTY HISTORICAL SOCIETY -
SCOTT ANDREW TREXLER II MEMORIAL
LIBRARY □ Allentown, PA
Allen, David, Libn.
FALLSVIEW PSYCHIATRIC HOSPITAL - STAFF
LIBRARY □ Cuyahoga Falls, OH
Allen, David, Libn.
SUNY AT STONY BROOK - ENVIRONMENTAL
INFORMATION SERVICE □ Stony Brook, NY
Allen, David, Dir.
TOYS 'N THINGS, TRAINING & RESOURCE
CENTER, INC. □ St. Paul, MN
Allen, Donna, Sec.
UNIVERSITY OF TORONTO - DEPARTMENT OF
CHEMISTRY LIBRARY □ Toronto, ON
Allen, Dorothy R., Libn.
INTERNATIONAL THOMSON EDUCATIONAL
PUBLISHING, INC. - EDITORIAL LIBRARY □
New York, NY

Allen, E., Libn.
WESTMINSTER PRESBYTERIAN CHURCH -
JOHN H. HOLMES LIBRARY □ Cincinnati, OH
Allen, Edna, Ref.Libn.
WARNER-LAMBERT CANADA, LTD. -
REFERENCE LIBRARY □ Scarborough, ON
Allen, Eleanor B., Hd.Libn.
UNIVERSITY OF PENNSYLVANIA - LIPPINCOTT
LIBRARY □ Philadelphia, PA
Allen, Farrell J., Sr.Tech.Libn.
MONSANTO TEXTILES COMPANY - TECHNICAL
LIBRARY □ Pensacola, FL
Allen, Gertrude M., Libn.
MASSACHUSETTS STATE DISTRICT COURT -
FOURTH EASTERN MIDDLESEX DIVISION -
LIBRARY □ Woburn, MA
Allen, Helen M., Libn.
UNION CLUB - LIBRARY □ New York, NY
Allen, J.H., Act.Dir.
WORLD DATA CENTER A - SOLAR-
TERRESTRIAL PHYSICS □ Boulder, CO
Allen, Jane D., Sr.Libn., Acq.
NEW YORK STATE DEPARTMENT OF HEALTH -
DIVISION OF LABORATORIES AND RESEARCH
LIBRARY □ Albany, NY
Allen, Janet S., Pres.
ART REFERENCE BUREAU, INC. □ Ancram, NY
Allen, Joyce S., Lib.Mgr.
METHODIST HOSPITAL OF INDIANA, INC. -
LIBRARY □ Indianapolis, IN
Allen, Louise M., Libn.
GREEN CLINIC - LIBRARY □ Ruston, LA
Allen, Luella, Asst.Libn., Media Rsrcs.
SUNY AT BUFFALO - HEALTH SCIENCES
LIBRARY □ Buffalo, NY
Allen, Marcia K., Libn.
CATHOLIC MEDICAL CENTER - HEALTH
SCIENCE LIBRARY □ Manchester, NH
Allen, Margaret A., Libn.
ST. JOSEPH'S HOSPITAL - SCHOOL OF
NURSING - LEARNING RESOURCE CENTER □
Marshfield, WI
Allen, Margaret C., Supv., Unpubl.Pict.
NATIONAL GEOGRAPHIC SOCIETY -
ILLUSTRATIONS LIBRARY □ Washington, DC
Allen, Mary Alice, Central Engr.Libn.
GEORGIA-PACIFIC CORPORATION -
TECHNICAL INFORMATION CENTER □ Atlanta,
GA
Allen, Mary Lou
ST. LOUIS PUBLIC LIBRARY - POPULAR
LIBRARY - MUSIC SECTION □ St. Louis, MO
Allen, Mary W., Libn.
WASHINGTON PSYCHOANALYTIC SOCIETY -
ERNEST E. HADLEY MEMORIAL LIBRARY □
Washington, DC
Allen, Nancy, Libn.
UNIVERSITY OF ILLINOIS - COMMUNICATIONS
LIBRARY □ Urbana, IL
Allen, Nancy S., Libn.
MUSEUM OF FINE ARTS - WILLIAM MORRIS
HUNT MEMORIAL LIBRARY □ Boston, MA
Allen, Pam, Asst.Libn.
PENINSULA TIMES TRIBUNE - LIBRARY □ Palo
Alto, CA
Allen, Pat, Instr.Techn.
BILLINGS PUBLIC SCHOOLS - INSTRUCTIONAL
MATERIALS CENTER □ Billings, MT
Allen, Pauline B., Libn.
NEBRASKA PSYCHIATRIC INSTITUTE -
LIBRARY† □ Omaha, NE
Allen, Ray, Folklorist
CENTER FOR SOUTHERN FOLKLORE -
ARCHIVES □ Memphis, TN
Allen, Reginald, Cur., Gilbert & Sullivan
PIERPONT MORGAN LIBRARY □ New York, NY
Allen, Robert L., Hd.
PENNSYLVANIA STATE UNIVERSITY -
AUDIOVISUAL SERVICES □ University Park, PA
Allen, Robert V., Act.Asst.Chf.
LIBRARY OF CONGRESS - EUROPEAN DIVISION
□ Washington, DC

PERSONNEL

Ameel, Henrietta
RILEY COUNTY HISTORICAL SOCIETY -
SEATON MEMORIAL LIBRARY □ Manhattan, KS

Amelung, Karen, Libn.
AMERICAN ECONOMIC DEVELOPMENT
COUNCIL - AEDC LIBRARY □ Kansas City, MO

Ames, Jan, Regional Libn.
SEATTLE PUBLIC LIBRARY - WASHINGTON
REGIONAL LIBRARY FOR THE BLIND AND
PHYSICALLY HANDICAPPED □ Seattle, WA

Ames, Patricia A., Libn.
U.S. ARMY - ARMAMENT RESEARCH &
DEVELOPMENT COMMAND - BENET WEAPONS
LABORATORY - TECHNICAL LIBRARY □
Watervliet, NY

Amirault, Mrs. Robert J., Libn.
NATURE CENTER FOR ENVIRONMENTAL
ACTIVITIES - REFERENCE LIBRARY □
Westport, CT

Ammen, Helen, Libn.
REPUBLICAN NATIONAL COMMITTEE -
RESEARCH LIBRARY □ Washington, DC

Ammer, William, Treas.
PICKAWAY COUNTY LAW LIBRARY □ Circleville,
OH

Ammons, Betty, Asst.Libn.
UNITED METHODIST HISTORICAL SOCIETY -
BALTIMORE ANNUAL CONFERENCE - LOVELY
LANE MUSEUM LIBRARY □ Baltimore, MD

Amnasan, Violet R., Libn.
GEAUGA COUNTY LAW LIBRARY □ Chardon, OH

Amon, Jane, Libn.
MORRISON AND FOERSTER - BRANCH LAW
LIBRARY □ Washington, DC

Amoriello, Lillian, Info.Sci.
AMERICAN HOME PRODUCTS CORPORATION -
WYETH LABORATORIES DIVISION LIBRARY □
Philadelphia, PA

Amos, D.M., Mgr.
CANADIAN THOROUGHBRED HORSE SOCIETY -
LIBRARY □ Rexdale, ON

Amrhein, John K., College Libn.
KUTZTOWN STATE COLLEGE - ROHRBACH
LIBRARY □ Kutztown, PA

Amsler, Clifford, Jr., Dir.
U.S. NATL. ARCHIVES & RECORDS SERVICE -
FEDERAL ARCHIVES AND RECORDS CENTER,
REGION 1 □ Waltham, MA

Amtzis, Selma, Med.Libn.
SEA VIEW HOSPITAL AND HOME - MEDICAL
LIBRARY □ Staten Island, NY

Amundson, Jean, Cat.
NAZARENE THEOLOGICAL SEMINARY -
WILLIAM BROADHURST LIBRARY □ Kansas City,
MO

Amy, Shirley, Per.Libn.
TEXAS STATE TECHNICAL INSTITUTE, WACO
CAMPUS - LEARNING RESOURCE CENTER □
Waco, TX

Anaclerio, C.R., Chf., Tech.Lib.
U.S. ARMY - CHEMICAL SYSTEMS LABORATORY
- TECHNICAL LIBRARY □ Aberdeen Proving
Ground, MD

Ananda, Peter, Hd.
UNIVERSITY OF CALIFORNIA, BERKELEY -
SOUTH/SOUTHEAST ASIA LIBRARY SERVICE □
Berkeley, CA

Anas, Roberta J., Hd.Libn.
SYMMERS, FISH AND WARNER - RESEARCH
LIBRARY □ New York, NY

Ancelet, Barry Jean
UNIVERSITY OF SOUTHWESTERN LOUISIANA -
CENTER FOR LOUISIANA STUDIES □ Lafayette,
LA

Anday, Betty, Lib.Asst.
VIRGINIA MUSEUM OF FINE ARTS - LIBRARY □
Richmond, VA

Anderjack, George M., Exec.Dir.
VENTURA COUNTY HISTORICAL SOCIETY -
LIBRARY & ARCHIVES □ Ventura, CA

Anderl, Susan, Spec.Coll.Libn.
UNIVERSITY OF NEVADA, LAS VEGAS -
GAMING RESEARCH CENTER □ Las Vegas, NV

Anders, Ora, Ref.
KENNEDY-KING COLLEGE - LIBRARY □ Chicago,
IL

Anders, Vicki, Hd., Biblog.Instr.
TEXAS A & M UNIVERSITY - REFERENCE
DIVISION □ College Station, TX

Andersen, Deborah, Asst.Libn.
NEW YORK STATE LIBRARY - HUMANITIES
REFERENCE SERVICE □ Albany, NY

Andersen, Hazel, Circ.Supv.
ASSOCIATION FOR RESEARCH AND
ENLIGHTENMENT - EDGAR CAYCE
FOUNDATION - LIBRARY □ Virginia Beach, VA

Andersen, Jeffrey W., Dir.
LYME HISTORICAL SOCIETY, INC. - ARCHIVES
□ Old Lyme, CT

Andersen, Lars, Archv.Coord.
SKAGIT COUNTY HISTORICAL MUSEUM -
HISTORICAL REFERENCE LIBRARY □ La Conner,
WA

Anderson, Albert G., Jr., Hd.Libn.
WORCESTER POLYTECHNIC INSTITUTE -
GEORGE C. GORDON LIBRARY □ Worcester, MA

Anderson, Anita, Chf., Ref.Dept.
ILLINOIS INSTITUTE OF TECHNOLOGY - JAMES
S. KEMPER LIBRARY □ Chicago, IL

Anderson, Anita, Libn.
MINNESOTA STATE ATTORNEY GENERAL -
LAW LIBRARY □ St. Paul, MN

Anderson, Anna Mary, Pres.
ALDRICH (Mariska) MEMORIAL FOUNDATION,
INC. - LIBRARY OF RARE MUSIC □ Pearl City, HI

Anderson, Beryl L., Chf.
NATIONAL LIBRARY OF CANADA - LIBRARY
DOCUMENTATION CENTRE □ Ottawa, ON

Anderson, Betty
KENOSHA ACHIEVEMENT CENTER - LIBRARY □
Kenosha, WI

Anderson, Beverly L., Project Dir.
NORTHWEST REGIONAL EDUCATIONAL
LABORATORY - CLEARINGHOUSE FOR APPLIED
PERFORMANCE TESTING (CAPT) □ Portland, OR

Anderson, Bruce, AV Prod.
ANOKA AREA VOCATIONAL TECHNICAL
INSTITUTE - MEDIA CENTER □ Anoka, MN

Anderson, Carolyn McCown, Dir.
MENNONITE HOSPITAL AND SCHOOL OF
NURSING - HEALTH SCIENCES LIBRARY □
Bloomington, IL

Anderson, Christine, Med.Res.Libn.
U.S. VETERANS ADMINISTRATION (CA-Los
Angeles) - MEDICAL RESEARCH LIBRARY □ Los
Angeles, CA

Anderson, Ms. D., Ref.Libn.
COVINGTON AND BURLING - LIBRARY □
Washington, DC

Anderson, David, Clinical Info.Spec.
WAKE FOREST UNIVERSITY - BOWMAN GRAY
SCHOOL OF MEDICINE - LIBRARY □ Winston-
Salem, NC

Anderson, David C., Tech.Serv.Libn.
UNIVERSITY OF CALIFORNIA, DAVIS - HEALTH
SCIENCES LIBRARY □ Davis, CA

Anderson, David N., Exec.Dir.
GEOTHERMAL RESOURCES COUNCIL - LIBRARY
□ Davis, CA

Anderson, Dixie, Lib.Asst.-Ref.
ALBERTA - DEPARTMENT OF EDUCATION -
LIBRARY □ Edmonton, AB

Anderson, Ellen, Libn.
UNIVERSITY OF NORTH CAROLINA, CHAPEL
HILL - SCHOOL OF LIBRARY SCIENCE LIBRARY
□ Chapel Hill, NC

Anderson, Elma, Ser.Libn.
MARYWOOD COLLEGE - LEARNING RESOURCES
CENTER □ Scranton, PA

Anderson, F. Helen, Libn.
CANADA - CANADIAN WILDLIFE SERVICE -
ATLANTIC REGION LIBRARY □ Sackville, NB

Anderson, Fiona, Libn.
FARRIS, VAUGHAN, WILLS & MURPHY -
LIBRARY □ Vancouver, BC

Anderson, Frank J., Libn.
WOFFORD COLLEGE - SANDOR TESZLER
LIBRARY - LITTLEJOHN RARE BOOK ROOM □
Spartanburg, SC

Anderson, Fred, Exec.Dir.
VIRGINIA BAPTIST HISTORICAL SOCIETY -
LIBRARY □ Richmond, VA

Anderson, G., Act.Libn.
NORTHWEST TERRITORIES - GOVERNMENT
IN-SERVICE LIBRARY □ Yellowknife, NT

Anderson, Glenda E., Res.Libn.
SAVANNAH (City) - MUNICIPAL RESEARCH
LIBRARY† □ Savannah, GA

Anderson, Glenda E., Res.Libn.
SAVANNAH (City) - POLICE DEPARTMENT -
LIBRARY □ Savannah, GA

Anderson, Grace, Libn.
SPARKS REGIONAL MEDICAL CENTER -
REGIONAL HEALTH SCIENCES LIBRARY □ Fort
Smith, AR

Anderson, Hattie T., Contracts Info.
JOHNS HOPKINS UNIVERSITY - APPLIED
PHYSICS LABORATORY - R.E. GIBSON LIBRARY
□ Laurel, MD

Anderson, Hermione, Libn.
ST. JOSEPH HOSPITAL AND HEALTH CARE
CENTER - MEDICAL LIBRARY □ Tacoma, WA

Anderson, James C., Cur.
UNIVERSITY OF LOUISVILLE - PHOTOGRAPHIC
ARCHIVES □ Louisville, KY

Anderson, James J., Hist.
U.S. NATL. PARK SERVICE - KINGS MOUNTAIN
NATL. MILITARY PARK - LIBRARY □ Kings
Mountain, NC

Anderson, Jan B., Mgr.
CITE RESOURCE CENTER □ Austin, TX

Anderson, Janet, Med.Rec.Adm.
DIVINE PROVIDENCE HOSPITAL - MEDICAL
LIBRARY □ Williamsport, PA

Anderson, Janet, Law.Libn.
TUOLUMNE COUNTY LAW LIBRARY □ Sonora,
CA

Anderson, Jean C., Chf.Libn.
SWEDISH HOSPITAL MEDICAL CENTER -
REFERENCE LIBRARY □ Seattle, WA

Anderson, Joan, Cat./Music Libn.
CALIFORNIA INSTITUTE OF THE ARTS -
LIBRARY □ Valencia, CA

Anderson, Joan, Libn.
CARNEGIE LIBRARY OF PITTSBURGH -
SCIENCE AND TECHNOLOGY DEPARTMENT □
Pittsburgh, PA

Anderson, Joan, Tech.Asst.
CHICAGO THEOLOGICAL SEMINARY -
HAMMOND LIBRARY □ Chicago, IL

Anderson, Jody, Libn.
ST. PATRICK HOSPITAL - LIBRARY □ Missoula,
MT

Anderson, John, Hd., Per.
SUNY - DOWNSTATE MEDICAL CENTER -
MEDICAL RESEARCH LIBRARY OF BROOKLYN†
□ Brooklyn, NY

Anderson, Joseph, Sr.Libn.
MERCANTILE LIBRARY ASSOCIATION -
MERCANTILE LIBRARY □ New York, NY

Anderson, Joseph J., State Libn.
NEVADA STATE LIBRARY □ Carson City, NV

Anderson, Joseph J., State Libn.
NEVADA STATE LIBRARY - DIVISION OF
STATE, COUNTY AND MUNICIPAL ARCHIVES □
Carson City, NV

Anderson, K.E., Mgr. of Engr.
MOBIL PIPE LINE COMPANY - ENGINEERING
LIBRARY □ Dallas, TX

Anderson, Kathie P., Corp.Libn.
REYNOLDS METALS COMPANY - CORPORATE
INFORMATION CENTER □ Richmond, VA

Anderson, L.V., Dir. of Lib.Serv.
WESTERN TEXAS COLLEGE - LEARNING
RESOURCE CENTER □ Snyder, TX

Anderson, Lawrence A., Libn.
CUNNINGHAM AND WALSH, INC. - LIBRARY □
New York, NY

Anderson, LeMoyne W., Dir. of Lib.
COLORADO STATE UNIVERSITY - WILLIAM E.
MORGAN LIBRARY □ Fort Collins, CO

Anderson, Lowell E., Cur., Hist. Sites
ILLINOIS STATE HISTORICAL LIBRARY □
Springfield, IL

Anderson, M. Sharon, Doc.Dept.Libn.
UNIVERSITY OF CALIFORNIA, SAN DIEGO -
UNIVERSITY LIBRARIES □ La Jolla, CA

Anderson, Marcia, Extramural Coord.
OHIO STATE UNIVERSITY - HEALTH SCIENCES
LIBRARY □ Columbus, OH

Anderson, Margaret, Libn.
SUN PRODUCTION COMPANY - INFORMATION
RESOURCES CENTER □ Richardson, TX

Anderson, Margaret J., Hd.Libn.
AUGSBURG COLLEGE - GEORGE SVERDRUP
LIBRARY AND MEDIA CENTER □ Minneapolis,
MN

Anderson, Margaret R., Mgr.
R & D ASSOCIATES - TECHNICAL
INFORMATION SERVICES □ Marina Del Rey, CA

Anderson, Marvin, Ref.
UNIVERSITY OF MINNESOTA - LAW LIBRARY □
Minneapolis, MN

Anderson, Marvin Roger, State Law Libn.
MINNESOTA STATE LAW LIBRARY □ St. Paul,
MN

Anderson, Mary Elizabeth, Libn.
U.S. NASA - HEADQUARTERS LIBRARY □
Washington, DC

Anderson, Michael, Archv.
U.S. NATL. ARCHIVES & RECORDS SERVICE -
FEDERAL ARCHIVES AND RECORDS CENTER,
REGION 9 □ Laguna Niguel, CA

Anderson, Nancy, Dir., Med.Rec.
MEMORIAL HOSPITAL - MEDICAL LIBRARY □
Lufkin, TX

Anderson, Nancy D., Libn.
UNIVERSITY OF ILLINOIS - MATHEMATICS
LIBRARY □ Urbana, IL

Anderson, Norman E., Assoc.Libn.
GORDON-CONWELL THEOLOGICAL SEMINARY -
GODDARD LIBRARY □ South Hamilton, MA

Anderson, Oriole, Libn.
MANUFACTURERS LIFE INSURANCE COMPANY
- BUSINESS LIBRARY □ Toronto, ON

Anderson, Orvis, Cur.
MERCER COUNTY HISTORICAL SOCIETY -
LIBRARY AND ARCHIVES □ Mercer, PA

Anderson, Patty, Archv.
U.S. NATL. ARCHIVES & RECORDS SERVICE -
FEDERAL ARCHIVES AND RECORDS CENTER,
REGION 9 □ Laguna Niguel, CA

Anderson, Paul, Archv.
WASHINGTON UNIVERSITY - SCHOOL OF
MEDICINE LIBRARY □ St. Louis, MO

Anderson, Peter G., Curric.Mtls.Libn.
CALIFORNIA STATE UNIVERSITY, CHICO -
MERIAM LIBRARY □ Chico, CA

Anderson, Phyllis P., Libn.
MC KEAN COUNTY LAW LIBRARY □ Smethport,
PA

Anderson, Richard, Cat.
NEW BRUNSWICK - LEGISLATIVE LIBRARY □
Fredericton, NB

Anderson, Ron, Field Serv.Libn./AV
SOUTH CAROLINA STATE LIBRARY □ Columbia,
SC

Anderson, Ross, Libn.
METROPOLITAN TORONTO LIBRARY - SOCIAL
SCIENCES DEPARTMENT □ Toronto, ON

Anderson, Sandra C., Tech.Libn.
UNION CARBIDE CORPORATION - LINDE
DIVISION - TECHNICAL LIBRARY □ Tonawanda,
NY

Anderson, Sharon, Ref.Libn.
DICKINSON SCHOOL OF LAW - SHEELY-LEE
LAW LIBRARY □ Carlisle, PA

Anderson, Sherrie, Libn.
GERBER PRODUCTS COMPANY - CORPORATE
LIBRARY □ Fremont, MI

Anderson, Sherry, Asst.Dir.Spec. Projects
EAST CAROLINA UNIVERSITY - HEALTH
SCIENCES LIBRARY □ Greenville, NC

Anderson, Stuart H., Libn.
NEW JERSEY STATE DEPARTMENT OF LABOR
AND INDUSTRY - LIBRARY □ Trenton, NJ

Anderson, Susan, Assoc.Libn.
COLUMBIA HOSPITAL - MEDICAL LIBRARY □
Milwaukee, WI

Anderson, T.J.B., Chf.Libn.
ONTARIO - MINISTRY OF CORRECTIONAL
SERVICES - LIBRARY SERVICES □ Toronto, ON

Anderson, Teresa J., Libn.
UNIVERSITY OF WISCONSIN, MADISON - LAND
TENURE CENTER - LIBRARY □ Madison, WI

Anderson, Terry L., Park Techn.
U.S. NATL. PARK SERVICE - ALLEGHENY
PORTAGE RAILROAD NATL. HISTORIC SITE -
LIBRARY □ Cresson, PA

Anderson, Thomas E., Asst.Libn.
SAN DIEGO COUNTY LAW LIBRARY □ San Diego,
CA

Anderson, Virginia, Asst.Libn.
INDIANA STATE UNIVERSITY - TEACHING
MATERIALS DIVISION □ Terre Haute, IN

Anderson, Virginia N., Libn.
CALIFORNIA INSTITUTE OF TECHNOLOGY -
AERONAUTICS LIBRARY □ Pasadena, CA

Anderson, Virginia N., Libn.
CALIFORNIA INSTITUTE OF TECHNOLOGY -
ENERGY RESEARCH LIBRARY □ Pasadena, CA

Anderson III, Yeatman, Cur.
PUBLIC LIBRARY OF CINCINNATI AND
HAMILTON COUNTY - DEPARTMENT OF RARE
BOOKS & SPECIAL COLLECTIONS □ Cincinnati,
OH

Andersson, Liselotte, Libn.
TULANE UNIVERSITY OF LOUISIANA -
MAXWELL MUSIC LIBRARY □ New Orleans, LA

Andersson, Meila, Libn.
SHELL CANADA RESOURCES LIMITED -
TECHNICAL LIBRARY □ Calgary, AB

Ando, Ester, Info.Techn.
SHELL DEVELOPMENT COMPANY -
WESTHOLLOW RESEARCH CENTER LIBRARY† □
Houston, TX

Andre, Dr. Leslie, Hd.Ser.Serv.
EASTERN ILLINOIS UNIVERSITY - BOOTH
LIBRARY □ Charleston, IL

Andre-Angers, Francine, Bibliotechnicienne
QUEBEC PROVINCE - MINISTERE DE
L'EDUCATION - CENTRALE DES
BIBLIOTHEQUES - CENTRE DOCUMENTAIRE □
Montreal, PQ

Andrejasich, Carol, Cat.
ELI LILLY AND COMPANY - SCIENTIFIC
LIBRARY □ Indianapolis, IN

Andres, Monica, Libn.
CENTER FOR NATIONAL SECURITY STUDIES -
CNSS LIBRARY □ Washington, DC

Andress, Loretta, Libn. I
ALASKA HEALTH SCIENCES LIBRARY □
Anchorage, AK

Andrew, Bruce, Hd., Rd.Serv.
SUNY - COLLEGE AT BUFFALO - EDWARD H.
BUTLER LIBRARY □ Buffalo, NY

Andrew, Gloria T., Mgr.
CONTROL DATA CORPORATION - LIBRARY/
INFORMATION CENTER □ Minneapolis, MN

Andrews, Mrs. C.B., Libn.
ERIE COUNTY HISTORICAL SOCIETY □ Erie, PA

Andrews, Claire, Ref.Libn.
KUTZTOWN STATE COLLEGE - ROHRBACH
LIBRARY □ Kutztown, PA

Andrews, Derwill F., Cat.
U.S. DEPT. OF COMMERCE - DEPARTMENTAL
LIBRARY □ Washington, DC

Andrews, Elizabeth, Asst.Libn.
NEW ENGLAND COLLEGE OF OPTOMETRY -
LIBRARY □ Boston, MA

Andrews, Elliott E., State Libn.
RHODE ISLAND STATE LIBRARY □ Providence,
RI

Andrews, James C., Dir. of Lib.
RENSSELAER POLYTECHNIC INSTITUTE -
FOLSOM LIBRARY □ Troy, NY

Andrews, Dr. John, Dir. of Res.
FOLGER SHAKESPEARE LIBRARY □ Washington,
DC

Andrews, John B., Exec.Dir.
NEW HAMPSHIRE MUNICIPAL ASSOCIATION -
LIBRARY □ Concord, NH

Andrews, Johnnie, Jr., Dir.
PRICHARD (Cleveland) MEMORIAL LIBRARY □
Prichard, AL

Andrews, Judy, Adm.Libn.
BOCA RATON COMMUNITY HOSPITAL - HEALTH
SCIENCES LIBRARY □ Boca Raton, FL

Andrews, Karen L., Hd.Libn.
UNIVERSITY OF CALIFORNIA, LOS ANGELES -
ENGINEERING & MATHEMATICAL SCIENCES
LIBRARY □ Los Angeles, CA

Andrews, Kate, Adm.
CLAY COUNTY HISTORICAL SOCIETY -
ARCHIVES □ Moorhead, MN

Andrews, Martha Shipman, Coord.
SMITHSONIAN INSTITUTION - NATL. MUSEUM
OF AMERICAN ART -INVENTORY OF AMERICAN
PAINTINGS EXECUTED BEFORE 1914 □
Washington, DC

Andrews, Mary, Libn.
ARCHIVES OF THE CANADIAN ROCKIES □
Banff, AB

Andrews, Michael W., Rd.Serv.Libn.
ELIZABETHTOWN COLLEGE - ZUG MEMORIAL
LIBRARY - ARCHIVES □ Elizabethtown, PA

Andrews, Nancy J., Libn.
FINE ARTS GALLERY OF SAN DIEGO - LIBRARY
□ San Diego, CA

Andrews, Patricia, Libn.
ENOCH PRATT FREE LIBRARY - MARYLAND
DEPARTMENT □ Baltimore, MD

Andrews, Patricia A., Libn.
U.S. NATL. ARCHIVES & RECORDS SERVICE -
NATL. ARCHIVES □ Washington, DC

Andrews, Patricia A., Act.Libn.
U.S. NATL. ARCHIVES & RECORDS SERVICE -
NATL. ARCHIVES LIBRARY □ Washington, DC

Andrews, Reid, Libn.
PAN AMERICAN SOCIETY OF NEW ENGLAND -
SHATTUCK LIBRARY □ Boston, MA

Andrews, Robert J., Pres.
INTERNATIONAL RAILROAD &
TRANSPORTATION POSTCARD COLLECTORS
CLUB - LIBRARY □ Providence, RI

Andrews, Roberta, Libn.
U.S. NATL. INSTITUTE FOR OCCUPATIONAL
SAFETY & HEALTH - CLEARINGHOUSE FOR
OCCUPATIONAL SAFETY & HEALTH INFO. □
Cincinnati, OH

Andrews, Sara, Ref.Hd.
UNIVERSITY OF VERMONT - DIVISION OF
HEALTH SCIENCES - CHARLES A. DANA
MEDICAL LIBRARY □ Burlington, VT

Andrews, Theodora, Libn.
PURDUE UNIVERSITY - PHARMACY LIBRARY □
West Lafayette, IN

Andrews, William M., Dir.
UNIVERSITY OF MINNESOTA TECHNICAL
COLLEGE, WASECA - LEARNING RESOURCES
CENTER □ Waseca, MN

Andrews-Zike, Lysbeth, Ref.Libn.
NEW HAVEN COLONY HISTORICAL SOCIETY -
LIBRARY □ New Haven, CT

Andrich, Betty, Chm.
CRAFTS GUILD OF MANITOBA - LIBRARY □
Winnipeg, MB

Andrle, Lorna, Ref.Libn.
U.S. ARMY POST - FORT LEWIS - LIBRARY
SYSTEM □ Fort Lewis, WA

Androlini, Karen, Info.Spec.
AMERICAN ASSOCIATION OF ADVERTISING
AGENCIES - MEMBER INFORMATION SERVICE
□ New York, NY

PERSONNEL

Androvics, Inara, Supv., Clipping Serv.
ONTARIO - LEGISLATIVE ASSEMBLY - LEGISLATIVE LIBRARY RESEARCH AND INFORMATION SERVICES □ Toronto, ON

Andrus, Kay, Asst.Dir.
OKLAHOMA CITY UNIVERSITY - LAW LIBRARY □ Oklahoma City, OK

Andrus, Roger, Libn.
OREGON STATE SUPREME COURT LIBRARY □ Salem, OR

Anduha, Isabel T., Court Libn.
U.S. DISTRICT COURT LIBRARY □ Honolulu, HI

Aneja, Kusum, Ser.Libn.
WIDENER UNIVERSITY - WOLFGRAM MEMORIAL LIBRARY □ Chester, PA

Anfang, Sandra, Volunteer Coord.
ARIZONA STATE REGIONAL LIBRARY FOR THE BLIND AND PHYSICALLY HANDICAPPED □ Phoenix, AZ

Ang, Wende, Ref.
SALISBURY STATE COLLEGE - BLACKWELL LIBRARY □ Salisbury, MD

Angel, Gilberte, Libn.
CONSOLIDATED-BATHURST INC. - RESEARCH CENTRE LIBRARY □ Grand Mere, PQ

Angeletti, Lois, Libn.
RICHMOND PUBLIC LIBRARY - ART AND MUSIC DEPARTMENT† □ Richmond, VA

Angelini, A., Hd.Cat.
EAST STROUDSBURG STATE COLLEGE - LIBRARY □ East Stroudsburg, PA

Angell, Mary, Mng.Ed./Libn.
WISCONSIN STATE MEDICAL SOCIETY - LIBRARY □ Madison, WI

Angevine, Martha Stanton, Coord.
LEXINGTON PUBLIC SCHOOLS - CURRICULUM RESOURCE CENTER □ Lexington, MA

Angier, Jennifer J., Ref. & Cat.Libn.
UNIVERSITY OF PITTSBURGH - WESTERN PSYCHIATRIC INSTITUTE AND CLINIC - LIBRARY □ Pittsburgh, PA

Angiletta, Anthony A., Social Sci.Biblog.
YALE UNIVERSITY - SOCIAL SCIENCE LIBRARY □ New Haven, CT

Angle, Nina K., Law Libn.
COLUMBIA GAS TRANSMISSION CORPORATION - LAW LIBRARY □ Charleston, WV

Angonese, A.N., Sr.Assoc.Mng.Engr.
UNDERWRITERS LABORATORIES INC. - STANDARDS REFERENCE CENTER □ Northbrook, IL

Anguilano, Michel, AV Dir.
MIAMI-DADE PUBLIC LIBRARY - AUDIO/VISUAL DEPARTMENT □ Miami, FL

Angus, H. Elizabeth, Libn.
CROWN LIFE INSURANCE COMPANY - LIBRARY □ Toronto, ON

Angus, Jacqueline, Supv., Lib.Sec.
GENERAL MILLS, INC. - JAMES FORD BELL TECHNICAL CENTER - TECHNICAL INFORMATION SERVICES □ Minneapolis, MN

Angus, Sheri, Ref.Libn.
BATTLE CREEK SANITARIUM HOSPITAL - MEDICAL LIBRARY □ Battle Creek, MI

Anish, Michele, Asst.Libn.
AMERICAN JEWISH COMMITTEE - BLAUSTEIN LIBRARY □ New York, NY

Anker, Anita, MULS Coord.
MINITEX □ Minneapolis, MN

Ankudowich, Mary M., Libn.
SMITH COLLEGE - WERNER JOSTEN LIBRARY FOR THE PERFORMING ARTS □ Northampton, MA

Annand, Stewart, Libn.
MC CUTCHEN, BLACK, VERLEGER AND SHEA - LAW LIBRARY □ Los Angeles, CA

Annenberg, Lester, Hd. of Sports Br.
TIME, INC. - LIBRARY □ New York, NY

Annenberg, Lester, Hd.Libn.
TIME, INC. - SPORTS LIBRARY □ New York, NY

Annett, Larry, Hd. of Lib.Oper.
CINCINNATI CITY PLANNING COMMISSION - PLANNING AND MANAGEMENT SUPPORT SYSTEM LIBRARY □ Cincinnati, OH

Annicharico, Ralph J., Asst. to Cur.
CATHOLIC UNIVERSITY OF AMERICA - OLIVEIRA LIMA LIBRARY □ Washington, DC

Annino, Harriet, Libn.
WOODWARD-CLYDE CONSULTANTS - ENVIRONMENTAL SYSTEMS DIVISION - LIBRARY □ San Francisco, CA

Annsan, Dan, Ref.Libn.
PALOMAR COLLEGE - PHIL H. PUTNAM MEMORIAL LIBRARY □ San Marcos, CA

Anolik, Ruth, Rd.Serv.Libn.
HOLY FAMILY COLLEGE - LIBRARY □ Philadelphia, PA

Ansari, Mary, Engr.Libn.
UNIVERSITY OF NEVADA, RENO - ENGINEERING LIBRARY □ Reno, NV

Anschutz, Ms. M.A., Libn.
CANADA - CANADIAN RADIO-TELEVISION AND TELECOMMUNICATIONS COMMISSION - LIBRARY □ Ottawa, ON

Ansel, Phyllis, Govt.Docs.Libn.
NEW ENGLAND SCHOOL OF LAW - LIBRARY □ Boston, MA

Ansley, Beth, Lib.Serv.Supv.
GEORGIA POWER COMPANY - LIBRARY □ Atlanta, GA

Ansley, Josephine, Govt.Doc.
OHIO NORTHERN UNIVERSITY - COLLEGE OF LAW - JAY P. TAGGART MEMORIAL LAW LIBRARY □ Ada, OH

Anson, Brooke, Coord., Pub.Serv.
UNIVERSITY OF WISCONSIN, STOUT - LIBRARY LEARNING CENTER - MEDIA RETRIEVAL SERVICES □ Menomonie, WI

Anson, Jack L., Exec.Dir.
NATIONAL INTERFRATERNITY CONFERENCE - LIBRARY □ Indianapolis, IN

Anstaett, Herbert B., Exec.Sec.
EVANGELICAL AND REFORMED HISTORICAL SOCIETY - LANCASTER CENTRAL ARCHIVES AND LIBRARY □ Lancaster, PA

Anstine, Francesca, Asst.Libn.
UNIVERSITY OF ILLINOIS MEDICAL CENTER - LIBRARY OF THE HEALTH SCIENCES □ Urbana, IL

Antes, E. Jean, Med.Ref.Libn.
PACKER (Robert) HOSPITAL - MEDICAL LIBRARY □ Sayre, PA

Anthony, Audree D., Lib.Supv.
LORILLARD RESEARCH CENTER LIBRARY □ Greensboro, NC

Anthony, Helen B., Libn.
UNIVERSITY OF VIRGINIA - EDUCATION LIBRARY □ Charlottesville, VA

Anthony, Kenneth H., LCDR, Hd.Libn.
MAINE MARITIME ACADEMY - NUTTING MEMORIAL LIBRARY □ Castine, ME

Anthony, Mary, Law Libn.
NEW YORK STATE SUPREME COURT - APPELLATE DIVISION, 4TH JUDICIAL DEPARTMENT - LAW LIBRARY □ Syracuse, NY

Anthony, Mary, Lib.Asst.II
TULARE COUNTY LAW LIBRARY □ Visalia, CA

Anthony, Peter, Hd.Libn.
UNIVERSITY OF MANITOBA - ARCHITECTURE & FINE ARTS LIBRARY □ Winnipeg, MB

Anthony, Peter, Adm.Hd.
UNIVERSITY OF MANITOBA - MUSIC READING ROOM □ Winnipeg, MB

Anthony, Robert, Lit.Res.Anl.
AEROSPACE CORPORATION - CHARLES C. LAURITSEN LIBRARY □ Los Angeles, CA

Anthony, Robert., Group Ldr.
GEORGE BROWN COLLEGE OF APPLIED ARTS & TECHNOLOGY □ Toronto, ON

Anthony, Susan, Hd., Info. Access
UNIVERSITY OF CINCINNATI - MEDICAL CENTER LIBRARIES - HEALTH SCIENCES LIBRARY □ Cincinnati, OH

Anthony, Walter, C.S.P., Dir.
OLD ST. MARY'S CHURCH - PAULIST LIBRARY □ San Francisco, CA

Antilla, Faith, Per.Libn.
FITCHBURG STATE COLLEGE - LIBRARY □ Fitchburg, MA

Antioco, Jurate, Libn.
PENNIE & EDMONDS - LAW LIBRARY □ New York, NY

Antipin, Rose, Libn.
UNITED ENGINEERS & CONSTRUCTORS, INC. - LIBRARY □ Philadelphia, PA

Antonelli, Claude, Ref.Libn.
UNIVERSITE DU QUEBEC A MONTREAL - BIBLIOTHEQUES DES SCIENCES JURIDIQUES □ Montreal, PQ

Antonietti, Reno, Dir. Media Serv.
ROCHESTER INSTITUTE OF TECHNOLOGY - WALLACE MEMORIAL LIBRARY □ Rochester, NY

Antos, Curtis, Info.Spec.
NATIONAL ACADEMY OF SCIENCES - NATIONAL RESEARCH COUNCIL - HIGHWAY RESEARCH INFORMATION SERVICE □ Washington, DC

Antworth, Simone
MAINE STATE LAW AND LEGISLATIVE REFERENCE LIBRARY □ Augusta, ME

Anzalone, Alfred M., Adm.Libn.
U.S. ARMY - PLASTICS TECHNICAL EVALUATION CENTER □ Dover, NJ

Anzul, Clement J., Libn.
FORDHAM UNIVERSITY - LIBRARY AT LINCOLN CENTER □ New York, NY

Aodette, Michele, Responsable
QUEBEC PROVINCE - MINISTERE DE L'AGRICULTURE, DES PECHERIES ET DE L'ALIMENTATION - CENTRE DE DOCUMENTATION □ Quebec, PQ

Aoki, Toshiyuki, Hd., Japanese Sect.
HARVARD UNIVERSITY - HARVARD YENCHING INSTITUTE - LIBRARY □ Cambridge, MA

Apante, Angel, Cat.
CUNY - CENTRO DE ESTUDIOS PUERTORRIQUENOS □ New York, NY

Apfel, Mrs. Jerome, Chm.
BETH DAVID REFORM CONGREGATION - JEWEL K. MARKOWITZ LIBRARY □ Philadelphia, PA

Api, Rose D., Off.Mgr.
SOAP AND DETERGENT ASSOCIATION - LIBRARY □ New York, NY

Apostolos, Margaret M., Micro. & Per.Libn.
KUTZTOWN STATE COLLEGE - ROHRBACH LIBRARY □ Kutztown, PA

Appel, Joan, Info.Spec.
NATIONAL REHABILITATION INFORMATION CENTER □ Washington, DC

Appel, Marsha, Staff Exec.
AMERICAN ASSOCIATION OF ADVERTISING AGENCIES - MEMBER INFORMATION SERVICE □ New York, NY

Appell, Frank C., Jr., Asst.Libn.
MIDDLETOWN PSYCHIATRIC CENTER - MEDICAL LIBRARY □ Middletown, NY

Appenzellar, Terry, Lib.Dir.
U.S. DEPT. OF JUSTICE - MAIN LIBRARY □ Washington, DC

Apperley, Ruby, Supv., Museum Serv.
SASKATCHEWAN MUSEUM OF NATURAL HISTORY - LIBRARY □ Regina, SK

Apple, Barbara, Libn.
WAUKEGAN NEWS-SUN - LIBRARY □ Waukegan, IL

Applebee, Arthur N., Assoc.Dir.
ERIC CLEARINGHOUSE ON READING AND COMMUNICATIONS SKILLS □ Urbana, IL

Appleby, J., Ref.Libn.
CONCORDIA UNIVERSITY - LOYOLA CAMPUS - GEORGES P. VANIER LIBRARY □ Montreal, PQ

Appleton, Margaret, Tech.Proc.
OHIO NORTHERN UNIVERSITY - COLLEGE OF LAW - JAY P. TAGGART MEMORIAL LAW LIBRARY □ Ada, OH

Apschnikat, Kenneth, Supt.
U.S. NATL. PARK SERVICE - MOUND CITY
GROUP NATL. MONUMENT - LIBRARY □
Chillicothe, OH

Aragon, Bill, Educ.Coord.
CHEYENNE MOUNTAIN ZOOLOGICAL PARK -
LIBRARY □ Colorado Springs, CO

Aragon, Lauren J., Libn.
U.S. AIR FORCE BASE - HOMESTEAD BASE
LIBRARY □ Homestead AFB, FL

Aranda-Coddou, Patricio, Assoc.Libn.
UNIVERSITY OF NEBRASKA, LINCOLN - LAW
LIBRARY □ Lincoln, NE

Arant-Cousins, Alice, Libn.
BARRETT, SMITH, SCHAPIRO, SIMON &
ARMSTRONG - LIBRARY □ New York, NY

Arbogast, Mrs. C.J., Libn.
POLYMER CORPORATION - LIBRARY □ Reading,
PA

Arbogast, Judy, Media Serv.Supv.
SAN DIEGO STATE UNIVERSITY - MEDIA &
CURRICULUM CENTER □ San Diego, CA

Arcari, Ralph, Dir. Of Libs.
UNIVERSITY OF CONNECTICUT - HEALTH
CENTER - LYMAN MAYNARD STOWE LIBRARY □
Farmington, CT

Archer, Edgar G., Dir.
LINCOLN MEMORIAL UNIVERSITY - ABRAHAM
LINCOLN LIBRARY AND MUSEUM □ Harrogate,
TN

Archer, Marian, Music Libn.
MADISON PUBLIC LIBRARY - ART AND MUSIC
DIVISION □ Madison, WI

Archibald, Genni, Lib.Off.
NOVA SCOTIA - DEPARTMENT OF CULTURE,
RECREATION AND FITNESS - LIBRARY □
Halifax, NS

Archibald, Jane, Coll.Dev.Off.
ST. MARY'S UNIVERSITY - PATRICK POWER
LIBRARY □ Halifax, NS

Archibald, Jean K., Dir.
MACALESTER COLLEGE - WEYERHAEUSER
LIBRARY □ St. Paul, MN

Arden, Sylvia, Hd.Libn.
SAN DIEGO HISTORICAL SOCIETY - LIBRARY
AND MANUSCRIPTS COLLECTION □ San Diego,
CA

Ardis, Susan B., Libn.
UNIVERSITY OF TEXAS, AUSTIN -
ENGINEERING LIBRARY □ Austin, TX

Arenberg, Henry X.
HIGHLAND PARK HISTORICAL SOCIETY -
LIBRARY □ Highland Park, IL

Arenz, Katherine, Adm.Asst.
UNIVERSITY OF WISCONSIN, LA CROSSE -
MURPHY LIBRARY □ La Crosse, WI

Arguimbau, Ellie, Asst.Archv.
MONTANA HISTORICAL SOCIETY - LIBRARY/
ARCHIVES □ Helena, MT

Argyropoulas, Nicholas, Act.Chf.Sup.Div.
U.S. DEFENSE MAPPING AGENCY -
HYDROGRAPHIC/TOPOGRAPHIC CENTER-
SUPPORT DIVISION - SCIENTIFIC DATA
DEPARTMENT □ Washington, DC

Arie, Barbara, Libn.
AMERICAN HEART ASSOCIATION - LIBRARY/
RECORDS CENTER □ Dallas, TX

Arkin, Cynthia R., Libn.
AMERICAN TELEPHONE & TELEGRAPH
COMPANY - LAW LIBRARY □ New York, NY

Arklie, Harriet, Dir.
NORTH CENTRAL COLLEGE - LIBRARY □
Naperville, IL

Arlen, Shelley, Photo Archv.
UNIVERSITY OF OKLAHOMA - WESTERN
HISTORY COLLECTIONS □ Norman, OK

Arleth, Hettie, Chf.Libn.
FORT WORTH STAR-TELEGRAM - LIBRARY □
Fort Worth, TX

Armeit, Marilyn, Libn.
FIDUCIARY TRUST COMPANY OF NEW YORK -
RESEARCH LIBRARY □ New York, NY

Armendt, Kathy E., Archv./Libn.
MARYLAND STATE HALL OF RECORDS
COMMISSION - LIBRARY □ Annapolis, MD

Armentrout, Sandra S., Dir.
BRICK STORE MUSEUM - EDITH CLEAVES
BARRY LIBRARY □ Kennebunk, ME

Armes, Patricia, Asst.Dir.Tech.Serv.
UNIVERSITY OF TEXAS HEALTH SCIENCE
CENTER, DALLAS - LIBRARY □ Dallas, TX

Armistead, Henry T., Hd., Coll.Dept.
JEFFERSON (Thomas) UNIVERSITY - SCOTT
MEMORIAL LIBRARY □ Philadelphia, PA

Armold, Caroline, Ref./ILL
SOUTHWESTERN OKLAHOMA STATE
UNIVERSITY - AL HARRIS LIBRARY □
Weatherford, OK

Armor, Robert D., Assoc.Libn.
SOUTHWEST RESEARCH INSTITUTE - THOMAS
BAKER SLICK MEMORIAL LIBRARY □ San
Antonio, TX

Armour, Mrs. Edward, Coord.Natl.Ref.Serv.
NATIONAL INSTITUTE ON MENTAL
RETARDATION - JOHN ORR FOSTER NATIONAL
REFERENCE LIBRARY □ Downsview, ON

Armour, James, Coord.Ref.
NORTHERN ARIZONA UNIVERSITY - LIBRARIES
□ Flagstaff, AZ

Armstead, Bernice, Act.Lib.Dir.
MEHARRY MEDICAL COLLEGE - MEDICAL
LIBRARY - LEARNING RESOURCES CENTER □
Nashville, TN

Armstrong, Alice, Libn.
EMR TELEMETRY-SANGAMO WESTON -
TECHNICAL INFORMATION CENTER □ Sarasota,
FL

Armstrong, B. June, Ref.Libn.
UNIVERSITY OF CALIFORNIA, LOS ANGELES -
ENGINEERING & MATHEMATICAL SCIENCES
LIBRARY □ Los Angeles, CA

Armstrong, Carole S., Sci.Br.Coord.
MICHIGAN STATE UNIVERSITY - ANIMAL
INDUSTRIES REFERENCE ROOM □ East Lansing,
MI

Armstrong, Carole S., Sci.Br.Coord.
MICHIGAN STATE UNIVERSITY - GEOLOGY
LIBRARY □ East Lansing, MI

Armstrong, Carole S., Sci.Br.Coord.
MICHIGAN STATE UNIVERSITY - PHYSICS-
ASTRONOMY LIBRARY □ East Lansing, MI

Armstrong, Carole S., Sci.Br.Coord.
MICHIGAN STATE UNIVERSITY - SCIENCE
LIBRARY □ East Lansing, MI

Armstrong, Dr. Cesar J., Res.Libn.
BLACKWELL, WALKER, GRAY, POWERS, FLICK
& HOEHL - LAW LIBRARY □ Miami, FL

Armstrong, Douglas, Hd.Libn.
ONTARIO - MINISTRY OF LABOUR - LIBRARY □
Toronto, ON

Armstrong, Elizabeth, Lib.Dir.
CALIFORNIA INSTITUTE OF THE ARTS -
LIBRARY □ Valencia, CA

Armstrong, Ellen J., Mgr.
MUSEUM OF CARTOON ART - LIBRARY □ Port
Chester, NY

Armstrong, Evelyn W., Mgr.
MERCK & COMPANY, INC. - MERCK SHARP &
DOHME RESEARCH LABORATORIES - LIBRARY
SERVICES □ West Point, PA

Armstrong, Dr. Helen Jane, Map Libn.
UNIVERSITY OF FLORIDA - MAP LIBRARY □
Gainesville, FL

Armstrong, Jane, Libn.
UNIVERSITY OF ILLINOIS - APPLIED LIFE
STUDIES LIBRARY □ Urbana, IL

Armstrong, Janice Gray, Libn.
MUSEUMS AT STONY BROOK - KATE STRONG
HISTORICAL LIBRARY □ Stony Brook, NY

Armstrong, John W., Selection Libn.
U.S. AIR FORCE - AIR FORCE SYSTEMS
COMMAND - AIR FORCE GEOPHYSICS
LABORATORY - RESEARCH LIBRARY† □
Bedford, MA

Armstrong, Joy A., Libn.
ABITIBI-PRICE INC. - RESEARCH CENTRE
LIBRARY □ Mississauga, ON

Armstrong, Lewis, Map Lib.Assoc.
UNIVERSITY OF KANSAS - MAP LIBRARY □
Lawrence, KS

Armstrong, Norma, Libn.
HANSON MATERIALS ENGINEERING (Western)
LTD. - BUSINESS LIBRARY □ Edmonton, AB

Armstrong, Rodney, Dir. & Libn.
BOSTON ATHENAEUM LIBRARY □ Boston, MA

Arndal, Robert E., Info.Spec.
GENERAL DYNAMICS CORPORATION -
CONVAIR DIVISION - RESEARCH LIBRARY □
San Diego, CA

Arndt, Clinton, Libn.
OAKLAND PUBLIC LIBRARY - HISTORY/
LITERATURE DIVISION □ Oakland, CA

Arndt, John, Ref./Coll.Libn.
WILFRID LAURIER UNIVERSITY - LIBRARY □
Waterloo, ON

Arner, Angela, Libn.
NEBRASKA METHODIST HOSPITAL - LIBRARY □
Omaha, NE

Arnesen, Sandra, Dir., LRC
CREIGHTON UNIVERSITY - HEALTH SCIENCES
LIBRARY □ Omaha, NE

Arneson, Arne, Music Libn.
UNIVERSITY OF COLORADO, BOULDER - MUSIC
LIBRARY □ Boulder, CO

Arnn, Judith A., Med.Libn.
U.S. AIR FORCE MEDICAL CENTER - WILFORD
HALL U.S.A.F. MEDICAL CENTER - MEDICAL
LIBRARY (SGEL) □ San Antonio, TX

Arnold, Carol W., Libn.
UNIVERSITY OF HAWAII - SCHOOL OF PUBLIC
HEALTH - REFERENCE ROOM □ Honolulu, HI

Arnold, Darlene, Sr.Libn.
MINNESOTA STATE DEPARTMENT OF
EDUCATION - OFFICE OF PUBLIC LIBRARIES
AND INTERLIBRARY COOPERATION □ St. Paul,
MN

Arnold, Doris, Res.Libn.
KENTUCKY STATE DEPARTMENT OF
COMMERCE - LIBRARY □ Frankfort, KY

Arnold, Elaine, Libn.
UNIVERSITY OF DETROIT - SCHOOL OF
ARCHITECTURE - LIBRARY □ Detroit, MI

Arnold, Gary J., Hd., Ref.
OHIO HISTORICAL SOCIETY - ARCHIVES-
LIBRARY □ Columbus, OH

Arnold, Glenda, Acq.Libn.
UNIVERSITY OF TENNESSEE - CENTER FOR
THE HEALTH SCIENCES LIBRARY □ Memphis,
TN

Arnold, Jessie, Dir.,Pub.Serv./Doc.
ALCORN STATE UNIVERSITY - JOHN DEWEY
BOYD LIBRARY □ Lorman, MS

Arnold, Joan, Cat.
SCHOOL OF VISUAL ARTS - LIBRARY □ New
York, NY

Arnold, Lee, Libn.
ADAMS ADVERTISING AGENCY, INC. -
LIBRARY □ Chicago, IL

Arnold, Lee, Libn.
WORLD ASSOCIATION OF DOCUMENT
EXAMINERS - WADE LIBRARY □ Chicago, IL

Arnold, Linda A., Hd., Cat.
SUNY - COLLEGE AT ONEONTA - JAMES M.
MILNE LIBRARY □ Oneonta, NY

Arnold, Lois, Med.Libn.
AKRON GENERAL MEDICAL CENTER - J.D.
SMITH MEMORIAL LIBRARY □ Akron, OH

Arnold, Mary Jo, Hd.Libn.
OHIO STATE UNIVERSITY - ENGINEERING
LIBRARY □ Columbus, OH

Arnold, Mary Jo, Hd.Libn.
OHIO STATE UNIVERSITY - MATERIALS
ENGINEERING LIBRARY □ Columbus, OH

Arnold, Nancy, Libn./Cur.
NEWCOMEN SOCIETY IN NORTH AMERICA -
THOMAS NEWCOMEN LIB. IN STEAM
TECHNOLOGY & INDUSTRIAL HISTORY □ Exton,
PA

Arnold, Nancy, Asst.Libn., Ref.
UNIVERSITY OF PENNSYLVANIA - BIDDLE LAW
LIBRARY □ Philadelphia, PA

Arnold, Rose, Libn.
WISCONSIN STATE LEGISLATIVE REFERENCE
BUREAU □ Madison, WI

Arnold, Ruth, Ref.Libn.
JERSEY CITY STATE COLLEGE - FORREST A.
IRWIN LIBRARY □ Jersey City, NJ

Arnold, S.K., Energy Info.Spec.
OKLAHOMA STATE DEPARTMENT OF ENERGY -
ENERGY INFORMATION CENTER □ Oklahoma
City, OK

Arnold, Stephen H., Sec.-Treas., Ed.
AFRICAN LITERATURE ASSOCIATION -
SECRETARIAT LIBRARY □ Edmonton, AB

Arnold, Wayne, Hd.
ROCHESTER PUBLIC LIBRARY - LOCAL
HISTORY DIVISION □ Rochester, NY

Arnot, Mr. J., Educ.Libn.
LAKEHEAD UNIVERSITY - EDUCATION LIBRARY
□ Thunder Bay, ON

Arnott, Barbara A., Adm.Libn.
U.S. NAVY - NAVAL AIR STATION (Alameda) -
LIBRARY □ Alameda, CA

Arnstein, Roslyn, Libn.
TAYLOR BUSINESS INSTITUTE - LIBRARY □
New York, NY

Arnwine, Jane, Info.Mgr.
NATIONAL ASSOCIATION OF RETAIL GROCERS
OF THE U.S., INC. - LIBRARY □ Washington, DC

Arny, Linda Ray, Ref./Asst.Br.Libn.
UNIVERSITY OF MASSACHUSETTS, AMHERST -
PHYSICAL SCIENCES LIBRARY □ Amherst, MA

Aroksaar, Richard, Cat.Libn.
UNIVERSITY OF SOUTHERN CALIFORNIA -
HEALTH SCIENCES CAMPUS - NORRIS
MEDICAL LIBRARY □ Los Angeles, CA

Aronson, Marcia, Libn.
NOVA SCOTIA - PUBLIC ARCHIVES OF NOVA
SCOTIA □ Halifax, NS

Aronson, Shirley C., Doc.Libn.
MARYLAND STATE LAW LIBRARY □ Annapolis,
MD

Arora, Ved P., Hd., Biblog.Serv.
SASKATCHEWAN - PROVINCIAL LIBRARY □
Regina, SK

Arostegui, Carlos, Asst.Cur.
HARVARD UNIVERSITY - DUMBARTON OAKS
CENTER FOR PRE-COLUMBIAN STUDIES -
LIBRARY □ Washington, DC

Arredondo, Gloria, Libn.
ST. BERNARDINE HOSPITAL - NORMAN F.
FELDHEYM LIBRARY □ San Bernardino, CA

Arrington, James, Chf., Circ. & ILL
U.S. DEPT. OF HEALTH AND HUMAN SERVICES -
DEPARTMENT LIBRARY □ Washington, DC

Arrington, Louis C., Prof.
UNIVERSITY OF WISCONSIN, MADISON -
POULTRY SCIENCE DEPARTMENT - HALPIN
MEMORIAL LIBRARY □ Madison, WI

Arrington, Susan J., Spec. Projects Libn.
U.S. CUSTOMS SERVICE - LIBRARY AND
INFORMATION CENTER □ Washington, DC

Arros, Jeno, Botanist
JARDIN BOTANIQUE DE MONTREAL -
BIBLIOTHEQUE □ Montreal, PQ

Arrowood, Nancy, Film Libn.
VIRGINIA STATE DEPARTMENT OF
TRANSPORTATION SAFETY - FILM LIBRARY □
Richmond, VA

Arroyo, Alicia, Hd., Music
UNIVERSITY OF PUERTO RICO - GENERAL
LIBRARY □ San Juan, PR

Arroyo-Carrion, Ramon, Dir.
CARIBBEAN REGIONAL LIBRARY □ San Juan, PR

Arsenoff, Mary M., Educ.Coord.
U.S. GENERAL SERVICES ADMINISTRATION -
CONSUMER INFORMATION CENTER □
Washington, DC

Arsic, Elinor B., Libn.
DE PAUL HOSPITAL - SCHOOL OF NURSING
LIBRARY □ Norfolk, VA

Arterbery, Vivian J., Lib.Dir.
RAND CORPORATION - LIBRARY □ Santa
Monica, CA

Arther, Richard O., Dir.
NATIONAL TRAINING CENTER OF POLYGRAPH
SCIENCE - TECHNICAL INFORMATION CENTER
□ New York, NY

Arthur, John, Info.Sci.
AMERICAN CYANAMID COMPANY -
AGRICULTURAL RESEARCH DIVISION -
TECHNICAL INFORMATION SERVICES □
Princeton, NJ

Artman, Loretta K., Sci.Ref.Libn.
UNIVERSITY OF WASHINGTON - NATURAL
SCIENCES LIBRARY □ Seattle, WA

Artz, Theodora, Hd.Acq.Dept.
UNIVERSITY OF DAYTON - LAW SCHOOL
LIBRARY □ Dayton, OH

Artzberger, John A., Dir. Mansion Musm.
OGLEBAY INSTITUTE - MANSION MUSEUM
LIBRARY □ Wheeling, WV

Arvidson, Aasa, Info.Off.
ROYAL SWEDISH EMBASSY - LIBRARY-
INFORMATION CENTER □ Washington, DC

Arwas, Clement, Libn.
UNIVERSITE DE MONTREAL - GEOLOGIE-
BIBLIOTHEQUE □ Montreal, PQ

Arzu, Bernard
U.S. BUREAU OF THE CENSUS - REGIONAL
DATA USER SERVICE - KANSAS CITY
REGIONAL OFFICE - LIBRARY □ Kansas City, KS

Asakawa, Mrs. George, Libn.
GLEN HELEN ASSOCIATION - LIBRARY □ Yellow
Springs, OH

Asawa, Edward E., Libn.
LOS ANGELES COUNTY - DEPARTMENT OF
MENTAL HEALTH - LIBRARY □ Los Angeles, CA

Asbell, Mary M., Ext.Libn.
UNIVERSITY OF TEXAS MEDICAL BRANCH -
MOODY MEDICAL LIBRARY □ Galveston, TX

Asbell, Mildred, Med.Libn.
CONNECTICUT VALLEY HOSPITAL - HALLOCK
MEDICAL LIBRARY □ Middletown, CT

Asbury, Herbert, Prog.Mgr., NASA
UNIVERSITY OF SOUTHERN CALIFORNIA -
NASA INDUSTRIAL APPLICATION CENTER
(NIAC) □ Los Angeles, CA

Asencio-Toro, Doris, Hd.Libn.
PUERTO RICO - SUPREME COURT - LAW
LIBRARY □ San Juan, PR

Ash, Joan, Assoc.Dir.
UNIVERSITY OF OREGON - HEALTH SCIENCES
CENTER - LIBRARY □ Portland, OR

Ash, Mary, Chf.Libn.
CANADA - NATIONAL DEFENCE - CANADIAN
FORCES COLLEGE - KEITH HODSON MEMORIAL
LIBRARY† □ Toronto, ON

Ashe, Kathleen, Tech.Serv.Libn.
UNIVERSITY OF MINNESOTA TECHNICAL
COLLEGE, WASECA - LEARNING RESOURCES
CENTER □ Waseca, MN

Asher, Doris H., Med.Libn.
SPARROW (Edward W.) HOSPITAL - MEDICAL
LIBRARY □ Lansing, MI

Asher, Mrs. Gunvanti, Tech.Serv.Libn.
HOLY FAMILY COLLEGE - LIBRARY □
Philadelphia, PA

Asher, Lester, Asst.Libn.
ILLINOIS RAILWAY MUSEUM - TECHNICAL
LIBRARY □ Union, IL

Ashford, C. Denise, Sr.Libn. & Mgr.
MOTOROLA, INC. - INTEGRATED CIRCUITS
DIVISION - TECHNICAL LIBRARY □ Phoenix, AZ

Ashford, C. Denise, Sr.Libn. & Mgr.
MOTOROLA, INC. - SEMICONDUCTOR
PRODUCTS DIVISION - TECHNICAL LIBRARY □
Phoenix, AZ

Ashford, Mrs. Freddye G., Univ.Libn.
LINCOLN UNIVERSITY OF MISSOURI - INMAN
E. PAGE LIBRARY □ Jefferson City, MO

Ashford, Marguerite, Ref.Libn.
BISHOP (Bernice P.) MUSEUM - LIBRARY □
Honolulu, HI

Ashin, Elizabeth R., Dental Ref.Libn.
LOUISIANA STATE UNIVERSITY MEDICAL
CENTER - LIBRARY □ New Orleans, LA

Ashley, Elizabeth, Dir. of Tech.Serv.
GOLDEN GATE BAPTIST THEOLOGICAL
SEMINARY - LIBRARY □ Mill Valley, CA

Ashley, Pamela, ILL
LOUISIANA STATE UNIVERSITY MEDICAL
CENTER - SCHOOL OF MEDICINE IN
SHREVEPORT - LIBRARY □ Shreveport, LA

Ashmon, Martha, Hd.Rd.Serv.Libn.
STANFORD UNIVERSITY - J. HUGH JACKSON
LIBRARY □ Stanford, CA

Ashton, Elizabeth H., Res.Libn.
CHEVRON OIL FIELD RESEARCH COMPANY -
TECHNICAL INFORMATION SERVICES □ La
Habra, CA

Ashton, Ray E., Dir. of Educ.
NORTH CAROLINA STATE MUSEUM - H.H.
BRIMLEY MEMORIAL LIBRARY □ Raleigh, NC

Ashworth, Margaret W., Libn.
CRANE PACKING COMPANY - TECHNICAL
LIBRARY □ Morton Grove, IL

Askew, Elizabeth Engle, Sr.Libn.
RICHMOND PUBLIC LIBRARY - BUSINESS,
SCIENCE & TECHNOLOGY DEPARTMENT† □
Richmond, VA

Asmundson, Michael, Hd., Loan Dept.
UNIVERSITY OF CALIFORNIA, DAVIS -
GENERAL LIBRARY □ Davis, CA

Asp, William G., Dir.
MINNESOTA STATE DEPARTMENT OF
EDUCATION - OFFICE OF PUBLIC LIBRARIES
AND INTERLIBRARY COOPERATION □ St. Paul,
MN

Aspry, Robert, Libn.
U.S. NAVY - NAVAL UNDERWATER SYSTEMS
CENTER - NEWPORT TECHNICAL LIBRARY □
Newport, RI

Assad, William, Govt.Doc.Libn.
ACADEMY OF AERONAUTICS - LIBRARY □
Flushing, NY

Astacio, Carmen, Archv.
PUERTO RICO - INSTITUTE OF PUERTO RICAN
CULTURE - ARCHIVO GENERAL DE PUERTO
RICO □ San Juan, PR

Astheimer, Bernice, Libn.
DUNLAP AND ASSOCIATES, INC. - LIBRARY □
Darien, CT

Aston, Charles E., Jr., Coord.
UNIVERSITY OF PITTSBURGH - DARLINGTON
MEMORIAL LIBRARY □ Pittsburgh, PA

Aston, Charles E., Jr., Coord.
UNIVERSITY OF PITTSBURGH - SPECIAL
COLLECTIONS DEPARTMENT □ Pittsburgh, PA

Aston, Jane, Supv., Graphics
OKLAHOMA STATE UNIVERSITY - AUDIO
VISUAL CENTER □ Stillwater, OK

Astraquillo, Divinia J., Law Libn.
MILWAUKEE COUNTY LAW LIBRARY □
Milwaukee, WI

Astroza, Maria Tereza, Ref.Libn.
PAN AMERICAN HEALTH ORGANIZATION -
DOCUMENTATION AND HEALTH INFORMATION
OFFICE† □ Washington, DC

Atallah, Shakeeb, Asst.Libn./Acq.
INTERNATIONAL MONETARY FUND/WORLD
BANK - JOINT BANK-FUND LIBRARY □
Washington, DC

Atcher, Tagalie, Dir.
GROUP HEALTH COOPERATIVE OF PUGET
SOUND - MEDICAL LIBRARY □ Seattle, WA

Atcheson, Pearl A., Dir., Med.Lib.
WASHOE MEDICAL CENTER - MEDICAL
LIBRARY □ Reno, NV

Atik, Shifra, Hd.Tech.Serv.
MEDICAL LIBRARY CENTER OF NEW YORK □
New York, NY

Atisanoe, Olive, Lib.Mgr.
FELETI PACIFIC LIBRARY† □ Pago Pago, AS

Atiyeh, George N., Hd. Near East Sect.
LIBRARY OF CONGRESS - AFRICAN & MIDDLE
EASTERN DIVISION □ Washington, DC

Atkins, Anita, Hd.Libn.
UNITED LODGE OF THEOSOPHISTS -
THEOSOPHY HALL - LIBRARY □ New York, NY

Atkins, Donna, Libn.
AMAX EXTRACTIVE RESEARCH &
DEVELOPMENT, INC. - TECHNICAL
INFORMATION CENTER □ Golden, CO

Atkins, Lenetta, Libn.
MERCY HOSPITAL - LEVITT HEALTH SCIENCES
LIBRARY □ Des Moines, IA

Atkins, Martha, Pub.Serv.Libn.
SUNY - COLLEGE AT CORTLAND - MEMORIAL
LIBRARY □ Cortland, NY

Atkins, Nancy F., Supv., Lib.Serv.
TENNESSEE VALLEY AUTHORITY - TECHNICAL
LIBRARY □ Chattanooga, TN

Atkins, Thomas, Hd., Instr.Serv.
BARUCH (Bernard M.) COLLEGE OF THE CITY
UNIVERSITY OF NEW YORK - LIBRARY □ New
York, NY

Atkinson, Calberta O., Libn.
RUST ENGINEERING COMPANY - LIBRARY □
Birmingham, AL

Atkinson, Jean, Chf.Med.Libn.
EISENHOWER MEDICAL CENTER - WALTER M.
LEUTHOLD MEDICAL LIBRARY □ Rancho Mirage,
CA

Atkinson, Judy, Mgr.
BURROUGHS CORPORATION - COMPUTER
SYSTEMS GROUP - TECHNICAL INFORMATION
RESOURCES CENTER† □ Pasadena, CA

Atlas, Aime, Sr.Libn.
PILGRIM PSYCHIATRIC CENTER - HEALTH
SCIENCES LIBRARY □ West Brentwood, NY

Atson, Elsa B., Asst.Libn.Tech.Serv.
JENKINS (Theodore F.) MEMORIAL LAW
LIBRARY COMPANY - LIBRARY □ Philadelphia,
PA

Attalai, Christine, Act.Chf.Libn.
UNIVERSITY OF TORONTO - FACULTY OF LAW
LIBRARY □ Toronto, ON

Attar, Carol, Lib.Dir.
COTTAGE HOSPITAL OF GROSSE POINTE -
MEDICAL LIBRARY □ Grosse Pointe Farms, MI

Attebery, D., Acq.Libn.
TRAVENOL LABORATORIES, INC. - LIBRARY □
Morton Grove, IL

Attebery, Joyce A., Lib.Techn.
U.S. NATL. PARK SERVICE - MESA VERDE
NATL. PARK - MUSEUM LIBRARY □ Mesa Verde
Natl. Park, CO

Attinello, Salvatore J., Ref.
KENNEDY-KING COLLEGE - LIBRARY □ Chicago,
IL

Attwood, Joan-Mary, Libn.
ARTHRITIS SOCIETY - NATIONAL OFFICE
LIBRARY □ Toronto, ON

Atwater, Virginia, Libn.
U.S. ARMY SERGEANTS MAJOR ACADEMY -
OTHON O. VALENT LEARNING RESOURCES
CENTER □ Ft. Bliss, TX

Atwood, Pamela C., Lib.Asst.
KRAUSE MILLING COMPANY - TECHNICAL
LIBRARY □ Milwaukee, WI

Atwood, Valdine C., Chm.
NATIONAL SOCIETY, DAUGHTERS OF THE
AMERICAN REVOLUTION - HANNAH WESTON
CHAPTER - BURNHAM TAVERN MUSEUM □
Machias, ME

Au, Eleanor C., Hd.Spec.Coll.
UNIVERSITY OF HAWAII - SPECIAL
COLLECTIONS - RARE BOOKS □ Honolulu, HI

Au, Jeannette Chin Chun, Hd., Tech.Serv.
ARIZONA STATE UNIVERSITY - COLLEGE OF
LAW - LIBRARY □ Tempe, AZ

Au, Marcia Learned, Hd.
TOLEDO-LUCAS COUNTY PUBLIC LIBRARY -
SOCIAL SCIENCE & GENERAL INFORMATION
DEPARTMENT □ Toledo, OH

Au, Vera, Biblog.
NATIONAL GEOGRAPHIC SOCIETY - LIBRARY □
Washington, DC

Aubry, John C., Archv./Libn.
AMERICAN INSTITUTE OF PHYSICS - CENTER
FOR HISTORY OF PHYSICS - NIELS BOHR
LIBRARY □ New York, NY

Aucker, Dr. John
TUSCULUM COLLEGE - INSTRUCTIONAL
MATERIALS CENTER □ Greeneville, TN

Audet, Louise, Asst. to Dir.
LA PRESSE, LTEE. - CENTRE DE
DOCUMENTATION □ Montreal, PQ

Audino, Nancy, Tech.Sys.Supv.
AMERICAN TELEPHONE & TELEGRAPH
COMPANY - LONG LINES DEPARTMENT -
INFORMATION RESEARCH CENTER □
Bedminster, NJ

Auducon, Lillian B.
FIRST PRESBYTERIAN CHURCH - LIBRARY □
Kalamazoo, MI

Auer, Grace, Coord. of Libs. & Archv.
COOK COUNTY HOSPITAL - HEALTH SCIENCE
LIBRARY □ Chicago, IL

Auer, Grace, Hd.Med.Libn.
COOK COUNTY HOSPITAL - TICE MEMORIAL
LIBRARY† □ Chicago, IL

Auerbach, Judith, Acq.Libn.
HARVARD UNIVERSITY - GRADUATE SCHOOL
OF DESIGN - FRANCES LOEB LIBRARY □
Cambridge, MA

Auerbach, Stevanne, Dir.
INSTITUTE FOR CHILDHOOD RESOURCES -
LIBRARY □ San Francisco, CA

Auerbach, Wanda, Ref.Libn.
UNIVERSITY OF WISCONSIN, MADISON -
CENTER FOR HEALTH SCIENCES LIBRARIES □
Madison, WI

Aufdenkamp, Jo Ann, Adm., Info.Serv.
LINCOLN NATIONAL LIFE INSURANCE
COMPANY - LAW LIBRARY □ Fort Wayne, IN

Aufiero, Joan, Ref.Libn.
BRITISH COLUMBIA LAW LIBRARY
FOUNDATION - VANCOUVER COURTHOUSE
LIBRARY □ Vancouver, BC

Augikos, Jan, Visual Coll.Cur.
ATLANTA COLLEGE OF ART - LIBRARY □
Atlanta, GA

August, Sidney, Dir.
COMMUNITY COLLEGE OF PHILADELPHIA -
EDUCATION RESOURCES CENTER □
Philadelphia, PA

Auh, Y. John, Hd.Libn.
WAGNER COLLEGE - HORRMANN LIBRARY □
Staten Island, NY

Auld, Jeffrey, Libn.
MARQUIS WHO'S WHO, INC. - RESEARCH
DEPARTMENT LIBRARY □ Chicago, IL

Aulf, Lydia
UNIVERSITY OF PUERTO RICO - NATURAL
SCIENCE LIBRARY □ Rio Piedras, PR

Aulffo, Pier, Asst.Libn.
BETZ LABORATORIES, INC. - RESEARCH
LIBRARY □ Trevose, PA

Ault, Betty, Lib.Asst.
DEACONESS HOSPITAL - DRUSCH
PROFESSIONAL LIBRARY □ St. Louis, MO

Austen, Loretta E., Tech.Lib.Asst.
CALIFORNIA STATE - COLORADO RIVER BOARD
OF CALIFORNIA - LIBRARY □ Los Angeles, CA

Austin, Ann, Dept.Hd.
LIBRARY ASSOCIATION OF PORTLAND -
GENERAL INFORMATION DEPARTMENT -
FOUNDATION CENTER □ Portland, OR

Austin, Sr. Ann Marie, R.S.M., Asst.Libn.
MERCY HOSPITAL - MEDICAL LIBRARY □
Wilkes-Barre, PA

Austin, Anne A., Manager
IBM CORPORATION - DP COMMUNICATIONS
LIBRARY† □ White Plains, NY

Austin, Beatrice B., Libn.
MOTOROLA, INC. - SEMICONDUCTOR
PRODUCTS DIVISION - TECHNICAL LIBRARY □
Phoenix, AZ

Austin, Carol, Lib.Techn.
U.S. AIR FORCE BASE - HOLLOMAN BASE
LIBRARY □ Alamogordo, NM

Austin, David L., Hd.
WICHITA STATE UNIVERSITY - THURLOW
LIEURANCE MEMORIAL MUSIC LIBRARY □
Wichita, KS

Austin, Dennis, Deputy Law Libn.
WISCONSIN STATE LAW LIBRARY □ Madison,
WI

Austin, Elizabeth B., Libn.
SAFEWAY STORES, INC. - LIBRARY □ Oakland,
CA

Austin, Jean, Supv., Indexing
BELL & HOWELL COMPANY - MICRO PHOTO
DIVISION - MICROFORMS ARCHIVE □ Wooster,
OH

Austin, John, Hd. of Cat.
MARSHALL (John) LAW SCHOOL - LIBRARY □
Chicago, IL

Austin, Judith, Res.Hist./Archv.
IDAHO STATE HISTORICAL SOCIETY -
LIBRARY AND ARCHIVES □ Boise, ID

Austin, Linda Swann, Libn.
THORNDIKE, DORAN, PAINE AND LEWIS INC. -
RESEARCH LIBRARY □ Atlanta, GA

Austin, Martha, Libn.
UNIVERSITY OF WASHINGTON - PHYSICS-
ASTRONOMY LIBRARY □ Seattle, WA

Austin, Nancy, Tech.Serv.
UNIVERSITY OF NORTH DAKOTA - SCHOOL OF
MEDICINE - HARLEY E. FRENCH MEDICAL
LIBRARY □ Grand Forks, ND

Austin, Phylis, Libn.
WILDERNESS LEADERSHIP INTERNATIONAL -
OUTDOOR LIVING LIBRARY □ North Fork, CA

Austin, William, Circ.Libn.
FORDHAM UNIVERSITY - LIBRARY AT LINCOLN
CENTER □ New York, NY

Austrins, Mudite, Pict.Libn.
HARCOURT BRACE JOVANOVICH, INC. -
PICTURE RESEARCH LIBRARY □ New York, NY

Avaloz, Faustino, Newspaper Cur.
MINNESOTA HISTORICAL SOCIETY -
REFERENCE LIBRARY □ St. Paul, MN

Avant, John Alfred, Fiction Libn.
BROOKLYN PUBLIC LIBRARY - LANGUAGE AND
LITERATURE DIVISION □ Brooklyn, NY

Avcin, Penelope F., Hd.Libn.
CHEVRON RESOURCES COMPANY - LIBRARY □
Golden, CO

Avdzej, Tamara, Acq.Libn.
KEAN COLLEGE OF NEW JERSEY - NANCY
THOMPSON LIBRARY □ Union, NJ

Avera, Victoria, Chf., Support Serv.
SMITHSONIAN INSTITUTION LIBRARIES □
Washington, DC

Averill, Harold A., Staff Archv.
UNIVERSITY OF TORONTO - UNIVERSITY
ARCHIVES □ Toronto, ON

Averill, Laurie, Rd.Serv.Libn.
RHODE ISLAND SCHOOL OF DESIGN - LIBRARY
□ Providence, RI

Aversa, Mary E., Mgr.
DOANE AGRICULTURAL SERVICE, INC. -
INFORMATION CENTER □ St. Louis, MO

Avery, Carol, Cat.
NORTH CAROLINA CENTRAL UNIVERSITY -
LAW LIBRARY □ Durham, NC

Avery, Galen, Tech.Lib.Asst.
UNIVERSITY OF MICHIGAN - DETROIT
BRANCH LIBRARY □ Detroit, MI

Avetria, Arsenia, Cat.
MEMORIAL SLOAN-KETTERING CANCER
CENTER - LEE COOMBE MEMORIAL LIBRARY □
New York, NY

Avey, Edward M., Tech.Serv.Libn.
CANADA - PUBLIC WORKS CANADA - ONTARIO
REGIONAL LIBRARY □ Willowdale, ON

Avila, Blanca, Libn.
HIGHWAY USERS FEDERATION - LIBRARY □
Washington, DC

Avila, Marian, Libn.
SAN DIEGO PUBLIC LIBRARY - SOCIAL
SCIENCES SECTION □ San Diego, CA

Avins, Wesley, Mgr.
PUBLIC LIBRARY OF FORT WAYNE AND ALLEN
COUNTY, INDIANA - BUSINESS AND
TECHNOLOGY DEPARTMENT □ Fort Wayne, IN

Avison, Liz, Hd.Libn.
UNIVERSITY OF TORONTO - AUDIO-VISUAL
LIBRARY □ Toronto, ON

Avlon, Mary, Libn.
CENTRAL ISLIP PSYCHIATRIC CENTER -
HEALTH SCIENCE LIBRARY □ Central Islip, NY

Avrett, Barbara, Libn.
GEORGIA REGIONAL HOSPITAL AT AUGUSTA -
HOSPITAL LIBRARY □ Augusta, GA

Avrin, Nancy F., Libn./Archv.
CENTER FOR MIGRATION STUDIES - LIBRARY
□ Staten Island, NY

Awad, Amal, Hd. of Tech.Serv.
COMMISSION DES ECOLES CATHOLIQUES DE
MONTREAL - BIBLIOTHEQUE CENTRALE □
Montreal, PQ

Axel-Lute, Paul, Hd., Pub.Serv./Online
RUTGERS UNIVERSITY, THE STATE
UNIVERSITY OF NEW JERSEY - JUSTICE
HENRY ACKERSON LIBRARY OF LAW &
CRIMINAL JUSTICE □ Newark, NJ

Axelrod, Velma, Med.Libn.
MAGEE-WOMENS HOSPITAL - HOWARD
ANDERSON POWER MEMORIAL LIBRARY □
Pittsburgh, PA

Axthelm, Kenneth W., Div.Chf.
BROOKLYN PUBLIC LIBRARY - AUDIO VISUAL
DIVISION □ Brooklyn, NY

Axtmann, Margaret Maes, Libn.
NATIONAL CENTER FOR STATE COURTS -
LIBRARY □ Williamsburg, VA

Axton, Janice, Ref.Libn.
PACE UNIVERSITY - LIBRARY □ New York, NY

Ayala, John L., Libn./Asst.Prof.
LONG BEACH CITY COLLEGE - PACIFIC COAST
CAMPUS LIBRARY □ Long Beach, CA

Ayala, Orietta, Hd., Acq.Dept.
UNIVERSITY OF PUERTO RICO - LAW SCHOOL
LIBRARY □ Rio Piedras, PR

Aycock, Margaret, Docs.Libn.
UNIVERSITY OF VIRGINIA - ARTHUR J.
MORRIS LAW LIBRARY □ Charlottesville, VA

Aycock, Martha, Ref.Libn.
UNION THEOLOGICAL SEMINARY IN VIRGINIA
- LIBRARY □ Richmond, VA

Ayer, Carol A., Libn.
U.S. FOREST SERVICE - PACIFIC NORTHWEST
FOREST & RANGE EXPERIMENT STATION -
FORESTRY SCIENCES LAB. LIBRARY □ Juneau,
AK

Ayers, Janet, Ref. & Coll.Dev.
NORTHWESTERN UNIVERSITY - SEELEY G.
MUDD LIBRARY FOR SCIENCE AND
ENGINEERING □ Evanston, IL

Aylward, James F., Adm.Libn.
U.S. NAVY - NAVAL EDUCATION AND TRAINING
CENTER - LIBRARY □ Newport, RI

Ayotte, Richard, Pub.Serv.Libn.
ORANGE COUNTY LAW LIBRARY □ Santa Ana,
CA

Ayoung, Miss R., Res.Libn.
IMPERIAL TOBACCO LTD. - RESEARCH
LIBRARY □ Montreal, PQ

Azzani, Eunice J., Libn.
DELOITTE, HASKINS & SELLS - AUDIT/MAS &
TAX LIBRARY† □ San Francisco, CA

Azzara, Elizabeth E., Assoc.Libn.
SETON HALL UNIVERSITY - MC LAUGHLIN
LIBRARY □ South Orange, NJ

B

Baacke, Ruth K., Asst.Libn.
MIDDLE EAST INSTITUTE - GEORGE CAMP
KEISER LIBRARY □ Washington, DC

Baaklini, Soumaya, Asst.Libn.
NEW YORK STATE LIBRARY - SCIENCES/
HEALTH SCIENCES/TECHNOLOGY REFERENCE
SERVICES □ Albany, NY

Baar, Hazel, Ref.Libn.
GRAND RAPIDS PUBLIC LIBRARY -
FOUNDATION CENTER REGIONAL COLLECTION
□ Grand Rapids, MI

Baas, Mary Ellen, Ref.Libn.
MEDICAL COLLEGE OF WISCONSIN - TODD
WEHR LIBRARY □ Milwaukee, WI

Baatz, Wilmer H., Hd.
INDIANA UNIVERSITY - EDUCATION LIBRARY
□ Bloomington, IN

Babb, Madeleine, Libn.
JRB ASSOCIATES, INC. - OCCUPATIONAL
HEALTH & SAFETY LIBRARY □ McLean, VA

Babcock, Marie, Corp. Files Mgr.
STANDARD & POOR'S CORPORATION -
LIBRARY □ New York, NY

Babcock, Sharon, Lib.Supv.
UNIVERSITY OF WASHINGTON - HEALTH
SCIENCES LIBRARY - K.K. SHERWOOD LIBRARY
□ Seattle, WA

Babeaux, Kathy A., Libn.
OHIOANA LIBRARY ASSOCIATION - OHIOANA
LIBRARY AND ARCHIVES □ Columbus, OH

Babian, Mary C., Supv./Acq.
GENERAL MOTORS CORPORATION - RESEARCH
LABORATORIES LIBRARY □ Warren, MI

Babilot, Dr. George, Dir.
SAN DIEGO STATE UNIVERSITY - CENTER FOR
PUBLIC ECONOMICS LIBRARY □ San Diego, CA

Babin, Joseph M., Dir. of Lib.
ST. JOSEPH SEMINARY COLLEGE - PERE
ROUQUETTE LIBRARY □ St. Benedict, LA

Babineau, Cietta M., Lib.Asst.
CHALMERS (Dr. Everett) HOSPITAL - DR.
GARFIELD MOFFATT HEALTH SCIENCES
LIBRARY □ Fredericton, NB

Babineau-Simenauer, Suzanne, Cur.
NEW YORK UNIVERSITY - INSTITUTE OF FINE
ARTS - PHOTOGRAPHIC ARCHIVE □ New York,
NY

Baca, Dan, Supv., Rpt.Lib.
UNIVERSITY OF CALIFORNIA - LOS ALAMOS
NATIONAL LABORATORY - LIBRARY □ Los
Alamos, NM

Bach, Barbara, Libn.
BETH EL SYNAGOGUE - MAX SHAPIRO LIBRARY
□ St. Louis Park, MN

Bachand, Michelle, Hd.Libn.
CANADIAN BROADCASTING CORPORATION -
LIBRARY □ Montreal, PQ

Bachman, Nancy, Res.Libn.
CONSUMERS UNION OF UNITED STATES, INC. -
LIBRARY □ Mount Vernon, NY

Bachmann, Joan, Lib. Aid
U.S. GEOLOGICAL SURVEY - WATER
RESOURCES DIVISION - NEW YORK
SUBDISTRICT - LIBRARY □ Syosset, NY

Bachrach, Joseph, Asst.Libn.
HEBREW THEOLOGICAL COLLEGE - SAUL
SILBER MEMORIAL LIBRARY □ Skokie, IL

Back, Julia G., Ref.Libn.
FEDERAL RESERVE SYSTEM - BOARD OF
GOVERNORS - RESEARCH LIBRARY □
Washington, DC

Backes, James C., Asst.Libn.
NEW YORK LAW INSTITUTE - LIBRARY □ New
York, NY

Backlund, Caroline H., Rd.Serv.
NATIONAL GALLERY OF ART - LIBRARY □
Washington, DC

Backman, Bob, AV Coord.
ST. LUKE'S HOSPITAL - LIBRARY† □ Fargo, ND

Backman, Robert E., Cur.
HANDWRITING ANALYSIS RESEARCH -
LIBRARY □ Greenfield, MA

Backovsky, Ljuba, Asst.Musm.Libn.
METROPOLITAN MUSEUM OF ART - THOMAS J.
WATSON LIBRARY □ New York, NY

Backsen, Marcella, Libn.
IMMACULATE HEART OF MARY - PARISH
LIBRARY □ Los Alamos, NM

Backus, Betty J.
UNION TEXAS PETROLEUM CORPORATION -
LIBRARY □ Houston, TX

Bacon, Agnes K., Dept.Hd.
NORDSON CORPORATION - TECHNICAL
INFORMATION DEPARTMENT □ Amherst, OH

Bacon, Charles, Founder
HOLY LAND MUSEUM & LIBRARY □ New York,
NY

Bacon, Ethel, Libn.
UNIVERSITY OF HARTFORD - HARTT SCHOOL
OF MUSIC - ALLEN MEMORIAL LIBRARY □ West
Hartford, CT

Badal, Jindriska, Info.Spec.
MASSACHUSETTS INSTITUTE OF TECHNOLOGY
- LABORATORY FOR COMPUTER SCIENCE -
READING ROOM □ Cambridge, MA

Badders, Hurley, Commn.Dir.
PENDLETON DISTRICT HISTORICAL AND
RECREATIONAL COMMISSION - REFERENCE
LIBRARY □ Pendleton, SC

Bader, Doris S., Libn.
LONG ISLAND CATHOLIC - RESEARCH LIBRARY
□ Hempstead, NY

Bader, Hazel, Libn.
RUTAN AND TUCKER - LIBRARY □ Santa Ana,
CA

Bader, Shelley A., Dir.
GEORGE WASHINGTON UNIVERSITY -
MEDICAL CENTER - PAUL HIMMELFARB
HEALTH SCIENCES LIBRARY □ Washington, DC

Badger, Harold, Libn.
FREEDOMS FOUNDATION AT VALLEY FORGE -
LIBRARY □ Valley Forge, PA

Bading, Kathryn E., Cat.
TRINITY UNIVERSITY - LIBRARY □ San Antonio,
TX

Badome, Jacqueline, Hd.Libn.
BRUNDAGE, STORY & ROSE, INVESTMENT
COUNSEL - LIBRARY □ New York, NY

Badr, Muhammad, Gen.Mgr.
NORTH AMERICAN ISLAMIC TRUST, INC. -
LIBRARY □ Indianapolis, IN

Badura, Jean, Tech.Libn.
NORLAND CORPORATION - TECHNICAL
LIBRARY □ Fort Atkinson, WI

Bae, Frank S.H., Law Libn.
NEW ENGLAND SCHOOL OF LAW - LIBRARY □
Boston, MA

Baer, E. Alex, Hd., Ref.Dept.
VIRGINIA POLYTECHNIC INSTITUTE AND
STATE UNIVERSITY - CAROL M. NEWMAN
LIBRARY □ Blacksburg, VA

Baer, Mark H., Dir. Of Libs.
HEWLETT-PACKARD COMPANY - CORPORATE
LIBRARY □ Palo Alto, CA

Baerwald, Dr. John, Dir., Coll. of Engr.
UNIVERSITY OF ILLINOIS - HIGHWAY TRAFFIC
SAFETY CENTER - LIBRARY □ Urbana, IL

Baez, Lourdes E., Libn.
PERSHING & CO. INC. - RESEARCH LIBRARY† □
New York, NY

Bagby, Felicia, Libn.
CLARK DIETZ ENGINEERS - LIBRARY □ Urbana,
IL

Bagdoyan, Helen, Pub.Serv.Libn.
GEORGETOWN UNIVERSITY - MEDICAL
CENTER - DAHLGREN MEMORIAL LIBRARY □
Washington, DC

Bagen, Rev. John J., C.M., Libn.
ST. MARY'S SEMINARY - ST. MARY'S OF THE
BARRENS LIBRARY □ Perryville, MO

Bagley, Marcy, Hd.Libn.
PHOENIX NEWSPAPERS, INC. - LIBRARY □
Phoenix, AZ

Bagnerise, Charles, Asst.Libn.
U.S. VETERANS ADMINISTRATION (LA-New
Orleans) - MEDICAL CENTER LIBRARY □ New
Orleans, LA

Bagwill, Alice, Libn.
U.S. COMPTROLLER OF THE CURRENCY -
LIBRARY □ Washington, DC

Baher-Simpon, Vaughn
UNIVERSITY OF SOUTHWESTERN LOUISIANA -
CENTER FOR LOUISIANA STUDIES □ Lafayette,
LA

Bahlke, Marianne, Archv.
SAN JOAQUIN COUNTY HISTORICAL MUSEUM □
Lodi, CA

Bahn, Gilbert S., Hd.
SCHUYLER TECHNICAL LIBRARY □ Newport
News, VA

Bahr, Christine, Libn.
UNITED HOSPITAL FUND OF NEW YORK -
REFERENCE LIBRARY □ New York, NY

Bahr, Edward, AV Distribution
UNIVERSITY OF WISCONSIN, STEVENS POINT
- JAMES H. ALBERTSON CENTER FOR
LEARNING RESOURCES □ Stevens Point, WI

Baier, C., Sec.
UNIVERSITY OF TORONTO - DEPARTMENT OF
MEDICAL RESEARCH LIBRARY □ Toronto, ON

Baier, Linda M., Asst.Libn.
INSTITUTE OF PAPER CHEMISTRY - LIBRARY □
Appleton, WI

Bailey, Beatrice I., Supv.
ST. PAUL PUBLIC LIBRARY - SCIENCE AND
INDUSTRY ROOM □ St. Paul, MN

Bailey, Bernadine, Asst.Med.Libn.
ARKANSAS STATE HOSPITAL - MEDICAL
LIBRARY □ Little Rock, AR

Bailey, Cheryl M., Dir.
MARY COLLEGE - LIBRARY □ Bismarck, ND

Bailey, Mr. Chris H., Cur. & Libn.
AMERICAN CLOCK AND WATCH MUSEUM -
EDWARD INGRAHAM LIBRARY □ Bristol, CT

Bailey, Donald K., Dir. Blind Div.
TEXAS STATE LIBRARY □ Austin, TX

Bailey, Edgar C., Jr., Ref.Libn.
PROVIDENCE COLLEGE - PHILLIPS MEMORIAL
LIBRARY □ Providence, RI

Bailey, F. Ruth, Asst.Libn./Rd.Serv.
NYACK COLLEGE - LIBRARY □ Nyack, NY

Bailey, Florence
MONTGOMERY COUNTY PLANNING
COMMISSION - RESEARCH LIBRARY □
Norristown, PA

Bailey, George M., Assoc.Dir. of Libs.
CLAREMONT COLLEGES - LIBRARY □ Claremont,
CA

Bailey, J.A., Dir.
UNIVERSITY OF TULSA - COLLEGE OF
ENGINEERING & PHYSICAL SCIENCES -
DIVISION OF INFORMATION SERVICES □ Tulsa,
OK

Bailey, J.H., Pres.
ERIE COUNTY HISTORICAL SOCIETY □ Erie, PA

Bailey, Prof. James F., III, Dir. Law Lib.
INDIANA UNIVERSITY - SCHOOL OF LAW
LIBRARY □ Indianapolis, IN

Bailey, Jean, Libn.
GLATFELTER (P.H.) COMPANY - RESEARCH
LIBRARY □ Spring Grove, PA

Bailey, Judith H., Libn.
FRENCH AMERICAN METALS CORPORATION -
LIBRARY □ Lakewood, CO

Bailey, Ms. Kay, Libn.
TEXAS EASTERN TRANSMISSION
CORPORATION - LIBRARY† □ Houston, TX

Bailey, Lois C., Adm.Asst.
UNIVERSITY OF DETROIT - LIBRARY MEDIA
CENTER □ Detroit, MI

Bailey, Marlene, Libn.
LAFAYETTE JOURNAL AND COURIER - LIBRARY
□ Lafayette, IN

Bailey, Martha J., Life Sci.Libn.
PURDUE UNIVERSITY - BIOCHEMISTRY
LIBRARY □ West Lafayette, IN

Bailey, Martha J., Life Sci.Libn.
PURDUE UNIVERSITY - LIFE SCIENCE LIBRARY
□ West Lafayette, IN

Bailey, Mary W., Ref.Libn.
VIRGINIA STATE UNIVERSITY - JOHNSTON
MEMORIAL LIBRARY □ Petersburg, VA

Bailey, Mercedes M., Chf.Libn.
INTER-AMERICAN DEFENSE COLLEGE -
LIBRARY □ Washington, DC

Bailey, Virginia S.
RENSSELAER POLYTECHNIC INSTITUTE -
ARCHITECTURE LIBRARY □ Troy, NY

Bailey, William M., Libn.
HILLSBOROUGH COUNTY LAW LIBRARY □
Tampa, FL

Baillargeon, Danielle, Ref.
CEGEP DE TROIS-RIVIERES - BIBLIOTHEQUE □
Trois-Rivieres, PQ

Baillie, Susan, Supv.
CONCORDIA UNIVERSITY - LOYOLA CAMPUS -
DRUMMOND SCIENCE LIBRARY □ Montreal, PQ

Baily, Prof. Dee, Music Libn.
BROOKLYN COLLEGE OF THE CITY UNIVERSITY
OF NEW YORK - MUSIC LIBRARY □ Brooklyn, NY

Bain, Christine A., Assoc.Libn.
NEW YORK STATE LIBRARY - SCIENCES/
HEALTH SCIENCES/TECHNOLOGY REFERENCE
SERVICES □ Albany, NY

Bain, Harry, Tax Mgr.
MURPHY OIL CORPORATION - TAX LIBRARY □
El Dorado, AR

Bain, Janice W., Libn.
NATIONAL ACADEMY OF SCIENCES -
NATIONAL RESEARCH COUNCIL -
TRANSPORTATION RESEARCH BOARD LIBRARY
□ Washington, DC

Baird, Bonnie, Hd.Ed.Serv.
DALHOUSIE UNIVERSITY - W.K. KELLOGG
HEALTH SCIENCES LIBRARY □ Halifax, NS

Baird, Dennis, Libn.
UNIVERSITY OF IDAHO - SOCIAL SCIENCE
LIBRARY □ Moscow, ID

Baird, M., Tech.Serv.
GOLDEY BEACOM COLLEGE - J. WILBUR
HIRONS LIBRARY □ Wilmington, DE

Baird, Nancy, Ref.Libn.
WESTERN KENTUCKY UNIVERSITY -
KENTUCKY LIBRARY AND MUSEUM/
UNIVERSITY ARCHIVES □ Bowling Green, KY

Bakcsy, Gabriel, Dir.
LONG ISLAND COLLEGE HOSPITAL - HOAGLAND
MEDICAL LIBRARY □ Brooklyn, NY

Bake, Maj. A.S.J., Hd., Hum./Soc.Sci.
ROYAL MILITARY COLLEGE OF CANADA -
MASSEY LIBRARY & SCIENCE/ENGINEERING
LIBRARY □ Kingston, ON

Baker, A. Albert, Hd.
UNIVERSITY OF SOUTHERN CALIFORNIA -
SCIENCE & ENGINEERING LIBRARY □ Los
Angeles, CA

Baker, Alberta, Libn.
CITIES SERVICE COMPANY - LEGAL DIVISION
LIBRARY □ Tulsa, OK

Baker, Alison, Med.Ref.Libn.
UNIVERSITY OF CHICAGO - DR. FRANK
BILLINGS LIBRARY □ Chicago, IL

Baker, Anna Lyon, Commun.Res.Coord.
INDIANAPOLIS POWER & LIGHT COMPANY -
CORPORATE COMMUNICATIONS SERVICES
REFERENCE LIBRARY □ Indianapolis, IN

Baker, Aurelia S., Libn.
CENTRAL STATE HOSPITAL - PROFESSIONAL
LIBRARY □ Indianapolis, IN

Baker, B. Gene, Dir.
FLORIDA STATE LEGISLATURE - DIVISION OF
LEGISLATIVE LIBRARY SERVICES □
Tallahassee, FL

Baker, Bradley, Doc.Libn.
NORTHEASTERN ILLINOIS UNIVERSITY -
LIBRARY □ Chicago, IL

Baker, Carl, Asst.Libn./Cat.
ART CENTER COLLEGE OF DESIGN - JAMES
LEMONT FOGG MEMORIAL LIBRARY □
Pasadena, CA

Baker, Carolyn, Asst.Libn.
OKLAHOMA REGIONAL LIBRARY FOR THE
BLIND AND PHYSICALLY HANDICAPPED □
Oklahoma City, OK

Baker, Connie, Chf.Libn.
U.S. VETERANS ADMINISTRATION (CA-San
Diego) - MEDICAL CENTER LIBRARY □ San
Diego, CA

Baker, Consuelo B., Libn.
PANAMA CANAL COMMISSION - LIBRARY-
MUSEUM □ APO Miami, FL

Baker, David, Bus.Mgr.
INDIANA STATE LIBRARY □ Indianapolis, IN

Baker, Dudley L., Exec.Sec.
SOCIETY OF ST. VINCENT DE PAUL - LIBRARY
□ St. Louis, MO

Baker, Elizabeth, Music Libn.
EASTERN KENTUCKY UNIVERSITY - JOHN
GRANT CRABBE LIBRARY □ Richmond, KY

Baker, Elizabeth K., Libn.
EASTERN KENTUCKY UNIVERSITY - MUSIC
LIBRARY □ Richmond, KY

Baker, Gayle, Circ.Supv.
VANDERBILT UNIVERSITY - MEDICAL CENTER
LIBRARY □ Nashville, TN

Baker, Grace E., Libn.
SOCIETY OF CALIFORNIA PIONEERS - JOSEPH
A. MOORE LIBRARY □ San Francisco, CA

Baker, J. Wayne, Lib.Dir.
OHIO NORTHERN UNIVERSITY - HETERICK
MEMORIAL LIBRARY □ Ada, OH

Baker, James D., Dir.
BROOME COMMUNITY COLLEGE - CECIL C.
TYRRELL LEARNING RESOURCES CENTER □
Binghamton, NY

Baker, James W., Res.Libn.
PLIMOTH PLANTATION, INC. - LIBRARY □
Plymouth, MA

Baker, Janet, Libn.
BANK OF AMERICA, NT & SA - REFERENCE
LIBRARY □ San Francisco, CA

Baker, Joanne T., Law Libn.
LAKE COUNTY LAW LIBRARY □ Waukegan, IL

Baker, Judith, Assoc.Dir.
HAHNEMANN MEDICAL COLLEGE & HOSPITAL -
WARREN H. FAKE LIBRARY □ Philadelphia, PA

Baker, Kay M., Field Rec.Libn.
U.S. GEOLOGICAL SURVEY - DENVER LIBRARY
□ Denver, CO

Baker, Letha, Law Libn.
NEVADA COUNTY LAW LIBRARY □ Nevada City,
CA

Baker, Linda, Adm.Libn.
SUTHERLAND, ASBILL & BRENNAN - LIBRARY □
Atlanta, GA

Baker, Marion F., Libn.
SUSQUEHANNA COUNTY HISTORICAL SOCIETY
AND FREE LIBRARY ASSOCIATION □ Montrose,
PA

Baker, Marion R., Info.Ret.
JET RESEARCH CENTER, INC. - TECHNICAL
INFORMATION AND SCIENCE LIBRARY □
Arlington, TX

Baker, Martha A., Libn.
HOBART BROTHERS COMPANY - TECHNICAL
CENTER - JOHN H. BLANKENBUEHLER
MEMORIAL LIBRARY □ Troy, OH

Baker, Mary E., Libn.
3M - MERTLE LIBRARY □ St. Paul, MN

Baker, Mary E., Libn.
3M - 235 LIBRARY □ St. Paul, MN

Baker, Maryann, Hd.
FREE LIBRARY OF PHILADELPHIA -
LITERATURE DEPARTMENT □ Philadelphia, PA

PERSONNEL

PERSONNEL

Baker, Myrna, Techn.
MANITOBA - DEPARTMENT OF ECONOMIC DEVELOPMENT AND TOURISM - LIBRARY □ Winnipeg, MB
Baker, Naydean L., Law Libn.
VENTURA COUNTY LAW LIBRARY □ Ventura, CA
Baker, Paula J., Hd.
TOLEDO-LUCAS COUNTY PUBLIC LIBRARY - FINE ARTS AND AUDIO SERVICE DEPARTMENT □ Toledo, OH
Baker, Mrs. Robert L., Jr., Res.Coord.
HISTORIC ANNAPOLIS, INC. - LIBRARY □ Annapolis, MD
Baker, Russell P., Archv.
ARKANSAS STATE HISTORY COMMISSION - ARCHIVES □ Little Rock, AR
Baker, Sara W., Dir.Lib.Serv.
HURON ROAD HOSPITAL - LIBRARY AND AUDIOVISUAL CENTER □ Cleveland, OH
Baker, Sharon P., Hd., Acq.Dept.
UNIVERSITY OF CALIFORNIA, DAVIS - GENERAL LIBRARY □ Davis, CA
Baker, Sylva, Hd.Libn.
ACADEMY OF NATURAL SCIENCES - LIBRARY □ Philadelphia, PA
Baker, Tracey, Asst.Libn.
MINNESOTA HISTORICAL SOCIETY - SPECIAL LIBRARIES □ St. Paul, MN
Baker, William A., Dir./Cur.of Musm.
MASSACHUSETTS INSTITUTE OF TECHNOLOGY - FRANCIS HART NAUTICAL MUSEUM - LIBRARY □ Cambridge, MA
Baker, Zachary, Asst.Libn.
YIVO INSTITUTE FOR JEWISH RESEARCH - LIBRARY AND ARCHIVES □ New York, NY
Baker-Batsel, John. D., Dir.
GRADUATE THEOLOGICAL UNION - LIBRARY □ Berkeley, CA
Bakken, Douglas A., Dir., Ford Archv.
HENRY FORD MUSEUM AND GREENFIELD VILLAGE - FORD ARCHIVES □ Dearborn, MI
Bakken, Douglas A., Dir.
HENRY FORD MUSEUM AND GREENFIELD VILLAGE - ROBERT H. TANNAHILL RESEARCH LIBRARY □ Dearborn, MI
Bakos, Dr. Edward, Med.Dir.
CLEVELAND PSYCHIATRIC INSTITUTE - KARNOSH LIBRARY □ Cleveland, OH
Balaban, Vivian, Asst.Libn.
HUNTER COLLEGE OF THE CITY UNIVERSITY OF NEW YORK - HUNTER COLLEGE SCHOOL OF SOCIAL WORK - LIBRARY □ New York, NY
Balachandran, M., Ref.Libn.
UNIVERSITY OF ILLINOIS - COMMERCE LIBRARY □ Urbana, IL
Balachandran, Mrs. Sarojini, Asst.Engr.Libn.
UNIVERSITY OF ILLINOIS - ENGINEERING LIBRARY □ Urbana, IL
Balaisis, Mary, Energy Enquiry Ctr.
CANADA - NATIONAL RESEARCH COUNCIL - CISTI - ENERGY BRANCH □ Ottawa, ON
Balanoff, Elizabeth, Dir.
ROOSEVELT UNIVERSITY - ORAL HISTORY PROJECT IN LABOR HISTORY □ Chicago, IL
Balassone, Bro. Gabriel, O.F.M., Dir., Lib.
DUNS SCOTUS COLLEGE - LIBRARY □ Southfield, MI
Balatti, Sheila, Chf.Libn.
BANK OF CANADA - LIBRARY □ Ottawa, ON
Balay, Robert, Hd., Ref.Dept.
YALE UNIVERSITY - CRAWFORD COLLECTION ON THE MODERN DRAMA □ New Haven, CT
Balazs, Andrew, Dept.Libn.
ALBERTA - DEPARTMENT OF THE ATTORNEY GENERAL - ATTORNEY GENERAL LAW LIBRARY □ Edmonton, AB
Baldauf, Gretchen, Hd.Curric.Lab.
SUNY - COLLEGE AT BUFFALO - EDWARD H. BUTLER LIBRARY □ Buffalo, NY
Baldini, Bernadette, Tech.Serv.
UNIVERSITY OF KENTUCKY - MEDICAL CENTER LIBRARY □ Lexington, KY

Baldock, Margaret, Libn.
UNIVERSITY OF SASKATCHEWAN - EDUCATION BRANCH LIBRARY □ Saskatoon, SK
Baldridge, Alan, Libn.
STANFORD UNIVERSITY - HOPKINS MARINE STATION - LIBRARY □ Pacific Grove, CA
Baldridge, Sheila, Libn.
CALIFORNIA STATE UNIVERSITY AND COLLEGES - MOSS LANDING MARINE LABORATORIES - LIBRARY □ Moss Landing, CA
Baldwin, Charlene M., Libn.
TETRA TECH, INC. - LIBRARY □ Pasadena, CA
Baldwin, Donald W., Chm., Bd. of Regt.
MONROE (James) MUSEUM AND MEMORIAL LIBRARY □ Fredericksburg, VA
Baldwin, Ella, Asst.Libn.
UNIVERSITY OF MINNESOTA - AMES LIBRARY OF SOUTH ASIA □ Minneapolis, MN
Baldwin, Jane, Music Ref.Libn.
UNIVERSITY OF WESTERN ONTARIO - MUSIC LIBRARY □ London, ON
Baldwin, Jerome C., Dir., Lib./Info.Serv
MINNESOTA STATE DEPARTMENT OF TRANSPORTATION - LIBRARY AND INFORMATION SERVICES SECTION □ St. Paul, MN
Baldwin, Mark F., Mgr., Tech.Info.Sys.
RAYTHEON COMPANY - SUBMARINE SIGNAL DIVISION - TECHNICAL INFORMATION CENTER □ Portsmouth, RI
Baldwin, Robert, Assoc.Libn.
YASODHARA ASHRAM SOCIETY - LIBRARY □ Kootenay Bay, BC
Baldwin, Dr. Ruth
UNIVERSITY OF FLORIDA - BALDWIN LIBRARY □ Gainesville, FL
Baldyga, Louise, Asst.Libn.
CONNECTICUT STATE LIBRARY - LAW LIBRARY AT BRIDGEPORT □ Bridgeport, CT
Bale, Marion C., Libn.
BRAUN (C.F.) COMPANY - MURRAY HILL DIVISION - ENGINEERING LIBRARY □ Murray Hill, NJ
Balent, Mary Z., Tech.Supv.
IFI/PLENUM DATA COMPANY - LIBRARY □ Alexandria, VA
Bales, Mrs. D.A., Sec.
GENSTAR CEMENT, LTD. - TECHNICAL LIBRARY □ Edmonton, AB
Balester, Vivian S., Hd.Libn.
SQUIRE, SANDERS & DEMPSEY - LAW LIBRARY □ Cleveland, OH
Balikos, Jeanne, Info.Res.
HUGHES AIRCRAFT COMPANY - INFORMATION RESOURCES SECTION □ Culver City, CA
Balio, Tino, Dir.
UNIVERSITY OF WISCONSIN, MADISON - WISCONSIN CENTER FOR FILM AND THEATER RESEARCH □ Madison, WI
Balius, Sharon, Hd., Ref./Spec.Coll.
UNIVERSITY OF MICHIGAN - ENGINEERING-TRANSPORTATION LIBRARY □ Ann Arbor, MI
Balkema, John B., Libn.
NATIONAL COUNCIL ON THE AGING - LIBRARY □ Washington, DC
Ball, Alice D., Exec.Dir.
UNIVERSAL SERIALS & BOOK EXCHANGE, INC. - DUPLICATE EXCHANGE CLEARINGHOUSE & INFORMATION CENTER □ Washington, DC
Ball, Darlene L., Mgr.
BURLINGTON INDUSTRIES, INC. - LIBRARY INFORMATION SERVICES □ Greensboro, NC
Ball, Evelyn
HARTFORD PUBLIC LIBRARY - REFERENCE AND GENERAL READING DEPARTMENT □ Hartford, CT
Ball, Mrs. Frank C., Cur.
CANADIAN COUNTY HISTORICAL MUSEUM - LIBRARY □ El Reno, OK
Ball, Helen, Cur. of Spec.Coll.
MIAMI UNIVERSITY - WALTER HAVIGHURST SPECIAL COLLECTIONS LIBRARY □ Oxford, OH

Ball, Lucile, Libn.
UNIVERSITY OF MIAMI - LOWE ART MUSEUM LIBRARY □ Coral Gables, FL
Ball, Susan Campbell, Libn.
PUGET SOUND POWER AND LIGHT COMPANY LIBRARY □ Bellevue, WA
Balla, Wesley G., Dir./Cur.
LE ROY HISTORICAL SOCIETY - LIBRARY □ Le Roy, NY
Ballard, Debbie, Tech.Libn.
SOUTHWIRE COMPANY - TECHNICAL LIBRARY □ Carrollton, GA
Ballard, Janet, Lib.Techn.
U.S. FISH & WILDLIFE SERVICE - LIBRARY† □ Anchorage, AK
Ballard, Jeannette E., Libn.
INA CORPORATION - LIBRARY □ Philadelphia, PA
Ballard, Natalie C., Libn.
LAWRENCE LAW LIBRARY □ Lawrence, MA
Ballard, Sharon, Search Serv.
WARNER-LAMBERT/PARKE-DAVIS - RESEARCH LIBRARY† □ Ann Arbor, MI
Ballasch, Sandra S., Libn.
UNIVERSITY OF IOWA - LIBRARY SCIENCE LIBRARY □ Iowa City, IA
Ballen, Marcia, Data Bank Mgr.
FRANKLIN RESEARCH CENTER - NATIONAL SOLAR HEATING & COOLING INFO. CTR. □ Rockville, MD
Ballendorf, Dirk A., Dir.
UNIVERSITY OF GUAM - MICRONESIAN AREA RESEARCH CENTER - PACIFIC COLLECTION □ Mangilao, GU
Ballentine, Frances D., Multi-Media Coord.
ORANGEBURG-CALHOUN TECHNICAL COLLEGE - GRESSETTE LEARNING RESOURCE CENTER □ Orangeburg, SC
Ballentine, Rebecca, Libn.
UNIVERSITY OF NORTH CAROLINA, CHAPEL HILL - INSTITUTE OF GOVERNMENT - LIBRARY □ Chapel Hill, NC
Balliet, Patrice, Children's Serv.
U.S. ARMY POST - FORT LEWIS - LIBRARY SYSTEM □ Fort Lewis, WA
Ballinger, Barbara, Hd.Libn.
OAK PARK PUBLIC LIBRARY - LOCAL AUTHOR AND HISTORY COLLECTIONS □ Oak Park, IL
Ballinger, Dr. Charles E., Exec.Sec.
NATIONAL COUNCIL FOR YEAR-ROUND EDUCATION - LIBRARY □ San Diego, CA
Ballowe, Pat, Hd.Libn.
CHURCH OF JESUS CHRIST OF LATTER-DAY SAINTS - TRI-CITIES BRANCH GENEALOGICAL LIBRARY □ Richland, WA
Balmer, Mary, Asst.Libn.Tech.Serv.
UNIVERSITY OF CONNECTICUT - LIBRARY □ Storrs, CT
Balogh, Cornelia O., Act.Hd.
CALIFORNIA STATE UNIVERSITY, LOS ANGELES - SCIENCE/TECHNOLOGY REFERENCE ROOM □ Los Angeles, CA
Balpataky, Susanne, Libn.
METROPOLITAN TORONTO LIBRARY - HISTORY DEPARTMENT □ Toronto, ON
Balshone, Cathy S., Hd.Libn.
BOSTON CONSERVATORY OF MUSIC - ALBERT ALPHIN MUSIC LIBRARY □ Boston, MA
Balsley, Susan, Libn.
VESTIGIA - LIBRARY □ Stanhope, NJ
Baltes, Jack, Dir., Info.Serv.
INTERNATIONAL FOUNDATION OF EMPLOYEE BENEFIT PLANS - INFORMATION CENTER □ Brookfield, WI
Balthazar, Luiza, Hd., ILL
NEW YORK MEDICAL COLLEGE AND THE WESTCHESTER ACADEMY OF MEDICINE - WESTCHESTER MEDICAL CENTER LIBRARY □ Valhalla, NY
Balthrop, Barry, Hd., Foreign Patents
U.S. PATENT & TRADEMARK OFFICE - SCIENTIFIC LIBRARY □ Arlington, VA

Baltis, Nancy, Mgr.
SYNTEX, U.S.A. - CORPORATE LIBRARY/ INFORMATION SERVICES □ Palo Alto, CA

Balz, Charles F., Project Mgr.
IBM CORPORATION - FEDERAL SYSTEMS DIVISION - AVIONICS SYSTEMS - LIBRARY □ Owego, NY

Balz, Elizabeth L., Assoc.Libn.
TRINITY LUTHERAN SEMINARY - LIBRARY □ Columbus, OH

Bamattre, Robert, Hd.Pub.Serv.
BIOLA COLLEGE, INC. - LIBRARY □ La Mirada, CA

Banash, Maxine Wisner, Dir.
HISTORICAL SOCIETY OF PALM BEACH COUNTY - LIBRARY AND ARCHIVES □ Palm Beach, FL

Banayo, Manny, Dir. of Info.Ctr.
SEARS, ROEBUCK AND CO. - ARCHIVES, BUSINESS HISTORY AND INFORMATION CENTER □ Chicago, IL

Bancone, Mary-Lynne, Asst.Libn.
TEACHERS INSURANCE AND ANNUITY ASSOCIATION OF AMERICA - BUSINESS LIBRARY □ New York, NY

Bancroft, David B., Staff Assoc.
WASHINGTON UNIVERSITY - DEPARTMENT OF TECHNOLOGY AND HUMAN AFFAIRS - LIBRARY □ St. Louis, MO

Bandel, Rubin, Adm.Asst.
SUNY AT BUFFALO - CHARLES B. SEARS LAW LIBRARY □ Buffalo, NY

Bandemer, June, Asst.Dir./Hd., Rd.Serv.
UNIVERSITY OF PITTSBURGH - FALK LIBRARY OF THE HEALTH SCIENCES □ Pittsburgh, PA

Bander, Edward, Law Libn.
SUFFOLK UNIVERSITY - LAW LIBRARY □ Boston, MA

Bandurraga, Peter L., Dir.
NEVADA HISTORICAL SOCIETY - LIBRARY† □ Reno, NV

Bandy, Charles, Dir.
UNIVERSITY OF COLORADO MEDICAL CENTER - DENISON MEMORIAL LIBRARY □ Denver, CO

Bandy, Margaret, Libn.
ST. JOSEPH HOSPITAL - HEALTH SCIENCES LIBRARY □ Denver, CO

Banek, Barbara Minne, Libn.
INLAND STEEL COMPANY - RESEARCH LABORATORIES - LIBRARY □ East Chicago, IN

Banerjee, Debra, Sec.
MASSACHUSETTS INSTITUTE OF TECHNOLOGY - DIVISION FOR STUDY AND RESEARCH IN EDUCATION - READING ROOM □ Cambridge, MA

Bangsberg, Nadine, Base Libn.
U.S. NAVY - NAVAL AMPHIBIOUS BASE (Coronado) - LIBRARY □ San Diego, CA

Banker, Sanford J., Chf., Lib.Serv.
U.S. VETERANS ADMINISTRATION (MN-St. Cloud) - MEDICAL CENTER LIBRARY □ St. Cloud, MN

Banker, Sharon, Lib.Asst.
MEMPHIS STATE UNIVERSITY LIBRARIES - CHEMISTRY LIBRARY □ Memphis, TN

Bankhead, Jean, Hd., Circ.Serv.
U.S. NATL. OCEANIC & ATMOSPHERIC ADMINISTRATION - ENVIRONMENTAL RESEARCH LABORATORIES - LIBRARY □ Boulder, CO

Banks, Ada E., Gen.Libn.
U.S. VETERANS ADMINISTRATION (CA-Palo Alto) - HOSPITAL MEDICAL LIBRARIES □ Palo Alto, CA

Banks, Brenda, Libn.
EDMONTON ART GALLERY - REFERENCE LIBRARY □ Edmonton, AB

Banks, Jane L., Cat.
FREDERICK CANCER RESEARCH CENTER - SCIENTIFIC LIBRARY □ Frederick, MD

Banks, Joyce, Rare Bks./Cons.Libn.
NATIONAL LIBRARY OF CANADA - RARE BOOKS AND MANUSCRIPTS DIVISION □ Ottawa, ON

Banks, Dr. Margaret A., Libn.
UNIVERSITY OF WESTERN ONTARIO - LAW LIBRARY □ London, ON

Banks, Mary Ellen, Libn.
SCHLUMBERGER-DOLL RESEARCH CENTER - LIBRARY □ Ridgefield, CT

Bannen, Carol, Libn.
REINHART, BOERNER, VAN DEUREN, NORRIS & RIESELBACH - LIBRARY □ Milwaukee, WI

Banner, Charla, Sci.Libn.
BUTLER UNIVERSITY - SCIENCE LIBRARY □ Indianapolis, IN

Banta, Alford J., Supt.
U.S. NATL. PARK SERVICE - PERRY'S VICTORY & INTERNATIONAL PEACE MEMORIAL - LIBRARY □ Put-In-Bay, OH

Banta, David A., Exec.Dir.
MARYLAND PHARMACEUTICAL ASSOCIATION - LIBRARY □ Baltimore, MD

Banta, John J., Chf. Law Libn.
WHITE AND CASE - LIBRARY □ New York, NY

Bantin, Philip C., Asst.Archv.
MARQUETTE UNIVERSITY - DEPARTMENT OF SPECIAL COLLECTIONS AND UNIVERSITY ARCHIVES □ Milwaukee, WI

Bantling, Bro. Cozen P.
INTERNATIONAL BROTHERHOOD OF OLD BASTARDS, INC. - SIR THOMAS CRAPPER MEMORIAL ARCHIVES □ St. Louis, MO

Baptist, Jean, Cons., Ref.Serv.
WINNIPEG SCHOOL DIVISION NO. 1 - TEACHERS LIBRARY AND RESOURCE CENTRE □ Winnipeg, MB

Baptiste, Renate, Purchases
DIGITAL EQUIPMENT CORPORATION - CORPORATE LIBRARY □ Maynard, MA

Bar-Tzur, Judy, Libn.
WESTERN STATES CHIROPRACTIC COLLEGE - W.A. BUDDEN MEMORIAL LIBRARY □ Portland, OR

Barad, Morton, Libn.
REID AND PRIEST - LAW LIBRARY □ New York, NY

Baradi, Edita R., Acq.Libn.
YALE UNIVERSITY - ECONOMIC GROWTH CENTER COLLECTION □ New Haven, CT

Baradi, Edita R., Acq.Libn.
YALE UNIVERSITY - SOCIAL SCIENCE LIBRARY □ New Haven, CT

Barager, Wendy, Asst.Lib.Supv.
ORLANDO SENTINEL STAR NEWSPAPER - LIBRARY □ Orlando, FL

Baran, Charlotte, Mgr., Prof.Info.
PFIZER, INC. - PFIZER PHARMACEUTICALS LIBRARY □ New York, NY

Baranski, F.D., Archv.
LONDON CLUB - ARCHIVES □ Topeka, KS

Barbalas, Louis X., Tech.Libn.
MOTOR VEHICLE MANUFACTURERS ASSOCIATION (MVMA) - TECHNICAL LIBRARY □ Detroit, MI

Barbash, Bronia, Libn.
MIAMI HEART INSTITUTE - MEDICAL LIBRARY □ Miami Beach, FL

Barbasiewicz, Kathryn, Libn. I
MILWAUKEE COUNTY LAW LIBRARY □ Milwaukee, WI

Barber, Angela, Asst.Cat.
U.S. AIR FORCE - AEROSPACE MEDICAL DIVISION - SCHOOL OF AEROSPACE MEDICINE - STRUGHOLD AEROMEDICAL LIBRARY □ Brooks AFB, TX

Barber, Catherine, Ser.Libn.
HENDERSON STATE UNIVERSITY - HUIE LIBRARY □ Arkadelphia, AR

Barber, Cyril, Hd.Libn.
INTERNATIONAL CHRISTIAN SCHOOL OF THEOLOGY - GRADUATE UNIVERSITY LIBRARY □ San Bernardino, CA

Barber, Dr. Elinore, Dir., Bach Inst.
BALDWIN-WALLACE COLLEGE - RIEMENSCHNEIDER BACH INSTITUTE - BACH LIBRARY □ Berea, OH

Barber, Frank T., Chf., Patent Counsel
GREYHOUND CORPORATION - PATENT LAW DEPARTMENT LIBRARY □ Scottsdale, AZ

Barber, Mary S., Extramural Libn.
UNIVERSITY OF LOUISVILLE - KORNHAUSER HEALTH SCIENCES LIBRARY □ Louisville, KY

Barber, Mildred, Hist.
CLOUD COUNTY HISTORICAL MUSEUM - LIBRARY □ Concordia, KS

Barber, Raymond R., Libn.
CORNING GLASS WORKS - TECHNICAL INFORMATION CENTER □ Corning, NY

Barber, Rhonda, Libn.
VARIAN CANADA INC. - TECHNICAL LIBRARY □ Georgetown, ON

Barber, Sylvia P., Cur.
SALISBURY HISTORICAL SOCIETY - ARCHIVES □ Salisbury, NH

Barbour, Harriet, Hd.Govt.Serv.
OKLAHOMA STATE DEPARTMENT OF LIBRARIES □ Oklahoma City, OK

Barbour, Jean, P.R.
AMERICAN MIME, INC. - LIBRARY □ New York, NY

Barbour, Wendell, Assoc.Dir./Rd.Serv.
GEORGIA SOUTHERN COLLEGE - ARCHIVES/ SPECIAL COLLECTIONS □ Statesboro, GA

Barbour-Talley, Donna, Libn.
NORTH MEMORIAL MEDICAL CENTER - MEDICAL LIBRARY □ Minneapolis, MN

Barbre, Betty, Asst.Libn.
UNION CARBIDE CORPORATION - NUCLEAR DIVISION - PADUCAH PLANT LIBRARY □ Paducah, KY

Barbula, Dr. Marvin, Director
SAN DIEGO COUNTY - DEPARTMENT OF EDUCATION - PROFESSIONAL RESOURCE AND DEVELOPMENT CENTER □ San Diego, CA

Barbuschak, Laurie A., Info.Spec.
NATIONAL RESTAURANT ASSOCIATION - INFORMATION RESOURCE CENTER □ Washington, DC

Barclay, Elisabeth, Libn.
FORBES HEALTH SYSTEM - EAST SUBURBAN HEALTH CENTER LIBRARY □ Monroeville, PA

Barclay, Morgan J., Hd., Local Hist.
TOLEDO-LUCAS COUNTY PUBLIC LIBRARY - LOCAL HISTORY & GENEALOGY DEPARTMENT □ Toledo, OH

Barclay, Susan, Chf.Libn.
DURHAM COLLEGE OF APPLIED ARTS AND TECHNOLOGY - LIBRARY □ Oshawa, ON

Bardenwerper, Fred L., Asst.Res.Dir.
DEFENSE RESEARCH INSTITUTE, INC. - BRIEF BANK □ Milwaukee, WI

Bardolphe, Anne D., Cat.Libn.
FLORIDA STATE UNIVERSITY - LAW LIBRARY □ Tallahassee, FL

Bardwell, John D., Dir.
UNIVERSITY OF NEW HAMPSHIRE - DEPARTMENT OF MEDIA SERVICES - FILM LIBRARY □ Durham, NH

Barefoot, Gary Fenton, Libn.
MOUNT OLIVE COLLEGE - FREE WILL BAPTIST HISTORICAL COLLECTION □ Mount Olive, NC

Barela, Lawrence, Legal Res.Libn.
UNIVERSITY OF NEW MEXICO - SCHOOL OF LAW LIBRARY □ Albuquerque, NM

Barensfeld, Thomas, Libn.
CLEVELAND PRESS - LIBRARY □ Cleveland, OH

Barham, Hugh, Hosp.Libn.
U.S. ARMY POST - FORT BENNING - RECREATION SERVICES LIBRARY BRANCH □ Ft. Benning, GA

Barich, Phyllis, Film Libn.
MANITOBA - DEPARTMENT OF EDUCATION - LIBRARY □ Winnipeg, MB

Baril, Raymond, Res.
UNIVERSITE DE MONTREAL - CENTRE DE RECHERCHES CARAIBES - BIBLIOTHEQUE □ Montreal, PQ

Barile, Frank F., Tech.Info.Spec.
U.S. NATL. INSTITUTES OF HEALTH - LIBRARY
□ Bethesda, MD

Barish, Larry, Res.Anl.
WISCONSIN STATE LEGISLATIVE REFERENCE
BUREAU □ Madison, WI

Barkdull, Margery K., Map Libn.
NATIONAL GEOGRAPHIC SOCIETY -
CARTOGRAPHIC DIVISION - MAP LIBRARY □
Washington, DC

Barker, Lytton T., Tech.Serv.Libn.
GUILFORD TECHNICAL INSTITUTE - LEARNING
RESOURCE CENTER □ Jamestown, NC

Barker, Sr. R. Mildred, Cur. of Mss.
UNITED SOCIETY OF BELIEVERS - THE SHAKER
LIBRARY □ Poland Spring, ME

Barker, Richard T., Libn.
APPALACHIAN STATE UNIVERSITY - BELK
LIBRARY □ Boone, NC

Barker, S.E., Mgr.
BRITISH COLUMBIA - MINISTRY OF FORESTS -
LIBRARY □ Victoria, BC

Barkey, Patrick, Dir.
CLAREMONT COLLEGES - LIBRARY □ Claremont,
CA

Barkley, Cynthia, Ref.Libn./Dance
LIBRARY OF CONGRESS - JOHN F. KENNEDY
CENTER FOR THE PERFORMING ARTS - THE
PERFORMING ARTS LIBRARY □ Washington, DC

Barkley, Marlene, Corp.Libn.
DANIEL, MANN, JOHNSON AND MENDENHALL -
LIBRARY □ Los Angeles, CA

Barkley, T.M., Cur. of Herbarium
KANSAS STATE UNIVERSITY - HERBARIUM
LIBRARY □ Manhattan, KS

Barkman, Yvonne, Health Sci.Libn.
HIALEAH HOSPITAL - HEALTH SCIENCE
LIBRARY □ Hialeah, FL

Barksdale, Kenneth, Acq.Libn.
EASTERN KENTUCKY UNIVERSITY - JOHN
GRANT CRABBE LIBRARY □ Richmond, KY

Barlas, Julie Sandall, Libn.
HARVARD UNIVERSITY - GORDON MC KAY
LIBRARY - DIVISION OF APPLIED SCIENCES □
Cambridge, MA

Barloga, Carolyn, Asst.Libn.
ST. FRANCIS HOSPITAL - HEALTH SCIENCE
LEARNING CENTER □ Milwaukee, WI

Barlow, Edward V., Law Libn.
RHODE ISLAND STATE LAW LIBRARY □
Providence, RI

Barlow, George, Chf.Libn.
MC GRAW-HILL, INC. - LIBRARY □ New York,
NY

Barmann, Edgar, Mng.Ed.
CATHOLIC UNIVERSE BULLETIN - LIBRARY □
Cleveland, OH

Barnaba, Eugenia M., Mgr., Tech.Serv.
CORNELL UNIVERSITY - RESOURCE
INFORMATION LABORATORY □ Ithaca, NY

Barnard, Delores, Libn.
STATE HISTORICAL SOCIETY OF NORTH
DAKOTA - RESEARCH AND REFERENCE
DIVISION □ Bismarck, ND

Barnard, Jean L., Rare Bks.Coord.
UNIVERSITY OF MICHIGAN - ALFRED
TAUBMAN MEDICAL LIBRARY □ Ann Arbor, MI

Barnard, Mary, Ref.
HARVARD UNIVERSITY - GRADUATE SCHOOL
OF BUSINESS ADMINISTRATION - BAKER
LIBRARY □ Boston, MA

Barnard, Richard E., Chf.Tech.Libn.
U.S. DEFENSE MAPPING AGENCY - AEROSPACE
CENTER - TECHNICAL LIBRARY □ St. Louis, MO

Barnard, Roy, Ser.Libn.
KEARNEY STATE COLLEGE - CALVIN T. RYAN
LIBRARY □ Kearney, NE

Barndt, Laura T., Libn./Media Techn.
COLUMBUS DEVELOPMENTAL CENTER - GOVE
SCHOOL LIBRARY □ Columbus, OH

Barner, Barry, Libn.
CANADA - CANADIAN FORESTRY SERVICE -
MARITIMES FOREST RESEARCH CENTRE -
LIBRARY □ Fredericton, NB

Barnes, Constance, Libn.
CRANBROOK ACADEMY OF ART - LIBRARY □
Bloomfield Hills, MI

Barnes, Esther, Libn.
ALTOONA MIRROR - LIBRARY □ Altoona, PA

Barnes, Norma, Libn.
PHILIPS ROXANE, INC. - TECHNICAL
INFORMATION CENTER □ St. Joseph, MO

Barnes, Patricia A., ILL Libn.
U.S. NATL. INSTITUTES OF HEALTH - LIBRARY
□ Bethesda, MD

Barnes, Robert, Hd.
ROCHESTER PUBLIC LIBRARY - REYNOLDS
AUDIO-VISUAL DEPARTMENT □ Rochester, NY

Barnes, Virginia, Info.Spec.
KERR-MC GEE CORPORATION - MC GEE
LIBRARY □ Oklahoma City, OK

Barnet, Holly, Acq.Sect.Hd.
UNIVERSITY OF CALIFORNIA, LOS ANGELES -
MANAGEMENT LIBRARY □ Los Angeles, CA

Barnett, Dorothy, Libn.
KANSAS STATE UNIVERSITY - ARCHITECTURE
AND DESIGN LIBRARY □ Manhattan, KS

Barnett, Janet K., Asst.Libn.
GREY ADVERTISING, INC. - RESEARCH
LIBRARY □ New York, NY

Barnett, Juanita, Libn.
OUACHITA BAPTIST UNIVERSITY - RILEY
LIBRARY □ Arkadelphia, AR

Barnett, Judith B., Asst.Libn.
UNIVERSITY OF RHODE ISLAND,
NARRAGANSETT BAY - PELL MARINE SCIENCE
LIBRARY □ Narragansett, RI

Barnett, Karen, Dp.Libn.
HUNTER COLLEGE OF THE CITY UNIVERSITY
OF NEW YORK - HEALTH PROFESSIONS
LIBRARY □ New York, NY

Barnett, Lynda, Design Libn.
CANADIAN BROADCASTING CORPORATION -
REFERENCE LIBRARY □ Toronto, ON

Barnett, Lynn, Asst.Dir.
ERIC CLEARINGHOUSE ON HIGHER EDUCATION
□ Washington, DC

Barnett, Lynn, Cat.Libn.
UNIVERSITY OF KENTUCKY - MEDICAL
CENTER LIBRARY □ Lexington, KY

Barnett, Patricia, Assoc.Musm.Libn.
METROPOLITAN MUSEUM OF ART - THOMAS J.
WATSON LIBRARY □ New York, NY

Barnett, Stanley, Libn.
FIRST BAPTIST CHURCH - LIBRARY □
Booneville, MS

Barnette, Donald C., Jr., Dept.Hd.
TOLEDO-LUCAS COUNTY PUBLIC LIBRARY -
HISTORY-TRAVEL-BIOGRAPHY DEPARTMENT □
Toledo, OH

Barney, Alan, Hd.Adm.Serv.Dept.
CENTER FOR RESEARCH LIBRARIES □ Chicago,
IL

Barney, Anita, Ref.Libn.
SACRED HEART UNIVERSITY - LIBRARY □
Bridgeport, CT

Barney, Frances J., Libn.
U.S. FOREST SERVICE - ROCKY MOUNTAIN
FOREST & RANGE EXPERIMENT STATION -
LIBRARY □ Fort Collins, CO

Barnhard, Neil K., Coord., Pub.Serv.
UNIVERSITY OF ARKANSAS MEDICAL
SCIENCES CAMPUS - MEDICAL SCIENCES
LIBRARY □ Little Rock, AR

Barnouw, Erik, Chf.
LIBRARY OF CONGRESS - MOTION PICTURE,
BROADCASTING & RECORDED SOUND
DIVISION □ Washington, DC

Barnum, Amy, Spec.Coll.
NEW YORK STATE HISTORICAL ASSOCIATION
- LIBRARY □ Cooperstown, NY

Barnum, Sally J., Dir.
UNITED WAY OF METROPOLITAN CHICAGO -
LIBRARY □ Chicago, IL

Baron, Ethelnel, Hospital Libn.
SHENANGO VALLEY OSTEOPATHIC HOSPITAL -
MEDICAL LIBRARY† □ Farrell, PA

Baron, Lorraine C., Libn.
IONICS, INC. - RESEARCH DEPARTMENT
LIBRARY □ Watertown, MA

Barone, Rita, Law Libn.
METROPOLITAN LIFE INSURANCE COMPANY -
LAW LIBRARY □ New York, NY

Barr, Douglas R., Mgr.
MC GILL UNIVERSITY - SUB-ARCTIC
RESEARCH STATION LIBRARY □ Schefferville,
PQ

Barr, Eleanor M., Archv./Ed.
SWARTHMORE COLLEGE - FRIENDS
HISTORICAL LIBRARY - PEACE COLLECTION □
Swarthmore, PA

Barr, John, Cat.
MEDICAL COLLEGE OF PENNSYLVANIA -
EASTERN PENNSYLVANIA PSYCHIATRIC
INSTITUTE - LIBRARY □ Philadelphia, PA

Barr, Mary P., Hd., Pub.Serv.
UNIVERSITY OF CALIFORNIA, SAN FRANCISCO
- LIBRARY □ San Francisco, CA

Barra, Carol H., Hd.Libn.
BREED, ABBOTT & MORGAN - LIBRARY □ New
York, NY

Barravecchia, Mary, Dir.
U.S. NAVY - NAVAL UNDERWATER SYSTEMS
CENTER - NEWPORT TECHNICAL LIBRARY □
Newport, RI

Barrera, Natalia, Lib.Asst.
SANTA ROSA MEDICAL CENTER - HEALTH
SCIENCE LIBRARY □ San Antonio, TX

Barret, Beth, Libn.
ST. MARY'S MEDICAL CENTER, INC. - SCHOOL
OF NURSING LIBRARY □ Knoxville, TN

Barrett, Ann, Libn.
HAWAII STATE CIRCUIT COURT - 2ND
CIRCUIT - LAW LIBRARY □ Wailuku, HI

Barrett, Carol A., Engr.Libn.
TEXTRON, INC. - BELL HELICOPTER COMPANY
- TECHNICAL LIBRARY □ Fort Worth, TX

Barrett, Darryl, Prof.Asst.
MINNEAPOLIS PUBLIC LIBRARY &
INFORMATION CENTER - ART, MUSIC & FILMS
DEPARTMENT □ Minneapolis, MN

Barrett, Donald J., Asst.Dir., Pub.Serv.
U.S. AIR FORCE ACADEMY - LIBRARY □ U.S. Air
Force Academy, CO

Barrett, Dorothy, Asst.Libn.
COMPUTER SCIENCES CORPORATION -
TECHNICAL LIBRARY □ Falls Church, VA

Barrett, Dorothy L., Chm., Lib.Comm.
UNITED DAUGHTERS OF THE CONFEDERACY -
CAROLINE MERIWETHER GOODLETT LIBRARY
□ Richmond, VA

Barrett, Elizabeth, Libn.
TRW, INC. - ENGINEERING LIBRARY □
Cleveland, OH

Barrett, Ellin, Sr.Libn.
INFORMATION HANDLING SERVICES - LIBRARY
□ Englewood, CO

Barrett, Jan, Libn.
FRASER AND BEATTY - LIBRARY □ Toronto, ON

Barrett, Jane R., Libn.
CANADIAN INSTITUTE OF INTERNATIONAL
AFFAIRS - LIBRARY □ Toronto, ON

Barrett, Laura, AV Libn.
COLLEGE OF MEDICINE AND DENTISTRY OF
NEW JERSEY AT NEWARK - GEORGE F. SMITH
LIBRARY □ Newark, NJ

Barrett, Melinda, Libn.
U.S. AIR FORCE HOSPITAL - MEDICAL LIBRARY
(CA-Mather AFB) □ Mather AFB, CA

Barrett, Rosemary, Libn.
FRITO-LAY, INC. - LIBRARY □ Dallas, TX

Barrett, Ruth Ann, Prog.Info.Coord.
ASSOCIATION OF JUNIOR LEAGUES -
RESOURCE CENTER† □ New York, NY

Barrette-Pilon, Nicole, Libn.
AYERST LABORATORIES - RESEARCH
LIBRARY† □ Montreal, PQ

Barrick, Susan O., Libn.
VIRGINIA INSTITUTE OF MARINE SCIENCE
LIBRARY □ Gloucester Point, VA

Barrie, Mary, Acq.Libn.
UNION UNIVERSITY - ALBANY LAW SCHOOL -
LIBRARY □ Albany, NY

Barringer, George M., Spec.Coll.Libn.
GEORGETOWN UNIVERSITY - SPECIAL
COLLECTION DIVISION - LAUINGER MEMORIAL
LIBRARY □ Washington, DC

Barrington, David S., Cur.
UNIVERSITY OF VERMONT - PRINGLE
HERBARIUM - LIBRARY □ Burlington, VT

Barriskill, Jennifer, Lib.Techn.
ALBERTA - WORKERS' HEALTH SAFETY &
COMPENSATION - OCCUPATIONAL HEALTH &
SAFETY DIVISION - LIBRARY □ Edmonton, AB

Barrois, Julie, Libn.
LOUISIANA STATE MUSEUM - LOUISIANA
HISTORICAL CENTER □ New Orleans, LA

Barron, Anne, Asst.Libn.
PENNIE & EDMONDS - LAW LIBRARY □ New
York, NY

Barron, Don L., Records Mgt.
SHELL OIL COMPANY - INFORMATION &
LIBRARY SERVICES □ Houston, TX

Barron, Edwina T., Libn.
PREFORMED LINE PRODUCTS COMPANY -
RESEARCH & ENGINEERING LIBRARY □
Cleveland, OH

Barrow, Sarilou A., Libn.
ORANGE COUNTY LAW LIBRARY □ Orlando, FL

Barrows, Allen F., Dir. of Pub.Serv.
UNIVERSITY OF WISCONSIN, STEVENS POINT
- JAMES H. ALBERTSON CENTER FOR
LEARNING RESOURCES □ Stevens Point, WI

Barrows, Richard S., Libn.
U.S. NAVY - OFFICE OF THE JUDGE ADVOCATE
GENERAL - LAW LIBRARY □ Alexandria, VA

Barrows, William, Info.Coord.
INTERNATIONAL FERTILITY RESEARCH
PROGRAM - LIBRARY □ Research Triangle Park,
NC

Barry, Ann, Dir. Of Res.
HANDY ASSOCIATES, INC. - RESEARCH
LIBRARY □ New York, NY

Barry, Colette, Libn.
QUEBEC PROVINCE - ARCHIVES NATIONALES
DU QUEBEC - BIBLIOTHEQUE □ Ste. Foy, PQ

Barry, Jane, Acq.Libn.
NEW YORK INSTITUTE OF TECHNOLOGY -
LIBRARY† □ Old Westbury, NY

Barry, Sr. Justin, O.P., Archv.
DOMINICAN SISTERS - CONGREGATION OF
THE HOLY NAME - ARCHIVES □ San Rafael, CA

Barry, Kevin, Res.Libn., Mgt.
METROPOLITAN LIFE INSURANCE COMPANY -
LIBRARY □ New York, NY

Barry, Kevin, Libn.
PRINCETON UNIVERSITY - INDUSTRIAL
RELATIONS LIBRARY □ Princeton, NJ

Barry, Sr. Martin, Asst.Archv.
DOMINICAN SISTERS - CONGREGATION OF
THE HOLY NAME - ARCHIVES □ San Rafael, CA

Barry, Richard A., Libn.
MANHATTAN COLLEGE - GROVER M. HERMANN
ENGINEERING LIBRARY □ Bronx, NY

Barry, Roger G., Dir.
WORLD DATA CENTER A - GLACIOLOGY □
Boulder CO

Barson, Betty, Asst.Libn.
CLEVELAND COLLEGE OF JEWISH STUDIES -
AARON GARBER LIBRARY □ Beachwood, OH

Barson, Dr. Norman, Supv.
CELANESE CORPORATION - SUMMIT
RESEARCH LABORATORIES - TECHNICAL
INFORMATION CENTER □ Summit, NJ

Bart, Hans, Musm.Libn.
UNIVERSITY OF ARIZONA - ARIZONA STATE
MUSEUM LIBRARY □ Tucson, AZ

Bartel, Bernice, Libn.
KANSAS STATE UNIVERSITY - PHYSICS
LIBRARY □ Manhattan, KS

Bartel, Betty, Rec.Mgmt.Asst.
KELLER (J.J.) & ASSOCIATES, INC. - RESEARCH
CENTER/LIBRARY SERVICES □ Neenah, WI

Bartel, Joan, Dept.Mgr.
LOS ANGELES PUBLIC LIBRARY - BUSINESS &
ECONOMICS DEPARTMENT □ Los Angeles, CA

Bartelli, Alice, Libn.
HAWAII STATE LIBRARY - EDNA ALLYN ROOM
□ Honolulu, HI

Bartels, Eileen, Libn.
U.S. FISH & WILDLIFE SERVICE - NORTHERN
PRAIRIE WILDLIFE RESEARCH CENTER
LIBRARY □ Jamestown, ND

Bartels, Kerry S., Hd., Archv.Div.
INDIANA STATE COMMISSION ON PUBLIC
RECORDS - ARCHIVES DIVISION □ Indianapolis,
IN

Bartenbach, Wilhelm, Exec.Dir.
PUBLIC AFFAIRS INFORMATION SERVICE □
New York, NY

Barth, Joseph M., Coll.Dev.Libn.
U.S. ARMY - MILITARY ACADEMY - LIBRARY □
West Point, NY

Barth, Miles, Cur.
INTERNATIONAL CENTER OF PHOTOGRAPHY -
ARCHIVES □ New York, NY

Barth, Miles, Cur., Archv. & Coll.
INTERNATIONAL CENTER OF PHOTOGRAPHY -
LIBRARY RESOURCE CENTER □ New York, NY

Barth, Sherrill, Libn.
DISADA PRODUCTIONS LTD. - WALT DISNEY
MEMORIAL LIBRARY □ Montreal, PQ

Bartholomew, Carol M., Geology Libn.
BRYN MAWR COLLEGE - GEOLOGY LIBRARY □
Bryn Mawr, PA

Bartkow, Michal, Libn.
POLISH SINGERS ALLIANCE OF AMERICA -
LIBRARY □ Brooklyn, NY

Bartkowski, Patricia, Archv.
WAYNE STATE UNIVERSITY - ARCHIVES OF
LABOR AND URBAN AFFAIRS/UNIVERSITY
ARCHIVES □ Detroit, MI

Bartlett, Eleanor A., Chf.
DISTRICT OF COLUMBIA PUBLIC LIBRARY -
HISTORY AND GEOGRAPHY DIVISION □
Washington, DC

Bartlett, Elinor, SDI Libn.
BELL CANADA - INFORMATION RESOURCE
CENTRE □ Montreal, PQ

Bartlett, Opal, Libn.
MEDICAL CENTER - SIMON SCHWOB MEDICAL
LIBRARY □ Columbus, GA

Bartlett, Pamila J., Lib.Asst.
NEW HAMPSHIRE PUBLIC UTILITIES
COMMISSION - LIBRARY □ Concord, NH

Bartlett, Vern, Info.Spec.
HONEYWELL, INC. - SYSTEMS & RESEARCH
CENTER - LIBRARY □ Minneapolis, MN

Bartley, Margaret, Asst.Libn.
BOSTON ARCHITECTURAL CENTER - ALFRED
SHAW AND EDWARD DURELL STONE LIBRARY □
Boston, MA

Bartman, Marie, Libn.
CONGREGATION AGUDAS ACHIM - BERNARD
RUBENSTEIN LIBRARY □ San Antonio, TX

Barto, Stephen C., Res.Assoc.
STATEN ISLAND HISTORICAL SOCIETY -
LIBRARY □ Staten Island, NY

Bartolme, Sr. Mary, Lib.Asst.
ST. FRANCIS SEMINARY - SALZMANN LIBRARY
□ Milwaukee, WI

Bartolo, Laura M., Libn.
PHILLIPS, LYTLE, HITCHCOCK, BLAINE AND
HUBER - LIBRARY □ Buffalo, NY

Barton, Barbara, Libn.
BANK OF CALIFORNIA - BUSINESS RESEARCH
LIBRARY □ San Francisco, CA

Barton, Bill, Chf., Hist.Res.Div.
WYOMING STATE ARCHIVES, MUSEUMS AND
HISTORICAL DEPARTMENT □ Cheyenne, WY

Barton, Carol P., Libn.
CANADA - MINISTRY OF STATE FOR SCIENCE
AND TECHNOLOGY - LIBRARY □ Ottawa, ON

Barton, Joan, Hd., Ref.
BRITISH COLUMBIA - LEGISLATIVE LIBRARY □
Victoria, BC

Barton, John, Media Circ.Serv.Libn.
WESTERN CONNECTICUT STATE COLLEGE -
RUTH A. HAAS LIBRARY □ Danbury, CT

Barton, Richard, Chf.
DETROIT PUBLIC LIBRARY - BUSINESS AND
FINANCE DEPARTMENT □ Detroit, MI

Barton, Richard, Hd., Pub.Serv.
NORTH DAKOTA STATE UNIVERSITY - LIBRARY
□ Fargo, ND

Barton, Ruth, Libn.
DETROIT PUBLIC LIBRARY - FINE ARTS
DEPARTMENT □ Detroit, MI

Bartosh, Eloise, Asst.Libn.
MERCY HOSPITAL - MEDICAL LIBRARY □
Scranton, PA

Bartoshesky, Florence, Mss. and Archv.
HARVARD UNIVERSITY - GRADUATE SCHOOL
OF BUSINESS ADMINISTRATION - BAKER
LIBRARY □ Boston, MA

Bartow, Martha M., Hd.Libn.
PUBLIC UTILITY COMMISSION OF TEXAS -
LIBRARY □ Austin, TX

Bartow, Sharon, Cat.
SALOMON BROTHERS - CORPORATE FINANCE
LIBRARY □ New York, NY

Bartram, Robert, Ref.Libn.
ENOCH PRATT FREE LIBRARY - GEORGE
PEABODY DEPARTMENT □ Baltimore, MD

Bartucca, Peter, Libn.
BURKE & BURKE - LAW LIBRARY □ New York,
NY

Bartz, Christine, Libn.
CRANBROOK INSTITUTE OF SCIENCE -
LIBRARY □ Bloomfield Hills, MI

Bartz, Christine, Med.Libn.
PLYMOUTH CENTER FOR HUMAN
DEVELOPMENT - MEDICAL LIBRARY □
Northville, MI

Baruth, Christopher M., Map Cat./Ref.Libn.
AMERICAN GEOGRAPHICAL SOCIETY
COLLECTION OF THE UNIVERSITY OF
WISCONSIN, MILWAUKEE - GOLDA MEIR
LIBRARY □ Milwaukee, WI

Barwicke, Ruth, Circ./Ref.
YESHIVA UNIVERSITY - LANDOWNE-BLOOM
LIBRARY† □ New York, NY

Basar, Dorothy L., Hd.Libn.
BEAVER COUNTY TIMES - LIBRARY □ Beaver,
PA

Baschnagel, Mrs. Robert, Libn.
GARDEN CENTER OF ROCHESTER - LIBRARY □
Rochester, NY

Basford, Terry, Asst.Hum.Libn.
OKLAHOMA STATE UNIVERSITY - HUMANITIES
DIVISION □ Stillwater, OK

Basile, Victor, Asst.Libn., Tech.Proc.
COLLEGE OF MEDICINE AND DENTISTRY OF
NEW JERSEY AT NEWARK - GEORGE F. SMITH
LIBRARY □ Newark, NJ

Basiuk, Emil, Assoc.Libn.
LOYOLA UNIVERSITY OF CHICAGO - MEDICAL
CENTER LIBRARY □ Maywood, IL

Baskin, Jeffrey, AV Libn.
UNIVERSITY OF ARKANSAS MEDICAL
SCIENCES CAMPUS - MEDICAL SCIENCES
LIBRARY □ Little Rock, AR

Baskin, Linda, Asst.Libn.
ERIC CLEARINGHOUSE ON ELEMENTARY AND
EARLY CHILDHOOD EDUCATION □ Champaign,
IL

Basler, Thomas G., Dir. of Libs.
MEDICAL COLLEGE OF GEORGIA - LIBRARY □
Augusta, GA

Baslock, Polly, Sr.Lib.Asst.
MASSACHUSETTS INSTITUTE OF TECHNOLOGY
- VON HIPPEL MATERIALS CENTER READING
ROOM □ Cambridge, MA

Bass, Mrs. Bohuslawa Z-P., Br.Supv.
DU PONT DE NEMOURS (E.I.) & COMPANY, INC. - TECHNICAL LIBRARY SYSTEM - PIONEERING RESEARCH LABORATORY BRANCH □ Wilmington, DE

Bass, Mrs. Bohuslawa Z-P., Br.Supv.
DU PONT DE NEMOURS (E.I.) & COMPANY, INC. - TECHNICAL LIBRARY SYSTEM - TEXTILE RESEARCH LABORATORY BRANCH □ Wilmington, DE

Bass, James, Asst. Law Libn.
ST. MARY'S UNIVERSITY - LAW LIBRARY □ San Antonio, TX

Bass, Kathy, Cat.
OKLAHOMA STATE DEPARTMENT OF LIBRARIES □ Oklahoma City, OK

Bassett, Barbara C., Libn.
CHURCH OF JESUS CHRIST OF LATTER-DAY SAINTS - LOVELL, WYOMING BRANCH GENEALOGICAL LIBRARY □ Lovell, WY

Bassett, Betty A., Mgr., Tech.Info.Ctr.
XEROX RESEARCH CENTRE OF CANADA - TECHNICAL INFORMATION CENTRE □ Mississauga, ON

Bassett, Mary, Sr. Staff Res.
INDIANA UNIVERSITY - INSTITUTE FOR URBAN TRANSPORTATION - RESOURCE CENTER □ Bloomington, IN

Bassett, Nell, Ref.Asst.
TROY STATE UNIVERSITY - LIBRARY □ Troy, AL

Bassett, Ruth, Libn.
BRANDYWINE CONSERVANCY, INC. - BRANDYWINE RIVER MUSEUM LIBRARY & STUDY CENTER □ Chadds Ford, PA

Bassist, Norma H., Libn.
BASSIST COLLEGE - LIBRARY □ Portland, OR

Bastien, Carol, Acq.Libn.
SOUTHWESTERN BAPTIST THEOLOGICAL SEMINARY - FLEMING LIBRARY □ Fort Worth, TX

Bastien, Juliette, Libn.
CANADA - NATIONAL FILM BOARD OF CANADA - EDMONTON DISTRICT OFFICE - FILM LIBRARY □ Edmonton, AB

Bastille, Jacqueline, Dir.
MASSACHUSETTS GENERAL HOSPITAL - TREADWELL AND PALMER-DAVIS LIBRARY □ Boston, MA

Bastone, Jessie, Cat.
UNIVERSITY OF TULSA - COLLEGE OF LAW LIBRARY □ Tulsa, OK

Batchelder, Robert, Map/Airphoto Libn.
UNIVERSITY OF CALGARY - ENVIRONMENT-SCIENCE-TECHNOLOGY LIBRARY □ Calgary, AB

Batchelor, Marcia I., Asst.Libn.
U.S. ARMY HOSPITALS - MADIGAN ARMY MEDICAL CENTER - MORALE SUPPORT LIBRARY □ Tacoma, WA

Bateman, Audray, Cur.
AUSTIN PUBLIC LIBRARY - AUSTIN-TRAVIS COUNTY COLLECTION □ Austin, TX

Bateman, Betty B., Ref.Libn.
IBM CORPORATION - LIBRARY □ Poughkeepsie, NY

Bateman, Mary Ruth, Tech.Libn.
CINTICHEM, INC. - LIBRARY □ Tuxedo, NY

Bates, Cathy, Med.Libn.
HOULTON REGIONAL HOSPITAL - LIBRARY □ Houlton, ME

Bates, Cynthia, Educ.Info.Dir.
NORTH DAKOTA STATE LIBRARY □ Bismarck, ND

Bates, D.M., Dir.
CORNELL UNIVERSITY - BAILEY HORTORIUM LIBRARY □ Ithaca, NY

Bates, David, Ref. & Copyright Libn.
GENERAL ELECTRIC COMPANY - CORPORATE RESEARCH & DEVELOPMENT - WHITNEY LIBRARY □ Schenectady, NY

Bates, Dr. George E., Jr., Dir.
MINNESOTA HISTORICAL SOCIETY - SOUTHEAST MINNESOTA HISTORICAL CENTER □ Winona, MN

Bates, Ken, Photographer
BRIGHAM AND WOMEN'S HOSPITAL - ABRAMSON CENTER FOR INSTRUCTIONAL MEDIA □ Boston, MA

Bates, Mabell S., Spec.Coll.Libn.
BRIDGEWATER STATE COLLEGE - CLEMENT C. MAXWELL LIBRARY □ Bridgewater, MA

Bates, Mariette, Resource Ctr.Coord.
ONE TO ONE - RESOURCE CENTER □ New York, NY

Bates, Marilyn Dee, Libn.
MISSISSIPPI STATE BOARD OF HEALTH - LIBRARY □ Jackson, MS

Bates, Peta, Libn.
LAW SOCIETY OF SASKATCHEWAN - BARRISTERS LIBRARY □ Saskatoon, SK

Bates, Peter J., Info.Spec.
SYNCRUDE CANADA, LTD. - RESEARCH DEPARTMENT LIBRARY □ Edmonton, AB

Bates, Ruthann, Proj.Dir.
CLEARINGHOUSE ON CHILD ABUSE AND NEGLECT INFORMATION □ Washington, DC

Bates, Mr. W.D., Lib.Supv.
MANITOBA - DEPARTMENT OF HEALTH - MANITOBA SCHOOL - MEMORIAL LIBRARY □ Portage La Prairie, MB

Batey, Deborah G., Med.Libn.
U.S. NAVY - NAVAL REGIONAL MEDICAL CENTER (Camp Pendleton) - MEDICAL LIBRARY □ Camp Pendleton, CA

Batey, Mary Elizabeth, Chf.Libn.
U.S. VETERANS ADMINISTRATION (MI-Ann Arbor) - HOSPITAL LIBRARY □ Ann Arbor, MI

Bathalon, Real, Lib.Techn.
CENTRE INTERCULTUREL MONCHANIN - BIBLIOTHEQUE □ Montreal, PQ

Batliner, Doris J., Chf.Libn.
COURIER-JOURNAL AND LOUISVILLE TIMES - LIBRARY □ Louisville, KY

Batson, Rebecca, Circ.Libn.
VIRGINIA UNION UNIVERSITY - WILLIAM J. CLARK LIBRARY □ Richmond, VA

Battaglia, Dr. Gioganni, Dir.
ITALIAN CULTURAL SERVICE - LIBRARY □ Montreal, PQ

Batterman, Rene, Libn.
TEMPLE EMANUEL - LIBRARY □ Cherry Hill, NJ

Battipaglia, Nicholas S., Jr., Math./Sci.Libn.
U.S. ARMY - MILITARY ACADEMY - LIBRARY □ West Point, NY

Battista, Dr. O.A., Pres.
RESEARCH SERVICES CORPORATION - INSTITUTE FOR MICROCRYSTAL POLYMER RESEARCH - LIBRARY □ Fort Worth, TX

Battiste, Anita L., Asst.Ref.Libn.
UNIVERSITY OF FLORIDA - HUME LIBRARY □ Gainesville, FL

Battisti, Josephine, Geology Lib.Mgr.
UNIVERSITY OF WYOMING - GEOLOGY LIBRARY □ Laramie, WY

Battle, Thomas C., Cur. of Mss.
HOWARD UNIVERSITY - MOORLAND-SPINGARN RESEARCH CENTER - MANUSCRIPT DIVISION □ Washington, DC

Battram, John V., Hd., AV Res.
UNIVERSITY OF WISCONSIN, WHITEWATER - LIBRARY & LEARNING RESOURCES □ Whitewater, WI

Batty, Ellen, Circ.Libn.
ATHENAEUM OF PHILADELPHIA □ Philadelphia, PA

Bau, Susan T., Prog.Libn.
NATIONAL PUBLIC RADIO - PROGRAM LIBRARY & AUDIO ARCHIVE □ Washington, DC

Bauer, Charles K., Mgr.
LOCKHEED-GEORGIA COMPANY - TECHNICAL INFORMATION DEPARTMENT □ Marietta, GA

Bauer, David C., Libn.
BRAINERD STATE HOSPITAL - LIBRARY† □ Brainerd, MN

Bauer, Frederick E., Jr., Assoc.Libn.
AMERICAN ANTIQUARIAN SOCIETY - LIBRARY □ Worcester, MA

Bauer, Roxy, Libn.
SCIENCE ASSOCIATES/INTERNATIONAL, INC. - LIBRARY □ New York, NY

Bauerle, Sharon, Sec./Libn.
UNIVERSITY OF MICHIGAN - AEROSPACE ENGINEERING DEPARTMENTAL LIBRARY □ Ann Arbor, MI

Baughman, Susan, Asst.Libn.
HARVARD UNIVERSITY - GRADUATE SCHOOL OF EDUCATION - GUTMAN LIBRARY □ Cambridge, MA

Baule, Betty A., Libn.
XAVIER HOSPITAL - DOCTOR'S LIBRARY □ Dubuque, IA

Baum, Inge, Libn.
SCOTTISH RITE SUPREME COUNCIL - LIBRARY □ Washington, DC

Baum, Judith, Libn.
PUBLIC EDUCATION ASSOCIATION - LIBRARY □ New York, NY

Baum, Mary, Libn.
CLEVELAND MUSEUM OF NATURAL HISTORY - HAROLD TERRY CLARK LIBRARY □ Cleveland, OH

Bauman, Joseph M., Chf., User Serv.
U.S. NATL. OCEANIC & ATMOSPHERIC ADM. - ENVIRONMENTAL DATA & INFO. SERV. - NATL. CLIMATIC CTR. LIBRARY □ Asheville, NC

Bauman, Dr. Richard, Dir.
UNIVERSITY OF TEXAS, AUSTIN - CENTER FOR INTERCULTURAL STUDIES IN FOLKLORE AND ETHNOMUSICOLOGY - LIBRARY □ Austin, TX

Baumann, Anne, Libn.
WOOD GUNDY LTD. - LIBRARY □ Toronto, ON

Baumann, Charles H., Univ.Libn.
EASTERN WASHINGTON UNIVERSITY - LIBRARY □ Cheney, WA

Baumann, Roland M., Div.Chf.
PENNSYLVANIA STATE HISTORICAL & MUSEUM COMMISSION - DIVISION OF ARCHIVES AND MANUSCRIPTS □ Harrisburg, PA

Baumeister, Yvonne, AV Coord.
FRENCH LIBRARY IN BOSTON, INC. □ Boston, MA

Baumruk, Robert, Div.Chf.
CHICAGO PUBLIC LIBRARY CENTRAL LIBRARY - SOCIAL SCIENCES & HISTORY DIVISION □ Chicago, IL

Bauner, Dr. Ruth, Educ.Div.Libn.
SOUTHERN ILLINOIS UNIVERSITY, CARBONDALE - EDUCATION DIVISION LIBRARY □ Carbondale, IL

Baur, Joyce E., Libn.
JENKINTOWN LIBRARY - PENNSYLVANIA COLLECTION □ Jenkintown, PA

Baurhenn, Etta, Tech.Serv.Libn.
CHARLES RIVER ASSOCIATES, INC. - LIBRARY □ Boston, MA

Baut, Donald V., Cur. of Res.
DEARBORN HISTORICAL MUSEUM - RESEARCH DIVISION - ARCHIVES AND LIBRARY □ Dearborn, MI

Bautista, Anne T., Libn.
MICHIGAN STATE LEGISLATIVE COUNCIL - LEGISLATIVE SERVICE BUREAU LIBRARY □ Lansing, MI

Bauza, Emma, Ser.Libn.
PUERTO RICO - SUPREME COURT - LAW LIBRARY □ San Juan, PR

Baver, Florence, Mgr.
PENNSYLVANIA DUTCH FOLK CULTURE SOCIETY, INC. - BAVER MEMORIAL LIBRARY □ Lenhartsville, PA

Baxter, Ann, Ref.Libn.
COLLEGE OF MEDICINE AND DENTISTRY OF NEW JERSEY AT NEWARK - GEORGE F. SMITH LIBRARY □ Newark, NJ

Baxter, Anne, Circ./AV Libn.
REFORMED THEOLOGICAL SEMINARY - LIBRARY □ Jackson, MS

Baxter, E., U.N. Doc.
WAYNE STATE UNIVERSITY - G. FLINT PURDY LIBRARY □ Detroit, MI

Baxter, Ellen P., Libn.
UNIVERSITY OF KENTUCKY - CHEMISTRY-PHYSICS LIBRARY □ Lexington, KY

Baxter, Marie, Lib.Supv.
U.S. NAVY - NAVAL AIR STATION (Pensacola) - LIBRARY □ Pensacola, FL

Baxter, Nancy, Dir.
PIONEER STUDY CENTER □ Traverse City, MI

Baxter, Pam, ILL Libn.
SUNY - COLLEGE AT GENESEO - MILNE LIBRARY □ Geneseo, NY

Baxter, Patricia, Libn.
ALBERTA HOSPITAL ASSOCIATION - RESOURCE CENTRE □ Edmonton, AB

Baxter, Susanna G., Libn.
SHRINERS HOSPITAL FOR CRIPPLED CHILDREN - ORTHOPEDIC LIBRARY □ Houston, TX

Baxtresser, Betty, Chf.
U.S. BUREAU OF THE CENSUS - LIBRARY & INFORMATION SERVICES BRANCH □ Suitland, MD

Bay, Sonja, Asst.Libn., Arch.
COOPER UNION FOR THE ADVANCEMENT OF SCIENCE AND ART - LIBRARY □ New York, NY

Bayard, Mary Ivy, Libn.
TEMPLE UNIVERSITY - CENTRAL LIBRARY SYSTEM - TYLER SCHOOL OF FINE ARTS - LIBRARY □ Philadelphia, PA

Bayer, Bernard, Hd.
OHIO STATE UNIVERSITY - MECHANIZED INFORMATION CENTER (MIC) □ Columbus, OH

Bayles, Anita, Circ.Libn.
UNIVERSITY OF SOUTH ALABAMA - LIBRARY - SPECIAL COLLECTIONS □ Mobile, AL

Bayles, Esther, Asst. to Libn.
UNIVERSITY OF HARTFORD - HARTT SCHOOL OF MUSIC - ALLEN MEMORIAL LIBRARY □ West Hartford, CT

Baylies, Zoe, Res.Dir.
TOBACCO MERCHANTS ASSOCIATION OF THE U.S. - HOWARD S. CULLMAN LIBRARY □ New York, NY

Baylo, Lesia Koro, Asst.Libn.
CLARKSON, GORDON /WOODS, GORDON - LIBRARY □ Toronto, ON

Bayne, Pauline S., Libn.
UNIVERSITY OF TENNESSEE - MUSIC LIBRARY □ Knoxville, TN

Bayne, T.M., Dir.
AMERICAN IRISH HISTORICAL SOCIETY - LIBRARY □ New York, NY

Bayorgeon, Mary M., Dir., Lib.Serv.
ST. ELIZABETH HOSPITAL - HEALTH SCIENCE LIBRARY □ Appleton, WI

Bayrak, Bettie, Libn.
ALBERTA - DEPARTMENT OF MUNICIPAL AFFAIRS - LIBRARY □ Edmonton, AB

Bayron, Vilma Rivera, Libn.
UNIVERSITY OF PUERTO RICO - GRADUATE SCHOOL OF LIBRARIANSHIPS - LIBRARY □ San Juan, PR

Bays, Diane, Chf.Libn.
CANADA - REGIONAL ECONOMIC EXPANSION - LIBRARY □ Ottawa, ON

Bays-Coutts, Eileen, Hd., Tech.Serv.
CANADA - DEPARTMENT OF FINANCE - FINANCE/TREASURY BOARD LIBRARY □ Ottawa, ON

Bazemore, Barbara, ILL
TENNESSEE VALLEY AUTHORITY - TECHNICAL LIBRARY □ Chattanooga, TN

Beaber, Patricia A., Ref.Libn.
TRENTON STATE COLLEGE - ROSCOE L. WEST LIBRARY □ Trenton, NJ

Beach, Alta, Sr.Libn.
NEW YORK STATE LIBRARY - SCIENCES/HEALTH SCIENCES/TECHNOLOGY REFERENCE SERVICES □ Albany, NY

Beach, Annabelle, Asst.Libn.
UNIVERSITY OF MISSOURI, KANSAS CITY - LAW LIBRARY □ Kansas City, MO

Beach, Linda, Libn.
ST. LUKE'S HOSPITAL OF BETHLEHEM, PENNSYLVANIA - TREXLER NURSES' LIBRARY □ Bethlehem, PA

Beach, R.M., Dir.
GOLDEY BEACOM COLLEGE - J. WILBUR HIRONS LIBRARY □ Wilmington, DE

Beach, Rosemary, Dir.
CEDAR FALLS HISTORICAL SOCIETY - ROWND HISTORICAL LIBRARY □ Cedar Falls, IA

Beach, Warren D., Supt.
U.S. NATL. PARK SERVICE - LINCOLN BOYHOOD NATL. MEMORIAL VISITOR CENTER □ Lincoln City, IN

Beachley, Joan, Asst.Cur.
COLUMBIA UNIVERSITY - DEPARTMENT OF ART HISTORY & ARCHAEOLOGY - PHOTOGRAPH COLLECTION □ New York, NY

Beadle, Carol, Pk.Techn.
U.S. NATL. PARK SERVICE - HALEAKALA NATL. PARK - LIBRARY □ Makawao, HI

Beaird, A. Michael, Law Libn.
UNIVERSITY OF MISSISSIPPI - SCHOOL OF LAW LIBRARY □ University, MS

Beal, Gretchen F., Libn.
KNOXVILLE-KNOX COUNTY METROPOLITAN PLANNING COMMISSION - LIBRARY □ Knoxville, TN

Beal, William C., Jr., Archv.
UNITED METHODIST CHURCH - GENERAL COMMISSION ON ARCHIVES AND HISTORY - LIBRARY AND ARCHIVES □ Lake Junaluska, NC

Beale, Joel A., Libn.
GULF OIL CHEMICALS COMPANY - BUSINESS INFORMATION CENTER □ Houston, TX

Beales, Carol, Asst. to the Cur.
COPLEY PRESS, INC. - JAMES S. COPLEY LIBRARY □ La Jolla, CA

Beall, Barbara A., Mgr.
NATIONAL FOREST PRODUCTS ASSOCIATION - INFORMATION CENTER □ Washington, DC

Bealmer, William, Dir.
SPRINGFIELD ART ASSOCIATION - MICHAEL VICTOR II ART LIBRARY □ Springfield, IL

Beaman, Barbara, Supv.
HERCULES, INC. - LIBRARY □ Wilmington, DE

Beaman, Patricia, Libn.
SAN ANTONIO STATE CHEST HOSPITAL - HEALTH SCIENCE LIBRARY □ San Antonio, TX

Bean, Betsy, Asst.Libn.
EAST TENNESSEE BAPTIST HOSPITAL - HEALTH SCIENCES LIBRARY □ Knoxville, TN

Bean, F., Tech.Info.Spec.
U.S. NATL. HIGHWAY TRAFFIC SAFETY ADMINISTRATION - TECHNICAL REFERENCE BRANCH □ Washington, DC

Bean, Margaret H., Online Serv.
DETROIT EDISON COMPANY - INFORMATION SERVICES LIBRARY† □ Detroit, MI

Bean, Pauline, Info.Spec.
OHIO STATE UNIVERSITY - MECHANIZED INFORMATION CENTER (MIC) □ Columbus, OH

Bean, Polly, Ref.
OHIO STATE UNIVERSITY - EDUCATION LIBRARY □ Columbus, OH

Bean, Vivienne, Ref.Serv.Supv.
HEWLETT-PACKARD COMPANY - CORPORATE LIBRARY □ Palo Alto, CA

Beard, Lucie, Libn.
DETROIT OSTEOPATHIC HOSPITAL CORPORATION - MEDICAL LIBRARY □ Detroit, MI

Beard, Wilma W.
TENNESSEE STATE DEPARTMENT OF HUMAN SERVICES - LIBRARY □ Nashville, TN

Bearden, E. Holmes, Mgr.
MOBIL OIL CORPORATION - PUBLIC AFFAIRS SECRETARIAT □ New York, NY

Bearden, Jacqueline K., Lib.Dir.
ST. AUGUSTINE HISTORICAL SOCIETY - LIBRARY □ St. Augustine, FL

Beardslee, Dr. R., Asst.Dir.Res.
BIO-SCIENCE LABORATORIES - LIBRARY □ Van Nuys, CA

Beardsley, Dr. Alan J., Lab.Dir.
U.S. NATL. MARINE FISHERIES SERVICE - W.F. THOMPSON MEMORIAL LIBRARY† □ Kodiak, AK

Beardsley, Barbara, Educ.Res.Off.
METROPOLITAN TORONTO SCHOOL BOARD - LIBRARY □ Toronto, ON

Beardsley, Mary Jane, Libn.
UNIVERSITY OF RHODE ISLAND - INTERNATIONAL CENTER FOR MARINE RESOURCE DEVELOPMENT - LIBRARY □ Kingston, RI

Beardsley, Sylvia, Info.Spec.
UNITED STATES GYPSUM COMPANY - RESEARCH CENTER LIBRARY □ Des Plaines, IL

Beardwood, L.B., Libn.
MONTGOMERY, MC CRACKEN, WALKER & RHOADS - LIBRARY □ Philadelphia, PA

Bearer, Annabeth, Tech.Res. Analyst
PHILLIPS PETROLEUM COMPANY - EXPLORATION & PRODUCTION GROUP - LIBRARY □ Bartlesville, OK

Bears, E., Supv.
STANDARD OIL COMPANY OF INDIANA - LIBRARY/INFORMATION CENTER □ Chicago, IL

Beary, Eugene G., Libn.
U.S. ARMY - NATICK RESEARCH AND DEVELOPMENT LABORATORIES - TECHNICAL LIBRARY □ Natick, MA

Beasley, Charles, Hd. Gifts
UNIVERSITY OF TEXAS, EL PASO - LIBRARY □ El Paso, TX

Beasley, Jonathan, Cat.
GENERAL THEOLOGICAL SEMINARY OF THE PROTESTANT EPISCOPAL CHURCH IN THE U.S.A. - ST. MARK'S LIBRARY □ New York, NY

Beasley, Lorna L., Libn.
AMERICAN INSURANCE ASSOCIATION - LAW LIBRARY† □ New York, NY

Beasley, Vivian, Ref.
KENTUCKY STATE LAW LIBRARY □ Frankfort, KY

Beaton, Patricia A., Ref./Govt.Doc.
NEW HAMPSHIRE COLLEGE - SHAPIRO LIBRARY □ Manchester, NH

Beatson, E.H.
PRINCETON UNIVERSITY - DEPARTMENT OF ART & ARCHAEOLOGY - INDEX OF CHRISTIAN ART □ Princeton, NJ

Beattie, Emily L., Hd., Tech.Serv.
BOSTON UNIVERSITY MEDICAL CENTER - ALUMNI MEDICAL LIBRARY □ Boston, MA

Beattie, Lorraine, Asst.Libn., Adm.
UNIVERSITY OF WATERLOO - DANA PORTER ARTS LIBRARY □ Waterloo, ON

Beattie, Lyn, Coord., Lib.Serv.
ESSO RESOURCES CANADA LIMITED - LIBRARY INFORMATION CENTRE □ Calgary, AB

Beatty, Betty, Hd., Tech.Serv.
WITTENBERG UNIVERSITY - THOMAS LIBRARY □ Springfield, OH

Beatty, Frank, Libn.
U.S. GEOLOGICAL SURVEY - NATIONAL MAPPING DIVISION ASSISTANCE FACILITY - LIBRARY □ NSTL Station, MS

Beatty, Suzanne D., Tech.Libn.
CHICAGO BRIDGE & IRON COMPANY - TECHNICAL LIBRARY □ Oak Brook, IL

Beatty, William K., Archival Assoc.
NORTHWESTERN UNIVERSITY - ARCHIVES □ Evanston, IL

Beatus, Helene, Libn.
CREEDMOOR PSYCHIATRIC CENTER - HEALTH SCIENCES LIBRARY □ Queens Village, NY

Beaty, M. Paul, Asst.Cat.
EAST STROUDSBURG STATE COLLEGE - LIBRARY □ East Stroudsburg, PA

Beaubien, Anne K., Mgr./Coord.
UNIVERSITY OF MICHIGAN - MICHIGAN INFORMATION TRANSFER SOURCE (MITS) □ Ann Arbor, MI

Beauchamp, Andrea, Prog.Coord.
UNIVERSITY OF MICHIGAN - HOPWOOD ROOM □ Ann Arbor, MI

Beauclair, Rene, Cat.Libn.
CINEMATHEQUE QUEBECOISE - CENTRE DE DOCUMENTATION CINEMATOGRAPHIQUE □ Montreal, PQ

Beaudet, Christian, Libn., Cat. Dept.
QUEBEC PROVINCE - MINISTERE DES COMMUNICATIONS - BIBLIOTHEQUE ADMINISTRATIVE □ Quebec, PQ

Beaudet, Francoise
UNIVERSITE DE MONTREAL - THEOLOGIE-PHILOSOPHIE BIBLIOTHEQUE □ Montreal, PQ

Beaudet, Louise, Hd. of Animation
CINEMATHEQUE QUEBECOISE - ARCHIVES & FILM MUSEUM □ Montreal, PQ

Beaudet, Normand, Bibliotechnicien
INSTITUT PHILIPPE PINEL - LIBRARY □ Montreal, PQ

Beaudoin, Kathleen, Libn.
CANADIAN MEDICAL ASSOCIATION - LIBRARY □ Ottawa, ON

Beaudoin, Linda
INSTITUT D'HISTOIRE DE L'AMERIQUE FRANCAISE (1970) - RESEARCH CENTRE LIBRARY □ Montreal, PQ

Beaudoin, Odette, Techn.
CONSERVATOIRE D'ART DRAMATIQUE DE QUEBEC - BIBLIOTHEQUE □ Quebec, PQ

Beaudoin, Yolande, Libn.
UNIVERSITE DE MONTREAL - PSYCHO-EDUCATION-BIBLIOTHEQUE □ Montreal, PQ

Beauford, Fred, Lib.Cons.
INNER CITY CULTURAL CENTER - LANGSTON HUGHES MEMORIAL LIBRARY □ Los Angeles, CA

Beaumier, Renald, Dir.
UNIVERSITE DU QUEBEC A MONTREAL - BIBLIOTHEQUE DE MUSIQUE □ Montreal, PQ

Beaumont, Jane, Coord.
CARLETON UNIVERSITY - NORMAN PATERSON SCHOOL OF INTERNATIONAL AFFAIRS - RESOURCE CENTRE □ Ottawa, ON

Beaumont, Mabel, Libn.
WOODWARD GOVERNOR CO. - WOODWARD LIBRARY □ Rockford, IL

Beaupre, Louis
MONTREAL URBAN COMMUNITY TRANSIT COMMISSION - LIBRARY □ Montreal, PQ

Beauregard, John, Dir.
GORDON COLLEGE - WINN LIBRARY □ Wenham, MA

Beaver, H.H., Chm.
BAYLOR UNIVERSITY - DEPARTMENT OF GEOLOGY - FERDINAND ROEMER GEOLOGICAL LIBRARY □ Waco, TX

Beaver, Lucile E., Lib.Dir.
U.S. DEPT. OF TRANSPORTATION - LIBRARY SERVICES DIVISION □ Washington, DC

Beavon, Constance, Art Libn.
CUNY - GRADUATE SCHOOL AND UNIVERSITY CENTER - LIBRARY □ New York, NY

Beazell, Tuula, Chf.Libn.
U.S. VETERANS ADMINISTRATION (PA-Pittsburgh) - MEDICAL LIBRARY □ Pittsburgh, PA

Bebb, Carol, Libn.
CHICAGO TRIBUNE - INFORMATION CENTER □ Chicago, IL

Bebbington, Marguerite, Tech.Info.Spec.
ENGELHARD CORPORATION - TECHNICAL INFORMATION CENTER □ Edison, NJ

Becham, Gerald C., Asst.Dir. Of Lib.
GEORGIA COLLEGE - INA DILLARD RUSSELL LIBRARY □ Milledgeville, GA

Bechanan, H. Gordon, Dir. of Libs.
VIRGINIA POLYTECHNIC INSTITUTE AND STATE UNIVERSITY - CAROL M. NEWMAN LIBRARY □ Blacksburg, VA

Bechor, Malvina, Cat.Libn.
EMORY UNIVERSITY - SCHOOL OF LAW LIBRARY† □ Atlanta, GA

Beck, Armin, Dean
NATIVE AMERICAN EDUCATIONAL SERVICES - NAES LIBRARY AND RESOURCE CENTER □ Chicago, IL

Beck, Beatrice M., Libn.
RANCHO SANTA ANA BOTANIC GARDEN - LIBRARY □ Claremont, CA

Beck, Carolyn, Cur. of Art
CARSON COUNTY SQUARE HOUSE MUSEUM - INFORMATION CENTER □ Panhandle, TX

Beck, Clare, Govt.Doc.Libn.
EASTERN MICHIGAN UNIVERSITY - CENTER OF EDUCATIONAL RESOURCES - GOVERNMENT DOCUMENTS COLLECTION □ Ypsilanti, MI

Beck, Clark L., Jr., Asst.Cur.
GENEALOGICAL SOCIETY OF NEW JERSEY - MANUSCRIPT COLLECTIONS □ New Brunswick, NJ

Beck, Clark L., Jr., Asst.Cur.
RUTGERS UNIVERSITY, THE STATE UNIVERSITY OF NEW JERSEY - SPECIAL COLLECTIONS DEPT.† □ New Brunswick, NJ

Beck, Holly, Pediatrics Libn.
HARTFORD HOSPITAL - HEALTH SCIENCE LIBRARIES □ Hartford, CT

Beck, J.M., Libn.
OHIO POWER COMPANY - LIBRARY □ Canton, OH

Beck, Jocelyne, Chf., Ref.
CANADA - SECRETARY OF STATE - TRANSLATION BUREAU - DOCUMENTATION DIRECTORATE □ Ottawa, ON

Beck, Kenneth L., Libn.
KENTUCKY CHRISTIAN COLLEGE - MEDIA CENTER □ Grayson, KY

Beck, Lois, Hd., Cat.
UNIVERSITY OF MINNESOTA, ST. PAUL - CENTRAL LIBRARY □ St. Paul, MN

Beck, Miriam R., Sec.
THOMAS COUNTY HISTORICAL SOCIETY - LIBRARY □ Colby, KS

Beck, Paul, Archival Libn.
DALLAS PUBLIC LIBRARY - ARCHIVES AND RESEARCH CENTER FOR TEXAS AND DALLAS HISTORY □ Dallas, TX

Beck, Sara R., Mgr., Financial/Marketing
MAY DEPARTMENT STORES COMPANY - INFORMATION CENTER □ St. Louis, MO

Beck, Dr. Shirley S., Chm., Div. of Prof.Educ.
TUSCULUM COLLEGE - INSTRUCTIONAL MATERIALS CENTER □ Greeneville, TN

Becker, Ann, Asst.Tech.Libn.
INSTITUTE OF GAS TECHNOLOGY - TECHNICAL INFORMATION CENTER □ Chicago, IL

Becker, Barbara K., Supv., INFoRM
WARNER-LAMBERT/PARKE-DAVIS - RESEARCH LIBRARY† □ Ann Arbor, MI

Becker, Daniel
AMERICAN AMBULANCE ASSOCIATION - INFORMATION CENTER† □ Youngstown, OH

Becker, Diane, Cur.
LATAH COUNTY HISTORICAL SOCIETY - LIBRARY □ Moscow, ID

Becker, Jacquelyn B., Corp.Libn.
HELENE CURTIS INDUSTRIES, INC. - CORPORATE LIBRARY □ Chicago, IL

Becker, Jeanne, Med.Libn.
CABRINI MEDICAL CENTER - DR. MASSIMO BAZZINI MEMORIAL LIBRARY □ New York, NY

Becker, Kate E., Asst.Libn.
UNIVERSITY OF NEBRASKA, LINCOLN - LAW LIBRARY □ Lincoln, NE

Becker, Philip, Asst.Libn.
U.S. COURT OF APPEALS, 2ND CIRCUIT - LIBRARY □ New York, NY

Becker, Ronald L., Asst.Cur.
GENEALOGICAL SOCIETY OF NEW JERSEY - MANUSCRIPT COLLECTIONS □ New Brunswick, NJ

Becker, Ronald L., Asst.Cur.
RUTGERS UNIVERSITY, THE STATE UNIVERSITY OF NEW JERSEY - SPECIAL COLLECTIONS DEPT.† □ New Brunswick, NJ

Becker, Solomon, Pub. Health Libn.
NEW YORK CITY - MUNICIPAL REFERENCE AND RESEARCH CENTER □ New York, NY

Becker, Solomon, Chf.Libn.
NEW YORK CITY - MUNICIPAL REFERENCE AND RESEARCH CENTER - HAVEN EMERSON PUBLIC HEALTH LIBRARY □ New York, NY

Becker, Stephen, Hist.
RIVERSIDE COUNTY HISTORICAL COMMISSION - LIBRARY □ Rubidoux, CA

Becker-Zawadowski, Iris, Libn.
ST. THOMAS PSYCHIATRIC HOSPITAL - LIBRARY SERVICES □ St. Thomas, ON

Beckman, Dennis D., Libn.
TOSCO CORPORATION - INFORMATION CENTER □ Los Angeles, CA

Beckman, Gary, Asst.Cur.
YALE UNIVERSITY - BABYLONIAN COLLECTION □ New Haven, CT

Beckman, Harold M., Exec.Dir.
PACKAGING INSTITUTE, USA - LIBRARY AND RESOURCE CENTER □ New York, NY

Beckman, Margaret L., Chf.Libn.
UNIVERSITY OF GUELPH - LIBRARY □ Guelph, ON

Beckwith, Herbert, Cat
NATIONAL MARITIME MUSEUM - J. PORTER SHAW LIBRARY □ San Francisco, CA

Beckwith, Margot L., Acq. & Cat.Libn.
ATOMIC ENERGY CONTROL BOARD - LIBRARY □ Ottawa, ON

Beckwith, Patricia, Tech.Libn.
LIQUID CARBONIC CORPORATION - RESEARCH AND DEVELOPMENT LIBRARY† □ Chicago, IL

Beckwith, Terry, Asst.Libn./Pub.Serv.
VERMONT LAW SCHOOL - LIBRARY □ South Royalton, VT

Bedell, Sylvia, Libn.
AMERICAN ASSOCIATION OF OCCUPATIONAL HEALTH NURSES - LIBRARY □ New York, NY

Bedford, Mary, Rsrcs./Reporting Coord.
NATIONAL 4-H COUNCIL - COMMUNICATIONS DIVISION □ Washington, DC

Bedikian, Elizabeth O., Div.Hd.
NEW ORLEANS PUBLIC LIBRARY - BUSINESS AND SCIENCE DIVISION □ New Orleans, LA

Bedke, Patrice, Media
ST. ANSELM'S COLLEGE - GEISEL LIBRARY □ Manchester, NH

Bedrosky, Nannette, Cat.Libn.
CREIGHTON UNIVERSITY - HEALTH SCIENCES LIBRARY □ Omaha, NE

Bedwell, Mrs. Moneta, Libn.
GRAHAM HOSPITAL ASSOCIATION - MEDICAL STAFF LIBRARY □ Canton, IL

Bedwell, Mrs. Moneta, Libn.
GRAHAM HOSPITAL ASSOCIATION - SCHOOL OF NURSING LIBRARY □ Canton, IL

Beech, Beatrice, Hd.Libn.
WESTERN MICHIGAN UNIVERSITY - INSTITUTE OF CISTERCIAN STUDIES LIBRARY □ Kalamazoo, MI

Beecher, John W., Libn.
UNIVERSITY OF ILLINOIS - AGRICULTURE LIBRARY □ Urbana, IL

Beecher, Raymond, Libn.
GREENE COUNTY HISTORICAL SOCIETY - VEDDER MEMORIAL LIBRARY □ Coxsackie, NY

Beechert, Edward, Dir.
UNIVERSITY OF HAWAII - DEPARTMENT OF HISTORY - PACIFIC REGIONAL ORAL HISTORY PROGRAM - LIBRARY □ Honolulu, HI

Beeching, Deanna, Hd.Libn.
PATRIOT NEWS COMPANY - NEWS LIBRARY □ Harrisburg, PA

Beedles, Sandra H., Asst.Libn.
INTERDENOMINATIONAL THEOLOGICAL CENTER - LIBRARY □ Atlanta, GA

Beeler, Richard, Bus./Econ.Libn.
COLORADO STATE UNIVERSITY - WILLIAM E. MORGAN LIBRARY □ Fort Collins, CO

Beer, Richard L., Law Libn.
ADAMS-PRATT OAKLAND COUNTY LAW
LIBRARY □ Pontiac, MI
Beerman, Mrs. Tibor
TEMPLE B'NAI ISRAEL - LASKER MEMORIAL
LIBRARY □ Galveston, TX
Beeson, Lone C., Hd.Libn.
WORLD AFFAIRS COUNCIL OF NORTHERN
CALIFORNIA - LIBRARY □ San Francisco, CA
Begg, Barbara A., Ref.Libn.
UNIVERSITY OF CALIFORNIA, SAN DIEGO -
SCIENCE & ENGINEERING LIBRARY □ La Jolla,
CA
Begg, Debra, Libn.
UNIVERSITY OF OTTAWA - MUSIC LIBRARY □
Ottawa, ON
Begg, Dr. Robert T., Hd.Libn.
OHIO NORTHERN UNIVERSITY - COLLEGE OF
LAW - JAY P. TAGGART MEMORIAL LAW
LIBRARY □ Ada, OH
Beggs, Alan, Art Libn.
YONKERS PUBLIC LIBRARY - FINE ARTS
DEPARTMENT □ Yonkers, NY
Begleiter, Ronni, Ref./Circ.Libn.
DRAKE UNIVERSITY - LAW LIBRARY □ Des
Moines, IA
Begos, Jane, Interp.Prog.Asst.
JAY (John) HOMESTEAD - JAY LIBRARY □
Katonah, NY
Behers, Janice, Libn.
U.S. BUREAU OF MINES - RENO METALLURGY
RESEARCH CENTER - LIBRARY □ Reno, NV
Behler, Patricia, Ch. & Young Adult
MISSOURI STATE LIBRARY □ Jefferson City,
MO
Behles, Patricia, Govt.Doc.Libn.
UNIVERSITY OF BALTIMORE - LAW LIBRARY □
Baltimore, MD
Behm, Leslie, Sci.Libn.
MICHIGAN STATE UNIVERSITY - SCIENCE
LIBRARY □ East Lansing, MI
Behr, Alice S., Tech.Libn.
UNION CARBIDE CORPORATION - RESEARCH
AND DEVELOPMENT LIBRARY □ South
Charleston, WV
Behrendt, Elizabeth, Ref./Circ.Libn.
U.S. GEOLOGICAL SURVEY - DENVER LIBRARY
□ Denver, CO
Behrens, Marge, Slavic/Orntl.Libn.
RAND CORPORATION - LIBRARY □ Santa
Monica, CA
Behringer, Nedra, Mgr., Corp.Lib.
WARNER-LAMBERT COMPANY - CORPORATE
LIBRARY† □ Morris Plains, NJ
Beier, Allison J., Asst.Libn.
CHADBOURNE, PARKE, WHITESIDE, & WOLFF -
LIBRARY □ New York, NY
Beil, Eloise, Asst.Archv.
STATEN ISLAND INSTITUTE OF ARTS AND
SCIENCES - LIBRARY □ Staten Island, NY
Beilby, Mary, Coll.Dev.Libn.
SUNY - COLLEGE AT CORTLAND - MEMORIAL
LIBRARY □ Cortland, NY
Beiler, Dorthea, Libn.
FIRST PRESBYTERIAN CHURCH - LIBRARY □ De
Land, FL
Beiman, Frances, Principal Libn.
NEWARK PUBLIC LIBRARY - EDUCATION
DIVISION □ Newark, NJ
Beinbrech, Pauline C., Libn.
PETROLITE CORPORATION - RESEARCH
LIBRARY □ St. Louis, MO
Beiner, Helen B., Coord.
ENCINO HISTORICAL SOCIETY, INC. - LIBRARY
□ Encino, CA
Beintema, William J., Law Libn.
OKLAHOMA CITY UNIVERSITY - LAW LIBRARY
□ Oklahoma City, OK
Bekassy, Eva, Sci.Div.Libn.
ST. JOHN'S UNIVERSITY - LIBRARY □ Jamaica,
NY

Beker, Janet M., Asst.Libn.
SAN DIEGO COUNTY LAW LIBRARY - VISTA
BRANCH □ Vista, CA
Bekiares, Susan, Doc.Libn.
UNIVERSITY OF ILLINOIS - DOCUMENTS
LIBRARY □ Urbana, IL
Beland, Andre, Ref.Libn.
COLLEGE DU NORD-OUEST - BIBLIOTHEQUE □
Rouyn, PQ
Beland, Andre, Ref.Libn.
UNIVERSITE DU QUEBEC - CEUAT
BIBLIOTHEQUE □ Rouyn, PQ
Belanger, Brien, Circ.Libn.
MOODY BIBLE INSTITUTE - LIBRARY □ Chicago,
IL
Belanger, Dolores A., Res.Libn.
COMBUSTION ENGINEERING, INC. - C-E
REFRACTORIES - RESEARCH & DEVELOPMENT
LIBRARY □ Valley Forge, PA
Belanger, Roland, Archv.
SOCIETE HISTORIQUE DU SAGUENAY -
BIBLIOTHEQUE □ Chicoutimi, PQ
Belastock, Tjalda, Hd.Ref.Libn.
BABSON COLLEGE - HORN LIBRARY □ Babson
Park, MA
Belch, Jean, Libn.
UNIVERSITY OF WASHINGTON - CURRICULUM
MATERIALS SECTION □ Seattle, WA
Belcher, C. Francis, Archv./Cons.
APPALACHIAN MOUNTAIN CLUB - LIBRARY □
Boston, MA
Belcher, Faye, Assoc.Dir.
MOREHEAD STATE UNIVERSITY - CAMDEN-
CARROLL LIBRARY □ Morehead, KY
Belford, Roz
COLLECTOR CIRCLE - LIBRARY □ Lake Park, FL
Belgado, Idalia, Dir., Graduate Libs.
UNIVERSITY OF PUERTO RICO - GENERAL
LIBRARY □ San Juan, PR
Belgrave, Michael V., Data User Serv.Off.
U.S. BUREAU OF THE CENSUS - REGIONAL
DATA USER SERVICE - NEW YORK REGIONAL
OFFICE - LIBRARY □ New York, NY
Belgum, Katherine, Asst. Law Libn.
UNIVERSITY OF IOWA - LAW LIBRARY □ Iowa
City, IA
Belina, Aniela, Documentalist
UNIVERSITE DE MONTREAL - CENTRE
INTERNATIONAL DE CRIMINOLOGIE
COMPAREE - DOCUMENTATION CENTRE □
Montreal, PQ
Beliveau, Karen D., Coord.
ALBERTA RESEARCH COUNCIL - SOLAR & WIND
ENERGY RESEARCH PROGRAM (SWERP)
INFORMATION CENTRE □ Edmonton, AB
Bell, Anne, Libn.
ABILENE REPORTER-NEWS - LIBRARY □
Abilene, TX
Bell, Barbara, Act.Hd.
VANCOUVER PUBLIC LIBRARY - BUSINESS &
ECONOMICS DIVISION □ Vancouver, BC
Bell, Carol A., Hd.Libn.
BECHTEL POWER CORPORATION - LIBRARY □
Gaithersburg, MD
Bell, Charlotte M., Dir., Media Serv.
FIRST BAPTIST CHURCH - LIBRARY □
Greensboro, NC
Bell, Christine L., Dir.Lib.Serv.
NEWTON-WELLESLEY HOSPITAL - PAUL
TALBOT BABSON MEMORIAL LIBRARY □ Newton
Lower Falls, MA
Bell, Doris, Mgr.
BARTON-ASCHMAN ASSOCIATES, INC. -
PLANNING LIBRARY† □ Evanston, IL
Bell, Elsie, Chf., Main Lib.
OKLAHOMA CITY METROPOLITAN LIBRARY
SYSTEM - BUSINESS-SCIENCE SECTION □
Oklahoma City, OK
Bell, Frances, Hd.
DALLAS PUBLIC LIBRARY - HUMANITIES
DIVISION □ Dallas, TX

Bell, Helen C., Hd.Ref.Dept.
UNIVERSITY OF TEXAS, EL PASO - LIBRARY □
El Paso, TX
Bell, Irena L., Asst.Chf.
NATIONAL LIBRARY OF CANADA -
MULTILINGUAL BIBLIOSERVICE □ Ottawa, ON
Bell, Dr. James B., Dir.
NEW ENGLAND HISTORIC GENEALOGICAL
SOCIETY - LIBRARY □ Boston, MA
Bell, JoAnn, Dir.
EAST CAROLINA UNIVERSITY - HEALTH
SCIENCES LIBRARY □ Greenville, NC
Bell, Joy Ann, Med.Libn.
ST. FRANCIS HOSPITAL - MEDICAL LIBRARY □
Miami Beach, FL
Bell, Kathy, Tech.Serv.Libn.
HONEYWELL, INC. - HONEYWELL
INFORMATION SYSTEMS - INFORMATION AND
LIBRARY SERVICES □ Waltham, MA
Bell, Lois, Rd.Adv.
DISTRICT OF COLUMBIA PUBLIC LIBRARY -
PHILOSOPHY, PSYCHOLOGY AND RELIGION
DIVISION □ Washington, DC
Bell, Marilyn, Lib.Supv.
PRINCE EDWARD ISLAND - DEPARTMENT OF
HEALTH AND SOCIAL SERVICES - HEALTH
BRANCH CENTRAL LIBRARY □ Charlottetown, PE
Bell, Mary, Asst.Libn.
OAK FOREST HOSPITAL - PROFESSIONAL
LIBRARY □ Oak Forest, IL
Bell, Marylin, Hd.Ref.
TENNESSEE STATE LIBRARY AND ARCHIVES -
ARCHIVES & MANUSCRIPTS SECTION □
Nashville, TN
Bell, Meg, Coll.Asst.
UNIVERSITY OF NORTH CAROLINA, CHAPEL
HILL - RARE BOOK COLLECTION □ Chapel Hill,
NC
Bell, Mertys W., Dean, LRC
GUILFORD TECHNICAL INSTITUTE - LEARNING
RESOURCE CENTER □ Jamestown, NC
Bell, Polly, Libn.
WATER AND WASTEWATER TECHNICAL
SCHOOL - LIBRARY □ Neosho, MO
Bell, Rebecca L., Tech.Serv.Libn.
SOUTH DAKOTA STATE LIBRARY □ Pierre, SD
Bell, Robert E., Hd., Ref.Dept./ILL
UNIVERSITY OF CALIFORNIA, DAVIS -
GENERAL LIBRARY □ Davis, CA
Bell, Sandra, Libn.
NORTH CENTRAL TEXAS COUNCIL OF
GOVERNMENTS - REGIONAL INFORMATION
SERVICE CENTER □ Arlington, TX
Bell, Sarah, Libn.
MIDRASHA COLLEGE OF JEWISH STUDIES -
LIBRARY □ Southfield, MI
Bell, Steven J., Ref.Libn.
PHILADELPHIA CORPORATION FOR AGING -
LIBRARY □ Philadelphia, PA
Bell, Susanne, Asst. Music Libn.
WASHINGTON UNIVERSITY - GAYLORD MUSIC
LIBRARY □ St. Louis, MO
Bell, Wanda R., Libn.
PENNSYLVANIA STATE DEPT. OF
ENVIRONMENTAL RESOURCES -
ENVIRONMENTAL PROTECTION TECHNICAL
REFERENCE LIBRARY □ Harrisburg, PA
Bellamy, Jane Young, Libn.
SAN BERNARDINO COUNTY - ENVIRONMENTAL
PUBLIC WORKS AGENCY - LIBRARY □ San
Bernardino, CA
Bellamy, Mrs. Shannon G., Supv.
SASKATCHEWAN - DEPARTMENT OF THE
ENVIRONMENT - LIBRARY □ Regina, SK
Bellamy, Dr. Virginia Nelle, Archv.
PROTESTANT EPISCOPAL CHURCH - ARCHIVES
□ Austin, TX
Bellefontaine, Edgar J., Libn.
SOCIAL LAW LIBRARY □ Boston, MA
Bellerose, Celine, Documentaliste
HYDRO-QUEBEC - DIRECTION RECHERCHE
ECONOMIQUE - CENTRE DE DOCUMENTATION
□ Montreal, PQ

**P
E
R
S
O
N
N
E
L**

Bellis, Gloria, Libn.
FUGRO GULF, INC. - LIBRARY □ Houston, TX
Bellis, Gloria, Libn.
WEINER'S STORES, INC. - LIBRARY □ Houston, TX
Belliveau, Gerard J., Jr., Libn.
RACQUET AND TENNIS CLUB - LIBRARY □ New York, NY
Bellomy, Anne, Libn.
MISSISSIPPI STATE BUREAU OF GEOLOGY - LIBRARY □ Jackson, MS
Bellotte, Doyle Ray, Libn.
LOUISIANA STATE DEPT. OF COMMERCE - OFFICE OF COMMERCE & INDUSTRY - INDUSTRIAL DEVELOPMENT REFERENCE LIBRARY □ Baton Rouge, LA
Belluomini, Michele A., Dir.
PLANNED PARENTHOOD OF SOUTHEASTERN PENNSYLVANIA - RESOURCE CENTER □ Philadelphia, PA
Belsterling, Jean I., Med.Libn.
WEST JERSEY HOSPITAL, EASTERN DIVISION - STAFF MEDICAL LIBRARY □ Voorhees, NJ
Belt, Jane, Libn.
CENTRAL WASHINGTON HOSPITAL - HEALTH SCIENCES LIBRARY □ Wenatchee, WA
Belt, Marva, Hd.
ENOCH PRATT FREE LIBRARY - SOCIAL SCIENCE AND HISTORY DEPARTMENT □ Baltimore, MD
Beltran, Lucrecia
UNIVERSITY OF PUERTO RICO - SCHOOL OF PUBLIC ADMINISTRATION - LIBRARY □ Rio Piedras, PR
Belyea, Kathy, Ref.Libn.
BELL TELEPHONE LABORATORIES, INC. - TECHNICAL LIBRARY □ Naperville, IL
Bemis, Michael F., Law Libn.
WISCONSIN STATE DEPARTMENT OF JUSTICE - LAW LIBRARY □ Madison, WI
Ben-Zvi, Mrs. Hava, Libn.
JEWISH FEDERATION COUNCIL OF GREATER LOS ANGELES - PETER M. KAHN JEWISH COMMUNITY LIBRARY □ Los Angeles, CA
Benally, Elaine, Info.Spec.
ERIC CLEARINGHOUSE ON RURAL EDUCATION AND SMALL SCHOOLS □ Las Cruces, NM
Benamati, Dennis C., Asst. Law Libn.
UNIVERSITY OF MAINE SCHOOL OF LAW - DONALD L. GARBRECHT LAW LIBRARY □ Portland, ME
Benchik, Barbara, Chf.Libn.
PEOPLES GAS LIGHT AND COKE COMPANY - LIBRARY □ Chicago, IL
Benda, Cathe, Libn.
ROCKWELL INTERNATIONAL - GRAPHIC SYSTEMS DIVISION - TECHNICAL INFORMATION CENTER □ Chicago, IL
Bendall, Teresa, Pub.Serv.Libn.
ALBERTA - DEPARTMENT OF LABOUR - LABOUR LIBRARY □ Edmonton, AB
Bendell, Beverley, Libn.
MONTREAL ENGINEERING COMPANY, LTD. - CALGARY LIBRARY □ Calgary, AB
Bender, Thomas R., Jr., Biolog.
PENNSYLVANIA STATE FISH COMMISSION LIBRARY - BENNER SPRING FISH RESEARCH STATION □ Bellefonte, PA
Bendes, Adele N., Mgr.
SALES & MARKETING EXECUTIVES INTERNATIONAL - MARKETING INFORMATION CENTER □ New York, NY
Benedetti, Joan M., Media Libn.
CRAFT AND FOLK ART MUSEUM - LIBRARY/MEDIA RESOURCE CENTER □ Los Angeles, CA
Benedetti, JoAnne, Tech.Asst. Film Coll
IDAHO STATE UNIVERSITY LIBRARY - AUDIO-VISUAL SERVICES □ Pocatello, ID
Benedict, Kay, Cur.
CASA GRANDE VALLEY HISTORICAL SOCIETY - MUSEUM LIBRARY □ Casa Grande, AZ

Benedict, Sr. Mary, O.S.B., Asst.Libn.
ST. BENEDICT'S ABBEY - BENET LIBRARY □ Benet Lake, WI
Benedict, Mary Jane, Libn.
LOUISVILLE SCHOOL OF ART - LIBRARY & MEDIA RESOURCE CENTER □ Anchorage, KY
Benedict, Mary Jane, Libn.
SPEED (J.B.) ART MUSEUM - LIBRARY □ Louisville, KY
Benefiel, Norma, Off.Serv.Supv.
PHILLIPS PETROLEUM COMPANY - ENGINEERING LIBRARY □ Bartlesville, OK
Benelisha, Eleanor, Dir., Lib.Serv.
ST. MARY'S HOSPITAL AND MEDICAL CENTER - MEDICAL LIBRARY □ San Francisco, CA
Benemann, William E., Tech.Serv.Libn.
GOLDEN GATE UNIVERSITY - SCHOOL OF LAW LIBRARY □ San Francisco, CA
Benenfeld, Alan R., Coord.
UNIVERSITY OF CALIFORNIA, LOS ANGELES - PHYSICAL SCIENCES & TECHNOLOGY LIBRARIES □ Los Angeles, CA
Benet, Sandra, Music Libn.
UNIVERSITY OF VICTORIA - MC PHERSON LIBRARY - MUSIC & AUDIO COLLECTION □ Victoria, BC
Benetz, Margaret D., Circ.
LOYOLA UNIVERSITY (New Orleans) - LAW LIBRARY □ New Orleans, LA
Benevich, Lauren A., Ref.Libn.
EMORY UNIVERSITY - SCHOOL OF MEDICINE - A.W. CALHOUN MEDICAL LIBRARY □ Atlanta, GA
Benford, Elizabeth S., Libn.
UNIVERSITY OF MICHIGAN - ENGLISH LANGUAGE INSTITUTE - LIBRARY □ Ann Arbor, MI
Benguiat, Vance, Exec.Dir.
CITIZENS UNION OF THE CITY OF NEW YORK - LIBRARY □ New York, NY
Benincasa, Anne, Circ.Supv.
YORK UNIVERSITY - STEACIE SCIENCE LIBRARY □ Downsview, ON
Benishek, Kristine, Circuit Libn.
CLEVELAND HEALTH SCIENCES LIBRARY - ALLEN MEMORIAL LIBRARY □ Cleveland, OH
Benjamin, Azalia, Branch Libn.
CHURCH OF JESUS CHRIST OF LATTER-DAY SAINTS - LANSING BRANCH GENEALOGICAL LIBRARY □ East Lansing, MI
Benjamin, Mrs. M., Libn.
CANADIAN MARCONI COMPANY - LIBRARY □ Montreal, PQ
Benjamin, Virginia, Pub.Serv.Libn.
UNIVERSITY OF GEORGIA - SCIENCE LIBRARY □ Athens, GA
Benka, Bonnie L., Cat.
TRENTON STATE COLLEGE - ROSCOE L. WEST LIBRARY □ Trenton, NJ
Benko, Jill, Res.Sec.
PENNSYLVANIA BLUE SHIELD - RESEARCH LIBRARY □ Camp Hill, PA
Benner, Dorothy, Archv.Asst.
CHAMPAIGN COUNTY HISTORICAL ARCHIVES □ Urbana, IL
Bennet, Christine, Tech.Libn.
KMS FUSION, INC. - FUSION LIBRARY □ Ann Arbor, MI
Bennett, A.L.
PRINCETON UNIVERSITY - DEPARTMENT OF ART & ARCHAEOLOGY - INDEX OF CHRISTIAN ART □ Princeton, NJ
Bennett, Barbara S., Asst.Dir.
GEORGIA HISTORICAL SOCIETY - LIBRARY □ Savannah, GA
Bennett, Charles Dana, Spec.Cons.
GRANGE-FARM FILM FOUNDATION - LIBRARY □ Washington, DC
Bennett, Charles G., Genealogical Libn.
BENNINGTON MUSEUM - GENEALOGICAL LIBRARY □ Bennington, VT

Bennett, Claire, Spec.Coll.
SOUTHERN CONNECTICUT STATE COLLEGE - H.C. BULEY LIBRARY □ New Haven, CT
Bennett, Donna, Rd.Serv.Libn.
NORTHERN KENTUCKY UNIVERSITY - SALMON P. CHASE COLLEGE OF LAW - LIBRARY □ Covington, KY
Bennett, Dorothea E., Chf., Lib.Serv.
U.S. VETERANS ADMINISTRATION (CA-Martinez) - HOSPITAL LIBRARY □ Martinez, CA
Bennett, Floyd, Cat.
SAM HOUSTON STATE UNIVERSITY - LIBRARY† □ Huntsville, TX
Bennett, Hilary, Dir. Of Pubn.
EARTHWATCH - LIBRARY □ Belmont, MA
Bennett, John M., Lib. Media Tech.Asst.
OHIO STATE UNIVERSITY - LATIN AMERICAN STUDIES READING ROOM AND LIBRARY □ Columbus, OH
Bennett, Josiah Q., Cat.
INDIANA UNIVERSITY - LILLY LIBRARY □ Bloomington, IN
Bennett, Joyce A., Dir.
BENTLEY COLLEGE - SOLOMON R. BAKER LIBRARY □ Waltham, MA
Bennett, K. Sharon, Libn.
CHARLESTON MUSEUM - LIBRARY □ Charleston, SC
Bennett, Mrs. M., Sec.
DIVERSEY WYANDOTTE INC. - RESEARCH CENTRE LIBRARY □ Mississauga, ON
Bennett, Madaleine, Libn.
RAYTHEON COMPANY - RESEARCH DIVISION - LIBRARY □ Waltham, MA
Bennett, Mary, Photographs Libn.
STATE HISTORICAL SOCIETY OF IOWA - LIBRARY □ Iowa City, IA
Bennett, Michael W., Musm.Dir.
SAN JOAQUIN COUNTY HISTORICAL MUSEUM □ Lodi, CA
Bennett, Dr. Myrtle C., Dir., Lib.Serv.
NORTH CAROLINA AGRICULTURAL & TECHNICAL STATE UNIVERSITY - F.D. BLUFORD LIBRARY □ Greensboro, NC
Bennett, Patricia, Sci.Biblog.
UNIVERSITY OF VIRGINIA - SCIENCE/TECHNOLOGY INFORMATION CENTER □ Charlottesville, VA
Bennett, Peggy, Cat.
SOUTHERN MISSIONARY COLLEGE - MC KEE LIBRARY - SPECIAL COLLECTIONS □ Collegedale, TN
Bennett, Phyllis, Dir., Med.Lib.
BAPTIST MEDICAL CENTER - WANN LANGSTON MEMORIAL LIBRARY □ Oklahoma City, OK
Bennett, Renee
UNITED NATIONS ASSOCIATION OF THE UNITED STATES OF AMERICA - GREATER ST. LOUIS CHAPTER - LIBRARY □ St. Louis, MO
Bennett, Richard E., Hd.
UNIVERSITY OF MANITOBA - ARCHIVES AND SPECIAL COLLECTIONS □ Winnipeg, MB
Bennett, Roy, Ref./ILL
IBM CORPORATION - GENERAL PRODUCTS DIVISION - INFORMATION/LIBRARY/LEARNING CENTER □ San Jose, CA
Bennett, Sandra, Libn.
UNIVERSITY OF VIRGINIA - BIOLOGY/PSYCHOLOGY LIBRARY □ Charlottesville, VA
Bennett, Valerie, Libn.
HORTICULTURAL SOCIETY OF NEW YORK - PUBLIC REFERENCE LIBRARY □ New York, NY
Benoit, Kenneth
MIAMI-DADE PUBLIC LIBRARY - ART AND MUSIC DIVISION □ Miami, FL
Benoit, Nicole, Data Dissemination Off.
CANADA - STATISTICS CANADA - ADVISORY SERVICES - MONTREAL REFERENCE CENTRE □ Montreal, PQ
Benoit, Rosemarie, Hd.Libn.
CENTRE DE SERVICES SOCIAUX DU MONTREAL METROPOLITAIN - BIBLIOTHEQUE □ Montreal, PQ

Bensinger, Hildred, Med.Ed.
U.S. AIR FORCE - AEROSPACE MEDICAL DIVISION - SCHOOL OF AEROSPACE MEDICINE - STRUGHOLD AEROMEDICAL LIBRARY □ Brooks AFB, TX

Benson, Harold W., Libn.
NEW YORK CITY HUMAN RESOURCES ADMINISTRATION - MC MILLAN LIBRARY □ New York, NY

Benson, Hazel B., Hd., Pub.Serv.
OHIO STATE UNIVERSITY - HEALTH SCIENCES LIBRARY □ Columbus, OH

Benson, Joseph, Dir.
CHICAGO TRANSIT AUTHORITY - HAROLD S. ANTHON MEMORIAL LIBRARY □ Chicago, IL

Benson, Judith, Libn.
MICHENER CENTRE - STAFF LIBRARY □ Red Deer, AB

Benson, Dr. Maxine, Cur.
COLORADO HISTORICAL SOCIETY - STEPHEN H. HART LIBRARY □ Denver, CO

Benson, Paula F., Chf., Lib.Serv.
U.S. VETERANS ADMINISTRATION (NY-Bath) - CENTER LIBRARY □ Bath, NY

Benson, Scott, Res.Lit.Anl.
OREGON STATE UNIVERSITY - SCHOOL OF OCEANOGRAPHY - NORTHWEST COASTAL INFORMATION CENTER (NCIC) □ Newport, OR

Bente, June, Mgr.
ORTHO PHARMACEUTICAL CORPORATION - HARTMAN LIBRARY □ Raritan, NJ

Bente, Dr. Paul F., Exec.Dir.
BIO-ENERGY COUNCIL - LIBRARY □ Washington, DC

Bentley, Carol, Hd., Mtls.Ctr.
CHICAGO STATE UNIVERSITY - DOUGLAS LIBRARY □ Chicago, IL

Bentley, Mrs. Charles M., Lib.Chm.
MONTEREY HISTORY & ART ASSOCIATION - MAYO HAYES O'DONNELL LIBRARY □ Monterey, CA

Bentley, Jane, Libn.
SAN DIEGO MUSEUM OF MAN - SCIENTIFIC LIBRARY □ San Diego, CA

Bentley, Janice B., Libn.
MAYER, BROWN & PLATT - LIBRARY □ Chicago, IL

Bentley, Lynn, Ref.Libn.
HUMBER COLLEGE OF APPLIED ARTS & TECHNOLOGY - LIBRARY □ Rexdale, ON

Bentley, Patsy A., Sr.Med.Libn.
AMERICAN HOSPITAL SUPPLY CORPORATION - DADE DIVISION LIBRARY □ Miami, FL

Benz, Allen, Libn.
AERIAL PHENOMENA RESEARCH ORGANIZATION, INC. - APRO LIBRARY □ Tucson, AZ

Benz, Delsa I., Corp.Libn.
BAUSCH & LOMB, INC. - CORPORATE LIBRARY □ Rochester, NY

Beraha, Dr. Louis, Res. Leader
U.S.D.A. - AGRICULTURAL RESEARCH SERVICE - NORTH CENTRAL REGION - MARKET PATHOLOGY RESEARCH LIBRARY □ Chicago, IL

Berberian, Kevork, Cat.Libn.
KEAN COLLEGE OF NEW JERSEY - NANCY THOMPSON LIBRARY □ Union, NJ

Berdahl, James N., Libn.
MINNESOTA ORCHESTRA - MUSIC LIBRARY □ Minneapolis, MN

Berdnikoff, Wm., Hd.
CANADA - CONSUMER AND CORPORATE AFFAIRS CANADA - PATENT AND COPYRIGHT OFFICE □ Ottawa, ON

Bereday, Patricia, Libn.
HOLLAND SOCIETY OF NEW YORK - LIBRARY □ New York, NY

Berenbaum, Adrienne, Libn.
COLLEGE OF MEDICINE AND DENTISTRY OF NEW JERSEY - RUTGERS MEDICAL SCHOOL - MEDIA LIBRARY □ Piscataway, NJ

Berens, Hazel, Lib.Asst., Supv.
LOS ANGELES COUNTY HARBOR UCLA MEDICAL CENTER - MEDICAL LIBRARY □ Torrance, CA

Beretz, Marilyn, Asst.Libn.
THEDA CLARK REGIONAL MEDICAL CENTER - HEALTH SCIENCES LIBRARY □ Neenah, WI

Berg, Ann, Libn.
TUCSON PUBLIC LIBRARY - TUCSON GOVERNMENTAL REFERENCE LIBRARY □ Tucson, AZ

Berg, Cristine, Circ.
UNIVERSITY OF WISCONSIN, LA CROSSE - MURPHY LIBRARY □ La Crosse, WI

Berg, Edith, Coord.
SASKATCHEWAN - DEPARTMENT OF CONSUMER AND COMMERICAL AFFAIRS - RESOURCE CENTRE □ Regina, SK

Berg, Florence R., Supv., Lit.Serv.
MERCK & COMPANY, INC. - MERCK SHARP & DOHME RESEARCH LABORATORIES - LIBRARY SERVICES □ West Point, PA

Berg, Frances, Br.Libn.
GENERAL ELECTRIC COMPANY - RSD BRANCH LIBRARY □ Philadelphia, PA

Berg, Frances, Br.Libn.
GENERAL ELECTRIC COMPANY - SPACE/RSD LIBRARIES □ Philadelphia, PA

Berg, Helen I., Circ.Libn.
KUTZTOWN STATE COLLEGE - ROHRBACH LIBRARY □ Kutztown, PA

Berg, Mrs. James, Supv.
BOB JONES UNIVERSITY - CHURCH MINISTRIES RESOURCE LAB □ Greenville, SC

Berg, Linda A., Lib.Techn.
CANADA - DEFENCE RESEARCH ESTABLISHMENT SUFFIELD - LIBRARY □ Ralston, AB

Berg, Margaret E., Rare Bk.Libn.
UNIVERSITY OF MICHIGAN - DEPARTMENT OF RARE BOOKS AND SPECIAL COLLECTIONS - LIBRARY □ Ann Arbor, MI

Berg, Richard R., Per./Lrng.Res.Libn.
UNITED THEOLOGICAL SEMINARY - LIBRARY □ Dayton, OH

Berg, Valborg Hansing, Libn.
FREEBORN COUNTY HISTORICAL SOCIETY - RESEARCH LIBRARY □ Albert Lea, MN

Bergamini, Sr. Rita, S.P., Archv.
SISTERS OF PROVIDENCE - SACRED HEART PROVINCE - ARCHIVES □ Seattle, WA

Bergan, Helen, Chf.
DISTRICT OF COLUMBIA PUBLIC LIBRARY - BIOGRAPHY DIVISION □ Washington, DC

Berge, Elsie
TRINITY LUTHERAN CHURCH - LIBRARY □ Moorhead, MN

Bergel, Wendy, Info.Spec.
GENERAL ELECTRIC COMPANY - COMPUTER MANAGEMENT OPERATION LIBRARY □ Bridgeport, CT

Bergen, John, Map Libn.
WESTERN ILLINOIS UNIVERSITY - LIBRARIES □ Macomb, IL

Bergen, John V., Map Libn.
WESTERN ILLINOIS UNIVERSITY - GEOGRAPHY & MAP LIBRARY □ Macomb, IL

Berger, Dr. Allen, Dir.
UNIVERSITY OF PITTSBURGH - READING/ COMMUNICATIONS RESOURCE CENTER □ Pittsburgh, PA

Berger, Alvin C., Act.Dir.
EAST STROUDSBURG STATE COLLEGE - LIBRARY □ East Stroudsburg, PA

Berger, Carol, Mgr., Lib./Info.Serv.
BEATRICE FOODS CO. - RESEARCH CENTER LIBRARY □ Chicago, IL

Berger, Clyde Cochran, Tech.Libn.
INSTITUTE OF LOGOPEDICS - TECHNICAL LIBRARY □ Wichita, KS

Berger, Edward, Cur.
RUTGERS UNIVERSITY, THE STATE UNIVERSITY OF NEW JERSEY - INSTITUTE OF JAZZ STUDIES □ Newark, NJ

Berger, L.W., Sr.Res.Info.Spec.
UNITED STATES STEEL CORPORATION - RESEARCH LABORATORY - TECHNICAL INFORMATION CENTER □ Monroeville, PA

Berger, Leslie, Ref./ILL Libn.
EAST STROUDSBURG STATE COLLEGE - LIBRARY □ East Stroudsburg, PA

Berger, Martin, Act.Dir.
U.S. NATL. BUREAU OF STANDARDS - PHOTON AND CHARGED PARTICLE DATA CENTER □ Washington, DC

Berger, Patricia W., Chf., Lib.Div.
U.S. NATL. BUREAU OF STANDARDS - LIBRARY □ Washington, DC

Berger, Paul, Group Mgr.
WITCO CHEMICAL CORPORATION - LIBRARY □ Houston, TX

Berger, Robert, Asst.Libn.
UNIVERSITY OF CALIFORNIA, SAN FRANCISCO - HASTINGS COLLEGE OF THE LAW - LEGAL INFORMATION CENTER □ San Francisco, CA

Bergeron, Arthur W., Jr., Archv.
LOUISIANA STATE OFFICE OF THE SECRETARY OF STATE - STATE ARCHIVES AND RECORDS SERVICE □ Baton Rouge, LA

Bergeron, Gilles, Rd.Serv.Libn.
UNIVERSITE DU QUEBEC A HULL - BIBLIOTHEQUE □ Hull, PQ

Berggren, Kathleen
BETTERLEY CONSULTING GROUP - TECHNICAL INFORMATION CENTER □ Boston, MA

Bergin, Dorothy C., Libn.
MOBIL TYCO SOLAR ENERGY CORPORATION - LIBRARY □ Waltham, MA

Berglund, Edean, Libn.
ST. LUKE'S HOSPITAL - MEDICAL LIBRARY □ Duluth, MN

Bergman, Bruce J., Lib.Dir./NY Campus
PACE UNIVERSITY - LIBRARY □ New York, NY

Bergman, Emily, Asst.Libn.
CALIFORNIA SCHOOL OF PROFESSIONAL PSYCHOLOGY - LOS ANGELES LIBRARY □ Los Angeles, CA

Bergman, Janet L., Libn.
JANUS FOUNDATION - LIBRARY □ San Francisco, CA

Bergmann, Emily, Libn.
CONDELL MEMORIAL HOSPITAL - FOHRMAN LIBRARY □ Libertyville, IL

Bergmann, L. James, Gen. Solicitor
UNION PACIFIC RAILROAD COMPANY - LAW LIBRARY □ Portland, OR

Bergmann, Randall W., Chf., Ref. & Circ.
U.S. AIR FORCE - AIR FORCE SYSTEMS COMMAND - AIR FORCE GEOPHYSICS LABORATORY - RESEARCH LIBRARY† □ Bedford, MA

Bergner, Clifford, Ref.Libn.
FLORIDA INSTITUTE OF TECHNOLOGY - SCHOOL OF APPLIED TECHNOLOGY - LIBRARY □ Jensen Beach, FL

Bergsten, Bebe, Libn.
LOCARE MOTION PICTURE RESEARCH GROUP - LIBRARY □ Los Angeles, CA

Berkemeier, Sr. Hildemar, Asst.Libn./ILL
CHRIST THE KING SEMINARY - LIBRARY □ East Aurora, NY

Berkey, Irene, Ref.Libn.
UNIVERSITY OF TEXAS SCHOOL OF LAW - TARLTON LAW LIBRARY □ Austin, TX

Berkey, Mary G., Libn.
U.S. FOOD & DRUG ADMINISTRATION - BUREAU OF RADIOLOGICAL HEALTH - LIBRARY □ Rockville, MD

Berkhofer, George H., Exec.Dir.
CLARK COUNTY HISTORICAL SOCIETY - LIBRARY □ Springfield, OH

Berkley, Audrey L., Libn.
ST. LOUIS METROPOLITAN MEDICAL SOCIETY - ST. LOUIS SOCIETY FOR MEDICAL AND SCIENTIFIC EDUCATION - LIBRARY □ St. Louis, MO

Berkman, Frank W., Exec.Dir.
HOTEL SALES MANAGEMENT ASSOCIATION -
SALES RESEARCH LIBRARY □ New York, NY

Berkner, Alice, Dir.
INTERNATIONAL BIRD RESCUE RESEARCH
CENTER - LIBRARY† □ Berkeley, CA

Berkowitz, Barbara, Ref.Libn.
BOARD OF COOPERATIVE EDUCATIONAL
SERVICES OF NASSAU COUNTY (BOCES) -
NASSAU EDUC. RSRCS. CTR. (NERC) □
Westbury, NY

Berkowitz, Dorothy J., Chf., Lib.Div.
U.S. INTERNATIONAL TRADE COMMISSION -
LIBRARY □ Washington, DC

Berkowitz, Joan, Media Coord.
BRIGHAM AND WOMEN'S HOSPITAL -
ABRAMSON CENTER FOR INSTRUCTIONAL
MEDIA □ Boston, MA

Berlin, Lenka, Libn.
DELOITTE HASKINS & SELLS - LIBRARY □
Philadelphia, PA

Berliner, Donna, Libn.
TEMPLE EMANU-EL - ALEX F. WEISBERG
LIBRARY □ Dallas, TX

Berliner, Mary Ann, Med.Libn.
LOS ANGELES COUNTY HARBOR UCLA MEDICAL
CENTER - MEDICAL LIBRARY □ Torrance, CA

Berman, Andrea B., Corp.Libn.
CONVERSE WARD DAVIS DIXON - CORPORATE
LIBRARY □ Pasadena, CA

Berman, Ellen L., Mgr.
TRW INC. - ENERGY SYSTEMS PLANNING
DIVISION - LIBRARY □ McLean, VA

Berman, Jenifer, Libn.
ARTHUR ANDERSEN & CO. - LIBRARY □
Hartford, CT

Berman, Leslie, Plan.Supv.
CONNECTICUT STATE LIBRARY □ Hartford, CT

Berman, Marsha, Assoc. Music Libn.
UNIVERSITY OF CALIFORNIA, LOS ANGELES -
MUSIC LIBRARY □ Los Angeles, CA

Bernaciak, Teresa, Lib.Techn.
MERCK & COMPANY, INC. - CALGON
CORPORATION - INFORMATION CENTER □
Pittsburgh, PA

Bernard, Arlys, Libn./Off.Mgr.
OREGON STATE UNIVERSITY - SCHOOL OF
OCEANOGRAPHY - NORTHWEST COASTAL
INFORMATION CENTER (NCIC) □ Newport, OR

Bernard, B.A., Res.Libn.
EMERY INDUSTRIES, INC. - RESEARCH
LIBRARY □ Cincinnati, OH

Bernard, Bobbi, Tech.Libn.
AMF, INC. - TECHNICAL INFORMATION
CENTER □ Stamford, CT

Bernard, David M., Area Dir.
U.S. DEPT. OF LABOR - OSHA - IDAHO AREA
OFFICE - LIBRARY □ Boise, ID

Bernard, Marielle, Lib.Techn.
QUEBEC PROVINCE - REGIE DE L'ELECTRICITE
ET DU GAZ - BIBLIOTHEQUE □ Montreal, PQ

Bernard, S.R., Dir.
U.S. OAK RIDGE NATL. LABORATORY -
INFORMATION CENTER FOR INTERNAL
EXPOSURE □ Oak Ridge, TN

Bernath, Kathleen, Interim Libn.
CLAREMONT GRADUATE SCHOOL -
EDUCATIONAL RESOURCE & INFORMATION
CENTER □ Claremont, CA

Bernath, Kathleen, Interim Libn.
CLAREMONT GRADUATE SCHOOL - GEORGE G.
STONE CENTER FOR CHILDREN'S BOOKS □
Claremont, CA

Bernauer, Peter, Libn./Info.Off.
CANADIAN PARAPLEGIC ASSOCIATION -
LIBRARY □ Toronto, ON

Berndt, Fred, Libn.
ST. PAUL TECHNICAL VOCATIONAL LIBRARY □
St. Paul, MN

Berner, Richard, Hd.Libn.
UNIVERSITY OF WASHINGTON - UNIVERSITY
ARCHIVES & MANUSCRIPT DIVISION -
MANUSCRIPT COLLECTION □ Seattle, WA

Berner, Richard C., Univ.Archv.
UNIVERSITY OF WASHINGTON - UNIVERSITY
ARCHIVES & MANUSCRIPT DIVISION -
UNIVERSITY ARCHIVES □ Seattle, WA

Bernhardt, Homer I., Hd.
UNIVERSITY OF PITTSBURGH - BEVIER
ENGINEERING LIBRARY □ Pittsburgh, PA

Bernhardt, Homer I., Hd.
UNIVERSITY OF PITTSBURGH - MATHEMATICS
LIBRARY □ Pittsburgh, PA

Bernhardt, Marcia, Exhibits Coord.
IRON COUNTY MUSEUM - ARCHIVES □ Caspian,
MI

Bernholdt, Jocelyn A., Med.Libn.
ALEXIAN BROTHERS MEDICAL CENTER -
MEDICAL LIBRARY □ Elk Grove Village, IL

Bernier, Leo R., Rec.Mgr.
NEW HAMPSHIRE STATE DEPARTMENT OF
STATE - DIVISION OF RECORDS MANAGEMENT
& ARCHIVES □ Concord, NH

Bernita, Sr. M., S.S.J., Lib.Dir.
BON SECOURS HOSPITAL - HEALTH SCIENCE
LIBRARY □ Grosse Pointe, MI

Bernstein, Bernice G., Asst.Libn.
MARYLAND STATE LAW LIBRARY □ Annapolis,
MD

Bernstein, Fran, Med.Libn.
U.S. VETERANS ADMINISTRATION (CT-West
Haven) - MEDICAL CENTER LIBRARY □ West
Haven, CT

Bernstein, Gloria S., Mgr., Lib.Info.Serv.
LIPTON (Thomas J.) INC. - RESEARCH LIBRARY
□ Englewood Cliffs, NJ

Bernstein, Joan, Asst.Libn.
UNIVERSITY OF PENNSYLVANIA - ANNENBERG
SCHOOL OF COMMUNICATIONS - LIBRARY □
Philadelphia, PA

Bernstein, Joan, Staff Res.Spec.Prog.
YALE UNIVERSITY - SOCIAL SCIENCE LIBRARY
□ New Haven, CT

Bernstein, Judith, Bus.Adm.Libn.
UNIVERSITY OF NEW MEXICO - WILLIAM J.
PARISH MEMORIAL LIBRARY □ Albuquerque, NM

Bernstein, Lillian, Libn.
NEWARK BETH ISRAEL MEDICAL CENTER - DR.
VICTOR PARSONNET MEMORIAL LIBRARY □
Newark, NJ

Bernstein, Lisbeth, Libn.
HARVARD UNIVERSITY - CENTER FOR SCIENCE
AND INTERNATIONAL AFFAIRS LIBRARY □
Cambridge, MA

Bernstein, Merle, Libn.
U.S. BUREAU OF MINES - TWIN CITIES
RESEARCH CENTER - LIBRARY □ Minneapolis,
MN

Bernstein, Pat, Tech.Lib.Asst.
BURNS AND ROE, INC. - TECHNICAL LIBRARY □
Oradell, NJ

Bernthaler, Jeanette, Act.Archv.
SAN BERNARDINO COUNTY HISTORICAL
ARCHIVES □ San Bernardino, CA

Berntsen, Patricia, ERIC/Per.Coord.
UNIVERSITY OF NORTH DAKOTA -
EDUCATIONAL RESOURCES INFORMATION
CENTER □ Grand Forks, ND

Berra, Marilyn, Circ.Supv.
EDEN THEOLOGICAL SEMINARY - LIBRARY □
Webster Groves, MO

Berrettini, JoEllen, Asst.Libn.
PEPPER, HAMILTON AND SCHEETZ - LAW
LIBRARY □ Philadelphia, PA

Berrien, Helen, Libn.
NEW ENGLAND FIRE & HISTORY MUSEUM -
LIBRARY AND ARCHIVE □ Brewster, MA

Berring, Robert C., Jr., Law Libn.
UNIVERSITY OF WASHINGTON - LAW SCHOOL
LIBRARY □ Seattle, WA

Berry, Corre, Fine Arts Ref.Libn.
SAM HOUSTON STATE UNIVERSITY - LIBRARY†
□ Huntsville, TX

Berry, Gayle C., ILL Libn.
CLARKSON COLLEGE OF TECHNOLOGY -
EDUCATIONAL RESOURCES CENTER □ Potsdam,
NY

Berry, James, Res.Coord.
HOUSING ASSOCIATION OF DELAWARE VALLEY
- LIBRARY □ Philadelphia, PA

Berry, Joy, Ref.Libn.
CALIFORNIA HISTORICAL SOCIETY -
SCHUBERT HALL LIBRARY □ San Francisco, CA

Berry, Marie, Hd.
SAN ANTONIO PUBLIC LIBRARY - HISTORY,
SOCIAL SCIENCE AND GENERAL REFERENCE
DEPARTMENT □ San Antonio, TX

Berry, Mary Jane, Libn.
PORTERVILLE STATE HOSPITAL - MEDICAL
LIBRARY □ Porterville, CA

Berry, Nancy, Ref.Libn.
ARTHUR D. LITTLE, INC. - RESEARCH LIBRARY
□ Cambridge, MA

Berry, Patricia A., Chf.Libn.
METROPOLITAN (Toronto) SEPARATE SCHOOL
BOARD - PROFESSIONAL LIBRARY† □ Toronto,
ON

Berry, Patrick, Libn.
LADISH CO. - METALLURGICAL DEPARTMENT
LIBRARY □ Cudahy, WI

Berry, Rachel, Mgr.
PILLSBURY COMPANY - MAIN OFFICE
MARKETING LIBRARY □ Minneapolis, MN

Berry, Robert H., Tech.Info.Spec.
GENERAL ELECTRIC COMPANY -
TRANSPORTATION TECHNOLOGY CENTER -
TECHNICAL INFORMATION CENTER □ Erie, PA

Berry, S.M., Pres.
NATIONAL ASSOCIATION OF HOSIERY
MANUFACTURERS - LIBRARY □ Charlotte, NC

Berry, Vernice W., Mgr.
FIRST PENNSYLVANIA BANK, N.A. -
MARKETING INFORMATION CENTER† □
Philadelphia, PA

Berryman, Dr. Bruce, Chm.
WILKES COLLEGE - EARTH AND
ENVIRONMENTAL SCIENCES READING ROOM □
Wilkes-Barre, PA

Bertalmio, Lynne, Dir.
STILLWATER PUBLIC LIBRARY - MINNESOTA
ROOM □ Stillwater, MN

Bertels, Henry J., S.J., Libn.
WOODSTOCK THEOLOGICAL CENTER -
LIBRARY □ Washington, DC

Berthelot, Benoit, Asst.Libn.
COLLEGE DOMINICAIN DE PHILOSOPHIE ET DE
THEOLOGIE - BIBLIOTHEQUE □ Ottawa, ON

Berthelsen, Barbara, Map Libn.
CORNELL UNIVERSITY - MAPS, MICROTEXT,
NEWSPAPERS DEPARTMENT □ Ithaca, NY

Berthold, Carol A., Libn.
CARNEGIE LIBRARY OF PITTSBURGH -
BUSINESS DIVISION □ Pittsburgh, PA

Bertholf, Robert J., Cur.
SUNY AT BUFFALO - POETRY/RARE BOOKS
COLLECTION □ Buffalo, NY

Bertley, Robert G., Libn.
SPERRY CORPORATION - SPERRY UNIVAC NEW
YORK TECHNICAL LIBRARY □ New York, NY

Bertolette, R.R., Mgr.
GIBBS AND COX, INC. - TECHNICAL
INFORMATION CONTROL DEPARTMENT □ New
York, NY

Bertolucci, Katherine, Consulting Libn.
WHALE CENTER - EXTINCT SPECIES
MEMORIAL FUND - LIBRARY □ Oakland, CA

Bertolucci, Ysabel R., Health Sci.Libn.
KAISER-PERMANENTE MEDICAL CENTER -
SOUTH SAN FRANCISCO HEALTH SCIENCES
LIBRARY □ South San Francisco, CA

Berton, Alberta D., Dir., Med.Doc.Serv.
COLLEGE OF PHYSICIANS OF PHILADELPHIA -
LIBRARY AND MEDICAL DOCUMENTATION
SERVICE □ Philadelphia, PA

Bertram, Lee Ann, Ref.Libn.
ELI LILLY AND COMPANY - SCIENTIFIC
LIBRARY □ Indianapolis, IN
Bertsch, Christine, Libn.
UNIVERSITY OF MAINE, PRESQUE ISLE -
LIBRARY □ Presque Isle, ME
Bertuccelli, Dr. Angela, Libn.
AMERICAN HYPNOTISTS' ASSOCIATION -
HYPNOSIS TECHNICAL CENTER □ San
Francisco, CA
Berube, Mrs. F., Ref.Techn.
ROYAL CANADIAN MOUNTED POLICE - LAW
ENFORCEMENT REFERENCE CENTRE □ Ottawa,
ON
Berube, Lorraine V., Docs.
UNIVERSITE LAVAL - BIBLIOTHEQUE
SCIENTIFIQUE† □ Ste. Foy, PQ
Besemer, Susan, Hd., Ind.Lrng.Ctr.
SUNY - COLLEGE AT BUFFALO - EDWARD H.
BUTLER LIBRARY □ Buffalo, NY
Beskid, Stephan J., Circ.Libn.
ST. VLADIMIR'S ORTHODOX THEOLOGICAL
SEMINARY - FR. GEORGES FLOROVSKY
LIBRARY □ Tuckahoe, NY
Beson, Carolyn, Supv., Tech.Info.Serv.
AMOCO PRODUCTION COMPANY - RESEARCH
CENTER LIBRARY† □ Tulsa, OK
Bessette, Irene, Libn.
QUEEN'S UNIVERSITY AT KINGSTON - LAW
LIBRARY □ Kingston, ON
Best, Carolyn, Ref.Libn.
U.S. NAVY - NAVAL AIR SYSTEMS COMMAND -
TECHNICAL LIBRARY □ Washington, DC
Best, Donna Jo, Chf., Circ.
WYOMING STATE LIBRARY □ Cheyenne, WY
Best, Edwin J., Hd.Ref.Libn.
TENNESSEE VALLEY AUTHORITY - TECHNICAL
LIBRARY □ Chattanooga, TN
Best, G. Ronnie, Assoc.Dir.
UNIVERSITY OF FLORIDA - CENTER FOR
WETLANDS REFERENCE LIBRARY □ Gainesville,
FL
Best, Margaret, Libn.
EASTERN MICHIGAN UNIVERSITY - CENTER OF
EDUCATIONAL RESOURCES - INSTRUCTIONAL
MATERIALS CENTER □ Ypsilanti, MI
Best, Reba A., Cat.
UNIVERSITY OF TENNESSEE - COLLEGE OF
LAW LIBRARY □ Knoxville, TN
Besterman, Elaine, Mgr.Lib.Serv.
DOW CHEMICAL COMPANY - MERRELL DOW
PHARMACEUTICALS, INC. - RESEARCH CENTER
LIBRARY □ Cincinnati, OH
Bethea, Frances S., Libn.
UNITED SERVICES AUTOMOBILE ASSOCIATION
- CORPORATE LIBRARY AND INFORMATION
CENTER □ San Antonio, TX
Bethel, Dorothy, Libn.
MIDWEST HISTORICAL & GENEALOGICAL
SOCIETY, INC. - LIBRARY □ Wichita, KS
Bethel, Gay, Info.Res.Spec.
TEXAS EMPLOYERS INSURANCE ASSOCIATION
- ENGINEERING INFORMATION CENTER □
Dallas, TX
Bethel, Kathleen, Asst.Libn.
JOHNSON PUBLISHING COMPANY, INC. -
LIBRARY □ Chicago, IL
Betsill, Joyce C., Supv., Proc.
NATIONAL GEOGRAPHIC SOCIETY -
ILLUSTRATIONS LIBRARY □ Washington, DC
Bettenberg, Julie, Rsrcs.Ed.
AMERICAN SOCIETY FOR AEROSPACE
EDUCATION □ Washington, DC
Bettendorf, Rev. James B., Dir.
FLINT NEWMAN CENTER - LIBRARY AND
CATHOLIC INFORMATION CENTER □ Flint, MI
Bettez, Jules, Dir.
SEMINAIRE DES TROIS RIVIERES - ARCHIVES
□ Trois-Rivieres, PQ
Bettis, Gary, Archv.
IDAHO STATE HISTORICAL SOCIETY -
LIBRARY AND ARCHIVES □ Boise, ID

Betts, Frances, Libn.
MERCY REGIONAL MEDICAL CENTER LIBRARY
□ Vicksburg, MS
Betz, Dr. Ellen, Supv. of Lib.
UNIVERSITY OF MINNESOTA - OCCUPATIONAL
INFORMATION LIBRARY □ Minneapolis, MN
Betz, Shirley M., Dir.
NAZARETH HOSPITAL - MEDICAL LIBRARY □
Philadelphia, PA
Bevan, Barbara H., Chf.Libn.
YORK HOSPITAL - LIBRARY □ York, PA
Bevan, David, Dir.Info.Serv.Div.
NORTH CAROLINA STATE DEPARTMENT OF
CULTURAL RESOURCES - DIVISION OF THE
STATE LIBRARY □ Raleigh, NC
Bevan, Leah, ILL
PITTSBURG STATE UNIVERSITY - LEONARD H.
AXE LIBRARY □ Pittsburg, KS
Bevens, Helen L., Asst.V.P. Supv./Libn.
FIRST HAWAIIAN BANK - RESEARCH DIVISION
LIBRARY □ Honolulu, HI
Beverage, John, Pub.Serv.Libn.
DALLAS THEOLOGICAL SEMINARY - MOSHER
LIBRARY □ Dallas, TX
Beversdorf, Anne, Libn.
AGENCY FOR INSTRUCTIONAL TELEVISION
(AIT) - RESEARCH LIBRARY □ Bloomington, IN
Bevilacqua, Ann. F., Doc.Libn.
FRANKLIN AND MARSHALL COLLEGE -
FACKENTHAL LIBRARY - SPECIAL
COLLECTIONS □ Lancaster, PA
Bevilalqua, Gina, Libn.
SOCIETE DE DEVELOPPEMENT DE LA BAIE
JAMES - SERVICE DOCUMENTATION □
Montreal, PQ
Beville, Mitchel, Assoc.Dir.
UNIVERSITY OF SOUTH DAKOTA -
GOVERNMENTAL RESEARCH LIBRARY □
Vermillion, SD
Bevington, Audrey, Libn.
COLD SPRING HARBOR LABORATORY - MAIN
LIBRARY □ Cold Spring Harbor, NY
Bewick, Brenda, Libn.
MC GILL UNIVERSITY - EXPERIMENTAL
SURGERY LIBRARY □ Montreal, PQ
Bey, Lois A., Mgr., Info.Ctr.
TRAVENOL LABORATORIES, INC. - LIBRARY □
Morton Grove, IL
Beyea, Marion, Prov.Archv.
NEW BRUNSWICK - PROVINCIAL ARCHIVES OF
NEW BRUNSWICK □ Fredericton, NB
Beyer, Ann, Ref.Libn.
UNIVERSITY OF CALIFORNIA - LOS ALAMOS
NATIONAL LABORATORY - LIBRARY □ Los
Alamos, NM
Beyer, Robyn, Libn.
PEPPER, HAMILTON AND SCHEETZ - LAW
LIBRARY □ Philadelphia, PA
Beymer, Charles R., Asst.Dir.
CALIFORNIA POLYTECHNIC STATE
UNIVERSITY - ROBERT E. KENNEDY LIBRARY □
San Luis Obispo, CA
Beynen, G. Koolemans, Slavic Biblog.
OHIO STATE UNIVERSITY - EAST EUROPEAN
AND SLAVIC READING ROOM □ Columbus, OH
Bezera, Elizabeth, Hd., Pub.Serv.
EMERSON COLLEGE - ABBOT MEMORIAL
LIBRARY □ Boston, MA
Bezugloff, Natalia B., Dept.Hd.
CLEVELAND PUBLIC LIBRARY - FOREIGN
LITERATURE DEPARTMENT □ Cleveland, OH
Bhan, Esme B., Mss.Res.Assoc.
HOWARD UNIVERSITY - MOORLAND-SPINGARN
RESEARCH CENTER - MANUSCRIPT DIVISION □
Washington, DC
Bhati, Pushpa, Sr.Libn.
CREEDMOOR PSYCHIATRIC CENTER - HEALTH
SCIENCES LIBRARY □ Queens Village, NY
Bial, Ray, Acq.Libn.
PARKLAND COLLEGE - LEARNING RESOURCE
CENTER □ Champaign, IL

Bialecki, Anthony G., Libn.
U.S. AIR FORCE - OFFICE OF SCIENTIFIC
RESEARCH - LIBRARY □ Bolling AFB, DC
Bianchini, Mr. L., Hd.Libn.
MOUNT SAINT VINCENT UNIVERSITY -
LIBRARY □ Halifax, NS
Biasiol, Rev. Virgilio, O.F.M., Dir.
SANTA BARBARA MISSION ARCHIVE-LIBRARY
□ Santa Barbara, CA
Bibbee, Robert, Per.Hd.
CHICAGO PUBLIC LIBRARY CENTRAL LIBRARY -
BUSINESS/SCIENCE/TECHNOLOGY DIVISION
□ Chicago, IL
Biblo, Herbert, Asst.Libn., Rd.Serv.
CRERAR (John) LIBRARY □ Chicago, IL
Biblo, Herbert, Libn.
ILLINOIS INSTITUTE OF TECHNOLOGY - JAMES
S. KEMPER LIBRARY □ Chicago, IL
Bick-Gregoire, Lorraine, Mgr.
RAYTHEON COMPANY - MISSILE SYSTEMS
DIVISION - BEDFORD LABORATORIES -
TECHNICAL INFORMATION CENTER □ Bedford,
MA
Bickford, Priscilla, Libn.
MAINE STATE DEPARTMENT OF
ENVIRONMENTAL PROTECTION &
DEPARTMENT OF CONSERVATION - DEP-DOC
JOINT LIBRARY □ Augusta, ME
Bickston, Devertt D., Libn.
SOUTHERN METHODIST UNIVERSITY -
SCIENCE/ENGINEERING LIBRARY □ Dallas, TX
Biddle, V., Asst.Libn.
SOUTH DAKOTA STATE SUPREME COURT -
LIBRARY □ Pierre, SD
Bidwell, John, Ref.Libn.
UNIVERSITY OF CALIFORNIA, LOS ANGELES -
WILLIAM ANDREWS CLARK MEMORIAL
LIBRARY □ Los Angeles, CA
Bidwell, Robert G., Assoc.Libn.
GEORGE WASHINGTON UNIVERSITY -
NATIONAL LAW CENTER - JACOB BURNS LAW
LIBRARY □ Washington, DC
Bidwell, Sharon, Supv./Lib.Ref.Serv.
COURIER-JOURNAL AND LOUISVILLE TIMES -
LIBRARY □ Louisville, KY
Bieber, Doris M., Libn.
VANDERBILT UNIVERSITY LAW LIBRARY □
Nashville, TN
Bieber, Ralph, Instr.Mtls.Spec.
COLUMBUS TECHNICAL INSTITUTE -
EDUCATIONAL RESOURCES CENTER† □
Columbus, OH
Bieble, Ruth, Libn.
CHEMICAL BANK - RESEARCH LIBRARY □ New
York, NY
Biefeld, Rebecca, Relg.Biblog.
SYRACUSE UNIVERSITY - E.S. BIRD LIBRARY -
HUMANITIES DEPARTMENT □ Syracuse, NY
Biehl, Nancy, Map Rm.
METROPOLITAN TORONTO LIBRARY - HISTORY
DEPARTMENT □ Toronto, ON
Bielecki, C., Asst.Info.Spec.
AIR PRODUCTS AND CHEMICALS, INC. -
INFORMATION SERVICES - TREXLERTOWN
LIBRARY □ Allentown, PA
Bielefield, Arlene F., Div.Hd.
CONNECTICUT STATE LIBRARY □ Hartford, CT
Bielenberg, W. Larry, Dir., Lib.Serv.
CONCORDIA SEMINARY - LIBRARY □ St. Louis,
MO
Bielmann, Lorraine, Hd.Libn.
CLINICAL RESEARCH INSTITUTE OF
MONTREAL - MEDICAL LIBRARY □ Montreal, PQ
Bienenstock, N.I., Cur.
FURNITURE LIBRARY ASSOCIATION □ High
Point, NC
Bienkowski, Alexander C., AV Libn.
UNIVERSITY OF TEXAS MEDICAL BRANCH -
MOODY MEDICAL LIBRARY □ Galveston, TX
Bier, Robert A., Jr., Chf.Libn.
U.S. GEOLOGICAL SURVEY - DENVER LIBRARY
□ Denver, CO

Bierbaum, Esther G., Libn.
PASADENA PRESBYTERIAN CHURCH - LIBRARY
□ St. Petersburg, FL
Bierlein, John Francis, Dir.Res.Dev.
DEMOCRATIC NATIONAL COMMITTEE -
RESEARCH LIBRARY □ Washington, DC
Biermann, W.W., Chf., Res.
ILLINOIS STATE DEPARTMENT OF COMMERCE
& COMMUNITY AFFAIRS - OFFICE OF POLICY &
PROGRAMS - LIBRARY □ Springfield, IL
Biersborn, Mary C., Mgr.
SPERRY CORPORATION - SPERRY UNIVAC
DIVISION - INFORMATION SERVICE CENTER □
Roseville, MN
Bierschenk, Nancy
TEXAS MEDICAL ASSOCIATION - MEMORIAL
LIBRARY □ Austin, TX
Biersteker, Ann, Pol.Sci.Biblog.
SYRACUSE UNIVERSITY - E.S. BIRD LIBRARY -
SOCIAL SCIENCES DEPARTMENT □ Syracuse,
NY
Biersteker, Ann J., African Biblog.
SYRACUSE UNIVERSITY - E.S. BIRD LIBRARY -
AREA STUDIES DEPARTMENT □ Syracuse, NY
Bigelow, Leonard, Mgr. of Lib.Serv.
MEDTRONIC, INC. - LIBRARY □ Minneapolis, MN
Biggins, Jeanne, Libn.
ONONDAGA COUNTY PUBLIC LIBRARY -
BUSINESS AND INDUSTRIAL DEPARTMENT □
Syracuse, NY
Biggio, Eugene, Dir.
KENT MEMORIAL LIBRARY - HISTORICAL
ROOM □ Suffield, CT
Biggs, Barbara, Libn.
LOUISIANA STATE DEPARTMENT OF NATURAL
RESOURCES - DIVISION OF RESEARCH &
DEVELOPMENT - LIBRARY □ Baton Rouge, LA
Biggs, Catherine, Libn.
HEWLETT-PACKARD COMPANY - CUPERTINO
LIBRARY □ Cupertino, CA
Biggs, Clyde, Off.Serv.Supv.
TEXAS STATE AIR CONTROL BOARD - LIBRARY
□ Austin, TX
Biggs, Deb R., Archv.
BOWLING GREEN STATE UNIVERSITY -
CENTER FOR ARCHIVAL COLLECTIONS □
Bowling Green, OH
Biggs, Donald W., Sr.Libn.
NEW JERSEY NEURO-PSYCHIATRIC INSTITUTE
- PROFESSIONAL LIBRARY □ Princeton, NJ
Bihon, Connie, Libn.
PENNZOIL PRODUCTS COMPANY - RESEARCH
DEPARTMENT LIBRARY □ Shreveport, LA
Bijlefeld, Willem, Supv., Lib.Comm.
HARTFORD SEMINARY FOUNDATION - CASE
MEMORIAL LIBRARY □ Hartford, CT
Bilbrey, Dale E., Libn./Musm.Coord.
UPPER ROOM DEVOTIONAL LIBRARY, MUSEUM
AND ARCHIVES □ Nashville, TN
Bileckyj, Peter, Acq./Ser.Libn.
DUKE UNIVERSITY - SCHOOL OF LAW LIBRARY
□ Durham, NC
Biles, Roberta F., Lib.Dir.
AMERICAN RED CROSS - NATIONAL
HEADQUARTERS LIBRARY □ Washington, DC
Bilgin, Deniz
JOHNS HOPKINS UNIVERSITY - CENTER FOR
METROPOLITAN PLANNING AND RESEARCH -
LIBRARY □ Baltimore, MD
Bilinski, Rev. Donald, O.F.M., Dir.
POLISH MUSEUM OF AMERICA - LIBRARY AND
ARCHIVES □ Chicago, IL
Bilk, Marjorie, Lib.Dir.
MOORE COLLEGE OF ART - LIBRARY □
Philadelphia, PA
Bill, Ruby, Libn.
LAKELAND COUNSELING CENTER - LIBRARY □
Elkhorn, WI
Billesbach, Ann E., Cur.
NEBRASKA STATE HISTORICAL SOCIETY -
WILLA CATHER HISTORICAL CENTER -
ARCHIVES □ Red Cloud, NE

Billhymer, Paul L., Libn.
UPPER COLORADO RIVER COMMISSION -
LIBRARY □ Salt Lake City, UT
Billiar, Joanne, Hd.Libn.
ST. VINCENT CHARITY HOSPITAL - LIBRARY □
Cleveland, OH
Billick, Pam, Dir.
ST. LUKE'S HOSPITAL - MEDICAL LIBRARY □
Cleveland, OH
Billings, Carol D., Dir.
LAW LIBRARY OF LOUISIANA □ New Orleans, LA
Billings, Pennie, Ref./Media Libn.
SCOTT & WHITE MEMORIAL HOSPITAL -
MEDICAL LIBRARY □ Temple, TX
Billings, Robert, Biblog.
CENTRAL CONNECTICUT STATE COLLEGE -
ELIHU BURRITT LIBRARY □ New Britain, CT
Bills, Tom, AV Serv.
WESTINGHOUSE ELECTRIC CORPORATION -
NUCLEAR ENERGY SYSTEMS - INFORMATION
RESOURCES† □ Pittsburgh, PA
Billups, Ann, Lib.Assoc.
UNIVERSITY OF GEORGIA - RICHARD B.
RUSSELL MEMORIAL LIBRARY □ Athens, GA
Billy, George J., Rd.Serv.Libn.
U.S. MERCHANT MARINE ACADEMY -
SCHUYLER OTIS BLAND MEMORIAL LIBRARY □
Kings Point, NY
Billyou, L.E., Libn.
TECHNICON INSTRUMENTS CORPORATION -
LIBRARY □ Tarrytown, NY
Bilodeau, Francoise, Bibliotechnicienne
QUEBEC PROVINCE - MINISTERE DE LA
JUSTICE - BIBLIOTHEQUE □ Ste. Foy, PQ
Bilsland, Ms. C., Supv., Lib.Res. & Tech.
TORONTO BOARD OF EDUCATION -
EDUCATION CENTRE LIBRARY □ Toronto, ON
Binder, Mitzi, Libn.
JOHNSON (Bernard) INC. - TECHNICAL LIBRARY
□ Houston, TX
Binder, Richard, Hum./Soc.Sci.Libn.
DREXEL UNIVERSITY LIBRARIES - GENERAL
LIBRARY □ Philadelphia, PA
Bingaman, Elizabeth, Films Spec.
MINNEAPOLIS PUBLIC LIBRARY &
INFORMATION CENTER - ART, MUSIC & FILMS
DEPARTMENT □ Minneapolis, MN
Bingaman, Joseph W., Cur., Latin Amer.Coll.
STANFORD UNIVERSITY - HOOVER
INSTITUTION ON WAR, REVOLUTION AND
PEACE - LIBRARY □ Stanford, CA
Bingham, Doris, Data Distr.Serv.
ESSO RESOURCES CANADA LIMITED - LIBRARY
INFORMATION CENTRE □ Calgary, AB
Bingham, Kathleen B., Libn.
NEW HAMPSHIRE HOSPITAL - SCHOOL OF
NURSING REFERENCE LIBRARY □ Concord, NH
Bingham, Kathleen S., Exec.V.P.
FIND/SVP - LIBRARY □ New York, NY
Bingham, Nancy, Asst.Coord/Info.Serv
EDUCATIONAL RESEARCH SERVICE - LIBRARY
□ Arlington, VA
Binion, Francie G.
ANALYTIC SERVICES, INC. - TECHNICAL
LIBRARY □ Arlington, VA
Binkley, Dorothy, Chf.Libn.
WESLEY MEDICAL CENTER - MC KIBBIN
PROFESSIONAL LIBRARY □ Wichita, KS
Binns, Mrs. W. Gordon, Libn.
REVEILLE UNITED METHODIST CHURCH -
REVEILLE MEMORIAL LIBRARY □ Richmond, VA
Bintliff, Barbara, Ref.Libn.
UNIVERSITY OF DENVER - COLLEGE OF LAW -
WESTMINSTER LAW LIBRARY □ Denver, CO
Birch, Tobeylynn, Hd.Libn.
CALIFORNIA SCHOOL OF PROFESSIONAL
PSYCHOLOGY - LOS ANGELES LIBRARY □ Los
Angeles, CA
Birchard, Jane M., Libn.
FLINT HILLS AREA VOCATIONAL-TECHNICAL
SCHOOL - LIBRARY □ Emporia, KS

Birchfield, Martha J., Dir.
LEXINGTON TECHNICAL INSTITUTE - LIBRARY
□ Lexington, KY
Bird, Judi, Hd.Acq.
SUNY - AGRICULTURAL AND TECHNICAL
COLLEGE AT FARMINGDALE - THOMAS D.
GREENLEY LIBRARY □ Farmingdale, NY
Bird, Shirlee A., Libn.
CHURCH OF JESUS CHRIST OF LATTER-DAY
SAINTS - EUGENE, OREGON BRANCH
GENEALOGICAL LIBRARY □ Eugene, OR
Bird, Viola A., Libn.
PRESTON, THORGRIMSON, ELLIS & HOLMAN -
LIBRARY □ Seattle, WA
Bird, Warren, Dir.
DUKE UNIVERSITY - MEDICAL CENTER
LIBRARY □ Durham, NC
Birdsall, Douglas, Hum.Libn.
IDAHO STATE UNIVERSITY LIBRARY -
HUMANITIES DIVISION □ Pocatello, ID
Birdwell, Effie N., Sr.Libn.
MONSANTO CHEMICAL INTERMEDIATES
COMPANY - PROCESS TECHNOLOGY
DEPARTMENT - LIBRARY □ Texas City, TX
Birdwell, Rebecca P., Libn.
UNIVERSITY OF TENNESSEE - SCIENCE-
ENGINEERING LIBRARY □ Knoxville, TN
Birkey, Grace L., Libn.
WABCO - CONSTRUCTION AND MINING
EQUIPMENT GROUP - ENGINEERING
TECHNICAL LIBRARY □ Peoria, IL
Birknes, Margaretha E.H., Law Libn.
NEW BEDFORD LAW LIBRARY □ New Bedford,
MA
Birks, Grant, Mgr.
BELL-NORTHERN RESEARCH LTD. - TECHNICAL
INFORMATION CENTRE □ Ottawa, ON
Birladeanu, Ludmila, Supv.
HARVARD UNIVERSITY - CHEMISTRY LIBRARY
□ Cambridge, MA
Birmingham, Judy, Info.Spec.
BABCOCK AND WILCOX COMPANY - RESEARCH
CENTER LIBRARY □ Alliance, OH
Birnbach, Melanie R., Med.Libn.
CHILDREN'S HOSPITAL - FORBES MEDICAL
LIBRARY □ Denver, CO
Birnbaum, Denise, Tech.Libn.
GARRETT CORPORATION - GARRETT TURBINE
ENGINE COMPANY - ENGINEERING LIBRARY □
Phoenix, AZ
Birnbaum, Henry, Univ.Libn.
PACE UNIVERSITY - LIBRARY □ New York, NY
Birnbaum, Melinda, Lib.Asst.
INSURANCE INSTITUTE FOR HIGHWAY SAFETY
- LIBRARY □ Washington, DC
Birney, Ann E., Libn.
JOSLYN ART MUSEUM - ART REFERENCE
LIBRARY □ Omaha, NE
Birschel, Dee, Assoc.Dir.
INTERNATIONAL FOUNDATION OF EMPLOYEE
BENEFIT PLANS - INFORMATION CENTER □
Brookfield, WI
Birula, Kay, Mgr.
AMP, INC. - TECHNICAL INFORMATION
CENTER □ Harrisburg, PA
Bisaillon, Blaise, Dir.
FORBES LIBRARY □ Northampton, MA
Bisch, Thelma, Libn.
KITCHENER-WATERLOO HOSPITAL - HEALTH
SCIENCES LIBRARY □ Kitchener, ON
Bischoff, Frances, Media Serv.Coord.
WISHARD (William N.) MEMORIAL HOSPITAL -
PROFESSIONAL LIBRARY/MEDIA SERVICES □
Indianapolis, IN
Bischoff, Mary, Coord.Tech.Serv.
CHRIST SEMINARY - SEMINEX LIBRARY □ St.
Louis, MO
Biscoe, Eleanor, Dir.
NATIONAL REHABILITATION INFORMATION
CENTER □ Washington, DC
Bishop, David, Univ.Libn.
UNIVERSITY OF CALIFORNIA, SAN FRANCISCO
- LIBRARY □ San Francisco, CA

Bishop, Delbert A., Asst.Dir., CPR
U.S. NATL. ARCHIVES & RECORDS SERVICE -
NATL. PERSONNEL RECORDS CENTER □ St.
Louis, MO
Bishop, Elizabeth, Sys. & Circ.Libn.
RYERSON POLYTECHNICAL INSTITUTE -
LEARNING RESOURCES CENTRE □ Toronto, ON
Bishop, Francis, Acq.Libn.
TENNESSEE VALLEY AUTHORITY - TECHNICAL
LIBRARY □ Chattanooga, TN
Bishop, Jean, Circ./ILL Libn.
MONTANA COLLEGE OF MINERAL SCIENCE AND
TECHNOLOGY - LIBRARY □ Butte, MT
Bishop, Mrs. Jesie, Tech.Serv.
ONTARIO - MINISTRY OF TRANSPORTATION
AND COMMUNICATIONS - LIBRARY AND
INFORMATION CENTRE □ Downsview, ON
Bishop, Lewis H.
WARSAW HISTORICAL SOCIETY - LIBRARY □
Warsaw, NY
Bishop, Richard, Sr.Rec.Anl.
TORONTO CITY RECORDS AND ARCHIVES
DIVISION □ Toronto, ON
Bishop, Susan E., Asst.Chf.
NATIONAL LIBRARY OF CANADA - COMPUTER-
BASED REFERENCE SERVICES □ Ottawa, ON
Bismuti, Gene, Chf.Info.Serv.Div.
WASHINGTON STATE LIBRARY □ Olympia, WA
Bisold, Dorothy
WASHINGTON STATE DEPARTMENT OF
COMMERCE AND ECONOMIC DEVELOPMENT -
TOURISM DEVELOPMENT DIVISION □ Seattle,
WA
Bitman, Leslie, Assoc.Libn.
SQUIRE, SANDERS & DEMPSEY - LAW LIBRARY
□ Cleveland, OH
Bitner, Harry, Legal Biblog.
COLUMBIA UNIVERSITY - LAW LIBRARY □ New
York, NY
Bitonti, Anthony J., Media Techn.
DETROIT INSTITUTE OF TECHNOLOGY - JAMES
C. GORDON MEMORIAL LIBRARY □ Detroit, MI
Bittel, Peter, Ref.Libn.
TEMPLE UNIVERSITY - CENTRAL LIBRARY
SYSTEM - ZAHN INSTRUCTIONAL MATERIALS
CENTER □ Philadelphia, PA
Bitter, Diane S., Cat.
UNIVERSITY OF TOLEDO - COLLEGE OF LAW
LIBRARY† □ Toledo, OH
Bitter, Jane L., Tech.Libn.
MOBIL RESEARCH & DEVELOPMENT
CORPORATION - PAULSBORO LABORATORY -
TECHNICAL INFORMATION SERVICES □
Paulsboro, NJ
Bitting, Judith C., Libn.
SMITH, KLINE & FRENCH LABORATORIES -
RESEARCH AND DEVELOPMENT LIBRARY □
Philadelphia, PA
Bitzer, June, Acq./Ref.Libn.
DELAWARE VALLEY COLLEGE OF SCIENCE AND
AGRICULTURE - JOSEPH KRAUSKOPF
MEMORIAL LIBRARY □ Doylestown, PA
Bivans, Margaret, Br./Ref.Libn.
U.S. NATL. OCEANIC & ATMOSPHERIC
ADMINISTRATION - ENVIRONMENTAL
RESEARCH LABORATORIES - LIBRARY □
Boulder, CO
Biwer, Terry, Res.Techn.
WAUKESHA COUNTY HISTORICAL MUSEUM -
RESEARCH CENTER □ Waukesha, WI
Bjarnar, Vilhjalmur, Cur.
CORNELL UNIVERSITY - ICELANDIC
COLLECTION □ Ithaca, NY
Bjerke, Cheryl A., Dir.
NORTHWESTERN COLLEGE OF CHIROPRACTIC
- LIBRARY □ St. Paul, MN
Bjerken, Lisa C., Libn.
FAIRVIEW SOUTHDALE HOSPITAL - MARY ANN
KING HEALTH SCIENCES LIBRARY □ Edina, MN
Bjorge, Gary, Asst.Libn.
UNIVERSITY OF KANSAS - EAST ASIAN
LIBRARY □ Lawrence, KS

Bjork, Carol, Libn.
MUSEUM OF FINE ARTS - SCHOOL LIBRARY □
Boston, MA
Bjorke, Wallace S., Music Libn.
UNIVERSITY OF MICHIGAN - MUSIC LIBRARY □
Ann Arbor, MI
Bjornberg, Linda, Libn.
WILLMAR STATE HOSPITAL - LIBRARY □
Willmar, MN
Black, B.A., Dir.
BRITISH COLUMBIA - MINISTRY OF
EDUCATION - PROVINCIAL EDUCATIONAL
MEDIA CENTRE □ Richmond, BC
Black, Bernice, Chf., Lib.Br.
U.S. ARMY - ENGINEER WATERWAYS
EXPERIMENT STATION - TECHNICAL
INFORMATION CENTER □ Vicksburg, MS
Black, Dorothy M., Asst. To Dir.
PHILADELPHIA COLLEGE OF BIBLE - SCOFIELD-
HILL MEMORIAL LIBRARY □ Langhorne, PA
Black, Elizabeth, Ref.Libn.
UNIVERSITY OF BRITISH COLUMBIA -
HUMANITIES DIVISION □ Vancouver, BC
Black, Ernest L., Mgr.
BURGESS INDUSTRIES - ENGINEERING
LIBRARY □ Dallas, TX
Black, George W., Jr., Sci.Libn.
SOUTHERN ILLINOIS UNIVERSITY,
CARBONDALE - SCIENCE DIVISION LIBRARY □
Carbondale, IL
Black, Hugh G., Pub.Serv.Mgr.
SOUTHWEST TEXAS STATE UNIVERSITY -
LEARNING RESOURCES CENTER □ San Marcos,
TX
Black, Isabella, Libn.
QUEENS CHILDREN'S PSYCHIATRIC CENTER -
LAURETTA BENDER CHILD PSYCHIATRY
LIBRARY □ Bellerose, NY
Black, Dr. J., Assoc.Libn.
UNIVERSITY OF GUELPH - LIBRARY □ Guelph,
ON
Black, Rev. J. Bernard, Libn.
UNIVERSITY OF TORONTO - ST. MICHAEL'S
COLLEGE - JOHN M. KELLY LIBRARY □ Toronto,
ON
Black, Kathy A., Doc.Libn.
GETTY OIL COMPANY, INC. - RESEARCH
CENTER LIBRARY □ Houston, TX
Black, Lawrence, Sr.Libn.
NEW YORK STATE INSTITUTE FOR BASIC
RESEARCH IN MENTAL RETARDATION -
LIBRARY □ Staten Island, NY
Black, Margaret
AMERICANS UNITED FOR LIFE - AUL LEGAL
DEFENSE FUND - INFORMATION CENTER □
Chicago, IL
Black, S., Libn.
GRANDE PRAIRIE GENERAL HOSPITAL -
LIBRARY □ Grande Prairie, AB
Black, Sandra M., Act.Chf.Libn.
MOHAWK COLLEGE OF APPLIED ARTS AND
TECHNOLOGY - MOHAWK LIBRARY RESOURCE
CENTRE □ Hamilton, ON
Black, Sophie K., Assoc.Libn.
NORTHEASTERN ILLINOIS UNIVERSITY -
LIBRARY □ Chicago, IL
Black, Thomas S., Div.Hd.
QUEENS BOROUGH PUBLIC LIBRARY -
LANGUAGE & LITERATURE DIVISION □
Jamaica, NY
Black, Valerie, Lib.Techn.
U.S. NATL. PARK SERVICE - YELLOWSTONE
LIBRARY AND MUSEUM ASSOCIATION □
Yellowstone National Park, WY
Blackbeard, Bill, Dir.
SAN FRANCISCO ACADEMY OF COMIC ART -
LIBRARY □ San Francisco, CA
Blackburn, A.S.T., Libn.
MARQUANDIA SOCIETY FOR STUDIES IN
HISTORY AND LITERATURE - LIBRARY □ Santa
Ana, CA

Blackburn, Frank M., Univ.Libn.
WEST TEXAS STATE UNIVERSITY - CORNETTE
LIBRARY □ Canyon, TX
Blackburn, Joy M., Libn.
WASHINGTON NATIONAL INSURANCE
COMPANY - INFORMATION RESOURCES
CENTER □ Evanston, IL
Blackburn, Linda, Ref.Libn.
GEORGETOWN UNIVERSITY - MEDICAL
CENTER - DAHLGREN MEMORIAL LIBRARY □
Washington, DC
Blackburn, Marie, Asst.Dir.
JACKSON COUNTY HISTORICAL SOCIETY -
RESEARCH LIBRARY & ARCHIVES □
Independence, MO
Blackford, James, Lib.Adm.
EL DORADO COUNTY LAW LIBRARY □
Placerville, CA
Blackstock, Dicksie C., Tech.Info.Mgr.
OCCIDENTAL RESEARCH CORPORATION -
TECHNICAL INFORMATION CENTER □ Irvine,
CA
Blackston, Jeanette, Lib.Serv.Adm.
METROPOLITAN PITTSBURGH PUBLIC
BROADCASTING, INC. - WQED LIBRARY □
Pittsburgh, PA
Blacquiere, Mrs. F., Sys.Libn.
CANADA - HEALTH AND WELFARE CANADA -
DEPARTMENTAL LIBRARY SERVICES □ Ottawa,
ON
Blain, Alice, Dir.
QUEBEC PROVINCE - OFFICE DES
COMMUNICATIONS SOCIALES - BIBLIOTHEQUE
□ Montreal, PQ
Blain-Juneau, Jocelyne, Chf.Libn.
CENTRE HOSPITALIER COTE-DES-NEIGES -
CENTRE DE DOCUMENTATION □ Montreal, PQ
Blain-Juneau, Jocelyne, Chf.Libn.
CENTRE HOSPITALIER JACQUES-VIGER -
BIBLIOTHEQUE MEDICALE □ Montreal, PQ
Blaine, Martha Royce, Hd.Archv.
OKLAHOMA HISTORICAL SOCIETY - DIVISION
OF LIBRARY RESOURCES □ Oklahoma City, OK
Blaine, Miles, Lib.Asst.
SAN DIEGO AERO-SPACE MUSEUM - N. PAUL
WHITTIER HISTORICAL AVIATION LIBRARY □
San Diego, CA
Blair, Beverlee A., Lib.Asst.
LEWIS (Elma) SCHOOL OF FINE ARTS -
LIBRARY† □ Dorchester, MA
Blair, Holley M., Asst. Law Libn.
WEST VIRGINIA UNIVERSITY - LAW LIBRARY
□ Morgantown, WV
Blair, John, Comp. Applications Libn.
TEXAS A & M UNIVERSITY - MEDICAL
SCIENCES LIBRARY □ College Station, TX
Blair, Marva, Asst.Libn.
AMERICAN EXPRESS COMPANY - SYSTEMS
LIBRARY □ Fort Lauderdale, FL
Blair, Rebecca, Pub.Serv.
HARVARD UNIVERSITY - DIVINITY SCHOOL -
ANDOVER-HARVARD THEOLOGICAL LIBRARY □
Cambridge, MA
Blair, Ruth, Mss.Cat.
CONNECTICUT HISTORICAL SOCIETY -
LIBRARY □ Hartford, CT
Blais, Pierre-Paul, Dir.
QUEBEC PROVINCE - MINISTERE DU REVENU -
BIBLIOTHEQUE □ Ste. Foy, PQ
Blaisdell, Dr. Doris, Assoc.Archv.
TEXAS TECH UNIVERSITY - SOUTHWEST
COLLECTION □ Lubbock, TX
Blaisdell, Robert, Govt.Doc.Libn.
WESTERN CONNECTICUT STATE COLLEGE -
RUTH A. HAAS LIBRARY □ Danbury, CT
Blaise, Sue Ann, Hd.Libn.
UNIVERSITY OF CALIFORNIA, SAN DIEGO -
MEDICAL CENTER LIBRARY □ San Diego, CA
Blake, Carol A., Asst.Libn.
PENNSYLVANIA STATE - LEGISLATIVE
REFERENCE BUREAU LIBRARY □ Harrisburg, PA

Blake, Deloris, Med.Libn.
BAPTIST HOSPITAL OF SOUTHEAST TEXAS -
MEDICAL LIBRARY □ Beaumont, TX
Blake, E. Sue., Libn.
GREATER LOS ANGELES ZOO ASSOCIATION -
ANDREW NORMAN EDUCATION CENTER □ Los
Angeles, CA
Blake, Martha A., Libn.
U.S. ARMY - CONSTRUCTION ENGINEERING
RESEARCH LABORATORY - H.B. ZACKRISON
MEMORIAL LIBRARY □ Champaign, IL
Blake, William R., Transl.
PHILLIPS PETROLEUM COMPANY - RESEARCH &
DEVELOPMENT DEPARTMENT - TECHNICAL
INFORMATION BRANCH □ Bartlesville, OK
Blakeley, Mary Lloyd, Hd. Map Libn.
UNIVERSITY OF ARIZONA - MAP COLLECTION
□ Tucson, AZ
Blalock, Mary Beth, Hd., Lib.Sci./Curric.Lab.
VANDERBILT UNIVERSITY LIBRARY -
EDUCATION LIBRARY □ Nashville, TN
Blanchard, Mary Gene, Libn.
CH2M HILL SOUTHEAST, INC. - INFORMATION
CENTER □ Gainesville, FL
Blanchard, Patricia A., Libn.
EDMUNDSON (Jennie) MEMORIAL HOSPITAL -
LIBRARY □ Council Bluffs, IA
Blanco, Jean, Cur./Cat.
UNIVERSITY OF PITTSBURGH - SPECIAL
COLLECTIONS DEPARTMENT □ Pittsburgh, PA
Bland, Catherine V., Dir., Lib.Serv.
VIRGINIA STATE UNIVERSITY - JOHNSTON
MEMORIAL LIBRARY □ Petersburg, VA
Bland, Donald G., Biologist Aide
ALABAMA STATE DEPARTMENT OF
CONSERVATION & NATURAL RESOURCES -
ALABAMA MARINE RESOURCES LAB. - LIBRARY
□ Dauphin Island, AL
Bland, G., Libn.
NORTH AMERICAN RADIO ARCHIVES (NARA) -
LENDING LIBRARY □ Reno, NV
Bland, Janet, Hd. Order Libn.
ARKANSAS STATE UNIVERSITY - DEAN B.
ELLIS LIBRARY □ State University, AR
Bland, Larry, Ed.
MARSHALL (George C.) RESEARCH
FOUNDATION - GEORGE C. MARSHALL
RESEARCH LIBRARY □ Lexington, VA
Bland, S., Tape Libn.
NORTH AMERICAN RADIO ARCHIVES (NARA) -
LENDING LIBRARY □ Reno, NV
Blandamer, Ann, Asst.Libn.
FOSTER ASSOCIATES, INC. - LIBRARY □
Washington, DC
Blanding, Sylvia J., Libn.
KANSAS STATE UNIVERSITY - RESOURCES ON
DEVELOPING COUNTRIES □ Manhattan, KS
Blandy, Susan, Ref.Libn.
HUDSON VALLEY COMMUNITY COLLEGE -
DWIGHT MARVIN LEARNING RESOURCES
CENTER □ Troy, NY
Blanton, Michael M., Chf.Libn.
U.S. VETERANS ADMINISTRATION (NC-Durham)
- MEDICAL CENTER LIBRARY □ Durham, NC
Blasband, David, Archv.
AMERICAN COLLEGE OF ORGONOMY, INC. -
LIBRARY □ New York, NY
Blaschak, M., Ref. & Cat.Libn.
BENDIX CORPORATION CENTER - LIBRARY □
Southfield, MI
Blase, Nancy G., Asst.Libn.
UNIVERSITY OF WASHINGTON - NATURAL
SCIENCES LIBRARY □ Seattle, WA
Blaser, Clare, Libn.
WEBSTER & SHEFFIELD - LIBRARY □ New York,
NY
Blaser, Kathleen, Libn.
ST. NICHOLAS HOSPITAL - HEALTH SCIENCES
LIBRARY □ Sheboygan, WI
Blasingame, Karen, Act.Clghse.Dir.
NATIONAL CLEARINGHOUSE FOR LEGAL
SERVICES - LIBRARY □ Chicago, IL

Blaskevica, Susan, Ref.Libn.
OHIO UNIVERSITY - HEALTH SCIENCES
LIBRARY □ Athens, OH
Blatecky, Barbara, Asst.Libn.
NATIONAL DAIRY COUNCIL - LIBRARY □
Rosemont, IL
Blatt, Jeannette, Asst.Libn.
JEWISH PUBLIC LIBRARY OF TORONTO □
Toronto, ON
Blattner, Julie M., Libn.
HARVARD UNIVERSITY - CENTER FOR MIDDLE
EASTERN STUDIES - LIBRARY □ Cambridge, MA
Blattner, Julie M., Libn.
HARVARD UNIVERSITY - INSTITUTE FOR
INTERNATIONAL DEVELOPMENT - LIBRARY □
Cambridge, MA
Blauer, Katherine, Asst.Libn.
GPU NUCLEAR - TMI TECHNICAL LIBRARY □
Middletown, PA
Blauet, Doris M., Libn.
FLINT OSTEOPATHIC HOSPITAL - DR. E.
HERZOG MEMORIAL MEDICAL LIBRARY □ Flint,
MI
Blaylock, James C., Libn.
BAPTIST MISSIONARY ASSOCIATION
THEOLOGICAL SEMINARY - KELLAR LIBRARY □
Jacksonville, TX
Blazer, Shirley C., Patent Coord.
GREYHOUND CORPORATION - PATENT LAW
DEPARTMENT LIBRARY □ Scottsdale, AZ
Blazina, Vesna, Libn.
UNIVERSITE DE MONTREAL - BIOLOGIE-
BIBLIOTHEQUE □ Montreal, PQ
Blechman, Burton M., Ref.Asst.
NEW YORK UNIVERSITY MEDICAL CENTER -
FREDERICK L. EHRMAN MEDICAL LIBRARY □
New York, NY
Bleecker, Constance, Libn./Archv.
WHALING MUSEUM SOCIETY, INC. - LIBRARY □
Cold Spring Harbor, NY
Bleecker, Ruth M., Cur. of Music
BOSTON PUBLIC LIBRARY - MUSIC
DEPARTMENT □ Boston, MA
Blenkhorn, Patricia J., Libn.
NEW BRUNSWICK TELEPHONE COMPANY, LTD.
- EDUCATIONAL LIBRARY □ Saint John, NB
Blenkush, Sharon, Cat.
OHIO NORTHERN UNIVERSITY - HETERICK
MEMORIAL LIBRARY □ Ada, OH
Blevins, Donald L., Libn.
U.S.D.A. - AGRICULTURAL RESEARCH SERVICE
- NORTHERN REGIONALRESEARCH CENTER
LIBRARY □ Peoria, IL
Blevins, Elliott, Asst.Libn.
GENERAL DYNAMICS CORPORATION - PUBLIC
AFFAIRS LIBRARY □ St. Louis, MO
Blewer, Sondra, Libn.
CENTER FOR THE STUDY OF THE PRESIDENCY
- LIBRARY □ New York, NY
Blinks, Doris, Lib.Supv.
OLMSTED COUNTY HISTORICAL SOCIETY -
LIBRARY AND ARCHIVES □ Rochester, MN
Bliss, Carey S., Cur. Rare Books
HUNTINGTON (Henry E.) LIBRARY, ART
GALLERY AND BOTANICAL GARDENS □ San
Marino, CA
Blixrud, Julia, OCLC Coord.
MINITEX □ Minneapolis, MN
Bloch, Judy, Cat.
INTERNATIONAL MUSEUM OF PHOTOGRAPHY
AT GEORGE EASTMAN HOUSE - LIBRARY □
Rochester, NY
Bloch, Maxene, Libn.
MINNEAPOLIS PUBLIC LIBRARY &
INFORMATION CENTER - BUSINESS AND
SCIENCE DEPARTMENT □ Minneapolis, MN
Blocher, Joan, Asst.Libn.
CHICAGO THEOLOGICAL SEMINARY -
HAMMOND LIBRARY □ Chicago, IL
Block, Eleanor, Hd.Libn.
OHIO STATE UNIVERSITY - JOURNALISM
LIBRARY □ Columbus, OH

Block, Miryam H.
AMERICAN JEWISH JOINT DISTRIBUTION
COMMITTEE - LIBRARY† □ New York, NY
Blocker, Martha G., Hd.Libn.
INDIANAPOLIS MUSEUM OF ART - REFERENCE
LIBRARY □ Indianapolis, IN
Blome, L.E., Doc. Control
TRW, INC. - DEFENSE & SPACE SYSTEMS
GROUP - TECHNICAL INFORMATION CENTER □
Redondo Beach, CA
Blommel, Henry H., Collector-Dir.
BLOMMEL HISTORIC AUTOMOTIVE DATA
COLLECTION - LIBRARY AND INFORMATION
CENTER □ Connersville, IN
Blomquist, Laura, Hd.Libn.
OHIO STATE UNIVERSITY - EDUCATION
LIBRARY □ Columbus, OH
Blomstrann, Lois L., Asst. to Dir.
NEW BRITAIN MUSEUM OF AMERICAN ART -
LIBRARY □ New Britain, CT
Blonde, Joseph, Ref.Libn.
FRASER-HICKSON INSTITUTE, MONTREAL -
FREE LIBRARY □ Montreal, PQ
Blondell, Lila, Film Lib.Mgr.
INDUSTRIAL MANAGEMENT SOCIETY - FILM
LIBRARY □ Des Plaines, IL
BloomBecker, Jay J., Dir.
NATIONAL CENTER FOR COMPUTER CRIME
DATA □ Los Angeles, CA
Bloomer, Jerry M., Libn.
NORTON (R.W.) ART GALLERY - REFERENCE-
RESEARCH LIBRARY □ Shreveport, LA
Bloomfield, Mr. Masse, Supv.
HUGHES AIRCRAFT COMPANY - TECHNICAL
LIBRARY □ Culver City, CA
Bloomgarden, Judy, Tech.Serv.Libn.
YALE UNIVERSITY - ART AND ARCHITECTURE
LIBRARY □ New Haven, CT
Bloomsburgh, Esther, Libn.
TEMPLE UNIVERSITY - CENTRAL LIBRARY
SYSTEM - AMBLER CAMPUS LIBRARY □ Ambler,
PA
Bloomstein, Carole, Gen.Libn.
BUREAU OF JEWISH EDUCATION - JEWISH
COMMUNITY LIBRARY □ San Francisco, CA
Blosmo, Lois, Cat.
BLACK HILLS STATE COLLEGE - E.Y. BERRY
LIBRARY-LEARNING CENTER □ Spearfish, SD
Blosser, Patricia, Assoc.Dir.
ERIC CLEARINGHOUSE FOR SCIENCE,
MATHEMATICS AND ENVIRONMENTAL
EDUCATION □ Columbus, OH
Blouch, Rev. Herbert R., Conf.Hist.
EVANGELICAL UNITED BRETHREN CHURCH -
HISTORICAL SOCIETY OF THE EASTERN
CONFERENCE - ARCHIVES ROOM □ Annville, PA
Blough, Keith, Asst. Law Libn.
CINCINNATI LAW LIBRARY ASSOCIATION □
Cincinnati, OH
Blouin, A.W.O., Hd. Field Serv.
CANADA - EMPLOYMENT & IMMIGRATION
CANADA - LIBRARY □ Ottawa, ON
Blouin, Francis, Assoc.Archv.
UNIVERSITY OF MICHIGAN - MICHIGAN
HISTORICAL COLLECTIONS - BENTLEY
HISTORICAL LIBRARY □ Ann Arbor, MI
Bluestein, Joseph C., Exec.Dir.
JEWISH COMMUNITY CENTER - LIBRARY □
Sioux City, IA
Bluestein, Patricia, Hd.Libn.
AMERICAN BANKER, INC. - LIBRARY† □ New
York, NY
Bluh, Fanny L., Adm.Asst.
UNITED CEREBRAL PALSY OF NEW YORK CITY,
INC. - LIBRARY □ New York, NY
Bluh, Pamela, Hd., Tech.Serv.
UNIVERSITY OF MARYLAND, BALTIMORE -
SCHOOL OF LAW - MARSHALL LAW LIBRARY □
Baltimore, MD
Blum, John P., Dir.
NEW MEXICO STATE SUPREME COURT - LAW
LIBRARY □ Santa Fe, NM

Blum, Phyllis R., Libn.
U.S. NAVY - NAVAL SCHOOL OF HEALTH
SCIENCES - LIBRARY □ Bethesda, MD
Blumberg, Janet, Chf.Cons.Serv.Div.
WASHINGTON STATE LIBRARY □ Olympia, WA
Blume, Peter F., Cur.
ALLENTOWN ART MUSEUM - RESEARCH
LIBRARY □ Allentown, PA
Blumenthal, Marcia, Chm., Lib.Comm.
ALL SOULS UNITARIAN CHURCH - E. BURDETTE
BACKUS LIBRARY □ Indianapolis, IN
Blums, Z.B., Transl.
HERCULES, INC. - RESEARCH CENTER -
TECHNICAL INFORMATION DIVISION □
Wilmington, DE
Blunt, Terry, Exec.Dir.
CONNECTICUT RIVER WATERSHED COUNCIL -
LIBRARY □ Easthampton, MA
Blust, Sandra, Libn.
PENNSYLVANIA STATE DEPARTMENT OF
ENVIRONMENTAL RESOURCES - BUREAU OF
TOPOGRAPHIC & GEOLOGIC SURVEY LIB. □
Harrisburg, PA
Boadt, Lawrence E., C.S.P., Libn.
ST. PAUL'S COLLEGE - LIBRARY □ Washington,
DC
Boardman, Charlotte K., Libn.
EDO CORPORATION - ENGINEERING LIBRARY □
College Point, NY
Boardman, Gerard, Res.Asst.
SOUTH STREET SEAPORT MUSEUM - LIBRARY
□ New York, NY
Boardman, June M., Supv., Lib./Files
ROSEWOOD CENTER - MEDICAL AND
PROFESSIONAL LIBRARY □ Owings Mills, MD
Boast, Carol, Act.Dir.
UNIVERSITY OF ILLINOIS - LAW LIBRARY □
Champaign, IL
Bobb, Frank W., Libn. & Cur.
GRAND LODGE OF FREE AND ACCEPTED
MASONS OF PENNSYLVANIA - LIBRARY □
Philadelphia, PA
Bobo, Jack E., Exec.V.P.
NATIONAL ASSOCIATION OF LIFE
UNDERWRITERS - LIBRARY† □ Washington, DC
Bobo, Mary, Archv.
UNIVERSITY OF LOUISVILLE - UNIVERSITY
ARCHIVES AND RECORDS CENTER - ORAL
HISTORY CENTER □ Louisville, KY
Bobrek, Nancy, Asst.Libn.
PITNEY BOWES - TECHNICAL INFORMATION
CENTER □ Stamford, CT
Bobula, Patty, Libn.
NEW HAMPSHIRE VOCATIONAL-TECHNICAL
COLLEGE - LIBRARY □ Laconia, NH
Bobvick, Mary, Chf., ADP Sect.
U.S. ARMY - ARMY LIBRARY □ Washington, DC
Bobzier, James, Supv.
HYSTER COMPANY - TECHNICAL
INFORMATION SERVICES □ Portland, OR
Boccaccio, Mary A., Hd./Univ.Archv.
UNIVERSITY OF MARYLAND, COLLEGE PARK -
LIBRARIES - ARCHIVES AND MANUSCRIPTS
DEPARTMENT □ College Park, MD
Boccetti, Louis G., Libn.
DU PONT DE NEMOURS (E.I.) & COMPANY, INC.
- DACRON RESEARCH LABORATORY -
TECHNICAL LIBRARY □ Kinston, NC
Boccieri, Kathryn A., Libn.
FRANKLIN GENERAL HOSPITAL - MEDICAL
LIBRARY □ Valley Stream, NY
Bock, Lori, Libn.
PILLSBURY COMPANY - MAIN OFFICE
MARKETING LIBRARY □ Minneapolis, MN
Bock, Rochelle, Sr.Ref.Libn.
UNIVERSITY OF CALIFORNIA, IRVINE -
BIOMEDICAL LIBRARY □ Irvine, CA
Bockelman, Sara, Libn.
FLETCHER, MAYO, ASSOCIATES, INC. -
LIBRARY □ St. Joseph, MO
Bocking, D.H., Assoc.Prov.Archv.
SASKATCHEWAN ARCHIVES BOARD □ Regina,
SK

Bockman, Marilyn M., V.P.
AMERICAN ASSOCIATION OF ADVERTISING
AGENCIES - MEMBER INFORMATION SERVICE
□ New York, NY
Bockstruck, Lloyd, Genealogy Libn.
DALLAS PUBLIC LIBRARY - HISTORY AND
SOCIAL SCIENCES DIVISION □ Dallas, TX
Bockstruck, Lloyd DeWitt, Head
DALLAS PUBLIC LIBRARY - GENEALOGY
COLLECTION □ Dallas, TX
Bodapati, R.A., Libn.
SVERDRUP & PARCEL AND ASSOCIATES, INC. -
TECHNICAL LIBRARY □ St. Louis, MO
Boddy, Michael P., Acq.
ASBURY THEOLOGICAL SEMINARY - B.L.
FISHER LIBRARY □ Wilmore, KY
Bodem, Dennis, Dir.
BESSER (Jesse) MUSEUM - LIBRARY □ Alpena,
MI
Bodine, Christine, State Doc.Libn.
RUTGERS UNIVERSITY, THE STATE
UNIVERSITY OF NEW JERSEY - JUSTICE
HENRY ACKERSON LIBRARY OF LAW &
CRIMINAL JUSTICE □ Newark, NJ
Bodine, Jean, Hd. of Files
TIME, INC. - LIBRARY □ New York, NY
Bodley, Margaret J., Dir.
NATIONAL COUNCIL ON FAMILY RELATIONS -
FAMILY RESOURCE & REFERRAL CENTER □
Minneapolis, MN
Bodnar, John, Dir.
INDIANA UNIVERSITY - ORAL HISTORY
RESEARCH PROJECT - LIBRARY □ Bloomington,
IN
Bodnar, Mrs. Marta, Libn.
ORTHO PHARMACEUTICAL (Canada), LTD. -
LIBRARY □ Don Mills, ON
Bodnariuk, Stefan, Supv. Film Ed.
AMERICAN CANCER SOCIETY - FILM LIBRARY
□ New York, NY
Bodoh, Lois C., Tech.Libn.
U.S. INDUSTRIAL CHEMICALS COMPANY -
TUSCOLA PLANT TECHNICAL LIBRARY AND
INFORMATION CENTER □ Tuscola, IL
Boede, Carol, Cat.
MORAINE PARK TECHNICAL INSTITUTE -
LEARNING RESOURCE CENTER □ Fond Du Lac,
WI
Boeder, Thelma, Archv./Exec.Dir.
UNITED METHODIST COMMN. ON ARCHIVES &
HIST. - MINNESOTA ANNUAL CONFERENCE -
ARCHIVES & HISTORICAL LIB. □ Minneapolis,
MN
Boegehold, Julie, Hd. of Pub.Serv.
PROVIDENCE ATHENAEUM - LIBRARY □
Providence, RI
Boehler, Kathleen, Order Libn.
INCO METALS COMPANY - BUSINESS LIBRARY
□ Toronto, ON
Boehm, Joanne, Libn.
REFORMED BIBLE COLLEGE - LIBRARY □ Grand
Rapids, MI
Boen, Daniel K.L., Cat.Libn.
UNIVERSITY OF WINDSOR - PAUL MARTIN
LAW LIBRARY □ Windsor, ON
Boer, Aileen C., Libn.
FEDERAL RESERVE BANK OF PHILADELPHIA -
LIBRARY □ Philadelphia, PA
Boeringer, James, Dir.
MORAVIAN MUSIC FOUNDATION, INC. -
LIBRARY □ Winston-Salem, NC
Boersema, Sally A., Lib.Ck.
MICHIGAN STATE UNIVERSITY - MICROFORMS
DIVISION □ East Lansing, MI
Boettcher, Glenn R., Dir.Libn.
PORTLAND STATE UNIVERSITY - COMMUNITY
SERVICES UNIT - CONTINUING EDUCATION
FILM LIBRARY □ Portland, OR
Boettcher, Ursula S., Libn.
MIDDLETOWN HOSPITAL ASSOCIATION - ADA
I. LEONARD MEMORIAL LIBRARY □ Middletown,
OH

Boevingloh, Vicki, Info.Spec.
SYNTEX, U.S.A. - CORPORATE LIBRARY/
INFORMATION SERVICES □ Palo Alto, CA
Bogan, Mary E., Spec.Coll.Libn.
EMPORIA STATE UNIVERSITY - WILLIAM
ALLEN WHITE LIBRARY - SPECIAL
COLLECTIONS □ Emporia, KS
Bogen, Betty, Chf., Lib.Serv.
U.S. VETERANS ADMINISTRATION (OH-Dayton)
- CENTER LIBRARY □ Dayton, OH
Bogen, Mitchell A., Libn.
METROPOLITAN HOSPITAL CENTER - DRAPER
HALL LIBRARY† □ New York, NY
Boggess, Jennylind C., Staff Libn.
U.S. NATL. INSTITUTES OF HEALTH - LIBRARY
□ Bethesda, MD
Boggess, John, Libn.
U.S. NASA - GODDARD SPACE FLIGHT CENTER
- LIBRARY† □ Greenbelt, MD
Bogie, Thomas M., Hd.
DALLAS PUBLIC LIBRARY - HISTORY AND
SOCIAL SCIENCES DIVISION □ Dallas, TX
Bogin, Fred, Ref./Acq.Libn.
BAECK (Leo) INSTITUTE - LIBRARY □ New York,
NY
Bognar, Dorothy McAdoo, Libn.
UNIVERSITY OF CONNECTICUT - MUSIC
LIBRARY □ Storrs, CT
Bogue, Annette G., Tech.Serv.
AMOCO INTERNATIONAL OIL COMPANY -
LIBRARY INFORMATION CENTER □ Houston, TX
Bogus, Elaine E., Info.Spec.
WESTINGHOUSE ELECTRIC CORPORATION -
NUCLEAR ENERGY SYSTEMS - INFORMATION
RESOURCES† □ Pittsburgh, PA
Bohack, Marge, Hd.Libn.
WICHITA GENERAL HOSPITAL - MEDICAL
LIBRARY □ Wichita Falls, TX
Bohall, William, Info.Spec.
MUSCATATUCK STATE HOSPITAL & TRAINING
CENTER - RESIDENT AND STAFF
DEVELOPMENT LIBRARY □ Butlerville, IN
Bohem, Hilda, Pub.Serv.Libn.
UNIVERSITY OF CALIFORNIA, LOS ANGELES -
DEPARTMENT OF SPECIAL COLLECTIONS □ Los
Angeles, CA
Bohlen, Jeanne, Dir.
FOUNDATION CENTER - CLEVELAND - KENT H.
SMITH LIBRARY □ Cleveland, OH
Bohley, Ronald, Libn.
UNIVERSITY OF MISSOURI, ROLLA - CURTIS
LAWS WILSON LIBRARY □ Rolla, MO
Bohley, Wilferd W., Archv.
EVANGELICAL AND REFORMED HISTORICAL
SOCIETY - EDEN ARCHIVES □ Webster Groves,
MO
Bohling, Raymond, Engr.Libn.
UNIVERSITY OF MINNESOTA - ENGINEERING
LIBRARY □ Minneapolis, MN
Bohne, Jean, Libn.
UNIVERSITY OF TORONTO - FACULTY OF
FORESTRY LIBRARY □ Toronto, ON
Bohr, Richard, Dir.
MIDWEST CHINA STUDY RESOURCE CENTER □
St. Paul, MN
Boilard, David W., Assoc.Dir.
UNIVERSITY OF SOUTH DAKOTA - CHRISTIAN
P. LOMMEN HEALTH SCIENCES LIBRARY □
Vermillion, SD
Boisvert, Danielle, Ref.Libn.
UNIVERSITE DU QUEBEC A HULL -
BIBLIOTHEQUE □ Hull, PQ
Boisvert, Donald J., Libn.
RHODE ISLAND STATE DEPARTMENT OF
COMMUNITY AFFAIRS - REFERENCE LIBRARY □
Providence, RI
Boisvert, Michel, Hd. of Ref.Serv.
RADIO QUEBEC - CENTRE DES RESSOURCES
DOCUMENTAIRES □ Montreal, PQ
Boite, Mary, Libn.
REGISTERED NURSES' ASSOCIATION OF
ONTARIO - LIBRARY □ Toronto, ON

Bolan, Suzanne, Dir.
ROSENBACH MUSEUM & LIBRARY† □
Philadelphia, PA

Boland, Miriam, Lib.Dir.
GEORGIA STATE DEPARTMENT OF HUMAN
RESOURCES - LIBRARY □ Atlanta, GA

Bolanos, Marie K., Dir.
ST. JOHN HOSPITAL - MEDICAL LIBRARY □
Detroit, MI

Bolas, Deborah W., Assoc.Libn.
MISSOURI HISTORICAL SOCIETY - RESEARCH
LIBRARY □ St. Louis, MO

Bolce, Frederica, Ref.Libn.
CLEVELAND HEALTH SCIENCES LIBRARY -
ALLEN MEMORIAL LIBRARY □ Cleveland, OH

Bolden, C.E., State Law Libn.
WASHINGTON STATE LAW LIBRARY □ Olympia,
WA

Bolden, Elizabeth C., Libn.
U.S. ARMY HOSPITALS - MADIGAN ARMY
MEDICAL CENTER - MEDICAL LIBRARY □
Tacoma, WA

Bolden, M. Scott, Asst.Libn.
NATIONAL GEOGRAPHIC SOCIETY -
ILLUSTRATIONS LIBRARY □ Washington, DC

Boldrick, S.J., Libn.
MIAMI-DADE PUBLIC LIBRARY - FLORIDA
COLLECTION □ Miami, FL

Bolduc, Estelle, Sec.
SEMINAIRE DE CHICOUTIMI - BIBLIOTHEQUE
□ Chicoutimi, PQ

Bolef, Doris, Dir.
RUSH UNIVERSITY AND MEDICAL CENTER -
LIBRARY □ Chicago, IL

Boles, Janice, Asst.Libn.
ERNST & WHINNEY - NATIONAL OFFICE
LIBRARY □ Cleveland, OH

Bolf, Marjorie, Resource Teacher
OREGON STATE SCHOOL FOR THE DEAF -
LIBRARY □ Salem, OR

Bolin, Nancy, Dir. Resource Serv.
CAMBRIDGE MENTAL HEALTH &
DEVELOPMENTAL CENTER - STAFF &
RESIDENT RESOURCE CENTER □ Cambridge, OH

Bolles, Charles, State Libn.
IDAHO STATE LIBRARY □ Boise, ID

Bolles, Shirley W., Libn.
RUTGERS UNIVERSITY, THE STATE
UNIVERSITY OF NEW JERSEY - LIBRARY OF
SCIENCE & MEDICINE □ Piscataway, NJ

Bollier, John, Pub.Serv.Libn.
YALE UNIVERSITY - DIVINITY SCHOOL
LIBRARY □ New Haven, CT

Bollinger, Thomas W., AV Coord.
NATIONAL COLLEGE OF CHIROPRACTIC -
LEARNING RESOURCE CENTER □ Lombard, IL

Bolshaw, Cynthia, Slide Libn.
WORCESTER ART MUSEUM - LIBRARY □
Worcester, MA

Bolstad, Bethel, Libn.
GREAT FALLS CLINIC - MEDICAL LIBRARY† □
Great Falls, MT

Bolster, Edward H., Pres.
CANTON HISTORICAL SOCIETY - LIBRARY† □
Canton, MA

Bolton, Barbara G., Libn.
DOMTAR, INC. - RESEARCH CENTRE LIBRARY □
Ste. Anne de Bellevue PQ

Bolton, Beth, Adm.Asst.
FOUNDATION FOR PUBLIC AFFAIRS -
RESOURCE CENTER □ Washington, DC

Bolton, Emily, Pub.Info.Asst.
U.S. NATL. PARK SERVICE - MIDWEST
REGIONAL OFFICE LIBRARY □ Omaha, NE

Bomar, Barbara R., Info.Mgr.
NATIONAL CRIME PREVENTION INSTITUTE -
INFORMATION CENTER □ Louisville, KY

Bomgardner, Barbara-Ann, Base Libn.
U.S. AIR FORCE BASE - MC GUIRE BASE
LIBRARY □ McGuire AFB, NJ

Bomgardner, Martha, Libn.
U.S. DEPT. OF JUSTICE - UNITED STATES
ATTORNEY, DISTRICT OF NEW JERSEY - LAW
LIBRARY □ Newark, NJ

Bommicino, Patricia
U.S. DEPT. OF LABOR - BUREAU OF LABOR
STATISTICS - INFORMATION AND ADVISORY
SECTION □ New York, NY

Bonacorda, James, Tax Libn.
WHITE AND CASE - LIBRARY □ New York, NY

Bonati, Christine S., Libn.
CONVALESCENT HOSPITAL FOR CHILDREN -
LIBRARY □ Rochester, NY

Bonchard, Charlotte, Bibliotechnicienne
QUEBEC PROVINCE - OFFICE DE
PLANIFICATION ET DE DEVELOPPEMENT DU
QUEBEC - BIBLIOTHEQUE □ Quebec, PQ

Bond, Beverly, Cat./Ser.
WEST LIBERTY STATE COLLEGE - ELBIN
LIBRARY □ West Liberty, WV

Bond, Marvin A., Chf., Res.Dev.
U.S. NATL. BUREAU OF STANDARDS - LIBRARY
□ Washington, DC

Bond, Mary, Libn.
COORS (Adolph) COMPANY - TECHNICAL
LIBRARY □ Golden, CO

Bond, Randall, Art Biblog.
SYRACUSE UNIVERSITY - E.S. BIRD LIBRARY -
FINE ARTS DEPARTMENT □ Syracuse, NY

Bond, William H., Libn.
HARVARD UNIVERSITY - HOUGHTON LIBRARY
□ Cambridge, MA

Bondarovich, Mary F., Mgr., Tech.Info.Ctr.
BRISTOL-MYERS PRODUCTS - TECHNICAL
INFORMATION CENTER □ Hillside, NJ

Bonds, Evan, Music Libn.
UNIVERSITY OF VIRGINIA - MUSIC LIBRARY □
Charlottesville, VA

Boner, Marian O., Dir.
TEXAS STATE LAW LIBRARY □ Austin, TX

Bonge, Barbara, Rd.Serv.Libn.
COOLEY (Thomas M.) LAW SCHOOL - LIBRARY □
Lansing, MI

Bongiorno, Mary E., Sr.Info.Spec.
AIR PRODUCTS AND CHEMICALS, INC. -
HOUDRY LABORATORIES - INFORMATION
SERVICES □ Marcus Hook, PA

Bonham, Miriam, Asst.Hd., Chem.Lib.
INDIANA UNIVERSITY - CHEMISTRY LIBRARY
□ Bloomington, IN

Bonhomme, Mary S., Mgr., Info./Commun.
CABOT CORPORATION - TECHNICAL
INFORMATION CENTER □ Kokomo, IN

Boni-Awotwi, Sekum, Asst.Libn.
HOWARD UNIVERSITY - HEALTH SCIENCES
LIBRARY □ Washington, DC

Bonin, Claude-Andre, Chf.Libn.
HYDRO-QUEBEC - BIBLIOTHEQUE □ Montreal,
PQ

Bonin, Lionel, Libn.
LAURENTIAN UNIVERSITY - SCHOOL OF
EDUCATION - LIBRARY □ Sudbury, ON

Bonin, Roger, Dir.
ECOLE POLYTECHNIQUE - BIBLIOTHEQUE □
Montreal, PQ

Bonis, Eva M., Res.Libn.
DENNISON MANUFACTURING COMPANY -
RESEARCH LIBRARY □ Framingham, MA

Bonn, Marie Jean, Supv.Libn.
EASTMAN KODAK COMPANY - KODAK
APPARATUS DIVISION - LIBRARY □ Rochester,
NY

Bonn, Thomas, Media Libn.
SUNY - COLLEGE AT CORTLAND - MEMORIAL
LIBRARY □ Cortland, NY

Bonnaffon, Anne, Med.Libn.
U.S. ARMY HOSPITALS - WALSON ARMY
HOSPITAL - MEDICAL LIBRARY □ Ft. Dix, NJ

Bonnelly, Claude, Dir. Adjoint
UNIVERSITE LAVAL - BIBLIOTHEQUE† □ Ste.
Foy, PQ

Bonner, Carol, V.P.
AIRCRAFT TECHNICAL PUBLISHERS - LIBRARY
□ San Francisco, CA

Bonner, Jean, Hospital Libn.
COMMUNITY HOSPITAL OF INDIANAPOLIS,
INC. - LIBRARY □ Indianapolis, IN

Bonner, Robert J., Dir. of Libs.
INDIANA UNIVERSITY/PURDUE UNIVERSITY
AT INDIANAPOLIS - UNIVERSITY LIBRARY □
Indianapolis, IN

Bonner, Sandra J., Dir. of Lib.Serv.
RECORDING FOR THE BLIND, INC. - MASTER
TAPE LIBRARY □ New York, NY

Bonner-Johnson, Patricia, Cat.Libn.
GONZAGA UNIVERSITY SCHOOL OF LAW -
LIBRARY □ Spokane, WA

Bonney, Ms. Frances, Libn.
CANADA - SCIENCE COUNCIL OF CANADA -
LIBRARY □ Ottawa, ON

Bonniwell, Cora
DELAWARE STATE OFFICE OF MANAGEMENT,
BUDGET & PLANNING - TECHNICAL LIBRARY □
Dover, DE

Bonomolo, Joan S., Asst.Libn.
BALTIMORE GAS AND ELECTRIC COMPANY -
LIBRARY □ Baltimore, MD

Bonsor, Nelda, Lib.Asst.
BRITISH COLUMBIA - MINISTRY OF HEALTH -
LIBRARY □ Victoria, BC

Bonthuis, Deborah, Ref.Libn.
BUENA VISTA COLLEGE - L.E. & E.L. BALLOU
LIBRARY □ Storm Lake, IA

Bontrager, Robert, Media Spec.
OREGON STATE SCHOOL FOR THE DEAF -
LIBRARY □ Salem, OR

Bonura, Larry S., Dir.
BIKELIBRARY □ Emporia, KS

Bonynge, Jeanne R., Libn.
U.S. TAX COURT - LIBRARY □ Washington, DC

Booher, Harold H., Libn.
EPISCOPAL THEOLOGICAL SEMINARY OF THE
SOUTHWEST - LIBRARY □ Austin, TX

Booher, Patricia M., Circ.Libn.
EPISCOPAL THEOLOGICAL SEMINARY OF THE
SOUTHWEST - LIBRARY □ Austin, TX

Booker, Nell, Libn.
BUTLER, BINION, RICE, COOK, & KNAPP - LAW
LIBRARY □ Houston, TX

Booker, Robert C., Supv.
MINNEAPOLIS INSTITUTE OF ARTS - ARTS
RESOURCE AND INFORMATION CENTER □
Minneapolis, MN

Booker, Susan, Tech.Serv.Libn.
MIDWESTERN BAPTIST THEOLOGICAL
SEMINARY - LIBRARY □ Kansas City, MO

Bookhout, Dr. Theodore A., Unit Leader
OHIO STATE UNIVERSITY - OHIO
COOPERATIVE WILDLIFE RESEARCH UNIT -
LIBRARY □ Columbus, OH

Bookmyer, Jane, Supv.
PPG INDUSTRIES, INC. - GLASS RESEARCH
CENTER - INFORMATION SERVICES □
Pittsburgh, PA

Boomgaarden, Wesley L., Hd., Circ.
MACALESTER COLLEGE - WEYERHAEUSER
LIBRARY □ St. Paul, MN

Boone, Beatrice, Visual Info.Spec.
U.S. FISH & WILDLIFE SERVICE - OFFICE OF
AUDIO-VISUAL - LIBRARY □ Washington, DC

Boone, Beth A., Libn.
UNIVERSITY OF NORTH CAROLINA, CHAPEL
HILL - HIGHWAY SAFETY RESEARCH CENTER -
LIBRARY □ Chapel Hill, NC

Boone, Mrs. Daniel
BOB JONES UNIVERSITY - CHURCH
MINISTRIES RESOURCE LAB □ Greenville, SC

Boone, Deborah, Libn.
ST. ELIZABETH HOSPITAL - HEALTH SCIENCES
LIBRARY □ Beaumont, TX

Boone, E.J., Archv.
MAC ARTHUR (General Douglas) MEMORIAL -
LIBRARY AND ARCHIVES □ Norfolk, VA

Boone, Emory, Libn.
U.S. VETERANS ADMINISTRATION (TN-Johnson City) - HOSPITAL LIBRARY □ Mountain Home, TN

Boone, Susan L., Cur.
SMITH COLLEGE - SOPHIA SMITH COLLECTION - WOMEN'S HISTORY ARCHIVE □ Northampton, MA

Boord, Kathryn, Cur. of Educ.
STUDENTS' MUSEUM, INC. - LIBRARY □ Knoxville, TN

Boorkman, Jo Anne, Asst.Dir., Pub.Serv.
UNIVERSITY OF NORTH CAROLINA, CHAPEL HILL - HEALTH SCIENCES LIBRARY □ Chapel Hill, NC

Booth, Helen, Libn.
ATOMIC ENERGY CONTROL BOARD - LIBRARY □ Ottawa, ON

Booth, Larry, Photo Archv.
SAN DIEGO HISTORICAL SOCIETY - PHOTOGRAPH ARCHIVES □ San Diego, CA

Booth, Lois, Ref.Libn.
U.S. ARMY POST - FORT BENNING - RECREATION SERVICES LIBRARY BRANCH □ Ft. Benning, GA

Booth, Phebe B., Libn.
WAUKEGAN HISTORICAL SOCIETY - JOHN RAYMOND MEMORIAL LIBRARY □ Waukegan, IL

Booth, Tom, Sys.Oper.Mgr.
DIGITAL EQUIPMENT CORPORATION - CORPORATE LIBRARY □ Maynard, MA

Booz, Cindy, Cat.Libn.
BETHANY AND NORTHERN BAPTIST THEOLOGICAL SEMINARIES - LIBRARY □ Oak Brook, IL

Boozer, Mary, Circ.
PRAIRIE VIEW A & M COLLEGE OF TEXAS - W.R. BANKS LIBRARY □ Prairie View, TX

Bopp, Richard, Project Libn.
UNIVERSITY OF ILLINOIS MEDICAL CENTER - LIBRARY OF THE HEALTH SCIENCES □ Urbana, IL

Boppert, Peter, Independent Stud.Ctr.
SOUTHERN CONNECTICUT STATE COLLEGE - H.C. BULEY LIBRARY □ New Haven, CT

Boram, Joan M., Libn.
CONSTRUCTION CONSULTANTS, INC. - LIBRARY □ Detroit, MI

Borbely, Jack, Mgr.
AMERICAN TELEPHONE & TELEGRAPH COMPANY - LONG LINES DEPARTMENT - INFORMATION RESEARCH CENTER □ Bedminster, NJ

Borchardt, Murle, Hd.Libn.
FOOTE CONE & BELDING - INFORMATION CENTER □ Chicago, IL

Borchert, Brenda L., Asst.Libn.
PENNWALT CORPORATION - LUCIDOL DIVISION - RESEARCH LIBRARY □ Buffalo, NY

Borda, Eva, Coll./Ref.Libn.
UNIVERSITY OF WESTERN ONTARIO - HEALTH SCIENCES LIBRARY □ London, ON

Borden, Ann, Exec.V.P.
NATIONAL ENERGY FOUNDATION - ENERGY REFERENCE AND RESOURCE CENTER □ New York, NY

Borden, Jeanne, Hd.Libn.
RHODE ISLAND SCHOOL OF DESIGN - LIBRARY □ Providence, RI

Borden, Marceia L., Asst. Planner
OAKLAND CITY PLANNING DEPARTMENT - LIBRARY □ Oakland, CA

Borden, Margaret, Libn.
U.S. ARMY - ELECTRONICS R & D COMMAND - TECHNICAL LIBRARY DIVISION □ Fort Monmouth, NJ

Borders, Delores, Info.Ctr.Mgr.
GARDNER ADVERTISING COMPANY - INFORMATION CENTER □ St. Louis, MO

Borders, Florence E., Sr.Archv.
AMISTAD RESEARCH CENTER - LIBRARY □ New Orleans, LA

Borders, Patrick, Ctr.Dir.
U.S. NATL. ARCHIVES & RECORDS SERVICE - FEDERAL ARCHIVES AND RECORDS CENTER, REGION 6 □ Kansas City, MO

Bordner, Ken, Dir.
FRANKLIN RESEARCH CENTER - NATIONAL SOLAR HEATING & COOLING INFO. CTR. □ Rockville, MD

Boren, Michael E., Libn.
COHEN AND URETZ - LAW LIBRARY □ Washington, DC

Borg, Anne W., Asst.Dir.
KENT MEMORIAL LIBRARY - HISTORICAL ROOM □ Suffield, CT

Borg, Joan, Libn.
FIRST PRESBYTERIAN CHURCH - THOMAS E. BOSWELL MEMORIAL LIBRARY □ Evanston, IL

Borgen, Wanda, Med.Libn.
VALLEY HOSPITAL - LIBRARY □ Ridgewood, NJ

Borger, Anna Louise, Libn.
BUTLER COUNTY HISTORICAL SOCIETY - OLIVE CLIFFORD STONE LIBRARY □ El Dorado, KS

Borgersen, Richard, Lib.Dir.
JEWISH BRAILLE INSTITUTE OF AMERICA, INC. - LIBRARY □ New York, NY

Borges, Ray, Automotive Res.
HARRAH'S AUTOMOTIVE LIBRARY □ Reno, NV

Borgeson, Earl C., Libn.
SOUTHERN METHODIST UNIVERSITY - UNDERWOOD LAW LIBRARY □ Dallas, TX

Borglund, Shirley, Hd.Libn.
STORMONT-VAIL REGIONAL MEDICAL CENTER AND SHAWNEE COUNTY MEDICAL SOCIETY - HEALTH SCIENCES LIBRARY □ Topeka, KS

Borgman, Betty, Ref.Libn.
WAYNE STATE UNIVERSITY - EDUCATION LIBRARY □ Detroit, MI

Borgmeyer, Sr. Raymond, Libn.
INCARNATE WORD HOSPITAL - MEDICAL LIBRARY □ St. Louis, MO

Boria, Marilyn, Div.Chf., Gen.Info.
CHICAGO PUBLIC LIBRARY CENTRAL LIBRARY - GENERAL INFORMATION SERVICES DIVISION- BIBLIOGRAPHIC & ILL CENTER □ Chicago, IL

Boria, Marilyn, Div.Chf.
CHICAGO PUBLIC LIBRARY CENTRAL LIBRARY - GENERAL INFORMATION SERVICES DIVISION - INFORMATION CENTER □ Chicago, IL

Boria, Marilyn, Div.Chf.
CHICAGO PUBLIC LIBRARY CENTRAL LIBRARY - GENERAL INFORMATION SERVICES DIV. - NEWSPAPERS & GEN. PERIODICALS CTR. □ Chicago, IL

Boris, Charry D., Asst.Libn.
AMAX, INC. - LIBRARY □ Greenwich, CT

Boris, Mary H., Libn.
NL BAROID PETROLEUM SERVICES - TECHNICAL LIBRARY □ Houston, TX

Boriss, Diana, Ref.Libn.
CHICAGO SUN-TIMES - EDITORIAL LIBRARY □ Chicago, IL

Borja, Beata C., Br.Lib.Supv.
FLORES (Nieves M.) MEMORIAL LIBRARY □ Agana, GU

Borner, Albert P., Libn.
DONOVAN, LEISURE, NEWTON & IRVINE - LIBRARY □ New York, NY

Bornfleth, Marcus, Hd.Info.Ctr.
SWIFT AND COMPANY - RESEARCH AND DEVELOPMENT INFORMATION CENTER □ Oak Brook, IL

Borntrager, Rev. Conrad M., O.S.M., Archv.
ORDER OF SERVANTS OF MARY - EASTERN PROVINCE LIBRARY - MORINI MEMORIAL COLLECTION □ Berwyn, IL

Borntrager, Rev. Conrad M., O.S.M., Archv.
OUR LADY OF SORROWS BASILICA - ARCHIVES □ Chicago, IL

Borock, Mrs. Freddie, Libn.
BROOKHAVEN MEMORIAL HOSPITAL - MEDICAL LIBRARY □ Patchogue, NY

Borodacz, Marusia, Libn.
ONTARIO - MINISTRY OF NATURAL RESOURCES - NATURAL RESOURCES LIBRARY □ Toronto, ON

Borodkin, Pauline, Hd. Music Libn.
MANSFIELD STATE COLLEGE - BUTLER MUSIC LIBRARY □ Mansfield, PA

Borrowman, Gerald L., Chf.
UNITED STATES SPACE EDUCATION ASSOCIATION - G.L. BORROWMAN ASTRONAUTICS LIBRARY □ Weyburn, SK

Borschell, Betty, Libn.
AMERICAN CONCRETE INSTITUTE - LIBRARY □ Detroit, MI

Borsuk, Elaine, Lib.Techn.
BUILT ENVIRONMENT COORDINATORS LIMITED - BEC INFORMATION SYSTEM (BIS) □ Toronto, ON

Borts, Dolly, Hd. of Tech.Serv.
PROVIDENCE ATHENAEUM - LIBRARY □ Providence, RI

Borys, Orest, Sr.Info.Spec.
COLONIAL PENN GROUP, INC. - INFORMATION RESEARCH CENTER □ Philadelphia, PA

Bosca, David T., Div.Chf.
CHICAGO PUBLIC LIBRARY CULTURAL CENTER - LITERATURE AND LANGUAGE DIVISION □ Chicago, IL

Bosch, Barbara, Supv. of Tech.Proc.
WASHTENAW COMMUNITY COLLEGE - LEARNING RESOURCE CENTER □ Ann Arbor, MI

Bosco, Julius C., Dir.
PHILADELPHIA COLLEGE OF BIBLE - SCOFIELD-HILL MEMORIAL LIBRARY □ Langhorne, PA

Bosco, Lillian, Libn.
IBM CORPORATION - SYSTEM COMMUNICATIONS DIVISION - SITE LIBRARY □ Kingston, NY

Boski, Marina M., Libn.
MONTREAL NEUROLOGICAL INSTITUTE - LIBRARY □ Montreal, PQ

Bosler, Lisa, Search Anl.
SUNY AT BUFFALO - HEALTH SCIENCES LIBRARY □ Buffalo, NY

Bosley, Jane M., Libn.
INSTITUTE FOR CANCER RESEARCH - LIBRARY □ Philadelphia, PA

Bosma, Elske, Libn.
ACRES CONSULTING SERVICES, LTD. - TORONTO LIBRARY □ Toronto, ON

Boss, Catherine M., Dir.
ELIZABETH GENERAL HOSPITAL & DISPENSARY - HEALTH SCIENCE LIBRARY □ Elizabeth, NJ

Boss, Lillian R., Law Libn.
SUTTER COUNTY LAW LIBRARY □ Yuba City, CA

Bossange, Hector, Dir.
MC LEAN HOSPITAL - MEDICAL LIBRARY □ Belmont, MA

Bosse, Maurice H., Dir. of Lib.Serv.
MASSACHUSETTS MARITIME ACADEMY - CAPTAIN CHARLES H. HURLEY LIBRARY □ Buzzards Bay, MA

Bossler, Kathryn C., Law Libn.
COLUMBIA GAS SYSTEM SERVICE CORPORATION - LAW LIBRARY □ Wilmington, DE

Bossong, Ken, Coord.
CITIZENS' ENERGY PROJECT, INC. - LIBRARY □ Washington, DC

Bossong, Ken, Coord.
CITIZENS' ENERGY PROJECT, INC. - PASSIVE SOLAR FOUNDATION - LIBRARY □ Washington, DC

Bostick, Sharon T., Libn.
OAKLAND UNIVERSITY - LIBRARY □ Rochester, MI

Boston, Barry E., Principal Libn.
BALTIMORE - DEPARTMENT OF LEGISLATIVE REFERENCE - LIBRARY □ Baltimore, MD

Bostwick, Elizabeth A., Libn.
HUNTINGTON GALLERIES - REFERENCE LIBRARY □ Huntington, WV

Bosveld, Harry, Park Supt.
FORT MALDEN NATIONAL HISTORIC PARK -
LIBRARY & ARCHIVES □ Amherstburg, ON
Boswell, Debbie, Lib.Coord.
VOLUNTEER/THE NATIONAL CENTER FOR
CITIZEN INVOLVEMENT - LIBRARY □ Boulder,
CO
Boswell, Roy V., Cur.
CALIFORNIA STATE UNIVERSITY, FULLERTON -
COLLECTION FOR THE HISTORY OF
CARTOGRAPHY □ Fullerton, CA
Bosworth, Lillian S., Coll.Dev./Circ.
ENVIRONMENTAL PROTECTION AGENCY -
ANDREW W. BREIDENBACH ENVIRONMENTAL
RESEARCH CTR., CINCINNATI - TECH.LIB. □
Cincinnati, OH
Botelho, John, Ref.-Transl.
U.P.E.C. CULTURAL CENTER - J.A. FREITAS
LIBRARY □ San Leandro, CA
Both, Stephanie, Libn.
MC GILL UNIVERSITY - LIBRARY SCIENCE
LIBRARY □ Montreal, PQ
Bothe, Jeane, Cur.Spec.Coll.
MUSEUM OF THE GREAT PLAINS - GREAT
PLAINS RESEARCH LIBRARY AND ARCHIVES □
Lawton, OK
Bothmer, A. James, Med.Libn.
MC KENNAN HOSPITAL - MEDICAL LIBRARY □
Sioux Falls, SD
Botnick, Rabbi Geoffery
CONGREGATION BRITH SHALOM - MORRIS P.
RADOV JEWISH CENTER LIBRARY □ Erie, PA
Bott, Audrey L., Dir. of Lib.Serv.
BUSINESS INTERNATIONAL - RESEARCH
LIBRARY □ New York, NY
Bott, Cynthia, Tech.Serv.Libn.
UNIVERSITY OF KENTUCKY - LAW LIBRARY □
Lexington, KY
Bott, Herbert, Asst. to the Coord.
COOPER UNION FOR THE ADVANCEMENT OF
SCIENCE AND ART - LIBRARY □ New York, NY
Botta, Gail, Ref. & Acq.
UNION UNIVERSITY - ALBANY MEDICAL
COLLEGE - SCHAFFER LIBRARY OF THE HEALTH
SCIENCES □ Albany, NY
Botto, Denise, Reserves
SOUTHERN CONNECTICUT STATE COLLEGE -
H.C. BULEY LIBRARY □ New Haven, CT
Bottoms, Jane R., Libn.
CHILDREN'S MEDICAL CENTER - LIBRARY □
Dayton, OH
Bottoms, Rita, Hd., Spec. Coll.
UNIVERSITY OF CALIFORNIA, SANTA CRUZ -
DEAN E. MC HENRY LIBRARY □ Santa Cruz, CA
Botts, Jean, Asst.Libn.
NORWALK HOSPITAL - R. GLEN WIGGANS
MEMORIAL LIBRARY □ Norwalk, CT
Bouchard, Helene H., Bibliotechnicienne
CENTRE HOSPITALIER COOKE - BIBLIOTHEQUE
MEDICALE ET ADMINISTRATIVE □ Trois-
Rivieres, PQ
Bouchard, Lucie, Documentaliste
UNIVERSITE DE MONTREAL - CENTRE
D'ETUDES ET DE DOCUMENTATION
EUROPEENNES □ Montreal, PQ
Bouchard, Nancy, Libn.
CHARETTE, FORTIN, HAWEY & COMPANY/
TOUCHE, ROSS & COMPANY - LIBRARY □
Montreal, PQ
Boucher, Miss B., Documentalist
ALCOHOLISM AND DRUG ADDICTION
RESEARCH FOUNDATION - LIBRARY □ Toronto,
ON
Boucher, Jean, Libn.
SHANNON & WILSON, INC. - TECHNICAL
LIBRARY □ Seattle, WA
Boucher, Mrs. L., Ref.Libn.
CONCORDIA UNIVERSITY - LOYOLA CAMPUS -
GEORGES P. VANIER LIBRARY □ Montreal, PQ
Boucher, Pauline A., Asst.Sci.Libn.
TUFTS UNIVERSITY - MATHEMATICS-PHYSICS
LIBRARY □ Medford, MA

Boucher, Pauline A., Asst.Sci.Libn.
TUFTS UNIVERSITY - ROCKWELL CHEMISTRY
LIBRARY □ Medford, MA
Boucher, Robert, Dir.
SEMINAIRE ST-ALPHONSE - BIBLIOTHEQUE □
Ste. Anne de Beaupre, PQ
Boucher, Shirley, Libn.
MISSOURI STATE CHEST HOSPITAL - MEDICAL
LIBRARY □ Mount Vernon, MO
Boudreau, Allan, Dir. & Cur.
GRAND LODGE OF NEW YORK, F. AND A.M. -
LIBRARY AND MUSEUM □ New York, NY
Boudreau, Berthe, Dir.
UNIVERSITE DE MONCTON - FACULTE DES
SCIENCES DE L'EDUCATION - CENTRE DE
RESSOURCES PEDAGOGIQUES □ Moncton, NB
Boudreau, Denis, Regional Adv.
CANADA - STATISTICS CANADA - ADVISORY
SERVICES - MONTREAL REFERENCE CENTRE □
Montreal, PQ
Boudreau, Gerald, Chf. Of Acq.Dept.
ECOLE DES HAUTES ETUDES COMMERCIALES
DE MONTREAL - BIBLIOTHEQUE □ Montreal, PQ
Boudreau, James A., Dir.
BABSON COLLEGE - HORN LIBRARY □ Babson
Park, MA
Boudreau, Richard A., Libn.
THOMAS COLLEGE - MARRINER LIBRARY □
Waterville, ME
Bougas, Stanley J., Dir.
U.S. DEPT. OF COMMERCE - DEPARTMENTAL
LIBRARY □ Washington, DC
Boulanger, Andre, Libn.
MANITOBA - CENTRE DE RESSOURCES
EDUCATIVES FRANCAISES DU MANITOBA □
Saint Boniface, MB
Boulet, Marcel, Hd.Libn.
COLLEGE UNIVERSITAIRE DE ST. BONIFACE -
BIBLIOTHEQUE UNIVERSITAIRE □ Saint-
Boniface, MB
Boulet, Mychelle, Ref.Libn.
UNIVERSITE DU QUEBEC A MONTREAL -
BIBLIOTHEQUE DES SCIENCES □ Montreal, PQ
Boulton, Earl M., Ref.Libn.
CREIGHTON UNIVERSITY - HEALTH SCIENCES
LIBRARY □ Omaha, NE
Bouniol, Eileen, Law Libn.
UNIVERSITY OF SOUTH DAKOTA - MC KUSICK
LAW LIBRARY □ Vermillion, SD
Bourassa, Lise D., Coord. AV Serv.
BIBLIOTHEQUE DE LA VILLE DE MONTREAL -
CINEMATHEQUE □ Montreal, PQ
Bourdages, Celine, Libn.
DOMINION ENGINEERING WORKS, LTD. -
LIBRARY □ Lachine, PQ
Bourdeau, Fernand, Supv., Adm.Serv.
CANADIAN BROADCASTING CORPORATION -
MUSIC SERVICES LIBRARY □ Montreal, PQ
Bourdon, Bonnie, Libn.
VERMONT INSTITUTE OF NATURAL SCIENCES
- LIBRARY □ Woodstock, VT
Bourdon, Don, Archv.
GLENBOW-ALBERTA INSTITUTE - LIBRARY &
ARCHIVES □ Calgary, AB
Bourg, Betty, Hd.Libn.
INTERNATIONAL BROTHERHOOD OF
TEAMSTERS, CHAUFFEURS, WAREHOUSEMEN
AND HELPERS OF AMERICA - RES./EDUC.
LIBRARY □ Washington, DC
Bourgeois, Miss A.E., Hd.Lib.Serv.
CANADA - GEOLOGICAL SURVEY OF CANADA -
LIBRARY □ Ottawa, ON
Bourke, Marion, Supv., Bks. For Blind
CALIFORNIA STATE LIBRARY □ Sacramento, CA
Bourke, Thomas, Chf.
NEW YORK PUBLIC LIBRARY - MICROFORM
DIVISION □ New York, NY
Bourque, Ernestine, Supv., Cat. & Acq.
CANADIAN PACIFIC, LTD. - CORPORATE
LIBRARY/INFORMATION CENTRE □ Montreal,
PQ

Bourque, Mureille, Documentaliste
CENTRE D'ETUDES DU TOURISME - TECHNICAL
INFORMATION CENTRE □ Montreal, PQ
Bourque, William A., Tech.Serv.Libn.
HARVARD UNIVERSITY - GODFREY LOWELL
CABOT SCIENCE LIBRARY □ Cambridge, MA
Boushe, Mary Sue, Law Libn.
MEMPHIS-SHELBY COUNTY BAR ASSOCIATION
LIBRARY □ Memphis, TN
Bousquet, Ann M., Med.Libn.
FANNY ALLEN HOSPITAL - INFORMATION
CENTER □ Winooski, VT
Bousquet, Jean, Supv.Mus./Art Serv.
BERKSHIRE ATHENAEUM - MUSIC AND ARTS
DEPARTMENT □ Pittsfield, MA
Boutchard, Deborah Davidson, Libn.
AMERICAN FILM INSTITUTE - RESOURCE
CENTER □ Washington, DC
Boutin, Jocelyne, Hd., Tech.Serv.
CANADA - PUBLIC SERVICE STAFF RELATIONS
BOARD - LIBRARY □ Ottawa, ON
Boutinon, Elizabeth R., Chf.Libn.
SHEARSON LOEB RHOADES, INC. - RESEARCH
LIBRARY □ New York, NY
Boutte, Carroll, Supv.Info.Spec.
U.S. DEFENSE AUDIOVISUAL AGENCY -
ARLINGTON STILL PHOTO DEPOSITORY □
Arlington, VA
Boutwell, Barbara, Libn.
MINE SAFETY APPLIANCES COMPANY - MSA
RESEARCH CORPORATION - CALLERY
CHEMICAL COMPANY - LIBRARY □ Evans City,
PA
Bouwens, Kathryn, Adult Serv.Libn.
MEMORIAL PRESBYTERIAN CHURCH - LIBRARY
□ Midland, MI
Bova, Adrienne M., Ed.
READER'S DIGEST - INDEX □ Pleasantville, NY
Bova, Patrick, Libn.
UNIVERSITY OF CHICAGO - NATIONAL
OPINION RESEARCH CENTER - LIBRARY AND
DATA ARCHIVES □ Chicago, IL
Bovee, Martha L., Assoc.Univ.Libn.
UNIVERSITY OF CALIFORNIA, SAN DIEGO -
UNIVERSITY LIBRARIES □ La Jolla, CA
Bovey, John A., Prov.Archv.
BRITISH COLUMBIA - PROVINCIAL ARCHIVES
□ Victoria, BC
Bovie, Christopher, Med.Libn.
U.S. VETERANS ADMINISTRATION (ME-
Augusta) - CENTER LIBRARY □ Augusta, ME
Bovo, Linda, Asst.Libn.
MERRILL LYNCH WHITE WELD - CAPITAL
MARKETS GROUP - LIBRARY □ New York, NY
Bow, Eric, Coord., Tech.Serv.
ONTARIO - MINISTRY OF CULTURE AND
RECREATION - LIBRARIES AND COMMUNITY
INFORMATION □ Toronto, ON
Bow, Jean, Libn.
NATHAN (Robert R.) ASSOCIATES, INC. -
LIBRARY □ Washington, DC
Bowar, Jean M., Law Libn.
MONTGOMERY COUNTY LAW LIBRARY □
Montgomery, AL
Bowden, Virginia, Assoc.Dir.
UNIVERSITY OF TEXAS HEALTH SCIENCE
CENTER, SAN ANTONIO - LIBRARY □ San
Antonio, TX
Bowdler, Debbie, Energy Info.Spec.
SOUTH CAROLINA STATE ENERGY EXTENSION
SERVICE - ENERGY INFORMATION CENTER □
Columbia, SC
Bowell, Daniel, Coll.Dev./Ref.
WHEATON COLLEGE - BILLY GRAHAM CENTER
LIBRARY □ Wheaton, IL
Bowen, Johanna, Ser./Per.Libn.
SUNY - COLLEGE AT CORTLAND - MEMORIAL
LIBRARY □ Cortland, NY
Bowen, Laurel, Cur. of Mss.
ILLINOIS STATE HISTORICAL LIBRARY □
Springfield, IL

Bowen, Louisa, Mss.
SOUTHERN ILLINOIS UNIVERSITY,
CARBONDALE - SPECIAL COLLECTIONS □
Carbondale, IL
Bowen, M.E., Libn.
FOSTER ADVERTISING COMPANY, LTD. -
INFORMATION CENTRE† □ Toronto, ON
Bowen, M. Rosalie, Legislative Ref.
RHODE ISLAND STATE LIBRARY □ Providence,
RI
Bowen, Nancy, Ref.
HARVARD UNIVERSITY - GRADUATE SCHOOL
OF BUSINESS ADMINISTRATION - BAKER
LIBRARY □ Boston, MA
Bower, Barbara, Tech.Info.Spec.
POPULATION REFERENCE BUREAU, INC. -
LIBRARY/INFORMATION SERVICE □
Washington, DC
Bower, Barbara A., Dir.
FORT LEWIS MILITARY MUSEUM - MUSEUM
RESEARCH LIBRARY □ Fort Lewis, WA
Bower, Cynthia E., Hd.Doc.Libn.
UNIVERSITY OF ARIZONA - GOVERNMENT
DOCUMENTS DEPARTMENT □ Tucson, AZ
Bower, Donald E., Dir.
NATIONAL WRITERS CLUB - LIBRARY □ Aurora,
CO
Bower, Janice, Info.Sci.
MASSACHUSETTS INSTITUTE OF TECHNOLOGY
- LINCOLN LABORATORY LIBRARY □ Lexington,
MA
Bower, Joan M., R.R.A.
ST. VINCENT HOSPITAL - MEDICAL LIBRARY □
Green Bay, WI
Bower, Mariya, Tech.Info.Spec.
ENGELHARD CORPORATION - TECHNICAL
INFORMATION CENTER □ Edison, NJ
Bower, Mary M., Dir.
FERRIS STATE COLLEGE - LIBRARY □ Big
Rapids, MI
Bower, Mary M., Dir.
FERRIS STATE COLLEGE - SCHOOL OF
PHARMACY - PERIODICAL READING ROOM □
Big Rapids, MI
Bower, Nancy, Archv.
RADCLIFFE COLLEGE - HENRY A. MURRAY
RESEARCH CENTER □ Cambridge, MA
Bower, Peter, Prov.Archv.
MANITOBA - PROVINCIAL ARCHIVES OF
MANITOBA □ Winnipeg, MB
Bowers, Ann M., Univ.Archv./Cur.
BOWLING GREEN STATE UNIVERSITY -
CENTER FOR ARCHIVAL COLLECTIONS □
Bowling Green, OH
Bowers, Gladys, Libn.
CALVERT MARINE MUSEUM - LIBRARY □
Solomons, MD
Bowers, Kent, Radio Rd.Serv.
OKLAHOMA REGIONAL LIBRARY FOR THE
BLIND AND PHYSICALLY HANDICAPPED □
Oklahoma City, OK
Bowers, Linda, Hd.Cat.
MUHLENBERG COLLEGE - JOHN A.W. HAAS
LIBRARY □ Allentown, PA
Bowers, Sandra, Hd.Ref.Libn.
U.S. BUREAU OF RECLAMATION - LIBRARY □
Denver, CO
Bowes, Winifred B., Libn.
ALCAN ALUMINUM CORPORATION -
CORPORATE LIBRARY □ Cleveland, OH
Bowie, Claire D., Chf.Rd.Serv.
CUNY - GRADUATE SCHOOL AND UNIVERSITY
CENTER - LIBRARY □ New York, NY
Bowker, P., Hd.Acq.
CANADA - TRANSPORT CANADA - LIBRARY &
INFORMATION CENTRE □ Ottawa, ON
Bowler, Mary-Lou, Serials Libn.
BABSON COLLEGE - HORN LIBRARY □ Babson
Park, MA
Bowler, Peter, Info.Spec., Bus.
GOODRICH (B.F.) COMPANY - AKRON
INFORMATION CENTER □ Akron, OH

Bowles, Garrett, Music Libn.
UNIVERSITY OF CALIFORNIA, SAN DIEGO -
UNIVERSITY LIBRARIES □ La Jolla, CA
Bowles, Nancy J., Libn.
DILLON, READ & COMPANY, INC. - LIBRARY □
New York, NY
Bowman, Dona, Med.Libn.
MADISON GENERAL HOSPITAL - MEMORIAL
LIBRARY □ Madison, WI
Bowman, Frances, Supv., Ref.Serv.
ATLANTIC-RICHFIELD COMPANY -
HEADQUARTERS LIBRARY □ Los Angeles, CA
Bowman, Dr. Inci A., Assoc.Cur., Hist./Med.
UNIVERSITY OF TEXAS MEDICAL BRANCH -
MOODY MEDICAL LIBRARY □ Galveston, TX
Bowman, Lois B., Asst.
EASTERN MENNONITE COLLEGE - MENNO
SIMONS HISTORICAL LIBRARY AND ARCHIVES
□ Harrisonburg, VA
Bowman, Lori Lee, Asst.Libn.
CENTRAL BAPTIST SEMINARY - DR. W.
GORDON BROWN MEMORIAL LIBRARY □
Toronto, ON
Bowman, Mary Jane, Ref.Libn.
AMERICAN COUNCIL OF LIFE INSURANCE -
LIBRARY □ Washington, DC
Bowne, Debra R.A., Res.Assoc.
PRUDENTIAL INSURANCE COMPANY OF
AMERICA - FINANCIAL LIBRARY □ Newark, NJ
Bowser, Mrs. Merle L., Pres.
CAMERON COUNTY HISTORICAL SOCIETY -
LITTLE MUSEUM □ Emporium, PA
Bowsfield, Hartwell, Univ.Archv.
YORK UNIVERSITY - UNIVERSITY ARCHIVES □
Downsview, ON
Bowyer, Valerie, Pub.Serv. & Info.
CONSULATE-GENERAL OF JAPAN - JAPANESE
CONSULATE LIBRARY □ Edmonton, AB
Box, Catherine J., Asst. Registrar
BAY COUNTY HISTORICAL SOCIETY - MUSEUM
OF THE GREAT LAKES - LIBRARY □ Bay City, MI
Boxer, Dr. Charles, Cons.
INDIANA UNIVERSITY - LILLY LIBRARY □
Bloomington, IN
Boyajian, Barbara, Med.Libn.
HOECHST-ROUSSEL PHARMACEUTICALS, INC. -
LIBRARY □ Somerville, NJ
Boyajian, J.G., Engr.Libn.
GENERAL DYNAMICS CORPORATION - POMONA
DIVISION - DIVISION LIBRARY MZ 4-20 □
Pomona, CA
Boyce, Barbara S., Asst.Libn./Cat.
TUFTS UNIVERSITY - FLETCHER SCHOOL OF
LAW & DIPLOMACY - EDWIN GINN LIBRARY □
Medford, MA
Boyce, Louise, Libn.
CHARLES RIVER BROADCASTING COMPANY -
WCRB LIBRARY □ Waltham, MA
Boyce, Richard D., Morale Sup.Coord.
U.S. ARMY POST - FORT STEWART/HUNTER
AAF LIBRARY SYSTEM □ Ft. Stewart, GA
Boyce, Ronald H., Hd., Lib.Serv.
LOYALIST COLLEGE OF APPLIED ARTS &
TECHNOLOGY - ANDERSON RESOURCE CENTRE
□ Belleville, ON
Boyd, Cheryl, Info.Spec.
RESEARCH INSTITUTE OF AMERICA -
INFORMATION SERVICES CENTER □ New York,
NY
Boyd, Effie W., Tech.Libn., Doc.Div.
ARNOLD ENGINEERING DEVELOPMENT CENTER
- LIBRARY □ Arnold Air Force Sta., TN
Boyd, Kathleen, Libn.
ST. ELIZABETH'S HOSPITAL - MEDICAL
LIBRARY □ Brighton, MA
Boyd, Kenneth A., Media Serv.
ASBURY THEOLOGICAL SEMINARY - B.L.
FISHER LIBRARY □ Wilmore, KY
Boyd, Louise, Supv.
U.S. NAVY - NAVAL AVIONICS CENTER -
TECHNICAL LIBRARY □ Indianapolis, IN

Boyd, Lynn D., Govt.Doc.Libn.
ALABAMA STATE SUPREME COURT - SUPREME
COURT AND STATE LAW LIBRARY □
Montgomery, AL
Boyd, Marge, Mgr.
INTEL-TECHNICAL INFORMATION CENTER □
Santa Clara, CA
Boyd, Marion, Info.Serv.Techn.
CANADA - REVENUE CANADA - CUSTOMS &
EXCISE - SCIENTIFIC AND TECHNICAL
INFORMATION CENTRE □ Ottawa, ON
Boyd, Mary T., Libn.
MADISON BUSINESS COLLEGE - LIBRARY □
Madison, WI
Boyd, Patricia, Libn.
BECHTEL - LEGAL DEPARTMENT LIBRARY □ San
Francisco, CA
Boyd, Ronald, First Asst.
DALLAS PUBLIC LIBRARY - HUMANITIES
DIVISION □ Dallas, TX
Boyd, Sandra, Ref.Libn.
WESTON SCHOOL OF THEOLOGY - LIBRARY □
Cambridge, MA
Boyd, Sandra H., Lib.Asst.
EASTMAN KODAK COMPANY - TENNESSEE
EASTMAN COMPANY - BUSINESS LIBRARY □
Kingsport, TN
Boyd, Shirley, Clerk
HEWLETT-PACKARD COMPANY - AVONDALE
DIVISION LIBRARY □ Avondale, PA
Boyd, Stanley E., Ref.Libn.
U.S. AIR FORCE INSTITUTE OF TECHNOLOGY -
LIBRARY □ Wright-Patterson AFB, OH
Boyd, Stephanie, Cat.Libn.
BELL CANADA - INFORMATION RESOURCE
CENTRE □ Montreal, PQ
Boyd, Trenton, Libn.
UNIVERSITY OF MISSOURI - VETERINARY
MEDICAL LIBRARY □ Columbia, MO
Boyden, Patrick C., Dir.
KENT STATE UNIVERSITY - COMPUTER
ASSISTED AND SELF INSTRUCTION CENTER □
Kent, OH
Boyer, Carol M., Med.Libn.
BOULDER VALLEY MEDICAL LIBRARY □ Boulder,
CO
Boyer, Fay E., Med.Libn.
GEORGIA BAPTIST MEDICAL CENTER -
MEDICAL LIBRARY □ Atlanta, GA
Boyer, Mrs. George F., Chairman
WILDWOOD HISTORICAL COMMISSION -
WILDWOOD LIBRARY OF NEW JERSEY
HISTORY □ Wildwood, NJ
Boyer, Ginette, Libn.
HOTEL-DIEU DE MONTREAL - CENTRE DE
DOCUMENTATION □ Montreal, PQ
Boyer, Harold N., Dir.
ST. FRANCIS MEDICAL CENTER - HEALTH
SCIENCES LIBRARY □ Trenton, NJ
Boyer, Jack K., Dir.
CARSON (Kit) MEMORIAL FOUNDATION -
HISTORICAL RESEARCH LIBRARY AND
ARCHIVES □ Taos, NM
Boyer, Margaret B., Libn.
ARMSTRONG WORLD INDUSTRIES, INC. -
MANAGEMENT REFERENCE SERVICES □
Lancaster, PA
Boykin, Carol, Libn.
MC GLADREY HENDRICKSON & COMPANY,
C.P.A. - CENTRAL LIBRARY □ Davenport, IA
Boykin, Joseph, Dir.
CLEMSON UNIVERSITY - ROBERT MULDROW
COOPER LIBRARY □ Clemson, SC
Boykin, Lucile, Local Hist.Spec.
DALLAS PUBLIC LIBRARY - ARCHIVES AND
RESEARCH CENTER FOR TEXAS AND DALLAS
HISTORY □ Dallas, TX
Boykiw, A.L., Asst.Libn.
ST. VLADIMIR'S UKRAINIAN GREEK
ORTHODOX CHURCH - LIBRARY OF ST.
VLADIMIR □ Calgary, AB

PERSONNEL

Boyko, Carol Richardson, Dir.
LOMA LINDA UNIVERSITY - NIELS BJORN
JORGENSEN MEMORIAL LIBRARY □ Loma Linda,
CA
Boylan, Lee, Ref.Libn.
BATTEN, BARTON, DURSTINE, OSBORN, INC. -
INFORMATION RETRIEVAL CENTER □ New
York, NY
Boylan, Ray, Asst.Dir.
CENTER FOR RESEARCH LIBRARIES □ Chicago,
IL
Boyle, C.S., Dir., Lib.Serv.
CANADA - FISHERIES & OCEANS - LIBRARY □
Ottawa, ON
Boyle, Eileen, Libn.
SAN DIEGO PUBLIC LIBRARY - LITERATURE &
LANGUAGE SECTION □ San Diego, CA
Boyle, Eileen, Libn.
SAN DIEGO PUBLIC LIBRARY - WANGENHEIM
ROOM □ San Diego, CA
Boyle, James E., Libn.
OVERSEAS DEVELOPMENT COUNCIL - LIBRARY
□ Washington, DC
Boyle, Joan, Circ.Libn.
PHILLIPS UNIVERSITY - GRADUATE SEMINARY
LIBRARY □ Enid, OK
Boyle, John, Dp.Dir.
U.S. DEPT. OF HEALTH AND HUMAN SERVICES -
DEPARTMENT LIBRARY □ Washington, DC
Boyle, Mary, AV/Publ.
UNIVERSITY OF WISCONSIN, MADISON -
WISCONSIN REGIONAL PRIMATE RESEARCH
CENTER - PRIMATE LIBRARY □ Madison, WI
Boyle, Sr. Mary David, C.S.A., Libn.
ST. AGNES HOSPITAL - LIBRARY □ Fond Du Lac,
WI
Boyle, Michael J., Dir.
WYOMING STATE ARCHIVES, MUSEUMS AND
HISTORICAL DEPARTMENT □ Cheyenne, WY
Boyle, Stephen O., Tech.Info.Spec.
TOSCO CORPORATION - TECHNICAL
INFORMATION CENTER □ Golden, CO
Boyles, Eleanor J., Doc.Libn.
MICHIGAN STATE UNIVERSITY - DOCUMENTS
DEPARTMENT □ East Lansing, MI
Boynes, Wynta, Ed.
AMERICAN COUNCIL OF VOLUNTARY
AGENCIES FOR FOREIGN SERVICE, INC. -
TECH. ASSISTANCE INFO. CLEARING HOUSE □
New York, NY
Boynton, Professor G.R., Dir.
UNIVERSITY OF IOWA - LABORATORY FOR
POLITICAL RESEARCH □ Iowa City, IA
Boynton, Yvonne, Med.Libn.
GALESBURG MENTAL HEALTH CENTER -
HIMWICH LIBRARY OF THE NEUROSCIENCES □
Galesburg, IL
Boysen, Jessica, Staff Libn.
COMMUNITY-GENERAL HOSPITAL OF GREATER
SYRACUSE - STAFF LIBRARY □ Syracuse, NY
Bozak, Paul, Libn.
MOOSE JAW LAW SOCIETY - LIBRARY† □
Moose Jaw, SK
Braatz, Karen K., Info.Spec.
SCHREIBER FOODS, INC. - LIBRARY □ Green
Bay, WI
Bracey, Maricia, Prts. & Photo Libn.
HOWARD UNIVERSITY - MOORLAND-SPINGARN
RESEARCH CENTER - MANUSCRIPT DIVISION □
Washington, DC
Bracker, Jeff, Counseling Coord.
GEORGIA STATE UNIVERSITY - SMALL
BUSINESS DEVELOPMENT CENTER □ Atlanta,
GA
Brackett, N. Scott, Tech.Libn.
LEAR SIEGLER, INC. - INSTRUMENT DIVISION
- ENGINEERING LIBRARY □ Grand Rapids, MI
Brackman, Arthur, Pres.
FREELANCE PHOTOGRAPHERS GUILD, INC. □
New York, NY

Brackney, William H., Exec.Dir.
AMERICAN BAPTIST HISTORICAL SOCIETY -
SAMUEL COLGATE BAPTIST HISTORICAL
LIBRARY □ Rochester, NY
Brackney, William H., Exec.Dir.
DANISH BAPTIST GENERAL CONFERENCE OF
AMERICA - ARCHIVES □ Rochester, NY
Bradberry, Helen, Libn.
CALIFORNIA STATE - COURT OF APPEAL, 4TH
APPELLATE DISTRICT, DIVISION TWO - LAW
LIBRARY □ San Bernardino, CA
Braddock, Betty, Asst.Dir.
KANSAS HERITAGE CENTER - LIBRARY □ Dodge
City, KS
Braddock, Virginia, Head, MGRC
BOULDER PUBLIC LIBRARY - MUNICIPAL
GOVERNMENT REFERENCE CENTER □ Boulder,
CO
Braddy, Mr. J.E., Mgr.
OWENS-ILLINOIS, INC. - TECHNICAL
INFORMATION SERVICES □ Toledo, OH
Braden, Jan, Asst.Libn.
WESLEY MEDICAL CENTER - MC KIBBIN
PROFESSIONAL LIBRARY □ Wichita, KS
Brader, Scott A., Supv., Publ.Pict.
NATIONAL GEOGRAPHIC SOCIETY -
ILLUSTRATIONS LIBRARY □ Washington, DC
Bradfield, Margaret, Lib.Techn.
ALBERTA - DEPARTMENT OF HOSPITALS AND
MEDICAL CARE - HOSPITAL SERVICES
LIBRARY □ Edmonton, AB
Bradford, Rae, Mgr.
CANADA - INDUSTRY, TRADE & COMMERCE -
CANADIAN GOVERNMENT OFFICE OF TOURISM
□ Ottawa, ON
Bradford, Roberta, Asst.Libn.
STOWE-DAY FOUNDATION - LIBRARY □
Hartford, CT
Bradley, Mrs. Alcyone B., Libn.
U.S. NATL. PARK SERVICE - EVERGLADES
NATL. PARK - REFERENCE LIBRARY □
Homestead, FL
Bradley, Annette, Hd., Ser.
LAURENTIAN UNIVERSITY - MAIN LIBRARY □
Sudbury, ON
Bradley, Barbara, Hd., AV Dept.
SOUTHEAST MICHIGAN REGIONAL FILM
LIBRARY □ Monroe, MI
Bradley, Dr. Carol June, Assoc.Dir.
SUNY AT BUFFALO - MUSIC LIBRARY □ Buffalo,
NY
Bradley, Catherine, Law Libn.
ILLINOIS STATE - SUPREME COURT LIBRARY □
Springfield, IL
Bradley, E., Lib.Techn.
U.S. VETERANS ADMINISTRATION (VA-
Hampton) - MEDICAL CENTER LIBRARY □
Hampton, VA
Bradley, Emily H., Asst.Libn.
CARNEGIE LIBRARY - HENDERSON ROOM □
Rome, GA
Bradley, Fran, Med.Libn.
U.S. VETERANS ADMINISTRATION (DC-
Washington) - MEDICAL CENTER LIBRARY† □
Washington, DC
Bradley, Helen, Patients' Libn.
U.S. VETERANS ADMINISTRATION (OH-Dayton)
- CENTER LIBRARY □ Dayton, OH
Bradley, Jana, Dir.
WISHARD (William N.) MEMORIAL HOSPITAL -
PROFESSIONAL LIBRARY/MEDIA SERVICES □
Indianapolis, IN
Bradley, Murray L., Hd., Rd.Serv.
U.S. NAVY - NAVAL WAR COLLEGE - LIBRARY □
Newport, RI
Bradley, Patricia V., Med.Libn.
U.S. PUBLIC HEALTH SERVICE HOSPITAL -
GALLUP INDIAN MEDICAL CENTER - MEDICAL
LIBRARY □ Gallup, NM
Bradley, Verdelle V., Libn.
VIRGINIA UNION UNIVERSITY - WILLIAM J.
CLARK LIBRARY □ Richmond, VA

Bradley, William M., Dir.
U.S. DEPT. OF COMMERCE - INTERNATIONAL
TRADE ADMINISTRATION - PITTSBURGH
DISTRICT OFFICE LIBRARY □ Pittsburgh, PA
Bradrick, Dolores, Law Libn.
BUTLER COUNTY LAW LIBRARY □ Butler, PA
Bradshaw, Belynda B., Mgt.Asst.
U.S. BUREAU OF LAND MANAGEMENT -
EASTERN STATES OFFICE LIBRARY □
Alexandria, VA
Bradshaw, Charles V., Pres., Bd.Chm.
CHURCH OF JESUS CHRIST OF LATTER-DAY
SAINTS - PRICE BRANCH GENEALOGICAL
LIBRARY □ Price, UT
Bradshaw, Janice, Supv.
CHICAGO DEPARTMENT OF HUMAN SERVICES
- LIBRARY □ Chicago, IL
Bradshaw, W.W., Ed. Newsletter
SOUTHWEST RESEARCH INSTITUTE -
NONDESTRUCTIVE TESTING INFORMATION
ANALYSIS CENTER □ San Antonio, TX
Bradt, Dona M. Sontag, Mgr.
ECONOMICS LABORATORY, INC. - CORPORATE
INFORMATION CENTER □ St. Paul, MN
Bradunas, Elena, Ethnic Spec.
LIBRARY OF CONGRESS - AMERICAN FOLKLIFE
CENTER □ Washington, DC
Brady, Ann, Hd.Biblog.Serv.
MECHANICS' INSTITUTE LIBRARY □ San
Francisco, CA
Brady, Ann, Cons.
NEVADA STATE LIBRARY □ Carson City, NV
Brady, Ann, Hd., Info.Ctr.
NEWSPAPER ADVERTISING BUREAU, INC. -
INFORMATION CENTER □ New York, NY
Brady, Bonnie, Law Libn.
INDIANA COUNTY LAW LIBRARY □ Indiana, PA
Brady, Brenda, Libn.
PRINCE EDWARD ISLAND - LEGISLATIVE
LIBRARY □ Charlottetown, PE
Brady, Carole S., Tech.Libn.
ENGINEERING-SCIENCE, INC. - TECHNICAL
LIBRARY □ Arcadia, CA
Brady, Colleen, Libn.
UNIVERSITY OF MINNESOTA - NEWMAN
CENTER LIBRARY □ Minneapolis, MN
Brady, Dorothy L., Libn.
GEOLOGICAL SURVEY OF ALABAMA - LIBRARY†
□ University, AL
Brady, Eugene, Libn.
MEMPHIS COMMERCIAL APPEAL - LIBRARY □
Memphis, TN
Brady, Frank B., Exec.Dir.
INSTITUTE OF NAVIGATION - LIBRARY □
Washington, DC
Brady, James J., Mgr.
GENERAL ELECTRIC COMPANY - AIRCRAFT
ENGINE GROUP - TECHNICAL INFORMATION
CENTER □ Cincinnati, OH
Brady, John D., Jr., Div.Hd.
QUEENS BOROUGH PUBLIC LIBRARY - SCIENCE
& TECHNOLOGY DIVISION □ Jamaica, NY
Brady, Joseph J., Pres.
ASSOCIATION OF CONSULTING MANAGEMENT
ENGINEERS - LIBRARY □ New York, NY
Brady, Josiah B., Libn.II
MEMPHIS-SHELBY COUNTY PUBLIC LIBRARY
AND INFORMATION CENTER - MEMPHIS ROOM
COLLECTIONS □ Memphis, TN
Brady, Mary, Telephone Ref.Serv.
NEW YORK PUBLIC LIBRARY - MID-
MANHATTAN LIBRARY - GENERAL REFERENCE
SERVICE/EDUCATION □ New York, NY
Brady, Mary Ann, Libn.
UNION CARBIDE CORPORATION - LINDE
DIVISION - TECHNICAL LIBRARY □ Indianapolis,
IN
Brady, Sr. Mary William, Archv.
COLLEGE OF ST. CATHERINE - LIBRARY - RUTH
SAWYER COLLECTION □ St. Paul, MN

Brady, Peggy M., Hd.Ref.Dept.
NORTH OLYMPIC LIBRARY SYSTEM - PORT ANGELES BRANCH - PACIFIC NORTHWEST ROOM □ Port Angeles, WA

Brady, Rose, Circ.
EDEN THEOLOGICAL SEMINARY - LIBRARY □ Webster Groves, MO

Brady, Ruth, Hd.Libn.
OUR LADY QUEEN OF MARTYRS - ST. LUCIAN LIBRARY □ Birmingham, MI

Bragdon, Lynn L., Chf., Lib.Serv.
U.S. VETERANS ADMINISTRATION (CO-Grand Junction) - HOSPITAL MEDICAL LIBRARY □ Grand Junction, CO

Brager, Beverly, Supv.
MADISON PUBLIC LIBRARY - ART AND MUSIC DIVISION □ Madison, WI

Brahms, Thomas W., Exec.Dir.
INSTITUTE OF TRANSPORTATION ENGINEERS - LIBRARY □ Washington, DC

Brail, Frederick R., Dir.
WESTERN MICHIGAN UNIVERSITY - EDUCATIONAL RESOURCES CENTER □ Kalamazoo, MI

Brajsa, Bogdana, Libn.
UNIVERSITY OF WESTERN ONTARIO - ENGINEERING LIBRARY □ London, ON

Braly, Shari, Ref.
MARTIN MARIETTA CORPORATION - DENVER DIVISION - RESEARCH LIBRARY □ Denver, CO

Brancato, Gale, Asst.Libn.
CONNECTICUT AGRICULTURAL EXPERIMENT STATION - OSBORNE LIBRARY □ New Haven, CT

Branch, Kathryn, Asst.Sci.Libn.
SAN DIEGO STATE UNIVERSITY - SCIENCE DEPARTMENT □ San Diego, CA

Brand, Alice, Chf.Libn.
MENNINGER FOUNDATION - PROFESSIONAL LIBRARY □ Topeka, KS

Brand, Dr. Charles, Dir.
UNIVERSITY OF MARYLAND, COLLEGE PARK - M. LUCIA JAMES CURRICULUM LIBRARY □ College Park, MD

Brandeis, Dr. Robert C., Libn.
UNIVERSITY OF TORONTO - VICTORIA UNIVERSITY - LIBRARY □ Toronto, ON

Brandel, Pamela, Cat.
MORAINE PARK TECHNICAL INSTITUTE - LEARNING RESOURCE CENTER □ Fond Du Lac, WI

Branden, Shirley, Hd.Ref.Libn.
UNIVERSITY OF TENNESSEE - CENTER FOR THE HEALTH SCIENCES LIBRARY □ Memphis, TN

Brandhorst, Wesley T., Dir.
ERIC PROCESSING AND REFERENCE FACILITY □ Bethesda, MD

Brandmeier, Donna L., Asst.Libn.
ST. LUKE'S HOSPITAL OF BETHLEHEM, PENNSYLVANIA - W.L. ESTES, JR. MEMORIAL LIBRARY □ Bethlehem, PA

Brandreth, Sr. Elizabeth Anne, Libn.
MERCY HOSPITAL - MEDICAL LIBRARY □ Scranton, PA

Brandt, Charles A.E., Chf.Consrv.
MANITOBA - PROVINCIAL ARCHIVES OF MANITOBA □ Winnipeg, MB

Brandt, Kandy B., Hd.
SEATTLE PUBLIC LIBRARY - MEDIA & PROGRAM SERVICES □ Seattle, WA

Brandt, Patricia, Soc.Sci./Hum. & Bus.
OREGON STATE UNIVERSITY - WILLIAM JASPER KERR LIBRARY □ Corvallis, OR

Branham, Gloria, Libn.
SOUTHWESTERN PUBLIC SERVICE COMPANY - LIBRARY □ Amarillo, TX

Branick, Rev. Vincent, S.M., Asst. to Dir.
UNIVERSITY OF DAYTON - MARIAN LIBRARY □ Dayton, OH

Brann, Andrew R., Acq.Libn.
UNIVERSITY OF KANSAS - SCHOOL OF LAW LIBRARY □ Lawrence, KS

Brann, Evelyn M., Libn.
EG&G, INC. - MASON RESEARCH INSTITUTE - LIBRARY □ Worcester, MA

Branstrator, Jon, Musm.Dir.
EARLHAM COLLEGE - JOSEPH MOORE MUSEUM - HADLEY LIBRARY □ Richmond, IN

Branton, Elsie B., Chf., Lib.Serv.
U.S. VETERANS ADMINISTRATION (TX-Kerrville) - HEALTH SCIENCES LIBRARY □ Kerrville, TX

Branton, Elsie B., Adm.Libn.
U.S. VETERANS ADMINISTRATION (TX-Marlin) - MEDICAL CENTER LIBRARY SERVICE (142D) □ Marlin, TX

Branton, Sharon, Hd. of Cat.
MC MASTER UNIVERSITY - HEALTH SCIENCES LIBRARY □ Hamilton, ON

Brantz, Malcolm, AV Libn.
UNIVERSITY OF CONNECTICUT - HEALTH CENTER - LYMAN MAYNARD STOWE LIBRARY □ Farmington, CT

Bras, Margarita, Ref.Dept.
UNIVERSITY OF PUERTO RICO - MEDICAL SCIENCES CAMPUS - LIBRARY □ Rio Piedras, PR

Brasche, Ann R., Tech.Libn
U.S. NAVY - NAVAL ELECTRONICS ENGINEERING CENTER (San Diego) - LIBRARY □ San Diego, CA

Brashear, Jan, Res.Libn.
PUBLIC AFFAIRS RESEARCH COUNCIL OF LOUISIANA - RESEARCH LIBRARY □ Baton Rouge, LA

Brasseaux, Carl A., Asst.Dir.
UNIVERSITY OF SOUTHWESTERN LOUISIANA - CENTER FOR LOUISIANA STUDIES □ Lafayette, LA

Braswell, Laura, Act.Dir. of LRC
COLUMBIA BIBLE COLLEGE - LEARNING RESOURCES CENTER □ Columbia, SC

Bratcher, Diane, Editor
NATIONAL COUNCIL OF CHURCHES - INTERFAITH CENTER ON CORPORATE RESPONSIBILITY □ New York, NY

Braten, Marlene, Asst.Libn.
ST. LUKE'S HOSPITAL CENTER - RICHARD WALKER BOLLING MEMORIAL MEDICAL LIBRARY □ New York, NY

Bratton, Rose J., Ref.Libn.
NATIONAL LEAGUE OF CITIES - MUNICIPAL REFERENCE SERVICE □ Washington, DC

Braucht, Karen, Tech.Serv. Law Libn.
UNIVERSITY OF MISSOURI - SCHOOL OF LAW LIBRARY □ Columbia, MO

Braude, Robert J., Dir.
UNIVERSITY OF NEBRASKA MEDICAL CENTER - MC GOOGAN LIBRARY OF MEDICINE □ Omaha, NE

Brault, M. Jean-Remi, Conservateur En Chef
QUEBEC PROVINCE - BIBLIOTHEQUE NATIONALE DU QUEBEC □ Montreal, PQ

Braun, Carl, Dept.Hd.
SYRACUSE UNIVERSITY - E.S. BIRD LIBRARY - SOCIAL SCIENCES DEPARTMENT □ Syracuse, NY

Braun, Jane D., Cat.
UNIVERSITY OF NORTH CAROLINA, CHAPEL HILL - LAW LIBRARY □ Chapel Hill, NC

Braun, Linda, Asst.Libn.
NEW YORK STATE LIBRARY - HUMANITIES REFERENCE SERVICE □ Albany, NY

Braun, Nancy R., Circ.Supv.
VANDERBILT UNIVERSITY LIBRARY - DIVINITY LIBRARY □ Nashville, TN

Braun, Nancy R., Circ.Supv.
VANDERBILT UNIVERSITY LIBRARY - DIVINITY LIBRARY - KESLER CIRCULATING LIBRARY □ Nashville, TN

Braun, Susan, Pres.
DANCE FILMS ASSOCIATION, INC. □ New York, NY

Braunger, Bunny, Med.Libn.
BETH ISRAEL HOSPITAL & GERIATRIC CENTER - HEALTH SCIENCE LIBRARY □ Denver, CO

Braunlein, John H., Dir.
MADISON COUNTY HISTORICAL SOCIETY - LIBRARY □ Oneida, NY

Brautigam, Patsy, Ref.Libn.
LAW LIBRARY OF LOUISIANA □ New Orleans, LA

Bravard, Robert S., Dir.
LOCK HAVEN STATE COLLEGE - GEORGE B. STEVENSON LIBRARY □ Lock Haven, PA

Braver, Norma, Ref.Libn.
UNIVERSITY OF LOUISVILLE - KORNHAUSER HEALTH SCIENCES LIBRARY □ Louisville, KY

Brawer, Dr. Florence B., Res.Educ.
ERIC CLEARINGHOUSE FOR JUNIOR COLLEGES □ Los Angeles, CA

Brawn, Iris M., Asst.Ref.Libn.
CINCINNATI MUNICIPAL REFERENCE LIBRARY □ Cincinnati, OH

Braxton, Ann B., Libn.
CIBA-GEIGY CORPORATION - TECHNICAL INFORMATION SERVICE □ Greensboro, NC

Braxton, Anne, Fine Arts Libn.
OHIO UNIVERSITY - FINE ARTS COLLECTION □ Athens, OH

Bray, Mary, Libn.
LAKELAND HOSPITAL - MEDICAL LIBRARY □ Elkhorn, WI

Bray, Mrs. O., Libn.
SPERRY CORPORATION - SPERRY MARINE SYSTEMS - ENGINEERING LIBRARY □ Charlottesville, VA

Brayfield, Mary Jane, Libn.
BENDIX CORPORATION - BENDIX ENERGY CONTROLS DIVISION - ENGINEERING LIBRARY □ South Bend, IN

Brazier, Donn P., Dir.
MUSEUM OF SCIENCE AND NATURAL HISTORY - LIBRARY □ St. Louis, MO

Brazil, Mary Jo, Libn.
AMERICAN JUSTICE INSTITUTE - LIBRARY □ Sacramento, CA

Brazin, Lillian, Res.Libn.
JEFFERSON (Thomas) UNIVERSITY - SCOTT MEMORIAL LIBRARY □ Philadelphia, PA

Braznytz, Helen C., Sr.Dept.Asst.
CASE WESTERN RESERVE UNIVERSITY - LAW LIBRARY □ Cleveland, OH

Breaden, Richard P., Lib.Dir.
ST. JOSEPH'S SEMINARY - ARCHBISHOP CORRIGAN MEMORIAL LIBRARY† □ Yonkers, NY

Breaden, Susannah, Libn.
UNIVERSITY OF UTAH - SPECIAL COLLECTIONS DEPARTMENT □ Salt Lake City, UT

Brecht, Albert, Dir.
UNIVERSITY OF SOUTHERN CALIFORNIA - LAW CENTER LIBRARY† □ Los Angeles, CA

Brede, Caroline, Asst. Law Libn.
UNIVERSITY OF MINNESOTA - LAW LIBRARY □ Minneapolis, MN

Bredemeier, V.B., Libn.
DU PONT DE NEMOURS (E.I.) & COMPANY, INC. - STINE LABORATORY LIBRARY □ Newark, DE

Breed, Patricia
NATIONAL COLLEGE OF EDUCATION - LEARNING RESOURCE CENTERS □ Evanston, IL

Breeden, Rebecca, Asst.Libn.
MENNINGER FOUNDATION - PROFESSIONAL LIBRARY □ Topeka, KS

Breedlove, Elizabeth, Hd., Tech.Serv.
NEW JERSEY STATE LIBRARY □ Trenton, NJ

Breen, Richard F., Jr., Law Libn.
WILLAMETTE UNIVERSITY - LAW LIBRARY □ Salem, OR

Breese, John K., Mgr.-RC/LS
KELLER (J.J.) & ASSOCIATES, INC. - RESEARCH CENTER/LIBRARY SERVICES □ Neenah, WI

Bregaint, Bernard, Mgr., Lib.Serv.
CAMBRIAN COLLEGE OF APPLIED ARTS AND TECHNOLOGY - LIBRARY □ Sudbury, ON

Bregault, C., Asst.Dir., Field
CANADA - AGRICULTURE CANADA - LIBRARIES DIVISION □ Ottawa, ON

Bregoli, Marilyn Smith, Libn.
SIMMONS COLLEGE - SCHOOL OF SOCIAL
WORK LIBRARY □ Boston, MA
Breinich, John A., Dir.
HAWAII MEDICAL LIBRARY, INC. □ Honolulu, HI
Breitbart, Joan, Sr.Libn.
FEDERAL RESERVE BANK OF NEW YORK -
RESEARCH LIBRARY □ New York, NY
Breitenstein, Paul R., Libn.
TREXLER (Harry C.) MASONIC LIBRARY □
Allentown, PA
Bremner, Margaret E., Lib.Res.Assoc.
HEIDRICK & STRUGGLES, INC. - LIBRARY
RESEARCH CENTER □ Chicago, IL
Bren, Nancy, Record Cat./Ref.Libn.
SUNY AT BUFFALO - MUSIC LIBRARY □ Buffalo,
NY
Breneau, Don, Ref.Coll.Dev.
WAYNE STATE UNIVERSITY - G. FLINT PURDY
LIBRARY □ Detroit, MI
Brennan, Ann M., Info.Spec.
WORLD DATA CENTER A - GLACIOLOGY □
Boulder CO
Brennan, David K., Libn.
UNIVERSITY OF TENNESSEE - COLLEGE OF
LAW LIBRARY □ Knoxville, TN
Brennan, Ellen, Libn.
PENNSYLVANIA ECONOMY LEAGUE - EASTERN
DIVISION - LIBRARY □ Philadelphia, PA
Brennan, Dr. John A., Cur.
UNIVERSITY OF COLORADO, BOULDER -
WESTERN HISTORICAL COLLECTION &
UNIVERSITY ARCHIVES □ Boulder, CO
Brennan, Kathleen, Archv.
ROCKEFELLER UNIVERSITY - ROCKEFELLER
ARCHIVE CENTER □ North Tarrytown, NY
Brennan, Margret, Supv., News Serv.
MOBIL OIL CORPORATION - PUBLIC AFFAIRS
SECRETARIAT □ New York, NY
Brennan, MaryLu, Supv.
SCARBOROUGH BOARD OF EDUCATION - A.B.
PATTERSON PROFESSIONAL LIBRARY □
Scarborough, ON
Brennan, Robert, Pres.
GREATER MADISON CHAMBER OF COMMERCE -
MATERIALS REFERENCE LIBRARY □ Madison,
WI
Brennan, Robert G., Asst.Dir.
CALIFORNIA STATE UNIVERSITY, CHICO -
MERIAM LIBRARY □ Chico, CA
Brennan, T. Patrick, Cur.
OGLEBAY INSTITUTE - MANSION MUSEUM
LIBRARY □ Wheeling, WV
Brenneise, Harvey, Assoc.Ref.Libn
ANDREWS UNIVERSITY - JAMES WHITE
LIBRARY □ Berrien Springs, MI
Brenneman, Betsey, Acq.
WORCESTER STATE COLLEGE - LEARNING
RESOURCES CENTER □ Worcester, MA
Brennen, Dolly M., Off.Mgr.
SWIGART MUSEUM - LIBRARY □ Huntingdon, PA
Brennen, Patrick W., Dir.
UNIVERSITY OF SOUTH DAKOTA - CHRISTIAN
P. LOMMEN HEALTH SCIENCES LIBRARY □
Vermillion, SD
Brenner, Ellen R., Libn.
NEW YORK CITY - OFFICE OF CHIEF MEDICAL
EXAMINER - MILTON HELPERN LIBRARY OF
LEGAL MEDICINE □ New York, NY
Brenner, Lawrence, Sr.Med.Libn.
BOSTON CITY HOSPITAL - MEDICAL LIBRARY □
Boston, MA
Brenner, M. Diane, Musm.Archv.
ANCHORAGE HISTORICAL AND FINE ARTS
MUSEUM - ARCHIVES □ Anchorage, AK
Brenner, Marilyn R., Libn.
TEMPLE BETH EL - PRENTIS MEMORIAL
LIBRARY □ Birmingham, MI
Brenny, Nancy, Libn.
PILLSBURY COMPANY - MAIN OFFICE
MARKETING LIBRARY □ Minneapolis, MN

Bresinger, Sheindel, Libn.
MAIMONIDES HOSPITAL & HOME FOR THE
AGED - POLLACK LIBRARY □ Montreal, PQ
Breslauer, Lester M., Chf.Libn.
BELL AEROSPACE TEXTRON - LAWRENCE D.
BELL MEMORIAL LIBRARY □ Buffalo, NY
Bresler, Geraldine J., Asst.Ref.Libn./ILL
TRENTON STATE COLLEGE - ROSCOE L. WEST
LIBRARY □ Trenton, NJ
Bresnahan, Alice, Libn.
3M - 209 LIBRARY □ St. Paul, MN
Bresnahan, Patti, Asst.Libn.
STARK COUNTY LAW LIBRARY ASSOCIATION -
LAW LIBRARY □ Canton, OH
Bressler, Nancy, Cur.Pub.Aff./Papers
PRINCETON UNIVERSITY - RARE BOOKS AND
SPECIAL COLLECTIONS □ Princeton, NJ
Breszee, Lorraine, Libn.
DANE COUNTY LAW LIBRARY □ Madison, WI
Bret-Harte, Margaret S., Hd.Libn.
ARIZONA HISTORICAL SOCIETY - LIBRARY □
Tucson, AZ
Brethauer, Thomas E., Libn.
INDIANA STATE HIGHWAY COMMISSION -
OFFICE OF HIGHWAY DEVELOPMENT -
TECHNICAL LIBRARY □ Indianapolis, IN
Brethour, Sherie, Libn.
ONTARIO FILM INSTITUTE - LIBRARY &
INFORMATION CENTRE □ Don Mills, ON
Breton, Francine, Bibliotechnicienne
QUEBEC PROVINCE - MINISTERE DES
CONSOMMATEURS, COOPERATIVES ET
INSTITUTIONS FINANCIERES - BIBLIOTHEQUE
□ Quebec, PQ
Brett, Lorraine E., Cat.
VIGO COUNTY SCHOOL CORPORATION -
INSTRUCTIONAL MATERIALS CENTER □ Terre
Haute, IN
Brett, Marianne E., Hosp.Libn.
NORTH YORK GENERAL HOSPITAL - W. KEITH
WELSH LIBRARY □ Willowdale, ON
Bretz, Randy, Dir.
UNIVERSITY OF NEBRASKA, LINCOLN -
INSTRUCTIONAL MEDIA CENTER □ Lincoln, NE
Breuer, Karin, Cur.
ROBERT GORE RIFKIND FOUNDATION - ART
LIBRARY AND GRAPHICS COLLECTION □
Beverly Hills, CA
Brewer, Annie M., Sr.Ed.
GALE RESEARCH COMPANY - LIBRARY □
Detroit, MI
Brewer, Calvin, Libn.
OKLAHOMA STATE UNIVERSITY - PHYSICAL
SCIENCES AND ENGINEERING DIVISION □
Stillwater, OK
Brewer, Christopher D., Musm.Techn.
KERN COUNTY MUSEUM - LIBRARY □
Bakersfield, CA
Brewer, Delores, Libn.
ST. LUKE'S MEMORIAL HOSPITAL - A.M.
JOHNSON MEMORIAL LIBRARY □ Spokane, WA
Brewer, Joan, Info.Serv.Off.
INSTITUTE FOR SEX RESEARCH, INC. -
LIBRARY AND INFORMATION SERVICE □
Bloomington, IN
Brewer, John, Lib. Contact
BUREAU OF GOVERNMENTAL RESEARCH -
LIBRARY† □ New Orleans, LA
Brewer, Karen, Dir.
NORTHEASTERN OHIO UNIVERSITIES COLLEGE
OF MEDICINE - BASIC MEDICAL SCIENCES
LIBRARY □ Rootstown, OH
Brewer, Martha, Dp.Dir.
LIFE PLANNING/HEALTH SERVICES -
LIBRARY/MEDIA SERVICES □ Dallas, TX
Brewer, Stanley E., Chf.Libn.
GULF REFINING & MARKETING COMPANY -
LIBRARY AND INFORMATION CENTER □
Houston, TX

Brewster, Olive N., Chf.Cat.
U.S. AIR FORCE - AEROSPACE MEDICAL
DIVISION - SCHOOL OF AEROSPACE MEDICINE
- STRUGHOLD AEROMEDICAL LIBRARY □ Brooks
AFB, TX
Brey, Frank, Hd.Libn./Pub.Serv.
INDIANA UNIVERSITY/PURDUE UNIVERSITY
AT INDIANAPOLIS - UNIVERSITY LIBRARY □
Indianapolis, IN
Breyley, Dorothy B., Libn.
STERLING DRUG, INC. - HILTON-DAVIS
CHEMICAL COMPANY DIVISION - LIBRARY □
Cincinnati, OH
Brian, Ray, Libn.
CALIFORNIA ACADEMY OF SCIENCES - J.W.
MAILLIARD, JR. LIBRARY □ San Francisco, CA
Brice, Ora, Cur.
SAUK COUNTY HISTORICAL SOCIETY, INC. -
HISTORICAL MUSEUM LIBRARY □ Baraboo, WI
Brichford, Maynard, Univ.Archv.
UNIVERSITY OF ILLINOIS - UNIVERSITY
ARCHIVES □ Urbana, IL
Bricker, Dorothy, Hd., Acq.
NATIONAL GEOGRAPHIC SOCIETY - LIBRARY □
Washington, DC
Bricker, Florence M., Dir. Of Archv.
EVANGELICAL AND REFORMED HISTORICAL
SOCIETY - LANCASTER CENTRAL ARCHIVES
AND LIBRARY □ Lancaster, PA
Bricker, Kathleen, Asst.Libn.
LAFAYETTE JOURNAL AND COURIER - LIBRARY
□ Lafayette, IN
Brickett, Dorothy
HARTFORD PUBLIC LIBRARY - REFERENCE AND
GENERAL READING DEPARTMENT □ Hartford,
CT
Bridgeford, Nancy J., CAPT Spec.
NORTHWEST REGIONAL EDUCATIONAL
LABORATORY - CLEARINGHOUSE FOR APPLIED
PERFORMANCE TESTING (CAPT) □ Portland, OR
Bridges, Barbara, Govt.Doc.Libn.
UNIVERSITY OF TEXAS SCHOOL OF LAW -
TARLTON LAW LIBRARY □ Austin, TX
Bridges, Kitty, Info.Spec.
EXXON BIOMEDICAL SCIENCES INC. - LIBRARY
□ East Millstone, NJ
Bridges, Laine, Libn.
COMMUNITY HOSPITAL OF BUNNELL -
MEDICAL LIBRARY □ Bunnell, FL
Bridges, Marian, ILL Libn.
CENTRAL CAROLINA TECHNICAL COLLEGE -
LEARNING RESOURCE CENTER □ Sanford, NC
Bridges, Dr. Roger D., Hd.Libn. & Dir., Res.
ILLINOIS STATE HISTORICAL LIBRARY □
Springfield, IL
Bridgman, Amy R., Libn.
AMERICAN OCCUPATIONAL THERAPY
ASSOCIATION - REFERENCE LIBRARY □
Rockville, MD
Bridgman, Kristina J., Law Libn.
MADISON COUNTY LAW LIBRARY □ London, OH
Bridgwater, Dorothy W., Asst.Libn.
YALE UNIVERSITY - BENJAMIN FRANKLIN
COLLECTION □ New Haven, CT
Brie-Berard, Marie, Documentaliste
CONFERENCE DES RECTEURS ET DES
PRINCIPAUX DES UNIVERSITES DU QUEBEC -
CENTRE DE DOCUMENTATION □ Montreal, PQ
Briegleb, Ann, Archv.
UNIVERSITY OF CALIFORNIA, LOS ANGELES -
MUSIC LIBRARY □ Los Angeles, CA
Brien, Therese, Exec.Sec.
INSTITUTE OF OCCUPATIONAL AND
ENVIRONMENTAL HEALTH - ARCHIVES □
Montreal, PQ
Briere, Jean-Marie, SDI
QUEBEC PROV. - MIN. DE L'ENERGIE ET DES
RESSOURCES - CENTRE DE DOCUMENTATION
ET DE RENSEIGNEMENTS □ Quebec, PQ
Brigandi, Carmen E., Law Libn.
NEW YORK STATE SUPREME COURT -
APPELLATE DIVISION, 4TH JUDICIAL
DEPARTMENT - LAW LIBRARY □ Syracuse, NY

Briggs, Barbara, Ref.Libn. & Cat.
BARRINGTON COLLEGE - LIBRARY □ Barrington, RI

Briggs, Frances M., Libn.
GENERAL ELECTRIC COMPANY - CARBOLOY SYSTEMS DEPARTMENT - CSD LIBRARY □ Detroit, MI

Briggs, Irene, Tech.Info.Spec.
U.S. GENERAL ACCOUNTING OFFICE - BOSTON REGIONAL OFFICE - TECHNICAL LIBRARY □ Boston, MA

Briggs, J.F.
3M - ENGINEERING INFORMATION SERVICES □ St. Paul, MN

Briggs, John, Biblog./Ref.Libn.
SUNY AT BINGHAMTON - FINE ARTS LIBRARY □ Binghamton, NY

Briggs, Margaret, Asst.Libn.
KANSAS STATE HISTORICAL SOCIETY - LIBRARY □ Topeka, KS

Briggs, Ramona, Mgr.Tech.Lib.
COMPUTER SCIENCES CORPORATION - TECHNICAL LIBRARY □ Falls Church, VA

Briggs, Robert L., Libn.
UNIVERSITY OF HOUSTON - SCHOOL OF MUSIC - WOODY HERMAN ARCHIVES □ Houston, TX

Briggs, Rose T., Dir. Emeritus
PILGRIM SOCIETY - PILGRIM HALL LIBRARY □ Plymouth, MA

Briggs, Shirley A., Exec.Dir.
RACHEL CARSON COUNCIL, INC. - LIBRARY □ Washington, DC

Briggs, Susan L., Assoc.Libn./Ref.
U.S. FOOD & DRUG ADMINISTRATION - NATIONAL CENTER FOR TOXICOLOGICAL RESEARCH - LIBRARY □ Jefferson, AK

Briggs, Veronica, Libn.
CHASE MANHATTAN BANK, N.A. - SYSTEMS LIBRARY □ New York, NY

Brigham, Florence C., Cur.
FALL RIVER HISTORICAL SOCIETY - LIBRARY □ Fall River, MA

Brigham, Jeffrey L., Asst.Libn./Tech.Serv
NYACK COLLEGE - LIBRARY □ Nyack, NY

Bright, Alice, Asst.Ref.
CARNEGIE-MELLON UNIVERSITY - ENGINEERING & SCIENCE LIBRARY □ Pittsburgh, PA

Bright, Charles D., Supv.
WYOMING STATE HOSPITAL - MEDICAL LIBRARY □ Evanston, WY

Bright, Elizabeth, Libn.
MINNESOTA STATE IRON RANGE RESOURCES & REHABILITATION BOARD - IRON RANGE RESEARCH CENTER □ Chisholm, MN

Bright, Martha, Asst.Libn.
MAHARISHI INTERNATIONAL UNIVERSITY - SCIENCE OF CREATIVE INTELLIGENCE COLLECTION □ Fairfield, IA

Brigl, Bob, Asst.Cur., Exhibits
WESTERN KENTUCKY UNIVERSITY - KENTUCKY LIBRARY AND MUSEUM/ UNIVERSITY ARCHIVES □ Bowling Green, KY

Briley, John B., Mgr.
OHIO HISTORICAL SOCIETY - CAMPUS MARTIUS MUSEUM - LIBRARY □ Marietta, OH

Brill, Faye, Mgr., Desk Res.
FOOTE CONE & BELDING - INFORMATION CENTER □ Chicago, IL

Brill, Martin, Info.Spec.
EUROPEAN COMMUNITY INFORMATION SERVICE - LIBRARY □ Washington, DC

Brill, Wesley A., Act.Adm.
COLT INDUSTRIES - FM ENGINE DIVISION LIBRARY □ Beloit, WI

Brindamour, Mary E., Libn.
DYNAMICS RESEARCH CORPORATION - LIBRARY □ Wilmington, MA

Brindle, John V., Cur. of Art
CARNEGIE-MELLON UNIVERSITY - HUNT INSTITUTE FOR BOTANICAL DOCUMENTATION - LIBRARY □ Pittsburgh, PA

Brink, Clarence, Coord., Ref.Serv.
VIGO COUNTY PUBLIC LIBRARY - SPECIAL COLLECTIONS □ Terre Haute, IN

Brinkley, Helen L., Lib.Techn.
U.S. AIR FORCE HOSPITAL MEDICAL CENTER - MEDICAL LIBRARY (OH-Wright-Patterson AFB) □ Wright-Patterson AFB, OH

Brinkley, Margaret, Adm.Asst.
UNIVERSITY OF PENNSYLVANIA - JOHN PENMAN WOOD MEMORIAL LIBRARY OF NATIONAL DEFENSE □ Philadelphia, PA

Brinkley, Margot, Dir.
FOUNDATION CENTER - WASHINGTON BRANCH LIBRARY □ Washington, DC

Brinkman, Carol, Ref.Libn.
UNIVERSITY OF LOUISVILLE - J.B. SPEED SCIENTIFIC SCHOOL - LIBRARY □ Louisville, KY

Brinkmeier, Hermina, Supv., Lib. & Rec.
MONSANTO RESEARCH CORPORATION - MOUND FACILITY - TECHNICAL INFORMATION CENTER □ Miamisburg, OH

Brinkmoeller, Elizabeth, Tech.Serv.Coord.
U.S. VETERANS ADMINISTRATION (OH-Cincinnati) - MEDICAL CENTER LIBRARY □ Cincinnati, OH

Brinks, Herbert, Cur., Heritage Hall
CALVIN COLLEGE AND SEMINARY - LIBRARY □ Grand Rapids, MI

Brinser, Jack W., Supv. Photographics
ARMSTRONG WORLD INDUSTRIES, INC. - TECHNICAL CENTER - TECHNICAL INFORMATION SERVICES □ Lancaster, PA

Brinsmead, Ann, Info.Spec.
HJK&A ADVERTISING & PUBLIC RELATIONS - INFORMATION CENTER □ Washington, DC

Brinson, Elizabeth, Assoc.Dir. LRC
FORT VALLEY STATE COLLEGE - HENRY ALEXANDER HUNT MEMORIAL LEARNING RESOURCES CENTER □ Fort Valley, GA

Brinton, Yuki T., Libn.
PENDLE HILL - QUAKER COLLECTION □ Wallingford, PA

Brisco, Valerie, Res.Asst.
NOVA SCOTIA - DEPARTMENT OF MINES & ENERGY - LIBRARY □ Halifax, NS

Briscoe, Georgia, Ser.
UNIVERSITY OF SAN DIEGO - MARVIN & LILLIAN KRATTER LAW LIBRARY □ San Diego, CA

Briscoe, Marianne G., Dir.Dev.
NEWBERRY LIBRARY □ Chicago, IL

Briski, Marlene, Res.Assoc.
KORN/FERRY INTERNATIONAL - LIBRARY □ Houston, TX

Brislin, Jane F., Dir.Info.Serv.
INDUSTRIAL HEALTH FOUNDATION, INC. - LIBRARY □ Pittsburgh, PA

Brister, Dorotha, Asst.Cat.
OKLAHOMA CITY UNIVERSITY - LAW LIBRARY □ Oklahoma City, OK

Bristor, Patricia, Acq.Libn.
WAYNE STATE UNIVERSITY - SCHOOL OF MEDICINE - VERA PARSHALL SHIFFMAN MEDICAL LIBRARY □ Detroit, MI

Brite, Agnes, Libn.
NEW ENGLAND MUTUAL LIFE INSURANCE COMPANY - BUSINESS LIBRARY □ Boston, MA

Britt, Terry, Assoc.Dir. of Libs.
U.S. NAVY - NAVAL POSTGRADUATE SCHOOL - DUDLEY KNOX LIBRARY □ Monterey, CA

Brittain, Barbara, Rd.Serv.Libn.
ORANGEBURG-CALHOUN TECHNICAL COLLEGE - GRESSETTE LEARNING RESOURCE CENTER □ Orangeburg, SC

Britton, Barbara S., Acq.Asst.
BRIDGEWATER STATE COLLEGE - CLEMENT C. MAXWELL LIBRARY □ Bridgewater, MA

Britton, Constance, Libn.
OHIO STATE AGRICULTURAL RESEARCH AND DEVELOPMENT CENTER - LIBRARY □ Wooster, OH

Britton, J.J., Libn.
CENTRAL PRESBYTERIAN CHURCH - LIBRARY □ Houston, TX

Britton, Jane P., Archv.
HISTORICAL FOUNDATION OF THE PRESBYTERIAN AND REFORMED CHURCHES - LIBRARY AND ARCHIVES □ Montreat, NC

Britton, Ruth, Libn.
UNIVERSITY OF SOUTHERN CALIFORNIA - SOCIAL WORK LIBRARY □ Los Angeles, CA

Britz, Daniel A., Biblog. of Africana
NORTHWESTERN UNIVERSITY - MELVILLE J. HERSKOVITS LIBRARY OF AFRICAN STUDIES □ Evanston, IL

Brkic, Beverly, Hd., Cat.Libn.
NORTH DAKOTA STATE UNIVERSITY - LIBRARY □ Fargo, ND

Broad, Julia, Libn.
HARRIS-STOWE STATE COLLEGE LIBRARY □ St. Louis, MO

Broaddus, Billie, Hd.
UNIVERSITY OF CINCINNATI - MEDICAL CENTER LIBRARIES - HEALTH SCIENCES LIBRARY □ Cincinnati, OH

Broaddus, Gloria H., Libn.
BABCOCK AND WILCOX COMPANY - FOSSIL POWER GENERATION DIVISION - TECHNICAL LIBRARY □ Barberton, OH

Broadhead, Barbara M., Supv.
INTERNATIONAL PAPER COMPANY - ERLING RIIS RESEARCH LABORATORY - INFORMATION SERVICES □ Mobile, AL

Broadnax, Lavonda, Asst.Libn.
HOWARD UNIVERSITY - HEALTH SCIENCES LIBRARY □ Washington, DC

Broadus, Laurie, Libn.
ST. MARY OF NAZARETH HOSPITAL - SCHOOL OF NURSING LIBRARY □ Chicago, IL

Brock, Jo Ann, Assoc.Libn.
UNIVERSITY OF CALIFORNIA, BERKELEY - GOVERNMENT DOCUMENTS DEPARTMENT □ Berkeley, CA

Brock, Lois, Libn.
GENERAL TIRE AND RUBBER COMPANY - RESEARCH DIVISION INFORMATION CENTER □ Akron, OH

Brockhurst, S., Lib.Techn.
CANADA - HEALTH AND WELFARE CANADA - HEALTH PROTECTION BRANCH - TORONTO REGIONAL LIBRARY □ Scarborough, ON

Brockman, Barbara, Tech.Proc./Circ.
EASTMAN KODAK COMPANY - RESEARCH LABORATORIES - RESEARCH LIBRARY □ Rochester, NY

Brockman, Mary, Libn.
VANDERBILT UNIVERSITY LIBRARY - CENTRAL DIVISION - SARAH SHANNON STEVENSON SCIENCE LIBRARY □ Nashville, TN

Brockway, Duncan, Dir., Lib.Serv.
SCHOOLS OF THEOLOGY IN DUBUQUE - LIBRARIES □ Dubuque, IA

Brockway, Paula, Libn.
U.S. AIR FORCE ACADEMY - MEDICAL LIBRARY □ U.S. Air Force Academy, CO

Brodman, Dr. Estelle, Libn. & Prof.
WASHINGTON UNIVERSITY - SCHOOL OF MEDICINE LIBRARY □ St. Louis, MO

Brodner, Larson, Supv.
ESSO RESOURCES CANADA LIMITED - LIBRARY INFORMATION CENTRE □ Calgary, AB

Brodnex, Cynthia M., Asst. Law Libn.
SAGINAW COUNTY LAW LIBRARY □ Saginaw, MI

Brodowski, Dr. Joyce, Assoc.Dir.
TRENTON STATE COLLEGE - ROSCOE L. WEST LIBRARY □ Trenton, NJ

Brody, Catherine T., Chf.Libn.
CUNY - NEW YORK CITY TECHNICAL COLLEGE LIBRARY/LEARNING RESOURCE CENTER □ Brooklyn, NY

Brody, Julia J., Chf.
NEW YORK PUBLIC LIBRARY - MID-MANHATTAN LIBRARY □ New York, NY

Brody, Leon, Ref.Libn.
U.S. OFFICE OF PERSONNEL MANAGEMENT -
LIBRARY □ Washington, DC
Broemmel, Ned, Pres.
HISTORICAL SOCIETY OF QUINCY AND ADAMS
COUNTY - LIBRARY □ Quincy, IL
Broenneke, Karen, Preservation Res.
LATAH COUNTY HISTORICAL SOCIETY -
LIBRARY □ Moscow, ID
Broering, Naomi C., Libn.
GEORGETOWN UNIVERSITY - MEDICAL
CENTER - DAHLGREN MEMORIAL LIBRARY □
Washington, DC
Brofft, Dottie F., Ref.Libn.
ENVIRONMENTAL PROTECTION AGENCY -
ANDREW W. BREIDENBACH ENVIRONMENTAL
RESEARCH CTR., CINCINNATI - TECH.LIB. □
Cincinnati, OH
Brogan, Linda, Asst.Dir., Res.
UNIVERSITY OF NORTH CAROLINA, CHAPEL
HILL - HEALTH SCIENCES LIBRARY □ Chapel
Hill, NC
Brokalakis, Melissa, Mgr., Info./Lib.Serv
HONEYWELL, INC. - HONEYWELL
INFORMATION SYSTEMS - INFORMATION AND
LIBRARY SERVICES □ Waltham, MA
Brombaugh, Susan, Cur.Asst.
YALE UNIVERSITY - COLLECTION OF MUSICAL
INSTRUMENTS - LIBRARY □ New Haven, CT
Bromberg, Johanna, Libn.
OMAHA PUBLIC LIBRARY - BUSINESS, SCIENCE
& TECHNOLOGY DEPARTMENT □ Omaha, NE
Bromer, A. Susan, Curric.Mtls.Libn.
EAST STROUDSBURG STATE COLLEGE -
LIBRARY □ East Stroudsburg, PA
Bromley, James R., Dir.
NORTHWOOD INSTITUTE OF TEXAS -
FREEDOM EDUCATION CENTER □ Cedar Hill, TX
Bromwich, G.R.E., V.P., Res. & Info.Dept.
REED STENHOUSE, LTD. - RESEARCH
DEPARTMENT LIBRARY □ Toronto, ON
Brong, Gerald R., Dir.
INFORMATION FUTURES - INFORMATION
CENTER □ Pullman, WA
Brong, Marlene A., Coord. Of Pubns.
INFORMATION FUTURES - INFORMATION
CENTER □ Pullman, WA
Brongers, Rein J., Hd.
UNIVERSITY OF BRITISH COLUMBIA -
MATHEMATICS LIBRARY □ Vancouver, BC
Brongers, Rein J., Hd.
UNIVERSITY OF BRITISH COLUMBIA - SCIENCE
DIVISION □ Vancouver, BC
Bronner, Edwin B., Cur.
HAVERFORD COLLEGE - TREASURE ROOM AND
QUAKER COLLECTION □ Haverford, PA
Bronson, Barbara, Libn.
WARREN COUNTY LAW LIBRARY □ Lebanon, OH
Brook, Dr. Barry S., Dir.
REPERTOIRE INTERNATIONAL
D'ICONOGRAPHIE MUSICALE - RESEARCH
CENTER FOR MUSICAL ICONOGRAPHY -
LIBRARY □ New York, NY
Brooke, Anna, Libn.
SMITHSONIAN INSTITUTION - HIRSHHORN
MUSEUM AND SCULPTURE GARDEN - LIBRARY
□ Washington, DC
Brooke, Marilyn, Media Libn.
RED RIVER COMMUNITY COLLEGE - LEARNING
RESOURCES CENTRE □ Winnipeg, MB
Brooker, Alice, Libn.
SPRINGFIELD ART MUSEUM - ART REFERENCE
LIBRARY □ Springfield, MO
Brookes, Betty, AV
EDEN THEOLOGICAL SEMINARY - LIBRARY □
Webster Groves, MO
Brookreson, Mrs. Frances, Libn.
HENDRICK MEDICAL CENTER - MARY MEEK
SCHOOL OF NURSING - LIBRARY □ Abilene, TX
Brooks, Beverly, Hd.Libn.
TRIDENT TECHNICAL COLLEGE - NORTH
CAMPUS LIBRARY □ North Charleston, SC

Brooks, Carolyn M., Libn.
EVANGELICAL COVENANT CHURCH - LIBRARY†
□ Muskegon, MI
Brooks, Charles, Educ.Cur.
BUFFALO & ERIE COUNTY HISTORICAL
SOCIETY - LIBRARY □ Buffalo, NY
Brooks, Elaine, Serials Libn.Asst.
BABSON COLLEGE - HORN LIBRARY □ Babson
Park, MA
Brooks, Frances, Circ./Order Libn.
STATE TECHNICAL INSTITUTE AT MEMPHIS -
GEORGE E. FREEMAN LIBRARY □ Memphis, TN
Brooks, Janet, Chf.Libn.
U.S. DEFENSE COMMUNICATIONS AGENCY -
TECHNICAL LIBRARY AND INFORMATION
CENTER □ Washington, DC
Brooks, Jean, Per.Ref.Libn.
PITTSBURG STATE UNIVERSITY - LEONARD H.
AXE LIBRARY □ Pittsburg, KS
Brooks, Jerrold Lee, Dir.
HISTORICAL FOUNDATION OF THE
PRESBYTERIAN AND REFORMED CHURCHES -
LIBRARY AND ARCHIVES □ Montreat, NC
Brooks, Judith, Prof.Coll.Dev.Libn.
OAKLAND SCHOOLS - EDUCATIONAL RESOURCE
CENTER □ Pontiac, MI
Brooks, Mary Ellen, Biblog.
UNIVERSITY OF GEORGIA - RARE BOOKS
DEPARTMENT □ Athens, GA
Brooks, Minette, Med.Libn.
HAMPTON GENERAL HOSPITAL - MEDICAL
LIBRARY □ Hampton, VA
Brooks, Peggy, Lib.Chm.
ANALYTICAL PSYCHOLOGY CLUB OF NEW YORK
- KRISTINE MANN LIBRARY □ New York, NY
Brooks, Robert E., Hd.Ref.Libn.
YALE UNIVERSITY - LAW LIBRARY □ New
Haven, CT
Brooks, Roger D., Law Libn.
KANSAS STATE SUPREME COURT - LAW
LIBRARY □ Topeka, KS
Brooks, Ruth H., Asst.Libn.
SOUTHWEST FOUNDATION FOR RESEARCH
AND EDUCATION - PRESTON G. NORTHROP
MEMORIAL LIBRARY □ San Antonio, TX
Brooks, Violette, Asst.Ref.Libn.
CHICAGO TRANSIT AUTHORITY - HAROLD S.
ANTHON MEMORIAL LIBRARY □ Chicago, IL
Brookshier, Doris, Educ.Libn.
CENTRAL MISSOURI STATE UNIVERSITY -
WARD EDWARDS LIBRARY □ Warrensburg, MO
Broomfield, Phyllis, Libn.
FLORIDA STATE UNIVERSITY - CTR. FOR
STUDIES IN VOCATIONAL EDUC. - FLORIDA
EDUCATORS INFO. SERV. □ Tallahassee, FL
Brophy, Cynthia, Project Dir.
CRIME & JUSTICE FOUNDATION -
MASCARELLO LIBRARY OF CRIMINAL JUSTICE
□ Boston, MA
Brophy, Jill, Hd.Cat.
RAND CORPORATION - LIBRARY □ Santa
Monica, CA
Brophy, Kathleen
HARTFORD PUBLIC LIBRARY - ART, MUSIC AND
RECREATION DEPARTMENT □ Hartford, CT
Brose, Jean M., Hd.Libn.
ROCHESTER METHODIST HOSPITAL -
METHODIST KAHLER LIBRARY □ Rochester, MN
Brosky, Catherine, Hd.
CARNEGIE LIBRARY OF PITTSBURGH -
SCIENCE AND TECHNOLOGY DEPARTMENT □
Pittsburgh, PA
Brosman, Geraldine Y., Libn.
U.S. AIR FORCE BASE - MINOT BASE LIBRARY □
Minot AFB, ND
Bross, Dorothy R., Sr.Libn., Rd.Serv.
NEW YORK STATE DEPARTMENT OF HEALTH -
DIVISION OF LABORATORIES AND RESEARCH
LIBRARY □ Albany, NY
Bross, Mary Louise, Circ.
MORAVIAN COLLEGE - REEVES LIBRARY □
Bethlehem, PA

Brosseau, Lise, Libn.
SIDBEC-DOSCO LTEE. - CENTRE DE
DOCUMENTATION □ Contrecoeur, PQ
Broughton, Clifford, AV Coord.
MICHIGAN OSTEOPATHIC MEDICAL CENTER,
INC. - HEALTH SCIENCE LIBRARY □ Detroit, MI
Broughton, Rita, Film Libn.
ST. LOUIS PUBLIC LIBRARY - FILM LIBRARY
SERVICE □ St. Louis, MO
Brouwer, Norman J., Ship Hist.
SOUTH STREET SEAPORT MUSEUM - LIBRARY
□ New York, NY
Brown, A., Jr., Hd., Engr.Serv.
HENRY (J.J.) CO., INC. - ENGINEERING
LIBRARY □ Moorestown, NJ
Brown, A.T., Libn.
TIMKEN COMPANY - RESEARCH LIBRARY □
Canton, OH
Brown, Adelaide Loretta, Libn.
U.S. DEPT. OF JUSTICE - LAND AND NATURAL
RESOURCES DIVISION LIBRARY □ Washington,
DC
Brown, Andrea, Per.
ST. LOUIS MERCANTILE LIBRARY
ASSOCIATION - LIBRARY □ St. Louis, MO
Brown, Anne, Judges' Libn.
ONTARIO - MINISTRY OF THE ATTORNEY
GENERAL - JUDGES' LIBRARY □ Toronto, ON
Brown, Rev. Arthur E., M.M., Libn.
MARYKNOLL SEMINARY - LIBRARY □ Maryknoll,
NY
Brown, Becky, Tech.Serv.Libn.
CENTRAL BIBLE COLLEGE - LIBRARY □
Springfield, MO
Brown, Bennie, Jr., Libn.
GUNSTON HALL PLANTATION - HOUSE MUSEUM
- LIBRARY □ Lorton, VA
Brown, Beth A., Dir., Tech.Info.Ctr.
NATIONAL CENTER FOR HOUSING
MANAGEMENT - TECHNICAL INFORMATION
CENTER† □ Washington, DC
Brown, Betty, Oklahoma Docs.
OKLAHOMA STATE DEPARTMENT OF
LIBRARIES □ Oklahoma City, OK
Brown, Beulah M., Libn.
SAN BERNARDINO COUNTY LAW LIBRARY† □
San Bernardino, CA
Brown, Dr. Bryce C., Musm.Dir.
BAYLOR UNIVERSITY - STRECKER MUSEUM
LIBRARY □ Waco, TX
Brown, Carmen, Hd., Pub.Serv./Ref.
WORCESTER POLYTECHNIC INSTITUTE -
GEORGE C. GORDON LIBRARY □ Worcester, MA
Brown, Carol A., Tech.Res.Libn.
CONSOLIDATED NATURAL GAS SERVICE CO.,
INC. - RESEARCH DEPARTMENT LIBRARY □
Cleveland, OH
Brown, Carolyn, Dir.
U.S. EXECUTIVE OFFICE OF THE PRESIDENT -
INFORMATION MANAGEMENT AND SERVICES
DIVISION □ Washington, DC
Brown, Charles A., Dir. of Lib.
MEMORIAL MEDICAL CENTER - HEALTH
SCIENCES LIBRARY □ Corpus Christi, TX
Brown, Charlotte, Asst.Ref.Libn.
STANFORD UNIVERSITY - J. HUGH JACKSON
LIBRARY □ Stanford, CA
Brown, Chris R., Spec. Events Coord.
BABSON COLLEGE - HORN LIBRARY □ Babson
Park, MA
Brown, Christine B., Trade Ref.Asst.
U.S. DEPT. OF COMMERCE - INTERNATIONAL
TRADE ADMINISTRATION - ATLANTA
DISTRICT OFFICE LIBRARY □ Atlanta, GA
Brown, Claire L., Spec.
HARVARD UNIVERSITY - LITTAUER LIBRARY □
Cambridge, MA
Brown, Connis O., Asst. State Archv.
VIRGINIA STATE LIBRARY □ Richmond, VA
Brown, Dale W., Dir.
ALEXANDRIA CITY PUBLIC SCHOOLS -
EDUCATIONAL MEDIA CENTER - NICHOLS
PROFESSIONAL LIBRARY □ Alexandria, VA

Brown, David, Libn.
UNIVERSITY OF CALIFORNIA, BERKELEY -
GRADUATE SCHOOL OF JOURNALISM -
LIBRARY □ Berkeley, CA

Brown, David C., Adm.Libn.
U.S. MARINE CORPS - EDUCATION CENTER -
JAMES CARSON BRECKINRIDGE LIBRARY &
AMPHIBIOUS WARFARE RESEARCH FACILITY □
Quantico, VA

Brown, Deborah L., Ext. Horticulturist
UNIVERSITY OF MINNESOTA - HORTICULTURE
EXTENSION CLINIC □ St. Paul, MN

Brown, Diana, Coord.
AMERICAN COLLEGE OF HOSPITAL
ADMINISTRATORS - RAY E. BROWN
MANAGEMENT COLLECTION □ Chicago, IL

Brown, Diane, Boettcher Libn.
COLORADO SCHOOL OF MINES - ARTHUR
LAKES LIBRARY □ Golden, CO

Brown, Donald, Mgr., Media Serv.
BABSON COLLEGE - HORN LIBRARY □ Babson
Park, MA

Brown, Donald, Coord., Mtls. Selection
PENNSYLVANIA STATE LIBRARY □ Harrisburg,
PA

Brown, Dorothy Eady, Sr.Libn.
UNIVERSITY OF ALABAMA - BUSINESS
LIBRARY □ University, AL

Brown, Dorothy L., Libn.
WILMINGTON NEWS-JOURNAL COMPANY -
LIBRARY □ Wilmington, DE

Brown, Dwight, Tax Libn.
MILBANK, TWEED, HADLEY & MC CLOY -
LIBRARY □ New York, NY

Brown, E.S.
UNIVERSITY OF TORONTO - FACULTY OF
ENGINEERING LIBRARY □ Toronto, ON

Brown, Eleanor, Musm.Cur.
SISKIYOU COUNTY MUSEUM - LIBRARY □
Yreka, CA

Brown, Eleanor T., Hd.
AMHERST COLLEGE - SCIENCE LIBRARY □
Amherst, MA

Brown, Elisabeth P., Asst.Libn.
AMERICAN COLLEGE - VANE B. LUCAS
MEMORIAL LIBRARY □ Bryn Mawr, PA

Brown, Elizabeth B., Libn.
MONTGOMERY MUSEUM OF FINE ARTS - ART
RESEARCH LIBRARY □ Montgomery, AL

Brown, Ellen, Tech.Serv.Supv.
CITY OF COMMERCE PUBLIC LIBRARY □
Commerce, CA

Brown, Ellen K., Hd.Archv./Hist.Mss.
BAYLOR UNIVERSITY - TEXAS COLLECTION □
Waco, TX

Brown, Eve, Records Mgt.Supv.
MOTT (Charles Stewart) FOUNDATION -
LIBRARY □ Flint, MI

Brown, Evelyn, Ed.
RILEY COUNTY GENEALOGICAL SOCIETY -
LIBRARY □ Manhattan, KS

Brown, G.H., Assoc.Libn.
MONTGOMERY, MC CRACKEN, WALKER &
RHOADS - LIBRARY □ Philadelphia, PA

Brown, George C., Music Dir.
CHARLES RIVER BROADCASTING COMPANY -
WCRB LIBRARY □ Waltham, MA

Brown, Gerald, Asst.Libn.
ST. LOUIS POST-DISPATCH - REFERENCE
DEPARTMENT □ St. Louis, MO

Brown, Gerald R., Chf.Libn.
WINNIPEG SCHOOL DIVISION NO. 1 -
TEACHERS LIBRARY AND RESOURCE CENTRE □
Winnipeg, MB

Brown, Geraldine McColgan, Hd.Libn.
XEROX CORPORATION - LAW LIBRARY □
Stamford, CT

Brown, Gordon, Asst.Archv.
MONTANA HISTORICAL SOCIETY - LIBRARY/
ARCHIVES □ Helena, MT

Brown, Grant, Libn.
ONTARIO GENEALOGICAL SOCIETY - LIBRARY
□ Willowdale, ON

Brown, Harold, Cur. Emeritus
MAINE MARITIME MUSEUM - LIBRARY/
ARCHIVES □ Bath, ME

Brown, Harold M., Asst.Libn.
NORTHROP UNIVERSITY - ALUMNI LIBRARY† □
Inglewood, CA

Brown, Helen-Ann, Med.Libn.
NATIONAL JEWISH HOSPITAL & RESEARCH
CENTER/NATIONAL ASTHMA CENTER -
MEDICAL LIBRARY □ Denver, CO

Brown, Helen G., Info.Anl.
GENERAL ELECTRIC COMPANY - AIRCRAFT
ENGINE GROUP - DR. C.W. SMITH TECHNICAL
INFORMATION CENTER □ Lynn, MA

Brown, Helene, Biomed.Br.Libn.
GENERAL MOTORS CORPORATION - RESEARCH
LABORATORIES LIBRARY □ Warren, MI

Brown, Howard C., Archv.
NEWFOUNDLAND - PROVINCIAL ARCHIVES OF
NEWFOUNDLAND AND LABRADOR □ St. John's,
NF

Brown, J. Robin, Dept.Libn.
ALBERTA - TREASURY DEPARTMENT - LIBRARY
SERVICES □ Edmonton, AB

Brown, J.T., Mgr.
BATTELLE-COLUMBUS LABORATORIES -
TACTICAL TECHNOLOGY CENTER □ Columbus,
OH

Brown, Jack Perry, Libn.
CLEVELAND MUSEUM OF ART - LIBRARY □
Cleveland, OH

Brown, James A., Hd., Rsrcs.
AMARILLO COLLEGE - LEARNING RESOURCE
CENTER □ Amarillo, TX

Brown, Jan, Doc.Libn.
WASHBURN UNIVERSITY OF TOPEKA - SCHOOL
OF LAW LIBRARY □ Topeka, KS

Brown, Jane, Assoc.Libn.
UNIVERSITY OF SASKATCHEWAN - ST.
THOMAS MORE COLLEGE - SHANNON LIBRARY
□ Saskatoon, SK

Brown, Janis, Pharmacy Libn.
UNIVERSITY OF SOUTHERN CALIFORNIA -
HEALTH SCIENCES CAMPUS - NORRIS
MEDICAL LIBRARY □ Los Angeles, CA

Brown, Jann Braudis
SETON HALL UNIVERSITY - SCHOOL OF LAW -
LAW LIBRARY □ Newark, NJ

Brown, Jay M., Chm., House Comm.
CONGREGATION MISHKAN ISRAEL - ADULT
LIBRARY □ Hamden, CT

Brown, Dr. Jeanette S., Dir.
CARNEGIE INSTITUTION OF WASHINGTON -
DEPARTMENT OF PLANT BIOLOGY - LIBRARY □
Stanford, CA

Brown, Julia, Mgr.
CALIFORNIA HISTORICAL SOCIETY - HISTORY
CENTER LIBRARY □ Los Angeles, CA

Brown, Dr. Katharine L., Exec.Dir.
WILSON (Woodrow) BIRTHPLACE
FOUNDATION, INC. - RESEARCH LIBRARY &
ARCHIVES □ Staunton, VA

Brown, Kathryn, Ed.
U.S. GENERAL SERVICES ADMINISTRATION -
CONSUMER INFORMATION CENTER □
Washington, DC

Brown, Kay, Cat.Libn.
SUNY - COLLEGE AT POTSDAM - FREDERICK W.
CRUMB MEMORIAL LIBRARY □ Potsdam, NY

Brown, Keith G., Tech.Info.Spec.
GENERAL DYNAMICS CORPORATION - FORT
WORTH DIVISION - RESEARCH LIBRARY □ Fort
Worth, TX

Brown, Laura Ferris, Chf.Libn.
AMERICAN ARBITRATION ASSOCIATION -
EASTMAN ARBITRATION LIBRARY □ New York,
NY

Brown, Mrs. Laure H., Libn.
U.S. NATL. CAPITAL PLANNING COMMISSION -
LIBRARY □ Washington, DC

Brown, Lauren R., Spec.Coll.Libn.
RICE UNIVERSITY - WOODSON RESEARCH
CENTER □ Houston, TX

Brown, Leslie, Act.Dir., Adm.Serv.
U.S. DEPT. OF HOUSING AND URBAN
DEVELOPMENT - REGION III - LIBRARY □
Philadelphia, PA

Brown, Linda, Libn.
NORTHEAST OHIO FOUR COUNTY REGIONAL
PLANNING & DEVELOPMENT ORGANIZATION -
TECHNICAL INFORMATION CENTER □ Akron,
OH

Brown, Linda, Assoc.Libn.
YALE UNIVERSITY - OBSERVATORY LIBRARY □
New Haven, CT

Brown, Lisle G., Cur.
MARSHALL UNIVERSITY - JAMES E. MORROW
LIBRARY - SPECIAL COLLECTIONS □
Huntington, WV

Brown, Lois, Braille Coord.
CANADIAN NATIONAL INSTITUTE FOR THE
BLIND - NATIONAL LIBRARY SERVICES □
Toronto, ON

Brown, Lorna, Libn.
ONTARIO - MINISTRY OF REVENUE - LIBRARY
□ Toronto, ON

Brown, Lucille W., Libn.
UNION UNIVERSITY - ALBANY COLLEGE OF
PHARMACY - LIBRARY □ Albany, NY

Brown, Mabel C., Dir., Lib.Serv.
OTTAWA CIVIC HOSPITAL - DR. GEORGE S.
WILLIAMSON HEALTH SCIENCES LIBRARY □
Ottawa, ON

Brown, Mabel E., Dir.
WESTON COUNTY HISTORICAL SOCIETY -
ANNA MILLER MUSEUM - LIBRARY □ Newcastle,
WY

Brown, Madeline A., Med.Libn.
CATHOLIC MEDICAL CENTER OF BROOKLYN &
QUEENS, INC. - ST. MARY'S HOSPITAL -
MEDICAL ADMINISTRATIVE LIBRARY □
Brooklyn, NY

Brown, Marguerite, Rec.Mgr.
SEVENTH-DAY ADVENTISTS - GENERAL
CONFERENCE - OFFICE OF ARCHIVES AND
STATISTICS □ Washington, DC

Brown, Marion, Libn.
U.S. ARMY SERGEANTS MAJOR ACADEMY -
OTHON O. VALENT LEARNING RESOURCES
CENTER □ Ft. Bliss, TX

Brown, Mary Anne, Asst.
NUCLEAR ASSURANCE CORPORATION -
INFORMATION CENTER □ Atlanta, GA

Brown, Mary E., Coll.Dev.
JOHNS HOPKINS UNIVERSITY - APPLIED
PHYSICS LABORATORY - R.E. GIBSON LIBRARY
□ Laurel, MD

Brown, Sister Mary Georgia, Libn.
LEILA HOSPITAL AND HEALTH CENTER -
MEDICAL LIBRARY □ Battle Creek, MI

Brown, Mary Grace H., Med.Libn./Media Serv.Dir.
PETERSBURG GENERAL HOSPITAL - MEDICAL
LIBRARY MEDIA SERVICES □ Petersburg, VA

Brown, Maxine, Asst.Libn.
LEXINGTON TECHNICAL INSTITUTE - LIBRARY
□ Lexington, KY

Brown, Milton H., Exec.Sec.
AMERICAN CAMELLIA SOCIETY - LIBRARY □
Fort Valley, GA

Brown, Milton M., Sec.
NATIONAL AERONAUTIC ASSOCIATION -
LIBRARY □ Washington, DC

Brown, Morton R., Libn.
SMITH BARNEY, HARRIS UPHAM & COMPANY,
INC. - LIBRARY □ New York, NY

Brown, Muriel, Children's Lit.Spec.
DALLAS PUBLIC LIBRARY - HUMANITIES
DIVISION □ Dallas, TX

Brown, Patricia, Dir.
NATIONAL COLLEGE OF CHIROPRACTIC -
LEARNING RESOURCE CENTER □ Lombard, IL

Brown, Patricia F., Libn.
ECUMENICAL LIBRARY □ New York, NY

Brown, Patricia I., Asst. Law Libn.
SUFFOLK UNIVERSITY - LAW LIBRARY □
Boston, MA

PERSONNEL

Brown, Patti, Info.Spec.
UNIVERSITY OF SOUTHERN CALIFORNIA - NASA INDUSTRIAL APPLICATION CENTER (NIAC) □ Los Angeles, CA

Brown, Paula, Mgr.
BATTEN, BARTON, DURSTINE, OSBORN, INC. - INFORMATION RETRIEVAL CENTER □ New York, NY

Brown, Mrs. Perry, Asst.Libn.
FIRST BAPTIST CHURCH - LIBRARY □ Brevard, NC

Brown, Philip, Pub.Serv.Libn.
SOUTH DAKOTA STATE UNIVERSITY - HILTON M. BRIGGS LIBRARY □ Brookings, SD

Brown, Regina, Hd.Libn.
OHIO STATE UNIVERSITY - ORTON MEMORIAL LIBRARY OF GEOLOGY □ Columbus, OH

Brown, Richard H., Dir.Res. & Educ.
NEWBERRY LIBRARY □ Chicago, IL

Brown, Richard L., Asst. Law Libn.
FLORIDA STATE UNIVERSITY - LAW LIBRARY □ Tallahassee, FL

Brown, Robert A., Chf.
U.S. DEFENSE LOGISTICS AGENCY - DEFENSE CONSTRUCTION SUPPLY CENTER - TECHNICAL DATA PROCESSING BRANCH □ Columbus, OH

Brown, Rev. Robert E., S.M., Archv.
SOCIETY OF MARY - CINCINNATI PROVINCE - ARCHIVES □ Dayton, OH

Brown, Ronald D., Group Supv.
JOHNS HOPKINS UNIVERSITY - APPLIED PHYSICS LABORATORY - CHEMICAL PROPULSION INFORMATION AGENCY □ Laurel, MD

Brown, Sharon, Libn.
CONOCO, INC. - MINERALS LIBRARY □ Denver, CO

Brown, Sharon, Asst.Libn.
NEW YORK SOCIETY LIBRARY □ New York, NY

Brown, Shelia E., Hd.
OWENSBORO-DAVIESS COUNTY PUBLIC LIBRARY - KENTUCKY ROOM □ Owensboro, KY

Brown, Sheryl J., Dir.
NORTHWOOD INSTITUTE OF TEXAS - ROSALIND KRESS HALEY LIBRARY □ Cedar Hill, TX

Brown, Shirley, Libn.
SHERWIN-WILLIAMS COMPANY OF CANADA, LTD. - TECHNICAL LIBRARY □ Montreal, PQ

Brown, Stanley W., Chf.Spec.Coll.
DARTMOUTH COLLEGE - SPECIAL COLLECTIONS □ Hanover, NH

Brown, Suzanne, Asst.Libn.
COLONIAL WILLIAMSBURG - AUDIO-VISUAL LIBRARY □ Williamsburg, VA

Brown, Yvonne, Hd., Art Sect.
CHICAGO PUBLIC LIBRARY CULTURAL CENTER - FINE ARTS DIVISION - ART SECTION □ Chicago, IL

Brown-Comment, Anna Mae, Supv., Info.Serv.
COLLEGE OF THE VIRGIN ISLANDS - CARIBBEAN RESEARCH INSTITUTE - LIBRARY □ St. Thomas, VI

Browne, Alice R., Ref.Libn.
RENSSELAER POLYTECHNIC INSTITUTE - FOLSOM LIBRARY □ Troy, NY

Browne, Cynthia E., Cat.
NEW JERSEY HISTORICAL SOCIETY - LIBRARY □ Newark, NJ

Browne, D.A., Pubn.Coord.
HERCULES, INC. - AEROSPACE DIVISION - MC GREGOR TECHNICAL INFORMATION CENTER □ McGregor, TX

Browne, Dr. Gary, Ed.
MARYLAND HISTORICAL SOCIETY - LIBRARY □ Baltimore, MD

Browne, Jane, Off.Mgr.
BOWLING GREEN STATE UNIVERSITY - CENTER FOR ARCHIVAL COLLECTIONS □ Bowling Green, OH

Browne, Mamie G., Act.Univ.Archv.
ALABAMA A & M UNIVERSITY - JOSEPH F. DRAKE MEMORIAL LEARNING RESOURCES CENTER □ Normal, AL

Browne, Robert, Pres.
BLACK ECONOMIC RESEARCH CENTER - REFERENCE LIBRARY □ New York, NY

Browne, Valerie, Archv.
WAYNE STATE UNIVERSITY - ARCHIVES OF LABOR AND URBAN AFFAIRS/UNIVERSITY ARCHIVES □ Detroit, MI

Brownell, Daphne, Cons.
HALIFAX HISTORICAL SOCIETY, INC. - LIBRARY □ Daytona Beach, FL

Browning, Donna, Med.Libn.
DEACONESS HOSPITAL - MEDICAL LIBRARY □ Buffalo, NY

Browning, Mary L., Chf., Rd.Serv.Engr.Div.
U.S. AIR FORCE INSTITUTE OF TECHNOLOGY - LIBRARY □ Wright-Patterson AFB, OH

Browning, Phyllis M., Sci.Info.Mgr.
BECKMAN INSTRUMENTS, INC. - SPINCO DIVISION - TECHNICAL LIBRARY □ Palo Alto, CA

Brownlee, Evelyn, Asst.Libn.
DELAWARE LAW SCHOOL OF WIDENER UNIVERSITY - LAW LIBRARY □ Wilmington, DE

Brownlee, Dr. Richard S., Dir.
STATE HISTORICAL SOCIETY OF MISSOURI - LIBRARY □ Columbia, MO

Brownlow, Frances, Libn. & Cat.
PUBLIC UTILITY COMMISSION OF TEXAS - LIBRARY □ Austin, TX

Brownlow, Judith, Libn.
U.S. NATL. MARINE FISHERIES SERVICE - NORTHEAST FISHERIES CENTER - LIBRARY □ Woods Hole, MA

Brozda, Wanda, Tech.Libn.
PPG INDUSTRIES, INC. - GLASS RESEARCH CENTER - INFORMATION SERVICES □ Pittsburgh, PA

Brubaker, Robert L., Cur., Spec.Coll.
CHICAGO HISTORICAL SOCIETY - SPECIAL COLLECTIONS □ Chicago, IL

Bruce, Ann M., Libn.
FLORIDA STATE HOSPITAL - PATIENT/STAFF LIBRARY □ Chattahoochee, FL

Bruce, Helen G., Libn.
BRITISH COLUMBIA - MINISTRY OF INDUSTRY & SMALL BUSINESS DEVELOPMENT - LIBRARY □ Victoria, BC

Bruce, Nancy, Lib.Supv.
TEXAS CHRISTIAN UNIVERSITY - INSTITUTE OF BEHAVIORAL RESEARCH - TECHNICAL LIBRARY □ Fort Worth, TX

Bruce, Nancy J., Lib.Supv.
TEXAS CHRISTIAN UNIVERSITY - INSTITUTE OF BEHAVIORAL RESEARCH - DRUG ABUSE COUNCIL LIBRARY □ Fort Worth, TX

Bruce, Pamela, Libn.
CANADA - PUBLIC ARCHIVES OF CANADA - NATL. FILM, TELEVISION & SOUND ARCHIVES - DOCUMENTATION & PUB. SERV. □ Ottawa, ON

Bruce, Robert K., Dept.Hd.
MINNEAPOLIS PUBLIC LIBRARY & INFORMATION CENTER - HISTORY DEPARTMENT □ Minneapolis, MN

Bruckman, Jan, Supv., Film Lib.
UNIVERSITY OF UTAH - INSTRUCTIONAL MEDIA SERVICES □ Salt Lake City, UT

Brude, Deborah J., Hd.Libn.
ANOKA AREA VOCATIONAL TECHNICAL INSTITUTE - MEDIA CENTER □ Anoka, MN

Brudvig, Glenn L., Dir.
UNIVERSITY OF MINNESOTA - BIOMEDICAL LIBRARY □ Minneapolis, MN

Brudvig, Karen, Libn.
MIDWAY HOSPITAL - HEALTH SCIENCES LIBRARY □ St. Paul, MN

Brue, Donald W., Libn.
LUTHERAN BRETHREN SCHOOLS - BIBLE COLLEGE AND SEMINARY LIBRARY □ Fergus Falls, MN

Brueck, Lora, Spec.Coll.
WORCESTER POLYTECHNIC INSTITUTE - GEORGE C. GORDON LIBRARY □ Worcester, MA

Brueck, Philip R., Chf., Park Oper.
U.S. NATL. PARK SERVICE - CAPE LOOKOUT NATL. SEASHORE - LIBRARY □ Beaufort, NC

Bruemner, Alice, Libn.
ALLSTATE INSURANCE COMPANY - LAW LIBRARY □ Northbrook, IL

Bruenjes, Alice, Hd.Libn.
JEWISH HOSPITAL OF ST. LOUIS - SCHOOL OF NURSING - MOSES SHOENBERG MEMORIAL LIBRARY □ St. Louis, MO

Brugera, Eva A., Ref.Libn.
U.S. VETERANS ADMINISTRATION (CA-Palo Alto) - HOSPITAL MEDICAL LIBRARIES □ Palo Alto, CA

Brugman, Mrs. T., Ref.Off.
ONTARIO - MINISTRY OF INDUSTRY AND TOURISM - INFORMATION CENTRE □ Toronto, ON

Bruhn, Mildred S., Supv.
UOP INC. - PATENT LIBRARY □ Des Plaines, IL

Bruins, Ella G., Asst.Libn.
SUNY AT ALBANY - LIBRARY SCIENCE BRANCH □ Albany, NY

Bruland, Rev. Osborne Y., Libn.
FAITH EVANGELICAL LUTHERAN SEMINARY - LIBRARY □ Tacoma, WA

Brule, Michel, Dir.Gen.
CINEMATHEQUE NATIONALE DU QUEBEC □ Montreal, PQ

Brumbaugh, Ted S., Dir.
MESA COUNTY VALLEY SCHOOL DISTRICT 51 - DEPARTMENT OF RESOURCES, RESEARCH AND DEVELOPMENT □ Grand Junction, CO

Brumgardt, John, Musm.Dir.
MUSEUM OF WESTERN COLORADO - ARCHIVES □ Grand Junction, CO

Brun, Christian, Dept.Hd.
UNIVERSITY OF CALIFORNIA, SANTA BARBARA - DEPARTMENT OF SPECIAL COLLECTIONS □ Santa Barbara, CA

Bruneau, Theresa, Libn.
CONFERENCE BOARD OF CANADA - LIBRARY & INFORMATION CENTER □ Ottawa, ON

Brunelle, Rev. Denis C., M.S.C., Libn.
MSC CENTER LIBRARY □ Shelby, OH

Bruner, Mrs. James G., Libn.
ST. THOMAS MORE HOSPITAL - MEDICAL LIBRARY □ Canon City, CO

Brunet, Fran, Libn.
ESHERICK, HOMSEY, DODGE & DAVIS - LIBRARY □ San Francisco, CA

Brunette, Mary J., Asst.Corp.Libn.
BAUSCH & LOMB, INC. - CORPORATE LIBRARY □ Rochester, NY

Brunka, Veronica, Lib.Supv.
ONTARIO - MINISTRY OF HEALTH - LIBRARY □ Toronto, ON

Brunke, Mrs. Conrad, Libn.
WARREN COUNTY HISTORICAL SOCIETY - LIBRARY AND ARCHIVES □ Warren, PA

Brunn, Carla, Search Coord.
MORRISON-KNUDSEN CO., INC. - RECORDS AND MICROGRAPHICS CENTER □ Boise, ID

Brunner, Karen B., Law Libn.
MORRIS COUNTY LAW LIBRARY □ Morristown, NJ

Brunnschweiler, Dr. Tamara, Biblog.Lat.Amer.Stud
MICHIGAN STATE UNIVERSITY - INTERNATIONAL LIBRARY □ East Lansing, MI

Brunson, Madelon, Archv.
REORGANIZED CHURCH OF JESUS CHRIST OF LATTER DAY SAINTS - LIBRARY & ARCHIVES □ Independence, MO

Brunson, Ruth, Dir.
UNIVERSITY OF ARKANSAS AT LITTLE ROCK - PULASKI COUNTY LAW LIBRARY □ Little Rock, AR

Brunstad, Mrs. Dera C., Libn.
CEDAR VALE REGIONAL HOSPITAL - LIBRARY □ Cedar Vale, KS

Brunton, Angela, Libn.
CALIFORNIA STATE DIVISION OF MINES AND
GEOLOGY - LIBRARY □ San Francisco, CA

Bryan, Betty A., Asst.Dir.
AMERICAN SOCIETY FOR METALS - METALS
INFORMATION □ Metals Park, OH

Bryan, Bonita, First Asst.
PUBLIC LIBRARY OF CINCINNATI AND
HAMILTON COUNTY - GOVERNMENT AND
BUSINESS DEPARTMENT □ Cincinnati, OH

Bryan, Bruce, Libn.
WELDING INSTITUTE OF CANADA - LIBRARY □
Oakville, ON

Bryan, Carla W., Libn.
NORTHWOOD INSTITUTE OF TEXAS - LIBRARY
□ Cedar Hill, TX

Bryan, Edwin H., Jr., Mgr.
PACIFIC SCIENTIFIC INFORMATION CENTER □
Honolulu, HI

Bryan, Libby, Libn.
WESTERN RESERVE PSYCHIATRIC
HABILITATION CENTER - STAFF LIBRARY □
Northfield, OH

Bryan, Rebecca, Hd., Ser.Dept.
SOUTH DAKOTA STATE UNIVERSITY - HILTON
M. BRIGGS LIBRARY □ Brookings, SD

Bryant, Betty, Libn.
CANADA - NATIONAL DEFENCE - NORTHERN
REGION REFERENCE LIBRARY □ Yellowknife, NT

Bryant, Charles R., Cur.
YALE UNIVERSITY - SOUTHEAST ASIA
COLLECTION □ New Haven, CT

Bryant, Fred D., Dir.
UNIVERSITY OF SOUTH FLORIDA - MEDICAL
CENTER LIBRARY □ Tampa, FL

Bryant, Lillian, Libn.
UNIVERSITY OF PENNSYLVANIA - SCHOOL OF
VETERINARY MEDICINE - C.J. MARSHALL
MEMORIAL LIBRARY □ Philadelphia, PA

Bryant, Paul F., Tech.Libn.
CHAMPION INTERNATIONAL - CHAMPION
PAPERS TECHNICAL LIBRARY □ Hamilton, OH

Bryant, Prudence W., Supv., Print Serv.
ALABAMA A & M UNIVERSITY - JOSEPH F.
DRAKE MEMORIAL LEARNING RESOURCES
CENTER □ Normal, AL

Brynes, Stephen, Sci. Correspondent
TRACOR JITCO, INC. - RESEARCH RESOURCES
INFORMATION CENTER □ Rockville, MD

Brysh, Janet F., Libn.
UNIVERSITY OF SOUTHERN MAINE - CENTER
FOR RESEARCH & ADVANCED STUDY -
RESEARCH CENTER LIBRARY □ Portland, ME

Bryson, Edna, Libn.
FIRST BAPTIST CHURCH - LIBRARY □ Brevard,
NC

Bryson, Emily Montez, Biblog.Instr.
CHICAGO STATE UNIVERSITY - DOUGLAS
LIBRARY □ Chicago, IL

Bryson, Shauna, Cat.
ICI AMERICAS INC. - ATLAS LIBRARY □
Wilmington, DE

Brzoska, Ellen, Libn.
YAKIMA VALLEY GENEALOGICAL SOCIETY -
LIBRARY □ Yakima, WA

Bube, Judith, Acq.Libn.
UNIVERSITY OF CALIFORNIA, IRVINE -
BIOMEDICAL LIBRARY □ Irvine, CA

Bubuc, Pierrette, Hd.
HOPITAL STE-JUSTINE - CENTRE
D'INFORMATION SUR LA SANTE DE L'ENFANT†
□ Montreal, PQ

Buch, Jane, Tech.Serv.Supv.
DELAWARE STATE - DIVISION OF LIBRARIES □
Dover, DE

Buch, Reid A., Libn.
FOUNDATION FOR STUDENT COMMUNICATION
- LIBRARY AND RESOURCE CENTER □ Princeton,
NJ

Buchan, Robert, Cur.
SHERIDAN COUNTY HISTORICAL SOCIETY,
INC. - AGNES & CLARENCE BENSCHOTER
MEMORIAL LIBRARY □ Rushville, NE

Buchanan, Barbara R., Libn.
DOW CHEMICAL OF CANADA, LTD. - LIBRARY □
Sarnia, ON

Buchanan, Gerald, Asst.Dir.Lib.Oper.
MISSISSIPPI STATE LIBRARY COMMISSION □
Jackson, MS

Buchanan, Holly S., Dir.
NORTON-CHILDREN'S HOSPITALS - MEDICAL
LIBRARY □ Louisville, KY

Buchanan, Jack T., Res.Libn.
EASTMAN KODAK COMPANY - TEXAS EASTMAN
COMPANY - RESEARCH LIBRARY □ Longview,
TX

Buchanan, Joel R., Asst.Dir.
U.S. OAK RIDGE NATL. LABORATORY -
NUCLEAR SAFETY INFORMATION CENTER □
Oak Ridge, TN

Buchanan, Karen E., Hd.Libn.
AMERICAN STOCK EXCHANGE - MARTIN J.
KEENA MEMORIAL LIBRARY □ New York, NY

Buchanan, Nancy, Rd.Serv.Libn.
NORTHERN KENTUCKY UNIVERSITY - SALMON
P. CHASE COLLEGE OF LAW - LIBRARY □
Covington, KY

Buchberg, Karl, Consrv.
PRINCETON UNIVERSITY - RARE BOOKS AND
SPECIAL COLLECTIONS □ Princeton, NJ

Buchheim, A.F. Gunther, Biblog.
CARNEGIE-MELLON UNIVERSITY - HUNT
INSTITUTE FOR BOTANICAL DOCUMENTATION
- LIBRARY □ Pittsburgh, PA

Buchheit, Mary E., Dir. of Med.Lib.
KINGSBROOK JEWISH MEDICAL CENTER -
MEDICAL LIBRARY □ Brooklyn, NY

Buchholz, Janis, Ref.Libn.
WAYNE STATE UNIVERSITY - SCIENCE
LIBRARY □ Detroit, MI

Buchholz, Margery
INDIANA STATE UNIVERSITY - CONTINUING
EDUCATION AND EXTENDED SERVICES -
LIBRARY □ Terre Haute, IN

Buchsen, Dolores M.
PENNSYLVANIA STATE HISTORICAL & MUSEUM
COMMISSION - PENNSYLVANIA LUMBER
MUSEUM - LIBRARY □ Galeton, PA

Buck, Aileen, Ref./Maps Libn.
NORTH DAKOTA STATE UNIVERSITY - LIBRARY
□ Fargo, ND

Buck, Ann M., Lib. Group Supv.
BELL TELEPHONE LABORATORIES, INC. &
WESTERN ELECTRIC, INC. - TECHNICAL
LIBRARY □ Reading, PA

Buck, Ivan L., AV Coord.
NORTHWEST HOSPITAL - EFFIE M. STOREY
LEARNING CENTER □ Seattle, WA

Buck, Joan, Lib.Res.Anl.
ROCKWELL INTERNATIONAL - SPACE
BUSINESSES - TECHNICAL INFORMATION
CENTER □ Downey, CA

Buck, Michael D., Dir. of Lib.
TEXAS STATE TECHNICAL INSTITUTE, RIO
GRANDE CAMPUS - LIBRARY □ Harlingen, TX

Buck, Patricia, Asst.Libn.
PHILADELPHIA BOARD OF EDUCATION -
PEDAGOGICAL LIBRARY □ Philadelphia, PA

Buck, Ron, Supv., Campus Serv.
OKLAHOMA STATE UNIVERSITY - AUDIO
VISUAL CENTER □ Stillwater, OK

Buck, S.A.
DOW CHEMICAL COMPANY - TECHNICAL
INFORMATION SERVICES - CENTRAL REPORT
INDEX □ Midland, MI

Buckardt, Dr. Henry L., Pres.
AMERICAN WORK HORSE MUSEUM - LIBRARY □
Paeonian Springs, VA

Buckel, William, Ref.Libn.
BATTELLE-COLUMBUS LABORATORIES -
LIBRARY □ Columbus, OH

Buckholtz, Donald E., Libn.
MASSACHUSETTS TAXPAYERS FOUNDATION,
INC. - LIBRARY □ Boston, MA

Buckley, Dr. Jay S., Jr., Dir.Tech.Info.
PFIZER, INC. - CENTRAL RESEARCH
TECHNICAL INFORMATION SERVICES □ Groton,
CT

Buckley, Keith, Ref.Libn.
INDIANA UNIVERSITY - LAW LIBRARY □
Bloomington, IN

Buckley, Margaret, Libn.
DES MOINES ART CENTER - LIBRARY □ Des
Moines, IA

Buckley, Martha F., Asst.Libn.
EMORY UNIVERSITY - DIVISION OF LIBRARY
AND INFORMATION MANAGEMENT LIBRARY □
Atlanta, GA

Buckley, Steven F., Hd. of Tech.Serv.
SUNY - COLLEGE AT BROCKPORT - DRAKE
MEMORIAL LIBRARY □ Brockport, NY

Buckwald, Joel, Chf., Archv.Br.
U.S. NATL. ARCHIVES & RECORDS SERVICE -
FEDERAL ARCHIVES AND RECORDS CENTER,
REGION 2 □ Bayonne, NJ

Buckwalter, Margaret, Ser.Libn.
CLARION STATE COLLEGE - RENA M. CARLSON
LIBRARY □ Clarion, PA

Buckwalter, Robert, Hd., Acq.
COLUMBIA UNIVERSITY - LAW LIBRARY □ New
York, NY

Budahn, Karen, Libn.
SOUTHEASTERN WISCONSIN HEALTH
SYSTEMS AGENCY - LIBRARY □ Milwaukee, WI

Buday, Magda, Bus.Libn.
WASHINGTON UNIVERSITY - BUSINESS
ADMINISTRATION LIBRARY □ St. Louis, MO

Budd, Mary N., Libn.
NORTH YORK PUBLIC LIBRARY - URBAN
AFFAIRS SECTION □ Willowdale, ON

Budde, Jacqueline, Libn.
UNIVERSITY OF MINNESOTA - HORMEL
INSTITUTE - LIBRARY □ Austin, MN

Budesen, Florence, Gen.Ref.Libn.
RHODE ISLAND STATE LIBRARY □ Providence,
RI

Budet, Ramon, Cat.
UNIVERSITY OF PUERTO RICO - HUMACAO
UNIVERSITY COLLEGE - LIBRARY □ Humacao,
PR

Budet, Virginia E., Patients Libn.
U.S. VETERANS ADMINISTRATION (PR-San
Juan) - HOSPITAL LIBRARY □ Rio Piedras, PR

Budington, William S., Exec.Dir./Libn.
CRERAR (John) LIBRARY □ Chicago, IL

Budny, Michael, V.P.
PILSUDSKI (Jozef) INSTITUTE OF AMERICA
FOR RESEARCH IN THE MODERN HISTORY OF
POLAND - LIBRARY □ New York, NY

Budny, Thomas, Circ.Mgr.
MARSHALL (John) LAW SCHOOL - LIBRARY □
Chicago, IL

Budrevics, Ms. D., Sr.Libn.
GULF CANADA LIMITED - LIBRARY □ Calgary,
AB

Budrew, John, Hd., Ser./Acq.
UNIVERSITY OF TEXAS HEALTH SCIENCE
CENTER, DALLAS - LIBRARY □ Dallas, TX

Budzol, Melvin, Supv., Info.Serv.
GOULD, INC. - GOULD INFORMATION CENTER □
Cleveland, OH

Buechler, John, Hd., Spec.Coll.
UNIVERSITY OF VERMONT - WILBUR
COLLECTION OF VERMONTIANA □ Burlington,
VT

Bueg, Emily J., Cat.Libn.
U.S. NATL. DEFENSE UNIVERSITY - LIBRARY □
Washington, DC

Buehler, Fred M., Asst.Ref.Libn.
UNIVERSITY OF WISCONSIN, STEVENS POINT
- JAMES H. ALBERTSON CENTER FOR
LEARNING RESOURCES □ Stevens Point, WI

Buell, Dr. Jesse H., Libn.
CLINTON HISTORICAL SOCIETY - LIBRARY □
Clinton, CT

PERSONNEL

Buelna, Joseph L., Chf., Tech.Lib.
U.S. ARMY - DUGWAY PROVING GROUND -
TECHNICAL LIBRARY □ Dugway, UT

Bueno, Luis, Lib.Dir.
MIAMI HERALD - LIBRARY □ Miami, FL

Buescher, Cynthia L., Libn.
IRISH-AMERICAN CULTURAL ASSOCIATION -
LIBRARY □ Chicago, IL

Bueschlen, Wava, Dir. of the Lib.
FORT WAYNE BIBLE COLLEGE - S.A. LEHMAN
MEMORIAL LIBRARY □ Fort Wayne, IN

Bueter, Rita Van Assche, Libn.
FRUEHAUF CORPORATION - RESEARCH AND
DEVELOPMENT DIVISION - LIBRARY □ Detroit,
MI

Bugeaud, Danielle, Libn.
ALBERTA - GOVERNMENT SERVICES -
INFORMATION SERVICES DIVISION LIBRARY □
Edmonton, AB

Bugman, Kathleen, Ref.Libn.
INDIANA STATE LIBRARY - INDIANA DIVISION
□ Indianapolis, IN

Buhman, Lesley, Pub.Serv.Ref.Libn.
LEWIS AND CLARK LAW SCHOOL -
NORTHWESTERN SCHOOL OF LAW - PAUL L.
BOLEY LAW LIBRARY □ Portland, OR

Buhr, L.R., Hd.Ref.Serv.
ALBERTA - LEGISLATIVE ASSEMBLY OF
ALBERTA - LEGISLATURE LIBRARY □ Edmonton,
AB

Buhr, Rosemary, Libn.
BARNES HOSPITAL - SCHOOL OF NURSING
LIBRARY & INSTRUCTIONAL RESOURCE
LABORATORY □ St. Louis, MO

Buie, Delinda Stephens, Asst.Cur.
UNIVERSITY OF LOUISVILLE - DEPARTMENT
OF RARE BOOKS AND SPECIAL COLLECTIONS □
Louisville, KY

Buika, Gina, Ph.D., Dir.Med.Lib.
BIRD S. COLER HOSPITAL - MEDICAL LIBRARY
□ New York, NY

Buitrago, Kerrie, Chf.Info.Spec.
EUROPEAN COMMUNITY INFORMATION
SERVICE - LIBRARY □ New York, NY

Bulerin, Josefina, Hd., Circ. & Ref.
UNIVERSITY OF PUERTO RICO - LAW SCHOOL
LIBRARY □ Rio Piedras, PR

Bulger, Janet, Act.Libn.
AMERICAN ELECTRIC POWER SERVICE CORP.
- LIBRARY □ New York, NY

Bull, Alice E., Libn.
BUREAU OF MUNICIPAL RESEARCH - LIBRARY
□ Toronto, ON

Bull, Ellen, Med.Libn.
WESTERN MISSOURI MENTAL HEALTH CENTER
- LIBRARY □ Kansas City, MO

Bull, Margery, Ref.Libn.
CANADA - REVENUE CANADA - TAXATION
LIBRARY □ Ottawa, ON

Bullard, Mrs. Jack, Cur.
JEFFERSON HISTORICAL SOCIETY AND
MUSEUM - ARCHIVES □ Jefferson, TX

Buller, Grace, Act.Dir.
ONTARIO - MINISTRY OF CULTURE AND
RECREATION - LIBRARIES AND COMMUNITY
INFORMATION □ Toronto, ON

Buller, Lillian T., Lib.Asst.
LONG ISLAND JEWISH-HILLSIDE MEDICAL
CENTER - HILLSIDE DIVISION - HEALTH
SCIENCES LIBRARY □ Glen Oaks, NY

Bulley, Joan S., Dir. of Lib.Serv.
WASHINGTON (Mary) HOSPITAL - LIBRARY □
Fredericksburg, VA

Bullion, Laura, Sr.Mss.Spec.
UNIVERSITY OF MISSOURI - WESTERN
HISTORICAL MANUSCRIPT COLLECTION/
STATE HISTORICAL SOCIETY OF MISSOURI □
Columbia, MO

Bullis, Barbara Olson, Libn.
GALESBURG COTTAGE HOSPITAL - HEALTH
SERVICES LIBRARY □ Galesburg, IL

Bullock, Ednita W., Hd.Libn.
BENNETT COLLEGE - THOMAS F. HOLGATE
LIBRARY - SPECIAL COLLECTIONS □
Greensboro, NC

Bullock, Sybil H., Libn.
U.S. ARMY - AEROMEDICAL RESEARCH
LABORATORY - SCIENTIFIC INFORMATION
CENTER □ Ft. Rucker, AL

Bulson, Christine, Hd., Ref.
SUNY - COLLEGE AT ONEONTA - JAMES M.
MILNE LIBRARY □ Oneonta, NY

Bult, Conrad J., Asst.Dir., Ref.
CALVIN COLLEGE AND SEMINARY - LIBRARY □
Grand Rapids, MI

Bunce, Peter W., Chf., Archv.Br.
U.S. NATL. ARCHIVES & RECORDS SERVICE -
FEDERAL ARCHIVES & RECORDS CENTER,
REGION 5 □ Chicago, IL

Bunce, William C., Dir. & Hd.Libn.
UNIVERSITY OF WISCONSIN, MADISON -
KOHLER ART LIBRARY □ Madison, WI

Bunch, Barry, Asst.Archv.
UNIVERSITY OF KANSAS - UNIVERSITY
ARCHIVES □ Lawrence, KS

Bunco, Merle, Per.
SOUTHERN CONNECTICUT STATE COLLEGE -
H.C. BULEY LIBRARY □ New Haven, CT

Bundy, Marlene, Supv.
ATLANTIC-RICHFIELD COMPANY - TECHNICAL
INFORMATION CENTER □ Denver, CO

Bunker, Neil, Biblog.Spec.
UNIVERSITY OF ROCHESTER - EASTMAN
SCHOOL OF MUSIC - SIBLEY MUSIC LIBRARY □
Rochester, NY

Bunker, Norman J., Libn.
MICHIGAN STATE DEPARTMENT OF
TRANSPORTATION - TRANSPORTATION
LIBRARY □ Lansing, MI

Bunker, Pamela, Cat./Tech.Serv.
WESTERN STATE UNIVERSITY - COLLEGE OF
LAW - LIBRARY □ San Diego, CA

Bunker, Phil, Law Libn.
WASHINGTON STATE ATTORNEY GENERAL'S
LIBRARY □ Olympia, WA

Bunnell, Chester S., Ref.Libn.
UNIVERSITY OF MISSISSIPPI - SCHOOL OF
LAW LIBRARY □ University, MS

Buntin, Steven Leslie, Bibliothecar
KXE6S VEREIN CHESS SOCIETY - SPECIAL/
RESEARCH LIBRARY - EAST DIVISION □ Chapel
Hill, NC

Bunting, Anne Carroll, Hd., Tech.Serv.Dept.
UNIVERSITY OF TENNESSEE - CENTER FOR
THE HEALTH SCIENCES LIBRARY □ Memphis,
TN

Bunyan, Linda E., Med.Libn.
ST. THOMAS HOSPITAL - MEDICAL LIBRARY □
Akron, OH

Buono, Irene, Asst.Libn.
RAYTHEON COMPANY - RESEARCH DIVISION -
LIBRARY □ Waltham, MA

Burbage, Mary L., Cat.
ENVIRONMENTAL PROTECTION AGENCY -
ANDREW W. BREIDENBACH ENVIRONMENTAL
RESEARCH CTR., CINCINNATI - TECH.LIB. □
Cincinnati, OH

Burbank, Frank, Coord.Instr.Rsrcs.
GATEWAY VOCATIONAL TECHNICAL & ADULT
EDUCATION DISTRICT - LEARNING
RESOURCES CENTER □ Kenosha, WI

Burbick, Doris, Libn.
BECHTEL - AUDIO-VISUAL LIBRARY □ San
Francisco, CA

Burch, Della C., Tech.Libn.Lib.Div.
ARNOLD ENGINEERING DEVELOPMENT CENTER
- LIBRARY □ Arnold Air Force Sta., TN

Burch, Mary B., Mss.Libn.
INDIANA STATE LIBRARY - INDIANA DIVISION
□ Indianapolis, IN

Burch, Mary S., Law Libn.
NEW YORK STATE SUPREME COURT - 3RD
JUDICIAL DISTRICT - LAW LIBRARY □ Troy, NY

Burcham, Cassandra, Info.Spec.
ATLANTIC-RICHFIELD COMPANY - ARCO
CHEMICAL COMPANY - RESEARCH &
ENGINEERING TECHNICAL INFORMATION
CENTER □ Newton Square, PA

Burchett, Glenn, Chf., Archv.Br.
U.S. NATL. ARCHIVES & RECORDS SERVICE -
FEDERAL ARCHIVES AND RECORDS CENTER,
REGION 9 □ San Bruno, CA

Burchill, Mary D., Cat.Libn.
UNIVERSITY OF KANSAS - SCHOOL OF LAW
LIBRARY □ Lawrence, KS

Burckel, Nicholas C., Dir.
UNIVERSITY OF WISCONSIN, PARKSIDE -
UNIVERSITY ARCHIVES AND AREA RESEARCH
CENTER □ Kenosha, WI

Burden, John, Per.Libn.
GRUMMAN AEROSPACE CORPORATION -
TECHNICAL INFORMATION CENTER □
Bethpage, NY

Burdett, Ollie Mae, Hd.Libn.
PHILLIPS PETROLEUM COMPANY - GAS & GAS
LIQUIDS DIVISION - LIBRARY† □ Bartlesville,
OK

Burdett, Thomas, Cur.
UNIVERSITY OF TEXAS, EL PASO - LIBRARY -
S.L.A. MARSHALL MILITARY HISTORY
COLLECTION □ El Paso, TX

Burdette, Eleanor, Act.Libn.
U.S. NASA - HEADQUARTERS LIBRARY □
Washington, DC

Burdick, Elizabeth B., Dir.
INTERNATIONAL THEATRE INSTITUTE OF THE
UNITED STATES, INC. - INTERNATIONAL
THEATRE COLLECTION □ New York, NY

Burdick, Oscar C., Assoc.Dir., Coll.Dev.
GRADUATE THEOLOGICAL UNION - LIBRARY □
Berkeley, CA

Burdick, Vanroy, Asst.Libn.
CALIFORNIA COLLEGE OF ARTS AND CRAFTS -
MEYER LIBRARY □ Oakland, CA

Burditt, Arthur K., Trustee & Libn.
CRANFORD HISTORICAL SOCIETY - MUSEUM
LIBRARY □ Cranford, NJ

Burel, Mary G., Acq.Libn.
GETTYSBURG COLLEGE - MUSSELMAN LIBRARY
- SPECIAL COLLECTIONS □ Gettysburg, PA

Buresh, Rev. Vitus, Spec.Coll.Libn.
ILLINOIS BENEDICTINE COLLEGE - THEODORE
LOWNIK LIBRARY □ Lisle, IL

Burg, Leon, Chf., Tech.Info.Off.
U.S. ARMY - TANK AUTOMOTIVE RESEARCH &
DEVELOPMENT COMMAND - TECHNICAL
LIBRARY SERVICES BRANCH □ Warren, MI

Burg, Nan C., Libn.
PENNSYLVANIA STATE DEPARTMENT OF
COMMUNITY AFFAIRS - LIBRARY† □ Harrisburg,
PA

Burger, Thomas C., Chf. Data Acq.Br.
U.S. GEOLOGICAL SURVEY - NATL.
CARTOGRAPHIC INFORMATION CENTER
(NCIC) □ Reston, VA

Burgess, A., Libn.
UNIVERSITY OF TORONTO - KNOX COLLEGE -
CAVEN LIBRARY □ Toronto, ON

Burgess, Barbara, Asst.Libn.
HOBE SOUND BIBLE COLLEGE - LIBRARY □ Hobe
Sound, FL

Burgess, Blanche, Supv., Local Hist.
ILLINOIS STATE HISTORICAL LIBRARY □
Springfield, IL

Burgess, Edwin B., Chf., Ref.Serv.
U.S. ARMY COMMAND AND GENERAL STAFF
COLLEGE - COMBINED ARMS RESEARCH
LIBRARY □ Fort Leavenworth, KS

Burgess, Dr. Larry E., Cur.
LINCOLN MEMORIAL SHRINE - LIBRARY □
Redlands, CA

Burgess, Mary Ellen, Exec.Sec.
AMERICAN COUNCIL OF VOLUNTARY
AGENCIES FOR FOREIGN SERVICE, INC. -
TECH. ASSISTANCE INFO. CLEARING HOUSE □
New York, NY

Burghardt, Klaus, Photographer
BRIGHAM AND WOMEN'S HOSPITAL - ABRAMSON CENTER FOR INSTRUCTIONAL MEDIA □ Boston, MA

Burgin, Barbara J., Adm.Sec.
KOSAIR CRIPPLED CHILDREN HOSPITAL - LIBRARY □ Louisville, KY

Burgmann, Walter S., Chf., Tech.Serv.
U.S. AIR FORCE ENVIRONMENTAL TECHNICAL APPLICATIONS CENTER - AIR WEATHER SERVICE TECHNICAL LIBRARY □ Scott AFB, IL

Burgoon, Robert, Park Techn.
U.S. NATL. PARK SERVICE - ORGAN PIPE CACTUS NATL. MONUMENT - LIBRARY □ Ajo, AZ

Burgos, Carmen Gloria, Libn.
OFFICE OF BILINGUAL EDUCATION - RESOURCE LIBRARY AND INFORMATION UNIT □ Brooklyn, NY

Burhans, Cynthia, Ref.Libn.
U.S. PUBLIC HEALTH SERVICE - PARKLAWN HEALTH LIBRARY □ Rockville, MD

Buri, Maura, Ser.Libn.
VILLANOVA UNIVERSITY - PULLING LAW LIBRARY □ Villanova, PA

Burich, Nancy J., Libn.
UNIVERSITY OF KANSAS REGENTS CENTER - LIBRARY □ Shawnee Mission, KS

Burich, Paula, Comp. Applications
MAYO FOUNDATION - MAYO CLINIC LIBRARY □ Rochester, MN

Burk, Alan, Libn.
UNIVERSITY OF WESTERN ONTARIO - SCHOOL OF BUSINESS ADMINISTRATION - BUSINESS LIBRARY & INFORMATION CENTRE □ London, ON

Burk, William R., Botany Libn.
UNIVERSITY OF NORTH CAROLINA, CHAPEL HILL - JOHN N. COUCH LIBRARY □ Chapel Hill, NC

Burkart, Jeff, AV Dir.
CONCORDIA COLLEGE - BUENGER MEMORIAL LIBRARY □ St. Paul, MN

Burke, Anna, Assoc.Libn.Pub.Serv.
SUNY - DOWNSTATE MEDICAL CENTER - MEDICAL RESEARCH LIBRARY OF BROOKLYN† □ Brooklyn, NY

Burke, Barbara L., Asst.Engr.Sci.Libn.
COLORADO STATE UNIVERSITY - ENGINEERING SCIENCES BRANCH LIBRARY □ Fort Collins, CO

Burke, Dorothy, Spec.Coll.Libn.
MINNEAPOLIS PUBLIC LIBRARY & INFORMATION CENTER - HISTORY DEPARTMENT □ Minneapolis, MN

Burke, Ellen, Circ.Libn.
STATE HISTORICAL SOCIETY OF WISCONSIN - LIBRARY □ Madison, WI

Burke, Frances M., Libn.
OVERBROOK SCHOOL FOR THE BLIND - LIBRARY □ Philadelphia, PA

Burke, Lois, Libn.
BENTON AND BOWLES, INC. - LIBRARY □ New York, NY

Burke, Margaret, Libn.
UNIVERSITY OF BRITISH COLUMBIA - SCHOOL OF LIBRARIANSHIP READING ROOM □ Vancouver, BC

Burke, Sherry, Lib.Techn.
CAMOSUN COLLEGE - LIBRARY/MEDIA SERVICES □ Victoria, BC

Burke, Vivienne C., Asst.V.P./Mgr.
RAINIER NATIONAL BANK - INFORMATION CENTER □ Seattle, WA

Burkey, Rev. Blaine, Archv./Hist.
ELLIS COUNTY HISTORICAL SOCIETY - ARCHIVES □ Hays, KS

Burkhard, Rev. John, Per.Libn.
ST. ANTHONY-ON-HUDSON THEOLOGICAL LIBRARY □ Rensselaer, NY

Burkhardt, Lillian, Adm.
SHERWIN-WILLIAMS COMPANY - COMMERCIAL INTELLIGENCE LIBRARY □ Cleveland, OH

Burkhart, Velda B., Hd., Prep.Dept.
VIRGINIA POLYTECHNIC INSTITUTE AND STATE UNIVERSITY - CAROL M. NEWMAN LIBRARY □ Blacksburg, VA

Burkholder, Sue B., Assoc.Libn.
OREGON STATE UNIVERSITY - WILLIAM JASPER KERR LIBRARY □ Corvallis, OR

Burks, Wanda L., Libn.
KANSAS CITY LIFE INSURANCE COMPANY - GENERAL LIBRARY AND ARCHIVES □ Kansas City, MO

Burleigh, Joan, Libn.
MENDOCINO ART CENTER - ART LIBRARY □ Mendocino, CA

Burlingham, Merry, South Asian Libn.
UNIVERSITY OF TEXAS, AUSTIN - ASIAN COLLECTION □ Austin, TX

Burlinson, John, Map Libn.
UNIVERSITY OF TEXAS, AUSTIN - PERRY-CASTANEDA LIBRARY - MAP COLLECTION □ Austin, TX

Burliuk, Penny, Lib.Supv.
ST. LAWRENCE COLLEGE OF APPLIED ARTS AND TECHNOLOGY - LEARNING RESOURCE CENTRE □ Kingston, ON

Burn, Barbara L., Libn.
GRAND VIEW COLLEGE - ARCHIVES □ Des Moines, IA

Burna, George, Mgr.
SCOTT PAPER COMPANY - RESEARCH LIBRARY & TECHNICAL INFORMATION SERVICE □ Philadelphia, PA

Burndorfer, Hans, Hd.
UNIVERSITY OF BRITISH COLUMBIA - MUSIC LIBRARY □ Vancouver, BC

Burnes, Aileen, Asst.Libn.
GEORGESON & COMPANY - LIBRARY □ New York, NY

Burnes, Richard, Supv., Tech.Proc.
MASSACHUSETTS INSTITUTE OF TECHNOLOGY - LINCOLN LABORATORY LIBRARY □ Lexington, MA

Burnett, Barbara J., Libn.
MONTGOMERY WARD AND CO. - CORPORATE LIBRARY □ Chicago, IL

Burnett, Betty, Supv., Main Lib.
UNIVERSITY OF CALIFORNIA - LOS ALAMOS NATIONAL LABORATORY - LIBRARY □ Los Alamos, NM

Burnett, Eustace, Jay St.Br.Libn.
CUNY - NEW YORK CITY TECHNICAL COLLEGE LIBRARY/LEARNING RESOURCE CENTER □ Brooklyn, NY

Burnett, Judy K., Libn.
CHAMPAIGN COUNTY LAW LIBRARY □ Urbana, OH

Burnett, Kathryn E., Assoc.Libn.
SMITH COLLEGE - WERNER JOSTEN LIBRARY FOR THE PERFORMING ARTS □ Northampton, MA

Burnett, Rosa S., Libn.
STATE TECHNICAL INSTITUTE AT MEMPHIS - GEORGE E. FREEMAN LIBRARY □ Memphis, TN

Burnett, Ruth, Hd., Acq.
SUNY - COLLEGE AT ONEONTA - JAMES M. MILNE LIBRARY □ Oneonta, NY

Burnett, Stephen J., Dir.
GEORGE MASON UNIVERSITY - SCHOOL OF LAW - LIBRARY† □ Arlington, VA

Burnett, Mrs. T.J., Jr., Chm.
HARRIS COUNTY HERITAGE SOCIETY - LIBRARY □ Houston, TX

Burnett, Torrey, Slides & Media
MASSACHUSETTS COLLEGE OF ART - LIBRARY □ Boston, MA

Burney, Dorothee, Hd.Libn.
GOETHE INSTITUTE BOSTON - LIBRARY □ Boston, MA

Burnham, Betty L., Libn.
BENDIX CORPORATION - ELECTRICAL COMPONENTS DIVISION - ENGINEERING LIBRARY □ Sidney, NY

Burnham, John P., Hd.Libn.
UNIVERSITY OF MAINE, FARMINGTON - MANTOR LIBRARY □ Farmington, ME

Burnham, Phyllis, Mss.Cat.
WESTERN MICHIGAN UNIVERSITY - ARCHIVES AND REGIONAL HISTORY COLLECTIONS □ Kalamazoo, MI

Burnham, Thomas
BRONSON (Silas) LIBRARY - BUSINESS, INDUSTRY, AND TECHNOLOGY DEPARTMENT† □ Waterbury, CT

Burns, Adele B., Res.Biblog.
UNIVERSITY OF PENNSYLVANIA - POPULATION STUDIES CENTER - DEMOGRAPHY LIBRARY □ Philadelphia, PA

Burns, Barrie, Act.Dir.Cat.
NATIONAL LIBRARY OF CANADA □ Ottawa, ON

Burns, Carol A., Asst.Libn.Pub.Serv.
EMORY UNIVERSITY - SCHOOL OF MEDICINE - A.W. CALHOUN MEDICAL LIBRARY □ Atlanta, GA

Burns, Mrs. D.J., Libn.
BIRMINGHAM BOTANICAL GARDENS - HORACE HAMMOND MEMORIAL LIBRARY □ Birmingham, AL

Burns, Dorothy, Ser.Libn.
LOYOLA UNIVERSITY OF CHICAGO - MEDICAL CENTER LIBRARY □ Maywood, IL

Burns, Glenda L., Libn.
PACIFIC COAST BANKING SCHOOL - LIBRARY □ Seattle, WA

Burns, Janice, Libn.
NESTLE ENTERPRISES, INC. - TECHNICAL SERVICE DIVISION - LIBRARY □ Fulton, NY

Burns, Jerry, Hist.Libn.
CREDIT UNION NATIONAL ASSOCIATION - INFORMATION RESOURCE CENTER □ Madison, WI

Burns, Jimmy, Libn.
IOWA STATE COMMISSION FOR THE BLIND - LIBRARY FOR THE BLIND & PHYSICALLY HANDICAPPED □ Des Moines, IA

Burns, Joan E., Principal Art Libn.
NEWARK PUBLIC LIBRARY - ART AND MUSIC DEPARTMENT □ Newark, NJ

Burns, John F., Chf. of Archv.
CALIFORNIA - STATE ARCHIVES □ Sacramento, CA

Burns, John T., Exec.Dir.
FOUNDATION FOR THE STUDY OF CYCLES INC. - LIBRARY □ Pittsburgh, PA

Burns, Karen, Dir., Info. & Res.
DIRECT MAIL/MARKETING ASSOCIATION, INC. - INFORMATION CENTER □ New York, NY

Burns, Keith P., Dir., Lib.Serv.
WEST VIRGINIA WESLEYAN COLLEGE - ANNIE MERNER PFEIFFER LIBRARY □ Buckhannon, WV

Burns, Lowell O., Dir.
U.S. DEPT. OF COMMERCE - INTERNATIONAL TRADE ADMINISTRATION - CHEYENNE DISTRICT OFFICE LIBRARY □ Cheyenne, WY

Burns, Lynn, Cat.
PHILADELPHIA COLLEGE OF TEXTILES AND SCIENCE - PASTORE LIBRARY □ Philadelphia, PA

Burns, Marie T., Libn./Rec.Mgr.
UNITED CHARITIES OF CHICAGO - LIBRARY □ Chicago, IL

Burns, Mary, Acq.
STANDARD & POOR'S CORPORATION - LIBRARY □ New York, NY

Burns, Mary Ada, Sr.Asst.Libn.
SAN DIEGO STATE UNIVERSITY - MEDIA & CURRICULUM CENTER □ San Diego, CA

Burns, Ruth S., Supv., Lib.Serv.
FRANKLIN MINT - INFORMATION RESEARCH SERVICES □ Franklin Center, PA

Burns, Susan, ILL Libn.
PALMER COLLEGE OF CHIROPRACTIC - LIBRARY □ Davenport, IA

PERSONNEL

Burns, Violanda O., Info.Anl.
MOBIL CHEMICAL COMPANY - PLASTICS
DIVISION - INFORMATION CENTER □ Macedon,
NY

Burr, Irma, Libn. Volunteer Coord.
OKLAHOMA REGIONAL LIBRARY FOR THE
BLIND AND PHYSICALLY HANDICAPPED □
Oklahoma City, OK

Burr, Robert L., Dir.
GONZAGA UNIVERSITY - CROSBY LIBRARY □
Spokane, WA

Burr, Samuel Engle, Jr., Act.Libn.
BURR (Aaron) ASSOCIATION - LIBRARY □
Hightstown, NJ

Burrell, Jon C., Exec.Dir.
MARYLAND MUNICIPAL LEAGUE - LIBRARY □
Annapolis, MD

Burrell, Lois, Chf.
NATIONAL LIBRARY OF CANADA - NEWSPAPER
DIVISION □ Ottawa, ON

Burress, Elaine, Libn.
U.S. DEFENSE TECHNICAL INFORMATION
CENTER - TECHNICAL LIBRARY □ Alexandria,
VA

Burris, Jim, Law Libn.
UTAH STATE - 3RD JUDICIAL DISTRICT - SALT
LAKE COUNTY LAW LIBRARY □ Salt Lake City,
UT

Burris, Ray, Chf., Tech.Serv.
U.S. PUBLIC HEALTH SERVICE - PARKLAWN
HEALTH LIBRARY □ Rockville, MD

Burris, Dr. Russell W., Dir.
UNIVERSITY OF MINNESOTA - CONSULTING
GROUP ON INSTRUCTIONAL DESIGN LIBRARY □
Minneapolis, MN

Burroughs, Charles, Asst.
DU SABLE MUSEUM OF AFRICAN AMERICAN
HISTORY - LIBRARY □ Chicago, IL

Burroughs, Sr. Louise, Archv.
DEACONESS COMMUNITY LUTHERAN CHURCH
OF AMERICA - LUTHERAN DEACONESS
COMMUNITY LIBRARY □ Gladwyne, PA

Burroughs, Dr. Margaret, Libn.
DU SABLE MUSEUM OF AFRICAN AMERICAN
HISTORY - LIBRARY □ Chicago, IL

Burroughs, Martha, Ref.Libn.
DENVER MEDICAL SOCIETY - LIBRARY □
Denver, CO

Burrows, Ann Lewis, Exec.Dir.
MARY BALL WASHINGTON MUSEUM AND
LIBRARY, INC. □ Lancaster, VA

Burrows, Diane S., Marketing Res.Coord.
REYNOLDS (R.J.) TOBACCO COMPANY -
MARKETING INTELLIGENCE LIBRARY □
Winston-Salem, NC

Burrows, Suzetta C., Assoc.Dir./Media Prog.
UNIVERSITY OF MIAMI - SCHOOL OF
MEDICINE - LOUIS CALDER MEMORIAL
LIBRARY □ Miami, FL

Burruss, Mildred, Ref.Libn.
U.S. NATL. DEFENSE UNIVERSITY - LIBRARY □
Washington, DC

Burstein, Joel, Assoc. Law Libn.
NEW MEXICO STATE SUPREME COURT - LAW
LIBRARY □ Santa Fe, NM

Burstein, Lee, Chf.Acq.Libn.
COOK COUNTY LAW LIBRARY □ Chicago, IL

Burston, Madeline H., Pub. Health Adm.
NASSAU COUNTY DEPARTMENT OF HEALTH -
DIVISION OF LABORATORIES & RESEARCH -
MEDICAL LIBRARY □ Hempstead, NY

Burt, DeVere, Musm.Dir.
CINCINNATI MUSEUM OF NATURAL HISTORY -
LIBRARY □ Cincinnati, OH

Burt, Eleanor J., Libn.
TENNESSEE STATE PLANNING OFFICE -
LIBRARY □ Nashville, TN

Burt, Karen, Circ.Libn.
CLEVELAND HEALTH SCIENCES LIBRARY -
HEALTH CENTER LIBRARY □ Cleveland, OH

Burt, Sandra, Libn.
CANADA - CANADIAN FORESTRY SERVICE -
GREAT LAKES FOREST RESEARCH CENTRE -
LIBRARY □ Sault Ste. Marie, ON

Burtnett, I.K., Hd.Libn.
U.S. NAVY - NAVAL AIR STATION - TECHNICAL
LIBRARY □ Point Mugu, CA

Burton, Elisabeth, Libn.
NOLAND (Lloyd) HOSPITAL - DAVID KNOX
MC KAMY MEDICAL LIBRARY □ Fairfield, AL

Burton, Mrs. F.H., Mgr.
CHURCH OF ENGLAND INSTITUTE - LIBRARY □
Saint John, NB

Burton, Faith, Hd., Lib.Mgt.Br. II
U.S. NAVY - NAVAL SURFACE WEAPONS
CENTER - WHITE OAK LIBRARY □ Silver Spring,
MD

Burton, Lois, Libn.
INDIANA ACADEMY OF SCIENCE - JOHN
SHEPARD WRIGHT MEMORIAL LIBRARY □
Indianapolis, IN

Burton, Nancy Lea, Cur.
ROLLINS COLLEGE - BEAL-MALTBIE SHELL
MUSEUM - LIBRARY □ Winter Park, FL

Burtschi, Josephine, Archv./Act.Libn.
VANDALIA HISTORICAL SOCIETY - JAMES
HALL LIBRARY □ Vandalia, IL

Burtschi, Mary, Dir.
VANDALIA HISTORICAL SOCIETY - JAMES
HALL LIBRARY □ Vandalia, IL

Bury, Ed, ILL
AYERST LABORATORIES - MEDICAL
INFORMATION CENTER □ New York, NY

Bury, Mary Ann, Info.Spec.
CELANESE CORPORATION - CELANESE
PLASTICS & SPECIALTIES COMPANY -
INFORMATION CENTER □ Chatham, NJ

Busch, B.J., Hd.
UNIVERSITY OF ALBERTA - H.T. COUTTS
EDUCATION LIBRARY □ Edmonton, AB

Busch, Betty, Libn.
DAYTON LAW LIBRARY† □ Dayton, OH

Busch, C.M., Engr.Libn.
GENERAL DYNAMICS CORPORATION - POMONA
DIVISION - DIVISION LIBRARY MZ 4-20 □
Pomona, CA

Busch, Margaret, Libn.
SYSTEM DEVELOPMENT CORPORATION - ARPA
RESEARCH LIBRARY □ Moffett Field, CA

Busenbark, Beverly V., Mgr.Lib.Serv.
BELL & HOWELL COMPANY - LIBRARY/
TECHNICAL INFORMATION SERVICES □
Pasadena, CA

Busey, Madge J., Dir.
U.S. ARMY POST - FORT BELVOIR - VAN NOY
LIBRARY □ Ft. Belvoir, VA

Bush, Alfred L., Cur., W. Americana
PRINCETON UNIVERSITY - RARE BOOKS AND
SPECIAL COLLECTIONS □ Princeton, NJ

Bush, Ann, Cur.
ATLANTA PUBLIC LIBRARY - FOUNDATION
COLLECTION □ Atlanta, GA

Bush, Ann, Libn.
ATLANTA PUBLIC LIBRARY - IVAN ALLEN, JR.
DEPARTMENT OF SCIENCE, INDUSTRY AND
GOVERNMENT □ Atlanta, GA

Bush, Carmel, TALON Coord.
UNIVERSITY OF TEXAS HEALTH SCIENCE
CENTER, DALLAS - LIBRARY □ Dallas, TX

Bush, Donna E., Dir.Lib.Serv.
FOREST INSTITUTE OF PROFESSIONAL
PSYCHOLOGY - LIBRARY □ Des Plaines, IL

Bush, Eileen, Libn.
CAPE COD MUSEUM OF NATURAL HISTORY -
LIBRARY AND INFORMATION CENTER □
Brewster, MA

Bush, Gail, Lib.Res.Mgr.
HEIDRICK & STRUGGLES, INC. - LIBRARY
RESEARCH CENTER □ Chicago, IL

Bush, Geneva, Sr.Hosp.Libn.
UNIVERSITY OF SOUTH ALABAMA - COLLEGE
OF MEDICINE - BIOMEDICAL LIBRARY □
Mobile, AL

Bush, Janet, Pres.
HENRY COUNTY HISTORICAL SOCIETY -
LIBRARY □ New Castle, IN

Bush, Janet E.N., Med.Rec.Adm.
CHILDREN'S HOSPITAL, INC. - MEDICAL
LIBRARY† □ Baltimore, MD

Bush, Lael Laning, Hd.Libn.
SONNENSCHEIN CARLIN NATH & ROSENTHAL -
LIBRARY □ Chicago, IL

Bush, Lois E., Asst.Libn.
VINSON & ELKINS - LAW LIBRARY □ Houston,
TX

Bush, Mary E., Libn.
BROUGHTON HOSPITAL - MEDICAL LIBRARY □
Morganton, NC

Bush, Mary H., Chf.Libn.
U.S. NASA - NATL. SPACE TECHNOLOGY
LABORATORIES - RESEARCH LIBRARY □ NSTL
Station, MS

Bush, Phyllis, Asst.Libn.
VETERANS HOME OF CALIFORNIA - LINCOLN
MEMORIAL LIBRARY □ Yountville, CA

Bush, R.A., Ref.Spec.
U.S. DEPT. OF ENERGY - PACIFIC NORTHWEST
LABORATORY - TECHNICAL INFO. SECT. □
Richland, WA

Bushman, Ted, Libn.
BUSHMAN (Ted) LAW OFFICES - LIBRARY □
Santa Maria, CA

Bushnell, Judith A., Libn., Fraser Lib.
SUNY - COLLEGE AT GENESEO - MILNE
LIBRARY □ Geneseo, NY

Bushnell, Marietta P., Libn.
PENNSYLVANIA ACADEMY OF THE FINE ARTS -
LIBRARY □ Philadelphia, PA

Bushy, Rebecca L., Asst.Ed.
INSTITUTE OF GAS TECHNOLOGY - TECHNICAL
INFORMATION CENTER □ Chicago, IL

Buske, A.G.
DOW CHEMICAL COMPANY - TECHNICAL
INFORMATION SERVICES - CHEMICAL
LIBRARY □ Midland, MI

Buske, Sue Miller, Exec.Dir.
NATIONAL FEDERATION OF LOCAL CABLE
PROGRAMMERS - LIBRARY† □ Kettering, OH

Buskirk, Mary, Libn.
CANADA - NATIONAL RESEARCH COUNCIL -
CISTI - PHYSICS BRANCH □ Ottawa, ON

Busquets, Carmen L., Libn.
UNIVERSITY OF PUERTO RICO - COLLEGE OF
EDUCATION - SELLES SOLA MEMORIAL
COLLECTION □ Rio Piedras, PR

Bussard, Marta Lee, Adm.
BOCKUS RESEARCH INSTITUTE - LIBRARY □
Philadelphia, PA

Busse, Miss S., Documentalist
ALCOHOLISM AND DRUG ADDICTION
RESEARCH FOUNDATION - LIBRARY □ Toronto,
ON

Busselle, Mrs. Pat, Leg.Ref.Libn.
NEW HAMPSHIRE STATE LIBRARY - DIVISION
OF LAW AND LEGISLATIVE REFERENCE
SERVICE □ Concord, NH

Bussey, Margaret, Med.Libn.
HIGHLAND HOSPITAL, INC. - MEDICAL
LIBRARY □ Lubbock, TX

Bussis, Leslie, Cur.
COLUMBIA UNIVERSITY - DEPARTMENT OF
ART HISTORY & ARCHAEOLOGY - PHOTOGRAPH
COLLECTION □ New York, NY

Bustamante, Suzanne, Sr.Info.Assoc.
ALLERGAN PHARMACEUTICALS, INC. -
PROFESSIONAL INFORMATION SERVICES □
Irvine, CA

Bustamante-Barron, Cecelia, Libn.
CONAC - LIBRARY □ Washington, DC

Busterna, Kathy, Libn.
UNIVERSITY OF MINNESOTA - ERIC SEVAREID
JOURNALISM LIBRARY □ Minneapolis, MN

Buswell, Christa, Chf., Lib.Serv.
U.S. VETERANS ADMINISTRATION (CA-Los
Angeles) - WADSWORTH MEDICAL LIBRARY □
Los Angeles, CA

Butcher, Patricia S., Rd.Adv./Educ.
TRENTON STATE COLLEGE - ROSCOE L. WEST LIBRARY □ Trenton, NJ

Buten, David, Dir.
BUTEN MUSEUM OF WEDGWOOD - LIBRARY □ Merion, PA

Buth, Olga, Music
UNIVERSITY OF TEXAS, AUSTIN - FINE ARTS LIBRARY □ Austin, TX

Buthod, J. Craig, Dept.Hd.
TULSA CITY-COUNTY LIBRARY SYSTEM - BUSINESS AND TECHNOLOGY DEPARTMENT □ Tulsa, OK

Butkovic, Margaret, AV Lib.Techn.
CANADIAN MEMORIAL CHIROPRACTIC COLLEGE - C.C. CLEMMER LIBRARY □ Toronto, ON

Butkovich, Margaret, Assoc.Dir.
UNIVERSITY OF COLORADO MEDICAL CENTER - DENISON MEMORIAL LIBRARY □ Denver, CO

Butler, Anne H., Libn.
ALSTON, MILLER AND GAINES - LAW LIBRARY □ Atlanta, GA

Butler, Mr. Beverley, Hd.Libn.
HUNTON & WILLIAMS - LAW LIBRARY □ Richmond, VA

Butler, Cynthia, Hd., Pub.Serv.
UNIVERSITY OF CALIFORNIA, IRVINE - BIOMEDICAL LIBRARY □ Irvine, CA

Butler, Dean, Sr.Libn.
IBM CORPORATION - BOULDER LIBRARY □ Boulder, CO

Butler, Eva K., Libn.
SCOTT PAPER COMPANY - MARKETING LIBRARY □ Philadelphia, PA

Butler, Evelyn, Libn.
UNIVERSITY OF PENNSYLVANIA - SCHOOL OF SOCIAL WORK - SMALLEY LIBRARY OF SOCIAL WORK □ Philadelphia, PA

Butler, Geoffrey J., Law Libn.
UTAH STATE LAW LIBRARY □ Salt Lake City, UT

Butler, Sr. Gertrude, Asst.Libn.
MERCY HOSPITAL - SCHOOL OF NURSING LIBRARY □ Pittsburgh, PA

Butler, Jane C., Info.Techn.
HOSPITAL CORPORATION OF AMERICA - RESEARCH/INFORMATION SERVICES □ Nashville, TN

Butler, Janice, Hd., Coll.Dev.
UNIVERSITY OF COLORADO MEDICAL CENTER - DENISON MEMORIAL LIBRARY □ Denver, CO

Butler, Lucy R., Chf., Lib.Serv.
U.S. VETERANS ADMINISTRATION (RI-Providence) - HOSPITAL LIBRARY □ Providence, RI

Butler, Margaret, Law Libn.
NEW YORK LIFE INSURANCE COMPANY - LAW LIBRARY □ New York, NY

Butler, Margaret, Supv.
RUTGERS UNIVERSITY, THE STATE UNIVERSITY OF NEW JERSEY - PHYSICS LIBRARY □ Piscataway, NJ

Butler, Margaret K., Dir.
ARGONNE NATIONAL LABORATORY - NATIONAL ENERGY SOFTWARE CENTER □ Argonne, IL

Butler, Marj, Asst.
HEWITT ASSOCIATES - LIBRARY □ Lincolnshire, IL

Butler, Ona C., Lib.Chm.
PENSACOLA MUSEUM OF ART - HARRY THORNTON MEMORIAL LIBRARY □ Pensacola, FL

Butler, Richard M., Dir., Medical Rec.
RIVERSIDE GENERAL HOSPITAL - MEDICAL LIBRARY □ Riverside, CA

Butler, Ruth G., Libn.
HOUGHTON COLLEGE - BUFFALO SUBURBAN CAMPUS - ADA M. KIDDER MEMORIAL LIBRARY □ West Seneca, NY

Butler, Sharon K., Sr.Libn., User Serv.
BETH ISRAEL MEDICAL CENTER - SEYMOUR J. PHILLIPS HEALTH SCIENCES LIBRARY □ New York, NY

Butler, Tyrone G., Asst.Archv.
SALVATION ARMY - ARCHIVES AND RESEARCH CENTER □ New York, NY

Butske, Carol L., Libn.
NORTHVILLE HISTORICAL SOCIETY - LIBRARY □ Northville, MI

Butson, Linda C., Libn.
MOUNTAIN AREA HEALTH EDUCATION CENTER - HEALTH SCIENCES LIBRARY □ Asheville, NC

Buttars, Gerald, Dir.
UTAH STATE LIBRARY - BLIND AND PHYSICALLY HANDICAPPED PROGRAM - REGIONAL LIBRARY □ Salt Lake City, UT

Butter, Karen, Pub.Serv.
UNIVERSITY OF UTAH - SPENCER S. ECCLES HEALTH SCIENCES LIBRARY □ Salt Lake City, UT

Butterfield, Cliff C., Coord., Tech.Data
LOCKHEED-CALIFORNIA COMPANY - TECHNICAL INFORMATION CENTER □ Burbank, CA

Butterill, Mary, Hd.Tech.Serv.
CANADA - REVENUE CANADA - TAXATION LIBRARY □ Ottawa, ON

Buttermore, Gregg, Archv.
AUBURN-CORD-DUESENBERG MUSEUM - TRI-KAPPA COLLECTION OF AUBURN AUTOMOTIVE LITERATURE □ Auburn, IN

Butterworth, Donald A., Tech.Serv.
ASBURY THEOLOGICAL SEMINARY - B.L. FISHER LIBRARY □ Wilmore, KY

Button, Carol J., Libn.
UNIVERSITY OF ALASKA - WILDLIFE LIBRARY □ Fairbanks, AK

Button, Katherine, MEDLINE Anl.
MASSACHUSETTS GENERAL HOSPITAL - TREADWELL AND PALMER-DAVIS LIBRARY □ Boston, MA

Button, Mary L., Med. Record Libn.
CLIFTON SPRINGS HOSPITAL AND CLINIC - MEDICAL LIBRARY □ Clifton Springs, NY

Butts, Theresa R., Chf.
U.S. ARMY - YUMA PROVING GROUND - FOREIGN INTELLIGENCE, SCIENTIFIC & TECHNICAL INFO.DIV. - TECHNICAL LIB. □ Yuma, AZ

Buurstra, Annette, Educ.Ref.Libn.
NORTHEASTERN ILLINOIS UNIVERSITY - LIBRARY □ Chicago, IL

Buyukmihci, Hope Sawyer, Sec.
UNEXPECTED WILDLIFE REFUGE - LIBRARY □ Newfield, NJ

Buzzetta, John, Publ.
PATERSON NEWS - LIBRARY/NEWSPAPER MORGUE □ Paterson, NJ

Bycio, Janet, Libn.
CANADA SYSTEMS GROUP - REFERENCE LIBRARY □ Mississauga, ON

Bye, John, Cur.
NORTH DAKOTA STATE UNIVERSITY - LIBRARY □ Fargo, ND

Bye, John E., Cur.Mss.
NORTH DAKOTA STATE UNIVERSITY - INSTITUTE FOR REGIONAL STUDIES □ Fargo, ND

Byers, Bertina, Chf., Doc.Ctr.
U.S. ARMY COMMAND AND GENERAL STAFF COLLEGE - COMBINED ARMS RESEARCH LIBRARY □ Fort Leavenworth, KS

Byers, Claudia J., RRA, Dir.Med.Rec.
OBICI (Louise) MEMORIAL HOSPITAL - LIBRARY □ Suffolk, VA

Byers, Dorothy F., Hd.
UNIVERSITY OF CINCINNATI - ENGINEERING LIBRARY □ Cincinnati, OH

Byers, Laura, Libn.
HARVARD UNIVERSITY - DUMBARTON OAKS GARDEN LIBRARY OF THE CENTER FOR STUDIES IN LANDSCAPE ARCHITECTURE □ Washington, DC

Byers, Montez, Rd.Serv.Libn.
BENNETT COLLEGE - THOMAS F. HOLGATE LIBRARY - SPECIAL COLLECTIONS □ Greensboro, NC

Bynagle, Hans, Dir., Lrng.Res.
FRIENDS UNIVERSITY - EDMUND STANLEY LIBRARY □ Wichita, KS

Bynon, George, Dir.
UNIVERSITY OF OREGON - INSTRUCTIONAL MEDIA CENTER □ Eugene, OR

Byock, Gayle, Assoc.Dir.
ERIC CLEARINGHOUSE FOR JUNIOR COLLEGES □ Los Angeles, CA

Byrd, Betty, Asst.Libn.
ST. JOSEPH HOSPITAL - INFORMATION SERVICES □ Alton, IL

Byrd, Caroline, Asst. Law Libn.
ST. MARY'S UNIVERSITY - LAW LIBRARY □ San Antonio, TX

Byrd, Dr. Cecil K., Cons.
INDIANA UNIVERSITY - LILLY LIBRARY □ Bloomington, IN

Byrd, Darlene F., Media Spec.
PRESBYTERIAN HOSPITAL - SCHOOL OF NURSING - LIBRARY □ Charlotte, NC

Byrd, Gary D., Chf.Libn.
UNIVERSITY OF MISSOURI, KANSAS CITY - HEALTH SCIENCES LIBRARY □ Kansas City, MO

Byrd, Jonda, ILL Libn.
ENVIRONMENTAL PROTECTION AGENCY - ANDREW W. BREIDENBACH ENVIRONMENTAL RESEARCH CTR., CINCINNATI - TECH.LIB. □ Cincinnati, OH

Byrd, Nancy, Govt.Doc.Spec.
AUSTIN PUBLIC LIBRARY - AUSTIN-TRAVIS COUNTY COLLECTION □ Austin, TX

Byrne, Christine C., Hd.
ATOMIC ENERGY OF CANADA, LTD. - ENGINEERING COMPANY LIBRARY □ Mississauga, ON

Byrne, Colleen, Asst.Libn.
MARINE MIDLAND BANK - LIBRARY □ New York, NY

Byrne, Elaine, Libn.
TEXAS STATE PARKS & WILDLIFE DEPARTMENT - LIBRARY □ Austin, TX

Byrne, Elizabeth D., Hd.Libn.
UNIVERSITY OF CINCINNATI - DESIGN, ARCHITECTURE & ART LIBRARY □ Cincinnati, OH

Byrne, Frank P., Jr., Chf.Libn.
U.S. MARINE CORPS - MARINE BAND LIBRARY □ Washington, DC

Byrne, Frederick, Libn.
COLUMBIA UNIVERSITY - BURGESS-CARPENTER LIBRARY □ New York, NY

Byrne, Frederick, Libn.
COLUMBIA UNIVERSITY - COLUMBIA COLLEGE LIBRARY □ New York, NY

Byrne, Frederick, Libn.
COLUMBIA UNIVERSITY - PHILOSOPHY LIBRARY □ New York, NY

Byrne, Margaret, Lib.Asst.
NATIONAL COUNCIL OF THE YOUNG MEN'S CHRISTIAN ASSOCIATIONS OF THE U.S. - YMCA HISTORICAL LIBRARY† □ New York, NY

Byrne, Margaret A., Libn.
U.S. AIR FORCE BASE - OFFUTT BASE LIBRARY □ Offutt AFB, NE

Byrne, Rusty Stieff, Pubn.
HARVARD UNIVERSITY - GRADUATE SCHOOL OF BUSINESS ADMINISTRATION - BAKER LIBRARY □ Boston, MA

Byrne, Therese E., Dir., Info.Serv.
LANDAUER ASSOCIATES, INC. - INFORMATION CENTER □ New York, NY

PERSONNEL

Byrnes, Mickey, Act. Law Libn.
WHITTIER COLLEGE - SCHOOL OF LAW -
LIBRARY □ Los Angeles, CA
Byrnes, Stephanie C., Libn.
AMERICAN INSTITUTE OF ARCHITECTS -
LIBRARY □ Washington, DC
Byrum, Lois, Sr.Libn.
MINNESOTA STATE DEPARTMENT OF
EDUCATION - INTERAGENCY RESOURCE AND
INFORMATION CENTER □ St. Paul, MN
Bysiewicz, Shirley R., Law Libn.
UNIVERSITY OF CONNECTICUT - LAW SCHOOL
LIBRARY □ West Hartford, CT
Bystram, Mrs. A.M., Dir., Lib.Serv.Br.
CANADA - ENVIRONMENT CANADA - LIBRARY
SERVICES BRANCH □ Ottawa, ON
Bystrom, Marcia M., Ref.Libn.
TENNESSEE VALLEY AUTHORITY - TECHNICAL
LIBRARY □ Muscle Shoals, AL
Byun, Il, Libn.
ADLER PLANETARIUM - LIBRARY □ Chicago, IL

C

C.-Lambert, Madeleine, Chf.Libn.
SNC GROUP - LIBRARY □ Montreal, PQ
Caballero, Cesar, Hd.Spec.Coll./Archv.
UNIVERSITY OF TEXAS, EL PASO - LIBRARY □
El Paso, TX
Caballero, Isabel S., Hist. of Med.Libn.
UNIVERSITY OF MIAMI - SCHOOL OF
MEDICINE - LOUIS CALDER MEMORIAL
LIBRARY □ Miami, FL
Cabana, Alice L., Libn.
ISOCHEM RESINS COMPANY - LIBRARY □
Lincoln, RI
Cabeen, S.K., Dir.
ENGINEERING SOCIETIES LIBRARY □ New
York, NY
Cable, Carole, Arch./Fine Arts Libn
UNIVERSITY OF TEXAS, AUSTIN -
ARCHITECTURE & PLANNING LIBRARY □ Austin,
TX
Cable, Carole, Arch./Fine Arts Libn
UNIVERSITY OF TEXAS, AUSTIN - FINE ARTS
LIBRARY □ Austin, TX
Cable, David, Adm.
SAGINAW COUNTY LAW LIBRARY □ Saginaw,
MI
Cable, Jan, Libn.
NEW YORK CITY BOARD OF EDUCATION -
DIVISION OF SPECIAL EDUCATION - SPECIAL
EDUC. TRAINING & RESOURCE CTR. □ New
York, NY
Cable, Leslie, Ref.Libn.
UNIVERSITY OF OREGON - HEALTH SCIENCES
CENTER - LIBRARY □ Portland, OR
Cabrera, Pablo, Hd., Binding
UNIVERSITY OF PUERTO RICO - GENERAL
LIBRARY □ San Juan, PR
Cabrita, Paul M., Hd.Libn.
MARIST COLLEGE - LIBRARY □ Washington, DC
Caccamo, James F., Archv.
HUDSON LIBRARY AND HISTORICAL SOCIETY □
Hudson, OH
Cadam, Ronnie, Libn.
STONE, MARRACCINI & PATTERSON -
RESEARCH & DEVELOPMENT LIBRARY □ San
Francisco, CA
Cadet, Janine, Libn.
UNIVERSITE DE MONTREAL - PHYSIQUE-
BIBLIOTHEQUE □ Montreal, PQ
Cadieux, J., Hd.Tech.Serv.
CANADA - TRANSPORT CANADA - LIBRARY &
INFORMATION CENTRE □ Ottawa, ON
Cadigan, Laurie A., Asst.Archv.
WEYERHAEUSER COMPANY - ARCHIVES □
Federal Way, WA
Cadwell, Annette, Hd. Marketing Libn.
CHICAGO TRIBUNE - MARKETING LIBRARY □
Chicago, IL

Cady, Jean L., Base Libn.
U.S. AIR FORCE BASE - MYRTLE BEACH BASE
LIBRARY □ Myrtle Beach AFB, SC
Caffrey, Margaret M., Libn.
ALLENTOWN STATE HOSPITAL - HEIM
MEMORIAL LIBRARY □ Allentown, PA
Cagle, William R., Libn.
INDIANA UNIVERSITY - LILLY LIBRARY □
Bloomington, IN
Cahalan, Sally S., Dir.
JAMES BUCHANAN FOUNDATION FOR THE
PRESERVATION OF WHEATLAND - LIBRARY □
Lancaster, PA
Cahall, Marcia, Libn.
PROCTER & GAMBLE COMPANY - LIBRARY □
Cincinnati, OH
Cahall, Michael, Dir.
CHAMPAIGN COUNTY HISTORICAL MUSEUM -
LIBRARY □ Champaign, IL
Cahill, George F., Pres.
NATIONAL FLAG FOUNDATION - FLAG PLAZA
LIBRARY □ Pittsburgh, PA
Cahill, Ms. L., Libn.
NESBITT, THOMSON AND COMPANY, LTD. -
RESEARCH LIBRARY □ Montreal, PQ
Cahill, Nan, Acq.
MARIANOPOLIS COLLEGE - LIBRARY □
Montreal, PQ
Cahoon, Herbert, Cur., Autog.Mss.
PIERPONT MORGAN LIBRARY □ New York, NY
Caiazzo, Ralph, Asst.Libn.
NEW YORK LAW INSTITUTE - LIBRARY □ New
York, NY
Caiger, Anne, Hist.Mss.Libn.
UNIVERSITY OF CALIFORNIA, LOS ANGELES -
DEPARTMENT OF SPECIAL COLLECTIONS □ Los
Angeles, CA
Cail, Nada, Cat.
VILLANOVA UNIVERSITY - PULLING LAW
LIBRARY □ Villanova, PA
Cain, Anne, Principal Libn.Ref.Serv.
PASADENA PUBLIC LIBRARY - BUSINESS-
TECHNOLOGY DIVISION □ Pasadena, CA
Cain, Charlene C., Archv.
LOUISIANA STATE OFFICE OF THE SECRETARY
OF STATE - STATE ARCHIVES AND RECORDS
SERVICE □ Baton Rouge, LA
Cain, Melissa, Libn.
UNIVERSITY OF ILLINOIS - ENGLISH LIBRARY
□ Urbana, IL
Cain, Melvin, Chm.
HOMOSEXUAL INFORMATION CENTER -
TANGENT GROUP □ Hollywood, CA
Cain, Myrna, Council Libn.
CANADIAN TOBACCO MANUFACTURERS
COUNCIL - SMOKING & HEALTH LIBRARY □
Montreal, PQ
Cain, Robert, Docs.Libn.
UNIVERSITY OF SOUTHERN COLORADO -
LIBRARY - SPECIAL COLLECTIONS □ Pueblo, CO
Caine, William C., Cat.
UNIVERSITY OF TEXAS, EL PASO - LIBRARY □
El Paso, TX
Cairns, Phyllis, Lib.Dir.
BRAILLE INSTITUTE OF AMERICA - LIBRARY □
Los Angeles, CA
Calabretta, Nancy, Ref.Libn.
JEFFERSON (Thomas) UNIVERSITY - SCOTT
MEMORIAL LIBRARY □ Philadelphia, PA
Calcese, Sarah L., Libn.
UNIVERSITY OF WISCONSIN, MADISON -
WATER RESOURCES CENTER - LIBRARY □
Madison, WI
Calderisi, Maria, Hd., Printed Coll.
NATIONAL LIBRARY OF CANADA - MUSIC
DIVISION □ Ottawa, ON
Caldwell, Denise, Area Libn.
BRITISH COLUMBIA LAW LIBRARY
FOUNDATION - KAMLOOPS COURTHOUSE
LIBRARY □ Kamloops, BC

Caldwell, Evelyn B., Libn.
AMERICAN ENTERPRISE INSTITUTE FOR
PUBLIC POLICY RESEARCH - LIBRARY □
Washington, DC
Caldwell, F.B., Dir. of Programmes
NAVY LEAGUE OF CANADA - NATIONAL OFFICE
- LIBRARY □ Ottawa, ON
Caldwell, John, Dir. of Lib.
AUGUSTANA COLLEGE - DENKMANN MEMORIAL
LIBRARY □ Rock Island, IL
Caldwell, John, Congressional Archv.
UNIVERSITY OF OKLAHOMA - WESTERN
HISTORY COLLECTIONS □ Norman, OK
Caldwell, Linda M., Med.Libn.
FREDERICK MEMORIAL HOSPITAL - WALTER F.
PRIOR MEDICAL LIBRARY† □ Frederick, MD
Calhoon, H. Joyce, Dir.-Archv.
TEXAS STATE LIBRARY - TEXAS ARCHIVES
DIVISION - SAM HOUSTON REGIONAL LIBRARY
AND RESEARCH CENTER □ Liberty, TX
Calhoon, William, Sci.Libn.
WESLEYAN UNIVERSITY - SCIENCE LIBRARY □
Middletown, CT
Calhoun, Catherine, Exec.Dir.
TORRINGTON HISTORICAL SOCIETY - LIBRARY
□ Torrington, CT
Calhoun, Clayne, Libn.
ROANOKE LAW LIBRARY □ Roanoke, VA
Calhoun, Hortense T., Res.Techn.
TUSKEGEE INSTITUTE - DIVISION OF
BEHAVIORAL SCIENCE RESEARCH - SCIENCE
INFORMATION CENTER □ Tuskegee Institute,
AL
Calhoun, James, Music Libn.
DALLAS PUBLIC LIBRARY - FINE ARTS
DIVISION □ Dallas, TX
Calhoun, Michele, Ref.Libn.
FIELD MUSEUM OF NATURAL HISTORY -
LIBRARY □ Chicago, IL
Caliendo, Lorraine, Dir.
AMERICAN MARKETING ASSOCIATION -
INFORMATION CENTER □ Chicago, IL
Calkins, Larry, Asst.Ref.Libn.
NEVADA STATE LIBRARY □ Carson City, NV
Callaghan, J. Claire, Dir.
CANADIAN MEMORIAL CHIROPRACTIC
COLLEGE - C.C. CLEMMER LIBRARY □ Toronto,
ON
Callaghan, Patrice, Hd.
PUBLIC LIBRARY OF CINCINNATI AND
HAMILTON COUNTY - FILMS AND RECORDINGS
CENTER □ Cincinnati, OH
Callaham, Betty E., State Libn.
SOUTH CAROLINA STATE LIBRARY □ Columbia,
SC
Callahan, Barbara A., Libn.
HARVARD UNIVERSITY - ARNOLD ARBORETUM
& GRAY HERBARIUM - LIBRARY □ Cambridge,
MA
Callahan, Daniel, Lib.Supv.
INSTITUTE OF SOCIETY, ETHICS & THE LIFE
SCIENCES - HASTINGS CENTER □ Hastings On
Hudson, NY
Callahan, Ellen, Hd. of Bk.Serv.
TIME, INC. - LIBRARY □ New York, NY
Callahan, Harriet, Libn./Louisiana Dept
LOUISIANA STATE LIBRARY □ Baton Rouge, LA
Callahan, John J., Pres.
TOLEDO LAW ASSOCIATION LIBRARY □ Toledo,
OH
Callahan, Kathleen E., Lib.Asst.
MICHIGAN STATE DEPARTMENT OF
AGRICULTURE - LIBRARY □ East Lansing, MI
Callahan, Linda A., Asst.Libn.
GCA CORPORATION - TECHNOLOGY DIVISION
- LIBRARY □ Bedford, MA
Callahan, Mary Helen, Accounts Adm.
UNIVERSITY OF DELAWARE, NEWARK -
COLLEGE OF URBAN AFFAIRS - LIBRARY† □
Newark, DE

Callahan, Nola Vanhoy, Assoc.Libn.
CHARLOTTE MEMORIAL HOSPITAL AND
MEDICAL CENTER - MEDICAL LIBRARY OF
MECKLENBURG COUNTY/LRC OF CHARLOTTE
AHEC □ Charlotte, NC

Callahan, Patricia, Cat.
UNIVERSITY OF PENNSYLVANIA - BIDDLE LAW
LIBRARY □ Philadelphia, PA

Callahan, Virginia C., Libn.
AMERICAN CETACEAN SOCIETY - NATIONAL
LIBRARY □ San Pedro, CA

Callard, Joanne, General Serv.
UNIVERSITY OF OKLAHOMA - HEALTH
SCIENCES CENTER LIBRARY □ Oklahoma City,
OK

Callarman, Barbara, Dir.
DOWNEY HISTORICAL SOCIETY MUSEUM -
LIBRARY □ Downey, CA

Callaway, Gwendolyn P., Info.Sci.
GEORGIA-PACIFIC CORPORATION -
TECHNICAL INFORMATION CENTER □ Atlanta,
GA

Callen, Rev. Robert V., S.J., Univ. Archv.
MARQUETTE UNIVERSITY - DEPARTMENT OF
SPECIAL COLLECTIONS AND UNIVERSITY
ARCHIVES □ Milwaukee, WI

Callen, Rev. Robert V., S.J., Univ.Archv.
MARQUETTE UNIVERSITY - MEMORIAL
LIBRARY □ Milwaukee, WI

Callery, Bernadette G., Libn.
CARNEGIE-MELLON UNIVERSITY - HUNT
INSTITUTE FOR BOTANICAL DOCUMENTATION
- LIBRARY □ Pittsburgh, PA

Callinan, Mary L., Mgr.
UNION DIME SAVINGS BANK - INFORMATION
CENTER □ New York, NY

Callow, Bette R., Slide Libn.
MEMPHIS ACADEMY OF ARTS - G. PILLOW
LEWIS MEMORIAL LIBRARY† □ Memphis, TN

Caluaresi, Frances, Libn.
GILBERT ASSOCIATES, INC. - CORPORATE
LIBRARY† □ Reading, PA

Calvert, Judy, Libn.
VIGO COUNTY HISTORICAL SOCIETY -
HISTORICAL MUSEUM OF THE WABASH VALLEY
- LIBRARY □ Terre Haute, IN

Calvert, Raymond, Tech.Serv.
FLORIDA STATE DIVISION OF BLIND SERVICES
- FLORIDA REGIONAL LIB. FOR THE BLIND &
PHYSICALLY HANDICAPPED □ Daytona Beach,
FL

Calvin, Betsy, Asst.Libn.
NEW YORK BOTANICAL GARDEN - CARY
ARBORETUM - LIBRARY □ Millbrook, NY

Calvort, Gale A., Interp.Serv.Libn.
MEDICAL COLLEGE OF GEORGIA - LIBRARY □
Augusta, GA

Camacho, Nancy, Libn.
PROCTOR COMMUNITY HOSPITAL - MEDICAL
LIBRARY □ Peoria, IL

Camacho, Wilfredo
UNIVERSITY OF PUERTO RICO - SCHOOL OF
PUBLIC ADMINISTRATION - LIBRARY □ Rio
Piedras, PR

Camarasana, Joanne, Libn.
WALTON LANTAFF SCHROEDER & CARSON -
LAW LIBRARY □ Miami, FL

Cambron, Carol, Acq.Libn.
CENTRAL MISSOURI STATE UNIVERSITY -
WARD EDWARDS LIBRARY □ Warrensburg, MO

Cameloford, Rumil of, Libn.
CK-PERMANENT PRESS - PARMAR ELDALIEVA
LIBRARY □ Scranton, PA

Camer, Richard, Res.
ZIFF-DAVIS PUBLISHING COMPANY -
PSYCHOLOGY TODAY - LIBRARY □ New York,
NY

Camero, Olga, Supv., Lib.Serv.
CONOCO, INC. - INTERNATIONAL
EXPLORATION AND PRODUCTION LIBRARY† □
Houston, TX

Cameron, A.K., Dir.
MARITIME MUSEUM OF BRITISH COLUMBIA -
LIBRARY □ Victoria, BC

Cameron, Connie, Asst.Libn.
BRYANT COLLEGE OF BUSINESS
ADMINISTRATION - EDITH M. HODGSON
MEMORIAL LIBRARY □ Smithfield, RI

Cameron, Dee B., Ref.Libn.
UNIVERSITY OF TEXAS, EL PASO - LIBRARY □
El Paso, TX

Cameron, Gwendolyn, Libn.
NORCEN ENERGY RESOURCES LIMITED -
LIBRARY □ Calgary, AB

Cameron, J., Res.Mgr.
CANADA - METRIC COMMISSION - SIM
RESEARCH UNIT □ Ottawa, ON

Cameron, Jean, Libn.
RAYTHEON SERVICE COMPANY - LIBRARY □
Burlington, MA

Cameron, Rev. Kenneth W., Archv./Histographer
PROTESTANT EPISCOPAL CHURCH -
EPISCOPAL DIOCESE OF CONNECTICUT -
DIOCESAN LIBRARY AND ARCHIVES □ Hartford,
CT

Cameron, Margaret, Asst.Libn.
CLARKSON GORDON - BUSINESS LIBRARY □
Montreal, PQ

Cameron, Marsha, Dir.Info.Serv.
CENTER FOR SOUTHERN FOLKLORE -
ARCHIVES □ Memphis, TN

Cameron, Mrs. Pat, Libn.
TRINITY MEMORIAL HOSPITAL - LIBRARY □
Cudahy, WI

Cameron, Richard A., Field Dir.
MINNESOTA HISTORICAL SOCIETY - DIVISION
OF ARCHIVES AND MANUSCRIPTS □ St. Paul,
MN

Camp, Paul Eugen, Exec.Sec.
FLORIDA HISTORICAL SOCIETY - LIBRARY □
Tampa, FL

Camp, Thomas E., Libn.
UNIVERSITY OF THE SOUTH - SCHOOL OF
THEOLOGY LIBRARY □ Sewanee, TN

Campaigne, Laura E., Libn.
ST. PETER'S HOSPITAL - MEDICAL STAFF
LIBRARY □ Albany, NY

Campbell, A., Libn.
CANADA - PUBLIC SERVICE COMMISSION -
LIBRARY SERVICES DIVISION □ Ottawa, ON

Campbell, Alexandra E., Chf., Preparations Br.
U.S. ARMY WAR COLLEGE - LIBRARY □ Carlisle
Barracks, PA

Campbell, Alma B., Mgr.
SPERRY CORPORATION - SPERRY UNIVAC
COMPUTER SYSTEMS - INFORMATION CENTER
□ Blue Bell, PA

Campbell, Arthur J., Jr., Libn.
WASHINGTON COUNTY LAW LIBRARY† □
Hagerstown, MD

Campbell, Billy W., Supv.
HUGHES AIRCRAFT COMPANY - COMPANY
TECHNICAL DOCUMENT CENTER □ Culver City,
CA

Campbell, C.D., Act.Mgr.
TRW, INC. - DEFENSE & SPACE SYSTEMS
GROUP - TECHNICAL INFORMATION CENTER □
Redondo Beach, CA

Campbell, Clara, Libn.
ROSICRUCIAN ORDER, AMORC - ROSICRUCIAN
RESEARCH LIBRARY □ San Jose, CA

Campbell, Corinne A., Libs.Mgr.
BOEING COMPANY - SEATTLE SERVICES
DIVISION - KENT TECHNICAL LIBRARY □
Seattle, WA

Campbell, Corinne A., Libs.Mgr.
BOEING COMPANY - SEATTLE SERVICES
DIVISION - RENTON LIBRARY □ Seattle, WA

Campbell, Deirdre A., Libn.
UNIVERSITY OF ARIZONA - INSTITUTE OF
ATMOSPHERIC PHYSICS LIBRARY □ Tucson, AZ

Campbell, Doris, Asst.Libn.
NATIONAL ASSOCIATION OF HOME BUILDERS -
NATIONAL HOUSING CENTER LIBRARY □
Washington, DC

Campbell, Dorothy M., Libn.
UNITED STATES TESTING COMPANY, INC. -
LIBRARY† □ Hoboken, NJ

Campbell, Douglas, Libn.
ASSOCIATION OF AVIATION & SPACE
MUSEOLOGISTS - INFORMATION CENTER □
Alexandria, VA

Campbell, Edward D.C., Jr., Dir.
CONFEDERATE MEMORIAL LITERARY SOCIETY
- MUSEUM OF THE CONFEDERACY - ELEANOR
S. BROCKENBROUGH LIBRARY □ Richmond, VA

Campbell, Frances D., Libn.
COLORADO STATE SUPREME COURT LIBRARY □
Denver, CO

Campbell, Francis D., Jr., Libn.
AMERICAN NUMISMATIC SOCIETY - LIBRARY
□ New York, NY

Campbell, Frank C., Chf.
NEW YORK PUBLIC LIBRARY - PERFORMING
ARTS RESEARCH CENTER - MUSIC DIVISION □
New York, NY

Campbell, Helen G., Media Spec.
PINELLAS COUNTY SCHOOL BOARD - MIRROR
LAKE/TOMLINSON EDUCATION CENTER -
LIBRARY/MEDIA CENTER □ St. Petersburg, FL

Campbell, Janet, Mgr.
LEWIS (Sinclair) INFORMATION &
INTERPRETIVE CENTRE □ Sauk Centre, MN

Campbell, Janis, Res.Libn.
BOARD OF TRADE OF METROPOLITAN
TORONTO - RESOURCE CENTRE □ Toronto, ON

Campbell, Jerry D., Libn.
SOUTHERN METHODIST UNIVERSITY -
PERKINS SCHOOL OF THEOLOGY - LIBRARY □
Dallas, TX

Campbell, Joan E., Info.Rsrcs.Ctr.Mgr.
NATIONAL RESTAURANT ASSOCIATION -
INFORMATION RESOURCE CENTER □
Washington, DC

Campbell, Joanne, Asst.Libn.-Cat.
AVCO CORPORATION - AVCO-EVERETT
RESEARCH LABORATORY - LIBRARY □ Everett,
MA

Campbell, Louisa, Bus.Spec.
FERGUSON LIBRARY - BUSINESS-TECHNOLOGY
DEPARTMENT □ Stamford, CT

Campbell, Louise, Asst.Libn.
HOUSTON OIL & MINERALS CORPORATION -
LIBRARY □ Houston, TX

Campbell, M.E., Libn.
MARITIME RESOURCE MANAGEMENT SERVICE
- INFORMATION CENTRE □ Amherst, NS

Campbell, Margaret, Libn.
CENTRAL SOYA COMPANY, INC. - FOOD
RESEARCH LIBRARY □ Fort Wayne, IN

Campbell, Martha, Asst.Libn.
COLORADO STATE SUPREME COURT LIBRARY □
Denver, CO

Campbell, Mary Jane, Libn.
FERRO CORPORATION - FERRO CHEMICAL
DIVISION - FERRO CHEMICAL LIBRARY □
Bedford, OH

Campbell, Neil, Asst.Dir./Tech.Serv.
TEXAS TECH UNIVERSITY - HEALTH SCIENCES
CENTER - LIBRARY OF THE HEALTH SCIENCES
□ Lubbock, TX

Campbell, Nina S., Assoc.Lib.Dir.
INDIANA UNIVERSITY - SCHOOL OF MEDICINE
LIBRARY □ Indianapolis, IN

Campbell, Paul R., Libn.
RHODE ISLAND HISTORICAL SOCIETY -
LIBRARY □ Providence, RI

Campbell, Sally, Info.Mgr.
BANK OF HAWAII - INFORMATION CENTER □
Honolulu, HI

Campbell, Sara, Cur.
NORTON SIMON MUSEUM OF ART AT
PASADENA - GALKA E. SCHEYER ARCHIVES □
Pasadena, CA

PERSONNEL

Campbell, Susan L., Libn./Res.
VANIER INSTITUTE OF THE FAMILY -
RESOURCE & INFORMATION CENTRE □ Ottawa,
ON

Campbell, Vivian L., Asst.Libn., Coll.Dev.
GEORGETOWN UNIVERSITY - LAW CENTER
LIBRARY □ Washington, DC

Campeau, Lucien, S.J., Res.
COMPAGNIE DE JESUS - JESUITS LIBRARY □
St. Jerome, PQ

Campeau, M., Hd. Curatorial Serv.
CANADA - PUBLIC ARCHIVES OF CANADA -
MANUSCRIPT DIVISION □ Ottawa, ON

Camper-Titsingh, Mary, Investment Res.Libn.
FORD FOUNDATION - INVESTMENT RESEARCH
LIBRARY □ New York, NY

Campese, Michael A., Lib.Dir.
ST. ELIZABETH'S HOSPITAL - HEALTH SCIENCE
LIBRARY □ Belleville, IL

Campfield, Mary, Dir. of Lib.Serv.
WINNEBAGO MENTAL HEALTH INSTITUTE -
MEDICAL LIBRARY □ Winnebago, WI

Campion, Serge G., Chf.Libn.
CANADA - TRANSPORT CANADA - LIBRARY &
INFORMATION CENTRE □ Ottawa, ON

Campo, L.D.
OLIN CORPORATION - RESEARCH CENTER/
INFORMATION CENTER □ New Haven, CT

Campo, Palma, Libn.
DYKEMA, GOSSETT, SPENCER, GOODNOW &
TRIGG - LAW LIBRARY □ Detroit, MI

Canada, Sally, Libn.
TITANIUM METALS CORPORATION OF
AMERICA - HENDERSON TECHNICAL LIBRARY
□ Henderson, NV

Canady, Virginia, Med.Libn.
WATSON CLINIC - MEDICAL LIBRARY □
Lakeland, FL

Canas, Yolanda, Cat.Libn.
DARGAN-CARVER LIBRARY □ Nashville, TN

Candau, Eugenie, Libn.
SAN FRANCISCO MUSEUM OF MODERN ART -
LOUISE S. ACKERMAN FINE ARTS LIBRARY □
San Francisco, CA

Candelmo, Emily, Libn.
TAMS ENGINEERS, ARCHITECTS & PLANNERS -
LIBRARY □ New York, NY

Canedo, Jeannine, Lib.Asst.
COLORADO SCHOOL FOR THE DEAF AND THE
BLIND - MEDIA CENTER □ Colorado Springs, CO

Canelake, Audrey, Libn.
MINNEAPOLIS PUBLIC LIBRARY &
INFORMATION CENTER - HISTORY
DEPARTMENT □ Minneapolis, MN

Canfanini, Margaret, Hd.Libn.
FRENCH LIBRARY IN BOSTON, INC. □ Boston,
MA

Cangialosi, Ruth, Asst.Libn.
MC GRAW-HILL, INC. - LIBRARY □ New York,
NY

Cann, Sharon, Libn.
NORTHSIDE HOSPITAL - WOODRUFF HEALTH
SCIENCE LIBRARY □ Atlanta, GA

Cannaday, Deborah J., Libn./Dir.
TOLEDO LAW ASSOCIATION LIBRARY □ Toledo,
OH

Cannan, Gisela Hill, Assoc.Libn.
GERMAN SOCIETY OF PENNSYLVANIA -
JOSEPH HORNER MEMORIAL LIBRARY □
Philadelphia, PA

Cannan, Julia, Coord.
KENT STATE UNIVERSITY - CHEMISTRY/
PHYSICS LIBRARY □ Kent, OH

Cannan, Julia, Coord.
KENT STATE UNIVERSITY - MAP LIBRARY □
Kent, OH

Canning, Ruby, Libn.
WEST VIRGINIA UNIVERSITY - CREATIVE
ARTS CENTER - MUSIC LIBRARY □ Morgantown,
WV

Cannon, F. Anne, Hd.
YORK UNIVERSITY - GOVERNMENT
DOCUMENTS/ADMINISTRATIVE STUDIES
LIBRARY □ Downsview, ON

Cannon, Joan D., Asst.Libn.
FLORIDA STATE SUPREME COURT LIBRARY □
Tallahassee, FL

Cannon, Linda L., Sec.
NEW YORK STATE COLLEGE OF CERAMICS,
ALFRED UNIVERSITY - SAMUEL R. SCHOLES
LIBRARY OF CERAMICS □ Alfred, NY

Cannon, Peter, Res.Anl.
WISCONSIN STATE LEGISLATIVE REFERENCE
BUREAU □ Madison, WI

Cannon, Ruth M.E., Libn.
FEDERAL RESERVE BANK OF RICHMOND -
RESEARCH LIBRARY □ Richmond, VA

Cantone, Sr. Paschal Marie, O.S.F., Libn.
ST. FRANCIS HOSPITAL, INC. - MEDICAL
LIBRARY □ Wilmington, DE

Cantor, Beverly L., Tech.Libn.
AMERICAN HOME PRODUCTS CORPORATION -
WYETH LABORATORIES DIVISION -
ANTIBIOTICS LABORATORIES LIBRARY† □
West Chester, PA

Cantrell, Barbi, Cons.
CENTER FOR HUMANE OPTIONS IN
CHILDBIRTH EXPERIENCES (CHOICE) -
LIBRARY □ Columbus, OH

Cantrell, Jacques, Libn.
M.P.K. OMEGA COMPANY - B.O.T.I. SPECIAL
RESEARCH COLLECTION □ Amarillo, TX

Cantrell, Jacques, Corp.Libn.
M.P.K. OMEGA COMPANY - BIOSCIENCE
LIBRARY □ Amarillo, TX

Cantrell, Jeanne D., Asst.Libn.
INSTITUTE OF LIVING - MEDICAL LIBRARY □
Hartford, CT

Cantrell, Marilyn, Dir.Med.Rec.
COMMUNITY HOSPITAL ASSOCIATION -
MEDICAL LIBRARY □ Battle Creek, MI

Cantwell, Barbara, Libn.
SKAGIT COUNTY HISTORICAL MUSEUM -
HISTORICAL REFERENCE LIBRARY □ La Conner,
WA

Capel, Gloria, Adm.
CROWN ZELLERBACH CORPORATION -
CORPORATE INFORMATION CENTER □ San
Francisco, CA

Capen, Karen, Distr.Rep.
NATIONAL FILM BOARD OF CANADA - FILM
LIBRARY □ New York, NY

Capers, Loretta, Libn.
COLLEGE FOR HUMAN SERVICES - LIBRARY □
New York, NY

Capitani, Cheryl A., Dir., Lib./Media Serv.
HARRISBURG HOSPITAL - HOSPITAL LIBRARY □
Harrisburg, PA

Caplan, Bernard, Res.Spec.
ENSANIAN PHYSICOCHEMICAL INSTITUTE -
INFORMATION CENTER FOR GRAVITATION
CHEMISTRY □ Eldred, PA

Capodagli, James, Ref.Libn.
SUNY - UPSTATE MEDICAL CENTER LIBRARY □
Syracuse, NY

Capolino, Ruth, Libn.
TRW, INC. - PHILADELPHIA LABORATORIES -
RESEARCH & DEVELOPMENT LIBRARY □
Philadelphia, PA

Caponigro, Angelina, Hd.Libn.
ST. AGNES MEDICAL CENTER - HEALTH
SCIENCES LIBRARY □ Philadelphia, PA

Capp, G.H., Supv.
ROCKWELL INTERNATIONAL - NORTH
AMERICAN AIRCRAFT DIVISION - TECHNICAL
INFORMATION CENTER □ Los Angeles, CA

Cappa-Rotunno, MaryAnn, Supv., Tech.Proc.
IRELL & MANELLA - LIBRARY □ Los Angeles, CA

Cappannari, Suzanne, ILL Asst.
VANDERBILT UNIVERSITY - MEDICAL CENTER
LIBRARY □ Nashville, TN

Cappiello, Deborah A., Tax Libn.
PRICE WATERHOUSE - TAX LIBRARY □ New
York, NY

Capps, Gene T., Dir., Dept. of Educ.
OLD SALEM, INC. - LIBRARY □ Winston-Salem,
NC

Capps, Marie T., Maps & Mss.Libn.
U.S. ARMY - MILITARY ACADEMY - LIBRARY □
West Point, NY

Capritta, Dianne, Assoc.Libn.Acq.
SUNY - COLLEGE OF ENVIRONMENTAL SCIENCE
AND FORESTRY - F. FRANKLIN MOON LIBRARY
□ Syracuse, NY

Capron, Shirley, Pub.Serv.Libn.
EXPERIMENT IN INTERNATIONAL LIVING -
SCHOOL FOR INTERNATIONAL TRAINING -
DONALD B. WATT LIBRARY □ Brattleboro, VT

Capute, Virginia B., Law Libn.
COLUMBUS LAW LIBRARY ASSOCIATION □
Columbus, OH

Caputo, Dr. Janette, Dir.
SAGINAW HEALTH SCIENCES LIBRARY □
Saginaw, MI

Caputo, Paul, Asst.Libn.
SUNY AT BUFFALO - HEALTH SCIENCES
LIBRARY □ Buffalo, NY

Caratenuto, Judith G., Law Libn.
FAIRFAX COUNTY LAW LIBRARY □ Fairfax, VA

Caravella, Joseph R., Dir., Prof.Serv.
NATIONAL COUNCIL OF TEACHERS OF
MATHEMATICS - TEACHER/LEARNING CENTER
□ Reston, VA

Caraway, Helen B., Libn.
U.S. NATIONAL MINE HEALTH AND SAFETY
ACADEMY - LEARNING RESOURCE CENTER □
Beckley, WV

Carbo, Dolores, Tech.Libn.
GENERAL ELECTRIC COMPANY - SPACE/RSD
LIBRARIES □ Philadelphia, PA

Carbonara, Dr. R.S.
BATTELLE-COLUMBUS LABORATORIES -
RAPIDLY SOLIDIFIED MATERIALS (RaSoMat) -
RESOURCE CENTER □ Columbus, OH

Carbone, Carmela, Dp.Dir.
ENGINEERING SOCIETIES LIBRARY □ New
York, NY

Carbonneau, Denis, Hd.Cat.
PRICE WATERHOUSE - NATIONAL
INFORMATION CENTER □ New York, NY

Cardace, Ann, Asst.Libn.
NATIONAL ASSOCIATION OF BROADCASTERS -
LIBRARY □ Washington, DC

Cardell, Betty, Acq.
U.S. CENTER FOR DISEASE CONTROL - CDC
LIBRARY □ Atlanta, GA

Cardell, Victor T., Asst. Music Libn.
CORNELL UNIVERSITY - MUSIC LIBRARY □
Ithaca, NY

Cardello, Patricia, Automated Serv.Libn.
AVCO CORPORATION - AVCO-EVERETT
RESEARCH LABORATORY - LIBRARY □ Everett,
MA

Carder, Robert W., Libn.
MADISON HISTORICAL SOCIETY, INC. -
LIBRARY □ Madison, CT

Cardew, Cecily, Lib.Dir. & Archv.
MOLESWORTH INSTITUTE - LIBRARY AND
ARCHIVES □ Storrs, CT

Cardillo, Wayne, Doc.Libn.
UNIVERSITY OF KANSAS - SCHOOL OF LAW
LIBRARY □ Lawrence, KS

Cardinal, J., Dir., Adm. & Personnel
CANADA - LIBRARY OF PARLIAMENT □ Ottawa,
ON

Cardinal, L., Chf., Modern Cart.Div
CANADA - PUBLIC ARCHIVES OF CANADA -
NATIONAL MAP COLLECTION □ Ottawa, ON

Cardinale, Susan, Coord.
UNIVERSITY OF MARYLAND, COLLEGE PARK -
LIBRARIES - WOMEN'S STUDIES PAMPHLET
COLLECTION □ College Park, MD

Cardoza, Donna, Lib.Ck.
EMANUEL MEDICAL CENTER - MEDICAL
LIBRARY □ Turlock, CA

Cardoza, Eleanor, Libn.
NOVA SCOTIA COMMISSION ON DRUG
DEPENDENCY - LIBRARY AND INFORMATION
CENTRE □ Halifax, NS

Cardozo, Manoel, Cur.
CATHOLIC UNIVERSITY OF AMERICA -
OLIVEIRA LIMA LIBRARY □ Washington, DC

Caren, Loretta, Hd.
UNIVERSITY OF ROCHESTER - PHYSICS-
OPTICS-ASTRONOMY LIBRARY □ Rochester, NY

Carestia, LTC Ralph R., MSC, Hd.
U.S. ARMY - ARMED FORCES PEST
MANAGEMENT BOARD - DEFENSE PEST
MANAGEMENT INFORMATION ANALYSIS
CENTER □ Washington, DC

Carew, Virginia, Ref.Libn.
AMERICAN BIBLE SOCIETY - LIBRARY □ New
York, NY

Carey, Cynthia, Program Libn.
PASADENA PUBLIC LIBRARY - BUSINESS-
TECHNOLOGY DIVISION □ Pasadena, CA

Carey, John, Asst.Hd.
ENOCH PRATT FREE LIBRARY - AUDIO-VISUAL
DEPARTMENT □ Baltimore, MD

Carey, John E., Gen.Mgr.
FOI SERVICES, INC. - LIBRARY □ Rockville, MD

Carey, Marsha, Act.Info.Spec.
U.S. FEDERAL JUDICIAL CENTER -
INFORMATION SERVICE □ Washington, DC

Caricone, Paul, Cat.
COLLEGE OF INSURANCE - INSURANCE
SOCIETY OF NEW YORK - LIBRARY □ New York,
NY

Carini, Helen, Tech.Libn.
GAF CORPORATION - TECHNICAL
INFORMATION SERVICES □ Wayne, NJ

Carkner, Mrs. J., ILL
BELL-NORTHERN RESEARCH LTD. - TECHNICAL
INFORMATION CENTRE □ Ottawa, ON

Carlburg, C. David, Asst.Libn.
CALIFORNIA STATE DEPARTMENT OF JUSTICE
- ATTORNEY GENERAL'S OFFICE - LAW
LIBRARY □ Los Angeles, CA

Carle, Patricia M., Lib.Cons.
ALLEGHENY COUNTY - DEPARTMENT OF
PLANNING - LIBRARY □ Pittsburgh, PA

Carleton, Dr. Don E., Hd.Libn./Archv.
UNIVERSITY OF TEXAS, AUSTIN - EUGENE C.
BARKER TEXAS HISTORY CENTER □ Austin, TX

Carlin, Christine, Maritime Info.Spec.
NATIONAL ACADEMY OF SCIENCES -
NATIONAL RESEARCH COUNCIL - MARITIME
RESEARCH INFORMATION SERVICE □
Washington, DC

Carlisle, Hilda, Lib.Chm.
FIRST UNITED METHODIST CHURCH -
GERTRUDE CALLIHAN MEMORIAL LIBRARY □
San Marcos, TX

Carlisle, William T., Assoc.Dir.
UNIVERSITY OF UTAH - CENTER FOR PUBLIC
AFFAIRS AND ADMINISTRATION - RESEARCH
LIBRARY □ Salt Lake City, UT

Carlock, Walter, Libn.
MINNEAPOLIS PUBLIC LIBRARY &
INFORMATION CENTER - BUSINESS AND
SCIENCE DEPARTMENT □ Minneapolis, MN

Carlsen, Robert, Teacher-Libn.
NORTHERN WISCONSIN CENTER FOR THE
DEVELOPMENTALLY DISABLED - LIBRARY/
INSTRUCTIONAL MATERIALS CENTER □
Chippewa Falls, WI

Carlson, Aileen A., Libn.
AMERICAN OPTICAL CORPORATION -
RESEARCH CENTER LIBRARY □ Southbridge, MA

Carlson, Bruce, Supv.
UNIVERSITY OF MANITOBA - MUSIC READING
ROOM □ Winnipeg, MB

Carlson, Gordon, Chf.Libn.
U.S. VETERANS ADMINISTRATION (ID-Boise) -
HOSPITAL LIBRARY (142D) □ Boise, ID

Carlson, Jacquelynn, Chf.Libn.
ST. MARY'S HOSPITAL - STAFF LIBRARY □
Minneapolis, MN

Carlson, Lillian V., Libn.
DUNWOODY INDUSTRIAL INSTITUTE - JOHN A.
BUTLER LEARNING CENTER □ Minneapolis, MN

Carlson, Linda, Rd.Serv.Libn.
JOHNS HOPKINS UNIVERSITY - SCHOOL OF
ADVANCED INTERNATIONAL STUDIES -
SYDNEY R. & ELSA W. MASON LIBRARY □
Washington, DC

Carlson, Livija, Libn.
UNIVERSITY OF MINNESOTA, ST. PAUL -
VETERINARY MEDICAL LIBRARY □ St. Paul, MN

Carlson, Lois O., Media Coord.
PHOENIX DAY SCHOOL FOR THE DEAF -
LIBRARY/MEDIA CENTER □ Phoenix, AZ

Carlson, Marilyn R., Libn.
NORTHWEST HOSPITAL - EFFIE M. STOREY
LEARNING CENTER □ Seattle, WA

Carlson, Mrs. Pat, Hd.Libn.
SOUTHERN CALIFORNIA COLLEGE OF
OPTOMETRY - M.B. KETCHUM MEMORIAL
LIBRARY □ Fullerton, CA

Carlson, Stan W., Dir. of Libs.
UNITY HOSPITAL - MEDICAL LIBRARY □ Fridley,
MN

Carlsson, Vera R., Hd. of Acq.
UNIVERSITY OF MINNESOTA - LAW LIBRARY □
Minneapolis, MN

Carlton, Gary, Hd., Circ.
UNIVERSITY OF CALIFORNIA, SANTA CRUZ -
DEAN E. MC HENRY LIBRARY □ Santa Cruz, CA

Carlton, William H., Personnel/Fiscal Off.
TEXAS STATE LIBRARY □ Austin, TX

Carlucci, April, Asst.Libn., Ref.Serv.
AMERICAN MUSEUM OF NATURAL HISTORY -
LIBRARY □ New York, NY

Carlucci, Nancy, Libn.
ONTARIO - MINISTRY OF THE SOLICITOR
GENERAL - OFFICE OF THE FIRE MARSHAL
LIBRARY □ Toronto, ON

Carmack, Norma, Ref.
TRINITY UNIVERSITY - LIBRARY □ San Antonio,
TX

Carman, Carol, Leg.Libn.
MARYLAND STATE DEPARTMENT OF
LEGISLATIVE REFERENCE - LIBRARY □
Annapolis, MD

Carmichael, Anne P., Corp.Libn.
CAROLINA POWER & LIGHT COMPANY -
CORPORATE LIBRARY □ Raleigh, NC

Carmichael, Dr. Ian
UNIVERSITY OF NOTRE DAME - RADIATION
LABORATORY - RADIATION CHEMISTRY DATA
CENTER □ Notre Dame, IN

Carmichael, Kathleen M., Asst.Libn.
HARPER-GRACE HOSPITALS - HARPER
HOSPITAL DIVISION - DEPARTMENT OF
LIBRARIES □ Detroit, MI

Carmichael, Mrs. M.F., Lib.Dir.
WATERBURY HOSPITAL HEALTH CENTER -
HEALTH CENTER LIBRARY □ Waterbury, CT

Carmichael, William C., Info.Sci.
GEORGIA-PACIFIC CORPORATION -
TECHNICAL INFORMATION CENTER □ Atlanta,
GA

Carmona-Treger, Rita, Hd., Ref.Serv.
FLORIDA INSTITUTE OF TECHNOLOGY -
LIBRARY □ Melbourne, FL

Carnahan, Joan A., Mgr., Lib. & Info.Ctr.
TENNECO CHEMICALS, INC. - LIBRARY □
Piscataway, NJ

Carneglia, A., ILL Libn.
PERKIN-ELMER CORPORATION - CORPORATE
LIBRARY □ Norwalk, CT

Carnell, Helen, Libn.
UNITED COOPERATIVES OF ONTARIO -
HARMAN LIBRARY □ Mississauga, ON

Carnes, Judith O., Ref.Libn. & Coll.Dev
YALE UNIVERSITY - SOCIAL SCIENCE LIBRARY
□ New Haven, CT

Carney, Eileen, Asst.Libn.
BRUNDAGE, STORY & ROSE, INVESTMENT
COUNSEL - LIBRARY □ New York, NY

Carney, Ellen, Res.Libn.
CONSUMERS UNION OF UNITED STATES, INC. -
LIBRARY □ Mount Vernon, NY

Carney, Patrick J., Lib.Dir.
U.S. MARINE CORPS - CAMP PENDLETON
LIBRARY SYSTEM† □ Camp Pendleton, CA

Caro, Eva K., Sr.Libn.
CALIFORNIA STATE DEPARTMENT OF
TRANSPORTATION - LABORATORY LIBRARY □
Sacramento, CA

Carol, Marcel C., Libn.
BAYLOR UNIVERSITY, DALLAS - LIBRARY □
Dallas, TX

Carolin, Janice, Asst.Libn.
MANUFACTURERS LIFE INSURANCE COMPANY
- BUSINESS LIBRARY □ Toronto, ON

Caron, G.
CANADA - PUBLIC ARCHIVES OF CANADA -
NATIONAL MAP COLLECTION □ Ottawa, ON

Caron, Mary, Info.Serv.Asst.
ILLINOIS BENEDICTINE COLLEGE - THEODORE
LOWNIK LIBRARY □ Lisle, IL

Caron, Monique
MAINE STATE LAW AND LEGISLATIVE
REFERENCE LIBRARY □ Augusta, ME

Caron, Theodore, Hd.Cat.
MAYO FOUNDATION - MAYO CLINIC LIBRARY □
Rochester, MN

Carpelan, Dr. Marian
UNIVERSITY OF CALIFORNIA, RIVERSIDE -
OFFICE OF TECHNICAL INFO. - STATEWIDE
AIR POLLUTION RESEARCH CTR. □ Riverside,
CA

Carpenter, Betty M., Libn.
SUFFOLK COUNTY HISTORICAL SOCIETY -
LIBRARY □ Riverhead, NY

Carpenter, Catherine B., Chf.Cat.
HARVARD UNIVERSITY - LITTAUER LIBRARY □
Cambridge, MA

Carpenter, Debbie, Ref.Libn.
U.S. ARMY - ENGINEER WATERWAYS
EXPERIMENT STATION - TECHNICAL
INFORMATION CENTER □ Vicksburg, MS

Carpenter, Esther M., Archv.
MUSEUM OF MODERN ART - DEPARTMENT OF
RIGHTS AND REPRODUCTIONS - AUDIOVISUAL
ARCHIVES □ New York, NY

Carpenter, Mrs. Forrest, Libn.
OAK GROVE LUTHERAN CHURCH - MEMORIAL
LIBRARY† □ Richfield, MN

Carpenter, Jean, Lib.Asst.
RAYTHEON COMPANY - SUBMARINE SIGNAL
DIVISION - TECHNICAL INFORMATION
CENTER □ Portsmouth, RI

Carpenter, Lester, Cur. of Programming
KINGMAN MUSEUM OF NATURAL HISTORY -
LIBRARY □ Battle Creek, MI

Carpenter, Lois, Hd.Ref.Serv.
MANITOBA - DEPARTMENT OF EDUCATION -
LIBRARY □ Winnipeg, MB

Carpenter, Tosca N., Hd.Libn.
NEWPORT HOSPITAL - INA MOSHER HEALTH
SCIENCES LIBRARY □ Newport, RI

Carpenter, Wendell, Coord., Rd.Serv.
CHRISTIAN RECORD BRAILLE FOUNDATION -
CHRISTIAN RECORD FREE LENDING LIBRARY □
Lincoln, NE

Carpentier, Louise, Govt.Doc.Libn.
CONCORDIA UNIVERSITY - SIR GEORGE
WILLIAMS CAMPUS - NORRIS LIBRARY □
Montreal, PQ

Carper, Anna M., Dir.
ELIZABETHTOWN COLLEGE - ZUG MEMORIAL
LIBRARY - ARCHIVES □ Elizabethtown, PA

Carper, Lee, Circ.Hd.
COLORADO SCHOOL OF MINES - ARTHUR
LAKES LIBRARY □ Golden, CO

PERSONNEL

Carr, Barbara, Ref.Libn.
ST. LAWRENCE COLLEGE OF APPLIED ARTS
AND TECHNOLOGY - LEARNING RESOURCE
CENTRE □ Kingston, ON

Carr, Barbara Z., Cons.
COLORADO STATE DEPARTMENT OF
EDUCATION - INSTRUCTIONAL MATERIALS
CENTER FOR THE VISUALLY HANDICAPPED □
Denver, CO

Carr, Sr. Frances A., Archv.
UNITED SOCIETY OF BELIEVERS - THE SHAKER
LIBRARY □ Poland Spring, ME

Carr, Irene, Rsrcs.Mtls.Asst.
EAST-WEST POPULATION INSTITUTE
RESOURCE MATERIALS COLLECTION □
Honolulu, HI

Carr, Jo Ann, Pub.Serv.
UNIVERSITY OF WISCONSIN, MADISON -
SCHOOL OF EDUCATION - INSTRUCTIONAL
MATERIALS CENTER □ Madison, WI

Carr, M., Libn.
UNIROYAL, INC. - CORPORATE LIBRARY □
Middlebury, CT

Carr, Margaret M., Info.Spec.
MARTIN MARIETTA LABORATORIES - LIBRARY
□ Baltimore, MD

Carr, W.L., Circ.
MC DONNELL DOUGLAS CORPORATION - MC
DONNELL AIRCRAFT LIBRARY □ St. Louis, MO

Carr, William, Chf.
PENNSYLVANIA STATE DEPT. OF
ENVIRONMENTAL RESOURCES -
ENVIRONMENTAL PROTECTION TECHNICAL
REFERENCE LIBRARY □ Harrisburg, PA

Carr-Harris, Ian, Dir.
ONTARIO COLLEGE OF ART - LIBRARY/
AUDIOVISUAL CENTRE □ Toronto, ON

Carrasquillo, Irma, Asst.Libn.
PUERTO RICO - ATENEO PUERTORRIQUENO -
BIBLIOTECA □ San Juan, PR

Carrick, Barbara J., Libn.
U.S. NATL. OCEANIC & ATMOSPHERIC
ADMINISTRATION - ENVIRONMENTAL DATA &
INFO. SERV. - GREAT LAKES LIBRARY† □ Ann
Arbor, MI

Carrick, Kathleen, Dir.
SUNY AT BUFFALO - CHARLES B. SEARS LAW
LIBRARY □ Buffalo, NY

Carrier, Esther Jane, ILL
LOCK HAVEN STATE COLLEGE - GEORGE B.
STEVENSON LIBRARY □ Lock Haven, PA

Carrier, John P., Chf.
U.S. ARMY - ELECTRONICS R & D COMMAND -
HARRY DIAMOND LABORATORIES-TECHNICAL
& VISUAL INFORMATION OFFICE □ Adelphi, MD

Carrier, Lois J., Hd.
UNIVERSITY OF BRITISH COLUMBIA - SOCIAL
SCIENCES DIVISION □ Vancouver, BC

Carriere, Mrs. Francoise, Tech.Info.Off.
ROADS AND TRANSPORTATION ASSOCIATION
OF CANADA - TECHNICAL INFORMATION
SERVICE □ Ottawa, ON

Carrigan, Jean, Chf.Libn.
EQUITABLE LIFE ASSURANCE SOCIETY OF THE
U.S. - GENERAL LIBRARY† □ New York, NY

Carrigan, John L., Dir.
CITY OF HOPE NATIONAL MEDICAL CENTER -
PINESS MEDICAL AND SCIENTIFIC LIBRARY □
Duarte, CA

Carrington, David K., Hd., Tech.Serv.
LIBRARY OF CONGRESS - GEOGRAPHY & MAP
DIVISION □ Washington, DC

Carrison, Dale K., Dean of Lib.
MANKATO STATE UNIVERSITY - LIBRARY □
Mankato, MN

Carro, Jorge L., Hd.Libn.
UNIVERSITY OF CINCINNATI - ROBERT S.
MARX LAW LIBRARY □ Cincinnati, OH

Carrol, Arthur L., Lib.Dir.
U.S. PUBLIC HEALTH SERVICE - PARKLAWN
HEALTH LIBRARY □ Rockville, MD

Carrol, J.N., Asst.
GULF OIL CHEMICALS COMPANY - HOUSTON
RESEARCH LIBRARY □ Houston, TX

Carroll, Angelica, Mgr.
MOODY'S INVESTORS SERVICE -
INFORMATION CENTER □ New York, NY

Carroll, Bonnie C., Asst.Mgr.
U.S. DEPT. OF ENERGY - TECHNICAL
INFORMATION CENTER - REFERENCE CENTER
□ Oak Ridge, TN

Carroll, C., Hd.Pub.Aff.Archv.
CANADA - PUBLIC ARCHIVES OF CANADA -
MANUSCRIPT DIVISION □ Ottawa, ON

Carroll, Rev. Clifford, S.J., Archv.
SOCIETY OF JESUS - OREGON PROVINCE
ARCHIVES □ Spokane, WA

Carroll, Diane J., Ref./Online Serv.
UNIVERSITY OF MINNESOTA, DULUTH -
HEALTH SCIENCE LIBRARY □ Duluth, MN

Carroll, Elizabeth J., Adm.Asst.
PENNSYLVANIA STATE UNIVERSITY - CENTER
FOR AIR ENVIRONMENT STUDIES -
INFORMATION CENTER □ University Park, PA

Carroll, Frank A., Cat.
U.S. ARMY POST - FORT RILEY - LIBRARIES† □
Fort Riley, KS

Carroll, J.E., Engr.Info.Anl.
LOCKHEED-GEORGIA COMPANY - TECHNICAL
INFORMATION DEPARTMENT □ Marietta, GA

Carroll, James, Asst.Libn.
WISCONSIN CONSERVATORY OF MUSIC -
LIBRARY □ Milwaukee, WI

Carroll, Larry, Asst.Adm.
INDIANAPOLIS - DEPARTMENT OF
METROPOLITAN DEVELOPMENT - DIVISION OF
PLANNING AND ZONING - LIBRARY □
Indianapolis, IN

Carroll, Linda J., Libn.
POPULATION CRISIS COMMITEE/DRAPER
FUND - LIBRARY □ Washington, DC

Carroll, Marian, Cat.
BROOKINGS INSTITUTION - LIBRARY □
Washington, DC

Carroll, Mary M., Med.Libn.
CALVARY HOSPITAL - MEDICAL LIBRARY □
Bronx, NY

Carroll, Ruth P., Dir.
ST. FRANCIS HOSPITAL AND MEDICAL CENTER
- SCHOOL OF NURSING LIBRARY □ Hartford, CT

Carroll, Virginia, Libn.
CAMP DRESSER & MC KEE, INC. - HERMAN G.
DRESSER LIBRARY □ Boston, MA

Carroll, Virginia D., Libn.
CALHOUN COUNTY MUSEUM - ARCHIVES AND
LIBRARY □ St. Matthews, SC

Carroon, Robert G., Cur.
MILWAUKEE COUNTY HISTORICAL SOCIETY -
LIBRARY AND ARCHIVES □ Milwaukee, WI

Carsch, Judith S., Libn.
WISE (Isaac M.) TEMPLE - RALPH COHEN
MEMORIAL LIBRARY □ Cincinnati, OH

Carson, Donald, Chf.Libn.
COLLEGE OF INSURANCE - INSURANCE
SOCIETY OF NEW YORK - LIBRARY □ New York,
NY

Carson, Donald E., Libn.
ASSOCIATION OF AVERAGE ADJUSTERS OF
THE UNITED STATES - LIBRARY □ New York,
NY

Carson, Mary Elizabeth, Libn.
GEO-TECH ARCHIVES LTD. -
PALEONTOLOGICAL RESEARCH LABORATORY -
LIBRARY □ Charlotte, NC

Carson, Roberta, Med.Rec.Libn.
CALIFORNIA STATE MEDICAL FACILITY -
STAFF LIBRARY □ Vacaville, CA

Carson, Theresa J., Hd.Circ.
DETROIT INSTITUTE OF TECHNOLOGY - JAMES
C. GORDON MEMORIAL LIBRARY □ Detroit, MI

Carstensen, Chris, Libn.
FIRST BAPTIST CHURCH - LIBRARY □ Sioux
Falls, SD

Carstensen, Helen, Libn.
MIAMI COUNTY LAW LIBRARY □ Troy, OH

Carswell, Mary Alice, Dir.
ACADEMY OF THE NEW CHURCH - LIBRARY □
Bryn Athyn, PA

Cartelli, Mary Anne, Lib.Asst.
ASIA SOCIETY - LIBRARY □ New York, NY

Carter, Allen, Libn.
U.S. NAVY - NAVAL REGIONAL MEDICAL
CENTER (Memphis) - GENERAL AND MEDICAL
LIBRARY† □ Millington, TN

Carter, Ann Hadley, Res.Asst./Libn.
SOUTHERN REGIONAL EDUCATION BOARD -
LIBRARY □ Atlanta, GA

Carter, Ann M., Libn.
DORSEY, WINDHORST, HANNAFORD, WHITNEY
& HALLADAY - LAW LIBRARY □ Minneapolis, MN

Carter, Bobby R., Dir. of Lib.Serv.
TEXAS COLLEGE OF OSTEOPATHIC MEDICINE -
MEDICAL LIBRARY □ Fort Worth, TX

Carter, Rev. D.J., Archv.
ANGLICAN CHURCH OF CANADA - DIOCESE OF
CALGARY - ANGLICAN ARCHIVES □ Calgary, AB

Carter, David C., Pres.
UNITED STATES BEET SUGAR ASSOCIATION -
LIBRARY □ Washington, DC

Carter, Donald, Supv., LRC
U.S. VETERANS ADMINISTRATION (MA-
Brockton) - MEDICAL CENTER LIBRARY □
Brockton, MA

Carter, Dr. Edward C., II, Libn.
AMERICAN PHILOSOPHICAL SOCIETY -
LIBRARY □ Philadelphia, PA

Carter, Eleanor M., Dir.
SUNY - AGRICULTURAL AND TECHNICAL
COLLEGE AT COBLESKILL - JARED VAN
WAGENEN, JR. LEARNING RESOURCE CENTER
□ Cobleskill, NY

Carter, Elizabeth, Pub.Serv.Libn.
UNIVERSITY OF CALIFORNIA, BERKELEY -
INSTITUTE OF TRANSPORTATION STUDIES
LIBRARY □ Berkeley, CA

Carter, Fay T., Acq.Libn.
LINCOLN UNIVERSITY OF MISSOURI - INMAN
E. PAGE LIBRARY □ Jefferson City, MO

Carter, Georgia Kay, Supv. Chemist
HERCULES, INC. - HATTIESBURG PLANT
LABORATORY - LIBRARY □ Hattiesburg, MS

Carter, Ida, Tech.Libn.
GARD, INC. - LIBRARY □ Niles, IL

Carter, Jackson, Ser.Libn.
EASTERN NEW MEXICO UNIVERSITY - GOLDEN
LIBRARY □ Portales, NM

Carter, James, Asst.Curric.Libn.
UNIVERSITY OF ALBERTA - H.T. COUTTS
EDUCATION LIBRARY □ Edmonton, AB

Carter, James W., Supv.
AMAX EXTRACTIVE RESEARCH &
DEVELOPMENT, INC. - TECHNICAL
INFORMATION CENTER □ Golden, CO

Carter, Jewell Alexander, Lib.Dir.
BAPTIST MEDICAL CENTERS-SAMFORD
UNIVERSITY - IDA V. MOFFETT SCHOOL OF
NURSING - L.R. JORDAN LIBRARY □
Birmingham, AL

Carter, John E., Cur., Photographs
NEBRASKA STATE HISTORICAL SOCIETY -
LIBRARY □ Lincoln, NE

Carter, Julia S., Libn.
INDIANA UNIVERSITY - MEDICAL SCIENCES
LIBRARY □ Bloomington, IN

Carter, Karen R., Mgr., Info.Rsrcs.Dept.
AMERICAN ACADEMY OF FAMILY PHYSICIANS
- INFORMATION RESOURCE DEPARTMENT □
Kansas City, MO

Carter, Kent, Chf., Archv.Br.
U.S. NATL. ARCHIVES & RECORDS SERVICE -
FEDERAL ARCHIVES AND RECORDS CENTER,
REGION 7 □ Fort Worth, TX

Carter, Mary, Hd., Acq.Libn.
NORTH DAKOTA STATE UNIVERSITY - LIBRARY
□ Fargo, ND

Carter, N.G., Ref.Spec.
U.S. DEPT. OF ENERGY - PACIFIC NORTHWEST LABORATORY - TECHNICAL INFO. SECT. □ Richland, WA

Carter, Nancy Carol, Dir.
GOLDEN GATE UNIVERSITY - SCHOOL OF LAW LIBRARY □ San Francisco, CA

Carter, Phillip, Hd.Circ.
MEDICAL LIBRARY CENTER OF NEW YORK □ New York, NY

Carter, Rick, Info.Spec.
HOLLINGSWORTH (John D.) ON WHEELS, INC. - INFORMATION SERVICES □ Greenville, SC

Carter, Rita A., Libn.
COMMUNICATIONS SATELLITE CORPORATION - CENTRAL LIBRARY □ Washington, DC

Carter, Robert Allan, Sr.Libn.
NEW YORK STATE LIBRARY - LEGISLATIVE AND GOVERNMENTAL SERVICES □ Albany, NY

Carter, Robert L., Asst.Libn.
INDIANA STATE UNIVERSITY - DEPARTMENT OF RARE BOOKS AND SPECIAL COLLECTIONS □ Terre Haute, IN

Carter, RoseMary, Med.Libn.
ST. JOSEPH HOSPITAL - HEALTH SCIENCES LIBRARY □ Flint, MI

Carter, Sharon, Tech.Info.Serv.Supv.
ST. PAUL FIRE & MARINE INSURANCE COMPANY - LOSS PREVENTION DEPT. - TECHNICAL INFORMATION SERVICES □ St. Paul, MN

Carter, Sharon C., Libn.
WORCESTER TELEGRAM AND GAZETTE, INC. - LIBRARY □ Worcester, MA

Carter, Susan Miller, Hist.Libn.
PLAINFIELD PUBLIC LIBRARY - GUILFORD TOWNSHIP HISTORICAL COLLECTION □ Plainfield, IN

Carter, Violet L., Adm.Off.
U.S. DEPT. OF HEALTH AND HUMAN SERVICES - DEPARTMENT LIBRARY □ Washington, DC

Carter, Wendy N., Rd.Serv.Spec.
U.S. VETERANS ADMINISTRATION (DC-Washington) - HEADQUARTERS CENTRAL OFFICE LIBRARY □ Washington, DC

Carter, William E., Chf.
LIBRARY OF CONGRESS - HISPANIC DIVISION □ Washington, DC

Cartier, Celine R., Dir.
UNIVERSITE LAVAL - BIBLIOTHEQUE† □ Ste. Foy, PQ

Cartledge, Ellen, Libn.
CONNECTICUT MUTUAL LIFE INSURANCE COMPANY - LIBRARY □ Hartford, CT

Cartmell, Ms. V.
CANADA - PUBLIC ARCHIVES OF CANADA - NATIONAL MAP COLLECTION □ Ottawa, ON

Carton, Vera, Sr.Libn., Open Lit.
U.S. ARMY - LOGISTICS LIBRARY □ Ft. Lee, VA

Cartwright, Joseph, Dir.
PUTNAM MUSEUM - LIBRARY □ Davenport, IA

Carty, Kevin J., Libn.
METROPOLITAN PROPERTY & LIABILITY INSURANCE COMPANY - LAW & BUSINESS LIBRARY □ Warwick, RI

Caruso, Joy-Louise, Info.Spec.
CPC INTERNATIONAL - MOFFETT TECHNICAL LIBRARY □ Argo, IL

Caruso, Karin, Dir., AV Serv.
NEW HAMPSHIRE COLLEGE - SHAPIRO LIBRARY □ Manchester, NH

Caruso, Mary Elsie, Adm.Libn.
U.S. ARMY HOSPITALS - LETTERMAN ARMY MEDICAL CENTER - MEDICAL LIBRARY □ San Francisco, CA

Caruso, Nicholas C., Libn.
UNIVERSITY OF PITTSBURGH - GRADUATE SCHOOL OF PUBLIC & INTERNATIONAL AFFAIRS LIBRARY □ Pittsburgh, PA

Caruthers, Judith A., Ref.Libn.
LOUISIANA STATE UNIVERSITY MEDICAL CENTER - LIBRARY □ New Orleans, LA

Carvalho, Eugene, Libn.
UNIVERSITY OF KANSAS - EAST ASIAN LIBRARY □ Lawrence, KS

Carvalho, Florina, ILL
ROCKWELL INTERNATIONAL - SCIENCE CENTER LIBRARY □ Thousand Oaks, CA

Carvalho, Joseph, III, Coll.Libn.
SPRINGFIELD CITY LIBRARY - WARTIME PROPAGANDA COLLECTION □ Springfield, MA

Carver, Joseph E., Dean of Lib.Serv.
BRITISH COLUMBIA INSTITUTE OF TECHNOLOGY - LIBRARY SERVICES DIVISION □ Burnaby, BC

Carver, Larry, Dept.Hd.
UNIVERSITY OF CALIFORNIA, SANTA BARBARA - MAP AND IMAGERY LABORATORY - LIBRARY □ Santa Barbara, CA

Carver, Richard, Chf., P.R. Off.
NATIONAL LIBRARY OF CANADA □ Ottawa, ON

Cary, Howard B., Dir.
HOBART BROTHERS COMPANY - TECHNICAL CENTER - JOHN H. BLANKENBUEHLER MEMORIAL LIBRARY □ Troy, OH

Cascio, Nina, AV Libn.
SUNY AT BUFFALO - CHARLES B. SEARS LAW LIBRARY □ Buffalo, NY

Case, Frances K., Handicapped Serv.
SOUTH CAROLINA STATE LIBRARY □ Columbia, SC

Case, Howard E.
SUSSEX COUNTY HISTORICAL SOCIETY - LIBRARY □ Newton, NJ

Casebier, Janet, Hd.Hum.Soc.Sci.Lib.
CALIFORNIA INSTITUTE OF TECHNOLOGY - ROBERT A. MILLIKAN MEMORIAL LIBRARY □ Pasadena, CA

Casella, Roberta, Libn., Core Coll.
TEXAS TECH UNIVERSITY - LIBRARY □ Lubbock, TX

Casement, Susan, Libn.
KANSAS STATE UNIVERSITY - RESOURCES ON DEVELOPING COUNTRIES □ Manhattan, KS

Casey, James B., Hd.Ref.Libn.
WESTERN RESERVE HISTORICAL SOCIETY - LIBRARY □ Cleveland, OH

Casey, Jeanne
NATIONAL HOME STUDY COUNCIL - LIBRARY □ Washington, DC

Casey, Joan A., Lib.Dir.
NATIONAL MUNICIPAL LEAGUE - LIBRARY □ New York, NY

Casey, Mark, Supv., Lib.Serv.
GOULD INC. - GOULD INFORMATION CENTER □ Rolling Meadows, IL

Casey, Phil, Chf.
U.S. ARMY - ARMAMENT MATERIAL READINESS COMMAND - TECHNICAL LIBRARY □ Rock Island, IL

Casey, S., Doc.Libn.
QUEEN'S UNIVERSITY AT KINGSTON - DOCUMENTS LIBRARY □ Kingston, ON

Casey, Verna, Libn.
EASTERN KENTUCKY UNIVERSITY - LAW ENFORCEMENT LIBRARY □ Richmond, KY

Casey, William T., Lib.Dir.
FITCHBURG STATE COLLEGE - LIBRARY □ Fitchburg, MA

Cash, Mary D., Libn.
STAMFORD CATHOLIC LIBRARY, INC. □ Stamford, CT

Cash, Michele, Ref./ILL
LEWIS UNIVERSITY - LIBRARY □ Romeoville, IL

Cash, Pamela J., Libn.
JOHNSON PUBLISHING COMPANY, INC. - LIBRARY □ Chicago, IL

Cashman, Norine Duncan, Cur.
BROWN UNIVERSITY - ART DEPARTMENT SLIDE ROOM □ Providence, RI

Cashore, Thomas, Asst.Soc.Stud.Libn.
SOUTHERN ILLINOIS UNIVERSITY, CARBONDALE - SOCIAL STUDIES DIVISION LIBRARY □ Carbondale, IL

Casile, Theresa K., Principal Libn.
NEW YORK PUBLIC LIBRARY - BELMONT REGIONAL LIBRARY - ENRICO FERMI CULTURAL CENTER □ Bronx, NY

Casino, Joseph J., Archv.
ST. CHARLES BORROMEO SEMINARY - RYAN MEMORIAL LIBRARY □ Philadelphia, PA

Cason, Cleo S., Libn.
MADISON COUNTY - ELBERT H. PARSONS PUBLIC LAW LIBRARY □ Huntsville, AL

Cason, Maidel, African Doc.Libn.
NORTHWESTERN UNIVERSITY - MELVILLE J. HERSKOVITS LIBRARY OF AFRICAN STUDIES □ Evanston, IL

Casper, Roderick J., Hd., Pub.Serv.
CALIFORNIA INSTITUTE OF TECHNOLOGY - ROBERT A. MILLIKAN MEMORIAL LIBRARY □ Pasadena, CA

Cass, D., Archv.
GLENBOW-ALBERTA INSTITUTE - LIBRARY & ARCHIVES □ Calgary, AB

Cass, Ed, Archv.
U.S. ARMY - MILITARY ACADEMY - ARCHIVES □ West Point, NY

Cass, Edward C., Archv.
U.S. ARMY - MILITARY ACADEMY - LIBRARY □ West Point, NY

Cassel, Debra, Ref.Libn.
MONTEFIORE HOSPITAL & MEDICAL CENTER - MEDICAL LIBRARY □ New York, NY

Cassell, Jo Anne S., Ref.Libn./Educ.
NATIONAL INSTITUTE OF EDUCATION - EDUCATIONAL RESEARCH LIBRARY □ Washington, DC

Cassell, Judy A., Libn.
COCA-COLA COMPANY - MARKETING INFORMATION CENTER □ Atlanta, GA

Cassels, Sheila E., Res.Libn.
ILLINOIS STATE INSTITUTE OF NATURAL RESOURCES - ENERGY INFORMATION LIBRARY □ Springfield, IL

Cassels, Sheila E., Res.Libn.
ILLINOIS STATE INSTITUTE OF NATURAL RESOURCES - ENVIRONMENTAL INFORMATION CENTER □ Chicago, IL

Cassidy, Eileen, Hd.Libn.
PALO ALTO MEDICAL FOUNDATION - BARNETT-HALL MEDICAL LIBRARY □ Palo Alto, CA

Cassidy, Helen, Tech.Proc.
MARIANOPOLIS COLLEGE - LIBRARY □ Montreal, PQ

Cassidy, Phoebe, Res.Libn.
SUN COMPANY - LIBRARY & INFORMATION SERVICE □ Marcus Hook, PA

Casstevens, Frances H., Pres.
YADKIN COUNTY HISTORICAL SOCIETY - LIBRARY □ Yadkinville, NC

Castalizo, Jorge, Ref.Libn.
BOSTON PUBLIC LIBRARY - GOVERNMENT DOCUMENTS, MICROTEXT, NEWSPAPERS □ Boston, MA

Castaneda, Liliana, Health Sci.Lib.Coord.
ST. JOSEPH HOSPITAL - LIBRARY □ Chicago, IL

Casteel, Kathleen, Hd.Ref.Libn.
CLEVELAND HEALTH SCIENCES LIBRARY - HEALTH CENTER LIBRARY □ Cleveland, OH

Castello, Virginia, Asst.Libn.
U.S. AIR FORCE - WESTERN SPACE AND MISSILE CENTER - WSMC TECHNICAL LIBRARY □ Vandenberg AFB, CA

Caster, Suzanne, Hd.Libn.
SAN FRANCISCO CHRONICLE - LIBRARY □ San Francisco, CA

Castle, Geoff, Archv.
BRITISH COLUMBIA - PROVINCIAL ARCHIVES - MAP DIVISION □ Victoria, BC

Castle, Gretchen, Career Counselor
UNIVERSITY OF MONTANA - CAREER PLANNING RESOURCE CENTER† □ Missoula, MT

Castle, Jewell C., Lib.Mgr.
IBM CORPORATION - INFORMATION SYSTEMS DIVISION - TECHNICAL LIBRARY □ Lexington, KY

Castle, Joseph, Spanish Mss. & Maps
LOUISIANA STATE MUSEUM - LOUISIANA HISTORICAL CENTER □ New Orleans, LA

Castricone, Robert A., Info.Spec.
U.S. DEPT. OF HEALTH AND HUMAN SERVICES - REGION I INFORMATION CENTER □ Boston, MA

Castro, J.M., Libn.
GENERAL REFRACTORIES COMPANY - U.S. REFRACTORIES DIVISION - RESEARCH CENTER LIBRARY □ Baltimore, MD

Castro, Susan M., Res.Libn.
CORPORATE-TECH PLANNING - RESEARCH LIBRARY □ Waltham, MA

Castro, Virginia, Lib.Tech.Asst.
CALIFORNIA STATE OFFICE OF LEGISLATIVE COUNSEL - LIBRARY □ Sacramento, CA

Castronis, Orlean, Archv.Assoc.
UNIVERSITY OF GEORGIA - RICHARD B. RUSSELL MEMORIAL LIBRARY □ Athens, GA

Catabia, Ronald, Sr.Ref.Libn.
SPRINGFIELD COLLEGE - BABSON LIBRARY □ Springfield, MA

Cate, L., Asst.Libn
AMERICAN GAS ASSOCIATION - LIBRARY □ Arlington, VA

Catelli, Carmen, Hd.
BIBLIOTHEQUE DE LA VILLE DE MONTREAL - COLLECTION GAGNON □ Montreal, PQ

Cater, Judy, Ref./Acq.Libn.
PALOMAR COLLEGE - PHIL H. PUTNAM MEMORIAL LIBRARY □ San Marcos, CA

Cates, Annette B., Libn.
COLUMBIA CHRISTIAN COLLEGE - LIBRARY □ Portland, OR

Cates, Jane, Rd.Adv.
DISTRICT OF COLUMBIA PUBLIC LIBRARY - BUSINESS, ECONOMICS & VOCATIONS DIVISION □ Washington, DC

Cathcart, John, Hd., Tech.Serv.
BENTLEY COLLEGE - SOLOMON R. BAKER LIBRARY □ Waltham, MA

Cathey, Eva M., Adm.Libn.
U.S. ARMY MISSILE & MUNITIONS CENTER & SCHOOL - MMCS TECHNICAL LIBRARY □ Redstone Arsenal, AL

Catlett, Stephen, Mss.Libn.
AMERICAN PHILOSOPHICAL SOCIETY - LIBRARY □ Philadelphia, PA

Catt, Valery, Unit Sec.
UNIVERSITY OF ARIZONA - ARIZONA COOPERATIVE WILDLIFE RESEARCH UNIT - RESEARCH COLLECTION □ Tucson, AZ

Caudle, Rebecca, AV & Ref.
UNION UNIVERSITY - ALBANY MEDICAL COLLEGE - SCHAFFER LIBRARY OF THE HEALTH SCIENCES □ Albany, NY

Caudron, John Armann, Pres.
FIREARMS RESEARCH AND IDENTIFICATION ASSOCIATION - LIBRARY □ Rowland Heights, CA

Caughman, Rudolph, Chf.Libn.
BENDER (Matthew) AND COMPANY, INC. - LIBRARY □ New York, NY

Caughran, Carol, Ref.Libn.
DE PAUL UNIVERSITY - LAW SCHOOL LIBRARY □ Chicago, IL

Caulker, Olive S., Asst.Dir./Tech.Serv.
MARQUETTE UNIVERSITY - MEMORIAL LIBRARY □ Milwaukee, WI

Causey, Elizabeth, AV Libn.
MEDICAL UNIVERSITY OF SOUTH CAROLINA - LIBRARY □ Charleston, SC

Cavacini, Giovina, Libn.
U.S. NAVY - NAVAL REGIONAL MEDICAL CENTER (Philadelphia) - MEDICAL LIBRARY □ Philadelphia, PA

Cavallari, Elfrieda L., Chf., Cat.
U.S. AIR FORCE - AIR FORCE SYSTEMS COMMAND - AIR FORCE GEOPHYSICS LABORATORY - RESEARCH LIBRARY† □ Bedford, MA

Cavanaugh, Philip M., Musm.Dir.
U.S. ARMY - PATTON MUSEUM OF CAVALRY & ARMOR - EMERT L. DAVIS MEMORIAL LIBRARY □ Ft. Knox, KY

Cavano, Joseph X., Info.Spec.
AMSTAR CORPORATION - RESEARCH AND DEVELOPMENT LIBRARY □ Brooklyn, NY

Cavasoz, Capt. J.P., Hd.
U.S. MARINE CORPS - CAMP H.M. SMITH LIBRARY† □ Honolulu, HI

Cave, Ginger, Dir., Community Rel.
PLANNED PARENTHOOD CENTER OF SAN ANTONIO - SOUTH CENTRAL REGIONAL LIBRARY □ San Antonio, TX

Caver, Joseph, Archv.
ALABAMA STATE DEPARTMENT OF ARCHIVES AND HISTORY □ Montgomery, AL

Caver, Katy, Cur.
TEXARKANA HISTORICAL SOCIETY & MUSEUM - LIBRARY □ Texarkana, TX

Cavin, Loutrell E.
U.S. AIR FORCE - STRATEGIC AIR COMMAND - LIBRARY SERVICES SAC (DPSO) □ Offutt AFB, NE

Cawley, Mrs. Inez, Govt.Doc.Libn.
WILFRID LAURIER UNIVERSITY - LIBRARY □ Waterloo, ON

Cawston, J.B., Principal
BRITISH COLUMBIA - MINISTRY OF FORESTS - TRAINING SCHOOL LIBRARY □ Surrey, BC

Caylor, L., Acq.Libn.
UNIVERSITY OF LOWELL, SOUTH CAMPUS - DANIEL H. O'LEARY LIBRARY □ Lowell, MA

Cazares, Edward A., City Attorney
HOUSTON - CITY LEGAL DEPARTMENT - LAW LIBRARY □ Houston, TX

Cebula, Theodore, Coord.Sci./Bus.Div.
MILWAUKEE PUBLIC LIBRARY - SCIENCE & BUSINESS DIVISION □ Milwaukee, WI

Cecere, Vikki, Libn.
U.S. VETERANS ADMINISTRATION (NY-Canandaigua) - MEDICAL CENTER LIBRARY (142D) □ Canandaigua, NY

Cederholm, Theresa D., Ref.Libn.
BOSTON PUBLIC LIBRARY - FINE ARTS DEPARTMENT □ Boston, MA

Ceibert, Mary, Asst.Libn.
UNIVERSITY OF ILLINOIS - RARE BOOK ROOM □ Urbana, IL

Cellers, Berta, Exec.Sec.
ARABIAN HORSE OWNERS FOUNDATION - W.R. BROWN MEMORIAL LIBRARY □ Tucson, AZ

Cellini, Nick, Libn.
BEVERLY HILLS PUBLIC LIBRARY - FINE ARTS DIVISION □ Beverly Hills, CA

Celona, Chris, Res.
BOOZ, ALLEN & HAMILTON, INC. - RESEARCH SERVICE □ New York, NY

Center, Sue, Dir., C.J.Ctr.
UNIVERSITY OF WISCONSIN, MADISON - LAW LIBRARY □ Madison, WI

Center, Sue L., Dir.
UNIVERSITY OF WISCONSIN, MADISON - LAW SCHOOL- CRIMINAL JUSTICE REFERENCE & INFORMATION CENTER □ Madison, WI

Centing, Richard, Hd.
OHIO STATE UNIVERSITY - ENGLISH, COMMUNICATION AND THEATRE GRADUATE LIBRARY □ Columbus, OH

Cepek, Larry, Media Libn.
OHIO DOMINICAN COLLEGE - LIBRARY □ Columbus, OH

Ceresa, Mario A., Hd.Libn.
DETROIT COLLEGE OF LAW - LIBRARY □ Detroit, MI

Cernat, Lucica, Exec.Sec.
ROMANIAN LIBRARY □ New York, NY

Cerny, Barbara, Principal Investigator
U.S. DEPT. OF ENERGY - LAWRENCE BERKELEY LABORATORY - LIBRARY □ Berkeley, CA

Certain, Prof. Phillip R.
UNIVERSITY OF WISCONSIN, MADISON - THEORETICAL CHEMISTRY INSTITUTE - LIBRARY □ Madison, WI

Cerutti, Elsie, Chf., Info.Serv.
U.S. NATL. BUREAU OF STANDARDS - LIBRARY □ Washington, DC

Cervera, Felipe, Supv.Exhibition Cat.
UNIVERSITY OF CALIFORNIA, SANTA BARBARA - ARTS LIBRARY □ Santa Barbara, CA

Chabot, Lizabeth, Cat.
BRIDGEWATER COLLEGE - ALEXANDER MACK MEMORIAL LIBRARY - SPECIAL COLLECTIONS □ Bridgewater, VA

Chabot, V., Hd. French Archv.
CANADA - PUBLIC ARCHIVES OF CANADA - MANUSCRIPT DIVISION □ Ottawa, ON

Chace, Laura L., Libn.
CINCINNATI HISTORICAL SOCIETY - LIBRARY □ Cincinnati, OH

Chach, Maryann, Film Ref.Libn.
EDUCATIONAL FILM LIBRARY ASSOCIATION - LIBRARY AND INFORMATION CENTER □ New York, NY

Chacon, Joan G., Alpine County Ck.
ALPINE COUNTY LAW LIBRARY □ Markleeville, CA

Chadbourn, Erika S., Cur. of Mss.
HARVARD UNIVERSITY - LAW SCHOOL LIBRARY □ Cambridge, MA

Chadbourne, Janice H., Ref.Libn.
BOSTON PUBLIC LIBRARY - FINE ARTS DEPARTMENT □ Boston, MA

Chadey, Henry F., Dir.
SWEETWATER COUNTY MUSEUM - INFORMATION CENTER □ Green River, WY

Chadwell, Patricia, Hd.
FORT WORTH PUBLIC LIBRARY - SOUTHWEST AND GENEALOGY DEPARTMENT □ Fort Worth, TX

Chadwick, Alena, Ref.Libn.
UNIVERSITY OF MASSACHUSETTS, AMHERST - MORRILL BIOLOGICAL & GEOLOGICAL SCIENCES LIBRARY □ Amherst, MA

Chadwick, Alena, Ref.Libn.
UNIVERSITY OF MASSACHUSETTS, AMHERST - PHYSICAL SCIENCES LIBRARY □ Amherst, MA

Chadwick, Leroy, Hd.Cat.Libn.
UNIVERSITY OF VIRGINIA MEDICAL CENTER - CLAUDE MOORE HEALTH SCIENCES LIBRARY □ Charlottesville, VA

Chadwick, Regina E., Hd.Libn.
CALIFORNIA MEDICAL ASSOCIATION - LIBRARY □ San Francisco, CA

Chaet, Mark, Dir., Instr. Media Ctr.
WESTERN STATES CHIROPRACTIC COLLEGE - W.A. BUDDEN MEMORIAL LIBRARY □ Portland, OR

Chaff, Sandra L., Dir.
MEDICAL COLLEGE OF PENNSYLVANIA - ARCHIVES AND SPECIAL COLLECTIONS ON WOMEN IN MEDICINE □ Philadelphia, PA

Chai, Julia, Asst.Libn.
AMERICAN CANCER SOCIETY - MEDICAL LIBRARY □ New York, NY

Challacombe, Elaine M., Libn.
STRONG (Margaret Woodbury) MUSEUM - LIBRARY □ Rochester, NY

Chalmers, John, Libn.
UNIVERSITY OF TEXAS, AUSTIN - HUMANITIES RESEARCH CENTER □ Austin, TX

Chalmers, V., Lib.Dir.
MANITOBA INDIAN CULTURAL EDUCATION CENTRE - PEOPLES LIBRARY □ Winnipeg, MB

Chamberlain, Betty, Dir.
ART INFORMATION CENTER, INC. □ New York, NY

Chamberlain, Ellen, Sec.
UNIVERSITY OF TORONTO - DEPARTMENT OF BOTANY LIBRARY □ Toronto, ON

Chamberlain, Erna, Sci.Ref.Libn.
SUNY AT BINGHAMTON - SCIENCE LIBRARY □
Binghamton, NY

Chamberlain, Ken, Hd.Libn.
CARR (Emily) COLLEGE OF ART - LIBRARY □
Vancouver, BC

Chamberlain, L. Carl, Rare Books Cat.
GEORGETOWN UNIVERSITY - SPECIAL
COLLECTION DIVISION - LAUINGER MEMORIAL
LIBRARY □ Washington, DC

Chamberlain, Sue, Archv.
SHARLOT HALL/PRESCOTT HISTORICAL
SOCIETIES - LIBRARY/ARCHIVES† □ Prescott,
AZ

Chamberlain, William R., Asst.Dir., Gen.Lib.
VIRGINIA STATE LIBRARY □ Richmond, VA

Chamberlain, Zella, Libn.
BOISE BIBLE COLLEGE - LIBRARY □ Boise, ID

Chamberlin, David, Archv.
BRITISH COLUMBIA - PROVINCIAL ARCHIVES -
MAP DIVISION □ Victoria, BC

Chamberlin, Richard, Asst.Libn.
INDIANA UNIVERSITY OF PENNSYLVANIA -
UNIVERSITY LIBRARY □ Indiana, PA

Chamberlin, Susan B., Asst.Dir.
UNIVERSITY OF NEW MEXICO - MEDICAL
CENTER LIBRARY □ Albuquerque, NM

Chambers, Eugene, Dir., Law Lib.
HARRIS COUNTY LAW LIBRARY □ Houston, TX

Chambers, Frances
CUNY - CITY COLLEGE LIBRARY - SCIENCE/
ENGINEERING DIVISION □ New York, NY

Chambers, Jeanette A., Lib.Techn.
U.S. ARMY HOSPITALS - LYSTER ARMY
HOSPITAL - MEDICAL LIBRARY □ Ft. Rucker, AL

Chambers, Joanna F., Coord., Lib.Serv.
TEXAS WOMAN'S UNIVERSITY - LIBRARY
SCIENCE LIBRARY - PROYECTO LEER □ Denton,
TX

Chambers, Martha, Cur.
NYLANDER MUSEUM - LIBRARY □ Caribou, ME

Chambers, Martha, Hd., Spec.Coll.
SUNY - COLLEGE AT ONEONTA - JAMES M.
MILNE LIBRARY □ Oneonta, NY

Chambers, Robert, Dir.
WAGNER FREE INSTITUTE OF SCIENCE -
LIBRARY □ Philadelphia, PA

Chambliss, Catherine F., Libn.
CHRISTIAN CHURCH (Disciples of Christ), INC. -
DIVISION OF HIGHER EDUCATION - LIBRARY □
St. Louis, MO

Champagne, Eric A., Libn.
CANADA - AGRICULTURE CANADA - RESEARCH
STATION, HARROW - LIBRARY □ Harrow, ON

Champeau, Louise, Supv., Music/Rec.Lib.
CANADIAN BROADCASTING CORPORATION -
MUSIC SERVICES LIBRARY □ Montreal, PQ

Champoux, Raymond J.
EG&G, INC. - CORPORATE HEADQUARTERS -
BUSINESS & FINANCIAL REFERENCE LIBRARY □
Wellesley, MA

Chan, Charlie, Supv., Tech.Serv.
CHINESE NATIONALIST LEAGUE OF CANADA -
LIBRARY† □ Vancouver, BC

Chan, Miss H.M., Libn.
ONTARIO - MINISTRY OF CORRECTIONAL
SERVICES - LIBRARY SERVICES □ Toronto, ON

Chan, John S.N., Libn.
CANADA - LABOUR CANADA - OCCUPATIONAL
SAFETY AND HEALTH BRANCH - TECHNICAL
RESOURCE CENTRE □ Ottawa, ON

Chan, Lillian, Sci.Libn.
SAN DIEGO STATE UNIVERSITY - SCIENCE
DEPARTMENT □ San Diego, CA

Chan, Mrs. Lu-Hwa, Asst.Libn.
WESTON RESEARCH CENTRE - LIBRARY □
Toronto, ON

Chan, M.L., Hd.Cat.
UNIVERSITY OF CALGARY - MEDICAL LIBRARY
□ Calgary, AB

Chan, Shirley S., Libn.
COLUMBIA HOSPITAL - SCHOOL OF NURSING
LIBRARY □ Milwaukee, WI

Chancellor, Betty, Acq./Ser.Asst.
TROY STATE UNIVERSITY - LIBRARY □ Troy, AL

Chander, Suneeta, Hd., Cat.Sect.
CANADA - REVENUE CANADA - CUSTOMS &
EXCISE LIBRARY □ Ottawa, ON

Chandik, Barbara V., Supv., Tech.Info.
VELSICOL CHEMICAL CORPORATION -
TECHNICAL INFORMATION CENTER □ Ann
Arbor, MI

Chandler, Deborah G., Info.Spec.
SCOTT PAPER COMPANY - S.D. WARREN
COMPANY - RESEARCH LIBRARY □ Westbrook,
ME

Chandler, Harold, Acq.Libn.
MEMPHIS THEOLOGICAL SEMINARY - LIBRARY
□ Memphis, TN

Chang, Albert M., Chf.Circ.Libn.
SOUTHWEST TEXAS STATE UNIVERSITY -
LEARNING RESOURCES CENTER □ San Marcos,
TX

Chang, Mrs. Chien Heh Y., Assoc.Libn.
SUNY - COLLEGE OF OPTOMETRY - HAROLD
KOHN MEMORIAL VISUAL SCIENCE LIBRARY □
New York, NY

Chang, Chun Chuan, Chf.Libn.
GROLIER INCORPORATED - LIBRARY □
Danbury, CT

Chang, Frances M., Libn.
U.S. NAVY - OFFICE OF NAVAL RESEARCH -
LIBRARY □ Arlington, VA

Chang, Dr. Henry C., Dir.
VIRGIN ISLANDS - DEPARTMENT OF
CONSERVATION & CULTURAL AFFAIRS -
BUREAU OF LIBRARIES AND MUSEUMS □ St.
Thomas, VI

Chang, Huei-Ju, Cat.Libn.
YALE UNIVERSITY - EAST ASIAN COLLECTION
□ New Haven, CT

Chang, Margaret, Archv.
NEWFOUNDLAND - PROVINCIAL ARCHIVES OF
NEWFOUNDLAND AND LABRADOR □ St. John's,
NF

Chang, Roy, Asst.Cat.Libn.
WESTERN ILLINOIS UNIVERSITY - LIBRARIES
□ Macomb, IL

Chang, Sherry, Libn.
SUNY AT STONY BROOK - MATHEMATICS-
PHYSICS LIBRARY □ Stony Brook, NY

Chang, Theresa, Ref.Libn.
BROOKINGS INSTITUTION - LIBRARY □
Washington, DC

Chang, Tohsook, Cat.Libn.
UNIVERSITY OF ALASKA, ANCHORAGE -
LIBRARY □ Anchorage, AK

Chang, Yeen-Mei Wu, China Libn.
UNIVERSITY OF WASHINGTON - EAST ASIA
LIBRARY □ Seattle, WA

Chanin, Leah F., Dir., Law Lib.
MERCER UNIVERSITY - LAW SCHOOL -
HALLIBURTON LAW LIBRARY □ Macon, GA

Channabasappa, Shantha, Assoc.Libn.
ENCYCLOPAEDIA BRITANNICA, INC. -
EDITORIAL LIBRARY □ Chicago, IL

Channing, Rhoda K., Libn.
BOSTON COLLEGE - SCHOOL OF MANAGEMENT
LIBRARY □ Chestnut Hill, MA

Channon, Geraldine, Dir.Res. & Info.Serv
CANADIAN TEACHERS' FEDERATION - GEORGE
G. CROSKERY MEMORIAL LIBRARY □ Ottawa,
ON

Chao, Gloria, Cat.Libn.
RUTGERS UNIVERSITY, THE STATE
UNIVERSITY OF NEW JERSEY - SCHOOL OF
LAW LIBRARY† □ Camden, NJ

Chao, Jennifer J., Libn.
BOSTON GLOBE NEWSPAPER COMPANY -
LIBRARY □ Boston, MA

Chao, Theresa, Per.Libn.
UNIVERSITY OF WISCONSIN, STEVENS POINT
- JAMES H. ALBERTSON CENTER FOR
LEARNING RESOURCES □ Stevens Point, WI

Chao, Mrs. Yen-Shew Lynn, Cur. of Rubel Coll.
HARVARD UNIVERSITY - FINE ARTS LIBRARY □
Cambridge, MA

Chapin, Debbie, Libn.
NATIONAL INVESTMENT SERVICES OF
AMERICA, INC. - LIBRARY □ Milwaukee, WI

Chapin, Merrible, Lib.Asst.
CANADIAN TROTTING ASSOCIATION -
STANDARDBRED CANADA LIBRARY □ Toronto,
ON

Chapin, Shirley, Libn.
NEW YORK CITY - PUBLIC HEALTH
LABORATORIES - WILLIAM HALLOCK PARK
MEMORIAL LIBRARY □ New York, NY

Chapis, Marilyn D., Med. Staff Libn.
POTTSTOWN MEMORIAL MEDICAL CENTER -
MEDICAL STAFF LIBRARY □ Pottstown, PA

Chaplan, Margaret A., Libn.
UNIVERSITY OF ILLINOIS - INSTITUTE OF
LABOR AND INDUSTRIAL RELATIONS LIBRARY
□ Champaign, IL

Chapman, Allan D., Musm.Libn.
METROPOLITAN MUSEUM OF ART - ROBERT
GOLDWATER LIBRARY OF PRIMITIVE ART □
New York, NY

Chapman, Bobby, Libn.
U.S. AIR FORCE HOSPITAL - EHRLING
BERGQUIST REGIONAL HOSPITAL - MEDICAL
LIBRARY □ Offutt AFB, NE

Chapman, Cynthia E., Supv.Info.Ctr.
CALGARY PLANNING DEPARTMENT -
INFORMATION SERVICES □ Calgary, AB

Chapman, David L., Assoc.Archv.
TEXAS A & M UNIVERSITY - ARCHIVES &
MANUSCRIPTS COLLECTIONS □ College Station,
TX

Chapman, Donald M., Chf., Info.Serv.Div.
U.S. DEPT. OF TRANSPORTATION - URBAN
MASS TRANSPORTATION ADM. -
TRANSPORTATION RESEARCH INFO. CENTER
(TRIC) □ Washington, DC

Chapman, Dorothy H., Cur.
TEXAS SOUTHERN UNIVERSITY - LIBRARY -
HEARTMAN COLLECTION □ Houston, TX

Chapman, Edith B., Sr.Lit.Sci.
WARNER-LAMBERT COMPANY - CORPORATE
LIBRARY† □ Morris Plains, NJ

Chapman, Janet, Info.Spec.
EXXON BIOMEDICAL SCIENCES INC. - LIBRARY
□ East Millstone, NJ

Chapman, Lynn M., Lib.Techn.
AKRON GENERAL MEDICAL CENTER - J.D.
SMITH MEMORIAL LIBRARY □ Akron, OH

Chapman, Marian L., Dir.
RESEARCH FOR BETTER SCHOOLS, INC. -
RESOURCE CENTER □ Philadelphia, PA

Chapman, Renee, Tech.Serv.Libn.
DRAKE UNIVERSITY - LAW LIBRARY □ Des
Moines, IA

Chapman, William, Libn.
CHAPMAN (Bruce) COMPANY - LIBRARY □
Grafton, VT

Chappel, Helen, Sec.
UNIVERSAL-CYCLOPS SPECIALTY STEEL
DIVISION - TECHNICAL INFORMATION
CENTER □ Bridgeville, PA

Chappell, Barbara A., Hd., Ref./Circ.
U.S. GEOLOGICAL SURVEY - LIBRARY □ Reston,
VA

Chappell, Gordon, Regional Hist.
U.S. NATL. PARK SERVICE - WESTERN
REGIONAL OFFICE - REGIONAL RESOURCES
LIBRARY □ San Francisco, CA

Chappell, Kate, Rsrcs.Anl.
SOUTHERN ILLINOIS UNIVERSITY,
EDWARDSVILLE - RESEARCH & PROJECTS
OFFICE LIBRARY □ Edwardsville, IL

Chappell, Susan, Med.Libn.
GREENVILLE GENERAL HOSPITAL - MEDICAL
LIBRARY □ Greenville, SC

Charbonneau, Monique, Lib.Dir.
QUEBEC PROVINCE - MINISTERE DES COMMUNICATIONS - BIBLIOTHEQUE ADMINISTRATIVE □ Quebec, PQ

Charest, Ginette, Audiovideotheque
HOPITAL STE-JUSTINE - CENTRE D'INFORMATION SUR LA SANTE DE L'ENFANT† □ Montreal, PQ

Charest, Ms. J., Tech.Serv.Supv.
BEDFORD INSTITUTE OF OCEANOGRAPHY - LIBRARY □ Dartmouth, NS

Charest, Nicole, Dir.
RADIO QUEBEC - CENTRE DES RESSOURCES DOCUMENTAIRES □ Montreal, PQ

Charette, Marcel, Ck. In Charge
CANADA - AGRICULTURE CANADA - NEATBY LIBRARY □ Ottawa, ON

Chariton, May, Libn.
SOUTHSIDE HOSPITAL - MEDICAL LIBRARY □ Bay Shore, NY

Charland, Diane
MONTREAL URBAN COMMUNITY TRANSIT COMMISSION - LIBRARY □ Montreal, PQ

Charlebois, Joyce, Libn.
PRATT AND WHITNEY AIRCRAFT OF CANADA, LTD. - LIBRARY □ Longueuil, PQ

Charles, John W., Spec.Coll.Libn.
UNIVERSITY OF ALBERTA - SPECIAL COLLECTIONS □ Edmonton, AB

Charlton, Barbara A., Assoc.Libn.
CALIFORNIA STATE UNIVERSITY, SACRAMENTO - LIBRARY - SCIENCE & TECHNOLOGY REFERENCE DEPARTMENT† □ Sacramento, CA

Charlton, Mary Lou, Libn.
HEALTH AND WELFARE PLANNING ASSOCIATION OF ALLEGHENY COUNTY - LIBRARY □ Pittsburgh, PA

Charlton, Dr. Thomas L., Chm. Texas Coll.Comm
BAYLOR UNIVERSITY - TEXAS COLLECTION □ Waco, TX

Charney, Jule G., Professor
MASSACHUSETTS INSTITUTE OF TECHNOLOGY - DYNAMICS OF ATMOSPHERES AND OCEANS LIBRARY □ Cambridge, MA

Charnow, Elaine, Libn.
NORTH SHORE SYNAGOGUE - CHARLES COHN MEMORIAL LIBRARY □ Syosset, NY

Charron, Sr. Irene, S.P., Med.Libn.
ST. ELIZABETH HOSPITAL - HEALTH SCIENCES LIBRARY □ Yakima, WA

Charron, Sylvie, Director
SOCIETE D'ENERGIE DE LA BAIE JAMES - CENTRE DE DOCUMENTATION-ENVIRONNEMENT □ Montreal, PQ

Chase, Angela, Govt.Doc.Libn.
HARTFORD PUBLIC LIBRARY - BUSINESS, SCIENCE & TECHNOLOGY DEPARTMENT □ Hartford, CT

Chase, Bradley, Tech.Asst.
SUNY AT BUFFALO - HEALTH SCIENCES LIBRARY □ Buffalo, NY

Chase, Doris E., Law Libn. I
NEW YORK STATE SUPREME COURT - 6TH JUDICIAL DISTRICT - LAW LIBRARY □ Binghamton, NY

Chase, Eleanor L., Hd.Libn.
UNIVERSITY OF WASHINGTON - GOVERNMENT PUBLICATIONS DIVISION □ Seattle, WA

Chase, Judith Wragg, Lib.Dir.
OLD SLAVE MART MUSEUM - LIBRARY □ Sullivan's Island, SC

Chase, Marcella, Libn.
MUTUAL OF OMAHA/UNITED OF OMAHA - LIBRARY □ Omaha, NE

Chase, Michael H., Dir.
UNIVERSITY OF CALIFORNIA, LOS ANGELES - BRAIN INFORMATION SERVICE □ Los Angeles, CA

Chase, Rory L., Corp.Libn.
CINCINNATI MILACRON, INC. - CORPORATE INFORMATION CENTER □ Cincinnati, OH

Chasen, Larry, Mgr.
GENERAL ELECTRIC COMPANY - SPACE/RSD LIBRARIES □ Philadelphia, PA

Chasse, Monique, Pub.Serv.Libn.
CAMBRIAN COLLEGE OF APPLIED ARTS AND TECHNOLOGY - LIBRARY □ Sudbury, ON

Chatfield, Mary V., Libn.
HARVARD UNIVERSITY - GRADUATE SCHOOL OF BUSINESS ADMINISTRATION - BAKER LIBRARY □ Boston, MA

Chaudet, Mae E., Libn.
UNIDYNAMICS/ST. LOUIS, INC. - LIBRARY □ St. Louis, MO

Chaudhuri, Binu, Res.Ctr.Coord.
NEW YORK STATE DIVISION OF SUBSTANCE ABUSE SERVICES - BUREAU OF TRAINING & RESOURCE DEVELOPMENT - RESOURCE CENTER □ New York, NY

Chavaria, Elvira, Mexican-Amer. Stud.Libn.
UNIVERSITY OF TEXAS, AUSTIN - BENSON LATIN AMERICAN COLLECTION □ Austin, TX

Chavez, Alice, Libn.
UNIVERSITY OF TEXAS, EL PASO - - NURSING/MEDICAL LIBRARY □ El Paso, TX

Chavis, Mr. C., Libn.
AMERICAN STANDARDS TESTING BUREAU, INC. - SAM TOUR LIBRARY □ New York, NY

Chawner, Brenda, Asst.Libn.
UNIVERSITY OF ALBERTA - BOREAL INSTITUTE FOR NORTHERN STUDIES - LIBRARY □ Edmonton, AB

Cheape, Kathleen, Asst. Law Libn.
UNIVERSITY OF NORTH CAROLINA, CHAPEL HILL - LAW LIBRARY □ Chapel Hill, NC

Checkovich, Peter, Dir.Educ. Media
SHENANDOAH COLLEGE & CONSERVATORY OF MUSIC - HOWE LIBRARY □ Winchester, VA

Cheek, Emory, Lib.Assoc.
UNIVERSITY OF GEORGIA - GEORGIA COASTAL PLAIN EXPERIMENT STATION LIBRARY □ Tifton, GA

Cheesman, Norman, Mgr.
CANADIAN GENERAL ELECTRIC COMPANY, LTD. - CORPORATE INFORMATION CENTRE □ Toronto, ON

Chen, Alice S., Supv.
ALBERTA - DEPARTMENT OF ENERGY AND NATURAL RESOURCES - MAP & AIR PHOTO REFERENCE LIBRARY □ Edmonton, AB

Chen, Catherine, Hd.Libn.
NORTHWOOD INSTITUTE - STROSACKER LIBRARY □ Midland, MI

Chen, Chi-Ping, Libn.
UNIVERSITY OF CALIFORNIA, BERKELEY - CENTER FOR CHINESE STUDIES - LIBRARY □ Berkeley, CA

Chen, Christina, Tech.Serv.Libn.
LOS ANGELES COUNTY/UNIVERSITY OF SOUTHERN CALIFORNIA MEDICAL CENTER - MEDICAL LIBRARIES □ Los Angeles, CA

Chen, David, Asst.Libn./Tech.Serv
EMORY UNIVERSITY - PITTS THEOLOGY LIBRARY □ Atlanta, GA

Chen, F., Libn.
PRINCETON UNIVERSITY - URBAN AND ENVIRONMENTAL STUDIES LIBRARY □ Princeton, NJ

Chen, Faustina, Libn.
DALHOUSIE UNIVERSITY - INSTITUTE OF PUBLIC AFFAIRS - LIBRARY □ Halifax, NS

Chen, Flora, Libn.
CANADA - NATIONAL RESEARCH COUNCIL - PRAIRIE REGIONAL LABORATORY LIBRARY □ Saskatoon, SK

Chen, Hsiao-Chiang, Sr.Cat.Libn.
YALE UNIVERSITY - EAST ASIAN COLLECTION □ New Haven, CT

Chen, Joanna, Libn.
BALCH, BINGHAM, BAKER, HAWTHORNE, WILLIAMS & WARD - LIBRARY† □ Birmingham, AL

Chen, Joanna, Cat.Libn.
SAMFORD UNIVERSITY - CUMBERLAND SCHOOL OF LAW - CORDELL HULL LAW LIBRARY† □ Birmingham, AL

Chen, John H.M., Gen.Dir.
INTERNATIONAL ASSOCIATION OF EDUCATORS FOR WORLD PEACE - IAEWP CENTER OF INTERCULTURAL INFORMATION □ Huntsville, AL

Chen, Mrs. Mai, Coord.Tech.Serv.
QUEEN'S UNIVERSITY AT KINGSTON - LAW LIBRARY □ Kingston, ON

Chen, Tung-Chu, Home Econ.Libn.
DREXEL UNIVERSITY LIBRARIES - GENERAL LIBRARY □ Philadelphia, PA

Cheney, M. Margaret, Med.Libn.
LEONARD MORSE HOSPITAL - MEDICAL LIBRARY □ Natick, MA

Cheng, Annie, Libn.
REVLON RESEARCH CENTER, INC. - LIBRARY □ Bronx, NY

Cheng, Catherine B., Ser.Libn.
TRENTON STATE COLLEGE - ROSCOE L. WEST LIBRARY □ Trenton, NJ

Cheng, Mrs. H.J., Asst.Libn.
NELSON GALLERY-ATKINS MUSEUM - SPENCER ART REFERENCE LIBRARY □ Kansas City, MO

Cheng, James K., Chf.Libn.
CHINESE NATIONALIST LEAGUE OF CANADA - LIBRARY† □ Vancouver, BC

Cheng, James K.M., Cur.
UNIVERSITY OF CHICAGO - FAR EASTERN LIBRARY □ Chicago, IL

Cheng, Juliana, Libn.
DELAWARE STATE DEPARTMENT OF TRANSPORTATION - LIBRARY □ Dover, DE

Cheng, Mu-Chin, Libn.
ADLER CENTER - LIBRARY □ Champaign, IL

Cheng, Nancy, Pub.Serv.Libn.
UNIVERSITY OF UTAH - LAW LIBRARY □ Salt Lake City, UT

Cheng, Paul P.W., East Asian Libn.
CORNELL UNIVERSITY - WASON COLLECTION □ Ithaca, NY

Chenier, Andre, Directeur
UNIVERSITE DU QUEBEC A HULL - BIBLIOTHEQUE □ Hull, PQ

Cheong, Kai-Limm, Cat.Libn.
O'MELVENY AND MYERS - INFORMATION SERVICES □ Los Angeles, CA

Cherellia, Peter P., Libn.
CITIZENS LAW LIBRARY □ Greensburg, PA

Chernega, Ann, Lib.Mgr.
WESTINGHOUSE ELECTRIC CORPORATION - NUCLEAR ENERGY SYSTEMS - ADVANCED REACTORS DIVISION - LIBRARY □ Madison, PA

Chernin, Bonnie, Archv.Libn.
METROPOLITAN LIFE INSURANCE COMPANY - LIBRARY □ New York, NY

Cherniv, Raisa, Dir.
LUTHERAN HOSPITAL OF FORT WAYNE, INC. - HEALTH SCIENCES LIBRARY □ Fort Wayne, IN

Chernofsky, Ellen, Libn.
AB BOOKMAN PUBLICATIONS, INC. - LIBRARY □ Clifton, NJ

Cheron, Theodore, Lit.Res.Anl.
AEROSPACE CORPORATION - CHARLES C. LAURITSEN LIBRARY □ Los Angeles, CA

Cherry, Cheryl A., Libn.
FISCHER & PORTER CO. - CORPORATE ENGINEERING LIBRARY □ Warminster, PA

Cherry, Ronald L., Dir.
UNIVERSITY OF ARIZONA - COLLEGE OF LAW LIBRARY □ Tucson, AZ

Cherry, Susan E., Mgr.
NATIONAL BANK OF DETROIT - MONEY MUSEUM LIBRARY □ Detroit, MI

Chervin, Shirley, Libn.
POMONA VALLEY COMMUNITY HOSPITAL - MEDICAL LIBRARY □ Pomona, CA

Cheshier, Robert G., Dir.
CLEVELAND HEALTH SCIENCES LIBRARY □ Cleveland, OH

Cheski, Richard M., State Libn.
STATE LIBRARY OF OHIO □ Columbus, OH

Cheslock, Rosalind P., Mgr.Info./Lib.Serv.
MARTIN MARIETTA LABORATORIES - LIBRARY □ Baltimore, MD

Chesney, Alison S. Ricker, Libn.
UNIVERSITY OF GEORGIA - SKIDAWAY INSTITUTE OF OCEANOGRAPHY - LIBRARY □ Savannah, GA

Chesney, Carolyn E., Libn.
HOUSE BEAUTIFUL - STAFF LIBRARY □ New York, NY

Chesney, Sandra, Lib.Asst.
FORT SANDERS REGIONAL MEDICAL CENTER - MEDICAL/NURSING LIBRARY □ Knoxville, TN

Chesnut, Linda, Lib.Sec.
COUNTRY MUSIC FOUNDATION - LIBRARY AND MEDIA CENTER □ Nashville, TN

Chestnut, Dr. Paul I., Asst. State Archv.
VIRGINIA STATE LIBRARY □ Richmond, VA

Chetner, S., Ref.Libn.
UNIVERSITY OF ALBERTA - HEALTH SCIENCES LIBRARY □ Edmonton, AB

Cheung, Anthony, Chf.Libn.
CANADA - DEFENCE AND CIVIL INSTITUTE OF ENVIRONMENTAL MEDICINE - SCIENTIFIC INFORMATION CENTRE □ Downsview, ON

Chewkanes, Michael W., Law Ck.
SALEM COUNTY LAW LIBRARY □ Salem, NJ

Chi, Alice, Asst.Libn.
PRINCETON UNIVERSITY - OFFICE OF POPULATION RESEARCH - LIBRARY □ Princeton, NJ

Chiang, Shu Shun, Mgr., Ref.Serv.
U.S. DEPT. OF JUSTICE - NATIONAL INSTITUTE OF JUSTICE - NATL. CRIMINAL JUSTICE REF. SERVICE □ Rockville, MD

Chiang, Win-Shin S., Law Libn.
LOYOLA UNIVERSITY (New Orleans) - LAW LIBRARY □ New Orleans, LA

Chiasson, Gilles, Mgr.
SPORT INFORMATION RESOURCE CENTRE □ Ottawa, ON

Chiavetta, Phyllis, Chf.Libn.
AMERICAN TELEPHONE & TELEGRAPH COMPANY - CORPORATE LIBRARY □ Basking Ridge, NJ

Chibnik, Katharine, Urban Plan.
COLUMBIA UNIVERSITY - AVERY ARCHITECTURAL AND FINE ARTS LIBRARY □ New York, NY

Chicco, Giuliano, Asst.Chf. Law Libn.
FEDERAL RESERVE BANK OF NEW YORK - LAW LIBRARY DIVISION □ New York, NY

Chichilla, Kay, Hd., ILL
UNIVERSITY OF TEXAS HEALTH SCIENCE CENTER, DALLAS - LIBRARY □ Dallas, TX

Chichura, Edward, Chf.Libn.
U.S. COURT OF APPEALS, 9TH CIRCUIT - LIBRARY □ San Francisco, CA

Chickanzeff, Sharon, Libn.
COLLEGE OF THE SAN FRANCISCO ART INSTITUTE - ANNE BREMER MEMORIAL LIBRARY □ San Francisco, CA

Chiesa, Adele M., Chf., Lrng.Rsrcs.Ctr.
NATIONAL FIRE ACADEMY - LIBRARY □ Emmitsburg, MD

Childs, Herbert E., Jr., Libn.
COGSWELL COLLEGE - LIBRARY □ San Francisco, CA

Childs, Martha C., Libn.
UNIVERSITY OF TENNESSEE - CENTER FOR THE HEALTH SCIENCES - PRESTON MEDICAL LIBRARY □ Knoxville, TN

Childs, Suse, Libn.
METROPOLITAN MUSEUM OF ART - CLOISTERS LIBRARY □ New York, NY

Childs, Ward, Asst.Archv.
PHILADELPHIA - CITY ARCHIVES □ Philadelphia, PA

Chillington, J.H., Asst.Dir.
BURNDY LIBRARY □ Norwalk, CT

Chillingworth, Maggie, Asst.Libn.
PRESTON, THORGRIMSON, ELLIS & HOLMAN - LIBRARY □ Seattle, WA

Chillman, Helen, Slide Libn.
YALE UNIVERSITY - ART AND ARCHITECTURE LIBRARY □ New Haven, CT

Chilson, Frances L., Hd. of Ser.
SUNY - COLLEGE AT POTSDAM - FREDERICK W. CRUMB MEMORIAL LIBRARY □ Potsdam, NY

Chilte, Janinn, Libn.
UTAH STATE HOSPITAL - LIBRARY □ Provo, UT

Chilton, Betty, Lib.Spec.
FAIRFAX COUNTY PUBLIC SCHOOLS - PROFESSIONAL REFERENCE LIBRARY IN EDUCATION □ Fairfax, VA

Chilton, Joan, Med.Libn.
COMMUNITY HOSPITAL - MEDICAL LIBRARY □ Santa Rosa, CA

Chimney, Mr. Lacy, Jr., Acq.Libn.
TEXAS SOUTHERN UNIVERSITY - LIBRARY - HEARTMAN COLLECTION □ Houston, TX

Chin, Ann M., Libn.
ONTARIO ECONOMIC COUNCIL - LIBRARY □ Toronto, ON

Chin, Cecilia, Assoc.Libn./Hd.Ref.
ART INSTITUTE OF CHICAGO - RYERSON AND BURNHAM LIBRARIES □ Chicago, IL

Chin, Elise, Hd., Cat.Sect.
UNIVERSITY OF WASHINGTON - EAST ASIA LIBRARY □ Seattle, WA

Chin, Ellen, Libn.
DANE COUNTY REGIONAL PLANNING COMMISSION - LIBRARY □ Madison, WI

Chin, Fred, Bus.Ref.Libn.
TRENTON STATE COLLEGE - ROSCOE L. WEST LIBRARY □ Trenton, NJ

Chin, Lily, Lib.Asst.
UNIVERSITY OF SASKATCHEWAN - THORVALDSON LIBRARY □ Saskatoon, SK

Chin, Loretta M., Libn.
ALAMEDA COUNTY OFFICE OF EDUCATION - TEACHERS' PROFESSIONAL LIBRARY □ Hayward, CA

Chin, Teruko Kyuma, Japan Libn.
UNIVERSITY OF WASHINGTON - EAST ASIA LIBRARY □ Seattle, WA

Chinea, Idalia, Cat.
UNIVERSITY OF PUERTO RICO - LAW SCHOOL LIBRARY □ Rio Piedras, PR

Chinn, Mr. D., Asst.Libn.
ST. THOMAS SEMINARY - LIBRARY □ Denver, CO

Chinn, Helen, Chm., Coll.Dev.
LOMA LINDA UNIVERSITY - DEL E. WEBB MEMORIAL LIBRARY □ Loma Linda, CA

Chinn, Lillian, Lib.Asst.
FAR WEST LABORATORY FOR EDUCATIONAL RESEARCH AND DEVELOPMENT - LIBRARY AND ARCHIVES □ San Francisco, CA

Chinnici, Lucille, Pres.
OUR LADY OF LIGHT LIBRARY □ Santa Barbara, CA

Chiodo, Genevieve R., Dir., Med.Rec.
BRADFORD HOSPITAL - DOCTORS' MEMORIAL LIBRARY □ Bradford, PA

Chiong, Anna, Libn.
UNIVERSITY OF WASHINGTON - GEOGRAPHY LIBRARY □ Seattle, WA

Chipman, Ernestine, Hd., Tech.Serv.
GRACE (W.R.) AND COMPANY - NATURAL RESOURCES GROUP - LIBRARY □ Dallas, TX

Chishti, Ghazala, Clinical Assoc.
LONG ISLAND UNIV. - ARNOLD & MARIE SCHWARTZ COLLEGE OF PHARMACY & HEALTH SCIENCES - INTERNATL. DRUG INFO.CTR. □ Brooklyn, NY

Chism, Harriet Jean, Sta.Libn.
U.S. NAVY - NAVAL AIR STATION (Lemoore) - LIBRARY† □ Lemoore, CA

Chittampalli, Ms. Padma, Med.Libn.
NORTH CENTRAL BRONX HOSPITAL - J. LEWIS AMSTER HEALTH SCIENCES LIBRARY □ Bronx, NY

Chitty, Mary G., Asst.Libn.
MASSACHUSETTS COLLEGE OF PHARMACY & ALLIED HEALTH SCIENCES - SHEPPARD LIBRARY □ Boston, MA

Chiu, Kai-Yun, Law Libn.
LIBRARY COMPANY OF THE BALTIMORE BAR - LIBRARY □ Baltimore, MD

Chiu, Liwa, Libn.
PAN AMERICAN WORLD AIRWAYS - CORPORATE LIBRARY □ New York, NY

Cho, Nammy M., Lib.Hd.
LOGICON, INC. - TECHNICAL LIBRARY □ San Pedro, CA

Cho, Yong-Ja, Hd.Libn.
UNIVERSITY OF MANITOBA - ENGINEERING LIBRARY □ Winnipeg, MB

Choe, Yoon-Whan, Korea Libn.
UNIVERSITY OF WASHINGTON - EAST ASIA LIBRARY □ Seattle, WA

Choi, Eunhee, Libn.
ILLINOIS STATE BUREAU OF EMPLOYMENT SECURITY - LABOR MARKET INFORMATION CENTER □ Chicago, IL

Choi, Jean, Cat.
TEMPLE UNIVERSITY - HEALTH SCIENCES CENTER - LIBRARY □ Philadelphia, PA

Chojenski, Peter P., Ref.Libn.
PURDUE UNIVERSITY - CALUMET LIBRARY □ Hammond, IN

Chojnacki, Stanislaw, Dir. of Lib.
UNIVERSITY OF SUDBURY - LIBRARY □ Sudbury, ON

Choma, Phil, Exec.Dir.
LEXINGTON-FAYETTE URBAN COUNTY PLANNING COMMISSION - TECHNICAL INFORMATION LIBRARY □ Lexington, KY

Chong, Nan S., Libn., Panama Coll.
PANAMA CANAL COMMISSION - LIBRARY-MUSEUM □ APO Miami, FL

Choppe, Elaine, Law Lib. Attendant
OCEAN COUNTY LAW LIBRARY □ Toms River, NJ

Chopra, Mrs. Swaran Lata, Dir., Med.Lib.
CHILDREN'S HOSPITAL OF PHILADELPHIA - MEDICAL LIBRARY □ Philadelphia, PA

Choquette-Habel, Monique, Sec./Archv.
SOCIETE D'HISTOIRE DES CANTONS DE L'EST - BIBLIOTHEQUE □ Sherbrooke, PQ

Chou, Chan-Shen, Asst.Libn.
CAHILL, GORDON, & REINDEL - LAW LIBRARY □ New York, NY

Chou, Min-Chih, Chinese Biblog.
PRINCETON UNIVERSITY - GEST ORIENTAL LIBRARY AND EAST ASIAN COLLECTIONS □ Princeton, NJ

Chou, Dr. Nelson, Libn.
RUTGERS UNIVERSITY, THE STATE UNIVERSITY OF NEW JERSEY - ALEXANDER LIBRARY - EAST ASIAN LIBRARY □ New Brunswick, NJ

Chouinard, Bernard, Responsable
UNIVERSITE DU QUEBEC A MONTREAL - CARTOTHEQUE □ Montreal, PQ

Chouinard, Germain, Dir.
UNIVERSITE DE SHERBROOKE - FACULTE DE MEDECINE - BIBLIOTHEQUE □ Sherbrooke, PQ

Chouinard, Joseph, Music Libn.
SUNY - COLLEGE AT FREDONIA - MUSIC LIBRARY □ Fredonia, NY

Chow, Mrs. Oi-Yung, Dir., State Lib.
HAWAII STATE LIBRARY - HAWAII AND PACIFIC SECTION I □ Honolulu, HI

Chowdhury, Mr. Man D., Libn.
HARLEM HOSPITAL CENTER - LIBRARY □ New York, NY

Chrestman, Mary, Jr.Libn.
UNIVERSITY OF MISSISSIPPI - ARCHIVES & SPECIAL COLLECTIONS/MISSISSIPPIANA □ University, MS

Chretien, Muriette, Ref. (Civil Law)
UNIVERSITY OF OTTAWA - LAW LIBRARY □ Ottawa, ON

PERSONNEL

Chrisant, Rosemarie, Lib.Dir.
AKRON LAW LIBRARY □ Akron, OH
Chrisman, Barbara, Ref.
BLACK HILLS STATE COLLEGE - E.Y. BERRY
LIBRARY-LEARNING CENTER □ Spearfish, SD
Christensen, Brian, Resource Off.
SASKATCHEWAN - DEPARTMENT OF TOURISM
AND RENEWABLE RESOURCES - FISH
MANAGEMENT DIVISION LIBRARY □ Prince
Albert, SK
Christensen, Connie, Libn.
DESERET NEWS - LIBRARY □ Salt Lake City, UT
Christensen, Gail, Musm.Asst.
BROWN COUNTY HISTORICAL SOCIETY -
MUSEUM LIBRARY □ New Ulm, MN
Christensen, John E., Dir.
WASHBURN UNIVERSITY OF TOPEKA - SCHOOL
OF LAW LIBRARY □ Topeka, KS
Christensen, Karen, Sec./Libn.
NEBRASKA STATE DEPARTMENT OF PUBLIC
WELFARE - LIBRARY □ Lincoln, NE
Christensen, Karl, Ref.Libn.
ST. JOHN'S UNIVERSITY - LAW LIBRARY □
Jamaica, NY
Christensen, Kate, Libn.
SUNRAE LEARNING RESOURCES CENTER □
Goleta, CA
Christensen, Kent, Libn.
PHILADELPHIA COLLEGE OF THE PERFORMING
ARTS - LIBRARY† □ Philadelphia, PA
Christensen, Laura A., Tech.Libn.
AMAX EXPLORATION, INC. - SCIENCE LIBRARY
□ Golden, CO
Christensen, Mary Ellen, Libn.
DOW CHEMICAL U.S.A. - WESTERN DIVISION -
LIBRARY □ Pittsburg, CA
Christensen, Pia, Ref.Libn.
UNIVERSITY OF BRITISH COLUMBIA -
CURRICULUM LABORATORY □ Vancouver, BC
Christensen, Ruth M., Libn.
SOUTHWEST MUSEUM - RESEARCH LIBRARY □
Los Angeles, CA
Christensen, Sheryl, Cat.Libn.
NORTH DAKOTA STATE SUPREME COURT LAW
LIBRARY □ Bismarck, ND
Christensen, Valerie, Res.Hist.
HALL COUNTY MUSEUM BOARD - STUHR
MUSEUM - LIBRARY AND ARCHIVES □ Grand
Island, NE
Christenson, Eugenia, Libn.
SHARON GENERAL HOSPITAL - MEDICAL STAFF
LIBRARY □ Sharon, PA
Christenson, Eugenia, Libn.
SHARON GENERAL HOSPITAL - SCHOOL OF
NURSING - LIBRARY □ Sharon, PA
Christenson, Phyllis, Chf., Law Lib.
U.S. GENERAL ACCOUNTING OFFICE -
TECHNICAL INFORMATION SOURCES AND
SERVICES BRANCH □ Washington, DC
Christenson, Virginia, Asst. to Dir.
SMITH COLLEGE - SOPHIA SMITH COLLECTION
- WOMEN'S HISTORY ARCHIVE □ Northampton,
MA
Christerisen, Terry, Dir. of LMC
KEARNEY STATE COLLEGE - CALVIN T. RYAN
LIBRARY □ Kearney, NE
Christerson, M.F., Coord. LRC
OKLAHOMA STATE UNIVERSITY - SCHOOL OF
TECHNICAL TRAINING - OKMULGEE BRANCH
LIBRARY □ Okmulgee, OK
Christian, A. Munro, Dir.
H.M.S. BOUNTY SOCIETY, INTERNATIONAL -
RESEARCH LIBRARY AND DEPOSITORY □
Tiburon, CA
Christiano, David, Libn.
MEIKLEJOHN CIVIL LIBERTIES INSTITUTE -
LIBRARY □ Berkeley, CA
Christiansen, Kay, Asst.Libn.
QUARLES & BRADY - LIBRARY □ Milwaukee, WI
Christianson, Elin B., Cur.
HOBART HISTORICAL SOCIETY, INC. -
MARIAM J. PLEAK MEMORIAL LIBRARY AND
ARCHIVE □ Hobart, IN

Christianson, Vicky, Med.Libn.
VALLEY MEDICAL CENTER OF FRESNO -
MEDICAL LIBRARY □ Fresno, CA
Christie, Edward F., Supv.
SRI INTERNATIONAL - BUSINESS
INTELLIGENCE PROGRAM - INFORMATION
CENTER □ Menlo Park, CA
Christie, Lucille, Dir.
LOMPOC MUSEUM - LIBRARY □ Lompoc, CA
Christman, Rebecca, Libn.
MERCY SCHOOL OF NURSING OF DETROIT -
LIBRARY □ Detroit, MI
Christoph, Peter R., Assoc.Libn.
NEW YORK STATE LIBRARY - MANUSCRIPTS
AND SPECIAL COLLECTION □ Albany, NY
Christopher, Edna, Cat.
UNIVERSITY OF CHICAGO - MUSIC
COLLECTION □ Chicago, IL
Christopher, Irene, Chf.Libn.
BOSTON UNIVERSITY MEDICAL CENTER -
ALUMNI MEDICAL LIBRARY □ Boston, MA
Christopher, Nick, Bus.Libn.
DAVIS POLK & WARDWELL - LIBRARY □ New
York, NY
Christopherson, Frances, Libn.
GREATER VANCOUVER REGIONAL DISTRICT -
LIBRARY □ Vancouver, BC
Chronister, Peg, Cur.
MUSEUM OF INDEPENDENT TELEPHONY -
ARCHIVES COLLECTION □ Abilene, KS
Chu, B., Libn.
UNIVERSITY OF TORONTO - DEPARTMENT OF
PHYSICS LIBRARY □ Toronto, ON
Chu, Eliza C., Asst.Libn.
BLUE CROSS OF SOUTHERN CALIFORNIA -
LEGAL AND BUSINESS LIBRARY □ Woodland
Hills, CA
Chu, Ellen M., Libn.
U.S. NATL. INSTITUTES OF HEALTH - DIVISION
OF COMPUTER RESEARCH & TECHNOLOGY -
LIBRARY □ Bethesda, MD
Chu, Insoo, Tech.Info.Spec.
STAUFFER CHEMICAL COMPANY - DE GUIGNE
TECHNICAL CENTER - RESEARCH LIBRARY □
Richmond, CA
Chu, Ruby, Hd.Libn.
ZENITH RADIO CORPORATION - ENGINEERING
LIBRARY □ Glenview, IL
Chu, Shih-Ping, Hd.Cat.Libn.
YALE UNIVERSITY - EAST ASIAN COLLECTION
□ New Haven, CT
Chu, Wendy, Mgr.
RCA CORPORATION - RCA LABORATORIES -
DAVID SARNOFF RESEARCH CENTER - LIBRARY
□ Princeton, NJ
Chuang, Felicia S., Libn.
TEXAS RESEARCH INSTITUTE OF MENTAL
SCIENCES - LIBRARY □ Houston, TX
Chui, Anita, Libn.
ONTARIO HYDRO - LIBRARY □ Toronto, ON
Chumak, O., Chf., Tech.Serv.
CANADA - AGRICULTURE CANADA - LIBRARIES
DIVISION □ Ottawa, ON
Chumas, Sophie J., Tech.Info.Spec.
U.S. NATL. BUREAU OF STANDARDS -
STANDARDS INFORMATION SERVICE □
Gaithersburg, MD
Chumney, Candes, Supv.
PIPER (Minnie Stevens) FOUNDATION -
FUNDING INFORMATION LIBRARY □ San
Antonio, TX
Chung, Catherine, Leg.Spec.
WILMER, CUTLER & PICKERING - LAW
LIBRARY □ Washington, DC
Chung, Helen, R&D Ref.Libn.
REYNOLDS (R.J.) TOBACCO COMPANY - R&D
INFORMATION SYSTEMS LIBRARY □ Winston-
Salem, NC
Chung, May, Libn.
ONTARIO HYDRO - LIBRARY □ Toronto, ON

Chung, Ms. Yun, Asst.Dir./Tech.Serv.
CHICAGO COLLEGE OF OSTEOPATHIC
MEDICINE - ALUMNI MEMORIAL LIBRARY □
Chicago, IL
Chunglo, Steve, Ref. & Doc.Libn.
WITTENBERG UNIVERSITY - THOMAS LIBRARY
□ Springfield, OH
Churan, Esther, Acq.
LAMAR UNIVERSITY - MARY AND JOHN GRAY
LIBRARY □ Beaumont, TX
Church, Miss C., Supv. of Tech.Serv.
ONTARIO BIBLE COLLEGE/ONTARIO
THEOLOGICAL SEMINARY - J. WILLIAM
HORSEY LIBRARY □ Willowdale, ON
Church, Mrs. C.A., Archv.
SCHENECTADY COUNTY HISTORICAL SOCIETY
- LIBRARY AND ARCHIVES □ Schenectady, NY
Church, Linda, Coord., Community Info.
ONTARIO - MINISTRY OF CULTURE AND
RECREATION - LIBRARIES AND COMMUNITY
INFORMATION □ Toronto, ON
Church, Velma Y., Med.Rec.Libn.
DAYTON CHILDREN'S PSYCHIATRIC HOSPITAL
- LIBRARY □ Dayton, OH
Churchfield, Beth, Info.Spec. II
KM&G INTERNATIONAL INC. - LIBRARY
SERVICES □ Pittsburgh, PA
Churchill, Barbara, Acq.Libn.
MAINE MARITIME ACADEMY - NUTTING
MEMORIAL LIBRARY □ Castine, ME
Churchill, Charles, Ref.Libn./Tech.Serv.
MASSACHUSETTS COLLEGE OF ART - LIBRARY
□ Boston, MA
Churchville, Lida H., Libn.
U.S. NATL. ARCHIVES & RECORDS SERVICE -
NATL. ARCHIVES LIBRARY □ Washington, DC
Churgin, James, Data Serv.
U.S. NATL. OCEANIC & ATMOSPHERIC
ADMINISTRATION - ENVIRONMENTAL DATA &
INFO. SERV. - NATL. OCEANOGRAPHIC DATA
CTR. □ Washington, DC
Churgin, James, Dir.
WORLD DATA CENTER A - OCEANOGRAPHY □
Washington, DC
Churgin, Sylvia, Libn.
SMITHSONIAN INSTITUTION LIBRARIES -
NATIONAL MUSEUM OF NATURAL HISTORY -
LIBRARY □ Washington, DC
Churney, Sarah, Cat.
LAW LIBRARY OF LOUISIANA □ New Orleans, LA
Chysh, Zola, Asst.Libn.
BEAVER COUNTY TIMES - LIBRARY □ Beaver,
PA
Ciacco, Catherine, Ref.
KUTAK, ROCK & HUIE - LAW LIBRARY □ Omaha,
NE
Ciampoli, Judy, Cur.
MISSOURI HISTORICAL SOCIETY - PICTORIAL
HISTORY COLLECTION □ St. Louis, MO
Ciaramella, Mary A., Chf.Libn.
LUMMUS COMPANY - LUMMUS TECHNICAL
CENTER - TECHNICAL INFORMATION
DEPARTMENT □ Bloomfield, NJ
Ciaravino, Anthony, Dept.Hd.
AUTOMATION INDUSTRIES, INC. - VITRO
LABORATORIES DIVISION - ADMINISTRATIVE
SUPPORT DEPARTMENT □ Silver Spring, MD
Ciarkowski, Elaine E., Circ.Libn.
HARVARD UNIVERSITY - SCHOOLS OF
MEDICINE, DENTAL MEDICINE AND PUBLIC
HEALTH - FRANCIS A. COUNTWAY LIBRARY □
Boston, MA
Ciarpelli, Kathy, Libn.
GENERAL RAILWAY SIGNAL CO. - TECHNICAL
LIBRARY □ Rochester, NY
Cibbarelli, Pamela, Pres.
CIBBARELLI & ASSOCIATES - INFORMATION
SERVICES □ Huntington Beach, CA
Cibulskis, Elizabeth R., Tech.Libn.
WRIGLEY (Wm., Jr.) COMPANY - QUALITY
ASSURANCE BRANCH LIBRARY □ Chicago, IL

Cibulskis, Elizabeth R., Tech.Libn.
WRIGLEY (Wm., Jr.) COMPANY - RESEARCH &
DEVELOPMENT LIBRARY □ Chicago, IL

Ciccone, Amy Navratil, Libn.
CHRYSLER MUSEUM - ART REFERENCE
LIBRARY □ Norfolk, VA

Ciccone, Barbara Gurdon, Marketing Res.Asst.
PRUDENTIAL INSURANCE COMPANY OF
AMERICA - CRISP MARKETING RESEARCH
LIBRARY □ Newark, NJ

Ciejka, Eleonora I., Per.Libn.
NEW JERSEY INSTITUTE OF TECHNOLOGY -
ROBERT W. VAN HOUTEN LIBRARY □ Newark,
NJ

Ciesielski, Joseph S., Dir.
UNIVERSITY OF SAN DIEGO - MARVIN &
LILLIAN KRATTER LAW LIBRARY □ San Diego,
CA

Ciko, Anthony, Sr.Med.Libn.
ERIE COUNTY MEDICAL CENTER - MEDICAL
LIBRARY □ Buffalo, NY

Cimon, Florence, Per.
ST. ANSELM'S COLLEGE - GEISEL LIBRARY □
Manchester, NH

Cimpl, Kay, Weston Lib.
UNIVERSITY OF WISCONSIN, MADISON -
CENTER FOR HEALTH SCIENCES LIBRARIES □
Madison, WI

Cintron, Carmelo Delgado, Law Libn.
UNIVERSITY OF PUERTO RICO - LAW SCHOOL
LIBRARY □ Rio Piedras, PR

Cioppa, Lawrence, Supv. Drama Libn.
NEW YORK PUBLIC LIBRARY - GENERAL
LIBRARY OF THE PERFORMING ARTS □ New
York, NY

Ciosek, Jane P., Libn.
INSTITUTE FOR DEFENSE ANALYSES -
COMMUNICATIONS RESEARCH DIVISION -
LIBRARY □ Princeton, NJ

Cipriani, Debra, Ser.Libn.
U.S. ARMY - MILITARY ACADEMY - LIBRARY □
West Point, NY

Cipriano, Rose M., Act.Libn.
CRAIG DEVELOPMENTAL CENTER - MARGARET
A. KENNGOTT MEMORIAL LIBRARY OF THE
HEALTH SCIENCES □ Sonyea, NY

Circiello, Jean, Libn.
ENVIRONMENTAL PROTECTION AGENCY -
REGION IX LIBRARY/INFORMATION CENTER □
San Francisco, CA

Ciskey, Debra J., Libn.
AMERICAN COLLECTORS ASSOCIATION, INC. -
ACA MEMORIAL LIBRARY □ Minneapolis, MN

Cisneros, Dorothy, Asst.Libn.
HUNTINGTON FREE LIBRARY - MUSEUM OF
THE AMERICAN INDIAN - LIBRARY □ Bronx, NY

Citron, Cary Graham, Hd.Libn.
DRAPER (Charles Stark) LABORATORY, INC. -
TECHNICAL INFORMATION CENTER □
Cambridge, MA

Ciurczak, Alexis, Pub./Tech.Serv.Libn.
PALOMAR COLLEGE - PHIL H. PUTNAM
MEMORIAL LIBRARY □ San Marcos, CA

Civille, Mary, Text Libn.
ATLANTA NEWSPAPERS - REFERENCE LIBRARY
□ Atlanta, GA

Civinskas, Anne Marie, Libn.
GENERAL FOODS CORPORATION - MAXWELL
HOUSE DIVISION - RESEARCH DEPARTMENT
LIBRARY □ Hoboken, NJ

Claffey, Joan M., Dir.
MICHIGAN STATE UNIVERSITY - NON-FORMAL
EDUCATION INFORMATION CENTER □ East
Lansing, MI

Claflin, David S., Dir./Adm.
INSTITUTE OF CERTIFIED TRAVEL AGENTS -
LIBRARY □ Wellesley, MA

Claggett, John, Mss.Spec.
UNIVERSITY OF MISSOURI - WESTERN
HISTORICAL MANUSCRIPT COLLECTION/
STATE HISTORICAL SOCIETY OF MISSOURI □
Columbia, MO

Clair, Gina Rabai, Leg.Libn.
MORRISON AND FOERSTER - BRANCH LAW
LIBRARY □ Washington, DC

Clancy, Jeanne M., Libn.
SASAKI ASSOCIATES, INC. - LIBRARY □
Watertown, MA

Clancy, Justine, Slide Cur.
UNIVERSITY OF SOUTHERN CALIFORNIA -
ARCHITECTURE & FINE ARTS LIBRARY □ Los
Angeles, CA

Clancy, Patricia, Libn.
LONG ISLAND LIGHTING COMPANY - LIBRARY
□ Hicksville, NY

Clancy, Stephen, Ref.Libn.
UNIVERSITY OF CALIFORNIA, IRVINE -
BIOMEDICAL LIBRARY □ Irvine, CA

Clancy, Steve, Asst.Dir.
SOUTHERN CALIFORNIA PERMANENTE
MEDICAL CENTER - HEALTH SCIENCES
LIBRARY/MEDIA CENTER □ Bellflower, CA

Clapp, Laurel R., Libn.
SAMFORD UNIVERSITY - CUMBERLAND
SCHOOL OF LAW - CORDELL HULL LAW
LIBRARY† □ Birmingham, AL

Clapp, Maxine B., Archv.
UNIVERSITY OF MINNESOTA - UNIVERSITY
ARCHIVES □ Minneapolis, MN

Clare, Sr. Lillian, Libn.
ST. JOHN'S HOSPITAL - MEDICAL LIBRARY □
Springfield, MO

Clare, Nancy, Cat.
CANADIAN INSTITUTE OF INTERNATIONAL
AFFAIRS - LIBRARY □ Toronto, ON

Claridge, Rev. G.G., Libn. & Archv.
ST. NORBERT ABBEY - AUGUSTINE LIBRARY □
De Pere, WI

Claridge, J.R., Exec.Dir.
ERIE COUNTY HISTORICAL SOCIETY □ Erie, PA

Clarie, Thomas, Ref.Libn.
SOUTHERN CONNECTICUT STATE COLLEGE -
H.C. BULEY LIBRARY □ New Haven, CT

Clark, Alfrieda, Chf., Spec.Projects
U.S. ARMY - ENGINEER WATERWAYS
EXPERIMENT STATION - TECHNICAL
INFORMATION CENTER □ Vicksburg, MS

Clark, Alice, Supv.
UNIVERSITY OF COLORADO, BOULDER -
BUREAU OF GOVERNMENTAL RESEARCH &
SERVICE LIBRARY □ Boulder, CO

Clark, Alson, Libn.
UNIVERSITY OF SOUTHERN CALIFORNIA -
ARCHITECTURE & FINE ARTS LIBRARY □ Los
Angeles, CA

Clark, Barton M., Libn.
UNIVERSITY OF ILLINOIS - EDUCATION AND
SOCIAL SCIENCE LIBRARY □ Urbana, IL

Clark, Betty, Acq.
BOEING MILITARY AIRPLANE COMPANY -
LIBRARY □ Wichita, KS

Clark, Blanche T., Dept.Hd.
BRONSON (Silas) LIBRARY - BUSINESS,
INDUSTRY, AND TECHNOLOGY DEPARTMENT†
□ Waterbury, CT

Clark, Carole, Libn.
ST. MARY'S HOSPITAL - LIBRARY □ Rochester,
MN

Clark, Dan O., Libn.
OHIO UNIVERSITY - MUSIC/DANCE LIBRARY □
Athens, OH

Clark, Edna W., Dir.
STUDENTS' MUSEUM, INC. - LIBRARY □
Knoxville, TN

Clark, Elaine, Asst.Libn.
NEW YORK STATE LIBRARY - LAW/SOCIAL
SCIENCE REFERENCE SERVICES □ Albany, NY

Clark, Elishia, Acq.Libn.
JACOBS ENGINEERING GROUP - TECHNICAL
INFORMATION SERVICES DEPARTMENT □
Houston, TX

Clark, Florence, Libn.
SUN CHEMICAL CORPORATION - RESEARCH
LIBRARY □ Carlstadt, NJ

Clark, George C., Hd.Libn.
MINOT STATE COLLEGE - MEMORIAL LIBRARY
□ Minot, ND

Clark, Georgia A., Law Libn.
WAYNE STATE UNIVERSITY - ARTHUR NEEF
LAW LIBRARY □ Detroit, MI

Clark, Greta, Dir.
PHILADELPHIA STATE HOSPITAL - STAFF
LIBRARY □ Philadelphia, PA

Clark, J.L., Base Libn.
U.S. AIR FORCE BASE - LITTLE ROCK BASE
LIBRARY† □ Jacksonville, AR

Clark, James M., Libn.
PHILADELPHIA COURT OF COMMON PLEAS -
LAW LIBRARY □ Philadelphia, PA

Clark, James P., Dir.
U.S. ARMY - MISSILE COMMAND & MARSHALL
SPACE FLIGHT CENTER - REDSTONE
SCIENTIFIC INFORMATION CENTER □
Redstone Arsenal, AL

Clark, Jane L., Dir., Med.Lib.Serv.
TIMKEN MERCY HOSPITAL - MEDICAL LIBRARY
□ Canton, OH

Clark, Jeff, Supv.
COLLEGE OF THE VIRGIN ISLANDS -
FOUNDATION CENTER REGIONAL COLLECTION
□ St. Thomas, VI

Clark, JoEvelyn, Libn.
MEAD JOHNSON AND COMPANY - MEAD
JOHNSON INSTITUTE - LIBRARY □ Evansville,
IN

Clark, John L.D., Dir.
ERIC CLEARINGHOUSE ON LANGUAGES AND
LINGUISTICS □ Washington, DC

Clark, Kit, Cat.
NOVA SCOTIA COLLEGE OF ART AND DESIGN -
LIBRARY □ Halifax, NS

Clark, Laura, Lib.Asst.
TACOMA NEWS TRIBUNE - LIBRARY □ Tacoma,
WA

Clark, Lois J., Libn.
KAISER FOUNDATION HOSPITALS - MEDICAL
LIBRARY □ Honolulu, HI

Clark, Lois O., Med.Libn.
LONG BEACH COMMUNITY HOSPITAL -
MEDICAL LIBRARY □ Long Beach, CA

Clark, M. Rosemary, Asst.Libn.
CHILDREN'S MEMORIAL HOSPITAL - JOSEPH
BRENNEMANN LIBRARY □ Chicago, IL

Clark, Margery M., Chf.Libn.
NATIONAL ASSOCIATION OF HOME BUILDERS -
NATIONAL HOUSING CENTER LIBRARY □
Washington, DC

Clark, Marianna Droescher, Hd.Libn.
U.S. NAVY - NAVAL SHIPYARD (Long Beach) -
TECHNICAL LIBRARY □ Long Beach, CA

Clark, Mary Ellen, Asst. to Cur.
SWARTHMORE COLLEGE - FRIENDS
HISTORICAL LIBRARY - PEACE COLLECTION □
Swarthmore, PA

Clark, Maryanne, Asst.Libn.
NEW YORK STATE SUPREME COURT -
APPELLATE DIVISION, 4TH JUDICIAL
DEPARTMENT - LAW LIBRARY □ Rochester, NY

Clark, Melba, Libn.
ST. JOSEPH HOSPITAL - MEDICAL LIBRARY □
Albuquerque, NM

Clark, Mercedes, Ser./ILL Libn.
TRW INC. - ENERGY SYSTEMS PLANNING
DIVISION - LIBRARY □ McLean, VA

Clark, Nancy, Libn.
U.S. VETERANS ADMINISTRATION (AZ-Phoenix)
- HOSPITAL LIBRARY □ Phoenix, AZ

Clark, Newton P., Rec. Retention Ctr.
MARTIN MARIETTA CORPORATION - DENVER
DIVISION - RESEARCH LIBRARY □ Denver, CO

Clark, Rae, Sr.Libn., Tech.Serv.
NEW YORK STATE DEPARTMENT OF HEALTH -
DIVISION OF LABORATORIES AND RESEARCH
LIBRARY □ Albany, NY

Clark, Robert, Hd.Libn.
MONTANA HISTORICAL SOCIETY - LIBRARY/
ARCHIVES □ Helena, MT

PERSONNEL

PERSONNEL

Clark, Robert L., Jr., Dir.
OKLAHOMA STATE DEPARTMENT OF
LIBRARIES □ Oklahoma City, OK

Clark, Susan, Libn.
LUTHERAN DEACONESS HOSPITAL - MEDICAL
LIBRARY □ Minneapolis, MN

Clark, Wendolyn, Ref.Libn.
TENNESSEE VALLEY AUTHORITY - TECHNICAL
LIBRARY □ Muscle Shoals, AL

Clark, Willie E., Film Libn.
U.S. DEPT. OF ENERGY - TECHNICAL
INFORMATION CENTER - FILM LIBRARY □ Oak
Ridge, TN

Clark, Winnifred, Libn.
DETROIT PUBLIC LIBRARY - FINE ARTS
DEPARTMENT □ Detroit, MI

Clarke, Barbara, Acq.Libn.
MEMORIAL SLOAN-KETTERING CANCER
CENTER - LEE COOMBE MEMORIAL LIBRARY □
New York, NY

Clarke, Barbara, Libn., CRC
SUNY - COLLEGE AT GENESEO - MILNE
LIBRARY □ Geneseo, NY

Clarke, Beverley, Sr.Libn.
IBM CORPORATION - RESEARCH LIBRARY □
San Jose, CA

Clarke, James P., Lib.Dir.
MARYWOOD COLLEGE - LEARNING RESOURCES
CENTER □ Scranton, PA

Clarke, Jane, Dir.
MERCY SCHOOL OF NURSING - E.O. MORROW
LIBRARY □ Canton, OH

Clarke, Jean B., Libn.
MOBIL RESEARCH & DEVELOPMENT
CORPORATION - CENTRAL RESEARCH
DIVISION LIBRARY □ Princeton, NJ

Clarke, Bro. Lewis N.
INTERNATIONAL BROTHERHOOD OF OLD
BASTARDS, INC. - SIR THOMAS CRAPPER
MEMORIAL ARCHIVES □ St. Louis, MO

Clarke, Robert F., Prog.Chf./Libn.
U.S. PUBLIC HEALTH SERVICE - NATL.
INSTITUTE OF MENTAL HEALTH - MENTAL
HEALTH STUDY CENTER LIBRARY □ Adelphi, MD

Clarke, Sarah H., Circ./Tchg.Res.Ctr.
NORTH ADAMS STATE COLLEGE - EUGENE L.
FREEL LIBRARY - SPECIAL COLLECTIONS □
North Adams, MA

Clarkson, Dorothy J., Supv.
POLYSAR, LTD. - INFORMATION CENTRE □
Sarnia, ON

Clarkson, Mary, Ref.
TRINITY UNIVERSITY - LIBRARY □ San Antonio,
TX

Clarkson, Teresa N., Libn.
DUANE, MORRIS & HECKSCHER - LAW LIBRARY
□ Philadelphia, PA

Clary, Alice, Libn.
CARNEGIE LIBRARY OF PITTSBURGH -
CENTRAL CHILDREN'S ROOM HISTORICAL
COLLECTION □ Pittsburgh, PA

Clary, Ann Roane, Chf.Libn.
FEDERAL RESERVE SYSTEM - BOARD OF
GOVERNORS - RESEARCH LIBRARY □
Washington, DC

Clary, Dorothy H., Libn.
CARRINGTON, COLEMAN, SLOMAN &
BLUMENTHAL - LIBRARY □ Dallas, TX

Clary, Kay, Res.Anl.
GREATER EGYPT REGIONAL PLANNING AND
DEVELOPMENT COMMISSION - LIBRARY-
RESEARCH CENTER □ Carbondale, IL

Clary, Lydia S., Coord.
ACCREDITING COMMISSION ON EDUCATION
FOR HEALTH SERVICES ADM. - RESOURCE CTR.
FOR HEALTH SERVICES ADM. EDUCATION □
Washington, DC

Clasper, James W., Asst.Corp.Libn.
CINCINNATI MILACRON, INC. - CORPORATE
INFORMATION CENTER □ Cincinnati, OH

Claspy, Lois, Music Libn.
BALDWIN-WALLACE COLLEGE -
RIEMENSCHNEIDER BACH INSTITUTE - BACH
LIBRARY □ Berea, OH

Classen, Joanne, Subject Spec.
DENVER PUBLIC LIBRARY - GENEALOGY
DIVISION □ Denver, CO

Clatanoff, Robert, Res.Assoc./Libn.
INTERNATIONAL ASSOCIATION OF ASSESSING
OFFICERS - RESEARCH AND TECHNICAL
SERVICES DEPT. - LIBRARY □ Chicago, IL

Claus, Robert, Archv.
CONNECTICUT STATE LIBRARY □ Hartford, CT

Clausen, Elizabeth, Chf.Libn.
AUGUSTANA HOSPITAL AND HEALTH CARE
CENTER - CARL A. HEDBERG HEALTH SCIENCE
LIBRARY □ Chicago, IL

Clausen, Esther M., Libn.
UNIVERSITY OF ILLINOIS - COMMERCE
LIBRARY □ Urbana, IL

Clausen, Nancy M., Mgr. of Info.Serv.
TRACY-LOCKE ADVERTISING AND PUBLIC
RELATIONS, INC. - LIBRARY □ Dallas, TX

Clausen, Rebecca, Lib.Supv.
PAYNE (Howard) UNIVERSITY - CURRICULUM
LIBRARY □ Brownwood, TX

Clausen, Sherry, Choral Music Libn.
WESTMINSTER CHOIR COLLEGE - TALBOTT
LIBRARY □ Princeton, NJ

Clausman, Gilbert J., Libn.
NEW YORK UNIVERSITY MEDICAL CENTER -
FREDERICK L. EHRMAN MEDICAL LIBRARY □
New York, NY

Claussen, Norma, Physical Sci.Libn.
UNIVERSITY OF CALIFORNIA, SANTA BARBARA
- SCIENCES-ENGINEERING LIBRARY □ Santa
Barbara, CA

Clausz, Joan A., Med.Libn.
WEST ALLIS MEMORIAL HOSPITAL - MEDICAL
LIBRARY □ West Allis, WI

Clay, Debra J., Tech.Lit.Libn.
GETTY OIL COMPANY, INC. - RESEARCH
CENTER LIBRARY □ Houston, TX

Clay, Genevieve J., Per.Libn.
EASTERN KENTUCKY UNIVERSITY - JOHN
GRANT CRABBE LIBRARY □ Richmond, KY

Clay, Katherine, Coord.Comp.Serv.
SAN MATEO COUNTY EDUCATIONAL
RESOURCES CENTER □ Redwood City, CA

Clayman, Ida, Cat.Libn.
VIRGINIA STATE UNIVERSITY - JOHNSTON
MEMORIAL LIBRARY □ Petersburg, VA

Claypool, Richard D., Res.
MORAVIAN MUSIC FOUNDATION, INC. -
LIBRARY □ Winston-Salem, NC

Clayton, Carla J., Mgr., Info.Serv.
WATERS ASSOCIATES INC. - INFORMATION
RESOURCE CENTER □ Milford, MA

Clayton, Dr. J. Glen, Spec.Coll.Libn.
FURMAN UNIVERSITY LIBRARY - SPECIAL
COLLECTIONS □ Greenville, SC

Clayton, John M., Jr., Archv.
UNIVERSITY OF DELAWARE, NEWARK -
ARCHIVES† □ Newark, DE

Clayton, Mary E., Law Libn.
LANE COUNTY LAW LIBRARY □ Eugene, OR

Clayton, Yvonne, Lib.Tech.
U.S.D.A. - AGRICULTURAL RESEARCH SERVICE
- WATER CONSERVATION LABORATORY
LIBRARY □ Phoenix, AZ

Clegg, Thomas J., Pres.
MUNCY HISTORICAL SOCIETY AND MUSEUM
OF HISTORY - HISTORICAL LIBRARY □ Muncy,
PA

Cleland, Carole, Chf.Libn.
U.S. FEDERAL DEPOSIT INSURANCE
CORPORATION - LIBRARY □ Washington, DC

Cleland, Monique C., Libn.
DARTMOUTH COLLEGE - KRESGE PHYSICAL
SCIENCES LIBRARY □ Hanover, NH

Clem, Marie, Teachers Res.Libn.
PRAIRIE VIEW A & M COLLEGE OF TEXAS -
W.R. BANKS LIBRARY □ Prairie View, TX

Clemen, Rudolf A., Jr., Info.Res.Spec.
AMERICAN RED CROSS - NATIONAL
HEADQUARTERS LIBRARY □ Washington, DC

Clemens, Joan, Retrieval Libn.
GRUMMAN AEROSPACE CORPORATION -
TECHNICAL INFORMATION CENTER □
Bethpage, NY

Clemens, Norman, Libn.
LEHMAN BROTHERS, KUHN, LOEB, INC. -
LIBRARY □ New York, NY

Clement, Charles, Mgr., Tech.Serv.
CHURCH OF JESUS CHRIST OF LATTER-DAY
SAINTS - GENEALOGICAL LIBRARY □ Salt Lake
City, UT

Clement, Emily, Asst.Libn.
BAKER & BOTTS - LAW LIBRARY □ Houston, TX

Clement, Hope, Assoc.Natl.Libn.
NATIONAL LIBRARY OF CANADA □ Ottawa, ON

Clement, R., ILL
CANADA - DEPARTMENT OF FINANCE -
FINANCE/TREASURY BOARD LIBRARY □
Ottawa, ON

Clement, Robert, Lit.Chem.
FERRO CORPORATION - LIBRARY □
Independence, OH

Clement, Russell, Ref./Lib.Instr.
BRIGHAM YOUNG UNIVERSITY, HAWAII
CAMPUS - JOSEPH F. SMITH LIBRARY AND
MEDIA CENTER □ Laie, HI

Clement, Susan D., Libn.
DETROIT EDISON COMPANY - INFORMATION
SERVICES LIBRARY† □ Detroit, MI

Clementine, Sister Mary, Libn.
ST. MARY HOSPITAL - MEDICAL LIBRARY □
Livonia, MI

Clements, Helen, Asst.Archv.
TEXAS TECH UNIVERSITY - SOUTHWEST
COLLECTION □ Lubbock, TX

Clements, Linda L., Libn.
RADIAN CORPORATION - LIBRARY □ Austin, TX

Clemmer, Dan O., Chf., Rd.Serv.
U.S. DEPT. OF STATE - LIBRARY □ Washington,
DC

Clemons, A.L.
DOW CHEMICAL COMPANY - TECHNICAL
INFORMATION SERVICES - CHEMICAL
LIBRARY □ Midland, MI

Clemson, Beverly C., Musm.Dir.
WALNUT CREEK HISTORICAL SOCIETY -
SHADELANDS RANCH HISTORICAL MUSEUM -
HISTORY ROOM □ Walnut Creek, CA

Clemson, Patrice, Asst.Libn.
UNIVERSITY OF PITTSBURGH - GRADUATE
SCHOOL OF PUBLIC & INTERNATIONAL
AFFAIRS LIBRARY □ Pittsburgh, PA

Clendaniel, Estella C., Supv., Lib. & Files
EASTERN SHORE HOSPITAL CENTER -
PROFESSIONAL LIBRARY □ Cambridge, MD

Clermont, Simonne, Law Libn.
UNIVERSITE DE MONCTON - BIBLIOTHEQUE DE
DROIT □ Moncton, NB

Cleveland, Dr. Ana, Dir.
TEXAS WOMAN'S UNIVERSITY - LIBRARY
SCIENCE LIBRARY - PROYECTO LEER □ Denton,
TX

Cleveland, Berniece, Act.Libn.
ALASKA STATE COURT SYSTEM - KETCHIKAN
LAW LIBRARY □ Ketchikan, AK

Cleveland, Mary Ann, Libn. I
FLORIDA STATE DEPT. OF NATURAL
RESOURCES - BUREAU OF GEOLOGY LIBRARY □
Tallahassee, FL

Cleveland, Susan, Dir.
UNIVERSITY OF PENNSYLVANIA - HERMAN
BEERMAN LIBRARY □ Philadelphia, PA

Cleveland, W.M., Hist.
ELEVENTH BOMBARDMENT GROUP (H)
ASSOCIATION - ARCHIVES □ Portsmouth, NH

Cleveland, W. M., Hist.
PEARL HARBOR SURVIVORS ASSOCIATION -
ARCHIVES □ Portsmouth, NH

Clever, Shannon, Hd., Ref.
UNIVERSITY OF SOUTH CAROLINA - SCHOOL OF MEDICINE LIBRARY □ Columbia, SC

Clevesy, Sandra, Dir.Lib.Serv.
FRAMINGHAM UNION HOSPITAL - CESARE GEORGE TEDESCHI LIBRARY □ Framingham, MA

Click, Mary A., Coord. LRC Adm.
SOUTHWEST TEXAS STATE UNIVERSITY - LEARNING RESOURCES CENTER □ San Marcos, TX

Cliffard, Paul M., Gen. Sales Mgr.
WIDE WORLD PHOTOS, INC. □ New York, NY

Clifford, Catherine J., Tech.Info.Spec.
U.S. NATL. INSTITUTES OF HEALTH - LIBRARY □ Bethesda, MD

Clifford, Esther B., Libn.
ORANGE AND ROCKLAND UTILITIES, INC. - LIBRARY □ Pearl River, NY

Clifford, Naomi, Natl.Off.Libn.
ERNST & WHINNEY - NATIONAL OFFICE LIBRARY □ Cleveland, OH

Clifford, Stanley, Coord.
HAYSTACK MOUNTAIN SCHOOL OF CRAFTS - LIBRARY □ Deer Isle, ME

Clifford, Susan G., Libn.
HUGHES AIRCRAFT COMPANY - EL SEGUNDO LIBRARY □ Los Angeles, CA

Clift, Evelyn S., Cur.
HENRY COUNTY HISTORICAL SOCIETY - LIBRARY □ New Castle, IN

Clifton, David L., Mgr., Info.Serv.
ROCKWELL INTERNATIONAL - ELECTRONICS OPERATIONS - DALLAS INFORMATION CENTER □ Dallas, TX

Clifton, Dorothy I., Dir.
VALDEZ HISTORICAL SOCIETY - VALDEZ HERITAGE ARCHIVES ALIVE □ Valdez, AK

Clifton, Joe Ann, Mgr., Tech.Libs.
LITTON INDUSTRIES - DATA SYSTEMS DIVISION - ENGINEERING LIBRARY □ Van Nuys, CA

Clifton, Joe Ann, Mgr., Info.Serv.
LITTON INDUSTRIES - GUIDANCE AND CONTROL SYSTEMS - LIBRARY □ Woodland Hills, CA

Cline, Caren T., Supv.Mgt.Asst.
U.S. BUREAU OF LAND MANAGEMENT - NEW MEXICO STATE OFFICE LIBRARY □ Santa Fe, NM

Cline, Fred A., Jr., Libn.
ASIAN ART MUSEUM OF SAN FRANCISCO - AVERY BRUNDAGE COLLECTION □ San Francisco, CA

Cline, Inez E., City/County Hist.
GARLAND COUNTY HISTORICAL SOCIETY - ARCHIVES □ Hot Springs, AR

Cline, Larry, Doc. Control
ENVIRONMENTAL PROTECTION AGENCY - ANDREW W. BREIDENBACH ENVIRONMENTAL RESEARCH CTR., CINCINNATI - TECH.LIB. □ Cincinnati, OH

Clinkenbeard, Beth A., Asst.Libn.
UNIVERSITY OF MICHIGAN - CENTER FOR RESEARCH ON ECONOMIC DEVELOPMENT □ Ann Arbor, MI

Clinkscales, C.C., III, Natl.Dir.
NATIONAL ALLIANCE OF SENIOR CITIZENS - LIBRARY† □ Falls Church, VA

Clinton, Janet, Chf. of Lib.Serv.
MERCY CATHOLIC MEDICAL CENTER - HEALTH SCIENCES LIBRARY □ Darby, PA

Clinton, Janet, Chf. of Lib.Serv.
MERCY CATHOLIC MEDICAL CENTER - MISERICORDIA DIVISION - HEALTH SCIENCES LIBRARY □ Philadelphia, PA

Clinton, Steve, Dir. of Lib.
INTERNATIONAL CHRISTIAN SCHOOL OF THEOLOGY - GRADUATE UNIVERSITY LIBRARY □ San Bernardino, CA

Clintworth, Bill, CME Project Libn.
UNIVERSITY OF SOUTHERN CALIFORNIA - HEALTH SCIENCES CAMPUS - NORRIS MEDICAL LIBRARY □ Los Angeles, CA

Clisby, Roger D., Cur.
CROCKER ART MUSEUM - RESEARCH LIBRARY □ Sacramento, CA

Clise, Eleanore R., Chf.Archv.
GENEVA HISTORICAL SOCIETY AND MUSEUM - JAMES D. LUCKETT MEMORIAL ARCHIVES □ Geneva, NY

Clissold, Penn, Libn.
LEHIGH-NORTHAMPTON COUNTIES JOINT PLANNING COMMISSION - LIBRARY □ Lehigh Valley, PA

Clist, Mary, Hd.Tech.Serv.
SUNY - AGRICULTURAL AND TECHNICAL COLLEGE AT COBLESKILL - JARED VAN WAGENEN, JR. LEARNING RESOURCE CENTER □ Cobleskill, NY

Cloakey, Gladys, Libn.
FLUKE (John) MANUFACTURING CO., INC. - LIBRARY □ Everett, WA

Close, Elizabeth G., Tech.Info.Spec.
U.S. FOREST SERVICE - INTERMOUNTAIN FOREST & RANGE EXPERIMENT STATION - LIBRARY □ Ogden, UT

Closson, Trudy, Rec.Mgr.
U.S. BUREAU OF LAND MANAGEMENT - CASPER DISTRICT OFFICE - LIBRARY† □ Casper, WY

Clotfelter, Cecil, Asst.Dir.Tech.Serv.
EASTERN NEW MEXICO UNIVERSITY - GOLDEN LIBRARY □ Portales, NM

Clouse, Jon, Dir.
UNIVERSITY OF MINNESOTA - DRUG INFORMATION SERVICE CENTER □ Minneapolis, MN

Clouser, Muriel, Tech.Serv.Libn.
CABRINI COLLEGE - HOLY SPIRIT LIBRARY □ Radnor, PA

Clouten, Keith H., Libn.
CANADIAN UNION COLLEGE - LIBRARY □ College Heights, AB

Cloutier, Jacques, Acq.
UNIVERSITE DU QUEBEC A HULL - BIBLIOTHEQUE □ Hull, PQ

Clow, Richard H., Libn.
EG&G, INC. - SANTA BARBARA DIVISION - LIBRARY □ Goleta, CA

Clow, Dr. Richmond L., Dir.
AMERICAN INDIAN RESEARCH PROJECT - LIBRARY □ Vermillion, SD

Clowers, Betty J., Assoc.Libn.
U.S. SUPREME COURT - LIBRARY □ Washington, DC

Cluff, Ervin, Libn.
CHURCH OF JESUS CHRIST OF LATTER-DAY SAINTS - SAFFORD-THATCHER STAKES - GENEALOGICAL LIBRARY □ Safford, AZ

Clulee, Charles R., Pres. Emeritus
WALLINGFORD HISTORICAL SOCIETY, INC. - LIBRARY □ Wallingford, CT

Clum, Audna T., Libn.
ST. MARY'S HOSPITAL - MEDICAL STAFF LIBRARY □ Troy, NY

Clunie, June A., Libn.
VETERANS HOME OF CALIFORNIA - LINCOLN MEMORIAL LIBRARY □ Yountville, CA

Clurman, E., Sr.Ck.
YESHIVA UNIVERSITY - ALBERT EINSTEIN COLLEGE OF MEDICINE - SURGERY LIBRARY □ Bronx, NY

Cluxton, Harriette M., Dir., Med.Lib.Serv.
ILLINOIS MASONIC MEDICAL CENTER - NOAH VAN CLEEF MEDICAL MEMORIAL LIBRARY □ Chicago, IL

Clyburn, Emily E., Staff Libn.
U.S. VETERANS ADMINISTRATION (SC-Columbia) - HOSPITAL LIBRARY □ Columbia, SC

Clyde, Arlene, Asst.Libn.
FREE METHODIST CHURCH OF NORTH AMERICA - HISTORICAL LIBRARY □ Winona Lake, IN

Clymer, Emerson M., Pres.
ROSICRUCIAN FRATERNITY - LIBRARY† □ Quakertown, PA

Clyne, Barbara A., Asst.Libn.
SULLIVAN AND CROMWELL - LIBRARY† □ New York, NY

Coakley, Gene, Hd., Circ.Dept.
YALE UNIVERSITY - LAW LIBRARY □ New Haven, CT

Coakley, Mary L., Lib. Group Supv.
BELL TELEPHONE LABORATORIES, INC. & WESTERN ELECTRIC, INC. - TECHNICAL LIBRARY □ Allentown, PA

Coar, John A., Adm.Libn.
ROSENMAN, COLIN, FREUND, LEWIS & COHEN - LAW LIBRARY □ New York, NY

Coates, Penny, Libn.
KITCHENER-WATERLOO RECORD - LIBRARY □ Kitchener, ON

Coates, Viona, Libn.
BRITISH COLUMBIA RESEARCH COUNCIL - LIBRARY □ Vancouver, BC

Coates, Viona, Res.Libn.
BRITISH COLUMBIA RESEARCH COUNCIL - URANIUM INFORMATION CENTRE □ Vancouver, BC

Coates, W. Paul, Mss.Libn.
HOWARD UNIVERSITY - MOORLAND-SPINGARN RESEARCH CENTER - MANUSCRIPT DIVISION □ Washington, DC

Coatsworth, Patricia, Hd.Libn.
MERRIAM CENTER LIBRARY □ Chicago, IL

Cobaugh, Stephen M., Intl.Pres.
UNITED STATES SPACE EDUCATION ASSOCIATION - USSEA MEDIA CENTER □ Elizabethtown, PA

Cobb, Bonita, Cat.
WINNIPEG SCHOOL DIVISION NO. 1 - TEACHERS LIBRARY AND RESOURCE CENTRE □ Winnipeg, MB

Cobb, David A., Libn.
UNIVERSITY OF ILLINOIS - MAP AND GEOGRAPHY LIBRARY □ Urbana, IL

Cobb, Helen, Lib.Asst.
QUEEN'S UNIVERSITY AT KINGSTON - PSYCHOLOGY LIBRARY □ Kingston, ON

Cobb, Jean, Ref.Libn.
SCHOOL OF THEOLOGY AT CLAREMONT - THEOLOGY LIBRARY □ Claremont, CA

Cobb, Sandra, Music Cat.
CLEVELAND INSTITUTE OF MUSIC - LIBRARY □ Cleveland, OH

Cobbett, Linda, Libn.
C-I-L INC. - CENTRAL LIBRARY □ Willowdale, ON

Cobbs, Lisa, Libn.
CENTER FOR WOMEN'S STUDIES AND SERVICES - CWSS LIBRARY □ San Diego, CA

Coberly, Jean, Hd., History Dept.
SEATTLE PUBLIC LIBRARY - HISTORY, GOVERNMENT AND BIOGRAPHY DEPARTMENT □ Seattle, WA

Cobey, Eleanor, Leg.Libn.
SHEA & GARDNER - LIBRARY □ Washington, DC

Coburn, Christine S., Libn.
MICROWAVE ASSOCIATES, INC. - LIBRARY □ Burlington, MA

Cocci, Mary Lou, Ref.Libn.
MITRE CORPORATION - CORPORATE LIBRARY† □ Bedford, MA

Cochran, Anita, Lib.Techn.
UNIVERSITY OF COLORADO, BOULDER - EARTH SCIENCES LIBRARY □ Boulder, CO

Cochran, Catherine F., Libn.
GENERAL MOTORS CORPORATION - PUBLIC RELATIONS STAFF LIBRARY □ Detroit, MI

Cochran, J. Wesley, Ref.Libn.
LOYOLA UNIVERSITY (New Orleans) - LAW LIBRARY □ New Orleans, LA

Cochran, Janet, Online Searcher
CONSUMER EDUCATION RESOURCE NETWORK (CERN) □ Rosslyn, VA

Cochran, Mary, Libn.
HIGHLAND PARK METHODIST CHURCH - LIBRARY □ Dallas, TX

Cochrane, Mary, Libn.
ELDORADO NUCLEAR, LTD. - RESEARCH &
DEVELOPMENT LIBRARY □ Ottawa, ON
Cochrane, Susan, Ref.
UNIVERSITY OF ALABAMA - SCHOOL OF LAW
LIBRARY □ University, AL
Cockhill, Brian, State Archv.
MONTANA HISTORICAL SOCIETY - LIBRARY/
ARCHIVES □ Helena, MT
Cockrum, Frances E., AHEC Libn.
TRINITY MEDICAL CENTER - ANGUS L.
CAMERON MEDICAL LIBRARY† □ Minot, ND
Cocks, J. Fraser, III, Cur., Spec.Coll.
COLBY COLLEGE - MILLER LIBRARY - SPECIAL
COLLECTIONS □ Waterville, ME
Coco, Alfred J., Libn.
UNIVERSITY OF DENVER - COLLEGE OF LAW -
WESTMINSTER LAW LIBRARY □ Denver, CO
Coco, Madeline A., Chf.Libn.
U.S. VETERANS ADMINISTRATION (NY-Batavia)
- MEDICAL CENTER LIBRARY □ Batavia, NY
Cody, Bruce, Pub.Info.Off.
ILLINOIS STATE HISTORICAL LIBRARY □
Springfield, IL
Cody, Jay, Dir./Cur.
LEACOCK (Stephen) MEMORIAL HOME -
LIBRARY □ Orillia, ON
Cody, Shirley A., Libn.
WALLA WALLA COLLEGE - SCHOOL OF NURSING
PROFESSIONAL LIBRARY □ Portland, OR
Coe, Corrine B., Acq.Libn.
YALE UNIVERSITY - KLINE SCIENCE LIBRARY □
New Haven, CT
Coe, Douglas, Res.Tech.
SAN DIEGO STATE UNIVERSITY - SOCIAL
SCIENCE RESEARCH LABORATORY - LIBRARY □
San Diego, CA
Coe, G., Ref.Libn.
GOLDEY BEACOM COLLEGE - J. WILBUR
HIRONS LIBRARY □ Wilmington, DE
Coe, Richard E., Lib.Dir.
SONS OF THE REVOLUTION IN THE STATE OF
CALIFORNIA SOCIETY - LIBRARY □ Glendale,
CA
Coello, Elizabeth, Ser.Cat.
TEACHERS COLLEGE - LIBRARY □ New York, NY
Coen, James L., Ref.Libn.
NEW YORK UNIVERSITY - GRADUATE SCHOOL
OF BUSINESS ADMINISTRATION - LIBRARY □
New York, NY
Coen, Jim, Ref.
STANDARD & POOR'S CORPORATION -
LIBRARY □ New York, NY
Cofer, Linda Landis, Supv., ERC
COLUMBUS TECHNICAL INSTITUTE -
EDUCATIONAL RESOURCES CENTER† □
Columbus, OH
Coffee, E. Guy, Hd.Libn.
KANSAS STATE UNIVERSITY - VETERINARY
MEDICAL LIBRARY □ Manhattan, KS
Coffee, Kathleen, Hd.Tech.Serv.
PITTSBURG STATE UNIVERSITY - LEONARD H.
AXE LIBRARY □ Pittsburg, KS
Coffey, Barbara, Assoc.Libn.
WENTWORTH INSTITUTE OF TECHNOLOGY -
LIBRARY □ Boston, MA
Coffey, Helen, Res.Ctr.Libn.
QUEEN'S UNIVERSITY AT KINGSTON -
EDUCATION LIBRARY □ Kingston, ON
Coffin, Mrs. Charles, Libn.
HISTORICAL SOCIETY OF EARLY AMERICAN
DECORATION, INC. - LIBRARY □ Albany, NY
Coffin, Shirley E., Libn.
PUBLIC LIBRARY OF CINCINNATI AND
HAMILTON COUNTY - ART AND MUSIC
DEPARTMENT □ Cincinnati, OH
Coffindaffer, Clarence L., State Libn.
SOUTH DAKOTA STATE LIBRARY □ Pierre, SD
Coffman, M. Hope, Mgr.
DRAPER (Charles Stark) LABORATORY, INC. -
TECHNICAL INFORMATION CENTER □
Cambridge, MA

Coffman, Mel, Supv.Clas. Loan Ctr.
MARTIN MARIETTA CORPORATION - DENVER
DIVISION - RESEARCH LIBRARY □ Denver, CO
Coffman, Ralph, Lib.Mgr.
DIGITAL EQUIPMENT CORPORATION -
CORPORATE LIBRARY □ Maynard, MA
Coffman, Randy, Ref.Libn.
TEXAS COLLEGE OF OSTEOPATHIC MEDICINE -
MEDICAL LIBRARY □ Fort Worth, TX
Coffroth, Irene, Libn.
SOMERSET COUNTY LAW LIBRARY† □
Somerset, PA
Cofta, Mary Ann, Asst.Libn.
ALCAN ALUMINUM CORPORATION -
CORPORATE LIBRARY □ Cleveland, OH
Cogan, Gale, Dir.
ST. JOHN'S HOSPITAL - HEALTH SCIENCE
LIBRARY □ Lowell, MA
Cogdell, William E., Asst. Law Libn.
TEXAS SOUTHERN UNIVERSITY - THURGOOD
MARSHALL SCHOOL OF LAW - LIBRARY† □
Houston, TX
Coggins, Timothy, Hd., Rd.Serv.
UNIVERSITY OF NORTH CAROLINA, CHAPEL
HILL - LAW LIBRARY □ Chapel Hill, NC
Coghlan, Gladys M., Dir. of Libs.
HISTORICAL SOCIETY OF DELAWARE -
LIBRARY† □ Wilmington, DE
Coghlan, Patricia M., Dir.
MEDICAL CENTER OF BEAVER COUNTY -
HEALTH SCIENCES LIBRARY □ Beaver, PA
Cogliano, Betsy, Cat.
MITRE CORPORATION - CORPORATE LIBRARY†
□ Bedford, MA
Cogswell, Robert E., Cat.
EPISCOPAL THEOLOGICAL SEMINARY OF THE
SOUTHWEST - LIBRARY □ Austin, TX
Cohan, Leonard, Dir. of Libs.
POLYTECHNIC INSTITUTE OF NEW YORK -
SPICER LIBRARY □ Brooklyn, NY
Cohan, Lois, Libn.
ROCKLAND RESEARCH INSTITUTE - ROCKLAND
HEALTH SCIENCES LIBRARY □ Orangeburg, NY
Cohen, Anne, Acq.Libn.
COMMUNITY COLLEGE OF BALTIMORE - BARD
LIBRARY - SPECIAL COLLECTIONS □ Baltimore,
MD
Cohen, Anne, Med.Libn.
SISTERS OF CHARITY HOSPITAL - MEDICAL
STAFF LIBRARY □ Buffalo, NY
Cohen, Ari, Hd.Cat.Dept.
ENGINEERING SOCIETIES LIBRARY □ New
York, NY
Cohen, Arthur M., Dir.
ERIC CLEARINGHOUSE FOR JUNIOR COLLEGES
□ Los Angeles, CA
Cohen, Barbara, Clinical Libn.
JEFFERSON (Thomas) UNIVERSITY - SCOTT
MEMORIAL LIBRARY □ Philadelphia, PA
Cohen, Barry L., MAP Libn.
NEW YORK CITY HUMAN RESOURCES
ADMINISTRATION - MEDICAL ASSISTANCE
PROGRAM - MEDICAID LIBRARY □ New York,
NY
Cohen, David, Prog.Dir.
QUEENS COLLEGE OF THE CITY UNIVERSITY
OF NEW YORK - ETHNIC MATERIALS
INFORMATION CENTER □ Flushing, NY
Cohen, Elinor, Adm., Tech.Info.Serv.
GENERAL FOODS CORPORATION - TECHNICAL
CENTER - TARRYTOWN TECHNICAL
INFORMATION CENTER □ White Plains, NY
Cohen, Elise, Cat.
EQUITABLE LIFE ASSURANCE SOCIETY OF THE
U.S. - GENERAL LIBRARY† □ New York, NY
Cohen, Harriet V., Ref.Libn.
U.S. NAVY - NAVAL REGIONAL MEDICAL
CENTER (Oakland) - MEDICAL LIBRARY □
Oakland, CA
Cohen, Jackson B., Hd., Sci.Lib.
QUEENS COLLEGE OF THE CITY UNIVERSITY
OF NEW YORK - SCIENCE LIBRARY □ Flushing,
NY

Cohen, Judith, Oral Hist.Libn.
NATIONAL MARITIME MUSEUM - J. PORTER
SHAW LIBRARY □ San Francisco, CA
Cohen, Leonard, Hd.Rd.Serv.
SUNY - COLLEGE AT CORTLAND - MEMORIAL
LIBRARY □ Cortland, NY
Cohen, Linda, Cat.
SUNY AT BUFFALO - CHARLES B. SEARS LAW
LIBRARY □ Buffalo, NY
Cohen, Madeline, Mgr., Lib.Serv.
AMERICAN BROADCASTING COMPANIES, INC.
- ABC NEWS INFORMATION CENTER □ New
York, NY
Cohen, Margery A., Libn.
CONNECTICUT STATE DEPARTMENT OF
HEALTH SERVICES - STANLEY H. OSBORN
MEDICAL LIBRARY □ Hartford, CT
Cohen, Marsha, Mgr., Info.Serv.
ALLY AND GARGANO, INC. - INFORMATION
CENTER □ New York, NY
Cohen, Matalie, Libn.
NORTH SHORE CONGREGATION ISRAEL -
OSCAR HILLEL PLOTKIN LIBRARY □ Glencoe, IL
Cohen, Morris L., Libn.
YALE UNIVERSITY - LAW LIBRARY □ New
Haven, CT
Cohen, Nancy, Med.Libn.
GRANT HOSPITAL - MEDICAL LIBRARY □
Columbus, OH
Cohen, Nancy, Asst.Libn.
PAINE WEBBER INC. - PAINE WEBBER BLYTH
EASTMAN - LIBRARY □ New York, NY
Cohen, Nancy B., Dir.
MOUNT SINAI HOSPITAL - HEALTH SCIENCES
LIBRARY† □ Hartford, CT
Cohen, Philip, Chf. Hydrologist
U.S. GEOLOGICAL SURVEY - WATER
RESOURCES DIVISION - NATL. WATER DATA
STORAGE & RETRIEVAL SYSTEM □ Reston, VA
Cohen, Roberta, Asst.Res.Libn.
ALCOLAC, INC. - RESEARCH LIBRARY □
Baltimore, MD
Cohen, Ronald D.
INDIANA UNIVERSITY NORTHWEST -
CALUMET REGIONAL ARCHIVES □ Gary, IN
Cohen, Rosemary, Hd., Cat.Sect.
U.S. DEPT. OF ENERGY - BROOKHAVEN NATL.
LABORATORY - TECHNICAL INFORMATION
DIVISION □ Upton, NY
Cohen, Samuel, Legal Res.Libn.
COLUMBIA UNIVERSITY - LAW LIBRARY □ New
York, NY
Cohen, Sharon, Dir. of Lib.Serv.
PROVIDENCE HOSPITAL - PANZNER MEMORIAL
LIBRARY† □ Southfield, MI
Cohen, Mrs. Shifra, Res.Anl.
BALTIMORE CITY DEPARTMENT OF HOUSING
AND COMMUNITY DEVELOPMENT - RESEARCH
LIBRARY □ Baltimore, MD
Cohler, Patricia, Libn.
NORTH SUBURBAN SYNAGOGUE BETH EL -
MAXWELL ABBELL LIBRARY □ Highland Park, IL
Cohn, Adele, Libn.
TEMPLE EMANU-EL - WILLIAM P. ENGEL
LIBRARY □ Birmingham, AL
Cohn, Alan M., Hum.Libn.
SOUTHERN ILLINOIS UNIVERSITY,
CARBONDALE - HUMANITIES DIVISION
LIBRARY □ Carbondale, IL
Cohn, Frieda S., Spec.
UNIVERSITY OF WISCONSIN, MADISON -
COMPUTER SCIENCES-COMPUTING CENTER-
STATISTICS STAFF COLLECTION □ Madison,
WI
Cohn, Jeannette, Ref.Libn.
TOBACCO INSTITUTE - LIBRARY □ Washington,
DC
Cohn, Dr. William L., Libn.
NICHOLS COLLEGE - CONANT LIBRARY □
Dudley, MA
Coil, Dorothy, Libn.
UNIVERSITY OF NOTRE DAME - LIFE SCIENCES
RESEARCH LIBRARY □ Notre Dame, IN

Coiner, Ann T., Ser.Libn.
TRINITY UNIVERSITY - LIBRARY □ San Antonio, TX

Coker, Sheila
CONTINENTAL TELEPHONE LABORATORIES - WALTER L. ROBERTS TECHNICAL LIBRARY □ Norcross, GA

Colabrese, Elizabeth, Libn.
DATA SYSTEMS ANALYSTS - TECHNICAL LIBRARY □ Pennsauken, NJ

Colavito, Greta, Lib.Hd.
THOMPSON (Boyce) INSTITUTE - LIBRARY □ Ithaca, NY

Colbeck, Lynda, Libn.
UNIVERSITY OF TORONTO - DAVID DUNLAP OBSERVATORY - LIBRARY □ Richmond Hill, ON

Colbert, Melissa, Libn.
BAKER & BOTTS - LAW LIBRARY □ Houston, TX

Colbert, R. Gary, Asst.Libn./Circ.
NATIONAL GEOGRAPHIC SOCIETY - ILLUSTRATIONS LIBRARY □ Washington, DC

Colburn, C.E., Libn.
GENERAL ELECTRIC COMPANY - APOLLO SYSTEMS - TECHNICAL AND SERVICES SUPPORT LIBRARY □ Houston, TX

Colby, Anita, Doc.Coord.
ERIC CLEARINGHOUSE FOR JUNIOR COLLEGES □ Los Angeles, CA

Colby, Anne, Dir.
RADCLIFFE COLLEGE - HENRY A. MURRAY RESEARCH CENTER □ Cambridge, MA

Colby, Autumn E., Res.Info.Spec.
GULF RESEARCH AND DEVELOPMENT COMPANY - TECHNICAL INFORMATION SERVICES □ Pittsburgh, PA

Colby, Charles C., III, Assoc.Libn.
HARVARD UNIVERSITY - SCHOOLS OF MEDICINE, DENTAL MEDICINE AND PUBLIC HEALTH - FRANCIS A. COUNTWAY LIBRARY □ Boston, MA

Colchin, Helen, Ref.Dept.Hd.
ALLEN COUNTY PUBLIC LIBRARY - INDIANA COLLECTION □ Fort Wayne, IN

Coldren, Sue, Libn.
PRESBYTERIAN DENVER HOSPITAL - BRADFORD MEMORIAL LIBRARY □ Denver, CO

Coldsmith, Elizabeth, Asst.Libn.
HARRISBURG HOSPITAL - HOSPITAL LIBRARY □ Harrisburg, PA

Cole, Beatrice, Libn.
AKWESASNE LIBRARY CULTURAL CENTER □ Hogansburg, NY

Cole, David C., Cur.
U.S. ARMY - FORT MEADE MUSEUM - LIBRARY □ Ft. George G. Meade, MD

Cole, Evelyn
UNIVERSITY OF NORTH DAKOTA - CHEMISTRY LIBRARY □ Grand Forks, ND

Cole, Georgia R., Coord.
VIGO COUNTY SCHOOL CORPORATION - INSTRUCTIONAL MATERIALS CENTER □ Terre Haute, IN

Cole, Georgina D., Lib.Dir.
CARLSBAD CITY LIBRARY - SPECIAL COLLECTIONS DEPARTMENT □ Carlsbad, CA

Cole, Glenore, Tech.Serv.
ARIZONA STATE REGIONAL LIBRARY FOR THE BLIND AND PHYSICALLY HANDICAPPED □ Phoenix, AZ

Cole, Herman, Jr., Dir.
ROSE-HULMAN INSTITUTE OF TECHNOLOGY - JOHN A. LOGAN LIBRARY □ Terre Haute, IN

Cole, Howson W., Libn.
VIRGINIA HISTORICAL SOCIETY - LIBRARY □ Richmond, VA

Cole, L.M., Internal Tech.Info.Serv.
BELL TELEPHONE LABORATORIES, INC. - LIBRARIES AND INFORMATION SYSTEMS CENTER □ Murray Hill, NJ

Cole, Lawrence, AV Supv.
KENT STATE UNIVERSITY - COMPUTER ASSISTED AND SELF INSTRUCTION CENTER □ Kent, OH

Cole, Lois H., Hd.Libn.
NORTHERN TRUST COMPANY - LIBRARY □ Chicago, IL

Cole, Lorna P., Libn.
UNIROYAL, LTD. - RESEARCH LABORATORIES LIBRARY □ Guelph, ON

Cole, Marsha, Hd.Libn.
MIDWEST RESEARCH INSTITUTE - PATTERSON REFERENCE LIBRARY AND ECONOMICS REFERENCE CENTER □ Kansas City, MO

Cole, Martha F., Libn.
BETH ISRAEL HOSPITAL - LASSOR AGOOS LIBRARY □ Boston, MA

Cole, Mary Elizabeth, Cons.Lib.Dev.
GEORGIA STATE DEPARTMENT OF EDUCATION - DIVISION OF PUBLIC LIBRARY SERVICES □ Atlanta, GA

Cole, Orin D., Hd.
PUBLIC LIBRARY OF YOUNGSTOWN AND MAHONING COUNTY - SCIENCE AND INDUSTRY DIVISION □ Youngstown, OH

Cole, Patricia N., Assoc.Libn.
FLORIDA HOSPITAL - DOCTORS' MEDICAL LIBRARY □ Orlando, FL

Cole, Sally M., Libn.
TINLEY PARK MENTAL HEALTH CENTER - INSTRUCTIONAL MEDIA LIBRARY □ Tinley Park, IL

Cole, Sara Turley, Law Libn.
MEMPHIS STATE UNIVERSITY LIBRARIES - SCHOOL OF LAW LIBRARY □ Memphis, TN

Cole, Terry, Cur.
ST. PETERSBURG HISTORICAL SOCIETY - LIBRARY AND ARCHIVES □ St. Petersburg, FL

Coleman, Angelique Banks, Asst.Libn.
AMERICAN BAPTIST THEOLOGICAL SEMINARY - T.L. HOLCOMB LIBRARY □ Nashville, TN

Coleman, Anna, Libn.
UNION CARBIDE CORPORATION - RESEARCH AND DEVELOPMENT LIBRARY □ Bound Brook, NJ

Coleman, Donna, Ref.Libn.
UNIVERSITY OF COLORADO MEDICAL CENTER - DENISON MEMORIAL LIBRARY □ Denver, CO

Coleman, Frances N., Act.Hd., Spec.Coll.
MISSISSIPPI STATE UNIVERSITY - MITCHELL MEMORIAL LIBRARY - SPECIAL COLLECTIONS □ Mississippi State, MS

Coleman, Joyce B., Libn.
BROWN UNIVERSITY - POPULATION STUDIES AND TRAINING CENTER - DEMOGRAPHY LIBRARY □ Providence, RI

Coleman, Merry J., Dir.
BECKER COUNTY HISTORICAL SOCIETY - WALTER D. BIRD MEMORIAL HISTORICAL LIBRARY □ Detroit Lakes, MN

Coleman, Mildred, Libn.
COLLEGE OF PREACHERS - LIBRARY □ Washington, DC

Coleman, Theodore H., Jr., Chf.Proc.Serv.
MEDICAL COLLEGE OF GEORGIA - LIBRARY □ Augusta, GA

Coleman, Virginia, Libn.
OHEV SHALOM SYNAGOGUE - RAY DOBLITZ MEMORIAL LIBRARY □ Wallingford, PA

Coles, Lynne L., Med.Libn.
MOUNT CLEMENS GENERAL HOSPITAL - STUCK MEDICAL LIBRARY □ Mt. Clemens, MI

Coles, Mary, Musm. Registrar
ARKANSAS STATE UNIVERSITY MUSEUM - HISTORICAL LIBRARY □ Jonesboro, AR

Coletti, Jeannette D., Libn.
NATIONAL ENDOWMENT FOR THE HUMANITIES - LIBRARY □ Washington, DC

Coletti, Margaret Hoekstra, Libn.
AMERICAN SOCIETY OF LAW & MEDICINE - SAGALL LIBRARY OF LAW, MEDICINE & HEALTH CARE □ Boston, MA

Coley, Betty A., Libn.
BAYLOR UNIVERSITY - ARMSTRONG BROWNING LIBRARY □ Waco, TX

Coley, Mildren S., Reader Serv.Libn.
ALABAMA STATE SUPREME COURT - SUPREME COURT AND STATE LAW LIBRARY □ Montgomery, AL

Coley, Robert E., Spec.Coll.Libn.
MILLERSVILLE STATE COLLEGE - HELEN A. GANSER LIBRARY □ Millersville, PA

Colfax, Leslie, Libn.
HOMOSEXUAL INFORMATION CENTER - TANGENT GROUP □ Hollywood, CA

Colgan, Dolores, Libn.
NATIONAL ECONOMIC RESEARCH ASSOCIATES, INC. - LIBRARY □ New York, NY

Colhoun, Jean, Hd. of Circ.
UNIVERSITY OF WESTERN ONTARIO - FACULTY OF EDUCATION LIBRARY □ London, ON

Collet, Lois W., Dir.
D'ARCY-MAC MANUS AND MASIUS - LIBRARY INFORMATION SERVICES □ Bloomfield Hills, MI

Collet, LCDR Mal J., Dir.
CITADEL - THE MILITARY COLLEGE OF SOUTH CAROLINA - ARCHIVES/MUSEUM □ Charleston, SC

Collett, Stewart, Mgr.
FALCONBRIDGE NICKEL MINES, LTD. - FALCONBRIDGE INFORMATION CENTRE □ Toronto, ON

Collette, Jacklyn, Libn.
SHRIVER (Eunice Kennedy) CENTER FOR MENTAL RETARDATION, INC. - LIBRARY □ Waltham, MA

Collette, Maria D., Med.Libn.
ST. LUKE'S HOSPITAL OF BETHLEHEM, PENNSYLVANIA - W.L. ESTES, JR. MEMORIAL LIBRARY □ Bethlehem, PA

Colley, Dr. Charles C., Dir.
UNIVERSITY OF TEXAS, ARLINGTON - LIBRARY - DIVISION OF SPECIAL COLLECTIONS AND ARCHIVES □ Arlington, TX

Colley, Marilyn, Program Lib.Asst.
UNIVERSITY OF MARYLAND, COLLEGE PARK - COMPUTER SCIENCE CENTER - PROGRAM LIBRARY □ College Park, MD

Collier, Alfred D., Cur.
COLLIER STATE PARK LOGGING MUSEUM - LIBRARY □ Klamath Falls, OR

Collier, Claire, Archv.
ROCKEFELLER UNIVERSITY - ROCKEFELLER ARCHIVE CENTER □ North Tarrytown, NY

Collier, Monica, Microforms
WAYNE STATE UNIVERSITY - G. FLINT PURDY LIBRARY □ Detroit, MI

Collier, Natalee, Dept.Hd.
LONG BEACH PUBLIC LIBRARY - FINE ARTS DEPARTMENT □ Long Beach, CA

Collier, Susan E., Tech.Libn.
INGERSOLL-RAND RESEARCH, INC. - TECHNICAL LIBRARY □ Princeton, NJ

Collier, Virginia, U.S.Govt.Doc.
OKLAHOMA STATE DEPARTMENT OF LIBRARIES □ Oklahoma City, OK

Colligan, Nancy, Info.Spec.
NATIONAL REHABILITATION INFORMATION CENTER □ Washington, DC

Collings, Wayne R., Professor
UNIVERSITY OF NEBRASKA, LINCOLN - C.Y. THOMPSON LIBRARY □ Lincoln, NE

Collins, Addie, Res.Libn.
SUTHERLAND, ASBILL & BRENNAN - LIBRARY □ Atlanta, GA

Collins, Catherine L., Cat.Libn.
CAPITAL DISTRICT LIBRARY COUNCIL FOR REFERENCE AND RESEARCH RESOURCES - BIBLIOGRAPHIC CENTER □ Latham, NY

Collins, Cheryl, Libn.
RILEY COUNTY HISTORICAL SOCIETY - SEATON MEMORIAL LIBRARY □ Manhattan, KS

Collins, Christiane C., Hd.Libn.
PARSONS SCHOOL OF DESIGN - ADAM L. GIMBEL DESIGN LIBRARY □ New York, NY

PERSONNE

PERSONNEL

Collins, Claire, Libn.
RESEARCH INSTITUTE FOR THE STUDY OF
MAN - LIBRARY □ New York, NY

Collins, D.L., Subdistrict Chf.
U.S. GEOLOGICAL SURVEY - WATER
RESOURCES LIBRARY □ Grand Junction, CO

Collins, Donald N., V.P.Commun.
FERTILIZER INSTITUTE □ Washington, DC

Collins, Donna I., Hd.Info.Serv. Group
CANADA - DEFENCE RESEARCH
ESTABLISHMENT ATLANTIC - LIBRARY □
Dartmouth, NS

Collins, Dorothy, Coord.
SAN DIEGO COUNTY - DEPARTMENT OF
EDUCATION - PROFESSIONAL RESOURCE AND
DEVELOPMENT CENTER □ San Diego, CA

Collins, Mrs. E., Hd.Circ.
UNIVERSITY OF TORONTO - ST. MICHAEL'S
COLLEGE - JOHN M. KELLY LIBRARY □ Toronto,
ON

Collins, Edward, Libn.
KETTERING COLLEGE OF MEDICAL ARTS -
LEARNING RESOURCES CENTER □ Kettering, OH

Collins, Elaine, Spec.Proj.
U.S. NATL. OCEANIC & ATMOSPHERIC
ADMINISTRATION - ENVIRONMENTAL DATA &
INFO. SERV. - NATL. OCEANOGRAPHIC DATA
CTR. □ Washington, DC

Collins, Frances W., Dir. of Musm.
ARTESIA HISTORICAL MUSEUM AND ART
CENTER - LIBRARY† □ Artesia, NM

Collins, Harry B., Jr., Pres.
BROWN BROTHERS - PHOTOGRAPH
COLLECTION □ Sterling, PA

Collins, Jane, Cat.
NATIONAL GALLERY OF ART - LIBRARY □
Washington, DC

Collins, Janet, Map Cur.
WESTERN WASHINGTON UNIVERSITY -
DEPARTMENT OF GEOGRAPHY AND REGIONAL
PLANNING - MAP LIBRARY □ Bellingham, WA

Collins, Jean, Assoc.Dir.
NORTHERN ARIZONA UNIVERSITY - LIBRARIES
□ Flagstaff, AZ

Collins, Jill
SASKATCHEWAN PIPING INDUSTRY JOINT
TRAINING BOARD - LIBRARY† □ Regina, SK

Collins, Kay, Libn.
U.S. RAILROAD RETIREMENT BOARD - LIBRARY
□ Chicago, IL

Collins, Linda S., Libn.
PORTSMOUTH RECEIVING HOSPITAL -
MEDICAL LIBRARY □ Portsmouth, OH

Collins, Lucie, Co-Dir.
SHARON HOSPITAL - HEALTH SCIENCES
LIBRARY □ Sharon, CT

Collins, M. Eileen, Doc.Libn.
U.S. ARMY - NATICK RESEARCH AND
DEVELOPMENT LABORATORIES - TECHNICAL
LIBRARY □ Natick, MA

Collins, Marlene F., Off.Mgr.
GEAUGA COUNTY HISTORICAL SOCIETY -
LIBRARY □ Burton, OH

Collins, Sr. Mary Agnella, S.C.N., Dir.
OUR LADY OF PEACE HOSPITAL - MEDICAL
LIBRARY □ Louisville, KY

Collins, Pat, Lib.Techn.
MANITOBA - DEPT. OF CONSUMER &
CORPORATE AFFAIRS & ENVIRONMENT -
DEPT. REF. SERV. - ENVIRONMENTAL MGT.
LIB. □ Winnipeg, MB

Collins, Patti Jill, Doc.Cat./Libn.
UNIVERSITY OF NEW BRUNSWICK - LAW
LIBRARY □ Fredericton, NB

Collins, Phyllis L., Libn.
TOBEY HOSPITAL - STILLMAN LIBRARY □
Wareham, MA

Collins, Rosemary, Mgr.
ASSOCIATION OF NATIONAL ADVERTISERS -
LIBRARY □ New York, NY

Collins, Sara, Virginiana Libn.
ARLINGTON COUNTY CENTRAL LIBRARY -
VIRGINIANA COLLECTION □ Arlington, VA

Collins, Sara, Virginiana Libn.
ARLINGTON COUNTY CENTRAL LIBRARY -
ZONTA ORAL HISTORY COLLECTION □
Arlington, VA

Collins, Sheila A., Libn.
DUFF AND PHELPS, INC. - RESEARCH LIBRARY
□ Chicago, IL

Collins, Sherri, Asst.Mgr.
NATIONAL COLLEGE OF DISTRICT ATTORNEYS
- RESOURCE CENTER □ Houston, TX

Collins-Williams, Jean, Hd., Ref.Serv.
ONTARIO - MINISTRY OF LABOUR - LIBRARY □
Toronto, ON

Collord, Kathryn, Libn.
FIRST UNITED METHODIST CHURCH - LIBRARY
□ Glen Ellyn, IL

Collyer, Dolores G., Adm.
AMERICAN SOCIETY FOR TESTING AND
MATERIALS - INFORMATION CENTER □
Philadelphia, PA

Collymore, Deborrah J., Asst. to Dir.
ERIC CLEARINGHOUSE ON URBAN EDUCATION
□ New York, NY

Colman, Gould, Univ.Archv.
CORNELL UNIVERSITY - DEPARTMENT OF
MANUSCRIPTS AND ARCHIVES □ Ithaca, NY

Colon, Carlos, Libn.
MEMPHIS-SHELBY COUNTY PUBLIC LIBRARY
AND INFO. CTR. - SCIENCE/BUSINESS/SOCIAL
SCIENCES DEPT. □ Memphis, TN

Colon, Felix, Asst.Dir.
UNIVERSITY OF PUERTO RICO - GRADUATE
SCHOOL OF PLANNING - LIBRARY □ Rio Piedras,
PR

Colon, Magda Rivera, Libn.
UNIVERSITY OF PUERTO RICO - SCHOOL OF
PUBLIC ADMINISTRATION - LIBRARY □ Rio
Piedras, PR

Colon, Mayra N.
UNIVERSITY OF PUERTO RICO - GRADUATE
SCHOOL OF PLANNING - LIBRARY □ Rio Piedras,
PR

Colston, Stephen A., Dir.
SAN DIEGO STATE UNIVERSITY - SAN DIEGO
HISTORY RESEARCH CENTER □ San Diego, CA

Colter, Carole, Health Sci.Libn.
MIDLAND HOSPITAL CENTER - HEALTH
SCIENCES LIBRARY □ Midland, MI

Colter, J. Elaine, Libn.
SAN DIEGO HALL OF SCIENCE - BERNICE
HARDING LIBRARY □ San Diego, CA

Colton, Margaret, Libn.
PHOENIX MUTUAL LIFE INSURANCE COMPANY
- LIBRARY □ Hartford, CT

Colucci, Patrick D., Base Libn.
U.S. AIR FORCE BASE - POPE BASE LIBRARY □
Pope AFB, NC

Colvig, Richard, Sr.Libn.
OAKLAND PUBLIC LIBRARY - ART, MUSIC,
RECREATION □ Oakland, CA

Colvin, Gloria, Assoc.Libn.
DURHAM HERALD-SUN NEWSPAPER - LIBRARY
□ Durham, NC

Colvin, Linda, Asst.
CHARLESTON GAZETTE-MAIL - LIBRARY □
Charleston, WV

Colwell, David, Ref.Libn.
SUSQUEHANNA COUNTY HISTORICAL SOCIETY
AND FREE LIBRARY ASSOCIATION □ Montrose,
PA

Colwell, Judith, Libn.
BAPTIST CONVENTION OF ONTARIO AND
QUEBEC - CANADIAN BAPTIST ARCHIVES □
Hamilton, ON

Colyer, Mrs. Neal
MADISON COUNTY HISTORICAL SOCIETY, INC.
- LIBRARY □ Richmond, KY

Coman, Patrick, Supv.Dept.Asst.
METROPOLITAN MUSEUM OF ART - THOMAS J.
WATSON LIBRARY □ New York, NY

Combe, David A., Libn.
TULANE UNIVERSITY OF LOUISIANA - LAW
LIBRARY □ New Orleans, LA

Combouzou, Mable T., Assoc.Dir.
LOUISIANA STATE OFFICE OF THE SECRETARY
OF STATE - STATE ARCHIVES AND RECORDS
SERVICE □ Baton Rouge, LA

Combs, Jim, Chf./Off.Serv.Sect.
IOWA STATE DEPARTMENT OF
ENVIRONMENTAL QUALITY - TECHNICAL
LIBRARY □ Des Moines, IA

Comeau, Eric, Dir.
CANADA - AGRICULTURE CANADA -
EXPERIMENTAL FARM LIBRARY □ La Pocatiere,
PQ

Commerton, B. Anne, Dir.
SUNY - COLLEGE AT OSWEGO - PENFIELD
LIBRARY □ Oswego, NY

Commes, Kristy, Chf.Spec.Serv.Div.
WASHINGTON STATE LIBRARY □ Olympia, WA

Compas, German, Ref.
CRAVATH, SWAINE, AND MOORE - LAW
LIBRARY □ New York, NY

Comport, Warren W., Libn.
GENERAL MOTORS CORPORATION - DIESEL
EQUIPMENT DIVISION - LIBRARY □ Grand
Rapids, MI

Compton, Carl B., Dir.
INSTITUTO INTERAMERICANO - LIBRARY† □
Denton, TX

Compton, Erlinda, Res.Hd.
BOEING COMPANY - SEATTLE SERVICES
DIVISION - RENTON LIBRARY □ Seattle, WA

Compton, Miles S., Hd.Libn.
SIMPSON COLLEGE - START-KILGOUR
MEMORIAL LIBRARY □ San Francisco, CA

Compton, Olga M., Mgr., TIC
CENTRAL VERMONT PUBLIC SERVICE
CORPORATION - TECHNICAL INFORMATION
CENTER □ Rutland, VT

Compton, Stephany R., Libn.
INSTITUTO INTERAMERICANO - LIBRARY† □
Denton, TX

Comptor, Anne, Coord.
JOHNS HOPKINS UNIVERSITY - POPULATION
INFORMATION PROGRAM □ Baltimore, MD

Conahan, J.E., Acq.Libn.
LOCKHEED MISSILES & SPACE COMPANY, INC.
- TECHNICAL INFORMATION CENTER □ Palo
Alto, CA

Conant, Margaret, Hd., Rd.Serv. & ILL
COLLEGE OF ST. CATHERINE - LIBRARY -
WOMAN'S COLLECTION □ St. Paul, MN

Conaway, Sr. Mary Christine, Libn.
ST. JOSEPH HOSPITAL - LIBRARY □ Ottumwa,
IA

Conde, Ana I., Hd.
INTER-AMERICAN DEVELOPMENT BANK -
TECHNICAL INFORMATION CENTER □
Washington, DC

Condon, Erika, Lib.Dir.
MOUNT ST. MARY'S COLLEGE - NEWMAN
SEMINAR □ Los Angeles, CA

Condon, Paulina, Acq.Libn.
U.S. AIR FORCE - AIR FORCE SYSTEMS
COMMAND - AIR FORCE GEOPHYSICS
LABORATORY - RESEARCH LIBRARY† □
Bedford, MA

Condron, Barbara J., Libn.
U.S. GEOLOGICAL SURVEY - WATER
RESOURCES DIVISION - COLORADO DISTRICT
LIBRARY □ Denver, CO

Conelley, Jean M., Asst.Dir.Tech.Serv.
UNIVERSITY OF MASSACHUSETTS MEDICAL
SCHOOL & WORCESTER DISTRICT MEDICAL
SOCIETY - LIBRARY □ Worcester, MA

Congdon, Robert, Media Spec.
DARGAN-CARVER LIBRARY □ Nashville, TN

Congdon, Rodney H., Chf. Law Libn.
FEDERAL RESERVE BANK OF NEW YORK - LAW
LIBRARY DIVISION □ New York, NY

Congleton, Caryl, Libn.
FLORIDA POWER & LIGHT COMPANY -
CORPORATE LIBRARY □ Miami, FL

Coniglio, Susan, Ref.Libn.
U.S. DEPT. OF ENERGY - SANDIA NATL.
LABORATORIES, LIVERMORE - TECHNICAL
LIBRARY □ Livermore, CA

Conklin, Annette, Rsrcs.Libn.
NOVATO UNIFIED SCHOOL DISTRICT -
INSTRUCTIONAL MATERIALS CENTER □
Novato, CA

Conklin, Charlotte L., Libn.
MC GEAN CHEMICAL COMPANY, INC. -
RESEARCH LABORATORY LIBRARY □ Cleveland,
OH

Conklin, Curt, Cat.Libn.
BRIGHAM YOUNG UNIVERSITY - J. REUBEN
CLARK LAW SCHOOL LIBRARY □ Provo, UT

Conklin, Michael, Ref.Libn.
WELLS FARGO BANK - LIBRARY □ San Francisco,
CA

Conklin, Susan L., Hist.
GENESEE COUNTY - DEPARTMENT OF HISTORY
- RESEARCH LIBRARY □ Batavia, NY

Conkling, Thomas W., Hd.
PENNSYLVANIA STATE UNIVERSITY -
ENGINEERING LIBRARY □ University Park, PA

Conkling, Thomas W., Libn.
PRINCETON UNIVERSITY - PLASMA PHYSICS
LIBRARY □ Princeton, NJ

Conlan, Ann A., Libn.
U.S. VETERANS ADMINISTRATION (FL-Bay
Pines) - CENTER LIBRARY □ Bay Pines, FL

Conley, John, Media Spec.
PARKLAND COLLEGE - LEARNING RESOURCE
CENTER □ Champaign, IL

Conley, Karen, Libn.
OCEANIC INSTITUTE LIBRARY □ Waimanalo, HI

Conley, Patricia, Ref.Libn.
MINNESOTA STATE LEGISLATIVE REFERENCE
LIBRARY □ St. Paul, MN

Conley, Philip, Libn.
ASSOCIATED GRANTMAKERS OF
MASSACHUSETTS, INC. - MASSACHUSETTS
REGIONAL FOUNDATION LIBRARY □ Boston, MA

Conley, Sharon A., Asst.Libn.
MIDDLESEX LAW LIBRARY ASSOCIATION -
LIBRARY □ Lowell, MA

Conlon, Rosa K., Sect.Mgr.
AVON PRODUCTS, INC. - TECHNICAL
INFORMATION CENTER LIBRARY □ Suffern, NY

Connaughton, Theresa, Asst.Supv., Tech.Proc.
UNIVERSITY OF CALIFORNIA - LOS ALAMOS
NATIONAL LABORATORY - LIBRARY □ Los
Alamos, NM

Connell, Carol, Asst.Libn.
INDIANA UNIVERSITY OF PENNSYLVANIA -
UNIVERSITY LIBRARY □ Indiana, PA

Connell, Michael, Dir.
MONTCLAIR PUBLIC LIBRARY - LOCAL
HISTORY FILE □ Montclair, NJ

Connell, Toni, Lib.Ck.
TEXAS STATE DEPARTMENT OF HEALTH -
LIBRARY □ Austin, TX

Connelley, Melba, Libn.
TEXAS ELECTRIC SERVICE COMPANY -
LIBRARY □ Fort Worth, TX

Connelly, John W., Leg. & Res.Asst.
ST. PAUL CITY COUNCIL - RESEARCH LIBRARY
□ St. Paul, MN

Conner, Carol N., Chf., Lib.Serv.
U.S. VETERANS ADMINISTRATION (WY-
Sheridan) - MEDICAL CENTER LIBRARY □
Sheridan, WY

Conner, Claire, Act.Div.Hd.
INDIANAPOLIS-MARION COUNTY PUBLIC
LIBRARY - ARTS DIVISION □ Indianapolis, IN

Connery, Susan E., Dir.
TRENTON TIMES - LIBRARY □ Trenton, NJ

Connick, Kathleen D., Med.Libn.
GOOD SAMARITAN HOSPITAL - MEDICAL
LIBRARY □ Cincinnati, OH

Conning, Carmela A., Libn.
NATIONAL CENTER FOR APPROPRIATE
TECHNOLOGY - LIBRARY □ Butte, MT

Connolly, Betty F., Chf., Lib.Serv.
U.S. VETERANS ADMINISTRATION (CA-Long
Beach) - MEDICAL CENTER LIBRARY □ Long
Beach, CA

Connolly, Bruce E., Hd., Tech.Serv.
NEW YORK STATE COLLEGE OF CERAMICS,
ALFRED UNIVERSITY - SAMUEL R. SCHOLES
LIBRARY OF CERAMICS □ Alfred, NY

Connolly, Elizabeth J., Rd.Adv.Libn.
U.S. ARMY - MILITARY ACADEMY - LIBRARY □
West Point, NY

Connolly, Florence, Cur.
BOSTON PUBLIC LIBRARY - FINE ARTS
DEPARTMENT □ Boston, MA

Connolly, Heather, Chf.Libn.
MECHANICS' INSTITUTE OF MONTREAL -
ATWATER LIBRARY □ Montreal, PQ

Connolly, Sr. Madeline, Libn.
ST. AUGUSTINE'S SEMINARY - LIBRARY □
Scarborough, ON

Connolly, Mary, Ref.Libn.
EASTMAN KODAK COMPANY - RESEARCH
LABORATORIES - RESEARCH LIBRARY □
Rochester, NY

Connolly, Patricia, Cur.
PRICE-POTTENGER NUTRITION FOUNDATION -
LIBRARY □ San Diego, CA

Connolly, Robert, Lib.Asst.
COLUMBIA UNIVERSITY - PATERNO LIBRARY □
New York, NY

Connor, A. Christine, Med.Libn.
ST. BARNABAS MEDICAL CENTER - MEDICAL
STAFF LIBRARY □ Livingston, NJ

Connor, Billie M., Principal Libn.
LOS ANGELES PUBLIC LIBRARY - SCIENCE &
TECHNOLOGY DEPARTMENT □ Los Angeles, CA

Connor, Elizabeth, Evening Serv.Libn.
JOHNS HOPKINS UNIVERSITY - WILLIAM H.
WELCH MEDICAL LIBRARY □ Baltimore, MD

Connor, Lynn S., Libn.
MARION COUNTY LAW LIBRARY □ Indianapolis,
IN

Connor, Nan, Info.Dir.
COMO ZOO - LIBRARY □ St. Paul, MN

Connor, Tina, Dir., of Pubns.
HISTORIC LANDMARKS FOUNDATION OF
INDIANA, INC. - INFORMATION CENTER □
Indianapolis, IN

Connors, John F., Adm.Libn.
U.S. VETERANS ADMINISTRATION (NY-Albany)
- MEDICAL CENTER LIBRARY (500/142-D) □
Albany, NY

Connors, Margaret, Libn.
SANTA BARBARA BOTANIC GARDEN - LIBRARY
□ Santa Barbara, CA

Connors, Matthew J., Sys.Anl.
U.S. DEPT. OF ENERGY - SANDIA NATL.
LABORATORIES, LIVERMORE - TECHNICAL
LIBRARY □ Livermore, CA

Conole, Philip, Music Record Cur.
SUNY AT BINGHAMTON - FINE ARTS LIBRARY □
Binghamton, NY

Conole, Philip, Cur.
SUNY AT BINGHAMTON - SPECIAL
COLLECTIONS □ Binghamton, NY

Conoley, Helen E., Libn.
U.S. NAVY - NAVAL SURFACE WEAPONS
CENTER - WHITE OAK LIBRARY □ Silver Spring,
MD

Conquest, Robert, Cur., Russia & Europe
STANFORD UNIVERSITY - HOOVER
INSTITUTION ON WAR, REVOLUTION AND
PEACE - LIBRARY □ Stanford, CA

Conrad, Agnes C., State Archv.
HAWAII STATE DEPARTMENT OF
ACCOUNTING AND GENERAL SERVICES -
PUBLIC ARCHIVES □ Honolulu, HI

Conrad, Glenn R., Dir.
UNIVERSITY OF SOUTHWESTERN LOUISIANA -
CENTER FOR LOUISIANA STUDIES □ Lafayette,
LA

Conrad, James, Coord.
EAST TEXAS STATE UNIVERSITY - ORAL
HISTORY PROGRAM □ Commerce, TX

Conrad, LaVerna J., Libn.
WHITE RIVER VALLEY HISTORICAL SOCIETY
MUSEUM - LIBRARY □ Auburn, WA

Conrad, Mary T., Trade Spec.
U.S. DEPT. OF COMMERCE - INTERNATIONAL
TRADE ADMINISTRATION - BALTIMORE
DISTRICT OFFICE LIBRARY □ Baltimore, MD

Conron, Frank, Sr.Libn.
NEW YORK STATE LIBRARY FOR THE BLIND
AND VISUALLY HANDICAPPED □ Albany, NY

Conroy, Audrey, Libn.
CANADA - FISHERIES & OCEANS -
NEWFOUNDLAND REGIONAL LIBRARY □ St.
John's, NF

Conroy, Marcia E., Cur. of Educ.
MASSACHUSETTS INSTITUTE OF TECHNOLOGY
- M.I.T. MUSEUM AND HISTORICAL
COLLECTIONS □ Cambridge, MA

Constantin, Celine, Ref. & Animation
COLLEGE DE JONQUIERE - CENTRE DE
RESSOURCES EDUCATIVES □ Jonquiere, PQ

Constantine, Marianne, Med.Libn.
MONTREAL CHEST HOSPITAL CENTRE -
MEDICAL LIBRARY □ Montreal, PQ

Conti, Gina, Lit.Chem.
GOODYEAR TIRE AND RUBBER COMPANY -
TECHNICAL INFORMATION CENTER □ Akron,
OH

Contreras, Rudolph R., Act.Libn.
U. S. GEOLOGICAL SURVEY - WATER
RESOURCES DIVISION - LIBRARY □
Indianapolis, IN

Convery, Thomas, Asst.Libn.
CAMDEN COUNTY BAR ASSOCIATION - LAW
LIBRARY† □ Camden, NJ

Conway, Claire E., Adm.
SCHWENKFELDER LIBRARY □ Pennsburg, PA

Conway, Jeanne, Hd., Pub.Serv.
GALLAUDET COLLEGE LIBRARY - SPECIAL
COLLECTIONS □ Washington, DC

Conway, John, Dir.
MONMOUTH MEDICAL CENTER - DR. FRANK J.
ALTSCHUL MEDICAL LIBRARY □ Long Branch, NJ

Conway, Mary E., Chf., Lib.Serv.
U.S. VETERANS ADMINISTRATION (WV-
Clarksburg) - MEDICAL CENTER LIBRARY
SERVICE □ Clarksburg, WV

Conway, Rita, Asst.Libn.
LEBOEUF, LAMB, LEIBY & MAC RAE - LIBRARY □
New York, NY

Conyne, Rita, Res.Libn.
PENNWALT CORPORATION - PENNWALT
PHARMACEUTICAL DIVISION - RESEARCH
LIBRARY □ Rochester, NY

Coogan, Helen M., Supv., Lib.
ROCKWELL INTERNATIONAL - SCIENCE
CENTER LIBRARY □ Thousand Oaks, CA

Cook, Alan, Asst.Libn.
PRINCETON UNIVERSITY - ENGINEERING
LIBRARY □ Princeton, NJ

Cook, Alan D., Horticulturist
DAWES ARBORETUM - LIBRARY □ Newark, OH

Cook, Cathy, Pub.Lib.Cons.
OKLAHOMA STATE DEPARTMENT OF
LIBRARIES □ Oklahoma City, OK

Cook, D. Louise, Archv.
KING (Martin Luther, Jr.) CENTER FOR SOCIAL
CHANGE - KING LIBRARY AND ARCHIVES □
Atlanta, GA

Cook, Elizabeth, Hd.Per.
INTERNATIONAL MONETARY FUND/WORLD
BANK - JOINT BANK-FUND LIBRARY □
Washington, DC

Cook, Elizabeth, Tech.Asst.
SAN DIEGO STATE UNIVERSITY - SOCIAL
SCIENCE RESEARCH LABORATORY - LIBRARY □
San Diego, CA

**P
E
R
S
O
N
N
E
L**

Cook, Elizabeth C., Park Techn.
U.S. NATL. PARK SERVICE - STONES RIVER
NATL. BATTLEFIELD - LIBRARY □ Murfreesboro,
TN
Cook, Ellen, Lib.Chf.
U.S. DEPT. OF THE INTERIOR - NATURAL
RESOURCES LIBRARY □ Washington, DC
Cook, Esther M., Libn.
WESTMINSTER PRESBYTERIAN CHURCH -
LIBRARY† □ Alexandria, VA
Cook, Florence, Cat.
WINEBRENNER THEOLOGICAL SEMINARY -
LIBRARY □ Findlay, OH
Cook, Miss Francis, Libn.
CENTRAL CHRISTIAN CHURCH - LIBRARY □
Lexington, KY
Cook, Guinevere, Asst.Libn.
HINSDALE SANITARIUM AND HOSPITAL - A.C.
LARSON LIBRARY† □ Hinsdale, IL
Cook, J. Frank, Dir.
UNIVERSITY OF WISCONSIN, MADISON -
ARCHIVES □ Madison, WI
Cook, Janice L., Legal Lit.Libn.
KANSAS STATE SUPREME COURT - LAW
LIBRARY □ Topeka, KS
Cook, Jean, Ser.
IOWA STATE UNIVERSITY - LIBRARY □ Ames,
IA
Cook, Kathy, Asst.Libn.
SOUTHERN ILLINOIS UNIVERSITY,
CARBONDALE - EDUCATION DIVISION LIBRARY
□ Carbondale, IL
Cook, Kevin L., Doc.Ref.Libn.
ARKANSAS STATE UNIVERSITY - DEAN B.
ELLIS LIBRARY □ State University, AR
Cook, Lawrence P., Dir.
U.S. NATL. BUREAU OF STANDARDS - PHASE
DIAGRAMS FOR CERAMISTS □ Washington, DC
Cook, Lucy, Asst.Libn.
PHILIP MORRIS, U.S.A. - RESEARCH CENTER
LIBRARY □ Richmond, VA
Cook, Margaret C., Cur., Mss./Rare Bks.
COLLEGE OF WILLIAM AND MARY - EARL
GREGG SWEM LIBRARY □ Williamsburg, VA
Cook, Marilyn, Dir.
WASHINGTON HOSPITAL CENTER - MEDICAL
LIBRARY □ Washington, DC
Cook, Marjorie E., Med.Libn.
WEST VOLUSIA MEMORIAL HOSPITAL -
MEDICAL LIBRARY □ De Land, FL
Cook, Mary Aline, Libn.
NEW HARMONY WORKINGMEN'S INSTITUTE -
LIBRARY AND MUSEUM □ New Harmony, IN
Cook, Mary E., Dir. Of Lib.Serv.
EAST TEXAS STATE UNIVERSITY - JAMES
GILLIAM GEE LIBRARY □ Commerce, TX
Cook, Nedra, Libn.
FORT SANDERS REGIONAL MEDICAL CENTER -
MEDICAL/NURSING LIBRARY □ Knoxville, TN
Cook, Pat, Coord. Media Ctr.
NORTHERN ARIZONA UNIVERSITY - LIBRARIES
□ Flagstaff, AZ
Cook, Patricia, Libn.
U.S. NATL. MARINE FISHERIES SERVICE -
NORTHWEST & ALASKA FISHERIES CENTER -
LIBRARY □ Seattle, WA
Cook, Patricia, ILL
U.S. NAVY - NAVAL RESEARCH LABORATORY -
RUTH H. HOOKER TECHNICAL LIBRARY □
Washington, DC
Cook, Paul, Lib.Dir.
PARADE PUBLICATIONS, INC. - LIBRARY □ New
York, NY
Cook, Richard L., Hosp.Libn.
HINSDALE SANITARIUM AND HOSPITAL - A.C.
LARSON LIBRARY† □ Hinsdale, IL
Cook, Romilda F., Libn.
BAPTIST MEDICAL CENTER - MEDICAL
LIBRARY □ Birmingham, AL
Cook, Sherry, Libn.
BECHTEL - DATA PROCESSING LIBRARY □ San
Francisco, CA

Cook, Sterling, Cur.
MC GUFFEY (William Holmes) HOUSE AND
MUSEUM - LIBRARY □ Oxford, OH
Cook, Sue E.G., Exec.Sec.
DAVIS (J.M.) GUN MUSEUM - RESEARCH
LIBRARY □ Claremore, OK
Cook, Virginia, Asst.Libn.
NORTH SHORE UNIVERSITY HOSPITAL -
DANIEL CARROLL PAYSON MEDICAL LIBRARY □
Manhasset, NY
Cook, Virginia I., Med.Libn.
NASSAU HOSPITAL - BENJAMIN WHITE
SEAMAN MEDICAL LIBRARY □ Mineola, NY
Cook, William, Libn.
ONONDAGA COUNTY PUBLIC LIBRARY - LOCAL
HISTORY AND GENEALOGY DEPARTMENT □
Syracuse, NY
Cooke, Mrs. A., Sr.Ref./SDI Libn.
CANADA - HEALTH AND WELFARE CANADA -
DEPARTMENTAL LIBRARY SERVICES □ Ottawa,
ON
Cooke, Mrs. Dudley S., Libn.
ROCKY HILL HISTORICAL SOCIETY - ACADEMY
HALL MUSEUM - LIBRARY □ Rocky Hill, CT
Cooke, Eileen D., Dir.
AMERICAN LIBRARY ASSOCIATION -
WASHINGTON OFFICE □ Washington, DC
Cooke, Mrs. G.A., Libn.
UNIVERSITY OF ALBERTA - BOREAL INSTITUTE
FOR NORTHERN STUDIES - LIBRARY □
Edmonton, AB
Cooke, Marcia Lynn, Libn.
UNIVERSITY OF WISCONSIN, MADISON -
WASHBURN OBSERVATORY - WOODMAN
ASTRONOMICAL LIBRARY □ Madison, WI
Cooke, Marischa B., Dir.
CALDWELL COMMUNITY COLLEGE AND
TECHNICAL INSTITUTE - LEARNING RESOURCE
CENTER □ Hudson, NC
Cooke, Mr. O.A., Chf.Cat.
CANADA - NATIONAL DEFENCE -
DIRECTORATE OF HISTORY LIBRARY □ Ottawa,
ON
Cooke, Sally, Circ. & Cat.Asst.
NORTH CENTRAL COLLEGE - LIBRARY □
Naperville, IL
Cooke, Sarah E., Archv.
TIPPECANOE COUNTY HISTORICAL
ASSOCIATION - ALAMEDA MC COLLOUGH
RESEARCH & GENEALOGY LIBRARY □ Lafayette,
IN
Cooklock, Richard A., Dir.
UNIVERSITY OF WISCONSIN, RIVER FALLS -
CHALMER DAVEE LIBRARY □ River Falls, WI
Cooks, Sondra Y., Libn.
AMERICAN BAPTIST THEOLOGICAL SEMINARY
- T.L. HOLCOMB LIBRARY □ Nashville, TN
Cooley, Dr. Everett L., Asst.Dir./Univ.Archv.
UNIVERSITY OF UTAH - SPECIAL COLLECTIONS
DEPARTMENT □ Salt Lake City, UT
Cooley, Terrence, Res.Anl.
MILWAUKEE COUNTY BOARD OF SUPERVISORS
- RESEARCH LIBRARY □ Milwaukee, WI
Cooling, Benjamin Franklin, Asst.Dir./Hist.Serv.
U.S. ARMY MILITARY HISTORY INSTITUTE □
Carlisle Barracks, PA
Coombe, Jane, Educ.Ext.Coord.
SASKATCHEWAN - DEPARTMENT OF LABOUR -
WOMEN'S DIVISION - RESOURCE CENTRE □
Regina, SK
Coombs, James A., Libn.
SOUTHWEST MISSOURI STATE UNIVERSITY -
MAP COLLECTION □ Springfield, MO
Coombs, Leonard, Asst.Archv.
UNIVERSITY OF MICHIGAN - MICHIGAN
HISTORICAL COLLECTIONS - BENTLEY
HISTORICAL LIBRARY □ Ann Arbor, MI
Coomes, Rev. J. Eugene, S.J., Libn.
ST. LOUIS UNIVERSITY - COLLEGE OF
PHILOSOPHY AND LETTERS - FUSZ MEMORIAL
LIBRARY □ St. Louis, MO

Coomes, Mildred, Cat.
OWENSBORO AREA MUSEUM - LIBRARY □
Owensboro, KY
Coon, Christa K., Exec.Dir.Lib.Serv.
JEFFERSON COUNTY PUBLIC SCHOOLS R1 -
PROFESSIONAL LIBRARY MEDIA CENTER □
Lakewood, CO
Coon, Velma, Ser.Cat.
U.S. DEPT. OF THE TREASURY - INFORMATION
SERVICES DIVISION - TREASURY DEPT.
LIBRARY □ Washington, DC
Coonce, Anne, Asst.Libn.
KEMPER GROUP - LIBRARY □ Long Grove, IL
Cooney, Jane, Mgr.
CANADIAN IMPERIAL BANK OF COMMERCE -
INFORMATION CENTRE □ Toronto, ON
Cooney, Jane, Chf., Oper.
U.S. ARMY - MISSILE COMMAND & MARSHALL
SPACE FLIGHT CENTER - REDSTONE
SCIENTIFIC INFORMATION CENTER □
Redstone Arsenal, AL
Cooney, Mary Ann, Circ.Libn.
MARYWOOD COLLEGE - LEARNING RESOURCES
CENTER □ Scranton, PA
Coonrod, Florence, Sr.Libn.
NEW YORK STATE LIBRARY - SCIENCES/
HEALTH SCIENCES/TECHNOLOGY REFERENCE
SERVICES □ Albany, NY
Cooper, Amy D., Libn.
CENTER FOR EARLY EDUCATION - LAURA M.
ELLIS MEMORIAL LIBRARY □ Los Angeles, CA
Cooper, Beverly Jane, Libn.
UNIVERSITY OF WASHINGTON - GRADUATE
SCHOOL - JOINT CENTER FOR GRADUATE
STUDY - LIBRARY □ Richland, WA
Cooper, Brian A., ILL Libn.
LEBOEUF, LAMB, LEIBY & MAC RAE - LIBRARY □
New York, NY
Cooper, Byron D., Assoc.Dir.
INDIANA UNIVERSITY - LAW LIBRARY □
Bloomington, IN
Cooper, Carolyn, Ref.
UNIVERSITY OF ALABAMA - SCHOOL OF LAW
LIBRARY □ University, AL
Cooper, Cathy, Assoc.Libn.
KEENELAND ASSOCIATION - LIBRARY □
Lexington, KY
Cooper, Diana, Fine Arts Ref.Libn.
UNIVERSITY OF BRITISH COLUMBIA - FINE
ARTS DIVISION □ Vancouver, BC
Cooper, Eileen, Asst.Libn.
DELAWARE LAW SCHOOL OF WIDENER
UNIVERSITY - LAW LIBRARY □ Wilmington, DE
Cooper, Hope, Adm.
CAMDEN DISTRICT HERITAGE FOUNDATION -
RESEARCH ARCHIVES □ Camden, SC
Cooper, Inez S., Spec.Coll.Libn.
SOUTHERN UTAH STATE COLLEGE - LIBRARY -
SPECIAL COLLECTIONS DEPARTMENT □ Cedar
City, UT
Cooper, Jane G., Asst.Libn.
MAINE MEDICAL CENTER - LIBRARY □ Portland,
ME
Cooper, John E., Lib. Group Supv.
BELL TELEPHONE LABORATORIES, INC. -
TECHNICAL LIBRARY □ Holmdel, NJ
Cooper, Joyce, Libn.
U.S. FISH & WILDLIFE SERVICE - FISH
FARMING EXPERIMENTAL STATION - LIBRARY
□ Stuttgart, AR
Cooper, Joyce R., Exec.Sec.
COUNTRY DOCTOR MUSEUM - LIBRARY □
Bailey, NC
Cooper, Mrs. M.R., Exec.Asst.
PHILADELPHIA PSYCHOANALYTIC INSTITUTE -
LIBRARY □ Philadelphia, PA
Cooper, Marguerite, Med.Libn.
ARIZONA STATE HOSPITAL - MEDICAL
LIBRARY □ Phoenix, AZ
Cooper, Mary Jo, Asst.Cur.
AUSTIN PUBLIC LIBRARY - AUSTIN-TRAVIS
COUNTY COLLECTION □ Austin, TX

Cooper, Mary L., Tech.Serv.Libn.
UNIVERSITY OF VIRGINIA - ARTHUR J.
MORRIS LAW LIBRARY □ Charlottesville, VA
Cooper, Nancy, Dir., Lib./Info.Serv.
GRUY (H.J.) & ASSOCIATES, INC. - LIBRARY □
Irving, TX
Cooper, Norma M., Music Libn.
PACIFIC UNIVERSITY - SCHOOL OF MUSIC -
LIBRARY □ Forest Grove, OR
Cooper, Richard S., Act.Hd.
UNIVERSITY OF CALIFORNIA, BERKELEY -
EAST ASIATIC LIBRARY □ Berkeley, CA
Cooper, Robert W., Exec.Sec.
AMERICAN FEDERATION OF ASTROLOGERS,
INC. - LIBRARY □ Tempe, AZ
Cooper, S. Jane, Hd.Med.Libn.
OKLAHOMA OSTEOPATHIC HOSPITAL - L.C.
BAXTER MEDICAL LIBRARY □ Tulsa, OK
Cooper, Sara E., Chf.Libn.
AMERICAN FEDERATION OF ASTROLOGERS,
INC. - LIBRARY □ Tempe, AZ
Cooper, Victoria L., Chf.Cat.
PANAMA CANAL COMMISSION - LIBRARY-
MUSEUM □ APO Miami, FL
Cooper, W., Hd., Docs.
U.S. NASA - JOHN F. KENNEDY SPACE CENTER
- LIBRARY □ Kennedy Space Center, FL
Cooper, William L., Dir.
DYKEMA, GOSSETT, SPENCER, GOODNOW &
TRIGG - LAW LIBRARY □ Detroit, MI
Cooperman, Susan, Patients' Libn.
U.S. VETERANS ADMINISTRATION (VA-Salem) -
MEDICAL CENTER LIBRARY □ Salem, VA
Coover, Diane, Libn.
TOSCO CORPORATION - TECHNICAL
INFORMATION CENTER □ Golden, CO
Coover, James, Dir.
SUNY AT BUFFALO - MUSIC LIBRARY □ Buffalo,
NY
Cooze, C.M., Libn.
AUSTRALIAN EMBASSY - LIBRARY □
Washington, DC
Cope, Alora, Asst. to Dir.
NORTH SUBURBAN LIBRARY SYSTEM &
SUBURBAN LIBRARY SYSTEM - SUBURBAN AV
SERVICE □ La Grange Park, IL
Copeland, Ella G., Libn.
STANDARD OIL COMPANY OF INDIANA -
CENTRAL RESEARCH LIBRARY □ Naperville, IL
Copeland, Julia, Env.Consrv.Libn.
MINNEAPOLIS PUBLIC LIBRARY &
INFORMATION CENTER - ENVIRONMENTAL
CONSERVATION LIBRARY OF MINNESOTA □
Minneapolis, MN
Copeley, William, Assoc.Libn.
NEW HAMPSHIRE HISTORICAL SOCIETY -
LIBRARY □ Concord, NH
Coplen, Ron, Libn.
HARCOURT BRACE JOVANOVICH, INC. -
EDITORIAL LIBRARY □ New York, NY
Coppel, Lynn M., Coord.
CALIFORNIA STATE UNIVERSITY, FULLERTON -
LIBRARY - FREEDOM CENTER □ Fullerton, CA
Coppens, P., Media Dir.
UNIVERSITY OF LOWELL, SOUTH CAMPUS -
DANIEL H. O'LEARY LIBRARY □ Lowell, MA
Coppin, Ann S., Supv.
CHEVRON OIL FIELD RESEARCH COMPANY -
TECHNICAL INFORMATION SERVICES □ La
Habra, CA
Coppinger, Fr. John W., S.A., Libn.
GRAYMOOR ECUMENICAL INSTITUTE -
CARDINAL SPELLMAN LIBRARY □ Garrison, NY
Coppola, Daniel, Libn.
ATLAS TRAFFIC CONSULTANTS CORPORATION
- TARIFF DEPARTMENT LIBRARY □ Flushing, NY
Coraggio, Mary, Hd., Acq.Br.
U.S. NAVY - NAVAL WEAPONS CENTER -
LIBRARY DIVISION □ China Lake, CA
Coral, Lenore, Libn.
UNIVERSITY OF WISCONSIN, MADISON -
MILLS MUSIC LIBRARY □ Madison, WI

Corber, Mrs. X., Sr.Info.Proc.
IBM CANADA, LTD. - EASTERN REGION
REFERENCE LIBRARY† □ Montreal, PQ
Corbett, B., Chf. Natural Res.Rec.
CANADA - PUBLIC ARCHIVES OF CANADA -
FEDERAL ARCHIVES DIVISION □ Ottawa, ON
Corbett, James, Libn.
HUGHES, HUBBARD, AND REED - LIBRARY □
New York, NY
Corbett, Patti K., Dir.
UNIVERSITY OF PITTSBURGH - GRADUATE
SCHOOL OF PUBLIC HEALTH LIBRARY □
Pittsburgh, PA
Corbin, Brenda G., Libn.
U.S. NAVY - NAVAL OBSERVATORY - MATTHEW
FONTAINE MAURY MEMORIAL LIBRARY □
Washington, DC
Corbin, Grace, Tech.Info.Spec.
U.S. ARMY COMPUTER SYSTEMS COMMAND -
TECHNICAL LIBRARY □ Ft. Belvoir, VA
Corcio, Ralph, Res.
TRENTON TIMES - LIBRARY □ Trenton, NJ
Corcoran, Virginia, Robinson Libn.
HARTFORD HOSPITAL - HEALTH SCIENCE
LIBRARIES □ Hartford, CT
Cordasci, Terry, Gen. Color Lib.
PHOTO RESEARCHERS, INC. - LIBRARY □ New
York, NY
Cordeiro, Daniel, Latin Amer.Biblog.
SYRACUSE UNIVERSITY - E.S. BIRD LIBRARY -
AREA STUDIES DEPARTMENT □ Syracuse, NY
Cordero, Aura S.
UNIVERSITY OF PUERTO RICO - NATURAL
SCIENCE LIBRARY □ Rio Piedras, PR
Cordner, Peg, Supv., Lib.Serv.
TOLEDO MENTAL HEALTH CENTER - LIBRARY
AND INFORMATION SERVICES† □ Toledo, OH
Cordova, Gregorio, Hd., Reserve
UNIVERSITY OF PUERTO RICO - GENERAL
LIBRARY □ San Juan, PR
Corey, D. Steven, Spec.Coll.Libn.
UNIVERSITY OF SAN FRANCISCO - SPECIAL
COLLECTIONS DEPT./DONOHUE RARE BOOK
ROOM □ San Francisco, CA
Corey, Karen M., Rd.Serv.Libn.
PURDUE UNIVERSITY - CALUMET LIBRARY □
Hammond, IN
Corey, Leslie N., Jr., Exec.Dir.
CONNECTICUT AUDUBON CENTER - LIBRARY □
Fairfield, CT
Corey, Susan, Libn.
LINN COUNTY BAR ASSOCIATION - LAW
LIBRARY† □ Cedar Rapids, IA
Corkran, Charles W., Asst.Dir.
U.S. PRESIDENTIAL LIBRARIES - LYNDON B.
JOHNSON LIBRARY† □ Austin, TX
Corkum, Myrtle, Exec.Asst.
HALIFAX BOARD OF TRADE - LIBRARY □ Halifax,
NS
Corless, Denise, Libn.
MALDEN HOSPITAL - MEDICAL LIBRARY □
Malden, MA
Corless, Isabel, Libn.
BURLINGTON COUNTY HISTORICAL SOCIETY -
DELIA BIDDLE PUGH LIBRARY □ Burlington, NJ
Corley, Jannis R., Law Libn.
SAGINAW COUNTY LAW LIBRARY □ Saginaw,
MI
Corley, Pamela, Ref.Libn.
UNIVERSITY OF SOUTHERN CALIFORNIA -
HEALTH SCIENCES CAMPUS - NORRIS
MEDICAL LIBRARY □ Los Angeles, CA
Corliss, Mary, Cur.Asst., Stills
MUSEUM OF MODERN ART - FILM STUDY
CENTER □ New York, NY
Corman, Gladys, Ck.
SNYDER COUNTY HISTORICAL SOCIETY, INC. -
LIBRARY □ Middleburg, PA
Corman, L., Libn.
UNIVERSITY OF TORONTO - UNIVERSITY OF
TRINITY COLLEGE - LIBRARY □ Toronto, ON

Cornacchia, Rocco, Reg.Libn.
CANADA - PUBLIC WORKS CANADA - ONTARIO
REGIONAL LIBRARY □ Willowdale, ON
Corneil, Charlotte, Pub.Serv.
LOUISIANA STATE UNIVERSITY - LAW
LIBRARY □ Baton Rouge, LA
Corneil, Dorothy, Asst. To Libn.
CANADA - LABOUR CANADA - OCCUPATIONAL
SAFETY AND HEALTH BRANCH - TECHNICAL
RESOURCE CENTRE □ Ottawa, ON
Cornell, Dr. George W., Dir. of Lib.Serv.
SUNY - COLLEGE AT BROCKPORT - DRAKE
MEMORIAL LIBRARY □ Brockport, NY
Cornell, Kim, Libn.
ONTARIO HYDRO - LIBRARY □ Toronto, ON
Cornett, Lloyd H., Jr., Dir.
U.S. AIR FORCE - ALBERT F. SIMPSON
HISTORICAL RESEARCH CENTER □ Maxwell
AFB, AL
Cornwell, Joy, Cat.
MAYO FOUNDATION - MAYO CLINIC LIBRARY □
Rochester, MN
Cornwell, Mary P., Chf.
U.S. PUBLIC HEALTH SERVICE HOSPITAL -
MEDICAL LIBRARY □ Baltimore, MD
Cornwell, Nancy W., Hd. of Pubn.
CLUB MANAGERS ASSOCIATION OF AMERICA -
INFORMATION, RESEARCH & STATISTICS
DEPARTMENT □ Washington, DC
Cornwell, Robena Eng, Asst.Univ.Libn.
UNIVERSITY OF FLORIDA - MUSIC LIBRARY □
Gainesville, FL
Cornwell, Sophy H., Spec.Coll.Libn.
LINCOLN UNIVERSITY - LANGSTON HUGHES
MEMORIAL LIBRARY - SPECIAL COLLECTIONS
□ Lincoln University, PA
Coronado, Barbara, Libn.
U.S. VETERANS ADMINISTRATION (TX-Temple)
- CENTER MEDICAL LIBRARY □ Temple, TX
Coronel, Ester, Asst.Tech.Serv.Libn.
WASHINGTON NATIONAL INSURANCE
COMPANY - INFORMATION RESOURCES
CENTER □ Evanston, IL
Corontzes, Arthur N., Assoc.Dir.
CITADEL - THE MILITARY COLLEGE OF SOUTH
CAROLINA - DANIEL LIBRARY □ Charleston, SC
Corrales, Helen M., Employee Serv.
WESTERN ELECTRIC COMPANY, INC. -
LIBRARY □ Phoenix, AZ
Corrin, Nancy, Mgr.
NATIONAL FIRE PROTECTION ASSOCIATION -
CHARLES S. MORGAN LIBRARY □ Quincy, MA
Corriveau, Conrad, Dir.
UNIVERSITE DU QUEBEC A MONTREAL -
BIBLIOTHEQUE DES SCIENCES □ Montreal, PQ
Corry, Ann Marie, Libn.
UNIVERSITY OF MISSOURI, KANSAS CITY -
SCHOOL OF DENTISTRY LIBRARY □ Kansas City,
MO
Corry, Ruth L., Hd., Ctrl.Res.
GEORGIA STATE DEPARTMENT OF ARCHIVES
AND HISTORY - CENTRAL RESEARCH LIBRARY
□ Atlanta, GA
Corsaro, James, Sr.Libn.
NEW YORK STATE LIBRARY - MANUSCRIPTS
AND SPECIAL COLLECTION □ Albany, NY
Corsello, Doris M. E., Cat.
DUQUESNE UNIVERSITY - LAW LIBRARY □
Pittsburgh, PA
Corsini, B. Andrew, Dir. of Pubn.
THEATRE HISTORICAL SOCIETY COLLECTION
□ Notre Dame, IN
Corso, H., TRW Doc.
TRW, INC. - DEFENSE & SPACE SYSTEMS
GROUP - TECHNICAL INFORMATION CENTER □
Redondo Beach, CA
Corson, David W., Hist. of Sci.Libn.
CORNELL UNIVERSITY - HISTORY OF SCIENCE
COLLECTIONS □ Ithaca, NY
Corson, Richard H., Libn.
SUNY - MARITIME COLLEGE - STEPHEN B.
LUCE LIBRARY □ Bronx, NY

PERSONNEL

Cort, Margaret M., Libn.
SPERRY CORPORATION - SPERRY GYROSCOPE
DIVISION - ENGINEERING LIBRARY □
Clearwater, FL

Cortelyou, Catherine, Pub.Serv.Libn.
UNIVERSITY OF CALIFORNIA, BERKELEY -
INSTITUTE OF TRANSPORTATION STUDIES
LIBRARY □ Berkeley, CA

Corth, Annette, Asst.Libn./Hd.Tech.Serv.
RUTGERS UNIVERSITY, THE STATE
UNIVERSITY OF NEW JERSEY - LIBRARY OF
SCIENCE & MEDICINE □ Piscataway, NJ

Cortina, Barbara, Asst.Chf.
U.S. GENERAL SERVICES ADMINISTRATION -
GSA LIBRARY □ Washington, DC

Corwin, L.A., Jr., Proj.Dir.
ORTHOPEDIC FOUNDATION FOR ANIMALS -
OFA HIP DYSPLASIA REGISTRY □ Columbia, MO

Cory, Kenneth A., Libn.
WESTERN MONTANA COLLEGE - LUCY CARSON
MEMORIAL LIBRARY □ Dillon, MT

Coscarelli, Mary, Prog.Adm.
AMERICAN ALLIANCE FOR HEALTH, PHYSICAL
EDUCATION, RECREATION & DANCE -
INFORMATION CENTER FOR THE
HANDICAPPED □ Reston, VA

Cose, Patricia, Ref.Libn.
PORT AUTHORITY OF NEW YORK AND NEW
JERSEY - LIBRARY □ New York, NY

Cosgrove, Barbara, Sr.Info.Assoc.
ALLERGAN PHARMACEUTICALS, INC. -
PROFESSIONAL INFORMATION SERVICES □
Irvine, CA

Cosimi, Ivan A., Dir.
U.S. DEPT. OF COMMERCE - INTERNATIONAL
TRADE ADMINISTRATION - MIAMI DISTRICT
OFFICE LIBRARY □ Miami, FL

Cossette, Joseph, S.J., Lib.Dir.
COMPAGNIE DE JESUS - JESUITS LIBRARY □
St. Jerome, PQ

Costa, Lerleen, Ser.Sect.Hd.
UNIVERSITY OF CALIFORNIA, LOS ANGELES -
MANAGEMENT LIBRARY □ Los Angeles, CA

Costa, Paulo, Libn.
BRAZILIAN-AMERICAN CULTURAL INSTITUTE,
INC. - HAROLD E. WIBBERLEY, JR. LIBRARY □
Washington, DC

Costanzo, Anthony J., Tech.Info.Supv.
ATLANTIC-RICHFIELD COMPANY - ARCO
CHEMICAL COMPANY - RESEARCH &
ENGINEERING TECHNICAL INFORMATION
CENTER □ Newton Square, PA

Costas, Dr. Aida R. Caro, Dir.
UNIVERSITY OF PUERTO RICO - HISTORICAL
RESEARCH CENTER □ Rio Piedras, PR

Costello, Rita, Bus.Adm.Libn.
DREXEL UNIVERSITY LIBRARIES - GENERAL
LIBRARY □ Philadelphia, PA

Costello, Robert C.
MERCER (William M.), INC. - LIBRARY
INFORMATION CENTER □ Los Angeles, CA

Cote, Gisele, Acq.
CINEMATHEQUE QUEBECOISE - ARCHIVES &
FILM MUSEUM □ Montreal, PQ

Cote, Leo, Libn.
LABRADOR CITY COLLEGIATE - LIBRARY □
Labrador City, NF

Cote, Lois, Libn.
ST. PETER'S SEMINARY - LIBRARY □ London,
ON

Cote, Michelle, Documentalist
UNIVERSITE DE MONTREAL - CENTRE DE
RECHERCHES CARAIBES - BIBLIOTHEQUE □
Montreal, PQ

Cote, Monique, Libn.
UNIVERSITE DU QUEBEC A MONTREAL -
CENTRE DE DOCUMENTATION ECONOMIE-
ADMINISTRATION □ Montreal, PQ

Cote, Nicole, Dir.
SOCIETE DE DEVELOPPEMENT DE LA BAIE
JAMES - SERVICE DOCUMENTATION □
Montreal, PQ

Cote, Paul, Asst.Libn.-Ref.
AVCO CORPORATION - AVCO-EVERETT
RESEARCH LABORATORY - LIBRARY □ Everett,
MA

Cote, Rene, Chf.Libn.
HOPITAL ST-LUC - BIBLIOTHEQUE MEDICALE†
□ Montreal, PQ

Cote-Thibodeau, Donna E., Libn.
CARY MEDICAL CENTER - HEALTH SCIENCE
LIBRARY □ Caribou, ME

Cotham, Steve, Tech.Serv./Ref.Libn.
KNOXVILLE-KNOX COUNTY PUBLIC LIBRARY
SYSTEM - MC CLUNG HISTORICAL
COLLECTION □ Knoxville, TN

Cotreau, Jane C., Libn.
MASSACHUSETTS COMPUTER ASSOCIATES,
INC. - LIBRARY □ Wakefield, MA

Cotten, Alice R., Asst.Cur.
UNIVERSITY OF NORTH CAROLINA, CHAPEL
HILL - NORTH CAROLINA COLLECTION □ Chapel
Hill, NC

Cotten, Mary Linda, Libn.
NATIONAL SOCIETY OF THE SONS OF THE
AMERICAN REVOLUTION - GENEALOGY
LIBRARY □ Louisville, KY

Cotter, Rev. Lawrence E., Archv.
DIOCESE OF OGDENSBURG - ARCHIVES □
Ogdensburg, NY

Cotter, Ray R., Libn.
CALTEX PETROLEUM CORPORATION -
PLANNING AND ECONOMICS DEPARTMENT -
LIBRARY □ New York, NY

Cotton, Karolyn, Libn.
RACINE JOURNAL TIMES - LIBRARY □ Racine,
WI

Cotton, Kenneth W., Lib.Dir.
WESTFIELD STATE COLLEGE - GOVERNOR
JOSEPH B. ELY MEMORIAL LIBRARY □
Westfield, MA

Cottrell, A.E., Info.Spec.
AIR PRODUCTS AND CHEMICALS, INC. -
INFORMATION SERVICES - TREXLERTOWN
LIBRARY □ Allentown, PA

Cottrell, Linda D., Map Cat.Libn.
UNIVERSITY OF ARIZONA - MAP COLLECTION
□ Tucson, AZ

Cottrell, W.B., Dir.
U.S. OAK RIDGE NATL. LABORATORY -
NUCLEAR SAFETY INFORMATION CENTER □
Oak Ridge, TN

Coty, Patricia, Hd., AV Serv.
JOHNS HOPKINS UNIVERSITY - WILLIAM H.
WELCH MEDICAL LIBRARY □ Baltimore, MD

Coughenour, Don R., Dir.
IOWA STATE DEPARTMENT OF HEALTH -
VITAL RECORDS - INFORMATION CENTER □
Des Moines, IA

Coughlin, Caroline M., Asst.Dir.
DREW UNIVERSITY - LIBRARY □ Madison, NJ

Coughlin, Janice, Lib.Supv.
SIR SANFORD FLEMING COLLEGE OF APPLIED
ARTS & TECHNOLOGY - LIBRARIES □
Peterborough, ON

Coughlin, Richard, Ref.Libn.
BOSTON COLLEGE - SCHOOL OF MANAGEMENT
LIBRARY □ Chestnut Hill, MA

Couillard, Merila, ILL
UNIVERSITE LAVAL - BIBLIOTHEQUE
SCIENTIFIQUE† □ Ste. Foy, PQ

Coulombe, Solange, Acq.
CEGEP DE TROIS-RIVIERES - BIBLIOTHEQUE □
Trois-Rivieres, PQ

Coulson, Rafael E., Dir.
U.S. ARMY SCHOOL OF THE AMERICAS -
LIBRARY/LEARNING CENTER □ APO Miami, FL

Coulter, Shirley, Coord.Sch.Libs.
NOVA SCOTIA - PROVINCIAL LIBRARY □
Halifax, NS

Coupe, Sandra, Libn.
U.S. DEPT. OF JUSTICE - FEDERAL BUREAU OF
INVESTIGATION - F.B.I. ACADEMY - LEARNING
RESOURCE CENTER □ Quantico, VA

Courage, Gordon, Hd.
WINNIPEG DEPARTMENT OF ENVIRONMENTAL
PLANNING - LIBRARY □ Winnipeg, MB

Cournoyea, Wende, Exec.Sec.
NORTON RESEARCH CORPORATION (Canada)
LTD. - LIBRARY □ Niagara Falls, ON

Court, Emily, Libn.
NORWICH HOSPITAL - HEALTH SCIENCES
LIBRARY □ Norwich, CT

Courtis, Shirley, Libn.
NORANDA RESEARCH CENTRE - LIBRARY □
Pointe Claire, PQ

Courtney, Marilyn G., Med.Libn.
FRANKLIN MEMORIAL HOSPITAL - TURNER
MEMORIAL LIBRARY □ Farmington, ME

Courtney, Mary E., Libn.
MEMORIAL HOSPITAL - MEDICAL AND
NURSING LIBRARY □ Cumberland, MD

Courtney, Vincent, Tech.Serv.
UNIVERSITY OF MAINE, FARMINGTON -
MANTOR LIBRARY □ Farmington, ME

Cousineau, J., Lib.Mgr.
CANADA - VETERANS AFFAIRS CANADA -
LIBRARY □ Ottawa, ON

Cousins, Lynne M., Libn.
CONFEDERATION LIFE INSURANCE COMPANY -
LIBRARY □ Toronto, ON

Coutin, Dr. Jose D., Dir.
UNIVERSITY OF DAYTON - LAW SCHOOL
LIBRARY □ Dayton, OH

Couts, Doris V., Libn.
TUSCARAWAS COUNTY LAW LIBRARY
ASSOCIATION □ New Philadelphia, OH

Couts, Mona, Info.Serv.Mgr.
WARNER-EDDISON ASSOCIATES, INC. -
INFORMATION SERVICE □ Cambridge, MA

Covalesky, Eleanor, Asst.Libn.
UNIVERSITY OF SAN FRANCISCO - SCHOOL OF
LAW LIBRARY □ San Francisco, CA

Covalt, Jeanie, Res.Libn.
KANSAS HERITAGE CENTER - LIBRARY □ Dodge
City, KS

Cover, Peggy, Sci.Tech.Agri.Serv.
CLEMSON UNIVERSITY - ROBERT MULDROW
COOPER LIBRARY □ Clemson, SC

Covert, Nadine, Exec.Dir.
EDUCATIONAL FILM LIBRARY ASSOCIATION -
LIBRARY AND INFORMATION CENTER □ New
York, NY

Covey, Carol, Ser.Libn.
WESTERN ILLINOIS UNIVERSITY - LIBRARIES
□ Macomb, IL

Covey, Gail, Libn.
ODESSA AMERICAN - EDITORIAL LIBRARY □
Odessa, TX

Covington, Louise, Tech.Serv.Libn.
TEXAS TECH UNIVERSITY - SCHOOL OF LAW
LIBRARY □ Lubbock, TX

Covington, Mary W., Supv.Tech.Info.
COPPER DEVELOPMENT ASSOCIATION, INC. -
COPPER DATA CENTER □ New York, NY

Covington, W.
OPTIKON LABORATORIES - LIBRARY □ West
Cornwall, CT

Covotsos, Louis J., Hd.Libn.
MC DERMOTT, WILL & EMERY - LIBRARY □
Chicago, IL

Cowan, Anita P., Dir.
NATIONAL CLEARINGHOUSE FOR FAMILY
PLANNING INFORMATION □ Rockville, MD

Cowan, Mrs. B.
CANADA - AGRICULTURE CANADA - RESEARCH
STATION, MORDEN - LIBRARY □ Morden, MB

Cowan, David G., Instr.Serv. Law Libn.
UNIVERSITY OF MISSOURI - SCHOOL OF LAW
LIBRARY □ Columbia, MO

Cowan, George A., Libn.
LINCOLN COUNTY LAW LIBRARY† □ Wiscasset,
ME

Cowan, Lenore, Cur.
NEW YORK PUBLIC LIBRARY - MID-
MANHATTAN LIBRARY - PICTURE COLLECTION
□ New York, NY

Coward, Robert Y., Hd.Libn.
FRANKLIN COLLEGE - SPECIAL COLLECTIONS □ Franklin, IN

Cowart, Cecilia, Dir., Commun.
AMERICAN BRAHMAN BREEDERS ASSOCIATION - LIBRARY □ Houston, TX

Cowe, Dorothy, Libn.
ITEK CORPORATION - OPTICAL SYSTEMS DIVISION - LIBRARY □ Lexington, MA

Cowe, Lind, Circ.Asst.
FITCHBURG STATE COLLEGE - LIBRARY □ Fitchburg, MA

Cowen, Sandra T., Res.Anl./Libn.
UNIVERSITY OF SOUTH CAROLINA - BUREAU OF GOVERNMENTAL RESEARCH AND SERVICE - LIBRARY □ Columbia, SC

Cowper, Mrs. D., Libn.
TORONTO GENERAL HOSPITAL - FUDGER MEDICAL LIBRARY □ Toronto, ON

Cowsert, Dale, Dir.
INTERNATIONAL INSTITUTE FOR ROBOTICS - LIBRARY □ Dallas, TX

Cox, Alice G., Libn.
MISSISSIPPI BAPTIST CONVENTION BOARD - MISSISSIPPI BAPTIST HISTORICAL COMMISSION □ Clinton, MS

Cox, Anne D., Cat.
EMORY UNIVERSITY - SPECIAL COLLECTIONS DEPARTMENT □ Atlanta, GA

Cox, Barbara, Map Libn.
UNIVERSITY OF UTAH - MAP LIBRARY □ Salt Lake City, UT

Cox, Brenda J., Libn.
HOWARD UNIVERSITY - SOCIAL WORK LIBRARY □ Washington, DC

Cox, Dwayne, Assoc.Univ.Archv.
UNIVERSITY OF LOUISVILLE - UNIVERSITY ARCHIVES AND RECORDS CENTER □ Louisville, KY

Cox, Dwayne, Co-Dir.
UNIVERSITY OF LOUISVILLE - UNIVERSITY ARCHIVES AND RECORDS CENTER - ORAL HISTORY CENTER □ Louisville, KY

Cox, Graham L., Dir., Eniviromental Educ.
NEW YORK STATE DEPARTMENT OF ENVIRONMENTAL CONSERVATION - OFFICE OF EDUC. SERV. - INFORMATION SERVICE □ Albany, NY

Cox, James C., Chf.Libn.
LOYOLA UNIVERSITY OF CHICAGO - MEDICAL CENTER LIBRARY □ Maywood, IL

Cox, Joan, Asst.
FALCONBRIDGE NICKEL MINES, LTD. - FALCONBRIDGE INFORMATION CENTRE □ Toronto, ON

Cox, Lynn, Prints & Photographs Cur.
PEALE MUSEUM - MUSEUM ARCHIVES □ Baltimore, MD

Cox, Mahala, Curric.Libn.
EDEN THEOLOGICAL SEMINARY - LIBRARY □ Webster Groves, MO

Cox, Marcia, AV Med.Libn.
UNIVERSITY OF MISSOURI, KANSAS CITY - HEALTH SCIENCES LIBRARY □ Kansas City, MO

Cox, Marjorie A.
NOVA SCOTIA HOSPITAL - HEALTH SCIENCE LIBRARY □ Dartmouth, NS

Cox, Martha M., Dir.
STARK COUNTY LAW LIBRARY ASSOCIATION - LAW LIBRARY □ Canton, OH

Cox, Phyllis A., Coll.Dev.Libn.
VIRGINIA COMMONWEALTH UNIVERSITY - MEDICAL COLLEGE OF VIRGINIA - TOMPKINS-MC CAW LIBRARY □ Richmond, VA

Cox, Mrs. Ralph, Asst.Libn.
FIRST BAPTIST CHURCH - LIBRARY □ Slocomb, AL

Cox, Shelley, Libn.
SOUTHERN ILLINOIS UNIVERSITY, CARBONDALE - SPECIAL COLLECTIONS □ Carbondale, IL

Coxe, Christine, Libn.
NORTH CAROLINA STATE DEPT. OF NATURAL RESOURCES & COMMUNITY DEVELOPMENT - DIV. OF COMMUNITY ASSISTANCE LIB. □ Raleigh, NC

Coyle, Mary, Ref.Libn.
MITRE CORPORATION - LIBRARY □ McLean, VA

Coyle, Michael P., Hd.
FREE LIBRARY OF PHILADELPHIA - LIBRARY FOR THE BLIND AND PHYSICALLY HANDICAPPED □ Philadelphia, PA

Coyle, Rosalie, Asst.Libn.
RAWLE AND HENDERSON - LAW LIBRARY □ Philadelphia, PA

Coyle, Sandy, Libn.
TEXAS STATE DEPARTMENT OF MENTAL HEALTH & MENTAL RETARDATION - CENTRAL OFFICE LIBRARY □ Austin, TX

Coyne, Joseph G., Mgr.
U.S. DEPT. OF ENERGY - TECHNICAL INFORMATION CENTER - REFERENCE CENTER □ Oak Ridge, TN

Cozzolino, Dorothy A., Libn.
U.S. COURT OF APPEALS, 3RD CIRCUIT - LIBRARY† □ Philadelphia, PA

Crabbe, John W., Dir. of Info.Serv.
SCIENCE APPLICATIONS, INC. - INFORMATION CENTER □ McLean, VA

Crabtree, Amy I., Libn.
GENERAL MOTORS CORPORATION - PUBLIC RELATIONS STAFF LIBRARY □ Detroit, MI

Crabtree, Dorothy T., Libn.
MONSANTO RESEARCH CORPORATION - DAYTON LABORATORY LIBRARY† □ Dayton, OH

Crabtree, Virginia, Circ./Ref. Libn.
NORTHROP CORPORATION - AIRCRAFT DIVISION - LIBRARY SERVICES □ Hawthorne, CA

Craft, D., Act.Libn.
FEDERAL RESERVE BANK OF CLEVELAND - PITTSBURGH BRANCH LIBRARY □ Pittsburgh, PA

Craft, Margaret E., Libn.
WYOMING HISTORICAL AND GEOLOGICAL SOCIETY - BISHOP MEMORIAL LIBRARY □ Wilkes-Barre, PA

Crager, Janet, Biomed.Ref.Libn.
BROWN UNIVERSITY - SCIENCES LIBRARY □ Providence, RI

Cragg, Ruth, Supv.Ref.Dept.
MOORE-COTTRELL SUBSCRIPTION AGENCIES - SERIALS REFERENCE LIBRARY □ North Cohocton, NY

Crago, Bonnie, Libn.
SOUTHERN OHIO GENEALOGICAL SOCIETY - REFERENCE LIBRARY □ Hillsboro, OH

Crahan, Elizabeth S., Dir.Lib.Serv.
LOS ANGELES COUNTY MEDICAL ASSOCIATION - LIBRARY □ Los Angeles, CA

Craig, Albert K., Libn.
ALABAMA STATE DEPARTMENT OF ARCHIVES AND HISTORY □ Montgomery, AL

Craig, Eugene, Libn.
ATLANTA HISTORICAL SOCIETY - ARCHIVES □ Atlanta, GA

Craig, Helen, Asst.Libn.
UNIVERSITY OF NEW BRUNSWICK - EDUCATION RESOURCE CENTRE □ Fredericton, NB

Craig, J.P., Mng.Dir.
FRANKLIN RESEARCH CENTER - SCIENCE INFORMATION SERVICES □ Philadelphia, PA

Craig, James H., Dir.
SYNERGY POWER INSTITUTE - LIBRARY □ Berkeley, CA

Craig, James L., Libn.
UNIVERSITY OF MASSACHUSETTS, AMHERST - MORRILL BIOLOGICAL & GEOLOGICAL SCIENCES LIBRARY □ Amherst, MA

Craig, James Pat, Hd.Libn.
U.S. FOOD & DRUG ADMINISTRATION - NATIONAL CENTER FOR TOXICOLOGICAL RESEARCH - LIBRARY □ Jefferson, AK

Craig, Marge, Co-Dir.
SYNERGY POWER INSTITUTE - LIBRARY □ Berkeley, CA

Craig, Sharon, Libn.
ERIE COUNTY LAW LIBRARY □ Erie, PA

Craig, Susan V., Art Libn.
UNIVERSITY OF KANSAS - MURPHY LIBRARY OF ART HISTORY □ Lawrence, KS

Crain, Deacon, Cur., Theater Arts
UNIVERSITY OF TEXAS, AUSTIN - HUMANITIES RESEARCH CENTER □ Austin, TX

Crain, John W., Dir.
DALLAS HISTORICAL SOCIETY - RESEARCH CENTER □ Dallas, TX

Crainey, M., Mgr.
STANDARDS COUNCIL OF CANADA - STANDARDS INFORMATION DIVISION □ Ottawa, ON

Crais, Mina L., Libn.
INTERNATIONAL HOUSE LIBRARY □ New Orleans, LA

Cram, Miss Kendall, Dir.
TENNESSEE STATE LIBRARY - STATE LIBRARY DIVISION □ Nashville, TN

Cram, Sandra, Asst.Libn.
FEDERAL RESERVE BANK OF BOSTON - RESEARCH LIBRARY† □ Boston, MA

Cramer, Anne, Dir.
EASTERN VIRGINIA MEDICAL SCHOOL - MOORMAN MEMORIAL LIBRARY □ Norfolk, VA

Cramer, Claudia M., Libn.
ROCK COUNTY HEALTH CARE CENTER - STAFF LIBRARY □ Janesville, WI

Cramer, Kenneth C., College Archv.
DARTMOUTH COLLEGE - SPECIAL COLLECTIONS □ Hanover, NH

Cramer, William S., Libn.
OAKLAND UNIVERSITY - LIBRARY □ Rochester, MI

Crampon, Jean, Hd.Ref.Libn.
SOUTHERN ILLINOIS UNIVERSITY - SCHOOL OF MEDICINE - MEDICAL LIBRARY □ Springfield, IL

Crampton, Mrs. M., Libn.
BOY SCOUTS OF CANADA - NATIONAL LIBRARY □ Ottawa, ON

Crandall, D.H., Dir.
U.S. OAK RIDGE NATL. LABORATORY - CONTROLLED FUSION ATOMIC DATA CENTER □ Oak Ridge, TN

Crandall, D.W., Libn.
BAKER & MC KENZIE - LAW LIBRARY □ New York, NY

Crandlemere, R. Wayne, Dir.
BRIGGS ENGINEERING & TESTING COMPANY, INC. - LIBRARY □ Norwell, MA

Crane, Joan S., Cur.Amer.Lit.
UNIVERSITY OF VIRGINIA - CLIFTON WALLER BARRETT LIBRARY □ Charlottesville, VA

Crane, Lois F., Libn.
WICHITA ART MUSEUM - LIBRARY □ Wichita, KS

Crane, Dr. Maurice A., Hd.
MICHIGAN STATE UNIVERSITY - G. ROBERT VINCENT VOICE LIBRARY □ East Lansing, MI

Cranford, Mrs. M.E., Libn.
CIP RESEARCH, LTD. - LIBRARY □ Hawkesbury, ON

Cranford, Nadine, Acq.
UNIVERSITY OF ARKANSAS, MONTICELLO - LIBRARY† □ Monticello, AR

Cranford, Theodore, Lib.Res.Anl.
ROCKWELL INTERNATIONAL - SPACE BUSINESSES - TECHNICAL INFORMATION CENTER □ Downey, CA

Cranor, Alice T., Hd., Info.Serv.Div.
U.S. NAVY - NAVAL INTELLIGENCE SUPPORT CENTER - INFORMATION SERVICES DIVISION □ Washington, DC

Crary, Jean K., Rec.Mgt.Anal.
UNIVERSITY OF DELAWARE, NEWARK - ARCHIVES† □ Newark, DE

PERSONNEL

Craven, James, Assoc.Archv.
UNIVERSITY OF MICHIGAN - MICHIGAN
HISTORICAL COLLECTIONS - BENTLEY
HISTORICAL LIBRARY □ Ann Arbor, MI

Craven, Pat, Libn.
WISCONSIN HOSPITAL ASSOCIATION -
MEMORIAL LIBRARY □ Madison, WI

Craven, R. Jayne, Hd., Art & Music
PUBLIC LIBRARY OF CINCINNATI AND
HAMILTON COUNTY - ART AND MUSIC
DEPARTMENT □ Cincinnati, OH

Cravets, Bertha, Libn.
TEMPLE B'RITH KODESH - LIBRARY □
Rochester, NY

Crawford, Anthony R., Asst.Dir./Lib. & Archv.
MISSOURI HISTORICAL SOCIETY - RESEARCH
LIBRARY □ St. Louis, MO

Crawford, Barbara L., Act.Dir.
HISTORIC LEXINGTON FOUNDATION -
GARLAND GRAY CENTER FOR JACKSON
STUDIES □ Lexington, VA

Crawford, Carter, Libn.
OPPENHEIMER & CO., INC. - LIBRARY† □ New
York, NY

Crawford, David S., Asst. Area Libn.
MC GILL UNIVERSITY - MEDICAL LIBRARY □
Montreal, PQ

Crawford, Doris L., Libn.
ST. ELIZABETH HOSPITAL MEDICAL CENTER -
SCHOOL OF NURSING LIBRARY □ Youngstown,
OH

Crawford, Dorothea, Acq.Libn.
CROWN ZELLERBACH CORPORATION -
CENTRAL RESEARCH LIBRARY □ Camas, WA

Crawford, Kristen Cooney, Libn.
SOHO CENTER FOR VISUAL ARTISTS - LIBRARY
□ New York, NY

Crawford, Marguerite C., Res.Spec.
CORNELL UNIVERSITY - JOHN M. ECHOLS
COLLECTION ON SOUTHEAST ASIA □ Ithaca, NY

Crawford, Marjorie, ILL/Circ.
RUTGERS UNIVERSITY, THE STATE
UNIVERSITY OF NEW JERSEY - JUSTICE
HENRY ACKERSON LIBRARY OF LAW &
CRIMINAL JUSTICE □ Newark, NJ

Crawford, Miriam I., Cur.
TEMPLE UNIVERSITY - CENTRAL LIBRARY
SYSTEM - CONWELLANA-TEMPLANA
COLLECTION □ Philadelphia, PA

Crawford, Paul C., Plan.Dir.
SAN LUIS OBISPO COUNTY PLANNING
DEPARTMENT - TECHNICAL INFORMATION
LIBRARY □ San Luis Obispo, CA

Crawford, Dr. Susan, Dir.
AMERICAN MEDICAL ASSOCIATION -
DIVISION OF LIBRARY AND ARCHIVAL
SERVICES □ Chicago, IL

Crawford, William, Lib.Techn.
DISTRICT OF COLUMBIA TEACHERS COLLEGE -
LIBRARY □ Washington, DC

Crawshaw, Mrs. E., Group Ldr.
GEORGE BROWN COLLEGE OF APPLIED ARTS &
TECHNOLOGY - LIBRARY □ Toronto, ON

Cray, Katherine, Asst.Libn.
GOLDMAN, SACHS AND COMPANY - LIBRARY □
New York, NY

Creager, William A., Pres.
CAPITAL SYSTEMS GROUP, INC. - LIBRARY □
Kensington, MD

Creaghe, Norma, Libn.
ST. ANSELM'S COLLEGE - GEISEL LIBRARY □
Manchester, NH

Creasey, J. Alex, State Law Libn.
WEST VIRGINIA STATE SUPREME COURT OF
APPEALS - STATE LAW LIBRARY □ Charleston,
WV

Creech, Heather E., Ref.Libn.
DALHOUSIE UNIVERSITY - LAW LIBRARY □
Halifax, NS

Creech, Mary, Archv.
MORAVIAN CHURCH IN AMERICA - SOUTHERN
PROVINCE - MORAVIAN ARCHIVES □ Winston-
Salem, NC

Creekmore, Cynthia, Asst.Libn.
INDIANA UNIVERSITY OF PENNSYLVANIA -
UNIVERSITY LIBRARY □ Indiana, PA

Creelman, Gwendolyn
MOUNT ALLISON UNIVERSITY - ALFRED
WHITEHEAD MEMORIAL MUSIC LIBRARY □
Sackville, NB

Creesy, Virginia, Cat.Libn.
COUDERT BROTHERS - LIBRARY □ New York,
NY

Cregar, Philip Berwick, Assoc. Law Libn.
UNIVERSITY OF TOLEDO - COLLEGE OF LAW
LIBRARY† □ Toledo, OH

Creighton, Alice S., Asst.Libn., Spec.Coll.
U.S. NAVAL ACADEMY - NIMITZ LIBRARY □
Annapolis, MD

Creighton, James, Recordings Archv.
UNIVERSITY OF TORONTO - FACULTY OF
MUSIC LIBRARY □ Toronto, ON

Creme, Francine, Tech.Libn.
BARR ENGINEERING COMPANY - LIBRARY □
Minneapolis, MN

Crenshaw, Tena L., Libn.
UNIVERSITY OF FLORIDA - EDUCATION
LIBRARY □ Gainesville, FL

Crepeau, Marguerite, Libn.
TWIN CITY FEDERAL SAVINGS & LOAN
ASSOCIATION - CORPORATE LIBRARY† □
Minneapolis, MN

Crespin, Christine Y., Supv.
ST. ANTHONY HOSPITAL - MEMORIAL MEDICAL
LIBRARY □ Denver, CO

Crespo, Donnie, Asst.Archv.
WEYERHAEUSER COMPANY - ARCHIVES □
Federal Way, WA

Cressman, Ruth, Asst.Libn.
UNIVERSITY OF MICHIGAN - DENTISTRY
LIBRARY □ Ann Arbor, MI

Cresto, Kathy, Ser.Libn.
PEPPERDINE UNIVERSITY - LIBRARY -
SPECIAL COLLECTIONS □ Malibu, CA

Crete, Line, Lib.Techn.
ST. VINCENT HOSPITAL - LIBRARY† □ Ottawa,
ON

Cretecos, Yvonne I., Med.Libn.
HUNT MEMORIAL HOSPITAL - GEORGE B.
PALMER MEMORIAL LIBRARY □ Danvers, MA

Creth, Sheila, Asst.Libn. Personnel
UNIVERSITY OF CONNECTICUT - LIBRARY □
Storrs, CT

Crews, B.C., Hd., Tech.Serv.
NORTH CAROLINA AGRICULTURAL &
TECHNICAL STATE UNIVERSITY - F.D.
BLUFORD LIBRARY □ Greensboro, NC

Crider, Carol, Cat.
ANDREWS UNIVERSITY - JAMES WHITE
LIBRARY □ Berrien Springs, MI

Criez, Diane, Cat.Hd.
BOEING COMPANY - SEATTLE SERVICES
DIVISION - RENTON LIBRARY □ Seattle, WA

Crippen, David R., Archv.
HENRY FORD MUSEUM AND GREENFIELD
VILLAGE - FORD ARCHIVES □ Dearborn, MI

Crisp, Carlotta, Lib.Techn.
BOSTON UNIVERSITY - CHEMISTRY LIBRARY □
Boston, MA

Crisp, Lynn, Lib.Asst./Slide Cur.
NORTH CAROLINA STATE UNIVERSITY -
HARRYE LYONS DESIGN LIBRARY □ Raleigh, NC

Crispen, Joanne, Dir. of Lib.Serv.
LUTHERAN GENERAL HOSPITAL - LIBRARY □
Park Ridge, IL

Crissey, Lois L., Principal Law Libn.
NEW YORK STATE SUPREME COURT - 8TH
JUDICIAL DISTRICT - LAW LIBRARY □ Buffalo,
NY

Crissman, Lois, Soc.Sci.Biblog.
NORTHWEST MISSOURI STATE UNIVERSITY -
WELLS LIBRARY □ Maryville, MO

Critchley, Alice, Mgr., Info.Ctr.
WESTERN UNION CORPORATION - LIBRARY† □
Upper Saddle River, NJ

Crocker, Anne, Law Libn.
UNIVERSITY OF NEW BRUNSWICK - LAW
LIBRARY □ Fredericton, NB

Crockett, M.C., Chf.Libn.
UNIVERSITY OF PRINCE EDWARD ISLAND -
ROBERTSON LIBRARY □ Charlottetown, PE

Crockett, Mary S., Libn.
CHARLESTON EVENING POST/NEWS AND
COURIER - LIBRARY □ Charleston, SC

Croft, Betty, Hd.Tech.Serv.
NORTHWEST MISSOURI STATE UNIVERSITY -
WELLS LIBRARY □ Maryville, MO

Croft, Betty, Cat.
PRICE WATERHOUSE - NEW YORK OFFICE
INFORMATION CENTER □ New York, NY

Croft, Rev. George, O.M.I., Hd.Libn.
OBLATE COLLEGE - LIBRARY □ Washington, DC

Croft, Martha, Doc.Libn.
CENTRAL CONNECTICUT STATE COLLEGE -
ELIHU BURRITT LIBRARY □ New Britain, CT

Croft, P.H., Pres.
AMERICAN SHORT LINE RAILROAD
ASSOCIATION - LIBRARY □ Washington, DC

Croft, Vicki F., Hd.
WASHINGTON STATE UNIVERSITY -
VETERINARY MEDICAL/PHARMACY LIBRARY □
Pullman, WA

Croix, Jean, Hd.
UNION CARBIDE CORPORATION - SOLVENTS &
INTERMEDIATES DIVISION - PLANT LIBRARY†
□ Texas City, TX

Crombie, Joanne, Asst.Libn.
RESURRECTION HOSPITAL - MEDICAL LIBRARY
& ALLIED HEALTH SCIENCES □ Chicago, IL

Crombie, Kenneth C., Tech.Libn.
GENERAL MOTORS CORPORATION - DELCO
ELECTRONICS DIVISION - TECHNICAL
LIBRARY† □ Goleta, CA

Crompton, Dianne, Lib.Techn.
CANADA WIRE AND CABLE, LTD. - TECHNICAL
LIBRARY □ Toronto, ON

Cromwell, Ann, Leg.Libn.
CAPLIN & DRYSDALE - LIBRARY □ Washington,
DC

Cronenwett, Philip N., Cur. of Mss.
DARTMOUTH COLLEGE - SPECIAL
COLLECTIONS □ Hanover, NH

Cronin, Constance, Res.Libn. Ref. & Ret.
WARNER-LAMBERT/PARKE-DAVIS -
RESEARCH LIBRARY† □ Ann Arbor, MI

Cronin, F.J., Res.Info.Spec.
LOCKHEED-GEORGIA COMPANY - TECHNICAL
INFORMATION DEPARTMENT □ Marietta, GA

Cronin, John, Chf.Libn.
BOSTON HERALD AMERICAN - REFERENCE
LIBRARY □ Boston, MA

Cronin, Kathleen, Asst.Libn.
BERLEX LABORATORIES, INC. - RESEARCH AND
DEVELOPMENT DIVISION LIBRARY □ Cedar
Knolls, NJ

Cronin, Mary J., Asst.Dir., Pub.Serv.
MARQUETTE UNIVERSITY - MEMORIAL
LIBRARY □ Milwaukee, WI

Crooks, Cal, AV Mtls.
BLACK HILLS STATE COLLEGE - E.Y. BERRY
LIBRARY-LEARNING CENTER □ Spearfish, SD

Crooks, James E., Data Base Coord./Ref.
UNIVERSITY OF MICHIGAN - ALFRED
TAUBMAN MEDICAL LIBRARY □ Ann Arbor, MI

Crosby, Ramona C.T., Supv.Info.Serv.
STAUFFER CHEMICAL COMPANY - EASTERN
RESEARCH CENTER INFORMATION SERVICES □
Dobbs Ferry, NY

Crosby, S., Info.Spec.
STANDARD OIL COMPANY OF INDIANA -
LIBRARY/INFORMATION CENTER □ Chicago, IL

Croslin, Kenneth, Dir.
TROY STATE UNIVERSITY - LIBRARY □ Troy, AL

Cross, Charlene, Ref. & Res.Spec.
WRIGHT STATE UNIVERSITY - ARCHIVES &
SPECIAL COLLECTIONS □ Dayton, OH

Cross, Dorothy, Chf., Rd.Serv.Br.
U.S. ARMY - ARMY LIBRARY □ Washington, DC

Cross, Jennie, Asst.Dir.
OAKLAND SCHOOLS - EDUCATIONAL RESOURCE
CENTER □ Pontiac, MI

Cross, Col. Leslie H., Libn.
NATIONAL GUARD ASSOCIATION OF THE
UNITED STATES - LIBRARY □ Washington, DC

Cross, Louise, Cur.
FRONTIER GATEWAY MUSEUM - LIBRARY □
Glendive, MT

Cross, Mary F., Libn.
SMATHERS & THOMPSON - LAW LIBRARY □
Miami, FL

Cross, Peggy, Hd.Libn.
CHAUTAUQUA COUNTY LAW LIBRARY □
Mayville, NY

Crossett, Dave, Libn.
GILA COUNTY LAW LIBRARY □ Globe, AZ

Crossfield, Nancy L., Libn.
UNIVERSITY OF WISCONSIN, MADISON -
GEOLOGY-GEOPHYSICS LIBRARY □ Madison, WI

Crossley, Virginia A., Asst.Med.Libn.
BEAUMONT (William) HOSPITAL - MEDICAL
LIBRARY □ Royal Oak, MI

Crossman, Muriel, Ref.Libn.
DUKES COUNTY HISTORICAL SOCIETY -
LIBRARY □ Edgartown, MA

Crosthwaite, E., Hd., AV Area
KELSEY INSTITUTE OF APPLIED ARTS AND
SCIENCES - LEARNING RESOURCES CENTRE □
Saskatoon, SK

Crotts, Martin L., Dir.
FLORIDA PUBLISHING CO. - EDITORIAL
LIBRARY □ Jacksonville, FL

Crouch, Howard E., Pres.
DAMIEN DUTTON SOCIETY FOR LEPROSY AID,
INC. - LIBRARY □ Bellmore, NY

Crouch, James, Libn.
U.S. NAVY - NAVAL SUPPLY SYSTEMS
COMMAND - LIBRARY □ Washington, DC

Crouch, James A., Jr., Hd.Circ.Dept.
UNIVERSITY OF TEXAS, EL PASO - LIBRARY □
El Paso, TX

Crouch, Judith Ann, Cat.
NORTHWESTERN OKLAHOMA STATE
UNIVERSITY - LIBRARY □ Alva, OK

Crouch, Keith, Chf.Libn.
ROYAL MILITARY COLLEGE OF CANADA -
MASSEY LIBRARY & SCIENCE/ENGINEERING
LIBRARY □ Kingston, ON

Crouse, Moses C., Cur.
AURORA COLLEGE - JENKS MEMORIAL
COLLECTION OF ADVENTUAL MATERIALS □
Aurora, IL

Croussouloudis, Despina, Sr.Libn.
NEW YORK PUBLIC LIBRARY - DONNELL
LIBRARY CENTER - CENTRAL CHILDREN'S
ROOM □ New York, NY

Crovatt, Alma, Libn.
ASSOCIATION FOR RESEARCH AND
ENLIGHTENMENT - ARE BRAILLE LIBRARY □
Virginia Beach, VA

Crow, Linda H., Libn.
BRIDGEWATER COURIER-NEWS - LIBRARY □
Bridgewater, NJ

Crowe, Richard T., Dir.
IRISH-AMERICAN CULTURAL ASSOCIATION -
LIBRARY □ Chicago, IL

Crowe, Susan, Supv., Tech.Serv.
AEROSPACE CORPORATION - CHARLES C.
LAURITSEN LIBRARY □ Los Angeles, CA

Crowell, David P., Ref. & Doc.Libn.
NEW JERSEY INSTITUTE OF TECHNOLOGY -
ROBERT W. VAN HOUTEN LIBRARY □ Newark,
NJ

Crowell, James P., Cur.
LONG BEACH PUBLIC LIBRARY - RANCHO LOS
CERRITOS MUSEUM - LIBRARY □ Long Beach,
CA

Crowell, Jo Lyn S., Adm.Libn.
MERCER UNIVERSITY - LAW SCHOOL -
HALLIBURTON LAW LIBRARY □ Macon, GA

Crowell, Mary, Libn.
NATIONAL ASSOCIATION OF PURCHASING
MANAGEMENT, INC. - PURCHASING
INFORMATION CENTER □ New York, NY

Crowers, Clifford P., Hd.
FREE LIBRARY OF PHILADELPHIA -
GOVERNMENT PUBLICATIONS DEPARTMENT □
Philadelphia, PA

Crowl, Virginia, Doc.Libn.
KENT STATE UNIVERSITY - DOCUMENTS
DEPARTMENT □ Kent, OH

Crowley, Rev. John A., Libn.
SEMINARY OF ST. VINCENT DE PAUL -
LIBRARY □ Boynton Beach, FL

Crowley, John V., Asst.Dir. of Libs.
SUNY - COLLEGE AT ONEONTA - JAMES M.
MILNE LIBRARY □ Oneonta, NY

Crowley, Patience L., Dir.
GIFFORD MEMORIAL HOSPITAL - HEALTH
INFORMATION CENTER □ Randolph, VT

Crowley, Sandra, Ref.Libn.
U.S. NASA - LEWIS RESEARCH CENTER -
LIBRARY □ Cleveland, OH

Crowley, Susan B., Law Libn.
SANTA BARBARA COUNTY LAW LIBRARY □
Santa Barbara, CA

Crowther, Janet, Asst.Libn.
U.S. COURT OF CLAIMS/U.S. COURT OF
CUSTOMS & PATENT APPEALS - COURTS'
LIBRARY □ Washington, DC

Crowther, Suzanne D., Railroad Info.Spec.
NATIONAL ACADEMY OF SCIENCES -
NATIONAL RESEARCH COUNCIL - RAILROAD
RESEARCH INFORMATION SERVICE □
Washington, DC

Croxford, Agnes M., Libn.
MACLAREN ENGINEERS PLANNERS &
SCIENTISTS INC. - LIBRARY □ Willowdale, ON

Crozier, Anne, Hospital Spec.
GEORGE WASHINGTON UNIVERSITY -
MEDICAL CENTER - PAUL HIMMELFARB
HEALTH SCIENCES LIBRARY □ Washington, DC

Crozier, Jean, Dir. Of Lib.Serv.
HARDY ASSOCIATES (1978) LTD. - LIBRARY □
Edmonton, AB

Crozier, Ron, Libn.
SANTA BARBARA MUSEUM OF ART - MUSEUM
LIBRARY AND ARCHIVES □ Santa Barbara, CA

Crozier, Ruth, Info.Spec.
COLONIAL PENN GROUP, INC. - INFORMATION
RESEARCH CENTER □ Philadelphia, PA

Cruikshank, Mrs. Eugene R.
DOUGLASS BOULEVARD CHRISTIAN CHURCH -
LIBRARY □ Louisville, KY

Crum, Norm, Lit. Search
LOCKHEED-CALIFORNIA COMPANY -
TECHNICAL INFORMATION CENTER □ Burbank,
CA

Crump, Dan, Libn.
PASADENA PUBLIC LIBRARY - REFERENCE
DIVISION □ Pasadena, CA

Crumpler, Ann P., Chf., Ref.Sec.
U.S. ARMY - OFFICE OF THE CHIEF OF
ENGINEERS - LIBRARY □ Washington, DC

Crumpler, Yvonne, Asst.Libn.
BIRMINGHAM PUBLIC AND JEFFERSON
COUNTY FREE LIBRARY - TUTWILER
COLLECTION OF SOUTHERN HISTORY AND
LITERATURE □ Birmingham, AL

Crutchfield, Benjamin F., Jr., Hd., Ref.
WEST VIRGINIA WESLEYAN COLLEGE - ANNIE
MERNER PFEIFFER LIBRARY □ Buckhannon, WV

Crutchfield, Mary Jane, Chf.Libn.
U.S. VETERANS ADMINISTRATION (TN-Johnson
City) - HOSPITAL LIBRARY □ Mountain Home,
TN

Crutchfield, Sharon R., Dir.
DAUGHTERS OF THE REPUBLIC OF TEXAS -
LIBRARY □ San Antonio, TX

Cruys, Mae, Hd.Libn.
HOLY TRINITY LUTHERAN CHURCH - LIBRARY†
□ Minneapolis, MN

Cruz, Joanne E., Lib.Coord.
COMPUTER AIDED MANUFACTURING-
INTERNATIONAL, INC. (CAM-I) - LIBRARY □
Arlington, TX

Cruze, Marianne H., Exec.Dir.
INTERNATIONAL VISITORS INFORMATION
SERVICE □ Washington, DC

Cryderman, Sandra A., Dir.
ST. JOSEPH HOSPITAL OF MT. CLEMENS -
MEDICAL LIBRARY □ Mt. Clemens, MI

Csaky, Susan D., Assoc.Prof./Law Libn.
UNIVERSITY OF MISSOURI - SCHOOL OF LAW
LIBRARY □ Columbia, MO

Cseh, Eugene, Acq.Libn.
UNIVERSITY OF CONNECTICUT - HEALTH
CENTER - LYMAN MAYNARD STOWE LIBRARY □
Farmington, CT

Csuros, Dr. Barna, Assoc.Dir.
KEAN COLLEGE OF NEW JERSEY - NANCY
THOMPSON LIBRARY □ Union, NJ

Cuadra, JoAnn, Med.Libn.
U.S. VETERANS ADMINISTRATION (MD-Fort
Howard) - HOSPITAL LIBRARY □ Fort Howard,
MD

Cubillas, Mary M., Reports
SHELL OIL COMPANY - INFORMATION &
LIBRARY SERVICES □ Houston, TX

Cubit, James, Asst.Dir., Tech.Serv.
UNIVERSITY OF MISSOURI, ROLLA - CURTIS
LAWS WILSON LIBRARY □ Rolla, MO

Cucchiara, Anthony M., Cur.
BRYANT LIBRARY - LOCAL HISTORY
COLLECTION □ Roslyn, NY

Cuddy, Joan, Slide Libn.
SOUTHERN ALBERTA INSTITUTE OF
TECHNOLOGY - ALBERTA COLLEGE OF ART -
LIBRARY □ Calgary, AB

Cuebas, Ana E., Hd., Rd.Serv.Div.
UNIVERSITY OF PUERTO RICO - MAYAGUEZ
CAMPUS - LIBRARY □ Mayaguez, PR

Cuesta, Emerita M., Res.Libn.
AMERIFIRST FEDERAL SAVINGS & LOAN -
LIBRARY □ Miami, FL

Culbert, Lorraine M., Libn.
SOHIO ALASKA PETROLEUM COMPANY -
TECHNICAL LIBRARY† □ Anchorage, AK

Culbertson, Diana, Libn.
NATIONAL DAIRY COUNCIL - LIBRARY □
Rosemont, IL

Culbertson, Lillian, Supv.Tech.Proc.
CHICAGO TRANSIT AUTHORITY - HAROLD S.
ANTHON MEMORIAL LIBRARY □ Chicago, IL

Culbertson, Margaret, Libn.
UNIVERSITY OF HOUSTON - FRANZHEIM
ARCHITECTURE LIBRARY □ Houston, TX

Culkin, Patricia, Assoc.Dir.
UNIVERSITY OF DENVER - PENROSE LIBRARY □
Denver, CO

Cullen, Arthur R., Dir.
IDAHO STATE UNIVERSITY - COLLEGE OF
EDUCATION - INSTRUCTIONAL MATERIALS
CENTER □ Pocatello, ID

Cullen, Martin, Libn.
OLWINE, CONNELLY, CHASE, O'DONNELL &
WEYHER - LAW LIBRARY □ New York, NY

Cullen, Matthew F., Hd., Lib.
U.S. DEPT. OF ENERGY - BONNEVILLE POWER
ADMINISTRATION - LIBRARY □ Portland, OR

Cullen, Rosemary L., Spec.Coll.Libn.
BROWN UNIVERSITY - SPECIAL
COLLECTIONS† □ Providence, RI

Culley, Paul T., Hd., Tech.Ref.
NEW YORK STATE COLLEGE OF CERAMICS,
ALFRED UNIVERSITY - SAMUEL R. SCHOLES
LIBRARY OF CERAMICS □ Alfred, NY

Cullison, William R., Cur., S.E. Arch.Archv.
TULANE UNIVERSITY OF LOUISIANA - SPECIAL
COLLECTIONS DIVISION □ New Orleans, LA

Culp, Paul, ILL Libn.
SAM HOUSTON STATE UNIVERSITY - LIBRARY†
□ Huntsville, TX

PERSONNEL

Culp, Robert, ILL Libn.
MOUNT SINAI SCHOOL OF MEDICINE OF THE CITY UNIVERSITY OF NEW YORK - GUSTAVE L. & JANET W. LEVY LIBRARY □ New York, NY

Culpepper, Betty M., Biblog./Hd., Ref.Dept.
HOWARD UNIVERSITY - MOORLAND-SPINGARN RESEARCH CENTER - LIBRARY DIVISION □ Washington, DC

Culver, Curtis, Exec.V.P.
DEBS (Eugene V.) FOUNDATION - LIBRARY □ Terre Haute, IN

Culver, Edward A., Tech.Asst.Oper.Prod.
IDAHO STATE UNIVERSITY LIBRARY - AUDIO-VISUAL SERVICES □ Pocatello, ID

Culverhouse, Gertrude, Chf., Ref./Pub.Serv.
U.S. SOCIAL SECURITY ADMINISTRATION - LIBRARY □ Baltimore, MD

Culwell, Marie, Staff Sec.
LAUREL GROVE HOSPITAL - MEDICAL & DENTAL STAFF LIBRARY □ Castro Valley, CA

Cummin, Mrs. R.I.
RADNOR HISTORICAL SOCIETY - RESEARCH LIBRARY □ Wayne, PA

Cumming, J., Hd.Ref.Rm.Serv.
CANADA - PUBLIC ARCHIVES OF CANADA - MANUSCRIPT DIVISION □ Ottawa, ON

Cumming, John, Dir.
CENTRAL MICHIGAN UNIVERSITY - CLARKE HISTORICAL LIBRARY □ Mt. Pleasant, MI

Cumming, Linda L., Subject Dept.Mgr.
DENVER PUBLIC LIBRARY - CONSERVATION LIBRARY & REGIONAL ENERGY/ENVIRONMENT INFORMATION CENTER □ Denver, CO

Cummings, Charles F., Supv.Libn.
NEWARK PUBLIC LIBRARY - NEW JERSEY REFERENCE DIVISION □ Newark, NJ

Cummings, Joe, Chf. of Res. & Stat.
TENNESSEE STATE DEPARTMENT OF EMPLOYMENT SECURITY - RESEARCH & STATISTICS SECTION □ Nashville, TN

Cummings, John J., Dir. of AIC
AYER (NW) INCORPORATED - AYER INFORMATION CENTER □ New York, NY

Cummings, John P., Assoc.Dir.
U.S. NAVAL ACADEMY - NIMITZ LIBRARY □ Annapolis, MD

Cummings, Judith, Ref.Libn.
PALO ALTO MEDICAL FOUNDATION - BARNETT-HALL MEDICAL LIBRARY □ Palo Alto, CA

Cummings, Martin M., M.D., Dir.
NATIONAL LIBRARY OF MEDICINE □ Bethesda, MD

Cummings, Nancy H., Libn.
U.S. ARMY - COLD REGIONS RESEARCH & ENGINEERING LABORATORY - LIBRARY □ Hanover, NH

Cummings, Patricia K., Libn.
RAMSEY COUNTY LAW LIBRARY □ St. Paul, MN

Cummings, Roberta, Acq.Libn.
SOUTHERN UNIVERSITY - LAW SCHOOL LIBRARY □ Baton Rouge, LA

Cummins, Darleen, Pres.
CHEROKEE COUNTY HISTORICAL SOCIETY - RESEARCH CENTER □ Cleghorn, IA

Cummins, Kathryn, Dir.
MIDLAND COUNTY HISTORICAL SOCIETY - ARCHIVES □ Midland, MI

Cumnock, Frances, Res.
MORAVIAN MUSIC FOUNDATION, INC. - LIBRARY □ Winston-Salem, NC

Cunha, Evano L., Chf.
U.S. AIR FORCE - AIR FORCE SYSTEMS COMMAND - AIR FORCE GEOPHYSICS LABORATORY - RESEARCH LIBRARY† □ Bedford, MA

Cunico, John A., Dir. of Comm.Educ.
PLANNED PARENTHOOD OF MINNESOTA - POPULATION RESOURCE CENTER □ St. Paul, MN

Cunkle, Elizabeth C., Cat., Asst.Libn.
SIERRA CLUB - WILLIAM E. COLBY MEMORIAL LIBRARY □ San Francisco, CA

Cunliffe, William H., Chf.
U.S. NATL. ARCHIVES & RECORDS SERVICE - NATL. ARCHIVES - CENTER FOR CARTOGRAPHIC & ARCHITECTURAL ARCHIVES □ Washington, DC

Cunningham, Carolyn, Asst.Libn.
COHEN AND URETZ - LAW LIBRARY □ Washington, DC

Cunningham, Charles, Asst.Libn.
TULSA WORLD-TULSA TRIBUNE - LIBRARY DEPARTMENT† □ Tulsa, OK

Cunningham, Clifford, Asst.Libn.
KITCHENER-WATERLOO RECORD - LIBRARY □ Kitchener, ON

Cunningham, Dr. David K., Tech.Info.Sci.
PILLSBURY COMPANY - TECHNICAL INFORMATION CENTER □ Minneapolis, MN

Cunningham, Eleanor, Lib.Techn.
NEW YORK STATE OFFICE OF MENTAL HEALTH - ST. LAWRENCE PSYCHIATRIC CENTER - LIBRARY □ Ogdensburg, NY

Cunningham, Esther
OLD CATHEDRAL PARISH CHURCH - BRUTE LIBRARY □ Vincennes, IN

Cunningham, Francis W., Mss.Cat.
ONEIDA HISTORICAL SOCIETY - LIBRARY □ Utica, NY

Cunningham, Jay, Supv., Tech.Serv.
CALIFORNIA STATE LIBRARY □ Sacramento, CA

Cunningham, Judith, Dir./Cur.
CALAVERAS COUNTY MUSEUM AND ARCHIVES □ San Andreas, CA

Cunningham, Julie, Ref.Libn.
ST. JOHN'S UNIVERSITY - LIBRARY □ Jamaica, NY

Cunningham, Lorraine, Asst.Libn.
REID AND PRIEST - LAW LIBRARY □ New York, NY

Cunningham, Lynda S., Assoc.Libn.
MARYLAND STATE DEPARTMENT OF LEGISLATIVE REFERENCE - LIBRARY □ Annapolis, MD

Cunningham, Margaret A., Libn.
HANCOCK COUNTY LAW LIBRARY, INC. □ Ellsworth, ME

Cunningham, Sharon, Media & Online Serv.
GEORGETOWN UNIVERSITY - LAW CENTER LIBRARY □ Washington, DC

Cunnington, Linda, Hd.Libn.
CLARKSON GORDON - BUSINESS LIBRARY □ Montreal, PQ

Cunnion, Rev. Theodore, S.J., Libn.
LOYOLA REFERENCE LIBRARY □ Bronx, NY

Cupp, Christopher, Libn.
U.S. AIR FORCE BASE - GRISSOM BASE LIBRARY □ Peru, IN

Cupryk, Robert, Cat.
COLLEGE OF MEDICINE AND DENTISTRY OF NEW JERSEY AT NEWARK - GEORGE F. SMITH LIBRARY □ Newark, NJ

Curci, Lucy, Law Libn.
FEDERAL RESERVE BANK OF NEW YORK - LAW LIBRARY DIVISION □ New York, NY

Curcio, Kathy, Dir.
HELENE FULD MEDICAL CENTER - HEALTH SCIENCES LIBRARY □ Trenton, NJ

Curlo, Bertha Mae, Supv., Oper.Sys.
WARNER-LAMBERT COMPANY - CORPORATE LIBRARY† □ Morris Plains, NJ

Curnes, Janice, Asst.Libn.
MOUNT SINAI MEDICAL CENTER - MEDICAL LIBRARY □ Milwaukee, WI

Curnoe, Glen, Libn.
LONDON PUBLIC LIBRARIES AND MUSEUMS - LONDON ROOM □ London, ON

Curnutt, Mandy, Data User Serv.Off.
U.S. BUREAU OF THE CENSUS - REGIONAL DATA USER SERVICE - SEATTLE REGIONAL OFFICE - LIBRARY □ Seattle, WA

Curran, Darryl, Pres.
LOS ANGELES CENTER FOR PHOTOGRAPHIC STUDIES - LIBRARY □ Los Angeles, CA

Curran, George L., III, Supv./Libn.
BOEHRINGER MANNHEIM CORPORATION - BMC INFORMATION CENTER □ Indianapolis, IN

Curran, Gertrude, Asst.Libn.
LUTHERAN GENERAL HOSPITAL - LIBRARY □ Park Ridge, IL

Curran, Peggy, Supv.Libn.
U.S. NAVY - NAVAL WEAPONS SUPPORT CENTER - LIBRARY □ Crane, IN

Curran, William, Asst.Libn.
ROYAL BANK OF CANADA - INFORMATION RESOURCES □ Montreal, PQ

Curren, J., Chf., Acq.Serv.
CANADA - AGRICULTURE CANADA - LIBRARIES DIVISION □ Ottawa, ON

Current, Phyllis, Supv.Libn.
NEW YORK PUBLIC LIBRARY - MID-MANHATTAN LIBRARY - HISTORY AND SOCIAL SCIENCES DEPARTMENT □ New York, NY

Currie, Clifford, Libn.
COLLEGE OF WILLIAM AND MARY - EARL GREGG SWEM LIBRARY □ Williamsburg, VA

Currie, June, Libn.
CANADA - FISHERIES & OCEANS - R&D DIRECTORATE - ARCTIC BIOLOGICAL STATION LIBRARY □ Ste. Anne-De-Bellevue, PQ

Currie, Kathleen, Acq. & Spec. Coll.
MOUNT SAINT VINCENT UNIVERSITY - LIBRARY □ Halifax, NS

Currie, Lyn, Libn.
UNIVERSITY OF BRITISH COLUMBIA - SOCIAL SCIENCES DIVISION □ Vancouver, BC

Curry, David R., Mgr.
BURROUGHS CORPORATION - CORPORATE INFORMATION RESEARCH CENTER □ Detroit, MI

Curry, David S., Libn.
UNIVERSITY OF IOWA - HEALTH SCIENCES LIBRARY □ Iowa City, IA

Curry, Frances, Libn.
AMERICAN ACADEMY OF PEDIATRICS - LIBRARY □ Evanston, IL

Curry, Frances, Libn.
WINDSOR STAR - LIBRARY □ Windsor, ON

Curry, Sr. Marilyn, Libn.
ST. MARTHA'S HOSPITAL - SCHOOL OF NURSING LIBRARY □ Antigonish, NS

Curtice, Claire B., Libn.
U.S. ARMY - LANGUAGE TRAINING FACILITY - LIBRARY □ Ft. Hood, TX

Curtin, Raymond W., Libn.
EASTMAN KODAK COMPANY - ENGINEERING LIBRARY □ Rochester, NY

Curtin-Stevenson, Mary, Hd.Cat.
EMERSON COLLEGE - ABBOT MEMORIAL LIBRARY □ Boston, MA

Curtis, Betty J.L., Med.Libn.
U.S. VETERANS ADMINISTRATION (PA-Lebanon) - MEDICAL CENTER LIBRARY □ Lebanon, PA

Curtis, Dr. George H., Asst.Dir.
U.S. PRESIDENTIAL LIBRARIES - HARRY S TRUMAN LIBRARY □ Independence, MO

Curtis, Gloria, Ref.Libn.
GENERAL ELECTRIC COMPANY - ADVANCED REACTOR SYSTEMS DEPT. - LIBRARY □ Sunnyvale, CA

Curtis, Howard W., Cur.
HAVERHILL PUBLIC LIBRARY - SPECIAL COLLECTIONS DIVISION □ Haverhill, MA

Curtis, Jim, AV Libn.
EAST TENNESSEE STATE UNIVERSITY, QUILLEN-DISHNER COLLEGE OF MEDICINE - DEPT. OF LEARNING RSRCS. - MEDICAL LIBRARY □ Johnson City, TN

Curtis, Karen, Libn.
TULSA CITY-COUNTY LIBRARY SYSTEM - BUSINESS AND TECHNOLOGY DEPARTMENT □ Tulsa, OK

Curtis, Marilyn D., Hd., Tech.Serv.
U.S. NAVY - NAVAL WAR COLLEGE - LIBRARY □ Newport, RI

Curtis, Marjorie B., Ref.Libn./ILL
MISSISSIPPI VALLEY STATE UNIVERSITY -
JAMES HERBERT WHITE LIBRARY □ Itta Bena,
MS

Curtis, Mary E., Chf., Lib.Serv.
U.S. VETERANS ADMINISTRATION (TX-Temple)
- CENTER MEDICAL LIBRARY □ Temple, TX

Curtis, Michael L., Libn.
ARNHOLD AND S. BLEICHROEDER, INC. -
LIBRARY □ New York, NY

Curtis, Paul J., Dir.
AMERICAN MIME, INC. - LIBRARY □ New York,
NY

Curtis, Peter H., Hd.Libn.
STATE HISTORICAL SOCIETY OF IOWA -
LIBRARY □ Iowa City, IA

Curtis, Ron, Asst.Dir.Tech.Serv.
CENTRAL STATE UNIVERSITY - LIBRARY □
Edmond, OK

Curtis-Kohrs, Charlotte, Supv., Lib.Serv.
PEAT, MARWICK, MITCHELL & COMPANY -
LIBRARY □ Houston, TX

Curtiss, Ruth E., Online Search
HERCULES, INC. - RESEARCH CENTER -
TECHNICAL INFORMATION DIVISION □
Wilmington, DE

Cusack, Edythe, Libn.
LONDON FREE PRESS PUBLISHING COMPANY,
LTD. - EDITORIAL LIBRARY □ London, ON

Cuseo, William J., Hd.
ROCHESTER PUBLIC LIBRARY - LITERATURE
AND RECREATION DIVISION □ Rochester, NY

Cushing, John D., Libn.
MASSACHUSETTS HISTORICAL SOCIETY -
RESEARCH LIBRARY □ Boston, MA

Cushing, Marie, Hd., Circ.
U.S. DEPT. OF ENERGY - LAWRENCE
LIVERMORE LAB. - TECHNICAL INFO. DEPT.
LIBRARY □ Livermore, CA

Cushing, Stanley E., Consrv.
BOSTON ATHENAEUM LIBRARY □ Boston, MA

Cushman, Helen M.B., Dir.
BAKER (H.M.) ASSOCIATES - RESEARCH
COLLECTION □ Westfield, NJ

Cushman, Robert, Photographic Serv.
ACADEMY OF MOTION PICTURE ARTS AND
SCIENCES - MARGARET HERRICK LIBRARY □
Beverly Hills, CA

Cussins, Marcia, Libn.
MISSOURI STATE DIVISION OF GEOLOGY AND
LAND SURVEY - LIBRARY □ Rolla, MO

Custer, Charles D., Exec.Dir.
CAPITAL DISTRICT LIBRARY COUNCIL FOR
REFERENCE AND RESEARCH RESOURCES -
BIBLIOGRAPHIC CENTER □ Latham, NY

Custer, Virginia, Libn.
WESTERN AND SOUTHERN LIFE INSURANCE
CO. - LIBRARY □ Cincinnati, OH

Cutberth, Mildred L., Sr.Libn.
NORTHEASTERN ILLINOIS PLANNING
COMMISSION - LIBRARY □ Chicago, IL

Cuthill, Dr. J.R., Metallurgist
U.S. NATL. BUREAU OF STANDARDS - ALLOY
DATA CENTER □ Washington, DC

Cutler, C.M., Area Coord.
CANADA - AGRICULTURE CANADA - RESEARCH
STATION, VANCOUVER - LIBRARY □ Vancouver,
BC

Cutler, Kirsten, Jr.Libn.
FIREMAN'S FUND INSURANCE COMPANIES -
LIBRARY† □ San Francisco, CA

Cutler, Phyllis, Asst.Univ.Libn.
BRANDEIS UNIVERSITY - GERSTENZANG
SCIENCE LIBRARY □ Waltham, MA

Cutlip, Arthur, Fed.Doc.Libn.
MIAMI-DADE PUBLIC LIBRARY - FEDERAL
DOCUMENTS DIVISION □ Miami, FL

Cutrell, Patricia A., Lib. Media Tech.Asst.
MC GILL & SMITH ENGINEERS, ARCHITECTS &
PLANNERS - LIBRARY □ Amelia, OH

Cutress, Bertha, Res.Assoc.
UNIVERSITY OF PUERTO RICO - MAYAGUEZ
CAMPUS - MARINE SCIENCES LIBRARY† □
Mayaguez, PR

Cutter, Margaret S., Libn.
LIMA MEMORIAL HOSPITAL - HEALTH
SCIENCES LIBRARY □ Lima, OH

Cylke, Frank Kurt, Dir.
LIBRARY OF CONGRESS - NATIONAL LIBRARY
SERVICE FOR THE BLIND AND PHYSICALLY
HANDICAPPED □ Washington, DC

Cyphers, James, Archv.
ROCKEFELLER UNIVERSITY - ROCKEFELLER
ARCHIVE CENTER □ North Tarrytown, NY

Cyr, Donald L., Ed.
STONEHENGE STUDY GROUP - LIBRARY □ Santa
Barbara, CA

Cyr, Helen W., Hd.
ENOCH PRATT FREE LIBRARY - AUDIO-VISUAL
DEPARTMENT □ Baltimore, MD

Cyr, Lucy L., Libn.
CONNECTICUT STATE LIBRARY - LAW LIBRARY
AT WATERBURY □ Waterbury, CT

Cyr, Mariann, Asst.Sci.Libn.
UNIVERSITY OF KANSAS - SCIENCE LIBRARY □
Lawrence, KS

Cyr, Paul, Libn.
NEW BEDFORD FREE PUBLIC LIBRARY -
GENEALOGY ROOM □ New Bedford, MA

Cyr, Paul, Cur.
NEW BEDFORD FREE PUBLIC LIBRARY -
MELVILLE WHALING ROOM □ New Bedford, MA

Czanyo, Mrs. M., Assoc.Dir.
CANADA - ENVIRONMENT CANADA - LIBRARY
SERVICES BRANCH □ Ottawa, ON

Czarnetzky, Lucille L., Cur.
MINER (Alice T.) COLONIAL COLLECTION -
LIBRARY □ Chazy, NY

Czechowicz, Maria, Dir.
FLUSHING HOSPITAL AND MEDICAL CENTER -
MEDICAL LIBRARY □ New York, NY

Cziffra, Peter, Libn.
PRINCETON UNIVERSITY - ASTRONOMY
LIBRARY □ Princeton, NJ

Cziffra, Peter, Libn.
PRINCETON UNIVERSITY - MATHEMATICS,
PHYSICS AND STATISTICS LIBRARY □
Princeton, NJ

Czike, Stephen F., Exec.Libn.
CHICAGO BAR ASSOCIATION - LIBRARY □
Chicago, IL

Czisny, Julie, Educ.Libn.
UNIVERSITY OF WISCONSIN, MILWAUKEE -
GOLDA MEIR LIBRARY - CURRICULUM
COLLECTION □ Milwaukee, WI

Czujak, Maureen, Hd., Rd.Serv.
NEW YORK MEDICAL COLLEGE AND THE
WESTCHESTER ACADEMY OF MEDICINE -
WESTCHESTER MEDICAL CENTER LIBRARY □
Valhalla, NY

D

Daane, Wilma A., Ref.Libn.
U.S. AIR FORCE - ACCOUNTING AND FINANCE
CENTER - TECHNICAL LIBRARY □ Denver, CO

Dabbs, Charlotte H., Libn.
U.S. NASA - MSFC LIBRARY □ Marshall Space
Flight Ctr., AL

Dabbs, Mary Lou, Hd.Libn.
CALLAWAY EDUCATIONAL ASSOCIATION -
COLEMAN LIBRARY □ LaGrange, GA

Dablemont, Maria, Libn.
INTERNATIONAL LIBRARY, ARCHIVES &
MUSEUM OF OPTOMETRY □ St. Louis, MO

Dacker, Paula, Fld.Serv.Libn.
BRAILLE INSTITUTE OF AMERICA - LIBRARY □
Los Angeles, CA

Dacko, A., Rpt.Supv.
ALUMINUM COMPANY OF AMERICA - ALCOA
LABORATORIES - INFORMATION DEPARTMENT
□ Alcoa Center, PA

Dada, Judy, Tech.Serv./Archv.
KENRICK SEMINARY LIBRARY □ St. Louis, MO

D'Adamo, Peggy, Pres.
ALTERNATIVE PRESS CENTER - LIBRARY □
Baltimore, MD

Dade, Mary J., Asst.Libn.
PACIFIC POWER AND LIGHT COMPANY -
LIBRARY □ Portland, OR

Daffe, Phyllis D., Asst. To Libn.
NORTHWEST BIBLE COLLEGE - LIBRARY □
Minot, ND

Daffern, A.M., Club Libn.
ALPINE CLUB OF CANADA - LIBRARY □ Banff,
AB

Daffron, Mary Ellen, Libn.
U.S. FEDERAL MARITIME COMMISSION -
LIBRARY† □ Washington, DC

Dagenhart, Nancy, Info.Spec.
NATIONAL ACADEMY OF SCIENCES -
NATIONAL RESEARCH COUNCIL - HIGHWAY
RESEARCH INFORMATION SERVICE □
Washington, DC

Daggy, Robert E., Cur.
BELLARMINE COLLEGE - THOMAS MERTON
STUDIES CENTER □ Louisville, KY

Dahl, Mr. E., Chf., Early Cart.Sect
CANADA - PUBLIC ARCHIVES OF CANADA -
NATIONAL MAP COLLECTION □ Ottawa, ON

Dahl, Richard C., Dir.
ARIZONA STATE UNIVERSITY - COLLEGE OF
LAW - LIBRARY □ Tempe, AZ

Dahlstrom, Ruth, Libn.
FIRST BAPTIST CHURCH - MEDIA LIBRARY □
Abilene, TX

Dahm, Frank, Dir.
DMS, INC. - TECHNICAL LIBRARY □ Greenwich,
CT

Dahm, Mary C., Libn.
ST. LOUIS COUNTY LAW LIBRARY □ Clayton,
MO

Dahms, Lester L., Exec.Dir.
AMERICAN INSTITUTE OF
PARLIAMENTARIANS - LIBRARY □ Des Moines,
IA

Daigle, Jean, Dir.
UNIVERSITE DE MONCTON - CENTRE
D'ETUDES ACADIENNES □ Moncton, NB

Daigle, Louise, Lib.Techn.
CENTRALE DE L'ENSEIGNEMENT DU QUEBEC -
CENTRE DE DOCUMENTATION □ Quebec, PQ

Dailey, Adelle G., Music Libn.
UNIVERSITY OF KENTUCKY - MUSIC LIBRARY/
LISTENING CENTER □ Lexington, KY

Dailey, Kazuko M., Asst.Univ.Libn/Tech.Serv.
UNIVERSITY OF CALIFORNIA, DAVIS -
GENERAL LIBRARY □ Davis, CA

Dailey, Linda D., Asst.Libn.
NORTH CENTRAL BIBLE COLLEGE - T.J. JONES
MEMORIAL LIBRARY □ Minneapolis, MN

Dainard, Norma, Asst. In Charge
METROPOLITAN TORONTO LIBRARY -
NEWSPAPER UNIT □ Toronto, ON

Dainauskas, Jonas, Cat. & Ref.Libn.
LIBRARY OF INTERNATIONAL RELATIONS □
Chicago, IL

Daines, Gladys D., Info.Off.
U.S. FOREST SERVICE - NORTHEASTERN
FOREST EXPERIMENT STATION LIBRARY □
Broomall, PA

Dais, Romeo, Libn.
MADISON PUBLIC LIBRARY - BUSINESS AND
SCIENCE DIVISION □ Madison, WI

Daitchman, Norman
ZITTRER, SIBLIN, STEIN, LEVINE - LIBRARY □
Montreal, PQ

Dakan, Tony, Dir., USAF Libs.
U.S. AIR FORCE - AIR FORCE MANPOWER AND PERSONNEL CENTER - MORALE, WELFARE & RECREATION DIVISION - LIBRARIES SECTION □ Randolph AFB, TX

Dakshinamurti, Ganga, Tech.Serv./Sys.Libn.
RED RIVER COMMUNITY COLLEGE - LEARNING RESOURCES CENTRE □ Winnipeg, MB

Dalby, Barbara M., Libn.
CHURCH OF JESUS CHRIST OF LATTER-DAY SAINTS - TAMPA BRANCH GENEALOGICAL LIBRARY □ Tampa, FL

Dale, David T., Libn.
YALE CLUB OF NEW YORK CITY - LIBRARY □ New York, NY

Dale, Marianne, Lib.Asst.
NORTH CAROLINA STATE UNIVERSITY - HARRYE LYONS DESIGN LIBRARY □ Raleigh, NC

Dalechek, Marjorie E., Photo Libn.
U.S. GEOLOGICAL SURVEY - DENVER LIBRARY □ Denver, CO

D'Aleo, Ruth P., Ref.Libn.
MORAVIAN COLLEGE - REEVES LIBRARY □ Bethlehem, PA

Dalesandro, Anne, Ref.Libn.
RUTGERS UNIVERSITY, THE STATE UNIVERSITY OF NEW JERSEY - SCHOOL OF LAW LIBRARY† □ Camden, NJ

D'Alessandro, Paul A., Assoc.Libn.
MAINE STATE LAW AND LEGISLATIVE REFERENCE LIBRARY □ Augusta, ME

Daley, Patricia, Libn.
ACCURAY CORPORATION - ENGINEERING LIBRARY □ Columbus, OH

Daley, Trudy, Chf.Libn.
UNITED STATES TRUST COMPANY - INVESTMENT LIBRARY □ New York, NY

Dallas, Larayne, Hd.Ref.Libn.
ARKANSAS STATE UNIVERSITY - DEAN B. ELLIS LIBRARY □ State University, AR

Dallas, Shirley, Info.Spec.
WASHINGTON STATE SUPERINTENDENT OF PUBLIC INSTRUCTION - RESOURCE INFORMATION CENTER □ Tumwater WA

Dallett, Francis James, Archv.
UNIVERSITY OF PENNSYLVANIA - ARCHIVES AND RECORDS CENTER □ Philadelphia, PA

Dalligan, Alice C., Chf.
DETROIT PUBLIC LIBRARY - BURTON HISTORICAL COLLECTION □ Detroit, MI

Dalphin, George R., Ref.Supv.
U.S. DEPT OF ENERGY - SANDIA NATL. LABORATORIES - TECHNICAL LIBRARY □ Albuquerque, NM

Dalrymple, Patricia A., Dir., Lib.Serv.
HAMOT MEDICAL CENTER - LIBRARY SERVICES □ Erie, PA

Dalrymple, Prudence, Hosp.Libn.
ROCKFORD MEMORIAL HOSPITAL - HEALTH SCIENCE LIBRARY □ Rockford, IL

Dalton, Deborah, Libn.
BASSETT (Mary Imogene) HOSPITAL - MEDICAL LIBRARY □ Cooperstown, NY

Dalton, Flora, Asst.Libn.
FIRST BAPTIST CHURCH - LIBRARY □ Slocomb, AL

Dalton, Richard R., Asst.Chf.Med.Libn.
UNIVERSITY OF MISSOURI, KANSAS CITY - HEALTH SCIENCES LIBRARY □ Kansas City, MO

Dalton, Susan, Assoc.Dir.
UNIVERSITY OF WISCONSIN, MADISON - WISCONSIN CENTER FOR FILM AND THEATER RESEARCH □ Madison, WI

Daly, Gail M., Ser.Libn.
UNIVERSITY OF MINNESOTA - LAW LIBRARY □ Minneapolis, MN

Daly, Jerry, Chm., Media Serv.
LOMA LINDA UNIVERSITY - DEL E. WEBB MEMORIAL LIBRARY □ Loma Linda, CA

Daly, John, Dir.
ILLINOIS STATE - OFFICE OF THE SECRETARY OF STATE - STATE ARCHIVES □ Springfield, IL

Daly, Rev. Lowrie J., Microfilm Projects
ST. LOUIS UNIVERSITY - KNIGHTS OF COLUMBUS VATICAN FILM LIBRARY □ St. Louis, MO

Daly, Richard, Asst.Dir./Tech.Proc.
TRENTON STATE COLLEGE - ROSCOE L. WEST LIBRARY □ Trenton, NJ

Daly, Susan, Libn.
BULL, HOUSSER AND TUPPER - LIBRARY □ Vancouver, BC

Dam, Mrs. Tran, Hd.Libn.
PROCTOR & REDFERN, CONSULTING ENGINEERS - LIBRARY □ Toronto, ON

Damaskos, James, Libn.
HARVARD UNIVERSITY - LITTAUER LIBRARY □ Cambridge, MA

D'Ambrosio, Ann Marie, Lib.Techn.
U.S. CUSTOMS SERVICE - REGION II - LAW LIBRARY □ New York, NY

D'Ambrosio, Margaret, Assoc.Libn.
AMERICAN NUMISMATIC SOCIETY - LIBRARY □ New York, NY

Dame, Fern Shrewsberry, Illus.Libn.
NATIONAL GEOGRAPHIC SOCIETY - ILLUSTRATIONS LIBRARY □ Washington, DC

Damkoehler, Mrs. Arthur, Libn.
HOPE LUTHERAN CHURCH - LIBRARY □ Milwaukee, WI

Damm, Robert L., Dir.
BUFFALO & ERIE COUNTY HISTORICAL SOCIETY - LIBRARY □ Buffalo, NY

Dammers, Kim, Musm.Dir.
BAY COUNTY HISTORICAL SOCIETY - MUSEUM OF THE GREAT LAKES - LIBRARY □ Bay City, MI

Damon, Cora M., Libn.
MID-MAINE MEDICAL CENTER - CLARA HODGKINS MEMORIAL HEALTH SCIENCES LIBRARY □ Waterville, ME

Damon, Gene, Asst.Libn., Sys.
UNIVERSITY OF WATERLOO - DANA PORTER ARTS LIBRARY □ Waterloo, ON

Damon, Janet R., Libn.
U.S. BUREAU OF ALCOHOL, TOBACCO AND FIREARMS - NATIONAL LABORATORY LIBRARY □ Rockville, MD

Damon, Sharon, Chf., Doc.Serv.
U.S. GENERAL ACCOUNTING OFFICE - TECHNICAL INFORMATION SOURCES AND SERVICES BRANCH □ Washington, DC

Damon, Shirley, Asst.Libn.
STONE AND WEBSTER MANAGEMENT CONSULTANTS, INC. - INFORMATION CENTER/LIBRARY† □ New York, NY

Danahar, Catherine M., Libn.
HARVARD UNIVERSITY - HARVARD FOREST LIBRARY □ Petersham, MA

Dance, Barbara, Libn.
TOUCHE, ROSS & COMPANY/TOUCHE ROSS & PARTNERS - LIBRARY □ Toronto, ON

Dance, Barbara, Libn.
UNIVERSITY OF TORONTO - FACULTY OF MANAGEMENT STUDIES LIBRARY □ Toronto, ON

Dancik, Deborah, Educ.Ref.Libn.
UNIVERSITY OF ALBERTA - H.T. COUTTS EDUCATION LIBRARY □ Edmonton, AB

D'Andrea, Julia, Cat.
UNIVERSITY OF PITTSBURGH - FALK LIBRARY OF THE HEALTH SCIENCES □ Pittsburgh, PA

Dandridge, Vonita, Ser.Libn.
VIRGINIA STATE UNIVERSITY - JOHNSTON MEMORIAL LIBRARY □ Petersburg, VA

Dandridge-Perry, C., Hd.
UNIVERSITY OF CALIFORNIA, LOS ANGELES - ENGLISH READING ROOM† □ Los Angeles, CA

Dandurand, Gary, AV Libn.
UNIVERSITY OF HEALTH SCIENCES/CHICAGO MEDICAL SCHOOL - LIBRARY □ North Chicago, IL

Dane, William J., Supv.
NEWARK PUBLIC LIBRARY - ART AND MUSIC DEPARTMENT □ Newark, NJ

Dang, Charlotte
LEEWARD COMMUNITY COLLEGE - LIBRARY □ Honolulu, HI

Dangerville, Marie, Transl./Receptionist
FRENCH LIBRARY IN BOSTON, INC. □ Boston, MA

Dangle-Killeen, Kathy, Ref.Libn.
NICHOLS COLLEGE - CONANT LIBRARY □ Dudley, MA

Daniel, E.L., Ref.Spec.
U.S. DEPT. OF ENERGY - PACIFIC NORTHWEST LABORATORY - TECHNICAL INFO. SECT. □ Richland, WA

Daniel, Eileen, Libn.
NORTHERN TELECOM CANADA, LTD. - NT LIBRARY □ Islington, ON

Daniel, Eleanor M., Hd.Libn.
OHIO STATE UNIVERSITY - BLACK STUDIES LIBRARY □ Columbus, OH

Daniel, Wayne, Libn./Archv.
FORT CONCHO REFERENCE LIBRARY □ San Angelo, TX

Daniels, Belinda, Act.Libn.
WINSTON-SALEM STATE UNIVERSITY - O'KELLY LIBRARY □ Winston-Salem, NC

Daniels, Bruce E., Deputy Dir.
RHODE ISLAND STATE DEPARTMENT OF STATE LIBRARY SERVICES □ Providence, RI

Daniels, Deborah, Info.Cons.
CITE RESOURCE CENTER □ Austin, TX

Daniels, Jerome P., Dir.
UNIVERSITY OF WISCONSIN, PLATTEVILLE - KARRMANN LIBRARY □ Platteville, WI

Danio, Mary, Asst.Libn.
UNIVERSITY OF MIAMI - DOROTHY & LEWIS ROSENSTIEL SCHOOL OF MARINE & ATMOSPHERIC SCIENCES - LIBRARY □ Miami, FL

Danker, Elizabeth, Circ./ILL
CHRIST SEMINARY - SEMINEX LIBRARY □ St. Louis, MO

Dankert, Phillip, Coll.Dev.
CORNELL UNIVERSITY - MARTIN P. CATHERWOOD LIBRARY OF INDUSTRIAL AND LABOR RELATIONS □ Ithaca, NY

Dankewych, Dr. Michael, Libn.
U.S. NAVY - DAVID W. TAYLOR NAVAL SHIP RESEARCH AND DEVELOPMENT CENTER - LIBRARY DIVISION □ Bethesda, MD

Danko, Diana M., Supv.Info.Serv.
PPG INDUSTRIES, INC. - CHEMICAL DIVISION - RESEARCH LIBRARY □ Barberton, OH

Dann, John C., Dir.
UNIVERSITY OF MICHIGAN - WILLIAM L. CLEMENTS LIBRARY □ Ann Arbor, MI

Danner, Mrs. Michael, Libn.
AMERICAN WATCHMAKERS INSTITUTE - LIBRARY □ Cincinnati, OH

Danner, Richard, Dir.
DUKE UNIVERSITY - SCHOOL OF LAW LIBRARY □ Durham, NC

Danner, Susan, Med.Libn.
ARCHBOLD (John D.) MEMORIAL HOSPITAL - RALPH PERKINS MEMORIAL LIBRARY □ Thomasville, GA

Danner, Susan T., Med.Libn.
SOUTH GEORGIA MEDICAL CENTER - MEDICAL LIBRARY □ Valdosta, GA

Dansereau, Heather, Med.Libn.
CIBA-GEIGY (Canada) LTD. - PHARMACEUTICAL LIBRARY □ Mississauga, ON

Dansker, Shirley E., Dir.
LENOX HILL HOSPITAL - HEALTH SCIENCES LIBRARY □ New York, NY

Danton, Lois King, Libn.
HERRICK HOSPITAL AND HEALTH CENTER - PSYCHIATRIC LIBRARY □ Berkeley, CA

Danziger, Beth, Asst. Law Libn.
UNIVERSITY OF CONNECTICUT - LAW SCHOOL LIBRARY □ West Hartford, CT

D'Aoust, J.G., D.D.S., Libn.
CANADIAN DENTAL ASSOCIATION - SYDNEY
WOOD BRADLEY MEMORIAL LIBRARY □ Ottawa,
ON

Daoust, Richard L., Hd.Libn.
MICHIGAN STATE DEPARTMENT OF LABOR -
MICHIGAN EMPLOYMENT SECURITY
COMMISSION - LIBRARY □ Detroit, MI

D'Aoust, Yolande, Lib.Asst.
CANADA - FARM CREDIT CORPORATION
CANADA - LIBRARY □ Ottawa, ON

Daptula, Joan, R.R.L., Libn.
SACRED HEART HOSPITAL - WILLIAM A.
HAUSMAN MEDICAL LIBRARY □ Allentown, PA

Darbee, Leigh, Ref.Libn.
INDIANA HISTORICAL SOCIETY - WILLIAM
HENRY SMITH MEMORIAL LIBRARY □
Indianapolis, IN

Darby, Dr. William J., Honor.Cur.
VANDERBILT UNIVERSITY - MEDICAL CENTER
LIBRARY □ Nashville, TN

Darcy, Kathy, Lib.Dev.Off.
WYOMING STATE LIBRARY □ Cheyenne, WY

Darcy, Madeleine A., Sr.Libn.
CALIFORNIA STATE RESOURCES AGENCY -
LIBRARY □ Sacramento, CA

Darcy, William, Base Libn.
U.S. AIR FORCE BASE - LAUGHLIN BASE
LIBRARY □ Del Rio, TX

Dardeau, Sr. Dorothy, Libn.
ST. FRANCES CABRINI HOSPITAL - MEDICAL
LIBRARY □ Alexandria, LA

Darknell, Edith, Libn.
CALIFORNIA STATE DEPARTMENT OF
TRANSPORTATION - TRANSPORTATION
LIBRARY □ Sacramento, CA

Darling, John, Libn.
UNIVERSITY OF NORTH CAROLINA, CHAPEL
HILL - ZOOLOGY LIBRARY □ Chapel Hill, NC

Darling, Mikell C., Dir.
EVANSTON HISTORICAL SOCIETY - CHARLES
GATES DAWES HOME - LIBRARY □ Evanston, IL

Darlington, Anne, Spec.Coll.Libn.
GEORGETOWN UNIVERSITY - MEDICAL
CENTER - DAHLGREN MEMORIAL LIBRARY □
Washington, DC

Darlington, Gerard, Libn.
QUEBEC PROVINCE - MINISTERE DES
AFFAIRES SOCIALES - BIBLIOTHEQUE† □
Montreal, PQ

Darnell, Linda, Libn.
CONWAY (E.A.) MEMORIAL HOSPITAL -
MEDICAL LIBRARY □ Monroe, LA

Darnell, Polly C., Libn.
SHELDON ART MUSEUM - GOVERNOR JOHN W.
STEWART & MR. & MRS. CHARLES M. SWIFT
RESEARCH CENTER LIBRARY □ Middlebury, VT

Darr, William, Asst.Dir.
GRACE THEOLOGICAL SEMINARY - LIBRARY □
Winona Lake, IN

Darrah, Elizabeth, Docs.Ref.Libn.
UNIVERSITY OF WASHINGTON - GOVERNMENT
PUBLICATIONS DIVISION □ Seattle, WA

Dart, Ann, Bookmobile Libn.
U.S. MARINE CORPS - CAMP PENDLETON
LIBRARY SYSTEM† □ Camp Pendleton, CA

Darveau, L., Loans
COMPLEXE SCIENTIFIQUE DU QUEBEC -
SERVICE DE DOCUMENTATION ET DE
BIBLIOTHEQUE □ Ste. Foy, PQ

Darvill, Eunice, Dir.
SKAGIT COUNTY HISTORICAL MUSEUM -
HISTORICAL REFERENCE LIBRARY □ La Conner,
WA

Darwick, Frances, Libn.
CONDIESEL MOBILE EQUIPMENT -
ENGINEERING LIBRARY □ Old Greenwich, CT

Darwin, Karen Lee, Projects Ed.
ENVIRONMENTAL EDUCATION GROUP -
LIBRARY □ Camarillo, CA

Das Gupta, Krishna, Tech.Serv.
WORCESTER STATE COLLEGE - LEARNING
RESOURCES CENTER □ Worcester, MA

Dasch, Jacqueline, Libn.
ENERGY IMPACT ASSOCIATES, INC. - LIBRARY
□ Pittsburgh, PA

Dashwar, Susan, Dir., Prog. & Proj.
NATIONAL ENERGY FOUNDATION - ENERGY
REFERENCE AND RESOURCE CENTER □ New
York, NY

Date, Sandra, Libn.
PILLSBURY COMPANY - MAIN OFFICE
MARKETING LIBRARY □ Minneapolis, MN

Dater, Lois, Cur.
STAMFORD HISTORICAL SOCIETY - LIBRARY □
Stamford, CT

D'Atri, Bianca G., Acq.Libn.
U.S. ARMY - NATICK RESEARCH AND
DEVELOPMENT LABORATORIES - TECHNICAL
LIBRARY □ Natick, MA

Daub, Peggy, Hd.Cat.
YALE UNIVERSITY - JOHN HERRICK JACKSON
MUSIC LIBRARY □ New Haven, CT

Daudelin, Lorraine M., Libn.
MONSANTO PLASTICS & RESINS COMPANY -
PLASTICS DIV. - SPRINGFIELD PLANT -
TECHNOLOGY LIBRARY □ Indian Orchard, MA

Daudelin, Robert, Exec.Dir.
CINEMATHEQUE QUEBECOISE - ARCHIVES &
FILM MUSEUM □ Montreal, PQ

Daugherty, Carolyn M., Libn.
UNION MEMORIAL HOSPITAL - NURSING
SCHOOL LIBRARY □ Baltimore, MD

Daugherty, John, Pk.Hist.
U.S. NATL. PARK SERVICE - GRAND TETON
NATL. PARK - LIBRARY □ Moose, WY

Daugherty, Norma A., Asst.Libn.
INSTITUTE OF LIVING - MEDICAL LIBRARY □
Hartford, CT

Daugherty, Verla, Tech.Libn.
NEW MEXICO STATE UNIVERSITY - PHYSICAL
SCIENCE LABORATORY - TECHNICAL LIBRARY
□ Las Cruces, NM

Daum, Tricia, Info.Spec.
COMINCO LTD. - INFORMATION SERVICES □
Vancouver, BC

Dauphinais, Edward, Libn.
UNIVERSITY OF NEW HAMPSHIRE -
CHEMISTRY LIBRARY □ Durham, NH

Dauphinais, Edward, Sci.Br.Libn.
UNIVERSITY OF NEW HAMPSHIRE - DAVID G.
CLARK MEMORIAL PHYSICS LIBRARY □ Durham,
NH

Dauphinais, Edward J., Libn.
UNIVERSITY OF NEW HAMPSHIRE -
ENGINEERING-MATH LIBRARY □ Durham, NH

Davenport, Barbara, Med.Libn.
CHILDREN'S HOSPITAL MEDICAL CENTER OF
NORTHERN CALIFORNIA - MEDICAL LIBRARY □
Oakland, CA

Davenport, Janet, Libn.
IOWA STATE COMMISSION FOR THE BLIND -
LIBRARY FOR THE BLIND & PHYSICALLY
HANDICAPPED □ Des Moines, IA

Davenport, John B., Spec.Coll.Libn.
COLLEGE OF ST. THOMAS - CELTIC LIBRARY □
St. Paul, MN

Davenport, Margaret J., Libn.
CAHILL, GORDON, & REINDEL - LAW LIBRARY □
New York, NY

Davenport, Mrs. Vanny, Libn. & Cur.
NATIONAL BANK OF ALASKA - HERITAGE
LIBRARY AND MUSEUM □ Anchorage, AK

Davern, Magge, Exec.Dir.
VOLUNTARY ACTION CENTER OF THE ST. PAUL
AREA - LIBRARY □ St. Paul, MN

David, Carol A., Libn.
CRAIN COMMUNICATIONS, INC. -
INFORMATION CENTER □ Chicago, IL

David, Martin, Dir.
UNIVERSITY OF WISCONSIN, MADISON - DATA
AND PROGRAM LIBRARY SERVICE □ Madison,
WI

David, Maureen Walsh, Asst.Libn.
SIMMONS COLLEGE - SCHOOL OF LIBRARY
SCIENCE - LIBRARY □ Boston, MA

David, Shirley H., Asst. State Law Libn.
MINNESOTA STATE LAW LIBRARY □ St. Paul,
MN

David, Zdenek, Libn.
WILSON (Woodrow) INTERNATIONAL CENTER
FOR SCHOLARS - LIBRARY □ Washington, DC

Davidoff, Donna J., Hd.Libn.
TEMPLE BETH ZION - LIBRARY □ Buffalo, NY

Davidson, B.J., Libn.
U.S. DEPT. OF ENERGY - LARAMIE ENERGY
TECHNOLOGY CENTER LIBRARY □ Laramie, WY

Davidson, Mrs. Elfa M., Libn.
CENTRE FOR CHRISTIAN STUDIES - LIBRARY†
□ Toronto, ON

Davidson, Gail, Lib.Prog.Off.
INTERNATIONAL COMMUNICATION AGENCY -
OFFICE OF THE ASSOCIATE DIRECTORATE
FOR EDUCATIONAL & CULTURAL AFFAIRS □
Washington, DC

Davidson, Gwen, Libn.
U.S. NATL. PARK SERVICE - LAKE MEAD NATL.
RECREATION AREA - LIBRARY □ Boulder City,
NV

Davidson, Janet, Religious Educ.Libn.
MC CORMICK THEOLOGICAL SEMINARY -
LIBRARY† □ Chicago, IL

Davidson, M., Libn.
ASSOCIATED ENGINEERING SERVICES, LTD. -
INFORMATION CENTRE □ Edmonton, AB

Davidson, Mary, Libn.
SOCIETY OF FRIENDS - PHILADELPHIA YEARLY
MEETING - LIBRARY □ Philadelphia, PA

Davidson, Mary V., Asst.Libn.
CHESTER COUNTY LAW AND MISCELLANEOUS
LIBRARY ASSOCIATION □ West Chester, PA

Davidson, Mary Wallace, Music Libn.
WELLESLEY COLLEGE - MUSIC LIBRARY □
Wellesley, MA

Davidson, Nancy, Libn.
FOOTE CONE & BELDING - INFORMATION
CENTER □ Chicago, IL

Davidson, R.B., Supv., R&D Info.Spec.
GOODRICH (B.F.) COMPANY - GOODRICH
CHEMICAL DIVISION TECHNICAL CENTER -
INFORMATION CENTER □ Avon Lake, OH

Davidson, Sarah, Info.Spec.
FARMLAND INDUSTRIES, INC. - J.W. CUMMINS
MEMORIAL LIBRARY □ Kansas City, MO

Davidson, Silvia, Libn.
YESHIVA UNIVERSITY - ALBERT EINSTEIN
COLLEGE OF MEDICINE - DEPT. OF
PSYCHIATRY - J. THOMPSON PSYCHIATRY LIB.
□ Bronx, NY

Davidson, Thomas M., Asst. to Libn.
WESTERN MONTANA COLLEGE - LUCY CARSON
MEMORIAL LIBRARY □ Dillon, MT

Davidson, Dr. William D., Sr.Res.Info.Sci.
GENERAL MILLS, INC. - JAMES FORD BELL
TECHNICAL CENTER - TECHNICAL
INFORMATION SERVICES □ Minneapolis, MN

Davies, Dennis B., Chf. Naturalist-Dir.
U.S. NATL. PARK SERVICE - DINOSAUR NATL.
MONUMENT - QUARRY VISITOR CENTER -
LIBRARY □ Jensen, UT

Davies, Lydia, Corp.Rec.Hd./Ref.Libn.
SALOMON BROTHERS - CORPORATE FINANCE
LIBRARY □ New York, NY

Davies, Patty, Ref.Libn.
UNIVERSITY OF OREGON - HEALTH SCIENCES
CENTER - LIBRARY □ Portland, OR

Davies, Richard L., Exec.Dir.
SILVER INSTITUTE - LIBRARY □ Washington,
DC

Davies, Thelma S., Spec.Serv.Libn.
FRANCIS BACON FOUNDATION - LIBRARY □
Claremont, CA

Davignon, Dr. Jean, Cons.
CLINICAL RESEARCH INSTITUTE OF
MONTREAL - MEDICAL LIBRARY □ Montreal, PQ

Davila, Carmen Alicia, Archv.
PUERTO RICO - INSTITUTE OF PUERTO RICAN
CULTURE - ARCHIVO GENERAL DE PUERTO
RICO □ San Juan, PR

PERSONNEL

Davila, Roberta, Chem.Info.Ctr.
INDIANA UNIVERSITY - CHEMISTRY LIBRARY
□ Bloomington, IN
Davini, Thurston, Libn.
UNIVERSITY OF WISCONSIN, MADISON -
SCHOOL OF SOCIAL WORK - VIRGINIA L.
FRANKS MEMORIAL LIBRARY □ Madison, WI
Davis, Al, Hd., Tech.Serv.
WINNIPEG SCHOOL DIVISION NO. 1 -
TEACHERS LIBRARY AND RESOURCE CENTRE □
Winnipeg, MB
Davis, Alta K., Act.Chf., Ref.Serv.
U.S. NATL. DEFENSE UNIVERSITY - LIBRARY □
Washington, DC
Davis, Alyce L., Sr.Libn.
CALIFORNIA STATE DEPARTMENT OF
TRANSPORTATION - DISTRICT 7 LIBRARY □
Los Angeles, CA
Davis, Anne C., Hd.Libn.
UNIVERSITY OF MICHIGAN - MENTAL HEALTH
RESEARCH INSTITUTE - LIBRARY □ Ann Arbor,
MI
Davis, Arthur, III, Data & Anl.Spec.
GREENSBORO PLANNING & COMMUNITY
DEVELOPMENT DEPARTMENT - LIBRARY □
Greensboro, NC
Davis, Barbara M., Hd., Tech.Info.Serv.
CABOT CORPORATION - TECHNICAL
INFORMATION CENTER □ Billerica, MA
Davis, Benjamin, Supt.
U.S. NATL. PARK SERVICE - CARL SANDBURG
HOME NATL. HISTORIC SITE - MUSEUM/
LIBRARY □ Flat Rock, NC
Davis, Betty, Marketing Dir.
LOCKHEED MISSILES & SPACE COMPANY, INC.
- LOCKHEED INFORMATION SYSTEMS □ Palo
Alto, CA
Davis, Betty L., Libn.
OKLAHOMA VETERANS CENTER - TALIHINA
DIVISION - LIBRARY □ Talihina, OK
Davis, Bill, Media Spec.
NEW MEXICO SCHOOL FOR THE VISUALLY
HANDICAPPED - LIBRARY □ Alamogordo, NM
Davis, Bonnie D., Adm.Libn.
U.S. NAVY - NAVAL EXPLOSIVE ORDNANCE
DISPOSAL TECHNOLOGY CENTER - TECHNICAL
LIBRARY □ Indian Head, MD
Davis, Prof. Carlos R., Dir.
INTERAMERICAN UNIVERSITY - SCHOOL OF
LAW - DOMINGO TOLEDO ALAMO LAW LIBRARY
□ Santurce, PR
Davis, Carol S., Sr.Cat.Libn.
WEST VIRGINIA UNIVERSITY - LAW LIBRARY
□ Morgantown, WV
Davis, Carolyn, Asst. To Div.Hd.
DALLAS PUBLIC LIBRARY - BUSINESS AND
TECHNOLOGY DIVISION □ Dallas, TX
Davis, Carolyn A., Mss.Libn.
SYRACUSE UNIVERSITY - GEORGE ARENTS
RESEARCH LIBRARY FOR SPECIAL
COLLECTIONS □ Syracuse, NY
Davis, Carrolyn, Archv./Libn.
WAYNE STATE UNIVERSITY - ARCHIVES OF
LABOR AND URBAN AFFAIRS/UNIVERSITY
ARCHIVES □ Detroit, MI
Davis, Charles E., Dir. of Libs./Archv.
SOUTHERN MISSIONARY COLLEGE - MC KEE
LIBRARY - SPECIAL COLLECTIONS □
Collegedale, TN
Davis, Chester L., Exec.Sec.
MARK TWAIN RESEARCH FOUNDATION -
LIBRARY □ Perry, MO
Davis, Mrs. Clayla, Lib.Dir.
NAPA VALLEY WINE LIBRARY ASSOCIATION -
LIBRARY □ St. Helena, CA
Davis, Clifton, Libn.
BANGOR THEOLOGICAL SEMINARY - MOULTON
LIBRARY □ Bangor, ME
Davis, Cullom, Dir.
SANGAMON STATE UNIVERSITY - ORAL
HISTORY OFFICE - LIBRARY □ Springfield, IL

Davis, Dale C., Chf., Lib.Serv.
U.S. VETERANS ADMINISTRATION (MO-
Columbia) - HOSPITAL LIBRARY □ Columbia, MO
Davis, David J., Prov.Archv.
NEWFOUNDLAND - PROVINCIAL ARCHIVES OF
NEWFOUNDLAND AND LABRADOR □ St. John's,
NF
Davis, Debra, Hd., Info.Ret.Serv.
BIBLIOGRAPHICAL CENTER FOR RESEARCH -
ROCKY MOUNTAIN REGION, INC. □ Denver, CO
Davis, Donna L., Med.Libn.
BAPTIST MEMORIAL HOSPITAL - JOHN L.
MC GEHEE LIBRARY □ Memphis, TN
Davis, Doris, Tech.Serv.Libn.
BENNETT COLLEGE - THOMAS F. HOLGATE
LIBRARY - SPECIAL COLLECTIONS □
Greensboro, NC
Davis, Elisabeth B., Libn.
UNIVERSITY OF ILLINOIS - BIOLOGY LIBRARY
□ Urbana, IL
Davis, Emma, Circ.Libn.
CENTER FOR RESEARCH LIBRARIES □ Chicago,
IL
Davis, Eric, Asst.Libn.
CINCINNATI POST - LIBRARY □ Cincinnati, OH
Davis, Estelle, Dir. of Lib.Serv.
SHARP (Donald N.) MEMORIAL COMMUNITY
HOSPITAL - HEALTH SCIENCE LIBRARY □ San
Diego, CA
Davis, Esther, Res.
FIRST BAPTIST CHURCH - I.C. ANDERSON
LIBRARY □ Waco, TX
Davis, Fannie M., Dir.
SUMTER AREA TECHNICAL COLLEGE -
LIBRARY† □ Sumter, SC
Davis, Frances, Hd., Stacks/Copy
U.S. NATL. INSTITUTES OF HEALTH - LIBRARY
□ Bethesda, MD
Davis, Frances F., Libn.
TUSKEGEE INSTITUTE - SCHOOL OF
ENGINEERING LIBRARY† □ Tuskegee Institute,
AL
Davis, Gentry, Supt.
U.S. NATL. PARK SERVICE - GEORGE
WASHINGTON CARVER NATIONAL MONUMENT
- LIBRARY □ Diamond, MO
Davis, George R., Chf.Libn.
PILLSBURY, MADISON AND SUTRO - LIBRARY □
San Francisco, CA
Davis, Gerald F., Lib.Dir.
SPRINGFIELD COLLEGE - BABSON LIBRARY □
Springfield, MA
Davis, Gwendolyn T., Info.Spec.
CHILD WELFARE LEAGUE OF AMERICA, INC. -
DOROTHY L. BERNHARD LIBRARY □ New York,
NY
Davis, Harold, Tech. Monitor
U. S. NASA - LYNDON B. JOHNSON SPACE
CENTER - SPACE LIFE SCIENCES ARCHIVAL
LIBRARY □ Houston, TX
Davis, Ilse, Lib.Techn.
UNIVERSITY OF OKLAHOMA - SCHOOL OF
ARCHITECTURE LIBRARY □ Norman, OK
Davis, Jacqueline Bass, Dir., Info.Serv.
MOTOROLA, INC. - MOS INTEGRATED
CIRCUITS DIVISION - INFORMATION CENTER
□ Austin, TX
Davis, James, Libn.
IDAHO STATE HISTORICAL SOCIETY -
LIBRARY AND ARCHIVES □ Boise, ID
Davis, James, Proc. & Cat.Libn.
JERSEY CITY STATE COLLEGE - FORREST A.
IRWIN LIBRARY □ Jersey City, NJ
Davis, Jean, Asst.Libn.
ROGERS CORPORATION - LURIE LIBRARY □
Rogers, CT
Davis, Joan N., Dir.
HUNTSVILLE MEMORIAL HOSPITAL - SCHOOL
OF VOCATIONAL NURSING - EARNESTINE
CANNON MEMORIAL LIBRARY □ Huntsville, TX
Davis, John H., Ref.Libn.
GONZAGA UNIVERSITY SCHOOL OF LAW -
LIBRARY □ Spokane, WA

Davis, Karen A., Med.Libn.
WINONA MEMORIAL HOSPITAL - HEALTH
SCIENCES LIBRARY □ Indianapolis, IN
Davis, Kathryn, Libn.
U.S. ARMY POST - FORT WAINWRIGHT -
LIBRARY □ Fairbanks, AK
Davis, Larry, Inst.Cons.
NORTH CAROLINA STATE DEPARTMENT OF
CULTURAL RESOURCES - LIBRARY FOR THE
BLIND AND PHYSICALLY HANDICAPPED □
Raleigh, NC
Davis, Linda, Asst.Cat.
GEORGETOWN UNIVERSITY - LAW CENTER
LIBRARY □ Washington, DC
Davis, Linda M., Info.Sci.
MORTON-NORWICH PRODUCTS, INC. -
NORWICH PHARMACAL COMPANY - R&D DEPT.
- LIBRARY INFORMATION GROUP □ Norwich, NY
Davis, Lulie, Sec.-Libn.
WASHINGTON COUNTY HISTORICAL SOCIETY
- LIBRARY □ Salem, IN
Davis, Lynda C., Act.Libn.
MARYLAND STATE DEPARTMENT OF
LEGISLATIVE REFERENCE - LIBRARY □
Annapolis, MD
Davis, Lynn, Photo Libn.
BISHOP (Bernice P.) MUSEUM - LIBRARY □
Honolulu, HI
Davis, Lynn, Asst.Libn.
WESTMINSTER THEOLOGICAL SEMINARY -
MONTGOMERY LIBRARY □ Philadelphia, PA
Davis, Madonna, Hum.Biblog.
NORTHWEST MISSOURI STATE UNIVERSITY -
WELLS LIBRARY □ Maryville, MO
Davis, Marc L., Libn.
WASHINGTON GAS LIGHT COMPANY - LIBRARY
□ Springfield, VA
Davis, Martha A., Libn.
U.S. ARMY COMMAND AND GENERAL STAFF
COLLEGE - COMBINED ARMS RESEARCH
LIBRARY □ Fort Leavenworth, KS
Davis, Mary A., Libn.
CHARLESTON AREA MEDICAL CENTER -
GENERAL DIVISION - MEDICAL LIBRARY □
Charleston, WV
Davis, Mary B., Libn.
HUNTINGTON FREE LIBRARY - MUSEUM OF
THE AMERICAN INDIAN - LIBRARY □ Bronx, NY
Davis, Mary B., Art Libn.
UNIVERSITY OF KENTUCKY - ART LIBRARY □
Lexington, KY
Davis, Mary M., Lib.Techn.
PIKES PEAK LIBRARY DISTRICT - LOCAL
HISTORY COLLECTION □ Colorado Springs, CO
Davis, Morris, Exec. Program Dir.
UNIVERSITY OF CALIFORNIA, BERKELEY -
INST. OF INDUSTRIAL RELATIONS - LABOR
OCCUPATIONAL HEALTH PROG.LIB. □ Berkeley,
CA
Davis, Nancy, Dir.
FRANKLIN MINT - INFORMATION RESEARCH
SERVICES □ Franklin Center, PA
Davis, Nancy, Asst.Libn.
UNIVERSITY OF ILLINOIS - AGRICULTURE
LIBRARY □ Urbana, IL
Davis, Odila Collazo de, Asst. to Law Libn.
INTERAMERICAN UNIVERSITY - SCHOOL OF
LAW - DOMINGO TOLEDO ALAMO LAW LIBRARY
□ Santurce, PR
Davis, Mrs. Ollye G., Res.Libn.
CLARK COLLEGE - SOUTHERN CENTER FOR
STUDIES IN PUBLIC POLICY - LIBRARY □
Atlanta, GA
Davis, Phyllis, Libn.
BENDIX CORPORATION - COMMUNICATIONS
DIVISION - ENGINEERING LIBRARY □
Baltimore, MD
Davis, Robert J., Hist.
INTERNATIONAL SOCIETY FOR
PHILOSOPHICAL ENQUIRY - ARCHIVES □
Belmont, MA
Davis, Robert J., Libn.
SEWARD & KISSEL - LIBRARY □ New York, NY

Davis, Ronald, Product Libn.
ELI LILLY AND COMPANY - SCIENTIFIC
LIBRARY □ Indianapolis, IN

Davis, Russell L., Dir.
UTAH STATE LIBRARY □ Salt Lake City, UT

Davis, Sally, Libn.
UNIVERSITY OF WISCONSIN, MADISON -
LIBRARY SCHOOL LIBRARY □ Madison, WI

Davis, Samuel A., Evening Libn.
JEFFERSON (Thomas) UNIVERSITY - SCOTT
MEMORIAL LIBRARY □ Philadelphia, PA

Davis, Sharon, Asst.Dir.Info.Serv.
UNIVERSITY OF COLORADO MEDICAL CENTER
- DENISON MEMORIAL LIBRARY □ Denver, CO

Davis, Susan, Ser.Ref.Libn.
ILLINOIS INSTITUTE OF TECHNOLOGY - JAMES
S. KEMPER LIBRARY □ Chicago, IL

Davis, Susan, Asst.Libn.
LUMMUS COMPANY - LUMMUS TECHNICAL
CENTER - TECHNICAL INFORMATION
DEPARTMENT □ Bloomfield, NJ

Davis, Trisha L., Mgr., Tech.Serv.Sect.
OCLC, INC. - LIBRARY □ Dublin, OH

Davis, Virginia, Ref.Libn.
CHICAGO SUN-TIMES - EDITORIAL LIBRARY □
Chicago, IL

Davis, Vonciel, Info.Spec.
ALABAMA STATE DEPARTMENT OF PUBLIC
HEALTH - REFERENCE LIBRARY □ Montgomery,
AL

Davis, Wendy A., Sr.Libn.
GULF CANADA LIMITED - CENTRAL LIBRARY □
Toronto, ON

Davis, William J., Exec.Dir.
NORFOLK AND PORTSMOUTH BAR
ASSOCIATION - LAW LIBRARY □ Norfolk, VA

Davis, Wylma P., Ref.Libn.
VIRGINIA MILITARY INSTITUTE - PRESTON
LIBRARY □ Lexington, VA

Davis-Millis, Nina, Libn.
MANHATTAN SCHOOL OF MUSIC - LIBRARY □
New York, NY

Davison, Enid, ILL
ACADIA UNIVERSITY - SCIENCE LIBRARY □
Wolfville, NS

Davison, Frieda, Hd., Tech.Serv.
EAST TENNESSEE STATE UNIVERSITY,
QUILLEN-DISHNER COLLEGE OF MEDICINE -
DEPT. OF LEARNING RSRCS. - MEDICAL
LIBRARY □ Johnson City, TN

Davisson, Lori, Res.Spec.
ARIZONA HISTORICAL SOCIETY - LIBRARY □
Tucson, AZ

Davy, Edgar W., Dewey Libn.
MASSACHUSETTS INSTITUTE OF TECHNOLOGY
- DEWEY LIBRARY □ Cambridge, MA

Dawkins, Mrs. B.T., Libn.
RAPIDES GENERAL HOSPITAL - MEDICAL
LIBRARY □ Alexandria, LA

Dawkins, Suzanne, Cat./Asst.Libn.
COMMODITY FUTURES TRADING COMMISSION
- LAW LIBRARY □ Washington, DC

Dawood, Rosemary, Asst. Chief
CHICAGO PUBLIC LIBRARY CENTRAL LIBRARY -
BUSINESS/SCIENCE/TECHNOLOGY DIVISION
□ Chicago, IL

Dawson, Bernice M., Lib.Asst.
UNIVERSITY OF TEXAS, AUSTIN - CLASSICS
LIBRARY □ Austin, TX

Dawson, Carole, Chf.Libn.
ALBERTA - DEPARTMENT OF ENERGY AND
NATURAL RESOURCES - LIBRARY† □ Edmonton,
AB

Dawson, Luther A., Lib.Dir.
UNITED STATES NEWS PUBLISHING, INC. -
LIBRARY □ Washington, DC

Dawson, Therese F., Chf.Libn.
ST. LOUIS PUBLIC LIBRARY - APPLIED
SCIENCE DEPARTMENT □ St. Louis, MO

Dawson, Victoria A., Hd.Libn.
EDUCATIONAL BROADCASTING CORPORATION
- CHANNEL 13 RESEARCH LIBRARY □ New York,
NY

Day, Duane R., Mgr.Lib.Serv.
GENERAL MILLS, INC. - GENERAL OFFICE
LIBRARY/INFORMATION CENTER □
Minneapolis, MN

Day, Elizabeth H., Med.Ref.Libn.
GOOD SAMARITAN HOSPITAL - RICHARD S.
BEINECKE MEDICAL LIBRARY □ West Palm
Beach, FL

Day, Jane, Hd., Ser.
SUNY AT BUFFALO - HEALTH SCIENCES
LIBRARY □ Buffalo, NY

Day, Joy A., Dir.
HOBE SOUND BIBLE COLLEGE - LIBRARY □ Hobe
Sound, FL

Day, Leslie, Libn.
MUTUAL LIFE ASSURANCE COMPANY OF
CANADA - LIBRARY □ Waterloo, ON

Day, Margaret, Info.Spec.
BURROUGHS WELLCOME COMPANY - LIBRARY
□ Research Triangle Park, NC

Day, Mario, Bibliothecaire
QUEBEC PROVINCE - MINISTERE DE
L'INDUSTRIE, DU COMMERCE ET DU
TOURISME - BIBLIOTHEQUE MINISTERIELLE □
Quebec, PQ

Day, Robert S., Exec.Dir.
INTERNATIONAL TENNIS HALL OF FAME AND
TENNIS MUSEUM - LIBRARY □ Newport, RI

Day, Ronald, Doc.Libn.
UNIVERSITY OF PENNSYLVANIA - BIDDLE LAW
LIBRARY □ Philadelphia, PA

Day, Serenna, Sr.Libn.
LOS ANGELES PUBLIC LIBRARY - CHILDREN'S
LITERATURE DEPARTMENT □ Los Angeles, CA

Day, Susan, Asst.Libn.
ROYAL ROADS MILITARY COLLEGE - LIBRARY □
Victoria, BC

Day, Viola Northrup, Hd.Cat.Libn.
YALE UNIVERSITY - DIVINITY SCHOOL
LIBRARY □ New Haven, CT

Dayhoff, Judy, Tech.Libn.
BALL AEROSPACE SYSTEMS DIVISION -
TECHNICAL LIBRARY □ Boulder, CO

Dayton, Donald W., Hd.Libn.
BETHANY AND NORTHERN BAPTIST
THEOLOGICAL SEMINARIES - LIBRARY □ Oak
Brook, IL

Dayton, Gary A., Libn./Archv.
SUNY - COLLEGE AT BUFFALO - BURCHFIELD
CENTER-WESTERN NEW YORK FORUM FOR
AMERICAN ART □ Buffalo, NY

Daze, Colleen J., Libn.
SCHENECTADY GAZETTE - LIBRARY □
Schenectady, NY

De, Maya, Ref.Asst.
MASSACHUSETTS REHABILITATION
COMMISSION - LIBRARY □ Boston, MA

De Bear, Estelle, Ref.Libn.
ST. JOHN'S PROVINCIAL SEMINARY - LIBRARY
□ Plymouth, MI

De Beaumont, J., Hd., Tech.Serv.
CANADA - PUBLIC SERVICE COMMISSION -
LIBRARY SERVICES DIVISION □ Ottawa, ON

de Bellefeville, Louise, Tech.Libn.
LAURENTIENNE COMPAGNIE D'ASSURANCE -
LIBRARY □ Quebec, PQ

De Bellis, Serena, Cur.
SAN FRANCISCO STATE UNIVERSITY - FRANK
V. DE BELLIS COLLECTION □ San Francisco, CA

de Benko, Dr. Eugene, Hd., Intl.Lib.
MICHIGAN STATE UNIVERSITY -
INTERNATIONAL LIBRARY □ East Lansing, MI

De Crenascol, Joan, Ref.Libn.
KEAN COLLEGE OF NEW JERSEY - NANCY
THOMPSON LIBRARY □ Union, NJ

de De Leon, Celia
UNIVERSITY OF PUERTO RICO - NATURAL
SCIENCE LIBRARY □ Rio Piedras, PR

De Fato, Elizabeth, Libn.
SEATTLE ART MUSEUM - LIBRARY □ Seattle,
WA

de Forest, Kellam, Dir.
DE FOREST RESEARCH SERVICE - LIBRARY □
Hollywood, CA

De Forest, Marjorie, Chf.Med.Libn.
MONTEFIORE HOSPITAL & MEDICAL CENTER -
MEDICAL LIBRARY □ New York, NY

De Gruson, Eugene, Spec.Coll.
PITTSBURG STATE UNIVERSITY - LEONARD H.
AXE LIBRARY □ Pittsburg, KS

de Jesus, A.M., Libn.
UNION CARBIDE CANADA, LTD. - PLASTICS &
CHEMICALS TECHNICAL CENTRE LIBRARY □
Pointe-Aux-Trembles, PQ

de Jong, N.J., Prov.Archv.
PRINCE EDWARD ISLAND - PUBLIC ARCHIVES
□ Charlottetown, PE

de Klerk, Ann, Assoc.Dir.
CARNEGIE-MELLON UNIVERSITY - HUNT
LIBRARY □ Pittsburgh, PA

De Klerk, Peter, Hd., Theological Div.
CALVIN COLLEGE AND SEMINARY - LIBRARY □
Grand Rapids, MI

De La Cruz, Estrella, Libn.
NORWEGIAN-AMERICAN HOSPITAL, INC. -
SEUFERT MEMORIAL LIBRARY □ Chicago, IL

De La Paz, Salvacion S., Assoc.Libn.Ser.
SUNY - COLLEGE OF ENVIRONMENTAL SCIENCE
AND FORESTRY - F. FRANKLIN MOON LIBRARY
□ Syracuse, NY

De La Rosa, Luis, Archv.
PUERTO RICO - INSTITUTE OF PUERTO RICAN
CULTURE - ARCHIVO GENERAL DE PUERTO
RICO □ San Juan, PR

de la Torre, David, Dev.Dir.
TRITON MUSEUM OF ART - LIBRARY □ Santa
Clara, CA

de la Vega, Amalia, ILL Coord.
UNIVERSITY OF MIAMI - SCHOOL OF
MEDICINE - LOUIS CALDER MEMORIAL
LIBRARY □ Miami, FL

De Laforest, Marcel, Hd., Adm.Br.
SASKATCHEWAN - PROVINCIAL LIBRARY □
Regina, SK

De Las Casas, Prof. Manuel Victor, Dir. & Med.Libn.
GORGAS MEMORIAL LABORATORY OF
TROPICAL AND PREVENTIVE MEDICINE, INC. -
BIO-MEDICAL RESEARCH LIBRARY □ APO
Miami, FL

De Las Casas, Prof. Manuel Victor, Dir. & Med.Libn.
GORGAS MEMORIAL LABORATORY OF
TROPICAL AND PREVENTIVE MEDICINE, INC. -
VIROLOGY UNIT LIBRARY □ APO Miami, FL

De Lergier, Clara S., Chf.Libn.
PUERTO RICO - ATENEO PUERTORRIQUENO -
BIBLIOTECA □ San Juan, PR

De Long, Kathleen, Asst.Educ.Ref.Libn.
UNIVERSITY OF ALBERTA - H.T. COUTTS
EDUCATION LIBRARY □ Edmonton, AB

De Martinez, Ileana D., Order Libn.
UNIVERSITY OF PUERTO RICO - MAYAGUEZ
CAMPUS - LIBRARY □ Mayaguez, PR

De Mund, Mary, Lib.Dir.
DENVER MEDICAL SOCIETY - LIBRARY □
Denver, CO

De Muro, Linda, Pub.Serv.Libn.
UNITED HOSPITALS MEDICAL CENTER OF
NEWARK - LIBRARY AND INFORMATION
SERVICES □ Newark, NJ

De Narvaez, Martha M., Mss./Rare Bks. Cur.
HISPANIC SOCIETY OF AMERICA - LIBRARY □
New York, NY

De Natale, Rose Marie, Libn.
DMS, INC. - TECHNICAL LIBRARY □ Greenwich,
CT

de Onis, Johanna, Ref.Libn.
U.S. NATL. DEFENSE UNIVERSITY - LIBRARY □
Washington, DC

de Ortiz, Oneida R., Dir.
UNIVERSITY OF PUERTO RICO - HUMACAO
UNIVERSITY COLLEGE - LIBRARY □ Humacao,
PR

De Petrillo, Michael, Libn.
ANTHROPOLOGY RESOURCE CENTER (ARC) -
CITIZENS INFORMATION CENTER □ Boston,
MA

De-Rouyn, Solange, Chf.
CENTRE HOSPITALIER ST-JOSEPH -
BIBLIOTHEQUE MEDICALE ET
ADMINISTRATIVE □ Trois-Rivieres, PQ

De Ruyt, Mr. Jean, Consul
BELGIAN CONSULATE GENERAL - LIBRARY □
New York, NY

De Saint-Rat, Catherine, Asst.Cur.
MIAMI UNIVERSITY - WALTER HAVIGHURST
SPECIAL COLLECTIONS LIBRARY □ Oxford, OH

de St. Remy, Barbara, Biblog.
QUEEN'S UNIVERSITY AT KINGSTON - SPECIAL
COLLECTIONS □ Kingston, ON

De Serio, Judith, Dir.
AMERICAN COUNCIL ON EDUCATION -
NATIONAL CENTER FOR HIGHER EDUCATION
(NCHE) - LIBRARY □ Washington, DC

De Tonnancour, P. Roger, Chf.Libn.
GENERAL DYNAMICS CORPORATION - FORT
WORTH DIVISION - RESEARCH LIBRARY □ Fort
Worth, TX

De Turk, William, Archv.
GUILD OF CARILLONNEURS IN NORTH
AMERICA - ARCHIVES □ Ann Arbor, MI

De Usabel, Frances, Inst.Serv.Libn.
WISCONSIN STATE DIVISION FOR LIBRARY
SERVICES - REFERENCE AND LOAN LIBRARY □
Madison, WI

De Varennes, Rosario, Cons., Sys.
UNIVERSITE LAVAL - BIBLIOTHEQUE† □ Ste.
Foy, PQ

De Vergie, Adrienne, Cat.
UNIVERSITY OF TEXAS SCHOOL OF LAW -
TARLTON LAW LIBRARY □ Austin, TX

De Voe, Stephen E., Assoc.Sci.Libn.
WAYNE STATE UNIVERSITY - SCIENCE
LIBRARY □ Detroit, MI

De-Vreeze, Beatrice, Hd.Libn.
NATIONAL THEATRE SCHOOL OF CANADA -
THEATRICAL LIBRARY □ Montreal, PQ

De Vries, Eileen, Libn.
CULINARY INSTITUTE OF AMERICA -
KATHARINE ANGELL LIBRARY □ Hyde Park, NY

De Young, J.A., Libn.
STELCO INC. - ENGINEERING SERVICES
LIBRARY □ Hamilton, ON

Deahl, Thomas F., Micropublisher
MICRODOC - TECHNICAL DOCUMENTATION
COLLECTION □ Philadelphia, PA

Deal, Andrew S., Dir.
UNIVERSITY OF CALIFORNIA - SAN JOAQUIN
VALLEY AGRICULTURAL RESEARCH &
EXTENSION CENTER □ Parlier, CA

DeAlleaume, William, Hd., Coll.Acq.
NEW YORK STATE LIBRARY □ Albany, NY

Deamer, Debra, Res.
TRENTON TIMES - LIBRARY □ Trenton, NJ

Dean, Alexis, Libn.
FLORIDA STATE HOSPITAL - PATIENT/STAFF
LIBRARY □ Chattahoochee, FL

Dean, Carole, Asst.Dir.
U.S. CENTER FOR DISEASE CONTROL - CDC
LIBRARY □ Atlanta, GA

Dean, Dr. Frederick C., Supv.
UNIVERSITY OF ALASKA - WILDLIFE LIBRARY
□ Fairbanks, AK

Dean, Grant, Asst.Cur.
CHICAGO HISTORICAL SOCIETY - SPECIAL
COLLECTIONS □ Chicago, IL

Dean, Kathryn, Cur. of Mss.
UNIVERSITY OF MANITOBA - ARCHIVES AND
SPECIAL COLLECTIONS □ Winnipeg, MB

Dean, Lee Ann, Info.Spec.
GIRARD BANK - INFORMATION CENTER □
Philadelphia, PA

Dean, Louise M., Libn.
UNIVERSITY OF MAINE, ORONO - IRA C.
DARLING CENTER LIBRARY† □ Walpole, ME

Dean, Marilyn W., Lib.Supv.
AROOSTOOK MEDICAL CENTER - A.R. GOULD
DIVISION - HEALTH SCIENCES LIBRARY □
Presque Isle, ME

Deane, Roxanne, Chf.
DISTRICT OF COLUMBIA PUBLIC LIBRARY -
WASHINGTONIANA DIVISION □ Washington,
DC

DeAngelis, Theresa
BRONSON (Silas) LIBRARY - BUSINESS,
INDUSTRY, AND TECHNOLOGY DEPARTMENT†
□ Waterbury, CT

Deans, Don J., Mgr.
SEAGRAM COMPANY, LTD. - INFORMATION
CENTRE, LIBRARY & ARCHIVES □ LaSalle, PQ

Dearborn, Josephine, Asst.Libn.
VIRGINIA THEOLOGICAL SEMINARY - BISHOP
PAYNE LIBRARY □ Alexandria, VA

Deathe, Frances, Acq.Libn.
OKLAHOMA CITY UNIVERSITY - LAW LIBRARY
□ Oklahoma City, OK

Deaven, Barbara E., Patients' Libn.
U.S. VETERANS ADMINISTRATION (PA-
Lebanon) - MEDICAL CENTER LIBRARY □
Lebanon, PA

Deaver, Sarah, Sch.Libn.
ST. LUKE'S HOSPITAL - SCHOOL OF NURSING
LIBRARY □ St. Louis, MO

Deavy, Elizabeth, Hd., Can.Off.Pubn.Sect
NATIONAL LIBRARY OF CANADA - OFFICIAL
PUBLICATIONS DIVISION □ Ottawa, ON

DeBardeleben, Marian Z., Res.Libn.
PHILIP MORRIS, U.S.A. - RESEARCH CENTER
LIBRARY □ Richmond, VA

DeBaun, Robert R., Base Libn.
U.S. AIR FORCE BASE - NORTON BASE LIBRARY
□ Norton AFB, CA

DeBell, Jeanne K., Cur.
SOMERS HISTORICAL SOCIETY - ARCHIVES □
Somers, CT

Deberry, Katie W., Libn.
U.S. VETERANS ADMINISTRATION (MO-St.
Louis) - HOSPITAL LIBRARY □ St. Louis, MO

DeBoer, Julie Farmar, Libn.
SIDLEY & AUSTIN - LIBRARY □ Chicago, IL

DeBois, Mildred, Cat.Libn.
STATE TECHNICAL INSTITUTE AT MEMPHIS -
GEORGE E. FREEMAN LIBRARY □ Memphis, TN

DeBolske, John J., Exec.Dir.
LEAGUE OF ARIZONA CITIES AND TOWNS -
LIBRARY □ Phoenix, AZ

deBruijn, Elsie, Hd.
UNIVERSITY OF BRITISH COLUMBIA -
MARJORIE SMITH LIBRARY □ Vancouver, BC

Debusman, Paul M., Ref./Ser.Libn.
SOUTHERN BAPTIST THEOLOGICAL SEMINARY
- JAMES P. BOYCE CENTENNIAL LIBRARY □
Louisville, KY

DeCamps, Alice L., Libn.
RICHMOND PUBLIC LIBRARY - BUSINESS,
SCIENCE & TECHNOLOGY DEPARTMENT† □
Richmond, VA

DeCandido, Grace Anne, Ref./Tech.Serv.Libn.
PARSONS SCHOOL OF DESIGN - ADAM L.
GIMBEL DESIGN LIBRARY □ New York, NY

DeCarufel, Gertrude S., Hd.Libn.
QUEBEC PROVINCE - MINISTERE DE
L'EDUCATION - CENTRALE DES
BIBLIOTHEQUES - CENTRE DOCUMENTAIRE □
Montreal, PQ

Dechow, Eileen M., Med.Libn.
BUTTERWORTH HOSPITAL - MEDICAL LIBRARY
□ Grand Rapids, MI

Decker, Debra, Instr.Mtls.Ctr.
CLARION STATE COLLEGE - RENA M. CARLSON
LIBRARY □ Clarion, PA

Decker, Geri, Libn.
UNIVERSITY OF NOTRE DAME -
ARCHITECTURE LIBRARY □ Notre Dame, IN

Decker, Leon, Cat.
CATERPILLAR TRACTOR COMPANY -
TECHNICAL INFORMATION CENTER □ Peoria,
IL

Decker, W., Libn.
SERVO CORPORATION OF AMERICA -
TECHNICAL LIBRARY □ Hicksville, NY

Deckert, Frank, Interp.Spec.
U.S. NATL. PARK SERVICE - ALASKA AREA
OFFICE - LIBRARY □ Anchorage, AK

DeClercq, Victor P., Chf.Ref.Libn.
COOK COUNTY LAW LIBRARY □ Chicago, IL

DeCora, Lambert, Asst.Libn.
UNIVERSITY OF ARKANSAS AT LITTLE ROCK -
PULASKI COUNTY LAW LIBRARY □ Little Rock,
AR

DeCorso, Deborah, Asst.Libn./Rd.Serv.
SACRED HEART UNIVERSITY - LIBRARY □
Bridgeport, CT

DeCosin, Marri
LEEWARD COMMUNITY COLLEGE - LIBRARY □
Honolulu, HI

DeCoux, Elizabeth A., Adm.Libn.
U.S. AIR FORCE BASE - KEESLER BASE -
MC BRIDE LIBRARY □ Keesler AFB, MS

Dederen, Louise, Cur., Heritage Rm.
ANDREWS UNIVERSITY - JAMES WHITE
LIBRARY □ Berrien Springs, MI

Dee, Cheryl, Med.Libn.
WATSON CLINIC - MEDICAL LIBRARY □
Lakeland, FL

Dee, Cheryl R., Med.Libn.
LAKELAND GENERAL HOSPITAL - MEDICAL
LIBRARY □ Lakeland, FL

Dee, Mathew F., Dir.
OHIO STATE UNIVERSITY - LAW LIBRARY □
Columbus, OH

Deegan, Joyce, Libn.
ROCKWELL INTERNATIONAL - ELECTRONICS
OPERATIONS - DALLAS INFORMATION CENTER
□ Dallas, TX

Deemer, Larry, Pub.Serv.Libn.
GONZAGA UNIVERSITY SCHOOL OF LAW -
LIBRARY □ Spokane, WA

Deering, Dr. Ronald F., Libn.
SOUTHERN BAPTIST THEOLOGICAL SEMINARY
- BILLY GRAHAM ROOM □ Louisville, KY

Deering, Dr. Ronald F., Libn.
SOUTHERN BAPTIST THEOLOGICAL SEMINARY
- JAMES P. BOYCE CENTENNIAL LIBRARY □
Louisville, KY

Dees, Anthony R., Dir.
GEORGIA HISTORICAL SOCIETY - LIBRARY □
Savannah, GA

Dees, Harry, Doc.Libn.
BRIGHAM YOUNG UNIVERSITY - J. REUBEN
CLARK LAW SCHOOL LIBRARY □ Provo, UT

Deese, Bill, Circ.Libn.
PEPPERDINE UNIVERSITY - LIBRARY -
SPECIAL COLLECTIONS □ Malibu, CA

DeFato, Joan, Plant Sci.Libn.
LOS ANGELES COUNTY DEPARTMENT OF
ARBORETA AND BOTANIC GARDENS - PLANT
SCIENCE LIBRARY □ Arcadia, CA

Deffenbaugh, Kay, Libn.
RIVERSIDE HOSPITAL - MEDICAL LIBRARY □
Toledo, OH

Degani, Edith, Adm.Libn.
JEWISH THEOLOGICAL SEMINARY OF
AMERICA - LIBRARY □ New York, NY

Degarme, Judy, Cat.
CHICAGO HISTORICAL SOCIETY - SPECIAL
COLLECTIONS □ Chicago, IL

Degenhardt, Judith, Asst.Libn.
LUTHERAN GENERAL HOSPITAL - LIBRARY □
Park Ridge, IL

DeGeus, Marilyn J., Dir. of Libs.
UNIVERSITY OF HEALTH SCIENCES - LIBRARY
□ Kansas City, MO

DeGolyer, Christine, Chem.Libn.
ROCHESTER INSTITUTE OF TECHNOLOGY -
CHEMISTRY GRADUATE RESEARCH LIBRARY □
Rochester, NY

DeGolyer, Christine, Hd. of Chem.Lib.
ROCHESTER INSTITUTE OF TECHNOLOGY -
WALLACE MEMORIAL LIBRARY □ Rochester, NY

DeGraff, Kathryn, Spec.Coll.Libn.
DE PAUL UNIVERSITY, LINCOLN PARK CAMPUS LIBRARY - SPECIAL COLLECTIONS DEPARTMENT □ Chicago, IL

Dehart, Odell, Cat.
BAKER & BOTTS - LAW LIBRARY □ Houston, TX

Deis, Louise, Info.Spec.
CPC INTERNATIONAL - BEST FOODS RESEARCH CENTER - INFORMATION CENTER† □ Union, NJ

Deitlen, Joann, Ser.Libn.
GENERAL ELECTRIC COMPANY - CORPORATE RESEARCH & DEVELOPMENT - WHITNEY LIBRARY □ Schenectady, NY

DeJarnatt, Jim, Cons.Lib. for Blind
GEORGIA STATE DEPARTMENT OF EDUCATION - DIVISION OF PUBLIC LIBRARY SERVICES □ Atlanta, GA

DeJarnatt, Jim, Dir.
GEORGIA STATE DEPARTMENT OF EDUCATION - LIBRARY FOR THE BLIND & PHYSICALLY HANDICAPPED □ Atlanta, GA

del Campo, Rosa
UNITED NATIONS ASSOCIATION OF THE UNITED STATES OF AMERICA - GREATER ST. LOUIS CHAPTER - LIBRARY □ St. Louis, MO

Del Cont, Mary, Libn.
WEST VIRGINIA STATE LEGISLATIVE REFERENCE LIBRARY □ Charleston, WV

del Fierro, Julie, Lib.Serv.Supv.
GTE PRODUCTS CORPORATION - SYLVANIA SYSTEMS GROUP - WESTERN DIVISION - LIBRARY □ Mountain View, CA

Del Pilar Barber, Giovanna, Hd.
UNIVERSITY OF PUERTO RICO - NATURAL SCIENCE LIBRARY □ Rio Piedras, PR

Del Signore, Louise, Libn.
DU PONT DE NEMOURS (E.I.) & COMPANY, INC. - CHEMICALS & PIGMENTS DEPT. - JACKSON LAB. LIBRARY □ Wilmington, DE

DeLa Pena, Rita, Tech.Asst.
IIT RESEARCH INSTITUTE - COMPUTER SEARCH CENTER □ Chicago, IL

DeLa Portilla, Diane, Libn.
CORPUS CHRISTI MUSEUM - STAFF LIBRARY □ Corpus Christi, TX

Delahanty, Hon. Thomas E., Libn.
ANDROSCOGGIN COUNTY LAW LIBRARY □ Auburn, ME

Delak, Carol, Assoc.Libn.
CAMPBELL-MITHUN, INC. - LIBRARY □ Minneapolis, MN

Delamarter, Ralph, Sr.Cons., Lib.Dev.
OREGON STATE LIBRARY □ Salem, OR

DeLancey, James, Assoc.Libn.
GEORGETOWN UNIVERSITY - BLOMMER SCIENCE LIBRARY □ Washington, DC

Delaney, Caldwell, Musm.Dir.
MUSEUMS OF THE CITY OF MOBILE - MUSEUM REFERENCE LIBRARY □ Mobile, AL

Delaney, Esther, Libn.
SAFECO INSURANCE COMPANY - LIBRARY □ Seattle, WA

Delaney, Oliver, Legislative Ref.
OKLAHOMA STATE DEPARTMENT OF LIBRARIES □ Oklahoma City, OK

Delaney, Dr. Robert W., Dir.
FORT LEWIS COLLEGE - CENTER OF SOUTHWEST STUDIES □ Durango, CO

Delaney, Verlean, Chf.Libn.
U.S. VETERANS ADMINISTRATION (OK-Oklahoma City) - HOSPITAL LIBRARY □ Oklahoma City, OK

Delap, James H., Chem. Professor
STETSON UNIVERSITY - CHEMISTRY LIBRARY □ De Land, FL

Delargy, Ann, Asst.Libn.
ROSS ROY, INC. - RESEARCH LIBRARY □ Detroit, MI

Delarm, Elaine, Cur.
COLEBROOK HISTORICAL SOCIETY - LIBRARY AND ARCHIVES □ Colebrook, CT

DeLashmitt, Eleanor, Libn.
MONTEREY COUNTY LAW LIBRARY □ Salinas, CA

Delavan, Carolyn, Leg.Libn.
MARYLAND STATE DEPARTMENT OF LEGISLATIVE REFERENCE - LIBRARY □ Annapolis, MD

Delbaum, Judith, Libn.
BLUE CROSS OF GREATER PHILADELPHIA - E.A. VAN STEENWYK MEMORIAL LIBRARY □ Philadelphia, PA

Delevich, Mrs. Biljana, Design Libn.
GENERAL MOTORS CORPORATION - DESIGN STAFF INFORMATION CENTER □ Warren, MI

DelFrate, Adelaide A., Hd., Lib.Br.
U.S. NASA - GODDARD SPACE FLIGHT CENTER - LIBRARY† □ Greenbelt, MD

Delfs, Jean, Cat.Libn.
ORAL ROBERTS UNIVERSITY - LAW LIBRARY □ Tulsa, OK

Delgado, Rafael R., Dir.
UNIVERSITY OF PUERTO RICO - GENERAL LIBRARY □ San Juan, PR

deLiesseline, Elizabeth, Info.Spec.
WESTVACO CORPORATION - INFORMATION SERVICES CENTER □ North Charleston, SC

DeLille, Carolyn, Libn.
UNIVERSITY OF ARKANSAS, FAYETTEVILLE - CHEMISTRY LIBRARY □ Fayetteville, AR

Deline, Phyllis, Mgr.
HOFFMANN-LA ROCHE, INC. - SCIENTIFIC LIBRARY □ Nutley, NJ

DeLissovoy, Mrs. Reymour, Hd., Slide/Photo Dept.
RHODE ISLAND SCHOOL OF DESIGN - LIBRARY □ Providence, RI

Dell, Geraldine, Circ.Libn.
CREIGHTON UNIVERSITY - HEALTH SCIENCES LIBRARY □ Omaha, NE

Dellenbach, Marcia, Archv.
ROOSEVELT UNIVERSITY - ARCHIVES □ Chicago, IL

Deller, Howard A., Lit.Anl.
AMERICAN GEOGRAPHICAL SOCIETY COLLECTION OF THE UNIVERSITY OF WISCONSIN, MILWAUKEE - GOLDA MEIR LIBRARY □ Milwaukee, WI

Dellinger, Doris, Libn.
BORG-WARNER CORPORATION - YORK DIVISION - ENGINEERING LIBRARY □ York, PA

Dellinger, Doris, Libn.
NATIONAL WRESTLING HALL OF FAME - LIBRARY □ Stillwater, OK

Delman, Dr. Bruce, Med.Libn.
U.S. VETERANS ADMINISTRATION (OH-Cleveland) - HOSPITAL LIBRARY □ Cleveland, OH

Delman, Farrell, Exec.Dir.
TOBACCO MERCHANTS ASSOCIATION OF THE U.S. - HOWARD S. CULLMAN LIBRARY □ New York, NY

Delnay, June, Libn.
DENVER THEOLOGICAL SEMINARY/BIBLE INSTITUTE - SAMUEL JAMES BRADFORD MEMORIAL LIBRARY □ Broomfield, CO

Delong, Charles J., Coord.Spec.Serv.
ALABAMA INSTITUTE FOR THE DEAF AND BLIND - LIBRARY FOR THE BLIND AND PHYSICALLY HANDICAPPED □ Talladega, AL

DeLong, Sharon, Eng.Info.Anl.
DIAMOND SHAMROCK CORPORATION - CORPORATE LIBRARY □ Painesville, OH

DeLorme, Margaret M., Mgr.
ITT CORPORATION - HEADQUARTERS LIBRARY □ New York, NY

Delozier, Mr. Lynn F., Chf.Libn.
U.S. VETERANS ADMINISTRATION (MD-Perry Point) - HOSPITAL MEDICAL LIBRARY □ Perry Point, MD

Deltieure, Henri, Pres.
SOCIETE CULINAIRE PHILANTHROPIQUE DE NEW YORK, INC. - LIBRARY □ New York, NY

Delvin, Robert C., Fine Arts Libn.
ILLINOIS WESLEYAN UNIVERSITY - THORPE MUSIC LIBRARY □ Bloomington, IL

DeMan, Thomas
FIRESTONE TIRE AND RUBBER COMPANY - DEFENSE RESEARCH AND PRODUCTS DIVISION - LIBRARY □ Akron, OH

Demarco, Elizabeth, Libn.
ONONDAGA COUNTY PUBLIC LIBRARY - ART AND MUSIC DEPARTMENT □ Syracuse, NY

Demaree, Marta, Ref.Libn.
SOUTHERN METHODIST UNIVERSITY - SCIENCE/ENGINEERING LIBRARY □ Dallas, TX

Demarest, Kenneth L., Jr., Pres.
HOLLAND SOCIETY OF NEW YORK - LIBRARY □ New York, NY

DeMarrais, Margaret F., Libn.
PASCACK VALLEY HOSPITAL - DAVID GOLDBERG MEMORIAL MEDICAL LIBRARY □ Westwood, NJ

DeMartin, Mary, Coord.Info. Center
DATA GENERAL CORPORATION - CORPORATE RESEARCH & DEVELOPMENT LIBRARY □ Westborough, MA

DeMayo, Rev. John B., Dir. of Libs.
ST. CHARLES BORROMEO SEMINARY - RYAN MEMORIAL LIBRARY □ Philadelphia, PA

Dembicki, Diane, Musm.Cur.
PONCA CITY CULTURAL CENTER MUSEUM - LIBRARY □ Ponca City, OK

Demchuck, Beverly, Lib.Asst.
MATHEMATICAL REVIEWS - LIBRARY □ Ann Arbor, MI

Demecour, Mary D., Libn.
ORANGE COUNTY ENVIRONMENTAL MANAGEMENT AGENCY - ADMINISTRATION/PLANNING LIBRARY □ Santa Ana, CA

Demeris, Nick C., Adm.Asst.
HOUSTON - CITY LEGAL DEPARTMENT - LAW LIBRARY □ Houston, TX

DeMerritt, Lynne, Libn.
MUNICIPAL RESEARCH AND SERVICES CENTER OF WASHINGTON - LIBRARY □ Seattle, WA

Demers, N., Sec.
INDUSTRIAL GENERAL INSURANCE COMPANY - LIBRARY† □ Quebec, PQ

Demes, Stanley B., Chf.Libn.
HUGHES AIRCRAFT COMPANY - GROUND SYSTEMS GROUP - TECHNICAL LIBRARY □ Fullerton, CA

Demlinger, Marlin, Lib.Chf.
CUNY - CITY COLLEGE LIBRARY - SCIENCE/ENGINEERING DIVISION □ New York, NY

DeMoss, Lucille G., Law Libn.
MAHONING LAW LIBRARY □ Youngstown, OH

Dempsey, Margie, Libn.
CHESHIRE HOSPITAL - MEDICAL LIBRARY □ Keene, NH

Dempsey, Vickie, Pubn.Coord.
INSTRUMENT SOCIETY OF AMERICA - LIBRARY □ Research Triangle Park, NC

DeMuth, Phyllis J., Libn.
ALASKA STATE DIVISION OF STATE LIBRARIES & MUSEUMS - HISTORICAL LIBRARY □ Juneau, AK

Denecke, Mildred F., Mgr.
ENVIRONMENTAL RESEARCH INSTITUTE OF MICHIGAN - INFRARED INFORMATION AND ANALYSIS CENTER (IRIA) □ Ann Arbor, MI

Denert, Gloria, Photograph Libn.
XEROX CORPORATION - XEROX EDUCATION PUBLICATIONS - LIBRARY □ Middletown, CT

Denfeld, Kay, Online Coord.
UNIVERSITY OF WASHINGTON - HEALTH SCIENCES LIBRARY □ Seattle, WA

Dengel, Lucy, Asst.Supv.
MONROE COUNTY LOCAL HISTORY ROOM & LIBRARY □ Sparta, WI

Dengler, Eartha, Ser.
MERRIMACK VALLEY TEXTILE MUSEUM - LIBRARY □ North Andover, MA

Dengler, Thomas P., Med.Libn.
LOS ANGELES COUNTY/LONG BEACH GENERAL HOSPITAL - MEDICAL LIBRARY □ Long Beach, CA

PERSONNEL

Denis, Leonard Rossiter, Libn.
GERMANTOWN HISTORICAL SOCIETY - LIBRARY □ Philadelphia, PA

Denker, Bert, DAPC Libn.
DU PONT (Henry Francis) WINTERTHUR MUSEUM - LIBRARY □ Winterthur, DE

Denney, Dorothy, Biomed.Libn.
U.S. DEPT. OF ENERGY - LAWRENCE BERKELEY LABORATORY - LIBRARY □ Berkeley, CA

Denney, Kathryn C., Libn.
VIRGINIA STATE DEPARTMENT OF CORRECTIONS - ACADEMY FOR STAFF DEVELOPMENT - LIBRARY □ Waynesboro, VA

Dennhardt, Lauren, Libn.
AMERICAN CONSERVATORY OF MUSIC - LIBRARY □ Chicago, IL

Dennis, Robert J., Recorded Sound Libn.
HARVARD UNIVERSITY - EDA KUHN LOEB MUSIC LIBRARY □ Cambridge, MA

Dennis, Rodney G., Cur. of Mss.
HARVARD UNIVERSITY - HOUGHTON LIBRARY □ Cambridge, MA

Dennis, Sandra, Mgr., Lib.Serv.
INFORONICS, INC. - TECHNICAL LIBRARY □ Littleton, MA

Dennison, Frances E., Asst.Libn.
BLACK & VEATCH CONSULTING ENGINEERS - CENTRAL LIBRARY □ Kansas City, MO

Dennison, Jacquelyn L., Coll.Dev.Libn.
MEDICAL COLLEGE OF GEORGIA - LIBRARY □ Augusta, GA

Dennison, Sam, Cur.
FREE LIBRARY OF PHILADELPHIA - EDWIN A. FLEISHER COLLECTION OF ORCHESTRAL MUSIC □ Philadelphia, PA

Denniston, Donna, Asst.Libn.
OKLAHOMA STATE UNIVERSITY - OKLAHOMA CITY BRANCH - TECHNICAL INSTITUTE LIBRARY □ Oklahoma City, OK

Denor, Judy, Lib.Spec.
MORAINE PARK TECHNICAL INSTITUTE - LEARNING RESOURCE CENTER □ Fond Du Lac, WI

Denson, Janeen, Circ.Libn.
DUKE UNIVERSITY - SCHOOL OF LAW LIBRARY □ Durham, NC

Denson, Mamie
MACON TELEGRAPH AND NEWS - LIBRARY† □ Macon, GA

Dent, Johnnie, Asst.Supv.
QUEENS BOROUGH PUBLIC LIBRARY - LANGSTON HUGHES COMMUNITY LIBRARY AND CULTURAL CENTER □ Corona, NY

Denton, Ramona, Rsrcs.Libn.
DARGAN-CARVER LIBRARY □ Nashville, TN

Denton, Richard, Ser.Libn.
SCHOOL OF THEOLOGY AT CLAREMONT - THEOLOGY LIBRARY □ Claremont, CA

Denyer, Janice, Libn.
METROPOLITAN TORONTO LIBRARY - SOCIAL SCIENCES DEPARTMENT □ Toronto, ON

Denzel, Justin, ILL Libn.
HOFFMANN-LA ROCHE, INC. - SCIENTIFIC LIBRARY □ Nutley, NJ

DePasquale, Mary, Ref.Libn.
MORGAN GUARANTY TRUST COMPANY OF NEW YORK - REFERENCE LIBRARY □ New York, NY

Deperrault, Jeanne, Ref.Libn.
MASSACHUSETTS INSTITUTE OF TECHNOLOGY - M.I.T. MUSEUM AND HISTORICAL COLLECTIONS □ Cambridge, MA

DePew, Doris, Adm.Asst.
WASHINGTON COUNTY HISTORICAL SOCIETY - LIBRARY □ Salem, IN

DePiesse, Larry, Hd.
WICHITA PUBLIC LIBRARY - BUSINESS AND TECHNOLOGY DIVISION □ Wichita, KS

DePlaen, Jacqueline, Hd., Doc.Serv.
UNIVERSITE DE MONTREAL - CENTRE INTERNATIONAL DE CRIMINOLOGIE COMPAREE - DOCUMENTATION CENTRE □ Montreal, PQ

DePopolo, Margaret, Rotch Libn.
MASSACHUSETTS INSTITUTE OF TECHNOLOGY - ROTCH LIBRARY OF ARCHITECTURE AND PLANNING □ Cambridge, MA

DePorte, Paul, Translator
U.S. NATL. INSTITUTES OF HEALTH - LIBRARY □ Bethesda, MD

DePuy, Rolfe, Hd., Order/Cat.
SUNY - DOWNSTATE MEDICAL CENTER - MEDICAL RESEARCH LIBRARY OF BROOKLYN† □ Brooklyn, NY

Der Manuelian, Dr. Lucy
ARMENIAN LIBRARY AND MUSEUM OF AMERICA □ Belmont, MA

Derby, Matthew I., Rabbi
CHICAGO SINAI CONGREGATION - EMIL G. HIRSCH LIBRARY □ Chicago, IL

Derbyshire, Joseph J., Libn.
BATES COLLEGE - LIBRARY - SPECIAL COLLECTIONS □ Lewiston, ME

Derfer, Marian M., Supv.Lib./Info.Serv.
SCM CORPORATION - ORGANIC CHEMICALS DIVISION - TECHNICAL LIBRARY □ Jacksonville, FL

Derge, Charlene C., Libn.
U.S. SECURITIES AND EXCHANGE COMMISSION - LIBRARY □ Washington, DC

DeRieux, Jackie, Asst.Libn./AV
AMERICAN INSTITUTE OF ARCHITECTS - LIBRARY □ Washington, DC

Derkach, Mary Ann, Libn.
OAKITE PRODUCTS INC. - CHEMICAL RESEARCH LIBRARY □ Berkeley Heights, NJ

Derksen, Charlotte R.M., Libn.
STANFORD UNIVERSITY - BRANNER EARTH SCIENCES LIBRARY □ Stanford, CA

Dermody, Rita R., Legal Libn.
CONTINENTAL ILLINOIS NATIONAL BANK AND TRUST COMPANY OF CHICAGO - INFORMATION SERVICES DIVISION □ Chicago, IL

Dermyer, A.L., Hd.Libn.
UNION PACIFIC RAILROAD COMPANY - LIBRARY □ Omaha, NE

DeRojas, Augustine, Asst.
LOCKWOOD, ANDREWS & NEWNAM, INC. - INFORMATION CENTER □ Houston, TX

Derrick, Louise S., Lib.Asst.
SACRED HEART HOSPITAL - HEALTH SCIENCE LIBRARY □ Cumberland, MD

Dershem, Larry, Asst.Libn.
SAN DIEGO COUNTY LAW LIBRARY □ San Diego, CA

Dertien, Elaine, Libn.
FONTENELLE FOREST NATURE CENTER - REFERENCE LIBRARY □ Bellevue, NE

Dery, Mary A., Asst.Libn.
HARPER-GRACE HOSPITALS - GRACE HOSPITAL DIVISION - OSCAR LE SEURE PROFESSIONAL LIBRARY □ Detroit, MI

DeRyke, DeLores, Pres.
AMERICAN OLD TIME FIDDLERS ASSOCIATION - ARCHIVES† □ Lincoln, NE

Des Chene, Dorice, Hd.
UNIVERSITY OF CINCINNATI - OESPER CHEMISTRY-BIOLOGY LIBRARY □ Cincinnati, OH

Des Jardins, Deedee Andrea, Libn.
BROCKTON ART MUSEUM - FULLER MEMORIAL LIBRARY □ Brockton, MA

Des Lauriers, Don, Cur.
KANKAKEE COUNTY HISTORICAL SOCIETY - LIBRARY □ Kankakee, IL

Desbarats, Aileen, Hd.
UNIVERSITY OF OTTAWA - MAP LIBRARY □ Ottawa, ON

Deschamps, N., Ref.Libn.
CANADIAN BROADCASTING CORPORATION - HEAD OFFICE LIBRARY □ Ottawa, ON

Deschatelets, Gilles, Chf., Sci.Coll.
UNIVERSITE LAVAL - BIBLIOTHEQUE† □ Ste. Foy, PQ

Deschatelets, Gilles, Chf.
UNIVERSITE LAVAL - BIBLIOTHEQUE SCIENTIFIQUE† □ Ste. Foy, PQ

DeSchryver, Victor, Libn.
UNIVERSITY OF DETROIT - SCHOOL OF DENTISTRY LIBRARY □ Detroit, MI

Desilets, Rita, Ck.
CANADA - REGIONAL ECONOMIC EXPANSION - GOVERNMENT DOCUMENTATION CENTRE □ Montreal, PQ

DeSimone, Elizabeth A., Ref.Libn.
U.S. DEPT. OF ENERGY - KNOLLS ATOMIC POWER LABORATORY - LIBRARIES □ Schenectady, NY

Desmarais, Christiane, Cartothecaire
UNIVERSITE DU QUEBEC A MONTREAL - INSTITUT NATIONAL DE LA RECHERCHE SCIENTIFIQUE - CARTOTHEQUE □ Montreal, PQ

Desmond, Bro. Scott, F.O.C., Libn.
NATIONAL ECUMENICAL COALITION, INC. - LIBRARY □ Washington, DC

Desoer, Bernard, Ref.Libn.
UNIVERSITY OF SASKATCHEWAN - EDUCATION BRANCH LIBRARY □ Saskatoon, SK

DeSouza, Y., Libn.
C-I-L INC. - PATENT AND LAW LIBRARY □ Willowdale, ON

Desrochers, Edmond E., Dir.
MAISON BELLARMIN LIBRARY □ Montreal, PQ

DesRoches, Amy, Libn.
VIRGINIA STATE TRUCK AND ORNAMENTALS RESEARCH STATION - LIBRARY □ Virginia Beach, VA

Desrosiers, Shirley, Libn.
BRITISH COLUMBIA - MINISTRY OF LANDS, PARKS AND HOUSING - PARKS LIBRARY □ Victoria, BC

Desruisseaux, Irene, Sec.
GRAND SEMINAIRE DES SAINTS APOTRES - BIBLIOTHEQUE □ Sherbrooke, PQ

Dessy, Blane, Pub.Lib.Cons.
OKLAHOMA STATE DEPARTMENT OF LIBRARIES □ Oklahoma City, OK

DeStefano, Rita A., Chf.Lib.
ST. CHARLES BORROMEO SEMINARY - RYAN MEMORIAL LIBRARY □ Philadelphia, PA

Destefano, Vicky, Hd., Ref.Br.
U.S. DEFENSE AUDIOVISUAL AGENCY - STILL PHOTO DEPOSITORY - ARMY COLLECTION □ Washington, DC

D'Estout, Marc, Asst.Dir.
TRITON MUSEUM OF ART - LIBRARY □ Santa Clara, CA

Detrich, R.D., Abstractor
MC DONNELL DOUGLAS CORPORATION - MC DONNELL AIRCRAFT LIBRARY □ St. Louis, MO

Detweiler, Gladys, Libn.
UNION NATIONAL BANK AND TRUST COMPANY - LIBRARY □ Souderton, PA

Detwiler, Doris, Chf.
DETROIT PUBLIC LIBRARY - LABOR COLLECTION □ Detroit, MI

Detwiler, Doris, Chf.
DETROIT PUBLIC LIBRARY - SOCIOLOGY AND ECONOMICS DEPARTMENT □ Detroit, MI

Deus, Seyem, Libn.
MANALYTICS, INC. - LIBRARY □ San Francisco, CA

Deuss, Jean, Chf.Libn.
FEDERAL RESERVE BANK OF NEW YORK - RESEARCH LIBRARY □ New York, NY

Deutch, Morton, Hand Binder
MISSOURI BOTANICAL GARDEN - LIBRARY □ St. Louis, MO

Deutsch, Gladys, Lib.Asst. IV/Supv.
MEMORIAL UNIVERSITY OF NEWFOUNDLAND - DEPARTMENT OF GEOGRAPHY - MAP LIBRARY □ St. John's, NF

Deutsch, Ruth C., Ref.Libn.
POLAROID CORPORATION - RESEARCH LIBRARY □ Cambridge, MA

Deutsch, Stewart F., Exec.Libn.
FRIED, FRANK, HARRIS, SHRIVER, JACOBSON - LIBRARY & INFORMATION CENTER □ New York, NY

Devan, Robert D., Consrv.
ARKANSAS STATE HISTORY COMMISSION - ARCHIVES □ Little Rock, AR

Devaney, James M., Dir.
BULOVA (Joseph) SCHOOL OF WATCHMAKING - LIBRARY □ Woodside, Queens, NY

Devault, Lillian A., Info.Spec.
GOODRICH (B.F.) COMPANY - RESEARCH AND DEVELOPMENT CENTER - BRECKSVILLE INFORMATION CENTER □ Brecksville, OH

Devendorf, Helen, Tech.Serv.Libn.
PIERCE JUNIOR COLLEGE - LIBRARY† □ Philadelphia, PA

DeVenney, Lorraine R., Libn.
SAMBORN, STEKETEE, OTIS & EVANS, INC. - RESOURCE & INFORMATION CENTER □ Toledo, OH

Devereux, Nancy L., Libn.
UNITED HOSPITAL - LIBRARY □ Grand Forks, ND

DeVilbiss, Mary Lee, Univ.Biblog.
CALIFORNIA STATE POLYTECHNIC UNIVERSITY, POMONA - LIBRARY □ Pomona, CA

DeVillier, Pat, Libn.
SPERRY CORPORATION - SPERRY FLIGHT SYSTEMS - ENGINEERING LIBRARY □ Phoenix, AZ

Devine, Eileen C., Dir.
IOWA STATE DEPARTMENT OF HEALTH - FILM LIBRARY □ Des Moines, IA

Devine, Judith W., Supv.
ST. PAUL PUBLIC LIBRARY - REFERENCE ROOM □ St. Paul, MN

Devlin, Margaret, Circ.Libn.
JEFFERSON (Thomas) UNIVERSITY - SCOTT MEMORIAL LIBRARY □ Philadelphia, PA

Devlin, Mary M., Dir., Spec.Serv.
AMERICAN MEDICAL ASSOCIATION - DIVISION OF LIBRARY AND ARCHIVAL SERVICES □ Chicago, IL

Devlin, Patricia B., Libn.
UNIVERSITY OF MICHIGAN - BIOLOGICAL STATION LIBRARY □ Pellston, MI

Devlin, Patricia B., Musm.Libn.
UNIVERSITY OF MICHIGAN - MUSEUMS LIBRARY □ Ann Arbor, MI

Devlin, Patricia B., Libn.
UNIVERSITY OF MICHIGAN - NATURAL SCIENCE AND NATURAL RESOURCES LIBRARY □ Ann Arbor, MI

Devlin, Violet K., Art Libn.
RIDER COLLEGE - FRANKLIN F. MOORE LIBRARY - ART ROOM □ Lawrenceville, NJ

DeVoe, Stanley E., Mgr., Lit.Serv.
AMERICAN CYANAMID COMPANY - LEDERLE LABORATORIES DIVISION - SUBBAROW MEMORIAL LIBRARY □ Pearl River, NY

Devyatkin, Paul, Libn.
YESHIVA UNIVERSITY - LANDOWNE-BLOOM LIBRARY† □ New York, NY

Dew, Roderick, Libn.
COLORADO SPRINGS FINE ARTS CENTER - REFERENCE LIBRARY AND TAYLOR MUSEUM LIBRARY □ Colorado Springs, CO

DeWaal, Ronald, Hum.Libn.
COLORADO STATE UNIVERSITY - WILLIAM E. MORGAN LIBRARY □ Fort Collins, CO

Dewald, Elmer J., Law Libn.
NORTH DAKOTA STATE SUPREME COURT LAW LIBRARY □ Bismarck, ND

DeWalt, Curtis W., Tech.Libn.
HERCULES, INC. - PICCO RESINS DIVISION - LIBRARY □ Clairton, PA

Dewberry, Betty, Asst.Libn.
JOHNSON SWANSON & BARBEE - LIBRARY □ Dallas, TX

DeWeerd, Barbara, Libn.
ST. MICHAEL'S HOSPITAL - HEALTH SCIENCES LIBRARY □ Stevens Point, WI

Dewey, Mrs. B.M., Cur.
SALMON BROOK HISTORICAL SOCIETY - REFERENCE AND EDUCATIONAL CENTER □ Granby, CT

Dewey, Cecelia, Info.Spec.
CONFERENCE BOARD, INC. - INFORMATION SERVICE □ New York, NY

Dewey, Wilma J., Libn.
LOS ANGELES PUBLIC LIBRARY - MUNICIPAL REFERENCE DEPARTMENT □ Los Angeles, CA

DeWitt, Donna, Asst.Libn.
INTERNATIONAL CHRISTIAN SCHOOL OF THEOLOGY - GRADUATE UNIVERSITY LIBRARY □ San Bernardino, CA

DeWitt, George
CITIES SERVICE COMPANY - LIBRARY □ Copperhill, TN

Dewitt, Martin, Dir./Cur.
BURPEE ART MUSEUM/ROCKFORD ART ASSOCIATION - KATHERINE PEARMAN MEMORIAL LIBRARY □ Rockford, IL

DeWitt, Zona, Libn.
MINNESOTA STATE LEGISLATIVE REFERENCE LIBRARY □ St. Paul, MN

Dewsnap, Barbara, Cons.
ETOBICOKE BOARD OF EDUCATION - RESOURCE LIBRARY □ Etobicoke, ON

Dexter, Joan, Libn.
RAYTHEON COMPANY - EQUIPMENT DIVISION - TECHNICAL INFORMATION CENTER □ Sudbury, MA

Dexter, Kathy H., Med.Lib.Dir.
SOUTHEAST ALABAMA MEDICAL CENTER - LIBRARY □ Dothan, AL

Dexter, Martha M., Mgr., Info.Serv.
U. S. OFFICE OF TECHNOLOGY ASSESSMENT - INFORMATION CENTER □ Washington, DC

Dexter, Patrick J., Info.Serv.Supv.
GILLETTE MEDICAL EVALUATION LABORATORIES - INFORMATION CENTER □ Rockville, MD

Deyoe, Dr. Charles
KANSAS STATE UNIVERSITY - FOOD AND FEED GRAIN INSTITUTE - SWANSON MEMORIAL LIBRARY □ Manhattan, KS

DeYoung, Marie, Libn.
NOVA SCOTIA - DEPARTMENT OF LABOUR AND MANPOWER - LIBRARY □ Halifax, NS

d'Hondt, Mary-Thadia, Archv./Libn.
SEATTLE & KING COUNTY HISTORICAL SOCIETY - SOPHIE FRYE BASS LIBRARY OF NORTHWEST AMERICANA □ Seattle, WA

Di Cesare, Annmaria, Mgr., Info.Serv.
MAGAZINE PUBLISHERS ASSOCIATION - MAGAZINE INFORMATION CENTER □ New York, NY

Di Giulio, Eva Maria, Libn.
AMAX, INC. - CLIMAX MOLYBDENUM COMPANY OF MICHIGAN - LIBRARY □ Ann Arbor, MI

Di Giusto, Bob, Cat.
MACALESTER COLLEGE - WEYERHAEUSER LIBRARY □ St. Paul, MN

Di Lisio, Roch-Josef, Assoc.Libn/Tech.Serv
SACRED HEART UNIVERSITY - LIBRARY □ Bridgeport, CT

Di Meglio, Arthur, Info.Spec.
CONFERENCE BOARD, INC. - INFORMATION SERVICE □ New York, NY

Di Roma, Edward, Div.Chf.
NEW YORK PUBLIC LIBRARY - ECONOMIC AND PUBLIC AFFAIRS DIVISION □ New York, NY

Di Salvi, Margaret, Libn.
NEWARK MUSEUM ASSOCIATION - MUSEUM LIBRARY □ Newark, NJ

Dial, Zona P., Libn.
AMERICAN COLLEGE OF NATURAL THERAPEUTICS & ARIZONA COLLEGE OF NATUROPATHIC MEDICINE - LIBRARY □ Mesa, AZ

Diamond, Ruth Y., Dir.
TEMPLE UNIVERSITY - HEALTH SCIENCES CENTER - LIBRARY □ Philadelphia, PA

Diamond, Shirley E., Corp.Libn.
DEWEY, BALLANTINE, BUSHBY, PALMER & WOOD - LIBRARY □ New York, NY

Diano, Anne, Libn.
VANCOUVER PUBLIC LIBRARY - BUSINESS & ECONOMICS DIVISION □ Vancouver, BC

Diatchun, Barbara, Ref.Libn.
MATHEMATICAL REVIEWS - LIBRARY □ Ann Arbor, MI

Diaz, Norka, Div.Hd.
NEW ORLEANS PUBLIC LIBRARY - FOREIGN LANGUAGE DIVISION □ New Orleans, LA

DiBartolomeis, Elizabeth, Spec.Coll.Cur.
BABSON COLLEGE - HORN LIBRARY □ Babson Park, MA

Dibner, Dr. Bern, Dir.
BURNDY LIBRARY □ Norwalk, CT

Dicaire, Mr. R., Ser.
UNIVERSITY OF OTTAWA - LAW LIBRARY □ Ottawa, ON

Dice, Carol, Libn.
AMAX, INC. - CLIMAX MOLYBDENUM COMPANY - TECHNICAL LIBRARY □ Climax, CO

Dicecco, M. Jane, Libn.
DU PONT DE NEMOURS (E.I.) & COMPANY, INC. - LEGAL DEPARTMENT LIBRARY □ Wilmington, DE

Dick, Anne C., Libn.
ST. JOSEPH'S HOSPITAL - HEALTH SCIENCE LIBRARY □ Lowell, MA

Dick, Daniel, Ref.
WORCESTER STATE COLLEGE - LEARNING RESOURCES CENTER □ Worcester, MA

Dicke, Karen, Economist
UNIVERSITY OF COLORADO, BOULDER - BUSINESS RESEARCH DIVISION - TRAVEL REFERENCE CENTER □ Boulder, CO

Dickens, Jane C., Act.Chf.
U.S. DEFENSE AUDIOVISUAL AGENCY - STILL PHOTO DEPOSITORY - ARMY COLLECTION □ Washington, DC

Dickens, Martha H., Libn.
ST. MARY'S MEDICAL CENTER, INC. - MEDICAL LIBRARY □ Knoxville, TN

Dickens, Pauline, AV Libn.
BLOOMFIELD COLLEGE - GEORGE TALBOT HALL LIBRARY □ Bloomfield, NJ

Dickensheet, Dean, Dir.
SAN FRANCISCO ACADEMY OF COMIC ART - LIBRARY □ San Francisco, CA

Dickensheet, Shirley, Dir.
SAN FRANCISCO ACADEMY OF COMIC ART - LIBRARY □ San Francisco, CA

Dickerson, Deborah J., Libn.
WEST VIRGINIA STATE ATTORNEY GENERAL - LAW LIBRARY □ Charleston, WV

Dickerson, Mary E., Hd., Info. & Ref.Serv.
ONTARIO - LEGISLATIVE ASSEMBLY - LEGISLATIVE LIBRARY RESEARCH AND INFORMATION SERVICES □ Toronto, ON

Dickerson, T. Jimmy, Libn.
UNIVERSITY OF NORTH CAROLINA, CHAPEL HILL - CHEMISTRY LIBRARY □ Chapel Hill, NC

Dickey, Dr. David S., Technical Dir.
CHEMINEER, INC. - LIBRARY □ Dayton, OH

Dickey, Jack W., Libn.
UNIVERSITY OF IOWA - PHYSICS LIBRARY □ Iowa City, IA

Dickey, Jack W., Libn.
UNIVERSITY OF IOWA - ZOOLOGY LIBRARY □ Iowa City, IA

Dickey, Loren L., Libn.
OZARK BIBLE COLLEGE - LIBRARY □ Joplin, MO

Dickinson, C. Harmon, Act.Hist.
SEVENTH DAY BAPTIST HISTORICAL SOCIETY - LIBRARY □ Plainfield, NJ

Dickinson, Fidelia, Coll.Dev.Libn.
SAN DIEGO STATE UNIVERSITY - MALCOLM A. LOVE LIBRARY □ San Diego, CA

Dickinson, Isabel, Hd.Libn.
UNIVERSITY OF CALIFORNIA, RIVERSIDE -
BIO-AGRICULTURAL LIBRARY □ Riverside, CA

Dickinson, Jean E., Chf., Tech.Lib.
U.S. AIR FORCE - FLIGHT TEST CENTER -
TECHNICAL LIBRARY □ Edwards AFB, CA

Dickinson, June M., Pres.
SCHUMANN MEMORIAL FOUNDATION, INC. -
LIBRARY □ Livonia, NY

Dickinson, Marjorie, Libn.
KINGWOOD CENTER - LIBRARY □ Mansfield, OH

Dickison, R.R., Chf.Libn.
U.S. OAK RIDGE NATL. LABORATORY -
LIBRARIES □ Oak Ridge, TN

Dickson, Elizabeth M., Ref.Libn.
U.S. ARMY FIELD ARTILLERY SCHOOL - MORRIS
SWETT LIBRARY □ Ft. Sill, OK

Dickson, Karolyn, Mgr.
WESTMINSTER COLLEGE - WINSTON
CHURCHILL MEMORIAL AND LIBRARY □ Fulton,
MO

Dickson, Katherine, Libn.
BUSINESS AND PROFESSIONAL WOMEN'S
FOUNDATION - LIBRARY □ Washington, DC

Dickson, Lance E., Dir.
LOUISIANA STATE UNIVERSITY - LAW
LIBRARY □ Baton Rouge, LA

Dickson, Margaret A., Libn. & Chm.Cat.
TEXAS TECH UNIVERSITY - LIBRARY □
Lubbock, TX

Dickson, Ruth, Libn.
LUTHER RICE SEMINARY - BERTHA SMITH
LIBRARY □ Jacksonville, FL

Dickson, Thomas A., Sr.Libn.
CALIFORNIA STATE HEALTH AND WELFARE
AGENCY - INTERDEPARTMENTAL LIBRARY □
Sacramento, CA

Didham, Reginald, Tech.Proc.
BOSTON CONSERVATORY OF MUSIC - ALBERT
ALPHIN MUSIC LIBRARY □ Boston, MA

Diehl, David J., Libn.
TEXAS STATE TECHNICAL INSTITUTE, RIO
GRANDE CAMPUS - LIBRARY □ Harlingen, TX

Diehl, John A., Libn.
OHIO COVERED BRIDGE COMMITTEE -
LIBRARY □ Cincinnati, OH

Diercks, John, Chm.
HOLLINS COLLEGE - MUSIC DEPARTMENT -
ERICH RATH LIBRARY - LISTENING CENTER □
Hollins College, VA

Diersen, Jean, Libn.
LUTHERAN BROTHERHOOD INSURANCE
SOCIETY - LB LIBRARY □ Minneapolis, MN

Dieter, Martin L., Info.Sys.Anl.
U.S. DEPT OF ENERGY - SANDIA NATL.
LABORATORIES - TECHNICAL LIBRARY □
Albuquerque, NM

Dieterich, M.F., Assoc. Law Libn.
UNIVERSITY OF WYOMING - LAW LIBRARY □
Laramie, WY

Dieterle, Diane, Dir.
GENEALOGICAL LIBRARY FOR THE BLIND &
PHYSICALLY HANDICAPPED, INC. -
GENEALOGICAL CENTER LIBRARY □ Atlanta, GA

Dieterle, John H., Treas.
GENEALOGICAL LIBRARY FOR THE BLIND &
PHYSICALLY HANDICAPPED, INC. -
GENEALOGICAL CENTER LIBRARY □ Atlanta, GA

Dietrich, Bruce L., Dir.
READING PUBLIC MUSEUM AND ART GALLERY -
REFERENCE LIBRARY □ Reading, PA

Dietrich, Bruce L., Dir. of Planetarium
READING SCHOOL DISTRICT PLANETARIUM -
LIBRARY □ Reading, PA

Dietrich, Peter James, Assoc.Libn.
CONSOLIDATED EDISON COMPANY OF NEW
YORK, INC. - LIBRARY □ New York, NY

Dietrich, Dr. R. Krystyna, Dir.
DIETRICH COLLECTION □ West Canaan, NH

Dietz, Dr. Charles, Dir.
ZANESVILLE ART CENTER - LIBRARY □
Zanesville, OH

Dietzel, Anita, Lib.Techn.
U.S. AIR FORCE BASE - BARKSDALE BASE
LIBRARY □ Barksdale AFB, LA

DiFelice, Clara J., Libn.
OAKLAND UNIVERSITY - LIBRARY □ Rochester,
MI

Diffendal, Anne P., Mss.Cur.
NEBRASKA STATE HISTORICAL SOCIETY -
ARCHIVES □ Lincoln, NE

Differding, Jane, Libn.
NIELSEN ENGINEERING & RESEARCH, INC. -
LIBRARY □ Mountain View, CA

Diffin, E. Marilyn, Asst.Libn.
CALAIS FREE LIBRARY □ Calais, ME

Diggin, Denise, Germantown Br.Chf.
U.S. DEPT. OF ENERGY - LIBRARY □
Washington, DC

DiGovanni, Beatrice M., Sr.Lib.Asst.
RAYTHEON COMPANY - SUBMARINE SIGNAL
DIVISION - TECHNICAL INFORMATION
CENTER □ Portsmouth, RI

DiGregorio, Marcia, Dept.Hd.
PROVIDENCE PUBLIC LIBRARY - BUSINESS-
INDUSTRY-SCIENCE DEPARTMENT □
Providence, RI

DiIorio, Anita, Res.Libn.
CANADIAN PACIFIC, LTD. - CORPORATE
LIBRARY/INFORMATION CENTRE □ Montreal,
PQ

Dike, Barbara, Libn.
EASTERN STATE HOSPITAL - PROFESSIONAL
LIBRARY □ Williamsburg, VA

Dillard, Douglas, Instr.Prog.
UNIVERSITY OF IOWA - LABORATORY FOR
POLITICAL RESEARCH □ Iowa City, IA

Dillard, Gerry, Libn. & Sec.
UNIVERSITY OF OKLAHOMA - OKLAHOMA
BIOLOGICAL STATION LIBRARY □ Norman, OK

Dillard, Julia, Cat.Libn.
TROY STATE UNIVERSITY - LIBRARY □ Troy, AL

Dillard, Lois, Ref.Libn.
GEOLOGICAL INFORMATION LIBRARY OF
DALLAS (GILD) - □ Dallas, TX

Dillard, Lura Ann, Mgr.Lib.Serv.Dept.
PLANNING RESEARCH CORPORATION -
LIBRARY SERVICES DEPARTMENT □ McLean,
VA

Dilley, Rick, Tech.Serv.Libn.
SOUTHERN ILLINOIS UNIVERSITY - SCHOOL OF
MEDICINE - MEDICAL LIBRARY □ Springfield, IL

Dilibe, Anne G., Libn.
CALIFORNIA HOSPITAL MEDICAL CENTER -
HEALTH SCIENCES LIBRARY □ Los Angeles, CA

Dillin, Dorothy B., Libn.
CARNEGIE INSTITUTION OF WASHINGTON -
TERRESTRIAL MAGNETISM DEPARTMENT
LIBRARY □ Washington, DC

Dilling, M.L.
DOW CHEMICAL COMPANY - TECHNICAL
INFORMATION SERVICES - CENTRAL REPORT
INDEX □ Midland, MI

Dillingham, Judith, Asst. to Dir.
ALFORD HOUSE/ANDERSON FINE ARTS
CENTER - ART REFERENCE LIBRARY □
Anderson, IN

Dillingham, Louise, Assoc.Cur.
TEXARKANA HISTORICAL SOCIETY & MUSEUM
- LIBRARY □ Texarkana, TX

Dillon, Eloise, Acq.Libn.
STATE LIBRARY OF FLORIDA □ Tallahassee, FL

Dillon, John H., Mgr.
ADISTRA CORPORATION - R & D LIBRARY □
Plymouth, MI

Dillon, Mary P., Assoc.Dir./Lib.Prog.
UNIVERSITY OF MIAMI - SCHOOL OF
MEDICINE - LOUIS CALDER MEMORIAL
LIBRARY □ Miami, FL

Dillon, Sue, Libn.
HANCOCK COUNTY LAW LIBRARY
ASSOCIATION □ Findlay, OH

Dillon, Susan L., Libn.
OCEANOGRAPHIC SERVICES, INC. -
TECHNICAL LIBRARY □ Goleta, CA

Dillon, William A., Dir.
JERVIS PUBLIC LIBRARY □ Rome, NY

Dilno, Dennis, Asst.Cat.
PRICE WATERHOUSE - NATIONAL
INFORMATION CENTER □ New York, NY

DiLoreto, Anne, Hd. Law Libn.
WIDETT, SLATER & GOLDMAN P.C. - LIBRARY □
Boston, MA

Dilts, Dottie, Libn.
SHEDD (John G.) AQUARIUM - LIBRARY □
Chicago, IL

Dimaguila, Jaime P., Libn.
U.S. NAVY - OFFICE OF THE GENERAL COUNSEL
- LAW LIBRARY □ Washington, DC

DiMarino, Joseph D., Mgr.Lib./Info.Ctr.
PHILADELPHIA NEWSPAPERS, INC. - INQUIRER
AND DAILY NEWS LIBRARY □ Philadelphia, PA

DiMauro, Paul, Coll.Dev.Libn.
RUSH UNIVERSITY AND MEDICAL CENTER -
LIBRARY □ Chicago, IL

Dimitroff, Lucienne Bloch, Sec.
BLOCH (Ernest) SOCIETY - ARCHIVES □ Gualala,
CA

Dimone, Vincent, Ref.
CRAVATH, SWAINE, AND MOORE - LAW
LIBRARY □ New York, NY

Dimsdale, Mrs. C., Mgr.
BELL-NORTHERN RESEARCH LTD. - TECHNICAL
INFORMATION CENTRE □ Ottawa, ON

DiMuccio, Mary-Jo, Prog.Mgr.
SUNNYVALE PATENT INFORMATION
CLEARINGHOUSE □ Sunnyvale, CA

Din, Munir U., Med.Libn.
HOSPITAL FOR SPECIAL SURGERY - KIM
BARRETT MEMORIAL LIBRARY □ New York, NY

Dincel, H.H., Cat./Supv.
ERTEC, WESTERN, INC. - LIBRARY □ Long
Beach, CA

Dincel, Misty Sis, Info.Dir.
ERTEC, WESTERN, INC. - LIBRARY □ Long
Beach, CA

Dinel, Guy, Chf., Archv.
UNIVERSITE LAVAL - BIBLIOTHEQUE† □ Ste.
Foy, PQ

Dingeman, Gaye M., Libn.
SAN DIEGO ECOLOGY CENTER - LIBRARY □ San
Diego, CA

Dingle-Cliff, Susan, Libn.
ALBERTA ALCOHOLISM AND DRUG ABUSE
COMMISSION - LIBRARY □ Edmonton, AB

Dingley, Doris A., Libn.
CONTROL DATA CORPORATION - LIBRARY/
INFORMATION CENTER □ Minneapolis, MN

Dingman, Nancy R., Chf.Libn.
U.S. VETERANS ADMINISTRATION (MI-
Saginaw) - MEDICAL CENTER LIBRARY □
Saginaw, MI

Dinkelacker, Mark, Circ.
UNIVERSITY OF CINCINNATI - ROBERT S.
MARX LAW LIBRARY □ Cincinnati, OH

Dinniman, Margo, Sr.Info.Spec.
WESTON (Roy F.), INC. - TECHNICAL
INFORMATION CENTER AND LIBRARY □ West
Chester, PA

Dinsmore, Mrs. Daniel, Libn.
ALLYN (Lyman) MUSEUM - LIBRARY □ New
London, CT

Dintrone, Charles, Doc.Libn.
SAN DIEGO STATE UNIVERSITY -
GOVERNMENT PUBLICATIONS DEPARTMENT □
San Diego, CA

Dinwiddie, Robert, Archv.Asst.
GEORGIA STATE UNIVERSITY - SOUTHERN
LABOR ARCHIVES □ Atlanta, GA

Dion, Chantale
ASSELIN, BENOIT, BOUCHER, DUCHARME,
LAPOINTE, INC. - LIBRARY DEPARTMENT □
Montreal, PQ

Dion, Gilles, Chf.
SOCIETE QUEBECOISE D'INITIATIVES
PETROLIERES - DOCUMENTATION CENTRE □
Ste. Foy, PQ

Dion, Kathleen, Libn.
NATIONAL JUDICIAL COLLEGE - LAW LIBRARY
□ Reno, NV
Dion, R.N., Supv.
DU PONT DE NEMOURS (E.I.) & COMPANY, INC.
- CHEMICALS & PIGMENTS DEPT. - JACKSON
LAB. LIBRARY □ Wilmington, DE
Dionne, JoAnn L., Ref. & Data Archv.
YALE UNIVERSITY - SOCIAL SCIENCE LIBRARY
□ New Haven, CT
Dionne, Richard J., Libn.
YALE UNIVERSITY - ANTHROPOLOGY LIBRARY
□ New Haven, CT
Dionne, Richard J., Sci.Libn.
YALE UNIVERSITY - KLINE SCIENCE LIBRARY □
New Haven, CT
DiPaolo, Joanna, Internal Coord.
ANTIOCH UNIVERSITY - LEARNING RESOURCE
CENTER □ Philadelphia, PA
Dipesa, Pamela
ALTERNATIVE PRESS CENTER - LIBRARY □
Baltimore, MD
DiPiazza, Anna, Chf.
DETROIT PUBLIC LIBRARY - HISTORY AND
TRAVEL DEPARTMENT □ Detroit, MI
Dirks, Laura E., Libn.
ALEXANDER & ALEXANDER, INC. - NATIONAL
PRODUCTION INFORMATION CENTER □
Minneapolis, MN
Dirks, Laura E., Libn.
PILOTS INTERNATIONAL ASSOCIATION -
LIBRARY □ Minneapolis, MN
Dirlam, Dona Mary, Info./Res.
GEMOLOGICAL INSTITUTE OF AMERICA -
RESEARCH LIBRARY □ Santa Monica, CA
Dirlik, Raja, Libn.
MC GILL UNIVERSITY - ISLAMIC STUDIES
LIBRARY □ Montreal, PQ
Discavage, Carol Lee, Libn.
MC CARTER & ENGLISH - LAW LIBRARY □
Newark, NJ
Diskin, Jill A., Adm.Mgr.
CARNEGIE-MELLON UNIVERSITY - HUNT
LIBRARY □ Pittsburgh, PA
Disrude, Elizabeth E., Supt.
U.S. NATL. PARK SERVICE - HOPEWELL
VILLAGE NATL. HISTORIC SITE - LIBRARY □
Birdsboro PA
Ditchey, Linnea, Supv.
ALLIED CORPORATION - TECHNICAL
INFORMATION SERVICE □ Morristown, NJ
Ditmer, Robert W., Dir. of Info.Res.
RAHENKAMP, SACHS, WELLS AND
ASSOCIATES, INC. - PLANNING LIBRARY □
Philadelphia, PA
Dittenhoffer, Mr. Tony, Ref.Coord.
CANADA - SOLICITOR GENERAL CANADA -
CRIMINOLOGY DOCUMENTATION CENTRE □
Ottawa, ON
Divilbiss, D.A., Hd.Libn.
MISSOURI STATE SUPREME COURT LIBRARY □
Jefferson City, MO
Divor, Joan C., Asst.Libn.
INA CORPORATION - LIBRARY □ Philadelphia,
PA
Dixon, Brian R., Assoc.Libn.
GEORGE WASHINGTON UNIVERSITY -
NATIONAL LAW CENTER - JACOB BURNS LAW
LIBRARY □ Washington, DC
Dixon, Harvey T., Libn.
U.S. NATL. PARK SERVICE - STATUE OF
LIBERTY NATL. MONUMENT - AMERICAN
MUSEUM OF IMMIGRATION - LIBRARY □ New
York, NY
Dixon, Rebecca Danforth, Dir.
CENTER FOR THE STUDY OF YOUTH
DEVELOPMENT, BOYS TOWN - LIBRARY
SERVICES DIVISION □ Boys Town, NE
Dixon, Thomas W., Jr., Pres.
CHESAPEAKE & OHIO HISTORICAL SOCIETY,
INC. - C & O ARCHIVAL COLLECTION □
Alderson, WV

Dixon, Yvette, Assoc.Libn.
MARYLAND STATE DEPARTMENT OF HEALTH &
MENTAL HYGIENE - LIBRARY† □ Baltimore, MD
Dize, Margaret A., Libn.
YORK COUNTY LAW LIBRARY □ York, PA
Dizon, Linda K., Libn.
UNIVERSITY OF HAWAII - WAIKIKI
AQUARIUM - LIBRARY □ Honolulu, HI
Doak, Wes, Chf. of Lib.Dev.
CALIFORNIA STATE LIBRARY □ Sacramento, CA
Doares, Wade A., Libn.
COLUMBIA UNIVERSITY - SULZBERGER
JOURNALISM LIBRARY □ New York, NY
Dobb, L. Bartley, State/Local Docs.Libn.
UNIVERSITY OF WASHINGTON - GOVERNMENT
PUBLICATIONS DIVISION □ Seattle, WA
Dobb, T.C. "Ted", Univ.Libn.
SIMON FRASER UNIVERSITY - LIBRARY -
SPECIAL COLLECTIONS □ Burnaby, BC
Dobbert, Irene A., Corp.Libn.
SENTRY LIBRARY □ Stevens Point, WI
Dobbin, Marie, Libn.
CHISHOLM TRAIL MUSEUM - ARCHIVES AND
LIBRARY □ Wellington, KS
Dobbs, George E., Law Libn.
NEW YORK STATE SUPREME COURT - 2ND
JUDICIAL DISTRICT - LAW LIBRARY □
Brooklyn, NY
Dobbs, Sr. M. Kathryn, C.S.F.N., Dir.
HOLY FAMILY COLLEGE - LIBRARY □
Philadelphia, PA
Dobi, Ellen K., Libn.
U.S. ARMY - COMMUNICATIONS-ELECTRONICS
COMMAND - TECHNICAL LIBRARY □ Fort
Monmouth, NJ
Dobkin, John H., Dir.
NATIONAL ACADEMY OF DESIGN - LIBRARY □
New York, NY
Dobrosky, Patricia M., Dir.
U.S. CUSTOMS SERVICE - LIBRARY AND
INFORMATION CENTER □ Washington, DC
Dobson, Christine B., Libn.
CORE LABORATORIES, INC. - LIBRARY □ Dallas,
TX
Dobson, Dawn, Libn.
CANADIAN LABOUR CONGRESS - LIBRARY □
Ottawa, ON
Dobson, Joanna, Libn.
AMERICAN CERAMIC SOCIETY - LIBRARY □
Columbus, OH
Dobson, John, Spec.Coll.Libn.
UNIVERSITY OF TENNESSEE - SPECIAL
COLLECTIONS □ Knoxville, TN
Dobson, Nancy H., Libn.
AUSTIN STATE HOSPITAL - STAFF LIBRARY □
Austin, TX
Dobur, Olga, Hd.
UNIVERSITY OF CINCINNATI - MATHEMATICS
LIBRARY □ Cincinnati, OH
Dochterman, Virginia
IOWA STATE DEPARTMENT OF HISTORY AND
ARCHIVES - IOWA HISTORICAL LIBRARY □ Des
Moines, IA
Dock, Gretchen M., Media Coord.
BRIGHAM AND WOMEN'S HOSPITAL -
ABRAMSON CENTER FOR INSTRUCTIONAL
MEDIA □ Boston, MA
Dockstader, Ray, Dp.Dir.
LIBRARY OF CONGRESS - AMERICAN FOLKLIFE
CENTER □ Washington, DC
Docktor, Robyn, AV Techn.
NATIONAL COLLEGE - THOMAS JEFFERSON
LIBRARY □ Rapid City, SD
Dodd, J.L., Supv.
TENNESSEE VALLEY AUTHORITY - MAPS AND
SURVEYS BRANCH - MAP INFORMATION AND
RECORDS UNIT □ Chattanooga, TN
Dodd, James B., Hd. User Serv.Div.
GEORGIA INSTITUTE OF TECHNOLOGY - PRICE
GILBERT MEMORIAL LIBRARY □ Atlanta, GA

Dodd, Jane, Sci.Ref.Libn.
TEXAS A & M UNIVERSITY - REFERENCE
DIVISION □ College Station, TX
Dodd, Phyllis, Supv.
DENVER PUBLIC SCHOOL DISTRICT 1 -
PROFESSIONAL LIBRARY □ Denver, CO
Dodd, Sue A., Data Libn.
UNIVERSITY OF NORTH CAROLINA, CHAPEL
HILL - INSTITUTE FOR RESEARCH IN SOCIAL
SCIENCE - DATA LIBRARY □ Chapel Hill, NC
Dodd, Virginia, Asst.
FALCONBRIDGE NICKEL MINES, LTD. -
FALCONBRIDGE INFORMATION CENTRE □
Toronto, ON
Dodge, Alice C., Libn.
ONEIDA HISTORICAL SOCIETY - LIBRARY □
Utica, NY
Dodge, Katherine, Supv.Lib.Serv.
MC CANN-ERICKSON, INC. - LIBRARY† □ New
York, NY
Dodge, Nancy L., Libn.
NEW HAMPSHIRE VOCATIONAL-TECHNICAL
COLLEGE - LIBRARY □ Portsmouth, NH
Dodge, Dr. Robert J., Local Govt.Rec.Spec.
KENT STATE UNIVERSITY - AMERICAN
HISTORY RESEARCH CENTER □ Kent, OH
Dodson, Ann T., Mgr.
OCLC, INC. - LIBRARY □ Dublin, OH
Dodson, Linda, Libn.
BOOZ, ALLEN APPLIED RESEARCH, INC. -
LIBRARY □ Bethesda, MD
Dodson, Max G., Chf. Law Libn.
U.S. COURT OF APPEALS, 5TH CIRCUIT -
LIBRARY □ New Orleans, LA
Dodson, Sherry, Libn.
GROUP HEALTH COOPERATIVE OF PUGET
SOUND - MEDICAL LIBRARY □ Seattle, WA
Dodson, Snowdy, Sci.Ref.Libn.
CALIFORNIA STATE UNIVERSITY,
NORTHRIDGE - LIBRARY - HEALTH SCIENCE
COLLECTION □ Northridge, CA
Dodson, Suzanne, Hd.
UNIVERSITY OF BRITISH COLUMBIA -
GOVERNMENT PUBLICATIONS & MICROFORMS
DIVISIONS □ Vancouver, BC
Doebel, Dr. Karl, Dir.
CIBA-GEIGY CORPORATION -
PHARMACEUTICALS DIVISION - SCIENTIFIC
INFORMATION CENTER† □ Summit, NJ
Doerr, Dean, Pub.Lib.Cons.
OKLAHOMA STATE DEPARTMENT OF
LIBRARIES □ Oklahoma City, OK
Doganges, Jacqueline, Asst.Dir.
U.S. COMMITTEE FOR UNICEF - INFORMATION
CENTER ON CHILDREN'S CULTURES □ New
York, NY
Dohan, Margaret, Libn.
INTERNATIONAL COMMUNICATION AGENCY,
UNITED STATES OF AMERICA - LIBRARY
SERVICE □ Ottawa, ON
Doherty, Amy S., Univ.Archv.Libn.
SYRACUSE UNIVERSITY - GEORGE ARENTS
RESEARCH LIBRARY FOR SPECIAL
COLLECTIONS □ Syracuse, NY
Doherty, Denis J., Hd.Libn. & Archv.
FRESNO DIOCESAN LIBRARY □ Fresno, CA
Doherty, Mr. G.J., Hd., Intl.Doc.
CANADA - INDUSTRY, TRADE & COMMERCE -
LIBRARY □ Ottawa, ON
Doherty, Janet, Libn.
MASSACHUSETTS STATE HOSPITAL SCHOOL -
MEDICAL LIBRARY □ Canton, MA
Doherty, Joseph H., Dir.
PROVIDENCE COLLEGE - PHILLIPS MEMORIAL
LIBRARY □ Providence, RI
Doherty, Marianne, Hd., Ref.Libn.
RUSH UNIVERSITY AND MEDICAL CENTER -
LIBRARY □ Chicago, IL
Doherty, Mary F., Assoc.Musm.Libn.
METROPOLITAN MUSEUM OF ART -
PHOTOGRAPH AND SLIDE LIBRARY □ New York,
NY

PERSONNEL

Doherty, Penny, Ref.Libn.
PHILADELPHIA COLLEGE OF PHARMACY AND SCIENCE - JOSEPH W. ENGLAND LIBRARY □ Philadelphia, PA

Doherty, R. Austin, Libn.
HOGAN & HARTSON - LIBRARY† □ Washington, DC

Doi, Masako, Libn.
HITTMAN ASSOCIATES, INC. - TECHNICAL INFORMATION DEPARTMENT - LIBRARY □ Columbia, MD

Doidge, Florence, Ref.Libn.
UNIVERSITY OF BRITISH COLUMBIA - WOODWARD BIOMEDICAL LIBRARY □ Vancouver, BC

Doikos, Helen, Libn.
SCUDDER, STEVENS & CLARK - LIBRARY □ Boston, MA

Dojka, John, Univ.Archv.
YALE UNIVERSITY - MANUSCRIPTS AND ARCHIVES □ New Haven, CT

Doksansky, Florence, Hd., Ref.
BROWN UNIVERSITY - SCIENCES LIBRARY □ Providence, RI

Dolan, Daphne, Chf.
CANADA - HEALTH AND WELFARE CANADA - DEPARTMENTAL LIBRARY SERVICES □ Ottawa, ON

Dolan, Janet, Health Info.Spec.
CLARK COUNTY DISTRICT HEALTH DEPARTMENT - LIBRARY □ Las Vegas, NV

Dolan, Patricia, Asst.Libn.Pub.Serv.
MITCHELL (William) COLLEGE OF LAW - JOHN B. SANBORN LIBRARY □ St. Paul, MN

Dolan, Robert, Libn.
CONNECTICUT STATE BOARD OF EDUCATION - J.M. WRIGHT TECHNICAL SCHOOL - LIBRARY □ Stamford, CT

Dole, Elizabeth, Ref.Libn.
UNIVERSITY OF VERMONT - CHEMISTRY/ PHYSICS LIBRARY □ Burlington, VT

Doleschal, Eugene, Libn.
NATIONAL COUNCIL ON CRIME AND DELINQUENCY - LIBRARY □ Hackensack, NJ

Dolinar, Mary M., Asst.Libn.
UNIVERSITY OF PITTSBURGH - GRADUATE SCHOOL OF PUBLIC HEALTH LIBRARY □ Pittsburgh, PA

Dolinsky, Beverly, Act.Dir.
INSTITUTE FOR PUBLIC TRANSPORTATION - LIBRARY □ New York, NY

Doliwa, Mrs. Zofia, Asst.Libn.
NEW YORK STATE DEPARTMENT OF LABOR - RESEARCH LIBRARY □ New York, NY

Dolores, Sister, S.C., Asst.Libn.
PENROSE HOSPITAL - WEBB MEMORIAL LIBRARY □ Colorado Springs, CO

Doloughty, Barbara, Ser.Libn.
UNIVERSITY OF PITTSBURGH - FALK LIBRARY OF THE HEALTH SCIENCES □ Pittsburgh, PA

Domabyl, Karen N., Libn.
U.S. NAVY - CENTER FOR NAVAL ANALYSES - LIBRARY □ Alexandria, VA

Doman, Shelley C., Chf., Lib.Serv.
U.S. VETERANS ADMINISTRATION (WV-Beckley) - MEDICAL CENTER LIBRARY □ Beckley, WV

Dombek, Lisa
SWEDENBORG LIBRARY AND BOOKSTORE □ Boston, MA

Domeck, L. Fay, Lib.Dir.
NORTH DAKOTA STATE HOSPITAL - DEPARTMENT OF LIBRARY SERVICES - HEALTH SCIENCE LIBRARY □ Jamestown, ND

Domenech, Helen J., Archv.
WIDENER UNIVERSITY - WOLFGRAM MEMORIAL LIBRARY □ Chester, PA

Domine, Kay J., Coll.Archv.
COLLEGE OF WILLIAM AND MARY - EARL GREGG SWEM LIBRARY □ Williamsburg, VA

Domingue, Goldie C., Dir., Info.Rsrcs.
3D/INTERNATIONAL - CORPORATE LIBRARY □ Houston, TX

Domini, Timothy, Map & Globe Cur.
BABSON COLLEGE - HORN LIBRARY □ Babson Park, MA

Dominitz, Linda, Res.Asst.
NEEDHAM, HARPER & STEERS OF CANADA, LTD. - INFORMATION SERVICES CENTRE □ Toronto, ON

Domino, Ms. Leslie Mirin, Mgr.
GOLD INFORMATION CENTER □ New York, NY

Dominy, Dr. Beryl W., Sr.Info.Sci.
PFIZER, INC. - CENTRAL RESEARCH TECHNICAL INFORMATION SERVICES □ Groton, CT

Domitz, Gary, Soc.Sci.Libn.
IDAHO STATE UNIVERSITY LIBRARY - SOCIAL SCIENCE DIVISION □ Pocatello, ID

Donahoe, Dorothy, Tech.Serv.
NAPA COUNTY HISTORICAL SOCIETY - GOODMAN LIBRARY □ Napa, CA

Donahue, Harold, Hd. Clerk
TENNESSEE VALLEY AUTHORITY - MAP SALES OFFICE □ Knoxville, TN

Donahue, Katharine E., Musm.Libn.
LOS ANGELES COUNTY MUSEUM OF NATURAL HISTORY - RESEARCH LIBRARY □ Los Angeles, CA

Donahue, Shirley, Hd., Tech.Serv.
CANADA - REGIONAL ECONOMIC EXPANSION - LIBRARY □ Ottawa, ON

Donaldson, David, Hd.Libn.
LEGAL AID SOCIETY - LIBRARIES □ New York, NY

Donaldson, George, Cur.
TEXAS STATE BUREAU OF ECONOMIC GEOLOGY - WELL SAMPLE AND CORE LIBRARY □ Austin, TX

Donaldson, Patrica B., Libn.
NEW YORK STATE SUPREME COURT - 5TH JUDICIAL DISTRICT - WATERTOWN LAW LIBRARY □ Watertown, NY

Donathan-Nordquist, Florence, Exec.Dir.
HALIFAX HISTORICAL SOCIETY, INC. - LIBRARY □ Daytona Beach, FL

Donati, Robert, Co.Rep., East Coast
LOCKHEED MISSILES & SPACE COMPANY, INC. - LOCKHEED INFORMATION SYSTEMS □ Palo Alto, CA

Donato, Anne, Cur., Waring Lib.
MEDICAL UNIVERSITY OF SOUTH CAROLINA - LIBRARY □ Charleston, SC

Donato, Ellen, Res.Libn.
INSIDE SPORTS MAGAZINE - LIBRARY □ New York, NY

Doncevic, Lois A., Sr.Libn.
ALLENTOWN CALL-CHRONICLE - NEWSPAPER LIBRARY □ Allentown, PA

Donelson, Frances A., Lib.Dir.
BACONE COLLEGE - LIBRARY □ Muskogee, OK

Donen, Jerome S., Dir.
EASTERN WASHINGTON UNIVERSITY - INSTRUCTIONAL MEDIA CENTER □ Cheney, WA

Donio, Dorothy
MIAMI-DADE PUBLIC LIBRARY - ART AND MUSIC DIVISION □ Miami, FL

Donkin, Kate, Map Cur.
MC MASTER UNIVERSITY - MAP LIBRARY □ Hamilton, ON

Donlan, Alberta F., Hd.Libn.
MUSEUM OF NEW MEXICO - MUSEUM OF FINE ARTS - LIBRARY □ Santa Fe, NM

Donley, Mary R., Coord., Tech.Serv.
UNIVERSITY OF WISCONSIN, STOUT - LIBRARY LEARNING CENTER - MEDIA RETRIEVAL SERVICES □ Menomonie, WI

Donnegan, Sr. Catherine, I.H.M., Acq.Libn.
MARYWOOD COLLEGE - LEARNING RESOURCES CENTER □ Scranton, PA

Donnell, Dr. H. Denny, Jr., Hist./Libn.
CHRISTMAS SEAL AND CHARITY STAMP SOCIETY - LIBRARY □ Columbia, MO

Donnell, Mary Ann, Libn.
PROVIDENCE HOSPITAL & SCHOOL OF NURSING - PROVIDENCE HEALTH SCIENCE LIBRARY □ Mobile, AL

Donnell, Robert, Dir.
UNIVERSITY OF SOUTH ALABAMA - COLLEGE OF MEDICINE - BIOMEDICAL LIBRARY □ Mobile, AL

Donnelly, Anna, Ref.Libn.
ST. JOHN'S UNIVERSITY - LIBRARY □ Jamaica, NY

Donoghue, Ruth H., Supv., Info.Serv.
EASTMAN KODAK COMPANY - PHOTOGRAPHIC TECHNOLOGY DIVISION - LIBRARY □ Rochester, NY

Donoghue, Simon, Ref.Libn.
BELMONT ABBEY COLLEGE - ABBOT VINCENT TAYLOR LIBRARY □ Belmont, NC

Donoho, Glenda
KENTUCKY STATE DEPARTMENT OF EDUCATION - RESOURCE CENTER □ Frankfort, KY

Donoho, Thomas A., Dept.Hd.
LOUISVILLE FREE PUBLIC LIBRARY - LIBRARY BROADCASTING □ Louisville, KY

Donohue, Evelyn, Lib.Techn.
ASHLAND CHEMICAL COMPANY - TECHNICAL INFORMATION CENTER □ Columbus, OH

Donohue, Joyce, Law Libn.
U.S. SOCIAL SECURITY ADMINISTRATION - LIBRARY □ Baltimore, MD

Donovan, Aileen M., Hd.
UNIVERSITY OF CALIFORNIA, BERKELEY - EARTHQUAKE ENGINEERING RESEARCH CENTER LIBRARY □ Richmond, CA

Donovan, Ann, Curriculum Libn.
CENTRAL WASHINGTON UNIVERSITY - LIBRARY - CURRICULUM LABORATORY □ Ellensburg, WA

Donovan, Catherine N., Sec.
PHOENIX PLANNING DEPARTMENT - LONG RANGE PLANNING DIVISION - LIBRARY □ Phoenix, AZ

Donovan, James, Sec.-Tres.
HENRY COUNTY LAW LIBRARY □ Napoleon, OH

Donovan, Kathryn M., Mgr.
PENNWALT CORPORATION - TECHNICAL DIVISION LIBRARY □ King Of Prussia, PA

Donovan, Maureen H., Japanese Cat.
OHIO STATE UNIVERSITY - EAST ASIAN COLLECTION □ Columbus, OH

Dontamsetti, Kumar, Hd.
UNIVERSITY OF CINCINNATI - MEDICAL CENTER LIBRARIES - MEDIA RESOURCES CENTER □ Cincinnati, OH

Doolen, Dr. Richard, Act.Dir.
UNIVERSITY OF MICHIGAN - MICHIGAN HISTORICAL COLLECTIONS - BENTLEY HISTORICAL LIBRARY □ Ann Arbor, MI

Dooley, Cynthia, Libn.
LITERARY AND HISTORICAL SOCIETY OF QUEBEC - LIBRARY† □ Quebec, PQ

Dooley, Maria, Libn.
BOARD OF COOPERATIVE EDUCATIONAL SERVICES OF NASSAU COUNTY (BOCES) - NASSAU EDUC. RSRCS. CTR. (NERC) □ Westbury, NY

Dooling, Marie, Asst.Libn.
ROCKEFELLER FOUNDATION - LIBRARY □ New York, NY

Doolittle, Carol, AV Coord.
CORNELL UNIVERSITY - AUDIO-VISUAL RESOURCE CENTER □ Ithaca, NY

Dopp, Bonnie Jo, Rd.Adv.
DISTRICT OF COLUMBIA PUBLIC LIBRARY - MUSIC & RECREATION DIVISION □ Washington, DC

Doran, Gary, Mgr.
AMERICAN TELEPHONE & TELEGRAPH COMPANY - EDITORIAL & HISTORICAL RESEARCH CENTER □ New York, NY

Doran, Sr. Maris Stella, O.S.B., Libn.
HOLY FAMILY CONVENT - LIBRARY □ Benet Lake, WI
Dordick, Beverly F., Libn.
NATIONAL ASSOCIATION OF REALTORS - HERBERT U. NELSON MEMORIAL LIBRARY □ Chicago, IL
Dore, Eleanor, Rd.Adv.
DISTRICT OF COLUMBIA PUBLIC LIBRARY - POPULAR LIBRARY □ Washington, DC
Dore, Louise, Techn.
CANADA - ENERGY, MINES & RESOURCES CANADA - EARTH PHYSICS BRANCH LIBRARY □ Ottawa, ON
Dorfman, Elaine, Oral Hist.Div.Hd.
MAGNES (Judah L.) MEMORIAL MUSEUM - WESTERN JEWISH HISTORY CENTER □ Berkeley, CA
Dorfman, Marcia, Asst.Libn.
GOOD SAMARITAN HOSPITAL - SHANK MEMORIAL LIBRARY □ Dayton, OH
Dorham, Barbara, Libn.
BROOKSIDE HOSPITAL - MEDICAL STAFF LIBRARY □ San Pablo, CA
Dorigan, M., Supv.
STANDARD OIL COMPANY OF INDIANA - LIBRARY/INFORMATION CENTER □ Chicago, IL
Dorilag, Lourdes (Ludy), Mgr.
AMDAHL CORPORATION - CORPORATE LIBRARY □ Sunnyvale, CA
Dorman, Louise, Act.Med.Libn.
WAYNE COUNTY GENERAL HOSPITAL - MEDICAL LIBRARY □ Westland, MI
Dorman, Nancy, Mgr./Lib. & Acq.
NATIONAL CLEARINGHOUSE FOR ALCOHOL INFORMATION - LIBRARY □ Rockville, MD
Dorman, Phae H., Supv.
DOW CHEMICAL U.S.A. - BUSINESS INFORMATION CENTER □ Midland, MI
Dorn, Georgette M., Spec./Hispanic Culture
LIBRARY OF CONGRESS - HISPANIC DIVISION □ Washington, DC
Dorner, Steven J., Mgr., Lib.Serv.
AMERICAN GAS ASSOCIATION - LIBRARY □ Arlington, VA
Dorney, G., Chf.Tech. Data Mgr.
U.S. DEFENSE LOGISTICS AGENCY - DEFENSE INDUSTRIAL SUPPLY CENTER - TECHNICAL DATA MANAGEMENT OFFICE □ Philadelphia, PA
Dorosh, Marion, Libn.
SOHIO PETROLEUM COMPANY - CENTRAL LIBRARY AND INFORMATION SERVICES □ San Francisco, CA
Dorris, Olive A., Asst.Libn.
CENTRAL NEW YORK ACADEMY OF MEDICINE - LIBRARY □ New Hartford, NY
Dorsey, B., Ref.
SOUTHWESTERN UNIVERSITY - SCHOOL OF LAW LIBRARY □ Los Angeles, CA
Dorsey, James C., Chf., Tech.Lib.
U.S. ARMY - CORPS OF ENGINEERS - SAVANNAH DISTRICT - TECHNICAL LIBRARY □ Savannah, GA
Dorst, Thomas, Asst.Archv.
NORTHWESTERN UNIVERSITY - ARCHIVES □ Evanston, IL
Dort, Donna, Libn.
PENNSYLVANIA STATE - JOINT STATE GOVERNMENT COMMISSION - LIBRARY □ Harrisburg, PA
Dort, Frances, Libn.
TEXAS INSTRUMENTS, INC. - NORTH BUILDING LIBRARY □ Dallas, TX
Dorval, Karen A., Fine Arts Supv.
SPRINGFIELD CITY LIBRARY - FINE ARTS DEPARTMENT □ Springfield, MA
Dossett, Jon, Tech. Staff Asst.
TEXAS STATE BUREAU OF ECONOMIC GEOLOGY - WELL SAMPLE AND CORE LIBRARY □ Austin, TX

Dote, Grace, Act.Hd.
UNIVERSITY OF CALIFORNIA, BERKELEY - GIANNINI FOUNDATION OF AGRICULTURAL ECONOMICS - RESEARCH LIBRARY □ Berkeley, CA
Dotson, James R., Libn.
SYMPHONY SOCIETY OF SAN ANTONIO - SYMPHONY LIBRARY □ San Antonio, TX
Dotterer, Ellen Castellan, Lib.Supv.
ROHM & HAAS COMPANY - HOME OFFICE LIBRARY □ Philadelphia, PA
Doty, Cheryl M., Libn.
BROWN AND WILLIAMSON TOBACCO CORPORATION - RESEARCH LIBRARY □ Louisville, KY
Doty, Jean S., Libn.
EASTERN MAINE MEDICAL CENTER - HEALTH SCIENCES LIBRARY □ Bangor, ME
Doty, Linda G., Lib.Adm.
INTERNATIONAL NICKEL COMPANY, INC. - LIBRARY □ New York, NY
Doucette, Sylvia, Info.Serv.
CANADIAN OLYMPIC ASSOCIATION - LIBRARY/INFORMATION SERVICES □ Montreal, PQ
Doud, Jess, Exec.Dir./Archv.
NAPA COUNTY HISTORICAL SOCIETY - GOODMAN LIBRARY □ Napa, CA
Doudera, A. Edward, J.D., Exec.Dir.
AMERICAN SOCIETY OF LAW & MEDICINE - SAGALL LIBRARY OF LAW, MEDICINE & HEALTH CARE □ Boston, MA
Doudna, Eileen B., Libn.
ST. JOSEPH HOSPITAL - HOSPITAL LIBRARY □ Lancaster, PA
Dougherty, Dorothy, Ref.Libn.
U.S. SOCIAL SECURITY ADMINISTRATION - LIBRARY □ Baltimore, MD
Dougherty, Joanne, Asst.Libn. & Archv.
AMHERST COLLEGE - SPECIAL COLLECTIONS DEPARTMENT AND ARCHIVES □ Amherst, MA
Dougherty, Phyllis K., Ref.Libn.
UNIVERSITY OF TENNESSEE - CENTER FOR THE HEALTH SCIENCES LIBRARY □ Memphis, TN
Doughtery, Nina, Info.Serv.
UNIVERSITY OF UTAH - SPENCER S. ECCLES HEALTH SCIENCES LIBRARY □ Salt Lake City, UT
Doughty, Barbara P., Med.Ref.Libn.
UNIVERSITY OF ALABAMA - COLLEGE OF COMMUNITY HEALTH SCIENCES - HEALTH SCIENCES LIBRARY □ University, AL
Douglas, Coreen, Libn.
EDMONTON CITY PLANNING DEPARTMENT - LIBRARY/RESOURCE CENTRE □ Edmonton, AB
Douglas, Katherine Meredith, Libn.
KNOX COUNTY GOVERNMENTAL LIBRARY □ Knoxville, TN
Douglas, Kimberly, Libn.
MAINE STATE DEPARTMENT OF MARINE RESOURCES - FISHERIES RESEARCH STATION - LIBRARY □ West Boothbay Harbor, ME
Douglas, Paula, Asst.Libn.
TACOMA NEWS TRIBUNE - LIBRARY □ Tacoma, WA
Douglas, Peter, Asst.Libn.
NEW YORK STATE LIBRARY FOR THE BLIND AND VISUALLY HANDICAPPED □ Albany, NY
Douglas, R. Alan, Cur.
WALKER (Hiram) HISTORICAL MUSEUM - REFERENCE LIBRARY □ Windsor, ON
Douglas, Dr. W.A.B., Dir.
CANADA - NATIONAL DEFENCE - DIRECTORATE OF HISTORY LIBRARY □ Ottawa, ON
Douglas-Hamilton, Lady Malcolm, Pres.
AMERICAN-SCOTTISH FOUNDATION, INC. - SCOTTISH RESEARCH LIBRARY □ New York, NY
Douglass, Adele S., Hd.Libn.
ILLINOIS STATE WATER SURVEY - LIBRARY □ Champaign, IL

Douglass, Elizabeth, Dir.
ASSOCIATION FOR GERONTOLOGY IN HIGHER EDUCATION - RESOURCE LIBRARY □ Washington, DC
Douglass, Renee, Libn.
BUCHANAN COUNTY LAW LIBRARY □ St. Joseph, MO
Doumato, Lamia, Ref.Libn.
NATIONAL GALLERY OF ART - LIBRARY □ Washington, DC
Dove, Janet, Dir.
UNIVERSITY OF DELAWARE, NEWARK - EDUCATION RESOURCE CENTER† □ Newark, DE
Dove, Louise E., Res.Asst.
URBAN WILDLIFE RESEARCH CENTER, INC. - LIBRARY □ Columbia, MD
Dow, Maynard Weston, Dir.
PLYMOUTH STATE COLLEGE - GEOGRAPHERS ON FILM COLLECTION □ Plymouth, NH
Dow, Ronald F., Dir.
NEW YORK UNIVERSITY - GRADUATE SCHOOL OF BUSINESS ADMINISTRATION - LIBRARY □ New York, NY
Dowd, Frank, Lib.Dir.
MAHARISHI INTERNATIONAL UNIVERSITY - SCIENCE OF CREATIVE INTELLIGENCE COLLECTION □ Fairfield, IA
Dowd, Judith A., Dept.Hd.
KAISER FOUNDATION HOSPITALS - MEDICAL LIBRARY □ Los Angeles, CA
Dowd, Bro. Philip, Lib.Dir.
MANHATTAN COLLEGE - SONNTAG LIBRARY □ Bronx, NY
Dowd, Sharon
WISCONSIN STATE OFFICE OF THE COMMISSIONER OF INSURANCE - LIBRARY □ Madison, WI
Dowd, W. Timothy, Exec.Dir.
INTERSTATE OIL AND GAS COMPACT COMMISSION - LIBRARY □ Oklahoma City, OK
Dowdell, Marlene S., Libn.
TELEDYNE CAE CORPORATION - ENGINEERING LIBRARY □ Toledo, OH
Dowdy, Mrs. Rae, Med. Staff Sec.
MEDICAL CENTER HOSPITAL - BELL-MARSH MEMORIAL LIBRARY □ Tyler, TX
Dowell, Gail E., Cat. & Music Libn.
HUDSON LIBRARY AND HISTORICAL SOCIETY □ Hudson, OH
Dowell, Wanda S., Cur.
FORT WARD MUSEUM - DOROTHY C.S. STARR CIVIL WAR RESEARCH LIBRARY □ Alexandria, VA
Dowie, Eve, Hd., Lib.Serv.
CANADA CENTRE FOR INLAND WATERS - LIBRARY □ Burlington, ON
Dowler, Lawrence, Act.Libn.
YALE UNIVERSITY - BEINECKE RARE BOOK AND MANUSCRIPT LIBRARY □ New Haven, CT
Dowler, Lawrence, Assoc.Libn.
YALE UNIVERSITY - MANUSCRIPTS AND ARCHIVES □ New Haven, CT
Dowling, Enos, Lib.Cons.
LINCOLN CHRISTIAN COLLEGE & SEMINARY - JESSIE C. EURY LIBRARY □ Lincoln, IL
Dowling, Jo A., Ref.Libn.
FLORIDA STATE SUPREME COURT LIBRARY □ Tallahassee, FL
Dowling, Karen, Curric.Libn.
MONTGOMERY COUNTY PUBLIC SCHOOLS - PROFESSIONAL LIBRARY □ Rockville, MD
Dowling, Kathleen, Ref.Supv.
BATTEN, BARTON, DURSTINE, OSBORN, INC. - INFORMATION RETRIEVAL CENTER □ New York, NY
Dowling, Shelley, Asst.Libn.
UNIVERSITY OF MISSOURI, KANSAS CITY - LAW LIBRARY □ Kansas City, MO
Downen, Madeline E., Supv.
ST. CATHERINE HOSPITAL - MC GUIRE MEMORIAL LIBRARY □ East Chicago, IN

PERSONNEL

Downey, Barbara, Asst.Libn.
BAYLOR UNIVERSITY, DALLAS - LIBRARY □
Dallas, TX

Downey, Bernard F., Libn.
RUTGERS UNIVERSITY, THE STATE
UNIVERSITY OF NEW JERSEY - INSTITUTE OF
MANAGEMENT/LABOR RELATIONS LIBRARY □
New Brunswick, NJ

Downey, Marcese W., Libn.
AUGUSTINIAN HISTORICAL INSTITUTE -
LIBRARY □ Villanova, PA

Downey, Myrna, Libn.
HARDWOOD PLYWOOD MANUFACTURERS
ASSOCIATION - LIBRARY □ Reston, VA

Downey, Patricia, Libn.
IOWA METHODIST SCHOOL OF NURSING -
MARJORIE GERTRUDE MORROW LIBRARY □
Des Moines, IA

Downie, Margaret, Assoc.Cur.
SHRINE TO MUSIC MUSEUM □ Vermillion, SD

Downing, Anthea, Chf.Libn.
ROYAL BANK OF CANADA - INFORMATION
RESOURCES □ Montreal, PQ

Downing, Bernas, Supv., Lit.Serv.
ELI LILLY AND COMPANY - GREENFIELD
LABORATORIES - LIBRARY AGRICULTURAL
SERVICE □ Greenfield, IN

Downing, Jeannette D., Libn.
NEW ORLEANS MUSEUM OF ART - FELIX J.
DREYOUS LIBRARY □ New Orleans, LA

Downs, Judy, Campus Libn.
CENTENNIAL COLLEGE OF APPLIED ARTS &
TECHNOLOGY - PROGRESS CAMPUS RESOURCE
CENTRE □ Scarborough, ON

Downs, Matthew P., Law Libn.
VALPARAISO UNIVERSITY - LAW LIBRARY □
Valparaiso, IN

Doyle, Dennis, Planner
ULSTER COUNTY PLANNING BOARD - LIBRARY
□ Kingston, NY

Doyle, Frances M., Supv.Libn.
U.S. ARMY - TRAINING AND DOCTRINE
COMMAND - TECHNICAL LIBRARY □ Ft. Monroe,
VA

Doyle, Francis R., Law Libn.
LOYOLA UNIVERSITY OF CHICAGO - LAW
LIBRARY □ Chicago, IL

Doyle, Jim L., Bus.Libn.
HIGHTOWER (Sara) REGIONAL LIBRARY -
BUSINESS LIBRARY □ Rome, GA

Doyle, John Timothy, Asst.Libn.
ALTOONA MIRROR - LIBRARY □ Altoona, PA

Doyle, Kevin, ILL
CANADA - AGRICULTURE CANADA - NEATBY
LIBRARY □ Ottawa, ON

Doyle, Leonard, Asst.Libn.
MIDDLESEX LAW LIBRARY ASSOCIATION -
LIBRARY† □ Cambridge, MA

Doyle, M. Bridget, Med.Libn.
HEPBURN (A. Barton) HOSPITAL - MEDICAL
LIBRARY □ Ogdensburg, NY

Draayer, Ingrid, Ref.Libn.
SPORT INFORMATION RESOURCE CENTRE □
Ottawa, ON

Drachkovitch, Milorad M., Archv.
STANFORD UNIVERSITY - HOOVER
INSTITUTION ON WAR, REVOLUTION AND
PEACE - LIBRARY □ Stanford, CA

Draganski, Donald, Libn.
ROOSEVELT UNIVERSITY - MUSIC LIBRARY □
Chicago, IL

Dragasevich, Diane, Libn./Supv.
NORTH YORK PUBLIC LIBRARY -
MULTILINGUAL MATERIALS DEPARTMENT† □
Downsview, ON

Draghi, Prof. Paul, Asst.Dir.
INDIANA UNIVERSITY - RESEARCH INSTITUTE
FOR INNER ASIAN STUDIES - LIBRARY □
Bloomington, IN

Dragotta, L., Supv., Lib.Serv.
AIR PRODUCTS AND CHEMICALS, INC. -
INFORMATION SERVICES - TREXLERTOWN
LIBRARY □ Allentown, PA

Dragutsky, Paula, Libn.
CANCER CARE, INC. - NATIONAL CANCER
FOUNDATION LIBRARY □ New York, NY

Drake, C.A.
CENTER FOR LIBERTARIAN STUDIES □ New
York, NY

Drake, Fr. Harold, Hd.
UNIVERSITY OF MANITOBA - ST. PAUL'S
COLLEGE - LIBRARY □ Winnipeg, MB

Drake, Jim, Libn.
REED LTD. - TECHNICAL INFORMATION
CENTRE □ Quebec, PQ

Drake, Keith A., Act.Med.Libn.
ALLIED HEALTH SCIENCES LIBRARY □ Austin,
TX

Drake, Mr. Mayo, Libn.
LOUISIANA STATE UNIVERSITY MEDICAL
CENTER - SCHOOL OF MEDICINE IN
SHREVEPORT - LIBRARY □ Shreveport, LA

Drake, Patricia J., Hd., Info.Serv.
CALGARY PLANNING DEPARTMENT -
INFORMATION SERVICES □ Calgary, AB

Drake, Randel Dean, Kpr./Ephemera
ARCANE ORDER - LIBRARY □ Falls Church, VA

Dralle, Dorothy, Libn.
ELLIS HOSPITAL - MEDICAL-NURSING LIBRARY
□ Schenectady, NY

Drancsak, Marina, Tech.Info.Spec.
U.S. DEPT. OF TRANSPORTATION - URBAN
MASS TRANSPORTATION ADM. -
TRANSPORTATION RESEARCH INFO. CENTER
(TRIC) □ Washington, DC

Drapeau, Micheline, Director
UNIVERSITE DU QUEBEC A MONTREAL -
BIBLIOTHEQUES DES SCIENCES JURIDIQUES □
Montreal, PQ

Draper, Jan, Act.Libn.
LEWIS COUNTY LAW LIBRARY □ Chehalis, WA

Draper, Linda, Hd., Tech.Serv.
INTERNATIONAL LIBRARY, ARCHIVES &
MUSEUM OF OPTOMETRY □ St. Louis, MO

Draper, Rosalie, Ck.
BETHANY COLLEGE - CHEMISTRY LIBRARY □
Bethany, WV

Drasgow, Laura S., Libn.
ASSOCIATED SPRING BARNES GROUP, INC. -
TECHNICAL CENTER LIBRARY □ Bristol, CT

Draughon, Dr. Ralph, Jr., Libn./Hist.
LEE (Robert E.) MEMORIAL ASSOCIATION, INC.
- JESSIE BALL DU PONT MEMORIAL LIBRARY □
Stratford, VA

Draves, William A., Natl.Coord.
FREE UNIVERSITY NETWORK - PUBLICATIONS
AND RESOURCES □ Manhattan, KS

Drawe, Kay, Libn.
WELDER (Rob & Bessie) WILDLIFE
FOUNDATION - LIBRARY □ Sinton, TX

Drayson, Pamela Kay, Libn.
ST. MARY'S HOSPITAL - LIBRARY □ Kansas
City, MO

Drayton, Anne Morddel, Libn.
SAN FRANCISCO PSYCHOANALYTIC INSTITUTE
- LIBRARY □ San Francisco, CA

Draz, Peter, Hd.Libn.
STATE HISTORICAL SOCIETY OF WISCONSIN -
LIBRARY □ Madison, WI

Drazba, Mary T., Sr.Dir.
BLUE CROSS AND BLUE SHIELD ASSOCIATIONS
- LIBRARY □ Chicago, IL

Drazniowsky, Roman, Cur.
AMERICAN GEOGRAPHICAL SOCIETY
COLLECTION OF THE UNIVERSITY OF
WISCONSIN, MILWAUKEE - GOLDA MEIR
LIBRARY □ Milwaukee, WI

Dreazen, Elizabeth, Info.Spec.
HARRIS TRUST AND SAVINGS BANK - LIBRARY
□ Chicago, IL

Dreher, Jeannette, Circ.Libn.
U.S. NASA - HEADQUARTERS LIBRARY □
Washington, DC

Drellich, Barbara, Hd., Tech.Info.Br.
U.S. NAVY - NAVAL SHIPYARD (Mare Island) -
TECHNICAL LIBRARY □ Vallejo, CA

Drenga, Steve, Supv.Lib.Asst.
BOSTON UNIVERSITY - LUTZ MEMORIAL
BIOLOGY LIBRARY □ Boston, MA

Dresner, Carol, Ref.Libn.
CLEVELAND HEALTH SCIENCES LIBRARY -
ALLEN MEMORIAL LIBRARY □ Cleveland, OH

Dresser, Betty, Libn.
LEWISTON TRIBUNE LIBRARY □ Lewiston, ID

Dresser, Sylvia, Acq.Libn.
UNIVERSITY OF ARKANSAS AT LITTLE ROCK -
PULASKI COUNTY LAW LIBRARY □ Little Rock,
AR

Drew, Dorothy, Libn.
CANADA - AGRICULTURE CANADA - LONDON
RESEARCH CENTRE LIBRARY □ London, ON

Drew, Frances, Arch.Libn.
GEORGIA INSTITUTE OF TECHNOLOGY - PRICE
GILBERT MEMORIAL LIBRARY -
ARCHITECTURE LIBRARY □ Atlanta, GA

Drews, Margaret A., Libn.
HENKEL CORPORATION - HENNEPIN
TECHNICAL CENTER LIBRARY □ Minneapolis,
MN

Driggers, Gerald, Pres.
L-5 SOCIETY - LIBRARY □ Tucson, AZ

Drinkard, Julia A., Info.Dir.
HARRISONBURG-ROCKINGHAM HISTORICAL
SOCIETY AND MUSEUM - JOHN W. WAYLAND
LIBRARY □ Harrisonburg, VA

Drinkhouse, Bruce, Pres.
NORTHAMPTON COUNTY HISTORICAL AND
GENEALOGICAL SOCIETY - HISTORICAL
MUSEUM AND LIBRARY □ Easton, PA

Driscoll, Eleanor A., Dir., Command Libs.
U.S. AIR FORCE - AIR FORCE SYSTEMS
COMMAND - LIBRARY DIVISION □ Washington,
DC

Dritschilo, Dr. William, Prof.
UNIVERSITY OF CALIFORNIA, LOS ANGELES -
ENVIRONMENTAL SCIENCE AND ENGINEERING
- LIBRARY □ Los Angeles, CA

Drittler, John, Chf.Libn.
OSSINING HISTORICAL SOCIETY MUSEUM -
LIBRARY □ Ossining, NY

Droessler, William F., Libn.
UNIVERSITY OF ARKANSAS, MONTICELLO -
LIBRARY† □ Monticello, AR

Drolet, Bernadette, Chf.Libn.
HOPITAL ST-SACREMENT - BIBLIOTHEQUE
MEDICALE □ Quebec, PQ

Drolet, Leon L., Jr., Dir.
NORTH SUBURBAN LIBRARY SYSTEM &
SUBURBAN LIBRARY SYSTEM - SUBURBAN AV
SERVICE □ La Grange Park, IL

Drong, Josephine V., Security & Storage
HUGHES AIRCRAFT COMPANY - COMPANY
TECHNICAL DOCUMENT CENTER □ Culver City,
CA

Drouin, Fernand, Dir.
LA PRESSE, LTEE. - CENTRE DE
DOCUMENTATION □ Montreal, PQ

Drouin, Rev. Georges, Archiviste
SEMINAIRE DE QUEBEC - ARCHIVES □ Quebec,
PQ

Drouin, Roger, Ref.Libn.
HYDRO-QUEBEC - INSTITUT DE RECHERCHE -
BIBLIOTHEQUE □ Varennes, PQ

Druck, Kitty, Hd.Transl.Dept.
HOECHST-ROUSSEL PHARMACEUTICALS, INC. -
LIBRARY □ Somerville, NJ

Druckman, Eleanor, Libn.
CENTER FOR THE ANALYSIS OF HEALTH
PRACTICES - LIBRARY □ Boston, MA

Druesedow, John E., Jr., Dir.
OBERLIN COLLEGE - CONSERVATORY OF
MUSIC - MARY M. VIAL MUSIC LIBRARY □
Oberlin, OH

Drum, Carol, Assoc.Libn.
UNIVERSITY OF FLORIDA - CHEMISTRY
LIBRARY □ Gainesville, FL

Drum, Claudia
ALSTON, MILLER AND GAINES - LAW LIBRARY
□ Atlanta, GA

Drum, Eunice, Dir., Tech.Serv.
NORTH CAROLINA STATE DEPARTMENT OF
CULTURAL RESOURCES - DIVISION OF THE
STATE LIBRARY □ Raleigh, NC

Drummond, Frances M., Supv.
AMOCO CANADA PETROLEUM COMPANY, LTD. -
LIBRARY INFORMATION CENTER □ Calgary, AB

Drummong, Dr. P.E., Mgr., Tech.Info.
FMC CORPORATION - AGRICULTURAL
CHEMICAL GROUP - RESEARCH AND
DEVELOPMENT DEPT. - TECHNICAL LIBRARY □
Middleport, NY

Drury, George H., Info.Chf.
KALMBACH PUBLISHING COMPANY -
INFORMATION CENTER □ Milwaukee, WI

Dryden, Deana, Libn.
ROYAL ALEXANDRA HOSPITAL - MEDICAL
LIBRARY □ Edmonton, AB

Dryden, Donna, Libn.
ALBERTA TEACHERS' ASSOCIATION - LIBRARY
□ Edmonton, AB

du Roy, Sherry, Libn.
ERNST & WHINNEY - LIBRARY □ Los Angeles,
CA

Duba, B.J., Mgr.
NORTHROP CORPORATION - ELECTRO-
MECHANICAL DIVISION - TECHNICAL
INFORMATION CENTER □ Anaheim, CA

Dubaz, Alice, Lib.Techn.
U.S. AIR FORCE BASE - KEESLER BASE - MC
BRIDE LIBRARY □ Keesler AFB, MS

Dube, Gilles, Map Div.
SOCIETE QUEBECOISE D'INITIATIVES
PETROLIERES - DOCUMENTATION CENTRE □
Ste. Foy, PQ

Duboczy, Julia T., Med.Libn.
ALAMEDA-CONTRA COSTA MEDICAL
ASSOCIATION - LIBRARY □ Oakland, CA

Dubois, Paul, Dir.
QUEBEC PROVINCE - MINISTERE DES
AFFAIRES SOCIALES - INFORMATHEQUE □
Quebec, PQ

DuBois, Dr. Paul Z., Dir. of Lib.Serv.
TRENTON STATE COLLEGE - ROSCOE L. WEST
LIBRARY □ Trenton, NJ

DuBow, Cathryn M., Supv., Lib.Serv.
COCA-COLA COMPANY - ARCHIVES &
BUSINESS INFORMATION SERVICES □ Atlanta,
GA

Dubreuil, Chantal, Documentaliste
UNIVERSITE LAVAL - CENTRE D'ETUDES
NORDIQUES (CEN) - CENTRE DE
DOCUMENTATION □ Ste. Foy, PQ

Dubreuil, Lorraine
MC GILL UNIVERSITY - MAP AND AIR PHOTO
LIBRARY □ Montreal, PQ

Dubson, Nadine A., Libn.
NEW YORK COUNTY SURROGATE'S COURT -
LAW LIBRARY† □ New York, NY

Dubuc, Richard, Assoc.Libn.
BARREAU DE MONTREAL - BIBLIOTHEQUE □
Montreal, PQ

Ducas, Ada M., Asst.Med.Libn.
ROYAL VICTORIA HOSPITAL - MEDICAL
LIBRARY† □ Montreal, PQ

Ducey, Richard, Asst.Libn./Rd.Serv.
NEW ENGLAND SCHOOL OF LAW - LIBRARY □
Boston, MA

Duchac, Gretchen N., Libn.
LUTHERAN MEDICAL CENTER - MEDICAL
LIBRARY □ Brooklyn, NY

Duchamp, Diane C., Info.Dir.
LOUISIANA STATE DEPARTMENT OF NATURAL
RESOURCES - DIVISION OF RESEARCH &
DEVELOPMENT - LIBRARY □ Baton Rouge, LA

Duchesne, Guy
CENTRALE DE L'ENSEIGNEMENT DU QUEBEC -
CENTRE DE DOCUMENTATION □ Quebec, PQ

Duchow, Sandra R., Chf.Med.Libn.
ROYAL VICTORIA HOSPITAL - MEDICAL
LIBRARY† □ Montreal, PQ

Duckett, Kenneth, Cur.
UNIVERSITY OF OREGON - SPECIAL
COLLECTIONS DIVISION □ Eugene, OR

Duckles, Vincent H., Hd.
UNIVERSITY OF CALIFORNIA, BERKELEY -
MUSIC LIBRARY □ Berkeley, CA

Duckworth, Janet, Libn.
LOGETRONICS, INC. - INFORMATION CENTER
□ Springfield, VA

Duclow, Geraldine, Libn.-In-Charge
FREE LIBRARY OF PHILADELPHIA - THEATRE
COLLECTION □ Philadelphia, PA

Duda, Sophia, Libn.
UNIVERSITY OF TORONTO - PATHOLOGY
LIBRARY □ Toronto, ON

Dudak, Helen Louise, Libn.
U.S.D.A. - AGRICULTURAL RESEARCH SERVICE
- HORTICULTURAL RESEARCH LABORATORY
LIBRARY □ Orlando, FL

Dudden, Rosalind, Dir. of Lib.Serv.
MERCY MEDICAL CENTER - LIBRARY AND
MEDIA RESOURCES DEPARTMENT □ Denver, CO

Duderwicz, Diana, Asst.Cat.Libn.
UNIVERSITY OF GEORGIA - LAW LIBRARY □
Athens, GA

Dudley, Annie L., Asst.Libn.
U.S. NAVY - NAVAL EXPLOSIVE ORDNANCE
DISPOSAL TECHNOLOGY CENTER - TECHNICAL
LIBRARY □ Indian Head, MD

Dudley, Durand S., Sr. Law Libn.
MARATHON OIL COMPANY - LAW LIBRARY □
Findlay, OH

Dudman, Mary K., Libn.
AUBURN UNIVERSITY - ARCHITECTURE AND
FINE ARTS LIBRARY □ Auburn, AL

Dudziak, Karen, Asst.Libn.
INDIANA UNIVERSITY - SCHOOL OF LIBRARY
AND INFORMATION SCIENCE LIBRARY □
Bloomington, IN

Dueck, Elizabeth, Asst.Libn.
CONFEDERATION LIFE INSURANCE COMPANY -
LIBRARY □ Toronto, ON

Dueker, Sarah, Asst.Chf., Lib.Br.
U.S. NASA - AMES RESEARCH CENTER -
LIBRARY □ Mountain View, CA

Dueltgen, Dr. Ronald R., Mgr.-Tech.Info.Serv.
HENKEL CORPORATION - HENNEPIN
TECHNICAL CENTER LIBRARY □ Minneapolis,
MN

Dueno, Rosa P., Spec.Cat.Off.
PUERTO RICO - ATENEO PUERTORRIQUENO -
BIBLIOTECA □ San Juan, PR

Duensing, Edward E., Jr., Info.Mgr.
RUTGERS UNIVERSITY, THE STATE
UNIVERSITY OF NEW JERSEY - CENTER FOR
URBAN POLICY RESEARCH LIBRARY □
Piscataway, NJ

Duerell, Anne M., Lib.Techn.
U.S. AIR FORCE BASE - HANSCOM BASE
LIBRARY □ Hanscom AFB, MA

Duerrehuhl, Ernest, Act.Libn.
LANCASTER THEOLOGICAL SEMINARY OF THE
UNITED CHURCH OF CHRIST - PHILIP SCHAFF
LIBRARY □ Lancaster, PA

Duesterbeck, Florance, Libn.
WASCANA INSTITUTE OF APPLIED ARTS AND
SCIENCES - RESOURCE & INFORMATION
CENTRE □ Regina, SK

Duff, Ann M., Res.Libn.
DOFASCO INC. - RESEARCH INFORMATION
CENTRE □ Hamilton, ON

Duff, Audrey O., Libn.
ATOMIC INDUSTRIAL FORUM - LIBRARY □
Washington, DC

Duff, David, Rd.Adv.
DISTRICT OF COLUMBIA PUBLIC LIBRARY -
AUDIOVISUAL DIVISION □ Washington, DC

Duff, Lucy W., Libn.
BUREAU OF SOCIAL SCIENCE RESEARCH -
LIBRARY □ Washington, DC

Duffany, Maureen B., Libn./Cur.Spec.Coll.
ST. JOHN'S SEMINARY - EDWARD LAURENCE
DOHENY MEMORIAL LIBRARY □ Camarillo, CA

Duffey, Mary S., Libn.
OHIO STATE LEGISLATIVE REFERENCE
BUREAU - LIBRARY† □ Columbus, OH

Duffey, Nona, Libn.
DETROIT GARDEN CENTER - LIBRARY □
Detroit, MI

Duffey, Polly Jean, Health Sci.Libn.
BAYFRONT MEDICAL CENTER, INC. - HEALTH
SCIENCES LIBRARY □ St. Petersburg, FL

Duffie, Judith, Info.Spec.
AMERICAN HOECHST - FILMS DIVISION -
TECHNICAL INFORMATION CENTER □ Greer,
SC

Duffy, Annette, Hd.Libn.
OKLAHOMA STATE UNIVERSITY - OKLAHOMA
CITY BRANCH - TECHNICAL INSTITUTE
LIBRARY □ Oklahoma City, OK

Duffy, L.
ATLANTIC PROVINCES ECONOMIC COUNCIL -
LIBRARY □ Halifax, NS

Duffy, Mark J., Archv.
PROTESTANT EPISCOPAL CHURCH -
EPISCOPAL DIOCESE OF MASSACHUSETTS -
DIOCESAN LIBRARY AND ARCHIVES □ Boston,
MA

Duffy, Richard, Sr.Libn.
IBM CORPORATION - FEDERAL SYSTEMS
DIVISION - AVIONICS SYSTEMS - LIBRARY □
Owego, NY

Duffy, William J., Res.Coord.
U.S. INTERAGENCY ADVANCED POWER GROUP
- POWER INFORMATION CENTER† □
Philadelphia, PA

Dufort, Robert, Ref.Libn.
CEGEP ST-JEAN SUR RICHELIEU -
BIBLIOTHEQUE† □ St. Jean, PQ

Dufour, Denise, Ref.Asst.
NATIONAL LIBRARY OF CANADA - CANADIAN
INDIAN RIGHTS COLLECTION □ Ottawa, ON

DuFour, Doris, Telereference
UNIVERSITE LAVAL - BIBLIOTHEQUE
SCIENTIFIQUE† □ Ste. Foy, PQ

Dufour, Jean-Pierre, Coord.
COLLEGE DE JONQUIERE - CENTRE DE
RESSOURCES EDUCATIVES □ Jonquiere, PQ

Dufresne, Daphne, Chf.Libn.
UNIVERSITE DU QUEBEC A MONTREAL -
BIBLIOTHEQUE DES ARTS □ Montreal, PQ

Duggan, Ann V., Mgr., Lib.Serv.
AMERICAN FOUNDRYMEN'S SOCIETY -
TECHNICAL INFORMATION CENTER† □ Des
Plaines, IL

Duggan, Elizabeth, Med.Libn.
GRACE GENERAL HOSPITAL - CHESLEY A.
PIPPY, JR. MEDICAL LIBRARY □ St. John's, NF

Dugger, Linda, Ser.
LAMAR UNIVERSITY - MARY AND JOHN GRAY
LIBRARY □ Beaumont, TX

Duggins, Lois
ST. LOUIS PUBLIC LIBRARY - ART
DEPARTMENT □ St. Louis, MO

Dugoff, Elizabeth, MRI Libn.
FLORIDA INSTITUTE OF TECHNOLOGY -
LIBRARY □ Melbourne, FL

Duhamel, Marie, Govt.Pubn.
UNIVERSITY OF OTTAWA - MORISSET
LIBRARY □ Ottawa, ON

Duignan, Peter, Cur., Africa Mid East
STANFORD UNIVERSITY - HOOVER
INSTITUTION ON WAR, REVOLUTION AND
PEACE - LIBRARY □ Stanford, CA

Duisin, Xenia W., Libn.
INSTITUTE OF PUBLIC ADMINISTRATION -
LIBRARY □ New York, NY

Dujsik, Gerald, Lib.Mgr.
CHRIST HOSPITAL - HOSPITAL LIBRARY □ Oak
Lawn, IL

Dujsik, Gerald, Lib.Mgr.
EVANGELICAL SCHOOL OF NURSING -
WOJNIAK MEMORIAL LIBRARY □ Oak Lawn, IL

**P
E
R
S
O
N
N
E
L**

Dukakis, Arthur G., Regional Dir.
U.S. BUREAU OF THE CENSUS - REGIONAL DATA USER SERVICE - BOSTON REGIONAL OFFICE - LIBRARY ◻ Boston, MA

Duke, Lucy L., Libn.
EMORY UNIVERSITY - SCHOOL OF DENTISTRY - SHEPPARD W. FOSTER LIBRARY ◻ Atlanta, GA

Duke, Suzanna, Libn.
LAW SOCIETY OF NEWFOUNDLAND - LIBRARY ◻ St. John's, NF

Dukes, Johanna Sheehy, AV Libn.
FLORIDA STATE UNIVERSITY - INSTRUCTIONAL SUPPORT CENTER - FILM LIBRARY ◻ Tallahassee, FL

Dukes, Morgan, Dir.Gen.Serv.
AMERICANS UNITED FOR SEPARATION OF CHURCH AND STATE - ARCHIVES ◻ Silver Spring, MD

Dukes, William H., Libn.
GIFFELS ASSOCIATES, INC. - LIBRARY ◻ Southfield, MI

Dula, Doron A., Tech.Libn.
ITEK CORPORATION - APPLIED TECHNOLOGY DIVISION - TECHNICAL LIBRARY ◻ Sunnyvale, CA

Dulaney, H.G., Lib.Dir.
RAYBURN (Sam) FOUNDATION - SAM RAYBURN LIBRARY ◻ Bonham, TX

Dulka, Michael, Map/Geog.Libn.
CLARK UNIVERSITY - GRADUATE SCHOOL OF GEOGRAPHY - GUY H. BURNHAM MAP-AERIAL PHOTOGRAPH LIBRARY ◻ Worcester, MA

Dull, Patricia J., Med.Libn.
TRUMBULL MEMORIAL HOSPITAL - WEAN MEDICAL LIBRARY ◻ Warren, OH

Dumais, Madeleine, Responsable
HOPITAL DE L'ENFANT-JESUS - BIBLIOTHEQUE MEDICALE ◻ Quebec, PQ

Dumbaugh, Hedda, Spec.Coll.
BETHANY AND NORTHERN BAPTIST THEOLOGICAL SEMINARIES - LIBRARY ◻ Oak Brook, IL

Dumbauld, Betty, Hd.Libn.
THOMPSON (J. Walter) COMPANY - INFORMATION CENTER ◻ Chicago, IL

Dumlao, Mercedes, Libn.
BECHTEL - DATA PROCESSING LIBRARY ◻ San Francisco, CA

Dumont, Ginette, Lib.Techn.
BEAUCHEMIN-BEATON-LAPOINTE, INC. - BBL LIBRARY ◻ Montreal, PQ

Dumont, Monique, Libn.
GESTAS INC. - DOCUMENTATION CENTER ◻ Montreal, PQ

Dumoulin, Real, Chf.
QUEBEC PROVINCE - MINISTERE DES AFFAIRES CULTURELLES - CENTRE DE DOCUMENTATION ◻ Quebec, PQ

Dunaway, Cleta, Cat.Libn.
COLUMBIA BIBLE COLLEGE - LEARNING RESOURCES CENTER ◻ Columbia, SC

Dunaway, Yvonne
MONROE, JUNEAU, JACKSON COUNTY, WISCONSIN GENEALOGY WORKSHOP - LIBRARY ◻ Black River Falls, WI

Dunbar, Barbara, Dir.
MC LEAN COUNTY HISTORICAL SOCIETY - MUSEUM AND LIBRARY ◻ Bloomington, IL

Dunbar, Linda, Lib.Techn.
VANCOUVER TEACHERS' PROFESSIONAL LIBRARY ◻ Vancouver, BC

Duncan, A.A., Ctr.Dir.
UNIVERSITY OF FLORIDA - AGRICULTURAL RESEARCH & EDUCATION CENTER - HOMESTEAD LIBRARY ◻ Homestead, FL

Duncan, Anita, Lib.Asst.
OHIO UNIVERSITY - MUSIC/DANCE LIBRARY ◻ Athens, OH

Duncan, Anita E., Lib.Techn.
ALBERTA - DEPARTMENT OF FEDERAL AND INTERGOVERNMENTAL AFFAIRS - LIBRARY ◻ Edmonton, AB

Duncan, Donnan, Circ.Libn.
LOGAN COLLEGE OF CHIROPRACTIC - LIBRARY ◻ Chesterfield, MO

Duncan, Margaret, Hd., Topside Br.
U.S. NAVY - NAVAL OCEAN SYSTEMS CENTER - TECHNICAL LIBRARY ◻ San Diego, CA

Duncan, Marian, Lib.Mgr.
MACLEAN-HUNTER, LTD. - LIBRARY ◻ Toronto, ON

Duncan, Martha D., Libn.
AUBURN UNIVERSITY - LEARNING RESOURCES CENTER ◻ Auburn, AL

Duncan, Ramona, Consrv.
INDIANA HISTORICAL SOCIETY - WILLIAM HENRY SMITH MEMORIAL LIBRARY ◻ Indianapolis, IN

Duncan, Sandra, Asst.Libn./Tech.Serv.
WISCONSIN STATE LAW LIBRARY ◻ Madison, WI

Duncombe, Sid, Dir.
UNIVERSITY OF IDAHO - BUREAU OF PUBLIC AFFAIRS RESEARCH - LIBRARY ◻ Moscow, ID

Dundon, Theresa, Libn.
UNIVERSITY OF CALIFORNIA, BERKELEY - NAVAL BIOSCIENCES LABORATORY - LIBRARY ◻ Oakland, CA

Dunfield, Everett R., Engr.Libn.
UNIVERSITY OF NEW BRUNSWICK - ENGINEERING LIBRARY ◻ Fredericton, NB

Dunham, Della M., Coord., Pub.Serv.
CHICAGO STATE UNIVERSITY - DOUGLAS LIBRARY ◻ Chicago, IL

Dunham, Randall B., Prof.
UNIVERSITY OF WISCONSIN, MADISON - WILLIAM A. SCOTT BUSINESS LIBRARY - JOHNSON FOUNDATION COLLECTION ◻ Madison, WI

Dunkel, Lisa M., Libn.
LANGLEY PORTER PSYCHIATRIC INSTITUTE - LIBRARY ◻ San Francisco, CA

Dunkle, William, Data Libn.
WOODS HOLE OCEANOGRAPHIC INSTITUTION - RESEARCH LIBRARY ◻ Woods Hole, MA

Dunkly, James, Libn.
NASHOTAH HOUSE - LIBRARY ◻ Nashotah, WI

Dunlap, Barbara J., Archv.
CUNY - CITY COLLEGE LIBRARY - COLLEGE ARCHIVES ◻ New York, NY

Dunlap, Barbara J., Libn.
CUNY - CITY COLLEGE LIBRARY - SPECIAL COLLECTIONS ◻ New York, NY

Dunlap, Betty
BONNER COUNTY HISTORICAL SOCIETY, INC. - RESEARCH LIBRARY ◻ Sandpoint, ID

Dunlap, Ellen S., Res.Libn.
UNIVERSITY OF TEXAS, AUSTIN - HUMANITIES RESEARCH CENTER ◻ Austin, TX

Dunlap, La Donna, Libn.
LEGAL SERVICES ORGANIZATION OF INDIANA, INC. - LIBRARY ◻ Indianapolis, IN

Dunleavy, Clara, Chf.Ref.Libn.
YESHIVA UNIVERSITY - ALBERT EINSTEIN COLLEGE OF MEDICINE - D. SAMUEL GOTTESMAN LIBRARY ◻ Bronx, NY

Dunlop, Alice W.
UNITED NATIONS ASSOCIATION OF THE UNITED STATES OF AMERICA - GREATER ST. LOUIS CHAPTER - LIBRARY ◻ St. Louis, MO

Dunn, Barbara E., Libn.
HAWAIIAN HISTORICAL SOCIETY - MISSION-HISTORICAL LIBRARY ◻ Honolulu, HI

Dunn, David W., Law Libn.
ORAL ROBERTS UNIVERSITY - LAW LIBRARY ◻ Tulsa, OK

Dunn, Diane M., Hd., Ref.Dept.
DETROIT NEWS - GEORGE B. CATLIN MEMORIAL LIBRARY ◻ Detroit, MI

Dunn, Donald J., Law Libn.
WESTERN NEW ENGLAND COLLEGE - SCHOOL OF LAW LIBRARY ◻ Springfield, MA

Dunn, George L., Jr., Libn.
MEMPHIS COMMERCIAL APPEAL - LIBRARY ◻ Memphis, TN

Dunn, Harriet, Asst. Professor
NASHVILLE STATE TECHNICAL INSTITUTE - EDUCATIONAL RESOURCE CENTER ◻ Nashville, TN

Dunn, Hedy M., Musm.Mgr.
LOS ALAMOS COUNTY HISTORICAL MUSEUM - ARCHIVES ◻ Los Alamos, NM

Dunn, Dr. Horton, Jr., Supv., Info.Serv.
LUBRIZOL CORPORATION - CHEMICAL LIBRARY ◻ Wickliffe, OH

Dunn, Jamie Niss, Asst.Libn.
DORSEY, WINDHORST, HANNAFORD, WHITNEY & HALLADAY - LAW LIBRARY ◻ Minneapolis, MN

Dunn, Mary B., Law Libn.
NEW YORK STATE SUPREME COURT - APPELLATE DIVISION, 4TH JUDICIAL DEPARTMENT - LAW LIBRARY ◻ Syracuse, NY

Dunn, Nancy, Libn.
CHILDREN'S HOSPITAL OF PITTSBURGH - BLAXTER MEMORIAL LIBRARY ◻ Pittsburgh, PA

Dunn, Pat, Ref.Libn.
UNIVERSITY OF BRITISH COLUMBIA - CURRICULUM LABORATORY ◻ Vancouver, BC

Dunn, Richard, Lib.Dir.
TECHNOMIC PUBLISHING CO., INC. - BUSINESS LIBRARY ◻ Westport, CT

Dunn, Sandra, Info.Serv.Off.
ONTARIO CRAFTS COUNCIL - CRAFT RESOURCE CENTRE ◻ Toronto, ON

Dunn, Susannah, Coord.
WEST VIRGINIA STATE DEPARTMENT OF EDUCATION - EDUCATIONAL MEDIA CENTER ◻ Charleston, WV

Dunnagan, Betsy, ILL Serv.
NORTH CAROLINA STATE DEPARTMENT OF CULTURAL RESOURCES - DIVISION OF THE STATE LIBRARY ◻ Raleigh, NC

Dunnigan, Brian Leigh, Exec.Dir.
OLD FORT NIAGARA ASSOCIATION - LIBRARY ◻ Youngstown, NY

Dunnigan, Mary C., Libn.
UNIVERSITY OF VIRGINIA - FISKE KIMBALL FINE ARTS LIBRARY ◻ Charlottesville, VA

Dunning, Carol J., Res.Assoc.
UNIVERSITY OF TEXAS, AUSTIN - CENTER FOR ENERGY STUDIES - ENERGY INFORMATION SERVICE ◻ Austin, TX

Dunwody, Lynn, Res.Libn.
HAY ASSOCIATES - RESEARCH LIBRARY ◻ Philadelphia, PA

Duong, Dr. Buu, Ref.Serv.
BRIDGEWATER COLLEGE - ALEXANDER MACK MEMORIAL LIBRARY - SPECIAL COLLECTIONS ◻ Bridgewater, VA

Dupont, Elizabeth D., Libn.
MERCER (George Jr.) MEMORIAL SCHOOL OF THEOLOGY - LIBRARY ◻ Garden City, NY

DuPont, Ginny, Med.Libn.
U.S. VETERANS ADMINISTRATION (DC-Washington) - MEDICAL CENTER LIBRARY† ◻ Washington, DC

Dupont, Richard, Asst.Libn.
COMBUSTION ENGINEERING, INC. - POWER SYSTEMS GROUP LIBRARY SERVICES ◻ Windsor, CT

Duppstadt, Mary Ann, Asst.Chf.Libn.
VOUGHT CORPORATION - TECHNICAL INFORMATION CENTER ◻ Dallas, TX

Dupree, Harry K., Dir.
U.S. FISH & WILDLIFE SERVICE - FISH FARMING EXPERIMENTAL STATION - LIBRARY ◻ Stuttgart, AR

Dupuis, Carmen, Materiatheque
HOPITAL STE-JUSTINE - CENTRE D'INFORMATION SUR LA SANTE DE L'ENFANT† ◻ Montreal, PQ, H3T 1C5 PQ

Dupuis, Marcel, Dir.
UNIVERSITE DU QUEBEC A MONTREAL - BIBLIOTHEQUE DES SCIENCES DE L'EDUCATION ◻ Montreal, PQ

Dupuis, Sylvie, Lib.Techn.
HOPITAL DE MONT-JOLI, INC. - BIBLIOTHEQUE ◻ Mont-Joli, PQ

Dupuy, Ronald J., Interpretive Ranger
LA PURISMA MISSION - ARCHIVES □ Lompoc,
CA

Duran, Frances, Per./Doc.
ADAMS STATE COLLEGE - LIBRARY □ Alamosa,
CO

Duran, Olga, Rsrcs. Facilitator
MEXICAN-AMERICAN OPPORTUNITY
FOUNDATION - INFORMATION AND REFERRAL
SERVICE - RESOURCE CENTER □ Monterey
Park, CA

Durance, Cynthia, Dir./Network Dev.Off.
NATIONAL LIBRARY OF CANADA □ Ottawa, ON

Durand, Joan W., Libn.
MOUNT ST. ALPHONSUS THEOLOGICAL
SEMINARY - LIBRARY □ Esopus, NY

Durand, Marielle, Libn.
UNIVERSITE DE MONTREAL - EDUCATION/
PSYCHOLOGIE/COMMUNICATION-
BIBLIOTHEQUE □ Montreal, PQ

Durant, Bene L., Libn.
CENTER FOR COMMUNITY ECONOMIC
DEVELOPMENT - LIBRARY □ Washington, DC

Durbin, Hugh A., Dir.
COLUMBUS PUBLIC SCHOOLS - TEACHERS'
PROFESSIONAL LIBRARY □ Columbus, OH

Durbrow, Mary C., Libn.
NEW CANAAN HISTORICAL SOCIETY -
LIBRARY □ New Canaan, CT

Durden, Jesse N., Dir.
U.S. DEPT. OF COMMERCE - INTERNATIONAL
TRADE ADMINISTRATION - DES MOINES
DISTRICT OFFICE LIBRARY □ Des Moines, IA

Durfey, William M., Exec.V.P.
NATIONAL ASSOCIATION OF ANIMAL
BREEDERS - LIBRARY† □ Columbia, MO

Durham, Eileen C., Libn.
PAGE COMMUNICATIONS ENGINEERS, INC. -
INFORMATION CENTER □ Vienna, VA

Durham, Vaida, Libn.
HARRIS HOSPITAL - MEDICAL LIBRARY □ Fort
Worth, TX

Durivage, Mary Jo, Med.Libn.
U.S. VETERANS ADMINISTRATION (MI-Allen
Park) - MEDICAL CENTER LIBRARY SERVICE
(142D) □ Allen Park, MI

Durkin, M.L., Chf.Libn.
U.S. ARMY AVIATION TRAINING LIBRARY □ Ft.
Rucker, AL

Durkin, Virginia, Med.Libn.
ST. VINCENT'S HOSPITAL - GARCEAU LIBRARY
□ Indianapolis, IN

Durling, Susanne, Info.Sci.
JOHNSON AND JOHNSON - RESEARCH CENTER
LIBRARY □ New Brunswick, NJ

Durnan, Mary L., Dir.
MARSHALL COUNTY HISTORICAL SOCIETY
MUSEUM - LIBRARY □ Plymouth, IN

Durning, Harry M., Exec.Dir.
BOSTON MUNICIPAL RESEARCH BUREAU -
LIBRARY □ Boston, MA

Durocher, Georges, Libn.
UNIVERSITY OF ALBERTA - FACULTE ST-JEAN
- BIBLIOTHEQUE □ Edmonton, AB

Durocher, Rene, Pres.
INSTITUT D'HISTOIRE DE L'AMERIQUE
FRANCAISE (1970) - RESEARCH CENTRE
LIBRARY □ Montreal, PQ

Durow, William, Asst.Libn.
GRAND LODGE OF IOWA, A.F. AND A.M. - IOWA
MASONIC LIBRARY □ Cedar Rapids, IA

Durr, W.T., Dir.
UNIVERSITY OF BALTIMORE - BALTIMORE
REGION INSTITUTIONAL STUDIES CENTER
(BRISC) □ Baltimore, MD

Durrett, Parthenia, Circ.
UNIVERSITY OF LOUISVILLE - KORNHAUSER
HEALTH SCIENCES LIBRARY □ Louisville, KY

Durso, Angie, Libn.
CHILDREN'S HOSPITAL OF SAN FRANCISCO -
EMGE MEDICAL LIBRARY □ San Francisco, CA

Durso, Michael P., Libn.
U.S. DEPT. OF ENERGY - HEALTH & SAFETY
LABORATORY LIBRARY □ New York, NY

Durst, Leslie, Libn.
WEST VIRGINIA SCHOOLS FOR THE DEAF AND
BLIND - WV SCHOOL FOR THE BLIND LIBRARY
□ Romney, WV

Durst, Marianna L., Staff Libn.
PRINCE WILLIAM COUNTY SCHOOLS - STAFF
LIBRARY □ Manassas, VA

Dusch, Margaret C., Asst.Dept.Hd.
CARNEGIE LIBRARY OF PITTSBURGH - MUSIC
AND ART DEPARTMENT □ Pittsburgh, PA

Duschenchuk, Judy, Engr.Libn.
GENERAL INSTRUMENT CORPORATION,
GOVERNMENT SYSTEMS DIVISION -
ENGINEERING LIBRARY □ Hicksville, NY

Dust, Steven, Dir.
MISSOURI STATE DIVISION OF COMMUNITY
AND ECONOMIC DEVELOPMENT - RESEARCH
LIBRARY □ Jefferson City, MO

Dustin, John, Hum.Libn.
SOUTHERN ILLINOIS UNIVERSITY,
EDWARDSVILLE - HUMANITIES & FINE ARTS
LIBRARY □ Edwardsville, IL

Dustin, M.J., Ref.Coord.
MINITEX □ Minneapolis, MN

Dutikow, Irene V., Dir.
RADIO FREE EUROPE/RADIO LIBERTY -
REFERENCE LIBRARY □ New York, NY

Dutil, Ghyslaine, Sec.
CENTRALE DE L'ENSEIGNEMENT DU QUEBEC -
CENTRE DE DOCUMENTATION □ Quebec, PQ

Dutt, Ann, Libn.
SKIDMORE, OWINGS & MERRILL - LIBRARY/
RESOURCE CENTER □ Chicago, IL

Dutton, Lee, Libn.
NORTHERN ILLINOIS UNIVERSITY -
SOUTHEAST ASIA COLLECTION □ DeKalb, IL

Dutton, Marilyn, Libn.
UNIVERSITY OF BRITISH COLUMBIA - SOCIAL
SCIENCES DIVISION □ Vancouver, BC

Duval, Barbara, Libn.
MERCY SCHOOL OF NURSING - LIBRARY □
Charlotte, NC

DuVal, Mary J., Libn.
ORGANIZATION RESOURCES COUNSELORS,
INC. - INFORMATION CENTER □ New York, NY

Duvall, Mary Lou, Ref.Libn.
KING COUNTY LAW LIBRARY □ Seattle, WA

Duvall, Scott, Asst.Cur.
BRIGHAM YOUNG UNIVERSITY - SPECIAL
COLLECTIONS □ Provo, UT

Duvally, Charlotte, Engr.Libn.
DREXEL UNIVERSITY LIBRARIES - SCIENCE
AND TECHNOLOGY LIBRARY □ Philadelphia, PA

DuWors, Elaine, Libn.
CRANE (J.W.) MEMORIAL LIBRARY □ Toronto,
ON

Duyka, Ann, Cat.
TEXAS A & M UNIVERSITY - MEDICAL
SCIENCES LIBRARY □ College Station, TX

Duyst, Jo, Acq.
CALVIN COLLEGE AND SEMINARY - LIBRARY □
Grand Rapids, MI

Duzy, Ken, Ref./CAI
IBM CORPORATION - GENERAL PRODUCTS
DIVISION - INFORMATION/LIBRARY/
LEARNING CENTER □ San Jose, CA

Dvorak, Dr. Anna, Libn.
NORTH CAROLINA MUSEUM OF ART - ART
REFERENCE LIBRARY □ Raleigh, NC

Dvorak, Jean, Per./Binding
BLACK HILLS STATE COLLEGE - E.Y. BERRY
LIBRARY-LEARNING CENTER □ Spearfish, SD

Dvorak, Robert, Dir.
GORDON-CONWELL THEOLOGICAL SEMINARY -
GODDARD LIBRARY □ South Hamilton, MA

Dvorzak, Marie, Libn.
UNIVERSITY OF MINNESOTA - GEOLOGY
LIBRARY □ Minneapolis, MN

Dwelley, Linda J., Media Resource Dir.
MAINE CRIMINAL JUSTICE ACADEMY - MEDIA
RESOURCES □ Waterville, ME

Dworaczek, Marian, Hd., Tech.Serv.
ONTARIO - MINISTRY OF LABOUR - LIBRARY □
Toronto, ON

Dworkin, Ellen, Sr.Libn.
GLENDALE PUBLIC LIBRARY - BRAND LIBRARY
□ Glendale, CA

Dworman, Thomas J.
DWORMAN (Thomas J.) - LIBRARY □ Detroit, MI

Dwoskin, Beth, Libn.
TEMPLE LIBRARY □ Cleveland, OH

Dwyer, Janet C., Libn.
JENSEN ASSOCIATES, INC. - LIBRARY □
Boston, MA

Dwyer, Mary, Musm.Serv.
NATIONAL SOARING MUSEUM - LIBRARY &
ARCHIVES □ Elmira, NY

Dwyer, Mary, Hd.Libn.
ST. PAUL RAMSEY MEDICAL CENTER -
MEDICAL LIBRARY □ St. Paul, MN

Dwyer, Melva J., Hd.
UNIVERSITY OF BRITISH COLUMBIA - FINE
ARTS DIVISION □ Vancouver, BC

Dwyer, William E., Dir.
U.S. DEPT. OF COMMERCE - INTERNATIONAL
TRADE ADMINISTRATION - ALBUQUERQUE
DISTRICT OFFICE LIBRARY† □ Albuquerque, NM

Dyal, Donald A., Hd., Spec.Coll.Div.
TEXAS A & M UNIVERSITY - SPECIAL
COLLECTIONS DIVISION □ College Station, TX

Dyches, Charlene, Asst., Microfilm
ALCOLAC, INC. - RESEARCH LIBRARY □
Baltimore, MD

Dyck, Marilyn, Ref.Libn.
CANADA - PUBLIC WORKS CANADA -
INFORMATION, RESEARCH & LIBRARY
SERVICES □ Ottawa, ON

Dye, Della, Mss.Libn.
UNIVERSITY OF UTAH - SPECIAL COLLECTIONS
DEPARTMENT □ Salt Lake City, UT

Dye, Glenn W., Sec.-Tres.
NATIONAL ASSOCIATION OF PRECANCEL
COLLECTORS, INC. - CHESTER DAVIS
MEMORIAL LIBRARY □ Wildwood, NJ

Dye, Margarette M., Libn.
POWELL, GOLDSTEIN, FRAZER & MURPHY -
LIBRARY† □ Atlanta, GA

Dye, Patricia, Hd.
METROPOLITAN TORONTO LIBRARY -
BUSINESS DEPARTMENT □ Toronto, ON

Dyer, Charles R., Law Libn.
UNIVERSITY OF MISSOURI, KANSAS CITY -
LAW LIBRARY □ Kansas City, MO

Dyer, Helen, Res.Libn.
BRISTOL-MYERS PRODUCTS - TECHNICAL
INFORMATION CENTER □ Hillside, NJ

Dyer, Judith C., Libn.
SAN DIEGO SOCIETY OF NATURAL HISTORY -
NATURAL HISTORY MUSEUM LIBRARY □ San
Diego, CA

Dyer, Ms. S.M., Libn.
SASKATCHEWAN TEACHERS' FEDERATION -
STEWART RESOURCES CENTRE □ Saskatoon,
SK

Dyer, Sue, Law Libn.
THELEN, MARRIN, JOHNSON & BRIDGES - LAW
LIBRARY □ San Francisco, CA

Dyess, Cynthia A., Libn.
IBM CORPORATION - ENGINEERING LIBRARY □
Austin, TX

Dyess, Dr. Stewart W., Asst.Dir./Lib.Serv.
TEXAS TECH UNIVERSITY - LIBRARY □
Lubbock, TX

Dyess, William, Dir.Rec.Mgt.Div.
TEXAS STATE LIBRARY □ Austin, TX

Dygert, James, Ref.Libn.
FEDERAL RESERVE BANK OF PHILADELPHIA -
LIBRARY □ Philadelphia, PA

Dykas, Lucille, Libn.
ST. JOSEPH HOSPITAL - MEDICAL LIBRARY □
St. Charles, MO

PERSONNEL

Dyki, Judy, Libn.
UNIVERSITY OF DETROIT - EVENING COLLEGE OF BUSINESS AND ADMINISTRATION - LIBRARY □ Detroit, MI

Dykstra, Stephanie, Ser.Libn.
UNIVERSITY OF BRITISH COLUMBIA - WOODWARD BIOMEDICAL LIBRARY □ Vancouver, BC

Dysart, Jane, Chf.Libn.
ROYAL BANK OF CANADA - INFORMATION RESOURCES □ Toronto, ON

Dysenchuk, Paul, Res.Asst./Libn.
UNITED NATIONS - CENTRE ON TRANSNATIONAL CORPORATIONS - LIBRARY □ New York, NY

Dyson, Allan J., Univ. Libn.
UNIVERSITY OF CALIFORNIA, SANTA CRUZ - DEAN E. MC HENRY LIBRARY □ Santa Cruz, CA

Dyson-Bonter, Peter, Dir., N.S.F.L.
CANADIAN FILM INSTITUTE - NATIONAL SCIENCE FILM LIBRARY □ Ottawa, ON

Dziedzina, Christine, Asst.Libn.
CLEVELAND METROPOLITAN GENERAL HOSPITAL - HAROLD H. BRITTINGHAM MEMORIAL LIBRARY □ Cleveland, OH

Dzierlenga, Donna, User Serv.Spec.
ERIC CLEARINGHOUSE FOR JUNIOR COLLEGES □ Los Angeles, CA

Dzierzak, Edward, AV Libn.
MARSHALL UNIVERSITY - SCHOOL OF MEDICINE - HEALTH SCIENCE LIBRARIES □ Huntington, WV

Dzurinko, Ms. M., Asst.Libn.
COVINGTON AND BURLING - LIBRARY □ Washington, DC

Dzwonkoski, Peter, Hd.
UNIVERSITY OF ROCHESTER - DEPARTMENT OF RARE BOOKS, MANUSCRIPTS & ARCHIVES □ Rochester, NY

E

Eads, Kathleen, Asst.Libn.
SOUTHERN ILLINOIS UNIVERSITY, CARBONDALE - HUMANITIES DIVISION LIBRARY □ Carbondale, IL

Eady, Lois A., Cur.
BIRMINGHAM PUBLIC AND JEFFERSON COUNTY FREE LIBRARY - COLLINS COLLECTION OF THE DANCE □ Birmingham, AL

Eagan, Deborah, Libn.
UNIVERSITY OF NEW MEXICO - TIREMAN LEARNING MATERIALS LIBRARY □ Albuquerque, NM

Eagles, D.E., Chem.-Libn.
IMPERIAL OIL, LTD. - RESEARCH TECHNICAL INFORMATION CENTRE □ Sarnia, ON

Eaglesfield, Jean, Lindgren Libn.
MASSACHUSETTS INSTITUTE OF TECHNOLOGY - LINDGREN LIBRARY □ Cambridge, MA

Eagleson, Laurie, Cat.Libn.
EASTERN NEW MEXICO UNIVERSITY - GOLDEN LIBRARY □ Portales, NM

Eagleton, Kathy, Dir.
BRANDON GENERAL HOSPITAL - LIBRARY SERVICES □ Brandon, MB

Eagon, Carrie W., Libn.
ESSO EASTERN, INC. - LIBRARY □ Houston, TX

Eakin, Dottie, Assoc.Dir., Tech.Serv.
HOUSTON ACADEMY OF MEDICINE - TEXAS MEDICAL CENTER LIBRARY □ Houston, TX

Eakin, Laurabelle, Dir.
UNIVERSITY OF PITTSBURGH - FALK LIBRARY OF THE HEALTH SCIENCES □ Pittsburgh, PA

Eames, Carol, Educ.Cur.
TULSA ZOOLOGICAL PARK - LIBRARY □ Tulsa, OK

Eandi, Eileen, Pub.Serv.Libn.
UNIVERSITY OF SOUTHERN CALIFORNIA - HEALTH SCIENCES CAMPUS - NORRIS MEDICAL LIBRARY □ Los Angeles, CA

Eannarino, Judith C., Rd.Serv.Libn.
MOHAWK VALLEY COMMUNITY COLLEGE - LIBRARY □ Utica, NY

Earl, Mitzi, Info.Dir.
NATIONAL GASOHOL COMMISSION - LIBRARY □ Lincoln, NE

Earley, Denise H., Info.Spec.
SOUTHEASTERN PENNSYLVANIA TRANSPORTATION AUTHORITY - LIBRARY □ Philadelphia, PA

Earls, Leone, Libn.
CANADIAN BROADCASTING CORPORATION - REFERENCE LIBRARY □ Toronto, ON

Early, Charles, Asst.Ref.Libn.
STANFORD UNIVERSITY - ENGINEERING LIBRARY □ Stanford, CA

Early, Mary, Info.Spec.
MILES LABORATORIES, INC. - LIBRARY RESOURCES AND SERVICES □ Elkhart, IN

Earnest, Kathryn, Asst.Acq.Libn.
U.S. ARMY - ADJUTANT GENERAL - LIBRARY DIVISION □ Alexandria, VA

Earnest, Marcia, Libn.
MERRILL (Charles E.) PUBLISHING COMPANY - LIBRARY □ Columbus, OH

Earnest, Ola May, Genealogist
LINN COUNTY HISTORICAL SOCIETY - LIBRARY □ Pleasanton, KS

Earwood, Janet, Spec.Coll.Libn.
CENTRAL BIBLE COLLEGE - LIBRARY □ Springfield, MO

Easley, Jane, Lib.Adm.
U.S. NAVY - NAVAL REGIONAL MEDICAL CENTER (Bremerton) - MEDICAL LIBRARY □ Bremerton, WA

Easley, Vi, Lib. Aide
FORT WORTH PUBLIC LIBRARY - BUSINESS AND TECHNOLOGY DEPARTMENT □ Fort Worth, TX

Eason, Nicholas J., Supt.
U.S. NATL. PARK SERVICE - ABRAHAM LINCOLN BIRTHPLACE NATL. HISTORIC SITE - LIBRARY □ Hodgenville, KY

Eason, Robert, Theater Libn.
DALLAS PUBLIC LIBRARY - FINE ARTS DIVISION □ Dallas, TX

Easson, Dr. Kay P., Exec.Dir.
AMERICAN BLAKE FOUNDATION - RESEARCH LIBRARY □ Memphis, TN

Easson, Dr. Roger R., Exec.Dir.
AMERICAN BLAKE FOUNDATION - RESEARCH LIBRARY □ Memphis, TN

East, Catherine, Sr.Libn., Ref.Serv.
U.S. POSTAL SERVICE - LIBRARY □ Washington, DC

East, Dr. Dennis, Hd.
OHIO HISTORICAL SOCIETY - ARCHIVES-LIBRARY □ Columbus, OH

Easter, Mona Jeanne, Hd., Tech.Serv.
NEBRASKA STATE LIBRARY COMMISSION □ Lincoln, NE

Easter, Ruth H., Libn.
AMERICAN ENKA COMPANY - BUSINESS AND TECHNICAL LIBRARY □ Enka, NC

Eastman, Betty-Jean, Med.Libn.
CENTRAL VERMONT HOSPITAL - MEDICAL LIBRARY □ Barre, VT

Eastman, Esther, Coord.
ATLANTIC-RICHFIELD COMPANY - GOVERNMENT RELATIONS INFORMATION RESOURCES CENTER □ Los Angeles, CA

Eaton, Casdiania P., Libn.
AMERICAN ACADEMY AND INSTITUTE OF ARTS AND LETTERS - LIBRARY □ New York, NY

Eaton, Conrad P., Libn.
U.S. DEPT. OF STATE - LIBRARY □ Washington, DC

Eaton, Elizabeth K., Assoc.Dir.Pub.Serv.
UNIVERSITY OF TEXAS MEDICAL BRANCH - MOODY MEDICAL LIBRARY □ Galveston, TX

Eaton, Eugenia, Hd.
UNIVERSITY OF CALIFORNIA, LOS ANGELES - PUBLIC AFFAIRS SERVICE □ Los Angeles, CA

Eaton, Mrs. James T., Libn.
CARMEL UNITED PRESBYTERIAN CHURCH - MEMORIAL LIBRARY □ Glenside, PA

Eaton, Jeanne Miller, Asst.Libn.
INSTITUTE OF GERONTOLOGY - LIBRARY □ Ann Arbor, MI

Eaton, Katherine G., Libn.
UNIVERSITY OF OREGON - BUREAU OF GOVERNMENTAL RESEARCH AND SERVICE LIBRARY □ Eugene, OR

Eaton, Lewis A., Park Techn.
U.S. NATL. PARK SERVICE - FORT LARAMIE NATL. HISTORIC SITE - LIBRARY □ Fort Laramie, WY

Eaton, Sharon, Info.Spec.
LOUISIANA STATE LEGISLATIVE COUNCIL - DIVISION OF INFORMATION SERVICES □ Baton Rouge, LA

Eatroff, Elaine B., Cur. of Rare Books
U.S. ARMY - MILITARY ACADEMY - LIBRARY □ West Point, NY

Ebanks, Hilma, Info.Spec.
CONFERENCE BOARD, INC. - INFORMATION SERVICE □ New York, NY

Ebbinghouse, Carol, Ref.
SOUTHWESTERN UNIVERSITY - SCHOOL OF LAW LIBRARY □ Los Angeles, CA

Ebbott, William, Docs./Per.Libn.
UNIVERSITY OF WISCONSIN, MADISON - LAW LIBRARY □ Madison, WI

Eben, Craig, Hd., Educ.Dev.Serv.
ILLINOIS BENEDICTINE COLLEGE - THEODORE LOWNIK LIBRARY □ Lisle, IL

Eben, J.P., Supv.
DOW CHEMICAL U.S.A. - TEXAS DIVISION - LIBRARY □ Freeport, TX

Eber, Beryl, Supv.Libn.
NEW YORK PUBLIC LIBRARY - DONNELL LIBRARY CENTER - NATHAN STRAUS YOUNG ADULT LIBRARY □ New York, NY

Eberhardt, Claire, Asst.Libn.
NEW YORK STATE LIBRARY - LAW/SOCIAL SCIENCE REFERENCE SERVICES □ Albany, NY

Eberhardt, Rev. N.C., C.M., Dir.Lib.Serv.
ST. JOHN'S SEMINARY - EDWARD LAURENCE DOHENY MEMORIAL LIBRARY □ Camarillo, CA

Eberhart, George M., Ser.Libn.
UNIVERSITY OF KANSAS - SCHOOL OF LAW LIBRARY □ Lawrence, KS

Eberhart, Martha, ILL Libn.
MEDICAL COLLEGE OF WISCONSIN - TODD WEHR LIBRARY □ Milwaukee, WI

Ebersole, W. Brian, Libn.
CLAREMONT COLLEGES - POMONA SCIENCE LIBRARIES □ Claremont, CA

Ebert, Catherine M., Cur.
CROW WING COUNTY HISTORICAL SOCIETY - MUSEUM LIBRARY □ Brainerd, MN

Ebner, William E., Chf.
TELEDYNE RYAN AERONAUTICAL - TECHNICAL INFORMATION SERVICES □ San Diego, CA

Ebro, Diana, Asst.Lib.Dir./Health Sci.
UNIVERSITY OF MINNESOTA, DULUTH - HEALTH SCIENCE LIBRARY □ Duluth, MN

Eby, Dr. Harold H., Dir.
CONOCO, INC. - RESEARCH AND DEVELOPMENT DEPARTMENT - TECHNICAL INFORMATION SERVICES □ Ponca City, OK

Echard, Dena, Ref.Libn.
MONTANA COLLEGE OF MINERAL SCIENCE AND TECHNOLOGY - LIBRARY □ Butte, MT

Eck, Robert F., Ref.Libn.
MICHIGAN STATE LIBRARY SERVICES - LAW LIBRARY □ Lansing, MI

Eckart, Daniel, Ref.Libn.
PROVIDENCE COLLEGE - PHILLIPS MEMORIAL LIBRARY □ Providence, RI

Eckel, Virginia E., Dir.
U.S. AIR FORCE INSTITUTE OF TECHNOLOGY - LIBRARY □ Wright-Patterson AFB, OH

Eckels, Diane, Assoc.Dir./Adm.Aff.
HOUSTON ACADEMY OF MEDICINE - TEXAS MEDICAL CENTER LIBRARY □ Houston, TX

Eckert, Dan, Libn.
HOLY FAMILY HOSPITAL - HEALTH SCIENCE
LIBRARY □ Manitowoc, WI

Eckert, Tim, Regional Archv.
WASHINGTON STATE OFFICE OF SECRETARY
OF STATE - DIVISION OF ARCHIVES AND
RECORD MANAGEMENT □ Olympia, WA

Eckert, Dr. William G., Dir.
INTERNATIONAL REFERENCE ORGANIZATION
IN FORENSIC MEDICINE AND SCIENCES -
LIBRARY AND REFERENCE CENTER □ Wichita,
KS

Eckes, Harold, Coord., Lrng.Rsrcs,Ctr.
LOS ANGELES TRADE-TECHNICAL COLLEGE -
LIBRARY □ Los Angeles, CA

Eckes, Mark, Adm.Coord.
MINITEX □ Minneapolis, MN

Eckey, Carol, Libn.
IOWA STATE COMMISSION FOR THE BLIND -
LIBRARY FOR THE BLIND & PHYSICALLY
HANDICAPPED □ Des Moines, IA

Eckhoff, Helga, Ser.Libn.
DORSEY, WINDHORST, HANNAFORD, WHITNEY
& HALLADAY - LAW LIBRARY □ Minneapolis, MN

Eckhouse, Elena, Libn.
SELIGMAN (J.&W.) & CO. INCORPORATED -
RESEARCH LIBRARY □ New York, NY

Eckl, Liz, Asst.Libn.
AMERICAN PUBLIC POWER ASSOCIATION -
LIBRARY □ Washington, DC

Eckley, Elena, Media Serv.Libn.
EMBRY RIDDLE AERONAUTICAL UNIVERSITY -
LEARNING RESOURCES CENTER □ Daytona
Beach, FL

Ecklund, Lynn, Tech.Info.Spec.
ATLANTIC-RICHFIELD COMPANY -
HEADQUARTERS LIBRARY □ Los Angeles, CA

Eckman, Charles, Libn.
PUBLIC LIBRARY OF FORT WAYNE AND ALLEN
COUNTY, INDIANA - BUSINESS AND
TECHNOLOGY DEPARTMENT □ Fort Wayne, IN

Edblom, Nancy, Ref.Libn.
SUNY - COLLEGE AT POTSDAM - FREDERICK W.
CRUMB MEMORIAL LIBRARY □ Potsdam, NY

Eddison, Elizabeth Bole, Pres.
WARNER-EDDISON ASSOCIATES, INC. -
INFORMATION SERVICE □ Cambridge, MA

Eddy, Barbara J., Educ.Libn.
MEMORIAL UNIVERSITY OF NEWFOUNDLAND -
EDUCATION LIBRARY □ St. John's, NF

Eddy, Dolores D., Regional Libn.
ENVIRONMENTAL PROTECTION AGENCY -
REGION VIII LIBRARY □ Denver, CO

Eddy, Donald, Libn.
CORNELL UNIVERSITY - RARE BOOKS
DEPARTMENT □ Ithaca, NY

Eddy, Holly H., Med.Libn.
SPRINGFIELD HOSPITAL - INFORMATION
CENTER LIBRARY □ Springfield, VT

Eddy, Leonard M., Dir.
UNIVERSITY OF LOUISVILLE - KORNHAUSER
HEALTH SCIENCES LIBRARY □ Louisville, KY

Edelman, Gayle S., Hd., Tech.Serv.
UNIVERSITY OF CHICAGO - LAW SCHOOL
LIBRARY □ Chicago, IL

Edelstein, Elizabeth, Libn.
GLADMAN (Everett A.) MEMORIAL HOSPITAL -
MEDICAL LIBRARY □ Oakland, CA

Edelstein, J.M., Chf.Libn.
NATIONAL GALLERY OF ART - LIBRARY □
Washington, DC

Edens, Marietta, Libn.
OZARK INSTITUTE - RURAL MEDIA CENTER
LIBRARY □ Eureka Springs, AR

Edgar, Martha, Pres.
NATIONAL WOMAN'S CHRISTIAN
TEMPERANCE UNION - FRANCES E. WILLARD
MEMORIAL LIBRARY □ Evanston, IL

Edgar, Neal, Assoc.Cur.
KENT STATE UNIVERSITY - DEPARTMENT OF
SPECIAL COLLECTIONS □ Kent, OH

Edge, Goode B., Hist. Site Mgr.
LOUISIANA STATE DEPT. OF CULTURE,
RECREATION & TOURISM - MANSFIELD STATE
COMMEMORATIVE AREA - MUSEUM & LIB. □
Mansfield, LA

Edgerly, Linda, Archv.
WEYERHAEUSER COMPANY - ARCHIVES □
Federal Way, WA

Edgerton, L.K., Libn.
SOCIETY OF THE FOUNDERS OF NORWICH,
CONNECTICUT - LEFFINGWELL INN LIBRARY □
Norwich, CT

Edie, Betty B., Libn.
COURIER - LIBRARY □ Findlay, OH

Edimont, T., Mgr.
WILLIAM-FREDERICK PRESS - PAMPHLET
LIBRARY □ New York, NY

Edinburg, Gloria L., Dir.
OXFORD MUSEUM - LIBRARY □ Oxford, MA

Edington, Dr. Everett D., Dir.
ERIC CLEARINGHOUSE ON RURAL EDUCATION
AND SMALL SCHOOLS □ Las Cruces, NM

Edkins, Barbara B., Libn.
PEABODY MUSEUM OF SALEM - PHILLIPS
LIBRARY □ Salem, MA

Edlhauser, June M., Coord. of Fine Arts
MILWAUKEE PUBLIC LIBRARY - ART, MUSIC
AND RECREATION SECTION □ Milwaukee, WI

Edmonds, Edmond P., Assoc. Law Libn.
COLLEGE OF WILLIAM AND MARY - MARSHALL-
WYTHE LAW LIBRARY □ Williamsburg, VA

Edmonson, James, Assoc.Cur.
CLEVELAND HEALTH SCIENCES LIBRARY -
HOWARD DITTRICK MUSEUM OF HISTORICAL
MEDICINE □ Cleveland, OH

Edmunds, S., Ref.Spec.
U.S. DEPT. OF ENERGY - PACIFIC NORTHWEST
LABORATORY - TECHNICAL INFO. SECT. □
Richland, WA

Edmundson, Henry, Mgr.
SCHLUMBERGER-DOLL RESEARCH CENTER -
LIBRARY □ Ridgefield, CT

Edsall, Shirley, Dir.
WILSON (Charles S.) MEMORIAL HOSPITAL -
LEARNING RESOURCES DEPARTMENT □
Johnson City, NY

Edson, Wendy B., Asst.Libn.
PHILLIPS, LYTLE, HITCHOCK, BLAINE AND
HUBER - LIBRARY □ Buffalo, NY

Edwards, Barbara, Hd.
MIAMI-DADE PUBLIC LIBRARY - ART AND
MUSIC DIVISION □ Miami, FL

Edwards, Cecilia C., Med.Libn.
U.S. ARMY HOSPITALS - WOMACK ARMY
HOSPITAL - MEDICAL LIBRARY □ Fort Bragg, NC

Edwards, Elizabeth, Circ.Supv.
WASHINGTON STATE UNIVERSITY -
VETERINARY MEDICAL/PHARMACY LIBRARY □
Pullman, WA

Edwards, Elizabeth D., Cat.
DRAPER (Charles Stark) LABORATORY, INC. -
TECHNICAL INFORMATION CENTER □
Cambridge, MA

Edwards, Fern, College Libn.
GALLAUDET COLLEGE LIBRARY - SPECIAL
COLLECTIONS □ Washington, DC

Edwards, G.P., Sr.Cur.
GILCREASE (Thomas) INSTITUTE OF
AMERICAN HISTORY AND ART - LIBRARY □
Tulsa, OK

Edwards, J. Duke, Law Libn.
UTAH STATE - 3RD JUDICIAL DISTRICT - SALT
LAKE COUNTY LAW LIBRARY □ Salt Lake City,
UT

Edwards, Dr. John Carver, Rec.Off./Archv.
UNIVERSITY OF GEORGIA - DEPARTMENT OF
RECORDS MANAGEMENT & UNIVERSITY
ARCHIVES □ Athens, GA

Edwards, John D., Assoc.Libn.
UNIVERSITY OF OKLAHOMA - LAW LIBRARY □
Norman, OK

Edwards, Kathleen, Libn.
CONTROL DATA CORPORATION - LIBRARY/
INFORMATION CENTER □ Minneapolis, MN

Edwards, Margo, Asst.Libn.
CAHILL, GORDON, & REINDEL - LAW LIBRARY □
New York, NY

Edwards, Mark T., Libn.
CALIFORNIA AIR RESOURCES BOARD -
LIBRARY □ Sacramento, CA

Edwards, Marsha, Libn.
BECHTEL POWER CORPORATION - TRUST &
THRIFT INVESTMENTS CENTER □ San
Francisco, CA

Edwards, Mary, Asst.Libn.
TORONTO CITY PLANNING AND DEVELOPMENT
DEPARTMENT - LIBRARY □ Toronto, ON

Edwards, Patricia A., Asst.Libn.
ARTHUR ANDERSEN & CO. - BUSINESS LIBRARY
□ Houston, TX

Edwards, Phil, Photo Archv.Spec.
SMITHSONIAN INSTITUTION LIBRARIES -
NATIONAL AIR AND SPACE MUSEUM - LIBRARY
□ Washington, DC

Edwards, Rita L., Dir./Lib. & AV Serv.
GEORGE BROWN COLLEGE OF APPLIED ARTS &
TECHNOLOGY - LIBRARY □ Toronto, ON

Edwards, Shirley L., Lib.Adm.
SPAR AEROSPACE LTD. - LIBRARY† □ Ste. Anne
De Bellevue, PQ

Edwards, Willie M., Hd.Libn.
INSTITUTE OF GERONTOLOGY - LIBRARY □ Ann
Arbor, MI

Effrat, Eileen, Ref.Libn.
MC GRAW-HILL, INC. - LIBRARY □ New York,
NY

Egan, Laura, Med.Libn.
ST. JOSEPH STATE HOSPITAL - PROFESSIONAL
LIBRARY □ St. Joseph, MO

Egan, Laurel, Docs.Libn.
MONTANA COLLEGE OF MINERAL SCIENCE AND
TECHNOLOGY - LIBRARY □ Butte, MT

Egan, Mrs. P., Lib.Asst.
QUEEN'S UNIVERSITY AT KINGSTON - CIVIL
ENGINEERING LIBRARY □ Kingston, ON

Egan, Rhonda R., Libn.
SACRAMENTO AREA COUNCIL OF
GOVERNMENTS - LIBRARY □ Sacramento, CA

Egbert, Elizabeth B., Libn.
U.S. NATL. PARK SERVICE - LONGFELLOW
NATL. HISTORIC SITE - LIBRARY □ Cambridge,
MA

Egertson, Yvonne L., Libn.
AMERICAN NEWSPAPER PUBLISHERS
ASSOCIATION - LIBRARY □ Washington, DC

Eggers, James, Info.Spec.
MITRE CORPORATION - TECHNICAL REPORT
CENTER† □ Bedford, MA

Eggert, Charlean, Law Libn.
DU PAGE COUNTY LAW LIBRARY □ Wheaton, IL

Eggert, Jean, Photo.Libn.
GREEN BAY PRESS-GAZETTE - LIBRARY □
Green Bay, WI

Eggleston, Gerald R., Acq.Libn.
STATE HISTORICAL SOCIETY OF WISCONSIN -
LIBRARY □ Madison, WI

Eggleston, Tom, Grand Sec.
GRAND LODGE OF IOWA, A.F. AND A.M. - IOWA
MASONIC LIBRARY □ Cedar Rapids, IA

Ehernberger, Nicolette
ST. LOUIS PUBLIC LIBRARY - HUMANITIES AND
SOCIAL SCIENCES DEPARTMENT □ St. Louis,
MO

Ehlers, William J., Libn.
SIMAT, HELLIESEN, AND EICHNER - LIBRARY □
New York, NY

Ehlert, Pat, Asst.Libn.
PLANNED PARENTHOOD ASSOCIATION OF
WISCONSIN - RESOURCE CENTER □ Milwaukee,
WI

Ehr, Patricia H., Hd.Libn.
NORTHWESTERN MUTUAL LIFE INSURANCE
COMPANY - REFERENCE LIBRARY □ Milwaukee,
WI

PERSONNEL

Ehrenberg, Ralph E., Asst.Chf.
LIBRARY OF CONGRESS - GEOGRAPHY & MAP DIVISION □ Washington, DC

Ehrenfried, Charles E., Tech.Dir.
IIT RESEARCH INSTITUTE - RELIABILITY ANALYSIS CENTER □ Rome, NY

Ehrhardt, Mr. Allyn, Libn.
FRANKLIN UNIVERSITY - LIBRARY □ Columbus, OH

Ehrig, Ellen, Chf.Ref./ILL Libn.
SUNY - AGRICULTURAL AND TECHNICAL COLLEGE AT ALFRED - WALTER C. HINKLE MEMORIAL LIBRARY □ Alfred, NY

Ehrke, Helen, Acq.Libn.
MEDICAL COLLEGE OF WISCONSIN - TODD WEHR LIBRARY □ Milwaukee, WI

Ehrlich, Nancy M., Dir.
JACKSON COUNTY HISTORICAL SOCIETY - RESEARCH LIBRARY & ARCHIVES □ Independence, MO

Ehrmann, Marie, Libn.-in-Charge
UNITED STATES GYPSUM COMPANY - RESEARCH CENTER LIBRARY □ Des Plaines, IL

Eiberson, Harold, Chf.Libn.
BARUCH (Bernard M.) COLLEGE OF THE CITY UNIVERSITY OF NEW YORK - LIBRARY □ New York, NY

Eichel, Nanette D., Info.Rsrcs.Coord.
COUNCIL OF STATE GOVERNMENTS - STATES INFORMATION CENTER □ Lexington, KY

Eichholz, Tanya, Info.Sci.
HOECHST-ROUSSEL PHARMACEUTICALS, INC. - LIBRARY □ Somerville, NJ

Eichinger, Ann, Ref.Libn.
SOUTH DAKOTA STATE LIBRARY □ Pierre, SD

Eichman, Barbara J., Libn.
AMERICAN CIVIL LIBERTIES UNION - LIBRARY/ARCHIVES† □ New York, NY

Eichstedt, Marie L., Acq.Libn.
U.S. AIR FORCE WEAPONS LABORATORY - TECHNICAL LIBRARY □ Kirtland AFB, NM

Eick, Barbara, Asst.Archv.
STANFORD UNIVERSITY - MUSIC LIBRARY □ Stanford, CA

Eickenhorst, Joanna W., Tech.Info.Spec.
STAUFFER CHEMICAL COMPANY - TECHNICAL INFORMATION CENTER □ Farmington, CT

Eickhoff, B.M., Physics Libn.
WASHINGTON UNIVERSITY - PFEIFFER PHYSICS LIBRARY □ St. Louis, MO

Eide, Margaret, Act.Archv.
EASTERN MICHIGAN UNIVERSITY - CENTER OF EDUCATIONAL RESOURCES - ARCHIVES/ SPECIAL COLLECTIONS □ Ypsilanti, MI

Eifling, Janice K., Libn.
U.S.D.A. - AGRICULTURAL RESEARCH SERVICE - NATL. ANIMAL DISEASE CENTER LIBRARY □ Ames, IA

Eifrig, Janice, Info.Anl./Spec.
DIGITAL EQUIPMENT CORPORATION - CORPORATE LIBRARY □ Maynard, MA

Eigner, Selma W., Libn.
WHIDDEN MEMORIAL HOSPITAL - LIBRARY □ Everett, MA

Einblau, Linda, Asst.Libn.
COLLEGE OF PHYSICIANS AND SURGEONS OF BRITISH COLUMBIA - MEDICAL LIBRARY SERVICE □ Vancouver, BC

Einowski, Ilona, Libn.
UNIVERSITY OF CALIFORNIA, BERKELEY - STATE DATA PROGRAM LIBRARY □ Berkeley, CA

Einstein, Dan, Archv.
UNIVERSITY OF CALIFORNIA, LOS ANGELES - ACADEMY OF TELEVISION ARTS & SCIENCES - TELEVISION ARCHIVES □ Los Angeles, CA

Eisen, David J., Dir. of Res. & Info.
NEWSPAPER GUILD - HEYWOOD BROUN LIBRARY □ Washington, DC

Eisen, Susan M., Libn.
ART INSTITUTE OF BOSTON - LIBRARY □ Boston, MA

Eisenberg, Debra S., Ref.Asst.
NEW YORK UNIVERSITY MEDICAL CENTER - FREDERICK L. EHRMAN MEDICAL LIBRARY □ New York, NY

Eisenberg, Peter, Cat.Libn.
PHILADELPHIA COLLEGE OF THE PERFORMING ARTS - LIBRARY† □ Philadelphia, PA

Eisenhauer, Jean, Hd.Tech.Serv.
WASHINGTON & LEE UNIVERSITY - LAW LIBRARY □ Lexington, VA

Eisenhut, Cheryl, Libn.
MEDTRONIC, INC. - LIBRARY □ Minneapolis, MN

Eisenman, Jean, Asst.Dir., Pub.Serv.
UNIVERSITY OF MISSOURI, ROLLA - CURTIS LAWS WILSON LIBRARY □ Rolla, MO

Eiser, Mary Jo, Libn.
SYBRON CORPORATION - TAYLOR INSTRUMENT PROCESS CONTROL DIVISION - TECHNICAL INFORMATION CENTER □ Rochester, NY

Eisner, Elyse, Libn.
BANK OF AMERICA, NT & SA - REFERENCE LIBRARY □ San Francisco, CA

Eiss, Merle I., Supv.
MC CORMICK & CO. - R & D INFORMATION CENTER □ Hunt Valley, MD

Ek, Jacqueline, Div.Hd.
INDIANAPOLIS-MARION COUNTY PUBLIC LIBRARY - FILM DIVISION □ Indianapolis, IN

Ekdahl, Janis, Asst.Dir.
MUSEUM OF MODERN ART - LIBRARY □ New York, NY

Ekdahl, Janis, Art Libn.
VASSAR COLLEGE - ART LIBRARY □ Poughkeepsie, NY

Ekendahl, James, Asst.Dir. Regional Dev.
UNIVERSITY OF WASHINGTON - HEALTH SCIENCES LIBRARY □ Seattle, WA

Ekers, Eric N., Hd.
ORGANIZATION FOR ECONOMIC COOPERATION AND DEVELOPMENT - PUBLICATIONS AND INFORMATION CENTER □ Washington, DC

Ekimov, Roza, Libn.
EXXON COMPANY, U.S.A. - EXPLORATION LIBRARY □ Houston, TX

Ekins, A. George, Asst.Libn.
CANADA - TRANSPORT CANADA - TRANSPORTATION DEVELOPMENT CENTRE - LIBRARY □ Montreal, PQ

Ekman, Sheila, Ref.Libn.
BENTLEY COLLEGE - SOLOMON R. BAKER LIBRARY □ Waltham, MA

Ekstrand, Nancy, Clinical Res.Libn.
WAKE FOREST UNIVERSITY - BOWMAN GRAY SCHOOL OF MEDICINE - LIBRARY □ Winston-Salem, NC

Elam, Craig, Assoc.Dir., Tech.Serv.
TEXAS COLLEGE OF OSTEOPATHIC MEDICINE - MEDICAL LIBRARY □ Fort Worth, TX

Elam, Joice, Doc.Libn.
EMORY UNIVERSITY - SCHOOL OF LAW LIBRARY† □ Atlanta, GA

Elbert, Dr. E. Duane, Musm.Cur.
COLES COUNTY HISTORICAL SOCIETY - GREENWOOD SCHOOL MUSEUM - LIBRARY □ Charleston, IL

Elchesen, Dennis, Hd., Res.Info. Group
U.S. DEPT. OF ENERGY - LAWRENCE LIVERMORE LAB. - TECHNICAL INFO. DEPT. LIBRARY □ Livermore, CA

Elder, Charles W., Hd.Libn.
HUNTER COLLEGE OF THE CITY UNIVERSITY OF NEW YORK - HUNTER COLLEGE SCHOOL OF SOCIAL WORK - LIBRARY □ New York, NY

Elder, Mrs. J.M., Libn.
C.L.S.C. METRO - FAMILY LIFE EDUCATION SERVICES - PEEL CENTRE LIBRARY† □ Montreal, PQ

Elder, K., Film Coord.
SCARBOROUGH PUBLIC LIBRARY - FILM SERVICES □ Scarborough, ON

Elder, Margaret
U.S. BUREAU OF RECLAMATION - LIBRARY □ Sacramento, CA

Elgee, Charlene, Hd. & Ref.Libn.
CANADA - PUBLIC SERVICE STAFF RELATIONS BOARD - LIBRARY □ Ottawa, ON

Elgood, William R., Dir.
GENERAL MOTORS INSTITUTE - LIBRARY† □ Flint, MI

Elias, Werner, Libn.
COLLECTORS CLUB - LIBRARY □ New York, NY

Elinoff, Linda S., Libn.
CAMP DRESSER & MC KEE, INC. - CDM ENVIRONMENTAL LIBRARY □ Wheat Ridge, CO

Eliot, Valerie J., Libn.
DEACONESS HOSPITAL - SCHOOL OF NURSING - RICHARD W. ANGERT MEMORIAL LIBRARY □ Cincinnati, OH

Elkin, Mary Ann, Supv., Health Educ.
MISSISSIPPI STATE BOARD OF HEALTH - FILM LIBRARY □ Jackson, MS

Elkins, Elizabeth A., Pub.Serv.Coord.
SUNY - COLLEGE OF ENVIRONMENTAL SCIENCE AND FORESTRY - F. FRANKLIN MOON LIBRARY □ Syracuse, NY

Elkins, Phyllis, Ref.Libn.
TENNESSEE VALLEY AUTHORITY - TECHNICAL LIBRARY □ Muscle Shoals, AL

Elledge, Dot, Dir., Lib.Serv.
WAYNE COMMUNITY COLLEGE - LEARNING RESOURCE CENTER □ Goldsboro, NC

Ellenberger, Jack S., Libn.
SHEARMAN & STERLING - LIBRARY □ New York, NY

Ellenwood, Dwight, Rec.Anl.
WASHINGTON STATE OFFICE OF SECRETARY OF STATE - DIVISION OF ARCHIVES AND RECORD MANAGEMENT □ Olympia, WA

Ellenwood, Rev. Lee K., Dir.
FIRST CHURCH OF CHRIST CONGREGATIONAL - JOHN P. WEBSTER LIBRARY □ West Hartford, CT

Elliker, Calvin, Music Libn.
INDIANA UNIVERSITY OF PENNSYLVANIA - COGSWELL MUSIC LIBRARY □ Indiana, PA

Elliker, Calvin, Asst.Libn.
INDIANA UNIVERSITY OF PENNSYLVANIA - UNIVERSITY LIBRARY □ Indiana, PA

Ellington, Ann W., Med.Libn.
CONE (Moses H.) MEMORIAL HOSPITAL - MEDICAL LIBRARY □ Greensboro, NC

Ellinwood, Sara, Asst.Libn.
KAMAN-TEMPO - TECHNICAL INFORMATION CENTER □ Santa Barbara, CA

Elliot, William T., Libn.
ONONDAGA COUNTY PUBLIC LIBRARY - BUSINESS AND INDUSTRIAL DEPARTMENT □ Syracuse, NY

Elliott, Barbara, Chf.Libn.
GENERAL DYNAMICS CORPORATION - PUBLIC AFFAIRS LIBRARY □ St. Louis, MO

Elliott, Beverly, Circ.Supv.
SAN DIEGO STATE UNIVERSITY - MEDIA & CURRICULUM CENTER □ San Diego, CA

Elliott, C. Danial, Cur.
UNIVERSITY OF CALIFORNIA, DAVIS - F. HAL HIGGINS LIBRARY OF AGRICULTURAL TECHNOLOGY □ Davis, CA

Elliott, Carol G., Cat.
UNIVERSITY OF ARIZONA - COLLEGE OF LAW LIBRARY □ Tucson, AZ

Elliott, Clark A., Assoc.Cur.
HARVARD UNIVERSITY - ARCHIVES □ Cambridge, MA

Elliott, Franki, Res.Asst.
ROYAL BANK OF CANADA - TAXATION LIBRARY □ Montreal, PQ

Elliott, Hamilton, Asst.Univ.Archv.
UNIVERSITY OF PENNSYLVANIA - ARCHIVES AND RECORDS CENTER □ Philadelphia, PA

Elliott, Kathleen, Sr.Libn.
CANADIAN NATIONAL RAILWAYS - DECHIEF LIBRARY □ Montreal, PQ

Elliott, Kay M., Chf.Libn.
IOWA STATE DEPARTMENT OF SOCIAL
SERVICES - LIBRARY □ Des Moines, IA

Elliott, Lois, Libn.
DELLCREST CHILDREN'S CENTRE - LIBRARY □
Downsview, ON

Elliott, Mrs. Lonnie J., Libn.
HUMAN RESOURCES RESEARCH
ORGANIZATION - VAN EVERA LIBRARY† □
Alexandria, VA

Elliott, Marilyn, Libn.
EDMONTON PUBLIC SCHOOL BOARD -
LEARNING RESOURCES PROFESSIONAL
LIBRARY □ Edmonton, AB

Elliott, Mary, Chf.
DISTRICT OF COLUMBIA PUBLIC LIBRARY -
MUSIC & RECREATION DIVISION □ Washington,
DC

Elliott, Shirley B., Legislative Libn.
NOVA SCOTIA - LEGISLATIVE LIBRARY □
Halifax, NS

Ellis, Bonnie J., Lib.Supv.
NEW BRUNSWICK RESEARCH AND
PRODUCTIVITY COUNCIL - LIBRARY □
Fredericton, NB

Ellis, Brenda M., Libn.
UMSTEAD (John) HOSPITAL - LEARNING
RESOURCE CENTER □ Butner, NC

Ellis, Charlotte, Sr.Asst.
WASHINGTON UNIVERSITY - BIOLOGY
LIBRARY □ St. Louis, MO

Ellis, Deborah, Asst.
MAIN (Chas. T.), INC. - LIBRARY □ Boston, MA

Ellis, Donna Burns, Mss.Libn.
MARYLAND HISTORICAL SOCIETY - LIBRARY □
Baltimore, MD

Ellis, Ellen, Libn.
VANDERBILT UNIVERSITY LIBRARY - DYER
OBSERVATORY □ Nashville, TN

Ellis, Ethel M., Cat.
HOWARD UNIVERSITY - MOORLAND-SPINGARN
RESEARCH CENTER - LIBRARY DIVISION □
Washington, DC

Ellis, Georgia, Chf.Libn.
CANADA - STATISTICS CANADA - LIBRARY □
Ottawa, ON

Ellis, Gloria B., Lib.Dir.
WALSH COLLEGE OF ACCOUNTANCY AND
BUSINESS ADMINISTRATION - LIBRARY □
Troy, MI

Ellis, Dr. Jack D., Dir.
MOREHEAD STATE UNIVERSITY - CAMDEN-
CARROLL LIBRARY □ Morehead, KY

Ellis, Joan, Coord.Ref.Serv.
UNIVERSITY OF LOWELL, NORTH CAMPUS -
ALUMNI/LYDON LIBRARY □ Lowell, MA

Ellis, John C., Dir.
ASSOCIATED GENERAL CONTRACTORS OF
AMERICA - JAMES L. ALLHANDS MEMORIAL
LIBRARY □ Washington, DC

Ellis, Juanita, Pres.
CITIZENS ASSOCIATION FOR SOUND ENERGY
(CASE) - LIBRARY □ Dallas, TX

Ellis, Larry, Cat.
ST. ELIZABETHS HOSPITAL - HEALTH
SCIENCES LIBRARY □ Washington, DC

Ellis, Margaret, Archv.
MISSISQUOI HISTORICAL SOCIETY - CORNELL
MILL MUSEUM - REFERENCE LIBRARY &
ARCHIVES □ Stanbridge East, PQ

Ellis, Mary Ann, Ref.Libn.
U.S. DEFENSE MAPPING AGENCY - AEROSPACE
CENTER - TECHNICAL LIBRARY □ St. Louis, MO

Ellis, Pearl, Asst.Dir.
SOUTHWESTERN ASSEMBLIES OF GOD
COLLEGE - P.C. NELSON MEMORIAL LIBRARY □
Waxahachie, TX

Ellis, Robert H., Jr.,Cur.
KENDALL WHALING MUSEUM - LIBRARY □
Sharon, MA

Ellis, Roy, Data User Serv.Off.
U.S. BUREAU OF THE CENSUS - REGIONAL
DATA USER SERVICE - SEATTLE REGIONAL
OFFICE - LIBRARY □ Seattle, WA

Ellis, William N., Exec.Dir.
TRANET - LIBRARY □ Rangeley, ME

Ellis, Y.A., Res.
U.S. OAK RIDGE NATL. LABORATORY -
NUCLEAR DATA PROJECT† □ Oak Ridge, TN

Ellison, Pat, Lib.Assoc.
SINGER (H. Douglas) MENTAL HEALTH CENTER -
LIBRARY □ Rockford, IL

Ellison, Sally H., Ref.Libn.
GENERAL MOTORS CORPORATION - RESEARCH
LABORATORIES LIBRARY □ Warren, MI

Ellison, Sandra, Pub.Lib.Cons.
OKLAHOMA STATE DEPARTMENT OF
LIBRARIES □ Oklahoma City, OK

Ellsworth, Daryl G., Libn.
WARREN STATE HOSPITAL - MEDICAL
LIBRARY □ Warren, PA

Ellsworth, Linda V., Hist.
HISTORIC PENSACOLA PRESERVATION BOARD
- LIBRARY □ Pensacola, FL

Ellsworth, Luramay, Law Libn.
LILLICK MC HOSE & CHARLES, ATTORNEYS AT
LAW - LAW LIBRARY† □ Los Angeles, CA

Ellsworth, Rudolph C., Libn.
METROPOLITAN SANITARY DISTRICT OF
GREATER CHICAGO - TECHNICAL LIBRARY □
Chicago, IL

Elman, Stanley A., Mgr.
LOCKHEED-CALIFORNIA COMPANY -
TECHNICAL INFORMATION CENTER □ Burbank,
CA

Elmer, Wilma, Per.
WESTERN EVANGELICAL SEMINARY - GEORGE
HALLAUER MEMORIAL LIBRARY □ Portland, OR

Elmore, Nigel, Musm.Spec.
SMITHSONIAN INSTITUTION - NATIONAL
ANTHROPOLOGICAL ARCHIVES □ Washington,
DC

Elmstrom, Dr. Gary W., Ctr.Dir.
UNIVERSITY OF FLORIDA - AGRICULTURAL
RESEARCH CENTER - LIBRARY □ Leesburg, FL

Elrod, James, Assoc.Libn.
CALIFORNIA INSTITUTE OF THE ARTS -
LIBRARY □ Valencia, CA

Elsaesser, Harvey, Info.Spec.
BUFFALO EVENING NEWS - LIBRARY □ Buffalo,
NY

Elsesser, Lionelle, Chf.Libn.
U.S. VETERANS ADMINISTRATION (MN-
Minneapolis) - HOSPITAL LIBRARY □
Minneapolis, MN

Elson, Mona, Hd., Cat.
MOUNT SINAI SCHOOL OF MEDICINE OF THE
CITY UNIVERSITY OF NEW YORK - GUSTAVE L.
& JANET W. LEVY LIBRARY □ New York, NY

Elston, Charles, Hd., Spec.Coll.
MARQUETTE UNIVERSITY - MEMORIAL
LIBRARY □ Milwaukee, WI

Elston, Charles B., Dept.Hd.
MARQUETTE UNIVERSITY - DEPARTMENT OF
SPECIAL COLLECTIONS AND UNIVERSITY
ARCHIVES □ Milwaukee, WI

Eltzroth, Richard T., Mss.Cur.
ATLANTA HISTORICAL SOCIETY - ARCHIVES □
Atlanta, GA

Elveson, Leon, Med.Libn.
JEWISH HOSPITAL AND MEDICAL CENTER OF
BROOKLYN - GREENPOINT HOSPITAL
AFFILIATION - MEDICAL LIBRARY □ Brooklyn,
NY

Elvidge, Mrs. M., Libn.
OGILVY, RENAULT - LIBRARY □ Montreal, PQ

Elvord, Zhita, School Libn.
WILSHIRE BOULEVARD TEMPLE - SIGMUND
HECHT LIBRARY □ Los Angeles, CA

Elwell, Pamela M., Libn.
MOUNT CARMEL MEDICAL CENTER - MOTHER
M. CONSTANTINE MEMORIAL LIBRARY □
Columbus, OH

Ely, Dr. Donald, Dir.
ERIC CLEARINGHOUSE ON INFORMATION
RESOURCES □ Syracuse, NY

Ely, Dwight C., Pres., Lib. Trustees
SOLANO COUNTY LAW LIBRARY □ Fairfield, CA

Embar, Indrani, Hd.Libn.
WORLD BOOK-CHILDCRAFT INTERNATIONAL,
INC.- RESEARCH LIBRARY □ Chicago, IL

Ember, George, Asst. to Dir.
CANADA - NATIONAL RESEARCH COUNCIL -
CANADA INSTITUTE FOR SCIENTIFIC AND
TECHNICAL INFORMATION (CISTI) □ Ottawa,
ON

Emberson, Eileen, Dir.Lib.Serv.
LUTHER HOSPITAL - MEDICAL LIBRARY □ Eau
Claire, WI

Embrey, Eliza E., Libn.
WAR MEMORIAL MUSEUM OF VIRGINIA -
RESEARCH LIBRARY □ Newport News, VA

Embry, Joan, Hd.Libn.
FLORIDA SCHOOL FOR THE DEAF AND BLIND -
LIBRARY FOR THE DEAF □ St. Augustine, FL

Embury, Sheila, Asst.Cur.
BROWN UNIVERSITY - ART DEPARTMENT
SLIDE ROOM □ Providence, RI

Emdad, Ali, Libn.
CLEVELAND HEARING AND SPEECH CENTER -
LUCILE DAUBY GRIES MEMORIAL LIBRARY □
Cleveland, OH

Emele, Russell J., Dir. Of Lib.
EAST STROUDSBURG STATE COLLEGE -
LIBRARY □ East Stroudsburg, PA

Emerick, Kenneth, Cat.
CLARION STATE COLLEGE - RENA M. CARLSON
LIBRARY □ Clarion, PA

Emerson, Katherine, Archv.
UNIVERSITY OF MASSACHUSETTS, AMHERST -
LIBRARY - DEPARTMENT OF ARCHIVES AND
MANUSCRIPTS □ Amherst, MA

Emerson, Maj. M.R., Lib.Off.
U.S. AIR FORCE ACADEMY - LAW LIBRARY □
U.S. Air Force Academy, CO

Emerson, R., Tech.Info.Spec.
U.S. DEFENSE MAPPING AGENCY - AEROSPACE
CENTER - TECHNICAL LIBRARY □ St. Louis, MO

Emerson, Ruth, Libn.
AMERICAN INSTITUTE OF BAKING - LIBRARY □
Manhattan, KS

Emerson, Susan, Hd.Libn.
OHIO STATE UNIVERSITY - AGRICULTURE
LIBRARY □ Columbus, OH

Emerson, Virginia B., Libn.
NEW SCHOOL OF MUSIC, INC. - ALICE TULLY
LIBRARY □ Philadelphia, PA

Emerson, William R., Dir.
U.S. PRESIDENTIAL LIBRARIES - FRANKLIN D.
ROOSEVELT LIBRARY □ Hyde Park, NY

Emery, Betty L., Libn.
ALLIED CORPORATION - CHEMICALS COMPANY
- SYRACUSE RESEARCH LABORATORY -
LIBRARY □ Solvay, NY

Emery, C. David, Assoc.Libn./Sup.Serv
UNIVERSITY OF WATERLOO - DANA PORTER
ARTS LIBRARY □ Waterloo, ON

Emery, Jean, Ref.Libn.
NORTHWESTERN UNIVERSITY - HEALTH
SCIENCES LIBRARY □ Chicago, IL

Emery, Louis E., Exec.Sec.
ASSOCIATION OF STUDENT INTERNATIONAL
LAW SOCIETIES - INFORMATION CENTER □
Washington, DC

Emery, Mark W., Ref.Libn.
UNIVERSITY OF UTAH - HUMAN RELATIONS
AREA FILES □ Salt Lake City, UT

Emery, Mary B., Libn.
UNIVERSITY OF SANTA CLARA - EDWIN A.
HEAFEY LAW LIBRARY □ Santa Clara, CA

Emery, Mary Louise, Libn. & Instr.
CLEVELAND MUSIC SCHOOL SETTLEMENT -
KULAS LIBRARY □ Cleveland, OH

Emish, Catherine A., Coord., Info.Serv.
KOPPERS COMPANY, INC. - ENGINEERING AND
CONSTRUCTION DIVISION - INFORMATION
SERVICE □ Pittsburgh, PA

Emmons, Paul, Music Libn.
CENTRAL WASHINGTON UNIVERSITY - MUSIC
LIBRARY □ Ellensburg, WA

Emond, Sr. Gemma, Med.Libn.
HOPITAL NOTRE DAME DE L'ESPERANCE -
BIBLIOTHEQUE† □ St. Laurent, PQ

Empey, Sharon, Tech.Serv.Libn.
UNIVERSITY OF ALBERTA - H.T. COUTTS
EDUCATION LIBRARY □ Edmonton, AB

Empey, Verla E., Libn.
WELLESLEY HOSPITAL - LIBRARY □ Toronto, ON

Enberg, Henry W., II, Legal Ed.
PRACTISING LAW INSTITUTE - LIBRARY □
New York, NY

Endicott, Judy G., Chf., Circ.
U.S. AIR FORCE - ALBERT F. SIMPSON
HISTORICAL RESEARCH CENTER □ Maxwell
AFB, AL

Endicott, Molly, Lib.Techn.
U.S. NATL. MARINE FISHERIES SERVICE - W.F.
THOMPSON MEMORIAL LIBRARY† □ Kodiak, AK

Endsley, Beverly J., Lib.Techn.
U.S. NAVY - NAVAL STATION LIBRARY (Guam) □
FPO San Francisco, CA

Eng, Adrienne, Info.Anl.
MC KINSEY & COMPANY, INC. - LIBRARY □
Washington, DC

Enge, Maureen, Mgr.
ONTARIO - MINISTRY OF INDUSTRY AND
TOURISM - INFORMATION CENTRE □ Toronto,
ON

Engel, Carl Thomas, Libn.
LAKE COUNTY HISTORICAL SOCIETY - PERCY
KENDALL SMITH LIBRARY FOR HISTORICAL
RESEARCH □ Mentor, OH

Engel, Catherine T., Ref.Libn.
COLORADO HISTORICAL SOCIETY - STEPHEN
H. HART LIBRARY □ Denver, CO

Engel, Claire, State Law Libn.
MONTANA STATE LAW LIBRARY† □ Helena, MT

Engel, Laura, Libn.
CRANFORD UNITED METHODIST CHURCH -
LIBRARY □ Cranford, NJ

Engel, M., Tech.Info.Spec.
U.S. NATL. HIGHWAY TRAFFIC SAFETY
ADMINISTRATION - TECHNICAL REFERENCE
BRANCH □ Washington, DC

Engelhardt, D. LeRoy, Libn.
NEW BRUNSWICK THEOLOGICAL SEMINARY -
GARDNER A. SAGE LIBRARY □ New Brunswick,
NJ

Engelmann, Hugo O., Ed.
CLEARINGHOUSE FOR SOCIOLOGICAL
LITERATURE □ Dekalb, IL

Engeman, Richard H., Libn.
SOUTHERN OREGON HISTORICAL SOCIETY -
RESEARCH LIBRARY □ Jacksonville, OR

Engen, Richard B., Dir.Lib. & Musm.Div.
ALASKA STATE DIVISION OF STATE LIBRARIES
& MUSEUMS - STATE LIBRARY □ Juneau, AK

Engerman, Jeanne, Asst.Libn.
WASHINGTON STATE HISTORICAL SOCIETY -
LIBRARY □ Tacoma, WA

Engfehr, Rev. William, Dir., Educ. Media
CONCORDIA SEMINARY - LIBRARY □ St. Louis,
MO

Engiles, Jim, Info.Spec.
INTEL-TECHNICAL INFORMATION CENTER □
Santa Clara, CA

England, Angela C., Med.Libn.
HOLSTON VALLEY HOSPITAL AND MEDICAL
CENTER - HEALTH SCIENCE LIBRARY □
Kingsport, TN

England, Kerry, Libn.
NORTHWEST MISSOURI STATE UNIVERSITY -
HORACE MANN LEARNING CENTER □ Maryville,
MO

Englander, Evelyn A., Libn.
U.S. MARINE CORPS - HISTORICAL CENTER
LIBRARY □ Washington, DC

Engle, June L., Libn.
EMORY UNIVERSITY - DIVISION OF LIBRARY
AND INFORMATION MANAGEMENT LIBRARY □
Atlanta, GA

Engle, Virginia H., Libn.
LANCASTER GENERAL HOSPITAL - MUELLER
HEALTH SCIENCES LIBRARY □ Lancaster, PA

Engleman, Roberta A., Asst.Cur./Cat.
UNIVERSITY OF NORTH CAROLINA, CHAPEL
HILL - RARE BOOK COLLECTION □ Chapel Hill,
NC

Engles, Joseph D., Dir.
MINNESOTA STATE IRON RANGE RESOURCES
& REHABILITATION BOARD - IRON RANGE
RESEARCH CENTER □ Chisholm, MN

Englese, Susan, Libn.
COLORADO STATE DEPARTMENT OF SOCIAL
SERVICE - LIBRARY □ Denver, CO

Engley, Beatrice, Info.Spec.
UNIVERSITY OF MISSOURI - HEALTH CARE
TECHNOLOGY CENTER - HCTC INFORMATION
CENTER □ Columbia, MO

English, Alison I., Libn.
ALABAMA POWER COMPANY - LIBRARY □
Birmingham, AL

English, Bernard L., Lib. Group Supv.
BELL TELEPHONE LABORATORIES, INC. &
WESTERN ELECTRIC, INC. - TECHNICAL
LIBRARY □ Indianapolis, IN

English, Cynthia, Hd.Ref.Libn.
BOSTON ATHENAEUM LIBRARY □ Boston, MA

English, Helen L., Libn.
MONROE COUNTY LAW LIBRARY □ Woodsfield,
OH

English, John, Dir., Nursing Educ.
SELKIRK MENTAL HEALTH CENTRE - CENTRAL
LIBRARY □ Selkirk, MB

English, Kathleen, Libn.
U.S. NATL. PARK SERVICE - HAWAII
VOLCANOES NATIONAL PARK - LIBRARY □
Honolulu, HI

English, Tom, Libn.
UNIVERSITY OF MINNESOTA - BELL MUSEUM
OF NATURAL HISTORY - LIBRARY □ Minneapolis,
MN

Englund, Catherine, Ref.Libn.
BRAILLE INSTITUTE OF AMERICA - LIBRARY □
Los Angeles, CA

Engro, Kathe., Asst.Dir.
NATIONAL INVESTMENT LIBRARY □ New York,
NY

Engst, Elaine, Asst.Archv.
CORNELL UNIVERSITY - DEPARTMENT OF
MANUSCRIPTS AND ARCHIVES □ Ithaca, NY

Engstrom, Karen, Dir. of Lib.Serv.
ST. FRANCIS HOSPITAL - COMMUNITY HEALTH
SCIENCE LIBRARY □ Breckenridge, MN

Enion, Pamela, Libn.
TECHNOLOGY & ECONOMICS, INC. - LIBRARY □
Cambridge, MA

Enis, Alma, Libn.
ALL SAINTS EPISCOPAL HOSPITAL - F.M.
CORSELIUS LIBRARY □ Fort Worth, TX

Ennerberg, Erik, Hd.Acq.Libn.
CALIFORNIA STATE POLYTECHNIC
UNIVERSITY, POMONA - LIBRARY □ Pomona,
CA

Ennis, Jerry, Staff Train.Supv.
CHURCH OF JESUS CHRIST OF LATTER-DAY
SAINTS - MT. WHITNEY BRANCH
GENEALOGICAL LIBRARY† □ Inyokern, CA

Ennis, Mary Jane, Res.Libn.
DRACKETT COMPANY - RESEARCH AND
DEVELOPMENT LIBRARY □ Cincinnati, OH

Ennis, Dr. William B., Jr., Ctr.Dir.
UNIVERSITY OF FLORIDA - AGRICULTURAL
RESEARCH CENTER - FORT LAUDERDALE
LIBRARY □ Fort Lauderdale, FL

Enola, John I., Libn.
AUSTINE SCHOOL - LIBRARY □ Brattleboro, VT

Ensanian, Armand O., Ref.Libn.
ENSANIAN PHYSICOCHEMICAL INSTITUTE -
INFORMATION CENTER FOR GRAVITATION
CHEMISTRY □ Eldred, PA

Ensanian, Elizabeth A., Chf.Libn.
ENSANIAN PHYSICOCHEMICAL INSTITUTE -
INFORMATION CENTER FOR GRAVITATION
CHEMISTRY □ Eldred, PA

Ensanian, Tamara, Res.Spec.
ENSANIAN PHYSICOCHEMICAL INSTITUTE -
INFORMATION CENTER FOR GRAVITATION
CHEMISTRY □ Eldred, PA

Ensign, David, Asst.Libn.
WASHBURN UNIVERSITY OF TOPEKA - SCHOOL
OF LAW LIBRARY □ Topeka, KS

Ensor, Sara U., Libn.
BLUE CROSS AND BLUE SHIELD OF NORTH
CAROLINA - INFORMATION CENTER □ Chapel
Hill, NC

Enyeart, James, Dir.
UNIVERSITY OF ARIZONA - CENTER FOR
CREATIVE PHOTOGRAPHY □ Tucson, AZ

Enz, Philip I., Adm.Libn.
CARTER (Larue D.) MEMORIAL HOSPITAL -
MEDICAL LIBRARY □ Indianapolis, IN

Epstein, B.E., V.P.
FRANKLIN RESEARCH CENTER - SCIENCE
INFORMATION SERVICES □ Philadelphia, PA

Epstein, Barbara A., Ref.Libn.
UNIVERSITY OF PITTSBURGH - WESTERN
PSYCHIATRIC INSTITUTE AND CLINIC -
LIBRARY □ Pittsburgh, PA

Epstein, Dena, Asst. Music Libn.
UNIVERSITY OF CHICAGO - MUSIC
COLLECTION □ Chicago, IL

Epstein, Elias, Dir. of Res.
NOVOCOL CHEMICAL MANUFACTURING
COMPANY, INC. - LIBRARY □ Brooklyn, NY

Epstein, Janet, Circ.Libn.
OHIO STATE SUPREME COURT LAW LIBRARY □
Columbus, OH

Epstein, Judith I., Libn.
SPRINGFIELD NEWSPAPERS - LIBRARY† □
Springfield, MA

Epstein, Michelle I., Libn.
NATIONAL AUDUBON SOCIETY - LIBRARY □
New York, NY

Epstein, Roni, Bus.Info.Libn.
GULF CANADA LIMITED - CENTRAL LIBRARY □
Toronto, ON

Epstein, Ruth, Ref.Libn.
UNIVERSITY OF CINCINNATI - MEDICAL
CENTER LIBRARIES - HEALTH SCIENCES
LIBRARY □ Cincinnati, OH

Erani, Karen, Asst.Libn.
PFIZER, INC. - PFIZER PHARMACEUTICALS
LIBRARY □ New York, NY

Erb, Peter C., Assoc.Dir.
SCHWENKFELDER LIBRARY □ Pennsburg, PA

Erbe, Edwin, Per.Libn.
KEAN COLLEGE OF NEW JERSEY - NANCY
THOMPSON LIBRARY □ Union, NJ

Erdican, Achilla I., Cat.Libn.
EMORY UNIVERSITY - PITTS THEOLOGY
LIBRARY □ Atlanta, GA

Erdmann, Charlotte A., Info.Serv.
SOUTH DAKOTA SCHOOL OF MINES &
TECHNOLOGY - DEVEREAUX LIBRARY □ Rapid
City, SD

Erganian, Richard, Info.Dir.
O.K. SUPERMARKET - REAL ESTATE &
SHOPPING CENTER DEVELOPMENT
INFORMATION CENTER □ Fresno, CA

Erhardt, Davis, Div.Hd.
QUEENS BOROUGH PUBLIC LIBRARY - LONG
ISLAND DIVISION □ Jamaica, NY

Erickson, Alan E., Sci.Spec.
HARVARD UNIVERSITY - GODFREY LOWELL
CABOT SCIENCE LIBRARY □ Cambridge, MA

Erickson, C.A., Libn.
YAKIMA COUNTY LAW LIBRARY □ Yakima, WA

Erickson, Carolyn A., Libn.
ZOECON CORPORATION - LIBRARY □ Palo Alto,
CA

Erickson, Donald, Dir.
ERIC CLEARINGHOUSE ON HANDICAPPED &
GIFTED CHILDREN - CEC INFORMATION
SERVICES □ Reston, VA

Erickson, Donald R., Hd., Tech.Lib.Sec.
U.S. NAVY - NAVAL SEA SYSTEMS COMMAND -
LIBRARY DOCUMENTATION BRANCH (SEA
9961) □ Washington, DC

Erickson, Jon, Co-Dir.
BIOMEDICAL COMPUTING TECHNOLOGY
INFORMATION CENTER □ Nashville, TN

Erickson, Kathy, Supv.
VIRGINIA STATE OFFICE OF EMERGENCY &
ENERGY SERVICES - ENERGY INFORMATION
AND SERVICES CENTER □ Richmond, VA

Erickson, Linda, Supv., Tech.Proc.
U.S. DEPT OF ENERGY - SANDIA NATL.
LABORATORIES - TECHNICAL LIBRARY □
Albuquerque, NM

Erickson, Marie K., Acq./Ser.
LOYOLA UNIVERSITY (New Orleans) - LAW
LIBRARY □ New Orleans, LA

Erickson, Nancy, Cat.Libn.
MINNESOTA HISTORICAL SOCIETY - SPECIAL
LIBRARIES □ St. Paul, MN

Erickson, Richard, Dir. of IMC
BAPTIST BIBLE COLLEGE OF PENNSYLVANIA -
RICHARD J. MURPHY MEMORIAL LIBRARY □
Clarks Summit, PA

Erickson, Rodney, Comm.Chm.
TRINITY LUTHERAN CHURCH - LIBRARY □
Moorhead, MN

Erickson, Stephanie, Asst.Libn.
OKLAHOMA STATE UNIVERSITY - PHYSICAL
SCIENCES AND ENGINEERING DIVISION □
Stillwater, OK

Erickson, Su, AV & Circ.
NORTH CENTRAL COLLEGE - LIBRARY □
Naperville, IL

Erickson, Tom, Graphic Artist
ANOKA AREA VOCATIONAL TECHNICAL
INSTITUTE - MEDIA CENTER □ Anoka, MN

Erickson, Dr. W. Edwin, Dir.
BLACK HILLS STATE COLLEGE - E.Y. BERRY
LIBRARY-LEARNING CENTER □ Spearfish, SD

Ericson, Christine, Cat.Libn.
COLORADO SCHOOL OF MINES - ARTHUR
LAKES LIBRARY □ Golden, CO

Ericson, Dale, Res.Libn.
HOLIDAY INNS, INC. - RESEARCH SERVICES
INFORMATION CENTER □ Memphis, TN

Ericson, Richard C., Exec.Dir.
CORRECTIONAL SERVICE OF MINNESOTA -
LIBRARY □ Minneapolis, MN

Ericson, Rick, Acq.Libn.
GEORGETOWN UNIVERSITY - LAW CENTER
LIBRARY □ Washington, DC

Ericson, Timothy L., Archv.
UNIVERSITY OF WISCONSIN, RIVER FALLS -
CHALMER DAVEE LIBRARY - AREA RESEARCH
CENTER □ River Falls, WI

Erisman, Kathryn, Govt.Doc.Libn.
CENTRAL MISSOURI STATE UNIVERSITY -
WARD EDWARDS LIBRARY □ Warrensburg, MO

Erlandson, Eileen M., Hd.Libn.
BETHESDA LUTHERAN MEDICAL CENTER -
MEDICAL-NURSING LIBRARY □ St. Paul, MN

Erlen, John, Med.Hist.Libn.
UNIVERSITY OF TEXAS HEALTH SCIENCE
CENTER, DALLAS - LIBRARY □ Dallas, TX

Ermatinger, Charles J., Vatican Film Libn.
ST. LOUIS UNIVERSITY - KNIGHTS OF
COLUMBUS VATICAN FILM LIBRARY □ St. Louis,
MO

Ermili, Nelly E., Hd., Acq.Dept.
YALE UNIVERSITY - LAW LIBRARY □ New
Haven, CT

Ernesaks, Sylvia, Sr.Libn.
ONTARIO HYDRO - LIBRARY □ Toronto, ON

Ernst, Dr. Joseph W., Dir.
ROCKEFELLER UNIVERSITY - ROCKEFELLER
ARCHIVE CENTER □ North Tarrytown, NY

Errickson, Betsy, Asst.Cur.
HOPEWELL MUSEUM - LIBRARY □ Hopewell, NJ

Erskine, Hilary, Tech.Info.Spec.
CIBA-GEIGY CORPORATION - TECHNICAL
INFORMATION SERVICE □ Greensboro, NC

Erslev, Allan J., M.D., Dir.
JEFFERSON (Thomas) UNIVERSITY - CARDEZA
FOUNDATION - TOCANTINS MEMORIAL
LIBRARY □ Philadelphia, PA

Ertel, Monica, Mgr.
MEMOREX CORPORATION - TECHNICAL
INFORMATION CENTER □ Santa Clara, CA

Ertl, Mary, Acq.
UNIVERSITY OF IOWA - LAW LIBRARY □ Iowa
City, IA

Ervin, Colleen S., Dir., Tech.Serv.
CALIFORNIA WESTERN LAW SCHOOL -
LIBRARY □ San Diego, CA

Ervin, Linda, Hd., Client Serv.
CANADA - DEPARTMENT OF FINANCE -
FINANCE/TREASURY BOARD LIBRARY □
Ottawa, ON

Ervin, Mary Lee, Asst.Archv.
OKLAHOMA HISTORICAL SOCIETY - DIVISION
OF LIBRARY RESOURCES □ Oklahoma City, OK

Ervin, Philip E., Corp.Libn.
UNITED WAY, INC., LOS ANGELES - LIBRARY □
Los Angeles, CA

Erwin, Clarissa, Div.Chf.
CHICAGO PUBLIC LIBRARY CULTURAL CENTER
- FINE ARTS DIVISION - ART SECTION □
Chicago, IL

Erwin, Clarissa, Div.Chf.
CHICAGO PUBLIC LIBRARY CULTURAL CENTER
- FINE ARTS DIVISION - MUSIC SECTION □
Chicago, IL

Erwin, Jacquelin, Libn.
ST. LUKE HOSPITAL - MEDICAL LIBRARY □
Pasadena, CA

Erwin, Patricia, Ref.Libn.
MAYO FOUNDATION - MAYO CLINIC LIBRARY □
Rochester, MN

Esau, Dwight B., Dir., Tech.Pubn.
AMERICAN SOCIETY OF SAFETY ENGINEERS -
TECHNICAL INFORMATION CENTER □ Park
Ridge, IL

Esbin, Martha, Law Libn.
SHUMAKER, LOOP & KENDRICK - LIBRARY □
Toledo, OH

Escalera, Digna C., Hd., Acq.
UNIVERSITY OF PUERTO RICO - GENERAL
LIBRARY □ San Juan, PR

Esch, Harold L., Hist.
AMERICAN LAWN BOWLS ASSOCIATION -
LIBRARY □ Orlando, FL

Eschenauer, L.A., Sec.
UNIVERSITY OF TORONTO - DEPARTMENT OF
GEOLOGY - COLEMAN LIBRARY □ Toronto, ON

Esckridge, Virginia C., Ref.Libn.
DUQUESNE UNIVERSITY - LAW LIBRARY □
Pittsburgh, PA

Escobar, Gabriel, Asst.Libn.
RACQUET AND TENNIS CLUB - LIBRARY □ New
York, NY

Escriu, Maria A., Libn.
CANADIAN ASSOCIATION - LATIN AMERICA
AND CARIBBEAN - INFORMATION CENTRE □
Toronto, ON

Escudero, Conrado A., U.S. Rep.
ASSOCIATION OF PHILIPPINE COCONUT
DESICCATORS - LIBRARY† □ New York, NY

Escudero, Estela, Libn.
COOK COUNTY HOSPITAL - HEALTH SCIENCE
LIBRARY □ Chicago, IL

Eshelman, Ralph, Dir.
CALVERT MARINE MUSEUM - LIBRARY □
Solomons, MD

Eskelson, B., Mgr.
BELL CANADA - INFORMATION RESOURCE
CENTRE □ Montreal, PQ

Eskind, Andrew, Act.Dir.
INTERNATIONAL MUSEUM OF PHOTOGRAPHY
AT GEORGE EASTMAN HOUSE - LIBRARY □
Rochester, NY

Eslick, Esther H., Med.Lib.Techn.
DIVINE PROVIDENCE HOSPITAL - MEDICAL
LIBRARY □ Williamsport, PA

Espenshade, Ralph S., Sci.Eng.Ref.Libn.
UNIVERSITY OF ARIZONA - SCIENCE-
ENGINEERING LIBRARY □ Tucson, AZ

Espinosa, Silvia
LOUISIANA STATE UNIVERSITY - REFERENCE
SERVICES □ Baton Rouge, LA

Espiritu, Trinidad, Libn.
SUN LIFE ASSURANCE COMPANY OF CANADA -
REFERENCE LIBRARY □ Toronto, ON

Esposito, Alice, Libn.
LIVINGSTON COUNTY LAW LIBRARY □
Geneseo, NY

Esposito, Michael, Adjunct Libn.
RENSSELAER POLYTECHNIC INSTITUTE -
FOLSOM LIBRARY □ Troy, NY

Esposito, Vicky, Clinical Data Coord.
SQUIBB CANADA INC. - MEDICAL LIBRARY □
Montreal, PQ

Esquibel, Sandra, Assoc. State Libn.
NEW MEXICO STATE LIBRARY □ Santa Fe, NM

Esquivel, Ricardo
SETON HALL UNIVERSITY - SCHOOL OF LAW -
LAW LIBRARY □ Newark, NJ

Esselborn, Albert, Esq., Libn.
NEW YORK STATE SUPREME COURT -
APPELLATE DIVISION, 2ND JUDICIAL
DEPARTMENT - LAW LIBRARY □ Brooklyn, NY

Essemann, Anette
DANISH CONSULATE GENERAL - INFORMATION
OFFICE □ New York, NY

Essex, Thomas, Asst.Libn.
WARREN COUNTY LAW LIBRARY □ Lebanon, OH

Essien, Obot A., Act. Law Libn.
HOWARD UNIVERSITY - SCHOOL OF LAW -
ALLEN MERCER DANIEL LAW LIBRARY □
Washington, DC

Esson, Beverly J., Libn.
UNITED TECHNOLOGIES CORPORATION -
PRATT & WHITNEY AIRCRAFT GROUP -
MATERIALS ENGINEERING RESEARCH LIB. □
Middletown, CT

Esson, Brenda M., Mgr.Info.Rsrcs. Group
CANADIAN STANDARDS ASSOCIATION -
INFORMATION CENTRE □ Toronto, ON

Esswein, Jeannine R., Libn.
CHADBOURNE, PARKE, WHITESIDE, & WOLFF -
LIBRARY □ New York, NY

Estes, Alice P., Lib.Mgr.
DRAVO CORPORATION - LIBRARY □ Pittsburgh,
PA

Estes, David E., Hd.
EMORY UNIVERSITY - SPECIAL COLLECTIONS
DEPARTMENT □ Atlanta, GA

Estoppey, Carol, Supv., Tech.Serv.
CONFERENCE BOARD, INC. - INFORMATION
SERVICE □ New York, NY

Estoppey, Joan, Sr.Libn.
COMBUSTION ENGINEERING, INC. - POWER
SYSTEMS GROUP LIBRARY SERVICES □
Windsor, CT

Estrada, James, Cat.Libn.
UNIVERSITY OF CONNECTICUT - HEALTH
CENTER - LYMAN MAYNARD STOWE LIBRARY □
Farmington, CT

Estry, Douna Seiler, Supv., Tech.Info.Sect.
FORD MOTOR COMPANY - TECHNICAL
INFORMATION SECTION & ENGINEERING &
RESEARCH LIBRARY □ Dearborn, MI

P
E
R
S
O
N
N
E
L

Eswein, Dorothy, Med.Rec.Dir./Libn.
GUADALUPE MEDICAL CENTER - MEDICAL
STAFF LIBRARY □ Carlsbad, NM

Esworthy, Robert S., Dir.
SCHOOL OF THE OZARKS - RALPH FOSTER
MUSEUM - LOIS BROWNELL RESEARCH
LIBRARY □ Point Lookout, MO

Eterovich, Adam S., Dir.
CROATIAN GENEALOGICAL SOCIETY - LIBRARY
□ San Carlos, CA

Etheredge, Helene K., Supv.Libn.
PORTLAND GENERAL ELECTRIC - CORPORATE
AND TECHNICAL LIBRARIES □ Portland, OR

Etheridge, Virginia, Cat.
COUNCIL ON FOREIGN RELATIONS - LIBRARY □
New York, NY

Etherington, Don, Asst.Dir./Consrv.Off.
UNIVERSITY OF TEXAS, AUSTIN - HUMANITIES
RESEARCH CENTER □ Austin, TX

Ethier, Patricia, Prof.Asst.
ST. PAUL PUBLIC LIBRARY - REFERENCE ROOM
□ St. Paul, MN

Etimov, Dimiter, Dir.
LORETTO HOSPITAL - HEALTH SCIENCES
LIBRARY □ Chicago, IL

Etler, Selma, Ref.Libn.
GEISINGER MEDICAL CENTER - MEDICAL
LIBRARY □ Danville, PA

Ettl, Lorraine, Pub.Serv.
UNIVERSITY OF NORTH DAKOTA - SCHOOL OF
MEDICINE - HARLEY E. FRENCH MEDICAL
LIBRARY □ Grand Forks, ND

Eubank, Larry, Lib.Info.Spec.
RCA CORPORATION - RCA LABORATORIES -
DAVID SARNOFF RESEARCH CENTER - LIBRARY
□ Princeton, NJ

Eubanks, Spanola, Dir., Lib.Serv.
DOROTHEA DIX HOSPITAL - F.T. FULLER STAFF
LIBRARY □ Raleigh, NC

Eugene, Robert, Cur.
PRINCETON ANTIQUES BOOKFINDERS - ART
MARKETING REFERENCE LIBRARY □ Atlantic
City, NJ

Evalds, Victoria, Libn.
BOSTON UNIVERSITY - AFRICAN STUDIES
LIBRARY □ Boston, MA

Evalds, Victoria K., Libn.
BELLET (Samuel) LIBRARY OF LAW, MEDICINE
AND BEHAVIORAL SCIENCE □ Philadelphia, PA

Evancho, Stephanie, Dir.
CARNEGIE-MELLON UNIVERSITY - AUDIO
VISUAL SERVICES □ Pittsburgh, PA

Evangelista, Caroline, Cur./Hist.
NUTLEY HISTORICAL SOCIETY MUSEUM -
ALICE J. BICKERS LIBRARY □ Nutley, NJ

Evankow, Lucy, Chf.Libn.
SCHOLASTIC MAGAZINES - EDITORIAL
DEPARTMENT - LIBRARY □ New York, NY

Evanoff, Ruthann, Info.Spec.
INSTITUTE OF INTERNATIONAL EDUCATION -
LIBRARY/COMMUNICATIONS □ New York, NY

Evans, Mrs. Adye Bel, Libn.
UNIVERSITY OF MICHIGAN - INSTITUTE FOR
SOCIAL RESEARCH - LIBRARY† □ Ann Arbor, MI

Evans, Al, Lrng.Rsrcs.Libn.
MOREHEAD STATE UNIVERSITY - CAMDEN-
CARROLL LIBRARY □ Morehead, KY

Evans, B.L., Asst.Chem.II
IOWA STATE UNIVERSITY - ENERGY AND
MINERAL RESOURCES RESEARCH INSTITUTE -
RARE EARTH INFORMATION CENTER □ Ames,
IA

Evans, David, Chm., Lib.Comm.
NEW CANAAN HISTORICAL SOCIETY -
LIBRARY □ New Canaan, CT

Evans, Dorothy, Asst.Libn.
CANADA - NATIONAL RESEARCH COUNCIL -
CISTI - ENERGY BRANCH □ Ottawa, ON

Evans, Douglas L., Libn.
WOLFE (Harvey G.) LIBRARY □ Glendale, CA

Evans, Elizabeth, Libn.
U.S. NAVY - FLEET ANTI-SUBMARINE
WARFARE TRAINING CENTER, ATLANTIC -
TACTICAL LIBRARY □ Norfolk, VA

Evans, Elizabeth, Network Coord.
UNIVERSITY OF SOUTH FLORIDA - MEDICAL
CENTER LIBRARY □ Tampa, FL

Evans, Emily, Libn.
PORTLAND ART MUSEUM - LIBRARY □ Portland,
OR

Evans, Everett, Microfilm Supv.
WASHINGTON STATE OFFICE OF SECRETARY
OF STATE - DIVISION OF ARCHIVES AND
RECORD MANAGEMENT □ Olympia, WA

Evans, Gloria B., Coord., Cat.Serv.
ALABAMA A & M UNIVERSITY - JOSEPH F.
DRAKE MEMORIAL LEARNING RESOURCES
CENTER □ Normal, AL

Evans, Jane, Govt.Doc.Libn.
UNIVERSITY OF CALIFORNIA, SAN FRANCISCO
- HASTINGS COLLEGE OF THE LAW - LEGAL
INFORMATION CENTER □ San Francisco, CA

Evans, Janet, Asst.Libn.
ACADEMY OF NATURAL SCIENCES - LIBRARY □
Philadelphia, PA

Evans, Linda J., Asst.Cur., Mss.
CHICAGO HISTORICAL SOCIETY - SPECIAL
COLLECTIONS □ Chicago, IL

Evans, Lois, Adm.Libn.
DIAMOND SHAMROCK CORPORATION -
CORPORATE LIBRARY □ Painesville, OH

Evans, Margaret J., Chf.Libn.
U.S. COURT OF APPEALS, 2ND CIRCUIT -
LIBRARY □ New York, NY

Evans, Margaret J., Libn.
U.S. CUSTOMS COURT - LIBRARY† □ New York,
NY

Evans, Marilyn L., Br.Supv.
DU PONT DE NEMOURS (E.I.) & COMPANY, INC.
- TECHNICAL LIBRARY SYSTEM - LOUVIERS
BRANCH □ Wilmington, DE

Evans, Mary, Asst.Libn.
EASTERN BAPTIST THEOLOGICAL SEMINARY -
LIBRARY □ Philadelphia, PA

Evans, Mary, Libn.
OHIO VALLEY GENERAL HOSPITAL -
PROFESSIONAL LIBRARY □ McKee's Rock, PA

Evans, Mary, Libn.
ST. JOSEPH HOSPITAL - HEALTH SCIENCE
LIBRARY □ Kansas City, MO

Evans, Max J., Asst.Dir.
STATE HISTORICAL SOCIETY OF WISCONSIN -
ARCHIVES DIVISION □ Madison, WI

Evans, Nancy H., Asst.Ref.Libn.
CARNEGIE-MELLON UNIVERSITY - HUNT
LIBRARY □ Pittsburgh, PA

Evans, Nelson H., Govt.Doc.Libn.
TRENTON STATE COLLEGE - ROSCOE L. WEST
LIBRARY □ Trenton, NJ

Evans, Patrick M.O., Cur.
BOY SCOUTS OF CANADA - MUSEUM &
ARCHIVES OF CANADIAN SCOUTING □ Ottawa,
ON

Evans, Peter, Libn.
UNIVERSITY OF CALIFORNIA, BERKELEY -
FOREST PRODUCTS LIBRARY □ Richmond, CA

Evans, Peter, Ref.Libn.
UNIVERSITY OF CALIFORNIA, BERKELEY -
FORESTRY LIBRARY □ Berkeley, CA

Evans, Renee, Chf.Libn.
LOCKHEED-CALIFORNIA COMPANY -
TECHNICAL INFORMATION CENTER □ Burbank,
CA

Evans, Professor Richard A., Lib.Dir.
U.S. NAVAL ACADEMY - NIMITZ LIBRARY □
Annapolis, MD

Evans, Rita
GULF OIL CORPORATION - BUSINESS
RESEARCH LIBRARY □ Pittsburgh, PA

Evans, Shirley, Bus.Libn.
MONSANTO COMPANY - INFORMATION
CENTER □ St. Louis, MO

Evansen, Michaeljohn, Media Techn.
EMMAUS BIBLE SCHOOL - LIBRARY □ Oak Park,
IL

Evanson, Beth, Libn.
BOEING VERTOL COMPANY - LYDIA RANKIN
TECHNICAL LIBRARY □ Philadelphia, PA

Eveland, Raymond E., Dir.
U.S. DEPT. OF COMMERCE - INTERNATIONAL
TRADE ADMINISTRATION - NEW ORLEANS
DISTRICT OFFICE LIBRARY □ New Orleans, LA

Evenson, Mariellen E., Tech.Serv.Libn.
MILWAUKEE AREA TECHNICAL COLLEGE -
RASCHE MEMORIAL LIBRARY □ Milwaukee, WI

Everall, Kathleen, Dir.
FLORIDA STATE DEPT. OF ENVIRONMENTAL
REGULATION - LIBRARY □ Tallahassee, FL

Everett, Dorothy M., Libn.
INDIANA STATE DEPT. OF PUBLIC
INSTRUCTION - PROFESSIONAL LIBRARY □
Indianapolis, IN

Evers, Donald J., Chf.Ref.Libn.
U.S. SECURITIES AND EXCHANGE
COMMISSION - PUBLIC REFERENCE LIBRARY □
Chicago, IL

Evers, Irene, Asst.Sci.Libn.
UNIVERSITY OF MONTANA - SCHOOL OF
FORESTRY - COOPERATIVE FOREST AND
CONSERVATION COLLECTION □ Missoula, MT

Evers, Jacques J., Mgr.
MOTOR VEHICLE MANUFACTURERS
ASSOCIATION (MVMA) - STATISTICS
INFORMATION CENTER □ Detroit, MI

Evers, Mary, Acq.Libn.
TENNESSEE VALLEY AUTHORITY - TECHNICAL
LIBRARY □ Muscle Shoals, AL

Eversole, Sharon, Libn.
ST. RITA'S MEDICAL CENTER - MEDICAL
LIBRARY □ Lima, OH

Everts, Helen L., Libn.
LANCASTER NEWSPAPERS - LIBRARY □
Lancaster, PA

Eves, Judith A., Libn.
PENNSYLVANIA ECONOMY LEAGUE - WESTERN
DIVISION - LIBRARY □ Pittsburgh, PA

Evetts, Rosemary, Libn.
SOUTH DAKOTA STATE HISTORICAL
RESOURCE CENTER □ Pierre, SD

Evich, Nancy, Act.Dir.
UNIVERSITY OF MICHIGAN - BUSINESS
ADMINISTRATION LIBRARY □ Ann Arbor, MI

Evitts, Beth A., Asst.Libn.
YORK HOSPITAL - LIBRARY □ York, PA

Evitts, Virginia, Libn.
AREA COOPERATIVE EDUCATIONAL SERVICES
- TEACHER RESOURCE LIBRARY □ New Haven,
CT

Ewald, Carlyn, Tech.Libn.
GPU NUCLEAR - OYSTER CREEK TECHNICAL
LIBRARY □ Forked River, NJ

Ewaskiw, Christine, Govt.Pubn./Ref.
UNIVERSITY OF ALBERTA - LAW LIBRARY □
Edmonton, AB

Ewbank, Lynn, Archv.
ARKANSAS STATE HISTORY COMMISSION -
ARCHIVES □ Little Rock, AR

Ewbank, Ralph L., Libn.
WESTERN EVANGELICAL SEMINARY - GEORGE
HALLAUER MEMORIAL LIBRARY □ Portland, OR

Ewell, Kathleen S., Dir.
PENNSYLVANIA RESOURCES AND
INFORMATION CENTER FOR SPECIAL
EDUCATION □ King of Prussia, PA

Ewen, Sylvia S., Chf.Libn.
SUNY - AGRICULTURAL AND TECHNICAL
COLLEGE AT FARMINGDALE - THOMAS D.
GREENLEY LIBRARY □ Farmingdale, NY

Ewens, Wilma, Hd.Cat.
GEORGETOWN UNIVERSITY - MEDICAL
CENTER - DAHLGREN MEMORIAL LIBRARY □
Washington, DC

Ewert, Thomas E., Dir.
UNIVERSITY OF VIRGINIA - BLANDY
EXPERIMENTAL FARM LIBRARY □ Boyce, VA

Fallows, Muriel, Hd. of Circ.
HARVARD UNIVERSITY - JOHN FITZGERALD
KENNEDY SCHOOL OF GOVERNMENT - LIBRARY
□ Cambridge, MA

Faltermeier, Jann, Law Libn.
FEDERAL RESERVE BANK OF KANSAS CITY -
LAW LIBRARY □ Kansas City, MO

Famularo, Sabiha, Cat.Libn.
JOHNS HOPKINS UNIVERSITY - SCHOOL OF
ADVANCED INTERNATIONAL STUDIES -
SYDNEY R. & ELSA W. MASON LIBRARY □
Washington, DC

Fancy, Margaret, Spec.Coll.Libn.
MOUNT ALLISON UNIVERSITY - WINTHROP P.
BELL COLLECTION OF ACADIANA □ Sackville, NB

Fanelli, Michelle, Hd.
FAIRLEIGH DICKINSON UNIVERSITY - WEINER
LIBRARY - REFERENCE/GOVERNMENT
DOCUMENTS DEPARTMENT □ Teaneck, NJ

Fangemann, Ruby, Tech.Serv.
CHASE MANHATTAN BANK, N.A. -
INFORMATION CENTER □ New York, NY

Fankhauser, Linda, Dir.
TOLEDO HOSPITAL - LIBRARY □ Toledo, OH

Fannin, Kathy, Res.Assoc.
MISSOURI STATE DIVISION OF COMMUNITY
AND ECONOMIC DEVELOPMENT - RESEARCH
LIBRARY □ Jefferson City, MO

Fannon, Elizabeth, Dept.Hd.
CLEVELAND PUBLIC LIBRARY - DOCUMENTS
COLLECTION □ Cleveland, OH

Fanta, David, Asst.Libn.
CHAPMAN AND CUTLER - LAW LIBRARY □
Chicago, IL

Fantozzi, Anthony J., Archv.
U.S. NATL. ARCHIVES & RECORDS SERVICE -
FEDERAL ARCHIVES AND RECORDS CENTER,
REGION 2 □ Bayonne, NJ

Farah, Priscilla, Assoc.Musm.Libn.
METROPOLITAN MUSEUM OF ART -
PHOTOGRAPH AND SLIDE LIBRARY □ New York,
NY

Fardig, Elsie, Music Libn.
UNIVERSITY OF MIAMI - SCHOOL OF MUSIC -
ALBERT PICK MUSIC LIBRARY □ Coral Gables,
FL

Farghal, Mahmoud, UN Spec.
LEAGUE OF ARAB STATES - ARAB
INFORMATION CENTER □ New York, NY

Farhat, Fred, Mgr., Lib.Serv.
KAISER ALUMINUM & CHEMICAL
CORPORATION - TECHNICAL INFORMATION
CENTER □ Pleasanton, CA

Farid, Mohsen M., Mgr., Info.Rsrcs.
ROCKWELL INTERNATIONAL - GENERAL
INDUSTRIES OPERATIONS - INFORMATION
CENTER □ Pittsburgh, PA

Farid, Susan L., Libn.
PARKVIEW MEMORIAL HOSPITAL -
PARKVIEW-METHODIST SCHOOL OF NURSING
- LIBRARY □ Fort Wayne, IN

Fariss, Linda, Pub.Serv.Libn.
INDIANA UNIVERSITY - LAW LIBRARY □
Bloomington, IN

Fark, Ronald, Hd., Circ.
BROWN UNIVERSITY - SCIENCES LIBRARY □
Providence, RI

Farkas, Eugene M., Chf., Educ.Rsrcs.Div.
U.S.D.A. - NATIONAL AGRICULTURAL LIBRARY
□ Beltsville, MD

Farkas, Susan, Asst.Libn.
EDISON ELECTRIC INSTITUTE - LIBRARY □
Washington, DC

Farley, Dr. A.L., Assoc.Prof. & Supv.
UNIVERSITY OF BRITISH COLUMBIA -
DEPARTMENT OF GEOGRAPHY - MAP AND AIR
PHOTO LIBRARY □ Vancouver, BC

Farley, David J., Asst.Dir. for Adm.
MARQUETTE UNIVERSITY - MEMORIAL
LIBRARY □ Milwaukee, WI

Farley, Earl, Dir.
UNIVERSITY OF KANSAS MEDICAL CENTER -
COLLEGE OF HEALTH SCIENCES AND HOSPITAL
- CLENDENING LIBRARY □ Kansas City, KS

Farley, James K., Tech.Info.Spec.
SETON, JOHNSON & ODELL, INC. - TECHNICAL
INFORMATION CENTER □ Portland, OR

Farley, Jeanette, Ref.Libn.
WESTERN KENTUCKY UNIVERSITY -
KENTUCKY LIBRARY AND MUSEUM/
UNIVERSITY ARCHIVES □ Bowling Green, KY

Farley, Joanne E., Mgr., Lib.Serv.
FEDERAL RESERVE BANK OF MINNEAPOLIS -
LIBRARY □ Minneapolis, MN

Farley, Patricia, Jr.Lib.Asst.
ESSEX COUNTY HOSPITAL CENTER -
HAMILTON MEMORIAL LIBRARY □ Cedar Grove,
NJ

Farley, Richard A., Adm.
U.S.D.A. - NATIONAL AGRICULTURAL LIBRARY
□ Beltsville, MD

Farman, Donna L., Libn.
PHOENIX DAY SCHOOL FOR THE DEAF -
LIBRARY/MEDIA CENTER □ Phoenix, AZ

Farmann, Kathleen, Law Libn.
UNIVERSITY OF NOTRE DAME - LAW SCHOOL
LIBRARY □ Notre Dame, IN

Farmer, Diana, Acq. & Ser.
KANSAS STATE UNIVERSITY - FARRELL
LIBRARY □ Manhattan, KS

Farmer, Don A., Sr. Planner
WASHTENAW COUNTY METROPOLITAN
PLANNING COMMISSION - LIBRARY □ Ann
Arbor, MI

Farmer, Gregory, Dir.
CONNECTICUT VALLEY HISTORICAL MUSEUM -
RESEARCH LIBRARY □ Springfield, MA

Farmer, Linda G., Med.Libn.
JACKSON-MADISON COUNTY GENERAL
HOSPITAL - LEARNING CENTER □ Jackson, TN

Farmer, Mabel, Libn.
COLLEGE OF FISHERIES, NAVIGATION,
MARINE ENGINEERING AND ELECTRONICS -
LIBRARY □ St. John's, NF

Farmer, Rebecca, Law Libn.
FIREMAN'S FUND INSURANCE COMPANIES -
LIBRARY† □ San Francisco, CA

Farnell, Mrs. M., Asst.Hd. & Ref.Hd.
UNIVERSITY OF ALBERTA - HUMANITIES AND
SOCIAL SCIENCES LIBRARY □ Edmonton, AB

Farnos, Lolita G., Asst.Dir.
UNIVERSITY OF PUERTO RICO - GENERAL
LIBRARY □ San Juan, PR

Farny, Diane M., Libn.
GRADUATE HOSPITAL - LIBRARY □ Philadelphia,
PA

Farooqui, S.A., Cat.
CANADA - FISHERIES & OCEANS - LIBRARY □
Ottawa, ON

Farrands, Jane E., Libn.
ORGANON, INC. - MEDICAL LIBRARY □ West
Orange, NJ

Farrar, Jennifer, Libn.
OGILVY & MATHER, INC. - RESEARCH LIBRARY
□ New York, NY

Farrell, Barbara D., Coord.
MOBIL EXPLORATION AND PRODUCING
SERVICES INC. - MEPSI LIBRARY □ Dallas, TX

Farrell, Barbara E., Map Libn.
CARLETON UNIVERSITY - MACODRUM LIBRARY
- MAP LIBRARY □ Ottawa, ON

Farrell, Helene S., Dir.
SCHOHARIE COUNTY HISTORICAL SOCIETY -
REFERENCE LIBRARY □ Schoharie, NY

Farrell, Lois, Hd.
UNIVERSITY OF CALIFORNIA, BERKELEY -
NATURAL RESOURCES LIBRARY □ Berkeley, CA

Farrell, Toni, Law Libn.
ST. PETERSBURG - MUNICIPAL REFERENCE
LIBRARY □ St. Petersburg, FL

Farrell-Duncan, Howertine, Libn./Supv., Ref.
HOWARD UNIVERSITY - HEALTH SCIENCES
LIBRARY □ Washington, DC

Farren, Donald, Hd.
UNIVERSITY OF NEW MEXICO - SPECIAL
COLLECTIONS DEPARTMENT □ Albuquerque, NM

Farrens, Mary, Libn.
UNIVERSITY OF CALIFORNIA, DAVIS -
AGRICULTURAL ECONOMICS BRANCH LIBRARY
□ Davis, CA

Farrers, Mary B., Hd., Agri.Econ.Lib.
UNIVERSITY OF CALIFORNIA, DAVIS -
GENERAL LIBRARY □ Davis, CA

Farrington, H., Orientation Libn.
CONCORDIA UNIVERSITY - SIR GEORGE
WILLIAMS CAMPUS - NORRIS LIBRARY □
Montreal, PQ

Farris, Donn Michael, Libn.
DUKE UNIVERSITY - DIVINITY SCHOOL
LIBRARY □ Durham, NC

Farris, Michael W., AV Prod.Serv.Mgr.
SOUTHWEST TEXAS STATE UNIVERSITY -
LEARNING RESOURCES CENTER □ San Marcos,
TX

Farris, Patricia, Office Mgr.
LEGAL SERVICES ORGANIZATION OF INDIANA,
INC. - LIBRARY □ Evansville, IN

Farrow, Mildred, Tech.Serv.Libn.
UNIVERSITY OF CHICAGO - HUMAN
RESOURCES CENTER - A.G. BUSH LIBRARY □
Chicago, IL

Farver, Jane, Photograph Lib.
CLEVELAND MUSEUM OF ART - LIBRARY □
Cleveland, OH

Farwell, Karen, Libn.
UNIVERSITY OF MINNESOTA - HAROLD SCOTT
QUIGLEY CENTER OF INTERNATIONAL
STUDIES LIBRARY □ Minneapolis, MN

Farwell, Robert D., Exec.Dir.
WHALING MUSEUM SOCIETY, INC. - LIBRARY □
Cold Spring Harbor, NY

Faryar, Jim, Libn.
KAISER FOUNDATION HOSPITAL -
MANAGEMENT EFFECTIVENESS LIBRARY □ Los
Angeles, CA

Fass, Evelyn M., Asst.Mgr.
INSTITUTE FOR DEFENSE ANALYSES -
TECHNICAL INFORMATION SERVICES □
Arlington, VA

Fassler, Bettifae, Assoc.Libn.
HOWARD UNIVERSITY - HEALTH SCIENCES
LIBRARY □ Washington, DC

Fast, Mrs. Lee, Lib.Ck.
WINFIELD STATE HOSPITAL AND TRAINING
CENTER - PROFESSIONAL AND MEDICAL
LIBRARY □ Winfield, KS

Fast, Stanley, Historic Site Adm.
MARK TWAIN BIRTHPLACE - RESEARCH
LIBRARY □ Stoutsville, MO

Fatcheric, J.P., Mgr., Info./Doc.
MILES LABORATORIES, INC.- DELBAY
PHARMACEUTICALS - RESEARCH LIBRARY □
West Haven, CT

Faubert, Ghyslaine, Lib.Techn.
CANADIAN TEACHERS' FEDERATION - GEORGE
G. CROSKERY MEMORIAL LIBRARY □ Ottawa,
ON

Faubion, Anita, Libn.
UNIVERSITY OF TEXAS, AUSTIN - HOGG
FOUNDATION FOR MENTAL HEALTH - LIBRARY
□ Austin, TX

Faucher, G., Asst. To The Ed.
ASSOCIATION DES MEDECINS DE LANGUE
FRANCAISE DU CANADA - UNION MEDICALE
DU CANADA - RESEARCH LIBRARY □ Montreal,
PQ

Fauhl, Ruth D., Lib.Asst.
UNIVERSITY OF KANSAS - WEALTHY BABCOCK
MATHEMATICS LIBRARY □ Lawrence, KS

Faul, Carol, Map Libn.
UNIVERSITY OF PENNSYLVANIA - GEOLOGY
MAP LIBRARY □ Philadelphia, PA

Faul, Mary A., Libn.
PINAL COUNTY HISTORICAL SOCIETY, INC. -
LIBRARY □ Florence, AZ

Faulkner, D.A., Meteorologist
CANADA - ATMOSPHERIC ENVIRONMENT
SERVICE - PACIFIC REGION - LIBRARY □
Vancouver, BC

Faupel, D. William, Dir., Lib. Serv.
ASBURY THEOLOGICAL SEMINARY - B.L.
FISHER LIBRARY □ Wilmore, KY

Faust, Julia B., Libn.
WEST SUBURBAN HOSPITAL - WALTER
LAWRENCE MEMORIAL LIBRARY □ Oak Park, IL

Faust, Kathy, Cat.Libn.
LEWIS AND CLARK LAW SCHOOL -
NORTHWESTERN SCHOOL OF LAW - PAUL L.
BOLEY LAW LIBRARY □ Portland, OR

Fauster, Carl U., Dir.
ANTIQUE AND HISTORIC GLASS FOUNDATION
- LIBRARY □ Toledo, OH

Faverty, Margaret, Archival Proc.
NORTHWESTERN UNIVERSITY - ARCHIVES □
Evanston, IL

Favorite, Miriam, Libn.
CAMDEN COUNTY HISTORICAL SOCIETY -
LIBRARY □ Camden, NJ

Favorite, Susan, Libn.
FAIRVIEW GENERAL HOSPITAL - HEALTH
MEDIA CENTER □ Cleveland, OH

Favreau, J.-Etienne, Ref.Libn.
UNIVERSITE DU QUEBEC A MONTREAL -
BIBLIOTHEQUE DES SCIENCES DE
L'EDUCATION □ Montreal, PQ

Fawcett, Braden S., Libn.
NORTHWEST BIBLE COLLEGE - J.C. COOKE
LIBRARY □ Edmonton, AB

Fawcett, George E., Hd., Acq./Ser.
UNIVERSITY OF NEBRASKA MEDICAL CENTER -
MC GOOGAN LIBRARY OF MEDICINE □ Omaha,
NE

Fawcett, Rosalie
HARTFORD PUBLIC LIBRARY - REFERENCE AND
GENERAL READING DEPARTMENT □ Hartford,
CT

Fawcett, W. Peyton, Hd.Libn.
FIELD MUSEUM OF NATURAL HISTORY -
LIBRARY □ Chicago, IL

Fawson, E. Curtis, Dir.
BRIGHAM YOUNG UNIVERSITY, HAWAII
CAMPUS - JOSEPH F. SMITH LIBRARY AND
MEDIA CENTER □ Laie, HI

Fay, C. Bradley, Mgr.
MARITIME RESOURCE MANAGEMENT SERVICE
- INFORMATION CENTRE □ Amherst, NS

Fay, Denise, Mgr.
NATIONAL INVESTIGATIONS COMMITTEE ON
UFOS - NEW AGE CENTER □ Van Nuys, CA

Fay, Mrs. Kevin J., Libn.
COTTAGE HOSPITAL - DAVID L. REEVES
MEDICAL LIBRARY □ Santa Barbara, CA

Fay, Peter J., Hd.Libn.
LIBRARY OF CONGRESS - JOHN F. KENNEDY
CENTER FOR THE PERFORMING ARTS - THE
PERFORMING ARTS LIBRARY □ Washington, DC

Fayette, Jos. A., Libn.
BANTAM BOOKS, INC. - LIBRARY □ New York,
NY

Fazzari, Francis, Asst.Libn.
INTERNATIONAL NUMISMATIC SOCIETY -
LIBRARY □ Washington, DC

Fazzone, Nancy, Dir., Lib.Serv.
SALEM HOSPITAL - MACK MEMORIAL HEALTH
SCIENCES LIBRARY □ Salem, MA

Featherstone, Thomas, Archv.
WAYNE STATE UNIVERSITY - ARCHIVES OF
LABOR AND URBAN AFFAIRS/UNIVERSITY
ARCHIVES □ Detroit, MI

Feder, Edith, Law Libn.
FEDERAL RESERVE BANK OF NEW YORK - LAW
LIBRARY DIVISION □ New York, NY

Feder, Helga, Hum.Ref.Libn.
CUNY - GRADUATE SCHOOL AND UNIVERSITY
CENTER - LIBRARY □ New York, NY

Feder, Maria, Tech. Processes
U.S. DEPT. OF ENERGY - LAWRENCE BERKELEY
LABORATORY - LIBRARY □ Berkeley, CA

Fedoroff, Nina, Asst.Libn.
BOOTH MEMORIAL MEDICAL CENTER -
MEDICAL LIBRARY □ Flushing, NY

Fedors, Carmel, Med.Libn.
GREENWICH HOSPITAL ASSOCIATION - GRAY
CARTER LIBRARY □ Greenwich, CT

Fedunok, Suzanne, Libn.
COLUMBIA UNIVERSITY - MATHEMATICS/
SCIENCE LIBRARY □ New York, NY

Fedunok, Suzanne, Libn.
COLUMBIA UNIVERSITY - PHYSICS LIBRARY □
New York, NY

Fedynsky, Alexander, Dir.
UKRAINIAN MUSEUM - ARCHIVES □ Cleveland,
OH

Feeley, James, Dir.
ALGONQUIN COLLEGE OF APPLIED ARTS &
TECHNOLOGY - RESOURCE CENTRES† □
Ottawa, ON

Feeney, Karen, Ref.Libn.
UNIVERSITY OF CALIFORNIA, SAN DIEGO -
SCIENCE & ENGINEERING LIBRARY □ La Jolla,
CA

Feeney, Kathryn, Libn.
UNIVERSITY OF BRITISH COLUMBIA - SOCIAL
SCIENCES DIVISION □ Vancouver, BC

Feeney, M. Patricia, Libn.
BURROUGHS CORPORATION - LIBRARY □
Mission Viejo, CA

Feeney, Mary E., Libn.
YALE UNIVERSITY - MEDICAL LIBRARY □ New
Haven, CT

Fehes, Leslie, Libn.
QUEENS CHILDREN'S PSYCHIATRIC CENTER -
LAURETTA BENDER CHILD PSYCHIATRY
LIBRARY □ Bellerose, NY

Fehl, Ken, Chm., Lib.Comm.
CONGREGATION BETH AM - LIBRARY □ Los
Altos Hills, CA

Fehlner, Rev. Peter D., Libn.
ST. ANTHONY-ON-HUDSON THEOLOGICAL
LIBRARY □ Rensselaer, NY

Feidt, Bill
U.S.D.A. - HUMAN NUTRITION INFORMATION
SERVICES - FOOD AND NUTRITION
INFORMATION CENTER □ Beltsville, MD

Feinberg, David, Libn.I
MEMPHIS-SHELBY COUNTY PUBLIC LIBRARY
AND INFORMATION CENTER - MEMPHIS ROOM
COLLECTIONS □ Memphis, TN

Feinberg, Dr. Hilda, Mgr., Lib./Info.Serv.
REVLON RESEARCH CENTER, INC. - LIBRARY □
Bronx, NY

Feinberg, Dr. Hilda, Chm., Lib.Comm.
SOCIETY OF COSMETIC CHEMISTS - LIBRARY
□ New York, NY

Feingold, Linda Marion, Sr.Cons., Info.
LAUTZE & LAUTZE ACCOUNTANCY
CORPORATION - RESOURCES DEVELOPMENT
CENTER □ San Francisco, CA

Feinstein, Joanne P., Libn.
SOUTHEASTERN PENNSYLVANIA
TRANSPORTATION AUTHORITY - LIBRARY □
Philadelphia, PA

Feinstein, Robert, Archv.
ANTIQUE PHONOGRAPH MONTHLY - APM
LIBRARY OF RECORDED SOUND □ Brooklyn, NY

Feitler, Lila, Ref.Libn.
IOWA STATE DEPARTMENT OF SOCIAL
SERVICES - LIBRARY □ Des Moines, IA

Felaco, Maja Bardot, Rd.Serv.Libn.
RHODE ISLAND SCHOOL OF DESIGN - LIBRARY
□ Providence, RI

Felcone, Joseph J., Libn.
DAVID LIBRARY OF THE AMERICAN
REVOLUTION □ Washington Crossing, PA

Feld, Maury D., Ref.Libn.
HARVARD UNIVERSITY - LITTAUER LIBRARY □
Cambridge, MA

Felder, Charletta P., Chf., Lib.Serv.
U.S. VETERANS ADMINISTRATION (SC-
Columbia) - HOSPITAL LIBRARY □ Columbia, SC

Feldick, Peggy, Ref. & ILL
MACALESTER COLLEGE - WEYERHAEUSER
LIBRARY □ St. Paul, MN

Feldman, Betsy, Info.Spec.I
KM&G INTERNATIONAL INC. - LIBRARY
SERVICES □ Pittsburgh, PA

Feldman, Caryl-Ann, Mgr., Rsrcs.Serv.
CHILDREN'S MUSEUM - RESOURCE CENTER □
Boston, MA

Feldman, Donald H., Mgr.
PLATT SACO LOWELL CORPORATION -
ENGINEERING LIBRARY □ Greenville, SC

Feldman, Eugene, Asst.
DU SABLE MUSEUM OF AFRICAN AMERICAN
HISTORY - LIBRARY □ Chicago, IL

Feldman, Fran, Libn.
ANDERSEN LABORATORIES, INC. - LIBRARY □
Bloomfield, CT

Feldman, Laurence, Br.Libn.
UNIVERSITY OF MASSACHUSETTS, AMHERST -
MORRILL BIOLOGICAL & GEOLOGICAL
SCIENCES LIBRARY □ Amherst, MA

Feldman, M.S., Libn.
U.S. DEPT. OF ENERGY - SAVANNAH RIVER
LAB. - TECHNICAL INFO. SERVICE LIBRARY □
Aiken, SC

Feldman, Marguerite S., Ser. & Circ.
ROSWELL PARK MEMORIAL INSTITUTE -
MEDICAL AND SCIENTIFIC LIBRARY □ Buffalo,
NY

Feldman, Mary, Chf., Hdq.Serv.Br.
U.S. DEPT. OF TRANSPORTATION - LIBRARY
SERVICES DIVISION □ Washington, DC

Feldman, Rayma, Sr.Info.Spec.
U.S. MARITIME ADMINISTRATION - NATL.
MARITIME RESEARCH CENTER - STUDY
CENTER □ Kings Point, NY

Feldman, T.K., Dir., Literary Arts Dept.
JEWISH COMMUNITY CENTER OF GREATER
WASHINGTON - KASS JUDAIC LIBRARY □
Rockville, MD

Feldstein, Dr. Arthur, Hd. of Lib.Comm.
SEA VIEW HOSPITAL AND HOME - MEDICAL
LIBRARY □ Staten Island, NY

Feldt, Candice, Music Cat.
SUNY AT STONY BROOK - MUSIC LIBRARY □
Stony Brook, NY

Feldt, Marna, Info.Off.
SWEDISH CONSULATE GENERAL - SWEDISH
INFORMATION SERVICE □ New York, NY

Felice, Michael, Hd.Ser.
UNIVERSITY OF ILLINOIS MEDICAL CENTER -
LIBRARY OF THE HEALTH SCIENCES □ Chicago,
IL

Felician, Bro., S.C., Libn.
UNION SAINT-JEAN-BAPTISTE - MALLET
LIBRARY □ Woonsocket, RI

Feliciano, Francisco
UNIVERSITY OF PUERTO RICO - NATURAL
SCIENCE LIBRARY □ Rio Piedras, PR

Felix, Donna, Asst.Libn.
CONNECTICUT COLLEGE - GREER MUSIC
LIBRARY □ New London, CT

Fell-Johnson, Barbara, Libn.
HAMPSHIRE COUNTY LAW LIBRARY □
Northampton, MA

Fellenberg, Annie, Stud. & Doc.Adm.
AIR FRANCE - PUBLIC RELATIONS
DEPARTMENT - LIBRARY □ New York, NY

Feller, Amy, Libn.
AMERICAN CAN COMPANY - TECHNICAL
INFORMATION CENTER □ Greenwich, CT

Feller, Judith M., Doc.Libn.
EAST STROUDSBURG STATE COLLEGE -
LIBRARY □ East Stroudsburg, PA

Fellows, Cynthia, Ref.Libn.
ALASKA STATE COURT SYSTEM - ALASKA
COURT LIBRARIES □ Anchorage, AK

Fellows, Paul E., Site Supt.
FORT MASSAC HISTORIC SITE - LIBRARY □
Metropolis, IL

Felo, Mary, Supv., Tech.Proc.
ATLANTIC-RICHFIELD COMPANY -
HEADQUARTERS LIBRARY □ Los Angeles, CA

Felsted, Carla Martindell, Libn.
AMERICAN AIRLINES, INC. - CORPORATE
LIBRARY □ Dallas/Ft. Worth Airport, TX

Felt, Margie, Med.Libn.
STANISLAUS COUNTY MEDICAL SOCIETY -
MEDICAL LIBRARY □ Modesto, CA

Feltes, Carol, Supv.
BATTELLE-COLUMBUS LABORATORIES -
LIBRARY □ Columbus, OH

Feltes, Gretchen, Circ.Libn.
GEORGETOWN UNIVERSITY - LAW CENTER
LIBRARY □ Washington, DC

Feltz, William, Res.Mtl.Spec.
EAST-WEST CULTURE LEARNING INSTITUTE -
RESOURCE MATERIALS COLLECTION □
Honolulu, HI

Fendry, Marie, Res.Libn.
PABST BREWING COMPANY - P-L
BIOCHEMICALS, INC. - RESEARCH LIBRARY □
Milwaukee, WI

Feng, Cyril C.H., Libn.
UNIVERSITY OF MARYLAND, BALTIMORE -
HEALTH SCIENCES LIBRARY □ Baltimore, MD

Feng, Grace, Supv.Libn.
U.S. ARMY - TROOP SUPPORT COMMAND -
STINFO AND REFERENCE LIBRARY □ St. Louis,
MO

Fenichel, Carol Hansen, Dir.Lib.Serv.
PHILADELPHIA COLLEGE OF PHARMACY AND
SCIENCE - JOSEPH W. ENGLAND LIBRARY □
Philadelphia, PA

Fenn, Dan H., Jr., Dir.
U.S. PRESIDENTIAL LIBRARIES - JOHN F.
KENNEDY LIBRARY □ Boston, MA

Fenn, Martha J., Libn.
BRATTLEBORO MEMORIAL HOSPITAL -
MEDICAL LIBRARY □ Brattleboro, VT

Fenn, Rosalyn F., Libn.
FLORIDA STATE LEGISLATURE - DIVISION OF
LEGISLATIVE LIBRARY SERVICES □
Tallahassee, FL

Fennell, Janice C., Lib.Dir.
GEORGIA COLLEGE - INA DILLARD RUSSELL
LIBRARY □ Milledgeville, GA

Fennell, Margene, Asst.Libn.
EASTERN MAINE MEDICAL CENTER - HEALTH
SCIENCES LIBRARY □ Bangor, ME

Fennewald, Joe, Circ.
KANSAS CITY ART INSTITUTE - LIBRARY □
Kansas City, MO

Fenske, Dr. David, Hd.Libn.
INDIANA UNIVERSITY - MUSIC LIBRARY □
Bloomington, IN

Fensom, Jean, Libn.
MC GILL UNIVERSITY - DENTISTRY LIBRARY □
Montreal, PQ

Fenster, Madeleine, Libn.
NEW YORK COUNTY - DISTRICT ATTORNEY'S
OFFICE LIBRARY □ New York, NY

Fenstermann, Duane, Acq.Libn.
LUTHER COLLEGE - PREUS LIBRARY □ Decorah,
IA

Fenton, Miss E.A.
CANADIAN TELEPHONE EMPLOYEES'
ASSOCIATION - LIBRARY □ Montreal, PQ

Fenton, Irene, Saltfleet Supv.
MOHAWK COLLEGE OF APPLIED ARTS AND
TECHNOLOGY - MOHAWK LIBRARY RESOURCE
CENTRE □ Hamilton, ON

Fenton, Mary Francis, Graphic Cons.
WESTERN MICHIGAN UNIVERSITY -
EDUCATIONAL RESOURCES CENTER □
Kalamazoo, MI

Fenton, N.A., Asst.Libn.
ECONOMICS LABORATORY, INC. - CORPORATE
INFORMATION CENTER □ St. Paul, MN

Fenton, Pat, Ref.Libn.
MINNESOTA STATE DEPARTMENT OF
EDUCATION - INTERAGENCY RESOURCE AND
INFORMATION CENTER □ St. Paul, MN

Ferber, Susan, Libn.
DISTILLED SPIRITS COUNCIL OF THE U.S.,
INC. - LIBRARY □ Washington, DC

Ferdinand, Miss I., Libn.
GEORGE BROWN COLLEGE OF APPLIED ARTS &
TECHNOLOGY - LIBRARY □ Toronto, ON

Ferenczy, Eleanora, Regional Libn.
CANADA - HEALTH AND WELFARE CANADA -
HEALTH PROTECTION BRANCH - REGIONAL
LIBRARY □ Longueuil, PQ

Ferens, Mariley, Libn.
U.S. GENERAL SERVICES ADMINISTRATION -
NORTHWEST FEDERAL REGIONAL COUNCIL -
LIBRARY □ Seattle, WA

Ferestad, Virginia, Hd.Libn.
CAMPBELL-MITHUN, INC. - LIBRARY □
Minneapolis, MN

Feret, Ronald E.
POPE, BALLARD, SHEPARD AND FOWLE -
LIBRARY □ Chicago, IL

Fergason, Dorinda, Fire Info.Spec.
NATIONAL FIRE PROTECTION ASSOCIATION -
CHARLES S. MORGAN LIBRARY □ Quincy, MA

Fergenson, Ruth, Libn.
WORLD ZIONIST ORGANIZATION - AMERICAN
SECTION - ZIONIST ARCHIVES AND LIBRARY □
New York, NY

Fergusan, Sarah Caroline, Hd.Libn.
UNIVERSITY OF FLORIDA - P.K. YONGE
LABORATORY SCHOOL - MEAD LIBRARY □
Gainesville, FL

Ferguson, C.T., Asst.Sec.
INTERNATIONAL JOINT COMMISSION -
LIBRARY □ Ottawa, ON

Ferguson, Connie, Libn.
BLUE CROSS OF WESTERN PENNSYLVANIA -
IN-HOUSE BUSINESS LIBRARY □ Pittsburgh, PA

Ferguson, Diane A., Libn.
U.S. ARMS CONTROL AND DISARMAMENT
AGENCY - LIBRARY □ Washington, DC

Ferguson, Earle, Cat.
UNIVERSITY OF MANITOBA - LAW LIBRARY □
Winnipeg, MB

Ferguson, Elizabeth E., Ref.Libn.
YALE UNIVERSITY - KLINE SCIENCE LIBRARY □
New Haven, CT

Ferguson, Emilia, Asst.Libn.
HOFFMANN-LA ROCHE, INC. - BUSINESS
INFORMATION CENTER □ Nutley, NJ

Ferguson, J. Ray, Assoc. Law Libn.
WASHINGTON UNIVERSITY - SCHOOL OF LAW
- FREUND LAW LIBRARY □ St. Louis, MO

Ferguson, Dr. John L., State Hist.
ARKANSAS STATE HISTORY COMMISSION -
ARCHIVES □ Little Rock, AR

Ferguson, John Philip, Dept.Hd.
CLEVELAND PUBLIC LIBRARY - POPULAR
LIBRARY DEPARTMENT □ Cleveland, OH

Ferguson, Lynn, Tech.Serv.
VANCOUVER SCHOOL OF THEOLOGY - LIBRARY
□ Vancouver, BC

Ferguson, Margaret, Talking Bks.Serv.
METROPOLITAN TORONTO LIBRARY - AUDIO
VISUAL SERVICES □ Toronto, ON

Ferguson, Patricia, Libn.
BENDIX CORPORATION - BENDIX AVIONICS
DIVISION - LIBRARY □ Fort Lauderdale, FL

Ferguson, Patricia, Pres.
DOCUMENTATION ASSOCIATES† □ Los Angeles,
CA

Ferguson, Paul F., Dir.
ST. MARY'S UNIVERSITY - LAW LIBRARY □ San
Antonio, TX

Ferguson, Sara, Libn.
UPDATA PUBLICATIONS, INC. - LIBRARY □ Los
Angeles, CA

Ferguson, Stanley, Spec.Proj.Libn.
UNIVERSITY OF TEXAS SCHOOL OF LAW -
TARLTON LAW LIBRARY □ Austin, TX

Ferguson, Stephen, Cur. of Rare Books
PRINCETON UNIVERSITY - RARE BOOKS AND
SPECIAL COLLECTIONS □ Princeton, NJ

Ferguson, Van, Proc.Archv.
ROSENBERG LIBRARY - ARCHIVES
DEPARTMENT □ Galveston, TX

Ferimer, Suzanne, Dir., Lrng.Rsrcs.
UNIVERSITY OF HOUSTON - COLLEGE OF
OPTOMETRY LIBRARY □ Houston, TX

Ferkull, Marion, Hd., Philosophy/Relg.Sect
CHICAGO PUBLIC LIBRARY CENTRAL LIBRARY -
SOCIAL SCIENCES & HISTORY DIVISION □
Chicago, IL

Ferland, Ronald J., Libn.
U.S. AIR FORCE BASE - BARKSDALE BASE
LIBRARY □ Barksdale AFB, LA

Fernandes, Y., Sec.
ONTARIO - LAND COMPENSATION BOARD -
LIBRARY† □ Toronto, ON

Fernandez, Nenita A., Cat.Libn.
YALE UNIVERSITY - ECONOMIC GROWTH
CENTER COLLECTION □ New Haven, CT

Fernandez, Olga M., Libn.
INTER-AMERICAN DEFENSE BOARD -
LIBRARY† □ Washington, DC

Fernandez, Raul P., Asst.Dir.
U.S. MARINE CORPS - CAMP PENDLETON
LIBRARY SYSTEM† □ Camp Pendleton, CA

Ferng, Hou Ran, Libn.
ST. JOHN'S UNIVERSITY - ASIAN COLLECTION
□ Jamaica, NY

Ferrall, Rebecca, Libn.
U.S. DEPT. OF JUSTICE - FEDERAL BUREAU OF
INVESTIGATION - F.B.I. ACADEMY - LEARNING
RESOURCE CENTER □ Quantico, VA

Ferrara, Mark M., Assoc.Dir.
KEAN COLLEGE OF NEW JERSEY - NANCY
THOMPSON LIBRARY □ Union, NJ

Ferree, G. Donald, Asst.Dir.Survey Res.
UNIVERSITY OF CONNECTICUT - INSTITUTE
FOR SOCIAL INQUIRY □ Storrs, CT

Ferrell, Mrs. Bernie, Libn.
ST. LOUIS MUNICIPAL MEDICAL LIBRARY -
CITY HOSPITAL 1 □ St. Louis, MO

Ferrell, Miss Jan, Ser.Acq.Supv.
FORD FOUNDATION - LIBRARY □ New York, NY

Ferrell, Patrice, Pk. Ranger
U.S. NATL. PARK SERVICE - RICHMOND NATL.
BATTLEFIELD PARK - LIBRARY □ Richmond, VA

Ferrell, Robert, Techn.
P.T. BOATS, INC. - LIBRARY, ARCHIVES &
TECHNICAL INFORMATION CENTER -
NATIONAL HEADQUARTERS □ Memphis, TN

Ferrer, Aida, Asst.Libn.
AMERICAN KENNEL CLUB - LIBRARY □ New
York, NY

Ferrerio, Joan, Libn.
O'CONNOR, CAVANAGH, ANDERSON,
WESTOVER, KILLINGSWORTH, BESHEARS -
LAW LIBRARY □ Phoenix, AZ

Ferrero, Carol, Foreign Lang.Spec.
DETROIT PUBLIC LIBRARY - FOREIGN
LANGUAGE COLLECTION □ Detroit, MI

Ferrier, Robert C., AV Spec.
IOWA STATE DEPARTMENT OF SOCIAL
SERVICES - LIBRARY □ Des Moines, IA

Ferriero, David S., Libn.
MASSACHUSETTS INSTITUTE OF TECHNOLOGY
- HUMANITIES LIBRARY □ Cambridge, MA

Ferrin, Paul, Libn.
MONSANTO COMPANY - RUBBER CHEMICALS
RESEARCH LIBRARY □ Akron, OH

Ferris, Bill, Dir.
CENTER FOR SOUTHERN FOLKLORE -
ARCHIVES □ Memphis, TN

Ferris, Patricia, Info.Spec.
NET ENERGY - ALTERNATIVE ENERGY LIBRARY
□ Arcata, CA

Ferris, S.E.
BRITISH COLUMBIA - MINISTRY OF ENERGY,
MINES AND PETROLEUM RESOURCES -
LIBRARY □ Victoria, BC

Ferry, Sheila, Ref.Coord.
BRITISH COLUMBIA INSTITUTE OF
TECHNOLOGY - LIBRARY SERVICES DIVISION
□ Burnaby, BC

Feryszka, Ida, Rd.Adv./Sci.Tech.
TRENTON STATE COLLEGE - ROSCOE L. WEST
LIBRARY □ Trenton, NJ

Feseler, Gene, AV Techn.
MANSFIELD STATE COLLEGE - AUDIOVISUAL
CENTER □ Mansfield, PA

Fesenmaier, Frani, Asst.Hd.
WEST VIRGINIA STATE LIBRARY COMMISSION
- FILM SERVICES DEPARTMENT □ Charleston,
WV

Fesenmaier, Steve, Film Libn.
WEST VIRGINIA STATE LIBRARY COMMISSION
- FILM SERVICES DEPARTMENT □ Charleston,
WV

Fessenden, Ann T., Tech.Serv.Libn.
UNIVERSITY OF MISSISSIPPI - SCHOOL OF
LAW LIBRARY □ University, MS

Fessenden, Jane, Libn.
MARINE BIOLOGICAL LABORATORY - LIBRARY
□ Woods Hole, MA

Festa, Daniel K., Circ.Libn.
UNIVERSITY OF SOUTH CAROLINA - SCHOOL
OF MEDICINE LIBRARY □ Columbia, SC

Fetherston, Lynn, Tech.Serv.
NEW BRUNSWICK THEOLOGICAL SEMINARY -
GARDNER A. SAGE LIBRARY □ New Brunswick,
NJ

Fetkovich, Malinda, Dir.
SHADYSIDE HOSPITAL - JAMES FRAZER
HILLMAN HEALTH SCIENCES LIBRARY □
Pittsburgh, PA

Fetterer, Rev. Raymond A., Libn. Emeritus
ST. FRANCIS SEMINARY - SALZMANN LIBRARY
□ Milwaukee, WI

Fetters, Linda K.
TEXAS MEDICAL ASSOCIATION - MEMORIAL
LIBRARY □ Austin, TX

Feuer, Sylvia, Extramural Coord.
CLEVELAND HEALTH SCIENCES LIBRARY -
ALLEN MEMORIAL LIBRARY □ Cleveland, OH

Few, Heather, Tech.Serv.
FLORIDA INSTITUTE OF TECHNOLOGY -
SCHOOL OF APPLIED TECHNOLOGY - LIBRARY □
Jensen Beach, FL

Few, John E., Libn.
HASSARD, BONNINGTON, ROGERS & HUBER -
LIBRARY □ San Francisco, CA

Fewell, Paulette C., Dir. of Info./Ed.
TENNESSEE STATE DEPARTMENT OF
AGRICULTURE - LOU WALLACE LIBRARY □
Nashville, TN

Fiasconaro, Jane, Libn.
HEWLETT-PACKARD COMPANY - DESKTOP
COMPUTER DIVISION - FORT COLLINS
FACILITY LIBRARY □ Fort Collins, CO

Fichtelberg, Doris, Supv.Libn., Music
FREE PUBLIC LIBRARY OF ELIZABETH, NJ - ART
AND MUSIC DEPARTMENT □ Elizabeth, NJ

Fichtenau, Lane E., Asst.Libn.
ADAMS-PRATT OAKLAND COUNTY LAW
LIBRARY □ Pontiac, MI

Fick, Barry W., Legal Techn., Libn.
MINNESOTA STATE DEPARTMENT OF REVENUE
- TAX LIBRARY □ St. Paul MN

Fick, Earl, Supv., Spec.Oper.
AUTOMATION INDUSTRIES, INC. - VITRO
LABORATORIES DIVISION - ADMINISTRATIVE
SUPPORT DEPARTMENT □ Silver Spring, MD

Fidelia, Sr. M., Med.Libn.
HOLY CROSS HOSPITAL - MEDICAL LIBRARY □
Salt Lake City, UT

Fidler, Linda M., Libn., Rd.Serv.
OBERLIN COLLEGE - CONSERVATORY OF
MUSIC - MARY M. VIAL MUSIC LIBRARY □
Oberlin, OH

Fieandt, Jayne, Asst. II
WICHITA PUBLIC LIBRARY - BUSINESS AND
TECHNOLOGY DIVISION □ Wichita, KS

Fiedler, Christine, Ref.
MUHLENBERG COLLEGE - JOHN A.W. HAAS
LIBRARY □ Allentown, PA

Fiedler, Grace, Asst.Libn.
ASCENSION LUTHERAN CHURCH - LIBRARY □
Milwaukee, WI

Fiedler, Katherine, Libn.
OWENSBORO MESSENGER-INQUIRER -
LIBRARY □ Owensboro, KY

Fiegelson, Amy, Acq.Techn.
NATIONAL COLLEGE - THOMAS JEFFERSON
LIBRARY □ Rapid City, SD

Field, Charles L., Asst. Law Libn.
NORTHEASTERN UNIVERSITY - LAW SCHOOL
LIBRARY □ Boston, MA

Field, Constance N., Asst. Music Libn.
NORTHWESTERN UNIVERSITY - MUSIC
LIBRARY □ Evanston, IL

Field, Judith J., Hd., Gen.Ref.
FLINT PUBLIC LIBRARY - MICHIGAN ROOM □
Flint, MI

Field, Natalie, Volunteer Hist.
SHARP (Ella) MUSEUM - LIBRARY □ Jackson, MI

Field, Whitney K., Circ.Supv.
UNIVERSITY OF MICHIGAN - ALFRED
TAUBMAN MEDICAL LIBRARY □ Ann Arbor, MI

Fielden, Alma Hall, Adm.Asst., Med. Staff
ST. ANTHONY HOSPITAL - MEDICAL LIBRARY □
Louisville, KY

Fielden, Marjorie M., Libn.
LIFE PLANNING/HEALTH SERVICES -
LIBRARY/MEDIA SERVICES □ Dallas, TX

Fieldhouse, Richard, Res.Libn.
FUND FOR PEACE - CENTER FOR DEFENSE
INFORMATION □ Washington, DC

Fields, Charles, AV Asst.
FIRST BAPTIST CHURCH - I.C. ANDERSON
LIBRARY □ Waco, TX

Fields, Patti, Cat.Libn.
MEDICAL UNIVERSITY OF SOUTH CAROLINA -
LIBRARY □ Charleston, SC

Fierke, Susan, Info.Spec.
UPJOHN COMPANY - CORPORATE TECHNICAL
LIBRARY □ Kalamazoo, MI

Fife, Dr. Jonathan D., Dir.
ERIC CLEARINGHOUSE ON HIGHER EDUCATION
□ Washington, DC

Fife, Sharon, Libn.
METROPOLITAN TORONTO LIBRARY - GENERAL
REFERENCE DEPARTMENT □ Toronto, ON

Fifer, Susan, Asst.Libn./Circ.Libn.
NATIONAL GEOGRAPHIC SOCIETY - LIBRARY □
Washington, DC

Figa, Dr. Felicia, Archv.
YIVO INSTITUTE FOR JEWISH RESEARCH -
LIBRARY AND ARCHIVES □ New York, NY

Figatner, Annette, Per.
KENNEDY-KING COLLEGE - LIBRARY □ Chicago,
IL

Figol, B., Lib.Mgr.
SPERRY UNIVAC COMPUTER SYSTEMS -
LIBRARY □ Mississauga, ON

Figueredo, Olga, Per.Libn.
FLORIDA INSTITUTE OF TECHNOLOGY -
SCHOOL OF APPLIED TECHNOLOGY - LIBRARY □
Jensen Beach, FL

Fike, Claude E., Dir.
UNIVERSITY OF SOUTHERN MISSISSIPPI - MC
CAIN LIBRARY □ Hattiesburg, MS

Fikes, Ann, Commun.Mgr.
NATIONAL COLLEGE OF DISTRICT ATTORNEYS
- RESOURCE CENTER □ Houston, TX

Filion, Dr. Paul-Emile, Dir. of Libs.
CONCORDIA UNIVERSITY - SIR GEORGE
WILLIAMS CAMPUS - NORRIS LIBRARY □
Montreal, PQ

Filipkowski, Mrs. J., Hd.Tech.Serv.
CANADA - HEALTH AND WELFARE CANADA -
DEPARTMENTAL LIBRARY SERVICES □ Ottawa,
ON

Filstrup, E. Christian, Hd.Libn.
CENTER FOR MODERN PSYCHOANALYTIC
STUDIES - LIBRARY □ New York, NY

Filstrup, E. Christian, Div.Chf.
NEW YORK PUBLIC LIBRARY - ORIENTAL
DIVISION □ New York, NY

Filupeit, Susan M., Tech.Proc.Libn.
MYSTIC SEAPORT, INC. - G.W. BLUNT WHITE
LIBRARY □ Mystic, CT

Finch, Jean L., Res. & Dev. Libn.
LEWIS AND CLARK LAW SCHOOL -
NORTHWESTERN SCHOOL OF LAW - PAUL L.
BOLEY LAW LIBRARY □ Portland, OR

Finch, Leroy, Sr. Metallurgist
ESCO CORP. - LIBRARY □ Portland, OR

Fincik, Virginia, Chf.
U.S. DEFENSE AUDIOVISUAL AGENCY -
ARLINGTON STILL PHOTO DEPOSITORY □
Arlington, VA

Findlay, Gail, Libn.
MEMPHIS STATE UNIVERSITY - PLANNING
LIBRARY □ Memphis, TN

Findlay, Dr. James, Professor of Hist.
UNIVERSITY OF RHODE ISLAND - RHODE
ISLAND ORAL HISTORY PROJECT □ Kingston, RI

Findlay, Stephen, Libn.I
MEMPHIS-SHELBY COUNTY PUBLIC LIBRARY
AND INFORMATION CENTER - MEMPHIS ROOM
COLLECTIONS □ Memphis, TN

Findley, Gail, Libn.
ST. JOSEPH HOSPITAL - HEALTH SCIENCE
LIBRARY □ Memphis, TN

Fine, Rabbi Arnold, Dir.
ASSOCIATED SYNAGOGUES OF
MASSACHUSETTS - LIBRARY □ Boston, MA

Fine, Jodie, Supv.
AMERICAN FEDERATION OF STATE, COUNTY
AND MUNICIPAL EMPLOYEES, AFL-CIO
(AFSCME) - INFORMATION CENTER □
Washington, DC

Finerly, Michele, Asst.Libn.
UNIVERSITY OF MISSOURI, KANSAS CITY -
LAW LIBRARY □ Kansas City, MO

Fingeret, Rose W., Chf.Libn.
U.S. VETERANS ADMINISTRATION (IL-Hines) -
MEDICAL LIBRARY □ Hines, IL

Fingerson, Ronald, Dean
UNIVERSITY OF WISCONSIN, WHITEWATER -
LIBRARY & LEARNING RESOURCES □
Whitewater, WI

Fingland, Geoffrey, Libn.
CHRISTIAN SCIENCE MONITOR - RESEARCH
LIBRARY □ Boston, MA

Fingold, Sydney, Libn.
HARVARD UNIVERSITY - NEW ENGLAND
REGIONAL PRIMATE RESEARCH CENTER -
LIBRARY □ Southborough, MA

Fink, Diana, Cat.
NORTH YORK PUBLIC LIBRARY - CANADIANA
COLLECTION □ Willowdale, ON

Fink, Eleanor E., Chf.
SMITHSONIAN INSTITUTION - NATL. MUSEUM
OF AMERICAN ART - OFFICE OF VISUAL
RSRCS. - SLIDE/PHOTOGRAPH ARCHIVE □
Washington, DC

Fink, Myron, Libn.
UNIVERSITY OF NEW MEXICO - SCHOOL OF
LAW LIBRARY □ Albuquerque, NM

Finkbiner, Earle P., Libn.
NATIONAL RAILWAY HISTORICAL SOCIETY -
LIBRARY OF AMERICAN TRANSPORTATION □
Jobstown, NJ

Finkel, Gertrude, Libn.
WORLD ZIONIST ORGANIZATION - AMERICAN
SECTION - ZIONIST ARCHIVES AND LIBRARY □
New York, NY

Finkel, Kenneth, Cur., Prints/Photog.
LIBRARY COMPANY OF PHILADELPHIA □
Philadelphia, PA

Finkel, Susan, Cur.
HISTORIC BETHLEHEM INC. - LIBRARY/
ARCHIVES □ Bethlehem, PA

Finkelpearl, Katherine D., Art Libn.
WELLESLEY COLLEGE - ART LIBRARY □
Wellesley, MA

Finlay, Rev. D.F., Libn.
UNIVERSITY OF TORONTO - PONTIFICAL
INSTITUTE OF MEDIAEVAL STUDIES - LIBRARY
□ Toronto, ON

PERSONNEL

Finlay, Sr. M. Catherine, CCVI, Dir.
ST. JOSEPH HOSPITAL - HOSPITAL HEALTH
SCIENCE LIBRARY □ Houston, TX
Finlayson, Janet, Hd.Libn.
MC GILL UNIVERSITY - MACDONALD COLLEGE
- LIBRARY □ Ste. Anne De Bellevue, PQ
Finlayson, Mary S., Libn.
SCIENCE MUSEUM OF MINNESOTA - LOUIS S.
HEADLEY MEMORIAL LIBRARY □ St. Paul, MN
Finley, John, Ref.Biblog.
MISSOURI STATE LIBRARY □ Jefferson City,
MO
Finn, Barbara L., Dir. of Med.Lib.
SINAI HOSPITAL OF DETROIT - SAMUEL FRANK
MEDICAL LIBRARY □ Detroit, MI
Finnan, Anne M., Ref.Libn.
FORDHAM UNIVERSITY - LIBRARY AT LINCOLN
CENTER □ New York, NY
Finnegan, Catherine, Law Libn.
NEVADA STATE SUPREME COURT - LIBRARY □
Carson City, NV
Finnegan, Nancy, Ref.Libn.
COLUMBUS TECHNICAL INSTITUTE -
EDUCATIONAL RESOURCES CENTER† □
Columbus, OH
Finnegan, Nancy, Pub.Serv.Spec.
OCLC, INC. - LIBRARY □ Dublin, OH
Finnemore, Alison, Libn.
PULP AND PAPER RESEARCH INSTITUTE OF
CANADA - LIBRARY □ Pointe Claire, PQ
Finney, Ann, Educ.Dir.
MARION COUNTY MEMORIAL HOSPITAL -
LIBRARY □ Marion, SC
Finster, Eileen E., Libn.
PITTSBURGH PRESS - LIBRARY □ Pittsburgh, PA
Fiore, Jannette, Libn.
MICHIGAN STATE UNIVERSITY - SPECIAL
COLLECTIONS DIVISION □ East Lansing, MI
Fiore, Jannette, Libn.
MICHIGAN STATE UNIVERSITY - SPECIAL
COLLECTIONS DIVISION - RUSSEL B. NYE
POPULAR CULTURE COLLECTION □ East
Lansing, MI
Fiorillo, Gina
BRITISH COLUMBIA - MINISTRY OF HUMAN
RESOURCES - LIBRARY† □ Vancouver, BC
Firestone, Sharon, Govt.Doc.Libn.
ARIZONA STATE UNIVERSITY - COLLEGE OF
LAW - LIBRARY □ Tempe, AZ
Firm, Christine K., Libn.
JEFFERSON COUNTY LAW LIBRARY □
Steubenville, OH
Firth, Edith G., Hd.
METROPOLITAN TORONTO LIBRARY -
CANADIAN HISTORY DEPARTMENT □ Toronto,
ON
Firth, Margaret A., Libn.
BEVERLY HOSPITAL - LIBRARY □ Beverly, MA
Fischer, Catherine, Libn.
COMBUSTION ENGINEERING, INC. - POWER
SYSTEMS GROUP LIBRARY SERVICES □
Windsor, CT
Fischer, Elizabeth, Libn.
AUDUBON HOSPITAL - MEDICAL LIBRARY □
Louisville, KY
Fischer, Howard E., Dir.
CENTER FOR NONPROFIT ORGANIZATION -
LIBRARY □ New York, NY
Fischer, James H., Sec.-Tres.
AMERICAN SOCIETY OF SUGAR BEET
TECHNOLOGISTS - LIBRARY □ Fort Collins, CO
Fischer, Norma L., Libn.
ST. JOHN UNITED CHURCH OF CHRIST -
LIBRARY □ Collinsville, IL
Fischer, P.E., Mgr., Tech.Info.Ctr.
CHEVRON RESEARCH COMPANY - TECHNICAL
INFORMATION CENTER □ Richmond, CA
Fischer, R.A., Sec.-Treas.
AMERICAN SOCIETY OF BAKERY ENGINEERS -
INFORMATION SERVICE AND LIBRARY† □
Chicago, IL

Fischier, Adrienne G., Libn.
HARVARD LIBRARY IN NEW YORK □ New York,
NY
Fischler, Barbara B., Hd., Pub.Serv.
INDIANA UNIVERSITY/PURDUE UNIVERSITY
AT INDIANAPOLIS - 38TH STREET CAMPUS
LIBRARY □ Indianapolis, IN
Fish, Arthur M., Doc.Libn.
UNIVERSITY OF WISCONSIN, STEVENS POINT
- JAMES H. ALBERTSON CENTER FOR
LEARNING RESOURCES □ Stevens Point, WI
Fish, James H., State Libn.
MASSACHUSETTS STATE LIBRARY □ Boston,
MA
Fish, Kaye M., Asst.Libn.
NORTON GALLERY AND SCHOOL OF ART -
LIBRARY □ West Palm Beach, FL
Fishe, Elizabeth A., Asst.Libn.
INSTITUTE OF LIVING - MEDICAL LIBRARY □
Hartford, CT
Fishel, Carolyn, Asst.Libn.
GLENDALE ADVENTIST MEDICAL CENTER -
LIBRARY □ Glendale, CA
Fishel, Leslie H., Jr., Dir.
HAYES (Rutherford B.) PRESIDENTIAL CENTER -
LIBRARY □ Fremont, OH
Fisher, Cynthia, Libn.
CANADIAN BROADCASTING CORPORATION -
TV CURRENT AFFAIRS LIBRARY □ Toronto, ON
Fisher, Elmer H., Supv., Info.Serv.
BABCOCK AND WILCOX COMPANY - RESEARCH
CENTER LIBRARY □ Alliance, OH
Fisher, Fran, Hd., Ser.Libn.
NORTH DAKOTA STATE UNIVERSITY - LIBRARY
□ Fargo, ND
Fisher, Frances, Hd., Ref. & Circ.Br.
U.S. NAVY - NAVAL WEAPONS CENTER -
LIBRARY DIVISION □ China Lake, CA
Fisher, George, Info.Asst./Libn.
AMERICAN COUNCIL OF VOLUNTARY
AGENCIES FOR FOREIGN SERVICE, INC. -
TECH. ASSISTANCE INFO. CLEARING HOUSE □
New York, NY
Fisher, George C., Hd.
ONTARIO - MINISTRY OF AGRICULTURE AND
FOOD - VETERINARY SERVICES LABORATORY
LIBRARY □ Kemptville, ON
Fisher, Dr. George W., Professor
JOHNS HOPKINS UNIVERSITY - DEPARTMENT
OF EARTH AND PLANETARY SCIENCES -
SINGEWALD READING ROOM □ Baltimore, MD
Fisher, Helen, Cons.Libn.
ST. THOMAS AQUINAS NEWMAN CENTER -
LIBRARY □ Albuquerque, NM
Fisher, Jane E.
BETHLEHEM STEEL CORPORATION - SCHWAB
MEMORIAL LIBRARY □ Bethlehem, PA
Fisher, Janet S., Asst. Dean
EAST TENNESSEE STATE UNIVERSITY,
QUILLEN-DISHNER COLLEGE OF MEDICINE -
DEPT. OF LEARNING RSRCS. - MEDICAL
LIBRARY □ Johnson City, TN
Fisher, Jean, Libn.
ARTHUR ANDERSEN & CO. - LIBRARY □ Boston,
MA
Fisher, Jocelyn, Lib.Dir.
BEYOND BAROQUE FOUNDATION - LIBRARY □
Venice, CA
Fisher, John M., Pres.
AMERICAN SECURITY COUNCIL EDUCATION
FOUNDATION - SOL FEINSTONE LIBRARY □
Boston, VA
Fisher, Kim, Hd., Hum.Div.
OKLAHOMA STATE UNIVERSITY - HUMANITIES
DIVISION □ Stillwater, OK
Fisher, Laura, Libn.
NEW YORK CITY COMMISSION ON HUMAN
RIGHTS - LIBRARY† □ New York, NY
Fisher, Lillian, Hd.Libn.
ALLEGHENY GENERAL HOSPITAL - MEDICAL
LIBRARY □ Pittsburgh, PA

Fisher, Patricia A., Asst.Dir., Pub.Serv.
UNIVERSITY OF DENVER - PENROSE LIBRARY □
Denver, CO
Fisher, Dr. Paul L., Dir.
UNIVERSITY OF MISSOURI - FREEDOM OF
INFORMATION CENTER □ Columbia, MO
Fisher, Perry G., Exec.Dir./Libn.
COLUMBIA HISTORICAL SOCIETY - LIBRARY □
Washington, DC
Fisher, William H., Hd.Libn.
WESTERN ELECTRIC COMPANY, INC. -
ENGINEERING RESEARCH CENTER -
TECHNICAL LIBRARY □ Princeton, NJ
Fisher-Fleming, Shirley D., Educ. Media Coord.
LANGLEY SCHOOL DISTRICT - RESOURCE
CENTRE □ Langley, BC
Fishman, Joel, Law Libn.
ALLEGHENY COUNTY LAW LIBRARY □
Pittsburgh, PA
Fishman, Michael J., Libn.
PACIFIC BIO-MARINE LABORATORIES, INC. -
LIBRARY □ Venice, CA
Fisk, Linda Fuerle, Libn.
BERKS COUNTY LAW LIBRARY □ Reading, PA
Fiske, Arthur W., Libn.
CLEVELAND LAW LIBRARY □ Cleveland, OH
Fisken, Patricia B., Spec.Subj.Asst.
DARTMOUTH COLLEGE - PADDOCK MUSIC
LIBRARY □ Hanover, NH
Fisler, Charlotte D., Libn.
ATLAS POWDER COMPANY - RESEARCH &
DEVELOPMENT LABORATORY - LIBRARY □
Tamaqua, PA
Fistrovic, Olivija, Med.Libn.
HOLY CROSS HOSPITAL - HEALTH SCIENCE
LIBRARY □ Chicago, IL
Fitak, Madge, Geologist
OHIO STATE DIVISION OF GEOLOGICAL
SURVEY - LIBRARY □ Columbus, OH
Fitch, Ann, Libn.
FIRST BAPTIST CHURCH - LIBRARY □ St. Paul,
MN
Fitt, Dr. Stephen D., Chm.
SAN DIEGO STATE UNIVERSITY - MEDIA &
CURRICULUM CENTER □ San Diego, CA
Fitting, Carol
HARTFORD PUBLIC LIBRARY - REFERENCE AND
GENERAL READING DEPARTMENT □ Hartford,
CT
Fitz Gerald, Sr. Constance, Archv.
CARMELITE MONASTERY - LIBRARY AND
ARCHIVES □ Baltimore, MD
Fitz Simmons, Eileen, Libn.
JESUIT SCHOOL OF THEOLOGY IN CHICAGO -
LIBRARY □ Chicago, IL
Fitzgerald, Carol, Soc.Sci.Ref.Libn.
CUNY - GRADUATE SCHOOL AND UNIVERSITY
CENTER - LIBRARY □ New York, NY
Fitzgerald, Catherine, Cat.
BOSTON COLLEGE - LAW SCHOOL LIBRARY □
Newton Centre, MA
Fitzgerald, Dorothy, Libn.
COLLEGE OF FAMILY PHYSICIANS OF CANADA -
CANADIAN LIBRARY OF FAMILY MEDICINE □
London, ON
Fitzgerald, Greg, Hd.Libn.
WESTERN MICHIGAN UNIVERSITY - MUSIC
LIBRARY □ Kalamazoo, MI
Fitzgerald, John, Asst.Libn.
HUGHES, HUBBARD, AND REED - LIBRARY □
New York, NY
FitzGerald, May, Libn.
WHITNEY MUSEUM OF AMERICAN ART -
LIBRARY □ New York, NY
Fitzgerald, Sandra, Hd.Libn.
INDIANAPOLIS NEWSPAPERS, INC. -
INDIANAPOLIS STAR AND INDIANAPOLIS
NEWS - REFERENCE LIBRARY □ Indianapolis, IN
FitzGerald, Sharron A., Dir., Tech.Serv.
U.S. SUPREME COURT - LIBRARY □ Washington,
DC

Fitzpatrick, Annette
NEW ZEALAND EMBASSY - LIBRARY □
Washington, DC
Fitzpatrick, Constance, Ref.Libn.
UNIVERSITY OF BRITISH COLUMBIA -
GOVERNMENT PUBLICATIONS & MICROFORMS
DIVISIONS □ Vancouver, BC
Fitzpatrick, Lois A., Dir.
CARROLL COLLEGE - LIBRARY □ Helena, MT
Fitzpatrick, M. Elaine, Libn.
C-I-L PAINTS INC. - PAINT RESEARCH
LABORATORY LIBRARY □ Toronto, ON
Fitzpatrick, Maureen, Gen.Serv.Mgr.
AMERICAN CAN COMPANY - BUTTERICK
FASHION MARKETING COMPANY - BUTTERICK
ARCHIVES/LIBRARY† □ New York, NY
Fitzpatrick, Roberta, Asst.Libn.
FLORIDA INSTITUTE OF TECHNOLOGY -
SCHOOL OF APPLIED TECHNOLOGY - LIBRARY □
Jensen Beach, FL
FitzPatrick, Terence, Libn.
SAN FRANCISCO EXAMINER - LIBRARY □ San
Francisco, CA
Fitzpayne, Elizabeth, Sr.Rd.Serv.Libn.
BRANDEIS UNIVERSITY - GERSTENZANG
SCIENCE LIBRARY □ Waltham, MA
Fitzsimmons, Joseph J., Pres.
XEROX CORPORATION - UNIVERSITY
MICROFILMS INTERNATIONAL - LIBRARY† □
Ann Arbor, MI
Flagg, Lucy, Sr.Libn.
CALIFORNIA STATE DEPARTMENT OF
DEVELOPMENTAL SERVICES - PROFESSIONAL
LIBRARY □ San Jose, CA
Flaherty, Barbara, Asst.Libn./Acq.
GEORGE MASON UNIVERSITY - SCHOOL OF
LAW - LIBRARY† □ Arlington, VA
Flaherty, Ellen, Asst.Chf.
DISTRICT OF COLUMBIA PUBLIC LIBRARY -
PHILOSOPHY, PSYCHOLOGY AND RELIGION
DIVISION □ Washington, DC
Flaherty, Shelagh, Libn.
VANCOUVER PUBLIC LIBRARY - BUSINESS &
ECONOMICS DIVISION □ Vancouver, BC
Flahiff, Sr. Margaret, Per.Libn.
ATLANTIC SCHOOL OF THEOLOGY - LIBRARY □
Halifax, NS
Flake, Chad, Cur.
BRIGHAM YOUNG UNIVERSITY - SPECIAL
COLLECTIONS □ Provo, UT
Flake, Mary E., Asst.Libn.
WHITE MEMORIAL MEDICAL CENTER -
COURVILLE-ABBOTT MEMORIAL LIBRARY □ Los
Angeles, CA
Flanagan, Ann B., Libn.
VIRGINIA ELECTRIC & POWER COMPANY -
LIBRARY □ Richmond, VA
Flanagan, Margaret, Libn.
EPISCOPAL HOSPITAL - MEDICAL LIBRARY □
Philadelphia, PA
Flanagan, Maureen D., Libn.
UNION CARBIDE CORPORATION - I.S.
INFORMATION CENTER □ Tarrytown, NY
Flannery, Louis, Chf.Libn.
OREGON HISTORICAL SOCIETY - LIBRARY □
Portland, OR
Flannery, Mary R., Supv.Libn., Rep.
U.S. AIR FORCE WEAPONS LABORATORY -
TECHNICAL LIBRARY □ Kirtland AFB, NM
Flath, Clara, Cat.
SOUTHERN CONNECTICUT STATE COLLEGE -
H.C. BULEY LIBRARY □ New Haven, CT
Flautz, Nan, Acq.
MUHLENBERG COLLEGE - JOHN A.W. HAAS
LIBRARY □ Allentown, PA
Flavin, Linda M., Hd.Cat.
MEDICAL COLLEGE OF GEORGIA - LIBRARY □
Augusta, GA
Flavin, Patricia A., Libn.
LONG ISLAND HISTORICAL SOCIETY - LIBRARY
□ Brooklyn, NY

Flax, Carol, Rsrcs,Ctr.Dir.
LOS ANGELES CENTER FOR PHOTOGRAPHIC
STUDIES - LIBRARY □ Los Angeles, CA
Flaxman, Dr. Erwin, Dir.
ERIC CLEARINGHOUSE ON URBAN EDUCATION
□ New York, NY
Fleckner, Maxine, Film Archv.
UNIVERSITY OF WISCONSIN, MADISON -
WISCONSIN CENTER FOR FILM AND THEATER
RESEARCH □ Madison, WI
Fledderus, Helen, Libn.
READER'S DIGEST - ADVERTISING AND
MARKETING LIBRARY □ New York, NY
Fleekner, John A., Coord.Res.Ctr.
STATE HISTORICAL SOCIETY OF WISCONSIN -
ARCHIVES DIVISION □ Madison, WI
Fleenor, Elisabeth J., Chf., Cat.Br.
U.S. AIR FORCE ACADEMY - LIBRARY □ U.S. Air
Force Academy, CO
Fleharty, Janet L., Media Spec.
COLORADO SCHOOL FOR THE DEAF AND THE
BLIND - MEDIA CENTER □ Colorado Springs, CO
Fleischer, Mary Beth, Asst.Libn.
UNIVERSITY OF TEXAS, AUSTIN - EUGENE C.
BARKER TEXAS HISTORY CENTER □ Austin, TX
Fleischhauer, Carl, Media Spec.
LIBRARY OF CONGRESS - AMERICAN FOLKLIFE
CENTER □ Washington, DC
Fleisher, Mary-Louise, Libn.
WOLF, BLOCK, SCHORR & SOLIS-COHEN -
LIBRARY† □ Philadelphia, PA
Fleming, Darlene, Sci.Libn.
ALCON LABORATORIES, INC. - RESEARCH &
DEVELOPMENT LIBRARY □ Fort Worth, TX
Fleming, Gail, Assoc.Libn.
UNIVERSITY OF CALIFORNIA, SAN FRANCISCO
- HASTINGS COLLEGE OF THE LAW - LEGAL
INFORMATION CENTER □ San Francisco, CA
Fleming, Herman, Rec./Rpt.Off.
NATIONAL SCIENCE FOUNDATION - LIBRARY □
Washington, DC
Fleming, John, Spec.Coll.Libn.
EDINBORO STATE COLLEGE - BARON-FORNESS
LIBRARY □ Edinboro, PA
Fleming, Paula J., Musm.Spec.
SMITHSONIAN INSTITUTION - NATIONAL
ANTHROPOLOGICAL ARCHIVES □ Washington,
DC
Fleming, Peter B., Chf., Lib.Serv.
U.S. VETERANS ADMINISTRATION (KS-Wichita)
- MEDICAL CENTER LIBRARY □ Wichita, KS
Fleming, Thomas, Chf., Law Br.
U.S. DEPT. OF COMMERCE - DEPARTMENTAL
LIBRARY □ Washington, DC
Flemister, Wilson N., Libn.
INTERDENOMINATIONAL THEOLOGICAL
CENTER - LIBRARY □ Atlanta, GA
Flemming, Tom, Hd. ILL
DALHOUSIE UNIVERSITY - W.K. KELLOGG
HEALTH SCIENCES LIBRARY □ Halifax, NS
Flener, Dr. Jane, Assoc.Dir., Pub.Serv.
UNIVERSITY OF MICHIGAN - LIBRARY
EXTENSION SERVICE □ Ann Arbor, MI
Flener, Jane G., Act.Hd.
UNIVERSITY OF MICHIGAN - DEPARTMENT OF
RARE BOOKS AND SPECIAL COLLECTIONS -
LIBRARY □ Ann Arbor, MI
Flesher, Ellen M., Libn.
TOPEKA STATE HOSPITAL - STAFF LIBRARY □
Topeka, KS
Flesher, Lorna J., Supv.Libn.
CALIFORNIA STATE DEPARTMENT OF
TRANSPORTATION - LAW LIBRARY □
Sacramento, CA
Fletcher, Herb, Libn.
ATOMIC ENERGY OF CANADA, LTD. -
COMMERCIAL PRODUCTS LIBRARY □ Ottawa,
ON
Fletcher, James R., Lib.Ck.
NORTHWEST GEORGIA REGIONAL HOSPITAL
AT ROME - MEDICAL LIBRARY □ Rome, GA

Fletcher, Joseph J., Ref.Libn.
NEW YORK UNIVERSITY - GRADUATE SCHOOL
OF BUSINESS ADMINISTRATION - LIBRARY □
New York, NY
Fletcher, Louise, Libn.
CANADA - NATIONAL RESEARCH COUNCIL -
CISTI - AERONAUTICAL & MECHANICAL
ENGINEERING BRANCH □ Ottawa, ON
Fletcher, Lyle, Archv.
WOOD COUNTY HISTORICAL SOCIETY -
HISTORICAL MUSEUM LIBRARY □ Bowling
Green, OH
Fletcher, Marjorie Amos, Dir.
AMERICAN COLLEGE - VANE B. LUCAS
MEMORIAL LIBRARY - ORAL HISTORY CENTER
& ARCHIVES □ Bryn Mawr, PA
Fletcher, P.A., Libn.
AMERICAN ALPINE CLUB - LIBRARY □ New
York, NY
Fletcher, R.M., Supv.
STEARNS-ROGER ENGINEERING
CORPORATION - TECHNICAL LIBRARY □
Denver, CO
Fletcher, Winston F., Res.Dir.
VICKERS & BENSON LTD. - RESOURCE CENTRE
□ Toronto, ON
Flewellen, Icabod, Dir.
AFRO-AMERICAN CULTURAL AND HISTORICAL
SOCIETY MUSEUM - LIBRARY† □ Cleveland, OH
Flexner, John, Acq.
HARWOOD FOUNDATION LIBRARY OF THE
UNIVERSITY OF NEW MEXICO □ Taos, NM
Flick, Roger C., Libn.
BRIGHAM YOUNG UNIVERSITY - UTAH VALLEY
BRANCH GENEALOGICAL LIBRARY □ Provo, UT
Flickinger, B. Floyd, Pres.
FLICKINGER FOUNDATION FOR AMERICAN
STUDIES, INC. - LIBRARY □ Baltimore, MD
Fling, M., Ref.Libn.
INDIANA UNIVERSITY - MUSIC LIBRARY □
Bloomington, IN
Flinn, Mary, Soc.Adm.
NORTH ANDOVER HISTORICAL SOCIETY -
LIBRARY □ North Andover, MA
Flint, J.G., Sec.
MINNESOTA STATE BOARD OF ANIMAL HEALTH
- LIBRARY □ St. Paul, MN
Flippin, Mrs. D.H., Chm.
AMELIA HISTORICAL LIBRARY - JACKSON
MEMORIAL LIBRARY □ Amelia, VA
Floerke, Sue, Consortium Coord.
MEMORIAL MEDICAL CENTER - HEALTH
SCIENCES LIBRARY □ Corpus Christi, TX
Flokstra, Gerard J., Jr., Libn.
CENTRAL BIBLE COLLEGE - LIBRARY □
Springfield, MO
Flood, Brian, Cat.
WILFRID LAURIER UNIVERSITY - LIBRARY □
Waterloo, ON
Flores, Clarita H., Libn.
AMERICAN CHEMICAL SOCIETY, INC. -
LIBRARY □ Washington, DC
Flores, Sr. Maria Carolina, CDP, Asst.Archv.
OUR LADY OF THE LAKE UNIVERSITY - OLD
SPANISH MISSIONS HISTORICAL RESEARCH
LIBRARY □ San Antonio, TX
Flores, Norman, Circ.Lib.
YESHIVA UNIVERSITY - ALBERT EINSTEIN
COLLEGE OF MEDICINE - D. SAMUEL
GOTTESMAN LIBRARY □ Bronx, NY
Flores, Santiago, Lib.Asst.
SAN DIEGO AERO-SPACE MUSEUM - N. PAUL
WHITTIER HISTORICAL AVIATION LIBRARY □
San Diego, CA
Florin, Carol C., Lib.Dir.
MITCHELL (William) COLLEGE OF LAW - JOHN B.
SANBORN LIBRARY □ St. Paul, MN
Florino, Joanne Volpe, Archv.
DEWITT HISTORICAL SOCIETY OF TOMPKINS
COUNTY - ARCHIVE/LIBRARY □ Ithaca, NY
Florio, Rosina A., Exec.Dir.
ART STUDENTS LEAGUE OF NEW YORK -
LIBRARY □ New York, NY

Flournoy, Donald B., Chf., Cartography
U.S. AIR FORCE - AIR UNIVERSITY - LIBRARY □
Maxwell AFB, AL

Flower, Eric S., Hd., Spec.Coll.
THOREAU FELLOWSHIP PAPERS† □ Orono, ME

Flower, Eric S., Dept.Hd.
UNIVERSITY OF MAINE, ORONO - RAYMOND H.
FOGLER LIBRARY - SPECIAL COLLECTIONS
DEPARTMENT† □ Orono, ME

Flower, Kenneth, Chf., Ref.Serv.
MASSACHUSETTS STATE LIBRARY □ Boston,
MA

Flower, Mrs. M.A., Libn.
MC GILL UNIVERSITY - NURSING LIBRARY □
Montreal, PQ

Flowers, Betty B., Acq.Libn.
NEW YORK UNIVERSITY MEDICAL CENTER -
FREDERICK L. EHRMAN MEDICAL LIBRARY □
New York, NY

Flowers, Kathryn, Libn.
ENVIRODYNE ENGINEERS, INC. - LIBRARY □ St.
Louis, MO

Fludd, Dorothy, Educ.Libn.
NEW YORK PUBLIC LIBRARY - MID-
MANHATTAN LIBRARY - GENERAL REFERENCE
SERVICE/EDUCATION □ New York, NY

Fludd, Marcella, ILL
ST. ELIZABETHS HOSPITAL - HEALTH
SCIENCES LIBRARY □ Washington, DC

Fluehr, Helen, Ref. & ILL Libn.
PIERCE JUNIOR COLLEGE - LIBRARY† □
Philadelphia, PA

Flukinger, Roy, Cur., Photog.
UNIVERSITY OF TEXAS, AUSTIN - HUMANITIES
RESEARCH CENTER □ Austin, TX

Flumiani, Dr. C.M., Dir.
AMERICAN CLASSICAL COLLEGE - LIBRARY □
Albuquerque, NM

Flumiani, Dr. C.M., Dir.
AMERICAN CLASSICAL COLLEGE - STOCK
MARKET LIBRARY □ Albuquerque, NM

Flynn, Barbara L., Hd.
CHICAGO PUBLIC LIBRARY CULTURAL CENTER
- AUDIOVISUAL CENTER □ Chicago, IL

Flynn, Debra, Asst.Mss.Libn.
INDIANA STATE LIBRARY - INDIANA DIVISION
□ Indianapolis, IN

Flynn, Elizabeth J., Mgr., Tech.Adm.
OLIN CORPORATION - FINE PAPER AND FILM
GROUP - TECHNICAL LIBRARY □ Pisgah Forest,
NC

Flynn, John C., Libn.
MOOSE LAKE STATE HOSPITAL - STAFF
LIBRARY □ Moose Lake, MN

Flynn, Kathleen M., Asst.Libn.
WESTERN NEW ENGLAND COLLEGE - SCHOOL
OF LAW LIBRARY □ Springfield, MA

Flynn, L., Tech.Info.Spec.
U.S. NATL. HIGHWAY TRAFFIC SAFETY
ADMINISTRATION - TECHNICAL REFERENCE
BRANCH □ Washington, DC

Flynn, Lauri R., Asst.Libn.
LEWIS AND CLARK LAW SCHOOL -
NORTHWESTERN SCHOOL OF LAW - PAUL L.
BOLEY LAW LIBRARY □ Portland, OR

Flynn, Lawrence E., Ck. of Courts
WISCONSIN STATE - RACINE COUNTY LAW
LIBRARY □ Racine, WI

Flynn, Libby, Hd., Tech.Serv.
GRADUATE THEOLOGICAL UNION - LIBRARY □
Berkeley, CA

Flynn, Maureen D., Libn.
U.S. POSTAL SERVICE - TRAINING &
DEVELOPMENT INSTITUTE - TECHNICAL
CENTER LIBRARY □ Norman, OK

Flynn, Patti, Med.Libn.
U.S. VETERANS ADMINISTRATION (CA-Long
Beach) - MEDICAL CENTER LIBRARY □ Long
Beach, CA

Flynn, Phyllis, Asst.Libn.
AMERICAN JEWISH COMMITTEE - BLAUSTEIN
LIBRARY □ New York, NY

Flynn, Richard M., Libn.
FOUNDATION OF THE FEDERAL BAR
ASSOCIATION - FEDERAL BAR FOUNDATION
LIBRARY □ Washington, DC

Flynn, Thomas, Dir.
NEW YORK STATE DEPARTMENT OF HEALTH -
DIVISION OF LABORATORIES AND RESEARCH
LIBRARY □ Albany, NY

Fodor, Elza O., Libn.
PUBLIC UTILITIES COMMISSION OF OHIO -
LIBRARY □ Columbus, OH

Fody, Barbara A., Hd.Libn.
PAINE WEBBER INC. - PAINE WEBBER BLYTH
EASTMAN - LIBRARY □ New York, NY

Foell, John F., Sr.Info.Spec.
CONOCO, INC. - RESEARCH AND
DEVELOPMENT DEPARTMENT - TECHNICAL
INFORMATION SERVICES □ Ponca City, OK

Foerstel, Herbert N., Hd.Libn.
UNIVERSITY OF MARYLAND, COLLEGE PARK -
LIBRARIES - ENGINEERING & PHYSICAL
SCIENCES LIBRARY □ College Park, MD

Fogarty, Catharine M., NJ Room Libn.
FAIRLEIGH DICKINSON UNIVERSITY -
MESSLER LIBRARY - NEW JERSEY ROOM □
Rutherford, NJ

Fogerty, James E., Dep. State Archv.
MINNESOTA HISTORICAL SOCIETY - DIVISION
OF ARCHIVES AND MANUSCRIPTS □ St. Paul,
MN

Fogg, Mrs. Donald, Curator
CHELMSFORD HISTORICAL SOCIETY -
BARRETT-BYAM HOMESTEAD LIBRARY □
Chelmsford, MA

Fogo, Eloise, Rd.Adv.
DISTRICT OF COLUMBIA PUBLIC LIBRARY -
SOCIOLOGY, GOVERNMENT & EDUCATION
DIVISION □ Washington, DC

Folen, Doris, Hd., Doc.Sect.
U.S. NAVY - NAVAL RESEARCH LABORATORY -
RUTH H. HOOKER TECHNICAL LIBRARY □
Washington, DC

Foley, Hila O., Libn.
CINCINNATI MUNICIPAL REFERENCE LIBRARY
□ Cincinnati, OH

Foley, Kathy, Chf.Libn.
HOUSTON POST - LIBRARY/INFORMATION
CENTER □ Houston, TX

Foley, Kenneth M., Chm.
CALAVERAS COUNTY LAW LIBRARY □ San
Andreas, CA

Foley, Marian, Off.Mgr.
INDIANA UNIVERSITY/PURDUE UNIVERSITY
AT INDIANAPOLIS - 38TH STREET CAMPUS
LIBRARY □ Indianapolis, IN

Foley, Marjorie A., Fld.Serv.
FLORIDA STATE DIVISION OF BLIND SERVICES
- FLORIDA REGIONAL LIB. FOR THE BLIND &
PHYSICALLY HANDICAPPED □ Daytona Beach,
FL

Foley, Mary Anne, Tech.Libn.
MOTOROLA, INC. - COMMUNICATION
PRODUCTS DIVISION - TECHNICAL LIBRARY □
Fort Lauderdale, FL

Foley, Nancy, Adult Serv.Libn.
SEATTLE PUBLIC LIBRARY - DOUGLASS-TRUTH
BRANCH LIBRARY □ Seattle, WA

Foley, Robert, ILL
FITCHBURG STATE COLLEGE - LIBRARY □
Fitchburg, MA

Foley, Sheila, Libn.
BRITISH COLUMBIA - COUNCIL OF FOREST
INDUSTRIES OF BRITISH COLUMBIA - LIBRARY
□ Vancouver, BC

Folk, Charlotte C., Libn.
ENVIRONMENTAL PROTECTION AGENCY -
ENVIRONMENTAL RESEARCH LABORATORY,
ATHENS - LIBRARY □ Athens, GA

Folke, Carolyn, Search Anl./Anl.
WISCONSIN STATE DEPARTMENT OF PUBLIC
INSTRUCTION - WISCONSIN DISSEMINATION
PROJECT (WDP) □ Madison, WI

Folkes, Tom, Health Sci.Libn.
MENTAL HEALTH INSTITUTE - HEALTH
SCIENCE LIBRARY □ Cherokee, IA

Folkestad, Patricia, Ser.Libn.
UNIVERSITY OF NORTH DAKOTA - OLAF H.
THORMODSGARD LAW LIBRARY □ Grand Forks,
ND

Folley, Patricia H., Bus.Libn.
UNIVERSITY OF IOWA - BUSINESS LIBRARY □
Iowa City, IA

Folmer, Jane, Dir.
COMMUNITY SERVICE, INC. - LIBRARY □
Yellow Springs, OH

Folter, Siegrun, Cat.
AMERICAN MUSIC CENTER - LIBRARY □ New
York, NY

Foltz, Faye, Hd., Ser.Sect.
WAKE FOREST UNIVERSITY - BOWMAN GRAY
SCHOOL OF MEDICINE - LIBRARY □ Winston-
Salem, NC

Foltz, Stephanie, Cur. of Educ.
CONFEDERATE MEMORIAL LITERARY SOCIETY
- MUSEUM OF THE CONFEDERACY - ELEANOR
S. BROCKENBROUGH LIBRARY □ Richmond, VA

Foltz, Susan, Libn.
GOOD SAMARITAN HOSPITAL - KROHN
MEMORIAL LIBRARY □ Lebanon, PA

Fones-Wolf, Kenneth, Asst.Cur.
TEMPLE UNIVERSITY - CENTRAL LIBRARY
SYSTEM - URBAN ARCHIVES □ Philadelphia, PA

Fonfa, Lynn, Asst.Archv.
CALIFORNIA HISTORICAL SOCIETY -
SCHUBERT HALL LIBRARY □ San Francisco, CA

Fong, Karina, Libn.
HUMBER COLLEGE OF APPLIED ARTS &
TECHNOLOGY - LIBRARY □ Rexdale, ON

Fong, Lawrence, Registrar
UNIVERSITY OF ARIZONA - CENTER FOR
CREATIVE PHOTOGRAPHY □ Tucson, AZ

Fontaine, Ronald G., Libn.
U.S. NATL. MARINE FISHERIES SERVICE -
MILFORD LABORATORY LIBRARY □ Milford, CT

Fontes, Geraldine I., Staff Serv.Anl.
CALIFORNIA STATE HEALTH & WELFARE
AGENCY DATA CENTER - TECHNICAL LIBRARY
UNIT □ Sacramento, CA

Fonvielle, Yvonne, Law Libn.
SOUTHERN UNIVERSITY - LAW SCHOOL
LIBRARY □ Baton Rouge, LA

Foohey, Mary Ann, Supv.Info.Proc.
AUTOMATION INDUSTRIES, INC. - VITRO
LABORATORIES DIVISION - ADMINISTRATIVE
SUPPORT DEPARTMENT □ Silver Spring, MD

Foote, J. Stevens, Ser.Cat.
EMORY UNIVERSITY - SCHOOL OF MEDICINE -
A.W. CALHOUN MEDICAL LIBRARY □ Atlanta,
GA

Foote, Martha, Asst.Libn.
CANADIAN INSTITUTE OF INTERNATIONAL
AFFAIRS - LIBRARY □ Toronto, ON

Footman, Annie B., Libn.
SIBLEY MEMORIAL HOSPITAL - MEDICAL
LIBRARY □ Washington, DC

Foran, Patricia, Libn.
SCIENCE CENTER OF PINELLAS - LIBRARY □ St.
Petersburg, FL

Forbes, Charles F., Hd.
UNIVERSITY OF BRITISH COLUMBIA -
HUMANITIES DIVISION □ Vancouver, BC

Forbes, Dr. John M., Dir. of Libs.
BAKER UNIVERSITY - QUAYLE RARE BIBLE
COLLECTION □ Baldwin City, KS

Forbes, Olive, Hd.Libn.
UNIVERSITY OF TEXAS, AUSTIN - LYNDON B.
JOHNSON SCHOOL OF PUBLIC AFFAIRS
LIBRARY □ Austin, TX

Forbes, Susan, West.Hist.Cat.
KANSAS STATE HISTORICAL SOCIETY -
LIBRARY □ Topeka, KS

Forbes, Zona Gale, Archv.
HISTORICAL SOCIETY OF LONG BEACH -
ARCHIVES □ Long Beach, CA

Force, Ronald, Asst.Dir.Pub.Serv.
WASHINGTON STATE UNIVERSITY - HOLLAND LIBRARY □ Pullman, WA

Forcht, Wanda, Libn.
WASHINGTON STATE SCHOOL FOR THE DEAF - LEARNING RESOURCE CENTER □ Vancouver, WA

Forcier, Ben R., Jr., Libn.
WALLA WALLA COUNTY LAW LIBRARY† □ Walla Walla, WA

Forcier, Lise, Chf.Tech.Serv.
CENTRE HOSPITALIER STE. JEANNE D'ARC - BIBLIOTHEQUE MEDICALE □ Montreal, PQ

Ford, Carolyn, Libn.
TUSKEGEE INSTITUTE - VETERINARY MEDICINE LIBRARY† □ Tuskegee Institute, AL

Ford, Constance, Chf.Libn.
UNION ELECTRIC COMPANY - LIBRARY □ St. Louis, MO

Ford, Jennifer, Libn.
ELGIN MENTAL HEALTH CENTER - ANTON BOISEN PROFESSIONAL LIBRARY □ Elgin, IL

Ford, Joseph M., Musm.Dir.
OWENSBORO AREA MUSEUM - LIBRARY □ Owensboro, KY

Ford, Karin E., Asst.Libn.
IDAHO STATE HISTORICAL SOCIETY - LIBRARY AND ARCHIVES □ Boise, ID

Ford, Mrs. M., Supv. of Rd.Serv.
ONTARIO BIBLE COLLEGE/ONTARIO THEOLOGICAL SEMINARY - J. WILLIAM HORSEY LIBRARY □ Willowdale, ON

Ford, Maria A., Libn.
CANADIAN NUMISMATIC ASSOCIATION - LIBRARY □ Collingwood, ON

Ford, Dr. Marjorie M., Libn.
CITY OF INDUSTRY - RALPH W. MILLER GOLF LIBRARY □ City of Industry, CA

Ford, Mary E., Lib.Techn.
U.S. BUREAU OF INDIAN AFFAIRS - OFFICE OF TECHNICAL ASSISTANCE & TRAINING (OTAT) - PROFESSIONAL LIBRARY† □ Brigham City, UT

Ford, Oscar, Asst. State Libn.
NEVADA STATE LIBRARY □ Carson City, NV

Ford, Patricia D., Asst. to Dir.
ALABAMA A & M UNIVERSITY - JOSEPH F. DRAKE MEMORIAL LEARNING RESOURCES CENTER □ Normal, AL

Ford, Peggy A., Musm.Coord.
GREELEY MUNICIPAL MUSEUM - LIBRARY □ Greeley, CO

Ford, Peter, Lib.Dir.
ROCHESTER TIMES-UNION AND ROCHESTER DEMOCRAT & CHRONICLE - LIBRARY □ Rochester, NY

Ford, Robert S., Asst.Libn.
CALIFORNIA RAILWAY MUSEUM - LIBRARY □ Suisun City, CA

Ford, Ruth, Med.Libn.
GAYLORD HOSPITAL - MEDICAL LIBRARY □ Wallingford, CT

Ford, Virginia, Lit.Res.Anl.
AEROSPACE CORPORATION - CHARLES C. LAURITSEN LIBRARY □ Los Angeles, CA

Forde, Ingrid F., Corp.Libn.
ONAN CORPORATION - LIBRARY □ Minneapolis, MN

Fordham, Joan, Adm.
INTERNATIONAL CRANE FOUNDATION - LIBRARY □ Baraboo, WI

Fordyce, Carol, Mgr.
ONTARIO - MINISTRY OF EDUCATION - INFORMATION CENTRE □ Toronto, ON

Foreman, Ann, Coll.Dev.
U.S. AIR FORCE - AERONAUTICAL LABORATORIES - TECHNICAL LIBRARY □ Dayton, OH

Foreman, Clifton M., Libn.
CHURCH OF JESUS CHRIST OF LATTER-DAY SAINTS - TACOMA BRANCH GENEALOGY LIBRARY □ Tacoma, WA

Foreman, Iona, Textbook Cons.
GEORGIA STATE DEPARTMENT OF EDUCATION - LIBRARY FOR THE BLIND & PHYSICALLY HANDICAPPED □ Atlanta, GA

Foreman, Robyn, Mgr.Rd.Serv.
SEATTLE PUBLIC LIBRARY - WASHINGTON REGIONAL LIBRARY FOR THE BLIND AND PHYSICALLY HANDICAPPED □ Seattle, WA

Forer, Daniel, Coord.
SAN FRANCISCO LIGHTHOUSE CENTER FOR THE BLIND - LIBRARY □ San Francisco, CA

Forester, Marilyn, Spec. Projects Coord.
BAKER CENTRE - SERVICES FOR THE HANDICAPPED - LIBRARY □ Calgary, AB

Forget, Louis, Dir.Lib.Sys.Ctr.
NATIONAL LIBRARY OF CANADA □ Ottawa, ON

Forgione, Nancy, Cat.
MARYLAND INSTITUTE, COLLEGE OF ART - DECKER LIBRARY □ Baltimore, MD

Forman, Mrs. Elmer, Ref.Libn.
CINCINNATI HISTORICAL SOCIETY - LIBRARY □ Cincinnati, OH

Formanek, Ellen, Libn.
SETTLEMENT MUSIC SCHOOL - BLANCHE WOLF KOHN LIBRARY □ Philadelphia, PA

Forrest, Elaine K.
FIRST PRESBYTERIAN CHURCH OF FLINT - PEIRCE MEMORIAL LIBRARY† □ Flint, MI

Forrest, Fred H., Libn.
WEBB INSTITUTE OF NAVAL ARCHITECTURE - LIVINGSTON LIBRARY □ Glen Cove, NY

Forrest, Joseph, Assoc.Dir.
HOWARD UNIVERSITY - HEALTH SCIENCES LIBRARY □ Washington, DC

Forsee, Joe. B., Dir.
GEORGIA STATE DEPARTMENT OF EDUCATION - DIVISION OF PUBLIC LIBRARY SERVICES □ Atlanta, GA

Forsman, Avis B., Libn.
KUTAK, ROCK & HUIE - LAW LIBRARY □ Omaha, NE

Forsman, Rick B., Assoc.Dir./Tech.Serv
UNIVERSITY OF ALABAMA IN BIRMINGHAM - LISTER HILL LIBRARY OF THE HEALTH SCIENCES □ Birmingham, AL

Forstall, Louise D., Hd.Libn.
TIME-LIFE BOOKS INC. - REFERENCE LIBRARY □ Alexandria, VA

Forstall, Philip L., Libn.
RAND MC NALLY AND COMPANY - LIBRARY □ Skokie, IL

Forsythe, Joan, Asst.Libn.
BROBECK, PHLEGER & HARRISON - LIBRARY □ San Francisco, CA

Fortado, Robert, Doc.Libn.
SOUTHERN ILLINOIS UNIVERSITY, EDWARDSVILLE - DOCUMENTS COLLECTION □ Edwardsville, IL

Fortenberry, Ann, Cat./Tech.Serv.Libn.
ALASKA STATE COURT SYSTEM - ALASKA COURT LIBRARIES □ Anchorage, AK

Fortier, B., Libn.
CATHOLIC UNIVERSITY OF AMERICA - ENGINEERING/ARCHITECTURE/ MATHEMATICS LIBRARY □ Washington, DC

Fortier, Bernard, Cat.
FRANCISCAN FRIARS OF THE ATONEMENT - ATONEMENT SEMINARY LIBRARY □ Washington, DC

Fortier, John W., Archv.
ONTARIO - MINISTRY OF CULTURE AND RECREATION - MAP LIBRARY □ Toronto, ON

Fortin, Jean-Marc, Lib.Techn./Asst.
SEMINAIRE DE CHICOUTIMI - BIBLIOTHEQUE □ Chicoutimi, PQ

Fortin, Sylvie, Techn.
HOPITAL RIVIERE-DES-PRAIRIES - BIBLIOTHEQUE DU PERSONNEL □ Montreal, PQ

Fortin, Mrs. V., Tech.Serv.Libn.
MC GILL UNIVERSITY - MACDONALD COLLEGE - LIBRARY □ Ste. Anne De Bellevue, PQ

Fortner, Roger L., Dir.
U.S. DEPT. OF COMMERCE - INTERNATIONAL TRADE ADMINISTRATION - CHARLESTON DISTRICT OFFICE LIBRARY □ Charleston, WV

Fortney, Lynn M., Chf.Med.Libn.
UNIVERSITY OF ALABAMA - COLLEGE OF COMMUNITY HEALTH SCIENCES - HEALTH SCIENCES LIBRARY □ University, AL

Fortney, Marie D., Libn.
HAMBURG CENTER FOR THE MENTALLY RETARDED - STAFF LIBRARY □ Hamburg, PA

Fortney, Mary, Map Libn.
NORTHWESTERN UNIVERSITY - MAP COLLECTION □ Evanston, IL

Fortney, V.J., Hd., Info.Serv.Dept.
BELL TELEPHONE LABORATORIES, INC. - LIBRARIES AND INFORMATION SYSTEMS CENTER □ Murray Hill, NJ

Fortunato, Eileen, Coll.Org.
MASSACHUSETTS GENERAL HOSPITAL - TREADWELL AND PALMER-DAVIS LIBRARY □ Boston, MA

Fortune, Joan, Mgr.
AMERICAN CRITICAL CARE - INFORMATION CENTER □ McGaw Park, IL

Fortvaler, Diana
FRANKLIN RESEARCH CENTER - NATIONAL SOLAR HEATING & COOLING INFO. CTR. □ Rockville, MD

Forwood, Connie, Libn.
U.S. AIR FORCE HOSPITAL - TECHNICAL LIBRARY □ Fairchild AFB, WA

Forys, John W., Libn.
UNIVERSITY OF IOWA - ENGINEERING LIBRARY □ Iowa City, IA

Forys, John W., Libn.
UNIVERSITY OF IOWA - MATHEMATICS LIBRARY □ Iowa City, IA

Fossum, Correne, Asst.Libn.
MINOT DAILY NEWS - LIBRARY □ Minot, ND

Fossum, Dennis, Monograph Libn.
UNIVERSITY OF NORTH DAKOTA - OLAF H. THORMODSGARD LAW LIBRARY □ Grand Forks, ND

Fostel, Donald, Principal Libn.
NEWARK PUBLIC LIBRARY - SOCIAL SCIENCE DIVISION □ Newark, NJ

Foster, A.M., County Ck.
JOSEPHINE COUNTY LAW LIBRARY† □ Grants Pass, OR

Foster, B.R.
YALE UNIVERSITY - BABYLONIAN COLLECTION □ New Haven, CT

Foster, Ms. D., Cat.
HURON COLLEGE - SILCOX MEMORIAL LIBRARY □ London, ON

Foster, Eileen, Lib.Mgr.
CANADA - TELESAT CANADA - COMPANY LIBRARY □ Ottawa, ON

Foster, Eleanor, Libn.
REPUBLICAN ASSOCIATES OF LOS ANGELES COUNTY - RESEARCH LIBRARY □ Glendale, CA

Foster, Eloise C., Dir.
AMERICAN HOSPITAL ASSOCIATION - ASA S. BACON MEMORIAL LIBRARY □ Chicago, IL

Foster, Eugenia, Cur.
UNIVERSITY OF CINCINNATI - JOHN MILLER BURNAM CLASSICAL LIBRARY □ Cincinnati, OH

Foster, Helen M., Hd.Libn.
GEE & JENSON ENGINEERS, ARCHITECTS, PLANNERS, INC. - LIBRARY □ West Palm Beach, FL

Foster, James, Ref.Libn.
STEAMSHIP HISTORICAL SOCIETY OF AMERICA - LIBRARY □ Baltimore, MD

Foster, Jane, Dir.
LENNOX AND ADDINGTON COUNTY MUSEUM - LIBRARY & ARCHIVES □ Napanee, ON

Foster, Jane N., Adm.Spec.
U.S. NASA - WALLOPS FLIGHT CENTER - TECHNICAL LIBRARY □ Wallops Island, VA

PERSONNEL

Foster, Jim, Dir.Lrng.Rsrc.Ctr.
CENTRAL CAROLINA TECHNICAL COLLEGE -
LEARNING RESOURCE CENTER □ Sanford, NC
Foster, Judie, Slide Libn.
PORTLAND ART MUSEUM - LIBRARY □ Portland,
OR
Foster, Keith, Cur.
LONG BEACH PUBLIC LIBRARY - RANCHO LOS
CERRITOS MUSEUM - LIBRARY □ Long Beach,
CA
Foster, Leslie A., Res.Asst.
DALHOUSIE UNIVERSITY - LAW LIBRARY □
Halifax, NS
Foster, Norma, Libn.
FIRST BAPTIST CHURCH - LIBRARY □ Slocomb,
AL
Foster, Norma Jean, Hd. of Lib.Serv.
UNIVERSITY OF TEXAS, DALLAS - CALLIER
CENTER FOR COMMUNICATIONS DISORDERS -
LIBRARY □ Dallas, TX
Foster, Olive S., Act. State Hist.
ILLINOIS STATE HISTORICAL LIBRARY □
Springfield, IL
Foster, Paul H., Cons.
OKLAHOMA GEOLOGICAL SURVEY - OKLAHOMA
GEOPHYSICAL OBSERVATORY LIBRARY □
Leonard, OK
Foster, Rita, Libn.
DOUGLAS OIL COMPANY OF CALIFORNIA -
RESEARCH AND TECHNOLOGY DEPARTMENT -
LIBRARY □ Paramount, CA
Foster, Robert, Ref.Libn.
NORTH OLYMPIC LIBRARY SYSTEM - PORT
ANGELES BRANCH - PACIFIC NORTHWEST
ROOM □ Port Angeles, WA
Foster, Saba L., Chf.Libn.
NATIONAL LIFE INSURANCE COMPANY -
LIBRARY □ Montpelier, VT
Foster, Sandra L., Libn.
INDIANAPOLIS BAR ASSOCIATION - LIBRARY†
□ Indianapolis, IN
Foster, Selma V., Hd. of Cat.
SUNY - COLLEGE AT POTSDAM - FREDERICK W.
CRUMB MEMORIAL LIBRARY □ Potsdam, NY
Foster, Shirley, Libn.
TORONTO STOCK EXCHANGE - LIBRARY □
Toronto, ON
Foster, Stephanie, ILL Libn.
NATIONAL ACADEMY OF SCIENCES -
NATIONAL ACADEMY OF ENGINEERING -
LIBRARY □ Washington, DC
Foster, Theodore, Map Libn.
OHIO UNIVERSITY - MAP COLLECTION □
Athens, OH
Foster, Thyra Jane, Cur.
SOCIETY OF FRIENDS - NEW ENGLAND YEARLY
MEETING OF FRIENDS - ARCHIVES □
Providence, RI
Foubert, E.L., Jr.
HOLLISTER-STIER LABORATORIES - LIBRARY □
Spokane, WA
Foudray, Rita, Libn.
DALLAS PUBLIC LIBRARY - HUMANITIES
DIVISION □ Dallas, TX
Fourchalk, Joy, Libn.
BRITISH COLUMBIA - MINISTRY OF HEALTH -
MENTAL HEALTH SERVICES LIBRARY □
Burnaby, BC
Fourmy, Frank, Archv.
CENTER FOR SOUTHERN FOLKLORE -
ARCHIVES □ Memphis, TN
Fourney, Norah, Hd.Libn.
ST. LAWRENCE COLLEGE OF APPLIED ARTS
AND TECHNOLOGY - LEARNING RESOURCE
CENTRE □ Cornwall, ON
Fournier, Cecile, Libn.
OTTAWA GENERAL HOSPITAL - MEDICAL
LIBRARY† □ Ottawa, ON
Fournier, Jacques, SDI
QUEBEC PROV. - MIN. DE L'ENERGIE ET DES
RESSOURCES - CENTRE DE DOCUMENTATION
ET DE RENSEIGNEMENTS □ Quebec, PQ

Fournier, Marc, Telereference & Publicity
QUEBEC PROVINCE - MINISTERE DES
COMMUNICATIONS - BIBLIOTHEQUE
ADMINISTRATIVE □ Quebec, PQ
Fournier, Michel, Chf., Cat.
UNIVERSITE LAVAL - BIBLIOTHEQUE† □ Ste.
Foy, PQ
Fouser, Jane G., Sr.Info.Anl.
CONTINENTAL ILLINOIS NATIONAL BANK AND
TRUST COMPANY OF CHICAGO -
INFORMATION SERVICES DIVISION □ Chicago,
IL
Foust, Donna, Asst.Hd.
ATLANTA PUBLIC LIBRARY - IVAN ALLEN, JR.
DEPARTMENT OF SCIENCE, INDUSTRY AND
GOVERNMENT □ Atlanta, GA
Foust, Judith, Coord., Tech.Serv.
PENNSYLVANIA STATE LIBRARY □ Harrisburg,
PA
Foutty, Kitty, Life Sci.Libn.
U.S. NASA - AMES RESEARCH CENTER -
LIBRARY □ Mountain View, CA
Fouty, Gary, Ref.
IOWA STATE UNIVERSITY - LIBRARY □ Ames,
IA
Foutz, Pauleen C., Hd.Libn.
CHURCH OF JESUS CHRIST OF LATTER-DAY
SAINTS - LAS VEGAS BRANCH GENEALOGICAL
LIBRARY □ Las Vegas, NV
Fow, Mark I., Act.Dir.
U.S. FOOD & DRUG ADMINISTRATION - NATL.
CLEARINGHOUSE FOR POISON CONTROL
CENTERS □ Rockville, MD
Fowler, Albert W., Assoc.Dir.
SWARTHMORE COLLEGE - FRIENDS
HISTORICAL LIBRARY □ Swarthmore, PA
Fowler, Ann, Coord.
NORTH CAROLINA STATE DEPARTMENT OF
PUBLIC INSTRUCTION - EDUCATION
INFORMATION CENTER □ Raleigh, NC
Fowler, Bessie, Cat.
HOWARD UNIVERSITY - MOORLAND-SPINGARN
RESEARCH CENTER - LIBRARY DIVISION □
Washington, DC
Fowler, Cary, Prog.Dir.
NATIONAL SHARECROPPERS FUND/RURAL
ADVANCEMENT FUND - F.P. GRAHAM
RESOURCE CENTER □ Wadesboro, NC
Fowler, Charles, Ref.Libn.
U.S. AIR FORCE - AIR FORCE SYSTEMS
COMMAND - AIR FORCE GEOPHYSICS
LABORATORY - RESEARCH LIBRARY† □
Bedford, MA
Fowler, Joseph R., Jr., Dir.
WEST VIRGINIA STATE GOVERNOR'S OFFICE
OF ECONOMIC & COMMUNITY DEVELOPMENT -
TRAVEL DEVELOPMENT DIVISION □ Charleston,
WV
Fowler, Rena, Asst.Dir., Tech.Serv.
UNIVERSITY OF DENVER - PENROSE LIBRARY □
Denver, CO
Fowler, Talbert B., Jr., Dir., Legal Res.
UNIVERSITY OF PITTSBURGH - LAW LIBRARY □
Pittsburgh, PA
Fowles, Margaret, Libn.
LEAGUE FOR INTERNATIONAL FOOD
EDUCATION - LIBRARY □ Washington, DC
Fowlie, Linda K., Ref.Libn.
GOVERNMENT RESEARCH CORPORATION -
LIBRARY □ Washington, DC
Fox, Barbara Jean, Ref./ILL
U.S.D.A. - AGRICULTURAL RESEARCH SERVICE
- SOUTHERN REGIONAL RESEARCH CENTER □
New Orleans, LA
Fox, Betty L., Chf., Tech.Lib.Div.
U.S. DEFENSE NUCLEAR AGENCY - TECHNICAL
LIBRARY DIVISION □ Washington, DC
Fox, Charles H., Chf.Spec.Serv.Sect.
NORTH CAROLINA STATE DEPARTMENT OF
CULTURAL RESOURCES - LIBRARY FOR THE
BLIND AND PHYSICALLY HANDICAPPED □
Raleigh, NC

Fox, Dexter, Chf./Tech.Serv.Sect.
U.S. ARMY - ARMY LIBRARY □ Washington, DC
Fox, Elizabeth, Cat.Libn.
QUEEN'S UNIVERSITY AT KINGSTON - LAW
LIBRARY □ Kingston, ON
Fox, Elizabeth F., Lib./Acq.
MERRILL LYNCH PIERCE FENNER & SMITH,
INC. - LIBRARY □ New York, NY
Fox, Gertrude, Curric.Res.Libn.
SALEM STATE COLLEGE - LIBRARY† □ Salem,
MA
Fox, Gertrude L., Libn.
SALEM STATE COLLEGE - CURRICULUM
RESOURCES CENTER† □ Salem, MA
Fox, H. Ronald, Chf., Lib.Serv.
U.S. VETERANS ADMINISTRATION (NE-Grand
Island) - HOSPITAL LIBRARY □ Grand Island, NE
Fox, James, Soc.Stud.Libn.
SOUTHERN ILLINOIS UNIVERSITY,
CARBONDALE - SOCIAL STUDIES DIVISION
LIBRARY □ Carbondale, IL
Fox, James R., Law Libn.
DICKINSON SCHOOL OF LAW - SHEELY-LEE
LAW LIBRARY □ Carlisle, PA
Fox, Jane G., Libn.
FOX CONSULTING AND LIBRARY SERVICE □
Swarthmore, PA
Fox, Janis M., Libn.
PONTIAC OSTEOPATHIC HOSPITAL - MEDICAL
LIBRARY □ Pontiac, MI
Fox, Jean J., Dir., Ref.Serv.
AMERICAN MEDICAL ASSOCIATION -
DIVISION OF LIBRARY AND ARCHIVAL
SERVICES □ Chicago, IL
Fox, Jeff, Plan.Dir.
NORTH DAKOTA STATE LIBRARY □ Bismarck,
ND
Fox, Jennifer B., Libn.
BARTHOLOMEW (Harland) AND ASSOCIATES,
INC. - LIBRARY □ Memphis, TN
Fox, Karl M., Info.Cons.
FOX CONSULTING AND LIBRARY SERVICE □
Swarthmore, PA
Fox, Lesley, Sec.
ZIMBABWE RHODESIAN INFORMATION OFFICE
- LIBRARY □ Washington, DC
Fox, Mark, Cat.Libn.
NEVADA STATE LIBRARY □ Carson City, NV
Fox, Maryfaith, Ref.Libn.
MADISON METROPOLITAN SCHOOL DISTRICT -
EDUCATION REFERENCE LIBRARY □ Madison,
WI
Fox, Priscilla, Reserve Rd.Rm.Libn.
CENTRAL CONNECTICUT STATE COLLEGE -
ELIHU BURRITT LIBRARY □ New Britain, CT
Fox, Rosmarie T., Asst.Libn
AKRON LAW LIBRARY □ Akron, OH
Fox, Wanda, Mgr.
ROCKWELL INTERNATIONAL - ELECTRONICS
OPERATIONS - DALLAS INFORMATION CENTER
□ Dallas, TX
Foxman, Carole, Med.Libn.
BROOKLINE HOSPITAL - MEDICAL LIBRARY □
Brookline, MA
Foxman, Diane, Hd., AV Serv.
UNIVERSITY OF NORTH CAROLINA, CHAPEL
HILL - HEALTH SCIENCES LIBRARY □ Chapel
Hill, NC
Foxworth, Jarrett, Med.Libn.
U.S. VETERANS ADMINISTRATION (TX-Dallas) -
MEDICAL CENTER LIBRARY SERVICE □ Dallas,
TX
Foy-McCarthy, Terry, Staff Libn.
BROOKLYN CHILDREN'S MUSEUM - STAFF
RESEARCH LIBRARY □ Brooklyn, NY
Fracasso, John, Automated Sys. & Serv.
UNIVERSITY OF WESTERN ONTARIO - SCHOOL
OF LIBRARY & INFORMATION SCIENCE -
LIBRARY □ London, ON
Fradkin, Louise G., Coord. of Pub.Serv./Ref.
TRENTON STATE COLLEGE - ROSCOE L. WEST
LIBRARY □ Trenton, NJ

Fragale, John, Jr., Chf.
U.S. ARMY - MATERIEL DEVELOPMENT &
READINESS COMMAND - HEADQUARTERS -
TECHNICAL LIBRARY □ Alexandria, VA

Frahm, Catharine C., Dir.
WASHINGTON COUNTY HISTORICAL
ASSOCIATION - MUSEUM LIBRARY □ Fort
Calhoun, NE

Fralish, Christine, Lib.Techn.
U.S. CENTER FOR DISEASE CONTROL - BUREAU
OF LABORATORIES - TECHNICAL
INFORMATION SERVICES LIBRARY □ Atlanta,
GA

Francaviglia, Michael, Mgr.
NATIONAL BROADCASTING COMPANY, INC. -
NEWS ARCHIVAL SERVICES LIBRARY □ New
York, NY

Franche, Yves, Libn.
INSTITUT CANADIEN-FRANCAIS D'OTTAWA -
LIBRARY □ Ottawa, ON

Francillon, W.H., Pres.
NATIONAL ASSOCIATION OF WATCH AND
CLOCK COLLECTORS MUSEUM - LIBRARY □
Columbia, PA

Francis, Carol A., Libn.
BRISTOL COUNTY LAW LIBRARY □ Taunton, MA

Francis, Mrs. F., Ref.Libn.
UNIVERSITY OF GUELPH - HUMANITIES AND
SOCIAL SCIENCES DIVISION - MAP
COLLECTION □ Guelph, ON

Francis, Frank, Gen.Mgr.
CRAVEN FOUNDATION - AUTOMOTIVE
REFERENCE LIBRARY □ Toronto, ON

Francis, Frank, Jr., Hd.Libn.
PRAIRIE VIEW A & M COLLEGE OF TEXAS -
W.R. BANKS LIBRARY □ Prairie View, TX

Francis, Gloria A., Chf.
DETROIT PUBLIC LIBRARY - RARE BOOK
DIVISION □ Detroit, MI

Francis, Mary
U.S. OAK RIDGE NATL. LABORATORY -
INFORMATION DIVISION - ENVIRONMENTAL
MUTAGEN INFORMATION CENTER □ Oak Ridge,
TN

Francis, Nancy, Libn.
KITCHENER-WATERLOO ART GALLERY -
ELEANOR CALVERT MEMORIAL LIBRARY □
Kitchener, ON

Francisco, Cecilia, Med.Cat.
UNIVERSITY OF NEVADA, RENO - SAVITT
MEDICAL LIBRARY □ Reno, NV

Franck, Dana, Asst.Libn.
CANADA - GEOLOGICAL SURVEY OF CANADA -
INSTITUTE OF SEDIMENTARY & PETROLEUM
GEOLOGY - LIBRARY □ Calgary, AB

Franck, Dr. Daniel H., Libn.
DENOYER-GEPPERT COMPANY - EDITORIAL
LIBRARY □ Chicago, IL

Franck, Jane P., Dir.
TEACHERS COLLEGE - LIBRARY □ New York, NY

Franco, Beverly, Libn.
JEWISH MUSEUM - LIBRARY □ New York, NY

Frandsen, Rex, Archv.
BRIGHAM YOUNG UNIVERSITY, HAWAII
CAMPUS - JOSEPH F. SMITH LIBRARY AND
MEDIA CENTER □ Laie, HI

Frank, Agnes T., Dir.
ST. VINCENT'S HOSPITAL AND MEDICAL
CENTER - MEDICAL LIBRARY □ New York, NY

Frank, Anita, Libn.
ROYAL TRUST CORPORATION OF CANADA -
INVESTMENT RESEARCH LIBRARY □ Toronto,
ON

Frank, Ann W., Fine Arts Libn.
MANCHESTER CITY LIBRARY - FINE ARTS
DEPARTMENT □ Manchester, NH

Frank, Bernice C., Law Libn.
BURROUGHS CORPORATION - LEGAL ACTIVITY
LIBRARY □ Detroit, MI

Frank, Catherine, Tech.Serv.Libn.
UNIVERSITY OF KENTUCKY - LAW LIBRARY □
Lexington, KY

Frank, Conie J., Libn.
ST. JOSEPH COUNTY LAW LIBRARY □ South
Bend, IN

Frank, Edwin, Lib.Asst.
MEMPHIS STATE UNIVERSITY LIBRARIES -
SPEECH AND HEARING CENTER LIBRARY □
Memphis, TN

Frank, Frances, Libn.
UNIVERSITY HOSPITAL (Louisville General) -
MEDICAL LIBRARY □ Louisville, KY

Frank, Linda, Asst.Libn.
BECKMAN INSTRUMENTS, INC. - SPINCO
DIVISION - TECHNICAL LIBRARY □ Palo Alto,
CA

Frank, Marion, Res.Libn.
INDUSTRIAL ACCIDENT PREVENTION
ASSOCIATION - LIBRARY □ Toronto, ON

Frank, Nessiah, Per.Asst.
SPERTUS COLLEGE OF JUDAICA - NORMAN AND
HELEN ASHER LIBRARY □ Chicago, IL

Frank, Richard E., Assoc.Dir.
UNIVERSITY OF NORTH DAKOTA - INSTITUTE
FOR ECOLOGICAL STUDIES - ENVIRONMENTAL
RESOURCE CENTER □ Grand Forks, ND

Frank, Robyn, Chf.
U.S.D.A. - HUMAN NUTRITION INFORMATION
SERVICES - FOOD AND NUTRITION
INFORMATION CENTER □ Beltsville, MD

Frank, Stuart, Dir.
KENDALL WHALING MUSEUM - LIBRARY □
Sharon, MA

Franke, Gail, ILL & Ref.Libn.
ROSWELL PARK MEMORIAL INSTITUTE -
MEDICAL AND SCIENTIFIC LIBRARY □ Buffalo,
NY

Frankel, Jean, Libn.
COMMUNICATIONS WORKERS OF AMERICA -
CWA INFORMATION LIBRARY □ Washington, DC

Frankel, Jessica, Ref.Libn.
PAINE WEBBER INC. - PAINE WEBBER BLYTH
EASTMAN - LIBRARY □ New York, NY

Frankel, Norma, Med.Libn., ILL
LONG ISLAND JEWISH-HILLSIDE MEDICAL
CENTER - HEALTH SCIENCES LIBRARY □ New
Hyde Park, NY

Frankel, Norman, Libn.
WESTERN MICHIGAN UNIVERSITY - SCHOOL
OF LIBRARIANSHIP - LABORATORY LIBRARY □
Kalamazoo, MI

Frankel, Vivian, Med.Libn.
LONG ISLAND JEWISH-HILLSIDE MEDICAL
CENTER - QUEENS HOSPITAL CENTER -
MEDICAL LIBRARY □ Jamaica, NY

Frankenberg, Celestine G., Dir. of Lib.Serv.
YOUNG AND RUBICAM INTERNATIONAL -
LIBRARY† □ New York, NY

Frankhouse, Dorothy M., Libn.
STOCKTON NEWSPAPERS INC. - STOCKTON
RECORD LIBRARY □ Stockton, CA

Franklin, Berenice, Mgr./Lib. Photo Serv.
COURIER-JOURNAL AND LOUISVILLE TIMES -
LIBRARY □ Louisville, KY

Franklin, Carole, Music Libn.
PENNSYLVANIA STATE UNIVERSITY - ARTS
LIBRARY □ University Park, PA

Franklin, Carolyn, Libn.
SOCIETY FOR NUTRITION EDUCATION - SNE
RESOURCE CENTER □ Berkeley, CA

Franklin, Elizabeth, Asst.
TUCSON MUSEUM OF ART - LIBRARY □ Tucson,
AZ

Franklin, Josephine, Coord., Info.Serv.
EDUCATIONAL RESEARCH SERVICE - LIBRARY
□ Arlington, VA

Franklin, Madeleine L'Engle, Writer in Residence
CATHEDRAL OF ST. JOHN THE DIVINE -
CATHEDRAL LIBRARY □ New York, NY

Franklin, Sandra Gallop, Asst.Libn.
MERCER UNIVERSITY - SOUTHERN COLLEGE
OF PHARMACY - H. CUSTER NAYLOR LIBRARY □
Atlanta, GA

Franks, JoAnn, Adm.Asst.
OHIO STATE UNIVERSITY - CENTER FOR LAKE
ERIE AREA RESEARCH - LAKE ERIE LIBRARY □
Columbus, OH

Franks, Robert, Libn.Asst.
IBM CANADA, LTD. - LABORATORY LIBRARY □
Don Mills, ON

Franks, Sharon, Libn.
UNIVERSITY OF CALIFORNIA - SAN JOAQUIN
VALLEY AGRICULTURAL RESEARCH &
EXTENSION CENTER □ Parlier, CA

Fransiszyn, M., Hd., Pub.Serv.
MC GILL UNIVERSITY - OSLER LIBRARY □
Montreal, PQ

Frantz, Barbara, Div.Hd.
INDIANAPOLIS-MARION COUNTY PUBLIC
LIBRARY - BUSINESS, SCIENCE AND
TECHNOLOGY DIVISION □ Indianapolis, IN

Franz, Donald, Exec.Sec.
STUDIO SUPPLIERS ASSOCIATION - BUSINESS
LIBRARY □ Hawthorne, NJ

Franzen, Monika, Res.Assoc.
HISTORICAL PICTURES SERVICE, INC. □
Chicago, IL

Franzman, Gene, Libn.
ROSICRUCIAN FELLOWSHIP - LIBRARY □
Oceanside, CA

Frasche, LTC Louis D.F., Dp.Dir.
U.S. ARMY MILITARY HISTORY INSTITUTE □
Carlisle Barracks, PA

Fraser, Alex W., Pres.
GLENGARRY GENEALOGICAL SOCIETY -
HIGHLAND HERITAGE LIBRARY □ Lancaster, ON

Fraser, C. William, Dir.
COLLEGE OF PHYSICIANS AND SURGEONS OF
BRITISH COLUMBIA - MEDICAL LIBRARY
SERVICE □ Vancouver, BC

Fraser, Christine A., Libn.
U.S. DEPT. OF HOUSING AND URBAN
DEVELOPMENT - REGION I - LIBRARY □ Boston,
MA

Fraser, Prof. Douglas, Rep.
COLUMBIA UNIVERSITY - DEPARTMENT OF
ART HISTORY & ARCHAEOLOGY - PHOTOGRAPH
COLLECTION □ New York, NY

Fraser, J.A., Archv.
TORONTO CITY RECORDS AND ARCHIVES
DIVISION □ Toronto, ON

Fraser, James A., Collective Member
CANADIAN GAY ARCHIVES - LIBRARY □
Toronto, ON

Fraser, Judith, Tech.Serv.Libn.
QUEEN'S UNIVERSITY AT KINGSTON -
DOCUMENTS LIBRARY □ Kingston, ON

Fraser, Nancy, Jr.Lib.Asst.
ESSEX COUNTY HOSPITAL CENTER -
HAMILTON MEMORIAL LIBRARY □ Cedar Grove,
NJ

Fraser, Sandra, Cat.
UNIVERSITY OF CALGARY - EDUCATION
MATERIALS CENTER □ Calgary, AB

Fraser, Terri, Musm.Dir.
DES PLAINES HISTORICAL SOCIETY - JOHN
BYRNE MEMORIAL LIBRARY □ Des Plaines, IL

Fraser, Walter J., Hd., Sys./Auto.Dept.
UNIVERSITY OF CALIFORNIA, DAVIS -
GENERAL LIBRARY □ Davis, CA

Frashier, Ann, Tech.Serv.Libn.
PEPPERDINE UNIVERSITY - LIBRARY -
SPECIAL COLLECTIONS □ Malibu, CA

Frasier, Mary, Info.Serv.Libn.
SOUTH DAKOTA STATE LIBRARY □ Pierre, SD

Fraulino, Philip, Libn.
U.S. NATL. OCEANIC & ATMOSPHERIC
ADMINISTRATION - GEOPHYSICAL FLUID
DYNAMICS LABORATORY - LIBRARY □
Princeton, NJ

Frayler, John M., Cur.
U.S. NATL. PARK SERVICE - SALEM MARITIME
NATL. HISTORIC SITE - LIBRARY □ Salem, MA

Frazee, Mary Louise, Libn.
U.S. DEPT. OF ENERGY - BETTIS ATOMIC
POWER LABORATORY - LIBRARY □ West Mifflin,
PA
Frazelle, Betty, Lib.Techn.
U.S. NAVY - NAVAL REGIONAL MEDICAL
CENTER (Camp Lejeune) - MEDICAL LIBRARY □
Camp Lejeune, NC
Frazier, Ken, Hd., Info.Serv.
UNIVERSITY OF WISCONSIN, MADISON -
STEENBOCK MEMORIAL LIBRARY □ Madison,
WI
Frebold, Mrs. E., Hd., Info.Serv.
CANADA - GEOLOGICAL SURVEY OF CANADA -
LIBRARY □ Ottawa, ON
Frechtling, Dr. Douglas, Dir.
U.S. TRAVEL DATA CENTER - LIBRARY □
Washington, DC
Frederick, Marsha, Asst.Libn.
U.S. COURT OF APPEALS, 3RD CIRCUIT -
LIBRARY† □ Philadelphia, PA
Frederick, Olivia, Cons.Archv.
JEFFERSON COUNTY OFFICE OF HISTORIC
PRESERVATION AND ARCHIVES □ Louisville, KY
Frederick, Pauline R., Lib.Asst.
UNIVERSITY OF CALIFORNIA, DAVIS -
CALIFORNIA PRIMATE RESEARCH CENTER -
REFERENCE SERVICES □ Davis, CA
Frederick, Tallulah, Tech.Libn.
LITTON INDUSTRIES - DATA SYSTEMS
DIVISION - ENGINEERING LIBRARY □ Van
Nuys, CA
Fredericks, Joreen, Asst.Libn.
EQUITABLE LIFE ASSURANCE SOCIETY OF THE
U.S. - TECHNICAL INFORMATION CENTER □
New York, NY
Fredericksen, Richard B., Dir.
UNIVERSITY OF ALABAMA IN BIRMINGHAM -
LISTER HILL LIBRARY OF THE HEALTH
SCIENCES □ Birmingham, AL
Frederickson, Joan A., Libn.
HAZELDEN FOUNDATION - STAFF & RESEARCH
LIBRARIES □ Center City, MN
Frederickson, Karen, Sr.Sec.
UNIVERSITY OF MINNESOTA - DEPARTMENT
OF LINGUISTICS - LINGUISTICS LIBRARY □
Minneapolis, MN
Fredrick, N.S., Chf.Libn.
GENERAL DYNAMICS CORPORATION - POMONA
DIVISION - DIVISION LIBRARY MZ 4-20 □
Pomona, CA
Fredrick, Tim, Regional Archv.
WASHINGTON STATE OFFICE OF SECRETARY
OF STATE - DIVISION OF ARCHIVES AND
RECORD MANAGEMENT □ Olympia, WA
Free, Opal M., Hd.
FLORIDA STATE UNIVERSITY - SPECIAL
COLLECTIONS □ Tallahassee, FL
Freed, Emil, Dir.
SOUTHERN CALIFORNIA LIBRARY FOR SOCIAL
STUDIES AND RESEARCH □ Los Angeles, CA
Freed, J. Arthur, Hd.Libn.
UNIVERSITY OF CALIFORNIA - LOS ALAMOS
NATIONAL LABORATORY - LIBRARY □ Los
Alamos, NM
Freedman, Arlene L., Dir. of Lib.Serv.
BETH ISRAEL MEDICAL CENTER - SEYMOUR J.
PHILLIPS HEALTH SCIENCES LIBRARY □ New
York, NY
Freedman, Lynn P., Mgr.
CONSUMERS UNION OF UNITED STATES, INC. -
LIBRARY □ Mount Vernon, NY
Freedman, Phyllis D., Libn.
ORLANDO MUNICIPAL REFERENCE LIBRARY □
Orlando, FL
Freeh, Mary Beth, Ref.
MUHLENBERG COLLEGE - JOHN A.W. HAAS
LIBRARY □ Allentown, PA

Freehling, Leonore, Libn.
REISS-DAVIS CHILD STUDY CENTER -
RESEARCH LIBRARY □ Los Angeles, CA
Freeman, Betty, Asst.Libn.
BAYLOR UNIVERSITY, DALLAS - LIBRARY □
Dallas, TX
Freeman, Corinne A., Soc.Serv.Libn.
FORDHAM UNIVERSITY - LIBRARY AT LINCOLN
CENTER □ New York, NY
Freeman, Doris, Per. & ILL Libn.
NEW ORLEANS BAPTIST THEOLOGICAL
SEMINARY - JOHN T. CHRISTIAN LIBRARY □
New Orleans, LA
Freeman, Elsa S., Dir.
U.S. DEPT. OF HOUSING AND URBAN
DEVELOPMENT - LIBRARY □ Washington, DC
Freeman, Frank H., Dir.
CENTER FOR CREATIVE LEADERSHIP -
LIBRARY □ Greensboro, NC
Freeman, George C., Hd.Biomed.Br.
UNIVERSITY OF BRITISH COLUMBIA -
BIOMEDICAL BRANCH LIBRARY □ Vancouver,
BC
Freeman, Homer W., Church Libn.
FIRST UNITED METHODIST CHURCH -
MEMORIAL LIBRARY □ Santa Barbara, CA
Freeman, Jane, Libn.
BELMONT ABBEY COLLEGE - ABBOT VINCENT
TAYLOR LIBRARY □ Belmont, NC
Freeman, Jane, Mgr.
GRACE (W.R.) AND COMPANY - NATURAL
RESOURCES GROUP - LIBRARY □ Dallas, TX
Freeman, Dr. John C., Hd.
INSTITUTE FOR STORM RESEARCH - LIBRARY
□ Houston, TX
Freeman, John Crosby, Dir.
AMERICAN LIFE FOUNDATION AND STUDY
INSTITUTE - AMERICANA RESEARCH LIBRARY
□ Watkins Glen, NY
Freeman, Larry, Cur.Dec. Arts Lib.
AMERICAN LIFE FOUNDATION AND STUDY
INSTITUTE - AMERICANA RESEARCH LIBRARY
□ Watkins Glen, NY
Freeman, Mary B., Staff Supv.-Lib.
AMERICAN TELEPHONE & TELEGRAPH
COMPANY - LONG LINES DEPARTMENT -
GOVERNMENT COMMUNICATIONS LIBRARY □
Washington, DC
Freeman, Mary Lee, Libn.
MOBIL EXPLORATION AND PRODUCING
SERVICES INC. - MEPSI LIBRARY □ Dallas, TX
Freeman, Nancy, Libn.
SCM CORPORATION - GLIDDEN-PIGMENTS
DIVISION - ADRIAN JOYCE WORKS RESEARCH
CENTER LIBRARY □ Baltimore, MD
Freeman, Peter, Chf.Libn.
CANADA - SUPREME COURT OF CANADA -
LIBRARY □ Ottawa, ON
Freeman, Ruth, Cur.Pict.Bk.Coll.
AMERICAN LIFE FOUNDATION AND STUDY
INSTITUTE - AMERICANA RESEARCH LIBRARY
□ Watkins Glen, NY
Freese, Robert, Area Libn.
MC GILL UNIVERSITY - NORTHERN STUDIES
LIBRARY □ Montreal, PQ
Freese, Robert, Libn.
MC GILL UNIVERSITY - PHYSICAL SCIENCES
LIBRARY □ Montreal, PQ
Freese, Robert, Area Libn.
MC GILL UNIVERSITY - RUTHERFORD PHYSICS
LIBRARY □ Montreal, PQ
Freese, Robert T., Area Libn.
MC GILL UNIVERSITY - MATHEMATICS
LIBRARY □ Montreal, PQ
Frehn, June, Asst.Libn.
HONEYWELL, INC. - CORPORATE TECHNOLOGY
CENTER LIBRARY □ Bloomington, MN
Freiherr, Gregory, Asst.Dir.
TRACOR JITCO, INC. - RESEARCH RESOURCES
INFORMATION CENTER □ Rockville, MD

Freitag, Doris, Consrv.
HARVARD UNIVERSITY - DIVINITY SCHOOL -
ANDOVER-HARVARD THEOLOGICAL LIBRARY □
Cambridge, MA
Freitag, Wolfgang, Libn.
HARVARD UNIVERSITY - FINE ARTS LIBRARY □
Cambridge, MA
French, A.F., Comp.Info.Supv.
BELL TELEPHONE LABORATORIES, INC. -
LIBRARIES AND INFORMATION SYSTEMS
CENTER □ Murray Hill, NJ
French, Beverlee, Libn.
UNIVERSITY OF CALIFORNIA, SAN DIEGO -
SCIENCE & ENGINEERING LIBRARY □ La Jolla,
CA
French, Catherine, Chf.Exec.Off.
AMERICAN SYMPHONY ORCHESTRA LEAGUE -
LIBRARY □ Vienna, VA
French, Evelyn G., Dir. Of Info.Sys.
AMERICAN BUSINESS PRESS, INC. - LIBRARY □
New York, NY
French, Frances, Libn.
MEMPHIS-SHELBY COUNTY PUBLIC LIBRARY
AND INFO. CTR. - SCIENCE/BUSINESS/SOCIAL
SCIENCES DEPT. □ Memphis, TN
French, Jean, Chf.Libn.
NATIONWIDE MUTUAL INSURANCE COMPANY -
LIBRARY □ Columbus, OH
French, John, Libn.
AMERICAN INSTITUTES FOR RESEARCH -
LIBRARY □ Palo Alto, CA
French, Linda L., Mgr.
COMPUTER SCIENCES CORPORATION -
TECHNICAL LIBRARY □ El Segundo, CA
French, Margaret A., Dir. of Res./Midwest
KORN/FERRY INTERNATIONAL - RESEARCH
LIBRARY □ Chicago, IL
French, Rae, Resource Ctr.Coord.
SASKATCHEWAN - DEPARTMENT OF CO-
OPERATION - LIBRARY □ Regina, SK
French, Robert B., Pres.
LOUISVILLE ACADEMY OF MUSIC - LIBRARY □
Louisville, KY
French, Sharon K., Libn.
BANK OF AMERICA, NT & SA - LAW LIBRARY □
San Francisco, CA
French, Thomas, Tech.Serv.Libn.
NORTHERN KENTUCKY UNIVERSITY - SALMON
P. CHASE COLLEGE OF LAW - LIBRARY □
Covington, KY
French, William D., Exec.Dir.
AMERICAN SOCIETY OF PHOTOGRAMMETRY -
HEINZ GRUNER LIBRARY □ Falls Church, VA
Frenette, Geraldine, Chf.
DETROIT PUBLIC LIBRARY - PHILOSOPHY,
RELIGION AND EDUCATION DEPARTMENT □
Detroit, MI
Frenze, Christopher, Res.Dir.
NATIONAL TAX EQUALITY ASSOCIATION -
LIBRARY □ Washington, DC
Frese, Irene, Lib. Aide
ATLANTIC-RICHFIELD COMPANY - ARCO
CHEMICAL COMPANY - RESEARCH &
ENGINEERING TECHNICAL INFORMATION
CENTER □ Newton Square, PA
Freshley, Katherine T., Libn.
TEXTILE MUSEUM - LIBRARY □ Washington, DC
Fretwell, Sara Barnett, Libn.
ANNE ARUNDEL GENERAL HOSPITAL -
MEMORIAL LIBRARY □ Annapolis, MD
Freudenberger, Elsie, Cat.Libn.
SCHOOL OF THEOLOGY AT CLAREMONT -
THEOLOGY LIBRARY □ Claremont, CA
Freund, Clare, Cat.
EASTMAN KODAK COMPANY - RESEARCH
LABORATORIES - RESEARCH LIBRARY □
Rochester, NY
Frewen, Mrs., Ref. Data Anl.
CANADA - INDUSTRY, TRADE & COMMERCE -
CANADIAN GOVERNMENT OFFICE OF TOURISM
□ Ottawa, ON

Frewin, C.C., Dir.
CONFEDERATION COLLEGE OF APPLIED ARTS & TECHNOLOGY - RESOURCE CENTRE □ Thunder Bay, ON

Frey, Agnes L., Chf., Rd.Serv.Br.
U.S. ARMY WAR COLLEGE - LIBRARY □ Carlisle Barracks, PA

Frey, Amy Louise, Libn.
PARK AVENUE SYNAGOGUE - ROTHSCHILD LIBRARY □ New York, NY

Frey, Charles, Dir.
PEORIA HISTORICAL SOCIETY - HARRY L. SPOONER MEMORIAL LIBRARY □ Peoria, IL

Frey, Charles J., Spec.Coll.Libn.
BRADLEY UNIVERSITY - VIRGINIUS H. CHASE SPECIAL COLLECTIONS CENTER - CHASE COLLECTION □ Peoria, IL

Frey, Charles J., Spec.Coll.Libn.
BRADLEY UNIVERSITY - VIRGINIUS H. CHASE SPECIAL COLLECTIONS CENTER - LINCOLN COLLECTIONS □ Peoria, IL

Frey, Charles J., Spec.Coll.Libn.
BRADLEY UNIVERSITY - VIRGINIUS H. CHASE SPECIAL COLLECTIONS CENTER - PEORIA HISTORICAL SOCIETY COLLECTIONS □ Peoria, IL

Frey, Emil F., Dir.
UNIVERSITY OF TEXAS MEDICAL BRANCH - MOODY MEDICAL LIBRARY □ Galveston, TX

Frey, Roxanne, Libn.
IROQUOIS COUNTY GENEALOGICAL SOCIETY - LIBRARY □ Watseka, IL

Freyermuth, Charlene, Lib.Techn.
U.S.D.A. - AGRICULTURAL RESEARCH SERVICE - STORED-PRODUCT INSECTS RESEARCH & DEVELOPMENT LAB. - LIBRARY □ Savannah, GA

Freyman, Marcelle, Asst. Dental Libn.
TEMPLE UNIVERSITY - HEALTH SCIENCES CENTER - LIBRARY □ Philadelphia, PA

Freytag, Mrs. Lindsay, Dir.
LICKING MEMORIAL HOSPITAL - MEDICAL LIBRARY □ Newark, OH

Frick, Joan, Libn.
FORD, BACON & DAVIS, INC. - LIBRARY □ New York, NY

Frideres, Dr. James S., Dir.
CANADIAN ETHNIC STUDIES ASSOCIATION - RESEARCH CENTRE □ Calgary, AB

Fridie, Stephanie, Ref.
SALISBURY STATE COLLEGE - BLACKWELL LIBRARY □ Salisbury, MD

Fridley, Bonnie, Search Analyst
U.S. AIR FORCE - AEROSPACE MEDICAL DIVISION - SCHOOL OF AEROSPACE MEDICINE - STRUGHOLD AEROMEDICAL LIBRARY □ Brooks AFB, TX

Frie, George, Engr.Adm.
CRANE COMPANY - HYDRO-AIRE DIVISION - TECHNICAL LIBRARY □ Burbank, CA

Fried, Arthur N., Supv.
LOCKHEED MISSILES & SPACE COMPANY, INC. - TECHNICAL INFORMATION CENTER □ Palo Alto, CA

Fried, Ava, Hd., Mtls. Access
UNIVERSITY OF CINCINNATI - MEDICAL CENTER LIBRARIES - HEALTH SCIENCES LIBRARY □ Cincinnati, OH

Frieday, Mrs. L.A., Hd. Automated Oper.
CANADA - GEOLOGICAL SURVEY OF CANADA - LIBRARY □ Ottawa, ON

Friede, John A., Pres.
VIDEO TAPE NETWORK, INC. - LIBRARY □ New York, NY

Friedel, Marie, Exec.Dir.
NATIONAL FOUNDATION FOR GIFTED AND CREATIVE CHILDREN - LIBRARY □ Warwick, RI

Friedenreich, Catherine J., Data User Serv.Off.
U.S. BUREAU OF THE CENSUS - REGIONAL DATA USER SERVICE - CHARLOTTE REGIONAL OFFICE - LIBRARY □ Charlotte, NC

Friedenstein, Hanna, Mgr.
CABOT CORPORATION - TECHNICAL INFORMATION CENTER □ Billerica, MA

Friedman, Arlene H., Libn.
ONONDAGA COUNTY PUBLIC LIBRARY - ART AND MUSIC DEPARTMENT □ Syracuse, NY

Friedman, Charlotte, Asst.Libn.
WORLD BOOK-CHILDCRAFT INTERNATIONAL, INC.- RESEARCH LIBRARY □ Chicago, IL

Friedman, Joan M., Cur. Of Rare Books
YALE UNIVERSITY - YALE CENTER FOR BRITISH ART - RARE BOOK COLLECTION □ New Haven, CT

Friedman, Joel I., Tech.Info.Spec.
NATIONAL INJURY INFORMATION CLEARINGHOUSE □ Washington, DC

Friedman, Judy, Mgr./Lib. & Ref.Serv.
NATIONAL BROADCASTING COMPANY, INC. - REFERENCE LIBRARY □ New York, NY

Friedman, Kathleen, Law Libn.
WAYNE COUNTY CIRCUIT COURT - LAW LIBRARY □ Detroit, MI

Friedman, Lori, Info.Spec.
PPG INDUSTRIES, INC. - CHEMICAL DIVISION - RESEARCH LIBRARY □ Barberton, OH

Friedman, Lydia, Chf.Med.Libn.
MAIMONIDES MEDICAL CENTER - MEDICAL LIBRARY □ Brooklyn, NY

Friedman, Martha, Libn.
UNIVERSITY OF ILLINOIS - HISTORY AND PHILOSOPHY LIBRARY □ Urbana, IL

Friedman, Roberta G., Sr. Law Libn.
FEDERAL RESERVE BANK OF NEW YORK - LAW LIBRARY DIVISION □ New York, NY

Friedman, Susan, Tech.Serv.Libn.
BATTEN, BARTON, DURSTINE, OSBORN, INC. - INFORMATION RETRIEVAL CENTER □ New York, NY

Fries, Victoria, Res.Libn.
ACTION - LIBRARY □ Washington, DC

Friesen, Eva, Tech.Serv.Libn.
RYERSON POLYTECHNICAL INSTITUTE - LEARNING RESOURCES CENTRE □ Toronto, ON

Friesen, Susan, Lib.Techn.
CAMOSUN COLLEGE - LIBRARY/MEDIA SERVICES □ Victoria, BC

Friewer, K.A.
DOW CHEMICAL COMPANY - TECHNICAL INFORMATION SERVICES - CHEMICAL LIBRARY □ Midland, MI

Frimel, J.W., Info.Spec.
GOODRICH (B.F.) COMPANY - GOODRICH CHEMICAL DIVISION TECHNICAL CENTER - INFORMATION CENTER □ Avon Lake, OH

Frimer, Baer M., Pres.
PICTORIAL PARADE INC. - LIBRARY □ New York, NY

Frins, Sarah L., Tech.Serv.Libn.
ALABAMA STATE SUPREME COURT - SUPREME COURT AND STATE LAW LIBRARY □ Montgomery, AL

Frisbie, Granville K., Chm., Lib.Comm.
SCOTTISH RITE BODIES, SAN DIEGO - SCOTTISH RITE MASONIC LIBRARY □ San Diego, CA

Frisby, Wilfred A., Dir. Of Lib.Serv.
PHILADELPHIA COLLEGE OF TEXTILES AND SCIENCE - PASTORE LIBRARY □ Philadelphia, PA

Frisch, Irene, Lib.Dir.
STERLING DRUG, INC. - WINTHROP LABORATORIES - MEDICAL LIBRARY □ New York, NY

Frisch, Sylvia, Libn.
MINNEAPOLIS PUBLIC LIBRARY & INFORMATION CENTER - MUNICIPAL INFORMATION LIBRARY □ Minneapolis, MN

Fritsche, Karen, Lib.Asst., Intl.
ARTHUR ANDERSEN & CO. - BUSINESS LIBRARY □ Houston, TX

Fritz, Al, Libn.
UNIVERSITY OF WASHINGTON - POLITICAL SCIENCE LIBRARY □ Seattle, WA

Fritz, Dr. Charles G., Dir.
ETHICON, INC. - SCIENTIFIC INFORMATION SERVICES □ Somerville, NJ

Fritz, William Richard, Sr., Libn.
LUTHERAN THEOLOGICAL SOUTHERN SEMINARY - LONEBERGER MEMORIAL LIBRARY □ Columbia, SC

Frobom, Jerome B., Chf., Govt.Pubn.
WYOMING STATE LIBRARY □ Cheyenne, WY

Froiland, Sven, Dir.
AUGUSTANA COLLEGE - CENTER FOR WESTERN STUDIES □ Sioux Falls, SD

Froman, Barry, Co-Owner
STOVE KING - LIBRARY □ Salt Lake City, UT

Froman, Clarence, Owner
STOVE KING - LIBRARY □ Salt Lake City, UT

Fromkes, Ruth, Info.Dir.
FOOTE CONE & BELDING - LIBRARY† □ New York, NY

Fromm, Esther, Archv./Dir.GPL
AMERICAN HISTORICAL SOCIETY OF GERMANS FROM RUSSIA - GREELEY PUBLIC LIBRARY □ Greeley, CO

Fromm, Ken, Asst.Dir./Media Ctr.
OHIO DOMINICAN COLLEGE - LIBRARY □ Columbus, OH

Fromm, Roger, Archv./Ref.Libn.
BLOOMSBURG STATE COLLEGE - HARVEY A. ANDRUSS LIBRARY □ Bloomsburg, PA

Frommer, Saul I., Sr.Musm.Sci.
UNIVERSITY OF CALIFORNIA, RIVERSIDE - DEPARTMENT OF ENTOMOLOGY - LIBRARY □ Riverside, CA

Frontz, Stephanie, Hd.
UNIVERSITY OF ROCHESTER - FINE ARTS LIBRARY □ Rochester, NY

Frosch, Paula, Libn.
METROPOLITAN MUSEUM OF ART - THOMAS J. WATSON LIBRARY □ New York, NY

Frost, Annette K., Hd., Lib.Serv.
FANSHAWE COLLEGE OF APPLIED ARTS AND TECHNOLOGY - MAIN LIBRARY □ London, ON

Frost, Bruce, Asst.Libn.
MISSOURI STATE SUPREME COURT LIBRARY □ Jefferson City, MO

Frost, E., Chf.Commun.Rec.
CANADA - PUBLIC ARCHIVES OF CANADA - FEDERAL ARCHIVES DIVISION □ Ottawa, ON

Frost, J. William, Dir.
SWARTHMORE COLLEGE - FRIENDS HISTORICAL LIBRARY □ Swarthmore, PA

Frost, Dr. John, Cur.
NEW YORK UNIVERSITY - ELMER HOLMES BOBST LIBRARY - FROST LIBRARY □ New York, NY

Frost, Judith G., Assoc.Libn.
CLEVELAND MUSEUM OF ART - LIBRARY □ Cleveland, OH

Frost, Dr. Shimon, Dir.
AMERICAN ASSOCIATION FOR JEWISH EDUCATION - LIBRARY □ New York, NY

Frost, Terrence P.
NEW HAMPSHIRE STATE WATER SUPPLY AND POLLUTION CONTROL COMMISSION - LIBRARY □ Concord, NH

Frost, William, Ref.Libn.
BLOOMSBURG STATE COLLEGE - HARVEY A. ANDRUSS LIBRARY □ Bloomsburg, PA

Frow, Richard G., Libn.
MIAMI-DADE PUBLIC LIBRARY - URBAN AFFAIRS LIBRARY □ Miami, FL

Fruehe, Margot, Libn.
MIDWEST COLLEGE OF ENGINEERING - JOSEPH M. HARRER LIBRARY □ Lombard, IL

Frump, John A., Mgr., Sci.Info.Serv.
INTERNATIONAL MINERALS & CHEMICALS CORPORATION - IMC RESEARCH & DEVELOPMENT LIBRARY □ Terre Haute, IN

P
E
R
S
O
N
N
E
L

Fry, Belle
MARYLAND STATE ENERGY OFFICE - LIBRARY
□ Baltimore, MD
Fry, Donald W., Dir.
U.S. DEPT. OF COMMERCE - INTERNATIONAL
TRADE ADMINISTRATION - PHOENIX
DISTRICT OFFICE LIBRARY □ Phoenix, AZ
Fry, Eileen, Slide Libn.
INDIANA UNIVERSITY - FINE ARTS LIBRARY □
Bloomington, IN
Fry, Eileen, Slide Libn.
INDIANA UNIVERSITY - FINE ARTS SLIDE
LIBRARY □ Bloomington, IN
Fry, Hazel, Area Hd.
UNIVERSITY OF CALGARY - ENVIRONMENT-
SCIENCE-TECHNOLOGY LIBRARY □ Calgary, AB
Fry, James W., Dp.Asst. State Libn.
STATE LIBRARY OF OHIO □ Columbus, OH
Fry, Stephen, Music Libn.
UNIVERSITY OF CALIFORNIA, LOS ANGELES -
MUSIC LIBRARY □ Los Angeles, CA
Frye, Florence, Chf.Libn.
SEATTLE POST-INTELLIGENCER - NEWSPAPER
LIBRARY □ Seattle, WA
Frye, Margaret, Asst.Libn.
NORTHWEST COLLEGE OF THE ASSEMBLIES OF
GOD - HURST LIBRARY □ Kirkland, WA
Frye, Dr. Roland Mushat, Cur.
UNIVERSITY OF PENNSYLVANIA - HORACE
HOWARD FURNESS MEMORIAL LIBRARY □
Philadelphia, PA
Fryer, William N., Chf.Psych.Serv.
ABILENE STATE SCHOOL - SPECIAL LIBRARY □
Abilene, TX
Frymark, Kathleen, Circ.Libn.
MARQUETTE UNIVERSITY - MEMORIAL
LIBRARY □ Milwaukee, WI
Fryshdorf, Hannah, Asst.Dir.
YIVO INSTITUTE FOR JEWISH RESEARCH -
LIBRARY AND ARCHIVES □ New York, NY
Fu, Paul S., Law Libn.
OHIO STATE SUPREME COURT LAW LIBRARY □
Columbus, OH
Fu, Tina, Asst.Dir., Pub.Serv.
UNIVERSITY OF WISCONSIN, OSHKOSH -
UNIVERSITY LIBRARIES AND LEARNING
RESOURCES □ Oshkosh, WI
Fuchs, C.
RESEARCH & EDUCATION ASSOCIATION -
LIBRARY □ New York, NY
Fuchs, Joe, Libn.
PASADENA PUBLIC LIBRARY - REFERENCE
DIVISION □ Pasadena, CA
Fuchs, Joseph L., Chf., Users' Serv.
UNITED NATIONS HEADQUARTERS - DAG
HAMMARSKJOLD LIBRARY □ New York, NY
Fuderer, Laura, Ref.Biblog.
FAIRLEIGH DICKINSON UNIVERSITY - WEINER
LIBRARY - REFERENCE/GOVERNMENT
DOCUMENTS DEPARTMENT □ Teaneck, NJ
Fuenfhausen, Ron, Cur.
CLAY COUNTY ARCHIVES □ Liberty, MO
Fugate, K.O., Pres. & Libn.
PANEL DISPLAYS, INC. - TECHNICAL LIBRARY†
□ Inglewood, CA
Fugate, Liz, Libn.
UNIVERSITY OF WASHINGTON - DRAMA
LIBRARY □ Seattle, WA
Fuge, Heidi A., Lib. & Musm.Dir.
HISTORICAL SOCIETY OF SARATOGA SPRINGS
- MUSEUM AND LIBRARY □ Saratoga Springs, NY
Fugle, Mary, Asst.Libn.
LUTHERAN MEDICAL CENTER - MEDICAL
LIBRARY □ Brooklyn, NY
Fuhr, J.R., Physicist
U.S. NATL. BUREAU OF STANDARDS - DATA
CENTER ON ATOMIC TRANSITION
PROBABILITIES □ Washington, DC
Fuhrmann, Debbie, Prog.Coord.
PLANNED PARENTHOOD ASSOCIATION OF ST.
LOUIS - FAMILY PLANNING LIBRARY □ St.
Louis, MO

Fujimoto, Patricia, Libn.
FOOTE CONE & BELDING - INFORMATION
CENTER □ Chicago, IL
Fujiwara, Susan, Info.Spec.
BNR INC. - INFORMATION RESOURCE CENTER
□ Mountain View, CA
Fukano, Yasuko T., Hd.Libn.
UNIVERSITY OF WASHINGTON - FISHERIES-
OCEANOGRAPHY LIBRARY □ Seattle, WA
Fukuji, Delia, Libn.
HAWAII STATE LIBRARY - EDNA ALLYN ROOM
□ Honolulu, HI
Fulcher, Jane M., Law Libn.
WASHINGTON COUNTY LAW LIBRARY □
Washington, PA
Fullam, Rev. Paul J., Libn.
PASSIONIST MONASTERY - LIBRARY □
Jamaica, NY
Fullam, R., Asst.Libn.
MC NEIL LABORATORIES - LIBRARY □ Fort
Washington, PA
Fuller, Mrs. Ben, Asst.
FIRST BAPTIST CHURCH - E.F. WALKER
MEMORIAL LIBRARY □ Luling, TX
Fuller, Dorothy C., Asst.Dir., Lib.Dev.
VIRGINIA STATE LIBRARY □ Richmond, VA
Fuller, Elizabeth G., Libn.
WESTCHESTER COUNTY HISTORICAL SOCIETY
- LIBRARY □ Tuckahoe, NY
Fuller, Jean, Libn.
ST. MARY'S HOSPITAL - FINKELSTEIN LIBRARY
□ Waterbury, CT
Fuller, John W., Dir.
UNIVERSITY OF IOWA - INSTITUTE OF URBAN
AND REGIONAL RESEARCH - LIBRARY □ Iowa
City, IA
Fuller, Kathleen, Hd.Libn.
FERRO CORPORATION - LIBRARY □
Independence, OH
Fuller, Linda P., Gen.Serv.Libn.
NORTH CAROLINA STATE UNIVERSITY - D.H.
HILL LIBRARY □ Raleigh, NC
Fuller, Ms. LoRene, Libn.
ENVIRONMENTAL PROTECTION AGENCY -
ROBERT S. KERR ENVIRONMENTAL RESEARCH
LABORATORY - LIBRARY □ Ada, OK
Fuller, Nancy F., Libn.
UNIVERSITY OF MISSISSIPPI - SCHOOL OF
PHARMACY - AUSTIN A. DODGE PHARMACY
LIBRARY □ University, MS
Fuller, Nell B., Hd.Tech.Serv.
UNIVERSITY OF VIRGINIA MEDICAL CENTER -
CLAUDE MOORE HEALTH SCIENCES LIBRARY □
Charlottesville, VA
Fuller, Stephan B., Music Libn.
HARVARD UNIVERSITY - RADCLIFFE COLLEGE -
MORSE MUSIC LIBRARY □ Cambridge, MA
Fullerton, Sylvia J., Asst.Univ.Libn.Sci.
DALHOUSIE UNIVERSITY - MACDONALD
SCIENCE LIBRARY □ Halifax, NS
Fullom, Agatha, Cur. in Residence
WATERVILLE HISTORICAL SOCIETY - LIBRARY
AND ARCHIVES □ Waterville, ME
Fullshire, Lynn C., Sr. Law Libn.
NEW YORK STATE SUPREME COURT - 10TH
JUDICIAL DISTRICT - LAW LIBRARY □
Riverhead, NY
Fullwood, Sallie, ILL
TRW, INC. - DEFENSE & SPACE SYSTEMS
GROUP - TECHNICAL LIBRARY† □ McLean, VA
Fulmer, Elisabeth S., Sec./Libn.
CLARION COUNTY HISTORICAL SOCIETY -
LIBRARY/MUSEUM □ Clarion, PA
Fulton, Elaine, Exec.Sec.
NATIONAL ASSOCIATION OF
PARLIAMENTARIANS - TECHNICAL
INFORMATION CENTER □ Kansas City, MO
Fulton, Elizabeth W., Sr.Res.Libn.
NATIONAL STEEL CORPORATION - RESEARCH
CENTER LIBRARY □ Weirton, WV

Fulton, June M., Dir., R.M.L.
COLLEGE OF PHYSICIANS OF PHILADELPHIA -
LIBRARY AND MEDICAL DOCUMENTATION
SERVICE □ Philadelphia, PA
Fulton, William A., Asst.Chf., Law Br.
U.S. DEPT. OF COMMERCE - DEPARTMENTAL
LIBRARY □ Washington, DC
Fultz, Gloria, Lib.Mgr.
FRANKLIN RESEARCH CENTER - NATIONAL
SOLAR HEATING & COOLING INFO. CTR. □
Rockville, MD
Funk, Mark E., Hd., Coll.Dev.
UNIVERSITY OF NEBRASKA MEDICAL CENTER -
MC GOOGAN LIBRARY OF MEDICINE □ Omaha,
NE
Funke, Rory, Hd.
UNIVERSITY OF OREGON - MICROFORMS AND
RECORDINGS DEPARTMENT □ Eugene, OR
Funkhouser, Richard L., Libn.
PURDUE UNIVERSITY - MATHEMATICAL
SCIENCES LIBRARY □ West Lafayette, IN
Funnell, Maureen D., Libn.
SOUTHWEST FOUNDATION FOR RESEARCH
AND EDUCATION - PRESTON G. NORTHROP
MEMORIAL LIBRARY □ San Antonio, TX
Funston, J. Arthur, Archv.
EARLHAM COLLEGE - QUAKER COLLECTION □
Richmond, IN
Fuqua, Ann, Site Mgr.
U.S. NATL. PARK SERVICE - ARLINGTON
HOUSE, THE ROBERT E. LEE MEMORIAL -
LIBRARY □ McLean, VA
Furbeyre, Mae L., Libn.
UNIVERSITY OF SOUTHERN CALIFORNIA -
SCHOOL OF LIBRARY & INFORMATION
MANAGEMENT - LIBRARY □ Los Angeles, CA
Furlan, Nancy J., Info.Serv.Adm.
ALUMINUM COMPANY OF AMERICA -
CORPORATE LIBRARY □ Pittsburgh, PA
Furlong, Robert E., Lib. Group Supv.
BELL TELEPHONE LABORATORIES, INC. -
TECHNICAL LIBRARY □ Naperville, IL
Furlow, Karen, Corp.Libn.
MC DERMOTT INC. - CORPORATE
INFORMATION CENTER □ New Orleans, LA
Furman, Evelyn E., Owner
TABOR OPERA HOUSE - LIBRARY □ Leadville, CO
Furnish, Carol, Ser.Libn.
OHIO NORTHERN UNIVERSITY - COLLEGE OF
LAW - JAY P. TAGGART MEMORIAL LAW
LIBRARY □ Ada, OH
Furnish, Jean, Ref.Libn.
UNIVERSITY OF CALIFORNIA - LOS ALAMOS
NATIONAL LABORATORY - LIBRARY □ Los
Alamos, NM
Furrer, Robert S.
AMUNDSON ASSOCIATES - PLANNING
REFERENCE LIBRARY† □ Springfield, OR
Furst, Kenneth W., Libn.
SUNY AT STONY BROOK - ENGINEERING
LIBRARY □ Stony Brook, NY
Furtick, Lorraine, Ser.Libn.
WESTERN CONNECTICUT STATE COLLEGE -
RUTH A. HAAS LIBRARY □ Danbury, CT
Furuli, Michael, Coord. Media
LORETTO HEIGHTS COLLEGE - MAY BONFILS
STANTON LIBRARY □ Denver, CO
Furushiro, Midori, Sec.
COLLEGE OF IDAHO - REGIONAL STUDIES
CENTER - LIBRARY □ Caldwell, ID
Fury, Laura D., Libn.
MADISON STATE HOSPITAL - CRAGMONT
MEDICAL LIBRARY □ Madison, IN
Fusco, Lucy, Asst.Libn.
BARRETT, SMITH, SCHAPIRO, SIMON &
ARMSTRONG - LIBRARY □ New York, NY
Fuscoe, James C., Chf.Libn.
ROHR INDUSTRIES - CORPORATE LIBRARY □
Chula Vista, CA
Fuseler, Elizabeth A., Libn.
TEXAS A & M UNIVERSITY AT GALVESTON -
LIBRARY □ Galveston, TX

Fuseler, Elizabeth A., Libn.
U.S. MERCHANT MARINE ACADEMY -
SCHUYLER OTIS BLAND MEMORIAL LIBRARY □
Kings Point, NY
Fuss, Janet R., Libn.
PARADISE VALLEY HOSPITAL - MEDICAL
LIBRARY □ National City, CA
Futrell, Gene, Curric.Lab.Libn.
EAST TEXAS BAPTIST COLLEGE - MAMYE
JARRETT LEARNING CENTER □ Marshall, TX

G

Gaar, Marcella C., Libn.
WASHINGTON MUTUAL SAVINGS BANK -
INFORMATION CENTER & DIETRICH SCHMITZ
MEMORIAL LIBRARY □ Seattle, WA
Gabarry, Suzanne A., Libn.
MERCY HOSPITAL - MEDICAL STAFF LIBRARY □
Pittsburgh, PA
Gabbard, Marilee, LRC Libn.
EASTERN KENTUCKY UNIVERSITY - JOHN
GRANT CRABBE LIBRARY □ Richmond, KY
Gabbert, Roy E., Libn.
ADAMS COUNTY LAW LIBRARY □ West Union,
OH
Gabel, E. Margaret
ELIZABETHTOWN COLLEGE - ZUG MEMORIAL
LIBRARY - ARCHIVES □ Elizabethtown, PA
Gaber, Lawrence, Art Libn.
MADISON PUBLIC LIBRARY - ART AND MUSIC
DIVISION □ Madison, WI
Gabert, Marjorie, Lib.Asst.
FERRIS STATE COLLEGE - SCHOOL OF
PHARMACY - PERIODICAL READING ROOM □
Big Rapids, MI
Gable, Ina, Lib.Comm.Chm.
FIRST SOUTHERN BAPTIST CHURCH - LIBRARY
□ Tucson, AZ
Gable, June R., Tech.Lib.Br.Hd.
U.S. NAVY - STRATEGIC SYSTEMS PROJECT
OFFICE - TECHNICAL LIBRARY □ Washington,
DC
Gable, Sarah, Ref.Libn.
UNIVERSITY OF SOUTH CAROLINA - SCHOOL
OF MEDICINE LIBRARY □ Columbia, SC
Gabriel, Andrea V., Libn.
TALL TIMBERS RESEARCH STATION - LIBRARY
□ Tallahassee, FL
Gabriel, Jennifer, Libn.
RECONSTRUCTIONIST RABBINICAL COLLEGE -
MORDECAI M. KAPLAN LIBRARY □ Philadelphia,
PA
Gadbois, Frank, Libn.
U.S. AIR FORCE - KEESLER TECHNICAL
TRAINING CENTER - ACADEMIC LIBRARY □
Keesler AFB, MS
Gadd, Wendy, Assoc.Libn.
KALAMAZOO INSTITUTE OF ARTS - ART
CENTER LIBRARY □ Kalamazoo, MI
Gaddis, Jane L., Libn.
LORD, BISSELL AND BROOK - LAW LIBRARY □
Chicago, IL
Gadker, Christine J., Res.Libn.
CARSTAB CORPORATION - RESEARCH LIBRARY
□ Cincinnati, OH
Gadreau, Rock, Dir.
ASSOCIATION DE PARALYSIE CEREBRALE DU
QUEBEC, INC. - CENTRE DE DOCUMENTATION
□ Quebec, PQ
Gadula, Marie, Libn.
MC LEOD YOUNG WEIR LIMITED -
INFORMATION CENTRE □ Toronto, ON
Gadwa, Candace E., Hd. Legal Asst./Libn.
SMITH, MIRO, HIRSCH & BRODY - LIBRARY □
Detroit, MI

Gadzikowski, Claire E., Spec.Proj.Coord., MCRMLP
UNIVERSITY OF NEBRASKA MEDICAL CENTER -
MC GOOGAN LIBRARY OF MEDICINE □ Omaha,
NE
Gaeddert, Kathryn, Cur.
SACRAMENTO CITY AND COUNTY MUSEUM -
LIBRARY □ Sacramento, CA
Gaffey, Debra, Asst.Libn.
NATIONAL ECONOMIC RESEARCH
ASSOCIATES, INC. - LIBRARY □ New York, NY
Gaffney, Thomas L., Dir.
MAINE HISTORICAL SOCIETY - LIBRARY □
Portland, ME
Gafford, Frank Hall, Jr., Dir.
CLARK COUNTY COMMUNITY COLLEGE -
LEARNING RESOURCES CENTER □ North Las
Vegas, NV
Gage, Dr. J. Fred, Dir.
UNIVERSITY OF PITTSBURGH - UNIVERSITY
CENTER FOR INSTRUCTIONAL RESOURCES □
Pittsburgh, PA
Gagliardi, Mr. Francis J., Assoc.Dir.
CENTRAL CONNECTICUT STATE COLLEGE -
ELIHU BURRITT LIBRARY □ New Britain, CT
Gagne, Jeannine, Responsable
JARDIN ZOOLOGIQUE DE QUEBEC -
BIBLIOTHEQUE □ Charlesbourg, PQ
Gagne, Joan, Educ.Libn.
MC GILL UNIVERSITY - EDUCATION LIBRARY □
Montreal, PQ
Gagne, Joan, Educ.Libn.
MC GILL UNIVERSITY - EDUCATION LIBRARY -
SAM RABINOVITCH MEMORIAL COLLECTION □
Montreal, PQ
Gagner, Ron
IBM CORPORATION - GENERAL TECHNOLOGY
DIVISION - INFORMATION CENTER/LEARNING
CENTER □ Essex Junction, VT
Gagnon, Claude, Hd. Music Serv.
CANADIAN BROADCASTING CORPORATION -
MUSIC SERVICES LIBRARY □ Montreal, PQ
Gagnon, Mr. R., Chf.Libn.
CANADA - PUBLIC WORKS CANADA -
INFORMATION, RESEARCH & LIBRARY
SERVICES □ Ottawa, ON
Gagnon, Richard, Libn.
AMERICAN-CANADIAN GENEALOGICAL
SOCIETY - LIBRARY □ Manchester, NH
Gagnon, Vernon N., Libn.
BOISE CASCADE CORPORATION - PULP &
PAPER RESEARCH LIBRARY □ Vancouver, WA
Gaines, James E., Hd.Libn.
VIRGINIA MILITARY INSTITUTE - PRESTON
LIBRARY □ Lexington, VA
Gaines, Lucille, Ref.Libn.
VIRGINIA STATE LIBRARY FOR THE VISUALLY
AND PHYSICALLY HANDICAPPED □ Richmond,
VA
Gaines, Paul, Proj.Dir.
NATIONAL CLEARINGHOUSE OF
REHABILITATION TRAINING MATERIALS -
REFERENCE COLLECTION □ Stillwater, OK
Gaines, Virginia, Cur.
MASON COUNTY HISTORICAL SOCIETY - ROSE
HAWLEY MUSEUM AND HISTORICAL LIBRARY □
Ludington, MI
Gaines, Willene J., Chf., Tech.Serv.
U.S. DEPT. OF COMMERCE - DEPARTMENTAL
LIBRARY □ Washington, DC
Gaines, William C., Pub.Serv.Libn.
PARKLAND COLLEGE - LEARNING RESOURCE
CENTER □ Champaign, IL
Gairiepy, Mme., Dir.
CINEMATHEQUE NATIONALE DU QUEBEC □
Montreal, PQ
Gaiser, Rosemary, Hd.
PUBLIC LIBRARY OF CINCINNATI AND
HAMILTON COUNTY - SCIENCE AND INDUSTRY
DEPARTMENT □ Cincinnati, OH
Gaither, Beryl, Lib.Techn.
UNIVERSITY OF KENTUCKY - BIOLOGICAL
SCIENCES LIBRARY □ Lexington, KY

Gal, Dr. Imre, Chf.Libn.
BLOOMFIELD COLLEGE - GEORGE TALBOT HALL
LIBRARY □ Bloomfield, NJ
Galal, Mrs. Horeya M., Asst. Law Libn.
UNIVERSITY OF PITTSBURGH - LAW LIBRARY □
Pittsburgh, PA
Galarneau, Pierrette, Libn.
HOPITAL JEAN-TALON - BIBLIOTHEQUE
MEDICALE □ Montreal, PQ
Galban, Victoria S., Asst.Cur., Res.
METROPOLITAN MUSEUM OF ART - ROBERT
LEHMAN COLLECTION - LIBRARY □ New York,
NY
Galbraith, Jeanne, Circ.Libn.
SUNY AT STONY BROOK - HEALTH SCIENCES
LIBRARY □ East Setauket, NY
Galbraith, Mr. Leslie R., Libn.
CHRISTIAN THEOLOGICAL SEMINARY -
LIBRARY □ Indianapolis, IN
Galbraith, Marc, Dir. of Ref.
KANSAS STATE LIBRARY □ Topeka, KS
Gale, Linda J., Libn.
EMHART INDUSTRIES, INC. - HARTFORD
DIVISION LIBRARY □ Windsor, CT
Gale, Margaret J., Libn.
BRITISH INFORMATION SERVICES - LIBRARY □
New York, NY
Gale, Virginia, Lib.Techn.
ST. JOSEPH HOSPITAL - HEALTH SCIENCE
LIBRARY □ Joliet, IL
Galejs, John E., Asst.Dir., Res.
IOWA STATE UNIVERSITY - LIBRARY □ Ames,
IA
Galipault, John B., Pres.
AVIATION SAFETY INSTITUTE - ASI
TECHNICAL LABS. - LIBRARY □ Worthington, OH
Galkowski, Patricia, Phys.Sci.Ref.Libn.
BROWN UNIVERSITY - SCIENCES LIBRARY □
Providence, RI
Gallagher, Sr. Annette, Ref.
MARYCREST COLLEGE - CONE LIBRARY† □
Davenport, IA
Gallagher, Barbara, Hd.Lib.Serv.
AMERICAN CHEMICAL SOCIETY, INC. -
LIBRARY □ Washington, DC
Gallagher, Connell, Mss.
UNIVERSITY OF VERMONT - WILBUR
COLLECTION OF VERMONTIANA □ Burlington,
VT
Gallagher, Elizabeth, Tech.Info.Spec.
U.S. NATL. INSTITUTES OF HEALTH - LIBRARY
□ Bethesda, MD
Gallagher, J.W., Act.Dir.
UNIVERSITY OF COLORADO, BOULDER - JOINT
INSTITUTE FOR LABORATORY ASTROPHYSICS
- INFO. ANALYSIS CENTER □ Boulder, CO
Gallagher, Joan, Libn.
AMERICAN CYANAMID COMPANY - STAMFORD
RESEARCH CENTER LIBRARY □ Stamford, CT
Gallagher, Joan L., Mgr.Tech.Info.
AMERICAN CYANAMID COMPANY - CHEMICAL
RESEARCH DIVISION - LIBRARY □ Bound Brook,
NJ
Gallagher, Kathy, Libn.
WASHINGTON UNIVERSITY - DENTISTRY
LIBRARY □ St. Louis, MO
Gallagher, Margaret M., Asst.Libn.
LIBBEY-OWENS-FORD COMPANY - TECHNICAL
CENTER - LIBRARY □ Toledo, OH
Gallagher, Mary Kaye, Mgr., Client Serv.
UNIVERSITY OF NEW MEXICO - TECHNOLOGY
APPLICATION CENTER □ Albuquerque, NM
Gallagher, Philip J., Libn.
JOHNSON (Robert Wood) FOUNDATION -
LIBRARY □ Princeton, NJ
Gallagher, R. Susan, Sys.Photo.Libn.
CANADIAN NATIONAL RAILWAYS -
PHOTOGRAPHIC LIBRARY □ Montreal, PQ
Gallagher, W.T., Mgr.
IBM CORPORATION - RESEARCH LIBRARY □
San Jose, CA

PERSONNEL

Gash, Anne Gail, Libn.
NEW YORK STATE SUPREME COURT - 11TH JUDICIAL DISTRICT - LAW LIBRARY □ Jamaica, NY

Gaskin, Annette C., Libn.
DESIGN PROFESSIONALS FINANCIAL CORPORATION - LIBRARY □ San Francisco, CA

Gaskins, Betty, Mgr.Lib.Serv.
DATA COURIER, INC. - LIBRARY SERVICES & ACQUISITIONS □ Louisville, KY

Gaspar, N.J., Hd., Info.Serv.
IMPERIAL OIL, LTD. - RESEARCH TECHNICAL INFORMATION CENTRE □ Sarnia, ON

Gaspari-Bridges, Patricia, Asst.Libn./Map Libn.
PRINCETON UNIVERSITY - GEOLOGY LIBRARY □ Princeton, NJ

Gasperini, Bonnie A., Med.Libn.
YPSILANTI REGIONAL PSYCHIATRIC HOSPITAL - LIBRARY □ Ypsilanti, MI

Gass, A. Beverley, Coord., Lib.Serv.
GUILFORD TECHNICAL INSTITUTE - LEARNING RESOURCE CENTER □ Jamestown, NC

Gast, Marie, Libn.
CORNELL UNIVERSITY - MAPS, MICROTEXT, NEWSPAPERS DEPARTMENT □ Ithaca, NY

Gaston, Howard J., Libn.
JAMAICA (B.W.I.) STUDY GROUP - LIBRARY □ West Granby, CT

Gaston, Judith A., Dir.
UNIVERSITY OF MINNESOTA - AUDIO VISUAL LIBRARY SERVICE □ Minneapolis, MN

Gately, Charles F., Dir.
U.S. DEPT. OF HEALTH AND HUMAN SERVICES - DEPARTMENT LIBRARY □ Washington, DC

Gately, Frank, Libn.
U.S. ARMY - CORPS OF ENGINEERS - GALVESTON DISTRICT - LIBRARY □ Galveston, TX

Gates, Earl, Libn.
UNIVERSITY OF KANSAS - THOMAS GORTON MUSIC LIBRARY □ Lawrence, KS

Gates, Prof. Francis, Law Libn.
COLUMBIA UNIVERSITY - LAW LIBRARY □ New York, NY

Gates, Harry
SOUTHERN OREGON STATE COLLEGE - LIBRARY □ Ashland, OR

Gates, Jane, Hd.Libn.
STRYBING ARBORETUM SOCIETY - HELEN CROCKER RUSSELL LIBRARY □ San Francisco, CA

Gates, Linda, Asst.Dir.Lib.Dev.
MISSISSIPPI STATE LIBRARY COMMISSION □ Jackson, MS

Gates, Lorena, Circ.
UNIVERSITY OF ARKANSAS, MONTICELLO - LIBRARY† □ Monticello, AR

Gates, Marylu, Act.Libn.
VIRGINIA STATE LIBRARY FOR THE VISUALLY AND PHYSICALLY HANDICAPPED □ Richmond, VA

Gates, Thomas, Hist.Spec.
CONTRA COSTA COUNTY - CENTRAL LIBRARY - LOCAL HISTORY COLLECTION □ Pleasant Hill, CA

Gates, Warren J., Pres.
CUMBERLAND COUNTY HISTORICAL SOCIETY & HAMILTON LIBRARY □ Carlisle, PA

Gatewood, Dr. George, Dir.
UNIVERSITY OF PITTSBURGH - ALLEGHENY OBSERVATORY - LIBRARY □ Pittsburgh, PA

Gatlin, Nancy, Libn.
SOUTHERN COLLEGE OF OPTOMETRY - WILLIAM P. MAC CRACKEN, JR. MEMORIAL LIBRARY □ Memphis, TN

Gatlin, Patricia F., Supv. of Lib.Serv.
UNION ELECTRIC COMPANY - LIBRARY □ St. Louis, MO

Gattinger, F. Eugene, Coord., Lib.Serv.
TORONTO BOARD OF EDUCATION - EDUCATION CENTRE LIBRARY □ Toronto, ON

Gatton, Frank D., Hd., Archival Serv.
NORTH CAROLINA STATE DEPT. OF CULTURAL RESOURCES - DIV. OF ARCHIVES AND HISTORY - ARCHIVES & RECORDS SECTION □ Raleigh, NC

Gauch, M. Lois, Libn.
EASTMAN KODAK COMPANY - BUSINESS LIBRARY □ Rochester, NY

Gaucher, Elaine M., Libn.
U.S. NAVY - NAVAL SUBMARINE MEDICAL RESEARCH LABORATORY - MEDICAL LIBRARY □ Groton, CT

Gaucher, Monique, Libn.
UNIVERSITE DU QUEBEC A MONTREAL - BIBLIOTHEQUE DES SCIENCES DE L'EDUCATION □ Montreal, PQ

Gaudette, Nancy, Worcester Coll.Libn.
WORCESTER FREE PUBLIC LIBRARY - REFERENCE AND RESEARCH □ Worcester, MA

Gault, Jean, Libn.
HUMBER COLLEGE OF APPLIED ARTS & TECHNOLOGY - LIBRARY □ Rexdale, ON

Gault, Robin R., Circ.Libn.
FLORIDA STATE UNIVERSITY - LAW LIBRARY □ Tallahassee, FL

Gause, Sharon, Libn.
UNIVERSITY OF COLORADO, BOULDER - AUDIOVISUAL/MICROFORMS DEPARTMENT □ Boulder, CO

Gauthier, Betty, Hd., Acq.
UNIVERSITY OF MICHIGAN - DEARBORN LIBRARY □ Dearborn, MI

Gauthier, Francine, Lib.Techn.
CANADA - LAW REFORM COMMISSION OF CANADA - LIBRARY □ Ottawa, ON

Gauthier, Ghislaine, Br.Libn.
BELL-NORTHERN RESEARCH LTD. - TECHNICAL INFORMATION CENTRE □ Verdun, PQ

Gautier, Alba S., Libn.
UNIVERSITY OF PUERTO RICO - COLLEGE OF EDUCATION - SELLES SOLA MEMORIAL COLLECTION □ Rio Piedras, PR

Gavin, Christine B., Instr. Media Spec.
ARLINGTON DEVELOPMENTAL CENTER - PROFESSIONAL LIBRARY □ Arlington, TN

Gavora, Eva, Libn.
CANADA - AGRICULTURE CANADA - PLANT RESEARCH LIBRARY □ Ottawa, ON

Gay, Jane E., Libn.
U.S. COURT OF APPEALS, 9TH CIRCUIT - LIBRARY □ Portland, OR

Gay, Jane E., Libn.
U.S. DISTRICT COURT - DISTRICT OF OREGON - LIBRARY □ Portland, OR

Gay, Paul, Assoc.Libn.
UNIVERSITY OF PENNSYLVANIA - BIDDLE LAW LIBRARY □ Philadelphia, PA

Gay, Ms. Zan, Libn.
UNIVERSITY OF MIAMI - LOWE ART MUSEUM LIBRARY □ Coral Gables, FL

Gaydosh, Mary E., Libn.
SAN LUIS OBISPO COUNTY LAW LIBRARY† □ San Luis Obispo, CA

Gaylor, Robert G., Libn.
OAKLAND UNIVERSITY - LIBRARY □ Rochester, MI

Gazillo, Mark, Pharmacy/Ref.
WESTERN NEW ENGLAND COLLEGE - JOHN D. CHURCHILL MEMORIAL LIBRARY □ Springfield, MA

Gazillo, Mark J., Pharmacy Libn.
MASSACHUSETTS COLLEGE OF PHARMACY & ALLIED HEALTH SCIENCES - HAMPDEN CAMPUS LIBRARY □ Springfield, MA

Geahigan, Priscilla C., Asst.Libn.
PURDUE UNIVERSITY - MANAGEMENT AND ECONOMICS LIBRARY □ West Lafayette, IN

Gearhart, Clara, Supv., Acq./Cat.
U.S. DEPT OF ENERGY - SANDIA NATL. LABORATORIES - TECHNICAL LIBRARY □ Albuquerque, NM

Geary, Dr. James W., Dir.
KENT STATE UNIVERSITY - AMERICAN HISTORY RESEARCH CENTER □ Kent, OH

Geary, James W., Univ.Archv.
KENT STATE UNIVERSITY - ARCHIVES □ Kent, OH

Gebben, Laurie, Llbn.
FOREMOST INSURANCE COMPANY - LIBRARY □ Grand Rapids, MI

Gebbie, A., Pres.
GEBBIE PRESS, INC. - HOUSE MAGAZINE LIBRARY □ New Paltz, NY

Gebhard, Mr. K.M., Hd., Sound Archv.
SASKATCHEWAN ARCHIVES BOARD □ Regina, SK

Gebhart, Jananne, Ser.Libn.
RINGLING SCHOOL OF ART AND DESIGN - LIBRARY □ Sarasota, FL

Gecas, Judith G., Hd., Pub.Serv.
UNIVERSITY OF CHICAGO - LAW SCHOOL LIBRARY □ Chicago, IL

Geddert, Jacob, Cat.
PRAIRIE BIBLE INSTITUTE - LIBRARY □ Three Hills, AB

Geddes, C.L., Dir.
AMERICAN INSTITUTE OF ISLAMIC STUDIES - MUSLIM BIBLIOGRAPHIC CENTER □ Denver, CO

Gee, Juanna I., Libn.
FLUOR OCEAN SERVICES, INC. - ENGINEERING LIBRARY □ Houston, TX

Gee, Kathleen, Cur., Iconography
UNIVERSITY OF TEXAS, AUSTIN - HUMANITIES RESEARCH CENTER □ Austin, TX

Gee, Sharon M., Chf.Libn.
ALBERTA RESEARCH COUNCIL - LIBRARY SERVICES □ Edmonton, AB

Geer, Mary Jane, Health Info.Spec.
MERCY HOSPITAL - HEALTH SCIENCES LIBRARY □ Portland, ME

Geering, Margaret B., Coord., Med. Staff Serv.
MONTICELLO MEDICAL CENTER - MEDICAL STAFF LIBRARY □ Longview, WA

Geers, Elmer L., Libn.
CINCINNATI POST - LIBRARY □ Cincinnati, OH

Gegan, Kathryn M., Libn.
COMMUNITY HOSPITAL AT GLEN COVE - MEDICAL LIBRARY □ Glen Cove, NY

Gegelys, Mary, Dir., Info.Ctr.
THOMPSON (J. Walter) COMPANY - INFORMATION CENTER □ New York, NY

Geggie, Susan, Dir.Lib.Serv.
CANADA - DEPARTMENT OF JUSTICE - LIBRARY □ Ottawa, ON

Gehani, Taro G., Acq.Libn.
DISTRICT OF COLUMBIA TEACHERS COLLEGE - LIBRARY □ Washington, DC

Gehres, Eleanor M., Hd.
DENVER PUBLIC LIBRARY - WESTERN HISTORY DEPARTMENT □ Denver, CO

Gehring, Adrian, Lib.Techn.
TORONTO TRANSIT COMMISSION - HEAD OFFICE LIBRARY □ Toronto, ON

Gehring, Donna G., Lib.Assoc.
UNIVERSITY OF NOTRE DAME - MATHEMATICS LIBRARY □ Notre Dame, IN

Gehringer, Michael E., Asst.Libn. for Res.
U.S. SUPREME COURT - LIBRARY □ Washington, DC

Geiger, Gene, Spec.Coll.Libn.
AUBURN UNIVERSITY - DEPARTMENT OF SPECIAL COLLECTIONS □ Auburn, AL

Geil, Jean, Assoc. Music Libn.
UNIVERSITY OF ILLINOIS - MUSIC LIBRARY □ Urbana, IL

Geiling, Carolyn S., Law Libn.
MONMOUTH COUNTY LAW LIBRARY □ Freehold, NJ

Geiser, Cherie, Post-Harvest Doc.Serv.
KANSAS STATE UNIVERSITY - FARRELL LIBRARY □ Manhattan, KS

Geiser, Marie, Hd. of Film Lib.
RADIO QUEBEC - CENTRE DES RESSOURCES DOCUMENTAIRES □ Montreal, PQ

Geiser, Mary LaRue, Libn.
PEAT, MARWICK, MITCHELL & COMPANY - AUDIT/MCD LIBRARY □ Chicago, IL

Geiser, Pat, Circ.
OHIO NORTHERN UNIVERSITY - COLLEGE OF LAW - JAY P. TAGGART MEMORIAL LAW LIBRARY □ Ada, OH

Geisser, Seymour, Dir.
UNIVERSITY OF MINNESOTA - STATISTICS LIBRARY □ Minneapolis, MN

Geist, John G., Exec.Dir.
HEALTH AND WELFARE COUNCIL OF CENTRAL MARYLAND, INC. - STAFF REFERENCE LIBRARY □ Baltimore, MD

Gelarden-Cooper, Diane, Med.Libn.
U.S. VETERANS ADMINISTRATION (KY-Lexington) - MEDICAL CENTER LIBRARY □ Lexington, KY

Gelber, Robert C., Asst.Libn.
NEW YORK STATE SUPREME COURT - APPELLATE DIVISION, 1ST JUDICIAL DEPARTMENT - LAW LIBRARY □ New York, NY

Geldon, Ruth, Asst.Libn.
FAUCETT (Jack) ASSOCIATES - LIBRARY □ Chevy Chase, MD

Gelinas, Gratien, Bibliothecaire
CENTRE HOSPITALIER CHRIST-ROI - BIBLIOTHEQUE MEDICALE □ Quebec, PQ

Gelinas, Michel, Libn.
UNIVERSITE DU QUEBEC - ECOLE NATIONALE D'ADMINISTRATION PUBLIQUE - CENTRE DE DOCUMENTATION □ Ste. Foy, PQ

Gelinas, Yvon-D., O.P., Hd.Libn.
DOMINICAINS DE ST-ALBERT-LE-GRAND, MONTREAL - INSTITUT D'ETUDES MEDIEVALES - BIBLIOTHEQUE □ Montreal, PQ

Geller, Marilyn, Cat.
HARVARD UNIVERSITY - TOZZER LIBRARY - PEABODY MUSEUM OF ARCHAEOLOGY AND ETHNOLOGY □ Cambridge, MA

Gelman, Marsha E., Med.Libn.
LATROBE AREA HOSPITAL - MEDICAL & NURSING LIBRARIES □ Latrobe, PA

Geltz, Elizabeth, Nursing Libn.
UNIVERSITY OF PITTSBURGH - FALK LIBRARY OF THE HEALTH SCIENCES □ Pittsburgh, PA

Gemeinhart, Ruth, Clerk
KENTUCKY CHRISTIAN COLLEGE - MEDIA CENTER □ Grayson, KY

Genco, Carol, Coord.Lib./Inquiry Serv.
MICHIGAN MUNICIPAL LEAGUE - LIBRARY □ Ann Arbor, MI

Gendler, Carol, Libn.
DOUGLAS COUNTY LAW LIBRARY □ Omaha, NE

Gendron, Ruth, Dir.
STS. MARY AND ELIZABETH HOSPITAL - MEDICAL LIBRARY □ Louisville, KY

Generao, Clarita M., Libn.
KNIGHT (Lester B.) & ASSOCIATES, INC. - MANAGEMENT CONSULTING LIBRARY □ Chicago, IL

Genesen, Judy, Ref.Libn.
CHICAGO TRANSIT AUTHORITY - HAROLD S. ANTHON MEMORIAL LIBRARY □ Chicago, IL

Genest, Sr. Marie-Paule, S.F.A., Chf.Libn.
HOPITAL ST-FRANCOIS D'ASSISE - MEDICAL & ADMINISTRATIVE LIBRARY □ Quebec, PQ

Genetti, Raynna Bowlby, Principal Investigator
CENTRAL MAINE MEDICAL CENTER - GERRISH-TRUE HEALTH SCIENCE LIBRARY □ Lewiston, ME

Gennett, Robert G., Spec.Coll.Libn.
LAFAYETTE COLLEGE - AMERICAN FRIENDS OF LAFAYETTE COLLECTION □ Easton, PA

Genovese, Robert, Cat.Libn.
COLGATE ROCHESTER/BEXLEY HALL/ CROZER THEOLOGICAL SEMINARIES - AMBROSE SWASEY LIBRARY □ Rochester, NY

Genrich, Mrs. Fran, Libn.
SUNDSTRAND AVIATION - ENGINEERING LIBRARY □ Rockford, IL

Gensel, Susan, Dir., Libs. & Marketing
COLD SPRING HARBOR LABORATORY - MAIN LIBRARY □ Cold Spring Harbor, NY

Gensler, Faith I., Libn.
G & W NATURAL RESOURCES GROUP - ZERBE RESEARCH CENTER - TECHNICAL LIBRARY □ Bethlehem, PA

Gent-Sandford, Louise, Libn.
LEHMAN BROTHERS, KUHN, LOEB, INC. - LIBRARY □ New York, NY

Gentien, P.V., Mgr., Tech.Lib.
DU PONT DE NEMOURS (E.I.) & COMPANY, INC. - TECHNICAL LIBRARY SYSTEM - LOUVIERS BRANCH □ Wilmington, DE

Gentner, Claudia A., Libn.
AMERICAN CYANAMID COMPANY - BUSINESS INFORMATION CENTER □ Wayne, NJ

Gentry, Mark, Ref.Libn.
CENTRAL BIBLE COLLEGE - LIBRARY □ Springfield, MO

Gentry, Susan K., Tech.Libn.
HUGHES AIRCRAFT COMPANY - SANTA BARBARA RESEARCH CENTER - TECHNICAL LIBRARY □ Goleta, CA

Gentzler, Lynn Wolf, Sr.Mss.Spec.
UNIVERSITY OF MISSOURI - WESTERN HISTORICAL MANUSCRIPT COLLECTION/ STATE HISTORICAL SOCIETY OF MISSOURI □ Columbia, MO

Genung, Marie, Hd., Educ.Serv.
UNIVERSITY OF CALIFORNIA, RIVERSIDE - EDUCATION SERVICES LIBRARY □ Riverside, CA

Georg, Kathleen R., Res.Hist.
U.S. NATL. PARK SERVICE - GETTYSBURG NATL. MILITARY PARK - CYCLORAMA CENTER LIBRARY □ Gettysburg, PA

George, Doris, Libn.
FALCONBRIDGE NICKEL MINES, LTD. - METALLURGICAL LABORATORIES INFORMATION SERVICES □ Thornhill, ON

George, Edna E., Libn.
WESTERN ELECTRIC COMPANY, INC. - GENERAL BUSINESS LIBRARY† □ New York, NY

George, Harvey F., Res.Dir.
GRAVURE RESEARCH INSTITUTE - LIBRARY □ Port Washington, NY

George, Mrs. Henrene, Supv.
AMERICAN BAPTIST CHURCHES IN THE U.S.A. - BOARD OF NATIONAL MINISTRIES - LIBRARY & RECORDS MANAGEMENT □ Valley Forge, PA

George, John, Govt.Pubn.Libn.
DALLAS PUBLIC LIBRARY - GOVERNMENT PUBLICATIONS DIVISION □ Dallas, TX

George, Melvin R., Dir.
NORTHEASTERN ILLINOIS UNIVERSITY - LIBRARY □ Chicago, IL

George, Pamela S., Social Worker
BETH ABRAHAM HOSPITAL - PATIENT'S LIBRARY □ Bronx, NY

George, Rachel, Libn.
REFORMED PRESBYTERIAN THEOLOGICAL SEMINARY - LIBRARY □ Pittsburgh, PA

George, Ralph, Asst.Libn.
SOCIETY OF MAYFLOWER DESCENDANTS IN THE STATE OF CALIFORNIA - LIBRARY □ San Francisco, CA

George, Twig C., Educ.Coord.
WHALE PROTECTION FUND - ENVIRONMENTAL EDUCATION RESOURCE LIBRARY □ Washington, DC

George, W.E., Res.Dir.
GEORGIA MUNICIPAL ASSOCIATION - LIBRARY □ Atlanta, GA

Georgenson, Gail S., Res.Libn.
UNIVERSITY OF ARIZONA - SPACE IMAGERY CENTER □ Tucson, AZ

Georges, Mary Ann, Staff Libn.
QUEEN STREET MENTAL HEALTH CENTRE - HEALTH SCIENCES LIBRARY† □ Toronto, ON

Gera, V. Lynn, Lib.Adm.
U.S. ARMY - WALTER REED ARMY INSTITUTE OF RESEARCH - LIBRARY □ Washington, DC

Geraghty, Miss E.M.L., Hist.
BELL CANADA - TELEPHONE HISTORICAL COLLECTION □ Montreal, PQ

Geraghty, Rev. James F., Archv.
DIOCESE OF LAFAYETTE, LOUISIANA - ARCHIVES □ Lafayette, LA

Geralds, Erika, Lib.Adm.Assoc.
UNIVERSITY OF LOUISVILLE - LIFE SCIENCES LIBRARY □ Louisville, KY

Gerard, Gary, Mgr.
KAISER ALUMINUM & CHEMICAL CORPORATION - TECHNICAL INFORMATION CENTER □ Pleasanton, CA

Gerbens, Martin L., Slide Cur.
RINGLING SCHOOL OF ART AND DESIGN - LIBRARY □ Sarasota, FL

Gerber, Anneke, Libn.
CALIFORNIA INSTITUTE OF TECHNOLOGY - MUNGER AFRICANA LIBRARY □ Pasadena, CA

Gerber, Frances, Supv.
MARYLAND GENERAL HOSPITAL - MEDICAL STAFF LIBRARY† □ Baltimore, MD

Gerber, Gloria, Media Spec.
WILSON (Charles S.) MEMORIAL HOSPITAL - LEARNING RESOURCES DEPARTMENT □ Johnson City, NY

Gerber, Judy, Chf.Libn., R & D
JOHNS-MANVILLE SALES CORPORATION - RESEARCH INFORMATION CENTER □ Denver, CO

Gerberg, Dr. Eugene J., Pres.
INSECT CONTROL AND RESEARCH, INC. - LIBRARY □ Baltimore, MD

Gerdes, Rev. Neil W., Libn.
CHICAGO THEOLOGICAL SEMINARY - HAMMOND LIBRARY □ Chicago, IL

Gerdes, Rev. Neil W., Libn.
MEADVILLE/LOMBARD THEOLOGICAL SCHOOL - LIBRARY □ Chicago, IL

Gerdine, Peter C., Acq. & Ser.Libn.
PLYMOUTH STATE COLLEGE - HERBERT H. LAMSON LIBRARY □ Plymouth, NH

Gerduk, Nettie, Libn.
TWENTIETH CENTURY FUND - LIBRARY □ New York, NY

Gergely, Emma, Med.Libn.
ALLIED CORPORATION - CORPORATE MEDICAL AFFAIRS LIBRARY □ Morristown, NJ

Gerhardt, Arlan, Ref.Libn.
INDIANA UNIVERSITY - EDUCATION LIBRARY □ Bloomington, IN

Gerhardt, Edwin L., Cur.
TOWSON STATE UNIVERSITY - GERHARDT LIBRARY OF MUSICAL INFORMATION □ Towson, MD

Gerhardt, Edwin L., Cur.
TOWSON STATE UNIVERSITY - GERHARDT MARIMBA & XYLOPHONE COLLECTION □ Towson, MD

Gerhardt, Robert, Sci.Libn.
SOUTHERN ILLINOIS UNIVERSITY, EDWARDSVILLE - SCIENCE LIBRARY □ Edwardsville, IL

Gericke, Dr. Paul, Dir. of Lib.
NEW ORLEANS BAPTIST THEOLOGICAL SEMINARY - JOHN T. CHRISTIAN LIBRARY □ New Orleans, LA

Gerken, C., Info.Spec.
BURROUGHS WELLCOME COMPANY - LIBRARY □ Research Triangle Park, NC

Gerl, Brian Jonathan, Dir.
WISCONSIN CONSERVATORY OF MUSIC - LIBRARY □ Milwaukee, WI

Gerlach, Gary G., Dir.
BIRMINGHAM BOTANICAL GARDENS - HORACE HAMMOND MEMORIAL LIBRARY □ Birmingham, AL

Gerling, Sally M., Chf.Libn.
GENESEE HOSPITAL - SAMUEL J. STABINS, M.D., HEALTH SCIENCES LIBRARY □ Rochester, NY

Germain, Claire, Sr.Ref.Libn.
DUKE UNIVERSITY - SCHOOL OF LAW LIBRARY □ Durham, NC

German, Barbara, Libn.
TRAPHAGEN SCHOOL OF FASHION - LIBRARY □
New York, NY

Germann, Malcolm, Asst.Libn.
WESLEY MEDICAL CENTER - MC KIBBIN
PROFESSIONAL LIBRARY □ Wichita, KS

Gern, Maria
FALKIRK HOSPITAL - LIBRARY □ Central Valley,
NY

Geron, Cary Ann, Libn.
SOUTHERN BAPTIST CONVENTION - FOREIGN
MISSION BOARD - MISSIONARY ORIENTATION
LIBRARY □ Pine Mountain, GA

Geroulo, Louise A., Chf., Lrng.Res.Serv.
U.S. VETERANS ADMINISTRATION (NJ-Lyons) -
HOSPITAL LIBRARY □ Lyons, NJ

Gerrard, Philip, Supv.Coord.Libn.
NEW YORK PUBLIC LIBRARY - DONNELL
LIBRARY CENTER □ New York, NY

Gerrety, Elizabeth, Hd., Circ.Dept.
GEORGE WASHINGTON UNIVERSITY -
MEDICAL CENTER - PAUL HIMMELFARB
HEALTH SCIENCES LIBRARY □ Washington, DC

Gerritts, Judy, Hd.Libn.
SAN FRANCISCO EXAMINER - LIBRARY □ San
Francisco, CA

Gersten, Karen, Assoc.Libn.Pub.Serv.
UNIVERSITY OF CALIFORNIA, LOS ANGELES -
MANAGEMENT LIBRARY □ Los Angeles, CA

Gerstner, Dr. Patsy A., Chf.Cur.
CLEVELAND HEALTH SCIENCES LIBRARY -
HOWARD DITTRICK MUSEUM OF HISTORICAL
MEDICINE □ Cleveland, OH

Gertrude, Sister, S.C., Libn.
ST. MARY'S HOSPITAL - MEDICAL ALLIED
HEALTH SCIENCE LIBRARY □ Passaic, NJ

Gervais, Antony, Dir.
INFORMATECH - CENTRE QUEBECOIS DE
BANQUES D'INFORMATION SCIENTIFIQUE ET
TECHNIQUE □ Montreal, PQ

Gervino, Joan, Dir.
AMERICAN BANKERS ASSOCIATION - LIBRARY
□ Washington, DC

Gerwing, Howard B., Rare Bks.Libn.
UNIVERSITY OF VICTORIA - MC PHERSON
LIBRARY - SPECIAL COLLECTIONS □ Victoria,
BC

Geske, Aina, Hd.Libn.
KENYON & ECKHARDT ADVERTISING -
INFORMATION CENTER □ New York, NY

Geske, Dulcie, Lib.Techn.
U.S. AIR FORCE BASE - LUKE BASE LIBRARY □
Luke AFB, AZ

Gesler, Sara, Hd.Libn.
CHARLOTTE OBSERVER AND THE CHARLOTTE
NEWS - LIBRARY □ Charlotte, NC

Gess, Catherine, Asst.Libn.
TAMPA TRIBUNE & TAMPA TIMES - LIBRARY □
Tampa, FL

Gesterfield, Kathryn J., Dir.
ILLINOIS STATE LIBRARY □ Springfield, IL

Getaz, Betsy
ALTERNATIVE PRESS CENTER - LIBRARY □
Baltimore, MD

Getrew, Ellen, Res.Libn.
CONSUMERS UNION OF UNITED STATES, INC. -
LIBRARY □ Mount Vernon, NY

Gettings, Holly, Lib.Hd.
EARTHWORM, INC. - RECYCLING
INFORMATION SERVICES □ Boston, MA

Getz, George F., Jr., Pres.
HALL OF FLAME - RICHARD S. FOWLER
MEMORIAL LIBRARY □ Phoenix, AZ

Getz, Oscar, Founder
BARTON MUSEUM OF WHISKEY HISTORY -
LIBRARY □ Bardstown, KY

Getze, Frederick B., Libn.
UNIVERSITY OF DELAWARE, NEWARK -
AGRICULTURAL LIBRARY† □ Newark, DE

Gex, Robert C., Libn.
STANFORD LINEAR ACCELERATOR CENTER -
LIBRARY □ Menlo Park, CA

Geyer, Barbara, Ref.Libn.
TEXAS TECH UNIVERSITY - LIBRARY -
DOCUMENTS DEPARTMENT □ Lubbock, TX

Geyer, Della M., Law Libn.
BAYLOR UNIVERSITY - LAW LIBRARY† □ Waco,
TX

Geyer, Enid, Cat.
UNION UNIVERSITY - ALBANY MEDICAL
COLLEGE - SCHAFFER LIBRARY OF THE HEALTH
SCIENCES □ Albany, NY

Geyger, Alexander, Rd.Adv.
DISTRICT OF COLUMBIA PUBLIC LIBRARY -
LANGUAGE, LITERATURE &FOREIGN LANGUAGE
DIVISION □ Washington, DC

Geyger, Barbara F., Chf.
DISTRICT OF COLUMBIA PUBLIC LIBRARY -
CHILDREN'S DIVISION □ Washington, DC

Ghali, Raouf, Assoc.Libn.
NEW YORK UNIVERSITY - DENTAL CENTER -
JOHN & BERTHA E. WALDMANN MEMORIAL
LIBRARY □ New York, NY

Ghering, Sr. M. Virgil, O.P., Libn.
ST. THOMAS INSTITUTE - LIBRARY □
Cincinnati, OH

Gherman, Paul, Asst.Dir., Adm.Serv.
IOWA STATE UNIVERSITY - LIBRARY □ Ames,
IA

Ghidotti, Pauline, Asst.Dir.
UNIVERSITY OF ARKANSAS AT LITTLE ROCK -
PULASKI COUNTY LAW LIBRARY □ Little Rock,
AR

Ghist, Ann, Libn.
ARTHUR ANDERSEN & CO. - BUSINESS LIBRARY
□ Houston, TX

Gholston, H.D., Supv.Tech.Lib.
CHEVRON RESEARCH COMPANY - TECHNICAL
INFORMATION CENTER □ Richmond, CA

Giacalone, Michael, Jr., Dir., Med.Educ.
MC LAREN GENERAL HOSPITAL - MEDICAL
LIBRARY □ Flint, MI

Giancott, E., Acq.
BENDIX CORPORATION CENTER - LIBRARY □
Southfield, MI

Giannini, Evelyn, Libn.
KEMPER GROUP - LIBRARY □ Long Grove, IL

Giannotti, Marshall, AV Libn..
NEW YORK COLLEGE OF PODIATRIC MEDICINE
- DR. SIDNEY DRUSKIN MEMORIAL LIBRARY† □
New York, NY

Giasi, Marie G., Libn.
BROOKLYN BOTANIC GARDEN - LIBRARY □
Brooklyn, NY

Gibbes, Catherine, Libn.
MASSACHUSETTS INSTITUTE OF TECHNOLOGY
- PSYCHOLOGY LIBRARY □ Cambridge, MA

Gibbons, Sr. Anna Marie, Lib.Asst.
ST. MARY'S HOSPITAL - HEALTH SCIENCES
LIBRARY □ West Palm Beach, FL

Gibbons, Dr. Barbara H., Assoc.Res.
UNIVERSITY OF HAWAII - PACIFIC BIO-
MEDICAL RESEARCH CENTER - LIBRARY □
Honolulu, HI

Gibbons, Susan Jane, Libn.
DECHERT, PRICE AND RHOADS - LIBRARY □
Philadelphia, PA

Gibbons, Susan K., Libn.
UNIVERSITY OF UTAH - CENTER FOR PUBLIC
AFFAIRS AND ADMINISTRATION - RESEARCH
LIBRARY □ Salt Lake City, UT

Gibbs, Andrea, Cat.
NATIONAL GALLERY OF ART - PHOTOGRAPHIC
ARCHIVES □ Washington, DC

Gibbs, Donald, Acq.
UNIVERSITY OF TEXAS, AUSTIN - BENSON
LATIN AMERICAN COLLECTION □ Austin, TX

Gibbs, Dr. Hyatt, Supv.
UNIVERSITY OF ARIZONA - OPTICAL
SCIENCES CENTER - READING ROOM □ Tucson,
AZ

Gibbs, John R., Asst.Libn.
UNIVERSITY OF WASHINGTON - MUSIC
LIBRARY □ Seattle, WA

Gibbs, K.L., Act.Dir.
BRITISH COLUMBIA - MINISTRY OF TOURISM -
PHOTOGRAPHIC LIBRARY □ Victoria, BC

Gibbs, Marilyn, Asst.Libn.
ATLANTA UNIVERSITY - SCHOOL OF LIBRARY &
INFORMATION STUDIES - LIBRARY □ Atlanta,
GA

Gibbs, Marilyn Osborne, Med.Libn.
DEKALB GENERAL HOSPITAL - MEDICAL
LIBRARY □ Decatur, GA

Gibbs, Mary M., Assoc.Info.Sci.
AYERST LABORATORIES - MEDICAL
INFORMATION CENTER □ New York, NY

Gibbs, Phyllis A., Med.Libn.
U.S. NAVY - NAVAL REGIONAL MEDICAL
CENTER (Great Lakes) - MEDICAL LIBRARY □
Great Lakes, IL

Gibson, Elizabeth, Libn.
SUN LIFE ASSURANCE COMPANY OF CANADA -
REFERENCE LIBRARY □ Toronto, ON

Gibson, Gladys, Chf.Libn.
ATOMIC ENERGY OF CANADA, LTD. - WNRE
LIBRARY □ Pinawa, MB

Gibson, Harold R., Libn.
GUEDEL MEMORIAL ANESTHESIA CENTER -
LIBRARY □ San Francisco, CA

Gibson, Harold R., Libn.
PACIFIC MEDICAL CENTER & UNIVERSITY OF
THE PACIFIC SCHOOL OF DENTISTRY - HEALTH
SCIENCES LIBRARY □ San Francisco, CA

Gibson, Helen R., Libn.
LEGAL SERVICES OF EASTERN MISSOURI, INC.
- LIBRARY □ St. Louis, MO

Gibson, Jannah, Libn.
ESOTERIC PHILOSOPHY CENTER, INC. -
LIBRARY □ Houston, TX

Gibson, Kay, Med.Libn.
ST. MARY'S HOSPITAL - MEDICAL LIBRARY □
Huntington, WV

Gibson, Louise, Lib.Dir.
CANADIAN HOSPITAL ASSOCIATION -
BLACKADER LIBRARY □ Ottawa, ON

Gibson, P., Asst.Hd., Pub.Serv.
CANADA - ENERGY, MINES & RESOURCES
CANADA - RESOURCE ECONOMICS LIBRARY □
Ottawa, ON

Gibson, Patricia, Libn.
ST. FRANCIS HOSPITAL - SCHOOL OF NURSING
LIBRARY □ Evanston, IL

Gibson, Phillip, AV
NORTHWEST CHRISTIAN COLLEGE - LEARNING
RESOURCE CENTER □ Eugene, OR

Gibson, Robert W., Jr., Dept.Hd.
GENERAL MOTORS CORPORATION - RESEARCH
LABORATORIES LIBRARY □ Warren, MI

Gibson-McDonald, N., Libn.
CANADA - AGRICULTURE CANADA - RESEARCH
STATION, VINELAND STATION - LIBRARY □
Vineland Station, ON

Giedinghagen, Dorothy, Libn.
WASHINGTON UNIVERSITY - SCHOOL OF
MEDICINE - DEPARTMENT OF PSYCHIATRY
LIBRARY □ St. Louis, MO

Giedrys, Ilona, Res.Libn.
MERCK & COMPANY, INC. - MERCK SHARP &
DOHME RESEARCH LABORATORIES -
RESEARCH LIBRARIES □ Rahway, NJ

Giefer, Gerald J., Libn.
UNIVERSITY OF CALIFORNIA, BERKELEY -
WATER RESOURCES CENTER ARCHIVES □
Berkeley, CA

Gieger, Geraldine, Res.Libn.
EXXON RESEARCH AND ENGINEERING
COMPANY - LIBRARY □ Baytown, TX

Giehl, Dudley, Pres.
ANIMAL LIBERATION, INC. - LIBRARY □ New
York, NY

Giella, Vicki C., Info.Ctr.Coord.
CARNATION COMPANY - LIBRARY □ Los
Angeles, CA

Giercuszkiewicz, Eva, Libn.
IOWA LAW ENFORCEMENT ACADEMY -
LIBRARY □ Johnston, IA

Gieryic, Michael, Hd.Libn.
SUNY - AGRICULTURAL AND TECHNICAL
COLLEGE AT MORRISVILLE - LIBRARY □
Morrisville, NY

Giesbrecht, Herbert, College Libn.
MENNONITE BRETHREN BIBLE COLLEGE -
LIBRARY □ Winnipeg, MB

Giesbrecht, J., Area Coord.
CANADA - AGRICULTURE CANADA - LONDON
RESEARCH CENTRE LIBRARY □ London, ON

Giesbrecht, John W., Asst.Libn.
MANITOBA - DEPARTMENT OF ECONOMIC
DEVELOPMENT AND TOURISM - LIBRARY □
Winnipeg, MB

Giet, G. Robert, Libn.
MARITIME MUSEUM (Allen Knight) - LIBRARY □
Monterey, CA

Giffen, Linda, Libn.
ALBERTA - DEPARTMENT OF ECONOMIC
DEVELOPMENT - LIBRARY □ Edmonton, AB

Gifford, Curtis, Sci.Libn.
COLORADO STATE UNIVERSITY - WILLIAM E.
MORGAN LIBRARY □ Fort Collins, CO

Gifford, Karlee, Libn.
YALE UNIVERSITY - COWLES FOUNDATION
FOR RESEARCH IN ECONOMICS - LIBRARY □
New Haven, CT

Gifford, R.A., Owner
HARRIS & GIFFORD - LIBRARY □ Alexandria, VA

Gigante, Marianne, Libn.
OHIO STATE ATTORNEY GENERAL'S OFFICE -
LAW LIBRARY □ Columbus, OH

Gigante, Vickilyn, Dir., Info.Sci.
GEOMET TECHNOLOGIES INC. - INFORMATION
CENTER □ Rockville, MD

Gignac, Solange G., Libn.
DENVER BOTANIC GARDENS - HELEN K.
FOWLER LIBRARY □ Denver, CO

Giguere, P. Raymond, O.P., Asst.Libn.
DOMINICAINS DE ST-ALBERT-LE-GRAND,
MONTREAL - INSTITUT D'ETUDES
MEDIEVALES - BIBLIOTHEQUE □ Montreal, PQ

Gilbaine, Miss E., Libn.
CRAFT CENTER MUSEUM - CRAFT CENTER
LIBRARY □ Wilton, CT

Gilbert, Anna S., Med.Libn.
U.S. VETERANS ADMINISTRATION (GA-
Augusta) - HOSPITAL LIBRARY □ Augusta, GA

Gilbert, Deborah D., Chf.Hosp.Libn.
CHILDREN'S HOSPITAL/NATIONAL MEDICAL
CENTER - HOSPITAL LIBRARY □ Washington,
DC

Gilbert, Elizabeth X., Sec.-Tres.
GEM VILLAGE MUSEUM - GREEN MEMORIAL
LIBRARY □ Bayfield, CO

Gilbert, Gail R., Hd., Art Lib.
UNIVERSITY OF LOUISVILLE - ALLEN R. HITE
ART INSTITUTE - MARGARET M. BRIDWELL
ART LIBRARY □ Louisville, KY

Gilbert, Harry, Libn.
UNIVERSITY OF KENTUCKY - HUNTER M.
ADAMS ARCHITECTURE LIBRARY □ Lexington,
KY

Gilbert, Jane C., Law Lib.Ck.
HERKIMER COUNTY LAW LIBRARY □ Herkimer,
NY

Gilbert, Leon, Translator
AMERICAN RED CROSS - NATIONAL
HEADQUARTERS LIBRARY □ Washington, DC

Gilbert, Mary, Libn.
NORTHEAST GEORGIA MEDICAL CENTER AND
HALL SCHOOL OF NURSING/BRENAU COLLEGE -
LIBRARY □ Gainesville, GA

Gilbert, Nancy L., Asst.Dir./Lib.Serv.
U.S. ARMY MILITARY HISTORY INSTITUTE □
Carlisle Barracks, PA

Gilbert, Ophelia, Lab. School Libn.
CENTRAL MISSOURI STATE UNIVERSITY -
WARD EDWARDS LIBRARY □ Warrensburg, MO

Gilbert, Ruth E., Med.Libn.
U.S. VETERANS ADMINISTRATION (CO-Denver)
- HOSPITAL LIBRARY □ Denver, CO

Gilbert, Thelma, Acq.Libn.
ANDREWS UNIVERSITY - JAMES WHITE
LIBRARY □ Berrien Springs, MI

Gilbert, Thomas F., Cat.Libn.
UNIVERSITY OF THE SOUTH - SCHOOL OF
THEOLOGY LIBRARY □ Sewanee, TN

Gilbertson, Helen J., Asst.Dept.Hd.
MINNEAPOLIS PUBLIC LIBRARY &
INFORMATION CENTER - SOCIOLOGY
DEPARTMENT □ Minneapolis, MN

Gilbertson, Jean, Libn.
UNIVERSITY OF WISCONSIN, MADISON -
COLLEGE OF ENGINEERING - TECHNICAL
REPORTS CENTER □ Madison, WI

Gilbertson, Kathi, Tech.Serv.
UNIVERSITY OF WISCONSIN, MADISON -
STEENBOCK MEMORIAL LIBRARY □ Madison,
WI

Gilbertson, Mary Edith, Acq.Libn.
WILLAMETTE UNIVERSITY - LAW LIBRARY □
Salem, OR

Gilborn, Craig, Dir.
ADIRONDACK HISTORICAL ASSOCIATION -
ADIRONDACK MUSEUM - RESEARCH LIBRARY □
Blue Mountain Lake, NY

Gilbreath, Marvin, Libn.
SAN FRANCISCO EXAMINER - LIBRARY □ San
Francisco, CA

Gildemeister, Enrique, Cat.
PORT AUTHORITY OF NEW YORK AND NEW
JERSEY - LIBRARY □ New York, NY

Gildemeister, Glen A., Dir.
NORTHERN ILLINOIS UNIVERSITY - REGIONAL
HISTORY CENTER □ DeKalb, IL

Gildemeister, Glen A., Archv.
NORTHERN ILLINOIS UNIVERSITY -
UNIVERSITY ARCHIVES □ DeKalb, IL

Gilden, Anita, Asst.Libn.
ALBRIGHT-KNOX ART GALLERY - ART
REFERENCE LIBRARY □ Buffalo, NY

Gilden, Mary Ellen, Libn.
SCHERER (R.P.) CORPORATION - LIBRARY □
Detroit, MI

Gildzen, Alex, Assoc.Cur.
KENT STATE UNIVERSITY - DEPARTMENT OF
SPECIAL COLLECTIONS □ Kent, OH

Giles, Charles E., Chf.Libn.
GENERAL DYNAMICS CORPORATION -
ELECTRIC BOAT DIVISION - DIVISION
LIBRARY □ Groton, CT

Giles, Esther L., Corp.Libn.
TRANS WORLD AIRLINES, INC. - CORPORATE
LIBRARY □ New York, NY

Giles, Garred, Scientific Serv.
CORNELL UNIVERSITY - ARECIBO
OBSERVATORY - LIBRARY □ Arecibo, PR

Giles, Margaret C., AV Cat.
ERIE COMMUNITY COLLEGE NORTH - LIBRARY
RESOURCES CENTER □ Buffalo, NY

Giles, Sondra, Ref.Libn.
PROVIDENCE COLLEGE - PHILLIPS MEMORIAL
LIBRARY □ Providence, RI

Giles, Sue, Coord.Lib.Serv.
RYERSON POLYTECHNICAL INSTITUTE -
LEARNING RESOURCES CENTRE □ Toronto, ON

Gilheany, Rosary S., Mgr./Lib. & Ref.Serv
UNITED HOSPITALS MEDICAL CENTER OF
NEWARK - LIBRARY AND INFORMATION
SERVICES □ Newark, NJ

Gilkes, Thelma, Cat.Libn.
CONNECTICUT COLLEGE - LIBRARY - SPECIAL
COLLECTIONS □ New London, CT

Gill, Barbara, Libn.
HISTORICAL SOCIETY OF BERKS COUNTY -
LIBRARY □ Reading, PA

Gill, Carol Winfield, Tech.Libn.
PHILLIPS PETROLEUM COMPANY - RESEARCH &
DEVELOPMENT DEPARTMENT - TECHNICAL
INFORMATION BRANCH □ Bartlesville, OK

Gill, Elizabeth D., Asst.Dir.
SRI INTERNATIONAL - LIBRARY AND
RESEARCH INFORMATION SERVICES
DEPARTMENT □ Menlo Park, CA

Gill, Gail P., Libn.
DELAWARE ACADEMY OF MEDICINE - LIBRARY
□ Wilmington, DE

Gill, Lynne N., Chf., Tech.Proc.
CONNECTICUT STATE LIBRARY □ Hartford, CT

Gill, Molly, Libn.
PINELLAS COUNTY JUVENILE WELFARE BOARD
- MAILANDE W. HOLLAND LIBRARY □ St.
Petersburg, FL

Gill, Norman N., Exec.Dir.
CITIZENS' GOVERNMENTAL RESEARCH
BUREAU, INC. □ Milwaukee, WI

Gill, Sam, Archv.
ACADEMY OF MOTION PICTURE ARTS AND
SCIENCES - MARGARET HERRICK LIBRARY □
Beverly Hills, CA

Gill, William R., Dir.
U.S.D.A. - AGRICULTURAL RESEARCH SERVICE
- NATL. TILLAGE MACHINERY LABORATORY
LIBRARY □ Auburn, AL

Gillan, Dr. Dennis, Hd.Tech.Serv.
BLOOMFIELD COLLEGE - GEORGE TALBOT HALL
LIBRARY □ Bloomfield, NJ

Gillard, Peter McCann, Act.Dir.
SMITHTOWN LIBRARY □ Smithtown, NY

Gillen, Thomas, Chf.Ref.Libn.
SMITHTOWN LIBRARY □ Smithtown, NY

Gillentine, Jane, Assoc. State Libn.
NEW MEXICO STATE LIBRARY □ Santa Fe, NM

Gilles, Debra L., Libn.
HOWARD YOUNG MEDICAL CENTER - HEALTH
SCIENCE LIBRARY □ Woodruff, WI

Gillesby, John D., Hd.Ref.Libn.
UNIVERSITY OF WISCONSIN, STEVENS POINT
- JAMES H. ALBERTSON CENTER FOR
LEARNING RESOURCES □ Stevens Point, WI

Gillespie, Harriet, Res.Libn.
HARBISON-WALKER REFRACTORIES COMPANY
- GARBER RESEARCH CENTER LIBRARY □
Pittsburgh, PA

Gillespie, J.C., Supv., Tech.Serv.
UNION CARBIDE CORPORATION - NUCLEAR
DIVISION - PADUCAH PLANT LIBRARY □
Paducah, KY

Gillespie, Norman, Asst.Libn.
MIAMI-DADE PUBLIC LIBRARY - FLORIDA
COLLECTION □ Miami, FL

Gillespie, Prentiss L., Libn.
LIBRARY OF CONGRESS - PRESERVATION
OFFICE □ Washington, DC

Gillette, Catherine H., Pub.Serv.Libn.
CLEVELAND STATE UNIVERSITY - JOSEPH W.
BARTUNEK III LAW LIBRARY □ Cleveland, OH

Gillette, Gerald W., Res.Hist.
UNITED PRESBYTERIAN CHURCH IN THE U.S.A.
- PRESBYTERIAN HISTORICAL SOCIETY -
LIBRARY □ Philadelphia, PA

Gillette, Martha, Adm.Asst.
NATIONAL STORYTELLING RESOURCE CENTER
□ Jonesboro, TN

Gillette, Michael, Chf., Oral Hist.Sect.
U.S. PRESIDENTIAL LIBRARIES - LYNDON B.
JOHNSON LIBRARY† □ Austin, TX

Gilliam, Dorothy, Cat.
UNION THEOLOGICAL SEMINARY IN VIRGINIA
- LIBRARY □ Richmond, VA

Gilliam, Susanne, Libn.
CORVA LIBRARY □ Cincinnati, OH

Gilliana, Concepcion V., Asst.Libn.
ILLINOIS COLLEGE OF OPTOMETRY - CARL F.
SHEPARD MEMORIAL LIBRARY □ Chicago, IL

Gilliana, Mr. Zia Solomon, Med.Libn.
RAVENSWOOD HOSPITAL MEDICAL CENTER -
MEDICAL-NURSING LIBRARY† □ Chicago, IL

Gillies, Elizabeth W., Libn.
HUEBNER (S.S.) FOUNDATION FOR INSURANCE
EDUCATION - LIBRARY □ Philadelphia, PA

Gillies, Ellen, Med.Libn.
UNIVERSITY OF VERMONT - DIVISION OF
HEALTH SCIENCES - CHARLES A. DANA
MEDICAL LIBRARY □ Burlington, VT

Gillies, Thomas D., Dir.
LINDA HALL LIBRARY □ Kansas City, MO

Gilligan, J. Joseph, Libn.
ESSEX COUNTY LAW LIBRARY □ Salem, MA

Gillis, Eileen W., Libn.
MERCY HOSPITAL - MC GLANNAN MEMORIAL LIBRARY □ Baltimore, MD

Gillis, Frank J., Dir.
INDIANA UNIVERSITY - ARCHIVES OF TRADITIONAL MUSIC □ Bloomington, IN

Gillis, Jeff, Hd.
DURANT FAMILY REGISTRY - LIBRARY □ Green Bay, WI

Gillis, P., Chf. Manpower Rec.
CANADA - PUBLIC ARCHIVES OF CANADA - FEDERAL ARCHIVES DIVISION □ Ottawa, ON

Gillmar, Dian, Info.Coord.
METROPOLITAN TRANSPORTATION COMMISSION - ASSOCIATION OF BAY AREA GOVERNMENTS (ABAG) - LIBRARY □ Berkeley, CA

Gillock, Oliver, Jr., Coord., Plan. & Dev.
NEW JERSEY STATE LIBRARY □ Trenton, NJ

Gilman, Jane, Res.Asst.
PENNEY (J.C.) COMPANY, INC. - LAW LIBRARY □ New York, NY

Gilman, Naomi P., Info.Dir.
GILMAN MUSEUM - LIBRARY □ Hellertown, PA

Gilman, Nelson J., Libn./Dir.
UNIVERSITY OF SOUTHERN CALIFORNIA - HEALTH SCIENCES CAMPUS - NORRIS MEDICAL LIBRARY □ Los Angeles, CA

Gilmer, Ann, Assoc.Dir./Pub.Serv.
TEXAS TECH UNIVERSITY - HEALTH SCIENCES CENTER - LIBRARY OF THE HEALTH SCIENCES □ Lubbock, TX

Gilmer, Wesley, Jr., State Law Libn.
KENTUCKY STATE LAW LIBRARY □ Frankfort, KY

Gilmore, Barbara A., Asst.Hd.
U.S. NAVY - NAVAL HISTORICAL CENTER - NAVAL HISTORY DIVISION - OPERATIONAL ARCHIVES □ Washington, DC

Gilmore, Larry D., Cur.
COLUMBIA RIVER MARITIME MUSEUM - LIBRARY □ Astoria, OR

Gilmore, Matt, Ref.
CRAVATH, SWAINE, AND MOORE - LAW LIBRARY □ New York, NY

Gilmore, Willard H., Asst.Libn.
MAINE MARITIME ACADEMY - NUTTING MEMORIAL LIBRARY □ Castine, ME

Gilner, David J., Ref./Pub.Serv.Libn.
HEBREW UNION COLLEGE - JEWISH INSTITUTE OF RELIGION - KLAU LIBRARY □ Cincinnati, OH

Gilreath, Charles, Hd., Automated Info.Ret.
TEXAS A & M UNIVERSITY - REFERENCE DIVISION □ College Station, TX

Gilroy, Dorothy A., Libn.
UNIVERSITY AFFILIATED CINCINNATI CENTER FOR DEVELOPMENTAL DISORDERS - RESEARCH LIBRARY □ Cincinnati, OH

Gilstrap, Max, Docs.Libn.
UNIVERSITY OF GEORGIA - GOVERNMENT REFERENCE/DOCUMENTS SECTION □ Athens, GA

Giltinan, Mary J., Rd.Serv.Libn.
ST. CHARLES BORROMEO SEMINARY - RYAN MEMORIAL LIBRARY □ Philadelphia, PA

Gilvin, Marjorie, Libn.
POLK PUBLIC MUSEUM - MEMORIAL LIBRARY □ Lakeland, FL

Gima, Marguerite, Libn.
ST. MARGARET HOSPITAL - SALLIE M. TYRRELL, M.D. MEMORIAL LIBRARY □ Hammond, IN

Gimelson, Deborah, Adm.Dir.
POETRY SOCIETY OF AMERICA - VAN VOORHIS LIBRARY □ New York, NY

Gimmi, Robert, Hd.Cat.
SHIPPENSBURG STATE COLLEGE - EZRA LEHMAN MEMORIAL LIBRARY □ Shippensburg, PA

Gindlesberger, Thomas D., Law Libn.
HOLMES COUNTY LAW LIBRARY □ Millersburg, OH

Ginger, Ann Fagan, Dir.
MEIKLEJOHN CIVIL LIBERTIES INSTITUTE - LIBRARY □ Berkeley, CA

Ginn, Marjorie, Acq.Libn.
MAYO FOUNDATION - MAYO CLINIC LIBRARY □ Rochester, MN

Gino, John, Prog.Dir.
STATEN ISLAND COOPERATIVE CONTINUUM - EDUCATIONAL RESOURCE CENTER □ Staten Island, NY

Ginsberg, Judy, Hd., Cat.
YORK UNIVERSITY - LAW LIBRARY □ Downsview, ON

Ginther, Bethany L., Libn.
NEW YORK STATE SUPREME COURT - 6TH JUDICIAL DISTRICT - LAW LIBRARY □ Norwich, NY

Gionfriddo, Jacquelin, Dir.
ST. JOSEPH'S HOSPITAL - JEROME MEDICAL LIBRARY □ St. Paul, MN

Gionfriddo, Jane, Circ.
BOSTON COLLEGE - LAW SCHOOL LIBRARY □ Newton Centre, MA

Giordano, Joan, Acq.Libn.
BLOOMFIELD COLLEGE - GEORGE TALBOT HALL LIBRARY □ Bloomfield, NJ

Giordano, Joan, Med.Libn.
WESTCHESTER COUNTY MEDICAL CENTER - HEALTH SCIENCES LIBRARY □ Valhalla, NY

Giovando, Elizabeth, Archv.
NANAIMO AND DISTRICT MUSEUM SOCIETY - ARCHIVES □ Nanaimo, BC

Giovannini, Kathleen A., Info.Sci.
AMERICAN CAN COMPANY - PRINCETON RESEARCH INFORMATION CENTER □ Princeton, NJ

Giral, Angela, Libn.
HARVARD UNIVERSITY - GRADUATE SCHOOL OF DESIGN - FRANCES LOEB LIBRARY □ Cambridge, MA

Giraldi, Alfred, Ref.Libn.
AMERICAN TELEPHONE & TELEGRAPH COMPANY - CORPORATE LIBRARY □ Basking Ridge, NJ

Girard, Guylaine, Lib.Techn.
SOCIETE DE DEVELOPPEMENT DE LA BAIE JAMES - SERVICE DOCUMENTATION □ Montreal, PQ

Girard, Louise H., Hd.Tech.Serv.
UNIVERSITY OF TORONTO - ST. MICHAEL'S COLLEGE - JOHN M. KELLY LIBRARY □ Toronto, ON

Girard, Roselle, Res.Sci.Assoc.
UNIVERSITY OF TEXAS, AUSTIN - BUREAU OF ECONOMIC GEOLOGY READING ROOM □ Austin, TX

Giratalla, Omnia, Sys.Anl.
ALBERTA RESEARCH COUNCIL - ALBERTA OIL SANDS INFORMATION CENTRE □ Edmonton, AB

Girill, Ruth, Ref.Libn.
BA INVESTMENT MANAGEMENT CORPORATION - LIBRARY □ San Francisco, CA

Giroux, Eutha F., Lib.Assoc.
MANTENO MENTAL HEALTH CENTER - STAFF LIBRARY □ Manteno, IL

Giroux, Paula, Lib.Techn.
U.S. DEPT. OF JUSTICE - UNITED STATES ATTORNEY, NORTHERN DISTRICT OF ILLINOIS - LIBRARY □ Chicago, IL

Girshick, David, Cat.Libn.
MONTANA HISTORICAL SOCIETY - LIBRARY/ ARCHIVES □ Helena, MT

Gisondi, Gary G., Libn.
NEW YORK PUBLIC LIBRARY - PERFORMING ARTS RESEARCH CENTER - RODGERS & HAMMERSTEIN ARCHIVES OF RECORDED SOUND □ New York, NY

Gissendanner, Cassandra S., Hd.
COLUMBIA MUSEUMS OF ART & SCIENCE - LIBRARY □ Columbia, SC

Gitner, Fred J., Libn.
FRENCH INSTITUTE/ALLIANCE FRANCAISE - LIBRARY □ New York, NY

Gitt, Joyce, Lib.Techn.
ETOBICOKE GENERAL HOSPITAL - MEDICAL LIBRARY □ Rexdale, ON

Gitt, Robert, Film Preservation
UNIVERSITY OF CALIFORNIA, LOS ANGELES - UCLA FILM ARCHIVES □ Los Angeles, CA

Gittelsohn, I. Marc, Undergraduate Libn.
UNIVERSITY OF CALIFORNIA, SAN DIEGO - UNIVERSITY LIBRARIES □ La Jolla, CA

Gittinger, Mrs. L.J., Chm.
UNITED DAUGHTERS OF THE CONFEDERACY - TEXAS CONFEDERATE MUSEUM LIBRARY □ Austin, TX

Gittings, Barbara, Coord.
GAY TASK FORCE (ALA-SRRT) - INFORMATION CENTER □ Philadelphia, PA

Gittings, Dan, Libn.
U.S. NATL. MARINE FISHERIES SERVICE - SOUTHWEST FISHERIES CENTER - LIBRARY □ La Jolla, CA

Gittings, Jeanne A., Libn.
LUTHERAN HOSPITAL - MEDICAL STAFF LIBRARY AND SCHOOL FOR NURSES LIBRARY □ Moline, IL

Gittins, A.R., Act.Dir.
UNIVERSITY OF IDAHO - IDAHO WATER RESOURCES RESEARCH INSTITUTE - TECHNICAL INFO. CENTER & READING ROOM □ Moscow, ID

Giustino, Emily L., Dir.
ST. MARY MEDICAL CENTER - - BELLIS MEDICAL LIBRARY □ Long Beach, CA

Givens, Mary K., ILL Libn.
UNIVERSITY OF TENNESSEE - CENTER FOR THE HEALTH SCIENCES LIBRARY □ Memphis, TN

Gjellstad, Rolfe, Cat.Libn.
YALE UNIVERSITY - DIVINITY SCHOOL LIBRARY □ New Haven, CT

Gjelten, Dan, Ref.Libn.
MINNESOTA STATE LEGISLATIVE REFERENCE LIBRARY □ St. Paul, MN

Gjeruldsen, Carol, Book Acq.Supv.
FORD FOUNDATION - LIBRARY □ New York, NY

Glad, Beverly J., V.P. & Dir.
SALOMON BROTHERS - CORPORATE FINANCE LIBRARY □ New York, NY

Gladis, Pat, Cat.
UNIVERSITY OF PITTSBURGH - SPECIAL COLLECTIONS DEPARTMENT □ Pittsburgh, PA

Gladish, Mary Louise, Biomed.Res.Serv.Libn.
VANDERBILT UNIVERSITY - MEDICAL CENTER LIBRARY □ Nashville, TN

Glardon, Carol, Adm.Asst.
MARSHALL (John) LAW SCHOOL - LIBRARY □ Chicago, IL

Glascock, Mary A., Libn.
SALVATION ARMY - ARCHIVES AND RESEARCH CENTER □ New York, NY

Glaser, June, Libn.
EASTMAN DENTAL CENTER - BASIL G. BIBBY LIBRARY □ Rochester, NY

Glasgow, Jean L., Spec.Coll.Libn.
TEXAS WOMAN'S UNIVERSITY - SPECIAL COLLECTIONS □ Denton, TX

Glasgow, Linda
RILEY COUNTY HISTORICAL SOCIETY - SEATON MEMORIAL LIBRARY □ Manhattan, KS

Glass, Catherine, Tech.Serv.Dir.
MILLERSVILLE STATE COLLEGE - HELEN A. GANSER LIBRARY □ Millersville, PA

Glass, Gary B., Deputy Dir.
GEOLOGICAL SURVEY OF WYOMING - PUBLIC RECORDS SECTION □ Laramie, WY

Glasser, Dorothy, Dept.Hd.
HOUSTON PUBLIC LIBRARY - TEXAS AND LOCAL HISTORY DEPARTMENT □ Houston, TX

Glasser, Leo G., Dir.
MOUNT CUBA ASTRONOMICAL OBSERVATORY - LAMBERT L. JACKSON MEMORIAL LIBRARY □ Wilmington, DE

Glassman, Roslyn S., Staff Libn.
LONG ISLAND COLLEGE HOSPITAL - HOAGLAND MEDICAL LIBRARY □ Brooklyn, NY

Glassmeyer, Anita M., Media Libn.
UNIVERSITY OF ARIZONA - ARIZONA HEALTH SCIENCES CENTER LIBRARY □ Tucson, AZ

Glatfelter, Dr. Charles, Dir.
ADAMS COUNTY HISTORICAL SOCIETY - LIBRARY □ Gettysburg, PA

Glatter, Vicki, Lib.Ck.
INTERNATIONAL JOINT COMMISSION - GREAT LAKES REGIONAL OFFICE LIBRARY □ Windsor, ON

Glazier, Joan W., Lib.Off.
MARINE MIDLAND BANK - LIBRARY □ New York, NY

Gleason, Burton J., Hd., Office of Info.
U.S. DEPT. OF ENERGY - AMES LABORATORY - DOCUMENT LIBRARY □ Ames, IA

Gleason, Joy, Hd.
CHICAGO PUBLIC LIBRARY CENTRAL LIBRARY - GENERAL INFORMATION SERVICES DIV. - NEWSPAPERS & GEN. PERIODICALS CTR. □ Chicago, IL

Gleason, Judith M., Tech.Info.Spec.
NORTON COMPANY - LIBRARY/TECHNICAL INFORMATION CENTER □ Worcester, MA

Gleason, Linda, Info.Serv.Libn.
MEMORIAL SLOAN-KETTERING CANCER CENTER - LEE COOMBE MEMORIAL LIBRARY □ New York, NY

Gleason, Wesley A., Libn.
CHURCH OF JESUS CHRIST OF LATTER-DAY SAINTS - LAIE, HAWAII STAKE BRANCH GENEALOGICAL LIBRARY □ Laie, HI

Gleboff, Nancy, Indexer
AMERICAN CHEMICAL SOCIETY, INC. - LIBRARY □ Washington, DC

Glen, Marlene, Libn.
CANADA - AGRICULTURE CANADA - RESEARCH STATION, SASKATOON - LIBRARY □ Saskatoon, SK

Glencross, L., Asst. to Lib.Supv.
SASKATCHEWAN - DEPARTMENT OF HEALTH - LIBRARY □ Regina, SK

Glendenning, Burton, Coord., Hist.Div.
NEW BRUNSWICK - PROVINCIAL ARCHIVES OF NEW BRUNSWICK □ Fredericton, NB

Glendon, Natasha, Ref.Libn.
BELL TELEPHONE LABORATORIES, INC. & WESTERN ELECTRIC, INC. - TECHNICAL LIBRARY □ North Andover, MA

Glenister, Peter, Cat.
MOUNT SAINT VINCENT UNIVERSITY - LIBRARY □ Halifax, NS

Glenn, James R., Dp.Dir.
SMITHSONIAN INSTITUTION - NATIONAL ANTHROPOLOGICAL ARCHIVES □ Washington, DC

Glenn, Jerry, Libn.
UPPER SNAKE RIVER VALLEY HISTORICAL SOCIETY - LIBRARY □ Rexburg, ID

Glenn, Leila S., Cat.
UNIVERSITY OF MIAMI - SCHOOL OF LAW LIBRARY □ Coral Gables, FL

Glenn, Lucy D., Chf.Med.Libn.
ROANOKE MEMORIAL HOSPITALS - MEDICAL LIBRARY □ Roanoke, VA

Glennon, Mary, Cat.
UNIVERSITY OF CALIFORNIA, SAN FRANCISCO - HASTINGS COLLEGE OF THE LAW - LEGAL INFORMATION CENTER □ San Francisco, CA

Glessner, Charles T., Dir.
U.S. NATL. ARCHIVES & RECORDS SERVICE - FEDERAL ARCHIVES AND RECORDS CENTER, REGION 3 □ Philadelphia, PA

Glessner, Debra, Asst.Libn.
HAWKINS, DELAFIELD & WOOD - LIBRARY □ New York, NY

Glick, Jacqueline, Ref.Libn.
MEDICAL COLLEGE OF WISCONSIN - TODD WEHR LIBRARY □ Milwaukee, WI

Glick, Robert, Hd., Pub. Programs
FOLGER SHAKESPEARE LIBRARY □ Washington, DC

Glickman, Linda S., Hd.Libn.
SYSTEM PLANNING CORPORATION - RESEARCH LIBRARY □ Arlington, VA

Glidden, Lt.Col. Benjaman C., Dir. of Libs.
U.S. AIR FORCE ACADEMY - LIBRARY □ U.S. Air Force Academy, CO

Globus, Sheila, Tech.Libn.
MOLSON BREWERIES OF CANADA, LTD. - INFORMATION CENTRE □ Montreal, PQ

Glock, Diane C., Cat.
GENERAL ELECTRIC COMPANY - MAIN LIBRARY □ Schenectady, NY

Glock, Jennie, Libn.
ST. MARY'S HOSPITAL - HEALTH SCIENCES LIBRARY □ West Palm Beach, FL

Glock, Martha, User Serv.Libn.
U.S. CUSTOMS SERVICE - LIBRARY AND INFORMATION CENTER □ Washington, DC

Glodek, C.J., Chf.Libn.
MICHIGAN CANCER FOUNDATION - LEONARD F. SIMONS RESEARCH LIBRARY □ Detroit, MI

Glodkowski, Susan, Info.Anl.
CONTINENTAL ILLINOIS NATIONAL BANK AND TRUST COMPANY OF CHICAGO - INFORMATION SERVICES DIVISION □ Chicago, IL

Gloeckner, Paul B., Chf.Libn.
PAUL, WEISS, RIFKIND, WHARTON AND GARRISON - LIBRARY □ New York, NY

Gloede, Yvonne, Info.Spec.
AMERICAN ASSOCIATION OF ADVERTISING AGENCIES - MEMBER INFORMATION SERVICE □ New York, NY

Gloger, Nancy, Cat.
BANK OF NOVA SCOTIA - LIBRARY □ Toronto, ON

Gloriod, Barbara, Rd.Adv.
DISTRICT OF COLUMBIA PUBLIC LIBRARY - LANGUAGE, LITERATURE &FOREIGN LANGUAGE DIVISION □ Washington, DC

Glover, Alice F., Cat.
NATIONAL SOCIETY OF THE SONS OF THE AMERICAN REVOLUTION - GENEALOGY LIBRARY □ Louisville, KY

Glover, Carol, Supv., Main Lib.
ROCKWELL INTERNATIONAL - ANAHEIM INFORMATION CENTER □ Anaheim, CA

Glover, Clara A., Dir.
COLORADO STATE HOME AND TRAINING SCHOOL - STAFF LIBRARY □ Wheat Ridge, CO

Glover, Erika, Assoc.Dir.
GRANGER COLLECTION □ New York, NY

Glover, Gwen L., Libn.
CENTRAL CAROLINA TECHNICAL COLLEGE - LEARNING RESOURCE CENTER □ Sanford, NC

Glover, J.M., Hd.Lib.Oper.
CANADA - ATMOSPHERIC ENVIRONMENT SERVICE - LIBRARY □ Downsview, ON

Glover, Jack, Owner
SUNSET TRADING POST-OLD WEST MUSEUM - LIBRARY □ Sunset, TX

Glover, William, Dir.
GRANGER COLLECTION □ New York, NY

Glueckert, John P., Asst.Libn.
UNIVERSITY OF SOUTHERN CALIFORNIA - DENTISTRY LIBRARY □ Los Angeles, CA

Glunz, Diane, Ref.Libn.
UNIVERSITY OF SOUTHERN CALIFORNIA - HEALTH SCIENCES CAMPUS - NORRIS MEDICAL LIBRARY □ Los Angeles, CA

Glushakow, Mildred, Dir.
SPRING GARDEN COLLEGE - LIBRARY □ Chestnut Hill, PA

Glynn, Cindy, Pub.Serv.Libn.
SALEM STATE COLLEGE - STUDENT GOVERNMENT ASSOCIATION & LIBRARY - LIBRARY OF SOCIAL ALTERNATIVES† □ Salem, MA

Glynn, Joseph M., Jr., Dir.
IRISH FAMILY HISTORY SOCIETY - LIBRARY □ Newton, MA

Glynn, William, Lib.Asst.
HARVARD UNIVERSITY - STATISTICS LIBRARY □ Cambridge, MA

Gnat, Jean M., Hd., Tech.Serv.
INDIANA UNIVERSITY/PURDUE UNIVERSITY AT INDIANAPOLIS - UNIVERSITY LIBRARY □ Indianapolis, IN

Gnatek, Victoria C., Adm.Asst.
SMITH COLLEGE - ARCHIVES □ Northampton, MA

Go, Fe Susan, Doc.Libn.
COMMUNITY SYSTEMS FOUNDATION - NUTRITION PLANNING INFORMATION SERVICE □ Ann Arbor, MI

Go, Ivonne K., Libn.
GOVERNOR BACON HEALTH CENTER - MEDICAL LIBRARY □ Delaware City, DE

Goble, Frank G., Pres.
JEFFERSON (Thomas) RESEARCH CENTER - LIBRARY □ Pasadena, CA

Godavari, S. Norma, Libn.
MANITOBA - DEPT. OF CONSUMER & CORPORATE AFFAIRS & ENVIRONMENT - DEPT. REFERENCE SERV. - CONSUMER AFF. LIB. □ Winnipeg, MB

Godbout-Mercure, Micheline, Hd. of Tech.Serv.
RADIO QUEBEC - CENTRE DES RESSOURCES DOCUMENTAIRES □ Montreal, PQ

Goddard, Susan, Faculty Libn.
UNIVERSITY OF TORONTO - FACULTY OF DENTISTRY LIBRARY □ Toronto, ON

Godden, Sharon, Adm.Supv.
NORWICH-EATON - FILM LIBRARY □ Paris, ON

Godel, Edith, Music Libn.
WESTERN CONNECTICUT STATE COLLEGE - RUTH A. HAAS LIBRARY □ Danbury, CT

Goderwis, Cherie L., R.N., Dir.
RUTLAND HOSPITAL - HEALTH SCIENCE LIBRARY □ Rutland, VT

Godfrey, Eleanor, Media Rsrcs.Dir.
UNION THEOLOGICAL SEMINARY IN VIRGINIA - LIBRARY □ Richmond, VA

Godfrey, Lois, Asst.Hd.Libn.
UNIVERSITY OF CALIFORNIA - LOS ALAMOS NATIONAL LABORATORY - LIBRARY □ Los Alamos, NM

Godin, Liz, Asst.Libn.
DOFASCO INC. - MAIN OFFICE LIBRARY □ Hamilton, ON

Godin, Roger A., Exec.Dir.
U.S. HOCKEY HALL OF FAME - LIBRARY □ Eveleth, MN

Godine, Anne, Asst.Libn.
COLLEGE OF ST. CATHERINE - PERFORMING ARTS LIBRARY □ St. Paul, MN

Goding, David, Hd.Libn.
CASE WESTERN RESERVE UNIVERSITY - SEARS LIBRARY □ Cleveland, OH

Godlove, C.J., Cat.
TRAVENOL LABORATORIES, INC. - LIBRARY □ Morton Grove, IL

Godoy, Alicia, Lang.Libn.
MIAMI-DADE PUBLIC LIBRARY - FOREIGN LANGUAGES DIVISION □ Miami, FL

Godwin, Gerrie, Asst.Libn.
MENNONITE HOSPITAL AND SCHOOL OF NURSING - HEALTH SCIENCES LIBRARY □ Bloomington, IL

Godwin, Bro. Roy, C.F.A., Prov.Archv.
CONGREGATION OF THE ALEXIAN BROTHERS - PROVINCIAL ARCHIVES □ Elk Grove Village, IL

Goebel, Heather L., Hd.
FORT WORTH PUBLIC LIBRARY - HUMANITIES DEPARTMENT □ Fort Worth, TX

Goecke, Wanda M., Base Libn.
U.S. AIR FORCE BASE - HOLLOMAN BASE
LIBRARY □ Alamogordo, NM

Goeckeler, Steve, Asst.Libn.
BURNS AND MC DONNELL ENGINEERING
COMPANY - TECHNICAL LIBRARY □ Kansas
City, MO

Goedecke, Jane L., Libn.
CANTON HISTORICAL SOCIETY - LIBRARY □
Collinsville, CT

Goedeker, Marianne C., Libn.
JOHNSON (George) ADVERTISING - LIBRARY □
St. Louis, MO

Goehner, Donna, Acq./Ser.Libn.
WESTERN ILLINOIS UNIVERSITY - LIBRARIES
□ Macomb, IL

Goekler, Lester A., Asst.Libn.
TEXAS RESEARCH INSTITUTE OF MENTAL
SCIENCES - LIBRARY □ Houston, TX

Goel, Krishan S., Libn.
U.S. ARMY - ENVIRONMENTAL HYGIENE
AGENCY - LIBRARY □ Aberdeen Proving Ground,
MD

Goeldner, C.R., Dir.
UNIVERSITY OF COLORADO, BOULDER -
BUSINESS RESEARCH DIVISION - BUSINESS &
ECONOMIC COLLECTION □ Boulder, CO

Goeldner, C.R., Dir.
UNIVERSITY OF COLORADO, BOULDER -
BUSINESS RESEARCH DIVISION - TRAVEL
REFERENCE CENTER □ Boulder, CO

Goerig, Janet, Dir. of Lib.Serv.
ST. VINCENT'S MEDICAL CENTER - DANIEL T.
BANKS HEALTH SCIENCE LIBRARY □ Bridgeport,
CT

Goertzen, Norma S., Dir.
NORTH PARK THEOLOGICAL SEMINARY -
MELLANDER LIBRARY □ Chicago, IL

Goertzen, Peter, Mgr.
MENNONITE VILLAGE MUSEUM (Canada) INC. -
LIBRARY □ Steinbach, MB

Goethert, Gay D., Lib.Supv.
ARNOLD ENGINEERING DEVELOPMENT CENTER
- LIBRARY □ Arnold Air Force Sta., TN

Goetsch, Rev. Ronald W., Archv.
LUTHERAN CHURCH - MISSOURI SYNOD -
NORTH WISCONSIN DISTRICT ARCHIVES □
Wausau, WI

Goetze, Pamela R., Libn.
INTERTECHNOLOGY/SOLAR CORPORATION -
LIBRARY □ Warrenton, VA

Goff, Sr. Dorothy, Libn.
DEACONESS COMMUNITY LUTHERAN CHURCH
OF AMERICA - LUTHERAN DEACONESS
COMMUNITY LIBRARY □ Gladwyne, PA

Goff, Karen E., Ref.Libn.
WEST VIRGINIA STATE LIBRARY COMMISSION
- REFERENCE LIBRARY □ Charleston, WV

Goff, William J., Libn.
UNIVERSITY OF CALIFORNIA, SAN DIEGO -
SCRIPPS INSTITUTION OF OCEANOGRAPHY
LIBRARY □ La Jolla, CA

Goguen, Alice, Statistician
ORDER OF DAEDALIANS - NATIONAL
HEADQUARTERS - LIBRARY AND INFORMATION
CENTER □ San Antonio, TX

Gohmann, Rev. Myron, C.P., Hd.Libn.
KENRICK SEMINARY LIBRARY □ St. Louis, MO

Gokahle, Shakuntala, Libn.
CARDINAL SPELLMAN PHILATELIC MUSEUM,
INC. - LIBRARY □ Weston, MA

Gold, Betty, Libn.
NATIONAL COUNCIL ON ALCOHOLISM, INC. -
LIBRARY† □ New York, NY

Gold, Dave, Dir. & Archv.
GOLD PARACHUTE LIBRARY, ARCHIVES &
TECHNICAL INFORMATION CENTER □
Ridgecrest, CA

Gold, Mrs. E.E., Libn.
COMINCO LTD. - SULLIVAN MINE LIBRARY □
Kimberley, BC

Gold, Ethel, Ref.
NEW YORK INSTITUTE OF TECHNOLOGY -
LIBRARY† □ Old Westbury, NY

Gold, James
HARTFORD PUBLIC LIBRARY - BUSINESS,
SCIENCE & TECHNOLOGY DEPARTMENT □
Hartford, CT

Gold, James
HARTFORD PUBLIC LIBRARY - REFERENCE AND
GENERAL READING DEPARTMENT □ Hartford,
CT

Gold, Leonard S., Div.Chf.
NEW YORK PUBLIC LIBRARY - JEWISH
DIVISION □ New York, NY

Gold, Suzanne, Libn./Asst.Hd.
UNIVERSITY OF CALIFORNIA, BERKELEY -
GOVERNMENT DOCUMENTS DEPARTMENT □
Berkeley, CA

Goldbeck, Gwendolyn, Asst.Sci.Libn.
MARQUETTE UNIVERSITY - SCIENCE LIBRARY
□ Milwaukee, WI

Goldberg, Barbara B., Chf.Libn.
U.S. VETERANS ADMINISTRATION (NY-
Brooklyn) - MEDICAL CENTER LIBRARY □
Brooklyn, NY

Goldberg, Eve M.
RHODE ISLAND STATE DEPARTMENT OF
ELDERLY AFFAIRS - LIBRARY □ Providence, RI

Goldberg, Joan E., Tech.Libn.
BETZ LABORATORIES, INC. - RESEARCH
LIBRARY □ Trevose, PA

Goldberg, Kay, Prog.Coord.
UNIVERSITY OF ILLINOIS MEDICAL CENTER -
LIBRARY OF THE HEALTH SCIENCES □ Chicago,
IL

Goldberg, Kenneth P., Pub.Serv.Libn.
CLEVELAND INSTITUTE OF ART - JESSICA R.
GUND MEMORIAL LIBRARY □ Cleveland, OH

Goldberg, Dr. Louise, Ref./Rare Books Libn.
UNIVERSITY OF ROCHESTER - EASTMAN
SCHOOL OF MUSIC - SIBLEY MUSIC LIBRARY □
Rochester, NY

Goldberg, Dr. Robert L., Dir.
WILLIAM PATERSON COLLEGE OF NEW JERSEY
- SARAH BYRD ASKEW LIBRARY - SPECIAL
COLLECTIONS □ Wayne, NJ

Goldberg, Ronnie, Search Spec.
SUNY AT BINGHAMTON - SCIENCE LIBRARY □
Binghamton, NY

Goldblatt, Margaret, Ser.Libn.
WASHINGTON UNIVERSITY - SCHOOL OF LAW
- FREUND LAW LIBRARY □ St. Louis, MO

Goldcamp, Alice, Libn.
BUTLER INSTITUTE OF AMERICAN ART -
LIBRARY □ Youngstown, OH

Golden, Barbara, Ref.Libn.
HENNEPIN COUNTY LAW LIBRARY □
Minneapolis, MN

Golden, Nancy J., Hd., Pub.Serv.
BOSTON UNIVERSITY MEDICAL CENTER -
ALUMNI MEDICAL LIBRARY □ Boston, MA

Golden, Patricia
NEW ZEALAND EMBASSY - LIBRARY □
Washington, DC

Goldenberg, Stephen, Video Libn.
SEATTLE PUBLIC LIBRARY - MEDIA &
PROGRAM SERVICES □ Seattle, WA

Golder, Melanie, Ref.Libn.
SOUTHERN METHODIST UNIVERSITY -
SCIENCE/ENGINEERING LIBRARY □ Dallas, TX

Goldhammer, Arlene, Asst.Libn.
MORGAN, LEWIS & BOCKIUS - LIBRARY □
Philadelphia, PA

Goldman, Arlene, Libn.
AMERICAN ASSOCIATION OF MEDICO-LEGAL
CONSULTANTS - LIBRARY □ Philadelphia, PA

Goldman, Ava, Corp.Libn.
FIRST FEDERAL SAVINGS & LOAN
ASSOCIATION OF BROWARD COUNTY -
CORPORATE LIBRARY □ Fort Lauderdale, FL

Goldman, Cynthia A., Libn.
U.S. NATL. BUREAU OF STANDARDS - OFFICE
OF STANDARD REFERENCE DATA - REFERENCE
CENTER □ Washington, DC

Goldman, Irene, Asst.Libn.
CONNECTICUT GENERAL LIFE INSURANCE
COMPANY - LIBRARY □ Hartford, CT

Goldman, Martha, Libn.
KELLEY, DRYE & WARREN - LAW LIBRARY □
New York, NY

Goldman, Viki, Ref.Libn.
BATTEN, BARTON, DURSTINE, OSBORN, INC. -
INFORMATION RETRIEVAL CENTER □ New
York, NY

Goldman, Wendy, Res.Libn.
CONSUMERS UNION OF UNITED STATES, INC. -
LIBRARY □ Mount Vernon, NY

Goldschmid, Johanna, Spec.Coll.Libn.
SAN FRANCISCO PUBLIC LIBRARY - SPECIAL
COLLECTIONS DEPARTMENT □ San Francisco,
CA

Goldsmith, Catherine, Hd., AV Ctr.
ART GALLERY OF ONTARIO - AUDIO-VISUAL
CENTRE □ Toronto, ON

Goldsmith, David, Asst.
LIMA STATE HOSPITAL - RESIDENTS &
PROFESSIONAL LIBRARY† □ Lima, OH

Goldsmith, Mrs. William, Libn.
AGUDAS ACHIM CONGREGATION - STEIN
MEMORIAL LIBRARY □ Columbus, OH

Goldstaub, Curt S., Cat.Libn.
KUTZTOWN STATE COLLEGE - ROHRBACH
LIBRARY □ Kutztown, PA

Goldstein, Arthur A.A., Chf.Cat.
KXE6S VEREIN CHESS SOCIETY - SPECIAL/
RESEARCH LIBRARY - EAST DIVISION □ Chapel
Hill, NC

Goldstein, Doris, Dir.Lib. & Info.Serv.
GEORGETOWN UNIVERSITY - KENNEDY
INSTITUTE OF ETHICS - CENTER FOR
BIOETHICS LIBRARY □ Washington, DC

Goldstein, Evelyn M., Dir.
AMERICAN ASSOCIATION OF MEDICO-LEGAL
CONSULTANTS - LIBRARY □ Philadelphia, PA

Goldstein, Harold S., Exec.Dir.
AMERICAN ROSE SOCIETY - LIBRARY □
Shreveport, LA

Goldstein, Helene, Reports Libn.
NATIONAL ACADEMY OF SCIENCES -
NATIONAL ACADEMY OF ENGINEERING -
LIBRARY □ Washington, DC

Goldstein, Dr. Kenneth, Hd.
UNIVERSITY OF PENNSYLVANIA -
DEPARTMENT OF FOLKLORE & FOLKLIFE -
ARCHIVE □ Philadelphia, PA

Goldstein, Laurence
LEEWARD COMMUNITY COLLEGE - LIBRARY □
Honolulu, HI

Goldstein, Rachael K., Libn.
COLUMBIA UNIVERSITY - HEALTH SCIENCES
LIBRARY □ New York, NY

Goldstein, Sidney, Dir.
BROWN UNIVERSITY - POPULATION STUDIES
AND TRAINING CENTER - DEMOGRAPHY
LIBRARY □ Providence, RI

Goldzwig, Jeanne B., Libn.
TEMPLE ISRAEL - RABBI LOUIS WITT
MEMORIAL LIBRARY □ Dayton, OH

Golembiewski, Terri M., Chf.Ref.Libn.
CHICAGO SUN-TIMES - EDITORIAL LIBRARY □
Chicago, IL

Golemboski, Dick, Supv., Info. Center
EG&G, INC. - WASHINGTON ANALYTICAL
SERVICES CENTER - INFORMATION CENTER □
Rockville, MD

Golightly, Bonnie, Asst.Libn.
SEAMEN'S CHURCH INSTITUTE OF NEW YORK
- JOSEPH CONRAD LIBRARY □ New York, NY

Gollop, Claudia J., Adm., Info.Serv.
MINORITY BUSINESS INFORMATION
INSTITUTE, INC. - LIBRARY □ New York, NY

Gollub, George A., Law Libn.
NORTHAMPTON COUNTY LAW LIBRARY □
Easton, PA

Golob, Mimi, Info.Sci.
AVON PRODUCTS, INC. - TECHNICAL
INFORMATION CENTER LIBRARY □ Suffern, NY

Golt, Lucille, Abstractor/Indexer
HERCULES, INC. - RESEARCH CENTER -
TECHNICAL INFORMATION DIVISION □
Wilmington, DE

Goltz, Eileen, Hd., Pub.Docs.
LAURENTIAN UNIVERSITY - MAIN LIBRARY □
Sudbury, ON

Gomez, Aurora, Libn.
UNIVERSIDAD BORICUA - PUERTO RICAN
RESEARCH & RESOURCES CENTER, INC. -
REFERENCE LIBRARY □ New York, NY

Gomez, Gerardo, Libn.
BRONX-LEBANON HOSPITAL CENTER -
CONCOURSE DIVISION MEDICAL LIBRARY □
Bronx, NY

Gomez, Teri, Adm.Asst.
BECHTEL CIVIL & MINERALS, INC. - MINING &
MINERALS BUSINESS DEVELOPMENT LIBRARY
□ San Francisco, CA

Gomien, Margaret, Libn.
BETHESDA HOSPITAL - INFORMATION
RESOURCE CENTER □ Cincinnati, OH

Gondy, Allie Wise, Music Libn.
WESTERN ILLINOIS UNIVERSITY - LIBRARIES
□ Macomb, IL

Gong, James G., Ref.Libn.
SEATTLE-FIRST NATIONAL BANK - LIBRARY □
Seattle, WA

Gongoll, Ward E., Hd.Libn.
DE SALES HALL SCHOOL OF THEOLOGY -
LIBRARY □ Hyattsville, MD

Gonnami, Tsuneharu, Japanese Libn.
UNIVERSITY OF BRITISH COLUMBIA - ASIAN
STUDIES LIBRARY □ Vancouver, BC

Gontrum, Barbara S., Dir.
UNIVERSITY OF MARYLAND, BALTIMORE -
SCHOOL OF LAW - MARSHALL LAW LIBRARY □
Baltimore, MD

Gonyon, Sr. Jeanne M., Libn.
CARMELITE MONASTERY - LIBRARY OF THE
IMMACULATE HEART OF MARY □ Barre, VT

Gonyou, James F., Dir.
GREAT WESTERN SUGAR COMPANY -
AGRICULTURAL RESEARCH CENTER -
RESEARCH LIBRARY □ Longmont, CO

Gonzales, Mrs. T.S., Libn.
BRANDON UNIVERSITY - CHRISTIE
EDUCATION LIBRARY □ Brandon, MB

Gonzalez, Carmen, Cat.
CATHOLIC UNIVERSITY OF PUERTO RICO -
MONSIGNOR JUAN FREMIOT TORRES OLIVER
LAW LIBRARY □ Ponce, PR

Gonzalez, Carmen A., Libn.
UNIVERSITY OF PUERTO RICO - NATURAL
SCIENCE LIBRARY □ Rio Piedras, PR

Gonzalez, Raphael, Libn.
ROGERS & WELLS - LAW LIBRARY □ New York,
NY

Gonzalez, Valentin, Acq.Libn.
INTERAMERICAN UNIVERSITY - SCHOOL OF
LAW - DOMINGO TOLEDO ALAMO LAW LIBRARY
□ Santurce, PR

Gonzalez, Victoria, Med.Libn.
BERGEN PINES COUNTY HOSPITAL - MEDICAL
LIBRARY □ Paramus, NJ

Gooch, Peggy, Dir.
PARK CITIES BAPTIST CHURCH - LIBRARY □
Dallas, TX

Gooch, William D., Asst. State Libn.
TEXAS STATE LIBRARY □ Austin, TX

Good, Julanne M., Libn.
ST. LOUIS PUBLIC LIBRARY - CHILDREN'S
LITERATURE ROOM □ St. Louis, MO

Good, Ruth, Hd.Libn.
TOCCOA FALLS COLLEGE - SEBY JONES
LIBRARY □ Toccoa Falls, GA

Goodale, Leslie, Dir.
CHILDREN'S MEMORIAL HOSPITAL - JOSEPH
BRENNEMANN LIBRARY □ Chicago, IL

Goodchild, Eleanor, Dir.Lib.Serv.
LOS ANGELES COUNTY HARBOR UCLA MEDICAL
CENTER - MEDICAL LIBRARY □ Torrance, CA

Goodchild, Eleanor, Libn.
UNIVERSITY OF PENNSYLVANIA - MEDICAL &
BIOLOGICAL SCIENCES LIBRARY □ Philadelphia,
PA

Goodding, Martha, Lib.Dir.
ST. JOSEPH STATE HOSPITAL - PROFESSIONAL
LIBRARY □ St. Joseph, MO

Goode, Allan, AV
OKLAHOMA STATE DEPARTMENT OF
LIBRARIES □ Oklahoma City, OK

Goode, Carol, Libn.
CONTINENTAL TELEPHONE LABORATORIES -
WALTER L. ROBERTS TECHNICAL LIBRARY □
Norcross, GA

Goodell, Lela, Asst.Libn.
HAWAIIAN MISSION CHILDREN'S SOCIETY -
MISSION-HISTORICAL LIBRARY □ Honolulu, HI

Goodemote, Rita L., Assoc.Dir.
SCHERING-PLOUGH CORPORATION -
PHARMACEUTICAL RESEARCH DIVISION -
LIBRARY INFORMATION CENTER □ Bloomfield,
NJ

Gooden, Gerald L., Dir.
BIOLA COLLEGE, INC. - LIBRARY □ La Mirada,
CA

Gooden, Kathryn, Libn.
GREENE COUNTY HISTORICAL SOCIETY -
LIBRARY AND MUSEUM □ Waynesburg, PA

Goodhartz, Gerald, Libn.
KAYE, SCHOLER, FIERMAN, HAYS & HANDLER -
LAW LIBRARY □ New York, NY

Goodhouse, Barbara A., Libn.
YORK RESEARCH CORPORATION - LIBRARY □
Stamford, CT

Goodlett, Doris, Hd., Adult Serv.
FERGUSON LIBRARY - BUSINESS-TECHNOLOGY
DEPARTMENT □ Stamford, CT

Goodman, A. Sue, Info.Spec.
INTERNATIONAL PAPER COMPANY - ERLING
RIIS RESEARCH LABORATORY - INFORMATION
SERVICES □ Mobile, AL

Goodman, Annie, Coll.Coord.
NILS PUBLISHING CO. - NATIONAL INSURANCE
LAW SERVICE - LIBRARY □ Chatsworth, CA

Goodman, Barbara W., Tech.Sec.-Libn.
THIELE KAOLIN COMPANY - RESEARCH &
DEVELOPMENT LIBRARY □ Sandersville, GA

Goodman, David
NATIONAL ACTION/RESEARCH ON THE
MILITARY-INDUSTRIAL COMPLEX - LIBRARY □
Philadelphia, PA

Goodman, Dr. David, Libn.
PRINCETON UNIVERSITY - CHEMISTRY &
BIOCHEMISTRY LIBRARY □ Princeton, NJ

Goodman, Delena, Hd.Libn.
ANDERSON COLLEGE - SCHOOL OF THEOLOGY -
BYRD MEMORIAL LIBRARY □ Anderson, IN

Goodman, Diane L., Dir.
IF EVERY FOOL, INC. - PERFORMING ARTS
LIBRARY □ New York, NY

Goodman, Edward, Educ.Biblog.
SYRACUSE UNIVERSITY - E.S. BIRD LIBRARY -
SOCIAL SCIENCES DEPARTMENT □ Syracuse,
NY

Goodman, Eva, Asst.Libn.
LAFAYETTE JOURNAL AND COURIER - LIBRARY
□ Lafayette, IN

Goodman, Joan T., Supv.
WARBURG PARIBAS BECKER, INC. - LIBRARY □
Chicago, IL

Goodman, Bro. L. Dennis, F.S.C.
MORAGA HISTORICAL SOCIETY - ARCHIVES □
Moraga, CA

Goodman, L. M., Coord.
PRANG-MARK SOCIETY - LIBRARY □ Watkins
Glen, NY

Goodman, Lois A., Hd.Pub.Serv.
ROCHESTER INSTITUTE OF TECHNOLOGY -
WALLACE MEMORIAL LIBRARY □ Rochester, NY

Goodman, Marcia M., Libn.
UNIVERSITY OF OKLAHOMA - HISTORY OF
SCIENCE COLLECTIONS □ Norman, OK

Goodman, Marcia M., Libn.
UNIVERSITY OF OKLAHOMA - LIMITED ACCESS
COLLECTION □ Norman, OK

Goodman, Marion, Libn.
MARYLAND NATIONAL CAPITAL PARK AND
PLANNING COMMISSION - LIBRARY □ Silver
Spring, MD

Goodman, Roy E., Reading Rm.Libn.
AMERICAN PHILOSOPHICAL SOCIETY -
LIBRARY □ Philadelphia, PA

Goodman, Ruth R., Libn.
FAR EAST MERCHANTS ASSOCIATION - FEMAS
TRADE LIBRARY □ Berkeley, CA

Goodrich, Jeanne, Dir., Lib.Dev.
NEVADA STATE LIBRARY □ Carson City, NV

Goodrich, Klara B., Med.Libn.
RESURRECTION HOSPITAL - MEDICAL LIBRARY
& ALLIED HEALTH SCIENCES □ Chicago, IL

Goodrich, Margaret, Libn.
DENVER ART MUSEUM - FREDERIC H. DOUGLAS
LIBRARY OF ANTHROPOLOGY AND ART □
Denver, CO

Goodridge, Betty, Info.Ctr.Coord.
CELANESE CORPORATION - CELANESE
CHEMICAL COMPANY, INC. - TECHNICAL
CENTER - LIBRARY □ Corpus Christi, TX

Goodsell, Joan, Cat.
THOMPSON (J. Walter) COMPANY -
INFORMATION CENTER □ New York, NY

Goodson, Stephen E., Dir.
FRESNO COUNTY DEPARTMENT OF EDUCATION
- IMC-LIBRARY □ Fresno, CA

Goodstein, Dr. Judith, Inst.Archv.
CALIFORNIA INSTITUTE OF TECHNOLOGY -
ROBERT A. MILLIKAN MEMORIAL LIBRARY □
Pasadena, CA

Goodwin, Cathy, Libn.
ROSENBERG CAPITAL MANAGEMENT -
LIBRARY □ San Francisco, CA

Goodwin, Deborah L., Cur.
CAPE ANN HISTORICAL ASSOCIATION -
LIBRARY □ Gloucester, MA

Goodwin, George H., Jr., Chf.Libn.
U.S. GEOLOGICAL SURVEY - LIBRARY □ Reston,
VA

Goodwin, Helen, Cur.
FIREFIGHTERS' MUSEUM OF NOVA SCOTIA -
LIBRARY & INFORMATION CENTER □ Yarmouth,
NS

Goodwin, J.H., Libn.
VIRGINIA THEOLOGICAL SEMINARY - BISHOP
PAYNE LIBRARY □ Alexandria, VA

Goodwin, Jack, Coll.Mgt.
SMITHSONIAN INSTITUTION LIBRARIES □
Washington, DC

Goodwin, Jane, Ref.Libn.
UNIVERSITY OF CONNECTICUT - SCHOOL OF
BUSINESS ADMINISTRATION LIBRARY □
Hartford, CT

Goodwin, Joann, Ref.Libn.
SAN DIEGO STATE UNIVERSITY -
GOVERNMENT PUBLICATIONS DEPARTMENT □
San Diego, CA

Goodwin, Julia, Techn.
U.S. BUREAU OF MINES - SALT LAKE CITY
RESEARCH CENTER - LIBRARY □ Salt Lake City,
UT

Goodwin, Vania, Reserve/ILL Assoc.
INDIANA UNIVERSITY/PURDUE UNIVERSITY
AT INDIANAPOLIS - UNIVERSITY LIBRARY □
Indianapolis, IN

Goodwin, Dr. William N., Dir.
YOUNG MEN'S CHRISTIAN ASSOCIATION OF
METROPOLITAN HARTFORD, INC. - CAREER
COUNSELING CENTER LIBRARY □ Hartford, CT

PERSONNEL

PERSONNEL

Goold, Karla P., Libn.
UNIVERSITY OF NOTRE DAME - CHEMISTRY/ PHYSICS LIBRARY □ Notre Dame, IN
Goolsby, Peggy B., Lib.Techn.
U.S. DEPT. OF DEFENSE - DEFENSE INDUSTRIAL PLANT EQUIPMENT CENTER - TECHNICAL DATA REPOSITORY & LIBRARY □ Memphis, TN
Goorough, Gary, Film Libn.
UNIVERSITY OF WISCONSIN, LA CROSSE - AUDIOVISUAL CENTER - FILM LIBRARY □ La Crosse, WI
Goot, Jacqueline, Act.Libn.
NEW YORK STATE DEPARTMENT OF TAXATION & FINANCE - TAX LIBRARY □ Albany, NY
Goote, Marinus, Theological Asst.
CALVIN COLLEGE AND SEMINARY - LIBRARY □ Grand Rapids, MI
Gor, Robert, ILL
STATE LIBRARY OF FLORIDA □ Tallahassee, FL
Gorchels, Dr. Clarence, Dir.
OREGON COLLEGE OF EDUCATION - LIBRARY □ Monmouth, OR
Gorden, Jan, Libn.
UNIVERSITY OF WASHINGTON - COMPUTING INFORMATION CENTER □ Seattle, WA
Gordon, Anne W., Libn.
UNIVERSITY OF PITTSBURGH - HENRY CLAY FRICK FINE ARTS LIBRARY □ Pittsburgh, PA
Gordon, Barbara B., Libn.
UNIVERSITY OF WASHINGTON - FOREST RESOURCES LIBRARY □ Seattle, WA
Gordon, Catherine, Libn.
UNIVERSITY OF CALIFORNIA, BERKELEY - EDUCATION/PSYCHOLOGY LIBRARY □ Berkeley, CA
Gordon, Constance G., Rare Book Cat.
CHICAGO PUBLIC LIBRARY CULTURAL CENTER - SPECIAL COLLECTIONS DIVISION □ Chicago, IL
Gordon, Donna M., Pub.Serv.Libn.
ALBERTA - DEPARTMENT OF ENERGY AND NATURAL RESOURCES - LIBRARY† □ Edmonton, AB
Gordon, Donna R., Ref.Libn.
BOSTON UNIVERSITY MEDICAL CENTER - ALUMNI MEDICAL LIBRARY □ Boston, MA
Gordon, Helen, Libn.
PLANNED PARENTHOOD ASSOCIATION OF WISCONSIN - RESOURCE CENTER □ Milwaukee, WI
Gordon, Ines Mora, Libn.
FESTIVAL CASALS, INC. - PUERTO RICO INDUSTRIAL DEVELOPMENT COMPANY - CONSERVATORIO DE MUSICA - LIBRARY □ Hato Rey, PR
Gordon, Dr. Irving, Supv.
HOOKER CHEMICAL CORPORATION - TECHNICAL INFORMATION CENTER □ Niagara Falls, NY
Gordon, James, Ref.Libn.
BROOKLYN LAW SCHOOL - LAW LIBRARY □ Brooklyn, NY
Gordon, Jean, Archv.Asst.
CHAMPAIGN COUNTY HISTORICAL ARCHIVES □ Urbana, IL
Gordon, Marjorie, Libn.
AMERICAN COUNCIL OF LIFE INSURANCE - LIBRARY □ Washington, DC
Gordon, Martin, Per.Libn.
FRANKLIN AND MARSHALL COLLEGE - FACKENTHAL LIBRARY - SPECIAL COLLECTIONS □ Lancaster, PA
Gordon, Mary Frances, Gifts & Exch.Libn.
TEXAS TECH UNIVERSITY - LIBRARY □ Lubbock, TX
Gordon, Phyllis, Libn.
CUYAHOGA COUNTY REGIONAL PLANNING COMMISSION - LIBRARY □ Cleveland, OH
Gordon, R.S., Dir.
CANADA - PUBLIC ARCHIVES OF CANADA - MANUSCRIPT DIVISION □ Ottawa, ON

Gordon, Rachael, Asst. Law Libn.
BANK OF AMERICA - SOUTHERN CALIFORNIA HEADQUARTERS - LAW LIBRARY □ Los Angeles, CA
Gordon, Richard, Lib.Mgr.
UNITED CEREBRAL PALSY OF NEW YORK CITY, INC. - LIBRARY □ New York, NY
Gordon, Robert N., Exec.Dir.
BRAILLE CIRCULATING LIBRARY, INC. □ Richmond, VA
Gordon, Robin Hughes, Econ. Planner
GREENVILLE COUNTY PLANNING COMMISSION - PLANNING TECHNICAL LIBRARY □ Greenville, SC
Gordon, Sgt. James, Res. & Trng.Asst.
AMERICAN FEDERATION OF POLICE RESEARCH CENTER AND LIBRARY □ North Miami, FL
Gordon, Sharon L., Tech.Serv.
LANCASTER BIBLE COLLEGE - STOLL MEMORIAL LIBRARY □ Lancaster, PA
Gordon, Terry, Non-print Cat.
COUNTRY MUSIC FOUNDATION - LIBRARY AND MEDIA CENTER □ Nashville, TN
Gordon, Vera N., Dp.Ck.
U.S. DISTRICT COURT - LIBRARY □ Juneau, AK
Gordon, Warren, Asst.Exec.Libn.
FRIED, FRANK, HARRIS, SHRIVER, JACOBSON - LIBRARY & INFORMATION CENTER □ New York, NY
Gordy, E. Dawn, Tech.Info.Spec.
U.S. NATL. HIGHWAY TRAFFIC SAFETY ADMINISTRATION - TECHNICAL REFERENCE BRANCH □ Washington, DC
Gore, Cheryl, Lib.Mgr.
BOEING COMPUTER SERVICES COMPANY - TECHNICAL LIBRARY □ Vienna, VA
Gore, Herbert, Acq.Libn.
PEPPERDINE UNIVERSITY - LIBRARY - SPECIAL COLLECTIONS □ Malibu, CA
Gore, LCDR M., Lib.Off.
U.S. NAVY - NAVAL AIR STATION (Key West) - LIBRARY □ Key West, FL
Gorecki, Danuta, Cat.
UNIVERSITY OF ILLINOIS - LAW LIBRARY □ Champaign, IL
Goren, Morton S., Libn.
U.S. DRUG ENFORCEMENT ADMINISTRATION - LIBRARY □ Washington, DC
Goren, Sheila Abbie, Sys.Libn.
AMERICAN EXPRESS COMPANY - SYSTEMS LIBRARY □ Fort Lauderdale, FL
Goren, Simon L., Law Libn.
CASE WESTERN RESERVE UNIVERSITY - LAW LIBRARY □ Cleveland, OH
Gorghan, Ann, Libn.
ST. JOSEPH'S MEDICAL CENTER - MEDICAL LIBRARY □ Yonkers, NY
Gorman, Alma, Hd.
CANADA - NATIONAL RESEARCH COUNCIL - CISTI - UPLANDS BRANCH □ Ottawa, ON
Gorman, Barbara M., Cur. of Hist.
KANSAS CITY MUSEUM OF HISTORY AND SCIENCE - ARCHIVES □ Kansas City, MO
Gorman, Evelyn S., Dir., Lib.Serv.
ST. JOSEPH'S HOSPITAL - MEDICAL LIBRARY □ Phoenix, AZ
Gorman, J.T., Info.Spec.
VALLEY NATIONAL BANK - FINANCIAL RESEARCH LIBRARY □ Phoenix, AZ
Gorman, Nancy, Chf., Cat.
COLLEGE OF MEDICINE AND DENTISTRY OF NEW JERSEY AT NEWARK - GEORGE F. SMITH LIBRARY □ Newark, NJ
Gormezano, K.S., Coord.
LE BEACON PRESSE - SMALL PRESS COLLECTION □ Iowa City, IA
Gormley, Mary T., Supv.
AMERICAN CAN COMPANY - BARRINGTON TECHNICAL CENTER - TECHNICAL INFORMATION CENTER □ Barrington, IL

Gorochow, Galina, Asst.Libn.
CHASE TRADE INFORMATION CORPORATION - LIBRARY □ New York, NY
Gorospe, Miss E., Techn.
ONTARIO - MINISTRY OF CORRECTIONAL SERVICES - LIBRARY SERVICES □ Toronto, ON
Gorse, Naomi S., Tech.Serv.Libn.
FRANCIS BACON FOUNDATION - LIBRARY □ Claremont, CA
Goshen, Ernest L., Cur.
PROWERS COUNTY HISTORICAL SOCIETY - BIG TIMBERS MUSEUM - LIBRARY □ Lamar, CO
Gosier, Doris, Coord.Pub.Serv.
FORT VALLEY STATE COLLEGE - HENRY ALEXANDER HUNT MEMORIAL LEARNING RESOURCES CENTER □ Fort Valley, GA
Goss, Anita B., Res.Libn.
PARADE PUBLICATIONS, INC. - LIBRARY □ New York, NY
Goss, Anne S., Hd.Libn.
OHIO UNIVERSITY - HEALTH SCIENCES LIBRARY □ Athens, OH
Goss, Dorothy K., Libn.
SUMMA CORPORATION - HUGHES HELICOPTERS - LIBRARY† □ Culver City, CA
Goss, Jessica S., Libn.
WORCESTER HISTORICAL MUSEUM - LIBRARY □ Worcester, MA
Goss, Laura L.
MAINE STATE LAW AND LEGISLATIVE REFERENCE LIBRARY □ Augusta, ME
Goss, Peggy L., Librarian
AMERICAN STATES INSURANCE COMPANY - LIBRARY □ Indianapolis, IN
Gosselin, Guy, Dir.
MOUNT WASHINGTON OBSERVATORY - LIBRARY □ Gorham, NH
Gosselin, Jean W., Res.Asst.
UNIVERSITY OF CONNECTICUT - INSTITUTE OF URBAN RESEARCH - LIBRARY □ Storrs, CT
Gossen, Eleanor A., Libn.
NEW YORK STATE MUSEUM AND SCIENCE SERVICE - MUSEUM LIBRARY □ Albany, NY
Gossett, D., Libn.
GEOSCIENCE, LTD. - LIBRARY □ Solana Beach, CA
Gosson, John F., Cur.
MARINE MUSEUM AT FALL RIVER, INC. - LIBRARY □ Fall River, MA
Gothberg, Loren A., Chm., Lib.Comm.
ST. LUKE'S MEMORIAL HOSPITAL - A.M. JOHNSON MEMORIAL LIBRARY □ Spokane, WA
Gotkowitz, Frances, Info.Spec.
MC KINSEY & COMPANY, INC. - LIBRARY □ Washington, DC
Gotsch, Lenard P., Ed.
RUTGERS UNIVERSITY, THE STATE UNIVERSITY OF NEW JERSEY - GOTTSCHO PACKAGING INFORMATION CENTER □ Piscataway, NJ
Gott, Gary, Multi-Media Libn.
BRIGHAM YOUNG UNIVERSITY - J. REUBEN CLARK LAW SCHOOL LIBRARY □ Provo, UT
Gottesman, Regina, Lib.Coord.
AVON PRODUCTS, INC. - CENTRAL LIBRARY† □ New York, NY
Gottlieb, Gerald, Cur., Early Ch. Books
PIERPONT MORGAN LIBRARY □ New York, NY
Gottlieb, Jane, Libn.
AMERICAN MUSIC CENTER - LIBRARY □ New York, NY
Gottlieb, Naomi, Bus.Mgr.
COMMUNITY SYSTEMS FOUNDATION - NUTRITION PLANNING INFORMATION SERVICE □ Ann Arbor, MI
Gottschalk, Dennis, Pres.
THEOSOPHICAL BOOK ASSOCIATION FOR THE BLIND, INC. □ Ojai, CA
Gottschalk, Libbie, Libn.
FRYE-SILLS, INC. - LIBRARY □ Englewood, CO
Gottselig, Leonard J., Chf.Libn.
GLENBOW-ALBERTA INSTITUTE - LIBRARY & ARCHIVES □ Calgary, AB

PERSONNEL

Granafei, Dinah, Hd.Libn.
UNIVERSITY OF WEST LOS ANGELES - LAW
LIBRARY □ Culver City, CA

Granat, Rhoda, Libn.
WAPORA, INC. - LIBRARY □ Washington, DC

Granberg, Margaret Daly, Libn.
DRAKE UNIVERSITY - COLLEGE OF PHARMACY
- LIBRARY □ Des Moines, IA

Grandage, Karen, Wake AHEC Libn.
WAKE COUNTY MEDICAL CENTER - MEDICAL
LIBRARY □ Raleigh, NC

Grande, Anne W., Hd.Libn.
HENNEPIN COUNTY LAW LIBRARY □
Minneapolis, MN

Grande, Professor D., Hd., Tech.Serv.
JOHN JAY COLLEGE OF CRIMINAL JUSTICE OF
THE CITY UNIVERSITY OF NEW YORK -
REISMAN MEMORIAL LIBRARY □ New York, NY

Grandon, Gary, Asst.Dir./Tech.Serv.
UNIVERSITY OF CONNECTICUT - INSTITUTE
FOR SOCIAL INQUIRY □ Storrs, CT

Grandstaff, Dr. E.C., Cur.
REHABILITATION RESEARCH FOUNDATION -
LIBRARY □ Canton, MO

Granek, Jacqueline, Libn.
BRIGER & ASSOCIATES - LIBRARY □ New York,
NY

Granese, Mary, Supv./Doc. & Archv.
MASSACHUSETTS INSTITUTE OF TECHNOLOGY
- LINCOLN LABORATORY LIBRARY □ Lexington,
MA

Granger, Carole A., Asst.Libn./Cat.
UNIVERSITY OF MONTANA - LAW SCHOOL
LIBRARY† □ Missoula, MT

Granger, Ethel M., Libn.
ST. MARY HOSPITAL - HEALTH SCIENCE
LIBRARY □ Port Arthur, TX

Granger, Michel, Chf.Libn.
CANADA - DEPARTMENT OF
COMMUNICATIONS - LIBRARY &
INFORMATION RETRIEVAL SERVICES □
Ottawa, ON

Granger, William S., Hd.
TOLEDO-LUCAS COUNTY PUBLIC LIBRARY -
LITERATURE/FICTION DEPARTMENT □ Toledo,
OH

Granquist, Ardene P., Asst.Libn.
CHURCH OF JESUS CHRIST OF LATTER-DAY
SAINTS - OAKLAND GENEALOGICAL BRANCH
LIBRARY □ Oakland, CA

Grant, Benjamin, Supv., Lib. Media Ctr.
LEXINGTON SCHOOL FOR THE DEAF - LIBRARY
MEDIA CENTER □ Jackson Heights, NY

Grant, Elizabeth, Info.Spec.
EUROPEAN COMMUNITY INFORMATION
SERVICE - LIBRARY □ New York, NY

Grant, G.E., Lib. Network Sup.Supv.
BELL TELEPHONE LABORATORIES, INC. -
LIBRARIES AND INFORMATION SYSTEMS
CENTER □ Murray Hill, NJ

Grant, George, Libn.
METROPOLITAN TORONTO LIBRARY - FINE
ART DEPARTMENT □ Toronto, ON

Grant, Jason C., III, Dir.
HAMPTON INSTITUTE - COLLIS P.
HUNTINGTON MEMORIAL LIBRARY □ Hampton,
VA

Grant, Katherine E., Dept.Mgr.
LOS ANGELES PUBLIC LIBRARY - ART, MUSIC &
RECREATION DEPARTMENT □ Los Angeles, CA

Grant, Marilyn A., Ref.Libn.
BOSTON COLLEGE - SCIENCE LIBRARY □
Chestnut Hill, MA

Grant, Marion, Libn.
SOLANO COUNTY LAW LIBRARY □ Fairfield, CA

Grant, Mary, ILL
UNIVERSITY OF LOUISVILLE - KORNHAUSER
HEALTH SCIENCES LIBRARY □ Louisville, KY

Grant, Mary A., Archv.
GEORGIA-PACIFIC CORPORATION - ARCHIVE
□ Portland, OR

Grant, Sharlane, Preservation Libn.
STATE HISTORICAL SOCIETY OF IOWA -
LIBRARY □ Iowa City, IA

Grantham, Glenna, ILL
MOHAWK COLLEGE OF APPLIED ARTS AND
TECHNOLOGY - MOHAWK LIBRARY RESOURCE
CENTRE □ Hamilton, ON

Grantham, Walter, Asst.Div.Chf.
CHICAGO PUBLIC LIBRARY CENTRAL LIBRARY -
SOCIAL SCIENCES & HISTORY DIVISION □
Chicago, IL

Grasgreen, Jodie, Market Anl.
PENTON/IPC - MARKETING INFORMATION
CENTER □ Cleveland, OH

Grasing, Kathleen, Asst. State Libn.
OREGON STATE LIBRARY □ Salem, OR

Grass, Charlene, OCLC
KANSAS STATE UNIVERSITY - FARRELL
LIBRARY □ Manhattan, KS

Grassi, Dawn S., Asst.Med.Libn.
WAKE COUNTY MEDICAL CENTER - MEDICAL
LIBRARY □ Raleigh, NC

Grassinger, John, Asst.Libn.
INDIANA UNIVERSITY OF PENNSYLVANIA -
UNIVERSITY LIBRARY □ Indiana, PA

Grater, Fred A., Cat.Libn.
EMORY UNIVERSITY - PITTS THEOLOGY
LIBRARY □ Atlanta, GA

Graterole, Nidia Miranda, Dir.
PUERTO RICO - GENERAL COURT OF JUSTICE -
OFFICE OF COURT ADMINISTRATION -
LIBRARY DIVISION □ Hato Rey, PR

Gration, Selby U., Dir. Of Libs.
SUNY - COLLEGE AT CORTLAND - MEMORIAL
LIBRARY □ Cortland, NY

Gratz, Delbert, Libn.
BLUFFTON COLLEGE - MENNONITE
HISTORICAL LIBRARY □ Bluffton, OH

Gratz, H. Tucker, Dir.
U.S. DEPT. OF COMMERCE - INTERNATIONAL
TRADE ADMINISTRATION - HONOLULU
DISTRICT OFFICE LIBRARY □ Honolulu, HI

Graubart, Marilyn, Mgr.Lib.Serv.
DIAMOND SHAMROCK CORPORATION -
CORPORATE LIBRARY □ Painesville, OH

Grauch, Maya, Acq.Asst.
EDEN THEOLOGICAL SEMINARY - LIBRARY □
Webster Groves, MO

Gravell, Helen, Asst.Libn.
ST. FRANCIS HOSPITAL, INC. - MEDICAL
LIBRARY □ Wilmington, DE

Graves, Carolyn, Chf., Tech.Serv.
U.S. ARMY POST - FORT BELVOIR - VAN NOY
LIBRARY □ Ft. Belvoir, VA

Graves, Dan W., Dir. of Libs.
CLARION STATE COLLEGE - RENA M. CARLSON
LIBRARY □ Clarion, PA

Graves, Dorothy P., Asst.Libn.
CUMBERLAND COUNTY LAW LIBRARY □
Bridgeton, NJ

Graves, Elaina, Libn.
STONEHENGE STUDY GROUP - LIBRARY □ Santa
Barbara, CA

Graves, Gail T., Sr.Libn.
UNIVERSITY OF ALABAMA - EDUCATION
LIBRARY □ University, AL

Graves, Geraldine N., Dir., Lib.Serv.
SOUTHERN CALIFORNIA PERMANENTE
MEDICAL CENTER - HEALTH SCIENCES
LIBRARY/MEDIA CENTER □ Bellflower, CA

Graves, Karen J., Hd., Educ.Serv.Dept.
UNIVERSITY OF TENNESSEE - CENTER FOR
THE HEALTH SCIENCES LIBRARY □ Memphis,
TN

Graves, Kristine, Libn.
U.S. DEPT. OF ENERGY - GRAND JUNCTION
OFFICE - TECHNICAL LIBRARY □ Grand
Junction, CO

Graves, Roberta
U.S. NAVY - NAVAL AIR ENGINEERING CENTER
- TECHNICAL LIBRARY, CODE 1115 □
Lakehurst, NJ

Gray, Audra, Libn.
CHAPARRAL GENEALOGICAL SOCIETY -
LIBRARY □ Tomball, TX

Gray, Beverly A., Hd. African Sect.
LIBRARY OF CONGRESS - AFRICAN & MIDDLE
EASTERN DIVISION □ Washington, DC

Gray, Carolyn, Cat.Libn.
WESTERN ILLINOIS UNIVERSITY - LIBRARIES
□ Macomb, IL

Gray, Donald P.
AMERICAN TEILHARD ASSOCIATION FOR THE
FUTURE OF MAN - LIBRARY □ Bronx, NY

Gray, Dorothy, Ref./Res.Libn.
UNIVERSITY OF CALIFORNIA, LOS ANGELES -
EDUCATION & PSYCHOLOGY LIBRARY □ Los
Angeles, CA

Gray, Gary, Coord.
OREGON INSTITUTE OF TECHNOLOGY -
LEARNING RESOURCES CENTER □ Klamath Falls,
OR

Gray, Gary B., Asst.Lib.Mgr./Media Ctr
METHODIST HOSPITAL OF INDIANA, INC. -
LIBRARY □ Indianapolis, IN

Gray, Gayl, Ref.Libn.
NATIONAL CENTER FOR ATMOSPHERIC
RESEARCH - MESA LIBRARY □ Boulder, CO

Gray, Heli, Lib.Asst.
UNIVERSITY CONGREGATIONAL CHURCH -
LIBRARY □ Seattle, WA

Gray, John E., Jr., Legislative Spec.
U.S.D.A. - NATIONAL AGRICULTURAL LIBRARY
- LAW LIBRARY □ Washington, DC

Gray, Kenneth E., Cur.
WABASH COUNTY HISTORICAL MUSEUM -
HISTORICAL LIBRARY □ Wabash, IN

Gray, Sr. Marie Albertus, O.P., Cons.Libn.
ST. THOMAS INSTITUTE - LIBRARY □
Cincinnati, OH

Gray, Mary Clare, Chf.Libn.
SMITHSONIAN INSTITUTION LIBRARIES -
CHESAPEAKE BAY CENTER FOR
ENVIRONMENTAL STUDIES - LIBRARY □
Edgewater, MD

Gray, Mary Clare, Chf.Libn.
SMITHSONIAN INSTITUTION LIBRARIES -
NATIONAL ZOOLOGICAL PARK - LIBRARY □
Washington, DC

Gray, Mary Clare, Libn.
SMITHSONIAN INSTITUTION LIBRARIES -
RADIATION BIOLOGY BRANCH LIBRARY □
Rockville, MD

Gray, Melvin, Pres.
BETTMANN ARCHIVE, INC. □ New York, NY

Gray, Paul D., Asst.Dir., MPR
U.S. NATL. ARCHIVES & RECORDS SERVICE -
NATL. PERSONNEL RECORDS CENTER □ St.
Louis, MO

Gray, Suzanne K., Coord.
BOSTON PUBLIC LIBRARY - SCIENCE
REFERENCE □ Boston, MA

Gray, Walter J., Dir.
UNIVERSITY OF RHODE ISLAND - SEA GRANT
MARINE ADVISORY SERVICE □ Narragansett, RI

Graydon, Elizabeth, Libn.
PRINCETON UNIVERSITY - PLASMA PHYSICS
LIBRARY □ Princeton, NJ

Grayson, Linda M., Chf., Leg.Res.Serv.
ONTARIO - LEGISLATIVE ASSEMBLY -
LEGISLATIVE LIBRARY RESEARCH AND
INFORMATION SERVICES □ Toronto, ON

Grayson, Virginia S., Libn.
AMAX, INC. - LAW LIBRARY □ Greenwich, CT

Grayson, Virginia S., Libn.
AMAX, INC. - LIBRARY □ Greenwich, CT

Graziani, Marta-Marie, Prof.Asst.
ENOCH PRATT FREE LIBRARY - FINE ARTS AND
RECREATION DEPARTMENT □ Baltimore, MD

Greager, Mrs. Giles, Hist.
WILSON COUNTY MUSEUM - LIBRARY □
Fredonia, KS

Greathouse, Stewart R., Info.Spec.
UNIVERSITY OF SOUTHERN CALIFORNIA -
ETHEL PERCY ANDRUS GERONTOLOGY CENTER
- GERONTOLOGICAL INFO. CENTER □ Los
Angeles, CA

Greathouse, Mrs. W.S., Pres.
FRYE (Charles and Emma) ART MUSEUM -
LIBRARY □ Seattle, WA

Greaves, F. Landon, Jr., Hd.Libn.
SOUTHEASTERN LOUISIANA UNIVERSITY - L.A.
SIMS MEMORIAL LIBRARY □ Hammond, LA

Greaves, H.P., Chf.Libn.
NORTH YORK BOARD OF EDUCATION - F.W.
MINKLER LIBRARY □ Willowdale, ON

Grech, Anthony P., Libn.
ASSOCIATION OF THE BAR OF THE CITY OF
NEW YORK - LIBRARY† □ New York, NY

Greear, Yvonne E., Asst.Dir.Pub.Serv.
UNIVERSITY OF TEXAS, EL PASO - LIBRARY □
El Paso, TX

Greehey, Barbara L., Asst.Libn.
MASSACHUSETTS COLLEGE OF PHARMACY &
ALLIED HEALTH SCIENCES - SHEPPARD
LIBRARY □ Boston, MA

Green, Alice, Hd.Libn.
AMARILLO GENEALOGICAL SOCIETY - LIBRARY
□ Amarillo, TX

Green, Alice, Sr.Lib.Asst.
STONE AND WEBSTER ENGINEERING
CORPORATION - TECHNICAL INFORMATION
CENTER □ Boston, MA

Green, Anna M., Libn.
MILWAUKEE COUNTY MENTAL HEALTH
COMPLEX - MICHAEL KASAK LIBRARY □
Milwaukee, WI

Green, Carol, Asst.Libn.
UNIVERSITY OF WASHINGTON - ENGINEERING
LIBRARY □ Seattle, WA

Green, Chuck, Dir.
MUSEUM OF CARTOON ART - LIBRARY □ Port
Chester, NY

Green, David B., Ed.
TRANET - LIBRARY □ Rangeley, ME

Green, David E., Assoc.Dir., Coll.Mgt.
GRADUATE THEOLOGICAL UNION - LIBRARY □
Berkeley, CA

Green, Dorothy, Res.Assoc.
SMITH COLLEGE - SOPHIA SMITH COLLECTION
- WOMEN'S HISTORY ARCHIVE □ Northampton,
MA

Green, Edith, Libn.
CALIFORNIA MISSIONARY BAPTIST
INSTITUTE - LIBRARY† □ Bellflower, CA

Green, Ellen Wilson, Med.Libn.
U.S. VETERANS ADMINISTRATION (CA-Los
Angeles) - WADSWORTH MEDICAL LIBRARY □
Los Angeles, CA

Green, Frank L., Libn.
WASHINGTON STATE HISTORICAL SOCIETY -
LIBRARY □ Tacoma, WA

Green, Freda, Lib.Techn.
CANADIAN TROTTING ASSOCIATION -
STANDARDBRED CANADA LIBRARY □ Toronto,
ON

Green, H., Info.Sci.
BURROUGHS WELLCOME COMPANY - LIBRARY
□ Research Triangle Park, NC

Green, Jeff, Tech.Asst.
SAN DIEGO STATE UNIVERSITY - SOCIAL
SCIENCE RESEARCH LABORATORY - LIBRARY □
San Diego, CA

Green, Judy, Ref.Libn.
HONEYWELL, INC. - HONEYWELL
INFORMATION SYSTEMS - INFORMATION AND
LIBRARY SERVICES □ Waltham, MA

Green, Julian, Libn.
HARVARD UNIVERSITY - GEOLOGICAL
SCIENCES LIBRARY □ Cambridge, MA

Green, Kim M., Libn.
TERRA-TEK - TECHNICAL LIBRARY □ Salt Lake
City, UT

Green, L., Libn.
INCO METALS COMPANY - J. ROY GORDON
RESEARCH LABORATORY □ Mississauga, ON

Green, Lois, Coord., Bk.Sel.
TROY STATE UNIVERSITY - LIBRARY □ Troy, AL

Green, Lynn, Asst.Chf.Libn.
PILLSBURY, MADISON AND SUTRO - LIBRARY □
San Francisco, CA

Green, Marion, Chf.Med.Ed.
U.S. AIR FORCE - AEROSPACE MEDICAL
DIVISION - SCHOOL OF AEROSPACE MEDICINE
- STRUGHOLD AEROMEDICAL LIBRARY □ Brooks
AFB, TX

Green, Mary, Act.Dir.
UNIVERSITY OF TEXAS, AUSTIN - NATURAL
FIBERS INFORMATION CENTER □ Austin, TX

Green, Nancy, Libn.
AMERICAN NUMISMATIC ASSOCIATION -
LIBRARY □ Colorado Springs, CO

Green, Patricia W., Lib.Supv.
AEROSPACE CORPORATION - WASHINGTON
LIBRARY □ Washington, DC

Green, Peggy, Asst.Libn.
UNIVERSITY OF WISCONSIN, MADISON -
LIBRARY SCHOOL LIBRARY □ Madison, WI

Green, Richard, Map Libn.
UNIVERSITY OF IOWA - SPECIAL
COLLECTIONS DEPARTMENT □ Iowa City, IA

Green, Rita, Libn.
COLORADO STATE DEPARTMENT OF GAME,
FISH AND PARKS - LIBRARY □ Denver, CO

Green, Roy E., Cur.
KOOTENAY LAKE HISTORICAL SOCIETY -
LIBRARY □ Kaslo, BC

Greenbaum, Rabbi Alan
TEMPLE B'NAI ISRAEL - LASKER MEMORIAL
LIBRARY □ Galveston, TX

Greenbaum, Diane, Libn.
MIDLAND-ROSS CORPORATION - LIBRARY □
Cleveland, OH

Greenberg, Adele, Rd.Adv.
NEW YORK PUBLIC LIBRARY - MID-
MANHATTAN LIBRARY - READERS' ADVISER'S
OFFICE □ New York, NY

Greenberg, Arlene, Libn.
SIR MORTIMER B. DAVIS JEWISH GENERAL
HOSPITAL - LADY DAVIS INSTITUTE FOR
MEDICAL RESEARCH - RESEARCH LIBRARY □
Montreal, PQ

Greenberg, Arlene, Chf.Med.Libn.
SIR MORTIMER B. DAVIS JEWISH GENERAL
HOSPITAL - MEDICAL LIBRARY □ Montreal, PQ

Greenberg, Bette R., Hd.Ref.Libn.
YALE UNIVERSITY - MEDICAL LIBRARY □ New
Haven, CT

Greenberg, Carolyn, Supv./Rd.Serv.
MASSACHUSETTS INSTITUTE OF TECHNOLOGY
- LINCOLN LABORATORY LIBRARY □ Lexington,
MA

Greenberg, Emily, Dir.
UNIVERSITY OF BALTIMORE - LAW LIBRARY □
Baltimore, MD

Greenberg, Gerald, Chf., Data Acq.
U.S. GEOLOGICAL SURVEY - NATL.
CARTOGRAPHIC INFORMATION CENTER
(NCIC) - WESTERN BRANCH □ Menlo Park, CA

Greenberg, Ida, Asst.Per.
JEWISH HOSPITAL AND MEDICAL CENTER OF
BROOKLYN - MEDICAL & NURSING LIBRARY □
Brooklyn, NY

Greenberg, J.
RESEARCH & EDUCATION ASSOCIATION -
LIBRARY □ New York, NY

Greenberg, Lenore R., Res.Libn.
HUMAN RESOURCES CENTER - RESEARCH
LIBRARY □ Albertson, NY

Greenberg, Ruth, Libn.
CHICAGO-READ MENTAL HEALTH CENTER -
PROFESSIONAL LIBRARY □ Chicago, IL

Greenberg, Stanley, Asst.Dir.
FORBES LIBRARY □ Northampton, MA

Greenbie, Vlasta K., Libn.
UNIVERSITY OF MASSACHUSETTS, AMHERST -
PHYSICAL SCIENCES LIBRARY □ Amherst, MA

Greenblatt, Melinda, Dir.-Libn.
U.S. COMMITTEE FOR UNICEF - INFORMATION
CENTER ON CHILDREN'S CULTURES □ New
York, NY

Greene, Adell, Libn.
MASSACHUSETTS STATE DEPARTMENT OF
COMMERCE AND DEVELOPMENT - RESEARCH
LIBRARY □ Boston, MA

Greene, Bill, Hist.
ALLEGANY COUNTY MUSEUM - LIBRARY □
Belmont, NY

Greene, Casey, Archv.
DALLAS HISTORICAL SOCIETY - RESEARCH
CENTER □ Dallas, TX

Greene, Christina, Asst.
BARNARD COLLEGE WOMEN'S CENTER -
BIRDIE GOLDSMITH AST RESOURCE
COLLECTION □ New York, NY

Greene, Debbie, Libn.
GOOD SAMARITAN HOSPITAL - HEALTH-
SCIENCE LIBRARY □ Mt. Vernon, IL

Greene, Edward J., Supv.Pk.Ranger
U.S. NATL. PARK SERVICE - BANDELIER NATL.
MONUMENT □ Los Alamos, NM

Greene, Frances G., Libn.
BAIRD CORPORATION - TECHNICAL LIBRARY □
Bedford, MA

Greene, Francis
ALTERNATIVE PRESS CENTER - LIBRARY □
Baltimore, MD

Greene, Harlan, Res.Cons.
SOUTH CAROLINA HISTORICAL SOCIETY -
LIBRARY □ Charleston, SC

Greene, Jane F., Dept.Hd.
BIRMINGHAM PUBLIC AND JEFFERSON
COUNTY FREE LIBRARY - ART AND MUSIC
DEPARTMENT □ Birmingham, AL

Greene, Jeremiah, Cat.
FITCHBURG STATE COLLEGE - LIBRARY □
Fitchburg, MA

Greene, Jon, Adv.Libn.
SOUTHERN CALIFORNIA LIBRARY FOR SOCIAL
STUDIES AND RESEARCH □ Los Angeles, CA

Greene, Jon S., Libn.
UNIVERSITY OF CALIFORNIA, LOS ANGELES -
ARCHITECTURE & URBAN PLANNING LIBRARY
□ Los Angeles, CA

Greene, Judith, Exec.Sec.
LIZZADRO MUSEUM OF LAPIDARY ART -
LIBRARY □ Elmhurst, IL

Greene, Kingsley, Hd. of Rd.Serv.
RENSSELAER POLYTECHNIC INSTITUTE -
FOLSOM LIBRARY □ Troy, NY

Greene, Lucy R., Sr.Libn., Cat.
U.S. ARMY - LOGISTICS LIBRARY □ Ft. Lee, VA

Greene, Mary P., Libn.
JOSLIN DIABETES FOUNDATION, INC. -
MEDICAL LIBRARY □ Boston, MA

Greene, Mildred R., Chf.
DISTRICT OF COLUMBIA PUBLIC LIBRARY -
POPULAR LIBRARY □ Washington, DC

Greene, Richard, Libn.
UNIVERSITE DE MONTREAL - SCIENCES
HUMAINES ET SOCIALES-BIBLIOTHEQUE □
Montreal, PQ

Greene, William T., Mgr.
3M - ENGINEERING INFORMATION SERVICES
□ St. Paul, MN

Greenfeld, Rhonda, Ref.Libn.
BELL CANADA - INFORMATION RESOURCE
CENTRE □ Montreal, PQ

Greenfield, Liga, Info.Spec.
UPJOHN COMPANY - CORPORATE TECHNICAL
LIBRARY □ Kalamazoo, MI

Greenfield, Marjorie, Libn.
METROPOLITAN HOSPITAL - LIBRARY □
Philadelphia, PA

Greenfield, Patricia J., Hd., Lib.Serv.
TOURO INFIRMARY - HOSPITAL LIBRARY □
New Orleans, LA

PERSONNEL

Greenfield, Richard, Internat'l Law Libn.
GEORGETOWN UNIVERSITY - LAW CENTER
LIBRARY □ Washington, DC
Greenhalgh, James A., Libn.
U.S. DEPT. OF LABOR - MINE SAFETY & HEALTH
ADMINISTRATION - INFORMATIONAL
SERVICES LIBRARY □ Denver, CO
Greenhalgh, Kathleen, Libn.
INDIAN AND COLONIAL RESEARCH CENTER,
INC. - EVA BUTLER LIBRARY □ Old Mystic, CT
Greenhall, Margaret Pyle, Supv.Libn.
NEW YORK PUBLIC LIBRARY - DONNELL
LIBRARY CENTER - RECORD LIBRARY □ New
York, NY
Greenholz, Carol, Hd.Tech.Serv./Cat.
SUNY - AGRICULTURAL AND TECHNICAL
COLLEGE AT FARMINGDALE - THOMAS D.
GREENLEY LIBRARY □ Farmingdale, NY
Greeniaus, Barbara, Dir., Lib.Serv.
WINNIPEG HEALTH SCIENCES CENTRE -
LIBRARY SERVICES □ Winnipeg, MB
Greening, Walter, Sr.Libn.
STOCKTON STATE HOSPITAL - PROFESSIONAL
LIBRARY □ Stockton, CA
Greenlaw, Evelyn A., Libn.
ST. MARY'S GENERAL HOSPITAL - HEALTH
SCIENCES LIBRARY □ Lewiston, ME
Greenmun, Janet, Coll.Dev.
BROOME COMMUNITY COLLEGE - CECIL C.
TYRRELL LEARNING RESOURCES CENTER □
Binghamton, NY
Greenshields, H., Chf.Libn.
ATOMIC ENERGY OF CANADA, LTD. -
TECHNICAL INFORMATION BRANCH - MAIN
LIBRARY □ Chalk River, ON
Greenslit, Ruth, Circ.
WORCESTER STATE COLLEGE - LEARNING
RESOURCES CENTER □ Worcester, MA
Greenspan, Susan, Libn.
HERNER AND COMPANY - LIBRARY □ Arlington,
VA
Greenstein, Mrs. Milton, Libn.
CONGREGATION KINS OF WEST ROGERS PARK
- JORDAN E. FEUER LIBRARY □ Chicago, IL
Greenwald, Camille Duer, Libn.
COLUMBIA GAS SYSTEM SERVICE
CORPORATION - RESEARCH LIBRARY □
Columbus, OH
Greenwald, Diane, ILL Cons.
DELAWARE STATE - DIVISION OF LIBRARIES □
Dover, DE
Greenwood, Dorothy, Libn.
MARISSA HISTORICAL & GENEALOGICAL
SOCIETY - LIBRARY □ Marissa, IL
Greenwood, Florine H., Libn.
NATIONAL SOCIETY, DAUGHTERS OF THE
AMERICAN REVOLUTION - ALOHA CHAPTER -
MEMORIAL LIBRARY □ Honolulu, HI
Greenwood, Jan, Libn.
ONTARIO MEDICAL ASSOCIATION - LIBRARY □
Toronto, ON
Greenwood, Mary M., Mgr.
IMPERIAL OIL, LTD. - BUSINESS INFORMATION
CENTRE □ Toronto, ON
Greenwood, Paula, Circuit Libn.
FISH MEMORIAL HOSPITAL - MEDICAL
LIBRARY □ De Land, FL
Greenwood, Rhonda Edonis, Law Libn.
GENERAL MILLS, INC. - LAW LIBRARY □
Minneapolis, MN
Greer, Brian J., Dir.
PALMER COLLEGE OF CHIROPRACTIC -
LIBRARY □ Davenport, IA
Greer, Kathleen M., Asst.Libn.
POLK COUNTY HISTORICAL AND
GENEALOGICAL LIBRARY □ Bartow, FL
Greer, Leslie K., Audio Libn.
TEMPLE UNIVERSITY - CENTRAL LIBRARY
SYSTEM - AUDIO UNIT □ Philadelphia, PA
Greer, Nancy, Hd.Tech.Serv.
SOLAR ENERGY RESEARCH INSTITUTE - SOLAR
ENERGY INFORMATION CENTER □ Golden, CO

Greer, Viola, Tech.Serv.Libn.
QUEEN'S UNIVERSITY AT KINGSTON -
BRACKEN LIBRARY □ Kingston, ON
Grefsheim, Suzanne, Chf.Tech.Serv.Div.
GEORGE WASHINGTON UNIVERSITY -
MEDICAL CENTER - PAUL HIMMELFARB
HEALTH SCIENCES LIBRARY □ Washington, DC
Gregg, Joseph, Hd., Acq.
NORTHEASTERN ILLINOIS UNIVERSITY -
LIBRARY □ Chicago, IL
Gregg, Martha C., Libn.
COMMUNITY SYSTEMS FOUNDATION -
NUTRITION PLANNING INFORMATION
SERVICE □ Ann Arbor, MI
Gregg, Richard N., Dir.
ALLENTOWN ART MUSEUM - RESEARCH
LIBRARY □ Allentown, PA
Gregg, Rosalie, Exec.Dir.
WISE COUNTY HISTORICAL COMMISSION
ARCHIVE □ Decatur, TX
Grego, Mrs. Noel R., Hd.
KENNEDY-KING COLLEGE - LIBRARY □ Chicago,
IL
Gregoire, Shirlie, Asst.Libn.
ST. AUGUSTINE'S SEMINARY - LIBRARY □
Scarborough, ON
Gregory, Alan, Music Cat.
UNIVERSITY OF NORTH CAROLINA, CHAPEL
HILL - MUSIC LIBRARY □ Chapel Hill, NC
Gregory, James P., Libn.
NEW YORK GENEALOGICAL AND
BIOGRAPHICAL SOCIETY - GENEALOGICAL
RESEARCH LIBRARY □ New York, NY
Gregory, Jean, Libn.
BECHTEL POWER CORPORATION - LIBRARY □
Los Angeles, CA
Gregory, Martha, Info. II Libn.
TULSA CITY-COUNTY LIBRARY SYSTEM -
BUSINESS AND TECHNOLOGY DEPARTMENT □
Tulsa, OK
Gregory, Pamela J., Law Libn.
PRINCE GEORGE'S COUNTY CIRCUIT COURT -
LAW LIBRARY □ Upper Marlboro, MD
Gregory, Ralph, Pres.
HEARST (Phoebe Apperson) HISTORICAL
SOCIETY, INC. - MUSEUM CENTER □ St. Clair,
MO
Greil, Barbara, Ser./Ref.Libn.
SUNY - AGRICULTURAL AND TECHNICAL
COLLEGE AT ALFRED - WALTER C. HINKLE
MEMORIAL LIBRARY □ Alfred, NY
Greist, Dr. John H., Co-Dir.
UNIVERSITY OF WISCONSIN, MADISON -
DEPARTMENT OF PSYCHIATRY - LITHIUM
INFORMATION CENTER □ Madison, WI
Grella, Susan, Gen.Serv.Libn.
PIERCE JUNIOR COLLEGE - LIBRARY† □
Philadelphia, PA
Grenda, Johanna, Info.Spec.
RAYTHEON COMPANY - RESEARCH DIVISION -
LIBRARY □ Waltham, MA
Grenier, M.T., Pres.
SEEK INFORMATION SERVICE □ San Dimas, CA
Grenier, Patricia, Coord., Info.Serv.
ONTARIO - MINISTRY OF EDUCATION -
INFORMATION CENTRE □ Toronto, ON
Gresack, Barbara, Libn.
CENTRAL SYNAGOGUE OF NASSAU COUNTY -
HELEN BLAU MEMORIAL LIBRARY □ Rockville
Centre, NY
Gresehover, Robert, Assoc.Dir.
JOHNS HOPKINS UNIVERSITY - WILLIAM H.
WELCH MEDICAL LIBRARY □ Baltimore, MD
Gresham, S.W., Libn.
UNIVERSITY OF ARIZONA - COLLEGE OF
ARCHITECTURE LIBRARY □ Tucson, AZ
Gresser, Marylyn E., Chf., Lib.Serv.
U.S. VETERANS ADMINISTRATION (FL-
Gainesville) - HOSPITAL LIBRARY □ Gainesville,
FL
Gresseth, Dale, Chm.
UNIVERSITY OF WISCONSIN, LA CROSSE -
MURPHY LIBRARY □ La Crosse, WI

Gressley, Gene M., Archv.
UNIVERSITY OF WYOMING - PETROLEUM
HISTORY AND RESEARCH CENTER LIBRARY □
Laramie, WY
Gressley, Gene M., Dir.
UNIVERSITY OF WYOMING - WESTERN
HISTORY RESEARCH CENTER LIBRARY □
Laramie, WY
Gretes, Frances C., Libn.
SKIDMORE, OWINGS & MERRILL - LIBRARY □
New York, NY
Greve, Edward, Ref./Archv./Doc.Libn.
UNIVERSITY OF WISCONSIN, SUPERIOR - JIM
DAN HILL LIBRARY □ Superior, WI
Greven, Maryanne, Proj.Libn.
CENTRAL MAINE MEDICAL CENTER - GERRISH-
TRUE HEALTH SCIENCE LIBRARY □ Lewiston,
ME
Grey, Catherine, Asst.Chf.
BROOKLYN PUBLIC LIBRARY - AUDIO VISUAL
DIVISION □ Brooklyn, NY
Grey, J. David, Pres.
AUSTEN (Jane) SOCIETY OF NORTH AMERICA -
ARCHIVES □ New York, NY
Gridley, Lyman D., Pres.
CHEMUNG COUNTY HISTORICAL SOCIETY,
INC. - MRS. ARTHUR W. BOOTH LIBRARY □
Elmira, NY
Grieder, Dr. Theodore, Cur.
NEW YORK UNIVERSITY - FALES LIBRARY -
DIVISION OF SPECIAL COLLECTIONS □ New
York, NY
Grier, Margot E., Per.Libn.
NATIONAL GALLERY OF ART - LIBRARY □
Washington, DC
Gries, Norma A., Libn.
CAMERON IRON WORKS, INC. - LIBRARY □
Houston, TX
Grieve, Isabel, Libn.
ANTHROPOSOPHICAL SOCIETY IN CANADA -
RUDOLPH STEINER LIBRARY □ Toronto, ON
Griffen, Charles S., Hd.
HARTFORD PUBLIC LIBRARY - BUSINESS,
SCIENCE & TECHNOLOGY DEPARTMENT □
Hartford, CT
Griffin, Ann, Adm.Asst.
INDIANA UNIVERSITY/PURDUE UNIVERSITY
AT INDIANAPOLIS - UNIVERSITY LIBRARY □
Indianapolis, IN
Griffin, Barbara, Lib.Asst.
MICHIGAN STATE DEPARTMENT OF
TRANSPORTATION - TRANSPORTATION
LIBRARY □ Lansing, MI
Griffin, Carol, Ref.Libn.
AMERICAN TELEPHONE & TELEGRAPH
COMPANY - CORPORATE RESEARCH LIBRARY □
New York, NY
Griffin, Gene C., Dir.
NORTH DAKOTA STATE UNIVERSITY - UPPER
GREAT PLAINS TRANSPORTATION INSTITUTE
- INFORMATION CENTER □ Fargo, ND
Griffin, Gerald T., Chf., Lib.Br.
U.S. AIR FORCE BASE - HANSCOM BASE
LIBRARY □ Hanscom AFB, MA
Griffin, Hillis L., Dir.
ARGONNE NATIONAL LABORATORY -
TECHNICAL INFORMATION SERVICES
DEPARTMENT □ Argonne, IL
Griffin, Janette, Cat.
NEW ORLEANS BAPTIST THEOLOGICAL
SEMINARY - JOHN T. CHRISTIAN LIBRARY □
New Orleans, LA
Griffin, Kathie, Libn.
SAN DIEGO PUBLIC LIBRARY - ART, MUSIC &
RECREATION SECTION □ San Diego, CA
Griffin, Linda, Libn.
SAN DIEGO PUBLIC LIBRARY - ART, MUSIC &
RECREATION SECTION □ San Diego, CA
Griffin, Lisa Carlson, Mss.Spec.
UNIVERSITY OF MISSOURI - WESTERN
HISTORICAL MANUSCRIPT COLLECTION/
STATE HISTORICAL SOCIETY OF MISSOURI □
Columbia, MO

Griffin, Marie, Libn.
RUTGERS UNIVERSITY, THE STATE
UNIVERSITY OF NEW JERSEY - INSTITUTE OF
JAZZ STUDIES □ Newark, NJ

Griffin, Olive L., Libn.
MERCER COUNTY LAW LIBRARY □ Mercer, PA

Griffin, Pamela, Asst.Med.Libn.
UNIVERSITY OF CALGARY - MEDICAL LIBRARY
□ Calgary, AB

Griffin, Stephanie, Cat.
BENTLEY COLLEGE - SOLOMON R. BAKER
LIBRARY □ Waltham, MA

Griffin, William H., Tech.Serv.Mgr.
SOUTHWEST TEXAS STATE UNIVERSITY -
LEARNING RESOURCES CENTER □ San Marcos,
TX

Griffis, Kathy E., Libn.
POLK COUNTY LAW LIBRARY □ Bartow, FL

Griffis, Miriam, Audio Supv/Cat.Spec.Coll.
BAYLOR UNIVERSITY - CROUCH MUSIC
LIBRARY □ Waco, TX

Griffiss, Keating, Libn.
HUNTER MUSEUM OF ART - REFERENCE
LIBRARY □ Chattanooga, TN

Griffith, Alice B., Lib.Dir.
MOHAWK VALLEY COMMUNITY COLLEGE -
LIBRARY □ Utica, NY

Griffith, Barrie, Sr.Libn.
CALIFORNIA STATE BOARD OF EQUALIZATION
- LAW LIBRARY □ Sacramento, CA

Griffith, Connie K., ILL
ROCKWELL INTERNATIONAL - ENERGY
SYSTEMS GROUP - LIBRARY □ Canoga Park, CA

Griffith, Devon, Chf.Libn.
NATIONAL SCIENCE TEACHERS ASSOCIATION
- GLENN O. BLOUGH LIBRARY □ Washington, DC

Griffith, Jack W., Libn., NLR Div.
U.S. VETERANS ADMINISTRATION (AR-Little
Rock) - HOSPITAL LIBRARIES □ Little Rock, AR

Griffith, Jerry, Libn.
U.S. ARMY - ENGINEER WATERWAYS
EXPERIMENT STATION - TECHNICAL
INFORMATION CENTER □ Vicksburg, MS

Griffith, Mona C., Chf.Libn.
MARTIN MARIETTA CORPORATION - ORLANDO
AEROSPACE DIVISION - INFORMATION
CENTER □ Orlando, FL

Griffith, Sheryl, Cat.Libn.
U.S. PRESIDENTIAL LIBRARIES - FRANKLIN D.
ROOSEVELT LIBRARY □ Hyde Park, NY

Griffith, Vicki L., Libn.
HANCOCK (Allan) FOUNDATION - HANCOCK
LIBRARY OF BIOLOGY & OCEANOGRAPHY □ Los
Angeles, CA

Griffiths, Philip A.
HARVARD UNIVERSITY - MATHEMATICAL
LIBRARY □ Cambridge, MA

Griffiths, Suzanne, Libn.
UNIVERSITY OF ILLINOIS - CLASSICS LIBRARY
□ Urbana, IL

Griffitts, Donna K., Adm.Libn.
U.S. ARMY/U.S. AIR FORCE - OFFICES OF THE
SURGEONS GENERAL - JOINT MEDICAL
LIBRARY □ Washington, DC

Grifhorst, James R., Data Archv.Mgr.
UNIVERSITY OF IOWA - LABORATORY FOR
POLITICAL RESEARCH □ Iowa City, IA

Grigg, Virginia C., Chf.Bur.Lib.Dev.
STATE LIBRARY OF FLORIDA □ Tallahassee, FL

Griggs, Charlotte, Libn.
PHILLIPS PETROLEUM COMPANY -
ENGINEERING LIBRARY □ Bartlesville, OK

Griggs, John B., Libn.
LLOYD LIBRARY AND MUSEUM □ Cincinnati, OH

Grilikhes, Sandra B., Hd.Libn.
UNIVERSITY OF PENNSYLVANIA - ANNENBERG
SCHOOL OF COMMUNICATIONS - LIBRARY □
Philadelphia, PA

Grill, Stanley, Libn.
PROGRAM PLANNERS, INC. - LIBRARY/
INFORMATION CENTER □ New York, NY

Grim, Mary C., Libn.
ADAMS COUNTY LAW LIBRARY† □ Gettysburg,
PA

Grim, Ronald E., Supv., Ref.Serv.
U.S. NATL. ARCHIVES & RECORDS SERVICE -
NATL. ARCHIVES - CENTER FOR
CARTOGRAPHIC & ARCHITECTURAL ARCHIVES
□ Washington, DC

Grimble, Heather, Lib.Techn.
GCG ENGINEERING PARTNERSHIP - LIBRARY □
Edmonton, AB

Grimes, Deirdre, Libn.
ROYAL BANK OF CANADA - INFORMATION
RESOURCES □ Toronto, ON

Grimes, Marie T., Asst.Libn.
GENERAL AMERICAN INVESTORS CO., INC. -
LIBRARY □ New York, NY

Grimes, Maxyne M., Asst.Dir.Tech.Serv.
UNIVERSITY OF SOUTH FLORIDA - MEDICAL
CENTER LIBRARY □ Tampa, FL

Grimm, Ann C., Libn.
UNIVERSITY OF MICHIGAN - HIGHWAY
SAFETY RESEARCH INSTITUTE - LIBRARY □
Ann Arbor, MI

Grimm, Ann C., Libn.
UNIVERSITY OF MICHIGAN - HIGHWAY
SAFETY RESEARCH INSTITUTE - PUBLIC
INFORMATION MATERIALS CENTER □ Ann
Arbor, MI

Grimm, Dorothy, Sr.Libn.
SAN DIEGO PUBLIC LIBRARY - SOCIAL
SCIENCES SECTION □ San Diego, CA

Grimshaw, Polly S., Libn./Cur.
INDIANA UNIVERSITY - FOLKLORE
COLLECTION □ Bloomington, IN

Grimsley, Judy L., Info.Rsrcs.Supv.
ORLANDO SENTINEL STAR NEWSPAPER -
LIBRARY □ Orlando, FL

Grincevicius, Ceslovas V.
LITHUANIAN AMERICAN COMMUNITY OF THE
U.S.A. - LITHUANIAN WORLD ARCHIVES □
Chicago, IL

Grinch, Mary Lou, Chf. of Lib.Serv.
ALTOONA HOSPITAL - GLOVER MEMORIAL
MEDICAL AND NURSING LIBRARY □ Altoona, PA

Grineff, Cecelia S., Registrar
MIAMI PURCHASE ASSOCIATION FOR
HISTORIC PRESERVATION - LIBRARY AND
INFORMATION CENTER □ Cincinnati, OH

Grinell, Sheila, Exec.Dir.
ASSOCIATION OF SCIENCE/TECHNOLOGY
CENTERS - LIBRARY □ Washington, DC

Griner, Lily, Libn.
AMERICAN INSTITUTES FOR RESEARCH -
LIBRARY □ Washington, DC

Griner, Mrs. Marina, Supv.Libn.
U.S. ARMY ADMINISTRATION CENTER - MAIN
LIBRARY □ Ft. Benjamin Harrison, IN

Grinnell, Margaret Tielke, Act.Dir.
MENDOTA MENTAL HEALTH INSTITUTE -
LIBRARY MEDIA CENTER □ Madison, WI

Grisak, Garry, Lib.Coord.
OLDS COLLEGE - LEARNING RESOURCES
CENTRE □ Olds, AB

Grisanti, Mary, Med.Libn.
U.S. VETERANS ADMINISTRATION (OH-
Brecksville) - HOSPITAL LIBRARY □ Brecksville,
OH

Grise, Anne S., Libn.
INDUSTRIAL RISK INSURERS - IRI LIBRARY □
Hartford, CT

Grise, Carol B., Supv., Info.Serv.
SCOTT (O.M.) AND SONS - INFORMATION
SERVICES □ Marysville, OH

Griskavich, Marcia, Cat., C.J.Ctr.
UNIVERSITY OF WISCONSIN, MADISON - LAW
LIBRARY □ Madison, WI

Griskavich, Marcia, Libn.
UNIVERSITY OF WISCONSIN, MADISON - LAW
SCHOOL- CRIMINAL JUSTICE REFERENCE &
INFORMATION CENTER □ Madison, WI

Grissett, Patty P., Tech.Serv.Libn
BAPTIST MEDICAL CENTERS-SAMFORD
UNIVERSITY - IDA V. MOFFETT SCHOOL OF
NURSING - L.R. JORDAN LIBRARY □
Birmingham, AL

Grissom, Bradley, Cat.
UNIVERSITY OF KENTUCKY - AGRICULTURE
LIBRARY □ Lexington, KY

Grissom, Marjorie, Children's Libn.
HUDSON LIBRARY AND HISTORICAL SOCIETY □
Hudson, OH

Gritton, James H., Law Libn.
IOWA STATE LAW LIBRARY □ Des Moines, IA

Gritzmacher, Lucy, Libn.
PHARMACEUTICAL MANUFACTURERS
ASSOCIATION - SCIENCE INFORMATION
SERVICES □ Washington, DC

Grix, Linda, Med.Libn.
ST. FRANCIS MEMORIAL HOSPITAL - WALTER
F. SCHALLER MEMORIAL LIBRARY □ San
Francisco, CA

Grobar, Bonnie, Hd., Ref. & Doc. Unit
TEXAS STATE LIBRARY - INFORMATION
SERVICES DIVISION □ Austin, TX

Grochowski, Barbara, Chf., Ref.Dept.
U.S. ARMY POST - FORT BELVOIR - VAN NOY
LIBRARY □ Ft. Belvoir, VA

Grodski, Renata, Libn.
ONTARIO - MINISTRY OF CULTURE AND
RECREATION - LIBRARY/RESOURCE CENTRE □
Toronto, ON

Grodzicky, Dr. Roman R., Chf.Libn.
MARIANOPOLIS COLLEGE - LIBRARY □
Montreal, PQ

Groen, Frances, Life Sci. Area Libn.
MC GILL UNIVERSITY - MEDICAL LIBRARY □
Montreal, PQ

Groen, Paulette, Libn.
SOCIETY OF MANUFACTURING ENGINEERS -
SME LIBRARY □ Dearborn, MI

Groesch, Dorthada, Dir.
ST. JOHN'S HOSPITAL - HEALTH SCIENCE
LIBRARY □ Springfield, IL

Grof-Iannelli, Martie, Coll.Dev.
UNIVERSITY OF WESTERN ONTARIO - SCHOOL
OF LIBRARY & INFORMATION SCIENCE -
LIBRARY □ London, ON

Grogan, Dorothy, Asst.Chf.
U.S. VETERANS ADMINISTRATION (ME-
Augusta) - CENTER LIBRARY □ Augusta, ME

Groman, Robert, Asst.Libn.
INTERNATIONAL CHRISTIAN SCHOOL OF
THEOLOGY - GRADUATE UNIVERSITY LIBRARY
□ San Bernardino, CA

Grondines, Louise, Cat.Libn.
UNIVERSITE DU QUEBEC A HULL -
BIBLIOTHEQUE □ Hull, PQ

Grooms, Carole, Assoc.Libn.
UNIVERSITY OF FLORIDA - LAW LIBRARY □
Gainesville, FL

Groot, Elizabeth H., Mgr., Tech.Info.Serv.
SCHENECTADY CHEMICALS, INC. - W.
HOWARD WRIGHT RESEARCH CENTER -
LIBRARY □ Schenectady, NY

Gropp, Dorothy, Assoc.Libn.
NATIONAL COUNCIL ON THE AGING - LIBRARY
□ Washington, DC

Grosh, Eileen, Libn.
CARNEGIE LIBRARY OF PITTSBURGH -
BUSINESS DIVISION □ Pittsburgh, PA

Grosjean, Margaretta, Cat.Libn.
BAPTIST BIBLE COLLEGE OF PENNSYLVANIA -
RICHARD J. MURPHY MEMORIAL LIBRARY □
Clarks Summit, PA

Gross, Alice, Corp.Libn.
SEAGRAM (Joseph E.) & SONS, INC. -
CORPORATE LIBRARY □ New York, NY

Gross, Edith, Med.Libn.
MONSOUR MEDICAL CENTER - HEALTH
SERVICES LIBRARY □ Jeannette, PA

Gross, Jerianne, Coll.Dev.-Ser.
CLEVELAND HEALTH SCIENCES LIBRARY -
HEALTH CENTER LIBRARY □ Cleveland, OH

PERSONNEL

Gross, John, Dir.
SALINAS PUBLIC LIBRARY - JOHN STEINBECK
LIBRARY □ Salinas, CA

Gross, Kenneth L., Lib.Serv.Dir.
NORTHWEST MUNICIPAL CONFERENCE -
GOVERNMENT INFORMATION CENTER □ Mt.
Prospect, IL

Gross, Leonard, Archv.
HISTORICAL COMMITTEE OF THE MENNONITE
CHURCH - ARCHIVES OF THE MENNONITE
CHURCH □ Goshen, IN

Gross, Marsha, Geology Libn.
NORTHWESTERN UNIVERSITY - GEOLOGY
LIBRARY □ Evanston, IL

Gross, Dr. Robert R., Archv.
BUCKNELL UNIVERSITY - ARCHIVES □
Lewisburg, PA

Gross, Robert V., Hd.
LIBRARY OF CONGRESS - GEN. READING
ROOMS DIV. - MICROFORM READING ROOM
SECTION □ Washington, DC

Grosse, Mrs. Alfred C., Lib.Chm.
EAST DALLAS CHRISTIAN CHURCH - HAGGARD
MEMORIAL LIBRARY† □ Dallas, TX

Grosse, June, Info.Sci.
AMERICAN CYANAMID COMPANY -
AGRICULTURAL RESEARCH DIVISION -
TECHNICAL INFORMATION SERVICES □
Princeton, NJ

Grosshans, Maxine, Ref.Libn.
UNIVERSITY OF MARYLAND, BALTIMORE -
SCHOOL OF LAW - MARSHALL LAW LIBRARY □
Baltimore, MD

Grossman, Dr. Burton J., Chf. of Med. Staff
LA RABIDA CHILDREN'S HOSPITAL AND
RESEARCH CENTER - LAWRENCE MERCER
PICK MEMORIAL LIBRARY □ Chicago, IL

Grossman, Charles, Libn.
RAILROAD ENTHUSIASTS NEW YORK
DIVISION, INC. - WILLIAMSON LIBRARY □ New
York, NY

Grossman, George S., Libn.
NORTHWESTERN UNIVERSITY - LAW SCHOOL
LIBRARY □ Chicago, IL

Grossman, Harriet, AV Libn.
COLUMBIA UNIVERSITY - HEALTH SCIENCES
LIBRARY □ New York, NY

Grossman, Robert, Libn.
PHILADELPHIA ORCHESTRA ASSOCIATION -
LIBRARY □ Philadelphia, PA

Grossmann, Maria, Libn.
HARVARD UNIVERSITY - DIVINITY SCHOOL -
ANDOVER-HARVARD THEOLOGICAL LIBRARY □
Cambridge, MA

Grosso, Pete, Automotive Res.
HARRAH'S AUTOMOTIVE LIBRARY □ Reno, NV

Grot-Zakrzewski, Zena C., Mgr.
COMBUSTION ENGINEERING, INC. - POWER
SYSTEMS GROUP LIBRARY SERVICES □
Windsor, CT

Groth, Paul E., Vice Pres.
MICROMEDEX, INC. - PAUL DE HAEN DRUG
INFORMATION SYSTEMS □ Englewood, CO

Groth, Virginia, Libn.
3M - LAW LIBRARY □ St. Paul, MN

Grotsky, Stephen R., Libn.
NEW YORK STATE SUPREME COURT -
APPELLATE DIVISION, 1ST JUDICIAL
DEPARTMENT - LAW LIBRARY □ New York, NY

Groulx, Denise, Supv.
CANADA - IMMIGRATION APPEAL BOARD -
LIBRARY □ Ottawa, ON

Grove, Brenda, Asst.Med.Libn.
METHODIST MEDICAL CENTER OF ILLINOIS -
MEDICAL LIBRARY □ Peoria, IL

Grove, Donna, Dept.Hd.
HOUSTON PUBLIC LIBRARY - SPECIAL
COLLECTIONS DEPARTMENT □ Houston, TX

Grove, Pearce S., Dir.
WESTERN ILLINOIS UNIVERSITY - LIBRARIES
□ Macomb, IL

Grove, Shari T., Pub.Serv.Libn.
HARVARD UNIVERSITY - TOZZER LIBRARY -
PEABODY MUSEUM OF ARCHAEOLOGY AND
ETHNOLOGY □ Cambridge, MA

Grover, Billie, Libn.
UNIVERSITY OF FLORIDA - AGRICULTURAL
RESEARCH CENTER - FORT LAUDERDALE
LIBRARY □ Fort Lauderdale, FL

Grover, Monica, Sect.Hd.
COLGATE PALMOLIVE COMPANY - TECHNICAL
INFORMATION CENTER □ Piscataway, NJ

Grover, Robert L., Chm.
BLUE SPRINGS HISTORICAL SOCIETY -
LIBRARY □ Independence, MO

Grover-Feild, Charlotte
INTERNATIONAL BACKPACKERS ASSOCIATION
- LIBRARY □ Lincoln Center, ME

Groves, Doris, LRC
SOUTHERN CONNECTICUT STATE COLLEGE -
H.C. BULEY LIBRARY □ New Haven, CT

Groves, Friederika, Libn.
BADISCHE CORPORATION - LIBRARY □
Williamsburg, VA

Grow, Neville L., Ref.Libn.
GENERAL MOTORS CORPORATION - RESEARCH
LABORATORIES LIBRARY □ Warren, MI

Gruben, Karl T., Libn.
VINSON & ELKINS - LAW LIBRARY □ Houston,
TX

Gruber, Dorothy H., Libn.
INSTITUTE FOR MEDICAL RESEARCH -
LIBRARY □ Camden, NJ

Grucan, Sally P., Tech.Serv.Libn.
RHODE ISLAND HISTORICAL SOCIETY -
LIBRARY □ Providence, RI

Gruenberg, Eden J., Libn.
CROUSE-IRVING MEMORIAL HOSPITAL -
LIBRARY □ Syracuse, NY

Gruenberg, Frederika, Asst.Div.Hd.
QUEENS BOROUGH PUBLIC LIBRARY -
LANGUAGE & LITERATURE DIVISION □
Jamaica, NY

Gruenert, Noal F., Info.Mgr.
SOUTHWESTERN ILLINOIS METROPOLITAN
AND REGIONAL PLANNING COMMISSION -
TECHNICAL LIBRARY □ Collinsville, IL

Gruenthal, Linda, Asst.Libn.
COLORADO STATE SUPREME COURT LIBRARY □
Denver, CO

Gruettner, Ruth, Lib.Adm.
AMERICAN CAN COMPANY - MARKETING
INFORMATION LIBRARY □ Greenwich, CT

Gruhn, Adolph M., Chm., Lib.Comm.
PSYCHOANALYTIC ASSOCIATION OF SEATTLE
- LIBRARY □ Seattle, WA

Grumet, Lori, Act.Hd.Libn.
U.S. NATL. PARK SERVICE - WESTERN
ARCHEOLOGICAL CENTER - LIBRARY □ Tucson,
AZ

Grunberger, Michael, Libn.
GRATZ COLLEGE - LIBRARY □ Philadelphia, PA

Grund, Henry J., II, Dir.
LIBRARY OF HENRY J. GRUND □ Mentor, OH

Grundke, Patricia J., Libn.
COMMUNITY MEMORIAL GENERAL HOSPITAL -
LIBRARY □ La Grange, IL

Grundset, Eric G., Asst.
FAIRFAX COUNTY PUBLIC LIBRARY - VIRGINIA
ROOM □ Fairfax, VA

Grundy, Ruth, Libn.
UNIVERSITY OF TEXAS - MARINE SCIENCE
LABORATORY - LIBRARY □ Port Aransas, TX

Grunewaldt, Lorraine, Supv.
ST. MARY'S HOSPITAL - MEDICAL LIBRARY □
Huntington, WV

Grunow, Millie H., Med.Libn.
DEACONESS HOSPITAL - HEALTH SCIENCE
LIBRARY □ Evansville, IN

Grunwald, Rabbi Binyomin, Hd.Libn.
OTZER HASFORIM OF TELSHE YESHIVA -
RABBI A.N. SCHWARTZ LIBRARY □ Wickliffe,
OH

Grutchfield, Martha, Cat.
AMERICAN MUSIC CENTER - LIBRARY □ New
York, NY

Gruver, Eilene, Asst. Law Libn.
CAPITAL UNIVERSITY - LAW SCHOOL LIBRARY
□ Columbus, OH

Grygo, Alice B., Ser.Libn.
MINNESOTA HISTORICAL SOCIETY -
REFERENCE LIBRARY □ St. Paul, MN

Gschneidner, Karl A., Jr., Dir.
IOWA STATE UNIVERSITY - ENERGY AND
MINERAL RESOURCES RESEARCH INSTITUTE -
RARE EARTH INFORMATION CENTER □ Ames,
IA

Guano, O.B., Bro. Jose "Bat"
INTERNATIONAL BROTHERHOOD OF OLD
BASTARDS, INC. - SIR THOMAS CRAPPER
MEMORIAL ARCHIVES □ St. Louis, MO

Guarducci, Elizabeth B., Med.Libn.
ESSEX COUNTY HOSPITAL CENTER -
HAMILTON MEMORIAL LIBRARY □ Cedar Grove,
NJ

Guarino, John, Asst.Libn.
HOWARD UNIVERSITY - ENGINEERING
LIBRARY □ Washington, DC

Guarracino, Joseph, Nonprint Hd.
DREXEL UNIVERSITY LIBRARIES - GENERAL
LIBRARY □ Philadelphia, PA

Guay, Alice, Hd., Intl.Pubn.
NATIONAL LIBRARY OF CANADA - OFFICIAL
PUBLICATIONS DIVISION □ Ottawa, ON

Guay, Maryrita, Asst.Libn.
MPR ASSOCIATES, INC. - LIBRARY □
Washington, DC

Gubeno, Leon, Hd., ILL
SUNY - DOWNSTATE MEDICAL CENTER -
MEDICAL RESEARCH LIBRARY OF BROOKLYN†
□ Brooklyn, NY

Gubiotti, R.A., Oper.Mgr.
BATTELLE-COLUMBUS LABORATORIES -
COPPER DATA CENTER □ Columbus, OH

Gubiotti, Ross, Data Proc.Mgr.
BATTELLE-COLUMBUS LABORATORIES -
MECHANICAL PROPERTIES DATA CENTER □
Columbus, OH

Gubman, Nancy, Dir.
NEW YORK UNIVERSITY - COURANT
INSTITUTE OF MATHEMATICAL SCIENCES -
LIBRARY □ New York, NY

Gucma, Mrs. Mina, Libn.
DOFASCO INC. - MAIN OFFICE LIBRARY □
Hamilton, ON

Gude, Gilbert, Dir.
LIBRARY OF CONGRESS - CONGRESSIONAL
RESEARCH SERVICE □ Washington, DC

Gudelsky, Jane M., Libn.
JONES, BIRD & HOWELL, ATTORNEYS AT LAW -
LIBRARY □ Atlanta, GA

Gudgen, Gretta, Circ.
PITTSBURG STATE UNIVERSITY - LEONARD H.
AXE LIBRARY □ Pittsburg, KS

Guelzow, D., Circ.
U.S. NASA - JOHN F. KENNEDY SPACE CENTER
- LIBRARY □ Kennedy Space Center, FL

Guerette, Jacques, RESORS Mgr.
CANADA - CANADA CENTRE FOR REMOTE
SENSING - TECHNICAL INFORMATION
SERVICE □ Ottawa, ON

Guerette, Normand, Dir.
QUEBEC PROV. - MIN. DE L'ENERGIE ET DES
RESSOURCES - CENTRE DE DOCUMENTATION
ET DE RENSEIGNEMENTS □ Quebec, PQ

Guerin, Betty B., Chf., Tech.Serv.
U.S. OFFICE OF PERSONNEL MANAGEMENT -
LIBRARY □ Washington, DC

Guerin-Place, Rosemary, Libn./Archv.
GIRL SCOUTS OF THE USA - LIBRARY/
ARCHIVES† □ New York, NY

Guerra, Elizabeth, Med.Rec.Dir.
SAN ANTONIO COMMUNITY HOSPITAL -
WEBER MEMORIAL LIBRARY □ Upland, CA

Guerrette, Mona, Libn.
YORK REGIONAL LIBRARY - BIBLIOTHEQUE DR.
MARGUERITE MICHAUD □ Fredericton, NB

Guertler, John T., Archv.
UNIVERSITY OF BALTIMORE - BALTIMORE
REGION INSTITUTIONAL STUDIES CENTER
(BRISC) □ Baltimore, MD

Guest, Rev. Francis F., O.F.M., Archv.-Hist.
SANTA BARBARA MISSION ARCHIVE-LIBRARY
□ Santa Barbara, CA

Guffey, Gloria, Libn.
U.S. AIR FORCE BASE - BOLLING BASE LIBRARY
□ Washington, DC

Gugisberg, Mercedes, Libn.
ST. THOMAS AQUINAS NEWMAN CENTER -
LIBRARY □ Albuquerque, NM

Guida, Pat, Mgr.
BOOZ ALLEN & HAMILTON, INC. - FOSTER D.
SNELL DIVISION - INFORMATION CENTER† □
Florham Park, NJ

Guido, John F., Hd.
WASHINGTON STATE UNIVERSITY -
MANUSCRIPTS, ARCHIVES, & SPECIAL
COLLECTIONS □ Pullman, WA

Guidotti, Annetta C., Law Libn.
WHITMAN & RANSOM - LIBRARY □ New York,
NY

Guignard, Alice, Coord.
ETOBICOKE BOARD OF EDUCATION -
RESOURCE LIBRARY □ Etobicoke, ON

Guilfoil, Elizabeth J., Dir.
SACRED HEART MEDICAL CENTER - HEALTH
SCIENCES LIBRARY □ Spokane, WA

Guillermard, Teresita, Ref. & Circ.Dept.Dir.
CATHOLIC UNIVERSITY OF PUERTO RICO -
MONSIGNOR JUAN FREMIOT TORRES OLIVER
LAW LIBRARY □ Ponce, PR

Guillet, Nancy M., Chf.Libn.
U.S. VETERANS ADMINISTRATION (LA-
Alexandria) - HOSPITAL MEDICAL LIBRARY □
Alexandria, LA

Guin, Marilyn, Libn.
OREGON STATE UNIVERSITY - MARINE
SCIENCE CENTER - LIBRARY □ Newport, OR

Guinee, Sr. Anne, Libn.
ST. ELIZABETH HOSPITAL - HEALTH SCIENCES
LIBRARY □ Elizabeth, NJ

Guitard, Florence, Libn.
ANDROSCOGGIN VALLEY HOSPITAL - MEDICAL
LIBRARY □ Berlin, NH

Guiu, Elizabeth, Libn.
NEW ENGLAND BAPTIST HOSPITAL - SCHOOL
OF NURSING LIBRARY □ Boston, MA

Guiu, Rafael, Mgr.
SWEDENBORG LIBRARY AND BOOKSTORE □
Boston, MA

Guleke, Kay, Hd.Libn.
AUSTIN AMERICAN STATESMAN - LIBRARY □
Austin, TX

Gulick, Melba, Ref.Libn.
SUNY - COLLEGE AT POTSDAM - FREDERICK W.
CRUMB MEMORIAL LIBRARY □ Potsdam, NY

Gulledge, A. Brandon, Hd.
YALE UNIVERSITY - STERLING CHEMISTRY
LIBRARY □ New Haven, CT

Gulledge, Dr. James L., Dir.
CORNELL UNIVERSITY - LABORATORY OF
ORNITHOLOGY - LIBRARY OF NATURAL
SOUNDS □ Ithaca, NY

Gulley, Larry, Mss. Libn.
UNIVERSITY OF GEORGIA - MANUSCRIPTS
COLLECTION □ Athens, GA

Gulliver, J.V., Libn./Adm.
MIDDLESEX LAW ASSOCIATION - LIBRARY □
London, ON

Gully, W., Libn.
CANADA - NATIONAL RESEARCH COUNCIL -
CISTI - DOMINION RADIO ASTROPHYSICAL
OBSERVATORY - LIBRARY □ Penticton, BC

Gulstad, Wilma, Mss.Spec.
UNIVERSITY OF MISSOURI - WESTERN
HISTORICAL MANUSCRIPT COLLECTION/
STATE HISTORICAL SOCIETY OF MISSOURI □
Columbia, MO

Gunby, Norma, Owner
COWETA GENEALOGICAL & HISTORICAL
SOCIETY - LIBRARY □ Sharpsburg, GA

Gundel, Lorraine, Libn.
QUEENS BOROUGH PUBLIC LIBRARY -
LANGSTON HUGHES COMMUNITY LIBRARY AND
CULTURAL CENTER □ Corona, NY

Gunderson, Nels, Libn.
INDIANA UNIVERSITY - SCHOOL OF PUBLIC
AND ENVIRONMENTAL AFFAIRS - LIBRARY □
Bloomington, IN

Gundlach, Alyne R., Chf.
PUBLIC LIBRARY OF NASHVILLE AND
DAVIDSON COUNTY - BUSINESS INFORMATION
SERVICE □ Nashville, TN

Gundry, L.D., Chf.Med.Libn.
BRYN MAWR HOSPITAL - MEDICAL LIBRARY □
Bryn Mawr, PA

Gundry, L.D., Chf.Med.Libn.
BRYN MAWR HOSPITAL - MEDICAL LIBRARY -
NURSING DIVISION □ Bryn Mawr, PA

Gunn, Diane, Slide Libn.
KENDALL SCHOOL OF DESIGN - LEARNING
RESOURCE CENTER □ Grand Rapids, MI

Gunn, Hazel D., Coord.
CORNELL UNIVERSITY - PROGRAM ON
PARTICIPATION AND LABOR-MANAGED
SYSTEMS - DOCUMENTATION CENTER □
Ithaca, NY

Gunn, Karen, Tech.Serv.Mgr.
MORGAN STANLEY & COMPANY, INC. -
LIBRARY □ New York, NY

Gunn, Leah M., Chf. Order Libn.
UNIVERSITY OF MICHIGAN - LAW LIBRARY □
Ann Arbor, MI

Gunner, Jean, Bookbinder & Consrv.
CARNEGIE-MELLON UNIVERSITY - HUNT
INSTITUTE FOR BOTANICAL DOCUMENTATION
- LIBRARY □ Pittsburgh, PA

Gunning, C., Asst.Libn.
NORTH BAY COLLEGE EDUCATION CENTRE -
LIBRARY □ North Bay, ON

Gunning, Ruth T., Mgr.
ROCKWELL INTERNATIONAL - BUSINESS
RESEARCH CENTER† □ Pittsburgh, PA

Gunning, W.S., Chm.Lib.Comm.
HISTORICAL SOCIETY OF PRINCETON -
LIBRARY □ Princeton, NJ

Gunnison, Foster, Jr., Adm.
INSTITUTE OF SOCIAL ETHICS - LIBRARY AND
ARCHIVES† □ Hartford, CT

Gunter, Linda, Cat.
UNIVERSITY OF LA VERNE - COLLEGE OF LAW -
LIBRARY □ La Verne, CA

Gunther, Barbara, Libn.
ANTHROPOSOPHICAL SOCIETY IN CANADA -
RUDOLPH STEINER LIBRARY □ Toronto, ON

Gunther, Barbara, Hd.
METROPOLITAN TORONTO LIBRARY -
LANGUAGES CENTRE □ Toronto, ON

Gunther, Ellen P., Libn.
ALBERTO-CULVER COMPANY - RESEARCH
LIBRARY □ Melrose Park, IL

Gupta, Marianne V., Chf.Libn.
AMERICAN TELEPHONE & TELEGRAPH
COMPANY - CORPORATE RESEARCH LIBRARY □
New York, NY

Gupta, Mrs. Pushpa, Libn.
CONSULATE GENERAL OF INDIA -
INFORMATION SERVICE OF INDIA LIBRARY† □
New York, NY

Guptill, Barbara, Mng.Libn.
SEATTLE PUBLIC LIBRARY - GOVERNMENTAL
RESEARCH ASSISTANCE LIBRARY □ Seattle,
WA

Gurn, Robert M., Hd.
BUFFALO & ERIE COUNTY PUBLIC LIBRARY -
FILM DEPARTMENT □ Buffalo, NY

Gurner, Richard, Lib.Adm.
POLAROID CORPORATION - RESEARCH
LIBRARY □ Cambridge, MA

Gurney, Susan, Ref.Libn.
SMITHSONIAN INSTITUTION - NATL. MUSEUM
OF AMERICAN ART/NATIONAL PORTRAIT
GALLERY - LIBRARY □ Washington, DC

Guske, Ellen, Res.Libn.
ILLINOIS BELL TELEPHONE COMPANY -
PIONEER HISTORICAL LIBRARY† □ Chicago, IL

Gusky, Laura, Supv.
MELDRUM AND FEWSMITH, INC. - BUSINESS
INFORMATION LIBRARY □ Cleveland, OH

Gustafson, Berdella, Libn.
EDGEWATER BAPTIST CHURCH - LIBRARY □
Minneapolis, MN

Gustafson, Mr. Lynn M., Supv.
NORTHERN STATES POWER COMPANY - "ASK
NSP" TAPE LIBRARY □ Minneapolis, MN

Gustafson, Maxine, Libn.
U.S. AIR FORCE HOSPITAL - SHEPPARD
REGIONAL HOSPITAL - MEDICAL LIBRARY □
Sheppard AFB, TX

Gustafson, Ruth, Adm.Sec.
MEMORIAL MEDICAL CENTER OF WEST
MICHIGAN - LIBRARY □ Ludington, MI

Gustin, Deborah A., Chf., Lib.Serv.
U.S. VETERANS ADMINISTRATION (MD-
Baltimore) - MEDICAL CENTER LIBRARY
SERVICE (142D) □ Baltimore, MD

Gustner, David L., Adm.
OAKLAND UNIVERSITY - LIBRARY □ Rochester,
MI

Guston, G. David, Archv.
BAPTIST GENERAL CONFERENCE - ARCHIVES □
St. Paul, MN

Gustow, Hazel, Dir.
PHILADELPHIA COLLEGE OF ART - LIBRARY □
Philadelphia, PA

Gutberlet, Grace R., Lib.Chm.
EMBROIDERERS' GUILD OF AMERICA, INC. -
LIBRARY □ New York, NY

Gutekunst, Blue K., Libn.
CATHOLIC UNIVERSITY OF AMERICA -
HUMANITIES LIBRARY □ Washington, DC

Gutenburg, U., Lib.Techn.
UNIVERSITY OF TORONTO - INSTITUTE FOR
POLICY ANALYSIS - LIBRARY □ Toronto, ON

Gutglass, Judith L., Ref.Libn.
WASHINGTON UNIVERSITY - SCHOOL OF LAW
- FREUND LAW LIBRARY □ St. Louis, MO

Gutglass, Judy, Ref.Libn.
U.S. COURT OF APPEALS, 8TH CIRCUIT -
LIBRARY □ St. Louis, MO

Gutheim, Janet L.
MAGNAVOX GOVERNMENT & INDUSTRIAL
ELECTRONICS COMPANY - ADVANCED
PRODUCTS DIVISION - LIBRARY† □ Torrance,
CA

Guthrie, Bill, Music Scores Cat.
UNIVERSITY OF WESTERN ONTARIO - MUSIC
LIBRARY □ London, ON

Guthrie, Isabella, Asst.Libn.
ROYAL ONTARIO MUSEUM - LIBRARY □
Toronto, ON

Guthrie, Mrs. William, Cat.
REVEILLE UNITED METHODIST CHURCH -
REVEILLE MEMORIAL LIBRARY □ Richmond, VA

Gutierrez, Carolyn, Libn.
DANCER FITZGERALD SAMPLE, INC. - LIBRARY
□ New York, NY

Gutierrez-Witt, Laura, Libn.
UNIVERSITY OF TEXAS, AUSTIN - BENSON
LATIN AMERICAN COLLECTION □ Austin, TX

Gutis, Mark, Media Serv.Libn.
WESTERN CONNECTICUT STATE COLLEGE -
RUTH A. HAAS LIBRARY □ Danbury, CT

Gutman, Riva, Info.Spec.
CONFERENCE BOARD, INC. - INFORMATION
SERVICE □ New York, NY

Gutowski, Jane E., Libn.
FIRST NATIONAL BANK OF BOSTON - LIBRARY
□ Boston, MA

PERSONNEL

Gutsch, Dr. William, Staff Astronomer
  ROCHESTER MUSEUM AND SCIENCE CENTER -
  STRASENBURGH PLANETARIUM - TODD
  LIBRARY □ Rochester, NY
Gutscher, Dianne M., Cur.
  BOWDOIN COLLEGE - LIBRARY - SPECIAL
  COLLECTIONS □ Brunswick, ME
Gutshall, Judy, Libn.
  PENNSYLVANIA STATE DEPARTMENT OF
  TRANSPORTATION - TRANSPORTATION
  INFORMATION CENTER □ Harrisburg, PA
Guttman, Renee, Libn.
  DIAMOND SHAMROCK CORPORATION -
  CORPORATE LIBRARY □ Painesville, OH
Gutz, Robert R., Asst.Libn.
  NEW YORK STATE SUPREME COURT -
  APPELLATE DIVISION, 4TH JUDICIAL
  DEPARTMENT - LAW LIBRARY □ Rochester, NY
Guy, C. Carol, Libn.
  CITIES SERVICE COMPANY - CHEMICALS AND
  MINERALS MARKET RESEARCH LIBRARY □
  Tulsa, OK
Guy, Nancy A., Law Libn.
  HUMBOLDT COUNTY LAW LIBRARY □ Eureka,
  CA
Guy, Wendell A., Dir.
  LONG ISLAND UNIV. - ARNOLD & MARIE
  SCHWARTZ COLLEGE OF PHARMACY & HEALTH
  SCIENCES - PHARMACEUTICAL STUDY CENTER
  □ Brooklyn, NY
Guyer, Mark, Coll.Dev.
  ANDERSON COLLEGE - SCHOOL OF THEOLOGY -
  BYRD MEMORIAL LIBRARY □ Anderson, IN
Guyotte, Linda, Libn.
  OAKLAND UNIVERSITY - LIBRARY □ Rochester,
  MI
Guze, Dr. Samuel B., Hd. of Dept.
  WASHINGTON UNIVERSITY - SCHOOL OF
  MEDICINE - DEPARTMENT OF PSYCHIATRY
  LIBRARY □ St. Louis, MO
Guzman, Alberto, Ref.Libn.
  INTERAMERICAN UNIVERSITY - SCHOOL OF
  LAW - DOMINGO TOLEDO ALAMO LAW LIBRARY
  □ Santurce, PR
Guzman, Diane, Libn.
  BROOKLYN MUSEUM - WILBOUR LIBRARY OF
  EGYPTOLOGY □ Brooklyn, NY
Gwinn, Mary Jane, Libn.
  WASHINGTON UNIVERSITY - CHEMISTRY
  LIBRARY □ St. Louis, MO
Gwyn, Ann S., Hd., Spec.Coll.
  TULANE UNIVERSITY OF LOUISIANA - SPECIAL
  COLLECTIONS DIVISION □ New Orleans, LA
Gydesen, S.P., Ref.Spec.
  U.S. DEPT. OF ENERGY - PACIFIC NORTHWEST
  LABORATORY - TECHNICAL INFO. SECT. □
  Richland, WA
Gyer, Jack, Cur.
  U.S. NATL. PARK SERVICE - YOSEMITE NATL.
  PARK - RESEARCH LIBRARY □ Yosemite National
  Park, CA
Gyorgy, R., Libn.
  UNIVERSITY OF SASKATCHEWAN - INSTITUTE
  FOR NORTHERN STUDIES - LIBRARY □
  Saskatoon, SK
Gyorgyey, Ferenc A., Hist.Libn.
  YALE UNIVERSITY - MEDICAL LIBRARY □ New
  Haven, CT
Gysin, Nellie, Adm.Asst.
  AIR TRANSPORT ASSOCIATION OF AMERICA -
  LIBRARY □ Washington, DC

H

Haab, Nancy J., Libn.
  WINTHROP, STIMSON, PUTNAM AND ROBERTS
  - LIBRARY □ New York, NY
Haag, Bill, Archv.
  WASHINGTON STATE OFFICE OF SECRETARY
  OF STATE - DIVISION OF ARCHIVES AND
  RECORD MANAGEMENT □ Olympia, WA

Haas, Al, Libn.
  COLORADO STATE DISTRICT COURT, 6TH
  JUDICIAL DISTRICT - LAW LIBRARY □ Durango,
  CO
Haas, Edward F., Dir.
  LOUISIANA STATE MUSEUM - LOUISIANA
  HISTORICAL CENTER □ New Orleans, LA
Haas, Janice L., Ref.Libn.
  HAYES (Rutherford B.) PRESIDENTIAL CENTER -
  LIBRARY □ Fremont, OH
Haas, Marynell, Libn.
  LOUISVILLE DEPARTMENT OF LAW - LIBRARY □
  Louisville, KY
Haas, Pamela, Asst.Libn., Photo Coll.
  AMERICAN MUSEUM OF NATURAL HISTORY -
  LIBRARY □ New York, NY
Haas, Dr. Samuel, Biblog.Libn.
  BLOOMFIELD COLLEGE - GEORGE TALBOT HALL
  LIBRARY □ Bloomfield, NJ
Haase, Gretchen, Libn.
  OPPENHEIMER, WOLFF, FOSTER, SHEPARD &
  DONNELLY - LIBRARY □ St. Paul, MN
Haase, Marion, Libn.
  AMERICAN CAN COMPANY - RESEARCH AND
  DEVELOPMENT LIBRARY □ Rothschild, WI
Habekost, Ulla, Libn.
  GOETHE INSTITUTE TORONTO - LIBRARY □
  Toronto, ON
Habel, Sue, Asst.Div.Chf.
  BROOKLYN PUBLIC LIBRARY - HISTORY,
  TRAVEL, RELIGION AND BIOGRAPHY DIVISION
  □ Brooklyn, NY
Habelman, Carolyn, Supv.
  MONROE COUNTY LOCAL HISTORY ROOM &
  LIBRARY □ Sparta, WI
Habelman, Carolyn, Pres.
  MONROE, JUNEAU, JACKSON COUNTY,
  WISCONSIN GENEALOGY WORKSHOP -
  LIBRARY □ Black River Falls, WI
Haber, Barbara, Cur. of Printed Bks.
  RADCLIFFE COLLEGE - ARTHUR AND
  ELIZABETH SCHLESINGER LIBRARY ON THE
  HISTORY OF WOMEN IN AMERICA □
  Cambridge, MA
Haber, Elinor, Info.Spec.
  U.S. MARITIME ADMINISTRATION - NATL.
  MARITIME RESEARCH CENTER - STUDY
  CENTER □ Kings Point, NY
Habermann, Margaret J., Cat.Libn.
  MINNESOTA HISTORICAL SOCIETY -
  REFERENCE LIBRARY □ St. Paul, MN
Habousha, Rachline, Asst.Ref.Libn.
  YESHIVA UNIVERSITY - ALBERT EINSTEIN
  COLLEGE OF MEDICINE - D. SAMUEL
  GOTTESMAN LIBRARY □ Bronx, NY
Hack, Leo M., Libn.
  BLACK & VEATCH CONSULTING ENGINEERS -
  CENTRAL LIBRARY □ Kansas City, MO
Hack, Rosalinda, Hd., Music Sect.
  CHICAGO PUBLIC LIBRARY CULTURAL CENTER
  - FINE ARTS DIVISION - MUSIC SECTION □
  Chicago, IL
Hacker, Lois, Chf.Tech.Serv.Libn.
  CUNY - GRADUATE SCHOOL AND UNIVERSITY
  CENTER - LIBRARY □ New York, NY
Hacker, Ray, Ref.Libn.
  MILLERSVILLE STATE COLLEGE - HELEN A.
  GANSER LIBRARY □ Millersville, PA
Hackett, Gabriel D., Owner, Ed.
  HACKETT (G.D.) PHOTOGRAPHY - ARCHIVES □
  New York, NY
Hackleman, Karen T., Reg.Dev.Coord., MCRMLP
  UNIVERSITY OF NEBRASKA MEDICAL CENTER -
  MC GOOGAN LIBRARY OF MEDICINE □ Omaha,
  NE
Hackleman, Michael A., Res.Dir.
  EARTHMIND - LIBRARY □ Mariposa, CA
Hackney, Carrie M., Libn.
  HOWARD UNIVERSITY - FINE ARTS LIBRARY □
  Washington, DC

Hadala, Paul F., Dir.
  U.S. ARMY - ENGINEER WATERWAYS
  EXPERIMENT STATION - SOIL MECHANICS
  INFORMATION ANALYSIS CENTER □ Vicksburg,
  MS
Haddad, Mushira, Hd., Gen.Serv.
  UNIVERSITY OF MISSOURI, ST. LOUIS -
  THOMAS JEFFERSON LIBRARY □ St. Louis, MO
Haddaway, William, Art Libn.
  DALLAS PUBLIC LIBRARY - FINE ARTS
  DIVISION □ Dallas, TX
Hadden, Robert Lee, Libn.
  BURROUGHS WELLCOME COMPANY - PLANT
  LIBRARY □ Greenville, NC
Haddick, Vern, Lib.Dir.
  CALIFORNIA INSTITUTE OF INTEGRAL
  STUDIES - LIBRARY □ San Francisco, CA
Hadidian, Dikran Y., Libn.
  PITTSBURGH THEOLOGICAL SEMINARY -
  CLIFFORD E. BARBOUR LIBRARY □ Pittsburgh,
  PA
Hadley, Rosemary J., Map Libn.
  UNIVERSITY OF BRITISH COLUMBIA -
  DEPARTMENT OF GEOGRAPHY - MAP AND AIR
  PHOTO LIBRARY □ Vancouver, BC
Hadsel, Dr. Fred L., Dir.
  MARSHALL (George C.) RESEARCH
  FOUNDATION - GEORGE C. MARSHALL
  RESEARCH LIBRARY □ Lexington, VA
Haeberle, Dr. Erwin J., Dir.
  INSTITUTE FOR ADVANCED STUDY OF HUMAN
  SEXUALITY - RESEARCH LIBRARY □ San
  Francisco, CA
Haefliger, Kathleen, Libn.
  UNIVERSITY OF IOWA - MUSIC LIBRARY □
  Iowa City, IA
Haertle, Robert J., Hd., Coll.Dept.
  MARQUETTE UNIVERSITY - MEMORIAL
  LIBRARY □ Milwaukee, WI
Haeussler, Margaretha
  U.S. DEPT. OF LABOR - BUREAU OF LABOR
  STATISTICS - INFORMATION AND ADVISORY
  SECTION □ New York, NY
Hafner, Dr. Arthur, Dir. of Libs.
  CHICAGO COLLEGE OF OSTEOPATHIC
  MEDICINE - ALUMNI MEMORIAL LIBRARY □
  Chicago, IL
Hafner, V. Kay, Med.Libn.
  U.S. AIR FORCE HOSPITAL - DAVID GRANT
  MEDICAL CENTER - LIBRARY □ Travis AFB, CA
Hagan, Arthur, Libn.
  SAN FRANCISCO EXAMINER - LIBRARY □ San
  Francisco, CA
Hagan, Jane, Lib.Serv.Supv.
  GLENDALE PUBLIC LIBRARY - BRAND LIBRARY
  □ Glendale, CA
Hagar, Alice, Media Libn.
  UNIVERSITY OF WISCONSIN, LA CROSSE -
  CURRICULUM AND INSTRUCTION CENTER □ La
  Crosse, WI
Hagberg, Betty, Mgr.
  DEERE & COMPANY - LIBRARY □ Moline, IL
Hagdu, Shirley, Ref.Libn.
  LAKEHEAD UNIVERSITY - CHANCELLOR
  PATERSON LIBRARY □ Thunder Bay, ON
Hagen, Beverly, Libn.
  ST. LUKE'S HOSPITAL MEDICAL CENTER -
  HEALTH-SCIENCES REFERENCE LIBRARY □
  Phoenix, AZ
Hagen, Carlos B., Hd.
  UNIVERSITY OF CALIFORNIA, LOS ANGELES -
  MAP LIBRARY □ Los Angeles, CA
Hagen, D.L., Info.Spec.
  AIR PRODUCTS AND CHEMICALS, INC. -
  INFORMATION SERVICES - TREXLERTOWN
  LIBRARY □ Allentown, PA
Hagen, William H., Libn.
  U.S. NAVY - REGIONAL DATA AUTOMATION
  CENTER - TECHNICAL LIBRARY □ Washington,
  DC
Hager, Mrs. Georgie, ILL Libn.
  MINOT STATE COLLEGE - MEMORIAL LIBRARY
  □ Minot, ND

Hager, Lucille, Dir.
CHRIST SEMINARY - SEMINEX LIBRARY □ St. Louis, MO

Hager, Mary Ann, Photo/Cart.Spec.
LUNAR AND PLANETARY INSTITUTE - PLANETARY IMAGE CENTER □ Houston, TX

Hagerman, Robert L., Asst.Ed.
VERMONT STATE OFFICE OF THE SECRETARY OF STATE - ARCHIVES AND STATE PAPERS DIVISION □ Montpelier, VT

Hagerstrand, M.A., Exec.V.P.
CHEROKEE NATIONAL HISTORICAL SOCIETY, INC. - LIBRARY AND ARCHIVES □ Tahlequah, OK

Hagerty, Fredericka A., Libn.
PENINSULA LIBRARY AND HISTORICAL SOCIETY □ Peninsula, OH

Haggart, Elizabeth M., Libn.
COLUMBIA HOSPITAL FOR WOMEN - MEDICAL LIBRARY □ Washington, DC

Haggerty, Gary, Asst.Libn.
BERKLEE COLLEGE OF MUSIC - LIBRARY □ Boston, MA

Haggerty, Thomas M., Chf., Rd.Serv.
U.S. DEPT. OF COMMERCE - DEPARTMENTAL LIBRARY □ Washington, DC

Haggin, June D., Libn.
EL PASO COUNTY LAW LIBRARY □ El Paso, TX

Haggstrom, David, AV Libn.
SUNY - AGRICULTURAL AND TECHNICAL COLLEGE AT ALFRED - WALTER C. HINKLE MEMORIAL LIBRARY □ Alfred, NY

Hagloch, Joseph, Circuit Libn.
CLEVELAND HEALTH SCIENCES LIBRARY - ALLEN MEMORIAL LIBRARY □ Cleveland, OH

Haglund, Doris Ellis, Base Libn.
U.S. AIR FORCE BASE - TINKER BASE LIBRARY □ Tinker AFB, OK

Hagopian, Alan, Supv.Prod.Lit.
MILES LABORATORIES, INC. - LIBRARY RESOURCES AND SERVICES □ Elkhart, IN

Hagopian, Shake, Libn.
CHAIT, SALOMON, GELBER, REIS, BRONSTEIN, LITVACK, ECHENBERG & LIPPER - LIBRARY □ Montreal, PQ

Hague, Linda, Sr. Lit.Sci.
WARNER-LAMBERT COMPANY - CORPORATE LIBRARY† □ Morris Plains, NJ

Hahn, Boksoon, Asst.Hd.Cat.Libn.
YALE UNIVERSITY - EAST ASIAN COLLECTION □ New Haven, CT

Hahn, Cora, Dir.
UNIVERSITY OF CONNECTICUT - LEARNING RESOURCES DIVISION - CENTER FOR INSTRUCTIONAL MEDIA & TECHNOLOGY □ Storrs, CT

Hahn, Ellen, Chf.
LIBRARY OF CONGRESS - GEN. READING ROOMS DIV. □ Washington, DC

Hahn, Ermina, Hd., Tech.Serv.
RUTGERS UNIVERSITY, THE STATE UNIVERSITY OF NEW JERSEY - JUSTICE HENRY ACKERSON LIBRARY OF LAW & CRIMINAL JUSTICE □ Newark, NJ

Hahn, Genevieve, Libn.
U.S. NATL. PARK SERVICE - POINT REYES NATL. SEASHORE - LIBRARY □ Point Reyes, CA

Hahn, Robert C., Libn.
UNIVERSITY OF MISSOURI - JOURNALISM LIBRARY □ Columbia, MO

Hahn, Susanne E., Libn.
SCHNADER, HARRISON, SEGAL & LEWIS - LIBRARY □ Philadelphia, PA

Haider, Ellen, Libn.
OHIO STATE DEPARTMENT OF TRANSPORTATION - LIBRARY □ Columbus, OH

Haig, Heather D., Lib.Techn.
SASKATCHEWAN - DEPARTMENT OF REVENUE, SUPPLY & SERVICES - SYSTEMS CENTRE LIBRARY □ Regina, SK

Haigh, H.W., Mgr.
WEYERHAEUSER COMPANY - TECHNICAL INFORMATION CENTER □ Tacoma, WA

Haight, Larry L., Libn.
ASSEMBLIES OF GOD GRADUATE SCHOOL - CORDAS C. BURNETT LIBRARY □ Springfield, MO

Hail, Christopher, Asst. And Ref.Libn.
HARVARD UNIVERSITY - GRADUATE SCHOOL OF DESIGN - FRANCES LOEB LIBRARY □ Cambridge, MA

Hail, Milta, Hd., Pub.Serv.
DE PAUL UNIVERSITY - LAW SCHOOL LIBRARY □ Chicago, IL

Haile, Dr. Getatchew, Mss.Cat.
ST. JOHN'S ABBEY AND UNIVERSITY - HILL MONASTIC MANUSCRIPT LIBRARY - BUSH CENTER □ Collegeville, MN

Haimson, Fima, Transl. & Interp.
PHILLIPS PETROLEUM COMPANY - RESEARCH & DEVELOPMENT DEPARTMENT - TECHNICAL INFORMATION BRANCH □ Bartlesville, OK

Haines, Ann H., Med.Libn.
KAISER SUNNYSIDE MEDICAL CENTER - LIBRARY □ Clackamas, OR

Haines, Mrs. D. Gale, Libn.
PETERSHAM HISTORICAL SOCIETY, INC. - LIBRARY □ Petersham, MA

Haines, Janice, Acq.Libn.
U.S. NATL. DEFENSE UNIVERSITY - LIBRARY □ Washington, DC

Haines, Mrs. Richard D., Cur./Libn.
RAILROAD AND PIONEER MUSEUM, INC. - LIBRARY □ Temple, TX

Hainston, Mildred, Ref.
CRAVATH, SWAINE, AND MOORE - LAW LIBRARY □ New York, NY

Hainsworth, Melody M., Libn.
ALBERTA - DEPARTMENT OF THE ATTORNEY GENERAL - JUDGES' LAW LIBRARY □ Calgary, AB

Hainsworth, Melody M., Libn.
LAW SOCIETY OF ALBERTA - CALGARY LIBRARY □ Calgary, AB

Hair, Jay D., Exec. V.P.
NATIONAL WILDLIFE FEDERATION - FRAZIER MEMORIAL LIBRARY □ Washington, DC

Hair, Sara J., Asst.Libn.
NATIONAL STEEL CORPORATION - RESEARCH CENTER LIBRARY □ Weirton, WV

Haire, Gloria, Hd.Libn.
U.S. DEPT. OF ENERGY - LAWRENCE BERKELEY LABORATORY - LIBRARY □ Berkeley, CA

Haire, Grace M., Cur.
INTERNATIONAL TENNIS HALL OF FAME AND TENNIS MUSEUM - LIBRARY □ Newport, RI

Haith, Dorothy, Libn.
FORT VALLEY STATE COLLEGE - HENRY ALEXANDER HUNT MEMORIAL LEARNING RESOURCES CENTER □ Fort Valley, GA

Haitz, M. Cherie, Dir.
MOUNT AUBURN HOSPITAL - HEALTH SCIENCES LIBRARY □ Cambridge, MA

Hakala, Bettina, Libn.
FASKEN & CALVIN, BARRISTERS AND SOLICITORS - LIBRARY □ Toronto, ON

Halasz, Marilynn, Mgr., Info.Serv.Sect.
PORTLAND CEMENT ASSOCIATION/ CONSTRUCTION TECHNOLOGY LABORATORIES - INFORMATION SERVICES SECTION □ Skokie, IL

Halberstam, Rabbi N., Libn.
MENORAH INSTITUTE - LIBRARY □ Brooklyn, NY

Halbfinger, Rabbi Abraham, Rabbinic Adm.
ASSOCIATED SYNAGOGUES OF MASSACHUSETTS - LIBRARY □ Boston, MA

Halbrook, Anne-Mieke, Hd.Libn.
GETTY (J. Paul) MUSEUM - RESEARCH LIBRARY □ Malibu, CA

Halbrook, Barbara, Assoc.Libn.
WASHINGTON UNIVERSITY - SCHOOL OF MEDICINE LIBRARY □ St. Louis, MO

Hale, Cheryl A., Chf., Lib.Serv.
U.S. VETERANS ADMINISTRATION (TX-Amarillo) - HOSPITAL LIBRARY □ Amarillo, TX

Hale, Dawn, OM Cat.
TEACHERS COLLEGE - LIBRARY □ New York, NY

Hale, Elizabeth, Rd.Adv.
DISTRICT OF COLUMBIA PUBLIC LIBRARY - BUSINESS, ECONOMICS & VOCATIONS DIVISION □ Washington, DC

Hale, Elizabeth, Archv.
MOBIL OIL CORPORATION - PUBLIC AFFAIRS SECRETARIAT □ New York, NY

Hale, Elizabeth F., Cons.
MONTREAL MILITARY AND MARITIME MUSEUM - MACDONALD STEWART LIBRARY □ Montreal, PQ

Hale, Judy, Mgr., Info.Serv.
GOODYEAR TIRE AND RUBBER COMPANY - BUSINESS INFORMATION CENTER □ Akron, OH

Hale, Judy E., Mgr., Info.Serv.
GOODYEAR TIRE AND RUBBER COMPANY - TECHNICAL INFORMATION CENTER □ Akron, OH

Hale, Kay K., Libn.
UNIVERSITY OF MIAMI - DOROTHY & LEWIS ROSENSTIEL SCHOOL OF MARINE & ATMOSPHERIC SCIENCES - LIBRARY □ Miami, FL

Hale, Kaycee, Dir.
FASHION INSTITUTE OF DESIGN & MERCHANDISING - RESOURCE AND RESEARCH CENTER □ Los Angeles, CA

Hale, Louis J., Standards Engr.
GARRETT MANUFACTURING, LTD. - ENGINEERING LIBRARY □ Rexdale, ON

Hale, Ruth, Hd.Biblog.Serv.Div.
GEORGIA INSTITUTE OF TECHNOLOGY - PRICE GILBERT MEMORIAL LIBRARY □ Atlanta, GA

Halevy, Professor B.J., Libn.
YORK UNIVERSITY - LAW LIBRARY □ Downsview, ON

Haley, Dan, Info.Spec.
UNIVERSITY OF SOUTHERN CALIFORNIA - NASA INDUSTRIAL APPLICATION CENTER (NIAC) □ Los Angeles, CA

Haley, Jack D., Assoc.Cur.
UNIVERSITY OF OKLAHOMA - WESTERN HISTORY COLLECTIONS □ Norman, OK

Haley, Jack D., Asst.Cur.
UNIVERSITY OF OKLAHOMA - WESTERN HISTORY COLLECTIONS - LIBRARY DIVISION □ Norman, OK

Haley, John, Circ. & ILL Techn.
PHILADELPHIA COLLEGE OF ART - LIBRARY □ Philadelphia, PA

Haley, June, Libn.
ATLANTIC COUNCIL OF THE UNITED STATES, INC. - LIBRARY □ Washington, DC

Haley, Roger K., Libn.
U.S. SENATE - LIBRARY □ Washington, DC

Haley, Sue, Tech.Asst.
MICHIGAN WISCONSIN PIPELINE COMPANY - LIBRARY □ Houston, TX

Halfpenny, Lucille S., Libn.
ST. THOMAS SEMINARY LIBRARY - ALUMNI COLLECTION □ Bloomfield, CT

Halgrimson, Andrea H., Hd.Libn.
FORUM PUBLISHING CO. - LIBRARY □ Fargo, ND

Halibey, Areta V., Hd.Libn.
INSTITUTE FOR JUVENILE RESEARCH - PROFESSIONAL LIBRARY □ Chicago, IL

Halicki, Kenneth C., Libn.
SEYFARTH, SHAW, FAIRWEATHER & GERALDSON - LIBRARY □ Chicago, IL

Halifax, R.A., Supv., Central Rec.
TORONTO CITY RECORDS AND ARCHIVES DIVISION □ Toronto, ON

Halkovic, Prof. Stephen, Dir.
INDIANA UNIVERSITY - RESEARCH INSTITUTE FOR INNER ASIAN STUDIES - LIBRARY □ Bloomington, IN

Hall, Agnez, Dir.Lib.Serv.
NEW BRUNSWICK - DEPARTMENT OF YOUTH, RECREATION & CULTURAL RESOURCES - NEW BRUNSWICK LIBRARY SERVICE □ Fredericton, NB

PERSONNEL

Hall, Ann Bowman, Libn.
U.S. NATL. MARINE FISHERIES SERVICE - SOUTHEAST FISHERIES CENTER - BEAUFORT LABORATORY LIBRARY† □ Beaufort, NC

Hall, Beverly A., Asst.Exec.Dir.
GEOTHERMAL RESOURCES COUNCIL - LIBRARY □ Davis, CA

Hall, Blaine H., Div.Coord.
BRIGHAM YOUNG UNIVERSITY - HUMANITIES AND ARTS DIVISION LIBRARY □ Provo, UT

Hall, Bonlyn G., Libn.
UNIVERSITY OF RICHMOND - MUSIC LIBRARY □ Richmond, VA

Hall, Carolyn, Lib.Techn.
BRITISH COLUMBIA HEALTH ASSOCIATION (BCHA) - LIBRARY □ Vancouver, BC

Hall, Carolyn, Libn.
FLORIDA STATE DEPT. OF HEALTH & REHABILITATIVE SERVICES - HRS RESOURCE CENTER □ Jacksonville, FL

Hall, Charla, Libn.
SHAKESPEARE SOCIETY OF AMERICA - NEW PLACE RARE BOOK LIBRARY† □ Los Angeles, CA

Hall, Cindy, Libn.
ZACHRY (H.B.) COMPANY - CENTRAL RECORDS AND LIBRARY □ San Antonio, TX

Hall, David, Libn., Leg.Lib.
MILWAUKEE - LEGISLATIVE REFERENCE BUREAU - LEGISLATIVE LIBRARY □ Milwaukee, WI

Hall, David, Chf.
NEW YORK PUBLIC LIBRARY - PERFORMING ARTS RESEARCH CENTER - RODGERS & HAMMERSTEIN ARCHIVES OF RECORDED SOUND □ New York, NY

Hall, Deanna Morrow, Mgr.Tech.Info.Rsrcs.
GEORGIA-PACIFIC CORPORATION - TECHNICAL INFORMATION CENTER □ Atlanta, GA

Hall, Deborah A., Dir.
MOUNT SINAI MEDICAL CENTER - MEDICAL LIBRARY □ Milwaukee, WI

Hall, Dorothy, Dir.
OKLAHOMA STATE DEPARTMENT OF HEALTH - INFORMATION & REFERRAL HEALTHLINE □ Oklahoma City, OK

Hall, Elede Toppy, Libn.
ADDISON-WESLEY PUBLISHING COMPANY - SCHOOL DIVISION LIBRARY □ Menlo Park, CA

Hall, Elizabeth, Libn. Emeritus
HORTICULTURAL SOCIETY OF NEW YORK - PUBLIC REFERENCE LIBRARY □ New York, NY

Hall, Elizabeth, Chf. Photographer
MINNESOTA HISTORICAL SOCIETY - SPECIAL LIBRARIES □ St. Paul, MN

Hall, Ellen F., Lib.Dir.
PRESENTATION COLLEGE - LIBRARY □ Aberdeen, SD

Hall, Esther, Order Libn.
BATTELLE-COLUMBUS LABORATORIES - LIBRARY □ Columbus, OH

Hall, Frances H., Libn.
NORTH CAROLINA STATE SUPREME COURT LIBRARY □ Raleigh, NC

Hall, George, Libn.
SOLAR TURBINES INTERNATIONAL - LIBRARY □ San Diego, CA

Hall, Gloria, Curric.Lab.Supv.
MC GILL UNIVERSITY - EDUCATION LIBRARY □ Montreal, PQ

Hall, H. Brent, Ref.Supv. & ILL
MAINE MARITIME ACADEMY - NUTTING MEMORIAL LIBRARY □ Castine, ME

Hall, Helen, Libn.
YARMOUTH COUNTY HISTORICAL SOCIETY - LIBRARY □ Yarmouth, NS

Hall, Holly, Hd.
WASHINGTON UNIVERSITY - DEPARTMENT OF SPECIAL COLLECTIONS □ St. Louis, MO

Hall, J.D., Mgr., R & D
EDDY (E.B.) FOREST PRODUCTS, LTD. - LIBRARY □ Hull, PQ

Hall, Jack, Med.Libn.
PUTNAM (Henry W.) MEMORIAL HOSPITAL - MEDICAL LIBRARY □ Bennington, VT

Hall, Jack C., Sr. Museum Sci.
UNIVERSITY OF CALIFORNIA, RIVERSIDE - DEPARTMENT OF ENTOMOLOGY - LIBRARY □ Riverside, CA

Hall, Jane, Circ. Reserve Supv.
CORNELL UNIVERSITY - ENGINEERING LIBRARY □ Ithaca, NY

Hall, Janet, Libn.
METROPOLITAN TORONTO LIBRARY - MUNICIPAL REFERENCE LIBRARY □ Toronto, ON

Hall, Jeffrey L., Data User Serv.Off.
U.S. BUREAU OF THE CENSUS - REGIONAL DATA USER SERVICE - NEW YORK REGIONAL OFFICE - LIBRARY □ New York, NY

Hall, Joan Ann, Libn.
COLLINS CANADA - TIC LIBRARY □ Toronto, ON

Hall, Dr. Joseph H., Libn.
COVENANT THEOLOGICAL SEMINARY - J. OLIVER BUSWELL, JR. LIBRARY □ St. Louis, MO

Hall, Juanita, Hd., Tech.Serv.
MOREHEAD STATE UNIVERSITY - CAMDEN-CARROLL LIBRARY □ Morehead, KY

Hall, Karen, Hd., Spec.Coll.
COLUMBIA UNIVERSITY - HEALTH SCIENCES LIBRARY □ New York, NY

Hall, Dr. Kenneth R., Dir.
TEXAS A & M UNIVERSITY - THERMODYNAMICS RESEARCH CENTER □ College Station, TX

Hall, Linda, Lib.Techn.
U.S. HERITAGE CONSERVATION AND RECREATION SERVICE - INFORMATION CLEARINGHOUSE† □ Atlanta, GA

Hall, Louise P., Dir.
SMITHTOWN HISTORICAL SOCIETY - LIBRARY □ Smithtown, NY

Hall, Lynda, Sci.Libn.
UNIVERSITY OF CALGARY - ENVIRONMENT-SCIENCE-TECHNOLOGY LIBRARY □ Calgary, AB

Hall, Lysa, Law Cat.
WILLAMETTE UNIVERSITY - LAW LIBRARY □ Salem, OR

Hall, Margaret, Asst.Libn.
HENNEPIN COUNTY LAW LIBRARY □ Minneapolis, MN

Hall, Martha, Rd.Serv.Libn.
PHILADELPHIA COLLEGE OF ART - LIBRARY □ Philadelphia, PA

Hall, Mary C., Act.Dir.
SUNY - COLLEGE AT BUFFALO - EDWARD H. BUTLER LIBRARY □ Buffalo, NY

Hall, Mary Joan, Libn.
GUGGENHEIM (Solomon R.) MUSEUM - LIBRARY □ New York, NY

Hall, R.J., Libn.
ALCOHOLISM AND DRUG ADDICTION RESEARCH FOUNDATION - LIBRARY □ Toronto, ON

Hall, Richard B., Cons.Bldg./Films
GEORGIA STATE DEPARTMENT OF EDUCATION - DIVISION OF PUBLIC LIBRARY SERVICES □ Atlanta, GA

Hall, Ruth, Acq.Libn.
PALMER COLLEGE OF CHIROPRACTIC - LIBRARY □ Davenport, IA

Hall, Sylvia, Dir., Lib.Dev.Div.
PENNSYLVANIA STATE LIBRARY □ Harrisburg, PA

Hall, Verona, Lib.Asst.
CAMP HILL HOSPITAL - HEALTH SCIENCES LIBRARY □ Halifax, NS

Hall, Virginia, Hd.Libn.
OHIO STATE UNIVERSITY - PHARMACY LIBRARY □ Columbus, OH

Hall, Virginia, Libn.
TEXAS STATE DEPARTMENT OF AGRICULTURE - LIBRARY □ Austin, TX

Hall, Vivian S., Libn.
UNIVERSITY OF KENTUCKY - GEOLOGY LIBRARY □ Lexington, KY

Hallblade, Shirley, Dir.
VANDERBILT UNIVERSITY LIBRARY - OWEN GRADUATE SCHOOL OF MANAGEMENT - MANAGEMENT LIBRARY □ Nashville, TN

Halle, Lucie, Lib.Techn.
CENTRALE DE L'ENSEIGNEMENT DU QUEBEC - CENTRE DE DOCUMENTATION □ Quebec, PQ

Haller, Blanche W., Dir. of Lib.Serv.
MONTCLAIR STATE COLLEGE - HARRY A. SPRAGUE LIBRARY - SPECIAL COLLECTIONS □ Upper Montclair, NJ

Hallett, Dessie M., Libn.
MOUNT VERNON PLACE UNITED METHODIST CHURCH - DESSIE M. HALLETT LIBRARY □ Washington, DC

Halliburton, Mary, Mgr.
AMERICAN HEART ASSOCIATION - LIBRARY/RECORDS CENTER □ Dallas, TX

Hallier, Sara, Libn.
REORGANIZED CHURCH OF JESUS CHRIST OF LATTER DAY SAINTS - LIBRARY & ARCHIVES □ Independence, MO

Hallo, William W., Cur.
YALE UNIVERSITY - BABYLONIAN COLLECTION □ New Haven, CT

Hallonquist, Lynne, Life Sci.Biblog.
UNIVERSITY OF BRITISH COLUMBIA - WOODWARD BIOMEDICAL LIBRARY □ Vancouver, BC

Halloran, Helen K., Hd.
SAN ANTONIO PUBLIC LIBRARY - LITERATURE, PHILOSOPHY AND RELIGION DEPARTMENT □ San Antonio, TX

Halloway, Hazel, Spec.Mtls.Techn.
MARICOPA TECHNICAL COMMUNITY COLLEGE - LIBRARY RESOURCE CENTER □ Phoenix, AZ

Hallowitz, Mildred, Hist. of Med.Libn.
SUNY AT BUFFALO - HEALTH SCIENCES LIBRARY □ Buffalo, NY

Hallstrom, Cheryl, Commun.Dir.
STEEL FOUNDERS' SOCIETY OF AMERICA - LIBRARY □ Rocky River, OH

Hallstrom, Dr. Curtis H., Info.Res. & Anl.
GENERAL MILLS, INC. - JAMES FORD BELL TECHNICAL CENTER - TECHNICAL INFORMATION SERVICES □ Minneapolis, MN

Hallstrom, Harlan, Asst.Libn.Pub.Serv.
DAKOTA STATE COLLEGE - KARL E. MUNDT LIBRARY □ Madison, SD

Hallwas, John, Dir., Regional Coll.
WESTERN ILLINOIS UNIVERSITY - LIBRARIES □ Macomb, IL

Halma, Linda, Ref.Libn.
KUTZTOWN STATE COLLEGE - ROHRBACH LIBRARY □ Kutztown, PA

Halma, Sidney, Dir.
CATAWBA COUNTY HISTORICAL MUSEUM - LIBRARY □ Newton, NC

Haloviak, Bert, Asst.Dir.
SEVENTH-DAY ADVENTISTS - GENERAL CONFERENCE - OFFICE OF ARCHIVES AND STATISTICS □ Washington, DC

Halper, Judith, Ref.Libn.
CHICAGO SUN-TIMES - EDITORIAL LIBRARY □ Chicago, IL

Halperen, Vivian Payne, Libn.
NORTH CAROLINA STATE LEGISLATIVE LIBRARY □ Raleigh, NC

Halperin, Michael, Hd., Gen.Lib.
DREXEL UNIVERSITY LIBRARIES - GENERAL LIBRARY □ Philadelphia, PA

Halpern, Meyer W., Hd. Law Libn.
MARIN COUNTY LAW LIBRARY □ San Rafael, CA

Halpern, R.P., Adm.
INTERNATIONAL MICROWAVE POWER INSTITUTE - REFERENCE LIBRARY† □ New York, NY

Halpin, Jerry, Cat.
ADAMS STATE COLLEGE - LIBRARY □ Alamosa, CO

Halsey, Kathleen, Asst.Ref.Libn.
UNIVERSITY OF WISCONSIN, STEVENS POINT
- JAMES H. ALBERTSON CENTER FOR
LEARNING RESOURCES □ Stevens Point, WI

Halsey, Wanda G., Libn.
ENQUIRER AND NEWS - EDITORIAL
REFERENCE LIBRARY □ Battle Creek, MI

Halstead, Bruce W., Lib.Dir.
WORLD LIFE RESEARCH INSTITUTE -
LIBRARY† □ Colton, CA

Halsted, Lawrence, Archv.
WAYNE STATE UNIVERSITY - ARCHIVES OF
LABOR AND URBAN AFFAIRS/UNIVERSITY
ARCHIVES □ Detroit, MI

Halttunen, Lisa, Ref.Libn.
MYSTIC SEAPORT, INC. - G.W. BLUNT WHITE
LIBRARY □ Mystic, CT

Halverson, Eric G., Proj.Mgr.
DENVER PUBLIC LIBRARY - FISH AND
WILDLIFE REFERENCE SERVICE □ Denver, CO

Halverson, Keith, Zoo Dir.
GREAT PLAINS ZOO - REFERENCE LIBRARY □
Sioux Falls, SD

Halvorson, Eric, Ref.Libn.
THOMPSON (J. Walter) COMPANY -
INFORMATION CENTER □ Chicago, IL

Halvorson, Vincent J., Supt.
U.S. NATL. PARK SERVICE - HOMESTEAD NATL.
MONUMENT - RESEARCH LIBRARY □ Beatrice,
NE

Halzel, Shirley, Asst.Libn.
ROGER WILLIAMS GENERAL HOSPITAL -
HEALTH SCIENCES LIBRARY □ Providence, RI

Ham, Arline, Med.Rec.Adm.
MID-VALLEY HOSPITAL ASSOCIATION -
PHYSICIAN'S MEDICAL LIBRARY □ Peckville, PA

Ham, F. Gerald, State Archv. & Dir.
STATE HISTORICAL SOCIETY OF WISCONSIN -
ARCHIVES DIVISION □ Madison, WI

Ham, Louraine, Pres.
DELTA COUNTY HISTORICAL SOCIETY
MUSEUM LIBRARY □ Escanaba, MI

Ham, Steven K., Pres.
NORTH AMERICAN RADIO ARCHIVES (NARA) -
LIBRARY □ Tucson, AZ

Hamberg, Cheryl, Ref.Libn. & ILL
MEHARRY MEDICAL COLLEGE - MEDICAL
LIBRARY - LEARNING RESOURCES CENTER □
Nashville, TN

Hambleton, James E., Asst.Libn.Pub.Serv.
UNIVERSITY OF TEXAS SCHOOL OF LAW -
TARLTON LAW LIBRARY □ Austin, TX

Hamblin, Alden, Dir.
DINOSAUR NATURAL HISTORY MUSEUM -
REFERENCE LIBRARY □ Vernal, UT

Hamblin, Jennifer, Archv.
GLENBOW-ALBERTA INSTITUTE - LIBRARY &
ARCHIVES □ Calgary, AB

Hambly, W.J., Registrar
CANADIAN CREDIT INSTITUTE - CREDIT
RESEARCH AND LENDING LIBRARY □ Toronto,
ON

Hambridge, Sally, Libn.
UNIVERSITY OF SOUTHERN CALIFORNIA -
INFORMATION SCIENCES INSTITUTE -
LIBRARY □ Marina Del Rey, CA

Hamburger, Roberta, Seminary Libn.
PHILLIPS UNIVERSITY - GRADUATE SEMINARY
LIBRARY □ Enid, OK

Hamburger, Susan, Asst.Libn.
FLORIDA STATE UNIVERSITY - SPECIAL
COLLECTIONS □ Tallahassee, FL

Hamby, Sharon, Dir.
BOSTON COLLEGE - LAW SCHOOL LIBRARY □
Newton Centre, MA

Hamer, Allegra, Asst. in Zoology
NEW YORK ZOOLOGICAL SOCIETY - LIBRARY □
Bronx, NY

Hamer, Collin B., Jr., Div.Hd.
NEW ORLEANS PUBLIC LIBRARY - LOUISIANA
DIVISION □ New Orleans, LA

Hamer, Jean, First Asst. & Cat.
PUBLIC LIBRARY OF CINCINNATI AND
HAMILTON COUNTY - DEPARTMENT OF RARE
BOOKS & SPECIAL COLLECTIONS □ Cincinnati,
OH

Hamerton, Irene, Libn.
MANITOBA - DEPARTMENT OF NATURAL
RESOURCES - LIBRARY □ Winnipeg, MB

Hamilton, Alice M., Libn.
PARSONS (Ralph M.) COMPANY - CENTRAL
LIBRARY □ Pasadena, CA

Hamilton, Ann H., Ref./Doc./Per.Libn.
BIRMINGHAM-SOUTHERN COLLEGE - CHARLES
ANDREW RUSH LEARNING CENTER/LIBRARY □
Birmingham, AL

Hamilton, Anne, Dir.
KENTUCKY STATE DEPARTMENT OF
EDUCATION - RESOURCE CENTER □ Frankfort,
KY

Hamilton, Aubrey N., Dept.Hd.
LOUISVILLE FREE PUBLIC LIBRARY - FILM
SERVICES □ Louisville, KY

Hamilton, Barbara U., Dir.
MEDICAL GROUP MANAGEMENT ASSOCIATION
- INFORMATION SERVICE □ Denver, CO

Hamilton, Beth A., Sr.Info.Sci.
TRIODYNE INC. CONSULTING ENGINEERS -
INFORMATION CENTER □ Skokie, IL

Hamilton, Brian C., Libn.
GREYSTONE PARK PSYCHIATRIC HOSPITAL -
HEALTH SCIENCE LIBRARY† □ Greystone Park,
NJ

Hamilton, Dennis O., Lib.Dir.
KZF, INC. - KZF LIBRARY □ Cincinnati, OH

Hamilton, Donald E., Educ.Libn.
UNIVERSITY OF VICTORIA - MC PHERSON
LIBRARY - CURRICULUM LABORATORY □
Victoria, BC

Hamilton, Eleanor, Lib.Supv.
ST. PAUL FIRE & MARINE INSURANCE
COMPANY - LIBRARY □ St. Paul, MN

Hamilton, Elizabeth, Res.Libn.
CONSUMERS UNION OF UNITED STATES, INC. -
LIBRARY □ Mount Vernon, NY

Hamilton, Jane Marie, Med.Libn.
CENTRAL STATE HOSPITAL - PROFESSIONAL
LIBRARY □ Norman, OK

Hamilton, Jeanette S., Supv., Info.Ctr.
GRACE (W.R.) AND COMPANY - RESEARCH
DIVISION LIBRARY □ Columbia, MD

Hamilton, Libby, Libn.
ALEXANDRIA HOSPITAL - HEALTH SCIENCES
LIBRARY† □ Alexandria, VA

Hamilton, Miss Ludovine, Libn.
LYNN HISTORICAL SOCIETY, INC. - LIBRARY □
Lynn, MA

Hamilton, Malcolm C., Libn.
HARVARD UNIVERSITY - JOHN FITZGERALD
KENNEDY SCHOOL OF GOVERNMENT - LIBRARY
□ Cambridge, MA

Hamilton, Nancy, Libn.
METROPOLITAN TORONTO LIBRARY -
MUNICIPAL REFERENCE LIBRARY □ Toronto,
ON

Hamilton, Prudence Harvey, Chf.Libn.
PENINSULA HOSPITAL AND MEDICAL CENTER -
MEDICAL STAFF LIBRARY □ Burlingame, CA

Hamilton, Simone, Supv.
LAURENTIAN HOSPITAL - MEDICAL LIBRARY □
Sudbury, ON

Hamilton, Sue, Libn.
MARITZ TRAVEL COMPANY - TRAVEL LIBRARY
□ Fenton, MO

Hamlin, Hope, Musm.Cur.
MOUNT WASHINGTON OBSERVATORY -
LIBRARY □ Gorham, NH

Hamlin, Omer, Jr., Dir.
UNIVERSITY OF KENTUCKY - MEDICAL
CENTER LIBRARY □ Lexington, KY

Hamm, Cassandra, Asst.Libn.
NEW YORK STATE LIBRARY FOR THE BLIND
AND VISUALLY HANDICAPPED □ Albany, NY

Hamm, Leta, Circ. & Per.
NORTHWEST CHRISTIAN COLLEGE - LEARNING
RESOURCE CENTER □ Eugene, OR

Hamm, Mary Ann, Libn.
PUBLIC SERVICE COMPANY OF COLORADO -
LIBRARY □ Denver, CO

Hammaker, Chuck, Hd., Coll.Dev.
UNIVERSITY OF MISSOURI, ST. LOUIS -
THOMAS JEFFERSON LIBRARY □ St. Louis, MO

Hammargren, Adelaide, Supv. of Lib.Serv.
CIBA-GEIGY CORPORATION -
PHARMACEUTICALS DIVISION - SCIENTIFIC
INFORMATION CENTER† □ Summit, NJ

Hammarskjold, Carolyn, Libn.
MICHIGAN STATE UNIVERSITY - W.K.
KELLOGG BIOLOGICAL STATION - WALTER F.
MOROFSKY MEMORIAL LIBRARY □ Hickory
Corners, MI

Hammell, Kathryn, ILL Libn.
UNIVERSITY OF ILLINOIS MEDICAL CENTER -
LIBRARY OF THE HEALTH SCIENCES □ Chicago,
IL

Hammer, Ann, Libn./Search Anl.
WISHARD (William N.) MEMORIAL HOSPITAL -
PROFESSIONAL LIBRARY/MEDIA SERVICES □
Indianapolis, IN

Hammer, Deborah, Div.Hd.
QUEENS BOROUGH PUBLIC LIBRARY -
HISTORY, TRAVEL & BIOGRAPHY DIVISION □
Jamaica, NY

Hammer, Stanley F., Asst.Libn.
CAMPBELL UNIVERSITY - SCHOOL OF LAW -
LAW LIBRARY □ Buies Creek, NC

Hammerlund, Barbara, Hd.Libn.
COOPER SCHOOL OF ART - LIBRARY† □
Cleveland, OH

Hammersmith, Ruth K., Dir.
NATIONAL SAFETY COUNCIL - LIBRARY □
Chicago, IL

Hammill, Roseann, Music Libn.
MICHIGAN STATE UNIVERSITY - MUSIC
LIBRARY □ East Lansing, MI

Hammond, Charles, Dir.
GORE PLACE SOCIETY, INC. - LIBRARY □
Waltham, MA

Hammond, Doris, Libn.
CANADIAN LIQUID AIR, LTD. - E & C LIBRARY □
Montreal, PQ

Hammond, Ellen H., Libn.
UNIVERSITY OF WISCONSIN, MADISON -
NIEMAN-GRANT JOURNALISM READING ROOM
□ Madison, WI

Hammond, Heather, Serials
FRANKLIN INSTITUTE - LIBRARY □ Philadelphia,
PA

Hammond, J. Samuel, Libn.
DUKE UNIVERSITY - MUSIC LIBRARY □ Durham,
NC

Hammond, Jane L., Law Libn.
CORNELL UNIVERSITY - LAW LIBRARY □
Ithaca, NY

Hammond, Karen, Libn.
NORANDA SALES CORPORATION, LTD. - SALES
LIBRARY □ Toronto, ON

Hammond, Lois D., Chf.Tech.Libn.
CINCINNATI ELECTRONICS CORPORATION -
TECHNICAL LIBRARY □ Cincinnati, OH

Hammond, Mrs. Luther C., Dir. of Lib.Serv.
FIRST BAPTIST CHURCH - MEDIA CENTER† □
Gainesville, FL

Hammond, Lyman H., Jr., Dir.
MAC ARTHUR (General Douglas) MEMORIAL -
LIBRARY AND ARCHIVES □ Norfolk, VA

Hammond, Ms. Lyn Smith, Med.Libn.
PARKVIEW EPISCOPAL HOSPITAL - MEDICAL
LIBRARY □ Pueblo, CO

Hammond, Robie, Sec.
PORTSMOUTH GENERAL HOSPITAL - MEDICAL
LIBRARY □ Portsmouth, VA

Hammond, Sue, Libn.
CAMPBELL TAGGART, INC. - RESEARCH
DIVISION - LIBRARY □ Dallas, TX

Hammond, Theresa M., Dir.Lib.Serv.
NEWPORT NEWS DAILY PRESS, INC. - LIBRARY
□ Newport News, VA
Hammond, Wayne G., Asst.Libn.
WILLIAMS COLLEGE - CHAPIN LIBRARY □
Williamstown, MA
Hamon, Peter, Dir.
WISCONSIN STATE DIVISION FOR LIBRARY
SERVICES - REFERENCE AND LOAN LIBRARY □
Madison, WI
Hamparzumian, Harry H., Mgr.
LOS ANGELES CHAMBER OF COMMERCE -
RESEARCH DEPARTMENT LIBRARY □ Los
Angeles, CA
Hampton, Martha N., Law Ser.Libn.
UNIVERSITY OF GEORGIA - LAW LIBRARY □
Athens, GA
Hamrick, Sharon R., Libn.
DYNAPOL - LIBRARY □ Palo Alto, CA
Hamson, Darryl, Med.Libn.
YORK HOSPITAL - MEDICAL LIBRARY □ York,
ME
Han, Chin-Soon, Hd.Libn.
BON SECOURS HOSPITAL - MEDICAL HEALTH
SCIENCE LIBRARY □ Methuen, MA
Hanafee, Valerie, Libn.
DICKINSON, WRIGHT, MC KEAN, CUDLIP &
MOON - LIBRARY □ Detroit, MI
Hanchett, Catherine, Doc.Proc.Libn.
SUNY - COLLEGE AT CORTLAND - MEMORIAL
LIBRARY □ Cortland, NY
Hanchett, Esther, Libn.
MATERNITY CENTER ASSOCIATION -
REFERENCE LIBRARY □ New York, NY
Hanchett, Mildred, Dir./Supv.
WAYNE HISTORICAL MUSEUM - HISTORICAL
COMMISSION ARCHIVES □ Wayne, MI
Hancock, Don, Info.Coord.
SOUTHWEST RESEARCH & INFORMATION
CENTER □ Albuquerque, NM
Hancock, Richard, Libn.
TIMES-WORLD CORPORATION - NEWSPAPER
LIBRARY □ Roanoke, VA
Hand, Anne T., Exec.Sec.
REXHAM CORPORATION - PACKAGING
TECHNICAL LIBRARY □ Flemington, NJ
Hand, Carolyn, Adm.Asst.
FLORIDA STATE LEGISLATURE - DIVISION OF
LEGISLATIVE LIBRARY SERVICES □
Tallahassee, FL
Hand, Linda, Libn.
JEFFERSON COUNTY LAW LIBRARY □
Birmingham, AL
Hand, Russ, Prog.
OHIO STATE UNIVERSITY - MECHANIZED
INFORMATION CENTER (MIC) □ Columbus, OH
Hande, Mr. D., Staff Archv.
SASKATCHEWAN ARCHIVES BOARD □ Regina,
SK
Handfield, F. Gerald, Field Agent
INDIANA STATE LIBRARY - INDIANA DIVISION
□ Indianapolis, IN
Handler, Marlene, Libn.
MICHIGAN PSYCHOANALYTIC INSTITUTE -
LIBRARY □ Southfield, MI
Handley, William, Hd.
FREE LIBRARY OF PHILADELPHIA - SOCIAL
SCIENCE & HISTORY DEPARTMENT □
Philadelphia, PA
Handman, Pamela, Asst.Libn.
CETUS CORPORATION - RESEARCH LIBRARY □
Berkeley, CA
Handrea, Mihai H., Libn.
PFORZHEIMER (Carl & Lily) FOUNDATION, INC. -
CARL H. PFORZHEIMER LIBRARY □ New York,
NY
Handy, Catherine, Ref.Libn.
WESTFIELD STATE COLLEGE - GOVERNOR
JOSEPH B. ELY MEMORIAL LIBRARY □
Westfield, MA

Handy, Riley, Hd., Spec.Coll.Dept.
WESTERN KENTUCKY UNIVERSITY -
KENTUCKY LIBRARY AND MUSEUM/
UNIVERSITY ARCHIVES □ Bowling Green, KY
Hanegraaf, Mary, Libn.
RIVERSIDE COMMUNITY MEMORIAL HOSPITAL
- HEALTH SCIENCE LIBRARY □ Waupaca, WI
Hanes, Fred W., Dir. Of Libs.
UNIVERSITY OF TEXAS, EL PASO - LIBRARY □
El Paso, TX
Hanfelder, Nancy, Libn.
STEIN ROE AND FARNHAM - LIBRARY □
Chicago, IL
Hanford, Sally, Asst.Libn./Tech.Serv.
AMERICAN INSTITUTE OF ARCHITECTS -
LIBRARY □ Washington, DC
Hanft, Margie, Film Libn.
CALIFORNIA INSTITUTE OF THE ARTS -
LIBRARY □ Valencia, CA
Hanger, Myrtle F., Libn.
DU PONT DE NEMOURS (E.I.) & COMPANY, INC.
- BENGER LABORATORY - LIBRARY □
Waynesboro, VA
Hanig, Mrs. Irving, Lib.Chm.
CONGREGATION SOLEL - LIBRARY† □ Highland
Park, IL
Hankamer, Roberta A., Libn.
GRAND LODGE OF MASSACHUSETTS, A.F. AND
A.M. - LIBRARY □ Boston, MA
Hankison, Jill, Libn.
UPJOHN COMPANY - BUSINESS LIBRARY 88-0
□ Kalamazoo, MI
Hanks, Ellen Todd, Hd., Ref.
UNIVERSITY OF TEXAS HEALTH SCIENCE
CENTER, SAN ANTONIO - LIBRARY □ San
Antonio, TX
Hanks, Janice, Asst.Libn.
UNIVERSITY OF SOUTHERN CALIFORNIA - VON
KLEINSMID LIBRARY □ Los Angeles, CA
Hanks, Mrs. John, Libn.
FIRST METHODIST CHURCH - BLISS MEMORIAL
LIBRARY □ Shreveport, LA
Hanley, Mr. Heschel, Hd.Tech.Serv.
CANADA - SOLICITOR GENERAL CANADA -
CRIMINOLOGY DOCUMENTATION CENTRE □
Ottawa, ON
Hanley, Patricia, Med.Libn.
KAISER PERMANENTE MEDICAL CENTER -
MEDICAL LIBRARY □ Portland, OR
Hanley, Thomas L., Assoc. Law Libn.
UNIVERSITY OF MISSOURI - SCHOOL OF LAW
LIBRARY □ Columbia, MO
Hanlon, A. Kathleen, Libn.
TISSUE CULTURE ASSOCIATION - W. ALTON
JONES CELL SCIENCE CENTER - GEORGE AND
MARGARET GEY LIBRARY □ Lake Placid, NY
Hanlon, Mary, Libn.
CHRIST HOSPITAL - HOSPITAL LIBRARY □ Oak
Lawn, IL
Hanlon, Mary T., Libn.
ROSELAND COMMUNITY HOSPITAL - HEALTH
SCIENCE LIBRARY □ Chicago, IL
Hanna, David L., Hd.Libn.
U.S. NAVY - NAVAL UNDERWATER SYSTEMS
CENTER - NEW LONDON TECHNICAL LIBRARY
□ New London, CT
Hanna, Jill, Tech.Serv.Libn.
MITRE CORPORATION - LIBRARY □ McLean, VA
Hanna, Katherine, Dir.
TAFT MUSEUM - LIBRARY □ Cincinnati, OH
Hanna, Mark, Hd.Ref.Libn.
AMARILLO GENEALOGICAL SOCIETY - LIBRARY
□ Amarillo, TX
Hannah, Catherina, Rec.Anl.
CHICAGO REGIONAL TRANSPORTATION
AUTHORITY - INFORMATION SERVICES -
LIBRARY □ Chicago, IL
Hannan, Joyce, Cat. & Clas.
FEDERAL RESERVE BANK OF BOSTON -
RESEARCH LIBRARY† □ Boston, MA
Hanne, Dan, Libn.
PASADENA PUBLIC LIBRARY - BUSINESS-
TECHNOLOGY DIVISION □ Pasadena, CA

Hannigan, Hilary, Ref.Libn.
PETRO-CANADA - LIBRARY SERVICES □
Calgary, AB
Hannigan, Sally, Principal Libn.
NEWARK PUBLIC LIBRARY - HUMANITIES
DIVISION □ Newark, NJ
Hannon, Dr. John P., Dir.
BRYANT COLLEGE OF BUSINESS
ADMINISTRATION - EDITH M. HODGSON
MEMORIAL LIBRARY □ Smithfield, RI
Hanowski, Laura M., Libn.
SASKATCHEWAN GENEALOGICAL SOCIETY -
LIBRARY □ Regina, SK
Hanrath, Linda, Corp.Libn.
WRIGLEY (Wm., Jr.) COMPANY - CORPORATE
LIBRARY □ Chicago, IL
Hansard, William, Lib.Dir.
ARKANSAS STATE UNIVERSITY - DEAN B.
ELLIS LIBRARY □ State University, AR
Hanscom, Marion, Spec.Coll./Fine Arts Libn
SUNY AT BINGHAMTON - FINE ARTS LIBRARY □
Binghamton, NY
Hanscom, Marion, Spec.Coll.Libn.
SUNY AT BINGHAMTON - SPECIAL
COLLECTIONS □ Binghamton, NY
Hansen, Alice, Supv.
SANDERS ASSOCIATES, INC. - TECHNICAL
LIBRARY □ Nashua, NH
Hansen, Alice E., Med.Libn.
WINTER PARK MEMORIAL HOSPITAL -
MEDICAL STAFF LIBRARY □ Winter Park, FL
Hansen, Asta, Libn.
UNIVERSITY OF WESTERN ONTARIO - CPRI
LIBRARY □ London, ON
Hansen, Clark B., Dir.
HANSEN (Clark Bradley) PRIVATE LIBRARY □
Minneapolis, MN
Hansen, Clark Bradley, Libn., Bookdealer
ORPHAN VOYAGE - KAMMANDALE LIBRARY □
St. Paul, MN
Hansen, Eric, Res.Anl.
ALASKA STATE DEPARTMENT OF COMMERCE
AND ECONOMIC DEVELOPMENT - ALASKA
PIPELINE COMMISSION - LIBRARY □
Anchorage, AK
Hansen, Erika M., Med.Libn.
HOLLYWOOD PRESBYTERIAN MEDICAL
CENTER - HEALTH SCIENCES LIBRARY □ Los
Angeles, CA
Hansen, Gladys, Archv.
SAN FRANCISCO PUBLIC LIBRARY - SAN
FRANCISCO HISTORY ROOM □ San Francisco,
CA
Hansen, James L., Ref./Genealogy Libn.
STATE HISTORICAL SOCIETY OF WISCONSIN -
LIBRARY □ Madison, WI
Hansen, Jim, Hd.
RELIGIOUS NEWS SERVICE - PHOTOGRAPH
LIBRARY □ New York, NY
Hansen, Joanne, Sci. & Tech.Libn.
EASTERN MICHIGAN UNIVERSITY - CENTER OF
EDUCATIONAL RESOURCES - MAP LIBRARY □
Ypsilanti, MI
Hansen, Lynn, Asst.Libn.
BUSINESS INTERNATIONAL - RESEARCH
LIBRARY □ New York, NY
Hansen, Mary E.
3M - 201 TECHNICAL LIBRARY □ St. Paul, MN
Hansen, Oda Bali, Libn.
FIREMAN'S FUND INSURANCE COMPANIES -
LIBRARY† □ San Francisco, CA
Hansen, Maj. Reed, Act.Chf., Res.Div.
U.S. AIR FORCE - ALBERT F. SIMPSON
HISTORICAL RESEARCH CENTER □ Maxwell
AFB, AL
Hansen, Richard H., Instr.Mtls.Libn.
ILLINOIS BENEDICTINE COLLEGE - THEODORE
LOWNIK LIBRARY □ Lisle, IL
Hansen, Robert C., Chf.Res.Asst.
U.S. NATL. OCEANIC & ATMOSPHERIC ADM. -
NATL. OCEAN SURVEY - PHYSICAL SCIENCE
SERVICES BRANCH - MAP LIB. □ Rockville, MD

Hansen, Thorvald, Archv.
GRAND VIEW COLLEGE - ARCHIVES □ Des Moines, IA
Hansen, Trudy J., Asst.Cur.
CHICAGO HISTORICAL SOCIETY - SPECIAL COLLECTIONS □ Chicago, IL
Hansen, William H., Libn.
U.S. ARMY ARMOR SCHOOL - LIBRARY □ Ft. Knox, KY
Hanson, Dr. Austin M., Mgr.
GRAIN PROCESSING CORPORATION - TECHNICAL INFORMATION CENTER, R&D □ Muscatine, IA
Hanson, Bruce, Circ./Ref.Libn.
DELAWARE VALLEY COLLEGE OF SCIENCE AND AGRICULTURE - JOSEPH KRAUSKOPF MEMORIAL LIBRARY □ Doylestown, PA
Hanson, Daniel, Ser./Ref.Libn.
ST. JOHN'S UNIVERSITY - LAW LIBRARY □ Jamaica, NY
Hanson, Diana, Asst. to Dir.
BROADCAST PIONEERS LIBRARY □ Washington, DC
Hanson, Diane, Prov. Law Libn.
BARRISTERS' SOCIETY OF NEW BRUNSWICK - LAW LIBRARY □ Fredericton, NB
Hanson, Grant Lee, Libn.
CHURCH OF JESUS CHRIST OF LATTER-DAY SAINTS - PRICE BRANCH GENEALOGICAL LIBRARY □ Price, UT
Hanson, Katherine, Mgr.
LESSER (Robert Charles) AND COMPANY - RESOURCE DEPARTMENT □ Beverly Hills, CA
Hanson, Kaye, Adm.Techn.
TEXAS STATE EMPLOYMENT COMMISSION - TEC LIBRARY □ Austin, TX
Hanson, Margaret, ILL Libn.
NEW ENGLAND NUCLEAR CORPORATION - TECHNICAL LIBRARY □ Boston, MA
Hanson, Mary, Jr.Libn.
ONTARIO HYDRO - LIBRARY □ Toronto, ON
Hanson, Mary A., Med.Libn.
ST. MARY'S HOSPITAL - LIBRARY □ Grand Rapids, MI
Hanson, Nancy A., Med.Libn.
WUESTHOFF MEMORIAL HOSPITAL - MEDICAL LIBRARY □ Rockledge, FL
Hanson, Nels, Asst.Libn.
TOSCO CORPORATION - INFORMATION CENTER □ Los Angeles, CA
Hanssen, Nancy E., Doc.Libn.
WILLIAMS COLLEGE - CENTER FOR ENVIRONMENTAL STUDIES - LIBRARY □ Williamstown, MA
Hanton, Rena C., Libn.
TULSA COUNTY LAW LIBRARY □ Tulsa, OK
Hanus, Otto, Libn./Cur.
SLAVONIC BENEVOLENT ORDER OF THE STATE OF TEXAS - LIBRARY, ARCHIVES, MUSEUM □ Temple, TX
Hanville, Kim, Asst.Libn.
BAPTIST CONVENTION OF ONTARIO AND QUEBEC - CANADIAN BAPTIST ARCHIVES □ Hamilton, ON
Happer, Alexandra, Asst.Libn./Tech.Serv.
ILIFF SCHOOL OF THEOLOGY - IRA J. TAYLOR LIBRARY □ Denver, CO
Harahan, Katherine, Libn.
U.S. LEAGUE OF SAVINGS ASSOCIATIONS - LIBRARY □ Washington, DC
Harasta, Catherine, Text Libn.
DALLAS MORNING NEWS - REFERENCE DEPARTMENT □ Dallas, TX
Harber, Catherine, Supt.
MARTIN COUNTY HISTORICAL SOCIETY - PIONEER MUSEUM - LIBRARY □ Fairmont, MN
Harber, Mr.P., French Lib.Cons.
TORONTO BOARD OF EDUCATION - EDUCATION CENTRE LIBRARY □ Toronto, ON
Harbert, Kathy, Ref.
GEORGE WASHINGTON UNIVERSITY - MEDICAL CENTER - PAUL HIMMELFARB HEALTH SCIENCES LIBRARY □ Washington, DC

Harbey, Mary Alice, Libn.
COOK COUNTY HISTORICAL SOCIETY - GRAND MARAIS LIBRARY □ Grand Marais, MN
Harbottle, Merry, Act.Prov.Libn.
SASKATCHEWAN - PROVINCIAL LIBRARY □ Regina, SK
Hardacre, Elizabeth, Lib.Techn.
CANADA - HEALTH AND WELFARE CANADA - HEALTH PROTECTION BRANCH - REGIONAL LIBRARY □ Vancouver, BC
Hardacre, Gracia, Archv.
AMISTAD RESEARCH CENTER - LIBRARY □ New Orleans, LA
Hardberger, Linda M., Libn.
SAN ANTONIO MUSEUM ASSOCIATION - WITTE MEMORIAL MUSEUM RESEARCH LIBRARY □ San Antonio, TX
Hardcastle, Barrie, Cur.
NANAIMO AND DISTRICT MUSEUM SOCIETY - ARCHIVES □ Nanaimo, BC
Hardee, Clara F., Tech.Info.Spec.
U.S. NATL. HIGHWAY TRAFFIC SAFETY ADMINISTRATION - TECHNICAL REFERENCE BRANCH □ Washington, DC
Hardee, Ethel R., Libn.
BALTIMORE ZOO - ARTHUR R. WATSON LIBRARY □ Baltimore, MD
Hardee, Martha G., Libn.
AVCO CORPORATION - AEROSTRUCTURES DIVISION - ENGINEERING LIBRARY □ Nashville, TN
Hardeman, Bernice
U.S. DEPT. OF COMMERCE - INTERNATIONAL TRADE ADMINISTRATION - HOUSTON DISTRICT OFFICE LIBRARY □ Houston, TX
Harden, Helen R., Dept.Supv.
FRITO-LAY, INC. - LIBRARY □ Dallas, TX
Hardgrove, David, Cat.
RUTGERS UNIVERSITY, THE STATE UNIVERSITY OF NEW JERSEY - JUSTICE HENRY ACKERSON LIBRARY OF LAW & CRIMINAL JUSTICE □ Newark, NJ
Hardham, Ann, Asst.Adm.
CROWN ZELLERBACH CORPORATION - CORPORATE INFORMATION CENTER □ San Francisco, CA
Hardies, Rod, Libn.
UNIVERSITY OF IDAHO - SCIENCE AND TECHNOLOGY LIBRARY □ Moscow, ID
Hardin, Al, Chf., Law Sect.
U.S. ARMY - ARMY LIBRARY □ Washington, DC
Hardin, Betty, Supv.Libn.
CASTLE & COOKE, INC. - LAW & GOVERNMENT DEPARTMENT INFORMATION CENTER □ San Francisco, CA
Hardin, Karl R., Libn.
KERN COUNTY SUPERINTENDENT OF SCHOOLS OFFICE - INSTRUCTIONAL RESOURCES CENTER □ Bakersfield, CA
Hardin, M.F.
U.S. ARMY POST - FORT HOOD - MSA DIVISION - CASEY MEMORIAL LIBRARY □ Ft. Hood, TX
Hardin, Mary, ILL
OKLAHOMA STATE DEPARTMENT OF LIBRARIES □ Oklahoma City, OK
Hardin, Nancy, Libn.
U.S. DEPT. OF ENERGY - TECHNICAL INFORMATION CENTER - REFERENCE CENTER □ Oak Ridge, TN
Harding, Dianne, Libn.
CANADA - TRANSPORT CANADA - TRAINING INSTITUTE - TECHNICAL INFORMATION CENTRE □ Cornwall, ON
Harding, Jean, Lib.Techn.
RYERSON POLYTECHNICAL INSTITUTE - LEARNING RESOURCES CENTRE □ Toronto, ON
Harding, Kathy, Lib.Asst.
QUEEN'S UNIVERSITY AT KINGSTON - MAP AND AIR PHOTO LIBRARY □ Kingston, ON
Harding, Mary, Ref.Libn.
FORD FOUNDATION - LIBRARY □ New York, NY

Hardison, Betty Jo, Chf.Libn.
BECHTEL - CENTRAL LIBRARY □ San Francisco, CA
Hardison, Mary S., Acq.Libn.
U.S. DEPT. OF COMMERCE - DEPARTMENTAL LIBRARY □ Washington, DC
Hardison, Dr. O.B., Jr., Dir.
FOLGER SHAKESPEARE LIBRARY □ Washington, DC
Hardnett, Carolyn J., Chf.Libn.
CHICAGO TRIBUNE PRESS SERVICE - WASHINGTON BUREAU - LIBRARY □ Washington, DC
Hardwick, Beth, Asst.Libn.
CALDWELL COMMUNITY COLLEGE AND TECHNICAL INSTITUTE - LEARNING RESOURCE CENTER □ Hudson, NC
Hardwick, Rev. John F., Dir., Plan/Prog.
PROTESTANT EPISCOPAL CHURCH - DIOCESE OF PENNSYLVANIA - INFORMATION CENTER □ Philadelphia, PA
Hardy, Carol L., Nonprint Media
CALIFORNIA STATE UNIVERSITY, CHICO - MERIAM LIBRARY □ Chico, CA
Hardy, Ethel
LOS ANGELES - DEPARTMENT OF WATER AND POWER - LEGAL DIVISION - LAW LIBRARY □ Los Angeles, CA
Hardy, Mr. J., Archivist
GEORGE BROWN COLLEGE OF APPLIED ARTS & TECHNOLOGY - LIBRARY □ Toronto, ON
Hardy, John L., Archv.
GEORGE BROWN COLLEGE OF APPLIED ARTS & TECHNOLOGY - ARCHIVES □ Toronto, ON
Hardy, Margaret C., Dir.
MIAMI VALLEY HOSPITAL - MEMORIAL MEDICAL LIBRARY □ Dayton, OH
Hardy, Patricia F., Libn.
COLUMBUS LEDGER-ENQUIRER - LIBRARY □ Columbus, GA
Hardy, Susanna, Libn.
SAN DIEGO PUBLIC LIBRARY - LITERATURE & LANGUAGE SECTION □ San Diego, CA
Hardy, Yvon, Chf., Proc.
UNIVERSITE LAVAL - BIBLIOTHEQUE† □ Ste. Foy, PQ
Hare, Evelyn, Libn.
STATEN ISLAND INSTITUTE OF ARTS AND SCIENCES - HIGH ROCK PARK CONSERVATION CENTER - LIBRARY □ Staten Island, NY
Hare, Frances A., Archv.
YAKIMA VALLEY MUSEUM AND HISTORICAL ASSOCIATION - LIBRARY □ Yakima, WA
Hare, John B., Sr.Info.Sci.
PFIZER, INC. - CENTRAL RESEARCH TECHNICAL INFORMATION SERVICES □ Groton, CT
Hargens, Amy, Assoc.Libn.
FEDERAL RESERVE BANK OF MINNEAPOLIS - LIBRARY □ Minneapolis, MN
Hargens, Amy, Libn.
UNIVERSITY OF MINNESOTA - FIRE CENTER □ Minneapolis, MN
Hargleroad, Bobbi Wells, Doc.Dir.
INSTITUTE ON THE CHURCH IN URBAN-INDUSTRIAL SOCIETY - LIBRARY □ Chicago, IL
Hargrave, Jean, Sr.Libn.
NEW YORK STATE LIBRARY - LEGISLATIVE AND GOVERNMENTAL SERVICES □ Albany, NY
Haring, Gayle, Mgr., Info.Serv.
BURSON-MARSTELLER - INFORMATION SERVICE □ New York, NY
Hark, Nellie F.
FLINT NEWMAN CENTER - LIBRARY AND CATHOLIC INFORMATION CENTER □ Flint, MI
Harke, Toby, Ref.Libn.
TEMPLE UNIVERSITY - HEALTH SCIENCES CENTER - LIBRARY □ Philadelphia, PA
Harker, Susan, Patient Educ.Libn.
U.S. VETERANS ADMINISTRATION (CA-Los Angeles) - WADSWORTH MEDICAL LIBRARY □ Los Angeles, CA

PERSONNEL

Harkins, Anna, Asst.Dir., Lib.Serv.
PITTSBURGH BOARD OF EDUCATION -
PROFESSIONAL LIBRARY □ Pittsburgh, PA
Harkins, John, Archv.
MEMPHIS-SHELBY COUNTY PUBLIC LIBRARY
AND INFORMATION CENTER - MEMPHIS ROOM
COLLECTIONS □ Memphis, TN
Harkins, William, Cat.
NATIONAL GALLERY OF ART - PHOTOGRAPHIC
ARCHIVES □ Washington, DC
Harkonen, Janine, Circuit Libn.
CLEVELAND HEALTH SCIENCES LIBRARY -
ALLEN MEMORIAL LIBRARY □ Cleveland, OH
Harkonen, Jeanine M., Circuit Libn.
WOMAN'S GENERAL HOSPITAL - MEDICAL
LIBRARY □ Cleveland, OH
Harlan, James H., Libn.
SAN PEDRO PENINSULA HOSPITAL - MEDICAL
LIBRARY □ San Pedro, CA
Harlan, Judi, Asst.Libn.
GREAT LAKES BASIN COMMISSION - GREAT
LAKES BASIN LIBRARY □ Ann Arbor, MI
Harlan, Lillian, Cur.
ELMHURST HISTORICAL COMMISSION -
LIBRARY □ Elmhurst, IL
Harlan, Renata W., Asst.Libn.
DAYTON ART INSTITUTE - LIBRARY □ Dayton,
OH
Harlem, Suzy, Br.Libn.
NATIONAL INSTITUTE OF EDUCATION -
EDUCATIONAL RESEARCH LIBRARY □
Washington, DC
Harlow, Ann K., User Serv.Libn.
U.S. ARMY - MILITARY ACADEMY - LIBRARY □
West Point, NY
Harlow, Carol, Circ./Per.Libn.
ATLANTA COLLEGE OF ART - LIBRARY □
Atlanta, GA
Harlow, Donald J., Dir
ESPERANTO LEAGUE FOR NORTH AMERICA -
ESPERANTO INFORMATION SERVICE □ El
Cerrito, CA
Harlow, Ethelyn, Libn.
ONTARIO - ARCHIVES OF ONTARIO - LIBRARY
□ Toronto, ON
Harlow, Jeanette, Libn.
IIT RESEARCH INSTITUTE - COMPUTER
SEARCH CENTER □ Chicago, IL
Harlow, Mary H., Libn.
ABILENE STATE SCHOOL - SPECIAL LIBRARY □
Abilene, TX
Harman, Anne L., Hd. Of Tech.Serv.
GEORGIA COLLEGE - INA DILLARD RUSSELL
LIBRARY □ Milledgeville, GA
Harman, Susan, Ref. & Circ.Libn.
MEDICAL AND CHIRURGICAL FACULTY OF THE
STATE OF MARYLAND - LIBRARY □ Baltimore,
MD
Harmatuck, Loretta, Coord.
WISCONSIN STATE DEPARTMENT OF PUBLIC
INSTRUCTION - WISCONSIN DISSEMINATION
PROJECT (WDP) □ Madison, WI
Harmatz, B., Res.
U.S. OAK RIDGE NATL. LABORATORY -
NUCLEAR DATA PROJECT† □ Oak Ridge, TN
Harmeling, Sr. Deborah, O.S.B., Hd.Libn.
MOUNT ST. MARY'S SEMINARY OF THE WEST -
LIBRARY □ Cincinnati, OH
Harmon, Angelina, Libn.
MEMORIAL SLOAN-KETTERING CANCER
CENTER - LEE COOMBE MEMORIAL LIBRARY □
New York, NY
Harmon, Dr. James S., Dir.
SOUTHEASTERN OKLAHOMA STATE
UNIVERSITY - KERR INDUSTRIAL
APPLICATIONS CENTER - LIBRARY □ Durant,
OK
Harmon, Merlynn S., Res.Libn.
BIBLIOGRAPHIC RESEARCH LIBRARY □ San
Jose, CA

Harmon, Patricia Ann, Libn.
UNIROYAL, INC. - UNIROYAL CHEMICAL
DIVISION - MANAGEMENT & TECHNICAL
INFORMATION SERVICES/LIBRARY □
Naugatuck, CT
Harmon, Robert B., Res.Biblog.
BIBLIOGRAPHIC RESEARCH LIBRARY □ San
Jose, CA
Harmony, Stephena, Libn.
UNIVERSITY OF CINCINNATI - MEDICAL
CENTER LIBRARIES - HEALTH SCIENCES
LIBRARY □ Cincinnati, OH
Harms, Herbert L.
EMMAUS LUTHERAN CHURCH - LIBRARY □
Denver, CO
Harms, Richard, Spec.
MICHIGAN STATE UNIVERSITY - UNIVERSITY
ARCHIVES AND HISTORICAL COLLECTIONS □
East Lansing, MI
Harms, Sally, Dir.
ST. LUKE'S METHODIST HOSPITAL - HEALTH
SCIENCE LIBRARY □ Cedar Rapids, IA
Harmsen, Mark S., Res.Dir.
REPUBLICAN ASSOCIATES OF LOS ANGELES
COUNTY - RESEARCH LIBRARY □ Glendale, CA
Harnack, Dr. Robert, Dir.
SUNY AT BUFFALO - CENTER FOR CURRICULUM
PLANNING □ Amherst, NY
Harnden, Donna J., Hd.Libn.
PEAT, MARWICK, MITCHELL & COMPANY -
LIBRARY □ Minneapolis, MN
Harnett, Patricia, Rec.Mgr.
NATIONAL DAIRY COUNCIL - LIBRARY □
Rosemont, IL
Harney, Nancy Lee, Libn.
HARTFORD SEMINARY FOUNDATION - CASE
MEMORIAL LIBRARY □ Hartford, CT
Harney, Roberta, Asst.
NEEDHAM, HARPER & STEERS ADVERTISING,
INC. - INFORMATION SERVICES □ Chicago, IL
Harnish, Rita, ILL Libn.
WITTENBERG UNIVERSITY - THOMAS LIBRARY
□ Springfield, OH
Harnly, Caroline, Sci.Libn.
MIAMI UNIVERSITY - SCIENCE LIBRARY □
Oxford, OH
Harnois, Helene, Lib.Techn.
MONTREAL CANCER INSTITUTE - LIBRARY □
Montreal, PQ
Harold, Steve, Musm.Dir.
MANISTEE COUNTY HISTORICAL MUSEUM -
FORTIER MEMORIAL LIBRARY □ Manistee, MI
Harper, Deidre, Hd. ILL
DREXEL UNIVERSITY LIBRARIES - GENERAL
LIBRARY □ Philadelphia, PA
Harper, Deidre, ILL
DREXEL UNIVERSITY LIBRARIES - SCIENCE
AND TECHNOLOGY LIBRARY □ Philadelphia, PA
Harper, Josephine L., Ref.Archv.
STATE HISTORICAL SOCIETY OF WISCONSIN -
ARCHIVES DIVISION □ Madison, WI
Harper, Judith, Hd.
UNIVERSITY OF MANITOBA - AGRICULTURE
LIBRARY □ Winnipeg, MB
Harper, Kathryn, Libn.
MEDFORD MAIL TRIBUNE - LIBRARY □ Medford,
OR
Harper, Marie F., Ref.Libn.
RHODE ISLAND HISTORICAL SOCIETY -
LIBRARY □ Providence, RI
Harper, Phyllis, Lib.Techn.
U.S. AIR FORCE HOSPITAL MEDICAL CENTER -
MEDICAL LIBRARY (MS-Keesler AFB) □ Keesler
AFB, MS
Harper, Robert L., Hd.Libn.
CALIFORNIA COLLEGE OF ARTS AND CRAFTS -
MEYER LIBRARY □ Oakland, CA
Harper, Shirley, Med.Libn.
ST. MARY-CORWIN HOSPITAL - FINNEY
MEMORIAL LIBRARY □ Pueblo, CO

Harper, Shirley F., Libn.
CORNELL UNIVERSITY - MARTIN P.
CATHERWOOD LIBRARY OF INDUSTRIAL AND
LABOR RELATIONS □ Ithaca, NY
Harpole, Patricia C., Chf. of Ref.Lib.
MINNESOTA HISTORICAL SOCIETY -
REFERENCE LIBRARY □ St. Paul, MN
Harpst, Elizabeth, Adm.Libn.
WINEBRENNER THEOLOGICAL SEMINARY -
LIBRARY □ Findlay, OH
Harpster, Robert W., Exec.Dir.
LEAGUE OF IOWA MUNICIPALITIES - LIBRARY
□ Des Moines, IA
Harrell, Alfonso, Supv.Rec.Ctr.
PHILADELPHIA - CITY ARCHIVES □ Philadelphia,
PA
Harrell, Helen C., Dir.
HERMANN HOSPITAL - SCHOOL OF
VOCATIONAL NURSING LIBRARY □ Houston, TX
Harren, Judith, Govt.Doc.Libn.
UNION UNIVERSITY - ALBANY LAW SCHOOL -
LIBRARY □ Albany, NY
Harrer, Rev. John A., Archv.
AMERICAN CONGREGATIONAL ASSOCIATION -
CONGREGATIONAL LIBRARY □ Boston, MA
Harrigan, Anne T., Libn.
WOODWARD-CLYDE CONSULTANTS, WESTERN
REGION - TECHNICAL LIBRARY □ San Francisco,
CA
Harrington, Moyra, Techn.
MANITOBA - DEPARTMENT OF ECONOMIC
DEVELOPMENT AND TOURISM - LIBRARY □
Winnipeg, MB
Harrington, Robert D., Dir.
SAN MATEO COUNTY LAW LIBRARY □ Redwood
City, CA
Harrington, Thomas, Media Libn.
GALLAUDET COLLEGE LIBRARY - SPECIAL
COLLECTIONS □ Washington, DC
Harris, Alice, Libn.
DOW CHEMICAL U.S.A. - ENGINEERING AND
CONSTRUCTION SERVICES LIBRARY† □
Houston, TX
Harris, Alice D., Pres.
ASSOCIATION FOR POPULATION/FAMILY
PLANNING LIBRARIES & INFORMATION
CENTERS INTERNATIONAL □ Chapel Hill, NC
Harris, Alice D., Rsrcs.Mtls.Spec.
EAST-WEST POPULATION INSTITUTE
RESOURCE MATERIALS COLLECTION □
Honolulu, HI
Harris, Angela, Ck.
EMR PHOTOELECTRIC-SCHLUMBERGER LTD. -
BUSINESS LIBRARY & TECHNICAL
INFORMATION □ Princeton Junction, NJ
Harris, Anna L., Libn.
CLEVELAND PSYCHIATRIC INSTITUTE -
KARNOSH LIBRARY □ Cleveland, OH
Harris, Barbara B., Libn.
CONTROL DATA CORPORATION -
GOVERNMENT SYSTEMS LIBRARY □ Alexandria,
VA
Harris, Mr. Carol, Cur.
JACKSONVILLE PUBLIC LIBRARY - FLORIDA
COLLECTION □ Jacksonville, FL
Harris, Carol A., Libn.
DEBORAH HEART AND LUNG CENTER -
MEDICAL LIBRARY □ Browns Mills, NJ
Harris, Cheryl, Health Sci.Libn.
U.S. VETERANS ADMINISTRATION (OH-Dayton)
- CENTER LIBRARY □ Dayton, OH
Harris, David C., Institute Mgr.
RESEARCH SERVICES CORPORATION -
INSTITUTE FOR MICROCRYSTAL POLYMER
RESEARCH - LIBRARY □ Fort Worth, TX
Harris, Elaine S., Info.Res.Anl.
SPERRY CORPORATION - SPERRY UNIVAC
COMPUTER SYSTEMS - INFORMATION CENTER
□ Blue Bell, PA
Harris, Eleanor, JBC Libn.
FLORIDA INSTITUTE OF TECHNOLOGY -
LIBRARY □ Melbourne, FL

Harris, Eleanor S., Br.Libn.
FLORIDA INSTITUTE OF TECHNOLOGY -
SCHOOL OF APPLIED TECHNOLOGY - LIBRARY □
Jensen Beach, FL

Harris, G.H., Supv.
BRITISH COLUMBIA - MINISTRY OF
ENVIRONMENT - MAPS LIBRARY □ Victoria, BC

Harris, Glenda, Libn.
LAS VEGAS REVIEW-JOURNAL - LIBRARY □ Las
Vegas, NV

Harris, Gregory P., Libn.
SHEPARD'S/MC GRAW-HILL - LIBRARY □
Colorado Springs, CO

Harris, Helen Y., Libn.
SEMMES, BOWEN & SEMMES - LAW LIBRARY □
Baltimore, MD

Harris, Hilda G., Assoc.Dir./Pub.Serv.
UNIVERSITY OF ALABAMA IN BIRMINGHAM -
LISTER HILL LIBRARY OF THE HEALTH
SCIENCES □ Birmingham, AL

Harris, J. Carver, Bus.Mgr.
ST. AUGUSTINE HISTORICAL SOCIETY -
LIBRARY □ St. Augustine, FL

Harris, Jack, Info.Spec.
MILES LABORATORIES, INC. - LIBRARY
RESOURCES AND SERVICES □ Elkhart, IN

Harris, Dr. Jan L., Supv.
VIRGINIA STATE DEPARTMENT OF
EDUCATION - DIVISION OF MANAGEMENT
INFORMATION SERVICES - LIBRARY □
Richmond, VA

Harris, Jane F., Asst.Libn.
SCOTT, FORESMAN & COMPANY, INC. -
EDITORIAL LIBRARY □ Glenview, IL

Harris, John, Libn.
PENNSYLVANIA COLLEGE OF PODIATRIC
MEDICINE - AUDIOVISUAL LIBRARY □
Philadelphia, PA

Harris, John M., Dir.
TIPPECANOE COUNTY HISTORICAL
ASSOCIATION - ALAMEDA MC COLLOUGH
RESEARCH & GENEALOGY LIBRARY □ Lafayette,
IN

Harris, Dr. Joseph, Res.Dir.
LABOR RESEARCH ASSOCIATION - LIBRARY □
New York, NY

Harris, Kathryn, User Serv.
SOUTHERN ILLINOIS UNIVERSITY - SCHOOL OF
MEDICINE - MEDICAL LIBRARY □ Springfield, IL

Harris, Linda K., Chm., Lib.Comm.
FIRST MERIDIAN HEIGHTS PRESBYTERIAN
CHURCH - HUDELSON LIBRARY □ Indianapolis,
IN

Harris, Lois, Spec.Coll.Libn.
VIGO COUNTY PUBLIC LIBRARY - SPECIAL
COLLECTIONS □ Terre Haute, IN

Harris, Lois E., Dir., Lib. & AV Serv.
PACIFIC HOSPITAL OF LONG BEACH - MEDICAL
STAFF LIBRARY □ Long Beach, CA

Harris, M.G., Division Libn.
MOBIL OIL CORPORATION - E & P DIVISION
LIBRARY □ Denver, CO

Harris, Madlynne, Ref.Libn.
UNIVERSITY OF PITTSBURGH - FALK LIBRARY
OF THE HEALTH SCIENCES □ Pittsburgh, PA

Harris, Margaret Jean, Asst.Libn.
HOUSTON PUBLIC LIBRARY - CLAYTON
LIBRARY CENTER FOR GENEALOGICAL
RESEARCH □ Houston, TX

Harris, Marinelle, Ser.Libn.
SOUTHWESTERN OKLAHOMA STATE
UNIVERSITY - AL HARRIS LIBRARY □
Weatherford, OK

Harris, Mark, Hd.
LOUISVILLE FREE PUBLIC LIBRARY -
KENTUCKY DIVISION □ Louisville, KY

Harris, Mary E., Asst.Sci.Libn.
SAN DIEGO STATE UNIVERSITY - SCIENCE
DEPARTMENT □ San Diego, CA

Harris, Mary Lou, Asst.Dir./Adm.Serv.
U.S. ARMY MILITARY HISTORY INSTITUTE □
Carlisle Barracks, PA

Harris, Mary R., Libn.
REYNOLDS METALS COMPANY - TECHNICAL
INFORMATION SERVICES LIBRARY □ Richmond,
VA

Harris, Maureen, Soc.Sci.Hum.Serv.
CLEMSON UNIVERSITY - ROBERT MULDROW
COOPER LIBRARY □ Clemson, SC

Harris, Melanie, Ref.Libn.
QUEEN'S UNIVERSITY AT KINGSTON -
EDUCATION LIBRARY □ Kingston, ON

Harris, Mildred, Staff Chm.
CUMBERLAND COUNTY HISTORICAL SOCIETY -
LIBRARY □ Greenwich, NJ

Harris, Mollie S., Hd.Libn.
JEWISH COMMUNITY CENTER - SAMUEL &
REBECCA ASTOR JUDAICA LIBRARY □ San
Diego, CA

Harris, N., Asst.Dir. of Instr.
NEWFOUNDLAND - DEPARTMENT OF
EDUCATION - INSTRUCTIONAL MATERIALS
LIBRARY □ St. John's, NF

Harris, Nancy, Libn.
MARSHALL, MELHORN, COLE, HUMMER &
SPITZER - LIBRARY □ Toledo, OH

Harris, Nancy S., Libn.
COLLEGE OF WILLIAM AND MARY - VIRGINIA
ASSOCIATED RESEARCH CAMPUS LIBRARY □
Newport News, VA

Harris, Mrs. R., Tech.Libn.
MIDLAND COUNTY PUBLIC LIBRARY - SCI-
TECH SECTION LIBRARY □ Midland, TX

Harris, Richard, Tech.Serv.Coord.
EASTERN VIRGINIA MEDICAL SCHOOL -
MOORMAN MEMORIAL LIBRARY □ Norfolk, VA

Harris, Robert L., Chf.Ref.Libn.
SOUTHWEST TEXAS STATE UNIVERSITY -
LEARNING RESOURCES CENTER □ San Marcos,
TX

Harris, Rosemary, Libn.
GALLO (E. & J.) WINERY - LIBRARY □ Modesto,
CA

Harris, Dr. S.J., Cat.
CANADA - NATIONAL DEFENCE -
DIRECTORATE OF HISTORY LIBRARY □ Ottawa,
ON

Harris, Mrs. Sina B., Adm.Asst.
UNIVERSITY OF LOUISVILLE - SEBASTIAN S.
KRESGE NATURAL SCIENCE LIBRARY □
Louisville, KY

Harris, Terri, Coord., Info.Spec.
ESSO RESOURCES CANADA LIMITED - LIBRARY
INFORMATION CENTRE □ Calgary, AB

Harris, William O., Asst.Libn.Rd.Serv.
CHRISTIAN THEOLOGICAL SEMINARY -
LIBRARY □ Indianapolis, IN

Harris, Dr. Woodfin G., Dir.
OKLAHOMA STATE UNIVERSITY - AUDIO
VISUAL CENTER □ Stillwater, OK

Harrison, Alice W., Libn.
ATLANTIC SCHOOL OF THEOLOGY - LIBRARY □
Halifax, NS

Harrison, Annie S., Libn.
KENTUCKY STATE DEPARTMENT OF LIBRARY &
ARCHIVES - KENTUCKIANA COLLECTION □
Frankfort, KY

Harrison, Carole, Lib.Coord.
OAKDALE REGIONAL CENTER FOR
DEVELOPMENTAL DISABILITIES - STAFF
LIBRARY □ Lapeer, MI

Harrison, Carolyn J., Asst.Libn.
NATIONAL GEOGRAPHIC SOCIETY -
ILLUSTRATIONS LIBRARY □ Washington, DC

Harrison, Dennis I., Cur. of Mss.
WESTERN RESERVE HISTORICAL SOCIETY -
LIBRARY □ Cleveland, OH

Harrison, Elaine, Ref.Libn.
MISSOURI STATE LIBRARY □ Jefferson City,
MO

Harrison, Elaine, Mss.Libn.
WESTERN KENTUCKY UNIVERSITY -
KENTUCKY LIBRARY AND MUSEUM/
UNIVERSITY ARCHIVES □ Bowling Green, KY

Harrison, Isom, Hd., Branches
U.S. DEPT. OF ENERGY - LAWRENCE
LIVERMORE LAB. - TECHNICAL INFO. DEPT.
LIBRARY □ Livermore, CA

Harrison, John, ILL
NEW YORK STATE OFFICE OF MENTAL HEALTH
- NEW YORK STATE PSYCHIATRIC INSTITUTE
- LIBRARY □ New York, NY

Harrison, John P., Hd.Cat.
BOSTON ATHENAEUM LIBRARY □ Boston, MA

Harrison, Jon, Fed.Doc.Libn.
MISSOURI STATE LIBRARY □ Jefferson City,
MO

Harrison, Marjorie T., Asst.Libn.
MAINE MARITIME ACADEMY - NUTTING
MEMORIAL LIBRARY □ Castine, ME

Harrison, Rayma, Assoc.Libn.
CALIFORNIA INSTITUTE OF TECHNOLOGY -
ENVIRONMENTAL ENGINEERING LIBRARY □
Pasadena, CA

Harrison, Steven D., Musm.Spec.
U.S. NATL. PARK SERVICE - JEFFERSON NATL.
EXPANSION MEMORIAL - LIBRARY □ St. Louis,
MO

Harrison, T., Hd., Print Area
KELSEY INSTITUTE OF APPLIED ARTS AND
SCIENCES - LEARNING RESOURCES CENTRE □
Saskatoon, SK

Harrison, Thomas J., Chf., Prof.Serv.
U.S. NATL. PARK SERVICE - GETTYSBURG
NATL. MILITARY PARK - CYCLORAMA CENTER
LIBRARY □ Gettysburg, PA

Harrison, Tom W., Mgr.
KERR-MC GEE CORPORATION - MC GEE
LIBRARY □ Oklahoma City, OK

Harrison, Veronica C., Libn.
MERCY HOSPITAL - SCHOOL OF NURSING
LIBRARY □ Pittsburgh, PA

Harrison, Zelda, Libn.
TEMPLE JUDEA - MEL HARRISON MEMORIAL
LIBRARY □ Coral Gables, FL

Harriss, Charlotte, Supv., Pub.Serv.
CALIFORNIA STATE LIBRARY □ Sacramento, CA

Harroff, William, Architecture Libn.
OKLAHOMA STATE UNIVERSITY - HUMANITIES
DIVISION □ Stillwater, OK

Harrsch, Reid, Acq.
WISCONSIN STATE DIVISION FOR LIBRARY
SERVICES - REFERENCE AND LOAN LIBRARY □
Madison, WI

Harry, Ms. D., Supv.
ALBERTA - OFFICE OF THE OMBUDSMAN -
OMBUDSMAN'S LIBRARY □ Edmonton, AB

Hart, Anne, Hd.
MEMORIAL UNIVERSITY OF NEWFOUNDLAND -
CENTRE FOR NEWFOUNDLAND STUDIES □ St.
John's, NF

Hart, B.F., Educ. Media Serv.
NOVA SCOTIA - DEPARTMENT OF EDUCATION
- EDUCATION MEDIA SERVICES □ Halifax, NS

Hart, Carroll, State Archv. & Dir.
GEORGIA STATE DEPARTMENT OF ARCHIVES
AND HISTORY - CENTRAL RESEARCH LIBRARY
□ Atlanta, GA

Hart, Dorothy, Base Libn.
U.S. AIR FORCE BASE - NELLIS BASE LIBRARY □
Las Vegas, NV

Hart, E.J., Adm.
ARCHIVES OF THE CANADIAN ROCKIES □
Banff, AB

Hart, George C., Biblog.
OHIO STATE UNIVERSITY - LATIN AMERICAN
STUDIES READING ROOM AND LIBRARY □
Columbus, OH

Hart, J. Robert, Dir.
HERTY FOUNDATION - LIBRARY □ Savannah, GA

Hart, James D., Dir.
UNIVERSITY OF CALIFORNIA, BERKELEY -
BANCROFT LIBRARY □ Berkeley, CA

Hart, Lyn, Dept.Hd.
ENOCH PRATT FREE LIBRARY - GEORGE
PEABODY DEPARTMENT □ Baltimore, MD

PERSONNEL

Hart, Marion L., AVP-Info.Serv.
UNITED VIRGINIA BANK - INFORMATION
CENTER □ Richmond, VA

Hart, Robert G., Gen.Mgr.
U.S. DEPT. OF THE INTERIOR - INDIAN ARTS
AND CRAFTS BOARD □ Washington, DC

Hart, William E., M.D., Libn.
HARTFORD MEDICAL SOCIETY - LIBRARY □
Hartford, CT

Hart, Winifred M., Libn.
U.S. DEPT. OF JUSTICE - CRIMINAL DIVISION -
LIBRARY □ Washington, DC

Hartbank, Betty, Hd.Ref.Serv.
EASTERN ILLINOIS UNIVERSITY - BOOTH
LIBRARY □ Charleston, IL

Harten, Lucille, Pubn.Ed.
IDAHO STATE UNIVERSITY - IDAHO MUSEUM
OF NATURAL HISTORY - LIBRARY □ Pocatello,
ID

Hartenstein, Jeanne L., Dir.Lib.Serv.
BRONSON METHODIST HOSPITAL - HEALTH
SCIENCES LIBRARY □ Kalamazoo, MI

Harter, Ann, Libn.
TAMPA BAY REGIONAL PLANNING COUNCIL -
RESEARCH & INFORMATION LIBRARY □ St.
Petersburg, FL

Harter, Elizabeth, Pub.Serv.Libn.
UNIVERSITY OF CALIFORNIA, LOS ANGELES -
ART LIBRARY □ Los Angeles, CA

Harter, Margaret, Lib.Asst.
RICHMOND PUBLIC LIBRARY - ART AND MUSIC
DEPARTMENT† □ Richmond, VA

Hartgen, David T., Hd. Data Anl.Bur.
NEW YORK STATE DEPARTMENT OF
TRANSPORTATION PLANNING DIVISION -
LIBRARY □ Albany, NY

Harthan, Stephen, Supv.Tech.Serv.
DALLAS THEOLOGICAL SEMINARY - MOSHER
LIBRARY □ Dallas, TX

Hartigan, Barry, Assoc.Libn.
UNIVERSITY OF FLORIDA - ENGINEERING &
PHYSICS LIBRARY □ Gainesville, FL

Hartinger, Bert, Mgr., City Rec.Ctr.
MILWAUKEE - LEGISLATIVE REFERENCE
BUREAU - LEGISLATIVE LIBRARY □ Milwaukee,
WI

Hartje, George N., Dir. of Lib.
NORTHEAST MISSOURI STATE UNIVERSITY -
PICKLER MEMORIAL LIBRARY - SPECIAL
COLLECTIONS □ Kirksville, MO

Hartke, Larry, Data User Serv.Off.
U.S. BUREAU OF THE CENSUS - REGIONAL
DATA USER SERVICE - SEATTLE REGIONAL
OFFICE - LIBRARY □ Seattle, WA

Hartke, Phyllis, Ref.Libn.
SQUIRE, SANDERS & DEMPSEY - LAW LIBRARY
□ Cleveland, OH

Hartley, Gloria R., Tech.Libn.
LUKENS STEEL COMPANY - TECHNICAL
LIBRARY □ Coatesville, PA

Hartley, Patty Y., Dir.
BETHESDA HOSPITAL - LIBRARY AND
EDUCATION SERVICES† □ Zanesville, OH

Hartman, Barbara, Med.Libn.
ST. MARGARET MEMORIAL HOSPITAL - PAUL
TITUS MEMORIAL LIBRARY AND SCHOOL OF
NURSING LIBRARY □ Pittsburgh, PA

Hartman, Eleanor C., Musm.Libn.
LOS ANGELES COUNTY MUSEUM OF ART -
RESEARCH LIBRARY □ Los Angeles, CA

Hartman, Gwen, Libn.
DELAVAN CORPORATION - ENGINEERING
LIBRARY □ West Des Moines, IA

Hartman, Marie, Map Libn.
DALLAS PUBLIC LIBRARY - GOVERNMENT
PUBLICATIONS DIVISION □ Dallas, TX

Hartman, Dr. Richard T., Dir.
UNIVERSITY OF PITTSBURGH - PYMATUNING
LABORATORY OF ECOLOGY - LIBRARY □
Linesville, PA

Hartman, Ruth Dahlgren, Hd.
CENTRAL WASHINGTON UNIVERSITY -
LIBRARY DOCUMENTS DEPARTMENT □
Ellensburg, WA

Hartman, Sherry, Ref. & Database
UNION UNIVERSITY - ALBANY MEDICAL
COLLEGE - SCHAFFER LIBRARY OF THE HEALTH
SCIENCES □ Albany, NY

Hartman, Wilma L., Libn., Pub.Serv.
LINDA HALL LIBRARY □ Kansas City, MO

Hartmere, Anne, Libn.
ARCHITECTS COLLABORATIVE - LIBRARY □
Cambridge, MA

Hartness-Kane, Ann, Pub.Serv.Libn.
UNIVERSITY OF TEXAS, AUSTIN - BENSON
LATIN AMERICAN COLLECTION □ Austin, TX

Hartnett, Mary, Indexer
WED ENTERPRISES - RESEARCH LIBRARY □
Glendale, CA

Hartshorne, Donna, Spec./Oral Hist.
UNIVERSITY OF WISCONSIN, MADISON -
ARCHIVES □ Madison, WI

Hartung, David D., Libn.
WISCONSIN INDIANHEAD TECHNICAL
INSTITUTE, NEW RICHMOND CAMPUS -
LEARNING RESOURCE CENTER □ New
Richmond, WI

Hartwell, Sarah L., Libn.
MOTE MARINE LABORATORY - DAVIS LIBRARY
□ Sarasota, FL

Hartwig, Deborah, Libn.
WASHINGTON UNIVERSITY - EARTH AND
PLANETARY SCIENCES LIBRARY □ St. Louis, MO

Hartwig, Karla, Lib.Techn.
TEXAS STATE TECHNICAL INSTITUTE, MID-
CONTINENT CAMPUS - LIBRARY† □ Amarillo, TX

Hartz, Mary K., Libn.
BUREAU OF SOCIAL SCIENCE RESEARCH -
LIBRARY □ Washington, DC

Hartzel, Mrs. Gerald F., Chm., Lib.Comm.
ZION MENNONITE CHURCH - LIBRARY □
Souderton, PA

Hartzer, Ronald B., Oral Hist.
INDIANA UNIVERSITY - ORAL HISTORY
RESEARCH PROJECT - LIBRARY □ Bloomington,
IN

Hartzler, Mary, Hd., Cat.Div.
INDIANA STATE LIBRARY □ Indianapolis, IN

Harvan, Christine, Libn.
LANCASTER LAW LIBRARY □ Lancaster, PA

Harvath, John, Dept.Hd.
HOUSTON PUBLIC LIBRARY - FINE ARTS &
RECREATION DEPARTMENT □ Houston, TX

Harvell, Gloria, Media Libn.
VIRGINIA STATE UNIVERSITY - JOHNSTON
MEMORIAL LIBRARY □ Petersburg, VA

Harvey, Avis E., Rsrcs./Info.Off.
PROTESTANT EPISCOPAL CHURCH EXECUTIVE
COUNCIL - HENRY KNOX SHERRILL RESOURCE
CENTER □ New York, NY

Harvey, C.G., Libn.
HUDSON'S BAY OIL & GAS COMPANY, LTD. -
CORPORATE LIBRARY □ Calgary, AB

Harvey, Charlie, Law Libn.
RUTGERS UNIVERSITY, THE STATE
UNIVERSITY OF NEW JERSEY - JUSTICE
HENRY ACKERSON LIBRARY OF LAW &
CRIMINAL JUSTICE □ Newark, NJ

Harvey, Charlie R., Libn./Asst.Prof.
VILLANOVA UNIVERSITY - PULLING LAW
LIBRARY □ Villanova, PA

Harvey, Diane K., Libn.
JOHNS HOPKINS UNIVERSITY - MILTON S.
EISENHOWER LIBRARY - GOVERNMENT
PUBN./MAPS/LAW LIBRARY □ Baltimore, MD

Harvey, Dorothy, Dept.Hd.
SACRAMENTO PUBLIC LIBRARY - BUSINESS &
MUNICIPAL DEPARTMENT □ Sacramento, CA

Harvey, Elaine, Acq.Libn.
EDEN THEOLOGICAL SEMINARY - LIBRARY □
Webster Groves, MO

Harvey, S/Sgt. F.C.
ONTARIO PROVINCIAL POLICE - TRAINING
BRANCH LIBRARY □ Brampton, ON

Harvey, Janet, Educ.Libn.
UNIVERSITY OF SOUTHERN CALIFORNIA -
EDUCATION LIBRARY □ Los Angeles, CA

Harvey, Judith, Ref.Libn.
MATHEMATICAL REVIEWS - LIBRARY □ Ann
Arbor, MI

Harvey, Karen J., Libn.
SMITH COLLEGE - HILLYER ART LIBRARY □
Northampton, MA

Harvey, Linda, Hd.Info.Serv.
DALHOUSIE UNIVERSITY - W.K. KELLOGG
HEALTH SCIENCES LIBRARY □ Halifax, NS

Harvey, Mabel E., Med.Libn.
SOUTH FLORIDA STATE HOSPITAL - MEDICAL
AND PROFESSIONAL LIBRARY □ Hollywood, FL

Harvey, Marie, Libn.
AMERICAN NATIONAL BUILDING - JOINT
VENTURE LAW LIBRARY □ Denver, CO

Harvey, Nancy, Asst.Chf.
CHICAGO PUBLIC LIBRARY CULTURAL CENTER
- FINE ARTS DIVISION - ART SECTION □
Chicago, IL

Harvey, Nancy, Asst.Div.Chf.
CHICAGO PUBLIC LIBRARY CULTURAL CENTER
- FINE ARTS DIVISION - MUSIC SECTION □
Chicago, IL

Harvey, Shirlee, Libn.
LOWNDES COUNTY LAW LIBRARY† □ Columbus,
MS

Harvey, Susan M., Tech.Libn.
METCUT RESEARCH ASSOCIATES, INC. -
MACHINABILITY DATA CENTER □ Cincinnati,
OH

Harvey, Suzanne, Cat.Libn.
UNIVERSITY OF PUGET SOUND - SCHOOL OF
LAW LIBRARY □ Tacoma, WA

Harvin, Marie, Res.Med.Libn.
UNIVERSITY OF TEXAS - M.D. ANDERSON
HOSPITAL AND TUMOR INSTITUTE -
RESEARCH MEDICAL LIBRARY □ Houston, TX

Harwood, Judith Ann, Libn.
SOUTHERN ILLINOIS UNIVERSITY,
CARBONDALE - UNDERGRADUATE LIBRARY □
Carbondale, IL

Harwood, Kay F., Libn.
RICHLAND MEMORIAL HOSPITAL - JOSEY
MEMORIAL MEDICAL LIBRARY □ Columbia, SC

Harwood, Rodene, Asst.Libn.
DENVER REGIONAL TRANSPORTATION
DISTRICT - LIBRARY □ Denver, CO

Hary, Edith L., State Law Libn.
MAINE STATE LAW AND LEGISLATIVE
REFERENCE LIBRARY □ Augusta, ME

Hasbrouck, Kenneth E., Dir.
HUGUENOT HISTORICAL SOCIETY, NEW PALTZ
- LIBRARY □ New Paltz, NY

Hasbury, Susan, Documentation
CANADA - NATIONAL GALLERY OF CANADA -
LIBRARY □ Ottawa, ON

Hasegawa, Kay, Libn.
SIOUX VALLEY HOSPITAL - MEDICAL LIBRARY
□ Sioux Falls, SD

Hasegawa, Raymond K., Att.
CARLSMITH, CARLSMITH, WICHMAN & CASE -
LIBRARY □ Hilo, HI

Hasenbalg, Ralph W., Mgr.
IBM CORPORATION - SYSTEM
COMMUNICATIONS DIVISION - SITE LIBRARY
□ Kingston, NY

Hasfjord, Nellie N., Dir.
ADAMS STATE COLLEGE - LIBRARY □ Alamosa,
CO

Hashim, Elinor, Asst.Mgr.Ref.
PERKIN-ELMER CORPORATION - CORPORATE
LIBRARY □ Norwalk, CT

Hasija, Mr. Gian C., Med.Libn.
JERSEY SHORE MEDICAL CENTER - MEDICAL LIBRARY □ Neptune, NJ

Hasil, Denise, Cat.Libn.
PROSKAUER, ROSE, GOETZ & MENDELSOHN - LIBRARY □ New York, NY

Haskell, Mary, Cat.
COLONIAL WILLIAMSBURG - RESEARCH LIBRARY & ARCHIVES □ Williamsburg, VA

Haskell, Peter C., Dir.
FRANKLIN AND MARSHALL COLLEGE - FACKENTHAL LIBRARY - SPECIAL COLLECTIONS □ Lancaster, PA

Hasker, Leslie A., Lib.Asst.
SHELBURNE MUSEUM, INC. - RESEARCH LIBRARY □ Shelburne, VT

Haskin, Peggy, Libn.
FLORIDA STATE UNIVERSITY - CTR. FOR STUDIES IN VOCATIONAL EDUC. - FLORIDA EDUCATORS INFO. SERV. □ Tallahassee, FL

Haskins, Charles, Libn.
U.S. ARMY POST - FORT MC PHERSON - LIBRARY SYSTEM □ Ft. McPherson, GA

Haskins, Katherine, Cat.Libn.
ART INSTITUTE OF CHICAGO - RYERSON AND BURNHAM LIBRARIES □ Chicago, IL

Haskins, Norma W., Chf., Lib.Serv.
U.S. VETERANS ADMINISTRATION (PA-Lebanon) - MEDICAL CENTER LIBRARY □ Lebanon, PA

Hass, Joan, Hd.Libn.
AKIN, GUMP, STRAUSS, HAUER & FELD LAW LIBRARY □ Dallas, TX

Hassan, Khan M., Asst.Libn./AV Serv.
IDAHO STATE UNIVERSITY LIBRARY - AUDIO-VISUAL SERVICES □ Pocatello, ID

Hassan, Dr. M.U., Libn.
SASKATCHEWAN - DEPARTMENT OF HIGHWAYS AND TRANSPORTATION - PLANNING BRANCH LIBRARY □ Regina, SK

Hassan, Steven, Pres.
EX-MOON INC. - BUSINESS LIBRARY □ Brookline, MA

Hasse, Glenn E., Chf.Libn.
U.S. VETERANS ADMINISTRATION (ND-Fargo) - CENTER LIBRARY □ Fargo, ND

Hassebrock, Erna, Libn. I/Tech.Serv.
U.S. FOOD & DRUG ADMINISTRATION - NATIONAL CENTER FOR TOXICOLOGICAL RESEARCH - LIBRARY □ Jefferson, AK

Hassell, Lorna, Libn.
UNIVERSITY OF TORONTO - WYCLIFFE COLLEGE - LEONARD LIBRARY □ Toronto, ON

Hassell, Willa, Libn.
ST. ELIZABETH COMMUNITY HEALTH CENTER - MEDICAL LIBRARY □ Lincoln, NE

Hassen, Marjorie, Record Libn.
PRINCETON UNIVERSITY - PHONOGRAPH RECORD LIBRARY □ Princeton, NJ

Hassert, Judith A., Res.Libn.
JOHNSON AND JOHNSON - CHICOPEE, INC. - RESEARCH DIVISION - LIBRARY □ Milltown, NJ

Hassett, Ann, Lib.Ck.
OUR LADY OF VICTORY HOSPITAL - HOSPITAL LIBRARY □ Lackawanna, NY

Hassler, William B., Base Libn.
U.S. AIR FORCE BASE - WHEELER BASE LIBRARY □ Wheeler AFB, HI

Hast, Adele, Editor-in-Chief
MARQUIS WHO'S WHO, INC. - RESEARCH DEPARTMENT LIBRARY □ Chicago, IL

Hastings, David, Asst. State Archv.
WASHINGTON STATE OFFICE OF SECRETARY OF STATE - DIVISION OF ARCHIVES AND RECORD MANAGEMENT □ Olympia, WA

Hastings, Joy, Mgr.Info.Ctr.
HUNT-WESSON FOODS - INFORMATION CENTER □ Fullerton, CA

Hastings, Margaret, Asst.Libn.
BRITISH COLUMBIA - LEGISLATIVE LIBRARY □ Victoria, BC

Haswell, Hollee, Libn.
SLEEPY HOLLOW RESTORATIONS, INC. - SPECIAL LIBRARY & ARCHIVES □ Tarrytown, NY

Haswell, Hollee, Libn.
WORCESTER ART MUSEUM - LIBRARY □ Worcester, MA

Hatcher, Danny R., Dir.
COUNTRY MUSIC FOUNDATION - LIBRARY AND MEDIA CENTER □ Nashville, TN

Hatcher, Linda, Lib. Staff Asst.
FLORIDA STATE HOSPITAL - HEALTH SCIENCE LIBRARY □ Chattahoochee, FL

Hatfield, Frances, Dir.
BROWARD COUNTY PUBLIC SCHOOLS - LEARNING RESOURCES - PROFESSIONAL LIBRARY □ Davie, FL

Hatfield, Katherine, Cat.Libn.
WITTENBERG UNIVERSITY - THOMAS LIBRARY □ Springfield, OH

Hatfield, Dr. Susan
HARPER-GRACE HOSPITALS - DRUG INFORMATION CENTER □ Detroit, MI

Hathaway, Joyce, Asst.Libn.
CHURCH OF JESUS CHRIST OF LATTER-DAY SAINTS - UPPER SNAKE RIVER BRANCH GENEALOGICAL LIBRARY □ Rexburg, ID

Hathaway, Kay, Asst.Libn.
JHK & ASSOCIATES - TECHNICAL LIBRARY - EAST □ Alexandria, VA

Hathorn, Isabel V., Libn.
SUFFOLK ACADEMY OF MEDICINE - LIBRARY □ Hauppauge, NY

Hathway, Judith, Cat.
UNIVERSITY OF WISCONSIN, MADISON - CENTER FOR HEALTH SCIENCES LIBRARIES □ Madison, WI

Hatmaker, N.A., Info.Spec.
U.S. OAK RIDGE NATL. LABORATORY - RADIATION SHIELDING INFORMATION CENTER □ Oak Ridge, TN

Hatten, Bob, Libn.
STANDARD OIL OF CALIFORNIA - CHEVRON U.S.A., INC. - EASTERN REGION LIBRARY □ New Orleans, LA

Hatten, Valerie, Libn.
MANITOBA MUSEUM OF MAN AND NATURE - LIBRARY □ Winnipeg, MB

Hattie, Mrs. Jean O., Libn.
DALHOUSIE UNIVERSITY - MARITIME SCHOOL OF SOCIAL WORK - LIBRARY □ Halifax, NS

Hatton, Bill, Sci.Libn.
IDAHO STATE UNIVERSITY LIBRARY - SCIENCE DIVISION □ Pocatello, ID

Hauck, Carolyn, AV Spec.
ENOCH PRATT FREE LIBRARY - AUDIO-VISUAL DEPARTMENT □ Baltimore, MD

Hauck, Bro. Damien, O.S.B., Act.Libn.
ST. JOSEPH ABBEY - LIBRARY □ St. Benedict, LA

Hauck, Philomena, Dir.
UNIVERSITY OF CALGARY - EDUCATION MATERIALS CENTER □ Calgary, AB

Hauerstein, Terry, Info.Off.
LEVER BROTHERS COMPANY - RESEARCH AND DEVELOPMENT DIVISION - RESEARCH LIBRARY □ Edgewater, NJ

Hauff, John H., Asst.Libn.
SAN FRANCISCO LAW LIBRARY □ San Francisco, CA

Haug, Barbara, Hist.
SMITH MEMORIAL LIBRARY □ Chautauqua, NY

Haug, Mary Ann, Asst.Dir.
MEDICAL GROUP MANAGEMENT ASSOCIATION - INFORMATION SERVICE □ Denver, CO

Haugen, Marsha, Libn.
HEWLETT-PACKARD COMPANY - LOVELAND FACILITY LIBRARY □ Loveland, CO

Haugen, Ruth D., Tech.Serv.Supv.
LIBERTY MUTUAL INSURANCE COMPANY - BUSINESS REFERENCE LIBRARY □ Boston, MA

Haumont, Corinne, Libn.
UNIVERSITE DE MONTREAL - CHIMIE-BIBLIOTHEQUE □ Montreal, PQ

Haun, Barbara, Libn.
ZELLER (George A.) MENTAL HEALTH CENTER - PROFESSIONAL LIBRARY □ Peoria, IL

Haury, David, Archv.
BETHEL COLLEGE - MENNONITE LIBRARY AND ARCHIVES □ North Newton, KS

Hause, Aaron, Act.Dir.
EASTERN MONTANA COLLEGE - LIBRARY - SPECIAL COLLECTIONS† □ Billings, MT

Hauser, William G., Visual Info.Off.
U.S. FOREST SERVICE - PERMANENT PHOTOGRAPHIC COLLECTION □ Washington, DC

Hauskin, Irene, Asst.Libn.
LUTHERAN BIBLE INSTITUTE - LIBRARY □ Issaquah, WA

Hausler, Donald, Libn.
OAKLAND PUBLIC LIBRARY - HISTORY/LITERATURE DIVISION □ Oakland, CA

Haussmann, Virginia, Lib.Asst.
PACIFIC LIGHTING CORPORATION - LAW LIBRARY □ Los Angeles, CA

Hauth, Allan, Ref.Coord.
JACKSON METROPOLITAN LIBRARY - INFORMATION AND REFERENCE DIVISION □ Jackson, MS

Hauw, Katherine, Libn.
TORONTO EAST GENERAL HOSPITAL - DOCTORS' LIBRARY □ Toronto, ON

Havens, Linda M., Libn.
BORGESS MEDICAL CENTER - LIBRARY □ Kalamazoo, MI

Haver, Richard, Chf.Libn.
U.S. VETERANS ADMINISTRATION (NC-Asheville) - MEDICAL CENTER LIBRARY □ Asheville, NC

Haveson, Cindy, Cur.
PERELMAN ANTIQUE TOY MUSEUM - LIBRARY □ Philadelphia, PA

Haviar, Jane, Res.Coord.
REYNOLDS (Russell) ASSOCIATES, INC. - LIBRARY □ Chicago, IL

Haviaras, Stratis, Cur.
HARVARD UNIVERSITY - WOODBERRY POETRY ROOM □ Cambridge, MA

Haviland, Virginia, Chf.
LIBRARY OF CONGRESS - CHILDREN'S LITERATURE CENTER □ Washington, DC

Havlena, Betty W., Chf.Libn.
DETROIT NEWS - GEORGE B. CATLIN MEMORIAL LIBRARY □ Detroit, MI

Havlik, Robert J., Engr.Libn.
UNIVERSITY OF NOTRE DAME - ENGINEERING LIBRARY □ Notre Dame, IN

Hawes, Rena E., Lib.Dir.
EINSTEIN (Albert) MEDICAL CENTER - DAROFF DIVISION - MEDICAL LIBRARY □ Philadelphia, PA

Hawke, Joseph H., Cur.
HOUGHTON COUNTY HISTORICAL SOCIETY - LIBRARY □ Lake Linden, MI

Hawke, Susan, Libn.
CONCORDIA UNIVERSITY - SIR GEORGE WILLIAMS CAMPUS - GUIDANCE INFORMATION CENTRE □ Montreal, PQ

Hawkes, Warren G., Asst.Libn.
NEW YORK STATE NURSES ASSOCIATION - LIBRARY □ Guilderland, NY

Hawkins, D.T., Info.Ret./Alerting Serv.
BELL TELEPHONE LABORATORIES, INC. - LIBRARIES AND INFORMATION SYSTEMS CENTER □ Murray Hill, NJ

Hawkins, Dave, Mgr.
SCARBOROUGH RESOURCE CENTRE □ Scarborough, ON

Hawkins, Dennis M., Pub.Serv.Libn.
BISHOP COLLEGE - ZALE LIBRARY - BANKS AFRO-AMERICAN HERITAGE COLLECTION □ Dallas, TX

Hawkins, Jean V., Med.Libn.
WAUKESHA MEMORIAL HOSPITAL - MEDICAL LIBRARY □ Waukesha, WI

P E R S O N N E L

Hawkins, Lyndsey, Lib.Asst.
 AUSTRALIAN INFORMATION SERVICE -
 REFERENCE LIBRARY/INFORMATION SERVICE
 □ New York, NY
Hawkins, Mary Ann, Archv.
 U.S. NATL. ARCHIVES & RECORDS SERVICE -
 FEDERAL ARCHIVES AND RECORDS CENTER,
 REGION 4 □ East Point, GA
Hawkins, Ronald A., Cat.
 UNITED THEOLOGICAL SEMINARY - LIBRARY □
 Dayton, OH
Hawkins, Verda M., Libn.
 KENNEDY/JENKS ENGINEERS, INC. - LIBRARY
 □ San Francisco, CA
Hawkins, Verna, Lib.Spec.
 WASHINGTON PUBLIC POWER SUPPLY SYSTEM
 - LIBRARY □ Richland, WA
Hawks, Beverly, Act.Dir.
 NEW MEXICO INSTITUTE OF MINING AND
 TECHNOLOGY - MARTIN SPEARE MEMORIAL
 LIBRARY □ Socorro, NM
Hawley, Robert A., Dir.
 SIMSBURY HISTORICAL SOCIETY - SIMSBURY
 RESEARCH LIBRARY □ Simsbury, CT
Haworth, Kent M., AV Rec.Prog.
 BRITISH COLUMBIA - PROVINCIAL ARCHIVES
 □ Victoria, BC
Hawryliuk, D.M., Libn.
 SUDBURY GENERAL HOSPITAL - HOSPITAL
 LIBRARY □ Sudbury, ON
Hawthorne, Flora L., Libn.
 MADDEN (John J.) ZONE CENTER -
 PROFESSIONAL LIBRARY □ Hines, IL
Hawthorne, Judy A., Adm.Libn.
 U.S. ARMY - TRADOC SYSTEMS ANALYSIS
 ACTIVITY - TRASANA TECHNICAL LIBRARY □
 White Sands Missile Range, NM
Hay, E. Patricia, Chf., Leg.Lib.Serv.
 ONTARIO - LEGISLATIVE ASSEMBLY -
 LEGISLATIVE LIBRARY RESEARCH AND
 INFORMATION SERVICES □ Toronto, ON
Hay, Gerald M., Libn.
 ITT NORTH - LIBRARY □ Columbus, OH
Hay, Patricia, Cat.
 ACADEMY OF THE NEW CHURCH - LIBRARY □
 Bryn Athyn, PA
Haycraft, Wilma, Lib.Ck.
 HOLZER MEDICAL CENTER - SCHOOL OF
 NURSING - LIBRARY □ Gallipolis, OH
Hayden, C.B., Adm. of Info.Serv.
 RESEARCH INSTITUTE OF AMERICA -
 INFORMATION SERVICES CENTER □ New York,
 NY
Hayden, Henry, Asst.Lib.Dir.
 BRAILLE INSTITUTE OF AMERICA - LIBRARY □
 Los Angeles, CA
Hayden, Lee, Asst.Supv.
 MADISON PUBLIC LIBRARY - BUSINESS AND
 SCIENCE DIVISION □ Madison, WI
Hayden, Marie, Acq.Libn.
 SAM HOUSTON STATE UNIVERSITY - LIBRARY†
 □ Huntsville, TX
Hayden, Sharon A., Libn.
 NIXON, HARGRAVE, DEVANS & DOYLE - LAW
 LIBRARY† □ Rochester, NY
Haydock, Eleanor, Libn.
 BRITISH COLUMBIA HYDRO & POWER
 AUTHORITY - LIBRARY □ Vancouver, BC
Hayes, Rev. Bonaventure F., O.F.M., Lib.Dir.
 CHRIST THE KING SEMINARY - LIBRARY □ East
 Aurora, NY
Hayes, Charles F., III, Res.Dir.
 NEW YORK STATE ARCHEOLOGICAL
 ASSOCIATION - LIBRARY □ Rochester, NY
Hayes, Cynthia, Libn.
 BUFFALO COURIER-EXPRESS - LIBRARY □
 Buffalo, NY
Hayes, Denise E., Tech.Info.Spec.
 U.S. DEPT. OF LABOR - OSHA - TECHNICAL
 DATA CENTER □ Washington, DC
Hayes, Eleanor, Libn.
 MOUNT SINAI HOSPITAL - SIDNEY LISWOOD
 LIBRARY □ Toronto, ON

Hayes, Elizabeth, Hd.
 YALE UNIVERSITY - ENGINEERING AND
 APPLIED SCIENCE LIBRARY □ New Haven, CT
Hayes, Eunice, Acq.Asst.
 EDEN THEOLOGICAL SEMINARY - LIBRARY □
 Webster Groves, MO
Hayes, Joan P., Libn.
 UNIVERSITY OF PUERTO RICO -
 AGRICULTURAL EXPERIMENT STATION -
 LIBRARY □ Rio Piedras, PR
Hayes, Katharine, District Libn.
 U.S. ARMY - CORPS OF ENGINEERS - ST. LOUIS
 DISTRICT - LIBRARY □ St. Louis, MO
Hayes, L. Susan, Info.Spec.
 SYSTEMS ENGINEERING LABORATORIES -
 TECHNICAL INFORMATION CENTER □ Fort
 Lauderdale, FL
Hayes, Lois F., Libn.
 CHICAGO COLLEGE OF OSTEOPATHIC
 MEDICINE - OLYMPIA FIELDS HOSPITAL
 LIBRARY □ Olympia Fields, IL
Hayes, Margaret L., Libn.
 AMERICAN PLAYERS THEATRE, INC. (APT) -
 LIBRARY □ Spring Green, WI
Hayes, Mary Beth, Libn.
 FASHION INSTITUTE OF DESIGN &
 MERCHANDISING - RESOURCE AND RESEARCH
 CENTER □ Los Angeles, CA
Hayes, Mary E., Ref.Libn.
 UNIVERSITY OF DETROIT - SCHOOL OF LAW
 LIBRARY □ Detroit, MI
Hayes, Patricia, Med.Libn.
 U.S. AIR FORCE HOSPITAL - MEDICAL LIBRARY
 (NY-Rome) □ Griffiss Air Force Base, NY
Hayes, Susan M., Regional Libn.
 U.S. DEPT. OF HOUSING AND URBAN
 DEVELOPMENT - REGION VI - LIBRARY □ Fort
 Worth, TX
Hayes, Suzanne, Ref.Libn.
 BATTEN, BARTON, DURSTINE, OSBORN, INC. -
 INFORMATION RETRIEVAL CENTER □ New
 York, NY
Hayes, William, Hist.
 OREGON ELECTRIC RAILWAY HISTORICAL
 SOCIETY, INC. - TROLLEY PARK - LIBRARY □
 Glenwood, OR
Hayes-Clabots, Katherine J., Libn.
 ECONOMICS LABORATORY, INC. - CORPORATE
 INFORMATION CENTER □ St. Paul, MN
Hayhurst, Ruth I., Libn.
 WEST VIRGINIA STATE GEOLOGICAL AND
 ECONOMIC SURVEY - LIBRARY □ Morgantown,
 WV
Haylock, Harry V., Supv.
 VARIAN CANADA INC. - TECHNICAL LIBRARY □
 Georgetown, ON
Haymond, Jay M., Libn.
 UTAH STATE HISTORICAL SOCIETY -
 RESEARCH LIBRARY □ Salt Lake City, UT
Haymond, Phillip M., Chf., Info./Lib.Serv.Dir.
 U.S. DEPT. OF THE INTERIOR - NATURAL
 RESOURCES LIBRARY □ Washington, DC
Haynes, Donald, State Libn.
 VIRGINIA STATE LIBRARY □ Richmond, VA
Haynes, Gene M., Med.Libn.
 U.S. VETERANS ADMINISTRATION (KY-
 Louisville) - HOSPITAL LIBRARY □ Louisville, KY
Haynes, Michael J., Libn.
 PARSONS STATE HOSPITAL AND TRAINING
 CENTER - MEDICAL LIBRARY □ Parsons, KS
Haynes, Stelma, Lib.Asst.
 FERGUSON BAPTIST CHURCH - LIBRARY □
 Ferguson, KY
Haynes-Esensten, Sandra, Pub.Serv.Libn.
 UNIVERSITY OF CALIFORNIA, LOS ANGELES -
 ART LIBRARY □ Los Angeles, CA
Hays, John T., Tech.Ed.
 HERCULES, INC. - RESEARCH CENTER -
 TECHNICAL INFORMATION DIVISION □
 Wilmington, DE
Hays, Mary J., Libn.
 COOLEY, GODWARD, CASTRO, HUDDLESON &
 TATUM - LIBRARY □ San Francisco, CA

Hays, Sherrill, Info.Spec., Tech.
 GOODRICH (B.F.) COMPANY - AKRON
 INFORMATION CENTER □ Akron, OH
Haysley, Mrs. Frances, Base Libn.
 U.S. AIR FORCE BASE - GEORGE BASE LIBRARY
 □ George AFB, CA
Hayter, Ursula, Libn.
 IMMACULATE HEART OF MARY - PARISH
 LIBRARY □ Los Alamos, NM
Haythorn, J. Denny, Dir., Law Lib.
 WHITTIER COLLEGE - SCHOOL OF LAW -
 LIBRARY □ Los Angeles, CA
Hayward, Christine, Hd.Ser.Serv.
 DALHOUSIE UNIVERSITY - W.K. KELLOGG
 HEALTH SCIENCES LIBRARY □ Halifax, NS
Hayward, Fredric, Dir.
 MEN'S RIGHTS, INC. - READING CENTER □
 Cambridge, MA
Hayward, Karen, Asst.Libn.
 LOYOLA UNIVERSITY OF CHICAGO - LAW
 LIBRARY □ Chicago, IL
Hayward, Mary Ellen, Archv.
 UNIVERSITY OF BALTIMORE - BALTIMORE
 REGION INSTITUTIONAL STUDIES CENTER
 (BRISC) □ Baltimore, MD
Hayward, Zita, Lib.Asst.
 NORTHWESTERN UNIVERSITY -
 MATHEMATICS LIBRARY □ Evanston, IL
Haywood, Henry, Asst.Libn.
 MILBANK, TWEED, HADLEY & MC CLOY -
 LIBRARY □ New York, NY
Hazelett, Barbara W., Adm.Libn.
 U.S. NATL. LABOR RELATIONS BOARD - LAW
 LIBRARY □ Washington, DC
Hazelton, Jane, Media Coord.
 UNIVERSITY OF TEXAS, AUSTIN - FILM
 LIBRARY □ Austin, TX
Hazelton, Penny A., Law Libn.
 UNIVERSITY OF MAINE SCHOOL OF LAW -
 DONALD L. GARBRECHT LAW LIBRARY □
 Portland, ME
Hazen, Natalie, Ser.Libn.
 PALO ALTO MEDICAL FOUNDATION -
 BARNETT-HALL MEDICAL LIBRARY □ Palo Alto,
 CA
Hazlett, Gwendolyn, Libn.
 WARNOCK HERSEY PROFESSIONAL SERVICES
 LTD. - LIBRARY† □ LaSalle, PQ
Haznedari, Ismail, Supv.Libn.
 U.S. ARMY - ARMAMENT RESEARCH &
 DEVELOPMENT COMMAND - SCIENTIFIC AND
 TECHNICAL INFORMATION DIVISION □ Dover,
 NJ
Head, Anita K., Libn.
 GEORGE WASHINGTON UNIVERSITY -
 NATIONAL LAW CENTER - JACOB BURNS LAW
 LIBRARY □ Washington, DC
Head, Jeanne M., Assoc., Staff-Lib.
 QUAKER OATS COMPANY - JOHN STUART
 RESEARCH LABORATORIES - RESEARCH
 LIBRARY □ Barrington, IL
Head, Judith, Hd.Libn.
 UNIVERSITY OF MANITOBA -
 ADMINISTRATIVE STUDIES LIBRARY □
 Winnipeg, MB
Headley, Ava Dell, Libn.
 U.S. ARMY OPERATIONAL TEST & EVALUATION
 AGENCY (OTEA) - TECHNICAL LIBRARY □ Falls
 Church, VA
Headley, Hope, Info.Serv.Asst.
 NATIONAL TRUST FOR HISTORIC
 PRESERVATION - INFORMATION SERVICES □
 Washington, DC
Headspeth, Dorothy W., Educ.Asst.Libn.
 CONNECTICUT STATE DEPARTMENT OF
 EDUCATION - CHARLES D. HINE LIBRARY □
 Hartford, CT
Heagy, Gayle Y., Libn.
 YORK COUNTY PLANNING COMMISSION -
 LIBRARY □ York, PA
Heagy, Jan B., Circ.-Ref.
 AMOCO INTERNATIONAL OIL COMPANY -
 LIBRARY INFORMATION CENTER □ Houston, TX

Healey, Charles F., Asst.Libn.
NEW JERSEY INSTITUTE OF TECHNOLOGY - ROBERT W. VAN HOUTEN LIBRARY □ Newark, NJ

Healey, Mary Catherine, Asst.Libn.
HALE AND DORR - LIBRARY □ Boston, MA

Healy, Sister Frances, Dir.
PROVIDENCE HOSPITAL - HEALTH SCIENCES LIBRARY □ Washington, DC

Healy, Helen J., Libn.
WESTERN MICHIGAN UNIVERSITY - EDUCATIONAL RESOURCES CENTER □ Kalamazoo, MI

Heaney, Howell J., Rare Book Libn.
FREE LIBRARY OF PHILADELPHIA - RARE BOOK DEPARTMENT □ Philadelphia, PA

Heard, Charlene, Libn.
ALTON TELEGRAPH PRINTING COMPANY - LIBRARY □ Alton, IL

Heard, Lt.Col. W.G., Cur.
ROYAL CANADIAN MILITARY INSTITUTE - LIBRARY □ Toronto, ON

Hearder-Moan, W., Libn.
HAMILTON LAW ASSOCIATION - LAW LIBRARY □ Hamilton, ON

Hearn, Barbara, Archv.
DU PONT (Henry Francis) WINTERTHUR MUSEUM - LIBRARY □ Winterthur, DE

Hearn, Helen O., Libn.
U.S. ARMY HOSPITALS - MC DONALD USA COMMUNITY HOSPITAL - MEDICAL LIBRARY □ Ft. Eustis, VA

Hearon, Pamela K., Asst.Libn.
UNIVERSITY OF FLORIDA - AGRICULTURAL RESEARCH & EDUCATION CENTER - LAKE ALFRED LIBRARY □ Lake Alfred, FL

Hearst, Nancy, Libn.
HARVARD UNIVERSITY - JOHN K. FAIRBANK CENTER FOR EAST ASIAN RESEARCH - LIBRARY □ Cambridge, MA

Heaser, Eileen, Sr.Asst.Ref.Libn.
CALIFORNIA STATE UNIVERSITY, SACRAMENTO - LIBRARY - SCIENCE & TECHNOLOGY REFERENCE DEPARTMENT† □ Sacramento, CA

Heaslip, Lloyd, Dir., Info. & Ref.Br.
CANADA - LIBRARY OF PARLIAMENT □ Ottawa, ON

Heath, Dr. Gordon G., Pres.
VISION INFORMATION PROGRAM, INC. □ Bloomington, IN

Heath, John Wright, Dir./Lib. & Info.Serv.
ATLANTA BUREAU OF PLANNING - LIBRARY □ Atlanta, GA

Heathfield, Cynthia A., Act.Chf.Libn.
U.S. VETERANS ADMINISTRATION (CA-San Francisco) - MEDICAL CENTER LIBRARY □ San Francisco, CA

Heaton, E.
PROCTER & GAMBLE COMPANY - MIAMI VALLEY LABORATORIES - TECHNICAL LIBRARY □ Cincinnati, OH

Heaton, Mrs. G., Hd.
UNIVERSITY OF TORONTO - GENERAL LIBRARY - SCIENCE AND MEDICINE DEPARTMENT □ Toronto, ON

Heaton, Mary B., Bus.Libn.
SUN COMPANY - LIBRARY & INFORMATION SERVICE □ Marcus Hook, PA

Hebert, Fernande, Med.Libn.
MARICOPA COUNTY GENERAL HOSPITAL - MEDICAL LIBRARY □ Phoenix, AZ

Hebert, Francoise, Exec.Dir.
CANADIAN NATIONAL INSTITUTE FOR THE BLIND - NATIONAL LIBRARY SERVICES □ Toronto, ON

Hebert, Gaetan, Media Coord.
COLLEGE LIONEL-GROULX - BIBLIOTHEQUE □ Ste. Therese, PQ

Hebert, John R., Asst.Chf.
LIBRARY OF CONGRESS - HISPANIC DIVISION □ Washington, DC

Hebert, Mary, Libn.
BLUE CROSS HOSPITAL SERVICE, INC. - LIBRARY □ St. Louis, MO

Hebert, R. Vivian, Law Libn.
U.S. ARMY - JUDGE ADVOCATE GENERAL'S SCHOOL - LIBRARY □ Charlottesville, VA

Hecht, Rachel R., Libn.
U.S. DEPT. OF JUSTICE - TAX DIVISION LIBRARY □ Washington, DC

Heck, Paula, Sr.Res.Info.Anl.
MERCK & COMPANY, INC. - MERCK SHARP & DOHME RESEARCH LABORATORIES - RESEARCH INFORMATION SYSTEMS □ Rahway, NJ

Heck, Thomas, Hd.Libn.
OHIO STATE UNIVERSITY - MUSIC LIBRARY □ Columbus, OH

Heckard, David C., Mgr.
ARMCO, INC. - TECHNICAL INFORMATION CENTER □ Middletown, OH

Heckel, J.W., Law Libn.
SANTA CLARA COUNTY LAW LIBRARY □ San Jose, CA

Hecker, Frances, Libn.
TULANE UNIVERSITY OF LOUISIANA - ARCHITECTURE LIBRARY □ New Orleans, LA

Heckman, Florence E., Ref.Libn.
NATIONAL SCIENCE FOUNDATION - LIBRARY □ Washington, DC

Hedderick, Alice Marie, Libn.
ANGLICAN CHURCH OF CANADA - CHURCH HOUSE LIBRARY □ Toronto, ON

Hedges, Barbara, Ref.Libn.
TEXAS A & M UNIVERSITY - REFERENCE DIVISION □ College Station, TX

Hedman, Kenneth W., Assoc.Dir.Libs.
UNIVERSITY OF TEXAS, EL PASO - LIBRARY □ El Paso, TX

Hedrick, David T., AV Libn.
GETTYSBURG COLLEGE - MUSSELMAN LIBRARY - SPECIAL COLLECTIONS □ Gettysburg, PA

Hedrick, Mildred S., Libn.
FIRST UNITED METHODIST CHURCH - ALLEN LIBRARY □ Kalamazoo, MI

Hedrick, Susan K., Libn.
OKLAHOMA STATE DEPARTMENT OF VOCATIONAL AND TECHNICAL EDUCATION - CURRICULUM DIVISION □ Stillwater, OK

Heelen, Catherine A., Libn.
ILLINOIS STATE BOARD OF EDUCATION - MEDIA AND RESOURCES CENTER □ Springfield, IL

Heer, Professor David M., Assoc.Dir.
UNIVERSITY OF SOUTHERN CALIFORNIA - POPULATION RESEARCH LABORATORY - LIBRARY □ Los Angeles, CA

Heeter, Judy, Libn.
ST. CLOUD HOSPITAL - HEALTH SCIENCES LIBRARY □ St. Cloud, MN

Heffernan, Steve, Libn.
CAMPBELL-MITHUN, INC. - RESEARCH INFORMATION CENTER □ Chicago, IL

Heffernan, T.L., Lab.Supv.
TEXAS STATE PARKS & WILDLIFE DEPARTMENT - MARINE LABORATORY LIBRARY □ Rockport, TX

Heffner, Susan R., Asst.Libn.
AMERICAN PSYCHOLOGICAL ASSOCIATION - ARTHUR W. MELTON LIBRARY □ Arlington, VA

Heffron, Paul T., Act.Chf.
LIBRARY OF CONGRESS - MANUSCRIPT DIVISION □ Washington, DC

Hefner, Sr. M. Xavier, Archv./Libn.
SISTERS OF ST. MARY OF NAMUR - MOUNT ST. MARY RESEARCH CENTER □ Kenmore, NY

Hefte, Pearl, Archv.
DAKOTA STATE COLLEGE - KARL E. MUNDT LIBRARY □ Madison, SD

Hegarty, Kevin, Dir.
TACOMA PUBLIC LIBRARY - SPECIAL COLLECTIONS □ Tacoma, WA

Hegel, Richard, Dir. of Lib.Serv.
SOUTHERN CONNECTICUT STATE COLLEGE - H.C. BULEY LIBRARY □ New Haven, CT

Hegenwald, Shirley B., Chf., Lib.Serv.
U.S. VETERANS ADMINISTRATION (LA-Shreveport) - MEDICAL CENTER LIBRARY □ Shreveport, LA

Hehl, Walter A., Hd.
CENTRAL CHRISTIAN CHURCH - LIBRARY □ Lexington, KY

Hehmeyer, Lauren, Ref.Libn.
MISSOURI STATE LIBRARY □ Jefferson City, MO

Hehr, Brenda C., Libn.
CABOT CORPORATION - READING RESEARCH & DEVELOPMENT LIBRARY □ Reading, PA

Heiberg, Dr. Elvin, Pres.
RICE COUNTY HISTORICAL SOCIETY - ARCHIVES □ Faribault, MN

Heidenreich, Rev. Francis J., Libn.
ST. LAWRENCE SEMINARY - LIBRARY □ Mount Calvary, WI

Heiderich, Kathleen, Prof.Asst.
ST. PAUL PUBLIC LIBRARY - CIRCULATION ROOM □ St. Paul, MN

Heidgerd, Lloyd H., Br.Libn.
UNIVERSITY OF NEW HAMPSHIRE - BIOLOGICAL SCIENCES LIBRARY □ Durham, NH

Heidlage, Robert, Lib.Asst.
UNIVERSITY OF MISSOURI - GEOLOGY LIBRARY □ Columbia, MO

Heidle, John, Per.Libn.
ERIE COMMUNITY COLLEGE NORTH - LIBRARY RESOURCES CENTER □ Buffalo, NY

Heidrick, Dana, Libn.
OAKLAND PUBLIC LIBRARY - SCIENCE/ SOCIOLOGY DIVISION □ Oakland, CA

Heigold, William G., Med.Libn.
BLISS (Malcolm) MENTAL HEALTH CENTER - ROBERT J. BROCKMAN MEMORIAL LIBRARY □ St. Louis, MO

Heikkila, Mrs. E., Dir., Med.Rec.
MINERAL SPRINGS HOSPITAL - MEDICAL LIBRARY □ Banff, AB

Heilakka, Dr. Edwin, Orchestra Libn.
CURTIS INSTITUTE OF MUSIC - LIBRARY □ Philadelphia, PA

Heile, Pat, Sec.
ARCHDIOCESE OF CINCINNATI - ARCHIVES □ Cincinnati, OH

Heileman, Gene, Tech.Libn.
WHIRLPOOL CORPORATION - TECHNICAL INFORMATION CENTER □ Benton Harbor, MI

Heim, Keith M., Coord., Spec.Coll.
MURRAY STATE UNIVERSITY - LIBRARY □ Murray, KY

Heiman, Paula, Libn.
CALIFORNIA STATE BANKING DEPARTMENT - LIBRARY □ San Francisco, CA

Hein, Mary, Libn.
NORTHEAST WISCONSIN TECHNICAL INSTITUTE - LEARNING RESOURCE CENTER □ Green Bay, WI

Heinbokel, Mary, Med.Libn.
SACRED HEART HOSPITAL - MEDICAL LIBRARY AND INFORMATION CENTER □ Yankton, SD

Heinbokel, Mary, Ref.Libn.
UNIVERSITY OF SOUTH DAKOTA - CHRISTIAN P. LOMMEN HEALTH SCIENCES LIBRARY □ Vermillion, SD

Heine, Aalbert, Musm.Dir.
CORPUS CHRISTI MUSEUM - STAFF LIBRARY □ Corpus Christi, TX

Heine, R. James
WESTINGHOUSE ELECTRIC CORPORATION - ELECTRICAL SYSTEMS DIVISION - TECHNICAL LIBRARY □ Lima, OH

Heineking, Genevieve, Staff Lit.Chem.
GOODYEAR TIRE AND RUBBER COMPANY - TECHNICAL INFORMATION CENTER □ Akron, OH

PERSONNEL

Heinen, Margaret, Rd.Serv.Libn.
WAYNE STATE UNIVERSITY - ARTHUR NEEF
LAW LIBRARY □ Detroit, MI

Heinonen, Valerie, Res.Mgr.
NATIONAL COUNCIL OF CHURCHES -
INTERFAITH CENTER ON CORPORATE
RESPONSIBILITY □ New York, NY

Heinrich, Dorothy L., Spec.Coll.Libn.
UNIVERSITY OF WISCONSIN, GREEN BAY -
AREA RESEARCH CENTER □ Green Bay, WI

Heinritz, Mrs. Robert, Hd.Libn.
PRINCE OF PEACE LUTHERAN CHURCH -
LIBRARY □ Milwaukee, WI

Heintzelman, Susan, Asst.Dir., Coll.
TEACHERS COLLEGE - LIBRARY □ New York, NY

Heinz, Catharine, Dir.
BROADCAST PIONEERS LIBRARY □ Washington,
DC

Heinz-Boewe, Karl, AV Libn.
UNIVERSITY OF KENTUCKY - MEDICAL
CENTER LIBRARY □ Lexington, KY

Heisa, Glenn, Libn.
WALKER MANUFACTURING CO. - LIBRARY □
Racine, WI

Heisch, John D., Hd.Libn.
OKLAHOMA HISTORICAL SOCIETY - DIVISION
OF LIBRARY RESOURCES □ Oklahoma City, OK

Heise, Dorothy, Tech.Info.Spec.
U.S. DEPT. OF AGRICULTURE - ECONOMICS
AND STATISTICS SERVICE - ESS REFERENCE
CENTER □ Washington, DC

Heise, Marlin L., Hd.Cat.Libn.
MINNESOTA HISTORICAL SOCIETY -
REFERENCE LIBRARY □ St. Paul, MN

Heiser, Lois, Act.Libn.
INDIANA UNIVERSITY - GEOLOGY LIBRARY □
Bloomington, IN

Heiser, Rev. W. Charles, S.J., Libn.
ST. LOUIS UNIVERSITY - DIVINITY LIBRARY □
St. Louis, MO

Heiser, Wilma, Lib.Spec.
PENNSYLVANIA STATE UNIVERSITY - APPLIED
RESEARCH LABORATORY - LIBRARY □ State
College, PA

Heisey, Terry M., Libn.
EVANGELICAL SCHOOL OF THEOLOGY -
ROSTAD LIBRARY □ Myerstown, PA

Heising, Anne S., Libn.
TIME-LIFE BOOKS INC. - REFERENCE LIBRARY
□ Alexandria, VA

Heisler, Helen P., Libn.
SARGENT & LUNDY ENGINEERS - TECHNICAL
LIBRARY □ Chicago, IL

Heiting, John R., Asst.Archv./Rec.Mgr.
UNIVERSITY OF SOUTH CAROLINA -
UNIVERSITY ARCHIVES □ Columbia, SC

Heitman, Roy K., Hd.Ref.Br.
U.S. DEFENSE AUDIOVISUAL AGENCY - STILL
PICTURE LIBRARY □ Washington, DC

Heitz, Thomas R., Chf., Lib.Serv.
NEW YORK STATE DEPARTMENT OF LAW -
LIBRARY □ Albany, NY

Hekman, Sharon, Info.Dir.
PIMA COUNTY JUVENILE COURT CENTER -
LIBRARY □ Tucson, AZ

Helander, Joel, Lib.Comm.Chm.
GUILFORD KEEPING SOCIETY, INC. - LIBRARY
□ Guilford, CT

Helde, Joan, Libn.
GEORGETOWN UNIVERSITY - CENTER FOR
POPULATION RESEARCH - LIBRARY □
Washington, DC

Helfter, Clyde, Cur. of Iconography
BUFFALO & ERIE COUNTY HISTORICAL
SOCIETY - LIBRARY □ Buffalo, NY

Helge, Brian, Assoc.Libn.
LUTHERAN SCHOOL OF THEOLOGY AT CHICAGO
- KRAUSS LIBRARY □ Chicago, IL

Helgeson, Duane, Hd., Physical Sci.
CALIFORNIA INSTITUTE OF TECHNOLOGY -
ROBERT A. MILLIKAN MEMORIAL LIBRARY □
Pasadena, CA

Helguera, Byrd S., Assoc.Dir.
VANDERBILT UNIVERSITY - MEDICAL CENTER
LIBRARY □ Nashville, TN

Helie, Caroline, Phys.Sci.Ref.Libn.
BROWN UNIVERSITY - SCIENCES LIBRARY □
Providence, RI

Heller, Betty, Ser.Libn.
BROWN UNIVERSITY - SCIENCES LIBRARY □
Providence, RI

Heller, James S., Libn.
U.S. DEPT. OF JUSTICE - CIVIL DIVISION
LIBRARY □ Washington, DC

Heller, Louise A., Libn.
TRI-STATE REGIONAL PLANNING COMMISSION
- LIBRARY □ New York, NY

Heller, Sharon, Western Jnl.Acq.Libn.
MATHEMATICAL REVIEWS - LIBRARY □ Ann
Arbor, MI

Heller, Susan J., Regional Libn.
U.S. DEPT. OF HOUSING AND URBAN
DEVELOPMENT - REGION II - LIBRARY □ New
York, NY

Hellickson, Michele, Interpretation Chf.
U.S. NATL. PARK SERVICE - THEODORE
ROOSEVELT NATL. PARK - LIBRARY □ Medora,
ND

Helling, James T., Chf., Rd.Serv.
U.S. AIR FORCE INSTITUTE OF TECHNOLOGY -
LIBRARY □ Wright-Patterson AFB, OH

Hellman, Donna, Lib.Techn.
CANADA - LAW REFORM COMMISSION OF
CANADA - LIBRARY □ Ottawa, ON

Hellwig, E. Nancy, AV Libn.
U.S. VETERANS ADMINISTRATION (NY-
Syracuse) - MEDICAL CENTER LIBRARY □
Syracuse, NY

Helman, Dr. W.P.
UNIVERSITY OF NOTRE DAME - RADIATION
LABORATORY - RADIATION CHEMISTRY DATA
CENTER □ Notre Dame, IN

Helmbold, F. Wilbur, Cur.
SAMFORD UNIVERSITY - BAPTIST HISTORICAL
COLLECTION □ Birmingham, AL

Helmbold, F. Wilbur, Univ.Libn.
SAMFORD UNIVERSITY - HARWELL GOODWIN
DAVIS LIBRARY □ Birmingham, AL

Helmer, Nancy L., Asst.Libn.
BINGHAMTON PSYCHIATRIC CENTER -
PROFESSIONAL LIBRARY □ Binghamton, NY

Helms, Frank Q., Dir. of Lib.Serv.
WEST CHESTER STATE COLLEGE - FRANCIS
HARVEY GREEN LIBRARY - SPECIAL
COLLECTIONS □ West Chester, PA

Helms, Susan, Asst.Libn.
U.S. VETERANS ADMINISTRATION (AL-
Montgomery) - MEDICAL CENTER LIBRARY
(142D) □ Montgomery, AL

Helmstetter, Jeanne G., Res.Assoc.
NEW JERSEY STATE LEAGUE OF
MUNICIPALITIES - LIBRARY □ Trenton, NJ

Helsabeck, Rosemary E., Libn.
FLORIDA STATE COURT OF APPEAL - 3RD
DISTRICT - LAW LIBRARY □ Miami, FL

Helser, Fred, Assoc.Libn.
FRANKLIN UNIVERSITY - LIBRARY □ Columbus,
OH

Helton, Helen, Chf., Tech.Serv.
U.S. AIR FORCE INSTITUTE OF TECHNOLOGY -
LIBRARY □ Wright-Patterson AFB, OH

Heltsley, Mary K., Libn.
FARIBAULT STATE HOSPITAL - LIBRARY □
Faribault, MN

Helyar, L.E.J., Cur. In Graphics
UNIVERSITY OF KANSAS - DEPARTMENT OF
SPECIAL COLLECTIONS □ Lawrence, KS

Helyar, Thelma, Libn.
UNIVERSITY OF KANSAS - CENTER FOR PUBLIC
AFFAIRS □ Lawrence, KS

Hembre, Sara, Asst. Law Libn.
WISCONSIN STATE DEPARTMENT OF JUSTICE
- LAW LIBRARY □ Madison, WI

Hemming, Richard, Prof.Asst.
ST. PAUL PUBLIC LIBRARY - ARTS AND AUDIO-
VISUAL SERVICES □ St. Paul, MN

Hemming, Terry, Circ.Libn.
BRIGHAM YOUNG UNIVERSITY - J. REUBEN
CLARK LAW SCHOOL LIBRARY □ Provo, UT

Hemperley, Mr. Marion R., Dp. Surveyor Gen.
GEORGIA STATE SURVEYOR GENERAL
DEPARTMENT - ARCHIVES □ Atlanta, GA

Hemphill, Piper L., Libn.
POLYMER INDUSTRIES - LIBRARY □ Greenville,
SC

Hench, Joan M., Coll.Dev.Libn.
U.S. ARMY WAR COLLEGE - LIBRARY □ Carlisle
Barracks, PA

Henderer, Carolyn, Libn.
BAHAI REFERENCE LIBRARY OF PEORIA □
Peoria, IL

Henderer, Edmond, Libn.
NATIONAL CAPITAL HISTORICAL MUSEUM OF
TRANSPORTATION - LIBRARY □ Silver Spring,
MD

Hendershot, Dr. Carl H., Publ.
HENDERSHOT BIBLIOGRAPHY & CONSULTANTS
- LIBRARY □ Bay City, MI

Hendershot, Carol, D.P. Specialist
INFORMATION TECHNOLOGY CENTER -
LIBRARY □ New York, NY

Henderson, Albert, Libn.
NEWMAN GROVE CREAMERY COMPANY -
LIBRARY □ Newman Grove, NE

Henderson, Beth, Libn.
LAKE CIRCUIT COURT - LIBRARY □ Crown
Point, IN

Henderson, Carolyn, Sr.Prof.
ALLERGAN PHARMACEUTICALS, INC. -
PROFESSIONAL INFORMATION SERVICES □
Irvine, CA

Henderson, Dan W., Circ./Ser.Libn.
UNIVERSITY OF ILLINOIS MEDICAL CENTER -
ROCKFORD SCHOOL OF MEDICINE - LIBRARY
OF THE HEALTH SCIENCES □ Rockford, IL

Henderson, Diane, Chf.Libn.
UNIVERSITY OF TORONTO - FACULTY OF
LIBRARY SCIENCE LIBRARY □ Toronto, ON

Henderson, E.M., Libn.
LITTON BIONETICS, INC. - SCIENTIFIC
LIBRARY □ Kensington, MD

Henderson, Edith G., Cur./Treasure Rm.
HARVARD UNIVERSITY - LAW SCHOOL
LIBRARY □ Cambridge, MA

Henderson, Ernest W., Chf.Libn.
CHURCH OF JESUS CHRIST OF LATTER-DAY
SAINTS - OAKLAND GENEALOGICAL BRANCH
LIBRARY □ Oakland, CA

Henderson, Fay J., Dir.Lib.Serv.
SPARTANBURG GENERAL HOSPITAL - HEALTH
SCIENCES LIBRARY □ Spartanburg, SC

Henderson, Floyd L., Libn.
U.S. FOREST SERVICE - NORTH CENTRAL
FOREST EXPERIMENT STATION LIBRARY □ St.
Paul, MN

Henderson, Helen H., Libn.
U.S. VETERANS ADMINISTRATION (MO-St.
Louis) - HOSPITAL LIBRARY □ St. Louis, MO

Henderson, Janice E., Libn.
MORGAN, LEWIS & BOCKIUS - LIBRARY □ New
York, NY

Henderson, Jon M., Mgr., Lib.Serv.
HALLMARK CARDS, INC. - CREATIVE
RESEARCH LIBRARY □ Kansas City, MO

Henderson, Katherine Slocum, Lib.Dir.
CLARK COUNTY LAW LIBRARY □ Las Vegas, NV

Henderson, Leonard, Hd., Tech.Serv. LRC
CHICAGO STATE UNIVERSITY - DOUGLAS
LIBRARY □ Chicago, IL

Henderson, Linda E., Info.Ctr.Coord.
ASSOCIATION OF GOVERNING BOARDS OF
UNIVERSITIES AND COLLEGES - TRUSTEE
INFORMATION CENTER □ Washington, DC

Henderson, Lois E., Lib.Supv.
FLORENCE CITY SCHOOLS - CENTRAL
RESOURCE CENTER □ Florence, AL

Henderson, Marjorie A., Mgr., Info.Serv./Lib.
XEROX CORPORATION - OFFICE SYSTEMS
DIVISION - INFORMATION SERVICES/
LIBRARY □ Dallas, TX

Henderson, Dr. Mary C., Cur.
MUSEUM OF THE CITY OF NEW YORK -
THEATRE COLLECTION □ New York, NY

Henderson, Mary Emma, Libn.
ABRAHAM BALDWIN AGRICULTURAL COLLEGE
- LIBRARY □ Tifton, GA

Henderson, Dr. Robbye R., Hd.Libn.
MISSISSIPPI VALLEY STATE UNIVERSITY -
JAMES HERBERT WHITE LIBRARY □ Itta Bena,
MS

Henderson, Ross M., Libn.
VANCOUVER VOCATIONAL INSTITUTE -
LIBRARY □ Vancouver, BC

Henderson, Ruth, Libn.
CUNY - CITY COLLEGE LIBRARY - MUSIC
LIBRARY □ New York, NY

Henderson, Mrs. S.H., Libn.
TRAVIS AVENUE BAPTIST CHURCH - MAURINE
HENDERSON LIBRARY □ Fort Worth, TX

Henderson, Shannon J., Assoc.Libn.
ARKANSAS TECH UNIVERSITY - TOMLINSON
LIBRARY □ Russellville, AR

Henderson, Dr. Sourya, Med.Libn.
AMERICAN CANCER SOCIETY - MEDICAL
LIBRARY □ New York, NY

Hendley, David D., Libn.
BETHLEHEM STEEL CORPORATION - BERNARD
D. BROEKER LAW LIBRARY □ Bethlehem, PA

Hendon, Pamela, Libn.
REYNOLDS METALS COMPANY - REDUCTION
RESEARCH LIBRARY □ Sheffield, AL

Hendrick, Agnes M., Sr.Lit.Sci.
MERCK & COMPANY, INC. - MERCK SHARP &
DOHME RESEARCH LABORATORIES - LIBRARY
SERVICES □ West Point, PA

Hendrick, Karen, Ref.Libn.
TEXAS TECH UNIVERSITY - LIBRARY -
DOCUMENTS DEPARTMENT □ Lubbock, TX

Hendricks, CPT Carl, Lib.Off.
U.S. ARMY HOSPITALS - BLISS ARMY HOSPITAL
- MEDICAL LIBRARY □ Fort Huachuca, AZ

Hendricks, D.R., Pres.
HAYES (Stanley W.) RESEARCH FOUNDATION -
LIBRARY □ Richmond, IN

Hendricks, Epsy Y., Lib.Dir.
ALCORN STATE UNIVERSITY - JOHN DEWEY
BOYD LIBRARY □ Lorman, MS

Hendricks, M., Lib.Ck.
TEHAMA COUNTY LAW LIBRARY □ Red Bluff,
CA

Hendricks, Vicki, British/Amer.Lit.Biblog.
SYRACUSE UNIVERSITY - E.S. BIRD LIBRARY -
HUMANITIES DEPARTMENT □ Syracuse, NY

Hendricks, Dr. William O., Dir.
SHERMAN RESEARCH LIBRARY □ Corona Del
Mar, CA

Hendrickson, Alice, Co-Chm.
LUTHERAN CHURCH LIBRARY ASSOCIATION -
BETHLEHEM LUTHERAN LIBRARY □ Aberdeen,
SD

Hendrickson, Sarah, Lib.Sys.Coord.
INSTITUTE FOR DEFENSE ANALYSES -
TECHNICAL INFORMATION SERVICES □
Arlington, VA

Hendry, Barbara L., Chf., Tech.Serv.Div.
U.S. AIR FORCE - ALBERT F. SIMPSON
HISTORICAL RESEARCH CENTER □ Maxwell
AFB, AL

Hendry, Helen I., Libn.
NOVA SCOTIA RESEARCH FOUNDATION
CORPORATION - LIBRARY† □ Dartmouth, NS

Hendsey, Susanne B., Lib.Dir.
U.S. FEDERAL TRADE COMMISSION - LIBRARY
□ Washington, DC

Heney, James, Asst.Libn.
GENERAL THEOLOGICAL LIBRARY □ Boston, MA

Henke, Dan F., Libn.
UNIVERSITY OF CALIFORNIA, SAN FRANCISCO
- HASTINGS COLLEGE OF THE LAW - LEGAL
INFORMATION CENTER □ San Francisco, CA

Henke, Esther Mae, Hd.Lib.Serv.
OKLAHOMA STATE DEPARTMENT OF
LIBRARIES □ Oklahoma City, OK

Henley, Atha Louise, Libn.
AUBURN UNIVERSITY - VETERINARY MEDICAL
LIBRARY □ Auburn University, AL

Henley, Carol, Info.Spec./Acq.
DIGITAL EQUIPMENT CORPORATION -
CORPORATE LIBRARY □ Maynard, MA

Henley, James E., Dir. of Musm.
SACRAMENTO CITY AND COUNTY MUSEUM -
LIBRARY □ Sacramento, CA

Henn, Barbara, Tech.Serv.Libn.
INDIANA UNIVERSITY - BUSINESS LIBRARY □
Bloomington, IN

Henneberry, Margaret, Exec.Dir.
WORLD PEACE THROUGH LAW CENTER -
INFORMATION CENTER □ Washington, DC

Hennemann, Jean, Tech.Libn.
BELL AEROSPACE TEXTRON - LAWRENCE D.
BELL MEMORIAL LIBRARY □ Buffalo, NY

Hennessy, Claire, Dir.
NEWTOWN HISTORIC ASSOCIATION, INC. -
LIBRARY □ Newtown, PA

Hennessy, Colm, Ref.Libn.
RUSH UNIVERSITY AND MEDICAL CENTER -
LIBRARY □ Chicago, IL

Hennesy, Janet, Prof.Asst.
MINNEAPOLIS PUBLIC LIBRARY &
INFORMATION CENTER - ART, MUSIC & FILMS
DEPARTMENT □ Minneapolis, MN

Henning, K. Louise, Asst.Libn.
UNIVERSITY OF WISCONSIN, MADISON -
KOHLER ART LIBRARY □ Madison, WI

Henning, Margaret, Ed.
CLEVELAND HEALTH SCIENCES LIBRARY -
HEALTH CENTER LIBRARY □ Cleveland, OH

Henning, Mary, Libn.
CANFIELD MEMORIAL LIBRARY - RUSSELL
VERMONTIANA COLLECTION □ Arlington, VT

Henning, Virginia, Ser. & Exchange Libn.
MINNESOTA STATE LAW LIBRARY □ St. Paul,
MN

Hennip, Susan, ILL
EDINBORO STATE COLLEGE - BARON-FORNESS
LIBRARY □ Edinboro, PA

Hennon, John G., Info.Ref.Spec.
UNIVERSITY OF PITTSBURGH - CENTER FOR
INTERNATIONAL STUDIES □ Pittsburgh, PA

Henri, Muriel, Libn.
INDUSTRIAL GRAIN PRODUCTS, LTD. -
RESEARCH & DEVELOPMENT LIBRARY □
Montreal, PQ

Henrich, Paul, Law Libn.
NEW YORK STATE SUPREME COURT - 2ND
JUDICIAL DISTRICT - LAW LIBRARY □
Brooklyn, NY

Henriksen, Astrid, Libn.
CHARLESTON EVENING POST/NEWS AND
COURIER - LIBRARY □ Charleston, SC

Henrikson, Gregor, Libn.
MINNEAPOLIS PUBLIC LIBRARY &
INFORMATION CENTER - GOVERNMENT
DOCUMENTS □ Minneapolis, MN

Henry, Anita, Cat.
BRIGHAM YOUNG UNIVERSITY, HAWAII
CAMPUS - JOSEPH F. SMITH LIBRARY AND
MEDIA CENTER □ Laie, HI

Henry, B. William, Jr., Park Hist.
U.S. NATL. PARK SERVICE - FORT LARNED
NATL. HISTORIC SITE - LIBRARY □ Larned, KS

Henry, Diane, Chf.
DISTRICT OF COLUMBIA PUBLIC LIBRARY -
AUDIOVISUAL DIVISION □ Washington, DC

Henry, Dr. Jeanette
AMERICAN INDIAN HISTORICAL SOCIETY -
LIBRARY† □ San Francisco, CA

Henry, Jeanie, Libn.
ALASKA STATE LEGISLATURE/LEGISLATIVE
AFFAIRS AGENCY - REFERENCE LIBRARY □
Juneau, AK

Henry, Judy G., Libn.
ST. JOSEPH'S HOSPITAL - MEDICAL LIBRARY†
□ Savannah, GA

Henry, Lawrence, Dir.
DELAWARE STATE ARCHIVES □ Dover, DE

Henry, Marcia, Libn.
ENVIRONMENTAL RESEARCH & TECHNOLOGY,
INC. - WESTERN REGIONAL OFFICE - LIBRARY
□ Westlake Village, CA

Henry, Margaret, Acq.
AYERST LABORATORIES - MEDICAL
INFORMATION CENTER □ New York, NY

Henry, Paula M., Acq.Libn.
SUNY - COLLEGE AT GENESEO - MILNE
LIBRARY □ Geneseo, NY

Henry, Sharon, Dp.Libn.
INTERNATIONAL DEVELOPMENT RESEARCH
CENTRE - LIBRARY □ Ottawa, ON

Hensel, Elizabeth, Lib.Ck.
UNIVERSITY HOSPITAL (Louisville General) -
MEDICAL LIBRARY □ Louisville, KY

Henseler, Barbara A., Ref.Libn.
U.S. NATL. DEFENSE UNIVERSITY - LIBRARY □
Washington, DC

Henshaw, Mrs. A., Libn.
SALVATION ARMY GRACE HOSPITAL - LIBRARY
□ Windsor, ON

Henson, Mrs. Gena R., Film Libn.
MISSISSIPPI STATE BOARD OF HEALTH - FILM
LIBRARY □ Jackson, MS

Henson, Jane E., Data Libn.
UNIVERSITY OF WISCONSIN, MADISON - DATA
AND PROGRAM LIBRARY SERVICE □ Madison,
WI

Henson, Judy, Assoc.Dir./Pub.Serv.
FLORIDA INSTITUTE OF TECHNOLOGY -
LIBRARY □ Melbourne, FL

Henson, Llewellyn L., Dir.
FLORIDA INSTITUTE OF TECHNOLOGY -
LIBRARY □ Melbourne, FL

Henzler, Martha, Cat.Libn.
LUTHER COLLEGE - PREUS LIBRARY □ Decorah,
IA

Hepler, Susan J., Chf. of Interpretation
U.S. NATL. PARK SERVICE - PETRIFIED
FOREST NATL. PARK - LIBRARY □ Petrified
Forest Natl. Park, AZ

Heppell, Shirley G., Libn.
CORTLAND COUNTY HISTORICAL SOCIETY -
LIBRARY □ Cortland, NY

Herb, Ben G., Tech. Staff Asst.
TEXAS STATE BUREAU OF ECONOMIC
GEOLOGY - WELL SAMPLE AND CORE LIBRARY
□ Austin, TX

Herbert, Annette F., Libn.-Supv.
KIDDER, PEABODY AND COMPANY, INC. -
LIBRARY† □ New York, NY

Herbert, Faith M., Lib.Techn.
ORANGE COUNTY DEPARTMENT OF
EDUCATION - LIBRARY □ Santa Ana, CA

Herczeg, Claire, Ref.Libn.
R & D ASSOCIATES - TECHNICAL
INFORMATION SERVICES □ Marina Del Rey, CA

Herdendorf, Charles E., Dir.
OHIO STATE UNIVERSITY - CENTER FOR LAKE
ERIE AREA RESEARCH - LAKE ERIE LIBRARY □
Columbus, OH

Herdendorf, Dr. Charles E., Dir.
OHIO STATE UNIVERSITY - FRANZ THEODORE
STONE LABORATORY - LIBRARY □ Put-In-Bay,
OH

Hergonson, Ruth, Ch.Serv.Supv.
CITY OF COMMERCE PUBLIC LIBRARY □
Commerce, CA

Heriot, Caroline C., Law Libn.
COLLEGE OF WILLIAM AND MARY - MARSHALL-
WYTHE LAW LIBRARY □ Williamsburg, VA

PERSONNEL

Heriot, Ruthanne, Spec.Coll.Lbn.
U.S. NATL. PARK SERVICE - HARPERS FERRY CENTER LIBRARY □ Harpers Ferry, WV

Herman, Dorothy W., Lbn.
MARLBOROUGH GALLERY - LIBRARY □ New York, NY

Herman, Georgianna, Lbn. & Supv.
UNIVERSITY OF MINNESOTA - INDUSTRIAL RELATIONS CENTER - REFERENCE ROOM □ Minneapolis, MN

Herman, Kelli J., Lbn.
BISMARCK TRIBUNE - LIBRARY □ Bismarck, ND

Herman, Linda, Med.Lbn.
MISERICORDIA HOSPITAL - WEINLOS MEDICAL LIBRARY □ Edmonton, AB

Herman, Linda E., Spec.Coll.Lbn.
CALIFORNIA STATE UNIVERSITY, FULLERTON - COLLECTION FOR THE HISTORY OF CARTOGRAPHY □ Fullerton, CA

Herman, Margaret, Coord., Coll.Dev.Serv.
ILLINOIS STATE LIBRARY □ Springfield, IL

Herman, Mari
NATIONAL COLLEGE OF EDUCATION - LEARNING RESOURCE CENTERS □ Evanston, IL

Herman, Miriam, Lib.Techn.
UNIVERSITY OF TORONTO - INSTITUTE OF CHILD STUDY - LIBRARY □ Toronto, ON

Hermann, Ann M., Dir.
SENECA FALLS HISTORICAL SOCIETY - LIBRARY □ Seneca Falls, NY

Hermanson, Joni M., Info.Sys.Dir.
FOREST PRODUCTS RESEARCH SOCIETY - ABSTRACT INFO. DIGEST SERVICE - INFORMATION CTR. □ Madison, WI

Hermesch, Monica, Chf.Lbn.
TRAVENOL LABORATORIES, INC. - HYLAND DIVISION - RESEARCH LIBRARY □ Glendale, CA

Hernandez, Arisleida, Lbn.
CORNELL UNIVERSITY - ARECIBO OBSERVATORY - LIBRARY □ Arecibo, PR

Hernandez, Carmen M., Hd., Cat.
UNIVERSITY OF PUERTO RICO - GENERAL LIBRARY □ San Juan, PR

Hernandez, Edna, Lbn.
CALIFORNIA STATE DEPARTMENT OF HEALTH SERVICES - VECTOR BIOLOGY AND CONTROL SECTION - LIBRARY □ Berkeley, CA

Hernandez, Jo Farb, Dir.
TRITON MUSEUM OF ART - LIBRARY □ Santa Clara, CA

Hernandez, Marilyn J., Health Lbn.
MANITOBA - DEPARTMENT OF HEALTH - ANNA E. WELLS MEMORIAL LIBRARY □ Winnipeg, MB

Hernandez, Tamsen M., Dir.
CONFERENCE BOARD, INC. - INFORMATION SERVICE □ New York, NY

Heron, David W., Hd., Rd.Serv.
STANFORD UNIVERSITY - HOOVER INSTITUTION ON WAR, REVOLUTION AND PEACE - LIBRARY □ Stanford, CA

Heron, Judith, Lbn.
NEW BRUNSWICK ASSOCIATION OF REGISTERED NURSES - LIBRARY □ Fredericton, NB

Heroux, Genevieve, Lib.Techn.
ABBOTT LABORATORIES, LTD. - COMPANY LIBRARY □ Montreal, PQ

Heroux, Mr. Rejean, Chf., Tech.Serv.
CANADA - SECRETARY OF STATE - TRANSLATION BUREAU - DOCUMENTATION DIRECTORATE □ Ottawa, ON

Heroux-Bouchard, Helene, Lib.Techn.
HOPITAL DU HAUT-RICHELIEU - BIBLIOTHEQUE MEDICALE □ St-Jean, PQ

Herperger, Mr. D., Staff Archv.
SASKATCHEWAN ARCHIVES BOARD □ Regina, SK

Herr, Marcianne, Cur. of Educ.
AKRON ART MUSEUM - LIBRARY □ Akron, OH

Herrera, Deborah D.
SETON HALL UNIVERSITY - SCHOOL OF LAW - LAW LIBRARY □ Newark, NJ

Herrgesell, Ron, Lbn.
AGWAY, INC. - CORPORATE LIBRARY □ Syracuse, NY

Herring, Geneva N., Med.Lbn.
FLORIDA STATE HOSPITAL - HEALTH SCIENCE LIBRARY □ Chattahoochee, FL

Herring, Dr. Jack W., Dir.
BAYLOR UNIVERSITY - ARMSTRONG BROWNING LIBRARY □ Waco, TX

Herrmann, Gretchen, Soc.Sci.Ref.-Biblog.
SUNY - COLLEGE AT CORTLAND - MEMORIAL LIBRARY □ Cortland, NY

Herrmann, Loretta, Lbn.
NEWMONT MINING CORPORATION - TECHNICAL ENGINEERING LIBRARY □ New York, NY

Herron, Margie E., Dir. of Field Serv.
SOUTH CAROLINA STATE LIBRARY □ Columbia, SC

Hersch, Gisela, Rare Books Lbn.
BUTLER UNIVERSITY - IRWIN LIBRARY □ Indianapolis, IN

Hersey, Dr. David F., Pres.
SMITHSONIAN SCIENCE INFORMATION EXCHANGE, INC. □ Washington, DC

Hershaft, Dr. Alex, Lbn.
VEGETARIAN INFORMATION SERVICE, INC. - INFORMATION CENTER □ Washington, DC

Hershberger, Richard, Assoc.Min.
WESTMINSTER PRESBYTERIAN CHURCH - LIBRARY □ Oklahoma City, OK

Hershcopf, Mrs. Marian, Lbn.
COLORADO STATE DIVISION OF WILDLIFE - RESEARCH CENTER LIBRARY □ Fort Collins, CO

Hershey, Robert A., Dir./State Geologist
TENNESSEE STATE DEPARTMENT OF CONSERVATION - DIVISION OF GEOLOGY - LIBRARY □ Nashville, TN

Hertel, Eugene S., Info.Sci.
UNIROYAL, INC. - UNIROYAL CHEMICAL DIVISION - MANAGEMENT & TECHNICAL INFORMATION SERVICES/LIBRARY □ Naugatuck, CT

Hertel, Maureen, Sec.
WATER QUALITY ASSOCIATION - RESEARCH COUNCIL LIBRARY† □ Lombard, IL

Hertzel, Laurie, Lbn.
DULUTH HERALD & NEWS-TRIBUNE - LIBRARY □ Duluth, MN

Hertzler, Mrs. James, Chm., Lib.Comm.
CUMBERLAND COUNTY HISTORICAL SOCIETY & HAMILTON LIBRARY □ Carlisle, PA

Hertzsprung, Colleen, Ref.Lbn.
PRAIRIE BIBLE INSTITUTE - LIBRARY □ Three Hills, AB

Herzberg, Elsie, Chf. of Circ.Dept.
YESHIVA UNIVERSITY - ALBERT EINSTEIN COLLEGE OF MEDICINE - D. SAMUEL GOTTESMAN LIBRARY □ Bronx, NY

Herzog, Diana E., Sec./Treas.
SMYTHE (R.M.) AND COMPANY - OBSOLETE AND INACTIVE SECURITIES LIBRARY □ New York, NY

Herzog, Kate S., Lbn.
MASSACHUSETTS INSTITUTE OF TECHNOLOGY - AERONAUTICS AND ASTRONAUTICS LIBRARY □ Cambridge, MA

Herzog, Melinda, Dir.
RAILROAD AND PIONEER MUSEUM, INC. - LIBRARY □ Temple, TX

Herzog, Susan, Lbn.
THOMAS, SNELL, JAMISON, RUSSELL, WILLIAMSON AND ASPERGER - LIBRARY □ Fresno, CA

Heseltine, Inez, Asst.Dir.
CANADA - NATIONAL RESEARCH COUNCIL - CANADA INSTITUTE FOR SCIENTIFIC AND TECHNICAL INFORMATION (CISTI) □ Ottawa, ON

Heslin, Catherine, Lbn.
WILLIAM H. RORER, INC. - RESEARCH LIBRARY □ Fort Washington, PA

Hess, Clare Marie, Lbn.
OXFORD UNIVERSITY PRESS, INC. - LIBRARY □ New York, NY

Hess, Gertrude D., Lbn.
HISTORICAL SOCIETY OF HADDONFIELD - LIBRARY □ Haddonfield, NJ

Hess, J. William, Assoc.Dir.
ROCKEFELLER UNIVERSITY - ROCKEFELLER ARCHIVE CENTER □ North Tarrytown, NY

Hess, Jane S., Hd., Tech.Lib.Br.
U.S. NASA - LANGLEY RESEARCH CENTER - TECHNICAL LIBRARY MS 185 □ Hampton, VA

Hess, Joseph, Dir.Educ.Serv.
ANNE ARUNDEL GENERAL HOSPITAL - MEMORIAL LIBRARY □ Annapolis, MD

Hess, Joyce, Art
UNIVERSITY OF TEXAS, AUSTIN - FINE ARTS LIBRARY □ Austin, TX

Hess, M. Cathern, Asst.Hd.Lbn.
INDIANAPOLIS NEWSPAPERS, INC. - INDIANAPOLIS STAR AND INDIANAPOLIS NEWS - REFERENCE LIBRARY □ Indianapolis, IN

Hess, Robert, Info.Off.
CENTER FOR NONPROFIT ORGANIZATION - LIBRARY □ New York, NY

Hess, Robert W., Chf., Tech.Serv.
U.S. DEPT. OF STATE - LIBRARY □ Washington, DC

Hess, Stanley W., Lbn.
NELSON GALLERY-ATKINS MUSEUM - SPENCER ART REFERENCE LIBRARY □ Kansas City, MO

Hess, Stephen H., Dir.
UNIVERSITY OF UTAH - INSTRUCTIONAL MEDIA SERVICES □ Salt Lake City, UT

Hesse, John A., Assoc.Cur.
MEMPHIS STATE UNIVERSITY LIBRARIES - C.H. NASH MUSEUM LIBRARY □ Memphis, TN

Hesse, Sharon, Office Mgr.
CENTER FOR SOUTHERN FOLKLORE - ARCHIVES □ Memphis, TN

Hessel, Carolyn S., Coord.
AMERICAN ASSOCIATION FOR JEWISH EDUCATION - NATIONAL EDUCATIONAL RESOURCE CENTER □ New York, NY

Hessel, William H., Semy.Lbn.
ANDREWS UNIVERSITY - JAMES WHITE LIBRARY □ Berrien Springs, MI

Hessenauer, Jean A., Govt.Doc./AV Lbn.
UNIVERSITY OF MARYLAND, BALTIMORE - SCHOOL OF LAW - MARSHALL LAW LIBRARY □ Baltimore, MD

Hesslein, Shirley B., Assoc.Dir.
SUNY AT BUFFALO - HEALTH SCIENCES LIBRARY □ Buffalo, NY

Hester, Bernice, Ref.Lbn.
U.S. MARINE CORPS - EDUCATION CENTER - JAMES CARSON BRECKINRIDGE LIBRARY & AMPHIBIOUS WARFARE RESEARCH FACILITY □ Quantico, VA

Hester, Helen, Res.Lbn.
MERCK & COMPANY, INC. - MERCK SHARP & DOHME RESEARCH LABORATORIES - RESEARCH LIBRARIES □ Rahway, NJ

Hester, Ralph, Tech.Info.Spec.
NATIONAL INSTITUTE OF ENVIRONMENTAL HEALTH SCIENCES - LIBRARY □ Research Triangle Park, NC

Hesz, Mrs. Bianka M., Med.Lbn.
UNIVERSITY OF PITTSBURGH - PRESBYTERIAN UNIVERSITY HOSPITAL - MEDICAL LIBRARY □ Pittsburgh, PA

Hettinger, Susan, First Asst.
PUBLIC LIBRARY OF CINCINNATI AND HAMILTON COUNTY - EDUCATION AND RELIGION DEPARTMENT □ Cincinnati, OH

Hetu, Sylvie, Lbn.
UNIVERSITE DE MONTREAL - CENTRE DE RECHERCHE SUR LES TRANSPORTS - DOCUMENTATION CENTRE □ Montreal, PQ

Hetzler, Rosemary, Hist.-Lbn.
PIONEERS' MUSEUM - LIBRARY AND ARCHIVES □ Colorado Springs, CO

Hetzner, Bernice M., Hist. of NE Med.
UNIVERSITY OF NEBRASKA MEDICAL CENTER -
MC GOOGAN LIBRARY OF MEDICINE □ Omaha,
NE

Heuer, Barry, Libn.
NOOTER CORPORATION - TECHNICAL LIBRARY
□ St. Louis, MO

Heuermann, Richard W., Lib.Info.Dir.
MC DONNELL PLANETARIUM - LIBRARY □ St.
Louis, MO

Heuser, Gustav, Patent Liason
ENGELHARD CORPORATION - TECHNICAL
INFORMATION CENTER □ Edison, NJ

Hevey, Kathleen G., Municipal Ref.Coord.
VIRGINIA BEACH PUBLIC LIBRARY SYSTEM -
MUNICIPAL REFERENCE LIBRARY □ Virginia
Beach, VA

Hewer, V.R., Group Mgr.
FRANKLIN RESEARCH CENTER - SCIENCE
INFORMATION SERVICES □ Philadelphia, PA

Hewings, Margot, Hd.
METROPOLITAN TORONTO LIBRARY -
MUNICIPAL REFERENCE LIBRARY □ Toronto,
ON

Hewison, Nancy, Hd.Ref.Libn.
UNIVERSITY OF OREGON - HEALTH SCIENCES
CENTER - LIBRARY □ Portland, OR

Hewitt, Helen, Libn.
VICTORY MEMORIAL HOSPITAL - MEDICAL
LIBRARY □ Waukegan, IL

Hewitt, Dr. Helen-Jo J.
UNIVERSITY OF TEXAS, AUSTIN -
LINGUISTICS RESEARCH CENTER - LIBRARY □
Austin, TX

Hewitt, Jan, Marketing Info.Spec.
LEVI STRAUSS & COMPANY - CORPORATE
MARKETING INFORMATION CENTER □ San
Francisco, CA

Hewitt, John H., Libn.
MASSACHUSETTS INSTITUTE OF TECHNOLOGY
- RESEARCH LABORATORY OF ELECTRONICS -
DOCUMENT ROOM □ Cambridge, MA

Hewitt, Julia, Mgr.
GENERAL ELECTRIC COMPANY - MAIN
LIBRARY □ Schenectady, NY

Hewitt, Margaret A., Libn.
HARVARD UNIVERSITY - SCHOOL OF PUBLIC
HEALTH - HEALTH SERVICES LIBRARY† □
Boston, MA

Hewitt, Margaret W., Dir.
NORTHWEST CHRISTIAN COLLEGE - LEARNING
RESOURCE CENTER □ Eugene, OR

Hewitt, Melanie A., Tech.Serv.Libn.
NEW YORK UNIVERSITY - GRADUATE SCHOOL
OF BUSINESS ADMINISTRATION - LIBRARY □
New York, NY

Hewitt, Raymond G., Dir. of Res.
RHODE ISLAND PUBLIC EXPENDITURE
COUNCIL - LIBRARY □ Providence, RI

Hewitt, Vivian D., Libn.
CARNEGIE ENDOWMENT FOR INTERNATIONAL
PEACE - LIBRARY - NEW YORK CENTER □ New
York, NY

Hewlett, Carol C., Libn.
MUNICIPAL TECHNICAL ADVISORY SERVICE -
LIBRARY □ Knoxville, TN

Hewlett, Frances A., Med.Libn.
U.S. NAVY - NAVAL REGIONAL MEDICAL
CENTER (Corpus Christi) - MEDICAL LIBRARY† □
Corpus Christi, TX

Hewlings, Charlotte H., Libn.
DELAWARE COUNTY LAW LIBRARY □ Media, PA

Heyck, H., SDI Libn.
CANADA - TRANSPORT CANADA - LIBRARY &
INFORMATION CENTRE □ Ottawa, ON

Heyd, Michael, Dir.
WILLIAMSPORT HOSPITAL - LEARNING
RESOURCES CENTER □ Williamsport, PA

Heyer, Mr. Terry L., Lib.Dir.
L.D.S. HOSPITAL - MEDICAL LIBRARY □ Salt
Lake City, UT

Heyman, Reba R., Info.Spec.
FOI SERVICES, INC. - LIBRARY □ Rockville, MD

Heyum, Renee, Cur.
UNIVERSITY OF HAWAII - SPECIAL
COLLECTIONS - PACIFIC COLLECTION □
Honolulu, HI

Hi-Choe, Young, Cat.Libn.
VALPARAISO UNIVERSITY - LAW LIBRARY □
Valparaiso, IN

Hibbard, Ms. R. Ashley, Asst.Libn.
NEW YORK STATE DEPARTMENT OF LABOR -
LABOR STAFF ACADEMY LIBRARY □ New York,
NY

Hibberd, Cynthia, Info.Spec.
ARTHUR D. LITTLE, INC. - MANAGEMENT
LIBRARY □ Cambridge, MA

Hibbs, A.C., Mgr.
ADAMS ADVERTISING AGENCY, INC. -
LIBRARY □ Chicago, IL

Hibpshman, Lawrence, State Archv.
SOUTH DAKOTA STATE DEPARTMENT OF
EDUCATION & CULTURAL AFFAIRS - ARCHIVES
RESOURCE CENTER □ Pierre, SD

Hick, Sharon, Assoc.Libn.
ROYAL ONTARIO MUSEUM - LIBRARY □
Toronto, ON

Hickerson, H. Thomas, Chm.
CORNELL UNIVERSITY - DEPARTMENT OF
MANUSCRIPTS AND ARCHIVES □ Ithaca, NY

Hickerson, Joseph C., Hd.
LIBRARY OF CONGRESS - AMERICAN FOLKLIFE
CENTER - ARCHIVE OF FOLK SONG □
Washington, DC

Hickerson, Mary, Report Libn.
VOUGHT CORPORATION - TECHNICAL
INFORMATION CENTER □ Dallas, TX

Hickey, Colleen M., Assoc.Dir.
UNIVERSITY OF DETROIT - SCHOOL OF LAW
LIBRARY □ Detroit, MI

Hickey, Damon D., Assoc.Lib.Dir./Cur.
GUILFORD COLLEGE - LIBRARY □ Greensboro,
NC

Hickey, Elaine, Libn.
ST. FRANCIS HOSPITAL - MEDICAL LIBRARY □
Honolulu, HI

Hickey, Gloria, Libn.
KEUFFEL AND ESSER COMPANY - CHEMICAL
RESEARCH AND DEVELOPMENT LIBRARY □
Morristown, NJ

Hickey, James, Libn.
ATLANTA PUBLIC LIBRARY - SPECIAL
COLLECTIONS DEPARTMENT □ Atlanta, GA

Hickey, Dr. James T., Cur., Lincoln Coll.
ILLINOIS STATE HISTORICAL LIBRARY □
Springfield, IL

Hickey, John, Vietnamese Cat.
CORNELL UNIVERSITY - JOHN M. ECHOLS
COLLECTION ON SOUTHEAST ASIA □ Ithaca, NY

Hickey, M. Eileen, Chf., Lib.Serv.
U.S. VETERANS ADMINISTRATION (VA-
Hampton) - MEDICAL CENTER LIBRARY □
Hampton, VA

Hickey, Margaret, Libn.
U.S. SMALL BUSINESS ADMINISTRATION -
REFERENCE LIBRARY □ Washington, DC

Hickling, Jeanne, Libn.
INDIANA INSTITUTE OF TECHNOLOGY - MC
MILLEN LIBRARY □ Fort Wayne, IN

Hickman, Marlene B., Libn.
SOUTHERN FOREST PRODUCTS ASSOCIATION -
LIBRARY □ New Orleans, LA

Hicks, Anita, Tech.Libn.
HITCO - TECHNICAL LIBRARY □ Gardena, CA

Hicks, Barbara, Libn.
CANADA - CANADIAN ADVISORY COUNCIL ON
THE STATUS OF WOMEN - DOCUMENTATION
CENTRE □ Ottawa, ON

Hicks, Charles, Rd.Adv.
DISTRICT OF COLUMBIA PUBLIC LIBRARY -
WASHINGTONIANA DIVISION □ Washington,
DC

Hicks, Clifford W., Assoc.Dir./Lib.Serv.
TEXAS TECH UNIVERSITY - LIBRARY □
Lubbock, TX

Hicks, Dorthea, Info.Spec.
HENKEL CORPORATION - HENNEPIN
TECHNICAL CENTER LIBRARY □ Minneapolis,
MN

Hicks, Francis P., Info.Anl.
SOUTHWEST RESEARCH INSTITUTE -
NONDESTRUCTIVE TESTING INFORMATION
ANALYSIS CENTER □ San Antonio, TX

Hicks, Kimberly, Lib.Asst.
CONTROL DATA CORPORATION - LIBRARY/
INFORMATION CENTER □ Minneapolis, MN

Hicks, Marilyn, Bus.Libn.
UNIVERSITY OF WISCONSIN, MADISON -
WILLIAM A. SCOTT BUSINESS LIBRARY □
Madison, WI

Hicks, Paul, Asst.Libn.
INDIANA UNIVERSITY OF PENNSYLVANIA -
UNIVERSITY LIBRARY □ Indiana, PA

Hicks, Pauline E., Asst.Univ.Libn.
FLORIDA A&M UNIVERSITY - SCHOOL OF
PHARMACY LIBRARY □ Tallahassee, FL

Hickson, Charlotte A., Libn. & Chm.Acq.
TEXAS TECH UNIVERSITY - LIBRARY □
Lubbock, TX

Hickson, Howard, Musm.Dir.
NORTHEASTERN NEVADA MUSEUM - LIBRARY
□ Elko, NV

Hidalgo, Florence, Hd., Pub.Serv.
MEDICAL COLLEGE OF OHIO AT TOLEDO -
RAYMON H. MULFORD LIBRARY □ Toledo, OH

Hidy, Paula, Ref.Libn.
CAPITAL UNIVERSITY - LAW SCHOOL LIBRARY
□ Columbus, OH

Hieb, Louis A., Hd., Spec.Coll.
UNIVERSITY OF ARIZONA - SPECIAL
COLLECTIONS DEPARTMENT □ Tucson, AZ

Hieb, Roland D., Exec.Dir.
NATIONAL CABLE TELEVISION INSTITUTE -
LIBRARY† □ Denver, CO

Hiebert, Erwin N.
HARVARD UNIVERSITY - HISTORY OF SCIENCE
LIBRARY □ Cambridge, MA

Hiestand, John P., Libn.
UNIVERSITY OF CINCINNATI - OMI COLLEGE
OF APPLIED SCIENCE - TIMOTHY C. DAY
TECHNICAL LIBRARY □ Cincinnati, OH

Hifner, William, Libn.
WASHINGTON POST - LIBRARY† □ Washington,
DC

Higa, Valerie T., Asst. Geographer
PACIFIC SCIENTIFIC INFORMATION CENTER □
Honolulu, HI

Higdon, Hattie, Dir., Tech.Serv./Acq.
ALCORN STATE UNIVERSITY - JOHN DEWEY
BOYD LIBRARY □ Lorman, MS

Higdon, Mary Ann, Doc.Libn.
TEXAS TECH UNIVERSITY - LIBRARY -
DOCUMENTS DEPARTMENT □ Lubbock, TX

Higdon, Thomas D., Libn.
UNIVERSITY OF ARIZONA - ARIZONA HEALTH
SCIENCES CENTER LIBRARY □ Tucson, AZ

Higgason, Elizabeth, Libn.
UNION OIL COMPANY OF CALIFORNIA -
INTERNATIONAL EXPLORATION LIBRARY □ Los
Angeles, CA

Higginbotham, Jay, Local Hist.Spec.
MOBILE PUBLIC LIBRARY - SPECIAL
COLLECTIONS DIVISION □ Mobile, AL

Higginbotham, Susan B., Med.Libn.
LUTHERAN MEDICAL CENTER - MEDICAL
LIBRARY □ Wheat Ridge, CO

Higgins, Bertha, Coord.Tech.Serv.
NOVA SCOTIA - PROVINCIAL LIBRARY □
Halifax, NS

Higgins, Clare, Sci.Libn.
PRATT INSTITUTE - LIBRARY □ Brooklyn, NY

Higgins, Evelyn L., Asst.Libn.
DAYTON ART INSTITUTE - LIBRARY □ Dayton,
OH

Higgins, Hazel M., Libn.
RAYTHEON DATA SYSTEMS COMPANY -
LIBRARY □ Norwood, MA

PERSONNEL

Higgins, James J., Dir.
PACKAGING CORPORATION OF AMERICA -
RESEARCH AND DEVELOPMENT LIBRARY □
Grand Rapids, MI

Higgins, Karen, Hd., Ref.Libn.
JOHNS HOPKINS UNIVERSITY - WILLIAM H.
WELCH MEDICAL LIBRARY □ Baltimore, MD

Higgins, Katherine, Hd.Cat.
WESTFIELD STATE COLLEGE - GOVERNOR
JOSEPH B. ELY MEMORIAL LIBRARY □
Westfield, MA

Higgins, Larry H., Mgr., Educ.
MEAD JOHNSON AND COMPANY - MEAD
JOHNSON INSTITUTE - LIBRARY □ Evansville,
IN

Higgins, Maripat, Res.Libn.
TWENTIETH CENTURY FOX FILM
CORPORATION - RESEARCH LIBRARY □ Beverly
Hills, CA

Higgins, Matthew, Chf., Plan. & Dev.
RHODE ISLAND STATE DEPARTMENT OF STATE
LIBRARY SERVICES □ Providence, RI

Higgins, Patricia, Cat.Libn.
MARICOPA COUNTY LAW LIBRARY □ Phoenix,
AZ

Higgins, Paula, Ref.Libn.
TEXAS A & M UNIVERSITY - REFERENCE
DIVISION □ College Station, TX

Higgins, Vicky L., Dir.Med.Rec.
DEAF SMITH GENERAL HOSPITAL - LIBRARY □
Hereford, TX

Higgins, William David, Asst.Dir.
PRICHARD (Cleveland) MEMORIAL LIBRARY □
Prichard, AL

Higgs, Ms. M.A., Hd., Ref. & Circ.
CANADA - NATIONAL DEFENCE - FORT
FRONTENAC LIBRARY □ Kingston, ON

Higgs, Norman C., Libn.
MACON COUNTY LAW LIBRARY □ Decatur, IL

Higgs, Patricia, Supv.
INSTITUTE OF EARLY AMERICAN HISTORY
AND CULTURE - KELLOCK LIBRARY □
Williamsburg, VA

High, Walter M., Hd. Monographic Cat.
NORTH CAROLINA STATE UNIVERSITY - D.H.
HILL LIBRARY □ Raleigh, NC

Highgas, William, Jr., Libn.
MIDDLESEX LAW LIBRARY ASSOCIATION -
LIBRARY† □ Cambridge, MA

Hihn, Nerisha, Libn.
BROWN & CALDWELL - LIBRARY □ Walnut
Creek, CA

Hiigel, Sharon, Archv.
FRESNO CITY AND COUNTY HISTORICAL
SOCIETY - ARCHIVES □ Fresno, CA

Hike, Clare, Asst.Libn.
BRONSON METHODIST HOSPITAL - HEALTH
SCIENCES LIBRARY □ Kalamazoo, MI

Hilbert-Price, Shirley, Anl.
ANTA CORPORATION - LIBRARY □ Oklahoma
City, OK

Hilborn, Allen C., Pub.Info.Off.
NEW JERSEY STATE MUSEUM - LIBRARY □
Trenton, NJ

Hildebrand, Janice, Libn.
SHEBOYGAN PRESS LIBRARY □ Sheboygan, WI

Hildebrand, Karen, Libn.
CALIFORNIA SCHOOL OF PROFESSIONAL
PSYCHOLOGY - BERKELEY LIBRARY □ Berkeley,
CA

Hildebrand, Linda L., Libn.
OAKLAND UNIVERSITY - LIBRARY □ Rochester,
MI

Hildebrand, N. Louise, Tech.Info.Spec.
U.S. DEFENSE MAPPING AGENCY - AEROSPACE
CENTER - TECHNICAL LIBRARY □ St. Louis, MO

Hildebrandt, Phyllis E., Chf., Lib.Serv.
U.S. VETERANS ADMINISTRATION (MI-Iron
Mountain) - MEDICAL CENTER LIBRARY □ Iron
Mountain, MI

Hildebrant, Kevin, Chf.Instr.
NATIONAL OUTDOOR LEADERSHIP SCHOOL -
OUTDOOR EDUCATION RESOURCE LIBRARY □
Lander, WY

Hildreth, John L., Supv.Rec.Libn.
NEW YORK PUBLIC LIBRARY - GENERAL
LIBRARY OF THE PERFORMING ARTS □ New
York, NY

Hildreth, Mildred, Ref.Libn.
MARSHALL UNIVERSITY - SCHOOL OF
MEDICINE - HEALTH SCIENCE LIBRARIES □
Huntington, WV

Hilgert, Earle, Coll.Dev.
MC CORMICK THEOLOGICAL SEMINARY -
LIBRARY† □ Chicago, IL

Hilgert, Elvire R., Libn.
MC CORMICK THEOLOGICAL SEMINARY -
LIBRARY† □ Chicago, IL

Hilgert, Dr. W. Earle, Act.Libn.
JESUIT SCHOOL OF THEOLOGY IN CHICAGO -
LIBRARY □ Chicago, IL

Hilke, Mary, Exec.Sec. & Cur.
KOOCHICHING COUNTY HISTORICAL SOCIETY
- MUSEUM □ International Falls, MN

Hilker, Emerson W., Dir.
FRANKLIN INSTITUTE - LIBRARY □ Philadelphia,
PA

Hill, Amelita, User.Serv.
ERIC CLEARINGHOUSE ON RURAL EDUCATION
AND SMALL SCHOOLS □ Las Cruces, NM

Hill, Arden G., Libn.
U.S. AIR FORCE BASE - MALMSTROM BASE
LIBRARY □ Malmstrom AFB, MT

Hill, Barbara L., Chf.Libn.
U.S. VETERANS ADMINISTRATION (MI-Battle
Creek) - HOSPITAL LIBRARY □ Battle Creek, MI

Hill, Barbara M., Libn.
MASSACHUSETTS COLLEGE OF PHARMACY &
ALLIED HEALTH SCIENCES - SHEPPARD
LIBRARY □ Boston, MA

Hill, Barbarie
UNIVERSITY AFFILIATED CINCINNATI CENTER
FOR DEVELOPMENTAL DISORDERS - RESEARCH
LIBRARY □ Cincinnati, OH

Hill, Brad S., Cur., Lowry Coll.
NATIONAL LIBRARY OF CANADA - RARE BOOKS
AND MANUSCRIPTS DIVISION □ Ottawa, ON

Hill, Connie, Tech.Libn.
GARRETT CORPORATION - AIRESEARCH
MANUFACTURING COMPANY - TECHNICAL
LIBRARY □ Torrance, CA

Hill, Deane W., Dir.
UNIVERSITY OF WISCONSIN, MADISON -
SCHOOL OF EDUCATION - INSTRUCTIONAL
MATERIALS CENTER □ Madison, WI

Hill, Diane E., Media Libn.
SUNY - UPSTATE MEDICAL CENTER LIBRARY □
Syracuse, NY

Hill, Dorothy, Hd., Acq.
MOUNT SINAI SCHOOL OF MEDICINE OF THE
CITY UNIVERSITY OF NEW YORK - GUSTAVE L.
& JANET W. LEVY LIBRARY □ New York, NY

Hill, Dorothy C., Supv. of Lib.
GTE - COMMUNICATION SYSTEMS DIVISION -
MAIN LIBRARY □ Needham Heights, MA

Hill, E., Spec.Coll.
UNIVERSITY OF WISCONSIN, LA CROSSE -
MURPHY LIBRARY □ La Crosse, WI

Hill, Edwin L., Spec.Coll.Libn.
UNIVERSITY OF WISCONSIN, LA CROSSE -
CENTER FOR CONTEMPORARY POETRY □ La
Crosse, WI

Hill, Eleanor, ILL Libn.
RUSH UNIVERSITY AND MEDICAL CENTER -
LIBRARY □ Chicago, IL

Hill, Elizabeth A., Ref.Libn.
U.S. AIR FORCE - ACCOUNTING AND FINANCE
CENTER - TECHNICAL LIBRARY □ Denver, CO

Hill, Mr. G.R., Chf.Libn.
MC MASTER UNIVERSITY - ARCHIVES AND
RESEARCH COLLECTIONS DIVISION □ Hamilton,
ON

Hill, Hazel, Acq.Libn.
MARSHALL (John) LAW SCHOOL - LIBRARY □
Chicago, IL

Hill, Helen, Libn.
SOCIETY OF MANAGEMENT ACCOUNTANTS OF
CANADA - RESOURCE CENTRE† □ Hamilton, ON

Hill, Howard, Hd.Cat.
OREGON COLLEGE OF EDUCATION - LIBRARY □
Monmouth, OR

Hill, John, Tech.Serv.
SOUTHERN CONNECTICUT STATE COLLEGE -
H.C. BULEY LIBRARY □ New Haven, CT

Hill, John J., Dir.
DALLAS CIVIC GARDEN CENTER - LIBRARY □
Dallas, TX

Hill, Judith, Asst.Libn.
MORGAN, LEWIS & BOCKIUS - LIBRARY □
Philadelphia, PA

Hill, Kenneth, Coord., AV Serv.
CLARK COUNTY COMMUNITY COLLEGE -
LEARNING RESOURCES CENTER □ North Las
Vegas, NV

Hill, Laurie, Libn.
ST. JOSEPH'S GENERAL HOSPITAL - MEDICAL
LIBRARY □ Thunder Bay, ON

Hill, Linda L., Mgr.
CITIES SERVICE COMPANY - ERG - RESEARCH
LIBRARY □ Tulsa, OK

Hill, Dr. Loren G., Dir.
UNIVERSITY OF OKLAHOMA - OKLAHOMA
BIOLOGICAL STATION LIBRARY □ Norman, OK

Hill, M., Libn.
ROSENBERG (Paul) ASSOCIATES - LIBRARY □
Pelham, NY

Hill, May Davis, Assoc.Archv.
UNIVERSITY OF MICHIGAN - MICHIGAN
HISTORICAL COLLECTIONS - BENTLEY
HISTORICAL LIBRARY □ Ann Arbor, MI

Hill, Nancy I., Lib.Techn.
U.S. ARMY - DEFENSE LANGUAGE INSTITUTE -
ACADEMIC LIBRARY □ Monterey, CA

Hill, Philip, Jr.Libn.
UNIVERSITY OF MISSISSIPPI - ARCHIVES &
SPECIAL COLLECTIONS/MISSISSIPPIANA □
University, MS

Hill, Richard L., First Asst., Annex
NEW YORK PUBLIC LIBRARY - ANNEX SECTION
- NEWSPAPERS AND OTHER RESEARCH
MATERIALS COLLECTION □ New York, NY

Hill, Richard L., First Asst., Annex
NEW YORK PUBLIC LIBRARY - ANNEX SECTION
- PATENTS COLLECTION □ New York, NY

Hill, Rowena, Res.Assoc.
LOUISIANA STATE UNIVERSITY - COASTAL
STUDIES INSTITUTE - REFERENCE ROOM □
Baton Rouge, LA

Hill, Ruth E., Oral Hist.Coord.
RADCLIFFE COLLEGE - ARTHUR AND
ELIZABETH SCHLESINGER LIBRARY ON THE
HISTORY OF WOMEN IN AMERICA □
Cambridge, MA

Hill, Susan, ILL Libn.
CLEVELAND HEALTH SCIENCES LIBRARY -
ALLEN MEMORIAL LIBRARY □ Cleveland, OH

Hill, Susan M., Libn.
NATIONAL ASSOCIATION OF BROADCASTERS -
LIBRARY □ Washington, DC

Hill, T.T., Libn.
MARQUETTE COPPERSMITHING COMPANY -
LIBRARY □ Philadelphia, PA

Hill, Vienda, Asst. Law Libn.
HARRIS COUNTY LAW LIBRARY □ Houston, TX

Hill-Masey, Mickey, Acq.Libn.
MEHARRY MEDICAL COLLEGE - MEDICAL
LIBRARY - LEARNING RESOURCES CENTER □
Nashville, TN

Hillard, Col. James M., Dir. Of Libs.
CITADEL - THE MILITARY COLLEGE OF SOUTH
CAROLINA - DANIEL LIBRARY □ Charleston, SC

Hillegas, James B., Pres.
TALLMADGE HISTORICAL SOCIETY - LIBRARY
& ARCHIVES □ Tallmadge, OH

Hillemeier, Edwinna C., Cur.
WINDSOR HISTORICAL SOCIETY - LIBRARY □ Windsor, CT

Hillen, Nancy, Lib.Mgr.
BROWN COUNTY MENTAL HEALTH CENTER - H.H. HUMPHREY MEMORIAL STAFF LIBRARY □ Green Bay, WI

Hillengas, Paul G., Libn.
NEW YORK STATE OFFICE OF MENTAL HEALTH - RESEARCH RESOURCE CENTER □ Albany, NY

Hiller, Steven Z., Libn.
UNIVERSITY OF WASHINGTON - MAP SECTION □ Seattle, WA

Hillerman, John, Mgr.
LA PURISIMA MISSION - ARCHIVES □ Lompoc, CA

Hilliard, Mrs. Howard, Cur.
BUREAU COUNTY HISTORICAL SOCIETY - MUSEUM & LIBRARY □ Princeton, IL

Hilligoss, Leland
ST. LOUIS PUBLIC LIBRARY - HISTORY AND GENEALOGY DEPARTMENT □ St. Louis, MO

Hilligoss, Martha, Chf.Libn.
ST. LOUIS PUBLIC LIBRARY - ART DEPARTMENT □ St. Louis, MO

Hillin, Bill, Supv., Tech.Serv.
UNIVERSITY OF COLORADO, BOULDER - EDUCATIONAL MEDIA CENTER □ Boulder, CO

Hillis, Janet B., Lib.Techn.
SMITH, KLINE & FRENCH CANADA, LTD. - MEDICAL/MARKETING LIBRARY □ Mississauga, ON

Hillman, Raymond W., Hist.Cur.
PIONEER MUSEUM AND HAGGIN GALLERIES - ALMEDA MAY CASTLE PETZINGER LIBRARY □ Stockton, CA

Hills, Virginia Carter, Libn.
NATIONAL GEOGRAPHIC SOCIETY - LIBRARY □ Washington, DC

Hillson, Muriel V., Libn.
NORFOLK REGIONAL CENTER AND NORTHEAST MENTAL HEALTH CLINIC - STAFF LIBRARY □ Norfolk, NE

Hillyer, Georgiana, Chf., Tech.Lib.
U.S. AIR FORCE WEAPONS LABORATORY - TECHNICAL LIBRARY □ Kirtland AFB, NM

Hillyer, Lila N., Libn.
WISCONSIN ALUMNI RESEARCH FOUNDATION - LIBRARY □ Madison, WI

Hilman, Catherine A., Health Sci.Libn.
PERTH AMBOY GENERAL HOSPITAL - MEDICAL LIBRARY □ Perth Amboy, NJ

Hilscher, Arthur, Dir.
CARTER-WALLACE, INC. - LIBRARY □ Cranbury, NJ

Hilt, Gerri, Dir. of Res.
REYNOLDS (Russell) ASSOCIATES, INC. - LIBRARY □ Chicago, IL

Hilt, Lyda, Genealogy Hd.
TIPPECANOE COUNTY HISTORICAL ASSOCIATION - ALAMEDA MC COLLOUGH RESEARCH & GENEALOGY LIBRARY □ Lafayette, IN

Hilt, Pamela S., Co.Libn.
ESTERLINE ANGUS INSTRUMENT CORPORATION - COMPANY LIBRARY □ Indianapolis, IN

Hilton, Beverly, Hd.Ref.
UNIVERSITY OF TEXAS HEALTH SCIENCE CENTER, DALLAS - LIBRARY □ Dallas, TX

Hilton, Pamela M., Libn.
U.S. NAVY - NAVAL AIR TEST CENTER - NAVAL AIR STATION - ENGINEERING & TECHNICAL LIBRARY □ Patuxent River, MD

Hilyard, Stevens W., Lib.Dir.
PITTSBURG STATE UNIVERSITY - LEONARD H. AXE LIBRARY □ Pittsburg, KS

Hinchliffe, Louise M., Lib.Techn.
U.S. NATL. PARK SERVICE - GRAND CANYON RESEARCH LIBRARY □ Grand Canyon, AZ

Hinden, Judee, Advertising
BELL & HOWELL COMPANY - MICRO PHOTO DIVISION - MICROFORMS ARCHIVE □ Wooster, OH

Hindmarsh, Douglas, Ref.Serv.Dir.
UTAH STATE LIBRARY □ Salt Lake City, UT

Hinds, Orlean, Libn.
WHITTAKER CORPORATION - TASKER SYSTEMS DIVISION - TECHNICAL LIBRARY □ Chatsworth, CA

Hines, Eugene E., Exec.Dir.
AMERICAN SOCIETY OF NOTARIES - LIBRARY □ Washington, DC

Hines, Lydia, Tech. Intelligence Sci.
UPJOHN COMPANY - CORPORATE TECHNICAL LIBRARY □ Kalamazoo, MI

Hines, Susie K., Libn.
U.S. NATL. MARINE FISHERIES SERVICE - NORTHEAST FISHERIES CENTER - OXFORD LAB. LIBRARY □ Oxford, MD

Hinkle, John, Outreach Serv.
OKLAHOMA STATE DEPARTMENT OF LIBRARIES □ Oklahoma City, OK

Hinkle, Patricia A., Libn.
WESTINGHOUSE ELECTRIC CORPORATION - TAMPA DIVISION - ENGINEERING LIBRARY □ Tampa, FL

Hinkle, Regina, Libn.
SOUTHERN NATURAL GAS COMPANY, INC. - CORPORATE LIBRARY □ Birmingham, AL

Hinks, Yvonne, Geology Libn.
UNIVERSITY OF CALGARY - ENVIRONMENT-SCIENCE-TECHNOLOGY LIBRARY □ Calgary, AB

Hinnov, Ann, Libn.
ALLENDALE MUTUAL INSURANCE COMPANY - LIBRARY □ Johnston, RI

Hinojosa, Mary Lou, Pharmacy Lib.Techn.
UNIVERSITY OF HOUSTON - COLLEGE OF PHARMACY LIBRARY □ Houston, TX

Hinrichs, Donald F., Sr.Libn.
LOS ANGELES PUBLIC LIBRARY - MUNICIPAL REFERENCE DEPARTMENT - WATER & POWER LIBRARY □ Los Angeles, CA

Hinrichs, Linda Keir, Spec.Coll.Libn.
UNIVERSITY OF DAYTON - ROESCH LIBRARY - SPECIAL COLLECTIONS □ Dayton, OH

Hinsey, Lois, Hist.
U.S. NATL. PARK SERVICE - CHEROKEE STRIP LIVING MUSEUM - RESEARCH LIBRARY □ Arkansas City, KS

Hinshaw, Janet G., Libn.
WILSON ORNITHOLOGICAL SOCIETY - JOSSELYN VAN TYNE MEMORIAL LIBRARY □ Ann Arbor, MI

Hinson, Jean, Act.Libn.
HISTORIC ST. AUGUSTINE PRESERVATION BOARD - HISPANIC RESEARCH LIBRARY □ St. Augustine, FL

Hinson, Maude R., Lib.Cons. & Res.
BIBLIOGRAPHIC SERVICE □ Downers Grove, IL

Hinton, Donald D., Jnl.Prod.Mgr.
NATIONAL TRANSLATIONS CENTER† □ Chicago, IL

Hinton, Floyd G., Mgr., Process Dev.
FRASER INC. - CENTRAL TECHNICAL DEPARTMENT LIBRARY □ Edmundston, NB

Hinton, Rebekah G., Libn.
U.S. PUBLIC HEALTH SERVICE HOSPITAL - PHOENIX INDIAN MEDICAL CENTER - LIBRARY □ Phoenix, AZ

Hinton, Theron D., Jr., Archv.
LOUISIANA STATE OFFICE OF THE SECRETARY OF STATE - STATE ARCHIVES AND RECORDS SERVICE □ Baton Rouge, LA

Hinz, Robert P., Dir.
JACKSONVILLE HEALTH EDUCATION PROGRAMS, INC. - BORLAND HEALTH SCIENCES LIBRARY □ Jacksonville, FL

Hinze, A.C., Law Libn.
EMORY UNIVERSITY - SCHOOL OF LAW LIBRARY† □ Atlanta, GA

Hippe, Erwin L., Libn.
KING COUNTY MASONIC LIBRARY ASSOCIATION - LIBRARY □ Seattle, WA

Hippensteel, Ann, Ref./Biblog.
UNIVERSITY OF MINNESOTA - EDUCATION-PSYCHOLOGY-LIBRARY SCIENCE LIBRARY □ Minneapolis, MN

Hirsch, Miriam, Med.Libn.
SAN FRANCISCO GENERAL HOSPITAL MEDICAL CENTER - BARNETT-BRIGGS LIBRARY □ San Francisco, CA

Hirsch, Patricia Ruth, Libn.
REVIEW & HERALD PUBLISHING ASSOCIATION - LIBRARY □ Washington, DC

Hirsch, Sarah, Asst.Libn.
GILCREASE (Thomas) INSTITUTE OF AMERICAN HISTORY AND ART - LIBRARY □ Tulsa, OK

Hirschfeld, Harriett, Hd.Libn.
LOGAN COLLEGE OF CHIROPRACTIC - LIBRARY □ Chesterfield, MO

Hirschfeld, Robert A., Ed./Publ.
SINGLE DAD'S LIFESTYLE MAGAZINE - LIBRARY □ Scottsdale, AZ

Hirsh, Barbara, Circ.Serv.Libn.
WESTERN CONNECTICUT STATE COLLEGE - RUTH A. HAAS LIBRARY □ Danbury, CT

Hirst, Donna, Tech.Serv.
UNIVERSITY OF IOWA - LAW LIBRARY □ Iowa City, IA

Hirzowski, Jacques, Marketing Mgr.
INFORMATECH - CENTRE QUEBECOIS DE BANQUES D'INFORMATION SCIENTIFIQUE ET TECHNIQUE □ Montreal, PQ

Hirtz, Carrie, Libn.
SKADDEN, ARPS, SLATE, MEAGHER & FLOM - LIBRARY □ New York, NY

Hiscock, Philip, Asst.Archv.
MEMORIAL UNIVERSITY OF NEWFOUNDLAND - FOLKLORE AND LANGUAGE ARCHIVE □ St. John's, NF

Hiscott, Lois, Libn.
NIAGARA HISTORICAL SOCIETY - LIBRARY □ Niagara on the Lake, ON

Hishida, Joan, Tech.Info.Spec.
STAUFFER CHEMICAL COMPANY - DE GUIGNE TECHNICAL CENTER - RESEARCH LIBRARY □ Richmond, CA

Hitchingham, Eileen E., Libn.
OAKLAND UNIVERSITY - LIBRARY □ Rochester, MI

Hitchings, Gladys, Libn.
DAVENPORT ART GALLERY - ART REFERENCE LIBRARY □ Davenport, IA

Hitchings, Sinclair H., Kpr. of Prints
BOSTON PUBLIC LIBRARY - PRINTS □ Boston, MA

Hitchman, Bevette, Registrar
NORTHEASTERN NEVADA MUSEUM - LIBRARY □ Elko, NV

Hite, Frank, Cat.Libn.
SOUTH CAROLINA STATE LIBRARY □ Columbia, SC

Hitt, Raymond W., Dir.Lib.Dev.Div.
TEXAS STATE LIBRARY □ Austin, TX

Hitt, Samuel, Dir.
UNIVERSITY OF NORTH CAROLINA, CHAPEL HILL - HEALTH SCIENCES LIBRARY □ Chapel Hill, NC

Hivale, K.R. Vihari, Asst.Libn. & Coord.
HUMBER COLLEGE OF APPLIED ARTS & TECHNOLOGY - LIBRARY □ Rexdale, ON

Hixon, Janet, Adm.Asst./Ref.
WESTERN STATE UNIVERSITY - COLLEGE OF LAW - LIBRARY □ San Diego, CA

Hixson, Constance, Libn.
UNIVERSITY OF OREGON - EDUCATIONAL POLICY AND MANAGEMENT DIVISION - RESOURCE CENTER □ Eugene, OR

Hixson, Janice, Animal Mgt.Sec.
WASHINGTON PARK ZOO - LIBRARY □ Portland, OR

PERSONNEL

Hiznay, Donna, Ref.Libn.
DIAMOND SHAMROCK CORPORATION -
CORPORATE LIBRARY ▢ Painesville, OH

Hizny, Annette, Assoc.Ser.Libn.
MARYWOOD COLLEGE - LEARNING RESOURCES
CENTER ▢ Scranton, PA

Hlatshwayo, Cecilia, Bus. & Econ.Libn.
U.S. CUSTOMS SERVICE - LIBRARY AND
INFORMATION CENTER ▢ Washington, DC

Hluchyj, N., Asst. for Govt.Aff.
ASBESTOS INFORMATION ASSOCIATION/
NORTH AMERICA - TECHNICAL AND MEDICAL
FILES ▢ Arlington, VA

Ho, Cora C., Assoc.Libn.
TUFTS UNIVERSITY - SCHOOLS OF MEDICINE,
DENTAL MEDICINE & VETERINARY MEDICINE -
HEALTH SCIENCES LIBRARY† ▢ Boston, MA

Ho, Don T., Lib. Group Supv.
BELL TELEPHONE LABORATORIES, INC. -
TECHNICAL LIBRARY ▢ Piscataway, NJ

Ho, Mr. J., Hd., Cat.Div.
CANADA - ENERGY, MINES & RESOURCES
CANADA - CANMET - LIBRARY ▢ Ottawa, ON

Ho, Leo, Media Acq.
WASHTENAW COMMUNITY COLLEGE -
LEARNING RESOURCE CENTER ▢ Ann Arbor, MI

Ho, Lucy, Assoc.Musm.Libn.
METROPOLITAN MUSEUM OF ART - THOMAS J.
WATSON LIBRARY ▢ New York, NY

Ho, Rosa, Libn.
UNIVERSITY OF SASKATCHEWAN - ST.
ANDREW'S COLLEGE - LIBRARY ▢ Saskatoon,
SK

Hoad, Linda, Mss.Libn.
NATIONAL LIBRARY OF CANADA - RARE BOOKS
AND MANUSCRIPTS DIVISION ▢ Ottawa, ON

Hoagland, Joan, Dept.Hd.
CLEVELAND PUBLIC LIBRARY - FINE ARTS
DEPARTMENT ▢ Cleveland, OH

Hoare, Mr. C.G.D., Supv., Sci.Info.
HOFFMANN-LA ROCHE, LTD. - CORPORATE
LIBRARY ▢ Vaudreuil, PQ

Hoare, Valerie E., Chf.Libn.
CANADA - ENERGY, MINES & RESOURCES
CANADA - SURVEYS & MAPPING BRANCH -
LIBRARY ▢ Ottawa, ON

Hobbs, Anna, Lib.Asst.
MINNEAPOLIS PUBLIC LIBRARY &
INFORMATION CENTER - HISTORY
DEPARTMENT ▢ Minneapolis, MN

Hobbs, Barbara H., Chf., Lib.Serv.
U.S. VETERANS ADMINISTRATION (TX-Waco) -
MEDICAL CENTER LIBRARY ▢ Waco, TX

Hobbs, Jim, Tech.Libn.
GULF SOUTH RESEARCH INSTITUTE - LIBRARY
▢ New Orleans, LA

Hobbs, John, Res.Assoc.
MISSOURI STATE DIVISION OF COMMUNITY
AND ECONOMIC DEVELOPMENT - RESEARCH
LIBRARY ▢ Jefferson City, MO

Hobbs, Mary, Trade Spec.
U.S. DEPT. OF COMMERCE - INTERNATIONAL
TRADE ADMINISTRATION - MINNEAPOLIS
DISTRICT OFFICE LIBRARY ▢ Minneapolis, MN

Hobby, Daniel T., Exec.Dir.
FORT LAUDERDALE HISTORICAL SOCIETY -
LIBRARY & ARCHIVES ▢ Fort Lauderdale, FL

Hobin, James R., Libn.
ALBANY INSTITUTE OF HISTORY AND ART -
MC KINNEY LIBRARY ▢ Albany, NY

Hobson, Alice, Asst.Libn.
GENERAL MOTORS CORPORATION - LEGAL
STAFF LIBRARY ▢ Detroit, MI

Hobson, Kitty A., Archv.
OSHKOSH PUBLIC MUSEUM - LIBRARY &
ARCHIVES ▢ Oshkosh, WI

Hobson, Kitty A., Archv./Hist.Libn.
UNITED METHODIST CHURCH - WISCONSIN
CONFERENCE - ARCHIVES ▢ Oshkosh, WI

Hobson, Pam, Assoc.Dir./Tech.Serv.
FLORIDA INSTITUTE OF TECHNOLOGY -
LIBRARY ▢ Melbourne, FL

Hoch, Minnie B., Dir.
COMMUNITY COLLEGE OF BALTIMORE - BARD
LIBRARY - SPECIAL COLLECTIONS ▢ Baltimore,
MD

Hoch, Sandy, Asst.Libn.
DISTRICT ONE TECHNICAL INSTITUTE -
LIBRARY - EDUCATIONAL RESOURCE CENTER ▢
Eau Claire, WI

Hochberg, Alan C., Asst.Chf.Libn.
SUNY - AGRICULTURAL AND TECHNICAL
COLLEGE AT FARMINGDALE - THOMAS D.
GREENLEY LIBRARY ▢ Farmingdale, NY

Hochstettler, June, Asst.Libn.
GRACE COLLEGE OF THE BIBLE - LIBRARY ▢
Omaha, NE

Hocker, Sarah H., Botany Libn.
UNIVERSITY OF KANSAS - DEPARTMENT OF
SPECIAL COLLECTIONS ▢ Lawrence, KS

Hodapp, Gladys, Asst.Libn.
COLLEGE OF INSURANCE - INSURANCE
SOCIETY OF NEW YORK - LIBRARY ▢ New York,
NY

Hodapp, Lawrence C., Controller
NEWBERRY LIBRARY ▢ Chicago, IL

Hodder, Alfred A., Pres.
MEDIC ALERT FOUNDATION INTERNATIONAL -
CENTRAL REFERENCE FILE OF MEMBERSHIP† ▢
Turlock, CA

Hodge, James, Jr., Partner
FULLER, HENRY, HODGE & SNYDER - LIBRARY†
▢ Toledo, OH

Hodge, Patricia, Libn.
EXXON BIOMEDICAL SCIENCES INC. - LIBRARY
▢ East Millstone, NJ

Hodge, Ruth E., Cat.Libn.
U.S. ARMY WAR COLLEGE - LIBRARY ▢ Carlisle
Barracks, PA

Hodges, Fletcher, Jr., Cur.
UNIVERSITY OF PITTSBURGH - FOSTER HALL
COLLECTION ▢ Pittsburgh, PA

Hodges, Kathy, Sr.Libn.
JOHNS-MANVILLE SALES CORPORATION -
CORPORATE INFORMATION CENTER ▢ Denver,
CO

Hodges, Susan, Hd., Ser.Serv.
INTERNATIONAL DEVELOPMENT RESEARCH
CENTRE - LIBRARY ▢ Ottawa, ON

Hodges, T. Mark, Dir.
VANDERBILT UNIVERSITY - MEDICAL CENTER
LIBRARY ▢ Nashville, TN

Hodges, Thelma F., Assoc.Libn.Tech.Serv
CHRISTIAN THEOLOGICAL SEMINARY -
LIBRARY ▢ Indianapolis, IN

Hodgins, R., Chf., Pub.Serv.
CANADA - AGRICULTURE CANADA - LIBRARIES
DIVISION ▢ Ottawa, ON

Hodgson, James, Acq.Libn.
HARVARD UNIVERSITY - FINE ARTS LIBRARY ▢
Cambridge, MA

Hodgson, John C., Chf.Libn.
NEW YORK DAILY NEWS - LIBRARY ▢ New
York, NY

Hodgson, Myra, Owner
ACQUIRE INFORMATION - INFORMATION
CENTER ▢ Palo Alto, CA

Hodina, Alfred, Hd.
UNIVERSITY OF CALIFORNIA, SANTA BARBARA
- SCIENCES-ENGINEERING LIBRARY ▢ Santa
Barbara, CA

Hodock, Irene, Libn.
INDIANA STATE SCHOOL FOR THE DEAF -
LIBRARY ▢ Indianapolis, IN

Hoeck, Albertha, Mgr.
MEIDINGER, INC. - INFORMATION CENTER ▢
Louisville, KY

Hoehn, Philip, Libn./Map Rm.
UNIVERSITY OF CALIFORNIA, BERKELEY -
GOVERNMENT DOCUMENTS DEPARTMENT ▢
Berkeley, CA

Hoehn, Philip, Map Libn.
UNIVERSITY OF CALIFORNIA, BERKELEY - MAP
ROOM ▢ Berkeley, CA

Hoelle, Dolores M., Libn.
PRINCETON UNIVERSITY - ENGINEERING
LIBRARY ▢ Princeton, NJ

Hoelle, Edith, Libn.
GLOUCESTER COUNTY HISTORICAL SOCIETY -
LIBRARY ▢ Woodbury, NJ

Hoeman, Mary Ann, Asst.Libn.
LOGAN COLLEGE OF CHIROPRACTIC - LIBRARY
▢ Chesterfield, MO

Hoerman, Heidi, Hd., Cat.
TEACHERS COLLEGE - LIBRARY ▢ New York, NY

Hoessle, Charles, Dp.Dir.
ST. LOUIS ZOOLOGICAL PARK - LIBRARY ▢ St.
Louis, MO

Hoetzer, Walter G., Sec./Treas.
INTERNATIONAL ASSOCIATION FOR
IDENTIFICATION - LIBRARY ▢ Utica, NY

Hoey, Evelyn L., Dir.
SUNY - UPSTATE MEDICAL CENTER LIBRARY ▢
Syracuse, NY

Hofer, Sherry, Hd., Circ.
UNIVERSITY OF WISCONSIN, WHITEWATER -
LIBRARY & LEARNING RESOURCES ▢
Whitewater, WI

Hoff, Carole, Sci.Info.Coord.
AMERICAN MC GAW - TECHNICAL
INFORMATION CENTER ▢ Santa Ana, CA

Hoff, Virginia, Libn.
RIGHT TO LIFE LEAGUE OF SOUTHERN
CALIFORNIA - LIBRARY† ▢ Los Angeles, CA

Hoffenberg, Bernice, Libn.
CONGREGATION BRITH SHALOM - MORRIS P.
RADOV JEWISH CENTER LIBRARY ▢ Erie, PA

Hoffenberg, Ruth, Asst. Libn.
LENOX HILL HOSPITAL - HEALTH SCIENCES
LIBRARY ▢ New York, NY

Hofferberth, Cindy, Dir. of Musm.
CARROLL COUNTY FARM MUSEUM - LANDON
BURNS MEMORIAL LIBRARY ▢ Westminster, MD

Hoffman, David, Chf.Libn.
NEWSDAY, INC. - LIBRARY ▢ Melville, NY

Hoffman, David R., Dir., Lib.Serv.Div.
PENNSYLVANIA STATE LIBRARY ▢ Harrisburg,
PA

Hoffman, Donna, Lib.Asst.
UNIVERSITY CONGREGATIONAL CHURCH -
LIBRARY ▢ Seattle, WA

Hoffman, Elliott W., Dir.
WEBSTER (Noah) FOUNDATION & HISTORICAL
SOCIETY OF WEST HARTFORD - LIBRARY ▢
West Hartford, CT

Hoffman, Gladys C., Cat.
AMERICAN PHILATELIC RESEARCH LIBRARY ▢
State College, PA

Hoffman, Helen, Libn.
RUTGERS UNIVERSITY, THE STATE
UNIVERSITY OF NEW JERSEY - WAKSMAN
INSTITUTE OF MICROBIOLOGY LIBRARY ▢
Piscataway, NJ

Hoffman, Jane, Tax Libn.
DEWEY, BALLANTINE, BUSHBY, PALMER &
WOOD - LIBRARY ▢ New York, NY

Hoffman, Margaret, Tech.Serv.Libn.
HAHNEMANN MEDICAL COLLEGE & HOSPITAL -
WARREN H. FAKE LIBRARY ▢ Philadelphia, PA

Hoffman, Mary Ann, Coord., Spec.Coll.
WRIGHT STATE UNIVERSITY - HEALTH
SCIENCES LIBRARY ▢ Dayton, OH

Hoffman, Michael, Dir. of Marketing
INTERNATIONAL FOODSERVICE
MANUFACTURERS ASSOCIATION -
INFORMATION SERVICE† ▢ Chicago, IL

Hoffman, Richard, Cat.
BIOLA COLLEGE, INC. - LIBRARY ▢ La Mirada,
CA

Hoffmann, John, Libn.
UNIVERSITY OF ILLINOIS - ILLINOIS
HISTORICAL SURVEY LIBRARY ▢ Urbana, IL

Hoffsis, Wallis D., Acq.Libn.
FLORIDA STATE UNIVERSITY - LAW LIBRARY ▢
Tallahassee, FL

Hollyer, Cameron, Doyle/Am.Lit.Spec.
METROPOLITAN TORONTO LIBRARY -
LITERATURE DEPARTMENT □ Toronto, ON

Holm, Carl B., Principal Planner
CUMBERLAND COUNTY PLANNING BOARD -
TECHNICAL REFERENCE LIBRARY □ Bridgeton,
NJ

Holman, Anna, Libn.
UNIVERSITY OF WESTERN ONTARIO -
FACULTY OF EDUCATION LIBRARY □ London,
ON

Holman, John M., Cur.
MEETING HOUSE GREEN MEMORIAL AND
HISTORICAL ASSOCIATION, INC. - TUCK
MEMORIAL MUSEUM - LIBRARY □ Hampton, NH

Holmen, Ginny, Law Libn.
MENDOCINO COUNTY LAW LIBRARY □ Ukiah,
CA

Holmer, Eileen, Ref.Libn.
DEERE & COMPANY - LIBRARY □ Moline, IL

Holmes, Andrew, Film Libn.
UNIVERSITY OF WISCONSIN, MADISON -
BUREAU OF AUDIOVISUAL INSTRUCTION -
LIBRARY □ Madison, WI

Holmes, Bettie S., Libn.
BALTIMORE COUNTY GENERAL HOSPITAL -
HEALTH SCIENCES LIBRARY □ Randallstown,
MD

Holmes, Bonnie M., Supv. Law Lib.Serv.
TENNESSEE VALLEY AUTHORITY - LAW
LIBRARY □ Knoxville, TN

Holmes, Dr. David, Dir.
UNIVERSITY OF OTTAWA - VANIER MEDICAL,
SCIENCE & ENGINEERING LIBRARY □ Ottawa,
ON

Holmes, Gabrielle, Libn.
SACRAMENTO PUBLIC LIBRARY - BUSINESS &
MUNICIPAL DEPARTMENT □ Sacramento, CA

Holmes, Hilda, Libn.
PRUDENTIAL INSURANCE COMPANY OF
AMERICA - WESTERN HOME OFFICE -
BUSINESS LIBRARY □ Van Nuys, CA

Holmes, James F., Prog.Coord.
U.S. BUREAU OF THE CENSUS - REGIONAL
DATA USER SERVICE - KANSAS CITY
REGIONAL OFFICE - LIBRARY □ Kansas City, KS

Holmes, Janet, Cur.Asst.
ROYAL ONTARIO MUSEUM - CANADIANA
GALLERY LIBRARY □ Toronto, ON

Holmes, Jill, Educ.Libn.
OKLAHOMA STATE UNIVERSITY - SOCIAL
SCIENCE DIVISION □ Stillwater, OK

Holmes, Johanne, Ser. & Circ.Libn.
DISTRICT OF COLUMBIA GENERAL HOSPITAL -
LIBRARY □ Washington, DC

Holmes, Kent
WESTERN STATE UNIVERSITY - COLLEGE OF
LAW - LIBRARY □ Fullerton, CA

Holmes, Linda, Asst.Libn.
BROOKLYN LAW SCHOOL - LAW LIBRARY □
Brooklyn, NY

Holmes, Lois A., Supv., Lib. & Files
U.S. DEPT. OF ENERGY - PACIFIC NORTHWEST
LABORATORY - TECHNICAL INFO. SECT. □
Richland, WA

Holmes, Marion C., Archv.
SAN MATEO COUNTY HISTORICAL
ASSOCIATION - LIBRARY □ San Mateo, CA

Holmes, W., Lib.Techn.
BRITISH COLUMBIA ALCOHOL AND DRUG
PROGRAMS - LIBRARY □ Vancouver, BC

Holmquist, Carolyn J., Hd.
SEATTLE PUBLIC LIBRARY - ART AND MUSIC
DEPARTMENT† □ Seattle, WA

Holobeck, Noel C., Chf.Libn.
ST. LOUIS PUBLIC LIBRARY - HISTORY AND
GENEALOGY DEPARTMENT □ St. Louis, MO

Holoch, Alan, Asst.Dir.
UNIVERSITY OF SOUTHERN CALIFORNIA - LAW
CENTER LIBRARY† □ Los Angeles, CA

Holohan, John S., Ref.Libn.
TUFTS UNIVERSITY - SCHOOLS OF MEDICINE,
DENTAL MEDICINE & VETERINARY MEDICINE -
HEALTH SCIENCES LIBRARY† □ Boston, MA

Holscher, Marilyn Reed, Dir.
HINCKLEY FOUNDATION MUSEUM - LIBRARY □
Ithaca, NY

Holsinger, Katherine, Film Lib.Mgr.
UNIVERSITY OF ARIZONA - DIVISION OF
MEDIA & INSTRUCTIONAL SERVICES - FILM
LIBRARY □ Tucson, AZ

Holst, Jerome A., Med.Libn.
GOOD SAMARITAN HOSPITAL OF ORANGE
COUNTY, INC. - MEDICAL LIBRARY □ Anaheim,
CA

Holst, Ruth, Med.Libn.
COLUMBIA HOSPITAL - MEDICAL LIBRARY □
Milwaukee, WI

Holston, Kim, Libn./Sec.
AMERICAN INSTITUTE FOR PROPERTY &
LIABILITY UNDERWRITERS - INSURANCE
INSTITUTE OF AMERICA - LIBRARY □ Malvern,
PA

Holt, Agnes M., Libn.
LOS ANGELES BAPTIST COLLEGE - ROBERT L.
POWELL MEMORIAL LIBRARY □ Newhall, CA

Holt, Barbara C., Assoc.Libn.
PERKINS, COIE, STONE, OLSEN & WILLIAMS -
LAW LIBRARY □ Seattle, WA

Holt, Daniel D., Hd., Field Serv.Sect.
ILLINOIS STATE HISTORICAL LIBRARY □
Springfield, IL

Holt, Janice C., Hd.Libn.
MARYLAND NATIONAL CAPITAL PARK AND
PLANNING COMMISSION - LIBRARY □ Silver
Spring, MD

Holt, June C., Libn.
MASSACHUSETTS REHABILITATION
COMMISSION - LIBRARY □ Boston, MA

Holt, Laura J., Libn.
MUSEUM OF NEW MEXICO - LABORATORY OF
ANTHROPOLOGY - LIBRARY □ Santa Fe, NM

Holt, Marian, Rd.Adv.
DISTRICT OF COLUMBIA PUBLIC LIBRARY -
BIOGRAPHY DIVISION □ Washington, DC

Holt, Mary, Libn.
CHARITY HOSPITAL - SCHOOL OF NURSING -
LIBRARY □ New Orleans, LA

Holt, Wendy M., Assoc.Libn.
CARPENTER TECHNOLOGY CORPORATION -
RESEARCH AND DEVELOPMENT CENTER
LIBRARY □ Reading, PA

Holtman, Eugene, Asst.Dir.
EASTERN MICHIGAN UNIVERSITY - CENTER OF
EDUCATIONAL RESOURCES - ARCHIVES/
SPECIAL COLLECTIONS □ Ypsilanti, MI

Holton, Alice K., Lib.Serv.Asst.
UNIVERSITY OF PENNSYLVANIA - NEW
BOLTON CENTER - JEAN AUSTIN DU PONT
LIBRARY □ Kennett Square, PA

Holton, Arthur A., Lib.Supv.
ARIZONA-SONORA DESERT MUSEUM - LIBRARY
□ Tucson, AZ

Holton, Charlotte, Libn.
AMERICAN MUSEUM OF NATURAL HISTORY -
OSBORN LIBRARY OF VERTEBRATE
PALEONTOLOGY† □ New York, NY

Holton, Edwin, Mgr./Comp. Searching
FLORIDA STATE UNIVERSITY - CTR. FOR
STUDIES IN VOCATIONAL EDUC. - FLORIDA
EDUCATORS INFO. SERV. □ Tallahassee, FL

Holton, Mark, Cur.
CONFEDERATION CENTRE ART GALLERY AND
MUSEUM - ART REFERENCE LIBRARY □
Charlottetown, PE

Holtz, Jerome, Hd., Biblog. Control
TEACHERS COLLEGE - LIBRARY □ New York, NY

Holtz, Virginia, Dir.
UNIVERSITY OF WISCONSIN, MADISON -
CENTER FOR HEALTH SCIENCES LIBRARIES □
Madison, WI

Holum, Katharine, Music Libn.
UNIVERSITY OF MINNESOTA - MUSIC LIBRARY
□ Minneapolis, MN

Holz, Carole, Asst.Libn.
SUN LIFE ASSURANCE COMPANY OF CANADA -
REFERENCE LIBRARY □ Wellesley Hills, MA

Holz, Gloria, Circ./Reserve Libn.
UNIVERSITY OF WISCONSIN, MADISON - LAW
LIBRARY □ Madison, WI

Holzbauer, H., Chief Libn.
U.S. DEFENSE INTELLIGENCE AGENCY -
LIBRARY RTS-ZA □ Washington, DC

Holzer, Francine, Hd.Libn.
METROMEDIA INC. - CORPORATE RESEARCH
LIBRARY □ New York, NY

Holzmann, Thomas, Libn.
PRINCETON UNIVERSITY - OFFICE OF
POPULATION RESEARCH - LIBRARY □ Princeton,
NJ

Hom, Kimiyo T., Libn.
UNIVERSITY OF CALIFORNIA, BERKELEY -
ASTRONOMY-MATHEMATICS-STATISTICS-
COMPUTER SCIENCES LIBRARY □ Berkeley, CA

Hom, Lily W., Tech.Info.Spec.
U.S. VETERANS ADMINISTRATION (NY-New
York) - OFFICE OF TECHNOLOGY TRANSFER -
REFERENCE COLLECTION □ New York, NY

Homan, Michael, Hd., Info.Serv.
UPJOHN COMPANY - CORPORATE TECHNICAL
LIBRARY □ Kalamazoo, MI

Homer, Ruth, Cat., ILL
PHILADELPHIA COLLEGE OF BIBLE - SCOFIELD-
HILL MEMORIAL LIBRARY □ Langhorne, PA

Homeyer, Mrs. Charles W., Jr., Libn.
FIRST CONGREGATIONAL CHURCH IN
WELLESLEY HILLS - LIBRARY† □ Wellesley Hills,
MA

Homrighausen, Carol L., Libn.
WOODSIDE RECEIVING HOSPITAL - STAFF
RESOURCE LIBRARY/PATIENTS' LIBRARY □
Youngstown, OH

Homsey, S., Libn.
DELAWARE MUSEUM OF NATURAL HISTORY -
LIBRARY □ Greenville, DE

Honeychurch, Deborah, Hd.
LOUISIANA STATE UNIVERSITY - NEWSPAPER-
MICROFORM ROOMS □ Baton Rouge, LA

Honeywell, Joan L., Libn.
BRITISH COLUMBIA LAW LIBRARY
FOUNDATION - VANCOUVER COURTHOUSE
LIBRARY □ Vancouver, BC

Honhart, Dr. Frederick L., Dir.
MICHIGAN STATE UNIVERSITY - UNIVERSITY
ARCHIVES AND HISTORICAL COLLECTIONS □
East Lansing, MI

Honig, Dale, Lib. Chairperson
CONGREGATION KENESETH ISRAEL - LIBRARY
□ Allentown, PA

Honjo, Miss Tatsuko, Dir., Info.Off.Serv.
CHAMBER OF COMMERCE OF HAWAII -
INFORMATION OFFICE □ Honolulu, HI

Honor, Naomi Goldberg, Libn.
ADATH JESHURUN CONGREGATION - JENNY
GROSS MEMORIAL LIBRARY □ Minneapolis, MN

Hood, Howard A., Legal Info.Spec.
VANDERBILT UNIVERSITY LAW LIBRARY □
Nashville, TN

Hood, Lawrence, Acq.Libn.
BRIGHAM YOUNG UNIVERSITY - J. REUBEN
CLARK LAW SCHOOL LIBRARY □ Provo, UT

Hood, Mary D., Hd., Pub.Serv.
UNIVERSITY OF SANTA CLARA - EDWIN A.
HEAFEY LAW LIBRARY □ Santa Clara, CA

Hood, Sandi, Cat.
DAUGHTERS OF THE REPUBLIC OF TEXAS -
LIBRARY □ San Antonio, TX

Hoogerhyde, L., Dir., Educ.
AMERICAN SOCIETY OF SAFETY ENGINEERS -
TECHNICAL INFORMATION CENTER □ Park
Ridge, IL

Hoogerwerf, Sharon, Libn.
GOETHE INSTITUTE ATLANTA - GERMAN
CULTURAL CENTER - LIBRARY □ Atlanta, GA

Hoogland, Sandra, Libn.
MOTOROLA, INC. - SYSTEMS DIVISION -
TECHNICAL LIBRARY □ Franklin Park, IL

Hook, Carolyn A., Hd.
WASHINGTON STATE UNIVERSITY -
EDUCATION LIBRARY □ Pullman, WA

Hook, Janet, Circ.Libn.
KENDALL SCHOOL OF DESIGN - LEARNING
RESOURCE CENTER □ Grand Rapids, MI

Hook, Sara Anne, Asst.Libn.
BLODGETT MEMORIAL MEDICAL CENTER -
RICHARD ROOT SMITH LIBRARY □ Grand
Rapids, MI

Hooker, Ida M., Libn.
MOUNTAIN BELL TELEPHONE COMPANY -
LIBRARY □ Denver, CO

Hooker, Lloyd W., Libn.
U.S. DEPT. OF JUSTICE - FEDERAL PRISON
SYSTEM - LIBRARY □ Washington, DC

Hooker, Marliss, Ref.Libn.
UNIVERSITY OF CONNECTICUT - HEALTH
CENTER - LYMAN MAYNARD STOWE LIBRARY □
Farmington, CT

Hooks, James, Asst.Libn.
INDIANA UNIVERSITY OF PENNSYLVANIA -
UNIVERSITY LIBRARY □ Indiana, PA

Hooks, Michael Q., Assoc.Archv.
TEXAS TECH UNIVERSITY - SOUTHWEST
COLLECTION □ Lubbock, TX

Hoolihan, Christopher, Rare Bk.Libn.
WASHINGTON UNIVERSITY - SCHOOL OF
MEDICINE LIBRARY □ St. Louis, MO

Hooper, Dorothy, Chm., Lib.Comm.
FIRST UNITED METHODIST CHURCH OF
ALHAMBRA - LIBRARY □ Alhambra, CA

Hooper, Ione, Libn.
ALBERTA - DEPARTMENT OF THE
ENVIRONMENT - LIBRARY □ Edmonton, AB

Hooper, Jimmie, Asst.Dept.Hd.
WICHITA PUBLIC LIBRARY - BUSINESS AND
TECHNOLOGY DIVISION □ Wichita, KS

Hooper, Judge Perry O., Dir.
MONTGOMERY COUNTY LAW LIBRARY □
Montgomery, AL

Hoopes, Mary Anne, Libn.
CLOROX COMPANY - TECHNICAL LIBRARY □
Pleasanton, CA

Hoops, Dr. Donald L., Exec.Dir.
AMERICAN OCCUPATIONAL MEDICAL
ASSOCIATION - LIBRARY □ Chicago, IL

Hooser, D.R., Cur.
SURREY MUSEUM - ARCHIVES □ Surrey, BC

Hootkin, Neil, Spec.Coll.Libn.
MEDICAL COLLEGE OF WISCONSIN - TODD
WEHR LIBRARY □ Milwaukee, WI

Hoover, Audrey, Libn.
EASTMAN KODAK COMPANY - COLORADO
DIVISION - ENGINEERING LIBRARY □ Windsor,
CO

Hoover, Esther, Asst.Libn.
REORGANIZED CHURCH OF JESUS CHRIST OF
LATTER DAY SAINTS - LIBRARY & ARCHIVES □
Independence, MO

Hoover, J.H., Hd., Bus.Adm./Govt.Doc
LOUISIANA STATE UNIVERSITY - CENTER FOR
ENGINEERING & BUSINESS ADMINISTRATION
READING ROOM □ Baton Rouge, LA

Hoover, James L., Asst. Law Libn.
COLUMBIA UNIVERSITY - LAW LIBRARY □ New
York, NY

Hoover, Kathryn M., Asst.Libn.
PINELLAS COUNTY LAW LIBRARY - ST.
PETERSBURG BRANCH □ St. Petersburg, FL

Hoover, Priscilla W., Libn.
DURHAM COUNTY HOSPITAL CORPORATION -
WATTS SCHOOL OF NURSING - LIBRARY □
Durham, NC

Hope, Monica, Doc.
INTERGOVERNMENTAL COMMITTEE ON URBAN
& REGIONAL RESEARCH (ICURR) □ Toronto, ON

Hope, Dr. Nelson W., Hd.Libn.
GARRETT CORPORATION - GARRETT TURBINE
ENGINE COMPANY - ENGINEERING LIBRARY □
Phoenix, AZ

Hopgood, Heather, Asst.Libn.
HAMILTON SPECTATOR - REFERENCE LIBRARY
□ Hamilton, ON

Hopkins, Alice, Libn.
U.S. NAVY - NAVAL SURFACE WEAPONS
CENTER - CENTER LIBRARY □ Dahlgren, VA

Hopkins, B., Doc.
WAYNE STATE UNIVERSITY - G. FLINT PURDY
LIBRARY □ Detroit, MI

Hopkins, Benjamin, Hd.Libn.
MASSACHUSETTS COLLEGE OF ART - LIBRARY
□ Boston, MA

Hopkins, Charles, Film Archv.
UNIVERSITY OF CALIFORNIA, LOS ANGELES -
UCLA FILM ARCHIVES □ Los Angeles, CA

Hopkins, Dorothy, Libn.
PITTSBURGH BOARD OF EDUCATION -
PROFESSIONAL LIBRARY □ Pittsburgh, PA

Hopkins, Frank Joy, Chf.Libn.
AMERICAN WORK HORSE MUSEUM - LIBRARY □
Paeonian Springs, VA

Hopkins, Isabella, Spec., Tech.Info.
GENERAL ELECTRIC COMPANY - SPACE/RSD
LIBRARIES □ Philadelphia, PA

Hopkins, Capt. James W., Asst.Dir., Tech.Serv.
U.S. AIR FORCE ACADEMY - LIBRARY □ U.S. Air
Force Academy, CO

Hopkins, Jan, Cat.Libn.
CROWN ZELLERBACH CORPORATION -
CENTRAL RESEARCH LIBRARY □ Camas, WA

Hopkins, Jean, Libn.
CONSOLIDATED HOSPITALS OF IDAHO FALLS -
MEDICAL LIBRARY □ Idaho Falls, ID

Hopkins, Joan, Info.Serv.Libn.
ILLINOIS BENEDICTINE COLLEGE - THEODORE
LOWNIK LIBRARY □ Lisle, IL

Hopkins, Judith, Rare Books Cat.
SUNY AT BUFFALO - POETRY/RARE BOOKS
COLLECTION □ Buffalo, NY

Hopkins, Linda Mitro, Mgr.
ROSS LABORATORIES - LIBRARY □ Columbus,
OH

Hopkins, Mary C., Libn.
WOODLAND PARK ZOOLOGICAL GARDENS -
LIBRARY □ Seattle, WA

Hopkins, Moreen
FINANCIAL EXECUTIVES RESEARCH
FOUNDATION - LIBRARY □ New York, NY

Hopman, Mark, Mgr.
BOOZ, ALLEN & HAMILTON, INC. - LIBRARY □
Chicago, IL

Hopper, Jean G., Libn.
GRAY PANTHERS - NATIONAL OFFICE LIBRARY
□ Philadelphia, PA

Hopper, Johanne, Libn.
UNIVERSITE DE MONTREAL - BIBLIOTHEQUE
PARA-MEDICALE □ Montreal, PQ

Hopper, Mildry S., Chf., Clas.Doc.
U.S. NATL. DEFENSE UNIVERSITY - LIBRARY □
Washington, DC

Hoppes, Muriel, Law Libn.
CALIFORNIA STATE LIBRARY □ Sacramento, CA

Hopson, Dallas C., Libn.
ST. JOHN'S EPISCOPAL HOSPITAL - NURSING
AND MEDICAL LIBRARY □ Brooklyn, NY

Hopson, Jean B., Lib.Dir.
WAKE FOREST UNIVERSITY - BABCOCK
GRADUATE SCHOOL OF MANAGEMENT -
LIBRARY □ Winston-Salem, NC

Hopwood, Susan, Found.Coll.Libn.
MARQUETTE UNIVERSITY - FOUNDATION
CENTER REGIONAL REFERENCE COLLECTION □
Milwaukee, WI

Horacek, Margot, Ref.Libn.
UNIVERSITY OF SOUTH FLORIDA - MEDICAL
CENTER LIBRARY □ Tampa, FL

Horan, Nancy, Asst.Libn.
NEW YORK STATE LIBRARY - LAW/SOCIAL
SCIENCE REFERENCE SERVICES □ Albany, NY

Hord, Patricia S., Libn.
INTERNATIONAL LABOR OFFICE -
WASHINGTON BRANCH LIBRARY □ Washington,
DC

Hores, Joseph, Per.Libn.
PACE UNIVERSITY - LIBRARY □ New York, NY

Horgan, Maureen, Asst. to the Dir.
TEACHERS COLLEGE - LIBRARY □ New York, NY

Horikawa, Emi K., Libn.
SWARTHMORE COLLEGE - DU PONT SCIENCE
LIBRARY □ Swarthmore, PA

Horikawa, Emi K., Libn.
SWARTHMORE COLLEGE - SPROUL
OBSERVATORY LIBRARY □ Swarthmore, PA

Horishny, Leo A., Asst.Libn.
PEDCO GROUP LIBRARY □ Cincinnati, OH

Hork, Lisa, Chf.Libn.
CALIFORNIA RAILWAY MUSEUM - LIBRARY □
Suisun City, CA

Horky, Lori, Lib.Asst.
UNIVERSITY OF SASKATCHEWAN - PHYSICS
BRANCH LIBRARY □ Saskatoon, SK

Horn, Barbara J., Lib.Dir.
U.S. NAVY - NAVAL SCHOOL - CIVIL ENGINEER
CORPS OFFICERS - MOREELL LIBRARY □ Port
Hueneme, CA

Horn, Betty L., Base Libn.
U.S. AIR FORCE BASE - LUKE BASE LIBRARY □
Luke AFB, AZ

Horn, David E., Archv.
DE PAUW UNIVERSITY - ARCHIVES OF DE
PAUW UNIVERSITY AND INDIANA UNITED
METHODISM □ Greencastle, IN

Horn, Harold E., Pres.
CABLE TELEVISION INFORMATION CENTER □
Arlington, VA

Horn, Janice, Hd.Cat.
CLARION STATE COLLEGE - RENA M. CARLSON
LIBRARY □ Clarion, PA

Horn, Karen, Cat.
NATIONAL GALLERY OF ART - PHOTOGRAPHIC
ARCHIVES □ Washington, DC

Horn, Larry, Libn.
ANTAEUS RESEARCH INSTITUTE - LIBRARY □
Fayetteville, AR

Horn, Margaret, Cat./Ref.Libn.
CONCORDIA COLLEGE - BUENGER MEMORIAL
LIBRARY □ St. Paul, MN

Horn, Maurine, Asst.Libn.
MISSISSIPPI STATE LAW LIBRARY □ Jackson,
MS

Horn, Roger, Circ.Libn.
CLARION STATE COLLEGE - RENA M. CARLSON
LIBRARY □ Clarion, PA

Horn, Zoia, Libn.
DATA CENTER - INVESTIGATIVE RESOURCE
CENTER □ Oakland, CA

Hornbach, Ruth, Hd.Libn.
KENDALL SCHOOL OF DESIGN - LEARNING
RESOURCE CENTER □ Grand Rapids, MI

Hornby, C., Res.Libn.
EDMONTON SEPARATE SCHOOL BOARD -
PROFESSIONAL LIBRARY □ Edmonton, AB

Horne, Ernest L., Cat.
GENERAL MOTORS CORPORATION - RESEARCH
LABORATORIES LIBRARY □ Warren, MI

Horne, Verne B., Archv.
MENNINGER FOUNDATION - ARCHIVES □
Topeka, KS

Horner, Marilyn, Libn.
FULTON COUNTY LAW LIBRARY ASSOCIATION
- LAW LIBRARY □ Wauseon, OH

Horner, William C., Systems Libn.
NORTH CAROLINA STATE UNIVERSITY - D.H.
HILL LIBRARY □ Raleigh, NC

Horney, Joyce, ILL Libn.
SOUTHERN ILLINOIS UNIVERSITY - SCHOOL OF
MEDICINE - MEDICAL LIBRARY □ Springfield, IL

Hornsby, Penelope, Asst. Regional Libn.
NORTH CAROLINA STATE DEPARTMENT OF
CULTURAL RESOURCES - LIBRARY FOR THE
BLIND AND PHYSICALLY HANDICAPPED □
Raleigh, NC

PERSONNEL

Horowitz, Cyma M., Dir.
AMERICAN JEWISH COMMITTEE - BLAUSTEIN LIBRARY □ New York, NY

Horowitz, Harvey P., Libn.
HEBREW UNION COLLEGE - JEWISH INSTITUTE OF RELIGION - FRANCES-HENRY LIBRARY □ Los Angeles, CA

Horrell, Jeffrey L., Art Libn.
DARTMOUTH COLLEGE - SHERMAN ART LIBRARY □ Hanover, NH

Horres, Mary, Assoc.Dir.
UNIVERSITY OF NORTH CAROLINA, CHAPEL HILL - HEALTH SCIENCES LIBRARY □ Chapel Hill, NC

Horsbrugh, Patrick, Chm.
ENVIRONIC FOUNDATION INTERNATIONAL, INC. - LIBRARY AND FILES □ Notre Dame, IN

Horst, Karen, Dir. of Lib.Serv.
ST. LUKE'S HOSPITAL OF KANSAS CITY - MEDICAL LIBRARY □ Kansas City, MO

Horton, Dorothy, Libn.
CLARINDA MENTAL HEALTH INSTITUTION - RESIDENTS AND STAFF LIBRARY □ Clarinda, IA

Horton, Gerry, Assoc., Staff-Lib.
QUAKER OATS COMPANY - JOHN STUART RESEARCH LABORATORIES - RESEARCH LIBRARY □ Barrington, IL

Horton, Gloria, Info.Tech.Asst.
LOUISIANA STATE LEGISLATIVE COUNCIL - DIVISION OF INFORMATION SERVICES □ Baton Rouge, LA

Horvath, David, Asst.Cur./Cat.
UNIVERSITY OF LOUISVILLE - PHOTOGRAPHIC ARCHIVES □ Louisville, KY

Horvath, Elizabeth, Ref.
NEW YORK CITY - MUNICIPAL REFERENCE AND RESEARCH CENTER □ New York, NY

Horvath, Dr. Janos, Pres.
KOSSUTH FOUNDATION - HUNGARIAN RESEARCH LIBRARY □ Indianapolis, IN

Horvath, Mary Ann E., Tech.Libn.
AVON PRODUCTS, INC. - TECHNICAL INFORMATION CENTER LIBRARY □ Suffern, NY

Horvitz, Eleanor F., Libn. & Archv.
RHODE ISLAND JEWISH HISTORICAL ASSOCIATION - LIBRARY □ Providence, RI

Horwitz, Ruth, Media Spec.
BENTLEY COLLEGE - SOLOMON R. BAKER LIBRARY □ Waltham, MA

Hoschek, John P., Pres.
MOTOR BUS SOCIETY, INC. - LIBRARY □ Trenton, NJ

Hosken, F.P., Coord.
WOMEN'S INTERNATIONAL NETWORK - LIBRARY □ Lexington, MA

Hoskin, Adele, Chf.Libn.
ELI LILLY AND COMPANY - SCIENTIFIC LIBRARY □ Indianapolis, IN

Hoskins, Anne
NATIONAL COLLEGE OF EDUCATION - LEARNING RESOURCE CENTERS □ Evanston, IL

Hoskins, Charles R., Info.Dir.
INTERNATIONAL NUMISMATIC SOCIETY - LIBRARY □ Washington, DC

Hoskins, Mrs. Pat S., Hd.Libn.
CONOCO, INC. - RESEARCH AND DEVELOPMENT DEPARTMENT - TECHNICAL INFORMATION SERVICES □ Ponca City, OK

Hosler, Dr. Robert M.
GREAT LAKES HISTORICAL SOCIETY - CLARENCE METCALF RESEARCH LIBRARY □ Vermilion, OH

Hospodka, Vera, Hd.Libn.
PENNSYLVANIA STATE UNIVERSITY, RADNOR CENTER FOR GRADUATE STUDIES AND CONTINUING EDUCATION - LIBRARY □ Radnor, PA

Hostetler, Karen, Per.Libn.
MOODY BIBLE INSTITUTE - LIBRARY □ Chicago, IL

Hotchkiss, Deborah, Asst.Ref.Libn.
SOUTH CAROLINA STATE LIBRARY □ Columbia, SC

Houck, Michael, Libn.
GREATER BALTIMORE MEDICAL CENTER - DR. JOHN E. SAVAGE MEDICAL STAFF LIBRARY □ Baltimore, MD

Houdek, Frank, Libn.
LAWLER, FELIX & HALL - LAW LIBRARY □ Los Angeles, CA

Hough, Beth A., Libn.
PSYCHOLOGICAL SERVICE OF PITTSBURGH - LIBRARY □ Pittsburgh, PA

Hough, Carolyn A., Mgr.Lib.Serv.
MICHIGAN OSTEOPATHIC MEDICAL CENTER, INC. - HEALTH SCIENCE LIBRARY □ Detroit, MI

Hough, Leslie S., Archv.
GEORGIA STATE UNIVERSITY - SOUTHERN LABOR ARCHIVES □ Atlanta, GA

Hough, Marianne, Dir., Med.Lib.
TAMPA GENERAL HOSPITAL - MEDICAL LIBRARY □ Tampa, FL

Houk, Mary Margaret, Dir.
BREVARD COLLEGE - JAMES A. JONES LIBRARY - FINE ARTS DIVISION □ Brevard, NC

Houkes, John M., Libn.
PURDUE UNIVERSITY - MANAGEMENT AND ECONOMICS LIBRARY □ West Lafayette, IN

Houle, F., Hd.Soc./Cult.Archv.
CANADA - PUBLIC ARCHIVES OF CANADA - MANUSCRIPT DIVISION □ Ottawa, ON

House, Barbara A, Eng.Info.Techn.
GEORGIA-PACIFIC CORPORATION - TECHNICAL INFORMATION CENTER □ Atlanta, GA

House, Dorothy A., Libn.
MUSEUM OF NORTHERN ARIZONA - HAROLD S. COLTON MEMORIAL LIBRARY □ Flagstaff, AZ

Householder, B., Bk.Cat./Ref.
U.S. NAVY - NAVAL COASTAL SYSTEMS CENTER - TECHNICAL LIBRARY □ Panama City, FL

Householder, Carolyn, Hd.
NASHVILLE STATE TECHNICAL INSTITUTE - EDUCATIONAL RESOURCE CENTER □ Nashville, TN

Housen, Mylo, Exec.Dir.
FRENCH LIBRARY IN BOSTON, INC. □ Boston, MA

Houser, Frederick N., Jr., RRIS Mgr.
NATIONAL ACADEMY OF SCIENCES - NATIONAL RESEARCH COUNCIL - RAILROAD RESEARCH INFORMATION SERVICE □ Washington, DC

Houser, Gloria W., Hd., Ser.Dept.
NORTH CAROLINA STATE UNIVERSITY - D.H. HILL LIBRARY □ Raleigh, NC

Houston, Diana Boardman, Libn.
TEXAS STATE DEPARTMENT OF HUMAN RESOURCES - LIBRARY □ Austin, TX

Houston, Grace, Libn.
COMMERCE CLEARING HOUSE, INC. - BUSINESS LIBRARY □ San Rafael, CA

Houston, Jeanne E., Libn.
BEAUMONT ENTERPRISE & JOURNAL - LIBRARY □ Beaumont, TX

Houze, Robert A., Lib.Dir.
TRINITY UNIVERSITY - LIBRARY □ San Antonio, TX

Hovde, Roberta, Libn.
MINNESOTA STATE ENERGY AGENCY - LIBRARY □ St. Paul, MN

Hover, Leila M., Libn.
HOLY NAME HOSPITAL - MEDICAL LIBRARY □ Teaneck, NJ

Hovorka, Diana, Asst.Ref.Libn.
SUNY - AGRICULTURAL AND TECHNICAL COLLEGE AT ALFRED - WALTER C. HINKLE MEMORIAL LIBRARY □ Alfred, NY

Howard, Alison, Hd.
UNIVERSITY OF CALIFORNIA, BERKELEY - OPTOMETRY LIBRARY □ Berkeley, CA

Howard, Ann, Dir.
MARSHALL UNIVERSITY - SCHOOL OF MEDICINE - HEALTH SCIENCE LIBRARIES □ Huntington, WV

Howard, Ann, Lib.Asst.
MICHIGAN STATE DEPARTMENT OF TRANSPORTATION - TRANSPORTATION LIBRARY □ Lansing, MI

Howard, B.D., Supv.Libn.
U.S. NAVY - NAVAL STATION LIBRARY (San Diego) □ San Diego, CA

Howard, Bill, Chf.
KENTUCKY STATE DEPARTMENT OF COMMERCE - DIVISION OF RESEARCH - MAP LIBRARY □ Frankfort, KY

Howard, Donald H., Div.Coord.
BRIGHAM YOUNG UNIVERSITY - RELIGION AND HISTORY DIVISION LIBRARY □ Provo, UT

Howard, Doris, Asst. Law Libn.
HARRIS COUNTY LAW LIBRARY □ Houston, TX

Howard, Eleanor, Med. Libn.
HAVERHILL MUNICIPAL (Hale) HOSPITAL - MEDICAL LIBRARY □ Haverhill, MA

Howard, Elizabeth B., Libn.
UNIVERSITY OF KENTUCKY - BIOLOGICAL SCIENCES LIBRARY □ Lexington, KY

Howard, Elizabeth Hicks, Tech.Libn.
HONEYWELL, INC. - RESIDENTIAL ENGINEERING LIBRARY □ St. Louis Park, MN

Howard, Elizabeth M., Libn.
AVCO CORPORATION - SYSTEMS DIVISION - RESEARCH LIBRARY □ Wilmington, MA

Howard, Ellen, Ref.Coord.
UNIVERSITY OF WASHINGTON - HEALTH SCIENCES LIBRARY □ Seattle, WA

Howard, Freddie S., Libn.
STANDARD & POOR'S COMPUSTAT SERVICES, INC. - DATA RESOURCE CENTER □ Denver, CO

Howard, Jeanne, Libn.
UNIVERSITY OF OKLAHOMA - PHYSICS-ASTRONOMY LIBRARY □ Norman, OK

Howard, Jeanne G., Libn.
UNIVERSITY OF OKLAHOMA - CHEMISTRY-MATHEMATICS LIBRARY □ Norman, OK

Howard, Jennie Meyer, Hd. of Tech.Serv.
HARVARD UNIVERSITY - JOHN FITZGERALD KENNEDY SCHOOL OF GOVERNMENT - LIBRARY □ Cambridge, MA

Howard, John, Assoc.Libn.
ROYAL ONTARIO MUSEUM - FAR EASTERN LIBRARY □ Toronto, ON

Howard, Mrs. M.B., Coord.
ONTARIO - MINISTRY OF CULTURE AND RECREATION - LIBRARY/RESOURCE CENTRE □ Toronto, ON

Howard, Milo B., Jr., Dir.
ALABAMA STATE DEPARTMENT OF ARCHIVES AND HISTORY □ Montgomery, AL

Howard, Norma, User.Serv.
ERIC CLEARINGHOUSE ON ELEMENTARY AND EARLY CHILDHOOD EDUCATION □ Champaign, IL

Howard, Patricia, Libn.
SISKIYOU COUNTY LAW LIBRARY† □ Yreka, CA

Howard, Polli, Dir. of Commun.
FUTURE HOMEMAKERS OF AMERICA - RESOURCE CENTER □ Washington, DC

Howard, Dr. Richard C., Act.Chf.
LIBRARY OF CONGRESS - ASIAN DIVISION □ Washington, DC

Howard, Roberta L., Tech.Libn.
DU PONT DE NEMOURS (E.I.) & COMPANY, INC. - POLYMER PRODUCTS LIBRARY □ Beaumont, TX

Howard, Sallie M., Staff Att.
KENTUCKY STATE LAW LIBRARY □ Frankfort, KY

Howard, Stephen R., Assoc.Archv.
FIRST CHURCH OF CHRIST SCIENTIST - ARCHIVES AND LIBRARY □ Boston, MA

Howard, Vivian S., Chf., Lrng.Rsrcs.
U.S. ARMY INFANTRY SCHOOL - LIBRARY □ Ft. Benning, GA

Howarth, Marna, Libn.
INSTITUTE OF SOCIETY, ETHICS & THE LIFE SCIENCES - HASTINGS CENTER □ Hastings On Hudson, NY

Howatt, Pauline T., Hd.Libn.
ALBERTA - DEPARTMENT OF ADVANCED
EDUCATION AND MANPOWER - LIBRARY □
Edmonton, AB

Howdle, Susan, Libn.
QUARLES & BRADY - LIBRARY □ Milwaukee, WI

Howe, Elizabeth, Prog.Dir.
HABITAT INSTITUTE - ENVIRONMENTAL
STUDIES LIBRARY □ Belmont, MA

Howe, Helen E., Hd.Libn.
PHILADELPHIA BOARD OF EDUCATION -
PEDAGOGICAL LIBRARY □ Philadelphia, PA

Howe, Linda L., Adm.Asst.
AMERICAN ACADEMY OF PSYCHOTHERAPISTS
- AAP TAPE LIBRARY □ Des Moines, IA

Howe, Robert, Asst.Libn., Docs.
UNIVERSITY OF FLORIDA - LATIN AMERICAN
COLLECTION □ Gainesville, FL

Howe, Robert W., Dir.
ERIC CLEARINGHOUSE FOR SCIENCE,
MATHEMATICS AND ENVIRONMENTAL
EDUCATION □ Columbus, OH

Howell, Alan, Acq.Libn.
BRIDGEWATER STATE COLLEGE - CLEMENT C.
MAXWELL LIBRARY □ Bridgewater, MA

Howell, Beth, Dir. of Lib.
WEST COAST UNIVERSITY - UNIVERSITY
CENTER LIBRARY □ Los Angeles, CA

Howell, Glen W., Act.Chf.Libn.
LAW SOCIETY OF UPPER CANADA - GREAT
LIBRARY □ Toronto, ON

Howell, Mrs. Joseph, Registrar
ZANESVILLE ART CENTER - LIBRARY □
Zanesville, OH

Howell, Josephine
MARSH AND MC LENNAN, INC. - INFORMATION
CENTER □ New York, NY

Howell, Dr. M.G., Hd., Tech.Info.Serv.
AMERICAN CYANAMID COMPANY - LEDERLE
LABORATORIES DIVISION - SUBBAROW
MEMORIAL LIBRARY □ Pearl River, NY

Howell, Rebecca, Per.Asst.
TROY STATE UNIVERSITY - LIBRARY □ Troy, AL

Howell, Sandra, Libn.
ATLANTA PUBLIC LIBRARY - IVAN ALLEN, JR.
DEPARTMENT OF SCIENCE, INDUSTRY AND
GOVERNMENT □ Atlanta, GA

Howells, Robert, V.P., Sales
ENVIRONMENT INFORMATION CENTER, INC. □
New York, NY

Howenstine, Barbara, Ref.Libn.
U.S. DEPT. OF COMMERCE - DEPARTMENTAL
LIBRARY □ Washington, DC

Howerton, Betty J., Hd.Libn.
WADDELL AND REED, INC. - RESEARCH
LIBRARY □ Kansas City, MO

Howes, Barbara, Asst.Sci.Libn.
BUTLER UNIVERSITY - SCIENCE LIBRARY □
Indianapolis, IN

Howes, Pat, Librarian
DAMES & MOORE - LIBRARY AND
INFORMATION CENTER □ Houston, TX

Howey, Marion L., Doc.Libn.
UNIVERSITY OF KANSAS - DOCUMENTS
COLLECTION □ Lawrence, KS

Howie, Robert L., Jr., Historiographer
PROTESTANT EPISCOPAL CHURCH -
EPISCOPAL DIOCESE OF MASSACHUSETTS -
DIOCESAN LIBRARY AND ARCHIVES □ Boston,
MA

Howk, Cynthia, Libn.
LANDMARK SOCIETY OF WESTERN NEW YORK
- WENRICH MEMORIAL LIBRARY □ Rochester,
NY

Howland, Margaret E.C., Cur.
MAC LEISH (Archibald) COLLECTION □
Greenfield, MA

Howland, Rosalie, Libn.
NEW MEXICO STATE COMMERCE AND
INDUSTRY DEPT. - ECONOMIC DEVELOPMENT
DIVISION - LIBRARY □ Santa Fe, NM

Howlett, JoAnn, Libn.
WISCONSIN STATE DEPARTMENT OF
ADMINISTRATION - LIBRARY □ Madison, WI

Howley, Helen, Assoc.Libn.
SAGINAW HEALTH SCIENCES LIBRARY □
Saginaw, MI

Howrey, Mary M., Lib.Dir.
AURORA COLLEGE - JENKS MEMORIAL
COLLECTION OF ADVENTUAL MATERIALS □
Aurora, IL

Howse, Beth M., Spec.Coll.Libn.
FISK UNIVERSITY - SPECIAL COLLECTIONS
DEPARTMENT □ Nashville, TN

Howson, Melba, Supv./Info.Coord.
BLUE CROSS/BLUE SHIELD OF GREATER NEW
YORK - REFERENCE LIBRARY □ New York, NY

Hoyer, Ed, Circ.
SOUTHERN CONNECTICUT STATE COLLEGE -
H.C. BULEY LIBRARY □ New Haven, CT

Hoyle, Dr. Karen Nelson, Cur.
UNIVERSITY OF MINNESOTA - CHILDREN'S
LITERATURE RESEARCH COLLECTIONS □
Minneapolis, MN

Hoyle, Pamela, Cur., Prints/Photographs
BOSTON ATHENAEUM LIBRARY □ Boston, MA

Hoyle, Stephen J., Libn.
U.S. NATIONAL MINE HEALTH AND SAFETY
ACADEMY - LEARNING RESOURCE CENTER □
Beckley, WV

Hoyt, Anne K., Hd.
OKLAHOMA STATE UNIVERSITY - CURRICULUM
MATERIALS LABORATORY □ Stillwater, OK

Hoyt, Dr. William D., Cur.
SANDY BAY HISTORICAL SOCIETY AND
MUSEUM - LIBRARY □ Rockport, MA

Hrabek, JoAnn, Ser.Asst.
MARSHALL (John) LAW SCHOOL - LIBRARY □
Chicago, IL

Hruby, Rev. B.S., Exec.Dir.
RESEARCH CENTER FOR RELIGION & HUMAN
RIGHTS IN CLOSED SOCIETIES -
INFORMATION CENTER □ New York, NY

Hruska, Dorothy, Co-Dir.&Cur.
LE SUEUR COUNTY HISTORICAL SOCIETY
MUSEUM - LIBRARY □ Elysian, MN

Hruska, James E., Dir.
LE SUEUR COUNTY HISTORICAL SOCIETY
MUSEUM - LIBRARY □ Elysian, MN

Hrycyna, Patricia, Per.Libn.
GULF CANADA LIMITED - CENTRAL LIBRARY □
Toronto, ON

Hsia, Tao-Tai, Chf.
LIBRARY OF CONGRESS - LAW LIBRARY - FAR
EASTERN LAW DIVISION □ Washington, DC

Hsieh, Lucia, Cat.
MORGAN GUARANTY TRUST COMPANY OF NEW
YORK - REFERENCE LIBRARY □ New York, NY

Hsieh, Teresa, Instr.-Libn.
UNIVERSITY OF TORONTO - EAST ASIAN
LIBRARY □ Toronto, ON

Hsiung, Lai-Ying, Hd. of Tech.Serv.
MEMORIAL UNIVERSITY OF NEWFOUNDLAND -
HEALTH SCIENCES LIBRARY □ St. John's, NF

Hsu, Bonnie, Libn.
LAKEVILLE HOSPITAL - HEALTH SCIENCES
LIBRARY □ Lakeville, MA

Hsu, Constance, Act.Hd., Cat.
SUNY - COLLEGE AT BUFFALO - EDWARD H.
BUTLER LIBRARY □ Buffalo, NY

Hsu, Veronica, Tech.Libn.
RCA CORPORATION - G & CS - AUTOMATED
SYSTEMS - ENGINEERING LIBRARY □
Burlington, MA

Hu, Chia-Yaung, Hd., Chinese Sect.
HARVARD UNIVERSITY - HARVARD YENCHING
INSTITUTE - LIBRARY □ Cambridge, MA

Hu, David Y., Biblog.
OHIO STATE UNIVERSITY - EAST ASIAN
COLLECTION □ Columbus, OH

Hu, Evelyn, Cat.Libn.
STANFORD UNIVERSITY - J. HUGH JACKSON
LIBRARY □ Stanford, CA

Hu, Shih-Sheng, Chf.Prov. Law Libn.
LAW SOCIETY OF ALBERTA - EDMONTON
LIBRARY □ Edmonton, AB

Hu, Shih-Sheng, Chf.Prov. Law Libn.
QUEEN'S BENCH - COURT OF APPEAL JUDGES'
LIBRARY □ Edmonton, AB

Huang, Anson, Asst.Libn.
U.S. COAST GUARD - TAMPA MEMORIAL
LIBRARY† □ New York, NY

Huang, Becky, Tech.Serv.Libn.
MICHIGAN OSTEOPATHIC MEDICAL CENTER,
INC. - HEALTH SCIENCE LIBRARY □ Detroit, MI

Huang, Mr. C.K., Dir.
SUNY AT BUFFALO - HEALTH SCIENCES
LIBRARY □ Buffalo, NY

Huang, Dora, Br.Hd.Libn.
U.S. NAVY - NAVAL AIR DEVELOPMENT
CENTER - TECHNICAL INFORMATION BRANCH
□ Warminster, PA

Huang, Liza, Asst.Libn.
SLOAN-KETTERING INSTITUTE FOR CANCER
RESEARCH - DONALD S. WALKER LABORATORY
- C.P. RHOADS MEMORIAL LIBRARY □ Rye, NY

Huang, Sam, Acq.
UNIVERSITY OF SOUTH DAKOTA - MC KUSICK
LAW LIBRARY □ Vermillion, SD

Huang, Shuchen, Engr.Libn.
WESTINGHOUSE ELECTRIC CORPORATION -
LAMP DIVISIONS - ENGINEERING LIBRARY □
Bloomfield, NJ

Huang, Steve, Asst. Law Libn.
UNIVERSITY OF SOUTH CAROLINA - COLEMAN
KARESH LAW LIBRARY □ Columbia, SC

Huang, Su-Lee, Assoc.Libn., Tech.Serv.
CLEVELAND MUSEUM OF ART - LIBRARY □
Cleveland, OH

Huang, Vicky S., Libn.
HUGHES AIRCRAFT COMPANY - EL SEGUNDO
LIBRARY □ Los Angeles, CA

Huang, Violet, Act.Ser./Ref.Libn.
ALABAMA A & M UNIVERSITY - JOSEPH F.
DRAKE MEMORIAL LEARNING RESOURCES
CENTER □ Normal, AL

Hubbard, Bede, Libn.
ST. PETER'S ABBEY & COLLEGE - LIBRARY □
Muenster, SK

Hubbard, Bruce, Libn.
BROWN & CALDWELL - LIBRARY □ Walnut
Creek, CA

Hubbard, Edwina M., Libn.
U.S. VETERANS ADMINISTRATION (WY-
Cheyenne) - CENTER LIBRARY □ Cheyenne, WY

Hubbard, Kathy, Hd.Libn.
BROWN & ROOT, INC. - TECHNICAL LIBRARY □
Houston, TX

Hubbard, M.B., Musm.Cur.
U.S. PRESIDENTIAL LIBRARIES - FRANKLIN D.
ROOSEVELT LIBRARY □ Hyde Park, NY

Hubbard, Marlis, Libn.
CONCORDIA UNIVERSITY - SIR GEORGE
WILLIAMS CAMPUS - GUIDANCE
INFORMATION CENTRE □ Montreal, PQ

Hubbard, Mary B., Hd.
TOLEDO-LUCAS COUNTY PUBLIC LIBRARY -
SCIENCE AND TECHNOLOGY DEPARTMENT □
Toledo, OH

Hubbard, Mary Kathryn, Mgr.
TURNER, COLLIE & BRADEN, INC. - LIBRARY
AND INFORMATION SERVICES □ Houston, TX

Hubbard, Terry, Soc.Sci.Libn.
COLORADO STATE UNIVERSITY - WILLIAM E.
MORGAN LIBRARY □ Fort Collins, CO

Hubbard, William J., Dir., Lib.Serv.
VIRGINIA STATE LIBRARY □ Richmond, VA

Huber, Bertha, Ref.Libn.
U.S. ARMY - ACADEMY OF HEALTH SCIENCES -
STIMSON LIBRARY† □ Ft. Sam Houston, TX

Huber, Donald L., Libn.
TRINITY LUTHERAN SEMINARY - LIBRARY □
Columbus, OH

Huber, George K., Music Libn.
SWARTHMORE COLLEGE - DANIEL UNDERHILL
MUSIC LIBRARY □ Swarthmore, PA

Huber, Kristina R., Asst.Libn.
UNIVERSITY OF MICHIGAN - HIGHWAY
SAFETY RESEARCH INSTITUTE - LIBRARY □
Ann Arbor, MI

Huber, Mildred, Lib.Asst.
WESTMORELAND HOSPITAL - HEALTH
EDUCATION CENTER □ Greensburg, PA

Huberdeau, Arsene, Dir.
MANITOBA - CENTRE DE RESSOURCES
EDUCATIVES FRANCAISES DU MANITOBA □
Saint Boniface, MB

Hubler, Mary Jane, Asst. to Dir.
LINCOLN NATIONAL LIFE FOUNDATION - LOUIS
A. WARREN LINCOLN LIBRARY AND MUSEUM □
Fort Wayne, IN

Huckins, Barbara W., Chf., Lib.Serv.
U.S. VETERANS ADMINISTRATION (TX-Dallas) -
MEDICAL CENTER LIBRARY SERVICE □ Dallas,
TX

Hucks, Herbert, Jr., Cur.
UNITED METHODIST COMMN. ON ARCHIVES &
HISTORY - SOUTH CAROLINA CONFERENCE -
HISTORICAL LIBRARY □ Spartanburg, SC

Hucks, Herbert, Jr., Archv.
WOFFORD COLLEGE - SANDOR TESZLER
LIBRARY - ARCHIVES □ Spartanburg, SC

Hudanick, Ann, Adm.Spec.
IBM CORPORATION - ENGINEERING LIBRARY □
Austin, TX

Huddleston, Ellen, Info.Serv.Libn.
IIT RESEARCH INSTITUTE -
ELECTROMAGNETIC COMPATIBILITY
ANALYSIS CENTER - TECHNICAL
INFORMATION SERVICES □ Annapolis, MD

Huddleston, Joann, Asst.Libn.
NEW ENGLAND MUTUAL LIFE INSURANCE
COMPANY - BUSINESS LIBRARY □ Boston, MA

Huddleston, Marsha, Libn.
CHICAGO PUBLIC LIBRARY CULTURAL CENTER
- THOMAS HUGHES CHILDREN'S LIBRARY □
Chicago, IL

Huddleston, Nancy, Per.Libn.
CROWN ZELLERBACH CORPORATION -
CENTRAL RESEARCH LIBRARY □ Camas, WA

Hudgin, Donald E., Info.Dir.
PRINCETON POLYMER LABORATORIES, INC. -
LIBRARY □ Plainsboro, NJ

Hudnut, Sophie, Act.Mgr.Customer Serv.
LOCKHEED MISSILES & SPACE COMPANY, INC.
- LOCKHEED INFORMATION SYSTEMS □ Palo
Alto, CA

Hudson, Anne, Hd., Cat.Sect.
UNIVERSITY OF MISSOURI - MEDICAL
LIBRARY† □ Columbia, MO

Hudson, Dale L., Music Libn.
FLORIDA STATE UNIVERSITY - WARREN D.
ALLEN MUSIC LIBRARY □ Tallahassee, FL

Hudson, Donna, Ref.Libn.
UNIVERSITY OF WISCONSIN, MADISON -
STEENBOCK MEMORIAL LIBRARY □ Madison,
WI

Hudson, Gary, Hd., Acq.Dept.
SOUTH DAKOTA STATE UNIVERSITY - HILTON
M. BRIGGS LIBRARY □ Brookings, SD

Hudson, Jean, Supv., Tech.Serv.
SCHERING-PLOUGH CORPORATION -
PHARMACEUTICAL RESEARCH DIVISION -
LIBRARY INFORMATION CENTER □ Bloomfield,
NJ

Hudson, Joan, Libn.
FRASER AND BEATTY - LIBRARY □ Toronto, ON

Hudson, Patricia H., Archv.
MONROE COUNTY HISTORICAL MUSEUM -
ARCHIVES □ Monroe, MI

Hudson, Paul, Hd.
PUBLIC LIBRARY OF CINCINNATI AND
HAMILTON COUNTY - GOVERNMENT AND
BUSINESS DEPARTMENT □ Cincinnati, OH

Hudson, Roberta L., Libn.
HAYES (Rutherford B.) PRESIDENTIAL CENTER -
LIBRARY □ Fremont, OH

Hudson, Thomas, Coord., Lib.Serv.
PENNHURST CENTER - STAFF LIBRARY □ Spring
City, PA

Hudson, Thomas G., Dir.
U.S. NATL. ARCHIVES & RECORDS SERVICE -
FEDERAL ARCHIVES AND RECORDS CENTER,
REGION 4 □ East Point, GA

Huebsch, Virginia, Libn.
SAMUEL ROBERTS NOBLE FOUNDATION, INC. -
BIOMEDICAL DIVISION LIBRARY □ Ardmore,
OK

Huecker, Celeste, Cat.Libn.
U.S. SOCIAL SECURITY ADMINISTRATION -
LIBRARY □ Baltimore, MD

Huefner, Robert P., Dir.
UNIVERSITY OF UTAH - CENTER FOR PUBLIC
AFFAIRS AND ADMINISTRATION - RESEARCH
LIBRARY □ Salt Lake City, UT

Huemer, Christina, Fine Arts
COLUMBIA UNIVERSITY - AVERY
ARCHITECTURAL AND FINE ARTS LIBRARY □
New York, NY

Huesing, Steven A., HCIB Secretariat
HEALTH COMPUTER INFORMATION BUREAU □
Edmonton, AB

Huestis, Jeffrey C., Coord./Res.Info.Serv
MICHIGAN TECHNOLOGICAL UNIVERSITY -
INSTITUTE OF WOOD RESEARCH
INFORMATION CENTER □ Houghton, MI

Huff, Ann, Ref.Libn.
FOUNDATION CENTER - NEW YORK - LIBRARY
□ New York, NY

Huff, Barbara, Ref.Libn.
LOYOLA LAW SCHOOL - LIBRARY □ Los Angeles,
CA

Huff, Carolyn W., Libn.
DELAWARE STATE DEPARTMENT OF PUBLIC
INSTRUCTION - LIBRARY □ Dover, DE

Huff, J. Roger, Sec./Ed.
BENTON COUNTY HISTORICAL SOCIETY -
LIBRARY □ Siloam Springs, AR

Huff, Kathryn F., Asst.Libn.
DISCIPLES OF CHRIST HISTORICAL SOCIETY -
LIBRARY □ Nashville, TN

Huff, Margaret F., Dean, LRC
ORANGEBURG-CALHOUN TECHNICAL COLLEGE
- GRESSETTE LEARNING RESOURCE CENTER □
Orangeburg, SC

Huff, Rose Marie, Libn.
TRIDENT TECHNICAL COLLEGE - NORTH
CAMPUS LIBRARY □ North Charleston, SC

Huffman, Donna, Asst.Dir.
INTERLOCHEN CENTER FOR THE ARTS - MUSIC
LIBRARY □ Interlochen, MI

Huffman, Gail, Libn.
WESTINGHOUSE ELECTRIC CORPORATION -
WESTINGHOUSE NUCLEAR TRAINING CENTER
- INSTRUCTIONAL MEDIA CENTER □ Zion, IL

Huffman, George E., Dir.
AMARILLO COLLEGE - LEARNING RESOURCE
CENTER □ Amarillo, TX

Huffman, Judy C., Libn.
INFORMATICS INC. - ISG LIBRARY □ Rockville,
MD

Hufford, Laurel, Children's Libn.
UNIVERSITY CONGREGATIONAL CHURCH -
LIBRARY □ Seattle, WA

Hug, Dr. Gordon
UNIVERSITY OF NOTRE DAME - RADIATION
LABORATORY - RADIATION CHEMISTRY DATA
CENTER □ Notre Dame, IN

Hugg, Corliss A., Asst.Res.Libn.
ENVIRONMENTAL RESEARCH INSTITUTE OF
MICHIGAN - ERIM INFORMATION CENTER □
Ann Arbor, MI

Huggins, Una D., Chf.Acq.Libn.
U.S. ARMY - ADJUTANT GENERAL - LIBRARY
DIVISION □ Alexandria, VA

Hugh, Yeon Jean, Chf. Indexer
ABELL (A.S.) COMPANY - BALTIMORE
SUNPAPERS - LIBRARY □ Baltimore, MD

Hughes, Rev. Canon M.A., Adm.Off.
ANGLICAN CHURCH OF CANADA - DIOCESE OF
MONTREAL - ARCHIVES† □ Montreal, PQ

Hughes, Charles Z., Libn.
BROADLAWNS MEDICAL CENTER - MEDICAL
LIBRARY □ Des Moines, IA

Hughes, Dorothy, Lib.Asst.
FERGUSON BAPTIST CHURCH - LIBRARY □
Ferguson, KY

Hughes, Dorothy S., Libn.
SEATTLE TRUST & SAVINGS BANK - LIBRARY □
Seattle, WA

Hughes, Fran, Micromedia
SOUTHERN CONNECTICUT STATE COLLEGE -
H.C. BULEY LIBRARY □ New Haven, CT

Hughes, Gay, Doc.Supv.
CURRY COLLEGE - LOUIS R. LEVIN MEMORIAL
LIBRARY □ Milton, MA

Hughes, Ivan W., O.S.B., Act.Libn.
CATHOLIC SEMINARY FOUNDATION OF
INDIANAPOLIS - LIBRARY □ Indianapolis, IN

Hughes, Dr. J. Marshal, II, Ctr.Libn.
U.S. NAVY - NAVAL SURFACE WEAPONS
CENTER - CENTER LIBRARY □ Dahlgren, VA

Hughes, Dr. J. Marshal, II, Act.Hd.
U.S. NAVY - NAVAL SURFACE WEAPONS
CENTER - WHITE OAK LIBRARY □ Silver Spring,
MD

Hughes, J. Michael, Asst.Ref.Libn.
YALE UNIVERSITY - LAW LIBRARY □ New
Haven, CT

Hughes, Janet, Lib.Mgr.
IBM CORPORATION - BOULDER LIBRARY □
Boulder, CO

Hughes, Jean, Libn.
SAN DIEGO PUBLIC LIBRARY - SOCIAL
SCIENCES SECTION □ San Diego, CA

Hughes, Judy L., Libn.
FIRST BAPTIST CHURCH OF LAKEWOOD -
CHURCH LIBRARY □ Long Beach, CA

Hughes, Kathy, Asst.Libn.
ST. LUKE'S HOSPITAL OF KANSAS CITY -
MEDICAL LIBRARY □ Kansas City, MO

Hughes, Mrs. Lealer, Libn.
U.S. ARMY - RESEARCH AND TECHNOLOGY
LABS (AVRADCOM) - APPLIED TECH.
LABORATORY - TECHNICAL LIB. □ Ft. Eustis, VA

Hughes, Marija Matich, Chf.Libn.
U.S. COMMISSION ON CIVIL RIGHTS - NATL.
CLEARINGHOUSE LIBRARY □ Washington, DC

Hughes, Norma, Dir.
MOHAVE MUSEUM OF HISTORY AND ARTS -
LIBRARY □ Kingman, AZ

Hughes, Peggy, Lib.Asst.
FOUNDATION FOR BLIND CHILDREN - LIBRARY
□ Scottsdale, AZ

Hughes, Raymond, Mus.Cur.
BUFFALO & ERIE COUNTY HISTORICAL
SOCIETY - LIBRARY □ Buffalo, NY

Hughes, Rita A., Chf. Libn.
MERRILL LYNCH PIERCE FENNER & SMITH,
INC. - LIBRARY □ New York, NY

Hughes, Mrs. Solon G., Dir.
HARRISON COUNTY HISTORICAL MUSEUM -
LIBRARY □ Marshall, TX

Hughes, Susan Kutscher, Info.Rsrcs.Coord.
MOBIL PRODUCING TEXAS & NEW MEXICO
INC. - INFORMATION RESOURCE CENTER □
Houston, TX

Hughes, Suzanne, Coord., Info.Serv.
LOUISIANA STATE LEGISLATIVE COUNCIL -
DIVISION OF INFORMATION SERVICES □ Baton
Rouge, LA

Hughes, Mr. Trevor, Info.Off.
NEW ZEALAND EMBASSY - LIBRARY □
Washington, DC

Hughes, Virginia, Ed., In The News
SCHERING-PLOUGH CORPORATION - BUSINESS
INFORMATION CENTER - LIBRARY □
Kenilworth, NJ

Hughes, Virginia C., Mgr.
U.S. DEPT. OF TRANSPORTATION - TRANSPORTATION SAFETY INSTITUTE - TECHNICAL REFERENCE SERVICE† □ Oklahoma City, OK

Hughes, Virginia C., Libn.
U.S. FEDERAL AVIATION ADMINISTRATION - AERONAUTICAL CENTER LIBRARY, AAC-44D □ Oklahoma City, OK

Hughston, Milan, Asst.Libn.
CARTER (Amon) MUSEUM OF WESTERN ART - LIBRARY □ Fort Worth, TX

Hugs, Theo D., Park Techn.
U.S. NATL. PARK SERVICE - BIGHORN CANYON NATL. RECREATION AREA - LIBRARY □ Fort Smith, MT

Hui, Timothy, Serials Libn.
DALLAS THEOLOGICAL SEMINARY - MOSHER LIBRARY □ Dallas, TX

Huie, Bruce Kin, Libn./Res.Asst.
HAMMER, SILER, GEORGE ASSOCIATES - LIBRARY† □ Washington, DC

Huijgen, Diane, Dir., Lib.Serv.
BANCROFT, AVERY AND MC ALISTER - LAW LIBRARY □ San Francisco, CA

Huitfeldt, Jennifer, Mgr., Info.Res.
CARRIER CORPORATION - LOGAN LEWIS LIBRARY □ Syracuse, NY

Huizar, Lois, Instr.Mtls.Ctr.Libn.
UNIVERSITY OF WISCONSIN, STEVENS POINT - JAMES H. ALBERTSON CENTER FOR LEARNING RESOURCES □ Stevens Point, WI

Hulbert, Linda, Assoc.Libn.Coll.Dev.
SUNY - UPSTATE MEDICAL CENTER LIBRARY □ Syracuse, NY

Hulbush, Dorothy, Libn.
U.S. AIR FORCE BASE - MC CHORD BASE LIBRARY □ Tacoma, WA

Hulett-Nelson, Fay, Supv.
BANK OF AMERICA - SYSTEMS LIBRARY □ San Francisco, CA

Hulkonen, David A., Chf. Clinical Med.Libn.
UNIVERSITY OF TEXAS MEDICAL BRANCH - MOODY MEDICAL LIBRARY □ Galveston, TX

Hull, David, Principal Libn.
NATIONAL MARITIME MUSEUM - J. PORTER SHAW LIBRARY □ San Francisco, CA

Hull, Doris M., Ref.Libn.
HOWARD UNIVERSITY - MOORLAND-SPINGARN RESEARCH CENTER - LIBRARY DIVISION □ Washington, DC

Hull, Nina M., Health Sci.Libn.
HOLY CROSS HOSPITAL - HEALTH SCIENCE LIBRARY □ San Fernando, CA

Hull, Thomas V., Libn.
AMERICAN LEGION - FILM LIBRARY □ Indianapolis, IN

Hull, Thomas V., Libn.
AMERICAN LEGION - NATIONAL HEADQUARTERS - LIBRARY □ Indianapolis, IN

Hull, Yvonne C., Libn.
XAVIER UNIVERSITY OF LOUISIANA - COLLEGE OF PHARMACY - LIBRARY □ New Orleans, LA

Hullihan, Ann, Res.Libn.
BBDO CHICAGO - INFORMATION CENTER □ Chicago, IL

Hulse, Granvyl, Libn.
NUMISMATICS INTERNATIONAL - LIBRARY □ Colebrook, NH

Hulse, Mary Ellen, Rec.Adm.
IOWA BEEF PROCESSORS, INC. - CORPORATE LIBRARY □ Dakota City, NE

Hulsizer, Bernice Lord, Libn.
UNIVERSITY OF ILLINOIS - PHYSICS/ASTRONOMY LIBRARY □ Urbana, IL

Hulsker, W., Found.Ctr.Coll.
WAYNE STATE UNIVERSITY - G. FLINT PURDY LIBRARY □ Detroit, MI

Hume, Howard N., Jr., Chf., Acq.
U.S. NATL. DEFENSE UNIVERSITY - LIBRARY □ Washington, DC

Humes, Aileen W., Libn.
NEW BRUNSWICK ELECTRIC POWER COMMISSION - LIBRARY □ Fredericton, NB

Humes, Durward, Mng.Dir.
METAL LATH/STEEL FRAMING ASSOCIATION - LIBRARY □ Chicago, IL

Hummel, Frances C., Res.Libn.
ALCOLAC, INC. - RESEARCH LIBRARY □ Baltimore, MD

Hummel, Pat, Govt.Docs.
UNIVERSITY OF UTAH - LAW LIBRARY □ Salt Lake City, UT

Hummer, Frank, Lib.Assoc.
IOWA STATE LAW LIBRARY □ Des Moines, IA

Hummer, Kathryn, Res.Libn.
PERSONAL PRODUCTS COMPANY - RESEARCH & DEVELOPMENT LIBRARY □ Milltown, NJ

Humnicky, Virginia, Ext.Libn.
INDIANA UNIVERSITY - SCHOOL OF MEDICINE LIBRARY □ Indianapolis, IN

Humphrey, Jean, Asst.Libn., Tech.Serv.
UNIVERSITY OF ARIZONA - COLLEGE OF LAW LIBRARY □ Tucson, AZ

Humphrey, Louise, Libn.
TRUE VINE MISSIONARY BAPTIST CHURCH - LIBRARY □ Alexandria, LA

Humphrey, Ms. M. Moss, Sr.Med.Libn.
KING (Martin Luther, Jr.) GENERAL HOSPITAL - MEDICAL LIBRARY □ Los Angeles, CA

Humphrey, Pat, Dir.Med.Rec.Dept.
RICHLAND MEMORIAL HOSPITAL - STAFF LIBRARY □ Olney, IL

Humphrey, Rita S., Adm.Asst.
BAYLOR UNIVERSITY - ARMSTRONG BROWNING LIBRARY □ Waco, TX

Humphreys, Jo Ann, Rd.Serv. Law Libn.
UNIVERSITY OF MISSOURI - SCHOOL OF LAW LIBRARY □ Columbia, MO

Humphreys, Kenneth K., Exec.Dir.
AMERICAN ASSOCIATION OF COST ENGINEERS - LIBRARY □ Morgantown, WV

Humphreys, N., Ref.Biblog.
UNIVERSITY OF WISCONSIN, LA CROSSE - MURPHY LIBRARY □ La Crosse, WI

Humphreys, Richard, Law Libn.
DELAWARE LAW SCHOOL OF WIDENER UNIVERSITY - LAW LIBRARY □ Wilmington, DE

Humphries, Donna I., Libn.
CANADIAN UTILITIES LIMITED - LIBRARY □ Edmonton, AB

Hunchar, Susan N., Libn.
U.S. DEPT. OF JUSTICE - ANTITRUST DIVISION LIBRARY □ Washington, DC

Hund, Flower, Bus. & Econ.Libn.
CENTRAL MISSOURI STATE UNIVERSITY - WARD EDWARDS LIBRARY □ Warrensburg, MO

Hung, Theresa, Rd.Adv.
DISTRICT OF COLUMBIA PUBLIC LIBRARY - TECHNOLOGY AND SCIENCE DIVISION □ Washington, DC

Hungate, Robert P., Act.Dir.
SAN DIEGO STATE UNIVERSITY - BUREAU OF BUSINESS & ECONOMIC RESEARCH LIBRARY □ San Diego, CA

Hunger, Charles, Dir., AV Serv.
KENT STATE UNIVERSITY - AUDIOVISUAL SERVICES □ Kent, OH

Hungerford, Anthos, Dir.
HURLEY MEDICAL CENTER - HAMADY HEALTH SCIENCES LIBRARY □ Flint, MI

Hunkler, Ann, Govt.Docs.Libn.
GOLDEN GATE UNIVERSITY - SCHOOL OF LAW LIBRARY □ San Francisco, CA

Hunn, Marvin, Ref.Libn.
DALLAS THEOLOGICAL SEMINARY - MOSHER LIBRARY □ Dallas, TX

Hunnewell, John J., Exec.Dir.
INTERNATIONAL INSTITUTE OF MUNICIPAL CLERKS - MANAGEMENT INFORMATION CENTER □ Pasadena, CA

Hunsberger, Albert I., Pres.
WATERLOO HISTORICAL SOCIETY - LIBRARY □ Kitchener, ON

Hunsberger, Barbara, Acq.Libn.
MILLERSVILLE STATE COLLEGE - HELEN A. GANSER LIBRARY □ Millersville, PA

Hunsecker, Helen L., Chf., Serv.Br.
U.S. ARMY WAR COLLEGE - LIBRARY □ Carlisle Barracks, PA

Hunsicker, Marya, Lib. for the Blind
NEW JERSEY STATE LIBRARY □ Trenton, NJ

Hunsicker, Susan
PENNWALT CORPORATION - TECHNICAL DIVISION LIBRARY □ King Of Prussia, PA

Hunsucker, Alice E., Asst.V.P./Mgr.
WELLS FARGO BANK - LIBRARY □ San Francisco, CA

Hunsucker, Miss Coy K., Hd.
PUBLIC LIBRARY OF CINCINNATI AND HAMILTON COUNTY - EXCEPTIONAL CHILDREN'S DIVISION □ Cincinnati, OH

Hunt, O.B., Bro. Mike
INTERNATIONAL BROTHERHOOD OF OLD BASTARDS, INC. - SIR THOMAS CRAPPER MEMORIAL ARCHIVES □ St. Louis, MO

Hunt, Alta N., Libn.
U.S. AIR FORCE BASE - GUNTER BASE LIBRARY □ Gunter AFS, AL

Hunt, Ann C., Libn.
TRANSAMERICA DE LAVAL INC. - TECHNICAL LIBRARY □ Trenton, NJ

Hunt, Barbara, Asst.Libn.Adm.
DADE COUNTY LAW LIBRARY □ Miami, FL

Hunt, Carol, Registrar
PUTNAM MUSEUM - LIBRARY □ Davenport, IA

Hunt, Charles, Law Libn.
LYCOMING COUNTY LAW LIBRARY □ Williamsport, PA

Hunt, Deborah, Asst.Libn./Circ.
LANCASTER BIBLE COLLEGE - STOLL MEMORIAL LIBRARY □ Lancaster, PA

Hunt, Debra, Coll.Libn.
NEVADA STATE LIBRARY □ Carson City, NV

Hunt, Diana E., Libn.
RUSSELL AND DUMOULIN - LIBRARY □ Vancouver, BC

Hunt, Dorothy, Lib.Asst.
NORTH CAROLINA STATE UNIVERSITY - HARRYE LYONS DESIGN LIBRARY □ Raleigh, NC

Hunt, Florine E., Corp.Libn.
PUBLIC SERVICE ELECTRIC AND GAS COMPANY - LIBRARY □ Newark, NJ

Hunt, Gary A., Hd.
OHIO UNIVERSITY - DEPARTMENT OF ARCHIVES AND SPECIAL COLLECTIONS □ Athens, OH

Hunt, Janet, Asst.Libn.
UNIVERSITY OF KING'S COLLEGE - KING'S COLLEGE LIBRARY □ Halifax, NS

Hunt, Lori A., Libn.
SHOOK, HARDY & BACON - LIBRARY □ Kansas City, MO

Hunt, Susan, Libn.
PUBLIC LIBRARY OF FORT WAYNE AND ALLEN COUNTY, INDIANA - BUSINESS AND TECHNOLOGY DEPARTMENT □ Fort Wayne, IN

Hunt-McCain, Pearl, Libn.
BOSTON REDEVELOPMENT AUTHORITY - STAFF LIBRARY† □ Boston, MA

Hunt-McCain, Pearl, Corp.Libn.
PEAVEY COMPANY - CORPORATE INFORMATION CENTER □ Minneapolis, MN

Hunter, Ann, Corp.Libn.
ANHEUSER-BUSCH COMPANIES, INC. - CORPORATE LIBRARY □ St. Louis, MO

Hunter, Beryl
CANADA - OFFICE OF THE COMMISSIONER OF OFFICIAL LANGUAGES - LIBRARY □ Ottawa, ON

Hunter, Diane C., Dir.Lib.Serv.
ATLANTA NEWSPAPERS - REFERENCE LIBRARY □ Atlanta, GA

Hunter, Glen, Libn
METROPOLITAN TORONTO LIBRARY - THEATRE DEPARTMENT □ Toronto, ON

PERSONNEL

PERSONNEL

Hunter, Isabel, Hd.Libn.
MEMORIAL UNIVERSITY OF NEWFOUNDLAND - HEALTH SCIENCES LIBRARY □ St. John's, NF
Hunter, J. A., Libn.
UNIVERSITY OF PENNSYLVANIA - WISTAR INSTITUTE OF ANATOMY & BIOLOGY - LIBRARY □ Philadelphia, PA
Hunter, J.E.B., Chf.Libn.
CANADA - NATIONAL GALLERY OF CANADA - LIBRARY □ Ottawa, ON
Hunter, James, Libn.
COLUMBUS DISPATCH - EDITORIAL LIBRARY □ Columbus, OH
Hunter, Josephine R., Lib.Cons.
HUMAN RESOURCES RESEARCH ORGANIZATION - VAN EVERA LIBRARY† □ Alexandria, VA
Hunter, M. Edward, Libn.
METHODIST THEOLOGICAL SCHOOL IN OHIO - LIBRARY □ Delaware, OH
Hunter, R.S., Libn.
WORCESTER HAHNEMANN HOSPITAL - SCHOOL OF NURSING LIBRARY† □ Worcester, MA
Huntington, Claire A., Libn.
GEISINGER MEDICAL CENTER - SCHOOL OF NURSING LIBRARY □ Danville, PA
Huntington, Nancy J., Adm.Asst.
UNITED SOCIETY OF BELIEVERS - THE SHAKER LIBRARY □ Poland Spring, ME
Huntzinger, David H., Chf. Interpreter
U.S. NATL. PARK SERVICE - LAKE MEAD NATL. RECREATION AREA - LIBRARY □ Boulder City, NV
Hunzeker, Dr. Jeanne, Dir.
CHILD WELFARE LEAGUE OF AMERICA, INC. - INFORMATIONAL RESOURCE SERVICES □ New York, NY
Hunziker, Rudi, Mgr., Customer Adm.
LOCKHEED MISSILES & SPACE COMPANY, INC. - LOCKHEED INFORMATION SYSTEMS □ Palo Alto, CA
Huppert, Ramona, Libn.
3M - 251 LIBRARY □ St. Paul, MN
Hurd, Christian P., District Libn.
U.S. ARMY - CORPS OF ENGINEERS - PORTLAND DISTRICT - LIBRARY □ Portland, OR
Hurd, Florence E., Cur.
CLARK COUNTY HISTORICAL SOCIETY - PIONEER MUSEUM - LIBRARY □ Ashland, KS
Hurd, Jean L., Sr.Info.Sys.Spec.
HONEYWELL, INC. - PROCESS CONTROLS DIVISION - INFORMATION CENTER, M.S. 221 □ Fort Washington, PA
Hurd, Julie M., Sci.Pub.Serv.Coord.
MICHIGAN STATE UNIVERSITY - SCIENCE LIBRARY □ East Lansing, MI
Hurd, Sr. Naomi, S.P., Libn.
ST. JOSEPH MEDICAL CENTER - HEALTH SCIENCE LIBRARY □ Burbank, CA
Hurd, Roger, Lib.Asst.
MINNEAPOLIS PUBLIC LIBRARY & INFORMATION CENTER - MUNICIPAL INFORMATION LIBRARY □ Minneapolis, MN
Hurd, Wenona, Lib. Attendant
ROCKWELL INTERNATIONAL - TECHNICAL INFORMATION CENTER □ Tulsa, OK
Hurlbert, Betty E., Libn.
ASARCO INC. - LIBRARY† □ South Plainfield, NJ
Hurley, Hazel, Libn.
NEW MEXICO STATE DEPARTMENT OF HOSPITALS - STATE HOSPITAL - ELLA P. KIEF MEMORIAL LIBRARY □ Las Vegas, NM
Hurley, Mrs. M.J., Mgr.
CANADA - NATIONAL ENERGY BOARD - LIBRARY □ Ottawa, ON
Hurley, Marianne, Hd. of Branches
CANADA - NATIONAL RESEARCH COUNCIL - CANADA INSTITUTE FOR SCIENTIFIC AND TECHNICAL INFORMATION (CISTI) □ Ottawa, ON
Hurn, Doris P., Libn.
SMITH (Frederick C.) CLINIC - MEDICAL LIBRARY □ Marion, OH

Hurst, Brenda, Ref.Libn.
MC GILL UNIVERSITY - ENGINEERING LIBRARY □ Montreal, PQ
Hurst, H., Dir., Info.Serv.
AUSTRALIAN INFORMATION SERVICE - REFERENCE LIBRARY/INFORMATION SERVICE □ New York, NY
Hurst, Martha, Libn.
PLOUGH, INC. - RESEARCH LIBRARY □ Memphis, TN
Hurt, Byrnice, Med.Libn.
ST. FRANCIS HOSPITAL - MEDICAL LIBRARY □ Roslyn, NY
Hurt, Howard, Hd.
UNIVERSITY OF BRITISH COLUMBIA - CURRICULUM LABORATORY □ Vancouver, BC
Hurt, Juanelle V., Act.Libn.
WINTER HAVEN HOSPITAL - J.G. CONVERSE MEMORIAL LIBRARY □ Winter Haven, FL
Hurtes, Reva, Libn.
UNIVERSITY OF MIAMI - SCHOOL OF MEDICINE - BASCOM PALMER EYE INSTITUTE - LIBRARY □ Miami, FL
Hurtt, James, Circ./ILL Libn.
MOUNT ST. MARY'S SEMINARY OF THE WEST - LIBRARY □ Cincinnati, OH
Hurwitz, Barbara, Libn.
TECHNOMIC PUBLISHING CO., INC. - BUSINESS LIBRARY □ Westport, CT
Huschen, Mary, Asst.Mgr.
CHICAGO TRIBUNE - INFORMATION CENTER □ Chicago, IL
Huseman, Dwight, Ser., Doc., Sys.Libn.
GETTYSBURG COLLEGE - MUSSELMAN LIBRARY - SPECIAL COLLECTIONS □ Gettysburg, PA
Huseman, Howard W., Assoc.Univ.Libn.
UNIVERSITY OF FLORIDA - ARCHITECTURE & FINE ARTS LIBRARY □ Gainesville, FL
Huson, Hobart, Owner
DAWGWOOD RESEARCH LIBRARY □ Refugio, TX
Hussain, Mohammad Riaz, Libn.
TECHNICAL UNIVERSITY OF NOVA SCOTIA - LIBRARY □ Halifax, NS
Hussey, Fr. M. Edmund, Archv.
ARCHDIOCESE OF CINCINNATI - ARCHIVES □ Cincinnati, OH
Hussey, Miss O., Commun.Sec.
ALCOHOL AND DRUG CONCERNS, INC. - AUDIOVISUAL LIBRARY □ Don Mills, ON
Hustad, Tina, Asst.Libn.
U.S. NATL. MARINE FISHERIES SERVICE - NORTHWEST & ALASKA FISHERIES CENTER - LIBRARY □ Seattle, WA
Husted, Albert, V.P.
INSTITUTE OF THE AMERICAN MUSICAL, INC. - LIBRARY □ Los Angeles, CA
Husted, Shirley C., County Hist.
MONROE COUNTY HISTORIAN'S DEPARTMENT - LIBRARY □ Rochester, NY
Huston, Jane, Branch Libn.
SHEARMAN & STERLING - LIBRARY □ New York, NY
Huston, Ralph D., Pres.
HISTORICAL SOCIETY OF DAUPHIN COUNTY - LIBRARY □ Harrisburg, PA
Huston, Ruth, Dir.
ALDERSGATE COLLEGE - WILSON MEMORIAL LIBRARY □ Moose Jaw, SK
Hustvedt, Lloyd, Exec.Sec.
NORWEGIAN-AMERICAN HISTORICAL ASSOCIATION - ARCHIVES □ Northfield, MN
Hutchason, Clark, Supv.
COEN COMPANY, INC. - TECHNICAL LIBRARY □ Burlingame, CA
Hutchens, Shirley, Archv.
SAMFORD UNIVERSITY - BAPTIST HISTORICAL COLLECTION □ Birmingham, AL
Hutchens, Shirley, Archv.
SAMFORD UNIVERSITY - HARWELL GOODWIN DAVIS LIBRARY □ Birmingham, AL
Hutchins, Andrea, Libn.
ANALYTIC SERVICES, INC. - TECHNICAL LIBRARY □ Arlington, VA

Hutchins, Barbara M., Exec.Sec.
RELIGIOUS ARTS GUILD - MUSIC LIBRARY □ Boston, MA
Hutchins, Betsy, Info.Off.
AMERICAN DONKEY AND MULE SOCIETY - INFORMATION OFFICE □ Denton, TX
Hutchins, Richard G., Dir.
SETON HALL UNIVERSITY - SCHOOL OF LAW - LAW LIBRARY □ Newark, NJ
Hutchinson, Ann P., Lib.Dir.
ROSWELL PARK MEMORIAL INSTITUTE - MEDICAL AND SCIENTIFIC LIBRARY □ Buffalo, NY
Hutchinson, Cindy, Chf.Libn.
ACUREX CORPORATION - TECHNICAL LIBRARY □ Mountain View, CA
Hutchinson, Susan, Diablo Tech.Info.Spec.
XEROX CORPORATION - PALO ALTO RESEARCH CENTER - TECHNICAL INFORMATION CENTER □ Palo Alto, CA
Hutchinson, William L., Mgr.Lib.& Files
PACIFIC POWER AND LIGHT COMPANY - LIBRARY □ Portland, OR
Hutchison, Jill, Res.Off.
AUSTRALIAN INFORMATION SERVICE - REFERENCE LIBRARY/INFORMATION SERVICE □ New York, NY
Hutchison, Mrs. Preston, Supv.
MORGAN COUNTY HISTORICAL SOCIETY - LIBRARY □ Versailles, MO
Hutchison, Mrs. R.L., Libn.
WESTMINSTER PRESBYTERIAN CHURCH - LIBRARY† □ Pittsburgh, PA
Huthnance, John R., Dir.
UNIVERSITY OF ALABAMA - JONES LAW INSTITUTE - LIBRARY □ Montgomery, AL
Hutson, Dorothy, Mgr., Tech.Serv.
GENERAL ELECTRIC COMPANY - ADVANCED REACTOR SYSTEMS DEPT. - LIBRARY □ Sunnyvale, CA
Huttner, Sidney F., Hd.
SYRACUSE UNIVERSITY - GEORGE ARENTS RESEARCH LIBRARY FOR SPECIAL COLLECTIONS □ Syracuse, NY
Hutton, J.F., Pres.
FRIENDS OF THE WESTERN PHILATELIC LIBRARY □ Sunnyvale, CA
Hutton, Marilyn, Hd.Mss.Acq. & Pubn.
TENNESSEE STATE LIBRARY AND ARCHIVES - ARCHIVES & MANUSCRIPTS SECTION □ Nashville, TN
Hutton, Mary Ann, Libn.
NATIONAL INSTITUTE ON MENTAL RETARDATION - JOHN ORR FOSTER NATIONAL REFERENCE LIBRARY □ Downsview, ON
Hutton, Richard, Chf.Cat.
NATIONAL GALLERY OF ART - PHOTOGRAPHIC ARCHIVES □ Washington, DC
Huwa, Elaine, Asst.Res.Libn.
GATES RUBBER COMPANY - TECHNICAL INFORMATION CENTER □ Denver, CO
Huygen, Michaele Lee, Info.Rsrcs.Libn.
BANCROFT, AVERY AND MC ALISTER - LAW LIBRARY □ San Francisco, CA
Huyke, Ena, Hd., Per.
UNIVERSITY OF PUERTO RICO - GENERAL LIBRARY □ San Juan, PR
Hyam, G., Hd.British Archv.
CANADA - PUBLIC ARCHIVES OF CANADA - MANUSCRIPT DIVISION □ Ottawa, ON
Hyatt, Mrs. Robert
FIRST BAPTIST CHURCH - MEDIA CENTER† □ Gainesville, FL
Hycnar, Barbara, Asst.Libn./Tech.Serv.
NORTHWESTERN UNIVERSITY - LAW SCHOOL LIBRARY □ Chicago, IL
Hyde, Ann, Mss.Libn.
UNIVERSITY OF KANSAS - DEPARTMENT OF SPECIAL COLLECTIONS □ Lawrence, KS
Hyde, Gail L., Libn.
CORNELL UNIVERSITY - NEW YORK STATE AGRICULTURAL EXPERIMENT STATION - LIBRARY† □ Geneva, NY

Hyde, Jerald
   ST. LOUIS PUBLIC LIBRARY - APPLIED
   SCIENCE DEPARTMENT □ St. Louis, MO
Hyde, Mary Lynn, Hd., Tech.Serv./Doc.
   UNIVERSITY OF SAN DIEGO - MARVIN &
   LILLIAN KRATTER LAW LIBRARY □ San Diego,
   CA
Hyde, Sam, Music Libn.
   UNIVERSITY OF HOUSTON - SCHOOL OF MUSIC
   - WOODY HERMAN ARCHIVES □ Houston, TX
Hyde, W.F.L., Grand Libn.
   GRAND LODGE OF MANITOBA, A.F. AND A.M. -
   MASONIC LIBRARY □ Winnipeg, MB
Hyer, David C., Exec.Dir.
   BUCK (Pearl S.) BIRTHPLACE FOUNDATION -
   LIBRARY □ Hillsboro, WV
Hyer, Susan, Asst.Libn.
   NEWSPAPER ADVERTISING BUREAU, INC. -
   INFORMATION CENTER □ New York, NY
Hylton, Marcia A., Corp.Libn.
   BERNSTEIN (Sanford C.) & COMPANY, INC. -
   RESEARCH LIBRARY □ New York, NY
Hyman, Barry E., Asst.Prov.Archv.
   MANITOBA - PROVINCIAL ARCHIVES OF
   MANITOBA □ Winnipeg, MB
Hyman, Laura, Asst.Libn.
   COLD SPRING HARBOR LABORATORY - MAIN
   LIBRARY □ Cold Spring Harbor, NY
Hymes, Fred, Mass Media Spec.
   CLARK COUNTY COMMUNITY COLLEGE -
   LEARNING RESOURCES CENTER □ North Las
   Vegas, NV
Hynek, C. Duke, Ct.Adm.
   KALAMAZOO COUNTY LAW LIBRARY - JUDGE
   RAYMOND FOX MEMORIAL LIBRARY □
   Kalamazoo, MI

I

Iamele, Richard T., Libn.
   LOS ANGELES COUNTY LAW LIBRARY □ Los
   Angeles, CA
Ibach, Robert, Dir.
   GRACE THEOLOGICAL SEMINARY - LIBRARY □
   Winona Lake, IN
Ichinose, Mitsuko, Cat./Ref.Libn.
   YALE UNIVERSITY - EAST ASIAN COLLECTION
   □ New Haven, CT
Ickes, Clark F., Chf.Libn.
   BALTIMORE NEWS AMERICAN LIBRARY □
   Baltimore, MD
Idema, Celene, Hd.
   GRAND RAPIDS PUBLIC LIBRARY - MICHIGAN
   ROOM □ Grand Rapids, MI
Idland, Myrtle, Libn.
   PHOENIX GENERAL HOSPITAL - MEDICAL
   LIBRARY □ Phoenix, AZ
Iemma, John A., Asst.Dir., DED
   RHODE ISLAND STATE DEPARTMENT OF
   ECONOMIC DEVELOPMENT - RESEARCH
   DIVISION LIBRARY □ Providence, RI
Ifshin, Steven L., Drug Info.Libn.
   UNIVERSITY OF CHICAGO HOSPITALS &
   CLINICS - PHARMACEUTICAL SERVICES -
   DRUG INFORMATION CENTER □ Chicago, IL
Ihlenfeldt, Kay, Dept.Hd.
   CHICAGO PUBLIC LIBRARY CENTRAL LIBRARY -
   GOVERNMENT PUBLICATIONS DEPARTMENT □
   Chicago, IL
Ikehara, Chris
   JOHNS HOPKINS UNIVERSITY - SCHOOL OF
   HYGIENE AND PUBLIC HEALTH -
   INTERDEPARTMENTAL LIBRARY □ Baltimore,
   MD
Iliff, Warren J., Dir.
   WASHINGTON PARK ZOO - LIBRARY □ Portland,
   OR
Ilisevich, Robert, Libn.
   CRAWFORD COUNTY HISTORICAL SOCIETY -
   LIBRARY AND ARCHIVES† □ Meadville, PA

Illman, Harry R., Libn.
   PRESS CLUB OF SAN FRANCISCO - WILL
   AUBREY MEMORIAL LIBRARY □ San Francisco,
   CA
Ilnicki, Henry, Hd., Gift Sect.
   NEW YORK STATE LIBRARY □ Albany, NY
Iltis, H.H., Dir. of Herbarium
   UNIVERSITY OF WISCONSIN, MADISON -
   BOTANY DEPARTMENT - HERBARIUM LIBRARY
   □ Madison, WI
Imbrie, Agnes, Libn.
   LOS ANGELES COUNTY DEPARTMENT OF
   HEALTH SERVICES-PREVENTIVE PUBLIC
   HEALTH - JOHN L. POMEROY MEMORIAL
   LIBRARY □ Los Angeles, CA
Imel, Susan, Asst.Dir.
   ERIC CLEARINGHOUSE ON ADULT, CAREER
   AND VOCATIONAL EDUCATION - NATL. CTR.
   FOR RESEARCH IN VOCATIONAL EDUC. □
   Columbus, OH
Imhof, Peter H., Libn.
   U.S. NAVY - NAVAL RESEARCH LABORATORY -
   RUTH H. HOOKER TECHNICAL LIBRARY □
   Washington, DC
Immel, Jean L., Archv.
   ARMSTRONG WORLD INDUSTRIES, INC. -
   MANAGEMENT REFERENCE SERVICES □
   Lancaster, PA
Inabinett, E.L., Libn.
   UNIVERSITY OF SOUTH CAROLINA - SOUTH
   CAROLINIANA LIBRARY □ Columbia, SC
Indra M., David, Asst. Dean
   OAKLAND UNIVERSITY - LIBRARY □ Rochester,
   MI
Indue, C., Libn.
   OHIO STATE UNIVERSITY - DISASTER
   RESEARCH CENTER - LIBRARY □ Columbus, OH
Ingalls, Bruce, Ref.Sect.
   ENVIRONMENTAL PROTECTION AGENCY -
   HEADQUARTERS LIBRARY □ Washington, DC
Ingalls, J., Music Libn.
   UNIVERSITY OF LOWELL, SOUTH CAMPUS -
   DANIEL H. O'LEARY LIBRARY □ Lowell, MA
Ingalls, Joan V., Libn.
   WINE INSTITUTE - LIBRARY □ San Francisco,
   CA
Ingalls, Nell, Asst.Libn.
   FRIEDMAN & KOVEN - LAW LIBRARY □ Chicago,
   IL
Ingber, Ellen Oberman, Info.Mgr.
   PURDUE FREDERICK COMPANY - RESEARCH
   LIBRARY □ Norwalk, CT
Ingersoll, Hilde, Lib.Asst.
   RIVERSIDE HOSPITAL - MEDICAL LIBRARY □
   Wilmington, DE
Ingersoll, Joan, Hd.
   U.S. NAVY - NAVAL OCEAN SYSTEMS CENTER -
   TECHNICAL LIBRARY □ San Diego, CA
Ingibergsson, Asgeir, Hd.Libn.
   CAMROSE LUTHERAN COLLEGE - LIBRARY □
   Camrose, AB
Inglis, Judith, Ext.Libn.
   UNIVERSITY OF MANITOBA - MEDICAL
   LIBRARY □ Winnipeg, MB
Inglis, Mike, Mgr., Nat.Rsrcs.Div.
   UNIVERSITY OF NEW MEXICO - TECHNOLOGY
   APPLICATION CENTER □ Albuquerque, NM
Inglis, Scottie, Tech.Serv.Libn.
   TUFTS UNIVERSITY - SCHOOLS OF MEDICINE,
   DENTAL MEDICINE & VETERINARY MEDICINE -
   HEALTH SCIENCES LIBRARY† □ Boston, MA
Ingmire, Mary, Libn.
   SILVER CROSS HOSPITAL - MEDICAL LIBRARY
   □ Joliet, IL
Ingraham, Beverly, Dir.
   OWYHEE COUNTY HISTORICAL COMPLEX
   MUSEUM - LIBRARY □ Murphy, ID
Ingraham, Leonoor, Circ.Libn.
   UNIVERSITY OF OREGON - HEALTH SCIENCES
   CENTER - LIBRARY □ Portland, OR

Ingram, Anne, Adm.Asst.
   WAKE FOREST UNIVERSITY - BOWMAN GRAY
   SCHOOL OF MEDICINE - LIBRARY □ Winston-
   Salem, NC
Ingram, Arlyn, Techn.
   CORNELL UNIVERSITY - RESOURCE
   INFORMATION LABORATORY □ Ithaca, NY
Ingram, Charles, Acq.Libn.
   SOUTHWESTERN OKLAHOMA STATE
   UNIVERSITY - AL HARRIS LIBRARY □
   Weatherford, OK
Ingram, Jeannine S., Res.
   MORAVIAN MUSIC FOUNDATION, INC. -
   LIBRARY □ Winston-Salem, NC
Ingram, John E., Archv.
   COLONIAL WILLIAMSBURG - RESEARCH
   LIBRARY & ARCHIVES □ Williamsburg, VA
Ingram, L. Marie, Law Libn.
   MANATEE COUNTY BAR ASSOCIATION - LAW
   LIBRARY □ Bradenton, FL
Ingram, LouElla, Libn.
   U.S. COURT OF CLAIMS/U.S. COURT OF
   CUSTOMS & PATENT APPEALS - COURTS'
   LIBRARY □ Washington, DC
Ingram, Mark A., Med.Libn.
   HOPKINS COUNTY - REGIONAL MEDICAL
   CENTER - LIBRARY □ Madisonville, KY
Ingui, Bette Jean, Ref.Libn.
   SUNY AT STONY BROOK - HEALTH SCIENCES
   LIBRARY □ East Setauket, NY
Iniguez, Eva B., Hd., Spec.Proj.
   UNIVERSITY OF PUERTO RICO - GENERAL
   LIBRARY □ San Juan, PR
Innerst, Betty, Libn.
   ST. THOMAS AQUINAS NEWMAN CENTER -
   LIBRARY □ Albuquerque, NM
Innes, Rosalind, Libn.
   ATKINS (Gordon) AND ASSOCIATES
   ARCHITECTS LTD. - LIBRARY □ Calgary, AB
Innes-Taylor, Catherine, Acq.Libn.
   UNIVERSITY OF ALASKA, ANCHORAGE -
   LIBRARY □ Anchorage, AK
Innis, Janet, Lib.Asst.
   QUEEN'S UNIVERSITY AT KINGSTON -
   CHEMISTRY LIBRARY □ Kingston, ON
Insetta, Patricia M., Libn.
   ABINGTON MEMORIAL HOSPITAL - WILMER
   MEMORIAL MEDICAL LIBRARY □ Abington, PA
Inskeep, Lois J., Chf., Lib.Serv.
   U.S. VETERANS ADMINISTRATION (NE-Omaha)
   - HOSPITAL LIBRARY □ Omaha, NE
Insler, Professor Stanley, Chm.
   YALE UNIVERSITY - INDOLOGICAL AND
   LINGUISTIC SEMINAR - LIBRARY □ New Haven,
   CT
Iobst, Barbara J., Med.Libn.
   ALLENTOWN HOSPITAL ASSOCIATION -
   HEALTH SCIENCES LIBRARY □ Allentown, PA
Iorio, Dr. E. James, Mgr.
   MARINE PRODUCTS COMPANY - LIBRARY □
   Boston, MA
Ipolito, Dorry, Video Libn.
   ENOCH PRATT FREE LIBRARY - AUDIO-VISUAL
   DEPARTMENT □ Baltimore, MD
Ippolito, Andrew V., Dir. of Lib. & Res.
   NEWSDAY, INC. - LIBRARY □ Melville, NY
Irelan, R.M., Tech.Spec.
   DU PONT DE NEMOURS (E.I.) & COMPANY, INC.
   - CHEMICALS & PIGMENTS DEPT. - JACKSON
   LAB. LIBRARY □ Wilmington, DE
Ireland, J., Libn.
   PRUDENTIAL LIFE INSURANCE COMPANY OF
   AMERICA - BUSINESS LIBRARY □ Toronto, ON
Ireland, Tessa J., Sec.
   UNIVERSITY OF TORONTO - ANTHROPOLOGY
   READING ROOM □ Toronto, ON
Irene, Sr. M., O.S.F., Libn.
   DIOCESE OF ALLENTOWN - PRO-LIFE LIBRARY
   □ Bethlehem, PA
Iriberry, Mildred, Asst.Libn. & Cat.
   BROOKLYN MUSEUM - ART REFERENCE
   LIBRARY □ Brooklyn, NY

Irish, Cathleen A., Tech.Info.Spec.
NATIONAL INJURY INFORMATION
CLEARINGHOUSE □ Washington, DC

Irish, Ned, Chm., Pubn.Comm.
AMERICAN HEMEROCALLIS SOCIETY -
LIBRARY □ Stone Mountain, GA

Irizany, Dadma, Lib.Asst.
ACADEMY OF THE STREET OF PUERTO RICAN
CONGRESS - LIBRARY □ Chicago, IL

Ironside, Eugenia, Asst.Libn.
FIREMAN'S FUND INSURANCE COMPANIES -
LIBRARY† □ San Francisco, CA

Irvine, Betty Jo, Hd.
INDIANA UNIVERSITY - FINE ARTS LIBRARY □
Bloomington, IN

Irvine, Deirdre, Libn.
MOTOROLA, INC. - SEMICONDUCTOR
PRODUCTS DIVISION - TECHNICAL LIBRARY □
Phoenix, AZ

Irvine, Dr. James S., Asst.Libn.Pub.Serv.
PRINCETON THEOLOGICAL SEMINARY - SPEER
LIBRARY† □ Princeton, NJ

Irvine, Joyce, Act.Leg.Libn.
MANITOBA - LEGISLATIVE LIBRARY □
Winnipeg, MB

Irvine, Kay, Asst.Libn.
WESTERN STATES CHIROPRACTIC COLLEGE -
W.A. BUDDEN MEMORIAL LIBRARY □ Portland,
OR

Irvine, Mary Helen, Assoc.Libn.
MAINE STATE LAW AND LEGISLATIVE
REFERENCE LIBRARY □ Augusta, ME

Irving, Ophelia M., Asst.Dir.Info.
NORTH CAROLINA STATE DEPARTMENT OF
CULTURAL RESOURCES - DIVISION OF THE
STATE LIBRARY □ Raleigh, NC

Irwin, Barbara Smith, Lib.Dir.
NEW JERSEY HISTORICAL SOCIETY - LIBRARY
□ Newark, NJ

Irwin, Ivan, Pres.
LINN COUNTY HISTORICAL SOCIETY -
LIBRARY □ Pleasanton, KS

Irwin, Lawrence L., Asst.Libn.
UNIVERSITY OF ARKANSAS, FAYETTEVILLE -
SPECIAL COLLECTIONS DIVISION □
Fayetteville, AR

Irwin, Ruth A., Libn.
DELAWARE STATE HOSPITAL - MEDICAL
LIBRARY □ New Castle, DE

Isa, Jacqueline, Acq.Libn.
CENTRAL CONNECTICUT STATE COLLEGE -
ELIHU BURRITT LIBRARY □ New Britain, CT

Isaac, Mrs. Torrey, Libn.
SMITH MEMORIAL LIBRARY □ Chautauqua, NY

Isaacs, Ann Fabe, Hd.
NATIONAL ASSOCIATION FOR CREATIVE
CHILDREN AND ADULTS (NACCA) - LIBRARY □
Cincinnati, OH

Isaacs, B.D., Lib.Dir.
GREENSBORO DAILY NEWS AND RECORD -
LIBRARY □ Greensboro, NC

Isaacson, Katherine Jones, Art Libn.
ROBERT GORE RIFKIND FOUNDATION - ART
LIBRARY AND GRAPHICS COLLECTION □
Beverly Hills, CA

Isaacson, Mel, Hd.Cat.
PACE UNIVERSITY - LIBRARY □ New York, NY

Isaacson, Richard T., Libn.
GARDEN CENTER OF GREATER CLEVELAND -
ELEANOR SQUIRE LIBRARY □ Cleveland, OH

Isaacson, Ruth
JEWISH COMMUNITY CENTER OF GREATER
MINNEAPOLIS - LIBRARY† □ Minneapolis, MN

Isabel, Yvon, Directeur
UNIVERSITE DU QUEBEC - MEDIATHEQUE □
Ste. Foy, PQ

Isadore, Harold W., Ref./Res.Libn.
SOUTHERN UNIVERSITY - LAW SCHOOL
LIBRARY □ Baton Rouge, LA

Isbell, Mary, Asst.Libn.
SOUTHERN ILLINOIS UNIVERSITY,
CARBONDALE - EDUCATION DIVISION LIBRARY
□ Carbondale, IL

Ische, John P., Dir.
LOUISIANA STATE UNIVERSITY MEDICAL
CENTER - LIBRARY □ New Orleans, LA

Isenberg, Helena, Libn.
JEWISH PUBLIC LIBRARY OF TORONTO □
Toronto, ON

Isenstein, Ellen, Ref.Libn.
BOSTON PUBLIC LIBRARY - GOVERNMENT
DOCUMENTS, MICROTEXT, NEWSPAPERS □
Boston, MA

Isetts, Charles, Hd.
UNIVERSITY OF CINCINNATI - MEDICAL
CENTER LIBRARIES - HISTORY OF HEALTH
SCIENCES LIBRARY AND MUSEUM □ Cincinnati,
OH

Ishee, Charles E., Libn.
PUBLIC LIBRARY OF CINCINNATI AND
HAMILTON COUNTY - ART AND MUSIC
DEPARTMENT □ Cincinnati, OH

Isherwood, Helen C., Libn.
NEW YORK INSTITUTE FOR THE EDUCATION
OF THE BLIND - WALTER BROOKS LIBRARY □
Bronx, NY

Isler, Sharon Louise, Med.Libn.
JOHN PETER SMITH HOSPITAL - MARIETTA
MEMORIAL MEDICAL LIBRARY □ Fort Worth, TX

Isley, Natelle, Mgr.
MISSISSIPPI STATE RESEARCH AND
DEVELOPMENT CENTER - INFORMATION
SERVICES DIVISION □ Jackson, MS

Ismail, Mrs. Fathia, Libn.
INTERNATIONAL CIVIL AVIATION
ORGANIZATION - LIBRARY □ Montreal, PQ

Ismarin, Corazon O'S., Libn.
ST. LUKE'S HOSPITAL - MEDICAL LIBRARY □
San Francisco, CA

Isom, Bill, Hd.Circ.Serv.
EASTERN ILLINOIS UNIVERSITY - BOOTH
LIBRARY □ Charleston, IL

Israel, Mrs. Kilja, Libn.
ST. FRANCIS MEDICAL CENTER - CAPE
COUNTY MEMORIAL MEDICAL LIBRARY □ Cape
Girardeau, MO

Itesco, Victor, Hd.Libn.
MONTREAL URBAN COMMUNITY TRANSIT
COMMISSION - LIBRARY □ Montreal, PQ

Itina, Irene, Hd., Govt.Doc.Sect.
NEW YORK PUBLIC LIBRARY - ECONOMIC AND
PUBLIC AFFAIRS DIVISION □ New York, NY

Ittelson, William, Dir.
UNIVERSITY OF ARIZONA ENVIRONMENTAL
PSYCHOLOGY PROGRAM - LIBRARY □ Tucson,
AZ

Ittner, Dwight, Libn.
UNIVERSITY OF ALASKA - BIO-MEDICAL
LIBRARY □ Fairbanks, AK

Iula, Jeff, Adm.Asst.
INTERNATIONAL SOAP BOX DERBY - LIBRARY
□ Akron, OH

Iva, Futrell, Libn.
ENVIRONMENTAL LAW INSTITUTE - LIBRARY □
Washington, DC

Ivain, Denise, Lib.Asst.
WATERBURY STATE TECHNICAL COLLEGE -
HELEN HAHLO LIBRARY □ Waterbury, CT

Ivanisevic, Vlatka, Libn.
CASE WESTERN RESERVE UNIVERSITY -
APPLIED SOCIAL SCIENCES LIBRARY □
Cleveland, OH

Ivanus, Theodore B., Hd.
UNIVERSITY OF NOTRE DAME -
INTERNATIONAL STUDIES LIBRARY □ Notre
Dame, IN

Ives, Mrs. A., Adm. & Info.Serv.
MC GILL UNIVERSITY - MACDONALD COLLEGE
- BRACE RESEARCH INSTITUTE LIBRARY □ Ste.
Anne De Bellevue, PQ

Ives, Colta Feller, Cur.
METROPOLITAN MUSEUM OF ART -
DEPARTMENT OF PRINTS AND PHOTOGRAPHS
□ New York, NY

Ives, Edward D., Dir.
UNIVERSITY OF MAINE, ORONO - NORTHEAST
ARCHIVES OF FOLKLORE AND ORAL HISTORY □
Orono, ME

Ives, Glen P., Musm.Dir.
SPRINGFIELD LIBRARY AND MUSEUMS
ASSOCIATION - CATHERINE E. HOWARD
MEMORIAL LIBRARY □ Springfield, MA

Ives, Sidney, Libn.
UNIVERSITY OF FLORIDA - BELKNAP
COLLECTION FOR THE PERFORMING ARTS □
Gainesville, FL

Ives, Sidney, Libn.
UNIVERSITY OF FLORIDA - RARE BOOKS &
MANUSCRIPTS □ Gainesville, FL

Ivey, Barbara M., Chf., Acq.Br.
U.S. AIR FORCE ACADEMY - LIBRARY □ U.S. Air
Force Academy, CO

Ivey, Donna M., Supv., Lib.Serv.
CONSUMERS' GAS COMPANY - LIBRARY
SERVICES □ Scarborough, ON

Ivey, Kathy, Libn.
MEMPHIS-SHELBY COUNTY PUBLIC LIBRARY
AND INFO. CTR. - SCIENCE/BUSINESS/SOCIAL
SCIENCES DEPT. □ Memphis, TN

Ivey, Robert, Libn.
GAINESVILLE SUN - LIBRARY □ Gainesville, FL

Ivory, Paul W., Adm. of Chesterwood
CHESTERWOOD - LIBRARY □ Stockbridge, MA

Ivy, Karen E., Libn.
COOPERS AND LYBRAND - LIBRARY □ San
Francisco, CA

Iwamoto, Margaret, Asst.Libn.
HAWAII NEWSPAPER AGENCY - LIBRARY □
Honolulu, HI

Iwanczyszyn, Martha, Ref.Libn.
DONALDSON, LUFKIN AND JENRETTE, INC. -
CORPORATE LIBRARY □ New York, NY

Iwanusa, Christine, Libn.
NEW YORK PUBLIC LIBRARY - DONNELL
LIBRARY CENTER - NATHAN STRAUS YOUNG
ADULT LIBRARY □ New York, NY

Izzicupo, Sunta, Cat.Hd.
CENTER FOR LAW AND EDUCATION -
VICTORIA GREGORIAN LIBRARY □ Cambridge,
MA

Izzo, Sami, Rsrcs.Ctr.Coord.
VERMONT INSTITUTE OF NATURAL SCIENCES
- LIBRARY □ Woodstock, VT

J

Jaansov-Boudreau, T., Hd., User Serv.
CANADA - PUBLIC SERVICE COMMISSION -
LIBRARY SERVICES DIVISION □ Ottawa, ON

Jabbour, Alan, Dir.
LIBRARY OF CONGRESS - AMERICAN FOLKLIFE
CENTER □ Washington, DC

Jablonowski, Christina, Libn.
CHANDLER EVANS, INC. - COMPANY LIBRARY □
West Hartford, CT

Jablonski, Mary, Acq.Libn.
OHIO STATE SUPREME COURT LAW LIBRARY □
Columbus, OH

Jackanicz, Donald W., Co-Libn.
BERTRAND RUSSELL SOCIETY, INC. - LIBRARY
□ Chicago, IL

Jacke, Edith, Libn.
MURRAY (Warren G.) DEVELOPMENTAL CENTER
- LIBRARY □ Centralia, IL

Jacklin, Kathleen, Archv.
CORNELL UNIVERSITY - DEPARTMENT OF
MANUSCRIPTS AND ARCHIVES □ Ithaca, NY

Jackonen, Felix V., Pres.
FINNISH AMERICAN HISTORICAL SOCIETY OF
MICHIGAN - LIBRARY □ Southfield, MI

Jackson, Andrew P., Supv.
QUEENS BOROUGH PUBLIC LIBRARY -
LANGSTON HUGHES COMMUNITY LIBRARY AND
CULTURAL CENTER □ Corona, NY

Jaffe, Rosalyn, Info.Serv.Libn.
NATIONAL ACADEMY OF SCIENCES - NATIONAL ACADEMY OF ENGINEERING - LIBRARY □ Washington, DC

Jaffe, Steven, Libn.
CONSOLIDATED EDISON COMPANY OF NEW YORK, INC. - LIBRARY □ New York, NY

Jaffee, Phyllis, Project Coord.
NATIONAL FEDERATION OF LOCAL CABLE PROGRAMMERS - LIBRARY† □ Kettering, OH

Jagels, Suellen, Asst.Libn.
EASTERN MAINE MEDICAL CENTER - HEALTH SCIENCES LIBRARY □ Bangor, ME

Jagoe, Katherine P., Hd., Res.Ctr.
DALLAS PUBLIC LIBRARY - ARCHIVES AND RESEARCH CENTER FOR TEXAS AND DALLAS HISTORY □ Dallas, TX

Jahnke, Ruth, Libn.
HYSTER COMPANY - TECHNICAL INFORMATION SERVICES □ Portland, OR

Jain, Dr. Nirmal K., Hd., Sci.Div.
ACADIA UNIVERSITY - SCIENCE LIBRARY □ Wolfville, NS

Jajko, Edward A., Near East Biblog.
YALE UNIVERSITY - SEMITIC REFERENCE LIBRARY □ New Haven, CT

Jajko, Pamela, Libn.
ST. FRANCIS HOSPITAL AND MEDICAL CENTER - SCHOOL OF NURSING LIBRARY □ Hartford, CT

Jakubczak, Dorothy, Tech.Libn.
DURO-TEST CORPORATION - TECHNICAL LIBRARY □ North Bergen, NJ

Jakus, Florence I., Ed.D., Med.Libn.
SUNRISE HOSPITAL MEDICAL CENTER - LIBRARY □ Las Vegas, NV

Jalenak, Natalie B., Libn.
MEMPHIS PINK PALACE MUSEUM - LIBRARY □ Memphis, TN

Jameikis, Brone, Kpr.
HONOLULU ACADEMY OF ARTS - AUDIOVISUAL CENTER □ Honolulu, HI

James, Ann, Libn.
EXPORT DEVELOPMENT CORPORATION - LIBRARY □ Ottawa, ON

James, Anna T., Libn.
TEXAS SOUTHERN UNIVERSITY - THURGOOD MARSHALL SCHOOL OF LAW - LIBRARY† □ Houston, TX

James, Billy M., Chf./Health Sci.Lib.
U.S. PUBLIC HEALTH SERVICE HOSPITAL - HEALTH SCIENCES LIBRARY □ New Orleans, LA

James, Bob, Info.Sys.Anl.
U.S. DEPT OF ENERGY - SANDIA NATL. LABORATORIES - TECHNICAL LIBRARY □ Albuquerque, NM

James, Craig, Docs.Libn.
SASKATCHEWAN - LEGISLATIVE LIBRARY □ Regina, SK

James, Geraldine R., Libn.
PQ CORPORATION - RESEARCH LIBRARY □ Lafayette Hill, PA

James, Henry
U.S.D.A. - HUMAN NUTRITION INFORMATION SERVICES - FOOD AND NUTRITION INFORMATION CENTER □ Beltsville, MD

James, John E., Supv., Lib.Serv.
AMERICAN HOME PRODUCTS CORPORATION - WYETH LABORATORIES DIVISION LIBRARY □ Philadelphia, PA

James, John V., Libn.
UNIVERSITY OF SASKATCHEWAN - WESTERN COLLEGE OF VETERINARY MEDICINE - LIBRARY □ Saskatoon, SK

James, Karin, Libn.
SCHUYLKILL VALLEY NATURE CENTER - LIBRARY □ Philadelphia, PA

James, Linda, Libn.
CORPUS CHRISTI CALLER-TIMES - LIBRARY □ Corpus Christi, TX

James, Mary, Libn.
EASTON HOSPITAL - MEDICAL LIBRARY □ Easton, PA

James, Olive C., Chf.
LIBRARY OF CONGRESS - LOAN DIVISION □ Washington, DC

James, R. Scott, Dir. of Rec./City Archv.
TORONTO CITY RECORDS AND ARCHIVES DIVISION □ Toronto, ON

James, William, Law Libn.
UNIVERSITY OF KENTUCKY - LAW LIBRARY □ Lexington, KY

James, Zoe S., Exec.Dir.
AMERICAN TRUCK HISTORICAL SOCIETY - LIBRARY □ Birmingham, AL

Jameson, V. Lloyd, Div.Coord.
BOSTON PUBLIC LIBRARY - GOVERNMENT DOCUMENTS, MICROTEXT, NEWSPAPERS □ Boston, MA

Jamison, Leila, Asst.Archv.
UNIVERSITY OF PITTSBURGH - ARCHIVES □ Pittsburgh, PA

Jamison, Tanya, Ext.Libn.
TEXAS TECH UNIVERSITY - HEALTH SCIENCES CENTER - LIBRARY OF THE HEALTH SCIENCES □ Lubbock, TX

Jandl, Nancy, Tech.Info.Mgr.
CHARLES RIVER ASSOCIATES, INC. - LIBRARY □ Boston, MA

Jane, Alberta, Cat.
OCTAMERON ASSOCIATES, INC. - RESEARCH LIBRARY □ Alexandria, VA

Janecek, K.L., Dir.
NORTH DAKOTA STATE UNIVERSITY - LIBRARY □ Fargo, ND

Janeway, R.C., Dir. of Lib.Serv.
TEXAS TECH UNIVERSITY - LIBRARY □ Lubbock, TX

Jang, Eugenia, Ser.Libn.
FIELD MUSEUM OF NATURAL HISTORY - LIBRARY □ Chicago, IL

Jang, Stephanie, Libn.
SIGNETICS CORPORATION - LIBRARY □ Sunnyvale, CA

Janiak, Jane M., Chf.Libn.
PORT AUTHORITY OF NEW YORK AND NEW JERSEY - LIBRARY □ New York, NY

Janicki, Sandra, Libn.
CARNEGIE LIBRARY OF PITTSBURGH - SCIENCE AND TECHNOLOGY DEPARTMENT □ Pittsburgh, PA

Janik, Toni, Hosp.Libn.
HOTEL-DIEU OF ST. JOSEPH HOSPITAL - MEDICAL LIBRARY □ Windsor, ON

Jankos, William, Cur.
UNIVERSITY OF SOUTHERN CALIFORNIA - LIBRARY - DEPARTMENT OF SPECIAL COLLECTIONS - AMERICAN LITERATURE COLLECTION □ Los Angeles, CA

Jankovics, Esther M., Mgr.
SCHERING-PLOUGH CORPORATION - BUSINESS INFORMATION CENTER - LIBRARY □ Kenilworth, NJ

Jankowski, Dorothy, Supv.Tech.Info.
DIAMOND SHAMROCK CORPORATION - CORPORATE LIBRARY □ Painesville, OH

Janofsky, Stephen, Med.Libn.
CUNY - CITY COLLEGE LIBRARY - SCIENCE/ ENGINEERING DIVISION □ New York, NY

Jansen, Ann C., Per.Libn.
MOUNT ST. MARY'S SEMINARY OF THE WEST - LIBRARY □ Cincinnati, OH

Jansen, Robert H., Asst.Libn.
MINNEAPOLIS STAR AND TRIBUNE - LIBRARY □ Minneapolis, MN

Janss-Clary, Mary, Res.Assoc.
WORLD VISION INTERNATIONAL - INFORMATION RESOURCE CENTER □ Monrovia, CA

Janssen, Ruth S., Libn.
U.S. ARMY MEDICAL RESEARCH INSTITUTE OF INFECTIOUS DISEASES - MEDICAL LIBRARY □ Frederick, MD

Januszkiewicz, Joan, Info.Spec.
BUFFALO EVENING NEWS - LIBRARY □ Buffalo, NY

Jaques, Thomas F., State Libn.
LOUISIANA STATE LIBRARY □ Baton Rouge, LA

Jarabek, Leona, Ref.Libn.
U.S. NASA - LEWIS RESEARCH CENTER - LIBRARY □ Cleveland, OH

Jarasitis, Ute, ILL
U.S. ARMY POST - FORT LEWIS - LIBRARY SYSTEM □ Fort Lewis, WA

Jardine, Barbara, Asst.Libn.
CONFERENCE BOARD OF CANADA - LIBRARY & INFORMATION CENTER □ Ottawa, ON

Jarett, Nella L., Libn.
LOEB AND LOEB - LAW LIBRARY □ Los Angeles, CA

Jarman, Evelyn R., Hd.
U.S. AIR FORCE BASE - ROBINS BASE LIBRARY □ Robins AFB, GA

Jarman, James, Hd., Order Dept.
POLYTECHNIC INSTITUTE OF NEW YORK - SPICER LIBRARY □ Brooklyn, NY

Jarrell, Randall, Dir.
UNIVERSITY OF CALIFORNIA, SANTA CRUZ - REGIONAL HISTORY PROJECT □ Santa Cruz, CA

Jarsoz, Jean, Ref.Libn.
NORTHEASTERN OHIO UNIVERSITIES COLLEGE OF MEDICINE - BASIC MEDICAL SCIENCES LIBRARY □ Rootstown, OH

Jarvis, Katherine S., Tech.Info.Spec.
XEROX CORPORATION - PALO ALTO RESEARCH CENTER - TECHNICAL INFORMATION CENTER □ Palo Alto, CA

Jarvis, Mary J., Med.Libn.
METHODIST HOSPITALS OF DALLAS - MEDICAL LIBRARY □ Dallas, TX

Jarvis, Patricia
ELIASON (Frank) CENTRE - HEALTH SCIENCES LIBRARY □ Saskatoon, SK

Jasek, Paul, Res.Asst.
CENTRAL NEW YORK REGIONAL PLANNING & DEVELOPMENT BOARD - LIBRARY & INFORMATION CENTER □ Syracuse, NY

Jasken, Eloise M., Libn.
3M - 270 LIBRARY □ St. Paul, MN

Jasko, Sr. Agnese, P.H.J.C., Libn.
SACRED HEART MONASTERY - LEO DEHON LIBRARY □ Hales Corners, WI

Jasnich, Adrienne, Assoc., Staff-Lib.
QUAKER OATS COMPANY - JOHN STUART RESEARCH LABORATORIES - RESEARCH LIBRARY □ Barrington, IL

Jason, Nora H., Project Ldr.
U. S. NATL. BUREAU OF STANDARDS - FIRE RESEARCH INFORMATION SERVICES □ Washington, DC

Jason, Patricia, Archv.
ERIE COUNTY HISTORICAL SOCIETY □ Erie, PA

Jaspal, Lelita, Ref.Libn.
BANK STREET COLLEGE OF EDUCATION - LIBRARY □ New York, NY

Jassin, Raymond M., Ref.Libn.
ROGERS & WELLS - LAW LIBRARY □ New York, NY

Jastrem, Barbara, Res.Libn.
FEDERAL RESERVE BANK OF CHICAGO - LIBRARY □ Chicago, IL

Jaworski, Teresa M., Libn.
STEVENS (J.P.) AND CO., INC. - TECHNICAL CENTER LIBRARY □ Garfield, NJ

Jax, John J., Dir.
UNIVERSITY OF WISCONSIN, STOUT - LIBRARY LEARNING CENTER - MEDIA RETRIEVAL SERVICES □ Menomonie, WI

Jayaraman, H.R., Info.Spec.
PHILLIPS PETROLEUM COMPANY - RESEARCH & DEVELOPMENT DEPARTMENT - TECHNICAL INFORMATION BRANCH □ Bartlesville, OK

Jayne, JoAnn, Libn.
ACADEMY OF AERONAUTICS - LIBRARY □ Flushing, NY

Jazdyk, Arlene, Asst.Med.Libn.
ST. MARY OF NAZARETH HOSPITAL - SISTER STELLA LOUISE HEALTH SCIENCE LIBRARY □ Chicago, IL

Jazwinski, Wanda, Pres.
POLISH AMERICAN CONGRESS - SOUTHERN CALIFORNIA-ARIZONA DIVISION - POLAND'S MILLENIUM LIBRARY □ Los Angeles, CA

Jedeka, Julianne, Lib.Mgr.
TEKTRONIX, INC. - CORPORATE LIBRARY □ Beaverton, OR

Jedlicka, Janet, Libn./Res.Ck.
SOCIETY OF AUTOMOTIVE ENGINEERS - SAE LIBRARY □ Warrendale, PA

Jedrey, Micheline E., Assoc.Libn.
MASSACHUSETTS INSTITUTE OF TECHNOLOGY - ROTCH LIBRARY OF ARCHITECTURE AND PLANNING □ Cambridge, MA

Jeffcoat, Pamela, Accs.Libn.
JOHNS HOPKINS UNIVERSITY - WILLIAM H. WELCH MEDICAL LIBRARY □ Baltimore, MD

Jeffcott, Janet B., Tech.Libn.
MADISON AREA TECHNICAL COLLEGE - TECHNICAL CENTER LIBRARY □ Madison, WI

Jefferies, Marion, Ref.Spec.
ALCAN INTERNATIONAL, LTD. - TECHNICAL INFORMATION CENTRE □ Arvida, PQ

Jefferson, Dr. James W., Co-Dir.
UNIVERSITY OF WISCONSIN, MADISON - DEPARTMENT OF PSYCHIATRY - LITHIUM INFORMATION CENTER □ Madison, WI

Jefferson, Karen L., Sr.Mss.Libn.
HOWARD UNIVERSITY - MOORLAND-SPINGARN RESEARCH CENTER - MANUSCRIPT DIVISION □ Washington, DC

Jeffery, Dr. Peter, Mss.Cat.
ST. JOHN'S ABBEY AND UNIVERSITY - HILL MONASTIC MANUSCRIPT LIBRARY - BUSH CENTER □ Collegeville, MN

Jeffries, Mary, Cat.
LORAIN COUNTY HISTORICAL SOCIETY - GERALD HICKS MEMORIAL LIBRARY □ Elyria, OH

Jelks, Joyce, Libn.
ATLANTA PUBLIC LIBRARY - SPECIAL COLLECTIONS DEPARTMENT □ Atlanta, GA

Jelley, David, Hd.Libn.
GTE LABORATORIES - LIBRARY □ Waltham, MA

Jemison, Karen, Adm.Libn.
U.S. VETERANS ADMINISTRATION (CA-Palo Alto) - HOSPITAL MEDICAL LIBRARIES □ Palo Alto, CA

Jen, Albert, Hd., Cat.
NORTHEASTERN ILLINOIS UNIVERSITY - LIBRARY □ Chicago, IL

Jen, Neil T.H., Hd., Cat.
SALISBURY STATE COLLEGE - BLACKWELL LIBRARY □ Salisbury, MD

Jendryk, Elizabeth, Asst.Libn.
UNIVERSITY OF PENNSYLVANIA - SCHOOL OF DENTAL MEDICINE - LEON LEVY LIBRARY □ Philadelphia, PA

Jeng, Helene W., Libn.
WILSON (Thomas) CENTER - MEDICAL AND PROFESSIONAL LIBRARY □ Mount Wilson, MD

Jenkins, Ada, Lib.Asst.
UNIVERSITY OF ARKANSAS, PINE BLUFF - JOHN BROWN WATSON MEMORIAL LIBRARY† □ Pine Bluff, AR

Jenkins, Aileen, Libn.
SALES AND MARKETING MANAGEMENT - LIBRARY □ New York, NY

Jenkins, Ann A., Adm.
MERCK & COMPANY, INC. - KELCO DIVISION - LITERATURE AND INFORMATION SERVICES □ San Diego, CA

Jenkins, Betty, Asst.Dir., Serv.
TEACHERS COLLEGE - LIBRARY □ New York, NY

Jenkins, Carol G., Assoc.Dir.
UNIVERSITY OF VIRGINIA MEDICAL CENTER - CLAUDE MOORE HEALTH SCIENCES LIBRARY □ Charlottesville, VA

Jenkins, D.R., Libn.
COLEMAN AND COMPANY - LIBRARY □ Los Angeles, CA

Jenkins, Glen, Rare Bk.Libn./Archv.
CLEVELAND HEALTH SCIENCES LIBRARY - HOWARD DITTRICK MUSEUM OF HISTORICAL MEDICINE □ Cleveland, OH

Jenkins, Harriet, Asst.Hd.
ENOCH PRATT FREE LIBRARY - SOCIAL SCIENCE AND HISTORY DEPARTMENT □ Baltimore, MD

Jenkins, Janice, Music Libn.
STETSON UNIVERSITY - SCHOOL OF MUSIC LIBRARY □ De Land, FL

Jenkins, Kathy I., Acq.Libn.
HOWARD UNIVERSITY - MOORLAND-SPINGARN RESEARCH CENTER - LIBRARY DIVISION □ Washington, DC

Jenkins, Lawrence, Media/AV Serv.
BROOME COMMUNITY COLLEGE - CECIL C. TYRRELL LEARNING RESOURCES CENTER □ Binghamton, NY

Jenkins, Leola H., Asst.Chf.
U.S. VETERANS ADMINISTRATION (NC-Durham) - MEDICAL CENTER LIBRARY □ Durham, NC

Jenkins, Mary M., Hd.Libn.
WEST VIRGINIA STATE DEPARTMENT OF CULTURE AND HISTORY - ARCHIVES AND HISTORY LIBRARY □ Charleston, WV

Jenkins, Norma P.H., Libn.
CORNING MUSEUM OF GLASS - LIBRARY □ Corning, NY

Jenkins, Pamela U., Asst. to Coord.
SMITHSONIAN INSTITUTION - NATL. MUSEUM OF AMERICAN ART -INVENTORY OF AMERICAN PAINTINGS EXECUTED BEFORE 1914□ Washington, DC

Jenkins, Phyllis A., Lib.Techn.
U.S. VETERANS ADMINISTRATION (TN-Murfreesboro) - MEDICAL CENTER LIBRARY □ Murfreesboro, TN

Jenkins, Robert, Cat.
GRUMMAN AEROSPACE CORPORATION - TECHNICAL INFORMATION CENTER □ Bethpage, NY

Jenkins, Robert L., Cur.
MARINELAND, INC. - RESEARCH LABORATORY □ St. Augustine, FL

Jenneman, Eugene A., Interpretation Chf.
BESSER (Jesse) MUSEUM - LIBRARY □ Alpena, MI

Jenner, Elizabeth, Hd.Libn.
CANADIAN BROADCASTING CORPORATION - REFERENCE LIBRARY □ Toronto, ON

Jennings, David, Asst.Libn.
BOSTON GLOBE NEWSPAPER COMPANY - LIBRARY □ Boston, MA

Jennings, Gary, First Asst.
DALLAS PUBLIC LIBRARY - ARCHIVES AND RESEARCH CENTER FOR TEXAS AND DALLAS HISTORY □ Dallas, TX

Jennings, Hazel, Libn.
ROHR MARINE, INC. - TECHNICAL LIBRARY† □ Chula Vista, CA

Jennings, Jan, Mgr./Libn.
OKLAHOMA WELL LOG LIBRARY, INC. □ Tulsa, OK

Jennings, Kelly, Libn.
TULSA CITY-COUNTY LIBRARY SYSTEM - BUSINESS AND TECHNOLOGY DEPARTMENT □ Tulsa, OK

Jennings, Lucile H., Proj.Dir.
AMERICAN HARP SOCIETY REPOSITORY □ Athens, OH

Jennings, Marie D., Adm.Libn.
U.S. AIR FORCE BASE - PATRICK BASE LIBRARY† □ Patrick AFB, FL

Jennings, Vera, Cons.
AMERICAN CAN COMPANY - BUTTERICK FASHION MARKETING COMPANY - BUTTERICK ARCHIVES/LIBRARY† □ New York, NY

Jensen, Bro. Aaron, Asst.Libn.
ASSUMPTION ABBEY - LIBRARY □ Richardson, ND

Jensen, Barbara, Adm.Off.
U.S. PRESIDENTIAL LIBRARIES - LYNDON B. JOHNSON LIBRARY† □ Austin, TX

Jensen, Becky, Mgr., Info.Serv.
UNIVERSITY OF SOUTHERN CALIFORNIA - NASA INDUSTRIAL APPLICATION CENTER (NIAC) □ Los Angeles, CA

Jensen, Betty Jo, Med.Libn.
WHATCOM/ISLAND HEALTH SERVICES - LIBRARY □ Bellingham, WA

Jensen, Dennis F., Lib.Mgr.
STANDARD & POOR'S CORPORATION - LIBRARY □ New York, NY

Jensen, Donna, Hd.Circ.Serv.
DALHOUSIE UNIVERSITY - W.K. KELLOGG HEALTH SCIENCES LIBRARY □ Halifax, NS

Jensen, Gary D., Hd.
LIBRARY OF CONGRESS - GEN. READING ROOMS DIV. - THOMAS JEFFERSON READING ROOMS SECTION □ Washington, DC

Jensen, Gunvor, Asst.Libn.
WAGNER COLLEGE - HORRMANN LIBRARY □ Staten Island, NY

Jensen, Joan, Ref.
UNIVERSITY OF CONNECTICUT - LIBRARY □ Storrs, CT

Jensen, Joseph E., Libn.
MEDICAL AND CHIRURGICAL FACULTY OF THE STATE OF MARYLAND - LIBRARY □ Baltimore, MD

Jensen, Dr. Louis R., Asst. Dean
INDIANA STATE UNIVERSITY - CONTINUING EDUCATION AND EXTENDED SERVICES - LIBRARY □ Terre Haute, IN

Jensen, M. Wayne, Dir.
TILLAMOOK COUNTY PIONEER MUSEUM - LIBRARY □ Tillamook, OR

Jensen, Mary Ann, Cur. Theatre Coll.
PRINCETON UNIVERSITY - RARE BOOKS AND SPECIAL COLLECTIONS □ Princeton, NJ

Jensen, Mary Ann, Cur.
PRINCETON UNIVERSITY - WILLIAM SEYMOUR THEATER COLLECTION □ Princeton, NJ

Jensen, Oliver, Chf.
LIBRARY OF CONGRESS - PRINTS & PHOTOGRAPHS DIVISION □ Washington, DC

Jensen, Sally, Acq.
U.S. NASA - HEADQUARTERS LIBRARY □ Washington, DC

Jensen, Yvette M., Libn.
MASSACHUSETTS MUTUAL LIFE INSURANCE COMPANY - LIBRARY □ Springfield, MA

Jenson, Annette, Libn.
GRAY, PLANT, MOOTY, MOOTY, AND BENNETT - LAW LIBRARY† □ Minneapolis, MN

Jenson, David L., Libn.
MINNEAPOLIS TECHNICAL INSTITUTE - LIBRARY □ Minneapolis, MN

Jenson, John R., Rare Book Libn.
UNIVERSITY OF MINNESOTA - SPECIAL COLLECTIONS AND RARE BOOKS □ Minneapolis, MN

Jenyik, Rosemarie, Tech.Serv.Libn.
U.S. VETERANS ADMINISTRATION (KS-Topeka) - DR. KARL A. MENNINGER MEDICAL LIBRARY □ Topeka, KS

Jepps, Sheila J., Hd.Libn.
SHELL CANADA RESOURCES LIMITED - TECHNICAL LIBRARY □ Calgary, AB

Jepson, Mabel, Tech.Serv.Libn.
SUNY AT BUFFALO - CHARLES B. SEARS LAW LIBRARY □ Buffalo, NY

Jerde, Curtis D., Cur.
TULANE UNIVERSITY OF LOUISIANA - WILLIAM RANSOM HOGAN JAZZ ARCHIVE □ New Orleans, LA

Jeremy, Joseph J., Dir.
U.S. DEPT. OF COMMERCE - INTERNATIONAL TRADE ADMINISTRATION - RENO DISTRICT OFFICE LIBRARY □ Reno, NV

Jergens, Clare M., Chf., Lib.Serv.
U.S. VETERANS ADMINISTRATION (IA-Des Moines) - HOSPITAL LIBRARY □ Des Moines, IA

P E R S O N N E L

Jeri, Raymond A., Libn.Asst.
NATIONAL SOCIETY TO PREVENT BLINDNESS - CONRAD BERENS LIBRARY □ New York, NY

Jerkovich, George, Dir./Cur.
UNIVERSITY OF KANSAS - SLAVIC COLLECTION □ Lawrence, KS

Jernigan, Thomas, M.D., Med.Dir.
NEW YORK LIFE INSURANCE COMPANY - MEDICAL DEPARTMENT LIBRARY □ New York, NY

Jernigan, Dr. W.W., Dir.
ORAL ROBERTS UNIVERSITY - LIBRARY - HOLY SPIRIT RESEARCH CENTER □ Tulsa, OK

Jerousek, William, Libn.
OAK PARK PUBLIC LIBRARY - LOCAL AUTHOR AND HISTORY COLLECTIONS □ Oak Park, IL

Jerrido, Margaret, Archv.
MEDICAL COLLEGE OF PENNSYLVANIA - ARCHIVES AND SPECIAL COLLECTIONS ON WOMEN IN MEDICINE □ Philadelphia, PA

Jerse, Dorothy, Musm.Cur.
VIGO COUNTY HISTORICAL SOCIETY - HISTORICAL MUSEUM OF THE WABASH VALLEY - LIBRARY □ Terre Haute, IN

Jersey, Patricia J., Ref./ILL Libn.
EAST STROUDSBURG STATE COLLEGE - LIBRARY □ East Stroudsburg, PA

Jervis, Pam, Cat.Libn.
BETHEL THEOLOGICAL SEMINARY - RESOURCE CENTER □ St. Paul, MN

Jeryn, Irene, Libn.
HOSPITAL FOR SICK CHILDREN - HOSPITAL LIBRARY □ Toronto, ON

Jeschke, Channing R., Libn.
EMORY UNIVERSITY - PITTS THEOLOGY LIBRARY □ Atlanta, GA

Jeschke, Freya, Libn.
GOETHE HOUSE NEW YORK - LIBRARY† □ New York, NY

Jeske, Dale, Hd.Libn. for Blind
CONNECTICUT STATE LIBRARY □ Hartford, CT

Jeske, Dale, Dir.
CONNECTICUT STATE LIBRARY - LIBRARY FOR THE BLIND AND PHYSICALLY HANDICAPPED □ Hartford, CT

Jesmer, Michel R., Lib.Techn.
CANADA - PARKS CANADA, ONTARIO REGION LIBRARY □ Cornwall, ON

Jespersen, B., Libn.
CAMPBELL INSTITUTE FOR RESEARCH AND TECHNOLOGY - RESEARCH DEVELOPMENT LIBRARY □ Camden, NJ

Jesse, Frank H., Patients' Libn.
U.S. VETERANS ADMINISTRATION (KY-Louisville) - HOSPITAL LIBRARY □ Louisville, KY

Jessee, Gordon E., Asst.Libn.
BABCOCK AND WILCOX COMPANY - NUCLEAR POWER GENERATION DIVISION - LIBRARY □ Lynchburg, VA

Jessup, Helen C., Libn.
POTOMAC ELECTRIC POWER COMPANY - LIBRARY □ Washington, DC

Jessup, Libby F., Principal Law Libn.
NEW YORK STATE SUPREME COURT - 2ND JUDICIAL DISTRICT - LAW LIBRARY □ Brooklyn, NY

Jestes, Edward, Libn.
UNIVERSITY OF CALIFORNIA, DAVIS - PHYSICAL SCIENCES LIBRARY □ Davis, CA

Jeter, Ruby Newell, Libn.
FRESNO GENEALOGICAL SOCIETY - LIBRARY □ Fresno, CA

Jetmalani, Dr. Narain B., Dir., Ed. & Res.
OREGON STATE HOSPITAL - MEDICAL LIBRARY □ Salem, OR

Jett, Don, Hd.Libn.
UNIVERSITY OF TENNESSEE - SCIENCE-ENGINEERING LIBRARY □ Knoxville, TN

Jett, John H., Dir.
ARIZONA STATE DEPARTMENT OF MINERAL RESOURCES - LIBRARY □ Phoenix, AZ

Jette, Jean-Paul, Dir.
UNIVERSITE DE MONTREAL - MEDECINE VETERINAIRE-BIBLIOTHEQUE □ St-Hyacinthe, PQ

Jevnikar, Jana, Info.Coord.
CLEARINGHOUSE FOR ARTS INFORMATION - CENTER FOR ARTS INFORMATION □ New York, NY

Jewell, Frank, Cur., Printed Coll.
CHICAGO HISTORICAL SOCIETY - SPECIAL COLLECTIONS □ Chicago, IL

Jewell, Mary Ellen, Asst.Libn.
HURON ROAD HOSPITAL - LIBRARY AND AUDIOVISUAL CENTER □ Cleveland, OH

Jewett, Christine C., Libn.
FULLER THEOLOGICAL SEMINARY - MC ALISTER LIBRARY □ Pasadena, CA

Jewkes, Peggy, Ref./Doc.Libn.
BLOOMSBURG STATE COLLEGE - HARVEY A. ANDRUSS LIBRARY □ Bloomsburg, PA

Jhabvala, Wendy, Dir.
NATIONAL CLEARINGHOUSE FOR ALCOHOL INFORMATION - LIBRARY □ Rockville, MD

Jimerson, Randall, Libn./Archv.
MANSFIELD HISTORICAL SOCIETY - EDITH MASON LIBRARY □ Storrs, CT

Jimerson, Randall, Archv.
UNIVERSITY OF CONNECTICUT - LIBRARY □ Storrs, CT

Jirkovsky, Z., Hd.
CONCORDIA UNIVERSITY - SIR GEORGE WILLIAMS CAMPUS - SCIENCE & ENGINEERING LIBRARY □ Montreal, PQ

Jivraj, Mumtaz, Med.Libn.
HOLY CROSS HOSPITAL OF CALGARY - MEDICAL LIBRARY □ Calgary, AB

Jo, Julitta, Ser.Libn.
SUNY AT STONY BROOK - HEALTH SCIENCES LIBRARY □ East Setauket, NY

Joba, Judith, Info.Spec.
C.I. POWER SERVICES - INFORMATION CENTRE □ Montreal, PQ

Jobe, Shirley A., Libn.
U.S. PRESIDENTIAL LIBRARIES - JOHN F. KENNEDY LIBRARY □ Boston, MA

Jobin, L., Loans
COMPLEXE SCIENTIFIQUE DU QUEBEC - SERVICE DE DOCUMENTATION ET DE BIBLIOTHEQUE □ Ste. Foy, PQ

Jobson, Valerie, Mgr.
CALGARY ECO-CENTRE SOCIETY - ENVIRONMENTAL INFORMATION CENTRE □ Calgary, AB

Joffred, K.A., Libn.
GILBERT ASSOCIATES, INC. - CORPORATE LIBRARY† □ Reading, PA

Johannessen, Joanne, Libn.
WERTHEIM AND COMPANY, INC. - RESEARCH LIBRARY □ New York, NY

John, Margaret D., Tech.Info.Spec.
SCOTT PAPER COMPANY - RESEARCH LIBRARY & TECHNICAL INFORMATION SERVICE □ Philadelphia, PA

Johndahl, Dr. Thor, Lab.Dir.
KTA-TATOR ASSOCIATES, INC. - LIBRARY □ Coraopolis, PA

Johns, Alan, Asst.Libn./Cat.
UNIVERSITY OF TENNESSEE - JOINT RESEARCH CENTERS LIBRARY □ Knoxville, TN

Johns, Bernice, Hd.
OMAHA PUBLIC LIBRARY - BUSINESS, SCIENCE & TECHNOLOGY DEPARTMENT □ Omaha, NE

Johns, Fabienne R., Hd.Libn.
PAYNE THEOLOGICAL SEMINARY - R.C. RANSOM MEMORIAL LIBRARY □ Wilberforce, OH

Johns, Frank, Libn.
BLUE CROSS AND BLUE SHIELD OF VIRGINIA - PLANS LIBRARY □ Richmond, VA

Johns, Gerald, Asst.Sci.Libn.
SAN DIEGO STATE UNIVERSITY - SCIENCE DEPARTMENT □ San Diego, CA

Johns, Gloria F.L., Libn.
CANADA LIFE ASSURANCE COMPANY - LIBRARY □ Toronto, ON

Johns, John E., First Asst.
PUBLIC LIBRARY OF CINCINNATI AND HAMILTON COUNTY - SCIENCE AND INDUSTRY DEPARTMENT □ Cincinnati, OH

Johns, Michele, Br.Libn.
UNIVERSITY OF ILLINOIS MEDICAL CENTER - PEORIA SCHOOL OF MEDICINE - LIBRARY OF THE HEALTH SCIENCES □ Peoria, IL

Johns, Nellie, Lib.Coord.
EMORY UNIVERSITY - YERKES REGIONAL PRIMATE CENTER - LIBRARY □ Atlanta, GA

Johns, Dr. T.R., Dept.Chm.
UNIVERSITY OF VIRGINIA MEDICAL CENTER - DEPARTMENT OF NEUROLOGY - ELIZABETH J. OHRSTROM LIBRARY □ Charlottesville, VA

Johnsen, Maggi, Sr.Archv.
GEORGIA STATE SURVEYOR GENERAL DEPARTMENT - ARCHIVES □ Atlanta, GA

Johnson, A. Kristine, Libn.
UNIVERSITY OF MINNESOTA - ARCHITECTURE LIBRARY □ Minneapolis, MN

Johnson, Adele, Acq.Libn.
NEW YORK STATE HISTORICAL ASSOCIATION - LIBRARY □ Cooperstown, NY

Johnson, Alan, Archv.Mgr.
WAKE FOREST UNIVERSITY - BOWMAN GRAY SCHOOL OF MEDICINE - LIBRARY □ Winston-Salem, NC

Johnson, Alice K., Libn.
PPG INDUSTRIES, INC. - CHEMICAL DIVISION - NATRIUM RESEARCH AND DEVELOPMENT LIBRARY □ New Martinsville, WV

Johnson, Allan R., Libn.
BRIERCREST BIBLE INSTITUTE - ARCHIBALD LIBRARY† □ Caronport, SK

Johnson, Andrew F., Libn.
UNIVERSITY OF WASHINGTON - SPECIAL COLLECTIONS DIVISION - PACIFIC NORTHWEST COLLECTION □ Seattle, WA

Johnson, Andrew L., Libn.
SYSTEMATICS GENERAL CORPORATION - LIBRARY □ Falls Church, VA

Johnson, Ann Kinken, Hd.Libn.
VIRGINIAN-PILOT & LEDGER-STAR - LIBRARY □ Norfolk, VA

Johnson, Annelle, Med.Libn.
JACKSON HOSPITAL AND CLINIC - MEDICAL LIBRARY □ Montgomery, AL

Johnson, Audrey, Act. County Hist.
MONROE COUNTY LOCAL HISTORY ROOM & LIBRARY □ Sparta, WI

Johnson, B.G.H., Biologist
CANADA - FISHERIES & OCEANS - SEA LAMPREY CONTROL CENTRE - LIBRARY □ Sault Ste. Marie, ON

Johnson, Barbara Coe, Dir. Of Libs.
HARPER-GRACE HOSPITALS - HARPER HOSPITAL DIVISION - DEPARTMENT OF LIBRARIES □ Detroit, MI

Johnson, Bernice W., Hd.Libn.
BROCKTON DAILY ENTERPRISE AND BROCKTON TIMES-ENTERPRISE - LIBRARY† □ Brockton, MA

Johnson, Bethry, Libn.
STEARNS-ROGER ENGINEERING CORPORATION - TECHNICAL LIBRARY □ Denver, CO

Johnson, Betty R., Libn.
U.S. ARMY - CORPS OF ENGINEERS - LOWER MISSISSIPPI VALLEY DIV. - MISSISSIPPI RIVER COMMN. TECHNICAL LIB. □ Vicksburg, MS

Johnson, Bobbie, Hd.Libn.
PAUL, HASTINGS, JANOFSKY AND WALKER - LAW LIBRARY □ Los Angeles, CA

Johnson, Bruce L., Lib.Dir.
CALIFORNIA HISTORICAL SOCIETY - SCHUBERT HALL LIBRARY □ San Francisco, CA

Johnson, Bruce S., Chf.Ref.Libn.
UNIVERSITY OF MICHIGAN - LAW LIBRARY □
Ann Arbor, MI
Johnson, Buford, Transit Planner
SAN FRANCISCO MUNICIPAL RAILWAY -
PLANNING DIVISION LIBRARY □ San Francisco,
CA
Johnson, Candice M., Libn.
SYBRON CORPORATION - PFAUDLER COMPANY
- TECHNICAL LIBRARY □ Rochester, NY
Johnson, Carol, Sci.Info.Coord.
AMERICAN MC GAW - TECHNICAL
INFORMATION CENTER □ Santa Ana, CA
Johnson, Catherine, Lib.Asst.
QUEEN'S UNIVERSITY AT KINGSTON -
PHYSICS LIBRARY □ Kingston, ON
Johnson, Cecile, Libn.
HOFFMANN-LA ROCHE, LTD. - CORPORATE
LIBRARY □ Vaudreuil, PQ
Johnson, Rev. Charles B., Dir.
ST. THOMAS SEMINARY LIBRARY - ALUMNI
COLLECTION □ Bloomfield, CT
Johnson, Charles H., Supv. Of Lib.
SPRING GROVE HOSPITAL CENTER -
SULZBACHER MEMORIAL LIBRARY† □
Catonsville, MD
Johnson, Cindy, Asst.Libn.
UNIVERSITY OF HEALTH SCIENCES/CHICAGO
MEDICAL SCHOOL - LIBRARY □ North Chicago,
IL
Johnson, Clifton H., Exec.Dir.
AMISTAD RESEARCH CENTER - LIBRARY □ New
Orleans, LA
Johnson, Corlan Dokken, Sr.Libn.
NAPA STATE HOSPITAL - WRENSHALL A.
OLIVER PROFESSIONAL LIBRARY □ Imola, CA
Johnson, D., Libn.
U.S. COAST GUARD ACADEMY - LIBRARY □ New
London, CT
Johnson, D. Thomas, Cur./Exhibits
KINGMAN MUSEUM OF NATURAL HISTORY -
LIBRARY □ Battle Creek, MI
Johnson, Dale L., Archv.
UNIVERSITY OF MONTANA - MAUREEN & MIKE
MANSFIELD LIBRARY - ARCHIVES† □ Missoula,
MT
Johnson, David J., Libn./Archv.
ARICA INSTITUTE, INC. - LIBRARY AND
ARCHIVES □ New York, NY
Johnson, David L., Dir.
PARKLAND COLLEGE - LEARNING RESOURCE
CENTER □ Champaign, IL
Johnson, Dr. David P.
AMERICAN COLLEGE OF HERALDRY - LIBRARY
□ University, AL
Johnson, Deborah P., Distr.Rep.
NATIONAL FILM BOARD OF CANADA - FILM
LIBRARY □ New York, NY
Johnson, Dennis
U.S. BUREAU OF THE CENSUS - REGIONAL
DATA USER SERVICE - KANSAS CITY
REGIONAL OFFICE - LIBRARY □ Kansas City, KS
Johnson, Diana, Mgr.
SOUTHWEST TEXAS STATE UNIVERSITY -
LEARNING RESOURCES CENTER □ San Marcos,
TX
Johnson, Diana, Ref./ILL
WORCESTER POLYTECHNIC INSTITUTE -
GEORGE C. GORDON LIBRARY □ Worcester, MA
Johnson, Diane, Ser.Libn.
SUNY - COLLEGE AT GENESEO - MILNE
LIBRARY □ Geneseo, NY
Johnson, Donna, Resource Ctr.Dir.
ABBOTT-NORTHWESTERN HOSPITAL
CORPORATION - HEALTH SCIENCES RESOURCE
CENTER □ Minneapolis, MN
Johnson, Duane A., Command Libn.
U.S. AIR FORCE - AIR TRAINING COMMAND -
LIBRARY PROGRAM ATC/DPSOL □ Randolph
AFB, TX

Johnson, Eleanor, Libn.
ENGLISH-SPEAKING UNION OF THE U.S.A. -
WASHINGTON D.C. BRANCH LIBRARY □
Washington, DC
Johnson, Eleanor, Field Libn.
UNIVERSITY OF ARIZONA - ARIZONA HEALTH
SCIENCES CENTER LIBRARY □ Tucson, AZ
Johnson, Eleanor, Asst.Libn.
WISCONSIN INDIANHEAD TECHNICAL
INSTITUTE, SUPERIOR CAMPUS - LIBRARY □
Superior, WI
Johnson, Elizabeth, Cat.
INDIANA UNIVERSITY - LILLY LIBRARY □
Bloomington, IN
Johnson, Elizabeth Anne, Dept.Hd.
LIBRARY ASSOCIATION OF PORTLAND -
LITERATURE AND HISTORY DEPARTMENT □
Portland, OR
Johnson, Elizabeth Anne
LIBRARY ASSOCIATION OF PORTLAND -
OREGON COLLECTION □ Portland, OR
Johnson, Ellen, Assoc.Libn.
UNIVERSITY OF KANSAS - THOMAS GORTON
MUSIC LIBRARY □ Lawrence, KS
Johnson, Ellen M., Libn.
FEDERAL RESERVE BANK OF KANSAS CITY -
RESEARCH LIBRARY □ Kansas City, MO
Johnson, Elly, Music Cat.
UNIVERSITY OF WISCONSIN, MILWAUKEE -
MUSIC COLLECTION □ Milwaukee, WI
Johnson, Esther, Libn.
UNIVERSITY OF CALIFORNIA, BERKELEY -
FORESTRY LIBRARY □ Berkeley, CA
Johnson, Eunice Bisbee, Sr.Lib.Asst.
UNIVERSITY OF MINNESOTA - PUBLIC
ADMINISTRATION LIBRARY □ Minneapolis, MN
Johnson, Eva, Adm.Asst.
FRENCH LIBRARY IN BOSTON, INC. □ Boston,
MA
Johnson, Mrs. Eyrle G., Libn.
SAN ANTONIO CONSERVATION SOCIETY -
LIBRARY □ San Antonio, TX
Johnson, F.T., Rec.Mgr.
UNIVERSITY OF UTAH - SPECIAL COLLECTIONS
DEPARTMENT □ Salt Lake City, UT
Johnson, Fannie, Circ.Libn.
LINCOLN UNIVERSITY OF MISSOURI - INMAN
E. PAGE LIBRARY □ Jefferson City, MO
Johnson, Fran, Center Libn.
MARICOPA TECHNICAL COMMUNITY COLLEGE
- LIBRARY RESOURCE CENTER □ Phoenix, AZ
Johnson, Fran R., Libn.
MARICOPA TECHNICAL COMMUNITY COLLEGE
- INDUSTRY EDUCATION CENTER LIBRARY □
Phoenix, AZ
Johnson, Gail W., Sr.Libn.
NEW YORK LIFE INSURANCE COMPANY - NEW
YORK LIFE LIBRARY □ New York, NY
Johnson, Garry, Dir.
LOUISVILLE BAPTIST HOSPITALS, INC. -
HAGAN LIBRARY □ Louisville, KY
Johnson, Genevieve L.
BELL TELEPHONE LABORATORIES, INC. &
WESTERN ELECTRIC, INC. - TECHNICAL
LIBRARY □ Reading, PA
Johnson, Glenn H., Jr., Dir.
WESTERN NEW ENGLAND COLLEGE - JOHN D.
CHURCHILL MEMORIAL LIBRARY □ Springfield,
MA
Johnson, Guela G., Libn.
UNIVERSITY OF WASHINGTON - SOCIAL WORK
LIBRARY □ Seattle, WA
Johnson, Harvey G., Info.Sci.
GENERAL MILLS, INC. - JAMES FORD BELL
TECHNICAL CENTER - TECHNICAL
INFORMATION SERVICES □ Minneapolis, MN
Johnson, Harvey J., Dir.
CATHOLIC CENTRAL UNION OF AMERICA -
CENTRAL BUREAU LIBRARY □ St. Louis, MO
Johnson, Hazel, Asst.Pub.Serv.Libn.
UNIVERSITY OF GEORGIA - LAW LIBRARY □
Athens, GA

Johnson, Herb, Dir., Media Ctr.
MC PHERSON COLLEGE - MILLER LIBRARY □
McPherson, KS
Johnson, Hilary C., Tech.Libn.
WESTINGHOUSE ELECTRIC CORPORATION -
STEAM TURBINE GENERATOR DIVISION -
TECHNICAL LIBRARY □ Philadelphia, PA
Johnson, Irma E., Lib.Coord.
WITCO CHEMICAL CORPORATION - GOLDEN
BEAR DIVISION - R & D LIBRARY □ Bakersfield,
CA
Johnson, Irma Y., Science Libn.
MASSACHUSETTS INSTITUTE OF TECHNOLOGY
- SCIENCE LIBRARY □ Cambridge, MA
Johnson, James, Libn.
ONTARIO BIBLE COLLEGE/ONTARIO
THEOLOGICAL SEMINARY - J. WILLIAM
HORSEY LIBRARY □ Willowdale, ON
Johnson, James, Assoc.Dir.
SLOAN (Alfred P., Jr.) MUSEUM - LIBRARY □
Flint, MI
Johnson, James, Jr., Dp. State Libn.
SOUTH CAROLINA STATE LIBRARY □ Columbia,
SC
Johnson, James P., Chf.Libn.
HOWARD UNIVERSITY - MOORLAND-SPINGARN
RESEARCH CENTER - LIBRARY DIVISION □
Washington, DC
Johnson, James R., Hd., Hist. & Travel
MEMPHIS-SHELBY COUNTY PUBLIC LIBRARY
AND INFORMATION CENTER - MEMPHIS ROOM
COLLECTIONS □ Memphis, TN
Johnson, Janice, Libn.
AMERICAN VETERINARY MEDICAL
ASSOCIATION - LIBRARY† □ Schaumburg, IL
Johnson, Janice, Libn.
FOOTE CONE & BELDING - INFORMATION
CENTER □ Chicago, IL
Johnson, Jean, Asst.Ref.Libn.
LEHIGH UNIVERSITY - MART SCIENCE AND
ENGINEERING LIBRARY □ Bethlehem, PA
Johnson, Jeffrey, Supv.Pub.Serv.
QUEEN'S UNIVERSITY AT KINGSTON - LAW
LIBRARY □ Kingston, ON
Johnson, Dr. Jerry, Dir.
UNIVERSITY OF SOUTH DAKOTA - BUSINESS
RESEARCH BUREAU □ Vermillion, SD
Johnson, Joan, Asst.Libn.
MC PHERSON COLLEGE - MILLER LIBRARY □
McPherson, KS
Johnson, JoAnn, Chf., Lib.Serv.
ENVIRONMENTAL PROTECTION AGENCY -
ANDREW W. BREIDENBACH ENVIRONMENTAL
RESEARCH CTR., CINCINNATI - TECH.LIB. □
Cincinnati, OH
Johnson, John, Doc.
KANSAS STATE UNIVERSITY - FARRELL
LIBRARY □ Manhattan, KS
Johnson, Judith, Archv.
PROTESTANT EPISCOPAL CHURCH -
EPISCOPAL DIOCESE OF NEW YORK -
ARCHIVES □ New York, NY
Johnson, Julia
MARSH AND MC LENNAN, INC. - INFORMATION
CENTER □ New York, NY
Johnson, Julie M., Assoc.Med.Libn.
UNIVERSITY OF SOUTH CAROLINA - SCHOOL
OF MEDICINE LIBRARY □ Columbia, SC
Johnson, June, Libn.
REDMOND (J.W.) COMPANY - LIBRARY □
Washington, DC
Johnson, Karen, Libn.
CENTRAL BAPTIST CHURCH - MEDIA CENTER □
St. Paul, MN
Johnson, Kathleen A.
UNIVERSITY OF NEBRASKA, LINCOLN -
ARCHITECTURE LIBRARY □ Lincoln, NE
Johnson, Kathrine E., Mgr., Lib.Serv.
VARIAN ASSOCIATES - TECHNICAL LIBRARY □
Palo Alto, CA

Johnson, Katie
ALTERNATIVE ENERGY RESOURCES
ORGANIZATION (AERO) - LIBRARY □ Billings,
MT

Johnson, Kay, South Reg.Libn.
SEATTLE PUBLIC LIBRARY - DOUGLASS-TRUTH
BRANCH LIBRARY □ Seattle, WA

Johnson, Kordillia C., Rare Bks.Libn.
UNIVERSITY OF WISCONSIN, PLATTEVILLE -
KARRMANN LIBRARY □ Platteville, WI

Johnson, Laura, Hd., Ext.Div.
INDIANA STATE LIBRARY □ Indianapolis, IN

Johnson, Laura M., Mgr.
BOZELL & JACOBS, INC. - CORPORATE
INFORMATION CENTER □ Chicago, IL

Johnson, Leanne, Tech.Serv.Libn.
CANADIAN MEMORIAL CHIROPRACTIC
COLLEGE - C.C. CLEMMER LIBRARY □ Toronto,
ON

Johnson, Lee Z., Archv.
FIRST CHURCH OF CHRIST SCIENTIST -
ARCHIVES AND LIBRARY □ Boston, MA

Johnson, Lenora I., Musm.Dir.
NORMAN COUNTY HISTORICAL SOCIETY -
MEMORIAL MUSEUM LIBRARY □ Ada, MN

Johnson, Linda, Res.Asst.
FOUNDATION FOR PUBLIC AFFAIRS -
RESOURCE CENTER □ Washington, DC

Johnson, Liz, Libn.
ALBERTA - ENERGY RESOURCES
CONSERVATION BOARD - LIBRARY □ Calgary,
AB

Johnson, Louise, Cur.
WASHINGTON COUNTY MUSEUM LIBRARY □
Stillwater, MN

Johnson, M. Malinda, Chf.Libn.
U.S. ARMY POST - FORT STEWART/HUNTER
AAF LIBRARY SYSTEM □ Ft. Stewart, GA

Johnson, Margaret, Hd., Coll.Proc.
UNIVERSITY OF MINNESOTA, ST. PAUL -
CENTRAL LIBRARY □ St. Paul, MN

Johnson, Margaret Ann, ILL Libn.
UNIVERSITY OF ARKANSAS MEDICAL
SCIENCES CAMPUS - MEDICAL SCIENCES
LIBRARY □ Little Rock, AR

Johnson, Margery, Hd., Instr.Mtls.Ctr.
CLARION STATE COLLEGE - RENA M. CARLSON
LIBRARY □ Clarion, PA

Johnson, Marguerite H., Law Libn.
PALM BEACH COUNTY - LAW LIBRARY □ West
Palm Beach, FL

Johnson, Marilyn K., Mgr.
SHELL OIL COMPANY - INFORMATION &
LIBRARY SERVICES □ Houston, TX

Johnson, Marion, Dir.Pub.Lib.Dev.
NORTH CAROLINA STATE DEPARTMENT OF
CULTURAL RESOURCES - DIVISION OF THE
STATE LIBRARY □ Raleigh, NC

Johnson, Mrs. Marion E., Libn.
FORINTEK CANADA CORP. - WESTERN
LABORATORY - LIBRARY □ Vancouver, BC

Johnson, Mark, Dir. of Educ.
CARSON COUNTY SQUARE HOUSE MUSEUM -
INFORMATION CENTER □ Panhandle, TX

Johnson, Marlys J., Tech.Libn.
FLUIDYNE ENGINEERING CORPORATION -
TECHNICAL LIBRARY □ Minneapolis, MN

Johnson, Mary E., Libn.
FOREST HISTORY SOCIETY, INC. - LIBRARY
AND ARCHIVES □ Santa Cruz, CA

Johnson, Mary E., Asst.Libn.
U.S. ARMY - CORPS OF ENGINEERS - SEATTLE
DISTRICT - LIBRARY □ Seattle, WA

Johnson, Mary H., Libn.
MENTAL HEALTH ASSOCIATION OF
WESTCHESTER COUNTY - LIBRARY □ White
Plains, NY

Johnson, Mary Jane, Sec.
PENNSYLVANIA STATE UNIVERSITY -
INSTITUTE FOR POLICY RESEARCH AND
EVALUATION - LIBRARY □ University Park, PA

Johnson, Mary Pat
VERMONT HISTORICAL SOCIETY - LIBRARY □
Montpelier, VT

Johnson, Millard F., Jr., Res.Assoc.
WASHINGTON UNIVERSITY - SCHOOL OF
MEDICINE LIBRARY □ St. Louis, MO

Johnson, Nan A., Libn.
TUFTS UNIVERSITY - FLETCHER SCHOOL OF
LAW & DIPLOMACY - EDWIN GINN LIBRARY □
Medford, MA

Johnson, Nancy, Doc./Ref.Libn.
UNIVERSITY OF ILLINOIS - LAW LIBRARY □
Champaign, IL

Johnson, Noel, Hd., Cat.Div.
U.S. NAVY - NAVAL POSTGRADUATE SCHOOL -
DUDLEY KNOX LIBRARY □ Monterey, CA

Johnson, Pam, Acq.
OHIO NORTHERN UNIVERSITY - COLLEGE OF
LAW - JAY P. TAGGART MEMORIAL LAW
LIBRARY □ Ada, OH

Johnson, Pamela, Comp.Serv.Coord.
UNIVERSITY OF CALIFORNIA, SANTA CRUZ -
SCIENCE LIBRARY □ Santa Cruz, CA

Johnson, Pat M., Corp.Libn.
MC CLELLAND ENGINEERS, INC. - CORPORATE
LIBRARY □ Houston, TX

Johnson, Patricia J., Asst.Libn.
NORTHWESTERN MUTUAL LIFE INSURANCE
COMPANY - REFERENCE LIBRARY □ Milwaukee,
WI

Johnson, Paula, Lib.Techn.
U.S. NATL. MARINE FISHERIES SERVICE -
AUKE BAY FISHERIES LABORATORY -
FISHERIES RESEARCH LIBRARY □ Auke Bay, AK

Johnson, Peggy B., Exec.Sec.
CLINTON RIVER WATERSHED COUNCIL -
LIBRARY □ Utica, MI

Johnson, Rachael, Cur.
NEW HAMPSHIRE ANTIQUARIAN SOCIETY -
LIBRARY □ Concord, NH

Johnson, Renita V., Court Libn.
NEW YORK STATE SUPREME COURT - 4TH
JUDICIAL DISTRICT - LAW LIBRARY □ Saratoga
Springs, NY

Johnson, Reta, Dp.Libn.
NEBRASKA STATE LIBRARY □ Lincoln, NE

Johnson, Richard D., Dir. of Libs.
SUNY - COLLEGE AT ONEONTA - JAMES M.
MILNE LIBRARY □ Oneonta, NY

Johnson, Dr. Robert N., Dir.
OAKLAND SCHOOLS - EDUCATIONAL RESOURCE
CENTER □ Pontiac, MI

Johnson, Robert O., Libn.
UNIVERSITY OF CINCINNATI - COLLEGE
CONSERVATORY OF MUSIC - GORNO
MEMORIAL MUSIC LIBRARY □ Cincinnati, OH

Johnson, Miss Roger Mae, Dept.Hd.
CLEVELAND PUBLIC LIBRARY - CHILDREN'S
LITERATURE DEPARTMENT □ Cleveland, OH

Johnson, Ronald D., Lib.Dir.
DANA COLLEGE - C.A. DANA-LIFE LIBRARY □
Blair, NE

Johnson, Roy C., Libn.
NEW YORK UNIVERSITY - DENTAL CENTER -
JOHN & BERTHA E. WALDMANN MEMORIAL
LIBRARY □ New York, NY

Johnson, Ruth H., Tech.Libn.
BABCOCK AND WILCOX COMPANY - NUCLEAR
POWER GENERATION DIVISION - LIBRARY □
Lynchburg, VA

Johnson, Sallie, Dept.Hd.
MEMPHIS-SHELBY COUNTY PUBLIC LIBRARY
AND INFO. CTR. - SCIENCE/BUSINESS/SOCIAL
SCIENCES DEPT. □ Memphis, TN

Johnson, Mrs. Sam E., Act.Libn.
ST. MATTHEW'S EPISCOPAL CATHEDRAL -
LIBRARY† □ Dallas, TX

Johnson, Samuel V., Hd. of Automation Serv.
RENSSELAER POLYTECHNIC INSTITUTE -
FOLSOM LIBRARY □ Troy, NY

Johnson, Sandra, Asst.Cur.
PENSACOLA HISTORICAL SOCIETY - LELIA
ABERCROMBIE HISTORICAL LIBRARY □
Pensacola, FL

Johnson, Sandra, Libn.
UNIVERSITY OF MINNESOTA - DRUG
INFORMATION SERVICE CENTER □ Minneapolis,
MN

Johnson, Sharon, Chf., Lib.Serv.
U.S. VETERANS ADMINISTRATION (NM-
Albuquerque) - MEDICAL CENTER LIBRARY □
Albuquerque, NM

Johnson, Sheila G., Biological Sci.Libn.
OKLAHOMA STATE UNIVERSITY - BIOLOGICAL
SCIENCES DIVISION □ Stillwater, OK

Johnson, Sigrid, Icelandic Libn.
UNIVERSITY OF MANITOBA - ARCHIVES AND
SPECIAL COLLECTIONS □ Winnipeg, MB

Johnson, Susan, Libn.
PILLSBURY COMPANY - MAIN OFFICE
MARKETING LIBRARY □ Minneapolis, MN

Johnson, Susan, Libn.
SASKATCHEWAN - DEPARTMENT OF LABOUR -
OCCUPATIONAL HEALTH AND SAFETY
DIVISION - LIBRARY □ Regina, SK

Johnson, Susan E., Asst.Libn.
MULTNOMAH SCHOOL OF THE BIBLE - JOHN
AND MARY MITCHELL LIBRARY □ Portland, OR

Johnson, Suzanne, Biomed.Sci.Libn.
COLORADO STATE UNIVERSITY - WILLIAM E.
MORGAN LIBRARY □ Fort Collins, CO

Johnson, Terry, Libn.
MARKEM CORPORATION - LIBRARY □ Keene,
NH

Johnson, Theodore E., Dir.
UNITED SOCIETY OF BELIEVERS - THE SHAKER
LIBRARY □ Poland Spring, ME

Johnson, Thomas L., Asst.Libn.
UNIVERSITY OF SOUTH CAROLINA - SOUTH
CAROLINIANA LIBRARY □ Columbia, SC

Johnson, W. Thomas, Law Libn.
LITTON INDUSTRIES - LAW LIBRARY □ Beverly
Hills, CA

Johnson, Wayne, State Libn.
WYOMING STATE LIBRARY □ Cheyenne, WY

Johnson, Willa H., Libn.
CHURCH OF THE INCARNATION - MARMION
LIBRARY □ Dallas, TX

Johnson, William E., Dir., AT/AV Lab.
TUSKEGEE INSTITUTE - VETERINARY
MEDICINE LIBRARY† □ Tuskegee Institute, AL

Johnson, William E., Law Libn./Professor
WEST VIRGINIA UNIVERSITY - LAW LIBRARY
□ Morgantown, WV

Johnson, William G., Div.Hd.
AKRON-SUMMIT COUNTY PUBLIC LIBRARY -
BUSINESS, LABOR AND GOVERNMENT
DIVISION □ Akron, OH

Johnsrud, Thomas, Ref.Libn.
SAN DIEGO COUNTY LAW LIBRARY □ San Diego,
CA

Johnston, Anne R., Pub.Info.Off.
WESTERN KENTUCKY UNIVERSITY -
KENTUCKY LIBRARY AND MUSEUM/
UNIVERSITY ARCHIVES □ Bowling Green, KY

Johnston, Bruce, Med.Libn.
EYE AND EAR HOSPITAL OF PITTSBURGH -
BLAIR-LIPPINCOTT LIBRARY □ Pittsburgh, PA

Johnston, D.L., Libn.
UNIVERSITY OF PITTSBURGH - LANGLEY HALL
LIBRARY □ Pittsburgh, PA

Johnston, Diane, Archv.
YUKON TERRITORY - DEPARTMENT OF
LIBRARY AND INFORMATION RESOURCES -
YUKON ARCHIVES □ Whitehorse, YT

Johnston, Dinnie K., Med.Libn.
VICKSBURG HOSPITAL, INC. - MEDICAL
LIBRARY □ Vicksburg, MS

Johnston, E.S., Libn.
EAST CHICAGO HISTORICAL SOCIETY -
LIBRARY □ East Chicago, IN

Johnston, Ellen A., Chf.Libn.
ALCAN ALUMINIUM, LTD. - GROUP
INFORMATION CENTRE □ Montreal, PQ

Johnston, Emilie G., Cur.
UNIVERSITY OF GUAM - MICRONESIAN AREA
RESEARCH CENTER - PACIFIC COLLECTION □
Mangilao, GU

Johnston, Francena, Med.Libn.
SAN ANTONIO COMMUNITY HOSPITAL -
WEBER MEMORIAL LIBRARY □ Upland, CA

Johnston, Georgann, Libn.
SACRAMENTO-EL DORADO MEDICAL SOCIETY
- PAUL H. GUTTMAN LIBRARY □ Sacramento, CA

Johnston, George F., Asst.Libn.
COVENANT THEOLOGICAL SEMINARY - J.
OLIVER BUSWELL, JR. LIBRARY □ St. Louis, MO

Johnston, Janelle D., Clerk
SASKATCHEWAN - DEPARTMENT OF TOURISM
AND RENEWABLE RESOURCES - FORESTRY
BRANCH LIBRARY □ Prince Albert, SK

Johnston, John W., Dir.
ASSOCIATION OF INTERNATIONAL COLLEGES
& UNIVERSITIES - AICU INTERNATIONAL
EDUCATION LIBRARY □ Independence, MO

Johnston, Judy, Jr.Hosp.Libn.
UNIVERSITY OF SOUTH ALABAMA - COLLEGE
OF MEDICINE - BIOMEDICAL LIBRARY □
Mobile, AL

Johnston, Louise C., Libn.
MOORE, GARDNER & ASSOCIATES, INC. -
LIBRARY □ Asheboro, NC

Johnston, Margaret E., Cur.
HAVERFORD TOWNSHIP HISTORICAL SOCIETY
- LIBRARY □ Havertown, PA

Johnston, Midge, Bus.Mgr.
U.S. NATL. PARK SERVICE - BADLANDS NATL.
MONUMENT - LIBRARY □ Interior, SD

Johnston, Nancy S., Dir.
NATIONAL INJURY INFORMATION
CLEARINGHOUSE □ Washington, DC

Johnston, Norma, Hd.Libn.
MC GILL UNIVERSITY - RELIGIOUS STUDIES
LIBRARY □ Montreal, PQ

Johnston, P.A., Cat.Hd.
BOEING COMPANY - SEATTLE SERVICES
DIVISION - KENT TECHNICAL LIBRARY □
Seattle, WA

Johnston, Rebecca, Hd.Cat.
WAKE FOREST UNIVERSITY - BOWMAN GRAY
SCHOOL OF MEDICINE - LIBRARY □ Winston-
Salem, NC

Johnston, Robert C., Ref.Libn.
WARREN LIBRARY ASSOCIATION - LIBRARY† □
Warren, PA

Johnston, Stanley, Exec.Sec.
ILLINOIS STATE LEGISLATIVE REFERENCE
BUREAU □ Springfield, IL

Johnston, Stephanie, Libn.
UNIVERSITY OF TORONTO - DEPARTMENT OF
COMPUTER SCIENCE LIBRARY □ Toronto, ON

Johnston, Susan H., Hd.Libn.
IBM CANADA, LTD. - DP CENTRAL LIBRARY □
Don Mills, ON

Johnstone, Betty Lu, Rd.Serv.Libn.
WESTERN CONSERVATIVE BAPTIST SEMINARY
- CLINE-TUNNELL LIBRARY □ Portland, OR

Johnstone, Lydia O., Hd.Libn.
WILLIAMS RESEARCH CORPORATION -
LIBRARY □ Walled Lake, MI

Johnting, Wendell E., Tech.Serv.Libn.
INDIANA UNIVERSITY - SCHOOL OF LAW
LIBRARY □ Indianapolis, IN

Joiner, E. Earl, Cur.
STETSON UNIVERSITY - FLORIDA BAPTIST
HISTORICAL COLLECTION □ De Land, FL

Joines, Vann, Pres.
SOUTHEAST INSTITUTE - LIBRARY† □ Chapel
Hill, NC

Joity, Donna, Assoc.Libn.
BAKER & BOTTS - LAW LIBRARY □ Houston, TX

Jolin, Louise, Libn.
HOPITAL STE-JUSTINE - CENTRE
D'INFORMATION SUR LA SANTE DE L'ENFANT†
□ Montreal, PQ

Jollie, Edward S., Jr., Supv., Circ.Serv.
CALIFORNIA INSTITUTE OF TECHNOLOGY -
JET PROPULSION LABORATORY - LIBRARY □
Pasadena, CA

Jolliff, Edna Lee, Assoc.Libn.
HARPER-GRACE HOSPITALS - HARPER
HOSPITAL DIVISION - DEPARTMENT OF
LIBRARIES □ Detroit, MI

Jolly, Wanda, Libn.
ATLANTA PUBLIC LIBRARY - IVAN ALLEN, JR.
DEPARTMENT OF SCIENCE, INDUSTRY AND
GOVERNMENT □ Atlanta, GA

Jonas, Mrs. Bill, Dir. of Lib.Serv.
CRESCENT HEIGHTS BAPTIST CHURCH -
LIBRARY □ Abilene, TX

Jonas, Eva, Libn.
HARVARD UNIVERSITY - MUSEUM OF
COMPARATIVE ZOOLOGY - LIBRARY □
Cambridge, MA

Jonas, Nellie G., Libn.
U.S. BUREAU OF MINES - ROLLA RESEARCH
CENTER - LIBRARY □ Rolla, MO

Jondro, Kim, Info.Spec.
UNIVERSITY OF DENVER AND DENVER
RESEARCH INSTITUTE - SOCIAL SYSTEMS
RESEARCH AND EVALUATION LIBRARY □
Denver, CO

Jones, Alfred H., Libn.
UNIVERSITY OF MISSOURI - ENGINEERING
LIBRARY □ Columbia, MO

Jones, Dr. Allen W., Archv.
AUBURN UNIVERSITY - ARCHIVES □ Auburn, AL

Jones, Andrea, Libn.
CARNEGIE LIBRARY OF PITTSBURGH -
CENTRAL CHILDREN'S ROOM HISTORICAL
COLLECTION □ Pittsburgh, PA

Jones, Anne, Libn.
AMERICAN MANAGEMENT ASSOCIATIONS -
LIBRARY □ New York, NY

Jones, Anne, Cat.
MERCER UNIVERSITY - LAW SCHOOL -
HALLIBURTON LAW LIBRARY □ Macon, GA

Jones, Dr. Arthur E., Jr., Dir.
DREW UNIVERSITY - LIBRARY □ Madison, NJ

Jones, Barbara A., Libn.
BETHANY UNITED METHODIST CHURCH -
LIBRARY □ Wauwatosa, WI

Jones, C.H., Lib.Supv.
BOEING MILITARY AIRPLANE COMPANY -
LIBRARY □ Wichita, KS

Jones, Mr. Carol D., Sci.Libn.
MICHIGAN STATE UNIVERSITY - SCIENCE
LIBRARY □ East Lansing, MI

Jones, Carol Y., Libn.
NORTHWESTERN COLLEGE OF CHIROPRACTIC
- LIBRARY □ St. Paul, MN

Jones, Carolyn G., Dir., Lib.Serv.
U.S. NAVY - NAVAL AMPHIBIOUS SCHOOL -
JOHN SIDNEY MC CAIN AMPHIBIOUS
WARFARE LIBRARY □ Norfolk, VA

Jones, Charlotte, Staff Assoc./Libn.
UNITED STATES TRADEMARK ASSOCIATION -
LAW LIBRARY □ New York, NY

Jones, Cheryl, Pub.Serv.Libn.
UNIVERSITY OF KENTUCKY - LAW LIBRARY □
Lexington, KY

Jones, Clarita, Asst.Libn.
FORBES, INC. - LIBRARY □ New York, NY

Jones, Clifton H., Dir.
SOUTHERN METHODIST UNIVERSITY - FIKES
HALL OF SPECIAL COLLECTIONS AND
DEGOLYER LIBRARY □ Dallas, TX

Jones, Clydia, Pict.Libn.
PLAYBOY ENTERPRISES, INC. - PHOTO
LIBRARY □ Chicago, IL

Jones, Daniel, ILL
UNIVERSITY OF TEXAS HEALTH SCIENCE
CENTER, SAN ANTONIO - LIBRARY □ San
Antonio, TX

Jones, Darlene, Dir.
WASCANA HOSPITAL - HEALTH SCIENCES
LIBRARY □ Regina, SK

Jones, David, Chm., Lib.Comm.
MIGRAINE FOUNDATION - LIBRARY □ Toronto,
ON

Jones, David, Act.Hd.
UNIVERSITY OF ALBERTA - SCIENCE LIBRARY
□ Edmonton, AB

Jones, DeAnna, Asst.Supv., Tech.Serv.
JOHNS HOPKINS UNIVERSITY - APPLIED
PHYSICS LABORATORY - R.E. GIBSON LIBRARY
□ Laurel, MD

Jones, Debra, Reader Serv.
DICKINSON SCHOOL OF LAW - SHEELY-LEE
LAW LIBRARY □ Carlisle, PA

Jones, Delores, Libn.
UNIVERSITY OF SOUTHERN MISSISSIPPI - MC
CAIN LIBRARY □ Hattiesburg, MS

Jones, Dixie E.A., Asst.Libn.
NORTHWESTERN STATE UNIVERSITY OF
LOUISIANA - EUGENE P. WATSON LIBRARY -
SHREVEPORT DIVISION □ Shreveport, LA

Jones, Donald, Dept.Hd.
COMMUNITY COLLEGE OF PHILADELPHIA -
EDUCATION RESOURCES CENTER □
Philadelphia, PA

Jones, Donald Bemis, Libn.
COLLEGE OF ST. CATHERINE - PERFORMING
ARTS LIBRARY □ St. Paul, MN

Jones, Dora, Spec.Coll.
BLACK HILLS STATE COLLEGE - E.Y. BERRY
LIBRARY-LEARNING CENTER □ Spearfish, SD

Jones, Dorothy K., Chf., Lib.Serv.
U.S. VETERANS ADMINISTRATION (GA-
Augusta) - HOSPITAL LIBRARY □ Augusta, GA

Jones, Douglas E., Sci.Eng.Ref.Libn.
UNIVERSITY OF ARIZONA - SCIENCE-
ENGINEERING LIBRARY □ Tucson, AZ

Jones, E. Paul, Hd.
BRIDGEPORT PUBLIC LIBRARY - TECHNOLOGY
AND BUSINESS DEPARTMENT □ Bridgeport, CT

Jones, Edlea, Libn.
BALTIMORE CITY HOSPITALS - HAROLD E.
HARRISON LIBRARY† □ Baltimore, MD

Jones, Edlea K., Libn.
MARYLAND STATE DEPARTMENT OF STATE
PLANNING - LIBRARY □ Baltimore, MD

Jones, Eleanor, Cat./Coord.
UNIVERSITY OF WESTERN ONTARIO - LAW
LIBRARY □ London, ON

Jones, Elizabeth, Libn.
LINDEMANN (Erich) MENTAL HEALTH CENTER -
LIBRARY □ Boston, MA

Jones, Elizabeth F., Adm.
JEFFERSON COUNTY OFFICE OF HISTORIC
PRESERVATION AND ARCHIVES □ Louisville, KY

Jones, Ellen, Supv., Info.Serv.
AMAX, INC. - CLIMAX MOLYBDENUM COMPANY
- TECHNICAL INFORMATION DEPARTMENT† □
Greenwich, CT

Jones, Esther, Pub.Serv.Libn.
UNIVERSITY OF FLORIDA - J. HILLIS MILLER
HEALTH CENTER LIBRARY □ Gainesville, FL

Jones, Mrs. Everette M., Asst.Libn.
TRINITY LUTHERAN CHURCH - LIBRARY □
Madison, WI

Jones, Florence, Order Libn.
UNIVERSITY OF KENTUCKY - MEDICAL
CENTER LIBRARY □ Lexington, KY

Jones, Mrs. G.B., Libn.
HILLSBOROUGH COUNTY HISTORICAL
COMMISSION - LIBRARY □ Tampa, FL

Jones, Grace M., Libn.
CHURCH OF JESUS CHRIST OF LATTER-DAY
SAINTS - EUREKA, CALIFORNIA STAKE
BRANCH GENEALOGICAL LIBRARY† □ Eureka,
CA

Jones, H.G., Cur.
UNIVERSITY OF NORTH CAROLINA, CHAPEL
HILL - NORTH CAROLINA COLLECTION □ Chapel
Hill, NC

PERSONNEL

PERSONNEL

Jones, Hugo W., Libn.
NORTHROP CORPORATION - AIRCRAFT
DIVISION - LIBRARY SERVICES □ Hawthorne,
CA
Jones, Jana, Sr.Libn.
GARRETT CORPORATION - AIRESEARCH
MANUFACTURING COMPANY - TECHNICAL
LIBRARY □ Torrance, CA
Jones, Jeanne, Asst.Libn.
OKLAHOMA STATE UNIVERSITY - BIOLOGICAL
SCIENCES DIVISION □ Stillwater, OK
Jones, Jeff
ALTERNATIVE PRESS CENTER - LIBRARY □
Baltimore, MD
Jones, Jennifer, Libn.
GENERAL AMERICAN INVESTORS CO., INC. -
LIBRARY □ New York, NY
Jones, John B., Ser.Libn.
BARUCH (Bernard M.) COLLEGE OF THE CITY
UNIVERSITY OF NEW YORK - LIBRARY □ New
York, NY
Jones, Joy B., Libn.
WEST VIRGINIA STATE DEPARTMENT OF
WELFARE - LIBRARY □ Charleston, WV
Jones, Joyce, Dir.
YORK-FINCH GENERAL HOSPITAL - DR.
THOMAS J. MALCHO MEMORIAL LIBRARY □
Downsview, ON
Jones, June D., Music Libn.
BRANDON UNIVERSITY - MUSIC LIBRARY† □
Brandon, MB
Jones, LaVerne K., Libn.
OKLAHOMA STATE UNIVERSITY - VETERINARY
MEDICINE LIBRARY □ Stillwater, OK
Jones, Leigh R., Historic Site Mgr.
SENATE HOUSE STATE HISTORIC SITE -
LIBRARY & ARCHIVES □ Kingston, NY
Jones, Leslie, Chf.Cat.Serv.
CANADA - MORTGAGE AND HOUSING
CORPORATION - CANADIAN HOUSING
INFORMATION CENTRE □ Ottawa, ON
Jones, Lesya, Libn.
METROPOLITAN TORONTO LIBRARY - GENERAL
REFERENCE DEPARTMENT □ Toronto, ON
Jones, Linda, Libn.
OPEN BIBLE COLLEGE - CARRIE HARDY
MEMORIAL LIBRARY □ Des Moines, IA
Jones, Linda, Acq.Libn.
SAMFORD UNIVERSITY - CUMBERLAND
SCHOOL OF LAW - CORDELL HULL LAW
LIBRARY† □ Birmingham, AL
Jones, Lois W., Dir. of Lib.
BERKSHIRE CHRISTIAN COLLEGE - DR. LINDEN
J. CARTER LIBRARY □ Lenox, MA
Jones, M. Frances, Assoc.Libn.
WEST TEXAS STATE UNIVERSITY - CORNETTE
LIBRARY □ Canyon, TX
Jones, Margaret
UNITED NATIONS ASSOCIATION OF THE
UNITED STATES OF AMERICA - GREATER ST.
LOUIS CHAPTER - LIBRARY □ St. Louis, MO
Jones, Marian, Libn.
CANADA - GEOLOGICAL SURVEY OF CANADA -
INSTITUTE OF SEDIMENTARY & PETROLEUM
GEOLOGY - LIBRARY □ Calgary, AB
Jones, Martha Ann, Cat.
UNIVERSITY OF DAYTON - SCHOOL OF
EDUCATION - CURRICULUM MATERIALS
CENTER □ Dayton, OH
Jones, Sr. Martin Joseph, Hd.Archv./Spec.Coll.
SUNY - COLLEGE AT BUFFALO - EDWARD H.
BUTLER LIBRARY □ Buffalo, NY
Jones, Mary M., Rd.Adv.
DISTRICT OF COLUMBIA PUBLIC LIBRARY -
ART DIVISION □ Washington, DC
Jones, Maureen, Asst.Libn.
SCHLUMBERGER-DOLL RESEARCH CENTER -
LIBRARY □ Ridgefield, CT
Jones, Millie, Tech.Libn.
LOS ANGELES COUNTY - DEPARTMENT OF
DATA PROCESSING - TECHNICAL LIBRARY □
Downey, CA

Jones, Miriam C., Archv.
ALABAMA STATE DEPARTMENT OF ARCHIVES
AND HISTORY □ Montgomery, AL
Jones, Miss Orlo, Genealogical Coord.
PRINCE EDWARD ISLAND HERITAGE
FOUNDATION - GENEALOGICAL COLLECTION □
Charlottetown, PE
Jones, Patricia, Prog.Coord.
UNIVERSITY OF ILLINOIS MEDICAL CENTER -
LIBRARY OF THE HEALTH SCIENCES □ Chicago,
IL
Jones, Patricia B., Corp.Libn.
LIBBEY-OWENS-FORD COMPANY - CORPORATE
LIBRARY □ Toledo, OH
Jones, Rendle, Libn.
KNOX COUNTY LAW LIBRARY □ Rockland, ME
Jones, Richard E., Music Libn.
UNIVERSITY OF WISCONSIN, MILWAUKEE -
MUSIC COLLECTION □ Milwaukee, WI
Jones, Robert, Darkroom Mgr.
CENTER FOR SOUTHERN FOLKLORE -
ARCHIVES □ Memphis, TN
Jones, Robert B., Hd., Microfilm Lab.
OHIO HISTORICAL SOCIETY - ARCHIVES-
LIBRARY □ Columbus, OH
Jones, Robert D., Lib.Techn.
U.S. AIR FORCE BASE - MARCH BASE LIBRARY
□ March AFB, CA
Jones, Robert E., Pres.
VESTIGIA - LIBRARY □ Stanhope, NJ
Jones, Roger C., Hd., Tech.Serv.Br.
NORTH CAROLINA STATE DEPT. OF CULTURAL
RESOURCES - DIV. OF ARCHIVES AND HISTORY
- ARCHIVES & RECORDS SECTION □ Raleigh, NC
Jones, Royden R., Asst.Libn.
U.S. AIR FORCE MEDICAL CENTER - WILFORD
HALL U.S.A.F. MEDICAL CENTER - MEDICAL
LIBRARY (SGEL) □ San Antonio, TX
Jones, Ruth A., Chf., Lib.Serv.
U.S. VETERANS ADMINISTRATION (WA-
Spokane) - MEDICAL CENTER LIBRARY □
Spokane, WA
Jones, Sarah C., Dir.Lib.Serv.
MORGAN STANLEY & COMPANY, INC. -
LIBRARY □ New York, NY
Jones, Suad, Med.Libn.
U.S. NAVY - NAVAL REGIONAL MEDICAL
CENTER (Portsmouth) - MEDICAL LIBRARY □
Portsmouth, VA
Jones, Susan S., Jrnl.Serv.Mgr.
INSTITUTE FOR SCIENTIFIC INFORMATION □
Philadelphia, PA
Jones, Terrance, Cat.
UNIVERSITY OF WISCONSIN, MADISON -
CENTER FOR HEALTH SCIENCES LIBRARIES □
Madison, WI
Jones, Thomasina, Chf./Control & Distr.
INSTITUTE FOR DEFENSE ANALYSES -
TECHNICAL INFORMATION SERVICES □
Arlington, VA
Jones, Timothy, Data User Serv.Off.
U.S. BUREAU OF THE CENSUS - REGIONAL
DATA USER SERVICE - DETROIT REGIONAL
OFFICE - LIBRARY □ Detroit, MI
Jones, Ursula M., Tech.Libn.
CITIES SERVICE COMPANY - PLASTICS
TECHNICAL CENTER - LIBRARY □ Lake Charles,
LA
Jones, Verdelle B., Asst.Lib., Tech.Proc.
WARNER-LAMBERT COMPANY - CORPORATE
LIBRARY† □ Morris Plains, NJ
Jones, Virgil L., Ref.Libn.
UNIVERSITY OF OKLAHOMA - HEALTH
SCIENCES CENTER LIBRARY □ Oklahoma City,
OK
Jones, Virginia Purefoy, Asst.Libn.
NORTH CAROLINA CENTRAL UNIVERSITY -
SCHOOL OF LIBRARY SCIENCE - LIBRARY □
Durham, NC
Jones, W. Marshall, Dir.
BILLINGS PUBLIC SCHOOLS - INSTRUCTIONAL
MATERIALS CENTER □ Billings, MT

Jones, William A., Spec.Coll.Libn.
CALIFORNIA STATE UNIVERSITY, CHICO -
MERIAM LIBRARY □ Chico, CA
Jonovich, Tina, Asst.Libn.
GILA COUNTY LAW LIBRARY □ Globe, AZ
Jonsberg, Judith P., Libn.
VINNELL CORPORATION - TECHNICAL
SERVICES DIVISION LIBRARY □ Alhambra, CA
Jonson, Joanne, Dir.
MINNESOTA STATE SERVICES FOR THE BLIND
AND VISUALLY HANDICAPPED -
COMMUNICATION CENTER □ St. Paul, MN
Jonynas, Alexandre, Asst.Dir.
UNIVERSITE DE MONTREAL - SCIENCES
HUMAINES ET SOCIALES-BIBLIOTHEQUE □
Montreal, PQ
Joorfetz, Clara, Libn.
ST. DOMINIC-JACKSON MEMORIAL HOSPITAL -
LUTHER MANSHIP MEDICAL LIBRARY □
Jackson, MS
Joost, Laura R., Chm., Lib.Comm.
CUMMER GALLERY OF ART - LIBRARY □
Jacksonville, FL
Joplin, James, Asst.Dir.Prod.Serv.
UNIVERSITY OF HOUSTON - AUDIOVISUAL
SERVICES □ Houston, TX
Joplin, Peggy J., Supv.
DU PONT DE NEMOURS (E.I.) & COMPANY, INC.
- PHOTO PRODUCTS DEPARTMENT -
INFORMATION CENTER □ Parlin, NJ
Jordahl, Anna
TRINITY LUTHERAN CHURCH - LIBRARY □
Moorhead, MN
Jordahl, Leigh D., Hd.Libn.
LUTHER COLLEGE - PREUS LIBRARY □ Decorah,
IA
Jordahl, Ron, Libn.
PRAIRIE BIBLE INSTITUTE - LIBRARY □ Three
Hills, AB
Jordan, Anne
UNIVERSITY OF TEXAS, AUSTIN -
ARCHITECTURE & PLANNING LIBRARY □ Austin,
TX
Jordan, B., Lib.Techn.
SYNCRUDE CANADA, LTD. - RESEARCH
DEPARTMENT LIBRARY □ Edmonton, AB
Jordan, Betty A.
HENRY FORD MUSEUM AND GREENFIELD
VILLAGE - FORD ARCHIVES □ Dearborn, MI
Jordan, Flo, Lib.Assoc.
MARION LABORATORIES, INC. - LIBRARY □
Kansas City, MO
Jordan, Florence E., Tech.Info.Spec.
NATIONAL INSTITUTE OF ENVIRONMENTAL
HEALTH SCIENCES - ENVIRONMENTAL
TERATOLOGY INFORMATION CENTER □
Research Triangle Park, NC
Jordan, Judy C., Lib.Techn.
U.S. BUREAU OF MINES - ADMINISTRATIVE
SERVICES - LIBRARY □ Washington, DC
Jordan, June, Assoc.Dir.
ERIC CLEARINGHOUSE ON HANDICAPPED &
GIFTED CHILDREN - CEC INFORMATION
SERVICES □ Reston, VA
Jordan, Katherine C., Sci.Ed.
FARNHAM (Frank C.) COMPANY, INC. - LIBRARY
□ Philadelphia, PA
Jordan, Louis, Hd.
UNIVERSITY OF NOTRE DAME - MEDIEVAL
INSTITUTE LIBRARY □ Notre Dame, IN
Jordan, Marie, Slide Libn.
ART CENTER COLLEGE OF DESIGN - JAMES
LEMONT FOGG MEMORIAL LIBRARY □
Pasadena, CA
Jordan, Mary K., Libn./Archv.
AMERICAN ASSOCIATION OF UNIVERSITY
WOMEN - EDUCATIONAL FOUNDATION
LIBRARY AND ARCHIVES □ Washington, DC
Jordan, P.L., Supv., Lib.Serv.
TRW, INC. - DEFENSE & SPACE SYSTEMS
GROUP - TECHNICAL INFORMATION CENTER □
Redondo Beach, CA

K

PERSONNEL

Kaczmarek, Mary F., Libn.
JOHNSON CONTROLS, INC. - CORPORATE INFO.
CTR./LIBRARY M47 □ Milwaukee, WI
Kadinger, Sharon, Libn.
U.S. GEOLOGICAL SURVEY - EROS DATA
CENTER - DON L. KULOW MEMORIAL LIBRARY
□ Sioux Falls, SD
Kadish, Elisa F., Libn.
SMITH, CURRIE & HANCOCK - LAW LIBRARY† □
Atlanta, GA
Kafes, Fred, Libn.
OUR LADY OF LOURDES HOSPITAL - MEDICAL
LIBRARY □ Camden, NJ
Kafiris, Toula, Archv.
INDIANA STATE COMMISSION ON PUBLIC
RECORDS - ARCHIVES DIVISION □ Indianapolis,
IN
Kafka, Miriam, Act.Libn.
LOS ANGELES COUNTY/OLIVE VIEW MEDICAL
CENTER - HEALTH SCIENCES LIBRARY □ Van
Nuys, CA
Kagan, Ilse E., Libn.
LEVY (W.J.) CONSULTANTS CORPORATION -
RESEARCH LIBRARY □ New York, NY
Kaganoff, Nathan M., Libn.
AMERICAN JEWISH HISTORICAL SOCIETY -
LIBRARY □ Waltham, MA
Kagehiro, Phyllis, Rsrcs.Mtls.Asst.
EAST-WEST POPULATION INSTITUTE
RESOURCE MATERIALS COLLECTION □
Honolulu, HI
Kahan, D.J., Metallurgist
U.S. NATL. BUREAU OF STANDARDS - ALLOY
DATA CENTER □ Washington, DC
Kahan, Nelida, Asst.Libn.
NEW YORK BOTANICAL GARDEN - LIBRARY □
Bronx, NY
Kahane, Betty, Libn.
TA ASSOCIATES - INFORMATION CENTER □
Montreal, PQ
Kahao, Mary Jane, Hd.
LOUISIANA STATE UNIVERSITY - LIBRARY
SCHOOL LIBRARY □ Baton Rouge, LA
Kahl, Julie, Libn.
MARIN GENERAL HOSPITAL - LIBRARY □ San
Rafael, CA
Kahla, Paula, Info.Spec.
NATIONAL CLEARINGHOUSE FOR FAMILY
PLANNING INFORMATION □ Rockville, MD
Kahles, John F., Dir.
METCUT RESEARCH ASSOCIATES, INC. -
MACHINABILITY DATA CENTER □ Cincinnati,
OH
Kahn, Helen, Ref.Libn.
INDIANA HISTORICAL SOCIETY - WILLIAM
HENRY SMITH MEMORIAL LIBRARY □
Indianapolis, IN
Kahn, Karen, ILL, Ref.Libn.
BENTLEY COLLEGE - SOLOMON R. BAKER
LIBRARY □ Waltham, MA
Kahn, Kathleen T., Libn.
CALIFORNIA FEDERAL SAVINGS AND LOAN
ASSOCIATION - MANAGEMENT LIBRARY □ Los
Angeles, CA
Kahn, Leybl, Libn.
YIDDISH LEAGUE - LIBRARY □ New York, NY
Kahn, Marilyn, Libn.
MC ADAMS (William Douglas), INC. - MEDICAL
LIBRARY □ New York, NY
Kahn, Nina, Law Libn.
U.S. VETERANS ADMINISTRATION (DC-
Washington) - GENERAL COUNSEL'S LAW
LIBRARY □ Washington, DC
Kahn, Tamar Joy, Libn.
OHR KODESH CONGREGATION - SISTERHOOD
LIBRARY □ Chevy Chase, MD
Kaighn, Anna Lee, Libn.
EG&G, INC. - TECHNICAL LIBRARY □ Las Vegas,
NV
Kaimowitz, Dr. Jeffrey H., Cur.
TRINITY COLLEGE - WATKINSON LIBRARY □
Hartford, CT

Kain, Joan, Sr.Libn.
NEW YORK STATE DEPARTMENT OF LAW -
NEW YORK CITY LIBRARY □ New York, NY
Kaiser, Clara, Libn./Genealogist
AUDRAIN COUNTY HISTORICAL SOCIETY -
ROSS HOUSE LIBRARY/AMERICAN SADDLE
HORSE MUSEUM LIBRARY □ Mexico, MO
Kaiser, Dorothy, Tech.Serv./Archv.
KENRICK SEMINARY LIBRARY □ St. Louis, MO
Kaiser, Elsa, Act.Dir.
SOCIETY OF PHOTO-TECHNOLOGISTS -
LIBRARY† □ Denver, CO
Kaiser, Joan, Med.Libn.
LOWELL GENERAL HOSPITAL - HEALTH
SCIENCE LIBRARY □ Lowell, MA
Kaiser, Michael N., Exec.Dir.
LEHIGH-NORTHAMPTON COUNTIES JOINT
PLANNING COMMISSION - LIBRARY □ Lehigh
Valley, PA
Kaisler, Dolores H., Libn.
MERCY HOSPITAL, INC. - NURSING LIBRARY □
Baltimore, MD
Kaiyalethe, Tamara, Sr.Lib.Asst.
UNIVERSITY OF MINNESOTA - MIDDLE EAST
LIBRARY □ Minneapolis, MN
Kajiwara, Sandra, Sr.Asst.Libn.
SAN JOSE STATE UNIVERSITY - LIBRARY -
SCIENCE/ENGINEERING DEPARTMENT† □ San
Jose, CA
Kaklamanos, Ann C., Libn.
FLORIDA STATE DEPT. OF LEGAL AFFAIRS -
ATTORNEY GENERAL'S LIBRARY □ Tallahassee,
FL
Kalaf, Laila, Info.Spec.
SOUTH FLORIDA REGIONAL PLANNING
COUNCIL - LIBRARY □ Miami, FL
Kalaitzis, Marla, Libn.
MIDDLESEX COUNTY PLANNING BOARD -
LIBRARY □ New Brunswick, NJ
Kalb, Mary, Info.Dir.
GREENWOOD PRESS - LIBRARY □ Westport, CT
Kaleem, Ata Ullah, Info.Dir.
AHMADIYYA MOVEMENT IN ISLAM - MUSLIM
LIBRARY □ Washington, DC
Kali, Lalitha, Libn.
CONNECTICUT STATE OFFICE OF POLICY AND
MANAGEMENT - LIBRARY □ Hartford, CT
Kalkanis, Agatha Pfeiffer, Chf.
DETROIT PUBLIC LIBRARY - MUSIC AND
PERFORMING ARTS DEPARTMENT □ Detroit, MI
Kalkbrenner, Jane, Libn.
ONONDAGA COUNTY PUBLIC LIBRARY -
BUSINESS AND INDUSTRIAL DEPARTMENT □
Syracuse, NY
Kalkus, Stanley, Dir.
U.S. NAVY - DEPARTMENT LIBRARY □
Washington, DC
Kallmann, Dr. Helmut, Chf.
NATIONAL LIBRARY OF CANADA - MUSIC
DIVISION □ Ottawa, ON
Kalloch, Phillip C., Jr., Supv., Info.Serv.
UNION MUTUAL LIFE INSURANCE COMPANY -
CORPORATE INFORMATION CENTER □ Portland,
ME
Kallop, Sharon M., Libn.
BIGHAM, ENGLAR, JONES AND HOUSTON -
LIBRARY □ New York, NY
Kallos, Olga, Tech.Proc.Serv.
HEWLETT-PACKARD COMPANY - CORPORATE
LIBRARY □ Palo Alto, CA
Kallusky, Barbara, Ref.
MITCHELL (William) COLLEGE OF LAW - JOHN B.
SANBORN LIBRARY □ St. Paul, MN
Kalman, Georgia, Libn.
TEMPLE ISRAEL - LIBRARY □ Minneapolis, MN
Kalsch, Alvina, Assoc.Libn.Tech.Serv.
SUNY - MARITIME COLLEGE - STEPHEN B.
LUCE LIBRARY □ Bronx, NY
Kalt, Kathleen L., Libn.
SKIDMORE, OWINGS & MERRILL - LIBRARY □
Washington, DC

Kalvonjian, Araxie, Tech.Proc./Acq.Libn.
GATEWAY VOCATIONAL TECHNICAL & ADULT
EDUCATION DISTRICT - LEARNING
RESOURCES CENTER □ Kenosha, WI
Kalyanpur, Yveline, Ref.Libn.
KEAN COLLEGE OF NEW JERSEY - NANCY
THOMPSON LIBRARY □ Union, NJ
Kameen, Karen, AV Libn.
UNIVERSITY OF PITTSBURGH - WESTERN
PSYCHIATRIC INSTITUTE AND CLINIC -
LIBRARY □ Pittsburgh, PA
Kamenoff, Lovisa, Mgr., Lib.Serv.
BROCKTON HOSPITAL - LIBRARY □ Brockton,
MA
Kamichaitis, Penelope H., Libn.
MONTREAL ENGINEERING COMPANY, LTD. -
LIBRARY □ Montreal, PQ
Kaminski, Edward, Mgr., Info. Retrieval
AMERICAN SOCIETY FOR METALS - METALS
INFORMATION □ Metals Park, OH
Kamm, Keith A., Biblog.
ATHENAEUM OF PHILADELPHIA □ Philadelphia,
PA
Kamman, Jeanette G., Dir.
ORPHAN VOYAGE - KAMMANDALE LIBRARY □
St. Paul, MN
Kammer, Jean, Libn.
D'ARCY-MAC MANUS AND MASIUS - LIBRARY†
□ St. Louis, MO
Kammerer, Kay, Health Sci.Libn.
ALTA BATES HOSPITAL - STUART MEMORIAL
LIBRARY □ Berkeley, CA
Kamra, Mr. S.K., Chf.Libn.
CANADA - NATIONAL DEFENCE - FORT
FRONTENAC LIBRARY □ Kingston, ON
Kamrud, Sylvia, Libn.
AMERICAN HARDWARE MUTUAL INSURANCE
COMPANY - LIBRARY □ Minneapolis, MN
Kan, Halina, Libn.
NL INDUSTRIES, INC. - MARKETING &
TECHNICAL INFORMATION SERVICE □
Hightstown, NJ
Kanabrodzki, Christina C., Commun.Libn.
MOTOR VEHICLE MANUFACTURERS
ASSOCIATION (MVMA) - COMMUNICATIONS
LIBRARY □ Detroit, MI
Kanafani, Marwan, Info.Off.
LEAGUE OF ARAB STATES - ARAB
INFORMATION CENTER □ New York, NY
Kanarek, Evelyn S., Libn.
MORTON-NORWICH PRODUCTS, INC. -
LIBRARY □ Chicago, IL
Kancel, Rita Hollecker, Libn.
WYANDOTTE COUNTY BAR LIBRARY □ Kansas
City, KS
Kane, Casey, Libn.
RAND CORPORATION - LIBRARY □ Washington,
DC
Kane, John F., Coord., Info.Serv.
ALUMINUM COMPANY OF AMERICA - ALCOA
LABORATORIES - INFORMATION DEPARTMENT
□ Alcoa Center, PA
Kane, Marie, Libn.
MARSCHALK COMPANY, INC. - LIBRARY □
Cleveland, OH
Kane, Sr. Mary Edith, Curric.Libn.
MARYCREST COLLEGE - CONE LIBRARY† □
Davenport, IA
Kane, William E., Chf.Libn.
U.S. VETERANS ADMINISTRATION (NY-Castle
Point) - MEDICAL CENTER LIBRARY □ Castle
Point, NY
Kaneko, Hideo, Cur.
YALE UNIVERSITY - EAST ASIAN COLLECTION
□ New Haven, CT
Kanen, Ronald A., Chf.Bur.Lib.Serv.
STATE LIBRARY OF FLORIDA □ Tallahassee, FL
Kang, Nam Hee, Tech.Info.Spec.
OCCIDENTAL RESEARCH CORPORATION -
TECHNICAL INFORMATION CENTER □ Irvine,
CA

Kangas, Jill, Musm.Dir.
LEWIS COUNTY HISTORICAL MUSEUM -
LIBRARY □ Chehalis, WA

Kanner, Ruth C., Dir. of Info.Serv.
MOORE-COTTRELL SUBSCRIPTION AGENCIES -
SERIALS REFERENCE LIBRARY □ North
Cohocton, NY

Kanocz, Otto, Chf.Libn.
BERNHARD (Richard J.) MEMORIAL LIBRARY OF
FEDERATION EMPLOYMENT & GUIDANCE
SERVICE □ New York, NY

Kansfield, Norman J., Libn.
WESTERN THEOLOGICAL SEMINARY -
BEARDSLEE LIBRARY □ Holland, MI

Kanter, Dorothy, Ser.Libn.
UNIVERSITY OF WISCONSIN, MADISON -
CENTER FOR HEALTH SCIENCES LIBRARIES □
Madison, WI

Kantor, Judith, Hd.Libn.
UNIVERSITY OF CALIFORNIA, LOS ANGELES -
UNIVERSITY ELEMENTARY SCHOOL LIBRARY □
Los Angeles, CA

Kantrow, Judith, Asst.Libn.
NATIONAL ASSOCIATION OF MUTUAL SAVINGS
BANKS - LIBRARY† □ New York, NY

Kanu, Ahmed H., AV & Doc.Libn.
OHIO STATE SUPREME COURT LAW LIBRARY □
Columbus, OH

Kao, Angela H., Orientalia Libn.
U.S. ARMY - MILITARY ACADEMY - LIBRARY □
West Point, NY

Kapadia, Sushila, Info.Sys.Libn.
COLLEGE OF MEDICINE AND DENTISTRY OF
NEW JERSEY AT NEWARK - GEORGE F. SMITH
LIBRARY □ Newark, NJ

Kapecky, Michele Ann, Chief Libn.
DETROIT FREE PRESS - LIBRARY □ Detroit, MI

Kaplan, Amy, Libn.
KENNEDY (John F.) MEMORIAL HOSPITAL -
CHERRY HILL DIVISION - MEDICAL LIBRARY □
Cherry Hill, NJ

Kaplan, Bess D., Materials Coord.
FOUNDATION FOR BLIND CHILDREN - LIBRARY
□ Scottsdale, AZ

Kaplan, Doris, Libn.
DINSMORE, SHOHL, COATES & DEUPREE -
LIBRARY □ Cincinnati, OH

Kaplan, Judith M., Hd.Libn.
AMERICAN FOUNDATION FOR THE BLIND -
M.C. MIGEL MEMORIAL LIBRARY □ New York,
NY

Kaplan, Leslie, Media Serv.
UNIVERSITY OF LOWELL, NORTH CAMPUS -
ALUMNI/LYDON LIBRARY □ Lowell, MA

Kaplan, Richard, Asst.Libn.Cat.
SUNY AT BUFFALO - HEALTH SCIENCES
LIBRARY □ Buffalo, NY

Kapnick, Laura, Mgr.Lib.Serv.
CBS INC. - CBS NEWS - REFERENCE LIBRARY □
New York, NY

Kapnick, Laura, Chf.Libn.
CBS INC. - CBS TECHNOLOGY CENTER □
Stamford, CT

Kapp, David, Asst.Libn.Pub.Serv.
UNIVERSITY OF CONNECTICUT - LIBRARY □
Storrs, CT

Kappenberg, Alice W., Archv.
SUFFOLK COUNTY HISTORICAL SOCIETY -
LIBRARY □ Riverhead, NY

Kapur, Umesh, Asst.Dir.Tech.Serv.
UNIVERSITY OF HOUSTON - AUDIOVISUAL
SERVICES □ Houston, TX

Karaczewsky, Oksana, Hd.Libn.
NEW YORK COLLEGE OF PODIATRIC MEDICINE
- DR. SIDNEY DRUSKIN MEMORIAL LIBRARY† □
New York, NY

Karan, Audette, Supv., Spec.Coll.
BELL & HOWELL COMPANY - MICRO PHOTO
DIVISION - MICROFORMS ARCHIVE □ Wooster,
OH

Karbal, Albert E., Dir.
CONGREGATION SHAAREY ZEDEK - LEARNING
RESOURCE CENTER □ Southfield, MI

Karch, Linda S., Libn.
MERCY HOSPITAL - MEDICAL LIBRARY □
Buffalo, NY

Karchmer, N., Evening Libn.
PACE UNIVERSITY, PLEASANTVILLE/
BRIARCLIFF - LIBRARY □ Pleasantville, NY

Karcz, JoAnn, AV Coord.
ST. PETER'S MEDICAL CENTER - LIBRARY □
New Brunswick, NJ

Karcz, Polly G., Tech.Info.Spec.
U.S. NATL. INSTITUTES OF HEALTH - LIBRARY
□ Bethesda, MD

Kardell, May, Libn.
CHEVY CHASE BAPTIST CHURCH - SEBRING
MEMORIAL LIBRARY □ Washington, DC

Karesh, Maxine S., Libn.
DAMES & MOORE - LIBRARY □ Cranford, NJ

Karg, Anita L., Asst.Archv.
CARNEGIE-MELLON UNIVERSITY - HUNT
INSTITUTE FOR BOTANICAL DOCUMENTATION
- LIBRARY □ Pittsburgh, PA

Karic, Seid, Cat.
INDIANA UNIVERSITY - NEAR EASTERN
COLLECTION □ Bloomington, IN

Karius, Jan, Cat.
CONCORDIA THEOLOGICAL SEMINARY -
LIBRARY □ Fort Wayne, IN

Karklins, Vija L., Assoc.Dir.
SMITHSONIAN INSTITUTION LIBRARIES □
Washington, DC

Karlen, Ann, Libn.
WASHINGTON COUNTY LAW LIBRARY† □
Hillsboro, OR

Karlin, Estelle, Libn.
HARVARD UNIVERSITY - OBSERVATORY
LIBRARY □ Cambridge, MA

Karlin, Martin, Chf.
U.S. DEPT. OF LABOR - BUREAU OF LABOR
STATISTICS - INFORMATION AND ADVISORY
SECTION □ New York, NY

Karner, Rita, Libn.
LITTLE COMPANY OF MARY HOSPITAL -
EDUCATION BUILDING LIBRARY □ Evergreen
Park, IL

Karnig, Jack J., Forest Mgr.
HARVARD UNIVERSITY - HARVARD BLACK
ROCK FOREST LIBRARY □ Cornwall, NY

Karonis, Mary, Coord.
SALEM STATE COLLEGE - STUDENT
GOVERNMENT ASSOCIATION & LIBRARY -
LIBRARY OF SOCIAL ALTERNATIVES† □ Salem,
MA

Karow, Betty, Libn.
MILWAUKEE ART CENTER - LIBRARY □
Milwaukee, WI

Karp, Margot, Lib.Sci.Libn.
PRATT INSTITUTE - LIBRARY □ Brooklyn, NY

Karpinski, Leszek M., Ref.Libn.
UNIVERSITY OF BRITISH COLUMBIA -
HUMANITIES DIVISION □ Vancouver, BC

Karpisek, Marion, Hd.
SALT LAKE CITY SCHOOLS - INSTRUCTIONAL
MEDIA CENTER □ Salt Lake City, UT

Karr, Ronald, Pub.Serv.Libn.
NORTHWESTERN UNIVERSITY -
TRANSPORTATION LIBRARY □ Evanston, IL

Karras, Thomas, Ref.Libn.
SAN DIEGO PUBLIC LIBRARY - SCIENCE &
INDUSTRY SECTION □ San Diego, CA

Kars, Marge, Dir.
HOLLAND COMMUNITY HOSPITAL - HOSPITAL
AND MEDICAL STAFF LIBRARY □ Holland, MI

Karten, Leona, Asst.Chf.
BROOKLYN PUBLIC LIBRARY - SOCIAL SCIENCE
DIVISION □ Brooklyn, NY

Karukin, Mildred, Assoc.Libn.
MOUNT SINAI MEDICAL CENTER OF GREATER
MIAMI - MEDICAL LIBRARY □ Miami Beach, FL

Kasakaitis, Jurgis, Hd.Libn.
BALZEKAS MUSEUM OF LITHUANIAN CULTURE
- RESEARCH LIBRARY □ Chicago, IL

Kasalko, Sally, Ref.Libn.
UNIVERSITY OF ARKANSAS MEDICAL
SCIENCES CAMPUS - MEDICAL SCIENCES
LIBRARY □ Little Rock, AR

Kaschsins, Elizabeth, Ref.Libn.
LUTHER COLLEGE - PREUS LIBRARY □ Decorah,
IA

Kascus, Marie, Ser.Libn.
CENTRAL CONNECTICUT STATE COLLEGE -
ELIHU BURRITT LIBRARY □ New Britain, CT

Kasher, Lynn, Assoc.Libn.
NEW YORK ACADEMY OF MEDICINE - LIBRARY
□ New York, NY

Kashyap, Ms. Meera, Circ./Tech.Serv.Libn.
HOWARD UNIVERSITY - SCHOOL OF LAW -
ALLEN MERCER DANIEL LAW LIBRARY □
Washington, DC

Kasman, Dorothy, Chf.Libn.
COOPERS AND LYBRAND - NATIONAL LIBRARY†
□ New York, NY

Kasner, Betsie, Hd., Info.Serv.
UNIVERSITY OF NEW MEXICO - BUREAU OF
BUSINESS & ECONOMIC RESEARCH DATA BANK
□ Albuquerque, NM

Kasner, Sr. M. Dolores, O.P., Dir.
TEXAS CATHOLIC HISTORICAL SOCIETY -
CATHOLIC ARCHIVES OF TEXAS □ Austin, TX

Kasow, Nadine, Ref.Libn.
THOMPSON (J. Walter) COMPANY -
INFORMATION CENTER □ New York, NY

Kasparian, Lucy, Pub.Serv.Libn.
CLARK COUNTY COMMUNITY COLLEGE -
LEARNING RESOURCES CENTER □ North Las
Vegas, NV

Kasper, Nancy, Educ.Libn.
YORK UNIVERSITY - FACULTY OF EDUCATION -
EDUCATION CENTRE □ Downsview, ON

Kass, Adelaide, Lit. Searcher
UOP INC. - RESEARCH TECHNICAL
INFORMATION CENTER □ Des Plaines, IL

Kass, Kenneth J., Chm.Bd. Of Dir.
CONTINENTAL CHEMISTE CORPORATION -
LIBRARY □ Chicago, IL

Kasses, Carol D., Hd. Access Sup.Serv.
COLUMBIA UNIVERSITY - HEALTH SCIENCES
LIBRARY □ New York, NY

Kasten, Lloyd, Prof.
UNIVERSITY OF WISCONSIN, MADISON -
SEMINARY OF MEDIEVAL SPANISH STUDIES -
LIBRARY □ Madison, WI

Kasten, Ulla, Musm.Ed.
YALE UNIVERSITY - BABYLONIAN COLLECTION
□ New Haven, CT

Kastens, Theana Y., V.P., Pub.Rel.
AIRPORT OPERATORS COUNCIL
INTERNATIONAL - LIBRARY □ Washington, DC

Kastner, James F., Chf.Libn.
U.S. VETERANS ADMINISTRATION (KY-
Louisville) - HOSPITAL LIBRARY □ Louisville, KY

Kastner, Margaret N., Hd. of Index
TIME, INC. - LIBRARY □ New York, NY

Katagiri, George, Coord., Instr.Tech.
OREGON STATE DEPARTMENT OF EDUCATION
- RESOURCE/DISSEMINATION CENTER □
Salem, OR

Katayama, Jane H., Lib.Mgr.
MASSACHUSETTS INSTITUTE OF TECHNOLOGY
- LINCOLN LABORATORY LIBRARY □ Lexington,
MA

Kates, Jacqueline R., Corp.Libn.
INSTRUMENTATION LABORATORY, INC. -
ANALYTICAL INSTRUMENTS DIVISION -
LIBRARY □ Wilmington, MA

Kates, Jacqueline R., Corp.Libn.
INSTRUMENTATION LABORATORY, INC. -
LIBRARY □ Lexington, MA

Katherman, Agnete V., Libn.
IBM CORPORATION - DP LIBRARY □ Houston,
TX

Kato, Stacia, Hd.Libn.
BECHTEL POWER CORPORATION - LIBRARY □
San Francisco, CA

PERSONNEL

Katopis, Beverly, Music Libn.
YONKERS PUBLIC LIBRARY - FINE ARTS
DEPARTMENT □ Yonkers, NY
Katre, Helen, Acq.Libn.
HELLENIC COLLEGE AND HOLY CROSS GREEK
ORTHODOX SCHOOL OF THEOLOGY -
COTSIDAS-TONNA LIBRARY □ Brookline, MA
Kats, Natasha, Exec.Sec.
BAY AREA COUNCIL ON SOVIET JEWRY -
ARCHIVES □ San Francisco, CA
Katsh, Sara, Libn.
ASSOCIATION OF OPERATING ROOM NURSES -
LIBRARY □ Denver, CO
Kattlove, Rose W., Hd.Libn.
XEROX CORPORATION - LIBRARY □ El Segundo,
CA
Katz, Annelise, Libn.
HARVARD UNIVERSITY - PSYCHOLOGY
RESEARCH LIBRARY □ Cambridge, MA
Katz, Annelise
HARVARD UNIVERSITY - SOCIAL RELATIONS/
SOCIOLOGY LIBRARY □ Cambridge, MA
Katz, Mrs. Barry
TEMPLE ISRAEL - PAUL PELTASON LIBRARY □
Creve Coeur, MO
Katz, Doris B., Mgr.
NATIONAL BROADCASTING COMPANY, INC. -
INFORMATION UNIT - RESEARCH
DEPARTMENT □ New York, NY
Katz, Helen, Sr.Ref.Libn.
CANADIAN IMPERIAL BANK OF COMMERCE -
INFORMATION CENTRE □ Toronto, ON
Katz, Jane, Asst.Libn.
JOHNS HOPKINS UNIVERSITY - JOHN WORK
GARRETT LIBRARY □ Baltimore, MD
Katz, Janet, Sr.Ref.Libn.
SUFFOLK UNIVERSITY - LAW LIBRARY □
Boston, MA
Katz, Janet Rocklin, Clas.Doc.Supv.
R & D ASSOCIATES - TECHNICAL
INFORMATION SERVICES □ Marina Del Rey, CA
Katz, Lilian G., Dir.
ERIC CLEARINGHOUSE ON ELEMENTARY AND
EARLY CHILDHOOD EDUCATION □ Champaign,
IL
Katz, Linda M.G., Archv.
YESHIVA UNIVERSITY - ALBERT EINSTEIN
COLLEGE OF MEDICINE - D. SAMUEL
GOTTESMAN LIBRARY □ Bronx, NY
Katz, Marilyn, Libn.
CHILD WELFARE LEAGUE OF AMERICA, INC. -
DOROTHY L. BERNHARD LIBRARY □ New York,
NY
Katz-Hyman, Martha, Asst.Libn.
AMERICAN JEWISH HISTORICAL SOCIETY -
LIBRARY □ Waltham, MA
Katzung, Alice C., Dir.
MARIN WILDLIFE CENTER - LIBRARY □ San
Rafael, CA
Katzung, Judith, Hd.Libn.
ST. PAUL DISPATCH-PIONEER PRESS -
LIBRARY □ St. Paul, MN
Kaubris-Kowalzyk, S.A., Asst.Libn.
BANGOR THEOLOGICAL SEMINARY - MOULTON
LIBRARY □ Bangor, ME
Kauff, Joan L., Chf.Med.Libn.
LONG ISLAND JEWISH-HILLSIDE MEDICAL
CENTER - HILLSIDE DIVISION - HEALTH
SCIENCES LIBRARY □ Glen Oaks, NY
Kauffman, Betty, Supv.Libn.
AMERICAN TELEPHONE & TELEGRAPH
COMPANY - MORRISTOWN CORPORATE
MARKETING LIBRARY □ Morristown, NJ
Kauffman, Betty J., Hd.Libn.
AMERICAN TELEPHONE & TELEGRAPH
COMPANY - BUSINESS & TECHNICAL
RESOURCE CENTER □ Piscataway, NJ
Kauffman, H.A., Dir. of Res.
BAKER (J.T.) CHEMICAL COMPANY - RESEARCH
LIBRARY □ Phillipsburg, NJ
Kauffman, Inge, Libn.
CALIFORNIA SCHOOL OF PROFESSIONAL
PSYCHOLOGY - FRESNO LIBRARY □ Fresno, CA

Kauffmann, Laura, Libn.
OWENS-ILLINOIS, INC. - BUSINESS
INFORMATION SERVICES □ Toledo, OH
Kaufman, David, Asst.Libn.
INDIANA UNIVERSITY OF PENNSYLVANIA -
UNIVERSITY LIBRARY □ Indiana, PA
Kaufman, Debra R., Info.Spec.
AMERICAN CAN COMPANY - BUSINESS
INFORMATION CENTER □ Greenwich, CT
Kaufman, Ivy, Libn.
MARSHALL, BRATTER, GREENE, ALLISON &
TUCKER - LIBRARY □ New York, NY
Kaufman, Judith, Libn.
SUNY AT STONY BROOK - MUSIC LIBRARY □
Stony Brook, NY
Kaufman, Margaret, Asst.Cur.
VALENTINE MUSEUM - LIBRARY □ Richmond,
VA
Kaufman, Nancy Jo, Asst.Med.Libn.
EQUITABLE LIFE ASSURANCE SOCIETY OF THE
U.S. - MEDICAL LIBRARY† □ New York, NY
Kaufman, Paula T., Libn.
COLUMBIA UNIVERSITY - THOMAS J. WATSON
LIBRARY OF BUSINESS AND ECONOMICS □ New
York, NY
Kaufman, Ruth, Ref.Libn.
WAYNE STATE UNIVERSITY - EDUCATION
LIBRARY □ Detroit, MI
Kaufman, Sonya, Hd., Ref.Serv.
UNIVERSITY OF CALIFORNIA, BERKELEY -
EDUCATION/PSYCHOLOGY LIBRARY □
Berkeley, CA
Kaufmann, Robert C., Libn.
SMITHSONIAN INSTITUTION LIBRARIES -
COOPER-HEWITT MUSEUM OF DESIGN - DORIS
& HENRY DREYFUSS MEMORIAL STUDY
CENTER □ New York, NY
Kaul, K.L., Hd.
WAYNE STATE UNIVERSITY - G. FLINT PURDY
LIBRARY □ Detroit, MI
Kaupa, Joyce, Patient Libn.
U.S. VETERANS ADMINISTRATION (NY-Buffalo)
- MEDICAL CENTER LIBRARY SERVICE □
Buffalo, NY
Kaushagen, Beverly A., Lib. Group Supv.
BELL TELEPHONE LABORATORIES, INC. &
WESTERN ELECTRIC, INC. - TECHNICAL
LIBRARY □ Columbus, OH
Kaushansky, Rosalie, Cat.
BANK OF MONTREAL - HEAD OFFICE LIBRARY □
Montreal, PQ
Kautz, George, Asst.Libn.
KING COUNTY LAW LIBRARY □ Seattle, WA
Kavass, Igor I., Dir.
VANDERBILT UNIVERSITY LAW LIBRARY □
Nashville, TN
Kawakami, Toyo S., Asst.Hd.
OHIO STATE UNIVERSITY - EDUCATION
LIBRARY □ Columbus, OH
Kawakami, Mrs. Toyo S., Hd.Libn.
OHIO STATE UNIVERSITY - SOCIAL WORK
LIBRARY □ Columbus, OH
Kay, Ella W., Cur.
CAPE MAY COUNTY HISTORICAL/
GENEALOGICAL SOCIETY AND MUSEUM -
LIBRARY □ Cape May Court House, NJ
Kay, Janice
DALHOUSIE UNIVERSITY - INSTITUTE OF
PUBLIC AFFAIRS - LIBRARY □ Halifax, NS
Kay, Mrs. Sidney R.
TEMPLE B'NAI ISRAEL - LASKER MEMORIAL
LIBRARY □ Galveston, TX
Kaya, Beatrice S., Chf.Libn.
HAWAII NEWSPAPER AGENCY - LIBRARY □
Honolulu, HI
Kaya, Kathryn, Libn.
MONTANA STATE UNIVERSITY - VETERINARY
RESEARCH LABORATORY - HUIDEKOPER
LIBRARY □ Bozeman, MT
Kaye, Barbara, Cat.
CANADA - PUBLIC ARCHIVES OF CANADA -
NATL. FILM, TELEVISION & SOUND ARCHIVES -
DOCUMENTATION & PUB. SERV. □ Ottawa, ON

Kaye, Doug, Hd.
UNIVERSITY OF BRITISH COLUMBIA - WILSON
RECORDINGS COLLECTION □ Vancouver, BC
Kaye, Geraldine C., Libn.
HARVARD UNIVERSITY - FARLOW REFERENCE
LIBRARY □ Cambridge, MA
Kaye, Margit E., Sr.Lib.Spec.
YALE UNIVERSITY - MAP COLLECTION □ New
Haven, CT
Kayne, Carolyn, Coord.
BROWARD COUNTY HISTORICAL COMMISSION
- LIBRARY & ARCHIVES □ Fort Lauderdale, FL
Kazimer, Mary Ellen, Asst.Libn.
LOYOLA UNIVERSITY OF CHICAGO - LAW
LIBRARY □ Chicago, IL
Kazymyra-Dzioba, Ms. N.
CANADA - PUBLIC ARCHIVES OF CANADA -
NATIONAL MAP COLLECTION □ Ottawa, ON
Kealey, Dorothy, Asst.Archv.
ANGLICAN CHURCH OF CANADA - GENERAL
SYNOD ARCHIVES □ Toronto, ON
Kealty, Diane, Pres.
HISTORIC WALKER'S POINT, INC. - LIBRARY □
Milwaukee, WI
Kean, Manuel, Owner
KEAN ARCHIVES □ Philadelphia, PA
Kean, Randolph, Archv.
CHESAPEAKE & OHIO HISTORICAL SOCIETY,
INC. - C & O ARCHIVAL COLLECTION □
Alderson, WV
Kear, Becky, Librarian
DAMES & MOORE - LIBRARY □ Atlanta, GA
Kearley, David, Dir.
VANDERBILT UNIVERSITY LIBRARY -
EDUCATION LIBRARY □ Nashville, TN
Kearley, Timothy, Foreign Law Libn.
UNIVERSITY OF ILLINOIS - LAW LIBRARY □
Champaign, IL
Kearney, Eileen, Tech.Proc.Libn.
ST. CHARLES BORROMEO SEMINARY - RYAN
MEMORIAL LIBRARY □ Philadelphia, PA
Kearney, Kate
UNIVERSITY OF PITTSBURGH - GRADUATE
SCHOOL OF PUBLIC HEALTH LIBRARY □
Pittsburgh, PA
Kearney, Lorraine, Coord., Lib.Serv.
DISTRICT ONE TECHNICAL INSTITUTE -
LIBRARY - EDUCATIONAL RESOURCE CENTER □
Eau Claire, WI
Kearney, Robert D., Asst.Dir.
CALIFORNIA COLLEGE OF PODIATRIC
MEDICINE - SCHMIDT MEDICAL LIBRARY □ San
Francisco, CA
Kearns, Glenn, Supv.Rec.Ctr.
MORRISON-KNUDSEN CO., INC. - RECORDS
AND MICROGRAPHICS CENTER □ Boise, ID
Kearns, Nancy J., Info.Dir.
SILVERWOOD INDUSTRIES, LTD. - RESEARCH
& DEVELOPMENT LIBRARY □ London, ON
Keate, Heather, Pub.Serv.
UNIVERSITY OF BRITISH COLUMBIA -
WOODWARD BIOMEDICAL LIBRARY □
Vancouver, BC
Keathley, Allen, Spec.Serv.Libn.
INDIANA STATE UNIVERSITY - SPECIAL
SERVICES AREA □ Terre Haute, IN
Keating, Michael, Sr. Market Anl.
PENTON/IPC - MARKETING INFORMATION
CENTER □ Cleveland, OH
Keating, Shirley, Asst.Dir.
MC GRAW-HILL PUBLICATIONS COMPANY -
MARKETING INFORMATION CENTER† □ New
York, NY
Keaveney, Sydney, Art & Arch.Libn.
PRATT INSTITUTE - LIBRARY □ Brooklyn, NY
Keck, Dr. C. William, Dir. of Health
AKRON CITY HEALTH DEPARTMENT - PUBLIC
HEALTH LIBRARY □ Akron, OH
Keck, Kerry A., Libn.
UNIVERSITY OF ILLINOIS - COORDINATED
SCIENCE LABORATORY LIBRARY □ Urbana, IL

Keck, Mary Ellen, Chf., Tech.Serv.
U.S. DEPT. OF THE INTERIOR - NATURAL
RESOURCES LIBRARY □ Washington, DC

Keckley, Mary W., Hd.Ser.Dept.
UNIVERSITY OF TEXAS, EL PASO - LIBRARY □
El Paso, TX

Keddle, David G., Dir.Med.Lib.
INGHAM MEDICAL CENTER - JOHN W. CHI
MEMORIAL MEDICAL LIBRARY □ Lansing, MI

Keddy, Linda M., Libn.
NOVA SCOTIA BARRISTERS' SOCIETY -
LIBRARY □ Halifax, NS

Kedigh, Kini, Editorial Prod.
CENTER FOR SOUTHERN FOLKLORE -
ARCHIVES □ Memphis, TN

Kedl, Aloysius
ST. CHARLES SCHOLASTICATE - LIBRARY □
Battleford, SK

Kee, Danny, Asst.Archv.
OKLAHOMA HISTORICAL SOCIETY - DIVISION
OF LIBRARY RESOURCES □ Oklahoma City, OK

Keefe, Margaret, Libn.
METROPOLITAN TORONTO LIBRARY - SOCIAL
SCIENCES DEPARTMENT □ Toronto, ON

Keefer, Elaine, Searcher & Ref.
UNIVERSITY OF SOUTH ALABAMA - COLLEGE
OF MEDICINE - BIOMEDICAL LIBRARY □
Mobile, AL

Keefer, Ruth L., Lit.Spec.
MOBIL RESEARCH & DEVELOPMENT
CORPORATION - FIELD RESEARCH
LABORATORY LIBRARY □ Dallas, TX

Keegan, Carol, Asst.Libn.
CHILTON COMPANY - MARKETING &
ADVERTISING INFORMATION CENTER □
Radnor, PA

Keelan, Mary F., Libn.
GREAT-WEST LIFE ASSURANCE COMPANY -
LIBRARY □ Winnipeg, MB

Keeler, Elizabeth, Asst.Engr.Libn.
PURDUE UNIVERSITY - ENGINEERING LIBRARY
□ West Lafayette, IN

Keeler, Dr. Robert W., Cur.
WASHINGTON COUNTY MUSEUM - LIBRARY □
Hillsboro, OR

Keeley, Kurt M., Tech.Libn.
AMERICAN WATER WORKS ASSOCIATION -
TECHNICAL LIBRARY AND INFORMATION
CENTER □ Denver, CO

Keeling, Alfreida, Libn.
U.S. VETERANS ADMINISTRATION (MO-St.
Louis) - HOSPITAL LIBRARY □ St. Louis, MO

Keenan, Elizabeth L., Rec.Libn.
CHICAGO PUBLIC LIBRARY CULTURAL CENTER
- FINE ARTS DIVISION - MUSIC SECTION □
Chicago, IL

Keenan, Gloria, Hd.Libn.
BINGHAMTON PRESS AND SUN BULLETIN -
LIBRARY □ Binghamton, NY

Keenan, Grace G., Asst.Libn.
JOSLYN ART MUSEUM - ART REFERENCE
LIBRARY □ Omaha, NE

Keene, Catherine, Dir.
PASSAIC COUNTY HISTORICAL SOCIETY -
LIBRARY □ Paterson, NJ

Keener, Donald S., Asst.Dir.Gen.Serv.
NORTH CAROLINA STATE UNIVERSITY - D.H.
HILL LIBRARY □ Raleigh, NC

Keener, Edison W., Att.
PEOPLES NATURAL GAS COMPANY - LAW
LIBRARY □ Pittsburgh, PA

Keeney, Ann, Med.Libn.
FRESNO COMMUNITY HOSPITAL - MEDICAL
LIBRARY □ Fresno, CA

Kees, Stephen J., Chf.Libn.
NIAGARA COLLEGE OF APPLIED ARTS AND
TECHNOLOGY - LEARNING RESOURCE CENTRE
□ Welland, ON

Keesee, R. Eugene, Owner
PHOTO TRENDS - LIBRARY □ New York, NY

Keeter, Alice, Hd., Index Unit
ORGANIZATION OF AMERICAN STATES -
COLUMBUS MEMORIAL LIBRARY □ Washington,
DC

Keeth, Kent, Dir.
BAYLOR UNIVERSITY - TEXAS COLLECTION □
Waco, TX

Kegerise, Antoinette, Asst.Libn.
HERCULES, INC. - RESEARCH CENTER -
TECHNICAL INFORMATION DIVISION □
Wilmington, DE

Kegg, Janet, Libn.
AMERICAN ASSOCIATION FOR THE
ADVANCEMENT OF SCIENCE - LIBRARY □
Washington, DC

Kehde, Edward, Assoc.Archv.
UNIVERSITY OF KANSAS - UNIVERSITY
ARCHIVES □ Lawrence, KS

Kehoe, Patrick E., Dir.
AMERICAN UNIVERSITY - WASHINGTON
COLLEGE OF LAW - LIBRARY □ Washington, DC

Kehrein, James E., Libn.
ILLINOIS RAILWAY MUSEUM - TECHNICAL
LIBRARY □ Union, IL

Kehrer, Mrs. Shelby J., Asst.Libn.
CINCINNATI ELECTRONICS CORPORATION -
TECHNICAL LIBRARY □ Cincinnati, OH

Keighley, David, Media Spec.
UNIVERSITY OF CONNECTICUT - PHARMACY
LIBRARY AND LEARNING CENTER □ Storrs, CT

Keim, Julia, Ref.Libn.
ROCKWELL INTERNATIONAL - ROCKETDYNE
DIVISION - TECHNICAL INFORMATION
CENTER □ Canoga Park, CA

Keister, Martha, Ref./Doc.Libn.
PACE UNIVERSITY - SCHOOL OF LAW LIBRARY
□ White Plains, NY

Keiter, Linda S., Coord., Sci.Lib.Serv.
UNIVERSITY OF WYOMING - SCIENCE AND
TECHNOLOGY LIBRARY □ Laramie, WY

Keith, Diana, Doc.Libn.
KEARNEY STATE COLLEGE - CALVIN T. RYAN
LIBRARY □ Kearney, NE

Keith, Marie C., Asst.Libn.
FRICK ART REFERENCE LIBRARY □ New York,
NY

Keith, Narinder, Hd.Ref. & Circ.
INTERNATIONAL MONETARY FUND/WORLD
BANK - JOINT BANK-FUND LIBRARY □
Washington, DC

Keith, Susan, Info.Spec.
PRIME COMPUTER, INC. - INFORMATION
CENTER □ Framingham, MA

Keitzer, Geri K., Libn.
CARRIER CORPORATION - ELLIOTT COMPANY -
ENGINEERING LIBRARY □ Jeannette, PA

Keizur, Berta, Hd., Info.Proc.
U.S. DEPT. OF ENERGY - LAWRENCE
LIVERMORE LAB. - TECHNICAL INFO. DEPT.
LIBRARY □ Livermore, CA

Keklock, Donna, Chf.Libn.
CHARLOTTE MEMORIAL HOSPITAL AND
MEDICAL CENTER - MEDICAL LIBRARY OF
MECKLENBURG COUNTY/LRC OF CHARLOTTE
AHEC □ Charlotte, NC

Kelenson, Dora, Libn.
AMERICAN FEDERATION OF LABOR AND
CONGRESS OF INDUSTRIAL ORGANIZATIONS -
LIBRARY □ Washington, DC

Kelham, Thomas, Cat. Clerk
MARSHALL (John) LAW SCHOOL - LIBRARY □
Chicago, IL

Kelker, Signe, Hd.Ref.Libn.
SHIPPENSBURG STATE COLLEGE - EZRA
LEHMAN MEMORIAL LIBRARY □ Shippensburg,
PA

Kelleher, Kathleen, Libn.
TEACHERS INSURANCE AND ANNUITY
ASSOCIATION OF AMERICA - BUSINESS
LIBRARY □ New York, NY

Kellen, James D., Cat.
COLLEGE OF ST. THOMAS - CELTIC LIBRARY □
St. Paul, MN

Keller, Arlene R., Libn.
TEMPLE UNIVERSITY - CENTRAL LIBRARY
SYSTEM - COLLEGE OF ENGINEERING -
TECHNOLOGY LIBRARY □ Philadelphia, PA

Keller, Daniel, Photo Cat.
NATIONAL MARITIME MUSEUM - J. PORTER
SHAW LIBRARY □ San Francisco, CA

Keller, Dean H., Cur.
KENT STATE UNIVERSITY - DEPARTMENT OF
SPECIAL COLLECTIONS □ Kent, OH

Keller, Gary, Dir.
LAKE COUNTY MUSEUM - LIBRARY AND
INFORMATION CENTER □ Wauconda, IL

Keller, George, Sci.Ref.Libn.
UNIVERSITY OF CALIFORNIA, SANTA CRUZ -
SCIENCE LIBRARY □ Santa Cruz, CA

Keller, Jean I., Asst.Libn.
HEINZ (H.J.) COMPANY - LIBRARY □ Pittsburgh,
PA

Keller, Joan R., Ext.Serv.Libn.
U.S. ARMY POST - PRESIDIO OF SAN
FRANCISCO - POST LIBRARY SYSTEM □
Presidio of San Francisco, CA

Keller, Madeline, Ref.Libn.
MANUFACTURERS HANOVER TRUST COMPANY
- CORPORATE LIBRARY/INVESTMENT LIBRARY
DIVISION □ New York, NY

Keller, Michael A., Music Libn.
CORNELL UNIVERSITY - MUSIC LIBRARY □
Ithaca, NY

Keller, Mildred, Mgr./Tech.Info.Serv.
DURACELL INTERNATIONAL, INC. - TECHNICAL
INFORMATION CENTER □ Burlington, MA

Keller, Pat, Acq.
UNIVERSITY OF CINCINNATI - ROBERT S.
MARX LAW LIBRARY □ Cincinnati, OH

Keller, Paula, Info.Spec.
AMERICAN SOYBEAN ASSOCIATION - LIBRARY
□ St. Louis, MO

Keller, Richard, Asst.Div.Chf.
BROOKLYN PUBLIC LIBRARY - ART AND MUSIC
DIVISION □ Brooklyn, NY

Keller, Mrs. T.G., Libn.
NEWSPAPER COMICS COUNCIL - LIBRARY AND
INFORMATION CENTER □ New York, NY

Keller, Wanda, Libn.
ALLEGANY COUNTY CIRCUIT COURT - LIBRARY
□ Cumberland, MD

Keller, William B., Hd.Libn.
MARYLAND HISTORICAL SOCIETY - LIBRARY □
Baltimore, MD

Keller, William E., Adm.Asst.
ILLINOIS STATE HISTORICAL LIBRARY □
Springfield, IL

Kellerman, Frank, Bio./Psych.Ref.Libn.
BROWN UNIVERSITY - SCIENCES LIBRARY □
Providence, RI

Kelley, Mrs., Asst. Genealogist
LEBANON COUNTY HISTORICAL SOCIETY -
LIBRARY □ Lebanon, PA

Kelley, Ann T., Info.Spec.
BONNER & MOORE ASSOCIATES, INC. -
LIBRARY □ Houston, TX

Kelley, Bruce, Dir./Cur.
ANTIQUE WIRELESS ASSOCIATION, INC. -
LIBRARY □ Holcomb, NY

Kelley, Elizabeth, Libn.
HAMLINE UNIVERSITY SCHOOL OF LAW -
LIBRARY □ St. Paul, MN

Kelley, Elizabeth, Dir.
MARICOPA COUNTY LAW LIBRARY □ Phoenix,
AZ

Kelley, Lorain, Libn.
CHAMPION INTERNATIONAL - CORPORATE
INFORMATION CENTER □ Stamford, CT

Kelley, Marianne, Ref.Libn.
ABBOTT-NORTHWESTERN HOSPITAL
CORPORATION - HEALTH SCIENCES RESOURCE
CENTER □ Minneapolis, MN

Kelley, Marilyn, Asst.Libn.
STURGIS LIBRARY □ Barnstable, MA

P E R S O N N E L

Kelley, Mary C., Br. Genealogy Libn.
CHURCH OF JESUS CHRIST OF LATTER-DAY
SAINTS - JACKSONVILLE, FLORIDA BRANCH
GENEALOGICAL LIBRARY □ Jacksonville, FL

Kelley, Pamela, Info.Tech.
UNIVERSITY OF PITTSBURGH - CENTER FOR
INTERNATIONAL STUDIES □ Pittsburgh, PA

Kelley, Peter, Coord.
PRATT INSTITUTE - PRATT/PHOENIX SCHOOL
OF DESIGN LIBRARY □ New York, NY

Kelley, Rosemary, Med.Libn.
UNIVERSITY OF NEW ENGLAND - LIBRARY† □
Biddeford, ME

Kelley, Rosemary G., Med.Libn.
UNIVERSITY OF NEW ENGLAND - NEW
ENGLAND COLLEGE OF OSTEOPATHIC
MEDICINE - NECOM LIBRARY □ Biddeford, ME

Kelley, Stephanie, Supv.
REORGANIZED CHURCH OF JESUS CHRIST OF
LATTER DAY SAINTS - SERVICES TO THE
BLIND □ Independence, MO

Kelley, Rev. Thomas C., Rector
ST. MARK'S SEMINARY - LIBRARY □ Erie, PA

Kellie, Mary, Inservice Coord.
NOTRE DAME HOSPITAL - LIBRARY □ Hearst,
ON

Kellman, Amy, Hd. Of Ch.Dept.
CARNEGIE LIBRARY OF PITTSBURGH -
CENTRAL CHILDREN'S ROOM HISTORICAL
COLLECTION □ Pittsburgh, PA

Kellogg, Eleanore, Asst.Libn.
CRANBROOK INSTITUTE OF SCIENCE -
LIBRARY □ Bloomfield Hills, MI

Kellogg, Pat, Supv.
CANADIAN BROADCASTING CORPORATION -
PROGRAM ARCHIVES (Sound) □ Toronto, ON

Kells, Shirley, Lib.Asst.
FOUNDATION FOR BLIND CHILDREN - LIBRARY
□ Scottsdale, AZ

Kelly, Agnes, Asst.Libn.
ERNST & WHINNEY - LIBRARY □ New York, NY

Kelly, Albert F., Chf., Tech.Lib.Br.
U.S. NASA - LYNDON B. JOHNSON SPACE
CENTER - TECHNICAL LIBRARY □ Houston, TX

Kelly, Ann M., Libn.
ST. ELIZABETH'S HOSPITAL - NURSING
SCHOOL LIBRARY □ Utica, NY

Kelly, Anthony, Bus.Libn.
BRITISH COLUMBIA INSTITUTE OF
TECHNOLOGY - LIBRARY SERVICES DIVISION
□ Burnaby, BC

Kelly, Ardie L., Libn.
MARINERS MUSEUM - LIBRARY □ Newport
News, VA

Kelly, Barbara R., Libn.
COMMONWEALTH EDISON COMPANY -
LIBRARY □ Chicago, IL

Kelly, Callista, Libn.
CANADA - DEPARTMENT OF
COMMUNICATIONS - COMMUNICATIONS
RESEARCH CENTRE LIBRARY □ Ottawa, ON

Kelly, Claire B., Res.Libn.
MERCK FROSST LABORATORIES - RESEARCH
LIBRARY □ Pointe Claire-Dorval, PQ

Kelly, Claudia, Libn.
MASSACHUSETTS STATE DEPARTMENT OF
LABOR & INDUSTRIES - REFERENCE LIBRARY □
Boston, MA

Kelly, Deborah M., Corp.Libn.
BRINCO LIMITED - LIBRARY □ Toronto, ON

Kelly, Donald, Art Gallery
BOSTON ATHENAEUM LIBRARY □ Boston, MA

Kelly, Eleanor M., Libn.
OUR LADY OF LOURDES HOSPITAL - SCHOOL OF
NURSING - LIBRARY □ Camden, NJ

Kelly, Elinor C., Libn.
EASTERN WASHINGTON STATE HISTORICAL
SOCIETY - LIBRARY □ Spokane, WA

Kelly, Elizabeth, Asst.Libn., Access Serv.
WASHINGTON UNIVERSITY - SCHOOL OF
MEDICINE LIBRARY □ St. Louis, MO

Kelly, Elizabeth C., Assoc.Dir.
CREIGHTON UNIVERSITY - LAW SCHOOL -
KLUTZNICK LIBRARY □ Omaha, NE

Kelly, Elizabeth C., Dir., Med.Lib.
U.S. FOOD & DRUG ADMINISTRATION -
BUREAU OF DRUGS - MEDICAL LIBRARY HFD-
630† □ Rockville, MD

Kelly, Elizabeth Slusser, Law Lib.Dir.
SOUTHERN ILLINOIS UNIVERSITY,
CARBONDALE - SCHOOL OF LAW LIBRARY □
Carbondale, IL

Kelly, Glen, Hd., Acq.
LAURENTIAN UNIVERSITY - MAIN LIBRARY □
Sudbury, ON

Kelly, Rev. James, Cat.
ST. ANTHONY-ON-HUDSON THEOLOGICAL
LIBRARY □ Rensselaer, NY

Kelly, James W., Cur.
HIGHLAND PARK HERBARIUM - LIBRARY □
Rochester, NY

Kelly, Janice, Ref.Libn.
CHICAGO COLLEGE OF OSTEOPATHIC
MEDICINE - ALUMNI MEMORIAL LIBRARY □
Chicago, IL

Kelly, Joanne, Lib.Dir.
VIDEO FREE AMERICA - LIBRARY □ San
Francisco, CA

Kelly, John, Asst.Cur.
UNIVERSITY OF SOUTHERN MISSISSIPPI - MC
CAIN LIBRARY □ Hattiesburg, MS

Kelly, John J., Libn.
HAMPDEN COUNTY LAW LIBRARY □ Springfield,
MA

Kelly, Karon M., Libn.
WESTERN INTERSTATE COMMISSION FOR
HIGHER EDUCATION - LIBRARY □ Boulder, CO

Kelly, Kay, Med.Libn.
BURNS (Dean C.) HEALTH SCIENCES LIBRARY □
Petoskey, MI

Kelly, Lorraine P., Libn.
ST. OLAF LUTHERAN CHURCH - CARLSEN
MEMORIAL LIBRARY† □ Minneapolis, MN

Kelly, Margaret, Ser.Libn.
BLOOMSBURG STATE COLLEGE - HARVEY A.
ANDRUSS LIBRARY □ Bloomsburg, PA

Kelly, Mary
3M - BUSINESS INFORMATION SERVICE □ St.
Paul, MN

Kelly, Sr. Mary Clarentia, Dir.
DOMINICAN EDUCATION CENTER - LIBRARY □
Sinsinawa, WI

Kelly, Michael, Libn./Archv.
BUFFALO BILL HISTORICAL CENTER - HAROLD
MC CRACKEN RESEARCH LIBRARY □ Cody, WY

Kelly, Patrick, Asst.Libn.
BRYANT COLLEGE OF BUSINESS
ADMINISTRATION - EDITH M. HODGSON
MEMORIAL LIBRARY □ Smithfield, RI

Kelly, Richard, Ref. & Acq.
NORTHWEST CHRISTIAN COLLEGE - LEARNING
RESOURCE CENTER □ Eugene, OR

Kelly, Robert Q., Dir.
CREIGHTON UNIVERSITY - LAW SCHOOL -
KLUTZNICK LIBRARY □ Omaha, NE

Kelly, Ruth, Libn.
JEWISH HOSPITAL OF ST. LOUIS -
ROTHSCHILD MEDICAL LIBRARY □ St. Louis,
MO

Kelly, Tyler, Libn.
MEXICAN AMERICAN LEGAL DEFENSE AND
EDUCATIONAL FUND - LIBRARY □ San
Francisco, CA

Kelner, Loretta, Hd., Ref.&Loan Div.
INDIANA STATE LIBRARY □ Indianapolis, IN

Kelsay, Susan M., Asst.Dir.
MORRIS (Robert) ASSOCIATES - LIBRARY □
Philadelphia, PA

Kelsey, Dorothea, Patients' Libn.
U.S. VETERANS ADMINISTRATION (CA-Long
Beach) - MEDICAL CENTER LIBRARY □ Long
Beach, CA

Kelso, Mark A., First Asst.
PUBLIC LIBRARY OF CINCINNATI AND
HAMILTON COUNTY - EXCEPTIONAL
CHILDREN'S DIVISION □ Cincinnati, OH

Kelty, Linda, Libn.
INDIANA UNIVERSITY - SOCIAL STUDIES
DEVELOPMENT CENTER - CURRICULUM
RESOURCE CENTER □ Bloomington, IN

Kemble, Harold E., Mss.Cur.
RHODE ISLAND HISTORICAL SOCIETY -
LIBRARY □ Providence, RI

Kemen, J.R., Spec.
GENERAL ELECTRIC COMPANY - METER
BUSINESS DEPARTMENT - LIBRARY & DATA
BUREAU □ Somersworth, NH

Kemp, Charles H., Dir.
OREGON INSTITUTE OF TECHNOLOGY -
LEARNING RESOURCES CENTER □ Klamath Falls,
OR

Kemp, Diana, Info.Spec.
CONSUMER EDUCATION RESOURCE NETWORK
(CERN) □ Rosslyn, VA

Kemp, Jeanne, Asst.Dir.
CENTRAL OPERA SERVICE - INFORMATION
CENTER AND LIBRARY □ New York, NY

Kemp, Kathryn, Dir.
UNIVERSITY OF THE PACIFIC - STUART
LIBRARY OF WESTERN AMERICANA □ Stockton,
CA

Kemp, Leatrice, Asst.Libn.
ROCHESTER MUSEUM AND SCIENCE CENTER -
LIBRARY □ Rochester, NY

Kemp, Lenore, Hd., Tech.Serv.
SUNY - COLLEGE AT BUFFALO - EDWARD H.
BUTLER LIBRARY □ Buffalo, NY

Kemp, Leora, Tech.Proc.Libn.
TEXAS STATE TECHNICAL INSTITUTE, WACO
CAMPUS - LEARNING RESOURCE CENTER □
Waco, TX

Kemp, Linda, Libn.
TEXAS EDUCATION AGENCY - RESOURCE
CENTER LIBRARY □ Austin, TX

Kemp, Wanda D., Mgr., Info.Serv.
SPECIAL LIBRARIES ASSOCIATION -
INFORMATION SERVICES □ New York, NY

Kempel, Harold, Mss.Libn.
SOCIETY OF FRIENDS - NEW ENGLAND YEARLY
MEETING OF FRIENDS - ARCHIVES □
Providence, RI

Kempel, Peter M., Dir., Res.Serv.
COOLEY (Thomas M.) LAW SCHOOL - LIBRARY □
Lansing, MI

Kempen, Carrie, Libn.
MERCANTILE TRUST COMPANY -
INTERNATIONAL LIBRARY □ St. Louis, MO

Kemper, Robert E., Dir.
NORTHERN ARIZONA UNIVERSITY - LIBRARIES
□ Flagstaff, AZ

Kemper, Suzanne, Libn.
ONTARIO LOTTERY CORPORATION - LIBRARY
□ Toronto, ON

Kemper, Suzanne W., Acq. & Ref.
NORTH ADAMS STATE COLLEGE - EUGENE L.
FREEL LIBRARY - SPECIAL COLLECTIONS □
North Adams, MA

Kenagy, Roy, Hd. Adult Serv.
CEDAR RAPIDS PUBLIC LIBRARY - BUSINESS
CENTER □ Cedar Rapids, IA

Kenamore, Jane A., Archv.
ROSENBERG LIBRARY - ARCHIVES
DEPARTMENT □ Galveston, TX

Kenan, Charlotte, Libn.
TUCSON CITIZEN - LIBRARY □ Tucson, AZ

Kendall, Nellie, Libn.
DALLAS PUBLIC LIBRARY - HISTORY AND
SOCIAL SCIENCES DIVISION □ Dallas, TX

Kenderson, Ann M., Coord., Pub.Rel.
UNIVERSITY OF PITTSBURGH - AFRO-
AMERICAN COLLECTION □ Pittsburgh, PA

Kendig, Barbara, Br.Libn.
HONEYWELL, INC. - HONEYWELL
INFORMATION SYSTEMS - INFORMATION AND
LIBRARY SERVICES □ Waltham, MA

Kendrick, Alice M., Dir.
LUTHERAN COUNCIL IN THE U.S.A. - RECORDS
AND INFORMATION CE NTER - REFERENCE
LIBRARY □ New York, NY

Keng, Mr. Hsiu-Yun, Dir.
SOUTH CAROLINA STATE DEPARTMENT OF
MENTAL RETARDATION - WHITTEN CENTER
LIBRARY & MEDIA RESOURCE SERVICES □
Clinton, SC

Kenneally, Louise M., Archv.
STONEHILL COLLEGE - ARNOLD B. TOFIAS
INDUSTRIAL ARCHIVES □ North Easton, MA

Kennedy, Doris Autrey, Libn.
CHRISTIAN CHURCH (Disciples of Christ), INC. -
LIBRARY □ Indianapolis, IN

Kennedy, Eileen M., Libn.
SCHERING-PLOUGH CORPORATION - BUSINESS
INFORMATION CENTER - LIBRARY □
Kenilworth, NJ

Kennedy, Mrs. Gene, Res.Libn.
BASF WYANDOTTE CORPORATION -
CORPORATE LIBRARY □ Wyandotte, MI

Kennedy, Harva, Cat.
MISSOURI BOTANICAL GARDEN - LIBRARY □
St. Louis, MO

Kennedy, Helen, Dir.
PACIFICA TAPE LIBRARY □ Los Angeles, CA

Kennedy, Jane, Libn.
BAUDER FASHION COLLEGE - LIBRARY □
Arlington, TX

Kennedy, Jane F., Gen.Mgr.
U.S. POSTAL SERVICE - LIBRARY □ Washington,
DC

Kennedy, Jean A., Chf.Libn.
U.S. VETERANS ADMINISTRATION (VA-Salem) -
MEDICAL CENTER LIBRARY □ Salem, VA

Kennedy, Joanne, Libn.
ST. JOHN'S HOSPITAL - HEALTH SCIENCE
LIBRARY □ Oxnard, CA

Kennedy, Katherine, Tech.Info.Spec.
U.S. ARMY - ENGINEER WATERWAYS
EXPERIMENT STATION - TECHNICAL
INFORMATION CENTER □ Vicksburg, MS

Kennedy, Kathleen, Educ.Libn.
GLASSBORO STATE COLLEGE - SAVITZ
LIBRARY - LLOYD V. MANWILLER CURRICULUM
LABORATORY □ Glassboro, NJ

Kennedy, Lynn J., Mgr.
AMERICAN PUBLIC TRANSIT ASSOCIATION -
LIBRARY □ Washington, DC

Kennedy, Marsha, Coord., Film Distr.
UNIVERSITY OF NEW HAMPSHIRE -
DEPARTMENT OF MEDIA SERVICES - FILM
LIBRARY □ Durham, NH

Kennedy, Martha, Cur. of Photographs
CALIFORNIA HISTORICAL SOCIETY -
SCHUBERT HALL LIBRARY □ San Francisco, CA

Kennedy, P., Preconfederation Archv.
CANADA - PUBLIC ARCHIVES OF CANADA -
MANUSCRIPT DIVISION □ Ottawa, ON

Kennedy, Pat, Asst.Libn.
MIDDLESEX COUNTY LAW LIBRARY† □ New
Brunswick, NJ

Kennedy, R.A., Dir.
BELL TELEPHONE LABORATORIES, INC. -
LIBRARIES AND INFORMATION SYSTEMS
CENTER □ Murray Hill, NJ

Kennedy, Scott, Hd., Phys.Sci.Lib.
UNIVERSITY OF CALIFORNIA, DAVIS -
GENERAL LIBRARY □ Davis, CA

Kennedy, Scott, Hd.Libn.
UNIVERSITY OF CALIFORNIA, DAVIS -
PHYSICAL SCIENCES LIBRARY □ Davis, CA

Kennedy, Theodore C., Supv.Libn.
U.S. AIR FORCE SCHOOL OF HEALTH CARE
SCIENCES - ACADEMIC LIBRARY □ Sheppard
AFB, TX

Kennedy, Win, Regional Mgr.
CANADA - EMPLOYMENT & IMMIGRATION
CANADA - PUBLIC AFFAIRS LIBRARY □
Winnipeg, MB

Kenney, Anne R., Assoc.Dir.
UNIVERSITY OF MISSOURI, ST. LOUIS -
WESTERN HISTORICAL MANUSCRIPT
COLLECTION/STATE HISTORICAL SOC. OF
MISSOURI □ St. Louis, MO

Kenney, Edward D., Libn.
U.S. DEPT. OF JUSTICE - FEDERAL BUREAU OF
INVESTIGATION - F.B.I. ACADEMY - LEARNING
RESOURCE CENTER □ Quantico, VA

Kenney, Evelyn, Med.Libn.
RIVERSIDE HOSPITAL - HEALTH SCIENCES
LIBRARY □ Newport News, VA

Kenney, Nancy Beth, Libn.
CH2M HILL, INC. - LIBRARY □ Portland, OR

Kenney, Noreen M., Regional Libn.
BROADVIEW DEVELOPMENTAL CENTER -
REGIONAL STAFF LIBRARY □ Broadview
Heights, OH

Kenney, W.J., Law Ck.
CANADA - NATIONAL DEFENCE - OFFICE OF
THE JUDGE ADVOCATE GENERAL - LIBRARY □
Ottawa, ON

Kenny, Kathryn A., Hd. of Circ.
U.S. AIR FORCE BASE - HANSCOM BASE
LIBRARY □ Hanscom AFB, MA

Kensmoe, Christine L., Libn.
STERLING DRUG, INC. - ZIMPRO INC. -
REFERENCE AND RESOURCE CENTER □
Rothschild, WI

Kent, Beverley, Chf.Libn.
BANK OF NOVA SCOTIA - LIBRARY □ Toronto,
ON

Kent, Caroline, Rd.Serv.Libn.
BRANDEIS UNIVERSITY - GERSTENZANG
SCIENCE LIBRARY □ Waltham, MA

Kent, Diana, Ref.Libn.
UNIVERSITY OF BRITISH COLUMBIA -
WOODWARD BIOMEDICAL LIBRARY □
Vancouver, BC

Kent, Frederick J., Hd.
FREE LIBRARY OF PHILADELPHIA - MUSIC
DEPARTMENT □ Philadelphia, PA

Kent, Frederick J., Hd.
FREE LIBRARY OF PHILADELPHIA - MUSIC
DEPARTMENT - DRINKER LIBRARY OF CHORAL
MUSIC □ Philadelphia, PA

Kent, Ron, Info.Anl.
ALLERGAN PHARMACEUTICALS, INC. -
PROFESSIONAL INFORMATION SERVICES □
Irvine, CA

Kenworthy, Eleanora M., Dir.
HAHNEMANN MEDICAL COLLEGE & HOSPITAL -
WARREN H. FAKE LIBRARY □ Philadelphia, PA

Kenyon, Carleton W., Law Libn.
LIBRARY OF CONGRESS - LAW LIBRARY □
Washington, DC

Kenyon, Cynthia, Dir.
U.S. DEPT. OF AGRICULTURE - ECONOMICS
AND STATISTICS SERVICE - ESS REFERENCE
CENTER □ Washington, DC

Kenyon, Kay, Asst.Libn.
SMITHSONIAN INSTITUTION LIBRARIES -
NATIONAL ZOOLOGICAL PARK - LIBRARY □
Washington, DC

Kenyon, Kenneth, Hd. of Res.Dept.
TWENTIETH CENTURY FOX FILM
CORPORATION - RESEARCH LIBRARY □ Beverly
Hills, CA

Kenyon, Lowell Anson, Dir.
INTERNATIONAL MILITARY ARCHIVES □
Washington, DC

Kenyon, Sharon, Libn.
TRINITY LUTHERAN CHURCH - LIBRARY □
Madison, WI

Kenyon, Sylvaine L., Chf.
NATIONAL CLEARINGHOUSE FOR MENTAL
HEALTH INFORMATION □ Rockville, MD

Kenyon, Xena, Libn.
U.S. VETERANS ADMINISTRATION (WI-Tomah)
- HOSPITAL LIBRARY □ Tomah, WI

Keogh, James, Cartographer
U.S. GEOLOGICAL SURVEY - NATL.
CARTOGRAPHIC INFORMATION CENTER
(NCIC) □ Denver, CO

Keogh, Jeanne M., Libn.
LIBBEY-OWENS-FORD COMPANY - TECHNICAL
CENTER - LIBRARY □ Toledo, OH

Keough, Doreen B., Libn.
ST. VINCENT MEDICAL CENTER - HEALTH
SCIENCES LIBRARY □ Los Angeles, CA

Keough, Kristin, Act.Chf./Interp.
BUFFALO & ERIE COUNTY HISTORICAL
SOCIETY - LIBRARY □ Buffalo, NY

Kepes, Katherine, Libn.
CARNEGIE LIBRARY OF PITTSBURGH - MUSIC
AND ART DEPARTMENT □ Pittsburgh, PA

Kepes, Lois, Lib.Assoc. I
UNIVERSITY OF PITTSBURGH - GRADUATE
SCHOOL OF PUBLIC & INTERNATIONAL
AFFAIRS LIBRARY □ Pittsburgh, PA

Keplinger, Michael, Chf.Info./Ref.Div.
LIBRARY OF CONGRESS - COPYRIGHT PUBLIC
INFORMATION OFFICE □ Washington, DC

Kepner, Frances, Cat.
INDIANA STATE UNIVERSITY - DEPARTMENT
OF RARE BOOKS AND SPECIAL COLLECTIONS □
Terre Haute, IN

Keppel, B.J., Ref.Libn.
UNIVERSITY OF OREGON - HEALTH SCIENCES
CENTER - LIBRARY □ Portland, OR

Kepper, Anna Dean, Cur.
UNIVERSITY OF NEVADA, LAS VEGAS -
GAMING RESEARCH CENTER □ Las Vegas, NV

Kepple, Robert J., Libn.
WESTMINSTER THEOLOGICAL SEMINARY -
MONTGOMERY LIBRARY □ Philadelphia, PA

Kepple, Robert R., Libn.
JOHNS HOPKINS UNIVERSITY - APPLIED
PHYSICS LABORATORY - R.E. GIBSON LIBRARY
□ Laurel, MD

Kerbel, Sandra S., Asst.Bus.Libn.
UNIVERSITY OF PITTSBURGH - GRADUATE
SCHOOL OF BUSINESS LIBRARY □ Pittsburgh, PA

Keresztesy, Frances, Sect.Hd., Res.Info.
MERCK & COMPANY, INC. - MERCK SHARP &
DOHME RESEARCH LABORATORIES -
RESEARCH INFORMATION SYSTEMS □ Rahway,
NJ

Kerfoot, Barbara, Ref./Cont.Educ.Libn.
RED RIVER COMMUNITY COLLEGE - LEARNING
RESOURCES CENTRE □ Winnipeg, MB

Kerka, Sandra, Acq.Coord.
ERIC CLEARINGHOUSE ON ADULT, CAREER
AND VOCATIONAL EDUCATION - NATL. CTR.
FOR RESEARCH IN VOCATIONAL EDUC. □
Columbus, OH

Kern, Betty, Acq. & Ser.
LAW LIBRARY OF LOUISIANA □ New Orleans, LA

Kern-Simirenko, Cheryl, Slavic Biblog.
SYRACUSE UNIVERSITY - E.S. BIRD LIBRARY -
AREA STUDIES DEPARTMENT □ Syracuse, NY

Kern-Simirenko, Cheryl, Biblog.
SYRACUSE UNIVERSITY - E.S. BIRD LIBRARY -
SOCIAL SCIENCES DEPARTMENT □ Syracuse,
NY

Kerndt, Miriam E., Libn.
UNIVERSITY OF WISCONSIN, MADISON -
GEOGRAPHY LIBRARY □ Madison, WI

Kerr, Agnes, Cat.Libn.
LUTHER-NORTHWESTERN SEMINARY -
LIBRARY □ St. Paul, MN

Kerr, Audrey M., Hd.Med.Libn.
UNIVERSITY OF MANITOBA - MEDICAL
LIBRARY □ Winnipeg, MB

Kerr, Donald R., Asst.Dir./Tech.Serv.
EAST TEXAS STATE UNIVERSITY - JAMES
GILLIAM GEE LIBRARY □ Commerce, TX

Kerr, Jean, Cat.
CALVARY BAPTIST THEOLOGICAL SEMINARY -
LIBRARY □ Lansdale, PA

Kerr, Jeannette A., Libn.
U.S. MARINE CORPS - EL TORO AIR STATION
LIBRARY □ Santa Ana, CA

Kerr, Kevin P., Res.Dir.
BOSTON MUNICIPAL RESEARCH BUREAU - LIBRARY □ Boston, MA

Kerr, M. Ruth, Libn.
COMPARATIVE ANIMAL RESEARCH LABORATORY - CARL REFERENCE LIBRARY □ Oak Ridge, TN

Kerr, Miriam, Libn.
UNION COLLEGE - DEPARTMENT OF NURSING LIBRARY† □ Denver, CO

Kerridge, Dr. Kenneth A., Hd., Lit.Sect.
BRISTOL-MYERS COMPANY - BRISTOL LABORATORIES - LIBRARY AND INFORMATION SERVICES □ Syracuse, NY

Kerrigan, Ms. J., Lib.Cons.
TORONTO BOARD OF EDUCATION - EDUCATION CENTRE LIBRARY □ Toronto, ON

Kerschner, Joan G., Dir., Pub.Serv.
NEVADA STATE LIBRARY □ Carson City, NV

Kersey, Marion C., Asst.Libn.
PLANNING RESEARCH CORPORATION - LIBRARY SERVICES DEPARTMENT □ McLean, VA

Kerstetter, John P., Supv.Acq./Cat.
KENT STATE UNIVERSITY - AUDIOVISUAL SERVICES □ Kent, OH

Kerstetter, Virginia, Coord.
EASTERN VIRGINIA MEDICAL SCHOOL - MOORMAN MEMORIAL LIBRARY □ Norfolk, VA

Kerwin, Maryann, Libn.
MIXING EQUIPMENT COMPANY, INC. - MIXCO R&D LIBRARY □ Rochester, NY

Kerwood, John, Dir.
ATLANTA HISTORICAL SOCIETY - ARCHIVES □ Atlanta, GA

Kesler, Cynthia J., Libn.
MAC KENZIE, SMITH, LEWIS, MICHELL & HUGHES - LAW LIBRARY □ Syracuse, NY

Kessenich, Judy, Ref.Libn.
U.S. FOREST SERVICE - FOREST PRODUCTS LABORATORY LIBRARY □ Madison, WI

Kessler, Barbara R., Ref.Libn.
COLUMBIA UNIVERSITY - LAW LIBRARY □ New York, NY

Kessler, Ben, Slide Libn.
PHILADELPHIA MUSEUM OF ART - SLIDE LIBRARY □ Philadelphia, PA

Kessler, Beverly, Libn.
OHIO STATE SCHOOL FOR THE BLIND - LIBRARY □ Columbus, OH

Kessler, Carl, Chf.
U.S. DEPT. OF THE INTERIOR - CENTER FOR INFORMATION AND LIBRARY SERVICES - LAW BRANCH □ Washington, DC

Kessler, Ruth, Asst.Dir.
OHIO STATE UNIVERSITY - LAW LIBRARY □ Columbus, OH

Ketcham, Hertha, Libn.
MACKAY - SHIELDS FINANCIAL CORPORATION - RESEARCH LIBRARY □ New York, NY

Ketchell, Debra, Pub.Serv.Coord.
EASTERN VIRGINIA MEDICAL SCHOOL - MOORMAN MEMORIAL LIBRARY □ Norfolk, VA

Kethley, Sue, Libn.
WACO-MC LENNAN COUNTY LIBRARY - SPECIAL COLLECTIONS DEPARTMENT† □ Waco, TX

Kettner, Judith, Sys.Libn.
AMERICAN EXPRESS COMPANY - CARD DIVISION - WESTERN REGION OPERATIONS CENTER - SYSTEMS LIBRARY □ Phoenix, AZ

Kevil, Hunter, Acq.Libn.
RENSSELAER POLYTECHNIC INSTITUTE - FOLSOM LIBRARY □ Troy, NY

Key, Betty, Oral Hist.Dir.
MARYLAND HISTORICAL SOCIETY - LIBRARY □ Baltimore, MD

Key, G.R.F., Rd.Adv.
DISTRICT OF COLUMBIA PUBLIC LIBRARY - WASHINGTONIANA DIVISION □ Washington, DC

Key, Jack D., Libn.
MAYO FOUNDATION - MAYO CLINIC LIBRARY □ Rochester, MN

Keys, Dr. Marshall, Dir.
CURRY COLLEGE - LOUIS R. LEVIN MEMORIAL LIBRARY □ Milton, MA

Keyserling, Leon H., Pres./Dir.
CONFERENCE ON ECONOMIC PROGRESS - LIBRARY □ Washington, DC

Khairallah, Lois M., Libn.
MIDDLE EAST INSTITUTE - GEORGE CAMP KEISER LIBRARY □ Washington, DC

Khalsa, Parmatma Singh, Pub.
SPIRITUAL COMMUNITY PUBLICATIONS - INFORMATION CENTER □ San Rafael, CA

Khan, Erwyn, Libn.
NEW YORK STATE METROPOLITAN TRANSPORTATION AUTHORITY - LIBRARY □ New York, NY

Khan, Syed, Asst. Life Sci.Libn.
PURDUE UNIVERSITY - LIFE SCIENCE LIBRARY □ West Lafayette, IN

Kharbas, Datta S., Hd.
UNIVERSITY OF ROCHESTER - ASIA LIBRARY □ Rochester, NY

Khavari, Sue, Hd.Cat.
MARQUETTE UNIVERSITY - LEGAL RESEARCH CENTER □ Milwaukee, WI

Kho, Miss Lian Tie, Libn.
YALE UNIVERSITY - SOUTHEAST ASIA COLLECTION □ New Haven, CT

Kibat, Betty, Asst.Libn.
MUTUAL OF OMAHA/UNITED OF OMAHA - LIBRARY □ Omaha, NE

Kibbey, Mark H., Hd.Eng./Sci.Libn.
CARNEGIE-MELLON UNIVERSITY - ENGINEERING & SCIENCE LIBRARY □ Pittsburgh, PA

Kibbey, Ray Anne
SOUTHERN OREGON STATE COLLEGE - LIBRARY □ Ashland, OR

Kibildis, Melba, Libn.
UNITED AUTOMOBILE, AEROSPACE & AGRICULTURAL IMPLEMENT WORKERS OF AMERICA - RESEARCH LIBRARY □ Detroit, MI

Kice, Carmella, Asst.
BIOSCIENCES INFORMATION SERVICE - BIOLOGICAL ABSTRACTS - LIBRARY □ Philadelphia, PA

Kiczek, Steven, Libn.
ST. MARY SEMINARY - LIBRARY □ Cleveland, OH

Kidd, Betty, Dir.
CANADA - PUBLIC ARCHIVES OF CANADA - NATIONAL MAP COLLECTION □ Ottawa, ON

Kidd, Claren M., Libn.
UNIVERSITY OF OKLAHOMA - GEOLOGY LIBRARY □ Norman, OK

Kidd, Mary Jean
ALTERNATIVE PRESS CENTER - LIBRARY □ Baltimore, MD

Kidder, Audrey J., Assoc.Dir.
SOUTHERN ILLINOIS UNIVERSITY - SCHOOL OF MEDICINE - MEDICAL LIBRARY □ Springfield, IL

Kidney, Ann, Asst.Libn.
POPE JOHN XXIII NATIONAL SEMINARY - LIBRARY □ Weston, MA

Kiefer, Rosemary, Libn.
BAPTIST HOSPITAL - MEDICAL LIBRARY □ Pensacola, FL

Kiefer, Rosemary Milner, Libn.
UNIVERSITY HOSPITAL AND CLINIC - HERBERT L. BRYANS MEMORIAL LIBRARY □ Pensacola, FL

Kiefer, Shirley
HARTFORD PUBLIC LIBRARY - REFERENCE AND GENERAL READING DEPARTMENT □ Hartford, CT

Kieffer, Karen, Info.Spec.
INTEL-TECHNICAL INFORMATION CENTER □ Santa Clara, CA

Kielly, Marion, Libn.
PRINCE EDWARD ISLAND - PLANNING LIBRARY □ Charlottetown, PE

Kienholz, Marian, Music Cat.
UNIVERSITY OF MINNESOTA - MUSIC LIBRARY □ Minneapolis, MN

Kiernan, Ellen, Hd., Circ.
SUNY - DOWNSTATE MEDICAL CENTER - MEDICAL RESEARCH LIBRARY OF BROOKLYN† □ Brooklyn, NY

Kiernan, John, Jr., Hd.Libn.
WATERBURY STATE TECHNICAL COLLEGE - HELEN HAHLO LIBRARY □ Waterbury, CT

Kiersky, Loretta J., Supv.
AIRCO, INC. - CENTRAL RESEARCH LABORATORIES - INFORMATION CENTER □ Murray Hill, NJ

Kieselbach, Karen, Ref.Libn.
COLORADO SCHOOL OF MINES - ARTHUR LAKES LIBRARY □ Golden, CO

Kiessling, Dr. E.C., Pres.
WATERTOWN HISTORICAL SOCIETY - ARCHIVES □ Watertown, WI

Kietzman, Mary W., Cat. & Music Spec.
PLYMOUTH STATE COLLEGE - HERBERT H. LAMSON LIBRARY □ Plymouth, NH

Kietzman, William, Slide & Art Spec.
PLYMOUTH STATE COLLEGE - HERBERT H. LAMSON LIBRARY □ Plymouth, NH

Kiger, Robert W., Dir.
CARNEGIE-MELLON UNIVERSITY - HUNT INSTITUTE FOR BOTANICAL DOCUMENTATION - LIBRARY □ Pittsburgh, PA

Kight, Myra L., Hd.
RICHMOND PUBLIC LIBRARY - ART AND MUSIC DEPARTMENT† □ Richmond, VA

Kightlinger, Margret, Libn./Techn.
U.S. ARMY - LANGUAGE TRAINING FACILITY - LIBRARY □ Fort George G. Meade, MD

Kilbourne, John D., Dir.
SOCIETY OF THE CINCINNATI - ANDERSON HOUSE LIBRARY AND MUSEUM □ Washington, DC

Kilburn, Gudrun, Lit.Cat./Ref.Libn.
SUNY AT BUFFALO - MUSIC LIBRARY □ Buffalo, NY

Kile, Barbara, Hd.
RICE UNIVERSITY - GOVERNMENT DOCUMENTS AND MICROFORMS DEPARTMENT □ Houston, TX

Kilfoyle, Barbara C., Asst.Libn.
ROPES & GRAY - CENTRAL LIBRARY □ Boston, MA

Kilgore, J.D., Dir.
U.S. NATL. ARCHIVES & RECORDS SERVICE - NATL. PERSONNEL RECORDS CENTER □ St. Louis, MO

Kilkenny, Angela, Asst.Libn.
CANADIAN EMBASSY - LIBRARY □ Washington, DC

Killinger, Karol, Bioscience Libn.
ICI AMERICAS INC. - ATLAS LIBRARY □ Wilmington, DE

Kilpatrick, Norman, Dir.
SURFACE MINING RESEARCH LIBRARY □ Charleston, WV

Kilrain, John J., Libn.
NEW YORK STATE DEPARTMENT OF COMMERCE - LIBRARY □ Albany, NY

Kim, Bang, Hd., Doc.
SOUTH DAKOTA STATE UNIVERSITY - HILTON M. BRIGGS LIBRARY □ Brookings, SD

Kim, Chin, Lib.Dir.
CALIFORNIA WESTERN LAW SCHOOL - LIBRARY □ San Diego, CA

Kim, Chung N., Cat.Libn.
CORNELL UNIVERSITY - MARTIN P. CATHERWOOD LIBRARY OF INDUSTRIAL AND LABOR RELATIONS □ Ithaca, NY

Kim, D., Coll.Dev.Libn.
UNIVERSITY OF LOWELL, SOUTH CAMPUS - DANIEL H. O'LEARY LIBRARY □ Lowell, MA

Kim, Mr. Ik-Sam, Hd.
UNIVERSITY OF CALIFORNIA, LOS ANGELES -
ORIENTAL LIBRARY □ Los Angeles, CA
Kim, Mr. Jei Whan, Libn.
HOWARD UNIVERSITY - HEALTH SCIENCES
LIBRARY - PHARMACY ANNEX □ Washington,
DC
Kim, K.J., Asst.Dir.
WIDENER UNIVERSITY - WOLFGRAM
MEMORIAL LIBRARY □ Chester, PA
Kim, Ke Chung, Cur.
PENNSYLVANIA STATE UNIVERSITY - FROST
ENTOMOLOGICAL MUSEUM - TAXONOMIC
RESEARCH LIBRARY □ University Park, PA
Kim, Keok, Patent Lit.Chem.
UOP INC. - PATENT LIBRARY □ Des Plaines, IL
Kim, Moon H., Libn.
NISSAN MOTOR CORPORATION - CORPORATE
LIBRARY† □ Carson, CA
Kim, Mrs. Myung-Jha, AV Libn.
HOWARD UNIVERSITY - SCHOOL OF LAW -
ALLEN MERCER DANIEL LAW LIBRARY □
Washington, DC
Kim, Mrs. San Oak, Asst.Hd.
UNIVERSITY OF CALIFORNIA, LOS ANGELES -
EDUCATION & PSYCHOLOGY LIBRARY □ Los
Angeles, CA
Kim, Soowan Y., Hd., Japanese/Korean Sect
PRINCETON UNIVERSITY - GEST ORIENTAL
LIBRARY AND EAST ASIAN COLLECTIONS □
Princeton, NJ
Kim, Stella P., Hd.Tech.Proc.
BIOLA COLLEGE, INC. - LIBRARY □ La Mirada,
CA
Kim, Sungha, Hd., Korean Sect.
HARVARD UNIVERSITY - HARVARD YENCHING
INSTITUTE - LIBRARY □ Cambridge, MA
Kimball, Joan E., Pres./Cur.
WOLFEBORO HISTORICAL SOCIETY -
PLEASANT VALLEY SCHOOLHOUSE - LIBRARY □
Wolfeboro, NH
Kimberlin, Robert, FERC Br.Chf.
U.S. DEPT. OF ENERGY - LIBRARY □
Washington, DC
Kimberly, Laura, Acq./Ser.Libn.
INDIANA UNIVERSITY - SCHOOL OF LAW
LIBRARY □ Indianapolis, IN
Kimbro, Jo, Cat.
SAM HOUSTON STATE UNIVERSITY - LIBRARY†
□ Huntsville, TX
Kimbro, L.W., Tech.Libn.
LOCKHEED-GEORGIA COMPANY - TECHNICAL
INFORMATION DEPARTMENT □ Marietta, GA
Kin, June C., Cat./Ser.
INSTITUTE FOR ADVANCED STUDIES OF
WORLD RELIGIONS - LIBRARY □ Stony Brook,
NY
Kincaid, Judith D., Cat.
SALISBURY STATE COLLEGE - BLACKWELL
LIBRARY □ Salisbury, MD
Kinch, Michael, Agriculture-Forestry
OREGON STATE UNIVERSITY - WILLIAM
JASPER KERR LIBRARY □ Corvallis, OR
Kindlin, Jean, Dir., Lib. & Media Serv.
UNIVERSITY OF PITTSBURGH - SCHOOL OF
LIBRARY & INFORMATION SCIENCE - INTL.
LIB. INFO. CTR. □ Pittsburgh, PA
Kindlin, Jean, Dir., Lib. & Media Serv.
UNIVERSITY OF PITTSBURGH - SCHOOL OF
LIBRARY & INFORMATION SCIENCE - LIBRARY
□ Pittsburgh, PA
Kindrachuk, F.J., Rector
MOHYLA INSTITUTE - LIBRARY AND ARCHIVES
□ Saskatoon, SK
Kindzerske, Marcia J., Libn.
ARTHUR D. LITTLE, INC. - BURLINGTON
LIBRARY □ Cambridge, MA
Kinevan, Col. M.E., Prof. of Law
U.S. AIR FORCE ACADEMY - LAW LIBRARY □
U.S. Air Force Academy, CO
King, Ann H., Asst.Ref.Libn.
UNIVERSITY OF FLORIDA - HUME LIBRARY □
Gainesville, FL

King, Annie G., Hd.Libn.
TUSKEGEE INSTITUTE - HOLLIS BURKE
FRISSELL LIBRARY-ARCHIVES† □ Tuskegee
Institute, AL
King, Betty Claire, Hd.
SAN ANTONIO PUBLIC LIBRARY - HARRY
HERTZBERG CIRCUS COLLECTION □ San
Antonio, TX
King, Carol S., Coord., Ser.Acq.
SOUTHWEST TEXAS STATE UNIVERSITY -
LEARNING RESOURCES CENTER □ San Marcos,
TX
King, Charles H., Jr., Cat.
SMITHSONIAN INSTITUTION - NATL. MUSEUM
OF AMERICAN ART/NATIONAL PORTRAIT
GALLERY - LIBRARY □ Washington, DC
King, Charles L., Hd., Ref.
SUNY - DOWNSTATE MEDICAL CENTER -
MEDICAL RESEARCH LIBRARY OF BROOKLYN†
□ Brooklyn, NY
King, Christee, Med.Libn.
TUCSON MEDICAL CENTER - MEDICAL
LIBRARY □ Tucson, AZ
King, Cornelia, Rare Book Biblog.
TEMPLE UNIVERSITY - CENTRAL LIBRARY
SYSTEM - RARE BOOK & MANUSCRIPT
COLLECTION □ Philadelphia, PA
King, Cornelia, Libn.
TEMPLE UNIVERSITY - CENTRAL LIBRARY
SYSTEM - SCIENCE FICTION COLLECTION □
Philadelphia, PA
King, Cyrus B., Asst.Dir.Coll.Dev.
NORTH CAROLINA STATE UNIVERSITY - D.H.
HILL LIBRARY □ Raleigh, NC
King, David E., Libn.
STANDARD EDUCATIONAL CORPORATION -
EDITORIAL LIBRARY □ Chicago, IL
King, Dorothy T., Libn.
EAST HAMPTON FREE LIBRARY - LONG ISLAND
COLLECTION □ East Hampton, NY
King, F. Wayne, Dir.
UNIVERSITY OF FLORIDA - FLORIDA STATE
MUSEUM LIBRARY □ Gainesville, FL
King, Geraldine L., Libn.
NEW BRUNSWICK - DEPARTMENT OF THE
ENVIRONMENT - LIBRARY □ Fredericton, NB
King, Hannah M., Ref.
FREDERICK CANCER RESEARCH CENTER -
SCIENTIFIC LIBRARY □ Frederick, MD
King, Jane Savage, Asst. Law Libn.
DU PONT DE NEMOURS (E.I.) & COMPANY, INC.
- LEGAL DEPARTMENT LIBRARY □ Wilmington,
DE
King, Joseph A. Cutshall, Dir.
GLENS FALLS-QUEENSBURY HISTORICAL
ASSN., INC. - CHAPMAN HISTORICAL MUSM. -
RUSSELL M.L. CARSON MEMORIAL LIB. □ Glens
Falls, NY
King, Kamla J., Libn.
WILKINSON, CRAGUN AND BARKER - LIBRARY
□ Washington, DC
King, Kathryn E., Libn.
LOS ANGELES COUNTY MUSEUM OF NATURAL
HISTORY - RESEARCH LIBRARY □ Los Angeles,
CA
King, Katie, Libn.
AMERICAN PUBLIC POWER ASSOCIATION -
LIBRARY □ Washington, DC
King, Laurie, Asst. to Dir.
PRICE WATERHOUSE - INFORMATION CENTER
□ Boston, MA
King, Linda, Search Anl.
UNIVERSITY OF TEXAS HEALTH SCIENCE
CENTER, DALLAS - LIBRARY □ Dallas, TX
King, Linda G., Libn.
TOUCHE, ROSS AND COMPANY - LIBRARY AND
INFORMATION CENTER □ Vancouver, BC
King, Luci, Lib.Chm.
GRAND RAPIDS ART MUSEUM - MC BRIDE
LIBRARY □ Grand Rapids, MI

King, Dr. Margot, Libn.
UNIVERSITY OF SASKATCHEWAN - ST.
THOMAS MORE COLLEGE - SHANNON LIBRARY
□ Saskatoon, SK
King, Maryde Fahey, Mgr.
GENERAL ELECTRIC COMPANY - CORPORATE
RESEARCH & DEVELOPMENT - WHITNEY
LIBRARY □ Schenectady, NY
King, Muriel
LEEWARD COMMUNITY COLLEGE - LIBRARY □
Honolulu, HI
King, Dr. Patricia M., Dir.
RADCLIFFE COLLEGE - ARTHUR AND
ELIZABETH SCHLESINGER LIBRARY ON THE
HISTORY OF WOMEN IN AMERICA □
Cambridge, MA
King, Paula C., Asst.Libn.
U.S. NASA - DRYDEN FLIGHT RESEARCH
CENTER - LIBRARY □ Edwards, CA
King, Peggy, Leg.Libn.
KENTUCKY STATE LEGISLATIVE RESEARCH
COMMISSION - LIBRARY □ Frankfort, KY
King, R.T., Oral Hist.
INDIANA UNIVERSITY - ORAL HISTORY
RESEARCH PROJECT - LIBRARY □ Bloomington,
IN
King, Radford G., Dir.
UNIVERSITY OF SOUTHERN CALIFORNIA -
NASA INDUSTRIAL APPLICATION CENTER
(NIAC) □ Los Angeles, CA
King, Shelden S., Engr.Libn.
WESTINGHOUSE ELECTRIC CORPORATION -
ENGINEERING LIBRARY □ Horseheads, NY
King, William E., Univ.Archv.
DUKE UNIVERSITY - ARCHIVES □ Durham, NC
Kingery, Rita, Libn.
SOUTHERN OHIO GENEALOGICAL SOCIETY -
REFERENCE LIBRARY □ Hillsboro, OH
Kinghorn, Edward J., Jr., Staff Assoc.
MUNICIPAL ASSOCIATION OF SOUTH
CAROLINA - LIBRARY AND REFERENCE CENTER
□ Columbia, SC
Kingman, Elizabeth Y., Libn.
SCHOOL OF AMERICAN RESEARCH - LIBRARY □
Santa Fe, NM
Kingman, Winifred, Libn.
JACK LONDON MUSEUM AND RESEARCH
CENTER □ Glen Ellen, CA
Kingsbury, Mildred E., Lib.Dir.
MARQUETTE GENERAL HOSPITAL - KEVIN F.
O'BRIEN HEALTH SCIENCES LIBRARY □
Marquette, MI
Kingsley, Thomas C., Libn.
SYRACUSE UNIVERSITY - LAW LIBRARY □
Syracuse, NY
Kingston, Betty, Libn.
ROYAL ONTARIO MUSEUM - FAR EASTERN
LIBRARY □ Toronto, ON
Kinne, Jane S., Pres.
PHOTO RESEARCHERS, INC. - LIBRARY □ New
York, NY
Kinnear, Sharlon, Ref.Libn., Br.
IBM CORPORATION - LIBRARY □ Poughkeepsie,
NY
Kinnett, David, Mss.Libn.
STATE HISTORICAL SOCIETY OF IOWA -
LIBRARY □ Iowa City, IA
Kinnett, David, Mss.Spec.
UNIVERSITY OF MISSOURI - WESTERN
HISTORICAL MANUSCRIPT COLLECTION/
STATE HISTORICAL SOCIETY OF MISSOURI □
Columbia, MO
Kinney, Elizabeth, Libn.
CARNEGIE LIBRARY OF PITTSBURGH -
SCIENCE AND TECHNOLOGY DEPARTMENT □
Pittsburgh, PA
Kinney, John M., State Archv.
ALASKA STATE DEPARTMENT OF
ADMINISTRATION - STATE ARCHIVES □
Juneau, AK
Kinney, Margaret M., Chf.Libn.
U.S. VETERANS ADMINISTRATION (NY-Bronx) -
MEDICAL CENTER LIBRARY □ Bronx, NY

PERSONNEL

Kinney, Marnelle, Supv., Br.Libs.
ROCKWELL INTERNATIONAL - ANAHEIM INFORMATION CENTER □ Anaheim, CA

Kinney, Nancy S., Dir.
WESTERN COSTUME COMPANY - RESEARCH LIBRARY □ Los Angeles, CA

Kinnison, Anna, Natl.Tres.
DAUGHTERS OF UNION VETERANS OF THE CIVIL WAR - NATIONAL HEADQUARTERS LIBRARY □ Springfield, IL

Kinsella, Peggy, Arts & Lit.Libn.
RYERSON POLYTECHNICAL INSTITUTE - LEARNING RESOURCES CENTRE □ Toronto, ON

Kinsella, Wendy, Hd.Libn.
ALBERTA - DEPARTMENT OF LABOUR - LABOUR LIBRARY □ Edmonton, AB

Kinslow, Barbara A., Libn.
KAMAN SCIENCES CORPORATION - LIBRARY □ Colorado Springs, CO

Kinsman, Marilyn G.
U.S. DEPT. OF COMMERCE - INTERNATIONAL TRADE ADMINISTRATION - BUFFALO DISTRICT OFFICE LIBRARY □ Buffalo, NY

Kinsman, Mary Jean, Res.
JEFFERSON COUNTY OFFICE OF HISTORIC PRESERVATION AND ARCHIVES □ Louisville, KY

Kinstdahl, Bob, Libn.
U.S. NAVY - NAVAL SUPPORT ACTIVITY - LIBRARY □ Seattle, WA

Kinucan, John, Hist.Spec.
RIVERSIDE COUNTY HISTORICAL COMMISSION - LIBRARY □ Rubidoux, CA

Kinzel, Mrs. M., Libn.
UNIVERSITY OF SASKATCHEWAN - LUTHERAN THEOLOGICAL SEMINARY - OTTO OLSON MEMORIAL LIBRARY† □ Saskatoon, SK

Kipilii, Mary Lu, Libn./AV Spec.
HAWAII STATE LIBRARY - FINE ARTS AND AUDIOVISUAL SECTION □ Honolulu, HI

Kipp, Elaine, Ref.Libn.
NORTHERN MONTANA COLLEGE - LIBRARY† □ Havre, MT

Kiprick, Mrs. J., Libn.
ALBERTA - DEPARTMENT OF THE ATTORNEY GENERAL - LAW SOCIETY LIBRARY □ Lethbridge, AB

Kiraldi, Louis, Hd.
WESTERN MICHIGAN UNIVERSITY - DOCUMENTS LIBRARY □ Kalamazoo, MI

Kiraldi, Dr. Louis, Hd.
WESTERN MICHIGAN UNIVERSITY - MAP LIBRARY □ Kalamazoo, MI

Kirby, A., Ref.Libn.
QUEEN'S UNIVERSITY AT KINGSTON - DOCUMENTS LIBRARY □ Kingston, ON

Kirby, Mr. C.
CANADA - NATIONAL MUSEUMS OF CANADA - PHOTOGRAPHIC DIVISION LIBRARY □ Ottawa, ON

Kirby, Colleen, ILL
BLACK HILLS STATE COLLEGE - E.Y. BERRY LIBRARY-LEARNING CENTER □ Spearfish, SD

Kirby, Don, Chf., Ref.Sect.
U.S. ARMY - ENGINEER WATERWAYS EXPERIMENT STATION - TECHNICAL INFORMATION CENTER □ Vicksburg, MS

Kirby, Robert, Asst.Libn.
INDIANA UNIVERSITY OF PENNSYLVANIA - UNIVERSITY LIBRARY □ Indiana, PA

Kirchenberger, Felicitas, Act.Libn.
MC GILL UNIVERSITY - ALLAN MEMORIAL INSTITUTE OF PSYCHIATRY - LIBRARY □ Montreal, PQ

Kircher, Roland E., Dir.
UNITED METHODIST CHURCH - WESLEY THEOLOGICAL SEMINARY - LIBRARY □ Washington, DC

Kirchfeld, Friedhelm, Libn.
NATIONAL COLLEGE OF NATUROPATHIC MEDICINE - LIBRARY □ Portland, OR

Kirchner, Andras, Med.Libn.
UNIVERSITY OF CALGARY - MEDICAL LIBRARY □ Calgary, AB

Kirchner, Elizabeth, Chf.Med.Libn.
CALGARY GENERAL HOSPITAL - LIBRARY SERVICES □ Calgary, AB

Kirchner, Elizabeth, Hd.Libn.
ST. LOUIS MERCANTILE LIBRARY ASSOCIATION - LIBRARY □ St. Louis, MO

Kirchner, William N., Dir.
CHEROKEE REGIONAL LIBRARY - GEORGIA HISTORY & GENEALOGICAL ROOM □ LaFayette, GA

Kirchoff, Diana, Rec.Mgr.
MORGAN STANLEY & COMPANY, INC. - LIBRARY □ New York, NY

Kiriazis, Judy, Adm.Dir.
LAKE MICHIGAN FEDERATION - ENVIRONMENTAL LIBRARY □ Chicago, IL

Kirk, Darcy, Tech.Serv.
BOSTON COLLEGE - LAW SCHOOL LIBRARY □ Newton Centre, MA

Kirk, Denise L., Libn.
MISERICORDIA HOSPITAL - SCHOOL OF NURSING LIBRARY □ Bronx, NY

Kirk, Jay H., Science Libn.
MARQUETTE UNIVERSITY - MEMORIAL LIBRARY □ Milwaukee, WI

Kirk, Jay H., Sci.Libn.
MARQUETTE UNIVERSITY - SCIENCE LIBRARY □ Milwaukee, WI

Kirk, Muriel M., Libn.
NATIONAL PRESBYTERIAN CHURCH - WILLIAM S. CULBERTSON LIBRARY □ Washington, DC

Kirk, Muriel S., Coord. for Lib.
MUSEUM OF FINE ARTS - ART REFERENCE LIBRARY □ St. Petersburg, FL

Kirk, Patricia A., Dir.
OREGON STATE LIBRARY - SERVICES FOR THE BLIND AND PHYSICALLY HANDICAPPED □ Salem, OR

Kirk, Sherwood, Assoc.Dir., Lib.Oper.
ILLINOIS STATE LIBRARY □ Springfield, IL

Kirk, Tom L., Chf.Libn.
U.S. AIR FORCE BASE - VANCE BASE LIBRARY □ Vance AFB, OK

Kirkbride, Becky, Libn.
OKLAHOMA STATE UNIVERSITY - SCHOOL OF TECHNICAL TRAINING - OKMULGEE BRANCH LIBRARY □ Okmulgee, OK

Kirkbride, Susan, Ref.Libn.
UNIVERSITY OF WISCONSIN, MADISON - CENTER FOR HEALTH SCIENCES LIBRARIES □ Madison, WI

Kirking, Clayton, Libn.
PHOENIX ART MUSEUM - LIBRARY □ Phoenix, AZ

Kirkland, James A., Libn.
TEXAS BAPTIST INSTITUTE/SEMINARY - LIBRARY □ Henderson, TX

Kirkland, Mr. N.L., Libn.
TACOMA NEWS TRIBUNE - LIBRARY □ Tacoma, WA

Kirkland, Talley, Hist.
U.S. NATL. PARK SERVICE - FORT PULASKI NATL. MONUMENT - LIBRARY □ Tybee Island, GA

Kirklin, Linda, Jr.Libn.
IBM CORPORATION - BOULDER LIBRARY □ Boulder, CO

Kirklin, Mary J., Adm.Asst.
INSTITUTE ON THE CHURCH IN URBAN-INDUSTRIAL SOCIETY - LIBRARY □ Chicago, IL

Kirkman, Jacqueline N., Tech.Libn.
MARTIN MARIETTA CHEMICALS - SODYECO DIVISION - TECHNICAL LIBRARY □ Charlotte, NC

Kirkpatrick, Brett A., Libn.
NEW YORK ACADEMY OF MEDICINE - LIBRARY □ New York, NY

Kirkpatrick, Mrs. Gabriel W., Med.Libn.
KENNEBEC VALLEY MEDICAL CENTER - MEDICAL LIBRARY □ Augusta, ME

Kirkpatrick, Mel, Libn.
INVESTORS DIVERSIFIED SERVICES, INC. - INVESTMENT LIBRARY □ Minneapolis, MN

Kirkpatrick, Nancy, Hd., Slide Dept.
ART INSTITUTE OF CHICAGO - RYERSON AND BURNHAM LIBRARIES □ Chicago, IL

Kirks, Ruth, Asst.Libn.
GULF COAST BIBLE COLLEGE - CHARLES EWING BROWN LIBRARY □ Houston, TX

Kirkwood, Isabell, Restorationist
FLORIDA STATE DIVISION OF ARCHIVES, HISTORY & RECORDS MANAGEMENT - FLORIDA STATE ARCHIVES □ Tallahassee, FL

Kirlin, George S., Libn.
KIRKLAND & ELLIS - LIBRARY □ Washington, DC

Kirn, Judith, Asst.Libn.
ST. MARY'S SEMINARY - ST. MARY'S OF THE BARRENS LIBRARY □ Perryville, MO

Kirner, Clara, Spec.Coll.Libn.
GLASSBORO STATE COLLEGE - SAVITZ LEARNING RESOURCES CENTER □ Glassboro, NJ

Kirsch, Anne, Libn.
CENTRAL SUFFOLK HOSPITAL - MEDICAL LIBRARY □ Riverhead, NY

Kirsch, Mary, Spec. Projects
HUDSON VALLEY COMMUNITY COLLEGE - DWIGHT MARVIN LEARNING RESOURCES CENTER □ Troy, NY

Kirschenbaum, Harold L., Asst.Dir.
LONG ISLAND UNIV. - ARNOLD & MARIE SCHWARTZ COLLEGE OF PHARMACY & HEALTH SCIENCES - INTERNATL. DRUG INFO.CTR. □ Brooklyn, NY

Kirsh, Julie, Chf.Libn.
TORONTO SUN - LIBRARY □ Toronto, ON

Kirshenbaum, Anna S., Libn.
TEMPLE BETH EL - LIBRARY □ Rochester, NY

Kirtley, Marjorie D., Law Libn.
VIRGINIA STATE LAW LIBRARY □ Richmond, VA

Kirven, Marian, Libn.
SWEDENBORG SCHOOL OF RELIGION - LIBRARY □ Newton, MA

Kirwan, Judith, Libn.
UNIVERSITY OF VIRGINIA - PHYSICS LIBRARY □ Charlottesville, VA

Kirwin, Florence M., Libn.
ASPEN INSTITUTE FOR HUMANISTIC STUDIES - DAVID MAYER LIBRARY □ Aspen, CO

Kishchuk, Marie, Act.Dir.
UKRAINIAN WOMEN'S ASSOCIATION OF CANADA - UKRAINIAN MUSEUM OF CANADA - LIBRARY □ Saskatoon, SK

Kishi, Mabel, Adm.Asst.
UNIVERSITY OF SOUTHERN CALIFORNIA - LAW CENTER LIBRARY† □ Los Angeles, CA

Kiss, Marian S., Cat.
NEW JERSEY INSTITUTE OF TECHNOLOGY - ROBERT W. VAN HOUTEN LIBRARY □ Newark, NJ

Kiss, Terry, Ref.Libn.
U.S. ARMY - ENGINEER WATERWAYS EXPERIMENT STATION - TECHNICAL INFORMATION CENTER □ Vicksburg, MS

Kisthardt, James N., Dept.Hd.
TRENTON FREE PUBLIC LIBRARY - ART & MUSIC DEPARTMENT □ Trenton, NJ

Kistler, Winifred E., Pub.Serv.Libn.
UNIVERSITY OF CALIFORNIA, DAVIS - HEALTH SCIENCES LIBRARY □ Davis, CA

Kistner, Glen, Hd., Circ.
NORTHEASTERN ILLINOIS UNIVERSITY - LIBRARY □ Chicago, IL

Kitajo, Gary K., Ref.Libn.
ALAMEDA COUNTY LAW LIBRARY □ Oakland, CA

Kitchen, Bettie, Files Supv.
PHILLIPS PETROLEUM COMPANY - RESEARCH & DEVELOPMENT DEPARTMENT - TECHNICAL INFORMATION BRANCH □ Bartlesville, OK

Kitchen, Nancy J., Law Libn.
PEPPERDINE UNIVERSITY - LAW LIBRARY □ Malibu, CA

Kitchens, Caroline, Pub.Info.Off.
ATLANTA BUREAU OF PLANNING - LIBRARY □ Atlanta, GA

Kitchens, Phil, Sr.Libn.
UNIVERSITY OF ALABAMA - ENGINEERING
LIBRARY □ University, AL

Kitchin, Luanne, Libn.
PENSION BENEFIT GUARANTY CORPORATION -
OFFICE OF THE GENERAL COUNSEL - LIBRARY
□ Washington, DC

Kitko, Robert, Ref.Libn.
BLOOMFIELD COLLEGE - GEORGE TALBOT HALL
LIBRARY □ Bloomfield, NJ

Kitt, Sandra, Libn.
AMERICAN MUSEUM OF NATURAL HISTORY -
HAYDEN PLANETARIUM - RICHARD S. PERKIN
LIBRARY □ New York, NY

Kittelson, David, Cur.
UNIVERSITY OF HAWAII - SPECIAL
COLLECTIONS - HAWAIIAN COLLECTION □
Honolulu, HI

Kittle, Dr. Arthur, Assoc.Dir.
GEORGIA INSTITUTE OF TECHNOLOGY - PRICE
GILBERT MEMORIAL LIBRARY □ Atlanta, GA

Kittrell, Carol Ann, Assoc.Ref.Libn.
UNIVERSITY OF ARKANSAS MEDICAL
SCIENCES CAMPUS - MEDICAL SCIENCES
LIBRARY □ Little Rock, AR

Kittrell, Kay, Dir.
WILLIAMS BROTHERS ENGINEERING COMPANY
- TECHNICAL INFORMATION CENTER □ Tulsa,
OK

Kittrick, Lucy, Libn.
WASHINGTON STATE UNIVERSITY -
VETERINARY MEDICAL/PHARMACY LIBRARY □
Pullman, WA

Kiviluoma, Roberta, Libn.
SAN DIEGO PUBLIC LIBRARY - LITERATURE &
LANGUAGE SECTION □ San Diego, CA

Kizis, Carol A., Tech.Libn.
WESTINGHOUSE ELECTRIC CORPORATION -
NUCLEAR ENERGY SYSTEMS - ADVANCED
REACTORS DIVISION - LIBRARY □ Madison, PA

Kjellberg, Betty J., Libn.
GOOD SAMARITAN HOSPITAL - HEALTH
SCIENCE LIBRARY □ Phoenix, AZ

Klaasen, David, Cur.
UNIVERSITY OF MINNESOTA - SOCIAL
WELFARE HISTORY ARCHIVES □ Minneapolis,
MN

Kladko, Joseph, Hd., Tech.Oper.
STANFORD UNIVERSITY - HOOVER
INSTITUTION ON WAR, REVOLUTION AND
PEACE - LIBRARY □ Stanford, CA

Klammer, Paul, Musm.Dir.
BROWN COUNTY HISTORICAL SOCIETY -
MUSEUM LIBRARY □ New Ulm, MN

Klammer, Werner, Coord., AV Serv.
CONCORDIA TEACHERS COLLEGE - LINK
LIBRARY □ Seward, NE

Klapthor, Robert, Sci.
KANSAS STATE UNIVERSITY - FARRELL
LIBRARY □ Manhattan, KS

Klass, Lionel, Ed. & Libn.
BROOKLYN DAILY LIBRARY □ Brooklyn, NY

Klassen, Georgeen, Asst.Chf.Archv.
GLENBOW-ALBERTA INSTITUTE - LIBRARY &
ARCHIVES □ Calgary, AB

Klauck, Karl D., Dp.Gen.Couns.
FOREIGN CLAIMS SETTLEMENT COMMISSION
OF THE UNITED STATES - LIBRARY □
Washington, DC

Klaw, Paula, Pres.
MOVIE STAR NEWS - PHOTOGRAPH
COLLECTION □ New York, NY

Klecker, Anita N., Dir. of Lib.Serv.
TORRANCE MEMORIAL HOSPITAL MEDICAL
CENTER - HEALTH SCIENCES LIBRARY □
Torrance, CA

Kleedorfer, Marsha L., Cur.
PENNSYLVANIA CANAL SOCIETY - CANAL
MUSEUM - RESEARCH LIBRARY □ Easton, PA

Kleehammer, Anne Farley, Adm.Libn.
U.S. NAVY - NAVAL AIR STATION (North Island)
- LIBRARY □ San Diego, CA

Kleiber, Michael C., Hd.Libn.
UNIVERSITY OF CALIFORNIA, BERKELEY -
INSTITUTE OF TRANSPORTATION STUDIES
LIBRARY □ Berkeley, CA

Klein, Francine R., Off.Mgr.
FOI SERVICES, INC. - LIBRARY □ Rockville, MD

Klein, Francis, Pres.
CARVER COUNTY HISTORICAL SOCIETY, INC. -
LIBRARY □ Waconia, MN

Klein, Henry, Libn.
AMERICAN INSTITUTE FOR MARXIST STUDIES
- LIBRARY □ New York, NY

Klein, Jeff, Energy Projects Dir.
SAVANNAH SCIENCE MUSEUM - ENERGY
LIBRARY □ Savannah, GA

Klein, Joanne S., Tech.Libn.
JONES AND LAUGHLIN STEEL CORPORATION -
GRAHAM LIBRARY □ Pittsburgh, PA

Klein, Leanne A., Libn.
MINNESOTA MUSEUM OF ART - LIBRARY □ St.
Paul, MN

Klein, Leslie, Info.Spec.
FOI SERVICES, INC. - LIBRARY □ Rockville, MD

Klein, Mary M., Libn.
WASHINGTON THEOLOGICAL UNION - LIBRARY
□ Silver Spring, MD

Klein, Mary S., Libn.
SQUIBB (E.R.) & SONS, INC. - SQUIBB INST.
FOR MEDICAL RES. - SCIENCE INFO. DEPT. -
NEW BRUNSWICK LIBRARY □ New Brunswick,
NJ

Klein, Michele S., Dir., Lib.Serv.
CHILDREN'S HOSPITAL OF MICHIGAN -
MEDICAL LIBRARY □ Detroit, MI

Klein, Pip, Coord.
ROARING FORK ENERGY CENTER - LIBRARY □
Aspen, CO

Klein, Richard S., Dir., Lib.Serv.
ILLINOIS COLLEGE OF PODIATRIC MEDICINE -
LIBRARY □ Chicago, IL

Klein, Robert, Libn.
U.S. VETERANS ADMINISTRATION (MO-St.
Louis) - HOSPITAL LIBRARY □ St. Louis, MO

Klein, Sami, Chf.
ENVIRONMENTAL PROTECTION AGENCY -
HEADQUARTERS LIBRARY □ Washington, DC

Klein, Susan, Lib.Instr.
UNIVERSITY OF WISCONSIN, LA CROSSE -
MURPHY LIBRARY □ La Crosse, WI

Klein, Susan R., Hd.Libn.
STURGIS LIBRARY □ Barnstable, MA

Klein, Wells C., Exec.Dir.
AMERICAN COUNCIL FOR NATIONALITIES
SERVICE - LIBRARY AND INFORMATION
CENTER □ New York, NY

Kleindienst, John, Mgr. of Res.
MISSOURI STATE DIVISION OF COMMUNITY
AND ECONOMIC DEVELOPMENT - RESEARCH
LIBRARY □ Jefferson City, MO

Kleiner, Jane
LOUISIANA STATE UNIVERSITY - REFERENCE
SERVICES □ Baton Rouge, LA

Kleinman, Cheryl, Supv., Data Banks
EG&G, INC. - WASHINGTON ANALYTICAL
SERVICES CENTER - INFORMATION CENTER □
Rockville, MD

Kleinman, Elsa C., Libn.
CALIFORNIA STATE DEPARTMENT OF
EDUCATION - SCHOOL FOR THE DEAF LIBRARY
□ Fremont, CA

Kleinmuntz, Dalia S., Lib.Dir.
GRANT HOSPITAL OF CHICAGO - LIBRARY □
Chicago, IL

Kleinschmidt, Betty, Asst.Libn
BETHEL THEOLOGICAL SEMINARY - RESOURCE
CENTER □ St. Paul, MN

Klekner, Paul M., Libn.
HONEYWELL, INC. - COMMERCIAL DIVISION -
LIBRARY □ Arlington Heights, IL

Kleman, Eleanor, Med.Libn.
PRINCE GEORGE'S GENERAL HOSPITAL &
MEDICAL CENTER - SAUL SCHWARTZBACH
MEMORIAL LIBRARY □ Cheverly, MD

Klemt, Calvin, Libn.
AUSTIN PRESBYTERIAN THEOLOGICAL
SEMINARY - STITT LIBRARY □ Austin, TX

Klepfisz, Rose, Dir., Archv.
AMERICAN JEWISH JOINT DISTRIBUTION
COMMITTEE - ARCHIVES □ New York, NY

Klepich, David, Hd., Tech.Serv.
U.S. DEPT. OF ENERGY - IDAHO NATL.
ENGINEERING LABORATORY - TECHNICAL
LIBRARY □ Idaho Falls, ID

Klepper, Michael, Media Serv.Libn.
UNIVERSITY OF VIRGINIA - ARTHUR J.
MORRIS LAW LIBRARY □ Charlottesville, VA

Kleptach, Sharon M., Tech.Serv.Libn.
SHENANDOAH COLLEGE & CONSERVATORY OF
MUSIC - HOWE LIBRARY □ Winchester, VA

Klesczewski, Mrs. Stephen, Libn.
ST. BERNARD'S PARISH - HAZARDVILLE
CATHOLIC LIBRARY □ Enfield, CT

Klesney, S.P.
DOW CHEMICAL COMPANY - TECHNICAL
INFORMATION SERVICES - CENTRAL REPORT
INDEX □ Midland, MI

Klieman, Janet S., Med.Libn.
ST. MARY OF NAZARETH HOSPITAL - SISTER
STELLA LOUISE HEALTH SCIENCE LIBRARY □
Chicago, IL

Klimiades, Mario N., Libn.
AMERIND FOUNDATION, INC. - FULTON-
HAYDEN MEMORIAL LIBRARY □ Dragoon, AZ

Klimley, Susan, Libn.
COLUMBIA UNIVERSITY - GEOLOGY LIBRARY □
New York, NY

Klimley, Susan, Libn.
COLUMBIA UNIVERSITY - LAMONT-DOHERTY
GEOLOGICAL OBSERVATORY - GEOSCIENCE
LIBRARY □ Palisades, NY

Klinck, Patricia E., State Libn.
VERMONT STATE DEPARTMENT OF LIBRARIES
□ Montpelier, VT

Kline, Eve, Libn./Dir.
PENNSYLVANIA STATE DEPARTMENT OF
PUBLIC WELFARE - SOMERSET STATE
HOSPITAL - LIBRARY □ Somerset, PA

Kline, Janet F., Libn.
UNIVERSITY OF WISCONSIN, MADISON -
DEPARTMENT OF URBAN AND REGIONAL
PLANNING - GRADUATE RESEARCH CENTER □
Madison, WI

Kline, Dr. Milton V., Dir. of Institute
INSTITUTE FOR RESEARCH IN HYPNOSIS -
BERNARD B. RAGINSKY RESEARCH LIBRARY □
New York, NY

Kline, Nancy, Orientation/Info.
UNIVERSITY OF CONNECTICUT - LIBRARY □
Storrs, CT

Kline, Susan A., Libn.
PENNSYLVANIA STATE - LEGISLATIVE
REFERENCE BUREAU LIBRARY □ Harrisburg, PA

Klinebriel, Sheila, Libn.
ATHENS COUNTY LAW LIBRARY □ Athens, OH

Kling, Harriet, Med.Libn.
QUAIN AND RAMSTAD CLINIC - MEDICAL
LIBRARY □ Bismarck, ND

Kling, Susan, Hd., Ref./Info.Serv.
NEBRASKA STATE LIBRARY COMMISSION □
Lincoln, NE

Klingeman, Peter C., Dir.
OREGON STATE UNIVERSITY - WATER
RESOURCES RESEARCH INSTITUTE - LIBRARY
□ Corvallis, OR

Klinger, Robert A., Grand Libn.
GRAND LODGE OF FREE AND ACCEPTED
MASONS OF CALIFORNIA - LIBRARY AND
MUSEUM □ San Francisco, CA

Klingle, Philip, Libn.
INSTITUTE OF JUDICIAL ADMINISTRATION -
LIBRARY □ New York, NY

Klingler, Evelyn L., Ref.Libn.
MORRIS COUNTY FREE LIBRARY - NEW JERSEY
ROOM □ Whippany, NJ

Klingman, Fred E., Pres.
CHURCH OF JESUS CHRIST OF LATTER-DAY SAINTS - SOUTHERN CALIFORNIA AREA GENEALOGICAL LIBRARY □ Los Angeles, CA

Kloberdanz, Timothy J., Hd.Archv.
INDIANA UNIVERSITY - FOLKLORE ARCHIVES □ Bloomington, IN

Klones, Stephanie, Sr.Res.Libn.
FEDERAL RESERVE BANK OF CHICAGO - LIBRARY □ Chicago, IL

Klor, Robin, Ref.Libn.
FOUNDATION CENTER - NEW YORK - LIBRARY □ New York, NY

Klosky, Patricia W., Libn.
INTERNATIONAL FOOD POLICY RESEARCH INSTITUTE - LIBRARY □ Washington, DC

Kluever, Connie L., Libn.
BROWN, WOOD, IVEY, MITCHELL & PETTY - LIBRARY □ New York, NY

Kluger, Mrs. J.A., Libn.
GAF CORPORATION - PROCESS DEVELOPMENT DEPARTMENT - RESEARCH LIBRARY† □ Binghamton, NY

Kluger, Joyce, Map/Sci.Ref.Libn.
SUNY AT BINGHAMTON - SCIENCE LIBRARY □ Binghamton, NY

Kluss, Esther, Ref.Libn.
QUEENS BOROUGH PUBLIC LIBRARY - HISTORY, TRAVEL & BIOGRAPHY DIVISION □ Jamaica, NY

Kluttz, Arletta M., Libn.
CONE MILLS CORPORATION - LIBRARY □ Greensboro, NC

Klyberg, Albert, Dir., RIHS
SOCIETY OF FRIENDS - NEW ENGLAND YEARLY MEETING OF FRIENDS - ARCHIVES □ Providence, RI

Klyve, Cordell, Libn.
WISCONSIN STATE DEPARTMENT OF TRANSPORTATION - LIBRARY □ Madison, WI

Knachel, Dr. Philip A., Assoc.Dir.
FOLGER SHAKESPEARE LIBRARY □ Washington, DC

Knapik, Robert, Ref.Libn.
SACRED HEART UNIVERSITY - LIBRARY □ Bridgeport, CT

Knapik, Robert M., Libn.
UNITED TECHNOLOGIES CORPORATION - SIKORSKY AIRCRAFT DIVISION - DIVISION LIBRARY □ Stratford, CT

Knapp, David, Libn., Tech.Serv.
OBERLIN COLLEGE - CONSERVATORY OF MUSIC - MARY M. VIAL MUSIC LIBRARY □ Oberlin, OH

Knapp, Paul L., Sci.Libn.
NORTHERN ILLINOIS UNIVERSITY - FARADAY LIBRARY† □ DeKalb, IL

Knarr, Linda, Libn.
JOHNS HOPKINS UNIVERSITY-SCHOOL OF HYGIENE & PUBLIC HEALTH-MATERNAL & CHILD HEALTH/POPULATION DYNAMICS LIB. □ Baltimore, MD

Knasiak, Theresa J., Adm.Libn.
U.S. AIR FORCE BASE - WRIGHT-PATTERSON GENERAL LIBRARY† □ Wright-Patterson AFB, OH

Knauff, Elisabeth S., Mgr., Info.Serv.Div.
U.S. DEPT. OF THE TREASURY - INFORMATION SERVICES DIVISION - TREASURY DEPT. LIBRARY □ Washington, DC

Knecht, Fred W., Tech.Serv.Libn.
KANSAS STATE SUPREME COURT - LAW LIBRARY □ Topeka, KS

Knecht, Paula, Cat.
PEPPERDINE UNIVERSITY - LAW LIBRARY □ Malibu, CA

Kneil, Gertrude M., Asst.Libn./Cat.
MELLON BANK, N.A. - LIBRARY □ Pittsburgh, PA

Knezek, Dr. LaVerne D., Assoc.Dir.
TEXAS CHRISTIAN UNIVERSITY - INSTITUTE OF BEHAVIORAL RESEARCH - DRUG ABUSE EPIDEMIOLOGY DATA CENTER □ Fort Worth, TX

Knier, Timothy, Hd., Acq.
MARQUETTE UNIVERSITY - LEGAL RESEARCH CENTER □ Milwaukee, WI

Kniesner, Dan L., Libn.
OHIO INSTITUTE OF TECHNOLOGY - LIBRARY □ Columbus, OH

Knight, Alice E., Libn.
WEST VIRGINIA STATE ATTORNEY GENERAL - LAW LIBRARY □ Charleston, WV

Knight, Anne, Libn.
BIRMINGHAM PUBLIC AND JEFFERSON COUNTY FREE LIBRARY - TUTWILER COLLECTION OF SOUTHERN HISTORY AND LITERATURE □ Birmingham, AL

Knight, Barbara, Libn.
ST. LUKE'S MEDICAL CENTER - LIBRARY □ Sioux City, IA

Knight, Dorothy H., LR Coord.
PASSAVANT MEMORIAL AREA HOSPITAL ASSOCIATION - SIBERT LIBRARY □ Jacksonville, IL

Knight, Helen, Univ.Archv.
WESTERN KENTUCKY UNIVERSITY - KENTUCKY LIBRARY AND MUSEUM/ UNIVERSITY ARCHIVES □ Bowling Green, KY

Knight, John, Comp.Prog.Techn.
ENVIRONMENTAL PROTECTION AGENCY - LIBRARY SERVICES □ Research Triangle Park, NC

Knight, Jym, Chf.Libn.
TENNESSEE BOTANICAL GARDENS & FINE ARTS CENTER - MINNIE RITCHEY & JOEL OWSLEY CHEEK LIBRARY □ Nashville, TN

Knight, Marie, Tech.Libn.
LOCKHEED ELECTRONICS COMPANY, INC. - TECHNICAL DOCUMENT CENTER AND LIBRARY† □ Plainfield, NJ

Knight, Marjorie, Acq.Hd.
BOEING COMPANY - SEATTLE SERVICES DIVISION - KENT TECHNICAL LIBRARY □ Seattle, WA

Knight, Mary Jane, Libn.
HAWAIIAN MISSION CHILDREN'S SOCIETY - MISSION-HISTORICAL LIBRARY □ Honolulu, HI

Knight, Olga, Mgr.
UNIVERSITY OF CALIFORNIA - EXTENSION MEDIA CENTER □ Berkeley, CA

Knitter, Judy, Pres.
DEL NORTE COUNTY HISTORICAL SOCIETY - LIBRARY □ Crescent City, CA

Knobil, Carole W., Assoc.Libn.
UNIVERSITY OF TEXAS SCHOOL OF LAW - TARLTON LAW LIBRARY □ Austin, TX

Knobloch, Shirley, Asst.Libn.
CHILDREN'S HOSPITAL/NATIONAL MEDICAL CENTER - HOSPITAL LIBRARY □ Washington, DC

Knoeppel, Helga K., Libn.
INTERNATIONAL MILITARY ARCHIVES □ Washington, DC

Knop, Judy, Cat.
MC CORMICK THEOLOGICAL SEMINARY - LIBRARY† □ Chicago, IL

Knopf, Carol L., Libn.
BROWN UNIVERSITY - POPULATION STUDIES AND TRAINING CENTER - DEMOGRAPHY LIBRARY □ Providence, RI

Knor, Frank, Sys.Libn.
BRITISH COLUMBIA INSTITUTE OF TECHNOLOGY - LIBRARY SERVICES DIVISION □ Burnaby, BC

Knorr, Martin, Dir.
HARRIS-STOWE STATE COLLEGE LIBRARY □ St. Louis, MO

Knoth, Carol, Assoc.Ref.Libn.
UNIVERSITY OF ARKANSAS MEDICAL SCIENCES CAMPUS - MEDICAL SCIENCES LIBRARY □ Little Rock, AR

Knott, Judith, Asst.Libn.
AMERICAN HOME PRODUCTS CORPORATION - WYETH LABORATORIES DIVISION LIBRARY □ Philadelphia, PA

Knott, Marie A., Libn.
SOUTHERN OHIO GENEALOGICAL SOCIETY - REFERENCE LIBRARY □ Hillsboro, OH

Knott, Martha E., Chf.Libn.
BAPTIST MEMORIAL HOSPITAL SYSTEM - BRUCE A. GARRETT MEMORIAL LIBRARY & MEDIA CENTER □ San Antonio, TX

Knotts, Mary Ann, Chf., Lib.Serv.
U.S. VETERANS ADMINISTRATION (AL-Birmingham) - HOSPITAL MEDICAL LIBRARY □ Birmingham, AL

Knowles, Caroline M., Libn.
CONCORDIA UNIVERSITY - LOYOLA CAMPUS - DRUMMOND SCIENCE LIBRARY □ Montreal, PQ

Knowles, Elizabeth W., Chm., Lib.Comm.
INDIAN RIVER MEMORIAL HOSPITAL - PROFESSIONAL LIBRARY □ Vero Beach, FL

Knowlton, David L., Exec.Dir.
NEW JERSEY OPTOMETRIC ASSOCIATION - DR. E.C. NUROCK LIBRARY □ Trenton, NJ

Knowlton, Deborah, Corp.Libn.
HAWAIIAN ELECTRIC CO., INC. - CORPORATE LIBRARY □ Honolulu, HI

Knowlton, Deborah, Corp.Libn.
HAWAIIAN ELECTRIC CO., INC. - ENGINEERING LIBRARY □ Honolulu, HI

Knowlton, Ruth, Cat.
NEW HAVEN COLONY HISTORICAL SOCIETY - LIBRARY □ New Haven, CT

Knox, Elizabeth B., Sec./Libn./Cur.
NEW LONDON COUNTY HISTORICAL SOCIETY - LIBRARY □ New London, CT

Knox, Miss M., Bookbinder & Consrv.
GLENBOW-ALBERTA INSTITUTE - LIBRARY & ARCHIVES □ Calgary, AB

Knubel, Helen, Archv.Cons.
LUTHERAN COUNCIL IN THE U.S.A. - RECORDS AND INFORMATION CE NTER - REFERENCE LIBRARY □ New York, NY

Knudsen, Helen Z., Libn.
CALIFORNIA INSTITUTE OF TECHNOLOGY - ASTROPHYSICS LIBRARY □ Pasadena, CA

Knudsen, Patricia, Dp.Dir.
UNIVERSITY OF MARYLAND, BALTIMORE - HEALTH SCIENCES LIBRARY □ Baltimore, MD

Knup, Marie, Assoc.Libn.
UNITED ENGINEERS & CONSTRUCTORS, INC. - LIBRARY □ Philadelphia, PA

Knupp, Valerie, Supv., Tech.Serv.
MC KINSEY & COMPANY, INC. - INFORMATION SERVICES □ New York, NY

Knutson, Jean, Ref.Serv.Hd.
BOEING COMPANY - SEATTLE SERVICES DIVISION - RENTON LIBRARY □ Seattle, WA

Knutson, LaVaughn S., Libn.
U.S. NAVY - FLEET ANALYSIS CENTER (FLTAC) - LIBRARY □ Corona, CA

Knutson, Maurice C., Chf., Lib.Serv.
U.S. VETERANS ADMINISTRATION (MT-Fort Harrison) - CENTER LIBRARY □ Fort Harrison, MT

Knutson, Robert, Hd., Dept.Spec.Coll.
UNIVERSITY OF SOUTHERN CALIFORNIA - LIBRARY - CINEMA LIBRARY □ Los Angeles, CA

Knutson, Robert, Hd.
UNIVERSITY OF SOUTHERN CALIFORNIA - LIBRARY - DEPARTMENT OF SPECIAL COLLECTIONS □ Los Angeles, CA

Ko, Dong, Gen.Ref.Libn.
SAM HOUSTON STATE UNIVERSITY - LIBRARY† □ Huntsville, TX

Kobayashi, Hanako, Res.Libn.
HAWAII STATE - LEGISLATIVE REFERENCE BUREAU LIBRARY □ Honolulu, HI

Kober, Gary Lee, Asst.Libn.
MONTREAL GENERAL HOSPITAL - MEDICAL LIBRARY □ Montreal, PQ

Kober, Mary J., Dir.
CATALYTIC, INC. - LIBRARY □ Philadelphia, PA

Kobialka, Nancy, Music Cat.
UNIVERSITY OF MIAMI - SCHOOL OF MUSIC - ALBERT PICK MUSIC LIBRARY □ Coral Gables, FL

Kobrynska, Anna, Acq.
SHEVCHENKO SCIENTIFIC SOCIETY, INC. -
LIBRARY AND ARCHIVES □ New York, NY

Kobulnicky, Paul, Libn.
UNIVERSITY OF PITTSBURGH - COMPUTER
SCIENCE LIBRARY □ Pittsburgh, PA

Kobulnicky, Paul J., Libn.
UNIVERSITY OF PITTSBURGH - ALLEGHENY
OBSERVATORY - LIBRARY □ Pittsburgh, PA

Kobulnicky, Paul J., Libn.
UNIVERSITY OF PITTSBURGH - CHEMISTRY
LIBRARY □ Pittsburgh, PA

Kobulnicky, Paul J., Libn.
UNIVERSITY OF PITTSBURGH - PHYSICS
LIBRARY □ Pittsburgh, PA

Kobus, Julia, Docs.
SOUTHERN CONNECTICUT STATE COLLEGE -
H.C. BULEY LIBRARY □ New Haven, CT

Koch, Charles W., Dir.Lrng.Rsrcs.
NORTHWEST MISSOURI STATE UNIVERSITY -
WELLS LIBRARY □ Maryville, MO

Koch, David V., Cur./Archv.
SOUTHERN ILLINOIS UNIVERSITY,
CARBONDALE - SPECIAL COLLECTIONS □
Carbondale, IL

Koch, Dr. Erwin T., Treas.
SCHUMANN MEMORIAL FOUNDATION, INC. -
LIBRARY □ Livonia, NY

Koch, Janet W., Conservator
NEW JERSEY HISTORICAL SOCIETY - LIBRARY
□ Newark, NJ

Koch, Jean, Asst.Libn.
UNIVERSITY OF ILLINOIS - COMMERCE
LIBRARY □ Urbana, IL

Koch, Laura D., Staff Libn., SERMLP
EMORY UNIVERSITY - SCHOOL OF MEDICINE -
A.W. CALHOUN MEDICAL LIBRARY □ Atlanta,
GA

Koch, Patricia A., Libn.
U.S. ADVISORY COMMISSION ON
INTERGOVERNMENTAL RELATIONS - LIBRARY
□ Washington, DC

Koch, Rev. R. David, Libn.
EASTERN BAPTIST THEOLOGICAL SEMINARY -
LIBRARY □ Philadelphia, PA

Kocher, Ardelle, Ref.Libn.
EASTMAN KODAK COMPANY - RESEARCH
LABORATORIES - RESEARCH LIBRARY □
Rochester, NY

Koda, Paul S., Cur.
UNIVERSITY OF NORTH CAROLINA, CHAPEL
HILL - RARE BOOK COLLECTION □ Chapel Hill,
NC

Koder, Sr. Alma, Libn.
LANKENAU HOSPITAL - SCHOOL OF NURSING
LIBRARY □ Philadelphia, PA

Koehler, Boyd, Rd.Serv. & Ref.Libn.
AUGSBURG COLLEGE - GEORGE SVERDRUP
LIBRARY AND MEDIA CENTER □ Minneapolis,
MN

Koehler, Dorothy, Hon.Libn.
THE WHEELMEN - LIBRARY† □ Warrington, PA

Koehler, Rev. Theodore, S.M., Dir.
UNIVERSITY OF DAYTON - MARIAN LIBRARY □
Dayton, OH

Koek, Eva B., Info.Spec.
SEARLE (G.D.) & CO. - RESEARCH LIBRARY □
Skokie, IL

Koel, Ottilia, Libn. & Cur. of Mss.
NEW HAVEN COLONY HISTORICAL SOCIETY -
LIBRARY □ New Haven, CT

Koelle, Joyce G., Mgr.
SANDOZ PHARMACEUTICALS - INFORMATION
SERVICES □ East Hanover, NJ

Koenig, Daniel D., Dir.Lrng.Rscrs.
PIEDMONT TECHNICAL COLLEGE - LIBRARY □
Greenwood, SC

Koenig, Dorothy A., Libn.
UNIVERSITY OF CALIFORNIA, BERKELEY -
ANTHROPOLOGY LIBRARY □ Berkeley, CA

Koenig, E., Info.Sys.Mgr.
UNIVERSITY OF LOWELL, SOUTH CAMPUS -
DANIEL H. O'LEARY LIBRARY □ Lowell, MA

Koenig, Dr. Roman T., Info.Dir.
FRITZSCHE, DODGE AND OLCOTT, INC. -
RESEARCH LIBRARY □ New York, NY

Koenigsberg, Allen, Dir.
ANTIQUE PHONOGRAPH MONTHLY - APM
LIBRARY OF RECORDED SOUND □ Brooklyn, NY

Koenke, Karl, Assoc.Dir.
ERIC CLEARINGHOUSE ON READING AND
COMMUNICATIONS SKILLS □ Urbana, IL

Koert, Catherine F., ILL Libn.
BRIDGEPORT PUBLIC LIBRARY - TECHNOLOGY
AND BUSINESS DEPARTMENT □ Bridgeport, CT

Koetitz, Edward A., Ref.Libn.
BETHANY BIBLE COLLEGE - LIBRARY □ Scotts
Valley, CA

Kohl, Arlene F., Tech.Libn.
FAIRCHILD-WESTON SYSTEMS INC. - WESTON
CONTROLS DIVISION - TECHNICAL LIBRARY □
Archbald, PA

Kohler, Barbara, Libn.
GREAT LAKES BASIN COMMISSION - GREAT
LAKES BASIN LIBRARY □ Ann Arbor, MI

Kohler, Dale, Tech. Staff Asst.
TEXAS STATE BUREAU OF ECONOMIC
GEOLOGY - WELL SAMPLE AND CORE LIBRARY
□ Austin, TX

Kohlhorst, Gail L., Chf.
U.S. GENERAL SERVICES ADMINISTRATION -
GSA LIBRARY □ Washington, DC

Kohli, Kathryn, Libn.
MINNEAPOLIS PUBLIC LIBRARY &
INFORMATION CENTER - BUSINESS AND
SCIENCE DEPARTMENT □ Minneapolis, MN

Kohlrieser, Lillian
U.S. DEPT. OF LABOR - BUREAU OF LABOR
STATISTICS - INFORMATION AND ADVISORY
SECTION □ New York, NY

Kohlrus, Anthony, Adm.Off.
SMITHSONIAN INSTITUTION LIBRARIES □
Washington, DC

Kohn, Ira, Cur. of Exhibits
WESTERN KENTUCKY UNIVERSITY -
KENTUCKY LIBRARY AND MUSEUM/
UNIVERSITY ARCHIVES □ Bowling Green, KY

Kohn, Mary, Ref.Serv.Libn.
WESTERN CONNECTICUT STATE COLLEGE -
RUTH A. HAAS LIBRARY □ Danbury, CT

Kohn, Vicky, Asst.Cur. of Educ.
WESTERN KENTUCKY UNIVERSITY -
KENTUCKY LIBRARY AND MUSEUM/
UNIVERSITY ARCHIVES □ Bowling Green, KY

Kohse, Vicki, Res.Dept.Libn.
ESSO RESOURCES CANADA LIMITED -
RESEARCH DEPARTMENT LIBRARY □ Calgary,
AB, AB

Kohut, Dr. J.J., Sci.Libn.
PORTLAND STATE UNIVERSITY - SCIENCE
LIBRARY □ Portland, OR

Kojelis, Daina, Hd. Multimedia Serv.
UNIVERSITY OF ILLINOIS MEDICAL CENTER -
LIBRARY OF THE HEALTH SCIENCES □ Chicago,
IL

Kok, Fr. Bede, O.C.S.O., Libn.
GETHSEMANI ABBEY - LIBRARY† □ Trappist, KY

Kok, John, Dir.
FOOTE CONE & BELDING - INFORMATION
CENTER □ Chicago, IL

Kolaczek, Jan, Libn.
UNIVERSITY OF OTTAWA - TEACHER
EDUCATION LIBRARY □ Ottawa, ON

Kolaczek, Marta, Lib.Techn.
CITADEL GENERAL ASSURANCE COMPANY -
INFORMATION CENTRE □ Toronto, ON

Kolb, C. Haven, Sec.
NATURAL HISTORY SOCIETY OF MARYLAND -
LIBRARY □ Baltimore, MD

Kolb, Lawrence, Hd.
CALIFORNIA STATE REGIONAL WATER
QUALITY CONTROL BOARD, SAN FRANCISCO
BAY REGION - LIBRARY □ Oakland, CA

Kolby, Shirley, Coord./Acq.
BAYSTATE MEDICAL CENTER - LIBRARY □
Springfield, MA

Kolesar, Pat, Libn.
REGISTERED NURSES' ASSOCIATION OF
BRITISH COLUMBIA - LIBRARY □ Vancouver, BC

Kollegger, James G., Pres. & Pub.
ENVIRONMENT INFORMATION CENTER, INC. □
New York, NY

Kolling, Harold, Univ.Cur.
BAKER UNIVERSITY - ARCHIVES AND
HISTORICAL LIBRARY □ Baldwin City, KS

Kolloge, Sandra, Act.Libn.
HAWAII STATE LIBRARY - LANGUAGE,
LITERATURE AND HISTORY SECTION □
Honolulu, HI

Kolman, Roberta, Hd.Ref.Libn.
UNIVERSITY OF CONNECTICUT - HEALTH
CENTER - LYMAN MAYNARD STOWE LIBRARY □
Farmington, CT

Kolmes, Bea, Info.Sci.
AMERICAN CYANAMID COMPANY -
AGRICULTURAL RESEARCH DIVISION -
TECHNICAL INFORMATION SERVICES □
Princeton, NJ

Kolner, Stuart J., Br.Libn.
UNIVERSITY OF ILLINOIS MEDICAL CENTER -
ROCKFORD SCHOOL OF MEDICINE - LIBRARY
OF THE HEALTH SCIENCES □ Rockford, IL

Kolp, John, Prog.Assoc.
UNIVERSITY OF IOWA - LABORATORY FOR
POLITICAL RESEARCH □ Iowa City, IA

Komadina, Kristi, Asst.Libn.
ILLINOIS STATE GEOLOGICAL SURVEY -
LIBRARY □ Champaign, IL

Kommer, Joen, Info.Spec.
WED ENTERPRISES - RESEARCH LIBRARY □
Glendale, CA

Kommers, Donald P., Dir.
UNIVERSITY OF NOTRE DAME - CENTER FOR
THE STUDY OF HUMAN RIGHTS - READING
ROOM □ Notre Dame, IN

Komoto, David T., Database Dev.Coord.
UNIVERSITY OF SOUTHERN CALIFORNIA -
NASA INDUSTRIAL APPLICATION CENTER
(NIAC) □ Los Angeles, CA

Konjevich, M., Lib.Mgr.
U.S. NASA - JOHN F. KENNEDY SPACE CENTER
- LIBRARY □ Kennedy Space Center, FL

Konop, Arthur J., Dir.-Archv.
ST. FRANCIS COLLEGE - JAMES A. KELLY
INSTITUTE FOR LOCAL HISTORICAL STUDIES -
LIBRARY □ Brooklyn, NY

Konrad, Joan, Cat.Libn.
JEFFERSON (Thomas) UNIVERSITY - SCOTT
MEMORIAL LIBRARY □ Philadelphia, PA

Konrath, Rose, Pub.Serv.Libn.
HUGHES AIRCRAFT COMPANY - TECHNICAL
LIBRARY □ Culver City, CA

Konstantinow, George, Lit.Sci.
REYNOLDS (R.J.) TOBACCO COMPANY - R&D
INFORMATION SYSTEMS LIBRARY □ Winston-
Salem, NC

Koo, S., Sr.Res.Libn.
FIRESTONE TIRE AND RUBBER COMPANY -
CENTRAL RESEARCH LIBRARY □ Akron, OH

Koob, Marion, Tech.Serv.
HOFFMANN-LA ROCHE, INC. - SCIENTIFIC
LIBRARY □ Nutley, NJ

Koon, Karol, Libn.
PORTLAND BUREAU OF PLANNING - LIBRARY □
Portland, OR

Koons, Bonnie, Acq.Dept.Dir.
CATHOLIC UNIVERSITY OF PUERTO RICO -
MONSIGNOR JUAN FREMIOT TORRES OLIVER
LAW LIBRARY □ Ponce, PR

Koons, Jane Baker, Coord.
MIDWEST CHINA CENTER - MIDWEST CHINA
ORAL HISTORY AND ARCHIVES COLLECTION □
St. Paul, MN

Kooperman, Evelyn, Libn.
SAN DIEGO PUBLIC LIBRARY - ART, MUSIC &
RECREATION SECTION □ San Diego, CA

Koozer, Donald E., Supv.
UNIVERSITY OF OKLAHOMA - ART LIBRARY □
Norman, OK

Kowalewski, Denis S., Libn.
CHAPMAN AND CUTLER - LAW LIBRARY □
Chicago, IL

Kowalewski, R., Sr.Ref.Libn.
UNIVERSITY OF LOWELL, SOUTH CAMPUS -
DANIEL H. O'LEARY LIBRARY □ Lowell, MA

Kowalewski, Dr. Thadeus, Libn.
FMC CORPORATION - AGRICULTURAL
CHEMICAL GROUP - RESEARCH AND
DEVELOPMENT DEPT. - TECHNICAL LIBRARY □
Middleport, NY

Kowalkowski, Carolyn, Dir.
ST. JOSEPH'S HOSPITAL - HEALTH SCIENCE
LIBRARY □ Chippewa Falls, WI

Kowalski, Cheryl K., Libn.
WALTHAM HOSPITAL - MEDICAL LIBRARY □
Waltham, MA

Kowitz, Aletha A., Dir.
AMERICAN DENTAL ASSOCIATION - BUREAU
OF LIBRARY SERVICES □ Chicago, IL

Kowrach, Rev. Edward J., Archv.
DIOCESE OF SPOKANE - DIOCESAN CHANCERY
ARCHIVES □ Spokane, WA

Kozak, Marlene Galante, Sr.Info.Anl.
AMERICAN CRITICAL CARE - INFORMATION
CENTER □ McGaw Park, IL

Kozak, Reka, Circ.Reserve Asst.
WASHINGTON UNIVERSITY - BIOLOGY
LIBRARY □ St. Louis, MO

Kozelka, Cathy Collins, Mgr.
DE SOTO, INC. - INFORMATION CENTER □ Des
Plaines, IL

Koziol, Jeanette R., Tech.Libn.
SINGER COMPANY - SPG ENGINEERING -
SEWING PRODUCTS GROUP - ENGINEERING
LIBRARY □ Elizabeth, NJ

Kozlowski, Anne, Coord.
CATHOLIC SOCIAL SERVICES - LIBRARY □
Milwaukee, WI

Kraemer, Linda L., Mgr., Info.Serv.
MC KINSEY & COMPANY, INC. - LIBRARY □ San
Francisco, CA

Krafchow, Edward, Libn.
UNIVERSITY OF ORIENTAL STUDIES -
INTERNATIONAL BUDDHIST MEDITATION
CENTER LIBRARY □ Los Angeles, CA

Kraft, Joan E., Chm., Lib.Comm.
ARCHAEOLOGICAL SOCIETY OF NEW JERSEY -
LIBRARY □ South Orange, NJ

Kraft, John L., Adm.
PENNSYLVANIA STATE HISTORICAL & MUSEUM
COMMISSION - EPHRATA CLOISTER - LIBRARY
□ Ephrata, PA

Kraft, Mary E., C.S.J., Archv.
SISTERS OF ST. JOSEPH OF CARONDELET - ST.
PAUL PROVINCE - ARCHIVES □ St. Paul, MN

Kraft, Sandra, Libn.
YOUNG RADIATOR COMPANY - LIBRARY □
Racine, WI

Krahn, Allan, Automation Libn.
LUTHER-NORTHWESTERN SEMINARY -
LIBRARY □ St. Paul, MN

Krajnak, Pat, Libn.
MILLER BREWING COMPANY - RESEARCH AND
TECHNICAL LIBRARY □ Milwaukee, WI

Krakauer, Eleanor, Libn.
AMC CANCER RESEARCH CENTER AND
HOSPITAL - GRACE & PHILIP LICHTENSTEIN
SCIENTIFIC LIBRARY □ Lakewood, CO

Krakora, Ed, Cat.Libn.
WASHINGTON UNIVERSITY - SCHOOL OF LAW
- FREUND LAW LIBRARY □ St. Louis, MO

Kralisz, Victor F., Adm.Mgr.
DALLAS PUBLIC LIBRARY - FILM SERVICE □
Dallas, TX

Kramer, Cecile E., Dir.
NORTHWESTERN UNIVERSITY - HEALTH
SCIENCES LIBRARY □ Chicago, IL

Kramer, D.A., Info.Spec.
GENERAL TIRE AND RUBBER COMPANY -
RESEARCH DIVISION INFORMATION CENTER □
Akron, OH

Kramer, Gretchen G., Libn.
CALIFORNIA JOCKEY CLUB AT BAY MEADOWS
- WILLIAM P. KYNE MEMORIAL LIBRARY □ San
Mateo, CA

Kramer, Helen, Ref.
PITTSBURG STATE UNIVERSITY - LEONARD H.
AXE LIBRARY □ Pittsburg, KS

Kramer, Joseph, Sr.Asst.Ref.Libn.
CALIFORNIA STATE UNIVERSITY,
SACRAMENTO - LIBRARY - SCIENCE &
TECHNOLOGY REFERENCE DEPARTMENT† □
Sacramento, CA

Kramer, K., Mtls. Control Libn.
SOUTHWESTERN UNIVERSITY - SCHOOL OF
LAW LIBRARY □ Los Angeles, CA

Kramer, Marcella, Asst. Law Libn.
NORTH DAKOTA STATE SUPREME COURT LAW
LIBRARY □ Bismarck, ND

Kramer, Margy L., Libn.
HOCKING TECHNICAL COLLEGE - LIBRARY □
Nelsonville, OH

Kramer, Raymond J., Asst.Libn.
U.S. SECURITIES AND EXCHANGE
COMMISSION - LIBRARY □ Washington, DC

Kramer, Rochelle P., Coord., Tech.Info.
WIRE ASSOCIATION INTERNATIONAL -
LIBRARY □ Guilford, CT

Kramer, Wendy H., Adm.Libn.
U.S.D.A. - AGRICULTURAL RESEARCH SERVICE
- EASTERN REGIONAL RESEARCH CENTER
LIBRARY □ Philadelphia, PA

Kramm, Pat, Ext.Spec.
UNIVERSITY OF MINNESOTA - AGRICULTURAL
EXTENSION SERVICE - EXTENSION HOME
EOCNOMICS - INFO. CTR. □ St. Paul, MN

Kramp, Robert, Ref.Serv.Libn.
OAKLAND SCHOOLS - EDUCATIONAL RESOURCE
CENTER □ Pontiac, MI

Kranish, Arthur, Hd.
SCIENCE TRENDS - LIBRARY □ Washington, DC

Kranz, Ralph, AV Libn.
ALCORN STATE UNIVERSITY - JOHN DEWEY
BOYD LIBRARY □ Lorman, MS

Krash, Ron, Dir.
UNIVERSITY OF MISSOURI, ST. LOUIS -
THOMAS JEFFERSON LIBRARY □ St. Louis, MO

Krasko, Nola G., Data User Serv.Off.
U.S. BUREAU OF THE CENSUS - REGIONAL
DATA USER SERVICE - NEW YORK REGIONAL
OFFICE - LIBRARY □ New York, NY

Krasner, Joan K., Natl.Libn.
LEVENTHAL (Kenneth) & COMPANY - LIBRARY □
Los Angeles, CA

Krasney, Rina, Ref.Libn.
UNIVERSITY OF MISSOURI, ST. LOUIS -
EDUCATION LIBRARY □ St. Louis, MO

Kratz, Eva, Dir. of Lib.Serv.
ST. FRANCIS MEDICAL CENTER - MOTHER
MACARIA HEALTH SCIENCE LIBRARY □
Lynwood, CA

Kratzenberg, W. Stephen, Exec.Sec.
HUGUENOT SOCIETY OF AMERICA - LIBRARY □
New York, NY

Kraulis, Ruth L., Libn.
CENTRAL BAPTIST SEMINARY - DR. W.
GORDON BROWN MEMORIAL LIBRARY □
Toronto, ON

Kraus, David H., Act.Chf.
LIBRARY OF CONGRESS - EUROPEAN DIVISION
□ Washington, DC

Kraus, Elizabeth W., Info.Assoc./Lib.Mgr.
EASTMAN KODAK COMPANY - RESEARCH
LABORATORIES - RESEARCH LIBRARY □
Rochester, NY

Kraus, Joe W., Dir.
ILLINOIS STATE UNIVERSITY - MILNER
LIBRARY† □ Normal, IL

Krause, Elizabeth R., Music Libn.
WASHINGTON UNIVERSITY - GAYLORD MUSIC
LIBRARY □ St. Louis, MO

Krause, Professor George, Dir. of Res.
MARINE PRODUCTS COMPANY - LIBRARY □
Boston, MA

Krause, Henrietta Park, Mss.Spec.
UNIVERSITY OF MISSOURI - WESTERN
HISTORICAL MANUSCRIPT COLLECTION/
STATE HISTORICAL SOCIETY OF MISSOURI □
Columbia, MO

Krauss, Alan J., Musm.Dir.
NEW BRITAIN YOUTH MUSEUM - RESOURCE
CENTER □ New Britain, CT

Krauss, Dina R., Med.Libn.
CUSHING HOSPITAL - MEDICAL LIBRARY† □
Framingham, MA

Krauss, Linda, Libn.
COLLEGE RETIREMENT EQUITIES FUND - CREF
RESEARCH LIBRARY □ New York, NY

Krawulski, Janet, Hd.Libn.
DETROIT INSTITUTE OF TECHNOLOGY - JAMES
C. GORDON MEMORIAL LIBRARY □ Detroit, MI

Krayewski, Frances, Supv., Tech.Serv.
IMPERIAL OIL, LTD. - BUSINESS INFORMATION
CENTRE □ Toronto, ON

Krcmar, Mrs. Jan, Chf.Libn.
BUNKER-RAMO CORPORATION - MAIN
LIBRARY □ Westlake, CA

Kreager, Sr. Kathryn, Circ.
MARYCREST COLLEGE - CONE LIBRARY† □
Davenport, IA

Krech, Betty
3M - PATENT INFORMATION CENTER □ St.
Paul, MN

Kredel, Olivia, Mgr.
NATIONAL LEAGUE OF CITIES - MUNICIPAL
REFERENCE SERVICE □ Washington, DC

Kregel, Charles E., Jr., Info.Mgr.
KIRKLAND & ELLIS - LIBRARY □ Washington, DC

Kregstein, Phyllis L., Biomed.Libn.
U.S. VETERANS ADMINISTRATION (NM-
Albuquerque) - MEDICAL CENTER LIBRARY □
Albuquerque, NM

Kreh, David, Dir.Tchg.Mtls.Ctr.
SUNY - COLLEGE AT CORTLAND - MEMORIAL
LIBRARY □ Cortland, NY

Kreider, Robert, Dir.
BETHEL COLLEGE - MENNONITE LIBRARY AND
ARCHIVES □ North Newton, KS

Kreiensieck, Julie, Mgr.
MORRISON-KNUDSEN CO., INC. - RECORDS
AND MICROGRAPHICS CENTER □ Boise, ID

Kreinbring, Mary, Tech.Serv.Libn.
CONTINENTAL ILLINOIS NATIONAL BANK AND
TRUST COMPANY OF CHICAGO -
INFORMATION SERVICES DIVISION □ Chicago,
IL

Kreissman, Bernard, Univ.Libn.
UNIVERSITY OF CALIFORNIA, DAVIS -
GENERAL LIBRARY □ Davis, CA

Kreiter, Marion A., Libn.
UNIVERSITY OF PENNSYLVANIA -
MATHEMATICS-PHYSICS-ASTRONOMY
LIBRARY □ Philadelphia, PA

Krekemeyer, Lynn, Libn.
ISI CORPORATION - RESEARCH LIBRARY □
Oakland, CA

Krell, H. Barbara, Libn.
STRAYER COLLEGE - WILKES LIBRARY □
Washington, DC

Kremer, Jill L., Dir.
JENKINS (Theodore F.) MEMORIAL LAW
LIBRARY COMPANY - LIBRARY □ Philadelphia,
PA

Kremer, Susan, Corp.Libn./Anl.
MEAD CORPORATION - CORPORATE LIBRARY □
Dayton, OH

Kremer, Teresa, Libn.
JEWISH BOARD OF FAMILY & CHILDREN
SERVICES - LIBRARY □ New York, NY

Krenta, Alicja, Hd.Acq.Libn.
YALE UNIVERSITY - MEDICAL LIBRARY □ New
Haven, CT

Krents, Irma Kopp, Dir.
AMERICAN JEWISH COMMITTEE - WILLIAM E.
WIENER ORAL HISTORY LIBRARY □ New York,
NY

Krents, Milton E., Natl.Bd.Chm.
AMERICAN JEWISH COMMITTEE - WILLIAM E.
WIENER ORAL HISTORY LIBRARY □ New York,
NY

Kresak, Vicki, Circuit Libn.
CLEVELAND HEALTH SCIENCES LIBRARY -
ALLEN MEMORIAL LIBRARY □ Cleveland, OH

Kreshka, Eva, Tech.Serv.Libn.
MILLS COLLEGE - MARGARET PRALL MUSIC
LIBRARY □ Oakland, CA

Kreslins, Janis, Ref.Asst.
COUNCIL ON FOREIGN RELATIONS - LIBRARY □
New York, NY

Kreta, Rev. Fr. Joseph P., Dean
ST. HERMAN'S ORTHODOX THEOLOGICAL
SEMINARY - LIBRARY □ Kodiak, AK

Kretschmann, Kate, AV Libn.
CLEVELAND CLINIC EDUCATION FOUNDATION
- MEDICAL LIBRARY/AUDIOVISUAL CENTER† □
Cleveland, OH

Kreuger, Miles M., Cur.
INSTITUTE OF THE AMERICAN MUSICAL, INC.
- LIBRARY □ Los Angeles, CA

Krichbaum, Mary, Asst.Libn.
HURON ROAD HOSPITAL - LIBRARY AND
AUDIOVISUAL CENTER □ Cleveland, OH

Krichmar, Albert, Linguistics/Commun.Libn.
UNIVERSITY OF CALIFORNIA, SANTA BARBARA
- SCIENCES-ENGINEERING LIBRARY □ Santa
Barbara, CA

Krick, Mary, Libn.
ILLINOIS STATE GEOLOGICAL SURVEY -
LIBRARY □ Champaign, IL

Krick, Robert K., Chf.Hist.
U.S. NATL. PARK SERVICE - FREDERICKSBURG
& SPOTSYLVANIA NATL. MILITARY PARK -
LIBRARY □ Fredericksburg, VA

Krieger, Leslie, Ref./Search Serv.
XEROX CORPORATION - TECHNICAL
INFORMATION CENTER □ Webster, NY

Krieger, Nava, Ref.Libn./Spec.Educ.
BOARD OF COOPERATIVE EDUCATIONAL
SERVICES OF NASSAU COUNTY (BOCES) -
NASSAU EDUC. RSRCS. CTR. (NERC) □
Westbury, NY

Krieger, Tikvah, Asst.Libn.
CLEVELAND COLLEGE OF JEWISH STUDIES -
AARON GARBER LIBRARY □ Beachwood, OH

Kriesel, Ronald W., Hd.Libn.
GULF COAST BIBLE COLLEGE - CHARLES
EWING BROWN LIBRARY □ Houston, TX

Kriigel, Barbara, Cat.
ANDREWS UNIVERSITY - JAMES WHITE
LIBRARY □ Berrien Springs, MI

Krinsky, Joan, Libn.
CITY OF HOPE NATIONAL MEDICAL CENTER -
PINESS MEDICAL AND SCIENTIFIC LIBRARY □
Duarte, CA

Krinsky, Santosh, Libn.
ATMANIKETAN ASHRAM - LIBRARY □ Pomona,
CA

Krisciunas, Kathy P., Tech.Serv.Libn.
UNIVERSITY OF DETROIT - SCHOOL OF LAW
LIBRARY □ Detroit, MI

Kritzman, Janie, Assoc.Dir.
BARNARD COLLEGE WOMEN'S CENTER -
BIRDIE GOLDSMITH AST RESOURCE
COLLECTION □ New York, NY

Krivanek, Judy M., Med.Libn.
U.S. ARMY HOSPITALS - D.D. EISENHOWER
ARMY MEDICAL CENTER - MEDICAL LIBRARY □
Ft. Gordon, GA

Krivatsy, Dr. Nati H., Ref.Libn.
FOLGER SHAKESPEARE LIBRARY □ Washington,
DC

Krivda, Marita J., Libn.
PENNSYLVANIA COLLEGE OF OPTOMETRY -
ALBERT FITCH MEMORIAL LIBRARY □
Philadelphia, PA

Kroah, Larry, Libn.
WILMINGTON COLLEGE - CURRICULUM
MATERIALS CENTER □ Wilmington, OH

Krodshen, Breta M., Law Libn.
UNITED BANK OF DENVER, N.A. - UNITED BANK
CENTER - LAW LIBRARY □ Denver, CO

Krofft, Lorraine, Libn.
CHURCH OF THE NAZARENE - HEADQUARTERS
LIBRARY □ Kansas City, MO

Kroft, Robin A., Libn.
JOHNS HOPKINS UNIVERSITY - SCHOOL OF
MEDICINE - JOSEPH L. LILIENTHAL LIBRARY □
Baltimore, MD

Krogh, Dave, Quality Control Mgr.
DAWE'S LABORATORIES, LTD. - TECHNICAL
AND AGRICULTURAL LIBRARIES □ Chicago, IL

Krogstad, Roland, Dir.
WISCONSIN STATE BOARD OF VOCATIONAL,
TECHNICAL & ADULT EDUCATION - RESEARCH
COORDINATING UNIT RESOURCE CTR. □
Madison, WI

Kroll, Mark, Tech.Serv.Libn.
ILLINOIS BENEDICTINE COLLEGE - THEODORE
LOWNIK LIBRARY □ Lisle, IL

Kroll, Susan M., Libn.
WARNER & SWASEY COMPANY - RESEARCH
DIVISION LIBRARY □ Solon, OH

Kromminga, Arlene, Libn.
MINNESOTA STATE INFORMATION SYSTEMS
DIVISION - LIBRARY □ St. Paul, MN

Krompart, Janet A., Libn.
OAKLAND UNIVERSITY - LIBRARY □ Rochester,
MI

Krompf, Steven Scott, Chf., Lib.Serv.
WILLARD PSYCHIATRIC CENTER -
PROFESSIONAL LIBRARY □ Willard, NY

Kronauer, Margaret L., Info.Spec.
UNIVERSITY OF SOUTHERN CALIFORNIA -
ETHEL PERCY ANDRUS GERONTOLOGY CENTER
- GERONTOLOGICAL INFO. CENTER □ Los
Angeles, CA

Kronenfeld, Michael, Dir.
SOUTH CAROLINA STATE DEPARTMENT OF
HEALTH & ENVIRONMENTAL CONTROL -
EDUCATIONAL RESOURCE CENTER □ Columbia,
SC

Kronick, Dr. David A., Libn.
UNIVERSITY OF TEXAS HEALTH SCIENCE
CENTER, SAN ANTONIO - LIBRARY □ San
Antonio, TX

Kronstedt, Richard, Hd.Libn.
MINNEAPOLIS COLLEGE OF ART AND DESIGN -
LIBRARY AND MEDIA CENTER □ Minneapolis,
MN

Kroon, Monique, Libn.
CANADA - CANADIAN FORESTRY SERVICE -
LAURENTIAN FOREST RESEARCH CENTRE -
LIBRARY □ Ste. Foy, PQ

Kropa, Jane, Cat.Libn.
EDEN THEOLOGICAL SEMINARY - LIBRARY □
Webster Groves, MO

Krost, Mary G., Libn.
FLORIDA STATE DEPT. OF NATURAL
RESOURCES - MARINE RESEARCH
LABORATORY - LIBRARY □ St. Petersburg, FL

Krubsack, Harold, Dir.
SOUTHWEST WISCONSIN VOCATIONAL-
TECHNICAL INSTITUTE - LEARNING
RESOURCES CENTER □ Fennimore, WI

Krucoff, Ella, Chf.Ref. & Doc.
EUROPEAN COMMUNITY INFORMATION
SERVICE - LIBRARY □ Washington, DC

Krueger, Carol A., Agency Libn.
NEBRASKA STATE GAME AND PARKS
COMMISSION - LIBRARY □ Lincoln, NE

Krueger, Geraldine L., Sr.Res.Assoc.
UNIVERSITY OF CINCINNATI - DEPARTMENT
OF ENVIRONMENTAL HEALTH LIBRARY □
Cincinnati, OH

Krueger, Kathleen, Registrar
BAY COUNTY HISTORICAL SOCIETY - MUSEUM
OF THE GREAT LAKES - LIBRARY □ Bay City, MI

Krueger, Lise, Photo Libn.
CANADA - NATIONAL FILM BOARD OF CANADA
- PHOTOTHEQUE □ Ottawa, ON

Kruger, Sheri, Hd.Ref.
LOS ANGELES COUNTY MEDICAL ASSOCIATION
- LIBRARY □ Los Angeles, CA

Kruk, Pauline A., Libn.
FAIRFIELD HILLS HOSPITAL - MEDICAL
LIBRARY □ Newtown, CT

Kruk, Valerie, Libn.
COOK COUNTY STATE'S ATTORNEY'S OFFICE
LIBRARY □ Chicago, IL

Krull, Dr. Charles F., V.P., Corn Res.
DEKALB AGRESEARCH INC. - CORN RESEARCH
CENTER - LIBRARY □ DeKalb, IL

Krumm, Roger V., Libn.
UNIVERSITY OF FLORIDA - ENGINEERING &
PHYSICS LIBRARY □ Gainesville, FL

Krummes, Daniel, Tech.Serv.Libn.
UNIVERSITY OF CALIFORNIA, BERKELEY -
INSTITUTE OF TRANSPORTATION STUDIES
LIBRARY □ Berkeley, CA

Krupp, Dr. E.C., Dir.
GRIFFITH OBSERVATORY - LIBRARY □ Los
Angeles, CA

Krupp, Mary, Corp.Libn.
GETTY OIL COMPANY, INC. - LIBRARY □ Los
Angeles, CA

Krupp, Robert G., Chf.
NEW YORK PUBLIC LIBRARY - SCIENCE AND
TECHNOLOGY RESEARCH CENTER □ New York,
NY

Krusas, Marilyn, Food Serv.Info.Spec.
TECHNOMIC CONSULTANTS - INFORMATION
CENTER □ Chicago, IL

Kruse, Carol M., Unit Mgr.
U.S. NATL. PARK SERVICE - FORT UNION NATL.
MONUMENT - LIBRARY □ Watrous, NM

Kruse, Gerald R., Dir.
RESEARCH MEDICAL CENTER - LOCKWOOD
MEMORIAL LIBRARY □ Kansas City, MO

Kruse, Ginny Moore, Dir.
UNIVERSITY OF WISCONSIN, MADISON -
COOPERATIVE CHILDREN'S BOOK CENTER
(CCBC) □ Madison, WI

Kruse, Harriet, Libn./Circ.
UNITED THEOLOGICAL SEMINARY OF THE
TWIN CITIES - LIBRARY □ New Brighton, MN

Kruse, Rhoda, Sr.Libn.
SAN DIEGO PUBLIC LIBRARY - GENEALOGY
ROOM □ San Diego, CA

Kruse, Rhoda E., Sr.Libn.
SAN DIEGO PUBLIC LIBRARY - CALIFORNIA
ROOM □ San Diego, CA

Kruse, Ted, Tech.Serv.Libn.
IIT RESEARCH INSTITUTE -
ELECTROMAGNETIC COMPATIBILITY
ANALYSIS CENTER - TECHNICAL
INFORMATION SERVICES □ Annapolis, MD

Krymkowski, Joseph, O.F.M., Libn.
FRANCISCAN FRIARS - ASSUMPTION FRIARY
LIBRARY □ Pulaski, WI

Krynicki, Marguerite J., Hd.Libn.
ILLINOIS BELL TELEPHONE COMPANY -
LIBRARY □ Chicago, IL

Kryszak, Wayne D., Chf.
DISTRICT OF COLUMBIA PUBLIC LIBRARY -
BUSINESS, ECONOMICS & VOCATIONS
DIVISION □ Washington, DC

Krzys, Dr. Richard, Dir.
UNIVERSITY OF PITTSBURGH - SCHOOL OF
LIBRARY & INFORMATION SCIENCE - INTL.
LIB. INFO. CTR. □ Pittsburgh, PA

Krzysiak, Patricia, Libn.
DAMES & MOORE - CHICAGO LIBRARY □ Park
Ridge, IL

Krzywkowski, Valerie, Ref.Libn.
KEARNEY STATE COLLEGE - CALVIN T. RYAN
LIBRARY □ Kearney, NE

Kuan, Jenny, Libn.
DAY & ZIMMERMANN, INC. - LIBRARY □
Philadelphia, PA

Kuba, Patricia H., Libn.
BINGHAM, DANA AND GOULD - LAW LIBRARY □
Boston, MA

Kubal, Gene, Chf., Gen.Ref.Sect.
U.S. ARMY - ARMY LIBRARY □ Washington, DC

Kubic, Criag, Act.Rd.Serv.Libn.
GOLDEN GATE BAPTIST THEOLOGICAL
SEMINARY - LIBRARY □ Mill Valley, CA

Kubinec, Janet, Cur., Hist.Coll.
UNIVERSITY OF PITTSBURGH - FALK LIBRARY
OF THE HEALTH SCIENCES □ Pittsburgh, PA

KuBinski, Barbara, Rd.Adv.
DISTRICT OF COLUMBIA PUBLIC LIBRARY -
TECHNOLOGY AND SCIENCE DIVISION □
Washington, DC

Kubisiak, Michael J., Hd., Exch./Order Sect.
U.S. GEOLOGICAL SURVEY - LIBRARY □ Reston,
VA

Kubjas, Anne, Health Sci.Libn.
SCARBOROUGH GENERAL HOSPITAL - HEALTH
SCIENCES LIBRARY □ Scarborough, ON

Kublin, Joyce A., Coord.Lib./AV Serv.
VICTORIA GENERAL HOSPITAL - HEALTH
SCIENCES LIBRARY □ Halifax, NS

Kubo, Hatsumi, Libn.
WALLA WALLA COLLEGE - CURRICULUM
LIBRARY □ College Place, WA

Kuchinsky, Saul, Libn.
BROOKLYN HOSPITAL - MEDICAL LIBRARY □
Brooklyn, NY

Kuchler, LaVerne, Act.Libn.
CONTEMPORARY CRAFTS ASSOCIATION -
LIBRARY □ Portland, OR

Kuchta, Irene, Res.Libn.
AMALGAMATED CLOTHING & TEXTILE
WORKERS UNION, AFL-CIO - RESEARCH
DEPARTMENT LIBRARY □ New York, NY

Kuchta, Linda, Cat.Libn.
PRATT AND WHITNEY AIRCRAFT OF CANADA,
LTD. - LIBRARY □ Longueuil, PQ

Kuck, Mary S., Libn.
U.S. COURT OF MILITARY APPEALS - LIBRARY†
□ Washington, DC

Kucsma, Susan, Mgr.
MARSH AND MC LENNAN, INC. - INFORMATION
CENTER □ New York, NY

Kuczynski, Kathleen, Lib.Dir.
HELEN HAYES HOSPITAL - LIBRARY □ West
Haverstraw, NY

Kuderling, Louise, Pubn.Mgr.
LEAGUE OF MINNESOTA CITIES - LIBRARY □
St. Paul, MN

Kudiesy, Norma M., Pub.Serv.Libn.
U.S. ARMY AIR DEFENSE SCHOOL - LIBRARY† □
Ft. Bliss, TX

Kudlaty, Ruth, Libn.
ORPHAN VOYAGE - KAMMANDALE LIBRARY □
St. Paul, MN

Kudo, Kathleen S., Libn.
HONOLULU (City And County) - MUNICIPAL
REFERENCE AND RECORDS CENTER □ Honolulu,
HI

Kuehling, Mary Alice, Libn.
METHODIST HOSPITAL - LIBRARY □ Madison,
WI

Kuehn, Claire R., Archv.-Libn.
PANHANDLE-PLAINS HISTORICAL MUSEUM -
HISTORIC RESEARCH CENTER □ Canyon, TX

Kuehne, Patricia A., Lib.Mgr.
WESTERN EVANGELICAL SEMINARY - GEORGE
HALLAUER MEMORIAL LIBRARY □ Portland, OR

Kueny, Suzanne, Ref.Libn.
U.S. ARMY CONCEPTS ANALYSIS AGENCY -
LIBRARY □ Bethesda, MD

Kufahl, Kathryn, Libn.
OLD AMERICAN INSURANCE COMPANY -
LIBRARY □ Kansas City, MO

Kugel, Betty, Libn./Cat.
UNITED METHODIST CHURCH - SOUTH
DAKOTA CONFERENCE - COMMITTEE ON
ARCHIVES AND HISTORY - LIBRARY □ Mitchell,
SD

Kugelman, Mary M., Libn.
U.S. VETERANS ADMINISTRATION (FL-Bay
Pines) - CENTER LIBRARY □ Bay Pines, FL

Kugler, Richard C., Dir.
OLD DARTMOUTH HISTORICAL SOCIETY AND
WHALING MUSEUM - LIBRARY □ New Bedford,
MA

Kugler, William J., Pres.
MUSICAL INSTRUMENT MUSEUM - LIBRARY □
St. Paul, MN

Kuhl, Danuta, Acq.Libn.
AMERICAN PETROLEUM INSTITUTE - LIBRARY
□ Washington, DC

Kuhn, Hannah R., Spec.Libn.
BRANDEIS-BARDIN INSTITUTE - HOUSE OF
THE BOOK □ Brandeis, CA

Kuhn, Keith, Interim Supv.
PUBLIC LIBRARY OF CINCINNATI AND
HAMILTON COUNTY - INSTITUTIONS/BOOKS
BY MAIL □ Cincinnati, OH

Kuhn, Martin A., Lib.Cons.
HOLOCAUST LIBRARY AND RESEARCH CENTER
OF SAN FRANCISCO □ San Francisco, CA

Kuhn, Warren B., Dean of Lib.Serv.
IOWA STATE UNIVERSITY - LIBRARY □ Ames,
IA

Kuhner, David, Asst.Dir., Sci.
CLAREMONT COLLEGES - LIBRARY □ Claremont,
CA

Kuhner, David, Libn.
CLAREMONT COLLEGES - NORMAN F. SPRAGUE
MEMORIAL LIBRARY □ Claremont, CA

Kuhns, Patricia J., Hd.Tech.Serv.
FREDERICK CANCER RESEARCH CENTER -
SCIENTIFIC LIBRARY □ Frederick, MD

Kuhr, Charmain, Circ.Asst.
MC CORMICK THEOLOGICAL SEMINARY -
LIBRARY† □ Chicago, IL

Kuhta, R., Per.Libn.
PACE UNIVERSITY, PLEASANTVILLE/
BRIARCLIFF - LIBRARY □ Pleasantville, NY

Kukainis, Irene P., Res.Assoc.
UNIVERSITY OF CINCINNATI - DEPARTMENT
OF ENVIRONMENTAL HEALTH LIBRARY □
Cincinnati, OH

Kukla, Dr. Jon K., Asst.Dir., Adm.Serv.
VIRGINIA STATE LIBRARY □ Richmond, VA

Kuklin, Susan Beverly, Dir.
DE PAUL UNIVERSITY - LAW SCHOOL LIBRARY
□ Chicago, IL

Kukreja, Neera, Cat.
ALEXIAN BROTHERS MEDICAL CENTER -
MEDICAL LIBRARY □ Elk Grove Village, IL

Kulberg, Lenore, Libn.
BUREAU OF JEWISH EDUCATION -
COMMUNITY LIBRARY □ Getzville, NY

Kulchar, Alexander, Med.Libn.
BRYN MAWR HOSPITAL - MEDICAL LIBRARY □
Bryn Mawr, PA

Kulchar, Alexander, Med.Libn.
BRYN MAWR HOSPITAL - MEDICAL LIBRARY -
NURSING DIVISION □ Bryn Mawr, PA

Kulhawy, Gloria, Tech.Serv.Libn.
CORNELL UNIVERSITY - ENGINEERING
LIBRARY □ Ithaca, NY

Kulhawy, Gloria, Libn.
PALEONTOLOGICAL RESEARCH INSTITUTION -
LIBRARY □ Ithaca, NY

Kulkarni, Janardan M., Sci.Libn.
UNIVERSITY OF LOUISVILLE - LIFE SCIENCES
LIBRARY □ Louisville, KY

Kulkarni, Janardan M., Sci.Libn.
UNIVERSITY OF LOUISVILLE - SEBASTIAN S.
KRESGE NATURAL SCIENCE LIBRARY □
Louisville, KY

Kulleseid, Eleanor, Lib.Dir.
BANK STREET COLLEGE OF EDUCATION -
LIBRARY □ New York, NY

Kulp, Mrs. Vlasta, Ref.Libn.
KANSAS STATE UNIVERSITY - VETERINARY
MEDICAL LIBRARY □ Manhattan, KS

Kulpa, Lorraine A., Legal Staff Libn.
GENERAL MOTORS CORPORATION - LEGAL
STAFF LIBRARY □ Detroit, MI

Kulys, Alfred, Cat.Libn.
COOK COUNTY LAW LIBRARY □ Chicago, IL

Kumar, Vijay, Coll./Ref.Libn.
UNIVERSITY OF WESTERN ONTARIO - HEALTH
SCIENCES LIBRARY □ London, ON

Kumatz, Cynthia C., Libn.
MORTON-NORWICH PRODUCTS, INC. -
NORWICH PHARMACAL COMPANY - R&D DEPT.
- LIBRARY INFORMATION GROUP □ Norwich, NY

Kumatz, Tad G., Asst.Dir.
PRATT INSTITUTE - LIBRARY □ Brooklyn, NY

Kunda, Vera, Ref.Libn.
UNIVERSITY OF ALBERTA - SCIENCE LIBRARY
□ Edmonton, AB

Kunde, Nancy, Archv./Rec.Mgr.
UNIVERSITY OF WISCONSIN, MADISON -
ARCHIVES □ Madison, WI

Kundzins, Ilga, Tech.Info.Spec.
U.S. DEPT. OF COMMERCE - INTERNATIONAL
TRADE ADMINISTRATION - NEW YORK
DISTRICT OFFICE LIBRARY □ New York, NY

Kunen, Eleanor, Libn.
MARLBOROUGH HOSPITAL - HEALTH SCIENCE
LIBRARY □ Marlborough, MA

Kunes, Ella R., Libn.-Cat.
GENERAL ELECTRIC COMPANY - CORPORATE
RESEARCH & DEVELOPMENT - WHITNEY
LIBRARY □ Schenectady, NY

Kung, Wen Kai, Cat.Libn. & Biblog.
UNIVERSITY OF OREGON - ORIENTALIA
COLLECTION □ Eugene, OR

Kuni, Dye, Dir., Lib.Serv.
SALEM HOSPITAL - HEALTH SCIENCES
LIBRARY AND INFORMATION CENTER □ Salem,
OR

Kunitz, Donald, Hd., Spec.Coll.
UNIVERSITY OF CALIFORNIA, DAVIS -
GENERAL LIBRARY □ Davis, CA

Kunsemiller, R. Lucille, Order Libn.
CALIFORNIA STATE UNIVERSITY, CHICO -
MERIAM LIBRARY □ Chico, CA

Kuntz, Helen H., Lib.Supv.
UNIVERSITY OF WISCONSIN, MADISON -
PLANT PATHOLOGY DEPARTMENT - MEMORIAL
LIBRARY □ Madison, WI

Kunz, Margaret, Libn.
U.S. NATL. INSTITUTES OF HEALTH - LIBRARY
□ Bethesda, MD

Kunzelman, Kathleen P., Film Libn.
TENNESSEE STATE DEPARTMENT OF PUBLIC
HEALTH - FILM LIBRARY □ Nashville, TN

Kuo, Andrew, Bible Cat.
AMERICAN BIBLE SOCIETY - LIBRARY □ New
York, NY

Kuo, Elaine, Res.Dir.
HOUZE, SHOURDS & MONTGOMERY, INC. -
RESEARCH LIBRARY □ Los Angeles, CA

Kuo, Elaine, Chf., Lib.Serv.
UNITED STATES RAILWAY ASSOCIATION -
USRA DOCUMENT CENTER □ Washington, DC

Kuo, Frank F., Dir.
PORTLAND STATE UNIVERSITY - AUDIO-
VISUAL SERVICES □ Portland, OR

Kuo, Margaret, Libn.
SCHLUMBERGER WELL SERVICES -
ENGINEERING LIBRARY □ Houston, TX

Kuo, Dr. Thomas, Cur.
UNIVERSITY OF PITTSBURGH - EAST ASIAN
LIBRARY □ Pittsburgh, PA

Kupers, Guntis, AV Spec.
ABBOTT-NORTHWESTERN HOSPITAL
CORPORATION - HEALTH SCIENCES RESOURCE
CENTER □ Minneapolis, MN

Kupstas, Kathryn, Hd., Tech.Serv.
AMERICAN BANKERS ASSOCIATION - LIBRARY
□ Washington, DC

Kuramoto, Mary I., Res.Libn.
FIRST HAWAIIAN BANK - RESEARCH DIVISION
LIBRARY □ Honolulu, HI

Kurbjun, Virginia, Libn.
U.S. ARMY - RESEARCH AND TECHNOLOGY
LABS (AVRADCOM) - APPLIED TECH.
LABORATORY - TECHNICAL LIB. □ Ft. Eustis, VA

PERSONNEL

Kurland, Mildred, Libn.
CONGREGATION RODEPH SHALOM - LIBRARY □
Philadelphia, PA

Kurtz, Diana, Assoc.
INSTITUTE FOR THEOLOGICAL &
PHILOSOPHICAL STUDIES - LIBRARY □
Bloomington, IL

Kurtz, Dr. James, Dir.
INSTITUTE FOR THEOLOGICAL &
PHILOSOPHICAL STUDIES - LIBRARY □
Bloomington, IL

Kurtz, Joan, Assoc.
INSTITUTE FOR THEOLOGICAL &
PHILOSOPHICAL STUDIES - LIBRARY □
Bloomington, IL

Kurtz, Mike, Hd., Clas.Info.Serv.
RAND CORPORATION - LIBRARY □ Santa
Monica, CA

Kurtz, Sharon, Info.Sys.Anl.
U.S. DEPT OF ENERGY - SANDIA NATL.
LABORATORIES - TECHNICAL LIBRARY □
Albuquerque, NM

Kurutz, Gary, Supv., Spec.Coll.
CALIFORNIA STATE LIBRARY □ Sacramento, CA

Kurutz, Gary F., Sutro Libn.
CALIFORNIA STATE LIBRARY - SUTRO LIBRARY
□ San Francisco, CA

Kurzig, Carol M., Dir.Pub.Serv.
FOUNDATION CENTER - NEW YORK - LIBRARY
□ New York, NY

Kusada, Haruyoshi, Dir.
INSTITUTE OF BUDDHIST STUDIES - LIBRARY
□ Berkeley, CA

Kusche, Genevieve, Libn.
KANKAKEE COUNTY HISTORICAL SOCIETY -
LIBRARY □ Kankakee, IL

Kushinka, Kerry L., Supv., Med./Sci.Info.
KNOLL PHARMACEUTICAL COMPANY -
RESEARCH LIBRARY □ Whippany, NJ

Kuskowski, Rev. Jerome, S.A.C., Libn.
PALLOTTINE PROVINCIALATE LIBRARY □
Milwaukee, WI

Kusmik, Cornell J., Acq.Libn.
CONCORDIA TEACHERS COLLEGE - KLINCK
MEMORIAL LIBRARY □ River Forest, IL

Kusnerz, Peggy Ann, Libn.
UNIVERSITY OF MICHIGAN - ART &
ARCHITECTURE LIBRARY □ Ann Arbor, MI

Kustelski, Jeanette, Libn.
CHAMPION INTERNATIONAL - HOERNER
WALDORF PACKAGING DIVISION - TECHNICAL
CENTER LIBRARY □ St. Paul, MN

Kuther, Patricia A., Med.Lib.Techn.
U.S. AIR FORCE HOSPITAL - MEDICAL LIBRARY
(AL-Montgomery) □ Montgomery, AL

Kutzner, Dr. Patricia L., Exec.Dir.
WORLD HUNGER EDUCATION SERVICE -
LIBRARY □ Washington, DC

Kuwamura, Frank K., Jr., Chf.Sci. Data Dept.
U.S. DEFENSE MAPPING AGENCY -
HYDROGRAPHIC/TOPOGRAPHIC CENTER-
SUPPORT DIVISION - SCIENTIFIC DATA
DEPARTMENT □ Washington, DC

Kwan, Patrick, Supv., Pub.Serv.
CHINESE NATIONALIST LEAGUE OF CANADA -
LIBRARY† □ Vancouver, BC

Kwiatkowski, Phillip C., Dir.
SLOAN (Alfred P., Jr.) MUSEUM - LIBRARY □
Flint, MI

Kwok, Rosita, Tech.Serv.Libn.
PEPPERDINE UNIVERSITY - LIBRARY -
SPECIAL COLLECTIONS □ Malibu, CA

Kwon, Sang-Hak, Coord., Tech.Serv.
CHICAGO STATE UNIVERSITY - DOUGLAS
LIBRARY □ Chicago, IL

Kwong, Bella, Med.Libn.
BAY HARBOR HOSPITAL - MEDICAL LIBRARY □
Harbor City, CA

Kwong, Bella, Women's Hosp.Libn.
LOS ANGELES COUNTY/UNIVERSITY OF
SOUTHERN CALIFORNIA MEDICAL CENTER -
MEDICAL LIBRARIES □ Los Angeles, CA

Kyed, James M., Hd., Engr.Libs.
MASSACHUSETTS INSTITUTE OF TECHNOLOGY
- BARKER ENGINEERING LIBRARY □ Cambridge,
MA

Kyle, J. Richard, Cur.
SWARTHMORE COLLEGE - FRIENDS
HISTORICAL LIBRARY - PEACE COLLECTION □
Swarthmore, PA

Kysely, Elizabeth, Chf., Ref.Br.
U.S. AIR FORCE ACADEMY - LIBRARY □ U.S. Air
Force Academy, CO

L

La Caille, Craig, Libn.
MORRIS CERULLO WORLD EVANGELISM, INC. -
SCHOOL OF MINISTRY LIBRARY □ San Diego,
CA

La Haye, Claude, Documentaliste
URBARC CANADA - LIBRARY □ Montreal, PQ

La Manna, Joan, Libn.
FOREMOST-MC KESSON - R & D CENTER
LIBRARY □ Dublin, CA

La Quay, Edwin G., Libn.
MOBAY CHEMICAL CORPORATION -
INFORMATION CENTER† □ Pittsburgh, PA

La Rocco, August, Spec. Projects Libn.
UNIVERSITY OF MIAMI - SCHOOL OF
MEDICINE - LOUIS CALDER MEMORIAL
LIBRARY □ Miami, FL

La Rose, Al, Hd.Ref.Libn.
WITTENBERG UNIVERSITY - THOMAS LIBRARY
□ Springfield, OH

La Rue, Robert, Libn.
UNIVERSITY OF VIRGINIA - CHEMISTRY
LIBRARY □ Charlottesville, VA

Laats, Armilda, Asst.Chf.Libn./Cat.
PORT AUTHORITY OF NEW YORK AND NEW
JERSEY - LIBRARY □ New York, NY

Laatz, Mary Jane, Dir.
INDIANA UNIVERSITY - SCHOOL OF MEDICINE
LIBRARY □ Indianapolis, IN

LaBau, Anthony F., Dir.
XAVIER SOCIETY FOR THE BLIND - NATIONAL
CATHOLIC PRESS AND LIBRARY FOR THE
VISUALLY HANDICAPPED □ New York, NY

Labault, Fernando
HARTFORD PUBLIC LIBRARY - REFERENCE AND
GENERAL READING DEPARTMENT □ Hartford,
CT

LaBay, Nancy, Tech.Info.Spec.
LEVENTHAL (Kenneth) & COMPANY - LIBRARY □
Los Angeles, CA

Laberge, Leo, Dir.
OBLATE FATHERS - BIBLIOTHEQUE
DESCHATELETS □ Ottawa, ON

Labib, Anita, User Serv.Coord.
ERIC CLEARINGHOUSE ON TESTS,
MEASUREMENT AND EVALUATION □ Princeton,
NJ

LaBissoniere, William, Libn.
UNIVERSITY OF MINNESOTA - GOVERNMENT
PUBLICATIONS DIVISION □ Minneapolis, MN

Labonte, Trish, Sys.Libn.
BRITISH COLUMBIA INSTITUTE OF
TECHNOLOGY - LIBRARY SERVICES DIVISION
□ Burnaby, BC

LaBorie, Timothy, Lib.Sci.Libn.
DREXEL UNIVERSITY LIBRARIES - GENERAL
LIBRARY □ Philadelphia, PA

Labovitz, Judy, Supv.
AMERICAN MC GAW - TECHNICAL
INFORMATION CENTER □ Santa Ana, CA

Labrie, Jean-Marc, Libn., Rd.Serv.
QUEBEC PROVINCE - MINISTERE DES
COMMUNICATIONS - BIBLIOTHEQUE
ADMINISTRATIVE □ Quebec, PQ

LaBrie, Rita, ILL Libn.
U.S. DEPT. OF ENERGY - LAWRENCE BERKELEY
LABORATORY - LIBRARY □ Berkeley, CA

Labrousse, Francois
CENTRE DE RECHERCHE INDUSTRIELLE DU
QUEBEC - DIRECTION DE L'INFORMATION
TECHNOLOGIQUE (DIT) □ Ste. Foy, PQ

Lacayo, Carmela G., Natl.Exec.Dir.
ASOCIACION NACIONAL PRO PERSONAS
MAYORES - LIBRARY □ Los Angeles, CA

LaChine, Guy L., Supv. Park Techn.
U.S. NATL. PARK SERVICE - DE SOTO NATL.
MEMORIAL - LIBRARY □ Bradenton, FL

Lachowicz, Audrey D., Med.Libn.
LEWIS-GALE HOSPITAL CORPORATION -
LEWIS-GALE MEDICAL LIBRARY □ Salem, VA

Lackner, Irene, Libn.
CANADA - ECONOMIC COUNCIL OF CANADA -
LIBRARY □ Ottawa, ON

Lacoste, Marie, Lib.Techn.
CANADA - SECRETARY OF STATE -
TRANSLATION BUREAU - LIBRARY □ Montreal,
PQ

LaCroix, Carla, Libn.
DALLAS PUBLIC LIBRARY - BUSINESS AND
TECHNOLOGY DIVISION □ Dallas, TX

Lacroix, Denise, Libn.
UNIVERSITE DE MONTREAL - OPTOMETRIE-
BIBLIOTHEQUE □ Montreal, PQ

LaCroix, Ghislain, Libn., Coll.Dev.
QUEBEC PROVINCE - MINISTERE DES
COMMUNICATIONS - BIBLIOTHEQUE
ADMINISTRATIVE □ Quebec, PQ

LaCroix, Michael J., Coord., Tech.Serv.
WRIGHT STATE UNIVERSITY - HEALTH
SCIENCES LIBRARY □ Dayton, OH

Lacy, Linda, Ser.Libn.
MARSHALL (John) LAW SCHOOL - LIBRARY □
Chicago, IL

Ladd, Anna, Asst.Libn.
TRINITY LUTHERAN CHURCH - LIBRARY □
Madison, WI

Ladd, Everett C., Jr., Exec.Dir.
UNIVERSITY OF CONNECTICUT - INSTITUTE
FOR SOCIAL INQUIRY □ Storrs, CT

Ladd, Everett C., Exec.Dir.
UNIVERSITY OF CONNECTICUT - ROPER
CENTER □ Storrs, CT

Ladd, Marcia, Biblog.Instr.
BENTLEY COLLEGE - SOLOMON R. BAKER
LIBRARY □ Waltham, MA

Laderman, Anne, Supv., Cat. Maintenance
SMITHSONIAN INSTITUTION LIBRARIES -
COOPER-HEWITT MUSEUM OF DESIGN - DORIS
& HENRY DREYFUSS MEMORIAL STUDY
CENTER □ New York, NY

Ladion, Gertrudes J., Law Libn.
SAN JOAQUIN COUNTY LAW LIBRARY □
Stockton, CA

Laes, Diane L., Libn.
GREEN BAY PRESS-GAZETTE - LIBRARY □
Green Bay, WI

Lafferty, LaVedi, Libn.
PHILOSOPHICAL HERITAGE INSTITUTE -
LIBRARY OF ESOTERIC STUDIES □ Fairbanks,
AK

LaFlare, Mary J., Mgr., Lib.Serv.
SPERRY AND HUTCHINSON COMPANY -
MARKET RESEARCH LIBRARY □ New York, NY

LaFon, S. Earl, Hd., Lib.Div.
U.S. NAVY - NAVAL WEAPONS CENTER -
LIBRARY DIVISION □ China Lake, CA

Lafortune, Francois, Chf.Libn.
MUSEE DU QUEBEC - BIBLIOTHEQUE □ Quebec,
PQ

Lafranchi, William E., Dir. of Libs./Media Rsrcs
INDIANA UNIVERSITY OF PENNSYLVANIA -
UNIVERSITY LIBRARY □ Indiana, PA

LaFrank, Kathleen, Libn.
NEW YORK STATE PARKS AND RECREATION -
DIVISION FOR HISTORIC PRESERVATION -
FIELD SERVICES BUREAU - LIBRARY □ Albany,
NY

Lagano, Vincent, Med.Libn.
KAISER-PERMANENTE MEDICAL CENTER - SAN FRANCISCO MEDICAL LIBRARY □ San Francisco, CA

Lagasse, Carol T., Cat.Libn.
RENSSELAER POLYTECHNIC INSTITUTE - FOLSOM LIBRARY □ Troy, NY

Lageson, Mary, Assoc.Libn.
STALEY (A.E.) MANUFACTURING COMPANY - TECHNICAL INFORMATION CENTER □ Decatur, IL

LaGory, Thomas W., Spec.Coll.Coord.
U.S. VETERANS ADMINISTRATION (OH-Cincinnati) - MEDICAL CENTER LIBRARY □ Cincinnati, OH

LaGrutta, Charles, Info.Ctr.Coord.
URBAN INVESTMENT AND DEVELOPMENT COMPANY - INFORMATION CENTER† □ Chicago, IL

Lahey, Judith A., Assoc.Libn.
UNIVERSITY OF CONNECTICUT - LAW SCHOOL LIBRARY □ West Hartford, CT

Lahr, Barbara J., Supv. of Educ.
LAKE COUNTY FOREST PRESERVE DISTRICT - RYERSON NATURE LIBRARY □ Libertyville, IL

Lahr, Mildred A., Supv., Info.Ctr.
ROCKWELL INTERNATIONAL - COLLINS DIVISIONS - INFORMATION CENTER □ Cedar Rapids, IA

Lai, John Yung-Hsiang, Assoc.Libn./Cat.
HARVARD UNIVERSITY - HARVARD YENCHING INSTITUTE - LIBRARY □ Cambridge, MA

Lai, Violet L., Hd.Libn.
HAWAII CHINESE HISTORY CENTER □ Honolulu, HI

Lain, Christine R., Libn.
U.S. AIR FORCE BASE - CARSWELL BASE LIBRARY □ Fort Worth, TX

Lain, Mildred, Hist.
COLUMBIA COUNTY HISTORICAL SOCIETY - MUSEUM □ St. Helens, OR

Laine, Esther, Lib.Asst.
UNIVERSITY OF CALIFORNIA, BERKELEY - ENTOMOLOGY LIBRARY □ Berkeley, CA

Laing, Gregory H., Genealogist
HAVERHILL PUBLIC LIBRARY - SPECIAL COLLECTIONS DIVISION □ Haverhill, MA

Laing, Michelle, Ref.Libn.
UNIVERSITY OF MANITOBA - ARCHITECTURE & FINE ARTS LIBRARY □ Winnipeg, MB

Laird, Marilyn Poe, Hd.Libn.
SOUTH SUBURBAN GENEALOGICAL & HISTORICAL SOCIETY - LIBRARY □ South Holland, IL

Laird, Mary Susan, Mgr., Lib.Serv.
ALZA CORPORATION - RESEARCH LIBRARY □ Palo Alto, CA

Laite, Berkley, Media/Curric.Libn.
SHIPPENSBURG STATE COLLEGE - EZRA LEHMAN MEMORIAL LIBRARY □ Shippensburg, PA

Lajara, Luz M., Libn.
UNIVERSITY OF PUERTO RICO - PUERTO RICAN COLLECTION □ Rio Piedras, PR

Lake, Carlton, Exec.Cur., French Coll.
UNIVERSITY OF TEXAS, AUSTIN - HUMANITIES RESEARCH CENTER □ Austin, TX

Lake, Don, Hd., Ref.Dept.
EASTERN WASHINGTON UNIVERSITY - LIBRARY □ Cheney, WA

Lake, Kay, Dir., Educ.Servs.
MARION GENERAL HOSPITAL - MEDICAL LIBRARY □ Marion, IN

Laki, Georgette, Bibliothecaire
CONSERVATOIRE D'ART DRAMATIQUE DE QUEBEC - BIBLIOTHEQUE □ Quebec, PQ

Lalande, Christine, Ser.Mgr.
SPORT INFORMATION RESOURCE CENTRE □ Ottawa, ON

Lalley, John B., Hd.Acq.
EAST STROUDSBURG STATE COLLEGE - LIBRARY □ East Stroudsburg, PA

Lallo, Joyce, Ref.Serv.Hd.
BOEING COMPANY - SEATTLE SERVICES DIVISION - KENT TECHNICAL LIBRARY □ Seattle, WA

Lalonde, Jules, Pub. Search Rm.
CANADA - CONSUMER AND CORPORATE AFFAIRS CANADA - PATENT AND COPYRIGHT OFFICE □ Ottawa, ON

Lamar, Doris M., Mgr., Info.Serv.
MC KINSEY & COMPANY, INC. - INFORMATION CENTER □ Los Angeles, CA

Lamarre, Andre, Hd.Libn.
QUEBEC PROVINCE - MINISTERE DE L'ENERGIE ET DES RESSOURCES - BIBLIOTHEQUE □ Quebec, PQ

Lamarre, Andre, SDI
QUEBEC PROV. - MIN. DE L'ENERGIE ET DES RESSOURCES - CENTRE DE DOCUMENTATION ET DE RENSEIGNEMENTS □ Quebec, PQ

Lamb, Alma, Asst.Libn.
SAN DIEGO STATE UNIVERSITY - MEDIA & CURRICULUM CENTER □ San Diego, CA

Lamb, Cheryl, Info.Sci.
AMERICAN CAN COMPANY - NEENAH TECHNICAL CENTER - TECHNICAL INFORMATION CENTER □ Neenah, WI

Lamb, Gertrude, Ph.D., Dir.
HARTFORD HOSPITAL - HEALTH SCIENCE LIBRARIES □ Hartford, CT

Lamb, John, Pub.Serv.Libn./ILL
WESTON SCHOOL OF THEOLOGY - LIBRARY □ Cambridge, MA

Lamb, John M., Info.Dir.
ILLINOIS CANAL SOCIETY - LIBRARY □ Lockport, IL

Lamb, Jolaine B., Base Libn.
U.S. AIR FORCE BASE - BEALE BASE LIBRARY □ Beale AFB, CA

Lamb, Ms. Lebby B., Bus.Libn.
GREENSBORO PUBLIC LIBRARY - BUSINESS LIBRARY □ Greensboro, NC

Lamb, Norma Jean, Hd.
BUFFALO & ERIE COUNTY PUBLIC LIBRARY - MUSIC DEPARTMENT □ Buffalo, NY

Lamb, Patricia, Law Libn.
DEL NORTE COUNTY LAW LIBRARY □ Crescent City, CA

Lamb, Seonaid, Ref.Libn.
UNIVERSITY OF BRITISH COLUMBIA - HUMANITIES DIVISION □ Vancouver, BC

Lamb, Una, Asst. to Libn.
GOLDEN VALLEY LUTHERAN COLLEGE - LIBRARY □ Minneapolis, MN

Lambers, Stephen, Govt.Doc./Info.Serv.
CALVIN COLLEGE AND SEMINARY - LIBRARY □ Grand Rapids, MI

Lambert, Dennis, Libn.
UNIVERSITY OF PITTSBURGH - DARLINGTON MEMORIAL LIBRARY □ Pittsburgh, PA

Lambert, Helene D., Med.Libn.
NEW ROCHELLE HOSPITAL MEDICAL CENTER - J. MARSHALL PERLEY HEALTH SCIENCE LIBRARY □ New Rochelle, NY

Lambert, Jeffrey, Asst.Libn.
COOPERS AND LYBRAND - LIBRARY □ Los Angeles, CA

Lambert, Lois, Libn.
PACIFIC TELEPHONE COMPANY - LIBRARY □ San Francisco, CA

Lambert, Nancy E., Supv.
3M - PATENT INFORMATION CENTER □ St. Paul, MN

Lambert, Nancy S., Libn.
YALE UNIVERSITY - ART AND ARCHITECTURE LIBRARY □ New Haven, CT

Lambert, Peggy B., Libn.
DUKE POWER COMPANY - DAVID NABOW LIBRARY □ Charlotte, NC

Lambert, Raymond, Owner
LAMBERT (Harold M.) STUDIOS - LIBRARY □ Philadelphia, PA

Lambert, Robert A., Asst.Libn., Tech.Serv.
U.S. NAVAL ACADEMY - NIMITZ LIBRARY □ Annapolis, MD

Lambert, Rose, Libn.
LOUISIANA STATE MUSEUM - LOUISIANA HISTORICAL CENTER □ New Orleans, LA

Lambkin, Claire A., Chf.Libn.
AMERICAN MANAGEMENT ASSOCIATIONS - LIBRARY □ New York, NY

Lambrou, Angella, Asst.Med.Libn.
MONTREAL CHILDREN'S HOSPITAL - MEDICAL LIBRARY □ Montreal, PQ

Lamers, Carl, Foreign Law Libn.
YALE UNIVERSITY - LAW LIBRARY □ New Haven, CT

Lamers, Claire, Asst.Libn.
NEW YORK GENEALOGICAL AND BIOGRAPHICAL SOCIETY - GENEALOGICAL RESEARCH LIBRARY □ New York, NY

Lamirande, Armand, Chf.Libn.
COLLEGE MILITAIRE ROYAL DE ST-JEAN - LIBRARY □ St. Jean, PQ

Lamonde, Professor Yvan, Dir.
MC GILL UNIVERSITY - FRENCH CANADA STUDIES PROGRAMME - REFERENCE LIBRARY □ Montreal, PQ

Lamont, Bridget, Assoc.Dir., Lib.Dev.
ILLINOIS STATE LIBRARY □ Springfield, IL

Lamont, John A., Info.Mgr.
NATIONAL MARINE MANUFACTURERS ASSOCIATION - INFORMATION CENTER □ New York, NY

Lamont, Joyce H., Cur.
UNIVERSITY OF ALABAMA - WILLIAM STANLEY HOOLE SPECIAL COLLECTIONS LIBRARY □ University, AL

Lamontagne, D., Libn.
PINELAND CENTER - MEDIA CENTER □ Pownal, ME

Lamontagne, Therese, Circ.Serv.Libn.
CALIFORNIA STATE POLYTECHNIC UNIVERSITY, POMONA - LIBRARY □ Pomona, CA

Lamos, Grant, III, Dir.
ASSOCIATED PRESS - NEWSPHOTO LIBRARY □ New York, NY

LaMotte, LuVerne, Chm., Lib.Comm.
GREENE AND GREENE LIBRARY □ Pasadena, CA

Lamoureux, Florence, Med.Libn.
BACKUS (William W.) HOSPITAL - MEDICAL/NURSING LIBRARY □ Norwich, CT

Lampen, Barbara, Archv.
NETHERLANDS MUSEUM - ARCHIVES AND LIBRARY □ Holland, MI

Lamphere, James J., Dir.Corp. Marketing Res.
GAF CORPORATION - LIBRARY □ New York, NY

Lampman, Wilma, Asst.Libn.
SOUTHERN ILLINOIS UNIVERSITY, CARBONDALE - UNDERGRADUATE LIBRARY □ Carbondale, IL

Lampson, Virginia, Dental Libn.
TEMPLE UNIVERSITY - HEALTH SCIENCES CENTER - LIBRARY □ Philadelphia, PA

Lamrey, Helen, Supv., Info.Serv.
PPG INDUSTRIES, INC. - COATINGS AND RESINS DIVISION - RESEARCH CENTER LIBRARY† □ Allison Park, PA

Lamstein, Sarah, Libn.
TEMPLE MISHKAN TEFILA - HARRY AND ANNA FEINBERG LIBRARY □ Chestnut Hill, MA

Lanahan, Rev. William F., Field Dir.
ST. JOHN'S ABBEY AND UNIVERSITY - HILL MONASTIC MANUSCRIPT LIBRARY - BUSH CENTER □ Collegeville, MN

Lancaster, John, Libn. & Archv.
AMHERST COLLEGE - SPECIAL COLLECTIONS DEPARTMENT AND ARCHIVES □ Amherst, MA

Lancaster, Kevin, Asst. Law Libn.
NEW MEXICO STATE SUPREME COURT - LAW LIBRARY □ Santa Fe, NM

Lancaster, Madeline E., Pres.
SPRINGFIELD HISTORICAL SOCIETY - LIBRARY □ Springfield, NJ

PERSONNEL

Lancaster, Olive V., Libn.
FAIRVIEW COLLEGE - LEARNING RESOURCES CENTRE □ Fairview, AB

Lanctot, Doris, Asst.Libn.
BECHTEL - CENTRAL LIBRARY □ San Francisco, CA

Land, Iris L., Mgr., Lib.Serv.
AIR CANADA - LIBRARY □ Montreal, PQ

Land, Phyllis M., Dir., Div.Instr. Media
INDIANA STATE DEPT. OF PUBLIC INSTRUCTION - PROFESSIONAL LIBRARY □ Indianapolis, IN

Land, R. Brian, Dir.
ONTARIO - LEGISLATIVE ASSEMBLY - LEGISLATIVE LIBRARY RESEARCH AND INFORMATION SERVICES □ Toronto, ON

Landau, Zuki, Chf.Libn.
SCHOOL OF VISUAL ARTS - LIBRARY □ New York, NY

Lande, Barbara P., Libn.
PORTER MEDICAL CENTER - MEDICAL LIBRARY AND INFORMATION SERVICE □ Middlebury, VT

Landeck, Mary E., Pub.Serv.Libn.
MILWAUKEE AREA TECHNICAL COLLEGE - RASCHE MEMORIAL LIBRARY □ Milwaukee, WI

Lander, James H., Lib.Mgr.
MERCY HEALTH CENTER - ANTHONY C. PFOHL HEALTH SCIENCE LIBRARY □ Dubuque, IA

Landers, Katherine, Libn.
EPISCOPAL CHURCH OF THE HOLY FAITH - PARISH LIBRARY □ Santa Fe, NM

Landfield, Jean, Chf.Libn.
U.S. VETERANS ADMINISTRATION (NE-Lincoln) - MEDICAL CENTER LIBRARY □ Lincoln, NE

Landis, Kay, Lit.Chem.
ASHLAND CHEMICAL COMPANY - TECHNICAL INFORMATION CENTER □ Columbus, OH

Landis, R.A., Info. Chemist
EL PASO PRODUCTS COMPANY - RESEARCH AND DEVELOPMENT LIBRARY □ Odessa, TX

Landon, Betty D., Dir.
SCHUYLER COUNTY HISTORICAL SOCIETY - OLD BRICK TAVERN MUSEUM - RESEARCH LIBRARY □ Montour Falls, NY

Landon, Richard G., Dept.Hd.
UNIVERSITY OF TORONTO - THOMAS FISHER RARE BOOK LIBRARY □ Toronto, ON

Landon, Rosemary, Found.Ctr.Coll.
JACKSON METROPOLITAN LIBRARY - INFORMATION AND REFERENCE DIVISION □ Jackson, MS

Landress, Sylvia, Dir. & Libn.
WORLD ZIONIST ORGANIZATION - AMERICAN SECTION - ZIONIST ARCHIVES AND LIBRARY □ New York, NY

Landrum, Hollis, Chf., Tech.Proc.Sect.
U.S. ARMY - ENGINEER WATERWAYS EXPERIMENT STATION - TECHNICAL INFORMATION CENTER □ Vicksburg, MS

Landrum, John H., Dir. of Rd.Serv.
SOUTH CAROLINA STATE LIBRARY □ Columbia, SC

Landry, William, Hd.Doc.Distr.Ctr.
RHODE ISLAND STATE LIBRARY □ Providence, RI

Lands, Karen, Libn.
U.S. VETERANS ADMINISTRATION (NY-Buffalo) - MEDICAL CENTER LIBRARY SERVICE □ Buffalo, NY

Lands, Rosemary J., Libn.
CHARLOTTE AND MECKLENBURG COUNTY PUBLIC LIBRARY - CAROLINA ROOM □ Charlotte, NC

Landwirth, Trudy, Dir.
METHODIST MEDICAL CENTER OF ILLINOIS - MEDICAL LIBRARY □ Peoria, IL

Lane, C.G., Jr., Dir.
PENOBSCOT MARINE MUSEUM - LIBRARY □ Searsport, ME

Lane, Carl, Keeper of Mss.
NEW JERSEY HISTORICAL SOCIETY - LIBRARY □ Newark, NJ

Lane, David, Libn.
MEMPHIS-SHELBY COUNTY PUBLIC LIBRARY AND INFO. CTR. - SCIENCE/BUSINESS/SOCIAL SCIENCES DEPT. □ Memphis, TN

Lane, David L., Supt.
U.S. NATL. PARK SERVICE - PIPESTONE NATL. MONUMENT - LIBRARY & ARCHIVES □ Pipestone, MN

Lane, David T., Adm.Asst./Info.Spec.
NEW YORK STATE OFFICE OF MENTAL HEALTH - NEW YORK STATE PSYCHIATRIC INSTITUTE - LIBRARY □ New York, NY

Lane, Diana, Act.Hd.
UNIVERSITY OF CALIFORNIA, IRVINE - MEDICAL CENTER LIBRARY □ Orange, CA

Lane, Eileen L., Libn.
GENERAL MOTORS CORPORATION - AC SPARK PLUG DIVISION - ENGINEERING LIBRARY □ Flint, MI

Lane, Faith M., Libn.
HERRICK AND SMITH - LAW LIBRARY □ Boston, MA

Lane, Mrs. J.E., Chf.Libn.
UNIVERSITY OF KING'S COLLEGE - KING'S COLLEGE LIBRARY □ Halifax, NS

Lane, Joyce, Libn.
CENTER FOR WOMEN'S STUDIES AND SERVICES - CWSS LIBRARY □ San Diego, CA

Lane, Joyce A., Libn.
U.S. NAVY - NAVAL MILITARY PERSONNEL COMMAND - TECHNICAL LIBRARY □ Washington, DC

Lane, Laura A., Dir., Res.
AMERICAN HERITAGE PUBLISHING COMPANY, INC. - LIBRARY □ New York, NY

Lane, Marie, Asst.Libn./Tech.Serv
GEORGE MASON UNIVERSITY - SCHOOL OF LAW - LIBRARY† □ Arlington, VA

Lane, Mary G., Sr.Libn.
HISTORICAL FOUNDATION OF THE PRESBYTERIAN AND REFORMED CHURCHES - LIBRARY AND ARCHIVES □ Montreat, NC

Lane, Nina M., Lib.Dir.
GROUP HEALTH ASSOCIATION OF AMERICA, INC. - GERTRUDE STURGES MEMORIAL LIBRARY □ Washington, DC

Lane, Dr. Richard, Archv.
NORTHEASTERN NEVADA MUSEUM - LIBRARY □ Elko, NV

Lane, Robert B., Dir.
U.S. AIR FORCE - AIR UNIVERSITY - LIBRARY □ Maxwell AFB, AL

Lane, William T., Hd., Info.Serv.
SUNY - COLLEGE AT GENESEO - MILNE LIBRARY □ Geneseo, NY

Lane-Lopez, Rose, Libn.
COMBUSTION ENGINEERING, INC. - POWER SYSTEMS GROUP LIBRARY SERVICES □ Windsor, CT

Lang, Elizabeth, Hd.
UNIVERSITY OF CALIFORNIA, RIVERSIDE - ENGLISH DEPARTMENT LIBRARY □ Riverside, CA

Lang, George W., Lib.Adm.
NORTH AMERICAN BAPTIST SEMINARY - KAISER-RAMAKER LIBRARY □ Sioux Falls, SD

Lang, Gyorgy, Ref.Libn.
BOSTON COLLEGE - LAW SCHOOL LIBRARY □ Newton Centre, MA

Lang, Janice, Tech.Serv.Supv.
WISCONSIN STATE DIVISION FOR LIBRARY SERVICES - REFERENCE AND LOAN LIBRARY □ Madison, WI

Lang, Leona, Dir.
PASQUA HOSPITAL - HEALTH SCIENCES LIBRARY □ Regina, SK

Lang, Sr. Regine, Libn.
ST. FRANCIS MEDICAL CENTER - HEALTH SCIENCES LIBRARY □ La Crosse, WI

Lang, Rev. Ron, Chm.
UNITED METHODIST CHURCH - YELLOWSTONE ANNUAL CONFERENCE - ARCHIVES □ Geraldine, MT

Lang, Saundra K., Lib.Techn.
PRO FOOTBALL HALL OF FAME - LIBRARY/ RESEARCH CENTER □ Canton, OH

Lang, Rev. Walter, Exec.Dir.
BIBLE SCIENCE ASSOCIATION - RESEARCH CENTER† □ Minneapolis, MN

Lange, Angie, Asst.Libn./Tech.Serv.
KUTAK, ROCK & HUIE - LAW LIBRARY □ Omaha, NE

Lange, Carla, Asst.Libn.
MISSOURI BOTANICAL GARDEN - LIBRARY □ St. Louis, MO

Lange, Clifford E., State Libn.
NEW MEXICO STATE LIBRARY □ Santa Fe, NM

Lange, R. Thomas, Chf.Med.Libn.
UNIVERSITY OF SOUTH CAROLINA - SCHOOL OF MEDICINE LIBRARY □ Columbia, SC

Langelier, G., Chf., Serv.Sect.
CANADA - PUBLIC ARCHIVES OF CANADA - NATIONAL MAP COLLECTION □ Ottawa, ON

Langen, John S., Sr.Libn.
UNIVERSITY OF ALABAMA - SCIENCE LIBRARY □ University, AL

Langer, Mrs. E., Libn.
WINNIPEG FREE PRESS - LIBRARY† □ Winnipeg, MB

Langerman, Lenore, Asst.Libn.
CENTER FOR THE STUDY OF THE PRESIDENCY - LIBRARY □ New York, NY

Langevin, G., Acq.
COMPLEXE SCIENTIFIQUE DU QUEBEC - SERVICE DE DOCUMENTATION ET DE BIBLIOTHEQUE □ Ste. Foy, PQ

Langhammer, E. Birgit, Libn.
HAMILTON BOARD OF EDUCATION - EDUCATION CENTRE LIBRARY □ Hamilton, ON

Langkau, Claire Marie, Libn.
UNION CARBIDE CORPORATION - BATTERY PRODUCTS DIVISION - TECHNICAL INFORMATION CENTER □ Cleveland, OH

Langlois, Janet L., Dir.
WAYNE STATE UNIVERSITY - FOLKLORE ARCHIVE □ Detroit, MI

Langlois, Rene-Daniel, Libn.
INSTITUT DE TECHNOLOGIE AGRICOLE - RESEARCH LIBRARY □ La Pocatiere, PQ

Langston, Gay, Hd., Circ.
UNIVERSITY OF TEXAS HEALTH SCIENCE CENTER, DALLAS - LIBRARY □ Dallas, TX

Langville, Alan, Libn.
WASHINGTON STATE UNIVERSITY - EDUCATION LIBRARY □ Pullman, WA

Lanham, Lois J., Hd.Ref.Libn.
U.S. DEPT. OF COMMERCE - DEPARTMENTAL LIBRARY □ Washington, DC

Lanier, Tish, Chf., Cat.Serv.
U.S. CENTER FOR DISEASE CONTROL - CDC LIBRARY □ Atlanta, GA

Lanigan, Janet, Libn.
FLORIDA STATE LEGISLATURE - DIVISION OF LEGISLATIVE LIBRARY SERVICES □ Tallahassee, FL

Lank, Dannette H., Info.Res.Spec.
AUTOTROL CORPORATION - BIO-SYSTEMS DIVISION - INFORMATION CENTER □ Milwaukee, WI

Lankford, Nancy, Asst.Dir.
UNIVERSITY OF MISSOURI - WESTERN HISTORICAL MANUSCRIPT COLLECTION/ STATE HISTORICAL SOCIETY OF MISSOURI □ Columbia, MO

Lannin, Sue, Ref.Libn.
MERRIAM CENTER LIBRARY □ Chicago, IL

Lannon, John, Acq.
BOSTON ATHENAEUM LIBRARY □ Boston, MA

Lansberg, Helen R., Dir.
INSTITUTE OF LIVING - MEDICAL LIBRARY □ Hartford, CT

Lansdale, Metta T., Jr., Mgr., Lib.Serv.
ST. JOSEPH MERCY HOSPITAL - RIECKER MEMORIAL LIBRARY □ Ann Arbor, MI

Lansing, James, Asst.Libn.
ROANOKE MEMORIAL HOSPITALS - MEDICAL LIBRARY □ Roanoke, VA

Lansky, Aaron, Exec.Dir.
NATIONAL YIDDISH BOOK EXCHANGE, INC. - LIBRARY □ Amherst, MA

Lanteri, Azarra, Asst.
UNIVERSITY OF ORIENTAL STUDIES - INTERNATIONAL BUDDHIST MEDITATION CENTER LIBRARY □ Los Angeles, CA

Lantz, Bonnie, Libn.
ALTOONA HOSPITAL - GLOVER MEMORIAL MEDICAL AND NURSING LIBRARY □ Altoona, PA

Lanzino, Catherine, Libn.
DAUPHIN COUNTY LAW LIBRARY □ Harrisburg, PA

Lao, Mary, Libn.
DOW CHEMICAL U.S.A. - WESTERN DIVISION RESEARCH LABORATORIES - LIBRARY □ Walnut Creek, CA

Lao, Niann, Asst.Libn. & Cat.
OHIO STATE SUPREME COURT LAW LIBRARY □ Columbus, OH

Lape, Jane M., Cur.-Libn.
FORT TICONDEROGA MUSEUM - LIBRARY □ Ticonderoga, NY

LaPerla, Susan, Libn.
U.S. DEPT. OF JUSTICE - NATIONAL INSTITUTE OF JUSTICE - NATL. CRIMINAL JUSTICE REF. SERVICE □ Rockville, MD

Laperle, Isabelle, Documentaliste
UNIVERSITE DE MONTREAL - DEPARTEMENT DE DEMOGRAPHIE - SERVICE DE LA RECHERCHE DOCUMENTATION □ Montreal, PQ

Laperriere, Jerome, Dir.
SEMINAIRE ST-JOSEPH - BIBLIOTHEQUE □ Trois-Rivieres, PQ

Laperriere, Jerome, Archv.
SEMINAIRE DES TROIS RIVIERES - ARCHIVES □ Trois-Rivieres, PQ

Lapham, Helen, Supv.
CORNELL UNIVERSITY - LABORATORY OF ORNITHOLOGY - LIBRARY □ Ithaca, NY

Lapidus, Marshall, Hd.Cat.
CLARK (Sterling and Francine) ART INSTITUTE - LIBRARY □ Williamstown, MA

LaPlante, Kathleen, Libn.
NEW MEXICO STATE ENERGY AND MINERALS DEPARTMENT - LIBRARY □ Santa Fe, NM

LaPlante, Mrs. Leroy H., Chm.
FIRST CONGREGATIONAL CHURCH OF AUBURN - LIBRARY □ Auburn, MA

Laplante, Louise, Regional Dir.
CANADIAN MUSIC CENTRE - LIBRARY† □ Montreal, PQ

LaPointe, Antoinette, Film Libn.
CANADA - NATIONAL FILM BOARD OF CANADA - FILM PREVIEW LIBRARY □ Montreal, PQ

Lapointe, JoAnne D., Cur.
LE CENTRE D'HERITAGE FRANCO-AMERICAIN - LIBRARY □ Lewiston, ME

Laponce, Iza, Libn.
UNIVERSITY OF BRITISH COLUMBIA - SOCIAL SCIENCES DIVISION □ Vancouver, BC

LaPorte, Sr. Margaret, Dir.
COLUMBUS HOSPITAL - HEALTH SCIENCES LIBRARY □ Great Falls, MT

Lapp, Dorothy, Lib.Techn.
CANADA - CANADIAN WILDLIFE SERVICE - PRAIRIE MIGRATORY BIRD RESEARCH CENTRE - LIBRARY □ Saskatoon, SK

Lapsansky, Phillip, Ref.Libn.
LIBRARY COMPANY OF PHILADELPHIA □ Philadelphia, PA

Larche, Thelma B., Assoc.Libn.
UNIVERSITY OF FLORIDA - P.K. YONGE LABORATORY SCHOOL - MEAD LIBRARY □ Gainesville, FL

Lareau, Carolyn A., Libn.
UNION CARBIDE CORPORATION - LAW DEPARTMENT LIBRARY □ New York, NY

Large, Deborah S., Dir.Lib.Serv.
UNIVERSITY OF TEXAS - INSTITUTE OF TEXAN CULTURES AT SAN ANTONIO - LIBRARY □ San Antonio, TX

Largen, Elsa, Proc.Ctr.
U.S. ARMY POST - FORT LEWIS - LIBRARY SYSTEM □ Fort Lewis, WA

Lariccia, Louise, Libn.
GOODYEAR AEROSPACE CORPORATION - LIBRARY □ Akron, OH

Larimer, Hugh, Map Libn.
UNIVERSITY OF MANITOBA - REFERENCE SERVICES DEPARTMENT - MAP AND ATLAS COLLECTION □ Winnipeg, MB

Larimer, John F., Assoc.Dir.
ARIZONA STATE UNIVERSITY - CENTER FOR METEORITE STUDIES - LIBRARY □ Tempe, AZ

Larimer, Lawrence M., Health Sci.Libn.
U.S. VETERANS ADMINISTRATION (TX-Kerrville) - HEALTH SCIENCES LIBRARY □ Kerrville, TX

Larison, Ruth A., Libn.
U.S. NATL. PARK SERVICE - ROCKY MOUNTAIN REGIONAL OFFICE - LIBRARY □ Denver, CO

Lariviere, Gemma, Libn.
MANITOBA - CENTRE DE RESSOURCES EDUCATIVES FRANCAISES DU MANITOBA □ Saint Boniface, MB

Lariviere, Mr. J., Chf.
NATIONAL LIBRARY OF CANADA - OFFICIAL PUBLICATIONS DIVISION □ Ottawa, ON

Lariviere, Jules, Libn.
UNIVERSITY OF OTTAWA - LAW LIBRARY □ Ottawa, ON

Larke, Tom, Ref.Libn.
ILLINOIS INSTITUTE OF TECHNOLOGY - JAMES S. KEMPER LIBRARY □ Chicago, IL

Larkin, Dorothy, Libn./Exec.Sec.
VESTIGIA - LIBRARY □ Stanhope, NJ

Larkins, Rosemary, Libn.
OHIO STATE INDUSTRIAL COMMISSION - DIVISION OF SAFETY AND HYGIENE - RESOURCE CENTER □ Columbus, OH

LaRoche, Christian, Musm.Dir.
HISTORICAL SOCIETY OF OKALOOSA & WALTON COUNTIES, INC. - MUSEUM LIBRARY □ Valparaiso, FL

LaRose, Helen, Supv., Archv.
EDMONTON CITY ARCHIVES □ Edmonton, AB

Larose, Helene, Ref.Libn.
COLLEGE LIONEL-GROULX - BIBLIOTHEQUE □ Ste. Therese, PQ

Larose, Luanne, Lib.Techn.
CANADA - DEPARTMENT OF INSURANCE - LIBRARY □ Ottawa, ON

Larouche, Irma, Biblog.
NATIONAL LIBRARY OF CANADA - REFERENCE AND BIBLIOGRAPHY SECTION □ Ottawa, ON

Laroussini, Donna H., Rd.Serv.Libn.
WAKE FOREST UNIVERSITY - LAW LIBRARY □ Winston-Salem, NC

Larriett, Freddie, Lib.Asst.
AMERICAN NATURAL RESOURCE COMPANY - SYSTEM ECONOMIC LIBRARY □ Detroit, MI

Larsen, Jeanne, Info.Spec.
WED ENTERPRISES - RESEARCH LIBRARY □ Glendale, CA

Larsen, K.
U.S. OAK RIDGE NATL. LABORATORY - INFORMATION DIVISION - ENVIRONMENTAL MUTAGEN INFORMATION CENTER □ Oak Ridge, TN

Larsen, Karen, Asst.Libn.
ROCHESTER METHODIST HOSPITAL - METHODIST KAHLER LIBRARY □ Rochester, MN

Larsen, Ms. Lotte, Ref./Ser.Libn.
OREGON COLLEGE OF EDUCATION - LIBRARY □ Monmouth, OR

Larsen, Mary, Libn.
DEKALB COUNTY BOARD OF EDUCATION - FERNBANK SCIENCE CENTER - LIBRARY □ Atlanta, GA

Larsen, Svend-Aage, Assoc.Prof.
UNIVERSITY OF WYOMING - ANIMAL SCIENCE DIVISION - WOOL LIBRARY □ Laramie, WY

Larsgaard, Mary, Map Libn.
COLORADO SCHOOL OF MINES - ARTHUR LAKES LIBRARY □ Golden, CO

Larson, Andre P., Dir.
SHRINE TO MUSIC MUSEUM □ Vermillion, SD

Larson, Arne B., Res.Cons.
SHRINE TO MUSIC MUSEUM □ Vermillion, SD

Larson, Butzer, Info.Spec.
MEALS FOR MILLIONS/FREEDOM FROM HUNGER FOUNDATION - LIBRARY □ Santa Monica, CA

Larson, Donald F., Counsel
NEW YORK STATE CONFERENCE OF MAYORS AND MUNICIPAL OFFICIALS - LIBRARY □ Albany, NY

Larson, E. Joseph, Pub.Info.Off.
U.S. SOIL CONSERVATION SERVICE - NATIONAL PHOTOGRAPHIC LIBRARY □ Washington, DC

Larson, Mrs. Einar M., Libn.
STRATFORD HISTORICAL SOCIETY - LIBRARY □ Stratford, CT

Larson, Evva L., Asst.State Libn.
IDAHO STATE LIBRARY - REGIONAL LIBRARY FOR THE BLIND AND PHYSICALLY HANDICAPPED □ Boise, ID

Larson, Gretchen S., Asst.Libn.
CASE WESTERN RESERVE UNIVERSITY - MATTHEW A. BAXTER SCHOOL OF LIBRARY & INFORMATION SCIENCE □ Cleveland, OH

Larson, Jean, Exec. V.P.
ROA FILMS - LIBRARY □ Milwaukee, WI

Larson, Joan, Hd., Circ.Dept.
SOUTH DAKOTA STATE UNIVERSITY - HILTON M. BRIGGS LIBRARY □ Brookings, SD

Larson, Joel D., Coord., Film Lib.
UNIVERSITY OF WISCONSIN, MADISON - BUREAU OF AUDIOVISUAL INSTRUCTION - LIBRARY □ Madison, WI

Larson, John Lauritz, Hist.
CONNER PRAIRIE PIONEER SETTLEMENT - RESEARCH DEPARTMENT LIBRARY □ Noblesville, IN

Larson, Julian, Libn.
OHIO STATE UNIVERSITY - CENTER FOR HUMAN RESOURCE RESEARCH - LIBRARY □ Worthington, OH

Larson, R., Info.Spec.
BURROUGHS WELLCOME COMPANY - LIBRARY □ Research Triangle Park, NC

Larson, Ronald, Principal Planner
GLENDALE CITY - PLANNING DIVISION - TECHNICAL LIBRARY □ Glendale, CA

Larson, Ronald J., Hd.Libn.
WISCONSIN STATE JOURNAL - LIBRARY □ Madison, WI

Larson, Signe, Chf., Info.Serv.
U.S. DEPT. OF HOUSING AND URBAN DEVELOPMENT - LIBRARY □ Washington, DC

Larson, Stanley, Ref.Libn.
AEROSPACE CORPORATION - CHARLES C. LAURITSEN LIBRARY □ Los Angeles, CA

Larson, Victor J., Info.Spec.
UNIVERSITY OF WISCONSIN, MILWAUKEE - GRADUATE SCHOOL - OFFICE OF RESEARCH - INFORMATION LIBRARY □ Milwaukee, WI

Larter, Cynthia A., Libn.
REED, SMITH, SHAW AND MC CLAY - LAW LIBRARY □ Pittsburgh, PA

LaRue, O. Jane, Coll. Botanist
UNIVERSITY OF MICHIGAN - MATTHAEI BOTANICAL GARDENS - LIBRARY □ Ann Arbor, MI

LaRue, Suzanne, Clinical Libn., Surgery
HARTFORD HOSPITAL - HEALTH SCIENCE LIBRARIES □ Hartford, CT

Larzelere, David W., Chf.Libn.
FLINT JOURNAL - EDITORIAL LIBRARY □ Flint, MI

PERSONNEL

Lasalle, D., ILL
CANADA - FISHERIES & OCEANS - LIBRARY □
Ottawa, ON

Lasater, Mary Charles, Monographs Libn.
VANDERBILT UNIVERSITY - MEDICAL CENTER
LIBRARY □ Nashville, TN

Lash, Barry, Hd.Libn.
SUNY - AGRICULTURAL AND TECHNICAL
COLLEGE AT ALFRED - WALTER C. HINKLE
MEMORIAL LIBRARY □ Alfred, NY

Lashley, Mark W., Med.Libn.
FLOYD MEDICAL CENTER - LIBRARY □ Rome,
GA

Laskovski, R. Peter, Musm.Dir. & Libn.
SHAKER MUSEUM FOUNDATION - EMMA B.
KING LIBRARY □ Old Chatham, NY

Lasky, Sylvia C., Children's Libn.
FLORES (Nieves M.) MEMORIAL LIBRARY □
Agana, GU

Lass, Dr. William E., Dir.
MINNESOTA HISTORICAL SOCIETY -
SOUTHERN MINNESOTA HISTORICAL CENTER
□ Mankato, MN

Lassanske, Vivian, Libn.
SAN LUIS OBISPO COUNTY PLANNING
DEPARTMENT - TECHNICAL INFORMATION
LIBRARY □ San Luis Obispo, CA

Lassleben, Lauren, Asst.Archv.
MAGNES (Judah L.) MEMORIAL MUSEUM -
WESTERN JEWISH HISTORY CENTER □
Berkeley, CA

Lasslo, Wilma R., Circ.Libn.
UNIVERSITY OF TENNESSEE - CENTER FOR
THE HEALTH SCIENCES LIBRARY □ Memphis,
TN

Lasworth, M. Louise, Ser.Supv.
SEARLE (G.D.) & CO. - RESEARCH LIBRARY □
Skokie, IL

Laszlo, George A., Mgr.
AYERST LABORATORIES - MEDICAL
INFORMATION CENTER □ New York, NY

Laszlo, Marcia, Asst.Musm.Libn.
METROPOLITAN MUSEUM OF ART - THOMAS J.
WATSON LIBRARY □ New York, NY

Lataniotis, Dolores, Libn.
FORBES, INC. - LIBRARY □ New York, NY

Latendresse, Raymond, Sr.Lit.Chem.
INTERNATIONAL FLAVORS AND FRAGRANCES,
INC. - TECHNICAL INFORMATION CENTER □
Union Beach, NJ

Latham, Ronald G., Dir.
EDWARDS (Jacob) LIBRARY □ Southbridge, MA

Lathey, Cambell, Asst.Libn.
NEW YORK STATE LIBRARY - SCIENCES/
HEALTH SCIENCES/TECHNOLOGY REFERENCE
SERVICES □ Albany, NY

Lathrop, Alan K., Cur.
UNIVERSITY OF MINNESOTA - MANUSCRIPTS
DIVISION □ St. Paul, MN

Lathrop, Ann, Coord.Lib.Serv.
SAN MATEO COUNTY EDUCATIONAL
RESOURCES CENTER □ Redwood City, CA

Lathrop, Irene, Dir. of Lib.Serv.
RHODE ISLAND HOSPITAL - PETERS HEALTH
SCIENCES LIBRARY □ Providence, RI

Lathrop, Mary Lou, Mgr.
LATHROP (Norman) ENTERPRISES - LIBRARY □
Wooster, OH

Latimer, Ira H., Exec. V.P.
AMERICAN FEDERATION OF SMALL BUSINESS -
INFORMATION CENTER □ Chicago, IL

Latour, Terry, Asst.Cur.
UNIVERSITY OF SOUTHERN MISSISSIPPI - MC
CAIN LIBRARY □ Hattiesburg, MS

Latta, Barbara, Hd.Libn.
ST. LOUIS PARK MEDICAL CENTER-RESEARCH
FOUNDATION - ARNESON LIBRARY □
Minneapolis, MN

Latus, Jane Keating, Hd.Libn.
BOSTON CITY HOSPITAL - NURSING - MORSE-
SLANGER LIBRARY □ Boston, MA

Latus, Sheila, Med.Libn.
KAISER-PERMANENTE MEDICAL CENTER -
HEALTH SCIENCES LIBRARY □ San Diego, CA

Latzke, Henry R., Dir., Lib.Serv.
CONCORDIA TEACHERS COLLEGE - KLINCK
MEMORIAL LIBRARY □ River Forest, IL

Lau, Anna, Coord., Info.Rsrcs.
ONTARIO - MINISTRY OF EDUCATION -
INFORMATION CENTRE □ Toronto, ON

Lau, Gene, Keyworder/Abstracter
ALBERTA RESEARCH COUNCIL - ALBERTA OIL
SANDS INFORMATION CENTRE □ Edmonton, AB

Lau, Ray D., Lib.Dir.
NORTHWESTERN OKLAHOMA STATE
UNIVERSITY - LIBRARY □ Alva, OK

Laub, Barbara, Instr./Liaison Libn.
STEVENS INSTITUTE OF TECHNOLOGY -
SAMUEL C. WILLIAMS LIBRARY □ Hoboken, NJ

Laubacher, Marilyn, User Serv.Libn.
ERIC CLEARINGHOUSE ON INFORMATION
RESOURCES □ Syracuse, NY

Laube, Lois, Act.Div.Hd.
INDIANAPOLIS-MARION COUNTY PUBLIC
LIBRARY - SOCIAL SCIENCE DIVISION □
Indianapolis, IN

Laubental, Min-Ja, Dir., Lib.Serv.
BRITISH COLUMBIA - MINISTRY OF HEALTH -
MENTAL HEALTH PROGRAMS - STAFF
REFERENCE LIBRARY □ Port Coquitlam, BC

Laudahn, Ruth, Act.Libn.
ALLEN COUNTY LAW LIBRARY □ Lima, OH

Laude, Walter, Asst.Libn.
INDIANA UNIVERSITY OF PENNSYLVANIA -
UNIVERSITY LIBRARY □ Indiana, PA

Lauderdale, Kenneth, Libn.
GENERAL ELECTRIC COMPANY - WILLIAM
STANLEY LIBRARY† □ Pittsfield, MA

Laue, Stephen, Data User Serv.Off.
U.S. BUREAU OF THE CENSUS - REGIONAL
DATA USER SERVICE - CHICAGO REGIONAL
OFFICE - LIBRARY □ Chicago, IL

Lauer, C.F., Ref.
MC DONNELL DOUGLAS CORPORATION - MC
DONNELL AIRCRAFT LIBRARY □ St. Louis, MO

Lauer, Jonathan, Hd., Pub.Serv.
WHEATON COLLEGE - LIBRARY □ Wheaton, IL

Lauer, Dr. Joseph, Libn. Sahel Doc.Ctr.
MICHIGAN STATE UNIVERSITY -
INTERNATIONAL LIBRARY □ East Lansing, MI

Lauer, Dr. Joseph J., Ed. & Libn.
MICHIGAN STATE UNIVERSITY -
INTERNATIONAL LIBRARY - SAHEL
DOCUMENTATION CENTER □ East Lansing, MI

Lauer, Judy A., Libn.
HANCOCK, ESTABROOK, RYAN, SHOVE & HUST
- LAW LIBRARY □ Syracuse, NY

Laufer, Marilyn, Educ.Cur.
SIOUX CITY ART CENTER ASSOCIATION -
LIBRARY □ Sioux City, IA

Laufer, Samuel, Asst.Libn.
YESHIVA TORAH VODAATH AND MESIFTA -
TORAH VODAATH LIBRARY □ Brooklyn, NY

Laughlin, Karen, Ref.Libn.
STATE HISTORICAL SOCIETY OF IOWA -
LIBRARY □ Iowa City, IA

Laughlin, M.C., Libn.
IDS LIFE INSURANCE COMPANY - LIBRARY □
Minneapolis, MN

Laughlin, Patricia, Libn.
MILWAUKEE PUBLIC MUSEUM - REFERENCE
LIBRARY □ Milwaukee, WI

Laughlin, Sarah B., Dir.
VERMONT INSTITUTE OF NATURAL SCIENCES
- LIBRARY □ Woodstock, VT

Laughlin, Winston M., Soil Sci.
UNIVERSITY OF ALASKA - ALASKA
AGRICULTURAL EXPERIMENT STATION -
LIBRARY □ Palmer, AK

Laughon, Barbara, Res.Libn.
OHIO STATE LEGISLATIVE SERVICE
COMMISSION - RESEARCH LIBRARY □
Columbus, OH

Laughton, Mary Frances, Hd.
CANADA - AIR POLLUTION TECHNICAL
INFORMATION SECTION □ Ottawa, ON

Laukaitis, Clarissa D., Libn.
WATERBURY AMERICAN-REPUBLICAN -
LIBRARY □ Waterbury, CT

Laukes, Jim, Ed.
OUTLOOK - OUTLOOK ACCESS CENTER □ Park
Forest, IL

Laundy, Philip A.C., Dir., Research Br.
CANADA - LIBRARY OF PARLIAMENT □ Ottawa,
ON

Lauria, Elaine, Circuit-Rider Libn.
UNIVERSITY OF SOUTHERN CALIFORNIA -
HEALTH SCIENCES CAMPUS - NORRIS
MEDICAL LIBRARY □ Los Angeles, CA

Laurin, Mala, Dir., Info.Serv.
GOULD INC. - GOULD INFORMATION CENTER □
Rolling Meadows, IL

Laurin, Michele, Tech.Libn.
GESTAS INC. - DOCUMENTATION CENTER □
Montreal, PQ

Laurinaitis, Bro. Bernard, S.M.
SOCIETY OF MARY - CINCINNATI PROVINCE -
ARCHIVES □ Dayton, OH

Laursen, Irene S., Science Libn.
WELLESLEY COLLEGE - SCIENCE LIBRARY □
Wellesley, MA

Lautaret, Ronald, Asst.Dir., Pub.Serv.
UNIVERSITY OF ALASKA, ANCHORAGE -
LIBRARY □ Anchorage, AK

Lautenschlager, Beth, Sr.Info.Spec.
WILLIAM H. RORER, INC. - RESEARCH LIBRARY
□ Fort Washington, PA

Lauterman, Frieda, Libn.
AGUDATH ISRAEL CONGREGATION - MALCA
PASS MEMORIAL LIBRARY □ Ottawa, ON

Lauver, Marvin E., Hd.Libn.
INTERNORTH - LIBRARY □ Omaha, NE

Laux, Barbara, Cat.Libn.
CHRIST THE KING SEMINARY - LIBRARY □ East
Aurora, NY

Lauzon, Helene, Hd.Libn.
HOPITAL MAISONNEUVE-ROSEMONT -
SERVICE DES BIBLIOTHEQUES □ Montreal, PQ

Lauzon, Helene, Documentalist
MONTREAL ASSOCIATION FOR THE MENTALLY
RETARDED - DOCUMENTATION CENTRE† □
Montreal, PQ

Lauzon, Maurice G., Libn.
NEW BEDFORD STANDARD-TIMES LIBRARY □
New Bedford, MA

Lavelli, Celeste, Asst.Libn.
AMERICAN LIBRARY ASSOCIATION -
HEADQUARTERS LIBRARY □ Chicago, IL

Lavendel, Giuliana A., Mgr.
XEROX CORPORATION - PALO ALTO RESEARCH
CENTER - TECHNICAL INFORMATION CENTER
□ Palo Alto, CA

Lavender, Jean, Asst.Libn.
UNIVERSITY OF TORONTO - FACULTY OF
MUSIC LIBRARY □ Toronto, ON

LaVerdi, Adelaide L., Hd.Cat.
SUNY - COLLEGE AT GENESEO - MILNE
LIBRARY □ Geneseo, NY

Lavergne, Rodolphe, Chf.Libn.
ECOLE DES HAUTES ETUDES COMMERCIALES
DE MONTREAL - BIBLIOTHEQUE □ Montreal, PQ

Lavery, Lucille, Sr.Lib.Asst.
CONNAUGHT LABORATORIES, LTD. - BALMER
NEILLY LIBRARY □ Willowdale, ON

Lavich, Norma, Music Libn.
CANADIAN BROADCASTING CORPORATION -
MUSIC & RECORD LIBRARY □ Winnipeg, MB

Lavigne, Leo, Cur.
ROYAL CANADIAN ORDNANCE CORPS MUSEUM
- LIBRARY □ Montreal, PQ

LaVigne, Norma, Asst.Libn.
NATIONAL ECUMENICAL COALITION, INC. -
LIBRARY □ Washington, DC

Lavigueur, Lucile, Libn.
ST. MARY'S HOSPITAL - MEDICAL LIBRARY □
Montreal, PQ

Lavilla, Sonia, ILL
HAHNEMANN MEDICAL COLLEGE & HOSPITAL - WARREN H. FAKE LIBRARY □ Philadelphia, PA

Lavine, Judy, Asst.Libn.
U.S. COURT OF APPEALS, 1ST CIRCUIT - LIBRARY □ Boston, MA

Laviolette, James, Ref.Libn.
RENSSELAER POLYTECHNIC INSTITUTE - FOLSOM LIBRARY □ Troy, NY

Lavoy, Constance J., Lib.Serv.Supv.
UNION CARBIDE AGRICULTURAL PRODUCTS COMPANY, INC. - LIBRARY □ Research Triangle Park, NC

Law, Daniel, Info.Spec.
MILES LABORATORIES, INC. - LIBRARY RESOURCES AND SERVICES □ Elkhart, IN

Law, Gordon T., Ref.Libn.
CORNELL UNIVERSITY - MARTIN P. CATHERWOOD LIBRARY OF INDUSTRIAL AND LABOR RELATIONS □ Ithaca, NY

Law, John W., Libn.
DECATUR MEMORIAL HOSPITAL - HEALTH SCIENCE LIBRARY □ Decatur, IL

Law, Leanne, Libn.
SELKIRK MENTAL HEALTH CENTRE - CENTRAL LIBRARY □ Selkirk, MB

Law, Libby, Field Serv.Libn.
SOUTH CAROLINA STATE LIBRARY □ Columbia, SC

Lawhon, Deborah D., Libn.
SOUTHERN BELL TELEPHONE AND TELEGRAPH COMPANY - LAW LIBRARY □ Atlanta, GA

Lawing, Hugh A., Hist.
U.S. NATL. PARK SERVICE - ANDREW JOHNSON NATL. HISTORIC SITE - LIBRARY □ Greeneville, TN

Lawler, Frances, Mgr.
CHURCH OF THE INCARNATION - MARMION LIBRARY □ Dallas, TX

Lawrance, D., Regional Adv.
CANADA - STATISTICS CANADA - ADVISORY SERVICES - REGINA REFERENCE CENTRE □ Regina, SK

Lawrence, A.R., Chf., Adm.Oper.Div.
U.S. NATL. HIGHWAY TRAFFIC SAFETY ADMINISTRATION - TECHNICAL REFERENCE BRANCH □ Washington, DC

Lawrence, Anne M., Med.Libn.
U.S. VETERANS ADMINISTRATION (NY-Syracuse) - MEDICAL CENTER LIBRARY □ Syracuse, NY

Lawrence, Deirdre, Cat.
MUSEUM OF FINE ARTS - WILLIAM MORRIS HUNT MEMORIAL LIBRARY □ Boston, MA

Lawrence, Duncan, Tech.Libn.
M.P.K. OMEGA COMPANY - BIOSCIENCE LIBRARY □ Amarillo, TX

Lawrence, Ellspath, Libn.
FOREIGN SERVICES RESEARCH INSTITUTE - LIBRARY □ Washington, DC

Lawrence, Essie, Site Mgr.
U.S. NATL. PARK SERVICE - FREDERICK DOUGLASS MEMORIAL HOME - LIBRARY □ Washington, DC

Lawrence, John P., Coord. Music Lib.
CANADIAN BROADCASTING CORPORATION - MUSIC LIBRARY □ Toronto, ON

Lawrence, John P., Coord.
CANADIAN BROADCASTING CORPORATION - RECORD LIBRARY† □ Toronto, ON

Lawrence, Lesley-Ann, Law Libn.
ROBINSON, CUTLER, SHEPPARD, BORENSTEIN, SHAPIRO, LANGLOIS & FLAM - LAW LIBRARY □ Montreal, PQ

Lawrence, Mollie, Info.Spec.-Bus.
POLYSAR, LTD. - INFORMATION CENTRE □ Sarnia, ON

Lawrence, Philip D., Jr., Supv., Info.Serv.
WESTPOINT PEPPERELL RESEARCH CENTER - INFORMATION SERVICES LIBRARY □ Shawmut, AL

Lawrence, Robert, Sci.-Tech.Ref.Libn.
OREGON STATE UNIVERSITY - WILLIAM JASPER KERR LIBRARY □ Corvallis, OR

Lawrence, Wendy, Pub.Serv.
OHIO NORTHERN UNIVERSITY - COLLEGE OF LAW - JAY P. TAGGART MEMORIAL LAW LIBRARY □ Ada, OH

Lawrenz-Miller, Dr. Susanne, Assoc.Dir.
LOS ANGELES - DEPARTMENT OF RECREATION AND PARKS - CABRILLO MARINE MUSEUM - LIBRARY □ San Pedro, CA

Lawson, Bennett F., Chf., Lib.Serv.
U.S. VETERANS ADMINISTRATION (KS-Leavenworth) - CENTER MEDICAL LIBRARY □ Leavenworth, KS

Lawson, C.
SPOTSYLVANIA HISTORICAL ASSOCIATION, INC. - RESEARCH MUSEUM AND LIBRARY □ Spotsylvania, VA

Lawson, Christina, Supv., Archv.
U.S. PRESIDENTIAL LIBRARIES - LYNDON B. JOHNSON LIBRARY† □ Austin, TX

Lawson, Constance, Res.Libn.
LONE STAR GAS COMPANY - RESEARCH LIBRARY □ Dallas, TX

Lawson, J.E., Chf. Geophysicist
OKLAHOMA GEOLOGICAL SURVEY - OKLAHOMA GEOPHYSICAL OBSERVATORY LIBRARY □ Leonard, OK

Lawson, James R., Libn.
SOCIETAS CAMPANARIORUM - LIBRARY □ New York, NY

Lawson, Jane A., Per.Libn.
EMORY UNIVERSITY - PITTS THEOLOGY LIBRARY □ Atlanta, GA

Lawson, Judith, Asst.Libn.
CONGREGATION BETH ACHIM - JOSEPH KATKOWSKY LIBRARY □ Livonia, MI

Lawson, Lonnie, Sci.Libn.
CENTRAL MISSOURI STATE UNIVERSITY - WARD EDWARDS LIBRARY □ Warrensburg, MO

Lawson, Mary, Libn.
MINNEAPOLIS PUBLIC LIBRARY & INFORMATION CENTER - BUSINESS AND SCIENCE DEPARTMENT □ Minneapolis, MN

Lawson, Roger, Cat.
NATIONAL GALLERY OF ART - LIBRARY □ Washington, DC

Lawson, Sandra L., Med.Libn.
FORSYTH MEMORIAL HOSPITAL - JOHN C. WHITAKER LIBRARY □ Winston-Salem, NC

Lawson, Wayne, Rec.Ctr.Mgr.
WASHINGTON STATE OFFICE OF SECRETARY OF STATE - DIVISION OF ARCHIVES AND RECORD MANAGEMENT □ Olympia, WA

Lawton, Elizabeth B., Libn.
AMERICAN PSYCHOLOGICAL ASSOCIATION - ARTHUR W. MELTON LIBRARY □ Arlington, VA

Lawton, Natalie V., Libn.
WESTERLY HOSPITAL - MEDICAL LIBRARY □ Westerly, RI

Lawton, P.A., Registrar
MUSEUM OF INDIAN HERITAGE - LIBRARY □ Indianapolis, IN

Laxer, Carol C., Dental Libn.
UNIVERSITY OF OREGON HEALTH SCIENCES CENTER - DENTAL LIBRARY† □ Portland, OR

Lay, Douglas H., Dir., Lib.Serv.
WAUSAU INSURANCE COMPANIES - LIBRARY □ Wausau, WI

Lay, William, Jr., Musm.Cur.
TIOGA COUNTY HISTORICAL SOCIETY MUSEUM - LIBRARY □ Owego, NY

Layaou, Cora, Govt.Doc.Libn.
OHIO NORTHERN UNIVERSITY - HETERICK MEMORIAL LIBRARY □ Ada, OH

Laycock, Dr. Anita, Libn.
HALIFAX INFIRMARY - HEALTH SERVICES LIBRARY† □ Halifax, NS

Layman, Mary F., Libn.
U.S. FISH & WILDLIFE SERVICE - WILDLIFE RESEARCH CENTER LIBRARY □ Denver, CO

Layman, Velma, Circ.Libn.
WITTENBERG UNIVERSITY - THOMAS LIBRARY □ Springfield, OH

Layne, Cathy, Libn.
TELEDYNE ENERGY SYSTEMS - LIBRARY □ Timonium, MD

Layton, Beth A., Libn.
WINCHESTER MEMORIAL HOSPITAL - HEALTH SCIENCES LIBRARY □ Winchester, VA

Layton, Mrs. S.A., Libn.
PEAT, MARWICK & PARTNERS - LIBRARY □ Toronto, ON

Lazar, Dr. David, Rabbi
OHEB ZEDECK SYNAGOGUE CENTER - LIBRARY □ Pottsville, PA

Lazar, Nancy, Libn.
U.S. COURT OF APPEALS, DISTRICT OF COLUMBIA CIRCUIT - LIBRARY □ Washington, DC

Lazar, Pamela L., Libn.
SOUTHEAST MICHIGAN COUNCIL OF GOVERNMENTS - LIBRARY □ Detroit, MI

Lazarevic, Martha, Tech.Serv.Libn.
FORD FOUNDATION - LIBRARY □ New York, NY

Lazewski, Barbara A., Tech.Libn.
RAY-O-VAC CORP. - TECHNOLOGY CENTER LIBRARY □ Madison, WI

Le Blanc, F.U., Hd., Rec.Mgt.Div.
NEW BRUNSWICK - PROVINCIAL ARCHIVES OF NEW BRUNSWICK □ Fredericton, NB

Le Blanc, J.-M., Hd., Res./Inq.Serv.
CANADA - PUBLIC ARCHIVES OF CANADA - MANUSCRIPT DIVISION □ Ottawa, ON

Le Borgne, Louis, Documentaliste
UNIVERSITE DU QUEBEC A MONTREAL - CENTRE DE DOCUMENTATION EN SCIENCES HUMAINES □ Montreal, PQ

Le Butt, Katherine, Regional Libn.
YORK REGIONAL LIBRARY - BIBLIOTHEQUE DR. MARGUERITE MICHAUD □ Fredericton, NB

Le Guern, Chuck, Info.Sci.
AMERICAN CYANAMID COMPANY - AGRICULTURAL RESEARCH DIVISION - TECHNICAL INFORMATION SERVICES □ Princeton, NJ

Le Veille, Linda L., Info.Spec.
REXNORD, INC. - TECHNICAL LIBRARY □ Milwaukee, WI

Lea, Keith F., Dir., Tech.Serv.
UNIVERSITY OF WISCONSIN, STEVENS POINT - JAMES H. ALBERTSON CENTER FOR LEARNING RESOURCES □ Stevens Point, WI

Leach, Lois V., Libn.
U.S. ARMED FORCES STAFF COLLEGE - LIBRARY □ Norfolk, VA

Leach, Sally, Asst. to the Dir.
UNIVERSITY OF TEXAS, AUSTIN - HUMANITIES RESEARCH CENTER □ Austin, TX

Leach, Sharon, Res.Dir.
WHITCOM INVESTMENT COMPANY - RESEARCH LIBRARY □ New York, NY

Leachman, James, Field Libn.
INDIANA HISTORICAL SOCIETY - WILLIAM HENRY SMITH MEMORIAL LIBRARY □ Indianapolis, IN

Leadbeater, David S., Sr.Rec.Libn.
CANADIAN BROADCASTING CORPORATION - MUSIC & RECORD LIBRARY □ Halifax, NS

Leadenham, Douglas J., Hd.
INDIANA UNIVERSITY - SWAIN HALL LIBRARY □ Bloomington, IN

Leaf, Donald, Hd., Tech.Proc.
MICHIGAN STATE LIBRARY SERVICES □ Lansing, MI

Leahy, Margaret T., Libn.
CANADA - SUPPLY & SERVICE CANADA - CANADIAN GOVERNMENT EXPOSITIONS CENTRE - TECHNICAL LIBRARY □ Ottawa, ON

PERSONNEL

Leahy, Mary Ann, Libn.
LATHROP, KOONTZ, RIGHTER, CLAGETT &
NORQUIST - LIBRARY □ Kansas City, MO

Leahy, Mary F., Supv./Libn.
MITRE CORPORATION - CORPORATE LIBRARY†
□ Bedford, MA

Learner, Robert, Musm.Dir.
KINGMAN MUSEUM OF NATURAL HISTORY -
LIBRARY □ Battle Creek, MI

Leary, Margaret A., Asst.Dir.
UNIVERSITY OF MICHIGAN - LAW LIBRARY □
Ann Arbor, MI

Leary, Suzanne, Asst. Law Libn.
NORTH CAROLINA CENTRAL UNIVERSITY -
LAW LIBRARY □ Durham, NC

Leavens, Bill, Chf.
U.S. VETERANS ADMINISTRATION (MI-Allen
Park) - MEDICAL CENTER LIBRARY SERVICE
(142D) □ Allen Park, MI

Leavitt, Donald L., Chf.
LIBRARY OF CONGRESS - MUSIC DIVISION □
Washington, DC

Leavitt, Edward P., Libn.
TUFTS UNIVERSITY - SCHOOLS OF MEDICINE,
DENTAL MEDICINE & VETERINARY MEDICINE -
HEALTH SCIENCES LIBRARY† □ Boston, MA

Lebans, Mrs. A.R., Archv.
ANGLICAN CHURCH OF CANADA - DIOCESE OF
MONTREAL - ARCHIVES† □ Montreal, PQ

LeBaron, B.B., Tech. Data Libn.
LOCKHEED MISSILES & SPACE COMPANY, INC.
- TECHNICAL INFORMATION CENTER □ Palo
Alto, CA

Lebbin, Lee J., Dir.
MICHIGAN TECHNOLOGICAL UNIVERSITY -
LIBRARY □ Houghton, MI

LeBeau, Constance J., Libn.
XEROX CORPORATION - GINN AND COMPANY
LIBRARY □ Lexington, MA

LeBel, Grace, Libn.
UNIVERSITY OF CALGARY - KANANASKIS
CENTRE FOR ENVIRONMENTAL RESEARCH -
LIBRARY □ Calgary, AB

LeBel, Jocelyn, Dir.
NEW BRUNSWICK - LEGISLATIVE LIBRARY □
Fredericton, NB

LeBlanc, Eric S., Libn.
CANADA - NATIONAL RESEARCH COUNCIL -
CISTI - DOMINION ASTROPHYSICAL
OBSERVATORY - LIBRARY □ Victoria, BC

LeBlanc, J., Hd., Rd.Serv.Sect.
CANADA - NATIONAL DEFENCE - NDHQ
LIBRARY □ Ottawa, ON

LeBlanc, Janice, Asst.Libn.
CANADA - NATIONAL DEFENCE - CANADIAN
FORCES COLLEGE - KEITH HODSON MEMORIAL
LIBRARY† □ Toronto, ON

LeBlanc, Jean, Coll.
UNIVERSITY OF OTTAWA - MORISSET
LIBRARY □ Ottawa, ON

Leblanc, Ronald, Libn.
UNIVERSITE DE MONCTON - CENTRE
D'ETUDES ACADIENNES □ Moncton, NB

Leblanc, Virginia, Asst.Med.Libn.
BRYN MAWR HOSPITAL - MEDICAL LIBRARY -
NURSING DIVISION □ Bryn Mawr, PA

Lebovitz, Ellen, Libn.
ATLANTIC RESEARCH CORPORATION -
LIBRARY □ Alexandria, VA

Lebron, Ruben Martinez, Adm.Asst. to Dir.
UNIVERSITY OF PUERTO RICO - MAYAGUEZ
CAMPUS - LIBRARY □ Mayaguez, PR

Lebrun, Louise, Tech.Serv.Libn.
CENTRE DE SERVICES SOCIAUX DU MONTREAL
METROPOLITAIN - BIBLIOTHEQUE □ Montreal,
PQ

LeBus, Betty V., Law Libn.
UNIVERSITY OF MIAMI - SCHOOL OF LAW
LIBRARY □ Coral Gables, FL

Lechner, Marian G., Libn.
CONNECTICUT GENERAL LIFE INSURANCE
COMPANY - LIBRARY □ Hartford, CT

Lechten, Walter, Principal, Relg.Sch.
TEMPLE SINAI - LIBRARY† □ Brookline, MA

Leckie, Rosemary W., Corp.Libn.
CRUM AND FORSTER CORPORATION -
CORPORATE LIBRARY □ Morristown, NJ

LeClair, Daniel P., Res.Spec.
MASSACHUSETTS STATE DEPARTMENT OF
CORRECTION - CENTRAL OFFICE STAFF
LIBRARY □ Boston, MA

LeClair, Micheline, Lib.Techn.
HOTEL-DIEU D'ARTHABASKA - MEDICAL
LIBRARY-DOCUMENTATION SERVICE □
Arthabaska, PQ

LeClaire, Ann, Dir., Lib.Serv.
MIRIAM HOSPITAL - MEDICAL LIBRARY □
Providence, RI

Leclerc, Helene
MONTREAL URBAN COMMUNITY TRANSIT
COMMISSION - LIBRARY □ Montreal, PQ

Leclerc, Michel, Chf.
HYDRO-QUEBEC - INSTITUT DE RECHERCHE -
BIBLIOTHEQUE □ Varennes, PQ

Leclerc, Nancy C., Chf.Libn./Mgr.
BANK OF MONTREAL - HEAD OFFICE LIBRARY □
Montreal, PQ

Leclerc, Ms. P., Chf.Libn.
ALCAN INTERNATIONAL, LTD. - TECHNICAL
INFORMATION CENTRE □ Arvida, PQ

Leclerc-Gauthier, Rita, Cons., Pubn.
UNIVERSITE LAVAL - BIBLIOTHEQUE† □ Ste.
Foy, PQ

Lecompte, Louis-Luc, Asst.
HOPITAL STE-JUSTINE - CENTRE
D'INFORMATION SUR LA SANTE DE L'ENFANT†
□ Montreal, PQ

Lecture, Anne, Dir.
SAN FRANCISCO ACADEMY OF COMIC ART -
LIBRARY □ San Francisco, CA

Ledbetter, Barbara A., Asst.Archv.
FORT BELKNAP ARCHIVES, INC. - LIBRARY □
Newcastle, TX

Ledden, Mildred, Assoc.Libn.
NEW YORK STATE LIBRARY - HUMANITIES
REFERENCE SERVICE □ Albany, NY

Leddy, Edward, Archv.
UNIVERSITY OF BALTIMORE - BALTIMORE
REGION INSTITUTIONAL STUDIES CENTER
(BRISC) □ Baltimore, MD

LeDell, Betty, Libn.
GRACE LUTHERAN CHURCH - LIBRARY □
Wayzata, MN

Ledford, Carole L., Libn.
UNIVERSITY OF GEORGIA - GEORGIA
AGRICULTURAL EXPERIMENT STATION
LIBRARY □ Experiment, GA

Ledford, Edith K., Med.Libn.
MEMORIAL HOSPITAL - MEDICAL LIBRARY □
Danville, VA

Ledford, Edith K., Libn.
MEMORIAL HOSPITAL - SCHOOL OF
PROFESSIONAL NURSING - LIBRARY □ Danville,
VA

Ledford, Elizabeth F., Libn.
CHARLOTTE LAW BUILDING ASSN. -
CHARLOTTE LAW LIBRARY □ Charlotte, NC

Leduc, Lise, Renseignements
HOPITAL STE-JUSTINE - CENTRE
D'INFORMATION SUR LA SANTE DE L'ENFANT†
□ Montreal, PQ

Ledwell, Bill, Chf. of Educ. Media
PRINCE EDWARD ISLAND - DEPARTMENT OF
EDUCATION - MEDIA CENTRE □ Charlottetown,
PE

Ledwell, Sr. Jean-Ann, Pub.Serv.Libn.
CANADIAN NATIONAL INSTITUTE FOR THE
BLIND - NATIONAL LIBRARY SERVICES □
Toronto, ON

Lee, Alice, Asst.Libn.
FAR EAST MERCHANTS ASSOCIATION - FEMAS
TRADE LIBRARY □ Berkeley, CA

Lee, Alice T., Libn.
U.S. AIR FORCE HOSPITAL - MEDICAL LIBRARY
(NM-Kirtland AFB) □ Kirtland AFB, NM

Lee, Alma, Libn.
KANSAS CITY - CITY DEVELOPMENT
DEPARTMENT - LIBRARY □ Kansas City, MO

Lee, Betty, Libn.
ETHYL CORPORATION - RESEARCH
LABORATORIES - RESEARCH LIBRARY □
Ferndale, MI

Lee, Beverly A., Libn.
UNIVERSITY OF MINNESOTA - CHEMISTRY
LIBRARY □ Minneapolis, MN

Lee, Mr. Boon T., Tech.Serv.Libn.
WINSTON-SALEM STATE UNIVERSITY -
O'KELLY LIBRARY □ Winston-Salem, NC

Lee, Carolyn T., Cur.
CATHOLIC UNIVERSITY OF AMERICA -
CLEMENTINE LIBRARY □ Washington, DC

Lee, Carolyn T., Cur.
CATHOLIC UNIVERSITY OF AMERICA -
SEMITICS - INSTITUTE OF CHRISTIAN
ORIENTAL RESEARCH (ICOR) LIBRARY □
Washington, DC

Lee, Charles E., Dir.
SOUTH CAROLINA STATE DEPARTMENT OF
ARCHIVES & HISTORY - ARCHIVES SEARCH
ROOM □ Columbia, SC

Lee, Charles W., Dir.
LIMA STATE HOSPITAL - RESIDENTS &
PROFESSIONAL LIBRARY† □ Lima, OH

Lee, Dennis, ILL
NORTHWEST COLLEGE OF THE ASSEMBLIES OF
GOD - HURST LIBRARY □ Kirkland, WA

Lee, Diane, Cat.
COLUMBIA UNIVERSITY - LAW LIBRARY □ New
York, NY

Lee, Edward, Cat.Libn.
WAYNE STATE UNIVERSITY - ARTHUR NEEF
LAW LIBRARY □ Detroit, MI

Lee, Ernest, Ref.Libn.
GEORGETOWN UNIVERSITY - MEDICAL
CENTER - DAHLGREN MEMORIAL LIBRARY □
Washington, DC

Lee, Esther, Asst.Div.Hd.
QUEENS BOROUGH PUBLIC LIBRARY - ART AND
MUSIC DIVISION □ Jamaica, NY

Lee, Frances, Ref.Libn.
GREENWICH LIBRARY - ORAL HISTORY
PROJECT □ Greenwich, CT

Lee, Fred, Libn.
DOW CORNING CORPORATION - BUSINESS
INFORMATION CENTER □ Midland, MI

Lee, Grace, Doc.Libn.
TEXAS TECH UNIVERSITY - SCHOOL OF LAW
LIBRARY □ Lubbock, TX

Lee, Helen, Libn.
UNION CAMP CORP. - R & D DIVISION LIBRARY
□ Princeton, NJ

Lee, Hyosoo, Tech.Serv.Libn.
CLEVELAND INSTITUTE OF ART - JESSICA R.
GUND MEMORIAL LIBRARY □ Cleveland, OH

Lee, J., Briarcliff Libn.
PACE UNIVERSITY, PLEASANTVILLE/
BRIARCLIFF - LIBRARY □ Pleasantville, NY

Lee, Jane Yu, Libn.
GTE AUTOMATIC ELECTRIC LABORATORIES -
LIBRARY† □ Northlake, IL

Lee, Jeannine, Act.Hd.
SUNY AT BUFFALO - ARCHITECTURE &
ENVIRONMENTAL DESIGN LIBRARY □ Buffalo,
NY

Lee, Joann H., Hd., Rd.Serv.
LAKE FOREST COLLEGE - THOMAS OSCAR
FREEMAN MEMORIAL LIBRARY □ Lake Forest, IL

Lee, Joel M., Libn.
AMERICAN LIBRARY ASSOCIATION -
HEADQUARTERS LIBRARY □ Chicago, IL

Lee, Josephine, Libn./Cat.
OLD ST. MARY'S CHURCH - PAULIST LIBRARY □
San Francisco, CA

Lee, Joyce, Ref.Libn.
NEVADA STATE LIBRARY □ Carson City, NV

Lee, Kathryn, Libn.
COLLEGE OF INSURANCE - WESTERN DIVISION
- LIBRARY □ Los Angeles, CA

Lee, L., Specifications
  U.S. NASA - JOHN F. KENNEDY SPACE CENTER
  - LIBRARY □ Kennedy Space Center, FL
Lee, Mrs. Lila J., Libn.
  HELD-POAGE MEMORIAL HOME & RESEARCH
  LIBRARY □ Ukiah, CA
Lee, Lydia H., Libn.
  EXXON NUCLEAR CO., INC. - RESEARCH &
  TECHNOLOGY CENTER LIBRARY □ Richland, WA
Lee, Malinda C., Assoc.Libn.
  GEORGE WASHINGTON UNIVERSITY -
  NATIONAL LAW CENTER - JACOB BURNS LAW
  LIBRARY □ Washington, DC
Lee, Margaret L., Dir.
  MILES LABORATORIES, INC. - LIBRARY
  RESOURCES AND SERVICES □ Elkhart, IN
Lee, Marianne S., Asst.Libn.
  NORTHERN TRUST COMPANY - LIBRARY □
  Chicago, IL
Lee, Marilyn
  SEARLE (G.D.) & CO. OF CANADA, LIMITED -
  LIBRARY □ Oakville, ON
Lee, Marilyn M., Law Libn.
  FRANKLIN COUNTY TRIAL COURT - LAW
  LIBRARIES □ Greenfield, MA
Lee, Marjorie, Lib.Asst.
  FLORIDA STATE LEGISLATURE - DIVISION OF
  LEGISLATIVE LIBRARY SERVICES □
  Tallahassee, FL
Lee, Martha Ann, Mgr., Tech.Proc.
  MISSISSIPPI STATE RESEARCH AND
  DEVELOPMENT CENTER - INFORMATION
  SERVICES DIVISION □ Jackson, MS
Lee, Minja, Tech.Serv.Libn.
  BARUCH (Bernard M.) COLLEGE OF THE CITY
  UNIVERSITY OF NEW YORK - LIBRARY □ New
  York, NY
Lee, Nadean, Hd.Circ.Libn.
  ARKANSAS STATE UNIVERSITY - DEAN B.
  ELLIS LIBRARY □ State University, AR
Lee, Nancy Craig, Hd., Tech.Serv.
  UNIVERSITY OF LOUISVILLE - KORNHAUSER
  HEALTH SCIENCES LIBRARY □ Louisville, KY
Lee, Oral, Prog.Adm.
  MOUNT DIABLO UNIFIED SCHOOL DISTRICT -
  TEACHERS' PROFESSIONAL LIBRARY □
  Concord, CA
Lee, Pamela, Acq.Libn.
  GEORGETOWN UNIVERSITY - MEDICAL
  CENTER - DAHLGREN MEMORIAL LIBRARY □
  Washington, DC
Lee, Patricia, Ref.Libn.
  UNIVERSITY OF TEXAS MEDICAL BRANCH -
  MOODY MEDICAL LIBRARY □ Galveston, TX
Lee, Paul J., Libn.
  CINCINNATI PUBLIC SCHOOLS -
  PROFESSIONAL LIBRARY† □ Cincinnati, OH
Lee, Penni, Sys.Libn.
  BANK OF NOVA SCOTIA - OPERATIONS
  LIBRARY □ Don Mills, ON
Lee, Richard, Libn.
  STANFORD UNIVERSITY - TANNER MEMORIAL
  PHILOSOPHY LIBRARY □ Stanford, CA
Lee, Rita, Regional Med.Lib.Coord.
  NEW YORK MEDICAL COLLEGE AND THE
  WESTCHESTER ACADEMY OF MEDICINE -
  WESTCHESTER MEDICAL CENTER LIBRARY □
  Valhalla, NY
Lee, Robert, Asst.Libn.
  JEFFERSON (Thomas) UNIVERSITY - SCOTT
  MEMORIAL LIBRARY □ Philadelphia, PA
Lee, Robert A., Hd., Res.Dept.
  UNIVERSAL CITY STUDIOS - RESEARCH
  DEPARTMENT LIBRARY □ Universal City, CA
Lee, Robert D.
  PENNSYLVANIA STATE UNIVERSITY -
  INSTITUTE OF PUBLIC ADMINISTRATION -
  LIBRARY □ University Park, PA
Lee, Rodney, Cur./Ref.
  QUEENS BOROUGH PUBLIC LIBRARY -
  LANGSTON HUGHES COMMUNITY LIBRARY AND
  CULTURAL CENTER □ Corona, NY

Lee, Sara Jane, Site Libn.
  TEXAS INSTRUMENTS, INC. - AUSTIN SITE
  LIBRARY □ Austin, TX
Lee, Shirley, Asst.Ref.Libn.
  RAND CORPORATION - LIBRARY □ Santa
  Monica, CA
Lee, Mrs. Soo, Assoc.Dir.
  WAKE FOREST UNIVERSITY - BOWMAN GRAY
  SCHOOL OF MEDICINE - LIBRARY □ Winston-
  Salem, NC
Lee, Stephen, Bagshaw Comm.Chm.
  TORONTO PUBLIC LIBRARY - MARGUERITE G.
  BAGSHAW COLLECTION □ Toronto, ON
Lee, Takika, Comparative Law Libn
  UNIVERSITY OF WASHINGTON - LAW SCHOOL
  LIBRARY □ Seattle, WA
Lee, Tsun Hai, Dir. of Health Educ.
  KERN COUNTY HEALTH DEPARTMENT - DR.
  MYRNIE A. GIFFORD PUBLIC HEALTH LIBRARY
  □ Bakersfield, CA
Lee, Mr. Wynn, Dir.
  MARK TWAIN MEMORIAL - LIBRARY □ Hartford,
  CT
Leech, Sara, Assoc.
  UNIVERSITY OF KENTUCKY - MEDICAL
  CENTER LIBRARY □ Lexington, KY
Leedale, Joan, Libn.
  DU PONT CANADA, INC. - PATENT DIVISION
  LIBRARY □ Mississauga, ON
Leeds, Edith H., Libn.
  SOCIETY OF FRIENDS - FRIENDS MEETING OF
  WASHINGTON - LIBRARY □ Washington, DC
Leeds, Pauline R., Libn.
  NEW ENGLAND NUCLEAR CORPORATION -
  TECHNICAL LIBRARY □ Boston, MA
Leen, Mary, Libn.
  BOSTONIAN SOCIETY - LIBRARY □ Boston, MA
Leeper, Mrs. Jacque, Resource Ctr.Libn.
  WAYNE PRESBYTERIAN CHURCH - LIBRARY □
  Wayne, PA
Leeper, Mrs. John P., Libn.
  MC NAY (Marion Koogler) ART INSTITUTE -
  LIBRARY □ San Antonio, TX
Leeper, Ruth, Lib.Asst.
  MERRITT (Samuel) HOSPITAL - MEDICAL
  LIBRARY □ Oakland, CA
Leerhoff, Ruth, Asst.Univ.Libn.
  SAN DIEGO STATE UNIVERSITY - MALCOLM A.
  LOVE LIBRARY □ San Diego, CA
Leese, Laura, Med.Libn.
  HORTON (Elizabeth A.) MEMORIAL HOSPITAL -
  MEDICAL LIBRARY □ Middletown, NY
Lefebvre, Diane, Lib.Techn.
  SOCIETE DE DEVELOPPEMENT DE LA BAIE
  JAMES - SERVICE DOCUMENTATION □
  Montreal, PQ
Lefebvre, Marie, Cartothecaire
  UNIVERSITE DU QUEBEC A TROIS-RIVIERES -
  CARTOTHEQUE □ Trois-Rivieres, PQ
LeFevre, Carol, Tech.Info.Spec.
  U.S. DEPT. OF LABOR - OSHA - TECHNICAL
  DATA CENTER □ Washington, DC
Leffingwell, Janna, Cat.Libn.
  STANFORD UNIVERSITY - J. HUGH JACKSON
  LIBRARY □ Stanford, CA
Leffler, Carolyn, Asst.Sec.
  MERCER COUNTY LAW LIBRARY □ Celina, OH
Leffler, Ruth E., Tech.Libn.
  ASSOCIATED TECHNICAL SERVICES, INC. -
  RESEARCH LIBRARY □ Glen Ridge, NJ
Lefkowitz, Robert J., Libn.
  ST. ANTHONY HOSPITAL - O'DONOGHUE
  MEDICAL LIBRARY □ Oklahoma City, OK
Lefkowski, Mary E., Govt.Doc.Libn.
  DICKINSON SCHOOL OF LAW - SHEELY-LEE
  LAW LIBRARY □ Carlisle, PA
Lefort, L., Data Off.
  CANADA - STATISTICS CANADA - ADVISORY
  SERVICES - EDMONTON REFERENCE CENTRE†
  □ Edmonton, AB

Legare, Paul J., Asst. Regional Dir.
  CANADA - STATISTICS CANADA - ADVISORY
  SERVICES - MONTREAL REFERENCE CENTRE □
  Montreal, PQ
Legenbauer, Heidi, Asst.
  TROY TIMES RECORD - LIBRARY □ Troy, NY
LeGendre, Elaine V., Health Sci.Libn.
  LAWRENCE MEMORIAL HOSPITAL OF MEDFORD
  - HEALTH SCIENCES LIBRARY □ Medford, MA
Legendre, Sally, Sr.Libn.
  NEW YORK STATE LIBRARY - LAW/SOCIAL
  SCIENCE REFERENCE SERVICES □ Albany, NY
Legere, Fr. Germain, C.P., Libn.
  CONGREGATION OF THE PASSION - HOLY
  CROSS PROVINCE - PROVINCIAL LIBRARY† □
  Louisville, KY
Legere, Monique, Dir.
  CANADA - CANADIAN INTERNATIONAL
  DEVELOPMENT AGENCY - DEVELOPMENT
  INFORMATION CENTRE □ Hull, PQ
Legett, Anne, Asst.Libn.
  BATON ROUGE STATE-TIMES & MORNING
  ADVOCATE NEWSPAPERS - LIBRARY □ Baton
  Rouge, LA
LeGette, Louise N., Chf.Libn.
  TAMPA TRIBUNE & TAMPA TIMES - LIBRARY □
  Tampa, FL
Legg, Patricia A., First Asst.
  FLINT PUBLIC LIBRARY - ART, MUSIC & DRAMA
  DEPARTMENT □ Flint, MI
Leggett, Lois, Cat.
  WINSTON-SALEM STATE UNIVERSITY -
  O'KELLY LIBRARY □ Winston-Salem, NC
LeGuern, Charles, Tech.Serv.Libn.
  MILES LABORATORIES, INC. - LIBRARY
  RESOURCES AND SERVICES □ Elkhart, IN
Leh, Carol S., Tech.Libn.
  SANDERS & THOMAS, INC. - LIBRARY □
  Pottstown, PA
Lehman, Carol A., Libn.
  GENERAL MOTORS CORPORATION - PUBLIC
  RELATIONS STAFF LIBRARY □ Detroit, MI
Lehman, Jane, Res.Anl., Lib.Sci.
  UNIVERSITY OF ALASKA, ANCHORAGE -
  ARCTIC ENVIRONMENTAL INFORMATION AND
  DATA CENTER □ Anchorage, AK
Lehman, Jane L., Libn.
  U.S. DISTRICT COURT - LAW LIBRARY □
  Anchorage, AK
Lehman, Lois J., Libn.
  PENNSYLVANIA STATE UNIVERSITY - COLLEGE
  OF MEDICINE - GEORGE T. HARRELL LIBRARY □
  Hershey, PA
Lehman, Melissa, Libn./Educ.Rep.
  MEMPHIS STATE UNIVERSITY LIBRARIES -
  C.H. NASH MUSEUM LIBRARY □ Memphis, TN
Lehmann, Lucile, Archv.
  UNIVERSITY OF FLORIDA - COASTAL &
  OCEANOGRAPHIC ENGINEERING DEPARTMENT
  - COASTAL ENGINEERING ARCHIVES □
  Gainesville, FL
Lehnert, Everett L., Pres.
  ST. PETERSBURG HISTORICAL SOCIETY -
  LIBRARY AND ARCHIVES □ St. Petersburg, FL
Lehnhardt, Kathy, Interp.Off.
  CALGARY ZOOLOGICAL SOCIETY - LIBRARY □
  Calgary, AB
Lehnig, Katharine P., Law Libn.
  BUCKS COUNTY LAW LIBRARY □ Doylestown,
  PA
Lehocky, Barbara, Hd., Inst./Res.Serv.
  UNIVERSITY OF MISSOURI, ST. LOUIS -
  THOMAS JEFFERSON LIBRARY □ St. Louis, MO
Lehrer, Susan Frisch, Cur.
  CHESTERWOOD - LIBRARY □ Stockbridge, MA
Lehwaldt, Marliese, Hd.Libn.
  LABATT BREWING COMPANY LIMITED -
  CENTRAL RESEARCH LIBRARY □ London, ON
Leibiger, I., Hd.
  LEIBIGER (O.W.) RESEARCH LABORATORIES,
  INC. - TECHNICAL INFORMATION CENTER† □
  Hoosick Falls, NY

PERSONNEL

Leibovici, Martin M., Libn.
GOLDWATER MEMORIAL HOSPITAL - HEALTH SCIENCES LIBRARY† □ Franklin D. Roosevelt Island, NY

Leibowitz, Margaret, Dp.Dir.
ALASKA STATE DIVISION OF STATE LIBRARIES & MUSEUMS - STATE LIBRARY □ Juneau, AK

Leibowitz, Martin, Asst.Chf.
BROOKLYN PUBLIC LIBRARY - SCIENCE AND INDUSTRY DIVISION □ Brooklyn, NY

Leibtag, Susan, Cat.
JOHNS HOPKINS UNIVERSITY-SCHOOL OF HYGIENE & PUBLIC HEALTH-MATERNAL & CHILD HEALTH/POPULATION DYNAMICS LIB. □ Baltimore, MD

Leiby, Zipora, Chf.Libn.
CLEVELAND COLLEGE OF JEWISH STUDIES - AARON GARBER LIBRARY □ Beachwood, OH

Leichter, Janice, Libn.
MOUNT ZION HEBREW CONGREGATION - TEMPLE LIBRARY □ St. Paul, MN

Leif, Mary D., Libn.
WASHINGTON HOSPITAL - MEDICAL-NURSES' LIBRARY □ Washington, PA

Leifer, Claire, Libn.Asst.
ANALYTIC SERVICES, INC. - TECHNICAL LIBRARY □ Arlington, VA

Leigh, Mrs. Jaroslava, Br.Libn./King's Park
SMITHTOWN LIBRARY □ Smithtown, NY

Leigh, Kathleen A., Libn.
GERMANTOWN HOSPITAL AND MEDICAL CENTER - MEDICAL STAFF LIBRARY □ Philadelphia, PA

Leigh, Kathleen A., Libn.
GERMANTOWN HOSPITAL AND MEDICAL CENTER - NURSING SCHOOL LIBRARY □ Philadelphia, PA

Leightly, Virginia, Acq.
UNIVERSITY OF LOUISVILLE - KORNHAUSER HEALTH SCIENCES LIBRARY □ Louisville, KY

Leighton, Helene, Hd., Comp.Serv.
MASSACHUSETTS GENERAL HOSPITAL - TREADWELL AND PALMER-DAVIS LIBRARY □ Boston, MA

Leighton, Lee W., Asst.Libn., Cat.Serv.
HARVARD UNIVERSITY - LAW SCHOOL LIBRARY □ Cambridge, MA

Leiphart, Patricia, Historic Site Mgr.
PENNSYLVANIA STATE HISTORICAL & MUSEUM COMMISSION - FORT LE BOEUF MUSEUM - LIBRARY □ Waterford, PA

Leipzig, Nancy, Info.Anl.
AMERICAN CRITICAL CARE - INFORMATION CENTER □ McGaw Park, IL

Leishman, Joan L., Libn.
C-I-L INC. - CHEMICALS RESEARCH LABORATORY LIBRARY □ Mississauga, ON

Leishman, Sara, Cur.
CAMBRIA COUNTY HISTORICAL SOCIETY - MUSEUM & LIBRARY □ Ebensburg, PA

Leishman, Wes, Interpretation Chf.
U.S. NATL. PARK SERVICE - CUMBERLAND GAP NATL. HISTORICAL PARK - LIBRARY □ Middlesboro, KY

Leisner, Edward, Med.Libn.
ERIE COUNTY MEDICAL CENTER - MEDICAL LIBRARY □ Buffalo, NY

Leister, Jack, Libn.
UNIVERSITY OF CALIFORNIA, BERKELEY - INSTITUTE OF GOVERNMENTAL STUDIES - LIBRARY □ Berkeley, CA

Leitch, Russell H., Dir.
U.S. DEPT. OF COMMERCE - INTERNATIONAL TRADE ADMINISTRATION - MILWAUKEE DISTRICT OFFICE LIBRARY □ Milwaukee, WI

Leith, Anna R., Hd.
UNIVERSITY OF BRITISH COLUMBIA - WOODWARD BIOMEDICAL LIBRARY □ Vancouver, BC

Leith, David A., Dir.
U.S. FISH & WILDLIFE SERVICE - ABERNATHY SALMON CULTURAL DEVELOPMENT CENTER - RESEARCH & INFO. CENTER □ Longview, WA

Leja, Ilga, Asst.Libn.
NOVA SCOTIA - LEGISLATIVE LIBRARY □ Halifax, NS

Lekisch, Barbara, Rsrcs.Libn.
SIERRA CLUB - WILLIAM E. COLBY MEMORIAL LIBRARY □ San Francisco, CA

Lem, Nancy E., Libn.
HEWLETT-PACKARD COMPANY - HP LABORATORIES - DEER CREEK LIBRARY □ Palo Alto, CA

LeMacher, Claire N., Asst.Cur.
PENSACOLA HISTORICAL SOCIETY - LELIA ABERCROMBIE HISTORICAL LIBRARY □ Pensacola, FL

Lemann, Susan, French Mss.
LOUISIANA STATE MUSEUM - LOUISIANA HISTORICAL CENTER □ New Orleans, LA

Lemaster, Gloria S., Libn.
ALABAMA INSTITUTE FOR THE DEAF AND BLIND - LIBRARY FOR THE BLIND AND PHYSICALLY HANDICAPPED □ Talladega, AL

Lemaster, Regina K., Microfilm Spec.
BOWLING GREEN STATE UNIVERSITY - CENTER FOR ARCHIVAL COLLECTIONS □ Bowling Green, OH

Lemay, Jeannette, Supv.
MONTREAL BOARD OF TRADE - INFORMATION CENTRE □ Montreal, PQ

Lemay, Louise, Chf.Libn.
CENTRE HOSPITALIER STE. JEANNE D'ARC - BIBLIOTHEQUE MEDICALE □ Montreal, PQ

Lembeck, Elaine, Asst.Libn.
GIVAUDAN CORPORATION - LIBRARY □ Clifton, NJ

Lemee, Loretta F., Libn.
RALSTON PURINA COMPANY - TECHNICAL INFORMATION CENTER □ St. Louis, MO

Lemelin, Evelina E., Libn.
CONNECTICUT STATE LIBRARY - LAW LIBRARY AT LITCHFIELD □ Litchfield, CT

Lemieux, Dr. Donald J., State Archv./Dir.
LOUISIANA STATE OFFICE OF THE SECRETARY OF STATE - STATE ARCHIVES AND RECORDS SERVICE □ Baton Rouge, LA

Lemieux, Francine, Ref., Edifice H.
QUEBEC PROVINCE - MINISTERE DES COMMUNICATIONS - BIBLIOTHEQUE ADMINISTRATIVE □ Quebec, PQ

Lemieux, Marcel, Asst.Libn.
COLLEGE UNIVERSITAIRE DE ST. BONIFACE - BIBLIOTHEQUE UNIVERSITAIRE □ Saint-Boniface, MB

Lemire, Camil, Med.Libn.
HOPITAL LOUIS H. LAFONTAINE - BIBLIOTHEQUE □ Montreal, PQ

Lemire, Diane, Aid Libn.
SOCIETE QUEBECOISE D'INITIATIVES PETROLIERES - DOCUMENTATION CENTRE □ Ste. Foy, PQ

Lemkau, Henry L., Jr., Dir.
UNIVERSITY OF MIAMI - SCHOOL OF MEDICINE - LOUIS CALDER MEMORIAL LIBRARY □ Miami, FL

Lemke, Susan, Chf., Spec.Coll.
U.S. NATL. DEFENSE UNIVERSITY - LIBRARY □ Washington, DC

Lemmon, Helen E., Libn.
JOHNSON BIBLE COLLEGE - GLASS MEMORIAL LIBRARY □ Kimberlin Heights Station, TN

Lemmon, Virginia, Ref.
RUTGERS UNIVERSITY, THE STATE UNIVERSITY OF NEW JERSEY - JUSTICE HENRY ACKERSON LIBRARY OF LAW & CRIMINAL JUSTICE □ Newark, NJ

Lemon, Kate, Info.Spec.
LOUISIANA STATE LEGISLATIVE COUNCIL - DIVISION OF INFORMATION SERVICES □ Baton Rouge, LA

Lenig, Wayne, Musm.Adm.
MOHAWK-CAUGHNAWAGA MUSEUM - LIBRARY □ Fonda, NY

Lenk, P.A., Spec.Coll.Asst.
COLBY COLLEGE - MILLER LIBRARY - SPECIAL COLLECTIONS □ Waterville, ME

Lenneberg, Hans, Music Libn.
UNIVERSITY OF CHICAGO - MUSIC COLLECTION □ Chicago, IL

Lenoski, C.G., Asst. Regional Dir.
CANADA - STATISTICS CANADA - ADVISORY SERVICES - VANCOUVER REFERENCE CENTRE □ Vancouver, BC

Lent, D.V., Tech.Info.Adm.
TECHNICAL ASSOCIATION OF THE PULP AND PAPER INDUSTRY - LIBRARY □ Atlanta, GA

Lent, Judith A., Libn.-Ref. & ILL
GENERAL ELECTRIC COMPANY - CORPORATE RESEARCH & DEVELOPMENT - WHITNEY LIBRARY □ Schenectady, NY

Lenthall, Franklyn, Cur.
BOOTHBAY THEATRE MUSEUM □ Boothbay, ME

Lentocha, Pat
ASSOCIATION OF NORTH AMERICAN DIRECTORY PUBLISHERS - PRICE & LEE COMPANY DIRECTORY LIBRARY □ Bellows Falls, VT

Lentz, Edward R., Hd., AV
OHIO HISTORICAL SOCIETY - ARCHIVES-LIBRARY □ Columbus, OH

Lentz, Joyce, Staff Libn.
ELWYN INSTITUTE - PROFESSIONAL LIBRARY □ Elwyn, PA

Lentz, Robert T., Archv.
JEFFERSON (Thomas) UNIVERSITY - SCOTT MEMORIAL LIBRARY □ Philadelphia, PA

Lenz, Ann
CONNECTICUT STATE LIBRARY - LAW LIBRARY AT NEW HAVEN □ New Haven, CT

Leo, May K., Libn.
NYACK COLLEGE - LIBRARY □ Nyack, NY

Leon, Eduardo, Archv.
PUERTO RICO - INSTITUTE OF PUERTO RICAN CULTURE - ARCHIVO GENERAL DE PUERTO RICO □ San Juan, PR

Leon, Judith Mae, Libn.
REED, SMITH, SHAW AND MC CLAY - LAW LIBRARY □ Pittsburgh, PA

Leon, Maurice, Dir.
UNIVERSITY OF WISCONSIN, MADISON - LAW LIBRARY □ Madison, WI

Leonard, Bill, Hd., Graphic Arts Serv.
UNIVERSITY OF OREGON - INSTRUCTIONAL MEDIA CENTER □ Eugene, OR

Leonard, Christine, Cat.
INCO METALS COMPANY - BUSINESS LIBRARY □ Toronto, ON

Leonard, Mrs. D.J., Libn.
SHAWINIGAN CONSULTANTS INC. - LIBRARY □ Montreal, PQ

Leonard, Diane, Supv., Cat.Serv.
CANADIAN BROADCASTING CORPORATION - MUSIC SERVICES LIBRARY □ Montreal, PQ

Leonard, Elsie A., Sect.Chf.
MARYLAND STATE DEPARTMENT OF EDUCATION - DIVISION OF LIBRARY DEVELOPMENT & SERVICES - MEDIA SERVICES CENTER □ Baltimore, MD

Leonard, Gloria, Serv.Dev.Libn.
SEATTLE PUBLIC LIBRARY - DOUGLASS-TRUTH BRANCH LIBRARY □ Seattle, WA

Leonard, Harriet, Ref.Libn.
DUKE UNIVERSITY - DIVINITY SCHOOL LIBRARY □ Durham, NC

Leonard, J.W., Mgr.
IBM CORPORATION - THOMAS J. WATSON RESEARCH CENTER LIBRARY □ Yorktown Heights, NY

Leonard, James B., Cat.
WAKE FOREST UNIVERSITY - LAW LIBRARY □ Winston-Salem, NC

Leonard, Jean, Med.Libn.
MERCY HOSPITAL OF NEW ORLEANS - MEDICAL LIBRARY □ New Orleans, LA

Leonard, Kevin B., Asst.Univ.Archv.
NORTHWESTERN UNIVERSITY - ARCHIVES □
Evanston, IL

Leonard, Lawrence, Chf., Tech.Proc.Br.
U.S. DEPT. OF TRANSPORTATION - LIBRARY
SERVICES DIVISION □ Washington, DC

Leonard, Michael, Info.Anl.
TRACY-LOCKE ADVERTISING AND PUBLIC
RELATIONS, INC. - LIBRARY □ Dallas, TX

Leonard, Nathalie B., Town Hist./Cur.
EDEN HISTORICAL SOCIETY - TOWN
HISTORIAN'S OFFICE AND HISTORICAL
SOCIETY LIBRARY □ Eden, NY

Leonard, Peter H., Dir.
METCO INC. - ENGINEERING LIBRARY □
Westbury, NY

Leonard, Rosalita J., Libn.
NATIONAL WOMAN'S CHRISTIAN
TEMPERANCE UNION - FRANCES E. WILLARD
MEMORIAL LIBRARY □ Evanston, IL

Leonard, Ruth S., Lib.Cons.
PROTESTANT EPISCOPAL CHURCH -
EPISCOPAL DIOCESE OF MASSACHUSETTS -
DIOCESAN LIBRARY AND ARCHIVES □ Boston,
MA

Leonard, Dr. W. Patrick, Dean
CHICAGO STATE UNIVERSITY - DOUGLAS
LIBRARY □ Chicago, IL

Leondar, Judith C., Mgr.
AMERICAN CYANAMID COMPANY -
AGRICULTURAL RESEARCH DIVISION -
TECHNICAL INFORMATION SERVICES □
Princeton, NJ

Leone, Dolores, Educ.Dir.
BETHESDA HOSPITAL - PROFESSIONAL
LIBRARY □ Denver, CO

Leone, Dorothy, Asst.Libn.
SEARS, ROEBUCK AND CO. - MERCHANDISE
DEVELOPMENT AND TESTING LABORATORY -
LIBRARY, DEPARTMENT 817† □ Chicago, IL

Leong, E.B., Sr.Libn.
LOCKHEED MISSILES & SPACE COMPANY, INC.
- TECHNICAL INFORMATION CENTER □ Palo
Alto, CA

Lerch, Barbara, Circ.
ST. ANSELM'S COLLEGE - GEISEL LIBRARY □
Manchester, NH

Lerch, Miriam S., Div.Hd.
CARNEGIE LIBRARY OF PITTSBURGH -
BUSINESS DIVISION □ Pittsburgh, PA

Leredu, Martha, Chf., Lib.Serv.
U.S. VETERANS ADMINISTRATION (WA-
Seattle) - HOSPITAL MEDICAL LIBRARY □
Seattle, WA

Lerner, Adele, Archv.
CORNELL UNIVERSITY - MEDICAL COLLEGE -
LIBRARY □ New York, NY

Lerner, Dr. Israel, Judaic Spec.
BOARD OF JEWISH EDUCATION OF GREATER
NEW YORK - EDUCATIONAL RESOURCE
LIBRARY □ New York, NY

Lerner, Leon L., Exec.Dir.
B'NAI B'RITH CAREER & COUNSELING
SERVICES - LIBRARY □ Baltimore, MD

LeRoy, Jean, Lib.Cons.
ST. PAUL'S EPISCOPAL CHURCH - LIBRARY □
Richmond, VA

Lesh, Dorothy L., Lit. Searcher
MERCK & COMPANY, INC. - CALGON
CORPORATION - INFORMATION CENTER □
Pittsburgh, PA

Lesh, Nancy, Asst.Dir., Tech.Serv.
UNIVERSITY OF ALASKA, ANCHORAGE -
LIBRARY □ Anchorage, AK

Leshendok, Maureen P., Cat.
U.S. INTERNATIONAL TRADE COMMISSION -
LIBRARY □ Washington, DC

LeSieur, B., Acq. & Coll.Libn.
MC GILL UNIVERSITY - MEDICAL LIBRARY □
Montreal, PQ

Lesley, Miriam L., Hd.
FREE LIBRARY OF PHILADELPHIA - ART
DEPARTMENT □ Philadelphia, PA

Leslie, G., Hd., Proc.
U.S. NASA - JOHN F. KENNEDY SPACE CENTER
- LIBRARY □ Kennedy Space Center, FL

Leslie, Gretchen K., Libn.
KRAMER CHIN AND MAYO INC. - LIBRARY □
Seattle, WA

Lesniak, Benjamin A., Libn.
CARBON COUNTY LAW LIBRARY □ Jim Thorpe,
PA

LeSourd, Jill, Libn.
GREENE COUNTY LAW LIBRARY □ Xenia, OH

LeSourd, Margaret S., Assoc.Univ.Libn.
UNIVERSITY OF FLORIDA - URBAN AND
REGIONAL PLANNING DOCUMENTS
COLLECTION □ Gainesville, FL

L'Esperance, Marcelle, Chf.Libn.
HOPITAL NOTRE DAME - MEDICAL LIBRARY □
Montreal, PQ

Lessard, Elizabeth, Libn.
MANCHESTER HISTORIC ASSOCIATION -
LIBRARY □ Manchester, NH

Lesser, Ann, Dir.
WARREN LIBRARY ASSOCIATION - LIBRARY† □
Warren, PA

Lesser, Charles H., Asst.Dir./Archv.
SOUTH CAROLINA STATE DEPARTMENT OF
ARCHIVES & HISTORY - ARCHIVES SEARCH
ROOM □ Columbia, SC

Lesser, Daniel, Dir.
NEW YORK UNIVERSITY - FILM LIBRARY □ New
York, NY

Lessing, Joan, Cur. Oral Hist.Coll.
RESEARCH FOUNDATION FOR JEWISH
IMMIGRATION, INC. - ARCHIVES □ New York,
NY

Lester, Lorraine, Assoc.Libn./Tech.Serv.
UNIVERSITY OF NEW MEXICO - SCHOOL OF
LAW LIBRARY □ Albuquerque, NM

Lester, Marilyn A., Dir. of Lrng.Rsrcs.
NATIONAL COLLEGE OF EDUCATION -
LEARNING RESOURCE CENTERS □ Evanston, IL

LeSueur, C. Robin, Libn.
HARVARD UNIVERSITY - SCHOOLS OF
MEDICINE, DENTAL MEDICINE AND PUBLIC
HEALTH - FRANCIS A. COUNTWAY LIBRARY □
Boston, MA

LeTendre, Louise A., Chf.Libn.
U.S. ARMY CONCEPTS ANALYSIS AGENCY -
LIBRARY □ Bethesda, MD

Lethbridge, Sheila M., Libn.
ORTHOPAEDIC AND ARTHRITIC HOSPITAL -
LIBRARY □ Toronto, ON

Letson, Ruth S., Libn.
TENNESSEE STATE DEPARTMENT OF
TRANSPORTATION - LIBRARY □ Nashville, TN

Lett, Marla, Asst.Libn.
YAVAPAI COUNTY LAW LIBRARY □ Prescott, AZ

Letterman, Lenore, ILL
LONG ISLAND JEWISH-HILLSIDE MEDICAL
CENTER - HILLSIDE DIVISION - HEALTH
SCIENCES LIBRARY □ Glen Oaks, NY

Leung, Joyce, Ref.Libn.
BRIDGEWATER STATE COLLEGE - CLEMENT C.
MAXWELL LIBRARY □ Bridgewater, MA

Leutenegger, Fr. Benedict, Archv.
OUR LADY OF THE LAKE UNIVERSITY - OLD
SPANISH MISSIONS HISTORICAL RESEARCH
LIBRARY □ San Antonio, TX

Leuzinger, Nancy J., Libn.
DRAVO CORPORATION - LIBRARY □ Pittsburgh,
PA

Lev, Yvonne, Libn.
ENVIRONMENTAL PROTECTION AGENCY -
REGION VI LIBRARY □ Dallas, TX

LeVan, Rose, Pres.
EAST CHICAGO HISTORICAL SOCIETY -
LIBRARY □ East Chicago, IN

Leve, L. Arless, Mgr.
UNION CARBIDE CORPORATION - BUSINESS
LIBRARY □ New York, NY

Levenberg, Charles M., Supv.
OPPENHEIMER, WOLFF, FOSTER, SHEPARD &
DONNELLY - LIBRARY □ St. Paul, MN

Levene, Lee-Allison, Info.Serv.
UNIVERSITY OF KANSAS MEDICAL CENTER -
COLLEGE OF HEALTH SCIENCES AND HOSPITAL
- CLENDENING LIBRARY □ Kansas City, KS

Levering, Philip, AV Cons.
SUFFOLK COOPERATIVE LIBRARY SYSTEM -
AUDIOVISUAL DEPT. □ Bellport, NY

Levesque, J. C., Asst.Libn.
CANADA - ENERGY, MINES & RESOURCES
CANADA - EARTH PHYSICS BRANCH LIBRARY □
Ottawa, ON

Levesque, Margaret
CANADAIR, LTD. - COMPANY LIBRARY† □
Montreal, PQ

Levesque, Raymond, Ref.
CEGEP DE TROIS-RIVIERES - BIBLIOTHEQUE □
Trois-Rivieres, PQ

Levi, Alla F., Dir. of Lib. Serv.
LINCOLN FIRST BANK, NA, INC. - LINCOLN
FIRST LIBRARY □ Rochester, NY

Levi, Dennis L., Chf., Lib.Serv.
U.S. VETERANS ADMINISTRATION (WA-
Tacoma) - MEDICAL CENTER LIBRARY □
Tacoma, WA

Levi, Penny G., Libn.
ST. MARY'S OF THE LAKE HOSPITAL - GIBSON
MEDICAL LIBRARY □ Kingston, ON

Levie, Jane H., Chf.Libn.
U.S. VETERANS ADMINISTRATION (CA-
Livermore) - MEDICAL LIBRARY □ Livermore, CA

Levin, Alvin, Libn.
WILLIAM-FREDERICK PRESS - PAMPHLET
LIBRARY □ New York, NY

Levin, Ann, Libn.
PENINSULA TEMPLE BETH EL - LIBRARY □ San
Mateo, CA

Levin, Arthur, Dir.
CENTER FOR MEDICAL CONSUMERS AND
HEALTH INFORMATION - LIBRARY □ New York,
NY

Levin, Mr. B., Chf.Res.Off.
PEEL COUNTY BOARD OF EDUCATION - J.A.
TURNER PROFESSIONAL LIBRARY □
Mississauga, ON

Levin, Barbara, Asst.Hd., Art Sect.
CHICAGO PUBLIC LIBRARY CULTURAL CENTER
- FINE ARTS DIVISION - ART SECTION □
Chicago, IL

Levin, Ellen J., Mgr., Info.Ctr.
ALUMINUM ASSOCIATION - INFORMATION
CENTER □ Washington, DC

Levin, Judy, Info.Mgr.
MORTON RESEARCH CORPORATION -
BUSINESS INFORMATION CENTER† □ Merrick,
NY

Levine, Amy M., Dir., Info.Serv.
REVLON HEALTH CARE GROUP - INFORMATION
SERVICES DEPARTMENT □ Tuckahoe, NY

Levine, Ellen, Libn.
CANADIAN BROADCASTING CORPORATION -
REFERENCE LIBRARY □ Toronto, ON

Levine, L., Sr.Tech.Info.Spec.
DOW CHEMICAL U.S.A. - TEXAS DIVISION -
LIBRARY □ Freeport, TX

Levine, Marion H., Hd., Ref.Dept.
HARVARD UNIVERSITY - SCHOOLS OF
MEDICINE, DENTAL MEDICINE AND PUBLIC
HEALTH - FRANCIS A. COUNTWAY LIBRARY □
Boston, MA

Levine, Ruth, Libn.
U.S. VETERANS ADMINISTRATION (NY-
Brooklyn) - MEDICAL CENTER LIBRARY □
Brooklyn, NY

Levine, Selma, Libn.
TEMPLE OHABEI SHALOM - LIBRARY □
Brookline, MA

Levinson, Debra, Mgr./Info.Ret.Serv.
NATIONAL BROADCASTING COMPANY, INC. -
REFERENCE LIBRARY □ New York, NY

Levinson, Marilyn I., Cat.
BOWLING GREEN STATE UNIVERSITY -
CENTER FOR ARCHIVAL COLLECTIONS □
Bowling Green, OH

Levinton, Juliette, Libn.
SCHRODER (J. Henry) BANK & TRUST COMPANY - LIBRARY □ New York, NY

Leviton, Elsie, Chm., Lib.Comm.
TEMPLE ISRAEL - LIBRARY □ West Palm Beach, FL

Levitt, Carole, Circ.Libn.
MARSHALL (John) LAW SCHOOL - LIBRARY □ Chicago, IL

Levkovitz, Susan, Chf.Cat.Libn.
CUNY - GRADUATE SCHOOL AND UNIVERSITY CENTER - LIBRARY □ New York, NY

Levstik, Frank R., State Archv.
OHIO HISTORICAL SOCIETY - ARCHIVES-LIBRARY □ Columbus, OH

Levstik, Joseph, Foreign Law Libn.
UNIVERSITY OF MINNESOTA - LAW LIBRARY □ Minneapolis, MN

Levy, Annette R., Dir.
JEWISH FEDERATION OF NASHVILLE AND MIDDLE TENNESSEE - ARCHIVES □ Nashville, TN

Levy, Arlene, Libn.
BLANEY, PASTERNAK, SMELA & WATSON - LAW LIBRARY □ Toronto, ON

Levy, Charlotte L., Libn.
BROOKLYN LAW SCHOOL - LAW LIBRARY □ Brooklyn, NY

Levy, James, Dir.
HARWOOD FOUNDATION LIBRARY OF THE UNIVERSITY OF NEW MEXICO □ Taos, NM

Levy, Jane, Libn./Archv.
MAGNES (Judah L.) MEMORIAL MUSEUM - MORRIS GOLDSTEIN LIBRARY □ Berkeley, CA

Levy, Judith, Lib.Dir.
SAN MATEO COUNTY DEPARTMENT OF PUBLIC HEALTH AND WELFARE - LIBRARY □ San Mateo, CA

Levy, Ralene, Info.Off.
CONSULATE GENERAL OF ISRAEL - LT. DAVID TAMIR LIBRARY AND READING ROOM □ New York, NY

Levy, Sarah N., Supv.Libn.
YESHIVA UNIVERSITY - MENDEL GOTTESMAN LIBRARY OF HEBRAICA AND JUDAICA □ New York, NY

Levy, Sharon, Libn.
NEW YORK PUBLIC LIBRARY - DONNELL LIBRARY CENTER - NATHAN STRAUS YOUNG ADULT LIBRARY □ New York, NY

Levy, Susan M., Libn.
DONORS FORUM OF CHICAGO - LIBRARY □ Chicago, IL

Levy, Suzanne S., Libn.
FAIRFAX COUNTY PUBLIC LIBRARY - VIRGINIA ROOM □ Fairfax, VA

Lew, Brenda, Assoc.Libn.
POLAROID CORPORATION - RESEARCH LIBRARY □ Cambridge, MA

Lew, Dr. Wasyl, Dir.
SHEVCHENKO SCIENTIFIC SOCIETY, INC. - LIBRARY AND ARCHIVES □ New York, NY

Lewallen, David, Br.Hd.
ALAMEDA COUNTY LIBRARY - BUSINESS & GOVERNMENT LIBRARY □ Oakland, CA

Lewandowski, Virginia, Libn.
HARLEM VALLEY PSYCHIATRIC CENTER - INTERDISCIPLINARY LIBRARY □ Wingdale, NY

Lewek, Deborah M., Chf., Lib.Serv.
U.S. VETERANS ADMINISTRATION (NY-Canandaigua) - MEDICAL CENTER LIBRARY (142D) □ Canandaigua, NY

Lewek, June B., Law Libn.
SONOMA COUNTY LAW LIBRARY □ Santa Rosa, CA

Lewis, Alan, Asst.Dir.
MINNESOTA STATE DEPARTMENT OF EDUCATION - OFFICE OF PUBLIC LIBRARIES AND INTERLIBRARY COOPERATION □ St. Paul, MN

Lewis, Alan M., Hd., Lib.Doc.Br.
U.S. NAVY - NAVAL SEA SYSTEMS COMMAND - LIBRARY DOCUMENTATION BRANCH (SEA 9961) □ Washington, DC

Lewis, Albert, Cur., Sci.Hist.Coll.
UNIVERSITY OF TEXAS, AUSTIN - HUMANITIES RESEARCH CENTER □ Austin, TX

Lewis, Alfred J., Asst. Law Libn.
UNIVERSITY OF CALIFORNIA, DAVIS - SCHOOL OF LAW - LAW LIBRARY □ Davis, CA

Lewis, Anne, Libn.
WESTRECO, INC. - TECHNICAL LIBRARY □ New Milford, CT

Lewis, Anne L., Ref.Libn.
ST. ELIZABETH MEDICAL CENTER - HEALTH SCIENCES LIBRARY □ Dayton, OH

Lewis, Annie May Alston, Libn.
HARDING GRADUATE SCHOOL OF RELIGION - L.M. GRAVES MEMORIAL LIBRARY □ Memphis, TN

Lewis, Anthony, Mng.Dir.
HOUSING ASSOCIATION OF DELAWARE VALLEY - LIBRARY □ Philadelphia, PA

Lewis, Miss Arel T., ILL Libn.
CENTRAL BAPTIST THEOLOGICAL SEMINARY - LIBRARY □ Kansas City, KS

Lewis, Audrey, Asst.Libn.
HOGAN & HARTSON - LIBRARY† □ Washington, DC

Lewis, Barbara B., Lib.Ck.
NEW YORK STATE SUPREME COURT - 6TH JUDICIAL DISTRICT - LAW LIBRARY □ Delhi, NY

Lewis, Betty K., Libn.
U.S. ARMY HOSPITALS - KENNER ARMY HOSPITAL - MEDICAL LIBRARY □ Ft. Lee, VA

Lewis, Betty Mae, Cur.
FOUNDATION HISTORICAL ASSOCIATION - SEWARD HOUSE □ Auburn, NY

Lewis, Blanche A., Libn.
SAN BERNARDINO SUN-TELEGRAM - LIBRARY □ San Bernardino, CA

Lewis, Brenda, Chf.Libn.
GREATER SOUTHEAST COMMUNITY HOSPITAL - LURA HEALTH SCIENCES LIBRARY □ Washington, DC

Lewis, Brigg, Libn.
CHURCH OF JESUS CHRIST OF LATTER-DAY SAINTS - MT. WHITNEY BRANCH GENEALOGICAL LIBRARY† □ Inyokern, CA

Lewis, C.P., Scientist-In-Charge
CANADA - INDIAN & NORTHERN AFFAIRS CANADA - INUVIK SCIENTIFIC RESOURCE CENTRE - LIBRARY □ Inuvik, NT

Lewis, Carol E., Ref.Libn.
VANDERBILT UNIVERSITY - MEDICAL CENTER LIBRARY □ Nashville, TN

Lewis, Charles F., Assoc.Cur.
ARIZONA STATE UNIVERSITY - CENTER FOR METEORITE STUDIES - LIBRARY □ Tempe, AZ

Lewis, Dale E., Ref.Libn.
BELL TELEPHONE LABORATORIES, INC. - TECHNICAL LIBRARY □ Holmdel, NJ

Lewis, David, Data User Serv.Off.
U.S. BUREAU OF THE CENSUS - REGIONAL DATA USER SERVICE - PHILADELPHIA REGIONAL OFFICE - LIBRARY □ Philadelphia, PA

Lewis, David W., Asst.Dir.Pub.Serv.
FRANKLIN AND MARSHALL COLLEGE - FACKENTHAL LIBRARY - SPECIAL COLLECTIONS □ Lancaster, PA

Lewis, E. Raymond, Libn.
U.S. HOUSE OF REPRESENTATIVES - LIBRARY □ Washington, DC

Lewis, Edith, Libn.
DISTRICT OF COLUMBIA PUBLIC LIBRARY - LIBRARY FOR THE BLIND AND PHYSICALLY HANDICAPPED □ Washington, DC

Lewis, Eleanor, Res.Assoc.
SMITH COLLEGE - SOPHIA SMITH COLLECTION - WOMEN'S HISTORY ARCHIVE □ Northampton, MA

Lewis, Elizabeth, Rare Book Libn.
MC GILL UNIVERSITY - DEPARTMENT OF RARE BOOKS & SPECIAL COLLECTIONS □ Montreal, PQ

Lewis, Eloise, Libn.
ROSS ROY, INC. - RESEARCH LIBRARY □ Detroit, MI

Lewis, Ethel M., Law Libn.
NEW YORK STATE SUPREME COURT - 7TH JUDICIAL DISTRICT - LAW LIBRARY □ Bath, NY

Lewis, Ethelene, Tech.Info.Spec.
U.S. NATL. BUREAU OF STANDARDS - STANDARDS INFORMATION SERVICE □ Gaithersburg, MD

Lewis, Florence E., Act.Hd.Libn.
HANCOCK (Allan) FOUNDATION - HANCOCK LIBRARY OF BIOLOGY & OCEANOGRAPHY □ Los Angeles, CA

Lewis, Fran, Libn.
ARIZONA STATE HIGHWAY DEPARTMENT - LIBRARY □ Phoenix, AZ

Lewis, Hal, Libn.
SCRANTON TRIBUNE AND SCRANTONIAN - LIBRARY □ Scranton, PA

Lewis, Helene, Ref.Libn.
ALCORN STATE UNIVERSITY - JOHN DEWEY BOYD LIBRARY □ Lorman, MS

Lewis, James, Ref.Libn.
CAROLINA POPULATION CENTER - LIBRARY □ Chapel Hill, NC

Lewis, Jean, Ref./Circ.Libn.
KIRKSVILLE COLLEGE OF OSTEOPATHIC MEDICINE - A.T. STILL MEMORIAL LIBRARY □ Kirksville, MO

Lewis, Joseph, Rd.Adv.
DISTRICT OF COLUMBIA PUBLIC LIBRARY - BLACK STUDIES DIVISION □ Washington, DC

Lewis, June, Acq.Libn.
FOSTER WHEELER DEVELOPMENT CORPORATION - RESEARCH INFORMATION CENTER AND LIBRARY □ Livingston, NJ

Lewis, Kathryn A., Libn., Spec.Coll.
TEXAS TECH UNIVERSITY - LIBRARY □ Lubbock, TX

Lewis, Kennard, Esq., Chm.Lib.Comm.
MONROE COUNTY LAW LIBRARY □ Stroudsburg, PA

Lewis, Larry C., Libn.
UNIVERSITY OF WESTERN ONTARIO - HEALTH SCIENCES LIBRARY □ London, ON

Lewis, Linda C., Musm.Dir.
SOUTHWEST MUSEUM OF SCIENCE & TECHNOLOGY/THE SCIENCE PLACE - LIBRARY □ Dallas, TX

Lewis, Louise, Chf., Pub.Serv.
U.S. CENTER FOR DISEASE CONTROL - CDC LIBRARY □ Atlanta, GA

Lewis, Margaret, Libn.
SUNY - COLLEGE OF OPTOMETRY - HAROLD KOHN MEMORIAL VISUAL SCIENCE LIBRARY □ New York, NY

Lewis, Marilyn, Marine Rsrcs.Libn.
SOUTH CAROLINA STATE WILDLIFE AND MARINE RESOURCES DEPT. - LIBRARY □ Charleston, SC

Lewis, Melba H., Libn.
NEW YORK STATE ELECTRIC AND GAS CORPORATION - CORPORATE TECHNICAL LIBRARY □ Binghamton, NY

Lewis, Merwin, Libn.
UNIVERSITY OF WESTERN ONTARIO - MUSIC LIBRARY □ London, ON

Lewis, Mona K., Asst.Info.Spec.
AMERICAN FOUNDATION FOR THE BLIND - M.C. MIGEL MEMORIAL LIBRARY □ New York, NY

Lewis, Nancy C., Libn.
ARKANSAS STATE ENERGY OFFICE LIBRARY □ Little Rock, AR

Lewis, Pam, Asst.Libn.
DAVIS, GRAHAM & STUBBS/COLORADO NATIONAL BUILDING - CNB LAW LIBRARY □ Denver, CO

Lewis, Ralph W., Chf., Lib.Br.
U.S. NASA - AMES RESEARCH CENTER -
LIBRARY □ Mountain View, CA

Lewis, Robert, Info.Sys.Mgr.
BLUE CROSS AND BLUE SHIELD ASSOCIATIONS
- LIBRARY □ Chicago, IL

Lewis, Robert F., Libn.
UNIVERSITY OF CALIFORNIA, SAN DIEGO -
BIOMEDICAL LIBRARY □ La Jolla, CA

Lewis, Robert G., Lib.Supv.
COMINCO LTD. - CENTRAL TECHNICAL
LIBRARY □ Trail, BC

Lewis, Roberta, Asst.Libn.
PFIZER, INC. - CENTRAL RESEARCH
TECHNICAL INFORMATION SERVICES □ Groton,
CT

Lewis, Ronald A., Univ.Libn.
ST. MARY'S UNIVERSITY - PATRICK POWER
LIBRARY □ Halifax, NS

Lewis, Rosalyn, Libn.
UNITED METHODIST PUBLISHING HOUSE -
LIBRARY □ Nashville, TN

Lewis, Shirley C., Dir.Lib.Serv.
PROVIDENCE HOSPITAL, EVERETT - HEALTH
INFORMATION NETWORK SERVICES (HINS) □
Everett, WA

Lewis, Susan, Hd.Libn.
BOSTON ARCHITECTURAL CENTER - ALFRED
SHAW AND EDWARD DURELL STONE LIBRARY □
Boston, MA

Lewis, William P., Exec.Dir.
LACKAWANNA HISTORICAL SOCIETY -
LIBRARY AND ARCHIVES □ Scranton, PA

Lewis, William R., Coord.
BOSTON PUBLIC LIBRARY - SOCIAL SCIENCES
□ Boston, MA

Lewis, Yvon, Dir.
SOCIETE NATIONALE DE DIFFUSION
EDUCATIVE ET CULTURELLE - SERVICE
D'INFORMATION SONDEC† □ Montreal, PQ

Leyerzapf, James W., Supv.Archv.
U.S. PRESIDENTIAL LIBRARIES - DWIGHT D.
EISENHOWER LIBRARY □ Abilene, KS

Leyshon, Frank, Libn.
GUERNSEY COUNTY LAW LIBRARY □
Cambridge, OH

Leyva, Judith Runyon, Law Libn.
WESTERN STATE UNIVERSITY - COLLEGE OF
LAW - LIBRARY □ San Diego, CA

Li, Dr. Ming-Yu, Doc.Spec.
UNIVERSITY OF CALIFORNIA, DAVIS -
ENVIRONMENTAL TOXICOLOGY LIBRARY □
Davis, CA

Li, Rose, Assoc.Libn.
NEW YORK BOTANICAL GARDEN - LIBRARY □
Bronx, NY

Li, Ruth H., Cat.
HOWARD UNIVERSITY - MOORLAND-SPINGARN
RESEARCH CENTER - LIBRARY DIVISION □
Washington, DC

Liardon, Carol, Asst.Libn.
ORAL ROBERTS UNIVERSITY - HEALTH
SCIENCES LIBRARY □ Tulsa, OK

Lias, Dr. Sharon G., Res.Chem.
U.S. NATL. BUREAU OF STANDARDS - ION
KINETICS AND ENERGETICS DATA CENTER □
Washington, DC

Liaw, Barbara, Cat.
ALABAMA A & M UNIVERSITY - JOSEPH F.
DRAKE MEMORIAL LEARNING RESOURCES
CENTER □ Normal, AL

Libbey, Elizabeth M., Music Libn.
CATHOLIC UNIVERSITY OF AMERICA - MUSIC
LIBRARY □ Washington, DC

Libbey, Frances T., Sci./Engr.Libn.
UNIVERSITY OF HARTFORD - DANA SCIENCE &
ENGINEERING LIBRARY □ West Hartford, CT

Libbey, Maurice, Hd.Acq.Serv.
EASTERN ILLINOIS UNIVERSITY - BOOTH
LIBRARY □ Charleston, IL

Libbey, Miriam H., Libn.
EMORY UNIVERSITY - SCHOOL OF MEDICINE -
A.W. CALHOUN MEDICAL LIBRARY □ Atlanta,
GA

Libby, Eileen, Libn.
UNIVERSITY OF CHICAGO - SOCIAL SERVICES
ADMINISTRATION LIBRARY □ Chicago, IL

Libby, Shirley E., Lib.Sec.
BRIDGEWATER STATE COLLEGE - CLEMENT C.
MAXWELL LIBRARY □ Bridgewater, MA

Liberman, Susan, Asst. to Gen. Counsel
NATIONAL ENDOWMENT FOR THE ARTS - LAW
LIBRARY □ Washington, DC

Liberno, Ceil, Act.Libn.
CEDARCREST REGIONAL HOSPITAL AND
DEPARTMENT OF MENTAL HEALTH - LIBRARY □
Newington, CT

Libhart, Myles, Dir. of Pubn.
U.S. DEPT. OF THE INTERIOR - INDIAN ARTS
AND CRAFTS BOARD □ Washington, DC

Licht, Juanita, Lib.Supv.
SHAPIRO (Samuel H.) DEVELOPMENTAL CENTER
- PROFESSIONAL LIBRARY □ Kankakee, IL

Lichtenberg, Elsa, Acq.Libn.
VILLANOVA UNIVERSITY - PULLING LAW
LIBRARY □ Villanova, PA

Lichtenstein, Aniela, Libn.
FILLMORE (Millard) HOSPITAL - KIDENEY
HEALTH SCIENCES LIBRARY □ Buffalo, NY

Lichtenstein, Mrs. Kineret, Libn.
ILLINOIS STATE PSYCHIATRIC INSTITUTE -
PROFESSIONAL LIBRARY □ Chicago, IL

Lichtenstein, Michela, Asst.Libn.
NEW YORK PUBLIC LIBRARY - BELMONT
REGIONAL LIBRARY - ENRICO FERMI
CULTURAL CENTER □ Bronx, NY

Licitis, Margot B., Transl.
ROHM & HAAS COMPANY - RESEARCH
DIVISION - INFORMATION SERVICES
DEPARTMENT □ Spring House, PA

Liddiard, Karen, Chf.Libn.
CALGARY HERALD - LIBRARY □ Calgary, AB

Lidster, Rita M., Libn.
SASKATCHEWAN - DEPARTMENT OF THE
ATTORNEY GENERAL - COURT OF APPEAL
LIBRARY □ Regina, SK

Lieb, Genette P., Libn.
GREY ADVERTISING, INC. - RESEARCH
LIBRARY □ New York, NY

Lieb, Louise Laughlin, Hd.Libn.
IRELL & MANELLA - LIBRARY □ Los Angeles, CA

Lieber, Winifred, Libn.
ROOSEVELT HOSPITAL - MEDICAL LIBRARY □
New York, NY

Lieberman, E. James, Dir.
ESPERANTIC STUDIES FOUNDATION - LIBRARY
□ Washington, DC

Lieberman, Jan, Libn.
CONGREGATION BETH AM - LIBRARY □ Los
Altos Hills, CA

Lieberman, Sherri, Ref.Libn.
MITRE CORPORATION - LIBRARY □ McLean, VA

Lieberman, Susan, Circ./Ref.Libn.
MOUNT SINAI SCHOOL OF MEDICINE OF THE
CITY UNIVERSITY OF NEW YORK - GUSTAVE L.
& JANET W. LEVY LIBRARY □ New York, NY

Liebert, Sharon, Asst.Libn.
U.S. VETERANS ADMINISTRATION (VT-White
River Jct.) - ALLIED HEALTH SCIENCES
LIBRARY □ White River Junction, VT

Liebig, James, Archv./Assoc.Dir.
UNIVERSITY OF WISCONSIN, MADISON -
ARCHIVES □ Madison, WI

Liebler, Rita V., Hosp.Libn.
BUTLER COUNTY MEMORIAL HOSPITAL - RUTH
ARMSTRONG MEMORIAL MEDICAL LIBRARY □
Butler, PA

Lieblich, Jerome H., Pres.
GLOBAL ENGINEERING DOCUMENTS - LIBRARY
□ Santa Ana, CA

Liegl, Dorothy, Cons.
SOUTH DAKOTA STATE LIBRARY □ Pierre, SD

Liem, Frieda, ILL
MEDICAL COLLEGE OF PENNSYLVANIA -
EASTERN PENNSYLVANIA PSYCHIATRIC
INSTITUTE - LIBRARY □ Philadelphia, PA

Liem, Yvonne, Hd.Biblog.
INTERNATIONAL MONETARY FUND/WORLD
BANK - JOINT BANK-FUND LIBRARY □
Washington, DC

Lien, Dennis, Contact Person
MINNESOTA SCIENCE FICTION SOCIETY -
LIBRARY □ Minneapolis, MN

Lien, Kent, Act. Media Supv.
NORTH DAKOTA STATE UNIVERSITY - LIBRARY
□ Fargo, ND

Lieneke, Francine, Serv.Dir.
LUTHERAN CHURCH - MISSOURI SYNOD -
LUTHERAN LIBRARY FOR THE BLIND □ St. Louis,
MO

Lieser, Robert, Libn.
TULSA CITY-COUNTY LIBRARY SYSTEM -
BUSINESS AND TECHNOLOGY DEPARTMENT □
Tulsa, OK

Lietman, Margaret C., Dir.
FORBES HEALTH SYSTEM - COLUMBIA HEALTH
CENTER LIBRARY □ Pittsburgh, PA

Lietman, Margaret C., Dir., Lib.Sci.Dept.
FORBES HEALTH SYSTEM - CORPORATE
OFFICE LIBRARY □ Pittsburgh, PA

Lietman, Margaret C., Dir. of Libs.
FORBES HEALTH SYSTEM - EAST SUBURBAN
HEALTH CENTER LIBRARY □ Monroeville, PA

Lietman, Margaret C., Dir./Dept. for Sys.
FORBES HEALTH SYSTEM - PITTSBURGH
SKILLED NURSING CENTER LIBRARY □
Pittsburgh, PA

Lievsay, Lilly, Hd.Cat. & Cur.
FOLGER SHAKESPEARE LIBRARY □ Washington,
DC

Lifland, Donna Z., Libn.
TEMPLE ISRAEL - LIBRARY† □ Lawrence, NY

Lifsey, J., V.P.
FRANKLIN RESEARCH CENTER - SCIENCE
INFORMATION SERVICES □ Philadelphia, PA

Light, Bette M., Med.Libn.
ST. BENEDICT'S HOSPITAL - HEALTH
SCIENCES LIBRARY □ Ogden, UT

Lightman, Benjamin, Chf.Libn.
TIME, INC. - LIBRARY □ New York, NY

Lightwood, Martha, Asst.Libn.
UNIVERSITY OF PENNSYLVANIA - LIPPINCOTT
LIBRARY □ Philadelphia, PA

Ligibel, Ted J., Preservation Off.
BOWLING GREEN STATE UNIVERSITY -
CENTER FOR ARCHIVAL COLLECTIONS □
Bowling Green, OH

Lignell, Ellen, Lib.Dir.
KANSAS CITY ART INSTITUTE - LIBRARY □
Kansas City, MO

Ligrani, Nancy, Sci./Tech.Libn.
UNIVERSITY OF TEXAS, AUSTIN -
ENGINEERING LIBRARY □ Austin, TX

Liivak, Arno, Law Libn.
RUTGERS UNIVERSITY, THE STATE
UNIVERSITY OF NEW JERSEY - SCHOOL OF
LAW LIBRARY† □ Camden, NJ

Likness, Craig, Ref.
TRINITY UNIVERSITY - LIBRARY □ San Antonio,
TX

Liles, Martha, Libn.
SYSTEMS CONTROL, INC. - TECHNICAL
LIBRARY □ Palo Alto, CA

Lilja, Lorraine, R.N. in AV Lab.
MIDWAY HOSPITAL - HEALTH SCIENCES
LIBRARY □ St. Paul, MN

Liljequist, Orval, Coord. of Hum.
MILWAUKEE PUBLIC LIBRARY - HUMANITIES
DIVISION - LOCAL HISTORY AND MARINE
ROOM □ Milwaukee, WI

Lilley, D.A., Hist.
U.S. NATL. PARK SERVICE - FREDERICKSBURG
& SPOTSYLVANIA NATL. MILITARY PARK -
LIBRARY □ Fredericksburg, VA

PERSONNEL

Lillis, Susan, Libn.
PUBLIC CITIZEN - CONGRESS WATCH -
LIBRARY □ Washington, DC

Lilly, Mary Jo, Asst.Biblog.
CARNEGIE-MELLON UNIVERSITY - HUNT
INSTITUTE FOR BOTANICAL DOCUMENTATION
- LIBRARY □ Pittsburgh, PA

Lilly, Roberta, Asst.Ed.
CARNEGIE-MELLON UNIVERSITY - HUNT
INSTITUTE FOR BOTANICAL DOCUMENTATION
- LIBRARY □ Pittsburgh, PA

Lim, Elsie, Asst.Libn.
CHEMISTS' CLUB LIBRARY - CHEMICAL
INTERNATIONAL INFORMATION CENTER □
New York, NY

Lim, Mr. Hoong, Libn.
BURNABY GENERAL HOSPITAL - DR. H.H.W.
BROOKE MEMORIAL LIBRARY □ Burnaby, BC

Lim, Josie, Hd., Tech.Serv.
CORNELL UNIVERSITY - MEDICAL COLLEGE -
LIBRARY □ New York, NY

Lim, Lourdes P., Libn.
GENERAL MOTORS CORPORATION -
ECONOMICS STAFF LIBRARY □ New York, NY

Lim, Mary, Libn.
MASSACHUSETTS STATE DIVISION OF
OCCUPATIONAL HYGIENE - SPECIAL
TECHNICAL LIBRARY □ Boston, MA

Lim, Sue C., Act.Hd.Cat.Libn.
CALIFORNIA STATE POLYTECHNIC
UNIVERSITY, POMONA - LIBRARY □ Pomona,
CA

Lima, Constance M., Libn.
EXXON CORPORATION - MEDICAL LIBRARY □
New York, NY

Limvere, Karl, Info.Asst.
NORTH DAKOTA FARMERS UNION - LULU
EVANSON RESOURCE LIBRARY □ Jamestown,
ND

Lin, Agnes, Tech.Serv.Div.
NEW YORK INSTITUTE OF TECHNOLOGY -
LIBRARY† □ Old Westbury, NY

Lin, Emily C., Libn.
LIQUID PAPER CORPORATION - EMPLOYEE
LIBRARY □ Dallas, TX

Lin, Kevin, Libn.
UNIVERSITY OF TEXAS, AUSTIN - ASIAN
COLLECTION □ Austin, TX

Lin, Louise, Coord., Lib.Serv.
ST. JOSEPH'S HOSPITAL - MEDICAL LIBRARY □
London, ON

Lin, Mei-Ying, Chinese Cat.
UNIVERSITY OF MICHIGAN - ASIA LIBRARY □
Ann Arbor, MI

Lin, Raymond, Tech.Serv.
SPRINGFIELD COLLEGE - BABSON LIBRARY □
Springfield, MA

Lin, Shu-Fang, Govt.Docs.Libn.
ST. JOHN'S UNIVERSITY - LIBRARY □ Jamaica,
NY

Lin, Tung-Fen, Libn.
AMERICAN MANAGEMENT ASSOCIATIONS -
LIBRARY □ New York, NY

Linard, James L., Res.Libn.
FAIRFAX COUNTY - COMPREHENSIVE
PLANNING LIBRARY □ Fairfax, VA

Lincks, Linda S., Mgr.
RALSTON PURINA COMPANY - TECHNICAL
INFORMATION CENTER □ St. Louis, MO

Lincoln, Christine L., Res.Libn.
PACIFIC-SIERRA RESEARCH CORPORATION -
LIBRARY □ Santa Monica, CA

Lincoln, Elizabeth G., Dir., Med.Rec.
SUNLAND CENTER AT ORLANDO - MEDICAL
LIBRARY □ Orlando, FL

Lincourt, Ghislaine, Adm.
FEDERATION DES MEDECINS
OMNIPRACTICIENS DU QUEBEC - TECHNICAL
INFORMATION CENTRE □ Montreal, PQ

Lind, Donna, Exec.Dir.
HENNEPIN COUNTY HISTORICAL SOCIETY -
ARCHIVES □ Minneapolis, MN

Lindahl, Charles, Assoc.Libn.
UNIVERSITY OF ROCHESTER - EASTMAN
SCHOOL OF MUSIC - SIBLEY MUSIC LIBRARY □
Rochester, NY

Lindauer, George, Libn.
UNIVERSITY OF LOUISVILLE - J.B. SPEED
SCIENTIFIC SCHOOL - LIBRARY □ Louisville, KY

Lindberg, Lottie, Libn.
DOW JONES & CO. - LIBRARY □ New York, NY

Lindberg, Lottie, Libn.
WALL STREET JOURNAL - LIBRARY □ New York,
NY

Lindberg, Martha, Asst.Libn.
WORLD ASSOCIATION OF DOCUMENT
EXAMINERS - WADE LIBRARY □ Chicago, IL

Lindblom, Freda, Acq.Libn.
PROVIDENCE COLLEGE - PHILLIPS MEMORIAL
LIBRARY □ Providence, RI

Lindblom, Joseph H., Libn.
CHURCH OF JESUS CHRIST OF LATTER-DAY
SAINTS - MESA BRANCH GENEALOGICAL
LIBRARY □ Mesa, AZ

Lindeken, Carl, Hist.Res.
WALNUT CREEK HISTORICAL SOCIETY -
SHADELANDS RANCH HISTORICAL MUSEUM -
HISTORY ROOM □ Walnut Creek, CA

Lindemann, James A., Libn.
OLD YORK ROAD HISTORICAL SOCIETY -
ARCHIVES □ Jenkintown, PA

Lindemon, Agnes M., Libn.
BALTIMORE GAS AND ELECTRIC COMPANY -
LIBRARY □ Baltimore, MD

Linden, Barbara, Adm.Asst.
MASSACHUSETTS INSTITUTE OF TECHNOLOGY
- M.I.T. MUSEUM AND HISTORICAL
COLLECTIONS □ Cambridge, MA

Linden, Margaret J., Chf.Libn.
STANDARD OIL COMPANY OF CALIFORNIA -
LIBRARY □ San Francisco, CA

Linden, Michael, Dir. of Res.
MOTION PICTURE ASSOCIATION OF AMERICA
- LIBRARY† □ New York, NY

Linden, Will, Libn.
AMERICAN COUNCIL FOR THE ARTS - LIBRARY
□ New York, NY

Linder, Gloria, Hd.Ref.Libn.
STANFORD UNIVERSITY - LANE MEDICAL
LIBRARY □ Stanford, CA

Linder, L.H., Mgr.Tech.Info.Serv.
FORD AEROSPACE & COMMUNICATIONS CORP.
- AERONUTRONIC DIVISION - TECHNICAL
INFORMATION SERVICES □ Newport Beach, CA

Linder, Robert A., Sr.Libn.
UNIVERSITY OF MISSISSIPPI - ARCHIVES &
SPECIAL COLLECTIONS/MISSISSIPPIANA □
University, MS

Linderman, Jim, Selection Spec.
UPJOHN COMPANY - CORPORATE TECHNICAL
LIBRARY □ Kalamazoo, MI

Linderman, Mrs. Marion, Pub.Serv. & ILL
SOUTHERN MISSIONARY COLLEGE - MC KEE
LIBRARY - SPECIAL COLLECTIONS □
Collegedale, TN

Lindgren, Arla, Hd., Acq.
TEACHERS COLLEGE - LIBRARY □ New York, NY

Lindgren, Dallas, Hd., Ref.Serv.
MINNESOTA HISTORICAL SOCIETY - DIVISION
OF ARCHIVES AND MANUSCRIPTS □ St. Paul,
MN

Lindgren, Mary, Libn.
COURAGE CENTER LIBRARY □ Golden Valley, MN

Lindloff, Kay, Libn.
(The) INSTITUTE FOR REHABILITATION AND
RESEARCH (TIRR) - INFORMATION SERVICES
CENTER □ Houston, TX

Lindner, Charlotte K., Dir. of Lib.
YESHIVA UNIVERSITY - ALBERT EINSTEIN
COLLEGE OF MEDICINE - D. SAMUEL
GOTTESMAN LIBRARY □ Bronx, NY

Lindner, Katherine L., Dir.
ENGLEWOOD HOSPITAL - MEDICAL LIBRARY □
Englewood, NJ

Lindner, Scott-Eric, Cat.
OTTAWA INSTITUTE - IRENE HOLM MEMORIAL
LIBRARY □ Columbus, OH

Lindquist, Charles N., Cur.
LENAWEE COUNTY HISTORICAL MUSEUM -
LIBRARY □ Adrian, MI

Lindquist, George, Assoc.Archv.
GUITAR FOUNDATION OF AMERICA - ARCHIVE
□ Milwaukee, WI

Lindquist, Susan O., Libn.
STAGECOACH HOUSE MUSEUM - LIBRARY □
Wyoming, RI

Lindquist, Dr. Vernon, Dir.
UNIVERSITY OF MAINE, PRESQUE ISLE -
LIBRARY □ Presque Isle, ME

Lindqvist, June A.V., Cur., Spec.Coll.
VIRGIN ISLANDS - DEPARTMENT OF
CONSERVATION & CULTURAL AFFAIRS -
BUREAU OF LIBRARIES AND MUSEUMS □ St.
Thomas, VI

Lindsay, Carol, Chf.Libn.
TORONTO STAR, LTD. - LIBRARY □ Toronto, ON

Lindsay, Louise, Ref.Libn., Edifice G.
QUEBEC PROVINCE - MINISTERE DES
COMMUNICATIONS - BIBLIOTHEQUE
ADMINISTRATIVE □ Quebec, PQ

Lindsay, Merrill K., Pres.
WHITNEY (Eli) MUSEUM - LIBRARY □ North
Branford, CT

Lindsay, Muriel, Libn.
AUTOMOBILE CLUB OF MISSOURI -
INFORMATION RESOURCE CENTER □ St. Louis,
MO

Lindsey, John, Law Professor/Law Libn.
TEMPLE UNIVERSITY - LAW LIBRARY □
Philadelphia, PA

Lindsey, Thomas K., Libn.
ELKEM METALS COMPANY - TECHNOLOGY
CENTER - HAYNES-BECKET MEMORIAL
LIBRARY □ Niagara Falls, NY

Lindstrand, Margaret A., Libn.
ST. JAMES HOSPITAL - MEDICAL LIBRARY □
Chicago Heights, IL

Lindt, Theodora L.D., Dir.
JEWISH MEMORIAL HOSPITAL - IRVING
DORFMAN MEMORIAL MEDICAL LIBRARY □
New York, NY

Lineback, Corrie T., Libn.
SCIENTIFIC-ATLANTA, INC. - LIBRARY □
Atlanta, GA

Linebaugh, Ruth, Mgr.
BATTELLE-COLUMBUS LABORATORIES - DIVER
EQUIPMENT INFORMATION CENTER □
Columbus, OH

Liner, Maureen, Circ.Hd.
CENTER FOR LAW AND EDUCATION -
VICTORIA GREGORIAN LIBRARY □ Cambridge,
MA

Lines, Adelia, Supv.
OAKLAND PUBLIC LIBRARY - INTERTRIBAL
LIBRARY PROJECT □ Oakland, CA

Lines, Jack, Pres.
WASHINGTON STATE HERITAGE COUNCIL -
INFORMATION CENTER □ Yakima, WA

Linfield, Hadassah, Dir.
U.S. DEPT. OF TRANSPORTATION -
TRANSPORTATION SYSTEMS CENTER -
TECHNICAL REFERENCE CENTER □ Cambridge,
MA

Linforth, Margit L., Libn.
GREAT LAKES COLLEGES ASSOCIATION -
PHILADELPHIA URBAN SEMESTER - LIBRARY □
Philadelphia, PA

Ling, Mrs. Robert E., Libn.
HIGH STREET CHRISTIAN CHURCH - H.A.
VALENTINE MEMORIAL LIBRARY □ Akron, OH

Lingelbach, Helen A., Fine Arts Libn.
CARNEGIE-MELLON UNIVERSITY - HUNT
LIBRARY □ Pittsburgh, PA

Lingelbach, Lorene, Libn.
BERLEX LABORATORIES, INC. - RESEARCH AND
DEVELOPMENT DIVISION LIBRARY □ Cedar
Knolls, NJ

Linger, Paul, Asst.Dir.
DENVER ZOOLOGICAL GARDEN - LIBRARY □ Denver, CO

Link, Margaret M., Engr. & Bus.Libn.
DARTMOUTH COLLEGE - FELDBERG LIBRARY □ Hanover, NH

Link, Noreen, Libn.
FOLEY & LARDNER - LIBRARY □ Milwaukee, WI

Linke, Frances Baur, Hd.Libn.
BLUE CROSS OF SOUTHERN CALIFORNIA - LEGAL AND BUSINESS LIBRARY □ Woodland Hills, CA

Linkins, Germaine C., Hd., Ser.Dept.
VIRGINIA POLYTECHNIC INSTITUTE AND STATE UNIVERSITY - CAROL M. NEWMAN LIBRARY □ Blacksburg, VA

Linkletter, Esther C., Hd.
SUNY AT STONY BROOK - CHEMISTRY LIBRARY □ Stony Brook, NY

Linn, D.C., Chf., Lib.Serv.
U.S. VETERANS ADMINISTRATION (TX-Bonham) - SAM RAYBURN MEMORIAL VETERANS CENTER MEDICAL LIBRARY □ Bonham, TX

Linn, Mary Jane, Chf., Cat.Serv.
SMITHSONIAN INSTITUTION LIBRARIES □ Washington, DC

Linn, Suellen, Lib.Dir.
LAKE PLACID ASSOCIATION FOR MUSIC, DRAMA & ART - NETTIE MARIE JONES FINE ARTS LIBRARY □ Lake Placid, NY

Linnamaa, Mari M., Cat.Dept.Hd.
NEW JERSEY INSTITUTE OF TECHNOLOGY - ROBERT W. VAN HOUTEN LIBRARY □ Newark, NJ

Linnane, Mary Lu, Hd., Tech.Serv.
DE PAUL UNIVERSITY - LAW SCHOOL LIBRARY □ Chicago, IL

Linneman, Mark, Ref.
UNIVERSITY OF IOWA - LAW LIBRARY □ Iowa City, IA

Lintner, Mary Kaye, Health Sci.Libn.
MEMORIAL HOSPITAL AT OCONOMOWOC - HEALTH SCIENCES LIBRARY □ Oconomowoc, WI

Linton, Barbara, Asst.Libn.
NATIONAL AUDUBON SOCIETY - LIBRARY □ New York, NY

Linton, Helen, Libn.
RIGGS (Austen) CENTER, INC. - AUSTEN FOX RIGGS LIBRARY □ Stockbridge, MA

Lioce, Carol A., Mgr., Info.Ctr.
GOODRICH (B.F.) COMPANY - RESEARCH AND DEVELOPMENT CENTER - BRECKSVILLE INFORMATION CENTER □ Brecksville, OH

Lipa, Dr. Jiri, Libn.
SEMINARY OF THE IMMACULATE CONCEPTION - LIBRARY □ Huntington, NY

Lipfert, Nathan, Asst.Cur.Res.
MAINE MARITIME MUSEUM - LIBRARY/ ARCHIVES □ Bath, ME

Lipinski, Mary E.
U.S. DEPT. OF COMMERCE - INTERNATIONAL TRADE ADMINISTRATION - BOSTON DISTRICT OFFICE LIBRARY □ Boston, MA

Lipinsky, Lino S., Cur.
JAY (John) HOMESTEAD - JAY LIBRARY □ Katonah, NY

Lipinsky de Orlov, Lino S., Dir.
GARIBALDI AND MEUCCI MEMORIAL MUSEUM - LIBRARY OF THE ITALIAN RISORGIMENTO □ Katonah, NY

Lipkin, Hilda, Dir.
TEANECK PUBLIC LIBRARY - ORAL AND LOCAL HISTORY PROJECT □ Teaneck, NJ

Lipman, Paula, Asst.Libn.
U.S. DEPT. OF ENERGY - HEADQUARTERS LAW LIBRARY □ Washington, DC

Lipman, Penny, Libn.
RIO ALGOM, LTD. - LIBRARY □ Toronto, ON

Lippman, Anne, Ref.Libn.
BOSTON COLLEGE - SCHOOL OF NURSING LIBRARY □ Chestnut Hill, MA

Lipscomb, Anne, Libn.
MISSISSIPPI STATE DEPARTMENT OF ARCHIVES AND HISTORY - ARCHIVES AND LIBRARY DIVISION □ Jackson, MS

Lipscomb, Carolyn, Hd., Circ.Serv.
UNIVERSITY OF NORTH CAROLINA, CHAPEL HILL - HEALTH SCIENCES LIBRARY □ Chapel Hill, NC

Lishan, Merrill H., Libn.
BESSEMER TRUST COMPANY, N.A. - INVESTMENT LIBRARY □ New York, NY

Lisker, Carol, Ser.Libn.
INDIANA UNIVERSITY - LAW LIBRARY □ Bloomington, IN

Liskow, Charles, Libn.
HUDSON ESSEX TERRAPLANE CLUB, INC. - LIBRARY □ Ypsilanti, MI

Liss, Ingrid A., Theater Sch.Asst.
CHILDREN'S THEATRE COMPANY AND SCHOOL - LIBRARY □ Minneapolis, MN

Lister, Judy, Group Ldr.
GEORGE BROWN COLLEGE OF APPLIED ARTS & TECHNOLOGY - LIBRARY □ Toronto, ON

Liszewski, Edward H., Asst.Chf.Libn.
U.S. GEOLOGICAL SURVEY - LIBRARY □ Reston, VA

Litchauer, Frances, Libn.
CURTISS-WRIGHT CORPORATION - LIBRARY SERVICES† □ Wood-Ridge, NJ

Litchfield, Meredith C., Asst.Dir., Adm.
KANSAS STATE UNIVERSITY - FARRELL LIBRARY □ Manhattan, KS

Little, Ann, Libn.
MANUFACTURERS HANOVER TRUST COMPANY - CORPORATE LIBRARY/FINANCIAL LIBRARY DIVISION □ New York, NY

Little, Ann, Libn.
MANUFACTURERS HANOVER TRUST COMPANY - CORPORATE LIBRARY/INVESTMENT LIBRARY DIVISION □ New York, NY

Little, Doris P., Libn.
U.S. FEDERAL AVIATION ADMINISTRATION - SOUTHERN REGION LIBRARY □ East Point, GA

Little, Grace, Libn.
LUTHERAN CHURCH IN AMERICA - FLORIDA SYNOD - MULTI-MEDIA LIBRARY □ Tampa, FL

Little, Karen M., Dir.
ST. LUKE'S HOSPITAL - MEDICAL LIBRARY □ Boise, ID

Little, Nancy C., Libn.
KNOEDLER (M.) AND COMPANY, INC. - LIBRARY □ New York, NY

Little, Rosemary Allen, Libn.
PRINCETON UNIVERSITY - PUBLIC ADMINISTRATION COLLECTION □ Princeton, NJ

Littlefield, Frederick, TV Producer-Dir.
UNIVERSITY OF NEW HAMPSHIRE - DEPARTMENT OF MEDIA SERVICES - FILM LIBRARY □ Durham, NH

Littlefield, Mary L., Sec.Lib.Comm.
LUTHERAN HOSPITALS AND HOMES SOCIETY OF AMERICA - LIBRARY □ Fargo, ND

Littlejohn, Nancy, Ser.Libn.
CENTRAL MISSOURI STATE UNIVERSITY - WARD EDWARDS LIBRARY □ Warrensburg, MO

Littlemeyer, Mary H., Archv.
ASSOCIATION OF AMERICAN MEDICAL COLLEGES - ARCHIVES □ Washington, DC

Littlepage, Sue E., Res.Libn.
ENSCO, INC. - TECHNICAL LIBRARY □ Springfield, VA

Littleton, Harold J., Pres.
LOMBARDY HALL FOUNDATION - LIBRARY □ Wilmington, DE

Littleton, Isaac T., Dir.
NORTH CAROLINA STATE UNIVERSITY - D.H. HILL LIBRARY □ Raleigh, NC

Littleton, Tucker R., Hist.
SWANSBORO HISTORICAL ASSOCIATION, INC. - RESEARCH FILES □ Swansboro, NC

Littlewood, John, Doc.Libn.
UNIVERSITY OF ILLINOIS - DOCUMENTS LIBRARY □ Urbana, IL

Littman, Rosette, Cat.
VILLANOVA UNIVERSITY - PULLING LAW LIBRARY □ Villanova, PA

Litvinoff, Ana, Acq.
LOUISIANA STATE UNIVERSITY - LAW LIBRARY □ Baton Rouge, LA

Litzenberger, Margaret, Asst.Libn.
BUFFALO PSYCHIATRIC CENTER - BPC LIBRARY □ Buffalo, NY

Litzinger, Sr. Caritas, Libn.
COLUMBUS DOMINICAN EDUCATION CENTER □ Columbus, OH

Liu, David C., Libn.
CHINESE CULTURAL CENTER - INFORMATION & COMMUNICATION DIVISION - LIBRARY □ New York, NY

Liu, Ellen, Monographs Acq.Libn.
UNIVERSITY OF ARKANSAS MEDICAL SCIENCES CAMPUS - MEDICAL SCIENCES LIBRARY □ Little Rock, AR

Liu, Eugene E., Bilingual Res.Libn.
EVALUATION, DISSEMINATION & ASSESSMENT CENTER - EDAC RESEARCH LIBRARY □ Cambridge, MA

Liu, Frank Yining, Law Libn.
DUQUESNE UNIVERSITY - LAW LIBRARY □ Pittsburgh, PA

Liu, Judy, Hd., Ref.Sect./ILL/Circ.
U.S. DEPT. OF ENERGY - BROOKHAVEN NATL. LABORATORY - TECHNICAL INFORMATION DIVISION □ Upton, NY

Liu, Shari Y., Libn.
BALLARD, SPAHR, ANDREWS AND INGERSOLL - LAW LIBRARY† □ Philadelphia, PA

Liu, Susan I-Man, Cat.
GIBSON, DUNN & CRUTCHER - LAW LIBRARY □ Los Angeles, CA

Liu, Wentsing, Dir.
BUFFALO GENERAL HOSPITAL, INC. - A.H. AARON MEDICAL LIBRARY □ Buffalo, NY

Lively, Eileen T., Libn.
SOUTHWEST TEXAS METHODIST HOSPITAL - MEDICAL-NURSING & PATIENT LIBRARY □ San Antonio, TX

Lively, Mildred L., Dir. of Lib.Serv.
FIRST BAPTIST CHURCH OF DALLAS - FIRST BAPTIST ACADEMY - GEORGE W. TRUETT MEMORIAL LIBRARY □ Dallas, TX

Lively, Nina
ALTERNATIVE PRESS CENTER - LIBRARY □ Baltimore, MD

Lively, William O., Libn.
ARINC RESEARCH CORPORATION - TECHNICAL LIBRARY □ Annapolis, MD

Livengood, Shirley, Tech. Data Libn.
STANFORD LINEAR ACCELERATOR CENTER - LIBRARY □ Menlo Park, CA

Livermore, Jane M., Libn.
SCIENCE SERVICE, INC. - LIBRARY □ Washington, DC

Livesay, Donetta, Lib.Techn.
U.S. NATL. PARK SERVICE - CAPE HATTERAS NATL. SEASHORE LIBRARY □ Manteo, NC

Livingston, Marilyn, Off.Mgr.
PSYNETICS FOUNDATION - LIBRARY □ Anaheim, CA

Livingstone, Bertha, Libn.
DUKE UNIVERSITY - BIOLOGY-FORESTRY LIBRARY □ Durham, NC

Liwang, Crisencia, Lit. Searcher
UOP INC. - RESEARCH TECHNICAL INFORMATION CENTER □ Des Plaines, IL

Lizotte, Jeanette S., Libn.
LANDELS, RIPLEY & DIAMOND - LIBRARY □ San Francisco, CA

Llewellyn, Teresa, Dp.Dir.
WILMER, CUTLER & PICKERING - LAW LIBRARY □ Washington, DC

Llorens, Ms. Ana R., Hd.Libn.
OHIO STATE UNIVERSITY - FOREIGN LANGUAGES GRADUATE LIBRARY □ Columbus, OH

PERSONNEL

Lloyd, Elizabeth, Cat.
UNIVERSITY OF TEXAS SCHOOL OF LAW -
TARLTON LAW LIBRARY □ Austin, TX

Lloyd, Heather M., Ref.Libn.
OKLAHOMA STATE UNIVERSITY - SPECIAL
COLLECTIONS AND MAPS □ Stillwater, OK

Lloyd, Janice L., Libn.
GRAPHIC ARTS TECHNICAL FOUNDATION -
E.H. WADEWITZ MEMORIAL LIBRARY □
Pittsburgh, PA

Lloyd, Leah R., Libn.
AULTMAN HOSPITAL - MEDICAL LIBRARY □
Canton, OH

Lloyd, Priscilla, Med.Libn.
NORTHEAST ALABAMA REGIONAL MEDICAL
CENTER - MEDICAL LIBRARY □ Anniston, AL

Llull, Harry P., Hd.Libn./Biblog.
STANFORD UNIVERSITY - MATHEMATICAL
AND COMPUTER SCIENCES LIBRARY □
Stanford, CA

Lo, C., Hd.Cat.
CANADA - TRANSPORT CANADA - LIBRARY &
INFORMATION CENTRE □ Ottawa, ON

Lo, Karl, Hd.
UNIVERSITY OF WASHINGTON - EAST ASIA
LIBRARY □ Seattle, WA

Lo, Mary, Res. Facility Libn.
UNIVERSITY OF TENNESSEE - SPACE
INSTITUTE LIBRARY □ Tullahoma, TN

Lo, Maryanne, Libn.
MEDTRONIC, INC. - LIBRARY □ Minneapolis, MN

Lo, Sara de Mundo, Libn.
UNIVERSITY OF ILLINOIS - MODERN
LANGUAGES AND LINGUISTICS LIBRARY □
Urbana, IL

Lobenstine, Joy, Adm.Asst.
ASSOCIATION FOR GERONTOLOGY IN HIGHER
EDUCATION - RESOURCE LIBRARY □
Washington, DC

Lober, Robin L., Dir.
LOS ANGELES COLLEGE OF CHIROPRACTIC -
HENRY G. HIGHLY LIBRARY □ Glendale, CA

Lobingier, Christopher, Sound Recordings Libn.
PEABODY CONSERVATORY OF MUSIC -
LIBRARY □ Baltimore, MD

Locas, Lise, Libn.
INDUSTRIAL ACCIDENT PREVENTION
ASSOCIATION - TECHNICAL INFORMATION
LIBRARY □ Montreal, PQ

Locatelli, Janet, ILL
MICHIGAN TECHNOLOGICAL UNIVERSITY -
LIBRARY □ Houghton, MI

Lochary, Ruth, Ser.Libn.
BLOOMFIELD COLLEGE - GEORGE TALBOT HALL
LIBRARY □ Bloomfield, NJ

Lochner, Mrs. P., Libn.
YARDNEY ELECTRIC CORPORATION -
TECHNICAL INFORMATION CENTER □
Pawcatuck, CT

Lockard, Karen S., Law Libn.
MONTGOMERY COUNTY CIRCUIT COURT - LAW
LIBRARY □ Rockville, MD

Locke, Carolyn, Ref.Libn.
NATIONAL GEOGRAPHIC SOCIETY - LIBRARY □
Washington, DC

Locke, Mamie, Archv.
ATLANTA HISTORICAL SOCIETY - ARCHIVES □
Atlanta, GA

Locker, Frank J., Supv.
BAXTER TRAVENOL LABORATORIES, INC. -
BUSINESS AND LAW LIBRARY/INFORMATION
CENTER □ Deerfield, IL

Locker, Mary Anne, Sci.Biblog.
NORTHWEST MISSOURI STATE UNIVERSITY -
WELLS LIBRARY □ Maryville, MO

Lockerby, Robert L., Eng.Libn.
PORTLAND STATE UNIVERSITY - SCIENCE
LIBRARY □ Portland, OR

Lockett, Sandra, Docs.
UNIVERSITY OF IOWA - LAW LIBRARY □ Iowa
City, IA

Lockhart, Deborah, Rd.Adv.
DISTRICT OF COLUMBIA PUBLIC LIBRARY -
BLACK STUDIES DIVISION □ Washington, DC

Lockhart, Hugh, Libn.
LAW SOCIETY OF BRITISH COLUMBIA -
VICTORIA LIBRARY† □ Victoria, BC

Lockhart, Virginia, Dir.
KANSAS STATE DEPARTMENT OF HEALTH &
ENVIRONMENT - BUREAU OF HEALTH &
ENVIRONMENTAL EDUCATION LIBRARY □
Topeka, KS

Lockrem, Jane, Libn.
SOUTHERN ILLINOIS UNIVERSITY,
CARBONDALE - SPECIAL COLLECTIONS □
Carbondale, IL

Lockstedt, Barbara, Mgr.
INTERNATIONAL OIL SCOUTS ASSOCIATION -
LIBRARY □ Austin, TX

Lockwood, A.W., Info.Spec.
NORTH CAROLINA STATE SCIENCE AND
TECHNOLOGY RESEARCH CENTER □ Research
Triangle Park, NC

Lockwood, DeLauna, Editor CINAHL
GLENDALE ADVENTIST MEDICAL CENTER -
LIBRARY □ Glendale, CA

Lockwood, Joyce, Info.Anl.
CANADA - INDUSTRY, TRADE & COMMERCE -
CANADIAN GOVERNMENT OFFICE OF TOURISM
□ Ottawa, ON

Lockwood, Lillie A., Libn.
U.S. VETERANS ADMINISTRATION (GA-
Augusta) - HOSPITAL LIBRARY □ Augusta, GA

Lockwood, Linda, Law Libn.
WINSTON & STRAWN - LIBRARY □ Chicago, IL

Lodato, James J., Principal Law Libn.
NASSAU COUNTY SUPREME COURT - 10TH
JUDICIAL DISTRICT - LAW LIBRARY □ Mineola,
NY

Loe, Nancy E., Hd.Libn.
PIKES PEAK LIBRARY DISTRICT - LOCAL
HISTORY COLLECTION □ Colorado Springs, CO

Loechell, Jan, Libn.
DESERT BOTANICAL GARDEN - RICHTER
LIBRARY □ Phoenix, AZ

Loeffler, Mildred, Libn.
RILEY COUNTY GENEALOGICAL SOCIETY -
LIBRARY □ Manhattan, KS

Loeffler, Mildred
RILEY COUNTY HISTORICAL SOCIETY -
SEATON MEMORIAL LIBRARY □ Manhattan, KS

Loeppky, S., Libn.
WINNIPEG CLINIC - LIBRARY □ Winnipeg, MB

Loepprich, Joyce, Ser.Libn.
UNIVERSITY OF CALIFORNIA, IRVINE -
BIOMEDICAL LIBRARY □ Irvine, CA

Loerke, Jean Penn, Musm.Dir./Hist.
WAUKESHA COUNTY HISTORICAL MUSEUM -
RESEARCH CENTER □ Waukesha, WI

Loesel, Louise, Libn.
FIRST UNITED PRESBYTERIAN CHURCH OF
THE COVENANT - BRITTAIN LIBRARY □ Erie,
PA

Loewry, Kate Naomi, Judaica Libn.
BUREAU OF JEWISH EDUCATION - JEWISH
COMMUNITY LIBRARY □ San Francisco, CA

Lofas, Jeannette, Exec.Dir.
STEP FAMILY FOUNDATION, INC. - LIBRARY □
New York, NY

Lofchie, Dr. Michael, Dir.
UNIVERSITY OF CALIFORNIA, LOS ANGELES -
AFRICAN STUDIES CENTER - RESEARCH
WORKSHOP & READING ROOM □ Los Angeles,
CA

Lofthouse, Norma, Libn.
BRITISH COLUMBIA - MINISTRY OF
EDUCATION - LIBRARY □ Victoria, BC

Loftiss, Floyd A., Supv., Tech.Serv.
OKLAHOMA STATE UNIVERSITY - AUDIO
VISUAL CENTER □ Stillwater, OK

Loftus, Helen E., Dept.Hd.
ELI LILLY AND COMPANY - BUSINESS LIBRARY
□ Indianapolis, IN

Log, Sara, Libn.
U.S. NATL. INSTITUTES OF HEALTH - LIBRARY
□ Bethesda, MD

Logan, Dr. Anne-Marie, Libn./Photo Archv.
YALE UNIVERSITY - YALE CENTER FOR
BRITISH ART - PHOTO ARCHIVE □ New Haven,
CT

Logan, Dr. Anne-Marie, Libn./Photo Archv.
YALE UNIVERSITY - YALE CENTER FOR
BRITISH ART - REFERENCE LIBRARY □ New
Haven, CT

Logan, Charles, Cat.
U.S. NAVY - NAVAL UNDERWATER SYSTEMS
CENTER - NEW LONDON TECHNICAL LIBRARY
□ New London, CT

Logan, Darryl, Med.Libn.
ST. FRANCIS HOSPITAL - HEALTH SCIENCES
LIBRARY □ Tulsa, OK

Logan, Eileen Y., Hd.
MIDLANTIC NATIONAL BANK - TRUST
DEPARTMENT LIBRARY □ Edison, NJ

Logan, Jeannette, Sec.
LOUISIANA TECH UNIVERSITY - COLLEGE OF
EDUCATION - EDUCATIONAL RESEARCH
LIBRARY □ Ruston, LA

Logan, John P., Info.Sys.Anl.
U.S. DEPT OF ENERGY - SANDIA NATL.
LABORATORIES - TECHNICAL LIBRARY □
Albuquerque, NM

Logan, Kathryn P., Asst. Music Libn.
UNIVERSITY OF NORTH CAROLINA, CHAPEL
HILL - MUSIC LIBRARY □ Chapel Hill, NC

Logan, Kenneth R., South Asia Libn.
UNIVERSITY OF CALIFORNIA, BERKELEY -
SOUTH/SOUTHEAST ASIA LIBRARY SERVICE □
Berkeley, CA

Logan, Marie V., Sr.Libn.
ATASCADERO STATE HOSPITAL -
PROFESSIONAL LIBRARY □ Atascadero, CA

Logan, Michael, Cat.Libn.
WENTWORTH INSTITUTE OF TECHNOLOGY -
LIBRARY □ Boston, MA

Logan, Wilda D., Mss.Libn.
HOWARD UNIVERSITY - MOORLAND-SPINGARN
RESEARCH CENTER - MANUSCRIPT DIVISION □
Washington, DC

Logsdon, Paul, Ref.Libn.
OHIO NORTHERN UNIVERSITY - HETERICK
MEMORIAL LIBRARY □ Ada, OH

Loh, Eudora, Foreign Docs.Libn.
UNIVERSITY OF CALIFORNIA, LOS ANGELES -
PUBLIC AFFAIRS SERVICE □ Los Angeles, CA

Lohf, Kenneth A., Libn.
COLUMBIA UNIVERSITY - RARE BOOK AND
MANUSCRIPT LIBRARY □ New York, NY

Lohman, William E., Mgr.
ILLINOIS STATE BOARD OF EDUCATION -
MEDIA AND RESOURCES CENTER □ Springfield,
IL

Lohr, Linda, Adm.Asst.
SUNY AT BUFFALO - HEALTH SCIENCES
LIBRARY □ Buffalo, NY

Lohr, Louise, Libn.
SYVA COMPANY - RESEARCH LIBRARY □ Palo
Alto, CA

Lohrer, Fred E., Libn.
ARCHBOLD BIOLOGICAL STATION OF THE
AMERICAN MUSEUM OF NATURAL HISTORY -
LIBRARY □ Lake Placid, FL

Lohse, Alice L., Libn.
NEVADA MENTAL HEALTH INSTITUTE -
MEDICAL LIBRARY □ Reno, NV

Lokets, Dina, Libn.
KENNECOTT CORPORATION - CORPORATE
PLANNING LIBRARY □ Stamford, CT

Lola, J.A., Asst. in Chg.
UNIVERSITY OF CHICAGO - YERKES
OBSERVATORY LIBRARY □ Williams Bay, WI

Lolley, Dr. John L., Dir. of Lib.Serv.
CENTRAL STATE UNIVERSITY - LIBRARY □
Edmond, OK

Lom, Jerome A., Stuart Libn.
ILLINOIS INSTITUTE OF TECHNOLOGY -
HAROLD LEONARD STUART SCHOOL OF
MANAGEMENT & FINANCE - LIBRARY □
Chicago, IL

Loman, Scott Steven, Libn.
CHILDREN'S MUSEUM OF INDIANAPOLIS -
RAUH MEMORIAL LIBRARY □ Indianapolis, IN

Lomax, Helen, Libn.
INDUSTRIAL HOME FOR THE BLIND - NASSAU-
SUFFOLK BRAILLE LIBRARY □ Hempstead, NY

Lomax, Ronald C., Ref.Libn.
ALAMEDA COUNTY LAW LIBRARY □ Oakland, CA

Lombardi, Dr. John, Res.Educ.
ERIC CLEARINGHOUSE FOR JUNIOR COLLEGES
□ Los Angeles, CA

Lombardi, Ralph G., Assoc.Libn.
SHEARMAN & STERLING - LIBRARY □ New York,
NY

Lomen, Nancy L., Libn.
U.S. VETERANS ADMINISTRATION (IA-Des
Moines) - HOSPITAL LIBRARY □ Des Moines, IA

Lonabaugh, Helen, Asst.Med.Libn.
BRYN MAWR HOSPITAL - MEDICAL LIBRARY □
Bryn Mawr, PA

Lonabaugh, Helen, Asst.Med.Libn.
BRYN MAWR HOSPITAL - MEDICAL LIBRARY -
NURSING DIVISION □ Bryn Mawr, PA

Loncaric, Inge, Supv.
ATLANTIC-RICHFIELD COMPANY - ARCO OIL
AND GAS COMPANY - RESEARCH &
DEVELOPMENT TECHNICAL INFORMATION
CENTER □ Dallas, TX

London, Frank M., Libn.
U.S. ARMY - MATERIEL DEVELOPMENT &
READINESS COMMAND (DARCOM) - INTERN
TRAINING CENTER LIBRARY □ Texarkana, TX

Loner, Anne S., Med.Libn.
WHEELING HOSPITAL, INC. - HENRY G. JEPSON
MEMORIAL LIBRARY □ Wheeling, WV

Lonergan, Rev. Lawrence A., C.M., Dir. of Libs.
ST. JOHN'S UNIVERSITY - LIBRARY □ Jamaica,
NY

Long, Aram, Staff Libn.
O.K. SUPERMARKET - REAL ESTATE &
SHOPPING CENTER DEVELOPMENT
INFORMATION CENTER □ Fresno, CA

Long, Caroline C., Health Sci.Biblog.
SYRACUSE UNIVERSITY - ENGINEERING & LIFE
SCIENCES LIBRARY □ Syracuse, NY

Long, Catherine, Cat.
LINCOLN UNIVERSITY OF MISSOURI - INMAN
E. PAGE LIBRARY □ Jefferson City, MO

Long, Charles R., Adm.Libn.
NEW YORK BOTANICAL GARDEN - CARY
ARBORETUM - LIBRARY □ Millbrook, NY

Long, Charles R., Dir.
NEW YORK BOTANICAL GARDEN - LIBRARY □
Bronx, NY

Long, Dorothy A., Pub.Serv.Libn.
DALHOUSIE UNIVERSITY - LAW LIBRARY □
Halifax, NS

Long, Elizabeth, Sr. Children's Libn.
NEW YORK PUBLIC LIBRARY - GENERAL
LIBRARY OF THE PERFORMING ARTS □ New
York, NY

Long, F. Raymond, Asst.Univ.Libn.
UNIVERSITY OF CALIFORNIA, IRVINE -
BIOMEDICAL LIBRARY □ Irvine, CA

Long, Irma R., Lib.Asst.
NEW BRUNSWICK - DEPARTMENT OF NATURAL
RESOURCES - FORESTS BRANCH LIBRARY □
Fredericton, NB

Long, Jane Sennett, Dir.
FOUNDATION FOR PUBLIC AFFAIRS -
RESOURCE CENTER □ Washington, DC

Long, Jean, Med.Libn.
NEWINGTON CHILDREN'S HOSPITAL -
PROFESSIONAL LIBRARY □ Newington, CT

Long, Rev. John F., S.J., Dir.
JOHN XXIII ECUMENICAL CENTER, INC. -
CENTER FOR EASTERN CHRISTIAN STUDIES □
Bronx, NY

Long, Kathleen A., Asst.Hd.Libn.
ARTHUR D. LITTLE, INC. - RESEARCH LIBRARY
□ Cambridge, MA

Long, Kathleen A., Mgr., Tech.Info.Serv
HONEYWELL, INC. - ELECTRO-OPTICS CENTER
- TECHNICAL LIBRARY □ Lexington, MA

Long, Kenneth, Mgr.
PENTON/IPC - MARKETING INFORMATION
CENTER □ Cleveland, OH

Long, Loretto M., Hd.
TEXAS A & M UNIVERSITY - TECHNICAL
REPORTS DEPARTMENT □ College Station, TX

Long, Margery, Archv.
WAYNE STATE UNIVERSITY - ARCHIVES OF
LABOR AND URBAN AFFAIRS/UNIVERSITY
ARCHIVES □ Detroit, MI

Long, Patricia Ann, Libn.
MINORITY BUSINESS INFORMATION
INSTITUTE, INC. - LIBRARY □ New York, NY

Long, Mrs. Robyn, Cat.
ALABAMA A & M UNIVERSITY - JOSEPH F.
DRAKE MEMORIAL LEARNING RESOURCES
CENTER □ Normal, AL

Long, Rosalee, Assoc. Law Libn.
STANFORD UNIVERSITY - LAW LIBRARY □
Stanford, CA

Long, Susan, Libn.
KALISPELL REGIONAL HOSPITAL - MEDICAL
LIBRARY □ Kalispell, MT

Long, Susan, Dir., Info.Ctr.
SAN MATEO COUNTY EDUCATIONAL
RESOURCES CENTER □ Redwood City, CA

Long, Tyrone, Media Spec.
ANTIOCH UNIVERSITY - LEARNING RESOURCE
CENTER □ Philadelphia, PA

Long, Walter K., Dir.
CAYUGA MUSEUM OF HISTORY AND ART -
LIBRARY & ARCHIVES □ Auburn, NY

Longacker, N., AV Spec.
HUDSON VALLEY COMMUNITY COLLEGE -
DWIGHT MARVIN LEARNING RESOURCES
CENTER □ Troy, NY

Longan, Louise, Libn.
SEQUOIA GENEALOGICAL SOCIETY - INEZ L.
HYDE MEMORIAL COLLECTION □ Tulare, CA

Longenecker, Lois, Asst.Libn.
ASSOCIATED MENNONITE BIBLICAL
SEMINARIES - MENNONITE BIBLICAL
SEMINARY - LIBRARY □ Elkhart, IN

Longenecker, Susan, Chf.Libn.
VERMONT STATE HOSPITAL - AGENCY OF
HUMAN SERVICES LIBRARY □ Waterbury, VT

Longland, Jean R., Cur.
HISPANIC SOCIETY OF AMERICA - LIBRARY □
New York, NY

Longley, Fred N., Asst.Libn./Hd.Ref.
CANADA - LABOUR CANADA - LIBRARY □
Ottawa, ON

Longo, Joy, Libn.
KEY BANK N.A. - INFORMATION CENTER □
Albany, NY

Longstreth, Ronald L., Exec.Sec.
INTERNATIONAL THESPIAN SOCIETY -
LIBRARY □ Cincinnati, OH

Longwell, Helen B., Libn.
UPJOHN COMPANY - PATENT LAW
DEPARTMENT - LIBRARY □ Kalamazoo, MI

Longworth, J. George, Asst.Commnr.
NEW YORK STATE DIVISION OF HUMAN
RIGHTS - REFERENCE LIBRARY □ New York, NY

Longyear, Douglas, Engr.Dir.
CRANE COMPANY - HYDRO-AIRE DIVISION -
TECHNICAL LIBRARY □ Burbank, CA

Lonnberg, Julia, Libn.
COLLEGE CENTER OF THE FINGER LAKES -
LIBRARY □ Corning, NY

Lonney, J., Sect.Chf.Tech.Lib.
WESTERN ELECTRIC COMPANY, INC. -
CORPORATE EDUCATION CENTER - LIBRARY □
Hopewell, NJ

Loomer, Robert F., Mgr.
BEIHOFF MUSIC CORPORATION - SHEET
MUSIC DEPARTMENT □ Milwaukee, WI

Loomis, Joan E., Cat.
VINSON & ELKINS - LAW LIBRARY □ Houston,
TX

Loomis, K., Libn.
INTERNATIONAL BIRD RESCUE RESEARCH
CENTER - LIBRARY† □ Berkeley, CA

Looney, Pat, Libn.
MERCHANTS NATIONAL BANK OF MOBILE -
EMPLOYEES LIBRARY† □ Mobile, AL

Looney, Robert F., Cur.
FREE LIBRARY OF PHILADELPHIA - PRINT AND
PICTURE COLLECTION □ Philadelphia, PA

Loop, Jacqueline, Libn.
ENERGY, INC. - TECHNICAL LIBRARY □ Idaho
Falls, ID

Loos, Patricia R., Dir.
LINCOLN JOURNAL-STAR - LIBRARY □ Lincoln,
NE

Loos, William H., Cur.
BUFFALO & ERIE COUNTY PUBLIC LIBRARY -
RARE BOOK ROOM □ Buffalo, NY

Lopez, George A., Asst.Libn.
ROSENMAN, COLIN, FREUND, LEWIS & COHEN -
LAW LIBRARY □ New York, NY

Lopez, Heriberto, Selection Libn.
UNIVERSITY OF PUERTO RICO - HUMACAO
UNIVERSITY COLLEGE - LIBRARY □ Humacao,
PR

Lopez, Juanita, Asst.Libn.
ITT CORPORATION - GILFILLAN ENGINEERING
LIBRARY† □ Van Nuys, CA

Lopez, Robert A., Hd.Libn.
MINNEAPOLIS STAR AND TRIBUNE - LIBRARY □
Minneapolis, MN

Lopez, Vicente, Libn.
UNIVERSITY OF PUERTO RICO - MAYAGUEZ
CAMPUS - MARINE SCIENCES LIBRARY† □
Mayaguez, PR

Lopez De Heredia, Maria, Libn.
DIVINE WORD INTERNATIONAL RELIGIOUS
EDUCATION CENTRE - LIBRARY □ London, ON

Lopez-Pritchard, Beatriz, Info.Spec.
OFFICE OF BILINGUAL EDUCATION -
RESOURCE LIBRARY AND INFORMATION UNIT
□ Brooklyn, NY

Lopiano, Rosemary, Ref./Cat.Libn.
ART INSTITUTE OF CHICAGO - RYERSON AND
BURNHAM LIBRARIES □ Chicago, IL

LoPresti, Maryellen, Libn.
NORTH CAROLINA STATE UNIVERSITY -
HARRYE LYONS DESIGN LIBRARY □ Raleigh, NC

Loranth, Alice N., Hd.
CLEVELAND PUBLIC LIBRARY - JOHN G. WHITE
COLLECTION OF FOLKLORE, ORIENTALIA, &
CHESS □ Cleveland, OH

Lord, Anne, Libn., Media Spec.
CALIFORNIA SCHOOL FOR THE BLIND -
LIBRARY MEDIA CENTER □ Fremont, CA

Lord, Arthur C., Chm.Lib.Comm.
LANCASTER COUNTY HISTORICAL SOCIETY -
LIBRARY □ Lancaster, PA

Lord, Marjorie, ILL
SUNY - COLLEGE AT BUFFALO - EDWARD H.
BUTLER LIBRARY □ Buffalo, NY

Lordi, Joseph A., Dir.
TAYLOR (Bayard) MEMORIAL LIBRARY □ Kennett
Square, PA

Lordi, Michael, Lib.Dir.
NEW SCHOOL FOR SOCIAL RESEARCH -
RAYMOND FOGELMAN LIBRARY □ New York, NY

Lorenz, Stella, Libn.
AMERICAN APPRAISAL COMPANY - LIBRARY □
Milwaukee, WI

Loria, Joan, Cur. of Exhibits
MASSACHUSETTS INSTITUTE OF TECHNOLOGY
- M.I.T. MUSEUM AND HISTORICAL
COLLECTIONS □ Cambridge, MA

Lorimer, Nicholas, Info. Officer
NEW ZEALAND CONSULATE GENERAL -
LIBRARY □ New York, NY

Lorimer, Suzanne, Art Libn.
UNIVERSITY OF CHICAGO - ART LIBRARY □
Chicago, IL

Loring, Lynn, Circ., Per.
BOSTON CONSERVATORY OF MUSIC - ALBERT ALPHIN MUSIC LIBRARY □ Boston, MA

Lorne, Lorraine K., Assoc.Libn.
DETROIT COLLEGE OF LAW - LIBRARY □ Detroit, MI

Lorrig, Judith, Mayo Med.Sch.Libn.
MAYO FOUNDATION - MAYO CLINIC LIBRARY □ Rochester, MN

Lort, June, Lib.Techn.
COMINCO LTD. - INFORMATION SERVICES □ Vancouver, BC

Losch, Marianne, Libn.
FINANCIAL ACCOUNTING STANDARDS BOARD (FASB) - LIBRARY □ Stamford, CT

Lose, Mary Louise P., Libn.
PEAT, MARWICK, MITCHELL & COMPANY - LIBRARY □ Minneapolis, MN

Losi, Jan J., Cur.
NIAGARA COUNTY HISTORICAL SOCIETY - LIBRARY AND ARCHIVES □ Lockport, NY

Loso, Donald R., Dir.
U.S. DEPT. OF COMMERCE - INTERNATIONAL TRADE ADMINISTRATION - ST. LOUIS DISTRICT OFFICE LIBRARY □ St. Louis, MO

Lospinuso, Margaret F., Music Libn.
UNIVERSITY OF NORTH CAROLINA, CHAPEL HILL - MUSIC LIBRARY □ Chapel Hill, NC

Lothian, Christina R.N., Archv./Libn.
LYMAN HOUSE MEMORIAL MUSEUM - KATHRYN E. LYLE MEMORIAL LIBRARY □ Hilo, HI

Lothyan, Phillip E., Chf., Archv.Br.
U.S. NATL. ARCHIVES & RECORDS SERVICE - FEDERAL ARCHIVES AND RECORDS CENTER, REGION 10 □ Seattle, WA

Lotz, John W., Gen.Mgr.
IFI/PLENUM DATA COMPANY - LIBRARY □ Alexandria, VA

Loubiere, Sue, Libn.
LOUISIANA STATE UNIVERSITY - SCHOOL OF VETERINARY MEDICINE - LIBRARY □ Baton Rouge, LA

Loucka, Patricia A., Libn.
GENERAL ELECTRIC COMPANY - REFRACTORY METAL PRODUCTS DEPARTMENT - LIBRARY† □ Cleveland, OH

Loucks, Cami L., Dir.
TRINITY LUTHERAN HOSPITAL - FLORENCE L. NELSON MEMORIAL LIBRARY □ Kansas City, MO

Loucks, Donald R., Chf. Depository Branch
U.S. DEFENSE AUDIOVISUAL AGENCY - DEPOSITORY BRANCH (DAVA-N-LGD) □ Norton AFB, CA

Loucks, Donna, Libn.
WEYERHAEUSER COMPANY - WESTERN FORESTRY RESEARCH CENTER - LIBRARY □ Centralia, WA

Loud, Robert L., Libn.
ST. ELIZABETH'S HOSPITAL - SCHOOL OF NURSING - LIBRARY □ Brighton, MA

Louden, Kristin, Hd., Circ.
UNIVERSITY OF COLORADO MEDICAL CENTER - DENISON MEMORIAL LIBRARY □ Denver, CO

Louderback, Patricia A., Chf.Libn.
U.S. ARMY POST - FORT LEWIS - LIBRARY SYSTEM □ Fort Lewis, WA

Louet, Sandra, Mgr.
ONTARIO - MINISTRY OF NATURAL RESOURCES - NATURAL RESOURCES LIBRARY □ Toronto, ON

Louet, Sandra, Mgr.
ONTARIO - MINISTRY OF NATURAL RESOURCES - NATURAL RESOURCES LIBRARY - MAPLE □ Maple, ON

Loughin, J. Curtis, Mgr., Info.Serv.
AMERICAN NEWSPAPER PUBLISHERS ASSOCIATION - LIBRARY □ Washington, DC

Loughlin, Beverly, Adm.Asst.
HARTFORD PUBLIC LIBRARY - REFERENCE AND GENERAL READING DEPARTMENT □ Hartford, CT

Loughran, Joan, Dir.Med.Rec. & Lib.
MEDICAL CENTER AT PRINCETON - MEDICAL CENTER LIBRARY □ Princeton, NJ

Louie, Thelma, Subject Anl.
AEROSPACE CORPORATION - CHARLES C. LAURITSEN LIBRARY □ Los Angeles, CA

Lounberg, Joyce, Cat.
UNIVERSITY OF UTAH - SPENCER S. ECCLES HEALTH SCIENCES LIBRARY □ Salt Lake City, UT

Lounder, Shirley A., Dir. of Res.
CANADIAN LAW INFORMATION COUNCIL - RESOURCE CENTRE FOR COMPUTERS AND LAW □ Ottawa, ON

Lounsbury, Loretta, Act.Libn.
STIEFEL LABORATORIES, INC. - RESEARCH INSTITUTE LIBRARY □ Oak Hill, NY

Loup, Jean, Libn.
UNIVERSITY OF MICHIGAN - LIBRARY SCIENCE LIBRARY □ Ann Arbor, MI

Louton, Arlene, Libn.
DONALDSON COMPANY, INC. - INFORMATION CENTER □ Minneapolis, MN

Louviere, Pauline, Dir.
SOUTHERN BAPTIST HOSPITAL - LEARNING RESOURCE CENTER □ New Orleans, LA

Lovari, John, Libn.
ADVERTISING RESEARCH FOUNDATION - LIBRARY □ New York, NY

Lovas, Irene, AV Libn.
U.S. VETERANS ADMINISTRATION (CA-Long Beach) - MEDICAL CENTER LIBRARY □ Long Beach, CA

Lovas, Irene, Med.Libn.
U.S. VETERANS ADMINISTRATION (NY-New York) - MEDICAL CENTER LIBRARY† □ New York, NY

Lovas, Paula M., Hd.
NATIONAL RETIRED TEACHERS ASSN.- AMERICAN ASSN. OF RETIRED PERSONS - NATL. GERONTOLOGY RESOURCE CTR. □ Washington, DC

Love, Barbara, Ref.Libn.
ST. LAWRENCE COLLEGE OF APPLIED ARTS AND TECHNOLOGY - LEARNING RESOURCE CENTRE □ Kingston, ON

Love, Erika, Dir.
UNIVERSITY OF NEW MEXICO - MEDICAL CENTER LIBRARY □ Albuquerque, NM

Love, Grace, Lib.Spec.
UNIVERSITY OF DELAWARE, NEWARK - CHEMISTRY/CHEMICAL ENGINEERING LIBRARY† □ Newark, DE

Love, Kathleen, Res.Dir.
PROJECT FOR PUBLIC SPACES - LIBRARY □ New York, NY

Love, M.J., Libn.
BRITISH COLUMBIA - MINISTRY OF HUMAN RESOURCES - LIBRARY† □ Vancouver, BC

Lovell, Bonnie, Night Libn.
DALLAS MORNING NEWS - REFERENCE DEPARTMENT □ Dallas, TX

Lovelock, Marty H., Libn.
CANADA - CANADIAN TRANSPORT COMMISSION - LIBRARY □ Ottawa, ON

Lovely, Norman E., Hd., Ref. & Res.
WORCESTER FREE PUBLIC LIBRARY - REFERENCE AND RESEARCH □ Worcester, MA

Lovett, Carol B., Archv.
MARSHALL HISTORICAL SOCIETY - ARCHIVES □ Marshall, MI

Lovett, Lovell K., Asst.Libn.
CHURCH OF JESUS CHRIST OF LATTER-DAY SAINTS - EL PASO BRANCH GENEALOGICAL LIBRARY □ El Paso, TX

Loving, Betty, Hd.Libn.
YAVAPAI COUNTY LAW LIBRARY □ Prescott, AZ

Loving, Lloyd, Libn.
DALLAS PUBLIC LIBRARY - BUSINESS AND TECHNOLOGY DIVISION □ Dallas, TX

Low, Betty P., Res. & Ref.Libn.
ELEUTHERIAN MILLS HISTORICAL LIBRARY □ Wilmington, DE

Low, Erick Baker, Assoc.Libn.
NATIONAL CENTER FOR STATE COURTS - LIBRARY □ Williamsburg, VA

Lowden, Arlene M., Libn.
SIEMENS GAMMASONICS, INC. - NUCLEAR MEDICAL DIVISION - RESEARCH LIBRARY □ Des Plaines, IL

Lowe, Cynthia A., Libn.
FRIEDMAN & KOVEN - LAW LIBRARY □ Chicago, IL

Lowe, David, Ref./Docs.
UNIVERSITY OF ALABAMA - SCHOOL OF LAW LIBRARY □ University, AL

Lowe, Doris, Hd., Ref.Dept.
CORNELL UNIVERSITY - MEDICAL COLLEGE - LIBRARY □ New York, NY

Lowe, James L., Dir.
DELTIOLOGISTS OF AMERICA - LIBRARY □ Newtown Square, PA

Lowe, May, Libn.
MOBILE COUNTY PUBLIC LAW LIBRARY □ Mobile, AL

Lowe, Peggy, Sec.Asst.
EL MONTE HISTORICAL SOCIETY - MUSEUM LIBRARY □ El Monte, CA

Lowe, William C., Asst.Dir.Ref.Serv.
NORTH CAROLINA STATE UNIVERSITY - D.H. HILL LIBRARY □ Raleigh, NC

Lowell, Amy, Pubn.Coord.
ANTHROPOLOGY RESOURCE CENTER (ARC) - CITIZENS INFORMATION CENTER □ Boston, MA

Lowell, Marcia, State Libn.
OREGON STATE LIBRARY □ Salem, OR

Lowell, Waverly, Cur. of Mss.
CALIFORNIA HISTORICAL SOCIETY - SCHUBERT HALL LIBRARY □ San Francisco, CA

Lowenstein, Florence, Ed.Assoc.
AMERICAN COUNCIL OF VOLUNTARY AGENCIES FOR FOREIGN SERVICE, INC. - TECH. ASSISTANCE INFO. CLEARING HOUSE □ New York, NY

Lowich, Donna, Asst.Libn.
AMERICAN TELEPHONE & TELEGRAPH COMPANY - BUSINESS & TECHNICAL RESOURCE CENTER □ Piscataway, NJ

Lowrey, Carol, Tech.Serv.Libn.
ART GALLERY OF ONTARIO - EDWARD P. TAYLOR REFERENCE LIBRARY □ Toronto, ON

Lowrie, A. Lucille, Libn.
U.S. AIR FORCE BASE - ALTUS BASE LIBRARY □ Altus AFB, OK

Lowry, Andree, Libn.
ENVIRONMENTAL PROTECTION AGENCY - ENVIRONMENTAL RESEARCH LABORATORY, GULF BREEZE - LIBRARY □ Gulf Breeze, FL

Lowry, Barbara, Asst.Ref.Libn.
PHILADELPHIA COLLEGE OF TEXTILES AND SCIENCE - PASTORE LIBRARY □ Philadelphia, PA

Lowry, Viola, Asst.Cur.
MERCER COUNTY HISTORICAL SOCIETY - LIBRARY AND ARCHIVES □ Mercer, PA

Lowy, George, Dir.
PRATT INSTITUTE - LIBRARY □ Brooklyn, NY

Loyal, Janice, Ser.Libn.
O'MELVENY AND MYERS - INFORMATION SERVICES □ Los Angeles, CA

Loyd, Ann M., Ref.Libn.
CARNEGIE LIBRARY OF PITTSBURGH - PENNSYLVANIA DIVISION □ Pittsburgh, PA

Loyd, Rev. Roger L., Cur.
SOUTHERN METHODIST UNIVERSITY - METHODIST HISTORICAL COLLECTIONS □ Dallas, TX

Loyd, Roger L., Assoc.Libn.
SOUTHERN METHODIST UNIVERSITY - PERKINS SCHOOL OF THEOLOGY - LIBRARY □ Dallas, TX

Lozano, Eduardo, Biblog.
UNIVERSITY OF PITTSBURGH - LATIN AMERICAN COLLECTION □ Pittsburgh, PA

Lu, C.H., Tech.Dir.
UNIVERSITY OF IOWA - LABORATORY FOR POLITICAL RESEARCH □ Iowa City, IA
Lu, James, Soc.Sci./Hum.
KANSAS STATE UNIVERSITY - FARRELL LIBRARY □ Manhattan, KS
Lu, Joseph, Doc.Libn.
IDAHO STATE UNIVERSITY LIBRARY - DOCUMENTS DIVISION □ Pocatello, ID
Lu, Dr. Po-Yung, Dir.
NATIONAL LIBRARY OF MEDICINE - TOXICOLOGY DATA BANK □ Oak Ridge, TN
Lu, Teresa Y., Libn.
VALLEY GENERAL HOSPITAL - LIBRARY □ Renton, WA
Lubek, Noreen, Asst.Libn.
ROCKWELL INTERNATIONAL - GRAPHIC SYSTEMS DIVISION - TECHNICAL INFORMATION CENTER □ Chicago, IL
Luberda, Robert G., Hd.Libn.
REAL ESTATE RESEARCH CORPORATION - LIBRARY □ Chicago, IL
Lubetski, Edith, Hd.Libn.
YESHIVA UNIVERSITY - HEDI STEINBERG LIBRARY □ New York, NY
Lucas, Barbara, Pub.Serv.
UNIVERSITY OF KENTUCKY - MEDICAL CENTER LIBRARY □ Lexington, KY
Lucas, Beth, Pk.Libn.
U.S. NATL. PARK SERVICE - GLACIER NATL. PARK - GEORGE C. RUHLE LIBRARY □ West Glacier, MT
Lucas, Darla L.W.
BETHLEHEM STEEL CORPORATION - SCHWAB MEMORIAL LIBRARY □ Bethlehem, PA
Lucas, Dorothy B., Libn.
AMERICAN BAPTIST THEOLOGICAL SEMINARY - T.L. HOLCOMB LIBRARY □ Nashville, TN
Lucas, Rev. Glenn, Archv./Hist.
UNITED CHURCH OF CANADA - CENTRAL ARCHIVES □ Toronto, ON
Lucas, Holly C.K.S., Libn.
UNIVERSITY OF PENNSYLVANIA - MOORE SCHOOL OF ELECTRICAL ENGINEERING LIBRARY □ Philadelphia, PA
Lucas, Holly C.K.S., Act.Hd.
UNIVERSITY OF PENNSYLVANIA - TOWNE SCIENTIFIC LIBRARY □ Philadelphia, PA
Lucas, Leonard, Hd., Soc.Sci. & Hist.
WORCESTER FREE PUBLIC LIBRARY - REFERENCE AND RESEARCH □ Worcester, MA
Lucas, Leora E., Hd., Tchg.Mtl.Ctr.
SUNY - COLLEGE AT ONEONTA - JAMES M. MILNE LIBRARY □ Oneonta, NY
Lucas, Lydia, Hd., Tech.Serv.
MINNESOTA HISTORICAL SOCIETY - DIVISION OF ARCHIVES AND MANUSCRIPTS □ St. Paul, MN
Lucas, Lynn, Asst.Libn.
INDIANA UNIVERSITY OF PENNSYLVANIA - UNIVERSITY LIBRARY □ Indiana, PA
Lucas, R.M., Med.Libn.
U.S. AIR FORCE HOSPITAL - MEDICAL LIBRARY (IL-Rantoul) □ Rantoul, IL
Lucas, Rosemary, Libn.
WISCONSIN STATE LEGISLATIVE REFERENCE BUREAU □ Madison, WI
Lucas, Susan M., Libn.
UNIVERSITY HOSPITALS OF CLEVELAND & CASE WESTERN RESERVE UNIVERSITY - DEPT. OF PATHOLOGY - LIBRARY □ Cleveland, OH
Lucas, Valeeta, Cat.Libn.
BURNS AND MC DONNELL ENGINEERING COMPANY - TECHNICAL LIBRARY □ Kansas City, MO
Lucchetti, Stephen C., Libn.
UNIVERSITY OF MICHIGAN - CHEMISTRY LIBRARY □ Ann Arbor, MI
Luce, Gordon R., Jr., Libn.
UNIVERSITY OF WISCONSIN, MADISON - BIOLOGY LIBRARY □ Madison, WI
Luceno, Jean M., Gold Info.Coord.
GOLD INFORMATION CENTER □ New York, NY

Lucey, Jean E., Dir.
INSURANCE LIBRARY ASSOCIATION OF BOSTON □ Boston, MA
Luchars, Margaret O., Techn.
SMITHSONIAN INSTITUTION LIBRARIES - COOPER-HEWITT MUSEUM OF DESIGN - DORIS & HENRY DREYFUSS MEMORIAL STUDY CENTER □ New York, NY
Luchechko, John, Hd.Rd.Serv.
JERSEY CITY STATE COLLEGE - FORREST A. IRWIN LIBRARY □ Jersey City, NJ
Lucht, Irma M., Dir.
METROPOLITAN PERIODICAL SERVICE □ Chicago, IL
Lucier, Donna, Libn.
NORTH CAROLINA STATE DEPT. OF NATURAL RESOURCES & COMMUNITY DEVELOPMENT - ENVIRONMENTAL MGT. LIBRARY □ Raleigh, NC
Luddy, Evangeline, Libn.
CONNECTICUT STATE LIBRARY - HARTFORD LAW BRANCH □ Hartford, CT
Ludewig, Bernice B., Libn.
ST. JOSEPH MEMORIAL HOSPITAL - HEALTH SCIENCE LIBRARY □ Kokomo, IN
Ludmer, Joyce, Art Libn./Dir.
UNIVERSITY OF CALIFORNIA, LOS ANGELES - ART LIBRARY - ELMER BELT LIBRARY OF VINCIANA □ Los Angeles, CA
Ludmer, Joyce P., Art Libn.
UNIVERSITY OF CALIFORNIA, LOS ANGELES - ART LIBRARY □ Los Angeles, CA
Ludovici, Ann, Ref.Libn.
TEMPLE UNIVERSITY - HEALTH SCIENCES CENTER - LIBRARY □ Philadelphia, PA
Ludt, Bonnie, Hd.Acq.Dept.
CALIFORNIA INSTITUTE OF TECHNOLOGY - ROBERT A. MILLIKAN MEMORIAL LIBRARY □ Pasadena, CA
Ludvigsen, Margaret, Mgr., Info.Serv.
FARMERS UNION CENTRAL EXCHANGE, INC. - INFORMATION CENTER □ St.Paul, MN
Ludwig, Logan, AV Libn.
ST. LOUIS UNIVERSITY - MEDICAL CENTER LIBRARY □ St. Louis, MO
Ludwig, Richard M., Asst.Libn.
PRINCETON UNIVERSITY - RARE BOOKS AND SPECIAL COLLECTIONS □ Princeton, NJ
Ludwikowski, Stella E., Adm.Libn.
U.S. AIR FORCE BASE - EIELSON BASE LIBRARY □ Eielson AFB, AK
Ludwin, Vivien, Pub.Serv.Libn.
QUEEN'S UNIVERSITY AT KINGSTON - BRACKEN LIBRARY □ Kingston, ON
Luebbe, Mary, Ref.Libn.
UNIVERSITY OF BRITISH COLUMBIA - GOVERNMENT PUBLICATIONS & MICROFORMS DIVISIONS □ Vancouver, BC
Luebbert, Nancy, Hist.Rec. Surveyor
LATAH COUNTY HISTORICAL SOCIETY - LIBRARY □ Moscow, ID
Luebke, Margaret F., Med.Libn.
DOCTORS' MEDICAL CENTER - PROFESSIONAL LIBRARY □ Modesto, CA
Lueck, Antoinette, Physical Sci.Libn.
COLORADO STATE UNIVERSITY - WILLIAM E. MORGAN LIBRARY □ Fort Collins, CO
Lueders, Julie A., Chf., Lib.Serv.
U.S. VETERANS ADMINISTRATION (CT-Newington) - HOSPITAL HEALTH SCIENCES LIBRARY □ Newington, CT
Luetge, Elvie Lou, Act.Exec.Dir.
ASSOCIATION FOR CHILDHOOD EDUCATION INTERNATIONAL - LIBRARY □ Washington, DC
Lufkin, Patricia, Info.Spec.
ECOLOGY & ENVIRONMENT, INC. - LIBRARY □ Buffalo, NY
Luger, Herbert, Regional Libn.
ENVIRONMENTAL PROTECTION AGENCY - REGION II LIBRARY □ New York, NY
Luhde, Jutta, Libn.
BERKSHIRE MEDICAL CENTER - MEDICAL LIBRARY □ Pittsfield, MA

Luik, Asta, Libn.
UNIVERSITY OF TORONTO - INSTITUTE FOR AEROSPACE STUDIES - LIBRARY □ Downsview, ON
Lukas, Carla M., Libn.
YALE UNIVERSITY - CLASSICS LIBRARY □ New Haven, CT
Lukas, Marilyn, Res.
BOOZ, ALLEN & HAMILTON, INC. - RESEARCH SERVICE □ New York, NY
Lukasiewich, Halina, Coord.Biblog.Control
CANADA - CANADIAN INTERNATIONAL DEVELOPMENT AGENCY - DEVELOPMENT INFORMATION CENTRE □ Hull, PQ
Lukasiewicz, Barbara, Hd., Ser.
UNIVERSITY OF MICHIGAN - DEARBORN LIBRARY □ Dearborn, MI
Lukasiewicz, Paul J., Mathematics Libn.
YALE UNIVERSITY - MATHEMATICS LIBRARY □ New Haven, CT
Luke, Keye L., Libn.
FMC CORPORATION - CENTRAL ENGINEERING LABORATORIES - LIBRARY □ Santa Clara, CA
Luke, Lisbeth L., Libn.
APPALACHIAN REGIONAL COMMISSION - LIBRARY □ Washington, DC
Lukens, Beatrice L., Libn.
UNIVERSITY OF CALIFORNIA, BERKELEY - EARTH SCIENCES LIBRARY □ Berkeley, CA
Lukes, Frank, Law Libn.
BAKER & MC KENZIE - LIBRARY □ Chicago, IL
Lukowycz, J.P., Chf.Ref. & Info.Proc
CANADA - PUBLIC ARCHIVES OF CANADA - FEDERAL ARCHIVES DIVISION □ Ottawa, ON
Luks, Lewis F., Cons.
MARIST COLLEGE - LIBRARY □ Washington, DC
Luksik, Joan, Dir.
MOUNT CARMEL MERCY HOSPITAL AND MEDICAL CENTER - MEDICAL LIBRARY □ Detroit, MI
Lull, David, Cat.Libn.
UNIVERSITY OF WISCONSIN, SUPERIOR - JIM DAN HILL LIBRARY □ Superior, WI
Lum, Raymond D., Hd., Western Sect.
HARVARD UNIVERSITY - HARVARD YENCHING INSTITUTE - LIBRARY □ Cambridge, MA
Lumia, Carol A., Asst.Dir.
HISTORICAL SOCIETY OF SARATOGA SPRINGS - MUSEUM AND LIBRARY □ Saratoga Springs, NY
Lumm, Jane, Adm.Asst.
UNIVERSITY OF MICHIGAN - MAP ROOM □ Ann Arbor, MI
Lummer, Florence, Libn.
ANTI-DEFAMATION LEAGUE OF B'NAI B'RITH - JACOB ALSON MEMORIAL LIBRARY □ New York, NY
Lummis, G.H., Mgr.
HALIFAX BOARD OF TRADE - LIBRARY □ Halifax, NS
Lumpkin, Hazel, Acq.Libn.
NORTH CAROLINA CENTRAL UNIVERSITY - LAW LIBRARY □ Durham, NC
Lumsden, Sharmyn, Photo.Cur.
AUSTIN PUBLIC LIBRARY - AUSTIN-TRAVIS COUNTY COLLECTION □ Austin, TX
Lunak, Louise, Libn.
CHICAGO ACADEMY OF SCIENCES - MATTHEW LAUGHLIN MEMORIAL LIBRARY □ Chicago, IL
Lund, Ann, Libn.
CAPITAL TIMES NEWSPAPER - LIBRARY □ Madison, WI
Lund, Mr. Chris, Photo Ed.
CANADA - NATIONAL FILM BOARD OF CANADA - PHOTOTHEQUE □ Ottawa, ON
Lund, Robert, Owner
AMERICAN MUSEUM OF MAGIC - LIBRARY □ Marshall, MI
Lundahl, Margaret, Libn.
ISHAM, LINCOLN & BEALE - LIBRARY □ Chicago, IL
Lundberg, Mrs. Erveen C., Hd.
HIGGINS (John Woodman) ARMORY, INC. - MEMORIAL LIBRARY □ Worcester, MA

PERSONNEL

Lunde, Daniel, Ref./Circ.Libn.
MINNESOTA STATE LAW LIBRARY □ St. Paul,
MN

Lundeen, Joel W., Assoc.Archv.
LUTHERAN CHURCH IN AMERICA - ARCHIVES □
Chicago, IL

Lundholm, Eugene T., Hd.Libn.
UNIVERSITY OF WISCONSIN, SUPERIOR - JIM
DAN HILL LIBRARY □ Superior, WI

Lundquist, Barbara, Chf.
DISTRICT OF COLUMBIA PUBLIC LIBRARY -
TECHNOLOGY AND SCIENCE DIVISION □
Washington, DC

Lundquist, Mrs. Duane, Hd.
WOODLAKE LUTHERAN CHURCH - LIBRARY† □
Richfield, MN

Lundsted, James E., Dir. Of Musm.
DOUGLAS COUNTY HISTORICAL MUSEUM -
LIBRARY □ Superior, WI

Lundstrom, Lynn, Asst.Libn.
BANCROFT, AVERY AND MC ALISTER - LAW
LIBRARY □ San Francisco, CA

Lundy, Mack, Libn.
TRIDENT TECHNICAL COLLEGE - NORTH
CAMPUS LIBRARY □ North Charleston, SC

Lung, Chung-Ming, Asst.Libn.
SMITHSONIAN INSTITUTION - FREER GALLERY
OF ART - LIBRARY □ Washington, DC

Lung, Vivian, Libn.
BELL CANADA - O.R. INFORMATION RESOURCE
CENTRE □ Toronto, ON

Lunk, William A., Chm. of Lib.Comm.
WILSON ORNITHOLOGICAL SOCIETY -
JOSSELYN VAN TYNE MEMORIAL LIBRARY □
Ann Arbor, MI

Lunt, Wilhelmina V., Cur.
HISTORICAL SOCIETY OF OLD NEWBURY -
LIBRARY □ Newburyport, MA

Luostari, Ken, Lib.Dir.
NATIONAL SKI HALL OF FAME AND MUSEUM -
ROLAND PALMEDO NATIONAL SKI LIBRARY □
Ishpeming, MI

Lupianez De Gonzalez, Ana Mercedes, Libn.
PUERTO RICO - OFFICE OF PERSONNEL -
LIBRARY □ Santurce, PR

Lupo, Mona C., Tech.Libn.
REYNOLDS ELECTRICAL AND ENGINEERING
COMPANY, INC. - TECHNICAL LIBRARY □ Las
Vegas, NV

Lupp, Denise, Lib.Serv.Coord.
WASHINGTON COUNTY HOSPITAL - LIBRARY □
Hagerstown, MD

Luquire, Wilson, Dean., Lib.Serv.
EASTERN ILLINOIS UNIVERSITY - BOOTH
LIBRARY □ Charleston, IL

Lurye, Joan B., Mgr.
AMERICAN EXPRESS COMPANY - CARD
INFORMATION CENTER □ New York, NY

Lusardi, Frank, Asst.Libn.
TOBACCO MERCHANTS ASSOCIATION OF THE
U.S. - HOWARD S. CULLMAN LIBRARY □ New
York, NY

Lusas, Dr. E.W., Dir.
FOOD PROTEIN RESEARCH AND DEVELOPMENT
CENTER - LIBRARY □ College Station, TX

Luse, Nancy, Info.Spec.
NATIONAL CAR RENTAL SYSTEM, INC. -
BUSINESS INFORMATION CENTER □
Minneapolis, MN

Lussier, Claudine, Dir.
CANADA - EMPLOYMENT & IMMIGRATION
CANADA - QUEBEC REGIONAL LIBRARY □
Montreal, PQ

Lust, Vernon G., Hd., Coll.Dev.Dept.
UNIVERSITY OF CALIFORNIA, DAVIS -
GENERAL LIBRARY □ Davis, CA

Lustig, Ingrid, Office Mgr.
FAIRBANKS ENVIRONMENTAL CENTER -
LIBRARY □ Fairbanks, AK

Lustig, Joanne, Info.Spec.
KNOLL PHARMACEUTICAL COMPANY -
RESEARCH LIBRARY □ Whippany, NJ

Luszczynska, Barbara, Asst.Libn.
WASHINGTON UNIVERSITY - CHEMISTRY
LIBRARY □ St. Louis, MO

Luther, M. Judy, Dir./Learning Rsrcs.
EMBRY RIDDLE AERONAUTICAL UNIVERSITY -
LEARNING RESOURCES CENTER □ Daytona
Beach, FL

Lutovsky, Margaret, Lrng.Res.Libn.
MILWAUKEE AREA TECHNICAL COLLEGE -
RASCHE MEMORIAL LIBRARY □ Milwaukee, WI

Lutz, Diane, Dir., Info.Serv.
CONFERENCE BOARD OF CANADA - LIBRARY &
INFORMATION CENTER □ Ottawa, ON

Lutz, Heidi, Adm.Asst./Libn.
SANTA CLARA COUNTY PLANNING
DEPARTMENT - LIBRARY □ San Jose, CA

Lutz, Sharon E., Asst.Libn.
GENERAL ELECTRIC COMPANY -
TRANSPORTATION TECHNOLOGY CENTER -
TECHNICAL INFORMATION CENTER □ Erie, PA

Lutz, Susan E., Lib.Techn.
OKLAHOMA WATER RESOURCES BOARD -
LIBRARY □ Oklahoma City, OK

Lutzker, David, Pres.
HASHOMER HATZAIR-ZIONIST YOUTH
MOVEMENT - LIBRARY □ New York, NY

Lutzker, Professor M., Hd., Rd.Serv.
JOHN JAY COLLEGE OF CRIMINAL JUSTICE OF
THE CITY UNIVERSITY OF NEW YORK -
REISMAN MEMORIAL LIBRARY □ New York, NY

LuValle, Jean L., Asst.Libn.
ZOECON CORPORATION - LIBRARY □ Palo Alto,
CA

Luxenberg, Alan H., Res.Libn.
FOREIGN POLICY RESEARCH INSTITUTE -
LIBRARY □ Philadelphia, PA

Luxner, Richard, Voorhees Br.Libn.
CUNY - NEW YORK CITY TECHNICAL COLLEGE
LIBRARY/LEARNING RESOURCE CENTER □
Brooklyn, NY

Luzader, JoAnn, Asst.Libn., Pub.Serv.
COLUMBUS TECHNICAL INSTITUTE -
EDUCATIONAL RESOURCES CENTER† □
Columbus, OH

Lwin, U Myo, Burmese Cat.
CORNELL UNIVERSITY - JOHN M. ECHOLS
COLLECTION ON SOUTHEAST ASIA □ Ithaca, NY

Lyau, Christine F.G., Asst.Libn.
SOUTHERN CALIFORNIA EDISON COMPANY -
LIBRARY □ Rosemead, CA

Lybeck, Marti, Asst.Br.Libn.
ST. PAUL PUBLIC LIBRARY - HIGHLAND PARK
BRANCH - PERRIE JONES MEMORIAL ROOM □
St. Paul, MN

Lyders, Richard, Exec.Dir.
HOUSTON ACADEMY OF MEDICINE - TEXAS
MEDICAL CENTER LIBRARY □ Houston, TX

Lydigsen, Mildred, Libn.
MAC NEAL MEMORIAL HOSPITAL - FRANK C.
BECHT MEMORIAL LIBRARY □ Berwyn, IL

Lydon, Mary E., Corp.Libn.
METCALF & EDDY, INC. - LIBRARY □ Boston,
MA

Lyerla, Gloria, Libn., ILL
TEXAS TECH UNIVERSITY - LIBRARY □
Lubbock, TX

Lyle, Cindy, Adm.
WOMEN ARTISTS NEWS - ARCHIVES □ New
York, NY

Lyle, Martha, Libn.
CARNEGIE LIBRARY OF PITTSBURGH -
SCIENCE AND TECHNOLOGY DEPARTMENT □
Pittsburgh, PA

Lyle, Robert S., Libn.
U.S. VETERANS ADMINISTRATION (PA-
Coatesville) - MEDICAL CENTER LIBRARY □
Coatesville, PA

Lyle, Royster, Cur. of Coll.
MARSHALL (George C.) RESEARCH
FOUNDATION - GEORGE C. MARSHALL
RESEARCH LIBRARY □ Lexington, VA

Lyles, Gloria, Adm.
JOHNS HOPKINS UNIVERSITY - WILLIAM H.
WELCH MEDICAL LIBRARY □ Baltimore, MD

Lyman, Norma Jane, Asst. Law Libn.
NEW HAMPSHIRE STATE LIBRARY - DIVISION
OF LAW AND LEGISLATIVE REFERENCE
SERVICE □ Concord, NH

Lynagh, Pat, Media Ctr.Libn.
CLEVELAND INSTITUTE OF ART - JESSICA R.
GUND MEMORIAL LIBRARY □ Cleveland, OH

Lynas, Lothian, Assoc.Libn.
NEW YORK BOTANICAL GARDEN - LIBRARY □
Bronx, NY

Lynch, Cheryl, Libn.
LAWRENCE EAGLE TRIBUNE - LIBRARY □
Lawrence, MA

Lynch, Evangeline M., Libn.
LOUISIANA STATE UNIVERSITY - RARE BOOK
COLLECTION □ Baton Rouge, LA

Lynch, Evangeline Mills, Libn.
LOUISIANA STATE UNIVERSITY - LOUISIANA
ROOM □ Baton Rouge, LA

Lynch, Mrs. Florence, Cat.
HARVARD UNIVERSITY - EDA KUHN LOEB
MUSIC LIBRARY □ Cambridge, MA

Lynch, Frances H., Asst.Dir.Tech.Serv.
VANDERBILT UNIVERSITY - MEDICAL CENTER
LIBRARY □ Nashville, TN

Lynch, James R., Archv.
CHURCH OF THE BRETHREN GENERAL BOARD -
BRETHREN HISTORICAL LIBRARY AND
ARCHIVES □ Elgin, IL

Lynch, Sr. M. Dennis, S.H.C.J., Lib.Dir.
ROSEMONT COLLEGE - GERTRUDE KISTLER
MEMORIAL LIBRARY - SPECIAL COLLECTIONS
□ Rosemont, PA

Lynch, Martha, Asst.Med.Libn.
METHODIST HOSPITAL - HEALTH SCIENCES
LIBRARY □ Brooklyn, NY

Lynch, Mollie S., Dir., Educ.Rsrcs.
ST. JOSEPH MERCY HOSPITAL - EDUCATIONAL
RESOURCES □ Pontiac, MI

Lynch, William L., Mng.Dir.
TAX EXECUTIVES INSTITUTE, INC. - TEI
INFORMATION SYSTEM □ Arlington, VA

Lynn, Carol, Med.Libn.
ANCLOTE PSYCHIATRIC CENTER - MEDICAL
LIBRARY† □ Tarpon Springs, FL

Lynn, Daphne, Dir.
MC KEESPORT HOSPITAL - HEALTH SERVICES
LIBRARY □ McKeesport, PA

Lynn, Deanna C., Asst.Libn.
ENVIRONMENTAL RESEARCH & TECHNOLOGY,
INC. - INFORMATION CENTER □ Concord, MA

Lynn, Edna, Exec.Sec.
COLUMBIA COUNTY HISTORICAL SOCIETY -
LIBRARY □ Orangeville, PA

Lynn, Mary Evelyn, Libn.
EAST TENNESSEE BAPTIST HOSPITAL -
HEALTH SCIENCES LIBRARY □ Knoxville, TN

Lynott, Nancy, Tech.Libn.
PERKIN-ELMER TECHNICAL SYSTEMS
DIVISION - LIBRARY □ Tinton Falls, NJ

Lyon, Eunice M., Med.Libn.
U.S. AIR FORCE HOSPITAL - MALCOLM GROW
MEDICAL CENTER - LIBRARY □ Washington, DC

Lyon, Frances, Dir. of Lib.Serv.
MEMORIAL HOSPITAL MEDICAL CENTER OF
LONG BEACH - MEDICAL LIBRARY □ Long
Beach, CA

Lyon, Grace, Hd.Libn.
LYON'S BUSINESS COLLEGE - LIBRARY □ New
Castle, PA

Lyon, James M., Dir.
FEDERAL RESERVE BANK OF MINNEAPOLIS -
LAW LIBRARY □ Minneapolis, MN

Lyon, R. Donald, Coord.
BURNABY AND NEW WESTMINSTER SCHOOL
BOARDS - REGIONAL FILM LIBRARY SERVICES
□ Burnaby, BC

Lyon, R. Donald, Coord.
BURNABY SCHOOL BOARD - DISTRICT
RESOURCE CENTRE □ Burnaby, BC

Lyon-Hartmann, Becky, Asst./Network Dev.
U.S. VETERANS ADMINISTRATION (DC-Washington) - HEADQUARTERS CENTRAL OFFICE LIBRARY □ Washington, DC

Lyon-Hartmann, Becky, Asst./Network Dev.
U.S. VETERANS ADMINISTRATION (DC-Washington) - HEADQUARTERS LIBRARY DIVISION □ Washington, DC

Lyons, Amy, Hd., Circ.
SUNY AT BUFFALO - HEALTH SCIENCES LIBRARY □ Buffalo, NY

Lyons, Clare-Marie, Libn.
CAMPBELL, GODFREY & LEWTAS - LIBRARY □ Toronto, ON

Lyons, Evelyn, ILL Libn.
MILLERSVILLE STATE COLLEGE - HELEN A. GANSER LIBRARY □ Millersville, PA

Lyons, Grace, Chf.
DISTRICT OF COLUMBIA PUBLIC LIBRARY - LIBRARY FOR THE BLIND AND PHYSICALLY HANDICAPPED □ Washington, DC

Lyons, Lois, Hd., Cat.
UNIVERSITY OF WISCONSIN, WHITEWATER - LIBRARY & LEARNING RESOURCES □ Whitewater, WI

Lyons, Lucy, Tech.Asst.
SAN DIEGO STATE UNIVERSITY - SOCIAL SCIENCE RESEARCH LABORATORY - LIBRARY □ San Diego, CA

Lyons, Sarah, Libn.
CONSERVATIVE BAPTIST THEOLOGICAL SEMINARY - CAREY S. THOMAS LIBRARY □ Denver, CO

Lyons, Susan, Dir.
BURLINGTON COUNTY LYCEUM OF HISTORY AND NATURAL SCIENCE - MOUNT HOLLY LIBRARY □ Mt. Holly, NJ

Lyons, Valerie, Photo Libn.
ATLANTA NEWSPAPERS - REFERENCE LIBRARY □ Atlanta, GA

Lyons, Virginia, ILL Libn.
BATTELLE-COLUMBUS LABORATORIES - LIBRARY □ Columbus, OH

Lysdahl, Ellie, Supv. Tape Textbook Sect.
MINNESOTA STATE SERVICES FOR THE BLIND AND VISUALLY HANDICAPPED - COMMUNICATION CENTER □ St. Paul, MN

Lysiuk, Alina, Asst.Med.Libn.
HOECHST-ROUSSEL PHARMACEUTICALS, INC. - LIBRARY □ Somerville, NJ

Lysyk, Pat, Ref.Libn.
UNIVERSITY OF BRITISH COLUMBIA - WOODWARD BIOMEDICAL LIBRARY □ Vancouver, BC

Lytle, Judy K., Libn.
MATTHEWS & NOWLIN - LIBRARY □ San Antonio, TX

Lytle, Myrtle L., Asst. to Dir.
WAKE FOREST UNIVERSITY - BAPTIST COLLECTION □ Winston-Salem, NC

Lytle, Steve, Archv.
HARTFORD HOSPITAL - HEALTH SCIENCE LIBRARIES □ Hartford, CT

Lytle, Susan S., Map Libn.
TEXAS A & M UNIVERSITY - MAP DEPARTMENT □ College Station, TX

M

Ma, Margaret C., Libn.
QUADREX CORPORATION - INFORMATION & RESOURCE CENTER LIBRARY □ Campbell, CA

Ma, Tai-loi, Hd., Cat.
UNIVERSITY OF CHICAGO - FAR EASTERN LIBRARY □ Chicago, IL

Ma, Vilia, Ref.Libn.
IBM CORPORATION - RESEARCH LIBRARY □ San Jose, CA

Ma, Wei-Yi, Chinese Biblog.
UNIVERSITY OF MICHIGAN - ASIA LIBRARY □ Ann Arbor, MI

Maack, David, Intl./Foreign Docs.Libn.
UNIVERSITY OF WASHINGTON - GOVERNMENT PUBLICATIONS DIVISION □ Seattle, WA

Maag, Albert F., Univ.Libn.
CAPITAL UNIVERSITY - CHEMISTRY LIBRARY □ Columbus, OH

Mabry, Raymond, Libn.
RICHMOND PUBLIC LIBRARY - ART AND MUSIC DEPARTMENT† □ Richmond, VA

Mabry, Shirley, Chf., Lib.Serv.
U.S. VETERANS ADMINISTRATION (FL-Lake City) - MEDICAL CENTER LIBRARY □ Lake City, FL

MacAdam, Bonnie, Cur.
LYME HISTORICAL SOCIETY, INC. - ARCHIVES □ Old Lyme, CT

McAdam, Eileen, Libn.
KAISER-PERMANENTE MEDICAL CENTER - HEALTH LIBRARY □ Oakland, CA

McAdams, B.A., Tech.Libn.
LOCKHEED-GEORGIA COMPANY - TECHNICAL INFORMATION DEPARTMENT □ Marietta, GA

McAlister, George L., Assoc.Dir.
LOMA LINDA UNIVERSITY - DEL E. WEBB MEMORIAL LIBRARY □ Loma Linda, CA

McAllister, Sr. Coletta, Archv./Cat.
ST. VINCENT HOSPITAL AND MEDICAL CENTER - HEALTH SCIENCE LIBRARY □ Toledo, OH

MacAllister, Edith, Libn.
OLD MANSE LIBRARY □ Newcastle, NB

McAllister, Lois, Asst.Cat.
NEW YORK STATE HISTORICAL ASSOCIATION - LIBRARY □ Cooperstown, NY

McAllister, Lowell, Dir.
MASSACHUSETTS AUDUBON SOCIETY - BERKSHIRE SANCTUARIES - LIBRARY □ Lenox, MA

McAlpin, Sidney, State Archv.
WASHINGTON STATE OFFICE OF SECRETARY OF STATE - DIVISION OF ARCHIVES AND RECORD MANAGEMENT □ Olympia, WA

McAnanama, Judith, Chf.Libn.
HAMILTON PUBLIC LIBRARY - SPECIAL COLLECTIONS □ Hamilton, ON

McAndrew, Marie, Libn.
MERCY HOSPITAL - SCHOOL OF NURSING - LIBRARY □ Scranton, PA

McAninch, Glen, Archv.Assoc.
UNIVERSITY OF GEORGIA - RICHARD B. RUSSELL MEMORIAL LIBRARY □ Athens, GA

McAninch, Sandra, Docs.Libn.
UNIVERSITY OF GEORGIA - GOVERNMENT REFERENCE/DOCUMENTS SECTION □ Athens, GA

McArdle, James J., Libn.
KING COUNTY LAW LIBRARY □ Seattle, WA

Macaree, Mary W., Hd.
UNIVERSITY OF BRITISH COLUMBIA - MAC MILLAN FORESTRY/AGRICULTURE LIBRARY □ Vancouver, BC

McArthur, David, Libn.
CANADIAN NUCLEAR ASSOCIATION - CNA LIBRARY □ Toronto, ON

McArthur, Dr. Priscilla, Educ.Coord.
ARKANSAS TERRITORIAL RESTORATION - LIBRARY □ Little Rock, AR

MacArthur, William J., Jr., Hd.
KNOXVILLE-KNOX COUNTY PUBLIC LIBRARY SYSTEM - MC CLUNG HISTORICAL COLLECTION □ Knoxville, TN

McAteer, Mary M., Law Libn.
HERCULES, INC. - LAW DEPARTMENT LIBRARY □ Wilmington, DE

McAuliffe, James R., Hd.Libn.
PIERCE JUNIOR COLLEGE - LIBRARY† □ Philadelphia, PA

McAuliffe, Phyllis M., Libn.
MALDEN HOSPITAL - SCHOOL OF NURSING LIBRARY □ Malden, MA

McAvity, Margaret, Libn.
PEARSON (Lester B.) COLLEGE OF THE PACIFIC - LIBRARY □ Victoria, BC

McAvoy, Kathleen C., Libn.
ST. JOSEPH HOSPITAL, OUR LADY OF FATIMA UNIT - HEALTH SCIENCE LIBRARY □ North Providence, RI

MacAyeal, Bettina R., Libn.
CASE WESTERN RESERVE UNIVERSITY - MATTHEW A. BAXTER SCHOOL OF LIBRARY & INFORMATION SCIENCE □ Cleveland, OH

McBeth, Deborah, Co-Libn.
NAVAJO NATION LIBRARY □ Window Rock, AZ

Macbeth, Eileen M., Libn.
CHESTER COUNTY LAW AND MISCELLANEOUS LIBRARY ASSOCIATION □ West Chester, PA

McBirney, Constance, Mss.Libn.
INDIANA HISTORICAL SOCIETY - WILLIAM HENRY SMITH MEMORIAL LIBRARY □ Indianapolis, IN

McBride, Barbara L., Mgr., Info.Serv.
FOOD MARKETING INSTITUTE - INFORMATION SERVICE □ Washington, DC

McBride, Deborah, Res. Staff
JEFFERSON COUNTY HISTORICAL SOCIETY - RESEARCH CENTER □ Port Townsend, WA

McBride, Delbert J., Cur.
STATE CAPITOL HISTORICAL ASSOCIATION - LIBRARY AND PHOTO ARCHIVES □ Olympia, WA

McBride, Elizabeth A., Doc.Libn.
EMORY UNIVERSITY - DOCUMENTS DEPARTMENT □ Atlanta, GA

McBride, Jerry, Asst.Archv.
ARNOLD SCHOENBERG INSTITUTE - ARCHIVES □ Los Angeles, CA

McBride, Patricia, Cat.Libn.
ST. THOMAS MORE CENTER - TIMOTHY PARKMAN MEMORIAL LIBRARY □ Tucson, AZ

McBride, Peggy, Planning Ref.Libn.
UNIVERSITY OF BRITISH COLUMBIA - FINE ARTS DIVISION □ Vancouver, BC

McBryde, Sarah E., Rd.Adv.
DISTRICT OF COLUMBIA PUBLIC LIBRARY - ART DIVISION □ Washington, DC

McCabe, C.R., Archv.
DELAWARE STATE ARCHIVES □ Dover, DE

McCabe, Patrick P., Dir.
U.S. DEPT. OF COMMERCE - INTERNATIONAL TRADE ADMINISTRATION - PHILADELPHIA DISTRICT OFFICE LIBRARY □ Philadelphia, PA

McCabe, Richard E., Pub.Dir.
WILDLIFE MANAGEMENT INSTITUTE - LIBRARY □ Washington, DC

McCabe, Roy, Mgr.
SYSTEM DEVELOPMENT CORPORATION - ARPA RESEARCH LIBRARY □ Moffett Field, CA

McCain, Bettye D., Hd., Media Spec.
CHARLOTTE-MECKLENBURG SCHOOLS - CURRICULUM RESEARCH CENTER □ Charlotte, NC

McCain, Diana, Book Cat.
CONNECTICUT HISTORICAL SOCIETY - LIBRARY □ Hartford, CT

McCain, Margaret, Asst.Libn.
ANDOVER COLLEGE - LIBRARY □ Portland, ME

McCall, Mr. Beauford, Ser.Libn.
FRANKLIN UNIVERSITY - LIBRARY □ Columbus, OH

McCall, Kevin, Libn.
PATTON BOGGS AND BLOW - LAW LIBRARY □ Washington, DC

McCall, William J., Sr.Tech.Libn.
NEW ENGLAND POWER COMPANY - TECHNICAL INFORMATION CENTER □ Westborough, MA

McCallister, Ellen, Libn.
MOUNT VERNON LADIES' ASSOCIATION OF THE UNION - RESEARCH AND REFERENCE LIBRARY □ Mount Vernon, VA

McCallum, Dorothy T., Libn.
REX HOSPITAL - LIBRARY □ Raleigh, NC

McCallum, Fred, Res.Ed.
UNIVERSITY OF ALABAMA - SCHOOL OF LAW - ALABAMA LAW REVIEW - LIBRARY □ University, AL

PERSONNEL

McCallum, Heather, Hd.
METROPOLITAN TORONTO LIBRARY -
THEATRE DEPARTMENT □ Toronto, ON
McCallum, John, Ref./Coll.Libn.
WILFRID LAURIER UNIVERSITY - LIBRARY □
Waterloo, ON
McCandless, Nancy P., Tech.Libn.
TRACOR, INC. - TECHNICAL LIBRARY □ Austin,
TX
McCann, Judy, Libn
METROPOLITAN TORONTO LIBRARY - SOCIAL
SCIENCES DEPARTMENT □ Toronto, ON
McCanna, Charlotte S.
DARTMOUTH COLLEGE - SANBORN ENGLISH
HOUSE LIBRARY □ Hanover, NH
McCants, Lt.Col. Arthur W., Jr., Chf.Oral Hist.
U.S. AIR FORCE - ALBERT F. SIMPSON
HISTORICAL RESEARCH CENTER □ Maxwell
AFB, AL
McCarley, Carol, Libn.
MEMPHIS-SHELBY COUNTY PUBLIC LIBRARY
AND INFO. CTR. - SCIENCE/BUSINESS/SOCIAL
SCIENCES DEPT. □ Memphis, TN
McCarroll, Colleen, Asst.Libn.
SONNENSCHEIN CARLIN NATH & ROSENTHAL -
LIBRARY □ Chicago, IL
McCarron, Judith B., Music Lib.Coord.
KENT STATE UNIVERSITY - MUSIC LIBRARY □
Kent, OH
McCarron, Mary M., Libn.
SEARS, ROEBUCK AND CO. - MERCHANDISE
DEVELOPMENT AND TESTING LABORATORY -
LIBRARY, DEPARTMENT 817† □ Chicago, IL
McCarthy, Catherine, Hd., Ref. & Res.Lib.
MASSACHUSETTS STATE BOARD OF LIBRARY
COMMISSIONERS - REFERENCE AND
RESEARCH LIBRARY □ Boston, MA
McCarthy, Dan, Pres.
NEBRASKA TESTING LABORATORIES - LIBRARY
□ Omaha, NE
McCarthy, Jane, Libn.
MUHLENBERG HOSPITAL - E. GORDON GLASS,
M.D., MEMORIAL LIBRARY □ Plainfield, NJ
McCarthy, Juanita, Corp.Libn.
MALLINCKRODT, INC. - LIBRARY □ St. Louis,
MO
McCarthy, Paul H., Archv./Cur. of Mss.
UNIVERSITY OF ALASKA - RARE BOOKS,
ARCHIVES & MANUSCRIPTS COLLECTIONS □
Fairbanks, AK
McCarthy, Susan, Ref.Libn.
UNIVERSITY OF COLORADO MEDICAL CENTER
- DENISON MEMORIAL LIBRARY □ Denver, CO
McCarthy, Thomas R., Asst.Dir.
IRISH-AMERICAN CULTURAL ASSOCIATION -
LIBRARY □ Chicago, IL
McCarthy, Thomas R., Dir.
NATIONAL YOUTH WORK ALLIANCE, INC. -
CLEARINGHOUSE/LIBRARY □ Washington, DC
McCarthy, Virginia, Dept.Libn.
NEW YORK STATE DEPARTMENT OF CIVIL
SERVICE - LIBRARY □ Albany, NY
McCarthy, William G., Lib.Prog.Dir.
MINNESOTA STATE DEPARTMENT OF PUBLIC
WELFARE - LIBRARY □ St. Paul, MN
McCartney, Jule, Ref.Libn.
U.S. OFFICE OF PERSONNEL MANAGEMENT -
LIBRARY □ Washington, DC
McCarty, Sally, Cat.Libn.
TROY STATE UNIVERSITY - LIBRARY □ Troy, AL
McCauley, Betty M., Libn.
ENVIRONMENTAL PROTECTION AGENCY -
ENVIRONMENTAL RESEARCH LABORATORY,
CORVALLIS - LIBRARY □ Corvallis, OR
McCauley, C. Cameron, Media Rep.
UNIVERSITY OF CALIFORNIA - EXTENSION
MEDIA CENTER □ Berkeley, CA
McCauley, Carolyn S., Libn.
OKLAHOMA SCHOOL OF BUSINESS - LIBRARY □
Tulsa, OK

McCauley, Cynthia, Libn.
U.S. FISH & WILDLIFE SERVICE - JOHN VAN
OOSTEN GREAT LAKES FISHERY RESEARCH
LIBRARY □ Ann Arbor, MI
McCauley, JoAnn, Info.Coord.
LANE COUNCIL OF GOVERNMENTS - LIBRARY □
Eugene, OR
McCauley, M.
CANADA - PUBLIC ARCHIVES OF CANADA -
NATIONAL MAP COLLECTION □ Ottawa, ON
McCauley, Philip F., Cur./Archv.
SOUTH DAKOTA SCHOOL OF MINES &
TECHNOLOGY - DEVEREAUX LIBRARY □ Rapid
City, SD
McCawley, Clemma Rita, Asst.Dir.Pub.Serv.
CENTRAL STATE UNIVERSITY - LIBRARY □
Edmond, OK
McChristian, Douglas C., Supt.
U.S. NATL. PARK SERVICE - FORT DAVIS NATL.
HISTORIC SITE - LIBRARY □ Fort Davis, TX
McClain, Ardina M., Lib.Techn.
U.S. NAVY - NAVAL AIR STATION (Key West) -
LIBRARY □ Key West, FL
McClain, David C., Hd.Libn.
BAPTIST BIBLE COLLEGE OF PENNSYLVANIA -
RICHARD J. MURPHY MEMORIAL LIBRARY □
Clarks Summit, PA
McClain, Gail, Hd.Tech.Serv.
INTERNATIONAL MUSEUM OF PHOTOGRAPHY
AT GEORGE EASTMAN HOUSE - LIBRARY □
Rochester, NY
McClain, Gerald M., Libn.
CITIZENS LAW LIBRARY □ Greensburg, PA
McClamma, C., Doc.Libn.
SOUTHWESTERN UNIVERSITY - SCHOOL OF
LAW LIBRARY □ Los Angeles, CA
McClanahan, Roger, Ed.Res.Assoc.
AMERICAN COUNCIL OF VOLUNTARY
AGENCIES FOR FOREIGN SERVICE, INC. -
TECH. ASSISTANCE INFO. CLEARING HOUSE □
New York, NY
McClane, Joseph C., Assoc.Libn.
UNITED ENGINEERS & CONSTRUCTORS, INC. -
LIBRARY □ Philadelphia, PA
McClary, Maryon, Cat.
UNIVERSITY OF ALBERTA - H.T. COUTTS
EDUCATION LIBRARY □ Edmonton, AB
McClaughry, Helen C., Base Libn.
U.S. AIR FORCE BASE - LOWRY BASE LIBRARY
□ Lowry AFB, CO
McClean, Ann, Law Lib.Ck.
NEW YORK STATE SUPREME COURT - 9TH
JUDICIAL DISTRICT - LAW LIBRARY □
Newburgh, NY
McCleary, G. Louise, Lib. Unit Hd.
GULF RESEARCH AND DEVELOPMENT
COMPANY - TECHNICAL INFORMATION
SERVICES □ Pittsburgh, PA
McClellan, Edna, Cat.
ARKANSAS STATE UNIVERSITY - DEAN B.
ELLIS LIBRARY □ State University, AR
McClellan, Jane, Asst.Dir.
ERIC CLEARINGHOUSE ON READING AND
COMMUNICATIONS SKILLS □ Urbana, IL
McClellan, Michael, Libn.
HONEYWELL, INC. - CORPORATE TECHNOLOGY
CENTER LIBRARY □ Bloomington, MN
McClellan, William M., Music Libn.
UNIVERSITY OF ILLINOIS - MUSIC LIBRARY □
Urbana, IL
McClenaghan, Norma, Hd., Acq.Dept.
WILFRID LAURIER UNIVERSITY - LIBRARY □
Waterloo, ON
McClennahan, Nancy, Libn.
BRONX-LEBANON HOSPITAL CENTER - FULTON
DIVISION MEDICAL LIBRARY □ Bronx, NY
McClintock, Marsha, Middle East Libn.
OHIO STATE UNIVERSITY - MIDDLE EAST/
ISLAMICA READING ROOM □ Columbus, OH
McClish, Lois E., Dir.
CITY OF COMMERCE PUBLIC LIBRARY □
Commerce, CA

McCloat, Elizabeth, Libn.
METROPOLITAN LIFE INSURANCE COMPANY -
LIBRARY □ New York, NY
McClory, Eugene, Pres.
ADLER (Alfred) INSTITUTE - LIBRARY □
Chicago, IL
McClory, Kathleen, Ref.Libn.
VIRGINIA UNION UNIVERSITY - WILLIAM J.
CLARK LIBRARY □ Richmond, VA
McCloskey, Brian, Adm.
UNITED METHODIST CHURCH - PHILADELPHIA
ANNUAL CONFERENCE - HISTORICAL SOCIETY
LIBRARY □ Philadelphia, PA
McCloskey, Maxine, Exec.Dir.
WHALE CENTER - EXTINCT SPECIES
MEMORIAL FUND - LIBRARY □ Oakland, CA
McCloskey, Richard G., Dir.
HAKLUYT MINOR - LIBRARY □ Bothell, WA
McClov, William B., Chinese Cat.
INDIANA UNIVERSITY - EAST ASIAN
COLLECTION □ Bloomington, IN
McClung, Ellen, English Lit.Spec.
METROPOLITAN TORONTO LIBRARY -
LITERATURE DEPARTMENT □ Toronto, ON
McClure, Aylene, Tech.Serv.Libn.
U.S. COURT OF APPEALS, 4TH CIRCUIT -
LIBRARY □ Richmond, VA
McClure, Betsy A., Supv.
UNIVERSITY OF MICHIGAN - DEPARTMENT OF
RARE BOOKS AND SPECIAL COLLECTIONS -
LIBRARY □ Ann Arbor, MI
McClure, Lola W., Tech.Libn.
HUNTINGTON ALLOYS, INC. - TECHNOLOGY
LIBRARY □ Huntington, WV
McClure, Lucretia, Med.Libn.
UNIVERSITY OF ROCHESTER - SCHOOL OF
MEDICINE & DENTISTRY - EDWARD G. MINER
LIBRARY □ Rochester, NY
McClure, Margaret, Libn.
MICHIGAN STATE DEPARTMENT OF NATURAL
RESOURCES - INSTITUTE FOR FISHERIES
RESEARCH - LIBRARY □ Ann Arbor, MI
McClure, Patricia Harlan, Dir.
NEW TRANSCENTURY FOUNDATION -
SECRETARIAT FOR WOMEN IN DEVE LOPMENT
- DOCUMENTATION CENTER □ Washington, DC
McCluskey, Dorothy A., Adm.Asst.
THATCHER GLASS MANUFACTURING CO. -
RESEARCH CENTER LIBRARY □ Elmira, NY
McClymont, I., Prime Min.Archv.
CANADA - PUBLIC ARCHIVES OF CANADA -
MANUSCRIPT DIVISION □ Ottawa, ON
McColley, Verna L., Lib.Techn.
GENESEE-LAPEER-SHIAWASSEE REGION V
PLANNING & DEVELOPMENT COMMISSION -
LIBRARY □ Flint, MI
McColloch, Mark, Archv.
UNIVERSITY OF PITTSBURGH - ARCHIVES OF
INDUSTRIAL SOCIETY □ Pittsburgh, PA
McComb, Ronald G., Hd.Libn.
CORNISH INSTITUTE - LIBRARY □ Seattle, WA
McConagha, John, Hd., Plan./Res.
STATE LIBRARY OF OHIO □ Columbus, OH
McConahey, Thomas M., Dir.Dev. & Training
ALTON MENTAL HEALTH CENTER -
PROFESSIONAL LIBRARY □ Alton, IL
McConkey, Joan, Res. & Plan.Libn.
UNIVERSITY OF COLORADO, BOULDER - ART
AND ARCHITECTURE LIBRARY □ Boulder, CO
McConnel, J. Patrick, Dp.Libn.
U.S. NAVY - NAVAL RESEARCH LABORATORY -
RUTH H. HOOKER TECHNICAL LIBRARY □
Washington, DC
McConnell, Dorothy D., Libn.
LOUISIANA STATE DEPARTMENT OF
TRANSPORTATION DEVELOPMENT - OFFICE OF
PUBLIC WORKS - TECHNICAL LIBRARY □ Baton
Rouge, LA
McConnell, Karen S., Corp.Libn.
GULF STATES UTILITIES COMPANY -
CORPORATE LIBRARY □ Beaumont, TX

McConnell, Loretta U., Libn.
AMERICAN LAW INSTITUTE - LIBRARY □ Philadelphia, PA

McConnell, Mary, Libn.
INTERNATIONAL CHRISTIAN SCHOOL OF THEOLOGY - GRADUATE UNIVERSITY LIBRARY □ San Bernardino, CA

McConnell, Sharon, Townsend Rm.
EASTERN KENTUCKY UNIVERSITY - JOHN GRANT CRABBE LIBRARY □ Richmond, KY

McConnell, Sherrill, Dir., Hist.Coll.
UNIVERSITY OF LOUISVILLE - UNIVERSITY ARCHIVES AND RECORDS CENTER □ Louisville, KY

McConnville, Richard, Res.Libn.
MELLON BANK, N.A. - LIBRARY □ Pittsburgh, PA

MacConomy, Edward N., Chf.
LIBRARY OF CONGRESS - NATIONAL REFERRAL CENTER □ Washington, DC

McCooey, Ellen B., Health Sci.Libn.
OAKLAND COUNTY HEALTH DIVISION - LIBRARY □ Pontiac, MI

McCook, Katherine, Hd.
METROPOLITAN TORONTO LIBRARY - LITERATURE DEPARTMENT □ Toronto, ON

McCool, Gary A., Educ.Ctr.Libn.
PLYMOUTH STATE COLLEGE - HERBERT H. LAMSON LIBRARY □ Plymouth, NH

McCorison, Marcus A., Dir.
AMERICAN ANTIQUARIAN SOCIETY - LIBRARY □ Worcester, MA

McCorkle, Barbara B., Cur. of Maps
YALE UNIVERSITY - MAP COLLECTION □ New Haven, CT

McCormack, Margaret, Hd.Cat.
SMITHTOWN LIBRARY □ Smithtown, NY

McCormack, W.B., R&D Libn.
DU PONT DE NEMOURS (E.I.) & COMPANY, INC. - CHEMICALS & PIGMENTS DEPT. - JACKSON LAB. LIBRARY □ Wilmington, DE

McCormick, B. Jack
WICHITA STATE UNIVERSITY - DEPARTMENT OF CHEMISTRY - LLOYD MC KINLEY MEMORIAL CHEMISTRY LIBRARY □ Wichita, KS

McCormick, Becky, Asst.Libn.
MERCY REGIONAL MEDICAL CENTER LIBRARY □ Vicksburg, MS

McCormick, Donald, First Asst.
NEW YORK PUBLIC LIBRARY - PERFORMING ARTS RESEARCH CENTER - RODGERS & HAMMERSTEIN ARCHIVES OF RECORDED SOUND □ New York, NY

McCormick, Dorcas M.C., Div.Hd.
NORTHWESTERN STATE UNIVERSITY OF LOUISIANA - EUGENE P. WATSON LIBRARY - SHREVEPORT DIVISION □ Shreveport, LA

MacCormick, Kristina, Cat.Libn.
RENSSELAER POLYTECHNIC INSTITUTE - FOLSOM LIBRARY □ Troy, NY

McCormick, Lisa L., Res.Libn.
CHRIST HOSPITAL INSTITUTE OF MEDICAL RESEARCH - LIBRARY □ Cincinnati, OH

McCormick, Marga, Assoc.Libn.
FRENCH LIBRARY IN BOSTON, INC. □ Boston, MA

McCormick, Mary, Desk Res.
FOOTE CONE & BELDING - INFORMATION CENTER □ Chicago, IL

McCormick, Maureen B., Exec.Dir.
BRITISH COLUMBIA LAW LIBRARY FOUNDATION - VANCOUVER COURTHOUSE LIBRARY □ Vancouver, BC

McCormick, Nancy, Circ.
UNIVERSITY OF MINNESOTA - LAW LIBRARY □ Minneapolis, MN

McCormick, Regina, Staff Assoc.
ERIC CLEARINGHOUSE FOR SOCIAL STUDIES/ SOCIAL SCIENCE EDUCATION - RESOURCE & DEMONSTRATION CENTER □ Boulder, CO

McCown, Julie J., Leg.Libn.
TENNESSEE STATE LEGISLATIVE LIBRARY □ Nashville, TN

McCown, Robert A., Mss.Libn.
UNIVERSITY OF IOWA - SPECIAL COLLECTIONS DEPARTMENT □ Iowa City, IA

McCoy, Amber, Sr.Ref.Libn.
CAMPBELL-EWALD COMPANY - REFERENCE CENTER □ Warren, MI

McCoy, Barbara S., Libn.
RCA CORPORATION - SOLID STATE DIVISION - LIBRARY □ Somerville, NJ

McCoy, Evelyn, Libn.
ARKANSAS ARTS CENTER - ELIZABETH PREWITT TAYLOR MEMORIAL LIBRARY □ Little Rock, AR

McCoy, Jacqueline M., Libn.
NUTRILITE PRODUCTS, INC. - RESEARCH LIBRARY □ Buena Park, CA

McCoy, James F., Dir.
HUDSON VALLEY COMMUNITY COLLEGE - DWIGHT MARVIN LEARNING RESOURCES CENTER □ Troy, NY

McCoy, Laueen, Res.
DISNEY (Walt) PRODUCTIONS - LIBRARY □ Burbank, CA

McCoy, Pamela
ADVANCED MICRO DEVICES, INC. - TECHNICAL LIBRARY □ Sunnyvale, CA

McCoy, William F., Assoc.Univ.Libn.
UNIVERSITY OF CALIFORNIA, DAVIS - GENERAL LIBRARY □ Davis, CA

McCracken, M.B., Libn.
INTERNATIONAL GAME FISH ASSOCIATION - INTERNATIONAL LIBRARY OF FISHES □ Fort Lauderdale, FL

McCrae, Sally, Coll.Libn.
UNIVERSITY OF WESTERN ONTARIO - FACULTY OF EDUCATION LIBRARY □ London, ON

McCray, Jeanette C., Asst.Libn./Pub.Serv.
UNIVERSITY OF ARIZONA - ARIZONA HEALTH SCIENCES CENTER LIBRARY □ Tucson, AZ

McCray, Maceo, Assoc.Libn.
HOWARD UNIVERSITY - HEALTH SCIENCES LIBRARY □ Washington, DC

McCray, Winn, Hd.
ROCHESTER PUBLIC LIBRARY - HISTORY AND TRAVEL DIVISION □ Rochester, NY

McCray, Yvonne, Ref.Libn.
KEAN COLLEGE OF NEW JERSEY - NANCY THOMPSON LIBRARY □ Union, NJ

McCrea, Graydon, Distribution Rep.
CANADA - NATIONAL FILM BOARD OF CANADA - EDMONTON DISTRICT OFFICE - FILM LIBRARY □ Edmonton, AB

McCrea, Katherine L., Libn.
NESBITT MEMORIAL HOSPITAL - LIBRARY □ Kingston, PA

McCrea, Maureen, Libn.
KENWORTH TRUCK CO. - DIVISION LIBRARY □ Kirkland, WA

McCready, R.R., Libn.
UNIVERSITY OF OREGON - ARCHITECTURE AND ALLIED ARTS BRANCH LIBRARY □ Eugene, OR

McCreary, Diane M., Libn.
ENVIRONMENTAL PROTECTION AGENCY - REGION III LIBRARY □ Philadelphia, PA

McCreary, Frances G., Libn.
UNIVERSITY OF COLORADO MEDICAL CENTER - RENE A. SPITZ PSYCHIATRIC LIBRARY □ Denver, CO

McCreary, Mary Louise, Libn.
ILLINOIS STATE LEGISLATIVE REFERENCE BUREAU □ Springfield, IL

McCrory, Mary M., Libn.
EINSTEIN (Albert) MEDICAL CENTER - SCHOOL OF NURSING LIBRARY □ Philadelphia, PA

McCuaig, Helen, Database Serv.
CANADA - ENVIRONMENT CANADA - LIBRARY SERVICES BRANCH □ Ottawa, ON

Maccubbin, Patricia G., Chf.Libn.
COLONIAL WILLIAMSBURG - AUDIO-VISUAL LIBRARY □ Williamsburg, VA

McCulley, Geraldine E., Asst.Libn., Tech.Proc.
UNIVERSITY OF PENNSYLVANIA - LIPPINCOTT LIBRARY □ Philadelphia, PA

McCulloch, William L., Exec.Dir.
AMERICAN ORTHOTIC AND PROSTHETIC ASSOCIATION - LIBRARY □ Alexandria, VA

McCullough, Barbara, Health Educ.
ESCAMBIA COUNTY HEALTH DEPARTMENT - LIBRARY □ Pensacola, FL

McCullough, Coyla, Hd., Res.Lit.Sect.
BURROUGHS WELLCOME COMPANY - LIBRARY □ Research Triangle Park, NC

McCullough, Frances, Libn.
MERCY NORTH HOSPITAL - HEALTH SCIENCES LIBRARY □ Hamilton, OH

McCullough, John, Libn.
DIVINE WORD SEMINARY - LIBRARY □ Bordentown, NJ

McCullough, Mabel B., Hd.Libn.
U.S. NAVY - NAVAL AIR STATION (Pensacola) - LIBRARY □ Pensacola, FL

McCullough, Mireille, Asst.Libn.
CANADA - LABOUR RELATIONS BOARD - LIBRARY □ Ottawa, ON

McCullough, Ruth R., Supv.
WESTINGHOUSE ELECTRIC CORPORATION - DEFENSE & ELECTRONIC SYSTEMS CENTER - TECHNICAL INFORMATION CENTER □ Baltimore, MD

McCullum, Anne, Circ.
VANCOUVER SCHOOL OF THEOLOGY - LIBRARY □ Vancouver, BC

McCully, Nancy B., Libn.
CATERPILLAR TRACTOR COMPANY - BUSINESS LIBRARY □ Peoria, IL

McCurdy, Scott, Legal Ref.Libn.
U.S. DEPT. OF THE TREASURY - INFORMATION SERVICES DIVISION - TREASURY DEPT. LIBRARY □ Washington, DC

McCurley, Karen, Libn.Asst.
ST. PAUL HOSPITAL - C.B. SACHER LIBRARY □ Dallas, TX

McCurry, Stephanie, AV Libn.
DELAWARE VALLEY COLLEGE OF SCIENCE AND AGRICULTURE - JOSEPH KRAUSKOPF MEMORIAL LIBRARY □ Doylestown, PA

McCutcheon, Ethel J., Musm.Cur.
UNITED DAUGHTERS OF THE CONFEDERACY - TEXAS CONFEDERATE MUSEUM LIBRARY □ Austin, TX

McDaniel, Dennis K., Dir.
PEALE MUSEUM - MUSEUM ARCHIVES □ Baltimore, MD

McDaniel, George, Dir. of Res.
CENTER FOR SOUTHERN FOLKLORE - ARCHIVES □ Memphis, TN

McDaniel, James, Instr.Mtls.Cat.
CLARION STATE COLLEGE - RENA M. CARLSON LIBRARY □ Clarion, PA

McDaniel, Jean, Libn.
ST. MARY'S HOSPITAL - LIBRARY □ Enid, OK

McDaniel, Sonja, Cat.
NATIONAL ECONOMIC RESEARCH ASSOCIATES, INC. - LIBRARY □ New York, NY

McDavid, Michael, Corp.Libn.
EQUIFAX, INC. - CORPORATE LIBRARY □ Atlanta, GA

McDavid, Sara June, Libn.
FEDERAL RESERVE BANK OF ATLANTA - RESEARCH LIBRARY □ Atlanta, GA

McDermand, Robert V., Coord. of Pub.Serv.
PLYMOUTH STATE COLLEGE - HERBERT H. LAMSON LIBRARY □ Plymouth, NH

McDermott, Dorothy, Asst.Libn.
MIAMI NEWS - LIBRARY □ Miami, FL

McDermott, Marilyn, Ref. & Circ.Libn.
MOHAWK COLLEGE OF APPLIED ARTS AND TECHNOLOGY - MOHAWK LIBRARY RESOURCE CENTRE □ Hamilton, ON

McDermott, Marjorie, Standards Libn.
DUKE POWER COMPANY - DAVID NABOW LIBRARY □ Charlotte, NC

McDermott, Patricia, Asst.Libn.
U.S. INTERNAL REVENUE SERVICE - LAW LIBRARY □ Washington, DC

McDevitt, J.F., Tech.Info.Prog.Engr.
GENERAL ELECTRIC COMPANY - AIRCRAFT ENGINE GROUP - TECHNICAL INFORMATION CENTER □ Cincinnati, OH

McDonald, Alice P., Libn.
SACRAMENTO COUNTY LAW LIBRARY† □ Sacramento, CA

McDonald, Ann M., Dir.
LIBERTY MUTUAL INSURANCE COMPANY - BUSINESS REFERENCE LIBRARY □ Boston, MA

McDonald, Arlys L., Music Libn.
ARIZONA STATE UNIVERSITY - MUSIC LIBRARY □ Tempe, AZ

McDonald, Barbara, Ref.Libn.
COLORADO SCHOOL OF MINES - ARTHUR LAKES LIBRARY □ Golden, CO

McDonald, Barbara, Info.Spec.
WESTVACO CORPORATION - INFORMATION SERVICES CENTER □ North Charleston, SC

MacDonald, Barbara J., Supv.
LITERACY VOLUNTEERS OF AMERICA, INC. - LIBRARY □ Syracuse, NY

McDonald, Brenda, Act.Hd.
UNIVERSITY OF TEXAS, EL PASO - LIBRARY - DOCUMENTS/MAPS LIBRARY □ El Paso, TX

McDonald, C., Hd., Circ.
UNIVERSITY OF WATERLOO - ENGINEERING, MATHEMATICS & SCIENCE DIVISIONAL LIBRARY □ Waterloo, ON

Macdonald, Christine, Libn.
CITADEL GENERAL ASSURANCE COMPANY - INFORMATION CENTRE □ Toronto, ON

MacDonald, Christine, Legislative Libn.
SASKATCHEWAN - LEGISLATIVE LIBRARY □ Regina, SK

McDonald, Clark E., Mng.Dir.
HARDWOOD PLYWOOD MANUFACTURERS ASSOCIATION - LIBRARY □ Reston, VA

McDonald, D.L., Dir.
CANADA - PUBLIC ARCHIVES OF CANADA - FEDERAL ARCHIVES DIVISION □ Ottawa, ON

McDonald, Dana M., Dir.
SOUTHERN ILLINOIS UNIVERSITY - SCHOOL OF MEDICINE - MEDICAL LIBRARY □ Springfield, IL

MacDonald, Duncan J., Res.Coord.
ONTARIO FEDERATION OF LABOUR - RESOURCE CENTRE □ Don Mills, ON

MacDonald, Elizabeth, Coord.Pub.Libs.
NOVA SCOTIA - PROVINCIAL LIBRARY □ Halifax, NS

McDonald, Eloise E., Hd.
UNIVERSITY OF ARKANSAS, FAYETTEVILLE - FINE ARTS LIBRARY □ Fayetteville, AR

McDonald, Gloria Dean, Asst.Libn.
DILLON, READ & COMPANY, INC. - LIBRARY □ New York, NY

McDonald, Isabel, Libn.
OREGON REGIONAL PRIMATE RESEARCH CENTER - LIBRARY □ Beaverton, OR

MacDonald, Capt. J.A., Lib.Off.
CANADA - NATIONAL DEFENCE - NORTHERN REGION REFERENCE LIBRARY □ Yellowknife, NT

McDonald, J. William, Dir.
COLORADO STATE WATER CONSERVATION BOARD - LIBRARY □ Denver, CO

MacDonald, Jacqueline, Libn.
UNIVERSITY OF SASKATCHEWAN - HEALTH SCIENCES LIBRARY □ Saskatoon, SK

McDonald, John P., Dir. of Libs.
UNIVERSITY OF CONNECTICUT - LIBRARY □ Storrs, CT

McDonald, John "Stu", Supv.
UNIVERSITY OF MICHIGAN - DEPARTMENT OF GEOLOGICAL SCIENCES - SUBSURFACE LABORATORY LIBRARY □ Ann Arbor, MI

McDonald, Judith, Dir.
MINNESOTA HISTORICAL SOCIETY - NORTH CENTRAL MINNESOTA HISTORICAL CENTER □ Bemidji, MN

McDonald, Judith, Circ. & Ref.
MOUNT SAINT VINCENT UNIVERSITY - LIBRARY □ Halifax, NS

McDonald, Lany W., Libn.
NEWS AND OBSERVER PUBLISHING COMPANY - LIBRARY □ Raleigh, NC

McDonald, Lois E., Asst.Cur.
EUGENE O'NEILL MEMORIAL THEATER CENTER, INC. - THEATER COLLECTION AND LIBRARY □ Waterford, CT

Macdonald, Lorna, Libn.
NEW YORK MEDICAL COLLEGE - DEPARTMENT OF PSYCHIATRY - LIBRARY □ New York, NY

McDonald, Marie, Libn.
PROCUREMENT ASSOCIATES - LIBRARY □ Covina, CA

McDonald, Nathan A., Dir., Tech.Serv.
MISSISSIPPI VALLEY STATE UNIVERSITY - JAMES HERBERT WHITE LIBRARY □ Itta Bena, MS

McDonald, Sekiko, Sr.Cat.Libn.
YALE UNIVERSITY - EAST ASIAN COLLECTION □ New Haven, CT

MacDonald, Stephen, Rec.Anl.
TORONTO CITY RECORDS AND ARCHIVES DIVISION □ Toronto, ON

McDonald, Susan, Supv., Info.Serv.
IMPERIAL OIL, LTD. - BUSINESS INFORMATION CENTRE □ Toronto, ON

MacDonald, W. James, Ref.Libn.
CONNECTICUT COLLEGE - LIBRARY - SPECIAL COLLECTIONS □ New London, CT

McDonald, William H., Arch.Serv.Dir.
INDIANA LIMESTONE INSTITUTE OF AMERICA, INC. - LIBRARY AND INFORMATION CENTER □ Bedford, IN

McDonell, Ellen, Ser.Libn.
UNIVERSITY OF TENNESSEE - CENTER FOR THE HEALTH SCIENCES LIBRARY □ Memphis, TN

McDonnell, Anne, Lib.Mgr.
KENTUCKY HISTORICAL SOCIETY - LIBRARY □ Frankfort, KY

McDonnell, Claire R., Mgr.Info.Serv.
JOHNSON AND JOHNSON - RESEARCH CENTER LIBRARY □ New Brunswick, NJ

McDonnell, Geraldine, Res.Libn.
FEDERAL RESERVE BANK OF CHICAGO - LIBRARY □ Chicago, IL

McDonnell, Janice P., Libn.
TENNESSEE VALLEY AUTHORITY - DIVISION OF FORESTRY, FISHERIES AND WILDLIFE DEVELOPMENT - LIBRARY □ Norris, TN

McDonnell, Julia, Cat.
BELMONT ABBEY COLLEGE - ABBOT VINCENT TAYLOR LIBRARY □ Belmont, NC

McDonough, Irma, Coord., Ch.Lib.Serv.
ONTARIO - MINISTRY OF CULTURE AND RECREATION - LIBRARIES AND COMMUNITY INFORMATION □ Toronto, ON

McDonough, M., Asst.Libn.
GILLETTE COMPANY - PERSONAL CARE DIVISION - INFORMATION CENTER □ Boston, MA

McDonough, Martin P., Hd.Libn.
U.S. NASA - LYNDON B. JOHNSON SPACE CENTER - TECHNICAL LIBRARY □ Houston, TX

McDonough, Mary A., Asst.Libn.
UNIVERSITY OF PITTSBURGH - THEODORE M. FINNEY MUSIC LIBRARY □ Pittsburgh, PA

McDougall, D.B., Legislative Libn.
ALBERTA - LEGISLATIVE ASSEMBLY OF ALBERTA - LEGISLATURE LIBRARY □ Edmonton, AB

MacDougall, Frank C., Libn.
MICHIGAN STATE UNIVERSITY - HIGHWAY TRAFFIC SAFETY CENTER - LIBRARY† □ East Lansing, MI

MacDougall, Frank C., Libn.
MICHIGAN STATE UNIVERSITY - UNIVERSITY EXTENSION LIBRARY† □ East Lansing, MI

McDowell, Agnes, Selection
UNIVERSITY OF KENTUCKY - AGRICULTURE LIBRARY □ Lexington, KY

McDowell, Barbara, Chf., Lib.Serv.
U.S. VETERANS ADMINISTRATION (SD-Sioux Falls) - HOSPITAL LIBRARY† □ Sioux Falls, SD

McDowell, George D., Lib.Dir.
PHILADELPHIA BULLETIN - NEWS LIBRARY □ Philadelphia, PA

McDowell, Judy, Ref.Libn./Educ.
NATIONAL INSTITUTE OF EDUCATION - EDUCATIONAL RESEARCH LIBRARY □ Washington, DC

McDowell, Julie H., Libn.
NEW YORK STATE SUPREME COURT - 6TH JUDICIAL DISTRICT - LAW LIBRARY □ Elmira, NY

McDowell, Marie D., Libn.
U.S. NAVY - NAVY PERSONNEL RESEARCH & DEVELOPMENT CENTER - TECHNICAL LIBRARY □ San Diego, CA

McDowell, William L., Jr., Dp.Dir.
SOUTH CAROLINA STATE DEPARTMENT OF ARCHIVES & HISTORY - ARCHIVES SEARCH ROOM □ Columbia, SC

McDuffee, Diana, Dir.
UNIVERSITY OF NORTH CAROLINA, CHAPEL HILL - INSTITUTE FOR RESEARCH IN SOCIAL SCIENCE - DATA LIBRARY □ Chapel Hill, NC

McDugle, Marcia B., Per.Libn.
EASTMAN KODAK COMPANY - RESEARCH LABORATORIES - RESEARCH LIBRARY □ Rochester, NY

Mace, Florence, Circ.Libn.
SAN DIEGO COUNTY LAW LIBRARY □ San Diego, CA

Mace, Mary B., Libn.
SPRAGUE ELECTRIC COMPANY - RESEARCH LIBRARY □ North Adams, MA

McEachern, Virginia S., Libn.
BRYAN (G. Werber) PSYCHIATRIC HOSPITAL - PROFESSIONAL LIBRARY □ Columbia, SC

Macek, Ruth
IBM CORPORATION - GENERAL TECHNOLOGY DIVISION - INFORMATION CENTER/LEARNING CENTER □ Essex Junction, VT

McElfresh, Melvin P., Libn.
U.S. AIR FORCE BASE - KELLY BASE - SPECIAL SERVICES LIBRARY □ San Antonio, TX

McElligott, Mary Ellen, Supv., Ed.Sect.
ILLINOIS STATE HISTORICAL LIBRARY □ Springfield, IL

McElligott, Paul, Assoc.Cartographer
NEW YORK STATE DEPARTMENT OF TRANSPORTATION - MAP INFORMATION UNIT □ Albany, NY

MacEliven, Douglass T., Dir.
LAW SOCIETY OF SASKATCHEWAN - LIBRARY □ Regina, SK

McElroy, Elizabeth W., Libn.
UNIVERSITY OF MARYLAND, COLLEGE PARK - LIBRARIES - CHARLES E. WHITE MEMORIAL LIBRARY □ College Park, MD

McElroy, F. Clifford, Sci.Libn.
BOSTON COLLEGE - SCIENCE LIBRARY □ Chestnut Hill, MA

McElroy, F. Clifford, Sci.Libn.
BOSTON COLLEGE - WESTON OBSERVATORY - CATHERINE B. O'CONNOR LIBRARY □ Weston, MA

McElroy, Shirley, Subject Anl.
AEROSPACE CORPORATION - CHARLES C. LAURITSEN LIBRARY □ Los Angeles, CA

McEnroe, Nancy F., Asst.Libn.
TRAVELERS INSURANCE COMPANIES - CORPORATE LIBRARY □ Hartford, CT

McEnulty, Kay, Energy Info./Educ.Coord.
KANSAS STATE ENERGY OFFICE - INFORMATION CENTER □ Topeka, KS

McGuire, Michael, Coord.
UNIVERSITY OF NEW BRUNSWICK - LAW
LIBRARY □ Fredericton, NB

McGuire, Ross, Cur.
BROOME COUNTY HISTORICAL SOCIETY -
LIBRARY AND ARCHIVES □ Binghamton, NY

McGuirl, Marlene C., Chf.
LIBRARY OF CONGRESS - LAW LIBRARY -
AMERICAN-BRITISH LAW DIVISION □
Washington, DC

McGurrin, Brian, Hd.
CANADA - CANADA CENTRE FOR REMOTE
SENSING - TECHNICAL INFORMATION
SERVICE □ Ottawa, ON

Machado, Cindy, Acq.Spec.
GENERAL RESEARCH CORPORATION - LIBRARY
□ Santa Barbara, CA

MacHaffie, Dr. Barbara, Ref. Libn.
PRINCETON THEOLOGICAL SEMINARY - SPEER
LIBRARY† □ Princeton, NJ

McHenry, Dorothy R., Hd.
TOLEDO-LUCAS COUNTY PUBLIC LIBRARY -
BUSINESS DEPARTMENT □ Toledo, OH

McHollin, Mattie, Ser.Libn.
MEHARRY MEDICAL COLLEGE - MEDICAL
LIBRARY - LEARNING RESOURCES CENTER □
Nashville, TN

Machowski, Edward J., Mgr.
ST. LOUIS - COMPTROLLERS OFFICE -
MICROFILM DEPARTMENT □ St. Louis, MO

McHugh, F. Joseph, Bureau Libn.
NEWSWEEK, INC. - WASHINGTON BUREAU
LIBRARY □ Washington, DC

McHugh, Mary Teresa, Law Libn.
FIDELITY & DEPOSIT COMPANY OF MARYLAND
- LAW LIBRARY □ Baltimore, MD

McHugh, Patricia, First Asst.
DETROIT PUBLIC LIBRARY - FINE ARTS
DEPARTMENT □ Detroit, MI

McHugo, Ann, Asst.Libn./Tech.Serv.
VERMONT LAW SCHOOL - LIBRARY □ South
Royalton, VT

Maciejewski, Richard, Chf.
DETROIT PUBLIC LIBRARY - MUNICIPAL
REFERENCE LIBRARY □ Detroit, MI

McIlroy, N.J., Libn.
ONTARIO - MINISTRY OF THE ENVIRONMENT -
LIBRARY □ Toronto, ON

McIlvain, Bill, Adm.Libn.
OKLAHOMA REGIONAL LIBRARY FOR THE
BLIND AND PHYSICALLY HANDICAPPED □
Oklahoma City, OK

McIlvaine, Betsy, Hd.Libn.
NORTH AMERICAN PHILIPS CORPORATION -
PHILIPS LABORATORIES RESEARCH LIBRARY □
Briarcliff Manor, NY

McIlvaine, Paul M., Assoc.Libn.
CIBA-GEIGY CORPORATION - CORPORATE
LIBRARY □ Ardsley, NY

McIlwain, William, Hd., Lang.Sect.
CHICAGO PUBLIC LIBRARY CULTURAL CENTER
- LITERATURE AND LANGUAGE DIVISION □
Chicago, IL

McInnes, Joan, Med.Libn.
U.S. VETERANS ADMINISTRATION (MA-Boston)
- HOSPITAL MEDICAL LIBRARY □ Boston, MA

McInnis, Alice M., Supv.Biblog.Dept.
MOORE-COTTRELL SUBSCRIPTION AGENCIES -
SERIALS REFERENCE LIBRARY □ North
Cohocton, NY

McInnis, Jacqueline Revel, Libn.
SPEARS, LUBERSKY, CAMPBELL, & BLEDSOE -
LIBRARY □ Portland, OR

McInroy, Moira, AV Libn.
TEXAS COLLEGE OF OSTEOPATHIC MEDICINE -
MEDICAL LIBRARY □ Fort Worth, TX

McIntire, James W., Dir.
U.S. DEPT. OF COMMERCE - INTERNATIONAL
TRADE ADMINISTRATION - SAVANNAH
DISTRICT OFFICE LIBRARY □ Savannah, GA

McIntosh, Cam, Libn.
PUGET SOUND COUNCIL OF GOVERNMENTS -
LIBRARY □ Seattle, WA

McIntosh, Julia E., Hd.Libn.
FEDERAL BUSINESS DEVELOPMENT BANK -
LIBRARY □ Montreal, PQ

McIntosh, Karen F., Cat.
AMARILLO COLLEGE - LEARNING RESOURCE
CENTER □ Amarillo, TX

McIntosh, Linda, Dir.
FAIRVIEW COMMUNITY HOSPITALS - HEALTH
SCIENCES LIBRARY □ Minneapolis, MN

MacIntosh, M.J., Asst.Dir., Hdq.
CANADA - AGRICULTURE CANADA - LIBRARIES
DIVISION □ Ottawa, ON

McInturff, Mary Jane, Med.Libn.
SCHICK SHADEL HOSPITAL - MEDICAL
LIBRARY □ Seattle, WA

McIntyre, Kathleen, Sr.Mss.Spec.
UNIVERSITY OF MISSOURI - WESTERN
HISTORICAL MANUSCRIPT COLLECTION/
STATE HISTORICAL SOCIETY OF MISSOURI □
Columbia, MO

McIntyre, Sandra, Data Off.
CANADA - STATISTICS CANADA - ADVISORY
SERVICES - TORONTO REFERENCE CENTRE □
Toronto, ON

McIntyre, Sharon R., Libn.
JONES, DAY, REAVIS & POGUE - LIBRARY □
Cleveland, OH

McIntyre, Solange V., Lib.Mgr.
BOEING COMPANY - SEATTLE SERVICES
DIVISION - KENT TECHNICAL LIBRARY □
Seattle, WA

McIntyre, Susan J., Med.Libn.
MOUNT SINAI HOSPITAL - MEDICAL LIBRARY □
Minneapolis, MN

McIntyre, William A., Libn.
NEW HAMPSHIRE VOCATIONAL-TECHNICAL
COLLEGE - LIBRARY □ Nashua, NH

McIsaac, Charles A., Dir., Lib.Serv.
NORTH ADAMS STATE COLLEGE - EUGENE L.
FREEL LIBRARY - SPECIAL COLLECTIONS □
North Adams, MA

McIsaac, John, Asst.Archv.
EDMONTON CITY ARCHIVES □ Edmonton, AB

MacIver, Anna M.
YORK COUNTY LAW ASSOCIATION - COURT
HOUSE LIBRARY □ Toronto, ON

Mack, Ann, Educ.Coord.
COMMUNITY ENVIRONMENTAL COUNCIL, INC.
- ECOLOGY CENTER LENDING LIBRARY □ Santa
Barbara, CA

Mack, Anne, Hd.
METROPOLITAN TORONTO LIBRARY - GENERAL
REFERENCE DEPARTMENT □ Toronto, ON

Mack, Barbara A.
SYSTEM PLANNING CORPORATION -
RESEARCH LIBRARY □ Arlington, VA

Mack, Bonnie R., Dept.Mgr./Lib.Serv.
RAPID CITY REGIONAL HOSPITAL - HEALTH
SCIENCES LIBRARY □ Rapid City, SD

Mack, James E., Pres. & Gen.Coun.
NATIONAL CONFECTIONERS ASSOCIATION OF
THE U.S. - LIBRARY† □ Chicago, IL

Mack, Sr. M. Theron, I.H.M., Cat.Libn.
MARYWOOD COLLEGE - LEARNING RESOURCES
CENTER □ Scranton, PA

Mack, Marilyn, Supv., Info.Serv.
NEEDHAM, HARPER & STEERS ADVERTISING,
INC. - INFORMATION SERVICES □ Chicago, IL

Mackaman, Frank H., II, Exec.Dir.
DIRKSEN (Everett McKinley) CONGRESSIONAL
LEADERSHIP RESEARCH CENTER - LIBRARY □
Pekin, IL

Mackars, J., Info.Spec.
BURROUGHS WELLCOME COMPANY - LIBRARY
□ Research Triangle Park, NC

McKay, Mrs. A., Libn.
ACRES CONSULTING SERVICES, LTD. -
LIBRARY □ Niagara Falls, ON

McKay, Alberta, Libn.
NORTH CAROLINA GEOLOGICAL SURVEY -
LIBRARY □ Raleigh, NC

Mc Kay, Ann, Staff Libn./Tech.Serv
CENTRAL MAINE MEDICAL CENTER - GERRISH-
TRUE HEALTH SCIENCE LIBRARY □ Lewiston,
ME

McKay, David, Dir./State Libn.
NORTH CAROLINA STATE DEPARTMENT OF
CULTURAL RESOURCES - DIVISION OF THE
STATE LIBRARY □ Raleigh, NC

McKay, Dorothy, Adm.Asst.
ONTARIO PUPPETRY ASSOCIATION - LIBRARY
□ Willowdale, ON

McKay, Eleanor, Cur.
MEMPHIS STATE UNIVERSITY LIBRARIES -
MISSISSIPPI VALLEY COLLECTION □ Memphis,
TN

Mackay, Jane, Doc.Libn.
TRINITY UNIVERSITY - LIBRARY □ San Antonio,
TX

McKay, Pamela, Per.
WORCESTER STATE COLLEGE - LEARNING
RESOURCES CENTER □ Worcester, MA

McKay, Rosalie, Libn.
UNIVERSITY OF CALIFORNIA, BERKELEY -
NATIVE AMERICAN STUDIES LIBRARY □
Berkeley, CA

McKay, Sharon E., Info.Dir.
DEUTZ DIESEL (Canada) LIMITED - BUSINESS
LIBRARY □ Montreal, PQ

Mackay-Smith, A., Cur. & Chm. of Bd.
NATIONAL SPORTING LIBRARY, INC. □
Middleburg, VA

McKean, Joan Maier, Chf., Lib.Serv.
U.S. NATL. OCEANIC & ATMOSPHERIC
ADMINISTRATION - ENVIRONMENTAL
RESEARCH LABORATORIES - LIBRARY □
Boulder, CO

McKearn, Anne B., Asst.Libn.
WORLD BOOK-CHILDCRAFT INTERNATIONAL,
INC.- RESEARCH LIBRARY □ Chicago, IL

McKee, David, Hd.Libn.
WESTERN MICHIGAN UNIVERSITY - BUSINESS
LIBRARY □ Kalamazoo, MI

McKee, George, Biblog./Ref.Libn.
SUNY AT BINGHAMTON - FINE ARTS LIBRARY □
Binghamton, NY

McKee, James E., Lib.Techn.
ALBERTA - PUBLIC UTILITIES BOARD -
LIBRARY □ Edmonton, AB

McKee, Jay R., Chf.Libn.
MARTIN MARIETTA CORPORATION - DENVER
DIVISION - RESEARCH LIBRARY □ Denver, CO

McKee, Marshall, Libn.
AMERICAN HUMANE EDUCATION SOCIETY -
HUMANE EDUCATION LIBRARY □ Framingham,
MA

McKee, Nancy, Hd.Ref.Libn.
CLARION STATE COLLEGE - RENA M. CARLSON
LIBRARY □ Clarion, PA

McKee, R., Dir.
MUSIC AND ARTS INSTITUTE OF SAN
FRANCISCO - COLLEGE LIBRARY □ San
Francisco, CA

McKee, William C., Chf.Archv.
GLENBOW-ALBERTA INSTITUTE - LIBRARY &
ARCHIVES □ Calgary, AB

McKeehan, Nancy, Coord., Tech.Serv.
MEDICAL UNIVERSITY OF SOUTH CAROLINA -
LIBRARY □ Charleston, SC

McKegney, Michael, Cat.
COLLEGE OF INSURANCE - INSURANCE
SOCIETY OF NEW YORK - LIBRARY □ New York,
NY

McKell, Linda, Hd.Libn.
FOUR-PHASE SYSTEMS - CORPORATE LIBRARY
□ Cupertino, CA

McKelvey, Sandra S., Sci.Info.Mgt.Coord.
MERCK & COMPANY, INC. - MERCK SHARP &
DOHME RESEARCH LABORATORIES - LIBRARY
SERVICES □ West Point, PA

MacKelvie, V.S., Chf.Libn.
CANADA - LABOUR CANADA - LIBRARY □
Ottawa, ON

Maclay, Veronica, Govt.Doc.Libn.
UNIVERSITY OF CALIFORNIA, SAN FRANCISCO - HASTINGS COLLEGE OF THE LAW - LEGAL INFORMATION CENTER □ San Francisco, CA

McLean, Ann Elizabeth, Coord. Media Serv.
CENTRAL WASHINGTON UNIVERSITY - MEDIA LIBRARY SERVICES □ Ellensburg, WA

McLean, Austin J., Chf., Spec.Coll.
UNIVERSITY OF MINNESOTA - SPECIAL COLLECTIONS AND RARE BOOKS □ Minneapolis, MN

MacLean, D. Louise, Libn.
U.S. ARMY - TACOM SUPPORT ACTIVITY-SELFRIDGE - RECREATION SERVICES LIBRARY □ Selfridge Air Natl. Guard Base, MI

McLean, Rev. Edward J., Exec.Dir.
ARCHDIOCESE OF HARTFORD - CATHOLIC INFORMATION CENTER† □ Hartford, CT

MacLean, Eleanor, Libn.
MC GILL UNIVERSITY - BLACKER/WOOD LIBRARY OF ZOOLOGY AND ORNITHOLOGY □ Montreal, PQ

McLean, J. Craig, Libn.
VIRGINIA COMMONWEALTH UNIVERSITY - MEDICAL COLLEGE OF VIRGINIA - TOMPKINS-MC CAW LIBRARY □ Richmond, VA

McLean, John, Dir.
U.S. NATL. ARCHIVES & RECORDS SERVICE - NATL. AUDIOVISUAL CENTER - INFORMATION SERVICES SECTION □ Washington, DC

MacLean, John C., Dir.
BEVERLY HISTORICAL SOCIETY - LIBRARY AND ARCHIVES □ Beverly, MA

McLean, Linda E., Dir./Site Mgr.
JAY (John) HOMESTEAD - JAY LIBRARY □ Katonah, NY

McLean, Marilyn, Ref.Libn.
BOSTON PUBLIC LIBRARY - GOVERNMENT DOCUMENTS, MICROTEXT, NEWSPAPERS □ Boston, MA

McLean, Nancy, Libn.
TALMUD TORAH SCHOOL - LIBRARY □ Vancouver, BC

MacLean, Paul, Hd., Circ.
SUNY - COLLEGE AT GENESEO - MILNE LIBRARY □ Geneseo, NY

McLean, Mrs. S.M., Hd., Purchasing
CANADA - INDUSTRY, TRADE & COMMERCE - LIBRARY □ Ottawa, ON

McLellan, Arnold, Hd.Libn.
BETHANY BIBLE COLLEGE - LIBRARY □ Scotts Valley, CA

MacLellan, Audrey, Chf.Libn.
HUMBER COLLEGE OF APPLIED ARTS & TECHNOLOGY - LIBRARY □ Rexdale, ON

McLellan, Mary, Legislative Ref.
MASSACHUSETTS STATE LIBRARY □ Boston, MA

McLellan-Breidenthal, Judy, Rd.Serv.Libn.
CURRY COLLEGE - LOUIS R. LEVIN MEMORIAL LIBRARY □ Milton, MA

McLemore, Nancy, Nursing Div.Libn.
ALCORN STATE UNIVERSITY - JOHN DEWEY BOYD LIBRARY □ Lorman, MS

McLendon, Wallace, Hd., Acq./Ser.Serv.
UNIVERSITY OF NORTH CAROLINA, CHAPEL HILL - HEALTH SCIENCES LIBRARY □ Chapel Hill, NC

McLeod, A.D., Res.Dir.
SASKATCHEWAN WHEAT POOL - REFERENCE LIBRARY □ Regina, SK

McLeod, John G., Libn.
ASSOCIATION OF AMERICAN RAILROADS - ECONOMICS AND FINANCE DEPARTMENT - LIBRARY □ Washington, DC

Mac Leod, June F., Law Libn.
GRAY, CARY, AMES & FRYE - LAW LIBRARY □ San Diego, CA

McLeod, Marj, Health Libn.
BRITISH COLUMBIA INSTITUTE OF TECHNOLOGY - LIBRARY SERVICES DIVISION □ Burnaby, BC

MacLeod, Rev. Neil A., Archv.
UNITED CHURCH OF CANADA - MARITIME CONFERENCE ARCHIVES □ Halifax, NS

MacLeod, Ronald K., Asst.Libn.
CANADIAN TAX FOUNDATION - LIBRARY □ Toronto, ON

McLeod, Sherry Ann
SOUTHERN OREGON STATE COLLEGE - LIBRARY □ Ashland, OR

MacLeod, Stephen, Assoc.Libn.
STANFORD UNIVERSITY - CUBBERLEY EDUCATION LIBRARY □ Stanford, CA

McLeod, Trina, Libn.
CHATTANOOGA TIMES - LIBRARY† □ Chattanooga, TN

McLeod, Walter H., Libn.
UNIVERSITY OF IDAHO - LAW LIBRARY □ Moscow, ID

McLoughlin, Catherine J., Libn.
STRATHY, ARCHIBALD AND SEAGRAM - LAW LIBRARY □ Toronto, ON

McMahon, Beverly M., Libn.
WESTMORELAND HOSPITAL - HEALTH EDUCATION CENTER □ Greensburg, PA

McMahon, Carolyn H., Libn.
NATIONAL COUNCIL OF TEACHERS OF ENGLISH - CURRICULUM LIBRARY □ Urbana, IL

MacMahon, Dr. Hugh, Chm., Lib.Comm.
VALLEY GENERAL HOSPITAL - LIBRARY □ Renton, WA

McMahon, Nathalie G., Asst.Dir., USAF Libs.
U.S. AIR FORCE - AIR FORCE MANPOWER AND PERSONNEL CENTER - MORALE, WELFARE & RECREATION DIVISION - LIBRARIES SECTION □ Randolph AFB, TX

McMahon, Rosemary, Cat.Libn.
COLUMBUS TECHNICAL INSTITUTE - EDUCATIONAL RESOURCES CENTER† □ Columbus, OH

McManimon, M. Frances, Med.Libn.
ST. JOSEPH'S HOSPITAL - SAMUEL ROSENTHAL MEMORIAL LIBRARY □ Milwaukee, WI

McManus, Marie R., Chf.Libn.
U.S. PUBLIC HEALTH SERVICE HOSPITAL - CHARLES FERGUSON MEDICAL LIBRARY □ Staten Island, NY

McManus, Mary, Libn.
ONTARIO - MINISTRY OF HEALTH - PSYCHIATRIC BRANCH - LIBRARY RESOURCE CENTRE □ Hamilton, ON

McManus, Maureen J., Libn.
AVANTEK, INC. - CORPORATE SERVICES LIBRARY □ Santa Clara, CA

McMartin, Mary, Pub.Serv.Libn.
UNIVERSITY OF VIRGINIA - SCIENCE/TECHNOLOGY INFORMATION CENTER □ Charlottesville, VA

McMaster, Deborah, Coord., Pub.Serv.
WAKE FOREST UNIVERSITY - BOWMAN GRAY SCHOOL OF MEDICINE - LIBRARY □ Winston-Salem, NC

McMaster, Jane, Ref.Libn.
OHIO STATE UNIVERSITY - ENGINEERING LIBRARY □ Columbus, OH

McMaster, Nina, Libn.
HARVARD UNIVERSITY - PHYSICS RESEARCH LIBRARY □ Cambridge, MA

McMearty, Mabbie, Tech.Libn.
GENERAL ELECTRIC COMPANY - SPACE/RSD LIBRARIES □ Philadelphia, PA

McMeekan, Dorothy B., Asst. Law Libn.
NEW YORK STATE SUPREME COURT - 10TH JUDICIAL DISTRICT - LAW LIBRARY □ Riverhead, NY

MacMillan, Christie, Libn.
HURONIA REGIONAL CENTRE - LIBRARY □ Orillia, ON

MacMillan, Mrs. Donald P., Libn.
UNITED CHURCH OF LOS ALAMOS - LIBRARY □ Los Alamos, NM

McMillan, Dorothy, Photo Libn.
SASKATCHEWAN - PHOTOGRAPHIC AND ART DIVISION - LIBRARY □ Regina, SK

McMillan, Elizabeth, Med.Libn.
U.S. VETERANS ADMINISTRATION (MD-Perry Point) - HOSPITAL MEDICAL LIBRARY □ Perry Point, MD

McMillan, Gary, Res.Spec.
COMMUNITY RELATIONS-SOCIAL DEVELOPMENT COMMISSION - RESEARCH LIBRARY □ Milwaukee, WI

MacMillan, Gary D., Dir.
ROCHESTER INSTITUTE OF TECHNOLOGY - WALLACE MEMORIAL LIBRARY □ Rochester, NY

McMillan, Helen, Lib.Techn.
U.S. AIR FORCE BASE - LAUGHLIN BASE LIBRARY □ Del Rio, TX

McMillan, Janice, Hosp.Libn.
BRANT (Joseph) MEMORIAL HOSPITAL - HOSPITAL LIBRARY □ Burlington, ON

McMillan, Judith L., Doc.
LOYOLA UNIVERSITY (New Orleans) - LAW LIBRARY □ New Orleans, LA

McMillan, Lenora W., Rd.Serv.
U.S. COMMISSION ON CIVIL RIGHTS - NATL. CLEARINGHOUSE LIBRARY □ Washington, DC

McMillen, John, Cat.
AMERICAN PETROLEUM INSTITUTE - LIBRARY □ Washington, DC

McMillin, Carol, Ref.Libn.
U.S. ARMY - ENGINEER WATERWAYS EXPERIMENT STATION - TECHNICAL INFORMATION CENTER □ Vicksburg, MS

McMonigal, Elizabeth, Br.Libn.
ST. PAUL PUBLIC LIBRARY - HIGHLAND PARK BRANCH - PERRIE JONES MEMORIAL ROOM □ St. Paul, MN

McMorrow, Kathleen, Libn.
UNIVERSITY OF TORONTO - FACULTY OF MUSIC LIBRARY □ Toronto, ON

MacMullen, Charmaine L., Act.Dir.
NORTHEASTERN BIBLE COLLEGE - LINCOLN MEMORIAL LIBRARY □ Essex Fells, NJ

McMullen, Elizabeth, Hosp.Libn.
ST. PETER'S MEDICAL CENTER - LIBRARY □ New Brunswick, NJ

MacMullen, Kenneth E., Libn.
PLYMOUTH COUNTY LAW LIBRARY ASSOCIATION - BROCKTON LAW LIBRARY □ Brockton, MA

McMullen, Patricia, Sec.
SPORTS RESEARCH INSTITUTE - LIBRARY □ University Park, PA

MacMullin, Margaret, Libn.
FORTRESS OF LOUISBOURG NATIONAL HISTORIC PARK - LIBRARY □ Louisbourg, NS

McMullin, P.W., Exec.Dir.
WHO AM I - LIBRARY □ Salt lake City, UT

MacMurray, A. Christine, Ed./Libn.
ANIMAL MEDICAL CENTER - LIBRARY □ New York, NY

MacMurray, Gwen, Per.Supv.
HAHNEMANN MEDICAL COLLEGE & HOSPITAL - WARREN H. FAKE LIBRARY □ Philadelphia, PA

McMurrough, Barbara L., Lib.Asst.
KENNEDY (Joseph P., Jr.) MEMORIAL HOSPITAL FOR CHILDREN - MEDICAL LIBRARY □ Brighton, MA

McMurtry, Geraldine, Asst.Libn.
HITTMAN ASSOCIATES, INC. - TECHNICAL INFORMATION DEPARTMENT - LIBRARY □ Columbia, MD

McMurtry, Maria Emma, Mgr.
AMERICAN PUBLIC HEALTH ASSOCIATION - INTERNATIONAL HEALTH PROGRAMS - RESOURCE CENTER □ Washington, DC

McNair, Marian B., Libn.
WESTWOOD FIRST PRESBYTERIAN CHURCH - WALTER LORENZ MEMORIAL LIBRARY □ Cincinnati, OH

McNally, Merrie Jo, Med.Lib.Techn.
ST. ANTHONY HOSPITAL - MEMORIAL MEDICAL LIBRARY □ Denver, CO

McNally, R.F., Supv.Tech.Info.
SPECIAL METALS CORPORATION - INFORMATION FACILITY □ New Hartford, NY

McNamara, Alice, Libn.
MPR ASSOCIATES, INC. - LIBRARY □
Washington, DC
McNamara, Charles B., Assoc.Libn.
CORNELL UNIVERSITY - RARE BOOKS
DEPARTMENT □ Ithaca, NY
McNamara, Darrell, Dir., Lib.Serv.
NORTH DAKOTA STATE LIBRARY □ Bismarck,
ND
McNamara, G.A., Libn.
MEMORIAL HOSPITAL - MEDICAL LIBRARY □
Albany, NY
McNamara, John N., Libn.
U.S. COURT OF APPEALS, 10TH CIRCUIT -
LIBRARY □ Denver, CO
McNamara, Julia I., Law Libn.
VENANGO COUNTY LAW LIBRARY □ Franklin, PA
McNamara, Mary E., Network Coord.
WAYNE STATE UNIVERSITY - SCHOOL OF
MEDICINE - VERA PARSHALL SHIFFMAN
MEDICAL LIBRARY □ Detroit, MI
McNamee, Donald W., Chf.Cat.
CALIFORNIA INSTITUTE OF TECHNOLOGY -
ROBERT A. MILLIKAN MEMORIAL LIBRARY □
Pasadena, CA
McNamee, Gil, Principal Libn.
SAN FRANCISCO PUBLIC LIBRARY - BUSINESS
LIBRARY □ San Francisco, CA
McNamee, Mary S., Cur., Coll.
EVANSVILLE MUSEUM OF ARTS AND SCIENCE -
LIBRARY □ Evansville, IN
McNealy, Terry A., Lib.Dir.
BUCKS COUNTY HISTORICAL SOCIETY -
SPRUANCE LIBRARY □ Doylestown, PA
McNee, John C., Asst.Dir., Pub.Serv.
IOWA STATE UNIVERSITY - LIBRARY □ Ames,
IA
McNeely, Kathleen V., Libn.
MOBIL OIL CANADA, LTD. - LIBRARY □ Calgary,
AB
McNeil, Ann, Asst.Dir.
WEST VIRGINIA STATE SUPREME COURT OF
APPEALS - STATE LAW LIBRARY □ Charleston,
WV
MacNeil, Bruce, Assoc.Libn./Rd.Serv.
UNIVERSITY OF WATERLOO - DANA PORTER
ARTS LIBRARY □ Waterloo, ON
McNeil, Don
LEEWARD COMMUNITY COLLEGE - LIBRARY □
Honolulu, HI
MacNeil, W.R., Sec.
CANADA - NATIONAL DEFENCE - CAMBRIDGE
MILITARY LIBRARY □ Halifax, NS
MacNeill, Margery, Med.Libn.
U.S. VETERANS ADMINISTRATION (MN-
Minneapolis) - HOSPITAL LIBRARY □
Minneapolis, MN
McNeill, Patrick D., Adm.
OAKLAND UNIVERSITY - LIBRARY □ Rochester,
MI
MacNeish, Dr. Richard S., Dir.
PEABODY (Robert S.) FOUNDATION FOR
ARCHEOLOGY - LIBRARY □ Andover, MA
McNerlin, Elizabeth A., Asst.Libn.
DECHERT, PRICE AND RHOADS - LIBRARY □
Philadelphia, PA
McNerney, Christine, Cartographer
NEW YORK STATE DEPARTMENT OF
TRANSPORTATION - MAP INFORMATION UNIT
□ Albany, NY
McNicol, Barbara A.
FLINT NEWMAN CENTER - LIBRARY AND
CATHOLIC INFORMATION CENTER □ Flint, MI
McNicoll, Lise
INSTITUT D'HISTOIRE DE L'AMERIQUE
FRANCAISE (1970) - RESEARCH CENTRE
LIBRARY □ Montreal, PQ
McNiece, Joan, First Asst.
NEW YORK PUBLIC LIBRARY - RARE BOOKS &
MANUSCRIPTS DIVISION - MANUSCRIPTS AND
ARCHIVES COLLECTION □ New York, NY
McNinch, Thomas C., Staff Attorney
HOLLAND & HART - LIBRARY □ Denver, CO

MacNintch, Dr. John E., Asst.Dir.Res.
BRISTOL-MYERS COMPANY - BRISTOL
LABORATORIES - LIBRARY AND INFORMATION
SERVICES □ Syracuse, NY
McNitt, Helen, Libn.
MIFFLIN COUNTY HISTORICAL SOCIETY -
LIBRARY AND MUSEUM □ Lewistown, PA
McNitt, Virginia A., Libn.
AMERICAN TEXTILE MANUFACTURERS
INSTITUTE (ATMI) - LIBRARY □ Washington, DC
McNulty, Patricia J., Supv.
MITRE CORPORATION - TECHNICAL REPORT
CENTER† □ Bedford, MA
McNutt, Eleanor, Assoc.Libn.
UNION UNIVERSITY - ALBANY MEDICAL
COLLEGE - SCHAFFER LIBRARY OF THE HEALTH
SCIENCES □ Albany, NY
McNutt, Dr. James C., Assoc. Professor
MC GILL UNIVERSITY - SCHOOL OF HUMAN
COMMUNICATION DISORDERS - LIBRARY □
Montreal, PQ
McNutt, Lawrence E., Data User Serv.Off.
U.S. BUREAU OF THE CENSUS - REGIONAL
DATA USER SERVICE - CHARLOTTE REGIONAL
OFFICE - LIBRARY □ Charlotte, NC
Macoll, Agathe, ILL
CANADA - CANADIAN TRANSPORT
COMMISSION - LIBRARY □ Ottawa, ON
Macomber, Ann Hodge, Libn.
LOUISIANA STATE UNIVERSITY MEDICAL
CENTER - LIBRARY □ New Orleans, LA
Macomber, Mary M., Libn.
BEREAN BIBLE COLLEGE - LIBRARY □ Calgary,
AB
Macomber, Nancy, Ref.Libn.
ST. JOHN'S UNIVERSITY - LIBRARY □ Jamaica,
NY
Macomber, Dr. William F., Mss.Cat.
ST. JOHN'S ABBEY AND UNIVERSITY - HILL
MONASTIC MANUSCRIPT LIBRARY - BUSH
CENTER □ Collegeville, MN
Macon, Mrs. James, Children's Libn.
REVEILLE UNITED METHODIST CHURCH -
REVEILLE MEMORIAL LIBRARY □ Richmond, VA
McPhaden, Mary, Per.Asst.
BANK OF MONTREAL - HEAD OFFICE LIBRARY □
Montreal, PQ
MacPhail, Ian, Libn.
MORTON ARBORETUM - STERLING MORTON
LIBRARY □ Lisle, IL
McPhail, Sunny, Libn.
ROCKY MOUNTAIN ENERGY CO. - LIBRARY □
Denver, CO
Macpherson, John, Libn.
UNIVERSITY OF WESTERN ONTARIO -
NATURAL SCIENCES LIBRARY □ London, ON
McPherson, Joy, Ref.Libn./Coll.Dev.
HARVARD UNIVERSITY - JOHN FITZGERALD
KENNEDY SCHOOL OF GOVERNMENT - LIBRARY
□ Cambridge, MA
MacPherson, Lillian, Law Libn.
UNIVERSITY OF ALBERTA - LAW LIBRARY □
Edmonton, AB
McPherson, Marion White, Assoc.Dir.
UNIVERSITY OF AKRON - ARCHIVES OF THE
HISTORY OF AMERICAN PSYCHOLOGY □ Akron,
OH
McPherson, Mary, Asst.Libn.
UNION CARBIDE CORPORATION - BUSINESS
LIBRARY □ New York, NY
MacPherson, Walter S., Libn.
WESTERN MEMORIAL REGIONAL HOSPITAL -
HEALTH SCIENCE LIBRARY □ Corner Brook, NF
McQuaid, Ann R., Libn.
TRA ARCHITECTURE ENGINEERING PLANNING
INTERIORS - LIBRARY □ Seattle, WA
McQuarle, Robert J., Dir.
LITTLETON AREA HISTORICAL MUSEUM -
LIBRARY† □ Littleton, CO
McQueen, Lorraine, Coord.Ref.Serv.
NOVA SCOTIA - PROVINCIAL LIBRARY □
Halifax, NS

MacQueen, S.B., Ref.Libn.
WESTERN ELECTRIC COMPANY, INC. -
CORPORATE EDUCATION CENTER - LIBRARY □
Hopewell, NJ
McQueen, William F., Med.Libn.
METROPOLITAN HOSPITAL - MEDICAL
LIBRARY □ Detroit, MI
McQuillan, David C., Map Libn.
UNIVERSITY OF SOUTH CAROLINA - MAP
LIBRARY □ Columbia, SC
McQuillen, Mary, Libn.
WOODBURY COUNTY BAR ASSOCIATION -
LIBRARY □ Sioux City, IA
McRae, Elizabeth, Cat.
YORK UNIVERSITY - LAW LIBRARY □
Downsview, ON
Macrae, Georgia, Asst. Law Libn.
UNIVERSITY OF CALGARY - LAW LIBRARY □
Calgary, AB
MacRae, Ruth, Lib.Asst.
FOOTHILLS HOSPITAL SCHOOL OF NURSING -
LIBRARY □ Calgary, AB
McRaith, Sr. M. Padraig, O.P., Libn. Emeritus
CARROLL COLLEGE - LIBRARY □ Helena, MT
McRory, Mary, Florida Libn.
STATE LIBRARY OF FLORIDA □ Tallahassee, FL
Macsali, Franceska, Site Libn.
U.S. NATL. PARK SERVICE - ROOSEVELT-
VANDERBILT NATL. HISTORIC SITES -
MUSEUMS □ Hyde Park, NY
McShane, Carol Brown, Libn./Archv.
CURTIS PUBLISHING COMPANY - ARCHIVES □
Indianapolis, IN
McShane, Karen, Tax Libn.
FRIED, FRANK, HARRIS, SHRIVER, JACOBSON -
LIBRARY & INFORMATION CENTER □ New York,
NY
McSheehey, Bruce, Ref.Libn.
FITCHBURG STATE COLLEGE - LIBRARY □
Fitchburg, MA
McSorley, Rev. Aidan, Asst.Libn.
CONCEPTION ABBEY AND SEMINARY -
LIBRARY □ Conception, MO
McSpedon, Frances M., Libn.
WHITE HAVEN CENTER - STAFF LIBRARY □
White Haven, PA
McSpiritt, Margaret, Circ.Supv.
BELL TELEPHONE LABORATORIES, INC. -
TECHNICAL LIBRARY □ Murray Hill, NJ
McSwain, Christy, Libn.
ATLANTIC-RICHFIELD COMPANY - ARCO
CHEMICAL COMPANY - RESEARCH &
ENGINEERING TECHNICAL INFORMATION
CENTER □ Newton Square, PA
MacSween, David N., Libn.
CANADA - TRANSPORT CANADA - CANADIAN
COAST GUARD COLLEGE - LIBRARY □ Sydney,
NS
McSweeney, Audrey B., Libn.
NOVA SCOTIA - DEPARTMENT OF EDUCATION
- EDUCATION MEDIA SERVICES □ Halifax, NS
McSweeney, Josephine, Ref.Libn.
PRATT INSTITUTE - LIBRARY □ Brooklyn, NY
McSweeney, Maria Jones, Mgr.
SCM CORPORATION - GLIDDEN COATINGS &
RESINS DIV./DURKEE FOODS DIV. -
TECHNICAL INFORMATION SERVICES □
Strongsville, OH
McTaggart, John B., Dir., Lib.Serv.
METHODIST THEOLOGICAL SCHOOL IN OHIO -
LIBRARY □ Delaware, OH
McTague, Timothy, Info.Spec.
AMERICAN ASSOCIATION OF ADVERTISING
AGENCIES - MEMBER INFORMATION SERVICE
□ New York, NY
McTiernan, Miriam, Territorial Archv.
YUKON TERRITORY - DEPARTMENT OF
LIBRARY AND INFORMATION RESOURCES -
YUKON ARCHIVES □ Whitehorse, YT
McTyre, J., Cat.Libn.
LOS ANGELES TRADE-TECHNICAL COLLEGE -
LIBRARY □ Los Angeles, CA

PERSONNEL

Maher, Priscilla, Asst.Libn.
AMERICAN SOCIETY OF ABDOMINAL
SURGEONS - DONALD COLLINS MEMORIAL
LIBRARY □ Melrose, MA

Maher, William J., Libn.
UNIVERSITY OF ILLINOIS - NEWSPAPER
LIBRARY □ Urbana, IL

Mahon, Cornelia E., Law Libn.
NEW YORK TELEPHONE COMPANY - LAW
LIBRARY □ New York, NY

Mahon, Linda, Adm.Sec.
CORNELL UNIVERSITY - SHOALS MARINE
LABORATORY - LIBRARY □ Ithaca, NY

Mahon, Patricia, Hd., Acq.
SMITHTOWN LIBRARY □ Smithtown, NY

Mahoney, James J.B., Asst.Dir.
ST. JOSEPH'S SEMINARY - ARCHBISHOP
CORRIGAN MEMORIAL LIBRARY† □ Yonkers, NY

Mahoney, James R., Rd.Adv./Soc.Sci.
TRENTON STATE COLLEGE - ROSCOE L. WEST
LIBRARY □ Trenton, NJ

Mahoney, Katherine L., Libn.
CANADA - CANADIAN WILDLIFE SERVICE -
ONTARIO REGION LIBRARY □ Ottawa, ON

Mahoney, R., Hd./Pub.Lib. Program
MICHIGAN STATE LIBRARY SERVICES □
Lansing, MI

Mahoney, Rebecca E., Libn.
INDIANA STATE DEPARTMENT OF COMMERCE
- ENERGY GROUP - LIBRARY □ Indianapolis, IN

Mahoney, Ronald J., Hd.
CALIFORNIA STATE UNIVERSITY, FRESNO -
DEPARTMENT OF SPECIAL COLLECTIONS □
Fresno, CA

Mahony, Doris M., Ref.Coll.Coord.
UNIVERSITY OF MICHIGAN - ALFRED
TAUBMAN MEDICAL LIBRARY □ Ann Arbor, MI

Maier, Charles, Archv.
YUKON TERRITORY - DEPARTMENT OF
LIBRARY AND INFORMATION RESOURCES -
YUKON ARCHIVES □ Whitehorse, YT

Maier, Rita S., Lib.Dir.
BOOTH MEMORIAL MEDICAL CENTER -
MEDICAL LIBRARY □ Flushing, NY

Maier, Virginia L., Libn.
DU PONT DE NEMOURS (E.I.) & COMPANY, INC.
- MARSHALL LABORATORY LIBRARY □
Philadelphia, PA

Mailhot, Denise, Libn.
ORDRE DES INFIRMIERES ET DES INFIRMIERS
DU QUEBEC - CENTRE DE DOCUMENTATION □
Montreal, PQ

Mailloux, Elizabeth N., Mgr.
MOBIL RESEARCH & DEVELOPMENT
CORPORATION - ENGINEERING DEPARTMENT -
INFORMATION CENTER □ Princeton, NJ

Mailloux, Prof. Noel
CENTRE DE RECHERCHES EN RELATIONS
HUMAINES - BIBLIOTHEQUE □ Montreal, PQ

Main, Mrs. Gale, Libn.
PARKER MEMORIAL BAPTIST CHURCH -
LIBRARY □ Anniston, AL

Maina, William, Asst.Dir.Pub.Serv.
UNIVERSITY OF TEXAS HEALTH SCIENCE
CENTER, DALLAS - LIBRARY □ Dallas, TX

Maine, John S., Lib.Dir.
MILLERSVILLE STATE COLLEGE - HELEN A.
GANSER LIBRARY □ Millersville, PA

Maines, Rachel, Dir.
CENTER FOR THE HISTORY OF AMERICAN
NEEDLEWORK - LIBRARY □ Ambridge, PA

Mains, Cheryl M. Ronning, Libn.
CANADA - AGRICULTURE CANADA - RESEARCH
STATION, LETHBRIDGE - LIBRARY □ Lethbridge,
AB

Maizell, Dr. R.E., Mgr.
OLIN CORPORATION - RESEARCH CENTER/
INFORMATION CENTER □ New Haven, CT

Maja, Yolanda, Health Sci.Lib.Techn.
ST. JOSEPH HOSPITAL - LIBRARY □ Chicago, IL

Majcher, Michael D., Mgr.
XEROX CORPORATION - TECHNICAL
INFORMATION CENTER □ Webster, NY

Majeski, Lila, Acq.
CAMROSE LUTHERAN COLLEGE - LIBRARY □
Camrose, AB

Major, Kristin, Tech.Serv.
ADAMS-PRATT OAKLAND COUNTY LAW
LIBRARY □ Pontiac, MI

Major, Susan, Libn.
UNIVERSITY OF ALBERTA - POPULATION
RESEARCH LIBRARY □ Edmonton, AB

Mak, Ms. J., ILL
TORONTO BOARD OF EDUCATION -
EDUCATION CENTRE LIBRARY □ Toronto, ON

Mak, Loretta, Libn.
HELLER, EHRMAN, WHITE & MC AULIFFE -
LIBRARY □ San Francisco, CA

Makar, Ragai N., Hd.Libn.
ADELPHI UNIVERSITY - SOCIAL WORK
LIBRARY □ Garden City, NY

Makeever, Virginia, Lib.Techn.
UNIVERSITY OF DELAWARE, NEWARK - MATH-
PHYSICS READING ROOM □ Newark, DE

Makepeace, Peggy H., Libn.
MURPHY OIL CORPORATION - LIBRARY □ El
Dorado, AR

Maki, G.W., Hd.Libn.
CONFEDERATION COLLEGE OF APPLIED ARTS &
TECHNOLOGY - RESOURCE CENTRE □ Thunder
Bay, ON

Makinen, Winifred, Tech.Libn.
UNION CARBIDE CORPORATION - PARMA
TECHNICAL CENTER - TECHNICAL
INFORMATION SERVICE □ Cleveland, OH

Makino, Yasuko, East Asian Cat.
UNIVERSITY OF ILLINOIS - ASIAN LIBRARY □
Urbana, IL

Makler, Stephanie, Dp.Dir.
NEW YORK CITY - MUNICIPAL REFERENCE
AND RESEARCH CENTER □ New York, NY

Malach, Mrs. J., Hd., Tech.Proc.
CANADA - NATIONAL DEFENCE - FORT
FRONTENAC LIBRARY □ Kingston, ON

Malamud, Edith, Circ.Libn.
WORLD AFFAIRS COUNCIL OF NORTHERN
CALIFORNIA - LIBRARY □ San Francisco, CA

Malamud, Judie, Asst.Libn., Pub.Serv.
UNIVERSITY OF PENNSYLVANIA - MEDICAL &
BIOLOGICAL SCIENCES LIBRARY □ Philadelphia,
PA

Malan, Harrison, Sr.Libn.
OAKLAND PUBLIC LIBRARY - HISTORY/
LITERATURE DIVISION □ Oakland, CA

Maland, David J., Libn.
U.S. COURT OF APPEALS, 8TH CIRCUIT -
RESEARCH LIBRARY □ St. Paul, MN

Malburg, Dorothy, Lib.Tech.
LUTHERAN MEDICAL CENTER - C. W. NEVEL
MEMORIAL LIBRARY □ Cleveland, OH

Malcom, Wilberta M., Libn.
AMES (A.E.) AND COMPANY, LTD. - LIBRARY □
Toronto, ON

Malden, Joyce, Libn.
CHICAGO MUNICIPAL REFERENCE LIBRARY □
Chicago, IL

Male, Cathy, Asst.Libn.
JONES, DAY, REAVIS & POGUE - LIBRARY □
Cleveland, OH

Malecki, Virginia
UTICA OBSERVER DISPATCH & UTICA DAILY
PRESS - LIBRARY† □ Utica, NY

Malik, Nailah, Tech.Libn.
BURROUGHS CORPORATION - SANTA BARBARA
PLANT - LIBRARY □ Goleta, CA

Malikyar, Rahella, Asst.Libn.
SAFECO INSURANCE COMPANY - LIBRARY □
Seattle, WA

Malinowski, Theresa, Supv.Tech.Serv.
MOORE-COTTRELL SUBSCRIPTION AGENCIES -
SERIALS REFERENCE LIBRARY □ North
Cohocton, NY

Malinsky, Barbara, Cur., Photographs
MEDICAL COLLEGE OF PENNSYLVANIA -
ARCHIVES AND SPECIAL COLLECTIONS ON
WOMEN IN MEDICINE □ Philadelphia, PA

Malisheski, Linda M., Libn.
CONTINENTAL CARBON COMPANY -
TECHNICAL LIBRARY† □ Houston, TX

Malison, Louise, AV Techn.
CONESTOGA COLLEGE OF APPLIED ARTS &
TECHNOLOGY, GUELPH CENTRE - HEALTH
SCIENCES DIV. LEARNING RESOURCE CENTRE
□ Guelph, ON

Malkin, Mrs. Audree, Libn.
UNIVERSITY OF CALIFORNIA, LOS ANGELES -
THEATER ARTS LIBRARY □ Los Angeles, CA

Malkowski, Eugene, Acq.Libn.
U.S. SOCIAL SECURITY ADMINISTRATION -
LIBRARY □ Baltimore, MD

Mallach, Stanley, Biblog.
UNIVERSITY OF WISCONSIN, MILWAUKEE -
MORRIS FROMKIN MEMORIAL COLLECTION □
Milwaukee, WI

Maller, Alma, Spec. Projects Libn.
BABSON COLLEGE - HORN LIBRARY □ Babson
Park, MA

Mallett, Dana D., Corp.Libn.
BDM CORPORATION - CORPORATE LIBRARY □
McLean, VA

Mallett, Doyce, Law Libn.
TEXAS STATE - COURT OF APPEALS - 7TH
SUPREME JUDICIAL DISTRICT AND POTTER
COUNTY - LAW LIBRARY □ Amarillo, TX

Mallette, Danielle, Ref.Libn.
UNIVERSITE DU QUEBEC A MONTREAL -
BIBLIOTHEQUE DES SCIENCES DE
L'EDUCATION □ Montreal, PQ

Malley, Eileen, Libn.
MAIN HURDMAN - LIBRARY† □ San Francisco,
CA

Mallick, Jerry, Cat./Adm.
NATIONAL GALLERY OF ART - PHOTOGRAPHIC
ARCHIVES □ Washington, DC

Mallino, Kathryne, Asst.Libn.
INDIANA UNIVERSITY OF PENNSYLVANIA -
UNIVERSITY LIBRARY □ Indiana, PA

Mallinson, Gwyneth Heynes, Mgr.Tech.Info.Serv.
AMPEX CORPORATION - TECHNICAL LIBRARY
MS 3-10 □ Redwood City, CA

Mallio, Osee, Cat.Oper., Projects
NEW ENGLAND WILD FLOWER SOCIETY, INC. -
LIBRARY □ Framingham, MA

Mallis, Genevieve, Libn.
CANDLER GENERAL HOSPITAL - PROFESSIONAL
LIBRARY □ Savannah, GA

Mallison, Irene K., Hd.Sci.Libn.
EMORY UNIVERSITY - SCIENCE LIBRARY □
Atlanta, GA

Mallon, Connie, Asst.Libn.
MARINE ENVIRONMENTAL SCIENCES
CONSORTIUM - LIBRARY† □ Dauphin Island, AL

Mallon, Capt. N.F., Hon.Libn.
ROYAL CANADIAN MILITARY INSTITUTE -
LIBRARY □ Toronto, ON

Mallos, Diane, Slide & Photo Libn.
SMITHSONIAN INSTITUTION - NATL. MUSEUM
OF AMERICAN ART - OFFICE OF VISUAL
RSRCS. - SLIDE/PHOTOGRAPH ARCHIVE □
Washington, DC

Malloy, Lois
UNIVERSITY OF CALIFORNIA, RIVERSIDE -
EDUCATION SERVICES LIBRARY □ Riverside,
CA

Malmberg, Carol, Ref.Libn.
UNIVERSITY OF CALIFORNIA - LOS ALAMOS
NATIONAL LABORATORY - LIBRARY □ Los
Alamos, NM

Malmgren, Terri L., Libn.
UNIVERSITY OF CALIFORNIA, DAVIS - HEALTH
SCIENCES LIBRARY □ Davis, CA

Malmgren, Terri L., Libn.
UNIVERSITY OF CALIFORNIA, DAVIS -
MEDICAL CENTER LIBRARY □ Sacramento, CA

Malone, Jackie, Libn.
SCUDDER, STEVENS & CLARK - LIBRARY □ New
York, NY

PERSONNEL

Malone, Kathy, Libn.
FORT WORTH PUBLIC LIBRARY - HUMANITIES DEPARTMENT □ Fort Worth, TX

Malone, Rosemary, Cat.
NEW ENGLAND REGIONAL COMMISSION (NERCOM) - REFERENCE LIBRARY □ Boston, MA

Maloney, Edmund P., Circ.Libn.
FORDHAM UNIVERSITY - MULCAHY LIBRARY □ Bronx, NY

Maloney, Margaret Crawford, Hd.
TORONTO PUBLIC LIBRARY - CANADIANA COLLECTION OF CHILDREN'S BOOKS □ Toronto, ON

Maloney, Margaret Crawford, Hd.
TORONTO PUBLIC LIBRARY - LILLIAN H. SMITH COLLECTION OF CHILDREN'S BOOKS □ Toronto, ON

Maloney, Margaret Crawford, Hd.
TORONTO PUBLIC LIBRARY - OSBORNE COLLECTION OF EARLY CHILDREN'S BOOKS □ Toronto, ON

Maloy, Robert, Dir.
SMITHSONIAN INSTITUTION LIBRARIES □ Washington, DC

Maltby, Dr. William, Exec.Dir.
CENTER FOR REFORMATION RESEARCH - LIBRARY □ St. Louis, MO

Malyk, M., Libn.
CANADA - AGRICULTURE CANADA - RESEARCH STATION, WINNIPEG - LIBRARY □ Winnipeg, MB

Malzer, Marietta, Archv.
OKLAHOMA STATE DEPARTMENT OF LIBRARIES □ Oklahoma City, OK

Mamarchev, Helen L., Coord.LRC
ERIC CLEARINGHOUSE ON COUNSELING AND PERSONNEL SERVICES - LEARNING RESOURCES CENTER □ Ann Arbor, MI

Mamchur, Natalia J., Mgr., Lib.Res.
RCA CORPORATION - ENGINEERING LIBRARY □ Moorestown, NJ

Mamdani, Zenny, Engr.Adm.Asst.
KOBE, INC. - ENGINEERING LIBRARY □ Huntington Park, CA

Mamoulides, Aphrodite, Lib.Supv.
SHELL DEVELOPMENT COMPANY - BELLAIRE RESEARCH CENTER LIBRARY □ Houston, TX

Managhan, Peter, Staff Libn.
ALBERTA HOSPITAL PONOKA - STAFF LIBRARY □ Ponoka, AB

Managhi, Dr. Russell M., Archv.-Chf.Libn.
NATIONAL SKI HALL OF FAME AND MUSEUM - ROLAND PALMEDO NATIONAL SKI LIBRARY □ Ishpeming, MI

Manaley, Shirley K., Libn.
IBM CORPORATION - SYSTEM PRODUCTS DIVISION - LIBRARY □ Endicott, NY

Manarin, Dr. Louis H., State Archv.
VIRGINIA STATE LIBRARY □ Richmond, VA

Manbeck, John B., Archv.
KINGSBOROUGH COMMUNITY COLLEGE - KINGSBOROUGH HISTORICAL SOCIETY □ Brooklyn, NY

Mancebo, Olga, Libn.
BECTON, DICKINSON IMMUNODIAGNOSTICS - TECHNICAL RESEARCH AND DEVELOPMENT LIBRARY† □ Orangeburg, NY

Mancevice, Mark F., Dir., Resource Ctr.
NEW ENGLAND TELEPHONE LEARNING CENTER - RESOURCE CENTER □ Marlborough, MA

Mancina, E., Chf.Libn.
DOUGLAS HOSPITAL CENTRE - STAFF LIBRARY □ Montreal, PQ

Mancini, John F., Res.Assoc.
FOUNDATION FOR PUBLIC AFFAIRS - RESOURCE CENTER □ Washington, DC

Mandel, Marie, Res.Libn.
TELEDYNE ISOTOPES - RESEARCH LIBRARY □ Westwood, NJ

Mandel, Ruth B., Dir.
CENTER FOR THE AMERICAN WOMAN & POLITICS - LIBRARY □ New Brunswick, NJ

Mandel, Tobyann, Libn.
HUGHES AIRCRAFT COMPANY - HUGHES RESEARCH LABORATORIES LIBRARY □ Malibu, CA

Mandel-Kent, Linda, Ref.Libn.
O'MELVENY AND MYERS - INFORMATION SERVICES □ Los Angeles, CA

Mandelman, Ellen, Libn.
CONGREGATION SHALOM - SHERMAN PASTOR MEMORIAL LIBRARY □ Milwaukee, WI

Mandeville, Mrs. Andree N., Libn.
CENTRE HOSPITALIER DE VERDUN - BIBLIOTHEQUE MEDICALE □ Verdun, PQ

Mandeville, Joanne, Libn.
CRANE COMPANY - HYDRO-AIRE DIVISION - TECHNICAL LIBRARY □ Burbank, CA

Mandeville, Nancy J., Tech.Libn.
GNOSTIC CONCEPTS, INC. - TECHNICAL LIBRARY □ Menlo Park, CA

Mandikos, George J., Tech.Dir.
AMERICAN ASSOCIATION OF TEXTILE CHEMISTS AND COLORISTS - LIBRARY □ Research Triangle Park, NC

Mandl, Patricia, Info.Spec./Tech.Serv.
GENERAL FOODS CORPORATION - MARKETING INFORMATION CENTER □ White Plains, NY

Mandle, Mark, Asst.Libn.
TECHNOMIC CONSULTANTS - INFORMATION CENTER □ Chicago, IL

Mandley, Catherine, Asst.Libn.
DU PONT CANADA, INC. - PATENT DIVISION LIBRARY □ Mississauga, ON

Mandracchia, James, Libn.
AKIN HALL ASSOCIATION - AKIN FREE LIBRARY □ Pawling, NY

Manes, Esther, Libn.
MEDICAL LETTER - LIBRARY □ New Rochelle, NY

Manet, Lyn, Libn.
U.S. AIR FORCE BASE - BLYTHEVILLE BASE LIBRARY □ Blytheville AFB, AR

Maney, James, Lib.Dir.
OBLATE COLLEGE OF THE SOUTHWEST - LIBRARY □ San Antonio, TX

Maney, James, Asst.Libn.
SEMINARY OF ST. VINCENT DE PAUL - LIBRARY □ Boynton Beach, FL

Maney, Marilyn, Asst.Libn.
WILLKIE FARR & GALLAGHER - LIBRARY □ New York, NY

Mang, Jeffery, Libn.
PATTON BOGGS AND BLOW - LAW LIBRARY □ Washington, DC

Mangieri, C.N., Dir.
SOUTH MOUNTAIN LABORATORIES, INC. - LIBRARY □ South Orange, NJ

Mangine, Brenda, Libn.
INDIANAPOLIS - DEPARTMENT OF METROPOLITAN DEVELOPMENT - DIVISION OF PLANNING AND ZONING - LIBRARY □ Indianapolis, IN

Mangion, Barbara E., Libn.
BIRD MACHINE COMPANY, INC. - LIBRARY □ South Walpole, MA

Mangum, Kathy, Ext.Spec.
UNIVERSITY OF MINNESOTA - AGRICULTURAL EXTENSION SERVICE - EXTENSION HOME EOCNOMICS - INFO. CTR. □ St. Paul, MN

Mangum, Neil, Hist.
U.S. NATL. PARK SERVICE - CUSTER BATTLEFIELD NATL. MONUMENT - LIBRARY □ Crow Agency, MT

Manheim, Theodore, Hd.
WAYNE STATE UNIVERSITY - EDUCATION LIBRARY □ Detroit, MI

Maniece, Olivia S., Chf.Libn.
U.S. VETERANS ADMINISTRATION (AL-Tuscaloosa) - HOSPITAL MEDICAL LIBRARY □ Tuscaloosa, AL

Manilla, George, Coord.
ELKO MEDICAL CLINIC - LIBRARY □ Elko, NV

Manion, Martha L., Assoc.Libn.
STAUFFER CHEMICAL COMPANY - MOUNTAIN VIEW RESEARCH CENTER LIBRARY □ Mountain View, CA

Manjula, Yaramakala, Libn.
ATLANTA PUBLIC LIBRARY - IVAN ALLEN, JR. DEPARTMENT OF SCIENCE, INDUSTRY AND GOVERNMENT □ Atlanta, GA

Mankell, Carolyn, Asst.Libn.
UNIVERSITY OF WISCONSIN, MADISON - NIEMAN-GRANT JOURNALISM READING ROOM □ Madison, WI

Mankin, Carole, Res. Project Libn.
MASSACHUSETTS GENERAL HOSPITAL - TREADWELL AND PALMER-DAVIS LIBRARY □ Boston, MA

Mankin, Charles J., Dir.
OKLAHOMA GEOLOGICAL SURVEY - OKLAHOMA GEOPHYSICAL OBSERVATORY LIBRARY □ Leonard, OK

Mankowitz, Gloria, Assoc.Dir.
MOTION PICTURE SERVICES □ Livingston, NJ

Mankowitz, Murray, Dir.
MOTION PICTURE SERVICES □ Livingston, NJ

Manley, Irwin G., Adm., Info.Serv.
GIBSON, DUNN & CRUTCHER - LAW LIBRARY □ Los Angeles, CA

Manlove, Patricia A., Libn.
WESTERN MONTANA CLINIC - LIBRARY □ Missoula, MT

Mann, Brenda, Libn.
U.S. ARMY RESEARCH OFFICE - TECHNICAL LIBRARY □ Research Triangle Park, NC

Mann, Deborah, Ref.
LOUISIANA STATE UNIVERSITY - LAW LIBRARY □ Baton Rouge, LA

Mann, I., Res.Libn.
FORD AEROSPACE & COMMUNICATIONS CORP. - AERONUTRONIC DIVISION - TECHNICAL INFORMATION SERVICES □ Newport Beach, CA

Mann, Ian, ILL
ONTARIO - MINISTRY OF TRANSPORTATION AND COMMUNICATIONS - LIBRARY AND INFORMATION CENTRE □ Downsview, ON

Mann, John B., Coord., AV Serv.
GUILFORD TECHNICAL INSTITUTE - LEARNING RESOURCE CENTER □ Jamestown, NC

Mann, Joyce A., Tech.Info.Off.
U.S. FISH & WILDLIFE SERVICE - NATIONAL FISHERIES CENTER - TECHNICAL INFORMATION SERVICE □ Kearneysville, WV

Mann, Lorne, Dir.
COMMONWEALTH MICROFILM LIBRARY □ Willowdale, ON

Mann, Ruth, Hist. of Med.Libn.
MAYO FOUNDATION - MAYO CLINIC LIBRARY □ Rochester, MN

Mann, Wayne C., Dir.
WESTERN MICHIGAN UNIVERSITY - ARCHIVES AND REGIONAL HISTORY COLLECTIONS □ Kalamazoo, MI

Manne, Elizabeth, Libn.
SKIDMORE, OWINGS & MERRILL - LIBRARY □ Denver, CO

Manning, Helen, Libn.
TEXAS INSTRUMENTS - HOUSTON SITE LIBRARY □ Houston, TX

Manning, John, Media Serv.Coord.
COLUMBUS TECHNICAL INSTITUTE - EDUCATIONAL RESOURCES CENTER† □ Columbus, OH

Manning, Kathryn, Libn.
WADLEY INSTITUTES OF MOLECULAR MEDICINE - RESEARCH INSTITUTE LIBRARY □ Dallas, TX

Manning, Leo W., Exec.Dir.
SOCIETY FOR ACADEMIC ACHIEVEMENT - LIBRARY □ Quincy, IL

Manning, Martha, Hd., Info.Serv.
SUNY AT BUFFALO - HEALTH SCIENCES LIBRARY □ Buffalo, NY

Manning, Mary G., Libn.
MERCY HOSPITAL - MEDICAL & HOSPITAL INSERVICE LIBRARIES □ Springfield, MA

Manning, Ralph, Asst.Libn., Tech.Serv.
UNIVERSITY OF OTTAWA - MORISSET LIBRARY □ Ottawa, ON

Manning, Robert N., Mgr.
HERCULES, INC. - RESEARCH CENTER - TECHNICAL INFORMATION DIVISION □ Wilmington, DE

Manning, T.M.
OLIN CORPORATION - RESEARCH CENTER/ INFORMATION CENTER □ New Haven, CT

Mannion, Lynette, Film Libn.
UNIVERSITY OF TORONTO - AUDIO-VISUAL LIBRARY □ Toronto, ON

Mannion, Mary, Asst.Libn.
MANUFACTURERS HANOVER TRUST COMPANY - CORPORATE LIBRARY/FINANCIAL LIBRARY DIVISION □ New York, NY

Manocchio, Rita F., Libn.
LEESONA CORPORATION - LIBRARY □ Warwick, RI

Manoogian, Sylva N., Principal Libn.
LOS ANGELES PUBLIC LIBRARY - FOREIGN LANGUAGES DEPARTMENT □ Los Angeles, CA

Manos, Eleanor V., Libn.
U.S. NAVY - NAVAL CONSTRUCTION BATTALION CENTER - LIBRARY □ Port Hueneme, CA

Mansbach, Carolyn, Med.Libn.
JAMAICA HOSPITAL - MEDICAL LIBRARY □ Jamaica, NY

Mansfield, Fred, Biblog.
UNIVERSITY OF ILLINOIS - LAW LIBRARY □ Champaign, IL

Mansfield, Jerry, Asst.Engr.Libn.
PURDUE UNIVERSITY - ENGINEERING LIBRARY □ West Lafayette, IN

Mansfield, Juliet I., Libn.
STURDY MEMORIAL HOSPITAL - HEALTH SCIENCES LIBRARY □ Attleboro, MA

Manson, Connie J., Libn.
WASHINGTON STATE DEPARTMENT OF NATURAL RESOURCES - DIVISION OF GEOLOGY AND EARTH RESOURCES - LIBRARY □ Lacey WA

Manson-Smith, Pamela, Libn.
UNIVERSITY OF TORONTO - SCHOOL OF ARCHITECTURE AND PLANNING LIBRARY □ Toronto, ON

Manss, Jacqualin, Hd., Circ.
UNIVERSITY OF CALIFORNIA, SANTA CRUZ - SCIENCE LIBRARY □ Santa Cruz, CA

Mansur, Jeannell, Drug Info. Pharmacist
UNIVERSITY OF CHICAGO HOSPITALS & CLINICS - PHARMACEUTICAL SERVICES - DRUG INFORMATION CENTER □ Chicago, IL

Mansur, Ruth, Rec. Preservation Techn.
LOUISIANA STATE OFFICE OF THE SECRETARY OF STATE - STATE ARCHIVES AND RECORDS SERVICE □ Baton Rouge, LA

Manton, Kenneth G., Asst.Dir.
DUKE UNIVERSITY - CENTER FOR DEMOGRAPHIC STUDIES - REFERENCE LIBRARY □ Durham, NC

Mantzel, Lois B., Libn.
TEXACO CHEMICAL COMPANY, INC. - TECHNICAL LITERATURE SECTION □ Austin, TX

Mantzoros, Tessie, Libn.
MC GRAW-HILL, INC. - BUSINESS WEEK MAGAZINE LIBRARY† □ New York, NY

Manuel, Melbarose, Assoc.Libn. & Cat.
SOUTHERN UNIVERSITY - LAW SCHOOL LIBRARY □ Baton Rouge, LA

Manville, Christine
SOCIETY OF FRIENDS - FRIENDS HOUSE LIBRARY □ Toronto, ON

Manwaring, Bob, Sr. AV Techn.
CENTENNIAL COLLEGE OF APPLIED ARTS & TECHNOLOGY - ASHTONBEE CAMPUS RESOURCE CENTRE □ Scarborough, ON

Manwaring, Mrs. S., Govt.Pubn.Libn.
UNIVERSITY OF ALBERTA - HUMANITIES AND SOCIAL SCIENCES LIBRARY □ Edmonton, AB

Manwaring, Sally, Hd., Govt.Pubn.Lib.
UNIVERSITY OF ALBERTA - GOVERNMENT PUBLICATIONS □ Edmonton, AB

Mao, Shelley Giak, Asst.Libn.
ST. JOSEPH HOSPITAL - HOSPITAL HEALTH SCIENCE LIBRARY □ Houston, TX

Maonnis, John, Photo Libn.
NATIONAL MARITIME MUSEUM - J. PORTER SHAW LIBRARY □ San Francisco, CA

Mapel, John, Unit Mgr.
U.S. NATL. PARK SERVICE - RUSSELL CAVE NATL. MONUMENT - LIBRARY □ Bridgeport, AL

Mapes, Martha, Libn.
TULSA CITY-COUNTY LIBRARY SYSTEM - BUSINESS AND TECHNOLOGY DEPARTMENT □ Tulsa, OK

Maples, Carol, Br.Libn.
U.S. AIR FORCE - FLIGHT TEST CENTER - TECHNICAL LIBRARY □ Edwards AFB, CA

Mar, Norma B., Libn.
CHEMISTS' CLUB LIBRARY - CHEMICAL INTERNATIONAL INFORMATION CENTER □ New York, NY

Maracek, Robert, Coord. ILL
NATIONAL SAFETY COUNCIL - LIBRARY □ Chicago, IL

Marafioti, Mrs. Armida M., Libn.
NEW YORK STATE SUPREME COURT - 3RD JUDICIAL DISTRICT - EMORY A. CHASE MEMORIAL LIBRARY □ Catskill, NY

Marano, Ray, Br.Libn.
WHITE AND CASE - LIBRARY □ New York, NY

Marasco, Bernadette, Sr.Tech.Info.Spec.
INTERNATIONAL PAPER COMPANY - CORPORATE RESEARCH & DEVELOPMENT DIVISION - TECHNICAL INFORMATION CENTER □ Tuxedo, NY

Marble, Beatrice N., Dept.Hd.
ONONDAGA COUNTY PUBLIC LIBRARY - ART AND MUSIC DEPARTMENT □ Syracuse, NY

Marboe, Peter C., Dir.
AUSTRIAN PRESS AND INFORMATION SERVICE □ New York, NY

Marcano, Enriqueta, Hd.Cat.
UNIVERSITY OF PUERTO RICO - LAW SCHOOL LIBRARY □ Rio Piedras, PR

Marcello, Dr. Ronald E., Coord.
NORTH TEXAS STATE UNIVERSITY - ORAL HISTORY COLLECTION □ Denton, TX

March, Frieda O., Chf.Libn.
IDAHO STATE HISTORICAL SOCIETY - GENEALOGICAL LIBRARY □ Boise, ID

Marchand, Miss M., Hd.Coll.Dev.
CANADA - HEALTH AND WELFARE CANADA - DEPARTMENTAL LIBRARY SERVICES □ Ottawa, ON

Marchese, Laverna, Libn.
FOOTHILLS PIPE LINES (Yukon) LTD. - LIBRARY □ Calgary, AB

Marchese, Marie-Ann, Lib.Coord.
LEXINGTON SCHOOL FOR THE DEAF - LIBRARY MEDIA CENTER □ Jackson Heights, NY

Marchessault, Ellen, Ser.Libn.
UNIVERSITY OF HEALTH SCIENCES/CHICAGO MEDICAL SCHOOL - LIBRARY □ North Chicago, IL

Marchfield, R.L., Pres.
VOLTAIRE SOCIETY - LIBRARY □ Okeechobee, FL

Marchiafava, Dr. Louis J., Archv.
HOUSTON PUBLIC LIBRARY - ARCHIVES AND MANUSCRIPT DEPARTMENT □ Houston, TX

Marcin, Arlene, Lib.Supv.
HARVARD UNIVERSITY - TICKNOR LIBRARY □ Cambridge, MA

Marcolina, Ruth, Dir.
SUNY AT STONY BROOK - HEALTH SCIENCES LIBRARY □ East Setauket, NY

Marcuccio, Phyllis, Tech.Cons.
NATIONAL SCIENCE TEACHERS ASSOCIATION - GLENN O. BLOUGH LIBRARY □ Washington, DC

Marcus, Frances, Asst.Libn.
ANDOVER COLLEGE - LIBRARY □ Portland, ME

Marcus, Professor Jacob R., Dir.
HEBREW UNION COLLEGE - JEWISH INSTITUTE OF RELIGION - AMERICAN JEWISH ARCHIVES □ Cincinnati, OH

Marcus, Jacob R., Dir.
HEBREW UNION COLLEGE - JEWISH INSTITUTE OF RELIGION - AMERICAN JEWISH PERIODICAL CENTER □ Cincinnati, OH

Marcus, Joyce, Ref.Asst.
BRIDGEWATER STATE COLLEGE - CLEMENT C. MAXWELL LIBRARY □ Bridgewater, MA

Marcus, Linda, Clghse.Dept.
NATIONAL RESOURCE CENTER FOR CONSUMERS OF LEGAL SERVICES - CLEARINGHOUSE □ Washington, DC

Marcus, Richard W., Hd.Libn.
SPERTUS COLLEGE OF JUDAICA - NORMAN AND HELEN ASHER LIBRARY □ Chicago, IL

Marcus, Ronald, Libn.
STAMFORD HISTORICAL SOCIETY - LIBRARY □ Stamford, CT

Marcus, Sharon, Libn.
UNIVERSITY OF CALIFORNIA, LOS ANGELES - MATHEMATICS READING ROOM □ Los Angeles, CA

Marcus, Terry, Libn.
MILWAUKEE INSTITUTE OF ART & DESIGN - LIBRARY □ Milwaukee, WI

Marcus, Tybe, Ref.
CANADA - ECONOMIC COUNCIL OF CANADA - LIBRARY □ Ottawa, ON

Marcy, Susan, Circuit Libn.
CLEVELAND HEALTH SCIENCES LIBRARY - ALLEN MEMORIAL LIBRARY □ Cleveland, OH

Marczak, Judith, Libn.
TYMSHARE, INC. - TECHNICAL LIBRARY □ Cupertino, CA

Mardney, Patrick, Media Serv.Spec.
OAKLAND SCHOOLS - EDUCATIONAL RESOURCE CENTER □ Pontiac, MI

Marek, Vera, Hd., Cat.Dept.
POLYTECHNIC INSTITUTE OF NEW YORK - SPICER LIBRARY □ Brooklyn, NY

Mares, Claire, Ed.
EASTERN NEBRASKA GENEALOGICAL SOCIETY - LIBRARY □ Fremont, NE

Margeton, Stephen G., Libn.
STEPTOE AND JOHNSON - LIBRARY □ Washington, DC

Margolis, Bernard, Dir., Lib.Sys.
MONROE COUNTY LIBRARY SYSTEM - GENERAL GEORGE ARMSTRONG CUSTER COLLECTION □ Monroe, MI

Margolis, Bernard A., Dir.
SOUTHEAST MICHIGAN REGIONAL FILM LIBRARY □ Monroe, MI

Margolis, Nancy H., Libn.
WESTMINSTER INSTITUTE FOR ETHICS AND HUMAN VALUES - LIBRARY □ London, ON

Margoshes, Miriam, Libn.
PERGAMON INSTITUTE - LIBRARY □ Elmsford, NY

Marics, Joseph, Hd. of Circ.
ASSEMBLIES OF GOD GRADUATE SCHOOL - CORDAS C. BURNETT LIBRARY □ Springfield, MO

Marie, Sr. Francis, Libn.
ST. JOSEPH HOSPITAL - OTTO C. BRANTIGAN MEDICAL LIBRARY □ Towson, MD

Marier, Donald, Dir.
ALTERNATIVE SOURCES OF ENERGY MAGAZINE - ENERGY INFORMATION REFERRAL SERVICE (EIRS) □ Milaca, MN

Marifke, Linda, Sr.Asst.Libn.
QUARLES & BRADY - LIBRARY □ Milwaukee, WI

Marin, Carmen M., Dir.
NORTH CAROLINA STATE UNIVERSITY - TOBACCO LITERATURE SERVICE □ Raleigh, NC

Marin, Christine N., Chicano Biblog.
ARIZONA STATE UNIVERSITY - CHICANO
STUDIES COLLECTION □ Tempe, AZ

Marin, Federico, Spec.Proj.
UNIVERSITY OF PUERTO RICO - MAYAGUEZ
CAMPUS - LIBRARY □ Mayaguez, PR

Marin, Regina F., Hd., Doc. & Maps
UNIVERSITY OF PUERTO RICO - GENERAL
LIBRARY □ San Juan, PR

Marinaccio, Alexander T., Supv.Lib./Tech.Serv.
INVENTORS CLUB OF AMERICA - INVENTORS
REFERENCE CENTER □ Springfield, MA

Marino, Samuel J., Act.Libn.
TEXAS WOMAN'S UNIVERSITY - LIBRARY
SCIENCE LIBRARY □ Denton, TX

Marion, Don, Libn.
UNIVERSITY OF MINNESOTA - PHYSICS
LIBRARY □ Minneapolis, MN

Marion, Frieda, Cur.
WHITTIER HOME ASSOCIATION - LIBRARY □
Amesbury, MA

Marion, Phyllis C., Hd. of Cat.
UNIVERSITY OF MINNESOTA - LAW LIBRARY □
Minneapolis, MN

Maritz, Cynthia A., Libn.
KRUPNICK & ASSOCIATES, INC. - LIBRARY □
St. Louis, MO

Marix, Mary L., Asst.Libn.
TOURO INFIRMARY - HOSPITAL LIBRARY □
New Orleans, LA

Mark, Lillian, Med.Libn.
CLEVELAND CLINIC EDUCATION FOUNDATION
- MEDICAL LIBRARY/AUDIOVISUAL CENTER† □
Cleveland, OH

Mark, Martha, Libn.
TULANE UNIVERSITY OF LOUISIANA -
MATHEMATICS RESEARCH LIBRARY □ New
Orleans, LA

Mark, Ronnie Joan, Dir.
CONEY ISLAND HOSPITAL - HAROLD FINK
MEMORIAL LIBRARY □ Brooklyn, NY

Mark, Ruth, Res.Anl.
CALIFORNIA STATE DEPARTMENT OF
INDUSTRIAL RELATIONS - DIVISION OF LABOR
STATISTICS AND RESEARCH LIBRARY □ San
Francisco, CA

Marke, Julius J., Law Libn.
NEW YORK UNIVERSITY - SCHOOL OF LAW
LIBRARY □ New York, NY

Markewicz, Frank J., Act. State Geologist
NEW JERSEY STATE DEPARTMENT OF
ENVIRONMENTAL PROTECTION - GEOLOGICAL
SURVEY - INFORMATION CENTER □ Trenton, NJ

Markey, Patricia, Cat.
MERRIMACK VALLEY TEXTILE MUSEUM -
LIBRARY □ North Andover, MA

Markham, Ann, Coord.
ILLINOIS MASONIC MEDICAL CENTER -
SCHOOL OF NURSING - DR. JOSEPH DEUTSCH
MEMORIAL LIBRARY □ Chicago, IL

Markham, Susan, Lib.Techn.
U.S. BUREAU OF MINES - TUSCALOOSA
RESEARCH CENTER - REFERENCE LIBRARY □
University, AL

Markham, Valiera, Lib.Techn.
U.S. AIR FORCE BASE - MC CLELLAN BASE
LIBRARY □ McClellan AFB, CA

Markle, Linda S., Asst.Libn.
ST. JOSEPH HOSPITAL OF MT. CLEMENS -
MEDICAL LIBRARY □ Mt. Clemens, MI

Markowetz, M., Asst.Dir./Hd., Pub.Serv.
UNIVERSITY OF WISCONSIN, MILWAUKEE -
GOLDA MEIR LIBRARY - CURRICULUM
COLLECTION □ Milwaukee, WI

Markowski, Benedict, Fld.Archv.
DETROIT PUBLIC LIBRARY - BURTON
HISTORICAL COLLECTION □ Detroit, MI

Marks, Becky, Asst.Libn.
KERR-MC GEE CORPORATION - MC GEE
LIBRARY □ Oklahoma City, OK

Marks, Carol, Libn.
JOHNSON SWANSON & BARBEE - LIBRARY □
Dallas, TX

Marks, Caroline, Hd.Libn.
CITIBANK, N.A. - INVESTMENT LIBRARY □ New
York, NY

Marks, Cicely P., Tech.Serv.Spec.
U.S. VETERANS ADMINISTRATION (DC-
Washington) - HEADQUARTERS CENTRAL
OFFICE LIBRARY □ Washington, DC

Marks, Coralyn, Lib.Dir.
NORTHWEST GENERAL HOSPITAL - MEDICAL
LIBRARY □ Milwaukee, WI

Marks, Ruth, Harmony Found.Adm.
SOCIETY FOR THE PRESERVATION AND
ENCOURAGEMENT OF BARBER SHOP QUARTET
SINGING IN AMERICA - OLD SONGS LIBRARY □
Kenosha, WI

Markush, Catherine, ILL
HEBREW UNION COLLEGE - JEWISH
INSTITUTE OF RELIGION - KLAU LIBRARY □
New York, NY

Markwell, Linda Garr, Grady Br.Libn.
EMORY UNIVERSITY - SCHOOL OF MEDICINE -
A.W. CALHOUN MEDICAL LIBRARY □ Atlanta,
GA

Markwood, Carolyn K., Libn.
DU PONT DE NEMOURS (E.I.) & COMPANY, INC.
- TECHNICAL LIBRARY SYSTEM - SPRUANCE
RESEARCH LABORATORY BRANCH □ Richmond,
VA

Markworth, Lawrence, Asst.Engr.Libn.
STANFORD UNIVERSITY - ENGINEERING
LIBRARY □ Stanford, CA

Marlaire, Michael, Mss.
SOUTHERN ILLINOIS UNIVERSITY,
CARBONDALE - SPECIAL COLLECTIONS □
Carbondale, IL

Marley, Carol, Map Cur.-Libn.
MC GILL UNIVERSITY - DEPARTMENT OF RARE
BOOKS & SPECIAL COLLECTIONS □ Montreal,
PQ

Marlow, Kathryn E., Libn.
NUS CORPORATION - TECHNICAL LIBRARY □
Pittsburgh, PA

Marose, Doris, Dir., Med.Lib.
MEMORIAL HOSPITAL - MEDICAL LIBRARY □
Sarasota, FL

Marousek, Kathy, Act. Dental Libn.
FAIRLEIGH DICKINSON UNIVERSITY - SCHOOL
OF DENTISTRY LIBRARY □ Hackensack, NJ

Marquardt, Jack, Chf.
SMITHSONIAN INSTITUTION LIBRARIES -
CENTRAL REFERENCE SERVICES □ Washington,
DC

Marquette, Carl G., Jr., First Asst.
PUBLIC LIBRARY OF CINCINNATI AND
HAMILTON COUNTY - HISTORY AND
LITERATURE DEPARTMENT □ Cincinnati, OH

Marquette, Carl G., Jr., Map Libn.
PUBLIC LIBRARY OF CINCINNATI AND
HAMILTON COUNTY - HISTORY AND
LITERATURE DEPARTMENT - MAP UNIT □
Cincinnati, OH

Marquette, Margaret, Coord.
LOS ANGELES COUNTY SUPERINTENDENT OF
SCHOOLS - PROFESSIONAL REFERENCE
CENTER □ Downey, CA

Marquez-Sterling, Carlos, Asst.Soc.Stud.Libn.
SOUTHERN ILLINOIS UNIVERSITY,
CARBONDALE - SOCIAL STUDIES DIVISION
LIBRARY □ Carbondale, IL

Marquis, Kay, Tech.Libn.
NASHUA CORPORATION - TECHNICAL LIBRARY
□ Nashua, NH

Marr, Antony, Assoc.Cur.
YALE UNIVERSITY - EAST ASIAN COLLECTION
□ New Haven, CT

Marr, Lisa, Cat.
SOUTHERN CONNECTICUT STATE COLLEGE -
H.C. BULEY LIBRARY □ New Haven, CT

Marra, Ruth, Asst.Archv.
NAPA COUNTY HISTORICAL SOCIETY -
GOODMAN LIBRARY □ Napa, CA

Marren, Janet C., Libn.
EDMONTON POWER - LIBRARY □ Edmonton, AB

Marrero, Betty-Ruth, Asst.Libn.
SOUTHERN ILLINOIS UNIVERSITY,
CARBONDALE - UNDERGRADUATE LIBRARY □
Carbondale, IL

Marron, Betsy, Prog.Serv.Dir.
GIRL SCOUTS OF RACINE COUNTY, INC. -
LIBRARY □ Racine, WI

Mars, Maline, Sec./Libn.
SOUTH SHORE HOSPITAL - MEDICAL STAFF
LIBRARY □ Chicago, IL

Marsala, Kathryn, Mgr., Tech.Info.Ctr.
EQUITABLE LIFE ASSURANCE SOCIETY OF THE
U.S. - TECHNICAL INFORMATION CENTER □
New York, NY

Marsden, Dorothy E., Libn.
VALLEJO NAVAL AND HISTORIC MUSEUM -
LIBRARY □ Vallejo, CA

Marsden, Tom, Info.Serv.Libn.
STEVENS INSTITUTE OF TECHNOLOGY -
SAMUEL C. WILLIAMS LIBRARY □ Hoboken, NJ

Marsh, Henry, Cur.
HOLY LAND MUSEUM & LIBRARY □ New York,
NY

Marsh, John S., Libn.
SIMPSON, THACHER & BARTLETT - LIBRARY† □
New York, NY

Marsh, Josephine, Data Proc.
UNIVERSITY OF NORTH CAROLINA, CHAPEL
HILL - INSTITUTE FOR RESEARCH IN SOCIAL
SCIENCE - DATA LIBRARY □ Chapel Hill, NC

Marsh, Sharon, Doc.Libn.
EASTERN KENTUCKY UNIVERSITY - JOHN
GRANT CRABBE LIBRARY □ Richmond, KY

Marsh, Sheila J., Media Libn.
CALIFORNIA STATE UNIVERSITY,
SACRAMENTO - LIBRARY - MEDIA SERVICES
CENTER □ Sacramento, CA

Marshall, A., Hd., Tech.Proc.
CARNEGIE-MELLON UNIVERSITY - HUNT
LIBRARY □ Pittsburgh, PA

Marshall, A.P., Act.Dir.
EASTERN MICHIGAN UNIVERSITY - CENTER OF
EDUCATIONAL RESOURCES - ARCHIVES/
SPECIAL COLLECTIONS □ Ypsilanti, MI

Marshall, Denis, Hd.Libn.
UNIVERSITY OF MANITOBA - LAW LIBRARY □
Winnipeg, MB

Marshall, Douglas, Maps Libn.
UNIVERSITY OF MICHIGAN - WILLIAM L.
CLEMENTS LIBRARY □ Ann Arbor, MI

Marshall, Gerald L., Libn.
LUTHER RICE SEMINARY - BERTHA SMITH
LIBRARY □ Jacksonville, FL

Marshall, Gordon M., Asst.Libn.
LIBRARY COMPANY OF PHILADELPHIA □
Philadelphia, PA

Marshall, Herbert, Dir.
U.S. NATL. PARK SERVICE - CHEROKEE STRIP
LIVING MUSEUM - RESEARCH LIBRARY □
Arkansas City, KS

Marshall, Howard W., Folklife Spec.
LIBRARY OF CONGRESS - AMERICAN FOLKLIFE
CENTER □ Washington, DC

Marshall, Jane, Law Libn.
NORTHWESTERN MUTUAL LIFE INSURANCE
COMPANY - LAW LIBRARY □ Milwaukee, WI

Marshall, Jane R., Cat.Libn.
BABSON COLLEGE - HORN LIBRARY □ Babson
Park, MA

Marshall, Joanne, Pub.Serv.Libn.
MC MASTER UNIVERSITY - HEALTH SCIENCES
LIBRARY □ Hamilton, ON

Marshall, Joseph W., Supv.Libn.
U.S. PRESIDENTIAL LIBRARIES - FRANKLIN D.
ROOSEVELT LIBRARY □ Hyde Park, NY

Marshall, K. Eric, Libn.
CANADA - FISHERIES & OCEANS -
FRESHWATER INSTITUTE LIBRARY □ Winnipeg,
MB

Marshall, Kathryn E., Chf., Lib.Serv.Sec.
U.S. AIR FORCE ENVIRONMENTAL TECHNICAL
APPLICATIONS CENTER - AIR WEATHER
SERVICE TECHNICAL LIBRARY □ Scott AFB, IL

Marshall, Laelle B., Exec.Sec.
ELECTRO-MECHANICS COMPANY - LIBRARY† □
Austin, TX

Marshall, Marion, Libn.
TAX FOUNDATION - LIBRARY □ Washington, DC

Marshall, Myrra N., Libn.
LIONS GATE HOSPITAL - DR. H. CARSON
GRAHAM MEMORIAL LIBRARY □ North
Vancouver, BC

Marshall, Patricia, Chf.Libn.
AMERICAN INSTITUTE OF AERONAUTICS AND
ASTRONAUTICS - TECHNICAL INFORMATION
SERVICE □ New York, NY

Marshall, Patricia K., Mgr., Res.Serv.
MOBIL OIL CORPORATION - PUBLIC AFFAIRS
SECRETARIAT □ New York, NY

Marshall, Rosita, Acq.
MARYCREST COLLEGE - CONE LIBRARY† □
Davenport, IA

Marshall, Ruth, Libn.
EMMAUS BIBLE SCHOOL - LIBRARY □ Oak Park,
IL

Marshall, Shirley, Tech.Info.Spec.
U.S. DEPT. OF LABOR - OSHA - TECHNICAL
DATA CENTER □ Washington, DC

Marshall, Thelma L., Libn.
GREAT FALLS GENEALOGY SOCIETY - LIBRARY
□ Great Falls, MT

Marshall, Bro. Thomas A., S.J., Libn.
CALIFORNIA PROVINCE OF THE SOCIETY OF
JESUS - JESUIT CENTER LIBRARY □ Los Gatos,
CA

Marshall, Warren, Supv. Reprographics
FRANKLIN INSTITUTE - LIBRARY □ Philadelphia,
PA

Marshment, Patrick R., Tech.Libn.
GTE LENKURT, INC. - TECHNICAL LIBRARY,
M679 □ San Carlos, CA

Marsick, Daniel, Tech.Info.Spec.
U.S. DEPT. OF LABOR - OSHA - TECHNICAL
DATA CENTER □ Washington, DC

Marson, Joyce, Dir.
WHITE MEMORIAL MEDICAL CENTER -
COURVILLE-ABBOTT MEMORIAL LIBRARY □ Los
Angeles, CA

Marson, Joyce, Dir.
WHITE MEMORIAL MEDICAL CENTER -
NEUROLOGY LIBRARY □ Los Angeles, CA

Marsteller, Ann L., Libn.
YEE (Alfred A.) & ASSOCIATES INC. - LIBRARY
□ Honolulu, HI

Marston, Claire, Lib.Asst.
UNIVERSITY CONGREGATIONAL CHURCH -
LIBRARY □ Seattle, WA

Martel, Christian, Lib.Techn.
HOTEL-DIEU DU SACRE-COEUR DE JESUS -
BIBLIOTHEQUE MEDICALE† □ Quebec, PQ

Martel, Elizabeth, Libn.
DUNHAM TAVERN MUSEUM - LIBRARY □
Cleveland, OH

Martha, Sr., Libn.
SACRED HEART HOSPITAL - HEALTH SCIENCE
LIBRARY □ Cumberland, MD

Marti, Hanna, Spec.Coll.Libn.
UNIVERSITY OF WESTERN ONTARIO - SCHOOL
OF LIBRARY & INFORMATION SCIENCE -
LIBRARY □ London, ON

Martin, Alvia D., Cur.
MADISON TOWNSHIP HISTORICAL SOCIETY -
THOMAS WARNE HISTORICAL MUSEUM AND
LIBRARY □ Matawan, NJ

Martin, Andree, Hd., Pub.Serv.
COLLEGE LIONEL-GROULX - BIBLIOTHEQUE □
Ste. Therese, PQ

Martin, Anita, Archv.
ELI LILLY AND COMPANY - LILLY ARCHIVES □
Indianapolis, IN

Martin, Anne F., GBG Libn.
IBM CANADA, LTD. - GENERAL BUSINESS
GROUP LIBRARY □ Don Mills, ON

Martin, Archie, AV Libn.
EMORY UNIVERSITY - SCHOOL OF MEDICINE -
A.W. CALHOUN MEDICAL LIBRARY □ Atlanta,
GA

Martin, B., Circ.Libn.
UNIVERSITY OF LOWELL, SOUTH CAMPUS -
DANIEL H. O'LEARY LIBRARY □ Lowell, MA

Martin, Bennie E., Chf.Libn.
COOK COUNTY LAW LIBRARY - CRIMINAL
COURT BRANCH □ Chicago, IL

Martin, Betty, Sr.Libn.
ONTARIO HYDRO - LIBRARY □ Toronto, ON

Martin, Beverly B., Libn.
JEWISH VOCATIONAL SERVICE - LIBRARY □
Chicago, IL

Martin, Carle, Doc.Cat./Circ.
U.S. NAVY - NAVAL COASTAL SYSTEMS
CENTER - TECHNICAL LIBRARY □ Panama City,
FL

Martin, Carol, Asst.Libn.
UNIVERSITY OF ARKANSAS, FAYETTEVILLE -
MEDICAL CENTER - NORTHWEST ARKANSAS
HEALTH EDUCATION CENTER □ Fayetteville, AR

Martin, Daniel, Asst.Adm.Libn.
UNIVERSITY OF TEXAS SCHOOL OF LAW -
TARLTON LAW LIBRARY □ Austin, TX

Martin, Rev. David L., Sec./Archv.
LUTHERAN CHURCH IN AMERICA - NORTH
CAROLINA SYNOD - ARCHIVES □ Salisbury, NC

Martin, Delores, Libn.
CABOT CORPORATION - LIBRARY □ Pampa, TX

Martin, Dolores M., Ed.
LIBRARY OF CONGRESS - HISPANIC DIVISION
□ Washington, DC

Martin, Donald L., Law Libn.
U.S. DEPT. OF LABOR - LIBRARY - LAW
LIBRARY DIVISION □ Washington, DC

Martin, Dorothy, Libn.
UNIVERSITY OF BRITISH COLUMBIA - SOCIAL
SCIENCES DIVISION □ Vancouver, BC

Martin, Dorothy A., Libn.
AMERICAN BAPTIST CHURCHES IN THE U.S.A.
- BOARD OF EDUCATIONAL MINISTRIES -
EDITORIAL LIBRARY □ Valley Forge, PA

Martin, Douglas W., Law Libn.
NORTH CAROLINA CENTRAL UNIVERSITY -
LAW LIBRARY □ Durham, NC

Martin, E.J., Mgr.
KAMAN-TEMPO - TECHNICAL INFORMATION
CENTER □ Santa Barbara, CA

Martin, Miss E.J.V., Hd., Info.Serv.
CANADA - INDUSTRY, TRADE & COMMERCE -
LIBRARY □ Ottawa, ON

Martin, Elese, Circ.Libn.
WHITTIER COLLEGE - SCHOOL OF LAW -
LIBRARY □ Los Angeles, CA

Martin, Fay D.
MASSACHUSETTS INSTITUTE OF TECHNOLOGY
- PHYSICS READING ROOM □ Cambridge, MA

Martin, Faye J., Lib.Tech.Asst.
UNIVERSITY OF NORTH CAROLINA, CHAPEL
HILL - MATHEMATICS-PHYSICS-STATISTICS
LIBRARY □ Chapel Hill, NC

Martin, Frances Patton, Res.Cur.
EVANSVILLE MUSEUM OF ARTS AND SCIENCE -
LIBRARY □ Evansville, IN

Martin, Fred, Asst.Libn.
MIAMI-DADE PUBLIC LIBRARY - BUSINESS,
SCIENCE AND TECHNOLOGY DEPARTMENT □
Miami, FL

Martin, Fred W., Dir.
UNIVERSITY OF COLORADO, BOULDER -
THERAPEUTIC RECREATION INFORMATION
CENTER (TRIC) □ Boulder, CO

Martin, G.A., Physicist
U.S. NATL. BUREAU OF STANDARDS - DATA
CENTER ON ATOMIC TRANSITION
PROBABILITIES □ Washington, DC

Martin, Gabrielle, Supv., Internal Doc.
IRELL & MANELLA - LIBRARY □ Los Angeles, CA

Martin, Harry, Libn.
HARVARD UNIVERSITY - LAW SCHOOL
LIBRARY □ Cambridge, MA

Martin, Sr. Helen, Ref.Libn.
WADHAMS HALL SEMINARY - COLLEGE
LIBRARY □ Ogdensburg, NY

Martin, I. Margareta, Info.Sci.
COCA-COLA COMPANY - TECHNICAL
INFORMATION SERVICES □ Atlanta, GA

Martin, Irmgarde, Libn.
ANDERSON CLAYTON FOODS - W.L. CLAYTON
RESEARCH CENTER □ Richardson, TX

Martin, J.C., Dir.
SAN JACINTO MUSEUM OF HISTORY
ASSOCIATION - LIBRARY □ La Porte, TX

Martin, Jack L., Dir.
INDIANAPOLIS MOTOR SPEEDWAY HALL OF
FAME MUSEUM - LIBRARY □ Indianapolis, IN

Martin, Jana, Med.Libn.
NORTH GENERAL HOSPITAL - MEDICAL
LIBRARY □ New York, NY

Martin, Jean, Libn.
VANCOUVER ART GALLERY - LIBRARY □
Vancouver, BC

Martin, Jean K., Lib.Mgr.
MOLYCORP, INC. - LIBRARY □ Los Angeles, CA

Martin, Jess A., Dir.
UNIVERSITY OF TENNESSEE - CENTER FOR
THE HEALTH SCIENCES LIBRARY □ Memphis,
TN

Martin, John, Pres.
WOODSTOCK HISTORICAL SOCIETY, INC. -
JOHN COTTON DANA LIBRARY □ Woodstock,
VT

Martin, Dr. John H., Dir.
CORNING MUSEUM OF GLASS - LIBRARY □
Corning, NY

Martin, Judith R., Cat.
WEST VIRGINIA WESLEYAN COLLEGE - ANNIE
MERNER PFEIFFER LIBRARY □ Buckhannon, WV

Martin, June, Circ.Libn.
EASTERN KENTUCKY UNIVERSITY - JOHN
GRANT CRABBE LIBRARY □ Richmond, KY

Martin, Karin E., Libn.
FIRST PRESBYTERIAN CHURCH - LIBRARY □
Upland, CA

Martin, Katherine R., Dir.
LLOYD (Alice) COLLEGE - APPALACHIAN ORAL
HISTORY PROJECT □ Pippa Passes, KY

Martin, Kathryn W., Libn.
DALLAS MANAGEMENT SERVICES LIBRARY □
Dallas, TX

Martin, Lawrence W., Libn.
BATTELLE NEW ENGLAND RESEARCH
LABORATORY - WILLIAM F. CLAPP
LABORATORIES, INC. - LIBRARY □ Duxbury, MA

Martin, Linda, Libn.
PLACER DEVELOPMENT, LTD. - LIBRARY □
Vancouver, BC

Martin, M.J., Dir.
U.S. OAK RIDGE NATL. LABORATORY -
NUCLEAR DATA PROJECT† □ Oak Ridge, TN

Martin, Margaret D., Law Libn.
FULTON COUNTY LAW LIBRARY □ Atlanta, GA

Martin, Marie A., Exec.Sec.
BISHOP'S MILL HISTORICAL INSTITUTE - SOL
FEINSTONE LIBRARY □ Edgemont, PA

Martin, Mary, Pub.Serv.
GENERAL MOTORS INSTITUTE - LIBRARY† □
Flint, MI

Martin, Mary, Doc. Delivery Coord.
MINITEX □ Minneapolis, MN

Martin, Mary Alice, Slide Cur.
MEMPHIS STATE UNIVERSITY LIBRARIES -
ART SLIDE LIBRARY □ Memphis, TN

Martin, Mary Dell, Chf., Pub.Distr.Sect.
U.S. ARMY - ENGINEER WATERWAYS
EXPERIMENT STATION - TECHNICAL
INFORMATION CENTER □ Vicksburg, MS

Martin, MaryLou T., Libn.
OAKLAND PUBLIC LIBRARY - CITYLINE
INFORMATION SERVICE □ Oakland, CA

Martin, Michael G., Jr., Asst.Cur./Archv.
UNIVERSITY OF NORTH CAROLINA, CHAPEL
HILL - SOUTHERN HISTORICAL COLLECTION &
MANUSCRIPTS DEPARTMENT □ Chapel Hill, NC

PERSONNEL

Martin, Mildred E., Libn.
SPRINGFIELD ACADEMY OF MEDICINE -
HEALTH SCIENCE LIBRARY □ Springfield, MA

Martin, Mona, Info.Spec.
WED ENTERPRISES - RESEARCH LIBRARY □
Glendale, CA

Martin, Norman, Hd., Ref. & ILL
UNIVERSITY OF WISCONSIN, WHITEWATER -
LIBRARY & LEARNING RESOURCES □
Whitewater, WI

Martin, Peggy, Libn.
HAWKINS, DELAFIELD & WOOD - LIBRARY □
New York, NY

Martin, R. Lawrence, Archv.
FERRIS STATE COLLEGE - LIBRARY □ Big
Rapids, MI

Martin, Ray D., Dir. of Legal Res.
UNIVERSITY OF ALABAMA - SCHOOL OF LAW
LIBRARY □ University, AL

Martin, Rebecca, Hd.Libn.
UNIVERSITY OF CALIFORNIA, BERKELEY -
BIOCHEMISTRY LIBRARY □ Berkeley, CA

Martin, Rebecca, Hd.Libn.
UNIVERSITY OF CALIFORNIA, BERKELEY -
BIOLOGY LIBRARY □ Berkeley, CA

Martin, Robert, Leg.Spec.
WILMER, CUTLER & PICKERING - LAW
LIBRARY □ Washington, DC

Martin, Roger, Hd., Rd.Serv.Div.
U.S. NAVY - NAVAL POSTGRADUATE SCHOOL -
DUDLEY KNOX LIBRARY □ Monterey, CA

Martin, Rosary H., Med.Libn.
LUTHERAN MEDICAL CENTER - C. W. NEVEL
MEMORIAL LIBRARY □ Cleveland, OH

Martin, Sandra I., Asst.Libn.
HARPER-GRACE HOSPITALS - HARPER
HOSPITAL DIVISION - DEPARTMENT OF
LIBRARIES □ Detroit, MI

Martin, Sara, Asst.Libn.
HOUSTON INTERNATIONAL MINERALS
CORPORATION - LIBRARY □ Denver, CO

Martin, Sarah S., Libn.
NATIONAL RADIO ASTRONOMY OBSERVATORY
- LIBRARY □ Charlottesville, VA

Martin, Sherrill, Ref./Acq. Libn.
FLORIDA STATE UNIVERSITY - CTR. FOR
STUDIES IN VOCATIONAL EDUC. - FLORIDA
EDUCATORS INFO. SERV. □ Tallahassee, FL

Martin, Shirley A., Ref.Libn.
UNIVERSITY OF MAINE, FARMINGTON -
MANTOR LIBRARY □ Farmington, ME

Martin, Teresa, Med.Libn.
PORTER MEMORIAL HOSPITAL - HARLEY E.
RICE MEMORIAL LIBRARY □ Denver, CO

Martin, Vernon, Dir.
CLOUD COUNTY HISTORICAL MUSEUM -
LIBRARY □ Concordia, KS

Martin, Vernon, Hd.
HARTFORD PUBLIC LIBRARY - ART, MUSIC AND
RECREATION DEPARTMENT □ Hartford, CT

Martin, Dr. William C., Physicist
U.S. NATL. BUREAU OF STANDARDS - ATOMIC
ENERGY LEVELS DATA CENTER □ Washington,
DC

Martin, Z.C., ILL
GEORGIA STATE DEPARTMENT OF HUMAN
RESOURCES - GEORGIA MENTAL HEALTH
INSTITUTE - ADDISON M. DUVAL LIBRARY □
Atlanta, GA

Martina, Sr. M., Dir.
MADONNA COLLEGE - CURRICULUM LIBRARY □
Livonia, MI

Martineau, A., Chf.Pub.Serv.
CANADA - PUBLIC ARCHIVES OF CANADA -
FEDERAL ARCHIVES DIVISION □ Ottawa, ON

Martineau, Colette, Hd., Acq.
CANADA - CANADIAN INTERNATIONAL
DEVELOPMENT AGENCY - DEVELOPMENT
INFORMATION CENTRE □ Hull, PQ

Martineau, Denise, Bibliotechnicienne
QUEBEC PROVINCE - MINISTERE DES
CONSOMMATEURS, COOPERATIVES ET
INSTITUTIONS FINANCIERES - BIBLIOTHEQUE
□ Quebec, PQ

Martineau, Noella, Med.Libn.
HOPITAL RIVIERE-DES-PRAIRIES -
BIBLIOTHEQUE DU PERSONNEL □ Montreal, PQ

Martinello, Gilda, Info.Serv.Libn.
CANADIAN NATIONAL RAILWAYS - DECHIEF
LIBRARY □ Montreal, PQ

Martinez, Angelina, Asst.Dir.
CALIFORNIA POLYTECHNIC STATE
UNIVERSITY - ROBERT E. KENNEDY LIBRARY □
San Luis Obispo, CA

Martinez, Anna, Sr.Libn.
SAN DIEGO PUBLIC LIBRARY - LITERATURE &
LANGUAGE SECTION □ San Diego, CA

Martinez, Bernice, Circ.
UNIVERSITY OF UTAH - LAW LIBRARY □ Salt
Lake City, UT

Martinez, Carole, Mgr.
SOUTHEAST METROPOLITAN BOARD OF
COOPERATIVE SERVICES - PROFESSIONAL
INFORMATION CENTER □ Denver, CO

Martinez, Donna, Asst.Libn.
BROBECK, PHLEGER & HARRISON - LIBRARY □
San Francisco, CA

Martinez, Eloise F., Supv.
AMOCO INTERNATIONAL OIL COMPANY -
LIBRARY INFORMATION CENTER □ Houston, TX

Martinez, Gladys L., Ref.Libn.
UNIVERSITY OF PUERTO RICO - MAYAGUEZ
CAMPUS - LIBRARY □ Mayaguez, PR

Martinez, Grace, Ref.Libn.
U.S. NASA - LYNDON B. JOHNSON SPACE
CENTER - TECHNICAL LIBRARY □ Houston, TX

Martinez, Katharine, Chf.Libn.
SMITHSONIAN INSTITUTION - NATL. MUSEUM
OF AMERICAN ART/NATIONAL PORTRAIT
GALLERY - LIBRARY □ Washington, DC

Martinez, Martha, Cat.
INTERAMERICAN UNIVERSITY - SCHOOL OF
LAW - DOMINGO TOLEDO ALAMO LAW LIBRARY
□ Santurce, PR

Martinez, Dr. Oscar J., Dir.
UNIVERSITY OF TEXAS, EL PASO - INSTITUTE
OF ORAL HISTORY □ El Paso, TX

Martinez, Victor L., Hd., Tech.Serv.
UNIVERSITY OF PUERTO RICO - MAYAGUEZ
CAMPUS - LIBRARY □ Mayaguez, PR

Martinke, Thomas L., Libn.
HERCULES, INC. - RESEARCH CENTER -
TECHNICAL INFORMATION DIVISION □
Wilmington, DE

Martino, Lt.Col. Frank, Hd.Sup.Br.
U.S. MARINE CORPS - HISTORICAL CENTER
LIBRARY □ Washington, DC

Martinsek, Catherine, Asst.Soc.Stud.Libn.
SOUTHERN ILLINOIS UNIVERSITY,
CARBONDALE - SOCIAL STUDIES DIVISION
LIBRARY □ Carbondale, IL

Martinsen, Deborah, Exec.Sec.
CENTER FOR THE STUDY OF HUMAN RIGHTS -
LIBRARY □ New York, NY

Martinsen, Elizabeth A., Chf., Ref.Serv./Br.
U.S. PUBLIC HEALTH SERVICE - PARKLAWN
HEALTH LIBRARY □ Rockville, MD

Martinson, Gayle, Area Res.Ctr.
UNIVERSITY OF WISCONSIN, STOUT -
LIBRARY LEARNING CENTER - MEDIA
RETRIEVAL SERVICES □ Menomonie, WI

Martinson, Sheila, Supv.Lib.Serv.
OTTER TAIL POWER COMPANY - LIBRARY □
Fergus Falls, MN

Martir, Noelia, Ser.Libn.
UNIVERSITY OF PUERTO RICO - MEDICAL
SCIENCES CAMPUS - LIBRARY □ Rio Piedras, PR

Martison, Jennifer, Libn.
BENNETT JONES - LIBRARY □ Calgary, AB

Marton, Victor, Supv., Info. Unit
LIBRARY OF CONGRESS - COPYRIGHT PUBLIC
INFORMATION OFFICE □ Washington, DC

Martone, Helen, Asst. to the Libn.
BLUE CROSS/BLUE SHIELD OF GREATER NEW
YORK - REFERENCE LIBRARY □ New York, NY

Marty, Jeanette Valentin, Asst.Libn.
CENTER FOR ENERGY AND ENVIRONMENT
RESEARCH - READING ROOM □ Mayaguez, PR

Martyn, Dorian, Cat.
UNIVERSITY OF MIAMI - SCHOOL OF
MEDICINE - LOUIS CALDER MEMORIAL
LIBRARY □ Miami, FL

Martz, David J., Jr., Dir.
UNIVERSITY OF TOLEDO - WARD M. CANADAY
CENTER □ Toledo, OH

Martz, James, Acq.Libn.
DICKINSON STATE COLLEGE - STOXEN
LIBRARY □ Dickinson, ND

Maru, Olavi, Libn.
AMERICAN BAR FOUNDATION - WILLIAM
NELSON CROMWELL LIBRARY □ Chicago, IL

Marvel, Dorothy, Libn.
ADAMS EXPRESS COMPANY - LIBRARY □
Baltimore, MD

Marvel, Estelle, Asst.Libn.
INSTITUTE FOR JUVENILE RESEARCH -
PROFESSIONAL LIBRARY □ Chicago, IL

Marwood, Alice, Libn.
BRITISH COLUMBIA GENEALOGICAL SOCIETY -
REFERENCE LIBRARY □ Richmond, BC

Marx, Amy, Docs.Libn.
UNIVERSITY OF GEORGIA - GOVERNMENT
REFERENCE/DOCUMENTS SECTION □ Athens,
GA

Marx, C., Cat.
UNIVERSITY OF WISCONSIN, LA CROSSE -
MURPHY LIBRARY □ La Crosse, WI

Marx, Karen, Lib.Asst.
BROOKHAVEN MEMORIAL HOSPITAL -
MEDICAL LIBRARY □ Patchogue, NY

Marz, Sandra, Pub.Serv.Libn.
WASHOE COUNTY LAW LIBRARY □ Reno, NV

Marzec, Mr. R.J., Mgr., Tech.Trng.Serv
DUKE POWER COMPANY - STEAM
PRODUCTION DEPARTMENT - INFORMATION
RESOURCE CENTER (IRC) □ Cornelius, NC

Masak, Phyllis, Cat. & Ref.Libn.
CONCORDIA TEACHERS COLLEGE - KLINCK
MEMORIAL LIBRARY □ River Forest, IL

Masar, H. Jane, Libn.
GENERAL DRAFTING COMPANY, INC. - MAP
LIBRARY □ Convent Station, NJ

Masar, Steve, Archv./Processor
UNIVERSITY OF WISCONSIN, MADISON -
ARCHIVES □ Madison, WI

Mascio, Clemente, Libn.
FASHION INSTITUTE OF DESIGN &
MERCHANDISING - RESOURCE AND RESEARCH
CENTER □ Los Angeles, CA

Masek, Linda, Hd.Libn.
ELYRIA MEMORIAL HOSPITAL - LIBRARY □
Elyria, OH

Mashbaum, Jesse, Dir.
BALTIMORE HEBREW COLLEGE - JOSEPH
MEYERHOFF LIBRARY □ Baltimore, MD

Mashburn, Martha, Doc./Tech.Serv.Libn.
GEORGIA STATE LIBRARY □ Atlanta, GA

Masin, Anton C., Hd.
UNIVERSITY OF NOTRE DAME - RARE BOOKS
AND SPECIAL COLLECTIONS DEPARTMENT □
Notre Dame, IN

Maskewitz, Betty F., Dir.
U.S. OAK RIDGE NATL. LABORATORY -
RADIATION SHIELDING INFORMATION
CENTER □ Oak Ridge, TN

Maslansky, Hannah V., Asst.Libn.
UNION CARBIDE CORPORATION - LIBRARY &
TECHNICAL INFORMATION SERVICE† □
Tarrytown, NY

Masling, Annette, Libn.
ALBRIGHT-KNOX ART GALLERY - ART
REFERENCE LIBRARY □ Buffalo, NY

Maslyn, David C., Hd.
UNIVERSITY OF RHODE ISLAND - SPECIAL
COLLECTIONS □ Kingston, RI

Mason, Alexandra, Spec.Coll.Libn.
UNIVERSITY OF KANSAS - DEPARTMENT OF
SPECIAL COLLECTIONS □ Lawrence, KS
Mason, David B., Archv. & Lib.Prog.
BRITISH COLUMBIA - PROVINCIAL ARCHIVES
□ Victoria, BC
Mason, Dorothy, Hd.Libn.
NEW PROVIDENCE HISTORICAL SOCIETY -
LIBRARY □ New Providence, NJ
Mason, E., Acq.Libn.
LOS ANGELES TRADE-TECHNICAL COLLEGE -
LIBRARY □ Los Angeles, CA
Mason, Eleanor, Hist. of Med./Archv.
MEDICAL AND CHIRURGICAL FACULTY OF THE
STATE OF MARYLAND - LIBRARY □ Baltimore,
MD
Mason, Elizabeth B., Act.Dir.
COLUMBIA UNIVERSITY - ORAL HISTORY
COLLECTION □ New York, NY
Mason, Ellsworth, Hd.
UNIVERSITY OF COLORADO, BOULDER -
SPECIAL COLLECTIONS DEPARTMENT □
Boulder, CO
Mason, Francis S., Jr., Asst.Dir.
PIERPONT MORGAN LIBRARY □ New York, NY
Mason, Frank O., Libn.
UNIVERSITY OF SOUTHERN CALIFORNIA -
DENTISTRY LIBRARY □ Los Angeles, CA
Mason, Glenn, Musm.Dir.
LANE COUNTY MUSEUM - SPECIAL
COLLECTIONS & ARCHIVES □ Eugene, OR
Mason, Hayden, Libn.
MAIN (Chas. T.), INC. - LIBRARY □ Boston, MA
Mason, Helen B., Res. Facility Libn.
UNIVERSITY OF TENNESSEE - SPACE
INSTITUTE LIBRARY □ Tullahoma, TN
Mason, Helen F., Adult Serv.Libn.
WARREN LIBRARY ASSOCIATION - LIBRARY† □
Warren, PA
Mason, John T., Jr., Dir.
U.S. NAVAL INSTITUTE - ORAL HISTORY
OFFICE □ Annapolis, MD
Mason, Martha A., Sr.Libn.
BINGHAMTON PSYCHIATRIC CENTER -
PROFESSIONAL LIBRARY □ Binghamton, NY
Mason, Mildred, Dir.
BUREAU OF NATIONAL AFFAIRS, INC. -
LIBRARY AND INFORMATION CENTER □
Washington, DC
Mason, Pauline M., Chf., Lib.Serv.
U.S. VETERANS ADMINISTRATION (PA-
Pittsburgh) - HOSPITAL LIBRARY □ Pittsburgh,
PA
Mason, Philip P., Dir.
WAYNE STATE UNIVERSITY - ARCHIVES OF
LABOR AND URBAN AFFAIRS/UNIVERSITY
ARCHIVES □ Detroit, MI
Mason, Sally, Lib.Res.Asst.
PRC VOORHEES - LIBRARY □ McLean, VA
Mason, Sharon, Cat.Libn.
KEARNEY STATE COLLEGE - CALVIN T. RYAN
LIBRARY □ Kearney, NE
Mason, Timothy, Cat.Libn.
TEXAS COLLEGE OF OSTEOPATHIC MEDICINE -
MEDICAL LIBRARY □ Fort Worth, TX
Massa, Paul P., Pres.
CONGRESSIONAL INFORMATION SERVICE,
INC. □ Washington, DC
Massari, Loretta, Libn.
ALLIED CORPORATION - BUSINESS LIBRARY □
Morristown, NJ
Massengale, Linda, Clerical Asst.
U.S. BUREAU OF LAND MANAGEMENT - ALASKA
OUTER-CONTINENTAL SHELF OFFICE -
LIBRARY □ Anchorage, AK
Massie, Juanita J., Med.Rec.Adm./Libn.
EVANSVILLE PSYCHIATRIC CHILDREN'S
CENTER - STAFF LIBRARY □ Evansville, IN
Massie, Larry B., Asst.Dir.
WESTERN MICHIGAN UNIVERSITY - ARCHIVES
AND REGIONAL HISTORY COLLECTIONS □
Kalamazoo, MI

Massis, Bruce E., Dir.
JEWISH GUILD FOR THE BLIND - YOUNG MEN'S
PHILANTHROPIC LEAGUE - CASSETTE LIBRARY
□ New York, NY
Massman, Virgil F., Exec.Dir.
HILL (James Jerome) REFERENCE LIBRARY □ St.
Paul, MN
Massmann, Robert E., Dir.
CENTRAL CONNECTICUT STATE COLLEGE -
ELIHU BURRITT LIBRARY □ New Britain, CT
Masson, Sandra, Libn.
CNA INSURANCE - LIBRARY □ Chicago, IL
Masson, Winifred, Res.Libn.
GOODYEAR TIRE AND RUBBER COMPANY -
TECHNICAL INFORMATION CENTER □ Akron,
OH
Mast, Joanne, Asst.Libn., Tech.Serv.
AMERICAN PHILATELIC RESEARCH LIBRARY □
State College, PA
Mast, Tammy, Libn.
SPERRY CORPORATION - SPERRY NEW
HOLLAND - ENGINEERING LIBRARY □ New
Holland, PA
Mastalir, Janet, Cat., Asst.Libn.
NATIONAL COLLEGE - THOMAS JEFFERSON
LIBRARY □ Rapid City, SD
Masters, Donna L., Archv.
LOUISIANA STATE OFFICE OF THE SECRETARY
OF STATE - STATE ARCHIVES AND RECORDS
SERVICE □ Baton Rouge, LA
Masters, Fred N., Jr., Mgr.Tech.Info.Rsrcs.
DEXTER CORPORATION - C.H. DEXTER
DIVISION - TECHNICAL LIBRARY □ Windsor
Locks, CT
Masters, Linda J., Lib.Tech.Asst.
MINER INSTITUTE FOR MAN AND
ENVIRONMENT - MINER CENTER LIBRARY □
Chazy, NY
Masterson, Lynne, Cat.
NATIONAL RETIRED TEACHERS ASSN.-
AMERICAN ASSN. OF RETIRED PERSONS -
NATL. GERONTOLOGY RESOURCE CTR. □
Washington, DC
Mastrian, Louis, Lib. Consultant
SHENANGO VALLEY OSTEOPATHIC HOSPITAL -
MEDICAL LIBRARY† □ Farrell, PA
Mastropierro, Rae, Law Libn.
VOLUSIA COUNTY LAW LIBRARY □ Daytona
Beach, FL
Mastrovita, Frank, Cat.
MITRE CORPORATION - TECHNICAL REPORT
CENTER† □ Bedford, MA
Masur, Nancy, Res.Libn.
SEAGRAM (Joseph E.) & SONS, INC. -
CORPORATE LIBRARY □ New York, NY
Matcher, Rita, Dir., Lib.Serv.
SINAI HOSPITAL OF BALTIMORE, INC. -
EISENBERG MEDICAL STAFF LIBRARY □
Baltimore, MD
Matchinski, William L., Inst.Prog.Lib.Spec.
WYOMING STATE HOSPITAL - MEDICAL
LIBRARY □ Evanston, WY
Matejka, Marcella, Dept.Hd.
CLEVELAND PUBLIC LIBRARY - BUSINESS,
ECONOMICS & LABOR DEPARTMENT □
Cleveland, OH
Matera, L., Info.Spec.
STANDARD OIL COMPANY OF INDIANA -
LIBRARY/INFORMATION CENTER □ Chicago, IL
Matesic, Kathleen, Asst.Dir., Media Serv.
UNIVERSITY OF PITTSBURGH - UNIVERSITY
CENTER FOR INSTRUCTIONAL RESOURCES □
Pittsburgh, PA
Mateyak, Karen, Ser.Ed.
MODERN LANGUAGE ASSOCIATION - CENTER
FOR BIBLIOGRAPHICAL SERVICES □ New York,
NY
Math, Sandra, Libn.
ASSOCIATION OF AMERICAN PUBLISHERS -
PUBLISHING EDUCATION INFORMATION
SERVICE □ New York, NY

Matheisen, Alice, Hd. of Acq.
TRENTON STATE COLLEGE - ROSCOE L. WEST
LIBRARY □ Trenton, NJ
Mather, Bryant, Dir.
U.S. ARMY - ENGINEER WATERWAYS
EXPERIMENT STATION - CONCRETE
TECHNOLOGY INFORMATION ANALYSIS
CENTER □ Vicksburg, MS
Mather, Florence, Hd., Cat.
ERIE COMMUNITY COLLEGE NORTH - LIBRARY
RESOURCES CENTER □ Buffalo, NY
Mather, Leonard J., Kpr./Memorabilia
ARCANE ORDER - LIBRARY □ Falls Church, VA
Mather, Virginia A., Libn.
U.S. AIR FORCE BASE - FAIRCHILD BASE
LIBRARY □ Fairchild AFB, WA
Matheson, Joyce, Dir., Lib.Serv.
HAVERFORD STATE HOSPITAL - MEDICAL
LIBRARY □ Upper Darby, PA
Matheson, Kirk, Hd.
UTAH STATE LIBRARY - FILM PROGRAM □ Salt
Lake City, UT
Matheson, William, Chf.
LIBRARY OF CONGRESS - RARE BOOK &
SPECIAL COLLECTIONS DIVISION □
Washington, DC
Mathews, James, Hd., Acq.
UNIVERSITY OF WISCONSIN, WHITEWATER -
LIBRARY & LEARNING RESOURCES □
Whitewater, WI
Mathews, Janet, Libn.
ALBANY BUSINESS COLLEGE - LIBRARY □
Albany, NY
Mathews, Karen, Sys.Anl.
UNIVERSITY OF CALIFORNIA - LOS ALAMOS
NATIONAL LABORATORY - LIBRARY □ Los
Alamos, NM
Mathews, Lorrayne, Libn.
WAUKESHA FREEMAN - NEWSPAPER LIBRARY
□ Waukesha, WI
Mathews, Marilyn, Libn.
ST. MARY'S HOSPITAL - MEDICAL LIBRARY □
Kitchener, ON
Mathews, Robert C., Act.Libn.
U.S. AIR FORCE BASE - KIRTLAND BASE
LIBRARY □ Kirtland AFB, NM
Mathewson, Donald R., Tourism Coord.
DELAWARE STATE TRAVEL SERVICE - LIBRARY
□ Dover, DE
Mathias, Barbara, Libn.
ONTARIO - MINISTRY OF LABOUR - ONTARIO
LABOUR RELATIONS BOARD - LIBRARY □
Toronto, ON
Mathies, Dr. Lorraine, Hd.
UNIVERSITY OF CALIFORNIA, LOS ANGELES -
EDUCATION & PSYCHOLOGY LIBRARY □ Los
Angeles, CA
Mathieu, Marie, Documentaliste
UNIVERSITE DE MONTREAL - ECOLE DE
TRADUCTION - CENTRE DE DOCUMENTATION
TERMINOLOGIQUE BILINGUE □ Montreal, PQ
Mathieu, Pierre, Dir.
SOLEIL LIMITEE - CENTRE DE
DOCUMENTATION □ Quebec, PQ
Mathieu, Richard, Chf.Libn.
QUEBEC PROVINCE - MINISTERE DU LOISIR,
DE LA CHASSE ET DE LA PECHE -
BIBLIOTHEQUE DE LA FAUNE □ Montreal, PQ
Mathis, Meyer, Dir., Off.Gen.Adm.
AMERICAN RED CROSS - NATIONAL
HEADQUARTERS LIBRARY □ Washington, DC
Mathis, Wes, Lib.Dir.
NATIONAL LIBRARY OF SPORTS □ San Jose, CA
Mathison, Ruby, Asst.Libn.
INTERNORTH - LIBRARY □ Omaha, NE
Mathys, Nel, Chf., Tech.Lib.
U.S. AIR FORCE - ROME AIR DEVELOPMENT
CENTER - TECHNICAL LIBRARY □ Griffiss AFB,
NY
Matiisen, Tina, Hd.Info.Serv.
CANADA - DEFENCE RESEARCH
ESTABLISHMENT OTTAWA - LIBRARY □
Ottawa, ON

Matkovic, Patricia, State Doc.Libn.
INDIANA STATE LIBRARY - INDIANA DIVISION □ Indianapolis, IN

Matlack, Robert, Libn.
CARNEGIE LIBRARY OF PITTSBURGH - SCIENCE AND TECHNOLOGY DEPARTMENT □ Pittsburgh, PA

Matous, Naomi L., Libn.
RESEARCH SERVICES CORPORATION - INSTITUTE FOR MICROCRYSTAL POLYMER RESEARCH - LIBRARY □ Fort Worth, TX

Matsinger, Jane, Index Ed.
MODERN LANGUAGE ASSOCIATION - CENTER FOR BIBLIOGRAPHICAL SERVICES □ New York, NY

Matson, JoAnne, Sec.
RANGE MENTAL HEALTH CENTER - LIBRARY □ Virginia, MN

Matson, Kathleen, Libn.
LOS ANGELES PSYCHOANALYTIC SOCIETY AND INSTITUTE - SIMMEL-FENICHEL LIBRARY □ Los Angeles, CA

Matson, Madeline, Coord., Pubn.
MISSOURI STATE LIBRARY □ Jefferson City, MO

Matson, Sheldon, Libn.
PATERSON NEWS - LIBRARY/NEWSPAPER MORGUE □ Paterson, NJ

Matsuda, Pegi, Film Libn.
GENERAL TELEPHONE OF CALIFORNIA - FILM LIBRARY □ Santa Monica, CA

Matsuda, Shizue, Libn.
INDIANA UNIVERSITY - EAST ASIAN COLLECTION □ Bloomington, IN

Matsumiya, Don, Hd., Ref.Serv.
HUGHES AIRCRAFT COMPANY - GROUND SYSTEMS GROUP - TECHNICAL LIBRARY □ Fullerton, CA

Matsumiya, Hisao, Pubn. Clearance
HUGHES AIRCRAFT COMPANY - INFORMATION RESOURCES SECTION □ Culver City, CA

Matsumoto, Hisao, Hd., Japanese Sect.
LIBRARY OF CONGRESS - ASIAN DIVISION □ Washington, DC

Matsuoka, Mary O., Libn.
HAWAIIAN SUGAR PLANTERS' ASSOCIATION EXPERIMENT STATION - LIBRARY □ Aiea, HI

Matsushige, Hatsue, Section Hd.
HAWAII STATE LIBRARY - HAWAII AND PACIFIC SECTION I □ Honolulu, HI

Matsuura, Les, Educ.Coord.
UNIVERSITY OF HAWAII - WAIKIKI AQUARIUM - LIBRARY □ Honolulu, HI

Matt, Salinda M., Libn.
LANCASTER COUNTY HISTORICAL SOCIETY - LIBRARY □ Lancaster, PA

Matta, Paula, Libn.
PRINCETON LIBRARY IN NEW YORK □ New York, NY

Mattei, Janet A., Dir.
AMERICAN ASSOCIATION OF VARIABLE STAR OBSERVERS - MC ATEER LIBRARY □ Cambridge, MA

Mattern, Joanne A., Supv.
DELAWARE STATE ARCHIVES □ Dover, DE

Matthes, Dolly, Rec.Coord.
DAIRYLAND POWER COOPERATIVE - LIBRARY □ La Crosse, WI

Matthew, Jeannette, Archv.
INDIANA UNIVERSITY/PURDUE UNIVERSITY AT INDIANAPOLIS - UNIVERSITY LIBRARY □ Indianapolis, IN

Matthewman, Anne, Libn.
ESSEX LAW ASSOCIATION - LIBRARY □ Windsor, ON

Matthews, Ann M., Historic Site Adm.
WATKINS WOOLEN MILL STATE HISTORIC SITE - RESEARCH LIBRARY □ Lawson, MO

Matthews, Catherine J., Libn.
UNIVERSITY OF TORONTO - CENTRE OF CRIMINOLOGY - LIBRARY □ Toronto, ON

Matthews, Donald N., Libn.
LUTHERAN THEOLOGICAL SEMINARY - A.R. WENTZ LIBRARY □ Gettysburg, PA

Matthews, Dorrie, Libn.
WRIGHT INSTITUTE - GRADUATE DIVISION LIBRARY □ Berkeley, CA

Matthews, Eileen M., Libn.
LEHN & FINK PRODUCTS GROUP - LIBRARY† □ Montvale, NJ

Matthews, Dr. Elizabeth W., Cat.Libn.
SOUTHERN ILLINOIS UNIVERSITY, CARBONDALE - SCHOOL OF LAW LIBRARY □ Carbondale, IL

Matthews, Janice Drumm, Law Lib.Ck.
NEW YORK STATE SUPREME COURT - 4TH JUDICIAL DISTRICT - LAW LIBRARY □ Oswego, NY

Matthews, Jaxon K., Libn.
CONTROL DATA CORPORATION - LIBRARY □ Sunnyvale, CA

Matthews, Jessie, Night Ref.Libn.
RUTGERS UNIVERSITY, THE STATE UNIVERSITY OF NEW JERSEY - SCHOOL OF LAW LIBRARY† □ Camden, NJ

Matthews, Leah, Supv./Libn.
SOUTHWESTERN BELL TELEPHONE COMPANY - BUSINESS INFORMATION RESOURCE SERVICE □ St. Louis, MO

Matthews, Linda Fink, Adm.Dir.
AFRICAN BIBLIOGRAPHIC CENTER - STAFF RESOURCE LIBRARY □ Washington, DC

Matthews, Linda M., Ref.Archv./Asst.Hd.
EMORY UNIVERSITY - SPECIAL COLLECTIONS DEPARTMENT □ Atlanta, GA

Matthews, Paula, Hd., Biblog. Search
TEACHERS COLLEGE - LIBRARY □ New York, NY

Matthews, Mrs. Raymond, Libn.
FIRST BAPTIST CHURCH - E.F. WALKER MEMORIAL LIBRARY □ Luling, TX

Matthews, Richard P., Spec.Coll.Libn.
TRENTON STATE COLLEGE - ROSCOE L. WEST LIBRARY □ Trenton, NJ

Matthews, Sandra S., Ref.
U.S. ARMED FORCES RADIOBIOLOGY RESEARCH INSTITUTE (AFRRI) - LIBRARY SERVICES □ Bethesda, MD

Matthews, Shelley B., Exec.Sec.
PLANNED PARENTHOOD OF CLEVELAND, INC. - LIBRARY □ Cleveland, OH

Mattice, Virginia S., Asst.Libn.
RCA CORPORATION - GSD - GOVERNMENT COMMUNICATIONS SYSTEMS - LIBRARY □ Camden, NJ

Mattick, Paul, Jr., Libn.
HARVARD UNIVERSITY - CENTER FOR EUROPEAN STUDIES - LIBRARY □ Cambridge, MA

Mattimore, Maryanne, Med.Libn.
BINGHAMTON GENERAL HOSPITAL - STUART B. BLAKELY MEMORIAL LIBRARY □ Binghamton, NY

Mattingly, John F., Dir.
ST. PATRICK'S SEMINARY - MC KEON MEMORIAL LIBRARY □ Menlo Park, CA

Mattison, Helen S., Educ.Spec., Media
BROWARD COUNTY PUBLIC SCHOOLS - LEARNING RESOURCES - PROFESSIONAL LIBRARY □ Davie, FL

Mattivi, Rebecca, Libn.
AIRCO CARBON - RESEARCH AND DEVELOPMENT LIBRARY □ St. Marys, PA

Mattocks, Geoffrey L., Dir.
FARMINGDALE PUBLIC SCHOOLS - PROFESSIONAL LIBRARY □ Farmingdale, NY

Mattoon, Bruce P., V.P.
FACTORY MUTUAL SYSTEM - FACTORY MUTUAL RESEARCH CORPORATION - LIBRARY □ Norwood, MA

Mattson, Margaret J., Libn.
U.S. BUREAU OF MINES - ALASKA FIELD OPERATIONS CENTER LIBRARY □ Juneau, AK

Mattson, Ruth, Ref.Libn.
EASTERN VIRGINIA MEDICAL SCHOOL - MOORMAN MEMORIAL LIBRARY □ Norfolk, VA

Mattson, Virginia, Circuit Libn.
CLEVELAND HEALTH SCIENCES LIBRARY - ALLEN MEMORIAL LIBRARY □ Cleveland, OH

Matty, Paul, Libn.
PIMA COUNTY PLANNING DEPARTMENT - LIBRARY □ Tucson, AZ

Matulka, Carol, Med.Libn.
ST. JOSEPH MEDICAL CENTER - MEDICAL LIBRARY □ Wichita, KS

Matusak, Susan, Hd.Libn.
INSTITUTE FOR SEX RESEARCH, INC. - LIBRARY AND INFORMATION SERVICE □ Bloomington, IN

Matz, Ruth G., Chf.Libn.
MASSACHUSETTS STATE DEPARTMENT OF THE ATTORNEY GENERAL - LIBRARY □ Boston, MA

Matz, Sandra, Asst.Dir.
SINAI HOSPITAL OF DETROIT - SAMUEL FRANK MEDICAL LIBRARY □ Detroit, MI

Matzka, Liselotte, Hd., Sci.Lib.
ADELPHI UNIVERSITY - SCIENCE LIBRARY □ Garden City, NY

Mauck, Virginia, Asst.Cur. of Mss.
INDIANA UNIVERSITY - LILLY LIBRARY □ Bloomington, IN

Mauerhoff, Joy, Hd., Coll.Dev.
ONTARIO - LEGISLATIVE ASSEMBLY - LEGISLATIVE LIBRARY RESEARCH AND INFORMATION SERVICES □ Toronto, ON

Maughan, Patricia Davitt, Engr.Libn.
COLUMBIA UNIVERSITY - AMBROSE MONELL ENGINEERING LIBRARY □ New York, NY

Maura, Mariano, Libn.
UNIVERSITY OF PUERTO RICO - NATURAL SCIENCE LIBRARY □ Rio Piedras, PR

Maurer, Esther J., Hd.
FREE LIBRARY OF PHILADELPHIA - EDUCATION, PHILOSOPHY, RELIGION DEPARTMENT □ Philadelphia, PA

Maurer, Louise, Sci.Libn.
MIAMI-DADE PUBLIC LIBRARY - BUSINESS, SCIENCE AND TECHNOLOGY DEPARTMENT □ Miami, FL

Maurice, Leatrice, Libn.
VILLE MARIE SOCIAL SERVICE CENTRE - LIBRARY □ Montreal, PQ

Maurin, Raissa, Chf.Libn.
U.S. VETERANS ADMINISTRATION (FL-Miami) - HOSPITAL MEDICAL LIBRARY □ Miami, FL

Mauter, George A., Supv.
FAIRCHILD INDUSTRIES - FAIRCHILD REPUBLIC COMPANY - ENGINEERING LIBRARY □ Farmingdale, NY

Mautner, Robert W., Sci.Eng.Ref.Libn.
UNIVERSITY OF ARIZONA - SCIENCE-ENGINEERING LIBRARY □ Tucson, AZ

Mautner, Susan L., Libn.
TEMPLE DE HIRSCH SINAI - LIBRARY □ Seattle, WA

Mavroleon, Mace G., Exec.Dir.
AMERICAN MERCHANT MARINE LIBRARY ASSOCIATION - PUBLIC LIBRARY OF THE HIGH SEAS □ New York, NY

Mawdsley, Katherine F., Hd., Govt.Doc.Dept.
UNIVERSITY OF CALIFORNIA, DAVIS - GENERAL LIBRARY □ Davis, CA

Mawn, Dr. Geoffrey P., Hist./Archv.
ARIZONA HISTORICAL FOUNDATION - HAYDEN LIBRARY □ Tempe, AZ

Mawn, Dr. Geoffrey P., Cur.
ARIZONA STATE UNIVERSITY - ARIZONA COLLECTIONS □ Tempe, AZ

Maxey, Barbara J., Sr.Libn.
RADIAN CORPORATION - LIBRARY □ Austin, TX

Maxham, Mrs. Donald G., Libn.
BRAINTREE HISTORICAL SOCIETY, INC. - LIBRARY □ Braintree, MA

Maximena, Delores E., Trans.Libn.
GENERAL MOTORS CORPORATION - RESEARCH LABORATORIES LIBRARY □ Warren, MI

Maxin, Jacqueline A., Supv.Info.Serv.
PPG INDUSTRIES, INC. - FIBER GLASS RESEARCH CENTER - LIBRAR Y □ Pittsburgh, PA

Maxon, Bill, Ref.Libn.
GEORGETOWN UNIVERSITY - LAW CENTER
LIBRARY □ Washington, DC

Maxwell, A., Project Dir.
HARVARD UNIVERSITY - RADIO ASTRONOMY
STATION - LIBRARY □ Fort Davis, TX

Maxwell, Miss B., Asst.Libn.
FALCONBRIDGE NICKEL MINES, LTD. -
METALLURGICAL LABORATORIES
INFORMATION SERVICES □ Thornhill, ON

Maxwell, Claude S., Supv., Photo Serv.
OKLAHOMA STATE UNIVERSITY - AUDIO
VISUAL CENTER □ Stillwater, OK

Maxwell, Daisy D., Libn.
FAYETTEVILLE PUBLISHING COMPANY -
NEWSPAPER LIBRARY □ Fayetteville, NC

Maxwell, Dolores M., Biblog.
TEXAS TECH UNIVERSITY - LIBRARY □
Lubbock, TX

Maxwell, Grover, Dir.
UNIVERSITY OF MINNESOTA - MINNESOTA
CENTER FOR PHILOSOPHY OF SCIENCE -
DEPARTMENTAL LIBRARY □ Minneapolis, MN

May, Arlee, Dir./NERMLS
HARVARD UNIVERSITY - SCHOOLS OF
MEDICINE, DENTAL MEDICINE AND PUBLIC
HEALTH - FRANCIS A. COUNTWAY LIBRARY □
Boston, MA

May, Barbara C., Ref.Ed.
DALLAS MORNING NEWS - REFERENCE
DEPARTMENT □ Dallas, TX

May, Bryan, Hd., Doc.Serv.Ctr.
COLUMBIA UNIVERSITY - HERBERT LEHMAN
LIBRARY □ New York, NY

May, Charles, Assoc. Professor
NASHVILLE STATE TECHNICAL INSTITUTE -
EDUCATIONAL RESOURCE CENTER □ Nashville,
TN

May, Cindy, Cat.Libn.
UNIVERSITY OF WISCONSIN, MADISON - LAW
LIBRARY □ Madison, WI

May, Dr. Curtis, Dir., Lib.Serv.
SAN MATEO COUNTY EDUCATIONAL
RESOURCES CENTER □ Redwood City, CA

May, Dolores A., Ref.Libn.
EBASCO SERVICES, INC. - CORPORATE
ADMINISTRATION LIBRARY □ New York, NY

May, J.A.
DOW CHEMICAL COMPANY - TECHNICAL
INFORMATION SERVICES - CHEMICAL
LIBRARY □ Midland, MI

May, Joanne M., Libn.
U.S. NAVY - NAVAL ENVIRONMENTAL
PREDICTION RESEARCH FACILITY -
TECHNICAL LIBRARY □ Monterey, CA

May, Lynn E., Joint Lib.Dir.
DARGAN-CARVER LIBRARY □ Nashville, TN

May, Patricia T., Asst.Libn.
ST. JOSEPH'S HOSPITAL AND MEDICAL
CENTER - HEALTH SCIENCES LIBRARY □
Paterson, NJ

May, Ruby S., Assoc.Dir.
UNIVERSITY OF ILLINOIS MEDICAL CENTER -
LIBRARY OF THE HEALTH SCIENCES □ Chicago,
IL

May, Sallie, Cat.Supv.
OUR LADY OF LIGHT LIBRARY □ Santa Barbara,
CA

Maybin, Arthur
SOUTH CAROLINA STATE GEOLOGICAL SURVEY
- LIBRARY □ Columbia, SC

Maycock, Susan E., Survey Dir.
CAMBRIDGE HISTORICAL COMMISSION -
LIBRARY □ Cambridge, MA

Mayden, Priscilla M., Dir.
UNIVERSITY OF UTAH - SPENCER S. ECCLES
HEALTH SCIENCES LIBRARY □ Salt Lake City,
UT

Mayer, Charles A., Lib.Cons.
ASPHALT INSTITUTE - RESEARCH LIBRARY □
College Park, MD

Mayer, Elizabeth Cohen, Libn.
WENDER, MURASE & WHITE - LIBRARY □ New
York, NY

Mayer, Eric, Law Libn.
HUDSON COUNTY LAW LIBRARY† □ Jersey City,
NJ

Mayer, George L., Coord.
NEW YORK PUBLIC LIBRARY - GENERAL
LIBRARY OF THE PERFORMING ARTS □ New
York, NY

Mayer, Harriet, Libn.
PUBLIC SERVICE ELECTRIC AND GAS
COMPANY - LIBRARY □ Newark, NJ

Mayer, Miga, Desk Res.
FOOTE CONE & BELDING - INFORMATION
CENTER □ Chicago, IL

Mayer, Robert, Hd.Cat.Libn.
STANFORD UNIVERSITY - J. HUGH JACKSON
LIBRARY □ Stanford, CA

Mayer, Vera, V.P., Info. & Archv.
NATIONAL BROADCASTING COMPANY, INC. -
REFERENCE LIBRARY □ New York, NY

Mayer, Dr. William J., Mgr.Tech.Info.Serv.
GENERAL MILLS, INC. - JAMES FORD BELL
TECHNICAL CENTER - TECHNICAL
INFORMATION SERVICES □ Minneapolis, MN

Mayers, Bernard J., Supv.
INTERNATIONAL FLAVORS AND FRAGRANCES,
INC. - TECHNICAL INFORMATION CENTER □
Union Beach, NJ

Mayers, Claire, Ref.Libn.
COLUMBIA UNIVERSITY - CENTER FOR
POPULATION & FAMILY HEALTH - LIBRARY/
INFORMATION PROGRAM □ New York, NY

Mayers, Karen A., Libn.
MORRISON & FOERSTER - LIBRARY □ Los
Angeles, CA

Mayeski, John, Dir. of Lib.
KEARNEY STATE COLLEGE - CALVIN T. RYAN
LIBRARY □ Kearney, NE

Mayfield, David M., Dir.
CHURCH OF JESUS CHRIST OF LATTER-DAY
SAINTS - GENEALOGICAL LIBRARY □ Salt Lake
City, UT

Mayfield, John S., Libn.
ARMY AND NAVY CLUB - LIBRARY □
Washington, DC

Mayfield, Mike, Chf., Musm.
WYOMING STATE ARCHIVES, MUSEUMS AND
HISTORICAL DEPARTMENT □ Cheyenne, WY

Mayfield, Vada, AV Libn.
MADISON PUBLIC LIBRARY - ART AND MUSIC
DIVISION □ Madison, WI

Mayhall, Pauline, Med.Libn.
U.S. ARMY HOSPITALS - NOBLE ARMY
HOSPITAL - MEDICAL LIBRARY □ Ft. McClellan,
AL

Maykuth, Daniel J., Mgr.
TIN RESEARCH INSTITUTE, INC. - LIBRARY &
INFORMATION CENTER □ Columbus, OH

Mayles, William F., Sci./Tech.Libn.
INDIANA UNIVERSITY/PURDUE UNIVERSITY
AT INDIANAPOLIS - 38TH STREET CAMPUS
LIBRARY □ Indianapolis, IN

Maynard, Elizabeth, Libn.
FEDERAL RESERVE BANK OF CLEVELAND -
RESEARCH LIBRARY □ Cleveland, OH

Maynerd, J. Edmund, Circ.Libn.
CITADEL - THE MILITARY COLLEGE OF SOUTH
CAROLINA - DANIEL LIBRARY □ Charleston, SC

Mayo, Harriett E., Asst.Libn.
ABRAHAM BALDWIN AGRICULTURAL COLLEGE
- LIBRARY □ Tifton, GA

Mayo, Dr. Hope, Mss.Cat.
ST. JOHN'S ABBEY AND UNIVERSITY - HILL
MONASTIC MANUSCRIPT LIBRARY - BUSH
CENTER □ Collegeville, MN

Mayo, Julia C., Ref.Libn.
U.S. NATL. DEFENSE UNIVERSITY - LIBRARY □
Washington, DC

Mayo, Kathleen, Inst.Cons.
STATE LIBRARY OF FLORIDA □ Tallahassee, FL

Mayo, Martha, Spec.Coll.Libn.
UNIVERSITY OF LOWELL, NORTH CAMPUS -
ALUMNI/LYDON LIBRARY □ Lowell, MA

Mayo, Martha, Hd., Spec.Coll.
UNIVERSITY OF LOWELL, NORTH CAMPUS -
UNIVERSITY LIBRARIES - SPECIAL
COLLECTIONS □ Lowell, MA

Mayor, Carol, Libn.
ST. FRANCIS-ST. GEORGE HOSPITAL - HEALTH
SCIENCES LIBRARY □ Cincinnati, OH

Mayover, Steven J., Lib. Film Oper.Supv.
FREE LIBRARY OF PHILADELPHIA - FILMS
DEPARTMENT □ Philadelphia, PA

Mayr, Ingrid C.D., Libn.
DITTBERNER ASSOCIATES, INC. - LIBRARY □
Bethesda, MD

Mayrand, F., Asst.Hd., Tech.Serv.
CANADA - ENERGY, MINES & RESOURCES
CANADA - RESOURCE ECONOMICS LIBRARY □
Ottawa, ON

Mayrand, Lise, Libn.
UNIVERSITE DE MONTREAL - EDUCATION
PHYSIQUE-BIBLIOTHEQUE □ Montreal, PQ

Mayti, Peggy, Hd. of Info. Bureau
MARYKNOLL SEMINARY - LIBRARY □ Maryknoll,
NY

Mayton, Regina A., Chf., Sys.Div.
U.S. AIR FORCE - AIR UNIVERSITY - LIBRARY □
Maxwell AFB, AL

Mazareas, Helen, Libn.
NEW ENGLAND MERCHANTS NATIONAL BANK -
LIBRARY □ Boston, MA

Mazeral, Ms. A., Lib.Info.Off.
BEDFORD INSTITUTE OF OCEANOGRAPHY -
LIBRARY □ Dartmouth, NS

Mazorol, Louise N., Chf.Libn.
CHARLESTON EVENING POST/NEWS AND
COURIER - LIBRARY □ Charleston, SC

Mazsick, Frank J., Lib.Dir.
SEMINARY OF ST. PIUS X - LIBRARY □ Erlanger,
KY

Mazur, Cole, Info.Tech.
UNIVERSITY OF PITTSBURGH - CENTER FOR
INTERNATIONAL STUDIES □ Pittsburgh, PA

Mazur, Diane, Cat.
BAYSTATE MEDICAL CENTER - LIBRARY □
Springfield, MA

Mazur, Marjorie, Dir. of Tech.Serv.
SOUTH CAROLINA STATE LIBRARY □ Columbia,
SC

Mazzini, Elsie, Dir.
MARIN COUNTY HISTORICAL SOCIETY -
LIBRARY □ San Rafael, CA

Mead, Catherine, Asst. State Libn.
STATE LIBRARY OF OHIO □ Columbus, OH

Mead, Clifford S., Libn.
KEENE STATE COLLEGE - WALLACE E. MASON
LIBRARY □ Keene, NH

Mead, John H., Musm.Supv.
BEAR MOUNTAIN TRAILSIDE MUSEUMS -
LIBRARY □ Bear Mountain, NY

Mead, Ken, Dir.Med.Lib.
HALIFAX HOSPITAL MEDICAL CENTER -
MEDICAL LIBRARY □ Daytona Beach, FL

Mead, Patricia, Asst.Med.Libn.
GORGAS ARMY HOSPITAL - SAMUEL TAYLOR
DARLING MEMORIAL LIBRARY □ APO Miami, FL

Mead, Thomas, Asst.Libn.
ROCHESTER GENERAL HOSPITAL - LILLIE B.
WERNER HEALTH SCIENCES LIBRARY □
Rochester, NY

Meade, B.R., Supv.
SINGER COMPANY - KEARFOTT DIVISION -
TECHNICAL INFORMATION CENTER† □ Wayne,
NJ

Meade, Robert, Bus.Libn.
MILES LABORATORIES, INC. - LIBRARY
RESOURCES AND SERVICES □ Elkhart, IN

Meader, Robert F.W., Libn.
SHAKER COMMUNITY, INC. - LIBRARY □
Pittsfield, MA

PERSONNEL

Meadow, C.Z., Dir.
CENTER FOR MODERN PSYCHOANALYTIC
STUDIES - LIBRARY □ New York, NY
Meadows, Barbara A., Chf.Libn.
U.S. VETERANS ADMINISTRATION (TN-
Nashville) - MEDICAL CENTER LIBRARY
SERVICE □ Nashville, TN
Meadows, Dorothy, ILL
EAST TEXAS BAPTIST COLLEGE - MAMYE
JARRETT LEARNING CENTER □ Marshall, TX
Meadows, Janice, Cat./ILL
VIRGINIA INSTITUTE OF MARINE SCIENCE
LIBRARY □ Gloucester Point, VA
Meadows, Judy, Info.Mgr.
ASPEN SYSTEMS CORPORATION - LAW
LIBRARY & INFORMATION CENTER □ Rockville,
MD
Meadows, Mark D., Hd., Cat.
ARKANSAS STATE UNIVERSITY - DEAN B.
ELLIS LIBRARY □ State University, AR
Meadows, Maryan, Hd.Libn.
PETRO-CANADA - LIBRARY SERVICES □
Calgary, AB
Meagher, Marian, Supv.Circ.
QUEEN'S UNIVERSITY AT KINGSTON -
EDUCATION LIBRARY □ Kingston, ON
Meahl, Darren, Libn.
MICHIGAN STATE UNIVERSITY - G. ROBERT
VINCENT VOICE LIBRARY □ East Lansing, MI
Meakin, Faith, Hd., Pub.Serv.
UNIVERSITY OF CALIFORNIA, SAN DIEGO -
BIOMEDICAL LIBRARY □ La Jolla, CA
Mealey, Catherine, Law Libn./Prof.
UNIVERSITY OF WYOMING - LAW LIBRARY □
Laramie, WY
Means, Ray B., Dir.
CREIGHTON UNIVERSITY - ALUMNI MEMORIAL
LIBRARY □ Omaha, NE
Meares, Carol Ann, Prog.Mgr.
U.S. DEPT. OF COMMERCE - NATL. TECHNICAL
INFORMATION SERVICE - PRODUCTIVITY
INFORMATION CENTER □ Washington, DC
Mears, William F., Assoc.Dir.
SOUTHWEST TEXAS STATE UNIVERSITY -
LEARNING RESOURCES CENTER □ San Marcos,
TX
Mechanic, Sylvia, Bus.Libn.
BROOKLYN PUBLIC LIBRARY - BUSINESS
LIBRARY □ Brooklyn, NY
Mecke, William M., Asst.Dir.
FOUNDATION FOR THE STUDY OF
PRESIDENTIAL AND CONGRESSIONAL TERMS -
LIBRARY □ Washington, DC
Mecklenburg, Ruth, Tech.Lib.Spec.
U.S. DEPT. OF TRANSPORTATION -
TRANSPORTATION TEST CENTER - TECHNICAL
LIBRARY □ Pueblo, CO
Meckly, Eugene P., Libn.
KOPPERS COMPANY, INC. - TECHNICAL
INFORMATION GROUP □ Monroeville, PA
Meconitas, Beth, Asst.Libn.
U.S. AIR FORCE BASE - KEESLER BASE -
MC BRIDE LIBRARY □ Keesler AFB, MS
Mecray, Frieda S., Info.Spec.
PHILADELPHIA QUARTZ COMPANY -
BUSINESS/ENGINEERING INFORMATION
CENTER □ Valley Forge, PA
Medaris, Linda, Ref.Libn.
CENTRAL MISSOURI STATE UNIVERSITY -
WARD EDWARDS LIBRARY □ Warrensburg, MO
Medearis, Mary, Dir.
SOUTHWEST ARKANSAS REGIONAL ARCHIVES
(SARA) □ Washington, AR
Medeiros, Marie A., Libn.
ICI AMERICAS INC. - WORKS EXPERIMENTAL
DEPARTMENT LIBRARY □ Dighton, MA
Meder, Rev. Stephen A., S.J., Libn.
COLOMBIERE COLLEGE - LIBRARY □ Clarkston,
MI
Medford, Roberta, State Docs.Libn.
UNIVERSITY OF CALIFORNIA, LOS ANGELES -
PUBLIC AFFAIRS SERVICE □ Los Angeles, CA

Medici, Marie C., Libn.
ST. VINCENT'S HOSPITAL - SCHOOL OF
NURSING LIBRARY □ New York, NY
Medigovich, Stella A., Libn.
MC DONNELL DOUGLAS CORPORATION -
ACTRON TECHNICAL LIBRARY† □ Monrovia, CA
Medina, Rubens, Chf.
LIBRARY OF CONGRESS - LAW LIBRARY -
HISPANIC LAW DIVISION □ Washington, DC
Medley, Larry, Libn.
SMITH (A.O.) CORPORATION - TECHNICAL
LIBRARY □ Milwaukee, WI
Medley, Nora, Asst.Libn.
MIAMI HERALD - LIBRARY □ Miami, FL
Medlicott, Mary Alice, Cur.
FRANKLIN COLLEGE - SPECIAL COLLECTIONS □
Franklin, IN
Medvedow, Jill, Archv.
FRANKLIN FURNACE ARCHIVE, INC. - LIBRARY
□ New York, NY
Medzie, Deena, Acq.Libn.
WIDENER UNIVERSITY - WOLFGRAM
MEMORIAL LIBRARY □ Chester, PA
Meece, Patricia, Res.Info.Spec.
UNIVERSITY OF ILLINOIS - SURVEY RESEARCH
LABORATORY - SRL DATA ARCHIVE □ Urbana,
IL
Meehan, Charles R., Dir.
UNIVERSITY OF LOWELL, SOUTH CAMPUS -
DANIEL H. O'LEARY LIBRARY □ Lowell, MA
Meehan, Margaret, Info.Spec.
DIGITAL EQUIPMENT CORPORATION -
CORPORATE LIBRARY □ Maynard, MA
Meehan, Thomas J., Libn.
HOME MISSIONERS OF AMERICA - GLENMARY
NOVITIATE LIBRARY □ Cincinnati, OH
Meek, LeRoy, Sr., Lit.Sci.
REYNOLDS (R.J.) TOBACCO COMPANY - R&D
INFORMATION SYSTEMS LIBRARY □ Winston-
Salem, NC
Meeks, Marilyn A., Libn.
MEMPHIS-SHELBY COUNTY OFFICE OF
PLANNING AND DEVELOPMENT - LIBRARY □
Memphis, TN
Meerdink, Richard E., District Libn.
MILWAUKEE AREA TECHNICAL COLLEGE -
RASCHE MEMORIAL LIBRARY □ Milwaukee, WI
Meernik, Mary, Libn.
ANN ARBOR NEWS - LIBRARY □ Ann Arbor, MI
Meese, Frances, Libn.
MEMORIAL HOSPITAL AND BETH-EL SCHOOL
OF NURSING - MEDICAL-NURSING LIBRARY □
Colorado Springs, CO
Meglis, Anne L., Libn.
DISTRICT OF COLUMBIA DEPARTMENT OF
HOUSING AND COMMUNITY DEVELOPMENT
LIBRARY □ Washington, DC
Mehalick, Joann, Supv. Of Lib.Serv.
EAST ORANGE GENERAL HOSPITAL - MEDICAL
LIBRARY □ East Orange, NJ
Mehegan, Doris, Hd.
TORONTO PUBLIC LIBRARY - SPACED-OUT
LIBRARY □ Toronto, ON
Mehl, Judy, Libn.
OHIO COLLEGE OF PODIATRIC MEDICINE -
LIBRARY □ Cleveland, OH
Mehl, Rev. Warren R., Libn.
EDEN THEOLOGICAL SEMINARY - LIBRARY □
Webster Groves, MO
Mehr, Joseph O., Libn.
PROVIDENCE JOURNAL COMPANY - NEWS
LIBRARY □ Providence, RI
Mehrabian, Dr. R.M., Dir.
U.S. NATL. BUREAU OF STANDARDS - ALLOY
DATA CENTER □ Washington, DC
Mehta, D., V.P.
MEDICAL RESEARCH LABORATORIES -
LIBRARY □ Niles, IL
Mei, Chiang C., Prof.Civ.Engr.
MASSACHUSETTS INSTITUTE OF TECHNOLOGY
- CIVIL ENGINEERING DEPT. - RALPH M.
PARSONS LABORATORY - REF. RM. □
Cambridge, MA

Meiboom, Esther, Clinical Libn.
COLLEGE OF MEDICINE AND DENTISTRY OF
NEW JERSEY AT NEWARK - GEORGE F. SMITH
LIBRARY □ Newark, NJ
Meier, Kathleen, Libn.
BAPTIST MEMORIAL HOSPITAL - SCHOOL OF
NURSING - LIBRARY □ Memphis, TN
Meikle, Alison, Libn.
KEMPTVILLE COLLEGE OF AGRICULTURAL
TECHNOLOGY - LIBRARY □ Kemptville, ON
Meinhardt, Cynthia, Libn.
OUTBOARD MARINE CORPORATION -
RESEARCH CENTER LIBRARY □ Milwaukee, WI
Meischeid, Richard C., Dir.
KOLLSMAN INSTRUMENT COMPANY -
TECHNICAL ENGINEERING LIBRARY □
Merrimack, NH
Meiss, Harriet, Res.Libn.
MOUNT SINAI SCHOOL OF MEDICINE OF THE
CITY UNIVERSITY OF NEW YORK - GUSTAVE L.
& JANET W. LEVY LIBRARY □ New York, NY
Meister, Anabel
CUNY - CITY COLLEGE LIBRARY - SCIENCE/
ENGINEERING DIVISION □ New York, NY
Meizner, Karen, Cat./Ref.Libn.
ART INSTITUTE OF CHICAGO - RYERSON AND
BURNHAM LIBRARIES □ Chicago, IL
Mejill, Gregorio, Cat.Dept.Dir.
CATHOLIC UNIVERSITY OF PUERTO RICO -
MONSIGNOR JUAN FREMIOT TORRES OLIVER
LAW LIBRARY □ Ponce, PR
Mekkawi, Mod, Libn.
HOWARD UNIVERSITY - ARCHITECTURE &
PLANNING LIBRARY □ Washington, DC
Mekos, Katherine F., Libn.
ARNOT-OGDEN MEMORIAL HOSPITAL - WEY
MEMORIAL LIBRARY □ Elmira, NY
Mela, Doris K., Libn.
NATIONAL BIOMEDICAL RESEARCH
FOUNDATION - LIBRARY □ Washington, DC
Melamed, Dorothy, Libn.
CARNEGIE LIBRARY OF PITTSBURGH -
SCIENCE AND TECHNOLOGY DEPARTMENT □
Pittsburgh, PA
Melamed, Dorothy B., Libn.
HEALTH EDUCATION CENTER LIBRARY □
Pittsburgh, PA
Melanson, Lloyd J., Tech.Serv.Libn.
ATLANTIC SCHOOL OF THEOLOGY - LIBRARY □
Halifax, NS
Melcher, Marlene
HARTFORD PUBLIC LIBRARY - BUSINESS,
SCIENCE & TECHNOLOGY DEPARTMENT □
Hartford, CT
Melde, F.B., Libn.
SHELL DEVELOPMENT COMPANY - BELLAIRE
RESEARCH CENTER LIBRARY □ Houston, TX
Meldrum, Lawrie G., Archv.
INDIANA STATE COMMISSION ON PUBLIC
RECORDS - ARCHIVES DIVISION □ Indianapolis,
IN
Melech, Laura, Asst.Libn.
ARTHUR YOUNG & COMPANY - LIBRARY □ New
York, NY
Melendez, Carmen M., Circ.
UNIVERSITY OF PUERTO RICO - LAW SCHOOL
LIBRARY □ Rio Piedras, PR
Melican, Robert L., Exec.Dir.
JOCKEY CLUB - LIBRARY □ New York, NY
Melius, Charlotte, Circ.
LOUISIANA STATE UNIVERSITY - LAW
LIBRARY □ Baton Rouge, LA
Mell, Ann, Libn.
CARROLL (John) UNIVERSITY -
SEISMOLOGICAL LIBRARY □ Cleveland, OH
Mellichamp, Freddie Ann, Chf., Lib.Sup.Serv.
STATE LIBRARY OF FLORIDA □ Tallahassee, FL
Mellinger, Selma, Libn.
CARNEGIE LIBRARY OF PITTSBURGH -
BUSINESS DIVISION □ Pittsburgh, PA
Mellon, Jeanne F., Libn.
ARTHUR YOUNG & COMPANY - LIBRARY □ New
York, NY

Mellon, Scott, Hd., Tech.Proc.
CANADA - NATIONAL RESEARCH COUNCIL - CISTI - AERONAUTICAL & MECHANICAL ENGINEERING BRANCH □ Ottawa, ON

Mellor, Davis G., MRIS Mgr.
NATIONAL ACADEMY OF SCIENCES - NATIONAL RESEARCH COUNCIL - MARITIME RESEARCH INFORMATION SERVICE □ Washington, DC

Melnikoff, Valerie, Info.Off.
CANADIAN HUNGER FOUNDATION - LIBRARY SERVICE □ Ottawa, ON

Melnizek, William, Jr., Res.Lit.Chem.
MOBIL CHEMICAL COMPANY - RESEARCH & DEVELOPMENT - TECHNICAL INFORMATION CENTER □ Edison, NJ

Melnychuk, Dianne, Ser.
MUHLENBERG COLLEGE - JOHN A.W. HAAS LIBRARY □ Allentown, PA

Melroy, Virginia, Cat.
UNIVERSITY OF IOWA - LAW LIBRARY □ Iowa City, IA

Melski, Diane, Cat.
CANADA - ECONOMIC COUNCIL OF CANADA - LIBRARY □ Ottawa, ON

Melton, Becky, Lib.Mgr.
DRISCOLL FOUNDATION CHILDREN'S HOSPITAL - MEDICAL LIBRARY† □ Corpus Christi, TX

Melton, Janet, Asst.Libn.
MASONIC GRAND LODGE OF TEXAS - LIBRARY AND MUSEUM □ Waco, TX

Melton, Sr. Marie, R.S.M., Asst.Dir.
ST. JOHN'S UNIVERSITY - LIBRARY □ Jamaica, NY

Meltzer, Lester, Hd.Libn.
PHILLIPS PETROLEUM COMPANY - RESEARCH & DEVELOPMENT DEPARTMENT - TECHNICAL INFORMATION BRANCH □ Bartlesville, OK

Meltzer, Morton, Mgr.
MARTIN MARIETTA CORPORATION - ORLANDO AEROSPACE DIVISION - INFORMATION CENTER □ Orlando, FL

Meltzer, Phyllis, Regional Loan Coord.
NATIONAL GALLERY OF ART - DEPARTMENT OF EXTENSION PROGRAMS □ Washington, DC

Melville, Dr. S. Donald, Dir.
ERIC CLEARINGHOUSE ON TESTS, MEASUREMENT AND EVALUATION □ Princeton, NJ

Melville, Suzanne, Ref.Libn.
PRATT AND WHITNEY AIRCRAFT OF CANADA, LTD. - LIBRARY □ Longueuil, PQ

Memmott, Roger, Dir. of Oper.
BUSINESS COMMUNICATIONS CO., INC. - LIBRARY □ Stamford, CT

Menanteaux, Bob, Ref.Libn.
UNIVERSITY OF PUGET SOUND - SCHOOL OF LAW LIBRARY □ Tacoma, WA

Menard, Real, Chf.Libn.
CANADA - DEFENCE RESEARCH ESTABLISHMENT VALCARTIER - LIBRARY □ Courcelette, PQ

Menashian, Ms. L.S., Mgr.
BNR INC. - INFORMATION RESOURCE CENTER □ Mountain View, CA

Mendell, Stefanie, Assoc.Libn.
PHILIP MORRIS, U.S.A. - RESEARCH CENTER LIBRARY □ Richmond, VA

Mendelsohn, David, Graphic Designer
UNIVERSITY OF NEW HAMPSHIRE - DEPARTMENT OF MEDIA SERVICES - FILM LIBRARY □ Durham, NH

Mendenhall, Bethany, Assoc.Libn.
GETTY (J. Paul) MUSEUM - RESEARCH LIBRARY □ Malibu, CA

Mendenhall, Donna, Info.Spec.
ATLANTIC-RICHFIELD COMPANY - ARCO CHEMICAL COMPANY - RESEARCH & ENGINEERING TECHNICAL INFORMATION CENTER □ Newton Square, PA

Mendenhall, Mary, Lrng.Mtl.Coll.Assoc.
KEARNEY STATE COLLEGE - CALVIN T. RYAN LIBRARY □ Kearney, NE

Mendez, Gloria, Cat.
INTERAMERICAN UNIVERSITY - SCHOOL OF LAW - DOMINGO TOLEDO ALAMO LAW LIBRARY □ Santurce, PR

Mendez, Ivan
UNIVERSITY OF PUERTO RICO - NATURAL SCIENCE LIBRARY □ Rio Piedras, PR

Mendl, Dido, Selection & Res.Off.
CANADIAN BROADCASTING CORPORATION - PROGRAM ARCHIVES (Sound) □ Toronto, ON

Mendola, Frank, Ref.
ORANGE COUNTY HISTORICAL COMMISSION - MUSEUM LIBRARY □ Orlando, FL

Mendola, James, Med.Libn.
U.S. VETERANS ADMINISTRATION (NY-Buffalo) - MEDICAL CENTER LIBRARY SERVICE □ Buffalo, NY

Mendonca, Francisco J., Supreme Sec.-Libn.
PORTUGUESE CONTINENTAL UNION OF THE U.S.A. - LIBRARY □ Boston, MA

Mendoza, R., Res.Asst.
WESTERN BEHAVIORAL SCIENCES INSTITUTE - LIBRARY □ La Jolla, CA

Mendro, Donna, Recordings Libn.
DALLAS PUBLIC LIBRARY - FINE ARTS DIVISION □ Dallas, TX

Menechian, Ludovic, Acq./Cat.
UNIVERSITY OF OTTAWA - LAW LIBRARY □ Ottawa, ON

Menegaux, Sandra, Asst.Libn.
CORNELL UNIVERSITY - MARTIN P. CATHERWOOD LIBRARY OF INDUSTRIAL AND LABOR RELATIONS □ Ithaca, NY

Meneray, Wilbur E., Mss.Libn.
TULANE UNIVERSITY OF LOUISIANA - SPECIAL COLLECTIONS DIVISION □ New Orleans, LA

Menewitch, Myron E., Tech.Libn.
MALCOLM PIRNIE, INC. - TECHNICAL LIBRARY □ White Plains, NY

Menke, Mary, Bookkeeping Libn.
UNIVERSITY OF TEXAS SCHOOL OF LAW - TARLTON LAW LIBRARY □ Austin, TX

Menne, Pamela M., Pediatrics Libn.
ST. LOUIS CHILDREN'S HOSPITAL - BORDEN S. VEEDER LIBRARY □ St. Louis, MO

Mennie, Elizabeth, Ref.Libn.
MC GILL UNIVERSITY - EDUCATION LIBRARY □ Montreal, PQ

Mennie, Elizabeth, Ref.Libn.
MC GILL UNIVERSITY - EDUCATION LIBRARY - SAM RABINOVITCH MEMORIAL COLLECTION □ Montreal, PQ

Menninger, Dr. Robert G., Dir. of Musm.
MENNINGER FOUNDATION - ARCHIVES □ Topeka, KS

Mensch, H.L., Assoc.Dir.
INSTITUTE OF GAS TECHNOLOGY - TECHNICAL INFORMATION CENTER □ Chicago, IL

Mentha, T., Mgr., Hist.Rec.
BELL CANADA - TELEPHONE HISTORICAL COLLECTION □ Montreal, PQ

Menz, William W., Vice-Pres., Res.
DAIRY RESEARCH, INC. - TECHNICAL INFORMATION SERVICE □ Rosemont, IL

Menzies, Neal, Hd.Libn.
PARSONS SCHOOL OF DESIGN - OTIS ART INSTITUTE - LIBRARY □ Los Angeles, CA

Merala, Marjan, Asst.Univ.Libn.
UNIVERSITY OF CALIFORNIA, DAVIS - GENERAL LIBRARY □ Davis, CA

Merala, Marjan, Libn.
UNIVERSITY OF CALIFORNIA, DAVIS - HEALTH SCIENCES LIBRARY □ Davis, CA

Meranda, Helen F., Journal Coord.
UNIVERSITY OF MICHIGAN - ALFRED TAUBMAN MEDICAL LIBRARY □ Ann Arbor, MI

Mercado, Awilda, Auxiliar de Biblioteca
PUERTO RICO DEPARTMENT OF HEALTH - RAMON EMETERIO BETANCES MEDICAL LIBRARY □ Mayaguez, PR

Mercado, Gloria M.
EVANGELICAL SEMINARY OF PUERTO RICO - JUAN DE VALDES LIBRARY □ Hato Rey, PR

Mercado, Heidi, Libn.
UNIVERSITY OF WASHINGTON - MATHEMATICS RESEARCH LIBRARY □ Seattle, WA

Mercer, Mrs. E., Act.Libn.
CANADIAN BROADCASTING CORPORATION - ENGINEERING HEADQUARTERS LIBRARY □ Montreal, PQ

Mercer, Elizabeth D., Libn.
SPRINGFIELD HOSPITAL CENTER - MEDICAL LIBRARY □ Sykesville, MD

Mercer, Marjorie, Coord., ONTERIS
ONTARIO - MINISTRY OF EDUCATION - INFORMATION CENTRE □ Toronto, ON

Merchant, Jacqueline M., Libn.
BALTIMORE CITY PUBLIC SCHOOLS - PROFESSIONAL MEDIA CENTER □ Baltimore, MD

Merchant, Jo Ann, Hd.Libn.
NUS CORPORATION - LIBRARY □ Rockville, MD

Mercieca, Charles, Exec. V.P.
INTERNATIONAL ASSOCIATION OF EDUCATORS FOR WORLD PEACE - IAEWP CENTER OF INTERCULTURAL INFORMATION □ Huntsville, AL

Mercier, Pierre, Libn.
METROPOLITAN TORONTO LIBRARY - SOCIAL SCIENCES DEPARTMENT □ Toronto, ON

Mercier, Roch, Libn.
QUEBEC PROVINCE - MINISTERE DU TRAVAIL ET DE LA MAIN-D'OEUVRE - BIBLIOTHEQUE □ Montreal, PQ

Mercure, Anne-Marie, Asst.Dir./Archv.Dev.
UNIVERSITY OF CONNECTICUT - INSTITUTE FOR SOCIAL INQUIRY □ Storrs, CT

Mercury, Jill, Doc.Libn.
TRW, INC. - DEFENSE & SPACE SYSTEMS GROUP - TECHNICAL LIBRARY† □ McLean, VA

Meredith, Don, Assoc.Libn.
HARDING GRADUATE SCHOOL OF RELIGION - L.M. GRAVES MEMORIAL LIBRARY □ Memphis, TN

Meredith, Jeanne D., Libn.
ELYRIA CHRONICLE-TELEGRAM - LIBRARY □ Elyria, OH

Meredith, M.H., Bus.Libn.
CUMMINS ENGINE CO., INC. - LIBRARIES □ Columbus, IN

Meredith, Pamela, Ser.
GEORGE WASHINGTON UNIVERSITY - MEDICAL CENTER - PAUL HIMMELFARB HEALTH SCIENCES LIBRARY □ Washington, DC

Meredith, Ruth, Supv.Libn.
U.S. ARMY - ARMAMENT RESEARCH & DEVELOPMENT COMMAND - SCIENTIFIC AND TECHNICAL INFORMATION DIVISION □ Dover, NJ

Merenda, Jean L., Law Libn.
CBS INC. - CBS LAW LIBRARY □ New York, NY

Mericle, Kim, Libn.
TEXAS STATE FOREST SERVICE - TEXAS FOREST PRODUCTS LABORATORY - LIBRARY □ Lufkin, TX

Merkel, Florence V., Lib.Supv.
KM&G INTERNATIONAL INC. - LIBRARY SERVICES □ Pittsburgh, PA

Merlo, Vincent V., Dir., Media & Tech.
KEAN COLLEGE OF NEW JERSEY - INSTRUCTIONAL RESOURCE CENTER □ Union, NJ

Merrell, Beth, Asst.Libn.
DISTRICT ONE TECHNICAL INSTITUTE - LIBRARY - EDUCATIONAL RESOURCE CENTER □ Eau Claire, WI

Merrell, Max J., Chf.Libn.
U.S. VETERANS ADMINISTRATION (WA-Walla Walla) - HOSPITAL LIBRARY □ Walla Walla, WA

Merrell, Sheila, Dir., Div. for Blind
KANSAS STATE LIBRARY □ Topeka, KS

Merriam, Louise A., Libn.
COLONIAL WILLIAMSBURG - RESEARCH
LIBRARY & ARCHIVES □ Williamsburg, VA

Merriam, Robert W.
NEW ENGLAND WIRELESS & STEAM MUSEUM,
INC. - LIBRARY □ East Greenwich, RI

Merrick, Nancy P., Ref./AV Libn.
UNIVERSITY OF NEBRASKA MEDICAL CENTER -
MC GOOGAN LIBRARY OF MEDICINE □ Omaha,
NE

Merrick, Thomas W., Dir.
GEORGETOWN UNIVERSITY - CENTER FOR
POPULATION RESEARCH - LIBRARY □
Washington, DC

Merriman, Sandra Elizabeth H., Cur.
ARCANE ORDER - LIBRARY □ Falls Church, VA

Merritt, Mrs. B., Film & ILL Libn.
ALCOHOLISM AND DRUG ADDICTION
RESEARCH FOUNDATION - LIBRARY □ Toronto,
ON

Merritt, Betty A., Asst.Libn.
PACIFIC GAS AND ELECTRIC COMPANY - LAW
LIBRARY □ San Francisco, CA

Merritt, C. Allen, Mgr.
IBM CORPORATION - GENERAL TECHNOLOGY
DIVISION - INFORMATION CENTER/LEARNING
CENTER □ Essex Junction, VT

Merritt, Clinton E., Hd.,Info.Rsrcs.
HUGHES AIRCRAFT COMPANY - INFORMATION
RESOURCES SECTION □ Culver City, CA

Merritt, Pat, Libn.
U.S. NAVY - NAVAL SUPERVISOR OF
SHIPBUILDING, CONVERSION AND REPAIR -
TECHNICAL LIBRARY □ San Diego, CA

Merritt, Paula, Tech.Serv.Libn.
AMERICAN ARBITRATION ASSOCIATION -
EASTMAN ARBITRATION LIBRARY □ New York,
NY

Merritt, Russell, Libn.
AMERICAN MUSIC CENTER - LIBRARY □ New
York, NY

Merry, Sue, Tech.Serv.Libn.
CANADIAN IMPERIAL BANK OF COMMERCE -
INFORMATION CENTRE □ Toronto, ON

Merryman, John, Chf., Ref.Serv. B
U.S. GENERAL ACCOUNTING OFFICE -
TECHNICAL INFORMATION SOURCES AND
SERVICES BRANCH □ Washington, DC

Merryman, Virginia, Libn.
CH2M HILL, INC. - INFORMATION CENTER □
Redding, CA

Mersky, Roy M., Dir. Of Res.
UNIVERSITY OF TEXAS SCHOOL OF LAW -
TARLTON LAW LIBRARY □ Austin, TX

Merte, Otto, Sr.Res.Supv.
MOTOR VEHICLE MANUFACTURERS
ASSOCIATION (MVMA) - PATENT RESEARCH
LIBRARY □ Detroit, MI

Mervine, Frank S., Tech.Info.Spec.
U.S. NATL. INSTITUTES OF HEALTH - LIBRARY
□ Bethesda, MD

Merz, Mildred H., Libn.
OAKLAND UNIVERSITY - LIBRARY □ Rochester,
MI

Mesa, Dr. Rosa Q., Dir.
UNIVERSITY OF FLORIDA - LATIN AMERICAN
COLLECTION □ Gainesville, FL

Mese, Gladys, Med.Libn.
NORTH SHORE HOSPITAL - MEDICAL LIBRARY
□ Miami, FL

Meserve, Leslie, Libn.
MILLER, NASH, YERKE, WIENER & HAGER -
LIBRARY □ Portland, OR

Mesh, Rosemary, Doc.Libn.
BROOKLYN PUBLIC LIBRARY - SOCIAL SCIENCE
DIVISION □ Brooklyn, NY

Meskel, Thomas J., Adm.
AMERICAN INSTITUTE OF AERONAUTICS AND
ASTRONAUTICS - TECHNICAL INFORMATION
SERVICE □ New York, NY

Meskin, Amy, Asst.Libn.
DIAMOND SHAMROCK CORPORATION -
PROCESS CHEMICALS DIVISION - LIBRARY† □
Morristown, NJ

Mess, M. Diane, Lib.Supv.
ST. ANTHONY HOSPITAL - MEDICAL LIBRARY □
Columbus, OH

Messer, Joyce, Dir., Finance/Adm.
METROPLAN, A COUNCIL OF GOVERNMENTS -
PLANNING LIBRARY □ Little Rock, AR

Messerle, Judith, Dir.
ST. JOSEPH HOSPITAL - INFORMATION
SERVICES □ Alton, IL

Messick, Karen J., Supv., Tech.Proc.
MERCK & COMPANY, INC. - MERCK SHARP &
DOHME RESEARCH LABORATORIES - LIBRARY
SERVICES □ West Point, PA

Messier, Elaine, Libn.
MISSION RESEARCH CORPORATION -
TECHNICAL LIBRARY □ Santa Barbara, CA

Messimer, Jean D., Libn.
UNIVERSITY OF COLORADO, BOULDER -
ENGINEERING LIBRARY □ Boulder, CO

Messmer, Jamie, Asst.Libn.
NEW YORK STATE LIBRARY - MANUSCRIPTS
AND SPECIAL COLLECTION □ Albany, NY

Messner, Ed, TV Prod.Coord.
CLARK COUNTY COMMUNITY COLLEGE -
LEARNING RESOURCES CENTER □ North Las
Vegas, NV

Messner, Eunice, Cat.
CATHOLIC SEMINARY FOUNDATION OF
INDIANAPOLIS - LIBRARY □ Indianapolis, IN

Mest, Belle, Mgr.Info.Serv.
NEEDHAM, HARPER & STEERS ADVERTISING,
INC. - INFORMATION SERVICES □ Chicago, IL

Meszaros, Gary A., Libn.
BELL & HOWELL EDUCATION GROUP - DE VRY
INSTITUTE OF TECHNOLOGY - LEARNING
RESOURCE CENTER □ Chicago, IL

Meszaros, Imre, Libn.
WASHINGTON UNIVERSITY - ART &
ARCHITECTURE LIBRARY □ St. Louis, MO

Metcalf, Judy, Asst.Ref.Ed.
DALLAS MORNING NEWS - REFERENCE
DEPARTMENT □ Dallas, TX

Metcalf, Kent E., Dir.
JEFFERSON COUNTY PUBLIC LAW LIBRARY □
Louisville, KY

Metcalf, Marjorie, Libn.
GRACE (W.R.) AND COMPANY - INDUSTRIAL
CHEMICALS GROUP - LIBRARY □ Cambridge, MA

Metcalfe, Helen M., Libn.
UNDERWOOD-MEMORIAL HOSPITAL -
LIBRARY† □ Woodbury, NJ

Metcalfe, R.E., Info. Chemist
GULF CANADA LIMITED - RESEARCH &
DEVELOPMENT DEPARTMENT - LIBRARY □
Mississauga, ON

Metcoff, Donald, Libn.
AMERICAN SOCIETY OF ARTISTS, INC. -
RESOURCE CENTER □ Chicago, IL

Methlie-Spitzer, Linda, Hd., Circ.
CORNELL UNIVERSITY - MEDICAL COLLEGE -
LIBRARY □ New York, NY

Metter, M.M., Mgr., Info.Serv.
NORTH CAROLINA STATE SCIENCE AND
TECHNOLOGY RESEARCH CENTER □ Research
Triangle Park, NC

Metts, Dena, Libn.
SOUTH HIGHLANDS HOSPITAL - MEDICAL
LIBRARY □ Birmingham, AL

Metz, Allan, Libn.
TEMPLE BETH-EL - WILLIAM G. BRAUDE
LIBRARY □ Providence, RI

Metz, Carolyn J., Dir.
INDIANAPOLIS MUSEUM OF ART - SLIDE
COLLECTION □ Indianapolis, IN

Metz, Janice R., Asst.Libn.
ILLINOIS AGRICULTURAL ASSOCIATION - IAA
AND AFFILIATED COMPANIES LIBRARY □
Bloomington, IL

Metz, Paul D., Hd., User Serv.Dept.
VIRGINIA POLYTECHNIC INSTITUTE AND
STATE UNIVERSITY - CAROL M. NEWMAN
LIBRARY □ Blacksburg, VA

Metzenbacher, Gary, Cat.
WESTERN EVANGELICAL SEMINARY - GEORGE
HALLAUER MEMORIAL LIBRARY □ Portland, OR

Metzger, Eva C., Dir.
CAROLINA LIBRARY SERVICES □ Chapel Hill, NC

Metzger, Janice M., Libn.
CONOCO COAL DEVELOPMENT COMPANY -
TECHNICAL LIBRARY □ Library, PA

Metzger, Judy, Asst.Libn.
LONG ISLAND HISTORICAL SOCIETY - LIBRARY
□ Brooklyn, NY

Metzger, Kurt, Data User Serv.Off.
U.S. BUREAU OF THE CENSUS - REGIONAL
DATA USER SERVICE - DETROIT REGIONAL
OFFICE - LIBRARY □ Detroit, MI

Metzinger, Sylvia, Rare Bk.Libn.
TULANE UNIVERSITY OF LOUISIANA - SPECIAL
COLLECTIONS DIVISION □ New Orleans, LA

Meucci, Joyce E., Lib.Assoc.
PRINCE GEORGE'S COUNTY SCHOOLS -
PROFESSIONAL LIBRARY □ Landover, MD

Meurer, Sonia D., Libn.
NABISCO, INC. - RESEARCH CENTER LIBRARY†
□ Fair Lawn, NJ

Mevers, Frank C., Archv./Dir.
NEW HAMPSHIRE STATE DEPARTMENT OF
STATE - DIVISION OF RECORDS MANAGEMENT
& ARCHIVES □ Concord, NH

Mewes, Mary, Ref.Libn.
ST. LOUIS MERCANTILE LIBRARY
ASSOCIATION - LIBRARY □ St. Louis, MO

Mewshaw, Robyn, Asst. Economist
UNIVERSITY OF NEW MEXICO - BUREAU OF
BUSINESS & ECONOMIC RESEARCH DATA BANK
□ Albuquerque, NM

Meyer, Barbara, Pub.Serv.Libn.
UNIVERSITY OF WISCONSIN, MADISON - LAW
LIBRARY □ Madison, WI

Meyer, Barbara, Libn.
UNIVERSITY OF WISCONSIN, MADISON - LAW
SCHOOL- CRIMINAL JUSTICE REFERENCE &
INFORMATION CENTER □ Madison, WI

Meyer, Carol E., Hd.Libn.
CINCINNATI LAW LIBRARY ASSOCIATION □
Cincinnati, OH

Meyer, Cynthia K., Chf., Lib.Serv.
U.S. VETERANS ADMINISTRATION (CA-Fresno)
- HOSPITAL MEDICAL LIBRARY □ Fresno, CA

Meyer, Francis, Asst.Libn.
TRINITY LUTHERAN CHURCH - LIBRARY □
Madison, WI

Meyer, G.C., R&D Chemist
DU PONT DE NEMOURS (E.I.) & COMPANY, INC.
- CHEMICALS & PIGMENTS DEPT. - JACKSON
LAB. LIBRARY □ Wilmington, DE

Meyer, Geraldine, Med.Lib.Techn.
U.S. VETERANS ADMINISTRATION (WV-
Martinsburg) - CENTER MEDICAL LIBRARY □
Martinsburg, WV

Meyer, Jerry, Adm.Libn.
U.S. NAVY - EDWARD RHODES STITT LIBRARY
□ Bethesda, MD

Meyer, Joe, Dir.Adm.Div.
TEXAS STATE LIBRARY □ Austin, TX

Meyer, Karen M., Law Libn.
CAPLIN & DRYSDALE - LIBRARY □ Washington,
DC

Meyer, Marc, Ref.Libn.
SMITHSONIAN INSTITUTION LIBRARIES -
NATIONAL AIR AND SPACE MUSEUM - LIBRARY
□ Washington, DC

Meyer, Marianne M., Promotion Mgr.
EXCERPTA MEDICA - DATABASE DIVISION □
Princeton, NJ

Meyer, Marvin P., Dir.
U.S. ARMY - ENGINEER WATERWAYS
EXPERIMENT STATION - PAVEMENTS & SOIL
TRAFFICABILITY INFO. ANALYSIS CTR. □
Vicksburg, MS

Meyer, Mary K., Genealogical Libn.
MARYLAND HISTORICAL SOCIETY - LIBRARY □ Baltimore, MD
Meyer, Mary T., Libn.
TENNESSEE BOTANICAL GARDENS & FINE ARTS CENTER - MINNIE RITCHEY & JOEL OWSLEY CHEEK LIBRARY □ Nashville, TN
Meyer, Phillip, Asst.Libn.Coll.Dev.
JENKINS (Theodore F.) MEMORIAL LAW LIBRARY COMPANY - LIBRARY □ Philadelphia, PA
Meyer, R.W., Assoc.Dir.
CLEMSON UNIVERSITY - ROBERT MULDROW COOPER LIBRARY □ Clemson, SC
Meyer, Roger L., Mgr.Tech.Info.Serv.
ENGELHARD CORPORATION - TECHNICAL INFORMATION CENTER □ Edison, NJ
Meyer, Sandra, Asst.Dir.
UNIVERSITY OF NEW MEXICO - MEDICAL CENTER LIBRARY □ Albuquerque, NM
Meyer, Sharon I., Corp.Libn.
AMERICAN HOSPITAL SUPPLY CORPORATION - CORPORATE INFORMATION CENTER □ Evanston, IL
Meyer, Valerie, Libn.
UNIVERSITY OF MICHIGAN - FINE ARTS LIBRARY □ Ann Arbor, MI
Meyerend, Maude H., Libn.
CHESTNUT HILL HOSPITAL - SCHOOL OF NURSING LIBRARY □ Philadelphia, PA
Meyerhoff, Erich, Libn.
CORNELL UNIVERSITY - MEDICAL COLLEGE - LIBRARY □ New York, NY
Meyerhoff, Laurel D., Libn.
EATON CORPORATION - AIL DIVISION - RESEARCH LIBRARY □ Melville, NY
Meyers, Patricia, Asst.Libn.
STOCKTON NEWSPAPERS INC. - STOCKTON RECORD LIBRARY □ Stockton, CA
Miasek, Meryl A., Vet.Med./Sci.Libn.
MICHIGAN STATE UNIVERSITY - SCIENCE LIBRARY □ East Lansing, MI
Michael, Ann B., Chf.Libn.
JOHNS-MANVILLE SALES CORPORATION - CORPORATE INFORMATION CENTER □ Denver, CO
Michael, Anna, Libn.
SACRAMENTO BEE - REFERENCE LIBRARY □ Sacramento, CA
Michael, Dr. James Robert, Dir.
LOUISIANA TECH UNIVERSITY - RESEARCH DIVISION/COLLEGE OF ADMINISTRATION AND BUSINESS - LIBRARY □ Ruston, LA
Michael, Shirley, Sr.Libn.
TRENTON FREE PUBLIC LIBRARY - ART & MUSIC DEPARTMENT □ Trenton, NJ
Michaelieu, Janet, Libn.
CENTRAL ARIZONA MUSEUM - LIBRARY & ARCHIVES □ Phoenix, AZ
Michaels, Bess, Hd., Access Serv.
COLUMBIA UNIVERSITY - LAW LIBRARY □ New York, NY
Michaels, Carolyn Leopold, Staff Libn.
NATIONAL SOCIETY, DAUGHTERS OF THE AMERICAN REVOLUTION - LIBRARY □ Washington, DC
Michaels, Rebecca, Field Serv.Libn.
U.S. ARMY - ADJUTANT GENERAL - LIBRARY DIVISION □ Alexandria, VA
Michaelson, Robert, Hd.Libn.
NORTHWESTERN UNIVERSITY - SEELEY G. MUDD LIBRARY FOR SCIENCE AND ENGINEERING □ Evanston, IL
Michalak, Dolores, Biblog.Asst.
TEMPLE UNIVERSITY - CENTRAL LIBRARY SYSTEM - CHEMISTRY LIBRARY □ Philadelphia, PA
Michalak, Jo-Ann, Libn.
COLUMBIA UNIVERSITY - LIBRARY SERVICE LIBRARY □ New York, NY
Michalak, Naomi, Patients' Libn.
U.S. VETERANS ADMINISTRATION (MA-Boston) - HOSPITAL MEDICAL LIBRARY □ Boston, MA

Michalak, Sarah C., Hd.Libn.
UNIVERSITY OF WASHINGTON - NATURAL SCIENCES LIBRARY □ Seattle, WA
Michalak, Thomas J., Dir.Univ.Libs.
CARNEGIE-MELLON UNIVERSITY - HUNT LIBRARY □ Pittsburgh, PA
Michalova, Dagmar, Assoc.Libn.
NEW YORK STATE DEPARTMENT OF HEALTH - DIVISION OF LABORATORIES AND RESEARCH LIBRARY □ Albany, NY
Michalowski, Daniel R., Park Dir.
SENECA ZOOLOGICAL SOCIETY - LIBRARY □ Rochester, NY
Michals, Mary, Iconographer
ILLINOIS STATE HISTORICAL LIBRARY □ Springfield, IL
Michalski, Ann, AV Libn.
MADISON PUBLIC LIBRARY - ART AND MUSIC DIVISION □ Madison, WI
Michaud, Lise, Circ. & ILL
BANK OF MONTREAL - HEAD OFFICE LIBRARY □ Montreal, PQ
Michaud, Margaret, Tech.Serv.Libn.
ANDOVER NEWTON THEOLOGICAL SCHOOL - TRASK LIBRARY □ Newton Centre, MA
Michaud, Robert, Libn.
MAINE STATE OFFICE OF ENERGY RESOURCES - LIBRARY □ Augusta, ME
Michaud, Yves, Map Libn.
UNIVERSITE DU QUEBEC A RIMOUSKI - CARTOTHEQUE □ Rimouski, PQ
Michel, Doris, Supv.Ck. Staff
SUNY - AGRICULTURAL AND TECHNICAL COLLEGE AT COBLESKILL - JARED VAN WAGENEN, JR. LEARNING RESOURCE CENTER □ Cobleskill, NY
Michel, Ginette, Info.Off.
CANADA - FARM CREDIT CORPORATION CANADA - LIBRARY □ Ottawa, ON
Michel, Maurice M., Law Libn.
UNIVERSITY OF MONTANA - LAW SCHOOL LIBRARY† □ Missoula, MT
Michel, Victor J., Mgr.
ROCKWELL INTERNATIONAL - ANAHEIM INFORMATION CENTER □ Anaheim, CA
Michelin, Claire, Circ.
UNIVERSITE LAVAL - BIBLIOTHEQUE SCIENTIFIQUE† □ Ste. Foy, PQ
Michels, Dr. Frederick A., Dir.
LAKE SUPERIOR STATE COLLEGE - MICHIGAN COLLECTION □ Sault Ste. Marie, MI
Michelson, Donald, Exec.Dir.
AMERICAN SOCIETY OF MILITARY HISTORY - LIBRARY □ Los Angeles, CA
Michniewski, Henry J., Hd., Lib.Dev.
NEW JERSEY STATE LIBRARY □ Trenton, NJ
Miciotta, Robert J., Hist. of Med.
LOUISIANA STATE UNIVERSITY MEDICAL CENTER - LIBRARY □ New Orleans, LA
Mickelson, Peter, Ref.Libn.
CALIFORNIA LUTHERAN COLLEGE - LIBRARY □ Thousand Oaks, CA
Mickey, Melissa B., Libn.
KRAFT, INC. - BUSINESS RESEARCH CENTER □ Glenview, IL
Micuda, Martha, Asst.Libn., Pub.Serv.
AMERICAN PHILATELIC RESEARCH LIBRARY □ State College, PA
Middendorf, Donna L., Libn.
KINNEY (A.M.) INC. - LIBRARY □ Cincinnati, OH
Middendorf, Gertrude, Libn.
WILSON (Woodrow) BIRTHPLACE FOUNDATION, INC. - RESEARCH LIBRARY & ARCHIVES □ Staunton, VA
Middendorf, Dr. Jack, Dir.
WAYNE STATE COLLEGE - U.S. CONN LIBRARY □ Wayne, NE
Middendorf, Mary Ann, Asst.Libn.
ST. ELIZABETH MEDICAL CENTER - SOUTH - LIBRARY □ Edgewood, KY
Middleton, Anne K., Ref.Libn.
SOUTH CAROLINA STATE LIBRARY □ Columbia, SC

Middleton, Dale, Assoc.Dir., PNRHSL
UNIVERSITY OF WASHINGTON - HEALTH SCIENCES LIBRARY □ Seattle, WA
Middleton, Harry J., Dir.
U.S. PRESIDENTIAL LIBRARIES - LYNDON B. JOHNSON LIBRARY† □ Austin, TX
Middleton, Lily, Hd., Circ.Dept.
POLYTECHNIC INSTITUTE OF NEW YORK - SPICER LIBRARY □ Brooklyn, NY
Midgley, John D., Asst.Libn.
ARTHUR YOUNG & COMPANY - LIBRARY □ New York, NY
Midson, Anthony, Asst.Dir.
PORTLAND STATE UNIVERSITY - AUDIO-VISUAL SERVICES □ Portland, OR
Miech, Rev. Lawrence, Lib.Dir.
ST. FRANCIS SEMINARY - SALZMANN LIBRARY □ Milwaukee, WI
Miedzinska, Krystyna, Ser.
UNIVERSITY OF OTTAWA - MORISSET LIBRARY □ Ottawa, ON
Migliacci, Jeanne, Sr.Libn.
MEDFIELD STATE HOSPITAL - MEDICAL LIBRARY □ Medfield, MA
Mignault, Marcel, Hd.
COLLEGE DE STE-ANNE-DE-LA-POCATIERE - BIBLIOTHEQUE □ La Pocatiere, PQ
Mihalism, Rhea, Biblog.Asst.
TEMPLE UNIVERSITY - CENTRAL LIBRARY SYSTEM - PHYSICS LIBRARY □ Philadelphia, PA
Mikalonis, Sandra, Libn./Cat. AV Serv.
ALBERTA - DEPARTMENT OF EDUCATION - LIBRARY □ Edmonton, AB
Mikel, Sarah A., Chf., Tech.Info.Div.
U.S. ARMY - OFFICE OF THE CHIEF OF ENGINEERS - LIBRARY □ Washington, DC
Mikell, William T., Sr. Clerk
NEW YORK STATE DIVISION OF HOUSING AND COMMUNITY RENEWAL - REFERENCE ROOM □ New York, NY
Mikkelson, Dwight, Pres.
BLACKFORD COUNTY HISTORICAL SOCIETY - MUSEUM AND BEESON LIBRARY □ Hartford City, IN
Miklas, Josephine, Tech.Serv.Libn.
ORANGE COUNTY LAW LIBRARY □ Santa Ana, CA
Miklus, Kathy, Rec.Spec.
FLORIDA STATE DEPT. OF NATURAL RESOURCES - DIV. OF STATE LANDS - BUREAU OF STATE LAND MANAGEMENT - TITLE SECTION □ Tallahassee, FL
Miko, Chris J., Sci.Libn.
MICHIGAN STATE UNIVERSITY - SCIENCE LIBRARY □ East Lansing, MI
Mikol, Kathryn L., Res.Libn.
GATES RUBBER COMPANY - TECHNICAL INFORMATION CENTER □ Denver, CO
Milam, Vicki, Hd., Acq.
UNIVERSITY OF COLORADO MEDICAL CENTER - DENISON MEMORIAL LIBRARY □ Denver, CO
Milanich, Melanie, Libn.
METROPOLITAN TORONTO LIBRARY - SOCIAL SCIENCES DEPARTMENT □ Toronto, ON
Milburn, Richard, Hd., Pub.Serv.
ONTARIO COLLEGE OF ART - LIBRARY/AUDIOVISUAL CENTRE □ Toronto, ON
Milch, Pauline, Libn.
HEBREW INSTITUTE OF PITTSBURGH - SOL ROSENBLOOM LIBRARY □ Pittsburgh, PA
Milek, Valerie, Cat.
BLACK HILLS STATE COLLEGE - E.Y. BERRY LIBRARY-LEARNING CENTER □ Spearfish, SD
Miles, Allan J., Asst. to Dir.
ATLANTA BUREAU OF PLANNING - LIBRARY □ Atlanta, GA
Miles, Carole W., Libn.
U.S. VETERANS ADMINISTRATION (PA-Coatesville) - MEDICAL CENTER LIBRARY □ Coatesville, PA
Miles, Colin, Regional Dir.
CANADIAN MUSIC CENTRE - LIBRARY □ Vancouver, BC

PERSONNEL

PERSONNEL

Miles, Dione, Archv.
WAYNE STATE UNIVERSITY - ARCHIVES OF LABOR AND URBAN AFFAIRS/UNIVERSITY ARCHIVES □ Detroit, MI

Miles, Don, Res.Libn.
MILLIKEN RESEARCH CORPORATION - RESEARCH LIBRARY □ Spartanburg, SC

Miles, Elizabeth T., Lib.Techn.
U. S. NAVY - NAVAL ORDNANCE STATION - TECHNICAL LIBRARY □ Louisville, KY

Miles, Gary, Resource Ctr.Dir.
TENNESSEE STATE DEPARTMENT OF PUBLIC HEALTH - MCH/HWP RESOURCE CENTER □ Nashville, TN

Miles, George, Cur./W.Amer.
YALE UNIVERSITY - BEINECKE RARE BOOK AND MANUSCRIPT LIBRARY □ New Haven, CT

Miles, Michele L., Libn.
GOODMAN AND GOODMAN - LIBRARY □ Toronto, ON

Miles, Sally J., Libn.
WEINBERG & GREEN, ATTORNEYS-AT-LAW - LIBRARY □ Baltimore, MD

Miles, Susan, Ref.Libn.
FEDERAL RESERVE BANK OF RICHMOND - RESEARCH LIBRARY □ Richmond, VA

Miles, William, Biblog.
CENTRAL MICHIGAN UNIVERSITY - CLARKE HISTORICAL LIBRARY □ Mt. Pleasant, MI

Miletich, Ivo, Hd., Acq.Dept.
CHICAGO STATE UNIVERSITY - DOUGLAS LIBRARY □ Chicago, IL

Miletich, John, Ref.Libn.
UNIVERSITY OF ALBERTA - SCIENCE LIBRARY □ Edmonton, AB

Miley, Rachel, Dir., Lib.Serv.
LE TOURNEAU COLLEGE - MARGARET ESTES LIBRARY □ Longview, TX

Milford, Charles C., Libn.
STANFORD UNIVERSITY - FOOD RESEARCH INSTITUTE - LIBRARY □ Stanford, CA

Milfred, Jeff, AV Tech.
WISCONSIN INDIANHEAD TECHNICAL INSTITUTE, NEW RICHMOND CAMPUS - LEARNING RESOURCE CENTER □ New Richmond, WI

Milholland, Elizabeth, Libn.
HIGHLAND UNITED PRESBYTERIAN CHURCH - LIBRARY □ New Castle, PA

Milinovich, Michele, Libn.
DULUTH BAR LIBRARY ASSOCIATION □ Duluth, MN

Miljenovik, Susan, Asst.Libn.
BAKER AND HOSTETLER - LIBRARY □ Cleveland, OH

Milkins, Ronald J.
NEW YORK STATE SUPREME COURT - APPELLATE DIVISION, 3RD JUDICIAL DEPARTMENT - LAW LIBRARY □ Albany, NY

Milkovich, Michael, Dir.
DIXON GALLERY AND GARDENS - LIBRARY □ Memphis, TN

Millar, Barbara, Asst.Dir.Tech.Serv.
UNIVERSITY OF ILLINOIS MEDICAL CENTER - LIBRARY OF THE HEALTH SCIENCES □ Chicago, IL

Millar, Cynthia
ST. LOUIS PUBLIC LIBRARY - HISTORY AND GENEALOGY DEPARTMENT □ St. Louis, MO

Mille, Martha, Circ.
UNIVERSITY OF SANTA CLARA - EDWIN A. HEAFEY LAW LIBRARY □ Santa Clara, CA

Millen, George, Hd.Cat.Libn.
CENTRAL MISSOURI STATE UNIVERSITY - WARD EDWARDS LIBRARY □ Warrensburg, MO

Miller, Alan V., Collective Member
CANADIAN GAY ARCHIVES - LIBRARY □ Toronto, ON

Miller, Alice, Lib.Chm.
VIZCAYA GUIDES LIBRARY □ Miami, FL

Miller, Ann, Lib./AV Techn.
ST. JOSEPH MEDICAL CENTER - HEALTH SCIENCE LIBRARY □ Burbank, CA

Miller, Ann P., Hd.
BUFFALO & ERIE COUNTY PUBLIC LIBRARY - EDUCATION, SOCIOLOGY, PHILOSOPHY & RELIGION DEPARTMENT □ Buffalo, NY

Miller, Ann P., Hd.
BUFFALO & ERIE COUNTY PUBLIC LIBRARY - LANGUAGE, LITERATURE AND ARTS DEPARTMENT □ Buffalo, NY

Miller, Annie, Asst.Libn.
BLUE CROSS/BLUE SHIELD OF GREATER NEW YORK - REFERENCE LIBRARY □ New York, NY

Miller, Arlene, Hd., Circ.
NEW YORK MEDICAL COLLEGE AND THE WESTCHESTER ACADEMY OF MEDICINE - WESTCHESTER MEDICAL CENTER LIBRARY □ Valhalla, NY

Miller, Arthur H., Jr., Coll.Libn.
LAKE FOREST COLLEGE - THOMAS OSCAR FREEMAN MEMORIAL LIBRARY □ Lake Forest, IL

Miller, B.J., Scientific Asst.
U.S. NATL. BUREAU OF STANDARDS - DATA CENTER ON ATOMIC TRANSITION PROBABILITIES □ Washington, DC

Miller, Barbara, Doc.Asst.
COUNCIL ON FOREIGN RELATIONS - LIBRARY □ New York, NY

Miller, Barbara, Corp.Libn.
DAYTON HUDSON CORPORATION LIBRARY □ Minneapolis, MN

Miller, Barbara, Ref.
UNIVERSITY OF TEXAS HEALTH SCIENCE CENTER, DALLAS - LIBRARY □ Dallas, TX

Miller, Barry K., Corp.Libn.
REYNOLDS (R.J.) INDUSTRIES, INC. - MANAGEMENT INFORMATION LIBRARY □ Winston-Salem, NC

Miller, Benjamin, Media Libn.
BOARD OF JEWISH EDUCATION OF GREATER NEW YORK - EDUCATIONAL RESOURCE LIBRARY □ New York, NY

Miller, Beth, Asst.Mgr.
UNIVERSITY OF MICHIGAN - SCHOOL OF ED. & SCHOOL OF LIB.SCI. - INSTR. RESOURCES UNIT OF INSTR. STRATEGY SERV. □ Ann Arbor, MI

Miller, Beth, Libn.
UNIVERSITY OF WESTERN ONTARIO - D.B. WELDON LIBRARY - DEPARTMENT OF SPECIAL COLLECTIONS □ London, ON

Miller, Betty, Lib.Supv.
CALSPAN CORPORATION - TECHNICAL LIBRARY □ Buffalo, NY

Miller, Betty, Pub.Lib.Cons.
STATE LIBRARY OF FLORIDA □ Tallahassee, FL

Miller, Beverly J., Tech.Info.Spec.
U.S. NATL. BUREAU OF STANDARDS - DATA CENTER ON ATOMIC LINE SHAPES AND SHIFTS □ Washington, DC

Miller, Bryan M., Chf., Archv.Serv.Div.
NEW MEXICO STATE RECORDS CENTER AND ARCHIVES - DOROTHY WOODWARD RESEARCH ROOM □ Santa Fe, NM

Miller, Carol, Libn.
HEWLETT-PACKARD COMPANY - ANDOVER DIVISION LIBRARY □ Andover, MA

Miller, Carolyn, Sci.Libn.
UNIVERSITY OF CALIFORNIA, SANTA CRUZ - SCIENCE LIBRARY □ Santa Cruz, CA

Miller, Carolynne, Hd., Genealogy Div.
INDIANA STATE LIBRARY □ Indianapolis, IN

Miller, David, Asst.Libn.
OHIO UNIVERSITY - SOUTHEAST ASIA COLLECTION □ Athens, OH

Miller, David M., Pres.
MERCER COUNTY HISTORICAL SOCIETY - LIBRARY AND ARCHIVES □ Mercer, PA

Miller, David W., Pres.
WATER INFORMATION CENTER, INC. □ Syosset, NY

Miller, Diane, Lib.Dir.
BLOOMINGTON-NORMAL DAILY PANTAGRAPH - NEWSPAPER LIBRARY □ Bloomington, IL

Miller, Dick R., Assoc.Libn.
NORTHEASTERN OHIO UNIVERSITIES COLLEGE OF MEDICINE - BASIC MEDICAL SCIENCES LIBRARY □ Rootstown, OH

Miller, Donald, Libn.
ELIZABETH GENERAL HOSPITAL & DISPENSARY - HEALTH SCIENCE LIBRARY □ Elizabeth, NJ

Miller, Dwight, Instr.Dev.
BRIGHAM YOUNG UNIVERSITY, HAWAII CAMPUS - JOSEPH F. SMITH LIBRARY AND MEDIA CENTER □ Laie, HI

Miller, Edith, Hum.Libn.
MIAMI UNIVERSITY - MUSIC LIBRARY □ Oxford, OH

Miller, Eileen M., Libn.
ST. LUKE'S HOSPITAL OF BETHLEHEM, PENNSYLVANIA - AUDIOVISUAL LIBRARY □ Bethlehem, PA

Miller, Elaine, Asst.Libn.
DELOITTE HASKINS & SELLS - EXECUTIVE OFFICE LIBRARY □ New York, NY

Miller, Elizabeth Jane, Cur.
COLUMBIA HISTORICAL SOCIETY - LIBRARY □ Washington, DC

Miller, Elizabeth R., Hd.Libn.
PENINSULA TIMES TRIBUNE - LIBRARY □ Palo Alto, CA

Miller, Ellen L., Mgr.Res.Serv.
BOOZ, ALLEN & HAMILTON, INC. - RESEARCH SERVICE □ New York, NY

Miller, Elsa A., Acq./Circ.Libn.
SOUTHERN BAPTIST THEOLOGICAL SEMINARY - JAMES P. BOYCE CENTENNIAL LIBRARY □ Louisville, KY

Miller, Dr. Elwood E., Dir.
UNIVERSITY OF COLORADO, BOULDER - EDUCATIONAL MEDIA CENTER □ Boulder, CO

Miller, F., Dir., Wash., DC
FRANKLIN RESEARCH CENTER - SCIENCE INFORMATION SERVICES □ Philadelphia, PA

Miller, Frances, Dir.
DAKOTA COUNTY HISTORICAL SOCIETY - LIBRARY AND MUSEUM □ South St. Paul, MN

Miller, Frances A., Sr.Libn.
NEW YORK STATE DEPARTMENT OF MOTOR VEHICLES - RESEARCH LIBRARY □ Albany, NY

Miller, Dr. Fredric, Cur.
TEMPLE UNIVERSITY - CENTRAL LIBRARY SYSTEM - URBAN ARCHIVES □ Philadelphia, PA

Miller, G., Libn.
CANADA - FISHERIES & OCEANS - PACIFIC BIOLOGICAL STATION - LIBRARY □ Nanaimo, BC

Miller, Gail, Circ.Hd.
BROOKS INSTITUTE OF PHOTOGRAPHY - LIBRARY □ Santa Barbara, CA

Miller, Gail, Libn.
LINCOLN PARK ZOOLOGICAL GARDENS - LIBRARY □ Chicago, IL

Miller, Gary, Archv.
U.S. NATL. ARCHIVES & RECORDS SERVICE - FEDERAL ARCHIVES AND RECORDS CENTER, REGION 9 □ Laguna Niguel, CA

Miller, George H., Cur.
RIPON HISTORICAL SOCIETY - LIBRARY □ Ripon, WI

Miller, Glenn E., Libn.
CHICAGO INSTITUTE FOR PSYCHOANALYSIS - MC LEAN LIBRARY □ Chicago, IL

Miller, Harold W., Chf.Libn.
TOUCHE ROSS AND COMPANY - BUSINESS LIBRARY □ New York, NY

Miller, Helen, Ref./Cat.Libn.
HOWARD UNIVERSITY - SCHOOL OF LAW - ALLEN MERCER DANIEL LAW LIBRARY □ Washington, DC

Miller, Helen, Night Supv.
LE TOURNEAU COLLEGE - MARGARET ESTES LIBRARY □ Longview, TX

Miller, Herbert, Libn.
MEIDINGER, INC. - INFORMATION CENTER □ Louisville, KY

Miller, Howard, Asst.Mgr.
SWEDENBORG LIBRARY AND BOOKSTORE □
Boston, MA

Miller, I.C.
U.S. OAK RIDGE NATL. LABORATORY -
INFORMATION DIVISION - ENVIRONMENTAL
MUTAGEN INFORMATION CENTER □ Oak Ridge,
TN

Miller, Inabeth, Libn.
HARVARD UNIVERSITY - GRADUATE SCHOOL
OF EDUCATION - GUTMAN LIBRARY □
Cambridge, MA

Miller, Irene, Libn.
WARNACO, INC. - MARKET RESEARCH
LIBRARY† □ Bridgeport, CT

Miller, Irene K., Libn.
FAIRFIELD HISTORICAL SOCIETY - REFERENCE
AND RESEARCH LIBRARY □ Fairfield, CT

Miller, Dr. James Q., Chm., Lib.Comm.
UNIVERSITY OF VIRGINIA MEDICAL CENTER -
DEPARTMENT OF NEUROLOGY - ELIZABETH J.
OHRSTROM LIBRARY □ Charlottesville, VA

Miller, Jan P., Gen.Mgr.
UNIVERSITY OF PITTSBURGH - CENTER FOR
INTERNATIONAL STUDIES □ Pittsburgh, PA

Miller, Janet, Circ.Supv.
NORTH DAKOTA STATE UNIVERSITY - LIBRARY
□ Fargo, ND

Miller, Janice, Asst.Libn.
CARLETON COUNTY LAW LIBRARY □ Ottawa,
ON

Miller, Jean J., Libn.
UNIVERSITY OF HARTFORD - ANNE BUNCE
CHENEY LIBRARY □ West Hartford, CT

Miller, Jean K., Dir.
UNIVERSITY OF TEXAS HEALTH SCIENCE
CENTER, DALLAS - LIBRARY □ Dallas, TX

Miller, Jean R., Chf.Libn.
BECKMAN INSTRUMENTS, INC. - RESEARCH
LIBRARY □ Fullerton, CA

Miller, Jeannine, Dir. of Media Ctr.
FIRST BAPTIST CHURCH - MEDIA CENTER† □
Roswell, NM

Miller, John, Act.Chf.
NEW YORK PUBLIC LIBRARY - SCHOMBURG
CENTER FOR RESEARCH IN BLACK CULTURE □
New York, NY

Miller, Joseph A., Libn.
YALE UNIVERSITY - FORESTRY LIBRARY □ New
Haven, CT

Miller, Joseph S., Adm.
MENNONITE HISTORICAL LIBRARY OF
EASTERN PENNSYLVANIA □ Lansdale, PA

Miller, Sr. Joy, I.B.V.M., Libn.
ST. JOHN'S PROVINCIAL SEMINARY - LIBRARY
□ Plymouth, MI

Miller, Juanita A., Libn.
INDIANA STATE SUPREME COURT - LAW
LIBRARY □ Indianapolis, IN

Miller, Judith A., Exec.Dir.
INTERFAITH FORUM ON RELIGION, ART AND
ARCHITECTURE - LIBRARY □ Washington, DC

Miller, Julia E., Libn.
INTERNATIONAL FOUNDATION OF EMPLOYEE
BENEFIT PLANS - INFORMATION CENTER □
Brookfield, WI

Miller, Juliet V., Dir.
ERIC CLEARINGHOUSE ON ADULT, CAREER
AND VOCATIONAL EDUCATION - NATL. CTR.
FOR RESEARCH IN VOCATIONAL EDUC. □
Columbus, OH

Miller, Karen, Libn.
CLEVELAND INSTITUTE OF MUSIC - LIBRARY □
Cleveland, OH

Miller, Karen, Info.Serv./ILL
SUNY AT BUFFALO - HEALTH SCIENCES
LIBRARY □ Buffalo, NY

Miller, Kathleen, Res.Assoc.
MOBIL OIL CORPORATION - PUBLIC AFFAIRS
SECRETARIAT □ New York, NY

Miller, Kathy, Libn.
WORLD MODELING ASSOCIATION - WMA
LIBRARY □ Croton-On-Hudson, NY

Miller, Kim M., Libn.
ANTIQUE AUTOMOBILE CLUB OF AMERICA -
AACA AUTOMOBILE REFERENCE COLLECTION □
Hershey, PA

Miller, Lester L., Jr., Supv.Libn.
U.S. ARMY FIELD ARTILLERY SCHOOL - MORRIS
SWETT LIBRARY □ Ft. Sill, OK

Miller, Lidie, Libn.
GHOST RANCH CONFERENCE CENTER - GHOST
RANCH LIBRARY† □ Abiquiu, NM

Miller, Lorraine K., Hd.Libn.
JEWISH COMMUNITY CENTERS ASSOCIATION
(JCCA) - TANNIE LEWIN JUDAICA LIBRARY □
St. Louis, MO

Miller, Lynne, Libn.
HERMAN MILLER, INC. - RESOURCE CENTER □
Zeeland, MI

Miller, M. Stone, Jr., Hd.
LOUISIANA STATE UNIVERSITY -
DEPARTMENT OF ARCHIVES AND
MANUSCRIPTS □ Baton Rouge, LA

Miller, Marcia A., Asst.Libn.
NEW YORK HOSPITAL - CORNELL MEDICAL
CENTER, WESTCHESTER DIVISION - MEDICAL
LIBRARY □ White Plains, NY

Miller, Margaret E., Asst.Libn.
GENERAL ATOMIC COMPANY - LIBRARY □ San
Diego, CA

Miller, Marilyn, Ref.Libn.
LOUISIANA STATE UNIVERSITY MEDICAL
CENTER - SCHOOL OF MEDICINE IN
SHREVEPORT - LIBRARY □ Shreveport, LA

Miller, Marjorie, Art Ref.Libn.
FASHION INSTITUTE OF TECHNOLOGY -
LIBRARY/MEDIA SERVICES □ New York, NY

Miller, Marjorie M., Doc.Libn.
PRINCE GEORGE'S COUNTY MEMORIAL
LIBRARY SYSTEM - PUBLIC DOCUMENTS
REFERENCE LIBRARY □ Upper Marlboro, MD

Miller, Marsha, Ref./Per.Libn.
ARKANSAS STATE UNIVERSITY - DEAN B.
ELLIS LIBRARY □ State University, AR

Miller, Mary, Cat.
HONEYWELL, INC. - SYSTEMS & RESEARCH
CENTER - LIBRARY □ Minneapolis, MN

Miller, Mary, Cat.Libn.
MINNEAPOLIS COLLEGE OF ART AND DESIGN -
LIBRARY AND MEDIA CENTER □ Minneapolis,
MN

Miller, Mary, Ser./Acq.Libn.
SUNY AT BUFFALO - CHARLES B. SEARS LAW
LIBRARY □ Buffalo, NY

Miller, Mary Jane, Lib. Group Supv.
BELL TELEPHONE LABORATORIES, INC. -
TECHNICAL LIBRARY □ Whippany, NJ

Miller, Mary Lee, Hd.
ROCHESTER PUBLIC LIBRARY - ART DIVISION
□ Rochester, NY

Miller, Mary McG., Chm. of Lib.Comm.
SPRINGFIELD ART CENTER - LIBRARY □
Springfield, OH

Miller, Maryrose, Ref.Libn.
COLUMBIA UNIVERSITY - THOMAS J. WATSON
LIBRARY OF BUSINESS AND ECONOMICS □ New
York, NY

Miller, Maureen, Subject Anl.
AEROSPACE CORPORATION - CHARLES C.
LAURITSEN LIBRARY □ Los Angeles, CA

Miller, Michael, Ref.Libn.
NORTH DAKOTA STATE UNIVERSITY - LIBRARY
□ Fargo, ND

Miller, Michael S., Dir.
MARYLAND STATE LAW LIBRARY □ Annapolis,
MD

Miller, Nancy E., Asst.Dir.
OHIO STATE UNIVERSITY - LAW LIBRARY □
Columbus, OH

Miller, Nancy R., Dir., Lib.Serv.
GOVERNMENT RESEARCH CORPORATION -
LIBRARY □ Washington, DC

Miller, Nell, Libn.
ROGERS ENVIRONMENTAL EDUCATION
CENTER - GEORGE W. HOTCHKIN MEMORIAL
LIBRARY □ Sherburne, NY

Miller, Oscar, Law Libn.
UNIVERSITY OF COLORADO, BOULDER - LAW
LIBRARY □ Boulder, CO

Miller, P., Cat.Libn.
OHIO DOMINICAN COLLEGE - LIBRARY □
Columbus, OH

Miller, Pat, Circ.
NORTHWESTERN OKLAHOMA STATE
UNIVERSITY - LIBRARY □ Alva, OK

Miller, Pauline M., Hd.Sci. & Tech.Dept.
SYRACUSE UNIVERSITY - ENGINEERING & LIFE
SCIENCES LIBRARY □ Syracuse, NY

Miller, Philip E., Libn.
HEBREW UNION COLLEGE - JEWISH
INSTITUTE OF RELIGION - KLAU LIBRARY □
New York, NY

Miller, R.B., Libn.
CATHOLIC UNIVERSITY OF AMERICA -
THEOLOGY/PHILOSOPHY/CANON LAW/
RELIGIOUS EDUCATION LIBRARY □
Washington, DC

Miller, Rhoda, Tech.Info. Aide
WATER POLLUTION CONTROL FEDERATION -
LIBRARY □ Washington, DC

Miller, Richard, Coord.Spec.Lib.Serv.
MISSOURI STATE LIBRARY □ Jefferson City,
MO

Miller, Rita, Libn.
SHELBY COUNTY LAW LIBRARY □ Sidney, OH

Miller, Robert, First Asst.
MEMPHIS-SHELBY COUNTY PUBLIC LIBRARY
AND INFORMATION CENTER - MEMPHIS ROOM
COLLECTIONS □ Memphis, TN

Miller, Dr. Robert, Hd.
SANTA BARBARA HISTORICAL SOCIETY -
GLEDHILL LIBRARY □ Santa Barbara, CA

Miller, Robert L., Libn.
UNIVERSITY CITY PUBLIC LIBRARY - RECORD
COLLECTION □ University City, MO

Miller, Robert P., Jr., Law Lib.Coord.
VIRGINIA BEACH PUBLIC LIBRARY SYSTEM -
ROBERT S. WAHAB, JR. PUBLIC LAW LIBRARY
□ Virginia Beach, VA

Miller, Roger, Ref.Libn.
UNION CARBIDE CORPORATION - BUSINESS
LIBRARY □ New York, NY

Miller, Roger M., Lib.Dir.
U.S. ARMY POST - FORT CARSON - LIBRARY □
Ft. Carson, CO

Miller, Ron, Attorney
AUGLAIZE COUNTY LAW LIBRARY □
Wapakoneta, OH

Miller, Ron, Hd.Libn.
CHARLESTON GAZETTE-MAIL - LIBRARY □
Charleston, WV

Miller, Ron, Dir.
WORLD ARCHEOLOGICAL SOCIETY -
INFORMATION CENTER □ Hollister, MO

Miller, Rose M., Libn.
RETINA FOUNDATION - JOINT RESEARCH
LIBRARY □ Boston, MA

Miller, Ruby B., Tech.Serv.
TRINITY UNIVERSITY - LIBRARY □ San Antonio,
TX

Miller, Scott, Rd.Serv.Libn.
BLOOMSBURG STATE COLLEGE - HARVEY A.
ANDRUSS LIBRARY □ Bloomsburg, PA

Miller, Scott, Musm.Dir.
NEVADA STATE MUSEUM □ Carson City, NV

Miller, Mrs. Seymour, Libn.
K.K. BENE ISRAEL/ROCKDALE TEMPLE -
SIDNEY G. ROSE MEMORIAL LIBRARY □
Cincinnati, OH

Miller, Mrs. Steve, Asst.Dir.
WORLD ARCHEOLOGICAL SOCIETY -
INFORMATION CENTER □ Hollister, MO

Miller, Stuart W., Info.Spec.
INTERNATIONAL ASSOCIATION OF ASSESSING OFFICERS - RESEARCH AND TECHNICAL SERVICES DEPT. - LIBRARY □ Chicago, IL

Miller, Sue, ILL
U.S. NASA - LANGLEY RESEARCH CENTER - TECHNICAL LIBRARY MS 185 □ Hampton, VA

Miller, Susan A., Libn.
LOO MERIDETH & MC MILLAN - LAW LIBRARY □ Los Angeles, CA

Miller, Suzanne, Law Libn.
UNIVERSITY OF LA VERNE - COLLEGE OF LAW - LIBRARY □ La Verne, CA

Miller, Terry, Ed.Libn.
ENCYCLOPAEDIA BRITANNICA, INC. - EDITORIAL LIBRARY □ Chicago, IL

Miller, Thomas, Cat.
CAPE BRETON MINERS' MUSEUM - LIBRARY □ Glace Bay, NS

Miller, Mrs. Tony
BOB JONES UNIVERSITY - CHURCH MINISTRIES RESOURCE LAB □ Greenville, SC

Miller, Tracey, Bus.Libn.
UNIVERSITY OF COLORADO, BOULDER - WILLIAM M. WHITE BUSINESS LIBRARY □ Boulder, CO

Miller, Veronica, Asst.Libn./Rsrcs.
TEMPLE UNIVERSITY - CENTRAL LIBRARY SYSTEM - AMBLER CAMPUS LIBRARY □ Ambler, PA

Miller, Virginia, Computerized Serv.
MEDICAL UNIVERSITY OF SOUTH CAROLINA - LIBRARY □ Charleston, SC

Miller, Vivian K., Res.Coord.
COLLEGE OF MEDICINE & DENTISTRY OF NEW JERSEY - RUTGERS MEDICAL SCHOOL - OFFICE OF CONSUMER HEALTH EDUCATION □ Piscataway, NJ

Miller, Mrs. W., Children's Libn.
FRASER-HICKSON INSTITUTE, MONTREAL - FREE LIBRARY □ Montreal, PQ

Miller, W. Everett, Libn. & Owner
LIBRARY OF VEHICLES □ Garden Grove, CA

Miller, Wayne, Libn.
HARRISBURG STATE HOSPITAL - STAFF LIBRARY† □ Harrisburg, PA

Miller, William B., Sec.
UNITED PRESBYTERIAN CHURCH IN THE U.S.A. - PRESBYTERIAN HISTORICAL SOCIETY - LIBRARY □ Philadelphia, PA

Miller, William C., Libn.
NAZARENE THEOLOGICAL SEMINARY - WILLIAM BROADHURST LIBRARY □ Kansas City, MO

Miller-Hartnett, Ms. Lee, Libn./Archv.
UNDERWOOD (William) COMPANY - LIBRARY □ Westwood, MA

Millican, Beatrice, Spec.Coll.Libn.
CARNEGIE LIBRARY - HENDERSON ROOM □ Rome, GA

Millich, E., Ref.
UNIVERSITY OF WISCONSIN, LA CROSSE - MURPHY LIBRARY □ La Crosse, WI

Milligan, Edna H., Libn.
FORBES HEALTH SYSTEM - COLUMBIA HEALTH CENTER LIBRARY □ Pittsburgh, PA

Milligan, Patricia M., Sr.Cat.
UNIVERSITY OF MAINE SCHOOL OF LAW - DONALD L. GARBRECHT LAW LIBRARY □ Portland, ME

Milligan, Stuart, Circ.Libn.
UNIVERSITY OF ROCHESTER - EASTMAN SCHOOL OF MUSIC - SIBLEY MUSIC LIBRARY □ Rochester, NY

Mills, Amy, Info.Spec.
AMERICAN ASSOCIATION OF ADVERTISING AGENCIES - MEMBER INFORMATION SERVICE □ New York, NY

Mills, Elaine L., Ed.
SMITHSONIAN INSTITUTION - NATIONAL ANTHROPOLOGICAL ARCHIVES □ Washington, DC

Mills, Emilie, Spec.Coll.Libn.
UNIVERSITY OF NORTH CAROLINA, GREENSBORO - DANCE COLLECTION □ Greensboro, NC

Mills, Jamie S., Asst. Professor
MISSISSIPPI UNIVERSITY FOR WOMEN - SCHOOL OF EDUCATION - LIBRARY SCIENCE DIVISION □ Columbus, MS

Mills, Jeanne M., Cur.Mss. & Bk.
PILGRIM SOCIETY - PILGRIM HALL LIBRARY □ Plymouth, MA

Mills, Jesse C., Chf.Libn.
TENNESSEE VALLEY AUTHORITY - TECHNICAL LIBRARY □ Knoxville, TN

Mills, Mary Alice, Dir.
U.S. CENTER FOR DISEASE CONTROL - CDC LIBRARY □ Atlanta, GA

Mills, Theresa, Inst.Cons.
SOUTH CAROLINA STATE LIBRARY □ Columbia, SC

Mills, William T., Pres.
MADISON HISTORICAL SOCIETY, INC. - LIBRARY □ Madison, CT

Millward, Dr. A.E., Libn.
UNIVERSITY OF MANITOBA - ST. JOHN'S COLLEGE - LIBRARY □ Winnipeg, MB

Milner, Zelda W., Dir.
U.S. DEPT. OF COMMERCE - INTERNATIONAL TRADE ADMINISTRATION - CLEVELAND DISTRICT OFFICE LIBRARY □ Cleveland, OH

Milnes, Victoria, Hd., Tech.Serv.
CANADA - LABOUR CANADA - LIBRARY □ Ottawa, ON

Milo, Susan, Tech.Libn.
FIBER MATERIALS, INC. - TECHNICAL LIBRARY □ Biddeford, ME

Milton, Ardyce, Asst.Libn.
EATON CORPORATION - CUTLER-HAMMER LIBRARY □ Milwaukee, WI

Milton, Dr. Sybil, Chf.Archv.
BAECK (Leo) INSTITUTE - LIBRARY □ New York, NY

Mimeault, Alice, Documentaliste
LE DROIT - CENTRE DE DOCUMENTATION □ Ottawa, ON

Mims, Dorothy H., Spec.Coll.Libn.
MEDICAL COLLEGE OF GEORGIA - LIBRARY □ Augusta, GA

Mims, Gloria, Hd., Spec.Coll.
ATLANTA UNIVERSITY - TREVOR ARNETT LIBRARY - SPECIAL COLLECTIONS† □ Atlanta, GA

Mims, Mrs. M.H., Libn.
TOMPKINS (D.A.) MEMORIAL LIBRARY □ Edgefield, SC

Mims, Susan, Libn.
BRACEWELL & PATTERSON - LAW LIBRARY □ Houston, TX

Minailo, Christine, Lib.Techn.
ALBERTA - TREASURY DEPARTMENT - BUREAU OF STATISTICS LIBRARY □ Edmonton, AB

Minckler, Jane T., Res.Libn.
ETHICON, INC. - SCIENTIFIC INFORMATION SERVICES □ Somerville, NJ

Mindeman, George A., Tech.Serv.Libn.
HISTORICAL FOUNDATION OF THE PRESBYTERIAN AND REFORMED CHURCHES - LIBRARY AND ARCHIVES □ Montreat, NC

Mindlin, Harold, Dir.
BATTELLE-COLUMBUS LABORATORIES - MECHANICAL PROPERTIES DATA CENTER □ Columbus, OH

Mindlin, Harold, Dir.
BATTELLE-COLUMBUS LABORATORIES - METALS AND CERAMICS INFORMATION CENTER □ Columbus, OH

Miner, Elizabeth D., Chf.Libn.
ARIZONA DAILY STAR - LIBRARY □ Tucson, AZ

Miner, Irene, Chf., Per.Sect.
U.S. ARMY - ARMY LIBRARY □ Washington, DC

Miner, Jerry, Libn.
CANADA - AGRICULTURE CANADA - RESEARCH STATION, KENTVILLE - LIBRARY □ Kentville, NS

Minesinger, Joan, Chf.Libn.
RIVERSIDE PRESS-ENTERPRISE COMPANY - EDITORIAL LIBRARY □ Riverside, CA

Ming, Virginia H., Hd.Ser. & Pub.Serv.
BAYLOR UNIVERSITY - TEXAS COLLECTION □ Waco, TX

Ming, William L., Hd.Acq. & Biblog.
BAYLOR UNIVERSITY - TEXAS COLLECTION □ Waco, TX

Mingmongkol, Santi, Res.Assoc.
SOUTHEAST ASIA RESOURCE CENTER □ Berkeley, CA

Mininni, Linda, Libn., Tech.Serv.
BETH ISRAEL MEDICAL CENTER - SEYMOUR J. PHILLIPS HEALTH SCIENCES LIBRARY □ New York, NY

Minjiras, Andrew, Post Libn.
U.S. ARMY POST - PRESIDIO OF SAN FRANCISCO - POST LIBRARY SYSTEM □ Presidio of San Francisco, CA

Mink, James V., Hd./Univ.Archv.
UNIVERSITY OF CALIFORNIA, LOS ANGELES - DEPARTMENT OF SPECIAL COLLECTIONS □ Los Angeles, CA

Mink, Shirley, Libn.
WEYERHAEUSER COMPANY - SOUTHERN FORESTRY RESEARCH LIBRARY □ Hot Springs, AR

Minkel, Vera, Mgr., Lib.Serv.
HONEYWELL, INC. - HONEYWELL INFORMATION SYSTEMS - TECHNICAL LIBRARY □ Phoenix, AZ

Minnerath, Janet, Med.Libn.
ALTON OCHSNER MEDICAL FOUNDATION - MEDICAL LIBRARY □ New Orleans, LA

Minney, Mary Alice, Dir., Dept. of Educ.
INTERNATIONAL CONSUMER CREDIT ASSOCIATION - DEPARTMENT OF EDUCATION LIBRARY □ St. Louis, MO

Minnich, Ann, Asst.
CHARLESTON GAZETTE-MAIL - LIBRARY □ Charleston, WV

Minns, Edith, Ch.Libn.
PENINSULA LIBRARY AND HISTORICAL SOCIETY □ Peninsula, OH

Minor, Carol, Info.Ctr./Lib.Mgr.
UNITED BANK OF DENVER, N.A. - INFORMATION CENTER LIBRARY □ Denver, CO

Minor, Charlotte, Coll.Dev.Libn.
EMBRY RIDDLE AERONAUTICAL UNIVERSITY - LEARNING RESOURCES CENTER □ Daytona Beach, FL

Minor, Dr. John T., Sr.Info.Spec.
CONOCO, INC. - RESEARCH AND DEVELOPMENT DEPARTMENT - TECHNICAL INFORMATION SERVICES □ Ponca City, OK

Minott, Laurel, Libn.
MICHIGAN STATE DEPARTMENT OF MENTAL HEALTH - LIBRARY □ Lansing, MI

Minsky, Norman, Sec./Tres.
PENOBSCOT BAR LIBRARY ASSOCIATION - LIBRARY □ Bangor, ME

Mintel, Richard H., Asst.Libn.
TRINITY LUTHERAN SEMINARY - LIBRARY □ Columbus, OH

Minter, Nancy, Ed.
NATIONAL LEAGUE OF CITIES - MUNICIPAL REFERENCE SERVICE □ Washington, DC

Minton, Bonny, Asst.Chf.
DISTRICT OF COLUMBIA PUBLIC LIBRARY - TECHNOLOGY AND SCIENCE DIVISION □ Washington, DC

Minton, James O., Map Libn.
UNIVERSITY OF MICHIGAN - MAP ROOM □ Ann Arbor, MI

Mintz, Anne, Libn.
LAZARD FRERES AND COMPANY - FINANCIAL LIBRARY† □ New York, NY

Mintz, Edith B., Hd. Libn.
ARTHUR D. LITTLE, INC. - MANAGEMENT LIBRARY □ Cambridge, MA

Mirabal, Alfonso, Data User Serv.Off.
U.S. BUREAU OF THE CENSUS - REGIONAL DATA USER SERVICE - DALLAS REGIONAL OFFICE - LIBRARY □ Dallas, TX

Mirabel, Lorraine M., Project Dir.
MEXICAN-AMERICAN OPPORTUNITY FOUNDATION - INFORMATION AND REFERRAL SERVICE - RESOURCE CENTER □ Monterey Park, CA

Mirabello, Vincent J., Lib.Ck.
WESTINGHOUSE ELECTRIC CORPORATION - LIBRARY 3-S-14 □ East Pittsburgh, PA

Miracle, Laura J., Libn.
CHICAGO BOARD OF TRADE - LIBRARY □ Chicago, IL

Miranda, Altagracia, Hd., Tech.Serv.
UNIVERSITY OF PUERTO RICO - LAW SCHOOL LIBRARY □ Rio Piedras, PR

Miranda, Cecilia, Libn.
SACRAMENTO PEAK OBSERVATORY - LIBRARY □ Sunspot, NM

Mirell, Sandee, Libn.
LOS ANGELES CITY ATTORNEY - LAW LIBRARY □ Los Angeles, CA

Mirly, Joann, Coord., Lib.Rsrcs.
CONCORDIA SEMINARY - LIBRARY □ St. Louis, MO

Miron, Jacques, Off.-In-Charge
CANADA - ATMOSPHERIC ENVIRONMENT SERVICE - QUEBEC REGION - BIBLIOTHEQUE REGIONALE □ St. Laurent, PQ

Mironeullo, Rimma, Tech.Libn.
AEROJET-CHEMICAL CORPORATION - AEROJET TACTICAL PROPULSION COMPANY - TECHNICAL INFORMATION CENTER □ Sacramento, CA

Mirsky, Phyllis, Libn.
TEMPLE ADATH ISRAEL - RUBEN LIBRARY† □ Merion, PA

Mirsky, Sonya Wohl, Libn./Cur., Spec.Coll.
ROCKEFELLER UNIVERSITY - LIBRARY □ New York, NY

Mirth, Karlo J., Mgr.
FOSTER WHEELER DEVELOPMENT CORPORATION - RESEARCH INFORMATION CENTER AND LIBRARY □ Livingston, NJ

Misaghi, Patricia, Acq.
UNIVERSITY OF ARIZONA - COLLEGE OF LAW LIBRARY □ Tucson, AZ

Mishkin, Leah, Libn. & Cur.
HEBREW THEOLOGICAL COLLEGE - SAUL SILBER MEMORIAL LIBRARY □ Skokie, IL

Miska, John P., Area Coord.
CANADA - AGRICULTURE CANADA - RESEARCH STATION, LETHBRIDGE - LIBRARY □ Lethbridge, AB

Miskin, Rose, Libn.
JEWISH PUBLIC LIBRARY OF TORONTO □ Toronto, ON

Miskowski, Bro. Timothy, Cat./AV Libn.
MOUNT ST. MARY'S SEMINARY OF THE WEST - LIBRARY □ Cincinnati, OH

Mislavitz, MaryAnn J., Mgr., Tech.Info.
AMERICAN CAN COMPANY - TECHNICAL INFORMATION CENTER □ Greenwich, CT

Missar, Charles D., Lib.Dir.
NATIONAL INSTITUTE OF EDUCATION - EDUCATIONAL RESEARCH LIBRARY □ Washington, DC

Missoff, Christine, Asst.Libn.
NEW YORK STATE LIBRARY - MANUSCRIPTS AND SPECIAL COLLECTION □ Albany, NY

Mistaras, Evangeline, Hd., Ref.
NORTHEASTERN ILLINOIS UNIVERSITY - LIBRARY □ Chicago, IL

Mistrik, Mrs. Marion, Libn.
AIR TRANSPORT ASSOCIATION OF AMERICA - LIBRARY □ Washington, DC

Mitchel, Nonie, Libn.
TEXAS STATE AERONAUTICS COMMISSION - LIBRARY & INFORMATION CENTER □ Austin, TX

Mitchell, Alice, Libn.
LEVENTHAL (Kenneth) & COMPANY - LIBRARY □ Los Angeles, CA

Mitchell, Ann M., Hd.Pub.Serv.
UNIVERSITY OF CALIFORNIA, LOS ANGELES - LAW LIBRARY† □ Los Angeles, CA

Mitchell, Aubrey H., Libn.
UNIVERSITY OF TENNESSEE - AGRICULTURE-VETERINARY MEDICINE LIBRARY □ Knoxville, TN

Mitchell, Bonnie J., Circ.Libn.
MOHAWK VALLEY COMMUNITY COLLEGE - LIBRARY □ Utica, NY

Mitchell, Carolyn, Libn.
MEDICAL PLANNING ASSOCIATES - LIBRARY □ Malibu, CA

Mitchell, Carolyn W., Hd.Libn.
ENVIRONMENTAL PROTECTION AGENCY - REGION IV LIBRARY □ Atlanta, GA

Mitchell, David, Asst.Libn.
CALIFORNIA RAILWAY MUSEUM - LIBRARY □ Suisun City, CA

Mitchell, Doris, Sci. & Tech.Libn.
HOWARD UNIVERSITY - CHEMISTRY LIBRARY □ Washington, DC

Mitchell, Doris, Sci. & Tech.Libn.
HOWARD UNIVERSITY - ENGINEERING LIBRARY □ Washington, DC

Mitchell, Edward S., Jr., Libn.
CHRONICLE-HERALD NEWS - LIBRARY □ Augusta, GA

Mitchell, Elaine, Dir. of Info.
WILMER, CUTLER & PICKERING - LAW LIBRARY □ Washington, DC

Mitchell, Herbert
COLUMBIA UNIVERSITY - AVERY ARCHITECTURAL AND FINE ARTS LIBRARY □ New York, NY

Mitchell, J.B., Hd.Libn.
FRANKLIN COUNTY HISTORICAL SOCIETY - STANLEY LIBRARY □ Ferrum, VA

Mitchell, J.G., Legislative Libn.
BRITISH COLUMBIA - LEGISLATIVE LIBRARY □ Victoria, BC

Mitchell, Joan, Biblog.
WILFRID LAURIER UNIVERSITY - LIBRARY □ Waterloo, ON

Mitchell, Joanna, Tech.Serv.
NORTHWESTERN UNIVERSITY - SEELEY G. MUDD LIBRARY FOR SCIENCE AND ENGINEERING □ Evanston, IL

Mitchell, Judy, Hd.Libn.
SOUTHERN BIBLE COLLEGE - WORDEN MC DONALD LIBRARY □ Houston, TX

Mitchell, June M., Chf., Lib.Serv.
U.S. VETERANS ADMINISTRATION (NY-Syracuse) - MEDICAL CENTER LIBRARY □ Syracuse, NY

Mitchell, Larry G., Cur.
CLASSIC AMX CLUB, INTERNATIONAL - AMX LIBRARY □ Loves Park, IL

Mitchell, Lynn M., Lib.Techn.
U.S. NATL. PARK SERVICE - MIDWEST ARCHEOLOGICAL CENTER - RESEARCH LIBRARY □ Lincoln, NE

Mitchell, Marcus J., Pub.Rel.Dir.
METROPOLITAN COUNCIL FOR EDUCATIONAL OPPORTUNITY - LIBRARY □ Roxbury, MA

Mitchell, Margaret, Libn.
TORONTO INSTITUTE OF MEDICAL TECHNOLOGY - LIBRARY □ Toronto, ON

Mitchell, Marian, Libn.
TRINITY UNIVERSITY - DALLAS THEATER CENTER LIBRARY □ Dallas, TX

Mitchell, Martha L., Univ.Archv.
BROWN UNIVERSITY - SPECIAL COLLECTIONS† □ Providence, RI

Mitchell, Martha M., Libn.
CHEMED CORPORATION - DEARBORN CHEMICAL (U.S.) LIBRARY □ Lake Zurich, IL

Mitchell, Mary E., Ref.Libn.
UNIVERSITY OF BRITISH COLUMBIA - LAW LIBRARY □ Vancouver, BC

Mitchell, Robert P., Intl.Doc.Libn.
UNIVERSITY OF ARIZONA - GOVERNMENT DOCUMENTS DEPARTMENT □ Tucson, AZ

Mitchell, Shannon, Libn.
WARNER, NORCROSS & JUDD - LIBRARY □ Grand Rapids, MI

Mitchell, Sonya, Dir.
MEAD CORPORATION - MEAD PAPERS - MEAD LIBRARY OF IDEAS □ Dayton, OH

Mitchell, Susan, Res.Libn., Med.
METROPOLITAN LIFE INSURANCE COMPANY - LIBRARY □ New York, NY

Mitchell, T.W., Chf.
NORTH CAROLINA STATE DEPT. OF CULTURAL RESOURCES - DIV. OF ARCHIVES AND HISTORY - ARCHIVES & RECORDS SECTION □ Raleigh, NC

Mitchell, Terry H., Park Techn.
U.S. NATL. PARK SERVICE - MOORES CREEK NATL. BATTLEFIELD - LIBRARY □ Currie, NC

Mitchell, William L., Consrv.Libn.
UNIVERSITY OF KANSAS - DEPARTMENT OF SPECIAL COLLECTIONS □ Lawrence, KS

Mittelbach, Frank G., Dir.
UNIVERSITY OF CALIFORNIA, LOS ANGELES - HOUSING, REAL ESTATE & URBAN LAND STUDIES PROGRAM COLLECTION □ Los Angeles, CA

Mittelberger, Ernest G., Musm.Dir.
WINE MUSEUM OF SAN FRANCISCO - CHRISTIAN BROTHERS RARE WINE BOOKS LIBRARY □ San Francisco, CA

Miu, Anna, Cat.
TEXAS SOUTHERN UNIVERSITY - LIBRARY - HEARTMAN COLLECTION □ Houston, TX

Miura, Verna K., Libn.
HONOLULU (City And County) - MUNICIPAL REFERENCE AND RECORDS CENTER □ Honolulu, HI

Mixer, Robert, Asst.Dir.
UNIVERSITY OF SOUTHERN CALIFORNIA - NASA INDUSTRIAL APPLICATION CENTER (NIAC) □ Los Angeles, CA

Mixter, Janet K., Med.Biblog.Libn.
LOYOLA UNIVERSITY OF CHICAGO - MEDICAL CENTER LIBRARY □ Maywood, IL

Miyamoto, Jean, Lib.Asst.
UNIVERSITY OF CALIFORNIA, LOS ANGELES - UNIVERSITY ELEMENTARY SCHOOL LIBRARY □ Los Angeles, CA

Mlotek, Eleanor, Archv.
YIVO INSTITUTE FOR JEWISH RESEARCH - LIBRARY AND ARCHIVES □ New York, NY

Moak, Harold, Dir./Eng.Plan.
CURTISS-WRIGHT CORPORATION - LIBRARY SERVICES† □ Wood-Ridge, NJ

Moake, Virginia H., Chf., Lib.Serv.
U.S. VETERANS ADMINISTRATION (IL- Marion) - HOSPITAL LIBRARY □ Marion, IL

Mobley, Arthur B., HRIS Mgr.
NATIONAL ACADEMY OF SCIENCES - NATIONAL RESEARCH COUNCIL - HIGHWAY RESEARCH INFORMATION SERVICE □ Washington, DC

Mobley, Emily R., Supv./Reader Serv.
GENERAL MOTORS CORPORATION - RESEARCH LABORATORIES LIBRARY □ Warren, MI

Mobley, Sara, Libn.
ARGUS RESEARCH CORPORATION - LIBRARY □ New York, NY

Mobley, Sara, Asst.Libn./Pub.Serv.
EMORY UNIVERSITY - PITTS THEOLOGY LIBRARY □ Atlanta, GA

Mochedlover, Helene, Dept.Mgr.
LOS ANGELES PUBLIC LIBRARY - LITERATURE & PHILOLOGY DEPARTMENT □ Los Angeles, CA

Mochedlover, Helene G., Dept.Mgr.
LOS ANGELES PUBLIC LIBRARY - FICTION DEPARTMENT □ Los Angeles, CA

Mochizuki, Tomie, Libn.
JAPAN SOCIETY, INC. - LIBRARY □ New York, NY

Modien, Rean, Lib.Techn.
ALBERTA - DEPARTMENT OF CONSUMER AND
CORPORATE AFFAIRS - RESOURCE CENTRE □
Edmonton, AB

Moeckel, Nancy, Sci.Libn.
MIAMI UNIVERSITY - SCIENCE LIBRARY □
Oxford, OH

Moedritzer, Anne, Ref.Libn.
EDEN THEOLOGICAL SEMINARY - LIBRARY □
Webster Groves, MO

Moeller, Dr. Henry R., Libn.
CENTRAL BAPTIST THEOLOGICAL SEMINARY -
LIBRARY □ Kansas City, KS

Moeller, Kathleen A., Dir., Lib.Serv.
OVERLOOK HOSPITAL - HEALTH SCIENCES
LIBRARY □ Summit, NJ

Moeny, Christine, Spec.Coll.
ADAMS STATE COLLEGE - LIBRARY □ Alamosa,
CO

Moeny, Don, AV
ADAMS STATE COLLEGE - LIBRARY □ Alamosa,
CO

Moffa, Monica A., Pub.Serv.Libn.
INDIANA UNIVERSITY - SCHOOL OF
DENTISTRY LIBRARY □ Indianapolis, IN

Moffat, Patricia A., Libn.
BENEFICIAL MANAGEMENT CORPORATION -
LIBRARY □ Morristown, NJ

Moffatt, Pattie, Per.
UNIVERSITY OF ARKANSAS, MONTICELLO -
LIBRARY† □ Monticello, AR

Moffeit, Tony, Hd., Pub. & Tech.Serv.
UNIVERSITY OF SOUTHERN COLORADO -
LIBRARY - SPECIAL COLLECTIONS □ Pueblo, CO

Moffett, Claire, Bus.Libn.
PRUDENTIAL INSURANCE COMPANY OF
AMERICA - BUSINESS LIBRARY □ Houston, TX

Moffett, Maggie, Asst.Libn.
HONEYWELL, INC. - CORPORATE TECHNOLOGY
CENTER LIBRARY □ Bloomington, MN

Moffitt, Fran, Libn.
DEERE & COMPANY - LAW LIBRARY □ Moline, IL

Moffitt, Mary, Libn.
WASHINGTON STATE SCHOOL FOR THE DEAF -
LEARNING RESOURCE CENTER □ Vancouver,
WA

Moger, Elizabeth Haas, Kpr.
SOCIETY OF FRIENDS - NEW YORK YEARLY
MEETING - RECORDS COMMITTEE - HAVILAND
RECORDS ROOM □ New York, NY

Mogford, Astrid, Transl.Coord.
BELL TELEPHONE LABORATORIES, INC. -
TECHNICAL LIBRARY □ Murray Hill, NJ

Mohlhenrich, John S., Chf.Pk. Interpreter
U.S. NATL. PARK SERVICE - NATCHEZ TRACE
PARKWAY - LIBRARY & VISITOR CENTER □
Tupelo, MS

Mohlke, Catherine M., Dir., Lib.Serv.
WESTVILLE CORRECTIONAL CENTER - STAFF
LIBRARY □ Westville, IN

Mohn, Doris, Cat.
BRYN MAWR HOSPITAL - MEDICAL LIBRARY □
Bryn Mawr, PA

Moholt, Mrs. E. Perry, Tech.Proc.Libn.
CARROLL COLLEGE - LIBRARY □ Helena, MT

Mohr, Carolyn, Libn.
MEIKLEJOHN CIVIL LIBERTIES INSTITUTE -
LIBRARY □ Berkeley, CA

Mohr, Elizabeth, Adm.Libn.
U.S. DEPT. OF ENERGY - BARTLESVILLE
ENERGY TECHNOLOGY CENTER LIBRARY □
Bartlesville, OK

Mohrer, Fruma, Archv.
YIVO INSTITUTE FOR JEWISH RESEARCH -
LIBRARY AND ARCHIVES □ New York, NY

Mohrman, Betty J., Libn.
AMERICAN GENERAL CAPITAL MANAGEMENT,
INC. - RESEARCH LIBRARY □ Houston, TX

Mohrman, Robert, Patients' Libn.
U.S. VETERANS ADMINISTRATION (NY-
Montrose) - HOSPITAL LIBRARY □ Montrose, NY

Mohundro, Jenny, AV Libn.
TEXAS STATE TECHNICAL INSTITUTE, WACO
CAMPUS - LEARNING RESOURCE CENTER □
Waco, TX

Moinester, Nina, Circ.Libn.
PACE UNIVERSITY - LIBRARY □ New York, NY

Moir, Lindsay, Asst.Libn.
GLENBOW-ALBERTA INSTITUTE - LIBRARY &
ARCHIVES □ Calgary, AB

Moise, C., Ref.
CANADA - FISHERIES & OCEANS - LIBRARY □
Ottawa, ON

Moist, Sherman, Libn.
DELAWARE COUNTY LAW LIBRARY □ Delaware,
OH

Mok, Vicky, Tech.Serv.Libn.
FANSHAWE COLLEGE OF APPLIED ARTS AND
TECHNOLOGY - MAIN LIBRARY □ London, ON

Mokry, Frantisek, Cat.
COLUMBIA UNIVERSITY - LAW LIBRARY □ New
York, NY

Moldenhauer, Hans, Dir.
MOLDENHAUER ARCHIVES □ Spokane, WA

Moldenhauer, Rosaleen, Dir.
MOLDENHAUER ARCHIVES □ Spokane, WA

Moles, Jean Ann, Ser.Libn.
UNIVERSITY OF ARKANSAS MEDICAL
SCIENCES CAMPUS - MEDICAL SCIENCES
LIBRARY □ Little Rock, AR

Molholt, Pat, Assoc.Dir.
RENSSELAER POLYTECHNIC INSTITUTE -
FOLSOM LIBRARY □ Troy, NY

Molieri, Loren, Libn.
IBM CORPORATION - GENERAL PRODUCTS
DIVISION - TECHNICAL INFORMATION
CENTER □ San Jose, CA

Molieri, Loren, Sr.Asst.Libn.
SAN JOSE STATE UNIVERSITY - LIBRARY -
SCIENCE/ENGINEERING DEPARTMENT† □ San
Jose, CA

Moline, Sandra, Hd.
UNIVERSITY OF WISCONSIN, MADISON -
PHYSICS LIBRARY □ Madison, WI

Molitor, Mary Ann, Asst.Libn.
MC DERMOTT, WILL & EMERY - LIBRARY □
Chicago, IL

Moll, Marita, Prog.Asst.
CANADIAN TEACHERS' FEDERATION - GEORGE
G. CROSKERY MEMORIAL LIBRARY □ Ottawa,
ON

Moll, Mary Ellen, Libn.
ENGLISH-SPEAKING UNION OF THE U.S.A. -
BOOKS ACROSS THE SEA LIBRARY □ New York,
NY

Moll, Sheila, Libn.
YORK BOROUGH BOARD OF EDUCATION -
PROFESSIONAL LIBRARY □ Toronto, ON

Molloy, Bridget, Libn.
UNIVERSITY OF SOUTHERN CALIFORNIA -
PHILOSOPHY LIBRARY □ Los Angeles, CA

Molod, Samuel E., Dp. State Libn.
CONNECTICUT STATE LIBRARY □ Hartford, CT

Moloney, Louis C., Dir., LRC
SOUTHWEST TEXAS STATE UNIVERSITY -
LEARNING RESOURCES CENTER □ San Marcos,
TX

Moloney, Walter, Dir.
MEMPHIS BOTANIC GARDEN FOUNDATION,
INC. - GOLDSMITH CIVIC GARDEN CTR. -
SYBIL MALLOY MEMORIAL LIBRARY □
Memphis, TN

Mols, Kathleen B., Asst.Libn.
ST. MARY'S HOSPITAL - LIBRARY □ Grand
Rapids, MI

Molson, Jean, Libn.
REGISTERED NURSES' ASSOCIATION OF
BRITISH COLUMBIA - LIBRARY □ Vancouver, BC

Molter, Maureen, Libn.
MEMORIAL HOSPITAL - HEALTH SCIENCES
LIBRARY □ Easton, MD

Moltke-Hansen, David, Archv.
SOUTH CAROLINA HISTORICAL SOCIETY -
LIBRARY □ Charleston, SC

Moltz, Sandra S., Tech.Libn.
GENERAL ELECTRIC COMPANY - AIRCRAFT
ENGINE GROUP - DR. C.W. SMITH TECHNICAL
INFORMATION CENTER □ Lynn, MA

Momjian, Edmond J., Supv., Info.Serv.
CALIFORNIA INSTITUTE OF TECHNOLOGY -
JET PROPULSION LABORATORY - LIBRARY □
Pasadena, CA

Momosor, Stetson P., Res.Anl., Lib.Sci.
UNIVERSITY OF ALASKA, ANCHORAGE -
ARCTIC ENVIRONMENTAL INFORMATION AND
DATA CENTER □ Anchorage, AK

Monaco, Ralph, Asst. Law Libn.
ST. JOHN'S UNIVERSITY - LAW LIBRARY □
Jamaica, NY

Monahon, Ruth, Med.Biblog.
UNIVERSITY OF SOUTHERN CALIFORNIA -
HEALTH SCIENCES CAMPUS - NORRIS
MEDICAL LIBRARY □ Los Angeles, CA

Mondou, Cecile, Hd.Libn.
CANADA - SECRETARY OF STATE -
TRANSLATION BUREAU - LIBRARY □ Montreal,
PQ

Monette, Gerard, Asst. to Dir.
LA PRESSE, LTEE. - CENTRE DE
DOCUMENTATION □ Montreal, PQ

Money, David, Asst.Libn.
OKLAHOMA COLLEGE OF OSTEOPATHIC
MEDICINE & SURGERY - LIBRARY □ Tulsa, OK

Monger, GeorgeAnne, Pub.Serv./Assoc.Dir.
LAMAR UNIVERSITY - MARY AND JOHN GRAY
LIBRARY □ Beaumont, TX

Monical, Ruth
SOUTHERN OREGON STATE COLLEGE -
LIBRARY □ Ashland, OR

Monighetti, Kathleen, Asst.Libn.
COMBUSTION ENGINEERING, INC. - POWER
SYSTEMS GROUP LIBRARY SERVICES □
Windsor, CT

Monk, Patricia Rodi, Chf.Libn.
U.S. COURT OF APPEALS, 8TH CIRCUIT -
LIBRARY □ St. Louis, MO

Monkhouse, R.E., Educ. Media Cons.
WELLINGTON COUNTY BOARD OF EDUCATION
- EDUCATION LIBRARY □ Guelph, ON

Monkhouse, Valerie, Chf.Lib.Div.
CANADA - NATIONAL MUSEUMS OF CANADA -
LIBRARY □ Ottawa, ON

Monkmeyer, Hilde R., Hd.
MONKMEYER PRESS PHOTO SERVICE □ New
York, NY

Monnot, Anne, Libn.
PRO FOOTBALL HALL OF FAME - LIBRARY/
RESEARCH CENTER □ Canton, OH

Monroe, Alden N., Mss.Supv.
CINCINNATI HISTORICAL SOCIETY - LIBRARY
□ Cincinnati, OH

Monroe, J., Ch.Info.Serv.Ctr.
WAYNE STATE UNIVERSITY - G. FLINT PURDY
LIBRARY □ Detroit, MI

Monroe, Jean, Ref.Libn.
WAYNE STATE UNIVERSITY - SCIENCE
LIBRARY □ Detroit, MI

Monroe, Linda, Info.Spec.
ARMOUR RESEARCH CENTER - LIBRARY □
Scottsdale, AZ

Monsivais, Jean, Secretary
LUTHERAN MEDICAL CENTER - MEDICAL
LIBRARY □ St. Louis, MO

Monsma, Marvin E., Dir.
CALVIN COLLEGE AND SEMINARY - LIBRARY □
Grand Rapids, MI

Monson, Cleo, Asst.Cur.
HOLY LAND MUSEUM & LIBRARY □ New York,
NY

Monta, Thelma, Asst.Libn.
SAN DIEGO MUSEUM OF MAN - SCIENTIFIC
LIBRARY □ San Diego, CA

Montag, Hermina, Asst.Div.Hd.
QUEENS BOROUGH PUBLIC LIBRARY - SCIENCE
& TECHNOLOGY DIVISION □ Jamaica, NY

Montag, Janet, Tech.Rsrcs.
WAYNE STATE COLLEGE - U.S. CONN LIBRARY
□ Wayne, NE

Montague, Katherine, Libn.
MEMPHIS-SHELBY COUNTY PUBLIC LIBRARY
AND INFO. CTR. - SCIENCE/BUSINESS/SOCIAL
SCIENCES DEPT. □ Memphis, TN

Montague, M.E., Lib.Techn.
PROTESTANT SCHOOL BOARD OF GREATER
MONTREAL - PROFESSIONAL LIBRARY □
Montreal, PQ

Montee, Monty L., Hd.Cat.Libn.
YALE UNIVERSITY - MEDICAL LIBRARY □ New
Haven, CT

Montekio, Abraham, Law Libn.
NEW YORK STATE SUPREME COURT - 2ND
JUDICIAL DISTRICT - LAW LIBRARY □
Brooklyn, NY

Montesinos, Mary Jane, Sr.Info.Sci.
COCA-COLA COMPANY - TECHNICAL
INFORMATION SERVICES □ Atlanta, GA

Montgomery, Dale, Dir.
UNIVERSITY OF WISCONSIN, LA CROSSE -
AUDIOVISUAL CENTER - FILM LIBRARY □ La
Crosse, WI

Montgomery, Dianne, Adm. Aide
FLINT DEPARTMENT OF COMMUNITY
DEVELOPMENT - LIBRARY □ Flint, MI

Montgomery, Dorothy, Govt.Pub.Libn.
WESTERN ILLINOIS UNIVERSITY - LIBRARIES
□ Macomb, IL

Montgomery, James W., Dir.
NEW YORK STATE OFFICE OF MENTAL HEALTH
- NEW YORK STATE PSYCHIATRIC INSTITUTE
- LIBRARY □ New York, NY

Montgomery, John E., Dir.
WEST VIRGINIA STATE SUPREME COURT OF
APPEALS - STATE LAW LIBRARY □ Charleston,
WV

Montgomery, Jon, Supt.
U.S. NATL. PARK SERVICE - APPOMATTOX
COURT HOUSE NATL. HISTORICAL PARK -
LIBRARY □ Appomattox, VA

Montgomery, Linda F., Dir.
MINNESOTA STATE LEGISLATIVE REFERENCE
LIBRARY □ St. Paul, MN

Montgomery, Mary E., Res.Libn.
EATON CORPORATION - ENGINEERING &
RESEARCH CENTER LIBRARY □ Southfield, MI

Montgomery, Sherry, Hd. AV Dept.
PHILADELPHIA COLLEGE OF PHARMACY AND
SCIENCE - JOSEPH W. ENGLAND LIBRARY □
Philadelphia, PA

Montgomery, Susan J., Mgr.
CONTINENTAL ILLINOIS NATIONAL BANK AND
TRUST COMPANY OF CHICAGO -
INFORMATION SERVICES DIVISION □ Chicago,
IL

Monti, Dr. Laura V., Keeper
BOSTON PUBLIC LIBRARY - RARE BOOKS AND
MANUSCRIPTS □ Boston, MA

Montijo, Maria E., Tech.Serv.Dir.
PUERTO RICO - SUPREME COURT - LAW
LIBRARY □ San Juan, PR

Montplaisir, Isabelle, Libn.
MUSEE D'ART CONTEMPORAIN - CENTRE DE
DOCUMENTATION □ Montreal, PQ

Monty, Vivienne, Asst.Hd.
YORK UNIVERSITY - GOVERNMENT
DOCUMENTS/ADMINISTRATIVE STUDIES
LIBRARY □ Downsview, ON

Moody, Kenneth E., Dir.
SUNY - DOWNSTATE MEDICAL CENTER -
MEDICAL RESEARCH LIBRARY OF BROOKLYN†
□ Brooklyn, NY

Moomaw, Judith, Hd., Ser.Dept.
UNIVERSITY OF CALIFORNIA, DAVIS -
GENERAL LIBRARY □ Davis, CA

Moon, Margaret, Libn.
MUSKEGON BUSINESS COLLEGE - LIBRARY □
Muskegon, MI

Mooney, Aidan, Chf. Indexer
NEWSWEEK, INC. - LIBRARY □ New York, NY

Mooney, Margaret, Asst.Libn.
UNIVERSITY OF CALIFORNIA, RIVERSIDE -
GOVERNMENT PUBLICATIONS DEPARTMENT -
LIBRARY □ Riverside, CA

Mooney, Philip F., Mgr.
COCA-COLA COMPANY - ARCHIVES &
BUSINESS INFORMATION SERVICES □ Atlanta,
GA

Mooney, Sandra
LOUISIANA STATE UNIVERSITY - REFERENCE
SERVICES □ Baton Rouge, LA

Mooney, Shirley E., Libn.
PACIFIC PRESS, LTD. - PRESS LIBRARY □
Vancouver, BC

Mooneyham, Kate, Asst.Libn.
DURHAM HERALD-SUN NEWSPAPER - LIBRARY
□ Durham, NC

Moore, Aletta, Supv.
3M - BUSINESS INFORMATION SERVICE □ St.
Paul, MN

Moore, Ann, Hd., Ref.Dept.
CHICAGO STATE UNIVERSITY - DOUGLAS
LIBRARY □ Chicago, IL

Moore, Barbara, Sys.Libn.
UNIVERSITY OF WISCONSIN, WHITEWATER -
LIBRARY & LEARNING RESOURCES □
Whitewater, WI

Moore, Betty Rose, Lib.Serv.Coord.
COLUMBIA UNIVERSITY CANCER CENTER -
INSTITUTE OF CANCER RESEARCH □ New York,
NY

Moore, Beverly A., Dir.
UNIVERSITY OF SOUTHERN COLORADO -
LIBRARY - SPECIAL COLLECTIONS □ Pueblo, CO

Moore, Carleton B., Dir.
ARIZONA STATE UNIVERSITY - CENTER FOR
METEORITE STUDIES - LIBRARY □ Tempe, AZ

Moore, Catherine, Libn.
MASSACHUSETTS STATE DEPARTMENT OF
PUBLIC HEALTH - CENTRAL LIBRARY □ Boston,
MA

Moore, Celia L., Res.Asst.
PICKWICK INTERNATIONAL, INC. - RESOURCE
CENTER □ Minneapolis, MN

Moore, Cheryl, Sr.Ref.Libn.
HUMBER COLLEGE OF APPLIED ARTS &
TECHNOLOGY - LIBRARY □ Rexdale, ON

Moore, Dale, Libn.
METROPOLITAN TORONTO LIBRARY -
MUNICIPAL REFERENCE LIBRARY □ Toronto,
ON

Moore, David G., Libn.
ONE, INC. - BLANCHE M. BAKER MEMORIAL
LIBRARY □ Los Angeles, CA

Moore, Dorothy W., Dir.
PEPPERDINE UNIVERSITY - LIBRARY -
SPECIAL COLLECTIONS □ Malibu, CA

Moore, Edythe, Mgr.Lib.Serv.
AEROSPACE CORPORATION - CHARLES C.
LAURITSEN LIBRARY □ Los Angeles, CA

Moore, Elaine, Children's Libn.
CLARION STATE COLLEGE - RENA M. CARLSON
LIBRARY □ Clarion, PA

Moore, Dr. Everett L., Dir., Lib.Serv.
WOODBURY UNIVERSITY - LIBRARY □ Los
Angeles, CA

Moore, Florence, Libn.
XEROX CORPORATION - XEROX EDUCATION
PUBLICATIONS - LIBRARY □ Middletown, CT

Moore, Florence A., Dir., Tech.Serv.Br.
CANADA - LIBRARY OF PARLIAMENT □ Ottawa,
ON

Moore, Frances, Asst.Cur.
AUSTIN PUBLIC LIBRARY - AUSTIN-TRAVIS
COUNTY COLLECTION □ Austin, TX

Moore, Harriet, Libn.
ANOKA STATE HOSPITAL - LIBRARY □ Anoka,
MN

Moore, Heather, Tech.Serv.Libn.
CANADA - DEPARTMENT OF JUSTICE -
LIBRARY □ Ottawa, ON

Moore, Heather, Chf.
CANADA - SOLICITOR GENERAL CANADA -
CRIMINOLOGY DOCUMENTATION CENTRE □
Ottawa, ON

Moore, Helga, Libn.
SAN DIEGO PUBLIC LIBRARY - SCIENCE &
INDUSTRY SECTION □ San Diego, CA

Moore, Henrietta, Circ.Supv.
TUFTS UNIVERSITY - FLETCHER SCHOOL OF
LAW & DIPLOMACY - EDWIN GINN LIBRARY □
Medford, MA

Moore, J.D., Sec.
CANADIAN EXPORT ASSOCIATION - LIBRARY □
Ottawa, ON

Moore, James, Regional Archv.
WASHINGTON STATE OFFICE OF SECRETARY
OF STATE - DIVISION OF ARCHIVES AND
RECORD MANAGEMENT □ Olympia, WA

Moore, James C., Dir.
MUSEUM OF ALBUQUERQUE - LIBRARY □
Albuquerque, NM

Moore, Jane R., Chf.Libn.
CUNY - GRADUATE SCHOOL AND UNIVERSITY
CENTER - LIBRARY □ New York, NY

Moore, Jean, Dir.
SHARON HOSPITAL - HEALTH SCIENCES
LIBRARY □ Sharon, CT

Moore, John, Engr.Sect.Hd.
CHICAGO PUBLIC LIBRARY CENTRAL LIBRARY -
BUSINESS/SCIENCE/TECHNOLOGY DIVISION
□ Chicago, IL

Moore, John M., Br.Libn.
SAN FRANCISCO LAW LIBRARY □ San Francisco,
CA

Moore, Joleta, Supv.
E-SYSTEMS, INC. - DIVISION LIBRARY □
Greenville, TX

Moore, Julie L., Bibliographer
MOORE (Julie) & ASSOCIATES - LIBRARY □
Riverside, CA

Moore, Karen L., Tech.Libn.
SINGER COMPANY - HRB-SINGER, INC. -
TECHNICAL INFORMATION CENTER □ State
College, PA

Moore, Kate H., Libn.
U.S. FISH & WILDLIFE SERVICE - NATL.
RESERVOIR RESEARCH LIBRARY □ Fayetteville,
AR

Moore, Katherine, Asst.Libn.
KNOEDLER (M.) AND COMPANY, INC. - LIBRARY
□ New York, NY

Moore, Lennis, Adm.
MIDWEST OLD SETTLERS AND THRESHERS
ASSOCIATION - OLD THRESHERS OFFICE -
LIBRARY □ Mount Pleasant, IA

Moore, Linda, Libn.
CYRUS J. LAWRENCE, INC. - LIBRARY □ New
York, NY

Moore, Lou Ann, Med.Libn.
U.S. VETERANS ADMINISTRATION (IL-North
Chicago) - HOSPITAL LIBRARY □ North Chicago,
IL

Moore, M. Elizabeth, Human Rsrcs.Supv.
MICHIGAN BELL TELEPHONE COMPANY -
CORPORATE REFERENCE CENTER □ Detroit, MI

Moore, Mae Frances, Libn.
WESTERN HIGHWAY INSTITUTE - RESEARCH
LIBRARY □ San Bruno, CA

Moore, Marilyn, Coord., Ref.Serv.
MISSISSIPPI STATE RESEARCH AND
DEVELOPMENT CENTER - INFORMATION
SERVICES DIVISION □ Jackson, MS

Moore, Mary, Sr.Info.Spec., Mgt.
CONFERENCE BOARD, INC. - INFORMATION
SERVICE □ New York, NY

Moore, Mary, Media Libn.
TEXAS TECH UNIVERSITY - HEALTH SCIENCES
CENTER - LIBRARY OF THE HEALTH SCIENCES
□ Lubbock, TX

Moore, Mary L., Libn.
EXXON COMPANY, U.S.A. - GENERAL SERVICES
- LIBRARY □ Houston, TX

PERSONNEL

Moore, Maureen M., Libn.
INTERNATIONAL MONETARY FUND/WORLD
BANK - JOINT BANK-FUND LIBRARY □
Washington, DC
Moore, Melissa, Cat.
KENTUCKY STATE LAW LIBRARY □ Frankfort,
KY
Moore, Mike, Parts & Res.Supv.
HARRAH'S AUTOMOTIVE LIBRARY □ Reno, NV
Moore, Mildred, Libn.
UNIVERSITY OF KENTUCKY - MATHEMATICS
LIBRARY □ Lexington, KY
Moore, Nancy H., Adm.Libn.
SHENANDOAH COLLEGE & CONSERVATORY OF
MUSIC - HOWE LIBRARY □ Winchester, VA
Moore, Patricia, Ref.Libn.
SAN DIEGO STATE UNIVERSITY -
GOVERNMENT PUBLICATIONS DEPARTMENT □
San Diego, CA
Moore, Patricia, Hd.Tech.Serv./Acq.
UNIVERSITY OF CALIFORNIA, LOS ANGELES -
ART LIBRARY □ Los Angeles, CA
Moore, Ramona L., Ser.Libn.
UNIVERSITY OF MAINE SCHOOL OF LAW -
DONALD L. GARBRECHT LAW LIBRARY □
Portland, ME
Moore, Richard D., Dir.
INTERNATIONAL COMMUNICATION AGENCY -
OFFICE OF THE ASSOCIATE DIRECTORATE
FOR EDUCATIONAL & CULTURAL AFFAIRS □
Washington, DC
Moore, Richard E., Lib.Dir.
SOUTHERN OREGON STATE COLLEGE -
LIBRARY □ Ashland, OR
Moore, Russell J., Dir.
LONG BEACH MUSEUM OF ART - LIBRARY □
Long Beach, CA
Moore, Sara L., Libn.
DISTRICT OF COLUMBIA GENERAL HOSPITAL -
LIBRARY □ Washington, DC
Moore, Viola M.
INDIANA NORTHERN GRADUATE SCHOOL OF
PROFESSIONAL MANAGEMENT - LIBRARY □ Gas
City, IN
Moore, Vivian, Lib.Asst.
ACADEMY OF MEDICINE OF THE COUNTY OF
QUEENS, INC. - CARL M. BOETTIGER
MEMORIAL LIBRARY† □ Forest Hills, NY
Moore, Wanda Lucia, Libn./Ed.
NASHVILLE AND DAVIDSON COUNTY
METROPOLITAN PLANNING COMMISSION -
LIBRARY □ Nashville, TN
Moore, William, Asst.Libn.
SYMPHONY SOCIETY OF SAN ANTONIO -
SYMPHONY LIBRARY □ San Antonio, TX
Moore, William J., Dir. of Mus.
GREENSBORO HISTORICAL MUSEUM □
Greensboro, NC
Moore, William L., Exec.Dir.
GREATER DALLAS PLANNING COUNCIL -
LIBRARY AND INFORMATION CENTER □ Dallas,
TX
Moorhead, Katharine, Libn.
MADISON COUNTY HISTORICAL SOCIETY -
MUSEUM LIBRARY □ Edwardsville, IL
Moorhouse, Rose, Lib.Techn.
U.S. AIR FORCE BASE - GRISSOM BASE
LIBRARY □ Peru, IN
Moorman, Thomas R., Libn.
PUBLIC LIBRARY OF CINCINNATI AND
HAMILTON COUNTY - ART AND MUSIC
DEPARTMENT □ Cincinnati, OH
Moossy, Yvonne R., Libn.
NATIONAL STANDARDS COUNCIL OF
AMERICAN EMBROIDERERS - NSCAE LIBRARY
□ Carnegie, PA
Moppett, Martha, Res.Libn.
NATIONAL ENQUIRER - RESEARCH
DEPARTMENT LIBRARY □ Lantana, FL

Morain, Stanley A., Dir.
UNIVERSITY OF NEW MEXICO - TECHNOLOGY
APPLICATION CENTER □ Albuquerque, NM
Morales, Lina B., Hd.Libn.
UNIVERSITY OF PUERTO RICO - COLLEGE OF
EDUCATION - SELLES SOLA MEMORIAL
COLLECTION □ Rio Piedras, PR
Morales, Louis M. Rodriguez, Dir. Cultural Inst.
PUERTO RICAN CULTURE INSTITUTE - LUIS
MUNOZ RIVERA LIBRARY AND MUSEUM† □
Barranquitas, PR
Morales, Olga, Circ./Lib.Asst.
UNIVERSITY OF CALIFORNIA, LOS ANGELES -
ART LIBRARY □ Los Angeles, CA
Morales, Phyllis S., Finance Libn.
BECHTEL - FINANCE LIBRARY □ San Francisco,
CA
Moran, Dick, Hd. of Data Serv.
CINCINNATI CITY PLANNING COMMISSION -
PLANNING AND MANAGEMENT SUPPORT
SYSTEM LIBRARY □ Cincinnati, OH
Moran, John, Asst.Div.Hd.
QUEENS BOROUGH PUBLIC LIBRARY -
HISTORY, TRAVEL & BIOGRAPHY DIVISION □
Jamaica, NY
Moran, John C., Dir.
CRAWFORD (F. Marion) MEMORIAL SOCIETY -
BIBLIOTHECA CRAWFORDIANA □ Nashville, TN
Moran, M.M., Doc.Acq.
TRW, INC. - DEFENSE & SPACE SYSTEMS
GROUP - TECHNICAL INFORMATION CENTER □
Redondo Beach, CA
Moran, Marguerite K., Dir.
M AND T CHEMICALS, INC. - TECHNICAL &
BUSINESS INFORMATION CENTER □ Rahway,
NJ
Moran, Paul F., Libn.
U.S. BUREAU OF MINES - AVONDALE RESEARCH
CENTER LIBRARY □ Avondale, MD
Moran, Peter P., Archv.
SIMCOE COUNTY ARCHIVES □ Minesing, ON
Moran, Robert
INDIANA UNIVERSITY NORTHWEST -
CALUMET REGIONAL ARCHIVES □ Gary, IN
Moran, Sally P., Libn.
NASHVILLE BANNER - LIBRARY □ Nashville, TN
Moran, Sylvia J., Coord.
ERIE COMMUNITY COLLEGE NORTH - LIBRARY
RESOURCES CENTER □ Buffalo, NY
Moran, Terry, Assoc.Libn.
HOUGHTON MIFFLIN COMPANY - LIBRARY □
Boston, MA
Moran, Thomas R., Libn.
GEORGIA STATE SUPREME COURT LIBRARY† □
Atlanta, GA
Moravec, Georgina, Libn.
TORONTO CITY PLANNING AND DEVELOPMENT
DEPARTMENT - LIBRARY □ Toronto, ON
Morden, David Wayne, Lib.Techn.
CARLETON MEMORIAL HOSPITAL - HEALTH
SCIENCES LIBRARY □ Woodstock, NB
More, Hazel M., Tech.Libn.
FAIRCHILD INDUSTRIES - TECHNICAL
INFORMATION SERVICE - LIBRARY □
Germantown, MD
More, Susan L., Acq.Libn.
UNIVERSITY OF TEXAS SCHOOL OF LAW -
TARLTON LAW LIBRARY □ Austin, TX
Moreau, Evelyn M., Sec.
NEWTON PUBLIC SCHOOLS - TEACHERS'
PROFESSIONAL LIBRARY □ Newton, MA
Moreau, Vivian, Ref.Libn.
BOSTON COLLEGE - GRADUATE SCHOOL OF
SOCIAL WORK LIBRARY □ Chestnut Hill, MA
Moreland, Rachel, Circ.
KANSAS STATE UNIVERSITY - FARRELL
LIBRARY □ Manhattan, KS
Morell de Ramirez, Lueny, Dir.
UNIVERSITY OF PUERTO RICO - MAYAGUEZ
CAMPUS - TECHNICAL INFORMATION CENTER
□ Mayaguez, PR

Morency, Anita, Asst.Libn.
LIFE INSURANCE MARKETING AND RESEARCH
ASSOCIATION - LIBRARY □ Hartford, CT
Moreno, Esperanza A., Hd. Nursing/Med.Lib.
UNIVERSITY OF TEXAS, EL PASO - LIBRARY □
El Paso, TX
Moreno, Esperanza A., Hd.Libn.
UNIVERSITY OF TEXAS, EL PASO - - NURSING/
MEDICAL LIBRARY □ El Paso, TX
Moreno, Pierrette, Circ.Libn.
UNIVERSITY OF TEXAS SCHOOL OF LAW -
TARLTON LAW LIBRARY □ Austin, TX
Moretti, Patricia C., Dir.Lib.Serv.
EAGLEVILLE HOSPITAL AND REHABILITATION
CENTER - HENRY S. LOUCHHEIM MEDICAL
LIBRARY □ Eagleville, PA
Moretto, Kathleen J., Asst.Libn.
YALE UNIVERSITY - JOHN HERRICK JACKSON
MUSIC LIBRARY □ New Haven, CT
Morey, T.J., Tech.Serv.
XEROX CORPORATION - TECHNICAL
INFORMATION CENTER □ Webster, NY
Morf, Elisabeth, Libn.
GOETHE INSTITUTE MONTREAL - GERMAN
CULTURAL CENTRE - LIBRARY □ Montreal, PQ
Morgan, Mrs. Almarine, Libn.
MORGAN (J. Harris) LAW OFFICE - LAW
LIBRARY □ Greenville, TX
Morgan, Alyce, Asst.Libn.
NATIONAL TRUST FOR HISTORIC
PRESERVATION - INFORMATION SERVICES □
Washington, DC
Morgan, Charlotte M., Libn.
MANTENO MENTAL HEALTH CENTER - STAFF
LIBRARY □ Manteno, IL
Morgan, Cyril C., Supv.
NEWFOUNDLAND LIGHT & POWER COMPANY,
LTD. - CENTRAL RECORDS LIBRARY □ St.
John's, NF
Morgan, Dennis R., Dir., Leg.Ref.Bur.
OHIO STATE LEGISLATIVE REFERENCE
BUREAU - LIBRARY† □ Columbus, OH
Morgan, Dotty, Pub.Educ.Dir.
AMERICAN CANCER SOCIETY - HAWAII
DIVISION - LIBRARY □ Honolulu, HI
Morgan, Mr. E.C., Staff Archv.
SASKATCHEWAN ARCHIVES BOARD □ Regina,
SK
Morgan, Elizabeth, Libn.
ONTARIO - MINISTRY OF CONSUMER AND
COMMERCIAL RELATIONS - LIBRARY □
Toronto, ON
Morgan, F.P., Chf., Lib.Br.
U.S. AIR FORCE BASE - EGLIN BASE LIBRARY □
Eglin AFB, FL
Morgan, Harriette, Ser.
U.S. CENTER FOR DISEASE CONTROL - CDC
LIBRARY □ Atlanta, GA
Morgan, James E., Dir.
UNIVERSITY OF OREGON - HEALTH SCIENCES
CENTER - LIBRARY □ Portland, OR
Morgan, John, Hd.Res.Lit.Anl.
OREGON STATE UNIVERSITY - SCHOOL OF
OCEANOGRAPHY - NORTHWEST COASTAL
INFORMATION CENTER (NCIC) □ Newport, OR
Morgan, Julia B., Archv.
JOHNS HOPKINS UNIVERSITY - FERDINAND
HAMBURGER, JR. ARCHIVES □ Baltimore, MD
Morgan, Kathryn, Cur.
LOUISIANA STATE UNIVERSITY - E.A. MC
ILHENNY NATURAL HISTORY COLLECTION □
Baton Rouge, LA
Morgan, M.
RCA CORPORATION - PICTURE TUBE DIVISION
- LIBRARY □ Marion, IN
Morgan, Mrs. Madel J., Dir., Archv. & Lib.Div.
MISSISSIPPI STATE DEPARTMENT OF
ARCHIVES AND HISTORY - ARCHIVES AND
LIBRARY DIVISION □ Jackson, MS
Morgan, Mildred A., Libn.
TRINITY MEDICAL CENTER - SCHOOL OF
NURSING LIBRARY □ Minot, ND

Morgan, Nancy L., Lib.Asst.
PEABODY INSTITUTE LIBRARY - DANVERS ARCHIVAL CENTER □ Danvers, MA

Morgan, Paula, Music Libn.
PRINCETON UNIVERSITY - MUSIC COLLECTION† □ Princeton, NJ

Morgan, Dr. R.J., Dir.
COLLEGE OF CAPE BRETON - BEATON INSTITUTE ARCHIVES □ Sydney, NS

Morgan, R.P., Libn.
CANADA - PARKS CANADA, WESTERN REGION - LIBRARY □ Calgary, AB

Morgan, Vivian, Hd.
U.S. NATL. INSTITUTE FOR OCCUPATIONAL SAFETY & HEALTH - CLEARINGHOUSE FOR OCCUPATIONAL SAFETY & HEALTH INFO. □ Cincinnati, OH

Morgan-Meskill, Jane, Info. & Res. Assoc.
AMERICAN COUNCIL OF VOLUNTARY AGENCIES FOR FOREIGN SERVICE, INC. - TECH. ASSISTANCE INFO. CLEARING HOUSE □ New York, NY

Morganti, Mary L., P.R.Off./Asst.Corp.Archv.
WELLS FARGO BANK - HISTORY DEPARTMENT 921 □ San Francisco, CA

Morgenstern, Dan, Dir.
RUTGERS UNIVERSITY, THE STATE UNIVERSITY OF NEW JERSEY - INSTITUTE OF JAZZ STUDIES □ Newark, NJ

Moriarty, Paul V., Asst.Dir.
UNIVERSITY OF WISCONSIN, PLATTEVILLE - KARRMANN LIBRARY □ Platteville, WI

Morin, Denise Paquet, Lib.Techn.
HOPITAL ST-FRANCOIS D'ASSISE - MEDICAL & ADMINISTRATIVE LIBRARY □ Quebec, PQ

Morin, Jeannine, Tech.Serv.
QUEBEC PROVINCE - MINISTERE DES AFFAIRES CULTURELLES - CENTRE DE DOCUMENTATION □ Quebec, PQ

Moris, Mary Lee, Cat.Libn.
EASTERN NEW MEXICO UNIVERSITY - GOLDEN LIBRARY □ Portales, NM

Morison, William J., Dir./Univ.Archv.
UNIVERSITY OF LOUISVILLE - UNIVERSITY ARCHIVES AND RECORDS CENTER □ Louisville, KY

Moritz, Thomas D., Asst.Libn.
UNIVERSITY OF WASHINGTON - FISHERIES-OCEANOGRAPHY LIBRARY □ Seattle, WA

Moritz, Thomas D., Libn.
UNIVERSITY OF WASHINGTON - FRIDAY HARBOR LABORATORIES - LIBRARY □ Friday Harbor, WA

Morley, Mae, Libn.
KINGSTON PSYCHIATRIC HOSPITAL - STAFF LIBRARY □ Kingston, ON

Morley, Nancy G., Libn.
INTERNATIONAL COUNCIL OF SHOPPING CENTERS - LIBRARY □ New York, NY

Morley, Sarah Knox, Libn.
LOS LUNAS HOSPITAL AND TRAINING SCHOOL - LIBRARY AND RESOURCE CENTER □ Los Lunas, NM

Morley, William F.E., Cur., Spec.Coll.
QUEEN'S UNIVERSITY AT KINGSTON - SPECIAL COLLECTIONS □ Kingston, ON

Morneau, Francine, Bibliotechnicienne
QUEBEC PROVINCE - MINISTERE DU LOISIR, DE LA CHASSE ET DE LA PECHE - BIBLIOTHEQUE DE LA FAUNE □ Orsainville, PQ

Morotte, Anne Marie, Exec.Dir.
FRENCH AMERICAN CULTURAL SERVICES AND EDUCATIONAL AID (FACSEA) □ New York, NY

Morphet, Norman D., Sect.Chf.
SUN COMPANY - LIBRARY & INFORMATION SERVICE □ Marcus Hook, PA

Morrell, Stephanie, Corp.Tech.Libn.
AMERICAN EXPRESS COMPANY - CORPORATE SYSTEMS & COMMUNICATIONS INFORMATION CENTER □ New York, NY

Morrill, Juanita H., Libn.
EASTERN STATE HOSPITAL - RESOURCE LIBRARY □ Lexington, KY

Morrill, Katherine, Asst.Libn.
NEW HAMPSHIRE HISTORICAL SOCIETY - LIBRARY □ Concord, NH

Morris, Beth, Res.Dept.Libn.
DEAN WITTER REYNOLDS, INC. - RESEARCH DEPARTMENT LIBRARY □ New York, NY

Morris, Bonnie, Lib.Adm.
MOUNT OLIVET LUTHERAN CHURCH - LIBRARY □ Minneapolis, MN

Morris, Caroline, Libn.-Archv.
PENNSYLVANIA HOSPITAL - DEPARTMENT FOR SICK AND INJURED - HISTORICAL LIBRARY □ Philadelphia, PA

Morris, Caroline, Libn.-Archv.
PENNSYLVANIA HOSPITAL - DEPARTMENT FOR SICK AND INJURED - MEDICAL LIBRARY □ Philadelphia, PA

Morris, Charlene, Tech.Libn.
E-SYSTEMS, INC. - GARLAND DIVISION - TECHNICAL LIBRARY □ Dallas, TX

Morris, Dilys E., Monographs
IOWA STATE UNIVERSITY - LIBRARY □ Ames, IA

Morris, Dorothy, Chf., Lib.
U.S. NASA - LEWIS RESEARCH CENTER - LIBRARY □ Cleveland, OH

Morris, Dorothy G., Libn.
FRESNO COUNTY LAW LIBRARY □ Fresno, CA

Morris, Gerald E., Libn.
MYSTIC SEAPORT, INC. - G.W. BLUNT WHITE LIBRARY □ Mystic, CT

Morris, Jacquelyn, Ref.Libn.
CORNELL UNIVERSITY - ALBERT R. MANN LIBRARY □ Ithaca, NY

Morris, Jean, Libn.
ALAMEDA COUNTY LIBRARY - BUSINESS & GOVERNMENT LIBRARY □ Oakland, CA

Morris, Jo Ann, Dir.
STAMFORD HOSPITAL - HEALTH SCIENCES LIBRARY □ Stamford, CT

Morris, Joan, Hd., Photo.Archv.
FLORIDA STATE UNIVERSITY - SPECIAL COLLECTIONS □ Tallahassee, FL

Morris, Joan L., Hd., Photo Archives
FLORIDA STATE UNIVERSITY - FLORIDA PHOTOGRAPHIC ARCHIVES □ Tallahassee, FL

Morris, Joann, Libn.
HALIFAX REGIONAL VOCATIONAL SCHOOL - LIBRARY □ Halifax, NS

Morris, Louise A., Libn.
AKRON - DEPARTMENT OF PLANNING AND URBAN RENEWAL AND METROPOLITAN AREA TRANSPORTATION STUDY - LIBRARY □ Akron, OH

Morris, Lynne D., Chf., Lib.Serv.
U.S. VETERANS ADMINISTRATION (IL-Chicago) - WESTSIDE HOSPITAL LIBRARY □ Chicago, IL

Morris, Mrs. M., Asst.Libn.
FALCONBRIDGE NICKEL MINES, LTD. - METALLURGICAL LABORATORIES INFORMATION SERVICES □ Thornhill, ON

Morris, Mae, Med.Libn.
U.S. VETERANS ADMINISTRATION (VA-Hampton) - MEDICAL CENTER LIBRARY □ Hampton, VA

Morris, Marge, Asst.Mgr.
AMERICAN ASSOCIATION OF ADVERTISING AGENCIES - MEMBER INFORMATION SERVICE □ New York, NY

Morris, Mary, ILL & Ref.Libn.
CANADA - CONSUMER AND CORPORATE AFFAIRS CANADA - PATENT AND COPYRIGHT OFFICE □ Ottawa, ON

Morris, Meg, Asst.Libn.
PENINSULA TIMES TRIBUNE - LIBRARY □ Palo Alto, CA

Morris, Col. (Ret.) Robert, Ed.
ORDER OF DAEDALIANS - NATIONAL HEADQUARTERS - LIBRARY AND INFORMATION CENTER □ San Antonio, TX

Morris, Robert, Hd., Spec.Coll.
TEACHERS COLLEGE - LIBRARY □ New York, NY

Morris, Sharon, Hd.Libn.
LUTHERAN HOSPITAL OF MARYLAND - CHARLES G. REIGNER MEDICAL LIBRARY □ Baltimore, MD

Morris, Sharon, Info.Mgr.
UNIVERSITY OF BALTIMORE - BALTIMORE REGION INSTITUTIONAL STUDIES CENTER (BRISC) □ Baltimore, MD

Morris, Stephanie A., Cur.
TEMPLE UNIVERSITY - CENTRAL LIBRARY SYSTEM - NATIONAL IMMIGRATION ARCHIVES □ Philadelphia, PA

Morris, Thelma J., Dept.Hd.
CLEVELAND PUBLIC LIBRARY - SOCIAL SCIENCES DEPT. □ Cleveland, OH

Morris, Theodore A., Sr.Lib.Assoc./Spec.
UNIVERSITY OF CINCINNATI - DEPARTMENT OF ENVIRONMENTAL HEALTH LIBRARY □ Cincinnati, OH

Morrison, Alan E., Libn.
UNIVERSITY OF PENNSYLVANIA - FINE ARTS LIBRARY □ Philadelphia, PA

Morrison, Carol, Chf.Libn.
CLEVELAND METROPOLITAN GENERAL HOSPITAL - HAROLD H. BRITTINGHAM MEMORIAL LIBRARY □ Cleveland, OH

Morrison, Carol A., Libn.
ONTARIO CANCER INSTITUTE - LIBRARY □ Toronto, ON

Morrison, Daryl, Libn.
UNIVERSITY OF OKLAHOMA - WESTERN HISTORY COLLECTIONS □ Norman, OK

Morrison, Daryl, Libn.
UNIVERSITY OF OKLAHOMA - WESTERN HISTORY COLLECTIONS - LIBRARY DIVISION □ Norman, OK

Morrison, Gary R., Dir.
U.S. NAVY - SUBMARINE BASE - SUBMARINE FORCE LIBRARY AND MUSEUM □ Groton, CT

Morrison, John, Ck.
CIP INC. NATURE CENTRE - LIBRARY □ Calumet, PQ

Morrison, Leland, Tech.Ed.
(Boston) CENTRAL TRANSPORTATION PLANNING STAFF - LIBRARY SERVICES □ Boston, MA

Morrison, M. Christine, Arts Libn.
NATIONAL ENDOWMENT FOR THE ARTS - ARTS LIBRARY/INFORMATION CENTER □ Washington, DC

Morrison, Marcia, Libn.
BUFFALO SOCIETY OF NATURAL SCIENCES - RESEARCH LIBRARY □ Buffalo, NY

Morrison, Mary, Cat.
BROOKLYN LAW SCHOOL - LAW LIBRARY □ Brooklyn, NY

Morrison, Mary, Ref.Libn.
HARVARD UNIVERSITY - GODFREY LOWELL CABOT SCIENCE LIBRARY □ Cambridge, MA

Morrison, Ralph, Tech.Libn.
M.P.K. OMEGA COMPANY - BIOSCIENCE LIBRARY □ Amarillo, TX

Morrison, Ray, Biblog.Instr.Libn.
PITTSBURG STATE UNIVERSITY - LEONARD H. AXE LIBRARY □ Pittsburg, KS

Morrison, Shirley A., Libn.
DUNLOP RESEARCH CENTRE - LIBRARY □ Mississauga, ON

Morrison, Shirley R., Assoc.Libn.
SANTA BARBARA MUSEUM OF NATURAL HISTORY - LIBRARY □ Santa Barbara, CA

Morrison, Sibyl A., Assoc.Dir./Lib.Serv.
TEXAS TECH UNIVERSITY - LIBRARY □ Lubbock, TX

Morrison, Mrs. William M., Jr., Dir.
WILTON HISTORICAL SOCIETY, INC. - LIBRARY □ Wilton, CT

Morrissett, Elizabeth, Hd.Libn.
MONTANA COLLEGE OF MINERAL SCIENCE AND TECHNOLOGY - LIBRARY □ Butte, MT

PERSONNEL

Morrissey, Jennifer, Libn.
FANSHAWE COLLEGE OF APPLIED ARTS AND TECHNOLOGY - LEARNING RESOURCE CENTRE - VICTORIA CAMPUS LIBRARY □ London, ON

Morrow, Alison, Libn.
SLOAN-KETTERING INSTITUTE FOR CANCER RESEARCH - DONALD S. WALKER LABORATORY - C.P. RHOADS MEMORIAL LIBRARY □ Rye, NY

Morrow, Darrell R., Dir.
RUTGERS UNIVERSITY, THE STATE UNIVERSITY OF NEW JERSEY - GOTTSCHO PACKAGING INFORMATION CENTER □ Piscataway, NJ

Morrow, Ellen B., Mgr.
QUAKER CHEMICAL CORPORATION - TECHNICAL INFORMATION CENTER □ Conshohocken, PA

Morrow, Glenn, ILL
NORTHWEST MISSOURI STATE UNIVERSITY - WELLS LIBRARY □ Maryville, MO

Morrow, Jean, Libn.
NEW ENGLAND CONSERVATORY OF MUSIC - HARRIET M. SPAULDING LIBRARY □ Boston, MA

Morrow, Lory, Photo Archv.
MONTANA HISTORICAL SOCIETY - LIBRARY/ ARCHIVES □ Helena, MT

Morse, Anita L., Prof., Dir. Law Lib.
CLEVELAND STATE UNIVERSITY - JOSEPH W. BARTUNEK III LAW LIBRARY □ Cleveland, OH

Morse, Carol F., Libn.
PUTNAM COUNTY HISTORICAL SOCIETY - FOUNDRY SCHOOL MUSEUM - REFERENCE LIBRARY □ Cold Spring, NY

Morse, David, Tech.Serv.Libn.
UNIVERSITY OF SOUTHERN CALIFORNIA - HEALTH SCIENCES CAMPUS - NORRIS MEDICAL LIBRARY □ Los Angeles, CA

Morse, Dolph, Pres.
REFERENCE PICTURES, INC. □ New York, NY

Morse, Kenneth T., Chf.Libn.
UNIVERSITY OF RHODE ISLAND, NARRAGANSETT BAY - PELL MARINE SCIENCE LIBRARY □ Narragansett, RI

Morse, Lorraine, Info.Spec.
HONEYWELL, INC. - HONEYWELL INFORMATION SYSTEMS - CIC INFORMATION CENTER □ Wellesley, MA

Morse, Nora, Ref.Libn.
UTICA MUTUAL INSURANCE COMPANY - REFERENCE AND LAW LIBRARY □ Utica, NY

Morse, Dr. Richard E., Chf., Ref.Div.
U.S. AIR FORCE - ALBERT F. SIMPSON HISTORICAL RESEARCH CENTER □ Maxwell AFB, AL

Morse, Robert, Libn.
FLORIDA STATE DEPT. OF TRANSPORTATION - CENTRAL REFERENCE LIBRARY □ Tallahassee, FL

Morse, Yvonne L., Chf., Lib.Serv.
U.S. VETERANS ADMINISTRATION (NC-Fayetteville) - HOSPITAL LIBRARY □ Fayetteville, NC

Morshead, Sheila, Libn./Media Spec.
CAMBRIDGE SCHOOL DEPARTMENT - TEACHERS' RESOURCE CENTER □ Cambridge, MA

Mortensen, Joan D., Law Libn.
U.S. DEPT. OF ENERGY - BONNEVILLE POWER ADMINISTRATION - LIBRARY □ Portland, OR

Mortensen, Ruth V., Libn.
LEBOEUF, LAMB, LEIBY & MAC RAE - LIBRARY □ New York, NY

Mortensen, Susan, Map Libn.
UTAH STATE HISTORICAL SOCIETY - RESEARCH LIBRARY □ Salt Lake City, UT

Mortimer, Dorothy, Libn.
METHODIST MEDICAL CENTER OF ILLINOIS - LEARNING RESOURCE CENTER □ Peoria, IL

Mortimer, Roger, Hd., Spec.Coll.
UNIVERSITY OF SOUTH CAROLINA - THOMAS COOPER LIBRARY - RARE BOOKS & SPECIAL COLLECTIONS DEPARTMENT □ Columbia, SC

Mortimer, Ruth, Cur.
SMITH COLLEGE - RARE BOOK ROOM □ Northampton, MA

Mortimer, William J., Mgr., Lib./Ref.Serv.
LIFE INSURANCE MARKETING AND RESEARCH ASSOCIATION - LIBRARY □ Hartford, CT

Mortner, Denise J., Libn. & Off.Mgr.
JULIEN AND SCHLESINGER, P.C., ATTORNEYS-AT-LAW - LIBRARY† □ New York, NY

Morton, Barbara, Libn.
INLAND STEEL COMPANY - INDUSTRIAL RELATIONS LIBRARY □ Chicago, IL

Morton, Donald J., Dir.
UNIVERSITY OF MASSACHUSETTS MEDICAL SCHOOL & WORCESTER DISTRICT MEDICAL SOCIETY - LIBRARY □ Worcester, MA

Morton, Judith, Libn.
UNIVERSITY OF CALIFORNIA, BERKELEY - SEBASTIAN S. KRESGE ENGINEERING LIBRARY □ Berkeley, CA

Morton, Dr. Julia F., Dir.
UNIVERSITY OF MIAMI - MORTON COLLECTANEA □ Coral Gables, FL

Morton, Kathleen, Libn.
ABCOR, INC. - LIBRARY □ Wilmington, MA

Morton, M.L., Dir., Lib.Div.
CANADA - AGRICULTURE CANADA - LIBRARIES DIVISION □ Ottawa, ON

Morton, Natalie G., Asst.Libn., Rd.Serv.
U.S. DEPT. OF LABOR - LIBRARY □ Washington, DC

Morton, Patricia Y., Asst.Libn.Hd.Cat.
PENNSYLVANIA STATE UNIVERSITY - COLLEGE OF MEDICINE - GEORGE T. HARRELL LIBRARY □ Hershey, PA

Morton, Thomas, Hd., Tech.Serv.
UNIVERSITY OF CALIFORNIA, SAN DIEGO - BIOMEDICAL LIBRARY □ La Jolla, CA

Morton, Walter, Cat.Libn.
LOUISIANA STATE UNIVERSITY MEDICAL CENTER - SCHOOL OF MEDICINE IN SHREVEPORT - LIBRARY □ Shreveport, LA

Morwood, Shari, Dir.
HEWLETT-PACKARD COMPANY - CORVALLIS DIVISION TECHNICAL INFORMATION CENTER □ Corvallis, OR

Mosca, Carlo A., Corp.Dir., Educ.
SEA WORLD, INC. - LIBRARY □ San Diego, CA

Moscatt, Angeline, Supv.Libn.
NEW YORK PUBLIC LIBRARY - DONNELL LIBRARY CENTER - CENTRAL CHILDREN'S ROOM □ New York, NY

Moscoso, Ana, Circ.Libn.
UNIVERSITY OF PUERTO RICO - MEDICAL SCIENCES CAMPUS - LIBRARY □ Rio Piedras, PR

Moseley, Eva, Cur. of Mss.
RADCLIFFE COLLEGE - ARTHUR AND ELIZABETH SCHLESINGER LIBRARY ON THE HISTORY OF WOMEN IN AMERICA □ Cambridge, MA

Moseley, Sally, Hd., Microfilm Lib.
GEORGIA STATE DEPARTMENT OF ARCHIVES AND HISTORY - CENTRAL RESEARCH LIBRARY □ Atlanta, GA

Moser, Edward R., Serials Libn.
CALIFORNIA INSTITUTE OF TECHNOLOGY - ROBERT A. MILLIKAN MEMORIAL LIBRARY □ Pasadena, CA

Moser, Margaret L., Libn.
ALLEGHENY COLLEGE - WALTER M. SMALL GEOLOGY LIBRARY □ Meadville, PA

Moser, Max L., Dir.
INDIANA STATE CHAMBER OF COMMERCE - RESEARCH LIBRARY □ Indianapolis, IN

Moses, Eva W., Asst.Libn.
NORTON (R.W.) ART GALLERY - REFERENCE-RESEARCH LIBRARY □ Shreveport, LA

Moses, Larry S., Exec.Dir.
BUREAU OF JEWISH EDUCATION - JEWISH COMMUNITY LIBRARY □ San Francisco, CA

Moses, Paula B., Mgr.
DOW CHEMICAL COMPANY - TECHNICAL INFORMATION SERVICES - CENTRAL REPORT INDEX □ Midland, MI

Moses, Paula B., Mgr.
DOW CHEMICAL COMPANY - TECHNICAL INFORMATION SERVICES - CHEMICAL LIBRARY □ Midland, MI

Mosher, Jeanette, Med.Libn.
MANATEE MEMORIAL HOSPITAL - WENTZEL MEDICAL LIBRARY □ Bradenton, FL

Mosher, Lisa, Asst.Libn.
ACADEMY OF MOTION PICTURE ARTS AND SCIENCES - MARGARET HERRICK LIBRARY □ Beverly Hills, CA

Mosigien, Rose, Circ./Coll.Dev.Libn.
UNIVERSITY OF WISCONSIN, MADISON - CENTER FOR HEALTH SCIENCES LIBRARIES □ Madison, WI

Mosimann, Elizabeth, Asst.Libn.
CARNEGIE-MELLON UNIVERSITY - HUNT INSTITUTE FOR BOTANICAL DOCUMENTATION - LIBRARY □ Pittsburgh, PA

Mosiniak, Judith, Lib.Asst.
MINNEAPOLIS PUBLIC LIBRARY & INFORMATION CENTER - HISTORY DEPARTMENT □ Minneapolis, MN

Moskal, Fredereike, Tech.Serv.Libn.
LEWIS UNIVERSITY - LIBRARY □ Romeoville, IL

Moske, Marjorie, Libn.
OKLAHOMA SCHOOL FOR THE BLIND - PARKVIEW LIBRARY □ Muskogee, OK

Moskowitz, Laura, Asst.Res.
DISNEY (Walt) PRODUCTIONS - LIBRARY □ Burbank, CA

Moskowitz, Michael Ann, Libn.
SIMMONS COLLEGE - SCHOOL OF LIBRARY SCIENCE - LIBRARY □ Boston, MA

Mosley, Doris O.R., Sys.Libn./Dp.
U.S. ARMY WAR COLLEGE - LIBRARY □ Carlisle Barracks, PA

Mosley, Lee J., Asst.Univ.Libn.
UNIVERSITY OF CALIFORNIA, SAN FRANCISCO - LIBRARY □ San Francisco, CA

Mosley, Madison, Mgr./Manual Searches
FLORIDA STATE UNIVERSITY - CTR. FOR STUDIES IN VOCATIONAL EDUC. - FLORIDA EDUCATORS INFO. SERV. □ Tallahassee, FL

Mosley, Mary F., Coord., Circ.Serv.
ALABAMA A & M UNIVERSITY - JOSEPH F. DRAKE MEMORIAL LEARNING RESOURCES CENTER □ Normal, AL

Mosnat, Jacalyn E., Libn.
NORMAN MUNICIPAL HOSPITAL - HEALTH SCIENCE LIBRARY □ Norman, OK

Moss, George H., Jr.
MOSS ARCHIVES □ Sea Bright, NJ

Moss, Dr. Jerome, Dir.
UNIVERSITY OF MINNESOTA, ST. PAUL - DEPARTMENT OF VOCATIONAL & TECHNICAL EDUCATION - LIBRARY □ St. Paul, MN

Moss, Jocelyn, Ref.Libn.
CALIFORNIA HISTORICAL SOCIETY - SCHUBERT HALL LIBRARY □ San Francisco, CA

Moss, Karen M., Chf.Libn.
U.S. COURT OF APPEALS, 1ST CIRCUIT - LIBRARY □ Boston, MA

Moss, Lucy, Staff Att.
NATIONAL CLEARINGHOUSE FOR LEGAL SERVICES - LIBRARY □ Chicago, IL

Moss, Dr. Roger W., Jr., Exec.Dir.
ATHENAEUM OF PHILADELPHIA □ Philadelphia, PA

Moss, William, Chf.Archv.
U.S. PRESIDENTIAL LIBRARIES - JOHN F. KENNEDY LIBRARY □ Boston, MA

Mosser, M.F., Libn.
SOCIETY OF COSTA RICA COLLECTORS (SOCORICO) - EARL FOSSOM MEMORIAL LIBRARY □ Perkasie, PA

Most, Marguerite, Asst. Law Libn.
UNIVERSITY OF SAN DIEGO - MARVIN &
LILLIAN KRATTER LAW LIBRARY □ San Diego,
CA

Motley, Archie, Cur. of Mss.
CHICAGO HISTORICAL SOCIETY - SPECIAL
COLLECTIONS □ Chicago, IL

Mott, Dorothy Williams, Libn./Cur.
MOTT RESEARCH GROUP - LIBRARY □
Washington, DC

Motta, Camille, Chf., Tech.Serv.
MASSACHUSETTS STATE LIBRARY □ Boston,
MA

Motteler, Lee S., Geographer
PACIFIC SCIENTIFIC INFORMATION CENTER □
Honolulu, HI

Mottweiler, Evelyn, Libn.
FREE METHODIST CHURCH OF NORTH
AMERICA - HISTORICAL LIBRARY □ Winona
Lake, IN

Motzkus, Gisela, Libn.
ILLINOIS STATE DEPARTMENT OF
TRANSPORTATION - TECHNICAL REFERENCE
LIBRARY □ Springfield, IL

Moubayed, Sylvia, Hd.Libn.
PROVIDENCE ATHENAEUM - LIBRARY □
Providence, RI

Moul, Professor Gail A., Libn.
BAPTIST BIBLE INSTITUTE - IDA J. MC MILLAN
LIBRARY □ Graceville, FL

Moulder, Cathy, Documentalist
MC MASTER UNIVERSITY - URBAN
DOCUMENTATION CENTRE □ Hamilton, ON

Moulik, Amal, Info.Spec.
SYNTEX, U.S.A. - CORPORATE LIBRARY/
INFORMATION SERVICES □ Palo Alto, CA

Moulton, David A., Asst.Libn.
STRAYER COLLEGE - WILKES LIBRARY □
Washington, DC

Moulton, James C., Sr.Info.Anl.
CONTINENTAL ILLINOIS NATIONAL BANK AND
TRUST COMPANY OF CHICAGO -
INFORMATION SERVICES DIVISION □ Chicago,
IL

Moulton, Ronald, TV Sys.Techn.
VANDERBILT UNIVERSITY LIBRARY -
TELEVISION NEWS ARCHIVE □ Nashville, TN

Mounce, Carolyn, Libn.
BLUE MOUNTAIN COLLEGE - MUSIC LIBRARY □
Blue Mountain, MS

Mounce, Marvin, Pub.Lib.Cons.
STATE LIBRARY OF FLORIDA □ Tallahassee, FL

Mount, Albertina F., Lib.Supv.
HARKNESS (Edward S.) EYE INSTITUTE - JOHN
M. WHEELER LIBRARY □ New York, NY

Mount, Joan, Hd., Ref. & Circ.
LAURENTIAN UNIVERSITY - MAIN LIBRARY □
Sudbury, ON

Mountain, Pat, Libn.
CHEVRON USA INC. - CENTRAL REGION -
TECHNICAL LIBRARY □ Denver, CO

Mounts, Earl, Comp.Sci.Libn.
CARNEGIE-MELLON UNIVERSITY -
ENGINEERING & SCIENCE LIBRARY □
Pittsburgh, PA

Moushey, Eugene, Asst.Ref.Libn.
WESTERN ILLINOIS UNIVERSITY - LIBRARIES
□ Macomb, IL

Moutinho, Betty, ILL
MONSANTO PLASTICS & RESINS COMPANY -
PLASTICS DIV. - SPRINGFIELD PLANT -
TECHNOLOGY LIBRARY □ Indian Orchard, MA

Moutseous, Margaret L., Lib.Dir.
CHILDREN'S HOSPITAL RESEARCH
FOUNDATION - RESEARCH LIBRARY □
Cincinnati, OH

Mover, Holly, Res.Spec.
VIRGINIA STATE OFFICE OF EMERGENCY &
ENERGY SERVICES - ENERGY INFORMATION
AND SERVICES CENTER □ Richmond, VA

Mowat, Vaila S., Hd., Engr.Doc.
HERMES ELECTRONICS LTD. - LIBRARY □
Dartmouth, NS

Mowers, Larry G., Asst.Libn.
HARVARD UNIVERSITY - EDA KUHN LOEB
MUSIC LIBRARY □ Cambridge, MA

Mowery, Bob Lee, Dir.
WITTENBERG UNIVERSITY - THOMAS LIBRARY
□ Springfield, OH

Moy, Gene P., Circ.Libn.
UNIVERSITY OF DETROIT - SCHOOL OF LAW
LIBRARY □ Detroit, MI

Moyal, Marjorie, Libn.
MAIN HURDMAN - LIBRARY □ New York, NY

Moye, Mary, AV Libn.
STATE LIBRARY OF FLORIDA □ Tallahassee, FL

Moyer, Anna Jane, ILL Libn.
GETTYSBURG COLLEGE - MUSSELMAN LIBRARY
- SPECIAL COLLECTIONS □ Gettysburg, PA

Moyer, O.M., Libn.
U.S. AIR FORCE BASE - EDWARDS BASE
LIBRARY† □ Edwards AFB, CA

Moyer, Patricia, Asst. Law Libn.
UNIVERSITY OF PITTSBURGH - LAW LIBRARY □
Pittsburgh, PA

Moyer, Mrs. Roland S., Libn.
NORTHAMPTON COUNTY HISTORICAL AND
GENEALOGICAL SOCIETY - HISTORICAL
MUSEUM AND LIBRARY □ Easton, PA

Moyers, June G., Base Libn.
U.S. AIR FORCE BASE - VANDENBERG BASE
LIBRARY □ Lompoc, CA

Moyle, Albert
OGLESBY HISTORICAL SOCIETY - LIBRARY □
Oglesby, IL

Moynihan, Mary K., Libn.
EXXON CORPORATION - LAW-TAX LIBRARY □
New York, NY

Moynihan, Patricia, Acq.Asst.
MARSHALL (John) LAW SCHOOL - LIBRARY □
Chicago, IL

Mozes, Dr. George, Dir.
MICHAEL REESE HOSPITAL & MEDICAL CTR. -
DEPT. OF LIBRARY & MEDIA RSRCS. □ Chicago,
IL

Mozorosky, Terry, Tech.Info.Spec.
LORAL ELECTRONIC SYSTEMS - TECHNICAL
INFORMATION CENTER □ Yonkers, NY

Mrozewski, Andrzej H., Chf.Libn.
LAURENTIAN UNIVERSITY - MAIN LIBRARY □
Sudbury, ON

Mu, Chungling, East Asian Cat.
CORNELL UNIVERSITY - WASON COLLECTION □
Ithaca, NY

Mucha, Margaret, Ref.Libn.
HOFFMANN-LA ROCHE, INC. - SCIENTIFIC
LIBRARY □ Nutley, NJ

Muchin, John, Hd., Slavic Coll.
UNIVERSITY OF MANITOBA - SLAVIC
COLLECTION □ Winnipeg, MB

Mudd, Isabelle, Adm.Libn.
U.S. ARMY POST - FORT WAINWRIGHT -
LIBRARY □ Fairbanks, AK

Mudloff, Cherrie M., Libn.
DETROIT RECEIVING HOSPITAL & UNIVERSITY
HEALTH CENTER - LIBRARY □ Detroit, MI

Mueckler, Rev. Edwin A., Archv.
LUTHERAN CHURCH - MISSOURI SYNOD -
MICHIGAN DISTRICT ARCHIVES □ Ann Arbor,
MI

Mueller, Bonita, Chf., Tech.Serv.
U.S. GENERAL ACCOUNTING OFFICE -
TECHNICAL INFORMATION SOURCES AND
SERVICES BRANCH □ Washington, DC

Mueller, Dorothy H., Libn.
PHILADELPHIA MARITIME MUSEUM - LIBRARY
□ Philadelphia, PA

Mueller, George John, Dir., Seward Sta.
UNIVERSITY OF ALASKA - INSTITUTE OF
MARINE SCIENCE - SEWARD MARINE STATION
LIBRARY □ Seward, AK

Mueller, Heinz Peter, Assoc. Law Libn.
BRIGHAM YOUNG UNIVERSITY - J. REUBEN
CLARK LAW SCHOOL LIBRARY □ Provo, UT

Mueller, Jane, Chf.Libn.
JIM WALTER RESEARCH CORPORATION -
LIBRARY □ St. Petersburg, FL

Mueller, Jean E., Libn.
UNIVERSITY OF SOUTHERN CALIFORNIA -
ETHEL PERCY ANDRUS GERONTOLOGY CENTER
- GERONTOLOGICAL INFO. CENTER □ Los
Angeles, CA

Mueller, Jeanne G., Tech.Serv.Libn.
INDIANA UNIVERSITY - SCHOOL OF MEDICINE
LIBRARY □ Indianapolis, IN

Mueller, Lynne, Ref.Libn.
MISSISSIPPI STATE UNIVERSITY - MITCHELL
MEMORIAL LIBRARY - SPECIAL COLLECTIONS
□ Mississippi State, MS

Mueller, Martha A., Hd., Rd.Serv./ILL
NEW YORK STATE COLLEGE OF CERAMICS,
ALFRED UNIVERSITY - SAMUEL R. SCHOLES
LIBRARY OF CERAMICS □ Alfred, NY

Mueller, Rev. Peter F., C.S.C., Dir.
CONGREGATION OF HOLY CROSS - MOREAU
SEMINARY - LIBRARY □ Notre Dame, IN

Muffs, Lauren, Ref.Libn.
BENTLEY COLLEGE - SOLOMON R. BAKER
LIBRARY □ Waltham, MA

Muhlberger, Richard, Dir.
SMITH (George Walter Vincent) ART MUSEUM -
LIBRARY □ Springfield, MA

Muir, Daniel T., Cur. Pictorial Coll.
ELEUTHERIAN MILLS HISTORICAL LIBRARY □
Wilmington, DE

Muir, Rodney Anne, Libn.
HOME OIL COMPANY, LTD. - LIBRARY □
Calgary, AB

Muir, Scott, Asst.Libn.
GEORGIA POWER COMPANY - LIBRARY □
Atlanta, GA

Muise, Charmaine, Teacher/Libn.
ALBERTA SCHOOL FOR THE DEAF - L.A.
BROUGHTON LIBRARY □ Edmonton, AB

Mukherjee, Yolande, Corp.Libn.
IMPERIAL TOBACCO LTD. - CORPORATE
LIBRARY □ Montreal, PQ

Mukhopadhyay, Christel, Libn.
FOREST ENGINEERING RESEARCH INSTITUTE
OF CANADA - LIBRARY □ Pointe Claire, PQ

Mulder, Marjorie, Libn.
GILFORD INSTRUMENT LABORATORIES, INC. -
TECHNICAL LIBRARY† □ Oberlin, OH

Muldrow, James C., Libn.
WASHINGTON METROPOLITAN AREA TRANSIT
AUTHORITY - OFFICE OF PUBLIC AFFAIRS -
LIBRARY □ Washington, DC

Mulkey, Jack, Dir.
JACKSON METROPOLITAN LIBRARY -
INFORMATION AND REFERENCE DIVISION □
Jackson, MS

Mull, Brenda, Asst.Libn.
DAUPHIN COUNTY LAW LIBRARY □ Harrisburg,
PA

Mull, Suzanne, Doc.Ret.Libn.
UNIVERSITY OF SOUTHERN CALIFORNIA -
NASA INDUSTRIAL APPLICATION CENTER
(NIAC) □ Los Angeles, CA

Mullaly, Sr. Columba, Archv.
TRINITY COLLEGE - ARCHIVES □ Washington,
DC

Mullaly, Edward J., S.J., Assoc.Dir.
ST. JOSEPH'S UNIVERSITY - INSTITUTE OF
INDUSTRIAL RELATIONS - LIBRARY □
Philadelphia, PA

Mullan, Carolie R., Assoc.Libn.
TEXAS TECH UNIVERSITY - SCHOOL OF LAW
LIBRARY □ Lubbock, TX

Mullan, Ms. S.L., Lib.Techn.
QUEEN ELIZABETH HOSPITAL OF MONTREAL -
HOSPITAL LIBRARY □ Montreal, PQ

Mullane, Bill, Spec.Coll.Libn.
NORTHERN ARIZONA UNIVERSITY - LIBRARIES
- SPECIAL COLLECTIONS DIVISION □ Flagstaff,
AZ

Mullane, Ruth, Tech.Serv.Br.
U.S. ARMY - ARMY LIBRARY □ Washington, DC

P E R S O N N E L

Mullaney, Judith L., Tech.Info.Spec.
OFFICE ON SMOKING AND HEALTH -
TECHNICAL INFORMATION CENTER □ Rockville,
MD

Mullen, Cecilia, Sr.Asst.Libn.
SAN JOSE STATE UNIVERSITY - LIBRARY -
SCIENCE/ENGINEERING DEPARTMENT† □ San
Jose, CA

Mullen, Grace, Archv.
WESTMINSTER THEOLOGICAL SEMINARY -
MONTGOMERY LIBRARY □ Philadelphia, PA

Mullen, Kathy, Libn.
ST. LUKE'S HOSPITAL - LIBRARY □ St. Louis,
MO

Mullen, Robert, Exec.Dir.
UNIONTOWN HOSPITAL ASSOCIATION -
MEDICAL LIBRARY □ Uniontown, PA

Mullen, Ruth, Libn.
REYNOLDA HOUSE, INC. - LIBRARY □ Winston-
Salem, NC

Mullendore, Betty
HARTFORD PUBLIC LIBRARY - REFERENCE AND
GENERAL READING DEPARTMENT □ Hartford,
CT

Muller, Beverly, Libn.
BRAUN (C.F.) COMPANY - REFERENCE LIBRARY
□ Alhambra, CA

Muller, Mrs. Frankie, Dir., Tech.Proc.
TROY STATE UNIVERSITY - LIBRARY □ Troy, AL

Muller, Karen, Hd., Tech.Serv.
ART INSTITUTE OF CHICAGO - RYERSON AND
BURNHAM LIBRARIES □ Chicago, IL

Muller, Robert Donald, Dir.
ONTARIO COUNTY HISTORICAL SOCIETY, INC.
- ARCHIVES □ Canandaigua, NY

Mullett, Philip I., Info.Spec.
NEWFOUNDLAND - DEPARTMENT OF RURAL
DEVELOPMENT - RESOURCE CENTRE □ St.
John's, NF

Mulligan, Kathleen, Cat.
ST. LOUIS MERCANTILE LIBRARY
ASSOCIATION - LIBRARY □ St. Louis, MO

Mulligan, Margaret, Asst.Supv., Lib.Serv.
CIBA-GEIGY CORPORATION -
PHARMACEUTICALS DIVISION - SCIENTIFIC
INFORMATION CENTER† □ Summit, NJ

Mullin, James J., Coord.Anl.Sys.
MICHIGAN STATE UNIVERSITY - UNIVERSITY
CENTER FOR INTERNATIONAL
REHABILITATION (UCIR) - RESOURCE LIBRARY
□ East Lansing, MI

Mullin, Marsha, Cur.
DISCOVERY HALL MUSEUM - RESEARCH
LIBRARY □ South Bend, IN

Mullinix, Charlotte, Libn.
U.S. NAVY - NAVAL SURFACE WEAPONS
CENTER - WHITE OAK LIBRARY □ Silver Spring,
MD

Mullins, Betty Ruth, Asst.Libn.
MISSISSIPPI STATE DEPARTMENT OF PUBLIC
WELFARE - JEAN GUNTER SOCIAL WELFARE
LIBRARY □ Jackson, MS

Mullins, Ethel F., Chf., Lib.Serv.
U.S. VETERANS ADMINISTRATION (KY-
Lexington) - MEDICAL CENTER LIBRARY □
Lexington, KY

Mullins, Linda, Ref.Libn.
HEWLETT-PACKARD COMPANY - CORPORATE
LIBRARY □ Palo Alto, CA

Mulloney, Paul F., Chf., Lib.Br.
U.S. BUREAU OF RECLAMATION - LIBRARY □
Denver, CO

Mullooly, Elnora E., Libn.
FAYETTE COUNTY LAW LIBRARY □ Uniontown,
PA

Mullooly, John P., M.D., Libn.
MILWAUKEE ACADEMY OF MEDICINE -
LIBRARY □ Milwaukee, WI

Mulloy, Betty, Libn.
ROGERS (Lauren) LIBRARY AND MUSEUM OF
ART □ Laurel, MS

Mulloy, Mary, Cat.Libn.
TROY STATE UNIVERSITY - LIBRARY □ Troy, AL

Multer, Ell-Piret, Tech.Info.Spec.
U.S. FISH & WILDLIFE SERVICE - COLUMBIA
NATIONAL FISHERIES RESEARCH LABORATORY
LIBRARY □ Columbia, MO

Mulvaney, Carol E., Tech.Libn.
CATERPILLAR TRACTOR COMPANY -
TECHNICAL INFORMATION CENTER □ Peoria,
IL

Mulvihill, JoAnn, Hd.Ref.Libn.
VANDERBILT UNIVERSITY LIBRARY -
EDUCATION LIBRARY □ Nashville, TN

Mulvihill, JoAnn, Libn.
VANDERBILT UNIVERSITY LIBRARY -
EDUCATION LIBRARY - PEABODY COLLECTION
OF BOOKS ON CHILDREN □ Nashville, TN

Mulvihill, John, Dir.
AMERICAN GEOLOGICAL INSTITUTE - GEO-REF
RETROSPECTIVE SEARCH SERVICE □ Falls
Church, VA

Mulvihill, Sylvia, Br.Asst.
ALAMEDA COUNTY LAW LIBRARY □ Hayward,
CA

Munchak, Irene, ILL & Ref.Libn.
MARYWOOD COLLEGE - LEARNING RESOURCES
CENTER □ Scranton, PA

Mundstock, Aileen, Tech.Info.Spec.
UNIVERSAL FOODS CORPORATION -
TECHNICAL INFORMATION SERVICES □
Milwaukee, WI

Mundy, Dulcie T., Lib.Asst.
UNIVERSITY OF MISSOURI - MATH SCIENCES
LIBRARY □ Columbia, MO

Mundy, James G., Jr., Libn.
UNION LEAGUE OF PHILADELPHIA - LIBRARY □
Philadelphia, PA

Munford, Norva, Hd.Rd.Serv.
SUNY - AGRICULTURAL AND TECHNICAL
COLLEGE AT COBLESKILL - JARED VAN
WAGENEN, JR. LEARNING RESOURCE CENTER
□ Cobleskill, NY

Munger, Dr. Edwin S., Dir.
CALIFORNIA INSTITUTE OF TECHNOLOGY -
MUNGER AFRICANA LIBRARY □ Pasadena, CA

Munger, Nancy Terry, Mgr., Info.Serv.
THOMPSON (J. Walter) COMPANY -
INFORMATION CENTER □ New York, NY

Mungro, Shirley, Doc.Anl.
MOBIL RESEARCH & DEVELOPMENT
CORPORATION - ENGINEERING DEPARTMENT -
INFORMATION CENTER □ Princeton, NJ

Munke, Margaret Pittman, Libn.
OUR LADY OF THE LAKE UNIVERSITY -
WORDEN SCHOOL OF SOCIAL SERVICE -
LIBRARY □ San Antonio, TX

Munoz, Patricia, Cat. & Acq.Libn.
MEDICAL AND CHIRURGICAL FACULTY OF THE
STATE OF MARYLAND - LIBRARY □ Baltimore,
MD

Munro, Dale, Libn.
ONTARIO SCIENCE CENTRE - LIBRARY □ Don
Mills, ON

Munro, J.D., Info.Spec.
CELANESE CORPORATION - SUMMIT
RESEARCH LABORATORIES - TECHNICAL
INFORMATION CENTER □ Summit, NJ

Munro, Margaret, Libn.
ENVIRONMENTAL PROTECTION AGENCY -
CENTRAL REGIONAL LABORATORY - LIBRARY □
Annapolis, MD

Munro, Robert, Assoc.Libn.
UNIVERSITY OF FLORIDA - LAW LIBRARY □
Gainesville, FL

Munson, Harold E., Supv. Project
TRW, INC. - BEARINGS DIVISION - RESEARCH
& DEVELOPMENT TECHNICAL LIBRARY □
Jamestown, NY

Munson, Stephen Edward, Law Libn.
STANISLAUS COUNTY LAW LIBRARY □
Modesto, CA

Munson, Thomas A., Supt.
U.S. NATL. PARK SERVICE - EFFIGY MOUNDS
NATL. MONUMENT - LIBRARY □ McGregor, IA

Muraska, Ms. Danute M., Med.Libn.
U.S. VETERANS ADMINISTRATION (PA-
Philadelphia) - MEDICAL CENTER LIBRARY □
Philadelphia, PA

Murata, L.R., Libn.
INDUSTRIAL INDEMNITY COMPANY - LIBRARY
□ San Francisco, CA

Muratori, Robin A., Libn.
ERIE COUNTY LAW LIBRARY† □ Sandusky, OH

Murch, Luella, Asst. Program Libn.
UNIVERSITY OF MARYLAND, COLLEGE PARK -
COMPUTER SCIENCE CENTER - PROGRAM
LIBRARY □ College Park, MD

Murchie, John, Lib.Dir.
NOVA SCOTIA COLLEGE OF ART AND DESIGN -
LIBRARY □ Halifax, NS

Murdoch, A.W., Asst.Prov.Archv.
ONTARIO - ARCHIVES OF ONTARIO - LIBRARY
□ Toronto, ON

Murdoch, Laurel, Libn.
TORY, TORY, DESLAURIERS & BINNINGTON -
LIBRARY □ Toronto, ON

Murdoch, S.K., Base Libn.
U.S. AIR FORCE BASE - HOWARD BASE
LIBRARY □ APO Miami, FL

Murdoch, Sue, Asst.Archv.
SIMCOE COUNTY ARCHIVES □ Minesing, ON

Murdock, David, Libn.
CARNEGIE LIBRARY OF PITTSBURGH -
SCIENCE AND TECHNOLOGY DEPARTMENT □
Pittsburgh, PA

Murdock, David A., Visual Info.Spec.
U.S. DEPT. OF HOUSING & URBAN
DEVELOPMENT - PHOTOGRAPHY LIBRARY □
Washington, DC

Murdock, Everlyne K., Act.Dir.
CONSUMER PRODUCT SAFETY COMMISSION -
LIBRARY INFORMATION SERVICES BRANCH □
Washington, DC

Murdock, Lynn, Libn.
BERKELEY PUBLIC LIBRARY - ART AND MUSIC
DIVISION □ Berkeley, CA

Murdock, Mary-Elizabeth, Coll.Archv.
SMITH COLLEGE - ARCHIVES □ Northampton,
MA

Murdock, Mary-Elizabeth, Dir.
SMITH COLLEGE - SOPHIA SMITH COLLECTION
- WOMEN'S HISTORY ARCHIVE □ Northampton,
MA

Murdock, William J., Lib.Dir.
PACE UNIVERSITY, PLEASANTVILLE/
BRIARCLIFF - LIBRARY □ Pleasantville, NY

Murley, Karen Ashkar, Sr.Libn.
IBM CORPORATION - GENERAL TECHNOLOGY
DIVISION - EAST FISHKILL FACILITY -
LIBRARY □ Hopewell Junction, NY

Muroga, Professor S., Chm.Lib.Comm.
UNIVERSITY OF ILLINOIS - DEPARTMENT OF
COMPUTER SCIENCE LIBRARY □ Urbana, IL

Murphey, Jane C., Asst.Libn.
UNITED AUTOMOBILE, AEROSPACE &
AGRICULTURAL IMPLEMENT WORKERS OF
AMERICA - RESEARCH LIBRARY □ Detroit, MI

Murphey, John M., Assoc.Dir. TALON
UNIVERSITY OF TEXAS HEALTH SCIENCE
CENTER, DALLAS - LIBRARY □ Dallas, TX

Murphy, Barbara, Adm.Asst.
U.S. PUBLIC HEALTH SERVICE - WINCHESTER
ENGINEERING & ANALYTICAL CENTER -
LIBRARY □ Winchester, MA

Murphy, Barbara G., Assoc. Law Libn.
UNIVERSITY OF VIRGINIA - ARTHUR J.
MORRIS LAW LIBRARY □ Charlottesville, VA

Murphy, Bernard F., Dir.
BALTIMORE - DEPARTMENT OF LEGISLATIVE
REFERENCE - LIBRARY □ Baltimore, MD

Murphy, Beth, Mgr., Lib. & Curric.Res.
HARPER & ROW, PUBLISHERS, INC. - SCHOOL
DIVISION LIBRARY □ New York, NY

Murphy, C. Edwin, Cur.
UNITED METHODIST CHURCH - NEBRASKA
CONFERENCE - HISTORICAL CENTER □ Lincoln,
NE

Murphy, Charles G., Sr.Asst.Libn.
PENNSYLVANIA STATE UNIVERSITY - APPLIED
RESEARCH LABORATORY - LIBRARY □ State
College, PA

Murphy, Charles J., Pub.Info.Off.
DUTCHESS COUNTY DEPARTMENT OF
PLANNING - INFORMATION CENTER □
Poughkeepsie, NY

Murphy, Colleen, Hd., Media Serv.
BENTLEY COLLEGE - SOLOMON R. BAKER
LIBRARY □ Waltham, MA

Murphy, Donna, Circ.Asst.
BABSON COLLEGE - HORN LIBRARY □ Babson
Park, MA

Murphy, Ellen M., Map/Gift Cat.
AMERICAN GEOGRAPHICAL SOCIETY
COLLECTION OF THE UNIVERSITY OF
WISCONSIN, MILWAUKEE - GOLDA MEIR
LIBRARY □ Milwaukee, WI

Murphy, Helen King, Dir.
HIGHLAND HOSPITAL OF ROCHESTER - THE
WILLIAMS HEALTH SCIENCES LIBRARY □
Rochester, NY

Murphy, Henry, Coll.Dev./Acq.Libn.
CORNELL UNIVERSITY - ALBERT R. MANN
LIBRARY □ Ithaca, NY

Murphy, Joseph P., Chf.Tech.Info.Serv.
AVCO CORPORATION - LYCOMING DIVISION -
LIBRARY & INFORMATION CENTER □ Stratford,
CT

Murphy, Joyce
BRITISH COLUMBIA - MINISTRY OF
ENVIRONMENT - LIBRARY □ Victoria, BC

Murphy, Larraine P., Off.Serv.Supv.-Lib.Serv.
STELCO INC. - CENTRAL LIBRARY □ Hamilton,
ON

Murphy, M., Lib. Custodian
JACKSON COUNTY LAW LIBRARY □ Jackson, OH

Murphy, Margaret, Libn.
NOVA SCOTIA - ATTORNEY GENERAL'S
LIBRARY □ Halifax, NS

Murphy, Margaret M., Chf., Tech.Lib.
U.S. ARMY - MATERIALS & MECHANICS
RESEARCH CENTER - TECHNICAL LIBRARY □
Watertown, MA

Murphy, Marilyn, Libn.
NEW ENGLAND AQUARIUM - LIBRARY □ Boston,
MA

Murphy, Marilyn L., Libn.
INDIANA UNIVERSITY/PURDUE UNIVERSITY
AT FORT WAYNE - FINE ARTS LIBRARY† □ Fort
Wayne, IN

Murphy, Mary A., Open Lit.Libn.
U.S. AIR FORCE - ARMAMENT DIVISION, AIR
FORCE ARMAMENT LABORATORY - TECHNICAL
LIBRARY □ Eglin AFB, FL

Murphy, Mary Engelmann, Libn.
DUN AND BRADSTREET, INC. - BUSINESS
LIBRARY □ New York, NY

Murphy, Maryanne, Libn.
U.S. COURT OF APPEALS, 3RD CIRCUIT -
BRANCH LIBRARY† □ Newark, NJ

Murphy, Pat, Res./Writer
SEA WORLD, INC. - LIBRARY □ San Diego, CA

Murphy, Patrick, Libn.
MEDICAL RESEARCH LABORATORIES -
LIBRARY □ Niles, IL

Murphy, Paul, Libn.
VANDERBILT UNIVERSITY LIBRARY - CENTRAL
DIVISION - SARAH SHANNON STEVENSON
SCIENCE LIBRARY □ Nashville, TN

Murphy, Paul T., Law Libn.
UNIVERSITY OF WINDSOR - PAUL MARTIN
LAW LIBRARY □ Windsor, ON

Murphy, Mrs. R.P., Libn.
ALLIED CORPORATION - FIBERS & PLASTICS
COMPANY - TECHNICAL CENTER LIBRARY □
Petersburg, VA

Murphy, Robert, Libn.
WEST VIRGINIA UNIVERSITY - MEDICAL
CENTER LIBRARY □ Morgantown, WV

Murphy, Robert B., Mgr.
IBM CORPORATION - GENERAL TECHNOLOGY
DIVISION - EAST FISHKILL FACILITY -
LIBRARY □ Hopewell Junction, NY

Murphy, Robert D., Hd.
ROCHESTER PUBLIC LIBRARY - EDUCATION
AND RELIGION DIVISION □ Rochester, NY

Murphy, Sara L., Sr.Libn.
U.S. DEPT. OF ENERGY - GRAND JUNCTION
OFFICE - TECHNICAL LIBRARY □ Grand
Junction, CO

Murphy, Susan F. , Cat.
GEORGIA HISTORICAL SOCIETY - LIBRARY □
Savannah, GA

Murphy, Terry, Info.Spec.
GOULD INC. - GOULD INFORMATION CENTER □
Rolling Meadows, IL

Murphy, Virginia, Med.Libn.
NORTHWESTERN MUTUAL LIFE INSURANCE
COMPANY - MEDICAL LIBRARY □ Milwaukee,
WI

Murphy, William D., Libn.
KIRKLAND & ELLIS - LIBRARY □ Chicago, IL

Murrah, David, Univ.Archv.
TEXAS TECH UNIVERSITY - SOUTHWEST
COLLECTION □ Lubbock, TX

Murray, Alice J., Law Libn.
MC GEORGE SCHOOL OF LAW - LAW LIBRARY □
Sacramento, CA

Murray, Alice R., Libn.
U.S. NAVY - NAVAL SHIPYARD (Philadelphia) -
TECHNICAL LIBRARY □ Philadelphia, PA

Murray, Anne, Libn.
U.S. ARMY AND AIR FORCE EXCHANGE
SERVICE - CENTRAL LIBRARY AD-M □ Dallas,
TX

Murray, Bill, Dir.
AURORA PUBLIC SCHOOLS - PROFESSIONAL
LIBRARY □ Aurora, CO

Murray, Bonnie Meyer, Park Techn.
U.S. NATL. PARK SERVICE - MOUND CITY
GROUP NATL. MONUMENT - LIBRARY □
Chillicothe, OH

Murray, Carol Ann, Libn.
CELANESE PLASTICS & SPECIALTIES COMPANY
- TECHNICAL CENTER - RESEARCH LIBRARY □
Jeffersontown, KY

Murray, Deborah M., Law Libn.
DISTRICT OF COLUMBIA - CORPORATION
COUNSEL LAW LIBRARY □ Washington, DC

Murray, Miss E.B., Libn.
BRITISH COLUMBIA TELEPHONE COMPANY -
BUSINESS LIBRARY □ Burnaby, BC

Murray, George, Mgr.
CHAMBER OF MINES OF EASTERN BRITISH
COLUMBIA - BUREAU OF INFORMATION □
Nelson, BC

Murray, James, Ref.Libn.
UNIVERSITY OF TEXAS SCHOOL OF LAW -
TARLTON LAW LIBRARY □ Austin, TX

Murray, James T., Tech.Libn.
UNIVERSITY OF TULSA - SIDNEY BORN
TECHNICAL LIBRARY □ Tulsa, OK

Murray, Dr. Joanne L., Metallurgist
U.S. NATL. BUREAU OF STANDARDS - ALLOY
DATA CENTER □ Washington, DC

Murray, Johnny F., Chf., Lib.
U.S. DEPT. OF DEFENSE - DEFENSE
INDUSTRIAL PLANT EQUIPMENT CENTER -
TECHNICAL DATA REPOSITORY & LIBRARY □
Memphis, TN

Murray, Kathleen, Tech.Serv./Assoc.Dir.
LAMAR UNIVERSITY - MARY AND JOHN GRAY
LIBRARY □ Beaumont, TX

Murray, Kathleen, Med.Libn.
PROVIDENCE MEDICAL CENTER - MEDICAL
LIBRARY □ Seattle, WA

Murray, Laura, AV Coord.
METROPOLITAN TORONTO LIBRARY - AUDIO
VISUAL SERVICES □ Toronto, ON

Murray, Lee M., Pub.Serv.Libn.
SYRACUSE UNIVERSITY - ENGINEERING & LIFE
SCIENCES LIBRARY □ Syracuse, NY

Murray, Lorraine, Health Rec.Adm.
WAINWRIGHT GENERAL HOSPITAL - MEDICAL
LIBRARY □ Wainwright, AB

Murray, Mrs. M., Libn.
NORTHERN MINER - LIBRARY □ Toronto, ON

Murray, Marijean, Supv.Libn.
U.S. ARMY SERGEANTS MAJOR ACADEMY -
OTHON O. VALENT LEARNING RESOURCES
CENTER □ Ft. Bliss, TX

Murray, Marilyn R., Libn.
ARTHUR ANDERSEN & CO. - LIBRARY □ Chicago,
IL

Murray, Mary P., Libn.
MERCY CENTER FOR HEALTH CARE SERVICES -
MEDICAL LIBRARY □ Aurora, IL

Murray, Patricia, Libn./Tech.Ed.
INTERNATIONAL JOINT COMMISSION - GREAT
LAKES REGIONAL OFFICE LIBRARY □ Windsor,
ON

Murray, Richard N., Dir.
BIRMINGHAM MUSEUM OF ART - REFERENCE
LIBRARY □ Birmingham, AL

Murray, Mr. Robin R.B., Dir.
NEW YORK STATE COLLEGE OF CERAMICS,
ALFRED UNIVERSITY - SAMUEL R. SCHOLES
LIBRARY OF CERAMICS □ Alfred, NY

Murray, Robinson, III, Assoc.Libn.
ESSEX INSTITUTE - JAMES DUNCAN PHILLIPS
LIBRARY □ Salem, MA

Murray, Ruth, Lit.Chem.
AMERICAN CHEMICAL SOCIETY, INC. -
RUBBER DIVISION - JOHN H. GIFFORD
MEMORIAL LIBRARY & INFORMATION CTR. □
Akron, OH

Murray, Sabina J., Asst.Libn.
CHURCH OF JESUS CHRIST OF LATTER-DAY
SAINTS - JACKSONVILLE, FLORIDA BRANCH
GENEALOGICAL LIBRARY □ Jacksonville, FL

Murray, Susan, Libn.
UNIVERSITY OF TORONTO - FACULTY OF
DENTISTRY LIBRARY □ Toronto, ON

Murray, Suzanne, Assoc.Dir.
SUNY - UPSTATE MEDICAL CENTER LIBRARY □
Syracuse, NY

Murrell, Irvin, Circ.-Ref.Libn.
NEW ORLEANS BAPTIST THEOLOGICAL
SEMINARY - JOHN T. CHRISTIAN LIBRARY □
New Orleans, LA

Murrin, Nancy, Ref.Libn.
AMERICAN BANKERS ASSOCIATION - LIBRARY
□ Washington, DC

Murry, Joye, Dir.
FIRST ASSEMBLY OF GOD - LIBRARY □ North
Little Rock, AR

Mursec, Ljudmila, Asst.Sci.Libn.
MARQUETTE UNIVERSITY - SCIENCE LIBRARY
□ Milwaukee, WI

Murway, Mark, Ref.Libn.
RUSH UNIVERSITY AND MEDICAL CENTER -
LIBRARY □ Chicago, IL

Musa, Dr. Byron, Chm., Lib. Committee
EUGENE HOSPITAL AND CLINIC - DOCTORS'
LIBRARY† □ Eugene, OR

Musante, Louis, Mgr.Tech.Anl.
UNIVERSITY OF PITTSBURGH - NASA
INDUSTRIAL APPLICATIONS CENTER □
Pittsburgh, PA

Muse, Winnie, Tech.Info.Spec.
U.S. DEPT. OF TRANSPORTATION - URBAN
MASS TRANSPORTATION ADM. -
TRANSPORTATION RESEARCH INFO. CENTER
(TRIC) □ Washington, DC

Musgrave, Myles T., Asst. to V.P.
ACHESON INDUSTRIES, INC. - CORPORATE
INFORMATION CENTER □ Port Huron, MI

Musgrove, Nancy, Libn.
ONTARIO - MINISTRY OF ENERGY - LIBRARY†
□ Toronto, ON

Muskat, Beatrice T., Libn.
TEMPLE ISRAEL OF GREATER MIAMI - LIBRARY
□ Miami, FL

PERSONNEL

Muskus, Elizabeth A., Mgr.Info./Res.Serv.
REDDY COMMUNICATIONS, INC. - INFORMATION/RESEARCH SERVICES □ Greenwich, CT

Musser, Geraldyne J., Asst.Libn.
GENERAL MOTORS CORPORATION - TAX SECTION LIBRARY □ Detroit, MI

Mustain, Anne, Cat.Libn.
UNIVERSITY OF VIRGINIA - ARTHUR J. MORRIS LAW LIBRARY □ Charlottesville, VA

Mustain, Jim, Info.Anl.
UNIVERSITY OF CALIFORNIA, LOS ANGELES - BRAIN INFORMATION SERVICE □ Los Angeles, CA

Mutale, Elaine, Ref.Libn.
ANDREWS UNIVERSITY - JAMES WHITE LIBRARY □ Berrien Springs, MI

Mutch, A. Douglas
LIVESTOCK FEED BOARD OF CANADA - LIBRARY □ Montreal, PQ

Muth, Ross E., Municipal Prog.Spec.
NEW YORK STATE CONFERENCE OF MAYORS AND MUNICIPAL OFFICIALS - LIBRARY □ Albany, NY

Muto, Albert, Asst.Libn.
FIREMAN'S FUND INSURANCE COMPANIES - LIBRARY† □ San Francisco, CA

Mutsaers, H.A., Libn.
CANADIAN MUSIC CENTRE - LIBRARY □ Toronto, ON

Muzzo, Joseph, Dir.
DOCTORS HOSPITAL - MEDICAL LIBRARY □ Columbus, OH

Mycio, Luba, Pub. Affairs
CANADIAN WILDLIFE FEDERATION - REFERENCE LIBRARY & INFORMATION CENTRE □ Ottawa, ON

Myer, Nancy E., Chf.Libn.
U.S. VETERANS ADMINISTRATION (AZ-Tucson) - MEDICAL CENTER LIBRARY □ Tucson, AZ

Myers, Agnes M., Dir.
LORETTO HEIGHTS COLLEGE - MAY BONFILS STANTON LIBRARY □ Denver, CO

Myers, Anna J., Libn.
PUBLIC LIBRARY OF CINCINNATI AND HAMILTON COUNTY - ART AND MUSIC DEPARTMENT □ Cincinnati, OH

Myers, Claryse D., Libn.
U.S. NATL. PARK SERVICE - GREAT SMOKY MOUNTAINS NATL. PARK - SUGARLANDS VISITOR CENTER □ Gatlinburg, TN

Myers, Darlene, Mgr.
UNIVERSITY OF WASHINGTON - COMPUTING INFORMATION CENTER □ Seattle, WA

Myers, Diana, Hd., Tech.Serv.
ONTARIO COLLEGE OF ART - LIBRARY/AUDIOVISUAL CENTRE □ Toronto, ON

Myers, Elissa Matulis, Dir., Res. & Info.
AMERICAN SOCIETY OF ASSOCIATION EXECUTIVES - INFORMATION CENTRAL □ Washington, DC

Myers, Elizabeth
RIVERSIDE PRESBYTERIAN CHURCH - JEAN MILLER LIBRARY □ Jacksonville, FL

Myers, Elizabeth, Hd.
UNIVERSITY OF CALIFORNIA, BERKELEY - GOVERNMENT DOCUMENTS DEPARTMENT □ Berkeley, CA

Myers, G. Richard, Libn.
GENERAL DYNAMICS CORPORATION - QUINCY SHIPBUILDING DIVISION LIBRARY □ Quincy, MA

Myers, George C., Dir. of Ctr.
DUKE UNIVERSITY - CENTER FOR DEMOGRAPHIC STUDIES - REFERENCE LIBRARY □ Durham, NC

Myers, Harriet J., Lib.Techn.
ENVIRONMENTAL PROTECTION AGENCY - LIBRARY SERVICES □ Research Triangle Park, NC

Myers, Irene L., Sect.Hd.
PROCTER & GAMBLE COMPANY - WINTON HILL TECHNICAL CENTER - TECHNICAL LIBRARY □ Cincinnati, OH

Myers, Joan B., Dir.
PHILADELPHIA BOARD OF EDUCATION - PEDAGOGICAL LIBRARY □ Philadelphia, PA

Myers, John R., Chf., Info.Sys.Div.
U.S.D.A. - NATIONAL AGRICULTURAL LIBRARY □ Beltsville, MD

Myers, Judith, Asst.Dir.
NEW YORK MEDICAL COLLEGE AND THE WESTCHESTER ACADEMY OF MEDICINE - WESTCHESTER MEDICAL CENTER LIBRARY □ Valhalla, NY

Myers, Kathy, Programmer
UNIVERSITY OF PITTSBURGH - CENTER FOR INTERNATIONAL STUDIES □ Pittsburgh, PA

Myers, Linda, Hd. Media Serv.
SUNY - AGRICULTURAL AND TECHNICAL COLLEGE AT COBLESKILL - JARED VAN WAGENEN, JR. LEARNING RESOURCE CENTER □ Cobleskill, NY

Myers, Linda K., Dir., LRC
TEXAS STATE TECHNICAL INSTITUTE, WACO CAMPUS - LEARNING RESOURCE CENTER □ Waco, TX

Myers, Marie-Anna, Hd., Lib.Dept.
CANATOM INC. - LIBRARY □ Montreal, PQ

Myers, Mary, Per.Libn.
BRIDGEWATER STATE COLLEGE - CLEMENT C. MAXWELL LIBRARY □ Bridgewater, MA

Myers, Mildred S., Dir.
UNIVERSITY OF PITTSBURGH - GRADUATE SCHOOL OF BUSINESS LIBRARY □ Pittsburgh, PA

Myers, Nancy Jane, Libn.
WILLIAMS-KUEBELBECK & ASSOCIATES, INC. - LIBRARY □ Redwood City, CA

Myers, Pamela A., Mgr.Info.Serv.
BELL & HOWELL COMPANY - MICRO PHOTO DIVISION - MICROFORMS ARCHIVE □ Wooster, OH

Myers, Peggy J., Corp.Libn.
ANCHOR HOCKING CORPORATION - CORPORATE LIBRARY □ Lancaster, OH

Myers, Ramon H., Cur., E. Asia Coll.
STANFORD UNIVERSITY - HOOVER INSTITUTION ON WAR, REVOLUTION AND PEACE - LIBRARY □ Stanford, CA

Myers, W.Z., Libn.
HAMMOND, INC. - EDITORIAL DEPARTMENT LIBRARY □ Maplewood, NJ

Myers, William, Hd., Mss.
OHIO HISTORICAL SOCIETY - ARCHIVES-LIBRARY □ Columbus, OH

Myhre, Margaret, Libn.
OAKLAND PUBLIC LIBRARY - HANDICAPPED SERVICES □ Oakland, CA

Mykleby, Elaine V., Libn.
FIRST LUTHERAN CHURCH - MEMORIAL LIBRARY □ Cedar Rapids, IA

Mykrantz, Barbara, Archv.
MISSOURI BOTANICAL GARDEN - LIBRARY □ St. Louis, MO

Mylenki, Mary, Sr.Asst.Libn.
NEW YORK HOSPITAL-CORNELL MEDICAL CENTER - OSKAR DIETHELM HISTORICAL LIBRARY □ New York, NY

Mylenki, Mary, Sr.Asst.Libn.
PAYNE WHITNEY PSYCHIATRIC CLINIC LIBRARY □ New York, NY

Myles, Colette, Hd.
UNIVERSITY OF CALIFORNIA, BERKELEY - INSTITUTE OF INTERNATIONAL STUDIES LIBRARY □ Berkeley, CA

Mylin, Dorothy J., Libn.
U.S. ARMY HOSPITALS - FITZSIMONS ARMY MEDICAL CENTER - MEDICAL-TECHNICAL LIBRARY □ Aurora, CO

Myong, Jae Hwi, Cat.Libn.
UNIVERSITY OF CALIFORNIA, IRVINE - BIOMEDICAL LIBRARY □ Irvine, CA

Myrick, Carole J., Med.Libn.
ANAHEIM MEMORIAL HOSPITAL - MEDICAL LIBRARY □ Anaheim, CA

Mysak, Basil
UKRAINIAN ENGINEERS SOCIETY OF AMERICA - LIBRARY □ New York, NY

Mysko, Bohdan W., Hd.
FREE LIBRARY OF PHILADELPHIA - MICROFORMS AND NEWSPAPERS DEPARTMENT □ Philadelphia, PA

N

Nabors, Cecile, Doc.Libn.
NEVADA STATE LIBRARY □ Carson City, NV

Nacheman, Elinor, Hd., Cat.Dept.
RHODE ISLAND SCHOOL OF DESIGN - LIBRARY □ Providence, RI

Nachlas, Irva B., Libn.
REGIONAL PLANNING COUNCIL - LIBRARY □ Baltimore, MD

Nachod, Katherine, Govt.Doc.Libn.
NEW ORLEANS PUBLIC LIBRARY - BUSINESS AND SCIENCE DIVISION □ New Orleans, LA

Nadal, Antonio, Hd. Law Libn.
PUERTO RICO - DEPARTMENT OF JUSTICE - LIBRARY □ San Juan, PR

Nadeau, Claude-Roger, S.J., Dir.
COMPAGNIE DE JESUS - BIBLIOTHEQUE DE THEOLOGIE □ Montreal, PQ

Nadeau, Lucienne, Dir.
COLLEGE DE MUSIQUE SAINTE-CROIX - BIBLIOTHEQUE □ St. Laurent, PQ

Nadkarni, Meena, Hd., Acq.
YORK UNIVERSITY - LAW LIBRARY □ Downsview, ON

Naegeli, Bruce, Asst.Dir.
MARICOPA COUNTY LAW LIBRARY □ Phoenix, AZ

Naese, Ann, Map Cur.
UNIVERSITY OF WATERLOO - UNIVERSITY MAP LIBRARY □ Waterloo, ON

Naeseth, Gerhard B., Libn.
VESTERHEIM GENEALOGICAL CENTER/NORWEGIAN-AMERICAN MUSEUM - LIBRARY □ Madison, WI

Naftalin, Mortimer, Asst. Law Libn.
U.S.D.A. - NATIONAL AGRICULTURAL LIBRARY - LAW LIBRARY □ Washington, DC

Nagata, K. Martha, Libn.
UNION CARBIDE CANADA, LTD. - REFERENCE LIBRARY □ Toronto, ON

Nagel, Paul C., Dir.
VIRGINIA HISTORICAL SOCIETY - LIBRARY □ Richmond, VA

Nagg, Shirley, Libn.
ROCHESTER BUSINESS INSTITUTE - BETTY CRONK MEMORIAL LIBRARY □ Rochester, NY

Nagle, Ellen, Hd., Ref.Sect.
COLUMBIA UNIVERSITY - HEALTH SCIENCES LIBRARY □ New York, NY

Nagle, Georgia M., Rd.Rm.Adm.
MASSACHUSETTS INSTITUTE OF TECHNOLOGY - INFORMATION PROCESSING SERVICES - READING ROOM □ Cambridge, MA

Nagpal, Regina, Hd., Instr.Serv.
WITTENBERG UNIVERSITY - THOMAS LIBRARY □ Springfield, OH

Nagy, Bernice L., Libn.
KENOSHA NEWS - NEWSPAPER LIBRARY† □ Kenosha, WI

Nagy, Mrs. K., Hd., Rd.Serv.
CANADA - ENERGY, MINES & RESOURCES CANADA - CANMET - LIBRARY □ Ottawa, ON

Nagy, Karen N., Asst. Music Libn.
NORTHWESTERN UNIVERSITY - MUSIC LIBRARY □ Evanston, IL

Nagy, Dr. Louis N., Dir.
KEAN COLLEGE OF NEW JERSEY - NANCY THOMPSON LIBRARY □ Union, NJ

Nagy, Robert, Cat.
ST. JOHN'S UNIVERSITY - LAW LIBRARY □
Jamaica, NY

Nagy, T., Ref.Coord.
CANADA - PUBLIC ARCHIVES OF CANADA -
NATIONAL MAP COLLECTION □ Ottawa, ON

Nahley, Duane G., Supv.Libn.
U.S. ARMY IN EUROPE (USAREUR) - LIBRARY
AND RESOURCE CENTER □ APO New York, NY

Nail, K., Archv.
U.S. NASA - JOHN F. KENNEDY SPACE CENTER
- LIBRARY □ Kennedy Space Center, FL

Nair, Lola, Cat.
ORAL ROBERTS UNIVERSITY - HEALTH
SCIENCES LIBRARY □ Tulsa, OK

Nair, Vijay, Libn.
ADIRONDACK HISTORICAL ASSOCIATION -
ADIRONDACK MUSEUM - RESEARCH LIBRARY □
Blue Mountain Lake, NY

Nairn, Charles E., Ref.Libn.
LAKE SUPERIOR STATE COLLEGE - MICHIGAN
COLLECTION □ Sault Ste. Marie, MI

Naisbitt, Jane, Libn.
SASKATCHEWAN - DEPARTMENT OF
EDUCATION - RESOURCE CENTRE □ Regina, SK

Naish, Mary, First Asst.
PUBLIC LIBRARY OF CINCINNATI AND
HAMILTON COUNTY - ART AND MUSIC
DEPARTMENT □ Cincinnati, OH

Naito, Shirley S., Oahu Ch.Coord.
HAWAII STATE LIBRARY - EDNA ALLYN ROOM
□ Honolulu, HI

Najar, Pamela, Consrv.
INDIANA HISTORICAL SOCIETY - WILLIAM
HENRY SMITH MEMORIAL LIBRARY □
Indianapolis, IN

Nakada, Ayako, Res.Asst.
METROPOLITAN MUSEUM OF ART - THOMAS J.
WATSON LIBRARY □ New York, NY

Nakamura, Hanako, Hd.
HAWAII STATE LIBRARY - BUSINESS,
SCIENCE, TECHNOLOGY UNIT □ Honolulu, HI

Namath, Nardina L., Dir., Lib./AV Serv.
HENRY FORD HOSPITAL - FRANK J. SLADEN
LIBRARY □ Detroit, MI

Namer, Sr. Rosella, Fine Arts Libn.
VITERBO COLLEGE - ZOELLER FINE ARTS
LIBRARY □ La Crosse, WI

Nanayakkara, D., Libn.
NEWFOUNDLAND - DEPARTMENT OF
EDUCATION - INSTRUCTIONAL MATERIALS
LIBRARY □ St. John's, NF

Nance, Marian O., Libn.
U.S. ARMY INSTITUTE FOR MILITARY
ASSISTANCE - MARQUAT MEMORIAL LIBRARY†
□ Fort Bragg, NC

Nance, Mrs. Patsy S., Libn.
TEXAS STATE - RAILROAD COMMISSION OF
TEXAS - CENTRAL RECORDS □ Austin, TX

Nangle, Karen, Black/White Lib.
PHOTO RESEARCHERS, INC. - LIBRARY □ New
York, NY

Nanstiel, Barbara, Coord. of Lib.Serv.
MERCY HOSPITAL - MEDICAL LIBRARY □
Wilkes-Barre, PA

Napier, Lucile, Acq.Libn.
U.S. AIR FORCE - AEROSPACE MEDICAL
DIVISION - SCHOOL OF AEROSPACE MEDICINE
- STRUGHOLD AEROMEDICAL LIBRARY □ Brooks
AFB, TX

Napoli, Gloria, Chf.Libn.
BERNHARD (Arnold) AND COMPANY, INC. -
BUSINESS LIBRARY □ New York, NY

Naquib, Moustafa, Ref.
NEW YORK CITY - MUNICIPAL REFERENCE
AND RESEARCH CENTER □ New York, NY

Naraine, Mrs. I., Libn.
DALLAS POWER AND LIGHT COMPANY -
RESEARCH LIBRARY □ Dallas, TX

Narang, Mr. Sat, Hd.Cat.Serv.
EASTERN ILLINOIS UNIVERSITY - BOOTH
LIBRARY □ Charleston, IL

Naranjo, Antonio, Foreign Law Libn.
COOK COUNTY LAW LIBRARY □ Chicago, IL

Naraynsingh, Miss T., Map Libn.
CANADA - GEOLOGICAL SURVEY OF CANADA -
LIBRARY □ Ottawa, ON

Narbut, Keltah T., Libn.
BANCROFT-WHITNEY COMPANY - EDITORIAL
LIBRARY† □ San Francisco, CA

Nardin, Doris, Major Lib.Ck.
PENN MUTUAL LIFE INSURANCE COMPANY -
LAW LIBRARY □ Philadelphia, PA

Nardini, Hannah, Libn.
CARLSMITH, CARLSMITH, WICHMAN & CASE -
LIBRARY □ Hilo, HI

Nardo, Mr. Helio, Asst.Cat.Libn.
WESTERN ILLINOIS UNIVERSITY - LIBRARIES
□ Macomb, IL

Nardone, Ernest, Ref.Libn.
RUTGERS UNIVERSITY, THE STATE
UNIVERSITY OF NEW JERSEY - JUSTICE
HENRY ACKERSON LIBRARY OF LAW &
CRIMINAL JUSTICE □ Newark, NJ

Narducci, Frances, Ref.Libn.
MC GRAW-HILL, INC. - LIBRARY □ New York,
NY

Nareff, Margaret W., Cur.Asst.
CRANDALL (Prudence) MEMORIAL MUSEUM -
LIBRARY □ Canterbury, CT

Narvaez, Peter, Archv.
MEMORIAL UNIVERSITY OF NEWFOUNDLAND -
FOLKLORE AND LANGUAGE ARCHIVE □ St.
John's, NF

Nase, Lois, Asst.Ref.Libn.
LEHIGH UNIVERSITY - MART SCIENCE AND
ENGINEERING LIBRARY □ Bethlehem, PA

Nash, C.C., Mgr.
FRANKLIN (H.H.) CLUB - LIBRARY† □ Cazenovia,
NY

Nash, Jeanne C., Hd.Cat.
INTERNATIONAL MONETARY FUND/WORLD
BANK - JOINT BANK-FUND LIBRARY □
Washington, DC

Nash, M.L., Attorney, Libn.
U.S. DEPT. OF STATE - OFFICE OF THE LEGAL
ADVISER - LAW LIBRARY □ Washington, DC

Nash, Martha C., Law Libn.
GULF COMPANIES - LAW LIBRARY □ Houston,
TX

Nash, N. Frederick, Libn.
UNIVERSITY OF ILLINOIS - RARE BOOK ROOM
□ Urbana, IL

Nash, Richard M., Assoc. Law Libn.
ARIZONA STATE UNIVERSITY - COLLEGE OF
LAW - LIBRARY □ Tempe, AZ

Nashu, A. Munim, EPA Coord./Libn.
UPJOHN COMPANY - D.S. GILMORE RESEARCH
LABORATORIES - RESEARCH LIBRARY □ North
Haven, CT

Naslund, Cheryl T., Spec. Subject Asst.
DARTMOUTH COLLEGE - MAP SECTION □
Hanover, NH

Nass, Dr. David L., Dir.
MINNESOTA HISTORICAL SOCIETY -
SOUTHWEST MINNESOTA HISTORICAL
CENTER □ Marshall, MN

Nast, Jo Anne, Supv., Sch.Serv.
ILLINOIS STATE HISTORICAL LIBRARY □
Springfield, IL

Nath, Capt. Herbert T., Ref.Libn.
CITADEL - THE MILITARY COLLEGE OF SOUTH
CAROLINA - DANIEL LIBRARY □ Charleston, SC

Nathanson, David, Chf.Libn.
U.S. NATL. PARK SERVICE - HARPERS FERRY
CENTER LIBRARY □ Harpers Ferry, WV

Nathanson, Paul, Libn.
VANCOUVER SCHOOL OF THEOLOGY - LIBRARY
□ Vancouver, BC

Nation, James R., Libn.
U.S. GEOLOGICAL SURVEY - FLAGSTAFF FIELD
CENTER - BRANCH LIBRARY □ Flagstaff, AZ

Naulty, Deborah, Ref.Libn.
FEDERAL RESERVE BANK OF PHILADELPHIA -
LIBRARY □ Philadelphia, PA

Navaretta, Cynthia, Dir.
WOMEN ARTISTS NEWS - ARCHIVES □ New
York, NY

Navarre, Sally, Asst.Libn.
KALAMAZOO INSTITUTE OF ARTS - ART
CENTER LIBRARY □ Kalamazoo, MI

Nawyn, John P., Libn.
BUCKS COUNTY PLANNING COMMISSION
STAFF LIBRARY □ Doylestown, PA

Naylor, Barbara, Sr.Libn.
FAIRVIEW STATE HOSPITAL - STAFF LIBRARY
□ Costa Mesa, CA

Naylor, David L., Assoc.Libn./Pub.Serv.
SYRACUSE UNIVERSITY - LAW LIBRARY □
Syracuse, NY

Naylor, Eleanor R., Libn.
BARIUM AND CHEMICALS, INC. - RESEARCH
LIBRARY □ Steubenville, OH

Nazario, Idalia, Archv.
PUERTO RICO - INSTITUTE OF PUERTO RICAN
CULTURE - ARCHIVO GENERAL DE PUERTO
RICO □ San Juan, PR

Nazarro, B., Cat.
SOUTHWESTERN UNIVERSITY - SCHOOL OF
LAW LIBRARY □ Los Angeles, CA

Naznitsky, Ira, Supv.
GAF CORPORATION - TECHNICAL
INFORMATION SERVICES □ Wayne, NJ

Nazzaro, Lorraine T., Libn.
AVCO CORPORATION - AVCO-EVERETT
RESEARCH LABORATORY - LIBRARY □ Everett,
MA

Neafus, S., Libn.
ICI AMERICAS INC. - DARCO EXPERIMENTAL
LABORATORY LIBRARY □ Marshall, TX

Neal, Anna, Libn.
MEMPHIS STATE UNIVERSITY LIBRARIES -
MUSIC LIBRARY □ Memphis, TN

Neal, Berna E., Libn.
UNIVERSITY OF MARYLAND, COLLEGE PARK -
LIBRARIES - ARCHITECTURE LIBRARY □
College Park, MD

Neal, Christina W., Libn.
UNIVERSITY OF MICHIGAN - SOCIAL WORK
LIBRARY □ Ann Arbor, MI

Neal, Kathryn B., Coord., Ref.Serv.
ALABAMA A & M UNIVERSITY - JOSEPH F.
DRAKE MEMORIAL LEARNING RESOURCES
CENTER □ Normal, AL

Neal, Margaret, Coord. & Info.Spec.
CANADIAN TROTTING ASSOCIATION -
STANDARDBRED CANADA LIBRARY □ Toronto,
ON

Neale, Judith, Sr.Libn.
JOHNS-MANVILLE SALES CORPORATION -
CORPORATE INFORMATION CENTER □ Denver,
CO

Neargardner, Linda, Dir.
SPOHN HOSPITAL - MEDICAL LIBRARY □ Corpus
Christi, TX

Neary, Sharon E., Libn.
SASKATCHEWAN RESEARCH COUNCIL -
LIBRARY □ Saskatoon, SK

Necht, Toby E., Tech.Libn.
GPU NUCLEAR - TECHNICAL LIBRARY □
Parsippany, NJ

Nedderman, Bob, State Doc.Libn.
MISSOURI STATE LIBRARY □ Jefferson City,
MO

Nee, William R., Vice Pres.
STANFORD ENVIRONMENTAL LAW SOCIETY -
LIBRARY □ Stanford, CA

Needham, Paul, Cur., Printed Bks.
PIERPONT MORGAN LIBRARY □ New York, NY

Neel, Suzanne Pickering, Dir.Prof.Prog./Serv.
ALEXANDER GRAHAM BELL ASSOCIATION FOR
THE DEAF - VOLTA BUREAU LIBRARY □
Washington, DC

Neeland, Ellen, Asst.Libn.
PEAT, MARWICK, MITCHELL & COMPANY -
LIBRARY □ Houston, TX

Neeley, Kathleen, Asst.Sci.Libn.
UNIVERSITY OF KANSAS - SCIENCE LIBRARY □
Lawrence, KS
Neely, Ann, Ref.Libn.
PARKLAND COLLEGE - LEARNING RESOURCE
CENTER □ Champaign, IL
Neely, Jesse G., Libn.
SCRIPPS CLINIC & RESEARCH FOUNDATION -
KRESGE MEDICAL LIBRARY □ La Jolla, CA
Neely, Mark E., Jr., Dir.
LINCOLN NATIONAL LIFE FOUNDATION - LOUIS
A. WARREN LINCOLN LIBRARY AND MUSEUM □
Fort Wayne, IN
Neeri, Elizabeth P., Libn.
XEROX ELECTRO-OPTICAL SYSTEMS -
TECHNICAL LIBRARY □ Pasadena, CA
Neese, Janet A., Hd., Coll.Dev.
SUNY - COLLEGE AT GENESEO - MILNE
LIBRARY □ Geneseo, NY
Neff, Jerry, Dir.
WAGNALLS MEMORIAL - LIBRARY □ Lithopolis,
OH
Nefsky, Judith, Archv.
CANADIAN JEWISH CONGRESS - LIBRARY &
ARCHIVES □ Montreal, PQ
Negaard, Chere, Dir., Lib.Serv.
NORTHROP UNIVERSITY - ALUMNI LIBRARY† □
Inglewood, CA
Negaard, Gordon R., Dir.
U.S. AIR FORCE - WRIGHT AERONAUTICAL
LABORATORIES - AEROSPACE STRUCTURES
INFORMATIONAL ANALYSIS CENTER □ Wright-
Patterson AFB, OH
Negin, Arthur W., Libn./V.P.
RICHLAND COUNTY LAW LIBRARY □ Mansfield,
OH
Negrych, Love, Cat.
UNIVERSITY OF MANITOBA - MEDICAL
LIBRARY □ Winnipeg, MB
Nehlig, Mary E., Asst.Dir., Lib.Serv.
WEST CHESTER STATE COLLEGE - FRANCIS
HARVEY GREEN LIBRARY - SPECIAL
COLLECTIONS □ West Chester, PA
Neiderheiser, Clodaugh, Asst.Archv.
UNIVERSITY OF MINNESOTA - UNIVERSITY
ARCHIVES □ Minneapolis, MN
Neiderkorn, Annette, Libn.
WESTERN WISCONSIN TECHNICAL INSTITUTE
- LIBRARY □ La Crosse, WI
Neidhardt, B.M., ILL
GOODRICH (B.F.) COMPANY - GOODRICH
CHEMICAL DIVISION TECHNICAL CENTER -
INFORMATION CENTER □ Avon Lake, OH
Neiger, James I., Adm./Coll.Dev.Libn.
HEBREW UNION COLLEGE - JEWISH
INSTITUTE OF RELIGION - KLAU LIBRARY □
Cincinnati, OH
Neigh, Pat, Circ.Libn.
BLOOMFIELD COLLEGE - GEORGE TALBOT HALL
LIBRARY □ Bloomfield, NJ
Neighbours, K.F., Archv.
FORT BELKNAP ARCHIVES, INC. - LIBRARY □
Newcastle, TX
Neikirk, Jody, Info.Asst.
UNIVERSITY OF MISSOURI - HEALTH CARE
TECHNOLOGY CENTER - HCTC INFORMATION
CENTER □ Columbia, MO
Neill, Charlotte, Asst.Dir.Tech.Serv.
TEXAS A & M UNIVERSITY - MEDICAL
SCIENCES LIBRARY □ College Station, TX
Neill, Desmond G., Libn.
MASSEY COLLEGE - LIBRARY □ Toronto, ON
Neilon, Madeline, Libn.
MIDDLESEX LAW LIBRARY ASSOCIATION -
LIBRARY □ Lowell, MA
Neilson, Ann, Libn.
GULF CANADA LIMITED - RESEARCH &
DEVELOPMENT DEPARTMENT - LIBRARY □
Mississauga, ON
Neilson, Marjorie, Documentalist
MC GILL UNIVERSITY - CENTRE FOR
DEVELOPING AREA STUDIES -
DOCUMENTATION CENTRE □ Montreal, PQ

Neiman, Susan, Asst.Libn.
HARVARD UNIVERSITY - ROBBINS LIBRARY □
Cambridge, MA
Neistein, Dr. Jose, Exec.Dir.
BRAZILIAN-AMERICAN CULTURAL INSTITUTE,
INC. - HAROLD E. WIBBERLEY, JR. LIBRARY □
Washington, DC
Neitz, Cordelia M., Libn.
CUMBERLAND COUNTY HISTORICAL SOCIETY
& HAMILTON LIBRARY □ Carlisle, PA
Nelken, Annabella B., Exec.Adm.
NATIONAL PSYCHOLOGICAL ASSOCIATION FOR
PSYCHOANALYSIS - GEORGE LAWTON
MEMORIAL LIBRARY □ New York, NY
Nelson, Ann, Hd.
UNIVERSITY OF BRITISH COLUMBIA -
INSTITUTE OF ANIMAL RESOURCE ECOLOGY -
LIBRARY □ Vancouver, BC
Nelson, April, Tech.Proc.Serv.Libn.
ROSEMONT COLLEGE - GERTRUDE KISTLER
MEMORIAL LIBRARY - SPECIAL COLLECTIONS
□ Rosemont, PA
Nelson, Barbara, Sr.Lib.Tech.Asst.
GOULD INC. - GOULD INFORMATION CENTER □
Rolling Meadows, IL
Nelson, Brent A., Libn.
UNIVERSITY OF ARKANSAS, FAYETTEVILLE -
TECHNOLOGY CAMPUS LIBRARY □ Little Rock,
AR
Nelson, Carolyn, Libn.
WESTERNERS INTERNATIONAL, A
FOUNDATION - LIBRARY □ Tucson, AZ
Nelson, Carolyn M., Libn.
U.S. BUREAU OF LAND MANAGEMENT -
MONTANA STATE OFFICE LIBRARY □ Billings,
MT
Nelson, Catharine E., Consrv.
HAVERHILL PUBLIC LIBRARY - SPECIAL
COLLECTIONS DIVISION □ Haverhill, MA
Nelson, Cecelia H., Cur.
OCEAN CITY HISTORICAL MUSEUM - LIBRARY
□ Ocean City, NJ
Nelson, Cecilia, Lib.Assoc.
IOWA STATE DEPARTMENT OF
ENVIRONMENTAL QUALITY - TECHNICAL
LIBRARY □ Des Moines, IA
Nelson, Charles L., Sr.Libn.
ARIZONA STATE DEPARTMENT OF HEALTH
SERVICES - PUBLIC HEALTH LIBRARY □
Phoenix, AZ
Nelson, Cheryl, Cat./AV Libn.
NICHOLS COLLEGE - CONANT LIBRARY □
Dudley, MA
Nelson, Clark, ILL Libn.
MAYO FOUNDATION - MAYO CLINIC LIBRARY □
Rochester, MN
Nelson, Dalmas H., Assoc.Dir.
UNIVERSITY OF UTAH - CENTER FOR PUBLIC
AFFAIRS AND ADMINISTRATION - RESEARCH
LIBRARY □ Salt Lake City, UT
Nelson, David M., Dir.
UNIVERSITY OF MINNESOTA - AGRICULTURAL
EXTENSION SERVICE - MINNESOTA ANALYSIS
& PLANNING SYSTEM □ St. Paul, MN
Nelson, Dwayne, Libn.
MARSTELLER, INC. - LIBRARY □ Chicago, IL
Nelson, Edward, Archv.
MINNESOTA STATE IRON RANGE RESOURCES
& REHABILITATION BOARD - IRON RANGE
RESEARCH CENTER □ Chisholm, MN
Nelson, Ellen, Info.Spec.
RAINIER NATIONAL BANK - INFORMATION
CENTER □ Seattle, WA
Nelson, Esther, Asst.Ref.Libn.
WESTERN ILLINOIS UNIVERSITY - LIBRARIES
□ Macomb, IL
Nelson, Gabrielle S., Mgr.
IBM CORPORATION - LIBRARY □ Poughkeepsie,
NY
Nelson, Dr. Gareth, Cur.
AMERICAN MUSEUM OF NATURAL HISTORY -
DEPARTMENT OF ICHTHYOLOGY - DEAN
MEMORIAL LIBRARY □ New York, NY

Nelson, Gerald O., Libn.
CALIFORNIA STATE REHABILITATION CENTER
- RESIDENT LIBRARY □ Norco, CA
Nelson, Gretchen, Hd., Cat.Dept.
SOUTH DAKOTA STATE UNIVERSITY - HILTON
M. BRIGGS LIBRARY □ Brookings, SD
Nelson, Helene W., Libn.
PARKER, CHAPIN, FLATTAU AND KLIMPL -
LIBRARY† □ New York, NY
Nelson, Hildegard, Per.Libn.
FULLER THEOLOGICAL SEMINARY -
MC ALISTER LIBRARY □ Pasadena, CA
Nelson, Jan, Act.Libn.
ROYAL COMMISSION ON THE NORTHERN
ENVIRONMENT - LIBRARY □ Thunder Bay, ON
Nelson, Jane, Staff Libn.
TRAVERSE CITY REGIONAL PSYCHIATRIC
HOSPITAL - STAFF LIBRARY □ Traverse City, MI
Nelson, Jane Gray, Hd.Libn.
FINE ARTS MUSEUMS OF SAN FRANCISCO -
LIBRARY □ San Francisco, CA
Nelson, Janie Jones, Libn.
U.S. GEOLOGICAL SURVEY - WATER
RESOURCES DIVISION - READING ROOM □
Albuquerque, NM
Nelson, Jeannette H., Sr.Libn.
COMPUTER SCIENCES CORPORATION -
TECHNICAL LIBRARY □ El Segundo, CA
Nelson, John D., Law Libn.
UNIVERSITY OF NEBRASKA, LINCOLN - LAW
LIBRARY □ Lincoln, NE
Nelson, Josephus, Hd. Main Reading Rm.
LIBRARY OF CONGRESS - GEN. READING
ROOMS DIV. □ Washington, DC
Nelson, L.E.
DOW CHEMICAL COMPANY - TECHNICAL
INFORMATION SERVICES - CENTRAL REPORT
INDEX □ Midland, MI
Nelson, Linda, Libn.
MUSEUM OF FINE ARTS, HOUSTON - LIBRARY □
Houston, TX
Nelson, Marcia, Libn.
ILLINOIS STATE WATER SURVEY - LIBRARY □
Champaign, IL
Nelson, Margaret V., Per. & Music
CAMROSE LUTHERAN COLLEGE - LIBRARY □
Camrose, AB
Nelson, Mariann, Ref.Anl.
UNIVERSITY OF MINNESOTA - INDUSTRIAL
RELATIONS CENTER - REFERENCE ROOM □
Minneapolis, MN
Nelson, Marie, AV Libn.
U.S. VETERANS ADMINISTRATION (MN-
Minneapolis) - HOSPITAL LIBRARY □
Minneapolis, MN
Nelson, Melanie, Cat.
UNIVERSITY OF ARKANSAS AT LITTLE ROCK -
PULASKI COUNTY LAW LIBRARY □ Little Rock,
AR
Nelson, Mona R., Program Coord.
KANDIYOHI COUNTY HISTORICAL SOCIETY -
VICTOR E. LAWSON RESEARCH LIBRARY □
Willmar, MN
Nelson, Nora, Cur.
STILL WATERS FOUNDATION - LIBRARY □
Pensacola, FL
Nelson, Norma, Asst.Ref.Libn.
YESHIVA UNIVERSITY - ALBERT EINSTEIN
COLLEGE OF MEDICINE - D. SAMUEL
GOTTESMAN LIBRARY □ Bronx, NY
Nelson, P.J., Regional Libn.
CANADA - TRANSPORT CANADA - CANADIAN
AIR TRANSPORTATION ADMINISTRATION -
WESTERN REGIONAL LIBRARY □ Edmonton, AB
Nelson, Peg, Libn.
BALL CORPORATION - BALL INFORMATION
CENTER AND LAW LIBRARY □ Muncie, IN
Nelson, Phyllis, Desk Res.
FOOTE CONE & BELDING - INFORMATION
CENTER □ Chicago, IL
Nelson, Ron, Pres.
PINE COUNTY HISTORICAL SOCIETY -
LIBRARY □ Askov, MN

Nelson, Ruth, Ref.Libn.
MARSHALL (John) LAW SCHOOL - LIBRARY □
Chicago, IL
Nelson, Shirley, AV Libn.
U.S. VETERANS ADMINISTRATION (IL- Marion)
- HOSPITAL LIBRARY □ Marion, IL
Nelson, Vance E., Cur.
NEBRASKA STATE HISTORICAL SOCIETY -
FORT ROBINSON MUSEUM - RESEARCH
LIBRARY □ Crawford, NE
Nelson, Vernon H., Archv.
MORAVIAN CHURCH IN AMERICA - NORTHERN
PROVINCE - MORAVIAN ARCHIVES □
Bethlehem, PA
Nelton, Bill, Libn.
MICHIGAN STATE DEPARTMENT OF PUBLIC
HEALTH - LIBRARY □ Lansing, MI
Nemec, Dolores, Libn.
UNIVERSITY OF WISCONSIN, MADISON - F.B.
POWER PHARMACEUTICAL LIBRARY □ Madison,
WI
Nemeth, Martha C., Tech.Libn.
SUNKIST GROWERS, INC. - RESEARCH
LIBRARY □ Ontario, CA
Nemiccolo, Harriet, Chf.Libn.
BOSTON COLLEGE - GRADUATE SCHOOL OF
SOCIAL WORK LIBRARY □ Chestnut Hill, MA
Nemoitin, Bernard O., Pres.
STAMFORD HISTORICAL SOCIETY - LIBRARY □
Stamford, CT
Nesbit, Beryl, Libn.
UNIVERSITY OF ROCHESTER - CHARLOTTE
WHITNEY ALLEN LIBRARY □ Rochester, NY
Nesbit, Jennifer, Hd., Educ.Sect.
CHICAGO PUBLIC LIBRARY CENTRAL LIBRARY -
SOCIAL SCIENCES & HISTORY DIVISION □
Chicago, IL
Nesbitt, Ina L., Med.Libn.
U.S. ARMY HOSPITALS - FORT POLK ARMY
HOSPITAL - MEDICAL LIBRARY □ Fort Polk, LA
Nesthus, Marie, Principal Libn.
NEW YORK PUBLIC LIBRARY - DONNELL
LIBRARY CENTER - FILM LIBRARY □ New York,
NY
Nesvig, Lorraine, Libn.
ARMOUR RESEARCH CENTER - LIBRARY □
Scottsdale, AZ
Neswick, Robert A., Mgr.
SPOKANE SPOKESMAN-REVIEW AND DAILY
CHRONICLE - NEWSPAPER REFERENCE
LIBRARY □ Spokane, WA
Nethers, Betty, Mgr.
OWENS-CORNING FIBERGLAS CORPORATION -
TECHNICAL DATA CENTER □ Granville, OH
Nettles, Joyce, Res.Libn.
TEXAS MID-CONTINENT OIL & GAS
ASSOCIATION - LIBRARY □ Dallas, TX
Nettleton, Helen, Libn.
OWYHEE COUNTY HISTORICAL COMPLEX
MUSEUM - LIBRARY □ Murphy, ID
Nettleton, Lavonne, Asst.Libn.
REFORMED BIBLE COLLEGE - LIBRARY □ Grand
Rapids, MI
Netz, David, E.R.C. Coord.
WESTERN MICHIGAN UNIVERSITY -
EDUCATIONAL RESOURCES CENTER □
Kalamazoo, MI
Netzow, Mary, Chf.Libn.
U.S. VETERANS ADMINISTRATION (DC-
Washington) - MEDICAL CENTER LIBRARY† □
Washington, DC
Neubauer, Carol J., Circ.Libn.
BRIDGEWATER STATE COLLEGE - CLEMENT C.
MAXWELL LIBRARY □ Bridgewater, MA
Neubig, P., Ref.Sys.Supv.
EXXON CORPORATION - COMMUNICATIONS
AND COMPUTER SCIENCE - TECHNICAL
LIBRARY □ Florham Park, NJ
Neuburger, Dorothy A., Chem.Info.Spec.
ECONOMICS LABORATORY, INC. - CORPORATE
INFORMATION CENTER □ St. Paul, MN

Neuendorf, Klaus, Libn.
OREGON STATE DEPARTMENT OF GEOLOGY
AND MINERAL INDUSTRIES - LIBRARY □
Portland, OR
Neuendorffer, Ruth, Libn.
HISTORICAL SOCIETY OF THE TARRYTOWNS -
HEADQUARTERS LIBRARY □ Tarrytown, NY
Neufeld, Irving H., Chf., Lib.Sys.
UNITED TECHNOLOGIES CORPORATION -
LIBRARY □ East Hartford, CT
Neufeld, Judith, Asst. to the Dir.
LONG ISLAND LIBRARY RESOURCES COUNCIL,
INC. (LILRC) □ Bellport, NY
Neufeld, M. Lynne, Exec.Dir.
NATIONAL FEDERATION OF ABSTRACTING
AND INDEXING SERVICES □ Philadelphia, PA
Neuman, Susan, Libn.
UNIVERSITY OF PITTSBURGH - ECONOMICS/
COLLECTION IN REGIONAL ECONOMICS □
Pittsburgh, PA
Neumann, Alice W., Instr./Media Coord.
JEWISH HOSPITAL OF CINCINNATI SCHOOL OF
NURSING - NURSE'S REFERENCE LIBRARY □
Cincinnati, OH
Neumann, D., Data Anl.
U.S. NATL. BUREAU OF STANDARDS -
CHEMICAL THERMODYNAMICS DATA CENTER
□ Washington, DC
Neumann, Diane G., Asst.Libn.
HARTFORD MEDICAL SOCIETY - LIBRARY □
Hartford, CT
Neumann, Evelyn, Lib.Adm.
LIBRARY ASSOCIATION OF LA JOLLA -
ATHENAEUM MUSIC AND ARTS LIBRARY □ La
Jolla, CA
Neuschafer, Ann, Membership Serv.Ck.
GOLF COURSE SUPERINTENDENTS
ASSOCIATION OF AMERICA - GCSAA LIBRARY
□ Lawrence, KS
Neutel, W., Natl. Ethnic Archv.
CANADA - PUBLIC ARCHIVES OF CANADA -
MANUSCRIPT DIVISION □ Ottawa, ON
Neutel, Walter, Chf.
CANADA - PUBLIC ARCHIVES OF CANADA -
NATIONAL ETHNIC ARCHIVES □ Ottawa, ON
Nevai, Maria, Tech.Serv.Libn.
COOLEY (Thomas M.) LAW SCHOOL - LIBRARY □
Lansing, MI
Neves, Donna, Asst.Libn.
KAISER-PERMANENTE MEDICAL CENTER -
PANORAMA CITY HEALTH SCIENCE LIBRARY □
Panorama City, CA
Neveu, Alfred J., Hd.Plan.Res. Unit
NEW YORK STATE DEPARTMENT OF
TRANSPORTATION PLANNING DIVISION -
LIBRARY □ Albany, NY
Neveu, Wilma B., Chf.Libn.
U.S. VETERANS ADMINISTRATION (LA-New
Orleans) - MEDICAL CENTER LIBRARY □ New
Orleans, LA
Nevill, Ann, Health Sci.Libn.
DALHOUSIE UNIVERSITY - W.K. KELLOGG
HEALTH SCIENCES LIBRARY □ Halifax, NS
Neville, Doris, Supv.Libn.
NEW YORK PUBLIC LIBRARY - MID-
MANHATTAN LIBRARY - HISTORY AND SOCIAL
SCIENCES DEPARTMENT □ New York, NY
Neville, Timothy, Photo Libn.
UTAH STATE HISTORICAL SOCIETY -
RESEARCH LIBRARY □ Salt Lake City, UT
Nevins, Joyce, Asst.Libn.
DONORS FORUM OF CHICAGO - LIBRARY □
Chicago, IL
New, Joel B., Dir.
U.S. DEPT. OF COMMERCE - INTERNATIONAL
TRADE ADMINISTRATION - GREENSBORO
DISTRICT OFFICE LIBRARY □ Greensboro, NC
New, Lillian R., Hd.
CHICAGO PUBLIC LIBRARY CULTURAL CENTER
- THOMAS HUGHES CHILDREN'S LIBRARY □
Chicago, IL

Newberry, J.M. "Boats", Founder & Dir.
P.T. BOATS, INC. - LIBRARY, ARCHIVES &
TECHNICAL INFORMATION CENTER -
NATIONAL HEADQUARTERS □ Memphis, TN
Newburg, Helen, Asst.Libn.
LANDMARK SOCIETY OF WESTERN NEW YORK
- WENRICH MEMORIAL LIBRARY □ Rochester,
NY
Newburger, Adele, Assoc.Dir.
UNIVERSITY OF BALTIMORE - BALTIMORE
REGION INSTITUTIONAL STUDIES CENTER
(BRISC) □ Baltimore, MD
Newby, Nella, Lib.Asst. & Ser.Libn.
CATHOLIC MEDICAL CENTER OF BROOKLYN &
QUEENS, INC. - CENTRAL MEDICAL LIBRARY □
Jamaica, NY
Newcom, Kirk, Soc.Sci.Libn.
CENTRAL MISSOURI STATE UNIVERSITY -
WARD EDWARDS LIBRARY □ Warrensburg, MO
Newcomb, Dorothy, Asst.Dir.
SALISBURY STATE COLLEGE - BLACKWELL
LIBRARY □ Salisbury, MD
Newcomb, Ruth, Hd., Tech.Serv.
MACALESTER COLLEGE - WEYERHAEUSER
LIBRARY □ St. Paul, MN
Newcombe, Barbara T., Mgr.
CHICAGO TRIBUNE - INFORMATION CENTER □
Chicago, IL
Newell, Anita, Mgr.
WESTINGHOUSE ELECTRIC CORPORATION -
RESEARCH LABORATORIES - LIBRARY† □
Pittsburgh, PA
Newell, Charles, Statistician
TEXAS STATE INDUSTRIAL COMMISSION -
RESEARCH LIBRARY □ Austin, TX
Newell, Elizabeth
NEW PROVIDENCE HISTORICAL SOCIETY -
LIBRARY □ New Providence, NJ
Newell, Vera C., Libn.
HERCULES, INC. - LIBRARY □ Wilmington, DE
Newgaard, JoAlyce, Ref.Libn.
FOUNDATION CENTER - NEW YORK - LIBRARY
□ New York, NY
Newhall, George, Film Libn.
SANDY CORPORATION - RESEARCH &
RETRIEVAL CENTER □ Southfield, MI
Newhams, Susan, Libn.
STONE AND WEBSTER ENGINEERING
CORPORATION - TECHNICAL INFORMATION
CENTER □ Denver, CO
Newhouse, Frances F., Libn.
SEBASTIAN COUNTY LAW LIBRARY □ Fort
Smith, AR
Newins, Nancy, Libn.
TEXAS INSTRUMENTS, INC. - RESEARCH
BUILDING LIBRARY □ Dallas, TX
Newlin, Jeanne, Cur., Theater Coll.
HARVARD UNIVERSITY - HOUGHTON LIBRARY
□ Cambridge, MA
Newlin, Jeanne T., Cur.
HARVARD UNIVERSITY - THEATRE
COLLECTION □ Cambridge, MA
Newlon, Kent, First Asst.
PUBLIC LIBRARY OF CINCINNATI AND
HAMILTON COUNTY - FILMS AND RECORDINGS
CENTER □ Cincinnati, OH
Newman, Carol, Libn.
BOULDER VALLEY PUBLIC SCHOOLS, REGION 2
- PROFESSIONAL LIBRARY □ Boulder, CO
Newman, Cheryl, Med.Libn.
RIVERVIEW HOSPITAL - MEDICAL LIBRARY† □
Red Bank, NJ
Newman, David, Res.Assoc
MOBIL OIL CORPORATION - PUBLIC AFFAIRS
SECRETARIAT □ New York, NY
Newman, David, Ref.Libn.
UNIVERSITY OF WESTERN ONTARIO -
FACULTY OF EDUCATION LIBRARY □ London,
ON
Newman, Fletcher C., Hd.Sci.Lib.
UNIVERSITY OF TEXAS, EL PASO - LIBRARY □
El Paso, TX

**P
E
R
S
O
N
N
E
L**

Newman, Fletcher C., Hd.
UNIVERSITY OF TEXAS, EL PASO - SCIENCE/
ENGINEERING/MATHEMATICS LIBRARY □ El
Paso, TX

Newman, Gerald L., Asst.Hum.Libn.
OKLAHOMA STATE UNIVERSITY - HUMANITIES
DIVISION □ Stillwater, OK

Newman, Jeannette, Asst.Libn.
DEBEVOISE, PLIMPTON, LYONS AND GATES -
LAW LIBRARY □ New York, NY

Newman, Joanne, Supv., AV
COCA-COLA COMPANY - ARCHIVES &
BUSINESS INFORMATION SERVICES □ Atlanta,
GA

Newman, John, Proj.Archv.
COLORADO STATE UNIVERSITY - GERMANS
FROM RUSSIA PROJECT LIBRARY □ Fort Collins,
CO

Newman, John J., Dp.Dir./Archv.
INDIANA STATE COMMISSION ON PUBLIC
RECORDS - ARCHIVES DIVISION □ Indianapolis,
IN

Newman, Linda P., Act. Mines Libn.
UNIVERSITY OF NEVADA, RENO - MACKAY
SCHOOL OF MINES LIBRARY □ Reno, NV

Newman, Patricia E., Transl.
U.S. DEPT OF ENERGY - SANDIA NATL.
LABORATORIES - TECHNICAL LIBRARY □
Albuquerque, NM

Newman, Susan T., Libn.
FORD FOUNDATION - LIBRARY □ New York, NY

Newman, Wilda B., Supv., Tech.Serv.
JOHNS HOPKINS UNIVERSITY - APPLIED
PHYSICS LABORATORY - R.E. GIBSON LIBRARY
□ Laurel, MD

Newman, William, Asst. Law Libn.
CAPITAL UNIVERSITY - LAW SCHOOL LIBRARY
□ Columbus, OH

Newnham, Rita, Leg.Libn.
MARYLAND STATE DEPARTMENT OF
LEGISLATIVE REFERENCE - LIBRARY □
Annapolis, MD

Newsom, Keith R., Supv.Libn., Open Lit.
U.S. AIR FORCE WEAPONS LABORATORY -
TECHNICAL LIBRARY □ Kirtland AFB, NM

Newsome, Margaret, Libn.
UNIVERSITY OF IDAHO - HUMANITIES
LIBRARY □ Moscow, ID

Newstead, Deborah, Lib.Techn.
SHAUGHNESSY HOSPITAL - HEALTH SCIENCES
LIBRARY □ Vancouver, BC

Newton, Barbara, Chf./Army Stud.Sect.
U.S. ARMY - ARMY LIBRARY □ Washington, DC

Newton, Charles, Libn.
BALTIMORE CITY DEPARTMENT OF PLANNING
- LIBRARY □ Baltimore, MD

Newton, Craig A., Cur.
COLUMBIA COUNTY HISTORICAL SOCIETY -
LIBRARY □ Orangeville, PA

Newton, Deborah A., District Libn.
U.S. ARMY - CORPS OF ENGINEERS -
SACRAMENTO DISTRICT - TECHNICAL
INFORMATION CENTER □ Sacramento, CA

Newton, Earle W., Dir.
MUSEUM OF THE AMERICAS - LIBRARY □
Brookfield, VT

Newton, Ellen, Libn.
UNITED FOOD AND COMMERCIAL WORKERS
INTERNATIONAL UNION - LIBRARY □
Washington, DC

Newton, Joan, Libn.
WINROCK INTERNATIONAL LIVESTOCK
RESEARCH AND TRAINING CENTER -
INTERNATIONAL CENTER LIBRARY □ Morrilton,
AR

Newton, Joyce, Info.Spec.
CORNING GLASS WORKS/CORNING MEDICAL &
SCIENTIFIC - DAVID R. STEINBERG MEMORIAL
LIBRARY & INFO. CENTER □ Medfield, MA

Newton, Karen W., Libn.
AEROSPACE CORPORATION - GERMANTOWN
LIBRARY □ Germantown, MD

Newton, Phyllis, Supv.Libn.
CALIFORNIA STATE DEPARTMENT OF
TRANSPORTATION - TRANSPORTATION
LIBRARY □ Sacramento, CA

Newton, Terra, Libn.
LOGANSPORT STATE HOSPITAL - MEDICAL
LIBRARY† □ Logansport, IN

Newton, William R., Supv., Res.Serv.
COCA-COLA COMPANY - ARCHIVES &
BUSINESS INFORMATION SERVICES □ Atlanta,
GA

Neyland, Cynthia K., Libn.
U.S. NAVY - NAVAL FACILITIES ENGINEERING
COMMAND - TECHNICAL LIBRARY □ Alexandria,
VA

Ng, Bok, Asst.Libn.
BECHTEL POWER CORPORATION - LIBRARY □
San Francisco, CA

Ng, Eva, Ch.Libn.
OAKLAND PUBLIC LIBRARY - ASIAN LIBRARY □
Oakland, CA

Ng, Hwei Wen, Libn.
CUTTER LABORATORIES - LIBRARY □ Berkeley,
CA

Ng, Pauline, Dir.
MEMORIAL HOSPITAL OF DU PAGE COUNTY -
MEDICAL & HEALTH SCIENCES LIBRARY □
Elmhurst, IL

Ng, Miss Tung-King, Hd.
UNIVERSITY OF BRITISH COLUMBIA - ASIAN
STUDIES LIBRARY □ Vancouver, BC

Nguyen, Janet, Cat.
U.S. PUBLIC HEALTH SERVICE - PARKLAWN
HEALTH LIBRARY □ Rockville, MD

Niblick, Patricia, Med.Libn.
CAYLOR-NICKEL CLINIC AND HOSPITAL -
MEDICAL LIBRARY □ Bluffton, IN

Nicely, Jane W., Mgr.
MAC FARLANE & COMPANY, INC. - FRY
CONSULTANTS INCORPORATED -
MANAGEMENT CENTRE □ Atlanta, GA

Nicely, Marilyn K., Acq.Libn.
UNIVERSITY OF OKLAHOMA - LAW LIBRARY □
Norman, OK

Nicholas, Paul T., Dir. of Engr.Serv.
AMERICAN INSTITUTE OF TIMBER
CONSTRUCTION - LIBRARY □ Englewood, CO

Nicholls, Pat, Chf.Libn.
UNIVERSITY OF WESTERN ONTARIO - SCHOOL
OF LIBRARY & INFORMATION SCIENCE -
LIBRARY □ London, ON

Nicholls, Dr. R.V.V., Archv./Libn.
CANADIAN RAILROAD HISTORICAL
ASSOCIATION - LIBRARY □ Montreal, PQ

Nichols, Barbara Best, Libn.
MONSANTO COMPANY - TRIANGLE PARK
DEVELOPMENT CENTER, INC. - LIBRARY □
Research Triangle Park, NC

Nichols, Carol, Libn.
RICHMOND PUBLIC LIBRARY - BUSINESS,
SCIENCE & TECHNOLOGY DEPARTMENT† □
Richmond, VA

Nichols, Diane, Ref.Libn.
UNIVERSITY OF LOUISVILLE - KORNHAUSER
HEALTH SCIENCES LIBRARY □ Louisville, KY

Nichols, Emmet A., Chf. Interpreter
U.S. NATL. PARK SERVICE - KENNESAW
MOUNTAIN NATL. BATTLEFIELD PARK -
LIBRARY □ Marietta, GA

Nichols, Gail, Libn.
UNIVERSITY OF CALIFORNIA, BERKELEY -
GOVERNMENT DOCUMENTS DEPARTMENT □
Berkeley, CA

Nichols, Gail A., Adm.Asst.
NORTH CENTRAL TEXAS COUNCIL OF
GOVERNMENTS - REGIONAL INFORMATION
SERVICE CENTER □ Arlington, TX

Nichols, J. Gary, State Libn.
MAINE STATE LIBRARY □ Augusta, ME

Nichols, Jacquelyn, Libn.
HEWLETT-PACKARD COMPANY - COLORADO
SPRINGS DIVISION - ENGINEERING RESOURCE
CENTER □ Colorado Springs, CO

Nichols, Joyce, Br.Libn./Nesconset
SMITHTOWN LIBRARY □ Smithtown, NY

Nichols, Julia, Coord., LRC
MEDICAL UNIVERSITY OF SOUTH CAROLINA -
LIBRARY □ Charleston, SC

Nichols, Ruby H., Patients' Libn.
U.S. VETERANS ADMINISTRATION (TN-
Murfreesboro) - MEDICAL CENTER LIBRARY □
Murfreesboro, TN

Nichols, Shirley G., Supv.Libn.
TENNESSEE VALLEY AUTHORITY - TECHNICAL
LIBRARY □ Muscle Shoals, AL

Nichols, William, Libn.
U.S. VETERANS ADMINISTRATION (AL-
Tuskegee) - MEDICAL CENTER LIBRARY □
Tuskegee, AL

Nichols, William J., Libn.
ASTOR HOME FOR CHILDREN - PROFESSIONAL
LIBRARY □ Rhinebeck, NY

Nicholsen, Margaret, Libn.
EVANSTON HISTORICAL SOCIETY - CHARLES
GATES DAWES HOME - LIBRARY □ Evanston, IL

Nicholson, Elizabeth S., Libn.
MC CUTCHEN, DOYLE, BROWN & ENERSEN -
LAW LIBRARY □ San Francisco, CA

Nicholson, Lillian, Libn.
SHRINERS HOSPITAL FOR CRIPPLED CHILDREN
- ORTHOPEDIC LIBRARY □ Houston, TX

Nicholson, Maurice, Cat.
SYSTEM DEVELOPMENT CORPORATION -
LIBRARY □ Santa Monica, CA

Nicholson, Millie, Libn.
MARTIN (Albert C.) & ASSOCIATES -
INFORMATION RESEARCH CENTER □ Los
Angeles, CA

Nickie, Edna, Libn.
ONTARIO - MINISTRY OF NATURAL
RESOURCES - NATURAL RESOURCES LIBRARY □
Toronto, ON

Nicklas, Linda Cheves, Spec.Coll.Libn.
STEPHEN F. AUSTIN STATE UNIVERSITY -
STEEN LIBRARY - SPECIAL COLLECTIONS
DEPARTMENT □ Nacogdoches, TX

Nicol, Jean M., Libn.
TOYS 'N THINGS, TRAINING & RESOURCE
CENTER, INC. □ St. Paul, MN

Nicol, Julie, Libn. for the Blind
MICHIGAN STATE LIBRARY SERVICES □
Lansing, MI

Niebuhr, Mary M., Asst.Dir.
ERIC CLEARINGHOUSE ON LANGUAGES AND
LINGUISTICS □ Washington, DC

Niehaus, Thomas, Dir.
TULANE UNIVERSITY OF LOUISIANA - LATIN
AMERICAN LIBRARY □ New Orleans, LA

Niekamp, Dorothy, Libn.
NINETY-NINES, INC. - LIBRARY □ Oklahoma
City, OK

Nielsen, Marian, Abstractor
KUTAK, ROCK & HUIE - LAW LIBRARY □ Omaha,
NE

Nielsen, Sonja M., Corp.Libn.
PAYETTE ASSOCIATES - LIBRARY □ Boston, MA

Nielsen, William E., Chf.Libn.
U.S. VETERANS ADMINISTRATION (WI-Tomah)
- HOSPITAL LIBRARY □ Tomah, WI

Niemann, John M., Dir.
INDIANA VOCATIONAL-TECHNICAL COLLEGE -
RESOURCE CENTER □ Gary, IN

Niemeyer, Dan, Supv., Prod.
UNIVERSITY OF COLORADO, BOULDER -
EDUCATIONAL MEDIA CENTER □ Boulder, CO

Niemeyer, Kay, Coord.
SAN DIEGO COUNTY - DEPARTMENT OF
EDUCATION - PROFESSIONAL RESOURCE AND
DEVELOPMENT CENTER □ San Diego, CA

Niemyer, Elizabeth, Acq.Libn.
FOLGER SHAKESPEARE LIBRARY □ Washington,
DC

Nier, Paula, Asst.Libn.
SELIGMAN (J.&W.) & CO. INCORPORATED -
RESEARCH LIBRARY □ New York, NY

Nies, Elizabeth A., Info.Sci.
MORTON-NORWICH PRODUCTS, INC. -
NORWICH PHARMACAL COMPANY - R&D DEPT.
- LIBRARY INFORMATION GROUP □ Norwich, NY

Nieves, Miguel Angel, Dir.
PUERTO RICO - INSTITUTE OF PUERTO RICAN
CULTURE - ARCHIVO GENERAL DE PUERTO
RICO □ San Juan, PR

Nieweg, Clinton F., Principal Libn.
PHILADELPHIA ORCHESTRA ASSOCIATION -
LIBRARY □ Philadelphia, PA

Nightingale, Margaret A., Libn.
PINELLAS COUNTY LAW LIBRARY -
CLEARWATER BRANCH □ Clearwater, FL

Nikirk, Robert, Libn.
GROLIER CLUB OF NEW YORK - LIBRARY □ New
York, NY

Nilan, Roxanne-Louise, Univ.Archv.
STANFORD UNIVERSITY - UNIVERSITY
ARCHIVES □ Stanford, CA

Niles, Carrie, Music/Media Cat.
SUNY - COLLEGE AT FREDONIA - MUSIC
LIBRARY □ Fredonia, NY

Niles, Joyce, Children's Libn.
BUREAU OF JEWISH EDUCATION - JEWISH
COMMUNITY LIBRARY □ San Francisco, CA

Nilsson, Frances S., Ref.Libn.
BABSON COLLEGE - HORN LIBRARY □ Babson
Park, MA

Nim, Myrtle, Music Libn.
CARNEGIE-MELLON UNIVERSITY - HUNT
LIBRARY □ Pittsburgh, PA

Nimer, Gilda, Libn.
AMERICAN UNIVERSITY - FOREIGN AREA
STUDIES LIBRARY □ Washington, DC

Nimmo, Fran, Libn.
AEROJET ORDNANCE COMPANY - TECHNICAL
LIBRARY □ Downey, CA

Nisbet, William, Supv.Ref.
NATIONAL SAFETY COUNCIL - LIBRARY □
Chicago, IL

Nisenoff, Sylvia, Prof.Info.Spec.
AMERICAN PERSONNEL AND GUIDANCE
ASSOCIATION - HEADQUARTERS OFFICE
LIBRARY □ Falls Church, VA

Nish, Susan, Techn.
ATOMIC ENERGY OF CANADA, LTD. -
ENGINEERING COMPANY LIBRARY □ Montreal,
PQ

Nishimura, Hazel S., Libn.
U.S. NATL. MARINE FISHERIES SERVICE -
WESTERN PACIFIC PROGRAMS OFFICE -
LIBRARY† □ Honolulu, HI

Nishizaki, Colette, Libn.
READER'S DIGEST MAGAZINES LIMITED -
EDITORIAL LIBRARY □ Montreal, PQ

Nispel, David, Res.Anl.
WISCONSIN STATE LEGISLATIVE REFERENCE
BUREAU □ Madison, WI

Nissly, Carl W., Pres.
IOWA GENEALOGICAL SOCIETY - LIBRARY □
Des Moines, IA

Niswander, Richard E., Dir., Lib.Serv.
NATIONAL COAL ASSOCIATION - LIBRARY □
Washington, DC

Nita, Mania, Ref.Libn.
PANAMA CANAL COMMISSION - LIBRARY-
MUSEUM □ APO Miami, FL

Nitz, Kathryn, Tech.Libn.
BENDIX CORPORATION - INSTRUMENTS & LIFE
SUPPORT DIVISION - ENGINEERING LIBRARY □
Davenport, IA

Niven, Garth, Chf.Libn.
LAW SOCIETY OF MANITOBA - LIBRARY □
Winnipeg, MB

Nix, Frances, Assoc.Dir.
ARKANSAS STATE LIBRARY† □ Little Rock, AR

Nix, Rev. J.E., Asst.Archv.
UNITED CHURCH OF CANADA - CENTRAL
ARCHIVES □ Toronto, ON

Nix, James R., Chm., Archv./Res.
LOMA LINDA UNIVERSITY - DEL E. WEBB
MEMORIAL LIBRARY □ Loma Linda, CA

Nixon, Diane S., Hd., Acq.Div.
U.S. NAVY - NAVAL POSTGRADUATE SCHOOL -
DUDLEY KNOX LIBRARY □ Monterey, CA

Nixon, Mrs. Eugene, Libn.
DELAWARE ART MUSEUM - LIBRARY □
Wilmington, DE

Nixon, Judith M., Ref.Coord.
UNIVERSITY OF WISCONSIN, PLATTEVILLE -
KARRMANN LIBRARY □ Platteville, WI

Nixon, Nancy, Libn.
FIRST PRESBYTERIAN CHURCH - LIBRARY □
Roseburg, OR

Nixon, Stuart, Gen.Mgr.
REDWOOD EMPIRE ASSOCIATION - LIBRARY □
San Francisco, CA

Nixon, Walter, Govt.Docs.Spec.
STANDARD & POOR'S CORPORATION -
LIBRARY □ New York, NY

Nobari, Nuchine, Chf.Libn.
DAVIS POLK & WARDWELL - LIBRARY □ New
York, NY

Nobbe, Nancy, Libn.
ST. LOUIS UNIVERSITY - PARKS COLLEGE OF
AERONAUTICAL TECHNOLOGY - LIBRARY □
Cahokia, IL

Noble, David, Libn.
CANCER CONTROL AGENCY OF BRITISH
COLUMBIA - LIBRARY □ Vancouver, BC

Noble, Donald J., Supv.
CATERPILLAR TRACTOR COMPANY - TRAINING
LIBRARY □ East Peoria, IL

Noble, Doris E., Ed.
TENNESSEE STATE DEPARTMENT OF
CONSERVATION - DIVISION OF GEOLOGY -
LIBRARY □ Nashville, TN

Noble, James, Doc.Cat./Ref.
U.S. NAVY - NAVAL COASTAL SYSTEMS
CENTER - TECHNICAL LIBRARY □ Panama City,
FL

Noble, Jean C., Ed.Libn.
PARADE PUBLICATIONS, INC. - LIBRARY □ New
York, NY

Noble, Valerie, Hd.
UPJOHN COMPANY - BUSINESS LIBRARY 88-0
□ Kalamazoo, MI

Noble, Vicki J., Asst.Libn.
U.S. ARMY HOSPITALS - MADIGAN ARMY
MEDICAL CENTER - MORALE SUPPORT
LIBRARY □ Tacoma, WA

Noblet, Chloris, Libn.
SACRAMENTO PUBLIC LIBRARY - BUSINESS &
MUNICIPAL DEPARTMENT □ Sacramento, CA

Noe Field, Rev. William, Libn.
SETON HALL UNIVERSITY - MAC MANUS
COLLECTION □ South Orange, NJ

Noel, Ann, Tech.Supv.
PRUDENTIAL INSURANCE COMPANY OF
AMERICA - FINANCIAL LIBRARY □ Newark, NJ

Noel, Nancy L., Cur.
BOSTON UNIVERSITY - DEPARTMENT OF
SPECIAL COLLECTIONS - NURSING ARCHIVES
□ Boston, MA

Nofi, Antonia, Asst.Libn.
PROGRESSIVE GROCER - RESEARCH LIBRARY □
New York, NY

Nogrady, Judith, Hd.
CANADA - TRANSPORT CANADA -
TRANSPORTATION DEVELOPMENT CENTRE -
LIBRARY □ Montreal, PQ

Nogueras, German, Cat.Libn.
PUERTO RICO - SUPREME COURT - LAW
LIBRARY □ San Juan, PR

Noia, Cynthia, Libn.
MONMOUTH COUNTY SOCIAL SERVICES -
LIBRARY □ Freehold, NJ

Nolan, Edward, Archv.
LANE COUNTY MUSEUM - SPECIAL
COLLECTIONS & ARCHIVES □ Eugene, OR

Nolan, Elaine, Cat./ILL Supv.
CURRY COLLEGE - LOUIS R. LEVIN MEMORIAL
LIBRARY □ Milton, MA

Nolan, Margaret P., Chf.Libn.
METROPOLITAN MUSEUM OF ART -
PHOTOGRAPH AND SLIDE LIBRARY □ New York,
NY

Nolan, Martha D., Hd.
HARTFORD PUBLIC LIBRARY - REFERENCE AND
GENERAL READING DEPARTMENT □ Hartford,
CT

Nolan, Dr. Patrick B., Hd.
WRIGHT STATE UNIVERSITY - ARCHIVES &
SPECIAL COLLECTIONS □ Dayton, OH

Noland, Jon, Circ.
IOWA STATE UNIVERSITY - LIBRARY □ Ames,
IA

Nolf, Nancy, Info./Referral Mgr.
CONSUMER EDUCATION RESOURCE NETWORK
(CERN) □ Rosslyn, VA

Nolf, Richard A., Dir.
ST. JOSEPH MUSEUM - LIBRARY □ St. Joseph,
MO

Nolin, Carolyn J., Asst. State Libn.
MAINE STATE LIBRARY □ Augusta, ME

Noling, A.W., Libn.
HURTY-PECK LIBRARY OF BEVERAGE
LITERATURE† □ Irvine, CA

Noll, Carol, Ser.Libn.
UNIVERSITY OF SOUTH CAROLINA - SCHOOL
OF MEDICINE LIBRARY □ Columbia, SC

Noll, Eleanor, Asst.Libn., Acq.
HAMLINE UNIVERSITY SCHOOL OF LAW -
LIBRARY □ St. Paul, MN

Noll, Mary K., Libn.
RCA CORPORATION - LIBRARY □ Lancaster, PA

Noller, David C., Tech.Info.Spec.
PENNWALT CORPORATION - LUCIDOL
DIVISION - RESEARCH LIBRARY □ Buffalo, NY

Nolte, Alice I., Field Serv.Libn.
SOUTH CAROLINA STATE LIBRARY □ Columbia,
SC

Nonack, Stephen, ILL
BOSTON ATHENAEUM LIBRARY □ Boston, MA

Nook, Cathy, Hd., Tech.Serv.
U.S. OAK RIDGE NATL. LABORATORY -
LIBRARIES □ Oak Ridge, TN

Noonan, F. Thomas, Cur., Reading Rm.
HARVARD UNIVERSITY - HOUGHTON LIBRARY
□ Cambridge, MA

Norberg, Lorraine, Libn.
UNITED CHURCH OF RELIGIOUS SCIENCE -
LIBRARY □ Los Angeles, CA

Norbie, Dorothy, Law Libn.
ROATH & BREGA, P.C. - LAW LIBRARY □
Denver, CO

Norcia, Hope, Dental Cat.
TEMPLE UNIVERSITY - HEALTH SCIENCES
CENTER - LIBRARY □ Philadelphia, PA

Nordby, Carol, Lib.Ck.
GOLDEN VALLEY HEALTH CENTER - MEDICAL
LIBRARY □ Golden Valley, MN

Nordby, Kenneth E., Lay Asst.
OUR SAVIOR'S LUTHERAN CHURCH - LIBRARY
□ Milwaukee, WI

Nordee, Robin, Ref.
LONG BEACH CITY COLLEGE - PACIFIC COAST
CAMPUS LIBRARY □ Long Beach, CA

Norden, Margaret, Ref.Libn.
UNIVERSITY OF PITTSBURGH - FALK LIBRARY
OF THE HEALTH SCIENCES □ Pittsburgh, PA

Nordeng, Diane, Libn.
NEUROPSYCHIATRIC INSTITUTE - LIBRARY □
Fargo, ND

Nordhaus, Kathy, Libn.
TEXAS INSTRUMENTS, INC. -
SEMICONDUCTOR BUILDING LIBRARY □ Dallas,
TX

Nordin, Paula H., Libn.
MOLLOY, JONES, DONAHUE, TRACHTA,
CHILDERS & MALLAMO - LIBRARY† □ Tucson,
AZ

Nordine, Ed, AV Libn.
WESTERN ILLINOIS UNIVERSITY - LIBRARIES
□ Macomb, IL

**P
E
R
S
O
N
N
E
L**

Nordquest, Corrine, Cat.Libn.
YALE UNIVERSITY - DIVINITY SCHOOL
LIBRARY □ New Haven, CT
Noreau, Patricia, Per.Libn.
UNIVERSITY OF LOWELL, NORTH CAMPUS -
ALUMNI/LYDON LIBRARY □ Lowell, MA
Norell, Angie, Libn.
MINNESOTA ZOOLOGICAL GARDEN - LIBRARY
□ Apple Valley, MN
Norelli, Barbara, Circ./ILL
UNION UNIVERSITY - ALBANY LAW SCHOOL -
LIBRARY □ Albany, NY
Norfleet, Phillip, Botanist
MEMPHIS BOTANIC GARDEN FOUNDATION,
INC. - GOLDSMITH CIVIC GARDEN CTR. -
SYBILE MALLOY MEMORIAL LIBRARY □
Memphis, TN
Noriega, Olivia, Hd. Descriptive Cat.
U.S. NAVY - NAVAL WEAPONS CENTER
LIBRARY DIVISION □ China Lake, CA
Norlander, Jaxine Thompson, Lib.Coord.
UNIVERSITY OF MINNESOTA - OCCUPATIONAL
INFORMATION LIBRARY □ Minneapolis, MN
Norman, Anita, Ref.Libn.
KEARNEY STATE COLLEGE - CALVIN T. RYAN
LIBRARY □ Kearney, NE
Norman, Elaine, Libn.
ONTARIO - MINISTRY OF THE ATTORNEY
GENERAL - LIBRARY □ Toronto, ON
Norman, Ranulph F., Dir.
MC GRAW-HILL PUBLICATIONS COMPANY -
MARKETING INFORMATION CENTER† □ New
York, NY
Norman, Wayne, Libn.
PARAPSYCHOLOGY FOUNDATION - EILEEN J.
GARRETT LIBRARY □ New York, NY
Normandin, Judy, Supv. Braille Sect.
MINNESOTA STATE SERVICES FOR THE BLIND
AND VISUALLY HANDICAPPED -
COMMUNICATION CENTER □ St. Paul, MN
Norris, Carole, Asst.Dir.
PENNSYLVANIA RESOURCES AND
INFORMATION CENTER FOR SPECIAL
EDUCATION □ King of Prussia, PA
Norris, Edmond J., Dir.
U.S. ARMY - COMMUNICATIONS SYSTEMS
CENTER - ELECTRONICS MUSEUM □ Fort
Monmouth, NJ
Norris, Elizabeth D., Libn./Hist.
YOUNG WOMEN'S CHRISTIAN ASSOCIATION -
NATIONAL BOARD - LIBRARY □ New York, NY
Norris, Leon M., Exec.Sec. & Cur.
ANDROSCOGGIN HISTORICAL SOCIETY -
CLARENCE E. MARCH LIBRARY □ Auburn, ME
Norris, Loretta, Chf., Law Serv.Br.
U.S. DEPT. OF TRANSPORTATION - LIBRARY
SERVICES DIVISION □ Washington, DC
Norris, Vernal, Chf.Lib.Asst.
UNIVERSITY OF CALIFORNIA, RIVERSIDE -
PHYSICAL SCIENCES LIBRARY □ Riverside, CA
Norster, Rayna Lee, Librarian
ANALYTICAL SYSTEMS ENGINEERING
CORPORATION - LIBRARY □ Burlington, MA
North, Dawn L., Libn.
KOKOMO TRIBUNE - LIBRARY □ Kokomo, IN
North, Jan, Cat.Libn.
UNIVERSITY OF ARKANSAS MEDICAL
SCIENCES CAMPUS - MEDICAL SCIENCES
LIBRARY □ Little Rock, AR
North, Jean, Reports Libn.
U.S. NASA - AMES RESEARCH CENTER -
LIBRARY □ Mountain View, CA
North, John, Dir.
RYERSON POLYTECHNICAL INSTITUTE -
LEARNING RESOURCES CENTRE □ Toronto, ON
North, Paul, Libn.
ACUREX CORPORATION - TECHNICAL LIBRARY
□ Mountain View, CA
Northcott, Dr. J., Supv.
ALLIED CORPORATION - CHEMICALS COMPANY
- LIBRARY □ Buffalo, NY

Northington, Elizabeth, Med.Libn.
U.S. VETERANS ADMINISTRATION (GA-
Augusta) - HOSPITAL LIBRARY □ Augusta, GA
Northrop, Ruth B., Oral Hist.
NAPA COUNTY HISTORICAL SOCIETY -
GOODMAN LIBRARY □ Napa, CA
Northup, Ruth A., Libn.
SOCIETY OF PHILATICIANS - LIBRARY □ St.
Augustine, FL
Norton, Deborah, Health Rec.Adm.
PRINCE EDWARD HEIGHTS - RESIDENT
RECORDS LIBRARY □ Picton, ON
Norton, Evelyn L., Act.Libn.
U.S. COAST GUARD/AIR STATION - BASE
LIBRARY □ Cape Cod, MA
Norton, Frank M., Med.Libn.
U.S. ARMY HOSPITALS - DARNALL ARMY
HOSPITAL - MEDICAL LIBRARY □ Ft. Hood, TX
Norton, Maryanne C., Libn.
MARATHON COUNTY HISTORICAL MUSEUM -
LIBRARY □ Wausau, WI
Norton, Myra, Libn.
OVERSEAS PRIVATE INVESTMENT
CORPORATION - LIBRARY □ Washington, DC
Norton, Nancy, Hd., User Serv.
U.S. OAK RIDGE NATL. LABORATORY -
LIBRARIES □ Oak Ridge, TN
Norton, Robert P., V.P.
FIRST FEDERAL SAVINGS AND LOAN
ASSOCIATION OF FORT WAYNE - LIBRARY □
Fort Wayne, IN
Norton, Thomas E., Dir.
DUKES COUNTY HISTORICAL SOCIETY -
LIBRARY □ Edgartown, MA
Norvell, Geneva N., Libn.
ST. JOHN MEDICAL CENTER - HEALTH
SCIENCES LIBRARY □ Tulsa, OK
Norwood, Claudia, Ref.Sect.
ENVIRONMENTAL PROTECTION AGENCY -
HEADQUARTERS LIBRARY □ Washington, DC
Noskowitz, Laura, Ref.Libn.
PRATT INSTITUTE - LIBRARY □ Brooklyn, NY
Nothdurft, Dr. Ivan H., Supv.Off.
AMERICAN BIBLE SOCIETY - LIBRARY □ New
York, NY
Notheisen, Margaret, Hd.Acq.
UNIVERSITY OF ILLINOIS MEDICAL CENTER -
LIBRARY OF THE HEALTH SCIENCES □ Chicago,
IL
Notrica, Anita, Libn.
CONGREGATION SHEARITH ISRAEL - SOPHIE
AND IVAN SALOMON LIBRARY COLLECTION □
New York, NY
Nott, Ysolde, Doc.
INTERGOVERNMENTAL COMMITTEE ON URBAN
& REGIONAL RESEARCH (ICURR) □ Toronto, ON
Novack, Allen R., Rare Bk. & Print Cur.
RINGLING SCHOOL OF ART AND DESIGN -
LIBRARY □ Sarasota, FL
Novak, Gregory M., Attorney/Libn.
ALLEN COUNTY LAW LIBRARY □ Lima, OH
Novak, Mr. J.L., Fire Res.Off.
CANADA - PUBLIC WORKS CANADA - OFFICE
OF THE DOMINION FIRE COMMISSIONER -
RESOURCE CENTRE □ Ottawa, ON
Novak, Jan Ryan, Dept.Hd.
CLEVELAND - DEPARTMENT OF LAW LIBRARY†
□ Cleveland, OH
Novak, Jan Ryan, Dept.Hd.
CLEVELAND PUBLIC LIBRARY - PUBLIC
ADMINISTRATION LIBRARY □ Cleveland, OH
Novick, Amy R., Adm.Asst.
INTERNATIONAL HUMAN RIGHTS LAW GROUP -
LIBRARY □ Washington, DC
Novinger, Margaret H., Adm.Libn.
U.S. ARMY SIGNAL CENTER & FORT GORDON -
CONRAD TECHNICAL LIBRARY □ Ft. Gordon, GA
Nowacki, Paul, Sect.Supv.
ALLERGAN PHARMACEUTICALS, INC. -
PROFESSIONAL INFORMATION SERVICES □
Irvine, CA

Nowak, Mrs. Ildiko D., Chf.
NATIONAL TRANSLATIONS CENTER† □
Chicago, IL
Nowell, Howard C., Jr., Div.Chf.
NEW HAMPSHIRE STATE FISH AND GAME
DEPARTMENT - MANAGEMENT AND RESEARCH
DIVISION - LIBRARY □ Concord, NH
Nowicki, Leonard, Hd., Ref.
SUNY - COLLEGE AT BUFFALO - EDWARD H.
BUTLER LIBRARY □ Buffalo, NY
Nowlan, Henri, Documentalist
UNIVERSITE DE MONCTON - FACULTE DES
SCIENCES DE L'EDUCATION - CENTRE DE
RESSOURCES PEDAGOGIQUES □ Moncton, NB
Nowosielski, Mrs. M., Hd.Tech.Serv.
CANADA - EMPLOYMENT & IMMIGRATION
CANADA - LIBRARY □ Ottawa, ON
Noyes, Dan, Staff Writer/Libn.
CENTER FOR INVESTIGATIVE REPORTING -
LIBRARY □ Oakland, CA
Noyes, Suzanne, Chf., Lib.Serv.
U.S. VETERANS ADMINISTRATION (MA-
Brockton) - MEDICAL CENTER LIBRARY □
Brockton, MA
Nucera, Jean, Govt.Doc.Libn.
RHODE ISLAND STATE LIBRARY □ Providence,
RI
Nuernberg, Donna S., Ref./Acq.Libn.
WAUSAU INSURANCE COMPANIES - LIBRARY □
Wausau, WI
Nuffer, R., Ref.
WAYNE STATE UNIVERSITY - G. FLINT PURDY
LIBRARY □ Detroit, MI
Nuffer, Stan, Supv.
PORTLAND STATE UNIVERSITY - AUDIO-
VISUAL SERVICES □ Portland, OR
Nugent, Alice, Lib.Asst.
UNIVERSITY CONGREGATIONAL CHURCH -
LIBRARY □ Seattle, WA
Nugent, Barbara, Regional Br.Libn.
NEW YORK PUBLIC LIBRARY - REGIONAL
LIBRARY FOR THE BLIND AND PHYSICALLY
HANDICAPPED □ New York, NY
Nugent, James
FOREST PRODUCTS ACCIDENT PREVENTION
ASSOCIATION - LIBRARY □ North Bay, ON
Nugent, John M., Univ.Archv.
UNIVERSITY OF KANSAS - UNIVERSITY
ARCHIVES □ Lawrence, KS
Nugent, Martha
PRICE WATERHOUSE - LIBRARY† □ Montreal,
PQ
Nugent, Robert S., Dir.
JERSEY CITY STATE COLLEGE - FORREST A.
IRWIN LIBRARY □ Jersey City, NJ
Nugent, Roberta F., Chf.Libn.
GIVAUDAN CORPORATION - LIBRARY □ Clifton,
NJ
Nunes, Martha, Lib.Techn.
ONTARIO - MINISTRY OF HEALTH - PUBLIC
HEALTH LABORATORIES - LIBRARY □ Toronto,
ON
Nunn, Jeri, Adm.Asst.
COLUMBIA UNIVERSITY - ORAL HISTORY
COLLECTION □ New York, NY
Nunn, Theodore J., Jr., Hd.
DAYTON AND MONTGOMERY COUNTY PUBLIC
LIBRARY - NON-PRINT MEDIA CENTER □
Dayton, OH
Nunno, Barbara J., Med.Libn.
SOUTH BALTIMORE GENERAL HOSPITAL -
MEDICAL LIBRARY □ Baltimore, MD
Nuquist, Mrs. Reidun D., Asst.Libn.
VERMONT HISTORICAL SOCIETY - LIBRARY □
Montpelier, VT
Nurmela, Lillian, Libn.
ALAMEDA COUNTY LIBRARY - BUSINESS &
GOVERNMENT LIBRARY □ Oakland, CA
Nurmi, Anne M., Libn.
VIRGINIA BAPTIST HOSPITAL - BARKSDALE
MEDICAL LIBRARY AND SCHOOL OF NURSING
LIBRARY □ Lynchburg, VA

Nuttall, Mrs. D., Lib.Asst.
QUEEN'S UNIVERSITY AT KINGSTON -
MATHEMATICS LIBRARY □ Kingston, ON

Nuttall, Deborah, Acq.Libn.
TRW INC. - ENERGY SYSTEMS PLANNING
DIVISION - LIBRARY □ McLean, VA

Nuttall, Deborah J., Libn.
METROPOLITAN WASHINGTON COUNCIL OF
GOVERNMENTS - LIBRARY □ Washington, DC

Nuttall, R.L., Data Anl.
U.S. NATL. BUREAU OF STANDARDS -
CHEMICAL THERMODYNAMICS DATA CENTER
□ Washington, DC

Nutting, Anne C., Supv.Prog.Libn.
BERKELEY PUBLIC LIBRARY - ART AND MUSIC
DIVISION □ Berkeley, CA

Nyberg, Cheryl, Circ./Ref.Libn.
UNIVERSITY OF ILLINOIS - LAW LIBRARY □
Champaign, IL

Nyberg, Nancy, Libn.
NYBERG CARTOGRAPHIC COLLECTION □
Shorewood, MN

Nycum, Prof. Peter S., Law Libn.
LEWIS AND CLARK LAW SCHOOL -
NORTHWESTERN SCHOOL OF LAW - PAUL L.
BOLEY LAW LIBRARY □ Portland, OR

Nydegger, Marion, Assoc.Libn.
TRINITY EPISCOPAL CHURCH - LIBRARY □
Santa Barbara, CA

Nykolyshyn, Helen, Cat.
UNIVERSITY OF DAYTON - MARIAN LIBRARY □
Dayton, OH

Nylander, Robert H., Arch.Hist.
CAMBRIDGE HISTORICAL COMMISSION -
LIBRARY □ Cambridge, MA

Nyquist, Bro. Paul, Hd.Libn.
ASSUMPTION ABBEY - LIBRARY □ Richardson,
ND

O

Oak, Dorothy M. Rich, Libn.
GTE SYLVANIA - ENGINEERING LIBRARY □
Danvers, MA

Oak, Lydia, Coord.Ref./Coll.Dev.
CANADA - CANADIAN INTERNATIONAL
DEVELOPMENT AGENCY - DEVELOPMENT
INFORMATION CENTRE □ Hull, PQ

Oakes, Bessie, Braille Libn.
UTAH STATE LIBRARY - BLIND AND
PHYSICALLY HANDICAPPED PROGRAM -
REGIONAL LIBRARY □ Salt Lake City, UT

Oakley, Edna M., Libn.
BERGEN COUNTY LAW LIBRARY □ Hackensack,
NJ

Oakley, Madeleine Cohen, Asst.Dir.
INSURANCE LIBRARY ASSOCIATION OF
BOSTON □ Boston, MA

Oakley, Robert L., Dir.
BOSTON UNIVERSITY - PAPPAS LAW LIBRARY
□ Boston, MA

Oakley, Yvonne H., Ctr.Libn.
U.S. DEFENSE LOGISTICS AGENCY - DEFENSE
GENERAL SUPPLY CENTER - CENTER LIBRARY
□ Richmond, VA

Oaksford, Margaret J., Libn.
CORNELL UNIVERSITY - SCHOOL OF HOTEL
ADMINISTRATION LIBRARY □ Ithaca, NY

Oates, Coby, Techn.-In-Charge
CANADA - NATIONAL DEFENCE - CANADIAN
FORCES COLLEGE - STAFF SCHOOL LIBRARY □
Toronto, ON

Oathout, Melvin C., Libn.
CAMARILLO STATE HOSPITAL - PROFESSIONAL
LIBRARY □ Camarillo, CA

O'Bannon, Paul W., Sr.Libn.
CALIFORNIA MARITIME ACADEMY LIBRARY† □
Vallejo, CA

O'Bar, Jack, Dir.
UNIVERSITY OF ALASKA, ANCHORAGE -
LIBRARY □ Anchorage, AK

Obecny, Nancy C., Law Libn.
OHIO COUNTY LAW LIBRARY □ Wheeling, WV

Obenhaus, Adah M., Chf.Cat.Libn.
SOUTHWEST TEXAS STATE UNIVERSITY -
LEARNING RESOURCES CENTER □ San Marcos,
TX

Oberbrunner, Marianne, Proj.Coord.
WISCONSIN INFORMATION SERVICE □
Milwaukee, WI

Oberc, Susanne, Ref.Libn.
U.S. NASA - LEWIS RESEARCH CENTER -
LIBRARY □ Cleveland, OH

Oberg, Richard, Libn.
UNIVERSITY OF WASHINGTON - COMPUTING
INFORMATION CENTER □ Seattle, WA

Oberhamer, Douglas R., Exec.Dir.
WATER QUALITY ASSOCIATION - RESEARCH
COUNCIL LIBRARY† □ Lombard, IL

Oberhausen, Judy, Act.Dir./Cur.
ART CENTER, INC. - LIBRARY □ South Bend, IN

Oberlander, Barbara, Law Lib.Ck.
NASSAU COUNTY SUPREME COURT - 10TH
JUDICIAL DISTRICT - LAW LIBRARY □ Mineola,
NY

Oberts, Kristin K., Supv.
3M - 201 TECHNICAL LIBRARY □ St. Paul, MN

O'Boyce, Edward J., Res.Assoc.
LOUISIANA TECH UNIVERSITY - RESEARCH
DIVISION/COLLEGE OF ADMINISTRATION AND
BUSINESS - LIBRARY □ Ruston, LA

O'Brien, Alberta T., Med.Libn.
MONTGOMERY HOSPITAL - MEDICAL LIBRARY
□ Norristown, PA

O'Brien, Barbara, Asst.Libn.
PRC CONSOER, TOWNSEND, INC. - LIBRARY
AND INFORMATION CENTER □ Chicago, IL

O'Brien, Betty A., Lib.Dir.
FRANCISCAN FATHERS OF CINCINNATI, OHIO
- ST. LEONARD COLLEGE - LIBRARY □ Dayton,
OH

O'Brien, Carol, Asst.
D'ARCY-MAC MANUS AND MASIUS - LIBRARY □
New York, NY

O'Brien, Elmer J., Libn.
UNITED THEOLOGICAL SEMINARY - LIBRARY □
Dayton, OH

O'Brien, Frances E., Med.Libn.
CARNEY HOSPITAL - MEDICAL LIBRARY □
Dorchester, MA

O'Brien, Hugh, Acq.Libn.
SHIPPENSBURG STATE COLLEGE - EZRA
LEHMAN MEMORIAL LIBRARY □ Shippensburg,
PA

O'Brien, J.W., Chf. State & Mil.Rec.
CANADA - PUBLIC ARCHIVES OF CANADA -
FEDERAL ARCHIVES DIVISION □ Ottawa, ON

O'Brien, Joan, Info.Spec.
PHILLIPS PETROLEUM COMPANY - RESEARCH &
DEVELOPMENT DEPARTMENT - TECHNICAL
INFORMATION BRANCH □ Bartlesville, OK

O'Brien, Sister Judith, Cat.
PRESENTATION COLLEGE - LIBRARY □
Aberdeen, SD

O'Brien, Julie M., Libn.
U.S. AIR FORCE BASE - PEASE BASE LIBRARY†
□ Pease AFB, NH

O'Brien, Linda, Ref.Libn.
AMERICAN TELEPHONE & TELEGRAPH
COMPANY - MORRISTOWN CORPORATE
MARKETING LIBRARY □ Morristown, NJ

O'Brien, Mary Frances, Libn.
NORTHERN RESEARCH & ENGINEERING
CORPORATION - LIBRARY □ Woburn, MA

O'Brien, Mary J., Libn.
LINCOLN INSTITUTE OF LAND POLICY -
LIBRARY □ Cambridge, MA

O'Brien, Nancy, Libn.
HASKINS LABORATORIES - LIBRARY □ New
Haven, CT

O'Brien, Patricia Marsh, Mgr., Sci.Info.Serv.
PHARMACEUTICAL MANUFACTURERS
ASSOCIATION - SCIENCE INFORMATION
SERVICES □ Washington, DC

O'Brien, Rita H., Info.Off.
HISTORIC ST. AUGUSTINE PRESERVATION
BOARD - HISPANIC RESEARCH LIBRARY □ St.
Augustine, FL

Obrochta, Gerald, Hd., Soc.Sci.Sect.
CHICAGO PUBLIC LIBRARY CENTRAL LIBRARY -
SOCIAL SCIENCES & HISTORY DIVISION □
Chicago, IL

O'Bryant, J. Frederick, Hd., AV Ctr.
UNIVERSITY OF VIRGINIA MEDICAL CENTER -
CLAUDE MOORE HEALTH SCIENCES LIBRARY □
Charlottesville, VA

Obsniuk, Rebecca, Libn.
GENERAL MOTORS CORPORATION -
TECHNICAL INFORMATION CENTER □ Warren,
MI

Obus, Harriet, Ref.
EDUCATIONAL BROADCASTING CORPORATION
- CHANNEL 13 RESEARCH LIBRARY □ New York,
NY

Ocain, Charlotte, Doc.Libn.
UNIVERSITY OF WISCONSIN, MADISON -
STEENBOCK MEMORIAL LIBRARY □ Madison,
WI

Ochal, Bethany J., Dir.
ORANGE COUNTY LAW LIBRARY □ Santa Ana,
CA

Ochoa, James J., Hd.Tech.Proc.
LOS ANGELES COUNTY MEDICAL ASSOCIATION
- LIBRARY □ Los Angeles, CA

Ochs, Mrs. Merle, Med.Libn.
DOMINICAN SANTA CRUZ HOSPITAL -
MEDICAL LIBRARY □ Santa Cruz, CA

Ochs, Michael, Libn.
HARVARD UNIVERSITY - EDA KUHN LOEB
MUSIC LIBRARY □ Cambridge, MA

Ockenfels, Katherine, OM Cat.
TEACHERS COLLEGE - LIBRARY □ New York, NY

Ockert, Dr. Karl F., Adm.Asst.
ROHM & HAAS COMPANY - RESEARCH
DIVISION - INFORMATION SERVICES
DEPARTMENT □ Spring House, PA

O'Coin, Vickie, Ser.Techn.
INTERNATIONAL BROTHERHOOD OF
TEAMSTERS, CHAUFFEURS, WAREHOUSEMEN
AND HELPERS OF AMERICA - RES./EDUC.
LIBRARY □ Washington, DC

O'Connell, Colette, Ref.Libn.
RENSSELAER POLYTECHNIC INSTITUTE -
FOLSOM LIBRARY □ Troy, NY

O'Connell, Edward M., Law Libn.
NEW YORK COUNTY LAWYERS' ASSOCIATION -
LIBRARY □ New York, NY

O'Connell, George E., Dir.
UNIVERSITY OF CONNECTICUT - LABOR
EDUCATION CENTER - INFORMATION CENTER
□ Storrs, CT

O'Connell, James J., III, Cur.
UNCAP INTERNATIONAL, INC. - PROJECT
COLLECTORS RESEARCH LIBRARY □ Los
Angeles, CA

O'Connell, Sr. Marguerite, Ph.D., Libn.
ST. FRANCIS HOSPITAL - MEDICAL LIBRARY □
Miami Beach, FL

O'Connell, Michelle D., Chf., Lib.Serv.
U.S. VETERANS ADMINISTRATION (NY-Buffalo)
- MEDICAL CENTER LIBRARY SERVICE □
Buffalo, NY

O'Connell, Monica, Rd.Adv.
DISTRICT OF COLUMBIA PUBLIC LIBRARY -
SOCIOLOGY, GOVERNMENT & EDUCATION
DIVISION □ Washington, DC

O'Connor, Ann E., Law Libn.
FITCHBURG LAW LIBRARY □ Fitchburg, MA

O'Connor, Beth, Libn.
NORTHWESTERN NATIONAL LIFE INSURANCE
COMPANY - LIBRARY □ Minneapolis, MN

O'Connor, Betsy, Libn.
BURLINGTON COUNTY MEMORIAL HOSPITAL -
HEALTH SCIENCES LIBRARY □ Mt. Holly, NJ

O'Connor, Denis R., Libn.
DEBEVOISE, PLIMPTON, LYONS AND GATES -
LAW LIBRARY □ New York, NY

O'Connor, Elaine P., Dir.
LONG (Earl K.) MEMORIAL HOSPITAL - MEDICAL
LIBRARY □ Baton Rouge, LA

O'Connor, Marihelen, Med.Libn.
SCOTTSDALE MEMORIAL HOSPITAL - HEALTH
SCIENCES LIBRARY □ Scottsdale, AZ

O'Connor, Patricia, Coll.Dev.Libn.
NORTH DAKOTA STATE UNIVERSITY - LIBRARY
□ Fargo, ND

O'Connor, Sister Susan Marie, C.S.J., Archv.
SISTERS OF ST. JOSEPH OF CARONDELET -
ALBANY PROVINCE - ARCHIVES □ Latham, NY

O'Connor, Sylvia N., Coord.Med.Lib.Serv.
RIVERSIDE MEDICAL CENTER - MEDICAL
LIBRARY □ Kankakee, IL

Oda, Phyllis, Libn.
RAYCHEM CORPORATION - TECHNICAL
LIBRARY □ Menlo Park, CA

Oddan, Linda, Assoc.Dir./Info.Serv.
MEDICAL COLLEGE OF WISCONSIN - TODD
WEHR LIBRARY □ Milwaukee, WI

O'Dell, Charles A., Libn.
ELLIS FISCHEL STATE CANCER HOSPITAL AND
CANCER RESEARCH CENTER - LIBRARY &
INFORMATION CENTER □ Columbia, MO

O'Dell, Harold, Libn.
MARYCREST COLLEGE - CONE LIBRARY† □
Davenport, IA

Odell, Joan, Law Libn.
SHASTA COUNTY LAW LIBRARY □ Redding, CA

Odell, Tobe, Libn., Lib.Serv.
ESSO RESOURCES CANADA LIMITED - LIBRARY
INFORMATION CENTRE □ Calgary, AB

Oderberg, I. Manuel, Res.Libn.
THEOSOPHICAL UNIVERSITY - LIBRARY □
Altadena, CA

Odermann, Anita, Dir./Christian Educ.
FIRST UNITED PRESBYTERIAN CHURCH -
LIBRARY □ Albuquerque, NM

Odien, Jean, Libn.
ST. MARY'S SCHOOL FOR THE DEAF -
PROFESSIONAL LIBRARY □ Buffalo, NY

Odman, Charlotte J., Libn.
LUTHERAN CHURCH IN AMERICA - BOARD OF
PUBLICATION - LIBRARY □ Philadelphia, PA

Od'Neal, Mary, Libn.
INTERNATIONAL CITY MANAGEMENT
ASSOCIATION - LIBRARY □ Washington, DC

Odom, Katherine C., Clinical Med.Libn.
UNIVERSITY OF TEXAS MEDICAL BRANCH -
MOODY MEDICAL LIBRARY □ Galveston, TX

O'Donnell, Dr. Bernard, Dir.
ERIC CLEARINGHOUSE ON READING AND
COMMUNICATIONS SKILLS □ Urbana, IL

O'Donnell, Ellen, Ref.Libn.
ST. JOHN HOSPITAL - MEDICAL LIBRARY □
Detroit, MI

O'Donnell, Gerald, Data User Serv.Off.
U.S. BUREAU OF THE CENSUS - REGIONAL
DATA USER SERVICE - DENVER REGIONAL
OFFICE - LIBRARY □ Denver, CO

O'Donnell, Holly, User Serv.Coord.
ERIC CLEARINGHOUSE ON READING AND
COMMUNICATIONS SKILLS □ Urbana, IL

O'Donnell, Jim, Act.Libn.
UNIVERSITY OF CALIFORNIA, LOS ANGELES -
GEOLOGY-GEOPHYSICS LIBRARY □ Los Angeles,
CA

O'Donnell, Kathleen M., Acq.Libn.
ROHM & HAAS COMPANY - RESEARCH
DIVISION - INFORMATION SERVICES
DEPARTMENT □ Spring House, PA

O'Donnell, Linda, Curric.Serv.Spec.
OAKLAND SCHOOLS - EDUCATIONAL RESOURCE
CENTER □ Pontiac, MI

O'Donnell, Maryann, Cat.
WILLKIE FARR & GALLAGHER - LIBRARY □ New
York, NY

O'Donnell, Maureen, Asst.Libn.
CHEMICAL BANK - RESEARCH LIBRARY □ New
York, NY

O'Donnell, Phyllis H., AMA Pubn. Indexing
AMERICAN MEDICAL ASSOCIATION -
DIVISION OF LIBRARY AND ARCHIVAL
SERVICES □ Chicago, IL

O'Donnell, Rosemary, Info.Spec.-Tech.
POLYSAR, LTD. - INFORMATION CENTRE □
Sarnia, ON

O'Donovan, Phyllis H., Libn.
CTB/MC GRAW-HILL - LIBRARY □ Monterey, CA

Odum, Mark, Info.Off.
NATIONAL REHABILITATION INFORMATION
CENTER □ Washington, DC

Odyniec, Mary T., Assoc.Ref.Libn.
CONNECTICUT COLLEGE - LIBRARY - SPECIAL
COLLECTIONS □ New London, CT

Oermann, Bob, Hd., Tech.Serv.
COUNTRY MUSIC FOUNDATION - LIBRARY AND
MEDIA CENTER □ Nashville, TN

Oestreich, Kathleen P., Mgr., Info.Serv.
BORG-WARNER CORPORATION - ROY C.
INGERSOLL RESEARCH CENTER - LIBRARY □
Des Plaines, IL

Oetting, Frieda R., Libn.
CHEMPLEX COMPANY - LIBRARY □ Rolling
Meadows, IL

Oey, Giok Po, Cur.
CORNELL UNIVERSITY - JOHN M. ECHOLS
COLLECTION ON SOUTHEAST ASIA □ Ithaca, NY

Offe, Hans Laf, Ref.Libn.
KXE6S VEREIN CHESS SOCIETY - SPECIAL/
RESEARCH LIBRARY - EAST DIVISION □ Chapel
Hill, NC

Offermann, Glenn W., Hd.Libn.
CONCORDIA COLLEGE - BUENGER MEMORIAL
LIBRARY □ St. Paul, MN

Officer, Michael B., Nutritionist
M.F.A. MILLING COMPANY - LIBRARY □
Springfield, MO

Ogata, Kay, Libn.
HAWAII STATE LIBRARY - SOCIAL SCIENCE
AND PHILOSOPHY SECTION □ Honolulu, HI

Ogden, Alan, Law Libn.
UNIVERSITY OF TULSA - COLLEGE OF LAW
LIBRARY □ Tulsa, OK

Ogden, Dale T., Libn.
U.S. AIR FORCE - ELECTRONIC SECURITY
COMMAND - GENERAL LIBRARY □ San Antonio,
TX

Ogden, G., Tech.Info.Spec.
U.S. NATL. HIGHWAY TRAFFIC SAFETY
ADMINISTRATION - TECHNICAL REFERENCE
BRANCH □ Washington, DC

Ogden, Helen, Libn.
RICHMOND PUBLIC LIBRARY - ART AND MUSIC
DEPARTMENT† □ Richmond, VA

Ogden, Nina, Libn.
FRANK, BERNSTEIN, CONAWAY & GOLDMAN -
LIBRARY □ Baltimore, MD

Ogg, Harold, Libn.
HAMMOND HISTORICAL SOCIETY - CALUMET
ROOM □ Hammond, IN

Ogilvie, Dolores, Libn.
ALBERTA - DEPARTMENT OF HOUSING AND
PUBLIC WORKS - HOUSING LIBRARY □
Edmonton, AB

Ogletree, Lisa, Mgr., Res./Info.Serv.
HOSPITAL CORPORATION OF AMERICA -
RESEARCH/INFORMATION SERVICES □
Nashville, TN

O'Grady, J., Ref.Libn.
PACE UNIVERSITY, PLEASANTVILLE/
BRIARCLIFF - LIBRARY □ Pleasantville, NY

O'Grady, R., Sec.
UNIVERSITY OF TORONTO - DEPARTMENT OF
ZOOLOGY LIBRARY □ Toronto, ON

Ogura, Irene, Hd.Cat.Libn.
UNIVERSITY OF COLORADO MEDICAL CENTER
- DENISON MEMORIAL LIBRARY □ Denver, CO

Oh, Song Ja, Dir.
STATEN ISLAND HOSPITAL - MEDICAL STAFF
LIBRARY □ Staten Island, NY

Oh, Soo Ok, Evening Libn.
ST. JOSEPH'S UNIVERSITY - ACADEMY OF
FOOD MARKETING - CAMPBELL LIBRARY □
Philadelphia, PA

Oh, Timothy T., Dir. of Lib.
MERCY HOSPITAL & MEDICAL CENTER -
MEDICAL LIBRARY □ Chicago, IL

O'Hair, Madalyn Murray, Archv.
STEVENS (Charles E.) AMERICAN ATHEIST
LIBRARY AND ARCHIVES INC.† □ Austin, TX

O'Halloran, Charles, State Libn.
MISSOURI STATE LIBRARY □ Jefferson City,
MO

O'Hara, Edward J., Univ.Libn.
SACRED HEART UNIVERSITY - LIBRARY □
Bridgeport, CT

O'Hara, Kathy, Lib.Techn.
ONTARIO NURSES ASSOCIATION - ONA
LIBRARY □ Toronto, ON

Ohlmann, Glenn, Tech.Serv.Libn.
CONCORDIA TEACHERS COLLEGE - LINK
LIBRARY □ Seward, NE

Ohmer, Roberta, Tech.Libn.
ST. LOUIS COLLEGE OF PHARMACY - O.J.
CLOUGHLY ALUMNI LIBRARY □ St. Louis, MO

Ohst, Alice, Libn.
DAMES & MOORE - LIBRARY □ Los Angeles, CA

Oh'Uiginn, Hon. Sean, Consul Gen.
IRELAND CONSULATE GENERAL - LIBRARY □
New York, NY

Oihus, Colleen, Asst.Cur.
UNIVERSITY OF NORTH DAKOTA -
DEPARTMENT OF SPECIAL COLLECTIONS □
Grand Forks, ND

Oilworth, Kirby, Libn.
CARNEGIE LIBRARY OF PITTSBURGH - MUSIC
AND ART DEPARTMENT □ Pittsburgh, PA

Oitzinger, Harvada, Dir.
ELMBROOK MEMORIAL HOSPITAL - MARY BETH
CURTIS HEALTH SCIENCE LIBRARY □
Brookfield, WI

Oiye, F.G., Supv., Doc.Serv.
TRW, INC. - DEFENSE & SPACE SYSTEMS
GROUP - TECHNICAL INFORMATION CENTER □
Redondo Beach, CA

Oiye, Julie Ann, Libn.
KING COUNTY YOUTH SERVICE CENTER -
LIBRARY □ Seattle, WA

Ojala, Marydee, Lib.Mgr.
BANK OF AMERICA, NT & SA - REFERENCE
LIBRARY □ San Francisco, CA

Oka, Susan, Asst.Libn.
ACADEMY OF MOTION PICTURE ARTS AND
SCIENCES - MARGARET HERRICK LIBRARY □
Beverly Hills, CA

Okada, Connie, Asst.Art Libn.
UNIVERSITY OF CALIFORNIA, SANTA BARBARA
- ARTS LIBRARY □ Santa Barbara, CA

Okajima, Michael, Ref.Libn.
HEWLETT-PACKARD COMPANY - CORPORATE
LIBRARY □ Palo Alto, CA

Okasako-Oshiro, Gloria, Info.Chem.
UNION OIL COMPANY OF CALIFORNIA -
TECHNICAL INFORMATION CENTER □
Placentia, CA

O'Keefe, Laura, Photographs Asst.
CALIFORNIA HISTORICAL SOCIETY -
SCHUBERT HALL LIBRARY □ San Francisco, CA

Okey, R. Anne, Labadie Coll.Libn.
UNIVERSITY OF MICHIGAN - DEPARTMENT OF
RARE BOOKS AND SPECIAL COLLECTIONS -
LIBRARY □ Ann Arbor, MI

Okim, Victor, Libn.
CATHOLIC UNIVERSITY OF AMERICA -
LIBRARY SCIENCE LIBRARY □ Washington, DC

Oko, Andrew J., Cur., Hist.Coll.
ART GALLERY OF HAMILTON - MURIEL ISABEL
BOSTWICK LIBRARY □ Hamilton, ON

Oksner, Claire, Hd.Libn.
JUNG (C.G.) INSTITUTE OF LOS ANGELES, INC.
- LIBRARY □ Los Angeles, CA

O'Laughlin, Mary, Chf.Libn.
U.S. ARMY POST - FORT RILEY - LIBRARIES† □ Fort Riley, KS

Oldenburg, Joseph F., Chf.
DETROIT PUBLIC LIBRARY - GENERAL INFORMATION DEPARTMENT □ Detroit, MI

Oldenquist, Riek A., Libn.
OHIO STATE DEPARTMENT OF ENERGY - ODOE LIBRARY □ Columbus, OH

Oldham, Ellen, Asst.Kpr./Rare Books
BOSTON PUBLIC LIBRARY - RARE BOOKS AND MANUSCRIPTS □ Boston, MA

Oldman, Vera, Pres., Musm.Corp.
GRAND ENCAMPMENT MUSEUM, INC. - LIBRARY □ Encampment, WY

Olds, Karen, Ref.Libn.
AEROSPACE CORPORATION - CHARLES C. LAURITSEN LIBRARY □ Los Angeles, CA

Oldsen, Diana, Lib.Techn.
UNIVERSITY OF COLORADO, BOULDER - INSTITUTE OF BEHAVIORAL SCIENCE - IBS RESEARCH LIBRARY □ Boulder, CO

O'Leary, Francis, Libn.
ST. LOUIS UNIVERSITY - MEDICAL CENTER LIBRARY □ St. Louis, MO

O'Leary, Patrick, Libn.
CROSBY, HEAFEY, ROACH & MAY - LAW LIBRARY □ Oakland, CA

O'Leary, Timothy J., Dir., File Res.
HUMAN RELATIONS AREA FILES, INC. □ New Haven, CT

Olek, Susan M., Circ.
ERIE COMMUNITY COLLEGE NORTH - LIBRARY RESOURCES CENTER □ Buffalo, NY

Olenick, Monte, Div.Chf.
BROOKLYN PUBLIC LIBRARY - LANGUAGE AND LITERATURE DIVISION □ Brooklyn, NY

Oler, Christine, Ref.Libn.
METHODIST HOSPITAL OF INDIANA, INC. - LIBRARY □ Indianapolis, IN

Oles, Steve, Libn.
O'CONNOR (Lindsay A. & Olive B.) HOSPITAL - LIBRARY □ Delhi, NY

Olesen, Sine, Libn.
IOWA STATE COMMISSION FOR THE BLIND - LIBRARY FOR THE BLIND & PHYSICALLY HANDICAPPED □ Des Moines, IA

Oleson, Sherry A., Dir.Med.Lib.Serv.
NORTH MEMORIAL MEDICAL CENTER - MEDICAL LIBRARY □ Minneapolis, MN

Olian, Irving, Libn.
TEMPLE BETH EL - LIBRARY □ Plainfield, NJ

Olin, Ferris, Art Libn.
RUTGERS UNIVERSITY, THE STATE UNIVERSITY OF NEW JERSEY - ART LIBRARY □ New Brunswick, NJ

Olin, Joyce, Govt.Docs./Ref.Libn.
DE PAUL UNIVERSITY - LAW SCHOOL LIBRARY □ Chicago, IL

Olivas, Arthur L., Archv.
MUSEUM OF NEW MEXICO - PHOTOGRAPHIC ARCHIVES □ Santa Fe, NM

Olive, Betsy Ann, Libn.
CORNELL UNIVERSITY - GRADUATE SCHOOL OF BUSINESS AND PUBLIC ADMINISTRATION - LIBRARY □ Ithaca, NY

Oliver, Anthony M., Libn.
HAWAII STATE DEPARTMENT OF PLANNING & ECONOMIC DEVELOPMENT - LIBRARY □ Honolulu, HI

Oliver, Bobbie E., Adm.Libn.
MEMPHIS THEOLOGICAL SEMINARY - LIBRARY □ Memphis, TN

Oliver, Diane, Act.Libn.
FLINT INSTITUTE OF ARTS - LIBRARY† □ Flint, MI

Oliver, Florence S., Archv.
SOMERS HISTORICAL SOCIETY - LIBRARY AND ARCHIVES □ Somers, NY

Oliver, Helen R., Libn.
CALAIS FREE LIBRARY □ Calais, ME

Oliver, Mary W., Law Libn.
UNIVERSITY OF NORTH CAROLINA, CHAPEL HILL - LAW LIBRARY □ Chapel Hill, NC

Oliver, P.A., Mgr.
GENERAL ELECTRIC COMPANY - TECHNICAL INFORMATION EXCHANGE □ Schenectady, NY

Oliver, Shirley, Ref.Libn.
UNIVERSITY OF KENTUCKY - MEDICAL CENTER LIBRARY □ Lexington, KY

Olivera, Guido, Foreign Libn.
UNIVERSITY OF TEXAS SCHOOL OF LAW - TARLTON LAW LIBRARY □ Austin, TX

Olivera, Ruth, Asst.Mss.Cat.
TULANE UNIVERSITY OF LOUISIANA - LATIN AMERICAN LIBRARY □ New Orleans, LA

Olivere, Michael, Adm.Asst.
PACIFIC SCIENCE CENTER FOUNDATION - LIBRARY □ Seattle, WA

Olivier, Daniel, Dept.Hd.
BIBLIOTHEQUE DE LA VILLE DE MONTREAL - COLLECTION GAGNON □ Montreal, PQ

Olivier, Suzanne, Directrice
INSTITUT NAZARETH ET LOUIS-BRAILLE - BIBLIOTHEQUE PUBLIQUE □ Longueuil, PQ

Olm, Jane G., Law Libn.
TEXAS TECH UNIVERSITY - SCHOOL OF LAW LIBRARY □ Lubbock, TX

Olmsted, Colleen, Res.Asst.
KELLER (J.J.) & ASSOCIATES, INC. - RESEARCH CENTER/LIBRARY SERVICES □ Neenah, WI

Olmsted, Wilma, Lib.Techn.
SASKATCHEWAN - DEPARTMENT OF EDUCATION - RESOURCE CENTRE □ Regina, SK

Olney, Elaine, Asst.Libn.
RILEY COUNTY GENEALOGICAL SOCIETY - LIBRARY □ Manhattan, KS

Olsen, Carla, Asst.Libn.
PRC CONSOER, TOWNSEND, INC. - LIBRARY AND INFORMATION CENTER □ Chicago, IL

Olsen, James L., Jr., Libn.
NATIONAL ACADEMY OF SCIENCES - NATIONAL ACADEMY OF ENGINEERING - LIBRARY □ Washington, DC

Olsen, Janet, Preparations Libn.
BLOOMSBURG STATE COLLEGE - HARVEY A. ANDRUSS LIBRARY □ Bloomsburg, PA

Olsen, Judith, Rd.Serv.Libn.
CABRINI COLLEGE - HOLY SPIRIT LIBRARY □ Radnor, PA

Olsen, Merlin, Dir.
CHURCH OF JESUS CHRIST OF LATTER-DAY SAINTS - CALGARY INSTITUTE OF RELIGION - LIBRARY □ Calgary, AB

Olsen, Patricia, Ser.
LE TOURNEAU COLLEGE - MARGARET ESTES LIBRARY □ Longview, TX

Olsen, Robert A., Jr., Libn.
TEXAS CHRISTIAN UNIVERSITY - MARY COUTS BURNETT LIBRARY - BRITE DIVINITY SCHOOL COLLECTION □ Fort Worth, TX

Olsen, Rowena, Libn.
MC PHERSON COLLEGE - MILLER LIBRARY □ McPherson, KS

Olsen, Mrs. Sigurd, Musm.Dir.
KITSAP COUNTY HISTORICAL MUSEUM - LIBRARY† □ Silverdale, WA

Olsen, Ted, Libn.
PASADENA PUBLIC LIBRARY - BUSINESS-TECHNOLOGY DIVISION □ Pasadena, CA

Olsen, Thomas M., Pres.
UFO INFORMATION RETRIEVAL CENTER, INC. □ Phoenix, AZ

Olsgaard, Jane K., Ref./Ext.Serv.Libn.
UNIVERSITY OF SOUTH DAKOTA - CHRISTIAN P. LOMMEN HEALTH SCIENCES LIBRARY □ Vermillion, SD

Olsgaard, John N., Archv.
UNIVERSITY OF SOUTH DAKOTA - I.D. WEEKS LIBRARY - RICHARDSON ARCHIVES □ Vermillion, SD

Olson, Anton, Asst.Cat.
NORTHWESTERN UNIVERSITY - HEALTH SCIENCES LIBRARY □ Chicago, IL

Olson, Carol, Order Libn.
LUTHER-NORTHWESTERN SEMINARY - LIBRARY □ St. Paul, MN

Olson, Carol R., Asst.Libn.
NEW YORK STATE DEPARTMENT OF TRANSPORTATION PLANNING DIVISION - LIBRARY □ Albany, NY

Olson, Darlene, Supv.Adm.Serv.
CROWN ZELLERBACH CORPORATION - CENTRAL RESEARCH LIBRARY □ Camas, WA

Olson, David, Asst.Libn.
DISTRICT ONE TECHNICAL INSTITUTE - LIBRARY - EDUCATIONAL RESOURCE CENTER □ Eau Claire, WI

Olson, David J., State Archv.
MICHIGAN STATE HISTORY DIVISION - ARCHIVES □ Lansing, MI

Olson, Donald D., Tech.Serv.Libn.
UNIVERSITY OF NORTH DAKOTA - OLAF H. THORMODSGARD LAW LIBRARY □ Grand Forks, ND

Olson, Douglas, Asst.Libn.
EASTERN WASHINGTON STATE HISTORICAL SOCIETY - LIBRARY □ Spokane, WA

Olson, Eric, Dir of Lib.Serv.
REID AND PRIEST - LAW LIBRARY □ New York, NY

Olson, Guni, Hd.Libn.
GRACE BIBLE COLLEGE - BULTEMA MEMORIAL LIBRARY □ Grand Rapids, MI

Olson, Ivy, Asst., Pub.Serv.
WHEATON COLLEGE - LIBRARY □ Wheaton, IL

Olson, James, AV Libn.
AUGSBURG COLLEGE - GEORGE SVERDRUP LIBRARY AND MEDIA CENTER □ Minneapolis, MN

Olson, Joann, Hum.Libn.
MIAMI UNIVERSITY - ART AND ARCHITECTURE LIBRARY □ Oxford, OH

Olson, Karen, Hd.
EASTERN WASHINGTON UNIVERSITY - MUSIC LIBRARY □ Cheney, WA

Olson, Kent C., Bus.Ref.Libn.
FORDHAM UNIVERSITY - LIBRARY AT LINCOLN CENTER □ New York, NY

Olson, Leona, Libn.
CO-OPERATIVE COLLEGE OF CANADA - LIBRARY SERVICES □ Saskatoon, SK

Olson, Margaret, Libn.
MINNESOTA STATE DEPARTMENT OF PUBLIC WELFARE - LIBRARY □ St. Paul, MN

Olson, Nancy S., Libn.
PENINSULA CONSERVATION FOUNDATION - LIBRARY OF THE ENVIRONMENT □ Palo Alto, CA

Olson, Neil B., Dir. of Libs.
SALEM STATE COLLEGE - LIBRARY† □ Salem, MA

Olson, Orville K., Cur. of Musm.
GOODHUE COUNTY HISTORICAL SOCIETY - LIBRARY □ Red Wing, MN

Olson, Paula, Asst.Libn.
AMERICAN COLLEGE OF OBSTETRICIANS AND GYNECOLOGISTS - RESOURCE CENTER □ Washington, DC

Olson, Ray, Ref.Libn.
LUTHER-NORTHWESTERN SEMINARY - LIBRARY □ St. Paul, MN

Olson, Robert
PASADENA FOUNDATION FOR MEDICAL RESEARCH - FILM LIBRARY □ Pasadena, CA

Olson, Robert, Info.Ret.Spec.
UTAH STATE BOARD OF EDUCATION - U-CRIS PROGRAM □ Salt Lake City, UT

Olson, Rue E., Libn.
ILLINOIS AGRICULTURAL ASSOCIATION - IAA AND AFFILIATED COMPANIES LIBRARY □ Bloomington, IL

Olson, Ruth, Archv.
FORT LARNED HISTORICAL SOCIETY, INC. - SANTA FE TRAIL CENTER LIBRARY □ Larned, KS

Olson, Sally, Libn.
GREEN GIANT / PILLSBURY COMPANY - LIBRARY □ Le Sueur, MN

**P
E
R
S
O
N
N
E
L**

Olson, Virgil J., Chf. Naturalist
U.S. NATL. PARK SERVICE - DEATH VALLEY NATL. MONUMENT - LIBRARY □ Death Valley, CA

Olsson, Diane T., Ref.Libn.
AMERICAN ARBITRATION ASSOCIATION - EASTMAN ARBITRATION LIBRARY □ New York, NY

Olstead, Patricia B., Chf., Lib.Serv.
U.S. ARMY - NATICK RESEARCH AND DEVELOPMENT LABORATORIES - TECHNICAL LIBRARY □ Natick, MA

Olver, Meredith, Ref.Libn.
THOMPSON (J. Walter) COMPANY - INFORMATION CENTER □ New York, NY

O'Mahoney, Elizabeth, Libn.
GOLDMAN, SACHS AND COMPANY - LIBRARY □ New York, NY

O'Malley, Rev. Kenneth, C.P., Lib.Dir.
CATHOLIC THEOLOGICAL UNION - LIBRARY □ Chicago, IL

O'Malley, William
COLUMBIA UNIVERSITY - AVERY ARCHITECTURAL AND FINE ARTS LIBRARY □ New York, NY

O'Meara, Kathleen C., Hd.
CHICAGO PUBLIC LIBRARY CENTRAL LIBRARY - GENERAL INFORMATION SERVICES DIVISION- BIBLIOGRAPHIC & ILL CENTER □ Chicago, IL

Ondriska, Rev. Albert, Pub.Serv.Libn.
ILLINOIS BENEDICTINE COLLEGE - THEODORE LOWNIK LIBRARY □ Lisle, IL

O'Neal, Ellis E., Jr., Libn.
ANDOVER NEWTON THEOLOGICAL SCHOOL - TRASK LIBRARY □ Newton Centre, MA

O'Neal, Pat, Circ.Libn.
MERCER UNIVERSITY - LAW SCHOOL - HALLIBURTON LAW LIBRARY □ Macon, GA

O'Neil, Gary, Dir. Of Res.
WASHINGTON STATE DEPARTMENT OF REVENUE - RESEARCH AND INFORMATION DIVISION - LIBRARY □ Olympia, WA

O'Neil, John, Specifier
PERKINS AND WILL ARCHITECTS, INC. - RESOURCE CENTER □ Chicago, IL

O'Neil, Julia, Dir.
MAY DEPARTMENT STORES COMPANY - INFORMATION CENTER □ St. Louis, MO

O'Neil, Kathy, Ecology Ctr.Coord.
COMMUNITY ENVIRONMENTAL COUNCIL, INC. - ECOLOGY CENTER LENDING LIBRARY □ Santa Barbara, CA

O'Neill, Dr. A.D.J., Chf., Sci.Serv.
CANADA - ATMOSPHERIC ENVIRONMENT SERVICE - ATLANTIC REGIONAL LIBRARY □ Bedford, NS

O'Neill, Jean, Dir., Lib.Serv.
SOUTHERN NEVADA MEMORIAL HOSPITAL - MEDICAL LIBRARY □ Las Vegas, NV

O'Neill, Marta G., Asst.Cur.
CHICAGO PUBLIC LIBRARY CULTURAL CENTER - SPECIAL COLLECTIONS DIVISION □ Chicago, IL

O'Neill, Mary, Libn.
ARTHUR ANDERSEN & CO. - LIBRARY □ Toronto, ON

O'Neill, Mary E., Res.Libn.
SYRACUSE RESEARCH CORPORATION - LIBRARY □ Syracuse, NY

O'Neill, Mary Jo, Musm.Dir.
EDWARD-DEAN MUSEUM ART REFERENCE LIBRARY □ Cherry Valley, CA

O'Neill, Dr. Robert K., Dept.Hd.
INDIANA STATE UNIVERSITY - DEPARTMENT OF RARE BOOKS AND SPECIAL COLLECTIONS □ Terre Haute, IN

O'Neill, Susan, Cat.Libn.
MEDICAL COLLEGE OF WISCONSIN - TODD WEHR LIBRARY □ Milwaukee, WI

O'Neill, Suzanne, Pub.Serv.Libn.
FANSHAWE COLLEGE OF APPLIED ARTS AND TECHNOLOGY - MAIN LIBRARY □ London, ON

Onesto, Dr. Serene, Coord., Lrng.Rsrcs.
CHICAGO STATE UNIVERSITY - DOUGLAS LIBRARY □ Chicago, IL

Oniewski, Rose, Doc.Libn.
SOUTH DAKOTA STATE LIBRARY □ Pierre, SD

Onoffrey, Jodi, Rec.Mgr.
SEVENTH-DAY ADVENTISTS - GENERAL CONFERENCE - OFFICE OF ARCHIVES AND STATISTICS □ Washington, DC

Onsi, Patricia, Assoc.Libn.Tech.Serv
SUNY - UPSTATE MEDICAL CENTER LIBRARY □ Syracuse, NY

Onufrock, Jack, Database Serv.Libn.
MARQUETTE UNIVERSITY - MEMORIAL LIBRARY □ Milwaukee, WI

Opar, Barbara, Arch.Biblog.
SYRACUSE UNIVERSITY - E.S. BIRD LIBRARY - FINE ARTS DEPARTMENT □ Syracuse, NY

Opas, Margaret, Asst.Libn.
THOMPSON (J. Walter) COMPANY - INFORMATION CENTER □ Chicago, IL

Opatrny, Judith T., Libn.
WILLKIE FARR & GALLAGHER - LIBRARY □ New York, NY

Opel, Julia, Asst.Libn.
COLONIAL WILLIAMSBURG - AUDIO-VISUAL LIBRARY □ Williamsburg, VA

Opel, William, Exec.Dir.
PASADENA FOUNDATION FOR MEDICAL RESEARCH - FILM LIBRARY □ Pasadena, CA

Operhall, Anthony, Assoc.Libn.
UNIVERSITY OF CALIFORNIA, DAVIS - PHYSICAL SCIENCES LIBRARY □ Davis, CA

Oppedal, Teresa, Assoc. Law Libn.
MORRISON & FOERSTER - LAW LIBRARY □ San Francisco, CA

Oppenheim, Linda, Libn.
PRINCETON UNIVERSITY - WOODROW WILSON SCHOOL OF PUBLIC AND INTERNATIONAL AFFAIRS - LIBRARY† □ Princeton, NJ

Oppenheim, Ralph G., Dir.
CENTER FOR LAW AND EDUCATION - VICTORIA GREGORIAN LIBRARY □ Cambridge, MA

Oppenheim, Roberta, Libn.
FORSYTH DENTAL CENTER - PERCY HOWE MEMORIAL LIBRARY □ Boston, MA

Oppenheimer, Gerald J., Dir.
UNIVERSITY OF WASHINGTON - HEALTH SCIENCES LIBRARY □ Seattle, WA

Oquita, Paula, Libn.
LOGICON, INC. - TACTICAL & TRAINING SYSTEMS DIVISION LIBRARY □ San Diego, CA

Oraha, Paul, Libn.
BECHTEL CIVIL & MINERALS, INC. - MINING & MINERALS BUSINESS DEVELOPMENT LIBRARY □ San Francisco, CA

Orbach, Mr. M., Ref.Libn.
CONCORDIA UNIVERSITY - LOYOLA CAMPUS - GEORGES P. VANIER LIBRARY □ Montreal, PQ

Orchard, Linea, Lib.Ck.
SHERRITT GORDON MINES, LTD. - RESEARCH CENTRE LIBRARY □ Fort Saskatchewan, AB

Orcutt, Roberta K., D.R.I. Libn.
UNIVERSITY OF NEVADA, RENO - DESERT RESEARCH INSTITUTE - LIBRARY □ Reno, NV

Orcutt, Roberta K., D.R.I. Libn.
UNIVERSITY OF NEVADA, RENO - DESERT RESEARCH INSTITUTE - WATER RESOURCES COLLECTION □ Sparks, NV

Orcutt, Roberta K., Physical Sci.Libn.
UNIVERSITY OF NEVADA, RENO - PHYSICAL SCIENCES LIBRARY □ Reno, NV

Order, Michele, Public Relations
BOSTON'S MUSEUM OF TRANSPORTATION - LIBRARY □ Boston, MA

Ordonez, Maria Elisa, Archv.
PUERTO RICO - INSTITUTE OF PUERTO RICAN CULTURE - ARCHIVO GENERAL DE PUERTO RICO □ San Juan, PR

O'Reilly, Mary C., Libn.
UNIVERSITY OF MINNESOTA - MINES, METALLURGY, & CHEMICAL ENGINEERING LIBRARY □ Minneapolis, MN

O'Reilly, Nancy, Attendant
YORK UNIVERSITY - RARE BOOKS AND SPECIAL COLLECTIONS □ Downsview, ON

Orfanos, Minnie, Libn.
NORTHWESTERN UNIVERSITY - DENTAL SCHOOL LIBRARY □ Chicago, IL

Orfe, Lynn, Asst.Libn.
BARRETT, SMITH, SCHAPIRO, SIMON & ARMSTRONG - LIBRARY □ New York, NY

Orfirer, Lenore F., Librarian
SANTA MONICA HOSPITAL MEDICAL CENTER - MEDICAL LIBRARY □ Santa Monica, CA

O'Riordan, Georgeanne M., Libn.
COLUMBIA UNIVERSITY - BIOLOGICAL SCIENCES LIBRARY □ New York, NY

O'Riordan, Georgeanne M., Libn.
COLUMBIA UNIVERSITY - PSYCHOLOGY LIBRARY □ New York, NY

Orlando, Richard, Res.Libn.
BANK OF MONTREAL - HEAD OFFICE LIBRARY □ Montreal, PQ

Orlino, Demetrio, Evening Pub.Serv.
LOYOLA LAW SCHOOL - LIBRARY □ Los Angeles, CA

Orloske, Margaret Q., Libn.
TIMEX CORPORATION - LEGAL & CORPORATE LIBRARY □ Waterbury, CT

Orlov, Vladimir, Dir.
UNITED NATIONS HEADQUARTERS - DAG HAMMARSKJOLD LIBRARY □ New York, NY

Orman, Margaret, Ref.Libn.
U.S. VETERANS ADMINISTRATION (MD-Perry Point) - HOSPITAL MEDICAL LIBRARY □ Perry Point, MD

Orman, Reba, Libn.
MEMPHIS-SHELBY COUNTY PUBLIC LIBRARY AND INFO. CTR. - SCIENCE/BUSINESS/SOCIAL SCIENCES DEPT. □ Memphis, TN

Ormerod, Barbara, Res.Mgr.
MORGAN STANLEY & COMPANY, INC. - LIBRARY □ New York, NY

Ormsby, Eric, Cur.
PRINCETON UNIVERSITY - NEAR EAST COLLECTIONS □ Princeton, NJ

Orosz, Barbara J., Hd.Libn.
UNION OIL COMPANY OF CALIFORNIA - TECHNICAL INFORMATION CENTER □ Placentia, CA

O'Rourke, Carol, Lib.Asst.
CANADA - MINISTRY OF STATE FOR SCIENCE AND TECHNOLOGY - LIBRARY □ Ottawa, ON

O'Rourke, Linda R., Med.Libn.
UNIVERSITY OF OKLAHOMA - HEALTH SCIENCES CENTER - DEPARTMENT OF SURGERY LIBRARY □ Oklahoma City, OK

O'Rourke, Margaret M., Libn.
REES-STEALY MEDICAL GROUP - LIBRARY □ San Diego, CA

O'Rourke, Peg
GEORGETOWN UNIVERSITY - BLOMMER SCIENCE LIBRARY □ Washington, DC

Orr, Adelaide L., Circ.Libn.
WARNER-PACIFIC COLLEGE - OTTO F. LINN LIBRARY □ Portland, OR

Orr, Elizabeth, Libn.
FIRST PRESBYTERIAN CHURCH - EWING MEMORIAL LIBRARY □ Houston, TX

Orr, Judy, Ref.Libn.
VANDERBILT UNIVERSITY - MEDICAL CENTER LIBRARY □ Nashville, TN

Orr, Laurie, Hd.Libn.
BIRMINGHAM NEWS - REFERENCE LIBRARY □ Birmingham, AL

Orr, Margaret, Order
IOWA STATE UNIVERSITY - LIBRARY □ Ames, IA

Orr, Sr. Mary Mark, Hd., Spec.Coll.Dept.
ST. MARY COLLEGE - LIBRARY - SPECIAL COLLECTIONS □ Leavenworth, KS

Orr, Maryruth, Libn.
WED ENTERPRISES - RESEARCH LIBRARY □
Glendale, CA
Orr, Valorie, Asst. Area Hd.
UNIVERSITY OF CALGARY - ENVIRONMENT-
SCIENCE-TECHNOLOGY LIBRARY □ Calgary, AB
Orr, Dr. William M., Gen.Lib.Adm.
WARNER-PACIFIC COLLEGE - OTTO F. LINN
LIBRARY □ Portland, OR
Orr-Cahall, Christina, Chf.Cur. of Art
ARCHIVES OF CALIFORNIA ART □ Oakland, CA
Orraca, Sadako, Acq.
ICI AMERICAS INC. - ATLAS LIBRARY □
Wilmington, DE
Orser, Lawan, Cat.Libn.
UNIVERSITY OF FLORIDA - HUME LIBRARY □
Gainesville, FL
Orth, Kathy, Racine & Elkhorn Libn.
GATEWAY VOCATIONAL TECHNICAL & ADULT
EDUCATION DISTRICT - LEARNING
RESOURCES CENTER □ Kenosha, WI
Ortiz, Angie, Lib.Ck.
TAUB (Ben) GENERAL HOSPITAL - DOCTOR'S
MEDICAL LIBRARY □ Houston, TX
Ortiz, Cynthia, Libn.
U.S. DEPT. OF ENERGY - NEVADA OPERATIONS
OFFICE - TECHNICAL LIBRARY □ Las Vegas, NV
Ortiz, Daniel
UNIVERSITY OF PUERTO RICO - SCHOOL OF
PUBLIC ADMINISTRATION - LIBRARY □ Rio
Piedras, PR
Ortiz, Jose J., Hd., Rm. for Blind
UNIVERSITY OF PUERTO RICO - GENERAL
LIBRARY □ San Juan, PR
Ortiz, Josefina Santiago, Libn.
PUERTO RICO - DEPARTMENT OF HEALTH -
MEDICAL LIBRARY □ San Juan, PR
Ortiz, Miguel Angel, Dir.
UNIVERSITY OF PUERTO RICO - MAYAGUEZ
CAMPUS - LIBRARY □ Mayaguez, PR
Ortuno, Daniel, Tech. Staff Asst.
TEXAS STATE BUREAU OF ECONOMIC
GEOLOGY - WELL SAMPLE AND CORE LIBRARY
□ Austin, TX
Ortutay, Phyllis A., Tech.Serv.Libn.
U.S. ARMY - MATERIEL DEVELOPMENT &
READINESS COMMAND - HEADQUARTERS -
TECHNICAL LIBRARY □ Alexandria, VA
Ortynsky, Vera, Hd., Cat.Sect.
COLUMBIA UNIVERSITY - HEALTH SCIENCES
LIBRARY □ New York, NY
Osborn, Carol, Sec./Libn.
GEORGIA KRAFT COMPANY - TECHNICAL
DEVELOPMENT CENTER LIBRARY □ Rome, GA
Osborn, Linda Raye, Cons.Ch.Serv.
GEORGIA STATE DEPARTMENT OF EDUCATION
- DIVISION OF PUBLIC LIBRARY SERVICES □
Atlanta, GA
Osborn, Margaret, Ref.Libn.
CLAREMONT COLLEGES - NORMAN F. SPRAGUE
MEMORIAL LIBRARY □ Claremont, CA
Osborn, Russell, Chf. Ranger
U.S. NATL. PARK SERVICE - SCOTTS BLUFF
NATL. MONUMENT - OREGON TRAIL MUSEUM
ASSOCIATION - LIBRARY □ Gerling, NE
Osborn, Walter, Ref.Libn.
MOODY BIBLE INSTITUTE - LIBRARY □ Chicago,
IL
Osborn, Walter, Ref.Libn.
MOODY BIBLE INSTITUTE - MOODYANA
COLLECTION □ Chicago, IL
Osborne, Cynthia L., Asst.Libn.
TRANSCONTINENTAL GAS PIPE LINE
CORPORATION - LIBRARY □ Houston, TX
Osborne, James W., Libn.
NORTHEASTERN HOSPITAL - SCHOOL OF
NURSING LIBRARY □ Philadelphia, PA
Osborne, Robin Ahrendt, Asst.Libn.
U.S. ARMY - CORPS OF ENGINEERS - FORT
WORTH DISTRICT - TECHNICAL LIBRARY □
Fort Worth, TX

Osburn, Harriet S., Hd.Libn.
XEROX CORPORATION - XEROX EDUCATION
PUBLICATIONS - LIBRARY □ Middletown, CT
Osburn, Joan, Libn.
ST. PETER'S HOSPITAL - PROFESSIONAL
LIBRARY □ Hamilton, ON
Osgood, James B., Asst.Hd./Cat.
KENNEDY-KING COLLEGE - LIBRARY □ Chicago,
IL
Osgood, Ronald, AV Spec.
BLACKHAWK TECHNICAL INSTITUTE,
JANESVILLE - LEARNING MATERIALS CENTER
□ Janesville, WI
O'Shea, Patricia R., Corp.Libn.
TEXASGULF, INC. - RESEARCH LIBRARY □
Stamford, CT
Osheroff, Sheila Keil, Cat.Libn.
UNIVERSITY OF OREGON - HEALTH SCIENCES
CENTER - LIBRARY □ Portland, OR
Oshiro, Ruby, Supv., User Serv.
AEROSPACE CORPORATION - CHARLES C.
LAURITSEN LIBRARY □ Los Angeles, CA
Osler, R., Coord., Boys & Girls Serv
TORONTO PUBLIC LIBRARY - MARGUERITE G.
BAGSHAW COLLECTION □ Toronto, ON
Osmanson, Fleur C., Libn.
HILL, FARRER & BURRILL - LAW LIBRARY† □
Los Angeles, CA
Osmundsen, L., Pres.
WENNER-GREN FOUNDATION FOR
ANTHROPOLOGICAL RESEARCH - LIBRARY □
New York, NY
Ossenkop, David, Assoc.Libn.
SUNY - COLLEGE AT POTSDAM - CRANE MUSIC
LIBRARY □ Potsdam, NY
Ossont, Jere R., Chf.
U.S. ARMY - LANGUAGE TRAINING FACILITY -
LIBRARY □ Fort George G. Meade, MD
Oster, E.H., Mgr., Info.Serv.
AMES RUBBER CORPORATION - TECHNICAL
INFORMATION CENTER† □ Hamburg, NJ
Ostraco, Delores, Chf., Circ.Serv.
U.S. ARMY POST - FORT BELVOIR - VAN NOY
LIBRARY □ Ft. Belvoir, VA
Ostrander, Dona, Curric.Libn.
CENTRAL CONNECTICUT STATE COLLEGE -
ELIHU BURRITT LIBRARY □ New Britain, CT
Ostrander, Sheila, Sr.Libn.
NEW YORK STATE LIBRARY - HUMANITIES
REFERENCE SERVICE □ Albany, NY
Ostrem, Walter M., Libn.
ST. PAUL PUBLIC SCHOOLS INDEPENDENT
SCHOOL DISTRICT 625 - DISTRICT
PROFESSIONAL LIBRARY □ St. Paul, MN
Ostrove, Geraldine, Dir.
NEW ENGLAND CONSERVATORY OF MUSIC -
HARRIET M. SPAULDING LIBRARY □ Boston, MA
O'Sullivan, Jane C., Adm.Libn.
U.S. NAVY - NAVAL REGIONAL MEDICAL
CENTER (Oakland) - MEDICAL LIBRARY □
Oakland, CA
Osvald, Karen, Archv.Asst.
GEORGIA HISTORICAL SOCIETY - LIBRARY □
Savannah, GA
Oswald, Edward, Bus.Libn.
MIAMI-DADE PUBLIC LIBRARY - BUSINESS,
SCIENCE AND TECHNOLOGY DEPARTMENT □
Miami, FL
Oswald, Genevieve, Cur.
NEW YORK PUBLIC LIBRARY - PERFORMING
ARTS RESEARCH CENTER - DANCE
COLLECTION □ New York, NY
Oswald, Rev. Robert M., Cat.
WISCONSIN LUTHERAN SEMINARY - LIBRARY
□ Mequon, WI
Osysko, Halina, Libn.
MANUFACTURERS HANOVER TRUST COMPANY
- INTERNATIONAL ECONOMICS DEPARTMENT -
LIBRARY □ New York, NY
Ota, Diane, First Asst.
BOSTON PUBLIC LIBRARY - MUSIC
DEPARTMENT □ Boston, MA

Otness, Harold
SOUTHERN OREGON STATE COLLEGE -
LIBRARY □ Ashland, OR
O'Toole, Susan, Asst.Libn.
FOLEY & LARDNER - LIBRARY □ Milwaukee, WI
Ott, John H., Dir.
SHAKER COMMUNITY, INC. - LIBRARY □
Pittsfield, MA
Ott, Kathleen Galiher, Mgr.
TRW, INC. - INFORMATION CENTER □
Arlington, VA
Ott, Kathy, Lib.Supv.
HONEYWELL, INC. - HONEYWELL
INFORMATION SYSTEMS - CIC INFORMATION
CENTER □ Wellesley, MA
Ott, Linda, Hd., Ref.Dept.
MORRIS COUNTY FREE LIBRARY - NEW JERSEY
ROOM □ Whippany, NJ
Ott, Retha Z., Mgr.
ALLERGAN PHARMACEUTICALS, INC. -
PROFESSIONAL INFORMATION SERVICES □
Irvine, CA
Ott, Wendell, Dir.
ROSWELL MUSEUM AND ART CENTER - ART
LIBRARY □ Roswell, NM
Ottesen, Carol, Libn.
ALASKA STATE DEPARTMENT OF
TRANSPORTATION & PUBLIC FACILITIES -
TECHNICAL LIBRARY □ Juneau, AK
Otting, Martha F., Libn.
PINELLAS COUNTY LAW LIBRARY - ST.
PETERSBURG BRANCH □ St. Petersburg, FL
Otto, A. Stuart, Dir.
INVISIBLE MINISTRY - COMMITTEE FOR AN
EXTENDED LIFESPAN - LIBRARY □ San Marcos,
CA
Otto, Betty J., Libn./Cur.
U.S. NATL. PARK SERVICE - ANTIETAM NATL.
BATTLEFIELD - VISITOR CENTER LIBRARY □
Sharpsburg, MD
Otto, Milton H., Libn.
BETHANY LUTHERAN THEOLOGICAL SEMINARY
- LIBRARY □ Mankato, MN
Otto, Theophil, Asst.Libn.
SOUTHERN ILLINOIS UNIVERSITY,
CARBONDALE - HUMANITIES DIVISION
LIBRARY □ Carbondale, IL
Ottosen, Charlie, Technologist
ALBERTA - DEPARTMENT OF ENERGY AND
NATURAL RESOURCES - MAP & AIR PHOTO
REFERENCE LIBRARY □ Edmonton, AB
Ouellet, Angelo, Asst.Libn.
COLLEGE DOMINICAIN DE PHILOSOPHIE ET DE
THEOLOGIE - BIBLIOTHEQUE □ Ottawa, ON
Ouellette, Billie Jean, Dir.
FLORIDA REGIONAL LIBRARY FOR THE BLIND
AND PHYSICALLY HANDICAPPED -
MULTISTATE CENTER FOR THE SOUTH □
Daytona Beach, FL
Ouellette, Billie Jean, Assoc.Dir.
FLORIDA STATE DIVISION OF BLIND SERVICES
- FLORIDA REGIONAL LIB. FOR THE BLIND &
PHYSICALLY HANDICAPPED □ Daytona Beach,
FL
Ouellette, Gabriele, Cat.
ROBERT GORE RIFKIND FOUNDATION - ART
LIBRARY AND GRAPHICS COLLECTION □
Beverly Hills, CA
Ounan, Francis X., Per.Libn.
ST. CHARLES BORROMEO SEMINARY - RYAN
MEMORIAL LIBRARY □ Philadelphia, PA
Ousley, Eloise, Supt.
ROOSEVELT'S (Franklin D.) LITTLE WHITE
HOUSE AND MUSEUM - ARCHIVES □ Warm
Springs, GA
Oussoren, Mary-Jane, Asst.Libn.
MC CARTHY AND MC CARTHY - LIBRARY □
Toronto, ON
Ouyang, Ellen, Tech.Serv.Libn.
UNIVERSITY OF UTAH - LAW LIBRARY □ Salt
Lake City, UT

PERSONNEL

Ouyang, Joseph, Asst.Libn.
UNIVERSITY OF MISSOURI, KANSAS CITY -
LAW LIBRARY □ Kansas City, MO

Ouzts, Philip A., Dir.
U.S. DEPT. OF COMMERCE - INTERNATIONAL
TRADE ADMINISTRATION - RICHMOND
DISTRICT OFFICE LIBRARY □ Richmond, VA

Ovas, Mary A., Lib.Techn.
CANADIAN NATIONAL RAILWAYS - CANADIAN
NATIONAL TELECOMMUNICATIONS - GREAT
LAKES REGION LIBRARY† □ Toronto, ON

Overbay, Kathleen G., Dir., Lib.Serv.
SOUTHWESTERN STATE HOSPITAL -
PROFESSIONAL LIBRARY □ Marion, VA

Overbeck, Dr. James A., Lib.Dir.
COLUMBIA THEOLOGICAL SEMINARY - JOHN
BULOW CAMPBELL LIBRARY □ Decatur, GA

Overby, Mary E., Spec.Coll.Asst.
GEORGIA BAPTIST HISTORICAL SOCIETY -
LIBRARY □ Macon, GA

Overby, Osmund, Dir. of Musm.
UNIVERSITY OF MISSOURI - MUSEUM LIBRARY
□ Columbia, MO

Overfield, Peggy A., Circ. & Archv.
SUNY - COLLEGE AT POTSDAM - FREDERICK W.
CRUMB MEMORIAL LIBRARY □ Potsdam, NY

Overman, Dorothy, Chf.Ref.Libn.
ST. LOUIS UNIVERSITY - MEDICAL CENTER
LIBRARY □ St. Louis, MO

Overstad, Beth, Coord.
TOYS 'N THINGS, TRAINING & RESOURCE
CENTER, INC. □ St. Paul, MN

Overstreet, Vickie, Libn.
BAPTIST HOSPITAL - LIBRARY □ Nashville, TN

Overton, Julie M., Coord., Local Hist.
GREENE COUNTY DISTRICT LIBRARY - GREENE
COUNTY ROOM □ Xenia, OH

Overwein, Martha A., Hd.
DAYTON AND MONTGOMERY COUNTY PUBLIC
LIBRARY - INDUSTRY AND SCIENCE DIVISION
□ Dayton, OH

Ovitsky, Margaret, Hd.Info.Serv.
UNIVERSITY OF ILLINOIS MEDICAL CENTER -
LIBRARY OF THE HEALTH SCIENCES □ Chicago,
IL

Owbird, S.N., Libn.
SCHOOL OF LIVING - RALPH BORSODI
MEMORIAL LIBRARY □ York, PA

Owen, Alice G., Libn.
NEIGHBORHOOD PLAYHOUSE SCHOOL OF THE
THEATRE - IRENE LEWISOHN LIBRARY □ New
York, NY

Owen, Amy, Deputy Dir.
UTAH STATE LIBRARY □ Salt Lake City, UT

Owen, Eleen M., Libn.
KANSAS TECHNICAL INSTITUTE - TULLIS
RESOURCE CENTER □ Salina, KS

Owen, Katherine, Mgr., INFoRM
WARNER-LAMBERT/PARKE-DAVIS - RESEARCH
LIBRARY† □ Ann Arbor, MI

Owen, Mildred B., Med.Libn.
U.S. ARMY HOSPITALS - FORT CARSON ARMY
HOSPITAL - MEDICAL LIBRARY □ Ft. Carson, CO

Owen, Myra, Libn.
UNIVERSITY OF OTTAWA - SCHOOL OF
NURSING LIBRARY □ Ottawa, ON

Owen, Thomas, Asst.Dir.
UNIVERSITY OF LOUISVILLE - UNIVERSITY
ARCHIVES AND RECORDS CENTER □ Louisville,
KY

Owens, Betty J., Libn.
U.S. BUREAU OF THE CENSUS - REGIONAL DATA
USER SERVICE - SEATTLE REGIONAL OFFICE -
LIBRARY □ Seattle, WA

Owens, Billie A., Libn.
U.S. AIR FORCE BASE - SHEPPARD BASE
LIBRARY □ Wichita Falls, TX

Owens, David, Dp. State Archv.
WASHINGTON STATE OFFICE OF SECRETARY
OF STATE - DIVISION OF ARCHIVES AND
RECORD MANAGEMENT □ Olympia, WA

Owens, Debra A., Asst.Tech.Dir.
AMERICAN SOCIETY FOR QUALITY CONTROL -
LIBRARY □ Milwaukee, WI

Owens, Dorothy M., Info.Spec.
GULF REFINING & MARKETING COMPANY -
LIBRARY AND INFORMATION CENTER □
Houston, TX

Owens, Dr. Frederick H., Mgr.
ROHM & HAAS COMPANY - RESEARCH
DIVISION - INFORMATION SERVICES
DEPARTMENT □ Spring House, PA

Owens, Geraldine H., Lib.Asst.
WALKER ART CENTER - STAFF REFERENCE
LIBRARY □ Minneapolis, MN

Owens, H. Jean, Lib.Dir.
INSTITUTE OF GERONTOLOGY - GERONTOLOGY
LEARNING RESOURCES CENTER □ Detroit, MI

Owens, Irene, Libn.
HOWARD UNIVERSITY - SCHOOL OF RELIGION
LIBRARY □ Washington, DC

Owens, James K., Chf.Archv.
U.S. NATL. ARCHIVES & RECORDS SERVICE -
FEDERAL ARCHIVES AND RECORDS CENTER,
REGION 1 □ Waltham, MA

Owens, Marillyn
MICHIGAN STATE UNIVERSITY - DOCUMENTS
DEPARTMENT □ East Lansing, MI

Owens, Nancy, Libn.
JONES AND LAUGHLIN STEEL CORPORATION -
COMMERCIAL LIBRARY □ Pittsburgh, PA

Owens, Virginia, Hd. Oklahoma Rsrcs.
OKLAHOMA STATE DEPARTMENT OF
LIBRARIES □ Oklahoma City, OK

Owings, Erma, Dir.
BITTER ROOT VALLEY HISTORICAL SOCIETY -
RAVALLI COUNTY MUSEUM □ Hamilton, MT

Ownby, Joanna, Asst. to Dir.
CROCKER ART MUSEUM - RESEARCH LIBRARY
□ Sacramento, CA

Owsley, Lucile C., Chf., Lib.Serv.
U.S. VETERANS ADMINISTRATION (NC-
Salisbury) - HOSPITAL LIBRARY □ Salisbury, NC

Oxley, Anna, Regional Libn.
CANADA - FISHERIES & OCEANS - SCOTIA-
FUNDY REGIONAL LIBRARY □ Halifax, NS

Oxley, Joseph H., Mgr.
BATTELLE-COLUMBUS LABORATORIES - STACK
GAS EMISSION CONTROL COORDINATION
CENTER - LIBRARY □ Columbus, OH

Oxley, Philip, Ref.Libn.
COLUMBIA UNIVERSITY - LAW LIBRARY □ New
York, NY

Oxtoby, Lowell, Circ.Libn.
WESTERN ILLINOIS UNIVERSITY - LIBRARIES
□ Macomb, IL

Oyer, John S., Dir.
MENNONITE HISTORICAL LIBRARY □ Goshen,
IN

Oyer, Ken, Libn.
ARCHBISHOP BERGAN MERCY HOSPITAL -
MEDICAL STAFF LIBRARY □ Omaha, NE

Ozawa, Ritsuko T., Asst.Cur.
SMITH COLLEGE - RARE BOOK ROOM □
Northampton, MA

Ozden, Faye, Supv.
SENECA COLLEGE OF APPLIED ARTS AND
TECHNOLOGY - RESOURCE CENTRE □
Willowdale, ON

Ozeroff, Carole G., Libn.
CONGREGATION ADATH JESHURUN - GOTTLIEB
MEMORIAL LIBRARY □ Elkins Park, PA

Ozment, Judith, Libn.
NATIONAL SPORTING LIBRARY, INC. □
Middleburg, VA

Ozolins, Sulamit, Tech.Serv.Libn.
LUTHER-NORTHWESTERN SEMINARY -
LIBRARY □ St. Paul, MN

P

Paarlberg, Mildred, Cur. of Coll.
TIPPECANOE COUNTY HISTORICAL
ASSOCIATION - ALAMEDA MC COLLOUGH
RESEARCH & GENEALOGY LIBRARY □ Lafayette,
IN

Paas, Dot, Libn.
ROSS, HARDIES, O'KEEFE, BABCOCK &
PARSONS - LAW LIBRARY □ Chicago, IL

Pabst, Kathleen T., Lib.Dir.
MECHANICS' INSTITUTE LIBRARY □ San
Francisco, CA

Pace, Barbara D., Med.Libn.
ST. PAUL HOSPITAL - C.B. SACHER LIBRARY □
Dallas, TX

Pace, Mary, Ref.Libn.
NORTHWESTERN UNIVERSITY - DENTAL
SCHOOL LIBRARY □ Chicago, IL

Pacetti, Esther, Libn.
PPG INDUSTRIES, INC. - GENERAL OFFICE
LIBRARY □ Pittsburgh, PA

Pacetti, Kifren, Asst.Libn.
ARMAK COMPANY - RESEARCH LIBRARY □
McCook, IL

Pacey, Margaret, Ref. & Ser.Libn.
NEW BRUNSWICK - LEGISLATIVE LIBRARY □
Fredericton, NB

Pachefsky, Reva
TREE OF LIFE PRESS - LIBRARY AND ARCHIVES
□ Gainesville, FL

Pachoca, L., Cat./Acq.Libn.
LIBRARY COMPANY OF THE BALTIMORE BAR -
LIBRARY □ Baltimore, MD

Pachtman, Robin, Biblog.Asst.
TEMPLE UNIVERSITY - CENTRAL LIBRARY
SYSTEM - BIOLOGY LIBRARY □ Philadelphia, PA

Pack, Annisteen, Mgt.Asst.
U.S. BUREAU OF LAND MANAGEMENT -
CALIFORNIA STATE OFFICE - LIBRARY □
Sacramento, CA

Package, John A., Chf., Lib.Serv.
U.S. VETERANS ADMINISTRATION (VT-White
River Jct.) - ALLIED HEALTH SCIENCES
LIBRARY □ White River Junction, VT

Packard, Agnes K., Libn.
HUNTINGTON HISTORICAL SOCIETY - LIBRARY
□ Huntington, NY

Packard, Barbara, Tech.Serv.Libn.
RECORDING FOR THE BLIND, INC. - MASTER
TAPE LIBRARY □ New York, NY

Packard, Tom, Engr.Libn.
GENERAL DYNAMICS CORPORATION -
DATAGRAPHIX, INC. - ENGINEERING LIBRARY
□ San Diego, CA

Packer, June, Rec.Mgr.
AMERICAN PLYWOOD ASSOCIATION -
INFORMATION CENTER □ Tacoma, WA

Padala, Patricia, Libn.
UNIVERSITY OF MICHIGAN - CENTER FOR
CONTINUING EDUCATION OF WOMEN -
LIBRARY □ Ann Arbor, MI

Padden, Barbara K., Hd.
LIBRARY ASSOCIATION OF PORTLAND - ART
AND MUSIC DEPARTMENT □ Portland, OR

Padgett, LaCona Raines, Hist.Libn.
POLK COUNTY HISTORICAL AND
GENEALOGICAL LIBRARY □ Bartow, FL

Padgett, Mary
MC LENNAN COUNTY LAW LIBRARY □ Waco, TX

Padnos, Mark, Dir.
ANTHOLOGY FILM ARCHIVES - LIBRARY □ New
York, NY

Padua, Noelia, Dir.
CATHOLIC UNIVERSITY OF PUERTO RICO -
MONSIGNOR JUAN FREMIOT TORRES OLIVER
LAW LIBRARY □ Ponce, PR

Paesani, Judith B.
UNIVERSITY OF CONNECTICUT - CENTER FOR REAL ESTATE & URBAN ECONOMIC STUDIES - REFERENCE & DOCUMENTS ROOM □ Storrs, CT

Paeth, Ms. Zillah, Hd.Acq.Libn.
OREGON COLLEGE OF EDUCATION - LIBRARY □ Monmouth, OR

Page, E.J., Chf. Chemist
BELDING HEMINWAY COMPANY - BELDING CORTICELLI RESEARCH CENTER - LIBRARY □ Putnam, CT

Page, Evelyn, Asst.Libn.
LUTHERAN HOSPITAL - MEDICAL STAFF LIBRARY AND SCHOOL FOR NURSES LIBRARY □ Moline, IL

Page, G. Wilson, Asst.Rec.Off.
UNIVERSITY OF GEORGIA - DEPARTMENT OF RECORDS MANAGEMENT & UNIVERSITY ARCHIVES □ Athens, GA

Page, John F., Dir.
NEW HAMPSHIRE HISTORICAL SOCIETY - LIBRARY □ Concord, NH

Page, Lori, Educ.Serv.Coord.
ONTARIO - MINISTRY OF GOVERNMENT SERVICES - TECHNICAL REFERENCE LIBRARY □ Toronto, ON

Page, Margareth, Techn.,Docs.
HOPITAL DU SACRE COEUR - PAVILLON ALBERT-PREVOST - MEDICAL LIBRARY □ Montreal, PQ

Page, Melda W., Chf.Libn.
U.S. VETERANS ADMINISTRATION (ME-Augusta) - CENTER LIBRARY □ Augusta, ME

Page, Penny B., Act.Libn.
RUTGERS UNIVERSITY, THE STATE UNIVERSITY OF NEW JERSEY - RUTGERS CENTER OF ALCOHOL STUDIES - LIBRARY □ Piscataway, NJ

Page, Vera, Foreign Law Libn.
UNIVERSITY OF WISCONSIN, MADISON - LAW LIBRARY □ Madison, WI

Page, William, Hd.Sci. & Tech.Lib.
DREXEL UNIVERSITY LIBRARIES - SCIENCE AND TECHNOLOGY LIBRARY □ Philadelphia, PA

Pages, Jose R., Acq.Libn.
UNIVERSITY OF GEORGIA - LAW LIBRARY □ Athens, GA

Paget, Mrs. K., Lib.Asst.
QUEEN'S UNIVERSITY AT KINGSTON - MECHANICAL ENGINEERING LIBRARY □ Kingston, ON

Paghis, Miriam, Libn.
JEWISH COMMUNITY CENTRE - LIBRARY □ Ottawa, ON

Pahl, Denise, Sr.Lib.Techn.
NORTH DAKOTA STATE HOSPITAL - DEPARTMENT OF LIBRARY SERVICES - HEALTH SCIENCE LIBRARY □ Jamestown, ND

Paik, Nan, Lib.Res.Anl.
ROCKWELL INTERNATIONAL - SPACE BUSINESSES - TECHNICAL INFORMATION CENTER □ Downey, CA

Paine, F. Helen, Libn.
MANITOBA - DEPARTMENT OF ECONOMIC DEVELOPMENT AND TOURISM - LIBRARY □ Winnipeg, MB

Paine, Jennie, Film Libn.
UNIVERSITY OF CALGARY - FILM LIBRARY □ Calgary, AB

Paine, Roberta M., Musm. Educator
METROPOLITAN MUSEUM OF ART - JUNIOR MUSEUM LIBRARY □ New York, NY

Paine, Thelma, Ref.Dept.Hd.
NEW BEDFORD FREE PUBLIC LIBRARY - GENEALOGY ROOM □ New Bedford, MA

Painter, Conrad, Asst.Libn.Tech.Serv.
DADE COUNTY LAW LIBRARY □ Miami, FL

Painter, Conrad L., Br.Libn.
FLORIDA STATE SUPREME COURT - 11TH JUDICIAL CIRCUIT - DADE COUNTY AUXILIARY LAW LIBRARY □ Miami Beach, FL

Painter, Patricia, Archv.
WAYNE STATE UNIVERSITY - ARCHIVES OF LABOR AND URBAN AFFAIRS/UNIVERSITY ARCHIVES □ Detroit, MI

Pak, Usok, Info.Rsrcs.Coord.
MOBIL RESEARCH & DEVELOPMENT CORPORATION - ENGINEERING DEPARTMENT - INFORMATION CENTER □ Princeton, NJ

Pakala, James C., Libn.
BIBLICAL THEOLOGICAL SEMINARY - LIBRARY □ Hatfield, PA

Palafox, Maria, Lib.Asst.
PACIFIC TELEPHONE COMPANY - LIBRARY □ San Francisco, CA

Palant, Celia, Libn.
GATEWAYS HOSPITAL AND COMMUNITY MENTAL HEALTH CENTER - PROFESSIONAL LIBRARY □ Los Angeles, CA

Palatsky, Celine, Asst.Musm.Libn.
METROPOLITAN MUSEUM OF ART - THOMAS J. WATSON LIBRARY □ New York, NY

Palevsky, Esther, Libn.
VISTRON CORPORATION - LIBRARY □ Cleveland, OH

Paliani, Mary Ann, Lib.Mgr.
ROCKWELL INTERNATIONAL - ATOMICS INTERNATIONAL DIVISION - ROCKY FLATS PLANT - TECHNICAL LIBRARY† □ Golden, CO

Palincsar, Stephen, Ref.Libn.
U.S. OFFICE OF PERSONNEL MANAGEMENT - LIBRARY □ Washington, DC

Pallay, Steven, Cat.Libn.
UNIVERSITY OF TORONTO - FACULTY OF MUSIC LIBRARY □ Toronto, ON

Palling, Dr. Barbara R., Hd.Libn.
BUENA VISTA COLLEGE - L.E. & E.L. BALLOU LIBRARY □ Storm Lake, IA

Pallman, Loma, Dir.
GRANDVIEW HOSPITAL - MEDICAL LIBRARY □ Dayton, OH

Palme, Natalie, Libn.
HARVARD MUSICAL ASSOCIATION - LIBRARY □ Boston, MA

Palmer, Beverly, Serv.Spec.
OAKLAND SCHOOLS - EDUCATIONAL RESOURCE CENTER □ Pontiac, MI

Palmer, Bruce, Cat.
UNIVERSITY OF ARIZONA - COLLEGE OF LAW LIBRARY □ Tucson, AZ

Palmer, Charlotte, Cat.Libn.
DE PAUL UNIVERSITY - LAW SCHOOL LIBRARY □ Chicago, IL

Palmer, David C., Asst. State Libn.
NEW JERSEY STATE LIBRARY □ Trenton, NJ

Palmer, Edith, Assoc.Libn.
STAUFFER CHEMICAL COMPANY - EASTERN RESEARCH CENTER INFORMATION SERVICES □ Dobbs Ferry, NY

Palmer, James, User Serv.Spec.
ERIC CLEARINGHOUSE FOR JUNIOR COLLEGES □ Los Angeles, CA

Palmer, Lorraine, Libn.
NEW YORK CHIROPRACTIC COLLEGE - LIBRARY □ Glen Head, NY

Palmer, Marg, Ministerial Libn.
BRITISH COLUMBIA - MINISTRY OF ENVIRONMENT - LIBRARY □ Victoria, BC

Palmer, Martha L., Asst. Law Libn.
UNIVERSITY OF MAINE SCHOOL OF LAW - DONALD L. GARBRECHT LAW LIBRARY □ Portland, ME

Palmer, Miriam, Med.Libn.
PROVIDENCE MEDICAL CENTER - MEDICAL LIBRARY □ Portland, OR

Palmer, Pamela, Libn.
MEMPHIS STATE UNIVERSITY LIBRARIES - ENGINEERING LIBRARY □ Memphis, TN

Palmer, Paul R., Cur.
COLUMBIA UNIVERSITY - COLUMBIANA □ New York, NY

Palmer, Raymond A., Libn.
WRIGHT STATE UNIVERSITY - HEALTH SCIENCES LIBRARY □ Dayton, OH

Palmer, Raymond M., Tech.Libn.
GENERAL ELECTRIC COMPANY - AIRCRAFT EQUIPMENT DIVISION - ARMAMENT SYSTEMS DEPT. ENGINEERING LIBRARY □ Burlington, VT

Palmer, Richard J., Libn.
MACOMB INTERMEDIATE SCHOOL DISTRICT - BEAL LIBRARY □ Mt. Clemens, MI

Palmer, Shirley, Res.Libn.
PROGRESSIVE GROCER - RESEARCH LIBRARY □ New York, NY

Palmer, Susan J., Tech.Proc.Libn.
WILLIAM PENN COLLEGE - WILCOX LIBRARY - SPECIAL COLLECTIONS □ Oskaloosa, IA

Palmieri, Dr. Lucien E., Hd., Coll.Dev.
SUNY - COLLEGE AT BUFFALO - EDWARD H. BUTLER LIBRARY □ Buffalo, NY

Palmquist, Beth, Cat.
AMERICAN GEOGRAPHICAL SOCIETY COLLECTION OF THE UNIVERSITY OF WISCONSIN, MILWAUKEE - GOLDA MEIR LIBRARY □ Milwaukee, WI

Palmquist, David W., Hd., Hist.Coll.
BRIDGEPORT PUBLIC LIBRARY - HISTORICAL COLLECTIONS □ Bridgeport, CT

Palmquist, Joan A., Libn.
UNIVERSITY OF ILLINOIS - HIGHWAY TRAFFIC SAFETY CENTER - LIBRARY □ Urbana, IL

Palms, Rev. Roger C., Ed.
GRAHAM (Billy) EVANGELISTIC ASSOCIATION - LIBRARY □ Minneapolis, MN

Paloma, Karen, Libn.
IOWA STATE COMMISSION FOR THE BLIND - LIBRARY FOR THE BLIND & PHYSICALLY HANDICAPPED □ Des Moines, IA

Palomo, Gerard, Circ.
UNIVERSITY OF TEXAS HEALTH SCIENCE CENTER, SAN ANTONIO - LIBRARY □ San Antonio, TX

Palsson, Gerald, Asst.Univ.Libn.
SAN DIEGO STATE UNIVERSITY - MALCOLM A. LOVE LIBRARY □ San Diego, CA

Paluka, Frank, Hd.
UNIVERSITY OF IOWA - SPECIAL COLLECTIONS DEPARTMENT □ Iowa City, IA

Palumbo, Richard
AESTHETIC REALISM FOUNDATION, INC. - LIBRARY □ New York, NY

Palumbo, Richard, Ref.Libn.
WAGNER COLLEGE - HORRMANN LIBRARY □ Staten Island, NY

Pan, Chi-Wei, Cat.
FIELD MUSEUM OF NATURAL HISTORY - LIBRARY □ Chicago, IL

Pana, Lucy M., Dept.Libn.
ALBERTA - DEPARTMENT OF CULTURE - DEPARTMENTAL LIBRARY □ Edmonton, AB

Pancake, Edwina H., Dir.
UNIVERSITY OF VIRGINIA - SCIENCE/TECHNOLOGY INFORMATION CENTER □ Charlottesville, VA

Panchita, Frometa, Lib.Pres.
ACADEMY OF THE STREET OF PUERTO RICAN CONGRESS - LIBRARY □ Chicago, IL

Panczyszyn, Dr. Marian, Sec.
UKRAINIAN MEDICAL ASSOCIATION OF NORTH AMERICA - MEDICAL ARCHIVES AND LIBRARY† □ Chicago, IL

Pandiri, Ananda, Asian Mtls.
SOUTHERN CONNECTICUT STATE COLLEGE - H.C. BULEY LIBRARY □ New Haven, CT

Pandolfi, Rosemary, Cat.
SCHOOL OF VISUAL ARTS - LIBRARY □ New York, NY

Panella, Nancy Mary, Libn.
ST. LUKE'S HOSPITAL CENTER - RICHARD WALKER BOLLING MEMORIAL MEDICAL LIBRARY □ New York, NY

Panepinto, Aura J., Dir.
UNIVERSITY OF PUERTO RICO - MEDICAL SCIENCES CAMPUS - LIBRARY □ Rio Piedras, PR

Panero, Sr. Elizabeth, Health Sci.Libn.
HOLY CROSS HOSPITAL - HEALTH SCIENCE LIBRARY □ San Fernando, CA

Panian, Linda, Res.Asst.
BISHOP BARAGA ASSOCIATION - ARCHIVES □
Marquette, MI
Pankey, Marilyn R., Dir., Med.Rec.
SIERRA VIEW DISTRICT HOSPITAL - MEDICAL
LIBRARY □ Porterville, CA
Pankiewicz, Cynthia A., Cur.
UNIVERSITY OF RHODE ISLAND - ART
DEPARTMENT - SLIDE LIBRARY □ Kingston, RI
Pankow, David, Libn.
ROCHESTER INSTITUTE OF TECHNOLOGY -
MELBERT B. CARY, JR. GRAPHIC ARTS
COLLECTION □ Rochester, NY
Panneton, Jacques, Consrv.
BIBLIOTHEQUE DE LA VILLE DE MONTREAL -
COLLECTION GAGNON □ Montreal, PQ
Panofsky, Hans E., Cur. of Africana
NORTHWESTERN UNIVERSITY - MELVILLE J.
HERSKOVITS LIBRARY OF AFRICAN STUDIES □
Evanston, IL
Pantano, Richard, Dir.
NEW HAMPSHIRE COLLEGE - SHAPIRO LIBRARY
□ Manchester, NH
Pantazis, Fotoula, Asst.Libn.
HAMILTON BOARD OF EDUCATION -
EDUCATION CENTRE LIBRARY □ Hamilton, ON
Panton, Linda, Hosp.Lib.Coord.
MC MASTER UNIVERSITY - HEALTH SCIENCES
LIBRARY □ Hamilton, ON
Pantridge, Barbara B., Libn.
DUTCHESS COUNTY MENTAL HEALTH LIBRARY
□ Poughkeepsie, NY
Pany, Diane, Hum.Ref.Libn.
SAM HOUSTON STATE UNIVERSITY - LIBRARY†
□ Huntsville, TX
Panzarella, Meg, Ref.Libn.
NORTHWESTERN UNIVERSITY - HEALTH
SCIENCES LIBRARY □ Chicago, IL
Paolucci, Anne, Exec.Dir.
COUNCIL ON NATIONAL LITERATURES -
INFORMATION CENTER □ Whitestone, NY
Papa, Angelo R., Lib.Asst.
NEW JERSEY STATE DEPARTMENT OF
ENVIRONMENTAL PROTECTION - DIVISION OF
WATER RESOURCES - LIBRARY □ Trenton, NJ
Papa, Leo, Libn.
GRUY (H.J.) & ASSOCIATES, INC. - LIBRARY □
Irving, TX
Papakhian, A. Ralph, Tech.Serv.Libn.
INDIANA UNIVERSITY - MUSIC LIBRARY □
Bloomington, IN
Paparelli, Marita E., Law Libn.
LACKAWANNA BAR ASSOCIATION - LAW
LIBRARY □ Scranton, PA
Pape, Renee, Libn.
GLENWOOD STATE HOSPITAL SCHOOL - STAFF
LIBRARY □ Glenwood, IA
Pape, Ruth P., Libn.
ST. ELIZABETH HOSPITAL MEDICAL CENTER -
MEMORIAL MEDICAL LIBRARY† □ Lafayette, IN
Papenfuse, Dr. Edward C., Archv.
MARYLAND STATE HALL OF RECORDS
COMMISSION - LIBRARY □ Annapolis, MD
Papermaster, Cynthia, Libn.
ORRICK, HERRINGTON, ROWLEY & SUTCLIFFE -
LIBRARY □ San Francisco, CA
Papillon, Lucien, Dir., Tech.Serv.
UNIVERSITE LAVAL - BIBLIOTHEQUE† □ Ste.
Foy, PQ
Paquette, Claire-Marie, Bus. & Mgt.Libn.
RYERSON POLYTECHNICAL INSTITUTE -
LEARNING RESOURCES CENTRE □ Toronto, ON
Paquette, Melinda R., Med.Libn.
READING HOSPITAL - MEDICAL LIBRARY □
Reading, PA
Paquette, Rita, Libn.
UNIVERSITE DE MONTREAL -
MATHEMATIQUES-BIBLIOTHEQUE □ Montreal,
PQ
Paquin, Marcel, Hd., Tech.Serv.
COLLEGE LIONEL-GROULX - BIBLIOTHEQUE □
Ste. Therese, PQ

Paquin, Nicole, Libn.
QUEBEC PROVINCE - REGIE DES RENTES -
CENTRE DE DOCUMENTATION □ Quebec, PQ
Paquin, Pierre, Ref.Libn.
BIBLIOTHEQUE DE LA VILLE DE MONTREAL -
COLLECTION GAGNON □ Montreal, PQ
Paradis, Olivier, Proc.Libn.
ECOLE POLYTECHNIQUE - BIBLIOTHEQUE □
Montreal, PQ
Pararas-Carayannis, Dr. George, Dir.
INTERNATIONAL TSUNAMI INFORMATION
CENTER □ Honolulu, HI
Parch, Grace D., Lib.Dir.
PLAIN DEALER PUBLISHING COMPANY -
LIBRARY □ Cleveland, OH
Parchman, June, Libn.
LUMMUS COMPANY - TECHNICAL LIBRARY □
Houston, TX
Pare, Gilles, Libn.
LE DEVOIR - CENTRE DE DOCUMENTATION □
Montreal, PQ
Pare, Richard, Assoc.Libn.
CANADA - LIBRARY OF PARLIAMENT □ Ottawa,
ON
Pareanen, Rosanne, Hd., Ref.Serv.
CANADA - REGIONAL ECONOMIC EXPANSION -
LIBRARY □ Ottawa, ON
Paredes, Miss Milagros M., Med.Libn.
LINCOLN HOSPITAL - MEDICAL LIBRARY □
Bronx, NY
Parent, Jacques, Dir., Acq.
CINEMATHEQUE NATIONALE DU QUEBEC □
Montreal, PQ
Parhad, Brian, Patients' Libn.
U.S. VETERANS ADMINISTRATION (IL-Chicago)
- WESTSIDE HOSPITAL LIBRARY □ Chicago, IL
Parhad, Bronwyn, Hd.
CHICAGO PUBLIC LIBRARY CENTRAL LIBRARY -
GENERAL INFORMATION SERVICES DIVISION -
INFORMATION CENTER □ Chicago, IL
Parham, Arthur R., Coord./Academic Comp.
CHICAGO STATE UNIVERSITY - DOUGLAS
LIBRARY □ Chicago, IL
Parham, Robert Bruce, Archv./Libn.
BOULDER HISTORICAL SOCIETY - PIONEER
MUSEUM - LIBRARY □ Boulder, CO
Parham, Sandra Heath, Libn.
ST. MARY'S HOSPITAL - HEALTH SCIENCES
LIBRARY □ Richmond, VA
Paris, Chantel, Libn.
SANATANA DHARMA FOUNDATION - GERTRUDE
C. BERNER MEMORIAL LIBRARY OF SPIRITUAL
SCIENCES □ St. Helena, CA
Paris, Kay, Musm.Dir.
BEAUMONT ART MUSEUM - LIBRARY □
Beaumont, TX
Paris, Shirley, Ref.
NEW YORK CITY - MUNICIPAL REFERENCE AND
RESEARCH CENTER □ New York, NY
Parish, David W., Gov.Doc.Libn.
SUNY - COLLEGE AT GENESEO - MILNE LIBRARY
□ Geneseo, NY
Parish, Gina, Mgr.
ARLINGTON PUBLIC SCHOOLS - PROFESSIONAL
LIBRARY □ Arlington, VA
Parish, Marisa, Children's Libn.
NEW YORK PUBLIC LIBRARY - BELMONT
REGIONAL LIBRARY - ENRICO FERMI
CULTURAL CENTER □ Bronx, NY
Parisky, Helen, Asst.Libn. & Cat.
CALIFORNIA LUTHERAN COLLEGE - LIBRARY □
Thousand Oaks, CA
Parisot, Beverly, Libn.
OMAHA PUBLIC LIBRARY - BUSINESS, SCIENCE
& TECHNOLOGY DEPARTMENT □ Omaha, NE
Park, Mrs. A. Belva, Med.Libn.
REGINA GENERAL HOSPITAL - MEDICAL
LIBRARY □ Regina, SK
Park, Helen, Cat.Libn.
SUNY AT STONY BROOK - HEALTH SCIENCES
LIBRARY □ East Setauket, NY

Park, Heo, Sr.Libn.
BERKELEY PUBLIC LIBRARY - ART AND MUSIC
DIVISION □ Berkeley, CA
Park, Robert C., Dir. of Lib. Serv.
ST. LUKE'S EPISCOPAL & TEXAS CHILDREN'S
HOSPITALS - MEDICAL LIBRARY □ Houston, TX
Park, Yoon S., Cat.
LIBRARY OF INTERNATIONAL RELATIONS □
Chicago, IL
Parker, Annette, Govt.Doc.
NORTHWESTERN OKLAHOMA STATE
UNIVERSITY - LIBRARY □ Alva, OK
Parker, C. Gerald, Hd., Sound Coll.
NATIONAL LIBRARY OF CANADA - MUSIC
DIVISION □ Ottawa, ON
Parker, Candace, Ref.Libn.
U.S. NAVY - NAVAL AIR SYSTEMS COMMAND -
TECHNICAL LIBRARY □ Washington, DC
Parker, Carolyn, AV Libn.
WAKE FOREST UNIVERSITY - BOWMAN GRAY
SCHOOL OF MEDICINE - LIBRARY □ Winston-
Salem, NC
Parker, Carroll T., State Libn.
GEORGIA STATE LIBRARY □ Atlanta, GA
Parker, Charlotte E., Dir.
GIRL SCOUTS OF THE USA - JULIETTE GORDON
LOW GIRL SCOUT NATIONAL CENTER □
Savannah, GA
Parker, Cut, Libn.
INVESTMENT COMPANY INSTITUTE - LIBRARY
□ Washington, DC
Parker, Edward D., Jr., Public Serv.
TRINITY UNIVERSITY - LIBRARY □ San Antonio,
TX
Parker, Elizabeth L., Libn.
COASTAL ECOSYSTEMS MANAGEMENTS, INC. -
LIBRARY □ Fort Worth, TX
Parker, Evelyn, New Bks.Libn.
VOUGHT CORPORATION - TECHNICAL
INFORMATION CENTER □ Dallas, TX
Parker, Jean, Libn.
MERCY HOSPITAL - HEALTH SCIENCES
LIBRARY □ Muskegon, MI
Parker, Jeanne
GENERAL ELECTRIC COMPANY - LAMP GLASS &
COMPONENTS LIBRARY □ Richmond Heights, OH
Parker, John, Cur.
UNIVERSITY OF MINNESOTA - JAMES FORD
BELL LIBRARY □ Minneapolis, MN
Parker, Kenneth, Libn.
STANFORD UNIVERSITY - CUBBERLEY
EDUCATION LIBRARY □ Stanford, CA
Parker, Leonard, Mgr., Tech.Info.Serv.
CIBA-GEIGY CORPORATION - TECHNICAL
INFORMATION SERVICE □ Greensboro, NC
Parker, M., Info.Spec.
BURROUGHS WELLCOME COMPANY - LIBRARY
□ Research Triangle Park, NC
Parker, Marian, Assoc.Dir.
SUNY AT BUFFALO - CHARLES B. SEARS LAW
LIBRARY □ Buffalo, NY
Parker, Mary L., Libn.
SOUTHERN CALIFORNIA EDISON COMPANY -
LIBRARY □ Rosemead, CA
Parker, Nancy Boothe, Dir.
RICE UNIVERSITY - WOODSON RESEARCH
CENTER □ Houston, TX
Parker, Peter J., Chf. of Mss.
HISTORICAL SOCIETY OF PENNSYLVANIA -
LIBRARY □ Philadelphia, PA
Parker, Stephen B., Libn.
ELECTRIC POWER RESEARCH INSTITUTE -
TECHNICAL LIBRARY □ Palo Alto, CA
Parker, Sybil P., Supv.Libn.
U.S. ARMY MILITARY POLICE SCHOOL -
LIBRARY □ Ft. McClellan, AL
Parker, Thomas W., Dir.
BOSTONIAN SOCIETY - LIBRARY □ Boston, MA
Parker, V., Libn.
AQUATIC RESEARCH INSTITUTE - LIBRARY □
Hayward, CA

Parker, Ms. V.
CANADA - PUBLIC ARCHIVES OF CANADA -
NATIONAL MAP COLLECTION □ Ottawa, ON

Parker, Virginia, Libn.
QUEEN'S UNIVERSITY AT KINGSTON -
BRACKEN LIBRARY □ Kingston, ON

Parker, Vivian B., Sr. Data Anl.
U.S. NATL. BUREAU OF STANDARDS -
CHEMICAL THERMODYNAMICS DATA CENTER
□ Washington, DC

Parker, William, Ref.Libn.
UNIVERSITY OF BRITISH COLUMBIA -
WOODWARD BIOMEDICAL LIBRARY □
Vancouver, BC

Parkes, Darla, Ref.Libn.
MISSOURI STATE LIBRARY □ Jefferson City, MO

Parkes, Katherine, Libn.
NATIONAL HOUSING LAW PROJECT/NATIONAL
ECONOMIC DEVELOPMENT AND LAW CENTER -
LIBRARY □ Berkeley, CA

Parkin, Derral, Libn.
UNIVERSITY OF HOUSTON - COLLEGE OF
PHARMACY LIBRARY □ Houston, TX

Parkinson, George, Cur.
WEST VIRGINIA UNIVERSITY - WEST
VIRGINIA COLLECTION □ Morgantown, WV

Parkinson, Greg T., Asst.Libn. & Hist.
CIRCUS WORLD MUSEUM - LIBRARY □ Baraboo,
WI

Parkinson, Howard, Circ.Libn.
WILFRID LAURIER UNIVERSITY - LIBRARY □
Waterloo, ON

Parkinson, Janet A., Libn.
PRICE WATERHOUSE - AUDIT LIBRARY □
Vancouver, BC

Parkinson, Mike, Lib.Supv.
SOUTHERN ALBERTA INSTITUTE OF
TECHNOLOGY - ALBERTA COLLEGE OF ART -
LIBRARY □ Calgary, AB

Parkinson, Patricia, Tech.Libn.
PPG INDUSTRIES, INC. - GLASS RESEARCH
CENTER - INFORMATION SERVICES □
Pittsburgh, PA

Parkinson, Robert L., Chf.Libn. & Hist.
CIRCUS WORLD MUSEUM - LIBRARY □ Baraboo,
WI

Parkman, Helen, Cur.
STEELE COUNTY HISTORICAL SOCIETY -
ARCHIVES □ Hope, ND

Parks, Ms. B.C., Libn.
CESSNA AIRCRAFT COMPANY - WALLACE
DIVISION - ENGINEERING LIBRARY □ Wichita,
KS

Parks, Dennis H., Libn.
PURDUE UNIVERSITY - AVIATION
TECHNOLOGY LIBRARY □ West Lafayette, IN

Parks, Dennis H., Act.Libn.
PURDUE UNIVERSITY - GEOSCIENCES LIBRARY
□ West Lafayette, IN

Parks, Dennis H., Act.Libn.
PURDUE UNIVERSITY - PHYSICS LIBRARY □
West Lafayette, IN

Parks, Dorothy Ruth, Dir.
VANDERBILT UNIVERSITY LIBRARY - DIVINITY
LIBRARY □ Nashville, TN

Parks, Dorothy Ruth, Dir.
VANDERBILT UNIVERSITY LIBRARY - DIVINITY
LIBRARY - KESLER CIRCULATING LIBRARY □
Nashville, TN

Parks, Gordon, Assoc.Dir.
UNIVERSITY OF WISCONSIN, WHITEWATER -
LIBRARY & LEARNING RESOURCES □
Whitewater, WI

Parks, Robert E., Music Libn.
VASSAR COLLEGE - GEORGE SHERMAN
DICKINSON MUSIC LIBRARY □ Poughkeepsie,
NY

Parks, Sandra, Lib.Techn.
MICHIGAN STATE UNIVERSITY - URBAN
POLICY AND PLANNING LIBRARY □ East Lansing,
MI

Parks, Stephen R., Cur./Osborn Coll.
YALE UNIVERSITY - BEINECKE RARE BOOK AND
MANUSCRIPT LIBRARY □ New Haven, CT

Parks, Stephen R., Libn.
YALE UNIVERSITY - ELIZABETHAN CLUB
COLLECTION □ New Haven, CT

Parming, Marju, Mgr.
U.S. GENERAL ACCOUNTING OFFICE -
TECHNICAL INFORMATION SOURCES AND
SERVICES BRANCH □ Washington, DC

Parnell, Ellen, Libn.
RICHMOND PUBLIC LIBRARY - BUSINESS,
SCIENCE & TECHNOLOGY DEPARTMENT† □
Richmond, VA

Parnell, Gertrude, Tech.Proc.
TROY STATE UNIVERSITY - LIBRARY □ Troy, AL

Paro, Kathleen, Instr.Serv.Libn.
EMBRY RIDDLE AERONAUTICAL UNIVERSITY -
LEARNING RESOURCES CENTER □ Daytona
Beach, FL

Parr, Mary Anne, Med.Libn.
ST. FRANCIS HOSPITAL - MEDICAL CENTER -
MEDICAL LIBRARY □ Peoria, IL

Parratt, Pat, Libn.
CARNEGIE INSTITUTION OF WASHINGTON -
LIBRARY □ Washington, DC

Parratt, Ruth W., Libn.
MC KEE (Davy) CORPORATION - INFORMATION
RESOURCE CENTER □ Cleveland, OH

Parrick, Joan L., Tech.Libn.
GPU NUCLEAR - TMI TECHNICAL LIBRARY □
Middletown, PA

Parris, Fred, Mgr., Info.Serv.
CLEARINGHOUSE ON CHILD ABUSE AND
NEGLECT INFORMATION □ Washington, DC

Parris, Pat, Libn.
KANSAS STATE UNIVERSITY - WILLARD
LIBRARY □ Manhattan, KS

Parrish, James, Extramural Prog.
UNIVERSITY OF ILLINOIS MEDICAL CENTER -
LIBRARY OF THE HEALTH SCIENCES □ Chicago,
IL

Parrish, Jenni, Dir.
UNIVERSITY OF PITTSBURGH - LAW LIBRARY □
Pittsburgh, PA

Parrish, Laryne, Musm.Cur.
WHEELRIGHT MUSEUM - LIBRARY □ Santa Fe,
NM

Parrish, Laura, Ser.Libn.
SAMFORD UNIVERSITY - CUMBERLAND
SCHOOL OF LAW - CORDELL HULL LAW
LIBRARY† □ Birmingham, AL

Parrish, Michael, Hd.
INDIANA UNIVERSITY - SCHOOL OF PUBLIC
AND ENVIRONMENTAL AFFAIRS - LIBRARY □
Bloomington, IN

Parrish, Octavia, Lib.Asst.
PORTSMOUTH PUBLIC LIBRARY - LOCAL
HISTORY ROOM □ Portsmouth, VA

Parrish, Ramona C., Libn.
DE PAUL HOSPITAL - DR. HENRY BOONE
MEMORIAL LIBRARY □ Norfolk, VA

Parrish, Sandra, Libn.
PIERSON, BALL & DOWD - LAW LIBRARY □
Washington, DC

Parriss, Mrs. Jean, Libn.
CLARKSON, GORDON /WOODS, GORDON -
LIBRARY □ Toronto, ON

Parrott, Mrs. D., Lib.Techn.
COLLEGE OF TRADES AND TECHNOLOGY -
MEDICAL LIBRARY □ St. John's, NF

Parry, David R., Dir.
LAKE COUNTY PUBLIC LIBRARY - SPECIAL
COLLECTIONS □ Leadville, CO

Parry, Hilda, Libn.
ATLANTIC-RICHFIELD COMPANY - ANACONDA
ALUMINUM COMPANY - COLUMBIA FALLS
REDUCTION DIVISION - LIBRARY □ Columbia
Falls, MT

Parry, Robert, Dp.Dir.
CUYAHOGA COUNTY REGIONAL PLANNING
COMMISSION - LIBRARY □ Cleveland, OH

Parsch, Janet, Sci.Libn.
MICHIGAN STATE UNIVERSITY - SCIENCE
LIBRARY □ East Lansing, MI

Parsonage, Dianne L., Dept.Libn.
CANADA - REVENUE CANADA - CUSTOMS &
EXCISE LIBRARY □ Ottawa, ON

Parsons, Mrs. C., Libn.
DE HAVILLAND AIRCRAFT OF CANADA, LTD. -
ENGINEERING LIBRARY □ Downsview, ON

Parsons, Charles, Govt.Doc.
UNIVERSITY OF CINCINNATI - ROBERT S.
MARX LAW LIBRARY □ Cincinnati, OH

Parsons, Donna, Dir.
COLLEGE OF IDAHO - REGIONAL STUDIES
CENTER - LIBRARY □ Caldwell, ID

Parsons, Frances E., Lib.Supv.
DU PONT DE NEMOURS (E.I.) & COMPANY, INC.
- LAVOISIER LIBRARY □ Wilmington, DE

Parsons, Gerald J., Dept.Hd.
ONONDAGA COUNTY PUBLIC LIBRARY - LOCAL
HISTORY AND GENEALOGY DEPARTMENT □
Syracuse, NY

Parsons, Joan, Hum.Libn.
RYERSON POLYTECHNICAL INSTITUTE -
LEARNING RESOURCES CENTRE □ Toronto, ON

Parsons, Karen, Libn.
SAGAMORE HILLS CHILDREN'S PSYCHIATRIC
HOSPITAL - STAFF MEDICAL LIBRARY □
Northfield, OH

Parsons, Kevin, Dir.
JUSTICE SYSTEM TRAINING ASSOCIATION -
PSYCHO-MOTOR SKILL DESIGN ARCHIVE □
Appleton, WI

Partlow, Richard V., Dept.Mgr.
LOS ANGELES PUBLIC LIBRARY - AUDIO-
VISUAL DEPARTMENT □ Los Angeles, CA

Partridge, Charles V., Libn.
DETROIT PUBLIC SCHOOLS - PROFESSIONAL
LIBRARY □ Detroit, MI

Pascarelli, Anne M., Asst.Libn.
NEW YORK ACADEMY OF MEDICINE - LIBRARY
□ New York, NY

Pascavage, Barbara Ann, Libn.
U.S. VETERANS ADMINISTRATION (TX-Waco) -
MEDICAL CENTER LIBRARY □ Waco, TX

Paschal, Janetta, ILL Libn.
WEST TEXAS STATE UNIVERSITY - CORNETTE
LIBRARY □ Canyon, TX

Paschall, Jo Anne, Hd.Libn.
ATLANTA COLLEGE OF ART - LIBRARY □ Atlanta,
GA

Pascoe, Frank, Ref. & Loan Serv.
MISSOURI STATE LIBRARY □ Jefferson City, MO

Pascucci, Joseph T., Libn.
NEW YORK STATE SUPREME COURT -
APPELLATE DIVISION, 4TH JUDICIAL
DEPARTMENT - LAW LIBRARY □ Rochester, NY

Pashley, Anne, Ref.Spec.
CANADIAN GENERAL ELECTRIC COMPANY,
LTD. - CORPORATE INFORMATION CENTRE □
Toronto, ON

Pasini, S. Elaine, Libn.
U.S. DEPT. OF ENERGY - MORGANTOWN
ENERGY TECHNOLOGY CENTER LIBRARY □
Morgantown, WV

Pask, Judith M., Asst.Libn.
PURDUE UNIVERSITY - MANAGEMENT AND
ECONOMICS LIBRARY □ West Lafayette, IN

Paskar, Joanne M., Hd.
U.S. AGENCY FOR INTERNATIONAL
DEVELOPMENT - DEVELOPMENT INFORMATION
CENTER □ Washington, DC

Pasmik, Eleonor E., Assoc.Libn., Hd.Ref.
NEW YORK UNIVERSITY MEDICAL CENTER -
FREDERICK L. EHRMAN MEDICAL LIBRARY □
New York, NY

Pasquarella, Kathryn, Med.Libn.
OHIO VALLEY HOSPITAL - HEALTH SCIENCES
LIBRARY □ Steubenville, OH

Pasquariella, Susan K., Hd.Libn.
COLUMBIA UNIVERSITY - CENTER FOR
POPULATION & FAMILY HEALTH - LIBRARY/
INFORMATION PROGRAM □ New York, NY

PERSONNEL

Pasquis-Audant, Colette, Libn.
HOTEL-DIEU DE LEVIS - BIBLIOTHEQUE
MEDICALE □ Levis, PQ
Pass, E., Libn.
ROYAL ALEXANDRA HOSPITAL - SCHOOL OF
NURSING LIBRARY □ Edmonton, AB
Passarelli, Anne B., Hd.Libn.
UNIVERSITY OF WASHINGTON - BUSINESS
ADMINISTRATION BRANCH LIBRARY □ Seattle,
WA
Passidomo, Don, Chf.Libn.
U.S. VETERANS ADMINISTRATION (DE-
Wilmington) - CENTER MEDICAL LIBRARY† □
Wilmington, DE
Pastan, Barbara P., Lib.Dir.
FAULKNER HOSPITAL - INGERSOLL BOWDITCH
LIBRARY □ Jamaica Plain, MA
Pastan, Herbert M., Libn.
U.S. ARMY INSTITUTE OF HERALDRY - LIBRARY
□ Alexandria, VA
Paster, J.G., Libn.
RHODE ISLAND STATE DEPARTMENT OF
HEALTH - GERTRUDE E. STURGES MEMORIAL
LIBRARY □ Providence, RI
Patail, George, Ref.Libn.
U.S. ARMY IN EUROPE (USAREUR) - LIBRARY
AND RESOURCE CENTER □ APO New York, NY
Patchett, Dr. J.E., Asst.Dir. of Res.
NORTON RESEARCH CORPORATION (Canada)
LTD. - LIBRARY □ Niagara Falls, ON
Pate, Pam, Med.Libn.
U.S. VETERANS ADMINISTRATION (AL-
Birmingham) - HOSPITAL MEDICAL LIBRARY □
Birmingham, AL
Paterakis, Diane, Act.Dir. Of Lib.
HELLENIC COLLEGE AND HOLY CROSS GREEK
ORTHODOX SCHOOL OF THEOLOGY -
COTSIDAS-TONNA LIBRARY □ Brookline, MA
Paterson, Ellen, Sci.Ref.-Biblog.
SUNY - COLLEGE AT CORTLAND - MEMORIAL
LIBRARY □ Cortland, NY
Patmon, Marian, Hd.Lib.Rsrcs.
OKLAHOMA STATE DEPARTMENT OF
LIBRARIES □ Oklahoma City, OK
Patrias, Karen, Chf., Ref.Biblog.
U.S. NATL. INSTITUTES OF HEALTH - LIBRARY
□ Bethesda, MD
Patricia, Coffey, Libn.
OAKLAND PUBLIC LIBRARY - SCIENCE/
SOCIOLOGY DIVISION □ Oakland, CA
Patricius, Sister Mary, Dir.
ST. MARY HOSPITAL - HEALTH SCIENCE
LIBRARY □ Port Arthur, TX
Patrick, Carolyn, Assoc.Dir.
TEXAS TECH UNIVERSITY - HEALTH SCIENCES
CENTER - REGIONAL ACADEMIC HEALTH
CENTER LIBRARY □ Amarillo, TX
Patrick, Lucia, Cons.Rd.Serv.
GEORGIA STATE DEPARTMENT OF EDUCATION
- DIVISION OF PUBLIC LIBRARY SERVICES □
Atlanta, GA
Patrick, Susan, Info.Ctr.Libn.
RYERSON POLYTECHNICAL INSTITUTE -
LEARNING RESOURCES CENTRE □ Toronto, ON
Patrick, W., Pub.Serv.Libn.
MC GILL UNIVERSITY - MEDICAL LIBRARY □
Montreal, PQ
Patrick, Wendy, Libn.
MC GILL UNIVERSITY - BOTANY-GENETICS
LIBRARY □ Montreal, PQ
Patsy, Janet E., Law Libn.
GENESEE COUNTY CIRCUIT COURT - LAW
LIBRARY □ Flint, MI
Patten, David J., Art Libn.
OBERLIN COLLEGE - CLARENCE WARD ART
LIBRARY □ Oberlin, OH
Patten, Frederick W., Cat.Libn.
HUGHES AIRCRAFT COMPANY - COMPANY
TECHNICAL DOCUMENT CENTER □ Culver City,
CA

Patterson, Mrs. Bobbie J., Coord.
WASHINGTON STATE SUPERINTENDENT OF
PUBLIC INSTRUCTION - RESOURCE
INFORMATION CENTER □ Tumwater WA
Patterson, D.K., Tech.Libn.
LOCKHEED-GEORGIA COMPANY - TECHNICAL
INFORMATION DEPARTMENT □ Marietta, GA
Patterson, Dewey F., Lib.Dir.
VERMONT TECHNICAL COLLEGE - HARTNESS
LIBRARY □ Randolph Center, VT
Patterson, Flora E., Dir.Pub.Serv.
NATIONAL LIBRARY OF CANADA □ Ottawa, ON
Patterson, Gregory R., Med.Libn.
UTAH VALLEY HOSPITAL - MEDICAL LIBRARY □
Provo, UT
Patterson, Jack M., Mgr.
BRITISH COLUMBIA AND YUKON CHAMBER OF
MINES - LIBRARY □ Vancouver, BC
Patterson, Jacque, Libn.
U.S. ARMY - CORPS OF ENGINEERS - MEMPHIS
DISTRICT - LIBRARY □ Memphis, TN
Patterson, Jenny, Libn.
NASHVILLE - METROPOLITAN DEPARTMENT OF
PUBLIC HEALTH - LENTZ HEALTH CENTER
LIBRARY □ Nashville, TN
Patterson, Judy, Libn.
CAMBRIA COUNTY FREE LAW LIBRARY □
Ebensburg, PA
Patterson, Julia A., Libn.
U.S. AIR FORCE BASE - MC CLELLAN BASE
LIBRARY □ McClellan AFB, CA
Patterson, Kim, AV Supv.
OUACHITA BAPTIST UNIVERSITY - RILEY
LIBRARY □ Arkadelphia, AR
Patterson, Laura, AV/Per.Libn.
LEWIS UNIVERSITY - LIBRARY □ Romeoville, IL
Patterson, Margaret, Patents
WARNER-LAMBERT/PARKE-DAVIS - RESEARCH
LIBRARY† □ Ann Arbor, MI
Patterson, Maureen L. P., Biblog./Hd.
UNIVERSITY OF CHICAGO - SOUTH ASIA
COLLECTION □ Chicago, IL
Patterson, Melvin, Libn.
SAN FRANCISCO EXAMINER - LIBRARY □ San
Francisco, CA
Patterson, Myron B., Lib.Res.
BRITISH COLUMBIA TELEPHONE COMPANY -
BUSINESS LIBRARY □ Burnaby, BC
Patterson, Robert, Hd., Pub.Serv.
MICHIGAN TECHNOLOGICAL UNIVERSITY -
LIBRARY □ Houghton, MI
Patterson, Shannon, Ref.
ADAMS STATE COLLEGE - LIBRARY □ Alamosa,
CO
Patterson, Thomas D., Libn.
SOUTHEASTERN WISCONSIN REGIONAL
PLANNING COMMISSION - REFERENCE
LIBRARY □ Waukesha, WI
Patterson, Vanessa, Supv., Res.Serv.
HOLIDAY INNS, INC. - RESEARCH SERVICES
INFORMATION CENTER □ Memphis, TN
Patterson, Virginia, Libn.
FIRST BAPTIST CHURCH - LIBRARY □ San
Antonio, TX
Patterson, William C., Dir.
SPERRY CORPORATION - BUSINESS PLANNING
LIBRARY □ New York, NY
Pattie, Miko, Cat.
EASTERN KENTUCKY UNIVERSITY - JOHN
GRANT CRABBE LIBRARY □ Richmond, KY
Pattillo, John W., Dir.
SOUTHERN TECHNICAL INSTITUTE - LIBRARY
□ Marietta, GA
Pattison, Fredrick W., Asst.Libn. & Indexer
AMERICAN JOURNAL OF NURSING COMPANY -
SOPHIA F. PALMER MEMORIAL LIBRARY □ New
York, NY
Pattison, Jane, Sr.Res.Libn.
HOOKER CHEMICAL CORPORATION -
TECHNICAL INFORMATION CENTER □ Niagara
Falls, NY

Patton, Bob, Coord.Curric.Div.
OKLAHOMA STATE DEPARTMENT OF
VOCATIONAL AND TECHNICAL EDUCATION -
CURRICULUM DIVISION □ Stillwater, OK
Patton, L.K., Exec.Dir.
KENTUCKY COVERED BRIDGE ASSOCIATION -
LIBRARY □ Fort Thomas, KY
Patton, Mary, Spec.
MICHIGAN STATE UNIVERSITY - UNIVERSITY
ARCHIVES AND HISTORICAL COLLECTIONS □
East Lansing, MI
Patton, Nicholas W., Principal Libn.
NEWARK PUBLIC LIBRARY - SCIENCE AND
TECHNOLOGY DIVISION □ Newark, NJ
Patton, Robert A., Interp.Spec.
U.S. NATL. PARK SERVICE - LAVA BEDS NATL.
MONUMENT - LIBRARY □ Tulelake, CA
Patton, Sandy, Libn.
COLORADO SPRINGS PUBLIC SCHOOLS -
DISTRICT NO. 11 - TEACHERS' PROFESSIONAL
LIBRARY □ Colorado Springs, CO
Patzwald, Gari-Anne, Libn.
NATIONAL COLLEGE OF CHIROPRACTIC -
LEARNING RESOURCE CENTER □ Lombard, IL
Paul, Andrea I., Mss.Cur.
NEBRASKA STATE HISTORICAL SOCIETY -
ARCHIVES □ Lincoln, NE
Paul, Bani, Cat.Libn.
ALCORN STATE UNIVERSITY - JOHN DEWEY
BOYD LIBRARY □ Lorman, MS
Paul, Donald C., Libn.
HUGHES AIRCRAFT COMPANY - CANOGA PARK
LIBRARY □ Canoga Park, CA
Paul, Donald T., Hd.
DAYTON AND MONTGOMERY COUNTY PUBLIC
LIBRARY - LITERATURE AND FINE ARTS
DIVISION □ Dayton, OH
Paul, Elizabeth, Ref.Libn.
SACRED HEART UNIVERSITY - LIBRARY □
Bridgeport, CT
Paul, George P., Circ.Libn.
UNIVERSITY OF VIRGINIA MEDICAL CENTER -
CLAUDE MOORE HEALTH SCIENCES LIBRARY □
Charlottesville, VA
Paul, Jacquelin, Asst.Libn.
DELAWARE LAW SCHOOL OF WIDENER
UNIVERSITY - LAW LIBRARY □ Wilmington, DE
Paul, Miss Jean, Chf.Libn.
NORTHERN ALBERTA INSTITUTE OF
TECHNOLOGY - LEARNING RESOURCE CENTRE
□ Edmonton, AB
Paul, Nancy, Hd., Tech.Serv.
UNIVERSITY OF WISCONSIN, MADISON - LAW
LIBRARY □ Madison, WI
Paul, Patricia, Hd.Cat.
UNIVERSITY OF WISCONSIN, STEVENS POINT
- JAMES H. ALBERTSON CENTER FOR LEARNING
RESOURCES □ Stevens Point, WI
Paul, Patty, Doc.Libn.
STATE LIBRARY OF FLORIDA □ Tallahassee, FL
Paul, Richard, Circ.
NEW YORK UNIVERSITY - GRADUATE SCHOOL
OF BUSINESS ADMINISTRATION - LIBRARY □
New York, NY
Paul, Sherri, Cat.
SLEEPY HOLLOW RESTORATIONS, INC. -
SPECIAL LIBRARY & ARCHIVES □ Tarrytown, NY
Paulaitis, Arthur, Sci. & Tech.Libn.
RYERSON POLYTECHNICAL INSTITUTE -
LEARNING RESOURCES CENTRE □ Toronto, ON
Pauli, Dan, Info.Spec.
ESSO RESOURCES CANADA LIMITED - LIBRARY
INFORMATION CENTRE □ Calgary, AB
Paull, Frank O., Jr., Dir.
MARQUETTE COUNTY HISTORICAL SOCIETY -
J.M. LONGYEAR RESEARCH LIBRARY □
Marquette, MI
Pauls, Adonijah, Libn.
MENNONITE BRETHREN BIBLICAL SEMINARY -
HIEBERT LIBRARY □ Fresno, CA
Paulsen, Dorothy, Musm. Registrar
NEVADA STATE MUSEUM □ Carson City, NV

Paulsen, Dorothy J., Cat. & Ser.Libn.
U.S. FOREST SERVICE - PACIFIC SOUTHWEST
FOREST & RANGE EXPERIMENT STATION -
WESTFORNET-BERKELEY □ Berkeley, CA
Paulson, Gale, Dir.
SAN FRANCISCO ACADEMY OF COMIC ART -
LIBRARY □ San Francisco, CA
Paulson, Peter, Dir.
NEW YORK STATE LIBRARY □ Albany, NY
Paulukonis, Joseph T., Dir.
DAKOTA STATE COLLEGE - KARL E. MUNDT
LIBRARY □ Madison, SD
Pauth, Patricia R., Adm.
PRICE WATERHOUSE - NEW YORK OFFICE
INFORMATION CENTER □ New York, NY
Pautz, Martin R., Dean, Lrng.Rsrcs.
GREENVILLE TECHNICAL COLLEGE - LEARNING
RESOURCES CENTER □ Greenville, SC
Pauwels, Colleen K., Dir.
INDIANA UNIVERSITY - LAW LIBRARY □
Bloomington, IN
Pavelko, Charlotte, Libn.
LANTERMAN (Frank J.) STATE HOSPITAL -
STAFF LIBRARY □ Pomona, CA
Pavetti, Sally Thomas, Cur.
EUGENE O'NEILL MEMORIAL THEATER CENTER,
INC. - THEATER COLLECTION AND LIBRARY □
Waterford, CT
Pavlich, Josephine, Asst.Libn.
MUSKEGON BUSINESS COLLEGE - LIBRARY □
Muskegon, MI
Pavlin, Stefanie A., Hd., Lib.Serv.
ONTARIO - MINISTRY OF TRANSPORTATION
AND COMMUNICATIONS - LIBRARY AND
INFORMATION CENTRE □ Downsview, ON
Pavlovsky, Olga, European Lit.Spec.
METROPOLITAN TORONTO LIBRARY -
LITERATURE DEPARTMENT □ Toronto, ON
Pawelek, Stephanie, Tech.Ck.
ITT CORPORATION - ITT AVIONICS/DEFENSE
COMMUNICATIONS DIVISION - TECHNICAL
LIBRARY† □ Nutley, NJ
Pawlik, Bernadette, Libn.
FOOTE CONE & BELDING - INFORMATION
CENTER □ Chicago, IL
Pawloski, Barbara, Doc.Libn.
GEORGETOWN UNIVERSITY - LAW CENTER
LIBRARY □ Washington, DC
Pawluk, Mr. W.S., Asst. Regional Dir.
CANADA - STATISTICS CANADA - ADVISORY
SERVICES - WINNIPEG REFERENCE CENTRE □
Winnipeg, MB
Payette, Serge, Dir.
UNIVERSITE LAVAL - CENTRE D'ETUDES
NORDIQUES (CEN) - CENTRE DE
DOCUMENTATION □ Ste. Foy, PQ
Paylor, Barbara Stagg, Libn.
HUGHES (Thomas) LIBRARY □ Rugby, TN
Paymer, Natalie S., Libn.
MARYLAND STATE LAW DEPARTMENT -
ATTORNEY GENERAL'S OFFICE - LIBRARY □
Baltimore, MD
Payne, Ben, Libn.
PENN VIRGINIA CORPORATION - LIBRARY □
Philadelphia, PA
Payne, Bernetta, Libn.
HOLY CROSS HOSPITAL OF SILVER SPRING -
MEDICAL LIBRARY □ Silver Spring, MD
Payne, Carolyn B., Rd.Serv.Libn.
U.S. ARMY POST - FORT JACKSON - LIBRARY □
Ft. Jackson, SC
Payne, Frank, Libn.
U.S. COURT OF APPEALS, 6TH CIRCUIT -
LIBRARY □ Cincinnati, OH
Payne, John R., Asst. to the Dir.
UNIVERSITY OF TEXAS, AUSTIN - HUMANITIES
RESEARCH CENTER □ Austin, TX
Payne, Lou D., Info.Spec.
PHILLIPS PETROLEUM COMPANY - RESEARCH &
DEVELOPMENT DEPARTMENT - TECHNICAL
INFORMATION BRANCH □ Bartlesville, OK
Payne, Robert, Dir. W.L.N.
WASHINGTON STATE LIBRARY □ Olympia, WA

Payne, Willene L., Libn.
BAPTIST MEMORIAL HOSPITAL - MEDICAL
LIBRARY □ Gadsden, AL
Payson, Evelyn, Asst.Libn.
NASHOTAH HOUSE - LIBRARY □ Nashotah, WI
Payson, Patricia, Libn.
SOUTHWEST WISCONSIN VOCATIONAL-
TECHNICAL INSTITUTE - LEARNING
RESOURCES CENTER □ Fennimore, WI
Paysse, James L., Ed.Asst.
TULANE UNIVERSITY OF LOUISIANA - DELTA
REGIONAL PRIMATE RESEARCH CENTER -
SCIENCE INFORMATION SERVICE □ Covington,
LA
Pazen, Dick, Res.Anl.
WISCONSIN STATE LEGISLATIVE REFERENCE
BUREAU □ Madison, WI
Pazienza, Lois, Libn.
METASCIENCE FOUNDATION - LIBRARY □
Kingston, RI
Peabody, Elaine, Asst.Ref.Libn.
SAN DIEGO COUNTY LAW LIBRARY □ San Diego,
CA
Peacock, Dr. Edward, Res.Dir.
AMERICAN INSTITUTE OF FAMILY RELATIONS
- ROSWELL H. JOHNSON RESEARCH LIBRARY □
Los Angeles, CA
Peacock, Joyce F., Libn.
AAI CORPORATION - TECHNICAL LIBRARY □
Baltimore, MD
Pearce, Dwain H., V.P., Gen.Mgr.
BELL & HOWELL COMPANY - MICRO PHOTO
DIVISION - MICROFORMS ARCHIVE □ Wooster,
OH
Pearce, Edward D., Libn.
MUSEUM OF SCIENCE - LIBRARY □ Boston, MA
Pearce, Karen E., Res.Libn.
ENVIRONMENTAL RESEARCH INSTITUTE OF
MICHIGAN - ERIM INFORMATION CENTER □
Ann Arbor, MI
Pearce, Kathy, Ser.Libn.
BRIGHAM YOUNG UNIVERSITY - J. REUBEN
CLARK LAW SCHOOL LIBRARY □ Provo, UT
Pearce, M.T., Mgr., Legal/Tax
MAY DEPARTMENT STORES COMPANY -
INFORMATION CENTER □ St. Louis, MO
Pearce, Mona B., Libn.
NEWFOUNDLAND - DEPARTMENT OF JUSTICE -
LAW LIBRARY □ St. John's, NF
Pearce, Stanley, Dir., Info.Serv.
O'MELVENY AND MYERS - INFORMATION
SERVICES □ Los Angeles, CA
Pearlman, Meyer, Lib.Comm.
RAILROAD ENTHUSIASTS NEW YORK
DIVISION, INC. - WILLIAMSON LIBRARY □ New
York, NY
Pearlman, Nancy, Exec.Dir.
ECOLOGY CENTER OF SOUTHERN CALIFORNIA
□ Los Angeles, CA
Pearlman, Sandy, Mng.Ed.
CRC PRESS, INC. - LIBRARY □ Boca Raton, FL
Pearlstein, Ms. Toby, Libn.
(Boston) CENTRAL TRANSPORTATION
PLANNING STAFF - LIBRARY SERVICES □
Boston, MA
Pearman, Sara J., Slide Lib.
CLEVELAND MUSEUM OF ART - LIBRARY □
Cleveland, OH
Pearson, Barbara, Water Res.Info.Spec.
WASHINGTON STATE DEPARTMENT OF
ECOLOGY - TECHNICAL LIBRARY □ Olympia, WA
Pearson, Ellen M., Asst.Libn.
UNIVERSITY OF GUELPH - LIBRARY □ Guelph,
ON
Pearson, Florence, Tech.Info.Spec.
ENVIRONMENTAL PROTECTION AGENCY -
REGION IX LIBRARY/INFORMATION CENTER □
San Francisco, CA
Pearson, Frances, Libn.
CALIFORNIA STATE DEPARTMENT OF WATER
RESOURCES - LAW LIBRARY □ Sacramento, CA

Pearson, Fred W., Ref.Libn. & Asst.Prof.
LANCASTER BIBLE COLLEGE - STOLL
MEMORIAL LIBRARY □ Lancaster, PA
Pearson, Frederic C., Circ.Libn.
COOK COUNTY LAW LIBRARY □ Chicago, IL
Pearson, Janice, Archv.
AMERICAN BIBLE SOCIETY - LIBRARY □ New
York, NY
Pearson, Louise, Cat.
DICKINSON STATE COLLEGE - STOXEN
LIBRARY □ Dickinson, ND
Pearson, Marjorie, Res.Chm.
GENEALOGICAL ASSOCIATION OF
SOUTHWESTERN MICHIGAN - MAUD PRESTON
PALENSKE MEMORIAL LIBRARY □ St. Joseph, MI
Pearson, Michael, Hd.
METROPOLITAN TORONTO LIBRARY - HISTORY
DEPARTMENT □ Toronto, ON
Pearson, Sherry, Tech.Info.Spec.
U.S. NATL. MARINE FISHERIES SERVICE -
NATIONAL MARINE MAMMAL LABORATORY -
LIBRARY □ Seattle, WA
Pearson, Virginia, Ref.Libn.
WESTERN KENTUCKY UNIVERSITY -
KENTUCKY LIBRARY AND MUSEUM/
UNIVERSITY ARCHIVES □ Bowling Green, KY
Pease, William, Cat.Dept.
SAN DIEGO STATE UNIVERSITY - MALCOLM A.
LOVE LIBRARY □ San Diego, CA
Peat, W. Leslie, Law Libn.
VERMONT LAW SCHOOL - LIBRARY □ South
Royalton, VT
Peatross, Elizabeth, Requisitions Libn.
LOUISIANA STATE UNIVERSITY MEDICAL
CENTER - SCHOOL OF MEDICINE IN
SHREVEPORT - LIBRARY □ Shreveport, LA
Peay, Wayne, Media/Tech. Serv.
UNIVERSITY OF UTAH - SPENCER S. ECCLES
HEALTH SCIENCES LIBRARY □ Salt Lake City, UT
Pecha, Janet, Supv., Archv.
COCA-COLA COMPANY - ARCHIVES &
BUSINESS INFORMATION SERVICES □ Atlanta,
GA
Peck, Dr.Abraham J., Assoc.Dir.
HEBREW UNION COLLEGE - JEWISH INSTITUTE
OF RELIGION - AMERICAN JEWISH ARCHIVES
□ Cincinnati, OH
Peck, Betty A., Adm.Asst.
UNIVERSITY OF MICHIGAN - ALFRED TAUBMAN
MEDICAL LIBRARY □ Ann Arbor, MI
Peck, David A., Personnel
CONNECTICUT STATE LIBRARY □ Hartford, CT
Peck, Elsie, Sr. Dance Libn.
NEW YORK PUBLIC LIBRARY - GENERAL
LIBRARY OF THE PERFORMING ARTS □ New
York, NY
Peck, Jane, Hd., Hum. & Fine Arts
WORCESTER FREE PUBLIC LIBRARY -
REFERENCE AND RESEARCH □ Worcester, MA
Peck, John G., Jr., Dir., Lib.Serv.
WESTMINSTER CHOIR COLLEGE - TALBOTT
LIBRARY □ Princeton, NJ
Peck, Joyce E., Dept.Hd.
FLINT PUBLIC LIBRARY - AUTOMOTIVE
HISTORY COLLECTION □ Flint, MI
Peck, Joyce E., Dept.Hd.
FLINT PUBLIC LIBRARY - BUSINESS AND
INDUSTRY DEPARTMENT □ Flint, MI
Peck, Margaret, Asst.
TUCSON MUSEUM OF ART - LIBRARY □ Tucson,
AZ
Peck, Mary J., AHEC Libn./Coord.
ROWAN MEMORIAL HOSPITAL - MC KENZIE
MEMORIAL LIBRARY □ Salisbury, NC
Peck, Theodore, Libn.
UNIVERSITY OF MINNESOTA, ST. PAUL -
BIOCHEMISTRY LIBRARY □ St. Paul, MN
Peck, Thomas D., Educ.Cons.
CALIFORNIA STATE DEPARTMENT OF ALCOHOL
AND DRUG PROGRAMS - INFORMATION
CLEARINGHOUSE □ Sacramento, CA

PERSONNEL

Peckham, Gloria M., Chf.Libn.
CANADA - ENERGY, MINES & RESOURCES
CANADA - CANMET - LIBRARY □ Ottawa, ON
Peckham, Harry, Asst.
TIME, INC. - SPORTS LIBRARY □ New York, NY
Peddle, Heddy M., Libn.
NEWFOUNDLAND AND LABRADOR
DEVELOPMENT CORPORATION LTD. - LIBRARY
□ St. John's, NF
Pedersen, Lila, Asst.Dir.
UNIVERSITY OF NORTH DAKOTA - SCHOOL OF
MEDICINE - HARLEY E. FRENCH MEDICAL
LIBRARY □ Grand Forks, ND
Pedersen/Vogel, Karen, Hd., Ref.Libn.
NORTH DAKOTA STATE UNIVERSITY - LIBRARY
□ Fargo, ND
Pederson, Virgil, Asst.Libn.
TECHNOMIC CONSULTANTS - INFORMATION
CENTER □ Chicago, IL
Pederson, Wayne A., Dir. of Lib.Serv.
IOWA LUTHERAN HOSPITAL - DEPARTMENT OF
LIBRARY SERVICES □ Des Moines, IA
Peebles, Harvey, Ref.Libn.
HENDERSON STATE UNIVERSITY - HUIE
LIBRARY □ Arkadelphia, AR
Peebles, Josephine, Proofreader
ASSOCIATION FOR RESEARCH AND
ENLIGHTENMENT - ARE BRAILLE LIBRARY □
Virginia Beach, VA
Peel, Richard C., Adm.Libn.
ARIZONA STATE REGIONAL LIBRARY FOR THE
BLIND AND PHYSICALLY HANDICAPPED □
Phoenix, AZ
Peele, Bonnie, Spec. Projects Libn.
NORTH CAROLINA STATE DEPARTMENT OF
CULTURAL RESOURCES - LIBRARY FOR THE
BLIND AND PHYSICALLY HANDICAPPED □
Raleigh, NC
Peelman, Marie A., Hd.Libn.
SAN DIEGO GAS AND ELECTRIC COMPANY -
LIBRARY □ San Diego, CA
Peery, Karen, Libn.
STEVENS CLINIC HOSPITAL - LIBRARY □ Welch,
WV
Peffer, Margery, Asst.Hd.
CARNEGIE LIBRARY OF PITTSBURGH -
SCIENCE AND TECHNOLOGY DEPARTMENT □
Pittsburgh, PA
Pefley, Lynn
OXY METAL INDUSTRIES CORPORATION -
ELECTROCHEMICAL LIBRARY† □ Warren, MI
Pegram, J. Wally, Libn.
UNIVERSITY OF CALIFORNIA, LOS ANGELES -
PHYSICS LIBRARY □ Los Angeles, CA
Peirce, Jane, Ref. & ILL
UNIVERSITY OF WISCONSIN, RIVER FALLS -
CHALMER DAVEE LIBRARY □ River Falls, WI
Peischl, Dr. Thomas M., Dir. of Libs.
SUNY - COLLEGE AT POTSDAM - FREDERICK W.
CRUMB MEMORIAL LIBRARY □ Potsdam, NY
Peiser, Judy, Dir.
CENTER FOR SOUTHERN FOLKLORE - ARCHIVES
□ Memphis, TN
Peitso, Joyce, Ser.
KANSAS CITY ART INSTITUTE - LIBRARY □
Kansas City, MO
Pekarski, Mary L., Libn.
BOSTON COLLEGE - SCHOOL OF NURSING
LIBRARY □ Chestnut Hill, MA
Pekkala, Esther, Archv.Sec.
FINNISH-AMERICAN HISTORICAL ARCHIVES □
Hancock, MI
Peladeau, Marius B., Dir.
FARNSWORTH (William A.) - LIBRARY AND ART
MUSEUM □ Rockland, ME
Pelchat, Eugene, Hd.Cat.Serv.
DALHOUSIE UNIVERSITY - W.K. KELLOGG
HEALTH SCIENCES LIBRARY □ Halifax, NS
Pella, Diane, Ref.Libn.
PRICE WATERHOUSE - NATIONAL
INFORMATION CENTER □ New York, NY

Pellan, Laurence, Libn.
MERCER (William M.) LTD. - LIBRARY/
INFORMATION CENTRE □ Toronto, ON
Pelletier, Charles, Chf., Acq.
UNIVERSITE LAVAL - BIBLIOTHEQUE† □ Ste.
Foy, PQ
Pelletier, Claire, Acq.Libn.
ECOLE POLYTECHNIQUE - BIBLIOTHEQUE □
Montreal, PQ
Pelletier, Daniel, Asst.Libn.
DEWEY, BALLANTINE, BUSHBY, PALMER &
WOOD - LIBRARY □ New York, NY
Pelletier, Jacqueline, Libn.
UNIVERSITE DE MONTREAL - AMENAGEMENT-
BIBLIOTHEQUE □ Montreal, PQ
Pelletier, Paul, Hd., Bus., Sci. & Tech.
WORCESTER FREE PUBLIC LIBRARY -
REFERENCE AND RESEARCH □ Worcester, MA
Pellini, Nancy M., Mgr.
STONE AND WEBSTER ENGINEERING
CORPORATION - TECHNICAL INFORMATION
CENTER □ Boston, MA
Pellitier, Suzanne I., Acq.Libn.
UNIVERSITY OF MAINE SCHOOL OF LAW -
DONALD L. GARBRECHT LAW LIBRARY □
Portland, ME
Pelly, John, Pict.Libn.
ST. LOUIS POST-DISPATCH - REFERENCE
DEPARTMENT □ St. Louis, MO
Pelote, Vincent, Asst.Cur.
RUTGERS UNIVERSITY, THE STATE
UNIVERSITY OF NEW JERSEY - INSTITUTE OF
JAZZ STUDIES □ Newark, NJ
Peltier, Jane, Acq.Libn.
EAGLEVILLE HOSPITAL AND REHABILITATION
CENTER - HENRY S. LOUCHHEIM MEDICAL
LIBRARY □ Eagleville, PA
Peluso, Kathleen, Asst.Libn.
STOCKTON NEWSPAPERS INC. - STOCKTON
RECORD LIBRARY □ Stockton, CA
Peluso, Sal, Sr.Lit.Sci.
WARNER-LAMBERT COMPANY - CORPORATE
LIBRARY† □ Morris Plains, NJ
Pelz, Bruce, Act.Hd., ILL
UNIVERSITY OF CALIFORNIA, LOS ANGELES -
PHYSICAL SCIENCES & TECHNOLOGY
LIBRARIES □ Los Angeles, CA
Pelz, Bruce E., Acq.Libn.
UNIVERSITY OF CALIFORNIA, LOS ANGELES -
ENGINEERING & MATHEMATICAL SCIENCES
LIBRARY □ Los Angeles, CA
Pelz, Craig L., Libn.
U.S. ARMY - CORPS OF ENGINEERS - FORT
WORTH DISTRICT - TECHNICAL LIBRARY □
Fort Worth, TX
Pence, Judy, Asst.Hd.
UNIVERSITY OF NEW MEXICO - SPECIAL
COLLECTIONS DEPARTMENT □ Albuquerque, NM
Pendell, Robert L., Mgr.Info.Ctrl.
RYDER SYSTEM, INC. - INFORMATION
CENTRAL □ Miami, FL
Pendleton, Eldridge H., Dir.
OLD GAOL MUSEUM - LIBRARY □ York, ME
Pendleton, Thomas H., Mgr.
WEST VIRGINIA STATE GOVERNOR'S OFFICE
OF ECON. & COMMUNITY DEV. - GOECD
COMMUNITY DEVELOPMENT DIV. - LIBRARY □
Charleston, WV
Peng, Lily, Info./Circ.Libn.
BAYSTATE MEDICAL CENTER - LIBRARY □
Springfield, MA
Penix, Cindy, Libn.
ROCKY MOUNT HISTORICAL ASSOCIATION -
LIBRARY □ Piney Flats, TN
Penix, Holly A., Lib.Asst.
UNIVERSITY OF ARIZONA - DIVISION OF
ECONOMIC AND BUSINESS RESEARCH -
LIBRARY □ Tucson, AZ
Penman, Elizabeth H., Libn.
MERCK & COMPANY, INC. - LAW LIBRARY □
Rahway, NJ

Penn, Miriam E., Cat.Libn.
VIRGINIA UNION UNIVERSITY - WILLIAM J.
CLARK LIBRARY □ Richmond, VA
Penne, Carol, Hd., Pub.Serv.
AMERICAN BANKERS ASSOCIATION - LIBRARY
□ Washington, DC
Pennell, Peggy, Libn.
CHEMICAL BANK - RESEARCH LIBRARY □ New
York, NY
Penney, Pearce J., Chf.Prov.Libn.
NEWFOUNDLAND - PUBLIC LIBRARY SERVICES
□ St. John's, NF
Pennington, David N., Chf., Lib.Serv.
U.S. VETERANS ADMINISTRATION (TN-
Murfreesboro) - MEDICAL CENTER LIBRARY □
Murfreesboro, TN
Pennington, David N., Asst.Libn.
U.S. VETERANS ADMINISTRATION (TN-
Nashville) - MEDICAL CENTER LIBRARY
SERVICE □ Nashville, TN
Pennock, Mary F., Lib.Assoc.
MANUFACTURERS ASSOCIATION OF CENTRAL
NEW YORK - LIBRARY □ Syracuse, NY
Penny, Jennifer, Libn.
UNIVERSITY OF ALBERTA - COMPUTING
SCIENCE READING ROOM □ Edmonton, AB
Penny, Laura, Asst.Libn.
PIKES PEAK LIBRARY DISTRICT - LOCAL
HISTORY COLLECTION □ Colorado Springs, CO
Penprase, Catherine, Adult Serv.Supv.
CITY OF COMMERCE PUBLIC LIBRARY □
Commerce, CA
Penrose, Anna Mae, Libn.
ST. JOSEPH'S UNIVERSITY - ACADEMY OF
FOOD MARKETING - CAMPBELL LIBRARY □
Philadelphia, PA
Penson, Andrew, Asst.Ref.Libn.
GEORGIA SOUTHERN COLLEGE - ARCHIVES/
SPECIAL COLLECTIONS □ Statesboro, GA
Pensyl, Janette L., Libn.
MONROE COUNTY LAW LIBRARY □ Stroudsburg,
PA
Pensyl, Ornella L., Chf.
U.S. ARMY INTELLIGENCE SCHOOL, DEVENS -
LIBRARY/LEARNING CENTER □ Ft. Devens, MA
Pentecost, Peggy, Info.Coord.
AUTOMOTIVE INFORMATION COUNCIL -
LIBRARY □ Southfield, MI
Pepin, Patricia, Chf., Lib.Br.
U.S. ARMY MEDICAL RESEARCH INSTITUTE OF
CHEMICAL DEFENSE - WOOD TECHNICAL
LIBRARY □ Aberdeen Proving Ground, MD
Pepin, Robert, Hd.
COLUMBIA UNIVERSITY - BUTLER LIBRARY
CIRCULATION DEPARTMENT □ New York, NY
Pepmueller, Calla Ann, Mgr.
U.S. DEPT OF ENERGY - SANDIA NATL.
LABORATORIES - TECHNICAL LIBRARY □
Albuquerque, NM
Peppel, Martha, Hd.Libn.
EBASCO SERVICES, INC. - CORPORATE
ADMINISTRATION LIBRARY □ New York, NY
Pepper, Alice, Asst.Libn.
MOTOR VEHICLE MANUFACTURERS
ASSOCIATION (MVMA) - TECHNICAL LIBRARY □
Detroit, MI
Pepper, Mrs. C., Libn.
CANADIAN RED CROSS SOCIETY - LIBRARY □
Toronto, ON
Pepper, David A., Chf.Libn.
COMINCO LTD. - INFORMATION SERVICES □
Vancouver, BC
Pepper, Sheila, Bus.Libn.
MC MASTER UNIVERSITY - BUSINESS LIBRARY
□ Hamilton, ON
Peralta, Lydia, Libn.
MAGNAVOX COMPANY - ENGINEERING
LIBRARY† □ Fort Wayne, IN
Perazza, Louis L., Libn.
PHILADELPHIA ORCHESTRA ASSOCIATION -
LIBRARY □ Philadelphia, PA

Perch, Dr. Robert, Lib.Chm.
MONTGOMERY HOSPITAL - MEDICAL LIBRARY
□ Norristown, PA
Percival, Marjorie, Hd.Libn.
INDIANAPOLIS PUBLIC SCHOOLS - TEACHERS
LIBRARY □ Indianapolis, IN
Percival, Mary, Libn.
MC CARTHY AND MC CARTHY - LIBRARY □
Toronto, ON
Percy, Nancy W., Asst. State Libn.
CALIFORNIA STATE LIBRARY □ Sacramento, CA
Percy, Theresa R., Asst.Libn.
OLD STURBRIDGE VILLAGE - RESEARCH
LIBRARY □ Sturbridge, MA
Pereira, Priscilla M., Educ.Ref.Libn.
CUNY - GRADUATE SCHOOL AND UNIVERSITY
CENTER - LIBRARY □ New York, NY
Pereny, Evelyn, Libn.
AULLWOOD AUDUBON CENTER AND FARM -
LIBRARY □ Dayton, OH
Peresich, Sr. Mary Giles, R.S.M., Assoc.Libn.
ST. JOHN'S MERCY MEDICAL CENTER - JOHN
YOUNG BROWN MEMORIAL LIBRARY □ St. Louis,
MO
Perez, Carlos, Ref.Libn.
UNIVERSITY OF PUERTO RICO - HUMACAO
UNIVERSITY COLLEGE - LIBRARY □ Humacao,
PR
Perez, Denise, Libn.
UNIVERSITY OF PUERTO RICO - PUERTO
RICAN COLLECTION □ Rio Piedras, PR
Perez, Ernest, Chf.Libn.
CHICAGO SUN-TIMES - EDITORIAL LIBRARY □
Chicago, IL
Perez, Maria Luisa, Libn.
METROPOLITAN DADE COUNTY PLANNING
DEPARTMENT - LIBRARY/INFORMATION
CENTER □ Miami, FL
Perez, Marjory Allen, County Hist.
WAYNE COUNTY HISTORICAL SOCIETY
MUSEUM - LIBRARY □ Lyons, NY
Perez, Marta E., Hd., Doc.Dept.
UNIVERSITY OF PUERTO RICO - LAW SCHOOL
LIBRARY □ Rio Piedras, PR
Perez, Nelida, Libn.
CUNY - CENTRO DE ESTUDIOS
PUERTORRIQUENOS □ New York, NY
Perham, Constance B., Owner-Cur.
NEW ALMADEN MERCURY MINING MUSEUM -
LIBRARY □ New Almaden, CA
Peritore, Laura, Ser./Ref.Libn.
UNIVERSITY OF CALIFORNIA, SAN FRANCISCO
- HASTINGS COLLEGE OF THE LAW - LEGAL
INFORMATION CENTER □ San Francisco, CA
Perkins, Angela
NORFOLK STATE COLLEGE - W.K. KELLOGG
SOCIAL SCIENCE RESEARCH CENTER -
LIBRARY □ Norfolk, VA
Perkins, Don, Libn.
SASKATOON STAR-PHOENIX - LIBRARY □
Saskatoon, SK
Perkins, Rev. Louis L., Hist.
PROTESTANT EPISCOPAL CHURCH -
EPISCOPAL DIOCESE OF EASTERN OREGON -
ARCHIVES □ Cove, OR
Perkins, Shirley, Hd.
UNIVERSITY OF SASKATCHEWAN - SPECIAL
COLLECTIONS - SHORTT LIBRARY OF
CANADIANA □ Saskatoon, SK
Perkins, Steve, Ref.
UNIVERSITY OF CINCINNATI - ROBERT S.
MARX LAW LIBRARY □ Cincinnati, OH
Perkins, Timothy, Media Ctr.Dir.
MINNEAPOLIS COLLEGE OF ART AND DESIGN -
LIBRARY AND MEDIA CENTER □ Minneapolis,
MN
Perkons, Caroline, Info.Serv.Spec.
BEECHAM PRODUCTS - WESTERN HEMISPHERE
RESEARCH - LIBRARY □ Parsippany, NJ
Perl, Ruth, Dir. of Res.
ACKERMAN INSTITUTE FOR FAMILY THERAPY,
INC. - LIBRARY □ New York, NY

Perlin, Ruth R., Cur.-in-Charge
NATIONAL GALLERY OF ART - DEPARTMENT OF
EXTENSION PROGRAMS □ Washington, DC
Perlman, Michael, Ref.Libn.
CHICAGO SUN-TIMES - EDITORIAL LIBRARY □
Chicago, IL
Perlman, Stephen, Libn.
U.S.D.A. - AGRICULTURAL RESEARCH SERVICE
- PLUM ISLAND ANIMAL DISEASE CENTER
LIBRARY □ Greenport, NY
Perlman, V., Supv.
STANDARD OIL COMPANY OF INDIANA -
LIBRARY/INFORMATION CENTER □ Chicago, IL
Perlroth, Irving, Data Preparation
U.S. NATL. OCEANIC & ATMOSPHERIC
ADMINISTRATION - ENVIRONMENTAL DATA &
INFO. SERV. - NATL. OCEANOGRAPHIC DATA
CTR. □ Washington, DC
Perno, Helen, Libn.
U.S. NATL. INSTITUTES OF HEALTH - LIBRARY
□ Bethesda, MD
Pernotto, Dennis A., Dir., Lrng.Rsrcs.
WRIGHT STATE UNIVERSITY - HEALTH
SCIENCES LIBRARY □ Dayton, OH
Perona, Gerald, Kenosha Campus Libn.
GATEWAY VOCATIONAL TECHNICAL & ADULT
EDUCATION DISTRICT - LEARNING
RESOURCES CENTER □ Kenosha, WI
Perot, Monica, Hd., Circ.
YORK UNIVERSITY - LAW LIBRARY □
Downsview, ON
Perrault, Arthur, Libn.
BARREAU DE MONTREAL - BIBLIOTHEQUE □
Montreal, PQ
Perreault, Mrs. C., ILL
SHAWINIGAN CONSULTANTS INC. - LIBRARY □
Montreal, PQ
Perreault, Robert, ILL
U.S. DEPT. OF TRANSPORTATION -
TRANSPORTATION SYSTEMS CENTER -
TECHNICAL REFERENCE CENTER □ Cambridge,
MA
Perreault, Robert B., Libn.
ASSOCIATION CANADO-AMERICAINE -
INSTITUT CANADO-AMERICAIN □ Manchester,
NH
Perrier, Monique, Hd., Ref.Serv.
CANADA - DEPARTMENT OF
COMMUNICATIONS - LIBRARY & INFORMATION
RETRIEVAL SERVICES □ Ottawa, ON
Perrin, Mrs. Lloyd W., Lib.Asst.
HISTORIC DEERFIELD, INC. - HENRY N. FLYNT
LIBRARY - POCUMTUCK VALLEY MEMORIAL
ASSOCIATION □ Deerfield, MA
Perrin, S.R., Spec. Projects Off.
CANADA - TAX REVIEW BOARD - TAX LIBRARY
□ Ottawa, ON
Perrine, Dr. Richard L., Chm.
UNIVERSITY OF CALIFORNIA, LOS ANGELES -
ENVIRONMENTAL SCIENCE AND ENGINEERING
- LIBRARY □ Los Angeles, CA
Perrine, Sue, Libn.
SHEA & GARDNER - LIBRARY □ Washington, DC
Perron, Mr. H., Ref.Libn.
CONCORDIA UNIVERSITY - LOYOLA CAMPUS -
GEORGES P. VANIER LIBRARY □ Montreal, PQ
Perron, Sylvie, Analyste
HYDRO-QUEBEC - DIRECTION RECHERCHE
ECONOMIQUE - CENTRE DE DOCUMENTATION
□ Montreal, PQ
Perrott, H.M., Libn.
DU PONT CANADA, INC. - MAITLAND WORKS
LIBRARY □ Maitland, ON
Perry, Alan F., Archv.
U.S. NATL. ARCHIVES & RECORDS SERVICE -
FEDERAL ARCHIVES AND RECORDS CENTER,
REGION 6 □ Kansas City, MO
Perry, Mrs. Billie Ann, Libn.
AEROSPACE INDUSTRIES ASSOCIATION OF
AMERICA - LIBRARY □ Washington, DC
Perry, Ceil, ILL Libn.
MOUNT ST. ALPHONSUS THEOLOGICAL
SEMINARY - LIBRARY □ Esopus, NY

Perry, Debra, Libn.
ATLANTA PUBLIC LIBRARY - SPECIAL
COLLECTIONS DEPARTMENT □ Atlanta, GA
Perry, Doris, Registrar
ALLEN COUNTY-FORT WAYNE HISTORICAL
SOCIETY - LIBRARY AND MANUSCRIPT
COLLECTIONS □ Fort Wayne, IN
Perry, Elizabeth, Act.Libn.
UNIVERSITY OF TORONTO - CENTRE FOR
INDUSTRIAL RELATIONS - INFORMATION
SERVICE □ Toronto, ON
Perry, Frances, Law Libn.
TARRANT COUNTY LAW LIBRARY □ Fort Worth,
TX
Perry, Gordon C., Exec.Dir.
NEW YORK STATE CONFERENCE OF MAYORS
AND MUNICIPAL OFFICIALS - LIBRARY □
Albany, NY
Perry, Guest, Libn.
HOUGHTON MIFFLIN COMPANY - LIBRARY □
Boston, MA
Perry, Helen, Assoc.Dir./Tape Coord.
CANADIAN NATIONAL INSTITUTE FOR THE
BLIND - NATIONAL LIBRARY SERVICES □
Toronto, ON
Perry, Irene, Asst.Libn., Engr./ILL
COOPER UNION FOR THE ADVANCEMENT OF
SCIENCE AND ART - LIBRARY □ New York, NY
Perry, Lee, Historical Coll.
UNIVERSITY OF BRITISH COLUMBIA -
WOODWARD BIOMEDICAL LIBRARY □
Vancouver, BC
Perry, Nena K., Ref.Libn.
EMORY UNIVERSITY - SCHOOL OF MEDICINE -
A.W. CALHOUN MEDICAL LIBRARY □ Atlanta, GA
Perry, Robin L., Dir. of Commun.
AMERICAN SYMPHONY ORCHESTRA LEAGUE -
LIBRARY □ Vienna, VA
Perry, Tessa, Order Libn.
GEORGETOWN UNIVERSITY - LAW CENTER
LIBRARY □ Washington, DC
Perry, W.M., Supv.
BETHLEHEM STEEL CORPORATION -
TECHNICAL INFORMATION □ Bethlehem, PA
Persempere, Dominic A., State Serv.Hd.
CONNECTICUT STATE LIBRARY □ Hartford, CT
Pershing, Laura M., Law Libn.
IDAHO STATE LAW LIBRARY □ Boise, ID
Persiani, Damon, Online Serv.
VIRGINIA COMMONWEALTH UNIVERSITY -
MEDICAL COLLEGE OF VIRGINIA - TOMPKINS-
MC CAW LIBRARY □ Richmond, VA
Perslin, Mrs. Clemence, Assoc.Libn.
HOWARD UNIVERSITY - ENGINEERING
LIBRARY □ Washington, DC
Person, Roland, Asst.Libn.
SOUTHERN ILLINOIS UNIVERSITY,
CARBONDALE - UNDERGRADUATE LIBRARY □
Carbondale, IL
Persons, Jerry, Hd.Libn.
STANFORD UNIVERSITY - MUSIC LIBRARY □
Stanford, CA
Persson, Dorothy M., Libn.
UNIVERSITY OF IOWA - PSYCHOLOGY LIBRARY
□ Iowa City, IA
Persson, Karin, Adm.Asst.
AMERICAN SWEDISH HISTORICAL MUSEUM -
NORD LIBRARY □ Philadelphia, PA
Pertell, Grace M., Asst.Libn.
COMMONWEALTH EDISON COMPANY -
LIBRARY □ Chicago, IL
Perton, David, Pres.
LEWIS (Frederic) INC. - PHOTOGRAPHIC
LIBRARY □ New York, NY
Pertz, Pat, Tech.Proc.
OHIO NORTHERN UNIVERSITY - COLLEGE OF
LAW - JAY P. TAGGART MEMORIAL LAW
LIBRARY □ Ada, OH
Pertzog, Betsy S., Med.Libn.
U.S. VETERANS ADMINISTRATION (AL-
Tuscaloosa) - HOSPITAL MEDICAL LIBRARY □
Tuscaloosa, AL

PERSONNEL

Perushek, Diane E., Cur.
CORNELL UNIVERSITY - WASON COLLECTION □
Ithaca, NY

Perussel, Jeanette, Hd., Cat. Maintenance
TEACHERS COLLEGE - LIBRARY □ New York, NY

Perussina, Mary Ann, Ref.Libn.
UNIVERSITY OF TEXAS MEDICAL BRANCH -
MOODY MEDICAL LIBRARY □ Galveston, TX

Peschel, Susan Ewart, Cat./Ref.Libn.
AMERICAN GEOGRAPHICAL SOCIETY
COLLECTION OF THE UNIVERSITY OF
WISCONSIN, MILWAUKEE - GOLDA MEIR
LIBRARY □ Milwaukee, WI

Peshel, Barbara B., Monograph Serv.
UNIVERSITY OF OKLAHOMA - HEALTH
SCIENCES CENTER LIBRARY □ Oklahoma City,
OK

Peternell, Therese, Libn.
UNIVERSITE DE MONTREAL - BIBLIOTHEQUE
DE LA SANTE □ Montreal, PQ

Peters, Alec, Dept.Dir.
FRANKLIN RESEARCH CENTER - SCIENCE
INFORMATION SERVICES □ Philadelphia, PA

Peters, Douglas E., Hist./Libn.
RAILWAYS TO YESTERDAY, INC. - LEHIGH
VALLEY TRANSPORTATION RESEARCH CENTER
□ Allentown, PA

Peters, E. Jean, Hd.Libn.
NEW MEXICO STATE LEGISLATIVE COUNCIL
SERVICE - LIBRARY □ Santa Fe, NM

Peters, Frances E., Libn.
PENNSYLVANIA COLLEGE OF PODIATRIC
MEDICINE - CHARLES E. KRAUSZ LIBRARY □
Philadelphia, PA

Peters, Francis Warren, Jr., Libn.
DETROIT INSTITUTE OF ARTS - RESEARCH
LIBRARY □ Detroit, MI

Peters, Gayle P., Chf., Archv.Br.
U.S. NATL. ARCHIVES & RECORDS SERVICE -
FEDERAL ARCHIVES AND RECORDS CENTER,
REGION 4 □ East Point, GA

Peters, Jean, Libn.
BOWKER (R.R.) COMPANY - FREDERIC G.
MELCHER LIBRARY □ New York, NY

Peters, Jeff, Res.Libn.
CARGILL, INC. - INFORMATION CENTER □
Minneapolis, MN

Peters, John A., Govt.Pub.Libn.
STATE HISTORICAL SOCIETY OF WISCONSIN -
LIBRARY □ Madison, WI

Peters, K. Scott, Acq.Libn.
ROCKWELL INTERNATIONAL - ROCKETDYNE
DIVISION - TECHNICAL INFORMATION
CENTER □ Canoga Park, CA

Peters, Margery, Libn.
GENERAL SOCIETY OF MECHANICS AND
TRADESMEN OF THE CITY OF NEW YORK -
LIBRARY □ New York, NY

Peters, Marion C., Libn.
UNIVERSITY OF CALIFORNIA, LOS ANGELES -
CHEMISTRY LIBRARY □ Los Angeles, CA

Peters, Muriel N., Libn.
DEDHAM HISTORICAL SOCIETY - LIBRARY □
Dedham, MA

Peters, R.F., Hd., LRC
SOUTHERN ALBERTA INSTITUTE OF
TECHNOLOGY - LEARNING RESOURCES CENTRE
□ Calgary, AB

Peters, Robert W., Interp.
U.S. NATL. PARK SERVICE - CARLSBAD
CAVERNS NATL. PARK - LIBRARY □ Carlsbad,
NM

Peters, Scott M., Cur. of Coll.
SLOAN (Alfred P., Jr.) MUSEUM - LIBRARY □
Flint, MI

Peters, William T., Lit.Coord.
SOCIETY OF FRIENDS - OHIO YEARLY MEETING
- WESTGATE FRIENDS LIBRARY □ Columbus, OH

Petersen, Karla D., Hd.Cat.Dept.
CENTER FOR RESEARCH LIBRARIES □ Chicago,
IL

Petersen, Keith, Dir.
LATAH COUNTY HISTORICAL SOCIETY -
LIBRARY □ Moscow, ID

Petersen, Mark A., Med.Libn.
U.S. VETERANS ADMINISTRATION (MO-Kansas
City) - MEDICAL CENTER LIBRARY □ Kansas
City, MO

Petersen, Marsha C., Dir.
HONOLULU (City And County) - MUNICIPAL
REFERENCE AND RECORDS CENTER □ Honolulu,
HI

Petersen, Philip V., Dir. of Info.
SOCIETY OF AMERICAN FORESTERS - LIBRARY
□ Bethesda, MD

Petersen, Phyllis, Hd. Of Tech.Serv.
SUNY - AGRICULTURAL AND TECHNICAL
COLLEGE AT MORRISVILLE - LIBRARY □
Morrisville, NY

Petersen, Robert, Rd.Serv.
UNIVERSITY OF CHICAGO - FAR EASTERN
LIBRARY □ Chicago, IL

Peterson, Agnes, Cur., W. Europe Coll.
STANFORD UNIVERSITY - HOOVER
INSTITUTION ON WAR, REVOLUTION AND
PEACE - LIBRARY □ Stanford, CA

Peterson, Amy K., Hd., Doc.Res.Coll.
UNIVERSITY OF WISCONSIN, WHITEWATER -
LIBRARY & LEARNING RESOURCES □
Whitewater, WI

Peterson, Arlene C., Mgr., Res.Info.Sys.
MERCK & COMPANY, INC. - MERCK SHARP &
DOHME RESEARCH LABORATORIES -
RESEARCH INFORMATION SYSTEMS □ Rahway,
NJ

Peterson, Barbara E., Libn.
AMERICAN OSTEOPATHIC ASSOCIATION -
ANDREW TAYLOR STILL MEMORIAL LIBRARY □
Chicago, IL

Peterson, Betty L., Exec.Dir.
INSTITUTE OF ENVIRONMENTAL SCIENCES -
LIBRARY □ Mt. Prospect, IL

Peterson, David F., Exec.Dir.
U.S. GENERAL SERVICES ADMINISTRATION -
CONSUMER INFORMATION CENTER □
Washington, DC

Peterson, Dennis, Pub.Serv.Libn.
PALMER COLLEGE OF CHIROPRACTIC -
LIBRARY □ Davenport, IA

Peterson, Elizabeth, Hd.Tech.Proc.
MINNESOTA STATE LAW LIBRARY □ St. Paul,
MN

Peterson, Erik, Coord.
OREGON INSTITUTE OF TECHNOLOGY -
LEARNING RESOURCES CENTER □ Klamath Falls,
OR

Peterson, Faye V., Supv.
SPERRY CORPORATION - SPERRY UNIVAC
DEFENSE SYSTEMS DIVISION - INFORMATION
SERVICE CENTER □ St. Paul, MN

Peterson, Gale E., Dir.
CINCINNATI HISTORICAL SOCIETY - LIBRARY
□ Cincinnati, OH

Peterson, Gerald L., Spec.Coll.Libn.
UNIVERSITY OF NORTHERN IOWA - LIBRARY -
SPECIAL COLLECTIONS □ Cedar Falls, IA

Peterson, Harold, Libn./Ed.-in-Chf.
MINNEAPOLIS INSTITUTE OF ARTS - LIBRARY -
EDITORIAL DEPARTMENT □ Minneapolis, MN

Peterson, Jean, Libn.
CAMBRIDGE STATE HOSPITAL - LIBRARY □
Cambridge, MN

Peterson, John, Cur. of the Archv.
LUTHERAN THEOLOGICAL SEMINARY - KRAUTH
MEMORIAL LIBRARY □ Philadelphia, PA

Peterson, Julia, Mgr.
CARGILL, INC. - INFORMATION CENTER □
Minneapolis, MN

Peterson, Julia J., Libn.
MASSACHUSETTS INSTITUTE OF TECHNOLOGY
- DEPARTMENT OF NUTRITION AND FOOD
SCIENCE - READING ROOM □ Cambridge, MA

Peterson, Karen, Cat.Libn.
WESTERN CONSERVATIVE BAPTIST SEMINARY
- CLINE-TUNNELL LIBRARY □ Portland, OR

Peterson, Linda E., Asst.Dir.
LIBERTY MUTUAL INSURANCE COMPANY -
BUSINESS REFERENCE LIBRARY □ Boston, MA

Peterson, Melva, Chf. Music Libn.
CUNY - CITY COLLEGE LIBRARY - MUSIC
LIBRARY □ New York, NY

Peterson, Peg, Corp.Libn.
MGIC INVESTMENT CORPORATION -
CORPORATE LIBRARY □ Milwaukee, WI

Peterson, Pennie D., Coord.
MISSOURI STATE LIBRARY - WOLFNER
MEMORIAL LIBRARY FOR THE BLIND &
PHYSICALLY HANDICAPPED □ St. Louis, MO

Peterson, Randall T., Dir.
MARSHALL (John) LAW SCHOOL - LIBRARY □
Chicago, IL

Peterson, Richard A., Ref.Libn.
UNIVERSITY OF VIRGINIA MEDICAL CENTER -
CLAUDE MOORE HEALTH SCIENCES LIBRARY □
Charlottesville, VA

Peterson, Ruth
UNIVERSITY OF NORTH DAKOTA -
ENGINEERING LIBRARY □ Grand Forks, ND

Peterson, Sara, Hd.Libn.
IOWA STATE UNIVERSITY - VETERINARY
MEDICAL LIBRARY □ Ames, IA

Peterson, Sharon R., Med.Libn.
JEWISH HOSPITAL AND MEDICAL CENTER OF
BROOKLYN - MEDICAL & NURSING LIBRARY □
Brooklyn, NY

Peterson, Stephen L., Libn.
YALE UNIVERSITY - DIVINITY SCHOOL
LIBRARY □ New Haven, CT

Peterson, Tim, Pict.Libn.
INDIANA HISTORICAL SOCIETY - WILLIAM
HENRY SMITH MEMORIAL LIBRARY □
Indianapolis, IN

Peterson, Vivian A., Dir., Lib.Serv.
CONCORDIA TEACHERS COLLEGE - LINK
LIBRARY □ Seward, NE

Petesch, John H., Cat.Libn.
UNIVERSITY OF TEXAS SCHOOL OF LAW -
TARLTON LAW LIBRARY □ Austin, TX

Petit, Michael J., Asst.Libn./Pub.Serv.
GEORGE MASON UNIVERSITY - SCHOOL OF
LAW - LIBRARY† □ Arlington, VA

Petit, Patrick, Assoc. Law Libn.
CATHOLIC UNIVERSITY OF AMERICA - ROBERT
J. WHITE LAW LIBRARY □ Washington, DC

Petitmermet, Jane F., Ref.Libn.
U.S. ARMY IN EUROPE (USAREUR) - LIBRARY
AND RESOURCE CENTER □ APO New York, NY

Petko, Charles M.
ENVIRONMENTAL PROTECTION AGENCY -
EASTERN ENVIRONMENTAL RADIATION LAB -
LIBRARY □ Montgomery, AL

Petrelli, Evelyn, Asst.Libn.
EDWARDS (Jacob) LIBRARY □ Southbridge, MA

Petrescu, Adrian, Dir.
ROMANIAN LIBRARY □ New York, NY

Petrescu, Danita, Libn.
ROMANIAN LIBRARY □ New York, NY

Petrie, Claire, Art & Arch.Libn.
PRATT INSTITUTE - LIBRARY □ Brooklyn, NY

Petrone, Anthony, Hd., Ref.Serv.
SEARLE (G.D.) & CO. - RESEARCH LIBRARY □
Skokie, IL

Petrov, Jane, Libn.
CENTRE DE READAPTATION LETHBRIDGE -
MEDICAL LIBRARY □ Montreal, PQ

Petrovics, Gabriella, Act.Libn.
OHIO STATE UNIVERSITY - HILANDAR ROOM □
Columbus, OH

Petrowicz, Mary Jane, Libn.
NEW ENGLAND BOARD OF HIGHER EDUCATION
- LIBRARY □ Wenham, MA

Petrowski, Carol, Ser.
LOYOLA LAW SCHOOL - LIBRARY □ Los Angeles,
CA

Petru, William C., Info. Network Coord.
HEWLETT-PACKARD COMPANY - CORPORATE
LIBRARY □ Palo Alto, CA

Petry, Dolores M., Libn.
CARNEGIE INSTITUTION OF WASHINGTON -
GEOPHYSICAL LABORATORY LIBRARY □
Washington, DC

Petry, Dr. John R., Libn.
MEMPHIS STATE UNIVERSITY LIBRARIES -
BUREAU OF EDUCATIONAL RESEARCH AND
SERVICES - LIBRARY □ Memphis, TN

Petry, Robyn, Asst.Libn.
ARMAK COMPANY - RESEARCH LIBRARY □
McCook, IL

Petschaft, Jane I., Libn.
DYNATECH CORPORATION LIBRARY □
Cambridge, MA

Pettengill, Helen M., Musm.Dir.
GRAFTON HISTORICAL MUSEUM □ Grafton, VT

Pettengill, Richard, Libn.
OAKLAND UNIVERSITY - LIBRARY □ Rochester,
MI

Petter, Christopher, Archv.
UNIVERSITY OF VICTORIA - MC PHERSON
LIBRARY - SPECIAL COLLECTIONS □ Victoria,
BC

Petteway, Alphonso B., Supv., Ref./Cat.
NATIONAL GEOGRAPHIC SOCIETY -
ILLUSTRATIONS LIBRARY □ Washington, DC

Pettis, Sue, Libn.
FIRST NATIONAL BANK OF OREGON - LIBRARY
□ Portland, OR

Pettit, Katherine D., Spec.Coll.Libn.
TRINITY UNIVERSITY - LIBRARY □ San Antonio,
TX

Pettit, Lorelei, Lib.Ck.
CANADA - ENVIRONMENTAL PROTECTION
SERVICE - LIBRARY □ West Vancouver, BC

Pettit, Martha, Libn.
DU PONT CANADA, INC. - CENTRAL LIBRARY □
Mississauga, ON

Pettway, Helen, Libn.
KRAFT, INC. - RESEARCH & DEVELOPMENT
LIBRARY □ Glenview, IL

Petty, Ruth, Libn.
NORTHWEST COLLEGE OF THE ASSEMBLIES OF
GOD - HURST LIBRARY □ Kirkland, WA

Pew, G., Hd.Cat.Libn.
UNIVERSITY OF LOWELL, SOUTH CAMPUS -
DANIEL H. O'LEARY LIBRARY □ Lowell, MA

Peyrat, Jean, Libn.
CENTER FOR CREATIVE STUDIES/COLLEGE OF
ART & DESIGN - LIBRARY □ Detroit, MI

Peyton, Daniel, Libn.
WATERFORD HOSPITAL - HEALTH SERVICES
LIBRARY □ St. John's, NF

Peyton, Gail, Inner City Stud.Libn
NORTHEASTERN ILLINOIS UNIVERSITY -
LIBRARY □ Chicago, IL

Peyton, Georgina C., Spec.Coll.
UNIVERSITY OF CALIFORNIA, SAN DIEGO -
UNIVERSITY LIBRARIES □ La Jolla, CA

Peyton, Madeleine A., Libn.
U.S. AIR FORCE BASE - MOODY BASE LIBRARY†
□ Moody AFB, GA

Peyton, Marguerite S., Asst.Libn.
MISSISSIPPI VALLEY STATE UNIVERSITY -
JAMES HERBERT WHITE LIBRARY □ Itta Bena,
MS

Pezzullo, Diane, Ref./Circ.Libn.
UNIVERSITY OF CALIFORNIA, LOS ANGELES -
EDUCATION & PSYCHOLOGY LIBRARY □ Los
Angeles, CA

Pfaff, Larry, Dp.Libn./Ref.Libn.
ART GALLERY OF ONTARIO - EDWARD P.
TAYLOR REFERENCE LIBRARY □ Toronto, ON

Pfaffenberger, Ann, Ref.Libn.
TEXAS COLLEGE OF OSTEOPATHIC MEDICINE -
MEDICAL LIBRARY □ Fort Worth, TX

Pfann, Mary L., Libn.
RCA CORPORATION - ASTRO-ELECTRONICS-
GOVERNMENT SYSTEMS DIVISION - LIBRARY □
Princeton, NJ

Pfannenstiel, Cynthia, Data Base Searches
PITTSBURG STATE UNIVERSITY - LEONARD H.
AXE LIBRARY □ Pittsburg, KS

Pfannenstiel, Tom A., Musm.Dir.
WYANDOTTE COUNTY MUSEUM - HARRY M.
TROWBRIDGE RESEARCH LIBRARY □ Bonner
Springs, KS

Pfanstiehl, Cody, Dir.Pub.Aff.
WASHINGTON METROPOLITAN AREA TRANSIT
AUTHORITY - OFFICE OF PUBLIC AFFAIRS -
LIBRARY □ Washington, DC

Pfeifer, Barbara J., Asst.Libn.
WEINBERG & GREEN, ATTORNEYS-AT-LAW -
LIBRARY □ Baltimore, MD

Pfeiffer, Anne, Sr.Res.Assoc.
MISSOURI STATE DIVISION OF COMMUNITY
AND ECONOMIC DEVELOPMENT - RESEARCH
LIBRARY □ Jefferson City, MO

Pfeiffer, Katherine, Licensing Libn.
GULF STATES UTILITIES COMPANY -
CORPORATE LIBRARY □ Beaumont, TX

Pfeiffer, Robert E., Act.Hd.
UNIVERSITY OF CALIFORNIA, BERKELEY -
MUSIC LIBRARY □ Berkeley, CA

Pfening, Fred D., Jr.
CIRCUS HISTORICAL SOCIETY - LIBRARY □
Columbus, OH

Pfingsten, C. Thomas, Dir.
PORTLAND STATE UNIVERSITY - MIDDLE EAST
STUDIES CENTER □ Portland, OR

Pfingston, Janet, Pub.Info.Asst.
HISTORIC LANDMARKS FOUNDATION OF
INDIANA, INC. - INFORMATION CENTER □
Indianapolis, IN

Pfister, Susan, Cat.Libn.
BRIDGEWATER STATE COLLEGE - CLEMENT C.
MAXWELL LIBRARY □ Bridgewater, MA

Pflueger, Kenneth, Dir., Lib.Serv.
CONCORDIA THEOLOGICAL SEMINARY -
LIBRARY □ Fort Wayne, IN

Pflug, Warner, Asst.Dir.
WAYNE STATE UNIVERSITY - ARCHIVES OF
LABOR AND URBAN AFFAIRS/UNIVERSITY
ARCHIVES □ Detroit, MI

Pfremmer, Patricia J., Law Libn.
SANTA CRUZ COUNTY LAW LIBRARY □ Santa
Cruz, CA

Phair, Mr. Arden, Adm./Cur.
ST. CATHARINES HISTORICAL MUSEUM -
LIBRARY □ St. Catharines, ON

Phelan, Dorcas, Media Tech.Asst.
FLOATING POINT SYSTEMS, INC. - TECHNICAL
LIBRARY □ Portland, OR

Phelan, Kathy, Cat.
MARYCREST COLLEGE - CONE LIBRARY† □
Davenport, IA

Phelps, Edward, Libn.
UNIVERSITY OF WESTERN ONTARIO - D.B.
WELDON LIBRARY - REGIONAL COLLECTION □
London, ON

Phelps, Evelyn B., Dept.Hd.
ONONDAGA COUNTY PUBLIC LIBRARY -
BUSINESS AND INDUSTRIAL DEPARTMENT □
Syracuse, NY

Phelps, Havilah, Libn.
KNOX COMMUNITY HOSPITAL - MEDICAL
LIBRARY □ Mount Vernon, OH

Phelps, Marion L., Cur. & Archv.
BROME COUNTY HISTORICAL SOCIETY -
ARCHIVES □ Knowlton, PQ

Phelps, Mary, Libn.
CHURCH OF JESUS CHRIST OF LATTER-DAY
SAINTS - CLEVELAND, OHIO STAKE BRANCH
GENEALOGICAL LIBRARY □ Westlake, OH

Phelps, Robert L., Ref.Libn.
U.S. NASA - LYNDON B. JOHNSON SPACE
CENTER - TECHNICAL LIBRARY □ Houston, TX

Phelps, Mrs. Willard, Dir. & Cur.
MAYVILLE HISTORICAL MUSEUM - LIBRARY □
Mayville, MI

Philbin, Margaret, Media Cat.Libn.
MARYWOOD COLLEGE - LEARNING RESOURCES
CENTER □ Scranton, PA

Philbin, Paul O., Ref.Libn.
OCLC, INC. - LIBRARY □ Dublin, OH

Philbrick, Ruth R., Cur.
NATIONAL GALLERY OF ART - PHOTOGRAPHIC
ARCHIVES □ Washington, DC

Philip, John, Supv., Field Serv.
STATE LIBRARY OF OHIO □ Columbus, OH

Philipp, Linda, Asst.Libn.
VINSON & ELKINS - LAW LIBRARY □ Houston,
TX

Philips, Arleen, Asst.Libn.
CLARINDA MENTAL HEALTH INSTITUTION -
RESIDENTS AND STAFF LIBRARY □ Clarinda, IA

Philips, Doris, Libn.
MORRIS COUNTY HISTORICAL SOCIETY -
VICTORIAN RESOURCE LIBRARY □ Morristown,
NJ

Philips, Rosemary B., Libn.
CHESTER COUNTY HISTORICAL SOCIETY -
LIBRARY □ West Chester, PA

Philips, Sandra, Libn.
D'ARCY-MAC MANUS AND MASIUS - LIBRARY □
New York, NY

Philley, H., Lib.Ck.
SASKATCHEWAN POWER CORPORATION -
LIBRARY □ Regina, SK

Phillips, Beverly R., Libn.
UNIVERSITY OF WISCONSIN, MADISON - LAND
TENURE CENTER - LIBRARY □ Madison, WI

Phillips, Bonnie A., Supv.
KELLOGG (M.W.) - RESEARCH INFORMATION
DIVISION □ Houston, TX

Phillips, Carol B., Chf.Ref.Libn.
UNIVERSITY OF TEXAS MEDICAL BRANCH -
MOODY MEDICAL LIBRARY □ Galveston, TX

Phillips, Dennis J., Pub.Serv.
MUHLENBERG COLLEGE - JOHN A.W. HAAS
LIBRARY □ Allentown, PA

Phillips, Don E., Ck. of Court
MARINETTE COUNTY LAW LIBRARY □
Marinette, WI

Phillips, Doris M., Lib.Serv.Coord.
BLACK HILLS STATE COLLEGE - E.Y. BERRY
LIBRARY-LEARNING CENTER □ Spearfish, SD

Phillips, Dorothy, Adm.
FEDERAL RESERVE BANK OF CHICAGO -
LIBRARY □ Chicago, IL

Phillips, Faye, Tech.Serv.Archv.
UNIVERSITY OF NORTH CAROLINA, CHAPEL
HILL - SOUTHERN HISTORICAL COLLECTION &
MANUSCRIPTS DEPARTMENT □ Chapel Hill, NC

Phillips, Frances M., Chf.Libn.
HARPER-GRACE HOSPITALS - GRACE HOSPITAL
DIVISION - OSCAR LE SEURE PROFESSIONAL
LIBRARY □ Detroit, MI

Phillips, Frank, Univ.Libn.
WESTERN STATE UNIVERSITY - COLLEGE OF
LAW - LIBRARY □ Fullerton, CA

Phillips, Ira, Asst. State Libn.
STATE LIBRARY OF OHIO □ Columbus, OH

Phillips, J. Richard, Rd.Serv.Libn.
STANFORD UNIVERSITY - DEPARTMENT OF
SPECIAL COLLECTIONS □ Stanford, CA

Phillips, James W., Cur.
SOUTHERN METHODIST UNIVERSITY - FIKES
HALL OF SPECIAL COLLECTIONS AND
DEGOLYER LIBRARY □ Dallas, TX

Phillips, Jane, Libn.
NOVA SCOTIA - DEPARTMENT OF SOCIAL
SERVICES - LIBRARY □ Halifax, NS

Phillips, Jerry C., Asst.Tech.Serv.Libn.
UNIVERSITY OF NEW MEXICO - SCHOOL OF
LAW LIBRARY □ Albuquerque, NM

Phillips, John, Asst.Doc.Libn.
OKLAHOMA STATE UNIVERSITY - DOCUMENTS
DIVISION □ Stillwater, OK

Phillips, John T., Lib.Supv.
UNION CARBIDE CORPORATION - NUCLEAR
DIVISION - OAK RIDGE GASEOUS DIFFUSION
PLANT LIBRARY □ Oak Ridge, TN

Phillips, Johnnie L., Ref.Dept.
SAN DIEGO STATE UNIVERSITY - MALCOLM A.
LOVE LIBRARY □ San Diego, CA

PERSONNEL

Phillips, Julia L., Res.Hd.
BOEING COMPANY - SEATTLE SERVICES DIVISION - KENT TECHNICAL LIBRARY □ Seattle, WA

Phillips, Julianne, Field Serv.Libn.
SOUTH CAROLINA STATE LIBRARY □ Columbia, SC

Phillips, Linda L., Tech.Info.Coord.
ROCHESTER GAS AND ELECTRIC CORPORATION - TECHNICAL INFORMATION CENTER □ Rochester, NY

Phillips, Marie, Hd.
ROCKFORD PUBLIC LIBRARY - BUSINESS, SCIENCE AND TECHNOLOGY DIVISION □ Rockford, IL

Phillips, Mary Louise, Local Hist.Libn.
CHARLOTTE AND MECKLENBURG COUNTY PUBLIC LIBRARY - CAROLINA ROOM □ Charlotte, NC

Phillips, Michael, Chf.Hist.
U.S. NATL. PARK SERVICE - SARATOGA NATL. HISTORICAL PARK - LIBRARY □ Stillwater, NY

Phillips, Michele, Documentarian
UNIVERSITY OF ARIZONA - OPTICAL SCIENCES CENTER - READING ROOM □ Tucson, AZ

Phillips, Nancy C., Libn.
U.S. VETERANS ADMINISTRATION (TN-Johnson City) - HOSPITAL LIBRARY □ Mountain Home, TN

Phillips, Phoebe F., Hd.Libn.
OHIO STATE UNIVERSITY - AGRICULTURAL TECHNICAL INSTITUTE - LIBRARY □ Wooster, OH

Phillips, R. Cody, Musm.Cur.
CASEMATE MUSEUM - LIBRARY □ Ft. Monroe, VA

Phillips, R.W., Asst.Libn.
U.S. VETERANS ADMINISTRATION (CA-Martinez) - HOSPITAL LIBRARY □ Martinez, CA

Phillips, Rajeana, Cat.Libn.
HUGHES AIRCRAFT COMPANY - COMPANY TECHNICAL DOCUMENT CENTER □ Culver City, CA

Phillips, Robert, Asst.Libn./Pub.Serv.
SOUTHWESTERN BAPTIST THEOLOGICAL SEMINARY - FLEMING LIBRARY □ Fort Worth, TX

Phillips, Rodney, Chf.
NEW YORK PUBLIC LIBRARY - GENERAL RESEARCH DIVISION □ New York, NY

Phillips, Roger, Hd., Spec.Serv.
WHEATON COLLEGE - LIBRARY □ Wheaton, IL

Phillips, Ruth M., Chm.
HUGUENOT-THOMAS PAINE HISTORICAL ASSOCIATION OF NEW ROCHELLE - HUFELAND MEMORIAL LIBRARY □ New Rochelle, NY

Phillips, Sharon A., Dir.
OAKWOOD HOSPITAL - MC LOUTH MEMORIAL HEALTH SCIENCE LIBRARY □ Dearborn, MI

Phillips, Shelley, Coord.Adm.Dept.
ST. LUKE'S HOSPITAL - SCHOOL OF NURSING LIBRARY □ St. Louis, MO

Phillips, Vicki W., Libn.
OKLAHOMA STATE UNIVERSITY - DOCUMENTS DIVISION □ Stillwater, OK

Phillips, Violet R., Hd.Libn.
LONG BEACH INDEPENDENT, PRESS-TELEGRAM - LIBRARY □ Long Beach, CA

Phillips, William F., Lit.Chem.
INTERNATIONAL MINERALS & CHEMICALS CORPORATION - IMC RESEARCH & DEVELOPMENT LIBRARY □ Terre Haute, IN

Phillpot, Clive, Dir.
MUSEUM OF MODERN ART - LIBRARY □ New York, NY

Philos, Helen S., Libn.
AMERICAN SOCIETY OF INTERNATIONAL LAW - LIBRARY □ Washington, DC

Philpott, Catherine E., Libn.
CANADA - CANADIAN FORESTRY SERVICE - NEWFOUNDLAND FOREST RESEARCH CENTRE - LIBRARY □ St. John's, NF

Phinney, Chad T., Musm.Asst.
PUEBLO GRANDE MUSEUM - RESEARCH LIBRARY □ Phoenix, AZ

Phinney, Hartley K., Jr., Dir.
COLORADO SCHOOL OF MINES - ARTHUR LAKES LIBRARY □ Golden, CO

Phinney, Jeannette, Ref.
DAUGHTERS OF THE REPUBLIC OF TEXAS - LIBRARY □ San Antonio, TX

Phyler, Frances, Lib.Techn.
U.S. BUREAU OF RECLAMATION - TECHNICAL LIBRARY† □ Boulder City, NV

Piatt, Gladys, Historic Site Asst.
JAY (John) HOMESTEAD - JAY LIBRARY □ Katonah, NY

Picard, Bethany, Libn.
EXXON COMPANY, U.S.A. - TECHNICAL SERVICES - ENGINEERING LIBRARY □ Baytown, TX

Picardo, Kathryn, Asst.Libn., Cat.
PHILADELPHIA COLLEGE OF OSTEOPATHIC MEDICINE - O.J. SNYDER MEMORIAL MEDICAL LIBRARY □ Philadelphia, PA

Picciano, Jacqueline, Libn.
AMERICAN JOURNAL OF NURSING COMPANY - SOPHIA F. PALMER MEMORIAL LIBRARY □ New York, NY

Piccinino, Rocco, Jr., Assoc.Libn.
UNITED ENGINEERS & CONSTRUCTORS, INC. - LIBRARY □ Philadelphia, PA

Piccoli, Roberta, Info.Spec.
THOMPSON (J. Walter) COMPANY - INFORMATION CENTER □ Chicago, IL

Pichet, Louise, Libn.
IMASCO FOODS, LTD. - LIBRARY □ Montreal, PQ

Pichi, Dr. Victor, Dir.
UNIVERSITE DE MONTREAL - CENTRE DE RECHERCHES CARAIBES - BIBLIOTHEQUE □ Montreal, PQ

Picini, Nancy, Asst.Libn.
EMMAUS BIBLE SCHOOL - LIBRARY □ Oak Park, IL

Pick, Paula, Hd.Cat.
BRITISH COLUMBIA INSTITUTE OF TECHNOLOGY - LIBRARY SERVICES DIVISION □ Burnaby, BC

Pickard, John C., Asst.Libn.
BIBLICAL THEOLOGICAL SEMINARY - LIBRARY □ Hatfield, PA

Pickenpaugh, Eileen, Res.Cons.
U.S. NAVY - NAVAL RESEARCH LABORATORY - RUTH H. HOOKER TECHNICAL LIBRARY □ Washington, DC

Pickens, Pamela E., Chem.Libn.
EMORY UNIVERSITY - CHEMISTRY LIBRARY □ Atlanta, GA

Pickett, Ellis B., Dir.
U.S. ARMY - ENGINEER WATERWAYS EXPERIMENT STATION - HYDRAULIC ENGINEERING INFORMATION ANALYSIS CENTER □ Vicksburg, MS

Pickett, Thomas E., Assoc.Dir.
DELAWARE STATE GEOLOGICAL SURVEY - LIBRARY □ Newark, DE

Picott, John B., Med.Libn.
BOSTON STATE HOSPITAL - MEDICAL LIBRARY □ Boston, MA

Picquet, D. Cheryn, Adm.Libn.
UNIVERSITY OF TENNESSEE - COLLEGE OF LAW LIBRARY □ Knoxville, TN

Picray, Pam, Med.Libn.
U.S. ARMY HOSPITALS - BASSETT ARMY HOSPITAL - MEDICAL LIBRARY □ Fort Wainwright, AK

Piechocki, Virginia, Acq.Libn.
SAN DIEGO COUNTY LAW LIBRARY □ San Diego, CA

Piel, Mark, Libn.
NEW YORK SOCIETY LIBRARY □ New York, NY

Piele, Philip K., Dir.
ERIC CLEARINGHOUSE ON EDUCATIONAL MANAGEMENT □ Eugene, OR

Pien, Arlene C., Libn.
ST. JOSEPH'S HOSPITAL - HELENE FULD LEARNING RESOURCE CENTER □ Elmira, NY

Pienitz, Eleanor, Libn., Info.Spec.
HARRIS CORPORATION - PRD ELECTRONICS DIVISION - INFORMATION CENTER □ Syosset, NY

Pieprzyk, Julie, Info.Spec.
SYNTEX, U.S.A. - CORPORATE LIBRARY/ INFORMATION SERVICES □ Palo Alto, CA

Pierce, Ann, Libn.
CUMBERLAND BAR ASSOCIATION - NATHAN AND HENRY B. CLEAVES LAW LIBRARY □ Portland, ME

Pierce, Anton R., Plan. & Res.Libn.
VIRGINIA POLYTECHNIC INSTITUTE AND STATE UNIVERSITY - CAROL M. NEWMAN LIBRARY □ Blacksburg, VA

Pierce, Barbara, Market Anl.
PENTON/IPC - MARKETING INFORMATION CENTER □ Cleveland, OH

Pierce, Charlotte G., Libn.
MISSISSIPPI STATE AGRICULTURAL & FORESTRY EXPERIMENT STATION - DELTA BR. EXPERIMENT STA. LIBRARY □ Stoneville, MS

Pierce, Eddist, Asst.Libn.
DOW CHEMICAL U.S.A. - ENGINEERING AND CONSTRUCTION SERVICES LIBRARY† □ Houston, TX

Pierce, Helen V., Libn.
GREENVILLE LAW LIBRARY □ Greenville, OH

Pierce, Irene R., Mgr., News Serv.
MOBIL OIL CORPORATION - PUBLIC AFFAIRS SECRETARIAT □ New York, NY

Pierce, Jerry, Pres.
INTERNATIONAL CLARINET SOCIETY - BURNET C. TUTHILL RESEARCH LIBRARY† □ Denver, CO

Pierce, Karen, Circ.
CALAIS FREE LIBRARY □ Calais, ME

Pierce, Linda, Index Ed.
AMERICAN INSTITUTE OF CERTIFIED PUBLIC ACCOUNTANTS - LIBRARY □ New York, NY

Pierce, M. Edith, Libn.
U.S. AIR FORCE BASE - CANNON BASE LIBRARY □ Cannon AFB, NM

Pierce, Mary J., Chf., Processing
SMITHSONIAN INSTITUTION LIBRARIES □ Washington, DC

Pierce, Marylou, Ref.Libn.
MECHANICS' INSTITUTE LIBRARY □ San Francisco, CA

Pierce, Miriam, Assoc.Libn.
PENNSYLVANIA STATE UNIVERSITY - LIFE SCIENCES LIBRARY □ University Park, PA

Pierce, Pauline D., Cur.
STOCKBRIDGE LIBRARY ASSOCIATION - HISTORICAL ROOM □ Stockbridge, MA

Pierce, Sally, Photodup.
BOSTON ATHENAEUM LIBRARY □ Boston, MA

Pierpoint, E., Cur.
ROSSLAND MUSEUM - ARCHIVES □ Rossland, BC

Pierrard, Jesse, Libn.
ST. JOSEPH HOSPITAL - MEDICAL AND NURSING LIBRARY □ Fort Worth, TX

Pierre, Margaret, Lib.Techn. (Supv.)
ALBERTA HOSPITAL - LIBRARY† □ Edmonton, AB

Pierson, Jeannie, Asst.
LOCKWOOD, ANDREWS & NEWNAM, INC. - INFORMATION CENTER □ Houston, TX

Pierson, Roscoe M., Libn.
LEXINGTON THEOLOGICAL SEMINARY - BOSWORTH MEMORIAL LIBRARY □ Lexington, KY

Pierstorff, Prof. Lola R., Dir.
UNIVERSITY OF WISCONSIN, MADISON - SCHOOL OF EDUCATION - HISTORICAL MATERIALS COLLECTION □ Madison, WI

Pieschel, Terri, Libn.
CHEVRON STANDARD, LTD. - LIBRARY □ Calgary, AB

Pietch, Eleanor E., Libn.
LORAIN COUNTY LAW LIBRARY ASSOCIATION -
LIBRARY □ Elyria, OH

Pietropaoli, Frank A., Br.Libn.
SMITHSONIAN INSTITUTION LIBRARIES -
NATIONAL MUSEUM OF AMERICAN HISTORY -
LIBRARY □ Washington, DC

Piety, Jean Z., Hd.
CLEVELAND PUBLIC LIBRARY - SCIENCE AND
TECHNOLOGY DEPARTMENT □ Cleveland, OH

Pifalo, Victoria G., Asst.Libn.
ELMIRA PSYCHIATRIC CENTER -
PROFESSIONAL LIBRARY □ Elmira, NY

Piggford, Roland, Act.Dir.
MASSACHUSETTS STATE BOARD OF LIBRARY
COMMISSIONERS - REFERENCE AND
RESEARCH LIBRARY □ Boston, MA

Piggott, Charla, Ref.Libn.
UNIVERSITY OF MISSOURI - MEDICAL
LIBRARY† □ Columbia, MO

Pignatello, Leonard J., Dept.Hd.
MINNEAPOLIS PUBLIC LIBRARY &
INFORMATION CENTER - BUSINESS AND
SCIENCE DEPARTMENT □ Minneapolis, MN

Pigno, Antonia, Minorities Res.Ctr.
KANSAS STATE UNIVERSITY - FARRELL
LIBRARY □ Manhattan, KS

Pigot, F.L., Ref.Libn.
UNIVERSITY OF PRINCE EDWARD ISLAND -
ROBERTSON LIBRARY □ Charlottetown, PE

Pigott, Louis I., Jr., Libn.
INTERNATIONAL ENGINEERING COMPANY,
INC. - LIBRARY □ San Francisco, CA

Piirto, John, Tech.Asst.
SAN DIEGO STATE UNIVERSITY - PUBLIC
ADMINISTRATION RESEARCH CENTER
LIBRARY □ San Diego, CA

Pike, Esther, Acq.Libn.
STANFORD UNIVERSITY - J. HUGH JACKSON
LIBRARY □ Stanford, CA

Pike, John R., Mng.Dir.
WISCONSIN ALUMNI RESEARCH FOUNDATION
- LIBRARY □ Madison, WI

Pike, Kermit J., Dir.
WESTERN RESERVE HISTORICAL SOCIETY -
LIBRARY □ Cleveland, OH

Pike, Lorraine, Libn.
ASCENSION LUTHERAN CHURCH - LIBRARY □
Milwaukee, WI

Pike, Mary L., Dp.Dir., Member Serv.
NATIONAL ASSOCIATION OF HOUSING AND
REDEVELOPMENT OFFICIALS - RESOURCE
CENTER □ Washington, DC

Pike, Vikki, Libn.
GTE PRODUCTS CORPORATION - SYLVANIA
SYSTEMS GROUP - WESTERN DIVISION -
LIBRARY □ Mountain View, CA

Pilikian, Helen M., Chf.Med.Libn.
LONG ISLAND JEWISH-HILLSIDE MEDICAL
CENTER - QUEENS HOSPITAL CENTER -
MEDICAL LIBRARY □ Jamaica, NY

Pilkington, James P., Adm.
VANDERBILT UNIVERSITY LIBRARY -
TELEVISION NEWS ARCHIVE □ Nashville, TN

Pillaert, E. Elizabeth, Cur.
UNIVERSITY OF WISCONSIN, MADISON -
ZOOLOGICAL MUSEUM LIBRARY □ Madison, WI

Pillai, Karley, Asst.Libn.
NEW YORK STATE LIBRARY - LAW/SOCIAL
SCIENCE REFERENCE SERVICES □ Albany, NY

Pillau, Estra R., Libn.
BROWARD COUNTY LAW LIBRARY □ Fort
Lauderdale, FL

Pillsbury, Elizabeth, Genealogist
FENTON HISTORICAL SOCIETY - LIBRARY □
Jamestown, NY

Pilon, Paul, Libn.
METROPOLITAN TORONTO LIBRARY - SOCIAL
SCIENCES DEPARTMENT □ Toronto, ON

Pimsler, Martin, Libn.
CENTER FOR THE STUDY OF ETHICS IN THE
PROFESSIONS - LIBRARY □ Chicago, IL

Pinckney, Cathey L., Libn.
ST. JOHN'S HOSPITAL AND HEALTH CENTER -
HOSPITAL LIBRARY† □ Santa Monica, CA

Pincoe, Ruth, Cat.
CANADIAN MUSIC CENTRE - LIBRARY □
Toronto, ON

Pincus, Lena, Libn.
SOUTHERN CALIFORNIA PSYCHOANALYTIC
INSTITUTE - FRANZ ALEXANDER LIBRARY □
Beverly Hills, CA

Pindar, Maia, Tech.Info.Spec.
XEROX CORPORATION - PALO ALTO RESEARCH
CENTER - TECHNICAL INFORMATION CENTER
□ Palo Alto, CA

Pine, Carol, Asst.Cur., Rare Bks.
HARVARD UNIVERSITY - SCHOOLS OF
MEDICINE, DENTAL MEDICINE AND PUBLIC
HEALTH - FRANCIS A. COUNTWAY LIBRARY □
Boston, MA

Pineda, Conchita J., Mgr.
CITIBANK, N.A. - FINANCIAL LIBRARY □ New
York, NY

Pineda, Lolly, Libn.
MOBIL LAND DEVELOPMENT CORPORATION -
LIBRARY □ San Francisco, CA

Pinero, Belsie C., Hd., Ref.
UNIVERSITY OF PUERTO RICO - GENERAL
LIBRARY □ San Juan, PR

Pines, Doralynn, Assoc.Musm.Libn.
METROPOLITAN MUSEUM OF ART - THOMAS J.
WATSON LIBRARY □ New York, NY

Pines, Philip A., Dir.
TROTTING HORSE MUSEUM - LIBRARY □
Goshen, NY

Pinkard, Inez C., Asst.Chf.Libn.
U.S. VETERANS ADMINISTRATION (AL-
Tuskegee) - MEDICAL CENTER LIBRARY □
Tuskegee, AL

Pinkerton, Barbara, Adm.Asst.
DEWITT HISTORICAL SOCIETY OF TOMPKINS
COUNTY - ARCHIVE/LIBRARY □ Ithaca, NY

Pinkerton, Robert L., Exec.Dir.
TRI-COUNTY REGIONAL PLANNING
COMMISSION - LIBRARY □ East Peoria, IL

Pinkneg, Mindy
UNIVERSITY OF NORTH DAKOTA - GEOLOGY
LIBRARY □ Grand Forks, ND

Pinkney, Elaine, Libn.
JOHNS HOPKINS HOSPITAL - DEPARTMENT OF
RADIOLOGY - LIBRARY □ Baltimore, MD

Pinkney, Helen L., Libn.
DAYTON ART INSTITUTE - LIBRARY □ Dayton,
OH

Pinnell, Jonalou M., Libn.
SEDGWICK COUNTY LAW LIBRARY† □ Wichita,
KS

Pinnell, Richard Hugh, Map Libn.
UNIVERSITY OF WATERLOO - UNIVERSITY
MAP LIBRARY □ Waterloo, ON

Pinney, Joyce, Libn.
PASADENA PUBLIC LIBRARY - REFERENCE
DIVISION □ Pasadena, CA

Pinsky, Susan, Pub.
STEREO PHOTOGRAPHERS, COLLECTORS &
ENTHUSIASTS CLUB - REEL THREE-D
ENTERPRISES - LIBRARY □ Duarte, CA

Pinson, Bob, Acq.Dir.
COUNTRY MUSIC FOUNDATION - LIBRARY AND
MEDIA CENTER □ Nashville, TN

Pinto, Rosalina G., Adm.Asst.
NORTHROP UNIVERSITY - ALUMNI LIBRARY† □
Inglewood, CA

Pinzelik, John, Chem.Libn.
PURDUE UNIVERSITY - CHEMISTRY LIBRARY □
West Lafayette, IN

Pinzl, Ann, Cur. Natural Hist.
NEVADA STATE MUSEUM □ Carson City, NV

Piorkowska, Janina, Per.Libn.
UNIVERSITY OF SOUTHERN COLORADO -
LIBRARY - SPECIAL COLLECTIONS □ Pueblo, CO

Piotrow, Dr. Phyllis T., Dir.
JOHNS HOPKINS UNIVERSITY - POPULATION
INFORMATION PROGRAM □ Baltimore, MD

Piotrowski, Thaddeus, Dir.Lrng.Res.Ctr.
BLOOMSBURG STATE COLLEGE - HARVEY A.
ANDRUSS LIBRARY □ Bloomsburg, PA

Pipe, Rebecca, Registrar
OVER (W.H.) MUSEUM - LIBRARY □ Vermillion,
SD

Piper, Clara, Libn.
NYLANDER MUSEUM - LIBRARY □ Caribou, ME

Piper, Mary C., Staff-Lib.
QUAKER OATS COMPANY - JOHN STUART
RESEARCH LABORATORIES - RESEARCH
LIBRARY □ Barrington, IL

Piper, Nelson A., Asst.Univ.Libn./Coll.
UNIVERSITY OF CALIFORNIA, DAVIS -
GENERAL LIBRARY □ Davis, CA

Piper, Oliva
CENTRAL OHIO TRANSIT AUTHORITY -
LIBRARY □ Columbus, OH

Piper, Mrs. Pat B., Asst. Law Libn.
UNIVERSITY OF CALIFORNIA, DAVIS - SCHOOL
OF LAW - LAW LIBRARY □ Davis, CA

Pipes, Alice, Med.Libn.
KAISER-PERMANENTE MEDICAL CENTER -
HAYWARD MEDICAL LIBRARY □ Hayward, CA

Pipes, Alice, Libn.
KAISER-PERMANENTE MEDICAL CENTER -
HEALTH INFORMATION CENTER □ Hayward, CA

Pipkin, Kathleen, Libn.
WILSON MEMORIAL HOSPITAL - LIBRARY/
LEARNING CENTER □ Wilson, NC

Piraino, Joan M., Libn.
SCIENCE RESEARCH ASSOCIATES, INC. -
LIBRARY □ Chicago, IL

Pirino, Karen, Dir.
ST. JOHN'S MERCY MEDICAL CENTER - JOHN
YOUNG BROWN MEMORIAL LIBRARY □ St. Louis,
MO

Pirus, Douglas I., Off.Mgr.
AMERICAN AVIATION HISTORICAL SOCIETY -
AAHS REFERENCE LIBRARY □ Garden Grove, CA

Piscadlo, Bruce S., Asst. Law Libn.
MONTGOMERY COUNTY LAW LIBRARY □
Norristown, PA

Pisciotta, Robert, Asst.Dir., Rd.Serv.
CHICAGO COLLEGE OF OSTEOPATHIC
MEDICINE - ALUMNI MEMORIAL LIBRARY □
Chicago, IL

Pistone, F.J., Pres.
HISTORICAL SOCIETY OF THE TOWN OF
NORTH HEMPSTEAD - LIBRARY □ Manhasset, NY

Pistorius, Nancy, Asst.Libn.
UNIVERSITY OF NEW MEXICO - FINE ARTS
LIBRARY □ Albuquerque, NM

Pita, Lorene S., Libn.
PROVIDENT HOSPITAL - HEALTH SCIENCES
LIBRARY □ Baltimore, MD

Pitcher, Beth E., Res.Libn.
PENICK CORPORATION RESEARCH LIBRARY □
Orange, NJ

Pitchford, Harriet, Cat.
U.S. ARMY POST - FORT BENNING -
RECREATION SERVICES LIBRARY BRANCH □ Ft.
Benning, GA

Pitchon A., Cindy
PROVIDENT MUTUAL LIFE INSURANCE
COMPANY OF PHILADELPHIA - LIBRARY □
Philadelphia, PA

Pitkin, Pat, Hd. of Tech.Serv.
ROCHESTER INSTITUTE OF TECHNOLOGY -
WALLACE MEMORIAL LIBRARY □ Rochester, NY

Pitschel, Barbara, Asst.Libn.
STRYBING ARBORETUM SOCIETY - HELEN
CROCKER RUSSELL LIBRARY □ San Francisco,
CA

Pittock, Thomas, Info.Tech.
UNIVERSITY OF PITTSBURGH - CENTER FOR
INTERNATIONAL STUDIES □ Pittsburgh, PA

Pitts, J.
OLIN CORPORATION - RESEARCH CENTER/
INFORMATION CENTER □ New Haven, CT

PERSONNEL

PERSONNEL

Pitts, Dr.James N., Jr., Dir. SAPRC
UNIVERSITY OF CALIFORNIA, RIVERSIDE -
OFFICE OF TECHNICAL INFO. - STATEWIDE
AIR POLLUTION RESEARCH CTR. □ Riverside,
CA

Pitts, Mary Louise, Chf., Rd.Serv.Div.
U.S. AIR FORCE - AIR UNIVERSITY - LIBRARY □
Maxwell AFB, AL

Pitts, Terence, Cur. of Photo Archv.
UNIVERSITY OF ARIZONA - CENTER FOR
CREATIVE PHOTOGRAPHY □ Tucson, AZ

Pitzer, Laura F., Libn.
GREENVILLE MENTAL HEALTH CENTER -
LIBRARY □ Greenville, SC

Pivnicki, Dr. D., Chm.Lib.Comm.
MC GILL UNIVERSITY - ALLAN MEMORIAL
INSTITUTE OF PSYCHIATRY - LIBRARY □
Montreal, PQ

Pivorun, Phyllis, Slide Cur.
CLEMSON UNIVERSITY - EMERY A. GUNNIN
ARCHITECTURAL LIBRARY □ Clemson, SC

Piwonka, Ruth, Exec.Dir.
COLUMBIA COUNTY HISTORICAL SOCIETY -
HOUSE OF HISTORY LIBRARY □ Kinderhook, NY

Pixley, Lorene, Asst.Libn.
SOUTHERN ILLINOIS UNIVERSITY,
CARBONDALE - EDUCATION DIVISION LIBRARY
□ Carbondale, IL

Pizer, Irwin H., Univ.Libn.
UNIVERSITY OF ILLINOIS MEDICAL CENTER -
LIBRARY OF THE HEALTH SCIENCES □ Chicago,
IL

Pizer, Laurence R., Dir.
PILGRIM SOCIETY - PILGRIM HALL LIBRARY □
Plymouth, MA

Pizzo, Anthony P., Chm.
HILLSBOROUGH COUNTY HISTORICAL
COMMISSION - LIBRARY □ Tampa, FL

Pla, Steven A., Libn.
AMERICAN PHILATELIC RESEARCH LIBRARY □
State College, PA

Plaisante, Gilbert, Libn.
QUEBEC PROVINCE - MINISTERE DES
AFFAIRES SOCIALES - INFORMATHEQUE □
Quebec, PQ

Plaiss, Mark, Lib.Asst.
ST. VINCENT'S HOSPITAL - GARCEAU LIBRARY
□ Indianapolis, IN

Plamann, Paul E., Hist.
U.S. NATL. PARK SERVICE - FORT MC HENRY
NATL. MONUMENT - LIBRARY □ Baltimore, MD

Plamondon, Yolande, Techn.
CENTRE HOSPITALIER ROBERT-GIFFARD -
BIBLIOTHEQUE PROFESSIONNELLE □ Beauport,
PQ

Plane, Daphne, Libn.
CALIFORNIA INSTITUTE OF TECHNOLOGY -
GEOLOGY LIBRARY □ Pasadena, CA

Plante, Dr. Julian G., Dir.
ST. JOHN'S ABBEY AND UNIVERSITY - HILL
MONASTIC MANUSCRIPT LIBRARY - BUSH
CENTER □ Collegeville, MN

Plante-Garneau, Suzanne
QUEBEC PROVINCE - OFFICE DE
PLANIFICATION ET DE DEVELOPPEMENT DU
QUEBEC - BIBLIOTHEQUE □ Quebec, PQ

Plaskacz, Mrs. Truus, Hd.Cat. Unit
NATIONAL LIBRARY OF CANADA -
MULTILINGUAL BIBLIOSERVICE □ Ottawa, ON

Plaso, Kathy, Consortium Libn.
PENNSYLVANIA STATE DEPARTMENT OF
PUBLIC WELFARE - SOMERSET STATE
HOSPITAL - LIBRARY □ Somerset, PA

Plaster, Joyce, Chf., Rd.Serv.
U.S. ARMY - MISSILE COMMAND & MARSHALL
SPACE FLIGHT CENTER - REDSTONE
SCIENTIFIC INFORMATION CENTER □
Redstone Arsenal, AL

Platou, J.S., Dir. of Info.
SULPHUR INSTITUTE - LIBRARY □ Washington,
DC

Platt, Jill Thomas, Corp.Libn.
SUNKIST GROWERS, INC. - CORPORATE
LIBRARY □ Sherman Oaks, CA

Platt, John H., Libn.
HISTORICAL SOCIETY OF PENNSYLVANIA -
LIBRARY □ Philadelphia, PA

Platt-Brown, Jane, Libn.
NATIONAL ECONOMIC RESEARCH
ASSOCIATES, INC. - LIBRARY □ Washington, DC

Platte, James P., Dean/Div.Lrng.Rsrcs.
LANSING COMMUNITY COLLEGE -
PROFESSIONAL RESOURCE CENTER □ Lansing,
MI

Platthy, Jeno, Ph.D., Libn.
HARVARD UNIVERSITY - CENTER FOR
HELLENIC STUDIES - LIBRARY □ Washington,
DC

Plattner, Steven, Photo Cur.
CINCINNATI HISTORICAL SOCIETY - LIBRARY
□ Cincinnati, OH

Player, Jewel A., Libn.
U.S. ARMY POST - FORT MC PHERSON -
LIBRARY SYSTEM □ Ft. McPherson, GA

Player, Julia, Assoc.Libn.
HOWARD UNIVERSITY - HEALTH SCIENCES
LIBRARY □ Washington, DC

Pleasant, Thella, Libn.
SONOMA STATE HOSPITAL - PROFESSIONAL
LIBRARY† □ Eldridge, CA

Plehaty, Phyllis, Cur. of Costumes
BOULDER HISTORICAL SOCIETY - PIONEER
MUSEUM - LIBRARY □ Boulder, CO

Plese, Pat, Asst.Techn.
INTERGALACTIC CORP. - LIBRARY □ Salt Lake
City, UT

Plessinger, Suzanne, Libn.
PAUL, HASTINGS, JANOFSKY AND WALKER -
LAW LIBRARY □ Los Angeles, CA

Pletscher, Josephine M., Libn., Fine Art Div.
PASADENA PUBLIC LIBRARY - ALICE COLEMAN
BATCHELDER MUSIC LIBRARY □ Pasadena, CA

Pletscher, Josephine M., Libn., Fine Arts Div.
PASADENA PUBLIC LIBRARY - FINE ARTS
DIVISION □ Pasadena, CA

Plewa, Michele M., Adm.Asst.
MARQUETTE UNIVERSITY - MEMORIAL
LIBRARY □ Milwaukee, WI

Plitt, Jeanne G., Dir.
ALEXANDRIA LIBRARY - LLOYD HOUSE □
Alexandria, VA

Ploch, Carol D., Med.Libn./Anl.
GOOD SAMARITAN HOSPITAL - RICHARD S.
BEINECKE MEDICAL LIBRARY □ West Palm
Beach, FL

Plockelman, Cynthia H., Ref.Libn.
FLORIDA STATE - SOUTH FLORIDA WATER
MANAGEMENT DISTRICT - REFERENCE
CENTER □ West Palm Beach, FL

Plotkin, Nathan, Libn.
CALIFORNIA MARITIME ACADEMY LIBRARY† □
Vallejo, CA

Plotkin, Susan, Info.Sys.Spec.
HONEYWELL, INC. - PROCESS CONTROLS
DIVISION - INFORMATION CENTER, M.S. 221 □
Fort Washington, PA

Plotnick, Robert Nathan, Libn.
CONNECTICUT STATE LIBRARY - LAW LIBRARY
AT BRIDGEPORT □ Bridgeport, CT

Plous, Ann L., Libn.
PANNELL KERR FORSTER - MANAGEMENT
ADVISORY SERVICES - LIBRARY □ Chicago, IL

Plowman, Mary K., Tech. Staff Asst.
TEXAS STATE BUREAU OF ECONOMIC GEOLOGY
- WELL SAMPLE AND CORE LIBRARY □ Austin,
TX

Plowman, Dr. Robert J., Chf., Archv.Br.
U.S. NATL. ARCHIVES & RECORDS SERVICE -
FEDERAL ARCHIVES AND RECORDS CENTER,
REGION 3 □ Philadelphia, PA

Plucinski, Veronica, Libn.
PFIZER, INC. - PFIZER PHARMACEUTICALS
LIBRARY □ New York, NY

Plum, Dorothy A., Libn.
ESSEX COUNTY HISTORICAL SOCIETY -
LIBRARY □ Elizabethtown, NY

Plumanis, Guna, Ref.Serv.
ONTARIO - MINISTRY OF TRANSPORTATION
AND COMMUNICATIONS - LIBRARY AND
INFORMATION CENTRE □ Downsview, ON

Plummer, Bill, III, Comm.Coord.
AMATEUR SOFTBALL ASSOCIATION - ASA
RESEARCH CENTER AND LIBRARY □ Oklahoma
City, OK

Plummer, Bruce, Act.Dir.
WORCESTER STATE COLLEGE - LEARNING
RESOURCES CENTER □ Worcester, MA

Plummer, John, Cur., Medv. & Ren.Mss.
PIERPONT MORGAN LIBRARY □ New York, NY

Plummer, Linda, Steinbeck Libn.
SALINAS PUBLIC LIBRARY - JOHN STEINBECK
LIBRARY □ Salinas, CA

Plunges, Gregory J., Libn.
MONMOUTH COUNTY HISTORICAL
ASSOCIATION - LIBRARY □ Freehold, NJ

Plungis, Joan, Mss.Libn.
INDIANA HISTORICAL SOCIETY - WILLIAM
HENRY SMITH MEMORIAL LIBRARY □
Indianapolis, IN

Plunket, Joy, Libn.
CHOATE, HALL AND STEWART - LAW LIBRARY
□ Boston, MA

Plunket, Linda, Proj.Coord.
CENTRAL MAINE MEDICAL CENTER - GERRISH-
TRUE HEALTH SCIENCE LIBRARY □ Lewiston,
ME

Pluscauskas, Martha, Coord.
EAST YORK BOARD OF EDUCATION -
PROFESSIONAL LIBRARY □ Toronto, ON

Pober, Susan J., Libn.
BROOKLYN CHILDREN'S MUSEUM - CHILDREN'S
RESOURCE LIBRARY □ Brooklyn, NY

Poburko, Mary Jo, Hd.Libn.
GOODWIN, PROCTER & HOAR - LAW LIBRARY □
Boston, MA

Pochert, Marjorie, Children's Libn.
MEMORIAL PRESBYTERIAN CHURCH - LIBRARY
□ Midland, MI

Podboy, Alvin M., Libn.
BAKER AND HOSTETLER - LIBRARY □ Cleveland,
OH

Poe, John E., Ref./Rd.Serv.Libn.
GEORGIA STATE LIBRARY □ Atlanta, GA

Poe, N., Tech.Rec.Anl.
SCM CORPORATION - GLIDDEN COATINGS &
RESINS DIV./DURKEE FOODS DIV. -
TECHNICAL INFORMATION SERVICES □
Strongsville, OH

Poehlman, Dorothy, Chf., 10A Serv.Br.
U.S. DEPT. OF TRANSPORTATION - LIBRARY
SERVICES DIVISION □ Washington, DC

Poethig, Richard P., Dir.
INSTITUTE ON THE CHURCH IN URBAN-
INDUSTRIAL SOCIETY - LIBRARY □ Chicago, IL

Poff, J.G., Hd.Libn.
NORTH BAY COLLEGE EDUCATION CENTRE -
LIBRARY □ North Bay, ON

Poffenroth, J., Lib.Asst., Engr.Lib.
ESSO RESOURCES CANADA LIMITED - LIBRARY
INFORMATION CENTRE □ Calgary, AB

Pogany, Ann M., Libn.
OAKLAND UNIVERSITY - LIBRARY □ Rochester,
MI

Pogue, Forrest C., Biographer
MARSHALL (George C.) RESEARCH FOUNDATION
- GEORGE C. MARSHALL RESEARCH LIBRARY □
Lexington, VA

Pogue, Laura, Ref.Libn.
SASKATCHEWAN - LEGISLATIVE LIBRARY □
Regina, SK

Pohl, Gunther E., Div.Chf.
NEW YORK PUBLIC LIBRARY - LOCAL HISTORY
AND GENEALOGY DIVISION □ New York, NY

Pohorecky, Natalia, Ref.Libn.
UNIVERSITY OF MANITOBA - MEDICAL
LIBRARY □ Winnipeg, MB

Points, Larry G., Chf.Interp.
U.S. NATL. PARK SERVICE - ASSATEAGUE
ISLAND NATL. SEASHORE - LIBRARY □ Berlin,
MD

Poirier, Linda, Cur. of Coll.
BATTLE CREEK ART CENTER LIBRARY -
MICHIGAN ART ARCHIVES □ Battle Creek, MI

Poisson, Beth C., Libn.
SHATTUCK (Lemuel) HOSPITAL - MEDICAL
LIBRARY □ Jamaica Plain, MA

Poitras, Lionel, Res.Off.
SASKATCHEWAN - DEPARTMENT OF INDUSTRY
AND COMMERCE - LIBRARY □ Regina, SK

Pojaujis, Irene, Sr.Lib.Techn.
CENTENNIAL COLLEGE OF APPLIED ARTS &
TECHNOLOGY - ASHTONBEE CAMPUS
RESOURCE CENTRE □ Scarborough, ON

Pokorny, George, Libn.
CHICAGO MOUNTAINEERING CLUB - JOHN
SPECK MEMORIAL LIBRARY □ Glen Ellyn, IL

Polach, Dr. Frank, Assoc.Libn.
RUTGERS UNIVERSITY, THE STATE
UNIVERSITY OF NEW JERSEY - LIBRARY OF
SCIENCE & MEDICINE □ Piscataway, NJ

Polacsek, John F., Cur.
GREAT LAKES MARITIME INSTITUTE - DOSSIN
GREAT LAKES MUSEUM INFORMATION CENTER
□ Detroit, MI

Polacsek, Richard A., M.D., Dir./Libn.
JOHNS HOPKINS UNIVERSITY - WILLIAM H.
WELCH MEDICAL LIBRARY □ Baltimore, MD

Polak, Virginia, Libn.
UNIVERSITY OF CALIFORNIA, BERKELEY -
UNIVERSITY EXTENSION - CONTINUING
EDUCATION OF THE BAR - LIBRARY □ Berkeley,
CA

Poland, Jean, Info.Serv.Mgr.
NATIONAL WATER WELL ASSOCIATION -
GROUND WATER LIBRARY/INFORMATION
CENTER □ Worthington, OH

Poland, Jean, Libn.
UNIVERSITY OF OKLAHOMA - ENGINEERING
LIBRARY □ Norman, OK

Poland, Ursula, Libn.
UNION UNIVERSITY - ALBANY MEDICAL
COLLEGE - SCHAFFER LIBRARY OF THE HEALTH
SCIENCES □ Albany, NY

Polardino, Linda S., Chf., Lib.Serv.
U.S. VETERANS ADMINISTRATION (NY-
Montrose) - HOSPITAL LIBRARY □ Montrose, NY

Poldoian, Jean, Supv.
NEW ENGLAND MUTUAL LIFE INSURANCE
COMPANY - BUSINESS LIBRARY □ Boston, MA

Polhill, Ruth B., Libn.
VAN WYCK HOMESTEAD MUSEUM - LIBRARY □
Fishkill, NY

Poli, Ross, Info.Spec.
OHIO STATE UNIVERSITY - MECHANIZED
INFORMATION CENTER (MIC) □ Columbus, OH

Polinsky, A.J., Libn.
BURNDY LIBRARY □ Norwalk, CT

Polinsky, Helga Brink, Exec.Ed.
AUTHENTICATED NEWS INTERNATIONAL -
PHOTO LIBRARY □ Katonah, NY

Polinsky, Sidney, Mng.Ed.
AUTHENTICATED NEWS INTERNATIONAL -
PHOTO LIBRARY □ Katonah, NY

Polito, Ruth, Libn.
LA SALLE STEEL COMPANY - RESEARCH AND
DEVELOPMENT LIBRARY† □ Hammond, IN

Polk, Diana, Ref.Libn.
DEERE & COMPANY - LIBRARY □ Moline, IL

Polk, Lorraine, Tech.Libn.
3M CANADA - TECHNICAL INFORMATION
CENTRE □ London, ON

Pollack, Barbara R., Dir., ACIM
BRIGHAM AND WOMEN'S HOSPITAL -
ABRAMSON CENTER FOR INSTRUCTIONAL
MEDIA □ Boston, MA

Pollack, Beth, Libn.
OGILVY & MATHER, INC. - RESEARCH LIBRARY
□ New York, NY

Pollack, Carol, Chf.Libn.
DETROITBANK CORPORATION - RESEARCH
LIBRARY □ Detroit, MI

Pollack, Cynthia, Park Ranger
U.S. NATL. PARK SERVICE - SAUGUS IRON
WORKS NATL. HISTORIC SITE - LIBRARY □
Saugus, MA

Pollack, Sally, Asst.Dir., Pub.Serv.
UNIVERSITY OF TEXAS HEALTH SCIENCE
CENTER, SAN ANTONIO - BRADY/GREEN
EDUCATIONAL RESOURCES CENTER □ San
Antonio, TX

Pollak, Sally, Asst.Dir.Pub.Serv.
UNIVERSITY OF TEXAS HEALTH SCIENCE
CENTER, SAN ANTONIO - LIBRARY □ San
Antonio, TX

Pollard, Mrs. G.E., Libn.
GEORGE (Henry) SCHOOL OF LOS ANGELES -
RESEARCH LIBRARY □ Tujunga, CA

Pollard, Greta
ALTERNATIVE PRESS CENTER - LIBRARY □
Baltimore, MD

Pollard, Russell, Tech.Serv.
HARVARD UNIVERSITY - DIVINITY SCHOOL -
ANDOVER-HARVARD THEOLOGICAL LIBRARY □
Cambridge, MA

Pollard, Stewart M.L., Exec.Sec.
MASONIC SERVICE ASSOCIATION OF THE
UNITED STATES - LIBRARY □ Silver Spring, MD

Pollard, W. Robert, Hd., Ref.Dept.
NORTH CAROLINA STATE UNIVERSITY - D.H.
HILL LIBRARY □ Raleigh, NC

Polley, Brian S., Libn.
FLORIDA STATE SUPREME COURT LIBRARY □
Tallahassee, FL

Pollis, Angela R., Staff Supv.
UNITED STATES STEEL CORPORATION -
RESEARCH LABORATORY - TECHNICAL
INFORMATION CENTER □ Monroeville, PA

Pollock, Ida C., Libn.
TEMPLE BETH-EL - ZISKIND MEMORIAL
LIBRARY □ Fall River, MA

Pollock, James W., Libn./Cat.
INDIANA UNIVERSITY - NEAR EASTERN
COLLECTION □ Bloomington, IN

Pollock, Miss M.Y., Mgr.
NORTHERN TELECOM CANADA, LTD. - LIBRARY
& TECHNICAL INFORMATION CENTRE □
Montreal, PQ

Poloniewicz, Tamara, Subj.Spec.
QUEENS BOROUGH PUBLIC LIBRARY - SCIENCE
& TECHNOLOGY DIVISION □ Jamaica, NY

Polonsky, Aaron, Acq.Libn.
BLOOMSBURG STATE COLLEGE - HARVEY A.
ANDRUSS LIBRARY □ Bloomsburg, PA

Polowy, Barbara C., Libn.
EVERSON MUSEUM OF ART - LIBRARY □
Syracuse, NY

Polowy, Barbara C., Libn.
MUNSON-WILLIAMS-PROCTOR INSTITUTE -
ART REFERENCE AND MUSIC LIBRARY □ Utica,
NY

Polster, Joanne, Libn.
AMERICAN CRAFT COUNCIL - LIBRARY □ New
York, NY

Poluy, Miriam, Assoc.Dir.
MILWAUKEE URBAN OBSERVATORY - URBAN
INFORMATION CENTER □ Milwaukee, WI

Pomerance, Deborah S., Libn.
DATA USE AND ACCESS LABORATORIES
(DUALABS) - LIBRARY □ Arlington, VA

Pomerantz, Barbara, Asst.Libn.
KENYON & ECKHARDT ADVERTISING -
INFORMATION CENTER □ New York, NY

Pomerantz, Julius, Libn.
CARTER, LEDYARD AND MILBURN - LIBRARY† □
New York, NY

Pomeroy, Cornelia, Circ.
WORCESTER POLYTECHNIC INSTITUTE -
GEORGE C. GORDON LIBRARY □ Worcester, MA

Pomiecko, Catherine A., Archv./Asst. Law Libn.
LIBERTY MUTUAL INSURANCE COMPANY - LAW
LIBRARY □ Boston, MA

Pommer, Michelle A., Libn.
HAWAIIAN TELEPHONE COMPANY - LIBRARY □
Honolulu, HI

Ponis, Roberta, Lib. Media Spec.
JEFFERSON COUNTY PUBLIC SCHOOLS R1 -
PROFESSIONAL LIBRARY MEDIA CENTER □
Lakewood, CO

Pool, Lucinda, Exec.Dir.
POLK (James K.) ANCESTRAL HOME - LIBRARY □
Columbia, TN

Pool, Rosemary, Med.Libn.
BON SECOURS HOSPITAL - HEALTH SCIENCES
LIBRARY □ Baltimore, MD

Pool, Susan, Info.Anl.
ALLERGAN PHARMACEUTICALS, INC. -
PROFESSIONAL INFORMATION SERVICES □
Irvine, CA

Poole, Ann, Libn.
UNIVERSITY OF TORONTO/YORK UNIVERSITY
JOINT PROGRAM IN TRANSPORTATION -
INFORMATION SERVICE □ Toronto, ON

Poole, Barbara, Chf. MEDDAC Libn.
GORGAS ARMY HOSPITAL - SAMUEL TAYLOR
DARLING MEMORIAL LIBRARY □ APO Miami, FL

Poole, Dr. Herbert, Dir.
GUILFORD COLLEGE - LIBRARY □ Greensboro,
NC

Poole, Judy, Prog.
UNIVERSITY OF NORTH CAROLINA, CHAPEL
HILL - INSTITUTE FOR RESEARCH IN SOCIAL
SCIENCE - DATA LIBRARY □ Chapel Hill, NC

Poole, Katherine, Lrng.Rsrcs.Libn.
HARVARD UNIVERSITY - GRADUATE SCHOOL
OF DESIGN - FRANCES LOEB LIBRARY □
Cambridge, MA

Poole-Kober, Evelyn M., Tech.Info.Ck.
ENVIRONMENTAL PROTECTION AGENCY -
DIVISION OF METEOROLOGY - INFORMATION
SERVICE CENTER □ Research Triangle Park, NC

Pooler, Margaret, Ref.Libn.
MATHEMATICAL REVIEWS - LIBRARY □ Ann
Arbor, MI

Pooley, Beverley J., Dir.
UNIVERSITY OF MICHIGAN - LAW LIBRARY □
Ann Arbor, MI

Poon, Mrs. Wei Chi, Hd.Libn.
UNIVERSITY OF CALIFORNIA, BERKELEY -
ASIAN AMERICAN STUDIES LIBRARY □
Berkeley, CA

Poor, W.E., Tech.Libn.
CUMMINS ENGINE CO., INC. - LIBRARIES □
Columbus, IN

Popa, Peggy L., Tech.Serv.Supv.
CONTINENTAL ILLINOIS NATIONAL BANK AND
TRUST COMPANY OF CHICAGO - INFORMATION
SERVICES DIVISION □ Chicago, IL

Pope, Andrew, Educ.Libn.
UNIVERSITY OF NEW BRUNSWICK -
EDUCATION RESOURCE CENTRE □ Fredericton,
NB

Pope, Cornelia C., Libn.
MERCY HOSPITAL - MEDICAL LIBRARY □ Miami,
FL

Pope, Mary, Chf., Tech.Serv.Br.
U.S. DEPT. OF THE TREASURY - INFORMATION
SERVICES DIVISION - TREASURY DEPT.
LIBRARY □ Washington, DC

Pope, Nancy, Cat.
NORTHWESTERN UNIVERSITY -
TRANSPORTATION LIBRARY □ Evanston, IL

Pope, Nannette M., Hd., Lib.Serv.
U.S. ARMED FORCES RADIOBIOLOGY
RESEARCH INSTITUTE (AFRRI) - LIBRARY
SERVICES □ Bethesda, MD

Pope, W. Nicholas, Assoc. Law Libn.
CLEVELAND STATE UNIVERSITY - JOSEPH W.
BARTUNEK III LAW LIBRARY □ Cleveland, OH

Pope, Wiley R., Ref.Libn.
MINNESOTA HISTORICAL SOCIETY -
REFERENCE LIBRARY □ St. Paul, MN

Popenoe, John, Dir.
FAIRCHILD TROPICAL GARDEN -
MONTGOMERY LIBRARY □ Miami, FL

Popescu, Dr. Constantin, Assoc.Libn.
MILWAUKEE SCHOOL OF ENGINEERING -
WALTER SCHROEDER LIBRARY ▢ Milwaukee, WI

Popik, Judith, Ref.Libn.
SHEARMAN & STERLING - LIBRARY ▢ New York,
NY

Poplau, Janice J., Cat.Libn.
BIRMINGHAM-SOUTHERN COLLEGE - CHARLES
ANDREW RUSH LEARNING CENTER/LIBRARY ▢
Birmingham, AL

Popoff, E.J., Per. & Microfilms
CANADA - LABOUR CANADA - LIBRARY ▢
Ottawa, ON

Popovich, Marjorie L., Hd., Info.Serv.
KENNECOTT CORPORATION - CARBORUNDUM
COMPANY - INFORMATION CENTER ▢ Niagara
Falls, NY

Popp, Richard H., Mgr., Corp. Training
WESTERN PUBLISHING COMPANY, INC. -
CORPORATE TRAINING CENTER LIBRARY ▢
Racine, WI

Poppalardo, Joetta, Dir. of Prof.Ed.
ALTOBELLO (Henry D.) CHILDREN AND YOUTH
CENTER - PROFESSIONAL COLLECTION ▢
Meriden, CT

Popplestone, John A., Dir.
UNIVERSITY OF AKRON - ARCHIVES OF THE
HISTORY OF AMERICAN PSYCHOLOGY ▢ Akron,
OH

Poray-Wybranowski, Dr. Anna, Chf.Libn.
POLISH INSTITUTE OF ARTS AND SCIENCES IN
CANADA - POLISH LIBRARY ▢ Montreal, PQ

Port, Jane S., Dir.
MOUNT SINAI SCHOOL OF MEDICINE OF THE
CITY UNIVERSITY OF NEW YORK - GUSTAVE L.
& JANET W. LEVY LIBRARY ▢ New York, NY

Port, Toby G., Adm.Libn.
ST. ELIZABETHS HOSPITAL - HEALTH
SCIENCES LIBRARY ▢ Washington, DC

Porte, Masha R., Film Spec.
DALLAS PUBLIC LIBRARY - FILM SERVICE ▢
Dallas, TX

Porter, Blaine D., Dir.
U.S. DEPT. OF COMMERCE - INTERNATIONAL
TRADE ADMINISTRATION - ANCHORAGE
DISTRICT OFFICE LIBRARY ▢ Anchorage, AK

Porter, Cynthia, V.P., Info.Serv.
BANK MARKETING ASSOCIATION -
INFORMATION CENTER ▢ Chicago, IL

Porter, Emma, Genealogist & Dir.
ST. CHARLES COUNTY HISTORICAL SOCIETY -
LIBRARY AND ARCHIVES ▢ St. Charles, MO

Porter, Helen, Libn.
MUSKINGUM LAW LIBRARY ▢ Zanesville, OH

Porter, Helen, Libn.
OSAWATOMIE STATE HOSPITAL - RAPAPORT
PROFESSIONAL LIBRARY - MENTAL HEALTH
LIBRARY† ▢ Osawatomie, KS

Porter, Jean M., Hd., Doc.Dept.
NORTH CAROLINA STATE UNIVERSITY - D.H.
HILL LIBRARY ▢ Raleigh, NC

Porter, Jean M., Supv.
NORTH CAROLINA STATE UNIVERSITY -
SOUTHERN WATER RESOURCES SCIENTIFIC
INFORMATION CENTER ▢ Raleigh, NC

Porter, Jonathan
HARTFORD PUBLIC LIBRARY - ART, MUSIC AND
RECREATION DEPARTMENT ▢ Hartford, CT

Porter, Kathryn W., Libn.
AETNA LIFE AND CASUALTY COMPANY -
LIBRARY ▢ Hartford, CT

Porter, Kitty, Libn.
DUKE UNIVERSITY - CHEMISTRY LIBRARY ▢
Durham, NC

Porter, Mr. L., Asst.Libn.
UNIVERSITY OF GUELPH - LIBRARY ▢ Guelph,
ON

Porter, Lee W., Chf.Libn.
U.S. ARMY POST - FORT MC PHERSON -
LIBRARY SYSTEM ▢ Ft. McPherson, GA

Porter, Lloyd R., Dir.
U.S. DEPT. OF COMMERCE - INTERNATIONAL
TRADE ADMINISTRATION - PORTLAND
DISTRICT OFFICE LIBRARY ▢ Portland, OR

Porter, Marguerite, Dir., Lib. Serv.
CANADIAN BIBLE COLLEGE/CANADIAN
THEOLOGICAL COLLEGE - ARCHIBALD
FOUNDATION LIBRARY ▢ Regina, SK

Porter, Mary, Asst.Libn.
LUTHERAN BIBLE INSTITUTE - LIBRARY ▢
Issaquah, WA

Porter, Patricia, Circ.Supv.
TROY STATE UNIVERSITY - LIBRARY ▢ Troy, AL

Porter, Patricia Bozyk, Chf.Libn.
RED RIVER COMMUNITY COLLEGE - LEARNING
RESOURCES CENTRE ▢ Winnipeg, MB

Porter, Robert, Mgr., Info.Serv.
AMERICAN COUNCIL FOR THE ARTS - LIBRARY
▢ New York, NY

Porter, Sandra, Adm.Asst.
OHIO VALLEY HEALTH SERVICES FOUNDATION,
INC. - LIBRARY ▢ Athens, OH

Porter, Shannon, Libn.
FORESTA INSTITUTE FOR OCEAN AND
MOUNTAIN STUDIES - ENVIRONMENTAL
STUDIES CENTER† ▢ Carson City, NV

Porter, Sheila C., Libn.
DALLAS COUNTY LAW LIBRARY ▢ Dallas, TX

Porter-Zadera, Suzanne, Dir.
PARK CITY HOSPITAL - CARLSON MEMORIAL
HEALTH SCIENCES LIBRARY ▢ Bridgeport, CT

Portlock, Lucile B., Hd.
NORFOLK PUBLIC LIBRARY - SARGEANT
MEMORIAL ROOM ▢ Norfolk, VA

Portmann, Douglas A., Tech.Libn.
MOBAY CHEMICAL CORPORATION - RESEARCH
LIBRARY ▢ New Martinsville, WV

Portsch, Joanne, Libn.
RAYTHEON COMPANY - EQUIPMENT DIVISION
- TECHNICAL INFORMATION CENTER ▢
Wayland, MA

Portugal, Carmelita Lavayna, Dir.
UNIVERSITY OF PITTSBURGH - SCHOOL OF
EDUCATION - INTERNATIONAL &
DEVELOPMENT EDUCATION PROGRAM
CLEARINGHOUSE ▢ Pittsburgh, PA

Poses, June A., Asst. to Libn.
COLLEGE OF PHYSICIANS OF PHILADELPHIA -
LIBRARY AND MEDICAL DOCUMENTATION
SERVICE ▢ Philadelphia, PA

Poses, Phyllis R., Div.Hd.
QUEENS BOROUGH PUBLIC LIBRARY - SOCIAL
SCIENCES DIVISION ▢ Jamaica, NY

Posey, Edwin D., Engr.Libn.
PURDUE UNIVERSITY - ENGINEERING LIBRARY
▢ West Lafayette, IN

Posey, Jewell, Archv.
UNITED METHODIST CHURCH - NORTHWEST
TEXAS ANNUAL CONFERENCE - COMMISSION
ON ARCHIVES AND HISTORY ▢ Abilene, TX

Posey, Linda L., Asst.Hd.Libn.
KNOXVILLE-KNOX COUNTY PUBLIC LIBRARY
SYSTEM - MC CLUNG HISTORICAL COLLECTION
▢ Knoxville, TN

Poshkus, Algirdas C., Tech.Info.Sci.
ARMSTRONG WORLD INDUSTRIES, INC. -
TECHNICAL CENTER - TECHNICAL
INFORMATION SERVICES ▢ Lancaster, PA

Posner, Shirley, Hd., Acq.
SUNY - COLLEGE AT BUFFALO - EDWARD H.
BUTLER LIBRARY ▢ Buffalo, NY

Posner, Walter, Ref.Libn.
SAN DIEGO STATE UNIVERSITY -
GOVERNMENT PUBLICATIONS DEPARTMENT ▢
San Diego, CA

Posniak, John R., Asst.Libn.
EXPORT-IMPORT BANK OF THE UNITED
STATES - LIBRARY ▢ Washington, DC

Post, Carl, Owner
THEATRE AND FILM ARTS - INFORMATION
CENTER ▢ Los Angeles, CA

Post, Doris, Dir.
GODFREY MEMORIAL LIBRARY ▢ Middletown,
CT

Post, Edward, Dir.
TRACOR JITCO, INC. - RESEARCH RESOURCES
INFORMATION CENTER ▢ Rockville, MD

Post, Helen, Med.Libn.
U.S. VETERANS ADMINISTRATION (DE-
Wilmington) - CENTER MEDICAL LIBRARY† ▢
Wilmington, DE

Post, J.B., Map Libn.
FREE LIBRARY OF PHILADELPHIA - SOCIAL
SCIENCE & HISTORY DEPARTMENT - MAP
COLLECTION ▢ Philadelphia, PA

Post, Linda, Info.Spec.
INTEL-TECHNICAL INFORMATION CENTER ▢
Santa Clara, CA

Post, Marilyn, Energy Info.Spec.
NORTHERN STATES POWER COMPANY - "ASK
NSP" TAPE LIBRARY ▢ Minneapolis, MN

Postell, William D., Jr., Med.Libn.
TULANE UNIVERSITY OF LOUISIANA - SCHOOL
OF MEDICINE - RUDOLPH MATAS MEDICAL
LIBRARY ▢ New Orleans, LA

Postlewait, Cheryl, Libn.
MOBAY CHEMICAL CORPORATION -
AGRICULTURAL CHEMICALS DIVISION -
LIBRARY ▢ Kansas City, MO

Potash, Loree E., Assoc.Libn.Pub.Serv.
CASE WESTERN RESERVE UNIVERSITY - LAW
LIBRARY ▢ Cleveland, OH

Poteat, James, Mgr., Res.Serv.
TELEVISION INFORMATION OFFICE OF THE
NATIONAL ASSOCIATION OF BROADCASTERS -
RESEARCH SERVICES† ▢ New York, NY

Poth, Lynn, Cat.
METROPOLITAN (Toronto) SEPARATE SCHOOL
BOARD - PROFESSIONAL LIBRARY† ▢ Toronto,
ON

Potter, Anne, Mgr., Comp.Serv.
FIND/SVP - LIBRARY ▢ New York, NY

Potter, Dorothy, Libn.
PASADENA PUBLIC LIBRARY - REFERENCE
DIVISION ▢ Pasadena, CA

Potter, George E., Pub.Serv.Libn.
HARVARD UNIVERSITY - HARVARD YENCHING
INSTITUTE - LIBRARY ▢ Cambridge, MA

Potter, James E., State Archv.
NEBRASKA STATE HISTORICAL SOCIETY -
ARCHIVES ▢ Lincoln, NE

Potter, Joyce A., Libn.
U.S. FEDERAL HOME LOAN BANK BOARD - LAW
LIBRARY ▢ Washington, DC

Potter, Marjorie P., Law Lib.Ck.
NEW YORK STATE SUPREME COURT - 4TH
JUDICIAL DISTRICT - LAW LIBRARY ▢ Lake
George, NY

Potter, Pamela A., Slide Libn.
MARYLAND INSTITUTE, COLLEGE OF ART -
DECKER LIBRARY ▢ Baltimore, MD

Potter, Rockwell H., Jr., Pub.Rec.Adm.
CONNECTICUT STATE LIBRARY ▢ Hartford, CT

Potter, S.
SPERRY CORPORATION - LAW LIBRARY ▢ New
York, NY

Potter, Sue, Dir., Directed Stud.
WAYNE COMMUNITY COLLEGE - LEARNING
RESOURCE CENTER ▢ Goldsboro, NC

Potter, T.R., Info.Spec.
NORTH CAROLINA STATE SCIENCE AND
TECHNOLOGY RESEARCH CENTER ▢ Research
Triangle Park, NC

Potter, Virginia, Ref.Supv.
WISCONSIN STATE DIVISION FOR LIBRARY
SERVICES - REFERENCE AND LOAN LIBRARY ▢
Madison, WI

Potthast, Cheryl, Med.Libn.
U.S. VETERANS ADMINISTRATION (IL-Chicago)
- LAKESIDE HOSPITAL MEDICAL LIBRARY ▢
Chicago, IL

Potts, Don, Hd. Automation Serv.
MEDICAL LIBRARY CENTER OF NEW YORK ▢
New York, NY

Potts, Ken, Libn.
MEMPHIS-SHELBY COUNTY PUBLIC LIBRARY
AND INFO. CTR. - SCIENCE/BUSINESS/SOCIAL
SCIENCES DEPT. □ Memphis, TN

Potts, Lesley S., Libn.
CLARKSVILLE LEAF-CHRONICLE COMPANY -
LIBRARY □ Clarksville, TN

Poucher, Lucy
SOUTHERN OREGON STATE COLLEGE - LIBRARY
□ Ashland, OR

Pouliott, Marianne K., Libn.
GENERAL ELECTRIC COMPANY - SILICONE
PRODUCTS DIVISION - LIBRARY □ Waterford,
NY

Pound, M.A., Supv.
U.S. DEPT. OF ENERGY - SANDIA NATL.
LABORATORIES, LIVERMORE - TECHNICAL
LIBRARY □ Livermore, CA

Pouzar, Frank, Libn.
DALLAS PUBLIC LIBRARY - BUSINESS AND
TECHNOLOGY DIVISION □ Dallas, TX

Povey, Cherryi M., Chf., Lib.Serv.
U.S. VETERANS ADMINISTRATION (UT-Salt
Lake City) - HOSPITAL MEDICAL LIBRARY □ Salt
Lake City, UT

Powell, Antoinette P., Libn.
UNIVERSITY OF KENTUCKY - AGRICULTURE
LIBRARY □ Lexington, KY

Powell, Mrs. Bobby H., Med.Libn.
CARRAWAY METHODIST MEDICAL CENTER -
MEDICAL LIBRARY □ Birmingham, AL

Powell, Camille M., Libn.
FLUOR ENGINEERS AND CONSTRUCTORS, INC.
- FLUOR HOUSTON LIBRARY □ Houston, TX

Powell, Claudia Lane, Doc.Consrv.Spec.
UNIVERSITY OF MISSOURI - WESTERN
HISTORICAL MANUSCRIPT COLLECTION/
STATE HISTORICAL SOCIETY OF MISSOURI □
Columbia, MO

Powell, Donald, Biblog.
TUCSON MUSEUM OF ART - LIBRARY □ Tucson,
AZ

Powell, Rev. Gary, Dir. of Lib.
BYZANTINE CATHOLIC SEMINARY OF SAINTS
CYRIL AND METHODIUS - BYZANTINE
SEMINARY LIBRARY □ Pittsburgh, PA

Powell, Rev. Gary, O.F.M.Cap., Libn.
ST. CYRIL AND METHODIUS BYZANTINE
CATHOLIC SEMINARY - LIBRARY □ Pittsburgh,
PA

Powell, James, Info.Sci.
UPJOHN COMPANY - CORPORATE TECHNICAL
LIBRARY □ Kalamazoo, MI

Powell, K.L., Lib.Serv.Coord.
ALBERTA - LEGISLATIVE ASSEMBLY OF
ALBERTA - LEGISLATURE LIBRARY □ Edmonton,
AB

Powell, Martha C., Church Music Libn.
SOUTHERN BAPTIST THEOLOGICAL SEMINARY
- CHURCH MUSIC LIBRARY □ Louisville, KY

Powell, Michael E., Dir.
WASHINGTON UNIVERSITY - GEORGE WARREN
BROWN SCHOOL OF SOCIAL WORK - LIBRARY &
LEARNING RESOURCES CENTER □ St. Louis, MO

Powell, N.L., Coord. Campus Libs.
CATHOLIC UNIVERSITY OF AMERICA -
CHEMISTRY LIBRARY □ Washington, DC

Powell, N.L., Libn.
CATHOLIC UNIVERSITY OF AMERICA -
NURSING/BIOLOGY LIBRARY □ Washington, DC

Powell, N.L., Coord., Campus Libs.
CATHOLIC UNIVERSITY OF AMERICA -
PHYSICS LIBRARY □ Washington, DC

Powell, Patricia, Libn.
WEST VIRGINIA UNIVERSITY MEDICAL
CENTER - CHARLESTON DIVISION - LEARNING
RESOURCES CENTER □ Charleston, WV

Powell, Patricia J., Libn.
FAYETTEVILLE AREA HEALTH EDUCATION
CENTER - LIBRARY □ Fayetteville, NC

Powell, Rebecca
MIAMI-DADE PUBLIC LIBRARY - ART AND
MUSIC DIVISION □ Miami, FL

Powell, Richard, Supv.Tchg.Mtls.Ctr.
ANDREWS UNIVERSITY - JAMES WHITE
LIBRARY □ Berrien Springs, MI

Powell, Richard M., Exec.Dir.
REFRIGERATION RESEARCH FOUNDATION -
LIBRARY □ Washington, DC

Powell, Russell H., Libn.
UNIVERSITY OF KENTUCKY - ENGINEERING
LIBRARY □ Lexington, KY

Powell, Sharon, Asst.Libn.
AEROSPACE INDUSTRIES ASSOCIATION OF
AMERICA - LIBRARY □ Washington, DC

Powell, Mr. T.D., Dir., Rec.& Tech.Serv.
SASKATCHEWAN ARCHIVES BOARD □ Regina,
SK

Powell, Virginia, Music/Educ./AV Libn.
WHEATON COLLEGE - LIBRARY □ Wheaton, IL

Powell, Wayne B., Sci./Engr.Libn.
TUFTS UNIVERSITY - RICHARD H. LUFKIN
LIBRARY □ Medford, MA

Power, Genie, Lib.Techn.
NEWFOUNDLAND - DEPARTMENT OF MINES
AND ENERGY - MINERAL DEVELOPMENT
DIVISION - LIBRARY □ St. John's, NF

Power, Mary, Coord., Ref.Serv.
NATIONAL RETIRED TEACHERS ASSN.-
AMERICAN ASSN. OF RETIRED PERSONS -
NATL. GERONTOLOGY RESOURCE CTR. □
Washington, DC

Power, Pauline V., Asst.Dir.Tech.Serv.
UNIVERSITY OF TEXAS MEDICAL BRANCH -
MOODY MEDICAL LIBRARY □ Galveston, TX

Powers, Anne, Libn.
UNIVERSITY OF CALIFORNIA, SANTA BARBARA
- BLACK STUDIES LIBRARY UNIT □ Santa
Barbara, CA

Powers, David F., Musm.Cur.
U.S. PRESIDENTIAL LIBRARIES - JOHN F.
KENNEDY LIBRARY □ Boston, MA

Powers, Jewett A., Tech.Info.Off.
U.S. DEPT. OF ENERGY - AMES LABORATORY -
DOCUMENT LIBRARY □ Ames, IA

Powers, Kathleen, Asst.Cat.
MARSHALL (John) LAW SCHOOL - LIBRARY □
Chicago, IL

Powers, Mrs. Louis L., Libn.
CONGREGATION BETH AM - DOROTHY G.
FELDMAN LIBRARY □ Cleveland Heights, OH

Powers, Thomas, Archv.
UNIVERSITY OF MICHIGAN - MICHIGAN
HISTORICAL COLLECTIONS - BENTLEY
HISTORICAL LIBRARY □ Ann Arbor, MI

Powers, William J., Jr., Exec. Law Libn.
COOK COUNTY LAW LIBRARY □ Chicago, IL

Powles, Laurence, Asst.Libn.
OAKLAND TRIBUNE - LIBRARY □ Oakland, CA

Poyer, Robert, Coord., Pub.Serv.
MEDICAL UNIVERSITY OF SOUTH CAROLINA -
LIBRARY □ Charleston, SC

Poyne, Ron G., AV Spec.
OKLAHOMA STATE UNIVERSITY - AUDIO
VISUAL CENTER □ Stillwater, OK

Pozzo, Joanne, Exec.Dir.
NATIONAL RESOURCE CENTER FOR
CONSUMERS OF LEGAL SERVICES -
CLEARINGHOUSE □ Washington, DC

Praemer, Victoria A., Hd.Libn.
ROOKS, PITTS, FULLAGAR & POUST - LIBRARY
□ Chicago, IL

Pragnell, Ruth, Libn.
GENERAL THEOLOGICAL LIBRARY □ Boston, MA

Pragnell, Terence, Law Libn.
PACIFIC LIGHTING CORPORATION - LAW
LIBRARY □ Los Angeles, CA

Prakash, Judith Middlebrook, Libn.
HAWAII STATE LIBRARY - SOCIAL SCIENCE
AND PHILOSOPHY SECTION □ Honolulu, HI

Pralle, Marilee, Ser.Libn.
PHILLIPS UNIVERSITY - GRADUATE SEMINARY
LIBRARY □ Enid, OK

Pratchett, Patricia A., Mgr., Lib.Serv.
UNITED SERVICES AUTOMOBILE ASSOCIATION
- CORPORATE LIBRARY AND INFORMATION
CENTER □ San Antonio, TX

Pratt, Annabelle, Jr.Libn.
OAKLAND PUBLIC LIBRARY - ART, MUSIC,
RECREATION □ Oakland, CA

Pratt, Kathleen L., Info.Dir.
ST. MARY'S HOSPITAL - MAX C. FLEISCHMANN
MEDICAL LIBRARY □ Reno, NV

Pratt, Leoma, Libn.
TYLER COURIER-TIMES-TELEGRAPH - LIBRARY
□ Tyler, TX

Pratt, Lydia S., Libn.
PORT AUTHORITY OF ALLEGHENY COUNTY -
TRANSIT RESEARCH LIBRARY □ Pittsburgh, PA

Pratt, M., Info.Spec.
BURROUGHS WELLCOME COMPANY - LIBRARY
□ Research Triangle Park, NC

Pratt, Mary S., Dept.Mgr.
LOS ANGELES PUBLIC LIBRARY - HISTORY
DEPARTMENT □ Los Angeles, CA

Pratt, Susan, Lib.Techn.
U.S. NAVY - NAVAL ORDNANCE STATION -
TECHNICAL LIBRARY □ Indian Head, MD

Pratt, V. Lorraine, Dir.
SRI INTERNATIONAL - LIBRARY AND
RESEARCH INFORMATION SERVICES
DEPARTMENT □ Menlo Park, CA

Pratt, Virginia, Libn.
UNIVERSITY OF CALIFORNIA, BERKELEY -
LIBRARY SCHOOL LIBRARY □ Berkeley, CA

Pray, Edna, Pharmacy Libn.
UNIVERSITY OF KENTUCKY - MEDICAL CENTER
LIBRARY □ Lexington, KY

Pray, Roberta, Res.Libn.
KANSAS STATE HISTORICAL SOCIETY -
LIBRARY □ Topeka, KS

Prchal, Dolly, Photo Serv.
NAPA COUNTY HISTORICAL SOCIETY -
GOODMAN LIBRARY □ Napa, CA

Prebisch, Eliana D., Libn.
INTERNATIONAL MONETARY FUND - LAW
LIBRARY □ Washington, DC

Preble, Leverett L., III, Hd. Law Libn./Prof.
CAPITAL UNIVERSITY - LAW SCHOOL LIBRARY
□ Columbus, OH

Precht, Rev. Dr. Fred L., Exec.Sec.
LUTHERAN CHURCH - MISSOURI SYNOD -
COMMISSION ON WORSHIP LIBRARY □ St.
Louis, MO

Preibish, Andre, Dir.Coll.Dev.
NATIONAL LIBRARY OF CANADA □ Ottawa, ON

Preisinger, George T., Adm.
OAKLAND UNIVERSITY - LIBRARY □ Rochester,
MI

Prelec, Antonija, Assoc.Dir./Coll.Dev.
SUNY AT STONY BROOK - HEALTH SCIENCES
LIBRARY □ East Setauket, NY

Premont, Jacques, Dir.
QUEBEC PROVINCE - LEGISLATURE DU QUEBEC
- BIBLIOTHEQUE† □ Quebec, PQ

Prendeville, Jet Marie, Art Libn.
RICE UNIVERSITY - ART LIBRARY □ Houston,
TX

Prepon, Leslie, Hd., Pub.Serv.
WESTERN NEW ENGLAND COLLEGE - SCHOOL
OF LAW LIBRARY □ Springfield, MA

Presby, Richard, Dir.
JHK & ASSOCIATES - TECHNICAL LIBRARY -
EAST □ Alexandria, VA

Presby, Richard, Libn.
JHK & ASSOCIATES - TECHNICAL LIBRARY -
WEST □ Emeryville, CA

Presho, Barbara, Libn.
CONSUMERS GLASS COMPANY LIMITED -
PLASTICS PACKAGING DIVISION LIBRARY □
Etobicoke, ON

Preslar, M. Gail, Asst.Res.Libn.
EASTMAN KODAK COMPANY - TENNESSEE
EASTMAN COMPANY - RESEARCH LIBRARY □
Kingsport, TN

Presley, Nancy, Hd., Rd.Serv.
SANTA MONICA PUBLIC LIBRARY -
CALIFORNIA SPECIAL COLLECTION □ Santa
Monica, CA

Preslock, Karen, Libn.
SMITHSONIAN INSTITUTION LIBRARIES -
CONSERVATION ANALYTICAL LABORATORY -
LIBRARY □ Washington, DC

Presser, Carolynne, Asst.Libn.
UNIVERSITY OF WATERLOO - ENGINEERING,
MATHEMATICS & SCIENCE DIVISIONAL
LIBRARY □ Waterloo, ON

Pressey, Heloise L., Asst.Archv.
METROPOLITAN OPERA ASSOCIATION -
ARCHIVES □ New York, NY

Pressley, Linda, Ref.Libn.
U.S. GENERAL SERVICES ADMINISTRATION -
GSA LIBRARY □ Washington, DC

Pressman, Nancy, Leader, Cat. Team
PRINCETON UNIVERSITY - NEAR EAST
COLLECTIONS □ Princeton, NJ

Pressman, Ruth, Asst.Dir.
STANFORD UNIVERSITY - LANE MEDICAL
LIBRARY □ Stanford, CA

Presson, Peggy F., Libn.
U.S. INDUSTRIAL CHEMICALS COMPANY -
LIBRARY □ New York, NY

Preston, Ann, Spec.Coll.Libn.
DREXEL UNIVERSITY LIBRARIES - GENERAL
LIBRARY □ Philadelphia, PA

Preston, Carol, Libn.
HUDSON'S BAY COMPANY - LIBRARY □
Winnipeg, MB

Preston, Caroline, Mss.Libn.
ESSEX INSTITUTE - JAMES DUNCAN PHILLIPS
LIBRARY □ Salem, MA

Preston, Douglas M., Dir., Hist.Soc.
ONEIDA HISTORICAL SOCIETY - LIBRARY □
Utica, NY

Preston, Elizabeth, Asst.Libn.
BRITISH COLUMBIA HYDRO & POWER
AUTHORITY - ENGINEERING LIBRARY □
Vancouver, BC

Preston, Gregor A., Hd., Cat.Dept.
UNIVERSITY OF CALIFORNIA, DAVIS -
GENERAL LIBRARY □ Davis, CA

Preston, Jean F., Cur. of Mss.
PRINCETON UNIVERSITY - RARE BOOKS AND
SPECIAL COLLECTIONS □ Princeton, NJ

Preston, John, Libn.
NEW YORK CITY POLICE DEPARTMENT -
POLICE ACADEMY LIBRARY □ New York, NY

Preston, K.H., Mgr.
ROCKWELL INTERNATIONAL - NEWPORT
BEACH INFORMATION CENTER □ Newport
Beach, CA

Preston, Linda D., Libn.
U.S. NATL. OCEANIC & ATMOSPHERIC ADM. -
ENVIRONMENTAL DATA & INFO. SERV. - NATL.
CLIMATIC CTR. LIBRARY □ Asheville, NC

Preston, Marcia, Hd., Biblog.
UNIVERSITY OF MICHIGAN - DEARBORN
LIBRARY □ Dearborn, MI

Preston, Margaret, Tech.Res.Assoc.
COMMERCIAL UNION INSURANCE COMPANIES
- RISK CONTROL TECHNICAL RESOURCE
CENTER □ Boston, MA

Preston, William, Chf.Libn.
U.S. VETERANS ADMINISTRATION (CT-West
Haven) - MEDICAL CENTER LIBRARY □ West
Haven, CT

Pretlow, Delores Z., Libn.
RICHMOND PUBLIC SCHOOLS - CURRICULUM
MATERIALS CENTER □ Richmond, VA

Prevaux, Carol, Supv.
FLORIDA POWER CORPORATION - CORPORATE
LIBRARY □ St. Petersburg, FL

Prever, Phil, Libn.
NEW HAMPSHIRE VOCATIONAL-TECHNICAL
COLLEGE - LIBRARY □ Claremont, NH

Prevratil, Judith, Hd.
ROCHESTER PUBLIC LIBRARY - SCIENCE AND
TECHNOLOGY DIVISION □ Rochester, NY

Prewitt, Barbara G., Libn.
ROHM & HAAS COMPANY - RESEARCH
DIVISION - INFORMATION SERVICES
DEPARTMENT □ Spring House, PA

Prewitt, Barbara G., Adm.Mgr.
ROHM & HAAS COMPANY - RESEARCH
DIVISION - INFORMATION SERVICES DEPT. -
LIBRARY □ Bristol, PA

Prewitt, Nancy C., Assoc.Dir.
UNIVERSITY OF MISSOURI - WESTERN
HISTORICAL MANUSCRIPT COLLECTION/
STATE HISTORICAL SOCIETY OF MISSOURI □
Columbia, MO

Price, Bernice H., Libn.
PROFESSIONAL GOLFERS' ASSOCIATION OF
AMERICA - LIBRARY □ Palm Beach Gardens, FL

Price, David, Info.Spec.
BURROUGHS WELLCOME COMPANY - LIBRARY
□ Research Triangle Park, NC

Price, George W., Supv.Doc.Ctr.
INSTITUTE OF GAS TECHNOLOGY - TECHNICAL
INFORMATION CENTER □ Chicago, IL

Price, J.A., Sect.Hd.
EXXON RESEARCH AND ENGINEERING
COMPANY - FLORHAM PARK INFORMATION
CENTER† □ Florham Park, NJ

Price, Jan, Libn.
HENNEPIN COUNTY LIBRARY SYSTEM -
GOVERNMENT CENTER INFORMATION LIBRARY
□ Minneapolis, MN

Price, Jane, Ref.Libn.
UNIVERSITY OF BRITISH COLUMBIA -
WOODWARD BIOMEDICAL LIBRARY □
Vancouver, BC

Price, John F., Act.Chf.
LIBRARY OF CONGRESS - SCIENCE &
TECHNOLOGY DIVISION □ Washington, DC

Price, Judy, Lib.Asst.
BRITISH COLUMBIA - MINISTRY OF HEALTH -
LIBRARY □ Victoria, BC

Price, Kathleen, Dir.
UNIVERSITY OF MINNESOTA - LAW LIBRARY □
Minneapolis, MN

Price, L.G., Archv.
TORONTO CITY RECORDS AND ARCHIVES
DIVISION □ Toronto, ON

Price, Margaret, Ref.Libn.
UNIVERSITY OF BRITISH COLUMBIA -
GOVERNMENT PUBLICATIONS & MICROFORMS
DIVISIONS □ Vancouver, BC

Price, May E., Cat.
UNIVERSITY OF CALIFORNIA, DAVIS - HEALTH
SCIENCES LIBRARY □ Davis, CA

Price, Patricia E., Libn.
HAWAII INSTITUTE OF GEOPHYSICS -
LIBRARY □ Honolulu, HI

Price, Ronald R., Co-Dir.
BIOMEDICAL COMPUTING TECHNOLOGY
INFORMATION CENTER □ Nashville, TN

Price, Rose M., Libn.
BRAKELEY, JOHN PRICE JONES, INC. -
LIBRARY† □ New York, NY

Price, Samuel W., Dir.
NATIONAL TOBACCO-TEXTILE MUSEUM -
LIBRARY AND INFORMATION CENTER □
Danville, VA

Price, Sophie, Hd., Cat.Sect.
NORTHWESTERN UNIVERSITY - HEALTH
SCIENCES LIBRARY □ Chicago, IL

Price, Stephanie, Libn.
BEECH-NUT FOODS CORPORATION -
TECHNICAL LIBRARY □ Canajoharie, NY

Price, Whit, Doc. Delivery
CAROLINA LIBRARY SERVICES □ Chapel Hill, NC

Price, William P., Chf., Lib.Serv.
U.S. VETERANS ADMINISTRATION (AZ-
Prescott) - HEALTH SCIENCES LIBRARY □
Prescott, AZ

Price, Wilma, Acq.Libn.
HUGHES AIRCRAFT COMPANY - GROUND
SYSTEMS GROUP - TECHNICAL LIBRARY □
Fullerton, CA

Prichard, Donald, Hd., Tech.Serv.
ERIE COMMUNITY COLLEGE NORTH - LIBRARY
RESOURCES CENTER □ Buffalo, NY

Prichard, Bro. Leo, Asst.Libn.
CONCEPTION ABBEY AND SEMINARY - LIBRARY
□ Conception, MO

Pride, Richard B., Assoc.Dir., MCRMLP
UNIVERSITY OF NEBRASKA MEDICAL CENTER -
MC GOOGAN LIBRARY OF MEDICINE □ Omaha,
NE

Prieditis, Dagnia, Libn.
OMAHA-COUNCIL BLUFFS METROPOLITAN
AREA PLANNING AGENCY (MAPA) - LIBRARY □
Omaha, NE

Priestly, Diana M., Law Libn.
UNIVERSITY OF VICTORIA - LAW LIBRARY† □
Victoria, BC

Prilop, Iona, Libn.
BLUE CROSS/BLUE SHIELD OF GREATER NEW
YORK - REFERENCE LIBRARY □ New York, NY

Primack, Alice, Assoc.Libn.
UNIVERSITY OF FLORIDA - ENGINEERING &
PHYSICS LIBRARY □ Gainesville, FL

Prime, Eugenie, Lib.Dir.
GLENDALE ADVENTIST MEDICAL CENTER -
LIBRARY □ Glendale, CA

Prince, Grace, Libn.
CANADIAN AMATEUR MUSICIANS-MUSICIENS
AMATEURS DU CANADA (CAMMAC) - MUSIC
LIBRARY □ Montreal, PQ

Prince, Grace, Ref.Libn.
MARIANOPOLIS COLLEGE - LIBRARY □ Montreal,
PQ

Prince, Mary R., Reader's Adviser
MISSISSIPPI VALLEY STATE UNIVERSITY -
JAMES HERBERT WHITE LIBRARY □ Itta Bena,
MS

Prince, Phyllis, Mgr.
CHAMPION INTERNATIONAL - CORPORATE
INFORMATION CENTER □ Stamford, CT

Prince, Ruth, Dir.
SHAVER HOSPITAL FOR CHEST DISEASES -
HEALTH SCIENCES LIBRARY □ St. Catharines,
ON

Prince, Wynona, Supv., Day Circ.
LE TOURNEAU COLLEGE - MARGARET ESTES
LIBRARY □ Longview, TX

Princz, Joseph, Assoc.Dir.
CONCORDIA UNIVERSITY - SIR GEORGE
WILLIAMS CAMPUS - NORRIS LIBRARY □
Montreal, PQ

Prine, Stephen, Dir., Div. of Blind
SOUTH CAROLINA STATE LIBRARY □ Columbia,
SC

Pringle, Anne, Hd., Sci. & Psych.Libs.
BRYN MAWR COLLEGE - GEOLOGY LIBRARY □
Bryn Mawr, PA

Pringle, Anne, Hd.Libn.
WAYNE PRESBYTERIAN CHURCH - LIBRARY □
Wayne, PA

Pringle, Robert M., Jr., Hd.Libn.
INTERCOLLEGIATE CENTER FOR NURSING
EDUCATION - LIBRARY □ Spokane, WA

Pringle, Yvonne, Info.Spec.
PPG INDUSTRIES, INC. - CHEMICAL DIVISION -
RESEARCH LIBRARY □ Barberton, OH

Prins, Johanna, Slide Cur.
SYRACUSE UNIVERSITY - E.S. BIRD LIBRARY -
FINE ARTS DEPARTMENT □ Syracuse, NY

Printz, Naomi, Asst.Libn.
XEROX CORPORATION - LIBRARY □ El Segundo,
CA

Prisco, Enzo, Libn.
IMMACULATE CONCEPTION SEMINARY -
LIBRARY □ Mahwah, NJ

Pristash, Kenneth, Audio Libn.
NEW ENGLAND CONSERVATORY OF MUSIC -
HARRIET M. SPAULDING LIBRARY □ Boston, MA

Pritchard, Doris, Hd.Libn.
UNIVERSITY OF MANITOBA - DENTAL LIBRARY
□ Winnipeg, MB

Pritchard, Joseph, Educ.Mtls.Libn.
UNIVERSITY OF WISCONSIN, SUPERIOR - JIM
DAN HILL LIBRARY □ Superior, WI

Pritchard, Mary, District Libn.
U.S. ARMY - CORPS OF ENGINEERS - SEATTLE
DISTRICT - LIBRARY □ Seattle, WA

Pritchard, Russ A., Dir.
MILITARY ORDER OF THE LOYAL LEGION OF
THE UNITED STATES - WAR LIBRARY AND
MUSEUM □ Philadelphia, PA

Pritcher, Pamela N., Libn. of Coll.
TOBACCO INSTITUTE - LIBRARY □ Washington,
DC

Pritchett, John C., Adm.Res.Libn.
UNIVERSITY OF ALABAMA - OFFICE OF
PLANNING AND OPERATIONS -
ADMINISTRATIVE RESEARCH LIBRARY □
University, AL

Pritchett, Margaret, Adm.Asst.
VANDERBILT UNIVERSITY LIBRARY -
TELEVISION NEWS ARCHIVE □ Nashville, TN

Pritchett, Morgan H., Hd.
ENOCH PRATT FREE LIBRARY - MARYLAND
DEPARTMENT □ Baltimore, MD

Pritchett, Myra S., Chf.Libn.
U.S. VETERANS ADMINISTRATION (NH-
Manchester) - MEDICAL CENTER LIBRARY □
Manchester, NH

Pritkin, Joel M., Cur.
MUSIC CENTER OPERATING COMPANY -
ARCHIVES □ Los Angeles, CA

Prival, Herbert, Per.
YESHIVA UNIVERSITY - LANDOWNE-BLOOM
LIBRARY† □ New York, NY

Privat, Jeannette M., A.V.P. & Mgr.
SEATTLE-FIRST NATIONAL BANK - LIBRARY □
Seattle, WA

Privette, Joylyn A., Adm. Clerk
COLORADO STATE DIVISION OF HIGHWAYS -
TECHNICAL LIBRARY □ Denver, CO

Procaccini, Kellie, 2nd Asst. Law Libn.
RHODE ISLAND STATE LAW LIBRARY □
Providence, RI

Prochovnick, Ammiel, Asst.Libn., Res.Serv.
CRERAR (John) LIBRARY □ Chicago, IL

Procopio, C.E., Dir. of Law Libs.
LIBERTY MUTUAL INSURANCE COMPANY - LAW
LIBRARY □ Boston, MA

Proctor, David, Asst.Libn.Pub.Serv.
JENKINS (Theodore F.) MEMORIAL LAW
LIBRARY COMPANY - LIBRARY □ Philadelphia, PA

Proctor, Esther W., Libn.
MANCHESTER HISTORICAL SOCIETY - LIBRARY
□ Manchester, MA

Proctor, Letitia B., Libn.
BROOKS MEMORIAL ART GALLERY - LIBRARY†
□ Memphis, TN

Proctor, Martha Jane, Pub.Lib.Cons.
STATE LIBRARY OF FLORIDA □ Tallahassee, FL

Proehl, Karl H., Map Libn.
PENNSYLVANIA STATE UNIVERSITY - MAPS
SECTION □ University Park, PA

Progar, James S., Asst.Dir.Adm.
MISSISSIPPI STATE LIBRARY COMMISSION □
Jackson, MS

Promen, Peter J., Libn.
JOHNS HOPKINS UNIVERSITY - SCHOOL OF
ADVANCED INTERNATIONAL STUDIES -
SYDNEY R. & ELSA W. MASON LIBRARY □
Washington, DC

Pront, Marsha, Hd.Libn.
PROSKAUER, ROSE, GOETZ & MENDELSOHN -
LIBRARY □ New York, NY

Proper, David R., Libn.
HISTORIC DEERFIELD, INC. - HENRY N. FLYNT
LIBRARY - POCUMTUCK VALLEY MEMORIAL
ASSOCIATION □ Deerfield, MA

Propp, Dale, Mgr.Pub.Serv.Dept.
TEXAS STATE LIBRARY - INFORMATION
SERVICES DIVISION □ Austin, TX

Proscino, Patricia, Ref./Acq.
BALCH INSTITUTE FOR ETHNIC STUDIES -
LIBRARY □ Philadelphia, PA

Pross, Cynthia, Asst.Libn.
MUTUAL OF NEW YORK - LIBRARY/
INFORMATION SERVICE □ New York, NY

Prosser, Judy, Archv./Registrar
MUSEUM OF WESTERN COLORADO - ARCHIVES
□ Grand Junction, CO

Prottsman, Mary Fran, Chf., Lib.Serv.
U.S. VETERANS ADMINISTRATION (AR-
Fayetteville) - MEDICAL CENTER LIBRARY □
Fayetteville, AR

Protzman, Lois, Libn.
FORT HAMILTON-HUGHES MEMORIAL
HOSPITAL CENTER - SOHN MEMORIAL HEALTH
SERVICES LIBRARY □ Hamilton, OH

Proudfit, Elisabeth R., Mgr., Info.Ctr.
ADVERTISING RESEARCH FOUNDATION -
LIBRARY □ New York, NY

Proulx, Agathe, Libn.
CANADIAN MUSIC CENTRE - LIBRARY† □
Montreal, PQ

Proulx, Steven, Chf.Libn.
OTTAWA CITIZEN - LIBRARY □ Ottawa, ON

Prout, Wilson, Asst. to Dir.
SUNY AT BUFFALO - HEALTH SCIENCES
LIBRARY □ Buffalo, NY

Prudhomme, Bernard, Mgr.
COCA-COLA COMPANY - TECHNICAL
INFORMATION SERVICES □ Atlanta, GA

Prue, Holly, Asst. Campus Libn.
CENTENNIAL COLLEGE OF APPLIED ARTS &
TECHNOLOGY - WARDEN WOODS CAMPUS
RESOURCE CENTRE □ Scarborough, ON

Pruett, Barbara J., Cat.
U.S. INTERNATIONAL TRADE COMMISSION -
LIBRARY □ Washington, DC

Pruett, Nancy, Subj.Spec.
U.S. DEPT OF ENERGY - SANDIA NATL.
LABORATORIES - TECHNICAL LIBRARY □
Albuquerque, NM

Prugh, Daniel F., Dir., Hist./Pub.Rel.
FRANKLIN COUNTY HISTORICAL SOCIETY -
CENTER OF SCIENCE & INDUSTRY - CLEMENTS
HISTORY MEMORIAL LIBRARY □ Columbus, OH

Pruhs, Sharon, Ref.Libn.
LOS ANGELES COUNTY/UNIVERSITY OF
SOUTHERN CALIFORNIA MEDICAL CENTER -
MEDICAL LIBRARIES □ Los Angeles, CA

Pruitt, John E., Jr.
SPOTSYLVANIA HISTORICAL ASSOCIATION,
INC. - RESEARCH MUSEUM AND LIBRARY □
Spotsylvania, VA

Pruna, Isabel, Cat.
INTER-AMERICAN DEFENSE COLLEGE -
LIBRARY □ Washington, DC

Pruter, Nancy, Supv.Cat.
NATIONAL SAFETY COUNCIL - LIBRARY □
Chicago, IL

Pruzin, Christine A., Libn.
INSURANCE INSTITUTE FOR HIGHWAY SAFETY
- LIBRARY □ Washington, DC

Ptak, T.M., Tech.Libn.
SCM CORPORATION - GLIDDEN COATINGS &
RESINS DIV./DURKEE FOODS DIV. -
TECHNICAL INFORMATION SERVICES □
Strongsville, OH

Puckett, E. Ann, Asst.Rd.Serv.Libn.
SOUTHERN ILLINOIS UNIVERSITY,
CARBONDALE - SCHOOL OF LAW LIBRARY □
Carbondale, IL

Puckett, Linda B., Asst.Libn.
LUTHERAN THEOLOGICAL SOUTHERN
SEMINARY - LONEBERGER MEMORIAL LIBRARY
□ Columbia, SC

Puckett, Marianne, Circ.Libn.
LOUISIANA STATE UNIVERSITY MEDICAL
CENTER - SCHOOL OF MEDICINE IN
SHREVEPORT - LIBRARY □ Shreveport, LA

Puckett, Robert A., Dir.
WICHITA-SEDGWICK COUNTY HISTORICAL
MUSEUM - LIBRARY & ARCHIVES □ Wichita, KS

Puffer, David B., Lib.Dir.
JOHNSON & WALES COLLEGE - PAUL
FRITZSCHE CULINARY LIBRARY □ Providence,
RI

Puffer, Karen J., Libn.
U.S. NASA - DRYDEN FLIGHT RESEARCH
CENTER - LIBRARY □ Edwards, CA

Pugh, Constance H., Libn.
SCHUYLKILL COUNTY LAW LIBRARY □ Pottsville,
PA

Pugh, M.J., Info.Spec.
NORTH CAROLINA STATE SCIENCE AND
TECHNOLOGY RESEARCH CENTER □ Research
Triangle Park, NC

Pugh, Mary Jo, Assoc.Archv.
UNIVERSITY OF MICHIGAN - MICHIGAN
HISTORICAL COLLECTIONS - BENTLEY
HISTORICAL LIBRARY □ Ann Arbor, MI

Pugh, Ronnie, Ref.Libn.
COUNTRY MUSIC FOUNDATION - LIBRARY AND
MEDIA CENTER □ Nashville, TN

Pughsley, Fran
ALSTON, MILLER AND GAINES - LAW LIBRARY □
Atlanta, GA

Pugiber, Genevieve, Documentaliste
FRENCH LIBRARY IN BOSTON, INC. □ Boston,
MA

Pugliano, Emilie, Libn.
SHAWMUT BANK OF BOSTON, N.A. - LIBRARY □
Boston, MA

Puhek, Esther L., Libn.
KENOSHA MEMORIAL HOSPITAL - HEALTH
SCIENCES LIBRARY □ Kenosha, WI

Pujat, Duressa, Libn.
HACKENSACK HOSPITAL - MEDICAL LIBRARY†
□ Hackensack, NJ

Pullen, Mary L., Lib.Mgr.
SOUTHERN RESEARCH INSTITUTE - THOMAS
W. MARTIN MEMORIAL LIBRARY □ Birmingham,
AL

Pulleyblank, Miss M., Libn.
GEORGE BROWN COLLEGE OF APPLIED ARTS &
TECHNOLOGY - LIBRARY □ Toronto, ON

Pullins, Melissa, Adm.Asst.
HAMMER, SILER, GEORGE ASSOCIATES -
LIBRARY† □ Washington, DC

Pullum, Thomas W., Dir.
UNIVERSITY OF WASHINGTON - CENTER FOR
STUDIES IN DEMOGRAPHY AND ECOLOGY -
LIBRARY □ Seattle, WA

Pulyk, Marcia, Ref. & Info.Libn.
CANADA - LABOUR CANADA - LIBRARY □
Ottawa, ON

Pumroy, Eric, Mss.Cur.
INDIANA HISTORICAL SOCIETY - WILLIAM
HENRY SMITH MEMORIAL LIBRARY □
Indianapolis, IN

Pun, Philomena, Ref.Libn.
CANADIAN IMPERIAL BANK OF COMMERCE -
INFORMATION CENTRE □ Toronto, ON

Pundy, Paul, Dir.
UKRAINIAN MEDICAL ASSOCIATION OF NORTH
AMERICA - MEDICAL ARCHIVES AND LIBRARY†
□ Chicago, IL

Pupius, Mrs. Nijole K., Tech.Libn.
UNION CARBIDE CORPORATION - FILMS-
PACKAGING DIVISION - TECHNICAL LIBRARY □
Chicago, IL

Purcell, Donald, Libn.
NOVA SCOTIA - DEPARTMENT OF
DEVELOPMENT - LIBRARY □ Halifax, NS

Purcell, John
SOUTHERN OREGON STATE COLLEGE - LIBRARY
□ Ashland, OR

Purcell, Judie, Ref./Res.Libn.
DUKE UNIVERSITY - SCHOOL OF LAW LIBRARY
□ Durham, NC

Purdy, James H., State Rec.Adm.
NEW MEXICO STATE RECORDS CENTER AND
ARCHIVES - DOROTHY WOODWARD RESEARCH
ROOM □ Santa Fe, NM

Purnell, O. James, III, Dir.
UNIVERSITY OF CONNECTICUT - PHARMACY
LIBRARY AND LEARNING CENTER □ Storrs, CT
Pursch, Lenore D., Med.Libn.
ST. ELIZABETH MEDICAL CENTER - HEALTH
SCIENCES LIBRARY □ Dayton, OH
Purse, Sheila, Hd.Libn.
CANADIAN CONSULATE GENERAL - LIBRARY □
New York, NY
Pursell, Joan, Life Sci.Ref.Libn.
UNIVERSITY OF CALIFORNIA, SANTA BARBARA
- SCIENCES-ENGINEERING LIBRARY □ Santa
Barbara, CA
Purser, Pat, Mgr., Tech.Lib.
CUBIC CORPORATION - LIBRARY □ San Diego,
CA
Purvis, Christine, Regional Dir.
CANADIAN MUSIC CENTRE - PRAIRIE REGION
LIBRARY □ Calgary, AB
Purvis, Harry, First Asst.
CHICAGO PUBLIC LIBRARY CULTURAL CENTER
- FINE ARTS DIVISION - MUSIC SECTION □
Chicago, IL
Purvis, Marjorie A., Commun.Res.Supv.
METROPOLITAN LIFE INSURANCE COMPANY -
LIBRARY □ Ottawa, ON
Puryear, Pamela E., Libn.
NORTH CAROLINA STATE UNIVERSITY -
FOREST RESOURCES LIBRARY □ Raleigh, NC
Purzycki, Mrs. M.H., Ref.Libn.
BELL TELEPHONE LABORATORIES, INC. -
TECHNICAL LIBRARY □ Piscataway, NJ
Pusey, Henry C., Hd.
U.S. NAVY - NAVAL RESEARCH LABORATORY -
SHOCK AND VIBRATION INFORMATION
CENTER □ Washington, DC
Putney, R. Taylor, Coord., Pub.Serv.
WRIGHT STATE UNIVERSITY - HEALTH
SCIENCES LIBRARY □ Dayton, OH
Puzzo, Phil, Ref.Libn.
PALOMAR COLLEGE - PHIL H. PUTNAM
MEMORIAL LIBRARY □ San Marcos, CA
Pyke, Carol J., Dir. of Lib.
URBAN INSTITUTE - LIBRARY □ Washington, DC
Pyles, Rodney A., Dir.
WEST VIRGINIA STATE DEPARTMENT OF
CULTURE AND HISTORY - ARCHIVES AND
HISTORY LIBRARY □ Charleston, WV
Pyne, Timothy, Libn.
AMERICAN JUDICATURE SOCIETY - RESEARCH
LIBRARY □ Chicago, IL
Pyrch, Mary Ellen, Ref.Libn.
UNIVERSITY OF ALBERTA - SCIENCE LIBRARY
□ Edmonton, AB

Q

Quah, Swee-Lan, Cat.
OHIO UNIVERSITY - SOUTHEAST ASIA
COLLECTION □ Athens, OH
Quam, Kirsten, Tech.Serv.Coord.
WISHARD (William N.) MEMORIAL HOSPITAL -
PROFESSIONAL LIBRARY/MEDIA SERVICES □
Indianapolis, IN
Quan, Alvina M., Ser.Libn.
FLORES (Nieves M.) MEMORIAL LIBRARY □
Agana, GU
Quantz, Sharon E., Libn.
MOUNTAIN VIEW BIBLE COLLEGE - LIBRARY □
Didsbury, AB
Quarterman, Lee, Assoc.Dir.
GEORGIA STATE UNIVERSITY - SMALL
BUSINESS DEVELOPMENT CENTER □ Atlanta,
GA
Quartey, Josephine, Info.Ret.Spec.
MERCK & COMPANY, INC. - CALGON
CORPORATION - INFORMATION CENTER □
Pittsburgh, PA
Quashen, Anne J., Exec.Dir.
NEW YORK STATE TRIAL LAWYERS
ASSOCIATION - LIBRARY □ New York, NY

Quay, Caren K., Regional Cons.
KAISER-PERMANENTE MEDICAL CENTERS,
NORTHERN CALIFORNIA REGION - REGIONAL
HEALTH LIBRARY SERVICES □ Oakland, CA
Quealey, Mrs. M., Supv., Lib.Serv.
HURONIA HISTORICAL PARKS - RESOURCE
CENTRE □ Midland, ON
Quebengco, Purificacion, Acq.Libn.
PACE UNIVERSITY - LIBRARY □ New York, NY
Queen, Margaret, Supv.Libn.
SAN DIEGO PUBLIC LIBRARY - HISTORY &
WORLD AFFAIRS SECTION □ San Diego, CA
Quement, Shirley, First Asst.
NEW YORK PUBLIC LIBRARY - MID-
MANHATTAN LIBRARY - HISTORY AND SOCIAL
SCIENCES DEPARTMENT □ New York, NY
Queripel, June, Staff Chm.
CUMBERLAND COUNTY HISTORICAL SOCIETY -
LIBRARY □ Greenwich, NJ
Quezada-Aragon, Manuela, Info.Spec.
ERIC CLEARINGHOUSE ON RURAL EDUCATION
AND SMALL SCHOOLS □ Las Cruces, NM
Quick, Linda M., Libn.
TEMPLE UNIVERSITY HOSPITAL - HEALTH
SCIENCES CENTER - DEPARTMENT OF
RADIOLOGY - LIBRARY □ Philadelphia, PA
Quick, Richard C., Dir. of Coll.Libs.
SUNY - COLLEGE AT GENESEO - MILNE LIBRARY
□ Geneseo, NY
Quick, Mrs. Young Hi, Ref.Libn.
WESTERN ELECTRIC COMPANY, INC. - PUBLIC
RELATIONS LIBRARY† □ New York, NY
Quigley, Elizabeth-Anne, Law Libn.
UNIVERSITY OF SAN FRANCISCO - SCHOOL OF
LAW LIBRARY □ San Francisco, CA
Quinlan, Nora J., Art/Irish Studies
UNIVERSITY OF KANSAS - DEPARTMENT OF
SPECIAL COLLECTIONS □ Lawrence, KS
Quinlivan, Mary, Libn.
ENVIRONMENTAL PROTECTION AGENCY -
NATIONAL ENFORCEMENT INVESTIGATIONS -
LIBRARY □ Denver, CO
Quinn, Al, Div.Dir.
TEXAS STATE LIBRARY - INFORMATION
SERVICES DIVISION □ Austin, TX
Quinn, Alicia, Libn.
HOUSTON LIGHTING & POWER COMPANY -
LIBRARY □ Houston, TX
Quinn, Allan, Dir.Info.Serv.Div.
TEXAS STATE LIBRARY □ Austin, TX
Quinn, Catherine, Cat.
NATIONAL GALLERY OF ART - LIBRARY □
Washington, DC
Quinn, Delores I., Libn.
OAK FOREST HOSPITAL - PROFESSIONAL
LIBRARY □ Oak Forest, IL
Quinn, Elizabeth, Asst.Libn.
GENERAL DYNAMICS CORPORATION - PUBLIC
AFFAIRS LIBRARY □ St. Louis, MO
Quinn, Frances M., Chf.
U.S. AIR FORCE - ARMAMENT DIVISION, AIR
FORCE ARMAMENT LABORATORY - TECHNICAL
LIBRARY □ Eglin AFB, FL
Quinn, Jane Taggart, Libn.
DELAWARE COUNTY PLANNING COMMISSION -
LIBRARY AND DATA SECTION □ Media, PA
Quinn, Karen Takle, Dir.
IBM CORPORATION - GENERAL PRODUCTS
DIVISION - INFORMATION/LIBRARY/
LEARNING CENTER □ San Jose, CA
Quinn, Kevin C., Act.Hd.
INDIANA UNIVERSITY - BIOLOGY LIBRARY □
Bloomington, IN
Quinn, Linda Sue, Asst.Cat.
UNION THEOLOGICAL SEMINARY IN VIRGINIA
- LIBRARY □ Richmond, VA
Quinn, Michael, Govt.Pubn.Libn.
GRACELAND COLLEGE - FREDERICK MADISON
SMITH LIBRARY □ Lamoni, IA
Quinn, Patrick M., Univ.Archv.
NORTHWESTERN UNIVERSITY - ARCHIVES □
Evanston, IL

Quinn, Susan, Tech.Info.Spec.
BAUSCH & LOMB, INC. - SOFLENS DIVISION -
SOFLENS TECHNICAL INFORMATION CENTER □
Rochester, NY
Quint, Barbara, Hd. of Ref.Serv.
RAND CORPORATION - LIBRARY □ Santa
Monica, CA
Quintal, Cecile C., Assoc.Dir.
UNIVERSITY OF NEW MEXICO - MEDICAL
CENTER LIBRARY □ Albuquerque, NM
Quintana, Emmanuel, Lib.Acq.
PAN AMERICAN HEALTH ORGANIZATION -
DOCUMENTATION AND HEALTH INFORMATION
OFFICE† □ Washington, DC
Quiring, Virginia M., Assoc. Dean Pub.Serv.
KANSAS STATE UNIVERSITY - FARRELL
LIBRARY □ Manhattan, KS
Quist, Edwin A., Libn.
PEABODY CONSERVATORY OF MUSIC -
LIBRARY □ Baltimore, MD
Qureshi, Mrs. Anwar S., Map Libn.
UNIVERSITY OF REGINA - MAP LIBRARY □
Regina, SK
Quy, Le Duy, Cat. & Clas.
CEGEP DE TROIS-RIVIERES - BIBLIOTHEQUE □
Trois-Rivieres, PQ

R

Rabasca, David L., Assoc.Libn.
MAINE STATE LAW AND LEGISLATIVE
REFERENCE LIBRARY □ Augusta, ME
Rabb, Mary, Libn.
CHICAGO ZOOLOGICAL PARK - BROOKFIELD
ZOO - LIBRARY □ Brookfield, IL
Rabek, Teresa, Libn.
POLISH INSTITUTE OF ARTS AND SCIENCES IN
CANADA - POLISH LIBRARY □ Montreal, PQ
Rabenstein, Bernard H., Acq.Libn.
HEBREW UNION COLLEGE - JEWISH INSTITUTE
OF RELIGION - KLAU LIBRARY □ Cincinnati, OH
Raber, Nevin W., Hd.
INDIANA UNIVERSITY - BUSINESS LIBRARY □
Bloomington, IN
Raber, Steve, Ref.Libn.
DAVIS POLK & WARDWELL - LIBRARY □ New
York, NY
Rabideau, Irvin, Mss.Spec.
DETROIT PUBLIC LIBRARY - BURTON
HISTORICAL COLLECTION □ Detroit, MI
Rabin, Judy, Asst. Music Libn.
UNIVERSITY OF ILLINOIS - MUSIC LIBRARY □
Urbana, IL
Rabin, Rose Marie, Info.Dir.
SOUTHERN CALIFORNIA INSTITUTE OF
ARCHITECTURE - ARCHITECTURE AND URBAN
PLANNING LIBRARY □ Santa Monica, CA
Rabins, Joan, Archv.
WAYNE STATE UNIVERSITY - ARCHIVES OF
LABOR AND URBAN AFFAIRS/UNIVERSITY
ARCHIVES □ Detroit, MI
Rabjohns, Ann, Chf.
DETROIT PUBLIC LIBRARY - LANGUAGE AND
LITERATURE DEPARTMENT □ Detroit, MI
Raby, Eva, Libn.
MC GILL UNIVERSITY - SOCIAL WORK LIBRARY
□ Montreal, PQ
Racca, Claudia F., Rec.Mgt.Off.
LOUISIANA STATE OFFICE OF THE SECRETARY
OF STATE - STATE ARCHIVES AND RECORDS
SERVICE □ Baton Rouge, LA
Racheter, Richard, Educ.Libn.
PACE UNIVERSITY - LIBRARY □ New York, NY
Rachlin, Deborah T., Asst.
MAIN (Chas. T.), INC. - LIBRARY □ Boston, MA
Rachow, Louis A., Cur.Libn.
WALTER HAMPDEN - EDWIN BOOTH THEATER
COLLECTION AND LIBRARY □ New York, NY
Racicot, L., Asst. & Cat.
COLLEGE MILITAIRE ROYAL DE ST-JEAN -
LIBRARY □ St. Jean, PQ

Racine, Rose, Libn.
CHAMBER OF COMMERCE OF THE UNITED
STATES OF AMERICA - LIBRARY □ Washington,
DC

Racioppo, Marie, Acq.Libn.
PACE UNIVERSITY - SCHOOL OF LAW LIBRARY
□ White Plains, NY

Raciti, Madeline L., Ref. & Cat.
GENERAL ELECTRIC COMPANY - CORPORATE
RESEARCH & DEVELOPMENT - WHITNEY
LIBRARY □ Schenectady, NY

Radatz, Clark, Res.Anl.
WISCONSIN STATE LEGISLATIVE REFERENCE
BUREAU □ Madison, WI

Radcliffe, Jane E., Musm. Registrar
MAINE STATE MUSEUM - RESOURCE CENTER □
Augusta, ME

Rader, Jennette, Libn.
UNIVERSITY OF CHICAGO - HUMAN
RESOURCES CENTER - A.G. BUSH LIBRARY □
Chicago, IL

Rader, Jennette S., Bus.Econ.Libn.
UNIVERSITY OF CHICAGO - BUSINESS/
ECONOMICS LIBRARY □ Chicago, IL

Rader, Margaret, Asst.Dir.
OREGON STATE LIBRARY - SERVICES FOR THE
BLIND AND PHYSICALLY HANDICAPPED □
Salem, OR

Rader, Robin, Ref.Libn.
SPRINGFIELD-GREENE COUNTY PUBLIC
LIBRARIES - EDWARD M. SHEPARD MEMORIAL
ROOM □ Springfield, MO

Radford, Elizabeth, Libn.
QUESTOR ASSOCIATES - LIBRARY □ San
Francisco, CA

Radha, Swami Sivananda
YASODHARA ASHRAM SOCIETY - LIBRARY □
Kootenay Bay, BC

Radigan, Patricia, Ref.Libn.
NEW YORK UNIVERSITY - GRADUATE SCHOOL
OF BUSINESS ADMINISTRATION - LIBRARY □
New York, NY

Rado, Stuart Alan, Exec.Dir.
NATIONAL NETWORK OF YOUTH ADVISORY
BOARDS, INC. - TECHNICAL ASSISTANCE
LIBRARY □ Miami Beach, FL

Radovancev, Estela, Lib./Media Spec.
NATIONAL COLLEGE OF EDUCATION - CHICAGO
CAMPUS LIBRARY □ Chicago, IL

Radvanyi, Helga, Mgr.
ALBERTA RESEARCH COUNCIL - ALBERTA OIL
SANDS INFORMATION CENTRE □ Edmonton, AB

Radwan, Eleanor, Sr. Principal Libn.
NEW YORK PUBLIC LIBRARY - MID-
MANHATTAN LIBRARY - GENERAL REFERENCE
SERVICE/EDUCATION □ New York, NY

Radway, Gerry, Libn.
GENERAL ELECTRIC COMPANY - ELECTRONICS
PARK LIBRARY □ Syracuse, NY

Radway, Mrs. Robert, Math/Natural Sci.Libn.
INSTITUTE FOR ADVANCED STUDY -
LIBRARIES □ Princeton, NJ

Rae, Ann, Asst. Law Libn.
UNIVERSITY OF ALBERTA - LAW LIBRARY □
Edmonton, AB

Rae, Jay, Regional Archv.
WASHINGTON STATE OFFICE OF SECRETARY
OF STATE - DIVISION OF ARCHIVES AND
RECORD MANAGEMENT □ Olympia, WA

Rafael, Ruth, Archv./Libn.
MAGNES (Judah L.) MEMORIAL MUSEUM -
WESTERN JEWISH HISTORY CENTER □
Berkeley, CA

Rafferty, Eve, Acq.Libn.
NATIONAL RETIRED TEACHERS ASSN.-
AMERICAN ASSN. OF RETIRED PERSONS -
NATL. GERONTOLOGY RESOURCE CTR. □
Washington, DC

Rafferty, Josephine, Tech.Libn.
U.S. NAVY - NAVAL SHIPYARD (Portsmouth) -
TECHNICAL LIBRARY □ Portsmouth, NH

Ragle, Mr. J.L., Lab.Dir.
ORANGE COUNTY SHERIFF/CORONER -
FORENSIC SCIENCE SERVICES LIBRARY □
Santa Ana, CA

Ragsdale, Jack, Co-Libn.
BERTRAND RUSSELL SOCIETY, INC. - LIBRARY
□ Chicago, IL

Ragsdale, Richard, Sr.Libn.
OAKLAND PUBLIC LIBRARY - SCIENCE/
SOCIOLOGY DIVISION □ Oakland, CA

Ragusa, Isa, Act.Dir.
PRINCETON UNIVERSITY - DEPARTMENT OF
ART & ARCHAEOLOGY - INDEX OF CHRISTIAN
ART □ Princeton, NJ

Rahal, Patricia, Libn.
COLLEGE OF TRADES AND TECHNOLOGY -
LIBRARY □ St. John's, NF

Rahal, Patricia, Libn.
COLLEGE OF TRADES AND TECHNOLOGY -
MEDICAL LIBRARY □ St. John's, NF

Rahe, Debbie, Lib.Ck.
LARNED STATE HOSPITAL - STAFF LIBRARY □
Larned, KS

Rahe, Emily, Lit. Searcher
DOW CHEMICAL COMPANY - MERRELL DOW
PHARMACEUTICALS, INC. - RESEARCH CENTER
LIBRARY □ Cincinnati, OH

Rahn, Rodney, Asst.
BEIHOFF MUSIC CORPORATION - SHEET MUSIC
DEPARTMENT □ Milwaukee, WI

Rai, Priya, Chf., Tech.Proc.
CENTRAL CONNECTICUT STATE COLLEGE -
ELIHU BURRITT LIBRARY □ New Britain, CT

Raiche, Steven J., Dir.
NEW YORK STATE PARKS AND RECREATION -
DIVISION FOR HISTORIC PRESERVATION -
FIELD SERVICES BUREAU - LIBRARY □ Albany,
NY

Raichman, Sherwin, Hd.
ST. LAWRENCE COLLEGE OF APPLIED ARTS
AND TECHNOLOGY - LEARNING RESOURCE
CENTRE □ Kingston, ON

Raidt, Mrs. Jack, Dir. of Lib.Serv.
NORTH PARK BAPTIST CHURCH - LIBRARY □
Sherman, TX

Raiford, Drusilla, Asst.Libn
ENERGY RESOURCES COMPANY - TECHNICAL
INFORMATION CENTER □ Cambridge, MA

Railo, Barbara, Hd.Libn.
MANNES COLLEGE OF MUSIC - HARRY
SCHERMAN LIBRARY □ New York, NY

Raine, Marjorie, Lib.Asst.Sr.
NORTHROP CORPORATION - VENTURA
DIVISION - TECHNICAL INFORMATION
CENTER □ Newbury Park, CA

Raines, Addie, Acq.Libn.
SIMPSON COLLEGE - START-KILGOUR
MEMORIAL LIBRARY □ San Francisco, CA

Raines, Elaine Y., Libn.
ARIZONA DAILY STAR - LIBRARY □ Tucson, AZ

Raines, Ruth, Adm.Asst.Gen.Serv.
UNIVERSITY OF CONNECTICUT - LIBRARY □
Storrs, CT

Raines, Sally, Libn.
U.S. DEPT. OF THE INTERIOR - OFFICE OF
REGIONAL SOLICITOR - LAW LIBRARY □
Denver, CO

Rainey, Laura J., Mgr.
ROCKWELL INTERNATIONAL - ROCKETDYNE
DIVISION - TECHNICAL INFORMATION
CENTER □ Canoga Park, CA

Rainey, Susan, Ranke Proj.Libn.
SYRACUSE UNIVERSITY - GEORGE ARENTS
RESEARCH LIBRARY FOR SPECIAL
COLLECTIONS □ Syracuse, NY

Rains, Marion E., Libn.
WILLIAM PENN COLLEGE - WILCOX LIBRARY -
SPECIAL COLLECTIONS □ Oskaloosa, IA

Raisor, Douglas, Supv.
KENTUCKY STATE DEPARTMENT FOR HUMAN
RESOURCES - LIBRARY □ Frankfort, KY

Rait, Ann, Libn.
BURNS FRY LIMITED - RESEARCH LIBRARY □
Toronto, ON

Raitt, Mildred, Chf., Acq.Serv.
SMITHSONIAN INSTITUTION LIBRARIES □
Washington, DC

Raker, Colleen, Hd.Cat.
UNIVERSITY OF PENNSYLVANIA - BIDDLE LAW
LIBRARY □ Philadelphia, PA

Ralston, Barbara, Chf.
U.S. DEFENSE LOGISTICS AGENCY -
HEADQUARTERS LIBRARY □ Alexandria, VA

Ralston, Charles A., Tech.Serv.Libn.
U.S. ARMY - MILITARY ACADEMY - LIBRARY □
West Point, NY

Ralston, Jack L., Libn.
UNIVERSITY OF MISSOURI, KANSAS CITY -
CONSERVATORY LIBRARY □ Kansas City, MO

Ramage, Patricia, Ser.Libn.
UNIVERSITY OF SOUTH ALABAMA - COLLEGE
OF MEDICINE - BIOMEDICAL LIBRARY □ Mobile,
AL

Ramage, Sue, Libn.
INDIANA UNIVERSITY - FINE ARTS LIBRARY □
Bloomington, IN

Raman, Arsella, Ser.Libn.
STANFORD LINEAR ACCELERATOR CENTER -
LIBRARY □ Menlo Park, CA

Raman, Dr. R.V.
BATTELLE-COLUMBUS LABORATORIES -
RAPIDLY SOLIDIFIED MATERIALS (RaSoMat) -
RESOURCE CENTER □ Columbus, OH

Ramavataram, S., Lit. Scanner
U.S. OAK RIDGE NATL. LABORATORY -
NUCLEAR DATA PROJECT† □ Oak Ridge, TN

Ramey, D., Cat.Libn.
LOS ANGELES TRADE-TECHNICAL COLLEGE -
LIBRARY □ Los Angeles, CA

Ramirez, Eriana, Acq.
ROCKWELL INTERNATIONAL - ENERGY
SYSTEMS GROUP - LIBRARY □ Canoga Park, CA

Ramirez, Irma, Music Libn.
UNIVERSITY OF PUERTO RICO - MAYAGUEZ
CAMPUS - LIBRARY □ Mayaguez, PR

Ramirez, Lilliam, Circ.Libn.
UNIVERSITY OF PUERTO RICO - MAYAGUEZ
CAMPUS - LIBRARY □ Mayaguez, PR

Ramirez, Myrna Y., Libn.
PUERTO RICO DEPARTMENT OF HEALTH -
RAMON EMETERIO BETANCES MEDICAL
LIBRARY □ Mayaguez, PR

Ramirez, Patricia
WESTERN PUBLISHING COMPANY, INC. -
CORPORATE TRAINING CENTER LIBRARY □
Racine, WI

Ramkey, Carol, Ref.
SALISBURY STATE COLLEGE - BLACKWELL
LIBRARY □ Salisbury, MD

Ramm, Dorothy, Per./Ref.Libn.
NORTHWESTERN UNIVERSITY -
TRANSPORTATION LIBRARY □ Evanston, IL

Ramma, Kamra, Hd.Libn.
CANADA - INDIAN & NORTHERN AFFAIRS
CANADA - DEPARTMENTAL LIBRARY □ Ottawa,
ON

Ramos, Anne, Libn.
TEXAS STATE LIBRARY - LIBRARY SCIENCE
COLLECTION □ Austin, TX

Ramsay, Jane, Rec.Res.
UNITED PRESBYTERIAN CHURCH IN THE U.S.A.
- PRESBYTERIAN HISTORICAL SOCIETY -
LIBRARY □ Philadelphia, PA

Ramsey, Carol, Cat.Libn.
UNIVERSITY OF GEORGIA - LAW LIBRARY □
Athens, GA

Ramulus, Carl, Libn.
ELECTRIC RAILROADERS' ASSOCIATION -
SPRAGUE MEMORIAL LIBRARY† □ New York, NY

Ranadive, Mrs. Ujwal, Tech.Libn.
BURNS AND ROE, INC. - TECHNICAL LIBRARY □
Oradell, NJ

Rand, Jane, Dir. of Lib.Serv.
BRATTLEBORO RETREAT - MEDICAL LIBRARY □ Brattleboro, VT

Rand, Paula, Libn.
MEMOREX CORPORATION - TECHNICAL INFORMATION CENTER □ Santa Clara, CA

Rand, Robin M., Dir., Lib.Serv.
MAINE MEDICAL CENTER - LIBRARY □ Portland, ME

Randall, Ann K., Asst.Univ.Libn.
BROWN UNIVERSITY - SCIENCES LIBRARY □ Providence, RI

Randall, Barbara, Coord.Instr.Sup.Serv.
PHOENIX ELEMENTARY SCHOOLS - DISTRICT NO. 1 - CURRICULUM MEDIA CENTER □ Phoenix, AZ

Randall, James, Dir.
WASHINGTON STATE SCHOOL FOR THE DEAF - LEARNING RESOURCE CENTER □ Vancouver, WA

Randall, Lilian M.C., Kpr. of Mss.
WALTERS ART GALLERY - LIBRARY □ Baltimore, MD

Randall, Phoebe, Circ.Libn.
MARSHALL UNIVERSITY - SCHOOL OF MEDICINE - HEALTH SCIENCE LIBRARIES □ Huntington, WV

Randel, Jo Stewart, Dir.
CARSON COUNTY SQUARE HOUSE MUSEUM - INFORMATION CENTER □ Panhandle, TX

Randich, Karla M., Dir., Pub.Serv.
CALIFORNIA WESTERN LAW SCHOOL - LIBRARY □ San Diego, CA

Randle, Melvia E., Bindery Asst.
SOUTHWEST TEXAS STATE UNIVERSITY - LEARNING RESOURCES CENTER □ San Marcos, TX

Randlett, Alice L., Acq.Libn.
UNIVERSITY OF WISCONSIN, STEVENS POINT - JAMES H. ALBERTSON CENTER FOR LEARNING RESOURCES □ Stevens Point, WI

Randolph, Adrijana Panoska, Dir./Libn.
MACEDONIAN ETHNIC LIBRARY □ Grosse Pointe Woods, MI

Randolph, Irene, Field Note Spec.
FLORIDA STATE DEPT. OF NATURAL RESOURCES - DIV. OF STATE LANDS - BUREAU OF STATE LAND MANAGEMENT - TITLE SECTION □ Tallahassee, FL

Randolph, Virginia, Hd.Libn.
PEPPERDINE UNIVERSITY - LIBRARY - SPECIAL COLLECTIONS □ Malibu, CA

Raney, Allan, Asst.Libn.
NEW YORK STATE LIBRARY - SCIENCES/ HEALTH SCIENCES/TECHNOLOGY REFERENCE SERVICES □ Albany, NY

Raney, Dr. Leon, Dean of Lib.
SOUTH DAKOTA STATE UNIVERSITY - HILTON M. BRIGGS LIBRARY □ Brookings, SD

Ranger, Lydia S., Hd.Libn.
HAWAII STATE LIBRARY - STATE LIBRARY FOR THE BLIND AND PHYSICALLY HANDICAPPED □ Honolulu, HI

Ranger, Paquerette, Libn.
UNIVERSITE DE MONTREAL - DROIT- BIBLIOTHEQUE □ Montreal, PQ

Ranger, William R., Libn.
U.S. FEDERAL AVIATION ADMINISTRATION - PACIFIC-ASIA REGION LIBRARY† □ Honolulu, HI

Ranieri, Marie, Libn.
U.S. ARMY - PLASTICS TECHNICAL EVALUATION CENTER □ Dover, NJ

Rankey, Bro. Edward, S.A., Libn.
FRANCISCAN FRIARS OF THE ATONEMENT - ATONEMENT SEMINARY LIBRARY □ Washington, DC

Rankin, Carol, Cat.
MC GRAW-HILL, INC. - LIBRARY □ New York, NY

Rankin, Eugenia, Libn.
ALABAMA STATE DEPARTMENT OF ARCHIVES AND HISTORY □ Montgomery, AL

Rankin, Jocelyn, Dir., Med.Lib.
MERCER UNIVERSITY - MEDICAL SCHOOL LIBRARY □ Macon, GA

Rankin, Joseph T., Cur.
NEW YORK PUBLIC LIBRARY - ARENTS COLLECTION OF BOOKS IN PARTS AND ASSOCIATED MATERIALS □ New York, NY

Rankin, Joseph T., Act.Chf.
NEW YORK PUBLIC LIBRARY - ART, PRINTS & PHOTOGRAPHS DIVISION - ART AND ARCHITECTURE COLLECTION □ New York, NY

Rankin, Joseph T., Act.Kpr.
NEW YORK PUBLIC LIBRARY - ART, PRINTS & PHOTOGRAPHS DIVISION - PRINT ROOM □ New York, NY

Rankin, Joseph T., Cur.
NEW YORK PUBLIC LIBRARY - SPENCER COLLECTION □ New York, NY

Rankin, Kiley, Info.Coord.
TRI-COUNTY REGIONAL PLANNING COMMISSION - INFORMATION RESOURCE CENTER □ Lansing, MI

Rankin, Rogers, Co-Cur.
HISTORICAL AND GENEALOGICAL SOCIETY OF INDIANA COUNTY - LIBRARY AND ARCHIVES □ Indiana, PA

Rannit, Tatiana, Cur.
YALE UNIVERSITY - SLAVIC & EAST EUROPEAN COLLECTIONS □ New Haven, CT

Ransom, Christina, Mgr.Info.Ctr.
AYERST LABORATORIES, INC. - INFORMATION CENTER □ Rouses Point, NY

Ransom, Mary Louise, Libn.
U.S. CIVIL AERONAUTICS BOARD - LIBRARY □ Washington, DC

Ranson, Lowell, Cat.
UNIVERSITY OF WISCONSIN, MADISON - CENTER FOR HEALTH SCIENCES LIBRARIES □ Madison, WI

Rantala, Donald, LRC Spec.
WISCONSIN INDIANHEAD TECHNICAL INSTITUTE, SUPERIOR CAMPUS - LIBRARY □ Superior, WI

Rao, Angelo, Hd., AV Serv.
ONTARIO COLLEGE OF ART - LIBRARY/ AUDIOVISUAL CENTRE □ Toronto, ON

Rao, G. Rani, Libn.
FOUNDATION FOR RESEARCH ON THE NATURE OF MAN - INSTITUTE FOR PARAPSYCHOLOGY - RESEARCH LIBRARY □ Durham, NC

Rao, Mr. Paladugu, Sys.Engr.
EASTERN ILLINOIS UNIVERSITY - BOOTH LIBRARY □ Charleston, IL

Raper, James E., Jr., Tech.Serv.Libn.
MOUNT SINAI SCHOOL OF MEDICINE OF THE CITY UNIVERSITY OF NEW YORK - GUSTAVE L. & JANET W. LEVY LIBRARY □ New York, NY

Rapetti, V.A., Chf.Libn.
U.S. NASA - JOHN F. KENNEDY SPACE CENTER - LIBRARY □ Kennedy Space Center, FL

Raphael, Dana, Dir.
HUMAN LACTATION CENTER, LTD. - LIBRARY □ Westport, CT

Raphelson, J., Tech.Serv.Libn.
HURLEY MEDICAL CENTER - HAMADY HEALTH SCIENCES LIBRARY □ Flint, MI

Rapisarda, Carl, Cat.
PERGAMON INSTITUTE - LIBRARY □ Elmsford, NY

Rapp, Brigid, Tech.Serv.Libn.
URBAN INSTITUTE - LIBRARY □ Washington, DC

Rapp, Ken, Asst.Archv.
U.S. ARMY - MILITARY ACADEMY - ARCHIVES □ West Point, NY

Rapp, William F., Libn.
J-B PUBLISHING COMPANY - RESEARCH LIBRARY □ Crete, NE

Rappaport, Gersten, Asst.Libn.
FORDHAM UNIVERSITY - SCHOOL OF LAW LIBRARY □ New York, NY

Rappaport, Susan, Press Sec.
FRENCH LIBRARY IN BOSTON, INC. □ Boston, MA

Rapske, Arnold, Libn.
NORTH AMERICAN BAPTIST COLLEGE - LIBRARY □ South Edmonton, AB

Raquet, Robin, ILL Libn.
EMORY UNIVERSITY - SCHOOL OF MEDICINE - A.W. CALHOUN MEDICAL LIBRARY □ Atlanta, GA

Rargus, Linda, Lib.Mgr.
OREGON RESEARCH INSTITUTE - LIBRARY □ Eugene, OR

Rasche, Richard R., Cur., Hist./Med.
UNIVERSITY OF TEXAS MEDICAL BRANCH - MOODY MEDICAL LIBRARY □ Galveston, TX

Raschella, Rosalie, Asst.Libn.
PUBLIC SERVICE ELECTRIC AND GAS COMPANY - LIBRARY □ Newark, NJ

Raser, Ed G., Cur./Hist.
W2ZI HISTORICAL WIRELESS MUSEUM - HISTORICAL WIRELESS LIBRARY □ Trenton, NJ

Rasmussen, Bette, Lib.Supv.
SANATANA DHARMA FOUNDATION - GERTRUDE C. BERNER MEMORIAL LIBRARY OF SPIRITUAL SCIENCES □ St. Helena, CA

Rasmussen, Bronwein, Libn.
FASHION INSTITUTE OF DESIGN & MERCHANDISING - LIBRARY □ San Francisco, CA

Rasmussen, Esther H., Asst.Libn.
PACKAGING CORPORATION OF AMERICA - RESEARCH AND DEVELOPMENT LIBRARY □ Grand Rapids, MI

Rasmussen, Gary C., Cat.Libn.
UNIVERSITY OF TEXAS MEDICAL BRANCH - MOODY MEDICAL LIBRARY □ Galveston, TX

Rasmussen, Jane, Libn.
CHEMICAL MANUFACTURERS ASSOCIATION - LIBRARY □ Washington, DC

Rasmussen, Ruth, Libn.
DANA COLLEGE - C.A. DANA-LIFE LIBRARY □ Blair, NE

Rasmussen, Steve, Lit. Searcher
MEDTRONIC, INC. - LIBRARY □ Minneapolis, MN

Rasmussen, Stuart, Libn.
SAN FRANCISCO EXAMINER - LIBRARY □ San Francisco, CA

Rassam, Dr. Ghassan N., Chf.Ed.
AMERICAN GEOLOGICAL INSTITUTE - GEO-REF RETROSPECTIVE SEARCH SERVICE □ Falls Church, VA

Ratcliff, Marcia G., Dir.
CBS INC. - CBS NEWS - REFERENCE LIBRARY □ New York, NY

Ratcliff, Roberta, Libn.
MINNEAPOLIS PUBLIC LIBRARY & INFORMATION CENTER - BUSINESS AND SCIENCE DEPARTMENT □ Minneapolis, MN

Ratesh, Ioana, Cat.
FEDERAL RESERVE SYSTEM - BOARD OF GOVERNORS - RESEARCH LIBRARY □ Washington, DC

Rathbun, Amanda, Acq.Tech.
MARICOPA TECHNICAL COMMUNITY COLLEGE - LIBRARY RESOURCE CENTER □ Phoenix, AZ

Rathgeb, William, Libn.
SANDOZ PHARMACEUTICALS - INFORMATION SERVICES □ East Hanover, NJ

Raths, H.W., Libn.
AMERICAN COUNCIL OF THE INTERNATIONAL INSTITUTE OF WELDING - LIBRARY □ Miami, FL

Ratliff, Neil, Fine Arts Libn.
UNIVERSITY OF MARYLAND, COLLEGE PARK - LIBRARIES - MUSIC LIBRARY □ College Park, MD

Ratliff, Priscilla, Supv.
ASHLAND CHEMICAL COMPANY - TECHNICAL INFORMATION CENTER □ Columbus, OH

Ratner, Rhoda, Libn.
SMITHSONIAN INSTITUTION LIBRARIES - MUSEUM REFERENCE CENTER □ Washington, DC

Rauch, Ann B., Tech.Libn.
GENERAL ELECTRIC COMPANY - ORDNANCE
SYSTEMS - ENGINEERING LIBRARY □ Pittsfield,
MA

Rauch, Marcella, Circulation Libn.
OUACHITA BAPTIST UNIVERSITY - RILEY
LIBRARY □ Arkadelphia, AR

Rauch, Marian, Tech.Libn.
JOHNSON CONTROLS - BATTERY DIVISION -
TECHNICAL LIBRARY □ Milwaukee, WI

Raue, Philip E., Hd.Cat.Dept.
UNIVERSITY OF TEXAS, EL PASO - LIBRARY □ El
Paso, TX

Raup, E. Ann, Libn.
PRICE WATERHOUSE - LIBRARY† □ Chicago, IL

Raus, E.J., Hist.
U.S. NATL. PARK SERVICE - FREDERICKSBURG
& SPOTSYLVANIA NATL. MILITARY PARK -
LIBRARY □ Fredericksburg, VA

Rausch, Carol-Ann, Med.Libn.
PAWTUCKET MEMORIAL HOSPITAL - HEALTH
SCIENCES LIBRARY □ Pawtucket, RI

Rausch, Rev. Ervin J., O.S.C., Hd.Libn.
CROSIER HOUSE OF STUDIES - LIBRARY □ Fort
Wayne, IN

Rauschenberg, Bradford L.
OLD SALEM, INC. - MUSEUM OF EARLY
SOUTHERN DECORATIVE ARTS (MESDA) -
LIBRARY □ Winston-Salem, NC

Rauschenberg, Dale E., Coord.
TOWSON STATE UNIVERSITY - GERHARDT
LIBRARY OF MUSICAL INFORMATION □
Towson, MD

Rauschenberg, Dale E., Assoc.Professor of Music
TOWSON STATE UNIVERSITY - GERHARDT
MARIMBA & XYLOPHONE COLLECTION □
Towson, MD

Ravdin, Susan B., Asst. to Cur.
BOWDOIN COLLEGE - LIBRARY - SPECIAL
COLLECTIONS □ Brunswick, ME

Ravenhall, Mary D., Libn.
UNIVERSITY OF ILLINOIS - CITY PLANNING
AND LANDSCAPE ARCHITECTURE LIBRARY □
Urbana, IL

Ravina, Doris M., Libn.
NEW YORK STATE SUPREME COURT - 5TH
JUDICIAL DISTRICT - LAW LIBRARY† □ Utica,
NY

Raviola, Edith M., Libn.
GENERAL ELECTRIC COMPANY - CORPORATE
RESEARCH & DEVELOPMENT - WHITNEY
LIBRARY □ Schenectady, NY

Rawles, Henry A., Jr., Mgr.Lib.Serv.
BATTELLE-COLUMBUS LABORATORIES -
LIBRARY □ Columbus, OH

Rawlins, Barbara, Asst.Libn.
SAN DIEGO MUSEUM OF MAN - SCIENTIFIC
LIBRARY □ San Diego, CA

Rawlinson, Jo Ann, Law Libn.
COCONINO COUNTY LAW LIBRARY □ Flagstaff,
AZ

Rawls, Andrew B., AV Libn.
SOUTHERN BAPTIST THEOLOGICAL SEMINARY
- AUDIOVISUAL CENTER □ Louisville, KY

Rawls, D.E., Lib.Supv.
NEWPORT NEWS SHIPBUILDING AND DRY
DOCK COMPANY - LIBRARY SERVICES
DEPARTMENT □ Newport News, VA

Rawls, Karen, Libn.
GEORGIA STATE DEPARTMENT OF OFFENDER
REHABILITATION - REFERENCE/RESOURCE
CENTER □ Atlanta, GA

Rawls, M., Hd., Rd./Ref.Serv.
U.S. NASA - JOHN F. KENNEDY SPACE CENTER -
LIBRARY □ Kennedy Space Center, FL

Rawoof, Jane, Acq. & Tech.Proc.
BROOME COMMUNITY COLLEGE - CECIL C.
TYRRELL LEARNING RESOURCES CENTER □
Binghamton, NY

Ray, Carol A., Med.Ref.Libn.
INDIANA UNIVERSITY - SCHOOL OF MEDICINE
LIBRARY □ Indianapolis, IN

Ray, Eleanor, Caretaker
WHITMAN (Walt) HOUSE - LIBRARY □ Camden,
NJ

Ray, Jean, Asst.Sci./Map Libn.
SOUTHERN ILLINOIS UNIVERSITY,
CARBONDALE - SCIENCE DIVISION LIBRARY □
Carbondale, IL

Ray, Joyce, Spec.Coll.
UNIVERSITY OF TEXAS HEALTH SCIENCE
CENTER, SAN ANTONIO - LIBRARY □ San
Antonio, TX

Ray, Kathryn, Asst.Chf.
DISTRICT OF COLUMBIA PUBLIC LIBRARY -
WASHINGTONIANA DIVISION □ Washington,
DC

Ray, Sr. Mary Dominic, Dir.
AMERICAN MUSIC RESEARCH CENTER -
LIBRARY □ San Rafael, CA

Ray, Mel, Libn.
U.S. NAVY - NAVAL RESEARCH LABORATORY -
UNDERWATER SOUND REFERENCE
DETACHMENT - TECHNICAL LIBRARY □ Orlando,
FL

Ray, Rebekah, Libn.
NATIONAL ACTION/RESEARCH ON THE
MILITARY-INDUSTRIAL COMPLEX - LIBRARY □
Philadelphia, PA

Ray, Sherry, Libn.
HOUSTON CHRONICLE - EDITORIAL LIBRARY □
Houston, TX

Ray-Crichton, Rebekah, Libn.
FELLOWSHIP OF RECONCILIATION - LIBRARY □
Nyack, NY

Raybon, Elaine, Cat.Libn.
HENDERSON STATE UNIVERSITY - HUIE
LIBRARY □ Arkadelphia, AR

Raybon, Jean, Hd., Tech. Proc.
OUACHITA BAPTIST UNIVERSITY - RILEY
LIBRARY □ Arkadelphia, AR

Raybourn, J.S., Staff V.P., Commun.
PRODUCE MARKETING ASSOCIATION - PMA
INFORMATION CENTER □ Newark, DE

Rayburn, June, Libn.
METHODIST HOSPITAL AND SCHOOL OF
NURSING - LIBRARY □ Lubbock, TX

Rayman, M. Ronald, Asst.Ref.Libn.
WESTERN ILLINOIS UNIVERSITY - LIBRARIES
□ Macomb, IL

Raymond, Estelle, Info.Ctr.Techn.
NORTH COUNTRY HOSPITAL AND HEALTH
CENTER, INC. - INFORMATION CENTER □
Newport, VT

Raymond, Lorraine, Pub.Serv.Libn.
UNIVERSITY OF WASHINGTON - HEALTH
SCIENCES LIBRARY □ Seattle, WA

Raynard, Carl, Mgr.
CALGARY ECO-CENTRE SOCIETY -
ENVIRONMENTAL INFORMATION CENTRE □
Calgary, AB

Raynard, Shirley M., Ref.Libn.
NEW ENGLAND REGIONAL COMMISSION
(NERCOM) - REFERENCE LIBRARY □ Boston, MA

Raynock, Jean, Libn.
MIDLAND-ROSS CORPORATION - THERMAL
SYSTEMS TECHNICAL CENTER - LIBRARY □
Toledo, OH

Raynor, Barbara A., Tech.Serv.Asst.
CAMPBELL UNIVERSITY - SCHOOL OF LAW -
LAW LIBRARY □ Buies Creek, NC

Raynor, Betty
HARTFORD PUBLIC LIBRARY - ART, MUSIC AND
RECREATION DEPARTMENT □ Hartford, CT

Razo, Richard, Interp.Spec.
U.S. NATL. PARK SERVICE - CHAMIZAL NATL.
MEMORIAL - LIBRARY □ El Paso, TX

Re, Armando, Asst.Libn., Tech.Serv.
SALEM STATE COLLEGE - LIBRARY† □ Salem,
MA

Rea, Jacqueline, Coord., Pict.Coll.
SMITHSONIAN INSTITUTION LIBRARIES -
COOPER-HEWITT MUSEUM OF DESIGN - DORIS
& HENRY DREYFUSS MEMORIAL STUDY CENTER
□ New York, NY

Rea, Jay, Archv.
EASTERN WASHINGTON UNIVERSITY -
LIBRARY □ Cheney, WA

Reaber, Raymond, Pres.
UNIVERSAL POSTAL UNION COLLECTORS -
LIBRARY □ Glendale, CA

Read, Cynthia, Asst.Cur., Graphics
HENRY FORD MUSEUM AND GREENFIELD
VILLAGE - ROBERT H. TANNAHILL RESEARCH
LIBRARY □ Dearborn, MI

Read, Linda D., Supv.Plan.Lib.
CALGARY PLANNING DEPARTMENT -
INFORMATION SERVICES □ Calgary, AB

Read, Margaret Anne, Asst.
ELKO MEDICAL CLINIC - LIBRARY □ Elko, NV

Read, Mary Margaret M., Sec.
AMERICAN SUFFOLK HORSE ASSOCIATION
(ASHA) - LIBRARY □ Wichita Falls, TX

Read, Ronald, Hd.
UNIVERSITY OF UTAH - NON-PRINT SERVICES
□ Salt Lake City, UT

Reade, Rita D., Libn.
LIFE SAVERS, INC. - RESEARCH AND
DEVELOPMENT DIVISION - TECHNICAL
INFORMATION CENTER □ Port Chester, NY

Reader, Elizabeth, Ref.Libn.
PRATT AND WHITNEY AIRCRAFT OF CANADA,
LTD. - LIBRARY □ Longueuil, PQ

Ready, Michael J., Hd.Libn.
PEAT, MARWICK, MITCHELL & COMPANY -
ACCOUNTING AND AUDITING LIBRARY □ New
York, NY

Reagan, Jan D., Legislative Libn.
FEDERAL RESERVE SYSTEM - BOARD OF
GOVERNORS - LAW LIBRARY □ Washington, DC

Ream, Diane F., Med.Libn.
BAPTIST HOSPITAL OF MIAMI - HEALTH
SCIENCES LIBRARY □ Miami, FL

Ream, Judith
NATIONAL COLLEGE OF EDUCATION -
LEARNING RESOURCE CENTERS □ Evanston, IL

Ream, Louise, Pres.
HEISEY COLLECTORS OF AMERICA, INC. - HCA
LIBRARY & ARCHIVES □ Newark, OH

Reams, Bernard D., Jr., Law Libn.
WASHINGTON UNIVERSITY - SCHOOL OF LAW -
FREUND LAW LIBRARY □ St. Louis, MO

Rearden, Phyllis, Pub.Serv.Coord.
EASTERN ILLINOIS UNIVERSITY - BOOTH
LIBRARY □ Charleston, IL

Reardon, Theodora J., Libn.
CLAIROL, INC. - RESEARCH LIBRARY □
Stamford, CT

Reaves, Alice Cameron, Asst.Libn.
NORTH CAROLINA STATE SUPREME COURT
LIBRARY □ Raleigh, NC

Reaves, Thelma, Media Ctr.Dir.
NORMANDALE BAPTIST CHURCH - MEDIA
CENTER □ Montgomery, AL

Rebecca, Richard D., Sr.Libn.
TRENTON FREE PUBLIC LIBRARY - BUSINESS
AND TECHNOLOGY DEPARTMENT □ Trenton, NJ

Rechard, Paul A., Dir.
UNIVERSITY OF WYOMING - WATER
RESOURCES RESEARCH INSTITUTE - LIBRARY
□ Laramie, WY

Recht, Judith, Abstract Writer
MONTCLAIR STATE COLLEGE - NATIONAL
ADULT EDUCATION CLEARINGHOUSE/
MULTIMEDIA CENTER □ Upper Montclair, NJ

Record, William J., Libn.
MISERICORDIA HOSPITAL - MEDICAL LIBRARY
□ Bronx, NY

Rector, A., Libn.
BRITISH COLUMBIA - JUDGES' LIBRARY -
SUPERIOR & COUNTY COURTS □ Vancouver, BC

Rector, Myrtle, Cur.
NORMAN COUNTY HISTORICAL SOCIETY -
MEMORIAL MUSEUM LIBRARY □ Ada, MN

Red, Lynn, Libn.
WASHINGTON STATE LIBRARY - RAINIER
SCHOOL STAFF LIBRARY □ Buckley, WA

PERSONNEL

Redalje, Susanne, Libn.
UNIVERSITY OF ILLINOIS - CHEMISTRY LIBRARY □ Urbana, IL

Redd, Gwendolyn L., Supv.Libn.
U.S. ARMY POST - FORT BENNING - RECREATION SERVICES LIBRARY BRANCH □ Ft. Benning, GA

Redding, Heather, Ref.
U.S. DEPT. OF ENERGY - IDAHO NATL. ENGINEERING LABORATORY - TECHNICAL LIBRARY □ Idaho Falls, ID

Redding, Helene, Ref.Libn.
UNIVERSITY OF BRITISH COLUMBIA - HUMANITIES DIVISION □ Vancouver, BC

Redding, John F., Libn.
NATIONAL BASEBALL HALL OF FAME AND MUSEUM - NATIONAL BASEBALL LIBRARY □ Cooperstown, NY

Redding, Julie, Libn.
BEAUMONT ART MUSEUM - LIBRARY □ Beaumont, TX

Reddy, Arjun, Hd.
UNIVERSITY OF MISSOURI - HEALTH CARE TECHNOLOGY CENTER - HCTC INFORMATION CENTER □ Columbia, MO

Redel, Judy, Libn.
CHICAGO TRIBUNE - INFORMATION CENTER □ Chicago, IL

Redhead, Ms. Pat, Libn.
CANADIAN COUNCIL ON SOCIAL DEVELOPMENT - LIBRARY □ Ottawa, ON

Redmond, Donald A., Geology Libn.
QUEEN'S UNIVERSITY AT KINGSTON - GEOLOGICAL SCIENCES LIBRARY □ Kingston, ON

Redmond, Elizabeth, Libn.
BURNETT (Leo) COMPANY, INC. - INFORMATION CENTER† □ Chicago, IL

Redmond, Mary, Hd., Leg./Govt.Serv.
NEW YORK STATE LIBRARY □ Albany, NY

Redmond, Mary, Principal Libn.
NEW YORK STATE LIBRARY - LEGISLATIVE AND GOVERNMENTAL SERVICES □ Albany, NY

Redrick, Miriam J., Mgr., Lib.Serv.
NATIONAL ASSOCIATION OF ACCOUNTANTS - LIBRARY □ New York, NY

Redston, Valerie, Libn.
BRITISH COLUMBIA CENTRAL CREDIT UNION - RESOURCE CENTRE □ Vancouver, BC

Redus, Mary H., Cur.
HISTORICAL SOCIETY OF DAUPHIN COUNTY - LIBRARY □ Harrisburg, PA

Reed, Bobby M., Hd., Cat.Sect.
U.S. GEOLOGICAL SURVEY - LIBRARY □ Reston, VA

Reed, Catherine
SWEDENBORG LIBRARY AND BOOKSTORE □ Boston, MA

Reed, Duane, Spec.Coll.Libn.
U.S. AIR FORCE ACADEMY - LIBRARY □ U.S. Air Force Academy, CO

Reed, E.G., Sect.Mgr.
MC DONNELL DOUGLAS CORPORATION - MC DONNELL DOUGLAS ASTRONAUTICS COMPANY - TECHNICAL LIBRARY SERVICES □ Huntington Beach, CA

Reed, Edith, Act.Libn.
SCHOOL OF FINE ARTS - LIBRARY □ Willoughby, OH

Reed, Howard B., Assoc.Dir., Musm.Coll.
FAIRBANKS MUSEUM AND PLANETARIUM - LIBRARY □ St. Johnsbury, VT

Reed, Ida, Hd.
CARNEGIE LIBRARY OF PITTSBURGH - MUSIC AND ART DEPARTMENT □ Pittsburgh, PA

Reed, James R., Dir. of Lib.
MISSOURI BOTANICAL GARDEN - LIBRARY □ St. Louis, MO

Reed, Jane, Libn.
UNION LEAGUE CLUB LIBRARY □ New York, NY

Reed, Janet S., Asst.Mgr.
CONTINENTAL ILLINOIS NATIONAL BANK AND TRUST COMPANY OF CHICAGO - INFORMATION SERVICES DIVISION □ Chicago, IL

Reed, Joanne, Prod.Info.Coord.
HOECHST-ROUSSEL PHARMACEUTICALS, INC. - LIBRARY □ Somerville, NJ

Reed, John F., Cur., Doc.
VALLEY FORGE HISTORICAL SOCIETY - LIBRARY □ Valley Forge, PA

Reed, Mabel, Sec. In Charge
HEARST (Phoebe Apperson) HISTORICAL SOCIETY, INC. - MUSEUM CENTER □ St. Clair, MO

Reed, Naomi, Circ. & Ref.Libn.
ARIZONA STATE UNIVERSITY - COLLEGE OF LAW - LIBRARY □ Tempe, AZ

Reed, R., Pub.
R & E RESEARCH ASSOCIATES - LIBRARY □ Palo Alto, CA

Reed, Renee, Libn.
MINNEAPOLIS PUBLIC LIBRARY & INFORMATION CENTER - LITERATURE AND LANGUAGE DEPARTMENT □ Minneapolis, MN

Reed, Richard S., Musm.Dir.
FRUITLANDS MUSEUMS - LIBRARY □ Harvard, MA

Reed, Roma, Libn.
UNIVERSITY OF VIRGINIA - MATHEMATICS-ASTRONOMY LIBRARY □ Charlottesville, VA

Reed, Rosalie, Med.Lib.Asst.
RIVERSIDE GENERAL HOSPITAL - MEDICAL LIBRARY □ Riverside, CA

Reed, Ruth S., Archv.
WESTERN PENNSYLVANIA GENEALOGICAL SOCIETY - LIBRARY □ Pittsburgh, PA

Reed, Stewart E., D.P.M.
REED LIBRARY OF FOOT & ANKLE □ Des Moines, IA

Reed, Virginia, Med.Libn.
MERCY HOSPITAL AND MEDICAL CENTER - JEAN FARB MEDICAL LIBRARY □ San Diego, CA

Reed, Virginia, Hd., Ser.Serv.
NORTHEASTERN ILLINOIS UNIVERSITY - LIBRARY □ Chicago, IL

Reeder, W.G., Dir.
TEXAS MEMORIAL MUSEUM - LIBRARY □ Austin, TX

Reedy, Judith El, Med.Libn.
CHAMPLAIN VALLEY - PHYSICIANS HOSPITAL MEDICAL CENTER - MEDICAL LIBRARY □ Plattsburgh, NY

Reepmeyer, Tina, Asst.Libn.
NEW YORK STATE DEPARTMENT OF LAW - LIBRARY □ Albany, NY

Rees, Marian, Assoc.Libn.
STANFORD UNIVERSITY - INSTITUTE FOR ENERGY STUDIES - ENERGY INFORMATION CENTER □ Stanford, CA

Rees, Pamela Clark, Dir.
IOWA STATE MEDICAL LIBRARY □ Des Moines, IA

Rees, Philip A., Art Libn.
UNIVERSITY OF NORTH CAROLINA, CHAPEL HILL - ART LIBRARY □ Chapel Hill, NC

Rees, Thomas, Ref.Libn.
SUNY AT STONY BROOK - HEALTH SCIENCES LIBRARY □ East Setauket, NY

Reese, Anne O., Hd.Libn.
TOLEDO MUSEUM OF ART - ART REFERENCE LIBRARY □ Toledo, OH

Reese, Bradley, Dir.
GEORGETOWN UNIVERSITY - EAST CAMPUS DATA LIBRARY □ Washington, DC

Reese, D. Andrews, Hd., Acq.
SALISBURY STATE COLLEGE - BLACKWELL LIBRARY □ Salisbury, MD

Reese, Faye L., Libn.
PIERCE COUNTY LAW LIBRARY □ Tacoma, WA

Reese, Gwynne H., Per.Libn.
EAST STROUDSBURG STATE COLLEGE - LIBRARY □ East Stroudsburg, PA

Reese, Mary E., Res.Libn.
TEXACO CHEMICAL COMPANY, INC. - TECHNICAL LITERATURE SECTION □ Austin, TX

Reese, Ray D., Libn.
U.S. BUREAU OF INDIAN AFFAIRS - OFFICE OF TECHNICAL ASSISTANCE & TRAINING (OTAT) - PROFESSIONAL LIBRARY† □ Brigham City, UT

Reeve, Elizabeth, Libn.
U.S. ARMY - SPECIAL SERVICES DIVISION - SHARPE ARMY DEPOT - LIBRARY □ Lathrop, CA

Reeve, Phyllis, Proc.Libn.
UNIVERSITY OF BRITISH COLUMBIA - GOVERNMENT PUBLICATIONS & MICROFORMS DIVISIONS □ Vancouver, BC

Reeves, Charles R., Archv.
U.S. NATL. ARCHIVES & RECORDS SERVICE - FEDERAL ARCHIVES AND RECORDS CENTER, REGION 4 □ East Point, GA

Reeves, Gayle
AMPEX CORPORATION - TECHNICAL LIBRARY MS 3-10 □ Redwood City, CA

Reeves, James H., Mgr.Tech.Serv.
AMERICAN INSTITUTE OF INDUSTRIAL ENGINEERS, INC. - LIBRARY □ Norcross, GA

Reeves, Mary Anna, Info.Sci.
AMERICAN CYANAMID COMPANY - AGRICULTURAL RESEARCH DIVISION - TECHNICAL INFORMATION SERVICES □ Princeton, NJ

Reeves, Pamela, Assoc.Dir.
EASTERN MICHIGAN UNIVERSITY - CENTER OF EDUCATIONAL RESOURCES - ARCHIVES/ SPECIAL COLLECTIONS □ Ypsilanti, MI

Reeves, Sharon Stewart, Dir., Lib.Serv.
SAN DIEGO UNION-TRIBUNE PUBLISHING COMPANY - LIBRARY □ San Diego, CA

Reeves, T.C., Pres.
MERRICK COUNTY HISTORICAL MUSEUM - LIBRARY □ Central City, NE

Rega, Christina, Libn.
FARM JOURNAL, INC. - MARKETING RESEARCH LIBRARY □ Philadelphia, PA

Regan, Charles Lee, Libn.
HUMAN RIGHTS INTERNET - LIBRARY □ Washington, DC

Regan, Helen, Libn.
PEPSICO, INC. - INFORMATION CENTER □ Valhalla, NY

Regan, Marguerite, Asst. to Dean
HOFSTRA UNIVERSITY - LIBRARY - SPECIAL COLLECTIONS □ Hempstead, NY

Regan, Muriel, Libn.
ROCKEFELLER FOUNDATION - LIBRARY □ New York, NY

Regan, Theresa, AV Matl.Instr.
PALO ALTO UNIFIED SCHOOL DISTRICT - TEACHERS' PROFESSIONAL LIBRARY □ Palo Alto, CA

Regenberg, Pat, Asst.Libn.
ST. PETER'S MEDICAL CENTER - LIBRARY □ New Brunswick, NJ

Regenberg, Patricia, Libn.
MOUNTAINSIDE HOSPITAL - SCHOOL OF NURSING LIBRARY □ Montclair, NJ

Regenstreif, Gene, Libn.
UNIVERSITY OF MICHIGAN - COOPERATIVE INFORMATION CENTER FOR HOSPITAL MANAGEMENT STUDIES □ Ann Arbor, MI

Regina, Ilme, Hd.
MIDLAND DOHERTY, LTD. - LIBRARY □ Toronto, ON

Regis, June, Staff Libn.
NEW BERLIN MEMORIAL HOSPITAL - LIBRARY □ New Berlin, WI

Regnier, Flora D., Hd. of Tech.Serv.
RENSSELAER POLYTECHNIC INSTITUTE - FOLSOM LIBRARY □ Troy, NY

Rehkopf, Charles F., Archv./Registrar
PROTESTANT EPISCOPAL CHURCH - MISSOURI DIOCESE - DIOCESAN ARCHIVES □ St. Louis, MO

Rehmar, Marie, Rd.Serv.Libn.
CLEVELAND STATE UNIVERSITY - JOSEPH W.
BARTUNEK III LAW LIBRARY □ Cleveland, OH

Reibel, Daniel B., Dir.
EARLY AMERICAN INDUSTRIES ASSOCIATION -
LIBRARY □ Washington Crossing, PA

Reibel, Lynn, Per.
HYSTER COMPANY - TECHNICAL
INFORMATION SERVICES □ Portland, OR

Reibman, Jean, Hd., Cat.Dept.
CORNELL UNIVERSITY - MEDICAL COLLEGE -
LIBRARY □ New York, NY

Reich, Marijane, Patients' Libn.
MENDOTA MENTAL HEALTH INSTITUTE -
LIBRARY MEDIA CENTER □ Madison, WI

Reich, Phyllis, Ref.Libn.
UNIVERSITY OF MINNESOTA, ST. PAUL -
CENTRAL LIBRARY □ St. Paul, MN

Reich, R.E., Cat. & Acq.Libn.
GRACE BIBLE COLLEGE - BULTEMA MEMORIAL
LIBRARY □ Grand Rapids, MI

Reichel, Deborah, C.S.R. Dept.Supv.
COLUMBIA BIBLE COLLEGE - LEARNING
RESOURCES CENTER □ Columbia, SC

Reicherter, Joan M., Libn.
NEWSOM (Earl) & COMPANY, INC. - LIBRARY □
New York, NY

Reichlin, Elinor, Libn.
SOCIETY FOR THE PRESERVATION OF NEW
ENGLAND ANTIQUITIES - LIBRARY □ Boston,
MA

Reichmann, A. Pamela, Libn.
SCHLITZ (Joseph) BREWING COMPANY -
MARKETING RESEARCH LIBRARY □ Milwaukee,
WI

Reid, Angea S., Rpt.Libn.
CABOT CORPORATION - TECHNICAL
INFORMATION CENTER □ Billerica, MA

Reid, Bruce D., Libn.
U.S. VETERANS ADMINISTRATION (PA-Wilkes-
Barre) - MEDICAL CENTER LIBRARY □ Wilkes-
Barre, PA

Reid, Carol L., Med.Libn.
MERCY HOSPITAL - MEDICAL LIBRARY □
Rockville Centre, NY

Reid, Carolyn A., Online Serv.Coord.
UNIVERSITY OF NEBRASKA MEDICAL CENTER -
MC GOOGAN LIBRARY OF MEDICINE □ Omaha,
NE

Reid, Douglas G., Hd.Libn.
BRIDGEPORT PUBLIC LIBRARY - TECHNOLOGY
AND BUSINESS DEPARTMENT □ Bridgeport, CT

Reid, Edge R., Volunteer Libn.
COLUMBUS MUSEUM OF ARTS AND SCIENCES -
CMAS RESEARCH LIBRARY □ Columbus, GA

Reid, Elizabeth A., Dir.
TORONTO WESTERN HOSPITAL - HEALTH
SCIENCES LIBRARY □ Toronto, ON

Reid, Frances, Gen.Cons.
NORTH CAROLINA STATE DEPARTMENT OF
CULTURAL RESOURCES - DIVISION OF THE
STATE LIBRARY □ Raleigh, NC

Reid, Jean-Paul, Libn.
UNIVERSITE DE MONTREAL - CENTRE
NATIONAL D'INFORMATION ET DE RECHERCHE
SUR L'AIDE JURIDIQUE □ Montreal, PQ

Reid, Jean-Paul, Ref.Libn.
UNIVERSITE DU QUEBEC A MONTREAL -
BIBLIOTHEQUES DES SCIENCES JURIDIQUES □
Montreal, PQ

Reid, Joan A., Legal Ed.
UNIVERSITY OF COLORADO, BOULDER -
SCHOOL OF LAW - ROCKY MOUNTAIN MINERAL
LAW FOUNDATION - RESEARCH LIBRARY □
Boulder, CO

Reid, JoAnne, Ref.Libn.
MITRE CORPORATION - LIBRARY □ McLean, VA

Reid, Linda L., Mgr., Checklist/Cat.
ONTARIO - LEGISLATIVE ASSEMBLY -
LEGISLATIVE LIBRARY RESEARCH AND
INFORMATION SERVICES □ Toronto, ON

Reid, M.H. (Lefty), Dir. & Cur.
HOCKEY HALL OF FAME - LIBRARY □ Toronto,
ON

Reid, Pat, Circ.Supv.
COLUMBIA BIBLE COLLEGE - LEARNING
RESOURCES CENTER □ Columbia, SC

Reid, Ronald, Assoc.Dir., Media Serv.
UNIVERSITY OF WISCONSIN, OSHKOSH -
UNIVERSITY LIBRARIES AND LEARNING
RESOURCES □ Oshkosh, WI

Reid, Ruth S., Archv./Rare Bk.Cur.
HISTORICAL SOCIETY OF WESTERN
PENNSYLVANIA - LIBRARY □ Pittsburgh, PA

Reid, Mr. T., Chf.Libn.
CANADA - DEPARTMENT OF FINANCE -
FINANCE/TREASURY BOARD LIBRARY □
Ottawa, ON

Reid, William K., Libn.
CRAWFORD COUNTY BAR ASSOCIATION - LAW
LIBRARY □ Meadville, PA

Reider, Mary Winn, Film Serv.Supv.
LOUISVILLE FREE PUBLIC LIBRARY - FILM
SERVICES □ Louisville, KY

Reidler, Celia, Educ.Dir.
COYOTE POINT MUSEUM - RESOURCE CENTER
□ San Mateo, CA

Reidy, Robin E., Libn.
SACRAMENTO UNION - EDITORIAL LIBRARY □
Sacramento, CA

Reifsteck, William E., Dir.
WAYNE COUNTY HISTORICAL MUSEUM -
LIBRARY □ Richmond, IN

Reilley, Elizabeth K., Libn.
PLANTING FIELDS ARBORETUM -
HORTICULTURAL LIBRARY □ Oyster Bay, NY

Reilly, Catherine, Mgr.
CHASE MANHATTAN BANK, N.A. -
INFORMATION CENTER □ New York, NY

Reilly, Cathy H., Libn.
ST. LOUIS - POLICE LIBRARY □ St. Louis, MO

Reilly, Joseph T., Data User Serv.Off.
U.S. BUREAU OF THE CENSUS - REGIONAL DATA
USER SERVICE - ATLANTA REGIONAL OFFICE -
LIBRARY □ Atlanta, GA

Reilly, Lois L., Libn.
OAKLAND UNIVERSITY - LIBRARY □ Rochester,
MI

Reilly, Lucille M., Med.Sec.
BISSELL (Emily P.) HOSPITAL - MEDICAL
LIBRARY □ Wilmington, DE

Reilly, Mary, Circ.
UNIVERSITY OF SAN DIEGO - MARVIN &
LILLIAN KRATTER LAW LIBRARY □ San Diego,
CA

Reilly, Michael M., Dir.
REILLY TRANSLATIONS - LIBRARY □ Fullerton,
CA

Reilly, Richard, Cur.
COPLEY PRESS, INC. - JAMES S. COPLEY
LIBRARY □ La Jolla, CA

Reilly, S. Kathleen, Libn.
CAPITAL RESEARCH COMPANY - RESEARCH
LIBRARY □ Los Angeles, CA

Reiman, Donald H., Ed., Shelley Project
PFORZHEIMER (Carl & Lily) FOUNDATION, INC. -
CARL H. PFORZHEIMER LIBRARY □ New York,
NY

Reiman, Eva, Rd.Serv.Libn.
PACE UNIVERSITY, PLEASANTVILLE/
BRIARCLIFF - LIBRARY □ Pleasantville, NY

Reimers, Ron, Photographer
UNIVERSITY OF CALIFORNIA, LOS ANGELES -
ART DEPARTMENT - VISUAL RESOURCE
COLLECTION & SERVICES □ Los Angeles, CA

Reinard, John R., Law Libn.
CUMBERLAND COUNTY LAW LIBRARY □
Bridgeton, NJ

Reiners, Margaret, Ser. & AV Libn.
NEW ENGLAND SCHOOL OF LAW - LIBRARY □
Boston, MA

Reinert, Ann, Libn.
NEBRASKA STATE HISTORICAL SOCIETY -
LIBRARY □ Lincoln, NE

Reinhardt, Alice, Chf., Lib.Serv.
LOS ANGELES COUNTY/UNIVERSITY OF
SOUTHERN CALIFORNIA MEDICAL CENTER -
MEDICAL LIBRARIES □ Los Angeles, CA

Reinhold, Edna J., Chf.Libn.
ST. LOUIS PUBLIC LIBRARY - HUMANITIES AND
SOCIAL SCIENCES DEPARTMENT □ St. Louis,
MO

Reinhold, Nancy G., Mgr.Info.Ctr.
NUCLEAR ASSURANCE CORPORATION -
INFORMATION CENTER □ Atlanta, GA

Reinig, Ellen T., Ext.Libn.
MEDICAL UNIVERSITY OF SOUTH CAROLINA -
LIBRARY □ Charleston, SC

Reinke, Bernnett, Lib.Dir.
DICKINSON STATE COLLEGE - STOXEN
LIBRARY □ Dickinson, ND

Reinmiller, Elinor, Coll.Dev.Libn.
UNIVERSITY OF TEXAS HEALTH SCIENCE
CENTER, DALLAS - LIBRARY □ Dallas, TX

Reinsch, Dorothy, Lib.Asst.
ST. ELIZABETH COMMUNITY HEALTH CENTER -
MEDICAL LIBRARY □ Lincoln, NE

Reischer, Bridget, Asst.Libn.
U.S. INTERNAL REVENUE SERVICE - LAW
LIBRARY □ Washington, DC

Reisinger, Landon Chas., Libn.
HISTORICAL SOCIETY OF YORK COUNTY -
LIBRARY AND ARCHIVES □ York, PA

Reiss, Nellie, Lande Libn.
MC GILL UNIVERSITY - DEPARTMENT OF RARE
BOOKS & SPECIAL COLLECTIONS □ Montreal, PQ

Reisse, Marilyn A., Doc.Coord.
MASSACHUSETTS INSTITUTE OF TECHNOLOGY
- CENTER FOR POLICY ALTERNATIVES -
DOCUMENTS COLLECTION □ Cambridge, MA

Reister, John F., Circ.Serv.Libn.
CALIFORNIA STATE UNIVERSITY, CHICO -
MERIAM LIBRARY □ Chico, CA

Reiter, Berle, Libn.
MICHIGAN STATE UNIVERSITY - V.G. GROVE
RESEARCH LIBRARY OF MATHEMATICS-
STATISTICS □ East Lansing, MI

Reith, Anita, Pub.Serv.Libn.
CONCORDIA TEACHERS COLLEGE - LINK
LIBRARY □ Seward, NE

Reith, Dr. Louis J., Rare Book Libn.
ST. BONAVENTURE UNIVERSITY - FRANCISCAN
INSTITUTE LIBRARY □ St. Bonaventure, NY

Reith-Winfhip, Laurie, Assoc.Libn./Tech.Serv.
SYRACUSE UNIVERSITY - LAW LIBRARY □
Syracuse, NY

Reitzel, Hilda M., Libn.
MINE SAFETY APPLIANCES COMPANY -
BUSINESS LIBRARY □ Pittsburgh, PA

Reitzel, Hilda M., Libn.
MINE SAFETY APPLIANCES COMPANY -
TECHNICAL LIBRARY □ Pittsburgh, PA

Relph, Matha H., Cat.Libn.
U.S. ARMY FIELD ARTILLERY SCHOOL - MORRIS
SWETT LIBRARY □ Ft. Sill, OK

Relyes, Donald P., Hd.
HOFFREL INSTRUMENTS, INC. - LIBRARY □
South Norwalk, CT

Remelts, Glenn, Hd.Pub.Serv./Br.Lib.
BELOIT COLLEGE - HERBERT V. KOHLER
SCIENCE LIBRARY □ Beloit, WI

Remillard, Juliette
INSTITUT D'HISTOIRE DE L'AMERIQUE
FRANCAISE (1970) - RESEARCH CENTRE
LIBRARY □ Montreal, PQ

Rempel, S. Patricia, Ser./Ref.
UNIVERSITY OF ALBERTA - LAW LIBRARY □
Edmonton, AB

Remy, Richard, Info.Sci.
SOUTHERN RESEARCH INSTITUTE - THOMAS
W. MARTIN MEMORIAL LIBRARY □ Birmingham,
AL

Remy, Ronald E., AV Dir.
MANSFIELD STATE COLLEGE - AUDIOVISUAL
CENTER □ Mansfield, PA

Renaud-Frigon, Claire, Chf.Libn.
CANADA - SECRETARY OF STATE - LIBRARY □
Hull, PQ

Renford, Beverly, Sr.Asst.Libn.Ref.
PENNSYLVANIA STATE UNIVERSITY - COLLEGE
OF MEDICINE - GEORGE T. HARRELL LIBRARY □
Hershey, PA

Renfro, Betty, Learning Lab.Coord.
NASHVILLE STATE TECHNICAL INSTITUTE -
EDUCATIONAL RESOURCE CENTER □ Nashville,
TN

Renfro, Sr. Jean Marie, Archv.
SISTERS OF SOCIAL SERVICE - ARCHIVES □ Los
Angeles, CA

Renn, Maryellen, Photograph Libn.
XEROX CORPORATION - XEROX EDUCATION
PUBLICATIONS - LIBRARY □ Middletown, CT

Rennebohm, Carolyn A., Libn.
WISCONSIN GAS COMPANY - CORPORATE AND
LAW LIBRARY □ Milwaukee, WI

Renner, Virginia J., Rd.Serv.Libn.
HUNTINGTON (Henry E.) LIBRARY, ART
GALLERY AND BOTANICAL GARDENS □ San
Marino, CA

Renninger, Karen, Chf., Lib.Div.
U.S. VETERANS ADMINISTRATION (DC-
Washington) - HEADQUARTERS CENTRAL
OFFICE LIBRARY □ Washington, DC

Renninger, Karen, Chf., Lib.Div.
U.S. VETERANS ADMINISTRATION (DC-
Washington) - HEADQUARTERS LIBRARY
DIVISION □ Washington, DC

Renouf, Nicholas, Asst.Cur.
YALE UNIVERSITY - COLLECTION OF MUSICAL
INSTRUMENTS - LIBRARY □ New Haven, CT

Rensel, Jeanne M., Hd.
WASHINGTON STATE DEPARTMENT OF
ECOLOGY - TECHNICAL LIBRARY □ Olympia, WA

Renshawe, Michael, Law Libn.
MC GILL UNIVERSITY - LAW LIBRARY □
Montreal, PQ

Renter, Lois, Hd.Libn.
AMERICAN COLLEGE TESTING PROGRAM -
LIBRARY □ Iowa City, IA

Rentof, Beryl, Evening Supv.Libn.
FASHION INSTITUTE OF TECHNOLOGY -
LIBRARY/MEDIA SERVICES □ New York, NY

Renz, Rev. Francis J., S.J., Mgr.
ARCHDIOCESE OF PHILADELPHIA - CATHOLIC
INFORMATION CENTER □ Philadelphia, PA

Renz, Marion C., Dir.
WHITE PLAINS HOSPITAL - BERTON LATTIN
MEMORIAL MEDICAL LIBRARY □ White Plains,
NY

Renzetti, V., Tech.Libn.
MICROTEL PACIFIC RESEARCH LTD. -
TECHNICAL LIBRARY □ Burnaby, BC

Rephann, Richard, Dir.
YALE UNIVERSITY - COLLECTION OF MUSICAL
INSTRUMENTS - LIBRARY □ New Haven, CT

Replansky, Lydia, Asst.Mgr.
SPORT INFORMATION RESOURCE CENTRE □
Ottawa, ON

Reppucci, Esther A., Supv., Lib./Rec.Ctr.
COM/ENERGY SERVICES CO. - LIBRARY □
Cambridge, MA

ReQua, Eloise, Dir.
LIBRARY OF INTERNATIONAL RELATIONS □
Chicago, IL

Requena, Linda, Chf., Med.Lib.
U.S. ARMY HOSPITALS - TRIPLER ARMY
MEDICAL CENTER - MEDICAL LIBRARY □ Tripler
AMC, HI

Resco, Carol, Ref.Libn.
UNIVERSITY OF CALIFORNIA, RIVERSIDE -
PHYSICAL SCIENCES LIBRARY □ Riverside, CA

Reser, Christine, Post Libn.
U.S. ARMY POST - FORT LEONARD WOOD -
LIBRARY SYSTEM □ Ft. Leonard Wood, MO

Reside, Karin, Ref.Libn.
FAYETTEVILLE AREA HEALTH EDUCATION
CENTER - LIBRARY □ Fayetteville, NC

Resnick, Gina, Libn.
MILBANK, TWEED, HADLEY & MC CLOY -
LIBRARY □ New York, NY

Resnik, Mary, Libn.
FOUNDATION CENTER - WASHINGTON BRANCH
LIBRARY □ Washington, DC

Ressler, Martin E., Owner
RESSLER (Martin E.) - PRIVATE MUSIC LIBRARY
□ Quarryville, PA

Resson, Ken, Info.Spec.
ESSO RESOURCES CANADA LIMITED - LIBRARY
INFORMATION CENTRE □ Calgary, AB

Restrepo, Fabio, Coord., Spec.Prog.
TEXAS WOMAN'S UNIVERSITY - LIBRARY
SCIENCE LIBRARY - PROYECTO LEER □ Denton,
TX

Retfalvi, Andrea, Libn.
UNIVERSITY OF TORONTO - FINE ARTS
LIBRARY □ Toronto, ON

Rettenmaier, Fred, Ref.Libn.
U.S. NAVY - NAVAL RESEARCH LABORATORY -
RUTH H. HOOKER TECHNICAL LIBRARY □
Washington, DC

Rettino, Janice, Mgr., Lib.Dev.
COLLEGE OF MEDICINE AND DENTISTRY OF
NEW JERSEY AT NEWARK - GEORGE F. SMITH
LIBRARY □ Newark, NJ

Reuben, Sylvia, Law Libn.
SOMERSET COUNTY LAW LIBRARY □ Somerville,
NJ

Reusch, Rita T., Dir.
UNIVERSITY OF NORTH DAKOTA - OLAF H.
THORMODSGARD LAW LIBRARY □ Grand Forks,
ND

Reuter, J. Robert, Libn.
MORGAN GUARANTY TRUST COMPANY OF NEW
YORK - REFERENCE LIBRARY □ New York, NY

Reuter, Mrs. Jack, Cur.
CANADIAN COUNTY HISTORICAL MUSEUM -
LIBRARY □ El Reno, OK

Revilla, Eugenio, Asst.Libn., Foreign
UNIVERSITY OF ARIZONA - COLLEGE OF LAW
LIBRARY □ Tucson, AZ

Rexroat, Richard, Hd., Ser.Sect.
UNIVERSITY OF MISSOURI - MEDICAL
LIBRARY† □ Columbia, MO

Rey, Joyce, Libn.
SMITHSONIAN INSTITUTION LIBRARIES -
ASTROPHYSICAL OBSERVATORY - LIBRARY† □
Cambridge, MA

Rey, Marguerite A., Hd., Tech.Serv.
LOYOLA UNIVERSITY (New Orleans) - LAW
LIBRARY □ New Orleans, LA

Reyering, Kathleen, Tech.Info.Spec.
U.S. DEPT. OF JUSTICE - NATIONAL INSTITUTE
OF JUSTICE - LIBRARY □ Washington, DC

Reyes, Helen M., Libn.
JOHN MUIR MEMORIAL HOSPITAL - HEALTH
SCIENCES LIBRARY □ Walnut Creek, CA

Reyes, Ruperta, Asst.Libn.
CALIFORNIA STATE - COURT OF APPEAL, 2ND
APPELLATE DISTRICT - LAW LIBRARY □ Los
Angeles, CA

Reyesmatos, Manuel, Adm.Asst.
PUERTO RICO - INSTITUTE OF PUERTO RICAN
CULTURE - ARCHIVO GENERAL DE PUERTO
RICO □ San Juan, PR

Reynard, Frank L., Libn.
MONSANTO COMPANY - ENGINEERING
INFORMATION CENTER - F1EE □ St. Louis, MO

Reynen, Richard G., Libn.
DELOITTE HASKINS & SELLS - LIBRARY □
Minneapolis, MN

Reynolds, Barbara J., M.D., Chm.Lib.Comm.
RICHLAND MEMORIAL HOSPITAL - STAFF
LIBRARY □ Olney, IL

Reynolds, Betty, Tech.Serv.
NEW MEXICO INSTITUTE OF MINING AND
TECHNOLOGY - MARTIN SPEARE MEMORIAL
LIBRARY □ Socorro, NM

Reynolds, Brewster C., Archv.
SAN DIEGO AERO-SPACE MUSEUM - N. PAUL
WHITTIER HISTORICAL AVIATION LIBRARY □
San Diego, CA

Reynolds, Catharine J., Hd., Govt.Pubn.
UNIVERSITY OF COLORADO, BOULDER -
GOVERNMENT PUBLICATIONS DIVISION □
Boulder, CO

Reynolds, Charlotte Teresa, Med.Libn.
CLARK COUNTY MEMORIAL HOSPITAL -
MEDICAL LIBRARY □ Jeffersonville, IN

Reynolds, Dennis, Hd., OCLC Serv.
BIBLIOGRAPHICAL CENTER FOR RESEARCH -
ROCKY MOUNTAIN REGION, INC. □ Denver, CO

Reynolds, Don L., Asst.Dir.
ST. JOSEPH MUSEUM - LIBRARY □ St. Joseph,
MO

Reynolds, Dorsey, Libn.
VALLEY FORGE CHRISTIAN COLLEGE - LIBRARY
□ Phoenixville, PA

Reynolds, Eleanor, Horace Mann Libn.
SALEM STATE COLLEGE - LIBRARY† □ Salem,
MA

Reynolds, Elinor, Med.Libn.
MONROE COMMUNITY HOSPITAL - HEALTH
SCIENCES LIBRARY □ Rochester, NY

Reynolds, Janice, Tech.Libn.
BANK OF MONTREAL - TECHNICAL
INFORMATION CENTRE □ Willowdale, ON

Reynolds, Janice C., Libn.
UNIVERSITY OF VIRGINIA MEDICAL CENTER -
DEPARTMENT OF NEUROLOGY - ELIZABETH J.
OHRSTROM LIBRARY □ Charlottesville, VA

Reynolds, Jeanne C., Genealogy Libn.
EL PASO PUBLIC LIBRARY - GENEALOGY
SECTION □ El Paso, TX

Reynolds, John, Cat.Libn.
NORTHROP CORPORATION - AIRCRAFT
DIVISION - LIBRARY SERVICES □ Hawthorne,
CA

Reynolds, Jon K., Univ.Archv.
GEORGETOWN UNIVERSITY - SPECIAL
COLLECTION DIVISION - LAUINGER MEMORIAL
LIBRARY □ Washington, DC

Reynolds, Joyce, Info.Spec.
CANADIAN RESTAURANT & FOODSERVICES
ASSOCIATION - RESOURCE CENTRE □ Toronto,
ON

Reynolds, Malcolm, Sr.Libn.
CALIFORNIA STATE DEPARTMENT OF JUSTICE
- ATTORNEY GENERAL'S OFFICE LIBRARY □ San
Francisco, CA

Reynolds, Norman, Supv. Campus Serv.
KENT STATE UNIVERSITY - AUDIOVISUAL
SERVICES □ Kent, OH

Reynolds, Stanley G., Cur.
REYNOLDS MUSEUM - LIBRARY □ Wetaskiwin,
AB

Reynolds, Wanetca, Libn.
HUBER (J.M.) CORPORATION - RESEARCH
LIBRARY □ Borger, TX

Rezab, Gordana, Archv./Spec.Coll.
WESTERN ILLINOIS UNIVERSITY - LIBRARIES
□ Macomb, IL

Rezak, Sheila A., Teacher Educ.Rscrs.
PURDUE UNIVERSITY - CALUMET LIBRARY □
Hammond, IN

Rezetka, Mary A., Mgr.Info.Ctr.
INTERNATIONAL DATA CORPORATION -
INFORMATION CENTER □ Framingham, MA

Reznack, Lauren, Law Libn.
HIGGS, FLETCHER & MACK - LAW LIBRARY† □
San Diego, CA

Rheam, Howard W., Doc. Control Off.
U.S. ARMY WAR COLLEGE - LIBRARY □ Carlisle
Barracks, PA

Rheaume, Paul, Assoc.Cur./Prog.
KINGMAN MUSEUM OF NATURAL HISTORY -
LIBRARY □ Battle Creek, MI

Rhee, Sue M., Cat.
NORTHWEST CHRISTIAN COLLEGE - LEARNING
RESOURCE CENTER □ Eugene, OR

Rhee, Susan, Cat.Libn.
UNIVERSITY OF CALIFORNIA, SAN DIEGO - UNIVERSITY LIBRARIES □ La Jolla, CA

Rhee, YangHoon, Libn.
JOHN DEERE PRODUCT ENGINEERING CENTER - LIBRARY □ Waterloo, IA

Rhein, Donna E., Dir.
DALLAS MUSEUM OF FINE ARTS - REFERENCE LIBRARY† □ Dallas, TX

Rhie, Schi-Zhin, Cat.Libn.
KEAN COLLEGE OF NEW JERSEY - NANCY THOMPSON LIBRARY □ Union, NJ

Rhine, Leonard, Tech.Serv.Libn.
UNIVERSITY OF FLORIDA - J. HILLIS MILLER HEALTH CENTER LIBRARY □ Gainesville, FL

Rhoades, Marjorie, Engr.Sci.Libn.
COLORADO STATE UNIVERSITY - WILLIAM E. MORGAN LIBRARY □ Fort Collins, CO

Rhoads, Donald, Ref.Libn.
P.T. BOATS, INC. - LIBRARY, ARCHIVES & TECHNICAL INFORMATION CENTER - NATIONAL HEADQUARTERS □ Memphis, TN

Rhode, Jim, Pres.
SEMANTODONTICS, INC. - LIBRARY □ Phoenix, AZ

Rhodehamel, John, Archv.
MOUNT VERNON LADIES' ASSOCIATION OF THE UNION - RESEARCH AND REFERENCE LIBRARY □ Mount Vernon, VA

Rhodes, Barbara, Asst.Ref.Libn.
OKLAHOMA STATE UNIVERSITY - SPECIAL COLLECTIONS AND MAPS □ Stillwater, OK

Rhodes, Barry, Dp.Dir.
NEW HAMPSHIRE STATE DEPARTMENT OF HEALTH & WELFARE - OFFICE OF ALCOHOL & DRUG ABUSE PREVENTION - LIBRARY □ Concord, NH

Rhodes, Dallas D., Cur.
WHITTIER COLLEGE - DEPARTMENT OF GEOLOGY - FAIRCHILD AERIAL PHOTOGRAPH COLLECTION □ Whittier, CA

Rhodes, Erroll, Sr.Res.
AMERICAN BIBLE SOCIETY - LIBRARY □ New York, NY

Rhodes, Frieda, Libn.
TEXAS GAS TRANSMISSION CORPORATION - LIBRARY □ Owensboro, KY

Rhodes, Jean, Govt.Doc.Libn.
FEDERAL RESERVE SYSTEM - BOARD OF GOVERNORS - RESEARCH LIBRARY □ Washington, DC

Rhodes, Joseph W., Dir.
BELOIT HISTORICAL SOCIETY - BARTLETT MEMORIAL MUSEUM - LIBRARY □ Beloit, WI

Rhodes, Myrtle J., Supv.Libn.
U.S. NAVY - NAVAL COASTAL SYSTEMS CENTER - TECHNICAL LIBRARY □ Panama City, FL

Rhodes, Ronald
WESTERN STATE UNIVERSITY - COLLEGE OF LAW - LIBRARY □ Fullerton, CA

Rhodes, Yvonne M., Adm.Libn.
U.S. ARMY HOSPITALS - FITZSIMONS ARMY MEDICAL CENTER - MEDICAL-TECHNICAL LIBRARY □ Aurora, CO

Rholes, Julia, Sci.Ref.Libn.
TEXAS A & M UNIVERSITY - REFERENCE DIVISION □ College Station, TX

Rhyne, Charles S., Gen.Couns.
NATIONAL INSTITUTE OF MUNICIPAL LAW OFFICES - LIBRARY □ Washington, DC

Ribback, Edgar G., Libn.
PORT OF SEATTLE - LIBRARY □ Seattle, WA

Ribera De Cambre, Iris, Dir., Tech.Serv.
UNIVERSITY OF PUERTO RICO - MEDICAL SCIENCES CAMPUS - LIBRARY □ Rio Piedras, PR

Ricard, Michel, Agent de Recherche
QUEBEC PROVINCE - MINISTERE DE LA JUSTICE - BIBLIOTHEQUE □ Ste. Foy, PQ

Riccardo-Markot, Vickie, Law Libn.
PRUDENTIAL INSURANCE COMPANY OF AMERICA - LAW LIBRARY □ Newark, NJ

Ricci, Mark, Owner
MEMORY SHOP, INC. - MOVIE MEMORABILIA STILLS □ New York, NY

Ricciardi, Dana D., Registrar/Archv.
MUSEUM OF THE AMERICAN CHINA TRADE - ARCHIVES □ Milton, MA

Rice, Agnes G., Libn.
ALLEN-BRADLEY COMPANY - CORPORATE LIBRARY □ Milwaukee, WI

Rice, Barbara, Hd., Ref.
NEW YORK STATE LIBRARY □ Albany, NY

Rice, Bradford H., Dir.
U.S. DEPT. OF COMMERCE - INTERNATIONAL TRADE ADMINISTRATION - MEMPHIS DISTRICT OFFICE LIBRARY □ Memphis, TN

Rice, Brenda, Libn.
UNIVERSITY OF CHICAGO - CHEMISTRY LIBRARY □ Chicago, IL

Rice, Carol A., Asst.Libn.
U.S. GEOLOGICAL SURVEY - NATIONAL MAPPING DIVISION ASSISTANCE FACILITY - LIBRARY □ NSTL Station, MS

Rice, Cecelia E., Pub.Serv.
XEROX CORPORATION - TECHNICAL INFORMATION CENTER □ Webster, NY

Rice, Cecelia E., Mgr.
XEROX CORPORATION - XEROX SQUARE LIBRARY† □ Rochester, NY

Rice, Chuck, Lib.Serv.Spec.
NATIONAL RURAL ELECTRIC COOPERATIVE ASSOCIATION - NORRIS MEMORIAL LIBRARY □ Washington, DC

Rice, Eleanor M., Libn.
RAYTHEON COMPANY - BADGER AMERICA, INC. - LIBRARY □ Cambridge, MA

Rice, Gwen, Chf., Ref. & ILL
WYOMING STATE LIBRARY □ Cheyenne, WY

Rice, Harvey, Pub.Serv.Libn.
OREGON INSTITUTE OF TECHNOLOGY - LEARNING RESOURCES CENTER □ Klamath Falls, OR

Rice, Marvin L., Libn.
GOODYEAR TIRE AND RUBBER COMPANY - GOODYEAR ATOMIC CORPORATION - TECHNICAL LIBRARY □ Piketon, OH

Rice, Sr. Mercia, Ref.Libn.
OHIO DOMINICAN COLLEGE - LIBRARY □ Columbus, OH

Rice, R. Curt, Lib.Dir.
WINNIPEG BIBLE COLLEGE/WINNIPEG THEOLOGICAL SEMINARY - LIBRARY □ Otterburne, MB

Rice, Ruth, Law Libn.
KLAMATH COUNTY - LOYD DELAP LAW LIBRARY □ Klamath Falls, OR

Rice, Sheila, Ref.Libn.
WASHTENAW COMMUNITY COLLEGE - LEARNING RESOURCE CENTER □ Ann Arbor, MI

Rich, A. Hester, Libn.
MARYLAND HISTORICAL SOCIETY - LIBRARY □ Baltimore, MD

Rich, Denise A., Info.Sys.Libn.
GENERAL ELECTRIC COMPANY - SPACE/RSD LIBRARIES □ Philadelphia, PA

Rich, Jessica, Chf.Libn.
U.S. AIR FORCE - WESTERN SPACE AND MISSILE CENTER - WSMC TECHNICAL LIBRARY □ Vandenberg AFB, CA

Rich, Maria F., Adm.Dir.
CENTRAL OPERA SERVICE - INFORMATION CENTER AND LIBRARY □ New York, NY

Rich, Patricia U., Hd. of Ref.
TIME, INC. - LIBRARY □ New York, NY

Richard, Rob, Assoc.Dir.-Main
LONG BEACH PUBLIC LIBRARY - FINE ARTS DEPARTMENT □ Long Beach, CA

Richards, Barbara G., Asst.Libn.
CARNEGIE-MELLON UNIVERSITY - MELLON INSTITUTE LIBRARY □ Pittsburgh, PA

Richards, Bud, Cur.
MADERA COUNTY HISTORICAL SOCIETY - MUSEUM/LIBRARY □ Madera, CA

Richards, Daniel, Assoc.Libn./Rsrcs. & Ref.
COLUMBIA UNIVERSITY - HEALTH SCIENCES LIBRARY □ New York, NY

Richards, James H., Jr., Libn.
GETTYSBURG COLLEGE - MUSSELMAN LIBRARY - SPECIAL COLLECTIONS □ Gettysburg, PA

Richards, Jean, Libn.
SHELL DEVELOPMENT COMPANY - WESTHOLLOW RESEARCH CENTER LIBRARY† □ Houston, TX

Richards, Katherine, Dir.
COOPER MEDICAL CENTER - REUBEN L. SHARP HEALTH-SCIENCE LIBRARY† □ Camden, NJ

Richards, Katherine, Asst.Libn.
NEW-YORK HISTORICAL SOCIETY - LIBRARY □ New York, NY

Richards, Louise W., Dept.Hd.
INDIANA STATE UNIVERSITY - TEACHING MATERIALS DIVISION □ Terre Haute, IN

Richards, N.J., Legislative Libn.
NEWFOUNDLAND - LEGISLATIVE LIBRARY† □ St. John's, NF

Richards, Robert B., Hd. of Academics
U.S. NAVY - NAVAL TEST PILOT SCHOOL - RESEARCH LIBRARY □ Patuxent River, MD

Richardson, Anne, Libn.
BLACK HILLS STATE COLLEGE - CURRICULUM LIBRARY □ Spearfish, SD

Richardson, Antona, Dir.
UNIVERSITY OF MINNESOTA - FIRE CENTER □ Minneapolis, MN

Richardson, Arlene, Dir.
UNIVERSITY OF NEW MEXICO - SLIDE LIBRARY □ Albuquerque, NM

Richardson, Christine E., Libn.
GERMAN SOCIETY OF PENNSYLVANIA - JOSEPH HORNER MEMORIAL LIBRARY □ Philadelphia, PA

Richardson, Deborra A., Music Libn.
HOWARD UNIVERSITY - MOORLAND-SPINGARN RESEARCH CENTER - MANUSCRIPT DIVISION □ Washington, DC

Richardson, Donald, Tech. Reports
WORCESTER POLYTECHNIC INSTITUTE - GEORGE C. GORDON LIBRARY □ Worcester, MA

Richardson, Donna, Asst.Dir. for Pub.Serv.
CENTER FOR THE STUDY OF YOUTH DEVELOPMENT, BOYS TOWN - LIBRARY SERVICES DIVISION □ Boys Town, NE

Richardson, Eleanor, Ref.Libn.
UNIVERSITY OF SOUTH CAROLINA - SOUTH CAROLINIANA LIBRARY □ Columbia, SC

Richardson, Gail, Libn.
LA JOLLA MUSEUM OF CONTEMPORARY ART - HELEN PALMER GEISEL LIBRARY □ La Jolla, CA

Richardson, Harry
CUSTER COUNTY HISTORICAL SOCIETY - LIBRARY □ Broken Bow, NE

Richardson, Iris W., Libn.
U.S. ARMY POST - FORT JACKSON - LIBRARY □ Ft. Jackson, SC

Richardson, Jeanne, Sci.Libn.
UNIVERSITY OF KANSAS - SCIENCE LIBRARY □ Lawrence, KS

Richardson, Jessie, Assoc.Libn.
UNIVERSITY OF MINNESOTA - BIOMEDICAL LIBRARY □ Minneapolis, MN

Richardson, Joseph, Asst.Doc.Libn.
UNIVERSITY OF KANSAS - DOCUMENTS COLLECTION □ Lawrence, KS

Richardson, Larry, Hd., Rd.Serv.
OREGON COLLEGE OF EDUCATION - LIBRARY □ Monmouth, OR

Richardson, Lynn, Search Anl.
CAROLINA POPULATION CENTER - LIBRARY □ Chapel Hill, NC

Richardson, Marie S., Libn.
UNITED ILLUMINATING COMPANY - LIBRARY □ New Haven, CT

Richardson, Mary, Libn.
CARNEGIE LIBRARY OF PITTSBURGH - CENTRAL CHILDREN'S ROOM HISTORICAL COLLECTION □ Pittsburgh, PA

Richardson, Rick, Prog.
UNIVERSITY OF IOWA - LABORATORY FOR POLITICAL RESEARCH □ Iowa City, IA

Richardson, Robert W., Exec.Dir.
COLORADO RAILROAD HISTORICAL FOUNDATION - LIBRARY □ Golden, CO

Richardson, Ruth, Libn.
FIRST BAPTIST CHURCH - LIBRARY □ Melrose, MA

Richardson, W.H., Libn.
GENERAL MOTORS CORPORATION - DETROIT DIESEL ALLISON DIVISION - LIBRARY □ Indianapolis, IN

Richardson-Tievi, Vicki, Desk Res.
FOOTE CONE & BELDING - INFORMATION CENTER □ Chicago, IL

Richer, Lillian, Doc.Libn.
GRUMMAN AEROSPACE CORPORATION - TECHNICAL INFORMATION CENTER □ Bethpage, NY

Richer, Suzanne, Dir.
CANADA - SECRETARY OF STATE - TRANSLATION BUREAU - DOCUMENTATION DIRECTORATE □ Ottawa, ON

Richer, Yvon, Univ.Chf.Libn.
UNIVERSITY OF OTTAWA - MORISSET LIBRARY □ Ottawa, ON

Richert, Paul, Law Libn.
UNIVERSITY OF AKRON - SCHOOL OF LAW - C. BLAKE MC DOWELL LAW LIBRARY □ Akron, OH

Richman, Linda, Info.Spec.
WESTINGHOUSE ELECTRIC CORPORATION - NUCLEAR ENERGY SYSTEMS - INFORMATION RESOURCES† □ Pittsburgh, PA

Richmond, Professor A.H.
YORK UNIVERSITY - INSTITUTE FOR BEHAVIOURAL RESEARCH - DATA BANK □ Downsview, ON

Richmond, Alice S., Libn.
NORTH CAROLINA CENTRAL UNIVERSITY - SCHOOL OF LIBRARY SCIENCE - LIBRARY □ Durham, NC

Richmond, Eero, Ref.Libn.
FAMILY SERVICE ASSOCIATION OF AMERICA - LIBRARY □ New York, NY

Richmond, Lynne E., Assoc.Libn.
MASSACHUSETTS MARITIME ACADEMY - CAPTAIN CHARLES H. HURLEY LIBRARY □ Buzzards Bay, MA

Richter, Adelaide, Sr.Libn.
ROYAL BANK OF CANADA - INFORMATION RESOURCES □ Montreal, PQ

Richter, Bernice, Libn.
MUSEUM OF SCIENCE & INDUSTRY - LIBRARY □ Chicago, IL

Richter, Edward, Hd.Ref.Libn.
EASTERN NEW MEXICO UNIVERSITY - GOLDEN LIBRARY □ Portales, NM

Richter, Heddy A., Acq.Libn.
ELEUTHERIAN MILLS HISTORICAL LIBRARY □ Wilmington, DE

Richter, Richard, Dir., Television
CONCORDIA TEACHERS COLLEGE - KLINCK MEMORIAL LIBRARY □ River Forest, IL

Richter, William, Asst.Archv.
UNIVERSITY OF TEXAS, AUSTIN - EUGENE C. BARKER TEXAS HISTORY CENTER □ Austin, TX

Rick, Tom, Libn.
HARRIS-STOWE STATE COLLEGE LIBRARY □ St. Louis, MO

Rickard, Ted, Libn.
ONTARIO CRAFTS COUNCIL - CRAFT RESOURCE CENTRE □ Toronto, ON

Rickards, Doris J., Med.Libn.
PAOLI MEMORIAL HOSPITAL - ROBERT M. WHITE MEMORIAL LIBRARY □ Paoli, PA

Rickerson, Connie, Libn.
HOLMES & NARVER, INC. - TECHNICAL LIBRARY □ Orange, CA

Rickett, Robert
3M - PATENT INFORMATION CENTER □ St. Paul, MN

Ricketts, Gail, Info.Ref.Spec.
UNIVERSITY OF PITTSBURGH - CENTER FOR INTERNATIONAL STUDIES □ Pittsburgh, PA

Ricketts, Lynne, Libn.
BEXAR COUNTY MEDICAL LIBRARY □ San Antonio, TX

Ricklefs, Katharine H., Lib.Techn.
ENI COMPANIES - INFORMATION CENTER □ Bellevue, WA

Rickles, Estelle, Libn.
DUNHILL COMPANY - BUSINESS RESEARCH LIBRARY □ Fort Lauderdale, FL

Rickling, Iraida B., Libn.
FLORIDA SOLAR ENERGY CENTER - LIBRARY □ Cape Canaveral, FL

Ricks, David, Planner
PACIFIC NORTHWEST RIVER BASINS COMMISSION - INFORMATION DEPARTMENT □ Vancouver, WA

Rickwald, Deborah, Res.Assoc.
OHIO STATE UNIVERSITY - THEATRE RESEARCH INSTITUTE □ Columbus, OH

Riddle, Louise, Supv., Film Lib.
UNIVERSITY OF COLORADO, BOULDER - EDUCATIONAL MEDIA CENTER □ Boulder, CO

Riddle, Peggy, Res.Asst.
DALLAS HISTORICAL SOCIETY - RESEARCH CENTER □ Dallas, TX

Rideout, Jean, Asst.Libn.
UNIVERSITY OF WISCONSIN, MADISON - LIBRARY SCHOOL LIBRARY □ Madison, WI

Ridge, Geraldine, Libn.
GOOD SAMARITAN SOCIETY - LIBRARY □ Edmonton, AB

Ridge, Hope S., Libn.
RAWLE AND HENDERSON - LAW LIBRARY □ Philadelphia, PA

Ridge, Marian, Libn.
YUKON TERRITORY - DEPARTMENT OF LIBRARY AND INFORMATION RESOURCES - YUKON ARCHIVES □ Whitehorse, YT

Ridgeway, Michel H., AV Libn.
U.S. ARMY - MILITARY ACADEMY - LIBRARY □ West Point, NY

Ridgway, Isabelle, Libn.
ONTARIO PAPER COMPANY, LTD. - LIBRARY □ Thorold, ON

Ridgway, Michelle, Marketing Info.Spec.
LEVI STRAUSS & COMPANY - CORPORATE MARKETING INFORMATION CENTER □ San Francisco, CA

Ridley, Edward, Dir.
U.S. NATL. OCEANIC & ATMOSPHERIC ADMINISTRATION - ENVIRONMENTAL DATA & INFO. SERV. - NATL. OCEANOGRAPHIC DATA CTR. □ Washington, DC

Ridley, Kathy, Libn.
CENTRAL STATE HOSPITAL - MENTAL HEALTH LIBRARY □ Milledgeville, GA

Riebel, Ellis F., Asst.Circ.Libn.
EAST STROUDSBURG STATE COLLEGE - LIBRARY □ East Stroudsburg, PA

Riedel, Louise D., Libn.
SOUTHWEST REGIONAL LABORATORY FOR EDUCATIONAL RESEARCH AND DEVELOPMENT - LIBRARY □ Los Alamitos, CA

Riedel, Sandi, Lib.Asst.
E-SYSTEMS, INC. - MELPAR DIVISION - TECHNICAL LIBRARY □ Falls Church, VA

Riegel, Mrs. Jo, Hd.Libn.
WAGNALLS MEMORIAL - LIBRARY □ Lithopolis, OH

Riehle, Dr. Hal F., Dir.
UNIVERSITY OF WISCONSIN, MADISON - BUREAU OF AUDIOVISUAL INSTRUCTION - LIBRARY □ Madison, WI

Rieke, Kenneth F., Chf., Rec.Ctr.
CONNECTICUT STATE LIBRARY □ Hartford, CT

Riemann, Frederick A., Asst.Libn.
GULF COMPANIES - LAW LIBRARY □ Houston, TX

Riese, Patricia, Libn.
RALTECH SCIENTIFIC SERVICES - LIBRARY □ Madison, WI

Riesgo, Raymond R., Dir.
U.S. DEPT. OF COMMERCE - INTERNATIONAL TRADE ADMINISTRATION - DETROIT DISTRICT OFFICE LIBRARY □ Detroit, MI

Riesmeyer, Mary Lynn, Natural Hist.Libn.
PHOTO RESEARCHERS, INC. - LIBRARY □ New York, NY

Riess, Al, Microforms
SUNY - COLLEGE AT BUFFALO - EDWARD H. BUTLER LIBRARY □ Buffalo, NY

Rife, C.D., Sci.Info.Coord.
LOCKHEED-GEORGIA COMPANY - TECHNICAL INFORMATION DEPARTMENT □ Marietta, GA

Rife, Mary L., Lib.Techn./Proc.Sect.
U.S. ARMY WAR COLLEGE - LIBRARY □ Carlisle Barracks, PA

Rife, Wanda, Asst.Libn.
INDIANA UNIVERSITY OF PENNSYLVANIA - UNIVERSITY LIBRARY □ Indiana, PA

Rigaud, Jeanne, Coord.
CANADIAN INSTITUTE OF HYPNOTISM - LIBRARY □ Montreal, PQ

Rigelhof, Karl, AV Techn.
SENECA COLLEGE OF APPLIED ARTS AND TECHNOLOGY - RESOURCE CENTRE □ Willowdale, ON

Rigelman, Mrs. Delma, Libn.
FIRST LUTHERAN CHURCH OF THE LUTHERAN CHURCH IN AMERICA - SCHENDEL MEMORIAL LIBRARY □ Red Wing, MN

Rigg, Cynthia, Ref.Libn.
NEWSWEEK, INC. - LIBRARY □ New York, NY

Riggle, Keven, Operational Serv.Supv.
MARQUETTE UNIVERSITY - SCIENCE LIBRARY □ Milwaukee, WI

Riggs, Dr. John B., Cur.Mss. & Archv.
ELEUTHERIAN MILLS HISTORICAL LIBRARY □ Wilmington, DE

Rights, Edith A., Libn.
MONTCLAIR ART MUSEUM - LE BRUN LIBRARY □ Montclair, NJ

Rigia, Violet, Libn.
BRIDGEPORT HOSPITAL - REEVES MEMORIAL LIBRARY □ Bridgeport, CT

Rigney, Janet, Libn.
COUNCIL ON FOREIGN RELATIONS - LIBRARY □ New York, NY

Riha, Otokar J., Transl.
PHILLIPS PETROLEUM COMPANY - RESEARCH & DEVELOPMENT DEPARTMENT - TECHNICAL INFORMATION BRANCH □ Bartlesville, OK

Riley, Edith M., Libn.
MAINE CHARITABLE MECHANIC ASSOCIATION - LIBRARY □ Portland, ME

Riley, Jacqueline R., Libn.
PUBLIC LIBRARY OF CINCINNATI AND HAMILTON COUNTY - ART AND MUSIC DEPARTMENT □ Cincinnati, OH

Riley, Margaret Crim, Libn.
WESTERN STATE HOSPITAL - PROFESSIONAL LIBRARY □ Hopkinsville, KY

Riley, Maria, Ed.
CENTER OF CONCERN - INFORMATION CENTER □ Washington, DC

Riley, Mary, Spec.Coll.Libn.
BATES COLLEGE - LIBRARY - SPECIAL COLLECTIONS □ Lewiston, ME

Riley, Mary, Chf.Ref.Libn.
FORDHAM UNIVERSITY - SPECIAL COLLECTIONS □ Bronx, NY

Riley, Patricia, Ref.
UNIVERSITY OF TEXAS HEALTH SCIENCE CENTER, SAN ANTONIO - LIBRARY □ San Antonio, TX

Riley, Sara J., Libn.
VENTURA COUNTY STAR-FREE PRESS - LIBRARY □ Ventura, CA

Riley, William M., Jr., Exec.Dir.
ARABIAN HORSE REGISTRY TRUST OF AMERICA - LIBRARY □ Denver, CO

Rimbach, Cynthia, Software Libn.
LITTON MELLONICS - PROGRAM LIBRARY □ Sunnyvale, CA

Rimmer, Anne, Asst.Libn.Tech.Serv.
UNIVERSITY OF TEXAS SCHOOL OF LAW - TARLTON LAW LIBRARY □ Austin, TX

Rinas, Mary E., Libn.
U.S. AIR FORCE BASE - REESE BASE LIBRARY □ Lubbock, TX

Rinden, Constance T., Law Libn.
NEW HAMPSHIRE STATE LIBRARY - DIVISION OF LAW AND LEGISLATIVE REFERENCE SERVICE □ Concord, NH

Rine, Marie, Libn.
MC FARLAND MENTAL HEALTH CENTER - STAFF LIBRARY □ Springfield, IL

Rinehart, Michael, Libn.
CLARK (Sterling and Francine) ART INSTITUTE - LIBRARY □ Williamstown, MA

Rinehart, Sarah, Cat.Libn.
UNIVERSITY OF OKLAHOMA - LAW LIBRARY □ Norman, OK

Rinehart, Ward, Ed.
JOHNS HOPKINS UNIVERSITY - POPULATION INFORMATION PROGRAM □ Baltimore, MD

Rinesmith, Mary E., Libn.
MC NEES, WALLACE AND NURICK - LIBRARY □ Harrisburg, PA

Ring, Daniel F., Libn.
OAKLAND UNIVERSITY - LIBRARY □ Rochester, MI

Ring, Joan, Acq./Cat.Libn.
STORMONT-VAIL REGIONAL MEDICAL CENTER AND SHAWNEE COUNTY MEDICAL SOCIETY - HEALTH SCIENCES LIBRARY □ Topeka, KS

Ring, Patricia M., Tech.Serv.Libn.
CLEVELAND STATE UNIVERSITY - JOSEPH W. BARTUNEK III LAW LIBRARY □ Cleveland, OH

Ringdal, June C., Law Libn.
BLAIR COUNTY LAW LIBRARY □ Hollidaysburg, PA

Ringstrom, Diana, Libn.
ALCOHOLISM FOUNDATION OF MANITOBA - WILLIAM POTOROKA MEMORIAL LIBRARY □ Winnipeg, MB

Rink, Evald, Imprints Libn.
ELEUTHERIAN MILLS HISTORICAL LIBRARY □ Wilmington, DE

Rinzel, Dennis, Media Dir.
UNIVERSITY OF WISCONSIN, MADISON - SCHOOL OF SOCIAL WORK - RESEARCH & INSTRUCTIONAL MEDIA CENTER □ Madison, WI

Riordan, Margaret B., Libn.
EMPLOYEE BENEFIT RESEARCH INSTITUTE - LIBRARY □ Washington, DC

Riordan, Patricia H., Libn.
MELLON BANK, N.A. - LIBRARY □ Pittsburgh, PA

Rios, Barbara J., Project Libn.
CENTER ON SOCIAL WELFARE POLICY AND LAW - LIBRARY □ New York, NY

Rios, Betty Rose, Asst.Dir.
ERIC CLEARINGHOUSE ON RURAL EDUCATION AND SMALL SCHOOLS □ Las Cruces, NM

Rioux, Gaston, O.M.I., Chf.Libn.
UNIVERSITE ST-PAUL D'OTTAWA - BIBLIOTHEQUE □ Ottawa, ON

Ripatti, Sally K., Spec.Mtls.Libn.
KNOXVILLE-KNOX COUNTY PUBLIC LIBRARY SYSTEM - MC CLUNG HISTORICAL COLLECTION □ Knoxville, TN

Ripin, Laura G., Libn.
DREXEL BURNHAM LAMBERT INC. - RESEARCH LIBRARY □ New York, NY

Ripley, Ann, Asst.
MURPHY OIL CORPORATION - LAW DEPARTMENT LIBRARY □ El Dorado, AR

Ripley, G. Birch, Libn.
ELRICK AND LAVIDGE, INC. - LIBRARY □ Chicago, IL

Ripley, Victoria, Chf.Libn.
HURON COLLEGE - SILCOX MEMORIAL LIBRARY □ London, ON

Rippeon, Janet D., Law Libn.
FREDERICK COUNTY LAW LIBRARY □ Frederick, MD

Ripper, Jean K., Asst. to Libn.
ST. LOUIS ART MUSEUM - RICHARDSON MEMORIAL LIBRARY □ St. Louis, MO

Rippy, Leo, Jr., Dir., Lib.Serv.
SCARRITT COLLEGE FOR CHRISTIAN WORKERS - VIRGINIA DAVIS LASKEY LIBRARY □ Nashville, TN

Ripy, Minnie Sue, Cat.
BROOKINGS INSTITUTION - LIBRARY □ Washington, DC

Riquier, Myrna D., Libn.
ROGERS CORPORATION - LURIE LIBRARY □ Rogers, CT

Risbrough, Ned, Exec.Dir.
EUGENE HEARING AND SPEECH CENTER - LIBRARY† □ Eugene, OR

Risk, James C., Mgr., Tech.Oper.
STACK'S RARE COIN COMPANY OF NEW YORK - TECHNICAL INFORMATION CENTER □ New York, NY

Rison, David, Graphic Designer
BRIGHAM AND WOMEN'S HOSPITAL - ABRAMSON CENTER FOR INSTRUCTIONAL MEDIA □ Boston, MA

Ristic, Jovanka, Map Cat./Ref.Libn.
AMERICAN GEOGRAPHICAL SOCIETY COLLECTION OF THE UNIVERSITY OF WISCONSIN, MILWAUKEE - GOLDA MEIR LIBRARY □ Milwaukee, WI

Ritcherson, Barbara, Pharmacy Libn.
TEXAS SOUTHERN UNIVERSITY - PHARMACY LIBRARY □ Houston, TX

Ritchey, Douglas, Ref.Libn.
MORTON ARBORETUM - STERLING MORTON LIBRARY □ Lisle, IL

Ritchie, David, Ref./Cat.Libn.
SUNY - COLLEGE AT CORTLAND - MEMORIAL LIBRARY □ Cortland, NY

Ritchie, David J., Libn.
SIMULATIONS PUBLICATIONS, INC. - SPI MILITARY LIBRARY □ New York, NY

Ritchie, Florence, Libn.
FIRST CONGREGATIONAL CHURCH - LIBRARY □ St. Joseph, MI

Ritchie, Mrs. Gaylan, Regional Marine Libn.
CANADA - TRANSPORT CANADA - CANADIAN COAST GUARD, MARITIMES REGION - MARINE LIBRARY □ Dartmouth, NS

Ritchie, Mark
EARTHWORK - CENTER FOR RURAL STUDIES □ San Francisco, CA

Rittenhouse, Robert J., Tech.Info.Spec.
GOULD, INC. - OCEAN SYSTEMS DIVISION - OCEAN SYSTEMS INFORMATION CENTER □ Cleveland, OH

Rittenhouse, Shirley A., Ref.Libn.
MARYLAND STATE LAW LIBRARY □ Annapolis, MD

Ritter, Audrey, Rsrcs.Spec.
ROCHESTER INSTITUTE OF TECHNOLOGY - NATIONAL TECHNICAL INSTITUTE FOR THE DEAF - STAFF RESOURCE CENTER □ Rochester, NY

Ritter, Clariss, Libn.
MILITARY ORDER OF THE LOYAL LEGION OF THE UNITED STATES - WAR LIBRARY AND MUSEUM □ Philadelphia, PA

Ritter, Darlyne, Libn.
MILWAUKEE PSYCHIATRIC HOSPITAL - LIBRARY □ Wauwatosa, WI

Ritter, Linda, Asst.Libn.
SAN DIEGO UNION-TRIBUNE PUBLISHING COMPANY - LIBRARY □ San Diego, CA

Ritter, Sheila, Exec.Dir.
NORTH AMERICAN STUDENTS OF COOPERATION - LIBRARY □ Ann Arbor, MI

Ritz, Jayne, Drug Info. Resident
LONG ISLAND UNIV. - ARNOLD & MARIE SCHWARTZ COLLEGE OF PHARMACY & HEALTH SCIENCES - INTERNATL. DRUG INFO.CTR. □ Brooklyn, NY

Rivas, Guillermo, Asst.Libn.
MOUNT SINAI HOSPITAL SERVICES - CITY HOSPITAL CENTER AT ELMHURST - MEDICAL LIBRARY □ Elmhurst, NY

Rivera, Adelaida, Hd., Circ.
UNIVERSITY OF PUERTO RICO - GENERAL LIBRARY □ San Juan, PR

Rivera, Agnes G.
UNIVERSITY OF PUERTO RICO - NATURAL SCIENCE LIBRARY □ Rio Piedras, PR

Rivera, Edmaris, Libn.
UNIVERSITY OF PUERTO RICO - PUERTO RICAN COLLECTION □ Rio Piedras, PR

Rivera, Flor P., Hd., Selection
UNIVERSITY OF PUERTO RICO - GENERAL LIBRARY □ San Juan, PR

Rivera, Israel, Libn.
PUERTO RICO - STATE DEPARTMENT OF CONSUMER AFFAIRS - LIBRARY □ Santurce, PR

Rivera, Lydia M., Libn.
CAMDEN COUNTY BAR ASSOCIATION - LAW LIBRARY† □ Camden, NJ

Rivera, Miguel A., Circ.
UNIVERSITY OF PUERTO RICO - LAW SCHOOL LIBRARY □ Rio Piedras, PR

Rivers, Barbara, Libn.
TRI-COUNTY HOSPITAL - MEDICAL LIBRARY □ Springfield, PA

Rivers, Richard D., Mgr.
AMERICAN AIR FILTER COMPANY, INC. - TECHNICAL LIBRARY □ Louisville, KY

Rizzuto, Carol, Res.Libn., Ins.
METROPOLITAN LIFE INSURANCE COMPANY - LIBRARY □ New York, NY

Roach, Lenore J., Sr.Libn.
KINGSBORO PSYCHIATRIC CENTER - MEDICAL LIBRARY □ Brooklyn, NY

Roach, Linda C., Libn.
MORGAN, LEWIS & BOCKIUS - LIBRARY □ Philadelphia, PA

Roach, Sue, Hd., Ref./Tech.Serv.
U.S. NAVY - OFFICE OF THE JUDGE ADVOCATE GENERAL - LAW LIBRARY □ Alexandria, VA

Roach, Terry T., Lib.Adm.
ACADEMY OF MOTION PICTURE ARTS AND SCIENCES - MARGARET HERRICK LIBRARY □ Beverly Hills, CA

Road, Rachel, Cur. of Photographs
TIPPECANOE COUNTY HISTORICAL ASSOCIATION - ALAMEDA MC COLLOUGH RESEARCH & GENEALOGY LIBRARY □ Lafayette, IN

Roadhouse, Mrs. I. R., Libn.
RIDGETOWN COLLEGE OF AGRICULTURAL TECHNOLOGY - LIBRARY □ Ridgetown, ON

Roake, Jo Ann, Ref.Libn.
PALOMAR COLLEGE - PHIL H. PUTNAM MEMORIAL LIBRARY □ San Marcos, CA

Robb, Darel J., Assoc.Dir./Coll.Dev.
MEDICAL COLLEGE OF WISCONSIN - TODD WEHR LIBRARY □ Milwaukee, WI

Robb, Deborah, Libn./Cat./Ref./Res.
KENTUCKY STATE DEPARTMENT FOR HUMAN RESOURCES - LIBRARY □ Frankfort, KY

Robb, Susan, Mgr., Res.Lib.
SEARLE (G.D.) & CO. - RESEARCH LIBRARY □ Skokie, IL

Robba, Diana, Lib.Spec.
HEWLETT-PACKARD COMPANY - SANTA CLARA DIVISION LIBRARY □ Santa Clara, CA

Robben, Dorothy D., Supv., Lib. & Rec.
AMERICAN BRANDS, INC. - AMERICAN TOBACCO COMPANY - DEPARTMENT OF RESEARCH & DEVELOPMENT LIBRARY □ Hopewell, VA

Robbin, Alice, Hd. of DPLS
UNIVERSITY OF WISCONSIN, MADISON - DATA AND PROGRAM LIBRARY SERVICE □ Madison, WI

Robbins, Allan, Libn.
ALEXANDRIA LIBRARY - LLOYD HOUSE □ Alexandria, VA

Robbins, Carol, Acq.
MARTIN MARIETTA CORPORATION - DENVER DIVISION - RESEARCH LIBRARY □ Denver, CO

Robbins, Irving, Libn.
MINNEAPOLIS PUBLIC LIBRARY & INFORMATION CENTER - BUSINESS AND SCIENCE DEPARTMENT □ Minneapolis, MN

Robbins, Jean, Libn.
BURROUGHS CORPORATION - COMPUTER SYSTEMS GROUP - TECHNICAL INFORMATION RESOURCES CENTER† □ Pasadena, CA

Robbins, Lora, Med.Libn.
U.S. PUBLIC HEALTH SERVICE HOSPITAL - MEDICAL LIBRARY □ Boston, MA

Robbins, Lynne, Dir.
PHILLIPS ACADEMY - OLIVER WENDELL HOLMES LIBRARY - SPECIAL COLLECTIONS □ Andover, MA

Robbins, Ortha D., Supv.
ST. PAUL PUBLIC LIBRARY - CIRCULATION ROOM □ St. Paul, MN

Robbins, Patricia V., Dir. of Ref. & Lib.
WISCONSIN STATE LEGISLATIVE REFERENCE BUREAU □ Madison, WI

Robbins, Rintha, Libn.
MADERA COUNTY HISTORICAL SOCIETY - MUSEUM/LIBRARY □ Madera, CA

Robbins, William R.
BRANT COUNTY MUSEUM - LIBRARY □ Brantford, ON

Robbs, Brett, Adm.Dir.
CENTER FOR SOUTHERN FOLKLORE - ARCHIVES □ Memphis, TN

Roberge, Monique, Audiovideotheque
CEGEP DE TROIS-RIVIERES - BIBLIOTHEQUE □ Trois-Rivieres, PQ

Roberson, Bernadine C., Libn.
U.S. DEPT. OF COMMERCE - INTERNATIONAL TRADE ADMINISTRATION - CHICAGO DISTRICT OFFICE LIBRARY □ Chicago, IL

Roberson, Suzanne, Asst.Libn.
ALBANY INSTITUTE OF HISTORY AND ART - MC KINNEY LIBRARY □ Albany, NY

Robert, Barry, Asst.Libn.
OTTAWA CITIZEN - LIBRARY □ Ottawa, ON

Robert, Cecile, Hd. of Pub.Serv.
COMMISSION DES ECOLES CATHOLIQUES DE MONTREAL - BIBLIOTHEQUE CENTRALE □ Montreal, PQ

Robert, Michel, Chf.Libn.
CEGEP ST-JEAN SUR RICHELIEU - BIBLIOTHEQUE† □ St. Jean, PQ

Roberts, Ammarette, Mgr., Tech.Info.Serv.
MOBIL RESEARCH & DEVELOPMENT CORPORATION - FIELD RESEARCH LABORATORY LIBRARY □ Dallas, TX

Roberts, Ann B., Libn.
MC GUIRE, WOODS AND BATTLE - LAW LIBRARY □ Richmond, VA

Roberts, Audrey, Per. & Curric.Libn.
CONCORDIA TEACHERS COLLEGE - KLINCK MEMORIAL LIBRARY □ River Forest, IL

Roberts, Barbara, Dir.
CHAMPAIGN COUNTY HISTORICAL ARCHIVES □ Urbana, IL

Roberts, Charlotte A., Law Libn.
ALLEN COUNTY LAW LIBRARY □ Fort Wayne, IN

Roberts, Cynthia, Slide Curator
SCHOOL OF VISUAL ARTS - LIBRARY □ New York, NY

Roberts, Don L., Hd.
NORTHWESTERN UNIVERSITY - MUSIC LIBRARY □ Evanston, IL

Roberts, Dr. Edward Graham, Dir.
GEORGIA INSTITUTE OF TECHNOLOGY - PRICE GILBERT MEMORIAL LIBRARY □ Atlanta, GA

Roberts, Elaine H., Libn.
PISCATAQUIS COUNTY LAW LIBRARY □ Dover-Foxcroft, ME

Roberts, Elizabeth P., Hd.
WASHINGTON STATE UNIVERSITY - OWEN SCIENCE AND ENGINEERING LIBRARY □ Pullman, WA

Roberts, Gerald F., Spec.Coll.Libn.
BEREA COLLEGE - HUTCHINS LIBRARY - SPECIAL COLLECTIONS □ Berea, KY

Roberts, Gerrard, Libn.
CLEVELAND ELECTRIC ILLUMINATING COMPANY - LIBRARY □ Cleveland, OH

Roberts, Glenda, Cat.
PITTSBURG STATE UNIVERSITY - LEONARD H. AXE LIBRARY □ Pittsburg, KS

Roberts, Gloria A., Hd. Libn.
PLANNED PARENTHOOD FEDERATION OF AMERICA, INC. - KATHARINE DEXTER MC CORMICK LIBRARY □ New York, NY

Roberts, Gretchen, Media Coord.
CROUSE-IRVING MEMORIAL HOSPITAL - LIBRARY □ Syracuse, NY

Roberts, H. Armstrong, III, Pres.
ROBERTS (H. Armstrong) COMPANY - STOCK PICTURE LIBRARY □ Philadelphia, PA

Roberts, Hazel J., Hd.Libn.
ASSOCIATION OF UNIVERSITIES AND COLLEGES OF CANADA - LIBRARY □ Ottawa, ON

Roberts, Helene, Cur. of Vis.Coll.
HARVARD UNIVERSITY - FINE ARTS LIBRARY □ Cambridge, MA

Roberts, Jean, Ed./Libn.
THORNDIKE LIBRARY □ Boston, MA

Roberts, Sr. Jean B., S.C.N., Med.Libn.
ST. VINCENT INFIRMARY - MEDICAL LIBRARY □ Little Rock, AR

Roberts, Joe, Ed.
NATIONAL RIFLE ASSOCIATION - TECHNICAL LIBRARY □ Washington, DC

Roberts, John, Rd.Adv./Music
TRENTON STATE COLLEGE - ROSCOE L. WEST LIBRARY □ Trenton, NJ

Roberts, Dr. John P., Sec.
NATIONAL MUSEUM OF TRANSPORT - TRANSPORTATION REFERENCE LIBRARY □ St. Louis, MO

Roberts, Juanita, Libn.
DARTNELL CORPORATION - PUBLISHING-RESEARCH LIBRARY □ Chicago, IL

Roberts, Karen, Libn.
ST. ANDREWS HOSPITAL - MEDICAL LIBRARY □ Boothbay Harbor, ME

Roberts, Kitty, Pub.Serv.Libn.
TEXAS A & M UNIVERSITY AT GALVESTON - LIBRARY □ Galveston, TX

Roberts, Linda L., Coll.Libn.
OKLAHOMA COLLEGE OF OSTEOPATHIC MEDICINE & SURGERY - LIBRARY □ Tulsa, OK

Roberts, Linda R., Cat. & Ref.Libn.
ROCKWELL INTERNATIONAL - SCIENCE CENTER LIBRARY □ Thousand Oaks, CA

Roberts, Patricia A.B., Res.Spec.
MONTANA STATE DEPARTMENT OF ADMINISTRATION - RESEARCH & INFORMATION SYSTEMS DIVISION - RESOURCE CENTER □ Helena, MT

Roberts, Phil, Sr.Res.Hist.
WYOMING STATE ARCHIVES, MUSEUMS AND HISTORICAL DEPARTMENT □ Cheyenne, WY

Roberts, Ruth, Mgt.Libn.
BRUNSWICK CORPORATION - MANAGEMENT LIBRARY □ Skokie, IL

Roberts, Sandra, Libn.
TENNESSEAN - LIBRARY □ Nashville, TN

Roberts, Susan K., Automation/Tech.Serv.
AMERICAN MEDICAL ASSOCIATION - DIVISION OF LIBRARY AND ARCHIVAL SERVICES □ Chicago, IL

Roberts, Victoria M., Res.Libn.
FEDERAL RESERVE BANK OF DALLAS - RESEARCH LIBRARY □ Dallas, TX

Robertson, Ann, Mgr., Info. & Anl.Serv.
MC KINSEY & COMPANY, INC. - LIBRARY □ Washington, DC

Robertson, Ann M., Info.Spec.
SAVAGE INFORMATION SERVICES □ Rolling Hills Estates, CA

Robertson, Bethany, Med.Libn.
LANSING GENERAL HOSPITAL - OSTEOPATHIC - K.M. BAKER MEMORIAL LIBRARY □ Lansing, MI

Robertson, Betty G., Info.Sec.
LEIGH INSTRUMENTS, LTD. - ENGINEERING & AEROSPACE DIVISION - TECHNICAL LIBRARY □ Carleton Place, ON

Robertson, Carolyn, Libn.
NATIONAL COTTON COUNCIL OF AMERICA - LIBRARY □ Memphis, TN

Robertson, D.F., Dir.
KELSEY INSTITUTE OF APPLIED ARTS AND SCIENCES - LEARNING RESOURCES CENTRE □ Saskatoon, SK

Robertson, David W., Asst.Mgr.
GENERAL REFRACTORIES COMPANY - U.S. REFRACTORIES DIVISION - RESEARCH CENTER LIBRARY □ Baltimore, MD

Robertson, Jack, Arts Libn.
VANDERBILT UNIVERSITY LIBRARY - CENTRAL DIVISION - ARTS LIBRARY □ Nashville, TN

Robertson, Jean, Dir., Info.Ctr.
NATIONAL SOCIETY OF PROFESSIONAL ENGINEERS - INFORMATION CENTER □ Washington, DC

Robertson, Jean, Ser.Libn.
STANFORD UNIVERSITY - J. HUGH JACKSON LIBRARY □ Stanford, CA

Robertson, Joyce, Lib.Asst.
ST. ALPHONSUS HOSPITAL - HEALTH SCIENCES LIBRARY □ Boise, ID

Robertson, Judith, Libn.
U.S. DEPT. OF LABOR - OSHA - REGIONAL LIBRARY □ Seattle, WA

Robertson, Lavonne D., Hd.Libn.
SALVATION ARMY SCHOOL FOR OFFICERS TRAINING - ELFTMAN MEMORIAL LIBRARY □ Rancho Palos Verdes, CA

Robertson, Lori, Circ.Libn.
SOUTHWESTERN BAPTIST THEOLOGICAL SEMINARY - FLEMING LIBRARY □ Fort Worth, TX

Robertson, Ms. M., Lib.Asst., Acq.
HURON COLLEGE - SILCOX MEMORIAL LIBRARY □ London, ON

Robertson, Mary, Asst.Dir.
CHEROKEE REGIONAL LIBRARY - GEORGIA HISTORY & GENEALOGICAL ROOM □ LaFayette, GA

Robertson, Mary, Cur. Of Mss.
HUNTINGTON (Henry E.) LIBRARY, ART GALLERY AND BOTANICAL GARDENS □ San Marino, CA

Robertson, Mary Kay, Circ.Libn.
VOUGHT CORPORATION - TECHNICAL INFORMATION CENTER □ Dallas, TX

Robertson, Mary Ruth, Libn.
CHESAPEAKE BAY MARITIME MUSEUM - LIBRARY □ St. Michaels, MD

Robertson, Retha, Libn.
HTB, INC. - TECHNICAL INFORMATION CENTER □ Oklahoma City, OK

Robertson, S. Donald, Hd.Libn.
SCOTT, FORESMAN & COMPANY, INC. - EDITORIAL LIBRARY □ Glenview, IL

Robertson, Susan T., Libn.
GRANT (Alexander) & COMPANY - CHICAGO OFFICE LIBRARY □ Chicago, IL

Robertson, W. Davenport, Hd.Libn.
NATIONAL INSTITUTE OF ENVIRONMENTAL HEALTH SCIENCES - LIBRARY □ Research Triangle Park, NC

Robichaux, Catherine, Libn.
HOUSTON LIGHTING & POWER COMPANY - LIBRARY □ Houston, TX

Robie, Nancy, Asst.Libn.
MASSACHUSETTS INSTITUTE OF TECHNOLOGY - NEUROSCIENCES RESEARCH PROGRAM - LIBRARY □ Boston, MA

Robillard, Jean-Jacques, Chf.Libn./Info.Dir.
COLLEGE DOMINICAIN DE PHILOSOPHIE ET DE THEOLOGIE - BIBLIOTHEQUE □ Ottawa, ON

Robinow, Beatrix H., Health Sci.Libn.
MC MASTER UNIVERSITY - HEALTH SCIENCES LIBRARY □ Hamilton, ON

Robins, Margaret, Med.Libn.
WOMEN'S COLLEGE HOSPITAL - MEDICAL LIBRARY □ Toronto, ON

Robinson, Agnes F., Asst. Law Libn.
DUQUESNE UNIVERSITY - LAW LIBRARY □ Pittsburgh, PA

Robinson, Alice B., Chf.
DISTRICT OF COLUMBIA PUBLIC LIBRARY - BLACK STUDIES DIVISION □ Washington, DC

Robinson, Anne, Media Serv.Libn.
DISTRICT OF COLUMBIA TEACHERS COLLEGE - LIBRARY □ Washington, DC

Robinson, Celia, Ref.Libn.
HENDERSON STATE UNIVERSITY - HUIE LIBRARY □ Arkadelphia, AR

Robinson, Chantal, Assoc.Dir.
QUEBEC PROVINCE - SERVICE GENERAL DES MOYENS D'ENSEIGNEMENT - CENTRE DE DOCUMENTATION □ Montreal, PQ

Robinson, Chris, Jr.Libn.
ONTARIO HYDRO - LIBRARY □ Toronto, ON

Robinson, D., Libn.
CANADA - CANADIAN FORESTRY SERVICE - NORTHERN FOREST RESEARCH CENTRE - LIBRARY □ Edmonton, AB

Robinson, Dean, ILL
TENNESSEE VALLEY AUTHORITY - TECHNICAL LIBRARY □ Chattanooga, TN

Robinson, Elizabeth A., Libn.
GOOD SAMARITAN HOSPITAL - SHANK MEMORIAL LIBRARY □ Dayton, OH

Robinson, Erika, Coord.
DISTRICT OF COLUMBIA PUBLIC SCHOOLS - DIVISION OF RESEARCH AND EVALUATION - RESEARCH INFORMATION CENTER □ Washington, DC

Robinson, Fay, Br.Libn.
U.S. ARMY POST - FORT LEWIS - LIBRARY SYSTEM □ Fort Lewis, WA

Robinson, Mrs. Halcyon S., Libn.
U.S. AIR FORCE BASE - CHARLESTON BASE LIBRARY □ Charleston AFB, SC

Robinson, Hank, Info.Sys.Spec.
MITRE CORPORATION - TECHNICAL REPORT CENTER† □ Bedford, MA

Robinson, Hannah G., Libn./S. Asia Coll.
INSTITUTE FOR ADVANCED STUDIES OF WORLD RELIGIONS - LIBRARY □ Stony Brook, NY

Robinson, James A., Asst.Libn.
WORCESTER TELEGRAM AND GAZETTE, INC. - LIBRARY □ Worcester, MA

Robinson, Josephine, Hd., Info. & Res.
U.S. DEPT. OF ENERGY - LAWRENCE BERKELEY LABORATORY - LIBRARY □ Berkeley, CA

Robinson, Judy, Hd.Libn.
SAN ANTONIO EXPRESS AND NEWS - LIBRARY □ San Antonio, TX

Robinson, Juliet, Libn.
MC CRONE (Walter C.) ASSOCIATES - LIBRARY □ Chicago, IL

Robinson, Karen, Libn.
ORAL ROBERTS UNIVERSITY - LIBRARY - HOLY SPIRIT RESEARCH CENTER □ Tulsa, OK

Robinson, Louise, Chf., Clipping Serv.
NATIONAL GEOGRAPHIC SOCIETY - LIBRARY □ Washington, DC

Robinson, Lowell M., Chf.Libn.
U.S. ARMY - ACADEMY OF HEALTH SCIENCES - STIMSON LIBRARY† □ Ft. Sam Houston, TX

Robinson, Lynn H., Libn.
WENTWORTH INSTITUTE OF TECHNOLOGY - LIBRARY □ Boston, MA

Robinson, Margaret, Act.Hd., Ref.
UNIVERSITY OF CALIFORNIA, SANTA CRUZ - DEAN E. MC HENRY LIBRARY □ Santa Cruz, CA

Robinson, Marjorie, Libn.
CANADIAN TAX FOUNDATION - LIBRARY □ Toronto, ON

Robinson, Michaele M., Libn.
ZOOLOGICAL SOCIETY OF SAN DIEGO - ERNST SCHWARZ LIBRARY □ San Diego, CA

Robinson, Nancy, Cat.
SOUTHERN BAPTIST THEOLOGICAL SEMINARY - JAMES P. BOYCE CENTENNIAL LIBRARY □ Louisville, KY

Robinson, Orvetta, Libn. & Registrar
ILLINOIS STATE MUSEUM OF NATURAL HISTORY AND ART - TECHNICAL LIBRARY □ Springfield, IL

Robinson, Pamela, Libn.
GIBSON, DUNN & CRUTCHER - LAW LIBRARY □ Los Angeles, CA

Robinson, Paul, Exec.Dir.
SOUTHWEST RESEARCH & INFORMATION CENTER □ Albuquerque, NM

Robinson, Pearl O., Libn.
U.S. NAVY - NAVAL SHIP SYSTEMS ENGINEERING STATION HEADQUARTERS - TECHNICAL LIBRARY □ Philadelphia, PA

Robinson, Miss R., Adm.Asst.
HORNER (Frank W.), LTD. - RESEARCH LIBRARY □ Montreal, PQ

Robinson, Renee, Info.Chem.
UNION OIL COMPANY OF CALIFORNIA - TECHNICAL INFORMATION CENTER □ Placentia, CA

Robinson, Richard, Ref.Libn.
U.S. DEPT. OF ENERGY - LAWRENCE BERKELEY LABORATORY - LIBRARY □ Berkeley, CA

Robinson, Shiela, Info.Spec.
WESTINGHOUSE ELECTRIC CORPORATION - NUCLEAR ENERGY SYSTEMS - INFORMATION RESOURCES† □ Pittsburgh, PA

Robinson, Shirley J., Per.Libn.
WINSTON-SALEM STATE UNIVERSITY - O'KELLY LIBRARY □ Winston-Salem, NC

Robinson, Teresa, Adm.Asst.
INTERNATIONAL VISITORS INFORMATION SERVICE □ Washington, DC

Robinson, Thomas J., Educ.Libn.
UNIVERSITY OF WINDSOR - FACULTY OF EDUCATION LIBRARY □ Windsor, ON

Robinson, Vera, Tech.Serv.Libn.
WESTERN THEOLOGICAL SEMINARY - BEARDSLEE LIBRARY □ Holland, MI

Robison, Jane R., Dir.
KANSAS HERITAGE CENTER - LIBRARY □ Dodge City, KS

Robitaille, Louise, Chf. Of Cat.Dept.
ECOLE DES HAUTES ETUDES COMMERCIALES DE MONTREAL - BIBLIOTHEQUE □ Montreal, PQ

Robitaille, Sylvie, Info.Off.
CANADA - PUBLIC ARCHIVES OF CANADA - NATL. FILM, TELEVISION & SOUND ARCHIVES - DOCUMENTATION & PUB. SERV. □ Ottawa, ON

Robson, Betty J., Res.Libn.
UNITED STATES BORAX RESEARCH CORPORATION - RESEARCH LIBRARY □ Anaheim, CA

Robson, Carolyn, Cat.Libn.
SUNY - COLLEGE AT POTSDAM - FREDERICK W. CRUMB MEMORIAL LIBRARY □ Potsdam, NY

Robson, Doreen, Ck.
CANADIAN JEWELLERS INSTITUTE - LIBRARY □ Toronto, ON

Robson, John M., Hd., Tech.Serv.
VIRGINIA MILITARY INSTITUTE - PRESTON LIBRARY □ Lexington, VA

Rocamora, Joel, Co-Dir.
SOUTHEAST ASIA RESOURCE CENTER □ Berkeley, CA

Rocco, Gail, Lib.Asst.
ST. JOSEPH MEDICAL CENTER - HEALTH SCIENCE LIBRARY □ Burbank, CA

Rocha, Guy, State Archv.
NEVADA STATE LIBRARY □ Carson City, NV

Rocha, Guy L., State Archv.
NEVADA STATE LIBRARY - DIVISION OF STATE, COUNTY AND MUNICIPAL ARCHIVES □ Carson City, NV

Rochette, L., Acq.
COMPLEXE SCIENTIFIQUE DU QUEBEC - SERVICE DE DOCUMENTATION ET DE BIBLIOTHEQUE □ Ste. Foy, PQ

Rock, Catherine, Adm.
LEVI STRAUSS & COMPANY - CORPORATE MARKETING INFORMATION CENTER □ San Francisco, CA

Rock, Dale, Naturalist
HENNEPIN COUNTY PARK RESERVE DISTRICT - LOWRY NATURE CENTER - LIBRARY □ Excelsior, MN

Rock, Susan, Ref.
KUTAK, ROCK & HUIE - LAW LIBRARY □ Omaha, NE

Rockefeller, Shirley J., Tech.Libn.
GENERAL ELECTRIC COMPANY - SPACE/RSD LIBRARIES □ Philadelphia, PA

Rocker, Willard L., Genealogy Libn.
MIDDLE GEORGIA REGIONAL LIBRARY - WASHINGTON MEMORIAL LIBRARY - GENEALOGICAL & HISTORICAL ROOM □ Macon, GA

Rockey, Steven W., Supv.
CORNELL UNIVERSITY - MATHEMATICS LIBRARY □ Ithaca, NY

Rockwell, Susan P., Lib.Techn.
U.S. NATL. MARINE FISHERIES SERVICE - NORTHEAST FISHERIES CENTER - LIBRARY □ Woods Hole, MA

Rocky, Helen K., Dir.Lib.Serv.
INTERNATIONAL ACADEMY AT SANTA BARBARA - LIBRARY □ Santa Barbara, CA

Rodda, Reddy, Libn.
UNIVERSITY OF TENNESSEE - SCIENCE-ENGINEERING LIBRARY □ Knoxville, TN

Rodeffer, Georgia H., Textiles Libn.
NORTH CAROLINA STATE UNIVERSITY - BURLINGTON TEXTILE LIBRARY □ Raleigh, NC

Roden, Jeanyce, Med.Libn.
U.S. VETERANS ADMINISTRATION (WA-Seattle) - HOSPITAL MEDICAL LIBRARY □ Seattle, WA

Rodenhauser, Paul C., Grand Recorder
RED CROSS OF CONSTANTINE - UNITED GRAND IMPERIAL COUNCIL - LIBRARY □ Chicago, IL

Rodenhaver, Dale Ann, Mgr.
BUDD COMPANY TECHNICAL LIBRARY □ Fort Washington, PA

Rodes, Barbara K., Libn.
CONSERVATION FOUNDATION - LIBRARY □ Washington, DC

Rodgers, Beth
STAGECOACH HOUSE MUSEUM - LIBRARY □ Wyoming, RI

Rodgers, Guy, Owner & Asst.Libn.
STAGECOACH HOUSE MUSEUM - LIBRARY □ Wyoming, RI

Rodgers, Jane C., Libn.
SHELL OIL COMPANY - INFORMATION & LIBRARY SERVICES □ Houston, TX

Rodgers, Jonathan H., Spec.Coll.Libn.
HEBREW UNION COLLEGE - JEWISH INSTITUTE OF RELIGION - KLAU LIBRARY □ Cincinnati, OH

Rodgers, Mary M., Libn.
WINE MUSEUM OF SAN FRANCISCO - CHRISTIAN BROTHERS RARE WINE BOOKS LIBRARY □ San Francisco, CA

Rodgers, Patricia, Coord., Tech.Serv.
UNIVERSITY OF SOUTH ALABAMA - COLLEGE OF MEDICINE - BIOMEDICAL LIBRARY □ Mobile, AL

Rodich, Lorraine E., Ref.
UNIVERSITY OF SANTA CLARA - EDWIN A. HEAFEY LAW LIBRARY □ Santa Clara, CA

PERSONNEL

Rodin, I., Coord., Online Ref.
UNIVERSITY OF WATERLOO - ENGINEERING,
MATHEMATICS & SCIENCE DIVISIONAL
LIBRARY □ Waterloo, ON

Rodkewich, Patricia, Doc.Libn.
UNIVERSITY OF MINNESOTA, ST. PAUL -
CENTRAL LIBRARY □ St. Paul, MN

Rodney, Mrs. Jamesie, Mgr.
PEABODY COLLEGE FOR TEACHERS - KENNEDY
CENTER - MATERIALS LIBRARY □ Nashville, TN

Rodriguez, Cesar, Acq.Libn.
YALE UNIVERSITY - SOCIAL SCIENCE LIBRARY
□ New Haven, CT

Rodriguez, Jose F., Circ. & Ref.Libn.
UNIVERSITY OF GEORGIA - LAW LIBRARY □
Athens, GA

Rodriguez, Narciso, Hd.Ser.
MEDICAL LIBRARY CENTER OF NEW YORK □
New York, NY

Rodwell, Mr. L.W., Staff Archv.
SASKATCHEWAN ARCHIVES BOARD □ Regina,
SK

Roe, Eunice, Project Assoc.
PENNSYLVANIA STATE UNIVERSITY -
INSTITUTE FOR RESEARCH ON LAND AND
WATER RESOURCES - LIBRARY □ University
Park, PA

Roe, Keith, Hd.
PENNSYLVANIA STATE UNIVERSITY - LIFE
SCIENCES LIBRARY □ University Park, PA

Roe, Ruth, Libn.
NEWPORT HARBOR ART MUSEUM - LIBRARY □
Newport Beach, CA

Roebroek, Roxanne, Info.Spec.
ESSO RESOURCES CANADA LIMITED - LIBRARY
INFORMATION CENTRE □ Calgary, AB

Roebuck, Edith V., Libn.
U.S. AIR FORCE BASE - DYESS BASE LIBRARY □
Abilene, TX

Roedell, Raymond Frank, Jr., Dir.
PENNSYLVANIA STATE DEPARTMENT OF
PUBLIC WELFARE - NORRISTOWN STATE
HOSPITAL - PROFESSIONAL/STAFF SERVICES
LIBRARY □ Norristown, PA

Roeder, Christine, Asst.Libn.
YOUNGSTOWN HOSPITAL ASSOCIATION -
HEALTH SCIENCES LIBRARY □ Youngstown, OH

Roeder, Walter, Hd.Ref.Libn.
CALIFORNIA STATE POLYTECHNIC
UNIVERSITY, POMONA - LIBRARY □ Pomona,
CA

Roehrich, James, Eng. Standards Supv.
SPECTROL ELECTRONICS CORPORATION -
LIBRARY □ Industry, CA

Roelker, Frank, Hd., Digester/Fld.Lib.Sec
U.S. NAVY - OFFICE OF THE JUDGE ADVOCATE
GENERAL - LAW LIBRARY □ Alexandria, VA

Roesch, Gay Ellen, Law Libn.
DAVIS, GRAHAM & STUBBS/COLORADO
NATIONAL BUILDING - CNB LAW LIBRARY □
Denver, CO

Roess, Anne C., Mgr.Tech.Info.Ctr.
INSTITUTE OF GAS TECHNOLOGY - TECHNICAL
INFORMATION CENTER □ Chicago, IL

Rogal, Patricia, Pict.Coll.
METROPOLITAN TORONTO LIBRARY - FINE ART
DEPARTMENT □ Toronto, ON

Rogalski, Leonore, Supv.
UOP INC. - RESEARCH TECHNICAL
INFORMATION CENTER □ Des Plaines, IL

Rogero, Thomas T., Libn.
UNIVERSITY OF MIAMI - SCIENCE/
ENGINEERING COLLECTION □ Coral Gables, FL

Rogers, Barbara, Lib.Supv.
OCCIDENTAL EXPLORATION & PRODUCTION
COMPANY - LIBRARY □ Bakersfield, CA

Rogers, Ben, Archv.
SOUTHWESTERN BAPTIST THEOLOGICAL
SEMINARY - FLEMING LIBRARY □ Fort Worth,
TX

Rogers, Bonnie L., Dean, Instr.Rsrcs.
PALOMAR COLLEGE - PHIL H. PUTNAM
MEMORIAL LIBRARY □ San Marcos, CA

Rogers, Brian D., Coll.Libn.
CONNECTICUT COLLEGE - LIBRARY - SPECIAL
COLLECTIONS □ New London, CT

Rogers, Carole, Libn.
UNITED GRAIN GROWERS LTD. - LIBRARY □
Winnipeg, MB

Rogers, Cissie, Coord.Pub.Serv.
NORTHERN ARIZONA UNIVERSITY - LIBRARIES
□ Flagstaff, AZ

Rogers, Mrs. Clyde, Hostess
DREW COUNTY HISTORICAL SOCIETY -
MUSEUM AND ARCHIVES □ Monticello, AR

Rogers, Dee, Libn.
AMERICAN CYANAMID COMPANY - SANTA
ROSA PLANT - LIBRARY □ Milton, FL

Rogers, Dori, Bus.Info.Spec.
GOODYEAR TIRE AND RUBBER COMPANY -
BUSINESS INFORMATION CENTER □ Akron, OH

Rogers, Dori, Staff Lit.Chem.
GOODYEAR TIRE AND RUBBER COMPANY -
TECHNICAL INFORMATION CENTER □ Akron,
OH

Rogers, Earl M., Asst.Mss.Libn.
UNIVERSITY OF IOWA - SPECIAL
COLLECTIONS DEPARTMENT □ Iowa City, IA

Rogers, Emilia, Acq.Asst.
EDEN THEOLOGICAL SEMINARY - LIBRARY □
Webster Groves, MO

Rogers, Helen, Chf.
NATIONAL LIBRARY OF CANADA - COMPUTER-
BASED REFERENCE SERVICES □ Ottawa, ON

Rogers, James, Dir.
BAYLOR UNIVERSITY - CONGRESSIONAL
COLLECTION □ Waco, TX

Rogers, Joe, Tech. Illustrator
NASHVILLE STATE TECHNICAL INSTITUTE -
EDUCATIONAL RESOURCE CENTER □ Nashville,
TN

Rogers, M. Margaret, Dir.Info.Serv.
NORTHWEST REGIONAL EDUCATIONAL
LABORATORY - INFORMATION CENTER/
LIBRARY □ Portland, OR

Rogers, Marian, Libn.
WISCONSIN STATE LEGISLATIVE REFERENCE
BUREAU □ Madison, WI

Rogers, Marianne, Ref.Libn.
YORK UNIVERSITY - LAW LIBRARY □
Downsview, ON

Rogers, Marilyn, Ser.Libn.
LOUISIANA STATE UNIVERSITY MEDICAL
CENTER - SCHOOL OF MEDICINE IN
SHREVEPORT - LIBRARY □ Shreveport, LA

Rogers, Marlin, Info.Sci.
ALCON LABORATORIES, INC. - RESEARCH &
DEVELOPMENT LIBRARY □ Fort Worth, TX

Rogers, NancyAnn, Res.Libn.
HASTINGS & SONS PUBLISHERS - DAILY
EVENING ITEM - NEWSPAPER MORGUE □ Lynn,
MA

Rogers, Peggy, Med.Libn.
RIVERSIDE HOSPITAL - HEALTH SCIENCES
LIBRARY □ Newport News, VA

Rogers, Peggy W., Cat.
NATIONAL CENTER FOR STATE COURTS -
LIBRARY □ Williamsburg, VA

Rogers, Ruth Reinstien, Kress Lib.
HARVARD UNIVERSITY - GRADUATE SCHOOL
OF BUSINESS ADMINISTRATION - BAKER
LIBRARY □ Boston, MA

Rogers, Ruth T., Adm.Libn.
U.S. NAVY - NAVAL AEROSPACE MEDICAL
INSTITUTE - LIBRARY □ Pensacola, FL

Rogers, Rutherford D., Libn.
YALE UNIVERSITY - AMERICAN ORIENTAL
SOCIETY LIBRARY □ New Haven, CT

Rogers, Mrs. S.
ST. JOSEPH'S HOSPITAL - HOSPITAL LIBRARY □
Hamilton, ON

Rogers, Susan, Acq.Libn.
STATE HISTORICAL SOCIETY OF IOWA -
LIBRARY □ Iowa City, IA

Rogers, Vicky, Chf.
DISTRICT OF COLUMBIA PUBLIC LIBRARY -
PHILOSOPHY, PSYCHOLOGY AND RELIGION
DIVISION □ Washington, DC

Rogerson, Mary F., Ref.Libn.
U.S. ARMY POST - FORT HOOD - MSA DIVISION
- CASEY MEMORIAL LIBRARY □ Ft. Hood, TX

Rogge, Rena, Ref.Libn.
KEAN COLLEGE OF NEW JERSEY - NANCY
THOMPSON LIBRARY □ Union, NJ

Rogier, June, Libn.
UNIVERSITY OF MINNESOTA - LANDSCAPE
ARBORETUM - ELMER L. & ELEANOR J.
ANDERSEN HORTICULTURAL LIBRARY □
Chaska, MN

Rogoff, June, Hd.
ROCHESTER PUBLIC LIBRARY - BUSINESS AND
SOCIAL SCIENCE DIVISION □ Rochester, NY

Rogowski, Alfreda, Acq.Libn.
FIELD MUSEUM OF NATURAL HISTORY -
LIBRARY □ Chicago, IL

Rogstad, Betty, Libn.
MINOT DAILY NEWS - LIBRARY □ Minot, ND

Rohan, William B., Asst.Libn.
SAN DIEGO COUNTY LAW LIBRARY □ San Diego,
CA

Rohira, Dr. L., Chm.Med.Lib.Comm.
CLEVELAND PSYCHIATRIC INSTITUTE -
KARNOSH LIBRARY □ Cleveland, OH

Rohles, Dr. F.H.
KANSAS STATE UNIVERSITY - INSTITUTE FOR
ENVIRONMENTAL RESEARCH - LIBRARY □
Manhattan, KS

Rohlf, Mark A., Asst.Libn.
COMMUNICATIONS SATELLITE CORPORATION
- CENTRAL LIBRARY □ Washington, DC

Rohm, Yvonne, Asst.Libn.
AID ASSOCIATION FOR LUTHERANS -
CORPORATE LIBRARY □ Appleton, WI

Rohman, Gloria, Libn.
MINNEAPOLIS PUBLIC LIBRARY &
INFORMATION CENTER - LITERATURE AND
LANGUAGE DEPARTMENT □ Minneapolis, MN

Rohn, Dorcas, Doc.Coord.
ERIC CLEARINGHOUSE ON READING AND
COMMUNICATIONS SKILLS □ Urbana, IL

Rohrbach, William P., Chm.
PARK COUNTY BAR ASSOCIATION - LAW
LIBRARY □ Cody, WY

Rohrbaugh, Bonnie, Chm.
POLK PUBLIC MUSEUM - MEMORIAL LIBRARY □
Lakeland, FL

Rohrer, Richard L., Dir.
UNIVERSITY OF MINNESOTA, ST. PAUL -
CENTRAL LIBRARY □ St. Paul, MN

Rohrig, Thomas T., Ref.Libn.
TEXAS TECH UNIVERSITY - LIBRARY -
DOCUMENTS DEPARTMENT □ Lubbock, TX

Rohrlick, Paula, Rsrcs.Dir.
ACTION FOR CHILDREN'S TELEVISION - ACT
RESOURCE LIBRARY □ Newtonville, MA

Rohrlick, Ruth, Hd., Norris Lib.
CONCORDIA UNIVERSITY - SIR GEORGE
WILLIAMS CAMPUS - NORRIS LIBRARY □
Montreal, PQ

Roith, Joann, Libn.
ROCKY MOUNTAIN HOSPITAL - C. LLOYD
PETERSON MEMORIAL LIBRARY □ Denver, CO

Roizman, Betty, Libn.
CHADWELL, KAYSER, RUGGLES, MC GEE &
HASTINGS - LAW LIBRARY □ Chicago, IL

Roland, Deborah
CALHOUN COUNTY MUSEUM - ARCHIVES AND
LIBRARY □ St. Matthews, SC

Rolen, Helen T., Libn.
PEAT, MARWICK, MITCHELL & COMPANY -
LIBRARY □ San Francisco, CA

Rolfs, Rodney D., Music Libn.
UNIVERSITY OF SOUTHERN CALIFORNIA -
MUSIC LIBRARY □ Los Angeles, CA

Roll, Kempton H., Exec.Dir.
METAL POWDER INDUSTRIES FEDERATION - TECHNICAL INFORMATION CENTER □ Princeton, NJ

Roll, Shirley, Libn.
VANDERBURGH COUNTY LAW LIBRARY □ Evansville, IN

Rollefson, John, Acq.Libn.
U.S. DEPT. OF ENERGY - LAWRENCE BERKELEY LABORATORY - LIBRARY □ Berkeley, CA

Roller, Duane H.D., Cur.
UNIVERSITY OF OKLAHOMA - HISTORY OF SCIENCE COLLECTIONS □ Norman, OK

Roller, Duane H.D., Cur.
UNIVERSITY OF OKLAHOMA - LIMITED ACCESS COLLECTION □ Norman, OK

Roller, Elizabeth A., Tech.Libn.
BURROUGHS CORPORATION - TECHNICAL INFORMATION CENTER □ Plymouth, MI

Rollheiser, Sandra K., Libn.
HAYES/HILL INCORPORATED - LIBRARY □ Chicago, IL

Rollin, Marian, AV
UNIVERSITY OF CONNECTICUT - LIBRARY □ Storrs, CT

Rollins, Alden, Govt.Doc.Libn.
UNIVERSITY OF ALASKA, ANCHORAGE - LIBRARY □ Anchorage, AK

Rollins, Betty A., Program Asst.
NATIONAL COUNCIL OF TEACHERS OF MATHEMATICS - TEACHER/LEARNING CENTER □ Reston, VA

Roilins, Elenor, Med.Libn.
U.S. VETERANS ADMINISTRATION (FL-Miami) - HOSPITAL MEDICAL LIBRARY □ Miami, FL

Rollins, Marilyn H., Ref.Dept.Mgr.
WINSTON-SALEM JOURNAL AND SENTINEL - LIBRARY □ Winston-Salem, NC

Rollins, Ottilie H., Assoc.Dir.
CLARKSON COLLEGE OF TECHNOLOGY - EDUCATIONAL RESOURCES CENTER □ Potsdam, NY

Rollins, William L., Info.Rep.
NEW HAMPSHIRE STATE DEPARTMENT OF PUBLIC WORKS AND HIGHWAYS - LIBRARY □ Concord, NH

Rolloff, C.A., Sec.
FOUR COUNTY LAW LIBRARY □ Montevideo, MN

Rolnicki, Tom, Exec.Dir.
ASSOCIATED COLLEGIATE PRESS/NATIONAL SCHOLASTIC PRESS ASSOCIATION - INFORMATION CENTER □ Minneapolis, MN

Roloff, Daphne C., Dir.
ART INSTITUTE OF CHICAGO - RYERSON AND BURNHAM LIBRARIES □ Chicago, IL

Romain, Joseph, Libn.
METROPOLITAN TORONTO LIBRARY - SOCIAL SCIENCES DEPARTMENT □ Toronto, ON

Romano, Rosemarie, Libn.
AUBURN MEMORIAL HOSPITAL - LIBRARY/ RESOURCE CENTER □ Auburn, NY

Romanoff, Julius S., Exec.Dir.
B'NAI B'RITH CAREER & COUNSELING SERVICES - LIBRARY □ Philadelphia, PA

Rombough, Dianne, Hd.
CANADA - ENERGY, MINES & RESOURCES CANADA - SURVEYS & MAPPING BRANCH - NATIONAL AIR PHOTO LIBRARY □ Ottawa, ON

Romero, Fr. Anthony E., O.P., Dir.
ST. THOMAS AQUINAS NEWMAN CENTER - LIBRARY □ Albuquerque, NM

Romero, Consuelo Serrano, Libn.
PUERTO RICO - DEPARTMENT OF HEALTH - MENTAL HEALTH LIBRARY □ San Juan, PR

Romero, Dorothy D., Libn.
OUR LADY OF THE LAKE REGIONAL MEDICAL CENTER - SCHOOL OF NURSING LIBRARY □ Baton Rouge, LA

Romero, Ray, Hd.Libn.
BERNALILLO COUNTY - DISTRICT COURT LAW LIBRARY† □ Albuquerque, NM

Romig, Joan L., Asst.Cur.
HISTORICAL SOCIETY OF DAUPHIN COUNTY - LIBRARY □ Harrisburg, PA

Rommelmeyer, Alberta, Archv.
CHIPPEWA VALLEY MUSEUM, INC. - LIBRARY □ Eau Claire, WI

Ronald, Dorothy Chesbro, Cur.
COLTON HALL MUSEUM - LIBRARY □ Monterey, CA

Ronan-Clark, Mary, Lib.Mgr.
TRW, INC. - DEFENSE & SPACE SYSTEMS GROUP - TECHNICAL LIBRARY† □ McLean, VA

Rondeau, Elaine, Libn.
ST. ANNE'S HOSPITAL - SULLIVAN MEDICAL LIBRARY □ Fall River, MA

Ronen, Naomi, Asst.Libn., Acq.
HARVARD UNIVERSITY - LAW SCHOOL LIBRARY □ Cambridge, MA

Rongone, Chris, Mss.Archv.
UNIVERSITY OF WISCONSIN, MADISON - WISCONSIN CENTER FOR FILM AND THEATER RESEARCH □ Madison, WI

Ronnermann, Gail, Sci.Libn.
QUEENS COLLEGE OF THE CITY UNIVERSITY OF NEW YORK - SCIENCE LIBRARY □ Flushing, NY

Rood, Edith, Dir., Info.Serv.
FIND/SVP - LIBRARY □ New York, NY

Rooney, Marsha, Dir./Cur.
ANDOVER HISTORICAL SOCIETY - CAROLINE M. UNDERHILL RESEARCH LIBRARY □ Andover, MA

Rooney, Marylynn, Lib.Asst.
SOUTHERN BAPTIST HOSPITAL - LEARNING RESOURCE CENTER □ New Orleans, LA

Rooney, Paul, Hd. AV Serv.
ST. MARY'S UNIVERSITY - PATRICK POWER LIBRARY □ Halifax, NS

Rooney, Robert, Circ.Libn.
TEMPLE UNIVERSITY - HEALTH SCIENCES CENTER - LIBRARY □ Philadelphia, PA

Roose, Walter R., Subj.Spec.
U.S. DEPT OF ENERGY - SANDIA NATL. LABORATORIES - TECHNICAL LIBRARY □ Albuquerque, NM

Root, Christine, Coll.Dev.Libn.
HUDSON VALLEY COMMUNITY COLLEGE - DWIGHT MARVIN LEARNING RESOURCES CENTER □ Troy, NY

Root, Clyde R., Hd.Libn.
NORTHWEST BIBLE COLLEGE - LIBRARY □ Minot, ND

Root, Nina J., Chairperson
AMERICAN MUSEUM OF NATURAL HISTORY - LIBRARY □ New York, NY

Roper, Donna, Reg./Cur.
PENDLETON DISTRICT HISTORICAL AND RECREATIONAL COMMISSION - REFERENCE LIBRARY □ Pendleton, SC

Roper, Janie, Circ.
BLACK HILLS STATE COLLEGE - E.Y. BERRY LIBRARY-LEARNING CENTER □ Spearfish, SD

Ropper, Sandra, Asst.Dir.
INSURANCE LIBRARY ASSOCIATION OF BOSTON □ Boston, MA

Rorabaugh, Francine, Libn.
CHEVRON GEOSCIENCES COMPANY - LIBRARY □ Houston, TX

Rosales, Emmanuel N., Cur.
LOS ANGELES - DEPARTMENT OF RECREATION AND PARKS - CABRILLO MARINE MUSEUM - LIBRARY □ San Pedro, CA

Rosario, Rosa M., AV Res.Libn.
UNIVERSITY OF PUERTO RICO - MEDICAL SCIENCES CAMPUS - LIBRARY □ Rio Piedras, PR

Rosborough, Brian, Pres.
EARTHWATCH - LIBRARY □ Belmont, MA

Roscoe, Donna, Supv.
SANDERS ASSOCIATES, INC. - TECHNICAL LIBRARY □ Nashua, NH

Rose, Mrs. C., Libn.
BUILDING PRODUCTS OF CANADA LTD. - LIBRARY† □ Lachine, PQ

Rose, Carol, Sec.
TRINITY COUNTY LAW LIBRARY □ Weaverville, CA

Rose, Deborah, Cur.
NIAGARA HISTORICAL SOCIETY - LIBRARY □ Niagara on the Lake, ON

Rose, Dianne, Med.Libn.
FRANKFORD HOSPITAL - SCHOOL OF NURSING - STUDENT LIBRARY □ Philadelphia, PA

Rose, Dianne E., Med.Libn.
FRANKFORD HOSPITAL - HOSPITAL LIBRARIES □ Philadelphia, PA

Rose, Donald, Hd., Cat.
TEXAS TECH UNIVERSITY - HEALTH SCIENCES CENTER - LIBRARY OF THE HEALTH SCIENCES □ Lubbock, TX

Rose, Isabel, Hd.
METROPOLITAN TORONTO LIBRARY - MUSIC DEPARTMENT □ Toronto, ON

Rose, Dr. Jack W., Exec.Dir.
NATIONAL TRACK AND FIELD HALL OF FAME OF THE U.S.A. - LIBRARY □ Charleston, WV

Rose, Jeanne, Sr.Info.Assoc.
ALLERGAN PHARMACEUTICALS, INC. - PROFESSIONAL INFORMATION SERVICES □ Irvine, CA

Rose, Marcene, Asst.Libn.
NEW YORK STATE LIBRARY FOR THE BLIND AND VISUALLY HANDICAPPED □ Albany, NY

Rose, Patricia A., Med.Libn.
ST. CHRISTOPHER'S HOSPITAL FOR CHILDREN - MEDICAL LIBRARY □ Philadelphia, PA

Rose, Robert F., Hd.Bus.Lib.
ARIZONA STATE UNIVERSITY - LLOYD BIMSON MEMORIAL LIBRARY □ Tempe, AZ

Rose, William, Dir.Lib./Media Serv.
SOUTH HILLS HEALTH SYSTEM - BEHAN HEALTH SCIENCE LIBRARY □ Pittsburgh, PA

Roseboro, Dagny, Circuit Libn.
CLEVELAND HEALTH SCIENCES LIBRARY - ALLEN MEMORIAL LIBRARY □ Cleveland, OH

Roseman, Esther, Libn.
GLENVIEW AREA HISTORICAL SOCIETY - LIBRARY □ Glenview, IL

Rosemeier, Libby, Per. & Govt.Doc.Libn.
MAINE MARITIME ACADEMY - NUTTING MEMORIAL LIBRARY □ Castine, ME

Rosen, Barry H., Dir./Archv.
UNIVERSITY OF SOUTH CAROLINA - UNIVERSITY ARCHIVES □ Columbia, SC

Rosen, Bettylou, Libn.
U.S. NATL. OCEANIC & ATMOSPHERIC ADMINISTRATION - LIBRARY & INFORMATION SERVICES DIVISION - MIAMI CENTER □ Miami, FL

Rosen, Jocelyn, Supv.Tech.Info.Serv.
ITT CONTINENTAL BAKING COMPANY - RESEARCH LABORATORIES LIBRARY □ Rye, NY

Rosen, Robert, Dir.
UNIVERSITY OF CALIFORNIA, LOS ANGELES - ACADEMY OF TELEVISION ARTS & SCIENCES - TELEVISION ARCHIVES □ Los Angeles, CA

Rosen, Robert, Dir.
UNIVERSITY OF CALIFORNIA, LOS ANGELES - UCLA FILM ARCHIVES □ Los Angeles, CA

Rosen, Robert, Dir.
UNIVERSITY OF CALIFORNIA, LOS ANGELES - UCLA RADIO ARCHIVES □ Los Angeles, CA

Rosenbaum, David, Ref.Libn.
WAYNE STATE UNIVERSITY - EDUCATION LIBRARY □ Detroit, MI

Rosenbaum, Rabbi Don, Libn.
HEBREW THEOLOGICAL COLLEGE - SAUL SILBER MEMORIAL LIBRARY □ Skokie, IL

Rosenbaum, Nathan, Sys.Libn.
U.S. AIR FORCE - AIR FORCE SYSTEMS COMMAND - AIR FORCE GEOPHYSICS LABORATORY - RESEARCH LIBRARY† □ Bedford, MA

Rosenbaum, Thomas, Archv.
ROCKEFELLER UNIVERSITY - ROCKEFELLER ARCHIVE CENTER □ North Tarrytown, NY

PERSONNEL

Rosenberg, E.H., Pres.
RETORT, INC. - LIBRARY □ Cambridge, MA
Rosenberg, Goldie, Mgr.
HOFFMANN-LA ROCHE, INC. - BUSINESS
INFORMATION CENTER □ Nutley, NJ
Rosenberg, Jack M., Dir.
LONG ISLAND UNIV. - ARNOLD & MARIE
SCHWARTZ COLLEGE OF PHARMACY & HEALTH
SCIENCES - INTERNATL. DRUG INFO.CTR. □
Brooklyn, NY
Rosenberg, Janice, Hosp.Libn.
CHICAGO COLLEGE OF OSTEOPATHIC
MEDICINE - ALUMNI MEMORIAL LIBRARY □
Chicago, IL
Rosenberg, Judith, Libn.
JOHNS HOPKINS UNIVERSITY - SCHOOL OF
MEDICINE - DEPARTMENT OF PEDIATRICS -
BAETJER MEMORIAL LIBRARY □ Baltimore, MD
Rosenberg, Linda, Asst.Dir./Res.
NATIONAL INVESTMENT LIBRARY □ New York,
NY
Rosenberg, Lois Gorr, Libn.
JENSEN (Rolf) & ASSOCIATES - LIBRARY □
Deerfield, IL
Rosenberg, Lucille, Libn.
LINCOLN GENERAL HOSPITAL - MEDICAL
LIBRARY □ Lincoln, NE
Rosenberg, Nancy H., Hd., Law Lib.
DRINKER, BIDDLE & REATH - LAW LIBRARY □
Philadelphia, PA
Rosenberg, Neil V., Dir.
MEMORIAL UNIVERSITY OF NEWFOUNDLAND -
FOLKLORE AND LANGUAGE ARCHIVE □ St.
John's, NF
Rosenberg, Steven, Libn.
REVLON RESEARCH CENTER, INC. - LIBRARY □
Bronx, NY
Rosenberger, Graham, Command Libn.
U.S. DEFENSE MAPPING AGENCY - AEROSPACE
CENTER - TECHNICAL LIBRARY □ St. Louis, MO
Rosenberger, H. Stephen, Circ. and ILL Serv.
TEACHERS COLLEGE - LIBRARY □ New York, NY
Rosenblatt, David J., Rec.Mgr.
AUBURN UNIVERSITY - ARCHIVES □ Auburn, AL
Rosenblum, Dr. Joseph, Ref./Info.Serv.Libn.
GUILFORD COLLEGE - LIBRARY □ Greensboro,
NC
Roseneder, Jan, Biblog.
UNIVERSITY OF CALGARY - SPECIAL
COLLECTIONS DIVISION □ Calgary, AB
Rosenfeld, Lillian, Ref.Libn.
AMERICAN INSTITUTE OF CERTIFIED PUBLIC
ACCOUNTANTS - LIBRARY □ New York, NY
Rosenfeld, Susan, Asst. Slide Curator
UNIVERSITY OF CALIFORNIA, LOS ANGELES -
ART DEPARTMENT - VISUAL RESOURCE
COLLECTION & SERVICES □ Los Angeles, CA
Rosenplot, David, Libn.
STELCO INC. - RESEARCH LIBRARY □ Hamilton,
ON
Rosenstein, Dr. Leon, Dir.
SAN DIEGO STATE UNIVERSITY - EUROPEAN
STUDIES CENTER - LIBRARY □ San Diego, CA
Rosenstein, Linda, Asst.Libn., .Tech.Serv.
UNIVERSITY OF PENNSYLVANIA - MEDICAL &
BIOLOGICAL SCIENCES LIBRARY □ Philadelphia,
PA
Rosenstein, Philip, Dir. of Libs.
COLLEGE OF MEDICINE AND DENTISTRY OF
NEW JERSEY AT NEWARK - GEORGE F. SMITH
LIBRARY □ Newark, NJ
Rosenstock, Susan, Per. & VF Techn.
PHILADELPHIA COLLEGE OF ART - LIBRARY □
Philadelphia, PA
Rosensweig, Ruth, Dir.
ST. JOSEPH'S HOSPITAL AND MEDICAL CENTER
- HEALTH SCIENCES LIBRARY □ Paterson, NJ
Rosenthal, Barbara G., Med.Libn.
ST. ELIZABETH HOSPITAL MEDICAL CENTER -
MEDICAL LIBRARY □ Youngstown, OH

Rosenthal, Francine, Lit. Searcher
DOW CHEMICAL COMPANY - MERRELL DOW
PHARMACEUTICALS, INC. - RESEARCH CENTER
LIBRARY □ Cincinnati, OH
Rosenthal, Patricia G., Hist./Genealogy Libn.
ROWAN PUBLIC LIBRARY - EDITH M. CLARK
HISTORY ROOM □ Salisbury, NC
Rosenthal, Robert, Cur.
UNIVERSITY OF CHICAGO - SPECIAL
COLLECTIONS □ Chicago, IL
Rosenwinkel, Heather, Acq.Libn.
UNIVERSITY OF OREGON - HEALTH SCIENCES
CENTER - LIBRARY □ Portland, OR
Rosenzweig, Nancy J., Reserve Supv.
UNIVERSITY OF MICHIGAN - ALFRED TAUBMAN
MEDICAL LIBRARY □ Ann Arbor, MI
Rosevear, Carol, Libn.
NEW BRUNSWICK MUSEUM - REFERENCE &
RESEARCH LIBRARIES □ Saint John, NB
Rosicky, Henry, Prog.Mgr.
U.S. PATENT & TRADEMARK OFFICE -
SCIENTIFIC LIBRARY □ Arlington, VA
Rosignolo, Beverly, Assoc.Libn.
COLLEGE OF INSURANCE - INSURANCE
SOCIETY OF NEW YORK - LIBRARY □ New York,
NY
Rosow, Stella M., Libn.
CARLSON COMPANIES - LIBRARY □ Minneapolis,
MN
Ross, Dr. Alberta B., Supv.
UNIVERSITY OF NOTRE DAME - RADIATION
LABORATORY - RADIATION CHEMISTRY DATA
CENTER □ Notre Dame, IN
Ross, Alexander D., Hd.Libn.
STANFORD UNIVERSITY - ART AND
ARCHITECTURE LIBRARY □ Stanford, CA
Ross, Ann K., Chf.
DISTRICT OF COLUMBIA PUBLIC LIBRARY -
SOCIOLOGY, GOVERNMENT & EDUCATION
DIVISION □ Washington, DC
Ross, Bonita, Western Bk.Acq.Libn.
MATHEMATICAL REVIEWS - LIBRARY □ Ann
Arbor, MI
Ross, Carol, Libn.
INGALLS MEMORIAL HOSPITAL - MEDICAL
LIBRARY □ Harvey, IL
Ross, Deborah, Tech.Serv.Libn.
NEW HAMPSHIRE COLLEGE - SHAPIRO LIBRARY
□ Manchester, NH
Ross, Delanie M., Libn.I
MEMPHIS-SHELBY COUNTY PUBLIC LIBRARY
AND INFORMATION CENTER - MEMPHIS ROOM
COLLECTIONS □ Memphis, TN
Ross, Dorothy M., Pres.
AUTOMOTIVE ORGANIZATION TEAM, INC. -
LIBRARY □ Midland, MI
Ross, Elizabeth, Asst.Med.Libn.
PIEDMONT HOSPITAL - SAULS MEMORIAL
LIBRARY □ Atlanta, GA
Ross, Jeanne, Asst.Libn.
BOLT BERANEK AND NEWMAN, INC. - LIBRARY
□ Cambridge, MA
Ross, Johanna, Assoc.Libn.
UNIVERSITY OF CALIFORNIA, DAVIS -
PHYSICAL SCIENCES LIBRARY □ Davis, CA
Ross, Joseph G., Jr., Hd., Info./Pubn.
LIBRARY OF CONGRESS - COPYRIGHT PUBLIC
INFORMATION OFFICE □ Washington, DC
Ross, Lillian, Community Serv.Dir.
CENTRAL AGENCY FOR JEWISH EDUCATION -
EDUCATIONAL RESOURCE CENTER/LIBRARY □
Miami, FL
Ross, Margaret, Res.Spec.
UNIVERSAL CITY STUDIOS - RESEARCH
DEPARTMENT LIBRARY □ Universal City, CA
Ross, Mary Ann, Libn.
CHICAGO BOARD OF EDUCATION - LIBRARY □
Chicago, IL
Ross, Maylene, Asst.Dir./Ref.
WESTERN NEW ENGLAND COLLEGE - JOHN D.
CHURCHILL MEMORIAL LIBRARY □ Springfield,
MA

Ross, Nancy, Libn.
CANADA - NATIONAL RESEARCH COUNCIL -
CISTI - CHEMISTRY BRANCH □ Ottawa, ON
Ross, Nancy, Libn.-Ed.
LAKE COUNTY REGIONAL PLANNING
COMMISSION - LIBRARY □ Waukegan, IL
Ross, Nancy, Ref.Libn.
U.S. ARMY IN EUROPE (USAREUR) - LIBRARY
AND RESOURCE CENTER □ APO New York, NY
Ross, Peggy, Libn.
MONTGOMERY ADVERTISER AND ALABAMA
JOURNAL - LIBRARY □ Montgomery, AL
Ross, Peggy, AV Libn.
ONTARIO - MINISTRY OF HEALTH -
PSYCHIATRIC BRANCH - LIBRARY RESOURCE
CENTRE □ Hamilton, ON
Ross, Philip, Acq.Libn.
WEST LIBERTY STATE COLLEGE - ELBIN
LIBRARY □ West Liberty, WV
Ross, Rhoda, V.P.
GLENGARRY GENEALOGICAL SOCIETY -
HIGHLAND HERITAGE LIBRARY □ Lancaster, ON
Ross, Rosalinda, Online Ref.Libn.
JEFFERSON (Thomas) UNIVERSITY - SCOTT
MEMORIAL LIBRARY □ Philadelphia, PA
Ross, Sidnie, Asst.Res.Libn.
CARGILL, INC. - INFORMATION CENTER □
Minneapolis, MN
Ross, Susan L., Libn.
WALSH YOUNG - LIBRARY □ Calgary, AB
Ross, Tina B., Dir.Tech.Info.Serv.
GULF RESEARCH AND DEVELOPMENT COMPANY
- TECHNICAL INFORMATION SERVICES □
Pittsburgh, PA
Rosse, Rosanna H., Hd., Rd.Serv.
CLARKSON COLLEGE OF TECHNOLOGY -
EDUCATIONAL RESOURCES CENTER □ Potsdam,
NY
Rosser, Helen, Libn.
BURLINGTON COUNTY TIMES - LIBRARY □
Willingboro, NJ
Rossi, Katherine P., Tech.Serv.Coord.
SUNY - COLLEGE OF ENVIRONMENTAL SCIENCE
AND FORESTRY - F. FRANKLIN MOON LIBRARY
□ Syracuse, NY
Rossi, Linda, Veterinary Med.Ref.Libn.
UNIVERSITY OF WISCONSIN, MADISON -
STEENBOCK MEMORIAL LIBRARY □ Madison, WI
Rossman, Kenneth F., Chf., Archv.Br.
U.S. NATL. ARCHIVES & RECORDS SERVICE -
FEDERAL ARCHIVES AND RECORDS CENTER,
REGION 9 □ Laguna Niguel, CA
Rossman, Seth, Photographer
INDIANA HISTORICAL SOCIETY - WILLIAM
HENRY SMITH MEMORIAL LIBRARY □
Indianapolis, IN
Rost, Betty, Cat.
ALBERTA - DEPARTMENT OF THE
ENVIRONMENT - LIBRARY □ Edmonton, AB
Rost, Grace A., Libn.
WEBER COUNTY LAW LIBRARY □ Ogden, UT
Rostad, Barbara, Res.Libn.
PILLSBURY COMPANY - MAIN OFFICE
MARKETING LIBRARY □ Minneapolis, MN
Rostock, Margit, Libn.
GOETHE INSTITUTE ATLANTA - GERMAN
CULTURAL CENTER - LIBRARY □ Atlanta, GA
Rosum, Judtih T., Lib.Asst.
FINANCIAL ACCOUNTING STANDARDS BOARD
(FASB) - LIBRARY □ Stamford, CT
Rotan, Jean B., Adm.Asst.
UNIVERSITY OF CALIFORNIA - SAN JOAQUIN
VALLEY AGRICULTURAL RESEARCH &
EXTENSION CENTER □ Parlier, CA
Roten, Paul, Libn.
ASSOCIATED MENNONITE BIBLICAL
SEMINARIES - MENNONITE BIBLICAL
SEMINARY - LIBRARY □ Elkhart, IN
Rotgin, Rheba, Libn.
TEMPLE EMANU-EL - LIBRARY □ Long Beach, NY

Roth, Beth, Ref.Libn.
U.S. VETERANS ADMINISTRATION (DC-
Washington) - HEADQUARTERS CENTRAL
OFFICE LIBRARY □ Washington, DC

Roth, Britain G., Mgr., Lib.Serv.
GEISINGER MEDICAL CENTER - MEDICAL
LIBRARY □ Danville, PA

Roth, Charles P., Hd.Tech.Serv./Cat.
PHILADELPHIA COLLEGE OF PHARMACY AND
SCIENCE - JOSEPH W. ENGLAND LIBRARY □
Philadelphia, PA

Roth, Claire J., Lib.Dir.
MERCANTILE LIBRARY ASSOCIATION -
MERCANTILE LIBRARY □ New York, NY

Roth, Dana L., Hd.Sci.Libn.
CALIFORNIA INSTITUTE OF TECHNOLOGY -
ROBERT A. MILLIKAN MEMORIAL LIBRARY □
Pasadena, CA

Roth, Dr. David M., Dir.
EASTERN CONNECTICUT STATE COLLEGE -
CENTER FOR CONNECTICUT STUDIES □
Willimantic, CT

Roth, Eris, Chf., Tech.Serv.
U.S. SOCIAL SECURITY ADMINISTRATION -
LIBRARY □ Baltimore, MD

Roth, Frank, Lib.Asst.
KANSAS STATE DEPARTMENT OF SOCIAL &
REHABILITATION SERVICES - STAFF
DEVELOPMENT TRAINING CENTER LIBRARY □
Topeka, KS

Roth, Helga, Chf., Clearinghouse
CLEARINGHOUSE ON THE HANDICAPPED □
Washington, DC

Roth, Dr. Herbert S., Dir.
AMERICAN ACADEMY OF PSYCHOTHERAPISTS
- AAP TAPE LIBRARY □ Des Moines, IA

Roth, Richard, Proj.Mgr.
CLEARINGHOUSE ON CHILD ABUSE AND
NEGLECT INFORMATION □ Washington, DC

Roth, Roslyn, Chf.Libn.
INSTITUTES OF RELIGION AND HEALTH -
LIBRARY □ New York, NY

Roth-Shomer, Forest, Dir.
ABUNDANT LIFE SEED FOUNDATION - LIBRARY
□ Port Townsend, WA

Rothbart, Bonnie, Mgr.
METRO-GOLDWYN-MAYER, INC. - PICTURE
RESEARCH LIBRARY □ Culver City, CA

Rothbart, Linda, Libn.
AMERICAN TRUCKING ASSOCIATIONS, INC. -
LIBRARY □ Washington, DC

Rothbart, Rise, Asst.Libn.
NEW YORK STATE LIBRARY - HUMANITIES
REFERENCE SERVICE □ Albany, NY

Rothberg, Marjorie, Govt.Doc.Libn.
DREXEL UNIVERSITY LIBRARIES - GENERAL
LIBRARY □ Philadelphia, PA

Rothe, Dorathy L., Cur.
MALDEN HISTORICAL SOCIETY - LIBRARY □
Malden, MA

Rothenberg, Dianne, Acq.
ERIC CLEARINGHOUSE ON ELEMENTARY AND
EARLY CHILDHOOD EDUCATION □ Champaign,
IL

Rothenberger, James, Dept.Hd.
UNIVERSITY OF CALIFORNIA, RIVERSIDE -
GOVERNMENT PUBLICATIONS DEPARTMENT -
LIBRARY □ Riverside, CA

Rothenberger, James, Gov.Pubn.Libn.
UNIVERSITY OF CALIFORNIA, RIVERSIDE -
MAP SECTION - LIBRARY □ Riverside, CA

Rothrock, Louise, Proofreader
ASSOCIATION FOR RESEARCH AND
ENLIGHTENMENT - ARE BRAILLE LIBRARY □
Virginia Beach, VA

Rothschild, Sieglinde H., Libn.
NEW YORK LAW INSTITUTE - LIBRARY □ New
York, NY

Rothstein, Galina, Hd.Cat.
NATIONAL YIDDISH BOOK EXCHANGE, INC. -
LIBRARY □ Amherst, MA

Rothwell, Dr. A., Chm., Lib.Comm.
SALVATION ARMY GRACE HOSPITAL - MEDICAL
STAFF LIBRARY □ Calgary, AB

Rotman, Elaine C., Libn.
HOSPITAL EDUCATIONAL AND RESEARCH FUND
- LILLIAN R. HAYT MEMORIAL LIBRARY □
Albany, NY

Rotman, Laurie D., Asst.Libn.
DRAPER (Charles Stark) LABORATORY, INC. -
TECHNICAL INFORMATION CENTER □
Cambridge, MA

Rottman, Anne, Libn.
MISSOURI STATE LEGISLATIVE LIBRARY □
Jefferson City, MO

Roughley, Jill, Asst.
BUILT ENVIRONMENT COORDINATORS
LIMITED - BEC INFORMATION SYSTEM (BIS) □
Toronto, ON

Roullard, June, AV Libn.
U.S. VETERANS ADMINISTRATION (ME-
Augusta) - CENTER LIBRARY □ Augusta, ME

Roumfort, Susan, Hd.
NEW JERSEY STATE LIBRARY - BUREAU OF
LAW AND REFERENCE □ Trenton, NJ

Rounds, Linn, Pub.Info.Off.
WYOMING STATE LIBRARY □ Cheyenne, WY

Roundtree, Beth, Media Spec.
CHARLOTTE-MECKLENBURG SCHOOLS -
CURRICULUM RESEARCH CENTER □ Charlotte,
NC

Roundtree, Elizabeth S., Coord., Tech.Serv.
LOUISIANA STATE LIBRARY □ Baton Rouge, LA

Roundtree, Ernestiene, Cur.
LOUISIANA STATE DEPT. OF CULTURE,
RECREATION & TOURISM - MANSFIELD STATE
COMMEMORATIVE AREA - MUSEUM & LIB. □
Mansfield, LA

Rountree, M.E., Hd.Libn.
MC NEIL LABORATORIES - LIBRARY □ Fort
Washington, PA

Rourke, Cynthia, Regional Ext.Libn.
COLLEGE OF PHYSICIANS OF PHILADELPHIA -
LIBRARY AND MEDICAL DOCUMENTATION
SERVICE □ Philadelphia, PA

Rourke, Doris, Tech.Serv.Libn.
WESTERN CONNECTICUT STATE COLLEGE -
RUTH A. HAAS LIBRARY □ Danbury, CT

Rouse, David, Bus.Info.Ctr.Hd.
CHICAGO PUBLIC LIBRARY CENTRAL LIBRARY -
BUSINESS/SCIENCE/TECHNOLOGY DIVISION
□ Chicago, IL

Rouse, Jeffrey P., Registrar
WESTMORELAND COUNTY MUSEUM OF ART -
ART REFERENCE LIBRARY □ Greensburg, PA

Rouse, John R., Dir.
WICHITA ART ASSOCIATION, INC. -
REFERENCE LIBRARY □ Wichita, KS

Rouse, Kendall, Libn.
UNIVERSITY OF WISCONSIN, MADISON -
CHEMISTRY LIBRARY □ Madison, WI

Rouse, M. Jean, Cat.
LOUISIANA STATE UNIVERSITY MEDICAL
CENTER - LIBRARY □ New Orleans, LA

Rouse, Myra J., Libn.
U.S. NAVY - NAVAL DENTAL RESEARCH
INSTITUTE - LIBRARY □ Great Lakes, IL

Roush, Dona, Assoc.Dir.
TEXAS TECH UNIVERSITY - HEALTH SCIENCES
CENTER - REGIONAL ACADEMIC HEALTH
CENTER LIBRARY □ El Paso, TX

Rousseau, Gratien, E.D.P. Mgr.
INFORMATECH - CENTRE QUEBECOIS DE
BANQUES D'INFORMATION SCIENTIFIQUE ET
TECHNIQUE □ Montreal, PQ

Rousseau, Juliana, Coord., Lib./Res.Serv
CONTRA COSTA COUNTY SUPERINTENDENT OF
SCHOOLS - ACCESS INFORMATION CENTER &
PROFESSIONAL LIBRARY □ Concord, CA

Roussin, R.W., Nuclear Engr.
U.S. OAK RIDGE NATL. LABORATORY -
RADIATION SHIELDING INFORMATION CENTER
□ Oak Ridge, TN

Roux, Helen M., Dir.
NEW CASTLE PUBLIC LIBRARY -
PENNSYLVANIA HISTORY ROOM □ New Castle,
PA

Rouzie, Katherine W., Dir., Lib.Serv.
EMANUEL HOSPITAL - LIBRARY SERVICES □
Portland, OR

Rovati, A., ILL Libn.
PAN AMERICAN HEALTH ORGANIZATION -
DOCUMENTATION AND HEALTH INFORMATION
OFFICE† □ Washington, DC

Rovig, Lorraine, Libn.
IOWA STATE COMMISSION FOR THE BLIND -
LIBRARY FOR THE BLIND & PHYSICALLY
HANDICAPPED □ Des Moines, IA

Rovner, Mr. J.
PRINCETON UNIVERSITY - NEAR EAST
COLLECTIONS □ Princeton, NJ

Rowan, Kim, Libn.
BEAK CONSULTANTS LTD. - LIBRARY □
Mississauga, ON

Rowe, David G., Cat.
FEDERAL BUSINESS DEVELOPMENT BANK -
LIBRARY □ Montreal, PQ

Rowe, Gladys E., Subj.Spec.
U.S. DEPT OF ENERGY - SANDIA NATL.
LABORATORIES - TECHNICAL LIBRARY □
Albuquerque, NM

Rowe, Glenn N., Mgr., Pub.Serv.
CHURCH OF JESUS CHRIST OF LATTER-DAY
SAINTS - HISTORICAL DEPARTMENT - CHURCH
LIBRARY-ARCHIVES □ Salt Lake City, UT

Rowe, Harold E., Libn.
SAN FRANCISCO LAW LIBRARY □ San Francisco,
CA

Rowe, Joyce, Libn.
MARSTELLER, INC. - LIBRARY □ Chicago, IL

Rowe, Kenneth E., Methodist Libn.
DREW UNIVERSITY - LIBRARY □ Madison, NJ

Rowe, LaDonna L., Libn.
SYSTEMS, SCIENCE AND SOFTWARE -
TECHNICAL LIBRARY □ La Jolla, CA

Rowe, Lauren C., Mgr., Info.Serv.
MC KINSEY & COMPANY, INC. - BUSINESS
RESEARCH LIBRARY □ Cleveland, OH

Rowe, Linda Jo, Libn.
ST. ANTHONY'S HOSPITAL, INC. - MEDICAL
LIBRARY □ St. Petersburg, FL

Rowe, Mason, Res.Anl.
TENNESSEE STATE COMMISSION ON AGING -
LIBRARY □ Nashville, TN

Rowe, Paola, Educ.Libn.
WELLINGTON COUNTY BOARD OF EDUCATION -
EDUCATION LIBRARY □ Guelph, ON

Rowe, W.C., Tech.Info.Prog.Engr.
GENERAL ELECTRIC COMPANY - AIRCRAFT
ENGINE GROUP - TECHNICAL INFORMATION
CENTER □ Cincinnati, OH

Rowell, Lois, Cat. & Ref.Libn.
OHIO STATE UNIVERSITY - MUSIC LIBRARY □
Columbus, OH

Rowland, Barbara, Libn.
CLARK COUNTY LAW LIBRARY □ Vancouver, WA

Rowland, Donald C., Dir.
BLACK HAWK COLLEGE - LEARNING
RESOURCES CENTER □ Moline, IL

Rowland, Professor Eileen, Chf.Libn.
JOHN JAY COLLEGE OF CRIMINAL JUSTICE OF
THE CITY UNIVERSITY OF NEW YORK -
REISMAN MEMORIAL LIBRARY □ New York, NY

Rowland, Helen M., Asst.Libn.
ASSOCIATION OF AMERICAN RAILROADS -
ECONOMICS AND FINANCE DEPARTMENT -
LIBRARY □ Washington, DC

Rowland, Shirley R., Media Supv.
BRYANT AND STRATTON BUSINESS INSTITUTE
- LIBRARY □ Buffalo, NY

Rowley, Ann, Asst.Tech.Libn.
UNIVERSITY OF TULSA - SIDNEY BORN
TECHNICAL LIBRARY □ Tulsa, OK

PERSONNEL

P E R S O N N E L

Rowley, Dennis, Info.Sys.Anl.
U.S. DEPT OF ENERGY - SANDIA NATL.
LABORATORIES - TECHNICAL LIBRARY □
Albuquerque, NM
Rowley, Gordon S., Music Libn.
NORTHERN ILLINOIS UNIVERSITY - MUSIC
LIBRARY† □ DeKalb, IL
Rowling, D.W., LRC Spec.
NORTHEAST WISCONSIN TECHNICAL
INSTITUTE - LEARNING RESOURCE CENTER □
Green Bay, WI
Rowling, Jim, Dir. of Tech.Serv.
KEARNEY STATE COLLEGE - CALVIN T. RYAN
LIBRARY □ Kearney, NE
Roy, Barbara, Cat.Libn.
UNITED PRESBYTERIAN CHURCH IN THE U.S.A.
- PRESBYTERIAN HISTORICAL SOCIETY -
LIBRARY □ Philadelphia, PA
Roy, Sr. Bibiane, O.P., Coord.
DIOCESE OF TUCSON - REGINA CLERI
RESOURCE LIBRARY □ Tucson, AZ
Roy, Claudette, SDI
QUEBEC PROV. - MIN. DE L'ENERGIE ET DES
RESSOURCES - CENTRE DE DOCUMENTATION
ET DE RENSEIGNEMENTS □ Quebec, PQ
Roy, Denis, Acq.Libn.
CINEMATHEQUE QUEBECOISE - CENTRE DE
DOCUMENTATION CINEMATOGRAPHIQUE □
Montreal, PQ
Roy, Donald E., Dir.
NEW YORK MEDICAL COLLEGE AND THE
WESTCHESTER ACADEMY OF MEDICINE -
WESTCHESTER MEDICAL CENTER LIBRARY □
Valhalla, NY
Roy, E. Irene, Libn.
CANADA - LAW REFORM COMMISSION OF
CANADA - LIBRARY □ Ottawa, ON
Roy, Ernest Bertrand, Responsable
QUEBEC PROVINCE - MINISTERE DES
AFFAIRES MUNICIPALES - CENTRE DE
DOCUMENTATION □ Quebec, PQ
Roy, Jean-Luc, Libn.
CENTRE D'ANIMATION, DE DEVELOPPEMENT
ET DE RECHERCHE EN EDUCATION -
BIBLIOTHEQUE □ Montreal, PQ
Roy, Jean-Pierre, Libn.
UNIVERSITE DU QUEBEC - MEDIATHEQUE □
Ste. Foy, PQ
Roy, Mary, Libn.
NORTHWESTERN UNIVERSITY -
TRANSPORTATION LIBRARY □ Evanston, IL
Roy, Robert, Dept.Hd.
BRITISH COLUMBIA INSTITUTE OF
TECHNOLOGY - LIBRARY SERVICES DIVISION □
Burnaby, BC
Royal, Linda G., Asst.Libn.
VIRGINIA ELECTRIC & POWER COMPANY -
LIBRARY □ Richmond, VA
Royce, Carol, Asst.Libn.
MAHARISHI INTERNATIONAL UNIVERSITY -
SCIENCE OF CREATIVE INTELLIGENCE
COLLECTION □ Fairfield, IA
Royce, Diana, Libn.
STOWE-DAY FOUNDATION - LIBRARY □
Hartford, CT
Roye, Josephine, Cat.
EVANGELICAL AND REFORMED HISTORICAL
SOCIETY - LANCASTER CENTRAL ARCHIVES
AND LIBRARY □ Lancaster, PA
Roylance, Dale, Cur. Graphic Arts
PRINCETON UNIVERSITY - RARE BOOKS AND
SPECIAL COLLECTIONS □ Princeton, NJ
Royle, Mary Anne, Law Lib.Dir.
WASHOE COUNTY LAW LIBRARY □ Reno, NV
Rozek, Dr. Sue, Hd.
SUNY - SCHOOL OF PHARMACY - DRUG
INFORMATION SERVICE - LIBRARY □ Buffalo,
NY
Rozen, Nineta, Rd.Adv.
DISTRICT OF COLUMBIA PUBLIC LIBRARY -
HISTORY AND GEOGRAPHY DIVISION □
Washington, DC

Rozmyslowska, Ewa, Cat.
KAYE, SCHOLER, FIERMAN, HAYS & HANDLER -
LAW LIBRARY □ New York, NY
Rozniatowski, David W., Libn.
WINNIPEG ART GALLERY - CLARA LANDER
LIBRARY □ Winnipeg, MB
Rozsypal, Hana, Acq.
FRANKLIN INSTITUTE - LIBRARY □ Philadelphia,
PA
Rubaloff, Marijoy, Libn.
EUGENE REGISTER-GUARD - NEWS LIBRARY □
Eugene, OR
Ruben, Janis M., Info.Spec.
AMERICAN STERILIZER COMPANY - LIBRARY □
Erie, PA
Rubens, Jane C., Libn.
COUDERT BROTHERS - LIBRARY □ New York, NY
Rubens, Larry, Mgr./Photography
KENT STATE UNIVERSITY - AUDIOVISUAL
SERVICES □ Kent, OH
Rubenstein, Beverly G., Libn.
HEALTH AND WELFARE COUNCIL OF CENTRAL
MARYLAND, INC. - STAFF REFERENCE LIBRARY
□ Baltimore, MD
Rubenstein, Natalie, Supv.Libn./Sci.Coll.
NEW YORK PUBLIC LIBRARY - MID-
MANHATTAN LIBRARY - SCIENCE/BUSINESS
DEPARTMENT □ New York, NY
Rubenstone, Jessie, Libn.
HAR ZION TEMPLE - IVA AND MATTHEW
RUZOSKER LIBRARY □ Philadelphia, PA
Rubin, Angela, Asst.Libn.
SOUTHERN ILLINOIS UNIVERSITY,
CARBONDALE - HUMANITIES DIVISION
LIBRARY □ Carbondale, IL
Rubin, Helen, Gen.Info.Libn.
FASHION INSTITUTE OF TECHNOLOGY -
LIBRARY/MEDIA SERVICES □ New York, NY
Rubin, Judith, Libn.
CANADA - LABOUR RELATIONS BOARD -
LIBRARY □ Ottawa, ON
Rubin, Karen, Libn.
ROOSEVELT HOSPITAL - HEALTH SCIENCE
LIBRARY □ Metuchen, NJ
Rubin, Phyliss, Coord. of Oper.
UNIVERSITY OF PENNSYLVANIA - ENERGY
CENTER - DRL BASEMENT ENERGY LIBRARY □
Philadelphia, PA
Rubin, Dr. Samuel, Chm.
NEW ORLEANS PSYCHOANALYTIC INSTITUTE,
INC. - LIBRARY □ New Orleans, LA
Rubin-Cohen, Ina M., Judaica Ref.
HEBREW UNION COLLEGE - JEWISH INSTITUTE
OF RELIGION - KLAU LIBRARY □ New York, NY
Rubino, Frank, Media Coord.
NEW YORK CITY BOARD OF EDUCATION -
DIVISION OF SPECIAL EDUCATION - SPECIAL
EDUC. TRAINING & RESOURCE CTR. □ New
York, NY
Rubinstein, Edith, Library Director
PENINSULA HOSPITAL CENTER - MEDICAL
LIBRARY □ Far Rockaway, NY
Rubinton, Phyllis, Libn.
NEW YORK HOSPITAL-CORNELL MEDICAL
CENTER - OSKAR DIETHELM HISTORICAL
LIBRARY □ New York, NY
Rubinton, Phyllis, Libn.
PAYNE WHITNEY PSYCHIATRIC CLINIC
LIBRARY □ New York, NY
Ruby, Florence V., Med.Libn.
SACRED HEART HOSPITAL - MEDICAL LIBRARY
□ Pensacola, FL
Rucker, Newton W., Chf.Libn.
U.S. ARMY HOSPITALS - WALTER REED ARMY
MEDICAL CENTER - MEDICAL LIBRARY □
Washington, DC
Ruda, Mildred, Lib.Techn., Ref.
U.S. NASA - HEADQUARTERS LIBRARY □
Washington, DC
Rudall, Diane, Mng.Ed.
MERRIAM CENTER LIBRARY □ Chicago, IL

Rudavsky, Arnona, Judaica Libn.
HEBREW UNION COLLEGE - JEWISH INSTITUTE
OF RELIGION - KLAU LIBRARY □ Cincinnati, OH
Rudberg, Peggy, Slide Libn.
MINNEAPOLIS COLLEGE OF ART AND DESIGN -
LIBRARY AND MEDIA CENTER □ Minneapolis,
MN
Ruddle, R.M., Mgr., Traffic Res.
CHESAPEAKE AND OHIO RAILROAD COMPANY -
TRAFFIC RESEARCH DEPARTMENT - LIBRARY □
Baltimore, MD
Rude, Nancy, Asst.Biblog.
SYRACUSE UNIVERSITY - MATHEMATICS
LIBRARY □ Syracuse, NY
Rudeen, Jacqueline, Chf.Tech.Serv.Div.
WASHINGTON STATE LIBRARY □ Olympia, WA
Rudin, Pearly, Med.Libn.
METHODIST HOSPITAL - MEDICAL LIBRARY □
St. Louis Park, MN
Rudisell, Carol, Mss.Libn.
STANFORD UNIVERSITY - DEPARTMENT OF
SPECIAL COLLECTIONS □ Stanford, CA
Rudisill, Horace Fraser, Hist.
DARLINGTON COUNTY HISTORICAL
COMMISSION - DARLINGTON COUNTY
ARCHIVES □ Darlington, SC
Rudisill, Richard, Hist.
MUSEUM OF NEW MEXICO - PHOTOGRAPHIC
ARCHIVES □ Santa Fe, NM
Rudkin, David W., Univ.Archv.
UNIVERSITY OF TORONTO - UNIVERSITY
ARCHIVES □ Toronto, ON
Rudolph, Sr. Catherine, OSF, Dir.
UNIVERSITY OF DAYTON - SCHOOL OF
EDUCATION - CURRICULUM MATERIALS
CENTER □ Dayton, OH
Rudolph, Dr. L.C., Cur. of Books
INDIANA UNIVERSITY - LILLY LIBRARY □
Bloomington, IN
Rudolph, Mary Jane, Acq.
KENNEDY-KING COLLEGE - LIBRARY □ Chicago,
IL
Rudy, Jack R., Chf.
U.S. HERITAGE CONSERVATION AND
RECREATION SERVICE - INTERAGENCY
ARCHEOLOGICAL SERVICE LIBRARY □ Denver,
CO
Rudzevicius, Diane, Law Cat.
CANADA - DEPARTMENT OF JUSTICE -
LIBRARY □ Ottawa, ON
Rueger, Brenda, Rare Bk.Ref.Libn.
STANFORD UNIVERSITY - DEPARTMENT OF
SPECIAL COLLECTIONS □ Stanford, CA
Ruess, Diane, Asst.Libn.Pub.Serv.
SUNY - COLLEGE OF ENVIRONMENTAL SCIENCE
AND FORESTRY - F. FRANKLIN MOON LIBRARY
□ Syracuse, NY
Rueth, Catherine M., Sec./Libn.
COUNTRYSIDE HOME - STAFF LIBRARY □
Jefferson, WI
Ruffier, Arthur J., Hd. of Ref.
WASHINGTON STATE LAW LIBRARY □ Olympia,
WA
Ruffner, Dr. James R., Adm.Serv.Off.
WAYNE STATE UNIVERSITY - SCIENCE
LIBRARY □ Detroit, MI
Ruffolo, Robert E., II, Pres.
PRINCETON ANTIQUES BOOKFINDERS - ART
MARKETING REFERENCE LIBRARY □ Atlantic
City, NJ
Rugge, Sue, Pres.
INFORMATION ON DEMAND □ Berkeley, CA
Ruggere, Christine, Cur./Hist.Coll.
COLLEGE OF PHYSICIANS OF PHILADELPHIA -
LIBRARY AND MEDICAL DOCUMENTATION
SERVICE □ Philadelphia, PA
Ruggieri, G.D., Ph.D., Dir.
OSBORN LABORATORIES OF MARINE SCIENCES
- NEW YORK AQUARIUM LIBRARY □ Brooklyn,
NY
Ruhl, Darrell, Exec.Dir.
SWEDENBORG FOUNDATION - LIBRARY □ New
York, NY

Ruhl, Taylor D., Libn.
PACIFIC UNION COLLEGE - PITCAIRN ISLANDS STUDY CENTER - LIBRARY □ Angwin, CA

Ruiz, Carlos C., Exec.Dir.
ACADEMY OF THE STREET OF PUERTO RICAN CONGRESS - LIBRARY □ Chicago, IL

Ruiz, Deborah, Libn.
OAKLAND PUBLIC LIBRARY - LATIN AMERICAN LIBRARY† □ Oakland, CA

Ruiz, Oralia R., Asst.Libn.
SOUTHWEST RESEARCH INSTITUTE - THOMAS BAKER SLICK MEMORIAL LIBRARY □ San Antonio, TX

Ruiz, Sandra, Libn.
ACADEMY OF THE STREET OF PUERTO RICAN CONGRESS - LIBRARY □ Chicago, IL

Ruiz de Nieves, Angela M., Hd., Cat.Sect.
UNIVERSITY OF PUERTO RICO - HUMACAO UNIVERSITY COLLEGE - LIBRARY □ Humacao, PR

Rukuts, Velga B., Libn.
ICI AMERICAS INC. - ATLAS LIBRARY □ Wilmington, DE

Ruland, Mary, Leg.Libn.
MARYLAND STATE DEPARTMENT OF LEGISLATIVE REFERENCE - LIBRARY □ Annapolis, MD

Rumack, Shirley, Libn.
CONGREGATION EMANU-EL B'NE JESHURUN - RABBI DUDLEY WEINBERG LIBRARY □ Milwaukee, WI

Rumage, Tim, Libn.
AUDUBON SOCIETY OF RHODE ISLAND - HARRY S. HATHAWAY LIBRARY OF NATURAL HISTORY AND CONSERVATION □ Providence, RI

Rumberger, Marian, Libn.
UNIVERSITY OF CALIFORNIA, DAVIS - INSTITUTE OF GOVERNMENTAL AFFAIRS - LIBRARY □ Davis, CA

Rumsey, Gary L., Dir.
U.S. FISH & WILDLIFE SERVICE - TUNISON LABORATORY OF FISH NUTRITION - LIBRARY □ Cortland, NY

Rumsey, Nancy S., Info.Spec.
ALADDIN INDUSTRIES - LIBRARY □ Nashville, TN

Runge, William H., Cur.
UNIVERSITY OF VIRGINIA - TRACY W. MC GREGOR LIBRARY □ Charlottesville, VA

Runkel, Phillip M., Asst.Archv.
MARQUETTE UNIVERSITY - DEPARTMENT OF SPECIAL COLLECTIONS AND UNIVERSITY ARCHIVES □ Milwaukee, WI

Runyan, Ann, Asst.Libn.
FIRST BAPTIST CHURCH - LIBRARY □ Brevard, NC

Runyon, Cynthia G., Cat.Libn.
EMORY UNIVERSITY - PITTS THEOLOGY LIBRARY □ Atlanta, GA

Ruocco, Patti, AV Libn.
NORTH SUBURBAN LIBRARY SYSTEM & SUBURBAN LIBRARY SYSTEM - SUBURBAN AV SERVICE □ La Grange Park, IL

Rupp, Fr. N. Daniel, Archv.
BISHOP BARAGA ASSOCIATION - ARCHIVES □ Marquette, MI

Rupprecht, Leslie P., Supv.
NEWARK PUBLIC LIBRARY - BUSINESS LIBRARY □ Newark, NJ

Ruschin, Siegfried, Libn., Coll.Dev.
LINDA HALL LIBRARY □ Kansas City, MO

Rush, Barbara, Program Libn.
UNIVERSITY OF MARYLAND, COLLEGE PARK - COMPUTER SCIENCE CENTER - PROGRAM LIBRARY □ College Park, MD

Rush, David E., Assoc.Libn.
MASSACHUSETTS COLLEGE OF PHARMACY & ALLIED HEALTH SCIENCES - SHEPPARD LIBRARY □ Boston, MA

Rush, Joseph, ILL Libn.
MITRE CORPORATION - CORPORATE LIBRARY† □ Bedford, MA

Rush, Mary, Libn.
MOUNT DESERT ISLAND BIOLOGICAL LABORATORY - LIBRARY □ Salsbury Cove, ME

Rush, Milagros R., Cat.
UNIVERSITY OF MINNESOTA - LAW LIBRARY □ Minneapolis, MN

Rush, Stephan, Chf.Libn.
CANADA - INDUSTRY, TRADE & COMMERCE - LIBRARY □ Ottawa, ON

Rushing, Kathryn K., Ed.
AUDUBON NATURALIST SOCIETY OF THE CENTRAL ATLANTIC STATES, INC. - LIBRARY □ Chevy Chase, MD

Rusin, Harriet, Lit. Searcher
ENVIRONMENTAL PROTECTION AGENCY - ANDREW W. BREIDENBACH ENVIRONMENTAL RESEARCH CTR., CINCINNATI - TECH.LIB. □ Cincinnati, OH

Rusk, Mike, Tech.Libn.
AMERICAN AIRLINES, INC. - ENGINEERING LIBRARY □ Tulsa, OK

Rusk, Susan, ILL
KANSAS STATE UNIVERSITY - FARRELL LIBRARY □ Manhattan, KS

Ruske, Martha, Cat.
WELLS FARGO BANK - LIBRARY □ San Francisco, CA

Russ, Evelyn, Libn.
STATE PARK HEALTH CENTER - PATIENTS' AND MEDICAL LIBRARY □ State Park, SC

Russ, Jon R., Chm., Lib.Comm.
PORTSMOUTH ATHENAEUM □ Portsmouth, NH

Russell, Amy J., Asst.Libn.
CABOT CORPORATION - TECHNICAL INFORMATION CENTER □ Kokomo, IN

Russell, B.G., Ref.Spec.
U.S. DEPT. OF ENERGY - PACIFIC NORTHWEST LABORATORY - TECHNICAL INFO. SECT. □ Richland, WA

Russell, Barbara, Cat.Libn.
SOUTHWESTERN BAPTIST THEOLOGICAL SEMINARY - FLEMING LIBRARY □ Fort Worth, TX

Russell, Beverly, Libn.
SEATTLE TIMES - LIBRARY† □ Seattle, WA

Russell, Carol N., Law Libn.
DELAWARE STATE LAW LIBRARY IN KENT COUNTY □ Dover, DE

Russell, Dan, Pres.
ST. JOSEPH HOSPITAL AND HEALTH CARE CENTER - MEDICAL LIBRARY □ Tacoma, WA

Russell, Fraser, Libn.
SASKATCHEWAN - DEPARTMENT OF LABOUR - LIBRARY □ Regina, SK

Russell, Gay R., Libn.
MONTGOMERY TECHNICAL INSTITUTE - LEARNING RESOURCES CENTER □ Troy, NC

Russell, George Ely, Genealogist
GENEALOGICAL PERIODICALS LIBRARY □ Middletown, MD

Russell, J. Thomas, Lib.Dir.
U.S. NATL. DEFENSE UNIVERSITY - LIBRARY □ Washington, DC

Russell, JoElla, Coord.Tech. Process
LORETTO HEIGHTS COLLEGE - MAY BONFILS STANTON LIBRARY □ Denver, CO

Russell, Lee, Sr.Libn.
AVCO CORPORATION - LYCOMING DIVISION - LIBRARY & INFORMATION CENTER □ Stratford, CT

Russell, Lockhart, Engr.Biblog.
SYRACUSE UNIVERSITY - ENGINEERING & LIFE SCIENCES LIBRARY □ Syracuse, NY

Russell, Lois B., Libn.
NORFOLK COUNTY LAW LIBRARY □ Dedham, MA

Russell, Phyllis, Libn.
MINT MUSEUM OF HISTORY - LASSITER LIBRARY □ Charlotte, NC

Russell, Phyllis J., Health Sci.Libn.
UNIVERSITY OF ALBERTA - HEALTH SCIENCES LIBRARY □ Edmonton, AB

Russell, Reba, Cur.
DIXON GALLERY AND GARDENS - LIBRARY □ Memphis, TN

Russell, Rhoda C., Libn.
TIME-LIFE BOOKS INC. - REFERENCE LIBRARY □ Alexandria, VA

Russell, Richard A., Libn.
BRODART, INC. - REFERENCE LIBRARY □ Williamsport, PA

Russell, Ruth, Hd., Ctrl.Lib.
CONTRA COSTA COUNTY - CENTRAL LIBRARY - LOCAL HISTORY COLLECTION □ Pleasant Hill, CA

Russell, Susan L., Mgr.
SAN JOSE HEALTH CENTER - HEALTH SCIENCE LIBRARY □ San Jose, CA

Russell, V.L., Supv., Archv.
TORONTO CITY RECORDS AND ARCHIVES DIVISION □ Toronto, ON

Russell, Violet, Coord.Lrng.Rsrcs.
AULTMAN HOSPITAL - SCHOOL OF NURSING LIBRARY □ Canton, OH

Russell, Volante H., Dir.
GRACELAND COLLEGE - FREDERICK MADISON SMITH LIBRARY □ Lamoni, IA

Russo, Barbara, Libn.
WASHINGTON STATE DEPARTMENT OF TRANSPORTATION - LIBRARY □ Olympia, WA

Russo, Edward J., Hd.
LINCOLN LIBRARY - SANGAMON VALLEY COLLECTION □ Springfield, IL

Russo, Elaine, Asst.Ref.Libn.
UNIVERSITY OF VIRGINIA MEDICAL CENTER - CLAUDE MOORE HEALTH SCIENCES LIBRARY □ Charlottesville, VA

Russo, Marcia S., Corp.Libn. & Hist.
TRAVELERS INSURANCE COMPANIES - CORPORATE LIBRARY □ Hartford, CT

Russo, Mary T., Spec.Coll.Libn.
BROWN UNIVERSITY - SPECIAL COLLECTIONS† □ Providence, RI

Ruth, Olivia, Hd., Comp.Serv.
FULLER THEOLOGICAL SEMINARY - MC ALISTER LIBRARY □ Pasadena, CA

Rutherford, Irmgard, Libn.
UNIVERSITY OF WASHINGTON - CHEMISTRY-PHARMACY LIBRARY □ Seattle, WA

Rutigliana, James P., Asst.Ct.Adm.
OCEAN COUNTY LAW LIBRARY □ Toms River, NJ

Rutledge, Aurora, Libn.
HIDALGO COUNTY LAW LIBRARY □ Edinburg, TX

Rutledge, Natalie, Asst.Libn.
SEATTLE PUBLIC LIBRARY - GOVERNMENTAL RESEARCH ASSISTANCE LIBRARY □ Seattle, WA

Rutledge, Patricia P., Libn.
CINCINNATI ART MUSEUM - LIBRARY □ Cincinnati, OH

Rutledge, Shirley, Libn.
DELTA WATERFOWL RESEARCH STATION - LIBRARY □ Portage La Prairie, MB

Rutowski, Pat, Educ.Asst.
COYOTE POINT MUSEUM - RESOURCE CENTER □ San Mateo, CA

Rutsis, Peggy, Med.Libn.
BEECHAM, INC. - BEECHAM LABORATORIES - MEDICAL LIBRARY □ Bristol, TN

Ruttenberg, Shirley W., Info.Anl.
TRIODYNE INC. CONSULTING ENGINEERS - INFORMATION CENTER □ Skokie, IL

Ruus, Ms. Laine, Hd., Data Lib.
UNIVERSITY OF BRITISH COLUMBIA - DATA LIBRARY □ Vancouver, BC

Ruus, Laine, Libn.
UNIVERSITY OF BRITISH COLUMBIA - SOCIAL SCIENCES DIVISION □ Vancouver, BC

Ruxin, Mrs. Olyn, Hd.Cat.Libn.
CLEVELAND HEALTH SCIENCES LIBRARY - HEALTH CENTER LIBRARY □ Cleveland, OH

Ruzicka, Aimee, Law Libn.
ALASKA STATE COURT SYSTEM - ALASKA COURT LIBRARIES □ Anchorage, AK

Ruzicka, Aimee
ALASKA STATE COURT SYSTEM - VALDEZ LAW LIBRARY □ Valdez, AK

PERSONNEL

Ryall, Doris, Libn.
ZOOLOGICAL SOCIETY OF PHILADELPHIA -
LIBRARY □ Philadelphia, PA

Ryan, Ann Miller, Med.Libn.
VALLEY PRESBYTERIAN HOSPITAL - LIBRARY
FOR MEDICAL AND HEALTH SCIENCES □ Van
Nuys, CA

Ryan, Barbara J., Med.Libn.
U.S. AIR FORCE HOSPITAL - MEDICAL LIBRARY
(OK-Tinker AFB) □ Tinker AFB, OK

Ryan, Bruce G., Asst.Chf.
NEW HAMPSHIRE STATE DEPARTMENT OF
EDUCATION - EDUCATIONAL INFORMATION
OFFICE AND LIBRARY □ Concord, NH

Ryan, Catherine, Libn.
GRACE GENERAL HOSPITAL - SCHOOL OF
NURSING LIBRARY □ St. John's, NF

Ryan, Christine, Libn.
CENTER FOR GOVERNMENTAL RESEARCH, INC.
- LIBRARY □ Rochester, NY

Ryan, Colleen A., Libn.
LOWENSTEIN (M.) CORPORATION - DESIGN
RESEARCH LIBRARY □ New York, NY

Ryan, David, Dir.
FORT WORTH ART MUSEUM - LIBRARY □ Fort
Worth, TX

Ryan, Donald F., Lab.Supt.
ATLANTIC-RICHFIELD COMPANY - ANACONDA
ALUMINUM COMPANY - COLUMBIA FALLS
REDUCTION DIVISION - LIBRARY □ Columbia
Falls, MT

Ryan, Elizabeth C., Sr.Res.Libn.
FEDERAL RESERVE BANK OF CHICAGO -
LIBRARY □ Chicago, IL

Ryan, Frederick W., Asst.Dir.
CALIFORNIA STATE UNIVERSITY, CHICO -
MERIAM LIBRARY □ Chico, CA

Ryan, James, Site Mgr.
OLANA STATE HISTORIC SITE - LIBRARY □
Hudson, NY

Ryan, Mrs. Jeri A., Libn.
AMERICAN COLLEGE OF SURGEONS - LIBRARY
□ Chicago, IL

Ryan, Joan I., Med.Rec.Libn.
VICTORIA UNION HOSPITAL - MEDICAL
LIBRARY □ Prince Albert, SK

Ryan, Karen J., Data Adm.Libn.
NORTHERN TELECOM CANADA, LTD. -
BUSINESS SYSTEMS LIBRARY □ Islington, ON

Ryan, Mary, Cat.
NORTH DAKOTA STATE LIBRARY □ Bismarck,
ND

Ryan, Mary, Coord., Tech.Serv.
UNIVERSITY OF ARKANSAS MEDICAL
SCIENCES CAMPUS - MEDICAL SCIENCES
LIBRARY □ Little Rock, AR

Ryan, Michael, Asst.Cur./Archv.
UNIVERSITY OF CHICAGO - SPECIAL
COLLECTIONS □ Chicago, IL

Ryan, Richard W., Rare Bk.Libn.
UNIVERSITY OF MICHIGAN - WILLIAM L.
CLEMENTS LIBRARY □ Ann Arbor, MI

Ryan, William, Media
LAMAR UNIVERSITY - MARY AND JOHN GRAY
LIBRARY □ Beaumont, TX

Ryan, William V., Dir.Lib.Serv.
BLOOMSBURG STATE COLLEGE - HARVEY A.
ANDRUSS LIBRARY □ Bloomsburg, PA

Ryans, Kathryn, Info.Spec.
IMPERIAL OIL, LTD. - BUSINESS INFORMATION
CENTRE □ Toronto, ON

Ryant, Carl G., Co-Dir.
UNIVERSITY OF LOUISVILLE - UNIVERSITY
ARCHIVES AND RECORDS CENTER - ORAL
HISTORY CENTER □ Louisville, KY

Ryder, Dorothy, Ref.Coll.Dev.Spec.
NATIONAL LIBRARY OF CANADA - REFERENCE
AND BIBLIOGRAPHY SECTION □ Ottawa, ON

Ryder, Suzanne M., Supv.Libn.
U.S. NAVY - NAVAL AIR TEST CENTER - NAVAL
AIR STATION - ENGINEERING & TECHNICAL
LIBRARY □ Patuxent River, MD

Rydesky, Mary, Hd., LRC
UNIVERSITY OF TEXAS HEALTH SCIENCE
CENTER, DALLAS - LIBRARY □ Dallas, TX

Ryken, Jorena, Asst. to Dir.
WHEATON COLLEGE - LIBRARY □ Wheaton, IL

Ryken, Margaret Green, Hd.Libn.
STANFORD UNIVERSITY - SWAIN LIBRARY OF
CHEMISTRY AND CHEMICAL ENGINEERING □
Stanford, CA

Rykoskey, Mary S., Libn.
CUMBERLAND COUNTY LAW LIBRARY □ Carlisle,
PA

Rylance, Dan, Cur.
UNIVERSITY OF NORTH DAKOTA -
DEPARTMENT OF SPECIAL COLLECTIONS □
Grand Forks, ND

Ryll, Judith A., Libn.
MC MILLAN, BINCH - LIBRARY □ Toronto, ON

Rynders, Kathryn, Ref.Libn.
UNIVERSITY OF MINNESOTA TECHNICAL
COLLEGE, WASECA - LEARNING RESOURCES
CENTER □ Waseca, MN

Ryoo, Heija, Acq.Libn.
SOUTHERN ILLINOIS UNIVERSITY,
CARBONDALE - SCHOOL OF LAW LIBRARY □
Carbondale, IL

Rys, J.L.
3M - ENGINEERING INFORMATION SERVICES □
St. Paul, MN

Ryskamp, Charles A., Dir.
PIERPONT MORGAN LIBRARY □ New York, NY

Ryweck, Morton W., Dir.
JEWISH COMMUNITY RELATIONS COUNCIL -
ANTI-DEFAMATION LEAGUE OF MINNESOTA-
DAKOTAS - LIBRARY □ Minneapolis, MN

Rzeczkowski, E. Matthew, O.P., Asst.Libn.
DOMINICAN COLLEGE LIBRARY □ Washington,
DC

Rzepecki, Arnold M., Libn.
SACRED HEART SEMINARY - COLLEGE LIBRARY
□ Detroit, MI

Rzepka, Donna M., Libn.
ROCKWELL INTERNATIONAL - AUTOMOTIVE
OPERATIONS DIVISION - REFERENCE CENTER
□ Troy, MI

Rzeszewski, Ted, Mgr., Advan. R & D
MATSUSHITA INDUSTRIAL COMPANY -
TECHNICAL INFORMATION SERVICES LIBRARY
□ Franklin Park, IL

S

Saar, Amanda, Circ.Libn.
UNIVERSITY OF ARKANSAS MEDICAL
SCIENCES CAMPUS - MEDICAL SCIENCES
LIBRARY □ Little Rock, AR

Sabella, Charles, Ref.Libn.
AMERICAN BANKERS ASSOCIATION - LIBRARY
□ Washington, DC

Sabin, James, Vice Pres., Ed.
GREENWOOD PRESS - LIBRARY □ Westport, CT

Sabo, Eleanor, Libn.
PANNELL KERR FORSTER - LIBRARY □ New
York, NY

Sabol, Lynn, Libn.
HALL-BROOKE HOSPITAL - PROFESSIONAL
LIBRARY □ Westport, CT

Sabonjian, Aznive, Libn.
CALBIOCHEM-BEHRING CORPORATION -
LIBRARY □ La Jolla, CA

Sabourin, Conrad, Delegate
CANADIAN BROADCASTING CORPORATION -
MUSIC SERVICES LIBRARY □ Montreal, PQ

Sabowitz, N.C., Systems Libn.
BEDFORD INSTITUTE OF OCEANOGRAPHY -
LIBRARY □ Dartmouth, NS

Sabre, Christine, Tech.Info.Spec.
OCCIDENTAL RESEARCH CORPORATION -
TECHNICAL INFORMATION CENTER □ Irvine,
CA

Sacchini, Martha, Med.Libn.
ST. JOSEPH'S HOSPITAL - LIBRARY □ Dickinson,
ND

Sacherek, Lynetta S., Asst.Libn.
SEATTLE-FIRST NATIONAL BANK - LIBRARY □
Seattle, WA

Sachs, Iris, Med.Libn.
WEISS (Louis A.) MEMORIAL HOSPITAL - L.
LEWIS COHEN MEMORIAL MEDICAL LIBRARY □
Chicago, IL

Sachse, Renate, Cat.Libn.
FRANKLIN AND MARSHALL COLLEGE -
FACKENTHAL LIBRARY - SPECIAL
COLLECTIONS □ Lancaster, PA

Sacks, Dr. Jonathan
MASSACHUSETTS INSTITUTE OF TECHNOLOGY
- DEPARTMENT OF MATHEMATICS - READING
ROOM □ Cambridge, MA

Sacks, Maj. Lorraine, Libn.
SALVATION ARMY SCHOOL FOR OFFICERS
TRAINING - BRENGLE MEMORIAL LIBRARY □
Suffern, NY

Sacks, Patricia Ann, Dir. of Libs.
MUHLENBERG COLLEGE - JOHN A.W. HAAS
LIBRARY □ Allentown, PA

Sadak, Luz, Cat.
INTER-AMERICAN DEVELOPMENT BANK -
TECHNICAL INFORMATION CENTER □
Washington, DC

Sadecki, Win, Corp.Libn.
HOUSEHOLD FINANCE CORPORATION -
CORPORATE LIBRARY □ Prospect Heights, IL

Sadler, Catherine E., Libn.
CHARLESTON LIBRARY SOCIETY □ Charleston,
SC

Sadler, Cynthia, Hd.Libn.
TEXAS STATE TECHNICAL INSTITUTE, MID-
CONTINENT CAMPUS - LIBRARY† □ Amarillo, TX

Sadler, Rowena S., Chf., Lib.Serv. & Info.Br
U.S. SOCIAL SECURITY ADMINISTRATION -
LIBRARY □ Baltimore, MD

Sadowski, Frank, Hd., Biblog.Serv.
UNIVERSITY OF MISSOURI, ST. LOUIS -
THOMAS JEFFERSON LIBRARY □ St. Louis, MO

Sadwith, Lucille, Dir.
CENTER FOR FARM AND FOOD RESEARCH, INC.
- LIBRARY □ Falls Village, CT

Saeed, Mr. Munawar Ahmad, Ref.Libn.
AHMADIYYA MOVEMENT IN ISLAM - MUSLIM
LIBRARY □ Washington, DC

Saenz, Mercedes, Hd., PR Coll.
UNIVERSITY OF PUERTO RICO - GENERAL
LIBRARY □ San Juan, PR

Saenz, Dr. Mercedes, Hd.
UNIVERSITY OF PUERTO RICO - PUERTO
RICAN COLLECTION □ Rio Piedras, PR

Safchuk, Alexandra Lobas, Tech.Serv.Libn.
ST. VLADIMIR'S ORTHODOX THEOLOGICAL
SEMINARY - FR. GEORGES FLOROVSKY
LIBRARY □ Tuckahoe, NY

Saferin, Ethel I., Libn.
PARK SYNAGOGUE LIBRARY □ Cleveland
Heights, OH

Saffer, Melinda, Lib.Dir.
WORCESTER FOUNDATION FOR
EXPERIMENTAL BIOLOGY - GEORGE F. FULLER
LIBRARY □ Shrewsbury, MA

Safley, Ann, Libn.
CARNEGIE LIBRARY OF PITTSBURGH - MUSIC
AND ART DEPARTMENT □ Pittsburgh, PA

Safranek, William, Libn.
MORGAN COUNTY BAR ASSOCIATION -
LIBRARY □ McConnelsville, OH

Sagar, Mary, Libn.
KALSEC, INC. - LIBRARY □ Kalamazoo, MI

Sager, Roberta, Tech.Libn.
WILPUTTE CORPORATION - LIBRARY □ Murray
Hill, NJ

Sahak, Judy Harvey, Libn.
CLAREMONT COLLEGES - ELLA STRONG
DENISON LIBRARY □ Claremont, CA

Sahak, Judy Harvey, Asst.Dir.
CLAREMONT COLLEGES - LIBRARY □ Claremont, CA

Sahu, Mrs. Krishna, Dir.
UNIVERSITY OF OSTEOPATHIC MEDICINE AND HEALTH SCIENCES - LIBRARY† □ Des Moines, IA

Sahyoun, Naim K., Dir. Of Libs.
PONTIAC GENERAL HOSPITAL - LIBRARY □ Pontiac, MI

Said, Josephine, Libn.
IOWA STATE DEPARTMENT OF TRANSPORTATION - LIBRARY □ Ames, IA

Saiet, Ronald, Assoc.Dir.Lrng.Serv.
NORTHEASTERN ILLINOIS UNIVERSITY - LIBRARY □ Chicago, IL

Saiki, Anne H., Libn.
LYON ASSOCIATES, INC. - BELT, COLLINS AND ASSOCIATES DIVISION - INFORMATION SERVICES □ Honolulu, HI

Saint, Barbara, Ref.Libn.
UNIVERSITY OF BRITISH COLUMBIA - BIOMEDICAL BRANCH LIBRARY □ Vancouver, BC

St. Amand, Sylvia, Mus.Libn.
SPRINGFIELD CITY LIBRARY - FINE ARTS DEPARTMENT □ Springfield, MA

St. Arnaud, Lise, Lib.Asst.
UNIVERSITY OF SASKATCHEWAN - GEOLOGY BRANCH LIBRARY □ Saskatoon, SK

St. Clair, Albert W., Law Libn.
WYOMING STATE LAW LIBRARY □ Cheyenne, WY

St. Clair, Geneva M., Acq.Hd.
BOEING COMPANY - SEATTLE SERVICES DIVISION - RENTON LIBRARY □ Seattle, WA

St. Clair, Guy, Dir.
UNIVERSITY CLUB LIBRARY □ New York, NY

St. Clair, Helen, Med.Libn.
WILMINGTON MEDICAL CENTER (Delaware Division) - MEDICAL STAFF LIBRARY □ Wilmington, DE

St. Clair, Jeffrey W., Med.Libn.
ST. MARY'S HOSPITAL & HEALTH CENTER - RALPH FULLER MEDICAL LIBRARY □ Tucson, AZ

St-Jacques, Suzanne, Hd., Ref.Serv.
UNIVERSITY OF OTTAWA - MORISSET LIBRARY □ Ottawa, ON

St. John, Esther, Hd.Libn.
FIRST BAPTIST CHURCH - LIBRARY □ North Kansas City, MO

St. John, Louise, Base Libn.
U.S. AIR FORCE BASE - BERGSTROM BASE LIBRARY □ Austin, TX

Saint-Martin, Lucienne, Libn.
HOPITAL STE-JUSTINE - CENTRE D'INFORMATION SUR LA SANTE DE L'ENFANT† □ Montreal, PQ, H3T 1C5 PQ

St. Pierre, Normand, Chf.Libn.
CANADA - PUBLIC ARCHIVES OF CANADA - LIBRARY □ Ottawa, ON

Saintcross, Eva M., Tech.Libn.
MARINE MIDLAND BANK - TECHNICAL INFORMATION CENTER □ Buffalo, NY

Saito, Masaei, Asst.Hd.
UNIVERSITY OF MICHIGAN - ASIA LIBRARY □ Ann Arbor, MI

Saiz, John T., Law Libn.
ST. JOHN'S UNIVERSITY - LAW LIBRARY □ Jamaica, NY

Sakamoto, Louise Y., Libn.
PUREX CORPORATION - TECHNICAL LIBRARY □ Carson, CA

Sakoian, Mary Ann, Libn.
BITUMINOUS COAL RESEARCH, INC. - LIBRARY □ Monroeville, PA

Salabiye, Velma S., Libn.
UNIVERSITY OF CALIFORNIA, LOS ANGELES - AMERICAN INDIAN STUDIES CENTER - LIBRARY □ Los Angeles, CA

Salam, Abdus, Hd.
METROPOLITAN TORONTO LIBRARY - SOCIAL SCIENCES DEPARTMENT □ Toronto, ON

Salama, Joe
INTERNATIONAL FABRICARE INSTITUTE - RESEARCH CENTER LIBRARY □ Silver Spring, MD

Salaman, David J., Libn.
BETH SHOLOM CONGREGATION - JOSEPH & ELIZABETH SCHWARTZ LIBRARY □ Elkins Park, PA

Salandy, Mrs. Pat, Libn.
EBERSTADT (F.) AND COMPANY - BUSINESS LIBRARY □ New York, NY

Salazar, Viola, Asst.Supv., Main Lib.
UNIVERSITY OF CALIFORNIA - LOS ALAMOS NATIONAL LABORATORY - LIBRARY □ Los Alamos, NM

Salber, Peter, Asst.Lib.Dir.
NEWSWEEK, INC. - LIBRARY □ New York, NY

Saldinger, J.P., Libn.
EXXON RESEARCH AND ENGINEERING COMPANY - FLORHAM PARK INFORMATION CENTER† □ Florham Park, NJ

Sale, E.T., Exec.Dir.
WINNIPEG SOCIAL PLANNING COUNCIL - LIBRARY □ Winnipeg, MB

Sale, Melanie Laura, Ser. & Doc.Libn.
COLLEGE OF WILLIAM AND MARY - MARSHALL-WYTHE LAW LIBRARY □ Williamsburg, VA

Saley, Stacey, Chf.Med.Libn.
MOUNT SINAI HOSPITAL SERVICES - CITY HOSPITAL CENTER AT ELMHURST - MEDICAL LIBRARY □ Elmhurst, NY

Salgat, Anne-Marie, Libn.
GENERAL THEOLOGICAL SEMINARY OF THE PROTESTANT EPISCOPAL CHURCH IN THE U.S.A. - ST. MARK'S LIBRARY □ New York, NY

Salisbury, Susan, Staff Libn.
UNIVERSITY OF CALIFORNIA, BERKELEY - INST. OF INDUSTRIAL RELATIONS - LABOR OCCUPATIONAL HEALTH PROG.LIB. □ Berkeley, CA

Salisz, Alexis L., Adm.
OAKLAND UNIVERSITY - LIBRARY □ Rochester, MI

Sall, Judy, Photo Libn.
DALLAS MORNING NEWS - REFERENCE DEPARTMENT □ Dallas, TX

Sally, Dana, Libn.
UNIVERSITY OF NORTH CAROLINA, CHAPEL HILL - MATHEMATICS-PHYSICS-STATISTICS LIBRARY □ Chapel Hill, NC

Salm, Kay E., Hd.Libn.
NORTHROP CORPORATION - RESEARCH AND TECHNOLOGY CENTER - LIBRARY SERVICES □ Palos Verdes Peninsula, CA

Salmon, R.R., Hist.
BROOKGREEN GARDENS - LIBRARY □ Murrells Inlet, SC

Salo, Anna B.
MANCHESTER MEMORIAL HOSPITAL - LIBRARY □ Manchester, CT

Salo, Annette, Libn.
ST. PAUL PUBLIC LIBRARY - VIDEO COMMUNICATIONS CENTER □ St. Paul, MN

Salovaara, Mary K., Asst.Libn.
KIRKLAND & ELLIS - LIBRARY □ Chicago, IL

Salscheider, Rosemary, Supv.
MACALESTER COLLEGE - OLIN SCIENCE LIBRARY □ St. Paul, MN

Saltalamachia, Joyce, Pub.Serv.Libn.
GOLDEN GATE UNIVERSITY - SCHOOL OF LAW LIBRARY □ San Francisco, CA

Salter, A., Asst.Archv.
ATLANTA HISTORICAL SOCIETY - ARCHIVES □ Atlanta, GA

Salter, Billie I., Libn. for Social Sci.
YALE UNIVERSITY - ECONOMIC GROWTH CENTER COLLECTION □ New Haven, CT

Salter, Billie I., Libn. for Social Sci.
YALE UNIVERSITY - SOCIAL SCIENCE LIBRARY □ New Haven, CT

Salumbides, Juliana C., Med.Libn.
GUAM MEMORIAL HOSPITAL AUTHORITY - MEDICAL LIBRARY □ Agana, GU

Salvail, Marthe Dumont, Hd.Libn.
CORPORATION PROFESSIONNELLE DES MEDECINS DU QUEBEC - INFORMATHEQUE □ Montreal, PQ

Salzman, Edith, Libn.
NORTHWEST COMMUNITY HOSPITAL - MEDICAL LIBRARY □ Arlington Heights, IL

Salzman, Edythe, Libn.
NASHOBA COMMUNITY HOSPITAL - MEDICAL LIBRARY □ Ayer, MA

Samard, Emiko, Assoc.Libn.
UNIVERSITY OF CALIFORNIA, IRVINE - MEDICAL CENTER LIBRARY □ Orange, CA

Samb, LaVerne, Libn.
LA CROSSE LUTHERAN HOSPITAL - HEALTH SCIENCES LIBRARY □ La Crosse, WI

Samek, Lois J., Med.Libn.
INDEPENDENCE MENTAL HEALTH INSTITUTE - MEDICAL LIBRARY □ Independence, IA

Samer, Marcia G., Info.Sci.
MORTON-NORWICH PRODUCTS, INC. - NORWICH PHARMACAL COMPANY - R&D DEPT. - LIBRARY INFORMATION GROUP □ Norwich, NY

Sameth, Marian, Assoc.Dir.
CITIZENS HOUSING AND PLANNING COUNCIL OF NEW YORK - LIBRARY □ New York, NY

Sammarco, Anthony Mitchell, Libn.
DORCHESTER HISTORICAL SOCIETY - ROBINSON-LEHANE LIBRARY □ Dorchester, MA

Sammis, Stewart, Archv.
COLLEGE OF MEDICINE AND DENTISTRY OF NEW JERSEY AT NEWARK - GEORGE F. SMITH LIBRARY □ Newark, NJ

Sammons, Christa A., Cur./German Coll.
YALE UNIVERSITY - BEINECKE RARE BOOK AND MANUSCRIPT LIBRARY □ New Haven, CT

Sammons, Pam, Tech.Libn.
FLUOR ENGINEERS AND CONSTRUCTORS, INC. - ENGINEERING LIBRARY □ Irvine, CA

Sample, C.A., Ref.Spec.
U.S. DEPT. OF ENERGY - PACIFIC NORTHWEST LABORATORY - TECHNICAL INFO. SECT. □ Richland, WA

Sams, Julie, Adm.Asst.
BAYLOR UNIVERSITY - J.M. DAWSON CHURCH-STATE RESEARCH CENTER - LIBRARY □ Waco, TX

Samson, Gary, Filmmaker
UNIVERSITY OF NEW HAMPSHIRE - DEPARTMENT OF MEDIA SERVICES - FILM LIBRARY □ Durham, NH

Samson, Lucila R., Med.Libn.
YONKERS GENERAL HOSPITAL - MEDICAL LIBRARY □ Yonkers, NY

Samuda, Madeleine, Ref.
COLLEGE UNIVERSITAIRE DE ST. BONIFACE - BIBLIOTHEQUE UNIVERSITAIRE □ Saint-Boniface, MB

Samuel, Evelyn, Hd.Libn.
NEW YORK UNIVERSITY - STEPHEN CHAN LIBRARY OF FINE ARTS □ New York, NY

Samuel, Harold E., Libn.
YALE UNIVERSITY - JOHN HERRICK JACKSON MUSIC LIBRARY □ New Haven, CT

Samuel, Kay, Cat.
NEW YORK COUNTY LAWYERS' ASSOCIATION - LIBRARY □ New York, NY

Samuel, Parkash, Chm., Lib.Comm.
NATIONAL PRESBYTERIAN CHURCH - WILLIAM S. CULBERTSON LIBRARY □ Washington, DC

Samuels, Joel L., Dir.Lib.Serv.
NEWBERRY LIBRARY □ Chicago, IL

Samuels, Lois, Info.Sci.
ETHICON, INC. - SCIENTIFIC INFORMATION SERVICES □ Somerville, NJ

Samuels, Ruth, Asst.
LOCKWOOD, ANDREWS & NEWNAM, INC. - INFORMATION CENTER □ Houston, TX

Samuels, William M., Exec.Dir.
NATIONAL SOCIETY FOR MEDICAL RESEARCH - NSMR DATA BANK □ Washington, DC

Samuelson, Eileen, Asst.Libn.
GRATZ COLLEGE - LIBRARY □ Philadelphia, PA

**P
E
R
S
O
N
N
E
L**

PERSONNEL

Sanborn, Helen W., Supv.Info.Serv.
CONSOLIDATED PAPERS, INC. - RESEARCH
AND DEVELOPMENT LIBRARY □ Wisconsin
Rapids, WI

Sanborn, K.J., Ed.Asst.
AMERICAN ASSOCIATION OF MUSEUMS -
MUSEUM RESOURCES AND INFORMATION
SERVICE □ Washington, DC

Sanborn, Richard, Libn.
CALIFORNIA SCHOOL OF PROFESSIONAL
PSYCHOLOGY - SAN DIEGO LIBRARY □ San
Diego, CA

Sanchez, Hector Ruben, Lib.Dir.
EVANGELICAL SEMINARY OF PUERTO RICO -
JUAN DE VALDES LIBRARY □ Hato Rey, PR

Sanchez, Margarita M., Doc.Libn.
UNIVERSITY OF PUERTO RICO - MAYAGUEZ
CAMPUS - LIBRARY □ Mayaguez, PR

Sand, Nanette O., Libn.
UNIVERSITY OF CALIFORNIA, BERKELEY -
INSTITUTE OF INDUSTRIAL RELATIONS
LIBRARY □ Berkeley, CA

Sandberg, Joy, Info.Ctr.Mgr.
MOUNTAIN STATES EMPLOYERS COUNCIL -
INFORMATION CENTER □ Denver, CO

Sandberg, Wanda H., Libn.
WORCESTER COUNTY HORTICULTURAL
SOCIETY - LIBRARY □ Worcester, MA

Sande, Betty, Spec.Proj.Libn.
MAYO FOUNDATION - MAYO CLINIC LIBRARY □
Rochester, MN

Sandel, Jean, Libn.
DEUTSCH, KERRIGAN AND STILES - LAW
LIBRARY □ New Orleans, LA

Sander, Leanne, Dir.
BOULDER HISTORICAL SOCIETY - PIONEER
MUSEUM - LIBRARY □ Boulder, CO

Sander, Phil, Musm.Dir.
KENOSHA COUNTY HISTORICAL SOCIETY -
HISTORICAL MUSEUM LIBRARY □ Kenosha, WI

Sanders, Aimee Devine, Lib.Cons.
HISTORICAL SOCIETY OF BERKS COUNTY -
LIBRARY □ Reading, PA

Sanders, Arthur H., Cur.
MUSICAL MUSEUM - RESEARCH LIBRARY □
Deansboro, NY

Sanders, Don, Hd.Cat./Ref.
UNIVERSITY OF CALGARY - LAW LIBRARY □
Calgary, AB

Sanders, Eleanor, Cat.
UNIVERSITY OF HEALTH SCIENCES - LIBRARY
□ Kansas City, MO

Sanders, Elizabeth
ALTERNATIVE PRESS CENTER - LIBRARY □
Baltimore, MD

Sanders, Elizabeth, Res.
EVANGELICAL AND REFORMED HISTORICAL
SOCIETY - LANCASTER CENTRAL ARCHIVES
AND LIBRARY □ Lancaster, PA

Sanders, Ethel, Assoc.Dir.
TROY STATE UNIVERSITY - LIBRARY □ Troy, AL

Sanders, James L., Asst.Ed.
SOIL CONSERVATION SOCIETY OF AMERICA -
H. WAYNE PRITCHARD LIBRARY □ Ankeny, IA

Sanders, James R., Dir.
TEXAS STATE LEGISLATIVE REFERENCE
LIBRARY □ Austin, TX

Sanders, John, Libn.
OAK HILLS BIBLE INSTITUTE - LIBRARY □
Bemidji, MN

Sanders, Regine, Tech.Libn.
U.S. AIR FORCE BASE - KEESLER BASE -
MC BRIDE LIBRARY □ Keesler AFB, MS

Sanders, Robin, Asst.Libn.
LANDAUER ASSOCIATES, INC. - INFORMATION
CENTER □ New York, NY

Sanders, William, Exhibits & Arts Libn.
WESTERN ILLINOIS UNIVERSITY - LIBRARIES
□ Macomb, IL

Sanderson, Barbara L., Libn.
BRITISH COLUMBIA - WORKER'S
COMPENSATION BOARD - LIBRARY □
Vancouver, BC

Sanderson, Harlan, Circ. & AV Libn.
LUTHER COLLEGE - PREUS LIBRARY □ Decorah,
IA

Sanderson, William, Non-Print
UNIVERSITY OF UTAH - LAW LIBRARY □ Salt
Lake City, UT

Sandine, Margaret, Tech.Serv.
SOUTH DAKOTA SCHOOL OF MINES &
TECHNOLOGY - DEVEREAUX LIBRARY □ Rapid
City, SD

Sandler, Gary, Asst.Cat.Libn.
ALCORN STATE UNIVERSITY - JOHN DEWEY
BOYD LIBRARY □ Lorman, MS

Sandler, Gary, Asst.Libn.
NEW YORK BOTANICAL GARDEN - LIBRARY □
Bronx, NY

Sandor, Eva, Libn.
ONTARIO HYDRO - LIBRARY □ Toronto, ON

Sandor, Ruth, Libn.
UNIVERSITY OF WISCONSIN, MADISON -
CENTER FOR DEMOGRAPHY - LIBRARY □
Madison, WI

Sandoval, Penny Ann, Photo Libn.
MARYKNOLL FATHERS - PHOTO LIBRARY □
Maryknoll, NY

Sands, Margaret, Circ.Libn.
SUNY - AGRICULTURAL AND TECHNICAL
COLLEGE AT ALFRED - WALTER C. HINKLE
MEMORIAL LIBRARY □ Alfred, NY

Sands, Nathan J., Mgr.
SINGER COMPANY - LIBRASCOPE DIVISION -
TECHNICAL INFORMATION CENTER □ Glendale,
CA

Sandstedt, P. Russann, Asst.Libn.
U.S. COURT OF APPEALS, 8TH CIRCUIT -
LIBRARY □ St. Louis, MO

Sandstrom, Judith, Chf., Rd.Serv.Br.
U.S. DEPT. OF THE TREASURY - INFORMATION
SERVICES DIVISION - TREASURY DEPT.
LIBRARY □ Washington, DC

Sandula, Margaretta, Chf.
DETROIT PUBLIC LIBRARY - NATIONAL
AUTOMOTIVE HISTORY COLLECTION □ Detroit,
MI

Sanduleak, Barbara, Supv., Lib.Serv.
GOULD, INC. - GOULD INFORMATION CENTER □
Cleveland, OH

Sandy, John H., Libn.
UNIVERSITY OF TEXAS, AUSTIN - PHYSICS-
MATHEMATICS-ASTRONOMY LIBRARY □ Austin,
TX

Sandy, Will, Lib.Coord.
AMERICAN JEWISH COMMITTEE - WILLIAM E.
WIENER ORAL HISTORY LIBRARY □ New York,
NY

Sanford, Clarke, Dir.Ed.Tech.
SUNY - AGRICULTURAL AND TECHNICAL
COLLEGE AT COBLESKILL - JARED VAN
WAGENEN, JR. LEARNING RESOURCE CENTER □
Cobleskill, NY

Sanford, Jaspyr, Sci.Ref.Libn.
SAM HOUSTON STATE UNIVERSITY - LIBRARY†
□ Huntsville, TX

Sanford, Judith, Ed.
HOFFMANN-LA ROCHE, INC. - BUSINESS
INFORMATION CENTER □ Nutley, NJ

Sanford, Lynda, Sci./Tech.Info.Hd.
CHICAGO PUBLIC LIBRARY CENTRAL LIBRARY -
BUSINESS/SCIENCE/TECHNOLOGY DIVISION
□ Chicago, IL

Sanford, Muriel A., Spec.Coll.Libn.
UNIVERSITY OF MAINE, ORONO - RAYMOND H.
FOGLER LIBRARY - SPECIAL COLLECTIONS
DEPARTMENT† □ Orono, ME

Sanger, Helen, Libn.
FRICK ART REFERENCE LIBRARY □ New York,
NY

Sangster, Collette, Dir.
ST. MARY'S SCHOOL FOR THE DEAF -
PROFESSIONAL LIBRARY □ Buffalo, NY

Sangster, Doris Mosdell, Cat.Off.
CANADIAN BROADCASTING CORPORATION -
PROGRAM ARCHIVES (Sound) □ Toronto, ON

Sankowski, Andrew, Lib. Planner
TEACHERS COLLEGE - LIBRARY □ New York, NY

Sano, Tony, Supv.
AMERICAN TELEPHONE & TELEGRAPH
COMPANY - EDITORIAL & HISTORICAL
RESEARCH CENTER □ New York, NY

Sansbury, Michele M., Mgr.
FREDERICK CANCER RESEARCH CENTER -
SCIENTIFIC LIBRARY □ Frederick, MD

Sansom, James F., Oper.Spec.
VOUGHT CORPORATION - TECHNICAL
INFORMATION CENTER □ Dallas, TX

Santa Lucia, Guy, Ref.Libn.
UNIVERSITY OF NEW ENGLAND - LIBRARY† □
Biddeford, ME

Santa Maria, Ofelia, Per.Libn.
WEST VIRGINIA INSTITUTE OF TECHNOLOGY -
VINING LIBRARY □ Montgomery, WV

Santella, Theresa, Asst.Libn.
U.S. COURT OF APPEALS, DISTRICT OF
COLUMBIA CIRCUIT - LIBRARY □ Washington,
DC

Santiago, Gladys, Hd.Libn.
PUERTO RICO - OFFICE OF BUDGET &
MANAGEMENT - LIBRARY □ San Juan, PR

Santoro, Louise, Asst.Libn.
WAGNER COLLEGE - HORRMANN LIBRARY □
Staten Island, NY

Santos, Ann
HARTFORD PUBLIC LIBRARY - BUSINESS,
SCIENCE & TECHNOLOGY DEPARTMENT □
Hartford, CT

Santos, Emerenciana S., Tech.Libn.
BURNS AND ROE, INC. - JAMES MACLEAN
TECHNICAL LIBRARY □ Woodbury, NY

Santos, Maria E.
UNIVERSITY OF PUERTO RICO - GRADUATE
SCHOOL OF PLANNING - LIBRARY □ Rio Piedras,
PR

Sanwald, Pat
BLAKE, CASSELS & GRAYDON - LIBRARY □
Toronto, ON

Sapienza, Diane G., Law Libn.
KADISON, PFAELZER, WOODARD, QUINN &
ROSSI - LAW LIBRARY □ Los Angeles, CA

Sapowith, Marcia K., Ref.Libn.
VILLANOVA UNIVERSITY - PULLING LAW
LIBRARY □ Villanova, PA

Sapp, Blossom, Libn.
U.S. NATL. PARK SERVICE - PU'UHONUA O
HONAUNAU NATL. HISTORICAL PARK -
LIBRARY □ Honaunau, HI

Sapp, V.J., Lib.Supv.
ALUMINUM COMPANY OF AMERICA - ALCOA
LABORATORIES - INFORMATION DEPARTMENT
□ Alcoa Center, PA

Sappers, Vernon J., Cur.
CALIFORNIA RAILWAY MUSEUM - LIBRARY □
Suisun City, CA

Saquet, Janette K., Libn.
SMITHSONIAN INSTITUTION LIBRARIES -
NATIONAL MUSEUM OF NATURAL HISTORY -
ANTHROPOLOGY BRANCH LIBRARY □
Washington, DC

Saraidaridis, Susan, Libn.
HEWLETT-PACKARD COMPANY - MEDICAL
ELECTRONICS DIVISION - LIBRARY □ Waltham,
MA

Sardeson, Vivian E., Libn.
BREVARD COLLEGE - JAMES A. JONES LIBRARY
- FINE ARTS DIVISION □ Brevard, NC

Sargent, Ann, Libn./Media Res.Asst.
HAYHURST (F.H.) COMPANY, LTD. - MEDIA
RESEARCH LIBRARY □ Toronto, ON

Sargent, Charles W., Ph.D., Dir.
TEXAS TECH UNIVERSITY - HEALTH SCIENCES
CENTER - LIBRARY OF THE HEALTH SCIENCES
□ Lubbock, TX

Sark, Sue, Acq.
UNIVERSITY OF TULSA - COLLEGE OF LAW
LIBRARY □ Tulsa, OK

Sarna, Helen, Asst.Libn.
HEBREW COLLEGE - JACOB AND ROSE GROSSMAN LIBRARY □ Brookline, MA

Sarophim, Tahani
CALGARY SOCIAL SERVICE DEPARTMENT - LIBRARY □ Calgary, AB

Sarr, John T., Pubn.Off.
AFRICAN-AMERICAN LABOR CENTER (AALC) - LIBRARY □ Washington, DC

Sarraga, Raquel, Hd., Spec.Coll.
UNIVERSITY OF PUERTO RICO - GENERAL LIBRARY □ San Juan, PR

Sarrasin, Louis, Libn.
UNIVERSITE DE MONTREAL - INFORMATIQUE-BIBLIOTHEQUE □ Montreal, PQ

Sarrazin, Jean, Act.Dir.
QUEBEC PROVINCE - SERVICE GENERAL DES MOYENS D'ENSEIGNEMENT - CENTRE DE DOCUMENTATION □ Montreal, PQ

Sartorius, R.C., Info.Anl.
GULF OIL CHEMICALS COMPANY - HOUSTON RESEARCH LIBRARY □ Houston, TX

Sass, Dr. Herman, Ref.Libn.
BUFFALO & ERIE COUNTY HISTORICAL SOCIETY - LIBRARY □ Buffalo, NY

Sassa, Reiko, Asst.Libn.
JAPAN SOCIETY, INC. - LIBRARY □ New York, NY

Sassaman, Judith A., Info.Spec.
GENERAL MILLS, INC. - MARKETING RESEARCH INFORMATION CENTER □ Minneapolis, MN

Sasse, Gary S., Exec.Dir.
RHODE ISLAND PUBLIC EXPENDITURE COUNCIL - LIBRARY □ Providence, RI

Sasseen, Elizabeth, Sr.Info.Spec./Ref.
GENERAL FOODS CORPORATION - MARKETING INFORMATION CENTER □ White Plains, NY

Sasser, Caroline A., Supv. of Lib.
GRACE (W.R.) AND COMPANY - RESEARCH DIVISION LIBRARY □ Columbia, MD

Sato, Beatrice, Chf.
CENTRE HOSPITALIER DE L'UNIVERSITE LAVAL - BIBLIOTHEQUE DES SCIENCES DE LA SANTE □ Quebec, PQ

Sato, Mrs. Fumi, Libn.
INTERNATIONAL PACIFIC SALMON FISHERIES COMMISSION - LIBRARY □ New Westminster, BC

Sato, Susie S., Libn./Asst.Archv.
ARIZONA HISTORICAL FOUNDATION - HAYDEN LIBRARY □ Tempe, AZ

Sattler, Alan H., Supv.Libn.
NEW YORK PUBLIC LIBRARY - GENERAL LIBRARY OF THE PERFORMING ARTS □ New York, NY

Saucier, Louise, Chf.Libn.
CENTRE HOSPITALIER HOTEL-DIEU DE SHERBROOKE - BIBLIOTHEQUE □ Sherbrooke, PQ

Sauer, Eloise A., Lib.Techn.
U.S. ARMY - CORPS OF ENGINEERS - SOUTH PACIFIC DIVISION - LIBRARY □ San Francisco, CA

Sauer, Joan Casson, Libn.
GREENVALE EDITORIAL SERVICES, INC. - LIBRARY □ Port Washington, NY

Sauer, Pauline, Hd.Lib.Asst.
FLORIDA PUBLISHING CO. - EDITORIAL LIBRARY □ Jacksonville, FL

Sauer, Serge A., Map Cur.
UNIVERSITY OF WESTERN ONTARIO - DEPARTMENT OF GEOGRAPHY - MAP LIBRARY □ London, ON

Saul, Marlene, Med.Libn.
KAISER FOUNDATION HOSPITALS - MEDICAL LIBRARY □ Parma, OH

Saunder, Joseph, Exhib.Coord.
PORT ADVENTURE, WRATHER PORT PROPERTIES, LTD. - ARCHIVES & RESOURCE CENTER □ Long Beach, CA

Saunders, J.L., Libn.
DEER LODGE HOSPITAL - MEDICAL REFERENCE LIBRARY □ Winnipeg, MB

Saunders, Jack
U.S. NATL. ARCHIVES & RECORDS SERVICE - WASHINGTON NATL. RECORDS CENTER □ Washington, DC

Saunders, Judith, Archv., Fine Arts
TORONTO CITY RECORDS AND ARCHIVES DIVISION □ Toronto, ON

Saunders, Juliet T., Asst.Libn.
PROVIDENCE ATHENAEUM - LIBRARY □ Providence, RI

Saunders, Larry N., Supv., Media Serv.
ALABAMA A & M UNIVERSITY - JOSEPH F. DRAKE MEMORIAL LEARNING RESOURCES CENTER □ Normal, AL

Saunders, Laurel B., Chf.
U.S. ARMY - WHITE SANDS MISSILE RANGE - TECHNICAL LIBRARY DIVISION □ White Sands Missile Range, NM

Saunders, Marjorie, Assoc.Dir.
CLEVELAND HEALTH SCIENCES LIBRARY - HEALTH CENTER LIBRARY □ Cleveland, OH

Saunders, Michael, Local Rec.
WASHINGTON STATE OFFICE OF SECRETARY OF STATE - DIVISION OF ARCHIVES AND RECORD MANAGEMENT □ Olympia, WA

Saunders, William B., Libn./External Coord.
ANTIOCH UNIVERSITY - LEARNING RESOURCE CENTER □ Philadelphia, PA

Sausedo, Ann E., Lib.Dir.
LOS ANGELES HERALD-EXAMINER - NEWSPAPER LIBRARY □ Los Angeles, CA

Sauter, Hubert E., Adm.
U.S. DEFENSE TECHNICAL INFORMATION CENTER □ Alexandria, VA

Savage, Blanche A., Med.Libn.
U.S. AIR FORCE HOSPITAL MEDICAL CENTER - MEDICAL LIBRARY (IL-Scott AFB) □ Scott AFB, IL

Savage, Gretchen Sue, Pres.
SAVAGE INFORMATION SERVICES □ Rolling Hills Estates, CA

Savage, Janice, Spec.Coll.
OUACHITA BAPTIST UNIVERSITY - RILEY LIBRARY □ Arkadelphia, AR

Savage, Katrina, Ref.Libn.
TEXAS TECH UNIVERSITY - LIBRARY - DOCUMENTS DEPARTMENT □ Lubbock, TX

Savage, Rosalind, Cur.
LANGSTON UNIVERSITY - MELVIN B. TOLSON BLACK HERITAGE CENTER† □ Langston, OK

Savard, Madeleine, Lib.Techn.
FEDERATION DES MEDECINS OMNIPRACTICIENS DU QUEBEC - TECHNICAL INFORMATION CENTRE □ Montreal, PQ

Savit, Madeleine Kolisch, Clinical Med.Libn.
SUNY AT STONY BROOK - HEALTH SCIENCES LIBRARY □ East Setauket, NY

Saviteer, Loretta, Asst.Libn.
MERIDEN-WALLINGFORD HOSPITAL - HEALTH SCIENCES LIBRARY □ Meriden, CT

Savitzky, E., Asst.Mgr.
PERKIN-ELMER CORPORATION - CORPORATE LIBRARY □ Norwalk, CT

Savory, Deborah, Supv.
MC GILL UNIVERSITY - MARINE SCIENCES LIBRARY □ Montreal, PQ

Sawaryn, Miss R.M., Ref.Libn.
WESTERN ELECTRIC COMPANY, INC. - TECHNICAL LIBRARY □ Baltimore, MD

Sawczuk, Marta, Acq.Libn.
JERSEY CITY STATE COLLEGE - FORREST A. IRWIN LIBRARY □ Jersey City, NJ

Sawhill, Mrs. John, Dir.
NEW CANAAN NATURE CENTER ASSOCIATION, INC. - LIBRARY† □ New Canaan, CT

Sawin, Philip Q., Coll.Dev.Libn.
UNIVERSITY OF WISCONSIN, STOUT - LIBRARY LEARNING CENTER - MEDIA RETRIEVAL SERVICES □ Menomonie, WI

Sawycky, Roman A., Supv.Libn.
FREE PUBLIC LIBRARY OF ELIZABETH, NJ - ART AND MUSIC DEPARTMENT □ Elizabeth, NJ

Sawyer, Ardis C., Libn.
MINNESOTA BIBLE COLLEGE - LIBRARY □ Rochester, MN

Sawyer, Larry, Media Prod.
KEARNEY STATE COLLEGE - CALVIN T. RYAN LIBRARY □ Kearney, NE

Sawyer, Marcy, News Libn.
ROCHESTER POST-BULLETIN - NEWS LIBRARY □ Rochester, MN

Sawyer, Warren A., Dir.
MEDICAL UNIVERSITY OF SOUTH CAROLINA - LIBRARY □ Charleston, SC

Sawyers, Elizabeth J., Dir.
OHIO STATE UNIVERSITY - HEALTH SCIENCES LIBRARY □ Columbus, OH

Sax, Margaret, Asst.Cur.
TRINITY COLLEGE - WATKINSON LIBRARY □ Hartford, CT

Saxe, Minna C., Chf.Ser.Libn.
CUNY - GRADUATE SCHOOL AND UNIVERSITY CENTER - LIBRARY □ New York, NY

Saxon, Gerald, Oral Hist.Libn.
DALLAS PUBLIC LIBRARY - ARCHIVES AND RESEARCH CENTER FOR TEXAS AND DALLAS HISTORY □ Dallas, TX

Saxon, Nancy Berry, Dir.
WASHINGTON COUNTY HISTORICAL AND MUSEUM SOCIETY - LE MOYNE HOUSE LIBRARY □ Washington, PA

Sayers, Winifred F., Libn.
GPU NUCLEAR - CORPORATE LIBRARY □ Parsippany, NJ

Sayers, Winifred F., Libn.
GPU NUCLEAR - LIBRARY □ Reading, PA

Sayler, Deb, ILL Supv.
NORTH DAKOTA STATE UNIVERSITY - LIBRARY □ Fargo, ND

Sayler, Terry Ann, Supv.Libn.
U.S. NAVY - NAVAL MEDICAL RESEARCH INSTITUTE - INFORMATION SERVICES BRANCH □ Bethesda, MD

Sayles, Adele, Libn.
TEMPLE ISRAEL - LIBRARY □ West Palm Beach, FL

Sayles, Eleanor G., Libn.
EDUCOM, INTERUNIVERSITY COMMUNICATIONS COUNCIL, INC. - LIBRARY □ Princeton, NJ

Sayles, Jeremy, Hd. Of Publ.Serv.
GEORGIA COLLEGE - INA DILLARD RUSSELL LIBRARY □ Milledgeville, GA

Saylik, Halim, Mgr.
AMERICAN ASSOCIATION OF CRIMEAN TURKS, INC. - ISMAIL GASPIRALI LIBRARY† □ Brooklyn, NY

Saylor, Helen, Med.Libn.
PRESBYTERIAN HOSPITAL - MEDICAL LIBRARY □ Albuquerque, NM

Saylor, John, Biblog./Ref.Libn.
CORNELL UNIVERSITY - ENGINEERING LIBRARY □ Ithaca, NY

Saylor, Linda, Lib.Supv.
STAUFFER CHEMICAL COMPANY - DE GUIGNE TECHNICAL CENTER - RESEARCH LIBRARY □ Richmond, CA

Sayre, John, Dir.
PHILLIPS UNIVERSITY - GRADUATE SEMINARY LIBRARY □ Enid, OK

Sayrs, Judith, Ref.Libn.
CREDIT UNION NATIONAL ASSOCIATION - INFORMATION RESOURCE CENTER □ Madison, WI

Sayus, Teresita D., Circ.Libn.
UNIVERSITY OF MIAMI - SCHOOL OF MEDICINE - LOUIS CALDER MEMORIAL LIBRARY □ Miami, FL

Sayward, Nick, Tech.Serv.Libn.
FORD FOUNDATION - INVESTMENT RESEARCH LIBRARY □ New York, NY

Sayyeau, Helen
PSYCHIATRIC CENTRE - STAFF LIBRARY □ Weyburn, SK

PERSONNEL

Scaccio, Ethel D., Hd., Cat. and Clas.
U.S. DEFENSE NUCLEAR AGENCY - TECHNICAL
LIBRARY DIVISION □ Washington, DC

Scala, H.A., Lib.Supv.
SINGER COMPANY - LINK DIVISION -
TECHNICAL LIBRARY □ Binghamton, NY

Scalf, Michael L., Supv. Contract Serv. Unit
TENNESSEE VALLEY AUTHORITY - MAP SALES
OFFICE □ Knoxville, TN

Scalice, Cathleen M., Tech.Libn.
ARGONNE NATIONAL LABORATORY -
ARGONNE-WEST TECHNICAL LIBRARY □ Idaho
Falls, ID

Scally, Sr. Anthony, Chf.Libn.
ASSOCIATION FOR THE STUDY OF AFRO-
AMERICAN LIFE AND HISTORY, INC. - CARTER
G. WOODSON LIBRARY □ Washington, DC

Scalzo, Geraldine, Hd.
UNIVERSITY OF CALIFORNIA, BERKELEY -
SOCIAL SCIENCE LIBRARY □ Berkeley, CA

Scalzo, Geraldine, Hd.
UNIVERSITY OF CALIFORNIA, BERKELEY -
SOCIAL WELFARE LIBRARY □ Berkeley, CA

Scammell, Harry D., Libn.
YALE UNIVERSITY - GEOLOGY LIBRARY □ New
Haven, CT

Scanlan, Jean M., Dir.
PRICE WATERHOUSE - INFORMATION CENTER
□ Boston, MA

Scanlon, Betty, Libn.
LOCKHEED CORPORATION - INTERNATIONAL
MARKETING LIBRARY □ Burbank, CA

Scanlon, Virginia, Libn.
CONNECTICUT STATE LIBRARY - LAW LIBRARY
AT ROCKVILLE □ Rockville, CT

Scannell, Elizabeth F.
BOSTON SCHOOL COMMITTEE OF THE CITY OF
BOSTON - ADMINISTRATION LIBRARY □
Boston, MA

Scannell, Francis X., State Libn.
MICHIGAN STATE LIBRARY SERVICES □
Lansing, MI

Scantland, Jean-Marie, Chf., Spec.Coll.
UNIVERSITE LAVAL - BIBLIOTHEQUE† □ Ste.
Foy, PQ

Scantlebury, Dorothea, Libn.
OAKLAND PUBLIC LIBRARY - ART, MUSIC,
RECREATION □ Oakland, CA

Scarborough, Ella B., Supv. IRC
DUKE POWER COMPANY - STEAM PRODUCTION
DEPARTMENT - INFORMATION RESOURCE
CENTER (IRC) □ Cornelius, NC

Scarborough, Mayra, Libn.
HOFFMANN-LA ROCHE, INC. - BUSINESS
INFORMATION CENTER □ Nutley, NJ

Scarborough, Rebecca, Hd., Govt.Doc.Dept.
BIRMINGHAM PUBLIC AND JEFFERSON COUNTY
FREE LIBRARY - GOVERNMENT DOCUMENTS
DEPARTMENT □ Birmingham, AL

Scardina, F., Educ.Dir.
KNOW, INC. □ Pittsburgh, PA

Scardinski, Irene, Libn.
GENERAL ELECTRIC COMPANY - DIRECT
CURRENT MOTOR AND GENERATOR
DEPARTMENT - LIBRARY □ Erie, PA

Scarlett, Robert M., Libn.
MEMPHIS ACADEMY OF ARTS - G. PILLOW
LEWIS MEMORIAL LIBRARY† □ Memphis, TN

Scarlett, Sharon, Archv.
LOS ALAMOS COUNTY HISTORICAL MUSEUM -
ARCHIVES □ Los Alamos, NM

Scarpato, Loann, Med.Libn.
LANKENAU HOSPITAL - MEDICAL LIBRARY □
Philadelphia, PA

Schaaf, Ray, Info.Off.
U.S. FOREST SERVICE - INYO NATL. FOREST -
INFORMATION SERVICE □ Bishop, CA

Schachter, Ms. Bert, Libn.
BATES (Ted) AND COMPANY - LIBRARY □ New
York, NY

Schachter, Dr. R., Dir.
WOMEN'S COLLEGE HOSPITAL - PSORIASIS
EDUCATION AND RESEARCH CENTRE □
Toronto, ON

Schade, Margaret, Libn.
CANADA - NATIONAL RESEARCH COUNCIL -
CISTI - SUSSEX BRANCH LIBRARY □ Ottawa, ON

Schader, Sondra E., Libn.
DETREX CHEMICAL INDUSTRIES, INC. -
RESEARCH LABORATORIES - LIBRARY □ Detroit,
MI

Schaefer, Helen, Chf. Indexer
MC GRAW-HILL, INC. - LIBRARY □ New York, NY

Schaefer, Dr. J.P., Dir.
PRINCE COUNTY HOSPITAL - MEDICAL
LIBRARY □ Summerside, PE

Schaefer, Lyle, District Archv.
LUTHERAN CHURCH - MISSOURI SYNOD -
COLORADO DISTRICT ARCHIVES □ Aurora, CO

Schaefer, Ruth, Asst.Chf.Libn.
FEDERAL RESERVE BANK OF NEW YORK -
RESEARCH LIBRARY □ New York, NY

Schaeffer, John L., Ed., Gas Abstracts
INSTITUTE OF GAS TECHNOLOGY - TECHNICAL
INFORMATION CENTER □ Chicago, IL

Schaeffer, Lorraine, Asst. State Libn.
STATE LIBRARY OF FLORIDA □ Tallahassee, FL

Schaeffer, Madeline, Libn.
EASTCHESTER HISTORICAL SOCIETY -
LIBRARY □ Eastchester NY

Schaeffer, Monica, Libn.
METASCIENCE FOUNDATION - LIBRARY □
Kingston, RI

Schafer, Jane, Cat.Libn.
UNIVERSITY OF SOUTH DAKOTA - CHRISTIAN
P. LOMMEN HEALTH SCIENCES LIBRARY □
Vermillion, SD

Schafer, Sue, Libn.
TOLEDO MENTAL HEALTH CENTER - LIBRARY
AND INFORMATION SERVICES† □ Toledo, OH

Schaffer, Evelyn J., Chf., Lib.Serv.
U.S. VETERANS ADMINISTRATION (WV-
Huntington) - MEDICAL CENTER LIBRARY □
Huntington, WV

Schair, Fern, Exec.Dir.
FUND FOR MODERN COURTS - LIBRARY □ New
York, NY

Schalit, Michael, Ref.Libn.
U.S. DEPT. OF ENERGY - SANDIA NATL.
LABORATORIES, LIVERMORE - TECHNICAL
LIBRARY □ Livermore, CA

Schalk-Greene, Katherine, Act.Dir.
SOUTH JERSEY REGIONAL FILM LIBRARY □
Voorhees, NJ

Schaller, Anne K., Dir.
NATICK HISTORICAL SOCIETY - LIBRARY □
South Natick, MA

Schallert, Ruth, Libn.
SMITHSONIAN INSTITUTION LIBRARIES -
NATIONAL MUSEUM OF NATURAL HISTORY -
BOTANY BRANCH LIBRARY □ Washington, DC

Schalow, Gertrude E., Asst.Libn.
U.S. BUREAU OF RECLAMATION - LIBRARY □
Denver, CO

Schalow, Mary J., Libn.
SALT RIVER PROJECT - LIBRARY □ Phoenix, AZ

Schanck, Peter C., Assoc.Prof./Lib.Dir.
UNIVERSITY OF DETROIT - SCHOOL OF LAW
LIBRARY □ Detroit, MI

Schapiro, Sue, Hd.Ref./Govt.Docs.
SUNY - AGRICULTURAL AND TECHNICAL
COLLEGE AT FARMINGDALE - THOMAS D.
GREENLEY LIBRARY □ Farmingdale, NY

Schappler, Rev. Norbert, Hd.Libn.
CONCEPTION ABBEY AND SEMINARY - LIBRARY
□ Conception, MO

Schara, Rita, Libn.
NORWALK STATE TECHNICAL COLLEGE -
LIBRARY □ Norwalk, CT

Scharf, Charlotte, Hd.Ser.
SUNY - AGRICULTURAL AND TECHNICAL
COLLEGE AT FARMINGDALE - THOMAS D.
GREENLEY LIBRARY □ Farmingdale, NY

Scharf, Mary E., Law Libn.
WISCONSIN STATE - FOND DU LAC COUNTY
LAW LIBRARY □ Fond Du Lac, WI

Scharf, Mimi, Data Proc.Spec.
SMITHSONIAN INSTITUTION LIBRARIES -
NATIONAL AIR AND SPACE MUSEUM - LIBRARY
□ Washington, DC

Scharmer, Roger, Libn.
U.S. FOREST SERVICE - FOREST PRODUCTS
LABORATORY LIBRARY □ Madison, WI

Schart, William L., Pk. Ranger
U.S. NATL. PARK SERVICE - AZTEC RUINS
NATL. MONUMENT - LIBRARY □ Aztec, NM

Schartner, Cindy, Libn.
GREENE, MANN, ROWE, STANTON, MASTRY &
BURTON - LIBRARY □ St. Petersburg, FL

Schaut, E.L., Tech.Mgr.
JOHNSON (S.C.) AND SON, INC. - TECHNICAL &
BUSINESS INFORMATION CENTER □ Racine, WI

Schechter, Sue
PASADENA HISTORICAL SOCIETY - LIBRARY □
Pasadena, CA

Schechtman, Joan, Mgr.
UNION CARBIDE CORPORATION - LIBRARY &
TECHNICAL INFORMATION SERVICE† □
Tarrytown, NY

Scheckter, Stella, Ref.Libn.
NEW HAMPSHIRE STATE LIBRARY □ Concord,
NH

Scheele, William E., Dir.
COLUMBUS MUSEUM OF ARTS AND SCIENCES -
CMAS RESEARCH LIBRARY □ Columbus, GA

Scheer, Anne B., Libn.
U.S. INTERNAL REVENUE SERVICE - LAW
LIBRARY □ Washington, DC

Scheer, Gladys E., Asst.Libn.
LEXINGTON THEOLOGICAL SEMINARY -
BOSWORTH MEMORIAL LIBRARY □ Lexington,
KY

Scheeren, Martha, Asst.Libn.
INDIANA UNIVERSITY OF PENNSYLVANIA -
UNIVERSITY LIBRARY □ Indiana, PA

Scheetz, Nicholas B., Mss.Libn.
GEORGETOWN UNIVERSITY - SPECIAL
COLLECTION DIVISION - LAUINGER MEMORIAL
LIBRARY □ Washington, DC

Scheetz, Stan, Libn.
MEDINA COUNTY LAW LIBRARY ASSOCIATION
□ Medina, OH

Scheffel, Kenneth, Assoc.Archv.
UNIVERSITY OF MICHIGAN - MICHIGAN
HISTORICAL COLLECTIONS - BENTLEY
HISTORICAL LIBRARY □ Ann Arbor, MI

Scheffler, Hannah N., Dir.
NEW YORK PUBLIC LIBRARY - EARLY
CHILDHOOD RESOURCE AND INFORMATION
CENTER □ New York, NY

Schefter, Anne, Tech.Serv.Asst.
NORTHWEST COLLEGE OF THE ASSEMBLIES OF
GOD - HURST LIBRARY □ Kirkland, WA

Scheiman, Royal, Chf.Libn.
GRUMMAN AEROSPACE CORPORATION -
TECHNICAL INFORMATION CENTER □
Bethpage, NY

Schein, Lorraine, Hd.Libn.
POLYTECHNIC INSTITUTE OF NEW YORK -
LONG ISLAND CENTER LIBRARY □ Long Island,
NY

Schelkopf, Nancy, Tech.Serv.
WHEATON COLLEGE - BILLY GRAHAM CENTER
LIBRARY □ Wheaton, IL

Schell, Rev. Edwin, Exec.Sec./Libn.
UNITED METHODIST HISTORICAL SOCIETY -
BALTIMORE ANNUAL CONFERENCE - LOVELY
LANE MUSEUM LIBRARY □ Baltimore, MD

Schell, Fran, Ref.Libn.
TENNESSEE STATE LIBRARY - STATE LIBRARY
DIVISION □ Nashville, TN

Schell, Norman, Media Spec.
CONCORDIA THEOLOGICAL SEMINARY -
LIBRARY □ Fort Wayne, IN

Schell, Rosalie, Dir., Rd.Serv.
CENTRAL MISSOURI STATE UNIVERSITY - WARD EDWARDS LIBRARY □ Warrensburg, MO

Schellpfeffer, Everett, Ref.Libn.
ILLINOIS INSTITUTE OF TECHNOLOGY - JAMES S. KEMPER LIBRARY □ Chicago, IL

Schemmel, Ms. D., Dept.Hd.
SPOHN HOSPITAL - MEDICAL LIBRARY □ Corpus Christi, TX

Schenk, Margaret, Hd., Coll.Dev.
SUNY AT BUFFALO - SCIENCE AND ENGINEERING LIBRARY □ Buffalo, NY

Schenk, Margot, Hd.Pub.Serv.
ST. MARY'S UNIVERSITY - PATRICK POWER LIBRARY □ Halifax, NS

Schepers, Agnes, Libn. II
MTS SYSTEMS CORPORATION - INFORMATION SERVICES □ Eden Prairie, MN

Schepis, Sandra, Libn.
MARCH OF DIMES BIRTH DEFECTS FOUNDATION - REFERENCE ROOM □ White Plains, NY

Scheps, Susan, Libn.
FAIRMOUNT TEMPLE - SAM AND EMMA MILLER LIBRARY □ Cleveland, OH

Scherdin, Mary Jane, Hd., L.M.C.
UNIVERSITY OF WISCONSIN, WHITEWATER - LIBRARY & LEARNING RESOURCES □ Whitewater, WI

Scherer, Alice, Libn.
MERRILL LYNCH WHITE WELD - CAPITAL MARKETS GROUP - LIBRARY □ New York, NY

Scherer, Elizabeth, Acq.Libn.
PITTSBURG STATE UNIVERSITY - LEONARD H. AXE LIBRARY □ Pittsburg, KS

Scherer, Herbert, Art Libn.
UNIVERSITY OF MINNESOTA - ART LIBRARY □ Minneapolis, MN

Schermetzler, Bernard, Archv./Iconographer
UNIVERSITY OF WISCONSIN, MADISON - ARCHIVES □ Madison, WI

Schertz, Morris, Dir.
UNIVERSITY OF DENVER - PENROSE LIBRARY □ Denver, CO

Scheuer, Caryl L., Dir., Lib.Serv.
HUTZEL HOSPITAL - MEDICAL LIBRARY □ Detroit, MI

Scheuerer, Elaine, Lib.Coord.
TRENTON PSYCHIATRIC HOSPITAL - MEDICAL LIBRARY □ Trenton, NJ

Scheufele, Iola, Cat., Proc.
NEW ENGLAND WILD FLOWER SOCIETY, INC. - LIBRARY □ Framingham, MA

Scheunemann, Janice, Adm.Ck.
ENVIRONMENTAL PROTECTION AGENCY - WENATCHEE PESTICIDES RESEARCH BRANCH - LIBRARY □ Wenatchee, WA

Schewe, Donald B., Asst.Dir.
U.S. PRESIDENTIAL LIBRARIES - FRANKLIN D. ROOSEVELT LIBRARY □ Hyde Park, NY

Schick, Renee, Project Dir.
ARTHRITIS INFORMATION CLEARINGHOUSE □ Bethesda, MD

Schiebel, Sarah R., Tech.Serv.Libn.
U.S. NATL. LABOR RELATIONS BOARD - LAW LIBRARY □ Washington, DC

Schiefelbein, Mrs. Gene, Libn.
DU PONT (Alfred I.) INSTITUTE OF THE NEMOURS FOUNDATION LIBRARY □ Wilmington, DE

Schifano, Ann M., Asst.Libn.
INSTITUTE FOR CANCER RESEARCH - LIBRARY □ Philadelphia, PA

Schiff, Arthur, Staff V.P.
AMERICAN SOCIETY OF TRAVEL AGENTS - LIBRARY† □ New York, NY

Schiff, Dorothy, Nursing Sch.Libn.
ST. MARGARET MEMORIAL HOSPITAL - PAUL TITUS MEMORIAL LIBRARY AND SCHOOL OF NURSING LIBRARY □ Pittsburgh, PA

Schiff, Judith A., Chf.Res.Archv.
YALE UNIVERSITY - MANUSCRIPTS AND ARCHIVES □ New Haven, CT

Schiffman, Genevieve N., Tech.Info.Spec.
U.S. NATL. INSTITUTES OF HEALTH - LIBRARY □ Bethesda, MD

Schildt, Sara K., Commun.Mgr.
U.S. FEED GRAINS COUNCIL - COMMUNICATIONS DEPARTMENT - LIBRARY □ Washington, DC

Schilke, John, AV Coord.
HOSPITAL OF ST. RAPHAEL - HEALTH SCIENCES LIBRARY □ New Haven, CT

Schiller, Joyce K., Asst.Libn./Tech.Serv.
ST. LOUIS ART MUSEUM - RICHARDSON MEMORIAL LIBRARY □ St. Louis, MO

Schilling, Irene, Cat.Libn.
AUGSBURG COLLEGE - GEORGE SVERDRUP LIBRARY AND MEDIA CENTER □ Minneapolis, MN

Schimansky, Dobrila-Donya, Musm.Libn.
METROPOLITAN MUSEUM OF ART - THOMAS J. WATSON LIBRARY □ New York, NY

Schimmelbusch, Johannes S.
U.S. DEPT. OF ENERGY - BONNEVILLE POWER ADMINISTRATION - LIBRARY □ Portland, OR

Schimmelpfeng, Richard P., Spec.Coll.Libn.
UNIVERSITY OF CONNECTICUT - LIBRARY □ Storrs, CT

Schindewolf, Trudy, Adm. Aide
HOUSTON CITY AVIATION DEPARTMENT - LIBRARY □ Houston, TX

Schindler, Merril, AV/CAI Libn.
MOUNT SINAI SCHOOL OF MEDICINE OF THE CITY UNIVERSITY OF NEW YORK - GUSTAVE L. & JANET W. LEVY LIBRARY □ New York, NY

Schipf, Robert, Sci.Libn.
UNIVERSITY OF MONTANA - SCHOOL OF FORESTRY - COOPERATIVE FOREST AND CONSERVATION COLLECTION □ Missoula, MT

Schipkowski, Frances, Sec.-Libn.
SOUTHERN ILLINOIS UNIVERSITY, EDWARDSVILLE - HUMAN SERVICES LIBRARY □ Edwardsville, IL

Schlachter, Gail A., Asst.Univ.Libn/Pub.Serv.
UNIVERSITY OF CALIFORNIA, DAVIS - GENERAL LIBRARY □ Davis, CA

Schlaerth, Sally G., Hd.Libn.
BUFFALO EVENING NEWS - LIBRARY □ Buffalo, NY

Schlee, Marilyn J., Lib.Serv.Off.
NORTHWEST BANCORPORATION - LIBRARY □ Minneapolis, MN

Schleg, M., Pub.Serv.Libn.
HURLEY MEDICAL CENTER - HAMADY HEALTH SCIENCES LIBRARY □ Flint, MI

Schleicher, Ben, Adm.Serv.Supv.
WOODWARD GOVERNOR CO. - WOODWARD LIBRARY □ Rockford, IL

Schleif, Julia Woodward, Libn.
GOOD SAMARITAN MEDICAL CENTER - DEACONESS HOSPITAL CAMPUS - HEALTH SCIENCE LIBRARY □ Milwaukee, WI

Schlenk, Pamela, Record Libn.
CLEVELAND INSTITUTE OF MUSIC - LIBRARY □ Cleveland, OH

Schlereth, Wendy C., Archv.
UNIVERSITY OF NOTRE DAME - ARCHIVES □ Notre Dame, IN

Schlesinger, Eloise, Libn.
JUNG (C.G.) INSTITUTE OF LOS ANGELES, INC. - LIBRARY □ Los Angeles, CA

Schlimgen, Joan B., Res.Libn.
NATIONAL ECONOMIC RESEARCH ASSOCIATES, INC. □ Los Angeles, CA

Schling, Dorothy T., Dir.
DANBURY SCOTT-FANTON MUSEUM AND HISTORICAL SOCIETY - LIBRARY □ Danbury, CT

Schlingman, Dorothy
WILKES COLLEGE - INSTITUTE OF REGIONAL AFFAIRS - LIBRARY† □ Wilkes-Barre, PA

Schloeder, Mary C., Libn.
U.S. DEPT. OF STATE - FOREIGN SERVICE INSTITUTE LIBRARY □ Arlington, VA

Schlosser, Anne G., Lib.Dir.
AMERICAN FILM INSTITUTE - CENTER FOR ADVANCED FILM STUDIES - CHARLES K. FELDMAN LIBRARY □ Beverly Hills, CA

Schlueter, R.A., Libn.
ALLIS-CHALMERS CORPORATION - ADVANCED TECHNOLOGY CENTER - LIBRARY □ Milwaukee, WI

Schluge, Vicki, Instr.Rsrcs.Mgr.
MADISON GENERAL HOSPITAL - NURSING EDUCATION - MAUDE WEBSTER MIDDLETON LIBRARY □ Madison, WI

Schluter, Helmi, Libn.
GOETHE INSTITUTE - LIBRARY □ San Francisco, CA

Schmelzer, Dr. Menaham, Libn.
JEWISH THEOLOGICAL SEMINARY OF AMERICA - LIBRARY □ New York, NY

Schmid, Josef, Jr., Libn.
MIDREX CORPORATION - LIBRARY □ Charlotte, NC

Schmid, Patricia, Asst. Law Libn.
UNIVERSITY OF PITTSBURGH - LAW LIBRARY □ Pittsburgh, PA

Schmid, Robert, Assoc.Libn.
UNIVERSITY OF HEALTH SCIENCES/CHICAGO MEDICAL SCHOOL - LIBRARY □ North Chicago, IL

Schmidgall, Judy, Circ.Dept.Hd.
HENDERSON STATE UNIVERSITY - HUIE LIBRARY □ Arkadelphia, AR

Schmidhammer, Jill, Exec.Dir.
NATIONAL ASSOCIATION OF QUICK PRINTERS - INTERNATIONAL QUICK PRINTING FOUNDATION LIBRARY □ Lafayette, IN

Schmidt, Barbara, ILL
OHIO STATE UNIVERSITY - HEALTH SCIENCES LIBRARY □ Columbus, OH

Schmidt, Carol, Lib.Techn.
ALBERTA - DEPARTMENT OF SOCIAL SERVICES & COMMUNITY HEALTH - LIBRARY □ Edmonton, AB

Schmidt, Carol, Tech.Asst.
MADONNA COLLEGE - CURRICULUM LIBRARY □ Livonia, MI

Schmidt, Carole, IMC
WAYNE STATE COLLEGE - U.S. CONN LIBRARY □ Wayne, NE

Schmidt, Dean, Dir.
UNIVERSITY OF MISSOURI - MEDICAL LIBRARY† □ Columbia, MO

Schmidt, Donald T., Dir., Lib.Archv.
CHURCH OF JESUS CHRIST OF LATTER-DAY SAINTS - HISTORICAL DEPARTMENT - CHURCH LIBRARY-ARCHIVES □ Salt Lake City, UT

Schmidt, Dorothy, Acq.
KRAFT, INC. - BUSINESS RESEARCH CENTER □ Glenview, IL

Schmidt, Erika, Libn.
BUTLER HOSPITAL - ISAAC RAY MEDICAL LIBRARY □ Providence, RI

Schmidt, Jean Marie, Libn.
U.S. ARMY - CORPS OF ENGINEERS - ST. PAUL DISTRICT - TECHNICAL LIBRARY □ St. Paul, MN

Schmidt, Kathleen, Lib.Supv.
WASHINGTON STATE UNIVERSITY - VETERINARY MEDICAL/PHARMACY LIBRARY □ Pullman, WA

Schmidt, Margaret, Mgr.
UNIVERSITY OF MICHIGAN - SCHOOL OF ED. & SCHOOL OF LIB.SCI. - INSTR. RESOURCES UNIT OF INSTR. STRATEGY SERV. □ Ann Arbor, MI

Schmidt, Marjorie A., Sec.
NICOLLET COUNTY HISTORICAL SOCIETY - MUSEUM □ St. Peter, MN

Schmidt, Martin F., Libn.
FILSON CLUB - LIBRARY □ Louisville, KY

Schmidt, Mary Ann, Libn.
MILWAUKEE SCHOOL OF ENGINEERING - WALTER SCHROEDER LIBRARY □ Milwaukee, WI

P E R S O N N E L

Schmidt, Mary Anne, Libn.
FIRST BAPTIST CHURCH OF DALLAS - FIRST
BAPTIST ACADEMY - GEORGE W. TRUETT
MEMORIAL LIBRARY □ Dallas, TX

Schmidt, Mary M., Libn.
PRINCETON UNIVERSITY - MARQUAND
LIBRARY □ Princeton, NJ

Schmidt, Nancy J., Libn.
HARVARD UNIVERSITY - TOZZER LIBRARY -
PEABODY MUSEUM OF ARCHAEOLOGY AND
ETHNOLOGY □ Cambridge, MA

Schmidt, Paula, Libn.
BAKER & DANIELS - LAW LIBRARY □
Indianapolis, IN

Schmidt, Robert R., Libn.
HALL OF JUSTICE LIBRARY □ San Francisco, CA

Schmidt, Sandra, Asst.Libn.
LUTHERAN HOSPITAL - MEDICAL STAFF
LIBRARY AND SCHOOL FOR NURSES LIBRARY □
Moline, IL

Schmidt, Valentine L., Libn.
RINGLING (John and Mable) MUSEUM OF ART -
ART RESEARCH LIBRARY □ Sarasota, FL

Schmiechen, Barbara, Ref./Ext.Libn.
UNIVERSITY OF WISCONSIN, MADISON -
CENTER FOR HEALTH SCIENCES LIBRARIES □
Madison, WI

Schmitt, Carol, Libn.
ALLEGHENY COUNTY HEALTH DEPARTMENT -
LIBRARY □ Pittsburgh, PA

Schmitt, Claudia, Hd., Ivan Allen Dept.
ATLANTA PUBLIC LIBRARY - FOUNDATION
COLLECTION □ Atlanta, GA

Schmitt, Claudia, Hd.
ATLANTA PUBLIC LIBRARY - IVAN ALLEN, JR.
DEPARTMENT OF SCIENCE, INDUSTRY AND
GOVERNMENT □ Atlanta, GA

Schmitt, Mary Leslie, Lib.Techn.
ROCKY MOUNTAIN ENERGY CO. - LIBRARY □
Denver, CO

Schmitt, Peter, Faculty Assoc.
WESTERN MICHIGAN UNIVERSITY - ARCHIVES
AND REGIONAL HISTORY COLLECTIONS □
Kalamazoo, MI

Schmitt, William C., Dir. of Educ.
FRANKLIN COUNTY HISTORICAL SOCIETY -
CENTER OF SCIENCE & INDUSTRY - CLEMENTS
HISTORY MEMORIAL LIBRARY □ Columbus, OH

Schmock, Fr. Hilarion, O.C.S.O., Libn.
GETHSEMANI ABBEY - LIBRARY† □ Trappist, KY

Schmorak, M.R., Res.
U.S. OAK RIDGE NATL. LABORATORY -
NUCLEAR DATA PROJECT† □ Oak Ridge, TN

Schmuck, Philip, Plan.Dir.
COLORADO STATE PLANNING LIBRARY □
Denver, CO

Schnaitter, Dr. Allene F., Dir. of Libs.
WASHINGTON STATE UNIVERSITY - HOLLAND
LIBRARY □ Pullman, WA

Schnall, Janet, Consulting Libn.
WALDO GENERAL HOSPITAL - MEDICAL
LIBRARY □ Seattle, WA

Schnare, MaryKay W., Libn.
UNIVERSITY OF CONNECTICUT - SCHOOL OF
BUSINESS ADMINISTRATION LIBRARY □
Hartford, CT

Schnare, Robert E., Spec.Coll.Libn.
U.S. ARMY - MILITARY ACADEMY - LIBRARY □
West Point, NY

Schnaubelt, Joseph C., O.S.A., Dir.
AUGUSTINIAN HISTORICAL INSTITUTE -
LIBRARY □ Villanova, PA

Schneberg, Ben, Law Libn.
BERLACK, ISRAELS AND LIBERMAN - LAW
LIBRARY □ New York, NY

Schneck, Mildred, Libn.
HUDSON INSTITUTE - LIBRARY □ Croton-On-
Hudson, NY

Schneider, E., Cat.Libn.
UNIVERSITY OF LOWELL, SOUTH CAMPUS -
DANIEL H. O'LEARY LIBRARY □ Lowell, MA

Schneider, Gail K., Adm.Libn.
STATEN ISLAND INSTITUTE OF ARTS AND
SCIENCES - LIBRARY □ Staten Island, NY

Schneider, Hennie R., Ref.Libn.
U.S. INTERNATIONAL TRADE COMMISSION -
LIBRARY □ Washington, DC

Schneider, Laura T., Supv., Ext.Serv.
NATIONAL GALLERY OF ART - DEPARTMENT OF
EXTENSION PROGRAMS □ Washington, DC

Schneider, Mary Jo, Asst.Libn.
THEOSOPHICAL SOCIETY IN AMERICA -
OLCOTT LIBRARY & RESEARCH CENTER □
Wheaton, IL

Schneider, Miriam, Libn.
MAINE AUDUBON SOCIETY - ENVIRONMENTAL
INFORMATION SERVICE □ Falmouth, ME

Schneider, Ralph, Hd., Hist.Sect.
CHICAGO PUBLIC LIBRARY CENTRAL LIBRARY -
SOCIAL SCIENCES & HISTORY DIVISION □
Chicago, IL

Schneller, Victoria, Hd., Ref.Serv.
U.S. NATL. OCEANIC & ATMOSPHERIC
ADMINISTRATION - ENVIRONMENTAL
RESEARCH LABORATORIES - LIBRARY □
Boulder, CO

Schnick, Rosalie A., Tech.Info.Spec.
U.S. FISH & WILDLIFE SERVICE - NATIONAL
FISHERY RESEARCH LABORATORY LIBRARY □
La Crosse, WI

Schnoor, Harriet E., Libn.
UNIVERSITY OF CHICAGO - ECKHART LIBRARY
□ Chicago, IL

Schobeloch, Jerry, AV Techn.
U.S. VETERANS ADMINISTRATION (IL-Chicago)
- WESTSIDE HOSPITAL LIBRARY □ Chicago, IL

Schock, Richard G., Dir.
MOODY BIBLE INSTITUTE - LIBRARY □ Chicago,
IL

Schock, Richard G., Dir.
MOODY BIBLE INSTITUTE - MOODYANA
COLLECTION □ Chicago, IL

Schoeler, Diane, Hd.Acq.Dept.
UNIVERSITY OF TEXAS, EL PASO - LIBRARY □ El
Paso, TX

Schoelkopf, R. Gerald, Spec.Coll.Libn.
WEST CHESTER STATE COLLEGE - FRANCIS
HARVEY GREEN LIBRARY - SPECIAL
COLLECTIONS □ West Chester, PA

Schoellkopf, Catharine, Libn.
FIDELITY MANAGEMENT & RESEARCH
COMPANY - LIBRARY □ Boston, MA

Schoelwer, Susan Prendergast, Cur.
CHICAGO PUBLIC LIBRARY CULTURAL CENTER
- SPECIAL COLLECTIONS DIVISION □ Chicago,
IL

Schoemann, Robert, Info.Spec.
BUFFALO EVENING NEWS - LIBRARY □ Buffalo,
NY

Schoen, Charlotte, Tech.Serv.
ASSOCIATION FOR RESEARCH AND
ENLIGHTENMENT - EDGAR CAYCE
FOUNDATION - LIBRARY □ Virginia Beach, VA

Schoen, Dr. John N., Sec.-Tres.
AMERICAN ACADEMY OF OPTOMETRY -
LIBRARY □ Owatonna, MN

Schoen, Marilyn, Adm.Asst.
RAND CORPORATION - LIBRARY □ Santa
Monica, CA

Schoen, Myron E., Dir.
UNION OF AMERICAN HEBREW
CONGREGATIONS - SYNAGOGUE
ARCHITECTURAL AND ART LIBRARY □ New
York, NY

Schoenberg, Jill, Fed.Doc.Libn.
RUTGERS UNIVERSITY, THE STATE
UNIVERSITY OF NEW JERSEY - JUSTICE HENRY
ACKERSON LIBRARY OF LAW & CRIMINAL
JUSTICE □ Newark, NJ

Schoenborn, Mrs. Rougean, Libn.
THERMO KING CORPORATION - LIBRARY □
Minneapolis, MN

Schoenbrun, Cyndi, Libn.
HAR ZION TEMPLE - IVA AND MATTHEW
RUZOSKER LIBRARY □ Philadelphia, PA

Schoenfelder, Marguerite, Libn.
POTTSVILLE HOSPITAL AND WARNE CLINIC -
MEDICAL LIBRARY □ Pottsville, PA

Schoenthaler, Jean A., Hd., Tech.Serv.
DREW UNIVERSITY - LIBRARY □ Madison, NJ

Schoenung, James G., Exec.Dir.
PENNSYLVANIA AREA LIBRARY NETWORK AND
UNION LIBRARY CATALOGUE OF
PENNSYLVANIA □ Philadelphia, PA

Scholberg, Henry, Libn.
UNIVERSITY OF MINNESOTA - AMES LIBRARY
OF SOUTH ASIA □ Minneapolis, MN

Scholnick, Ellin, Pres.
PIAGET (Jean) SOCIETY - LIBRARY □ Newark,
DE

Scholten, Frances, Libn.
AMERICAN CYANAMID COMPANY -
ENVIRONMENTAL SERVICES DIVISION
LIBRARY† □ Wayne, NJ

Scholtes, Hilda B., Univ.Archv.
MISSISSIPPI STATE UNIVERSITY - MITCHELL
MEMORIAL LIBRARY - SPECIAL COLLECTIONS □
Mississippi State, MS

Schomer, Elizabeth, Chf.Libn.
BARBER (Richard J.) ASSOCIATES, INC. -
LIBRARY □ Washington, DC

Schonbrun, Rena, Libn.
U.S.D.A. - AGRICULTURAL RESEARCH SERVICE
- WESTERN REGIONAL RESEARCH CENTER
LIBRARY □ Berkeley, CA

Schonlaw, Sandra, Tech.Serv.Libn.
U.S. VETERANS ADMINISTRATION (CA-Los
Angeles) - WADSWORTH MEDICAL LIBRARY □
Los Angeles, CA

Schoolfield, Dudley B., Cat.
MOBIL RESEARCH & DEVELOPMENT
CORPORATION - FIELD RESEARCH
LABORATORY LIBRARY □ Dallas, TX

Schoon, Margaret S., Cat.Libn.
PURDUE UNIVERSITY - CALUMET LIBRARY □
Hammond, IN

Schoonover, David E., Cur./Amer.Lit.
YALE UNIVERSITY - BEINECKE RARE BOOK AND
MANUSCRIPT LIBRARY □ New Haven, CT

Schoonover, Phyllis, Music Libn.
BUTLER UNIVERSITY - JORDAN COLLEGE OF
FINE ARTS MUSIC LIBRARY □ Indianapolis, IN

Schop, Edith, Libn.
NEW YORK STATE SUPREME COURT - 3RD
JUDICIAL DISTRICT - HAMILTON ODELL
LIBRARY □ Monticello, NY

Schor, Danielle
U.S.D.A. - HUMAN NUTRITION INFORMATION
SERVICES - FOOD AND NUTRITION
INFORMATION CENTER □ Beltsville, MD

Schorr, Jeanne, Libn.
DALLAS PUBLIC LIBRARY - HUMANITIES
DIVISION □ Dallas, TX

Schortman, Doris, Res.
PARADE PUBLICATIONS, INC. - LIBRARY □ New
York, NY

Schoyer, George P., Hd.Libn.
OHIO STATE UNIVERSITY - HISTORY,
POLITICAL SCIENCE, AND PHILOSOPHY
GRADUATE LIBRARY □ Columbus, OH

Schoyer, George P., Hd.Libn.
OHIO STATE UNIVERSITY - MAP GRADUATE
LIBRARY □ Columbus, OH

Schrader, Jane Marie, Hd.Libn.
SILVER BURDETT COMPANY - EDITORIAL
LIBRARY □ Morristown, NJ

Schrader, Marge, Libn.
DAWE'S LABORATORIES, LTD. - TECHNICAL
AND AGRICULTURAL LIBRARIES □ Chicago, IL

Schrag, Dale R., Cur.
WICHITA STATE UNIVERSITY - SPECIAL
COLLECTIONS □ Wichita, KS

Schrag, Ruth, Libn. & Church Archv.
ST. STEPHEN'S COLLEGE - LIBRARY □
Edmonton, AB

Schram, W., Lib.Instr.
WAYNE STATE UNIVERSITY - G. FLINT PURDY
LIBRARY □ Detroit, MI
Schramm, Jeanne, Ref.Libn.
WEST LIBERTY STATE COLLEGE - ELBIN
LIBRARY □ West Liberty, WV
Schramm, Mary T., Libn.-Dir.
PRC CONSOER, TOWNSEND, INC. - LIBRARY
AND INFORMATION CENTER □ Chicago, IL
Schreck, Kathleen A., Asst.Libn.
REPUBLIC STEEL CORPORATION - RESEARCH
CENTER LIBRARY □ Cleveland, OH
Schreder, Betsy S., Chf.Libn.
U.S. VETERANS ADMINISTRATION (PA-Wilkes-
Barre) - MEDICAL CENTER LIBRARY □ Wilkes-
Barre, PA
Schreibstein, Florence, Chf.Per.Libn.
YESHIVA UNIVERSITY - ALBERT EINSTEIN
COLLEGE OF MEDICINE - D. SAMUEL
GOTTESMAN LIBRARY □ Bronx, NY
Schreiner, Gwen R., Libn.
U.S. DEPT. OF ENERGY - NATIONAL ATOMIC
MUSEUM - LIBRARY □ Albuquerque, NM
Schreiner, Katherine J., Asst.Libn.
GEORGIA POWER COMPANY - LIBRARY □
Atlanta, GA
Schreiner, Lois, Docs.Libn.
UNIVERSITY OF OREGON - GOVERNMENT
DOCUMENTS SECTION □ Eugene, OR
Schroader, Vanessa R.L., Mgr.
EG&G, INC. - WASHINGTON ANALYTICAL
SERVICES CENTER - INFORMATION CENTER □
Rockville, MD
Schroeder, Edwin M., Law Libn.
FLORIDA STATE UNIVERSITY - LAW LIBRARY □
Tallahassee, FL
Schroeder, Dr. Eva I.A., Dir.
MONTEREY INSTITUTE OF INTERNATIONAL
STUDIES - WILLIAM TELL COLEMAN LIBRARY†
□ Monterey, CA
Schroeder, H.M., Tech.Info.Mgr.
TEXTRON, INC. - SPENCER KELLOGG DIVISION
- RESEARCH CENTER LIBRARY □ Buffalo, NY
Schroeder, Joseph R., Dir.
UNIVERSITY OF HOUSTON - AUDIOVISUAL
SERVICES □ Houston, TX
Schroeder, Patricia, Libn./Rec.Ck.
CALGARY ZOOLOGICAL SOCIETY - LIBRARY □
Calgary, AB
Schroeder, Penny, Hd.Cat.
CAPITAL UNIVERSITY - LAW SCHOOL LIBRARY
□ Columbus, OH
Schroeder, Sandy, Asst.Libn.
MISSOURI STATE SUPREME COURT LIBRARY □
Jefferson City, MO
Schroeder, W.R. Bill, Mng.Dir.
CITIZENS SAVINGS ATHLETIC FOUNDATION -
LIBRARY† □ Los Angeles, CA
Schroeppel, Donna Marie, Exec.Sec.
INSTITUTE FOR ADVANCED PERCEPTION -
LIBRARY □ Oak Park, IL
Schroeter, George, Assoc.Libn.
MOBILE PUBLIC LIBRARY - SPECIAL
COLLECTIONS DIVISION □ Mobile, AL
Schroff, Rebecca, Asst.Libn.
KIRKLAND & ELLIS - LIBRARY □ Chicago, IL
Schroh, Brenda, Info.Spec.
TRANSCANADA TELEPHONE SYSTEM -
INFORMATION CENTRE □ Ottawa, ON
Schrotberger, W. Buck, Sr.Cons.
COLORADO STATE DEPARTMENT OF
EDUCATION - INSTRUCTIONAL MATERIALS
CENTER FOR THE VISUALLY HANDICAPPED □
Denver, CO
Schroth, Thelma, Cur.
CLOUD COUNTY HISTORICAL MUSEUM -
LIBRARY □ Concordia, KS
Schryer, Michael, Fed.Lib. Liaison Off.
NATIONAL LIBRARY OF CANADA □ Ottawa, ON
Schuberg, Delphie, Libn.
OREGON STATE SCHOOL FOR THE BLIND -
MEDIA CENTER □ Salem, OR

Schuermann, Lois J., Asst.Libn
AMERICAN PETROLEUM INSTITUTE - LIBRARY
□ Washington, DC
Schuffels, Zenaida, Asst.Libn.
LUNDEBERG MARYLAND SEAMANSHIP SCHOOL
- LIBRARY □ Piney Point, MD
Schug, Janet J., Dir.
FRANKLIN COUNTY LAW LIBRARY □
Chambersburg, PA
Schuh, Walter, Asst.Mgr.
ROA FILMS - LIBRARY □ Milwaukee, WI
Schuhle, Jacob, Educ.Ref.-Biblog.
SUNY - COLLEGE AT CORTLAND - MEMORIAL
LIBRARY □ Cortland, NY
Schuler, Betty K., Libn.
WAYNE COUNTY LAW LIBRARY ASSOCIATION
□ Wooster, OH
Schuler, Linette, Lib.Instr.
UNIVERSITY OF WISCONSIN, STEVENS POINT
- JAMES H. ALBERTSON CENTER FOR LEARNING
RESOURCES □ Stevens Point, WI
Schulman, Jacque-Lynne, Hd., Biblog. & Ref.
GEORGE WASHINGTON UNIVERSITY -
MEDICAL CENTER - PAUL HIMMELFARB HEALTH
SCIENCES LIBRARY □ Washington, DC
Schulman, Rebecca, Acq.
LOYOLA LAW SCHOOL - LIBRARY □ Los Angeles,
CA
Schulmeyer, Alfred W., Supt.
U.S. NATL. PARK SERVICE - BIG HOLE NATL.
BATTLEFIELD - LIBRARY □ Wisdom, MT
Schulte, Linda, Act.Dir.
SOUTHWESTERN UNIVERSITY - SCHOOL OF
LAW LIBRARY □ Los Angeles, CA
Schulte, Lorraine, Mgr.
UPJOHN COMPANY - CORPORATE TECHNICAL
LIBRARY □ Kalamazoo, MI
Schulte, Stephanie, Libn.
MERCY HOSPITAL - HEALTH SERVICES
LIBRARY □ Cedar Rapids, IA
Schultis, Ann, Hd. ILL
UNIVERSITY OF TEXAS, EL PASO - LIBRARY □ El
Paso, TX
Schultz, Barbara A., Chf., Lib.Serv.
U.S. VETERANS ADMINISTRATION (OH-
Chillicothe) - HOSPITAL LIBRARY □ Chillicothe,
OH
Schultz, Dr. Charles R., Univ.Archv.
TEXAS A & M UNIVERSITY - ARCHIVES &
MANUSCRIPTS COLLECTIONS □ College Station,
TX
Schultz, Elaine, Info.Spec.
BANK OF HAWAII - INFORMATION CENTER □
Honolulu, HI
Schultz, Erich R.W., Univ.Libn.
WILFRID LAURIER UNIVERSITY - LIBRARY □
Waterloo, ON
Schultz, Glenda J., Libn.
ONTARIO - MINISTRY OF NORTHERN AFFAIRS -
LIBRARY □ Toronto, ON
Schultz, Henrietta, Libn.
CHICAGO SINAI CONGREGATION - EMIL G.
HIRSCH LIBRARY □ Chicago, IL
Schultz, Henrietta, Libn.
CONGREGATION RODFEI ZEDEK - J.S.
HOFFMAN MEMORIAL LIBRARY □ Chicago, IL
Schultz, Jon S., Dir.
UNIVERSITY OF HOUSTON - LAW LIBRARY □
Houston, TX
Schultz, Linda, Rsrcs.Ctrs.Supv.
NORTH DAKOTA STATE UNIVERSITY - LIBRARY
□ Fargo, ND
Schultz, Marion E., Med.Libn.
SALEM COUNTY MEMORIAL HOSPITAL - DAVID
W. GREEN MEDICAL LIBRARY □ Salem, NJ
Schultz, Mary Agnes, Asst.Libn.
ABELL (A.S.) COMPANY - BALTIMORE
SUNPAPERS - LIBRARY □ Baltimore, MD
Schultz, Dr. Peter, Staff Sci.
LUNAR AND PLANETARY INSTITUTE -
PLANETARY IMAGE CENTER □ Houston, TX

Schultz, Ruth, Asst.Dir.
AMERICAN DENTAL ASSOCIATION - BUREAU
OF LIBRARY SERVICES □ Chicago, IL
Schultz, Ursula, Act.Hd.
NATIONAL LIBRARY OF CANADA - REFERENCE
AND BIBLIOGRAPHY SECTION □ Ottawa, ON
Schultz-Writsel, Lynn, Act.Dir.
NATIONAL MENTAL HEALTH ASSOCIATION -
CLIFFORD BEERS MEMORIAL LIBRARY □
Arlington, VA
Schultze, Phyllis A., Assoc.Libn.
NATIONAL COUNCIL ON CRIME AND
DELINQUENCY - LIBRARY □ Hackensack, NJ
Schulz, Diana, Volunteer Coord.
FLORIDA STATE DIVISION OF BLIND SERVICES
- FLORIDA REGIONAL LIB. FOR THE BLIND &
PHYSICALLY HANDICAPPED □ Daytona Beach,
FL
Schulz, Judy, Rsrcs.Spec.
ORANGE COUNTY TRANSIT DISTRICT -
RESOURCE CENTER □ Garden Grove, CA
Schulz, Justine, Ref.Libn.
NATIONAL MARITIME MUSEUM - J. PORTER
SHAW LIBRARY □ San Francisco, CA
Schulz, Marilyn, Mgr., Acq. & Cat.
CANADIAN NATIONAL INSTITUTE FOR THE
BLIND - NATIONAL LIBRARY SERVICES □
Toronto, ON
Schulz, Mary, Group Leader
MERCK & COMPANY, INC. - MERCK SHARP &
DOHME RESEARCH LABORATORIES -
RESEARCH INFORMATION SYSTEMS □ Rahway,
NJ
Schulze, Richard, Lib.Assoc.
IOWA STATE LAW LIBRARY □ Des Moines, IA
Schumacher, Joan, QA Data Ck.
U.S. DEFENSE CONTRACT ADMINISTRATION -
SERVICES MANAGEMENT AREA LIBRARY □
Milwaukee, WI
Schumann, Mrs. E., Libn.
GEORGE BROWN COLLEGE OF APPLIED ARTS &
TECHNOLOGY - LIBRARY □ Toronto, ON
Schumm, R.H., Data Anl.
U.S. NATL. BUREAU OF STANDARDS -
CHEMICAL THERMODYNAMICS DATA CENTER
□ Washington, DC
Schupmann, Mildred, Med.Libn.
MISSOURI BAPTIST HOSPITAL - MEDICAL
LIBRARY □ St. Louis, MO
Schuster, Neil D., V.P., Res.
AMERICAN WATERWAYS OPERATORS, INC. -
LIBRARY □ Arlington, VA
Schutten, Marguerite, Ref.Spec.
KRAFT, INC. - RESEARCH & DEVELOPMENT
LIBRARY □ Glenview, IL
Schutz, Robert, Transl.
DOW CHEMICAL COMPANY - MERRELL DOW
PHARMACEUTICALS, INC. - RESEARCH CENTER
LIBRARY □ Cincinnati, OH
Schutzer, Cynthia, Assoc.Libn.
HACKENSACK HOSPITAL - MEDICAL LIBRARY†
□ Hackensack, NJ
Schwabl, Kathleen, Sec.
INSURANCE INSTITUTE OF SOUTHERN
ALBERTA - LIBRARY □ Calgary, AB
Schwager, Carleton, Biblog.Asst.
TEMPLE UNIVERSITY - CENTRAL LIBRARY
SYSTEM - RARE BOOK & MANUSCRIPT
COLLECTION □ Philadelphia, PA
Schwaller, Janet, Per.Libn.
LINCOLN UNIVERSITY OF MISSOURI - INMAN
E. PAGE LIBRARY □ Jefferson City, MO
Schwamb, Don F., Dir.
VALUATION RESEARCH CORPORATION -
CORPORATE RESEARCH AND REFERENCE
LIBRARY □ Milwaukee, WI
Schwanke, Dean A., User Serv.Spec.
ERIC CLEARINGHOUSE ON TEACHER
EDUCATION □ Washington, DC
Schwappach, Pat, Musm.Dir.
ANOKA COUNTY HISTORICAL GENEALOGICAL
SOCIETY - LIBRARY □ Anoka, MN

PERSONNEL

Schwartz, Alan M., Archv.
  PROTESTANT EPISCOPAL CHURCH -
  EPISCOPAL DIOCESE OF SOUTH DAKOTA -
  ARCHIVES □ Sioux Falls, SD
Schwartz, Amelia, Lib.Mgr.
  ZIFF-DAVIS PUBLISHING COMPANY - PUBLIC
  TRAVEL AND TRANSPORTATION DIVISION -
  LIBRARY □ New York, NY
Schwartz, April, Ref.Libn.
  MINNESOTA HISTORICAL SOCIETY -
  REFERENCE LIBRARY □ St. Paul, MN
Schwartz, Bernard D., Res.Asst.
  NEW YORK CITY BOARD OF EDUCATION -
  RESOURCE CENTER - CURRICULUM LIBRARY □
  Brooklyn, NY
Schwartz, Carol, Libn.
  INTERNATIONAL LONGSHOREMEN'S AND
  WAREHOUSEMEN'S UNION - ANNE RAND
  RESEARCH LIBRARY □ San Francisco, CA
Schwartz, Carole, Asst.Libn., Archv.
  CINCINNATI ART MUSEUM - LIBRARY □
  Cincinnati, OH
Schwartz, Daniel, Libn.
  CANADIAN BROADCASTING CORPORATION -
  REFERENCE LIBRARY □ Toronto, ON
Schwartz, Diane, Biblog.Instr.Coord.
  UNIVERSITY OF MICHIGAN - ALFRED TAUBMAN
  MEDICAL LIBRARY □ Ann Arbor, MI
Schwartz, Eugene P., Chm.
  MISSOURI COUNCIL FOR HANDGUN CONTROL -
  LIBRARY □ University City, MO
Schwartz, Gloria, Libn.
  TEMPLE BETH SHOLOM - LIBRARY □ Miami
  Beach, FL
Schwartz, Herbert, Res.Coord.
  BIOVIVAN RESEARCH INSTITUTE - LIBRARY □
  Vineland, NJ
Schwartz, Herbert, Sys.
  WILFRID LAURIER UNIVERSITY - LIBRARY □
  Waterloo, ON
Schwartz, Julie, Libn.
  SQUARE D COMPANY - LIBRARY □ Milwaukee,
  WI
Schwartz, Lillian, Libn.
  TEMPLE EMANU-EL - CONGREGATIONAL
  LIBRARY □ Providence, RI
Schwartz, Marilyn W., Chf.Libn.
  U.S. NAVY - NAVAL REGIONAL MEDICAL
  CENTER (San Diego) - THOMPSON MEDICAL
  LIBRARY □ San Diego, CA
Schwartz, Milton, Hist.
  PORT ADVENTURE, WRATHER PORT
  PROPERTIES, LTD. - ARCHIVES & RESOURCE
  CENTER □ Long Beach, CA
Schwartz, Mortimer D., Law Libn.
  UNIVERSITY OF CALIFORNIA, DAVIS - SCHOOL
  OF LAW - LAW LIBRARY □ Davis, CA
Schwartz, Pincus, Asst.Libn.
  YESHIVA TORAH VODAATH AND MESIFTA -
  TORAH VODAATH LIBRARY □ Brooklyn, NY
Schwartz, Rosaline, Dir., Spec. Project
  YIVO INSTITUTE FOR JEWISH RESEARCH -
  LIBRARY AND ARCHIVES □ New York, NY
Schwartz, Stephen H., Dir.
  KENOSHA PUBLIC MUSEUM - LIBRARY □
  Kenosha, WI
Schwartzbauer, Eileen, Dept.Hd.
  MINNEAPOLIS PUBLIC LIBRARY &
  INFORMATION CENTER - SOCIOLOGY
  DEPARTMENT □ Minneapolis, MN
Schwarz, Betsy, Libn.
  WOMEN'S RESOURCE AND ACTION CENTER -
  SOJOURNER TRUTH WOMEN'S RESOURCE
  LIBRARY □ Iowa City, IA
Schwarz, Betty Ann, Info.Sci.
  MERCK & COMPANY, INC. - CALGON
  CORPORATION - INFORMATION CENTER □
  Pittsburgh, PA
Schwarz, Carol V., Tech.Libn.
  SINGER COMPANY - LINK DIVISION -
  TECHNICAL LIBRARY □ Sunnyvale, CA

Schwarz, Joanne L., Hd.Libn., Sci. & Tech.
  MILLER BREWING COMPANY - RESEARCH AND
  TECHNICAL LIBRARY □ Milwaukee, WI
Schwarz, Martita, Dept.Hd.
  YONKERS PUBLIC LIBRARY - FINE ARTS
  DEPARTMENT □ Yonkers, NY
Schwass, Earl R., Dir.
  U.S. NAVY - NAVAL WAR COLLEGE - LIBRARY □
  Newport, RI
Schweitzer, Leland R., Mgr. Of Res.Lab.
  ASGROW SEED COMPANY - RESEARCH CENTER
  □ Twin Falls, ID
Schweizer, Linda, Asst.Bus.Libn.
  MICHIGAN STATE UNIVERSITY - BUSINESS
  LIBRARY □ East Lansing, MI
Schwellenbach, Sue, Asst.Libn.
  ROCKY MOUNTAIN NEWS - LIBRARY □ Denver,
  CO
Schwenk, B., Ref.Asst.
  AIR PRODUCTS AND CHEMICALS, INC. -
  INFORMATION SERVICES - TREXLERTOWN
  LIBRARY □ Allentown, PA
Schwenke, Ezster L.K., Libn.
  UNIVERSITY OF NEW BRUNSWICK - SCIENCE
  LIBRARY □ Fredericton, NB
Schwerin, Gertrude D., Libn.
  FLEXIBLE CAREERS - LIBRARY □ Chicago, IL
Schwerzel, Sharon, Hd.Libn.
  OHIO STATE UNIVERSITY - BIOLOGICAL
  SCIENCES LIBRARY □ Columbus, OH
Schworer, L.A., Sec./Christian Educ.
  FIRST PRESBYTERIAN CHURCH - CHRISTIAN
  EDUCATION DEPARTMENT - LIBRARY □ San
  Diego, CA
Sciamma, Leon Pierre, Cartothecaire
  UNIVERSITE DU QUEBEC A MONTREAL -
  CARTOTHEQUE □ Montreal, PQ
Sciolino, Elaine T., Asst.Libn.
  WHITE AND CASE - LIBRARY □ New York, NY
Sciotti, Angela M., Lib.Dir.
  SWAIN SCHOOL OF DESIGN - LIBRARY† □ New
  Bedford, MA
Scirica, Rosemarie, Lib.Adm.
  SPERRY CORPORATION - LAW LIBRARY □ New
  York, NY
Scofield, Constance, ILL
  SOUTH DAKOTA STATE LIBRARY □ Pierre, SD
Scofield, James S., Chf.Libn.
  ST. PETERSBURG TIMES AND EVENING
  INDEPENDENT - LIBRARY □ St. Petersburg, FL
Scoggins, Lillian, Cat.
  LUTHERAN THEOLOGICAL SEMINARY - KRAUTH
  MEMORIAL LIBRARY □ Philadelphia, PA
Scollie, F.B., Chf.Libn.
  CANADA - ENERGY, MINES & RESOURCES
  CANADA - RESOURCE ECONOMICS LIBRARY □
  Ottawa, ON
Scollin, Ruth, Libn.
  SANTA BARBARA COUNTY GENEALOGICAL
  SOCIETY - LIBRARY □ Goleta, CA
Scoones, Lori, Asst.Libn.
  GENERAL ELECTRIC COMPANY - AIRCRAFT
  EQUIPMENT DIVISION - INFORMATION
  RESOURCES □ Utica, NY
Scott, Adella B., Dir. of LRC
  WASHTENAW COMMUNITY COLLEGE -
  LEARNING RESOURCE CENTER □ Ann Arbor, MI
Scott, Alfredia A., Libn.
  GEORGIA STATE DEPARTMENT OF
  TRANSPORTATION - RESEARCH LIBRARY □
  Atlanta, GA
Scott, Andrue, Lib.Info.Mgr.
  NATIONAL EMPLOYMENT LAW PROJECT, INC. -
  LIBRARY □ New York, NY
Scott, Ann, Educ./Online Search Serv.
  KANSAS STATE UNIVERSITY - FARRELL
  LIBRARY □ Manhattan, KS
Scott, Barbara G., Dir.
  BIRMINGHAM-SOUTHERN COLLEGE - CHARLES
  ANDREW RUSH LEARNING CENTER/LIBRARY □
  Birmingham, AL
Scott, Betty Ann, Pub.Lib.Cons.
  STATE LIBRARY OF FLORIDA □ Tallahassee, FL

Scott, Brenda, Dir. of Libs.
  GEORGIA STATE DEPARTMENT OF HUMAN
  RESOURCES - GEORGIA MENTAL HEALTH
  INSTITUTE - ADDISON M. DUVAL LIBRARY □
  Atlanta, GA
Scott, Brenda, Supv.Lib. & Files
  MARYLAND STATE DEPARTMENT OF HEALTH &
  MENTAL HYGIENE - LIBRARY† □ Baltimore, MD
Scott, Carolyn, Libn.
  FAEGRE & BENSON - LAW LIBRARY □
  Minneapolis, MN
Scott, Catherine D., Libn.
  SMITHSONIAN INSTITUTION LIBRARIES -
  NATIONAL AIR AND SPACE MUSEUM - LIBRARY
  □ Washington, DC
Scott, Diane, Libn.
  NORTHWEST BAPTIST THEOLOGICAL COLLEGE
  AND SEMINARY - LIBRARY □ Vancouver, BC
Scott, Dorothy, Libn.
  CANADIAN HEARING SOCIETY - LIBRARY □
  Toronto, ON
Scott, Duscha S., Dir.
  JACKSON HOMESTEAD - LIBRARY & ARCHIVES
  □ Newton, MA
Scott, Dr. Edward A., Dir.
  CASTLETON STATE COLLEGE - CALVIN
  COOLIDGE LIBRARY - LEARNING RESOURCES
  CENTER □ Castleton, VT
Scott, Enid, Libn.
  KINGSTON GENERAL HOSPITAL - MEDICAL
  LIBRARY □ Kingston, ON
Scott, Floyd, Cur.
  CARSON COUNTY SQUARE HOUSE MUSEUM -
  INFORMATION CENTER □ Panhandle, TX
Scott, Gregory M., Pres.
  TRIGOM - RESEARCH LIBRARY □ Yarmouth, ME
Scott, James F., Hd.Libn.
  MULTNOMAH SCHOOL OF THE BIBLE - JOHN
  AND MARY MITCHELL LIBRARY □ Portland, OR
Scott, Dr. James W., Dir.
  WESTERN WASHINGTON UNIVERSITY -
  CENTER FOR PACIFIC NORTHWEST STUDIES □
  Bellingham, WA
Scott, Jean L., Cat./Ser.Libn.
  U.S. NASA - LYNDON B. JOHNSON SPACE
  CENTER - TECHNICAL LIBRARY □ Houston, TX
Scott, Jean M.
  SETON HALL UNIVERSITY - SCHOOL OF LAW -
  LAW LIBRARY □ Newark, NJ
Scott, Joseph
  UNIVERSITY OF CONNECTICUT - MUSIC
  LIBRARY □ Storrs, CT
Scott, Kathleen, Ref.Libn.
  WASHTENAW COMMUNITY COLLEGE -
  LEARNING RESOURCE CENTER □ Ann Arbor, MI
Scott, Kathryn, Chf.Cat.
  NATIONAL SOCIETY, DAUGHTERS OF THE
  AMERICAN REVOLUTION - LIBRARY □
  Washington, DC
Scott, Linda, Libn.
  TEAM FOUR INC. - LIBRARY □ St. Louis, MO
Scott, Mary Ellen, Cat./Archv.
  PITTSBURGH THEOLOGICAL SEMINARY -
  CLIFFORD E. BARBOUR LIBRARY □ Pittsburgh,
  PA
Scott, Michael D., Exec.Dir.
  CENTER FOR COMPUTER/LAW - LIBRARY □ Los
  Angeles, CA
Scott, Nancy, Archv.
  GETTYSBURG COLLEGE - MUSSELMAN LIBRARY
  - SPECIAL COLLECTIONS □ Gettysburg, PA
Scott, Phil, AV Archv.
  U.S. PRESIDENTIAL LIBRARIES - LYNDON B.
  JOHNSON LIBRARY† □ Austin, TX
Scott, Richard P., Cat.
  NATIONAL SCIENCE FOUNDATION - LIBRARY □
  Washington, DC
Scott, Sandra, Hd., Spec.Lib.Serv.
  NEBRASKA STATE LIBRARY COMMISSION □
  Lincoln, NE

Scott, Sharon, Asst.Cur.
CHICAGO PUBLIC LIBRARY CULTURAL CENTER - VIVIAN G. HARSH COLLECTION OF AFRO-AMERICAN HISTORY & LIT.† □ Chicago, IL

Scott, Sue, Circ.Libn.
NORTH CAROLINA STATE DEPARTMENT OF CULTURAL RESOURCES - LIBRARY FOR THE BLIND AND PHYSICALLY HANDICAPPED □ Raleigh, NC

Scott, Ursula, Asst.Ref.Libn.
TEXAS TECH UNIVERSITY - HEALTH SCIENCES CENTER - LIBRARY OF THE HEALTH SCIENCES □ Lubbock, TX

Scott, Virginia, Hd.Libn.
BIRMINGHAM PUBLIC AND JEFFERSON COUNTY FREE LIBRARY - TUTWILER COLLECTION OF SOUTHERN HISTORY AND LITERATURE □ Birmingham, AL

Scott, Wendy, Campus Libn.
CENTENNIAL COLLEGE OF APPLIED ARTS & TECHNOLOGY - ASHTONBEE CAMPUS RESOURCE CENTRE □ Scarborough, ON

Scott, Willie, Asst.Libn.
SOUTHERN ILLINOIS UNIVERSITY, CARBONDALE - UNDERGRADUATE LIBRARY □ Carbondale, IL

Scotti, Cecelia, Asst.Libn.
BREED, ABBOTT & MORGAN - LIBRARY □ New York, NY

Scougall, Jean, Dir.
BAYSTATE MEDICAL CENTER - LIBRARY □ Springfield, MA

Scovel, Cathy, Asst.Libn.
U.S. MARINE CORPS - KANEOHE AIR STATION LIBRARY □ Kaneohe Bay, HI

Scowen, Amy, Libn.
TOWERS, PERRIN, FORSTER & CROSBY - INFORMATION CENTRE □ Montreal, PQ

Scratch, Margaret, Coord., Info.Serv.
UNIVERSITY OF REGINA - CANADIAN PLAINS RESEARCH CENTER INFORMATION SYSTEM □ Regina, SK

Scribner, Mary L., Hd.Libn.
INSTITUTE OF PAPER CHEMISTRY - LIBRARY □ Appleton, WI

Scrimgeour, Andrew D., Libn.
ILIFF SCHOOL OF THEOLOGY - IRA J. TAYLOR LIBRARY □ Denver, CO

Scrofani, Robert, Exec. V.P.
GEORGE (Henry) SCHOOL OF SOCIAL SCIENCE - RESEARCH LIBRARY □ San Francisco, CA

Scroggins, Mary B., Libn.
OREGON STATE UNIVERSITY - SCHOOL OF FORESTRY - FRL LIBRARY □ Corvallis, OR

Scroggs, Marie, Adm.Asst.
U.S. DEPT. OF COMMERCE - DEPARTMENTAL LIBRARY □ Washington, DC

Scroggs, Marie, Spec.Coll.Asst.
UNIVERSITY OF WEST FLORIDA - JOHN C. PACE LIBRARY - SPECIAL COLLECTIONS □ Pensacola, FL

Scroggs, W.B., Res.Libn.
SURGIKOS - RESEARCH LIBRARY □ Arlington, TX

Scully, Mariwayne, Libn.
SOUTHEAST METROPOLITAN BOARD OF COOPERATIVE SERVICES - PROFESSIONAL INFORMATION CENTER □ Denver, CO

Scura, Georgia, Ref.Libn.
UNIVERSITY OF CONNECTICUT - HEALTH CENTER - LYMAN MAYNARD STOWE LIBRARY □ Farmington, CT

Seaberry, Ivy, Lib.Techn.
U.S. NAVY - NAVAL SUPPLY CENTER - TECHNICAL DIVISION - TECHNICAL LIBRARY □ San Diego, CA

Seabrooks, Nettie H., Mgr.
GENERAL MOTORS CORPORATION - PUBLIC RELATIONS STAFF LIBRARY □ Detroit, MI

Seaburg, Alan, Mss. and Archv.
HARVARD UNIVERSITY - DIVINITY SCHOOL - ANDOVER-HARVARD THEOLOGICAL LIBRARY □ Cambridge, MA

Seaburg, Carl, Info.Off./Archv.
UNITARIAN-UNIVERSALIST ASSOCIATION - ARCHIVES □ Boston, MA

Seager, Danielle, Sys.Supv.
U.S. DEPT OF ENERGY - SANDIA NATL. LABORATORIES - TECHNICAL LIBRARY □ Albuquerque, NM

Seagle, Janet, Libn./Musm.Cur.
UNITED STATES GOLF ASSOCIATION - GOLF HOUSE LIBRARY □ Far Hills, NJ

Seal, Robert, Cur.
FOOTHILL COLLEGE - ELECTRONICS MUSEUM - DE FOREST MEMORIAL ARCHIVES □ Los Altos Hills, CA

Seals, Houston, Libn. II
ANCORA PSYCHIATRIC HOSPITAL - HEALTH SCIENCES LIBRARY □ Hammonton, NJ

Seaman, Anne T., Libn.
HONOLULU ACADEMY OF ARTS - ROBERT ALLERTON LIBRARY □ Honolulu, HI

Seaman, Don D., Libn.
CHURCH OF JESUS CHRIST OF LATTER-DAY SAINTS - ALBUQUERQUE BRANCH GENEALOGICAL LIBRARY □ Albuquerque, NM

Seaman, Maureen G., Libn.
OREGON GRADUATE CENTER FOR STUDY AND RESEARCH - LIBRARY □ Beaverton, OR

Seaman, Sara, Tech.Libn.
WILLIAMS BROTHERS ENGINEERING COMPANY - TECHNICAL INFORMATION CENTER □ Tulsa, OK

Seamans, Nancy H., Libn.
HAYES, SEAY, MATTERN & MATTERN - TECHNICAL LIBRARY □ Roanoke, VA

Seamans, Warren A., Dir.
MASSACHUSETTS INSTITUTE OF TECHNOLOGY - M.I.T. MUSEUM AND HISTORICAL COLLECTIONS □ Cambridge, MA

Search, Roger M., V.P.Indus.Rel.
HUBBELL , INC. - LIBRARY □ Orange, CT

Searcy, Herbert, Cat.
UNIVERSITY OF WISCONSIN, LA CROSSE - MURPHY LIBRARY □ La Crosse, WI

Searle, JoAnne M., Dir.
MORRISTOWN MEMORIAL HOSPITAL - LATHROPE HEALTH SCIENCES LIBRARY □ Morristown, NJ

Searls, Eileen H., Law Libn.
ST. LOUIS UNIVERSITY - SCHOOL OF LAW - LIBRARY □ St. Louis, MO

Searls, Keith, Libn.
ASSOCIATION OF TRIAL LAWYERS OF AMERICA - ATLA LIBRARY □ Washington, DC

Sears, Linda A., Libn., Sr.
WEST CENTRAL GEORGIA REGIONAL HOSPITAL - STAFF/PATIENT LIBRARY □ Columbus, GA

Sears, Phyllis J., Supv.
CHRYSLER CORPORATION - ENGINEERING DIVISION - ENGINEERING LIBRARY □ Detroit, MI

Sears, Russell L., Acq.Libn.
AMERICAN GRADUATE SCHOOL OF INTERNATIONAL MANAGEMENT - LIBRARY □ Glendale, AZ

Seaton, Helen J., Libn.
MISSOURI BAPTIST HOSPITAL - SCHOOL OF NURSING LIBRARY □ St. Louis, MO

Seay, Patricia, Law Libn.
IMPERIAL COUNTY LAW LIBRARY □ El Centro, CA

Sebastian, Anne, Asst.Libn.
CURTIS INSTITUTE OF MUSIC - LIBRARY □ Philadelphia, PA

Sebestyen, Judith, Asst.Libn.
AMERICAN JEWISH HISTORICAL SOCIETY - LIBRARY □ Waltham, MA

Seboek, L.
CANADA - PUBLIC ARCHIVES OF CANADA - NATIONAL MAP COLLECTION □ Ottawa, ON

Sechrest, S., Doc.
UNIVERSITY OF WISCONSIN, LA CROSSE - MURPHY LIBRARY □ La Crosse, WI

Secunda, Jeannette L., Libn.
HOME LIFE INSURANCE COMPANY - LIBRARY □ New York, NY

Sedgwick, Dorothy L., Libn.
PRICE WATERHOUSE - NATIONAL RESEARCH LIBRARY □ Toronto, ON

Sedgwick, Frederica M., Dir.
LOYOLA LAW SCHOOL - LIBRARY □ Los Angeles, CA

Sedgwick, Gregory B., Libn.
LEEDS, HILL & JEWETT, INC. - LIBRARY □ San Francisco, CA

Sedgwick, Shirley, Chf., Acq.
WYOMING STATE LIBRARY □ Cheyenne, WY

Sedlacek, Marie, Cat.
JOSLYN ART MUSEUM - ART REFERENCE LIBRARY □ Omaha, NE

See, Donna, Asst.Libn.
WEST VIRGINIA SCHOOLS FOR THE DEAF AND BLIND - WV SCHOOL FOR THE BLIND LIBRARY □ Romney, WV

Seeber, Frances, Supv.Archv.
U.S. PRESIDENTIAL LIBRARIES - FRANKLIN D. ROOSEVELT LIBRARY □ Hyde Park, NY

Seebers, Barbara, Asst.Libn.
HOUSTON CHRONICLE - EDITORIAL LIBRARY □ Houston, TX

Seeds, Robert, Health Sci.Libn.
PENNSYLVANIA STATE UNIVERSITY - LIFE SCIENCES LIBRARY □ University Park, PA

Seeger, Leinaala, Asst.Law Libn.
MC GEORGE SCHOOL OF LAW - LAW LIBRARY □ Sacramento, CA

Seeger, Marjorie J., Libn.
MC KAY DEE HOSPITAL CENTER - EDUCATIONAL MEDIA CENTER □ Ogden, UT

Seegraber, Frank, Spec.Coll.Libn.
BOSTON COLLEGE - LIBRARY - IRISH COLLECTION □ Chestnut Hill, MA

Seegraber, Frank J., Spec.Coll.Libn.
BOSTON COLLEGE - LIBRARY - BREHAUT BOSTONIAN COLLECTION □ Chestnut Hill, MA

Seegraber, Frank J., Spec.Coll.Libn.
BOSTON COLLEGE - LIBRARY - FRANCIS THOMPSON COLLECTION □ Chestnut Hill, MA

Seegraber, Frank J., Spec.Coll.Libn.
BOSTON COLLEGE - LIBRARY - NICHOLAS M. WILLIAMS ETHNOLOGICAL COLLECTION □ Chestnut Hill, MA

Seekatz, Kathleen, Libn.
HONEYWELL, INC. - DEFENSE ELECTRONICS DIVISION, TRAINING AND CONTROL SYSTEMS OPERATION - TECHNICAL LIBRARY □ West Covina, CA

Seeley, Catherine, Ref.Libn.
SUNY - UPSTATE MEDICAL CENTER LIBRARY □ Syracuse, NY

Seeley, Elizabeth, Med.Libn.
HACKLEY HOSPITAL - MEDICAL LIBRARY □ Muskegon, MI

Seeley, Marianna, Libn.
BURROUGHS CORPORATION - RANCHO BERNARDO TECHNICAL INFORMATION CENTER □ San Diego, CA

Seelick, Beth, Libn.
DIEBOLD GROUP, INC. - LIBRARY □ New York, NY

Seeling, Sherri, Res.Spec.
UNIVERSAL CITY STUDIOS - RESEARCH DEPARTMENT LIBRARY □ Universal City, CA

Seely, Doris J., Asst.Libn., Cat.
MONTEREY INSTITUTE OF INTERNATIONAL STUDIES - WILLIAM TELL COLEMAN LIBRARY† □ Monterey, CA

Seer, Gitelle, Libn.
DEWEY, BALLANTINE, BUSHBY, PALMER & WOOD - LIBRARY □ New York, NY

Seery, John A., Pub.Serv.
ASBURY THEOLOGICAL SEMINARY - B.L. FISHER LIBRARY □ Wilmore, KY

Seevers, James, Adm.
ADLER PLANETARIUM - LIBRARY □ Chicago, IL

PERSONNEL

Sefcik, Sylvia J., Libn.
U.S. AIR FORCE BASE - LORING BASE LIBRARY
□ Loring AFB, ME
Sefton, Amelia K., Libn. I
U.S. ARMY POST - FORT HAMILTON - LIBRARY
□ Brooklyn, NY
Sefton, Shirley, Hd., Tech.Serv.
SASKATCHEWAN - PROVINCIAL LIBRARY □
Regina, SK
Segal, Harriet, Biblog.Asst.
TEMPLE UNIVERSITY - CENTRAL LIBRARY
SYSTEM - SCHOOL OF SOCIAL
ADMINISTRATION - LIBRARY □ Philadelphia, PA
Segal, JoAn S., Interim Exec.Dir.
BIBLIOGRAPHICAL CENTER FOR RESEARCH -
ROCKY MOUNTAIN REGION, INC. □ Denver, CO
Segal, Oreet, Asst.Libn.
WILLIAM J. CAMPBELL LIBRARY OF THE
UNITED STATES COURTS □ Chicago, IL
Segal, Sheryl A., Lib.Dir.
U.S. FEDERAL COMMUNICATIONS
COMMISSION - LIBRARY □ Washington, DC
Segall, Andrea, Law Libn.
LINCOLN UNIVERSITY - LAW LIBRARY □ San
Francisco, CA
Segel, James, Exec.Dir.
MASSACHUSETTS MUNICIPAL ASSOCIATION -
RESEARCH LIBRARY □ Boston, MA
Seger, Susan, Libn.
UNIVERSITY OF MICHIGAN - DENTISTRY
LIBRARY □ Ann Arbor, MI
Segger, Martin, Cur.
UNIVERSITY OF VICTORIA - KATHARINE
MALTWOOD COLLECTION □ Victoria, BC
Seglin, Adelia P., Dir.
ST. JOHN'S MEMORIAL HOSPITAL - HEALTH
SCIENCES LIBRARY □ Anderson, IN
Sego, Gary, Spec.Archv.
JEFFERSON COUNTY OFFICE OF HISTORIC
PRESERVATION AND ARCHIVES □ Louisville, KY
Seguin, Micheline, Documentaliste
INSTITUT CANADIEN D'EDUCATION DES
ADULTES - CENTRE DE DOCUMENTATION □
Montreal, PQ
Seh, Sandy, Libn.Asst.
ANALYTIC SERVICES, INC. - TECHNICAL
LIBRARY □ Arlington, VA
Seibels, Cynthia, Libn.
KENNEDY GALLERIES - ART LIBRARY □ New
York, NY
Seibert, Donald, Dept.Hd.
SYRACUSE UNIVERSITY - E.S. BIRD LIBRARY -
FINE ARTS DEPARTMENT □ Syracuse, NY
Seidel, Mrs. Leslie R., Med.Libn.
U.S. ARMY HOSPITALS - CUTLER ARMY
HOSPITAL - MEDICAL LIBRARY □ Ft. Devens,
MA
Seidler, Janice, Hd.Libn.
MATHEMATICAL REVIEWS - LIBRARY □ Ann
Arbor, MI
Seidler, Louise M., Supv.
AMOCO PRODUCTION COMPANY - NEW
ORLEANS REGION - LIBRARY INFORMATION
CENTER □ New Orleans, LA
Seidman, Ann M., Mgr.
STALEY (A.E.) MANUFACTURING COMPANY -
TECHNICAL INFORMATION CENTER □ Decatur,
IL
Seidman, Eleanor, Adm.Asst.
STONE AND WEBSTER ENGINEERING
CORPORATION - TECHNICAL INFORMATION
CENTER □ Boston, MA
Seidman, Ruth K., Libn.
ENVIRONMENTAL PROTECTION AGENCY -
REGION I LIBRARY □ Boston, MA
Seidwitz, J.A., Mgr.
ROCKWELL INTERNATIONAL - TECHNICAL
INFORMATION CENTER □ Columbus, OH
Seifer, Marc, Dir.
METASCIENCE FOUNDATION - LIBRARY □
Kingston, RI

Seifert, Jan, Fine Arts Libn.
UNIVERSITY OF OKLAHOMA - MUSIC LIBRARY
□ Norman, OK
Seifert, Jan, Fine Arts Libn.
UNIVERSITY OF OKLAHOMA - SCHOOL OF
DRAMA LIBRARY □ Norman, OK
Seiffer, Lynn, Ref.Libn.
NEWSWEEK, INC. - LIBRARY □ New York, NY
Seifullin, E.T., Supv.Engr.Adm.
UOP INC. - BOSTROM DIVISION -
ENGINEERING LIBRARY □ Milwaukee, WI
Seig, Mary, Asst.Libn.
NATIONAL SOCIETY, DAUGHTERS OF THE
AMERICAN REVOLUTION - LIBRARY □
Washington, DC
Seigelman, Lynn, Ref.Libn.
GEORGETOWN UNIVERSITY - MEDICAL
CENTER - DAHLGREN MEMORIAL LIBRARY □
Washington, DC
Seiglar, Barbara, Dir.
BAPTIST MEMORIAL HOSPITAL - LEARNING
RESOURCES CENTER □ Kansas City, MO
Seigle, Jeanne C., Law Libn.
ALLIED CORPORATION - LAW LIBRARY □
Morristown, NJ
Seigler, Michael E., Law Libn.
ATLANTA LAW SCHOOL - LIBRARY □ Atlanta, GA
Seinfeld, Evelyn, Libn.
AMERICAN FEDERATION OF STATE, COUNTY
AND MUNICIPAL EMPLOYEES, AFL-CIO
(AFSCME) - DC37 RESEARCH LIBRARY □ New
York, NY
Sekerak, Robert, Tech.Serv.Hd.
UNIVERSITY OF VERMONT - DIVISION OF
HEALTH SCIENCES - CHARLES A. DANA
MEDICAL LIBRARY □ Burlington, VT
Sekerka, Mrs. James, Cur.
LAKEWOOD HISTORICAL SOCIETY - LIBRARY □
Lakewood, OH
Seki, G., Acq.Libn.
TRW, INC. - DEFENSE & SPACE SYSTEMS
GROUP - TECHNICAL INFORMATION CENTER □
Redondo Beach, CA
Sekine, Gail, Braneida Supv.
MOHAWK COLLEGE OF APPLIED ARTS AND
TECHNOLOGY - MOHAWK LIBRARY RESOURCE
CENTRE □ Hamilton, ON
Sekler, Emily, Site Supv.
U.S. NASA - HEADQUARTERS LIBRARY □
Washington, DC
Sekula, Linda, Hd.Libn.
TEMPLE UNIVERSITY - CENTRAL LIBRARY
SYSTEM - ZAHN INSTRUCTIONAL MATERIALS
CENTER □ Philadelphia, PA
Selakoff, Judith, Libn.
RESEARCH INSTITUTE FOR THE STUDY OF MAN
- LIBRARY □ New York, NY
Selb, Robert, Museum Cur.
CANTON HISTORICAL SOCIETY - LIBRARY □
Collinsville, CT
Selby, Joan, Colbeck Libn.
UNIVERSITY OF BRITISH COLUMBIA - SPECIAL
COLLECTIONS DIVISION □ Vancouver, BC
Selby, Vickie, Libn.
MISSOURI STATE COURT OF APPEALS,
WESTERN DISTRICT - LIBRARY □ Kansas City,
MO
Selch, John, Newspaper Libn.
INDIANA STATE LIBRARY - INDIANA DIVISION
□ Indianapolis, IN
Seldin, Daniel, Hd.
INDIANA UNIVERSITY - GEOGRAPHY AND MAP
LIBRARY □ Bloomington, IN
Self, David, Libn.
UNIVERSITY OF ILLINOIS - VETERINARY
MEDICINE LIBRARY □ Urbana, IL
Self, Phyllis, Libn.
UNIVERSITY OF ILLINOIS MEDICAL CENTER -
LIBRARY OF THE HEALTH SCIENCES □ Urbana,
IL

Selfridge, Anna B., Asst.Cur./Mss., Archv.
ALLEN COUNTY HISTORICAL SOCIETY -
ELIZABETH M. MAC DONELL MEMORIAL
LIBRARY □ Lima, OH
Selgensen, Lou, Libn.
MASON AND COMPANY - LIBRARY □ Calgary, AB
Selgestad, Marcel, Asst.Libn.Acq./Cat.
DAKOTA STATE COLLEGE - KARL E. MUNDT
LIBRARY □ Madison, SD
Selig, Edith G., Adm.Asst.
NATIONAL CONFERENCE OF CHRISTIANS AND
JEWS - PAULA K. LAZRUS LIBRARY OF
INTERGROUP RELATIONS □ New York, NY
Selix, Harold, Asst.Dir.Lib.Serv.
EAGLEVILLE HOSPITAL AND REHABILITATION
CENTER - HENRY S. LOUCHHEIM MEDICAL
LIBRARY □ Eagleville, PA
Selke, Elaine, Libn.
CONNAUGHT LABORATORIES, LTD. - BALMER
NEILLY LIBRARY □ Willowdale, ON
Sell, David, Policy Anl.
SOUTH DAKOTA STATE OFFICE OF ENERGY
POLICY - LIBRARY □ Pierre, SD
Sellars, Judith, Libn.
MUSEUM OF NEW MEXICO - MUSEUM OF
INTERNATIONAL FOLK ART - LIBRARY □ Santa
Fe, NM
Sellers, Brenda A., Asst.Libn.
ABRAHAM BALDWIN AGRICULTURAL COLLEGE -
LIBRARY □ Tifton, GA
Sellers, Lee, Libn.
UNIVERSITY OF CONNECTICUT - SCHOOL OF
SOCIAL WORK - LIBRARY □ West Hartford, CT
Sellers, Martha M., Tech.Libn.
OLIN CORPORATION - FINE PAPER AND FILM
GROUP - TECHNICAL LIBRARY □ Pisgah Forest,
NC
Sellers, Norma, Ser./Doc.Libn.
U.S. AIR FORCE - AEROSPACE MEDICAL
DIVISION - SCHOOL OF AEROSPACE MEDICINE
- STRUGHOLD AEROMEDICAL LIBRARY □ Brooks
AFB, TX
Selmer, Marsha L., Map Libn.
UNIVERSITY OF ILLINOIS, CHICAGO CIRCLE -
LIBRARY - MAP SECTION □ Chicago, IL
Selph, Jana, Libn.
GENSTAR CORP. - LIBRARY □ San Francisco, CA
Seltzer, Ada M., Asst.Dir., Pub.Serv.
UNIVERSITY OF SOUTH FLORIDA - MEDICAL
CENTER LIBRARY □ Tampa, FL
Seltzer, Evelyn
HARTFORD PUBLIC LIBRARY - REFERENCE AND
GENERAL READING DEPARTMENT □ Hartford,
CT
Selz, Julia, Slide Libn.
BOSTON ARCHITECTURAL CENTER - ALFRED
SHAW AND EDWARD DURELL STONE LIBRARY □
Boston, MA
Selzer, Nancy S., Libn.
DU PONT DE NEMOURS (E.I.) & COMPANY, INC.
- HASKELL LABORATORY FOR TOXICOLOGY &
INDUSTRIAL MEDICINE - LIBRARY □ Newark,
DE
Semenuk, Dr. Nick, Sec.Hd.Lit. Search
SQUIBB (E.R.) AND SONS, INC. - SQUIBB
INSTITUTE FOR MEDICAL RESEARCH -
SCIENCE INFORMATION DEPARTMENT □
Princeton, NJ
Semick, Georgette, Prog.Dir.
U.S. DEPT. OF JUSTICE - NATIONAL INSTITUTE
OF JUSTICE - NATL. CRIMINAL JUSTICE REF.
SERVICE □ Rockville, MD
Semler, Karen, Asst. Music Libn.
UNIVERSITY OF VIRGINIA - MUSIC LIBRARY □
Charlottesville, VA
Semonche, Barbara P., Chf.Libn.
DURHAM HERALD-SUN NEWSPAPER - LIBRARY
□ Durham, NC
Sendek, Irene, Hd. Loyola Libs.
CONCORDIA UNIVERSITY - LOYOLA CAMPUS -
GEORGES P. VANIER LIBRARY □ Montreal, PQ

Sengstacken, R. Robert, Libn.
TOBACCO MERCHANTS ASSOCIATION OF THE
U.S. - HOWARD S. CULLMAN LIBRARY □ New
York, NY

Sentner, Sylvia, Hd., Per.Dept.
CORNELL UNIVERSITY - MEDICAL COLLEGE -
LIBRARY □ New York, NY

Sepehri, Abazar, Libn.
UNIVERSITY OF TEXAS, AUSTIN - MIDDLE
EAST COLLECTION □ Austin, TX

Sepessy, Joan L., Asst.Libn.
TOLEDO MUSEUM OF ART - ART REFERENCE
LIBRARY □ Toledo, OH

Sercombe, Laurel, Music Cat.
UNIVERSITY OF WASHINGTON - MUSIC
LIBRARY □ Seattle, WA

Serebrin, Ray, Prog.Libn.
SEATTLE PUBLIC LIBRARY - MEDIA &
PROGRAM SERVICES □ Seattle, WA

Serena, Richard, Libn.
GOLDEN VALLEY LUTHERAN COLLEGE -
LIBRARY □ Minneapolis, MN

Serette, David W., Cur. of Graphics
UNITED SOCIETY OF BELIEVERS - THE SHAKER
LIBRARY □ Poland Spring, ME

Sergott, Mary Anne, Libn. II
DETROIT PUBLIC LIBRARY - MUNICIPAL
REFERENCE LIBRARY □ Detroit, MI

Serguison, John, Reports Indexer
CATERPILLAR TRACTOR COMPANY -
TECHNICAL INFORMATION CENTER □ Peoria, IL

Serha, Liza, Libn.
U.S. NATL. INSTITUTES OF HEALTH - NATL.
INSTITUTE OF ALLERGY & INFECTIOUS
DISEASES - ROCKY MOUNTAIN LAB. LIB. □
Hamilton, MT

Serreno, Joanne, Cat.
HARVARD UNIVERSITY - TOZZER LIBRARY -
PEABODY MUSEUM OF ARCHAEOLOGY AND
ETHNOLOGY □ Cambridge, MA

Seruya, Flora, Cat.
AMERICAN CANCER SOCIETY - MEDICAL
LIBRARY □ New York, NY

Servis, Willie M., Subj.Spec.
U.S. DEPT OF ENERGY - SANDIA NATL.
LABORATORIES - TECHNICAL LIBRARY □
Albuquerque, NM

Sessa, Jane T., Libn.
CONGRESSIONAL BUDGET OFFICE - LIBRARY □
Washington, DC

Sethna, Mr. Nari, Exec.Mgr.
REFRIGERATION SERVICE ENGINEERS
SOCIETY - LIBRARY □ Des Plaines, IL

Setnosky, Julie, Sr.Libn.
HENNEPIN COUNTY LIBRARY SYSTEM -
GOVERNMENT CENTER INFORMATION LIBRARY
□ Minneapolis, MN

Settle, Joan, Libn.
BALTIMORE MUSEUM OF ART - REFERENCE
LIBRARY □ Baltimore, MD

Setton, Sarah, Asst. to the Pres.
SUGAR ASSOCIATION, INC. - LIBRARY □
Washington, DC

Seubert, David, Asst.Libn.
GOETHE INSTITUTE BOSTON - LIBRARY □
Boston, MA

Seulowitz, Lois, Mgr.
GENERAL FOODS CORPORATION - MARKETING
INFORMATION CENTER □ White Plains, NY

Seuss, Herbert J., Corp.Libn.
EATON CORPORATION - CUTLER-HAMMER
LIBRARY □ Milwaukee, WI

Severson, Daryl, Asst.Libn.
ALBANY INSTITUTE OF HISTORY AND ART - MC
KINNEY LIBRARY □ Albany, NY

Sevier, Jeffrey A., Tech.Proc.Libn.
HUGHES AIRCRAFT COMPANY - COMPANY
TECHNICAL DOCUMENT CENTER □ Culver City,
CA

Sevigny, Paul S., Pres.
AMERICAN SOCIETY OF DOWSERS, INC. -
LIBRARY □ Danville, VT

Sevy, Barbara, Libn.
PHILADELPHIA MUSEUM OF ART - LIBRARY □
Philadelphia, PA

Sewald, Beatrice R., Asst.Libn.
NASSAU COUNTY DEPARTMENT OF HEALTH -
DIVISION OF LABORATORIES & RESEARCH -
MEDICAL LIBRARY □ Hempstead, NY

Seward, Gerry, Info.Spec.
SYNTEX, U.S.A. - CORPORATE LIBRARY/
INFORMATION SERVICES □ Palo Alto, CA

Seward, Stephen, Dir. N.Y. Lib.
FOUNDATION CENTER - NEW YORK - LIBRARY
□ New York, NY

Seward, Sue, Hd., Ref.
U.S. NASA - LANGLEY RESEARCH CENTER -
TECHNICAL LIBRARY MS 185 □ Hampton, VA

Sewell, Georgia Gwin, Libn.
HOTEL DIEU HOSPITAL - LIBRARY □ New
Orleans, LA

Sewell, Kermit R., Exchange Slavic Libn.
UNIVERSITY OF KANSAS - SLAVIC COLLECTION
□ Lawrence, KS

Sewell, P.L., Hd.Libn.
GENERAL ELECTRIC COMPANY - AIRCRAFT
ENGINE GROUP - TECHNICAL INFORMATION
CENTER □ Cincinnati, OH

Sewell, Robert G., Japanese Biblog.
UNIVERSITY OF ILLINOIS - ASIAN LIBRARY □
Urbana, IL

Sexton, Ebba Jo, Circ.Libn.
UNIVERSITY OF KENTUCKY - LAW LIBRARY □
Lexington, KY

Sexton, Madeleine, Ref./Cat.
IBM CORPORATION - GENERAL PRODUCTS
DIVISION - INFORMATION/LIBRARY/
LEARNING CENTER □ San Jose, CA

Sexton, Mary, Ref.Libn.
TEXAS STATE TECHNICAL INSTITUTE, WACO
CAMPUS - LEARNING RESOURCE CENTER □
Waco, TX

Sexton, Mary E., Lib. Group Supv.
BELL TELEPHONE LABORATORIES, INC. &
WESTERN ELECTRIC, INC. - TECHNICAL
LIBRARY □ North Andover, MA

Seyffarth, Jeanne, Asst.Libn.
OPPENHEIMER & CO., INC. - LIBRARY† □ New
York, NY

Seymour, Bessie
U.S. COAST GUARD - TAMPA MEMORIAL
LIBRARY† □ New York, NY

Seymour, Jack D., Chf., Lib.Serv.
U.S. VETERANS ADMINISTRATION (SD-Fort
Meade) - MEDICAL CENTER LIBRARY □ Fort
Meade, SD

Seymour, Jill, Asst.Libn.
GRACELAND COLLEGE - FREDERICK MADISON
SMITH LIBRARY □ Lamoni, IA

Shaak, Graig D., Asst.Dir.
UNIVERSITY OF FLORIDA - FLORIDA STATE
MUSEUM LIBRARY □ Gainesville, FL

Shabowich, Stanley A., Acq.Libn.
PURDUE UNIVERSITY - CALUMET LIBRARY □
Hammond, IN

Shackelford, Bruce M., Cur./Dir.
CREEK INDIAN MEMORIAL ASSOCIATION -
CREEK COUNCIL HOUSE MUSEUM - LIBRARY □
Okmulgee, OK

Shackelford, Daria, Med.Libn./Dir.
REHABILITATION INSTITUTE, INC. - MC
PHERSON BROWNING MEMORIAL LIBRARY □
Detroit, MI

Shacklette, Lisa, Cat./Conversion Libn.
CARNEGIE-MELLON UNIVERSITY - HUNT
LIBRARY □ Pittsburgh, PA

Shaeffer, Margaret W.M., Dir.
JEFFERSON COUNTY HISTORICAL SOCIETY -
LIBRARY □ Watertown, NY

Shafer, Wade H., Asst.Dir.
PURDUE UNIVERSITY - CINDAS - ELECTRONIC
PROPERTIES INFORMATION CENTER □ West
Lafayette, IN

Shafer, Wade H., Asst.Dir.
PURDUE UNIVERSITY - CINDAS -
THERMOPHYSICAL PROPERTIES RESEARCH
CENTER - LIBRARY □ West Lafayette, IN

Shaffer, Dale E., Lib.Cons. & Dir.
JENNINGS LIBRARY □ Salem, OH

Shaffer, Ellen, Cur.
SILVERADO MUSEUM □ St. Helena, CA

Shaffer, Ethel V., Cat.Libn.
LUTHERAN THEOLOGICAL SEMINARY - A.R.
WENTZ LIBRARY □ Gettysburg, PA

Shaffer, Harold, Ser.Libn.
INDIANA UNIVERSITY - SCHOOL OF MEDICINE
LIBRARY □ Indianapolis, IN

Shaffer, Jack W., Dir.
ST. VINCENT HOSPITAL AND MEDICAL CENTER
- HEALTH SCIENCE LIBRARY □ Toledo, OH

Shaffer, Kenneth M., Jr., Acq.Libn.
BETHANY AND NORTHERN BAPTIST
THEOLOGICAL SEMINARIES - LIBRARY □ Oak
Brook, IL

Shaffer, Mary L., Dir.
U.S. ARMY - ARMY LIBRARY □ Washington, DC

Shah, Mrs. Neeta N., Chf.Med.Libn.
HALL (William S.) PSYCHIATRIC INSTITUTE -
PROFESSIONAL LIBRARY □ Columbia, SC

Shah, Ms. Shanta, Libn.
CRAWFORD W. LONG MEMORIAL HOSPITAL -
LIBRARY† □ Atlanta, GA

Shakelton, Mary A., Ref./Circ.Libn.
GORDON COLLEGE - WINN LIBRARY □ Wenham,
MA

Shalik, Adele, Asst.Adm.
PRICE WATERHOUSE - NEW YORK OFFICE
INFORMATION CENTER □ New York, NY

Shanahan, Pauline, Asst.Libn.
DURACELL INTERNATIONAL, INC. - TECHNICAL
INFORMATION CENTER □ Burlington, MA

Shand, Hope, Res.Assoc.
NATIONAL SHARECROPPERS FUND/RURAL
ADVANCEMENT FUND - F.P. GRAHAM
RESOURCE CENTER □ Wadesboro, NC

Shane, Mr. T.C., Jr., Tech.Libn.
INTERNATIONAL MINERALS & CHEMICALS
CORPORATION - IMC RESEARCH &
DEVELOPMENT LIBRARY □ Terre Haute, IN

Shanefield, Irene Deborah, Med.Libn.
JEWISH CONVALESCENT HOSPITAL CENTRE -
HEALTH SCIENCES INFORMATION CENTRE □
Chomedey, Laval, PQ

Shanholtz, Brenda W., Libn.
U.S. ARMY - ELECTRONICS R & D COMMAND -
TECHNICAL LIBRARY DIVISION □ Fort
Monmouth, NJ

Shank, William, Music Libn.
CUNY - GRADUATE SCHOOL AND UNIVERSITY
CENTER - LIBRARY □ New York, NY

Shanks, Doreen, Hd.Libn.
UNIVERSITY OF MANITOBA - EDUCATION
LIBRARY □ Winnipeg, MB

Shanks, Kathy, Libn.
AMERICAN ASSOCIATION OF PETROLEUM
GEOLOGISTS - LIBRARY □ Tulsa, OK

Shanks, Polly, Mgr., S.D.I.
MISSISSIPPI STATE RESEARCH AND
DEVELOPMENT CENTER - INFORMATION
SERVICES DIVISION □ Jackson, MS

Shanks, Robert, Exec.Asst.
CANADA - NATIONAL RESEARCH COUNCIL -
CANADA INSTITUTE FOR SCIENTIFIC AND
TECHNICAL INFORMATION (CISTI) □ Ottawa,
ON

Shanks, W. Kenneth, Archv.
U.S. NATL. ARCHIVES & RECORDS SERVICE -
FEDERAL ARCHIVES & RECORDS CENTER,
REGION 5 □ Chicago, IL

Shanley, Elaine, Hd.Cat.
PROVIDENCE COLLEGE - PHILLIPS MEMORIAL
LIBRARY □ Providence, RI

Shanman, Roberta, Lib.Res.Anl.
ROCKWELL INTERNATIONAL - SPACE
BUSINESSES - TECHNICAL INFORMATION
CENTER □ Downey, CA

PERSONNEL

Shannon, Dwight W., Assoc.Dir.
CALIFORNIA STATE UNIVERSITY, CHICO -
MERIAM LIBRARY □ Chico, CA

Shannon, Robert, Educ.Serv.Off., Supv.
U.S. NAVY - NAVAL AIR STATION (Alameda) -
LIBRARY □ Alameda, CA

Shapiro, Barbara, Supv.Libn.
NEW YORK PUBLIC LIBRARY - MID-
MANHATTAN LIBRARY - LEARNER'S ADVISORY
SERVICE □ New York, NY

Shapiro, Beth J., Libn.
MICHIGAN STATE UNIVERSITY - C.W. BARR
PLANNING AND DESIGN LIBRARY □ East
Lansing, MI

Shapiro, Beth J., Libn.
MICHIGAN STATE UNIVERSITY - URBAN
POLICY AND PLANNING LIBRARY □ East Lansing,
MI

Shapiro, Fred R., Hist.
NORTH AMERICAN TIDDLYWINKS
ASSOCIATION - ARCHIVES □ Silver Spring, MD

Shapiro, June R., Div.Hd.
CONNECTICUT STATE LIBRARY □ Hartford, CT

Shapiro, Leonard P., Dir.
CALIFORNIA COLLEGE OF PODIATRIC
MEDICINE - SCHMIDT MEDICAL LIBRARY □ San
Francisco, CA

Shapiro, Marsha, Asst.Libn.
MANUFACTURERS LIFE INSURANCE COMPANY -
BUSINESS LIBRARY □ Toronto, ON

Shapley, Ellen, Sr.Res.Libn.
TRACY-LOCKE ADVERTISING AND PUBLIC
RELATIONS, INC. - LIBRARY □ Dallas, TX

Sharav, Vera, Ref.Libn.
PROSKAUER, ROSE, GOETZ & MENDELSOHN -
LIBRARY □ New York, NY

Sharke, Ingrid, Libn.
TROY TIMES RECORD - LIBRARY □ Troy, NY

Sharma, Katherine, Libn.
CROSS CANCER INSTITUTE - LIBRARY □
Edmonton, AB

Sharma, Mohan, Hd.
UNIVERSITY OF ALBERTA - HUMANITIES AND
SOCIAL SCIENCES LIBRARY □ Edmonton, AB

Sharma, Ramesh, Hd., Tech.Serv.
GALLAUDET COLLEGE LIBRARY - SPECIAL
COLLECTIONS □ Washington, DC

Sharma, Sue, Div.Chf.
BROOKLYN PUBLIC LIBRARY - ART AND MUSIC
DIVISION □ Brooklyn, NY

Sharon, Dan, Libn.
SPERTUS COLLEGE OF JUDAICA - NORMAN AND
HELEN ASHER LIBRARY □ Chicago, IL

Sharp, Alice L., Cat.
COLORADO HISTORICAL SOCIETY - STEPHEN
H. HART LIBRARY □ Denver, CO

Sharp, Donald J., Act.Chf.Libn.
LAKEHEAD UNIVERSITY - CHANCELLOR
PATERSON LIBRARY □ Thunder Bay, ON

Sharp, Elaine, Tech.Serv.
UNIVERSITY OF WISCONSIN, MADISON -
WISCONSIN REGIONAL PRIMATE RESEARCH
CENTER - PRIMATE LIBRARY □ Madison, WI

Sharp, Rev. James C., Act.Univ.Libn.
SETON HALL UNIVERSITY - MC LAUGHLIN
LIBRARY □ South Orange, NJ

Sharp, Linda Carlson, Cat.
INDIANA HISTORICAL SOCIETY - WILLIAM
HENRY SMITH MEMORIAL LIBRARY □
Indianapolis, IN

Sharp, Mrs. Major Gordon
SALVATION ARMY - EDUCATION DEPARTMENT
LIBRARY □ New York, NY

Sharp, Marie, Mgr.
BOCES - ORLEANS-NIAGARA EDUCATIONAL
COMMUNICATIONS CENTER □ Sanborn, NY

Sharp, Valetta, Libn.
U.S. ARMY - CORPS OF ENGINEERS - OMAHA
DISTRICT - LIBRARY □ Omaha, NE

Sharpless, Mercedes Benitez, Libn.
LAFAYETTE COLLEGE - KIRBY LIBRARY OF
GOVERNMENT AND LAW† □ Easton, PA

Sharrett, Ruth, Entomology Res.Libn.
CANADA - AGRICULTURE CANADA -
ENTOMOLOGY RESEARCH LIBRARY □ Ottawa,
ON

Shasky, Florian J., Chf.
STANFORD UNIVERSITY - DEPARTMENT OF
SPECIAL COLLECTIONS □ Stanford, CA

Shatkin, Leon, Hd., ILL Ctr.
CONNECTICUT STATE LIBRARY □ Hartford, CT

Shattuck, Beverly, Asst.Dir.Pub.Serv.
UNIVERSITY OF MASSACHUSETTS MEDICAL
SCHOOL & WORCESTER DISTRICT MEDICAL
SOCIETY - LIBRARY □ Worcester, MA

Shatz, Norma, Lib.Coord.
SUNY AT BUFFALO - CENTER FOR CURRICULUM
PLANNING □ Amherst, NY

Shaver, Donna B., Info.Spec.
NORTHWEST REGIONAL EDUCATIONAL
LABORATORY - INFORMATION CENTER/
LIBRARY □ Portland, OR

Shaver, Helen, Resource Ctr.Supv.
MOHAWK COLLEGE OF APPLIED ARTS AND
TECHNOLOGY - MOHAWK LIBRARY RESOURCE
CENTRE □ Hamilton, ON

Shaver, Nancy B., Libn.
INTERNATIONAL FRANCHISE ASSOCIATION -
LIBRARY □ Washington, DC

Shaw, Andrew, Jr., Dir.
WILKES COLLEGE - INSTITUTE OF REGIONAL
AFFAIRS - LIBRARY† □ Wilkes-Barre, PA

Shaw, C., Data Off.
CANADA - STATISTICS CANADA - ADVISORY
SERVICES - EDMONTON REFERENCE CENTRE†
□ Edmonton, AB

Shaw, Courtney A., Libn.
UNIVERSITY OF MARYLAND, COLLEGE PARK -
LIBRARIES - ART LIBRARY □ College Park, MD

Shaw, Darline, Circ.
BOEING MILITARY AIRPLANE COMPANY -
LIBRARY □ Wichita, KS

Shaw, Donald C., Libn.
WESTERN NEW YORK GENEALOGICAL
SOCIETY, INC. - LIBRARY □ Hamburg, NY

Shaw, Col. Donald P., Dir.
U.S. ARMY MILITARY HISTORY INSTITUTE □
Carlisle Barracks, PA

Shaw, Elizabeth, Libn.
FLORENCE DEVELOPMENT DIVISION -
RESEARCH AND PLANNING LIBRARY □ Florence,
SC

Shaw, Ena, Med.Ed.
U.S. AIR FORCE - AEROSPACE MEDICAL
DIVISION - SCHOOL OF AEROSPACE MEDICINE
- STRUGHOLD AEROMEDICAL LIBRARY □ Brooks
AFB, TX

Shaw, J. Ned, Libn.
U.S. NAVY - NAVAL UNDERWATER SYSTEMS
CENTER - NEW LONDON TECHNICAL LIBRARY □
New London, CT

Shaw, Jean
BETHESDA HOSPITAL - CHILDBIRTH
EDUCATION LIBRARY† □ Zanesville, OH

Shaw, John Bennett, Owner
BROTHERS THREE OF MORIARTY - LIBRARY □
Santa Fe, NM

Shaw, John T., Lib. Group Supv.
BELL TELEPHONE LABORATORIES, INC. &
WESTERN ELECTRIC, INC. - TECHNICAL
LIBRARY □ Norcross, GA

Shaw, Kerrie, Ref.Libn.
EASTERN VIRGINIA MEDICAL SCHOOL -
MOORMAN MEMORIAL LIBRARY □ Norfolk, VA

Shaw, Mary Nell, Rec.Mgr.
ARKANSAS STATE HISTORY COMMISSION -
ARCHIVES □ Little Rock, AR

Shaw, Meg M.
UNIVERSITY OF KENTUCKY - ART LIBRARY □
Lexington, KY

Shaw, Priscilla B., Libn.
AMERICAN BAPTIST CHURCHES IN THE U.S.A. -
BOARD OF INTERNATIONAL MINISTRIES -
LIBRARY AND CENTRAL FILES □ Valley Forge, PA

Shaw, Rebecca, Circ.Supv.
OHIO NORTHERN UNIVERSITY - HETERICK
MEMORIAL LIBRARY □ Ada, OH

Shaw, Robert, Sr.Libn.
CALIFORNIA STATE DEPARTMENT OF JUSTICE
- ATTORNEY GENERAL'S OFFICE - LAW
LIBRARY □ San Diego, CA

Shaw, Susan, Asst.
SPARTANBURG GENERAL HOSPITAL - HEALTH
SCIENCES LIBRARY □ Spartanburg, SC

Shaw, Vivian, Libn.
JACKSON COUNTY LAW LIBRARY □ Kansas City,
MO

Shawcross, William H., Mgr. of Serv.
DECISIONS AND DESIGNS, INC. - LIBRARY □
McLean, VA

Shay, Lynn Rebbeor, Cur.
COLE COUNTY HISTORICAL SOCIETY -
MUSEUM AND LIBRARY □ Jefferson City, MO

Shaye, Marc K., General Counsel
SPILL CONTROL ASSOCIATION OF AMERICA -
LIBRARY □ Southfield, MI

Shayne, Mette, Francophone Africa
NORTHWESTERN UNIVERSITY - MELVILLE J.
HERSKOVITS LIBRARY OF AFRICAN STUDIES □
Evanston, IL

Shea, John D., Libn.
UNION BANK - LIBRARY □ Los Angeles, CA

Shea, Larry L., Chf., Lib.Serv.
U.S. VETERANS ADMINISTRATION (OK-
Muskogee) - MEDICAL CENTER LIBRARY □
Muskogee, OK

Shea, Linda Loring, Corp.Libn.
PRIME COMPUTER, INC. - INFORMATION
CENTER □ Framingham, MA

Shea, Mary M., Libn.
MORSE SCHOOL OF BUSINESS - LIBRARY □
Hartford, CT

Shearer, Linda, Dir.
ARTISTS SPACE - COMMITTEE FOR THE
VISUAL ARTS - UNAFFILIATED ARTISTS FILE □
New York, NY

Shearer, Marilyn, Libn.
ST. FRANCIS HOSPITAL - MEDICAL LIBRARY □
Santa Barbara, CA

Shearer, Susan, Info.Serv.Coord.
NATIONAL TRUST FOR HISTORIC
PRESERVATION - INFORMATION SERVICES □
Washington, DC

Shearin, Malcolm, Dir., Media Prod.
WAYNE COMMUNITY COLLEGE - LEARNING
RESOURCE CENTER □ Goldsboro, NC

Sheaves, David, Info.Serv.Coord.
UNIVERSITY OF NORTH CAROLINA, CHAPEL
HILL - CENTER FOR EARLY ADOLESCENCE -
INFORMATION SERVICES DIVISION □ Carrboro,
NC

Sheaves, Miriam, Dept.Libn.
UNIVERSITY OF NORTH CAROLINA, CHAPEL
HILL - GEOLOGY LIBRARY □ Chapel Hill, NC

Shedlarz, Ellen, Supv., Ref.Serv.
MC KINSEY & COMPANY, INC. - INFORMATION
SERVICES □ New York, NY

Shedlock, James, Doc. Delivery Libn.
WAYNE STATE UNIVERSITY - SCHOOL OF
MEDICINE - VERA PARSHALL SHIFFMAN
MEDICAL LIBRARY □ Detroit, MI

Shedlock, Mary L., Asst. to Res.Dir.
NEW YORK STATE ARCHEOLOGICAL
ASSOCIATION - LIBRARY □ Rochester, NY

Sheehan, Catherine, Ref.Libn.
MEMORIAL UNIVERSITY OF NEWFOUNDLAND -
HEALTH SCIENCES LIBRARY □ St. John's, NF

Sheehan, Joseph J., Archv.
U.S. NATL. ARCHIVES & RECORDS SERVICE -
FEDERAL ARCHIVES AND RECORDS CENTER,
REGION 3 □ Philadelphia, PA

Sheehan, Kathryn, Corp.Libn.
KEARNEY (A.T.), INC. - INFORMATION CENTER
□ Chicago, IL

Sheehan, Mary H., Libn.
MONSANTO PLASTICS & RESINS COMPANY -
RESINS DIVISION - TECHNOLOGY LIBRARY □
Indian Orchard, MA

Sheehan, Robert C., Sr. Principal Libn.
NEW YORK PUBLIC LIBRARY - MID-
MANHATTAN LIBRARY - HISTORY AND SOCIAL
SCIENCES DEPARTMENT □ New York, NY

Sheehan, William J., C.S.B., Asst.Libn.
WOODSTOCK THEOLOGICAL CENTER -
LIBRARY □ Washington, DC

Sheeley, Christine, Asst.Libn.
CHILTON COMPANY - MARKETING &
ADVERTISING INFORMATION CENTER □
Radnor, PA

Sheets, Elizabeth, Libn.
IOWA STATE COMMISSION FOR THE BLIND -
LIBRARY FOR THE BLIND & PHYSICALLY
HANDICAPPED □ Des Moines, IA

Sheets, Michael, Dir., Med.Lib.
ST. JOSEPH'S HOSPITAL - MEDICAL LIBRARY □
Fort Wayne, IN

Shefrin, Jill, Libn.
TORONTO PUBLIC LIBRARY - CANADIANA
COLLECTION OF CHILDREN'S BOOKS □ Toronto,
ON

Shefrin, Jill, Libn.
TORONTO PUBLIC LIBRARY - LILLIAN H. SMITH
COLLECTION OF CHILDREN'S BOOKS □ Toronto,
ON

Shefrin, Jill, Libn.
TORONTO PUBLIC LIBRARY - OSBORNE
COLLECTION OF EARLY CHILDREN'S BOOKS □
Toronto, ON

Sheible, Doris, Tech.Serv.Libn.
U.S. ARMY POST - FORT CARSON - LIBRARY □
Ft. Carson, CO

Sheil, Sr. Joan, Dir., Lib.Serv.
MARYCREST COLLEGE - CONE LIBRARY† □
Davenport, IA

Shekha, Sharon, Search Anl.
UNIVERSITY OF TEXAS HEALTH SCIENCE
CENTER, DALLAS - LIBRARY □ Dallas, TX

Shelar, James W., Libn.
ARNOLD AND PORTER - LIBRARY □ Washington,
DC

Shelden, Patricia, Hd.
UNIVERSITY OF HAWAII - PUBLIC SERVICES -
GOVERNMENT DOCUMENTS, MAPS &
MICROFORMS □ Honolulu, HI

Sheldon, Judy, Tech.Asst.
CALIFORNIA HISTORICAL SOCIETY -
SCHUBERT HALL LIBRARY □ San Francisco, CA

Sheldon, Kathleen, Libn.
METROPOLITAN MUSEUM OF ART -
PHOTOGRAPH AND SLIDE LIBRARY □ New York,
NY

Shelkrot, Elliot L., State Libn.
PENNSYLVANIA STATE LIBRARY □ Harrisburg,
PA

Shell, E.W., Dept.Hd.
AUBURN UNIVERSITY - INTERNATIONAL
CENTER FOR AQUACULTURE - LIBRARY □
Auburn University, AL

Shelley, Dr. Harry S., Honor.Cur.
VANDERBILT UNIVERSITY - MEDICAL CENTER
LIBRARY □ Nashville, TN

Shellhamer, Patricia, Asst.Libn.
SCHUYLKILL COUNTY LAW LIBRARY □ Pottsville,
PA

Shellhammer, Karen, Educ.Coord.
TRITON MUSEUM OF ART - LIBRARY □ Santa
Clara, CA

Shelstad, Kirsten R., Lib.Dir.
MEDICAL ASSOCIATES - HEALTH CENTER -
LIBRARY □ Menomonee Falls, WI

Shelton, Gayle C., Jr., Dir.
U.S. DEPT. OF COMMERCE - INTERNATIONAL
TRADE ADMINISTRATION - BIRMINGHAM
DISTRICT OFFICE LIBRARY □ Birmingham, AL

Shelton, J. Walter, Assoc.Libn., Tech.Serv
CRERAR (John) LIBRARY □ Chicago, IL

Shelton, Kathryn H., Libn.
ALASKA STATE LEGISLATURE/LEGISLATIVE
AFFAIRS AGENCY - REFERENCE LIBRARY □
Juneau, AK

Shelton, Lois, Dir.
UNIVERSITY OF ARIZONA - POETRY CENTER □
Tucson, AZ

Shelton, Pamela, Cat.
U.S. ARMY POST - FORT HOOD - MSA DIVISION
- CASEY MEMORIAL LIBRARY □ Ft. Hood, TX

Shelton, Peggy, Chf.Libn.
TELEDYNE BROWN ENGINEERING - TECHNICAL
LIBRARY □ Huntsville, AL

Shen, C.T., Pres./Libn.
INSTITUTE FOR ADVANCED STUDIES OF
WORLD RELIGIONS - LIBRARY □ Stony Brook,
NY

Shen, Chung-Tai, Chf.Libn.
TRANSPORTATION INSTITUTE - LIBRARY □
Washington, DC

Sheng, Jack T., Law Libn.
DUVAL COUNTY LAW LIBRARY □ Jacksonville, FL

Sheng, Katherine, Ref.Libn.
TEACHERS COLLEGE - LIBRARY □ New York, NY

Shepard, Eve, Info.Coord.
NATIONAL SCHOOL BOARDS ASSOCIATION -
RESOURCE CENTER □ Washington, DC

Shepard, Mrs. Finley, Cur.
CASTLETON HISTORICAL SOCIETY - MUSEUM
LIBRARY □ Castleton, VT

Shepard, Kevin, Dir.
CINCINNATI CITY PLANNING COMMISSION -
PLANNING AND MANAGEMENT SUPPORT
SYSTEM LIBRARY □ Cincinnati, OH

Shepard, Martha L., Libn.
U.S. DEPT. OF THE INTERIOR - ALASKA
RESOURCES LIBRARY □ Anchorage, AK

Shepard, Samuel P., Libn.
U.S. BUREAU OF MINES - CHARLES W.
HENDERSON MEMORIAL LIBRARY □ Denver, CO

Shephard-Lupo, Pamela, Lib.Mgr.
ENERGY RESOURCES COMPANY - TECHNICAL
INFORMATION CENTER □ Cambridge, MA

Shepherd, G. Frederick, Dir.
GEOLOGICAL INFORMATION LIBRARY OF
DALLAS (GILD) - □ Dallas, TX

Shepherd, Murray C., Univ.Libn.
UNIVERSITY OF WATERLOO - DANA PORTER
ARTS LIBRARY □ Waterloo, ON

Shepherd, Rae, Cat.Libn.
SUNY - COLLEGE AT CORTLAND - MEMORIAL
LIBRARY □ Cortland, NY

Shepherd, Raymond V., Jr., Adm.
CLIVEDEN - LIBRARY □ Philadelphia, PA

Shepherd, Suzanne, Bk.Cat.
U.S. BUREAU OF RECLAMATION - LIBRARY □
Denver, CO

Shepp, Lawrence R.
FITZGERALD, ABBOTT AND BEARDSLEY - LAW
LIBRARY □ Oakland, CA

Shere, Ken, U.S. Gen.Mgr.
NATIONAL FILM BOARD OF CANADA - FILM
LIBRARY □ New York, NY

Sheridan, Alice J., Dir.
FAIRFAX HOSPITAL - JACOB D. ZYLMAN
MEMORIAL LIBRARY □ Falls Church, VA

Sheridan, Connie, Supv., Tech.Proc.
UNIVERSITY OF CALIFORNIA - LOS ALAMOS
NATIONAL LABORATORY - LIBRARY □ Los
Alamos, NM

Sheridan, Helen, Hd.Libn.
KALAMAZOO INSTITUTE OF ARTS - ART
CENTER LIBRARY □ Kalamazoo, MI

Sherlock, Al, Chf., Tech.Info.Ctr.
U.S. ARMY - ENGINEER WATERWAYS
EXPERIMENT STATION - TECHNICAL
INFORMATION CENTER □ Vicksburg, MS

Sherman, Andrea, Hd./Media Consortium
CORNELL UNIVERSITY - MEDICAL COLLEGE -
LIBRARY □ New York, NY

Sherman, C. Neil, Dir.
U.S. DEPT. OF ENERGY - LIBRARY □ Washington,
DC

Sherman, Dorothy N., Libn.
PHILADELPHIA ELECTRIC COMPANY - LIBRARY
□ Philadelphia, PA

Sherman, Dottie, Info./Rec.Dir.
AMERICAN NUCLEAR INSURERS -
INFORMATION RECORDS CENTER □ Farmington,
CT

Sherman, Ellen, Asst.Libn.
BECHTEL - CENTRAL LIBRARY □ San Francisco,
CA

Sherman, Iva Jean, Dir.
ST. LUCIE COUNTY HISTORICAL MUSEUM -
LIBRARY □ Fort Pierce, FL

Sherman, James G., Lib.Dir.
SAN FERNANDO VALLEY COLLEGE OF LAW -
LAW LIBRARY □ Sepulveda, CA

Sherman, Janice, Asst.Libn.
AMERICAN AUTOMOBILE ASSOCIATION -
LIBRARY □ Falls Church, VA

Sherman, Judith Jones, Asst.Libn.
LOS ANGELES COUNTY MUSEUM OF ART -
RESEARCH LIBRARY □ Los Angeles, CA

Sherman, Marion, Libn.
ST. LOUIS CONSERVATORY OF MUSIC AND
SCHOOLS FOR THE ARTS - MAE M. WHITAKER
LIBRARY □ St. Louis, MO

Sherman, Paul T., Adm.Serv.
CUNY - NEW YORK CITY TECHNICAL COLLEGE
LIBRARY/LEARNING RESOURCE CENTER □
Brooklyn, NY

Sherman, Robert, Acq.Libn.
UNIVERSITY OF PITTSBURGH - FALK LIBRARY
OF THE HEALTH SCIENCES □ Pittsburgh, PA

Sherman, William F., Weekend Libn.
ILLINOIS BENEDICTINE COLLEGE - THEODORE
LOWNIK LIBRARY □ Lisle, IL

Sherr, Janet M., Group Ldr.
BIOSCIENCES INFORMATION SERVICE -
BIOLOGICAL ABSTRACTS - LIBRARY □
Philadelphia, PA

Sherr, Merrill F., Hd.Libn.
NEW YORK POST - LIBRARY □ New York, NY

Sherr, Mrs. Rubby, Soc.Sci.Libn.
INSTITUTE FOR ADVANCED STUDY -
LIBRARIES □ Princeton, NJ

Sherrard, Mary Alice, Libn.
MEMORIAL HOSPITAL OF MARTINSVILLE -
MEDICAL LIBRARY □ Martinsville, VA

Sherrill, Nancy, Genealogist
VIGO COUNTY PUBLIC LIBRARY - SPECIAL
COLLECTIONS □ Terre Haute, IN

Sherry, Joseph E., Libn.
VINELAND HISTORICAL AND ANTIQUARIAN
SOCIETY - LIBRARY □ Vineland, NJ

Sherson, Elizabeth, Med.Libn.
HOSPITAL OF THE GOOD SAMARITAN -
MEDICAL LIBRARY □ Los Angeles, CA

Shervey, George M., Pres.
GRANT COUNTY HISTORICAL SOCIETY -
LIBRARY □ Elbow Lake, MN

Sherwin, Dr. Charles, AV Libn.
THIRD BAPTIST CHURCH - LIBRARY □ St. Louis,
MO

Sherwin, Rosalie, Tech.Serv.Libn.
UNIVERSITY OF BALTIMORE - LAW LIBRARY □
Baltimore, MD

Sherwood, Betty, Libn.
BUTTERWORTH HOSPITAL - SCHOOL OF
NURSING LIBRARY† □ Grand Rapids, MI

Sherwood, Betty, ILL Libn./Biblog.
U.S. NASA - AMES RESEARCH CENTER -
LIBRARY □ Mountain View, CA

Sherwood, Gertrude, Info.Spec.
U.S. NATL. BUREAU OF STANDARDS - OFFICE
OF STANDARD REFERENCE DATA - REFERENCE
CENTER □ Washington, DC

Sherwood, Larry, Exec.Dir.
NEW ENGLAND SOLAR ENERGY ASSOCIATION -
LIBRARY □ Brattleboro, VT

Sherwood, Mildred K., Libn.
SEATTLE WEAVERS' GUILD - LIBRARY □
Seattle, WA

Sherwood, William F., Systems Anl.
UNIVERSITY OF TEXAS MEDICAL BRANCH -
MOODY MEDICAL LIBRARY ◻ Galveston, TX

Shetron, Stephen, Sr.Res.Sci.
MICHIGAN TECHNOLOGICAL UNIVERSITY -
FORD FORESTRY CENTER - LIBRARY ◻ L'Anse,
MI

Shevack, Hilda N., Logistics/Data Mgr.
GENERAL INSTRUMENT CORPORATION,
GOVERNMENT SYSTEMS DIVISION -
ENGINEERING LIBRARY ◻ Hicksville, NY

Sheviak, Jean K., Ser.Libn.
RENSSELAER POLYTECHNIC INSTITUTE -
FOLSOM LIBRARY ◻ Troy, NY

Shew, Anita K., Law Libn.
BUTLER COUNTY LAW LIBRARY ASSOCIATION
◻ Hamilton, OH

Shew, Anne, Med.Libn.
DAVIES (Ralph K.) MEDICAL CENTER -
FRANKLIN HOSPITAL MEDICAL LIBRARY ◻ San
Francisco, CA

Shewan, Elizabeth, Libn.
CANADIAN PRESS - LIBRARY ◻ Toronto, ON

Sheward, Helen C., Libn.
KAISER-PERMANENTE MEDICAL CENTER -
MEDICAL LIBRARY ◻ Oakland, CA

Shewbridge, Anna M., Libn.
OLD CHARLES TOWN LIBRARY, INC. ◻ Charles
Town, WV

Shewell, Margaret, Libn.
PINELLAS COUNTY LAW LIBRARY -
CLEARWATER BRANCH ◻ Clearwater, FL

Sheynin, Prof. Hayim Y., Lib.Dir.
DROPSIE UNIVERSITY - LIBRARY ◻ Philadelphia,
PA

Shiah, Aliena, Cat.
WIDENER UNIVERSITY - WOLFGRAM
MEMORIAL LIBRARY ◻ Chester, PA

Shibla, Julia B., Asst.V.P./ Hd.Libn.
FIRST BOSTON CORPORATION - LIBRARY ◻
New York, NY

Shieh, Monica, Res.Libn.
WASHINGTON UNIVERSITY - COMPUTER
LABORATORIES REFERENCE ROOM ◻ St. Louis,
MO

Shields, Andrew T., Lib.Coord.
SOUTHERN CALIFORNIA SOCIETY FOR
PSYCHICAL RESEARCH, INC. - LIBRARY ◻ Los
Angeles, CA

Shields, Brigid, Newspaper Ref.Libn.
MINNESOTA HISTORICAL SOCIETY -
REFERENCE LIBRARY ◻ St. Paul, MN

Shields, Caryl L., ILL Libn.
U.S. GEOLOGICAL SURVEY - DENVER LIBRARY ◻
Denver, CO

Shields, Ingrid, Archv.
GEORGIA STATE SURVEYOR GENERAL
DEPARTMENT - ARCHIVES ◻ Atlanta, GA

shields, larry, Exec.Dir.
NATIONAL RAILROAD CONSTRUCTION AND
MAINTENANCE ASSOCIATION, INC. -
TECHNICAL REFERENCE LIBRARY ◻ Highland, IN

Shields, Sr. M. Jean Ellen, BVM, Hd.Libn.
DON BOSCO TECHNICAL INSTITUTE - LEE
LIBRARY ◻ Rosemead, CA

Shields, Sarah, Cur.
VALENTINE MUSEUM - LIBRARY ◻ Richmond, VA

Shields, Valerie, Ref.Libn.
SACRED HEART UNIVERSITY - LIBRARY ◻
Bridgeport, CT

Shields, Velma, Libn.
UNDERWOOD, NEUHAUS & COMPANY INC. -
CORPORATE FINANCE DEPARTMENT - LIBRARY
◻ Houston, TX

Shiff, Linda Solomon, Libn.
CANADIAN NURSES ASSOCIATION - HELEN K.
MUSSALLEM LIBRARY ◻ Ottawa, ON

Shiff, Robert A., Pres.
NATIONAL RECORDS MANAGEMENT COUNCIL -
LIBRARY ◻ New York, NY

Shiffler, Mrs. Harrold, Libn.
FIRST PRESBYTERIAN CHURCH - LIBRARY ◻
Hastings, NE

Shiflet, Robert J., Exec. V.P.
PALOMINO HORSE BREEDERS OF AMERICA -
LIBRARY ◻ Mineral Wells, TX

Shifrin, Judy, Chf., Lib.Serv.
U.S. FEDERAL AVIATION ADMINISTRATION -
CENTRAL REGION LIBRARY ◻ Kansas City, MO

Shih, Maria, Supv., Res./Ref.
EG&G, INC. - WASHINGTON ANALYTICAL
SERVICES CENTER - INFORMATION CENTER ◻
Rockville, MD

Shilts, Dorothy, Libn.
WICHITA SCOUTING CO-OP, INC. - OIL
INFORMATION LIBRARY ◻ Wichita Falls, TX

Shimek, Ursula, Sr.Libn.
IBM CORPORATION - INFORMATION CENTER/
LIBRARY ◻ Rochester, MN

Shimomura, Mariko, Asst. Japanese Sect.
PRINCETON UNIVERSITY - GEST ORIENTAL
LIBRARY AND EAST ASIAN COLLECTIONS ◻
Princeton, NJ

Shin, Sun, Rd.Adv.
DISTRICT OF COLUMBIA PUBLIC LIBRARY -
BUSINESS, ECONOMICS & VOCATIONS
DIVISION ◻ Washington, DC

Shinbaum, Myrna, Assoc.Dir.
NATIONAL CONFERENCE ON SOVIET JEWRY
(NCSJ) - RESEARCH BUREAU ◻ New York, NY

Shiner, Gail, Sci. Correspondent
TRACOR JITCO, INC. - RESEARCH RESOURCES
INFORMATION CENTER ◻ Rockville, MD

Shiner, Sharon L., Libn.
INGERSOLL-RAND COMPANY - TECHNICAL
LIBRARY ◻ Phillipsburg, NJ

Shiotani, Nancy, Hd.Cat.Libn.
STANFORD UNIVERSITY - LANE MEDICAL
LIBRARY ◻ Stanford, CA

Shipe, Belle B., Libn.
BARNES ENGINEERING COMPANY - LIBRARY ◻
Stamford, CT

Shipley, Mary K., Staff Sec.
WARREN HOSPITAL - MEDICAL LIBRARY ◻
Phillipsburg, NJ

Shipley, Sally
AMOCO PRODUCTION COMPANY - LAW
DEPARTMENT LIBRARY ◻ Tulsa, OK

Shipman, Barbara L., ILL Hd.
UNIVERSITY OF MICHIGAN - ALFRED TAUBMAN
MEDICAL LIBRARY ◻ Ann Arbor, MI

Shipman, John, Tech.Res.
ONTARIO - MINISTRY OF CULTURE AND
RECREATION - PLANNING AND TECHNICAL
SERVICES ◻ Toronto, ON

Shipman, Patricia E., Hd.Libn.
CAROLINA POPULATION CENTER - LIBRARY ◻
Chapel Hill, NC

Shiramizu, Mary K., Libn.
ST. BENEDICT'S HOSPITAL - HEALTH
SCIENCES LIBRARY ◻ Ogden, UT

Shirato, Linda, Ref.Libn.
WASHTENAW COMMUNITY COLLEGE -
LEARNING RESOURCE CENTER ◻ Ann Arbor, MI

Shireman, Lydia, Libn.
OAKLAND PUBLIC LIBRARY - HANDICAPPED
SERVICES ◻ Oakland, CA

Shirk, Gertrude F., Ed.
FOUNDATION FOR THE STUDY OF CYCLES INC.
- LIBRARY ◻ Pittsburgh, PA

Shirk, Virginia R., Libn.
MINNESOTA GAS COMPANY - LIBRARY ◻
Minneapolis, MN

Shirley, Eileen P., Libn.
PARK RIDGE HOSPITAL - MEDICAL LIBRARY ◻
Rochester, NY

Shirley, Sherrilynne, Assoc.Dir.
UNIVERSITY OF SOUTHERN CALIFORNIA -
HEALTH SCIENCES CAMPUS - NORRIS MEDICAL
LIBRARY ◻ Los Angeles, CA

Shively, Daniel, Asst.Libn.
INDIANA UNIVERSITY OF PENNSYLVANIA -
UNIVERSITY LIBRARY ◻ Indiana, PA

Shively, John R., Pres.
JAPANESE-AMERICAN SOCIETY FOR
PHILATELY - LIBRARY ◻ El Cerrito, CA

Shlapak, Irene, Hd.Libn.
ONTARIO - MINISTRY OF COMMUNITY AND
SOCIAL SERVICES - MINISTRY LIBRARY† ◻
Toronto, ON

Shoaf, Patricia, Libn.
WILMINGTON STAR-NEWS NEWSPAPERS, INC.
- LIBRARY ◻ Wilmington, NC

Shocket, Phyllis B., ILL/Ref.
U.S. FEDERAL COMMUNICATIONS
COMMISSION - LIBRARY ◻ Washington, DC

Shockley, Ann Allen, Assoc.Libn./Archv.
FISK UNIVERSITY - SPECIAL COLLECTIONS
DEPARTMENT ◻ Nashville, TN

Shoemaker, Betty G., Church Libn.
FIRST CHRISTIAN REFORMED CHURCH -
LIBRARY ◻ Zeeland, MI

Shoemaker, Edward C., Tech.Serv.Libn.
OKLAHOMA HISTORICAL SOCIETY - DIVISION
OF LIBRARY RESOURCES ◻ Oklahoma City, OK

Shoengold, Nathan, Ref.Libn.
QUEENS BOROUGH PUBLIC LIBRARY - SOCIAL
SCIENCES DIVISION ◻ Jamaica, NY

Shoens, Claire, Oper.Mgr.
STANFORD UNIVERSITY - FALCONER BIOLOGY
LIBRARY ◻ Stanford, CA

Shoettger, Dr. Richard, Dir.
U.S. FISH & WILDLIFE SERVICE - COLUMBIA
NATIONAL FISHERIES RESEARCH LABORATORY
LIBRARY ◻ Columbia, MO

Shofner, Nancy S., Asst.Dir.
SOUTHERN TECHNICAL INSTITUTE - LIBRARY
◻ Marietta, GA

Sholtz, Katherine J., Dir. of Lib.Serv.
WESTERN CONNECTICUT STATE COLLEGE -
RUTH A. HAAS LIBRARY ◻ Danbury, CT

Shong, Glenn, Media Spec.
MENDOTA MENTAL HEALTH INSTITUTE -
LIBRARY MEDIA CENTER ◻ Madison, WI

Shong, Joy, Libn.
ST. FRANCIS HOSPITAL - HEALTH SCIENCE
LEARNING CENTER ◻ Milwaukee, WI

Shoniker, Rev. Fintan R., O.S.B., Dir.
ST. VINCENT COLLEGE AND ARCHABBEY -
LIBRARY ◻ Latrobe, PA

Shonkwiler, Paula, Libn.
ROCKY MOUNTAIN NEWS - LIBRARY ◻ Denver,
CO

Shonn, Eleanor, Med.Libn.
OHIO VALLEY MEDICAL CENTER - HUPP
MEDICAL LIBRARY† ◻ Wheeling, WV

Shook, Constance R., Hd.Libn.
DELAWARE VALLEY COLLEGE OF SCIENCE AND
AGRICULTURE - JOSEPH KRAUSKOPF
MEMORIAL LIBRARY ◻ Doylestown, PA

Shook, Dr. R.W., Dir.
VICTORIA COLLEGE - LIBRARY - TEXAS AND
LOCAL HISTORY COLLECTION ◻ Victoria, TX

Shopland, Donald R., Tech.Info.Off.
OFFICE ON SMOKING AND HEALTH -
TECHNICAL INFORMATION CENTER ◻ Rockville,
MD

Shore, Jenafred J., Libn.
NATIONAL WILDLIFE FEDERATION - FRAZIER
MEMORIAL LIBRARY ◻ Washington, DC

Shore, June, Libn.
MOHAWK COLLEGE OF APPLIED ARTS AND
TECHNOLOGY - HEALTH SCIENCES LIBRARY
RESOURCE CENTRE ◻ Hamilton, ON

Shore, June, Health Sci.Libn.
MOHAWK COLLEGE OF APPLIED ARTS AND
TECHNOLOGY - MOHAWK LIBRARY RESOURCE
CENTRE ◻ Hamilton, ON

Shore, Meta, Libn.
WELD COUNTY GENERAL HOSPITAL - STAFF
LIBRARY ◻ Greeley, CO

Shore, Michael S., Info.Spec.
RESEARCH FOR BETTER SCHOOLS, INC. -
RESOURCE CENTER ◻ Philadelphia, PA

Shore, Philip, Assoc.Libn.
EARLHAM COLLEGE - QUAKER COLLECTION ◻
Richmond, IN

Shores, Cecelia, Hd.Acq.Libn.
CENTER FOR RESEARCH LIBRARIES □ Chicago, IL

Shorr, Marilyn S., Assoc.Dir.
ERIC CLEARINGHOUSE ON HIGHER EDUCATION □ Washington, DC

Short, B.A., Libn.
EXXON RESEARCH AND ENGINEERING COMPANY - FLORHAM PARK INFORMATION CENTER† □ Florham Park, NJ

Short, Janet, Cat.
BISHOP (Bernice P.) MUSEUM - LIBRARY □ Honolulu, HI

Short, Linda K., Libn.
MAC FARLANE & COMPANY, INC. - FRY CONSULTANTS INCORPORATED - MANAGEMENT CENTRE □ Atlanta, GA

Short, Sylvia, State Libn.
DELAWARE STATE - DIVISION OF LIBRARIES □ Dover, DE

Shorthouse, Thomas J., Law Libn.
UNIVERSITY OF BRITISH COLUMBIA - LAW LIBRARY □ Vancouver, BC

Shortt, Mary, Chf.Libn.
UNIVERSITY OF TORONTO - FACULTY OF EDUCATION LIBRARY □ Toronto, ON

Shoup, Mary Agnes, Asst.Libn.
UNIVERSITY OF DETROIT - SCHOOL OF DENTISTRY LIBRARY □ Detroit, MI

Shoupe, Louisa M., Libn.
PACIFIC GAS AND ELECTRIC COMPANY - LIBRARY □ San Francisco, CA

Showalter, Esther, Co-Chm.
LUTHERAN CHURCH LIBRARY ASSOCIATION - BETHLEHEM LUTHERAN LIBRARY □ Aberdeen, SD

Showalter, Grace, Libn.
EASTERN MENNONITE COLLEGE - MENNO SIMONS HISTORICAL LIBRARY AND ARCHIVES □ Harrisonburg, VA

Showalter, J. Gordan, Physicist
U.S. NAVY - NAVAL RESEARCH LABORATORY - SHOCK AND VIBRATION INFORMATION CENTER □ Washington, DC

Showalter, Dr. Victor M., Dir.
FEDERATION FOR UNIFIED SCIENCE EDUCATION - FUSE CENTER LIBRARY† □ Columbus, OH

Shrader, Bette, Libn.
OMAHA WORLD-HERALD - LIBRARY □ Omaha, NE

Shrader, Richard A., Ref.Archv.
UNIVERSITY OF NORTH CAROLINA, CHAPEL HILL - SOUTHERN HISTORICAL COLLECTION & MANUSCRIPTS DEPARTMENT □ Chapel Hill, NC

Shrader, Steve, District Ranger
U.S. NATL. PARK SERVICE - COULEE DAM NATL. RECREATION AREA - FORT SPOKANE VISITOR CENTER □ Davenport, WA

Shriver, Rosalia, Prof.Asst.
ENOCH PRATT FREE LIBRARY - FINE ARTS AND RECREATION DEPARTMENT □ Baltimore, MD

Shriver, Stanley L., Dir.
OHIO STATE DEPARTMENT OF TAXATION - RESEARCH AND STATISTICS LIBRARY □ Columbus, OH

Shroder, Emelie, Division Chief
CHICAGO PUBLIC LIBRARY CENTRAL LIBRARY - BUSINESS/SCIENCE/TECHNOLOGY DIVISION □ Chicago, IL

Shub, Bertha J., Libn.
NORTH CHARLES GENERAL HOSPITAL - MEDICAL STAFF LIBRARY □ Baltimore, MD

Shubert, Joseph F., Asst.Commnr.
NEW YORK STATE LIBRARY □ Albany, NY

Shubnell, Penny, Tech.Libn.
DENNY'S INC. - COMPUTER SERVICES LIBRARY □ La Mirada, CA

Shulman, Frank Joseph, Libn.
UNIVERSITY OF MARYLAND, COLLEGE PARK - LIBRARIES - EAST ASIA COLLECTION □ College Park, MD

Shulman, Tikvah S., Libn.
PROVIDENT MUTUAL LIFE INSURANCE COMPANY OF PHILADELPHIA - LIBRARY □ Philadelphia, PA

Shultes, Dorothea, Hosp.Libn.
CROUSE-IRVING MEMORIAL HOSPITAL - LIBRARY □ Syracuse, NY

Shults, Linda, Libn.
TENNECO, INC. - CORPORATE LIBRARY □ Houston, TX

Shultz, Barbara, First Asst.
MEMPHIS-SHELBY COUNTY PUBLIC LIBRARY AND INFO. CTR. - SCIENCE/BUSINESS/SOCIAL SCIENCES DEPT. □ Memphis, TN

Shultz, Suzanne M., Libn.
POLYCLINIC MEDICAL CENTER - MEDICAL STAFF LIBRARY □ Harrisburg, PA

Shumake, Nora Lee, Tech.Serv.Libn.
UNIVERSITY OF DETROIT - SCHOOL OF DENTISTRY LIBRARY □ Detroit, MI

Shumaker, David, Ref.Libn.
MITRE CORPORATION - LIBRARY □ McLean, VA

Shumaker, Donna, Br.Libn.
SQUIRE, SANDERS & DEMPSEY - LAW LIBRARY □ Cleveland, OH

Shuman, Kristen, Sr. Music Libn.
NEW YORK PUBLIC LIBRARY - GENERAL LIBRARY OF THE PERFORMING ARTS □ New York, NY

Shung, Lily, Tech.Libn.
ROCHESTER INSTITUTE OF TECHNOLOGY - TECHNICAL & EDUCATION CENTER FOR THE GRAPHIC ARTS - GRAPHIC ARTS INFO.SERV. □ Rochester, NY

Shupe, Barbara A., Libn.
SUNY AT STONY BROOK - MAP LIBRARY □ Stony Brook, NY

Shuster, Helen, Hd., Tech.Serv.
WORCESTER POLYTECHNIC INSTITUTE - GEORGE C. GORDON LIBRARY □ Worcester, MA

Shuster, Susanna, Mgr., Search & Ret.
DOCUMENTATION ASSOCIATES† □ Los Angeles, CA

Shute, Rev. Daniel, Libn.
PRESBYTERIAN COLLEGE - LIBRARY □ Montreal, PQ

Shutt, Philip L., Registrar/Historiographer
PROTESTANT EPISCOPAL CHURCH - EPISCOPAL DIOCESE OF SPRINGFIELD, ILLINOIS - DIOCESAN CENTER LIBRARY □ Springfield, IL

Shutt, Thelma, Asst.Libn.
U.S. ARMY ADMINISTRATION CENTER - MAIN LIBRARY □ Ft. Benjamin Harrison, IN

Shutzer, Carole B., Libn.
HELIX TECHNOLOGY CORPORATION - LIBRARY □ Waltham, MA

Shy, Arlene P., Mss.Libn.
UNIVERSITY OF MICHIGAN - WILLIAM L. CLEMENTS LIBRARY □ Ann Arbor, MI

Siarny, William D., Jr., Dir.
NATIONAL LIVESTOCK AND MEAT BOARD - MEAT INDUSTRY INFORMATION CENTER □ Chicago, IL

Sibbett, Diane, Libn.
CANADIAN EDUCATION ASSOCIATION - LIBRARY □ Toronto, ON

Sibia, Tejinder S., Hd., Biol./Agri.Sci.
UNIVERSITY OF CALIFORNIA, DAVIS - GENERAL LIBRARY □ Davis, CA

Sibley, Anna Margaret, Libn.
YUMA COUNTY LAW LIBRARY □ Yuma, AZ

Sibley, Marjorie H., Ref.Libn.
AUGSBURG COLLEGE - GEORGE SVERDRUP LIBRARY AND MEDIA CENTER □ Minneapolis, MN

Sichel, Beatrice, Hd.Libn.
WESTERN MICHIGAN UNIVERSITY - PHYSICAL SCIENCES LIBRARY □ Kalamazoo, MI

Sickels, Merylin, Med.Rec.Libn.
ST. JOSEPH HOSPITAL - MEDICAL STAFF LIBRARY □ St. Joseph, MO

Sickels, Steven N., Tech.Serv.Libn.
BUENA VISTA COLLEGE - L.E. & E.L. BALLOU LIBRARY □ Storm Lake, IA

Sicking, Mary M., Libn.
CENTRAL INSTITUTE FOR THE DEAF - EDUCATIONAL RESEARCH LIBRARY □ St. Louis, MO

Sickles, Linda, Dir.
NORTH OAKLAND GENEALOGICAL SOCIETY - LIBRARY □ Lake Orion, MI

Sicotte, Evelyne, Indexer
CENTRE DE SERVICES SOCIAUX DU MONTREAL METROPOLITAIN - BIBLIOTHEQUE □ Montreal, PQ

Sidel, Dr. Victor W., Chm.Dept.Soc.Med.
MONTEFIORE HOSPITAL & MEDICAL CENTER - KARL CHERKASKY SOCIAL MEDICINE LIBRARY □ New York, NY

Sideman, Leonard, Libn.
PENNSYLVANIA STATE DEPARTMENT OF HEALTH - BUREAU OF LABORATORIES LIBRARY □ Lionville, PA

Siden, Harriet, Art Libn.
D'ARCY-MAC MANUS AND MASIUS - LIBRARY INFORMATION SERVICES □ Bloomfield Hills, MI

Sider, Dr. E. Morris, Archv.
BRETHREN IN CHRIST CHURCH AND MESSIAH COLLEGE - ARCHIVES □ Grantham, PA

Sidrow, Sigrid, Libn.
MARCHAIS (Jacques) CENTER OF TIBETAN ARTS, INC. - LIBRARY □ Staten Island, NY

Siebecker, Dorothy, Cat.
TUCSON MUSEUM OF ART - LIBRARY □ Tucson, AZ

Sieben, Gloria, Libn.
ST. MARY OF THE LAKE SEMINARY - FEEHAN MEMORIAL LIBRARY □ Mundelein, IL

Sieber, Robert L., Dir.
PENNSYLVANIA FARM MUSEUM OF LANDIS VALLEY - LIBRARY □ Lancaster, PA

Siebert, Mary Kay, Libn.
AMERICAN MEDICAL RECORD ASSOCIATION - FORE LIBRARY† □ Chicago, IL

Siebesma, Marcia K., Cat.
OHIO NORTHERN UNIVERSITY - COLLEGE OF LAW - JAY P. TAGGART MEMORIAL LAW LIBRARY □ Ada, OH

Siebold, Mrs. Leah, Hd., Rd.Serv.
SASKATCHEWAN - PROVINCIAL LIBRARY □ Regina, SK

Siedle, Veronica, Libn.
U.S. FISH & WILDLIFE SERVICE - SCIENCE REFERENCE LIBRARY □ Twin Cities, MN

Siedlecki, Adele A., Libn.
NASSAU COUNTY PLANNING COMMISSION - LIBRARY □ Mineola, NY

Siedschlaw, Betty, Inst.Cons.
SOUTH DAKOTA STATE LIBRARY □ Pierre, SD

Siefert, Donna, Libn.
HANDY ASSOCIATES, INC. - RESEARCH LIBRARY □ New York, NY

Siefred-Stewart, Joan, Asst.
HEWITT ASSOCIATES - LIBRARY □ Lincolnshire, IL

Siegel, Gladys E., Libn.
AMERICAN PETROLEUM INSTITUTE - LIBRARY □ Washington, DC

Siegel, Leonard M., Dir.
PACIFIC STUDIES CENTER - LIBRARY □ Mountain View, CA

Siegel, Shalva, Spec. Subjects Cat.
HEBREW COLLEGE - JACOB AND ROSE GROSSMAN LIBRARY □ Brookline, MA

Siegel, Steven W., Exec.Sec.
JEWISH HISTORICAL SOCIETY OF NEW YORK, INC. - LIBRARY □ New York, NY

Siegfried, Dorothy, Chf.
U.S. AIR FORCE - AERONAUTICAL LABORATORIES - TECHNICAL LIBRARY □ Dayton, OH

Siegler, Sharon, Hd., Pub.Serv.
LEHIGH UNIVERSITY - MART SCIENCE AND ENGINEERING LIBRARY □ Bethlehem, PA

PERSONNEL

Siekevitz, Rebecca, Supv.Libn.
NEW YORK PUBLIC LIBRARY - MID-MANHATTAN LIBRARY - ART LIBRARY □ New York, NY

Siemens, William, Jr., Ref.Libn.
UNIVERSITY OF ALASKA, ANCHORAGE - LIBRARY □ Anchorage, AK

Siemers, Lynne, Libn.
MINNESOTA STATE DEPARTMENT OF HEALTH - ROBERT N. BARR PUBLIC HEALTH LIBRARY □ Minneapolis, MN

Siemsen, David P., Dir., Lib.Serv.
WILLIAMSPORT AREA COMMUNITY COLLEGE - SLOAN FINE ARTS LIBRARY† □ Williamsport, PA

Siena, Sr. Margaret, S.C.N., Asst.Libn.
OUR LADY OF PEACE HOSPITAL - MEDICAL LIBRARY □ Louisville, KY

Siencewicz, Evelyn, Ref.Libn.
FAULKNER HOSPITAL - INGERSOLL BOWDITCH LIBRARY □ Jamaica Plain, MA

Sienda, Madeline, Libn.
SUNDSTRAND DATA CONTROL, INC. - LIBRARY □ Redmond, WA

Siener, William H., Exec.Dir.
WYOMING HISTORICAL AND GEOLOGICAL SOCIETY - BISHOP MEMORIAL LIBRARY □ Wilkes-Barre, PA

Sierecki, Joan J., Corp.Libn.
NESTE, BRUDIN & STONE, INC. - CORPORATE LIBRARY □ San Diego, CA

Sierp, Rev. Dieter G., Lib.Dir.
EPISCOPAL THEOLOGICAL SEMINARY IN KENTUCKY - BROWNING MEMORIAL LIBRARY □ Lexington, KY

Sievan, Lee, Resource Libn.
INTERNATIONAL CENTER OF PHOTOGRAPHY - LIBRARY RESOURCE CENTER □ New York, NY

Siever, Robert A., Asst.Dir.Tech.Serv.
FRANKLIN AND MARSHALL COLLEGE - FACKENTHAL LIBRARY - SPECIAL COLLECTIONS □ Lancaster, PA

Siewers, Iris J., Info.Sci.
UNION CARBIDE CORPORATION - LIBRARY & TECHNICAL INFORMATION SERVICE† □ Tarrytown, NY

Sifford, Harlan, Libn.
UNIVERSITY OF IOWA - ART LIBRARY □ Iowa City, IA

Sifleet, Inez, Libn.
DANA CORPORATION - WEATHERHEAD DIVISION - LIBRARY AND TECHNICAL INFORMATION CENTER □ Cleveland, OH

Sigari, Marie, Cat.
ROCKWELL INTERNATIONAL - ROCKETDYNE DIVISION - TECHNICAL INFORMATION CENTER □ Canoga Park, CA

Sigel, John A.
CALIFORNIA STATE SUPREME COURT LIBRARY† □ San Francisco, CA

Sigerson, Marjorie L., Libn.
MUSEUM OF ARTS AND SCIENCES - BRUCE EVERETT BATES MEMORIAL LIBRARY □ Daytona Beach, FL

Sigman, Paula M., Asst.Archv.
DISNEY (Walt) PRODUCTIONS - ARCHIVES □ Burbank, CA

Siiro, John R., Ref.Libn.
UNIVERSITY OF TENNESSEE - COLLEGE OF LAW LIBRARY □ Knoxville, TN

Sikes, Janice White, Cur.
ATLANTA PUBLIC LIBRARY - SPECIAL COLLECTIONS DEPARTMENT □ Atlanta, GA

Silberman, E., Professor/Dir.
FISK UNIVERSITY - MOLECULAR SPECTROSCOPY RESEARCH LABORATORY - LIBRARY □ Nashville, TN

Silberstein, Roy, Lit. Search
LOCKHEED-CALIFORNIA COMPANY - TECHNICAL INFORMATION CENTER □ Burbank, CA

Siler-Regan, Linda, Asst.Libn.Biblog.Control
GEORGETOWN UNIVERSITY - LAW CENTER LIBRARY □ Washington, DC

Silfen, Esther, Asst.Libn.
CABRINI MEDICAL CENTER - DR. MASSIMO BAZZINI MEMORIAL LIBRARY □ New York, NY

Sillius, Irene, Lib.Techn.
DURACELL INC. - RESEARCH LIBRARY □ Mississauga, ON

Silva, Don, Libn.
SAN DIEGO PUBLIC LIBRARY - HISTORY & WORLD AFFAIRS SECTION □ San Diego, CA

Silva, Mary, Libn.
ARIZONA STATE OFFICE OF ECONOMIC PLANNING AND DEVELOPMENT - RESEARCH LIBRARY □ Phoenix, AZ

Silva, Phyllis Peloquin, Dir.
RHODE ISLAND STATE ARCHIVES □ Providence, RI

Silva, Remedios, Hd.Cat.
SUNY AT BUFFALO - HEALTH SCIENCES LIBRARY □ Buffalo, NY

Silver, Charles, Supv.
MUSEUM OF MODERN ART - FILM STUDY CENTER □ New York, NY

Silver, Helene A., Dept.Hd.
LONG BEACH PUBLIC LIBRARY - LITERATURE AND HISTORY DEPARTMENT† □ Long Beach, CA

Silver, Lyn, Adm.Dir.
BAUDER FASHION COLLEGE - LIBRARY □ Arlington, TX

Silver, Martin, Music Libn.
UNIVERSITY OF CALIFORNIA, SANTA BARBARA - ARTS LIBRARY □ Santa Barbara, CA

Silverman, Elsa, Asst.Libn.
U.S. TAX COURT - LIBRARY □ Washington, DC

Silverman, Helen F., Libn.
ST. LOUIS COLLEGE OF PHARMACY - O.J. CLOUGHLY ALUMNI LIBRARY □ St. Louis, MO

Silverman, Judy, Sr.Info.Spec., Econ.
CONFERENCE BOARD, INC. - INFORMATION SERVICE □ New York, NY

Silverman, Marc, Asst. Law Libn.
UNIVERSITY OF PITTSBURGH - LAW LIBRARY □ Pittsburgh, PA

Silverman, Marion H., Dir.
EINSTEIN (Albert) MEDICAL CENTER - NORTHERN DIVISION - LURIA MEDICAL LIBRARY† □ Philadelphia, PA

Silverman, Susanne, Libn.
RICHARDSON-VICKS, INC. - VICK DIVISIONS RESEARCH & DEVELOPMENT - RESEARCH LIBRARY □ New Rochelle, NY

Silvernail, Barbara, Internatl.Docs.Libn.
UNIVERSITY OF CALIFORNIA, LOS ANGELES - PUBLIC AFFAIRS SERVICE □ Los Angeles, CA

Silvers, P.G., Hd., Lib.Serv.
AMERICAN SCIENCE FICTION ASSOCIATION - ASFA LIBRARY □ Port Neches, TX

Silvestro, Josephine, Libn.
GCA CORPORATION - TECHNOLOGY DIVISION - LIBRARY □ Bedford, MA

Silvin, John S., Dir.
BRISTOL-MYERS COMPANY - BRISTOL LABORATORIES - LIBRARY AND INFORMATION SERVICES □ Syracuse, NY

Silzer, Beth, Dir.
PLAINS HEALTH CENTRE - DR. W.A. RIDDELL HEALTH SCIENCES LIBRARY □ Regina, SK

Sim, J. Derek, Libn.
SHERRITT GORDON MINES, LTD. - RESEARCH CENTRE LIBRARY □ Fort Saskatchewan, AB

Sim, Patrick, Libn.
AMERICAN SOCIETY OF ANESTHESIOLOGISTS - WOOD LIBRARY-MUSEUM OF ANESTHESIOLOGY □ Park Ridge, IL

Simak, Andrew, Hd.Libn.
NEW YORK LAW SCHOOL - LIBRARY □ New York, NY

Simard, Clement-Jacques, Dir.
SEMINAIRE DE CHICOUTIMI - BIBLIOTHEQUE □ Chicoutimi, PQ

Simard, Denis, Dir.
CEGEP DE TROIS-RIVIERES - BIBLIOTHEQUE □ Trois-Rivieres, PQ

Simard, Miss Marjolaine, Archv.
SOCIETE QUEBECOISE D'INITIATIVES PETROLIERES - DOCUMENTATION CENTRE □ Ste. Foy, PQ

Simchovitch, Samuel, Libn.
BETH TZEDEC SYNAGOGUE - CONGREGATIONAL LIBRARY □ Toronto, ON

Simendinger, Anita, Info.Sys.Mgr.
CONSUMER EDUCATION RESOURCE NETWORK (CERN) □ Rosslyn, VA

Simmer, Ronald V., Libn.
LOCKHEED PETROLEUM SERVICES LTD. - ENGINEERING LIBRARY† □ New Westminster, BC

Simmonds, Dr. Richard C., Exec.Sec.
INTERNATIONAL HIBERNATION SOCIETY □ Rockville, MD

Simmons, Bill, Data User Serv.Off.
U.S. BUREAU OF THE CENSUS - REGIONAL DATA USER SERVICE - DETROIT REGIONAL OFFICE - LIBRARY □ Detroit, MI

Simmons, Brian, Med.Libn.
BLODGETT MEMORIAL MEDICAL CENTER - RICHARD ROOT SMITH LIBRARY □ Grand Rapids, MI

Simmons, Camille, Libn.
U.S. NATL. ARCHIVES & RECORDS SERVICE - NATL. ARCHIVES LIBRARY □ Washington, DC

Simmons, Diane, Exec.Sec.
FARMLAND INDUSTRIES, INC. - FARMLAND RESEARCH CENTER & FARMLAND AGRISERVICES □ Hutchinson, KS

Simmons, Donnalee L., Libn.
AUTOMOBILE CLUB OF SOUTHERN CALIFORNIA - HIGHWAY ENGINEERING DEPARTMENT LIBRARY □ Los Angeles, CA

Simmons, GeorJane, Libn.
PANHANDLE EASTERN PIPE LINE COMPANY - TECHNICAL INFORMATION CENTER □ Kansas City, MO

Simmons, Henry, Asst.Cur.
UNIVERSITY OF SOUTHERN MISSISSIPPI - MC CAIN LIBRARY □ Hattiesburg, MS

Simmons, Ida, Mgr. of Commun.
U.S. TRAVEL DATA CENTER - LIBRARY □ Washington, DC

Simmons, Joseph M., Mgr.
TOWERS, PERRIN, FORSTER & CROSBY, INC. - INFORMATION CENTER □ New York, NY

Simmons, Karen Hegge, Chf.Libn.
AMERICAN INSTITUTE OF CERTIFIED PUBLIC ACCOUNTANTS - LIBRARY □ New York, NY

Simmons, Lee, Libn.
AMERICAN PHARMACEUTICAL ASSOCIATION - FOUNDATION LIBRARY □ Washington, DC

Simmons, Robert M., Curric.Libn.
BRIDGEWATER STATE COLLEGE - CLEMENT C. MAXWELL LIBRARY □ Bridgewater, MA

Simmons, Walter T., Ck. of Court
ILLINOIS STATE - APPELLATE COURT, 5TH DISTRICT - LIBRARY† □ Mt. Vernon, IL

Simms, Betty B., Tech.Libn.
UNITED CATALYSTS, INC. - TECHNICAL LIBRARY □ Louisville, KY

Simms, Ruth R., Libn.
GENERAL COMMISSION ON CHAPLAINS AND ARMED FORCES PERSONNEL - CHAPLAINS MEMORIAL LIBRARY □ Washington, DC

Simon, Anabel, Sr.Libn.
BAPTIST HOSPITAL - MEDICAL LIBRARY □ Pensacola, FL

Simon, Andrea, Info.Spec.
FOI SERVICES, INC. - LIBRARY □ Rockville, MD

Simon, Edith, Libn.
AMERICAN CONTRACT BRIDGE LEAGUE - ALBERT H. MOREHEAD MEMORIAL LIBRARY □ Memphis, TN

Simon, Enid, Assoc.Dir.
UNIVERSITY OF WISCONSIN, MADISON - KURT F. WENDT ENGINEERING LIBRARY □ Madison, WI

Simon, Mr. J.L., Hd., Info.Proc.
CANADA - INDUSTRY, TRADE & COMMERCE - LIBRARY □ Ottawa, ON

Simon, Mary K., Libn.
AMERICAN PUBLIC WORKS ASSOCIATION - INFORMATION SERVICE □ Chicago, IL

Simon, Nancy, Med.Libn.
ROSE MEDICAL CENTER - LIBRARY □ Denver, CO

Simon, Paula, Teaching Spec.
UNIVERSITY OF MINNESOTA - CENTER FOR YOUTH DEVELOPMENT AND RESEARCH - RESOURCE ROOM □ St. Paul, MN

Simon, Susan H., Ref.Libn.
U.S. NATL. LABOR RELATIONS BOARD - LAW LIBRARY □ Washington, DC

Simonds, Patricia K., Ref.Libn.
FLORIDA STATE UNIVERSITY - LAW LIBRARY □ Tallahassee, FL

Simonds, Sandra, Director
AMERICAN PSYCHOTHERAPY ASSOCIATION - LIBRARY □ West Palm Beach, FL

Simonetta, Dr. L., Lib.Chm.
WILLIAMS (C.S.) CLINIC - LIBRARY □ Trail, BC

Simonetti, Martha, Assoc.Archv.
PENNSYLVANIA STATE HISTORICAL & MUSEUM COMMISSION - DIVISION OF ARCHIVES AND MANUSCRIPTS □ Harrisburg, PA

Simons, Bennie P., Adm.Asst.
SAM HOUSTON STATE UNIVERSITY - LIBRARY† □ Huntsville, TX

Simons, Eleanor, Libn.
NORTHEASTERN VERMONT REGIONAL HOSPITAL - INFORMATION CENTER/LIBRARY □ St. Johnsbury, VT

Simons, Gordon N., Cur.
PENSACOLA HISTORICAL SOCIETY - LELIA ABERCROMBIE HISTORICAL LIBRARY □ Pensacola, FL

Simons, Mrs. Ute, Med.Libn.
HOAG MEMORIAL HOSPITAL-PRESBYTERIAN - MEDICAL LIBRARY □ Newport Beach, CA

Simor, George, Chf. Book Acq.Libn.
CUNY - GRADUATE SCHOOL AND UNIVERSITY CENTER - LIBRARY □ New York, NY

Simor, Suzanna, Art Libn.
QUEENS COLLEGE OF THE CITY UNIVERSITY OF NEW YORK - PAUL KLAPPER LIBRARY - ART LIBRARY □ Flushing, NY

Simosko, Vladimir, Hd.Sci.Libn.
UNIVERSITY OF MANITOBA - SCIENCE LIBRARY □ Winnipeg, MB

Simpson, Ann W., Asst.Libn.
PIERSON, BALL & DOWD - LAW LIBRARY □ Washington, DC

Simpson, Anne, Cat.
INTERNATIONAL DEVELOPMENT RESEARCH CENTRE - LIBRARY □ Ottawa, ON

Simpson, Carol Robinson, Libn.
NORTH AMERICAN WEATHER CONSULTANTS - TECHNICAL LIBRARY □ Salt Lake City, UT

Simpson, Christine, Libn.
U.S. VETERANS ADMINISTRATION (NC-Salisbury) - HOSPITAL LIBRARY □ Salisbury, NC

Simpson, Donald B., Dir.
CENTER FOR RESEARCH LIBRARIES □ Chicago, IL

Simpson, Evelyn, Med.Libn.
WESTERN MEDICAL CENTER - MEDICAL LIBRARY □ Santa Ana, CA

Simpson, Heidi, Libn.
JOHNSON COUNTY MENTAL HEALTH CENTER - JOHN R. KEACH MEMORIAL LIBRARY □ Mission, KS

Simpson, Jerome, Libn.
OKLAHOMA REGIONAL LIBRARY FOR THE BLIND AND PHYSICALLY HANDICAPPED □ Oklahoma City, OK

Simpson, Joan, Cat.
DALHOUSIE UNIVERSITY - LAW LIBRARY □ Halifax, NS

Simpson, Joseph, Tech.Serv.
LOUISIANA STATE UNIVERSITY - LAW LIBRARY □ Baton Rouge, LA

Simpson, Leslie D., Supv.
INDIANA UNIVERSITY - LEARNING RESOURCE CENTER □ Bloomington, IN

Simpson, Mrs. M.A., Supt.
BATTLEFORD NATIONAL HISTORIC PARK - CAMPBELL INNES MEMORIAL LIBRARY □ Battleford, SK

Simpson, M. Ronald, Hd., Tech.Info.Ctr.
NORTH CAROLINA STATE UNIVERSITY - D.H. HILL LIBRARY □ Raleigh, NC

Simpson, Mary Ellen, Welfare Libn.
MISSISSIPPI STATE DEPARTMENT OF PUBLIC WELFARE - JEAN GUNTER SOCIAL WELFARE LIBRARY □ Jackson, MS

Simpson, Richard, Pub.Serv.Libn.
HARVARD UNIVERSITY - FINE ARTS LIBRARY □ Cambridge, MA

Simpson, Rolly L., Hd., Prod.Sect.
BURROUGHS WELLCOME COMPANY - LIBRARY □ Research Triangle Park, NC

Simpson, Mrs. S., Ck.
FALCONBRIDGE NICKEL MINES, LTD. - METALLURGICAL LABORATORIES INFORMATION SERVICES □ Thornhill, ON

Simpson, Seth, Libn.
OAKLAND TRIBUNE - LIBRARY □ Oakland, CA

Sims, Anne, Archv.
SOUTHERN ILLINOIS UNIVERSITY, CARBONDALE - SPECIAL COLLECTIONS □ Carbondale, IL

Sims, Edith
LOUISIANA STATE UNIVERSITY - REFERENCE SERVICES □ Baton Rouge, LA

Sims, Phil, Music Libn.
SOUTHWESTERN BAPTIST THEOLOGICAL SEMINARY - FLEMING LIBRARY □ Fort Worth, TX

Sims-Wood, Janet L., Ref.Libn.
HOWARD UNIVERSITY - MOORLAND-SPINGARN RESEARCH CENTER - LIBRARY DIVISION □ Washington, DC

Sina, Fran, Ref./Circ.Supv.
HAHNEMANN MEDICAL COLLEGE & HOSPITAL - WARREN H. FAKE LIBRARY □ Philadelphia, PA

Sinclair, Donald A., Cur. of Spec.Coll.
GENEALOGICAL SOCIETY OF NEW JERSEY - MANUSCRIPT COLLECTIONS □ New Brunswick, NJ

Sinclair, Donald A., Cur.
RUTGERS UNIVERSITY, THE STATE UNIVERSITY OF NEW JERSEY - SPECIAL COLLECTIONS DEPT.† □ New Brunswick, NJ

Sinclair, John, Dir.
DETROIT JAZZ CENTER - JAZZ ARCHIVE □ Detroit, MI

Sinclair, John M., Libn.
EDMONTON SUN - NEWSPAPER LIBRARY □ Edmonton, AB

Sinclair, Julianne, Libn.
ALABAMA LEAGUE OF MUNICIPALITIES - LIBRARY □ Montgomery, AL

Sinclair, Mary Jane T., Asst.Libn.
CANADA - SUPREME COURT OF CANADA - LIBRARY □ Ottawa, ON

Sinclair, Sabina, Hd.
INDIANA UNIVERSITY - OPTOMETRY BRANCH LIBRARY □ Bloomington, IN

Sinegal, Jayne, Ref.Libn.
U.S. OFFICE OF PERSONNEL MANAGEMENT - LIBRARY □ Washington, DC

Singer, Betsy, Chf.
NATIONAL INSTITUTE OF ARTHRITIS, METABOLISM & DIGESTIVE DISEASES - OFFICE OF HEALTH RESEARCH REPORTS □ Bethesda, MD

Singer, Blanche, ILL
UNIVERSITY OF WISCONSIN, MADISON - CENTER FOR HEALTH SCIENCES LIBRARIES □ Madison, WI

Singer, C., Assoc.Dir.
BUTLER INSTITUTE OF AMERICAN ART - LIBRARY □ Youngstown, OH

Singer, Carol, Ref.Coord.
WAYNE STATE COLLEGE - U.S. CONN LIBRARY □ Wayne, NE

Singer, L., Non-Print Libn.
CONCORDIA UNIVERSITY - SIR GEORGE WILLIAMS CAMPUS - NORRIS LIBRARY □ Montreal, PQ

Singerman, Donald, Cat.
MOUNT ZION HEBREW CONGREGATION - TEMPLE LIBRARY □ St. Paul, MN

Singerman, Donald, Cat.
ST. PAUL PUBLIC LIBRARY - HIGHLAND PARK BRANCH - PERRIE JONES MEMORIAL ROOM □ St. Paul, MN

Singerman, Robert, Hd.
UNIVERSITY OF FLORIDA - ISSER AND RAE PRICE LIBRARY OF JUDAICA □ Gainesville, FL

Singh, Miss, Libn.
WASCANA INSTITUTE OF APPLIED ARTS AND SCIENCES - RESOURCE & INFORMATION CENTRE □ Regina, SK

Singh, Gurnek, Dept.Hd./Asian Bibl.
SYRACUSE UNIVERSITY - E.S. BIRD LIBRARY - AREA STUDIES DEPARTMENT □ Syracuse, NY

Singh, Rana, Dir., Info.Anl.Div.
UNITED NATIONS - CENTRE ON TRANSNATIONAL CORPORATIONS - LIBRARY □ New York, NY

Singleton, Christine M., Res.Libn.
NEW YORK UNIVERSITY MEDICAL CENTER - INSTITUTE OF ENVIRONMENTAL MEDICINE - LIBRARY □ Tuxedo, NY

Singleton, Jean E., Hd.Libn.
INDIANA STATE LIBRARY - INDIANA DIVISION □ Indianapolis, IN

Singleton, M., Libn.
BERGEN COUNTY HISTORICAL SOCIETY - LIBRARY □ Hackensack, NJ

Sinha, Dr. E., Hd.
OCEAN ENGINEERING INFORMATION SERVICE □ La Jolla, CA

Sink, Thomas R., Dir. of Lib.Serv.
MERCY HOSPITAL - EDWARD L. BURNS HEALTH SCIENCES LIBRARY □ Toledo, OH

Sinko, Agnes, Ref.Libn.
NEW YORK CITY HUMAN RESOURCES ADMINISTRATION - MC MILLAN LIBRARY □ New York, NY

Sinkus, Raminta, Hd., Cat.Serv
DE PAUL UNIVERSITY - LAW SCHOOL LIBRARY □ Chicago, IL

Sinnette, Elinor D., Oral Hist.Libn.
HOWARD UNIVERSITY - MOORLAND-SPINGARN RESEARCH CENTER - MANUSCRIPT DIVISION □ Washington, DC

Sintz, Edward F., Dir.
MIAMI-DADE PUBLIC LIBRARY - GENEALOGY ROOM □ Miami, FL

Sipe, Gary, Libn.
FRANKLIN FURNACE ARCHIVE, INC. - LIBRARY □ New York, NY

Sipe, Mr. Lynn, Libn.
UNIVERSITY OF SOUTHERN CALIFORNIA - VON KLEINSMID LIBRARY □ Los Angeles, CA

Sipe, Mr. Lynn, Libn.
UNIVERSITY OF SOUTHERN CALIFORNIA - VON KLEINSMID LIBRARY - ORIENTALIA COLLECTION □ Los Angeles, CA

Sipit, Ibrahim, Dir.
TURKISH TOURISM AND INFORMATION OFFICE □ New York, NY

Sipkov, Ivan, Chf.
LIBRARY OF CONGRESS - LAW LIBRARY - EUROPEAN LAW DIVISION □ Washington, DC

Sipsma, Mary, Med.Libn.
ST. CATHERINE'S HOSPITAL - MEDICAL LIBRARY □ Kenosha, WI

Sirignano, Lynn, Acq.Libn.
CARNEGIE-MELLON UNIVERSITY - HUNT LIBRARY □ Pittsburgh, PA

Sirman, Margaret A., Libn.
GULF OIL CORPORATION - GS & T CORPORATE ENGINEERING LIBRARY □ Houston, TX

Sirois, Dorothy, Med.Libn.
MONTREAL CHILDREN'S HOSPITAL - MEDICAL LIBRARY □ Montreal, PQ

Siron, Catherine, Coord., Lib.Serv.
ST. JOSEPH HOSPITAL - HEALTH SCIENCE LIBRARY □ Joliet, IL

Siroonian, Harold, Sci. & Engr.Libn.
MC MASTER UNIVERSITY - THODE LIBRARY OF SCIENCE & ENGINEERING □ Hamilton, ON

Sirrocco, Angela, Chf., Commun.Ctr.
NATIONAL CLEARINGHOUSE FOR MENTAL HEALTH INFORMATION □ Rockville, MD

Sirrocco, Angela, Chief
U.S. PUBLIC HEALTH SERVICE - NATIONAL INSTITUTE OF MENTAL HEALTH - COMMUNICATION CENTER - LIBRARY □ Rockville, MD

Sirskyj, Dr. W., Cat.
WILFRID LAURIER UNIVERSITY - LIBRARY □ Waterloo, ON

Sisamis, Paul G., Supv.Mtls.
KENT STATE UNIVERSITY - AUDIOVISUAL SERVICES □ Kent, OH

Sisk, Rev. Richard, S.J., Asst.Archv.
SOCIETY OF JESUS - OREGON PROVINCE ARCHIVES □ Spokane, WA

Sisson, S. Gail, Asst.Libn.
GULF COMPANIES - LAW LIBRARY □ Houston, TX

Sistrunk, Carol, Chf.Libn.
U.S. VETERANS ADMINISTRATION (MS-Jackson) - CENTER LIBRARY □ Jackson, MS

Sitzmann, Glenn, Ser.Cat.
CLARION STATE COLLEGE - RENA M. CARLSON LIBRARY □ Clarion, PA

Sivers, Robert, Asst.Hd.
UNIVERSITY OF CALIFORNIA, SANTA BARBARA - SCIENCES-ENGINEERING LIBRARY □ Santa Barbara, CA

Sizemore, Nellie W., R&D Libn.
REYNOLDS (R.J.) TOBACCO COMPANY - R&D INFORMATION SYSTEMS LIBRARY □ Winston-Salem, NC

Sizer, Fred M., Libn.
GOULD, INC. - OCEAN SYSTEMS DIVISION - OCEAN SYSTEMS INFORMATION CENTER □ Cleveland, OH

Sizer, Samuel A., Cur., Spec.Coll.
UNIVERSITY OF ARKANSAS, FAYETTEVILLE - SPECIAL COLLECTIONS DIVISION □ Fayetteville, AR

Sjostrom, Eric A., Asst.Libn.
MINNESOTA ORCHESTRA - MUSIC LIBRARY □ Minneapolis, MN

Sjostrom, Joan, Libn.
NORWALK HOSPITAL - R. GLEN WIGGANS MEMORIAL LIBRARY □ Norwalk, CT

Skaggs, Betty A., Libn.
OKLAHOMA COUNTY LAW LIBRARY □ Oklahoma City, OK

Skaggs, Deborah, Access Archv.
UNIVERSITY OF LOUISVILLE - UNIVERSITY ARCHIVES AND RECORDS CENTER □ Louisville, KY

Skalstad, Doris, Asst.Hd.
MINNEAPOLIS PUBLIC LIBRARY & INFORMATION CENTER - HISTORY DEPARTMENT □ Minneapolis, MN

Skalton, Lawrence, Geologist & Mgr.
KANSAS STATE GEOLOGICAL SURVEY - WICHITA WELL SAMPLE LIBRARY □ Wichita, KS

Skaradzinski, Debra, Rd.Rm.Supv.
UNIVERSITY OF NORTH CAROLINA, CHAPEL HILL - RARE BOOK COLLECTION □ Chapel Hill, NC

Skarr, Robert J., Libn.
FAUCETT (Jack) ASSOCIATES - LIBRARY □ Chevy Chase, MD

Skau, Dorothy B., Libn.
U.S.D.A. - AGRICULTURAL RESEARCH SERVICE - SOUTHERN REGIONALRESEARCH CENTER □ New Orleans, LA

Skeele, Lillian, Libn.
WORTHINGTON HISTORICAL SOCIETY - LIBRARY □ Worthington, OH

Skeen, Douglas T., Ct.Libn.
BALTIMORE COUNTY CIRCUIT COURT - LAW LIBRARY □ Towson, MD

Skeen, Molly, Asst.Libn.
FIREMAN'S FUND INSURANCE COMPANIES - LIBRARY† □ San Francisco, CA

Skeen, Molly M., Libn.
FEDERAL HOME LOAN BANK OF SAN FRANCISCO - LIBRARY □ San Francisco, CA

Skelton, Mrs. Brooke, Cat.
WILFRID LAURIER UNIVERSITY - LIBRARY □ Waterloo, ON

Skelton, Peter, Policy & Plan.
CANADA - NATIONAL RESEARCH COUNCIL - CANADA INSTITUTE FOR SCIENTIFIC AND TECHNICAL INFORMATION (CISTI) □ Ottawa, ON

Skerrett, Claire, Lib.Dir.
CABRINI COLLEGE - HOLY SPIRIT LIBRARY □ Radnor, PA

Skerritt, Elizabeth, Corp.Libn.
INTERNATIONAL PAPER COMPANY - CORPORATE INFORMATION CENTER □ New York, NY

Skewis, Mrs. Paul
HISTORIC SCHAEFFERSTOWN, INC. - THOMAS R. BRENDLE MEMORIAL LIBRARY & MUSEUM □ Schaefferstown, PA

Skidmore, Carolyn R., Lib.Dir.
WEST VIRGINIA STATE DEPARTMENT OF EDUCATION - EDUCATIONAL MEDIA CENTER □ Charleston, WV

Skidmore, Janice, Assoc.
NEEDHAM, HARPER & STEERS ADVERTISING, INC. - INFORMATION SERVICES □ Chicago, IL

Skidmore, Kerry F., Libn.
ST. MARK'S HOSPITAL - LIBRARY □ Salt Lake City, UT

Skillings, Judith, Mgr., Info.Ctr.
CHILTON COMPANY - MARKETING & ADVERTISING INFORMATION CENTER □ Radnor, PA

Skillion, Anne, Ref.Libn.
COLUMBIA UNIVERSITY - BIOLOGICAL SCIENCES LIBRARY □ New York, NY

Skinner, Aubrey E., Libn.
UNIVERSITY OF TEXAS, AUSTIN - CHEMISTRY LIBRARY □ Austin, TX

Skinner, Connie, Libn.
KINO COMMUNITY HOSPITAL - LIBRARY† □ Tucson, AZ

Skinner, Elaine, Asst.Educ.Coord.
CALGARY ZOOLOGICAL SOCIETY - LIBRARY □ Calgary, AB

Skinner, George E., Dir.
UNIVERSITY OF ARKANSAS, FAYETTEVILLE - LAW LIBRARY □ Fayetteville, AR

Skinner, Linda, Libn.
MINT MUSEUM OF HISTORY - LASSITER LIBRARY □ Charlotte, NC

Skinner, Lois M., Libn.
ETHYL CORPORATION - CHEMICAL DEVELOPMENT LIBRARY □ Baton Rouge, LA

Skinner, Mary Ann, Libn.
NEWSDAY, INC. - LIBRARY □ Melville, NY

Skinner, Mary M., Chf.Lib.Serv.Div.
CANADA - ATMOSPHERIC ENVIRONMENT SERVICE - LIBRARY □ Downsview, ON

Skinner, Roger D., Dir.
FRIENDS OF THE WESTERN PHILATELIC LIBRARY □ Sunnyvale, CA

Skinner, Thomas, Hd., Tech.Serv.
SOUTHERN ALBERTA INSTITUTE OF TECHNOLOGY - LEARNING RESOURCES CENTRE □ Calgary, AB

Skirrow, Helen, Coord., Lib.Serv.
ALBERTA - DEPARTMENT OF EDUCATION - LIBRARY □ Edmonton, AB

Sklaar, Vera, Libn.
BRITISH CONSULATE-GENERAL - LIBRARY □ San Francisco, CA

Sklair, Terry, Asst.Libn.
MC DERMOTT, WILL & EMERY - LIBRARY □ Chicago, IL

Sklar, Hinda, Hd., Tech.Serv.
HARVARD UNIVERSITY - GRADUATE SCHOOL OF DESIGN - FRANCES LOEB LIBRARY □ Cambridge, MA

Skoglund, Susan E., Libn.
RIVERSIDE OSTEOPATHIC HOSPITAL - RALPH F. LINDBERG MEMORIAL LIBRARY □ Trenton, MI

Skold, Mrs. Gale W., Libn.
OUR REDEEMERS LUTHERAN CHURCH - LIBRARY □ Benson, MN

Skolnik, Esther, Med.Libn.
ST. JOHN'S EPISCOPAL HOSPITAL (South Shore Division) - MEDICAL LIBRARY □ Far Rockaway, NY

Skonecki, Leonard, Libn.
DAYTON MENTAL HEALTH CENTER - STAFF LIBRARY □ Dayton, OH

Skonezny, Nancie J., Libn.
BRUSH WELLMAN, INC. - TECHNICAL LIBRARY □ Cleveland, OH

Skoog, Anne C., Fine/Rare Bks.Libn.
CARNEGIE-MELLON UNIVERSITY - HUNT LIBRARY □ Pittsburgh, PA

Skop, Vera, Libn.
ST. VLADIMIR INSTITUTE - UKRAINIAN LIBRARY □ Toronto, ON

Skrukrud, Nora, Asst.Libn.
CROSBY, HEAFEY, ROACH & MAY - LAW LIBRARY □ Oakland, CA

Skuce, D., Map Resource Spec.
CANADA - ENERGY, MINES & RESOURCES CANADA - GEOGRAPHICAL SERVICES DIRECTORATE - MAP RESOURCE CENTRE □ Ottawa, ON

Skuja, Lucija, Art Libn.
GRAND RAPIDS PUBLIC LIBRARY - FURNITURE DESIGN COLLECTION □ Grand Rapids, MI

Skupien, Ronald, Data User Serv.Off.
U.S. BUREAU OF THE CENSUS - REGIONAL DATA USER SERVICE - CHICAGO REGIONAL OFFICE - LIBRARY □ Chicago, IL

Skyrm, Sally, Music Libn.
SUNY - COLLEGE AT POTSDAM - CRANE MUSIC LIBRARY □ Potsdam, NY

Slachta, Olga, Map Libn.
BROCK UNIVERSITY - DEPARTMENT OF GEOGRAPHY - MAP LIBRARY □ St. Catharines, ON

Slack, Jane G., Libn.
LAURELTON CENTER - LIBRARY □ Laurelton, PA

Slack, Lucille, Mgr., Lib.Serv.
DATACROWN, INC. - LIBRARY □ Willowdale, ON

Slade, Louise M., Staff Asst.
COLORADO STATE DEPARTMENT OF NATURAL RESOURCES - COLORADO GEOLOGICAL SURVEY LIBRARY □ Denver, CO

Slader, Genevieve, Libn./Cur.
WASHINGTON COUNTY HISTORICAL ASSOCIATION - MUSEUM LIBRARY □ Fort Calhoun, NE

Slager, Colleen, Pub.Serv.Libn.
WESTERN THEOLOGICAL SEMINARY - BEARDSLEE LIBRARY □ Holland, MI

Slagt, Joan, Translator
ONTARIO HYDRO - LIBRARY □ Toronto, ON

Slaight, Wilma R., Archv.
WELLESLEY COLLEGE - ARCHIVES □ Wellesley, MA

Slamkowski, Donna, Res.Libn.
MINNESOTA STATE ENERGY AGENCY - LIBRARY □ St. Paul, MN

Slansky, Jack, Chf. Cartographer
NEVADA STATE DEPARTMENT OF TRANSPORTATION - MAP INFORMATION LIBRARY □ Carson City, NV

Slate, Ted, Lib.Dir.
NEWSWEEK, INC. - LIBRARY □ New York, NY

Slater, David, Sec.
ADVISORY GROUP ON ELECTRON DEVICES - LIBRARY □ New York, NY

Slater, Diane, AV Libn.
UNIVERSITY OF WISCONSIN, MADISON - CENTER FOR HEALTH SCIENCES LIBRARIES □ Madison, WI

Slater, Robert O., Res.Ctr.Coord.
CENTER FOR NEW SCHOOLS - RESOURCE CENTER† □ Chicago, IL

Slater, Ronald, Cat.
LAURENTIAN UNIVERSITY - MAIN LIBRARY □ Sudbury, ON

Slattery, John M., Hist.
TWIRLY BIRDS ARCHIVE □ Oxon Hill, MD

Slawson, Elizabeth F., Engr.Libn.
U.S. ARMY ENGINEER SCHOOL - LIBRARY □ Ft. Belvoir, VA

Sleight, B.G., Libn.
FAIRFAX COUNTY PUBLIC LIBRARY - BUSINESS & TECHNICAL SECTION □ Fairfax, VA

Sleight, Wicky, Hd.Libn.
TEXAS STATE DEPARTMENT OF WATER RESOURCES - WATER RESOURCES RESEARCH LIBRARY □ Austin, TX

Slezak, Eva, Spec.
ENOCH PRATT FREE LIBRARY - MARYLAND DEPARTMENT □ Baltimore, MD

Slifer, Biljon, Adm.Asst.
LOUISVILLE AND JEFFERSON COUNTY PLANNING COMMISSION - LOUISVILLE METROPOLITAN PLANNING LIBRARY □ Louisville, KY

Slinn, Janet R., Info.Serv.Cons.
NEW ENGLAND BOARD OF HIGHER EDUCATION - LIBRARY □ Wenham, MA

Slivka, Enid Miller, Libn.
BECK (R.W.) & ASSOCIATES - LIBRARY □ Seattle, WA

Slivka, Jacqueline W., Libn.
U.S. NAVY - NAVAL WEAPONS STATION - LIBRARY □ Yorktown, VA

Sliwa, Shirley, Dir.
NATIONAL SOARING MUSEUM - LIBRARY & ARCHIVES □ Elmira, NY

Sloan, Barbara, Info.Spec.
EUROPEAN COMMUNITY INFORMATION SERVICE - LIBRARY □ Washington, DC

Sloan, Deloras, Asst.Libn.
MERCY HOSPITAL - LEVITT HEALTH SCIENCES LIBRARY □ Des Moines, IA

Sloan, R.D., Jr., Dir./Govt.Serv.
UNIVERSITY OF COLORADO, BOULDER - BUREAU OF GOVERNMENTAL RESEARCH & SERVICE LIBRARY □ Boulder, CO

Sloan, Virgene K., Libn.
WOODMEN ACCIDENT & LIFE COMPANY - LIBRARY □ Lincoln, NE

Sloane, Eleanor, Supv.
U.S. NATL. INSTITUTES OF HEALTH - NATIONAL CANCER INSTITUTE - DIVISION OF CANCER TREATMENT - LIBRARY □ Silver Spring, MD

Sloane, Richard, Libn.
UNIVERSITY OF PENNSYLVANIA - BIDDLE LAW LIBRARY □ Philadelphia, PA

Sloat, Helen, Church Libn.
NORTHMINSTER UNITED PRESBYTERIAN CHURCH - LIBRARY □ New Castle, PA

Slocombe, Patty S., Libn.
MARITZ, INC. - LIBRARY □ Fenton, MO

Slocum, Ann L., Med.Libn.
CHENANGO MEMORIAL HOSPITAL - MEDICAL LIBRARY □ Norwich, NY

Slocum, Leslie
TELEVISION INFORMATION OFFICE OF THE NATIONAL ASSOCIATION OF BROADCASTERS - RESEARCH SERVICES† □ New York, NY

Slomowitz, Lynn, Libn.
SAN DIEGO PUBLIC LIBRARY - HISTORY & WORLD AFFAIRS SECTION □ San Diego, CA

Sloshberg, Leah P., Dir. of Musm.
NEW JERSEY STATE MUSEUM - LIBRARY □ Trenton, NJ

Slotkin, Helen W., Archv./Spec.Coll.Hd.
MASSACHUSETTS INSTITUTE OF TECHNOLOGY - INSTITUTE ARCHIVES AND SPECIAL COLLECTIONS □ Cambridge, MA

Slotten, Martha Calvert, Cur.
DICKINSON COLLEGE - LIBRARY - SPECIAL COLLECTIONS □ Carlisle, PA

Slowinski, Rose, Dir.
EVANSTON HOSPITAL - WEBSTER MEDICAL LIBRARY □ Evanston, IL

Sluiter, Barbara, Hd. of Cat.
CALVIN COLLEGE AND SEMINARY - LIBRARY □ Grand Rapids, MI

Sly, Dale W., Pres.
SAN FRANCISCO COLLEGE OF MORTUARY SCIENCE - LIBRARY □ San Francisco, CA

Sly, Maureen, Hd., Tech.Serv.
INTERNATIONAL DEVELOPMENT RESEARCH CENTRE - LIBRARY □ Ottawa, ON

Slyhoff, Merle, Acq.Libn.
UNIVERSITY OF PENNSYLVANIA - BIDDLE LAW LIBRARY □ Philadelphia, PA

Smail, Laura, Spec./Oral Hist.
UNIVERSITY OF WISCONSIN, MADISON - ARCHIVES □ Madison, WI

Small, Doris, Hd., Tech.Serv.
RAND CORPORATION - LIBRARY □ Santa Monica, CA

Small, Jeffrey, AV Libn.
UNIVERSITY OF MAINE, PRESQUE ISLE - LIBRARY □ Presque Isle, ME

Small, Marion, Asst.Cur.Coll.
MAINE MARITIME MUSEUM - LIBRARY/ ARCHIVES □ Bath, ME

Small, Mindy Kaye, Archv.
U.S. DEFENSE AUDIOVISUAL AGENCY - ARLINGTON STILL PHOTO DEPOSITORY □ Arlington, VA

Small, Sally S., Hd.Libn.
PENNSYLVANIA STATE UNIVERSITY, BERKS CAMPUS - LIBRARY □ Reading, PA

Small, Wendell G., Jr., Libn.
STATE MUTUAL LIFE ASSURANCE COMPANY OF AMERICA - LIBRARY □ Worcester, MA

Smallen, Anna, Asst.Libn.
CHADBOURNE, PARKE, WHITESIDE, & WOLFF - LIBRARY □ New York, NY

Smallman, Mary H., Hist.
ST. LAWRENCE COUNTY HISTORY AND RESEARCH CENTER - LIBRARY □ Canton, NY

Smardo, Toni, Libn.
DALLAS PUBLIC LIBRARY - HISTORY AND SOCIAL SCIENCES DIVISION □ Dallas, TX

Smarjesse, Myrtle, Med.Libn.
SCHNEPP (Kenneth H.) MEDICAL LIBRARY □ Springfield, IL

Smart, John, Act.Chf., Lib.Br.
U.S. NATL. INSTITUTES OF HEALTH - LIBRARY □ Bethesda, MD

Smart, Margaret, Doc.Libn.
COLORADO SCHOOL OF MINES - ARTHUR LAKES LIBRARY □ Golden, CO

Smart, Marriott W., Libn.
GULF OIL CORPORATION - GULF MINERAL RESOURCES COMPANY - EXPLORATION LIBRARY □ Denver, CO

Smarte, Lynn, Asst.Dir./User Serv.
ERIC CLEARINGHOUSE ON HANDICAPPED & GIFTED CHILDREN - CEC INFORMATION SERVICES □ Reston, VA

Smeby, A.B., Cur.
DAKOTA COUNTY HISTORICAL SOCIETY - LIBRARY AND MUSEUM □ South St. Paul, MN

Smedlund, Ruth, Res.Libn.
INTERNATIONAL MINERALS & CHEMICAL CORPORATION - LIBRARY □ Mundelein, IL

Smejkal, Kenneth, Acq.Libn.
WESTERN ILLINOIS UNIVERSITY - LIBRARIES □ Macomb, IL

Smelkinson, Tenna, Mgr.
COMPUTER SCIENCES CORPORATION - SYSTEMS SCIENCES DIVISION - TECHNICAL INFORMATION CENTER □ Silver Spring, MD

Smeraldi, Florence, Sec.
HUDSON RIVER ENVIRONMENTAL SOCIETY - LIBRARY □ Bronx, NY

Smidt, Donna C., Assoc.Musm.Libn.
METROPOLITAN MUSEUM OF ART - PHOTOGRAPH AND SLIDE LIBRARY □ New York, NY

Smigarowski, M., Lib.Supv.
SASKATCHEWAN - DEPARTMENT OF HEALTH - LIBRARY □ Regina, SK

Smika, Dr. D.E., Location Leader
U.S.D.A. - AGRICULTURAL RESEARCH SERVICE - CENTRAL GREAT PLAINS RESEARCH STATION - LIBRARY □ Akron, CO

Smiley, Lucille B., Libn.
HOWARD UNIVERSITY - SCHOOL OF BUSINESS AND PUBLIC ADMINISTRATION - LIBRARY □ Washington, DC

Smink, June E., Libn.
VIRGINIA NATIONAL BANK - LIBRARY □ Norfolk, VA

Smisek, Thomas, Lib.Asst. Films
MINNEAPOLIS PUBLIC LIBRARY & INFORMATION CENTER - ART, MUSIC & FILMS DEPARTMENT □ Minneapolis, MN

Smiser, Mary Miller, Libn.
JOHNSON COUNTY HISTORICAL SOCIETY - HERITAGE LIBRARY □ Warrensburg, MO

Smisko, Marsha, Desk Res.
FOOTE CONE & BELDING - INFORMATION CENTER □ Chicago, IL

Smith, A., Libn.
U.S.D.A. - AGRICULTURAL RESEARCH SERVICE - SNAKE RIVER CONSERVATION RESEARCH CENTER - LIBRARY □ Kimberly, ID

Smith, Adelaide R., Cur.
HISTORICAL SOCIETY OF THE TARRYTOWNS - HEADQUARTERS LIBRARY □ Tarrytown, NY

Smith, Al, Hd.
GEORGIA STATE FORESTRY COMMISSION - LIBRARY† □ Macon, GA

Smith, Alice B., Asst.Libn.
SWEDISH MEDICAL CENTER - LIBRARY □ Englewood, CO

Smith, Amber Lee, Pub.Serv.Libn.
UNIVERSITY OF OKLAHOMA - LAW LIBRARY □ Norman, OK

Smith, Anita A., Hist.
MONTGOMERY COUNTY - DEPARTMENT OF HISTORY AND ARCHIVES □ Fonda, NY

Smith, Ann S., Hd., ILL Ctr.
NORTH CAROLINA STATE UNIVERSITY - D.H. HILL LIBRARY □ Raleigh, NC

Smith, Annie J., Med.Libn.
SAMARITAN HOSPITAL - MEDICAL LIBRARY □ Troy, NY

Smith, Audrey, Assoc.Libn.
NEW YORK STATE LIBRARY FOR THE BLIND AND VISUALLY HANDICAPPED □ Albany, NY

Smith, Ava, Libn.
KENTUCKY MOUNTAIN BIBLE INSTITUTE - GIBSON LIBRARY □ Vancleve, KY

Smith, Barbara, Asst.Libn.
BOLT BERANEK AND NEWMAN, INC. - LIBRARY □ Cambridge, MA

Smith, Barbara, Libn.
SNYDER (H.L.) MEMORIAL RESEARCH FOUNDATION - LIBRARY □ Winfield, KS

Smith, Barbara, Libn.
VIRGINIA CHEMICALS, INC. - LIBRARY □ Portsmouth, VA

Smith, Barbara D., Asst.Libn.
DREYFUS CORPORATION - LIBRARY □ New York, NY

Smith, Barbara J., Ck. To Jury Comm.
SUSSEX COUNTY LAW LIBRARY □ Newton, NJ

Smith, Barbara M., Prog.Dir.
GEORGIA CONSERVANCY, INC. - LIBRARY □ Atlanta, GA

Smith, Bernie Todd, Libn.
ROCHESTER GENERAL HOSPITAL - LILLIE B. WERNER HEALTH SCIENCES LIBRARY □ Rochester, NY

Smith, Bessie Hess, Libn.
BAYLOR UNIVERSITY - CROUCH MUSIC LIBRARY □ Waco, TX

Smith, Betty, Ck.
CANADIAN JEWELLERS INSTITUTE - LIBRARY □ Toronto, ON

Smith, Betty, Documentalist
UNIVERSITY OF WATERLOO - ONLINE INFORMATION RETRIEVAL SYSTEM FOR THE SOCIOLOGY OF LEISURE & SPORT (SIRLS) □ Waterloo, ON

Smith, Billy, Dir.
INDIANA STATE BOARD OF HEALTH - JACOB T. OLIPHANT LIBRARY □ Indianapolis, IN

Smith, C. Perry, Libn.
CHURCH OF JESUS CHRIST OF LATTER-DAY SAINTS - VENTURA BRANCH GENEALOGICAL LIBRARY □ Ventura, CA

Smith, Carol
BRITISH COLUMBIA - MINISTRY OF ENVIRONMENT - LIBRARY □ Victoria, BC

Smith, Carol T., Div.Coord.
BRIGHAM YOUNG UNIVERSITY - SCIENCE DIVISION LIBRARY □ Provo, UT

Smith, Mrs. Carter, Archv.
HISTORIC MOBILE PRESERVATION SOCIETY - MITCHELL ARCHIVES □ Mobile, AL

Smith, Catherine L., Asst.Libn.
EASTERN MAINE MEDICAL CENTER - HEALTH SCIENCES LIBRARY □ Bangor, ME

Smith, Mrs. Charles
BOB JONES UNIVERSITY - CHURCH MINISTRIES RESOURCE LAB □ Greenville, SC

Smith, Clifton F., Libn.
SANTA BARBARA MUSEUM OF NATURAL HISTORY - LIBRARY □ Santa Barbara, CA

Smith, Cloyd R., Tech.Libn.
ARMSTRONG WORLD INDUSTRIES, INC. - TECHNICAL CENTER - TECHNICAL INFORMATION SERVICES □ Lancaster, PA

Smith, Cynthia, Lit.Chem.
GOODYEAR TIRE AND RUBBER COMPANY - TECHNICAL INFORMATION CENTER □ Akron, OH

Smith, Cynthia M., Chf.Libn.
INCO METALS COMPANY - BUSINESS LIBRARY □ Toronto, ON

Smith, D., Libn.
ALBERTA - DEPARTMENT OF TRANSPORTATION - LIBRARY □ Edmonton, AB

Smith, D. Ryan, Dir.
STAR OF THE REPUBLIC MUSEUM - LIBRARY □ Washington, TX

Smith, David A.L., Libn.
U.S. AIR FORCE BASE - LANGLEY BASE LIBRARY □ Langley AFB, VA

Smith, David A.L., Chf.Libn.
U.S. AIR FORCE - TACTICAL AIR COMMAND - LANGLEY BASE LIBRARY □ Langley AFB, VA

Smith, David D., Ref.Libn.
BELL TELEPHONE LABORATORIES, INC. - TECHNICAL LIBRARY □ Naperville, IL

Smith, Mrs. David P., Chm.
HIGHLAND PARK PRESBYTERIAN CHURCH - MADELINE ROACH MEYERCORD LIBRARY □ Dallas, TX

Smith, David R., Archv.
DISNEY (Walt) PRODUCTIONS - ARCHIVES □ Burbank, CA

Smith, Debbie, Musm. Registrar
WESTERN KENTUCKY UNIVERSITY - KENTUCKY LIBRARY AND MUSEUM/ UNIVERSITY ARCHIVES □ Bowling Green, KY

Smith, Deborah, Asst.Rsrcs.Spec.
UNIVERSITY OF CALIFORNIA, IRVINE - INSTITUTE OF TRANSPORTATION STUDIES - RESOURCE CENTER† □ Irvine, CA

Smith, Diane, Libn.
PENNHURST CENTER - STAFF LIBRARY □ Spring City, PA

Smith, Don, Educ.Libn.
SOUTHERN ILLINOIS UNIVERSITY, EDWARDSVILLE - EDUCATION LIBRARY □ Edwardsville, IL

Smith, Mrs. Donald B., Chm. Of Lib.
DETROIT GARDEN CENTER - LIBRARY □ Detroit, MI

Smith, Donald R., Libn.
ST. ELIZABETH MEDICAL CENTER - NORTH - MEDICAL LIBRARY □ Covington, KY

Smith, Doris N., Chf.Libn.
OREGONIAN LIBRARY □ Portland, OR

Smith, Dorman H., Hd. Music Libn.
UNIVERSITY OF ARIZONA - MUSIC COLLECTION □ Tucson, AZ

Smith, Earl P., Prod.Supv.
AUBURN UNIVERSITY - LEARNING RESOURCES CENTER □ Auburn, AL

Smith, Eleanor, Libn.
CONGREGATION BETH SHALOM - RABBI MORDECAI S. HALPERN MEMORIAL LIBRARY □ Oak Park, MI

Smith, Elinore, Slide Libn.
TUCSON MUSEUM OF ART - LIBRARY □ Tucson, AZ

Smith, Elizabeth, Asst.Ed.
CARNEGIE-MELLON UNIVERSITY - HUNT INSTITUTE FOR BOTANICAL DOCUMENTATION - LIBRARY □ Pittsburgh, PA

Smith, Elizabeth, Cur., Hist.Dept.
SUSQUEHANNA COUNTY HISTORICAL SOCIETY AND FREE LIBRARY ASSOCIATION □ Montrose, PA

Smith, Elizabeth L., V.P. & Mgr.
CAMPBELL-EWALD COMPANY - REFERENCE CENTER □ Warren, MI

Smith, Elizabeth S.
3M - 201 TECHNICAL LIBRARY □ St. Paul, MN

Smith, Elliott, Dir.
MICHIGAN STATE LEGISLATIVE COUNCIL - LEGISLATIVE SERVICE BUREAU LIBRARY □ Lansing, MI

Smith, Elmer V., Dir.
CANADA - NATIONAL RESEARCH COUNCIL - CANADA INSTITUTE FOR SCIENTIFIC AND TECHNICAL INFORMATION (CISTI) □ Ottawa, ON

Smith, Eric J., Libn.
DUKE UNIVERSITY - SCHOOL OF ENGINEERING LIBRARY □ Durham, NC

Smith, Esther, Coll.Dev.Libn.
CENTER FOR RESEARCH LIBRARIES □ Chicago, IL

Smith, Evelyn L., Chf.Cat.Libn.
UNIVERSITY OF MICHIGAN - LAW LIBRARY □ Ann Arbor, MI

Smith, F. Hampton, Mss.Spec.
UNIVERSITY OF MISSOURI - WESTERN HISTORICAL MANUSCRIPT COLLECTION/ STATE HISTORICAL SOCIETY OF MISSOURI □ Columbia, MO

Smith, Frances, Cur.
WYANDOT COUNTY HISTORICAL SOCIETY - WYANDOT MUSEUM - LIBRARY □ Upper Sandusky, OH

Smith, Sr. Frances A., R.S.C.J., Libn.
CENTER FOR APPLIED RESEARCH IN THE APOSTOLATE - CARA RESEARCH LIBRARY† □ Washington, DC

Smith, Frances E., Libn.
U.S. NAVY - NAVAL AIR STATION (Memphis) - LIBRARY □ Millington, TN

Smith, Frances P., Libn.
STRAUB CLINIC & HOSPITAL, INC. - ARNOLD LIBRARY □ Honolulu, HI

Smith, Frank, Mgr. Correspondence Serv.
CHURCH OF JESUS CHRIST OF LATTER-DAY SAINTS - GENEALOGICAL LIBRARY □ Salt Lake City, UT

Smith, Frederick E., Law Libn.
UNIVERSITY OF CALIFORNIA, LOS ANGELES - LAW LIBRARY† □ Los Angeles, CA

Smith, Gary L., Asst.Libn.
SOUTHERN CALIFORNIA EDISON COMPANY - LIBRARY □ Rosemead, CA

Smith, George F., M.D., Cur. & Dir.
INTERNATIONAL COLLEGE OF SURGEONS HALL OF FAME - DR. JOSEPH MONTAGUE PROCTOLOGIC LIBRARY □ Chicago, IL

Smith, Dr. Gerald A., Dir.
SAN BERNARDINO COUNTY MUSEUM - WILSON C. HANNA LIBRARY/RESEARCH LIBRARY □ Redlands, CA

Smith, Gerald P., Cur.
MEMPHIS STATE UNIVERSITY LIBRARIES - C.H. NASH MUSEUM LIBRARY □ Memphis, TN

Smith, Gloria M., Libn.
INTERNATIONAL READING ASSOCIATION - LIBRARY □ Newark, DE

Smith, Grace E., Libn.
WICHITA FALLS STATE HOSPITAL - MEDICAL LIBRARY □ Wichita Falls, TX

Smith, Harold, Asst.Chf. & Ref.
GRUMMAN AEROSPACE CORPORATION - TECHNICAL INFORMATION CENTER □ Bethpage, NY

Smith, Harriet E., Principal Law Libn.
NEW YORK STATE SUPREME COURT - 9TH JUDICIAL DISTRICT - LAW LIBRARY □ White Plains, NY

Smith, Hazel, Chm., Lib.Comm.
PARK PLACE CHURCH OF GOD - CARL KARDATZKE MEMORIAL LIBRARY □ Anderson, IN

Smith, Helen, Educ.Rsrcs. & Ch.Coll.
WORCESTER STATE COLLEGE - LEARNING RESOURCES CENTER □ Worcester, MA

Smith, Helen L., Dir.
THOMAS COUNTY HISTORICAL SOCIETY - LIBRARY □ Colby, KS

Smith, Henry M., Dir.
UNITED WAY OF AMERICA - INFORMATION CENTER† □ Alexandria, VA

Smith, Hope, Libn.
AMERICAN BIBLIOGRAPHICAL CENTER - CLIO PRESS - THE INGE BOEHM LIBRARY □ Santa Barbara, CA

Smith, Ila J., Rec.Ck.
OKLAHOMA GEOLOGICAL SURVEY - OKLAHOMA GEOPHYSICAL OBSERVATORY LIBRARY □ Leonard, OK

Smith, Ilene N., Med.Libn.
ROCKINGHAM MEMORIAL HOSPITAL - HEALTH SCIENCES LIBRARY □ Harrisonburg, VA

Smith, Irene P., Cons.
RHODE ISLAND STATE DEPARTMENT OF EDUCATION - EDUCATION INFORMATION SERVICES □ Providence, RI

Smith, Jack, AV Spec.
NASHVILLE STATE TECHNICAL INSTITUTE - EDUCATIONAL RESOURCE CENTER □ Nashville, TN

Smith, Janet B., Libn.
U.S. FEDERAL HOME LOAN BANK BOARD - RESEARCH LIBRARY □ Washington, DC

Smith, Janet P., Libn.
SOMERVILLE HOSPITAL - CARR HEALTH SCIENCES LIBRARY □ Somerville, MA

Smith, Janice B., Tech.Serv.Libn.
UNION PACIFIC RAILROAD COMPANY - LIBRARY □ Omaha, NE

Smith, Janice E., Libn.
MAC FARLANE & COMPANY, INC. - FRY CONSULTANTS INCORPORATED - MANAGEMENT CENTRE □ Atlanta, GA

Smith, Jean, Libn.
PENNSYLVANIA STATE UNIVERSITY - ARCHITECTURE READING ROOM □ University Park, PA

Smith, Jean, Hd.Libn.
PENNSYLVANIA STATE UNIVERSITY - ARTS LIBRARY □ University Park, PA

Smith, Jean H., Law Libn.
KINGS COUNTY LAW LIBRARY □ Hanford, CA

Smith, Jerome, Info.Tech.
UNIVERSITY OF PITTSBURGH - CENTER FOR INTERNATIONAL STUDIES □ Pittsburgh, PA

Smith, Miss Jo Therese, Hd.
WITCO CHEMICAL CORPORATION - TECHNICAL CENTER LIBRARY† □ Oakland, NJ

Smith, Joan, Sr.Asst.Libn.
CORNELL UNIVERSITY - MAPS, MICROTEXT, NEWSPAPERS DEPARTMENT □ Ithaca, NY

Smith, Joan M.B., Med.Libn.
BEAUMONT (William) HOSPITAL - MEDICAL LIBRARY □ Royal Oak, MI

Smith, John M., Assoc.Dir.Tech.Serv.
UNIVERSITY OF TEXAS MEDICAL BRANCH - MOODY MEDICAL LIBRARY □ Galveston, TX

Smith, Juanita J., Spec.Coll.Libn.
BALL STATE UNIVERSITY - BRACKEN LIBRARY - SPECIAL COLLECTIONS □ Muncie, IN

Smith, Judith A., Libn.
BLAKE, CASSELS & GRAYDON - LIBRARY □ Toronto, ON

Smith, Judith K., Libn.
CARTER (Larue D.) MEMORIAL HOSPITAL - MEDICAL LIBRARY □ Indianapolis, IN

Smith, Julie, Med.Libn.
ST. JOSEPH HOSPITAL - BURLEW MEDICAL LIBRARY □ Orange, CA

Smith, Karen, Doc.Libn.
SUNY AT BUFFALO - CHARLES B. SEARS LAW LIBRARY □ Buffalo, NY

Smith, Kate, Libn.
ST. LUKE'S HOSPITAL - HEALTH SCIENCES LIBRARY □ Denver, CO

Smith, Katherine, Lib.Techn.
SOUTHEAST MICHIGAN COUNCIL OF GOVERNMENTS - LIBRARY □ Detroit, MI

Smith, L., Mgr., Info.Serv.
MC KINSEY & COMPANY, INC. - LIBRARY □ Chicago, IL

Smith, Larry G., Mgr., Anl.Serv.
UNITED MERCHANTS AND MANUFACTURING COMPANY - RESEARCH CENTER LIBRARY □ Langley, SC

Smith, Laura H., Libn.
MEDFIELD HISTORICAL SOCIETY - LIBRARY □ Medfield, MA

Smith, Laura J., Hd.
DAYTON AND MONTGOMERY COUNTY PUBLIC LIBRARY - SOCIAL SCIENCES DIVISION □ Dayton, OH

Smith, Libby, Libn.
ENVIRONMENTAL PROTECTION AGENCY - LIBRARY SERVICES □ Research Triangle Park, NC

Smith, Linda-Jean, Libn.
STRADLEY, RONON, STEVENS & YOUNG - LAW LIBRARY □ Philadelphia, PA

Smith, Linda L., Libn.
LEXINGTON HERALD-LEADER - LIBRARY □ Lexington, KY

Smith, Lisa S., Coord. of Vols.
INTERNATIONAL VISITORS INFORMATION SERVICE □ Washington, DC

Smith, Lois W., Libn.
BAPTIST MEDICAL CENTER - AMELIA WHITE PITTS MEMORIAL LIBRARY □ Columbia, SC

Smith, Lorraine, Lib.Asst.
TORONTO EAST GENERAL HOSPITAL - DOCTORS' LIBRARY □ Toronto, ON

Smith, Sr. Louise, Coll.Libn.
UNIVERSITY OF WESTERN ONTARIO - MUSIC LIBRARY □ London, ON

Smith, Louise H., Libn.
OHIO STATE UNIVERSITY - ENGLISH DEPARTMENT LIBRARY □ Columbus, OH

Smith, Lynn R., Acq.Libn.
INDIANA UNIVERSITY - SCHOOL OF MEDICINE LIBRARY □ Indianapolis, IN

Smith, Lytton, Asst.Chf.Libn.
SEATTLE POST-INTELLIGENCER - NEWSPAPER LIBRARY □ Seattle, WA

Smith, M., Dir.
FLAG RESEARCH CENTER - LIBRARY □ Winchester, MA

Smith, M.M., Supv., User Serv.
MC DONNELL DOUGLAS CORPORATION - DOUGLAS AIRCRAFT COMPANY - TECHNICAL LIBRARY □ Long Beach, CA

Smith, Margaretta W., Dir. of Libs.
NEW YORK INSTITUTE OF TECHNOLOGY - LIBRARY† □ Old Westbury, NY

Smith, Marian, Online Serv.
GENERAL ELECTRIC COMPANY - MAIN LIBRARY □ Schenectady, NY

Smith, Martha, Libn.
BURBANK HOSPITAL - SCHOOL OF NURSING - GRACE GUMMO LIBRARY □ Fitchburg, MA

Smith, Martin, Libn.
UNIVERSITY OF TEXAS, AUSTIN - GEOLOGY LIBRARY □ Austin, TX

Smith, Marvin, Lib.Dir.
NORTH CENTRAL BIBLE COLLEGE - T.J. JONES MEMORIAL LIBRARY □ Minneapolis, MN

Smith, Sr. Mary Elfreda, S.H.C.J., Per.Libn.
ROSEMONT COLLEGE - GERTRUDE KISTLER MEMORIAL LIBRARY - SPECIAL COLLECTIONS □ Rosemont, PA

Smith, Maryann D., Asst.Cur.
MUSEUM OF THE CITY OF NEW YORK - THEATRE COLLECTION □ New York, NY

Smith, Matthew, Archv.
PROVIDENCE COLLEGE - PHILLIPS MEMORIAL LIBRARY □ Providence, RI

Smith, Maureen, Cat.
TEMPLE UNIVERSITY - HEALTH SCIENCES CENTER - LIBRARY □ Philadelphia, PA

Smith, Maxine, Hostess/Libn.
CHAUTAUQUA COUNTY HISTORICAL SOCIETY - LIBRARY □ Westfield, NY

Smith, Maxine C., Libn.
U.S. ARMY - CORPS OF ENGINEERS - SOUTHWESTERN DIVISION - LIBRARY □ Dallas, TX

Smith, Maxine M., Lit. Searcher
ENVIRONMENTAL PROTECTION AGENCY - ANDREW W. BREIDENBACH ENVIRONMENTAL RESEARCH CTR., CINCINNATI - TECH.LIB. □ Cincinnati, OH

Smith, Michael K., Libn.
DALLAS PUBLIC LIBRARY - HISTORY AND SOCIAL SCIENCES DIVISION □ Dallas, TX

Smith, Mildred W., Hd.
U.S. NAVY - COMMAND OPERATIONAL TEST AND EVALUATION FORCE - TECHNICAL AND PROFESSIONAL LIBRARY □ Norfolk, VA

Smith, Murphy D., Assoc. Libn.
AMERICAN PHILOSOPHICAL SOCIETY - LIBRARY □ Philadelphia, PA

Smith, Nan, Acq.Libn.
WASHINGTON & LEE UNIVERSITY - LAW LIBRARY □ Lexington, VA

Smith, Nancy, Libn.
DALLAS PUBLIC LIBRARY - HUMANITIES DIVISION □ Dallas, TX

Smith, Nancy, Hd., Tech.Serv.
OKLAHOMA CITY UNIVERSITY - LAW LIBRARY □ Oklahoma City, OK

Smith, Nancy J., Libn.
PEE DEE AREA HEALTH EDUCATION CENTER LIBRARY □ Florence, SC

Smith, Nicole, Coord.Doc./Info.
CANADA - CANADIAN INTERNATIONAL DEVELOPMENT AGENCY - DEVELOPMENT INFORMATION CENTRE □ Hull, PQ

Smith, P.E., Tech.Serv.Adm.
NORTON COMPANY - COATED ABRASIVE DIVISION - TECHNICAL LIBRARY □ Troy, NY

Smith, Pamela J., Libn.
METROPOLITAN TORONTO PLANNING DEPARTMENT - LIBRARY □ Toronto, ON

Smith, Patricia M., Asst.Libn.
NATIONAL GEOGRAPHIC SOCIETY - LIBRARY □ Washington, DC

Smith, Patricia S., Asst.Libn.
KANSAS CITY TIMES-STAR - LIBRARY □ Kansas City, MO

Smith, Peg, Dir.
MARICOPA TECHNICAL COMMUNITY COLLEGE - LIBRARY RESOURCE CENTER □ Phoenix, AZ

Smith, Peggy, Adm.Coord.
ASOCIACION NACIONAL PRO PERSONAS MAYORES - LIBRARY □ Los Angeles, CA

Smith, Philip, Cat./Asst.Libn.
ACADEMY OF AERONAUTICS - LIBRARY □ Flushing, NY

Smith, Priscilla P., Libn.
SMITHSONIAN INSTITUTION - FREER GALLERY OF ART - LIBRARY □ Washington, DC

Smith, R.B., Supv./Database Serv.
AIR PRODUCTS AND CHEMICALS, INC. - INFORMATION SERVICES - TREXLERTOWN LIBRARY □ Allentown, PA

Smith, R.J.
3M - ENGINEERING INFORMATION SERVICES □ St. Paul, MN

Smith, Rebecca A., Libn.
HISTORICAL ASSOCIATION OF SOUTHERN FLORIDA - CHARLTON W. TEBEAU LIBRARY OF FLORIDA HISTORY □ Miami, FL

Smith, Regina A., Asst.Libn., Rd.Serv.
VILLANOVA UNIVERSITY - PULLING LAW LIBRARY □ Villanova, PA

Smith, Reginald W., Assoc.Dir. of Libs.
COLLEGE OF MEDICINE AND DENTISTRY OF NEW JERSEY AT NEWARK - GEORGE F. SMITH LIBRARY □ Newark, NJ

Smith, Richard T., Dir.
SOUTHWEST RESEARCH INSTITUTE - NONDESTRUCTIVE TESTING INFORMATION ANALYSIS CENTER □ San Antonio, TX

Smith, Rita, Res.Libn.
AIRCO CARBON - RESEARCH LIBRARY □ Niagara Falls, NY

Smith, Rita F., Adm.Libn.
U.S. AIR FORCE HOSPITAL MEDICAL CENTER - MEDICAL LIBRARY (MS-Keesler AFB) □ Keesler AFB, MS

Smith, Rita M., Cat.Libn.
CALIFORNIA STATE UNIVERSITY, CHICO - MERIAM LIBRARY □ Chico, CA

Smith, Robert, Asst.Libn.
UNIVERSITY CLUB LIBRARY □ New York, NY

Smith, Robert H., Jr., Archv.
WRIGHT STATE UNIVERSITY - ARCHIVES & SPECIAL COLLECTIONS □ Dayton, OH

Smith, Roberta, Pres.
MANSFIELD HISTORICAL SOCIETY - EDITH MASON LIBRARY □ Storrs, CT

Smith, Robin E., Leg.Hist.
KIRKLAND & ELLIS - LIBRARY □ Washington, DC

Smith, Rose-Anne, Libn.
VANCOUVER PUBLIC LIBRARY - BUSINESS & ECONOMICS DIVISION □ Vancouver, BC

Smith, Rosl, Cat.Libn.
CUNY - GRADUATE SCHOOL AND UNIVERSITY CENTER - LIBRARY □ New York, NY

Smith, Roxanne, Lib.Techn.
BRITISH COLUMBIA - MINISTRY OF FORESTS - LIBRARY □ Victoria, BC

Smith, Ruth P., Libn.
TORONTO DOMINION BANK - DEPARTMENT OF ECONOMIC RESEARCH - LIBRARY □ Toronto, ON

PERSONNEL

PERSONNEL

Smith, Ruth S., Mgr.
INSTITUTE FOR DEFENSE ANALYSES -
TECHNICAL INFORMATION SERVICES □
Arlington, VA

Smith, Sallie, Tech.Libn.
ST. JOE MINERALS CORPORATION - RESEARCH
DEPARTMENT INFORMATION CENTER □
Monaca, PA

Smith, Sandi, Asst.Libn.
OKLAHOMA HISTORICAL SOCIETY - DIVISION
OF LIBRARY RESOURCES □ Oklahoma City, OK

Smith, Sandra, Asst. to Libn.
INTERNATIONAL LIBRARY, ARCHIVES &
MUSEUM OF OPTOMETRY □ St. Louis, MO

Smith, Sharon, Libn.
ILLINOIS STATE - APPELLATE COURT, 3RD
DISTRICT - LIBRARY □ Ottawa, IL

Smith, Sheila, Coord., Pict.Coll.
SMITHSONIAN INSTITUTION LIBRARIES -
COOPER-HEWITT MUSEUM OF DESIGN - DORIS
& HENRY DREYFUSS MEMORIAL STUDY CENTER
□ New York, NY

Smith, Shirlee A., Kpr. Hudson's Bay Archv.
MANITOBA - PROVINCIAL ARCHIVES OF
MANITOBA □ Winnipeg, MB

Smith, Shirlee Anne, Kpr.
HUDSON'S BAY COMPANY ARCHIVES □
Winnipeg, MB

Smith, Shirley, Hd., Pub.Serv.
UNIVERSITY OF MICHIGAN - DEARBORN
LIBRARY □ Dearborn, MI

Smith, Shirley K., Libn.
CANADIAN NATIONAL RAILWAYS - CANADIAN
NATIONAL TELECOMMUNICATIONS - GREAT
LAKES REGION LIBRARY† □ Toronto, ON

Smith, Steve, Techn.
CORNELL UNIVERSITY - RESOURCE
INFORMATION LABORATORY □ Ithaca, NY

Smith, Stuart C., Asst.Dir. & Ed.
ERIC CLEARINGHOUSE ON EDUCATIONAL
MANAGEMENT □ Eugene, OR

Smith, Susan, Asst.Libn.
WEST GEORGIA COLLEGE - SPECIAL
COLLECTIONS DEPARTMENT† □ Carrollton, GA

Smith, Sweetman R., Bus.-Tech.Ref.Libn.
FASHION INSTITUTE OF TECHNOLOGY -
LIBRARY/MEDIA SERVICES □ New York, NY

Smith, Sylvia, Asst.Libn.
TEXAS STATE DEPARTMENT OF WATER
RESOURCES - WATER RESOURCES RESEARCH
LIBRARY □ Austin, TX

Smith, Thomas A., Mss.Cur.
HAYES (Rutherford B.) PRESIDENTIAL CENTER -
LIBRARY □ Fremont, OH

Smith, Thomas O., Libn.
U.S. NATL. PARK SERVICE - MORRISTOWN
NATIONAL HISTORICAL PARK - LIBRARY □
Morristown, NJ

Smith, Timothy H., Exec.Dir.
NATIONAL COUNCIL OF CHURCHES -
INTERFAITH CENTER ON CORPORATE
RESPONSIBILITY □ New York, NY

Smith, Mrs. Tom, Libn.
FIRST PRESBYTERIAN CHURCH OF GADSDEN -
LIBRARY □ Gadsden, AL

Smith, Toms E., Sr.Libn.
UTICA/MARCY PSYCHIATRIC CENTER - UTICA
CAMPUS LIBRARY SERVICES □ Utica, NY

Smith, Ms. V., Adm.Asst.
BARUCH (Belle W.) INSTITUTE FOR MARINE
BIOLOGY AND COASTAL RESEARCH - LIBRARY
□ Columbia, SC

Smith, V. Ruth, Hd.
STANISLAUS COUNTY SCHOOLS - TEACHERS'
PROFESSIONAL LIBRARY □ Modesto, CA

Smith, Virgie, Cat.
WASHBURN UNIVERSITY OF TOPEKA - SCHOOL
OF LAW LIBRARY □ Topeka, KS

Smith, Virginia R., Hd.Asst./Pict.Libn.
CHICAGO PUBLIC LIBRARY CULTURAL CENTER
- FINE ARTS DIVISION - ART SECTION □
Chicago, IL

Smith, Vivienne B., Libn.
CANADA - AGRICULTURE CANADA - RESEARCH
STATION, SUMMERLAND - LIBRARY □
Summerland, BC

Smith, W.I., Dominion Archv.
CANADA - PUBLIC ARCHIVES OF CANADA -
NATIONAL ETHNIC ARCHIVES □ Ottawa, ON

Smith, W. Louis, Pres.
FUTURE AVIATION PROFESSIONALS OF
AMERICA (FAPA) - INFORMATION CENTER □
Las Vegas, NV

Smith, W. Thomas, Exec.Dir.
HYMN SOCIETY OF AMERICA - LIBRARY □
Springfield, OH

Smith, Wanda B., Libn.
GREENE COUNTY LAW LIBRARY† □
Waynesburg, PA

Smith, Wayne, Libn.
COMMUNICATIONS SATELLITE CORPORATION
- TECHNICAL LIBRARY □ Clarksburg, MD

Smith, Mrs. William, Asst.
FIRST BAPTIST CHURCH - E.F. WALKER
MEMORIAL LIBRARY □ Luling, TX

Smith, William, Cat.Libn.
STATE LIBRARY OF FLORIDA □ Tallahassee, FL

Smith, Winston H., Asst.Libn.
HARKNESS (Edward S.) EYE INSTITUTE - JOHN
M. WHEELER LIBRARY □ New York, NY

Smith, Ybo, AV Techn.
CAMOSUN COLLEGE - LIBRARY/MEDIA
SERVICES □ Victoria, BC

Smithee, Jeannette, Libn.
LAUBACH LITERACY INTERNATIONAL, INC. -
LIBRARY □ Syracuse, NY

Smithson, Gisela, Tech.Libn.
CANADIAN CANNERS, LTD. - RESEARCH
CENTRE - LIBRARY □ Burlington, ON

Smits, Edward J., Dir.
NASSAU COUNTY MUSEUM REFERENCE
LIBRARY □ East Meadow, NY

Smoczynski, Louise, Adm.Asst.
DANE COUNTY REGIONAL PLANNING
COMMISSION - LIBRARY □ Madison, WI

Smokey, Sheila, Supv.Tech.Lib.
FMC CORPORATION - ORDNANCE
ENGINEERING DIVISION - TECHNICAL
LIBRARY □ San Jose, CA

Smolek, Janice McAteer, Act.Dir./Lib.Serv.
LUNDEBERG MARYLAND SEAMANSHIP SCHOOL
- LIBRARY □ Piney Point, MD

Smolin, Ronald P., Libn.
SPACE FUTURES SOCIETY - LIBRARY □
Philadelphia, PA

Smoot, Samille J., Hd., Circ.Serv.
MEDICAL COLLEGE OF GEORGIA - LIBRARY □
Augusta, GA

Smoot, Stephen P., Dir.
U.S. DEPT. OF COMMERCE - INTERNATIONAL
TRADE ADMINISTRATION - SALT LAKE CITY
DISTRICT OFFICE LIBRARY □ Salt Lake City, UT

Smoots, Charles, Mgr.
IIT RESEARCH INSTITUTE - GUIDANCE AND
CONTROL INFORMATION ANALYSIS CENTER
(GACIAC) □ Chicago, IL

Smrekar, Marian N., Law Libn.
KERN COUNTY LAW LIBRARY □ Bakersfield, CA

Smukler, Sherman, Pres.
THEOSOPHICAL SOCIETY - SAN FRANCISCO
LODGE LIBRARY □ San Francisco, CA

Smyth, Anna, Marketing Libn.
SMITH, KLINE & FRENCH LABORATORIES -
MARKETING RESEARCH LIBRARY □ Philadelphia,
PA

Smyth, Lilian, Res.Libn.
JOHNSON AND JOHNSON, LTD. - RESEARCH
LIBRARY □ Montreal, PQ

Smyth, Mary Anne, Lib.Techn.
GOLDER (H.Q.) & ASSOCIATES - LIBRARY† □
Mississauga, ON

Smyth, Mary B., Lib.Mgr.
CITY COLLEGE OF SAN FRANCISCO - HOTEL
AND RESTAURANT DEPARTMENT - ALICE
STATLER LIBRARY □ San Francisco, CA

Smythe, Alvetta D., Hd., Annapolis Lib.
U.S. NAVY - DAVID W. TAYLOR NAVAL SHIP
RESEARCH AND DEVELOPMENT CENTER -
LIBRARY DIVISION □ Bethesda, MD

Snead, Marie, Asst.Libn.
INDIANA UNIVERSITY OF PENNSYLVANIA -
UNIVERSITY LIBRARY □ Indiana, PA

Sneed, M., Libn.
NORTHROP CORPORATION - ELECTRO-
MECHANICAL DIVISION - TECHNICAL
INFORMATION CENTER □ Anaheim, CA

Sneid, M., Libn.
CONGOLEUM CORPORATION - RESILIENT
FLOORING DIVISION - TECHNICAL RESEARCH
LIBRARY □ Trenton, NJ

Snezek, P. Paul, Dir.
WHEATON COLLEGE - LIBRARY □ Wheaton, IL

Snider, David, Libn.
TENNESSEE STATE ENERGY AUTHORITY -
LIBRARY □ Nashville, TN

Snider, Edith, Libn.
TENNESSEE STATE DEPARTMENT OF
ECONOMIC & COMMUNITY DEVELOPMENT -
LIBRARY □ Nashville, TN

Sniderman, Gloria, Ref.Libn.
WAYNE STATE UNIVERSITY - EDUCATION
LIBRARY □ Detroit, MI

Sniderman, Lynn, Assoc.Libn.
FEDERAL RESERVE BANK OF CLEVELAND -
RESEARCH LIBRARY □ Cleveland, OH

Snitow, Emily L., Libn.
CHILDREN'S SPECIALIZED HOSPITAL -
MEDICAL LIBRARY □ Mountainside, NJ

Snoddy, Donald D., Asst. State Archv.
NEBRASKA STATE HISTORICAL SOCIETY -
ARCHIVES □ Lincoln, NE

Snodgrass, Becky S., Asst.Libn.
TEXAS STATE DEPARTMENT OF HUMAN
RESOURCES - LIBRARY □ Austin, TX

Snow, Bobbie, Chf.Circ.Libn.
UNIVERSITY OF MICHIGAN - LAW LIBRARY □
Ann Arbor, MI

Snow, C. Richard, Venango Campus Libn.
CLARION STATE COLLEGE - RENA M. CARLSON
LIBRARY □ Clarion, PA

Snow, Carl E., Film Libn.
PURDUE UNIVERSITY - FILM LIBRARY □ West
Lafayette, IN

Snowball, George, Hd., Budget Plan./Adm.
CONCORDIA UNIVERSITY - SIR GEORGE
WILLIAMS CAMPUS - NORRIS LIBRARY □
Montreal, PQ

Snowhite, Morton, Libn.
NEW JERSEY INSTITUTE OF TECHNOLOGY -
ROBERT W. VAN HOUTEN LIBRARY □ Newark,
NJ

Snyder, Ann B., Libn.
BRIGHAM AND WOMEN'S HOSPITAL - PETER
BENT BRIGHAM SCHOOL OF NURSING -
LIBRARY □ Boston, MA

Snyder, Charles, Libn.
HARVARD UNIVERSITY - SCHOOL OF MEDICINE
- LUCIEN HOWE LIBRARY OF
OPHTHALMOLOGY† □ Boston, MA

Snyder, Cynthia, Dir.
COUNCIL FOR ADVANCEMENT AND SUPPORT
OF EDUCATION - REFERENCE CENTER □
Washington, DC

Snyder, Mrs. E.R., Libn.
FIRST CHRISTIAN CHURCH - WINONA ROEHL
LIBRARY □ Knoxville, TN

Snyder, Edna M., Libn.
U.S. ARMY MEDICAL BIOENGINEERING
RESEARCH & DEVELOPMENT LABORATORY -
TECHNICAL REFERENCE LIBRARY □ Frederick,
MD

Snyder, Eileen, Libn.
SYRACUSE UNIVERSITY - GEOLOGY LIBRARY □
Syracuse, NY

Snyder, Eileen, Libn.
SYRACUSE UNIVERSITY - PHYSICS LIBRARY □
Syracuse, NY

Snyder, Ellie, Info.Spec.
NATIONAL SCIENCE TEACHERS ASSOCIATION
- GLENN O. BLOUGH LIBRARY □ Washington, DC
Snyder, June M., Asst.Libn.
VELSICOL CHEMICAL CORPORATION -
RESEARCH AND DEVELOPMENT DEPARTMENT -
LIBRARY† □ Chicago, IL
Snyder, Madge, Libn.
AMERICAN MANAGEMENT ASSOCIATIONS -
D.W. MITCHELL MEMORIAL LIBRARY □
Hamilton, NY
Snyder, Mary, Non-Print Libn.
NOVA SCOTIA COLLEGE OF ART AND DESIGN -
LIBRARY □ Halifax, NS
Snyder, Patt, Libn.
SHELL DEVELOPMENT COMPANY - BIOLOGICAL
SCIENCES RESEARCH CENTER - LIBRARY □
Modesto, CA
Snyder, Rena, Chf.Med.Libn.
UNION MEMORIAL HOSPITAL - DR. JOHN M.T.
FINNEY, JR. MEMORIAL MEDICAL LIBRARY □
Baltimore, MD
Snyder, Sally, Libn.
FORT MALDEN NATIONAL HISTORIC PARK -
LIBRARY & ARCHIVES □ Amherstburg, ON
Snyder, Shelli, Libn.
SOUTHERN CALIFORNIA ASSOCIATION OF
GOVERNMENTS - INFORMATION RESOURCE
CENTER □ Los Angeles, CA
Snyder, Sherrie, Ref.Libn.
UTAH STATE LIBRARY □ Salt Lake City, UT
Snyder, Thomas, Ref.Libn.
PACE UNIVERSITY - LIBRARY □ New York, NY
Snyder, Virginia J., Chf.Libn.
U.S. AIR FORCE BASE - ANDREWS BASE
LIBRARY □ Washington, DC
Snyder, W.A., Mgr., Tech.Info.
U.S. DEPT. OF ENERGY - PACIFIC NORTHWEST
LABORATORY - TECHNICAL INFO. SECT. □
Richland, WA
Sobel, Sharon G.S., Law Libn.
OWENS-CORNING FIBERGLAS CORPORATION -
LAW DEPARTMENT LIBRARY □ Toledo, OH
Sobel, Susan, Asst.Libn.
DROPSIE UNIVERSITY - LIBRARY □ Philadelphia,
PA
Soben, Phyllis, Med.Libn.
CEDARS-SINAI MEDICAL CENTER - HEALTH
SCIENCES INFORMATION CENTER □ Los
Angeles, CA
Sober, Annelie, Dir., Med.Lib.
MILLER-DWAN HOSPITAL AND MEDICAL
CENTER - TILDERQUIST MEMORIAL MEDICAL
LIBRARY □ Duluth, MN
Sobieski, Colleen Joy, Mgr., Info.Ctr.
RADER COMPANIES, INC. - INFORMATION
CENTER □ Portland, OR
Sobin, Maryann, Libn.
ENGELHARD CORPORATION - TECHNICAL
INFORMATION CENTER □ Edison, NJ
Sobkowiak, Emily, Med.Libn.
MOUNT SINAI HOSPITAL MEDICAL CENTER -
LEWISOHN MEMORIAL LIBRARY □ Chicago, IL
Sobon, Juliette L., Asst.Cur. of Lib.
HISPANIC SOCIETY OF AMERICA - LIBRARY □
New York, NY
Sobotka, John, Archv.
UNIVERSITY OF MISSISSIPPI - SCHOOL OF
LAW LIBRARY □ University, MS
Sochasky, Mrs. Lee, Prog.Coord.
INTERNATIONAL ATLANTIC SALMON
FOUNDATION - LIBRARY □ St. Andrews, NB
Soczka, Janice, Asst.Cur.
CHICAGO HISTORICAL SOCIETY - SPECIAL
COLLECTIONS □ Chicago, IL
Soderberg, Arlette, Hd. of Ref.
UNIVERSITY OF MINNESOTA - LAW LIBRARY □
Minneapolis, MN
Soderlund, Carl, Libn.
CLEARFIELD LAW LIBRARY □ Clearfield, PA
Sodhi, B., Libn.
NOVA SCOTIA AGRICULTURAL COLLEGE -
LIBRARY □ Truro, NS

Soenksen, Shirley, Ref.Libn.
AMERICAN HISTORICAL SOCIETY OF GERMANS
FROM RUSSIA - GREELEY PUBLIC LIBRARY □
Greeley, CO
Soete, George, Ref.Libn.
UNIVERSITY OF CALIFORNIA, SAN DIEGO -
UNIVERSITY LIBRARIES □ La Jolla, CA
Soiffer, Renee, Branch Libn.
NORTHROP CORPORATION - AIRCRAFT
DIVISION - LIBRARY SERVICES □ Hawthorne,
CA
Sokalzuk, Pauline M., Law Libn.
NORTHUMBERLAND COUNTY LAW LIBRARY □
Sunbury, PA
Sokkar, JoAnn, Libn.
UNIVERSITY OF MICHIGAN - BUSINESS
ADMINISTRATION LIBRARY - INDUSTRIAL
RELATIONS SECTION □ Ann Arbor, MI
Sokol, Karol M., Libn.
CLEARY, GOTTLIEB, STEEN & HAMILTON -
LIBRARY □ New York, NY
Sokolov, Barbara J., Ldr., Lib.Sci. Group
UNIVERSITY OF ALASKA, ANCHORAGE -
ARCTIC ENVIRONMENTAL INFORMATION AND
DATA CENTER □ Anchorage, AK
Sol, Ellen, Supv.Lib.Oper.
SYSTEM DEVELOPMENT CORPORATION -
LIBRARY □ Santa Monica, CA
Solbrig, Dorothy J., Libn.
HARVARD UNIVERSITY - BIOLOGICAL
LABORATORIES LIBRARY □ Cambridge, MA
Soldwisch, Marilyn, Lib.Techn.
U.S. NAVY - FLEET COMBAT DIRECTION
SYSTEMS SUPPORT ACTIVITY, SAN DIEGO -
DATA RESOURCE CENTER† □ San Diego, CA
Soler, Eleanor, Libn.
NEW YORK THEOLOGICAL SEMINARY -
LIBRARY □ New York, NY
Soles, Elizabeth L., Hd.Libn.
JACOBS ENGINEERING GROUP - TECHNICAL
INFORMATION SERVICES DEPARTMENT □
Houston, TX
Solis, Miguel, Ref.
INDIANA UNIVERSITY - LILLY LIBRARY □
Bloomington, IN
Solley, Nancy, Ref.Libn.
WESTERN KENTUCKY UNIVERSITY -
KENTUCKY LIBRARY AND MUSEUM/
UNIVERSITY ARCHIVES □ Bowling Green, KY
Soloman, Marvin, Soc.Sci./Map Libn.
SOUTHERN ILLINOIS UNIVERSITY,
EDWARDSVILLE - SOCIAL SCIENCE/
BUSINESS/MAP LIBRARY □ Edwardsville, IL
Solomon, Cliff, LRC Coord.
UNIVERSITY OF SOUTHERN CALIFORNIA -
HEALTH SCIENCES CAMPUS - NORRIS MEDICAL
LIBRARY □ Los Angeles, CA
Solomon, Joel L., Libn.
CASEY, LANE & MITTENDORF - LAW LIBRARY □
New York, NY
Solomon, Meredith, Circ./Pharmacy Libn.
SOUTHWESTERN OKLAHOMA STATE
UNIVERSITY - AL HARRIS LIBRARY □
Weatherford, OK
Solomon, Michelle, Tech.Ref.Libn.
NATIONAL PASSENGER RAILROAD
CORPORATION (AMTRAK) - COMPUTER
SERVICES DEPARTMENT LIBRARY □
Washington, DC
Solomon, Sue, Libn.
FIRST CHRISTIAN CHURCH - LIBRARY □
Alexandria, VA
Solomonoff, Sonia, Cat.
CASE WESTERN RESERVE UNIVERSITY - LAW
LIBRARY □ Cleveland, OH
Solow, Linda I., Music Libn.
MASSACHUSETTS INSTITUTE OF TECHNOLOGY
- MUSIC LIBRARY □ Cambridge, MA
Soltow, Martha Jane, Libn.
MICHIGAN STATE UNIVERSITY - LABOR AND
INDUSTRIAL RELATIONS LIBRARY □ East
Lansing, MI

Solvick, Shirley, Chf.
DETROIT PUBLIC LIBRARY - FINE ARTS
DEPARTMENT □ Detroit, MI
Solyma, Alice, Libn.
CANADA - CANADIAN FORESTRY SERVICE -
PACIFIC FOREST RESEARCH CENTRE -
LIBRARY □ Victoria, BC
Somerman, Nelly, Libn.
DICK (A.B.) COMPANY - LIBRARY □ Chicago, IL
Somers, Audrey D., Educ.Coord.
MIRAMICHI HOSPITAL - HEALTH SCIENCES
LIBRARY □ Newcastle, NB
Somers, Mrs. Carin, Dir.
NOVA SCOTIA - PROVINCIAL LIBRARY □
Halifax, NS
Somerville, Arleen, Hd.
UNIVERSITY OF ROCHESTER - CARLSON
LIBRARY □ Rochester, NY
Sommer, Deborah, Asst.Libn.
UNIVERSITY OF CALIFORNIA, BERKELEY -
GOVERNMENT DOCUMENTS DEPARTMENT □
Berkeley, CA
Sommer, Dr. Frank H., III, Hd. Of Lib.
DU PONT (Henry Francis) WINTERTHUR
MUSEUM - LIBRARY □ Winterthur, DE
Sommer, Ronald R., Hd., Rd.Serv.Dept.
UNIVERSITY OF TENNESSEE - CENTER FOR
THE HEALTH SCIENCES LIBRARY □ Memphis, TN
Sommerfeld, Marcia, Archv.
NORTHERN ILLINOIS UNIVERSITY - REGIONAL
HISTORY CENTER □ DeKalb, IL
Sommerfeld, Vi, Corp.Sec.
MC KINNON, ALLEN & ASSOCIATES (Western),
LTD. - RESEARCH LIBRARY □ Calgary, AB
Sommerville, James, Libn.
MOUNT PLEASANT MENTAL HEALTH
INSTITUTE - PROFESSIONAL LIBRARY □ Mt.
Pleasant, IA
Son, Bonnie, Asst.Libn.
HINSDALE SANITARIUM AND HOSPITAL - A.C.
LARSON LIBRARY† □ Hinsdale, IL
Sondag, Pauline, Libn.
MICHIGAN STATE UNIVERSITY -
AGRICULTURAL ECONOMICS REFERENCE
ROOM □ East Lansing, MI
Song, Ms. Seungja, Med.Libn.
U.S. PUBLIC HEALTH SERVICE HOSPITAL -
MEDICAL SERVICE LIBRARY† □ Seattle, WA
Sonnemann, Sabine, Asst.Chf.
NATIONAL LIBRARY OF CANADA - NEWSPAPER
DIVISION □ Ottawa, ON
Sonnet, Susan, Asst. Music Libn.
UNIVERSITY OF CALIFORNIA, SANTA BARBARA
- ARTS LIBRARY □ Santa Barbara, CA
Sonnier, Clytie, Asst. Law Libn.
HARRIS COUNTY LAW LIBRARY □ Houston, TX
Sook, Lois, Med.Libn.
NEW YORK INFIRMARY BEEKMAN DOWNTOWN
HOSPITAL - ELISHA WALKER STAFF LIBRARY □
New York, NY
Soong, Huey-Min, Ref.Libn.
UNIVERSITY OF WINDSOR - PAUL MARTIN LAW
LIBRARY □ Windsor, ON
Soong, Irma Tam, Exec.Dir. Emeritus
HAWAII CHINESE HISTORY CENTER □ Honolulu,
HI
Soong, Jean, Hd., Monographs Proc.
U.S. NATL. INSTITUTES OF HEALTH - LIBRARY
□ Bethesda, MD
Soos, Maria, Hd.Cat.
WAGNER COLLEGE - HORRMANN LIBRARY □
Staten Island, NY
Soper, F.A., Dir.
NARCOTICS EDUCATION, INC. -
SCHARFFENBERG MEMORIAL LIBRARY □
Washington, DC
Soper, Marley H., Act.Dir.
ANDREWS UNIVERSITY - JAMES WHITE
LIBRARY □ Berrien Springs, MI
Sor, Yvonne, Mgr.Info.Sci.
RUST-OLEUM CORPORATION - R & D LIBRARY □
Evanston, IL

PERSONNEL

Sorem, Janet, Hd.Libn.
ERNST & WHINNEY - DATA SYSTEMS LIBRARY □ New York, NY

Sorem, Janet, Hd.Libn.
ERNST & WHINNEY - INTERNATIONAL LIBRARY □ New York, NY

Sorem, Janet, Hd.Libn.
ERNST & WHINNEY - LIBRARY □ New York, NY

Sorensen, Edwin, Hd.
NORTHPORT PUBLIC SCHOOLS - TEACHERS' PROFESSIONAL LIBRARY □ Northport, NY

Sorensen, Janice H., Libn.
KANSAS STATE GEOLOGICAL SURVEY - MOORE HALL LIBRARY □ Lawrence, KS

Sorensen, Lynn A., Corp.Dir. of Libs.
DETROIT MACOMB HOSPITALS ASSOCIATION - HOSPITAL LIBRARY □ Detroit, MI

Sorenson, Barbara Rich, Archv.
UNITED METHODIST CHURCH - SOUTH DAKOTA CONFERENCE - COMMITTEE ON ARCHIVES AND HISTORY - LIBRARY □ Mitchell, SD

Sorg, Elizabeth, Libn.
EASTERN STATE SCHOOL AND HOSPITAL - STAFF LIBRARY □ Trevose, PA

Sorgen, Herbert J., Libn.
SUNY - AGRICULTURAL AND TECHNICAL COLLEGE AT DELHI - LIBRARY† □ Delhi, NY

Sorger, Joan L., Dept.Hd.
CLEVELAND PUBLIC LIBRARY - GENERAL REFERENCE DEPARTMENT □ Cleveland, OH

Sorieul, Francoise
ASSOCIATION DES UNIVERSITES PARTIELLEMENT OU ENTIEREMENT DE LANGUE FRANCAISE - BIBLIOTHEQUE □ Montreal, PQ

Sorkow, Janice, Mgr. Photographic Serv.
MUSEUM OF FINE ARTS - DEPARTMENT OF PHOTOGRAPHIC SERVICES - SLIDE & PHOTOGRAPH LIBRARY □ Boston, MA

Soroka, Allen H., Asst.Libn., Ref.
UNIVERSITY OF BRITISH COLUMBIA - LAW LIBRARY □ Vancouver, BC

Soroka, Zofia A., Hd.Biblog.
UNIVERSITY OF WISCONSIN, STEVENS POINT - JAMES H. ALBERTSON CENTER FOR LEARNING RESOURCES □ Stevens Point, WI

Sorrell, Laura L., Dir. of Res.
KORN/FERRY INTERNATIONAL - LIBRARY □ Houston, TX

Sorrell, Robin, Lib. Aid
U.S. ARMY RESEARCH OFFICE - TECHNICAL LIBRARY □ Research Triangle Park, NC

Sorrells, Dillman B., Arch.Lib.Spec.
CLEMSON UNIVERSITY - EMERY A. GUNNIN ARCHITECTURAL LIBRARY □ Clemson, SC

Sorrough, Gail, Libn.
BECHTEL - GEOLOGY LIBRARY □ San Francisco, CA

Sorvari, Karen C., Dir. of Res.
CAMPBELL UNIVERSITY - SCHOOL OF LAW - LAW LIBRARY □ Buies Creek, NC

Sosa, James, Hd.
SAN ANTONIO PUBLIC LIBRARY - BUSINESS, SCIENCE AND TECHNOLOGY DEPARTMENT □ San Antonio, TX

Sotendahl, Audrey B., Ref./ILL Libn.
MOHAWK VALLEY COMMUNITY COLLEGE - LIBRARY □ Utica, NY

Soucie, Jeannine, Info.Spec.
ARIZONA STATE ENERGY INFORMATION CENTER □ Phoenix, AZ

Souders, Marilyn, Chf. of Acq.
NEWSWEEK, INC. - LIBRARY □ New York, NY

Soulard, Claude, Libn.
UNIVERSITE DE MONTREAL - MUSIQUE-BIBLIOTHEQUE □ Montreal, PQ

Soullen, Marilyn, Asst.Libn., Govt.Doc.
HAMLINE UNIVERSITY SCHOOL OF LAW - LIBRARY □ St. Paul, MN

Sours, Nomeka B., Exec.Sec.
ROANOKE VALLEY HISTORICAL SOCIETY - LIBRARY □ Roanoke, VA

Souter, Thomas A., Assoc.Dir.
VIRGINIA POLYTECHNIC INSTITUTE AND STATE UNIVERSITY - CAROL M. NEWMAN LIBRARY □ Blacksburg, VA

Southern, G. Edwin, Jr., Asst.Univ.Archv.
DUKE UNIVERSITY - ARCHIVES □ Durham, NC

Southwell, Mary, Acq.
UTAH STATE LIBRARY □ Salt Lake City, UT

Southwick, Neal S., Libn.
CHURCH OF JESUS CHRIST OF LATTER-DAY SAINTS - UPPER SNAKE RIVER BRANCH GENEALOGICAL LIBRARY □ Rexburg, ID

Sowby, Laurene A., Libn.
SALT LAKE TRIBUNE - LIBRARY □ Salt Lake City, UT

Sowchek, Ellen, Libn.
NATIONAL COUNCIL OF THE YOUNG MEN'S CHRISTIAN ASSOCIATIONS OF THE U.S. - YMCA HISTORICAL LIBRARY† □ New York, NY

Sowell, Frank U., Jr., Assoc. Legal Anl.
CLEVELAND ELECTRIC ILLUMINATING COMPANY - LAW LIBRARY □ Cleveland, OH

Sowell, Joseph B., Med.Libn.
JACKSON MEMORIAL HOSPITAL - SCHOOL OF NURSING LIBRARY □ Miami, FL

Sowell, Steven, Assoc.Dir., Pub.Serv.
TEXAS COLLEGE OF OSTEOPATHIC MEDICINE - MEDICAL LIBRARY □ Fort Worth, TX

Sowicz, Eugenia V., Supv. Book & Journal Lib.
GENERAL ELECTRIC COMPANY - SPACE/RSD LIBRARIES □ Philadelphia, PA

Spaak, Albert, Exec.Dir.
PLASTICS INSTITUTE OF AMERICA - LIBRARY □ Hoboken, NJ

Spadaccini, Colleen, Libn.
OAK TERRACE NURSING HOME - DEPT. OF PUBLIC WELFARE MEDICAL LIBRARY □ Minnetonka, MN

Spaeth, Mary A., Res.Info.Coord.
UNIVERSITY OF ILLINOIS - SURVEY RESEARCH LABORATORY - SURVEY AND CENSUS DATA LIBRARY □ Urbana, IL

Spak, Nancy, Hd., Pub.Serv.
MARQUETTE UNIVERSITY - LEGAL RESEARCH CENTER □ Milwaukee, WI

Spang, L., Searcher
WAYNE STATE UNIVERSITY - G. FLINT PURDY LIBRARY □ Detroit, MI

Spangelo, Dr. L.P.S., Dir.
CANADA - AGRICULTURE CANADA - RESEARCH STATION, BEAVERLODGE - LIBRARY □ Beaverlodge, AB

Sparhawk, Mary B., Cat./Ref.Libn.
UNIVERSITY OF PENNSYLVANIA - SCHOOL OF SOCIAL WORK - SMALLEY LIBRARY OF SOCIAL WORK □ Philadelphia, PA

Sparks, Janelle, Ed.
CRC PRESS, INC. - LIBRARY □ Boca Raton, FL

Sparks, Marie, Lib.Dir.
INDIANA UNIVERSITY - SCHOOL OF DENTISTRY LIBRARY □ Indianapolis, IN

Sparks, Peter G., Chf.
LIBRARY OF CONGRESS - PRESERVATION OFFICE □ Washington, DC

Sparks, R.E., Tech.Libn.
GENERAL MOTORS CORPORATION - DELCO ELECTRONICS DIVISION - TECHNICAL LIBRARY □ Kokomo, IN

Sparks, Dr. William S., Libn.
ST. PAUL SCHOOL OF THEOLOGY - DANA DAWSON LIBRARY □ Kansas City, MO

Sparling, Tobin A., Cat.Libn.
YALE UNIVERSITY - YALE CENTER FOR BRITISH ART - RARE BOOK COLLECTION □ New Haven, CT

Sparrow, Dr. Glenn W., Dir.
SAN DIEGO STATE UNIVERSITY - PUBLIC ADMINISTRATION RESEARCH CENTER LIBRARY □ San Diego, CA

Sparrow, Mary N., Chf.Libn.
GANNETT (Guy) PUBLISHING COMPANY - PRESS HERALD-EVENING EXPRESS LIBRARY □ Portland, ME

Sparvier, David L., Coord.
SASKATCHEWAN INDIAN CULTURAL COLLEGE - LIBRARY □ Saskatoon, SK

Spaude, Milton P., Libn. & Professor
MICHIGAN LUTHERAN SEMINARY - LIBRARY □ Saginaw, MI

Spaulding, F.H., Hd., Lib.Oper.Dept.
BELL TELEPHONE LABORATORIES, INC. - LIBRARIES AND INFORMATION SYSTEMS CENTER □ Murray Hill, NJ

Spaulding, Mrs. J. Lloyd, Libn.
MENNONITE CHURCH - WESTERN DISTRICT CONFERENCE - WESTERN DISTRICT LOAN LIBRARY □ North Newton, KS

Spaulding, Leslie B., Libn.
MERCER COUNTY REGIONAL PLANNING COMMISSION - LIBRARY □ Sharpsville, PA

Spaulding, Patricia E., Libn.
PINELLAS COUNTY LAW LIBRARY - CLEARWATER BRANCH □ Clearwater, FL

Spayd, Cynthia, Libn.
PENNSYLVANIA DUTCH FOLK CULTURE SOCIETY, INC. - BAVER MEMORIAL LIBRARY □ Lenhartsville, PA

Speaks, Norita, ILL Libn.
GREENSBORO PUBLIC LIBRARY - BUSINESS LIBRARY □ Greensboro, NC

Spear, Louise S., Asst.Dir.
INDIANA UNIVERSITY - ARCHIVES OF TRADITIONAL MUSIC □ Bloomington, IN

Spears, Dave, Libn.
PORTSMOUTH BAR AND LAW LIBRARY □ Portsmouth, OH

Spector, Paul C.
HOLDEN ARBORETUM - WARREN H. CORNING LIBRARY □ Mentor, OH

Speed, Bert L., Chf.Pk. Interpreter
U.S. NATL. PARK SERVICE - CHICKASAW NATL. RECREATION AREA - TRAVERTINE NATURE CENTER LIBRARY □ Sulphur, OK

Speer, Alexander D., Planner
ANNE ARUNDEL COUNTY OFFICE OF PLANNING AND ZONING - LIBRARY □ Annapolis, MD

Speers, Gilda, Acq.Libn.
BABSON COLLEGE - HORN LIBRARY □ Babson Park, MA

Speeth, Sheridan, Tech.Info.Spec.
GOULD, INC. - GOULD INFORMATION CENTER □ Cleveland, OH

Speich, Carrol, Acq.Libn.
NORTHROP CORPORATION - AIRCRAFT DIVISION - LIBRARY SERVICES □ Hawthorne, CA

Speirs, Sr. Gilmary, I.H.M., Commun.Libn.
MARYWOOD COLLEGE - LEARNING RESOURCES CENTER □ Scranton, PA

Speirs, Margaret C., Asst.Libn.
EASTERN MAINE MEDICAL CENTER - HEALTH SCIENCES LIBRARY □ Bangor, ME

Spell, Cynthia, Cat./Ref.Libn.
DELAWARE VALLEY COLLEGE OF SCIENCE AND AGRICULTURE - JOSEPH KRAUSKOPF MEMORIAL LIBRARY □ Doylestown, PA

Spellman, Ann, Lrng.Ctr.Libn.
LINCOLN CHRISTIAN COLLEGE & SEMINARY - JESSIE C. EURY LIBRARY □ Lincoln, IL

Spellman, Lawrence E., Cur. of Maps
PRINCETON UNIVERSITY - RARE BOOKS AND SPECIAL COLLECTIONS □ Princeton, NJ

Spellman, Lawrence E., Cur. of Maps
PRINCETON UNIVERSITY - RICHARD HALLIBURTON MAP COLLECTION □ Princeton, NJ

Spence, Aurelia, Dir.
CENTRAL STATE HOSPITAL - MENTAL HEALTH LIBRARY □ Milledgeville, GA

Spence, Aurelia S., Lib.Dir.
CENTRAL STATE HOSPITAL - MEDICAL LIBRARY □ Milledgeville, GA

Spence, Gem, Per.
DELL PUBLISHING COMPANY, INC. - LIBRARY □ New York, NY

Spence, Linda, Info.Spec.
WESTINGHOUSE ELECTRIC CORPORATION -
NUCLEAR ENERGY SYSTEMS - INFORMATION
RESOURCES† □ Pittsburgh, PA
Spence, Marie Rose
MANITOBA INDIAN CULTURAL EDUCATION
CENTRE - PEOPLES LIBRARY □ Winnipeg, MB
Spence, Ruth S., Map Cur.
BIRMINGHAM PUBLIC AND JEFFERSON COUNTY
FREE LIBRARY - RUCKER AGEE
CARTOGRAPHICAL COLLECTION □ Birmingham,
AL
Spencer, Carol, Med.Libn.
LAHEY CLINIC MEDICAL CENTER - RICHARD B.
CATTELL MEMORIAL LIBRARY □ Burlington, MA
Spencer, Carol, Asst.Libn.
NEW YORK INSTITUTE OF TECHNOLOGY -
CENTER FOR ENERGY POLICY AND RESEARCH -
ENERGY INFORMATION CENTER □ Old
Westbury, NY
Spencer, Edward, Info.Coord.
ECOLOGY CENTER - LIBRARY □ Berkeley, CA
Spencer, Faye, Libn.
DECATUR HERALD AND REVIEW - LIBRARY □
Decatur, IL
Spencer, J. Rodgers, Assoc. Pastor
FIRST PRESBYTERIAN CHURCH - LIBRARY† □ El
Paso, TX
Spencer, Lorna, Cur.
CATTARAUGUS COUNTY MEMORIAL AND
HISTORICAL MUSEUM - LIBRARY □ Little Valley,
NY
Spencer, Marian H., Lib.Dir.
WILSON MEMORIAL HOSPITAL - LIBRARY/
LEARNING CENTER □ Wilson, NC
Spencer, Mima, Assoc.Dir.
ERIC CLEARINGHOUSE ON ELEMENTARY AND
EARLY CHILDHOOD EDUCATION □ Champaign,
IL
Spencer, Patricia A., Archv./Libn.
ST. JOSEPH HOSPITAL - LIBRARY □ Chicago, IL
Spengler, Kenneth C., Exec.Dir.
AMERICAN METEOROLOGICAL SOCIETY -
ABSTRACTS PROJECT - LIBRARY† □ Boston, MA
Spengler, Kenneth C., Exec.Dir.
AMERICAN METEOROLOGICAL SOCIETY -
BROOKS LIBRARY □ Boston, MA
Spenser, Rita, Act.Libn.
UNION UNIVERSITY - DUDLEY OBSERVATORY -
LIBRARY □ Schenectady, NY
Sperber, Jonathan, Asst.Archv.
BAECK (Leo) INSTITUTE - LIBRARY □ New York,
NY
Sperlbaum, Andrea, Ser.Libn.
WAYNE STATE UNIVERSITY - SCHOOL OF
MEDICINE - VERA PARSHALL SHIFFMAN
MEDICAL LIBRARY □ Detroit, MI
Sperling, Steve, Dir.
YOUTH NETWORK COUNCIL OF CHICAGO, INC.
- CLEARINGHOUSE □ Chicago, IL
Spernoga, Victoria, Ref.Libn.
OHIO STATE UNIVERSITY - HEALTH SCIENCES
LIBRARY □ Columbus, OH
Spicer, Claudia A., Cur.
WESTERN MUSEUM OF MINING & INDUSTRY -
LIBRARY □ Colorado Springs, CO
Spicer, Erik J., Parliamentary Libn.
CANADA - LIBRARY OF PARLIAMENT □ Ottawa,
ON
Spiegelman, Barbara, Cons.
WESTINGHOUSE ELECTRIC CORPORATION -
NUCLEAR ENERGY SYSTEMS - INFORMATION
RESOURCES† □ Pittsburgh, PA
Spier, Peggy, Ref.Libn.
MC GRAW-HILL, INC. - LIBRARY □ New York, NY
Spieth, Marsha, Cat.
NATIONAL GALLERY OF ART - LIBRARY □
Washington, DC
Spigelman, Cynthia, Assoc.Libn.
PORTLAND CEMENT ASSOCIATION/
CONSTRUCTION TECHNOLOGY LABORATORIES
- INFORMATION SERVICES SECTION □ Skokie,
IL

Spiker, Sue
NATIONAL ASSOCIATION OF QUICK PRINTERS
- INTERNATIONAL QUICK PRINTING
FOUNDATION LIBRARY □ Lafayette, IN
Spillman, Pamela, Lib.Asst.
U.S. AIR FORCE HOSPITAL MEDICAL CENTER -
MEDICAL LIBRARY (OH-Wright-Patterson AFB) □
Wright-Patterson AFB, OH
Spindler, Mary Anne, Libn.
MEDICAL CARE DEVELOPMENT, INC. - LIBRARY
□ Augusta, ME
Spindler, Ruth A., Sr.Info.Spec.
GOODRICH (B.F.) COMPANY - RESEARCH AND
DEVELOPMENT CENTER - BRECKSVILLE
INFORMATION CENTER □ Brecksville, OH
Spinelli, Frances M., Dir.
MONTCLAIR STATE COLLEGE - NATIONAL
ADULT EDUCATION CLEARINGHOUSE/
MULTIMEDIA CENTER □ Upper Montclair, NJ
Spinks, Paul, Dir. of Libs.
U.S. NAVY - NAVAL POSTGRADUATE SCHOOL -
DUDLEY KNOX LIBRARY □ Monterey, CA
Spirito, Mrs. S., Group Ldr.
GEORGE BROWN COLLEGE OF APPLIED ARTS &
TECHNOLOGY - LIBRARY □ Toronto, ON
Spiro, Elizabeth, Hd.Libn.
RESOURCE & RESEARCH CENTER FOR BEAVER
COUNTY & LOCAL HISTORY □ Beaver Falls, PA
Spitz, Herman H., Dir. of Res.
JOHNSTONE (E.R.) TRAINING & RESEARCH
CENTER - PROFESSIONAL LIBRARY □
Bordentown, NJ
Spitzen, Rosemary, Asst.Libn.
U.S. NAVY - EDWARD RHODES STITT LIBRARY
□ Bethesda, MD
Spitzer, Paul, Adm.
BOEING COMPANY - SEATTLE SERVICES
DIVISION - HISTORICAL SERVICES AND
ARCHIVES □ Seattle, WA
Spitzform, Dana, Cat.
DICKINSON SCHOOL OF LAW - SHEELY-LEE
LAW LIBRARY □ Carlisle, PA
Spivey, Ruth, Doc.Libn.
WOODS HOLE OCEANOGRAPHIC INSTITUTION
- RESEARCH LIBRARY □ Woods Hole, MA
Splichal, Mr. LaMoyne, Libn.
NORTH DAKOTA STATE HIGHWAY
DEPARTMENT - LIBRARY □ Bismarck, ND
Spoede, Mary H., Med.Libn.
SCOTT & WHITE MEMORIAL HOSPITAL -
MEDICAL LIBRARY □ Temple, TX
Spohn, Clarence E., Cur.
HISTORICAL SOCIETY OF THE COCALICO
VALLEY - MUSEUM AND LIBRARY □ Ephrata, PA
Spohn, Richard A., Hd.
UNIVERSITY OF CINCINNATI - GEOLOGY
LIBRARY □ Cincinnati, OH
Spolarich, Eleanor, Libn.
GENERAL MOTORS CORPORATION - ELECTRO-
MOTIVE DIVISION - ENGINEERING LIBRARY □
La Grange, IL
Sponholz, Judy, Dept.Libn.
ALBERTA - DEPARTMENT OF SOCIAL SERVICES
& COMMUNITY HEALTH - LIBRARY □ Edmonton,
AB
Spoo, Corinne H., Hd.
PAINE ART CENTER AND ARBORETUM -
LIBRARY □ Oshkosh, WI
Spoor, Richard D., Dir.
UNION THEOLOGICAL SEMINARY - LIBRARY □
New York, NY
Spradlin, Frances, ILL Libn.
UNIVERSITY OF OREGON - HEALTH SCIENCES
CENTER - LIBRARY □ Portland, OR
Spragens, John, Jr., Co-Dir.
SOUTHEAST ASIA RESOURCE CENTER □
Berkeley, CA
Sprague, Karol, Asst. to Libn.
MICHIGAN BELL TELEPHONE COMPANY -
CORPORATE REFERENCE CENTER □ Detroit, MI
Sprague, Mary M., Dir.
CARLETON MEMORIAL HOSPITAL - HEALTH
SCIENCES LIBRARY □ Woodstock, NB

Sprague, Roderick, Dir.
UNIVERSITY OF IDAHO - ARCHIVE OF PACIFIC
NORTHWEST ARCHAEOLOGY □ Moscow, ID
Spranger, Shirley L., Hd., Pub.Serv.Sect.
NEW YORK PUBLIC LIBRARY - ECONOMIC AND
PUBLIC AFFAIRS DIVISION □ New York, NY
Sprankle, Anita T., Non-Bk.Mtls.Libn.
KUTZTOWN STATE COLLEGE - ROHRBACH
LIBRARY □ Kutztown, PA
Sprinc, Fr. Nicholas, Sec.
SLOVAK WRITERS AND ARTISTS ASSOCIATION
- SLOVAK INSTITUTE - LIBRARY† □ Cleveland,
OH
Spring, Joan E., Cat.
EMORY UNIVERSITY - SCHOOL OF MEDICINE -
A.W. CALHOUN MEDICAL LIBRARY □ Atlanta, GA
Springenberg, Mrs. Vi
CENTRAL STATES INSTITUTE OF ADDICTIONS
- LIBRARY □ Chicago, IL
Springer, Jean M., Exec.Dir.
YOUNG MEN'S MERCANTILE LIBRARY
ASSOCIATION - LIBRARY □ Cincinnati, OH
Springer, John J., Libn.
KANSAS CITY TIMES-STAR - LIBRARY □ Kansas
City, MO
Springer, Nelson P., Cur.
MENNONITE HISTORICAL LIBRARY □ Goshen,
IN
Sprinkle, Michael D., Dir.
WAKE FOREST UNIVERSITY - BOWMAN GRAY
SCHOOL OF MEDICINE - LIBRARY □ Winston-
Salem, NC
Sprinzen, Scott, Ref.Libn.
UNIVERSITY OF CHICAGO - BUSINESS/
ECONOMICS LIBRARY □ Chicago, IL
Sprott, Elizabeth A., Libn.
SOUTH CAROLINA STATE SUPREME COURT -
LIBRARY □ Columbia, SC
Sprowl, Jody, Libn.
LEGAL SERVICES ORGANIZATION OF INDIANA,
INC. - DELAWARE COUNTY OFFICE - LIBRARY □
Muncie, IN
Sprung, George, Ref.Libn.
COLLEGE OF MEDICINE AND DENTISTRY OF
NEW JERSEY AT NEWARK - GEORGE F. SMITH
LIBRARY □ Newark, NJ
Sprung, Lori L., Info.Spec.
SAVAGE INFORMATION SERVICES □ Rolling Hills
Estates, CA
Spudeiko, George T., Hd.Libn.
TOLSTOY FOUNDATION CENTER - TOLSTOY
LIBRARY □ Valley Cottage, NY
Spula, Jack, Co-Hd., Cat.Dept.
UNIVERSITY OF ROCHESTER - EASTMAN
SCHOOL OF MUSIC - SIBLEY MUSIC LIBRARY □
Rochester, NY
Spurlock, Sandra, Dir.Lib.Serv.
LONG ISLAND JEWISH-HILLSIDE MEDICAL
CENTER - HEALTH SCIENCES LIBRARY □ New
Hyde Park, NY
Spyker, Elaine, AV Libn.
JEFFERSON (Thomas) UNIVERSITY - SCOTT
MEMORIAL LIBRARY □ Philadelphia, PA
Squire, Jeannette W., Libn.
PLYMOUTH CONGREGATIONAL CHURCH - VIDA
B. VAREY LIBRARY □ Seattle, WA
Squire, Richard J., Dir.
BEDFORD HISTORICAL SOCIETY - LIBRARY □
Bedford, OH
Squire, Stephen E., Libn.
VIRGINIA STATE DIVISION OF JUSTICE AND
CRIME PREVENTION - LIBRARY □ Richmond, VA
Squires, Lillian, Libn.
TERRELL STATE HOSPITAL - MEDICAL LIBRARY
□ Terrell, TX
Squires, Martha K., Libn., Res.Ck.
CHEMUNG COUNTY HISTORICAL SOCIETY, INC.
- MRS. ARTHUR W. BOOTH LIBRARY □ Elmira,
NY
Squyres, Barbara, Engr.Libn.
HUGHES AIRCRAFT COMPANY - ENGINEERING
LIBRARY □ Newport Beach, CA

Srinivasagam, Elizabeth, Hd., Rd.Serv.
YORK UNIVERSITY - LAW LIBRARY □
Downsview, ON
Srygley, Ted F., Dir.
UNIVERSITY OF FLORIDA - J. HILLIS MILLER
HEALTH CENTER LIBRARY □ Gainesville, FL
Staar, Richard F., Assoc.Dir.Lib.Oper.
STANFORD UNIVERSITY - HOOVER
INSTITUTION ON WAR, REVOLUTION AND
PEACE - LIBRARY □ Stanford, CA
Staats, Joan, Sr. Staff Sci.
JACKSON LABORATORY - RESEARCH LIBRARY □
Bar Harbor, ME
Staats, Mary, Libn.
PETTIT & MARTIN - LIBRARY □ San Francisco,
CA
Stachiewicz, Wanda, Hon.Cur.
POLISH INSTITUTE OF ARTS AND SCIENCES IN
CANADA - POLISH LIBRARY □ Montreal, PQ
Stachura, Irene A., Libn.
U.S. HERITAGE CONSERVATION AND
RECREATION SERVICE - PACIFIC SOUTHWEST
REGIONAL OFFICE - LIBRARY □ San Francisco,
CA
Stack, May, Asst.Libn./Cat.
WESTERN NEW ENGLAND COLLEGE - JOHN D.
CHURCHILL MEMORIAL LIBRARY □ Springfield,
MA
Stack, Rita B., Libn.
EASTMAN KODAK COMPANY - HEALTH, SAFETY
AND HUMAN FACTORS LABORATORY - LIBRARY
□ Rochester, NY
Stackpole, Edourd A., Hist.
NANTUCKET HISTORICAL ASSOCIATION -
PETER FOULGER LIBRARY □ Nantucket, MA
Stackpole, Laurie E., Chf., User Serv.Br.
U.S. NATL. OCEANIC & ATMOSPHERIC
ADMINISTRATION - LIBRARY AND
INFORMATION SERVICES DIVISION □ Rockville,
MD
Stacy, Betty A., Libn.
VIRGINIA MUSEUM OF FINE ARTS - LIBRARY □
Richmond, VA
Stacy, Donald K., Libn.
NORTH CAROLINA STATE JUSTICE ACADEMY -
LEARNING RESOURCE CENTER □ Salemburg, NC
Stad, Frederick, V.P.
AMERICAN SOCIETY OF ANCIENT
INSTRUMENTS - LIBRARY □ Drexel Hill, PA
Stadden, Richard C., Info.Ret.
ARMSTRONG WORLD INDUSTRIES, INC. -
TECHNICAL CENTER - TECHNICAL
INFORMATION SERVICES □ Lancaster, PA
Stafford, Barbara, Pres.
NORTH OAKLAND GENEALOGICAL SOCIETY -
LIBRARY □ Lake Orion, MI
Stafford, Helen, Asst.Libn.
U.S. NATL. INSTITUTE FOR OCCUPATIONAL
SAFETY & HEALTH - CLEARINGHOUSE FOR
OCCUPATIONAL SAFETY & HEALTH INFO. □
Cincinnati, OH
Stafford, Patsy, Info.Spec.
NATIONAL CLEARINGHOUSE OF
REHABILITATION TRAINING MATERIALS -
REFERENCE COLLECTION □ Stillwater, OK
Stafford, R.S.
U.S. OAK RIDGE NATL. LABORATORY -
INFORMATION DIVISION - ENVIRONMENTAL
MUTAGEN INFORMATION CENTER □ Oak Ridge,
TN
Stager, David C., Geology Libn.
PRINCETON UNIVERSITY - GEOLOGY LIBRARY
□ Princeton, NJ
Stagg, Debby, Cat./Tech.Serv.Libn.
PHILADELPHIA COLLEGE OF ART - LIBRARY □
Philadelphia, PA
Staggs, Edwin A., Sr.Lit.Sci./Hd.Libn.
3M - RIKER LABORATORIES, INC. -
NORTHRIDGE LIBRARY □ Northridge, CA
Staggs, Patty, Libn.
UNIVERSITY OF OKLAHOMA - CENTER FOR
ECONOMIC AND MANAGEMENT RESEARCH □
Norman, OK

Stagner, Adalene, Libn.
BURNS AND MC DONNELL ENGINEERING
COMPANY - TECHNICAL LIBRARY □ Kansas City,
MO
Stahl, J. Natalia, Ser. & Acq.Libn.
CLARKSON COLLEGE OF TECHNOLOGY -
EDUCATIONAL RESOURCES CENTER □ Potsdam,
NY
Stahl, Joan, Dept.Hd.
ENOCH PRATT FREE LIBRARY - FINE ARTS AND
RECREATION DEPARTMENT □ Baltimore, MD
Stahl, Ramona, Circ.
PEPPERDINE UNIVERSITY - LAW LIBRARY □
Malibu, CA
Stahl, Susan, Asst.Archv.
UNIVERSITY OF KANSAS - UNIVERSITY
ARCHIVES □ Lawrence, KS
Stahl, Thomas B., Law Libn.
SANDUSKY COUNTY LAW LIBRARY □ Fremont,
OH
Stair, Barbara, Asst.Libn.
PURDUE UNIVERSITY - AVIATION
TECHNOLOGY LIBRARY □ West Lafayette, IN
Stair, Fred, Libn.
CITIES SERVICE COMPANY - ERG - RESEARCH
LIBRARY □ Tulsa, OK
Stair, Hershall, Libn.
TRUNKLINE GAS COMPANY - GENERAL LIBRARY
□ Houston, TX
Stajniak, Elizabeth T., Libn.
DETROIT BAR ASSOCIATION FOUNDATION -
LIBRARY □ Detroit, MI
Stalbaum, Bertha, Musm.Cur.
HISTORICAL SOCIETY OF PORTER COUNTY -
LIBRARY □ Valparaiso, IN
Staley, Ronald, Radio Archv.
UNIVERSITY OF CALIFORNIA, LOS ANGELES -
UCLA RADIO ARCHIVES □ Los Angeles, CA
Staller, Betsy, Ref.Libn.
NEWSWEEK, INC. - LIBRARY □ New York, NY
Stallings, Elizabeth, Regional Liaison
U.S. DEPT. OF HOUSING AND URBAN
DEVELOPMENT - LIBRARY □ Washington, DC
Stalnaker, Enolia L., Chf., Lib.Serv.
U.S. VETERANS ADMINISTRATION (IN-Fort
Wayne) - HOSPITAL LIBRARY □ Fort Wayne, IN
Stalsitz, Emma, Asst.Libn.
SACRED HEART HOSPITAL - WILLIAM A.
HAUSMAN MEDICAL LIBRARY □ Allentown, PA
Stambaugh, Catherine T., Libn.
PENNSYLVANIA STATE DEPARTMENT OF
JUSTICE - OFFICE OF ATTORNEY GENERAL
LAW LIBRARY □ Harrisburg, PA
Stambaugh, Dorothy, Libn.
TRUMBULL MEMORIAL HOSPITAL - SCHOOL OF
NURSING LIBRARY □ Warren, OH
Stamey, Tom W., Mgr., R&D
REYNOLDS (R.J.) TOBACCO COMPANY - R&D
INFORMATION SYSTEMS LIBRARY □ Winston-
Salem, NC
Stamm, Geoffry, Dir., Advisory Serv.
U.S. DEPT. OF THE INTERIOR - INDIAN ARTS
AND CRAFTS BOARD □ Washington, DC
Stamoolis, Peter, Libn.
CONSOLIDATION COAL COMPANY -
EXPLORATION LIBRARY □ Pittsburgh, PA
Stamper, Nancy, Cat.
UNIVERSITY OF GEORGIA - RARE BOOKS
DEPARTMENT □ Athens, GA
Stampfle, Felice, Cur., Draw./Prints
PIERPONT MORGAN LIBRARY □ New York, NY
Stancil, C. Ira, Info.Spec.
MARYLAND STATE DEPARTMENT OF
EDUCATION - DIVISION OF LIBRARY
DEVELOPMENT & SERVICES - MEDIA SERVICES
CENTER □ Baltimore, MD
Stancu, S., Sound Recording Cat.
INDIANA UNIVERSITY - MUSIC LIBRARY □
Bloomington, IN
Stand, Lucy, Lib.Assoc. II
UNIVERSITY OF PITTSBURGH - GRADUATE
SCHOOL OF PUBLIC & INTERNATIONAL
AFFAIRS LIBRARY □ Pittsburgh, PA

Standifur, Kristine, Res.Asst.
MARSHALL UNIVERSITY - RESEARCH
COORDINATING UNIT FOR VOCATIONAL
EDUCATION □ Huntington, WV
Standing, Doris A., Libn.
ONTARIO - MINISTRY OF HEALTH - PUBLIC
HEALTH LABORATORIES - LIBRARY □ Toronto,
ON
Standish, Beulah I., Libn.
CONSUMERS POWER COMPANY - LAW LIBRARY
□ Jackson, MI
Standley, Grace, Soc.Sci.Ref.Libn.
SAM HOUSTON STATE UNIVERSITY - LIBRARY†
□ Huntsville, TX
Stanek, Agnes, Ck.
SASKATOON CANCER CLINIC - LIBRARY &
SIGGA COOK MEMORIAL LIBRARY □ Saskatoon,
SK
Stanek, E., Law Libn.
UNIVERSITY OF SASKATCHEWAN - LAW
LIBRARY □ Saskatoon, SK
Stanek, S., Clas. Reports Libn.
LOCKHEED MISSILES & SPACE COMPANY, INC.
- TECHNICAL INFORMATION CENTER □ Palo
Alto, CA
Stanfield, Barrie, Libn.
CANADA - AGRICULTURE CANADA - RESEARCH
STATION, CHARLOTTETOWN - LIBRARY □
Charlottetown, PE
Stange, Cheryl L., Asst.Libn.
FMC CORPORATION - CENTRAL ENGINEERING
LABORATORIES - LIBRARY □ Santa Clara, CA
Stangl, Peter, Dir.
STANFORD UNIVERSITY - LANE MEDICAL
LIBRARY □ Stanford, CA
Stangs, Loretta F., Mgr., Lib.Serv.
HOECHST-ROUSSEL PHARMACEUTICALS, INC. -
LIBRARY □ Somerville, NJ
Staniszewski, Victoria, Asst.Libn.
SOUTH MACOMB HOSPITAL - DETROIT-
MACOMB HOSPITALS ASSOCIATION MEDICAL
LIBRARY □ Warren, MI
Staniszewski, Victoria A., Asst.Libn.
DETROIT MACOMB HOSPITALS ASSOCIATION -
HOSPITAL LIBRARY □ Detroit, MI
Stankevich, Mary, Libn.
METROPOLITAN JEWISH GERIATRIC CENTER -
MAX B. & LOUISA S. MARKS MEMORIAL
MEDICAL LIBRARY† □ Brooklyn, NY
Stankiewicz, Carol, Ref.Libn.
DUN AND BRADSTREET, INC. - BUSINESS
LIBRARY □ New York, NY
Stankowski, Barbara, Exec.Sec.
HOLLAND SOCIETY OF NEW YORK - LIBRARY □
New York, NY
Stankus, Tony, Sci.Libn.
HOLY CROSS COLLEGE - SCIENCE LIBRARY □
Worcester, MA
Stanley, Frances, Asst.Libn.
BURNS AND MC DONNELL ENGINEERING
COMPANY - TECHNICAL LIBRARY □ Kansas City,
MO
Stanley, Janet L., Br.Libn.
SMITHSONIAN INSTITUTION LIBRARIES -
MUSEUM OF AFRICAN ART - BRANCH LIBRARY
□ Washington, DC
Stanley, Jean, Dir., Lib.Serv.
ST. ALEXIS HOSPITAL - HEALTH SCIENCES
LIBRARY □ Cleveland, OH
Stanley, John H., Spec.Coll.Libn.
BROWN UNIVERSITY - SPECIAL COLLECTIONS†
□ Providence, RI
Stanley, John R., Libn.
DALLAS BIBLE COLLEGE - GOULD MEMORIAL
LIBRARY† □ Dallas, TX
Stanley, Mr. Lee, Asst.Libn.
CONGREGATION RODEPH SHALOM - LIBRARY □
Philadelphia, PA
Stanley, Linda C., Libn.
ROXBOROUGH MEMORIAL HOSPITAL - SCHOOL
OF NURSING AND MEDICAL STAFF LIBRARY □
Philadelphia, PA

Stanley, William A., Chf.
U.S. NATL. OCEANIC & ATMOSPHERIC ADM. -
NATL. OCEAN SURVEY - PHYSICAL SCIENCE
SERVICES BRANCH - MAP LIB. □ Rockville, MD
Stanton, Mrs. James H., Med.Libn.
CAMBRIDGE HOSPITAL - MEDICAL LIBRARY □
Cambridge, MA
Stanton, Lee, Sr.Libn.
NEW YORK STATE LIBRARY - HUMANITIES
REFERENCE SERVICE □ Albany, NY
Stanton, R.O., Hd., Info.Sys.Dept.
BELL TELEPHONE LABORATORIES, INC. -
LIBRARIES AND INFORMATION SYSTEMS
CENTER □ Murray Hill, NJ
Stanway, Sondra, Libn.
ALASKA STATE DEPARTMENT OF FISH AND
GAME - LIBRARY □ Juneau, AK
Stanwick, Kathy, Asst.Dir.
CENTER FOR THE AMERICAN WOMAN &
POLITICS - LIBRARY □ New Brunswick, NJ
Stanwood, Cheryl, Law Libn.
CALIFORNIA STATE - COURT OF APPEAL, 2ND
APPELLATE DISTRICT - LAW LIBRARY □ Los
Angeles, CA
Stapele, Deborah A., Mgr., Info.Serv.
UNITED FRESH FRUIT AND VEGETABLE
ASSOCIATION - LIBRARY □ Alexandria, VA
Stapinsky, Berthe
INSTITUT D'HISTOIRE DE L'AMERIQUE
FRANCAISE (1970) - RESEARCH CENTRE
LIBRARY □ Montreal, PQ
Stapper, Antoinette, Libn.
NATIONAL ASSOCIATION OF MUTUAL SAVINGS
BANKS - LIBRARY† □ New York, NY
Stargard, William, Asst.Cur.
COLUMBIA UNIVERSITY - DEPARTMENT OF
ART HISTORY & ARCHAEOLOGY - PHOTOGRAPH
COLLECTION □ New York, NY
Stargardt, Betty, Film Libn.
VIRGINIA STATE DEPARTMENT OF
TRANSPORTATION SAFETY - FILM LIBRARY □
Richmond, VA
Stark, Dr. Bruce, Dir.
SUNY - COLLEGE AT PLATTSBURGH - SPECIAL
COLLECTIONS □ Plattsburgh, NY
Stark, Harold E., Sr.Libn., Tech.Serv.
U.S. POSTAL SERVICE - LIBRARY □ Washington,
DC
Stark, Janet M., Libn.
FISH AND NEAVE - LIBRARY □ New York, NY
Stark, Lucile S., Dir.
UNIVERSITY OF PITTSBURGH - WESTERN
PSYCHIATRIC INSTITUTE AND CLINIC -
LIBRARY □ Pittsburgh, PA
Stark, Marcella, History Biblog.
SYRACUSE UNIVERSITY - E.S. BIRD LIBRARY -
AREA STUDIES DEPARTMENT □ Syracuse, NY
Stark, Marilyn, Librarian
DAMES & MOORE - LIBRARY □ Golden, CO
Stark, Patricia, Ref./Biblog.
UNIVERSITY OF MINNESOTA - EDUCATION-
PSYCHOLOGY-LIBRARY SCIENCE LIBRARY □
Minneapolis, MN
Stark, Patricia, Ref.Archv.
YALE UNIVERSITY - MANUSCRIPTS AND
ARCHIVES □ New Haven, CT
Stark, Pearl, Screening
FRANKLIN INSTITUTE - LIBRARY □ Philadelphia,
PA
Stark, Peter, Asst.Doc.Libn.
CENTRAL WASHINGTON UNIVERSITY -
LIBRARY DOCUMENTS DEPARTMENT □
Ellensburg, WA
Stark, Peter, Map Libn.
CENTRAL WASHINGTON UNIVERSITY - MAP
LIBRARY □ Ellensburg, WA
Stark, Richard, Indexer
SPORT INFORMATION RESOURCE CENTRE □
Ottawa, ON
Stark, Sandra, Newspaper Libn.
ILLINOIS STATE HISTORICAL LIBRARY □
Springfield, IL

Starke, Ray, Med.Libn.
U.S. VETERANS ADMINISTRATION (MO-
Columbia) - HOSPITAL LIBRARY □ Columbia, MO
Starr, Cora, Circ.
TELEDYNE ISOTOPES - RESEARCH LIBRARY □
Westwood, NJ
Starr, Daniel A., Sr.Cat.
MUSEUM OF MODERN ART - LIBRARY □ New
York, NY
Starr, Gail, Law Libn.
UNIVERSITY OF CALGARY - LAW LIBRARY □
Calgary, AB
Starr, L., Ref.Libn.
UNIVERSITY OF ALBERTA - HEALTH SCIENCES
LIBRARY □ Edmonton, AB
Starr, M.J., Hd., Branch Lib.
CANADA - NATIONAL DEFENCE - NDHQ
LIBRARY □ Ottawa, ON
Starr, Marjorie L., Libn.
U.S. NAVY - NAVAL REGIONAL MEDICAL
CENTER (Quantico) - MEDICAL LIBRARY □
Quantico, VA
Start, Howard D., Dir.
WESTERN ONTARIO BREEDERS, INC. -
LIBRARY □ Woodstock, ON
Starz, Robert L., Law Libn.
MARQUETTE UNIVERSITY - LEGAL RESEARCH
CENTER □ Milwaukee, WI
Stasium, Bruce, Circ.Asst.
MARICOPA TECHNICAL COMMUNITY COLLEGE
- LIBRARY RESOURCE CENTER □ Phoenix, AZ
Statsky, William P., Libn.
ANTIOCH SCHOOL OF LAW - LIBRARY □
Washington, DC
Staubs, Hilda E., Musm.Techn.
U.S. NATL. PARK SERVICE - HARPERS FERRY
NATL. HISTORICAL PARK - LIBRARY □ Harpers
Ferry, WV
Stave, Thomas A., Hd.
UNIVERSITY OF OREGON - GOVERNMENT
DOCUMENTS SECTION □ Eugene, OR
Stavee, Kathleen, Ref.Libn.
NEW JERSEY HISTORICAL SOCIETY - LIBRARY
□ Newark, NJ
Stavetski, Norma K., Asst.Res.Libn.
ETHICON, INC. - SCIENTIFIC INFORMATION
SERVICES □ Somerville, NJ
Stavn, Virginia, Prof.Asst.
ST. PAUL PUBLIC LIBRARY - SCIENCE AND
INDUSTRY ROOM □ St. Paul, MN
Steagald, Sadie, Ref.Asst.
DARGAN-CARVER LIBRARY □ Nashville, TN
Stebbins, Marilyn F., Libn.
WILBUR SMITH AND ASSOCIATES - LIBRARY □
Columbia, SC
Stebelton, Marilyn, Prog.Coord.
WAGNALLS MEMORIAL - LIBRARY □ Lithopolis,
OH
Stecher, Bonnie, Lib.Dir.
DANVERS STATE HOSPITAL - MAC DONALD
MEDICAL LIBRARY □ Hathorne, MA
Stecher, Bonnie, Libn.
HOGAN (Charles V.) REGIONAL CENTER -
REGIONAL RESOURCE LIBRARY □ Hathorne, MA
Stecher, Bonnie, Libn.
HOGAN (Charles V.) REGIONAL CENTER - STAFF
LIBRARY □ Hathorne, MA
Steck, Roger, Exec.Sec.
CUMBERLAND COUNTY HISTORICAL SOCIETY &
HAMILTON LIBRARY □ Carlisle, PA
Steedman, Isobel M., Libn.
MANITOBA CANCER TREATMENT AND
RESEARCH FOUNDATION - LIBRARY □ Winnipeg,
MB
Steel, Joan, Libn.
SASKATOON GALLERY AND CONSERVATORY
CORPORATION - MENDEL ART GALLERY -
LIBRARY □ Saskatoon, SK
Steel, Lauri, Dir., Data Bank
AMERICAN INSTITUTES FOR RESEARCH -
PROJECT TALENT DATA BANK □ Palo Alto, CA

Steele, Anita M., Dir.
UNIVERSITY OF PUGET SOUND - SCHOOL OF
LAW LIBRARY □ Tacoma, WA
Steele, Apollonia, Spec.Coll.Libn.
UNIVERSITY OF CALGARY - SPECIAL
COLLECTIONS DIVISION □ Calgary, AB
Steele, Carole, Libn.
WESTERN LIFE INSURANCE COMPANY -
LIBRARY □ St. Paul, MN
Steele, Carole B., Asst.Libn.
U.S. AIR FORCE BASE - EGLIN BASE LIBRARY □
Eglin AFB, FL
Steele, Charles, Jr., Sci.Libn.
OHIO NORTHERN UNIVERSITY - HETERICK
MEMORIAL LIBRARY □ Ada, OH
Steele, Clara, Cat.Libn.
U.S. NATL. OCEANIC & ATMOSPHERIC
ADMINISTRATION - ENVIRONMENTAL
RESEARCH LABORATORIES - LIBRARY □
Boulder, CO
Steele, Dale, Map Ref.Libn.
UNIVERSITY OF ARIZONA - MAP COLLECTION □
Tucson, AZ
Steele, Eric, Sr. Principal Libn.
NEW YORK PUBLIC LIBRARY - MID-
MANHATTAN LIBRARY - LITERATURE AND
LANGUAGE DEPARTMENT □ New York, NY
Steele, Frances E., Tech.Libn.
BAKER (J.T.) CHEMICAL COMPANY - RESEARCH
LIBRARY □ Phillipsburg, NJ
Steele, Lee, Ref.Libn.
DELAWARE STATE - DIVISION OF LIBRARIES □
Dover, DE
Steele, Lina, Cur.
NATIONAL GALLERY OF ART - INDEX OF
AMERICAN DESIGN □ Washington, DC
Steele, Patricia, Br.Mgr.
INDIANA UNIVERSITY - HEALTH, PHYSICAL
EDUCATION & RECREATION LIBRARY □
Bloomington, IN
Steele, Phyllis, Local Rec.Spec.
WRIGHT STATE UNIVERSITY - ARCHIVES &
SPECIAL COLLECTIONS □ Dayton, OH
Steele, Robert B., Res. Chemist
ASBESTOS CORPORATION, LTD. - PRODUCT
RESEARCH & DEVELOPMENT LIBRARY □
Thetford Mines, PQ
Steele, Victoria, Belt Lib.Asst.
UNIVERSITY OF CALIFORNIA, LOS ANGELES -
ART LIBRARY □ Los Angeles, CA
Steele, Victoria, Belt Lib.Asst.
UNIVERSITY OF CALIFORNIA, LOS ANGELES -
ART LIBRARY - ELMER BELT LIBRARY OF
VINCIANA □ Los Angeles, CA
Steelman, Raylene, Rd.Serv.
UNIVERSITY OF ARKANSAS, MONTICELLO -
LIBRARY† □ Monticello, AR
Steelman, Robert F., Res.
MORAVIAN MUSIC FOUNDATION, INC. -
LIBRARY □ Winston-Salem, NC
Steen, Mrs. A.
UNION GAS, LTD. - LIBRARY SERVICE† □
Chatham, ON
Steen, Nancy, Hd.Libn.
BOWLING GREEN STATE UNIVERSITY -
POPULAR CULTURE LIBRARY □ Bowling Green,
OH
Steenblick, Dr. Ronald
UNIVERSITY OF PENNSYLVANIA - ENERGY
CENTER - DRL BASEMENT ENERGY LIBRARY □
Philadelphia, PA
Steenland, Sally, Info.Spec.
NATIONAL COMMISSION ON WORKING
WOMEN - RESOURCE CENTER □ Washington, DC
Steeves, Brenda Howitson, Chf., Spec.Coll.
MASSACHUSETTS STATE LIBRARY □ Boston,
MA
Steeves, H.A., Libn.
SPERRY CORPORATION - RESEARCH CENTER
LIBRARY □ Sudbury, MA
Stefanelli, Julia, Res.Assoc.
ALLIANCE TO SAVE ENERGY - LIBRARY □
Washington, DC

PERSONNEL

Steffen, Faith, Libn.
OREGON STATE DEPARTMENT OF
TRANSPORTATION - LIBRARY □ Salem, OR
Steffen, Ruth, Libn.
BAPTIST MEDICAL CENTER - MEDICAL
LIBRARY □ Montgomery, AL
Steffensen, Jean, Law Libn.
CONTRA COSTA COUNTY LAW LIBRARY □
Martinez, CA
Steffenson, Martin, Hd., Ref.Dept.
SOUTH DAKOTA STATE UNIVERSITY - HILTON
M. BRIGGS LIBRARY □ Brookings, SD
Steffey, Jane, Dir., Adv.Serv.
AMERICAN HORTICULTURAL SOCIETY -
HAROLD B. TUKEY MEMORIAL LIBRARY □ Mount
Vernon, VA
Stege Teleky, Elizabeth, Mss.Libn.
UNIVERSITY OF CHICAGO - SPECIAL
COLLECTIONS □ Chicago, IL
Steger, Albert P., Libn.
DETROIT SYMPHONY ORCHESTRA - LIBRARY □
Detroit, MI
Steger, Florence, Libn.
CARROLL COUNTY BAR LIBRARY □ Westminster,
MD
Stegh, Les, Archv.
DEERE & COMPANY - LIBRARY □ Moline, IL
Steglich, Sharon, Circ.Libn.
UTAH STATE LIBRARY - BLIND AND
PHYSICALLY HANDICAPPED PROGRAM -
REGIONAL LIBRARY □ Salt Lake City, UT
Stehlik-Kokker, Jane, Mgr., Sci.Info.Serv.
MARION LABORATORIES, INC. - LIBRARY □
Kansas City, MO
Steidl, Lola, Cat.
GOLDEN VALLEY LUTHERAN COLLEGE -
LIBRARY □ Minneapolis, MN
Steiger, Monte, Coord.Cat.
NORTHERN ARIZONA UNIVERSITY - LIBRARIES
□ Flagstaff, AZ
Steigner, Mary, Evening Supv.
NEW ENGLAND COLLEGE OF OPTOMETRY -
LIBRARY □ Boston, MA
Steimle, Claire L., Act.Libn.
U.S. NATL. MARINE FISHERIES SERVICE -
SANDY HOOK LABORATORY - LIONEL A.
WALFORD LIBRARY □ Highlands, NJ
Stein, Bessie A., Lib.Dir.
MEDICAL COLLEGE OF WISCONSIN - TODD
WEHR LIBRARY □ Milwaukee, WI
Stein, Douglas L., Mss.Libn.
MYSTIC SEAPORT, INC. - G.W. BLUNT WHITE
LIBRARY □ Mystic, CT
Stein, Elida B., Libn.
COLUMBIA UNIVERSITY - CHEMISTRY LIBRARY
□ New York, NY
Stein, Hadassah, Libn.
ROGER WILLIAMS GENERAL HOSPITAL -
HEALTH SCIENCES LIBRARY □ Providence, RI
Stein, Jerome D., Jr., Sr.Lit.Sci.
WARNER-LAMBERT COMPANY - CORPORATE
LIBRARY† □ Morris Plains, NJ
Stein, Judith, Dir. of Res.
CLARK (William H.) ASSOCIATES, INC. -
RESEARCH LIBRARY □ New York, NY
Stein, Julian U., Dir.
AMERICAN ALLIANCE FOR HEALTH, PHYSICAL
EDUCATION, RECREATION & DANCE -
INFORMATION CENTER FOR THE
HANDICAPPED □ Reston, VA
Stein, Karen, Res.Libn.
CHEM SYSTEMS INC. - INFORMATION CENTER
□ Tarrytown, NY
Stein, Virginia, Hd., Circ.
HARVARD UNIVERSITY - GRADUATE SCHOOL
OF EDUCATION - GUTMAN LIBRARY □
Cambridge, MA
Steinbach, Anna Belle, Med.Libn.
U.S. PUBLIC HEALTH SERVICE HOSPITAL -
MEDICAL LIBRARY† □ Carville, LA

Steinbach, Robert H., Sr.Musm.Cur.
HISTORIC ST. AUGUSTINE PRESERVATION
BOARD - HISPANIC RESEARCH LIBRARY □ St.
Augustine, FL
Steinbeck, Bertha A., Libn.
U.S. AIR FORCE BASE - CHANUTE BASE
TECHNICAL BRANCH LIBRARY† □ Chanute AFB,
IL
Steinberg, Celia, Ref.Libn.
UNIVERSITY OF MIAMI - SCHOOL OF
MEDICINE - LOUIS CALDER MEMORIAL
LIBRARY □ Miami, FL
Steinberg, Dr. Charles
MC GILL UNIVERSITY - LABOUR AGREEMENTS
DATA BANK □ Montreal, PQ
Steinberg, Lois, Libn.
URBAN LAND INSTITUTE - LIBRARY □
Washington, DC
Steinberger, Virginia, Mgr.
ENDO LABORATORIES, INC. - LIBRARY □ Garden
City, NY
Steiner, Bernadette, Libn.
SADTLER RESEARCH LABORATORIES, INC. -
LIBRARY □ Philadelphia, PA
Steiner, Carolyn, Office Mgr.
ENVIRONMENTAL ACTION COALITION -
LIBRARY/RESOURCE CENTER □ New York, NY
Steiner, Doris L., Supv.
DOW CHEMICAL COMPANY - LEGAL LIBRARY □
Midland, MI
Steiner, Mary Lou, Cat.
MACALESTER COLLEGE - WEYERHAEUSER
LIBRARY □ St. Paul, MN
Steiner, Ronald, Assoc.Dir.
INDIANA UNIVERSITY OF PENNSYLVANIA -
UNIVERSITY LIBRARY □ Indiana, PA
Steiner, Samuel, Libn. & Archv.
CONRAD GREBEL COLLEGE - LIBRARY/
ARCHIVES □ Waterloo, ON
Steinfeld, E.J. (Bud), Data User Serv.Off.
U.S. BUREAU OF THE CENSUS - REGIONAL DATA
USER SERVICE - LOS ANGELES REGIONAL
OFFICE - LIBRARY □ Los Angeles, CA
Steinhardt, Beth, Libn.
CRAWFORD AND RUSSELL, INC. - TECHNICAL
LIBRARY □ Stamford, CT
Steinhauer, Dale R., Libn.
UNIVERSITY OF MAINE, PRESQUE ISLE -
LIBRARY □ Presque Isle, ME
Steininger, Ellen, Hd.Libn.
MARSTELLER, INC. - LIBRARY □ Chicago, IL
Steinke, Cynthia A., Libn.
UNIVERSITY OF ILLINOIS, CHICAGO CIRCLE -
SCIENCE LIBRARY □ Chicago, IL
Steitz, June Harrison, Subject Spec.
NAISMITH MEMORIAL BASKETBALL HALL OF
FAME - EDWARD J. AND GENA G. HICKOX
LIBRARY □ Springfield, MA
Stell, Ann, Coord., Ch. Work
SMITHTOWN LIBRARY □ Smithtown, NY
Stell, Melvina, Hd.Libn.
GOOD SAMARITAN HOSPITAL AND MEDICAL
CENTER - LIBRARY □ Portland, OR
Stella, Colleen, Ref./ILL Libn.
SUNY - AGRICULTURAL AND TECHNICAL
COLLEGE AT MORRISVILLE - LIBRARY □
Morrisville, NY
Stembera, George, Cat.Libn.
FULLER THEOLOGICAL SEMINARY -
MC ALISTER LIBRARY □ Pasadena, CA
Stenberg, Beth M., Med.Libn.
SAN ANTONIO STATE HOSPITAL - STAFF
LIBRARY □ San Antonio, TX
Stenberg, Debora K., Lib.Dir.
NEW BRITAIN GENERAL HOSPITAL - HEALTH
SCIENCE LIBRARY □ New Britain, CT
Stender, Walter W., Assoc.Dir.
JOHNS HOPKINS UNIVERSITY - POPULATION
INFORMATION PROGRAM □ Baltimore, MD
Stenger, Marymina, Asst.Libn.Tech.Serv.
MITCHELL (William) COLLEGE OF LAW - JOHN B.
SANBORN LIBRARY □ St. Paul, MN

Stenstrom, Patricia, Libn.
UNIVERSITY OF ILLINOIS - LIBRARY AND
INFORMATION SCIENCE LIBRARY □ Urbana, IL
Stepan, Jan, Asst.Libn., Intl. Law
HARVARD UNIVERSITY - LAW SCHOOL LIBRARY
□ Cambridge, MA
Stepanian, Ellen M., Dir. of Lib. Media
SHAKER HEIGHTS CITY SCHOOL DISTRICT -
GARVIN LIBRARY □ Shaker Heights, OH
Stepek, Susan, Asst.Mgr.
CAMPBELL-EWALD COMPANY - REFERENCE
CENTER □ Warren, MI
Stephan, Evelyn B., Chf.Libn.
U.S. ARMY POST - FORT BRAGG - LIBRARY □
Fort Bragg, NC
Stephan, Susan L., Libn.
SUNLAND CENTER AT GAINESVILLE - LIBRARY
□ Gainesville, FL
Stephanian, Charles, Dir., Media Serv.
COLLEGE OF THE SAN FRANCISCO ART
INSTITUTE - ANNE BREMER MEMORIAL
LIBRARY □ San Francisco, CA
Stephans, Hildegard G., Asst.Libn. & Cat.
AMERICAN PHILOSOPHICAL SOCIETY -
LIBRARY □ Philadelphia, PA
Stephen, Baburaj, Libn.
INDIA - EMBASSY OF INDIA - LIBRARY OF THE
INFORMATION SERVICE OF INDIA □
Washington, DC
Stephen, Robert, Libn.
HAYES (Max S.) VOCATIONAL SCHOOL -
LIBRARY □ Cleveland, OH
Stephen, Ross, College Libn.
RIDER COLLEGE - FRANKLIN F. MOORE
LIBRARY □ Lawrenceville, NJ
Stephens, Alpha F.
FLORIDA STATE DEPT. OF STATE TREASURER -
DIVISION OF INSURANCE - LEGAL BUREAU
LIBRARY □ Tallahassee, FL
Stephens, Ann, Dir.
CUMBERLAND COUNTY HOSPITAL SYSTEM,
INC. - CAPE FEAR VALLEY HOSPITAL -
MEDICAL LIBRARY □ Fayetteville, NC
Stephens, Denny, Asst.Dir.
OKLAHOMA STATE DEPARTMENT OF
LIBRARIES □ Oklahoma City, OK
Stephens, Diana C., Med.Libn.
HAWAII STATE HOSPITAL - MEDICAL LIBRARY
□ Kaneohe, HI
Stephens, Gretchen, Libn.
PURDUE UNIVERSITY - VETERINARY MEDICAL
LIBRARY □ West Lafayette, IN
Stephens, Irving E., Hd. of Bldg.Serv.
RENSSELAER POLYTECHNIC INSTITUTE -
FOLSOM LIBRARY □ Troy, NY
Stephens, J. Kent, ILL
CALIFORNIA STATE UNIVERSITY, CHICO -
MERIAM LIBRARY □ Chico, CA
Stephens, Jim, Spec. Projects Libn.
SOUTHERN METHODIST UNIVERSITY -
SCIENCE/ENGINEERING LIBRARY □ Dallas, TX
Stephens, Kathleen Genuchi, Assoc.Dir., Lib.Serv.
WESTERN TEXAS COLLEGE - LEARNING
RESOURCE CENTER □ Snyder, TX
Stephens, Kenneth, Hd., Info.Serv.
CANADA - NATIONAL RESEARCH COUNCIL -
CISTI - AERONAUTICAL & MECHANICAL
ENGINEERING BRANCH □ Ottawa, ON
Stephens, Marcia, Dir. of Lib.Serv.
ST. LUKE'S HOSPITAL - LIBRARY† □ Fargo, ND
Stephens, Norris L., Libn.
UNIVERSITY OF PITTSBURGH - THEODORE M.
FINNEY MUSIC LIBRARY □ Pittsburgh, PA
Stephens, Dr. Robert, Dir., AV Ctr.
ARKANSAS STATE UNIVERSITY - DEAN B. ELLIS
LIBRARY □ State University, AR
Stephenson, Betty, Asst.Ref.Libn.
SAN DIEGO COUNTY LAW LIBRARY □ San Diego,
CA
Stephenson, Christie D., Biblog.
UNIVERSITY OF VIRGINIA - FISKE KIMBALL
FINE ARTS LIBRARY □ Charlottesville, VA

Stephenson, Clarence D., Co-Cur.
HISTORICAL AND GENEALOGICAL SOCIETY OF INDIANA COUNTY - LIBRARY AND ARCHIVES □ Indiana, PA

Stephenson, Joyce, Circ.
NOVA SCOTIA COLLEGE OF ART AND DESIGN - LIBRARY □ Halifax, NS

Stephenson, Judy, Lib.Techn.
U.S. ARMY ARMOR SCHOOL - LIBRARY □ Ft. Knox, KY

Stephenson, Laura, Off.Serv.Supv.
IOWA STATE DEPARTMENT OF ENVIRONMENTAL QUALITY - TECHNICAL LIBRARY □ Des Moines, IA

Stephenson, Patricia A., Indexer
MAY DEPARTMENT STORES COMPANY - INFORMATION CENTER □ St. Louis, MO

Stephenson, Richard W., Hd., Ref.Sect.
LIBRARY OF CONGRESS - GEOGRAPHY & MAP DIVISION □ Washington, DC

Stephenson, Robert E., Arch.Libn.
VIRGINIA POLYTECHNIC INSTITUTE AND STATE UNIVERSITY - ARCHITECTURE LIBRARY □ Blacksburg, VA

Stercho, June C., Doc.Libn.
U.S. AIR FORCE - ARMAMENT DIVISION, AIR FORCE ARMAMENT LABORATORY - TECHNICAL LIBRARY □ Eglin AFB, FL

Sterganos, Deena H., Hd., Pub.Serv
PENNSYLVANIA STATE UNIVERSITY, BERKS CAMPUS - LIBRARY □ Reading, PA

Sterlin, Annette, Tech.Serv.Libn.
HUGHES AIRCRAFT COMPANY - TECHNICAL LIBRARY □ Culver City, CA

Sterling, Cynthia R., Libn.
U.S. VETERANS ADMINISTRATION (OH-Cincinnati) - MEDICAL CENTER LIBRARY □ Cincinnati, OH

Sterling, Dr. Ray, Dir.
UNIVERSITY OF MINNESOTA - UNDERGROUND SPACE CENTER - LIBRARY □ Minneapolis, MN

Sterling, Sheila, Hd.Libn.
HUTTON (E.F.) & COMPANY, INC. - LIBRARY □ New York, NY

Stern, Annelore, Asst.Libn.
UNIVERSITY OF SOUTHERN CALIFORNIA - VON KLEINSMID LIBRARY □ Los Angeles, CA

Stern, Arlene, Asst.Libn.
CRAVATH, SWAINE, AND MOORE - LAW LIBRARY □ New York, NY

Stern, Grace, Libn.
TEMPLE SHAAREY ZEDEK - LIBRARY □ Amherst, NY

Stern, Jan
RACAL-MILGO, INC. - INFORMATION RESOURCES □ Miami, FL

Stern, Sandra, Info.Spec.
AMERICAN ASSOCIATION OF ADVERTISING AGENCIES - MEMBER INFORMATION SERVICE □ New York, NY

Stern, Stephanie, Libn.
BAECK (Leo) INSTITUTE - LIBRARY □ New York, NY

Sternberg, Susan, Info.Spec.
BURSON-MARSTELLER - INFORMATION SERVICE □ New York, NY

Sternik, Marsha, Libn.
U.S. DEPT. OF ENERGY - BARTLESVILLE ENERGY TECHNOLOGY CENTER LIBRARY □ Bartlesville, OK

Stesis, Karen, Clinical Libn.
GEORGETOWN UNIVERSITY - MEDICAL CENTER - DAHLGREN MEMORIAL LIBRARY □ Washington, DC

Stetz, Elizabeth A., Libn.
WATERLOO LIBRARY AND HISTORICAL SOCIETY† □ Waterloo, NY

Steuermann, Clara, Archv.
ARNOLD SCHOENBERG INSTITUTE - ARCHIVES □ Los Angeles, CA

Stevanovic, Bosiljka, Supv.Libn.
NEW YORK PUBLIC LIBRARY - DONNELL LIBRARY CENTER - FOREIGN LANGUAGE LIBRARY □ New York, NY

Stevens, Alan R., Act.Chf.
U.S. GEOLOGICAL SURVEY - NATL. CARTOGRAPHIC INFORMATION CENTER (NCIC) □ Reston, VA

Stevens, Barbara E., Dir.
U.S. ARMY WAR COLLEGE - LIBRARY □ Carlisle Barracks, PA

Stevens, Christine L., Ref.Libn.
INDIANA UNIVERSITY - SCHOOL OF LAW LIBRARY □ Indianapolis, IN

Stevens, Ms. H.
CANADA - PUBLIC ARCHIVES OF CANADA - NATIONAL MAP COLLECTION □ Ottawa, ON

Stevens, Helen E., Tech.Libn.
FOXBORO COMPANY - RD & E LIBRARY □ Foxboro, MA

Stevens, Icle Jean, Hd.Educ.Lib.
UNIVERSITY OF TEXAS, EL PASO - LIBRARY □ El Paso, TX

Stevens, Jane, Hd., LA Coll.
TULANE UNIVERSITY OF LOUISIANA - SPECIAL COLLECTIONS DIVISION □ New Orleans, LA

Stevens, Jean, Hd.
UNIVERSITY OF TEXAS, EL PASO - EDUCATION LIBRARY □ El Paso, TX

Stevens, Jeanne, Asst.Libn.
ANOKA AREA VOCATIONAL TECHNICAL INSTITUTE - MEDIA CENTER □ Anoka, MN

Stevens, Karen D., Libn.
UNIVERSITY OF PENNSYLVANIA - MORRIS ARBORETUM LIBRARY □ Philadelphia, PA

Stevens, Kay E., Libn.
CONSUMERS POWER COMPANY - PARNALL TECHNICAL LIBRARY □ Jackson, MI

Stevens, Lori, Dir.
STOCKPHOTOS, INC. - LIBRARY □ New York, NY

Stevens, Mary, Mgr.Lib.Serv.
SANDERS ASSOCIATES, INC. - TECHNICAL LIBRARY □ Nashua, NH

Stevens, Mary P., Musm.Libn.
MISSISSIPPI MUSEUM OF NATURAL SCIENCE - LIBRARY □ Jackson, MS

Stevens, Mike, Supv. of Res.
NATIONAL LIBRARY OF SPORTS □ San Jose, CA

Stevens, Milton, Dir./AWI Elm Trust
AMERICAN WATCHMAKERS INSTITUTE - LIBRARY □ Cincinnati, OH

Stevens, Norman D., Univ.Libn.
UNIVERSITY OF CONNECTICUT - LIBRARY □ Storrs, CT

Stevens, Robert, Libn.
ENOCH PRATT FREE LIBRARY - MARYLAND DEPARTMENT □ Baltimore, MD

Stevens, Robert R., Dir.
VINCENNES UNIVERSITY - BYRON R. LEWIS HISTORICAL LIBRARY □ Vincennes, IN

Stevens, Rosemary, Asst.Libn.
METROPOLITAN LIFE INSURANCE COMPANY - LIBRARY □ New York, NY

Stevens, Stanley D., Map Libn.
UNIVERSITY OF CALIFORNIA, SANTA CRUZ - MAP COLLECTION □ Santa Cruz, CA

Stevens, Tandy L., Info.Sys.Spec.
U.S. DEPT. OF TRANSPORTATION - URBAN MASS TRANSPORTATION ADM. - TRANSPORTATION RESEARCH INFO. CENTER (TRIC) □ Washington, DC

Stevenson, Dorothy, Sr.Rec.Techn.
GRACE (W.R.) AND COMPANY - NATURAL RESOURCES GROUP - LIBRARY □ Dallas, TX

Stevenson, Iris C., Chf.Libn.
U.S. COURT OF APPEALS, 4TH CIRCUIT - LIBRARY □ Richmond, VA

Stevenson, Mrs. J., Lib.Asst.
QUEEN'S UNIVERSITY AT KINGSTON - BIOLOGY LIBRARY □ Kingston, ON

Stevenson, Katherine, Libn.
NATIONAL CLEARINGHOUSE FOR LEGAL SERVICES - LIBRARY □ Chicago, IL

Stevenson, Marsha, Ref./Cat.Libn.
UNIVERSITY OF PITTSBURGH - HENRY CLAY FRICK FINE ARTS LIBRARY □ Pittsburgh, PA

Stevenson, Octave S., Chf.
DISTRICT OF COLUMBIA PUBLIC LIBRARY - LANGUAGE, LITERATURE &FOREIGN LANGUAGE DIVISION □ Washington, DC

Stevenson, Roberta B., Hd., Preservation
UNIVERSITY OF CALIFORNIA, DAVIS - GENERAL LIBRARY □ Davis, CA

Stevenson, Ruth, Law Libn.
SAN FRANCISCO - CITY ATTORNEY'S OFFICE - LIBRARY □ San Francisco, CA

Steves, Kathleen A., Asst.Libn.
SLEEPY HOLLOW RESTORATIONS, INC. - SPECIAL LIBRARY & ARCHIVES □ Tarrytown, NY

Steveson, Joy, Libn.
CH2M HILL CORP. - LIBRARY □ Sacramento, CA

Steward, Auburn, Libn.
BAPTIST MEDICAL CENTER SYSTEM - MARGARET CLARK GILBREATH MEMORIAL LIBRARY □ Little Rock, AR

Steward, Connie, Mgr.
GENERAL ELECTRIC COMPANY - ELECTRONICS PARK LIBRARY □ Syracuse, NY

Steward, Ouida, Libn.
SAN JUAN COUNTY ARCHAEOLOGICAL RESEARCH CENTER & LIBRARY □ Farmington, NM

Stewardson, Ms. D., Libn./Archv.
CLARKE INSTITUTE OF PSYCHIATRY - FARRAR LIBRARY □ Toronto, ON

Stewart, Anna, Info.Cons.
CITE RESOURCE CENTER □ Austin, TX

Stewart, Barbara Rose, Hd.Libn.
REED, SMITH, SHAW AND MC CLAY - LAW LIBRARY □ Pittsburgh, PA

Stewart, Beverly, Hd.Libn.
FULTON COUNTY HISTORICAL AND GENEALOGICAL SOCIETY - RESEARCH ROOM □ Canton, IL

Stewart, Charlotte, Dir., Res.Coll.
MC MASTER UNIVERSITY - ARCHIVES AND RESEARCH COLLECTIONS DIVISION □ Hamilton, ON

Stewart, Christine, Sci.Eng.Ref.Libn.
UNIVERSITY OF ARIZONA - SCIENCE-ENGINEERING LIBRARY □ Tucson, AZ

Stewart, Coy E., Libn.
WESTINGHOUSE ELECTRIC CORPORATION - NAVAL REACTOR FACILITY LIBRARY □ Idaho Falls, ID

Stewart, Cynthia, Mss.Spec.
UNIVERSITY OF MISSOURI - WESTERN HISTORICAL MANUSCRIPT COLLECTION/STATE HISTORICAL SOCIETY OF MISSOURI □ Columbia, MO

Stewart, Elizabeth, Asst.Cur.
UNIVERSITY OF KANSAS - KANSAS COLLECTION □ Lawrence, KS

Stewart, Emery, Museum Cur.
MASONIC GRAND LODGE OF TEXAS - LIBRARY AND MUSEUM □ Waco, TX

Stewart, Eugene L., Exec.Sec.
TRADE RELATIONS COUNCIL OF THE UNITED STATES - LIBRARY □ Washington, DC

Stewart, Frances S., Supv., Dept.Libs.
ALABAMA A & M UNIVERSITY - JOSEPH F. DRAKE MEMORIAL LEARNING RESOURCES CENTER □ Normal, AL

Stewart, Mrs. Francis, AV Libn.
WEST LIBERTY STATE COLLEGE - ELBIN LIBRARY □ West Liberty, WV

Stewart, Gary, Consrv.
SHRINE TO MUSIC MUSEUM □ Vermillion, SD

Stewart, Gwyn, Acq./Ser.
U.S. NAVY - NAVAL COASTAL SYSTEMS CENTER - TECHNICAL LIBRARY □ Panama City, FL

Stewart, Helene, Libn.
REGINA CITY - PLANNING DEPARTMENT - LIBRARY □ Regina, SK

Stewart, Hope, Res.
BOOZ ALLEN & HAMILTON, INC. - FOSTER D.
SNELL DIVISION - INFORMATION CENTER† □
Florham Park, NJ

Stewart, Jane, Librarian
PERKINS, COIE, STONE, OLSEN & WILLIAMS -
LAW LIBRARY □ Seattle, WA

Stewart, Jean, Res.Assoc.
ARGUS ARCHIVES, INC. □ New York, NY

Stewart, Jerald, Lib.Dir.
NORTH DAKOTA STATE SCHOOL OF SCIENCE -
MILDRED JOHNSON LIBRARY □ Wahpeton, ND

Stewart, Judy, Libn.
MOTOROLA, INC. - GOVERNMENT
ELECTRONICS DIVISION - TECHNICAL
LIBRARY □ Scottsdale, AZ

Stewart, Kathryn A., Libn.
CARNATION RESEARCH LABORATORIES -
LIBRARY □ Van Nuys, CA

Stewart, Lois, Libn.
MC KINNEY JOB CORPS - LIBRARY □ McKinney,
TX

Stewart, Louann, Libn.
SAMARITAN HEALTH CENTER - DEACONESS
HOSPITAL UNIT - MEDICAL LIBRARY □ Detroit,
MI

Stewart, Mae, Ser.Libn.
ILLINOIS BENEDICTINE COLLEGE - THEODORE
LOWNIK LIBRARY □ Lisle, IL

Stewart, Moyle D., Chf., Tech.Info.
U.S. GEOLOGICAL SURVEY - NATL.
CARTOGRAPHIC INFORMATION CENTER (NCIC)
- WESTERN BRANCH □ Menlo Park, CA

Stewart, P., Libn.
IMPERIAL LIFE ASSURANCE COMPANY -
LIBRARY □ Toronto, ON

Stewart, Polly, Libn.
RESEARCH AND REVIEW SERVICE OF AMERICA
- LIBRARY □ Indianapolis, IN

Stewart, Renee M., Lib.Techn.
U.S. DEPT. OF THE INTERIOR - OFFICE OF
SURFACE MINING - LIBRARY □ Kansas City, MO

Stewart, Sgt. Allan W., Adm.Spec.
U.S. AIR FORCE BASE - LAUGHLIN BASE
LIBRARY □ Del Rio, TX

Stewart, Susan, Hd.Libn.
IRVING TRUST COMPANY - BUSINESS LIBRARY
□ New York, NY

Stewart-Smith, Natalie, Lib.Asst.
MEMPHIS STATE UNIVERSITY LIBRARIES -
MISSISSIPPI VALLEY COLLECTION □ Memphis,
TN

Stibbe, H., Chf., Doc. Control
CANADA - PUBLIC ARCHIVES OF CANADA -
NATIONAL MAP COLLECTION □ Ottawa, ON

Stickel, Donald, Asst. Life Sci.Libn.
PURDUE UNIVERSITY - LIFE SCIENCE LIBRARY
□ West Lafayette, IN

Stickle, Cheryl R., Libn.
SCOTT PAPER COMPANY - RESEARCH LIBRARY
& TECHNICAL INFORMATION SERVICE □
Philadelphia, PA

Stickler, Merrill, Dir.
CURTISS (Glenn H.) MUSEUM OF LOCAL
HISTORY - MINOR SWARTHOUT MEMORIAL
LIBRARY □ Hammondsport, NY

Stickney, Edith P., Libn.
TRINITY EPISCOPAL CHURCH - LIBRARY □
Santa Barbara, CA

Stickney, Eleanor H., Sr.Musm.Asst.
YALE UNIVERSITY - ORNITHOLOGY LIBRARY □
New Haven, CT

Stieber, Michael T., Archv.
CARNEGIE-MELLON UNIVERSITY - HUNT
INSTITUTE FOR BOTANICAL DOCUMENTATION
- LIBRARY □ Pittsburgh, PA

Stieg, Gilbert D., Dir.
RACINE COUNTY HISTORICAL MUSEUM, INC. -
REFERENCE LIBRARY OF GENEALOGY AND
LOCAL HISTORY □ Racine, WI

Stielow, Dr. Frederick J., Archv.
UNIVERSITY OF SOUTHWESTERN LOUISIANA -
JEFFERSON CAFFERY LOUISIANA ROOM □
Lafayette, LA

Stiff, David G., Libn.
GRAHAM (Billy) EVANGELISTIC ASSOCIATION -
LIBRARY □ Minneapolis, MN

Stifflear, Allan J., Dir.
WESTON SCHOOL OF THEOLOGY - LIBRARY □
Cambridge, MA

Stiffler, Stuart, Lib.Dir.
CORNELL COLLEGE - CHEMISTRY LIBRARY □
Mount Vernon, IA

Stiggins, Richard J., Coord.
NORTHWEST REGIONAL EDUCATIONAL
LABORATORY - CLEARINGHOUSE FOR APPLIED
PERFORMANCE TESTING (CAPT) □ Portland, OR

Stiles, C. Carmon, Dir.
U.S. DEPT. OF COMMERCE - INTERNATIONAL
TRADE ADMINISTRATION - DALLAS DISTRICT
OFFICE LIBRARY □ Dallas, TX

Stiles, Lauren, Hum.Ref.-Biblog.
SUNY - COLLEGE AT CORTLAND - MEMORIAL
LIBRARY □ Cortland, NY

Stiles, Lois Kent, Chf.
DISTRICT OF COLUMBIA PUBLIC LIBRARY -
ART DIVISION □ Washington, DC

Stilley, Bettye W., Med.Libn.
U.S. NAVY - NAVAL REGIONAL MEDICAL
CENTER (Jacksonville) - MEDICAL LIBRARY† □
Jacksonville, FL

Stillings, Jayne, Lib.Asst.
UNIVERSITY OF HARTFORD - HARTT SCHOOL
OF MUSIC - ALLEN MEMORIAL LIBRARY □ West
Hartford, CT

Stillman, Charles, Libn.
KENNEBEC COUNTY LAW LIBRARY† □ Augusta,
ME

Stillman, Louise V., Pres.
SCHUYLER COUNTY HISTORICAL SOCIETY -
LEE SCHOOL MUSEUM □ Montour Falls, NY

Stilman, Ruth, Libn.
SIR MORTIMER B. DAVIS JEWISH GENERAL
HOSPITAL - INSTITUTE OF COMMUNITY &
FAMILY PSYCHIATRY - LIBRARY □ Montreal, PQ

Stilwell, Mary L., Cat.
CALIFORNIA ACADEMY OF SCIENCES - J.W.
MAILLIARD, JR. LIBRARY □ San Francisco, CA

Stimage, Joyce, Spec.Coll.
PRAIRIE VIEW A & M COLLEGE OF TEXAS -
W.R. BANKS LIBRARY □ Prairie View, TX

Stines, Joe R., Hd.Libn.
UNIVERSITY OF TENNESSEE - JOINT
RESEARCH CENTERS LIBRARY □ Knoxville, TN

Stinson, Judy, Doc./Ref.Libn.
WASHINGTON & LEE UNIVERSITY - LAW
LIBRARY □ Lexington, VA

Stinson, Patrick B., Exec.Dir.
NATIONAL INDUSTRIAL RECREATION
ASSOCIATION - INFORMATION CENTER □
Chicago, IL

Stirrat, Agnes, Cat.Libn.
EDEN THEOLOGICAL SEMINARY - LIBRARY □
Webster Groves, MO

Stith, Janet, Asst.
UNIVERSITY OF KENTUCKY - MEDICAL CENTER
LIBRARY □ Lexington, KY

Stith, Nina, Med.Libn.
UNIONTOWN HOSPITAL ASSOCIATION -
MEDICAL LIBRARY □ Uniontown, PA

Stithem, Naomi E., Lib.Spec.
WASHINGTON STATE UNIVERSITY -
EDUCATION LIBRARY □ Pullman, WA

Stitsworth, Karen, Ref.Libn.
UNIVERSITY OF ARKANSAS AT LITTLE ROCK -
PULASKI COUNTY LAW LIBRARY □ Little Rock,
AR

Stitzinger, James F., Libn.
CALVARY BAPTIST THEOLOGICAL SEMINARY -
LIBRARY □ Lansdale, PA

Stiverson, Dr. Gregory A., Asst.Archv.
MARYLAND STATE HALL OF RECORDS
COMMISSION - LIBRARY □ Annapolis, MD

Stjernholm, Kirstine, Ref.Libn.
UNIVERSITY OF SOUTHERN COLORADO -
LIBRARY - SPECIAL COLLECTIONS □ Pueblo, CO

Stock, Carole, Online Coord./Ref. PNRHSL
UNIVERSITY OF WASHINGTON - HEALTH
SCIENCES LIBRARY □ Seattle, WA

Stock, Kay, Sr.Lib.Asst.
LIONEL D. EDIE AND COMPANY, INC. -
LIBRARY† □ New York, NY

Stockdale, Judith M., Exec.Dir.
OPEN LANDS PROJECT - LIBRARY □ Chicago, IL

Stockdale, Kay L., Libn.
HISTORICAL FOUNDATION OF THE
PRESBYTERIAN AND REFORMED CHURCHES -
LIBRARY AND ARCHIVES □ Montreat, NC

Stocker, Anna T., Lib.Res.Asst.
GROUP HEALTH ASSOCIATION OF AMERICA,
INC. - GERTRUDE STURGES MEMORIAL
LIBRARY □ Washington, DC

Stockett, Lura, Circ.Libn.
FULLER THEOLOGICAL SEMINARY -
MC ALISTER LIBRARY □ Pasadena, CA

Stockey, Edward, Hd., Data Serv.Div.
INDIANA STATE LIBRARY □ Indianapolis, IN

Stocking, Carolyn, Govt.Pubn.
UNIVERSITY OF CONNECTICUT - LIBRARY □
Storrs, CT

Stockly, Elizabeth, Lib.Dir.
ART CENTER COLLEGE OF DESIGN - JAMES
LEMONT FOGG MEMORIAL LIBRARY □ Pasadena,
CA

Stocks, Lee, Lib.Serv.Mgr.
BA INVESTMENT MANAGEMENT CORPORATION
- LIBRARY □ San Francisco, CA

Stockton, Julie, Hd.
YORK UNIVERSITY - LISTENING ROOM □
Downsview, ON

Stoddard, Hillary, ILL
VIRGINIA COMMONWEALTH UNIVERSITY -
MEDICAL COLLEGE OF VIRGINIA - TOMPKINS-
MC CAW LIBRARY □ Richmond, VA

Stoddard, Nancy Williams, Libn.
ST. LOUIS POST-DISPATCH - REFERENCE
DEPARTMENT □ St. Louis, MO

Stoddard, Roger E., Assoc.Libn.
HARVARD UNIVERSITY - HOUGHTON LIBRARY
□ Cambridge, MA

Stoddard, William S., Bus.Libn.
MICHIGAN STATE UNIVERSITY - BUSINESS
LIBRARY □ East Lansing, MI

Stoddard, Wilma L., Plan.Div.Asst.
U.S. DEPT. OF ENERGY - ALASKA POWER
ADMINISTRATION - LIBRARY □ Juneau, AK

Stoddart, Joan, Info.Serv.
UNIVERSITY OF UTAH - SPENCER S. ECCLES
HEALTH SCIENCES LIBRARY □ Salt Lake City, UT

Stoeckenius, Kai, Asst.Hd.Libn.
SAN FRANCISCO EXAMINER - LIBRARY □ San
Francisco, CA

Stoey, Richard E., Ref.Libn.
GENERAL MOTORS CORPORATION - RESEARCH
LABORATORIES LIBRARY □ Warren, MI

Stoffel, Edna, Med.Lib.Techn.
WILCOX (G.N.) MEMORIAL HOSPITAL & HEALTH
CENTER - MEDICAL LIBRARY □ Lihue, HI

Stoia, Joseph, Med.Libn.
KETTERING COLLEGE OF MEDICAL ARTS -
LEARNING RESOURCES CENTER □ Kettering, OH

Stoia, Joseph P., Med.Libn.
KETTERING MEMORIAL HOSPITAL - MEDICAL
LIBRARY □ Kettering, OH

Stoker, Alan, Audio/Video Engr.
COUNTRY MUSIC FOUNDATION - LIBRARY AND
MEDIA CENTER □ Nashville, TN

Stokes, Alan H., Mss.Libn.
UNIVERSITY OF SOUTH CAROLINA - SOUTH
CAROLINIANA LIBRARY □ Columbia, SC

Stokes, Cornelia R., Coord., Rd.Serv.
HOWARD UNIVERSITY - MOORLAND-SPINGARN
RESEARCH CENTER - LIBRARY DIVISION □
Washington, DC

Stokes, Kathryne B., Asst. Law Libn.
UNIVERSITY OF MIAMI - SCHOOL OF LAW
LIBRARY □ Coral Gables, FL

Stokes, Ray, Cur., Spec.Coll.
TEXAS COLLEGE OF OSTEOPATHIC MEDICINE -
MEDICAL LIBRARY □ Fort Worth, TX

Stoksik, Pamela, Hd., Tech.Serv./Sys.
ONTARIO - LEGISLATIVE ASSEMBLY -
LEGISLATIVE LIBRARY RESEARCH AND
INFORMATION SERVICES □ Toronto, ON

Stokstad, Karen, Libn.
OCTAMERON ASSOCIATES, INC. - RESEARCH
LIBRARY □ Alexandria, VA

Stoll, Ilen, Tech.Serv.Libn.
MONTANA COLLEGE OF MINERAL SCIENCE AND
TECHNOLOGY - LIBRARY □ Butte, MT

Stoll, Karen, Cur.
MONROE COUNTY LIBRARY SYSTEM - GENERAL
GEORGE ARMSTRONG CUSTER COLLECTION □
Monroe, MI

Stoll, Karen, Dp.Hd.Libn.
UNIVERSITY OF CALIFORNIA - LOS ALAMOS
NATIONAL LABORATORY - LIBRARY □ Los
Alamos, NM

Stoller, Janet, Libn.
MUTUAL OF NEW YORK - LAW LIBRARY □ New
York, NY

Stoller, Janet, Libn.
MUTUAL OF NEW YORK - LIBRARY/
INFORMATION SERVICE □ New York, NY

Stolp, Marianne, Cat.Libn.
METROPOLITAN LIFE INSURANCE COMPANY -
LIBRARY □ New York, NY

Stolper, Gertrude, Libn.
UNIVERSITY OF MICHIGAN - BUREAU OF
GOVERNMENT LIBRARY □ Ann Arbor, MI

Stolt, Wilbur, Archv.
UNIVERSITY OF WISCONSIN, MILWAUKEE -
AREA RESEARCH CENTER □ Milwaukee, WI

Stolz, Martha R., Libn.
ST. ALPHONSUS HOSPITAL - HEALTH SCIENCES
LIBRARY □ Boise, ID

Stolz, Preble, Law Libn.
UNIVERSITY OF CALIFORNIA, BERKELEY - LAW
LIBRARY □ Berkeley, CA

Stone, Amy, Circ.Libn.
PIERCE JUNIOR COLLEGE - LIBRARY† □
Philadelphia, PA

Stone, Bernice N., Supv.Libn.
FORT LOGAN MENTAL HEALTH CENTER -
MEDICAL LIBRARY† □ Denver, CO

Stone, Dennis J., Law Libn.
GONZAGA UNIVERSITY SCHOOL OF LAW -
LIBRARY □ Spokane, WA

Stone, Elberta H., Libn.
NEWARK BOARD OF EDUCATION - TEACHERS'
PROFESSIONAL LIBRARY □ Newark, NJ

Stone, Emily G., Cat.Asst.
BRIDGEWATER STATE COLLEGE - CLEMENT C.
MAXWELL LIBRARY □ Bridgewater, MA

Stone, Gordon, Assoc.Musm.Libn.
METROPOLITAN MUSEUM OF ART - IRENE
LEWISOHN COSTUME REFERENCE LIBRARY □
New York, NY

Stone, Kathleen V., Lib.Ck.
SAN JOSE MEDICAL CLINIC - STAFF LIBRARY □
San Jose, CA

Stone, Leona P., Circ.Libn.
COLUMBIA UNION COLLEGE - THEOFIELD G.
WEIS LIBRARY □ Takoma Park, MD

Stone, Linda, Cur. of Art
PHILLIPS (FRANK) FOUNDATION, INC. -
WOOLAROC MUSEUM - LIBRARY □ Bartlesville,
OK

Stone, Margaret, Hd., Ref. & Info.
MOREHEAD STATE UNIVERSITY - CAMDEN-
CARROLL LIBRARY □ Morehead, KY

Stone, Martha, Act. Centre Libn.
INTERNATIONAL DEVELOPMENT RESEARCH
CENTRE - LIBRARY □ Ottawa, ON

Stone, Marvin H., Fine Coll.Libn.
DALLAS PUBLIC LIBRARY - RARE BOOK ROOM □
Dallas, TX

Stone, Pat, Hd.Libn.
U.S. NAVY - NAVAL AIR SYSTEMS COMMAND -
TECHNICAL LIBRARY □ Washington, DC

Stone, Patricia, Libn./Archv.
NORTH YORK PUBLIC LIBRARY - CANADIANA
COLLECTION □ Willowdale, ON

Stone, Rosalie, Hd., Tech.Serv.
NEW YORK MEDICAL COLLEGE AND THE
WESTCHESTER ACADEMY OF MEDICINE -
WESTCHESTER MEDICAL CENTER LIBRARY □
Valhalla, NY

Stone, Susan, Asst.Libn.
SUSQUEHANNA COUNTY HISTORICAL SOCIETY
AND FREE LIBRARY ASSOCIATION □ Montrose,
PA

Stone, William V., Libn.
ST. JOHN'S UNIVERSITY, NOTRE DAME
CAMPUS - LIBRARY □ Staten Island, NY

Stoneburg, Mary Jane, Hd., Per.Dept.
BUCKNELL UNIVERSITY - ELLEN CLARKE
BERTRAND LIBRARY □ Lewisburg, PA

Stoneham, John, Libn.
MARYLAND INSTITUTE, COLLEGE OF ART -
DECKER LIBRARY □ Baltimore, MD

Stonehill, Helen, Chf.Libn.
ICD REHABILITATION AND RESEARCH CENTER
- LIBRARY □ New York, NY

Stonehouse, Marie Louise, Mgr.
MERCK & COMPANY, INC. - CALGON
CORPORATION - INFORMATION CENTER □
Pittsburgh, PA

Stoner, Marla, Asst.Libn.
GILLETTE RESEARCH INSTITUTE - TECHNICAL
LIBRARY □ Rockville, MD

Stoner, Ruth, Lib.Techn.
NIAGARA PARKS COMMISSION - SCHOOL OF
HORTICULTURE - HORTICULTURAL LIBRARY □
Niagara Falls, ON

Stoops, Louise, Chf.Libn.
LEHMAN BROTHERS, KUHN, LOEB, INC. -
LIBRARY □ New York, NY

Stopard, Linda, Libn.
KINGSTON HOSPITAL - LIBRARY □ Kingston, NY

Stoppel, Kaye, Ser.Libn.
DRAKE UNIVERSITY - LAW LIBRARY □ Des
Moines, IA

Storbo, Larry, Libn.
SAN RAFAEL INDEPENDENT JOURNAL -
NEWSPAPER LIBRARY □ San Rafael, CA

Storch, Alison A., Mgr., Info.Serv.
IIT RESEARCH INSTITUTE -
ELECTROMAGNETIC COMPATIBILITY
ANALYSIS CENTER - TECHNICAL
INFORMATION SERVICES □ Annapolis, MD

Storck, Thomas, Asst.Doc.Cat.
OKLAHOMA STATE UNIVERSITY - DOCUMENTS
DIVISION □ Stillwater, OK

Storer, Maryruth, Asst. Law Libn.
O'MELVENY AND MYERS - INFORMATION
SERVICES □ Los Angeles, CA

Storey, Mrs. Theo H., Libn.
BAPTIST MEDICAL CENTER SYSTEM - CENTRAL
BAPTIST HOSPITAL LIBRARY □ Little Rock, AR

Storm, Herman, Tech.Serv.
UNIVERSITY OF WISCONSIN, RIVER FALLS -
CHALMER DAVEE LIBRARY □ River Falls, WI

Storm, Mary L., Libn.
MOULTRIE COUNTY HISTORICAL &
GENEALOGICAL SOCIETY - MOULTRIE COUNTY
HERITAGE CENTER □ Sullivan, IL

Storm, William, Asst.Cur. Audio Archv.
SYRACUSE UNIVERSITY - GEORGE ARENTS
RESEARCH LIBRARY FOR SPECIAL
COLLECTIONS □ Syracuse, NY

Storms, Katherine H., Info.Spec.
IN-FACT - RESEARCH AND INFORMATION
SERVICE □ Rensselaerville, NY

Storms, Kenneth, Info.Spec.
IN-FACT - RESEARCH AND INFORMATION
SERVICE □ Rensselaerville, NY

Story, Allen, Asst.Libn.
U.S. INTERNAL REVENUE SERVICE - LAW
LIBRARY □ Washington, DC

Story, Karen, Libn.
MEIGS COUNTY LAW LIBRARY □ Pomeroy, OH

Story, Steve, Media Coord.
SOUTHWESTERN BAPTIST THEOLOGICAL
SEMINARY - FLEMING LIBRARY □ Fort Worth,
TX

Stott, Paul, Loan Libn.
CORNELL UNIVERSITY - ALBERT R. MANN
LIBRARY □ Ithaca, NY

Stotz, Wendy A., Cat./Ref.
DANIEL WEBSTER COLLEGE - LIBRARY □
Nashua, NH

Stouder, Vicki, Libn.
NCR CORPORATION - TECHNICAL LIBRARY □
Dayton, OH

Stout, Billy D., Hist.
U.S. NATL. PARK SERVICE - PEA RIDGE NATL.
MILITARY PARK - LIBRARY □ Pea Ridge, AR

Stout, Cathy A., Libn.
NEW JERSEY STATE DEPARTMENT OF HEALTH
- LIBRARY □ Trenton, NJ

Stout, E.E., Engr.Adm.Coord.
MACK TRUCKS, INC. - TECHNICAL
INFORMATION CENTER - ENGINEERING
DIVISION LIBRARY □ Hagerstown, MD

Stout, Judy, Libn.
MARINE ENVIRONMENTAL SCIENCES
CONSORTIUM - LIBRARY† □ Dauphin Island, AL

Stout, Prentice K., Marine Educ.Spec.
UNIVERSITY OF RHODE ISLAND,
NARRAGANSETT BAY - DIVISION OF MARINE
RESOURCES - MARINE AWARENESS CENTER □
Narragansett Bay, RI

Stout, Richard A., Dir.
SCHIELE MUSEUM OF NATURAL HISTORY AND
PLANETARIUM - LIBRARY □ Gastonia, NC

Stout, Robert J., Hd.
OHIO STATE UNIVERSITY - CHILDREN'S
HOSPITAL LIBRARY □ Columbus, OH

Stovall, Juanita, Circ.
BOEING MILITARY AIRPLANE COMPANY -
LIBRARY □ Wichita, KS

Stowawy, M., Info.Spec.
STANDARD OIL COMPANY OF INDIANA -
LIBRARY/INFORMATION CENTER □ Chicago, IL

Stowe, Stephanie H., Libn.
DENVER MUSEUM OF NATURAL HISTORY -
LIBRARY □ Denver, CO

Stowe, Virginia, Libn.
UNITED CHURCH BOARD FOR WORLD
MINISTRIES - LIBRARY □ New York, NY

Strable, Edward G., V.P., Dir.Info.Serv.
THOMPSON (J. Walter) COMPANY -
INFORMATION CENTER □ Chicago, IL

Strachota, Nancy, Supv.
ALTERNATIVE SOURCES OF ENERGY
MAGAZINE - ENERGY INFORMATION REFERRAL
SERVICE (EIRS) □ Milaca, MN

Strada, Marta, Dir., Cat.
NATIONAL GEOGRAPHIC SOCIETY - LIBRARY □
Washington, DC

Strahan, Jean D., Libn.
NATIONAL GENEALOGICAL SOCIETY - LIBRARY
□ Washington, DC

Straight, Elsie H., Libn.
RINGLING SCHOOL OF ART AND DESIGN -
LIBRARY □ Sarasota, FL

Strain, Laura M., Law Libn.
LATHAM & WATKINS - LAW LIBRARY □ Los
Angeles, CA

Strain, Paula M., Mgr., Info.Serv.
MITRE CORPORATION - LIBRARY □ McLean, VA

Strait, George A., Dir.
UNIVERSITY OF IOWA - LAW LIBRARY □ Iowa
City, IA

Stramiello, Angela R., Libn.
ENGLISH, MC CAUGHAN AND O'BRYAN - LAW
LIBRARY □ Fort Lauderdale, FL

Stranberg, Patsy, Hd., ILL/Circ.
EAST TENNESSEE STATE UNIVERSITY,
QUILLEN-DISHNER COLLEGE OF MEDICINE -
DEPT. OF LEARNING RSRCS. - MEDICAL
LIBRARY □ Johnson City, TN

PERSONNEL

Strand, Kathryn, Libn.
NATIONAL CENTER FOR ATMOSPHERIC
RESEARCH - HIGH ALTITUDE OBSERVATORY
LIBRARY □ Boulder, CO

Strand, Marguerite, Libn.
COPLEY PRESS, INC. - JAMES S. COPLEY
LIBRARY □ La Jolla, CA

Strand, Paul J., Dir.
SAN DIEGO STATE UNIVERSITY - SOCIAL
SCIENCE RESEARCH LABORATORY - LIBRARY □
San Diego, CA

Strang, Mrs. Marian B., Med.Libn.
U.S. ARMY HOSPITALS - GENERAL LEONARD
WOOD ARMY COMMUNITY HOSPITAL -
MEDICAL LIBRARY □ Ft. Leonard Wood, MO

Stranick, Barbara E., Libn.
U.S. VETERANS ADMINISTRATION (PA-
Coatesville) - MEDICAL CENTER LIBRARY □
Coatesville, PA

Stranska, Hana, ILL
POLYTECHNIC INSTITUTE OF NEW YORK -
SPICER LIBRARY □ Brooklyn, NY

Strassberg, Richard, Dir., LMD Ctr.
CORNELL UNIVERSITY - MARTIN P.
CATHERWOOD LIBRARY OF INDUSTRIAL AND
LABOR RELATIONS □ Ithaca, NY

Strasser, Dennis
NATIONAL COLLEGE OF EDUCATION -
LEARNING RESOURCE CENTERS □ Evanston, IL

Strasser, Theresa, Asst.Libn.
NEW YORK STATE LIBRARY - SCIENCES/
HEALTH SCIENCES/TECHNOLOGY REFERENCE
SERVICES □ Albany, NY

Stratelak, Nadia, Acq.Libn.
WAYNE STATE UNIVERSITY - ARTHUR NEEF
LAW LIBRARY □ Detroit, MI

Strattis, Ella, Asst.Libn.
SPRING GARDEN COLLEGE - LIBRARY □
Chestnut Hill, PA

Stratton, Esther M., Br.Libn.
CHURCH OF JESUS CHRIST OF LATTER-DAY
SAINTS - HELENA BRANCH GENEALOGICAL
LIBRARY □ Helena, MT

Stratton, Frances M., Leader, Ref. Group
AMERICAN CYANAMID COMPANY - LEDERLE
LABORATORIES DIVISION - SUBBAROW
MEMORIAL LIBRARY □ Pearl River, NY

Stratton, Lucile, Libn.
BENDIX CORPORATION - KANSAS CITY
DIVISION - TECHNICAL INFORMATION
CENTER □ Kansas City, MO

Straub, Ronda, Asst.Libn.
LOUISVILLE BAPTIST HOSPITALS, INC. -
HAGAN LIBRARY □ Louisville, KY

Straub, William J., Circ.Mgr.
PUBLIC LAW EDUCATION INSTITUTE -
LIBRARY □ Washington, DC

Straughan, Virginia, Archv.
SPOKANE VALLEY PIONEER MUSEUM, INC. -
LIBRARY† □ Spokane, WA

Straus, Harriett, Libn.
NEW YORK STATE SUPREME COURT - 3RD
JUDICIAL DISTRICT - LAW LIBRARY □ Kingston,
NY

Strauss, Carol, Asst.Libn.
POSTGRADUATE CENTER FOR MENTAL HEALTH
- EMIL A. GUTHEIL MEMORIAL LIBRARY □ New
York, NY

Strauss, Carol D., Lib.Serv.Coord.
WESTLAKE COMMUNITY HOSPITAL - LIBRARY
□ Melrose Park, IL

Strauss, Herbert A., Coord. of Res.
RESEARCH FOUNDATION FOR JEWISH
IMMIGRATION, INC. - ARCHIVES □ New York,
NY

Strauss, Jeanne, Transl.
PHILLIPS PETROLEUM COMPANY - RESEARCH &
DEVELOPMENT DEPARTMENT - TECHNICAL
INFORMATION BRANCH □ Bartlesville, OK

Straw, Leilani, Asst.Dir.
SPENCE-CHAPIN SERVICES TO FAMILIES AND
CHILDREN - CHARLOTTE TOWLE MEMORIAL
LIBRARY □ New York, NY

Straw, Marian G., Cultural Arts Coord.
QUEENS BOROUGH PUBLIC LIBRARY -
LANGSTON HUGHES COMMUNITY LIBRARY AND
CULTURAL CENTER □ Corona, NY

Strawbridge, Frederic, Asst.Libn./Gen.Serv.
TEMPLE UNIVERSITY - CENTRAL LIBRARY
SYSTEM - AMBLER CAMPUS LIBRARY □ Ambler,
PA

Strawn, Mildred, Hd., Tech.Serv.
MARQUETTE UNIVERSITY - LEGAL RESEARCH
CENTER □ Milwaukee, WI

Strazdon, Maureen E., Libn.
AMERICAN COLLEGE - VANE B. LUCAS
MEMORIAL LIBRARY □ Bryn Mawr, PA

Streamer, William A., Jr., Info.Spec.
MARYLAND STATE DEPARTMENT OF
EDUCATION - DIVISION OF LIBRARY
DEVELOPMENT & SERVICES - MEDIA SERVICES
CENTER □ Baltimore, MD

Streb, Carrie
LOUISIANA STATE UNIVERSITY - REFERENCE
SERVICES □ Baton Rouge, LA

Strecker, Candi, Libn.
RICHARDSON COMPANY - LIBRARY/
INFORMATION CENTER □ Melrose Park, IL

Streeper, Mary Sue, Chf., Biblog.Serv.
WYOMING STATE LIBRARY □ Cheyenne, WY

Street, Jenny, Mgt.Asst.
OREGON INSTITUTE OF TECHNOLOGY -
LEARNING RESOURCES CENTER □ Klamath Falls,
OR

Streeter, David, Spec.Coll.Libn.
POMONA PUBLIC LIBRARY - SPECIAL
COLLECTIONS DEPARTMENT □ Pomona, CA

Strehl, Dan, Libn.
LOS ANGELES PUBLIC LIBRARY - NEWSPAPER
ROOM □ Los Angeles, CA

Streiff, Ann W., Dir.
BETHLEHEM STEEL CORPORATION - SCHWAB
MEMORIAL LIBRARY □ Bethlehem, PA

Streiff, Kwang Hee, Chf., Lib.Serv.
U.S. VETERANS ADMINISTRATION (MO-Poplar
Bluff) - MEDICAL CENTER LIBRARY (142D) □
Poplar Bluff, MO

Streit, Rev. David, Libn.
ST. MARK'S SEMINARY - LIBRARY □ Erie, PA

Streit, Samuel A., Spec.Coll.Libn.
BROWN UNIVERSITY - SPECIAL COLLECTIONS†
□ Providence, RI

Strelzoff, Claire, Libn.
ST. ANNE'S HOSPITAL - MEDICAL STAFF
LIBRARY □ Chicago, IL

Strelzoff, Claire, Libn.
ST. ELIZABETH'S HOSPITAL - LUKEN HEALTH
SCIENCES LIBRARY □ Chicago, IL

Strempek, Carol, Hd., Ser. & Cat.
CURRY COLLEGE - LOUIS R. LEVIN MEMORIAL
LIBRARY □ Milton, MA

Streuli, Huguette, Libn.
WINDELS, MARX, DAVIES & IVES - LIBRARY □
New York, NY

Strey, Geraldine, Libn.
UNIVERSITY OF WISCONSIN, MADISON -
VOCATIONAL EDUCATION RESOURCE
MATERIALS CENTER □ Madison, WI

Strharsky, Harry, Exec.Dir.
DATA CENTER - INVESTIGATIVE RESOURCE
CENTER □ Oakland, CA

Strickland, Albert C., Libn.
UNIVERSITY OF FLORIDA - HUME LIBRARY □
Gainesville, FL

Strickland, June M., Libn.
INSTITUTE OF THE PENNSYLVANIA HOSPITAL -
MEDICAL LIBRARY† □ Philadelphia, PA

Strickland, June M., Libn.
PHILADELPHIA ASSOCIATION FOR
PSYCHOANALYSIS - LOUIS S. KAPLAN
MEMORIAL LIBRARY □ Bala Cynwyd, PA

Strickland, Muriel, Map Cur.
SAN DIEGO STATE UNIVERSITY -
GOVERNMENT PUBLICATIONS DEPARTMENT □
San Diego, CA

Strickland, Nellie B., Div.Chf.
U.S. ARMY - ADJUTANT GENERAL - LIBRARY
DIVISION □ Alexandria, VA

Strickler, Merle
SPOTSYLVANIA HISTORICAL ASSOCIATION,
INC. - RESEARCH MUSEUM AND LIBRARY □
Spotsylvania, VA

Stricks, Jim, Coord.
UNIVERSITY OF ALASKA - CENTER FOR CROSS-
CULTURAL STUDIES - RESOURCE CENTER □
Fairbanks, AK

Strife, Janina, Sr.Libn.
UTICA/MARCY PSYCHIATRIC CENTER -
MARCY CAMPUS PROFESSIONAL LIBRARY □
Utica, NY

Stripnieks, L., Ref.Libn.
CANADA - ATMOSPHERIC ENVIRONMENT
SERVICE - LIBRARY □ Downsview, ON

Stroemgren, C., Libn.
Q.I.T. - FER ET TITANE INC. - BIBLIOTHEQUE □
Sorel, PQ

Stroh, Y., Info.Spec.
AIR PRODUCTS AND CHEMICALS, INC. -
INFORMATION SERVICES - TREXLERTOWN
LIBRARY □ Allentown, PA

Strohecker, Edwin C., Dean
MURRAY STATE UNIVERSITY - LIBRARY □
Murray, KY

Strohofer, Jean, Libn.
CRAVATH, SWAINE, AND MOORE - LAW
LIBRARY □ New York, NY

Strolle, Helen S., Mgr.
DU PONT DE NEMOURS (E.I.) & COMPANY, INC.
- TECHNICAL LIBRARY SYSTEM -
HEADQUARTERS □ Wilmington, DE

Stroman, Rosalie H., Chf., Rd.Serv.Sect.
U.S. NATL. INSTITUTES OF HEALTH - LIBRARY
□ Bethesda, MD

Stromei, Susan, Asst.Libn.
COLONIAL WILLIAMSBURG - RESEARCH
LIBRARY & ARCHIVES □ Williamsburg, VA

Stromme, Gary L., Law Libn.
PACIFIC GAS AND ELECTRIC COMPANY - LAW
LIBRARY □ San Francisco, CA

Stromstad, Ron, Libn.
UNIVERSITY OF NORTH DAKOTA - INSTITUTE
FOR ECOLOGICAL STUDIES - ENVIRONMENTAL
RESOURCE CENTER □ Grand Forks, ND

Strona, Mrs. Proserfina, Hd., Doc.Ctr.
HAWAII STATE LIBRARY - HAWAII AND
PACIFIC SECTION I □ Honolulu, HI

Strong, Bernice, Ref.
DAUGHTERS OF THE REPUBLIC OF TEXAS -
LIBRARY □ San Antonio, TX

Strong, Donald R., Libn.
WEST LIBERTY STATE COLLEGE - ELBIN
LIBRARY □ West Liberty, WV

Strong, Gary E., State Libn.
CALIFORNIA STATE LIBRARY □ Sacramento, CA

Strong, Jean, Libn.
ELMIRA STAR GAZETTE - LIBRARY □ Elmira, NY

Strong, M.A., Med.Libn.
ST. MICHAEL MEDICAL CENTER - AQUINAS
MEDICAL LIBRARY† □ Newark, NJ

Strong, Moira O., Chf.Libn.
NEW JERSEY STATE DEPARTMENT OF LAW
AND PUBLIC SAFETY - ATTORNEY GENERAL'S
LIBRARY □ Trenton, NJ

Strong, Pat, Libn.
SUNCOR INC. - LIBRARY □ Calgary, AB

Strong, Susan S., Hd., AV & Art Ref.
NEW YORK STATE COLLEGE OF CERAMICS,
ALFRED UNIVERSITY - SAMUEL R. SCHOLES
LIBRARY OF CERAMICS □ Alfred, NY

Strothers, Oscar E., Chf. Law Libn.
U.S. DEPT. OF ENERGY - HEADQUARTERS LAW
LIBRARY □ Washington, DC

Stroud, Ronald, Asst. Law Libn.
CINCINNATI LAW LIBRARY ASSOCIATION □
Cincinnati, OH

Stroud, Sandy, Asst.Libn.
BLOOMINGTON-NORMAL DAILY PANTAGRAPH -
NEWSPAPER LIBRARY □ Bloomington, IL

Stroup, Kay, Libn.
OREGON STATE DEPARTMENT OF REVENUE - LIBRARY □ Salem, OR

Stroup, Dr. M. Jane, Libn.
NANTUCKET MARIA MITCHELL ASSOCIATION - LIBRARY □ Nantucket, MA

Stroupe, Ray M., Pres.
NATIONAL TAX EQUALITY ASSOCIATION - LIBRARY □ Washington, DC

Strubel, Tamara, Asst.Libn.
MONROE DEVELOPMENTAL CENTER - STAFF/PARENT LIBRARY □ Rochester, NY

Struble, Elizabeth, Asst.Libn.
OKLAHOMA STATE UNIVERSITY - PHYSICAL SCIENCES AND ENGINEERING DIVISION □ Stillwater, OK

Struckmeyer, Mary, ILL
WISCONSIN STATE DIVISION FOR LIBRARY SERVICES - REFERENCE AND LOAN LIBRARY □ Madison, WI

Strupczewski, June, Info.Sci.
HOECHST-ROUSSEL PHARMACEUTICALS, INC. - LIBRARY □ Somerville, NJ

Struth, Dr. Alan H., Lib.Dir.
UNIVERSITY OF PENNSYLVANIA - ENERGY CENTER - DRL BASEMENT ENERGY LIBRARY □ Philadelphia, PA

Stryck, B. Camille, Staff Libn.
STANDARD OIL COMPANY OF INDIANA - CENTRAL RESEARCH LIBRARY □ Naperville, IL

Stuart, Joyce, Coord. of Tech.Serv.
ASSEMBLIES OF GOD GRADUATE SCHOOL - CORDAS C. BURNETT LIBRARY □ Springfield, MO

Stubbs, Linda M., Chf., Operations Br.
U.S. NATL. ARCHIVES & RECORDS SERVICE - FEDERAL ARCHIVES AND RECORDS CENTER, REGION 6 □ Kansas City, MO

Stubbs, Walter, Asst.Soc.Stud.Libn.
SOUTHERN ILLINOIS UNIVERSITY, CARBONDALE - SOCIAL STUDIES DIVISION LIBRARY □ Carbondale, IL

Stuckey, Kenneth A., Res.Libn.
PERKINS SCHOOL FOR THE BLIND - SAMUEL P. HAYES RESEARCH LIBRARY □ Watertown, MA

Stuckey, Dr. Ronald L., Cur.
OHIO STATE UNIVERSITY - FRANZ THEODORE STONE LABORATORY - LIBRARY □ Put-In-Bay, OH

Studaker, M., Tech.Serv.Libn.
HURLEY MEDICAL CENTER - HAMADY HEALTH SCIENCES LIBRARY □ Flint, MI

Studer, Ida, Libn.
SASKATCHEWAN - DEPARTMENT OF NORTHERN SASKATCHEWAN - LIBRARY □ La Ronge, SK

Studer, Louise E., Asst.Libn.
FISH AND NEAVE - LIBRARY □ New York, NY

Studt, Shirlee A., Art Libn.
MICHIGAN STATE UNIVERSITY - ART/MAPS DIVISION □ East Lansing, MI

Stuehrenberg, Suzanne E., Tech.Serv.Libn.
PILLSBURY COMPANY - TECHNICAL INFORMATION CENTER □ Minneapolis, MN

Stuiver, Chitra, Libn./Art Spec.
HAWAII STATE LIBRARY - FINE ARTS AND AUDIOVISUAL SECTION □ Honolulu, HI

Stuller, Lola, Libn.
ALVERNO COLLEGE - RESEARCH CENTER ON WOMEN □ Milwaukee, WI

Stultz, George, Libn.
U.S. DEPT. OF ENERGY - IDAHO NATL. ENGINEERING LABORATORY - TECHNICAL LIBRARY □ Idaho Falls, ID

Stumberg, Mary Sue, Libn.
PATTON STATE HOSPITAL - STAFF LIBRARY □ Patton, CA

Stump, Bonita, Acq.Libn.
LOCKHEED-CALIFORNIA COMPANY - TECHNICAL INFORMATION CENTER □ Burbank, CA

Stump, Dr. J.H., Mgr. R & D
REICHOLD CHEMICALS, INC. - NEWPORT DIVISION LIBRARY □ Pensacola, FL

Stumpf, Howard, Pres.
POINT OF PURCHASE ADVERTISING INSTITUTE - INFORMATION CENTER □ New York, NY

Stumpf, Phillip Q., Jr., Mgr.
MOBIL RESEARCH & DEVELOPMENT CORPORATION - PAULSBORO LABORATORY - TECHNICAL INFORMATION SERVICES □ Paulsboro, NJ

Sturgis, Lorenza, ILL
CHICAGO COLLEGE OF OSTEOPATHIC MEDICINE - ALUMNI MEMORIAL LIBRARY □ Chicago, IL

Sturm, Dana, ILL
NEVADA STATE LIBRARY □ Carson City, NV

Sturm, Marian, Libn.
CHICAGO PUBLIC LIBRARY CULTURAL CENTER - THOMAS HUGHES CHILDREN'S LIBRARY □ Chicago, IL

Sturm, William, Libn.
OAKLAND PUBLIC LIBRARY - HISTORY/LITERATURE DIVISION □ Oakland, CA

Sturtz, Rev. Richard S., Hd.Libn.
WADHAMS HALL SEMINARY - COLLEGE LIBRARY □ Ogdensburg, NY

Stutheit, Lois A., Libn.
U.S. BANCORP - RESOURCE LIBRARY □ Portland, OR

Stuve, William E., Govt.Pubn./Map Libn.
CALIFORNIA STATE UNIVERSITY, CHICO - MERIAM LIBRARY □ Chico, CA

Su, Julie C., Cat.
INDIANAPOLIS MUSEUM OF ART - REFERENCE LIBRARY □ Indianapolis, IN

Su, Meng-Fen, East Asian Cat.
OHIO STATE UNIVERSITY - EAST ASIAN COLLECTION □ Columbus, OH

Su, Siew Phek, Asst.Cat.Libn.
UNIVERSITY OF FLORIDA - HUME LIBRARY □ Gainesville, FL

Suarez, Diana W., Cur. of Educ.
HUNTER MUSEUM OF ART - REFERENCE LIBRARY □ Chattanooga, TN

Suarez, Douglas G., Corp.Libn.
ERCO INDUSTRIES, LTD. - LIBRARY □ Islington, ON

Suazo, Ernest J., Supt.
U.S. NATL. PARK SERVICE - SITKA NATL. HISTORICAL PARK - LIBRARY □ Sitka, AK

Sublette, Doris, Libn.
UNIVERSITY OF ILLINOIS - ILLINOIS STATE NATURAL HISTORY SURVEY - LIBRARY □ Champaign, IL

Suchoff, Dr. Benjamin, Trustee
NEW YORK BARTOK ARCHIVE □ Lynbrook, NY

Suchyta, Lillian, Hd.Proc.Dept.
DETROIT BAR ASSOCIATION FOUNDATION - LIBRARY □ Detroit, MI

Suddon, Alan, Hd.
METROPOLITAN TORONTO LIBRARY - FINE ART DEPARTMENT □ Toronto, ON

Suddon, Alan, Hd. of Unit
METROPOLITAN TORONTO LIBRARY - NEWSPAPER UNIT □ Toronto, ON

Suderow, Edwin, Hd., Lit.Sect.
CHICAGO PUBLIC LIBRARY CULTURAL CENTER - LITERATURE AND LANGUAGE DIVISION □ Chicago, IL

Suelflow, Dr. August R., Dir.
CONCORDIA HISTORICAL INSTITUTE - DEPARTMENT OF ARCHIVES AND HISTORY □ St. Louis, MO

Suessmuth, Charles, Chf.Libn.
TENNECO, INC. - CORPORATE LIBRARY □ Houston, TX

Sugimura, Sue, Circ.Libn.
HAWAII STATE LIBRARY - STATE LIBRARY FOR THE BLIND AND PHYSICALLY HANDICAPPED □ Honolulu, HI

Suh, Ann S., Ref.
UNIVERSITY OF MINNESOTA - LAW LIBRARY □ Minneapolis, MN

Suh, Choo, Sr. Japanese Libn.
UNIVERSITY OF MICHIGAN - ASIA LIBRARY □ Ann Arbor, MI

Suhadolnik, Susan, Ref.Libn.
VANDERBILT UNIVERSITY LIBRARY - OWEN GRADUATE SCHOOL OF MANAGEMENT - MANAGEMENT LIBRARY □ Nashville, TN

Suhr, Angie, AV Spec.
NORTH CAROLINA STATE DEPARTMENT OF CULTURAL RESOURCES - DIVISION OF THE STATE LIBRARY □ Raleigh, NC

Suhr, Paul A., Libn.
NORTH CAROLINA STATE UNIVERSITY - TOBACCO LITERATURE SERVICE □ Raleigh, NC

Suits, H.L., Dir.
WORLD DATA CENTER A - METEOROLOGY AND NUCLEAR RADIATION □ Asheville, NC

Suitts, Stephen T., Exec.Dir.
SOUTHERN REGIONAL COUNCIL, INC. - REFERENCE LIBRARY† □ Atlanta, GA

Suleiman, Jo-Ann D., Biomed.Libn.
U.S. AIR FORCE HOSPITAL MEDICAL CENTER - MEDICAL LIBRARY (OH-Wright-Patterson AFB) □ Wright-Patterson AFB, OH

Sulerud, Grace K., Acq. & Ref.Libn.
AUGSBURG COLLEGE - GEORGE SVERDRUP LIBRARY AND MEDIA CENTER □ Minneapolis, MN

Sulfridge, Nancy, Asst.Ed.
TRACOR JITCO, INC. - RESEARCH RESOURCES INFORMATION CENTER □ Rockville, MD

Suljak, Nedjelko Dinko, Hd.Libn.
UNIVERSITY OF CALIFORNIA, DAVIS - INSTITUTE OF GOVERNMENTAL AFFAIRS - LIBRARY □ Davis, CA

Sulkin, Danny, AV Spec.
VANDERBILT UNIVERSITY LIBRARY - OWEN GRADUATE SCHOOL OF MANAGEMENT - MANAGEMENT LIBRARY □ Nashville, TN

Sullivan, C.M., Libn.
UNIVERSITY OF FLORIDA - AGRICULTURAL RESEARCH & EDUCATION CENTER - HOMESTEAD LIBRARY □ Homestead, FL

Sullivan, Charles M., Exec.Dir.
CAMBRIDGE HISTORICAL COMMISSION - LIBRARY □ Cambridge, MA

Sullivan, Daniel, Hd.Cat.Libn.
UNIVERSITY OF SOUTHERN COLORADO - LIBRARY - SPECIAL COLLECTIONS □ Pueblo, CO

Sullivan, Deborah, Pres.
MARSHALL HISTORICAL SOCIETY - ARCHIVES □ Marshall, MI

Sullivan, Donna, Lib.Mgr.
MADISON COMMUNITY HOSPITAL - HEALTH-SCIENCE LIBRARY □ Madison, SD

Sullivan, Elaine, Leg.Hist./Cat./Ref.
U.S. FEDERAL COMMUNICATIONS COMMISSION - LIBRARY □ Washington, DC

Sullivan, Gina, Ck.
SAN ANTONIO EXPRESS AND NEWS - LIBRARY □ San Antonio, TX

Sullivan, Howard, Coll.Dev.
WAYNE STATE UNIVERSITY - G. FLINT PURDY LIBRARY □ Detroit, MI

Sullivan, James, Musm.Dir.
NORTHERN INDIANA HISTORICAL SOCIETY - FREDERICK ELBEL LIBRARY □ South Bend, IN

Sullivan, James G., Automated Proj.Libn.
STANFORD UNIVERSITY - J. HUGH JACKSON LIBRARY □ Stanford, CA

Sullivan, Kathryn, Libn.
PANDULLO QUIRK ASSOCIATES - LIBRARY □ Wayne, NJ

Sullivan, Dr. Larry E., Libn.
NEW-YORK HISTORICAL SOCIETY - LIBRARY □ New York, NY

Sullivan, Lester, Archv.
AMISTAD RESEARCH CENTER - LIBRARY □ New Orleans, LA

Sullivan, Marilyn, Assoc. Dir. for Adm.
MEDICAL COLLEGE OF WISCONSIN - TODD WEHR LIBRARY □ Milwaukee, WI

Sullivan, Marjorie E., Chf., Lib.Serv.
U.S. VETERANS ADMINISTRATION (MA-Northampton) - MEDICAL CENTER LIBRARY □ Northampton, MA

Sullivan, Martha J., Lib.Adm.
CONNECTICUT STATE LIBRARY - LAW LIBRARY AT NEW HAVEN □ New Haven, CT

Sullivan, Mary, Circ.
DANIEL WEBSTER COLLEGE - LIBRARY □ Nashua, NH

Sullivan, Mary L., Libn.
BRISTOL COUNTY BAR ASSOCIATION - FALL RIVER LAW LIBRARY □ Fall River, MA

Sullivan, Michael V., Hd.Libn.
STANFORD UNIVERSITY - FALCONER BIOLOGY LIBRARY □ Stanford, CA

Sullivan, Mike, Dir. of Pub. Affairs
INDUSTRIAL FORESTRY ASSOCIATION - LIBRARY □ Portland, OR

Sullivan, Mildred, Res.Spec.
MONTANA STATE DEPARTMENT OF NATURAL RESOURCES & CONSERVATION - RESEARCH & INFORMATION CENTER □ Helena, MT

Sullivan, Pat, Asst.Libn.
CORNELL UNIVERSITY - FINE ARTS LIBRARY □ Ithaca, NY

Sullivan, Patricia E., Ser.Libn.
CALIFORNIA STATE UNIVERSITY, CHICO - MERIAM LIBRARY □ Chico, CA

Sullivan, Philip, Supv.
MADISON PUBLIC LIBRARY - BUSINESS AND SCIENCE DIVISION □ Madison, WI

Sullivan, Rosemary, Asst.Libn.
PLYMOUTH COUNTY LAW LIBRARY ASSOCIATION - BROCKTON LAW LIBRARY □ Brockton, MA

Sullivan, Sarabeth, Div.Hd.
DALLAS PUBLIC LIBRARY - BUSINESS AND TECHNOLOGY DIVISION □ Dallas, TX

Sullivan, Suzanne, Ref. & ILL
BROOME COMMUNITY COLLEGE - CECIL C. TYRRELL LEARNING RESOURCES CENTER □ Binghamton, NY

Sullivan, Vicki, Dir., Lib.Rsrcs.
OKLAHOMA HISTORICAL SOCIETY - DIVISION OF LIBRARY RESOURCES □ Oklahoma City, OK

Sulyok, Agnes, Hd., Circ.
UNIVERSITY OF OTTAWA - MORISSET LIBRARY □ Ottawa, ON

Sumergrade, Rushel, Chf.Libn.
BRADFORD NATIONAL CORPORATION - LIBRARY □ New York, NY

Sumerlin, Katherine, Periodicals Libn.
OUACHITA BAPTIST UNIVERSITY - RILEY LIBRARY □ Arkadelphia, AR

Summar, Donald J., Libn.
NATIONAL ASSOCIATION OF WATCH AND CLOCK COLLECTORS MUSEUM - LIBRARY □ Columbia, PA

Summers, Brian, Libn.
FOUNDATION FOR ECONOMIC EDUCATION - LIBRARY □ Irvington-On-Hudson, NY

Summers, Carol A., Info.Mgr.
CANADIAN CONSULATE GENERAL - INFORMATION CENTER □ Chicago, IL

Summers, Robert L., Jr., Asst. Law Libn.
LOYOLA UNIVERSITY (New Orleans) - LAW LIBRARY □ New Orleans, LA

Summers, Sheryl H., Asst.Libn.
DETROIT COLLEGE OF LAW - LIBRARY □ Detroit, MI

Summit, Dr. Roger K., Mgr.
LOCKHEED MISSILES & SPACE COMPANY, INC. - LOCKHEED INFORMATION SYSTEMS □ Palo Alto, CA

Sumner, Gwen, Media Techn.
MANSFIELD STATE COLLEGE - BUTLER MUSIC LIBRARY □ Mansfield, PA

Sumner, Mark R., Dir.
UNIVERSITY OF NORTH CAROLINA, CHAPEL HILL - INSTITUTE OF OUTDOOR DRAMA - ARCHIVES □ Chapel Hill, NC

Sumner, Mary Ann, Assoc.Libn.
EDUCATIONAL TESTING SERVICE - CARL CAMPBELL BRIGHAM LIBRARY □ Princeton, NJ

Sumners, Bill, Asst.Archv.
AUBURN UNIVERSITY - ARCHIVES □ Auburn, AL

Sumpter, Ethel L., Rd.Adv.
DISTRICT OF COLUMBIA PUBLIC LIBRARY - HISTORY AND GEOGRAPHY DIVISION □ Washington, DC

Sumpter, Martha K., Libn.
U.S. AIR FORCE BASE - GOODFELLOW BASE LIBRARY □ Goodfellow AFB, TX

Sun, Aurora, Libn.
ST. JOHN'S HOSPITAL - SCHOOL OF NURSING LIBRARY □ Springfield, MO

Sun, Cossette T., Law Lib.Dir.
ALAMEDA COUNTY LAW LIBRARY □ Hayward, CA

Sun, Cossette T., Law Lib.Dir.
ALAMEDA COUNTY LAW LIBRARY □ Oakland, CA

Sun, Mr. Lan C., Libn.
SHELL CANADA LIMITED - OAKVILLE RESEARCH CENTRE - SHELL RESEARCH CENTRE LIBRARY □ Oakville, ON

Sun Chang, Kang-i, Cur.
PRINCETON UNIVERSITY - GEST ORIENTAL LIBRARY AND EAST ASIAN COLLECTIONS □ Princeton, NJ

Sund, Cheryl, Office Serv.Mgr.
U.S. GEOLOGICAL SURVEY - NATL. CARTOGRAPHIC INFORMATION CENTER (NCIC) □ Denver, CO

Sunday, Donald E., Ref.Libn.
GENERAL MOTORS CORPORATION - RESEARCH LABORATORIES LIBRARY □ Warren, MI

Sundberg, Carl, Res.Assoc.
WHITCOM INVESTMENT COMPANY - RESEARCH LIBRARY □ New York, NY

Sundborg, Laurie, Libn.
CONSERVATION DISTRICTS FOUNDATION - DAVIS CONSERVATION LIBRARY □ League City, TX

Sundbye, Delores, Supv.
ST. PAUL PUBLIC LIBRARY - ARTS AND AUDIO-VISUAL SERVICES □ St. Paul, MN

Sundeen, Dr. Daniel A., Assoc. Professor
UNIVERSITY OF SOUTHERN MISSISSIPPI - GEOLOGY DEPARTMENT - LIBRARY □ Hattiesburg, MS

Sunder-Raj, P.E., Chf.Libn.
CANADA - EMPLOYMENT & IMMIGRATION CANADA - LIBRARY □ Ottawa, ON

Sunderland, Edwin, Jr., Libn.
U.S. NATL. INSTITUTES OF HEALTH - LIBRARY □ Bethesda, MD

Sunderland, Edwin P., Ref.Libn.
U.S. PUBLIC HEALTH SERVICE - PARKLAWN HEALTH LIBRARY □ Rockville, MD

Sundermeyer, Ruth, Prof.Asst.
ENOCH PRATT FREE LIBRARY - FINE ARTS AND RECREATION DEPARTMENT □ Baltimore, MD

Sundgren, Gundula, Dir.
SCANDINAVIAN COUNCIL FOR APPLIED RESEARCH - SCANDINAVIAN DOCUMENTATION CENTER □ Washington, DC

Sundquist, Ken, Libn.
ONTARIO - MINISTRY OF AGRICULTURE AND FOOD - LIBRARY □ Toronto, ON

Sung, H.W., Media Libn.
MEHARRY MEDICAL COLLEGE - MEDICAL LIBRARY - LEARNING RESOURCES CENTER □ Nashville, TN

Superior, William J., Pres.
THORNTHWAITE (C.W.) ASSOCIATES LABORATORY OF CLIMATOLOGY - LIBRARY □ Elmer, NJ

Suprapto, R.M., Indonesian Cat.
CORNELL UNIVERSITY - JOHN M. ECHOLS COLLECTION ON SOUTHEAST ASIA □ Ithaca, NY

Suprapto, Sari Devi, Thai Cat.
CORNELL UNIVERSITY - JOHN M. ECHOLS COLLECTION ON SOUTHEAST ASIA □ Ithaca, NY

Surace, Cecily J., Lib.Dir.
LOS ANGELES TIMES - EDITORIAL LIBRARY □ Los Angeles, CA

Suran, Frank, Assoc.Archv.
PENNSYLVANIA STATE HISTORICAL & MUSEUM COMMISSION - DIVISION OF ARCHIVES AND MANUSCRIPTS □ Harrisburg, PA

Suretsky, Harold, Acq.
RUTGERS UNIVERSITY, THE STATE UNIVERSITY OF NEW JERSEY - JUSTICE HENRY ACKERSON LIBRARY OF LAW & CRIMINAL JUSTICE □ Newark, NJ

Surles, Richard H., Jr., Libn.
UNIVERSITY OF OREGON - LAW LIBRARY □ Eugene, OR

Surrency, Erwin C., Law Libn.
UNIVERSITY OF GEORGIA - LAW LIBRARY □ Athens, GA

Sussman, Jody, Ref.Libn.
MEDICAL COLLEGE OF WISCONSIN - TODD WEHR LIBRARY □ Milwaukee, WI

Sussman, Leonard R., Exec.Dir.
FREEDOM HOUSE - INFORMATION CENTER □ New York, NY

Sutcliffe, Ginger, Dir. of Lib.Serv.
FIRST BAPTIST CHURCH - I.C. ANDERSON LIBRARY □ Waco, TX

Sutcliffe, Priscilla H., Spec.Coll.Libn.
CLEMSON UNIVERSITY - ROBERT MULDROW COOPER LIBRARY □ Clemson, SC

Suter, Cindy, Asst.Libn.
ST. JUDE CHILDREN'S RESEARCH HOSPITAL - RESEARCH LIBRARY □ Memphis, TN

Suthard, Carol, Hd., Marketing Serv.
EG&G, INC. - WASHINGTON ANALYTICAL SERVICES CENTER - INFORMATION CENTER □ Rockville, MD

Suthard, Karl P., Archv.Spec.
SMITHSONIAN INSTITUTION LIBRARIES - NATIONAL AIR AND SPACE MUSEUM - LIBRARY □ Washington, DC

Sutherland, Mrs. D., Libn.
ROYAL CANADIAN MILITARY INSTITUTE - LIBRARY □ Toronto, ON

Sutherland, J. Elizabeth, Hd.
BEDFORD INSTITUTE OF OCEANOGRAPHY - LIBRARY □ Dartmouth, NS

Sutherland, John, Map Cur.
UNIVERSITY OF GEORGIA - SCIENCE LIBRARY - MAP COLLECTION □ Athens, GA

Sutherland, Michael C., Spec.Coll.Libn.
OCCIDENTAL COLLEGE - MARY NORTON CLAPP LIBRARY □ Los Angeles, CA

Sutherland, Mike, Spec.Coll.Libn.
ROUNCE AND COFFIN CLUB, LOS ANGELES - LIBRARY □ Los Angeles, CA

Sutherland, Ronald R., Dir.
MC DONNELL PLANETARIUM - LIBRARY □ St. Louis, MO

Sutliff, Mary E., Tech.Libn.
KIMBERLY-CLARK CORPORATION - LIBRARY □ Neenah, WI

Sutphin, Sue, Tech.Libn.
MASON & HANGER-SILAS MASON COMPANY, INC. - PANTEX PLANT - TECHNICAL LIBRARY □ Amarillo, TX

Sutrick, Anita, Asst.Libn.
OKLAHOMA COLLEGE OF OSTEOPATHIC MEDICINE & SURGERY - LIBRARY □ Tulsa, OK

Sutt, Joanne, Med.Libn.
ST. AGNES HOSPITAL - L.P. GUNDRY HEALTH SCIENCES LIBRARY □ Baltimore, MD

Sutter, Dr., Chm.
FRANKLIN AND MARSHALL COLLEGE - DEPARTMENT OF PHYSICS - LIBRARY □ Lancaster, PA

Sutter, Deborah, Media Coord.
PROVIDENCE HOSPITAL - SCHOOL OF NURSING LIBRARY □ Sandusky, OH

Suttles, Barbara C., Coord.
OLIN CORPORATION - CHEMICALS - CHARLESTON TECHNICAL INFORMATION CENTER □ Charleston, TN

Sutton, Amelia, Chf., Doc.
U.S. ARMY - WHITE SANDS MISSILE RANGE - TECHNICAL LIBRARY DIVISION □ White Sands Missile Range, NM

Sutton, Betty, Asst. to Libn.
UNIVERSITY OF KENTUCKY - EDUCATION LIBRARY □ Lexington, KY

Sutton, Evelyn, Libn.
UNITED METHODIST CHURCH - GENERAL COMMISSION ON ARCHIVES AND HISTORY - LIBRARY AND ARCHIVES □ Lake Junaluska, NC

Sutton, Gary C., Master Sgt.
U.S. AIR FORCE HOSPITAL - MEDICAL LIBRARY (TX-Reese AFB) □ Reese AFB, TX

Sutton, Mark, Br.Libn.
LAMAR UNIVERSITY - MARY AND JOHN GRAY LIBRARY □ Beaumont, TX

Sutton, Professor Robert M., Dir.
UNIVERSITY OF ILLINOIS - ILLINOIS HISTORICAL SURVEY LIBRARY □ Urbana, IL

Suvak, Nancy J., Res.Supv.
UNITED STATES STEEL CORPORATION - COMMERCIAL INFORMATION CENTER □ Pittsburgh, PA

Suvak, William A., Jr., Libn. II
PENNSYLVANIA STATE DEPARTMENT OF PUBLIC WELFARE - MENTAL HEALTH AND MEDICAL LIBRARY □ Bridgeville, PA

Suydam, Marilyn N., Dir./Prof.Math.Educ.
OHIO STATE UNIVERSITY - CALCULATOR INFORMATION CENTER □ Columbus, OH

Svarczkopf, Katherine
HARRISON (Benjamin) MEMORIAL HOME - LIBRARY □ Indianapolis, IN

Sved, Alexander, Asst.Libn.
LOYOLA UNIVERSITY OF CHICAGO - LAW LIBRARY □ Chicago, IL

Svengalis, Kendall, Asst. Law Libn.
RHODE ISLAND STATE LAW LIBRARY □ Providence, RI

Svetlik, Ms. S., Ref.Libn.
BEDFORD INSTITUTE OF OCEANOGRAPHY - LIBRARY □ Dartmouth, NS

Svoboda, Joseph G., Archv.
UNIVERSITY OF NEBRASKA, LINCOLN - UNIVERSITY ARCHIVES AND SPECIAL COLLECTIONS □ Lincoln, NE

Swadden, Patricia, Ref.Libn.
COMINCO LTD. - INFORMATION SERVICES □ Vancouver, BC

Swain, Barbara C., Libn.
UNIVERSITY OF ILLINOIS - HOME ECONOMICS LIBRARY □ Urbana, IL

Swain, Hannah K., Libn.
CAPE MAY COUNTY HISTORICAL/ GENEALOGICAL SOCIETY AND MUSEUM - LIBRARY □ Cape May Court House, NJ

Swan, Deloris J., Lib.Off.
U.S. NAVY - NAVAL AIR ENGINEERING CENTER - TECHNICAL LIBRARY, CODE 1115 □ Lakehurst, NJ

Swan, Janet, Assoc.Libn.
FEDERAL RESERVE BANK OF MINNEAPOLIS - LIBRARY □ Minneapolis, MN

Swanekamp, Joan, Co-Hd., Cat.Dept.
UNIVERSITY OF ROCHESTER - EASTMAN SCHOOL OF MUSIC - SIBLEY MUSIC LIBRARY □ Rochester, NY

Swanick, Eric L., Doc.Libn.
NEW BRUNSWICK - LEGISLATIVE LIBRARY □ Fredericton, NB

Swanigan, Meryl H., Corp.Libn.
ATLANTIC-RICHFIELD COMPANY - HEADQUARTERS LIBRARY □ Los Angeles, CA

Swann, Arthur, Dir. of Archv.
UNITED METHODIST CHURCH - NORTHERN CALIFORNIA-NEVADA CONFERENCE - J.A.B. FRY RESEARCH LIBRARY □ Stockton, CA

Swann, Arthur W., Sci.Libn.
UNIVERSITY OF THE PACIFIC - SCIENCE LIBRARY □ Stockton, CA

Swanner, Ronnie C., AV Serv.
TRINITY UNIVERSITY - LIBRARY □ San Antonio, TX

Swanner, Sallieann, Acq.
UNIVERSITY OF TEXAS HEALTH SCIENCE CENTER, SAN ANTONIO - LIBRARY □ San Antonio, TX

Swanson, Albert A., Archv.
(Boston) METROPOLITAN DISTRICT COMMISSION - LIBRARY □ Boston, MA

Swanson, Cynthia, Acq.
PEPPERDINE UNIVERSITY - LAW LIBRARY □ Malibu, CA

Swanson, Donna
KENTUCKY STATE DEPARTMENT OF EDUCATION - RESOURCE CENTER □ Frankfort, KY

Swanson, Dorothy, Libn.
NEW YORK UNIVERSITY - TAMIMENT LIBRARY □ New York, NY

Swanson, Duane P., Asst.Archv.Pub.Rec.
MINNESOTA HISTORICAL SOCIETY - DIVISION OF ARCHIVES AND MANUSCRIPTS □ St. Paul, MN

Swanson, Edward, Hd., Tech.Serv.
MINNESOTA HISTORICAL SOCIETY - REFERENCE LIBRARY □ St. Paul, MN

Swanson, Edward I., Dir.
GENERAL COMMISSION ON CHAPLAINS AND ARMED FORCES PERSONNEL - CHAPLAINS MEMORIAL LIBRARY □ Washington, DC

Swanson, Ellen, Chm.Lib.Comm.
AUGUSTANA LUTHERAN CHURCH - LIBRARY □ Denver, CO

Swanson, Lynn, Sr.Lib.Asst.
MINNESOTA GEOLOGICAL SURVEY - LIBRARY □ St. Paul, MN

Swanson, Martha, Asst.Cat.Libn.
WESTERN ILLINOIS UNIVERSITY - LIBRARIES □ Macomb, IL

Swanson, Patricia, Ed.
UNIVERSITY OF MINNESOTA - ST. ANTHONY FALLS HYDRAULIC LABORATORY - LORENZ G. STRAUB MEMORIAL LIBRARY □ Minneapolis, MN

Swanson, Ruth, Weston Lib.
UNIVERSITY OF WISCONSIN, MADISON - CENTER FOR HEALTH SCIENCES LIBRARIES □ Madison, WI

Swanson, Sheila, Libn.
ACADEMY OF MEDICINE, TORONTO - WILLIAM BOYD LIBRARY □ Toronto, ON

Swanton, James, Chf.Cat.
YESHIVA UNIVERSITY - ALBERT EINSTEIN COLLEGE OF MEDICINE - D. SAMUEL GOTTESMAN LIBRARY □ Bronx, NY

Swarm, Elsie, Libn.
THIRD BAPTIST CHURCH - LIBRARY □ St. Louis, MO

Swart, Hannah, Cur.
HOARD HISTORICAL MUSEUM - LIBRARY □ Fort Atkinson, WI

Swartman, R.K., Pres.
SOLCAN, LTD. - LIBRARY □ London, ON

Swartz, Cyndy
UNIVERSITY OF PITTSBURGH - GRADUATE SCHOOL OF PUBLIC HEALTH LIBRARY □ Pittsburgh, PA

Swartz, Roderick G., State Libn.
WASHINGTON STATE LIBRARY □ Olympia, WA

Sweaney, Dr. Wilma, Libn.
UNIVERSITY OF SASKATCHEWAN - HEALTH SCIENCES LIBRARY □ Saskatoon, SK

Swedenberg, Anne, Asst.Med.Libn. I
WASHINGTON HOSPITAL CENTER - MEDICAL LIBRARY □ Washington, DC

Sweek, Andree, Med.Rec.Libn.
HOLLEY (A.G.) STATE HOSPITAL - BENJAMIN L. BROCK MEDICAL LIBRARY □ Lantana, FL

Sweely, Edna, Cur., Hist.Soc.Lib.
WIDENER UNIVERSITY - WOLFGRAM MEMORIAL LIBRARY □ Chester, PA

Sweely, Edna S., Cur.
DELAWARE COUNTY HISTORICAL SOCIETY - LIBRARY □ Chester, PA

Sween, Jane C., Libn.
MONTGOMERY COUNTY HISTORICAL SOCIETY - LIBRARY □ Rockville, MD

Sweeney, Barbara, Libn.
LADISH CO. - METALLURGICAL DEPARTMENT LIBRARY □ Cudahy, WI

Sweeney, Carolyn, Info.Mgr.
DIGITAL EQUIPMENT CORPORATION - CORPORATE LIBRARY □ Maynard, MA

Sweeney, Del, Info.Spec.
PENNSYLVANIA STATE UNIVERSITY - TRANSPORTATION INSTITUTE WORKING COLLECTION □ University Park, PA

Sweeney, Grace, Libn.
BLACKHAWK TECHNICAL INSTITUTE, JANESVILLE - LEARNING MATERIALS CENTER □ Janesville, WI

Sweeney, Jean S., Supv.Info.Serv.
CELANESE CORPORATION - SUMMIT RESEARCH LABORATORIES - TECHNICAL INFORMATION CENTER □ Summit, NJ

Sweeney, Joan, Coord.Ref.Serv.
INSTITUTE FOR DEFENSE ANALYSES - TECHNICAL INFORMATION SERVICES □ Arlington, VA

Sweeney, Kathryn, Libn.
DENVER POST - LIBRARY □ Denver, CO

Sweeney, Mary Ellen, Hd. of Circ.
NEW ENGLAND CONSERVATORY OF MUSIC - HARRIET M. SPAULDING LIBRARY □ Boston, MA

Sweeney, Patsy, Libn.
BIRMINGHAM PUBLIC AND JEFFERSON COUNTY FREE LIBRARY - ART AND MUSIC DEPARTMENT □ Birmingham, AL

Sweeney, Urban J., Chf.Libn.
GENERAL DYNAMICS CORPORATION - CONVAIR DIVISION - RESEARCH LIBRARY □ San Diego, CA

Sweet, Douglas L., Dir., R. & D.
STATE BAR OF MICHIGAN - LIBRARY □ Lansing, MI

Sweet, Herman R., Libn.
HARVARD UNIVERSITY - OAKES AMES ORCHID LIBRARY □ Cambridge, MA

Sweet, Julia W., Libn.
CARTER & BURGESS, INC. ENGINEERS & PLANNERS - LIBRARY □ Fort Worth, TX

Sweet, Vickie, Circ./Acq.
U.S. NASA - LANGLEY RESEARCH CENTER - TECHNICAL LIBRARY MS 185 □ Hampton, VA

Sweet, Vivian, Libn.
MADISON PUBLIC LIBRARY - BUSINESS AND SCIENCE DIVISION □ Madison, WI

Sweeting, Sharon, Spec.Actv.Libn.
SMITHSONIAN INSTITUTION LIBRARIES □ Washington, DC

Sweetland, Lorraine, Libn./Supv.
WASHINGTON ADVENTIST HOSPITAL - MEDICAL LIBRARY □ Takoma Park, MD

Sweeton, Janice, Med.Libn.
CHILTON MEMORIAL HOSPITAL - MEDICAL LIBRARY □ Pompton Plains, NJ

Sweets, Henry, Cur.
MARK TWAIN MUSEUM - LIBRARY □ Hannibal, MO

Swenson, Elizabeth, Libn.
FERGUS FALLS STATE HOSPITAL - LIBRARY □ Fergus Falls, MN

Swenson, Evelyn J., Dir.
MINNESOTA HISTORICAL SOCIETY - NORTHWEST MINNESOTA HISTORICAL CENTER □ Moorhead, MN

Swenson, Perry, Libn.
SIOUX FALLS ARGUS-LEADER - LIBRARY □ Sioux Falls, SD

Sweny, Edward J., Libn.
NEW ENGLAND DEPOSIT LIBRARY, INC. □ Allston, MA

Swerbrick, B.F., Libn.
DU PONT CANADA, INC. - RESEARCH CENTRE
LIBRARY □ Kingston, ON
Swerdlove, Dorothy, Cur.
NEW YORK PUBLIC LIBRARY - PERFORMING
ARTS RESEARCH CENTER - BILLY ROSE
THEATRE COLLECTION □ New York, NY
Swetell, Marilyn, Libn.
DIAMOND SHAMROCK CORPORATION -
PROCESS CHEMICALS DIVISION - LIBRARY† □
Morristown, NJ
Sweton, Marian, Hd.Cat.
WESTERN RESERVE HISTORICAL SOCIETY -
LIBRARY □ Cleveland, OH
Swietek, Emily, GACIAC Coord.
IIT RESEARCH INSTITUTE - GUIDANCE AND
CONTROL INFORMATION ANALYSIS CENTER
(GACIAC) □ Chicago, IL
Swift, Barbara, Libn.
FMC CORPORATION - MARINE COLLOIDS
DIVISION - LIBRARY □ Rockland, ME
Swift-Rosenzweig, Leslie, Res.Assoc.
FOUNDATION FOR PUBLIC AFFAIRS -
RESOURCE CENTER □ Washington, DC
Swigart, Helen F., Mgr.
SWIGART MUSEUM - LIBRARY □ Huntingdon, PA
Swigart, William E., Jr., Exec.Dir.
SWIGART MUSEUM - LIBRARY □ Huntingdon, PA
Swijter, Sara, Ref.
MUHLENBERG COLLEGE - JOHN A.W. HAAS
LIBRARY □ Allentown, PA
Swim, Frances F., Field Libs.Coord.
U.S. NATL. OCEANIC & ATMOSPHERIC
ADMINISTRATION - LIBRARY AND
INFORMATION SERVICES DIVISION □ Rockville,
MD
Swinford, Jann, Media Dir.
NEW CASTLE STATE HOSPITAL - MEDICAL
LIBRARY □ New Castle, IN
Swingle, M.K., Ref.Libn.
CALIFORNIA HISTORICAL SOCIETY -
SCHUBERT HALL LIBRARY □ San Francisco, CA
Swingle, Ruth, Libn.
HASTINGS REGIONAL CENTER - MEDICAL
LIBRARY □ Hastings, NE
Swinton, Jeanne, Libn.
SANGER (Margaret) CENTER-PLANNED
PARENTHOOD NEW YORK CITY - ABRAHAM
STONE LIBRARY □ New York, NY
Swisher, Christopher, AV Libn.
WIDENER UNIVERSITY - WOLFGRAM
MEMORIAL LIBRARY □ Chester, PA
Swisher, Violet D., Libn.
U.S. OFFICE OF PERSONNEL MANAGEMENT -
LIBRARY □ Washington, DC
Swist, Anne C., Lit.Anl.
BRISTOL-MYERS PRODUCTS - TECHNICAL
INFORMATION CENTER □ Hillside, NJ
Switt, Karen J., Mgr., Info.Serv.
TECHNOMIC CONSULTANTS - INFORMATION
CENTER □ Chicago, IL
Swityk, Bill, Asst.Libn.
ST. VLADIMIR'S UKRAINIAN GREEK ORTHODOX
CHURCH - LIBRARY OF ST. VLADIMIR □ Calgary,
AB
Swoiskin, Lenore, Dir. of Archv.
SEARS, ROEBUCK AND CO. - ARCHIVES,
BUSINESS HISTORY AND INFORMATION
CENTER □ Chicago, IL
Swope, C. Hermas, Lib.Adm.
AMERICAN OPTICAL CORPORATION -
RESEARCH CENTER LIBRARY □ Southbridge, MA
Swope, Frances A., Archv.
GREENBRIER HISTORICAL SOCIETY -
ARCHIVES □ Lewisburg, WV
Sydij, Dianne D., Libn.
THOMSON, ROGERS, BARRISTERS &
SOLICITORS - LIBRARY† □ Toronto, ON
Syed, Mariam, Asst.Libn.
SEARS, ROEBUCK AND CO. - MERCHANDISE
DEVELOPMENT AND TESTING LABORATORY -
LIBRARY, DEPARTMENT 817† □ Chicago, IL

Syed, Shameem, Asst.Libn.
UNIVERSITY OF MASSACHUSETTS, AMHERST -
LABOR RELATIONS & RESEARCH CENTER
LIBRARY □ Amherst, MA
Sykas, Anna, Lib.Asst.
SPRINGFIELD HOSPITAL - INFORMATION
CENTER LIBRARY □ Springfield, VT
Sykes, Barbara A., Bus.Ref.Libn.
FORDHAM UNIVERSITY - LIBRARY AT LINCOLN
CENTER □ New York, NY
Sykes, Kathleen, Libn.
AUSTIN PUBLIC LIBRARY - AUSTIN-TRAVIS
COUNTY COLLECTION □ Austin, TX
Sykes, Shirley, Ser.Libn.
UNIVERSITY OF TEXAS SCHOOL OF LAW -
TARLTON LAW LIBRARY □ Austin, TX
Sykes, Stephanie, Tech.Serv.Libn.
BELL CANADA - INFORMATION RESOURCE
CENTRE □ Montreal, PQ
Sykora, Sylvia, Cur.
COTTONWOOD COUNTY HISTORICAL SOCIETY
- LIBRARY† □ Windom, MN
Sylvester, Jean, Musm. Docent
LINN COUNTY HISTORICAL SOCIETY - LIBRARY
□ Pleasanton, KS
Sylvestre, Dr. J.G., Natl.Libn.
NATIONAL LIBRARY OF CANADA □ Ottawa, ON
Symanski, Anna, Supt.
MADISON COUNTY HISTORICAL SOCIETY -
MUSEUM LIBRARY □ Edwardsville, IL
Symeonglou, Rheba, Libn.
ST. LOUIS PSYCHOANALYTIC INSTITUTE -
BETTY GOLDE SMITH MEMORIAL LIBRARY □ St.
Louis, MO
Symon, Carol, Supv., Info.Ctr.
GENERAL FOODS, LTD. - INFORMATION
CENTRE □ Toronto, ON
Symonds, Mrs. John, Pres.
HISTORIC ANNAPOLIS, INC. - LIBRARY □
Annapolis, MD
Synerholm, Chris, Info.Spec.
SYNTEX, U.S.A. - CORPORATE LIBRARY/
INFORMATION SERVICES □ Palo Alto, CA
Syverson, Kathy, Info.Anl.
AMERICAN CRITICAL CARE - INFORMATION
CENTER □ McGaw Park, IL
Szabo, Alesiz, Cat.Libn.
WESTERN CONNECTICUT STATE COLLEGE -
RUTH A. HAAS LIBRARY □ Danbury, CT
Szabo, Maria, Libn.
BECHTEL - DATA PROCESSING LIBRARY □ San
Francisco, CA
Szabo, Ruth E., Med.Libn.
ST. JOSEPH HOSPITAL, OUR LADY OF
PROVIDENCE UNIT - HEALTH SCIENCE
LIBRARY □ Providence, RI
Szach, Eugene, Ref.Libn.
UNIVERSITY OF MANITOBA - LAW LIBRARY □
Winnipeg, MB
Szachlewicz, Kalinka, Libn.
COMINCO LTD. - PRODUCT RESEARCH CENTRE
LIBRARY □ Mississauga, ON
Szarmach, Paul, Dir.
SUNY AT BINGHAMTON - CENTER FOR
MEDIEVAL AND EARLY RENAISSANCE STUDIES
□ Binghamton, NY
Szasz, Debbie, Acq.Techn.
COLUMBIA UNION COLLEGE - THEOFIELD G.
WEIS LIBRARY □ Takoma Park, MD
Szatkowski, Henry, Pub.Info.Off.
DELAWARE STATE TRAVEL SERVICE - LIBRARY
□ Dover, DE
Szczech, Bernadette, Marketing Libn.
CHICAGO TRIBUNE - MARKETING LIBRARY □
Chicago, IL
Szczepaniak, Adam, Asst.Libn.
MEDICAL AND CHIRURGICAL FACULTY OF THE
STATE OF MARYLAND - LIBRARY □ Baltimore,
MD
Szczepaniak, Frank J., P.T. Boat Coord.
P.T. BOATS, INC. - LIBRARY, ARCHIVES &
TECHNICAL INFORMATION CENTER □ Fall River,
MA

Sze, Melanie C., Libn.
STANDARD BRANDS INC. - LIBRARY □ Wilton,
CT
Szefczyk, Dorothy, Libn.
ENVIRONMENTAL PROTECTION AGENCY -
REGION II FIELD OFFICE - TECHNICAL
LIBRARY □ Edison, NJ
Szegedi, Laszlo, Cat.Libn.
LOYOLA LAW SCHOOL - LIBRARY □ Los Angeles,
CA
Szemes, Patricia, AV Serv.Libn.
GEORGETOWN UNIVERSITY - MEDICAL
CENTER - DAHLGREN MEMORIAL LIBRARY □
Washington, DC
Szentkiralyi, Irene, Asst.Libn.
LUTHERAN MEDICAL CENTER - C. W. NEVEL
MEMORIAL LIBRARY □ Cleveland, OH
Szesko, Gerald, Tech.Sect.Hd.
CHICAGO PUBLIC LIBRARY CENTRAL LIBRARY -
BUSINESS/SCIENCE/TECHNOLOGY DIVISION
□ Chicago, IL
Szewczuk, Stephen, Libn.
NEW YORK SOCIETY OF MODEL ENGINEERS -
LIBRARY □ Carlstadt, NJ
Szladits, Dr. Lola L., Cur.
NEW YORK PUBLIC LIBRARY - BERG
COLLECTION □ New York, NY
Szot, Irene, Lib.Asst.
ST. ANTHONY HOSPITAL - SPRAFKA MEMORIAL
HEALTH SCIENCE LIBRARY □ Chicago, IL
Szterenfeld, Helen, Hd.
INTERNATIONAL PLANNED PARENTHOOD
FEDERATION - WESTERN HEMISPHERE REGION
- LIBRARY □ New York, NY
Szucs, Frank, Libn.
ONTARIO - MINISTRY OF HOUSING - LIBRARY
□ Toronto, ON
Szumni, Wallace, Asst.Libn.
D'ARCY-MAC MANUS AND MASIUS - LIBRARY
INFORMATION SERVICES □ Bloomfield Hills, MI
Szymanski, Lucyna, Tech.Serv.Coord.
RUSH UNIVERSITY AND MEDICAL CENTER -
LIBRARY □ Chicago, IL

T

Tabachnik, Miriam, Libn.
ADLER (Alfred) INSTITUTE - LIBRARY □ Chicago,
IL
Tabakin, Rhea, Exec.Off.Libn.
DELOITTE HASKINS & SELLS - EXECUTIVE
OFFICE LIBRARY □ New York, NY
Tabb, Winston, Asst.Chf.
LIBRARY OF CONGRESS - GEN. READING
ROOMS DIV. □ Washington, DC
Taber, John, Ser.Libn.
TEXAS COLLEGE OF OSTEOPATHIC MEDICINE -
MEDICAL LIBRARY □ Fort Worth, TX
Tabit, Edith, Rd.Serv.Libn.
WEST VIRGINIA INSTITUTE OF TECHNOLOGY -
VINING LIBRARY □ Montgomery, WV
Tabler, Grayson, Libn.
U.S. FOOD & DRUG ADMINISTRATION - BUREAU
OF FOODS LIBRARY □ Washington, DC
Tabor, John, Prog.Dir.
UNIVERSITY OF CONNECTICUT - INSTITUTE
OF PUBLIC SERVICE - INTERNATIONAL
LIBRARY □ Hartford, CT
Tabor, Susan, Circ.
HEBREW UNION COLLEGE - JEWISH INSTITUTE
OF RELIGION - KLAU LIBRARY □ New York, NY
Taborsky, Theresa, Lib.Dir.
WIDENER UNIVERSITY - WOLFGRAM
MEMORIAL LIBRARY □ Chester, PA
Tabron, Lynda B., Per.Libn.
COMMUNITY COLLEGE OF BALTIMORE - BARD
LIBRARY - SPECIAL COLLECTIONS □ Baltimore,
MD

Taccarino, Paul, Libn.
U.S. ARMY - ENGINEER WATERWAYS
EXPERIMENT STATION - TECHNICAL
INFORMATION CENTER □ Vicksburg, MS

Tachuk, Roger, Hd., Ref.Sect.
NORTHWESTERN UNIVERSITY - HEALTH
SCIENCES LIBRARY □ Chicago, IL

Tack, A. Catherine, Libn.
CARNEGIE LIBRARY OF PITTSBURGH - MUSIC
AND ART DEPARTMENT □ Pittsburgh, PA

Taddeo, Joseph, Storage Mgr.
MARSHALL (John) LAW SCHOOL - LIBRARY □
Chicago, IL

Tadlock, Phyllis J., Libn.
SPERRY CORPORATION - SPERRY UNIVAC -
LIBRARY/TECHNICAL INFORMATION CENTER
□ Salt Lake City, UT

Taeger, Maureen, Libn.
NORTHERN COLLEGE - HAILEYBURY SCHOOL OF
MINES - LIBRARY □ Haileybury, ON

Taff, Edith, Libn.
SOUTHEASTERN BIBLE COLLEGE - ROWE
MEMORIAL LIBRARY □ Birmingham, AL

Tafoya, Herlinda, Libn.
COCHISE COUNTY LAW LIBRARY □ Bisbee, AZ

Taft, Lynne, Libn.
ERNST & WHINNEY - LIBRARY □ Detroit, MI

Tahirkheli, Sharon
AMERICAN GEOLOGICAL INSTITUTE - GEO-REF
RETROSPECTIVE SEARCH SERVICE □ Falls
Church, VA

Tai, Mildred C., Clerical Staff Supv.
FLORES (Nieves M.) MEMORIAL LIBRARY □
Agana, GU

Tai, Sidney, Supv., Rare Bks.Rm.
HARVARD UNIVERSITY - HARVARD YENCHING
INSTITUTE - LIBRARY □ Cambridge, MA

Tai, Wen-Pai, Chinese Libn.
UNIVERSITY OF CHICAGO - FAR EASTERN
LIBRARY □ Chicago, IL

Taillefer-Witty, Nicole, Libn.
UNIVERSITE DE MONTREAL - BOTANIQUE-
BIBLIOTHEQUE □ Montreal, PQ

Taillon, Micheline, Lib.Supv.
CANADIAN NATIONAL INSTITUTE FOR THE
BLIND - QUEBEC DIVISION LIBRARY† □
Montreal, PQ

Taira, B., Ser.Acq.Libn.
TRW, INC. - DEFENSE & SPACE SYSTEMS
GROUP - TECHNICAL INFORMATION CENTER □
Redondo Beach, CA

Taitano, Magdalena S., Territorial Libn.
FLORES (Nieves M.) MEMORIAL LIBRARY □
Agana, GU

Taitt, Rosalind, Linguistics Spec.
METROPOLITAN TORONTO LIBRARY -
LITERATURE DEPARTMENT □ Toronto, ON

Takakoshi, Gay, Libn.
QUEST RESEARCH CORPORATION - LIBRARY □
McLean, VA

Takemoto, Hazel M., Libn.
HILO HOSPITAL - FRED IRWIN MEDICAL
LIBRARY† □ Hilo, HI

Takis, Stephanie, Exec.Sec.
ASSOCIATION FOR EXPERIENTIAL EDUCATION
- LIBRARY □ Denver, CO

Takita, Jim, Dept.Hd.
LIBRARY ASSOCIATION OF PORTLAND -
SOCIAL SCIENCE AND SCIENCE DEPARTMENT
□ Portland, OR

Talalay, K., Ref.Libn.
INDIANA UNIVERSITY - MUSIC LIBRARY □
Bloomington, IN

Talat-Kielpsz, Janina, Hd.Libn.
OHIO STATE UNIVERSITY - MATHEMATICS
LIBRARY □ Columbus, OH

Talbot, Arlene, Ser. & Circ.Supv.
CALIFORNIA COLLEGE OF ARTS AND CRAFTS -
MEYER LIBRARY □ Oakland, CA

Talbot, George A., Archv. AV Coll.
STATE HISTORICAL SOCIETY OF WISCONSIN -
ARCHIVES DIVISION □ Madison, WI

Talcott, Ann W., Lib. Group Supv.
BELL TELEPHONE LABORATORIES, INC. -
TECHNICAL LIBRARY □ Murray Hill, NJ

Tallar, Georgia, Spec.Serv.Libn.
PALMER COLLEGE OF CHIROPRACTIC -
LIBRARY □ Davenport, IA

Tallentire, Tom, Cat.
UNIVERSITY OF CINCINNATI - ROBERT S.
MARX LAW LIBRARY □ Cincinnati, OH

Tallerico, Phyllis M., Cat.Libn.
KEAN COLLEGE OF NEW JERSEY - NANCY
THOMPSON LIBRARY □ Union, NJ

Talley, Loretta I.
MC LEAN COUNTY BAR ASSOCIATION -
ILLINOIS SUPREME COURT - LIBRARY □
Bloomington, IL

Tallman, Carol W., Lib.Techn.
PENNSYLVANIA STATE HISTORICAL & MUSEUM
COMMISSION - REFERENCE LIBRARY □
Harrisburg, PA

Tallman, Johanna E., Dir. of Libs.
CALIFORNIA INSTITUTE OF TECHNOLOGY -
ROBERT A. MILLIKAN MEMORIAL LIBRARY □
Pasadena, CA

Tallon, Jim, Rd.Serv.Coord.
CONCORDIA UNIVERSITY - SIR GEORGE
WILLIAMS CAMPUS - NORRIS LIBRARY □
Montreal, PQ

Talmage, Rev. J. Philip, Hd., Ref.Dept.
MARQUETTE UNIVERSITY - MEMORIAL
LIBRARY □ Milwaukee, WI

Tam, Miriam, Asst.Libn., Tech.Serv.
AMERICAN MUSEUM OF NATURAL HISTORY -
LIBRARY □ New York, NY

Tam, Vernon, Inst.Libn.
HAWAII STATE LIBRARY - STATE LIBRARY FOR
THE BLIND AND PHYSICALLY HANDICAPPED □
Honolulu, HI

Tamaribuchi, Franklin S., TAC Spec.
HAWAII STATE DEPARTMENT OF EDUCATION -
AUDIOVISUAL SERVICES □ Honolulu, HI

Tamayo, Daisy, Sr.Libn., Art
FREE PUBLIC LIBRARY OF ELIZABETH, NJ - ART
AND MUSIC DEPARTMENT □ Elizabeth, NJ

Tambo, David C., Cur.
BALL STATE UNIVERSITY - ALTHEA L.
STOECKEL DELAWARE COUNTY ARCHIVES &
LOCAL HISTORY COLLECTION □ Muncie, IN

Tamer, S.M., Libn.
RCA CORPORATION - RCA CONSUMER
ELECTRONICS LIBRARY □ Indianapolis, IN

Tammard, Marcella C., Libn.
OLIN CORPORATION - METALS RESEARCH
LABORATORIES - METALS INFORMATION
CENTER □ New Haven, CT

Tammen, Kathryn, Supv., Acq.
GENERAL RESEARCH CORPORATION - LIBRARY
□ Santa Barbara, CA

Tampold, Ana, Ref.Libn.
BANK OF NOVA SCOTIA - LIBRARY □ Toronto,
ON

Tamura, Catherine C., Learning Ctr.Coord.
AMERICAN LUNG ASSOCIATION OF HAWAII -
LEARNING CENTER FOR LUNG HEALTH □
Honolulu, HI

Tamura, Marsha N., FPIC Supv.
HAWAII PLANNED PARENTHOOD - FAMILY
PLANNING INFORMATION CENTER (FPIC) -
LIBRARY □ Honolulu, HI

Tan, Victoria, Circ.
MARIANOPOLIS COLLEGE - LIBRARY □ Montreal,
PQ

Tan Shen, Shirley, Libn.
UNIVERSITY OF WISCONSIN, MADISON -
MATHEMATICS LIBRARY □ Madison, WI

Tanaka, Momoe, State Law Libn.
HAWAII STATE SUPREME COURT - LAW
LIBRARY □ Honolulu, HI

Tanasescu, Elena, Info.Anl.
UNIVERSITY OF CALIFORNIA, LOS ANGELES -
BRAIN INFORMATION SERVICE □ Los Angeles,
CA

Tang, Mr. Chin-Shih, Ref. (Common Law)
UNIVERSITY OF OTTAWA - LAW LIBRARY □
Ottawa, ON

Tang, Eugenia, Cat.
TEXAS A & M UNIVERSITY - TECHNICAL
REPORTS DEPARTMENT □ College Station, TX

Taniguchi, Norma, Libn.
CANADA - AGRICULTURE CANADA - RESEARCH
STATION, FREDERICTON - LIBRARY □
Fredericton, NB

Tanin, Eleanore, Broadcast Supv.
UNIVERSITY OF CALIFORNIA, LOS ANGELES -
ACADEMY OF TELEVISION ARTS & SCIENCES -
TELEVISION ARCHIVES □ Los Angeles, CA

Tanin, Eleanore, Broadcast Supv.
UNIVERSITY OF CALIFORNIA, LOS ANGELES -
UCLA RADIO ARCHIVES □ Los Angeles, CA

Tannberg, Kersti, Fine Arts Libn.
WHEATON COLLEGE - LIBRARY - FINE ARTS
COLLECTION □ Norton, MA

Tannehill, Robert S., Jr., Lib.Mgr.
CHEMICAL ABSTRACTS SERVICE - LIBRARY □
Columbus, OH

Tanner, Anne, Diocesan Libn.
ANGLICAN CHURCH OF CANADA - DIOCESE OF
TORONTO - DIOCESAN LIBRARY & RESOURCE
CENTRE† □ Toronto, ON

Tanner, Elizabeth L., Libn.
GREELEY AND HANSEN - LIBRARY □ Chicago, IL

Tanner, Nancy, Asst.Libn.
AKIN, GUMP, STRAUSS, HAUER & FELD LAW
LIBRARY □ Dallas, TX

Tanner, Rebekkah, Cat.
U.S. COMMITTEE FOR UNICEF - INFORMATION
CENTER ON CHILDREN'S CULTURES □ New
York, NY

Tanner, Rose, Chm.
ANSHE HESED TEMPLE - LIBRARY □ Erie, PA

Tanner, Sandra H., Libn.
ARLINGTON BAPTIST COLLEGE - EARL K.
OLDHAM LIBRARY □ Arlington, TX

Tanner, Thomas M., Libn.
LINCOLN CHRISTIAN COLLEGE & SEMINARY -
JESSIE C. EURY LIBRARY □ Lincoln, IL

Tanno, John W., Music Libn.
UNIVERSITY OF CALIFORNIA, RIVERSIDE -
MUSIC LIBRARY □ Riverside, CA

Tanski, Henry M., Jr., Asst.Interp.
U.S. NATL. PARK SERVICE - CRATER LAKE
NATL. PARK - LIBRARY □ Crater Lake, OR

Tanzer, Barbara, Asst.Libn.
NEW YORK COUNTY LAWYERS' ASSOCIATION -
LIBRARY □ New York, NY

Taplinger, Beverly R., Lib.Techn.
U.S. DEPT. OF HOUSING AND URBAN
DEVELOPMENT - REGION III - LIBRARY □
Philadelphia, PA

Tapscott, Doug, Acq.
AIRCRAFT TECHNICAL PUBLISHERS - LIBRARY
□ San Francisco, CA

Taranta, Rene, Med.Libn.
WARREN GENERAL HOSPITAL - MEDICAL
STAFF LIBRARY □ Warren, OH

Tarbert, Anita W., Lib.Techn.
U.S. GEOLOGICAL SURVEY - WESTERN
MINERAL RESOURCES LIBRARY □ Spokane, WA

Tarbox, G.L., Jr., Dir.
BROOKGREEN GARDENS - LIBRARY □ Murrells
Inlet, SC

Targ, Fred, V.P.
CONTINENTAL CHEMISTE CORPORATION -
LIBRARY □ Chicago, IL

Tarman, Mary Sandra, Libn.
RAMSEY COUNTY MEDICAL SOCIETY -
BOECKMANN LIBRARY □ St. Paul, MN

Tarnawsky, Marta, Asst.Libn., Intl. Law
UNIVERSITY OF PENNSYLVANIA - BIDDLE LAW
LIBRARY □ Philadelphia, PA

Tarpley, Dr. Fred, Natl.Dir.
AMERICAN NAME SOCIETY - PLACE NAME
SURVEY OF THE UNITED STATES - LIBRARY □
Commerce, TX

Tarter, Theodore, Cur.
CONDE NAST PUBLICATIONS, INC. - LIBRARY □
New York, NY
Tashima, Marie, Supv., Info.Serv.
NALCO CHEMICAL COMPANY - TECHNICAL
CENTER - INFORMATION SERVICES □
Naperville, IL
Tashjean, Catherine, Ref.Libn.
U.S. OFFICE OF PERSONNEL MANAGEMENT -
LIBRARY □ Washington, DC
Tashjian, Sharon A., AV Libn.
EMANUEL HOSPITAL - LIBRARY SERVICES □
Portland, OR
Tate, Elaine A., Med.Libn.
U.S. ARMY HOSPITALS - MARTIN ARMY
COMMUNITY HOSPITAL - MEDICAL LIBRARY □
Ft. Benning, GA
Tate, R.W., Dir. Of Res.
DELAVAN CORPORATION - ENGINEERING
LIBRARY □ West Des Moines, IA
Tate, Sue, Ser. & Ref.Libn.
UNIVERSITY OF HEALTH SCIENCES - LIBRARY
□ Kansas City, MO
Tatian, Carol, Libn.
CARNEGIE LIBRARY OF PITTSBURGH - MUSIC
AND ART DEPARTMENT □ Pittsburgh, PA
Tatley, Orlette, Asst. to Libn.
GOLDEN VALLEY LUTHERAN COLLEGE -
LIBRARY □ Minneapolis, MN
Tatman, Mary Ann, Med.Libn.
U.S. VETERANS ADMINISTRATION (VA-Salem) -
MEDICAL CENTER LIBRARY □ Salem, VA
Tatman, Sandra, Arch.Libn.
ATHENAEUM OF PHILADELPHIA □ Philadelphia,
PA
Tattershall, Miss S., Hd., Lib.Sect.
SHELL CANADA LIMITED - TECHNICAL LIBRARY
□ Toronto, ON
Taub, Edith A., Dir. of Libs.
METHODIST HOSPITAL - HEALTH SCIENCES
LIBRARY □ Brooklyn, NY
Tauber, Anna R., Libn.
CARNEGIE MUSEUM OF NATURAL HISTORY -
LIBRARY □ Pittsburgh, PA
Tauber, Bonnie, Mgr.Info.Serv.
LEBER KATZ, INC. - MARKETING
INFORMATION CENTER LIBRARY □ New York,
NY
Tauber, M. Joan, Libn.
SUNY - CENTRAL ADMINISTRATION RESEARCH
LIBRARY □ Albany, NY
Taubman, Susan, Lrng.Rsrcs.Coord.
CREEDMOOR PSYCHIATRIC CENTER - HEALTH
SCIENCES LIBRARY □ Queens Village, NY
Taurytzky, Sary, Libn.
WASHINGTON STATE LIBRARY - WESTERN
STATE HOSPITAL - STAFF LIBRARY □ Fort
Steilacoom, WA
Tausky, Janice, Libn.
UNIVERSITY OF MASSACHUSETTS, AMHERST -
LABOR RELATIONS & RESEARCH CENTER
LIBRARY □ Amherst, MA
Tavino, Mrs. Ralph
CIRCLEVILLE PRESBYTERIAN CHURCH - BOOK
NOOK □ Circleville, NY
Tawyea, Edward, Hd., Circ. Media Libn.
NORTHWESTERN UNIVERSITY - HEALTH
SCIENCES LIBRARY □ Chicago, IL
Tax, Andrew, Asst.Sci.Libn.
SOUTHERN ILLINOIS UNIVERSITY,
CARBONDALE - SCIENCE DIVISION LIBRARY □
Carbondale, IL
Taylor, Mr. A.C., Exec.Dir.Dept.Adm.
NATIONAL LIBRARY OF CANADA □ Ottawa, ON
Taylor, Adrienne, Ref.Libn.
NORTH YORK PUBLIC LIBRARY - CANADIANA
COLLECTION □ Willowdale, ON
Taylor, Aline H., Libn.
GENERAL TELEPHONE COMPANY OF THE
SOUTHWEST - E.H. DANNER LIBRARY OF
TELEPHONY □ San Angelo, TX

Taylor, Annabelle, Libn.
CANADA - NATIONAL RESEARCH COUNCIL -
ATLANTIC RESEARCH LABORATORY - LIBRARY
□ Halifax, NS
Taylor, Anne, Chf., Lib.Serv.
U.S. VETERANS ADMINISTRATION (WI-
Madison) - WILLIAM S. MIDDLETON MEMORIAL
VETERANS HOSPITAL - LIBRARY □ Madison, WI
Taylor, Arthur, Photographer
MUSEUM OF NEW MEXICO - PHOTOGRAPHIC
ARCHIVES □ Santa Fe, NM
Taylor, Barb, Act.Libn.
GOULD, INC. - NAVCOM SYSTEMS DIVISION -
TECHNICAL LIBRARY† □ El Monte, CA
Taylor, Dr. Barry N., Chf.
U.S. NATL. BUREAU OF STANDARDS -
FUNDAMENTAL CONSTANTS DATA CENTER □
Washington, DC
Taylor, Beatrice K., Mss.Libn.
DU PONT (Henry Francis) WINTERTHUR
MUSEUM - LIBRARY □ Winterthur, DE
Taylor, Bernard H., Libn.
U.S. DEPT. OF HOUSING AND URBAN
DEVELOPMENT - REGION II - LIBRARY □ New
York, NY
Taylor, Betsy, Chf., Lib.Serv.
U.S. VETERANS ADMINISTRATION (IL-Danville)
- MEDICAL CENTER LIBRARY □ Danville, IL
Taylor, Betty W., Dir.
UNIVERSITY OF FLORIDA - LAW LIBRARY □
Gainesville, FL
Taylor, Blanche B., Libn.
UTAH WATER RESEARCH LABORATORY -
LIBRARY □ Logan, UT
Taylor, Byron C., Base Libn.
U.S. AIR FORCE BASE - WHITEMAN BASE
LIBRARY □ Whiteman AFB, MO
Taylor, Carol Lenz, Libn.
BORDEN INC. - RESEARCH CENTRE - LIBRARY □
Syracuse, NY
Taylor, Carolyn L., Asst.Libn.
ST. LOUIS UNIVERSITY - MEDICAL CENTER
LIBRARY □ St. Louis, MO
Taylor, Charles E., Supv., Projects
U.S. NATL. ARCHIVES & RECORDS SERVICE -
NATL. ARCHIVES - CENTER FOR
CARTOGRAPHIC & ARCHITECTURAL ARCHIVES
□ Washington, DC
Taylor, Christine, Libn.
SNOHOMISH COUNTY LAW LIBRARY □ Everett,
WA
Taylor, Dan, Ref.
UNIVERSITY OF TEXAS HEALTH SCIENCE
CENTER, SAN ANTONIO - LIBRARY □ San
Antonio, TX
Taylor, Deonna, Mgr., Lib.Serv.
FIND/SVP - LIBRARY □ New York, NY
Taylor, Donald R., Adm.
NORTH CAROLINA STATE DEPARTMENT OF
CULTURAL RESOURCES - TRYON PALACE
RESTORATION - LIBRARY □ New Bern, NC
Taylor, Doreen, Chf.Libn.
ONTARIO HYDRO - LIBRARY □ Toronto, ON
Taylor, Foli, Photograph Libn.
MINOT DAILY NEWS - LIBRARY □ Minot, ND
Taylor, Gay Le Cleire, Libn.
WHEATON HISTORICAL ASSOCIATION -
LIBRARY & RESEARCH OFFICE □ Millville, NJ
Taylor, Gertrude, Ed.
UNIVERSITY OF SOUTHWESTERN LOUISIANA -
CENTER FOR LOUISIANA STUDIES □ Lafayette,
LA
Taylor, Gladys, Archv.
ROCHESTER INSTITUTE OF TECHNOLOGY -
WALLACE MEMORIAL LIBRARY □ Rochester, NY
Taylor, H. Leroy, Libn.
CHURCH OF JESUS CHRIST OF LATTER-DAY
SAINTS - EL PASO BRANCH GENEALOGICAL
LIBRARY □ El Paso, TX
Taylor, Helen, Libn.
ST. LOUIS PUBLIC LIBRARY - POPULAR
LIBRARY - MUSIC SECTION □ St. Louis, MO

Taylor, Hugh A., Prov.Archv.
NOVA SCOTIA - PUBLIC ARCHIVES OF NOVA
SCOTIA □ Halifax, NS
Taylor, James B., Dept.Hd.
SEATTLE PUBLIC LIBRARY - BUSINESS AND
SCIENCE DEPARTMENT □ Seattle, WA
Taylor, Jimmizine, Ref. Libn.
PRAIRIE VIEW A & M COLLEGE OF TEXAS -
W.R. BANKS LIBRARY □ Prairie View, TX
Taylor, Joan R., Ref.Libn.
U.S. DEPT. OF COMMERCE - DEPARTMENTAL
LIBRARY □ Washington, DC
Taylor, Joann L., Dir.
U.S. DEPT. OF ENERGY - LABORATORY OF
BIOMEDICAL AND ENVIRONMENTAL SCIENCES
- LIBRARY □ Los Angeles, CA
Taylor, John, Asst. Law Libn.
ORAL ROBERTS UNIVERSITY - LAW LIBRARY □
Tulsa, OK
Taylor, Joyce, Educ.Libn.
UNIVERSITY OF MISSISSIPPI - SCHOOL OF
EDUCATION LIBRARY □ University, MS
Taylor, Juanita, Chf.Libn.
U.S. ARMY POST - PRESIDIO OF SAN
FRANCISCO - POST LIBRARY SYSTEM □ Presidio
of San Francisco, CA
Taylor, Karen, AV Libn.
UNIVERSITY OF TEXAS HEALTH SCIENCE
CENTER, DALLAS - LIBRARY □ Dallas, TX
Taylor, Kent J., Supv./Pk. Ranger
U.S. NATL. PARK SERVICE - FORT VANCOUVER
NATL. HISTORIC SITE - LIBRARY □ Vancouver,
WA
Taylor, Lidia, Ref.Libn.
CANADA - CANADA CENTRE FOR REMOTE
SENSING - TECHNICAL INFORMATION SERVICE
□ Ottawa, ON
Taylor, Lila, Asst.Libn.
PUTNAM COMPANIES - INVESTMENT
RESEARCH LIBRARY □ Boston, MA
Taylor, Madeline, Ser.Libn.
COLLEGE OF MEDICINE AND DENTISTRY OF
NEW JERSEY AT NEWARK - GEORGE F. SMITH
LIBRARY □ Newark, NJ
Taylor, Margaret Jean, Libn.
U.S. FOREST SERVICE - SOUTHEASTERN
FOREST EXPERIMENT STATION LIBRARY† □
Asheville, NC
Taylor, Margaret P.J., Dir., Lib.Serv.
CHILDREN'S HOSPITAL OF EASTERN ONTARIO -
MEDICAL LIBRARY □ Ottawa, ON
Taylor, Margaret R., Dir., Marketing Res.
BALTIMORE ECONOMIC DEVELOPMENT
CORPORATION - LIBRARY □ Baltimore, MD
Taylor, Marion, Hd.Coll.Plan.
UNIVERSITY OF CALIFORNIA, SANTA CRUZ -
DEAN E. MC HENRY LIBRARY □ Santa Cruz, CA
Taylor, Mark, Hd., Tech.Serv.
MASSACHUSETTS GENERAL HOSPITAL -
TREADWELL AND PALMER-DAVIS LIBRARY □
Boston, MA
Taylor, Mary-Stuart, Chf., Cat.
U.S. NATL. DEFENSE UNIVERSITY - LIBRARY □
Washington, DC
Taylor, Mary Virginia, Chf., Lib.Serv.
U.S. VETERANS ADMINISTRATION (TN-
Memphis) - MEDICAL CENTER LIBRARY □
Memphis, TN
Taylor, Maureen, Graphics Cur.
RHODE ISLAND HISTORICAL SOCIETY -
LIBRARY □ Providence, RI
Taylor, Molly, Lib.Techn.
ALBERTA ALCOHOLISM AND DRUG ABUSE
COMMISSION - LIBRARY □ Calgary, AB
Taylor, Nancy, Tech.Serv.Instr.Prog.
UNIVERSITY OF WISCONSIN, MADISON -
SCHOOL OF EDUCATION - INSTRUCTIONAL
MATERIALS CENTER □ Madison, WI
Taylor, Neda Marie, Libn.
U.S. COAST GUARD - OCEANOGRAPHIC UNIT -
LIBRARY □ Washington, DC

Taylor, Norma M., Assoc.Libn.
MASSACHUSETTS STATE DEPARTMENT OF THE
ATTORNEY GENERAL - LIBRARY □ Boston, MA

Taylor, Olga, Libn.
ARLINGTON HOSPITAL - DOCTORS' LIBRARY† □
Arlington, VA

Taylor, R. Thad, Pres.
SHAKESPEARE SOCIETY OF AMERICA - NEW
PLACE RARE BOOK LIBRARY† □ Los Angeles, CA

Taylor, Rita, Libn.
STANFORD LINEAR ACCELERATOR CENTER -
LIBRARY □ Menlo Park, CA

Taylor, Robert, Ref.Libn.
SAN DIEGO PUBLIC LIBRARY - SCIENCE &
INDUSTRY SECTION □ San Diego, CA

Taylor, Rosemarie Kazda, Dir., Lib.Serv.
WILKES-BARRE GENERAL HOSPITAL -
HOSPITAL LIBRARY □ Wilkes-Barre, PA

Taylor, Ruth, Assoc.Libn.
WAYNE STATE UNIVERSITY - SCHOOL OF
MEDICINE - VERA PARSHALL SHIFFMAN
MEDICAL LIBRARY □ Detroit, MI

Taylor, Saundra, Cur. of Mss.
INDIANA UNIVERSITY - LILLY LIBRARY □
Bloomington, IN

Taylor, Sharon, Asst.Dir.Pub.Serv.
JACKSON METROPOLITAN LIBRARY -
INFORMATION AND REFERENCE DIVISION □
Jackson, MS

Taylor, Sharon, Dir.
REFORMED THEOLOGICAL SEMINARY -
LIBRARY □ Jackson, MS

Taylor, Shirley, Co-Libn.
GREATER SOUTHEAST COMMUNITY HOSPITAL
- LURA HEALTH SCIENCES LIBRARY □
Washington, DC

Taylor, Shirley, Supv.
OWENS-ILLINOIS, INC. - TECHNICAL
INFORMATION SERVICES □ Toledo, OH

Taylor, Susan D., Act.Commn.
U.S. EQUAL EMPLOYMENT OPPORTUNITY
COMMISSION - LIBRARY □ Washington, DC

Taylor, Vickie, Hd.Libn.
PEAT, MARWICK, MITCHELL & COMPANY -
CENTRAL LIBRARY □ Los Angeles, CA

Taylor, W.D., Dir.
WASHINGTON STATE DEPARTMENT OF
COMMERCE AND ECONOMIC DEVELOPMENT -
TOURISM DEVELOPMENT DIVISION □ Seattle,
WA

Taylor, Wm.M., CAI Supv.
KENT STATE UNIVERSITY - COMPUTER
ASSISTED AND SELF INSTRUCTION CENTER □
Kent, OH

Tayyeb, Rashid, Hd.Tech.Serv.
ST. MARY'S UNIVERSITY - PATRICK POWER
LIBRARY □ Halifax, NS

Tchobanoff, James B., Mgr.
PILLSBURY COMPANY - TECHNICAL
INFORMATION CENTER □ Minneapolis, MN

Teach, Marian A., Tech.Info.Spec.
CHEVRON OIL FIELD RESEARCH COMPANY -
TECHNICAL INFORMATION SERVICES □ La
Habra, CA

Teahan, John, Asst.Libn.
WADSWORTH ATHENEUM - AUERBACH ART
LIBRARY □ Hartford, CT

Teal, Lee, Libn.
CANADA - AGRICULTURE CANADA - CANADIAN
GRAIN COMMISSION - LIBRARY □ Winnipeg, MB

Teare, Robert F., Asst.Dir., Tech.Serv.
CLAREMONT COLLEGES - LIBRARY □ Claremont,
CA

Tebbutt, Jean M., Chf.Libn.
HAMILTON SPECTATOR - REFERENCE LIBRARY
□ Hamilton, ON

Tebo, Jay, Leader, Ref. & Bk.Serv.
AUTOMATION INDUSTRIES, INC. - VITRO
LABORATORIES DIVISION - ADMINISTRATIVE
SUPPORT DEPARTMENT □ Silver Spring, MD

Tebo, Marlene, Asst.Dir.
SUNY AT BINGHAMTON - SCIENCE LIBRARY □
Binghamton, NY

Teclaff, Dr. Ludwik A., Professor/Libn.
FORDHAM UNIVERSITY - SCHOOL OF LAW
LIBRARY □ New York, NY

Tedesco, Eileen, Acq.Libn.
STONE AND WEBSTER ENGINEERING
CORPORATION - TECHNICAL INFORMATION
CENTER □ Boston, MA

Tedman, Vernelia, Libn.
HONEYWELL, INC. - MICRO SWITCH
ENGINEERING LIBRARY □ Freeport, IL

Teel, Cora, Archv.
MARSHALL UNIVERSITY - JAMES E. MORROW
LIBRARY - SPECIAL COLLECTIONS □ Huntington,
WV

Teeple, F.Diane, Exec.Asst. to the Dir.
ONTARIO - LEGISLATIVE ASSEMBLY -
LEGISLATIVE LIBRARY RESEARCH AND
INFORMATION SERVICES □ Toronto, ON

Teeter, Enola Jane N., Libn.
LONGWOOD GARDENS, INC. - LIBRARY □
Kennett Square, PA

Tega, Vasile, Ref.Libn.
ECOLE DES HAUTES ETUDES COMMERCIALES
DE MONTREAL - BIBLIOTHEQUE □ Montreal, PQ

Teich, Steve, OHIN Coord.
UNIVERSITY OF OREGON - HEALTH SCIENCES
CENTER - LIBRARY □ Portland, OR

Teichman, R., AV Archv.
U.S. PRESIDENTIAL LIBRARIES - FRANKLIN D.
ROOSEVELT LIBRARY □ Hyde Park, NY

Teigen, Philip, Osler Libn.
MC GILL UNIVERSITY - OSLER LIBRARY □
Montreal, PQ

Teigler, Elaine E., Asst.Libn./Pub.Serv.
NORTHWESTERN UNIVERSITY - LAW SCHOOL
LIBRARY □ Chicago, IL

Teitelbaum, Gene W., Libn.
UNIVERSITY OF LOUISVILLE - SCHOOL OF LAW
LIBRARY □ Louisville, KY

Teitelbaum, Marsha, Circ.
CASE WESTERN RESERVE UNIVERSITY - LAW
LIBRARY □ Cleveland, OH

Teller, Rev.Msgr. Raymond, Dir.
ARCHDIOCESE OF PHILADELPHIA - CATHOLIC
INFORMATION CENTER □ Philadelphia, PA

Tellier, Corinne, Ref.Libn.
WINNIPEG SCHOOL DIVISION NO. 1 -
TEACHERS LIBRARY AND RESOURCE CENTRE □
Winnipeg, MB

Teloh, Mary H., Spec.Coll.Libn.
VANDERBILT UNIVERSITY - MEDICAL CENTER
LIBRARY □ Nashville, TN

Tempkin, Mrs. Elliot, Libn.
TEMPLE BETH ISRAEL - LIBRARY □ Phoenix, AZ

Temple, Joy, Cat.
SOUTHERN OHIO GENEALOGICAL SOCIETY -
REFERENCE LIBRARY □ Hillsboro, OH

Temple, Nancy, Techn.
ALTOONA AREA PUBLIC LIBRARY & DISTRICT
CENTER - PENNSYLVANIA ROOM □ Altoona, PA

Tener, Jean, Archv.
UNIVERSITY OF CALGARY - SPECIAL
COLLECTIONS DIVISION □ Calgary, AB

Tennenhouse, Michael, Pub.Serv.Libn.
UNIVERSITY OF MANITOBA - MEDICAL
LIBRARY □ Winnipeg, MB

Tenner, Louise, Acq.Libn.
UNIVERSITY OF TEXAS, EL PASO - LIBRARY □ El
Paso, TX

Tenny, Dana, Libn.
TORONTO PUBLIC LIBRARY - CANADIANA
COLLECTION OF CHILDREN'S BOOKS □ Toronto,
ON

Tenny, Dana, Libn.
TORONTO PUBLIC LIBRARY - LILLIAN H. SMITH
COLLECTION OF CHILDREN'S BOOKS □ Toronto,
ON

Tenny, Dana, Libn.
TORONTO PUBLIC LIBRARY - OSBORNE
COLLECTION OF EARLY CHILDREN'S BOOKS □
Toronto, ON

Tepper, Herbert J., Cat.Libn.
STATE HISTORICAL SOCIETY OF WISCONSIN -
LIBRARY □ Madison, WI

Tepper, Jean, Lib.Asst.
GULF CANADA LIMITED - CENTRAL LIBRARY □
Toronto, ON

Teranis, Mara, Info.Sci.
JOHNSON (S.C.) AND SON, INC. - TECHNICAL &
BUSINESS INFORMATION CENTER □ Racine, WI

Terhune, R. Stanford, Cat.Libn.
GORDON COLLEGE - WINN LIBRARY □ Wenham,
MA

Termine, Jack E., Med.Libn.
NEW YORK ORTHOPAEDIC HOSPITAL -
RUSSELL A. HIBBS LIBRARY □ New York, NY

Ternberg, Milton G., Hd.
DALLAS PUBLIC LIBRARY - GOVERNMENT
PUBLICATIONS DIVISION □ Dallas, TX

Ternisien, Robert, Supv., Music Copyrights
CANADIAN BROADCASTING CORPORATION -
MUSIC SERVICES LIBRARY □ Montreal, PQ

Terpo, Mary A., Law Libn.
WORCESTER COUNTY LAW LIBRARY □
Worcester, MA

Terrell, Mary Jane, Distr.Rep.
NATIONAL FILM BOARD OF CANADA - FILM
LIBRARY □ New York, NY

Terrill, Marjorie L., Med.Libn.
MENORAH MEDICAL CENTER - ROBERT
UHLMAN MEDICAL LIBRARY □ Kansas City, MO

Terry, Anita, Hd., Info.Serv.
MAYO FOUNDATION - MAYO CLINIC LIBRARY □
Rochester, MN

Terry, Blanche, Res.Dir.
VICKSBURG & WARREN COUNTY HISTORICAL
SOCIETY - MC CARDLE LIBRARY □ Vicksburg,
MS

Terry, Carol, Libn.
FORT WORTH PUBLIC LIBRARY - HUMANITIES
DEPARTMENT □ Fort Worth, TX

Terry, Edward S., Dir.
JOHNS HOPKINS UNIVERSITY - SCHOOL OF
HYGIENE AND PUBLIC HEALTH -
INTERDEPARTMENTAL LIBRARY □ Baltimore,
MD

Terry, Forrest A., Deputy Archv.
UTAH STATE ARCHIVES □ Salt Lake City, UT

Terry, Gail, Asst.Archv.
COLONIAL WILLIAMSBURG - RESEARCH
LIBRARY & ARCHIVES □ Williamsburg, VA

Terry, Joan N., Libn.
NORTHEAST UTILITIES SERVICE COMPANY -
LIBRARY □ Hartford, CT

Terry, Mary Jo, Libn.
DISNEY (Walt) PRODUCTIONS - LIBRARY □
Burbank, CA

Terry, Maryeva W., Mgr.
UNIVERSITY OF WASHINGTON - REGIONAL
PRIMATE RESEARCH CENTER - PRIMATE
INFORMATION CENTER □ Seattle, WA

Terry, Nancy L., Asst.Med.Libn. II
WASHINGTON HOSPITAL CENTER - MEDICAL
LIBRARY □ Washington, DC

Terry, Roslyn M., Libn. Pro Tem
CONVERSE WARD DAVIS DIXON - LIBRARY □
Caldwell, NJ

Terry, Spurgeon D., Law Libn.
U.S.D.A. - NATIONAL AGRICULTURAL LIBRARY -
LAW LIBRARY □ Washington, DC

Terryberry, Ann B., Cat./Order
NORTH ADAMS STATE COLLEGE - EUGENE L.
FREEL LIBRARY - SPECIAL COLLECTIONS □
North Adams, MA

Terstegge, Mary Anne, Hist.Libn.
TULARE COUNTY FREE LIBRARY - CALIFORNIA
HISTORICAL RESEARCH COLLECTION □ Visalia,
CA

Tertell, Susan
MINNEAPOLIS PUBLIC LIBRARY &
INFORMATION CENTER - GOVERNMENT
DOCUMENTS □ Minneapolis, MN

Terzian, Sherry, Dir.
NEUROPSYCHIATRIC INSTITUTE - MENTAL
HEALTH INFORMATION SERVICE □ Los Angeles,
CA

Tesmer, Nancy S., Chf., Lib.Serv.
U.S. VETERANS ADMINISTRATION (OH-
Brecksville) - HOSPITAL LIBRARY □ Brecksville,
OH

Tesmer, Nancy S., Chf.Libn.
U.S. VETERANS ADMINISTRATION (OH-
Cleveland) - HOSPITAL LIBRARY □ Cleveland, OH

Tessler, Helene L., Cur.-Libn.
BRISTOL HISTORICAL AND PRESERVATION
SOCIETY - LIBRARY □ Bristol, RI

Testa, Dana D., AV Serv.
UNIVERSITY OF OKLAHOMA - HEALTH
SCIENCES CENTER LIBRARY □ Oklahoma City,
OK

Testa, Elizabeth, Sr.Libn.
CALIFORNIA STATE POSTSECONDARY
EDUCATION COMMISSION - LIBRARY □
Sacramento, CA

Teter, Cynthia A., Lrng.Ctr.Instr.
DALLAS SKILLS CENTER - LEARNING LAB □
Dallas, TX

Teter, Mrs. Roy, Jr., Libn.
ASBURY UNITED METHODIST CHURCH -
LIBRARY □ Tacoma, WA

Thackray, Dr. Arnold W., Cur.
UNIVERSITY OF PENNSYLVANIA - EDGAR FAHS
SMITH MEMORIAL COLLECTION IN THE
HISTORY OF CHEMISTRY □ Philadelphia, PA

Thaker, Bala, Govt.Doc. & Ser.
WHITTIER COLLEGE - SCHOOL OF LAW -
LIBRARY □ Los Angeles, CA

Thalken, Thomas, Dir.
U.S. PRESIDENTIAL LIBRARIES - HERBERT
HOOVER LIBRARY □ West Branch, IA

Thaper, Shashi P., Hd.Libn.
MARYLAND STATE DEPARTMENT OF NATURAL
RESOURCES - LIBRARY □ Annapolis, MD

Tharaud, Cynthia M., Med.Libn.
MESA COUNTY MEDICAL SOCIETY - DR. E.H.
MUNRO MEDICAL LIBRARY □ Grand Junction, CO

Tharp, Sonny, Asst.Libn.
COURIER-JOURNAL AND LOUISVILLE TIMES -
LIBRARY □ Louisville, KY

Thatcher, Linda, Acq.Libn.
UTAH STATE HISTORICAL SOCIETY -
RESEARCH LIBRARY □ Salt Lake City, UT

Thauberger, Marianne, Libn.
UNIVERSITY OF REGINA - EDUCATION BRANCH
LIBRARY □ Regina, SK

Thaxton, Carol J., Hd.Libn.
FEDERAL RESERVE BANK OF ST. LOUIS -
RESEARCH LIBRARY □ St. Louis, MO

Thayer, Candace W., Libn.
ST. MARY'S HEALTH CENTER - HEALTH
SCIENCES LIBRARY □ St. Louis, MO

The, Tjeng Sioe, Indonesian Cat.
CORNELL UNIVERSITY - JOHN M. ECHOLS
COLLECTION ON SOUTHEAST ASIA □ Ithaca, NY

The-Mulliner, Lian, Hd.Libn.
OHIO UNIVERSITY - SOUTHEAST ASIA
COLLECTION □ Athens, OH

Theall, John N., Asst.Dir.Pub.Serv.
UNIVERSITY OF ILLINOIS MEDICAL CENTER -
LIBRARY OF THE HEALTH SCIENCES □ Chicago,
IL

Theberge, Guy, Sec.
COLLEGE DE STE-ANNE-DE-LA-POCATIERE -
SOCIETE HISTORIQUE-DE-LA-COTE-DU-SUD -
BIBLIOTHEQUE □ La Pocatiere, PQ

Theil, Gordon, Asst. Music Libn.
UNIVERSITY OF CALIFORNIA, LOS ANGELES -
MUSIC LIBRARY □ Los Angeles, CA

Theisen, Rev. Wilfred, O.S.B., Asst.Dir.
ST. JOHN'S ABBEY AND UNIVERSITY - HILL
MONASTIC MANUSCRIPT LIBRARY - BUSH
CENTER □ Collegeville, MN

Theobald, H. Rupert, Chf.
WISCONSIN STATE LEGISLATIVE REFERENCE
BUREAU □ Madison, WI

Theodore, Sr. Mary, C.S.F.N., Libn.
MERCY HOSPITAL - SCHOOL OF NURSING
LIBRARY □ Altoona, PA

Theodos, Cytheria, Dir.Info.Serv.
DREYFUS CORPORATION - LIBRARY □ New
York, NY

Theodosette, Sr. M., Archv.
SISTERS OF THE HOLY FAMILY OF NAZARETH -
IMMACULATE CONCEPTION PROVINCE -
ARCHIVES □ Philadelphia, PA

Theologides, Maro, Supv.
HONEYWELL, INC. - SYSTEMS & RESEARCH
CENTER - LIBRARY □ Minneapolis, MN

Therien, Master Corporal, Libn.
CANADA - NATIONAL DEFENCE - MAPPING AND
CHARTING ESTABLISHMENT TECHNICAL
LIBRARY □ Ottawa, ON

Therrien, Elyse, Libn.
DOMTAR, INC. - CENTRAL LIBRARY □ Montreal,
PQ

Therrien, Kathy, AV Libn.
METROPOLITAN TORONTO LIBRARY - AUDIO
VISUAL SERVICES □ Toronto, ON

Thevenet, Susanne D., Libn.
DOW, LOHNES & ALBERTSON - LAW LIBRARY □
Washington, DC

Thews, Dorothy D., Dept.Hd.
MINNEAPOLIS PUBLIC LIBRARY &
INFORMATION CENTER - LITERATURE AND
LANGUAGE DEPARTMENT □ Minneapolis, MN

Thibault, Marie-Therese, Ref.
QUEBEC PROVINCE - MINISTERE DES
AFFAIRES CULTURELLES - CENTRE DE
DOCUMENTATION □ Quebec, PQ

Thibault, Solange, Per.
CEGEP DE TROIS-RIVIERES - BIBLIOTHEQUE □
Trois-Rivieres, PQ

Thibodeau, Johane, Asst.Libn.
CANADA - SUPREME COURT OF CANADA -
LIBRARY □ Ottawa, ON

Thibodeau, Patricia L., Dir.
WOMEN & INFANTS HOSPITAL OF RHODE
ISLAND - HEALTH SCIENCES INFORMATION
CENTER □ Providence, RI

Thiedeman, Mary P., Ref.Libn./Ser.
WEST VIRGINIA WESLEYAN COLLEGE - ANNIE
MERNER PFEIFFER LIBRARY □ Buckhannon, WV

Thiegs, Francis J., Hd., Tech.Serv.
NEW YORK UNIVERSITY MEDICAL CENTER -
FREDERICK L. EHRMAN MEDICAL LIBRARY □
New York, NY

Thiel, Ronald E., Dir.
SOD TOWN PIONEER HOMESTEAD MUSEUM -
LIBRARY† □ Colby, KS

Thiele, Judith C., Ref. & Coll.Libn.
UNIVERSITY OF BRITISH COLUMBIA - CHARLES
CRANE MEMORIAL LIBRARY □ Vancouver, BC

Thiele, Paul E., Libn. & Hd.
UNIVERSITY OF BRITISH COLUMBIA - CHARLES
CRANE MEMORIAL LIBRARY □ Vancouver, BC

Thielman, Pam, ILL
GEORGE WASHINGTON UNIVERSITY -
MEDICAL CENTER - PAUL HIMMELFARB HEALTH
SCIENCES LIBRARY □ Washington, DC

Thieme, Mary S., Cur. of Coll.
CUMBERLAND MUSEUM AND SCIENCE CENTER
- LIBRARY □ Nashville, TN

Thiesson, Mrs. A., Libn.
WINNIPEG DEPARTMENT OF ENVIRONMENTAL
PLANNING - LIBRARY □ Winnipeg, MB

Thiriar, J.P., Supt.
NORANDA MINES LTD. - CCR DIVISION -
PROCESS DEVELOPMENT LIBRARY □ Montreal,
PQ

Thirlwall, David, Ref.Libn.
UNIVERSITY OF MANITOBA - EDUCATION
LIBRARY □ Winnipeg, MB

Thodeson, Kathyrn, Asst.Libn.
ST. VINCENT CHARITY HOSPITAL - LIBRARY □
Cleveland, OH

Thoele, Sylvia, Media Libn.
U.S. VETERANS ADMINISTRATION (IL-North
Chicago) - HOSPITAL LIBRARY □ North Chicago,
IL

Thom, Rupert C., Libn.
U.S. AIR FORCE BASE - ENGLAND BASE
LIBRARY □ England AFB, LA

Thoman, Nancy, Reports Libn.
ICI AMERICAS INC. - ATLAS LIBRARY □
Wilmington, DE

Thomann, Dorothy, Libn.
HUFFMAN MEMORIAL UNITED METHODIST
CHURCH - LIBRARY □ St. Joseph, MO

Thomas, Alfred, Jr., Univ.Archv.
ARIZONA STATE UNIVERSITY - UNIVERSITY
ARCHIVES □ Tempe, AZ

Thomas, Anita, Lib.Techn.
SYNCRUDE CANADA, LTD. - OPERATIONS
LIBRARY □ Fort McMurray, AB

Thomas, Arthur, Ref./Res.Libn.
SOUTHERN UNIVERSITY - LAW SCHOOL
LIBRARY □ Baton Rouge, LA

Thomas, Barbara, Ref.
TEXAS A & M UNIVERSITY - MEDICAL
SCIENCES LIBRARY □ College Station, TX

Thomas, Becky C., Music Libn.
MOUNT UNION COLLEGE - STURGEON MUSIC
LIBRARY □ Alliance, OH

Thomas, Bettye J., Libn./Sec.
WASHINGTON UNIVERSITY - EDWARD
MALLINCKRODT INSTITUTE OF RADIOLOGY
LIBRARY □ St. Louis, MO

Thomas, Bruce E., Hd.Rd.Serv.Libn.
LOCK HAVEN STATE COLLEGE - GEORGE B.
STEVENSON LIBRARY □ Lock Haven, PA

Thomas, Charles R., Exec.Dir.
CAUSE - LIBRARY □ Boulder, CO

Thomas, Cherry, Spec.Coll.
UNIVERSITY OF ALABAMA - SCHOOL OF LAW
LIBRARY □ University, AL

Thomas, D.A., Tech.Serv.
UNIVERSITY OF KANSAS MEDICAL CENTER -
COLLEGE OF HEALTH SCIENCES AND HOSPITAL
- CLENDENING LIBRARY □ Kansas City, KS

Thomas, D.W., V.P.
THOMPSON (J. Walter) COMPANY - RESEARCH
LIBRARY □ Los Angeles, CA

Thomas, David, Cur.
CANFIELD MEMORIAL LIBRARY - RUSSELL
VERMONTIANA COLLECTION □ Arlington, VT

Thomas, David A., Law Libn.
BRIGHAM YOUNG UNIVERSITY - J. REUBEN
CLARK LAW SCHOOL LIBRARY □ Provo, UT

Thomas, David H., Hd., Tech.Serv.
MICHIGAN TECHNOLOGICAL UNIVERSITY -
LIBRARY □ Houghton, MI

Thomas, David L., Entomology Libn.
CORNELL UNIVERSITY - ENTOMOLOGY
LIBRARY □ Ithaca, NY

Thomas, Dr. Doris Byrd, Libn.
CARTER (William) COLLEGE & EVANGELICAL
THEOLOGICAL SEMINARY - WAGNER-
KEVETTER LIBRARY □ Goldsboro, NC

Thomas, Ellen, Libn.
CORNELL UNIVERSITY - PHYSICAL SCIENCES
LIBRARY □ Ithaca, NY

Thomas, Gordon B., Dir.
U.S. DEPT. OF COMMERCE - INTERNATIONAL
TRADE ADMINISTRATION - CINCINNATI
DISTRICT OFFICE LIBRARY □ Cincinnati, OH

Thomas, Hugh, Med.Libn.
EYE FOUNDATION HOSPITAL - JOHN E. MEYER
EYE FOUNDATION LIBRARY □ Birmingham, AL

Thomas, J., ILL
ALBERTA - DEPARTMENT OF THE
ENVIRONMENT - LIBRARY □ Edmonton, AB

Thomas, Ms. J., Supv., Ref.
TORONTO BOARD OF EDUCATION - EDUCATION CENTRE LIBRARY □ Toronto, ON

Thomas, Jan, Libn.
MARATHON OIL COMPANY - RESEARCH CENTER LIBRARY □ Littleton, CO

Thomas, Jeani P., Libn.
WYOMING STATE DEPARTMENT OF HEALTH & SOCIAL SERVICE - HEALTH INFORMATION LIBRARY □ Cheyenne, WY

Thomas, Jeanne F., Libn.
MERRILL-PALMER INSTITUTE - EDNA NOBLE WHITE LIBRARY □ Detroit, MI

Thomas, Jeanne F., Libn.
MERRILL-PALMER INSTITUTE - KRESGE HISTORICAL LIBRARY □ Detroit, MI

Thomas, Joan L., Libn.
COLLIN MEMORIAL HOSPITAL - MEDICAL LIBRARY □ McKinney, TX

Thomas, Karol, Libn.
SAN MATEO COUNTY EDUCATIONAL RESOURCES CENTER □ Redwood City, CA

Thomas, Katharine S., Info.Sci.
LAWLER MATUSKY & SKELLY ENGINEERS - LIBRARY □ Pearl River, NY

Thomas, Mrs. Kodell M., Chf., Lib.Serv.
U.S. VETERANS ADMINISTRATION (GA-Dublin) - CENTER LIBRARY □ Dublin, GA

Thomas, Linda Charlmyra, Med.Libn.
MERRITT (Samuel) HOSPITAL - MEDICAL LIBRARY □ Oakland, CA

Thomas, Mrs. Lou, Libn.
BATON ROUGE STATE-TIMES & MORNING ADVOCATE NEWSPAPERS - LIBRARY □ Baton Rouge, LA

Thomas, Lydia B., Libn.
IOWA STATE DEPARTMENT OF PUBLIC INSTRUCTION - RESOURCE CENTER □ Des Moines, IA

Thomas, Margaret, Hd., Coll.Dev.
UNIVERSITY OF MICHIGAN - DEARBORN LIBRARY □ Dearborn, MI

Thomas, Mary, Hd., Coll.Dev.
UNIVERSITY OF NORTH CAROLINA, CHAPEL HILL - HEALTH SCIENCES LIBRARY □ Chapel Hill, NC

Thomas, Mary Lou, Cur.
CANFIELD MEMORIAL LIBRARY - RUSSELL VERMONTIANA COLLECTION □ Arlington, VT

Thomas, Mary Lou, Assoc.Libn.
NEW YORK GENEALOGICAL AND BIOGRAPHICAL SOCIETY - GENEALOGICAL RESEARCH LIBRARY □ New York, NY

Thomas, Page, Tech.Serv.
SOUTHERN METHODIST UNIVERSITY - PERKINS SCHOOL OF THEOLOGY - LIBRARY □ Dallas, TX

Thomas, Paul W., Dir.
WESLEYAN CHURCH - ARCHIVES & HISTORICAL LIBRARY □ Marion, IN

Thomas, Pearl M., Libn.
PHILOSOPHICAL RESEARCH SOCIETY - RESEARCH LIBRARY □ Los Angeles, CA

Thomas, Robert M., Asst.Chf.
NEW YORK PUBLIC LIBRARY - MID-MANHATTAN LIBRARY □ New York, NY

Thomas, Ronald F., Libn./Treas.
YESTERYEARS MUSEUM ASSOCIATION, INC. - LIBRARY □ Sandwich, MA

Thomas, Sue, Circ.Asst.
MARICOPA TECHNICAL COMMUNITY COLLEGE - LIBRARY RESOURCE CENTER □ Phoenix, AZ

Thomas, Susan, Hd., Adm.Serv.
STATE LIBRARY OF OHIO □ Columbus, OH

Thomas, Terry B., Pres.
GARDEN GROVE HISTORICAL SOCIETY - E.G.WARE LIBRARY □ Garden Grove, CA

Thomas, Thedosia, Color Slide Ed.
U.S. DEPT. OF AGRICULTURE - PHOTOGRAPHY DIVISION - PHOTOGRAPH LIBRARY □ Washington, DC

Thomas, Vi, Libn.
WESTERN STATE HOSPITAL - MEDICAL LIBRARY □ Fort Supply, OK

Thomas-Jackson, Penny, Med.Libn.
HENROTIN HOSPITAL - MEDICAL LIBRARY □ Chicago, IL

Thomas-Jackson, Penny, Assoc.Dir.
ILLINOIS COLLEGE OF PODIATRIC MEDICINE - LIBRARY □ Chicago, IL

Thompson, Alleen, Mgr., Lib.
GENERAL ELECTRIC COMPANY - NUCLEAR ENERGY GROUP - LIBRARY □ San Jose, CA

Thompson, Anya, Ed.
ARGENTINE INFORMATION SERVICE CENTER† □ New York, NY

Thompson, B. Dolores, Exec.Dir.
FENTON HISTORICAL SOCIETY - LIBRARY □ Jamestown, NY

Thompson, Barbara J., Libn.
ECONOMICS RESEARCH ASSOCIATES - LIBRARY† □ Los Angeles, CA

Thompson, Benna Brodsky, Libn.
U.S.D.A. - AGRICULTURAL RESEARCH SERVICE - SOUTHERN REGION - RICHARD B. RUSSELL AGRICULTURAL RESEARCH CTR. LIB. □ Athens, GA

Thompson, Berneice, Libn.
HUSSON COLLEGE - LIBRARY □ Bangor, ME

Thompson, Bert A., Dir., Lib.Serv.
ILLINOIS BENEDICTINE COLLEGE - THEODORE LOWNIK LIBRARY □ Lisle, IL

Thompson, C.M., Dir.
UNIVERSITY OF OKLAHOMA - HEALTH SCIENCES CENTER LIBRARY □ Oklahoma City, OK

Thompson, Chris F., Regional Res.Off.
BRITISH COLUMBIA - MINISTRY OF FORESTS - NELSON FOREST REGION LIBRARY □ Nelson, BC

Thompson, Clare T., Libn.
SPERRY CORPORATION - BUSINESS PLANNING LIBRARY □ New York, NY

Thompson, Connie B., Assoc.Libn.
FEDERAL RESERVE BANK OF RICHMOND - RESEARCH LIBRARY □ Richmond, VA

Thompson, Mrs. Corley, Exec.Dir.
ST. LOUIS HEARING AND SPEECH CENTER - LIBRARY □ St. Louis, MO

Thompson, Mrs. D.A., Dir. of Pharm.Serv.
ST. JOSEPH'S HOSPITAL - DRUG INFORMATION CENTRE □ Hamilton, ON

Thompson, Debbie, Med.Libn.
U.S. VETERANS ADMINISTRATION (IN-Indianapolis) - MEDICAL CENTER LIBRARY □ Indianapolis, IN

Thompson, Donald, Bus.Libn.
SOUTHERN ILLINOIS UNIVERSITY, EDWARDSVILLE - SOCIAL SCIENCE/BUSINESS/MAP LIBRARY □ Edwardsville, IL

Thompson, Doris, Asst.Libn.
INDIANAPOLIS PUBLIC SCHOOLS - TEACHERS LIBRARY □ Indianapolis, IN

Thompson, Dorothea M., Asst.Ref.Libn.
CARNEGIE-MELLON UNIVERSITY - HUNT LIBRARY □ Pittsburgh, PA

Thompson, Edna S., Lib.Asst.
BAR ASSOCIATION OF THE DISTRICT OF COLUMBIA - LIBRARY □ Washington, DC

Thompson, Eleanor E., Dir.
WENHAM HISTORICAL ASSOCIATION AND MUSEUM - COLONEL TIMOTHY PICKERING LIBRARY □ Wenham, MA

Thompson, Eleanor M., Libn. Print Bk.
DU PONT (Henry Francis) WINTERTHUR MUSEUM - LIBRARY □ Winterthur, DE

Thompson, Elizabeth M., Media Serv.Libn.
DISTRICT OF COLUMBIA TEACHERS COLLEGE - LIBRARY □ Washington, DC

Thompson, F.H., Law Libn.
SOUTH TEXAS COLLEGE OF LAW - LIBRARY □ Houston, TX

Thompson, Frances, Libn.
ONTARIO - MINISTRY OF COMMUNITY AND SOCIAL SERVICES - RESOURCE LIBRARY □ Woodstock, ON

Thompson, Genevieve, Soc. Worker
ORPHAN VOYAGE - KAMMANDALE LIBRARY □ St. Paul, MN

Thompson, H. Jean, Libn.
U.S. VETERANS ADMINISTRATION (MI-Ann Arbor) - HOSPITAL LIBRARY □ Ann Arbor, MI

Thompson, Jane, Ref. Staff
UNIVERSITY OF DENVER - COLLEGE OF LAW - WESTMINSTER LAW LIBRARY □ Denver, CO

Thompson, Jane, Ser.Libn.
UNIVERSITY OF OREGON - HEALTH SCIENCES CENTER - LIBRARY □ Portland, OR

Thompson, Janice, Ref.Libn.
UNIVERSITY OF SOUTHERN CALIFORNIA - HEALTH SCIENCES CAMPUS - NORRIS MEDICAL LIBRARY □ Los Angeles, CA

Thompson, Jean, Supv.
PUBLIC SERVICE COMPANY OF OKLAHOMA - REFERENCE CENTER □ Tulsa, OK

Thompson, Jeanne, Info.Spec.
DIGITAL EQUIPMENT CORPORATION - CORPORATE LIBRARY □ Maynard, MA

Thompson, Johanna, Asst.Libn.
DELAWARE LAW SCHOOL OF WIDENER UNIVERSITY - LAW LIBRARY □ Wilmington, DE

Thompson, John, Tech.Serv.
WHEATON COLLEGE - BILLY GRAHAM CENTER LIBRARY □ Wheaton, IL

Thompson, Judy, Libn. A
FEDERAL RESERVE BANK OF ST. LOUIS - RESEARCH LIBRARY □ St. Louis, MO

Thompson, Kathleen, Libn.
ASSOCIATION OF INTERNATIONAL COLLEGES & UNIVERSITIES - AICU INTERNATIONAL EDUCATION LIBRARY □ Independence, MO

Thompson, Kathleen, Dir.
(The) INTERNATIONAL UNIVERSITY - INTERNATIONAL RELATIONS LIBRARY AND RESEARCH CENTER □ Independence, MO

Thompson, LaDonna M., Mgr.
MTS SYSTEMS CORPORATION - INFORMATION SERVICES □ Eden Prairie, MN

Thompson, Laura, DTIC Oper.
U.S. NAVY - NAVAL COASTAL SYSTEMS CENTER - TECHNICAL LIBRARY □ Panama City, FL

Thompson, Linda L., Law Libn.
WORLD BANK LAW LIBRARY □ Washington, DC

Thompson, Linda S., Libn.
MUSKEGON CHRONICLE - EDITORIAL LIBRARY □ Muskegon, MI

Thompson, Mary, Libn.
WOODVILLE STATE HOSPITAL - PROFESSIONAL LIBRARY □ Carnegie, PA

Thompson, O., Microreproduction
UNIVERSITY OF WISCONSIN, LA CROSSE - MURPHY LIBRARY □ La Crosse, WI

Thompson, Patricia, Tech.Info.Coord.
MARY KAY COSMETICS, INC. - TECHNICAL INFORMATION CENTER □ Dallas, TX

Thompson, Phillip, Archv.
BAYLOR UNIVERSITY - CONGRESSIONAL COLLECTION □ Waco, TX

Thompson, Mrs. R., Assoc.Dir.
CANADA - ENVIRONMENT CANADA - LIBRARY SERVICES BRANCH □ Ottawa, ON

Thompson, Ms. Rebecca, Ref./ILL
OREGON COLLEGE OF EDUCATION - LIBRARY □ Monmouth, OR

Thompson, Richard, Libn.
HAWAII STATE DEPARTMENT OF ACCOUNTING AND GENERAL SERVICES - PUBLIC ARCHIVES □ Honolulu, HI

Thompson, Richard M., Info.Spec./Musm.Mgr.
GEORGIA-PACIFIC CORPORATION - HISTORICAL MUSEUM □ Portland, OR

Thompson, Roger S., Libn.
FERMI NATIONAL ACCELERATOR LABORATORY - LIBRARY □ Batavia, IL

PERSONNEL

Thompson, Rose, Libn.
BARLOW HOSPITAL - ELKS LIBRARY □ Los Angeles, CA

Thompson, Rose F., Tech.Serv.Libn.
MAINE MEDICAL CENTER - LIBRARY □ Portland, ME

Thompson, Ruth Margaret, Dir.
CANADA - EXTERNAL AFFAIRS CANADA - LIBRARY □ Ottawa, ON

Thompson, Sandra, Biblog.Asst.
TEMPLE UNIVERSITY - CENTRAL LIBRARY SYSTEM - MATHEMATICAL SCIENCES LIBRARY □ Philadelphia, PA

Thompson, Sandra R., Libn.
INDIANA STATE PLANNING SERVICES AGENCY - LIBRARY† □ Indianapolis, IN

Thompson, Sheila, Libn.
VANCOUVER PUBLIC LIBRARY - BUSINESS & ECONOMICS DIVISION □ Vancouver, BC

Thompson, Shirley, Tech.Serv.
CHURCH OF JESUS CHRIST OF LATTER-DAY SAINTS - MT. WHITNEY BRANCH GENEALOGICAL LIBRARY† □ Inyokern, CA

Thompson, Shirley, Supv. of Lib.
SHELL DEVELOPMENT COMPANY - WESTHOLLOW RESEARCH CENTER LIBRARY† □ Houston, TX

Thompson, Terrence A., Dir. of Lib.
NORTHERN MONTANA COLLEGE - LIBRARY† □ Havre, MT

Thompson, Mrs. Terry, Archv.
ANGLICAN CHURCH OF CANADA - GENERAL SYNOD ARCHIVES □ Toronto, ON

Thompson, Mrs. Vernese B., Cons.
U.S. MARINE CORPS - CAMP PENDLETON LIBRARY SYSTEM† □ Camp Pendleton, CA

Thompson, William P., Libn.
PIEDMONT BIBLE COLLEGE - GEORGE M. MANUEL MEMORIAL LIBRARY □ Winston-Salem, NC

Thompson, Wilma, Asst.Libn.
WASHOE COUNTY LAW LIBRARY □ Reno, NV

Thompson-Larson, Jeanette, Libn.
MINNEAPOLIS PUBLIC LIBRARY & INFORMATION CENTER - HISTORY DEPARTMENT □ Minneapolis, MN

Thomsen, Linda, Lib.Techn.
U.S. VETERANS ADMINISTRATION (MT-Miles City) - MEDICAL CENTER LIBRARY □ Miles City, MT

Thomsen, Mary H., Libn.
PUTNAM COMPANIES - INVESTMENT RESEARCH LIBRARY □ Boston, MA

Thomsen, Odelta A., Libn.
BILLINGS GAZETTE - NEWS LIBRARY □ Billings, MT

Thomson, Ashley, Ref. & Circ.
LAURENTIAN UNIVERSITY - MAIN LIBRARY □ Sudbury, ON

Thomson, Carol, Lib.Asst.
ELKEM METALS COMPANY - TECHNOLOGY CENTER - HAYNES-BECKET MEMORIAL LIBRARY □ Niagara Falls, NY

Thomson, Diane, Lib.Dir.
CANADIAN HOSPITAL ASSOCIATION - BLACKADER LIBRARY □ Ottawa, ON

Thomson, Dorothy, Asst.Libn., Pub.Serv.
UNIVERSITY OF OTTAWA - MORISSET LIBRARY □ Ottawa, ON

Thomson, Linda, Dir.
TEL-MED HEALTH INFORMATION SERVICE □ Minneapolis, MN

Thomson, Mrs. Marion, Libn.
CANADA - NATIONAL DEFENCE - CANADIAN FORCES MEDICAL SERVICES SCHOOL - LIBRARY □ Borden, ON

Thomson, Sharon, Libn.
CANADA - FISHERIES & OCEANS - INSTITUTE OF OCEAN SCIENCES - LIBRARY □ Sidney, BC

Thorkilson, Terry A., Dir. & Assoc.Prof.
UNIVERSITY OF VIRGINIA MEDICAL CENTER - CLAUDE MOORE HEALTH SCIENCES LIBRARY □ Charlottesville, VA

Thorleifson, Mary Claire, Libn.
NORTH DAKOTA STATE UNIVERSITY - BOTTINEAU BRANCH AND INSTITUTE OF FORESTRY - LIBRARY □ Bottineau, ND

Thornbrough, Gayle, Dir.
INDIANA HISTORICAL SOCIETY - WILLIAM HENRY SMITH MEMORIAL LIBRARY □ Indianapolis, IN

Thornburgh, J.K., Libn.
RAYTHEON COMPANY - ELECTROMAGNETIC SYSTEMS DIVISION - ENGINEERING LIBRARY □ Goleta, CA

Thornbury, Sedgley, Pres.
PATRIOTIC EDUCATION, INC. - LIBRARY □ Daytona Beach, FL

Thorne, Nancy R., Dir.
MIDDLESEX MEMORIAL HOSPITAL - HEALTH SCIENCES LIBRARY □ Middletown, CT

Thorne, Shirley, Ref.
NORTHWESTERN OKLAHOMA STATE UNIVERSITY - LIBRARY □ Alva, OK

Thornell, Camille, Libn.
CHICAGO PUBLIC LIBRARY CULTURAL CENTER - THOMAS HUGHES CHILDREN'S LIBRARY □ Chicago, IL

Thornley, Phyllis, Asst.Dir.
MINNEAPOLIS PUBLIC SCHOOLS - SPECIAL SCHOOL DISTRICT 1 - BOARD OF EDUCATION LIBRARY □ Minneapolis, MN

Thornlow, Bruce, Ref./AV Libn.
U.S. VETERANS ADMINISTRATION (MA-Brockton) - MEDICAL CENTER LIBRARY □ Brockton, MA

Thornton, Anne R., Chf.Libn.
U.S. VETERANS ADMINISTRATION (MO-St. Louis) - HOSPITAL LIBRARY □ St. Louis, MO

Thornton, Glenda, Acq.Libn.
HENDERSON STATE UNIVERSITY - HUIE LIBRARY □ Arkadelphia, AR

Thornton, Jerry
UNIVERSITY OF MICHIGAN - MAP ROOM □ Ann Arbor, MI

Thornton, Josephine, Transl.
MELLON BANK, N.A. - LIBRARY □ Pittsburgh, PA

Thornton, Sheila F., Chf., State Lib.Serv.
CALIFORNIA STATE LIBRARY □ Sacramento, CA

Thorp, Milton K., Cur.
HACKETTSTOWN HISTORICAL SOCIETY - MUSEUM □ Hackettstown, NJ

Thorpe, Annette, Post Libn.
U.S. ARMY POST - FORT HOOD - MSA DIVISION - CASEY MEMORIAL LIBRARY □ Ft. Hood, TX

Thorpe, James, Dir.
HUNTINGTON (Henry E.) LIBRARY, ART GALLERY AND BOTANICAL GARDENS □ San Marino, CA

Thorpe, Marjorie V., Staff Libn.
COMMUNITY HOSPITAL OF THE MONTEREY PENINSULA - MEDICAL STAFF LIBRARY† □ Carmel, CA

Thorpe, Suzanne, Asst.Libn., Cat.
HAMLINE UNIVERSITY SCHOOL OF LAW - LIBRARY □ St. Paul, MN

Thorson, Mildred Ellquist, Preparator
UNIVERSITY OF WASHINGTON - ART SLIDE COLLECTION □ Seattle, WA

Thorton, Elizabeth, Info.Spec.
NATIONAL REHABILITATION INFORMATION CENTER □ Washington, DC

Thrash, James R., Dir.
SALISBURY STATE COLLEGE - BLACKWELL LIBRARY □ Salisbury, MD

Threadgill, Mary G., Ref.Libn.
U.S. NATL. DEFENSE UNIVERSITY - LIBRARY □ Washington, DC

Threatt, Thomas K., Asst.
FORT WORTH PUBLIC LIBRARY - HUMANITIES DEPARTMENT □ Fort Worth, TX

Threndyle, Shirley Anne, Libn.
NEWMAN THEOLOGICAL COLLEGE - LIBRARY† □ Edmonton, AB

Throckmorton, Edith H., Dir.
ST. VINCENT HOSPITAL AND MEDICAL CENTER - HEALTH SCIENCES LIBRARY† □ Portland, OR

Thurman, Carol, Lib.Asst.
UNIVERSITY OF TEXAS, ARLINGTON - LIBRARY - DIVISION OF SPECIAL COLLECTIONS AND ARCHIVES □ Arlington, TX

Thurman, Estelle, Libn.
NORDEN SYSTEMS, INC. - TECHNICAL LIBRARY □ Norwalk, CT

Thurman, John H., Libn.
TENNESSEE VALLEY BANCORP - LIBRARY □ Nashville, TN

Thurston, Eve, Cat.
NEW YORK CITY - MUNICIPAL REFERENCE AND RESEARCH CENTER □ New York, NY

Thurston, Minnie G., Supv., Lib.Serv.
WESTINGHOUSE ELECTRIC CORPORATION - OFFSHORE POWER SYSTEMS LIBRARY □ Jacksonville, FL

Thurston, Nancy, Libn.
ONTARIO - MINISTRY OF NATURAL RESOURCES - MINES LIBRARY □ Toronto, ON

Thweatt, Elizabeth, Doc./Acq.Libn.
GONZAGA UNIVERSITY SCHOOL OF LAW - LIBRARY □ Spokane, WA

Thweatt, John, Hd.Mss.Proc.
TENNESSEE STATE LIBRARY AND ARCHIVES - ARCHIVES & MANUSCRIPTS SECTION □ Nashville, TN

Tibbets, Kathie K., Circ./Ref.Libn.
UNIVERSITY OF MAINE SCHOOL OF LAW - DONALD L. GARBRECHT LAW LIBRARY □ Portland, ME

Tiberg, Ethel, Mgr.Lib.Serv.
EDISON ELECTRIC INSTITUTE - LIBRARY □ Washington, DC

Tibesar, Rev. Leo J., Dir.
ST. PAUL SEMINARY - JOHN IRELAND MEMORIAL LIBRARY □ St. Paul, MN

Tiblin, Mariann, Biblog.
UNIVERSITY OF MINNESOTA - SCANDINAVIAN COLLECTION □ Minneapolis, MN

Tiburtia, Sister M., F.S.S.J., Cons.
ST. JOSEPH INTERCOMMUNITY HOSPITAL - MEDICAL STAFF LIBRARY □ Cheektowaga, NY

Tice, Kathy, Libn.
TOUCHE ROSS AND COMPANY - LIBRARY □ Los Angeles, CA

Tice, Mary T., Mgr.
RAYTHEON COMPANY - BUSINESS INFORMATION CENTER □ Lexington, MA

Tichy, Linda, Tech.Libn.
UNION CARBIDE CORPORATION - PARMA TECHNICAL CENTER - TECHNICAL INFORMATION SERVICE □ Cleveland, OH

Tichy, Louise, Rec.Mgr.
U.S. BUREAU OF LAND MANAGEMENT - CALIFORNIA STATE OFFICE - LIBRARY □ Sacramento, CA

Tidwell, Janet P., Libn.
CURTIS, MALLET-PREVOST, COLT AND MOSLE - LIBRARY† □ New York, NY

Tieman, Joan M., Asst.Ref.Libn.
CARNEGIE-MELLON UNIVERSITY - HUNT LIBRARY □ Pittsburgh, PA

Tiemann, Sandy, Asst.Libn.
NATIONAL WILDLIFE FEDERATION - FRAZIER MEMORIAL LIBRARY □ Washington, DC

Tien, Mary Anna, Middletown Dir.
CONNECTICUT STATE COLLEGE □ Hartford, CT

Tierney, Catherine, Hd.Tech.Serv.
BOSTON UNIVERSITY - PAPPAS LAW LIBRARY □ Boston, MA

Tierney, Catherine M., Chf.Libn.
AKRON BEACON JOURNAL - REFERENCE LIBRARY □ Akron, OH

Tierney, Clifford L., Mgr.
WHIRLPOOL CORPORATION - TECHNICAL INFORMATION CENTER □ Benton Harbor, MI

Tierney, Diane F., Libn.
PHILADELPHIA COMMUNITY LEGAL SERVICES, INC. - LAW LIBRARY □ Philadelphia, PA

Tierney, Judith, Spec.Coll.Libn.
KING'S COLLEGE - D. LEONARD CORGAN LIBRARY □ Wilkes-Barre, PA
Tiff, Arthur, Media Spec.
PRESENTATION COLLEGE - LIBRARY □ Aberdeen, SD
Tiff, Georgiana, Dept.Hd.
DENVER PUBLIC LIBRARY - ARCHERY COLLECTION □ Denver, CO
Tiff, Georgiana, Dept.Hd.
DENVER PUBLIC LIBRARY - FRIENDS OF MUSIC FOLK-MUSIC COLLECTION □ Denver, CO
Tiff, John T., Hist.
U.S. NATL. PARK SERVICE - LYNDON B. JOHNSON NATL. HISTORICAL PARK - LIBRARY □ Johnson City, TX
Tiffany, Mrs. Keppel
CORRY AREA HISTORICAL SOCIETY - LIBRARY □ Corry, PA
Tighe, Pauline Jones, Libn.
CALIFORNIA STATE AUTOMOBILE ASSOCIATION - LIBRARY □ San Francisco, CA
Tillapaugh, Elizabeth, Hd. Serials
SUNY - AGRICULTURAL AND TECHNICAL COLLEGE AT COBLESKILL - JARED VAN WAGENEN, JR. LEARNING RESOURCE CENTER □ Cobleskill, NY
Tilles, Doris, ILL
OREGON STATE UNIVERSITY - WILLIAM JASPER KERR LIBRARY □ Corvallis, OR
Tillett, Barbara, Tech.Serv.Libn.
UNIVERSITY OF CALIFORNIA, SAN DIEGO - SCRIPPS INSTITUTION OF OCEANOGRAPHY LIBRARY □ La Jolla, CA
Tilley, Ms. Lou W., Regional Libn.
ENVIRONMENTAL PROTECTION AGENCY - REGION V LIBRARY □ Chicago, IL
Tillinger, Frances, Libn.
MORRISTOWN JEWISH COMMUNITY CENTER - LIBRARY □ Morristown, NJ
Tillman, James S., Cat.
UNIVERSITY OF SOUTH FLORIDA - MEDICAL CENTER LIBRARY □ Tampa, FL
Timberlake, Cynthia, Libn.
BISHOP (Bernice P.) MUSEUM - LIBRARY □ Honolulu, HI
Timberlake, Pat, Ref. & Loan Serv.
MISSOURI STATE LIBRARY □ Jefferson City, MO
Timian, Sylvia, Libn.
NORTH MEMORIAL MEDICAL CENTER - MEDICAL LIBRARY □ Minneapolis, MN
Timm, Marianne, Chf. Documentalist
INTERNATIONAL INSTITUTE OF STRESS - LIBRARY AND DOCUMENTATION CENTER □ Montreal, PQ
Timm, Nathan, Linker Trainer
WISCONSIN STATE DEPARTMENT OF PUBLIC INSTRUCTION - WISCONSIN DISSEMINATION PROJECT (WDP) □ Madison, WI
Timmerman, Mildred D., Libn.
CENTRAL NEW YORK ACADEMY OF MEDICINE - LIBRARY □ New Hartford, NY
Timms, Arthur M., Exec.Dir.
CONSERVATION COUNCIL OF ONTARIO - LIBRARY □ Toronto, ON
Timms, Timmy, Libn.
UNITED WAY OF THE LOWER MAINLAND - LIBRARY □ Vancouver, BC
Timour, John A., Libn.
JEFFERSON (Thomas) UNIVERSITY - SCOTT MEMORIAL LIBRARY □ Philadelphia, PA
Timperley, Doris, Cat.Libn.
KEARNEY STATE COLLEGE - CALVIN T. RYAN LIBRARY □ Kearney, NE
Ting, Ching-Cheng, R & D Libn.
WESTERN GEOPHYSICAL COMPANY OF AMERICA - R & D LIBRARY □ Houston, TX
Ting, Robert, Chf.Libn.
U.S. NATL. OCEANIC & ATMOSPHERIC ADMINISTRATION - LIBRARY & INFORMATION SERVICES DIV. - CORAL GABLES CENTER □ Coral Gables, FL

Ting, Robert N., Chf.Libn.
U.S. NATL. OCEANIC & ATMOSPHERIC ADMINISTRATION - LIBRARY & INFORMATION SERVICES DIVISION - MIAMI CENTER □ Miami, FL
Ting, Shirley C., Chf., Lib.Serv.
U.S. VETERANS ADMINISTRATION (MO-Kansas City) - MEDICAL CENTER LIBRARY □ Kansas City, MO
Tinio, Cecilia, Chf.Libn.
MC ADAMS (William Douglas), INC. - MEDICAL LIBRARY □ New York, NY
Tinkham, Natalie, Supv.Libn.
MADISON PUBLIC LIBRARY - LITERATURE AND SOCIAL SCIENCES □ Madison, WI
Tinner, Connie, Supv., Info.Serv.
CHICAGO REGIONAL TRANSPORTATION AUTHORITY - INFORMATION SERVICES - LIBRARY □ Chicago, IL
Tipka, Donald, Dept.Hd.
CLEVELAND PUBLIC LIBRARY - HISTORY AND GEOGRAPHY DEPARTMENT □ Cleveland, OH
Tipsword, Thomas, Cat./Ref.Libn.
U.S. ARMY - TROOP SUPPORT COMMAND - STINFO AND REFERENCE LIBRARY □ St. Louis, MO
Tipton, Jenny, Libn.
NATIONAL ORGANIZATION FOR WOMEN (NOW) - ACTION CENTER LIBRARY □ Washington, DC
Tipton, Roberta, Libn.
KENNEDY (John F.) MEDICAL CENTER - LIBRARY □ Edison, NJ
Tirado, Amilcar, Libn.
CUNY - CENTRO DE ESTUDIOS PUERTORRIQUENOS □ New York, NY
Tirrell, Brenda Peabody, Dept.Hd.
HOUSTON PUBLIC LIBRARY - BUSINESS, SCIENCE & TECHNOLOGY DEPARTMENT □ Houston, TX
Tirrell, Norma, Chf.
MONTANA STATE DEPARTMENT OF COMMERCE - TRAVEL PROMOTION BUREAU □ Helena, MT
Tisdale, Janice, Libn.
JORDAN (Edward C.) CO., INC. - LIBRARY □ Portland, ME
Tishler, Myra, Libn.
CONGREGATION BETH JACOB - GOODWIN FAMILY LIBRARY† □ Merchantville, NJ
Titterington, James L., Coord., Film Lib.
UNIVERSITY OF NEBRASKA, LINCOLN - INSTRUCTIONAL MEDIA CENTER □ Lincoln, NE
Titus, Elizabeth, Libn.
OAKLAND UNIVERSITY - LIBRARY □ Rochester, MI
Tkaczuk, Lydia, Chf., Lib.Serv.
U.S. VETERANS ADMINISTRATION (IL-Chicago) - LAKESIDE HOSPITAL MEDICAL LIBRARY □ Chicago, IL
Tobia, Rajia, Ref.
UNIVERSITY OF TEXAS HEALTH SCIENCE CENTER, SAN ANTONIO - LIBRARY □ San Antonio, TX
Tobia, Rajia C., Libn.
UNIVERSITY OF TEXAS HEALTH SCIENCE CENTER, SAN ANTONIO - BRADY/GREEN EDUCATIONAL RESOURCES CENTER □ San Antonio, TX
Tobias, Leslie, Info.Spec.
CONFERENCE BOARD, INC. - INFORMATION SERVICE □ New York, NY
Tobin, Jean E., Libn.
NEW YORK STOCK EXCHANGE - RESEARCH LIBRARY† □ New York, NY
Tobol, Carol, Res.Asst.
KENDALL WHALING MUSEUM - LIBRARY □ Sharon, MA
Todd, Mrs. Alma P., Acq.Libn.
MISSISSIPPI VALLEY STATE UNIVERSITY - JAMES HERBERT WHITE LIBRARY □ Itta Bena, MS
Todd, Barbara, Educ.Off.
RODMAN HALL ARTS CENTRE - ART LIBRARY □ St. Catharines, ON

Todd, Fred W., Chf.Libn.
U.S. AIR FORCE - AEROSPACE MEDICAL DIVISION - SCHOOL OF AEROSPACE MEDICINE - STRUGHOLD AEROMEDICAL LIBRARY □ Brooks AFB, TX
Todd, Kay Moller, Libn.
KILPATRICK & CODY - LIBRARY □ Atlanta, GA
Todd, Nancy C., Libn.
KLAUDER (Louis T.) & ASSOCIATES - LIBRARY □ Philadelphia, PA
Todd, Rose-Aimee, Chf.Libn.
CANADA - NATIONAL FILM BOARD OF CANADA - REFERENCE LIBRARY □ Montreal, PQ
Toelken, J. Barre
UNIVERSITY OF OREGON - DEPARTMENT OF ENGLISH - RANDALL V. MILLS ARCHIVES OF NORTHWEST FOLKLORE □ Eugene, OR
Toeppe, Joan, Lib.Sys.Coord.
DIAMOND SHAMROCK CORPORATION - CORPORATE LIBRARY □ Painesville, OH
Togman, Esther, Asst.Dir. & Libn.
WORLD ZIONIST ORGANIZATION - AMERICAN SECTION - ZIONIST ARCHIVES AND LIBRARY □ New York, NY
Tolar, Donna M.L., Tech.Serv.Libn.
ORANGEBURG-CALHOUN TECHNICAL COLLEGE - GRESSETTE LEARNING RESOURCE CENTER □ Orangeburg, SC
Tolchin, Judith, U.S.Docs.Libn.
UNIVERSITY OF CALIFORNIA, LOS ANGELES - PUBLIC AFFAIRS SERVICE □ Los Angeles, CA
Toll, Grace, Libn.
PARKVIEW HOSPITAL - LIBRARY □ Philadelphia, PA
Toll, Mary B., Doc.Libn.
SOUTH CAROLINA STATE LIBRARY □ Columbia, SC
Tolles, Bryant F., Jr., Libn.
ESSEX INSTITUTE - JAMES DUNCAN PHILLIPS LIBRARY □ Salem, MA
Tolmachev, Mirjana, Coord., User Serv.
PENNSYLVANIA STATE LIBRARY □ Harrisburg, PA
Tolman, Mrs. Arvilla C., Lib.Chm.
PETERBOROUGH HISTORICAL SOCIETY - LIBRARY □ Peterborough, NH
Tolman, Ruth, Pres.
WORLD MODELING ASSOCIATION - WMA LIBRARY □ Croton-On-Hudson, NY
Tolovi, Paul A., Info.Spec.
U.S. DEFENSE COMMUNICATIONS AGENCY - TECHNICAL LIBRARY AND INFORMATION CENTER □ Washington, DC
Toman, Vera, L.I. Coll.Libn.
SMITHTOWN LIBRARY □ Smithtown, NY
Tomaski, Michael, Libn.
HERNER AND COMPANY - LIBRARY □ Arlington, VA
Tomasovic, Evelyn, Libn.
ROSENN, JENKINS & GREENWALD, ATTORNEYS AT LAW - LIBRARY □ Wilkes-Barre, PA
Tomasulo, Patricia, Libn.
SUNY - DOWNSTATE MEDICAL CENTER - DEPARTMENT OF PSYCHIATRY LIBRARY □ Brooklyn, NY
Tombleson, Dr. Gary E., Coll.Libn.
ARMSTRONG COLLEGE - LIBRARY □ Berkeley, CA
Tome, Susan Rau, Tech.Libn.
3M - 230 LIBRARY □ St. Paul, MN
Tomich, Mrs. Marciel, Registrar
PACIFIC COAST BANKING SCHOOL - LIBRARY □ Seattle, WA
Tomko, Lucille A., Ref.Libn.
CARNEGIE LIBRARY OF PITTSBURGH - PENNSYLVANIA DIVISION □ Pittsburgh, PA
Tomlin, Anne Costello, Dir.
AUBURN MEMORIAL HOSPITAL - LIBRARY/ RESOURCE CENTER □ Auburn, NY
Tomlin, Kim J., Libn.
SMALL, CRAIG & WERKENTHIN - LIBRARY □ Austin, TX

Tomlin, Mary Evelyn, Ref. & Data Serv.Br.
MISSISSIPPI STATE RESEARCH AND
DEVELOPMENT CENTER - INFORMATION
SERVICES DIVISION □ Jackson, MS

Tomlin, Maxine, Libn.
DOW CHEMICAL COMPANY - RESEARCH
CENTER LIBRARY □ Indianapolis, IN

Tomlin, Ron, Archv.
MISSISSIPPI STATE DEPARTMENT OF
ARCHIVES AND HISTORY - ARCHIVES AND
LIBRARY DIVISION □ Jackson, MS

Tomlinson, Edwin W., Libn.
SHERMAN RESEARCH LIBRARY □ Corona Del
Mar, CA

Tomlinson, J., Chf., Lib. Network
CANADA - SECRETARY OF STATE -
TRANSLATION BUREAU - DOCUMENTATION
DIRECTORATE □ Ottawa, ON

Tomlinson, Leigh, Res.Ctr.Coord.
GIRL SCOUTS OF RACINE COUNTY, INC. -
LIBRARY □ Racine, WI

Tomlinson, Patricia A., Asst.Libn.
ST. JOSEPH HOSPITAL OF MT. CLEMENS -
MEDICAL LIBRARY □ Mt. Clemens, MI

Tomlinson, William D., Dir.
WESTERN MONTANA SCIENTISTS'
COMMITTEE FOR PUBLIC INFORMATION -
MONTANA ENVIRONMENTAL LIBRARY □
Missoula, MT

Tommey, Richard J., Libn.
GENERAL ATOMIC COMPANY - LIBRARY □ San
Diego, CA

Tompkins, Louise, Libn.
PRINCETON UNIVERSITY - PLINY FISK
LIBRARY OF ECONOMICS AND FINANCE □
Princeton, NJ

Tompkins, Steve, Libn.
U.S. ARMY - PLASTICS TECHNICAL
EVALUATION CENTER □ Dover, NJ

Tomposki, Philip, Ref.Libn.
U.S. NAVY - NAVAL UNDERWATER SYSTEMS
CENTER - NEWPORT TECHNICAL LIBRARY □
Newport, RI

Tondi, Lorraine, Dir./Res.
KINGSBOROUGH COMMUNITY COLLEGE -
KINGSBOROUGH HISTORICAL SOCIETY □
Brooklyn, NY

Toner, Mary Anne, Libn.
WORCESTER CITY HOSPITAL - MEDICAL
LIBRARY □ Worcester, MA

Toner, Michael P., Lib.Dir.
SCHEIE EYE INSTITUTE - LIBRARY □
Philadelphia, PA

Toney, Stephen, Sys. & Plan.Mgr.
SMITHSONIAN INSTITUTION LIBRARIES □
Washington, DC

Tong, Josephine, Mtls.Rsrcs.Ctr.
ALBERTA - DEPARTMENT OF EDUCATION -
LIBRARY □ Edmonton, AB

Tonge, Karyl, Map Libn.
STANFORD UNIVERSITY - CENTRAL MAP
COLLECTION □ Stanford, CA

Tongue, Marie, Dir. of Lib.Serv.
FIRST UNITED METHODIST CHURCH - LIBRARY
□ Tulsa, OK

Tooke, Elaine, Rd.Serv.Libn.
MC MASTER UNIVERSITY - THODE LIBRARY OF
SCIENCE & ENGINEERING □ Hamilton, ON

Tooker, G. Calvin, Libn.
METROPOLITAN STATE HOSPITAL - STAFF
LIBRARY □ Norwalk, CA

Tooker, Peggy, Ref.Libn.
TEXAS TECH UNIVERSITY - LIBRARY -
DOCUMENTS DEPARTMENT □ Lubbock, TX

Tooley, Bonita, Libn.
SETON MEMORIAL LIBRARY & MUSEUM □
Cimarron, NM

Toomey, Kathleen M., Libn.
MC GILL UNIVERSITY - MARVIN DUCHOW
MUSIC LIBRARY □ Montreal, PQ

Toon, Mrs. J., Libn.
ALBERTA - DEPARTMENT OF CULTURE -
HISTORICAL RESOURCES LIBRARY □ Edmonton,
AB

Tooth, John, Hd.Libn.
MANITOBA - DEPARTMENT OF EDUCATION -
LIBRARY □ Winnipeg, MB

Topp, Carole L., Asst.Libn.
BETHESDA LUTHERAN MEDICAL CENTER -
MEDICAL-NURSING LIBRARY □ St. Paul, MN

Toppan, Muriel, Ref.Libn.
WALTERS ART GALLERY - LIBRARY □ Baltimore,
MD

Topper, Judith M., Med.Libn.
LAWRENCE HOSPITAL - ASHLEY BAKER
MORRILL LIBRARY □ Bronxville, NY

Topping, Donald M., Dir.
UNIVERSITY OF HAWAII - SOCIAL SCIENCE
RESEARCH INSTITUTE □ Honolulu, HI

Topping, Gary, Mss.Cur.
UTAH STATE HISTORICAL SOCIETY -
RESEARCH LIBRARY □ Salt Lake City, UT

Toran, Karen, Circ.Libn.
UNIVERSITY OF CALIFORNIA, SAN FRANCISCO
- HASTINGS COLLEGE OF THE LAW - LEGAL
INFORMATION CENTER □ San Francisco, CA

Tordella, Stephen J., Spec.
UNIVERSITY OF WISCONSIN, MADISON -
DEPARTMENT OF RURAL SOCIOLOGY - APPLIED
POPULATION LAB. - LIBRARY □ Madison, WI

Torkelson, Norma R., Chf., Lib.Serv.
U.S. VETERANS ADMINISTRATION (KS-Topeka)
- DR. KARL A. MENNINGER MEDICAL LIBRARY □
Topeka, KS

Tormes, Leo, Film Lib.Dir.
EASTERN NEW MEXICO UNIVERSITY - GOLDEN
LIBRARY □ Portales, NM

Tornell, Helen M., Libn.
TEXTILE RESEARCH INSTITUTE - LIBRARY □
Princeton, NJ

Torode, William W., Libn.
NATIONAL SPELEOLOGICAL SOCIETY - NSS
LIBRARY □ Huntsville, AL

Torre, Dr. Louis P., Physical Sci.Libn.
RUTGERS UNIVERSITY, THE STATE
UNIVERSITY OF NEW JERSEY - CHEMISTRY
LIBRARY □ Piscataway, NJ

Torre, Dr. Louis P., Phys.Sci.Libn.
RUTGERS UNIVERSITY, THE STATE
UNIVERSITY OF NEW JERSEY - PHYSICS
LIBRARY □ Piscataway, NJ

Torrente, Michael J., Assoc.Dir., SERMLP
EMORY UNIVERSITY - SCHOOL OF MEDICINE -
A.W. CALHOUN MEDICAL LIBRARY □ Atlanta, GA

Torres, Cecilia C., Law Libn.
PIMA COUNTY LAW LIBRARY □ Tucson, AZ

Torres, Jesse Joseph, Libn.
ACADEMY OF AMERICAN FRANCISCAN
HISTORY - LIBRARY □ Washington, DC

Torres, Jesse Joseph, Asst.Libn.
PAN AMERICAN HEALTH ORGANIZATION -
DOCUMENTATION AND HEALTH INFORMATION
OFFICE† □ Washington, DC

Torres, Olga R., Dir., Tech.Serv.
UNIVERSITY OF PUERTO RICO - GENERAL
LIBRARY □ San Juan, PR

Torres, Patsy, Regional Libn.
U.S. DEPT. OF HOUSING AND URBAN
DEVELOPMENT - REGION VIII - LIBRARY □
Denver, CO

Torres-Irizarry, Martha, Libn.
UNIVERSITY OF PUERTO RICO - GRADUATE
SCHOOL OF PLANNING - LIBRARY □ Rio Piedras,
PR

Tortora, Eileen, Ser.Libn.
HOECHST-ROUSSEL PHARMACEUTICALS, INC. -
LIBRARY □ Somerville, NJ

Tortorelli, R.R., Sci.Serv.Techn.
CANADA - ATMOSPHERIC ENVIRONMENT
SERVICE - CENTRAL REGION LIBRARY □
Winnipeg, MB

Toscan, Joyce, Non-Govt.Org.Libn.
UNIVERSITY OF CALIFORNIA, LOS ANGELES -
PUBLIC AFFAIRS SERVICE □ Los Angeles, CA

Toscano, Lynn Schweitzer, Act.Cur.
UNIVERSITY OF MINNESOTA - IMMIGRATION
HISTORY RESEARCH CENTER □ St. Paul, MN

Toscano, Rita, Libn.
NATIONAL LEAGUE OF CITIES - MUNICIPAL
REFERENCE SERVICE □ Washington, DC

Tosi, Laura, Lib.Assoc.
BRONX COUNTY HISTORICAL SOCIETY -
LIBRARY† □ Bronx, NY

Tostevin, Patricia A., Libn.
ITT RAYONIER, INC. - OLYMPIC RESEARCH
DIVISION - LIBRARY □ Shelton, WA

Toth, Ethel, Libn.
BENDIX CORPORATION - ENGINEERING
REFERENCE LIBRARY □ Teterboro, NJ

Toth, Georgina Gy, Assoc.Ref.Libn.
CLEVELAND MUSEUM OF ART - LIBRARY □
Cleveland, OH

Toth, Paulette, Ref.
CRAVATH, SWAINE, AND MOORE - LAW
LIBRARY □ New York, NY

Touger, Mirel, Libn.
TEMPLE BETH EL - BUDDY BERMAN MEMORIAL
LIBRARY □ Cedarhurst, NY

Touhey, John F., Dir.
FASHION INSTITUTE OF TECHNOLOGY -
LIBRARY/MEDIA SERVICES □ New York, NY

Touloukian, Y.S., Dir.
PURDUE UNIVERSITY - CINDAS - ELECTRONIC
PROPERTIES INFORMATION CENTER □ West
Lafayette, IN

Touloukian, Y.S., Dir.
PURDUE UNIVERSITY - CINDAS -
THERMOPHYSICAL PROPERTIES RESEARCH
CENTER - LIBRARY □ West Lafayette, IN

Toupin, Carmen Delorme, Animator
MUSEE D'ART DE JOLIETTE - BIBLIOTHEQUE □
Joliette, PQ

Toupin, Juanita M., Libn.
MONTREAL MUSEUM OF FINE ARTS - LIBRARY†
□ Montreal, PQ

Toupin, Robert, Dir.
UNIVERSITY OF SUDBURY - ARCHIVES □
Sudbury, ON

Toups, Don, Libn.
FORT WORTH PUBLIC LIBRARY - BUSINESS
AND TECHNOLOGY DEPARTMENT □ Fort Worth,
TX

Toups, Patricia A., Libn.
LIFE OFFICE MANAGEMENT ASSOCIATION -
INFORMATION CENTER □ Atlanta, GA

Tousegnant, Laurent, Libn.
MONASTERE DES PERES REDEMPTORISTES -
BIBLIOTHEQUE† □ Sherbrooke, PQ

Toutant, Bernard L., Adm.
OAKLAND UNIVERSITY - LIBRARY □ Rochester,
MI

Tovsky, Annette, Libn.
TEMPLE ISRAEL - LEONARD M. SANDHAUS
MEMORIAL LIBRARY □ Sharon, MA

Towaij, Maureen, Mgr.
BELL-NORTHERN RESEARCH LTD. - TECHNICAL
INFORMATION CENTRE □ Ottawa, ON

Towell, Ann, Med.Libn.
GOOD SAMARITAN MEDICAL CENTER -
LUTHERAN CAMPUS - EVANS MEMORIAL
LIBRARY □ Milwaukee, WI

Towell, Jane, Br.Libn.
WHITE AND CASE - LIBRARY □ New York, NY

Towers, Suellen M., Hd. Marylandia Dept.
UNIVERSITY OF MARYLAND, COLLEGE PARK -
LIBRARIES - MARYLAND AND RARE BOOK
ROOM □ College Park, MD

Towers, Thomas A., Dir.
U.S. DEPT. OF LABOR - OSHA - TECHNICAL
DATA CENTER □ Washington, DC

Towery, Mrs. Dick, Libn.
FIRST METHODIST CHURCH - BLISS MEMORIAL
LIBRARY □ Shreveport, LA

Towle, Stephanie, Libn.
NASHVILLE GENERAL HOSPITAL - HEALTH
SCIENCE LIBRARY □ Nashville, TN

Towler, Naythell, Asst.Libn.
PRINCE GEORGE'S GENERAL HOSPITAL &
MEDICAL CENTER - SAUL SCHWARTZBACH
MEMORIAL LIBRARY □ Cheverly, MD

Towles, James, Tech.Info.Spec.
U.S. DEPT. OF LABOR - OSHA - TECHNICAL
DATA CENTER □ Washington, DC

Towles, Karen B., Tech.Info.Spec.
U.S. DEPT. OF LABOR - OSHA - TECHNICAL
DATA CENTER □ Washington, DC

Towner, Lawrence W., Pres./Libn.
NEWBERRY LIBRARY □ Chicago, IL

Townsend, E.J., Mgr.
WASHINGTON'S HEADQUARTERS AND MUSEUM
- LIBRARY □ Newburgh, NY

Townsend, Gloria, ILL
EASTERN NEW MEXICO UNIVERSITY - GOLDEN
LIBRARY □ Portales, NM

Townsend, Mary, Libn.
UNIVERSITY OF MICHIGAN - SCHOOL OF
PUBLIC HEALTH - PUBLIC HEALTH LIBRARY □
Ann Arbor, MI

Townsend, Robert J., Publishing Mgr.
QUESTOR ASSOCIATES - LIBRARY □ San
Francisco, CA

Townsend, Sherry, Tech.Libn.
REYNOLDS METALS COMPANY - ALUMINA
DIVISION - TECHNICAL INFORMATION
CENTER □ Little Rock, AR

Townshend, Linda S., Acq.Libn.
DALHOUSIE UNIVERSITY - LAW LIBRARY □
Halifax, NS

Towry, Lucy, Libn.
TULSA WORLD-TULSA TRIBUNE - LIBRARY
DEPARTMENT† □ Tulsa, OK

Tozer, Peggy M., Lib.Dir.
EASTERN NEW MEXICO UNIVERSITY - GOLDEN
LIBRARY □ Portales, NM

Tozer, Ronald G., Interp.Serv.Supv.
ALGONQUIN PARK MUSEUM - LIBRARY &
ARCHIVES □ Whitney, ON

Tozeski, Stanley, Archv.
U.S. NATL. ARCHIVES & RECORDS SERVICE -
FEDERAL ARCHIVES AND RECORDS CENTER,
REGION 1 □ Waltham, MA

Tracey, Kenneth D., Exec.Dir.
LEVERE MEMORIAL FOUNDATION - LIBRARY □
Evanston, IL

Tracy, Joan, Asst.Libn.Tech.Serv.
EASTERN WASHINGTON UNIVERSITY -
LIBRARY □ Cheney, WA

Tracy, Kenneth L., Hd.Libn.
SOUTHERN CALIFORNIA COLLEGE - O. COPE
BUDGE LIBRARY† □ Costa Mesa, CA

Tracz, Orysia, Libn.
UKRAINIAN CULTURAL AND EDUCATIONAL
CENTRE - LIBRARY □ Winnipeg, MB

Trafford, John E., Exec.Dir.
NEW JERSEY STATE LEAGUE OF
MUNICIPALITIES - LIBRARY □ Trenton, NJ

Trafford, Judy, Res.Lab.Libn.
PETRO-CANADA - LIBRARY SERVICES □
Calgary, AB

Traiman, Stephen, Exec.Dir.
RECORDING INDUSTRY ASSOCIATION OF
AMERICA - REFERENCE LIBRARY □ New York,
NY

Traina, Helen, Asst.Sec.
CHEMICAL BANK - RESEARCH LIBRARY □ New
York, NY

Trainer, Sally M., Sec.
WIGHT CONSULTING ENGINEERS, INC. -
TECHNICAL LIBRARY □ Barrington, IL

Trainor, Mary Anne, Ser. & Acq.Libn.
MC MASTER UNIVERSITY - HEALTH SCIENCES
LIBRARY □ Hamilton, ON

Tramdack, Phillip, Cat.
TRINITY UNIVERSITY - LIBRARY □ San Antonio,
TX

Tran, Mrs. Thuan T., Hd.Libn.
WESTERN WISCONSIN TECHNICAL INSTITUTE
- LIBRARY □ La Crosse, WI

Tranfaglia, Twyla, Asst.Libn.
TARRANT COUNTY LAW LIBRARY □ Fort Worth,
TX

Trani, Gertrude D., Asst.Libn.
CULINARY INSTITUTE OF AMERICA -
KATHARINE ANGELL LIBRARY □ Hyde Park, NY

Trapani, Jean, Mgr., Info.Serv.
WESTRECO, INC. - TECHNICAL LIBRARY □ New
Milford, CT

Trask, Carole, Libn.
POUDRE VALLEY MEMORIAL HOSPITAL - MEDIA
RESOURCES LIBRARY □ Fort Collins, CO

Trask, Richard B., Town Archv.
PEABODY INSTITUTE LIBRARY - DANVERS
ARCHIVAL CENTER □ Danvers, MA

Tratner, Alan A., Dir.
GEOTHERMAL WORLD CORPORATION -
INFORMATION CENTER □ Camarillo, CA

Tratner, Alan Arthur, Exec.Dir.
ENVIRONMENTAL EDUCATION GROUP -
LIBRARY □ Camarillo, CA

Tratt, G.M.T., Sec.
UNIVERSITY OF ALBERTA - NUCLEAR PHYSICS
LIBRARY □ Edmonton, AB

Traub, Dr. Hamilton P., Hd.
TRAUB PLANT SCIENCE LIBRARY □ La Jolla, CA

Traube, Rabbi Isaac M., Ph.D., Libn.
YESHIVA TORAH VODAATH AND MESIFTA -
TORAH VODAATH LIBRARY □ Brooklyn, NY

Trautman, Maryellen, Libn.
U.S. NATL. ARCHIVES & RECORDS SERVICE -
NATL. ARCHIVES LIBRARY □ Washington, DC

Travis, Julie, Supv.
DALLAS PUBLIC LIBRARY - FILM SERVICE □
Dallas, TX

Travis, Marguerite W., Libn.
ST. THOMAS SEMINARY - LIBRARY □ Denver,
CO

Travisono, Diana, Res.
AMERICAN CORRECTIONAL ASSOCIATION -
LIBRARY □ College Park, MD

Treadway, Ternan, Lib.Serv.Coord.
NATIONAL COUNCIL OF SENIOR CITIZENS,
INC. - LIBRARY □ Washington, DC

Tredwell, Irving, Jr., Asst.Libn.
PILGRIM PSYCHIATRIC CENTER - HEALTH
SCIENCES LIBRARY □ West Brentwood, NY

Treese, William R., Hd.
UNIVERSITY OF CALIFORNIA, SANTA BARBARA
- ARTS LIBRARY □ Santa Barbara, CA

Treggett, Janice, Hd. of Acq.
SUNY - COLLEGE AT POTSDAM - FREDERICK W.
CRUMB MEMORIAL LIBRARY □ Potsdam, NY

Treiman, Marilyn, Ref.Libn.
UNIVERSITY OF CALIFORNIA - LOS ALAMOS
NATIONAL LABORATORY - LIBRARY □ Los
Alamos, NM

Treimanis, Anna, Hd.Cat.
UNIVERSITY OF ILLINOIS MEDICAL CENTER -
LIBRARY OF THE HEALTH SCIENCES □ Chicago,
IL

Tremaine, Kenneth, Coord. of Media
LEXINGTON SCHOOL FOR THE DEAF - LIBRARY
MEDIA CENTER □ Jackson Heights, NY

Tremblay, Levis, Tech.Serv.
COLLEGE DU NORD-OUEST - BIBLIOTHEQUE □
Rouyn, PQ

Tremblay, Levis, Tech.Serv.
UNIVERSITE DU QUEBEC - CEUAT
BIBLIOTHEQUE □ Rouyn, PQ

Tremblay, Louise
CONFEDERATION DES CAISSES POPULAIRES
ET D'ECONOMIE DESJARDINS DU QUEBEC -
CENTRE DE DOCUMENTATION □ Levis, PQ

Tremblay, Monique, Cat. & Clas.
COLLEGE DE JONQUIERE - CENTRE DE
RESSOURCES EDUCATIVES □ Jonquiere, PQ

Tremblay, P., Ref.Libn.
COLLEGE MILITAIRE ROYAL DE ST-JEAN -
LIBRARY □ St. Jean, PQ

Tremblay, Ms. Virve M., MIRS Libn.
NCR CANADA LTD. - MIRS LIBRARY □
Mississauga, ON

Trenholme, Margery W., Chf.Libn.
FRASER-HICKSON INSTITUTE, MONTREAL -
FREE LIBRARY □ Montreal, PQ

Trepman, Paul, Dir.
JEWISH PUBLIC LIBRARY OF MONTREAL □
Montreal, PQ

Trescott, Virginia M., Spec.Coll.Libn.
BROWN UNIVERSITY - SPECIAL COLLECTIONS†
□ Providence, RI

Tretheway, Willeen, AV Libn.
WISCONSIN STATE DIVISION FOR LIBRARY
SERVICES - REFERENCE AND LOAN LIBRARY □
Madison, WI

Treude, J. Mai, Libn.
UNIVERSITY OF MINNESOTA - MAP DIVISION □
Minneapolis, MN

Treumuth, Sharon J., Adm.Asst.
NATIONAL BANK OF DETROIT - MONEY
MUSEUM LIBRARY □ Detroit, MI

Trevanion, Margaret U., Med.Libn.
NORTH HILLS PASSAVANT HOSPITAL -
MEDICAL LIBRARY □ Pittsburgh, PA

Trevaskis, Miss L., Libn.
CELANESE CANADA, INC. - LIBRARY □ Montreal,
PQ

Treves, Ralph, Owner
TREVES (Ralph) WORKSHOP FEATURES -
WORKSHOP PHOTOS □ West Palm Beach, FL

Tribble, Ed, Archv.Supv.
FLORIDA STATE DIVISION OF ARCHIVES,
HISTORY & RECORDS MANAGEMENT - FLORIDA
STATE ARCHIVES □ Tallahassee, FL

Tribull, Alice, Asst.Libn.
BENDIX CORPORATION - COMMUNICATIONS
DIVISION - ENGINEERING LIBRARY □ Baltimore,
MD

Triffin, Nicholas, Asst.Libn., Rd.Serv.
UNIVERSITY OF CONNECTICUT - LAW SCHOOL
LIBRARY □ West Hartford, CT

Triggs, Dr. Frances Oralind, Chm.
COMMITTEE ON DIAGNOSTIC READING TESTS,
INC. - LIBRARY □ Mountain Home, NC

Trimble, Bob, AV Libn.
SOUTHWESTERN BAPTIST THEOLOGICAL
SEMINARY - FLEMING LIBRARY □ Fort Worth,
TX

Trimble, Dr. George X., Dir.
ST. MARY'S HOSPITAL MEDICAL EDUCATION
FOUNDATION - MEDICAL LITERATURE
INFORMATION CENTER □ Kansas City, MO

Trimble, Jerri, Asst.Libn.
ST. JOSEPH HOSPITAL - MEDICAL LIBRARY □
Lexington, KY

Trimble, Kathleen L., Hd.Libn.
TOLEDO BLADE - LIBRARY □ Toledo, OH

Trimboli, Sr. Teresa, F.M.I., Assoc.Dir.
ST. MARY'S UNIVERSITY - LAW LIBRARY □ San
Antonio, TX

Trimmer, Elizabeth D., Techn.
U.S. NATL. ARCHIVES & RECORDS SERVICE -
FEDERAL ARCHIVES & RECORDS CENTER,
REGION 5 □ Chicago, IL

Trinkaus, Tanya, Asst.Cur.
BROWN UNIVERSITY - ART DEPARTMENT
SLIDE ROOM □ Providence, RI

Triplett, Billy, AV Libn.
LOUISIANA STATE UNIVERSITY MEDICAL
CENTER - SCHOOL OF MEDICINE IN
SHREVEPORT - LIBRARY □ Shreveport, LA

Triplett, Elizabeth, Libn.
RICHMOND PUBLIC LIBRARY - BUSINESS,
SCIENCE & TECHNOLOGY DEPARTMENT† □
Richmond, VA

Tripp, Donna, Dir.
EMERSON COLLEGE - ABBOT MEMORIAL
LIBRARY □ Boston, MA

Tripp, Jeffrey A., Mgr.
GENERAL REFRACTORIES COMPANY - U.S.
REFRACTORIES DIVISION - RESEARCH CENTER
LIBRARY □ Baltimore, MD

Tripp, Juanita S., Libn.
ILLINOIS STATE BOARD OF EDUCATION -
MEDIA AND RESOURCES CENTER □ Springfield,
IL

Tripp, Maureen, Hd., Media Serv.
EMERSON COLLEGE - ABBOT MEMORIAL
LIBRARY □ Boston, MA

Tripp, Wendell, Chf., Lib.Serv.
NEW YORK STATE HISTORICAL ASSOCIATION
- LIBRARY □ Cooperstown, NY

Trippett, Sandra, Dir.
FIRST BAPTIST CHURCH - JOHN L. WHORTON
MEDIA CENTER □ Longview, TX

Trisdale, Raymon, Chf.
U.S. ARMY - LOGISTICS LIBRARY □ Ft. Lee, VA

Trithart, David, Ref.Libn.
SUNY - COLLEGE AT POTSDAM - FREDERICK W.
CRUMB MEMORIAL LIBRARY □ Potsdam, NY

Tritz, Peter, Res.Dir.
LEAGUE OF MINNESOTA CITIES - LIBRARY □ St.
Paul, MN

Trivedi, Mr. Harish, Ref. & Res.Dir.
DAYTON NEWSPAPERS INC. - REFERENCE
LIBRARY □ Dayton, OH

Trocchia, Mary Ann, Sr.Asst.
ADELPHI UNIVERSITY - SOCIAL WORK
LIBRARY □ Garden City, NY

Troiano, Wendy, Libn.
BANGOR MENTAL HEALTH INSTITUTE - HEALTH
SCIENCES MEDIA CENTER □ Bangor, ME

Troise, Fred L., V.P. & Gen.Mgr.
WATER INFORMATION CENTER, INC. □
Syosset, NY

Trolander, Judith Ann, Dir.
MINNESOTA HISTORICAL SOCIETY -
NORTHEAST MINNESOTA HISTORICAL CENTER
□ Duluth, MN

Trolle, Larisa, Libn.
HARVARD UNIVERSITY - HARVARD UKRAINIAN
RESEARCH INSTITUTE - REFERENCE LIBRARY
□ Cambridge, MA

Trombello, Lawrence, Chf.
U.S. NATL. PARK SERVICE - ALLEGHENY
PORTAGE RAILROAD NATL. HISTORIC SITE -
LIBRARY □ Cresson, PA

Trombetta, Robert J., Dir.
PENNSYLVANIA STATE HISTORICAL & MUSEUM
COMMISSION - FORT PITT MUSEUM - LIBRARY
□ Pittsburgh, PA

Trombitas, Ildiko, Hd., Tech.Info.Dept.
BURROUGHS WELLCOME COMPANY - LIBRARY
□ Research Triangle Park, NC

Trombley, Ivan C., Libn.
PPG INDUSTRIES, INC. - CHEMICAL DIVISION -
RESEARCH LIBRARY □ Corpus Christi, TX

Tromley, Mercedes, Adm.Asst.
CONFEDERATE MEMORIAL LITERARY SOCIETY
- MUSEUM OF THE CONFEDERACY - ELEANOR S.
BROCKENBROUGH LIBRARY □ Richmond, VA

Troop, Anne, Mgr., Info.Serv.
CPC INTERNATIONAL - BEST FOODS RESEARCH
CENTER - INFORMATION CENTER† □ Union, NJ

Troph, Lucille R., Dept.Hd.
CLEVELAND PUBLIC LIBRARY - LITERATURE
DEPARTMENT □ Cleveland, OH

Trosset, Ruth P., Assoc.Prof.
UNIVERSITY OF CINCINNATI - DEPARTMENT
OF ENVIRONMENTAL HEALTH LIBRARY □
Cincinnati, OH

Trott, James, Archeo.
U.S. NATL. PARK SERVICE - CHACO CANYON
NATL. MONUMENT - VISITOR CENTER LIBRARY
□ Bloomfield, NM

Trott, Margaret, Campus & Coord.Libn.
HUMBER COLLEGE OF APPLIED ARTS &
TECHNOLOGY - LIBRARY □ Rexdale, ON

Trott, Mary B., Asst.Archv.
SMITH COLLEGE - ARCHIVES □ Northampton,
MA

Trott, Nancy, Ref.Libn.
PRICE WATERHOUSE - NATIONAL
INFORMATION CENTER □ New York, NY

Trotta, Victoria K., Hd., Tech.Serv.
UNIVERSITY OF SOUTHERN CALIFORNIA - LAW
CENTER LIBRARY† □ Los Angeles, CA

Trotti, Dr. John B., Libn.
UNION THEOLOGICAL SEMINARY IN VIRGINIA
- LIBRARY □ Richmond, VA

Trottier, Aime, Libn.
ORATOIRE ST-JOSEPH - CENTRE DE
DOCUMENTATION □ Montreal, PQ

Troup, Loretta, Cat.
TRW INC. - ENERGY SYSTEMS PLANNING
DIVISION - LIBRARY □ McLean, VA

Trout, Frank E., Cur.
HARVARD UNIVERSITY - MAP COLLECTION □
Cambridge, MA

Trout, Len L., Dir.
UNIVERSITY OF NEVADA, RENO - RESEARCH
AND EDUCATIONAL PLANNING CENTER □ Reno,
NV

Troy, Margaret H., Hd.Libn.
BOLT BERANEK AND NEWMAN, INC. - LIBRARY
□ Cambridge, MA

Troy, Terrance N., Group Leader
U.S. NATL. BUREAU OF STANDARDS -
STANDARDS INFORMATION SERVICE □
Gaithersburg, MD

Troyer, Alice, Asst.Libn.
CRAIN COMMUNICATIONS, INC. -
INFORMATION CENTER □ Chicago, IL

Troyer, Frederic L., Libn.
ROYAL ASTRONOMICAL SOCIETY OF CANADA -
NATIONAL LIBRARY □ Toronto, ON

Truax, Anne, Dir.
MINNESOTA WOMEN'S CENTER - RESOURCE
COLLECTION □ Minneapolis, MN

Trubey, Cornelia, Libn.
ROPES & GRAY - CENTRAL LIBRARY □ Boston,
MA

Trubey, D.K., Physicist
U.S. OAK RIDGE NATL. LABORATORY -
RADIATION SHIELDING INFORMATION CENTER
□ Oak Ridge, TN

Trueblood, Emily, Sr.Libn.
FEDERAL RESERVE BANK OF NEW YORK -
RESEARCH LIBRARY □ New York, NY

Trueblood, Jean, Asst.Libn.
VINNELL CORPORATION - TECHNICAL
SERVICES DIVISION LIBRARY □ Alhambra, CA

Trued, Mrs. Nymah L., Chf., Lib.Serv.
U.S. VETERANS ADMINISTRATION (OR-
Portland) - MEDICAL LIBRARY □ Portland, OR

Trued, Mrs. Nymah L., Chf., Lib.Serv.
U.S. VETERANS ADMINISTRATION (WA-
Vancouver) - HOSPITAL LIBRARY □ Vancouver,
WA

Truelson, Judith A., Dir.
UNIVERSITY OF SOUTHERN CALIFORNIA -
CROCKER BUSINESS LIBRARY □ Los Angeles, CA

Truelson, Stanley, Dir.
ALASKA HEALTH SCIENCES LIBRARY □
Anchorage, AK

Truesdell, Bill, Chf. Naturalist
U.S. NATL. PARK SERVICE - DENALI NATL.
PARK - LIBRARY □ McKinley Park, AK

Truesdell, Walter G., Libn.
REFORMED EPISCOPAL CHURCH -
THEOLOGICAL SEMINARY - KUEHNER
MEMORIAL LIBRARY □ Philadelphia, PA

Truex, William, Cur.
TALLMADGE HISTORICAL SOCIETY - LIBRARY
& ARCHIVES □ Tallmadge, OH

Truhan, Br. Luke, Libn.
ST. JOSEPH'S ABBEY - LIBRARY □ Spencer, MA

Truitt, Margaret H., ILL
MEDICAL COLLEGE OF GEORGIA - LIBRARY □
Augusta, GA

Trujillo, Roberto G., Assoc.Libn./Unit Hd.
UNIVERSITY OF CALIFORNIA, SANTA BARBARA
- LIBRARY - CHICANO STUDIES COLLECTION □
Santa Barbara, CA

Trull, JoAnn, Libn.
GULF RESOURCES AND CHEMICAL
CORPORATION - LITHIUM CORPORATION OF
AMERICA, INC. - RESEARCH LIBRARY □
Bessemer City, NC

Trunks, Mrs. Pat, ILL
ROYAL ONTARIO MUSEUM - LIBRARY □ Toronto,
ON

Truono, Leslie, Abstractor/Indexer
HERCULES, INC. - RESEARCH CENTER -
TECHNICAL INFORMATION DIVISION □
Wilmington, DE

Truscott, Jean M., Libn.
ST. MARY'S HOSPITAL - MEMORIAL LIBRARY □
Milwaukee, WI

Truscott, Myfanwy, Libn.
CAMPION COLLEGE - LIBRARY □ Regina, SK

Tryon, Mary J., Sec.
UNION UNIVERSITY - ALBANY LAW SCHOOL -
LIBRARY □ Albany, NY

Tryon, Roy H., Lib.Dir.
BALCH INSTITUTE FOR ETHNIC STUDIES -
LIBRARY □ Philadelphia, PA

Trzyna, T.C., Pres.
CALIFORNIA INSTITUTE OF PUBLIC AFFAIRS -
LIBRARY □ Claremont, CA

Tsai, Ernest J., Libn.
WASHINGTON UNIVERSITY - EAST ASIAN
LIBRARY □ St. Louis, MO

Tsai, Sheng Luen, Hd., Tech.Serv.
BRIGHAM YOUNG UNIVERSITY, HAWAII
CAMPUS - JOSEPH F. SMITH LIBRARY AND
MEDIA CENTER □ Laie, HI

Tsalos, George, Archv.
WAYNE STATE UNIVERSITY - ARCHIVES OF
LABOR AND URBAN AFFAIRS/UNIVERSITY
ARCHIVES □ Detroit, MI

Tsang, Kathryn, Photo Libn.
WORLD BOOK-CHILDCRAFT INTERNATIONAL,
INC.- RESEARCH LIBRARY □ Chicago, IL

Tsang, W.M., Chf.Libn.
CANADA - ENERGY, MINES & RESOURCES
CANADA - EARTH PHYSICS BRANCH LIBRARY □
Ottawa, ON

Tsangali, Sophia, Pub.Serv.Libn..
HELLENIC COLLEGE AND HOLY CROSS GREEK
ORTHODOX SCHOOL OF THEOLOGY -
COTSIDAS-TONNA LIBRARY □ Brookline, MA

Tsao, James, Chf. of Tech.Serv.
WASHINGTON STATE LAW LIBRARY □ Olympia,
WA

Tschinlsel, Andrew, Sr. Law Libn.
NEW YORK STATE SUPREME COURT - 2ND
JUDICIAL DISTRICT - LAW LIBRARY □ Brooklyn,
NY

Tschudy, Karen D., Lib.Dir.
CLEVELAND INSTITUTE OF ART - JESSICA R.
GUND MEMORIAL LIBRARY □ Cleveland, OH

Tse, Shui-Yim, Chinese Libn.
UNIVERSITY OF BRITISH COLUMBIA - ASIAN
STUDIES LIBRARY □ Vancouver, BC

Tseng, Chou-shia Y., Libn.
INSTITUTE FOR STORM RESEARCH - LIBRARY
□ Houston, TX

Tseng, Dr. Henry P., Law Libn.
UNION UNIVERSITY - ALBANY LAW SCHOOL -
LIBRARY □ Albany, NY

Tseou, Carolyn, Supv.Libn.
XEROX CORPORATION - XEROX SQUARE
LIBRARY† □ Rochester, NY

Tsilimos, Steve, Lit.Chem.
GOODYEAR TIRE AND RUBBER COMPANY -
TECHNICAL INFORMATION CENTER □ Akron,
OH

Tsui, Theresa, Per. & Doc.Libn.
JERSEY CITY STATE COLLEGE - FORREST A.
IRWIN LIBRARY □ Jersey City, NJ

Tsuneishi, David, Tech.Serv.
U.S. COMMISSION ON CIVIL RIGHTS - NATL.
CLEARINGHOUSE LIBRARY □ Washington, DC

Tu, C. Brian, Libn.
BRITISH COLUMBIA UTILITIES COMMISSION -
LIBRARY □ Vancouver, BC

Tubbs, Barbara, ILL
WARREN LIBRARY ASSOCIATION - LIBRARY† □
Warren, PA

Tubesing, Richard L., Lib.Dir.
LEWIS UNIVERSITY - LIBRARY □ Romeoville, IL

Tucci, Valerie K., Mgr., Info.Serv.
AIR PRODUCTS AND CHEMICALS, INC. -
INFORMATION SERVICES - TREXLERTOWN
LIBRARY □ Allentown, PA

Tuccinardi, Norma, Instr. Media Spec.
WASHINGTON STATE SCHOOL FOR THE DEAF -
LEARNING RESOURCE CENTER □ Vancouver,
WA

Tuchman, Maurice S., Libn.
HEBREW COLLEGE - JACOB AND ROSE
GROSSMAN LIBRARY □ Brookline, MA

Tucker, Bonita J., Adm.Libn.
U.S. ARMY HOSPITALS - MADIGAN ARMY
MEDICAL CENTER - MORALE SUPPORT LIBRARY
□ Tacoma, WA

Tucker, Bonnie, Main Post Libn.
U.S. ARMY POST - FORT LEWIS - LIBRARY
SYSTEM □ Fort Lewis, WA

Tucker, Cornelia, Libn.
TEMPLE UNIVERSITY - CENTRAL LIBRARY
SYSTEM - CENTER CITY LIBRARY □ Philadelphia,
PA

Tucker, Elizabeth, Info.Dir.
AGBABIAN ASSOCIATES - LIBRARY □ El
Segundo, CA

Tucker, Elizabeth, Libn.
U.S. NAVY - NAVAL SURFACE WEAPONS
CENTER - WHITE OAK LIBRARY □ Silver Spring,
MD

Tucker, Mrs. Hartley, Asst.Libn.
BETH ISRAEL CONGREGATION - LIBRARY □
Vineland, NJ

Tucker, Jane C., Sr.Sys.Libn.
U.S. NATL. BUREAU OF STANDARDS - LIBRARY
□ Washington, DC

Tucker, Laura, Libn.
AMERICAN INSTITUTE FOR ECONOMIC
RESEARCH - E.C. HARWOOD LIBRARY □ Great
Barrington, MA

Tucker, Louise K., Libn.
GARY POST-TRIBUNE - LIBRARY □ Gary, IN

Tucker, Mae S., Asst.Dir.Lib.Serv.
CHARLOTTE AND MECKLENBURG COUNTY
PUBLIC LIBRARY - TEXTILE COLLECTION □
Charlotte, NC

Tucker, Martha, Act. State Libn.
KANSAS STATE LIBRARY □ Topeka, KS

Tucker, Norman P., Res. & Prog.Off.
BOSTON ATHENAEUM LIBRARY □ Boston, MA

Tucker, Ms. Pat, Libn.
OKLAHOMA GAS AND ELECTRIC COMPANY -
LIBRARY □ Oklahoma City, OK

Tucker, Richard W., Archv.
NORTH AMERICAN TIDDLYWINKS
ASSOCIATION - ARCHIVES □ Silver Spring, MD

Tucker, Rose Ann, ILL
JACKSON METROPOLITAN LIBRARY -
INFORMATION AND REFERENCE DIVISION □
Jackson, MS

Tudiver, Lillian, Div.Chf.
BROOKLYN PUBLIC LIBRARY - SOCIAL SCIENCE
DIVISION □ Brooklyn, NY

Tudor, Dean, Chm.
RYERSON POLYTECHNICAL INSTITUTE -
LIBRARY ARTS DEPT. - LIBRARY □ Toronto, ON

Tull, Willis Clayton, Jr., Libn.
MILBOURNE & TULL RESEARCH CENTER -
LIBRARY □ Cockeysville, MD

Tull, Willis Clayton, Jr., Libn.
UNITARIAN AND UNIVERSALIST
GENEALOGICAL SOCIETY - LIBRARY □
Cockeysville, MD

Tullis, Carol, Ref.Libn.
INDIANA UNIVERSITY - BIOLOGY LIBRARY □
Bloomington, IN

Tumbler, Laurel J., Mgr.
GIRARD BANK - INFORMATION CENTER □
Philadelphia, PA

Tumpek, Theresa, Asst.Libn.
WHITMAN & RANSOM - LIBRARY □ New York,
NY

Tung, Cecilia, Libn.
TEXAS INSTRUMENTS, INC. - INFORMATION
SYSTEMS & SERVICES LIBRARY □ Dallas, TX

Tung, Sandra, Info.Spec.
UNIVERSITY OF SOUTHERN CALIFORNIA -
NASA INDUSTRIAL APPLICATION CENTER
(NIAC) □ Los Angeles, CA

Tung, Sophie, ILL Libn.
HUGHES AIRCRAFT COMPANY - GROUND
SYSTEMS GROUP - TECHNICAL LIBRARY □
Fullerton, CA

Tuohy, Donald R., Cur. Anthropology
NEVADA STATE MUSEUM □ Carson City, NV

Tuohy, Nancy, Asst.Libn.
LOYOLA UNIVERSITY OF CHICAGO - LAW
LIBRARY □ Chicago, IL

Tupper, Pat, Lib.Prog.Dir.
MINNESOTA STATE DEPARTMENT OF
EDUCATION - INTERAGENCY RESOURCE AND
INFORMATION CENTER □ St. Paul, MN

Turanski, Margaret K., Asst.Hd.
FREE LIBRARY OF PHILADELPHIA - FILMS
DEPARTMENT □ Philadelphia, PA

Turba, Jerry, Media Techn.
NORTHEAST WISCONSIN TECHNICAL
INSTITUTE - LEARNING RESOURCE CENTER □
Green Bay, WI

Turcotte, Mildred, Libn.
UNIVERSITY OF CINCINNATI - MEDICAL
CENTER LIBRARIES - COLLEGE OF NURSING &
HEALTH - LEVI MEMORIAL LIBRARY □
Cincinnati, OH

Turek, Robert O., Soc.Sci.Libn.
WESTERN KENTUCKY UNIVERSITY -
FOLKLORE, FOLKLIFE, & ORAL HISTORY
ARCHIVES □ Bowling Green, KY

Turgeon, Cynthia, Libn.
FORD AEROSPACE & COMMUNICATIONS CORP.
- WESTERN DEVELOPMENT LABORATORIES
(WDL) - TECHNICAL LIBRARY □ Palo Alto, CA

Turkington, Mrs. N., Hd., Sci./Engr.Div.
ROYAL MILITARY COLLEGE OF CANADA -
MASSEY LIBRARY & SCIENCE/ENGINEERING
LIBRARY □ Kingston, ON

Turkmen, Aydin Y., Ref.Lib.
GRAND LODGE OF NEW YORK, F. AND A.M. -
LIBRARY AND MUSEUM □ New York, NY

Turman, Barbara, Libn.
UNIVERSITY OF TEXAS, AUSTIN - PERRY-
CASTANEDA LIBRARY - DOCUMENTS
COLLECTION □ Austin, TX

Turman, Lynne, Libn.
RICHMOND MEMORIAL HOSPITAL - MEDICAL
AND NURSING SCHOOL LIBRARY □ Richmond,
VA

Turnage, Lorretta, Leg.Libn.
MARYLAND STATE DEPARTMENT OF
LEGISLATIVE REFERENCE - LIBRARY □
Annapolis, MD

Turnbull, Barbara, Assoc.Libn.
FEDERAL RESERVE BANK OF PHILADELPHIA -
LIBRARY □ Philadelphia, PA

Turnbull, Fiona, Tech.Serv.Libn.
U.S. COURT OF APPEALS, 8TH CIRCUIT -
LIBRARY □ St. Louis, MO

Turnbull, Krista, Cur.
UNIVERSITY OF WASHINGTON - SCHOOL OF
NUTRITION SCIENCES AND TEXTILES -
COSTUME AND TEXTILE STUDY CENTER □
Seattle, WA

Turnbull, M.A. Brian, Map Cur.
UNIVERSITY OF VICTORIA - MC PHERSON
LIBRARY - UNIVERSITY MAP COLLECTION □
Victoria, BC

Turner, Annetta, Campus Libn.
CENTENNIAL COLLEGE OF APPLIED ARTS &
TECHNOLOGY - WARDEN WOODS CAMPUS
RESOURCE CENTRE □ Scarborough, ON

Turner, Betty A., Hd.Libn.
ARKANSAS GAZETTE - NEWS LIBRARY □ Little
Rock, AR

Turner, Charles W., Libn.
ROCKBRIDGE HISTORICAL SOCIETY -
LIBRARY/ARCHIVES □ Lexington, VA

Turner, Decherd, Dir.
UNIVERSITY OF TEXAS, AUSTIN - HUMANITIES
RESEARCH CENTER □ Austin, TX

Turner, Dorothy S., Assoc.Cur. of Musm.
CITADEL - THE MILITARY COLLEGE OF SOUTH
CAROLINA - ARCHIVES/MUSEUM □ Charleston,
SC

Turner, Elnora H., Pub. Health Libn.
NORTH CAROLINA STATE DEPARTMENT OF
HUMAN RESOURCES - DIVISION OF HEALTH
SERVICES - PUBLIC HEALTH LIBRARY □ Raleigh,
NC

Turner, Evlyn L., Law Libn.
BUTTE COUNTY LAW LIBRARY □ Oroville, CA

Turner, Gurley, Dir. of Info.Serv.
CATALYST - INFORMATION CENTER □ New
York, NY

Turner, Judith Campbell, Sect.Hd., Libn.
MILWAUKEE PUBLIC MUSEUM - REFERENCE
LIBRARY □ Milwaukee, WI

Turner, Mary E., Med.Libn.
U.S. VETERANS ADMINISTRATION (NY-
Montrose) - HOSPITAL LIBRARY □ Montrose, NY

Turner, Mary Louise, Chf.Educ./Info.Serv.Dept.
MEDICAL COLLEGE OF GEORGIA - LIBRARY □
Augusta, GA

Turner, Rebecca, Ref.Libn.
EASTERN KENTUCKY UNIVERSITY - JOHN
GRANT CRABBE LIBRARY □ Richmond, KY

Turner, Ruth, Asst.Libn.
INTERNATIONAL MINERALS & CHEMICALS
CORPORATION - IMC RESEARCH &
DEVELOPMENT LIBRARY □ Terre Haute, IN

Turner, Mrs. S.L., Lib.Techn.
MONTREAL GENERAL HOSPITAL - NURSES
LIBRARY □ Montreal, PQ

Turner, Tamara A., Dir.
CHILDREN'S ORTHOPEDIC HOSPITAL &
MEDICAL CENTER - HOSPITAL LIBRARY □
Seattle, WA

Turner, Willie, Res.Asst.
CENTER FOR WOMEN POLICY STUDIES -
RESOURCE CENTER □ Washington, DC

Turnheim, Ilse, Archv.
BAECK (Leo) INSTITUTE - LIBRARY □ New York,
NY

Turnquist, Reba, Asst. Law Libn.
UNIVERSITY OF WASHINGTON - LAW SCHOOL
LIBRARY □ Seattle, WA

Turo, Sally, Libn.
TOMPKINS COMMUNITY HOSPITAL - ROBERT
BROAD MEDICAL LIBRARY □ Ithaca, NY

Turro, Rev. James C., Dir., Lib.Serv.
IMMACULATE CONCEPTION SEMINARY -
LIBRARY □ Mahwah, NJ

Turtell, Neal, Chf., Spec. Projects
SMITHSONIAN INSTITUTION LIBRARIES □
Washington, DC

Tuszynski, Dr. Frances, Libn.
POLISH AMERICAN CONGRESS - SOUTHERN
CALIFORNIA-ARIZONA DIVISION - POLAND'S
MILLENIUM LIBRARY □ Los Angeles, CA

Tuthill, Barbara, Supv.Libn.
SAN DIEGO PUBLIC LIBRARY - ART, MUSIC &
RECREATION SECTION □ San Diego, CA

Tutt, Celestine C., Libn.
COLUMBIA UNIVERSITY - WHITNEY M. YOUNG,
JR. MEMORIAL LIBRARY OF SOCIAL WORK □
New York, NY

Tuttle, Irene H., Libn.
ANDOVER COLLEGE - LIBRARY □ Portland, ME

Tuttle, Irma S., Libn.
MASONIC MEDICAL RESEARCH LABORATORY -
LIBRARY □ Utica, NY

Tuttle, Walter Alan, Libn.
NATIONAL HUMANITIES CENTER - LIBRARY □
Research Triangle Park, NC

U

Upton, Mildred, Libn.
MONSANTO TEXTILES COMPANY - LIBRARY □ Greenwood, SC

Urbankiewicz, Nancy L., Libn.
CANADA - ENVIRONMENTAL PROTECTION SERVICE - ONTARIO REGION LIBRARY† □ Toronto, ON

Ureneck, Dolores, Lib.Mgr.
CARTER-WALLACE, INC. - LIBRARY □ Cranbury, NJ

Urness, Carol, Asst.Cur.
UNIVERSITY OF MINNESOTA - JAMES FORD BELL LIBRARY □ Minneapolis, MN

Urquhart, Al, Dir.
UNIVERSITY OF OREGON - ENVIRONMENTAL STUDIES CENTER □ Eugene, OR

Urquhart, E., Libn.
GRAYS HARBOR COUNTY LAW LIBRARY □ Montesano, WA

Urquhart, Kenneth T., Hd.,Mss.Div. & Lib.
HISTORIC NEW ORLEANS COLLECTION - LIBRARY □ New Orleans, LA

Urwiler, Richard, IRC Rsrcs.
WAYNE STATE COLLEGE - U.S. CONN LIBRARY □ Wayne, NE

Usher, Esther, Libn.
UNITED ENGINEERS & CONSTRUCTORS, INC. - BOSTON OFFICE - LIBRARY □ Boston, MA

Usher, Roland G., Jr., Hist.
PROTESTANT EPISCOPAL CHURCH - DIOCESE OF INDIANAPOLIS, INDIANA - ARCHIVES □ Indianapolis, IN

Utterback, Martha, Asst.Dir.
DAUGHTERS OF THE REPUBLIC OF TEXAS - LIBRARY □ San Antonio, TX

Utterback, Nancy, Hd.Pub.Serv.
UNIVERSITY OF LOUISVILLE - KORNHAUSER HEALTH SCIENCES LIBRARY □ Louisville, KY

Utz, Lily, Techn.
U.S. NATL. ARCHIVES & RECORDS SERVICE - FEDERAL ARCHIVES & RECORDS CENTER, REGION 5 □ Chicago, IL

Uunila, Edith, Asst.Ed.
CHRONICLE OF HIGHER EDUCATION - LIBRARY □ Washington, DC

Uva, Peter, Asst.Libn.Pub.Serv.
SUNY - UPSTATE MEDICAL CENTER LIBRARY □ Syracuse, NY

Uyenaka, S., Japanese Biblog.
UNIVERSITY OF TORONTO - EAST ASIAN LIBRARY □ Toronto, ON

V

Vaagen, Marjorie, Libn./AV Spec.
WOODWARD STATE HOSPITAL SCHOOL - RESIDENT LIBRARY □ Woodward, IA

Vaagen, Marjorie, Libn.
WOODWARD STATE HOSPITAL SCHOOL - STAFF LIBRARY □ Woodward, IA

Vaccaro, M., Asst.Libn.
NEW ENGLAND INSTITUTE - LIBRARY □ Ridgefield, CT

Vachon, Florian, Lib.Dir.
FOREIGN MISSIONS SOCIETY OF QUEBEC - LIBRARY □ Laval, PQ

Vacula, Mary A., Libn.
WEIR (Paul) COMPANY - LIBRARY □ Chicago, IL

Vada, Ilse, Libn.
NATIONAL INSTITUTE ON DRUG ABUSE - RESOURCE CENTER □ Rockville, MD

Vader, Betty, Asst.Libn.
WYANDOTTE COUNTY BAR LIBRARY □ Kansas City, KS

Vago, Marianne, Libn.
NATIONAL STARCH AND CHEMICAL CORPORATION - LIBRARY □ Bridgewater, NJ

Vaiginas, Paul, Libn.
NEW ENGLAND DEACONESS HOSPITAL - HORRAX LIBRARY □ Boston, MA

Vail, Keith R., Assoc.Dir.
SALISBURY STATE COLLEGE - BLACKWELL LIBRARY □ Salisbury, MD

Vainauskas, Jack G., Med.Rec.Adm.
PALOS COMMUNITY HOSPITAL - MEDICAL LIBRARY □ Palos Heights, IL

Vajda, Elizabeth A., Coord. for Lib.Serv.
COOPER UNION FOR THE ADVANCEMENT OF SCIENCE AND ART - LIBRARY □ New York, NY

Vajda, John E.
U.S. NAVY - DEPARTMENT LIBRARY □ Washington, DC

Valaitis, Vakare, Info.Sci.
IIT RESEARCH INSTITUTE - GUIDANCE AND CONTROL INFORMATION ANALYSIS CENTER (GACIAC) □ Chicago, IL

Valencia, Maria L., Libn.
PUERTO RICAN CULTURE INSTITUTE - LUIS MUNOZ RIVERA LIBRARY AND MUSEUM† □ Barranquitas, PR

Valencia, Mercy, Sys.Coord.
UNIVERSITY OF ARIZONA - ARID LANDS INFORMATION CENTER □ Tucson, AZ

Valente, Rev. John Bosco, O.F.M., Libn.
ST. FRANCIS MONASTERY AND CHAPEL - ST. FRANCIS CHAPEL INFORMATION CENTER & FREE-LENDING LIBRARY □ Providence, RI

Valentine, Jean, Dir.
DOUGLASS HISTORICAL SOCIETY MUSEUM - MUSEUM ARCHIVES □ Douglass, KS

Valentine, Patrick M., Foreign Lang.Libn.
CUMBERLAND COUNTY PUBLIC LIBRARY - NORTH CAROLINA FOREIGN LANGUAGE CENTER □ Fayetteville, NC

Valeri, John R., Law Libn.
CATHOLIC UNIVERSITY OF AMERICA - ROBERT J. WHITE LAW LIBRARY □ Washington, DC

Valeriani, Joseph
MEDFORD HISTORICAL SOCIETY - LIBRARY □ Medford, MA

Valerio, Clement, Jr., Hd.
ANDERSEN LABORATORIES, INC. - LIBRARY □ Bloomfield, CT

Valerio, Eduarda C., Asst.Libn.
PORTUGUESE CONTINENTAL UNION OF THE U.S.A. - LIBRARY □ Boston, MA

Valescu, Frances, Libn.
ARKANSAS STATE HISTORY COMMISSION - ARCHIVES □ Little Rock, AR

Valint, Nancy, Libn.
FOSTER ASSOCIATES, INC. - LIBRARY □ Washington, DC

Vallancourt, Donna L., Libn.
GENRAD, INC. - LIBRARY □ Concord, MA

Valle, Barbara, Asst.Libn.
PACIFIC PRESS, LTD. - PRESS LIBRARY □ Vancouver, BC

Vallinos, Alice, Res.Libn.
NEEDHAM, HARPER & STEERS ADVERTISING, INC. - RESEARCH LIBRARY □ New York, NY

Valone, Gloria, Asst.Dir.
KEAN COLLEGE OF NEW JERSEY - NANCY THOMPSON LIBRARY □ Union, NJ

Valpy, Amanda, Chf.Libn.
TORONTO GLOBE AND MAIL, LTD. - LIBRARY □ Toronto, ON

Valunas, Madelyn, Ser.Libn.
SHIPPENSBURG STATE COLLEGE - EZRA LEHMAN MEMORIAL LIBRARY □ Shippensburg, PA

Van Allen, Russell E., Asst. Law Libn.
UTAH STATE LAW LIBRARY □ Salt Lake City, UT

Van Arsdale, M.J., Libn.
BEAL COLLEGE - LIBRARY □ Bangor, ME

Van Atta, Cathaleen, Libn.
KITT PEAK NATIONAL OBSERVATORY - LIBRARY □ Tucson, AZ

Van Berkel, Joyce, Subj.Spec.
U.S. DEPT OF ENERGY - SANDIA NATL. LABORATORIES - TECHNICAL LIBRARY □ Albuquerque, NM

Van Brocklin, Vincent, Ser.Libn.
HAWAII STATE LIBRARY - SERIALS SECTION □ Honolulu, HI

Van Brunt, Virginia, Info.Spec.
ARTHRITIS INFORMATION CLEARINGHOUSE □ Bethesda, MD

Van Buren, Rita, Intl.Spec.
PRICE WATERHOUSE - NATIONAL INFORMATION CENTER □ New York, NY

Van Buskirk, E. Lynne, Assoc.Dir.
NEW JERSEY EDUCATION ASSOCIATION - RESEARCH LIBRARY □ Trenton, NJ

Van Camp, Ann, Search Anl.
INDIANA UNIVERSITY - SCHOOL OF MEDICINE LIBRARY □ Indianapolis, IN

Van Dam, Thomas, Libn.
PINE REST CHRISTIAN HOSPITAL - VAN NOORD HEALTH SCIENCES LIBRARY □ Grand Rapids, MI

Van de Putte, Elizabeth, Info.Spec.
LOUISIANA STATE LEGISLATIVE COUNCIL - DIVISION OF INFORMATION SERVICES □ Baton Rouge, LA

Van De Velde, Catherine, Hd., Rd.Serv.
BENTLEY COLLEGE - SOLOMON R. BAKER LIBRARY □ Waltham, MA

Van De Voorde, Philip, Govt.Pubn.
IOWA STATE UNIVERSITY - LIBRARY □ Ames, IA

Van Den Berg, Mr. R., Dept.Libn.
CANADA - NATIONAL DEFENCE - NDHQ LIBRARY □ Ottawa, ON

Van der Bellen, Liana, Chf.
NATIONAL LIBRARY OF CANADA - RARE BOOKS AND MANUSCRIPTS DIVISION □ Ottawa, ON

Van Der Lyke, Barbara, Willimantic Dir.
CONNECTICUT STATE LIBRARY □ Hartford, CT

Van Der Voorn, Neal, Libn.
WASHINGTON STATE LIBRARY - EASTERN STATE HOSPITAL LIBRARY □ Medical Lake, WA

Van Der Voorn, Neal, Inst.Serv.Libn.
WASHINGTON STATE LIBRARY - LAKELAND VILLAGE BRANCH LIBRARY □ Medical Lake, WA

Van Dine, Ann, Asst.Mgr.Lib.Serv.
HOECHST-ROUSSEL PHARMACEUTICALS, INC. - LIBRARY □ Somerville, NJ

Van Dinter, Nancy, Chf.Libn.
IDAHO STATESMAN - LIBRARY □ Boise, ID

van Donkersgoed, Elbert, Res. & Policy Dir.
CHRISTIAN FARMERS FEDERATION OF ONTARIO - FOUND. FOR CHRISTIAN ALTERNATIVES IN AGRICULTURE-LIBRARY □ Harriston, ON

Van Dusen, Herbert, Libn.
AMERICAN ASSOCIATION OF CORRECTIONAL OFFICERS - LIBRARY □ Saginaw, MI

Van Dusen, Larry, Tech.Info.Spec.
U.S. FOREST SERVICE - ROCKY MOUNTAIN FOREST & RANGE EXPERIMENT STATION - LIBRARY □ Fort Collins, CO

Van Dyk, Stephen, Arch.Info.Ctr.Supv.
NEW JERSEY INSTITUTE OF TECHNOLOGY - ROBERT W. VAN HOUTEN LIBRARY □ Newark, NJ

Van Dyke, Ruth, Libn.
DAMES & MOORE - SEATTLE OFFICE LIBRARY □ Seattle, WA

Van Egdom, Deborah, Dir.Lib.Serv.
IOWA HOSPITAL ASSOCIATION - LIBRARY □ Des Moines, IA

Van Heurn, Helen S., Asst.Cat.
UNIVERSITY OF MIAMI - SCHOOL OF MEDICINE - LOUIS CALDER MEMORIAL LIBRARY □ Miami, FL

Van Hine, Pamela, Libn.
AMERICAN COLLEGE OF OBSTETRICIANS AND GYNECOLOGISTS - RESOURCE CENTER □ Washington, DC

Van Hoogenstyn, Parker, Hd. Media/Spec.Proj.
SUNY - AGRICULTURAL AND TECHNICAL COLLEGE AT FARMINGDALE - THOMAS D. GREENLEY LIBRARY □ Farmingdale, NY

Van Horn, Elizabeth K., Libn.
BAR ASSOCIATION OF THE DISTRICT OF
COLUMBIA - LIBRARY □ Washington, DC
Van Horn, Judy, Lib.Supv.
GULF OIL CORPORATION - BUSINESS
RESEARCH LIBRARY □ Pittsburgh, PA
Van Horn, Linda, Clinical Libn.
TUFTS UNIVERSITY - SCHOOLS OF MEDICINE,
DENTAL MEDICINE & VETERINARY MEDICINE -
HEALTH SCIENCES LIBRARY† □ Boston, MA
Van Horn, Robert B., Dir., Info.Serv.
MARTIN/WILLIAMS ADVERTISING AGENCY -
LIBRARY/INFORMATION CENTER □
Minneapolis, MN
Van Horn, Virginia, Libn.
SPERRY CORPORATION - SPERRY UNIVAC
DEFENSE SYSTEMS DIVISION - INFORMATION
SERVICE CENTER □ St. Paul, MN
Van Kleek, Rev. Laurence M., Libn.
WESTERN PENTECOSTAL BIBLE COLLEGE -
LIBRARY □ Clayburn, BC
Van Lare, Donald H., Great Lakes Archv.
BOWLING GREEN STATE UNIVERSITY -
CENTER FOR ARCHIVAL COLLECTIONS □
Bowling Green, OH
Van Leir, Lorraine, Libn.
HENRY (J.J.) CO., INC. - ENGINEERING LIBRARY
□ Moorestown, NJ
Van Lierde, Isobel, Ser.Libn.
CANADA - NATIONAL GALLERY OF CANADA -
LIBRARY □ Ottawa, ON
Van Linh, Tran, Comparative Law
LOUISIANA STATE UNIVERSITY - LAW LIBRARY
□ Baton Rouge, LA
Van Mater, John P., Libn.
THEOSOPHICAL UNIVERSITY - LIBRARY □
Altadena, CA
Van Mater, Sarah B., Asst.Libn.
THEOSOPHICAL UNIVERSITY - LIBRARY □
Altadena, CA
Van Meer, David J., Cur.
SKAGIT COUNTY HISTORICAL MUSEUM -
HISTORICAL REFERENCE LIBRARY □ La Conner,
WA
Van Meeveren, Dawn, Asst.Libn., Cat.
TOCCOA FALLS COLLEGE - SEBY JONES
LIBRARY □ Toccoa Falls, GA
Van Meter, Terry, Dir.
U.S. CAVALRY MUSEUM - LIBRARY □ Fort Riley,
KS
Van Nest, Dee T., Asst.Law Libn.
MARYLAND STATE LAW LIBRARY □ Annapolis,
MD
Van Nice, Dorothy, Sr.Libn.
SAN DIEGO PUBLIC LIBRARY - SCIENCE &
INDUSTRY SECTION □ San Diego, CA
Van Niel, Eloise, Act.Hd.
HAWAII STATE LIBRARY - FINE ARTS AND
AUDIOVISUAL SECTION □ Honolulu, HI
Van Nocker, Allison, Cur. of Coll.
KINGMAN MUSEUM OF NATURAL HISTORY -
LIBRARY □ Battle Creek, MI
Van Nortwick, Barbara, Lib.Dir.
NEW YORK STATE NURSES ASSOCIATION -
LIBRARY □ Guilderland, NY
Van Note, R., ILL
UNIVERSITY OF WISCONSIN, LA CROSSE -
MURPHY LIBRARY □ La Crosse, WI
Van Ornam, Nancy, Dept.Hd.
TRENTON FREE PUBLIC LIBRARY - BUSINESS
AND TECHNOLOGY DEPARTMENT □ Trenton, NJ
Van Pulis, Noelle, Info.Spec.
OHIO STATE UNIVERSITY - MECHANIZED
INFORMATION CENTER (MIC) □ Columbus, OH
van Reenen, Johann, Libn.
VICTORIA MEDICAL SOCIETY/ROYAL JUBILEE
HOSPITAL - LIBRARY □ Victoria, BC
Van Rooyen, Hilda, Med.Libn.
IZAAK WALTON KILLAM HOSPITAL FOR
CHILDREN - MEDICAL STAFF LIBRARY □ Halifax,
NS
Van Rossem, Karen, Res.
NEWSDAY, INC. - LIBRARY □ Melville, NY

Van Ryzin, Elizabeth M., Sr.Libn.
INSTITUTE OF GAS TECHNOLOGY - TECHNICAL
INFORMATION CENTER □ Chicago, IL
Van Sledright, Connie, Hd., Circ.
CALVIN COLLEGE AND SEMINARY - LIBRARY □
Grand Rapids, MI
Van Sluys, Loralie, Mgr.
HEWITT ASSOCIATES - LIBRARY □ Lincolnshire,
IL
Van Steen, Jeanne, Pres.
NUTLEY HISTORICAL SOCIETY MUSEUM -
ALICE J. BICKERS LIBRARY □ Nutley, NJ
Van Toll, Faith, Assoc.Dir. Network
WAYNE STATE UNIVERSITY - SCHOOL OF
MEDICINE - VERA PARSHALL SHIFFMAN
MEDICAL LIBRARY □ Detroit, MI
Van Velzer, Verna, Chf.Libn.
ESL, INC./SUBSIDIARY OF TRW - RESEARCH
LIBRARY □ Sunnyvale, CA
Van Vuren, Darcy D., AV Prog.Spec.
U.S. VETERANS ADMINISTRATION (DC-
Washington) - HEADQUARTERS CENTRAL
OFFICE LIBRARY □ Washington, DC
Van Weringh, Janet, Info.Ret.Libn.
CLARKSON COLLEGE OF TECHNOLOGY -
EDUCATIONAL RESOURCES CENTER □ Potsdam,
NY
Van Why, Carol, Asst.Dept.Hd.
MINNEAPOLIS PUBLIC LIBRARY &
INFORMATION CENTER - LITERATURE AND
LANGUAGE DEPARTMENT □ Minneapolis, MN
Van Why, Joseph S., Dir.
STOWE-DAY FOUNDATION - LIBRARY □
Hartford, CT
Van Winkle, Mary, Ref.Libn.
BENTLEY COLLEGE - SOLOMON R. BAKER
LIBRARY □ Waltham, MA
Vanags, Miss E.M., Hd.
ALCAN INTERNATIONAL LTD. - KINGSTON
LABORATORIES - LIBRARY □ Kingston, ON
VanAllen, Neil K., Gen.Supv./Info.Serv.
GENERAL MOTORS CORPORATION - RESEARCH
LABORATORIES LIBRARY □ Warren, MI
VanAuken, Richard, Dir.
INFORMATION TECHNOLOGY CENTER -
LIBRARY □ New York, NY
Vanberg, Bent, Cons.
SONS OF NORWAY - NORTH STAR LIBRARY □
Minneapolis, MN
Vance, Sandra, Libn.
SPRINGFIELD, ILLINOIS STATE JOURNAL &
REGISTER - EDITORIAL LIBRARY □ Springfield,
IL
Vance, Sharon, Hd., Tech.Serv.
WHEATON COLLEGE - LIBRARY □ Wheaton, IL
VandeBrink, Jake, Hd.Libn.
EDMONTON GENERAL HOSPITAL - HEALTH
SCIENCES LIBRARY □ Edmonton, AB
Vandegrift, Rev. J. Raymond, O.P., Libn.
DOMINICAN COLLEGE LIBRARY □ Washington,
DC
VandenBerge, Peter N., Dir. of Lib.Serv.
COLGATE ROCHESTER/BEXLEY HALL/ CROZER
THEOLOGICAL SEMINARIES - AMBROSE
SWASEY LIBRARY □ Rochester, NY
Vander Velde, John J., Spec.Proj. & Ed.Cons.
KANSAS STATE UNIVERSITY - FARRELL
LIBRARY □ Manhattan, KS
Vanderberg, Thelma, Libn.
REGIONAL PLAN ASSOCIATION, INC. - LIBRARY
□ New York, NY
Vanderburg, Patricia, Tech.Serv.Libn.
U.S. ARMY POST - FORT STEWART/HUNTER
AAF LIBRARY SYSTEM □ Ft. Stewart, GA
Vanderby, John, Libn.
SAN DIEGO PUBLIC LIBRARY - ART, MUSIC &
RECREATION SECTION □ San Diego, CA
Vanderhand, Pat
VIRGINIA STATE WATER CONTROL BOARD -
LIBRARY □ Richmond, VA

VanderMeer, Jon, Lrng.Lab.Supv.
WESTERN MICHIGAN UNIVERSITY -
EDUCATIONAL RESOURCES CENTER □
Kalamazoo, MI
VanderMeer, Patricia, Libn.
WESTERN MICHIGAN UNIVERSITY -
EDUCATIONAL RESOURCES CENTER □
Kalamazoo, MI
Vanderpoorten, Mary Beth, Acq.Libn.
COLORADO SCHOOL OF MINES - ARTHUR LAKES
LIBRARY □ Golden, CO
Vandersypen, Karla, Rare Bk.Libn.
UNIVERSITY OF MICHIGAN - DEPARTMENT OF
RARE BOOKS AND SPECIAL COLLECTIONS -
LIBRARY □ Ann Arbor, MI
VanDeusen, Toni, Libn.
JACKSON COUNTY LAW LIBRARY □ Medford, OR
Vandever, Mary, Asst.Tech.Libn.
GTE LENKURT, INC. - TECHNICAL LIBRARY,
M679 □ San Carlos, CA
Vandon, Gwen, Circ. & Ser.Libn.
BETHANY AND NORTHERN BAPTIST
THEOLOGICAL SEMINARIES - LIBRARY □ Oak
Brook, IL
Vandoros, Mrs. Z., Hd., Tech.Serv.
CANADA - DEPARTMENT OF
COMMUNICATIONS - LIBRARY & INFORMATION
RETRIEVAL SERVICES □ Ottawa, ON
Vaneck, Louisa, Circ.Tech.
ST. MARY'S UNIVERSITY - LAW LIBRARY □ San
Antonio, TX
Vanek, Eva, Mgr.Lib.Serv.
MERRILL LYNCH WHITE WELD - CAPITAL
MARKETS GROUP - LIBRARY □ New York, NY
Vangsness, Nellie, Per.Supv.
NORTH DAKOTA STATE UNIVERSITY - LIBRARY
□ Fargo, ND
Vaniman, Brinn, Libn.
SAN DIEGO PUBLIC LIBRARY - LITERATURE &
LANGUAGE SECTION □ San Diego, CA
Vann, J. Daniel, Exec.Dir.
UNIVERSITY OF WISCONSIN, OSHKOSH -
UNIVERSITY LIBRARIES AND LEARNING
RESOURCES □ Oshkosh, WI
Vann, J. Graves, Jr., Asst.Dir./Marketing
NORTH CAROLINA STATE SCIENCE AND
TECHNOLOGY RESEARCH CENTER □ Research
Triangle Park, NC
Vann, Dr. James E., Dir.
NORTH CAROLINA STATE SCIENCE AND
TECHNOLOGY RESEARCH CENTER □ Research
Triangle Park, NC
Vann, Joyce J., Dept.Libn.
ALABAMA A & M UNIVERSITY - JOSEPH F.
DRAKE MEMORIAL LEARNING RESOURCES
CENTER □ Normal, AL
Vann, Vicki, Libn.
KERR-MC GEE CORPORATION - MC GEE
LIBRARY □ Oklahoma City, OK
Vannorsdall, Mildred, Prof.Lib.Libn.
CHICAGO PUBLIC LIBRARY CENTRAL LIBRARY -
PROFESSIONAL LIBRARY □ Chicago, IL
VanPuffelen, John, Libn.
APPALACHIAN BIBLE COLLEGE - LIBRARY □
Bradley, WV
Vanston, John D., Law Libn.
MAGUIRE, VOORHIS AND WELLS - LIBRARY □
Orlando, FL
Vanstone, Ms. H.C., Lib.Techn.
CANADA - AGRICULTURE CANADA - REGIONAL
DEVELOPMENT & INTERNATIONAL AFFAIRS
LIBRARY □ Regina, SK
Vanstone, H.C., Lib.Techn.
CANADA - AGRICULTURE CANADA - RESEARCH
STATION, REGINA - LIBRARY □ Regina, SK
Vanstone, Sarah, Info.Spec.
IMPERIAL OIL, LTD. - BUSINESS INFORMATION
CENTRE □ Toronto, ON
Vanzant, Michelle, Law Libn.
HIGHLAND COUNTY LAW LIBRARY □ Hillsboro,
OH

Vargo, Mary O., Tech.Info.Spec.
U.S. GENERAL ACCOUNTING OFFICE - SAN
FRANCISCO REGIONAL OFFICE - LIBRARY □ San
Francisco, CA

Vargo, S.G., Mgr.
WESTINGHOUSE ELECTRIC CORPORATION -
MEDIUM POWER TRANSFORMER DIV. -
SHARON ENGINEERING LIBRARY □ Sharon, PA

Varieur, Normand L., Libn.
U.S. ARMY - ARMAMENT RESEARCH &
DEVELOPMENT COMMAND - SCIENTIFIC AND
TECHNICAL INFORMATION DIVISION □ Dover,
NJ

Vark, Mariamma, Coord., Ref.Serv.
WIDENER UNIVERSITY - WOLFGRAM
MEMORIAL LIBRARY □ Chester, PA

Varma, D.K., Adm.Stud.Libn.
YORK UNIVERSITY - GOVERNMENT
DOCUMENTS/ADMINISTRATIVE STUDIES
LIBRARY □ Downsview, ON

Varnado, Brien, Supt.
U.S. NATL. PARK SERVICE - FORT SUMTER
NATL. MONUMENT - LIBRARY □ Sullivan's Island,
SC

Varnardo, R. Brien, Pk.Supt.
U.S. NATL. PARK SERVICE - MANASSAS NATL.
BATTLEFIELD PARK - LIBRARY □ Manassas, VA

Varner, James H., Lib. Group Supv.
BELL TELEPHONE LABORATORIES, INC. &
WESTERN ELECTRIC, INC. - TECHNICAL
LIBRARY □ Denver, CO

Varnum, Virginia, Libn.
AMERICAN MANAGEMENT ASSOCIATIONS -
LIBRARY □ New York, NY

Vartian, Ross, Adm.Dir.
ARMENIAN ASSEMBLY CHARITABLE TRUST -
LIBRARY AND INFORMATION CENTER □
Washington, DC

Vasaturo, Ronald, Cat.
UNIVERSITY OF SAN DIEGO - MARVIN &
LILLIAN KRATTER LAW LIBRARY □ San Diego,
CA

Vasey, Lucille, Acq.
HYSTER COMPANY - TECHNICAL
INFORMATION SERVICES □ Portland, OR

Vasey, Maureen, Dir., Info.Serv.
CANADIAN REHABILITATION COUNCIL FOR
THE DISABLED - CRCD RESOURCE CENTRE □
Toronto, ON

Vashaw, Kathleen S., Tech.Info.Spec.
U.S. NATL. INSTITUTES OF HEALTH - LIBRARY
□ Bethesda, MD

Vasil, Nick P., Tech.Serv.Supv.
INDIANA VOCATIONAL-TECHNICAL COLLEGE -
RESOURCE CENTER □ Gary, IN

Vasilakis, Mary, Mgr.
WESTINGHOUSE ELECTRIC CORPORATION -
NUCLEAR ENERGY SYSTEMS - INFORMATION
RESOURCES† □ Pittsburgh, PA

Vaslef, Irene, Libn.
HARVARD UNIVERSITY - DUMBARTON OAKS
RESEARCH LIBRARY AND COLLECTION □
Washington, DC

Vasquez, Noris, Dir., Pub.Serv.
UNIVERSITY OF PUERTO RICO - GENERAL
LIBRARY □ San Juan, PR

Vastine, Ruth C., Lib.Mgr.
AIRCRAFT TECHNICAL PUBLISHERS - LIBRARY
□ San Francisco, CA

Vaughan, Anne, Libn.
LITTON INDUSTRIES - ELECTRON TUBE
DIVISION - LIBRARY □ San Carlos, CA

Vaughan, Stephanie, Hd., Ref.
UNIVERSITY OF WYOMING - SCIENCE AND
TECHNOLOGY LIBRARY □ Laramie, WY

Vaughn, Evelyn, Libn.
NASSAU COUNTY DEPARTMENT OF HEALTH -
CENTRAL RESEARCH LIBRARY □ Mineola, NY

Vaughn, Kathryn, Chf.Med.Libn.
MONTREAL GENERAL HOSPITAL - MEDICAL
LIBRARY □ Montreal, PQ

Vaughn, Nancy, Med.Libn.
U.S. VETERANS ADMINISTRATION (KS-Topeka)
- DR. KARL A. MENNINGER MEDICAL LIBRARY □
Topeka, KS

Vaughn, W.A., Libn.
ARKANSAS TECH UNIVERSITY - TOMLINSON
LIBRARY □ Russellville, AR

Vaught, Don, Libn.
SKAGIT COUNTY LAW LIBRARY† □ Mount
Vernon, WA

Vaught, Edwin F., Libn.
SOUTHWEST RESEARCH INSTITUTE - THOMAS
BAKER SLICK MEMORIAL LIBRARY □ San
Antonio, TX

Vaught, Rosalie, Libn.
U.S. NATL. MARINE FISHERIES SERVICE -
SOUTHEAST FISHERIES CENTER - PANAMA
CITY LABORATORY - LIBRARY □ Panama City,
FL

Vavra, Deborah Jones, Libn.
OHIO STATE UNIVERSITY - INSTITUTE OF
POLAR STUDIES - GOLDTHWAIT POLAR
LIBRARY □ Columbus, OH

Vavra, Janet, Tech.Dir.
UNIVERSITY OF MICHIGAN - INSTITUTE FOR
SOCIAL RESEARCH - ISR SOCIAL SCIENCE
ARCHIVE □ Ann Arbor, MI

Vdovin, George, Libn.
UNIVERSITY OF CALIFORNIA, BERKELEY -
CHEMISTRY LIBRARY □ Berkeley, CA

Veach, M. Jane, Asst. to Hd.
UNIVERSITY OF NEW BRUNSWICK -
ENGINEERING LIBRARY □ Fredericton, NB

Veasley, Mignon, Hd.Libn.
PRICE WATERHOUSE - LIBRARY □ Los Angeles,
CA

Veatch, James R., Assoc. Professor
NASHVILLE STATE TECHNICAL INSTITUTE -
EDUCATIONAL RESOURCE CENTER □ Nashville,
TN

Vecoli, Rudolph J., Dir.
UNIVERSITY OF MINNESOTA - IMMIGRATION
HISTORY RESEARCH CENTER □ St. Paul, MN

Veeder, George A., Pres.
KENILWORTH HISTORICAL SOCIETY - KILNER
LIBRARY □ Kenilworth, IL

Veenman, R., Lib.Supv.
SIR SANFORD FLEMING COLLEGE OF APPLIED
ARTS & TECHNOLOGY - LIBRARIES □
Peterborough, ON

Veit, Henri, Div.Chf.
BROOKLYN PUBLIC LIBRARY - HISTORY,
TRAVEL, RELIGION AND BIOGRAPHY DIVISION
□ Brooklyn, NY

Velantzas, Tina, Info.Sci.
COLGATE PALMOLIVE COMPANY - TECHNICAL
INFORMATION CENTER □ Piscataway, NJ

Velasco, Dolores
UNITED FARM WORKERS OF AMERICA, AFL-
CIO - I.C. LIBRARY† □ Keene, CA

Velasco, Peter Gines, Dir.
UNITED FARM WORKERS OF AMERICA, AFL-
CIO - I.C. LIBRARY† □ Keene, CA

Velez, Betsaida, Libn.
CARIBBEAN CENTER FOR ADVANCED STUDIES
- LIBRARY □ Santurce, PR

Velics, Laszlo, Univ.Biblog.
MICHIGAN TECHNOLOGICAL UNIVERSITY -
LIBRARY □ Houghton, MI

Velkas, Carmen L., Info.Spec.
OFFICE OF BILINGUAL EDUCATION -
RESOURCE LIBRARY AND INFORMATION UNIT
□ Brooklyn, NY

Velthuys, Paula, Prints & Photographs
MARYLAND HISTORICAL SOCIETY - LIBRARY □
Baltimore, MD

Veneziani, Pat, Adm.
ARMED FORCES COMMUNICATIONS AND
ELECTRONICS ASSOCIATION - LIBRARY □ Falls
Church, VA

Venne, Louise, Libn.
CANADA - NATIONAL RESEARCH COUNCIL -
CISTI - INDUSTRIAL MATERIALS RESEARCH
INSTITUTE LIBRARY □ Montreal, PQ

Venne, Paul R., Area Coord., Quebec
CANADA - AGRICULTURE CANADA - RESEARCH
STATION, STE-FOY - LIBRARY □ Ste. Foy, PQ

Verble, Frances, Cat.
UNIVERSITY OF TENNESSEE - CENTER FOR
THE HEALTH SCIENCES LIBRARY □ Memphis, TN

Verchomin, Mrs. J., Dir.
UKRAINIAN WOMEN'S ASSOCIATION OF
CANADA - UKRAINIAN MUSEUM OF CANADA -
LIBRARY □ Edmonton, AB

Vercio, Roseanne, Asst.Med.Libn.
PORTER MEMORIAL HOSPITAL - HARLEY E.
RICE MEMORIAL LIBRARY □ Denver, CO

Verdini, Gaetano, Foreign Lang.Spec.
BROOKLYN PUBLIC LIBRARY - LANGUAGE AND
LITERATURE DIVISION □ Brooklyn, NY

Verdugo, Karen, Pub.Serv.
LOYOLA LAW SCHOOL - LIBRARY □ Los Angeles,
CA

Vergamini, Thomas P., Act. Law Lib.Dir.
NORTHERN KENTUCKY UNIVERSITY - SALMON
P. CHASE COLLEGE OF LAW - LIBRARY □
Covington, KY

Verhaeren, Paul, Off.Mgr.
SWEDENBORG FOUNDATION - LIBRARY □ New
York, NY

Verhage, Erma L., Lib.Asst.
U.S. NAVY - NAVAL AIR STATION (Lemoore) -
LIBRARY† □ Lemoore, CA

Verich, Dr. Thomas M., Archv.
UNIVERSITY OF MISSISSIPPI - ARCHIVES &
SPECIAL COLLECTIONS/MISSISSIPPIANA □
University, MS

Verity, John B., Lib.Mgr.
U.S. DEPT. OF ENERGY - LAWRENCE
LIVERMORE LAB. - TECHNICAL INFO. DEPT.
LIBRARY □ Livermore, CA

Verma, Kamlesh, Ref.Libn.
COMPUTER SCIENCES CORPORATION -
TECHNICAL LIBRARY □ Falls Church, VA

Vermandere, Bertha, Ref.Libn.
COLLEGE DE MUSIQUE SAINTE-CROIX -
BIBLIOTHEQUE □ St. Laurent, PQ

Vermillion, Ann-Marie, Hd.Libn.
HOUSTON INTERNATIONAL MINERALS
CORPORATION - LIBRARY □ Denver, CO

Vermillion, Jane E., Libn.
ENGINEERS' CLUB OF DAYTON - LIBRARY □
Dayton, OH

Vermillion, Judy, Med.Libn.
CHILDREN'S MERCY HOSPITAL - MEDICAL
LIBRARY □ Kansas City, MO

Verrier, Philip, Res. Forester
NEW HAMPSHIRE STATE DIVISION OF
FORESTS AND LANDS - FOX FOREST LIBRARY □
Hillsboro, NH

Verrioli, P.C., Libn.
FRENCH (R.T.) COMPANY - TECHNICAL
LIBRARY □ Rochester, NY

Verstynen, Evelyn, Cons.Libn.
ST. THOMAS AQUINAS NEWMAN CENTER -
LIBRARY □ Albuquerque, NM

Vesely, Marilyn, Pub.Info.Off.
OKLAHOMA STATE DEPARTMENT OF
LIBRARIES □ Oklahoma City, OK

Vesley, Roberta A., Libn.
AMERICAN KENNEL CLUB - LIBRARY □ New
York, NY

Vest, Donald R., Libn.
PUEBLO REGIONAL PLANNING COMMISSION -
LIBRARY □ Pueblo, CO

Vest, Stephen, Assoc.Libn.
SHENANDOAH COLLEGE & CONSERVATORY OF
MUSIC - HOWE LIBRARY □ Winchester, VA

Vestal, Alice M., Hd.
UNIVERSITY OF CINCINNATI - SPECIAL
COLLECTIONS DEPARTMENT □ Cincinnati, OH

Vey, Jeff A., Info.Spec.
BUCKS COUNTY PLANNING COMMISSION
STAFF LIBRARY □ Doylestown, PA

Veysey, Arthur, Gen.Mgr.
CANTIGNY WAR MEMORIAL MUSEUM OF THE
FIRST DIVISION - ARCHIVES ROOM □ Wheaton,
IL

Via, Nancy, Info.
SOUTHERN CONNECTICUT STATE COLLEGE -
H.C. BULEY LIBRARY □ New Haven, CT

Vial, Susan, Libn.
ART GALLERY OF GREATER VICTORIA -
LIBRARY □ Victoria, BC

Viau, Mr. Rheal, Data Base Anl.
CANADA - INDUSTRY, TRADE & COMMERCE -
CANADIAN GOVERNMENT OFFICE OF TOURISM
□ Ottawa, ON

Vick, Kathy, Assoc.Info.Anl.
AMERICAN CRITICAL CARE - INFORMATION
CENTER □ McGaw Park, IL

Vickers, Donald, AV Cons.
WINNIPEG SCHOOL DIVISION NO. 1 -
TEACHERS LIBRARY AND RESOURCE CENTRE □
Winnipeg, MB

Vickers, Rebecca, Assoc.Dir./Tech.Serv.
LUBBOCK CHRISTIAN COLLEGE - MOODY
LIBRARY □ Lubbock, TX

Vickery, Kae, Lib.Supv.
BANK OF MONTREAL - OPERATIONS &
SYSTEMS LIBRARY □ Montreal, PQ

Vickery, Dr. Tom Rusk, Dir.
SYRACUSE UNIVERSITY - SCHOOL OF
EDUCATION - EDUCATIONAL RESOURCE
CENTER □ Syracuse, NY

Victor, Albert, Libn.
NATIONAL HAMILTONIAN PARTY -
HAMILTONIAN LIBRARY □ Flint, MI

Victor, Shirley, Asst.Libn.
NEW YORK BOTANICAL GARDEN - LIBRARY □
Bronx, NY

Victor, Stephen, Dp.Dir.
SLATER MILL HISTORIC SITE - RESEARCH
LIBRARY □ Pawtucket, RI

Victoria, Vicki, Asst.Libn.
AKRON BEACON JOURNAL - REFERENCE
LIBRARY □ Akron, OH

Vidor, David, Cat.Libn.
FEDERAL RESERVE BANK OF ATLANTA -
RESEARCH LIBRARY □ Atlanta, GA

Viehdorfer, Alreeta, Command Libn.
U.S. AIR FORCE - ACCOUNTING AND FINANCE
CENTER - TECHNICAL LIBRARY □ Denver, CO

Viel, Jocelyne, Asst.Libn.
CLINICAL RESEARCH INSTITUTE OF
MONTREAL - MEDICAL LIBRARY □ Montreal, PQ

Vielehr, Alice, Libn.
FOUNDATION FOR CITIZEN EDUCATION -
ANNA LORD STRAUSS LIBRARY □ New York, NY

Viergever, Dan W., Main Post Libn.
U.S. ARMY POST - FORT RILEY - LIBRARIES† □
Fort Riley, KS

Vierich, Richard W., Hd.Libn.
UNIVERSITY OF CALIFORNIA, RIVERSIDE -
PHYSICAL SCIENCES LIBRARY □ Riverside, CA

Vigars, Linda, Ref.Libn.
GENERAL ELECTRIC COMPANY - MAIN LIBRARY
□ Schenectady, NY

Viger, Rev. Jacques, S.S., Hd.Libn.
GRAND SEMINAIRE DE MONTREAL -
BIBLIOTHEQUE □ Montreal, PQ

Viger, Veronica, Ref.Libn.
EQUITABLE LIFE ASSURANCE SOCIETY OF THE
U.S. - GENERAL LIBRARY† □ New York, NY

Viggiano, F.X., Exec.Dir.
UNITED STATES STUDENT ASSOCIATION -
INFORMATION SERVICES □ Washington, DC

Vigil, Marcia, Ref. Staff
UNIVERSITY OF DENVER - COLLEGE OF LAW -
WESTMINSTER LAW LIBRARY □ Denver, CO

Vigil, Peter, Online Search Coord.
UNIVERSITY OF CALIFORNIA, DAVIS - HEALTH
SCIENCES LIBRARY □ Davis, CA

Vignapiano, Emma G., Circ./ILL
U.S. ARMY WAR COLLEGE - LIBRARY □ Carlisle
Barracks, PA

Vignone, Maria, D.C. Br.Chf.
U.S. DEPT. OF ENERGY - LIBRARY □ Washington,
DC

Vijay, Mrs. Girija, Dir., Med.Lib.
CRAWFORD W. LONG MEMORIAL HOSPITAL -
LIBRARY† □ Atlanta, GA

Vikre, David, Sci.Libn.
SMITH COLLEGE - CLARK SCIENCE LIBRARY □
Northampton, MA

Vilcins, Miss Maija, Ref.Serv.
CANADA - NATIONAL GALLERY OF CANADA -
LIBRARY □ Ottawa, ON

Vilella, Enrique, Dir.
U.S. DEPT. OF COMMERCE - INTERNATIONAL
TRADE ADMINISTRATION - SAN JUAN
DISTRICT OFFICE LIBRARY □ San Juan, PR

Viles, Ann, Music Libn.
MEMPHIS STATE UNIVERSITY LIBRARIES -
MUSIC LIBRARY □ Memphis, TN

Villafane, Aida G., Spec.Coll.Libn.
UNIVERSITY OF PUERTO RICO - MAYAGUEZ
CAMPUS - LIBRARY □ Mayaguez, PR

Villanti, Frances, Lib.Techn.
TORONTO TRANSIT COMMISSION -
ENGINEERING & CONSTRUCTION LIBRARY □
Toronto, ON

Villarreal, L. Guen, Asst.Libn.
WASHBURN UNIVERSITY OF TOPEKA - SCHOOL
OF LAW LIBRARY □ Topeka, KS

Villemaire, Sr. Gabrielle, S.S.A., Libn.
CANADIAN CENTRE FOR ECUMENISM -
LIBRARY □ Montreal, PQ

Villemi, Uko, Cat.
U.S. DEPT. OF COMMERCE - DEPARTMENTAL
LIBRARY □ Washington, DC

Villeneuve-Allaire, Mme. Lise, Libn., Cat.Dept.
QUEBEC PROVINCE - MINISTERE DES
COMMUNICATIONS - BIBLIOTHEQUE
ADMINISTRATIVE □ Quebec, PQ

Villere, Dawn N., Sr.Tech.Libn.
ITT CORPORATION - GILFILLAN ENGINEERING
LIBRARY† □ Van Nuys, CA

Vince, Thomas L., Libn. & Cur.
HUDSON LIBRARY AND HISTORICAL SOCIETY □
Hudson, OH

Vincelli, Sue, Libn.
GENERAL ELECTRIC COMPANY - LIGHTING
RESEARCH AND TECHNICAL SERVICES
OPERATIONS - LIBRARY □ Cleveland, OH

Vincent, Claire E., Legal Res.Libn.
KANSAS STATE SUPREME COURT - LAW
LIBRARY □ Topeka, KS

Vincent, Joseph G., Exec.Dir.
ROME HISTORICAL SOCIETY - ELAINE &
WILLIAM E. SCRIPTURE MEMORIAL LIBRARY □
Rome, NY

Vincent, Kathy, Acq.Libn.
WAKE FOREST UNIVERSITY - BOWMAN GRAY
SCHOOL OF MEDICINE - LIBRARY □ Winston-
Salem, NC

Vinces, Martine, Archv.
CBS RECORDS - ARCHIVES □ New York, NY

Vine, Naomi, Dir. of Educ.
MUSEUM OF CONTEMPORARY ART - LIBRARY □
Chicago, IL

Vinet, Bernard, Dir., Dev. & Pub.Serv.
UNIVERSITE LAVAL - BIBLIOTHEQUE† □ Ste.
Foy, PQ

Vining, John, Exec.Dir.
MIAMI VALLEY REGIONAL PLANNING
COMMISSION - LIBRARY □ Dayton, OH

Vinson, Charlotte W., Chf.Libn.
LONE STAR GAS COMPANY - RESEARCH
LIBRARY □ Dallas, TX

Viola, Dr. Herman J., Dir.
SMITHSONIAN INSTITUTION - NATIONAL
ANTHROPOLOGICAL ARCHIVES □ Washington,
DC

Violet, Jane, Libn.
COMMUNITY HOSPITAL OF SPRINGFIELD &
CLARK COUNTY - HEALTH SCIENCES LIBRARY □
Springfield, OH

Virtue, Joyce, Lib. Teaching Asst.
OREGON STATE SCHOOL FOR THE DEAF -
LIBRARY □ Salem, OR

Viskochil, Larry, Cur., Graphic Coll.
CHICAGO HISTORICAL SOCIETY - SPECIAL
COLLECTIONS □ Chicago, IL

Visscher, Helga, Ref.Libn.
UNIVERSITY OF ALABAMA - EDUCATION
LIBRARY □ University, AL

Visser, Murray R., Supv.Libn.
U.S. MARINE CORPS - KANEOHE AIR STATION
LIBRARY □ Kaneohe Bay, HI

Viswanatha, Hema, Info.Spec.
MASSACHUSETTS INSTITUTE OF TECHNOLOGY
- LINCOLN LABORATORY LIBRARY □ Lexington,
MA

Vitai, Jean, Coll./Ref.Libn.
UNIVERSITY OF WESTERN ONTARIO -
NATURAL SCIENCES LIBRARY □ London, ON

Vitek, Clement G., Chf.Libn.
ABELL (A.S.) COMPANY - BALTIMORE
SUNPAPERS - LIBRARY □ Baltimore, MD

Vitriol, Malvin, Chf.Libn.
U.S. VETERANS ADMINISTRATION (NY-New
York) - MEDICAL CENTER LIBRARY† □ New
York, NY

Viviano, Joseph, Adm.Asst.
ENOCH PRATT FREE LIBRARY - FINE ARTS AND
RECREATION DEPARTMENT □ Baltimore, MD

Vix, Laura, Off.Supv.
POPE COUNTY HISTORICAL SOCIETY &
MUSEUM - LIBRARY □ Glenwood, MN

Vixie, Anne, Bus.Res.Spec.
LAMB-WESTON - BUSINESS RESEARCH CENTER
□ Portland, OR

Vizoyan, Barbara B., Libn.
GEORGESON & COMPANY - LIBRARY □ New
York, NY

Vlantikas, Mary C., Libn.
FEDERAL RESERVE BANK OF BOSTON -
RESEARCH LIBRARY† □ Boston, MA

Vlasic, Ivan, Hd.Tech.Serv.
SUNY - COLLEGE AT CORTLAND - MEMORIAL
LIBRARY □ Cortland, NY

Vocasek, Helen A., Dir., Med.Rec.
ST. JOHN'S RIVERSIDE HOSPITAL - MEDICAL
LIBRARY □ Yonkers, NY

Vocelka, Mary, Lib.Techn.
U.S. NATL. PARK SERVICE - YOSEMITE NATL.
PARK - RESEARCH LIBRARY □ Yosemite National
Park, CA

Voci, F.K.
DOW CHEMICAL COMPANY - TECHNICAL
INFORMATION SERVICES - CHEMICAL LIBRARY
□ Midland, MI

Vodicka, Julia R., Musm.Dir.
OVER (W.H.) MUSEUM - LIBRARY □ Vermillion,
SD

Voelker, Linda, Coll./Ref.Libn.
UNIVERSITY OF WESTERN ONTARIO - HEALTH
SCIENCES LIBRARY □ London, ON

Voelker, Margie L., Libn.
UNIVERSITY OF MINNESOTA - MATHEMATICS
LIBRARY □ Minneapolis, MN

Voelker, Robert B., Asst.Libn.
UNIVERSITY OF NEBRASKA, LINCOLN - LAW
LIBRARY □ Lincoln, NE

Voeltz, Richard E., Assoc. Professor
UNIVERSITY OF NEBRASKA, LINCOLN -
CHEMISTRY LIBRARY □ Lincoln, NE

Voeltz, Richard E., Assoc. Professor
UNIVERSITY OF NEBRASKA, LINCOLN -
DENTISTRY LIBRARY □ Lincoln, NE

Voeltz, Richard E., Assoc. Professor
UNIVERSITY OF NEBRASKA, LINCOLN - LIFE
SCIENCES LIBRARY □ Lincoln, NE

Voge, Susan, Med.Libn.
EQUITABLE LIFE ASSURANCE SOCIETY OF THE
U.S. - MEDICAL LIBRARY† □ New York, NY

Vogel, Dorothy, Asst.Bus.Libn.
BROOKLYN PUBLIC LIBRARY - BUSINESS LIBRARY □ Brooklyn, NY

Vogel, Helen A., Libn.
ROCHESTER PSYCHIATRIC CENTER - PROFESSIONAL LIBRARY □ Rochester, NY

Vogel, Karen, Med.Libn.
U.S. VETERANS ADMINISTRATION (CA-Long Beach) - MEDICAL CENTER LIBRARY □ Long Beach, CA

Vogel, Marion L., Dean of Lrng.Rsrcs.
TRIDENT TECHNICAL COLLEGE - NORTH CAMPUS LIBRARY □ North Charleston, SC

Vogel, Thomas, Hd., Ref.
PHILADELPHIA COLLEGE OF TEXTILES AND SCIENCE - PASTORE LIBRARY □ Philadelphia, PA

Vogelstein, Susan, Lib.Dir.
92ND STREET YOUNG MEN'S AND YOUNG WOMEN'S HEBREW ASSOCIATION - BUTTENWIESER LIBRARY □ New York, NY

Voges, Mickie A., Hd., Ref.
UNIVERSITY OF TEXAS SCHOOL OF LAW - TARLTON LAW LIBRARY □ Austin, TX

Vogler, Cheryl, Lib.Tech.Asst.
ST. LOUIS ART MUSEUM - RICHARDSON MEMORIAL LIBRARY □ St. Louis, MO

Vogt, Sheryl, Hd.
UNIVERSITY OF GEORGIA - RICHARD B. RUSSELL MEMORIAL LIBRARY □ Athens, GA

Vogt, Viola, Cat.
FIRST LUTHERAN CHURCH OF THE LUTHERAN CHURCH IN AMERICA - SCHENDEL MEMORIAL LIBRARY □ Red Wing, MN

Vogt-O'Connor, Diane, Hd.Libn.
CRANBROOK ACADEMY OF ART - LIBRARY □ Bloomfield Hills, MI

Vohra, Pran, Supv./Chf.Libn.
WASCANA INSTITUTE OF APPLIED ARTS AND SCIENCES - RESOURCE & INFORMATION CENTRE □ Regina, SK

Voigt, Ann, Market Info.Ctr.
LOCKHEED-CALIFORNIA COMPANY - TECHNICAL INFORMATION CENTER □ Burbank, CA

Voigt, John, Libn.
BERKLEE COLLEGE OF MUSIC - LIBRARY □ Boston, MA

Voiland, Jeannette, Asst.Libn.
SEATTLE PUBLIC LIBRARY - GOVERNMENTAL RESEARCH ASSISTANCE LIBRARY □ Seattle, WA

Voit, Irene, Asst.Libn.
OREGON STATE UNIVERSITY - WILLIAM JASPER KERR LIBRARY □ Corvallis, OR

Volin, Rudolph H., Mechanical Engr.
U.S. NAVY - NAVAL RESEARCH LABORATORY - SHOCK AND VIBRATION INFORMATION CENTER □ Washington, DC

Volk, Mary J., Libn.
CARNEGIE-MELLON UNIVERSITY - MELLON INSTITUTE LIBRARY □ Pittsburgh, PA

Volkersz, Evert, Libn.
SUNY AT STONY BROOK - DEPARTMENT OF SPECIAL COLLECTIONS □ Stony Brook, NY

Vollenweider, Laura S., Libn.
REYNOLDS, SMITH & HILLS - LIBRARY □ Jacksonville, FL

Vollmer, Marguerite, Asst.Libn.
SAN DIEGO COUNTY LAW LIBRARY - VISTA BRANCH □ Vista, CA

Volz, Arlene, Ref.Libn.
UNIVERSITY OF MIAMI - SCHOOL OF MEDICINE - LOUIS CALDER MEMORIAL LIBRARY □ Miami, FL

Volz, Robert L., Custodian
WILLIAMS COLLEGE - CHAPIN LIBRARY □ Williamstown, MA

Von Boltenstern, W., Coord.
INTERNATIONAL POSTCARD COLLECTORS ASSOCIATION, INC. - LIBRARY† □ Los Angeles, CA

Von Brauchitsch, Ilse, Ref.Libn.
UNIVERSITY OF OKLAHOMA - HEALTH SCIENCES CENTER LIBRARY □ Oklahoma City, OK

von Gunst-Andersen, Jon A., Cur.
HISTORICAL SOCIETY OF PALM BEACH COUNTY - LIBRARY AND ARCHIVES □ Palm Beach, FL

Von Gunten, Louis E., Asst.Libn.
ALAMEDA COUNTY LAW LIBRARY □ Oakland, CA

Von Hake, Margaret J., Libn.
COLUMBIA UNION COLLEGE - THEOFIELD G. WEIS LIBRARY □ Takoma Park, MD

Von Halle, E.S.
U.S. OAK RIDGE NATL. LABORATORY - INFORMATION DIVISION - ENVIRONMENTAL MUTAGEN INFORMATION CENTER □ Oak Ridge, TN

Von Henning, Horst, Chm.Lib.Comm.
AMERICAN ALPINE CLUB - LIBRARY □ New York, NY

Von Nussbaumer, Dr. Aliyah, Res.Libn.
DRESSER INDUSTRIES, INC. - MAGCOBAR RESEARCH LIBRARY □ Houston, TX

von Rebhan, Anne, Chf. Slide Libn.
NATIONAL GALLERY OF ART - EDUCATION DIVISION SLIDE LIBRARY □ Washington, DC

von Schrader, Julie L., Libn.
PITNEY, HARDIN & KIPP - LAW LIBRARY □ Morristown, NJ

Von Uhlenhorst-Ziechmann, W.K., Dir.
INSTITUTE FOR CENTRAL EUROPEAN RESEARCH - LIBRARY □ Shaker Heights, OH

Von Wersch, Doreen, Lib.Asst.
VICTORIA GENERAL HOSPITAL - HEALTH SCIENCES LIBRARY† □ Victoria, BC

VonBruck, Ms. Marion, Medical Librarian
PIERCE COUNTY MEDICAL LIBRARY □ Tacoma, WA

VonderLindt, Alice M., Chf., Lib.Serv.
U.S. VETERANS ADMINISTRATION (PA-Coatesville) - MEDICAL CENTER LIBRARY □ Coatesville, PA

Vondrasek, Bets, Cur.
WHITMAN (Walt) BIRTHPLACE ASSOCIATION - LIBRARY AND MUSEUM □ Huntington Station, NY

Vondruska, Eloise, Tech.Serv.Libn.
PARKLAND COLLEGE - LEARNING RESOURCE CENTER □ Champaign, IL

Vongpaisal, Suvakorn, Ref. & Circ.
LAURENTIAN UNIVERSITY - MAIN LIBRARY □ Sudbury, ON

Vonka, Stephanie, Asst.Libn.
SNC GROUP - LIBRARY □ Montreal, PQ

VonRosen, Margaret, Libn.
CHRYSLER DEFENSE, INC. - ENGINEERING DIVISION - TECHNICAL LIBRARY □ Center Line, MI

VonRothkirch, Dr. Edward, Dir.
INTERNATIONAL ASSOCIATION OF INDEPENDENT PRODUCERS - LIBRARY† □ Washington, DC

Vork, Doris, Libn.
UNIROYAL, INC. - TECHNICAL LIBRARY □ Middlebury, CT

Vorse, Elinore, Ref.Libn.
SUNY - COLLEGE AT POTSDAM - FREDERICK W. CRUMB MEMORIAL LIBRARY □ Potsdam, NY

Vosburgh, Faith, Asst.Libn./Ref.
AMERICAN INSTITUTE OF ARCHITECTS - LIBRARY □ Washington, DC

Vosikovska, Jana, Chf.
CANADA - PUBLIC ARCHIVES OF CANADA - NATL. FILM, TELEVISION & SOUND ARCHIVES - DOCUMENTATION & PUB. SERV. □ Ottawa, ON

Vosper, Robert, Dir.
UNIVERSITY OF CALIFORNIA, LOS ANGELES - WILLIAM ANDREWS CLARK MEMORIAL LIBRARY □ Los Angeles, CA

Voss, Ingrid M., Libn.
NORTHERN PETROCHEMICAL COMPANY - TECHNICAL CENTER LIBRARY □ Morris, IL

Voss, Marjorie Anne, Cur.
TONGASS HISTORICAL SOCIETY, INC. - ROBBIE BARTHOLOMEW MEMORIAL LIBRARY □ Ketchikan, AK

Votaw, Floyd, Hd. Of Tech.Serv.
GRACE THEOLOGICAL SEMINARY - LIBRARY □ Winona Lake, IN

Vreeland, Ann, Ser. & Ref.Libn.
ST. PETER'S MEDICAL CENTER - LIBRARY □ New Brunswick, NJ

Vrooman, George K., Chf., Sci./Tech.Info.
U.S. ARMY - ARMAMENT RESEARCH & DEVELOPMENT COMMAND - BENET WEAPONS LABORATORY - TECHNICAL LIBRARY □ Watervliet, NY

Vrugtman, Ina, Botanical Libn.
ROYAL BOTANICAL GARDENS - LIBRARY □ Hamilton, ON

Vugrinecz, Anna-Elizabeth, Ref.Libn.
WESTERN ELECTRIC COMPANY, INC. - KEARNY INFORMATION RESOURCE CENTER □ Kearny, NJ

Vuturo, Susan, Sr. Clinical Med.Libn.
UNIVERSITY OF MISSOURI, KANSAS CITY - HEALTH SCIENCES LIBRARY □ Kansas City, MO

Vyas, Hansa S., Search Anl./Assoc.Libn.
PHILADELPHIA COLLEGE OF OSTEOPATHIC MEDICINE - O.J. SNYDER MEMORIAL MEDICAL LIBRARY □ Philadelphia, PA

Vyas, Dr. Shanker H., Dir. Of Libs.
PHILADELPHIA COLLEGE OF OSTEOPATHIC MEDICINE - O.J. SNYDER MEMORIAL MEDICAL LIBRARY □ Philadelphia, PA

Vyas, Umesh, Ref.Libn.
UNIVERSITY OF CALGARY - LAW LIBRARY □ Calgary, AB

Vyas, Veena N., Dir., Med.Lib.
ORTHOPAEDIC HOSPITAL - RUBEL MEMORIAL LIBRARY □ Los Angeles, CA

Vyzralek, Frank E., State Archv.
STATE HISTORICAL SOCIETY OF NORTH DAKOTA - RESEARCH AND REFERENCE DIVISION □ Bismarck, ND

W

Wachna, Jane, Libn.
FINANCIAL TIMES OF CANADA - LIBRARY □ Toronto, ON

Wachna, P., Gallery Asst.
TORONTO CITY RECORDS AND ARCHIVES DIVISION □ Toronto, ON

Wachs, Sharona, Libn.
SPERTUS COLLEGE OF JUDAICA - NORMAN AND HELEN ASHER LIBRARY □ Chicago, IL

Wachtel, Lee, Res.Libn.
NORTHEAST OHIO AREAWIDE COORDINATING AGENCY - RESEARCH LIBRARY □ Cleveland, OH

Wack, Helen, Libn.
COLORADO STATE HOSPITAL - PROFESSIONAL LIBRARY □ Pueblo, CO

Wacker, Jan, Staff Asst.
UNIVERSITY OF NEBRASKA, LINCOLN - INSTRUCTIONAL MEDIA CENTER □ Lincoln, NE

Wackerbarth, Carrie, Lib.Mgr.
UNIVERSITY OF NEW MEXICO - DEPARTMENT OF ANTHROPOLOGY - CLARK FIELD ARCHIVES □ Albuquerque, NM

Waddell, Carol N., Asst.Dir.
TIPPECANOE COUNTY HISTORICAL ASSOCIATION - ALAMEDA MC COLLOUGH RESEARCH & GENEALOGY LIBRARY □ Lafayette, IN

Waddell, Gene, Dir.
SOUTH CAROLINA HISTORICAL SOCIETY - LIBRARY □ Charleston, SC

Waddell, Samuel J., Chf.Libn.
HUNTER COLLEGE OF THE CITY UNIVERSITY OF NEW YORK - HEALTH PROFESSIONS LIBRARY □ New York, NY

PERSONNEL

Wadden, Emily E., Law Libn.
SPOKANE COUNTY LAW LIBRARY □ Spokane, WA

Waddington, Elaine, Libn.
ROYAL VICTORIA HOSPITAL - OBSTETRICS & GYNAECOLOGY LIBRARY □ Montreal, PQ

Waddington, Murray, Libn.
METROPOLITAN TORONTO LIBRARY - FINE ART DEPARTMENT □ Toronto, ON

Waddington, Susan R., Dept.Hd.
PROVIDENCE PUBLIC LIBRARY - ART AND MUSIC DEPARTMENT □ Providence, RI

Wade, Arthur, Hd., Journals Proc.
U.S. NATL. INSTITUTES OF HEALTH - LIBRARY □ Bethesda, MD

Wade, Carol, Libn.
FLORIDA STATE BOARD OF REGENTS - LIBRARY □ Tallahassee, FL

Wade, Diana M., Act.Hd.
U.S. NATL. ARCHIVES & RECORDS SERVICE - NATL. AUDIOVISUAL CENTER - INFORMATION SERVICES SECTION □ Washington, DC

Wade, Grace, Asst.Libn.
CHURCH OF JESUS CHRIST OF LATTER-DAY SAINTS - EL PASO BRANCH GENEALOGICAL LIBRARY □ El Paso, TX

Wade, L.E., Adm.
MOUNT CUBA ASTRONOMICAL OBSERVATORY - LAMBERT L. JACKSON MEMORIAL LIBRARY □ Wilmington, DE

Wadley, Carol, Nursing Sch.Libn.
STORMONT-VAIL REGIONAL MEDICAL CENTER AND SHAWNEE COUNTY MEDICAL SOCIETY - HEALTH SCIENCES LIBRARY □ Topeka, KS

Wadnizak, Lillian M., Lib.Mgr.
NORTH DAKOTA STATE UNIVERSITY - DIVISION OF INDEPENDENT STUDY - FILM LIBRARY □ Fargo, ND

Wadsack, Ronald L., Libn.
CHURCH OF JESUS CHRIST OF LATTER-DAY SAINTS - MORRISTOWN, NEW JERSEY BRANCH GENEALOGICAL LIBRARY □ Morristown, NJ

Waechter, Thomas, ILL
ST. LOUIS UNIVERSITY - MEDICAL CENTER LIBRARY □ St. Louis, MO

Wagener, Elsie, Circ.Libn.
U.S. AIR FORCE - AEROSPACE MEDICAL DIVISION - SCHOOL OF AEROSPACE MEDICINE - STRUGHOLD AEROMEDICAL LIBRARY □ Brooks AFB, TX

Wagener, Henry, Media Cons.
MINNESOTA STATE DEPARTMENT OF PUBLIC WELFARE - LIBRARY □ St. Paul, MN

Wagenveld, Linda M., Mgr.
HERMAN MILLER, INC. - RESOURCE CENTER □ Zeeland, MI

Wages, Orland (Jack), Libn.
BRIDGEWATER COLLEGE - ALEXANDER MACK MEMORIAL LIBRARY - SPECIAL COLLECTIONS □ Bridgewater, VA

Waggener, Lexie Jean Brown, Dir.
TENNESSEE STATE LIBRARY AND ARCHIVES - ARCHIVES & MANUSCRIPTS SECTION □ Nashville, TN

Waggoner, Phyllis A., Lib.Mgr.
FEDERAL RESERVE BANK OF SAN FRANCISCO - RESEARCH LIBRARY □ San Francisco, CA

Wagner, Betty L., Libn.
UNIVERSITY OF WASHINGTON - ARCHITECTURE - URBAN PLANNING LIBRARY □ Seattle, WA

Wagner, Carroll Sue, Ref.Libn.
UNIVERSITY OF CALIFORNIA - LOS ALAMOS NATIONAL LABORATORY - LIBRARY □ Los Alamos, NM

Wagner, Charlotte A., Asst.Libn.
GULF REFINING & MARKETING COMPANY - LIBRARY AND INFORMATION CENTER □ Houston, TX

Wagner, Durrett, Ed.Cons.
HISTORICAL PICTURES SERVICE, INC. □ Chicago, IL

Wagner, Edward C., Libn.
NEW YORK STATE SUPREME COURT - 2ND JUDICIAL DISTRICT - LAW LIBRARY □ Staten Island, NY

Wagner, Ellen, Photograph Archv.
BOULDER HISTORICAL SOCIETY - PIONEER MUSEUM - LIBRARY □ Boulder, CO

Wagner, Erig, Ref.Asst.
UNIVERSITY OF HOUSTON - COLLEGE OF PHARMACY LIBRARY □ Houston, TX

Wagner, Frank, Info.Spec.
CELANESE CORPORATION - CELANESE CHEMICAL COMPANY, INC. - TECHNICAL CENTER - LIBRARY □ Corpus Christi, TX

Wagner, Ilene M., Tech.Libn.
U.S. NAVY - NAVAL SHIPYARD (Norfolk) - TECHNICAL LIBRARY □ Portsmouth, VA

Wagner, J.A., Reports Acq.Libn.
LOCKHEED MISSILES & SPACE COMPANY, INC. - TECHNICAL INFORMATION CENTER □ Palo Alto, CA

Wagner, Jane E., Hd.
PUBLIC LIBRARY OF CINCINNATI AND HAMILTON COUNTY - EDUCATION AND RELIGION DEPARTMENT □ Cincinnati, OH

Wagner, Jean C., Libn.
METROPOLITAN MUSEUM OF ART - ROBERT GOLDWATER LIBRARY OF PRIMITIVE ART □ New York, NY

Wagner, John, Ref. Staff
UNIVERSITY OF DENVER - COLLEGE OF LAW - WESTMINSTER LAW LIBRARY □ Denver, CO

Wagner, Judy, User Serv.
ERIC CLEARINGHOUSE ON ADULT, CAREER AND VOCATIONAL EDUCATION - NATL. CTR. FOR RESEARCH IN VOCATIONAL EDUC. □ Columbus, OH

Wagner, Louise, Libn.
ARTHUR ANDERSEN & CO. - LIBRARY† □ New York, NY

Wagner, Murray L., Hd.Libn.
BETHANY AND NORTHERN BAPTIST THEOLOGICAL SEMINARIES - LIBRARY □ Oak Brook, IL

Wagner, Priscilla, Libn.
THISTLETOWN REGIONAL CENTRE - LIBRARY □ Rexdale, ON

Wagner, Rod, Dp.Dir.
NEBRASKA STATE LIBRARY COMMISSION □ Lincoln, NE

Wagner, Thomas M., Principal Planner
GEORGIA STATE OFFICE OF PLANNING AND BUDGET - STATE DATA CENTER □ Atlanta, GA

Wagoner, George D., Dir.
SOUTHOLD HISTORICAL SOCIETY MUSEUM - LIBRARY □ Southold, NY

Wahrow, Lillian A., Med.Libn.
NEW YORK HOSPITAL - CORNELL MEDICAL CENTER, WESTCHESTER DIVISION - MEDICAL LIBRARY □ White Plains, NY

Waidelich, Ann, Libn.
MADISON PUBLIC LIBRARY - MUNICIPAL REFERENCE SERVICE □ Madison, WI

Wainwright, Alexander D., Cur. Parrish Coll.
PRINCETON UNIVERSITY - RARE BOOKS AND SPECIAL COLLECTIONS □ Princeton, NJ

Wainwright, Tom A., Libn.
AMERICAN CYANAMID COMPANY - LEDERLE LABORATORIES DIVISION - SUBBAROW MEMORIAL LIBRARY □ Pearl River, NY

Wait, Carol D., Ser.Libn.
CAPITAL DISTRICT LIBRARY COUNCIL FOR REFERENCE AND RESEARCH RESOURCES - BIBLIOGRAPHIC CENTER □ Latham, NY

Waitz, Janet L., Libn.
TOWNSEND-GREENSPAN & COMPANY, INC. - LIBRARY □ New York, NY

Wake, Malcolm J.H., Dir.
ROYAL CANADIAN MOUNTED POLICE - CENTENNIAL MUSEUM LIBRARY □ Regina, SK

Wakefield, Elizabeth, Dir.
ST. JOSEPH HOSPITAL - MEDICAL STAFF LIBRARY □ Lorain, OH

Wakefield, June C., Info.Ctr.Dir.
NORTHWESTERN MEDICAL CENTER - INFORMATION CENTER □ St. Albans, VT

Wakefield, Marie, Libn.
HARRIS-STOWE STATE COLLEGE LIBRARY □ St. Louis, MO

Wakiji, Eileen, Ref.Libn.
UNIVERSITY OF SOUTHERN CALIFORNIA - HEALTH SCIENCES CAMPUS - NORRIS MEDICAL LIBRARY □ Los Angeles, CA

Walag, Stanley J., Asst.Libn.
NEW YORK LAW INSTITUTE - LIBRARY □ New York, NY

Walburg, Charles H., Chf.
U.S. FISH & WILDLIFE SERVICE - EAST CENTRAL RESERVOIR INVESTIGATIONS LIBRARY □ Bowling Green, KY

Walch, Dr. David B., Dir.
CALIFORNIA POLYTECHNIC STATE UNIVERSITY - ROBERT E. KENNEDY LIBRARY □ San Luis Obispo, CA

Walcoff, Michael P., Mgr.
AMERICAN SOCIETY FOR NONDESTRUCTIVE TESTING - LIBRARY AND INFORMATION CENTER □ Columbus, OH

Walcott, Rosalind, ESS Libn.
SUNY AT STONY BROOK - EARTH AND SPACE SCIENCES LIBRARY □ Stony Brook, NY

Walczak, Jean A., Asst.Libn.
CONSUMERS POWER COMPANY - PARNALL TECHNICAL LIBRARY □ Jackson, MI

Waldecker, Doris, Libn.
ACACIA MUTUAL LIFE INSURANCE COMPANY - LIBRARY □ Washington, DC

Walden, Elaine B., Libn.
DALLAS TIMES-HERALD - LIBRARY □ Dallas, TX

Walden, Glenn, Hd.
LOUISIANA STATE UNIVERSITY - LISTENING ROOMS □ Baton Rouge, LA

Waldern, D.E., Dir.
CANADA - AGRICULTURE CANADA - RESEARCH STATION, LACOMBE - LIBRARY □ Lacombe, AB

Waldie, Mina, Supv.Libn.
WISCONSIN STATE LEGISLATIVE REFERENCE BUREAU □ Madison, WI

Waldman, Elizabeth, Asst., Issue Desk
ST. LOUIS MERCANTILE LIBRARY ASSOCIATION - LIBRARY □ St. Louis, MO

Waldner, J. Dudley, Exec.Sec.
COMICS MAGAZINE ASSOCIATION OF AMERICA, INC. - LIBRARY □ New York, NY

Waldow, Betty J., Exec.Dir.
MC CARTHY (Walter T.) LAW LIBRARY† □ Arlington, VA

Waldron, Esther, Hd., Cat.Dept.
UNIVERSITY OF PITTSBURGH - FALK LIBRARY OF THE HEALTH SCIENCES □ Pittsburgh, PA

Waldron, Rodney K., Dir. Of Libs.
OREGON STATE UNIVERSITY - WILLIAM JASPER KERR LIBRARY □ Corvallis, OR

Wales, Patricia L., Dir., Lib.Serv.
HOSPITAL OF ST. RAPHAEL - HEALTH SCIENCES LIBRARY □ New Haven, CT

Walia, Rajinder S., Law Libn.
NORTHEASTERN UNIVERSITY - LAW SCHOOL LIBRARY □ Boston, MA

Walker, Aaron, Patron Serv.
CHURCH OF JESUS CHRIST OF LATTER-DAY SAINTS - MT. WHITNEY BRANCH GENEALOGICAL LIBRARY† □ Inyokern, CA

Walker, Annalise, Canadian Arch.Archv.
UNIVERSITY OF CALGARY - ENVIRONMENT-SCIENCE-TECHNOLOGY LIBRARY □ Calgary, AB

Walker, Anne, Coll./Ref.Libn.
UNIVERSITY OF WESTERN ONTARIO - HEALTH SCIENCES LIBRARY □ London, ON

Walker, Bernice B., Med.Libn.
U.S. VETERANS ADMINISTRATION (VA-Richmond) - HOSPITAL LIBRARY □ Richmond, VA

Walker, Brian, Dir.
MUSEUM OF CARTOON ART - LIBRARY □ Port Chester, NY

Walker, Ms. C.E.J., Hd.Lib.Info.Serv.
CANADA - EMPLOYMENT & IMMIGRATION
CANADA - LIBRARY □ Ottawa, ON

Walker, Celine F., Chf., Sci.Dept.
STANFORD UNIVERSITY - ENGINEERING
LIBRARY □ Stanford, CA

Walker, Charlotte, Asst.Libn.
WILMINGTON NEWS-JOURNAL COMPANY -
LIBRARY □ Wilmington, DE

Walker, Connie C., Cat./Ref.
U.S. NAVY - NAVAL AIR STATION (Pensacola) -
LIBRARY □ Pensacola, FL

Walker, Constance, Libn.
ST. MARY'S SEMINARY - CARDINAL BERAN
LIBRARY □ Houston, TX

Walker, Cynthia, Rec.Techn.
COX (Lester E.) MEDICAL CENTER - DOCTORS'
LIBRARY □ Springfield, MO

Walker, Diane E., Info.Ctr.Coord.
LOCKWOOD, ANDREWS & NEWNAM, INC. -
INFORMATION CENTER □ Houston, TX

Walker, Diane Parr, Music Cat./Ref.Libn.
SUNY AT BUFFALO - MUSIC LIBRARY □ Buffalo,
NY

Walker, Elaine, Circ.Libn.
SCHOOL OF THEOLOGY AT CLAREMONT -
THEOLOGY LIBRARY □ Claremont, CA

Walker, Elizabeth, Libn.
CURTIS INSTITUTE OF MUSIC - LIBRARY □
Philadelphia, PA

Walker, Eunice, Cat.Libn.
FASHION INSTITUTE OF TECHNOLOGY -
LIBRARY/MEDIA SERVICES □ New York, NY

Walker, F. Rebecca, Libn.
RICHMOND PUBLIC LIBRARY - BUSINESS,
SCIENCE & TECHNOLOGY DEPARTMENT† □
Richmond, VA

Walker, Gay, Cur.
YALE UNIVERSITY - ARTS OF THE BOOK
COLLECTION □ New Haven, CT

Walker, Gina R., Act.Archv.
INDIANA STATE UNIVERSITY, EVANSVILLE -
SPECIAL COLLECTIONS AND UNIVERSITY
ARCHIVES □ Evansville, IN

Walker, Henry, Gen. Counsel
TENNESSEE STATE PUBLIC SERVICE
COMMISSION - LEGAL DEPARTMENT - LIBRARY
□ Nashville, TN

Walker, John, Dir.
EAST CENTRAL OKLAHOMA STATE UNIVERSITY
- OKLAHOMA ENVIRONMENTAL
INFORMATION/MEDIA CENTER □ Ada, OK

Walker, Laura, Libn.
BROOKINGS INSTITUTION - LIBRARY □
Washington, DC

Walker, Lloanne, Libn.
ALBERTA ASSOCIATION OF REGISTERED
NURSES - LIBRARY □ Edmonton, AB

Walker, Luise E., Hd.Libn.
UNIVERSITY OF OREGON - SCIENCE BRANCH
LIBRARY □ Eugene, OR

Walker, Margaret B., Libn.
EL PASO COUNTY LAW LIBRARY □ Colorado
Springs, CO

Walker, Mary Edith, Med.Libn.
ST. JUDE CHILDREN'S RESEARCH HOSPITAL -
RESEARCH LIBRARY □ Memphis, TN

Walker, Mary Jo, Spec.Coll.
EASTERN NEW MEXICO UNIVERSITY - GOLDEN
LIBRARY □ Portales, NM

Walker, Mary M., Libn.
NEW ENGLAND WILD FLOWER SOCIETY, INC. -
LIBRARY □ Framingham, MA

Walker, Michael C., Sci./Ref.Libn.
ALABAMA A & M UNIVERSITY - JOSEPH F.
DRAKE MEMORIAL LEARNING RESOURCES
CENTER □ Normal, AL

Walker, Orrin M., Law Libn.
UNIVERSITY OF ALABAMA - SCHOOL OF LAW
LIBRARY □ University, AL

Walker, Paul A., Dir.
JANUS INFORMATION FACILITY □ San
Francisco, CA

Walker, R.G., Archv.
ANGLICAN CHURCH OF CANADA - PROVINCIAL
SYNOD OF BRITISH COLUMBIA AND THE YUKON
- ARCHIVES □ Vancouver, BC

Walker, Renee, Libn.
FIDELITY MUTUAL LIFE INSURANCE COMPANY
- LIBRARY ARCHIVES □ Philadelphia, PA

Walker, Stephen, Cat.Libn.
CENTRAL MISSOURI STATE UNIVERSITY -
WARD EDWARDS LIBRARY □ Warrensburg, MO

Walker, Theresa, Circ.Mgr.
CATHOLIC THEOLOGICAL UNION - LIBRARY □
Chicago, IL

Walker, William B., Chf.Libn.
METROPOLITAN MUSEUM OF ART - THOMAS J.
WATSON LIBRARY □ New York, NY

Walker, William D., Dir.
MEDICAL LIBRARY CENTER OF NEW YORK □
New York, NY

Walker-Atchison, Susan, Cur.
ART MUSEUM OF SOUTH TEXAS - LIBRARY □
Corpus Christi, TX

Walkup, Betsy, Assoc.Libn.
GEORGETOWN UNIVERSITY - KENNEDY
INSTITUTE OF ETHICS - CENTER FOR
BIOETHICS LIBRARY □ Washington, DC

Wall, C. Edward, Hd.Libn.
UNIVERSITY OF MICHIGAN - DEARBORN
LIBRARY □ Dearborn, MI

Wall, Colleen
3M - 201 TECHNICAL LIBRARY □ St. Paul, MN

Wall, Constance B., Cat.
DETROIT INSTITUTE OF ARTS - RESEARCH
LIBRARY □ Detroit, MI

Wall, Patricia, Acq.Libn.
UNIVERSITY OF NORTH CAROLINA, CHAPEL
HILL - LAW LIBRARY □ Chapel Hill, NC

Wall, Dr. Paul L., Dir.
TUSKEGEE INSTITUTE - DIVISION OF
BEHAVIORAL SCIENCE RESEARCH - SCIENCE
INFORMATION CENTER □ Tuskegee Institute,
AL

Wall, Philippa, Hd.
CANADA - IMMIGRATION APPEAL BOARD -
LIBRARY □ Ottawa, ON

Wallace, Atarrha, Hd.Tech.Serv.
MANITOBA - DEPARTMENT OF EDUCATION -
LIBRARY □ Winnipeg, MB

Wallace, Bernice, Libn.
MICHIGAN STATE UNIVERSITY - CHEMISTRY
LIBRARY □ East Lansing, MI

Wallace, Bruce, Multi-State Libn.
UTAH STATE LIBRARY - BLIND AND
PHYSICALLY HANDICAPPED PROGRAM -
REGIONAL LIBRARY □ Salt Lake City, UT

Wallace, Carolyn A., Dir./Cur.
UNIVERSITY OF NORTH CAROLINA, CHAPEL
HILL - SOUTHERN HISTORICAL COLLECTION &
MANUSCRIPTS DEPARTMENT □ Chapel Hill, NC

Wallace, Dee, Libn.
UNIVERSITY OF ILLINOIS - RICKER LIBRARY
OF ARCHITECTURE AND ART □ Urbana, IL

Wallace, Diane, Asst.Libn.
BROCKTON HOSPITAL - LIBRARY □ Brockton,
MA

Wallace, Mrs. I.W., Libn.
MONCTON HOSPITAL - HEALTH SCIENCES
LIBRARY □ Moncton, NB

Wallace, Ian, Libn.
CANADA - AGRICULTURE CANADA - RESEARCH
STATION, ST-JEAN - LIBRARY □ St. Jean-Sur-
Richelieu, PQ

Wallace, James O., Dir.
SAN ANTONIO COLLEGE - SPECIAL
COLLECTIONS □ San Antonio, TX

Wallace, Katharine, Libn.
U.S. NAVY - NAVAL OCEANOGRAPHIC OFFICE -
NAVY LIBRARY □ Bay St. Louis, MS

Wallace, Lorraine, Engr.Libn.
AVCO CORPORATION - LYCOMING DIVISION -
LIBRARY & INFORMATION CENTER □ Stratford,
CT

Wallace, Marie, Law Libn.
KINDEL & ANDERSON - LIBRARY □ Los Angeles,
CA

Wallace, Marla, Lib.Techn.
U.S. GEOLOGICAL SURVEY - WATER
RESOURCES DIVISION - LIBRARY □ Madison,
WI

Wallace, Marlene B., Archv. & Ed.
VERMONT STATE OFFICE OF THE SECRETARY
OF STATE - ARCHIVES AND STATE PAPERS
DIVISION □ Montpelier, VT

Wallace, Nancy, Lib.Cons. Young Adult
NORTH CAROLINA STATE DEPARTMENT OF
CULTURAL RESOURCES - DIVISION OF THE
STATE LIBRARY □ Raleigh, NC

Wallace, R. Stuart, Mss.Libn.
NEW HAMPSHIRE HISTORICAL SOCIETY -
LIBRARY □ Concord, NH

Wallace, Richard E., Mgr.Info.Serv.
ARCHER DANIELS MIDLAND COMPANY -
RESEARCH LIBRARY □ Decatur, IL

Wallace, Robert B., Libn.
DADE COUNTY LAW LIBRARY □ Miami, FL

Wallace, Tish, Libn.
FARMERS INSURANCE GROUP - LIBRARY □ Los
Angeles, CA

Wallach, Judy L., Asst.Libn.
NEW YORK LIFE INSURANCE COMPANY - NEW
YORK LIFE LIBRARY □ New York, NY

Walle, Dennis, Archv./Mss.Cur.
UNIVERSITY OF ALASKA, ANCHORAGE -
LIBRARY □ Anchorage, AK

Wallen, Regina T., Hd., Tech.Serv.
UNIVERSITY OF SANTA CLARA - EDWIN A.
HEAFEY LAW LIBRARY □ Santa Clara, CA

Wallen, Robert, Naturalist
WISCONSIN STATE DEPARTMENT OF NATURAL
RESOURCES - MAC KENZIE ENVIRONMENTAL
EDUCATION CENTER □ Poynette, WI

Waller, A.N.
SPOTSYLVANIA HISTORICAL ASSOCIATION,
INC. - RESEARCH MUSEUM AND LIBRARY □
Spotsylvania, VA

Waller, Carolyn A., Libn.
BRADLEY (Emma Pendleton) HOSPITAL - AUSTIN
T. AND JUNE ROCKWELL LEVY LIBRARY □
Riverside, RI

Waller, Elaine, Supv.Mus.Mtls.Ctr.
ANDREWS UNIVERSITY - JAMES WHITE
LIBRARY □ Berrien Springs, MI

Waller, Frances L.N., Libn.
SPOTSYLVANIA HISTORICAL ASSOCIATION,
INC. - RESEARCH MUSEUM AND LIBRARY □
Spotsylvania, VA

Waller, Georgeann, Assoc.Libn.
MARYLAND STATE DEPARTMENT OF
LEGISLATIVE REFERENCE - LIBRARY □
Annapolis, MD

Waller, Robert, Supv.Res.Spec.
U.S. DEFENSE AUDIOVISUAL AGENCY -
ARLINGTON STILL PHOTO DEPOSITORY □
Arlington, VA

Wallgren, Rex, Radio Prog.Mgr.
UTAH STATE LIBRARY - BLIND AND
PHYSICALLY HANDICAPPED PROGRAM -
REGIONAL LIBRARY □ Salt Lake City, UT

Wallin, Janet L., Law Libn.
UNIVERSITY OF TOLEDO - COLLEGE OF LAW
LIBRARY† □ Toledo, OH

Wallin, Karen, Mgr./Volunteer Serv.
SEATTLE PUBLIC LIBRARY - WASHINGTON
REGIONAL LIBRARY FOR THE BLIND AND
PHYSICALLY HANDICAPPED □ Seattle, WA

Wallin, Ragnhild, Libn.
SWEDISH CONSULATE GENERAL - SWEDISH
INFORMATION SERVICE □ New York, NY

Wallin, W.D., Dir., Finance
SOURIS VALLEY EXTENDED CARE HOSPITAL -
LIBRARY □ Weyburn, SK

Walls, Mrs. B., Lib.Asst.
QUEEN'S UNIVERSITY AT KINGSTON - DUPUIS
HALL LIBRARY □ Kingston, ON

PERSONNEL

Walls, Edwina, Hist. of Med.Libn.
UNIVERSITY OF ARKANSAS MEDICAL
SCIENCES CAMPUS - MEDICAL SCIENCES
LIBRARY □ Little Rock, AR

Walls, Nina, Cat.
BALCH INSTITUTE FOR ETHNIC STUDIES -
LIBRARY □ Philadelphia, PA

Wally, Margarette, Libn.
ST. LUKE'S HOSPITAL - MEDICAL LIBRARY† □
Jacksonville, FL

Walsh, Anne P., Asst.Libn.
WORCESTER ART MUSEUM - LIBRARY □
Worcester, MA

Walsh, Catherine, Supv.
GENERAL ELECTRIC COMPANY - AIRCRAFT
EQUIPMENT DIVISION - INFORMATION
RESOURCES □ Utica, NY

Walsh, Donald A., Gen.Counsel
NEW YORK STATE CONFERENCE OF MAYORS
AND MUNICIPAL OFFICIALS - LIBRARY □
Albany, NY

Walsh, Frank E., Dir.
CHARLTON PARK VILLAGE AND MUSEUM -
LIBRARY □ Hastings, MI

Walsh, Mrs. Frederick R., Dir.
RENSSELAER COUNTY HISTORICAL SOCIETY -
LIBRARY □ Troy, NY

Walsh, Gretchen, Hd.
BOSTON UNIVERSITY - AFRICAN STUDIES
LIBRARY □ Boston, MA

Walsh, Helen, Ldr., Res. Group
UNION CARBIDE CORPORATION - LINDE
DIVISION - COMMUNICATIONS LIBRARY □ New
York, NY

Walsh, James E., Kpr., Printed Bks.
HARVARD UNIVERSITY - HOUGHTON LIBRARY
□ Cambridge, MA

Walsh, Joseph E., Bus.Br.Libn.
BOSTON PUBLIC LIBRARY - KIRSTEIN
BUSINESS BRANCH □ Boston, MA

Walsh, K.L., Chm., Lib.Comm.
ALBERTA MENTAL HEALTH SERVICES -
LIBRARY □ Calgary, AB

Walsh, Karen, Ref.Libn.
BATTEN, BARTON, DURSTINE, OSBORN, INC. -
INFORMATION RETRIEVAL CENTER □ New
York, NY

Walsh, Kathleen E., Libn.
WANDERER PRESS - LIBRARY □ St. Paul, MN

Walsh, Lea, ILL Libn.
SOUTH CAROLINA STATE LIBRARY □ Columbia,
SC

Walsh, Mary, Chf.Libn.
SUN LIFE ASSURANCE COMPANY OF CANADA -
REFERENCE LIBRARY □ Toronto, ON

Walsh, Sandra, Ref.Libn.
ONTARIO - MINISTRY OF TREASURY AND
ECONOMICS - LIBRARY SERVICES BRANCH □
Toronto, ON

Walsh, Sylvia, Libn.
RUTGERS UNIVERSITY, THE STATE
UNIVERSITY OF NEW JERSEY -
MATHEMATICAL SCIENCES LIBRARY □
Piscataway, NJ

Walsh, Wanda T., Libn.
CARLETON COUNTY LAW LIBRARY □ Ottawa,
ON

Walshe, Margaret, Hd.
METROPOLITAN TORONTO LIBRARY - SCIENCE
& TECHNOLOGY DEPARTMENT □ Toronto, ON

Walstad, Ken, Mng.Dir.
INTERNATIONAL FESTIVALS ASSOCIATION -
LIBRARY □ Minneapolis, MN

Walstrom, Jon, Map Libn.
MINNESOTA HISTORICAL SOCIETY - SPECIAL
LIBRARIES □ St. Paul, MN

Walt, Anne, Circ./Biblog./Coord.
KEARNEY STATE COLLEGE - CALVIN T. RYAN
LIBRARY □ Kearney, NE

Walter, Dave, Ref.Libn.
MONTANA HISTORICAL SOCIETY - LIBRARY/
ARCHIVES □ Helena, MT

Walter, Gary D., Libn.
U.S. ARMY - DEFENSE LANGUAGE INSTITUTE -
ACADEMIC LIBRARY □ Monterey, CA

Walter, Georgia, Dir. of Lib.
KIRKSVILLE COLLEGE OF OSTEOPATHIC
MEDICINE - A.T. STILL MEMORIAL LIBRARY □
Kirksville, MO

Walter, Lily, Libn.
WASCANA HOSPITAL - HEALTH SCIENCES
LIBRARY □ Regina, SK

Walter, Pat L., Asst.Dir., Info.Serv.
UNIVERSITY OF CALIFORNIA, LOS ANGELES -
BRAIN INFORMATION SERVICE □ Los Angeles,
CA

Walter, Ruth, Ref.Libn.
EAST TENNESSEE STATE UNIVERSITY,
QUILLEN-DISHNER COLLEGE OF MEDICINE -
DEPT. OF LEARNING RSRCS. - MEDICAL
LIBRARY □ Johnson City, TN

Walter, Dr. Stephen B., Dir., L.R.C.
TRI-COUNTY TECHNICAL COLLEGE - LIBRARY □
Pendleton, SC

Walters, Bernard G., Pres.
INTERNATIONAL ROCK AND ROLL MUSIC
ASSOCIATION, INC. - LIBRARY □ Nashville, TN

Walters, Clarence R., State Libn.
CONNECTICUT STATE LIBRARY □ Hartford, CT

Walters, Corky, Chf., Coll.Dev.
WYOMING STATE LIBRARY □ Cheyenne, WY

Walters, Donna, Libn.
BAYVET - LIBRARY □ Shawnee, KS

Walters, Eartha, Asst.Libn.
ALLIS-CHALMERS CORPORATION - ADVANCED
TECHNOLOGY CENTER - LIBRARY □ Milwaukee,
WI

Walters, Elizabeth C., Libn.
SANTA CLARA COUNTY HEALTH DEPARTMENT -
LIBRARY □ San Jose, CA

Walters, Heather, Hd., Ser.Dept.
POLYTECHNIC INSTITUTE OF NEW YORK -
SPICER LIBRARY □ Brooklyn, NY

Walters, Mary L., Hd.Libn. & Asst.Prof.
LANCASTER BIBLE COLLEGE - STOLL
MEMORIAL LIBRARY □ Lancaster, PA

Walters, Raquel A., Chf., Lib.Serv.
U.S. VETERANS ADMINISTRATION (PR-San
Juan) - HOSPITAL LIBRARY □ Rio Piedras, PR

Walters, Roberta A., Tech.Serv.Libn.
ALAMEDA COUNTY LAW LIBRARY □ Oakland, CA

Walters, Sara Jane, Exhibits Dir.
BOULDER HISTORICAL SOCIETY - PIONEER
MUSEUM - LIBRARY □ Boulder, CO

Waltner, Nell L., Hd., Acq.Dept.
NORTH CAROLINA STATE UNIVERSITY - D.H.
HILL LIBRARY □ Raleigh, NC

Walton, Mrs. Artence, Tech.Dir.
MONARCH MARKING SYSTEMS - TECHNICAL
LIBRARY □ Miamisburg, OH

Walton, Cinda, Dir. of Med.Rec.
BIXBY (Emma L.) HOSPITAL - PATMOS
MEMORIAL LIBRARY □ Adrian, MI

Walton, Darrel, Exec.Dir.
AMERICAN LUNG ASSOCIATION OF KANSAS -
INFORMATION CENTER □ Topeka, KS

Walton, Helyn M., Tech.Libn.
U.S. DEPT. OF ENERGY - KNOLLS ATOMIC
POWER LABORATORY - LIBRARIES □
Schenectady, NY

Walton, Jan, Libn.
ST. JOHN'S HOSPITAL - FREDERICK J. PLONDKE
MEDICAL LIBRARY □ St. Paul, MN

Walton, Laurence R., Corp.Libn.
PET, INC. - CORPORATE INFORMATION
CENTER □ St. Louis, MO

Walton, Linda, Ref.Libn.
INDIANA STATE LIBRARY - INDIANA DIVISION
□ Indianapolis, IN

Walton, Lonita M., Dept.Hd.
SEATTLE PUBLIC LIBRARY - EDUCATION,
PSYCHOLOGY, SOCIOLOGY, SPORTS
DEPARTMENT □ Seattle, WA

Walton, Lynette, Archv.
GLENBOW-ALBERTA INSTITUTE - LIBRARY &
ARCHIVES □ Calgary, AB

Walton, Nancy Kay, Info./Rec.Ctr.Mgr.
AMERICAN MICROSYSTEMS, INC. -
INFORMATION CENTER □ Santa Clara, CA

Walton, Peggy, Independent Study Area
UNIVERSITY OF TENNESSEE - CENTER FOR
THE HEALTH SCIENCES LIBRARY □ Memphis, TN

Waltz, Mary Anne, Geog. & Map Biblog.
SYRACUSE UNIVERSITY - E.S. BIRD LIBRARY -
AREA STUDIES DEPARTMENT □ Syracuse, NY

Waluzyniec, H., Cat. & Proc.Libn.
MC GILL UNIVERSITY - MEDICAL LIBRARY □
Montreal, PQ

Wamsley, Mrs. Charles, Asst. to Hd.
ST. MARY COLLEGE - LIBRARY - SPECIAL
COLLECTIONS □ Leavenworth, KS

Wan, Weiying, Hd.
UNIVERSITY OF MICHIGAN - ASIA LIBRARY □
Ann Arbor, MI

Wanat, Camille, Hd.
UNIVERSITY OF CALIFORNIA, BERKELEY -
PHYSICS LIBRARY □ Berkeley, CA

Wandersee, Mary J., Libn.
MAINE STATE DEPARTMENT OF HUMAN
SERVICES - DEPARTMENTAL LIBRARY □
Augusta, ME

Wang, A., Tech. Reports Supv.
BELL TELEPHONE LABORATORIES, INC. -
LIBRARIES AND INFORMATION SYSTEMS
CENTER □ Murray Hill, NJ

Wang, Amy L., Libn.
JOHN HANCOCK MUTUAL LIFE INSURANCE
COMPANY - COMPANY LIBRARY □ Boston, MA

Wang, Anna K., Asst.Libn./Cat.
STRONG (Margaret Woodbury) MUSEUM -
LIBRARY □ Rochester, NY

Wang, Bonnie, Dir., Info.Serv.
BANK MARKETING ASSOCIATION -
INFORMATION CENTER □ Chicago, IL

Wang, Catherine, Libn.
STANLEY ASSOCIATES ENGINEERING, LTD. -
LIBRARY □ Edmonton, AB

Wang, Chi, Hd., Chinese/Korean Sect.
LIBRARY OF CONGRESS - ASIAN DIVISION □
Washington, DC

Wang, Chih, Libn.
ATLANTA UNIVERSITY - SCHOOL OF LIBRARY &
INFORMATION STUDIES - LIBRARY □ Atlanta,
GA

Wang, Doris, Libn.
AIRCO, INC. - CENTRAL RESEARCH
LABORATORIES - INFORMATION CENTER □
Murray Hill, NJ

Wang, Eunice, Cat.
ST. ANSELM'S COLLEGE - GEISEL LIBRARY □
Manchester, NH

Wang, Helen, Asst.Cat.
MARSHALL (John) LAW SCHOOL - LIBRARY □
Chicago, IL

Wang, Henry, Gov.Doc.Libn.
STANFORD UNIVERSITY - J. HUGH JACKSON
LIBRARY □ Stanford, CA

Wang, Jo S., Chf.Cat.
HARVARD UNIVERSITY - SCHOOLS OF
MEDICINE, DENTAL MEDICINE AND PUBLIC
HEALTH - FRANCIS A. COUNTWAY LIBRARY □
Boston, MA

Wang, Peter, Cat.
MORTON ARBORETUM - STERLING MORTON
LIBRARY □ Lisle, IL

Wang, Richard, Hd.
UNIVERSITY OF MINNESOTA - EAST ASIAN
LIBRARY □ Minneapolis, MN

Wang, Shu-Sheng, Chinese/Japanese Cat.
PRINCETON UNIVERSITY - GEST ORIENTAL
LIBRARY AND EAST ASIAN COLLECTIONS □
Princeton, NJ

Wangerin, Mark, Coord., Pub.Serv.
CONCORDIA SEMINARY - LIBRARY □ St. Louis,
MO

Wanio, Tanya, Info.Coord.
INTERGOVERNMENTAL COMMITTEE ON URBAN
& REGIONAL RESEARCH (ICURR) □ Toronto, ON

Wank, Paul
LOUISIANA STATE UNIVERSITY - REFERENCE
SERVICES □ Baton Rouge, LA

Wannarka, Marjorie, Dir.
CREIGHTON UNIVERSITY - HEALTH SCIENCES
LIBRARY □ Omaha, NE

Wannemacher, Jacqueline M., Mgr.
GENERAL ELECTRIC COMPANY - AIRCRAFT
ENGINE GROUP - DR. C.W. SMITH TECHNICAL
INFORMATION CENTER □ Lynn, MA

Wannemacher, Maxyne M., Law Libn.
RIVERSIDE COUNTY LAW LIBRARY □ Riverside,
CA

Wanner, Judith, Libn.
ONTARIO - MINISTRY OF AGRICULTURE AND
FOOD - HORTICULTURAL RESEARCH
INSTITUTE OF ONTARIO - LIBRARY □ Vineland
Station, ON

Want, Bob, Ref.Libn.
SOUTHERN METHODIST UNIVERSITY -
SCIENCE/ENGINEERING LIBRARY □ Dallas, TX

Waranius, Frances B., Lib./Info.Ctr.Mgr.
LUNAR AND PLANETARY INSTITUTE -
LIBRARY/INFORMATION CENTER □ Houston,
TX

Ward, Audrey, Leg.Ref.Spec.
NATIONAL ACADEMY OF SCIENCES -
NATIONAL ACADEMY OF ENGINEERING -
LIBRARY □ Washington, DC

Ward, Cheryl, Sys.Libn.
CAROLINA POPULATION CENTER - LIBRARY □
Chapel Hill, NC

Ward, Christine, Mss.Libn.
ALBANY INSTITUTE OF HISTORY AND ART -
MC KINNEY LIBRARY □ Albany, NY

Ward, Dederick C., Libn.
UNIVERSITY OF ILLINOIS - GEOLOGY LIBRARY
□ Urbana, IL

Ward, Diane, Pub.Serv.Libn.
UNIVERSITY OF BALTIMORE - LAW LIBRARY □
Baltimore, MD

Ward, Dorothy I., Ser.Libn.
U.S. ARMY - MISSILE COMMAND & MARSHALL
SPACE FLIGHT CENTER - REDSTONE
SCIENTIFIC INFORMATION CENTER □
Redstone Arsenal, AL

Ward, Edith, TNC Affairs Off.
UNITED NATIONS - CENTRE ON
TRANSNATIONAL CORPORATIONS - LIBRARY □
New York, NY

Ward, Eileen, Res.Spec.
HONEYWELL, INC. - HONEYWELL
INFORMATION SYSTEMS - INFORMATION AND
LIBRARY SERVICES □ Waltham, MA

Ward, Ella C., Cat.
ARKANSAS STATE UNIVERSITY - DEAN B. ELLIS
LIBRARY □ State University, AR

Ward, Jane, Libn.
THOMPSON & KNIGHT - LIBRARY □ Dallas, TX

Ward, Janet, Ref.Libn.
UNIVERSITY OF SOUTHERN CALIFORNIA -
HEALTH SCIENCES CAMPUS - NORRIS MEDICAL
LIBRARY □ Los Angeles, CA

Ward, Joyce, Libn.
TRUDEAU INSTITUTE IMMUNOBIOLOGICAL
RESEARCH LABORATORIES - LIBRARY □
Saranac Lake, NY

Ward, Loraine, Med.Libn.
U.S. AIR FORCE HOSPITAL - MEDICAL LIBRARY
(TX-Carswell AFB)† □ Carswell AFB, TX

Ward, Margaret, Fld.Archv.
DETROIT PUBLIC LIBRARY - BURTON
HISTORICAL COLLECTION □ Detroit, MI

Ward, Margery, Pubn.
UNIVERSITY OF UTAH - SPECIAL COLLECTIONS
DEPARTMENT □ Salt Lake City, UT

Ward, Marietta M., Libn.
UNIVERSITY OF WASHINGTON - ART LIBRARY
□ Seattle, WA

Ward, Nancy E., Libn.
LAFAYETTE CLINIC - LIBRARY □ Detroit, MI

Ward, Ruth M., Archv.
ARLINGTON HISTORICAL SOCIETY - ARCHIVES
□ Arlington, VA

Ward, Vera, Off.Libn.
KEARNEY (A.T.), INC. - INFORMATION CENTER
□ Chicago, IL

Ward, Victoria M., Law Libn.
MORGAN, LEWIS & BOCKIUS - LIBRARY □
Washington, DC

Ward, William D., Coord.
UNIVERSITY OF OTTAWA - INSTITUTE FOR
INTERNATIONAL COOPERATION -
DOCUMENTATION CENTRE □ Ottawa, ON

Warden, Carolyn, Libn.-Search & Ret.
GENERAL ELECTRIC COMPANY - CORPORATE
RESEARCH & DEVELOPMENT - WHITNEY
LIBRARY □ Schenectady, NY

Warden, Joan, Libn.
GREAT LAKES RESEARCH CORPORATION -
RESEARCH LIBRARY □ Elizabethton, TN

Wardlaw, Janet, Ser.
UNIVERSITY OF CINCINNATI - ROBERT S.
MARX LAW LIBRARY □ Cincinnati, OH

Wardrop, A.E.
3M - ENGINEERING INFORMATION SERVICES □
St. Paul, MN

Wardrop, Elaine L., Libn.
3M - 236 LIBRARY □ St. Paul, MN

Wardwell, Johnina, Libn.
WESLEY UNITED METHODIST CHURCH -
LIBRARY □ La Crosse, WI

Ware, Evelyn, Info.Anl.
ALLERGAN PHARMACEUTICALS, INC. -
PROFESSIONAL INFORMATION SERVICES □
Irvine, CA

Ware, Jennifer, Libn.
OREGON CENTER FOR GERONTOLOGY AT THE
UNIVERSITY OF OREGON - RESOURCE CENTER
□ Eugene, OR

Ware, Malcolm S., Sr.Libn.
GULF COAST RESEARCH LABORATORY -
GORDON GUNTER LIBRARY □ Ocean Springs, MS

Ware, Sharon
U.S. COURT OF APPEALS, 10TH CIRCUIT -
OKLAHOMA CITY GENERAL LIBRARY □
Oklahoma City, OK

Waren, Doris Jean, Libn.
KEENELAND ASSOCIATION - LIBRARY □
Lexington, KY

Wargo, Lucy, Med.Libn.
CHILDREN'S HOSPITAL OF BUFFALO - MEDICAL
LIBRARY □ Buffalo, NY

Warkentin, Katherine, Doc.Libn.
SHIPPENSBURG STATE COLLEGE - EZRA
LEHMAN MEMORIAL LIBRARY □ Shippensburg,
PA

Warlick, Mary, Libn.
METROPOLITAN MUSEUM OF ART -
PHOTOGRAPH AND SLIDE LIBRARY □ New York,
NY

Warlick, Rebecca
TEXAS MEDICAL ASSOCIATION - MEMORIAL
LIBRARY □ Austin, TX

Warmack, Geraldine, Libn.
WILL ROGERS LIBRARY □ Claremore, OK

Warman, James C., Dir.
AUBURN UNIVERSITY - WATER RESOURCES
RESEARCH INSTITUTE - INFORMATION
CENTER □ Auburn, AL

Warmann, Carolyn, Asst.Libn.
OKLAHOMA STATE UNIVERSITY - BIOLOGICAL
SCIENCES DIVISION □ Stillwater, OK

Warne, Jeri, PROBE Libn.
INDIANA UNIVERSITY - EDUCATION LIBRARY □
Bloomington, IN

Warnement, Judith, Regional Lib.Coord.
NORTHEASTERN OHIO UNIVERSITIES COLLEGE
OF MEDICINE - BASIC MEDICAL SCIENCES
LIBRARY □ Rootstown, OH

Warner, Betty, Acq.Libn.
UNIVERSITY OF PUGET SOUND - SCHOOL OF
LAW LIBRARY □ Tacoma, WA

Warner, Bruno, Libn.
SACRED HEART HOSPITAL - MEDICAL LIBRARY
□ Eau Claire, WI

Warner, Carol, Per./Doc.Libn.
WEST VIRGINIA STATE DEPARTMENT OF
CULTURE AND HISTORY - ARCHIVES AND
HISTORY LIBRARY □ Charleston, WV

Warner, Claudette S., Libn.
BANK ADMINISTRATION INSTITUTE -
INFORMATION CENTER □ Park Ridge, IL

Warner, David, Leg.Libn.
MARYLAND STATE DEPARTMENT OF
LEGISLATIVE REFERENCE - LIBRARY □
Annapolis, MD

Warner, Debra, Staff Libn./Ref.Serv
CENTRAL MAINE MEDICAL CENTER - GERRISH-
TRUE HEALTH SCIENCE LIBRARY □ Lewiston,
ME

Warner, Elizabeth R., Med.Libn.
CROZER CHESTER MEDICAL CENTER -
MEDICAL LIBRARY □ Chester, PA

Warner, F. Eleanor, Hd.Libn.
NEW ENGLAND COLLEGE OF OPTOMETRY -
LIBRARY □ Boston, MA

Warner, Heidi L., Cur.
MC HENRY MUSEUM - LIBRARY □ Modesto, CA

Warner, Helen J., Libn.
BETHESDA MEMORIAL HOSPITAL - MEDICAL
LIBRARY □ Boynton Beach, FL

Warner, Jan, Dir.
WEYERHAEUSER (Charles A.) MEMORIAL
MUSEUM - LIBRARY □ Little Falls, MN

Warner, Kathleen, Libn. I
MTS SYSTEMS CORPORATION - INFORMATION
SERVICES □ Eden Prairie, MN

Warner, Dr. Robert M., U.S.Archv.
U.S. NATL. ARCHIVES & RECORDS SERVICE -
NATL. ARCHIVES □ Washington, DC

Warner, Rosabelle, Circ.Libn.
WESTERN CONNECTICUT STATE COLLEGE -
RUTH A. HAAS LIBRARY □ Danbury, CT

Warner, Sarah L., Libn.
PARSONS, BRINCKERHOFF, QUADE & DOUGLAS
- LIBRARY □ New York, NY

Warner, W.C., Hd./Info.Ctr.
GENERAL TIRE AND RUBBER COMPANY -
RESEARCH DIVISION INFORMATION CENTER □
Akron, OH

Warnke, Nancy, Libn.
U.S. DISTRICT COURT - NORTHERN
CALIFORNIA DISTRICT - LOUIS E. GOODMAN
MEMORIAL LIBRARY □ San Francisco, CA

Warnken, Wendy, Assoc.Cur.
MUSEUM OF THE CITY OF NEW YORK -
THEATRE COLLECTION □ New York, NY

Warnow, Joan, Assoc.Dir.
AMERICAN INSTITUTE OF PHYSICS - CENTER
FOR HISTORY OF PHYSICS - NIELS BOHR
LIBRARY □ New York, NY

Waron, Olga, Assoc. Examiner
NEW YORK STATE DEPARTMENT OF LABOR -
WORKERS' COMPENSATION BOARD - LIBRARY
□ New York, NY

Warpeha, Rita C., Chf.Libn.
ACTION - LIBRARY □ Washington, DC

Warren, Bee, Libn.
DE CORDOVA MUSEUM - LIBRARY □ Lincoln, MA

Warren, Bonnie J., Asst.Libn.
MARION COUNTY LAW LIBRARY □ Indianapolis,
IN

Warren, Brenda G., Dir. of Lib.
CRISWELL CENTER FOR BIBLICAL STUDIES -
LIBRARY □ Dallas, TX

Warren, Carol A., Jr.Res.Assoc.
UNIVERSITY OF CINCINNATI - DEPARTMENT
OF ENVIRONMENTAL HEALTH LIBRARY □
Cincinnati, OH

PERSONNEL

Warren, Dave, Pict.Ed.
U.S. DEPT. OF AGRICULTURE - PHOTOGRAPHY DIVISION - PHOTOGRAPH LIBRARY □ Washington, DC

Warren, Dorothea, Ref.Libn.
WASHBURN UNIVERSITY OF TOPEKA - SCHOOL OF LAW LIBRARY □ Topeka, KS

Warren, E. Louise, Asst.Libn.Tech.Serv.
EMORY UNIVERSITY - SCHOOL OF MEDICINE - A.W. CALHOUN MEDICAL LIBRARY □ Atlanta, GA

Warren, Frank, Dir.
NATIONAL SOCIETY FOR AUTISTIC CHILDREN - INFORMATION & REFERRAL SERVICE □ Washington, DC

Warren, Dr. G. Garry, Dir.Lrng.Rsrcs.
HENDERSON STATE UNIVERSITY - HUIE LIBRARY □ Arkadelphia, AR

Warren, Gale, Res.
DISNEY (Walt) PRODUCTIONS - LIBRARY □ Burbank, CA

Warren, George E., State Archv.
COLORADO STATE DIVISION OF STATE ARCHIVES AND PUBLIC RECORDS □ Denver, CO

Warren, Henry C., Chf.Pk. Naturalist
U.S. NATL. PARK SERVICE - OLYMPIC NATL. PARK - PIONEER MEMORIAL MUSEUM - LIBRARY □ Port Angeles, WA

Warren, Karen, Asst.Cur.
AUSTIN PUBLIC LIBRARY - AUSTIN-TRAVIS COUNTY COLLECTION □ Austin, TX

Warren, Lucretia D., Libn.
MIAMI-DADE PUBLIC LIBRARY - GENEALOGY ROOM □ Miami, FL

Warren, Marlea R., Dept.Hd.
MINNEAPOLIS PUBLIC LIBRARY & INFORMATION CENTER - ART, MUSIC & FILMS DEPARTMENT □ Minneapolis, MN

Warren, Richard, Jr., Cur.
YALE UNIVERSITY - COLLECTION OF THE LITERATURE OF THE AMERICAN MUSICAL THEATRE □ New Haven, CT

Warren, Richard, Jr., Cur.
YALE UNIVERSITY - YALE COLLECTION OF HISTORICAL SOUND RECORDINGS □ New Haven, CT

Warren, Robert, Supt.
U.S. NATL. PARK SERVICE - FORT NECESSITY NATL. BATTLEFIELD - LIBRARY □ Farmington, PA

Warrick, R., Mgr.Tech.Serv.
AVIATION ELECTRIC, LTD. - TECHNICAL DATA SECTION LIBRARY† □ Montreal, PQ

Warro, Edward A., Chf.Acq.Libn.
SOUTHWEST TEXAS STATE UNIVERSITY - LEARNING RESOURCES CENTER □ San Marcos, TX

Warth, N., Sec.
SOCIETY FOR THE INVESTIGATION OF THE UNEXPLAINED - LIBRARY □ Little Silver, NJ

Warthen, Lee, Ref.Libn.
BRIGHAM YOUNG UNIVERSITY - J. REUBEN CLARK LAW SCHOOL LIBRARY □ Provo, UT

Wartluft, The Rev. David J., Lib.Dir.
LUTHERAN THEOLOGICAL SEMINARY - KRAUTH MEMORIAL LIBRARY □ Philadelphia, PA

Wartoe, Ellen, Libn.
FORT WORTH PUBLIC LIBRARY - BUSINESS AND TECHNOLOGY DEPARTMENT □ Fort Worth, TX

Wartzok, Susan, Cat.Libn.
COMMUNITY COLLEGE OF BALTIMORE - BARD LIBRARY - SPECIAL COLLECTIONS □ Baltimore, MD

Warwas, Elke M., Libn.
BECHTEL CANADA LIMITED - ENGINEERING CONSULTANTS - LIBRARY □ Toronto, ON

Waser, Grace M., Lib.Dir.
LA VINA HOSPITAL FOR RESPIRATORY DISEASES - MEDICAL LIBRARY† □ Altadena, CA

Wash, Eleanor E., Sr.Libn.
LANTERMAN (Frank J.) STATE HOSPITAL - STAFF LIBRARY □ Pomona, CA

Washburn, David B., Prof. Staff Libn.
NEW HAMPSHIRE HOSPITAL - PROFESSIONAL LIBRARY □ Concord, NH

Washburn, David L., Archv.
UNIVERSITY OF UTAH - SPECIAL COLLECTIONS DEPARTMENT □ Salt Lake City, UT

Washburn, Marion, Libn.
INTERNATIONAL SWIMMING HALL OF FAME - MUSEUM & LIBRARY □ Fort Lauderdale, FL

Washburn, Mary, Asst.Libn.
U.S. COURT OF APPEALS, 2ND CIRCUIT - LIBRARY □ New York, NY

Washington, Ada M., Libn./Ck.
NORFOLK BOTANICAL GARDENS - LIBRARY □ Norfolk, VA

Washington, Mrs. Clannie H., Libn.
SOUTH CAROLINA STATE DEPARTMENT OF MENTAL RETARDATION - MIDLANDS CENTER LIBRARY □ Columbia, SC

Washington, Dixie Lee, Exec.Sec.
WASHINGTON COUNTY MUSEUM OF FINE ARTS - LIBRARY □ Hagerstown, MD

Washington, Ruth, Libn.
HARVARD UNIVERSITY - W.E.B. DU BOIS INSTITUTE FOR AFRO-AMERICAN RESEARCH - LIBRARY □ Cambridge, MA

Wasowski, Maria, Libn.
DELOITTE HASKINS & SELLS - LIBRARY □ Washington, DC

Wass, Edward P., Act.Hd.
UNIVERSITY OF ROCHESTER - MANAGEMENT LIBRARY □ Rochester, NY

Wass, Janice Tauer, Libn.
ROCHESTER MUSEUM AND SCIENCE CENTER - LIBRARY □ Rochester, NY

Wasser, Leon, Libn.
B'NAI BRITH HILLEL FOUNDATION AT MC GILL UNIVERSITY - LIBRARY □ Montreal, PQ

Wasser, Solidelle
U.S. DEPT. OF LABOR - BUREAU OF LABOR STATISTICS - INFORMATION AND ADVISORY SECTION □ New York, NY

Wassom, John S., Dir.
U.S. OAK RIDGE NATL. LABORATORY - INFORMATION DIVISION - ENVIRONMENTAL MUTAGEN INFORMATION CENTER □ Oak Ridge, TN

Wasson, Diane G., Asst.Libn.
HISTORIC NEW ORLEANS COLLECTION - LIBRARY □ New Orleans, LA

Watanabe, Dr. Ruth, Libn.
UNIVERSITY OF ROCHESTER - EASTMAN SCHOOL OF MUSIC - SIBLEY MUSIC LIBRARY □ Rochester, NY

Watchke, Gary, Res.Anl.
WISCONSIN STATE LEGISLATIVE REFERENCE BUREAU □ Madison, WI

Waters, Betsy M., Lib.Supv.
MOORE BUSINESS FORMS, INC. - RESEARCH CENTER LIBRARY □ Grand Island, NY

Waters, Carol, Dir. of Educ.
NEW HAMPSHIRE GOVERNOR'S COUNCIL ON ENERGY - ENERGY INFORMATION CENTER □ Concord, NH

Waters, Mrs. Jack, Lib.Asst.
FIRST BAPTIST CHURCH - STINCEON IVEY MEMORIAL LIBRARY† □ Fairmont, NC

Waters, Samuel T., Dp.Adm.
U.S.D.A. - NATIONAL AGRICULTURAL LIBRARY □ Beltsville, MD

Waters, Shelia, Asst.
LOCKWOOD, ANDREWS & NEWNAM, INC. - INFORMATION CENTER □ Houston, TX

Watkins, Anne, Registrar/Libn.
ABBY ALDRICH ROCKEFELLER FOLK ART CENTER - LIBRARY □ Williamsburg, VA

Watkins, Betty E., Lib.Dir.
WISCONSIN SCHOOL FOR THE DEAF - JOHN R. GANT LIBRARY □ Delavan, WI

Watkins, Charlotte, Ed.
ERIC CLEARINGHOUSE ON ELEMENTARY AND EARLY CHILDHOOD EDUCATION □ Champaign, IL

Watkins, Dorcas, Acq.
GENERAL MOTORS INSTITUTE - LIBRARY† □ Flint, MI

Watkins, Gary N., Asst. to Dir.
TEXAS MUNICIPAL LEAGUE - LIBRARY □ Austin, TX

Watkins, Jessie B., Libn.
SENECA FALLS HISTORICAL SOCIETY - LIBRARY □ Seneca Falls, NY

Watkins, John F., Exec.Dir.
ALABAMA LEAGUE OF MUNICIPALITIES - LIBRARY □ Montgomery, AL

Watkins, Miriam, Cat.
UNIVERSITY OF ARKANSAS AT LITTLE ROCK - PULASKI COUNTY LAW LIBRARY □ Little Rock, AR

Watkins, Richard L., Electronic Techn.
OKLAHOMA GEOLOGICAL SURVEY - OKLAHOMA GEOPHYSICAL OBSERVATORY LIBRARY □ Leonard, OK

Watkins, Thomas T., Libn.
COLUMBIA UNIVERSITY - MUSIC LIBRARY □ New York, NY

Watley, Ann, Hd., Cat.
UNIVERSITY OF TEXAS HEALTH SCIENCE CENTER, DALLAS - LIBRARY □ Dallas, TX

Watson, Betty, Libn.
FIRESTONE TIRE AND RUBBER COMPANY - BUSINESS LIBRARY □ Akron, OH

Watson, Carol A., Dir. Of Lib.Serv.
WASHINGTON BIBLE COLLEGE/CAPITAL BIBLE SEMINARY - OYER MEMORIAL LIBRARY □ Lanham, MD

Watson, Cheryl L., Libn.
TRANSCONTINENTAL GAS PIPE LINE CORPORATION - LIBRARY □ Houston, TX

Watson, Chris, Libn.
WEBSTER (Noah) FOUNDATION & HISTORICAL SOCIETY OF WEST HARTFORD - LIBRARY □ West Hartford, CT

Watson, Clarice, Acq.Libn.
ERIC CLEARINGHOUSE ON EDUCATIONAL MANAGEMENT □ Eugene, OR

Watson, D. Floyd, Archv.
ALABAMA STATE DEPARTMENT OF ARCHIVES AND HISTORY □ Montgomery, AL

Watson, Eda C., Libn.
CLERMONT COUNTY LAW LIBRARY ASSOCIATION □ Batavia, OH

Watson, Ellen I., Ref.Libn.
COMMUNITY COLLEGE OF BALTIMORE - BARD LIBRARY - SPECIAL COLLECTIONS □ Baltimore, MD

Watson, Georgianna, Govt.Doc.Libn.
U.S. ARMY - MILITARY ACADEMY - LIBRARY □ West Point, NY

Watson, Halbert, Libn.
POMONA PUBLIC LIBRARY - SPECIAL COLLECTIONS DEPARTMENT □ Pomona, CA

Watson, Irene, Archv.
UNITED METHODIST CHURCH - KANSAS WEST CONFERENCE - ARCHIVES AND HISTORY DEPOSITORY □ Winfield, KS

Watson, Janice, Lib.Techn.
SASKATCHEWAN - DEPARTMENT OF SOCIAL SERVICES - LIBRARY □ Regina, SK

Watson, Jean, Libn.
BEAVER COUNTY BAR ASSOCIATION - LAW LIBRARY □ Beaver, PA

Watson, Kathy, Sr.Info.Anl.
TRACY-LOCKE ADVERTISING AND PUBLIC RELATIONS, INC. - LIBRARY □ Dallas, TX

Watson, Linda L., Dir.
NATIONAL COLLEGE - THOMAS JEFFERSON LIBRARY □ Rapid City, SD

Watson, Margaret, Libn.
U.S. BUREAU OF RECLAMATION - LIBRARY □ Denver, CO

Watson, Nancy C., Chf. of Genealogy
MIDDLE GEORGIA REGIONAL LIBRARY - WASHINGTON MEMORIAL LIBRARY - GENEALOGICAL & HISTORICAL ROOM □ Macon, GA

Watson, Paula, Hd.
UNIVERSITY OF ILLINOIS - DOCUMENTS LIBRARY □ Urbana, IL

Watson, Paulette Skirbunt, Dir.
MONROE (James) MUSEUM AND MEMORIAL LIBRARY □ Fredericksburg, VA

Watson, Peggy, Libn.
CANADA - AGRICULTURE CANADA - SAANICHTON RESEARCH & PLANT QUARANTINE STATION - LIBRARY □ Sidney, BC

Watson, Priscilla Mace, Libn.
UNIVERSITY OF CALIFORNIA, BERKELEY - SCIENCE & MATHEMATICS EDUCATION LIBRARY □ Berkeley, CA

Watson, Sharon D., Libn.
BORG-WARNER CORPORATION - CHEMICALS LIBRARY □ Washington, WV

Watstein, Sarah, Ref.Libn.
TEACHERS COLLEGE - LIBRARY □ New York, NY

Watt, Mr. C.R., Hd., Spec.Coll.Div.
ROYAL MILITARY COLLEGE OF CANADA - MASSEY LIBRARY & SCIENCE/ENGINEERING LIBRARY □ Kingston, ON

Watt, Donald, Libn.
METROPOLITAN TORONTO LIBRARY - GENERAL REFERENCE DEPARTMENT □ Toronto, ON

Watt, Mary Morris, Libn.
RICHMOND NEWSPAPERS, INC. - LIBRARY □ Richmond, VA

Watt, Rob, Chief Pk. Naturalist
POINT PELEE NATIONAL PARK - LIBRARY □ Leamington, ON

Watt, Ronald, Mgr.Tech.Serv.
CHURCH OF JESUS CHRIST OF LATTER-DAY SAINTS - HISTORICAL DEPARTMENT - CHURCH LIBRARY-ARCHIVES □ Salt Lake City, UT

Watterson, Jane, ILL Libn.
U.S. NATL. OCEANIC & ATMOSPHERIC ADMINISTRATION - ENVIRONMENTAL RESEARCH LABORATORIES - LIBRARY □ Boulder, CO

Watterson, Mickie, Assoc.Dir.Info.Sys.
NEW YORK INSTITUTE OF TECHNOLOGY - CENTER FOR ENERGY POLICY AND RESEARCH - ENERGY INFORMATION CENTER □ Old Westbury, NY

Watterson, R.M., Libn.
MEDICAL COLLEGE OF OHIO AT TOLEDO - RAYMON H. MULFORD LIBRARY □ Toledo, OH

Watts, Anne, Supv.
ST. LOUIS PUBLIC LIBRARY - READERS SERVICES/DOCUMENTS DEPARTMENT □ St. Louis, MO

Watts, Catherine B., Per. & Maps
ANDREWS UNIVERSITY - JAMES WHITE LIBRARY □ Berrien Springs, MI

Watts, Mrs. Doris E., Libn.
U.S. INTERSTATE COMMERCE COMMISSION - LIBRARY □ Washington, DC

Watts, Henrietta, Cat.Libn.
MOODY BIBLE INSTITUTE - LIBRARY □ Chicago, IL

Watts, Henrietta, Cat.Libn.
MOODY BIBLE INSTITUTE - MOODYANA COLLECTION □ Chicago, IL

Watts, Janice, Dir., Med. Records
PHOENIX GENERAL HOSPITAL - MEDICAL LIBRARY □ Phoenix, AZ

Watts, John, Pres.
COMPOSERS AND CHOREOGRAPHERS THEATRE, INC. - MASTER TAPE LIBRARY □ New York, NY

Watts, Shirley Marie, Libn.
VANDERBILT UNIVERSITY LIBRARY - MUSIC LIBRARY □ Nashville, TN

Waudby-Smith, Joyce, Libn.
CANADA - NATIONAL RESEARCH COUNCIL - CISTI - BUILDING RESEARCH BRANCH □ Ottawa, ON

Waugh, Arthur B., Hd.
UNIVERSITY OF CALIFORNIA, BERKELEY - ENVIRONMENTAL DESIGN LIBRARY □ Berkeley, CA

Waugh, Hillary, Exec. V.P.
MYSTERY WRITERS OF AMERICA, INC. - MYSTERY LIBRARY □ New York, NY

Waverchak, Gail, Med.Libn.
ST. JOSEPH'S HOSPITAL - RUSSELL BELLMAN LIBRARY □ Atlanta, GA

Wawrzonek, M.S., Info.Anl.
CHEVRON RESEARCH COMPANY - TECHNICAL INFORMATION CENTER □ Richmond, CA

Waxman, Joanne, Libn.
PORTLAND SCHOOL OF ART - LIBRARY □ Portland, ME

Way, Angelina, Ref.Libn.
EMORY UNIVERSITY - SCHOOL OF LAW LIBRARY† □ Atlanta, GA

Way, Harold E., Ref.Libn.
CORNELL UNIVERSITY - MARTIN P. CATHERWOOD LIBRARY OF INDUSTRIAL AND LABOR RELATIONS □ Ithaca, NY

Way, Susan, Asst.Libn.
PROVIDENCE MEDICAL CENTER - MEDICAL LIBRARY □ Seattle, WA

Waznis, Betty, Asst.Libn.
ARIZONA STATE REGIONAL LIBRARY FOR THE BLIND AND PHYSICALLY HANDICAPPED □ Phoenix, AZ

Wear, Byron, Exec.Dir.
UNITED STATES LIFESAVING ASSOCIATION - LIBRARY & INFORMATION CENTER □ Huntington Beach, CA

Weart, Spencer, Dir.
AMERICAN INSTITUTE OF PHYSICS - CENTER FOR HISTORY OF PHYSICS - NIELS BOHR LIBRARY □ New York, NY

Weary, Richard L., Map Libn.
U.S. ARMY WAR COLLEGE - LIBRARY □ Carlisle Barracks, PA

Weatherhead, Barbara, Dir.
ONTARIO - MINISTRY OF TREASURY AND ECONOMICS - LIBRARY SERVICES BRANCH □ Toronto, ON

Weatherhead, Peter, Pubn.Chm.
ANTIQUE AND CLASSIC CAR CLUB OF CANADA - LIBRARY □ Toronto, ON

Weatherhead, Shelley J., Libn.
CANADIAN WESTERN NATURAL GAS COMPANY LIMITED - LIBRARY □ Calgary, AB

Weatherill, Helene A., Libn.
SULLIVAN AND CROMWELL - LIBRARY† □ New York, NY

Weathers, Azilee, Rd.Serv.Libn.
SAMFORD UNIVERSITY - CUMBERLAND SCHOOL OF LAW - CORDELL HULL LAW LIBRARY† □ Birmingham, AL

Weatherwax, Mary Lynn, Libn.
CANADIAN REAL ESTATE ASSOCIATION - LIBRARY □ Don Mills, ON

Weaver, Mrs., Genealogist
LEBANON COUNTY HISTORICAL SOCIETY - LIBRARY □ Lebanon, PA

Weaver, Anna L., AFA Libn.
UNIVERSITY OF FLORIDA - ARCHITECTURE & FINE ARTS LIBRARY □ Gainesville, FL

Weaver, Barbara F., State Libn.
NEW JERSEY STATE LIBRARY □ Trenton, NJ

Weaver, Carolyn G., Assoc.Dir., Pub.Serv.
UNIVERSITY OF NEBRASKA MEDICAL CENTER - MC GOOGAN LIBRARY OF MEDICINE □ Omaha, NE

Weaver, Charles, Asst.Libn.
DETROIT SYMPHONY ORCHESTRA - LIBRARY □ Detroit, MI

Weaver, Connie, Ref.Libn.
NORTHWOOD INSTITUTE - STROSACKER LIBRARY □ Midland, MI

Weaver, Frances A., Asst.Univ.Archv.
UNIVERSITY OF NORTH CAROLINA, CHAPEL HILL - SOUTHERN HISTORICAL COLLECTION & MANUSCRIPTS DEPARTMENT □ Chapel Hill, NC

Weaver, John M., Chf., Res.Dev.
U.S. DEPT. OF HOUSING AND URBAN DEVELOPMENT - LIBRARY □ Washington, DC

Weaver, R. David, Libn.
ST. LOUIS PUBLIC LIBRARY - CAROL MC DONALD GARDNER RARE BOOK ROOM □ St. Louis, MO

Weaver, William B., Ref.Libn.
UNIVERSITY OF FLORIDA - HUME LIBRARY □ Gainesville, FL

Web, Marek, Chf.Archv.
YIVO INSTITUTE FOR JEWISH RESEARCH - LIBRARY AND ARCHIVES □ New York, NY

Webb, Doris G., Ref./ILL
DANIEL WEBSTER COLLEGE - LIBRARY □ Nashua, NH

Webb, Dorothy, Ed.Res.Supv.
CANADIAN NATIONAL RAILWAYS - PUBLIC AFFAIRS DEPARTMENT LIBRARY □ Montreal, PQ

Webb, Duncan C., Asst. State Law Libn.
MICHIGAN STATE LIBRARY SERVICES - LAW LIBRARY □ Lansing, MI

Webb, Glennie Ruth, Media Libn.
SEATTLE PUBLIC LIBRARY - MEDIA & PROGRAM SERVICES □ Seattle, WA

Webb, Jane, Libn.
CALGARY BOARD OF EDUCATION - PROFESSIONAL LIBRARY □ Calgary, AB

Webb, Judy, Libn.
CALHOUN COUNTY HISTORICAL MUSEUM - LIBRARY □ Rockwell City, IA

Webb, Linda H., Libn.
ABT ASSOCIATES INC. - LIBRARY □ Cambridge, MA

Webb, Lorrayne B., Libn.
UNIVERSITY OF TEXAS HEALTH SCIENCE CENTER, HOUSTON - DENTAL BRANCH LIBRARY □ Houston, TX

Webb, Michael, User Serv.Spec.
ERIC CLEARINGHOUSE ON URBAN EDUCATION □ New York, NY

Webb, Molly
ST. DAVID'S UNITED CHURCH - LIBRARY† □ Calgary, AB

Webb, Susan, Libn.
INGERSOLL-RAND COMPANY - ENGINEERING LIBRARY □ Nashua, NH

Webber, Catharine, Supv.
CENTRAL MAINE POWER COMPANY - LIBRARY SERVICES □ Augusta, ME

Webber, John P., Chf., Info.Res.Dev.Br.
U.S. NATL. OCEANIC & ATMOSPHERIC ADMINISTRATION - LIBRARY AND INFORMATION SERVICES DIVISION □ Rockville, MD

Webber, Lorraine E., Info.Spec./Law Libn.
UNION MUTUAL LIFE INSURANCE COMPANY - CORPORATE INFORMATION CENTER □ Portland, ME

Webber, Sylvia J., Chf.
U.S. ARMY INTELLIGENCE CENTER & SCHOOL - ACADEMIC LIBRARY □ Ft. Huachuca, AZ

Webbert, Charles A., Libn.
UNIVERSITY OF IDAHO - SPECIAL COLLECTIONS LIBRARY □ Moscow, ID

Weber, Beth, Lib.Asst.
TRINITY MEMORIAL HOSPITAL - LIBRARY □ Cudahy, WI

Weber, David, Libn.
ALAMEDA COUNTY LIBRARY - BUSINESS & GOVERNMENT LIBRARY □ Oakland, CA

Weber, David N., Info./Res.Ctr.Coord.
NATIONAL ASSOCIATION OF SOCIAL WORKERS - RESOURCE CENTER† □ Washington, DC

Weber, David S., Archv.
U.S. NATL. ARCHIVES & RECORDS SERVICE - FEDERAL ARCHIVES & RECORDS CENTER, REGION 5 □ Chicago, IL

Weber, Donald John, Dir.
FLORIDA STATE DIVISION OF BLIND SERVICES - FLORIDA REGIONAL LIB. FOR THE BLIND & PHYSICALLY HANDICAPPED □ Daytona Beach, FL

PERSONNEL

Weber, E. Sue, Asst.Dir.Tech.Serv.
UNIVERSITY OF TEXAS HEALTH SCIENCE
CENTER, SAN ANTONIO - LIBRARY □ San
Antonio, TX

Weber, Edward C., Labadie Coll.Libn.
UNIVERSITY OF MICHIGAN - DEPARTMENT OF
RARE BOOKS AND SPECIAL COLLECTIONS -
LIBRARY □ Ann Arbor, MI

Weber, Else, Asst.Lib.Supv.
UOP INC. - RESEARCH TECHNICAL
INFORMATION CENTER □ Des Plaines, IL

Weber, Janet, Libn.
MINNESOTA STATE DEPARTMENT OF PUBLIC
SAFETY - (MINNESOTA) STATE PATROL FILM
LIBRARY □ St. Paul, MN

Weber, Linda, Circ.Libn.
UNIVERSITY OF SOUTHERN CALIFORNIA -
SCIENCE & ENGINEERING LIBRARY □ Los
Angeles, CA

Weber, Louise, Lib.Techn.
MILWAUKEE AREA TECHNICAL COLLEGE -
SOUTH CAMPUS LIBRARY □ Oak Creek, WI

Weber, Nancy, Ref./Circ.
IBM CORPORATION - GENERAL PRODUCTS
DIVISION - INFORMATION/LIBRARY/
LEARNING CENTER □ San Jose, CA

Weber, Robert F., Asst.Ref.Libn.
VILLANOVA UNIVERSITY - PULLING LAW
LIBRARY □ Villanova, PA

Weber, Ron, Photo/Cart.Mgr.
LUNAR AND PLANETARY INSTITUTE -
PLANETARY IMAGE CENTER □ Houston, TX

Weber, Victoria, Asst.Libn./Acq.
VERMONT LAW SCHOOL - LIBRARY □ South
Royalton, VT

Weber, Warren R., Cur.
U.S. NATL. PARK SERVICE - CARL SANDBURG
HOME NATL. HISTORIC SITE - MUSEUM/
LIBRARY □ Flat Rock, NC

Weberg, Lorraine, Evening Art Ref.Libn.
FASHION INSTITUTE OF TECHNOLOGY -
LIBRARY/MEDIA SERVICES □ New York, NY

Webers, Leonard, Circ.
KANSAS CITY ART INSTITUTE - LIBRARY □
Kansas City, MO

Webre, Steve, Cur., Spanish Mss.
LOUISIANA STATE MUSEUM - LOUISIANA
HISTORICAL CENTER □ New Orleans, LA

Webster, Alma A., Supv. Of Lrng.Rsrcs.
EDMONTON PUBLIC SCHOOL BOARD -
LEARNING RESOURCES PROFESSIONAL
LIBRARY □ Edmonton, AB

Webster, David, Consrv.
TEACHERS COLLEGE - LIBRARY □ New York, NY

Webster, Deborah, Asst.Hd.
UNIVERSITY OF NORTH CAROLINA, CHAPEL
HILL - LAW LIBRARY □ Chapel Hill, NC

Webster, Donald F., Dir.
SUNY - COLLEGE OF ENVIRONMENTAL SCIENCE
AND FORESTRY - F. FRANKLIN MOON LIBRARY
□ Syracuse, NY

Webster, Harriet A., Info.Sci.
DUKE POWER COMPANY - DAVID NABOW
LIBRARY □ Charlotte, NC

Webster, J., Lib.Supv.
SIR SANFORD FLEMING COLLEGE OF APPLIED
ARTS & TECHNOLOGY - LIBRARIES □
Peterborough, ON

Webster, James K., Dir.
SUNY AT BUFFALO - SCIENCE AND
ENGINEERING LIBRARY □ Buffalo, NY

Webster, Kathryn, Tech.Serv.Libn.
UNIVERSITY OF ILLINOIS - LAW LIBRARY □
Champaign, IL

Webster, Leta, Tech.Serv.Supv.
UNIVERSITY OF MISSOURI, ST. LOUIS -
EDUCATION LIBRARY □ St. Louis, MO

Webster, Lois S., Libn.
AMERICAN NUCLEAR SOCIETY - LIBRARY □ La
Grange Park, IL

Webster, Monica, Ser.Libn.
QUEEN'S UNIVERSITY AT KINGSTON -
BRACKEN LIBRARY □ Kingston, ON

Wechsler, Joseph G., Dir.
CLEARINGHOUSE ON CHILD ABUSE AND
NEGLECT INFORMATION □ Washington, DC

Wecht, Donald, Libn.
BOTEIN, HAYS, SKLAR & HERZBERG - LIBRARY
□ New York, NY

Wecker, Steven, Mgr., Lib.Serv.
NATIONAL BANK OF DETROIT - LIBRARY □
Detroit, MI

Weddell, Priscilla, Libn.
TELEDYNE WATER PIK - INFORMATION
CENTER □ Fort Collins, CO

Wedig, Bro. Vincent, O.S.B., Libn.
ST. BENEDICT'S ABBEY - BENET LIBRARY □
Benet Lake, WI

Weech, Jane, Media Libn.
MARYCREST COLLEGE - CONE LIBRARY† □
Davenport, IA

Weedman, Parmula K., Med.Libn.
U.S. VETERANS ADMINISTRATION (IN-Marion) -
HOSPITAL MEDICAL LIBRARY □ Marion, IN

Weekes, Dr. K. David, Dir.
MIDWESTERN BAPTIST THEOLOGICAL
SEMINARY - LIBRARY □ Kansas City, MO

Weeks, Gerry, Forestry Libn.
BRITISH COLUMBIA INSTITUTE OF
TECHNOLOGY - LIBRARY SERVICES DIVISION □
Burnaby, BC

Weeks, Jane, Asst.Libn.
JORDAN (Edward C.) CO., INC. - LIBRARY □
Portland, ME

Weeks, Ruth, Cat.
UNIVERSITY OF ALABAMA - SCHOOL OF LAW
LIBRARY □ University, AL

Weeks, Susan, Spec.Coll.Libn.
UNIVERSITY OF NEW MEXICO - SCHOOL OF
LAW LIBRARY □ Albuquerque, NM

Weer, Mildred B., Lib.Spec.
UNIVERSITY OF DELAWARE, NEWARK -
COLLEGE OF MARINE STUDIES - MARINE
STUDIES COMPLEX LIBRARY† □ Lewes, DE

Wees, Dustin, Slide Libn.
CLARK (Sterling and Francine) ART INSTITUTE -
LIBRARY □ Williamstown, MA

Wegman, Marie A., Libn.
U.S. PUBLIC HEALTH SERVICE HOSPITAL -
MEDICAL LIBRARY† □ San Francisco, CA

Wegner, Mary, Dir., Med.Lib.
IOWA METHODIST MEDICAL CENTER - OLIVER
J. FAY MEMORIAL LIBRARY □ Des Moines, IA

Wehr, Myron P., Pres.
TREXLER (Harry C.) MASONIC LIBRARY □
Allentown, PA

Wei, Carl K., Libn.
ONTARIO RESEARCH FOUNDATION - LIBRARY □
Mississauga, ON

Wei, Esther, Ser.Libn.
OHIO STATE UNIVERSITY - HEALTH SCIENCES
LIBRARY □ Columbus, OH

Wei, Iping K., Hd., Chinese Sect.
PRINCETON UNIVERSITY - GEST ORIENTAL
LIBRARY AND EAST ASIAN COLLECTIONS □
Princeton, NJ

Wei, Karen, Chinese Cat.
UNIVERSITY OF ILLINOIS - ASIAN LIBRARY □
Urbana, IL

Weibel, Carol, Libn.
UNIVERSITY OF WASHINGTON - PHILOSOPHY
LIBRARY □ Seattle, WA

Weibell, Fred J., Chf./BECC
U.S. VETERANS ADMINISTRATION (CA-
Sepulveda) - BIOMEDICAL ENGINEERING &
COMPUTING CENTER - LIBRARY □ Sepulveda,
CA

Weiberg, Erling, Exec.Sec.
MINNESOTA STATE WATER RESOURCES
BOARD - LIBRARY □ St. Paul, MN

Weida, William A., Libn.
AMERICAN SOCIETY FOR METALS - METALS
INFORMATION □ Metals Park, OH

Weidenhamer, Rev. Bradley E., Libn.
ASHLAND THEOLOGICAL SEMINARY - ROGER
DARLING MEMORIAL LIBRARY □ Ashland, OH

Weidl, Beverly, Cur.
HOPEWELL MUSEUM - LIBRARY □ Hopewell, NJ

Weidner, Ruth, Music Libn.
WEST CHESTER STATE COLLEGE - MUSIC
LIBRARY □ West Chester, PA

Weigel, J.J., Supv., Automated Oper.
MC DONNELL DOUGLAS CORPORATION -
DOUGLAS AIRCRAFT COMPANY - TECHNICAL
LIBRARY □ Long Beach, CA

Weigel, Jack W., Libn.
UNIVERSITY OF MICHIGAN - MATHEMATICS
LIBRARY □ Ann Arbor, MI

Weigel, Jack W., Libn.
UNIVERSITY OF MICHIGAN - PHYSICS-
ASTRONOMY LIBRARY □ Ann Arbor, MI

Weigel, Patricia A., Cat.Libn.
BLOOMSBURG STATE COLLEGE - HARVEY A.
ANDRUSS LIBRARY □ Bloomsburg, PA

Weigold, George W., Mng.Dir.
DAIRY SOCIETY INTERNATIONAL - LIBRARY □
Washington, DC

Weihs, Mary, Libn.
ST. JOSEPH HOSPITAL - SISTER MARY ALVINA
NURSING LIBRARY □ Towson, MD

Weil, Peter E., Libn.
ILLINOIS COLLEGE OF OPTOMETRY - CARL F.
SHEPARD MEMORIAL LIBRARY □ Chicago, IL

Weimer, Ferne L., Act.Dir.
WHEATON COLLEGE - BILLY GRAHAM CENTER
LIBRARY □ Wheaton, IL

Weimer, Jane, Acq.Libn.
OHIO NORTHERN UNIVERSITY - HETERICK
MEMORIAL LIBRARY □ Ada, OH

Weimer, Jean, Hd., IN Div.
INDIANA STATE LIBRARY □ Indianapolis, IN

Weimer, Mark F., Rare Bk.Libn.
SYRACUSE UNIVERSITY - GEORGE ARENTS
RESEARCH LIBRARY FOR SPECIAL
COLLECTIONS □ Syracuse, NY

Wein, Sheldon, Libn.
PEAT, MARWICK, MITCHELL & COMPANY -
ACCOUNTING AND AUDITING LIBRARY □ New
York, NY

Weinbaum, Alex S., Hd.
FREE LIBRARY OF PHILADELPHIA - BUSINESS,
SCIENCE AND INDUSTRY DEPARTMENT □
Philadelphia, PA

Weinbaum, Paul O., Musm.Cur.
U.S. NATL. PARK SERVICE - STATUE OF
LIBERTY NATL. MONUMENT - AMERICAN
MUSEUM OF IMMIGRATION - LIBRARY □ New
York, NY

Weinberg, Allen, City Archv.
PHILADELPHIA - CITY ARCHIVES □ Philadelphia,
PA

Weinberg, Bella Hass, Libn.
YIVO INSTITUTE FOR JEWISH RESEARCH -
LIBRARY AND ARCHIVES □ New York, NY

Weinberg, Belle, Sr.Libn.
NEW YORK PUBLIC LIBRARY - MID-
MANHATTAN LIBRARY - PROJECT ACCESS □
New York, NY

Weinberg, Fleur, Dir.
WILLS EYE HOSPITAL AND RESEARCH
INSTITUTE - ARTHUR J. BEDELL MEMORIAL
LIBRARY □ Philadelphia, PA

Weinberg, Judith, Libn.
MASSACHUSETTS HORTICULTURAL SOCIETY -
LIBRARY □ Boston, MA

Weindling, Nelson, Info.Spec.
MILES LABORATORIES, INC. - LIBRARY
RESOURCES AND SERVICES □ Elkhart, IN

Weiner, Alan, Chf., Ref.
BARUCH (Bernard M.) COLLEGE OF THE CITY
UNIVERSITY OF NEW YORK - LIBRARY □ New
York, NY

Weiner, C., Circ.
SOUTHWESTERN UNIVERSITY - SCHOOL OF
LAW LIBRARY □ Los Angeles, CA

Weinert, Donald G., Exec.Dir.
NATIONAL SOCIETY OF PROFESSIONAL
ENGINEERS - INFORMATION CENTER □
Washington, DC

Weingartz, Emily, Info.Spec.
KELLOGG COMPANY - TECHNICAL LIBRARY
SERVICES □ Battle Creek, MI

Weinrich, Gloria, Sr.Libn.
NEW YORK STATE DEPARTMENT OF LABOR -
RESEARCH LIBRARY □ New York, NY

Weinroth, Rita, Ref.Libn./Occup.Info
BOARD OF COOPERATIVE EDUCATIONAL
SERVICES OF NASSAU COUNTY (BOCES) -
NASSAU EDUC. RSRCS. CTR. (NERC) □
Westbury, NY

Weinstein, Carol L., Judaica/Media Libn.
HEBREW UNION COLLEGE - JEWISH INSTITUTE
OF RELIGION - KLAU LIBRARY □ Cincinnati, OH

Weinstein, Dora D., Hd., User Serv.
U.S. PATENT & TRADEMARK OFFICE -
SCIENTIFIC LIBRARY □ Arlington, VA

Weinstein, Ellen, Hd.
LONG ISLAND UNIVERSITY - C.W. POST
CENTER - PALMER GRADUATE LIBRARY
SCHOOL LIBRARY† □ Greenvale, NY

Weinstein, Gertrude
NATIONAL COLLEGE OF EDUCATION -
LEARNING RESOURCE CENTERS □ Evanston, IL

Weinstein, Jeffrey, Cat.
WED ENTERPRISES - RESEARCH LIBRARY □
Glendale, CA

Weinstein, Jill, Intl.Libn.
SALOMON BROTHERS - CORPORATE FINANCE
LIBRARY □ New York, NY

Weinstein, Mitzi, Libn.
WILSHIRE BOULEVARD TEMPLE - SIGMUND
HECHT LIBRARY □ Los Angeles, CA

Weinstein, Myron, Act.Hd. Hebraic Sect.
LIBRARY OF CONGRESS - AFRICAN & MIDDLE
EASTERN DIVISION □ Washington, DC

Weinstein, Saul, Dir.
EDINBORO STATE COLLEGE - BARON-FORNESS
LIBRARY □ Edinboro, PA

Weinstein, Seymour, Asst.Dir./Circ.Bldg.Serv.
TRENTON STATE COLLEGE - ROSCOE L. WEST
LIBRARY □ Trenton, NJ

Weinstein, Sue, Assoc.Libn./Hd.Pub.Serv.
UNIVERSITY OF DENVER - COLLEGE OF LAW -
WESTMINSTER LAW LIBRARY □ Denver, CO

Weinstock, Joanna, Asst.Libn.
HELEN HAYES HOSPITAL - LIBRARY □ West
Haverstraw, NY

Weinstock, Nancy L., Rare Bk.Libn. & Cat.
PHILADELPHIA COLLEGE OF PHARMACY AND
SCIENCE - JOSEPH W. ENGLAND LIBRARY □
Philadelphia, PA

Weinthal, Edward, Libn.
BETH ABRAHAM HOSPITAL - PATIENT'S
LIBRARY □ Bronx, NY

Weintraub, Lilien, Libn.
TURTLE BAY MUSIC SCHOOL - LIBRARY □ New
York, NY

Weipert, Margaret, Sec.
MONROE COUNTY LAW LIBRARY □ Monroe, MI

Weir, Ms. Arvella, Regional Libn.
ENVIRONMENTAL PROTECTION AGENCY -
REGION X LIBRARY □ Seattle, WA

Weir, Dr. Birdie O., Dir.
ALABAMA A & M UNIVERSITY - JOSEPH F.
DRAKE MEMORIAL LEARNING RESOURCES
CENTER □ Normal, AL

Weir, Edward E., Hd.Adm.Serv.
UNIVERSITY OF TEXAS, EL PASO - LIBRARY □ El
Paso, TX

Weir, Gertrude B., Libn.
UNIVERSITY OF NEW ENGLAND - LIBRARY† □
Biddeford, ME

Weir, Janet, Asst. Law Libn.
UNIVERSITY OF WYOMING - LAW LIBRARY □
Laramie, WY

Weir, Katherine M., Hd.
ARIZONA STATE UNIVERSITY - HOWE
ARCHITECTURE LIBRARY □ Tempe, AZ

Weir, Linda, Ref.Libn.
UNIVERSITY OF CALIFORNIA, SAN FRANCISCO
- HASTINGS COLLEGE OF THE LAW - LEGAL
INFORMATION CENTER □ San Francisco, CA

Weir, Dr. Mary Jean, Sr.Asst.Libn.
SAN DIEGO STATE UNIVERSITY - MEDIA &
CURRICULUM CENTER □ San Diego, CA

Weirbach, Esq., James L., Law Libn.
LEHIGH COUNTY LAW LIBRARY □ Allentown, PA

Weis, Aimee, Interlibrary Loans
COMMUNITY COLLEGE OF PHILADELPHIA -
EDUCATION RESOURCES CENTER □ Philadelphia,
PA

Weis, Helene, Libn.
WILLET STAINED GLASS STUDIOS - LIBRARY □
Philadelphia, PA

Weisbard, Phyllis Holman, Libn.
TEMPLE SINAI - LIBRARY □ Washington, DC

Weisenburger, Pat, Asst.
KANSAS STATE UNIVERSITY - ARCHITECTURE
AND DESIGN LIBRARY □ Manhattan, KS

Weiser, David R., Mgr.
PHILLIPS PETROLEUM COMPANY - RESEARCH &
DEVELOPMENT DEPARTMENT - TECHNICAL
INFORMATION BRANCH □ Bartlesville, OK

Weiser, Virginia, Life Sci.Ref.Libn.
UNIVERSITY OF CALIFORNIA, SANTA BARBARA
- SCIENCES-ENGINEERING LIBRARY □ Santa
Barbara, CA

Weisgerber, Alberta, Lib.Mgr.
PROCTER & GAMBLE COMPANY - IVORYDALE
TECHNICAL CENTER - LIBRARY □ Cincinnati, OH

Weisling, Alice, Res.Ctr.Libn.
MEAD JOHNSON AND COMPANY - MEAD
JOHNSON RESEARCH CENTER - LIBRARY □
Evansville, IN

Weisman, Becky, Adm.Serv.Mgr.
INDIANAPOLIS CENTER FOR ADVANCED
RESEARCH - ARAC - NASA TECHNICAL
INFORMATION CENTER □ Indianapolis, IN

Weisman, Janet, Assignment Supv.
INDUSTRIAL HOME FOR THE BLIND - NASSAU-
SUFFOLK BRAILLE LIBRARY □ Hempstead, NY

Weiss, David, Law Libn.
UNIVERSITY OF FLORIDA - LAW LIBRARY □
Gainesville, FL

Weiss, Dianne Kovitz, Libn.
ST. CLARE'S HOSPITAL & HEALTH CENTER -
MEDICAL LIBRARY □ New York, NY

Weiss, Egon A., Libn.
U.S. ARMY - MILITARY ACADEMY - LIBRARY □
West Point, NY

Weiss, Harvey, Archaeology Adv.
YALE UNIVERSITY - BABYLONIAN COLLECTION
□ New Haven, CT

Weiss, Janet, Cat.
UNITED THEOLOGICAL SEMINARY OF THE
TWIN CITIES - LIBRARY □ New Brighton, MN

Weiss, Joy, Libn.
CONESTOGA COLLEGE OF APPLIED ARTS &
TECHNOLOGY, GUELPH CENTRE - HEALTH
SCIENCES DIV. LEARNING RESOURCE CENTRE
□ Guelph, ON

Weiss, Judith M., Law Libn.
FEDERAL RESERVE SYSTEM - BOARD OF
GOVERNORS - LAW LIBRARY □ Washington, DC

Weiss, Marcia, Libn.
SHULTON, INC. - RESEARCH AND
DEVELOPMENT LIBRARY □ Clifton, NJ

Weiss, Sabrina, Music Cat.
VASSAR COLLEGE - GEORGE SHERMAN
DICKINSON MUSIC LIBRARY □ Poughkeepsie,
NY

Weiss, Susan, Supv.
E-SYSTEMS, INC. - ECI DIVISION - TECHNICAL
INFORMATION CENTER □ St. Petersburg, FL

Weiss, Hon. Virginia, Libn.
LICKING COUNTY LAW LIBRARY ASSOCIATION
□ Newark, OH

Weitkemper, Harry, Asst.Chf./Lib.Oper.
U.S. VETERANS ADMINISTRATION (DC-
Washington) - HEADQUARTERS LIBRARY
DIVISION □ Washington, DC

Weitkemper, Harry D., Asst.Chf./Lib.Oper.
U.S. VETERANS ADMINISTRATION (DC-
Washington) - HEADQUARTERS CENTRAL
OFFICE LIBRARY □ Washington, DC

Weitkemper, Larry D., Chf., Lib.Serv.
U.S. VETERANS ADMINISTRATION (IN-
Indianapolis) - MEDICAL CENTER LIBRARY □
Indianapolis, IN

Weitkemper, Larry D., Chf.Libn.
U.S. VETERANS ADMINISTRATION (NY-
Northport) - HOSPITAL LIBRARY □ Northport, NY

Weitzel, Jacqueline, Dir.
PHILADELPHIA QUARTZ COMPANY -
BUSINESS/ENGINEERING INFORMATION
CENTER □ Valley Forge, PA

Weitzel, Sarah, Info.Sci.
MARION LABORATORIES, INC. - LIBRARY □
Kansas City, MO

Welborn, Doreen, Info.Spec.
MC KINSEY & COMPANY, INC. - INFORMATION
CENTER □ Los Angeles, CA

Welburn, Janice D., Psych.Libn.
PRINCETON UNIVERSITY - PSYCHOLOGY
LIBRARY □ Princeton, NJ

Welburn, Ron, Oral Hist.Coord.
RUTGERS UNIVERSITY, THE STATE
UNIVERSITY OF NEW JERSEY - INSTITUTE OF
JAZZ STUDIES □ Newark, NJ

Welch, Carolyn J., Med.Libn.
KNOLL PHARMACEUTICAL COMPANY -
RESEARCH LIBRARY □ Whippany, NJ

Welch, Eric, Ref.Libn.
UNIVERSITY OF ILLINOIS MEDICAL CENTER -
ROCKFORD SCHOOL OF MEDICINE - LIBRARY
OF THE HEALTH SCIENCES □ Rockford, IL

Welch, Jeanie, Asst.Libn.
AMERICAN GRADUATE SCHOOL OF
INTERNATIONAL MANAGEMENT - LIBRARY □
Glendale, AZ

Welch, Jeanne, ILL
ST. ANSELM'S COLLEGE - GEISEL LIBRARY □
Manchester, NH

Welch, Lawrence A., Adm.
WEST VOLUSIA MEMORIAL HOSPITAL -
MEDICAL LIBRARY □ De Land, FL

Welch, Marianne, Ref./Coll.Libn.
UNIVERSITY OF WESTERN ONTARIO - LAW
LIBRARY □ London, ON

Welch, Monica, Mgr.
CANADA - MORTGAGE AND HOUSING
CORPORATION - CANADIAN HOUSING
INFORMATION CENTRE □ Ottawa, ON

Welch, Oneta M., Lib.Techn.
AUTOMATED LOGISTIC MANAGEMENT
SYSTEMS AGENCY - LIBRARY □ St. Louis, MO

Welch, Sue, Cat.
COLLEGE OF WILLIAM AND MARY - MARSHALL-
WYTHE LAW LIBRARY □ Williamsburg, VA

Welch, Thomas L., Dir.
ORGANIZATION OF AMERICAN STATES -
COLUMBUS MEMORIAL LIBRARY □ Washington,
DC

Welch, Walter L., Audio Archv.Cur.
SYRACUSE UNIVERSITY - GEORGE ARENTS
RESEARCH LIBRARY FOR SPECIAL
COLLECTIONS □ Syracuse, NY

Welcome, Genice, Exec.Sec.
DEER ISLE-STONINGTON HISTORICAL
SOCIETY - LIBRARY □ Deer Isle, ME

Welden, Stephanie, State Law Libn.
NEW YORK STATE LIBRARY - LAW/SOCIAL
SCIENCE REFERENCE SERVICES □ Albany, NY

Welder, Mary Black, Ref.Libn.
MEDICAL COLLEGE OF WISCONSIN - TODD
WEHR LIBRARY □ Milwaukee, WI

Weldon, Shawn, Archv.
BALCH INSTITUTE FOR ETHNIC STUDIES -
LIBRARY □ Philadelphia, PA

Weliver, E. Delmer, Dir.
INTERLOCHEN CENTER FOR THE ARTS - MUSIC
LIBRARY □ Interlochen, MI

Welker, Betty, Ref.Libn.
PORT AUTHORITY OF NEW YORK AND NEW
JERSEY - LIBRARY □ New York, NY

Welker, Kathy J., Asst.Dir.
INDIANA UNIVERSITY - SCHOOL OF LAW
LIBRARY □ Indianapolis, IN

PERSONNEL

Well, Maureen D., Law Libn.
CONNECTICUT STATE LIBRARY □ Hartford, CT
Wellander, Joan, Adult Serv.Libn.
SMITHTOWN LIBRARY □ Smithtown, NY
Wellborn, Cecil W., Hd.Libn.
UNIVERSITY OF ARIZONA - LIBRARY SCIENCE
COLLECTION □ Tucson, AZ
Weller, Ann C., Hd. Clinical Med.
AMERICAN MEDICAL ASSOCIATION - DIVISION
OF LIBRARY AND ARCHIVAL SERVICES □
Chicago, IL
Weller, Verna A., Libn.
MOUNT CARMEL LUTHERAN CHURCH - LIBRARY
□ Milwaukee, WI
Welles, A.L., Dir.
LEARNING INCORPORATED - LIBRARY □
Manset-Seawall, ME
Wellheiser, J., Consrv.
TORONTO CITY RECORDS AND ARCHIVES
DIVISION □ Toronto, ON
Wellington, Carol S., Libn.
HILL AND BARLOW - LIBRARY □ Boston, MA
Wellington, Flora H., Hd.Tech.Serv.
UNIVERSITY OF MIAMI - SCHOOL OF
MEDICINE - LOUIS CALDER MEMORIAL
LIBRARY □ Miami, FL
Wellington, Jean Susorney, Classics Libn.
UNIVERSITY OF CINCINNATI - JOHN MILLER
BURNAM CLASSICAL LIBRARY □ Cincinnati, OH
Wellisch, Hans H., Dir.
UNIVERSITY OF MARYLAND, COLLEGE PARK -
U.S. INFORMATION CENTER FOR THE
UNIVERSAL DECIMAL CLASSIFICATION □
College Park, MD
Wellman, Earl H., Libn.
AEROPHILATELIC FEDERATION OF THE
AMERICAS - LIBRARY □ Brookfield, IL
Wellman, Loretto M., Info.Spec.
BORG-WARNER CORPORATION - ROY C.
INGERSOLL RESEARCH CENTER - LIBRARY □
Des Plaines, IL
Wells, Dr. A., Chf. of Doc.
LEE PHARMACEUTICALS - LIBRARY □ South El
Monte, CA
Wells, Anne S., Mss.Libn.
MISSISSIPPI STATE UNIVERSITY - MITCHELL
MEMORIAL LIBRARY - SPECIAL COLLECTIONS □
Mississippi State, MS
Wells, Dorothy, Local Docs.Libn.
UNIVERSITY OF CALIFORNIA, LOS ANGELES -
PUBLIC AFFAIRS SERVICE □ Los Angeles, CA
Wells, Elaine, Med.Libn.
KING (Martin Luther, Jr.) GENERAL HOSPITAL -
MEDICAL LIBRARY □ Los Angeles, CA
Wells, Elizabeth, Spec.Coll.Libn.
SAMFORD UNIVERSITY - HARWELL GOODWIN
DAVIS LIBRARY □ Birmingham, AL
Wells, Elizabeth C., Spec.Coll.Libn.
SAMFORD UNIVERSITY - BAPTIST HISTORICAL
COLLECTION □ Birmingham, AL
Wells, Ellen B., Chf.
SMITHSONIAN INSTITUTION LIBRARIES -
SPECIAL COLLECTIONS BRANCH □ Washington,
DC
Wells, Mrs. Hans, Dir.
FIRST BAPTIST CHURCH - LIBRARY □ McAllen,
TX
Wells, Harold F., Dir.
CALIFORNIA STATE POLYTECHNIC
UNIVERSITY, POMONA - LIBRARY □ Pomona,
CA
Wells, James M., V.P.
NEWBERRY LIBRARY □ Chicago, IL
Wells, Jane B., Libn.
UNIVERSITY HOSPITAL - HEALTH SCIENCES
LIBRARY □ Augusta, GA
Wells, Judy, Bus.Libn.
UNIVERSITY OF MINNESOTA - BUSINESS
REFERENCE SERVICE □ Minneapolis, MN
Wells, Judy, Bus.Libn.
UNIVERSITY OF MINNESOTA - DELOITTE
HASKINS & SELLS TAX RESEARCH ROOM □
Minneapolis, MN

Wells, Lois E., Libn.
JACKSONVILLE MENTAL HEALTH AND
DEVELOPMENTAL CENTER - LIBRARY □
Jacksonville, IL
Wells, Maria X., Cur., Italian Coll.
UNIVERSITY OF TEXAS, AUSTIN - HUMANITIES
RESEARCH CENTER □ Austin, TX
Wells, Marianna, Hd.
UNIVERSITY OF CINCINNATI - PHYSICS
LIBRARY □ Cincinnati, OH
Wells, Marianne, Libn.
UNIVERSITY OF CINCINNATI - OBSERVATORY
LIBRARY □ Cincinnati, OH
Wells, Mary Lou, Mgr.
RICHARDSON-VICKS, INC. - MARKETING
INFORMATION CENTER □ Wilton, CT
Wells, Dr. Merle, Hist. & Archv.
IDAHO STATE HISTORICAL SOCIETY - LIBRARY
AND ARCHIVES □ Boise, ID
Wells, Ruth, Cat.
ORAL ROBERTS UNIVERSITY - LIBRARY - HOLY
SPIRIT RESEARCH CENTER □ Tulsa, OK
Wells, Shirley, Libn.
ARMOUR PHARMACEUTICAL COMPANY -
LIBRARY† □ Kankakee, IL
Wells, Susan, Hd., Cat.Serv.
WESTERN NEW ENGLAND COLLEGE - SCHOOL
OF LAW LIBRARY □ Springfield, MA
Welsh, Eric, Ref.Libn.
DADE COUNTY LAW LIBRARY □ Miami, FL
Welsh, Harry E., Dir.
SOUTH DAKOTA SCHOOL OF MINES &
TECHNOLOGY - DEVEREAUX LIBRARY □ Rapid
City, SD
Welsh, John, Sys.Anl.
U.S. NATL. OCEANIC & ATMOSPHERIC
ADMINISTRATION - ENVIRONMENTAL
RESEARCH LABORATORIES - LIBRARY □
Boulder, CO
Welsh, Sue, Asst.Libn.
U.S. COURT OF APPEALS, 9TH CIRCUIT -
LIBRARY □ San Francisco, CA
Welshhans, Janice B., Libn.
KING & SPALDING - LAW LIBRARY† □ Atlanta,
GA
Welte, Gertrude, Registrar
SUFFOLK MARINE MUSEUM - HERVEY G. SMITH
RESEARCH LIBRARY □ West Sayville, NY
Welton, Marlene, Lib.Asst.
INSTITUTE OF LAW RESEARCH AND REFORM -
LIBRARY □ Edmonton, AB
Welty, J., Info.Spec.
AIR PRODUCTS AND CHEMICALS, INC. -
INFORMATION SERVICES - TREXLERTOWN
LIBRARY □ Allentown, PA
Welwood, Ronald J., Chm.
DAVID THOMPSON UNIVERSITY CENTRE -
SPECIAL COLLECTIONS □ Nelson, BC
Wember, Bertha, Libn.
TEMPLE ISRAEL - LIBRARY □ West Bloomfield,
MI
Wemhoff, Sr. Gertrude, O.S.B., Exec.Dir.
NATIONAL SISTERS VOCATION CONFERENCE -
LIBRARY □ Chicago, IL
Wender, Ruth W., Assoc. to Dir.
UNIVERSITY OF OKLAHOMA - HEALTH
SCIENCES CENTER LIBRARY □ Oklahoma City,
OK
Wendroff, Catriona, Ref.
GOLDEN GATE UNIVERSITY - LIBRARIES □ San
Francisco, CA
Wendt, Laurel A., Rd.Serv.Libn.
SOUTHERN ILLINOIS UNIVERSITY,
CARBONDALE - SCHOOL OF LAW LIBRARY □
Carbondale, IL
Wendt, Lillian, Libn.
MODESTO BEE - EDITORIAL LIBRARY □
Modesto, CA
Wengel, Linda, Hd.Libn.
EMERGENCY CARE RESEARCH INSTITUTE -
LIBRARY □ Plymouth Meeting, PA

Wenger, Carolyn C., Dir.
LANCASTER MENNONITE HISTORICAL
SOCIETY - LIBRARY □ Lancaster, PA
Wenger, Charles B., Chf.Libn.
NATIONAL CENTER FOR ATMOSPHERIC
RESEARCH - MESA LIBRARY □ Boulder, CO
Wenger, Larry B.
UNIVERSITY OF VIRGINIA - ARTHUR J.
MORRIS LAW LIBRARY □ Charlottesville, VA
Wenger, Milton B., Info.Spec.
CHEM SYSTEMS INC. - INFORMATION CENTER
□ Tarrytown, NY
Wengle, Annette, Libn.
METROPOLITAN TORONTO LIBRARY - THEATRE
DEPARTMENT □ Toronto, ON
Wenner, Marie, Supv.
TRINITY LUTHERAN CHURCH - LIBRARY □
Moorhead, MN
Wente, Norman G., Libn.
LUTHER-NORTHWESTERN SEMINARY -
LIBRARY □ St. Paul, MN
Wentworth, Jennifer M., Libn.
POLAR GAS PROJECT - LIBRARY □ Toronto, ON
Wentworth, T.T., Jr., Pres.
WENTWORTH (T.T., Jr.) MUSEUM - LIBRARY □
Pensacola, FL
Wenzel, Duane, Asst.Libn.
GRANT (Alexander) & COMPANY - CHICAGO
OFFICE LIBRARY □ Chicago, IL
Wenzl, Sr. Mary Louis, Lib.Ck.
ST. FRANCIS HOSPITAL - DOCTORS' LIBRARY □
Colorado Springs, CO
Werbel, Cherie, Sr.Libn.
LETCHWORTH VILLAGE DEVELOPMENTAL
CENTER - ISAAC N. WOLFSON LIBRARY □
Thiells, NY
Werbin, Ms. R.
CANADA - PUBLIC ARCHIVES OF CANADA -
NATIONAL MAP COLLECTION □ Ottawa, ON
Werbowyj, O., Hd., Tech.Serv.
MC GILL UNIVERSITY - OSLER LIBRARY □
Montreal, PQ
Werk, William R., Chf.
U.S. ARMY - ELECTRONICS R & D COMMAND -
TECHNICAL LIBRARY DIVISION □ Fort
Monmouth, NJ
Werling, Anita, Mgr.Coll.Dev.
XEROX CORPORATION - UNIVERSITY
MICROFILMS INTERNATIONAL - LIBRARY† □
Ann Arbor, MI
Werner, Gloria, Libn.
UNIVERSITY OF CALIFORNIA, LOS ANGELES -
BIOMEDICAL LIBRARY □ Los Angeles, CA
Werner, Janet, Coord., Info.
TOLEDO MENTAL HEALTH CENTER - LIBRARY
AND INFORMATION SERVICES† □ Toledo, OH
Werner, Joanne, Cat.Libn.
MOHAWK VALLEY COMMUNITY COLLEGE -
LIBRARY □ Utica, NY
Werner, Joyce C., Hd.
LOUISIANA STATE UNIVERSITY - REFERENCE
SERVICES □ Baton Rouge, LA
Werner, Lawrence W., Libn.
HONEYWELL, INC. - DEFENSE SYSTEMS
DIVISION - ENGINEERING LIBRARY □ Hopkins,
MN
Werner, O. James, Libn.
SAN DIEGO COUNTY LAW LIBRARY □ San Diego,
CA
Werner, O. James, Libn.
SAN DIEGO COUNTY LAW LIBRARY - VISTA
BRANCH □ Vista, CA
Werner, Stuart, Tech.Info.Spec.
U.S. DEPT. OF COMMERCE - INTERNATIONAL
TRADE ADMINISTRATION - NEW YORK
DISTRICT OFFICE LIBRARY □ New York, NY
Wernersbach, Geraldine, Hd.Circ.
UNIVERSITY OF DAYTON - LAW SCHOOL
LIBRARY □ Dayton, OH
Werry, Jim, Libn.
CANADA - NATIONAL FILM BOARD OF CANADA
- EDMONTON DISTRICT OFFICE - FILM
LIBRARY □ Edmonton, AB

Wert, Dr. Lucille, Chem.Libn.
UNIVERSITY OF ILLINOIS - CHEMISTRY
LIBRARY □ Urbana, IL

Wertheimer, Dr. Albert I., Dir.
UNIVERSITY OF MINNESOTA - SOCIAL AND
ADMINISTRATIVE PHARMACY READING ROOM
□ Minneapolis, MN

Weschcke, Carl L., Pres.
WESCHCKE (Carl L.) LIBRARY □ Woodbury, MN

Weseloh, Todd S., Libn./Archv.
CANAL MUSEUM - RESEARCH LIBRARY AND
DOCUMENTATION CENTER □ Syracuse, NY

Weselteer, Ruth, Libn.
LEBHAR-FRIEDMAN, INC. - CHAIN STORE AGE -
READER SERVICE RESEARCH LIBRARY □ New
York, NY

Wesley, Dianna L., Med.Libn.
NORTHVILLE REGIONAL PSYCHIATRIC
HOSPITAL - PROFESSIONAL LIBRARY □
Northville, MI

Wesley, Nancy M., Libn.
CHILDREN'S HOSPITAL, INC. - MEDICAL-
NURSING LIBRARY □ St. Paul, MN

Wesling, Angela Green, Med.Libn.
MOUNT ZION HOSPITAL AND MEDICAL CENTER
- HARRIS M. FISHBON MEMORIAL LIBRARY □
San Francisco, CA

Wessells, Robert S., Asst.Libn.
U.S. NAVY - NAVAL EDUCATION AND TRAINING
CENTER - LIBRARY □ Newport, RI

Wessels, Margie, Med.Libn.
NORTHWEST GENERAL HOSPITAL - MEDICAL
LIBRARY □ Milwaukee, WI

Wessenberg, Kristi, Asst.Libn.
PILLSBURY, MADISON AND SUTRO - LIBRARY □
San Francisco, CA

West, Barbara, Dir.
ANCHOR FOUNDATION - LIBRARY OF SOCIAL
HISTORY† □ New York, NY

West, Candy, Lib.Comm.
NORTH SHORE SYNAGOGUE - CHARLES COHN
MEMORIAL LIBRARY □ Syosset, NY

West, Carl, Libn.
CUMBERLAND COUNTY HISTORICAL SOCIETY -
LIBRARY □ Greenwich, NJ

West, Carol, Circ., Desk Supv.
NEW HAMPSHIRE COLLEGE - SHAPIRO LIBRARY
□ Manchester, NH

West, Dona L., Hd.
U-HAUL - RESEARCH AND LIBRARY SERVICES □
Phoenix, AZ

West, Eleanora F., Cur. of Musm.
FITCHBURG HISTORICAL SOCIETY - LIBRARY □
Fitchburg, MA

West, Heather, Libn.
SASKATCHEWAN INDIAN FEDERATED COLLEGE
- LIBRARY □ Regina, SK

West, J. Martin, Dir./Cur.
FORT LIGONIER MEMORIAL FOUNDATION -
HENRY BOUQUET ROOM □ Ligonier, PA

West, Linda L., Libn.
U.S. NATL. PARK SERVICE - DINOSAUR NATL.
MONUMENT - QUARRY VISITOR CENTER -
LIBRARY □ Jensen, UT

West, Lois A., Supv.
CENTER FOR WOMEN POLICY STUDIES -
RESOURCE CENTER □ Washington, DC

West, Mary Ellen, Lib.Techn.
U.S. VETERANS ADMINISTRATION (MA-Boston)
- OUTPATIENT CLINIC MEDICAL LIBRARY □
Boston, MA

West, May, Asst.Libn.
FERMI NATIONAL ACCELERATOR LABORATORY
- LIBRARY □ Batavia, IL

West, Richard Vincent, Dir.
CROCKER ART MUSEUM - RESEARCH LIBRARY
□ Sacramento, CA

West, Wanda, Libn.
NEW MEXICO SCHOOL FOR THE VISUALLY
HANDICAPPED - LIBRARY □ Alamogordo, NM

Westberg, Sigurd F., Archv.
EVANGELICAL COVENANT CHURCH OF
AMERICA - ARCHIVES AND HISTORICAL
LIBRARY □ Chicago, IL

Westbrook, E.E., Info.Ctr.Mgr.
BATTELLE-COLUMBUS LABORATORIES -
TACTICAL TECHNOLOGY CENTER □ Columbus,
OH

Westbrook, Josephine
NEW PROVIDENCE HISTORICAL SOCIETY -
LIBRARY □ New Providence, NJ

Westbrook, Patricia C., Libn.
MERIDEN-WALLINGFORD HOSPITAL - HEALTH
SCIENCES LIBRARY □ Meriden, CT

Westcott, Mr., Dir.
AFRAM ASSOCIATES, INC. - AFRAMAILIBRARY
□ Harlem, NY

Westelaken, W., Ref.Libn.
UNIVERSITY OF MANITOBA - SCIENCE
LIBRARY □ Winnipeg, MB

Wester, Karen, Tech.Libn.
GEOMET TECHNOLOGIES INC. - INFORMATION
CENTER □ Rockville, MD

Wester-House, Mary, Info.Spec.
HOSPITAL CORPORATION OF AMERICA -
RESEARCH/INFORMATION SERVICES □
Nashville, TN

Westergard, Marjorie D., Libn.
WISCONSIN STATE DEPARTMENT OF PUBLIC
INSTRUCTION - LIBRARY □ Madison, WI

Westerhaus, Rev. Martin O., Libn.
WISCONSIN LUTHERAN SEMINARY - LIBRARY □
Mequon, WI

Westermann, Mary L., Med.Libn.
NASSAU COUNTY MEDICAL SOCIETY - NASSAU
ACADEMY OF MEDICINE - JOHN N. SHELL
LIBRARY □ Garden City, NY

Westermeyer, Carroll, Chm., Tech.Serv.
LOMA LINDA UNIVERSITY - DEL E. WEBB
MEMORIAL LIBRARY □ Loma Linda, CA

Western, Susan, Subject Spec.
UNIVERSITY OF TORONTO - CENTRE FOR
INDUSTRIAL RELATIONS - INFORMATION
SERVICE □ Toronto, ON

Westhuis, Judith, Tech.Serv.Libn.
UNION UNIVERSITY - ALBANY LAW SCHOOL -
LIBRARY □ Albany, NY

Westlake, Paulette, Lib.Techn.
CANADA - FISHERIES & OCEANS - FISHERIES
MANAGEMENT REGIONAL LIBRARY □
Vancouver, BC

Westley, Donna, ILL Libn.
MARQUETTE UNIVERSITY - MEMORIAL
LIBRARY □ Milwaukee, WI

Westling, Ellen, Hd., Info.Serv.
MASSACHUSETTS GENERAL HOSPITAL -
TREADWELL AND PALMER-DAVIS LIBRARY □
Boston, MA

Westmoreland, Eva, Info.Cons.
CITE RESOURCE CENTER □ Austin, TX

Weston, Janice C., Chf.Libn.
U.S. ARMY ORDNANCE CENTER & SCHOOL -
LIBRARY □ Aberdeen Proving Ground, MD

Weston, Marian, ILL Libn.
AMERICAN HERITAGE PUBLISHING COMPANY,
INC. - LIBRARY □ New York, NY

Weston, Ruby D., Libn.
MARYLAND STATE HIGHWAY
ADMINISTRATION - LIBRARY □ Baltimore, MD

Westre, Tom, Libn.
FRESNO COUNTY DEPARTMENT OF EDUCATION
- IMC-LIBRARY □ Fresno, CA

Westwood, Anita F., Med. Subject Spec.
DENVER PUBLIC LIBRARY - DENVER GENERAL
HOSPITAL LIBRARY □ Denver, CO

Wethey, Connee Chandler, Med.Libn.
PIEDMONT HOSPITAL - SAULS MEMORIAL
LIBRARY □ Atlanta, GA

Wetts, Hazel, Libn.
UNIVERSITY OF SOUTHERN CALIFORNIA -
SCIENCE & ENGINEERING LIBRARY □ Los
Angeles, CA

Wetzel, Frank, Libn.
LINCOLN EDUCATIONAL FOUNDATION -
LIBRARY OF INDIVIDUAL BUSINESS HISTORIES
□ New York, NY

Weum, Colleen, Coll.Dev.Libn.
UNIVERSITY OF WASHINGTON - HEALTH
SCIENCES LIBRARY □ Seattle, WA

Wexler, Jacob, Libn.
NEW YORK CITY - LAW DEPARTMENT -
CORPORATION COUNSEL'S LIBRARY □ New
York, NY

Weyhmiller, Sue A., Libn.
VANDERCOOK COLLEGE OF MUSIC - HARRY
RUPPEL MEMORIAL LIBRARY □ Chicago, IL

Weyhrauch, Ernest E., Dean Of Libs.
EASTERN KENTUCKY UNIVERSITY - JOHN
GRANT CRABBE LIBRARY □ Richmond, KY

Whalen, A.G., Chf.Libn.
NATIONAL FILM BOARD OF CANADA - FILM
LIBRARY □ New York, NY

Whalen, George, Libn.
ONTARIO - MINISTRY OF EDUCATION -
EDUCATION CENTER LIBRARY □ Sudbury, ON

Whalen, Jane, Libn.
DEACONESS HOSPITAL - DRUSCH
PROFESSIONAL LIBRARY □ St. Louis, MO

Whalen, John J., Prog.Mgr., R&D Lib.
REYNOLDS (R.J.) TOBACCO COMPANY - R&D
INFORMATION SYSTEMS LIBRARY □ Winston-
Salem, NC

Whalen, Pauline K., Libn.
SALK INSTITUTE FOR BIOLOGICAL STUDIES -
LIBRARY □ San Diego, CA

Whalen, William F., Chf.
U.S. AIR FORCE - AIR FORCE SYSTEMS
COMMAND - TECHNICAL INFORMATION
CENTER □ Holloman AFB, NM

Whaley, Martha, Cat.Libn.
EAST TENNESSEE STATE UNIVERSITY,
QUILLEN-DISHNER COLLEGE OF MEDICINE -
DEPT. OF LEARNING RSRCS. - MEDICAL
LIBRARY □ Johnson City, TN

Whaley, Martha, Libn.
FIRST NATIONAL BANK OF CHICAGO - LIBRARY
□ Chicago, IL

Wharton, Valy, Libn.
FLORIDA STATE DEPT. OF HEALTH &
REHABILITATIVE SERVICES - RESOURCE
CENTER □ Tallahassee, FL

Whateley, Dorothy, Info.Sci.
JOHNSON AND JOHNSON - RESEARCH CENTER
LIBRARY □ New Brunswick, NJ

Whatley, Michael, Act.Chf., Interp.
U.S. NATL. PARK SERVICE - CAPE COD NATL.
SEASHORE - LIBRARY □ South Wellfleet, MA

Wheat, Helen, Spec.Coll.Libn.
NORTHEASTERN OKLAHOMA STATE
UNIVERSITY - JOHN VAUGHAN LIBRARY/
LEARNING RESOURCES CENTER □ Tahlequah,
OK

Wheat, Helen, Dir. of Tech.Proc.
SAM HOUSTON STATE UNIVERSITY - LIBRARY†
□ Huntsville, TX

Wheatley, Dr. William B.
BRISTOL-MYERS COMPANY - BRISTOL
LABORATORIES - LIBRARY AND INFORMATION
SERVICES □ Syracuse, NY

Wheaton, Leslie Anne, Hd.Libn.
DONALDSON, LUFKIN AND JENRETTE, INC. -
CORPORATE LIBRARY □ New York, NY

Wheeler, Beverly, Lib.Ck.
MOUNTAIN BELL TELEPHONE COMPANY -
LIBRARY □ Denver, CO

Wheeler, Claire L., Adm.Asst.
SHAKER MUSEUM FOUNDATION - EMMA B.
KING LIBRARY □ Old Chatham, NY

Wheeler, Constance, Dir.
BUILT ENVIRONMENT COORDINATORS
LIMITED - BEC INFORMATION SYSTEM (BIS) □
Toronto, ON

Wheeler, Diane L., Libn.
GRAND RAPIDS PRESS - REFERENCE LIBRARY □
Grand Rapids, MI

PERSONNEL

Wheeler, Doris A., Design Libn.
LOUISIANA STATE UNIVERSITY - COLLEGE OF DESIGN - DESIGN RESOURCE CENTER □ Baton Rouge, LA

Wheeler, Dr. Jane, Cur.
PEABODY (Robert S.) FOUNDATION FOR ARCHEOLOGY - LIBRARY □ Andover, MA

Wheeler, Joan E., Lib.Techn.
JANEWAY (Dr. Charles A.) CHILD HEALTH CENTRE - JANEWAY MEDICAL LIBRARY □ St. John's, NF

Wheeler, Linda, Ref.Libn.
SPORT INFORMATION RESOURCE CENTRE □ Ottawa, ON

Wheeler, Lora Jeanne, Libn.
AMERICAN GRADUATE SCHOOL OF INTERNATIONAL MANAGEMENT - LIBRARY □ Glendale, AZ

Wheeler, Margo, Music Lib.Asst.
GUSTAVUS ADOLPHUS COLLEGE - LUND MUSIC LIBRARY □ St. Peter, MN

Wheeler, Marjorie, Ref.Dept.Hd.
LAMAR UNIVERSITY - MARY AND JOHN GRAY LIBRARY □ Beaumont, TX

Wheeler, Nicholas A., Prof.
REED COLLEGE - PHYSICS LIBRARY† □ Portland, OR

Wheeler, Pat
ALTERNATIVE PRESS CENTER - LIBRARY □ Baltimore, MD

Wheeler, Ruth, Hd., Dissemination Serv.
SUNY AT BUFFALO - HEALTH SCIENCES LIBRARY □ Buffalo, NY

Wheeler, Verna Anne, Exec.Dir.
CROSBY COUNTY PIONEER MEMORIAL - CCPM HISTORICAL COLLECTION/MUSEUM LIBRARY □ Crosbyton, TX

Whelchel, Lloyd E., Rec.Libn.
WASHINGTON ARCHAEOLOGICAL RESEARCH CENTER - LIBRARY □ Pullman, WA

Whelihan, Annette, Asst.Libn.
SENTRY LIBRARY □ Stevens Point, WI

Wherley, Marilyn C., Dept.Hd.
LOS ANGELES PUBLIC LIBRARY - PHILOSOPHY & RELIGION DEPARTMENT □ Los Angeles, CA

Wherley, Marilyn C., Dept.Hd.
LOS ANGELES PUBLIC LIBRARY - SOCIAL SCIENCES DEPARTMENT □ Los Angeles, CA

Wherry, Mrs. Del, Libn.
EXXON COMPANY, U.S.A. - LAW LIBRARY □ Houston, TX

Whipkey, Harry E., State Archv.
PENNSYLVANIA STATE HISTORICAL & MUSEUM COMMISSION - DIVISION OF ARCHIVES AND MANUSCRIPTS □ Harrisburg, PA

Whipple, Dr. Caroline Becker, Dir.
SCHOOL OF THEOLOGY AT CLAREMONT - THEOLOGY LIBRARY □ Claremont, CA

Whipple, Marcia, Chf.Libn.
U.S. ARMY POST - FORT LEONARD WOOD - LIBRARY SYSTEM □ Ft. Leonard Wood, MO

Whipple, P. Michael, Ref.
PEPPERDINE UNIVERSITY - LAW LIBRARY □ Malibu, CA

Whipple, S. Lawrence, Archv.
LEXINGTON HISTORICAL SOCIETY, INC. - LIBRARY □ Lexington, MA

Whisenhunt, Sue, Sr.Libn.
VARIAN ASSOCIATES - TECHNICAL LIBRARY □ Palo Alto, CA

Whisenton, Andre C., Libn.
U.S. DEPT. OF LABOR - LIBRARY □ Washington, DC

Whistance-Smith, R., Univ. Map Curator
UNIVERSITY OF ALBERTA - UNIVERSITY MAP COLLECTION □ Edmonton, AB

Whitaker, Albert H., State Archv.
MASSACHUSETTS STATE ARCHIVES DIVISION □ Boston, MA

Whitaker, Carl, Law Libn.
MORRISON & FOERSTER - LAW LIBRARY □ San Francisco, CA

Whitaker, Lesley, Ref.Libn.
U.S. NASA - AMES RESEARCH CENTER - LIBRARY □ Mountain View, CA

Whitaker, R. Reed, Chf., Archv.Br.
U.S. NATL. ARCHIVES & RECORDS SERVICE - FEDERAL ARCHIVES AND RECORDS CENTER, REGION 6 □ Kansas City, MO

Whitaker, Susanne K., Libn.
CORNELL UNIVERSITY - FLOWER VETERINARY LIBRARY □ Ithaca, NY

Whitcomb, Dorothy, Hist.Coll.Libn.
UNIVERSITY OF WISCONSIN, MADISON - CENTER FOR HEALTH SCIENCES LIBRARIES □ Madison, WI

White, Andrea, Stat.Asst./Libn.
NCNB - LIBRARY □ Charlotte, NC

White, Barbara A., Spec.Coll.Libn.
UNIVERSITY OF NEW HAMPSHIRE - SPECIAL COLLECTIONS □ Durham, NH

White, Barbara C., Chf.Libn.
DEAN WITTER REYNOLDS, INC. - LIBRARY □ New York, NY

White, Barbara E., Supv.
ROCKWELL INTERNATIONAL - SPACE BUSINESSES - TECHNICAL INFORMATION CENTER □ Downey, CA

White, Beryl, Law Libn.
ITT CORPORATION - LEGAL DEPARTMENT LIBRARY □ New York, NY

White, Betty J., Libn.
UNIVERSITY OF TEXAS, AUSTIN - SCIENCE LIBRARY □ Austin, TX

White, Bruce, Coord., Educ. & Ext.
GALLERY/STRATFORD - JOHN MARTIN LIBRARY □ Stratford, ON

White, Ms. C., Asst.Libn.
COVINGTON AND BURLING - LIBRARY □ Washington, DC

White, Carol, Libn.
AKWESASNE LIBRARY CULTURAL CENTER □ Hogansburg, NY

White, Cecil R., Libn.
GOLDEN GATE BAPTIST THEOLOGICAL SEMINARY - LIBRARY □ Mill Valley, CA

White, Corinne, Libn.
AKWESASNE LIBRARY CULTURAL CENTER □ Hogansburg, NY

White, Donald G., Dir.
RUTGERS UNIVERSITY, THE STATE UNIVERSITY OF NEW JERSEY - COMPUTER REFERENCE CENTER □ Piscataway, NJ

White, Dorothy, Ser.Libn.
SOUTHERN TECHNICAL INSTITUTE - LIBRARY □ Marietta, GA

White, Edna, Asst.Ref.Libn.
SOUTH CAROLINA STATE LIBRARY □ Columbia, SC

White, Edward, Asst.Libn., Pub.Serv.
UNIVERSITY OF ARIZONA - COLLEGE OF LAW LIBRARY □ Tucson, AZ

White, Ernest M., Libn.
LOUISVILLE PRESBYTERIAN THEOLOGICAL SEMINARY - LIBRARY □ Louisville, KY

White, Evy, Art/Slide Libn.
CALIFORNIA INSTITUTE OF THE ARTS - LIBRARY □ Valencia, CA

White, Frank, Hd., Acq.Sect.
CANADA - DEPARTMENT OF FINANCE - FINANCE/TREASURY BOARD LIBRARY □ Ottawa, ON

White, Henry O., Hd.Cat.
MISSISSIPPI VALLEY STATE UNIVERSITY - JAMES HERBERT WHITE LIBRARY □ Itta Bena, MS

White, J.E., Mathematician
U.S. OAK RIDGE NATL. LABORATORY - RADIATION SHIELDING INFORMATION CENTER □ Oak Ridge, TN

White, James J., Asst.Cur. of Art
CARNEGIE-MELLON UNIVERSITY - HUNT INSTITUTE FOR BOTANICAL DOCUMENTATION - LIBRARY □ Pittsburgh, PA

White, Jane, Asst.Libn.
DISTRICT ONE TECHNICAL INSTITUTE - LIBRARY - EDUCATIONAL RESOURCE CENTER □ Eau Claire, WI

White, Jane M., Libn.
MEAD CORPORATION - LIBRARY □ Chillicothe, OH

White, Jane N., Libn.
UNIVERSITY OF KENTUCKY - EDUCATION LIBRARY □ Lexington, KY

White, Jeanne, Act.Libn.
CORNELL UNIVERSITY - ALBERT R. MANN LIBRARY □ Ithaca, NY

White, Jeronell, Lib.Dir.
FLORENCE-DARLINGTON TECHNICAL COLLEGE - LIBRARY □ Florence, SC

White, John, Pub.Serv.Libn.
HUDSON VALLEY COMMUNITY COLLEGE - DWIGHT MARVIN LEARNING RESOURCES CENTER □ Troy, NY

White, John C., Libn.
U.S. VETERANS ADMINISTRATION (OH-Brecksville) - HOSPITAL LIBRARY □ Brecksville, OH

White, Joyce G., M.D., Libn.
HUNTERDON MEDICAL CENTER - MEDICAL LIBRARY □ Flemington, NJ

White, Judith, Sr.Supv.
UNIVERSITY OF VICTORIA - MC PHERSON LIBRARY - MUSIC & AUDIO COLLECTION □ Victoria, BC

White, Lionel, AV
FASHION INSTITUTE OF TECHNOLOGY - LIBRARY/MEDIA SERVICES □ New York, NY

White, Mari, Law Libn.
CROWN LIFE INSURANCE COMPANY - LAW LIBRARY □ Toronto, ON

White, Marian, Libn.
DALLAS PUBLIC LIBRARY - BUSINESS AND TECHNOLOGY DIVISION □ Dallas, TX

White, Mary Jane, Info.Spec.
MICHIGAN EDUCATION ASSOCIATION - LIBRARY □ East Lansing, MI

White, Mary W., Doc.Libn.
SOUTHERN RESEARCH INSTITUTE - THOMAS W. MARTIN MEMORIAL LIBRARY □ Birmingham, AL

White, Maryellen, Asst.Res.Libn.
DENNISON MANUFACTURING COMPANY - RESEARCH LIBRARY □ Framingham, MA

White, Melvin, Chf., Circ.
COLLEGE OF MEDICINE AND DENTISTRY OF NEW JERSEY AT NEWARK - GEORGE F. SMITH LIBRARY □ Newark, NJ

White, Nancy, Asst.Libn.
PACIFIC GAS AND ELECTRIC COMPANY - LIBRARY □ San Francisco, CA

White, Neva L., Cat.
KANSAS STATE UNIVERSITY - FARRELL LIBRARY □ Manhattan, KS

White, Peggy, Ck.
PROVIDENCE MEDICAL CENTER - MEDICAL LIBRARY □ Seattle, WA

White, Rhea A., Cons.
AMERICAN SOCIETY FOR PSYCHICAL RESEARCH - LIBRARY □ New York, NY

White, Richard A., Supv., Archv.
NATIONAL GEOGRAPHIC SOCIETY - ILLUSTRATIONS LIBRARY □ Washington, DC

White, Tera B., Mgr., Corp.Info.Serv.
BLUE CROSS AND BLUE SHIELD OF NORTH CAROLINA - INFORMATION CENTER □ Chapel Hill, NC

White, Teresa, Cat.
ATLANTIC-RICHFIELD COMPANY - HEADQUARTERS LIBRARY □ Los Angeles, CA

White, Thomas E.
U.S. NATL. PARK SERVICE - WALNUT CANYON NATL. MONUMENT - LIBRARY □ Flagstaff, AZ

White, Virginia, Cat.
DIGITAL EQUIPMENT CORPORATION - CORPORATE LIBRARY □ Maynard, MA

White, Virginia, Libn.
LYNCHBURG TRAINING SCHOOL AND HOSPITAL - PROFESSIONAL LIBRARY □ Lynchburg, VA

White, Mrs. W.N., Libn.
RIVERSIDE HOSPITAL - SCOBIE MEMORIAL LIBRARY □ Ottawa, ON

White, Dr. Wayne, Pres.
NATIONAL COUNCIL FOR YEAR-ROUND EDUCATION - LIBRARY □ San Diego, CA

Whitehead, A.B., Supv., Tech.Sup.
U.S. BUREAU OF MINES - SALT LAKE CITY RESEARCH CENTER - LIBRARY □ Salt Lake City, UT

Whitehead, Merriel T., Libn.
VSE CORPORATION - TECHNICAL LIBRARY □ Alexandria, VA

Whitehead, Olive F., Mgr., Lib.Rsrcs.
RCA CORPORATION - GSD - GOVERNMENT COMMUNICATIONS SYSTEMS - LIBRARY □ Camden, NJ

Whitehead, Sue, Hd.Per.
BIOLA COLLEGE, INC. - LIBRARY □ La Mirada, CA

Whitehead, Thomas M., Hd., Spec.Coll.Dept.
TEMPLE UNIVERSITY - CENTRAL LIBRARY SYSTEM - RARE BOOK & MANUSCRIPT COLLECTION □ Philadelphia, PA

Whitehorne, Lorna Z., Libn.
BRANDON TRAINING SCHOOL - LIBRARY □ Brandon, VT

Whitehouse, Helen, Paraprofessional
WASHINGTON STATE LIBRARY - RAINIER SCHOOL STAFF LIBRARY □ Buckley, WA

Whitelock, O.R., Dir.
U.S. NATL. ARCHIVES & RECORDS SERVICE - FEDERAL ARCHIVES AND RECORDS CENTER, REGION 2 □ Bayonne, NJ

Whiteman, Maxwell, Cons./Archv.
UNION LEAGUE OF PHILADELPHIA - LIBRARY □ Philadelphia, PA

Whiteman, Merlin P., Readers Serv.Libn.
INDIANA UNIVERSITY - SCHOOL OF LAW LIBRARY □ Indianapolis, IN

Whitemarsh, Thomas R., Res.Libn.
MAYER (Oscar) & COMPANY - RESEARCH DEPARTMENT LIBRARY □ Madison, WI

Whiteside, Henrietta, Info.Serv.Coord.
EAST-WEST GATEWAY COORDINATING COUNCIL - REFERENCE AREA □ St. Louis, MO

Whiteside, Phyllis J., Med.Libn.
U.S. ARMY HOSPITALS - IRWIN ARMY HOSPITAL - MEDICAL LIBRARY □ Fort Riley, KS

Whiteside, S., Libn.
NOVA SCOTIA MUSEUM - LIBRARY □ Halifax, NS

Whiteway, Ken, Rd.Serv.Libn.
UNIVERSITY OF SASKATCHEWAN - LAW LIBRARY □ Saskatoon, SK

Whitfield, B.L.
U.S. OAK RIDGE NATL. LABORATORY - INFORMATION DIVISION - ENVIRONMENTAL MUTAGEN INFORMATION CENTER □ Oak Ridge, TN

Whitford, Jackie, Libn.
HONEYWELL, INC. - HONEYWELL INFORMATION SYSTEMS - TECHNICAL LIBRARY □ Phoenix, AZ

Whiting, Brooke, Literary Mss.Libn.
UNIVERSITY OF CALIFORNIA, LOS ANGELES - DEPARTMENT OF SPECIAL COLLECTIONS □ Los Angeles, CA

Whiting, David S., Coord.Libn./Media
NEWTON PUBLIC SCHOOLS - TEACHERS' PROFESSIONAL LIBRARY □ Newton, MA

Whiting, Marrin Y., Cur.
BIRMINGHAM PUBLIC AND JEFFERSON COUNTY FREE LIBRARY - J. HUBERT SCRUGGS, JR. COLLECTION OF PHILATELY □ Birmingham, AL

Whitinger, Elaine H., Nursing Libn.
INDIANA UNIVERSITY - SCHOOL OF MEDICINE LIBRARY □ Indianapolis, IN

Whitlock, C.C., Chf.Libn.
ROYAL ROADS MILITARY COLLEGE - LIBRARY □ Victoria, BC

Whitman, Beverly, Lib.Techn.
U.S. NATL. PARK SERVICE - YELLOWSTONE LIBRARY AND MUSEUM ASSOCIATION □ Yellowstone National Park, WY

Whitman, Joan T., Libn.
JAMESON MEMORIAL HOSPITAL - SCHOOL OF NURSING LIBRARY □ New Castle, PA

Whitmore, Dr. Marilyn P., Univ.Archv.
UNIVERSITY OF PITTSBURGH - ARCHIVES □ Pittsburgh, PA

Whitmore, Richard, Libn.
ST. PETER REGIONAL TREATMENT CENTER - STAFF LIBRARY □ St. Peter, MN

Whitney, Byron V., Hd., Tech.Serv.
CLARKSON COLLEGE OF TECHNOLOGY - EDUCATIONAL RESOURCES CENTER □ Potsdam, NY

Whitney, Janet T., Supv.Libn.
CALIFORNIA STATE DEPARTMENT OF JUSTICE - ATTORNEY GENERAL'S OFFICE - LAW LIBRARY □ Los Angeles, CA

Whitney, Josephine J., Tech.Libn.
UNITED AIR LINES, INC. - ENGINEERING DEPARTMENT - LIBRARY □ San Francisco, CA

Whitney, Kenneth, Co-Cur.
AURORA HISTORICAL SOCIETY - ELBERT HUBBARD LIBRARY AND MUSEUM □ East Aurora, NY

Whitney, Mrs. Kenneth, Co-Cur.
AURORA HISTORICAL SOCIETY - ELBERT HUBBARD LIBRARY AND MUSEUM □ East Aurora, NY

Whitney, Virginia B., Med.Libn.
WAKE COUNTY MEDICAL CENTER - MEDICAL LIBRARY □ Raleigh, NC

Whitson, Vivienne, Chf.Libn.
METROPOLITAN HOSPITAL CENTER - FREDERICK M. DEARBORN MEDICAL LIBRARY □ New York, NY

Whitt, Chester, Public Serv.
BROOME COMMUNITY COLLEGE - CECIL C. TYRRELL LEARNING RESOURCES CENTER □ Binghamton, NY

Whittemore, Dorothy, Dir.
TULANE UNIVERSITY OF LOUISIANA - SCHOOL OF BUSINESS ADMINISTRATION - NORMAN MAYER LIBRARY □ New Orleans, LA

Whitten, Alice, Lib.Tech.Asst.
CALIFORNIA STATE DEPARTMENT OF TRANSPORTATION - DISTRICT 4 LIBRARY □ San Francisco, CA

Whittick, Judith A., Info.Res.
MEMORIAL UNIVERSITY OF NEWFOUNDLAND - OCEAN ENGINEERING INFORMATION CENTRE □ St. John's, NF

Whittick, Susan, Libn.
ALCOHOLISM COMMISSION OF SASKATCHEWAN - LIBRARY □ Regina, SK

Whittier, Steve, Libn.
SOUTHEAST LOUISIANA HOSPITAL - PROFESSIONAL LIBRARY □ Mandeville, LA

Whittle, Susan, Pub.Lib.Cons.
STATE LIBRARY OF FLORIDA □ Tallahassee, FL

Whittock, John M., Jr., Libn.
UNIVERSITY OF PENNSYLVANIA - SCHOOL OF DENTAL MEDICINE - LEON LEVY LIBRARY □ Philadelphia, PA

Whitzman, Susan, Asst. Campus Libn.
CENTENNIAL COLLEGE OF APPLIED ARTS & TECHNOLOGY - PROGRESS CAMPUS RESOURCE CENTRE □ Scarborough, ON

Wholley, Diana, Asst.Libn.
CHOATE, HALL AND STEWART - LAW LIBRARY □ Boston, MA

Whyte, Lisa, Res.
CHASE MANHATTAN BANK, N.A. - INFORMATION CENTER □ New York, NY

Wiacek, Elma, Acq.
SOUTHERN CONNECTICUT STATE COLLEGE - H.C. BULEY LIBRARY □ New Haven, CT

Wiant, Sarah K., Dir.
WASHINGTON & LEE UNIVERSITY - LAW LIBRARY □ Lexington, VA

Wiberg, Gene, Exec.Sec.
REPUBLICAN ASSOCIATES OF LOS ANGELES COUNTY - RESEARCH LIBRARY □ Glendale, CA

Wichers, Dr. Willard, Musm.Dir.
NETHERLANDS MUSEUM - ARCHIVES AND LIBRARY □ Holland, MI

Wickens, Marjorie, Libn.
FORINTEK CANADA CORPORATION - EASTERN FOREST PRODUCTS LABORATORY - LIBRARY □ Ottawa, ON

Wicklund, Nancy A., Asst.Libn./Ref.
WESTMINSTER CHOIR COLLEGE - TALBOTT LIBRARY □ Princeton, NJ

Wickman, Dr. John E., Dir.
U.S. PRESIDENTIAL LIBRARIES - DWIGHT D. EISENHOWER LIBRARY □ Abilene, KS

Wickremeratne, Swarna, Lib.Hd.
THEOSOPHICAL SOCIETY IN AMERICA - OLCOTT LIBRARY & RESEARCH CENTER □ Wheaton, IL

Wickwire, Cynthia, Circuit Libn.
CLEVELAND HEALTH SCIENCES LIBRARY - ALLEN MEMORIAL LIBRARY □ Cleveland, OH

Widder, Keith R., Cur.
MACKINAC ISLAND STATE PARK COMMISSION - HISTORICAL RESEARCH COLLECTION □ Lansing, MI

Widdicombe, Richard P., Dir.
STEVENS INSTITUTE OF TECHNOLOGY - SAMUEL C. WILLIAMS LIBRARY □ Hoboken, NJ

Widdicombe, Ruth, Archv./Libn.
ROCK COUNTY HISTORICAL SOCIETY - ARCHIVES OF ROCK COUNTY HISTORY □ Janesville, WI

Widger, Betty J., Genealogist
PORTAGE COUNTY HISTORICAL SOCIETY, INC. - LIBRARY AND MUSEUM □ Ravenna, OH

Widner, Evelyn M., Sr.Res.Assoc.
UNIVERSITY OF CINCINNATI - DEPARTMENT OF ENVIRONMENTAL HEALTH LIBRARY □ Cincinnati, OH

Wiebusch, Larry, Musm.Chm.
BLUE SPRINGS HISTORICAL SOCIETY - LIBRARY □ Independence, MO

Wieckowski, Karen, Asst.Libn.
GREENVILLE GENERAL HOSPITAL - MEDICAL LIBRARY □ Greenville, SC

Wiedel, Ann E., Hd.Libn.
SECURITY PACIFIC NATIONAL BANK - BANK LIBRARY □ Los Angeles, CA

Wiederaenders, Robert C., Archv.
AMERICAN LUTHERAN CHURCH - ARCHIVES □ Dubuque, IA

Wiedersheim, William A., Archv.
NEW HAVEN COLONY HISTORICAL SOCIETY - LIBRARY □ New Haven, CT

Wiegand, Nancy M., Libn.
LEWIS, RICE, TUCKER, ALLEN AND CHUBB - LAW LIBRARY □ St. Louis, MO

Wieland, Larry, Libn.
U.S. DEPT. OF LABOR - EMPLOYMENT & TRAINING ADMINISTRATION - REGION 8 TECHNICAL RESOURCE LIBRARY □ Denver, CO

Wienberg, Beatrice, Asst.Libn.
INDUSTRIAL HOME FOR THE BLIND - NASSAU-SUFFOLK BRAILLE LIBRARY □ Hempstead, NY

Wiener, Alissa, ILL Asst.
MINNESOTA HISTORICAL SOCIETY - REFERENCE LIBRARY □ St. Paul, MN

Wiener, Dr. Israel, Lib.Chm./Libn.
CONGREGATION BETH ACHIM - JOSEPH KATKOWSKY LIBRARY □ Livonia, MI

Wiens, Elizabeth, Cat.
SOUTHERN CONNECTICUT STATE COLLEGE - H.C. BULEY LIBRARY □ New Haven, CT

Wierenga, Janice A., Libn.
BASF WYANDOTTE CORPORATION - PIGMENTS DIVISION LIBRARY □ Holland, MI

Wiers, Rita, Sr. Typist
NEW YORK STATE DEPARTMENT OF AUDIT CONTROL - LIBRARY □ Albany, NY

Wierzba, Heidemarie B., Sect.Supv.
ALLERGAN PHARMACEUTICALS, INC. -
PROFESSIONAL INFORMATION SERVICES □
Irvine, CA

Wiese, Patricia, Dir., Audio Ctr.
UNIVERSITY OF WISCONSIN, MILWAUKEE -
MUSIC COLLECTION □ Milwaukee, WI

Wiese, Dr. W.L., Dir.
U.S. NATL. BUREAU OF STANDARDS - DATA
CENTER ON ATOMIC LINE SHAPES AND SHIFTS
□ Washington, DC

Wiese, Dr. W.L., Hd.
U.S. NATL. BUREAU OF STANDARDS - DATA
CENTER ON ATOMIC TRANSITION
PROBABILITIES □ Washington, DC

Wiesenthal, Diane, Chf., Lib.Serv.
U.S. VETERANS ADMINISTRATION (AZ-Phoenix)
- HOSPITAL LIBRARY □ Phoenix, AZ

Wigent, Evelyn S., Libn.
ST. ELIZABETH MEDICAL CENTER - SCHOOL OF
NURSING LIBRARY □ Lafayette, IN

Wiggins, Gary, Hd.
INDIANA UNIVERSITY - CHEMISTRY LIBRARY □
Bloomington, IN

Wiggins, Lillian, Dir.-Cur.
EL MONTE HISTORICAL SOCIETY - MUSEUM
LIBRARY □ El Monte, CA

Wiggins, Terry, Hd.Libn.
MEDICAL COLLEGE OF PENNSYLVANIA -
EASTERN PENNSYLVANIA PSYCHIATRIC
INSTITUTE - LIBRARY □ Philadelphia, PA

Wight, Gudrun, Media Spec.
UNIVERSITY OF CALGARY - EDUCATION
MATERIALS CENTER □ Calgary, AB

Wightman, Mary Frances, Tech.Libn.
DELAWARE RIVER BASIN COMMISSION -
TECHNICAL LIBRARY □ Trenton, NJ

Wiist, Stephen R., Tech.Serv.Libn.
U.S. MERCHANT MARINE ACADEMY -
SCHUYLER OTIS BLAND MEMORIAL LIBRARY □
Kings Point, NY

Wijegoonawardena, Badra
NATIONAL FOUNDATION FOR CONSUMER
CREDIT - LIBRARY □ Washington, DC

Wikander, E. Marie, Asst.Libn.
CLARK (Sterling and Francine) ART INSTITUTE -
LIBRARY □ Williamstown, MA

Wiktor, Christian L., Law Libn.
DALHOUSIE UNIVERSITY - LAW LIBRARY □
Halifax, NS

Wilber, Kaylene B., Hd.Libn.
TRI-COUNTY TECHNICAL COLLEGE - LIBRARY □
Pendleton, SC

Wilbur, Helen L., Mgr., Info.Serv.
ZINC INSTITUTE - INFORMATION SERVICE □
New York, NY

Wilbur, Lowell R., Libn.
IOWA STATE DEPARTMENT OF HISTORY AND
ARCHIVES - IOWA HISTORICAL LIBRARY □ Des
Moines, IA

Wilbur, Marjorie
AMPEX CORPORATION - TECHNICAL LIBRARY
MS 3-10 □ Redwood City, CA

Wilbur, Ruth, Libn.
SOCIETY OF MAYFLOWER DESCENDANTS IN
THE STATE OF CALIFORNIA - LIBRARY □ San
Francisco, CA

Wilbur, Ruth E., Dir.
NORTHAMPTON HISTORICAL SOCIETY -
HISTORICAL COLLECTION □ Northampton, MA

Wilburn, Gene, Hd.Libn.
ROYAL ONTARIO MUSEUM - LIBRARY □ Toronto,
ON

Wilcox, Alice E., Dir.
MINITEX □ Minneapolis, MN

Wilcox, Bill, Chf., Interp.
U.S. NATL. PARK SERVICE - BOOKER T.
WASHINGTON NATL. MONUMENT - LIBRARY □
Hardy, VA

Wilcox, Harold E., Supv.
UNITED TECHNOLOGIES CORPORATION -
CHEMICAL SYSTEMS DIVISION - LIBRARY □
Sunnyvale, CA

Wilcox, June, Preparations Libn.
HUNTINGTON (Henry E.) LIBRARY, ART
GALLERY AND BOTANICAL GARDENS □ San
Marino, CA

Wilcox, Lloyd, Libn.
SOUTHERN OHIO GENEALOGICAL SOCIETY -
REFERENCE LIBRARY □ Hillsboro, OH

Wilcox, Marjorie C., Exec.Dir.
GRAND RAPIDS LAW LIBRARY □ Grand Rapids,
MI

Wild, Larry, Coord.Bus./Tech.Serv.
MARICOPA TECHNICAL COMMUNITY COLLEGE
- LIBRARY RESOURCE CENTER □ Phoenix, AZ

Wild, Norine E., Libn.
CLEVELAND PSYCHOANALYTIC SOCIETY -
LIBRARY □ Cleveland, OH

Wilde, Lucy, Gen.Ref.
KANSAS STATE UNIVERSITY - FARRELL
LIBRARY □ Manhattan, KS

Wildemuth, Barbara M., Assoc.Dir.
ERIC CLEARINGHOUSE ON TESTS,
MEASUREMENT AND EVALUATION □ Princeton,
NJ

Wilder, Carolyn, Info.Anl.
TOWERS, PERRIN, FORSTER & CROSBY, INC. -
INFORMATION CENTER □ New York, NY

Wilder, D. Adel, Mgr., Lib.
CALIFORNIA INSTITUTE OF TECHNOLOGY -
JET PROPULSION LABORATORY - LIBRARY □
Pasadena, CA

Wilder, David, Dir.
LONG ISLAND LIBRARY RESOURCES COUNCIL,
INC. (LILRC) □ Bellport, NY

Wilder, M. Alice, Tech.Info.Spec.
XEROX CORPORATION - PALO ALTO RESEARCH
CENTER - TECHNICAL INFORMATION CENTER
□ Palo Alto, CA

Wilder, Mary, Ref./Biblog.
UNIVERSITY OF COLORADO, BOULDER -
GOVERNMENT PUBLICATIONS DIVISION □
Boulder, CO

Wilder, Ulah, Hd.Libn.
OAKLAND CITY COLLEGE - FOUNDERS
MEMORIAL LIBRARY □ Oakland City, IN

Wilder-Jones, Robert, Info.Anl.
UNIVERSITY OF CALIFORNIA, LOS ANGELES -
BRAIN INFORMATION SERVICE □ Los Angeles,
CA

Wildey, Emily M., Libn.
NEW YORK STATE SUPREME COURT - 3RD
JUDICIAL DISTRICT - LAW LIBRARY □ Hudson,
NY

Wildgoose, N., Hd.Pub.Serv.
CANADA - HEALTH AND WELFARE CANADA -
DEPARTMENTAL LIBRARY SERVICES □ Ottawa,
ON

Wildin, Nancy, Hd.
SEATTLE PUBLIC LIBRARY - LITERATURE,
LANGUAGES, PHILOSOPHY & RELIGION
DEPARTMENT □ Seattle, WA

Wildman, Iris, Pub.Serv.Libn.
STANFORD UNIVERSITY - LAW LIBRARY □
Stanford, CA

Wildman, Joni, Dir.
BATTLE CREEK SANITARIUM HOSPITAL -
MEDICAL LIBRARY □ Battle Creek, MI

Wilensky, Elsie, Med.Libn.
NORTH SHORE UNIVERSITY HOSPITAL -
DANIEL CARROLL PAYSON MEDICAL LIBRARY □
Manhasset, NY

Wiley, Terese K., Acq.Libn.
KENRICK SEMINARY LIBRARY □ St. Louis, MO

Wiley, Theresa K., Lib.Mgr.
UNIVERSITY OF KENTUCKY - INSTITUTE FOR
MINING AND MINERALS RESEARCH - IMMR
LIBRARY □ Lexington, KY

Wiley, Wilda, Libn.
TENNECO, INC. - TENNECO OIL COMPANY -
GEOLOGICAL RESEARCH LIBRARY □ Houston,
TX

Wilford, Enid L., Base Libn.
U.S. AIR FORCE BASE - CASTLE BASE - BAKER
LIBRARY □ Castle AFB, CA

Wilgus, Sue, Musm.Dir.
BARTHOLOMEW COUNTY HISTORICAL
SOCIETY - MUSEUM LIBRARY □ Columbus, IN

Wilhelm, Diane, Ref.Libn.
ILLINOIS STATE HISTORICAL LIBRARY □
Springfield, IL

Wilhelm, Mara R., Chf., Lib.Serv.
U.S. VETERANS ADMINISTRATION (AL-
Montgomery) - MEDICAL CENTER LIBRARY
(142D) □ Montgomery, AL

Wilhelm, Paula, Assoc.Libn.
CLEVELAND ELECTRIC ILLUMINATING
COMPANY - LIBRARY □ Cleveland, OH

Wilhelm, Stephen, Media Oper.Coord.
BABSON COLLEGE - HORN LIBRARY □ Babson
Park, MA

Wilhide, Betsy
PENNWALT CORPORATION - TECHNICAL
DIVISION LIBRARY □ King Of Prussia, PA

Wilhite, Carolyn, Libn.
GRACE (W.R.) AND COMPANY - AGRICULTURAL
CHEMICALS GROUP - PLANNING SERVICES
LIBRARY □ Memphis, TN

Wilhoit, Frances
INDIANA UNIVERSITY - JOURNALISM LIBRARY
□ Bloomington, IN

Wilimovsky, Diana, Libn.
MAC MILLAN BLOEDEL RESEARCH LIMITED -
LIBRARY □ Vancouver, BC

Wilken, Madeleine, Assoc. Law Libn.
WESTERN NEW ENGLAND COLLEGE - SCHOOL
OF LAW LIBRARY □ Springfield, MA

Wilkens, Carol, Comp.Ref.Ctr.Hd.
CHICAGO PUBLIC LIBRARY CENTRAL LIBRARY -
BUSINESS/SCIENCE/TECHNOLOGY DIVISION
□ Chicago, IL

Wilkerson, Robert C., Mgr.Adm.Sys.
CELANESE CORPORATION - CELANESE
CHEMICAL COMPANY, INC. - TECHNICAL
CENTER - LIBRARY □ Corpus Christi, TX

Wilkerson, Stiefel J., Pres.
KNOX COUNTY HISTORICAL SOCIETY -
LIBRARY □ Edina, MO

Wilkes, Adeline W., Libn.
FLORIDA STATE UNIVERSITY - LIBRARY
SCIENCE LIBRARY □ Tallahassee, FL

Wilkes, Col. Quenten L., Commander
U.S. AIR FORCE ENVIRONMENTAL TECHNICAL
APPLICATIONS CENTER - AIR WEATHER
SERVICE TECHNICAL LIBRARY □ Scott AFB, IL

Wilkie, Elizabeth, Hd., Center Lib.
U.S. NAVY - NAVAL WEAPONS CENTER -
LIBRARY DIVISION □ China Lake, CA

Wilkins, Barratt, State Libn.
STATE LIBRARY OF FLORIDA □ Tallahassee, FL

Wilkins, Betty, Assoc. Law Libn.
UNIVERSITY OF WASHINGTON - LAW SCHOOL
LIBRARY □ Seattle, WA

Wilkins, Diane, Ref./Coll.Libn.
WILFRID LAURIER UNIVERSITY - LIBRARY □
Waterloo, ON

Wilkins, Eleanore E., Libn.
U.S. GEOLOGICAL SURVEY - LIBRARY □ Menlo
Park, CA

Wilkins, Ms. Lane, Dir.
UNIVERSITY OF UTAH - LAW LIBRARY □ Salt
Lake City, UT

Wilkins, Dr. Madeleine J., Mgr.
NATIONAL RECREATION AND PARK
ASSOCIATION - JOSEPH LEE MEMORIAL
LIBRARY AND INFORMATION CENTER □
Arlington, VA

Wilkins, Madge L., Libn.
HUGHES TOOL COMPANY - BUSINESS AND
TECHNICAL LIBRARY □ Houston, TX

Wilkins, Marilyn, Div.Hd.
NEW ORLEANS PUBLIC LIBRARY - ART, MUSIC
& RECREATION DIVISION □ New Orleans, LA

Wilkins, Mary Ann, Libn.
DUKE UNIVERSITY - MATH-PHYSICS LIBRARY □
Durham, NC

Williams, Janelle S., Libn.
U.S. ARMY TRANSPORTATION - TECHNICAL INFORMATION AND RESEARCH CENTER □ Newport News, VA

Williams, Janet, Libn.
EDUCATIONAL TESTING SERVICE - CARL CAMPBELL BRIGHAM LIBRARY □ Princeton, NJ

Williams, Janice, Libn.
KETTERING (Charles F.) RESEARCH LABORATORY - LIBRARY □ Yellow Springs, OH

Williams, Jean, Acq.Libn.
VIRGINIA STATE UNIVERSITY - JOHNSTON MEMORIAL LIBRARY □ Petersburg, VA

Williams, Jean C., Chf.Libn.
U.S. VETERANS ADMINISTRATION (IA-Iowa City) - HOSPITAL LIBRARY □ Iowa City, IA

Williams, Jean S., Sr.Lib.Asst.
DUKE UNIVERSITY - MARINE LABORATORY - A.S. PEARSE MEMORIAL LIBRARY □ Beaufort, NC

Williams, Jeane M., Archv.
HISTORICAL PICTURES SERVICE, INC. □ Chicago, IL

Williams, Jeanne, Circ.Supv.
UNIVERSITY OF PENNSYLVANIA - BIDDLE LAW LIBRARY □ Philadelphia, PA

Williams, Jill, Cat.
ATOMIC ENERGY OF CANADA, LTD. - TECHNICAL INFORMATION BRANCH - MAIN LIBRARY □ Chalk River, ON

Williams, John H., Sr. Law Libn.
FEDERAL RESERVE BANK OF NEW YORK - LAW LIBRARY DIVISION □ New York, NY

Williams, June B., Libn.
COOPERS AND LYBRAND - LIBRARY □ Los Angeles, CA

Williams, June B., Libn.
LUCE, FORWARD, HAMILTON & SCRIPPS - LIBRARY □ San Diego, CA

Williams, Karin H., Corp.Libn.
WEYERHAEUSER COMPANY - CORPORATE LIBRARY □ Tacoma, WA

Williams, Ken, Libn.
INSTITUTE FOR BEHAVIORAL RESEARCH - LIBRARY □ Silver Spring, MD

Williams, Kenneth, Per.Libn.
HUDSON VALLEY COMMUNITY COLLEGE - DWIGHT MARVIN LEARNING RESOURCES CENTER □ Troy, NY

Williams, Kerry, Libn.
TEXAS STATE AIR CONTROL BOARD - LIBRARY □ Austin, TX

Williams, Laurence, Media Ctr.Libn.
WEST LIBERTY STATE COLLEGE - ELBIN LIBRARY □ West Liberty, WV

Williams, Luester, Lib.Asst.
TUSKEGEE INSTITUTE - DEPARTMENT OF ARCHITECTURE LIBRARY† □ Tuskegee Institute, AL

Williams, Lynda Jane, Libn.
PRINCE GEORGE CITIZEN - NEWSPAPER LIBRARY □ Prince George, BC

Williams, M.L., ILL & Per.Libn.
SOUTHERN METHODIST UNIVERSITY - PERKINS SCHOOL OF THEOLOGY - LIBRARY □ Dallas, TX

Williams, Mae E., Libn.
MERCER MEDICAL CENTER - DAVID B. ACKLEY MEDICAL LIBRARY □ Trenton, NJ

Williams, Marcia J., Per.Libn.
HUGHES AIRCRAFT COMPANY - TECHNICAL LIBRARY □ Culver City, CA

Williams, Marvin, Hd.Cat.
TENNESSEE STATE LIBRARY - STATE LIBRARY DIVISION □ Nashville, TN

Williams, Mary, Libn.
CAMBRIDGE MENTAL HEALTH & DEVELOPMENTAL CENTER - STAFF & RESIDENT RESOURCE CENTER □ Cambridge, OH

Williams, Mary, Libn.
ONTARIO - CIVIL SERVICE COMMISSION - LIBRARY □ Toronto, ON

Williams, Mary E., Venango Campus Libn.
CLARION STATE COLLEGE - RENA M. CARLSON LIBRARY □ Clarion, PA

Williams, Mary E., Libn.
U.S. NAVY - OFFICE OF THE GENERAL COUNSEL - LAW LIBRARY □ Washington, DC

Williams, Mary-Lois, Cat.
CANADIAN IMPERIAL BANK OF COMMERCE - INFORMATION CENTRE □ Toronto, ON

Williams, Maudine B., Hd.Libn.
INDIANA UNIVERSITY - HERRON SCHOOL OF ART - LIBRARY □ Indianapolis, IN

Williams, Michael L., Cat.
U.S. COMMISSION ON CIVIL RIGHTS - NATL. CLEARINGHOUSE LIBRARY □ Washington, DC

Williams, Mildred, Hd.Asst.
CHICAGO PUBLIC LIBRARY CULTURAL CENTER - THOMAS HUGHES CHILDREN'S LIBRARY □ Chicago, IL

Williams, Millicent, Libn.
JOHN DEERE PRODUCT ENGINEERING CENTER - LIBRARY □ Waterloo, IA

Williams, Mitsuko, Asst.Libn.
UNIVERSITY OF ILLINOIS - BIOLOGY LIBRARY □ Urbana, IL

Williams, Nancy W., Ref.Libn.
INDIANA UNIVERSITY/PURDUE UNIVERSITY AT INDIANAPOLIS - 38TH STREET CAMPUS LIBRARY □ Indianapolis, IN

Williams, Dr. Nyal, Music Libn.
BALL STATE UNIVERSITY - MUSIC LIBRARY □ Muncie, IN

Williams, Pam, Assoc.Libn.
UNIVERSITY OF FLORIDA - LAW LIBRARY □ Gainesville, FL

Williams, Pat, Dir. of Planning
HARTFORD - CITY PLAN LIBRARY □ Hartford, CT

Williams, Patricia, Tech.Libn.
ABAM ENGINEERS, INC. - TECHNICAL LIBRARY □ Tacoma, WA

Williams, Patricia, Sr.Libn.
HOFFMANN-LA ROCHE, INC. - BUSINESS INFORMATION CENTER □ Nutley, NJ

Williams, Patricia A., Sr.Libn.
HENNEPIN COUNTY MEDICAL CENTER - HEALTH SCIENCES LIBRARY □ Minneapolis, MN

Williams, Randall, Dir.
SOUTHERN POVERTY LAW CENTER - KLANWATCH - LIBRARY □ Montgomery, AL

Williams, Dr. Richmond D., Lib.Dir.
ELEUTHERIAN MILLS HISTORICAL LIBRARY □ Wilmington, DE

Williams, Robert, Ref.Libn.
OHIO STATE UNIVERSITY - HEALTH SCIENCES LIBRARY □ Columbus, OH

Williams, Robert C.
FREE LIBRARY OF PHILADELPHIA - MUSIC DEPARTMENT - DRINKER LIBRARY OF CHORAL MUSIC □ Philadelphia, PA

Williams, Robert C., Libn.
UNIVERSITY OF ALASKA - INSTITUTE OF MARINE SCIENCE - LIBRARY □ Fairbanks, AK

Williams, Robert C., Inst.Libn.
UNIVERSITY OF ALASKA - INSTITUTE OF MARINE SCIENCE - SEWARD MARINE STATION LIBRARY □ Seward, AK

Williams, Roger, Jr., Libn.
STONINGTON HISTORICAL SOCIETY - WHITEHALL LIBRARY □ Stonington, CT

Williams, Roger M., Hd.Libn./Archv.
NAZARENE BIBLE COLLEGE - LIBRARY □ Colorado Springs, CO

Williams, Ruth J., Libn.
BAKER (Michael, Jr.), INC. - LIBRARY □ Beaver, PA

Williams, S., Health Educ.Libn.
HURLEY MEDICAL CENTER - HAMADY HEALTH SCIENCES LIBRARY □ Flint, MI

Williams, Sheryl K., Cur.
UNIVERSITY OF KANSAS - KANSAS COLLECTION □ Lawrence, KS

Williams, Sheryl K., Cur., Kansas Coll.
UNIVERSITY OF KANSAS - WILCOX COLLECTION OF CONTEMPORARY POLITICAL MOVEMENTS □ Lawrence, KS

Williams, Stephanie V., Hd., Tech.Doc.Sec.
U.S. NAVY - NAVAL SEA SYSTEMS COMMAND - LIBRARY DOCUMENTATION BRANCH (SEA 9961) □ Washington, DC

Williams, Sue, Libn.
AMERICAN AUTOMOBILE ASSOCIATION - LIBRARY □ Falls Church, VA

Williams, Ted L., Med.Lib.Off.
U.S. AIR FORCE HOSPITAL - MEDICAL LIBRARY (FL-Patrick AFB) □ Patrick AFB, FL

Williams, Veronica, Libn.
U.S. NATL. ARCHIVES & RECORDS SERVICE - NATL. ARCHIVES LIBRARY □ Washington, DC

Williams, W.A., Info.Spec.
GENERAL TIRE AND RUBBER COMPANY - RESEARCH DIVISION INFORMATION CENTER □ Akron, OH

Williamson, Anne K., Cur.
JONES LIBRARY □ Amherst, MA

Williamson, Harriet, Dir.
MERCY HOSPITAL - LIBRARY □ Urbana, IL

Williamson, J. Reid, Jr., Pres.
HISTORIC LANDMARKS FOUNDATION OF INDIANA, INC. - INFORMATION CENTER □ Indianapolis, IN

Williamson, James, Assoc.Libn.Pub.Serv.
SUNY - COLLEGE OF ENVIRONMENTAL SCIENCE AND FORESTRY - F. FRANKLIN MOON LIBRARY □ Syracuse, NY

Williamson, Jane, Ser.Libn.
MEMPHIS THEOLOGICAL SEMINARY - LIBRARY □ Memphis, TN

Williamson, Jane, Libn.
WOMEN'S ACTION ALLIANCE, INC. - LIBRARY □ New York, NY

Williamson, Miriam B., Libn.
BLOUNT MEMORIAL HOSPITAL - LESLIE R. LINGEMAN MEMORIAL MEDICAL LIBRARY □ Maryville, TN

Williamson, Nan, Supv.Doc. Delivery
CAROLINA LIBRARY SERVICES □ Chapel Hill, NC

Williamson, Wendy, Graduate Res.Asst.
UNIVERSITY OF MINNESOTA - ECONOMICS RESEARCH LIBRARY □ Minneapolis, MN

Williard, Raelen, Libn.
NATIONAL CENTER FOR APPROPRIATE TECHNOLOGY - LIBRARY □ Butte, MT

Willig, Maureen T., Libn.
TAFT, STETTINIUS & HOLLISTER - LAW LIBRARY □ Cincinnati, OH

Willingham, Jacqueline G., Asst.Hd.Cat.Dept.
UNIVERSITY OF TEXAS, EL PASO - LIBRARY □ El Paso, TX

Willingham, Robert M., Act.Asst.Dir.
UNIVERSITY OF GEORGIA - RARE BOOKS DEPARTMENT □ Athens, GA

Willis, Dorothy B., Libn.
IMMANUEL MEDICAL CENTER - PROFESSIONAL LIBRARY □ Omaha, NE

Willis, H.B., Dir.
ISOTTA FRASCHINI OWNERS ASSOCIATION - RESEARCH LIBRARY □ North Fort Meyers, FL

Willis, Jeffrey A., Hd.Libn.
TALLADEGA COUNTY LAW LIBRARY □ Talladega, AL

Willis, M., Med.Libn.
SCHUMPERT MEDICAL CENTER - MEDICAL LIBRARY □ Shreveport, LA

Willis, Melinda R., Lib.Techn.
UNIVERSITY OF OKLAHOMA - CHEMISTRY-MATHEMATICS LIBRARY □ Norman, OK

Willis, Paul J., Archv.
INTERNATIONAL FORTEAN ORGANIZATION - INFO RESEARCH LIBRARY □ College Park, MD

Willis, Dr. Stephen, Hd., Mss.Coll.
NATIONAL LIBRARY OF CANADA - MUSIC DIVISION □ Ottawa, ON

Willoughby, Nona C., Hd.Libn.
NORTHERN WESTCHESTER HOSPITAL CENTER - HEALTH SCIENCES LIBRARY □ Mount Kisco, NY

Wills, Alice, Tech.Serv.
ENVIRONMENTAL PROTECTION AGENCY - HEADQUARTERS LIBRARY □ Washington, DC

Wills, Duncan
NORTHERN PIGMENT LIMITED - TECHNICAL LIBRARY† □ Toronto, ON

Wills, Keith C., Dir. of Libs.
SOUTHWESTERN BAPTIST THEOLOGICAL SEMINARY - FLEMING LIBRARY □ Fort Worth, TX

Wills, Lisa, Libn.
GULF COAST WASTE DISPOSAL AUTHORITY - RESEARCH AND DEVELOPMENT LIBRARY □ Houston, TX

Wills, Richard D., Libn.
WESTERN STATE HOSPITAL - MEDICAL LIBRARY □ Staunton, VA

Willson, Gordon L., Society Pres.
SAUK COUNTY HISTORICAL SOCIETY, INC. - HISTORICAL MUSEUM LIBRARY □ Baraboo, WI

Willson, Katherine H., Mgr., Info.Serv.
FUTURES GROUP, INC. - LIBRARY □ Glastonbury, CT

Wilson, Ann M., Libn.
INTERMETRICS INC. - LIBRARY □ Cambridge, MA

Wilson, Barbara, Chf., Spec.Lib.Serv.
RHODE ISLAND STATE DEPARTMENT OF STATE LIBRARY SERVICES □ Providence, RI

Wilson, Barbara A., Med.Libn.
SANTA CLARA VALLEY MEDICAL CENTER - MEDICAL LIBRARY □ San Jose, CA

Wilson, Beth, Asst.Libn.
MISSOURI HISTORICAL SOCIETY - RESEARCH LIBRARY □ St. Louis, MO

Wilson, Beverly, Asst.Libn., Tech.Serv.
COLUMBUS TECHNICAL INSTITUTE - EDUCATIONAL RESOURCES CENTER† □ Columbus, OH

Wilson, Ms. Bobbi, Libn.
OTTAWA INSTITUTE - IRENE HOLM MEMORIAL LIBRARY □ Columbus, OH

Wilson, Bonnie, Hd.
MINNESOTA HISTORICAL SOCIETY - SPECIAL LIBRARIES □ St. Paul, MN

Wilson, Bonnie L., Libn.
FRANKLIN INSTITUTE OF BOSTON - LIBRARY □ Boston, MA

Wilson, Carol, Libn.
SANTA BARBARA NEWS PRESS - LIBRARY □ Santa Barbara, CA

Wilson, Carol R., Libn.
UNIVERSITY OF MICHIGAN - CENTER FOR RESEARCH ON ECONOMIC DEVELOPMENT □ Ann Arbor, MI

Wilson, Carole, Sr.Asst.Libn.
SAN DIEGO STATE UNIVERSITY - MEDIA & CURRICULUM CENTER □ San Diego, CA

Wilson, Catherine W., Libn.
WORKMEN'S COMPENSATION BOARD OF ONTARIO - HOSPITAL & REHABILITATION CENTRE - MEDICAL LIBRARY □ Downsview, ON

Wilson, Christopher, Asst.Cat.
CANADIAN MUSIC CENTRE - LIBRARY □ Toronto, ON

Wilson, Connie, Libn.
UNIVERSITY OF ARKANSAS, FAYETTEVILLE - MEDICAL CENTER - NORTHWEST ARKANSAS HEALTH EDUCATION CENTER □ Fayetteville, AR

Wilson, Cora R., Libn.
SPOKANE MEDICAL LIBRARY □ Spokane, WA

Wilson, D.H., Dir. of Educ.
CANADIAN WOOD COUNCIL - LIBRARY □ Ottawa, ON

Wilson, D. Keith, Pub.Serv./Automation
BRIGHAM YOUNG UNIVERSITY, HAWAII CAMPUS - JOSEPH F. SMITH LIBRARY AND MEDIA CENTER □ Laie, HI

Wilson, David K., Cur.
CUSTER COUNTY HISTORICAL SOCIETY - LIBRARY □ Broken Bow, NE

Wilson, Diane, Film Libn.
MICHIGAN STATE DEPARTMENT OF LABOR - MICHIGAN EMPLOYMENT SECURITY COMMISSION - LIBRARY □ Detroit, MI

Wilson, Dorothy, Libn.
WESTERN ELECTRIC COMPANY, INC. - TECHNICAL LIBRARY □ Shreveport, LA

Wilson, Dorothy I., Ed.Asst.
UNIVERSITY OF MISSISSIPPI - BUREAU OF GOVERNMENTAL RESEARCH LIBRARY □ University, MS

Wilson, Edna, Lib.Asst.
UNIVERSITY OF SASKATCHEWAN - ENGINEERING BRANCH LIBRARY □ Saskatoon, SK

Wilson, Rev. Edwin H., Hist.
FELLOWSHIP OF RELIGIOUS HUMANISTS - BRANCH LIBRARY† □ Cocoa Beach, FL

Wilson, Edwin H., Hist.
FELLOWSHIP OF RELIGIOUS HUMANISTS - LIBRARY □ Yellow Springs, OH

Wilson, Eleanor C., Libn.
BARRINGTON COLLEGE - LIBRARY □ Barrington, RI

Wilson, Fred L., Jr., Med. Staff Libn.
CONEMAUGH VALLEY MEMORIAL HOSPITAL - MEDICAL STAFF LIBRARY □ Johnstown, PA

Wilson, Greta S., Mss.Libn.
HOWARD UNIVERSITY - MOORLAND-SPINGARN RESEARCH CENTER - MANUSCRIPT DIVISION □ Washington, DC

Wilson, Guy, Chf., Ref.Serv. A
U.S. GENERAL ACCOUNTING OFFICE - TECHNICAL INFORMATION SOURCES AND SERVICES BRANCH □ Washington, DC

Wilson, Helen M., Libn.
HISTORICAL SOCIETY OF WESTERN PENNSYLVANIA - LIBRARY □ Pittsburgh, PA

Wilson, Helen M., Libn.
WESTERN PENNSYLVANIA GENEALOGICAL SOCIETY - LIBRARY □ Pittsburgh, PA

Wilson, Mrs. Howard, Med.Libn.
ST. FRANCIS HOSPITAL - MEDICAL LIBRARY □ Poughkeepsie, NY

Wilson, Mrs. Howard A., Med.Libn.
VASSAR BROTHERS HOSPITAL - MEDICAL LIBRARY □ Poughkeepsie, NY

Wilson, Ian E., Prov.Archv.
SASKATCHEWAN ARCHIVES BOARD □ Regina, SK

Wilson, J.A., Libn.
CANADA - DEFENCE RESEARCH ESTABLISHMENT PACIFIC - LIBRARY† □ Victoria, BC

Wilson, Jane
BLAKE, CASSELS & GRAYDON - LIBRARY □ Toronto, ON

Wilson, Jane, Libn.
VANDERBILT (R.T.) COMPANY, INC. - LIBRARY □ East Norwalk, CT

Wilson, Jeffrey L., Dir.
PACIFIC CHRISTIAN COLLEGE - HURST MEMORIAL LIBRARY □ Fullerton, CA

Wilson, John, Chf., Sys.Anl.
U.S. GEOLOGICAL SURVEY - NATL. CARTOGRAPHIC INFORMATION CENTER (NCIC) □ Reston, VA

Wilson, Joseph, Cat.Libn.
MERRIAM CENTER LIBRARY □ Chicago, IL

Wilson, Judith, Dir.
SANDY CORPORATION - RESEARCH & RETRIEVAL CENTER □ Southfield, MI

Wilson, Dr. Karen S., Music Libn.
BOB JONES UNIVERSITY - MUSIC LIBRARY □ Greenville, SC

Wilson, Kitty, Info.Spec.-Bus./Tech.
POLYSAR, LTD. - INFORMATION CENTRE □ Sarnia, ON

Wilson, Lorraine, Soc.Serv.Libn.
RYERSON POLYTECHNICAL INSTITUTE - LEARNING RESOURCES CENTRE □ Toronto, ON

Wilson, Margaret F., Asst.Univ.Libn.
FLORIDA A&M UNIVERSITY - ARCH/TECH LIBRARY □ Tallahassee, FL

Wilson, Mari, Assoc.Libn.
UNIVERSITY OF CALIFORNIA, BERKELEY - ENERGY AND RESOURCES PROGRAM - ENERGY INFORMATION CENTER □ Berkeley, CA

Wilson, Marietta, Libn.
MERCY MEDICAL CENTER - HEALTH SCIENCES LIBRARY □ Springfield, OH

Wilson, Marilyn J., Acq.Libn.
UNIVERSITY OF CALIFORNIA, SAN DIEGO - UNIVERSITY LIBRARIES □ La Jolla, CA

Wilson, Martha, Exec.Dir.
FRANKLIN FURNACE ARCHIVE, INC. - LIBRARY □ New York, NY

Wilson, Mary, Ref.Libn.
KEMPER GROUP - LIBRARY □ Long Grove, IL

Wilson, Mary D., Sec.
MIDDLEBURY HISTORICAL SOCIETY - MIDDLEBURY ACADEMY MUSEUM LIBRARY □ Wyoming, NY

Wilson, Mary W., Dir.
PUBLIC RELATIONS SOCIETY OF AMERICA - INFORMATION CENTER □ New York, NY

Wilson, Maureen F., Hd.
UNIVERSITY OF BRITISH COLUMBIA - MAP DIVISION □ Vancouver, BC

Wilson, Melanie, Ref.Libn.
UNIVERSITY OF ILLINOIS MEDICAL CENTER - PEORIA SCHOOL OF MEDICINE - LIBRARY OF THE HEALTH SCIENCES □ Peoria, IL

Wilson, Michael E., Asst.Archv.
ROSENBERG LIBRARY - ARCHIVES DEPARTMENT □ Galveston, TX

Wilson, Nancy L., Lib.Mgr.
BOEING COMPANY - SEATTLE SERVICES DIVISION - RENTON LIBRARY □ Seattle, WA

Wilson, Ms. P., Circ.
HURON COLLEGE - SILCOX MEMORIAL LIBRARY □ London, ON

Wilson, Peggy, Chf.Libn.
FIRST INTERSTATE BANK OF CALIFORNIA - LIBRARY □ Los Angeles, CA

Wilson, Mrs. R., Staff Archv.
SASKATCHEWAN ARCHIVES BOARD □ Regina, SK

Wilson, Robert, Hd., Pub.Serv.
SOUTHERN ALBERTA INSTITUTE OF TECHNOLOGY - LEARNING RESOURCES CENTRE □ Calgary, AB

Wilson, Robert M., Sci. & Engr.Libn.
LAURENTIAN UNIVERSITY - SCIENCE AND ENGINEERING LIBRARY □ Sudbury, ON

Wilson, Ron, Ref.Libn.
NEWSWEEK, INC. - LIBRARY □ New York, NY

Wilson, Ronald, Pk.Hist.
U.S. NATL. PARK SERVICE - APPOMATTOX COURT HOUSE NATL. HISTORICAL PARK - LIBRARY □ Appomattox, VA

Wilson, Susan W., Dir.
DANIEL FREEMAN HOSPITAL - VICTOR J. WACHA MEDICAL LIBRARY □ Inglewood, CA

Wilson, Susan W., Asst.Mgr.
FREDERICK CANCER RESEARCH CENTER - SCIENTIFIC LIBRARY □ Frederick, MD

Wilson, Theresa E., Asst.Libn.
CHARLESTON LIBRARY SOCIETY □ Charleston, SC

Wilson, Thomas F., Info.Mgr.
SEARCH GROUP, INC. - LIBRARY □ Sacramento, CA

Wilson, Dr. V. Chivers, Libn.
GLAXO CANADA, LTD. - REFERENCE LIBRARY† □ Toronto, ON

Wilson, Virginia M., Asst.Chf., Lib.Serv.
U.S. VETERANS ADMINISTRATION (GA-Atlanta) - HOSPITAL MEDICAL LIBRARY □ Decatur, GA

PERSONNEL

Wilson, Vivian L., Law Libn.
WAKE FOREST UNIVERSITY - LAW LIBRARY □
Winston-Salem, NC
Wilson, W.T., Res. Entomologist
U.S.D.A. - AGRICULTURAL RESEARCH SERVICE
- HONEY BEE PESTICIDES/DISEASES
RESEARCH LABORATORY - LIBRARY □ Laramie,
WY
Wilson, William G., Libn.
UNIVERSITY OF MARYLAND, COLLEGE PARK -
COLLEGE OF LIBRARY & INFORMATION
SERVICES - LIBRARY □ College Park, MD
Wilsted, Thomas, Archv./Adm.
SALVATION ARMY - ARCHIVES AND RESEARCH
CENTER □ New York, NY
Wilt, Charles, Circ. & Ref.
FRANKLIN INSTITUTE - LIBRARY □ Philadelphia,
PA
Wilt, Sue Ann, Libn.
MICHIGAN STATE UNIVERSITY -
INSTRUCTIONAL MEDIA CENTER - FILM
LIBRARY □ East Lansing, MI
Wilton, Elaine B., Libn.
CONGREGATION ADATH ISRAEL - LIBRARY □
Boston, MA
Wilton, Karen E., Libn.
CANADA - AGRICULTURE CANADA - RESEARCH
STATION, SWIFT CURRENT - LIBRARY □ Swift
Current, SK
Wiltshire, Denise A., Libn.
U. S. GEOLOGICAL SURVEY - WATER
RESOURCES DIVISION - NEW YORK DISTRICT -
LIBRARY □ Albany, NY
Wimbish, Emery, Jr., Hd.Libn.
LINCOLN UNIVERSITY - LANGSTON HUGHES
MEMORIAL LIBRARY - SPECIAL COLLECTIONS □
Lincoln University, PA
Wimmer, Katherine, Dir., Lib.Serv.
ST. JOSEPH HOSPITAL - LIBRARY □ Chicago, IL
Wimsatt, Theresa, Asst.Dir., Med.Rec.
COX (Lester E.) MEDICAL CENTER - DOCTORS'
LIBRARY □ Springfield, MO
Windels, Gene, Corp.Libn.
INFORMATION ACCESS CORPORATION -
LIBRARY □ Menlo Park, CA
Windes, Thomas C., Supv.Archeo.
U.S. NATL. PARK SERVICE - CHACO CENTER -
LIBRARY □ Albuquerque, NM
Windham, Carol, Hd.Libn.
MIDWAY HOSPITAL - HEALTH SCIENCES
LIBRARY □ St. Paul, MN
Windler, Jacqueline, Dir., Info.Rsrcs.Ctr.
CATHOLIC HEALTH ASSOCIATION OF THE
UNITED STATES - INFORMATION RESOURCE
CENTER □ St. Louis, MO
Windrem, Laurel, Med.Libn.
KAISER-PERMANENTE MEDICAL CENTER -
HEALTH SCIENCES LIBRARY □ San Diego, CA
Windsor, Donald A., Leader, Lib. & Info Group
MORTON-NORWICH PRODUCTS, INC. -
NORWICH PHARMACAL COMPANY - R&D DEPT.
- LIBRARY INFORMATION GROUP □ Norwich, NY
Winearls, Joan, Map Libn.
UNIVERSITY OF TORONTO - MAP LIBRARY □
Toronto, ON
Winfrey, Dr. Dorman H., Dir. & Libn.
TEXAS STATE LIBRARY □ Austin, TX
Wingate, Dawn A., Tech.Libn.
MAX FACTOR & COMPANY - R & D LIBRARY □
Hollywood, CA
Wingate, Gayla, Libn./P.R.
PORTMAN (John) & ASSOCIATES - LIBRARY □
Atlanta, GA
Wingate, Henry, Libn.
UNIVERSITY OF VIRGINIA - COLGATE DARDEN
GRADUATE SCHOOL OF BUSINESS
ADMINISTRATION - LIBRARY □ Charlottesville,
VA
Wingate, Margaret, Ref.Asst.
BROOME COMMUNITY COLLEGE - CECIL C.
TYRRELL LEARNING RESOURCES CENTER □
Binghamton, NY

Wingenroth, Janet, Ref.Libn.
CARROLL COLLEGE - LIBRARY □ Helena, MT
Winger, Anna K., Libn.
U.S. DEFENSE LOGISTICS AGENCY - DEFENSE
LOGISTICS SERVICES CENTER - LIBRARY □
Battle Creek, MI
Wingert, Carole, Law Libn.
MISSOURI STATE COURT OF APPEALS,
SOUTHERN DISTRICT - LAW LIBRARY □
Springfield, MO
Wingert, Ray, Media Spec.
HARRISBURG HOSPITAL - HOSPITAL LIBRARY □
Harrisburg, PA
Winiarski, Joanne, Hd.Libn.
OGILVY & MATHER, INC. - RESEARCH LIBRARY
□ New York, NY
Winick, Lester E., Lib.Comm.
COLLECTORS CLUB OF CHICAGO - LIBRARY □
Chicago, IL
Winik, Ruth, Mgr., Tech.Info.Ctr.
IBM CORPORATION - GENERAL PRODUCTS
DIVISION - TECHNICAL INFORMATION
CENTER □ San Jose, CA
Winkelman, Stuart, Lib.Asst.
SAN DIEGO AERO-SPACE MUSEUM - N. PAUL
WHITTIER HISTORICAL AVIATION LIBRARY □
San Diego, CA
Winkels, Mary, Mgr., Tech.Info.Div.
U.S. DEPT. OF ENERGY - BROOKHAVEN NATL.
LABORATORY - TECHNICAL INFORMATION
DIVISION □ Upton, NY
Winkler, Margaret, Coord.
FLORIDA STATE UNIVERSITY - CTR. FOR
STUDIES IN VOCATIONAL EDUC. - FLORIDA
EDUCATORS INFO. SERV. □ Tallahassee, FL
Winkler, Marianne, Libn.
CONGREGATION EMANU-EL - IVAN M.
STELTENHEIM LIBRARY† □ New York, NY
Winland, Jane E., Ref.Libn.
COLUMBIA UNIVERSITY - THOMAS J. WATSON
LIBRARY OF BUSINESS AND ECONOMICS □ New
York, NY
Winn, Carolyn P., Res.Libn.
WOODS HOLE OCEANOGRAPHIC INSTITUTION
- RESEARCH LIBRARY □ Woods Hole, MA
Winn, Christina, AV Libn.
KIRKSVILLE COLLEGE OF OSTEOPATHIC
MEDICINE - A.T. STILL MEMORIAL LIBRARY □
Kirksville, MO
Winn, Herbert E., Libn.
BARTLESVILLE PUBLIC LIBRARY - HISTORY
ROOM □ Bartlesville, OK
Winn, Karyl, Mss.Libn.
UNIVERSITY OF WASHINGTON - UNIVERSITY
ARCHIVES & MANUSCRIPT DIVISION -
MANUSCRIPT COLLECTION □ Seattle, WA
Winn, Sidney E., Sr.Info.Spec.
GULF RESEARCH AND DEVELOPMENT COMPANY
- TECHNICAL INFORMATION SERVICES □
Pittsburgh, PA
Winnacker, Martha, Res.Assoc.
SOUTHEAST ASIA RESOURCE CENTER □
Berkeley, CA
Winner, Marian C., Hd.Sci.Libn.
MIAMI UNIVERSITY - SCIENCE LIBRARY □
Oxford, OH
Winsborough, Shirley, Asst.Libn./Tech.Serv.
WISCONSIN STATE LAW LIBRARY □ Madison,
WI
Winsche, Richard A., Hist.
NASSAU COUNTY MUSEUM LIBRARY AT SANDS
POINT □ Sands Point, NY
Winsche, Richard A., Hist.
NASSAU COUNTY MUSEUM REFERENCE
LIBRARY □ East Meadow, NY
Winslow, D.H., Mgr.
UNIROYAL, INC. - TECHNICAL LIBRARY □
Middlebury, CT
Winslow, Lisa, Law Libn.
GREENBERG AND GLUSKER - LIBRARY □ Los
Angeles, CA

Winslow, N., Health Educ.Libn.
HURLEY MEDICAL CENTER - HAMADY HEALTH
SCIENCES LIBRARY □ Flint, MI
Winslow, Susan G., Dir.
U.S. OAK RIDGE NATL. LABORATORY -
TOXICOLOGY INFORMATION RESPONSE
CENTER □ Oak Ridge, TN
Winsor, George, Professor of Educ.
WILMINGTON COLLEGE - CURRICULUM
MATERIALS CENTER □ Wilmington, OH
Winstead, G. Alvis, Dir. & Libn.
TENNESSEE STATE LAW LIBRARY □ Nashville,
TN
Winstead, Mamie H., Libn.
TENNESSEE STATE SUPREME COURT - LAW
LIBRARY □ Knoxville, TN
Winston, Michael R., Dir. of Ctr.
HOWARD UNIVERSITY - MOORLAND-SPINGARN
RESEARCH CENTER - LIBRARY DIVISION □
Washington, DC
Winston, Dr. Michael R., Dir. of Ctr.
HOWARD UNIVERSITY - MOORLAND-SPINGARN
RESEARCH CENTER - MANUSCRIPT DIVISION □
Washington, DC
Winston, Sophie, Chf.Med.Libn.
BROOKDALE HOSPITAL MEDICAL CENTER -
MARIE SMITH SCHWARTZ MEDICAL LIBRARY □
Brooklyn, NY
Winstone, Larry, Meteorologist
CANADA - ATMOSPHERIC ENVIRONMENT
SERVICE - WESTERN REGION HEADQUARTERS
LIBRARY □ Edmonton, AB
Winter, Catherine, Coord.
CAMOSUN COLLEGE - LIBRARY/MEDIA
SERVICES □ Victoria, BC
Winter, Glenna, Dept.Libn.
ALBERTA - DEPARTMENT OF TOURISM AND
SMALL BUSINESS - LIBRARY □ Edmonton, AB
Winter, Madeline F., Libn.
BERKSHIRE EAGLE - LIBRARY □ Pittsfield, MA
Winter, Marjorie, Per.Asst.
GRACE COLLEGE OF THE BIBLE - LIBRARY □
Omaha, NE
Winter, Michael B., Lib.Dir.
WESTERN CONSERVATIVE BAPTIST SEMINARY
- CLINE-TUNNELL LIBRARY □ Portland, OR
Winter, Roland A., Libn.
MIDDLESEX COUNTY LAW LIBRARY† □ New
Brunswick, NJ
Winter, William O., Dir./Govt.Res.
UNIVERSITY OF COLORADO, BOULDER -
BUREAU OF GOVERNMENTAL RESEARCH &
SERVICE LIBRARY □ Boulder, CO
Winteregg, Candy, Asst.Dir./Med.Libn.
GRANDVIEW HOSPITAL - MEDICAL LIBRARY □
Dayton, OH
Winterhalter, Cynthia C., Cur.
ASHLAND HISTORICAL SOCIETY - LIBRARY □
Ashland, MA
Winternitz, Dr. Emanuel, Dir.
REPERTOIRE INTERNATIONAL
D'ICONOGRAPHIE MUSICALE - RESEARCH
CENTER FOR MUSICAL ICONOGRAPHY -
LIBRARY □ New York, NY
Winters, Michael, Lrng.Rsrcs.Spec.
OAKLAND PUBLIC SCHOOLS - PROFESSIONAL
LIBRARY □ Oakland, CA
Winters, Mr. Murl M., Dir.Info.Serv.
SOUTHWESTERN ASSEMBLIES OF GOD
COLLEGE - P.C. NELSON MEMORIAL LIBRARY □
Waxahachie, TX
Winters, Wilma E., Libn.
HARVARD UNIVERSITY - CENTER FOR
POPULATION STUDIES LIBRARY □ Boston, MA
Winthurst, Mrs. F.T., Lib.Chm.
BLACKHAWK GENEALOGICAL SOCIETY -
LIBRARY □ Rock Island, IL
Wiren, Harold N., Hd.Libn.
UNIVERSITY OF WASHINGTON - ENGINEERING
LIBRARY □ Seattle, WA
Wirth, Linda, Cat.Libn.
GEORGETOWN UNIVERSITY - LAW CENTER
LIBRARY □ Washington, DC

PERSONNEL

PERSONNEL

Worthley, Rev.Dr. Harold F., Libn.
AMERICAN CONGREGATIONAL ASSOCIATION -
CONGREGATIONAL LIBRARY □ Boston, MA

Wortis, Avi, Rd.Adv./Humanities
TRENTON STATE COLLEGE - ROSCOE L. WEST
LIBRARY □ Trenton, NJ

Wos, Midge, Hd.Libn.
ST. LUKE'S HOSPITAL - MEDICAL LIBRARY □
Milwaukee, WI

Wosh, Peter J., Univ.Arch.
SETON HALL UNIVERSITY - UNIVERSITY
ARCHIVES □ South Orange, NJ

Wostradowski, Jane, Libn.
MACRAE, MONTGOMERY & CUNNINGHAM -
LIBRARY □ Vancouver, BC

Wotherspoon, Shelagh, Hd. of Pub.Serv.
MEMORIAL UNIVERSITY OF NEWFOUNDLAND -
HEALTH SCIENCES LIBRARY □ St. John's, NF

Wou, Alice, Biblog.
AMERICAN CANCER SOCIETY - MEDICAL
LIBRARY □ New York, NY

Woy, James B., Hd.
FREE LIBRARY OF PHILADELPHIA -
MERCANTILE LIBRARY □ Philadelphia, PA

Woy, Sara G., Hd.Libn.
GERMANTOWN FRIENDS MEETING - FRIENDS
FREE LIBRARY □ Philadelphia, PA

Wraith, R.D., Res.Coord.
VICKERS & BENSON LTD. - RESOURCE CENTRE
□ Toronto, ON

Wray, Phoebe, Exec.Dir.
CENTER FOR ACTION ON ENDANGERED
SPECIES, INC. - LIBRARY □ Ayer, MA

Wreath, April, Hd., Cat.Serv.
UNIVERSITY OF NORTH CAROLINA, CHAPEL
HILL - HEALTH SCIENCES LIBRARY □ Chapel Hill,
NC

Wren, Dr. Daniel, Cur.
UNIVERSITY OF OKLAHOMA - HARRY W. BASS
COLLECTION IN BUSINESS HISTORY □ Norman,
OK

Wren, James A., Mgr.
MOTOR VEHICLE MANUFACTURERS
ASSOCIATION (MVMA) - PATENT RESEARCH
LIBRARY □ Detroit, MI

Wrenn, Christy J., Adm.Libn.
SHREVEPORT TIMES - LIBRARY □ Shreveport,
LA

Wrenn, R. Scott, Dp. Law Libn.
IDAHO STATE LAW LIBRARY □ Boise, ID

Wrenn, Teresa E., Law Libn.
PENNEY (J.C.) COMPANY, INC. - LAW LIBRARY
□ New York, NY

Wrenn, Tony, Archv.
AMERICAN INSTITUTE OF ARCHITECTS -
LIBRARY □ Washington, DC

Wright, Agnes, Lib.Techn.
SACRED HEART MEDICAL CENTER - HEALTH
SCIENCES LIBRARY □ Spokane, WA

Wright, Angie, Cat.
BOEING MILITARY AIRPLANE COMPANY -
LIBRARY □ Wichita, KS

Wright, AnnieLee, Libn.
HILL JUNIOR COLLEGE - CONFEDERATE
RESEARCH CENTER AND GUN MUSEUM □
Hillsboro, TX

Wright, Dr. C.D., Coord.
AUBURN UNIVERSITY - LEARNING RESOURCES
CENTER □ Auburn, AL

Wright, Clara M., Adm.Ck.
MEMPHIS BOTANIC GARDEN FOUNDATION,
INC. - GOLDSMITH CIVIC GARDEN CTR. -
SYBILE MALLOY MEMORIAL LIBRARY □
Memphis, TN

Wright, Mrs. D.O., Mgr.
STONE AND WEBSTER MANAGEMENT
CONSULTANTS, INC. - INFORMATION CENTER/
LIBRARY† □ New York, NY

Wright, Dorothy N., Libn.
SECURITY BENEFIT LIFE INSURANCE
COMPANY - LIBRARY □ Topeka, KS

Wright, Mrs. F. Gwendolyn, Chf.Educ.Libn.
QUEEN'S UNIVERSITY AT KINGSTON -
EDUCATION LIBRARY □ Kingston, ON

Wright, Frances, Libn.
FOURNIER NEWSPAPERS - LIBRARY □ Kent, WA

Wright, Frankie, Dir.
PHOTOPHILE - LIBRARY □ San Diego, CA

Wright, G. Ruth, Chm.Lib.Comm.
MOUNT VERNON PLACE UNITED METHODIST
CHURCH - DESSIE M. HALLETT LIBRARY □
Washington, DC

Wright, Mrs. G.W., Asst.Libn.
FIRST BAPTIST CHURCH - LIBRARY □ Slocomb,
AL

Wright, George E., Jr., Archv.
ASSOCIATION OF BALLOON & AIRSHIP
CONSTRUCTORS - TECHNICAL LIBRARY □
Rosemead, CA

Wright, Gerald D., Genealogist
CALIFORNIA HISTORICAL SOCIETY -
SCHUBERT HALL LIBRARY □ San Francisco, CA

Wright, Hanford D., Hd.
UNION COLLEGE CHARACTER RESEARCH
PROJECT - LIBRARY □ Schenectady, NY

Wright, Helena, Libn.
MERRIMACK VALLEY TEXTILE MUSEUM -
LIBRARY □ North Andover, MA

Wright, James B., Libn.
UNIVERSITY OF NEW MEXICO - FINE ARTS
LIBRARY □ Albuquerque, NM

Wright, Jan, Co-Libn.
NAVAJO NATION LIBRARY □ Window Rock, AZ

Wright, Janet, Tech.Serv.
U.S. ARMY IN EUROPE (USAREUR) - LIBRARY
AND RESOURCE CENTER □ APO New York, NY

Wright, Jill, Law Libn.
ESSEX COUNTY LAW LIBRARY □ Newark, NJ

Wright, Joseph F., Hd.Libn.
MIAMI NEWS - LIBRARY □ Miami, FL

Wright, Joyce, Hd.
UNIVERSITY OF HAWAII - ASIA COLLECTION □
Honolulu, HI

Wright, Joyce S., Musm.Dir.
LARAMIE PLAINS MUSEUM ASSOCIATION -
LIBRARY □ Laramie, WY

Wright, Judith M., Law Libn.
UNIVERSITY OF CHICAGO - LAW SCHOOL
LIBRARY □ Chicago, IL

Wright, Judy, Libn.
TEXAS RESEARCH LEAGUE - LIBRARY □ Austin,
TX

Wright, Kathy, Hd., Bayside Br.
U.S. NAVY - NAVAL OCEAN SYSTEMS CENTER -
TECHNICAL LIBRARY □ San Diego, CA

Wright, Kathy, Automation Spec.
U.S. NAVY - NAVAL OCEAN SYSTEMS CENTER -
TECHNICAL LIBRARY □ San Diego, CA

Wright, Linda
ST. LOUIS PUBLIC LIBRARY - APPLIED SCIENCE
DEPARTMENT □ St. Louis, MO

Wright, Loretta O., Media Spec.
VOLUSIA COUNTY SCHOOL BOARD - TEACHERS'
RESOURCE LIBRARY □ Daytona Beach, FL

Wright, Lottie, Supv.
DISTRICT OF COLUMBIA TEACHERS COLLEGE -
LIBRARY □ Washington, DC

Wright, Martha, Ref.Libn.
INDIANA STATE LIBRARY - INDIANA DIVISION
□ Indianapolis, IN

Wright, Mary, Asst.Libn.
PEAT, MARWICK, MITCHELL & COMPANY -
LIBRARY □ Houston, TX

Wright, Mary A., Hd.
SAN ANTONIO PUBLIC LIBRARY - ART, MUSIC
AND FILMS DEPARTMENT □ San Antonio, TX

Wright, Meredith S., Mgr.
UNION CARBIDE CORPORATION - PARMA
TECHNICAL CENTER - TECHNICAL
INFORMATION SERVICE □ Cleveland, OH

Wright, Myrna, Libn.
MINNESOTA LIBRARY FOR THE BLIND AND
PHYSICALLY HANDICAPPED □ Faribault, MN

Wright, Nan, Hd., Ref.Dept.
TRENTON FREE PUBLIC LIBRARY -
TRENTONIANA COLLECTION □ Trenton, NJ

Wright, Nancy D., V.P. for Lib.Serv.
HERNER AND COMPANY - LIBRARY □ Arlington,
VA

Wright, Nancy M., Libn.
HEINZ (H.J.) COMPANY - LIBRARY □ Pittsburgh,
PA

Wright, Nanette F., Asst.Libn.
DETROIT COLLEGE OF LAW - LIBRARY □
Detroit, MI

Wright, O.B., Leg. Liaison Off.
TORONTO CITY RECORDS AND ARCHIVES
DIVISION □ Toronto, ON

Wright, Patrick, Ref.Libn.
UNIVERSITY OF MANITOBA - EDUCATION
LIBRARY □ Winnipeg, MB

Wright, Patsy, Libn.
ST. CLAIRE MEDICAL CENTER - MEDICAL
LIBRARY □ Morehead, KY

Wright, Paula, Data User Serv.Off.
U.S. BUREAU OF THE CENSUS - REGIONAL DATA
USER SERVICE - DALLAS REGIONAL OFFICE -
LIBRARY □ Dallas, TX

Wright, Ray, Res.Dir.
NATIONAL CHAMBER OF COMMERCE FOR
WOMEN - ELIZABETH LEWIN BUSINESS
LIBRARY & INFORMATION CENTER □ New York,
NY

Wright, Raymond, Mgr., Patron Serv.
CHURCH OF JESUS CHRIST OF LATTER-DAY
SAINTS - GENEALOGICAL LIBRARY □ Salt Lake
City, UT

Wright, Rhona, Libn.
SASKATCHEWAN - DEPARTMENT OF
AGRICULTURE - LIBRARY □ Regina, SK

Wright, Dr. Richard J., Dir.
BOWLING GREEN STATE UNIVERSITY -
CENTER FOR ARCHIVAL COLLECTIONS □
Bowling Green, OH

Wright, Rita J., Soc.Sci./Res.Assoc.
UNIVERSITY OF TEXAS, AUSTIN - BUREAU OF
BUSINESS RESEARCH - INFORMATION
SERVICES □ Austin, TX

Wright, Rosa Gahn, Libn.
LAW LIBRARY ASSOCIATION OF ST. LOUIS □ St.
Louis, MO

Wright, Rosalee I., Tech.Rep./Ref.Libn.
UNIVERSITY OF CALIFORNIA, LOS ANGELES -
ENGINEERING & MATHEMATICAL SCIENCES
LIBRARY □ Los Angeles, CA

Wright, Sylvia H., Chf.Arch.Libn.
CUNY - CITY COLLEGE LIBRARY -
ARCHITECTURE LIBRARY □ New York, NY

Wright, Thomas F., Libn.
UNIVERSITY OF CALIFORNIA, LOS ANGELES -
WILLIAM ANDREWS CLARK MEMORIAL
LIBRARY □ Los Angeles, CA

Wright, Virginia, Asst.Libn.
CORNING MUSEUM OF GLASS - LIBRARY □
Corning, NY

Wright, W. Kenneth
U.S. BUREAU OF THE CENSUS - REGIONAL DATA
USER SERVICE - KANSAS CITY REGIONAL
OFFICE - LIBRARY □ Kansas City, KS

Wright, Wayne, Rd.Serv.
NEW YORK STATE HISTORICAL ASSOCIATION
- LIBRARY □ Cooperstown, NY

Wright, Dr. William, Hd.
NEW JERSEY STATE LIBRARY - BUREAU OF
ARCHIVES & HISTORY □ Trenton, NJ

Wright, William F., Ref.Libn.
BELL TELEPHONE LABORATORIES, INC. -
TECHNICAL LIBRARY □ Murray Hill, NJ

Wrightson, R., Hd. of Acq.
CONCORDIA UNIVERSITY - SIR GEORGE
WILLIAMS CAMPUS - NORRIS LIBRARY □
Montreal, PQ

Wrigley, Elizabeth S., Dir.-Libn.
FRANCIS BACON FOUNDATION - LIBRARY □
Claremont, CA

Wroblewski, Stephan, Ref.Libn.
QUEENS BOROUGH PUBLIC LIBRARY -
LANGUAGE & LITERATURE DIVISION □ Jamaica,
NY

Wroolie, Melvin S., Cur.
LAC QUI PARLE COUNTY HISTORICAL SOCIETY
- HISTORIC CENTER □ Madison, MN

Wrynn, Paul, Per.Libn.
NEW YORK UNIVERSITY MEDICAL CENTER -
FREDERICK L. EHRMAN MEDICAL LIBRARY □
New York, NY

Wu, Daisy T., Dir.
UNIVERSITY OF WISCONSIN, MADISON -
STEENBOCK MEMORIAL LIBRARY □ Madison, WI

Wu, Dorothea, Div.Hd.
QUEENS BOROUGH PUBLIC LIBRARY - ART AND
MUSIC DIVISION □ Jamaica, NY

Wu, Eugene, Libn.
HARVARD UNIVERSITY - HARVARD YENCHING
INSTITUTE - LIBRARY □ Cambridge, MA

Wu, J., Sys.Libn.
CANADA - AGRICULTURE CANADA - LIBRARIES
DIVISION □ Ottawa, ON

Wu, Lisa C., Chf., Tech.Serv.
U.S. NATL. INSTITUTES OF HEALTH - LIBRARY
□ Bethesda, MD

Wu, Margaret, WRISC
U.S. DEPT. OF ENERGY - LAWRENCE BERKELEY
LABORATORY - LIBRARY □ Berkeley, CA

Wu, Shirley, Libn.
U.S. VETERANS ADMINISTRATION (NC-
Salisbury) - HOSPITAL LIBRARY □ Salisbury, NC

Wu Tsiang, Ching-Fen, Libn.
WOODVIEW-CALABASAS PSYCHIATRIC
HOSPITAL - LIBRARY □ Calabasas, CA

Wudyka, Mark, Libn.
GOWANDA PSYCHIATRIC CENTER - HEALTH
SCIENCES LIBRARY □ Helmuth, NY

Wuertz, E. Lavonne, Tech.Serv./Ref.Libn.
UNIVERSITY OF SOUTHERN CALIFORNIA -
CROCKER BUSINESS LIBRARY □ Los Angeles, CA

Wulfekoetter, Gertrude, Libn.
UNIVERSITY CONGREGATIONAL CHURCH -
LIBRARY □ Seattle, WA

Wulff, Jacqueline, Libn.
NORTH MEMORIAL MEDICAL CENTER -
MEDICAL LIBRARY □ Minneapolis, MN

Wulff, L. Yvonne, Hd.
UNIVERSITY OF MICHIGAN - ALFRED TAUBMAN
MEDICAL LIBRARY □ Ann Arbor, MI

Wurfel, Clifford R., Assoc.Libn.
UNIVERSITY OF CALIFORNIA, RIVERSIDE -
SPECIAL COLLECTIONS □ Riverside, CA

Wurzburger, Marilyn, Hd., Spec.Coll.
ARIZONA STATE UNIVERSITY - SPECIAL
COLLECTIONS □ Tempe, AZ

Wyant, June F., Career Info.Spec.
UNIVERSITY OF OREGON - CAREER
INFORMATION CENTER □ Eugene, OR

Wyatt, Beverly J., Site Agent
OKLAHOMA HISTORICAL SOCIETY -
CHICKASAW COUNCIL HOUSE LIBRARY □
Tishomingo, OK

Wyatt, Mrs. G., Acq.Techn.
ROYAL CANADIAN MOUNTED POLICE - LAW
ENFORCEMENT REFERENCE CENTRE □ Ottawa,
ON

Wyatt, Susan, Assoc.Dir.
ARTISTS SPACE - COMMITTEE FOR THE
VISUAL ARTS - UNAFFILIATED ARTISTS FILE □
New York, NY

Wybenga, Helena, Hd.Ser.Libn.
UNIVERSITY OF OTTAWA - VANIER MEDICAL,
SCIENCE & ENGINEERING LIBRARY □ Ottawa,
ON

Wygant, Alice C., Ref.Libn.
UNIVERSITY OF TEXAS MEDICAL BRANCH -
MOODY MEDICAL LIBRARY □ Galveston, TX

Wygant, Larry, Assoc.Dir.Hist./Med.Archv
UNIVERSITY OF TEXAS MEDICAL BRANCH -
MOODY MEDICAL LIBRARY □ Galveston, TX

Wygnanski, Jadwiga, Libn.
MC GILL UNIVERSITY - ENGINEERING LIBRARY
□ Montreal, PQ

Wykes, Adrienne, Lib.Asst.
METROPOLITAN TORONTO ASSOCIATION FOR
THE MENTALLY RETARDED - HOWARD E.
BACON MEMORIAL LIBRARY □ Toronto, ON

Wykoff, Leslie Webb, Libn.
KAISER FOUNDATION HOSPITALS - HEALTH
SERVICES RESEARCH CENTER LIBRARY □
Portland, OR

Wyneken, Rev. Karl H.
LUTHERAN CHURCH - MISSOURI SYNOD -
CALIFORNIA, NEVADA AND HAWAII DISTRICT
ARCHIVES □ San Francisco, CA

Wyngaard, Susan, Hd.Libn.
OHIO STATE UNIVERSITY - FINE ARTS
LIBRARY □ Columbus, OH

Wynne, Allen, Dept.Hd.
UNIVERSITY OF COLORADO, BOULDER -
MATHEMATICS & PHYSICS LIBRARY □ Boulder,
CO

Wynne, Marjorie G., Res.Libn.
YALE UNIVERSITY - BEINECKE RARE BOOK AND
MANUSCRIPT LIBRARY □ New Haven, CT

Wynne, Nancy G., Libn.
CARTER (Amon) MUSEUM OF WESTERN ART -
LIBRARY □ Fort Worth, TX

Wypyski, Eugene M., Libn.
HOFSTRA UNIVERSITY - SCHOOL OF LAW
LIBRARY □ Hempstead, NY

Wyse, J. Kenneth, Cat.
CLARION STATE COLLEGE - RENA M. CARLSON
LIBRARY □ Clarion, PA

Wyser, Theresa A., Libn.
CONNECTICUT POLICE ACADEMY - RESOURCE
CENTER □ Meriden, CT

Wysong, Breena L., Libn.
MUNCIE STAR-PRESS LIBRARY □ Muncie, IN

X

X, Laura, Dir. & Pres.
WOMEN'S HISTORY RESEARCH CENTER, INC. -
WOMEN'S HISTORY LIBRARY □ Berkeley, CA

Xang, R., Acq.Libn.
PACE UNIVERSITY, PLEASANTVILLE/
BRIARCLIFF - LIBRARY □ Pleasantville, NY

Y

Yacavoni, John, Asst.Dir.
VERMONT STATE AGENCY OF
ADMINISTRATION - PUBLIC RECORDS
DIVISION □ Montpelier, VT

Yachnes, Eleanor, M.D., Chm., Lib.Comm.
IVIMEY (Muriel) LIBRARY □ New York, NY

Yackle, Jeanette, Ref.Libn.
UNIVERSITY OF TEXAS SCHOOL OF LAW -
TARLTON LAW LIBRARY □ Austin, TX

Yadon, Vernal L., Musm.Dir.
PACIFIC GROVE MUSEUM OF NATURAL
HISTORY - LIBRARY □ Pacific Grove, CA

Yaffee, Rachel, Libn.
KESHER ZION SYNAGOGUE SISTERHOOD -
LIBRARY □ Reading, PA

Yagello, Virginia E., Hd.Libn.
OHIO STATE UNIVERSITY - CHEMISTRY
LIBRARY □ Columbus, OH

Yagello, Virginia E., Hd.Libn.
OHIO STATE UNIVERSITY - COLE MEMORIAL
LIBRARY OF THE PHYSICS AND ASTRONOMY
DEPARTMENT □ Columbus, OH

Yager, Ellen, Asst.Libn.
WINTHROP, STIMSON, PUTNAM AND ROBERTS
- LIBRARY □ New York, NY

Yager, W.P., Asst.Dir.
MARITIME MUSEUM OF BRITISH COLUMBIA -
LIBRARY □ Victoria, BC

Yahya, M.A. Rashid, Asst.
AHMADIYYA MOVEMENT IN ISLAM - MUSLIM
LIBRARY □ Washington, DC

Yake, Neil, Dir., Health Inst.
SLOAN (Alfred P., Jr.) MUSEUM - LIBRARY □
Flint, MI

Yaller, Loretta O., Libn.
PIPER & MARBURY - LAW LIBRARY □ Baltimore,
MD

Yam, Helen, Hist. of Med.
UNIVERSITY OF NEBRASKA MEDICAL CENTER -
MC GOOGAN LIBRARY OF MEDICINE □ Omaha,
NE

Yamada, R.M., Ref.Libn.
TRW, INC. - DEFENSE & SPACE SYSTEMS
GROUP - TECHNICAL INFORMATION CENTER □
Redondo Beach, CA

Yamakawa, Takaharu, Japanese Cat.
UNIVERSITY OF MICHIGAN - ASIA LIBRARY □
Ann Arbor, MI

Yamamoto, Linda Y., Libn.
KAISER FOUNDATION HOSPITAL -
MANAGEMENT EFFECTIVENESS LIBRARY □ Los
Angeles, CA

Yamasaki, Bruce, Cat.
U.S. PUBLIC HEALTH SERVICE - PARKLAWN
HEALTH LIBRARY □ Rockville, MD

Yampolsky, Philip, Libn.
COLUMBIA UNIVERSITY - EAST ASIAN LIBRARY
□ New York, NY

Yan, Ms. R.H., Lab.Libn.
IBM CANADA, LTD. - LABORATORY LIBRARY □
Don Mills, ON

Yancey, Sarah B., Cur.
WAYNE COUNTY HISTORICAL SOCIETY
MUSEUM - LIBRARY □ Lyons, NY

Yanchisin, Daniel A., Spec.Coll.Libn.
VIRGINIA COMMONWEALTH UNIVERSITY -
JAMES BRANCH CABELL LIBRARY - SPECIAL
COLLECTIONS □ Richmond, VA

Yandle, Anne, Hd.
UNIVERSITY OF BRITISH COLUMBIA - SPECIAL
COLLECTIONS DIVISION □ Vancouver, BC

Yanes, Frank, Per.Coord.
UNIVERSITY OF MIAMI - SCHOOL OF
MEDICINE - LOUIS CALDER MEMORIAL
LIBRARY □ Miami, FL

Yang, Jackson, Engr./Sci.Libn.
MICHIGAN STATE UNIVERSITY - ENGINEERING
LIBRARY □ East Lansing, MI

Yang, Jackson, Engr./Sci.Libn.
MICHIGAN STATE UNIVERSITY - SCIENCE
LIBRARY □ East Lansing, MI

Yang, Lena L., Libn./E. Asia Coll.
INSTITUTE FOR ADVANCED STUDIES OF
WORLD RELIGIONS - LIBRARY □ Stony Brook,
NY

Yang, Lillian, Pub.Serv./Ref.Libn.
UNIVERSITY OF SOUTHERN CALIFORNIA -
CROCKER BUSINESS LIBRARY □ Los Angeles, CA

Yang, Sophia, Chf., Acq.
U.S. PUBLIC HEALTH SERVICE - PARKLAWN
HEALTH LIBRARY □ Rockville, MD

Yanicke, Joan, Dir., Lib.Serv.
ST. MICHAEL'S HOSPITAL - REGNER HEALTH
SCIENCES LIBRARY □ Milwaukee, WI

Yanover, Abraham F., Exec.Dir.
BUREAU OF JEWISH EDUCATION - COMMUNITY
LIBRARY □ Getzville, NY

Yao, Ta-Liang Daisy, Libn.
DIXMONT STATE HOSPITAL - PERSONNEL
LIBRARY □ Sewickley, PA

Yap, Janet, Ref./Govt.Doc.
BRIGHAM YOUNG UNIVERSITY, HAWAII
CAMPUS - JOSEPH F. SMITH LIBRARY AND
MEDIA CENTER □ Laie, HI

Yarbrough, Jerry, Chf.Pk. Ranger
U.S. NATL. PARK SERVICE - TIMPANOGOS
CAVE NATL. MONUMENT - LIBRARY □ American
Fork, UT

PERSONNEL

Yardley, Tommy M., Coord., Health Sci.Lib.
TEXAS WOMAN'S UNIVERSITY, DALLAS
CENTER - F.W. AND BESSIE DYE MEMORIAL
LIBRARY □ Dallas, TX

Yarrington, Gary, Musm.Cur.
U.S. PRESIDENTIAL LIBRARIES - LYNDON B.
JOHNSON LIBRARY† □ Austin, TX

Yasui, Bea, Sr.Libn.
LOS ANGELES PUBLIC LIBRARY - MUNICIPAL
REFERENCE DEPARTMENT - POLICE LIBRARY □
Los Angeles, CA

Yasukawa, Leilani P., Lib.Asst.
HAWAIIAN TELEPHONE COMPANY - LIBRARY □
Honolulu, HI

Yates, Eva, Hd.
BIRMINGHAM PUBLIC AND JEFFERSON COUNTY
FREE LIBRARY - YOUTH DEPARTMENT □
Birmingham, AL

Yates, Jane, Archv.
CITADEL - THE MILITARY COLLEGE OF SOUTH
CAROLINA - ARCHIVES/MUSEUM □ Charleston,
SC

Yates, Mary K., Libn.
KING RESEARCH, INC. - CENTER FOR
QUANTITATIVE SCIENCES - LIBRARY □
Rockville, MD

Yates, Melinda, Sr.Libn.
NEW YORK STATE LIBRARY - HUMANITIES
REFERENCE SERVICE □ Albany, NY

Yates, Stanley B., Asst.Libn.
PRINCETON UNIVERSITY - ENGINEERING
LIBRARY □ Princeton, NJ

Yates, Stanley M., Spec.Coll.
IOWA STATE UNIVERSITY - LIBRARY □ Ames,
IA

Yatsko, Cindy, Search Anl.
INTERNATIONAL MINERALS & CHEMICALS
CORPORATION - IMC RESEARCH &
DEVELOPMENT LIBRARY □ Terre Haute, IN

Yaver, Joseph, Exec.Dir.
SPIE - THE INTERNATIONAL SOCIETY FOR
OPTICAL ENGINEERING - LIBRARY □
Bellingham, WA

Yeager, Cynthia M., Libn.
MILITARY ORDER OF THE LOYAL LEGION OF
THE UNITED STATES - WAR LIBRARY AND
MUSEUM □ Philadelphia, PA

Yeager, Luke, Supv. School Lib.Serv.
ARLINGTON PUBLIC SCHOOLS - PROFESSIONAL
LIBRARY □ Arlington, VA

Yeaman, Ruth, Libn.
UNIVERSITY OF UTAH - SPECIAL COLLECTIONS
DEPARTMENT □ Salt Lake City, UT

Yeargain, Eloisa G., Act.Hd.
UNIVERSITY OF CALIFORNIA, LOS ANGELES -
MANAGEMENT LIBRARY □ Los Angeles, CA

Yeates, Elizabeth J., Chf., LISD
U.S. NATL. OCEANIC & ATMOSPHERIC
ADMINISTRATION - LIBRARY AND
INFORMATION SERVICES DIVISION □ Rockville,
MD

Yeates, Michael W., Registrar
MASSACHUSETTS INSTITUTE OF TECHNOLOGY
- M.I.T. MUSEUM AND HISTORICAL
COLLECTIONS □ Cambridge, MA

Yedlin, Deborah, Asst.Libn., Tech.Serv.
WASHINGTON UNIVERSITY - SCHOOL OF
MEDICINE LIBRARY □ St. Louis, MO

Yee, Sen, Patient Educ.Libn.
U.S. VETERANS ADMINISTRATION (CA-San
Francisco) - MEDICAL CENTER LIBRARY □ San
Francisco, CA

Yeg, Jean K., Lib.Asst.
HAWAII STATE DEPARTMENT OF HEALTH -
HASTINGS H. WALKER MEDICAL LIBRARY □
Honolulu, HI

Yeh, Emily, Vol.Coord.
GEORGIA STATE DEPARTMENT OF EDUCATION
- LIBRARY FOR THE BLIND & PHYSICALLY
HANDICAPPED □ Atlanta, GA

Yeh, Helen, Cat.
PRAIRIE VIEW A & M COLLEGE OF TEXAS -
W.R. BANKS LIBRARY □ Prairie View, TX

Yeh, Nah Lin, Hd., Tech.Serv.
LE TOURNEAU COLLEGE - MARGARET ESTES
LIBRARY □ Longview, TX

Yelich, Nolan T., Dir., Adm.Serv.
VIRGINIA STATE LIBRARY □ Richmond, VA

Yellis, Jo, Leg.Libn.
EDISON ELECTRIC INSTITUTE - LIBRARY □
Washington, DC

Yellowhammer, Joyce, Libn./Data Anl.
NATIONAL INDIAN EDUCATION ASSOCIATION
- LIBRARY □ Minneapolis, MN

Yelvington, Julia, Chf., Archv.
WYOMING STATE ARCHIVES, MUSEUMS AND
HISTORICAL DEPARTMENT □ Cheyenne, WY

Yenner, Connie J., Libn.
ARKANSAS STATE DEPARTMENT OF
POLLUTION CONTROL AND ECOLOGY - LIBRARY
□ Little Rock, AR

Yenney, Patricia A., Libn. I
ALASKA HEALTH SCIENCES LIBRARY □
Anchorage, AK

Yeno, Anne
BRONSON (Silas) LIBRARY - BUSINESS,
INDUSTRY, AND TECHNOLOGY DEPARTMENT†
□ Waterbury, CT

Yeoh, Josephine W., Dir.
RIVERSIDE METHODIST HOSPITAL - LIBRARY
RESOURCE CENTER □ Columbus, OH

Yerdon, Lawrence J., Musm.Dir./Cur.
QUINCY HISTORICAL SOCIETY - LIBRARY □
Quincy, MA

Yerington, Mr. A.P., Res. Entomologist
U.S.D.A. - AGRICULTURAL RESEARCH SERVICE
- STORED-PRODUCT INSECTS RESEARCH
LABORATORY □ Fresno, CA

Yerke, Theodor B., WESTFORNET Prog.Mgr.
U.S. FOREST SERVICE - PACIFIC SOUTHWEST
FOREST & RANGE EXPERIMENT STATION -
WESTFORNET-BERKELEY □ Berkeley, CA

Yetman, Jeanette, Tech.Proc.Asst.
NORTHEASTERN UNIVERSITY - LAW SCHOOL
LIBRARY □ Boston, MA

Yetman, Nancy, Tech.Libn.
DONNELLY MIRRORS, INC. - LIBRARY □ Holland,
MI

Yeung, Cecilia, Cat.
PLAINS HEALTH CENTRE - DR. W.A. RIDDELL
HEALTH SCIENCES LIBRARY □ Regina, SK

Yeung, E., Order Libn.
FULLER THEOLOGICAL SEMINARY - MC
ALISTER LIBRARY □ Pasadena, CA

Yew, June, Cat.
RUSH UNIVERSITY AND MEDICAL CENTER -
LIBRARY □ Chicago, IL

Ying, Sharon, Chinese Cat.Supv.
UNIVERSITY OF MICHIGAN - ASIA LIBRARY □
Ann Arbor, MI

Ying, Sun Chyi, Cat.Libn..
WHITTIER COLLEGE - SCHOOL OF LAW -
LIBRARY □ Los Angeles, CA

Yirka, Carl A., Hd., Acq.
NORTHWESTERN UNIVERSITY - LAW SCHOOL
LIBRARY □ Chicago, IL

Yoak, Stuart, Ref.Libn.
WAYNE STATE UNIVERSITY - ARTHUR NEEF
LAW LIBRARY □ Detroit, MI

Yocom, Laura, Law Libn.
CALAVERAS COUNTY LAW LIBRARY □ San
Andreas, CA

Yocum, Leah
PENNWALT CORPORATION - TECHNICAL
DIVISION LIBRARY □ King Of Prussia, PA

Yoder, Dr. Claude, Chm.
FRANKLIN AND MARSHALL COLLEGE -
CHEMISTRY DEPARTMENT - WILLIAM SHAND,
JR. MEMORIAL LIBRARY □ Lancaster, PA

Yoder, Robert A., Supv.Film Ctr.
KENT STATE UNIVERSITY - AUDIOVISUAL
SERVICES □ Kent, OH

Yoelson, Martin I., Chf.Pk.Hist.
U.S. NATL. PARK SERVICE - INDEPENDENCE
NATL. HISTORICAL PARK - LIBRARY □
Philadelphia, PA

Yon, Paul D., Assoc.Dir.
BOWLING GREEN STATE UNIVERSITY -
CENTER FOR ARCHIVAL COLLECTIONS □
Bowling Green, OH

Yoo, Yushin, Coord., Patron Serv.
MURRAY STATE UNIVERSITY - LIBRARY □
Murray, KY

Yoon, Steven I., Cur.
HOWARD UNIVERSITY - BERNARD B. FALL
COLLECTION □ Washington, DC

Yoon, Susan, Tech.Serv.Libn.
CATHOLIC THEOLOGICAL UNION - LIBRARY □
Chicago, IL

York, Jan, Libn.
NORTON COMPANY - CHAMBERLAIN
LABORATORIES - TECHNICAL LIBRARY □ Akron,
OH

York, Josefa A., Libn.
UNIVERSITY OF TEXAS, AUSTIN - MARINE
SCIENCE INSTITUTE - GEOPHYSICS
LABORATORY - LIBRARY □ Galveston, TX

York, Michael C., Asst.Dir.
CASTLETON STATE COLLEGE - CALVIN
COOLIDGE LIBRARY - LEARNING RESOURCES
CENTER □ Castleton, VT

Yorke, Louise M., Libn.
MEDICAL CENTER AT PRINCETON - MEDICAL
CENTER LIBRARY □ Princeton, NJ

Yorks, Melissa, Tech.Info.Spec.
OFFICE ON SMOKING AND HEALTH -
TECHNICAL INFORMATION CENTER □ Rockville,
MD

Yos, David, Ref.Libn.
EASTERN NEW MEXICO UNIVERSITY - GOLDEN
LIBRARY □ Portales, NM

Yoshinaga, Lucienne, Hd.Tech.Serv.
BROOKLYN LAW SCHOOL - LAW LIBRARY □
Brooklyn, NY

Yost, Bill, Supv.
BOB JONES UNIVERSITY - SCHOOL OF
EDUCATION - MEDIA CENTER □ Greenville, SC

Yost, Rev. Charles, S.C.J., Cons.
SACRED HEART MONASTERY - LEO DEHON
LIBRARY □ Hales Corners, WI

Yost, Dr. F. Donald, Archv.
SEVENTH-DAY ADVENTISTS - GENERAL
CONFERENCE - OFFICE OF ARCHIVES AND
STATISTICS □ Washington, DC

Yother, Larry W., Libn.
HARTFORD STATE TECHNICAL COLLEGE -
GROM HAYES LIBRARY □ Hartford, CT

You, Kathy, Libn.
GENERAL HOSPITAL - HEALTH SCIENCES
LIBRARY □ Sault Ste. Marie, ON

Younce, Rev. Loring, Hd.Libn.
LUTHERAN BIBLE INSTITUTE - LIBRARY □
Issaquah, WA

Youner, Sara
MARSH AND MC LENNAN, INC. - INFORMATION
CENTER □ New York, NY

Young, Abram Owen, Libn.
CHURCH OF JESUS CHRIST OF LATTER-DAY
SAINTS - ST. GEORGE BRANCH GENEALOGICAL
LIBRARY □ St. George, UT

Young, Alene, Hd., Rd.Serv.
NORTH CAROLINA AGRICULTURAL &
TECHNICAL STATE UNIVERSITY - F.D.
BLUFORD LIBRARY □ Greensboro, NC

Young, Carol, Musm.Adm.
LATAH COUNTY HISTORICAL SOCIETY -
LIBRARY □ Moscow, ID

Young, Colette F. H., Oahu YA Coord.
HAWAII STATE LIBRARY - YOUNG ADULT
SECTION □ Honolulu, HI

Young, David, Mgr., Comp.Sys.
IFI/PLENUM DATA COMPANY - LIBRARY □
Alexandria, VA

Young, Diana, Lib.Cons.Ch.Serv.
NORTH CAROLINA STATE DEPARTMENT OF
CULTURAL RESOURCES - DIVISION OF THE
STATE LIBRARY □ Raleigh, NC

Young, Dottie, Libn.
ARCAIR COMPANY - LIBRARY □ Lancaster, OH

Young, Ella Mae, Res.Hist.
DOUGLAS COUNTY MUSEUM - LAVOLA BAKKEN MEMORIAL LIBRARY ▢ Roseburg, OR

Young, Francis A., Dir.
WASHINGTON STATE UNIVERSITY - PRIMATE RESEARCH CENTER LIBRARY ▢ Pullman, WA

Young, Helen, Adm.Coord.
BARBERTON CITIZENS HOSPITAL - MEDICAL LIBRARY† ▢ Barberton, OH

Young, Jacqui, Ref.Libn.
ELI LILLY AND COMPANY - SCIENTIFIC LIBRARY ▢ Indianapolis, IN

Young, Jayne F., Engr.Libn.
COLUMBIA GULF TRANSMISSION COMPANY - ENGINEERING LIBRARY ▢ Houston, TX

Young, Judy, Lib.Asst.
QUEEN'S UNIVERSITY AT KINGSTON - ELECTRICAL ENGINEERING LIBRARY ▢ Kingston, ON

Young, Judy, Asst.Rpt.Libn.
UNIVERSITY OF CALIFORNIA - LOS ALAMOS NATIONAL LABORATORY - LIBRARY ▢ Los Alamos, NM

Young, Kathleen, Libn.
KEYSTONE CUSTODIAN FUNDS, INC. - LIBRARY ▢ Boston, MA

Young, Kay, Docs.Libn.
UNIVERSITY OF GEORGIA - GOVERNMENT REFERENCE/DOCUMENTS SECTION ▢ Athens, GA

Young, Maureen, Info./Res.Spec.
REDDY COMMUNICATIONS, INC. - INFORMATION/RESEARCH SERVICES ▢ Greenwich, CT

Young, Morris N., M.D., Dir.
YOUNG (Morris N. & Chesley V.) MNEMONICS LIBRARY ▢ New York, NY

Young, Patricia, Law Libn.
BELL CANADA - LAW LIBRARY ▢ Montreal, PQ

Young, Patricia, Libn.
ENGLEWOOD HOSPITAL - SCHOOL OF NURSING LIBRARY ▢ Englewood, NJ

Young, Paul M., Libn. & Chm.Ref.
TEXAS TECH UNIVERSITY - LIBRARY ▢ Lubbock, TX

Young, Pearl, Libn.
FIRST BAPTIST CHURCH - LIBRARY ▢ Kennett, MO

Young, Penny, Asst.Dir.
UNIVERSITY OF CINCINNATI - MEDICAL CENTER LIBRARIES - HISTORY OF HEALTH SCIENCES LIBRARY AND MUSEUM ▢ Cincinnati, OH

Young, Rita K., Hd.Cat.
WEST VIRGINIA INSTITUTE OF TECHNOLOGY - VINING LIBRARY ▢ Montgomery, WV

Young, Robert, Adm. & Core Libn.
BRITISH COLUMBIA INSTITUTE OF TECHNOLOGY - LIBRARY SERVICES DIVISION ▢ Burnaby, BC

Young, Sandra E., Hd., Ref./Info.Serv.
U.S. DEFENSE NUCLEAR AGENCY - TECHNICAL LIBRARY DIVISION ▢ Washington, DC

Young, Sherry, Libn.
BAPTIST MEMORIAL HOSPITAL - SCHOOL OF NURSING - LIBRARY ▢ Memphis, TN

Young, Susan, Libn.
OAKLAND PUBLIC LIBRARY - LATIN AMERICAN LIBRARY† ▢ Oakland, CA

Young, Thomas E., Libn.
SOUTHWESTERN ART ASSOCIATION - PHILBROOK ART CENTER - LIBRARY ▢ Tulsa, OK

Young, Victor D., Dir.
WEST VIRGINIA INSTITUTE OF TECHNOLOGY - VINING LIBRARY ▢ Montgomery, WV

Younger, William C., Dir.
ALABAMA STATE SUPREME COURT - SUPREME COURT AND STATE LAW LIBRARY ▢ Montgomery, AL

Youngholm, Philip, Music Libn.
CONNECTICUT COLLEGE - GREER MUSIC LIBRARY ▢ New London, CT

Youngquist, Ronald E., Hd., Rec.Serv.
NORTH CAROLINA STATE DEPT. OF CULTURAL RESOURCES - DIV. OF ARCHIVES AND HISTORY - ARCHIVES & RECORDS SECTION ▢ Raleigh, NC

Yount, Diana, Spec.Coll.Libn.
ANDOVER NEWTON THEOLOGICAL SCHOOL - TRASK LIBRARY ▢ Newton Centre, MA

Youssif, Nassif, Hd.
UNIVERSITY OF MINNESOTA - MIDDLE EAST LIBRARY ▢ Minneapolis, MN

Youster, Allan, Lib.Supv.
MC GILL UNIVERSITY - MATHEMATICS LIBRARY ▢ Montreal, PQ

Yow, Dr. Maude, Hd.
MISSISSIPPI UNIVERSITY FOR WOMEN - SCHOOL OF EDUCATION - LIBRARY SCIENCE DIVISION ▢ Columbus, MS

Yowell, Jerry, Mgr., Indus.Div.
UNIVERSITY OF NEW MEXICO - TECHNOLOGY APPLICATION CENTER ▢ Albuquerque, NM

Yu, Amanda, Libn.
YORK TECHNICAL COLLEGE - LIBRARY ▢ Rock Hill, SC

Yu, Chilin, Libn.
COLUMBUS COLLEGE OF ART AND DESIGN - PACKARD LIBRARY ▢ Columbus, OH

Yu, Hung-Chih, Spec.Coll.
TEXAS A & M UNIVERSITY - MEDICAL SCIENCES LIBRARY ▢ College Station, TX

Yu, Jeffrey C., Libn.
EASTMAN KODAK COMPANY - KODAK APPARATUS DIVISION - LIBRARY ▢ Rochester, NY

Yu, Kuang-Hu, Cat.
TRENTON STATE COLLEGE - ROSCOE L. WEST LIBRARY ▢ Trenton, NJ

Yu, Lincoln H.S., Libn.
U.S. NAVY - NAVAL SHIPYARD (Pearl Harbor) - TECHNICAL LIBRARY ▢ Pearl Harbor, HI

Yu, Robert H.S., Hd.
METROPOLITAN TORONTO LIBRARY - BIBLIOGRAPHIC CENTRE & INTERLOAN ▢ Toronto, ON

Yu, Winnie, Asst.Libn.
KAISER FOUNDATION HOSPITALS - MEDICAL LIBRARY ▢ Los Angeles, CA

Yuan, Christina, Ref.
WORCESTER POLYTECHNIC INSTITUTE - GEORGE C. GORDON LIBRARY ▢ Worcester, MA

Yucht, Rene, Hd.Libn.
NEW CASTLE COUNTY LAW LIBRARY ▢ Wilmington, DE

Yucuis, Gerald J., Mgr.
IIT RESEARCH INSTITUTE - COMPUTER SEARCH CENTER ▢ Chicago, IL

Yugo, Susan, Asst.Archv.
UNIVERSITY OF WISCONSIN, PARKSIDE - UNIVERSITY ARCHIVES AND AREA RESEARCH CENTER ▢ Kenosha, WI

Yung, Judy, Libn.
OAKLAND PUBLIC LIBRARY - ASIAN LIBRARY ▢ Oakland, CA

Yunker, J. Olivia, Supv.
U.S. DEPT. OF ENERGY - KNOLLS ATOMIC POWER LABORATORY - LIBRARIES ▢ Schenectady, NY

Yurkiw, P., Hd.Tech.Serv.
CANADA - PUBLIC ARCHIVES OF CANADA - MANUSCRIPT DIVISION ▢ Ottawa, ON

Yurschak, Beverly, Libn.
NORTHWEST HOSPITAL - MEDICAL LIBRARY ▢ Chicago, IL

Yuschak, Donna, Libn.
SOUTHWESTERN INDIANA MENTAL HEALTH CENTER - LIBRARY ▢ Evansville, IN

Z

Zabel, Jean, Libn., Leg.Lib.
MILWAUKEE - LEGISLATIVE REFERENCE BUREAU - LEGISLATIVE LIBRARY ▢ Milwaukee, WI

Zabel, Peggy, Info.Sci.
RALSTON PURINA COMPANY - TECHNICAL INFORMATION CENTER ▢ St. Louis, MO

Zabilansky, Dorothea M., Med.Libn.
ROCKVILLE GENERAL HOSPITAL - MEDICAL LIBRARY/RESOURCE ROOM ▢ Rockville, CT

Zaborowski, Mary Ann, Info.Res.Anl.
SPERRY CORPORATION - SPERRY UNIVAC COMPUTER SYSTEMS - INFORMATION CENTER ▢ Blue Bell, PA

Zabrosky, Frank A., Cur.
UNIVERSITY OF PITTSBURGH - ARCHIVES OF INDUSTRIAL SOCIETY ▢ Pittsburgh, PA

Zabrosky, Jackie, Asst.Libn.
GEE & JENSON ENGINEERS, ARCHITECTS, PLANNERS, INC. - LIBRARY ▢ West Palm Beach, FL

Zacher, Elaine, Libn.
KAISER ENGINEERS, INC. - ENGINEERING LIBRARY ▢ Oakland, CA

Zadarnowski, Jozef, Assoc.Acq.Libn.
SAN DIEGO COUNTY LAW LIBRARY ▢ San Diego, CA

Zadner, Paul, Hd., Circ./Per.
SUNY - COLLEGE AT BUFFALO - EDWARD H. BUTLER LIBRARY ▢ Buffalo, NY

Zadnikar, Vili, Assoc.Libn.Tech.Serv.
CASE WESTERN RESERVE UNIVERSITY - LAW LIBRARY ▢ Cleveland, OH

Zafren, Herbert C., Co-Dir.
HEBREW UNION COLLEGE - JEWISH INSTITUTE OF RELIGION - AMERICAN JEWISH PERIODICAL CENTER ▢ Cincinnati, OH

Zafren, Herbert C., Lib.Dir.
HEBREW UNION COLLEGE - JEWISH INSTITUTE OF RELIGION - KLAU LIBRARY ▢ Cincinnati, OH

Zahed, Hyder A., Info.Spec.
BURROUGHS WELLCOME COMPANY - LIBRARY ▢ Research Triangle Park, NC

Zaher, Claudia, Rd.Serv.Libn.
NORTHERN KENTUCKY UNIVERSITY - SALMON P. CHASE COLLEGE OF LAW - LIBRARY ▢ Covington, KY

Zahniser, Adrienne, Hd.Libn.
OHIO STATE UNIVERSITY - WOMEN'S STUDIES LIBRARY ▢ Columbus, OH

Zajac, Suzanne, Ref.Libn.
ROSWELL PARK MEMORIAL INSTITUTE - MEDICAL AND SCIENTIFIC LIBRARY ▢ Buffalo, NY

Zakrzewski, Dr. Richard J., Musm.Dir.
FORT HAYS STATE UNIVERSITY - STERNBERG MEMORIAL MUSEUM - LIBRARY ▢ Hays, KS

Zalben, Barry, Res.Coord.
MILWAUKEE - LEGISLATIVE REFERENCE BUREAU - LEGISLATIVE LIBRARY ▢ Milwaukee, WI

Zaletel, Hank, Ref.Libn.
IOWA STATE DEPARTMENT OF TRANSPORTATION - LIBRARY ▢ Ames, IA

Zalin, Fern, Libn.
PHILADELPHIA PSYCHIATRIC CENTER - PROFESSIONAL LIBRARY ▢ Philadelphia, PA

Zaloudek, Marjorie C., Archv.Libn.
ST. LOUIS - COMPTROLLERS OFFICE - MICROFILM DEPARTMENT ▢ St. Louis, MO

Zalubas, Dr. Romuald, Physicist
U.S. NATL. BUREAU OF STANDARDS - ATOMIC ENERGY LEVELS DATA CENTER ▢ Washington, DC

Zamarelli, Calvin A., Chf.Libn.
U.S. VETERANS ADMINISTRATION (NJ-East Orange) - MEDICAL CENTER LIBRARY† ▢ East Orange, NJ

PERSONNEL

Zambotti, Marguerite, Ref.Libn.
C.I.T. FINANCIAL CORPORATION - REFERENCE LIBRARY □ New York, NY

Zamonski, Stanley W., Cur.
BUFFALO BILL MEMORIAL MUSEUM - INFORMATION CENTER □ Golden, CO

Zamora, George, Acq.
NEW MEXICO INSTITUTE OF MINING AND TECHNOLOGY - MARTIN SPEARE MEMORIAL LIBRARY □ Socorro, NM

Zamora, Gloria, Subj.Spec.
U.S. DEPT OF ENERGY - SANDIA NATL. LABORATORIES - TECHNICAL LIBRARY □ Albuquerque, NM

Zanan, Arthur S., Law Libn.
MONTGOMERY COUNTY LAW LIBRARY □ Norristown, PA

Zapata, Alina
PUERTO RICO - ATENEO PUERTORRIQUENO - BIBLIOTECA □ San Juan, PR

Zapf, Cynthia, Libn.
POLYCHROME CORPORATION - RESEARCH & DEVELOPMENT LIBRARY† □ Yonkers, NY

Zaporozhetz, Laurene E., Ref.Libn., Educ.
UNIVERSITY OF OREGON - CURRICULUM AND JUVENILE COLLECTIONS □ Eugene, OR

Zappert, Fred, Mgr.,Oper.
LOCKHEED MISSILES & SPACE COMPANY, INC. - LOCKHEED INFORMATION SYSTEMS □ Palo Alto, CA

Zar, Kathleen A., Map Libn.
UNIVERSITY OF CHICAGO - MAP COLLECTION □ Chicago, IL

Zarabi, Ali, Tech.Serv.Libn.
UNIVERSITY CLUB LIBRARY □ New York, NY

Zaremba, Andrew, Libn.
CENTURY ASSOCIATION - LIBRARY □ New York, NY

Zartman, Geraldine, Mining Info.Spec.
ALASKA STATE DEPARTMENT OF NATURAL RESOURCES - DIVISION OF GEOLOGICAL SURVEY - INFORMATION CENTER □ Ketchikan, AK

Zavez, Elenore, Circ.Libn.
CENTRAL CONNECTICUT STATE COLLEGE - ELIHU BURRITT LIBRARY □ New Britain, CT

Zawadzki, Danuta M., Acq., Circ. & Ref.
HUGHES AIRCRAFT COMPANY - COMPANY TECHNICAL DOCUMENT CENTER □ Culver City, CA

Zawadzki, Danuta M., V.P.
POLISH AMERICAN CONGRESS - SOUTHERN CALIFORNIA-ARIZONA DIVISION - POLAND'S MILLENIUM LIBRARY □ Los Angeles, CA

Zbehlik, Jerry, Doc.Mgr.
CARTER-WALLACE, INC. - LIBRARY □ Cranbury, NJ

Zdenek, Lorraine, Libn.
AMERICAN SOKOL EDUCATION AND PHYSICAL CULTURE ORGANIZATION - LIBRARY □ Berwyn, IL

Zeck, Otto F., Musm.Cur.
BECKER COUNTY HISTORICAL SOCIETY - WALTER D. BIRD MEMORIAL HISTORICAL LIBRARY □ Detroit Lakes, MN

Zeender, Ruth, Lib.Tech.Asst.
UNIVERSITY OF MARYLAND, COLLEGE PARK - COLLEGE OF LIBRARY & INFORMATION SERVICES - LIBRARY □ College Park, MD

Zehery, Saeid, Cat.Libn.
HOOD THEOLOGICAL SEMINARY - LIVINGSTONE COLLEGE - LIBRARY □ Salisbury, NC

Zehnpfennig, Diane, Med.Libn.
U.S. VETERANS ADMINISTRATION (IL-Chicago) - WESTSIDE HOSPITAL LIBRARY □ Chicago, IL

Zeidner, Christine, Sci. & Engr.Libn.
UNIVERSITY OF UTAH - MATHEMATICS LIBRARY □ Salt Lake City, UT

Zeimetz, Mary, Asst.Dept.Hd.
MINNEAPOLIS PUBLIC LIBRARY & INFORMATION CENTER - BUSINESS AND SCIENCE DEPARTMENT □ Minneapolis, MN

Zeind, Samir, Dir.
HUNTINGTON MEMORIAL HOSPITAL - HEALTH SCIENCES LIBRARY □ Pasadena, CA

Zeitler, Karen, Ref.
ICI AMERICAS INC. - ATLAS LIBRARY □ Wilmington, DE

Zeitlin, Jacob Israel, Pres.
ZEITLIN & VER BRUGGE, BOOKSELLERS - LIBRARY □ Los Angeles, CA

Zeitlin, Stanley, Pres.
ZEITLIN PERIODICALS COMPANY, INC. - LIBRARY □ Los Angeles, CA

Zelenko, Barbara J., Hd.Libn.
U.S. DEPT. OF JUSTICE - UNITED STATES ATTORNEY, SOUTHERN DISTRICT OF NEW YORK - LIBRARY □ New York, NY

Zell, Diana, Asst.Libn.
NEW YORK STATE DEPARTMENT OF STATE - FIRE ACADEMY LIBRARY □ Montour Falls, NY

Zeller, Hortense, Libn.
HAIGHT, GARDNER, POOR AND HAVENS - LIBRARY □ New York, NY

Zeller, Lore, Libn.
JUNG (C.G.) INSTITUTE OF LOS ANGELES, INC. - LIBRARY □ Los Angeles, CA

Zeller, Marilou, Asst.Cat.Libn.
BLOOMSBURG STATE COLLEGE - HARVEY A. ANDRUSS LIBRARY □ Bloomsburg, PA

Zelman, Gerson, Ref.Libn.
NEWSWEEK, INC. - LIBRARY □ New York, NY

Zelnik, Barbara L., Asst.Dir.
JOHNS HOPKINS UNIVERSITY - SCHOOL OF HYGIENE AND PUBLIC HEALTH - INTERDEPARTMENTAL LIBRARY □ Baltimore, MD

Zeman, Eleanore, Cat./Ref.
U.S. ARMY MISSILE & MUNITIONS CENTER & SCHOOL - MMCS TECHNICAL LIBRARY □ Redstone Arsenal, AL

Zembicki, Christine R., Circ. & ILL Libn.
NEW JERSEY INSTITUTE OF TECHNOLOGY - ROBERT W. VAN HOUTEN LIBRARY □ Newark, NJ

Zenan, Joan S., Libn.
UNIVERSITY OF NEVADA, RENO - SAVITT MEDICAL LIBRARY □ Reno, NV

Zenelis, John, Hd., Law Cat.
COLUMBIA UNIVERSITY - LAW LIBRARY □ New York, NY

Zenner, Hans, Hd., Tech.Serv.
NORTH DAKOTA STATE UNIVERSITY - LIBRARY □ Fargo, ND

Zentner, Elise, Libn.
CONGREGATION BETH AM - LIBRARY □ Los Altos Hills, CA

Zerkow, Syma, Dept.Hd.
HOUSTON PUBLIC LIBRARY - FILM COLLECTION DEPARTMENT □ Houston, TX

Zerwekh, Charles E., Tech.Info.Sys.Mgr.
POLAROID CORPORATION - RESEARCH LIBRARY □ Cambridge, MA

Zerwekh, June, Circ.Libn.
RUSH UNIVERSITY AND MEDICAL CENTER - LIBRARY □ Chicago, IL

Zerwick, James W., Engr.Libn.
UNIVERSITY OF VIRGINIA - ENGINEERING LIBRARY □ Charlottesville, VA

Zeve, Ann R., Libn.
TEMPLE SHAREY TEFILO - EDWARD EHRENKRANTZ LIBRARY □ East Orange, NJ

Zevely, Sandra, Coord.
SAN DIEGO COUNTY - DEPARTMENT OF EDUCATION - PROFESSIONAL RESOURCE AND DEVELOPMENT CENTER □ San Diego, CA

Zeydel, Jeanne R., Agency Libn.
INTERNATIONAL COMMUNICATION AGENCY - LIBRARY □ Washington, DC

Zezulka, Linda, Asst.Cur.
AUSTIN PUBLIC LIBRARY - AUSTIN-TRAVIS COUNTY COLLECTION □ Austin, TX

Zgodava, Richard, Asst.Dept.Hd.
MINNEAPOLIS PUBLIC LIBRARY & INFORMATION CENTER - ART, MUSIC & FILMS DEPARTMENT □ Minneapolis, MN

Zia, Dora, Res.Libn.
BECTON, DICKINSON & COMPANY - RESEARCH CENTER LIBRARY □ Research Triangle Park, NC

Ziaian, Monir, Hd.Libn.
UNIVERSITY OF SOUTHERN CALIFORNIA - INSTITUTE OF SAFETY & SYSTEMS MANAGEMENT - LIBRARY □ Los Angeles, CA

Ziaya, Alana, Asst.Libn.
MARSHFIELD CLINIC - MEDICAL CENTER LIBRARY □ Marshfield, WI

Zibrat, Jan, Med.Libn.
SWEDISH COVENANT HOSPITAL - JOSEPH G. STROMBERG LIBRARY OF THE HEALTH SCIENCES □ Chicago, IL

Ziccardi, Gerald J., Med.Libn.
U.S. DEFENSE LOGISTICS AGENCY - DEFENSE PERSONNEL SUPPORT CTR. - DIRECTORATE OF MED. MATERIEL TECH. LIBRARY □ Philadelphia, PA

Zick, Kenneth A., II, Dir.
WAKE FOREST UNIVERSITY - LAW LIBRARY □ Winston-Salem, NC

Zickgraf, Sr. Therese, C.S.J., Libn.
LOYOLA MARYMOUNT COLLEGE - ORANGE CAMPUS - LIBRARY □ Orange, CA

Ziebold, Marilyn, Asst.Libn.
CATERPILLAR TRACTOR COMPANY - TECHNICAL INFORMATION CENTER □ Peoria, IL

Zieg, Gerald W., Dir.
HARPER-GRACE HOSPITALS - DRUG INFORMATION CENTER □ Detroit, MI

Ziegenfuss, Donald G., Dir.
CARLTON, FIELDS, WARD, EMMANUEL, SMITH & CUTLER, P.A. - LIBRARY □ Tampa, FL

Ziegler, Arthur P., Jr.
PITTSBURGH HISTORY & LANDMARKS FOUNDATION - JAMES D. VAN TRUMP LIBRARY □ Pittsburgh, PA

Ziegler, Dr. Georgianna, Asst.Cur.
UNIVERSITY OF PENNSYLVANIA - HORACE HOWARD FURNESS MEMORIAL LIBRARY □ Philadelphia, PA

Ziegler, Roma, Cat.Libn.
MORAVIAN COLLEGE - REEVES LIBRARY □ Bethlehem, PA

Zieleniewski, Janet L., Libn.
PEDCO GROUP LIBRARY □ Cincinnati, OH

Zielinska, Marie F., Chf.
NATIONAL LIBRARY OF CANADA - MULTILINGUAL BIBLIOSERVICE □ Ottawa, ON

Ziemer, Dixie, Libn.
OREGON STATE DEPARTMENT OF LAND CONSERVATION AND DEVELOPMENT - LIBRARY □ Salem, OR

Ziemke, Linda, Dir.
GOOD SAMARITAN HOSPITAL - LIBRARY □ Puyallup, WA

Ziesler, Peggy A., Libn.
CALIFORNIA STATE DEPARTMENT OF TRANSPORTATION - DISTRICT 11 LIBRARY □ San Diego, CA

Zietz, Robert J., Hd.
MOBILE PUBLIC LIBRARY - SPECIAL COLLECTIONS DIVISION □ Mobile, AL

Ziino, Adeline, Cat.Asst.
BRIDGEWATER STATE COLLEGE - CLEMENT C. MAXWELL LIBRARY □ Bridgewater, MA

Zilavy, Julie-Ann, Info.Spec.
AMERICAN ASSOCIATION OF ADVERTISING AGENCIES - MEMBER INFORMATION SERVICE □ New York, NY

Zimmer, Judith L., Libn.
RHODE ISLAND MEDICAL SOCIETY - LIBRARY □ Providence, RI

Zimmerberg, Helen Y., Libn.
PRINCETON UNIVERSITY - BIOLOGY LIBRARY □ Princeton, NJ

Zimmerman, Barbara, Asst.Libn.
WESLEY MEDICAL CENTER - MC KIBBIN PROFESSIONAL LIBRARY □ Wichita, KS

Zimmerman, Bernardine, Info.Spec.
ENVIRONMENTAL RESEARCH & TECHNOLOGY, INC. - LIFE SCIENCES INFORMATION CENTER □ Fort Collins, CO

Zimmerman, Carolee, Sec. II-Libn.
FLORIDA STATE MEDICAL ENTOMOLOGY LABORATORY LIBRARY □ Vero Beach, FL

Zimmerman, Carolyn, Hd., Circ. & Reserve
CORNELL UNIVERSITY - MARTIN P. CATHERWOOD LIBRARY OF INDUSTRIAL AND LABOR RELATIONS □ Ithaca, NY

Zimmerman, Carolyn, Libn.
HATBORO BAPTIST CHURCH - LIBRARY □ Hatboro, PA

Zimmerman, Cheryl, Chf.Libn.
ONTARIO EDUCATIONAL COMMUNICATIONS AUTHORITY - MEDIA RESOURCE CENTRE □ Toronto, ON

Zimmerman, Donna K., Libn.
INDIANA LAW ENFORCEMENT ACADEMY - DAVID F. ALLEN MEMORIAL LEARNING RESOURCES CENTER □ Plainfield, IN

Zimmerman, Gail, Asst. Law Libn.
SANDUSKY COUNTY LAW LIBRARY □ Fremont, OH

Zimmerman, Gaynelle, Hd.Cat.
PLYMOUTH STATE COLLEGE - HERBERT H. LAMSON LIBRARY □ Plymouth, NH

Zimmerman, Gerald, Asst.Chf.
CHICAGO PUBLIC LIBRARY CULTURAL CENTER - LITERATURE AND LANGUAGE DIVISION □ Chicago, IL

Zimmerman, H. Neil, Libn.
POPULATION COUNCIL - LIBRARY □ New York, NY

Zimmerman, Irene, Asst.Libn.
UNIVERSITY OF WISCONSIN, MADISON - PHYSICS LIBRARY □ Madison, WI

Zimmerman, Janet, Cat.Libn.
WAYNE STATE UNIVERSITY - SCHOOL OF MEDICINE - VERA PARSHALL SHIFFMAN MEDICAL LIBRARY □ Detroit, MI

Zimmerman, John, Lib.Dir.
FROSTBURG STATE COLLEGE - LIBRARY □ Frostburg, MD

Zimmerman, Kathleen, Libn.
NORTH DAKOTA STATE DEPARTMENT OF HEALTH - HEALTH EDUCATION FILM & STAFF JOURNAL LIBRARY □ Bismarck, ND

Zimmermann, Albert, Med.Ed., Libn.
MARSHFIELD CLINIC - MEDICAL CENTER LIBRARY □ Marshfield, WI

Zimpfer, William E., Libn.
BOSTON UNIVERSITY - SCHOOL OF THEOLOGY LIBRARY □ Boston, MA

Zimpfer, William E., Libn.
UNITED METHODIST CHURCH - SOUTHERN NEW ENGLAND CONFERENCE - HISTORICAL SOCIETY LIBRARY □ Boston, MA

Zimring, Vicki, Ref.Libn.
UNITED BANK OF DENVER, N.A. - INFORMATION CENTER LIBRARY □ Denver, CO

Zini, Maria, Hd.
CARNEGIE LIBRARY OF PITTSBURGH - PENNSYLVANIA DIVISION □ Pittsburgh, PA

Zinker, Selma, Lib.Supv.
TANDEM COMPUTERS, INC. - CORPORATE LIBRARY □ Cupertino, CA

Zinnato, Diana, Cat.Libn.
UNIVERSITY OF SOUTH CAROLINA - SCHOOL OF MEDICINE LIBRARY □ Columbia, SC

Zins, Gwendolyn, Docs.
UNIVERSITY OF UTAH - SPENCER S. ECCLES HEALTH SCIENCES LIBRARY □ Salt Lake City, UT

Zipin, Amnon, Jewish Stud.Libn.
OHIO STATE UNIVERSITY - JUDAICA LIBRARY □ Columbus, OH

Zipkowitz, Fay, Dir.
RHODE ISLAND STATE DEPARTMENT OF STATE LIBRARY SERVICES □ Providence, RI

Zipp, Louise, Libn.
UNIVERSITY OF IOWA - BOTANY-CHEMISTRY LIBRARY □ Iowa City, IA

Zipp, Louise, Libn.
UNIVERSITY OF IOWA - GEOLOGY LIBRARY □ Iowa City, IA

Zipper, Masha, Mgr.
PRICE WATERHOUSE - NATIONAL INFORMATION CENTER □ New York, NY

Zippert, Katherine, Asst.Libn.
NORTH SHORE UNIVERSITY HOSPITAL - DANIEL CARROLL PAYSON MEDICAL LIBRARY □ Manhasset, NY

Zislin, Phyllis, Act.Dir.
BETH ISRAEL CONGREGATION - LIBRARY □ Vineland, NJ

Zissis, George J., Dir.
ENVIRONMENTAL RESEARCH INSTITUTE OF MICHIGAN - INFRARED INFORMATION AND ANALYSIS CENTER (IRIA) □ Ann Arbor, MI

Zitkovich, Anne, Act.Hd., Cat.Dept.
NORTHWESTERN UNIVERSITY - LAW SCHOOL LIBRARY □ Chicago, IL

Zito, Dr. Anthony, Univ.Archv.
CATHOLIC UNIVERSITY OF AMERICA - DEPARTMENT OF ARCHIVES AND MANUSCRIPTS □ Washington, DC

Zizka, George E.A., Libn.
VICTORIA GENERAL HOSPITAL - HEALTH SCIENCES LIBRARY† □ Victoria, BC

Zlomke, Clay, Dir. of Engr.
BRUNSWICK CORPORATION - DEFENSE DIVISION - TECHNICAL LIBRARY □ Costa Mesa, CA

Zobrist, Dr. Benedict K., Dir.
U.S. PRESIDENTIAL LIBRARIES - HARRY S TRUMAN LIBRARY □ Independence, MO

Zoccola, Donna M., Libn.
FRIENDS HOSPITAL - NORMAN D. WEINER PROFESSIONAL LIBRARY □ Philadelphia, PA

Zoellick, Ruthann, Libn.
EAST CENTRAL OKLAHOMA STATE UNIVERSITY - OKLAHOMA ENVIRONMENTAL INFORMATION/MEDIA CENTER □ Ada, OK

Zoller, C.E., Mgr.
MC DONNELL DOUGLAS CORPORATION - MC DONNELL AIRCRAFT LIBRARY □ St. Louis, MO

Zoller, Victor, Info.Spec.
BABCOCK AND WILCOX COMPANY - RESEARCH CENTER LIBRARY □ Alliance, OH

Zonghi, Bertha, Jr.Cat.
BOSTON PUBLIC LIBRARY - RARE BOOKS AND MANUSCRIPTS □ Boston, MA

Zorach, Margaret B., Chf.Libn.
BROOKLYN MUSEUM - ART REFERENCE LIBRARY □ Brooklyn, NY

Zorbas, Elaine, Libn., Ref.Div.
PASADENA PUBLIC LIBRARY - REFERENCE DIVISION □ Pasadena, CA

Zorich, Philip, Asst.Libn.
INDIANA UNIVERSITY OF PENNSYLVANIA - UNIVERSITY LIBRARY □ Indiana, PA

Zoumer, R., Consul
SWEDISH CONSULATE - LIBRARY □ Calgary, AB

Zschunke, William J., Libn.
U.S. AIR FORCE - OFFICE OF JUDGE ADVOCATE GENERAL - LEGAL REFERENCE LIBRARY □ Washington, DC

Zub, Vera, Cat.
WILFRID LAURIER UNIVERSITY - LIBRARY □ Waterloo, ON

Zubkoff, Helene, Ref./Info.Serv.Spec.
AMERICAN COLLEGE OF NURSING HOME ADMINISTRATORS - LIBRARY □ Washington, DC

Zubrow, Marcia, Hd.Ref.Libn.
SUNY AT BUFFALO - CHARLES B. SEARS LAW LIBRARY □ Buffalo, NY

Zuck, Prof. Lowell H., Libn.
EVANGELICAL AND REFORMED HISTORICAL SOCIETY - EDEN ARCHIVES □ Webster Groves, MO

Zucker, Donna, Libn.
TEMPLE EMANU-EL - WILLIAM P. ENGEL LIBRARY □ Birmingham, AL

Zuckerman, Edith, Slide Cur.
TEMPLE UNIVERSITY - CENTRAL LIBRARY SYSTEM - TYLER SCHOOL OF FINE ARTS - SLIDE LIBRARY □ Philadelphia, PA

Zuehlke, Lois J., Lib.Dir.
MERCY HOSPITAL - MEDICAL LIBRARY □ Janesville, WI

Zuehlsdorf, Frances P., Libn.
AUTOMATIC SPRINKLER COMPANY - INTERSTATE ELECTRONICS DIVISION - LIBRARY □ Anaheim, CA

Zuetell, Marina H., Health Sci.Libn.
MORITZ COMMUNITY HOSPITAL - DEAN PIEROSE MEMORIAL HEALTH SCIENCES LIBRARY □ Sun Valley, ID

Zuger, Joy E., Chf., Lib.Serv.
U.S. VETERANS ADMINISTRATION (IN-Marion) - HOSPITAL MEDICAL LIBRARY □ Marion, IN

Zugschwert, John F., Exec.Dir.
AMERICAN HELICOPTER SOCIETY - TECHNICAL INFORMATION □ Washington, DC

Zukowski, Frances, Libn.
LAKE COUNTY SUPERIOR COURT LIBRARY □ Gary, IN

Zukowski, Stanley P., Hd.
BUFFALO & ERIE COUNTY PUBLIC LIBRARY - BUSINESS AND LABOR DEPARTMENT □ Buffalo, NY

Zukowski, Stanley P., Hd.
BUFFALO & ERIE COUNTY PUBLIC LIBRARY - SCIENCE AND TECHNOLOGY DEPARTMENT □ Buffalo, NY

Zukowsky, John, Arch.Archv.
ART INSTITUTE OF CHICAGO - RYERSON AND BURNHAM LIBRARIES □ Chicago, IL

Zultanky, Peggy A., Libn.
MARYVIEW HOSPITAL - DOCTORS' LIBRARY □ Portsmouth, VA

Zumstein, Marjorie A., Psych.Libn.
PURDUE UNIVERSITY - PSYCHOLOGICAL SCIENCES LIBRARY □ West Lafayette, IN

Zumwalt, George M., Chf., Lib.Serv.
U.S. VETERANS ADMINISTRATION (AR-Little Rock) - HOSPITAL LIBRARIES □ Little Rock, AR

Zupanick, Adina, Mgr., Lib.Serv.
LEEDS AND NORTHRUP COMPANY - TECHNICAL CENTER LIBRARY □ North Wales, PA

Zupko, Janet K., Mgr., Info.Serv.
CPC INTERNATIONAL - MOFFETT TECHNICAL LIBRARY □ Argo, IL

Zuppann, Edith, Pub.Chm.
GENEALOGICAL ASSOCIATION OF SOUTHWESTERN MICHIGAN - MAUD PRESTON PALENSKE MEMORIAL LIBRARY □ St. Joseph, MI

Zuraw, Cathy, Hd.Libn.
SHERIDAN COLLEGE OF APPLIED ARTS AND TECHNOLOGY - SCHOOL OF DESIGN - LIBRARY □ Mississauga, ON

Zussy, Nancy, Dp. State Libn.
WASHINGTON STATE LIBRARY □ Olympia, WA

Zuther-Kerr, Karen, Ser./ILL Libn.
UNIVERSITY OF SOUTH DAKOTA - CHRISTIAN P. LOMMEN HEALTH SCIENCES LIBRARY □ Vermillion, SD

Zuzick, Kathryn T., Libn.
U.S. DEFENSE COMMUNICATIONS AGENCY - NATL. MILITARY COMMAND SYSTEM SUPPORT CENTER - TECHNICAL LIBRARY □ Washington, DC

Zvejnieks, Laila, Ser.Libn.
ONTARIO - MINISTRY OF TRANSPORTATION AND COMMUNICATIONS - LIBRARY AND INFORMATION CENTRE □ Downsview, ON

Zvonchenko, Walter, Ref.Libn./Theater
LIBRARY OF CONGRESS - JOHN F. KENNEDY CENTER FOR THE PERFORMING ARTS - THE PERFORMING ARTS LIBRARY □ Washington, DC

Zweibach, Allan, Tech.Serv.
GRAND LODGE OF NEW YORK, F. AND A.M. - LIBRARY AND MUSEUM □ New York, NY

PERSONNEL

Zweifel, Prof. LeRoy G., Dir.
UNIVERSITY OF WISCONSIN, MADISON - KURT
F. WENDT ENGINEERING LIBRARY □ Madison,
WI

Zwick, Sharan, Libn.
ARNOLD, WHITE & DURKEE - LIBRARY □
Houston, TX

Zych, Carol, Sr.Info.Sci.
SCHERING-PLOUGH CORPORATION -
PHARMACEUTICAL RESEARCH DIVISION -
LIBRARY INFORMATION CENTER □ Bloomfield,
NJ

Zych, Freda, Libn.
METROPOLITAN TORONTO LIBRARY - HISTORY
DEPARTMENT □ Toronto, ON

Zynjuk, Nila, Info.Coord.
NATIONAL MICROGRAPHICS ASSOCIATION -
RESOURCE CENTER □ Silver Spring, MD